The Sports Encyclopedia:
Baseball 2007

27th Edition

David S. Neft • Richard M. Cohen • Michael L. Neft

ST. MARTIN'S GRIFFIN ⚡ NEW YORK

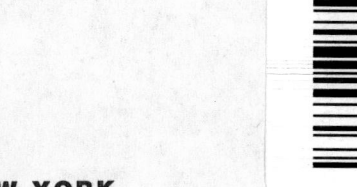

To Richard M. "Dick" Cohen
1938–1991
He spent much of his life researching sports history,
but he always believed that the best was yet to come.

www.stmartins.com

Library of Congress Cataloging-in-Publication Data

ISBN-13: 978-0-312-36359-8
ISBN-10: 0-312-36359-1

First Edition: February 2007

10 9 8 7 6 5 4 3 2 1

Contents

Preface

The Sports Encyclopedia: Baseball is the first reference book in a continuing series of major sports encyclopedias. This book, in particular, marks the first major reference book to appear on baseball since 1969. The previous effort, The Baseball Encyclopedia, represented, to that time, the most complete compendium on the subject ever offered. As we were proud to play a major role in the development of that effort, so are we proud to be the authors of this book. Yet beyond simply presenting baseball statistics again, it is our belief that we have presented a different format which adds yet another dimension to the study of the records and performances of former seasons. Instead of primarily presenting an alphabetical list of all ballplayers, we have placed the emphasis on the season so that the reader will be able to perceive baseball as a team sport from year to year and follow the ballplayers and their achievements in more direct relationship to one another.

In using such a format, we have also taken a certain license to arrange the history of baseball into various time periods, complete with its own lifetime registers, to give a truer perspective to the game of baseball as it has changed throughout the years. More importantly though, and perhaps out of a greater consideration for the economics of book buying, we planned the book in a way which makes it possible to purchase the greatest amount of information for the lowest price of any similar book in the marketplace.

This book, of course, could not have been accomplished by two individuals alone. Baseball is simply too expansive a subject to allow such an undertaking. It is, therefore appropriate that the organizations and individuals who assisted in the preparation of the manuscript not only receive the recognition they deserve, but also be given a rousing "thank you" for their fine and untiring efforts in our and all of baseball's behalf (with the previous positions they held):

Manuscript Preparation
Bob Carroll
Roland T. Johnson
Jordan A. Deutsch
Consultants in the preparation of the manuscript
John G. Hogrogian, N. Richard Anderson, Michael Rothstein, Doug Feinberg, Jeffrey Fox
Baseball Hall of Fame
Paul Kerr, President
Bill Guilfoile, Associate Director
Jack Redding, Librarian
Tom Heitz, Librarian
Bill Deane, Senior Research Director
Cliff Kachline, Historian, with special thanks for his continuing effort to collect demographic questionnaires for every man who ever played in the major leagues.
Society for American Baseball Research, a huge effort led by Bill Haber, Brooklyn, N.Y. included:
Arthue Ahrens, Chicago, Ill.
William Balza, Beaver Dam, Wis.
Rich Bozzone, Tolland, Conn.
Bob Brauner, Brookline, Mass.
Bill Carle, Grandview, Mo.
Frank Caruso, Olympia, Wash.
John Clark, Regina, Sask., Canada
Arthur Craig, Belmont, Mass.
Bob Davids, Washington, D.C.
Ted DiTullio, Bronx, N.Y.
Ron Liebman, Queens, N.Y.
John O'Malley, New York, N.Y.
Dan Dischley, Lake Ronkonkoma, N.Y.
John England, Fort Smith, Ark.
Paul Frisz, Terre Haute, Ind.
Larry Fritsch, Stevens Point, Wisc.
Vic Frolund, Youngstown, Ohio
Dan Ginsburg, Pittsburgh, Pa.

Ray Gonzalez, Woodside, N.Y.
Bill Gustafson, San Jose, Calif.
Tom Hufford, Pulaski, Va.
Larry Kelley, Meridan, Idaho
Stanley Kuminski, Brooklyn, N.Y.
Irv Lerner, Philadelphia, Pa.
Bill Loughman, Elmhurst, Ill.
Jim MacAlister, Philadelphia, Pa.
Stan Makowsky, Brooklyn, N.Y.
Bob McConnell, Wilmington, Del.
Wayne McElreavy, Claremont, N.H.
Fred McKie, Penns Grove, N.J.
Jim McLean, Rockford, Ill.
Doug McWilliams, Berkeley, Calif.
Peter Molin, Arlington, Va.
Ray Nemec, Downers Grove, Ill.
Robert Oliver, Salem Ore.
Pete Palmer, Lexington, Mass.
John Pardon, Croton-on-Hudson, N.Y.
Paul Quinn, Chicago, Ill.
Owen Ricker, Regina, Sask. , Canada
Emil Rothe, Chicago, Ill.
Vincent Russo, Queens, N.Y.
Tom Shea, Hingham, Mass.
Joe Simenic, Cleveland, Ohio
Jack Smalling, Ames, Iowa
David Stephan, Los Angeles, Calif.
John Stirling, Indianapolis, Ind.
Neil Sussman, Ft. Lauderdale, Fla.
John Tattersall, Havertown, Pa.
Bob Thing, Skowhegan, Maine
Bill Weiss, San Mateo, Calif.
Walt Wilson, Chicago, Ill.
Raphie Winnie, Seattle, Wash.
Daniel Woods, Hyde Park, Maine
R.H. Ziegler, Manhattan, Kan.
The Elias Sports Bureau
Seymour Siwoff
Steve Hirdt
Our Agent and Advisor
Robert Markel
Production
Land Systems
Fairfield, CT

The authors' wives, (a special thanks for their faith and cooperation throughout the project): Naomi Neft and Nancy Cohen.

In each section of the book, codes, unfamiliar abbreviations, and bold facing may be shown. The following, by section, is an explanation of this matter:
Yearly Statistical Sections
Age-The age shown for each player is as of July 1 of that year.

Codes and Explanations

For batters, the age shown is the average age based on those men who had at least 1 at bat per game scheduled. For pitchers, the age shown is the average age based on those men who appeared in an least 15 games.

Traded players-Whenever a number or numbers appear before a player's name, such as 1,2,3,4,5, or 13, 14,15,24,25, it indicates that he played for more than one team that year. For example, 2 would mean that the team he is shown with is his second team that year. On the other hand, 13 would mean that the player started the year with that team, was traded, and returned to that team again.

Bold Facing-Indicates league leaders.

Grouped Players-Certain players may be grouped together because of a lack of space on the page. When they do appear in such groupings, the information shown indicates the following:

Batters-Jones 24 L 3-7-Last Name, Age, Bats (Left or Right, or Both), Hits, At Bats.

Pitchers-Smith 21 R 0-1-Last Name, Age, Throws (Left or Right, Won and Lost Record.

Team Name Line-Shown alongside the name of each team is Position Finished, Won-Lost Record, Winning Percentage, Games Behind, and Manager. If a team had more than one manager, the won and lost record and the winning percentage for each manager is shown.

Partial Innings Pitched-Whenever a .1 is shown under in IP (Innings Pitched) Column, it indicates 1/3 of an inning pitched.

Career Interruptions-Whenever a symbol appears in parenthesis after a player's name, i.e., Jones (XX), it indicates a career interruption of 30 days or more duration, or a career ending injury or illness. The explanation to these symbols may be found under Career Interruption Codes on this page.

World Series Sections

Bold Facing-In the individual game line score totals, it indicates winning and losing pitchers and winning and losing team. In the composite box score totals, it indicates that the player led the Series in the indicated category.

Register Sections

Players have been assigned to the various register sections according to what time period they played the most. The only exception to this is that anybody who played mostly in the nineteenth century, would appear in the 1901-1919 Period Register Section.

Men who were primarily non-pitchers are included in the pitcher register only if they pitched in 5 or more games.

The information which appears in each Period Register Section, in addition to the player's lifetime statistics, is as follows:

Last name, Use name (name player was known as), Middle names, and Nicknames, the last of which appear in parenthesis ( ):

Ruth, Babe-George Herman (The Sultan of Swat)

For Latin ballplayers, where the mother's maiden name became part of the player's name, the information is indicated by brackets [ ] which appear between the middle name and the nickname. Such as in the case of Luis Aparicio:

Aparicio, Luis-Luis Ernesto [Monteil] (Little Louie)

If a player used another name other than that he was "born as", his real name is indicated in parenthesis ( ) after the last last name and use name. Such as in the case of Max Carey:

Carey (Carnarius), Max (Maxilian-Max George (Scoops)

Manager-Whenever an M appears before a year or years it indicates that a player was a manager.

League Abbreviations-Each of the league affiliations is abbreviated and stands for the following: AA-American Association, AL-American League, FL-Federal League, NL-National League, PL-Players League, UA-Union Association.

Other Major League Sports-Certain players also played professional basketball or football. Such information is indicated with the league in abbreviations. These abbreviations stand for the following: NBL-National Basketball League, NBA-National Basketball Association, NFL-National Football League, AAFC-All American Football Conference, BAA-Basketball Association of America, ABL-American Basketball League.

Career Interruptions-If an abbreviation other than a league follows the year played, it means a career end or full year missed because of certain prevailing reasons. The explanation of these abbreviations may be found under the Career Interruption Codes on this page.

Career Interruption Codes

AA	— Injured in automobile accident	BN	— Broken ankle
AJ	— Arm injury	BP	— Broken hip bone
AL	— Alcohol Problem	BR	— Broken rib or ribs
BA	— Broken or dislocated arm	BS	— Broken bone in shoulder
BC	— Broken or dislocated collarbone	BT	— Broken toe
BE	— Broken bone in elbow	BW	— Broken wrist
BF	— Broken bone in foot	BX	— Broken spine
BG	— Broken finger	BY	— Broken cheek bone
BH	— Broken bone in hand	BZ	— Broken Nose
BJ	— Broken jaw	CJ	— Face injury
BK	— Broken bone in knee	CN	— Concussion
BL	— Broken leg	CP	— Blood poisoning
DD	— Died during the season or the following off-season		
DE	— Declared ineligible by commissioner or league president		
DL	— Declared ineligible for life by commissioner		
DO	— Declared ineligible for playing in outlaw league		
DP	— On team for entire year but did not play		
DR	— Drug problem or other substance abuse		
DU	— Unofficially declared ineligible for life		
EJ	— Elbow injury		
FA	— Finger amputated		
FJ	— Foot or heel injury		
FP	— Fracture in pelvis		
FR	— Badly burned		
FS	— Fractured skull		
GJ	— Groin injury		
GW	— Gunshot wounds		
HJ	— Hand injury		
HO	— Holdout		
IB	— Injured buttocks		
IF	— Didn't play in order to be with a member of the family who was ill		
IJ	— Eye injury		
IL	— Illness		
IN	— Couldn't play because of injunction issued by Pennsylvania Court in suit brought by Phi. NL		
JA	— In jail for assault		
JJ	— Injury or on disabled list type of injury unknown		
JL	— Went to play in Japanese League		
JT	— Jumped team		
KB	— Killed by pitched ball		
KJ	— Knee injury		
KP	— Kept out of lineup as part of A.L.-N.L. peace agreement in 1903		
LA	— Leg amputated		
LF	— Left before the end of the season to play pro football		
LJ	— Leg or thigh injury - including achilles tendon		
MJ	— Abdominal muscle injury or stomach muscle injury		
ML	— Special military leave to play baseball		
MM	— Merchant marine		
MS	— Military service		
NJ	— Ankle injury		
PB	— Head injury from pitched ball		
PJ	— Hip injury		
PP	— Personal problems		
QJ	— Brain injury		
RB	— Retired to play pro basketball		
RC	— Retired to coach		
RF	— Retired to work in front office		
RJ	— Finger injury		
RL	— Reported late in order to finish school year or returned to school before the end of the baseball season		
RM	— Retired to manage		
RP	— Attended to personal business		
RR	— Refused to report		
SA	— Sore arm		
SC	— Barred by court injunction		
SD	— Suspended by commissioner for drug abuse		
SJ	— Shoulder injury or shoulder separation		
SL	— Suspended by commissioner or league president		
SM	— Suspended for playing in the Mexican League		
ST	— Suspended by team		
SU	— Suspended for hitting or abusing umpire		
TJ	— Chest injury		
UJ	— Side injury		
VJ	— Rib injury		
VR	— Voluntarily retired		
WJ	— Wrist injury		
WW	— Voluntarily retired or played only part time while working for the government or in plants producing war material		
XJ	— Back injury		
YJ	— Head injury		
ZJ	— Neck injury		

4

The Great Mississippi

For Lee Allen,
*who called one night
on his way back to Cooperstown
to say he had discovered the sun.*

The Great Mississippi

Up from the grasslands,
The plains, the cities,
Up from the vastness
of the land itself:
Up
Up
Up
To the Great Mississippi.

Up to that First Field
bathed in sun,
Basking in the glory
of its birth
Immersed in future time.

Further up slides the sun.

Up
To the Red Stockings from Cincinnati,
The original Magnificent Machine,
The dynasty without a future.
Up
To the National Association,
Swaying in its greatness.

Further up slides the sun.

Through the mouth of history
slide provocative names
Once breathed on the lips
of dreamers.

In what fine grave
do the
Elizabeth Resolutes
Troy Haymakers,
And
Lord Baltimores
   now rest?

Upmovingup
To expanding cities
   pocketed
In gray concrete.

(Can you hear the shrill and melodic chant
   of the Train Conductor
   calling out his roll?)

:NewYawkHartfordBosstonPhilaDELphia
LouievilleCINCINnatiShecargo and
   SaintLouieeeeee.

Up up up
Up
To the Great Mississippi.

The Grand Central Hotel

No sun,
Now rubble,
The collected debris
of memories
Echoes
An anquished ring
   through the corridors
of Manhattan Canyons:

Where are we going?

From where
To where
Do we step?

December...a month...a day...a time
logged on the fresh pages of history...
the first and only real entry...a league
...a new league...a microscopic legion of
men bearing witness to the birth, unfurling
its colors on an industrial land to detract

from the former failure...

The National Association is dead,
Long live the National League!

From rubble to rubble,
From dust to dust,
New fortresses
Stretch their fledgling arms
And puncture the sky
With abbreviated zeal.

Like so many transients
Awaiting a derailed train,
The others come
And never go.

The American Association is dead
The Union Association is dead
The Players League is dead.
All gone,
All dead,

Long live the National League!

The American League

After the rubble-
the dust,
The coat of dust
hovering over sidewalks,
Into the cracks of time.

Dust races in the sunlight.

Fresh footprints
Permanent steps
   on the floor of history.

The steps of giants,
Of circus performers,
And
Golden-armed magicians
   traipsing
Through sun-filled cities
And sunless nights
In search of permanence.

Brave Mack
Cornelius Alexander McGillicuddy
Mack
Mack the Master,
   the tall, lean visionary
   who led a white elephant
And
   of course
Notwithstandingnotwithout
   in center ring
The acrobat from Georgia
The acrobat who spelled
   his name
CAPITAL C
   little o
   little b
   little b
The frenzied acrobat
   who danced on the wall of greatness
With razor feet,
Who cut his image
   in swirls of blood.

O,
The sawdust stained with blood,
The dripping pattern
   of immortal footprints
Imprinted on the souls
   of ordinary men.

Dust races in the sunlight
But the sun cannot speak.

1919

Before the threat
And dismal cold gray
   of mourning
Came the sun.

And Charlie Comiskey
   should've turned in his sleep
   should've turned in his sleep
   should've turned...

Insane sun
Floating above the earth
Like some extravagant madman
Spending next year's allowance.

The same burning sun
In the same afternoons
In all the cities
East
   and somewhat
West
   of the
Great Mississippi.

   should've turned in his sleep
Too many
Suns
In too many
Cities

Too many faces
Faces
in the face of it
All.

How much grief?
Too
Much
Grief.
Too many faces
Too many suns
Far too many of too many things
Far too many of too many things.

   should've turned in his sleep

More like Dali,
   less Victoria.
The playing field becomes a landscape
Fixed and isolated and trapped
Between the borders of its own fabrication.

The stadium faces
Blur
   in the afternoon sun
The celebration
Ends
   in the afternoon sun
The victory becomes
Defeat
   in the afternoon sun.

Morality
Victoria Escaped
Insane sun.

How many of how many things?

The death of honor
The end of a fading
And final trust.

   should've turned in his sleep

And as
The unsettling dust
Settles in the throat of all men
There are not enough beers
In all the bars
In all the worlds
To flush out the stale bitterness
Of too many afternoons
In too many suns.

And Charlie Chomsky
   woke up
   and deposited the nightmare
   in the pillow of his dream.

The Babe

Jovial Giant squashed between
Greatness and an empty childhood;
Juxtaposed in time and play.

Mirthmaker,
Charmer,
Crowd-pleaser,
Lover,
King.

A crown of gold
A golden crown
A golden statue
A statue of gold.

We
Toast you with gauntlets of gold
And crown you with our passion.
We
Celebrate your proud head
Tipped upward and framed by a golden sun.

6

We
Chill in your stretching shadow
Which blocks the sun.

Can you remember
All the autographs inked in hysteria?
Or
The pennants
Nailed
On flagpoles atop the stadium roof?
Nailed
By the bludgeoning power of your power.

The wind makes those flags
Dance in the sky,
And their sound is the sound
Of seagulls-
Returning home to dine.

A Fisherman's Tale

Ernest
Hemingway
Immortalized
Joe
DiMaggio
and
Joe
DiMaggio
Immortalized
Himself
And
So
Did
Ted Williams
    that wonderful slugger from Boston.

Jackie

He waited
In the whiteness of the afternoon sun;
Black man on green ground.
He waited
In the silence of his tongue;
Black man on green ground.
He waited
In the path of his words
Which broke his bones;
Black man on green ground.
He waited
As few men have ever
waited
And endured
Before a multitude
as no man before,

O,
To have conquered the white sun,
    blinding
To have sailed the sun and ridden
    its joy
    in tears
And
    in laughter.

To have ridden the white sun,
    blinding
And to be
    struck
    struck
    struck
        by the rising

Of
Your
Own
Black
Sun.

Your crown was white;
...and waited.

Twenty-Six Years Now

After the war
After white on white on white
After Robinson

Yes,
Twenty-Six
years now
Twenty-Six
Twenty-Six
have come
And
Gone.

And the once empty rosters are no longer
Empty
as the face of my mother
That day
My father spoke.

I remember the gloom of my fathers words
And what they did to my mother's face
And what they did to my heart
—Those words my daddy spoke.

Daddy told us about
Josh Gibson
And how he was
Swatting white balls
In black parks
while Ruth and fellows
like Foxx
Were
Making hay.

Daddy told us about
Satch, Ole Satch
Lean and hummin'
Told about
Ole Satch
And how when Satch was
Striking black leather
In places
Like
Chattanooga
And Birmingham
And Pittsburgh
And Bismarck
And Cleveland
And Wichita
And Kansas City
And Havana and
Told when
Satch was doing all those things
How
Grove and Dean and Feller
Were
Making Hay.

Yes,
Twenty-six years
since my father's words
Twenty-six years
since his death

He had a belly laugh

My daddy did
And his laugh
 if ever such a sound could reach your ears
Would be filled with the
Loud
 and
Quiet joy
That men such as
 Mays and Robinson and Aaron
Could have given him.

Not their booming home rums and feats of magic

Just their faces
Just their faces
Just their faces
 now.

NO. 714

On the
21st of July
Henry Aaron
 slapped Home Run No. 700
And smiled
In the quiet way in which
He smiles.

On the
17th of August
Henry Aaron
 slapped Home Run No. 703
And wondered
if his wrists would not give way
And cheat him.

On the
3rd day of September
Henry Aaron
 slapped Home Run No. 707
 slapped Home Run No. 708
And thought
 of the stars.

On the
17th of September
Henry Aaron
 slapped Home Run No. 711
And said
 it wasn't important
anymore
There was
 time.

On the
22nd day of September
Henry Aaron
 slapped home run No. 712
And wondered
 if nature understood
 the struggle
Of men.

The sun is awesome and
 does not compromise.

On the
29th day of September
Henry Aaron
 slapped home run No. 713
And forgot
All the cruelty sent by mail.

A child walks
To the edge of the water
And efforts in the sand
 of the afternoon sun
 to save
Stale castles
Too illiterate
 to fall.

On the
30th day of September
Henry Aaron
 singled three times
And then went home
To wait
 the summer.

Beyond the Great Mississippi

After St. Louis
We crowded our caravans
And headed
West,
Uncautiously moving
Toward the sun.

Moved
Until
We reached
The waters of the Pacific,
Until
We seeded
Unknown soil.

And some of the seedlings took and some died.

Moved
Southward
And even
Northward
Beyond
Familiar borders.

And the land
Which once selfishly
 nestled its offspring
In limited embrace
Now
Extended its arms
To all
 who chanced the journey.

And the sun
No longer shone
In the same afternoons
In the same cities.

    —Jordan A. Deutsch
    October, 1973

1876-1900
A Journey Through a Once and Distant Time

If H.G. Wells actually built his time machine and one could be transported back in time, the chances are that any similarity between the game of the twentieth century and the game as played through 1892, would simply be an illusion in the eye of the beholder. While struggling to see which men, let alone a league could survive the rigors of implanting a new, national pastime, the playing rules, those necessary guidelines which were needed to bring continuity to the sport, were being changed continually. Beyond some of the rules, which are humorous in retrospect (such as before 1887, when the batter had the right to call for a high or low pitch), there are those rules which make it impossible to compare and judge the player performance pre-1893 with the standards of play as they are known today. The most relevant fact supporting this statement is the 1893 rule change which lengthened the pitching distance to 60 feet, 6 inches-a distance still used in all of professional baseball. Interestingly enough, in the search for an equitable separation of batter and pitcher, the distance started out at 45 feet. In 1881 five feet were tacked on and remained the same until the start of the 1893 season. Perhaps as important as the pitching distance was the pitcher's delivery which, until 1883, was underhanded. Getting to first base via a walk was a difficult chore for most of the seventies and eighties. It was not until 1989 that four balls got a batter to first. Before then it took anywhere from nine, in 1879, to five in 1887. Yet while the batter couldn't get a "cheap ticket" to the first sack, neither could he easily be victimized by the fast ball. The three-strike rule was not adopted until 1888, refined in 1895 (a strike being charged on a foul tip), and made uniform in 1903 when a foul tip caught after two strikes resulted in an out. It was not until 1891 that baseball instituted the substitution rule, which previously had only been allowed in the case of injury or permission by the other team.

Scoring rules also added to the distortion in early statistical tabulation. These include the 1887 rule which credited a base on balls as a hit and the 1876 rule which charged the batter with a time at bat on a base on balls (both of these distortions are not used in this book). Stolen base statistics, which began in 1886, credited a runner for each extra base advanced on another players' hit. It was not until 1898 that this rule was changed to the one used today. In trying to determine how to classify base on balls, wild pitch, hit batter, and balks, the poor moundsman got it all lumped in the single category of "error". This was the ruling established in 1883, reversed in 1887, reestablished in 1888, and finally abolished in 1889—the same year the sacrifice bunt was first recognized, although charging the batter with a time at bat.

But baseball in its youth was more than the evolution of rule changes. There were the individuals, and the leagues, of which four fought for dominance in the last quarter century of the 1800's. In 1876, following the demise of the National Association, a league simply classified as "professional" and not major due to its erratic scheduling, came the National League. Organized on February 2, 1876, and mostly due to the efforts of William A. Hulbert, owner of the Chicago team, a league constitution was drafted which called for a tight organization and a firm schedule of games. Hulbert took over the reins of league presidency in 1877 from Morgan G. Bulkeley, and although his iron fisted leadership was able to right scandal, end jumping franchises, and fatten the anemic coffers, it also led to the first rival league. Hulbert saw fit to throw Cincinnati out of the league after the 1880 season for permitting games on the Sabbath and liquor in the stands. It was this move which led to the formation of the American Association in 1882. Headed by Justin Thorner, of Cincinnati, and H.D. "Denny" Knight, of Pittsburgh, the new league not only succeeded in raiding players, but allowed the scheduling of Sunday games while cutting ticket prices from 50 to 25 cents. Hulbert died in 1882 and A.G. Mills, the new National League President, saw the inevitable and sued for peace in time to save his league from ruin. Out of the "laying down of arms" came the National Agreement, a document which not only led to mutual protection over player contracts, but brought about the first post-season championships between the two leagues in 1884.

That same year the Union Association headed by Henry V. Lucus, a St. Louis millionaire, came into being. But unlike the player raiding which led to the success of the American Association, the Union Association's tactics only resulted in their downfall. Both the other leagues raided enough of the new league's players so that at season's end only five of the original 12 franchises remained intact, and the Union Association was merely another page in baseball history. In 1890, as the result of an organization begun in 1885, baseball's newest league came into existence. Called the Players' League, and made up of mostly of available stars of the time, the new league was born out of the frustration of limited salaries, unjust fines, and the reserve clause. But a lack of administrative leadership and heavy gate competition ended their efforts after a year. It was their existence, as well as their demise, which consequently brought an end to the American Association after the 1891 season. Upset over the reassignment of Players' League personnel, the league withdrew from the National Agreement. This time, however, its 25 cent admission price could not support the finances which were needed for another war with the National League. Of the eight teams in the league, four went by the way of history and the other four joined the National League to bring their circuit to 12 clubs-an ill-devised structure which lasted through the 1899 season when four teams were dropped. It was a move which two years later led to the birth of the strongest rival the National League had ever known.

1876-1900 STARS

(Only those stars who did not appear in a single major league game after 1900, the 1876-1900 stars who played after 1900 are included in the 1901-1919 list)

BATTERS

USE NAME - GIVEN NAMES (NICKNAMES) / TEAM BY YEAR	BIRTH DATE	BIRTH PLACE	DEATH DATE	B	T	HGT	WGT	G	AB	R	H	2B	3B	HR	RBI	BB	BA	SA
Anson, Cap-Adrian Constantine (Pop)-1B 76-97, M79-97ChiN M98NYN	4-17-52	Marshalltown, Iowa	4-14-22	R	R	6'1	227	2268	9067	1728	3022	528	126	97	1879	952	.333	.451
Brown, Tom-Thomas Tarlton-OF 82BalAA 83-84 ColAA 85-86PitAA 87PittN 87IndN 88-89BosN 90BosP 91 BosAA 92-94LouN 95StlN 95-98, M97-98WasN	9-21-60	Liverpool, England	10-27-27	L	R	5'10	168	1783	7338	1524	1952	238	137	65		749	.266	.362
Browning, Pete-Louis Rogers (The Gladiator)-OF 82-89LouAA 90CleP 91PitN 91CinN 92LouN 92CinN 93 LouN 94StlN 94BrnN	6-17-61	Louisville, Ky.	9-10-05	R	R	6'	180	1180	4795	950	1664	292	89	46		465	.347	.474
Burns, Oyster-Thomas P.-OF 84WilU 84-88BalAA 88-89BknAA 9095BKn	9-6-64	Philadelphia, Pa.	11-11-28	R	R	5'8	183	1178	4615	876	1388	228	131	65	834	464	.301	.464
Comiskey, Charlie-Charles Albert (Commy, The Old Roman)-1B 82-89, M83, 85-89StLAA	8-15-59	Chicago, Ill.	10-26-31	R	R	6'	180	1385	5801	981	1543	199	69	29	883	197	.266	.339
Connor, Roger-Roger-1B 80-82TroyN 83-89, 91,93-94NYN 90NYP 92PhiN 94-97,M96StLN	7-1-57	Waterbury, Conn.	1-4-31	L	L	6'3	220	1987	7732	1607	2460	429	227	137	1323	1002	.318	.486
Dalrymple, Abner-Abner Frank-OF 78MilN 79-86ChiN 87-88PittN 91C-MAA 93-94LouN	9-9-57	Warren, Ill.	1-25-39	L	R	5'10	175	941	4131	812	1195	216	81	43	407	204	.289	.412
Denny, Jerry-Jeremiah, Dennis-3B 81-85ProvN 86StLN 87-89IndN 90-91NYN 91CleN 91PhiN	3-16-59	New York, N.Y.	8-16-27	R	R	5'11	180	1234	4925	709	1284	238	74	74	667	173	.261	.384
Dunlap, Fred-Frederick C. (Sure Shot)-2B 80-83CleN 84StLU 85-86StLN 86-87DetN 88-90, M89DetN 91WasAA	5-21-59	Philadelphia, Pa.	12-1-02	R	R	5'8	165	955	3939	750	1176	224	53	41		283	.299	.414
Ewing, Buck-William-C, 1B, OF 80-82 TroyN 83-39NYN 90,M90NYP 91-92NYN 93-94CinN 95-97, M95-99CinN MOONYN	10-17-59	Hoagland, Ohio	10-20-06	R	R	5'10	188	1281	5318	1118	1633	237	179	71	884	392	.307	.459
Glasscock, Jack-John Wesley (Pebbly Jack)-SS 79-84 CleN 85-89, M89ClbN 90-91NYN 92-93StLN 93-94PitN 95 LouN 95WasN	7-22-59	Wheeling, W.Va.	2-24-47	R	R	5'8	160	1721	6955	1150	2038	309	95	27	847	439	.293	.376
Gore, George-George F.-OF 79-86ChiN 87-89NYN 90NYP 91-92NYN 92StLN	5-3-57	Saccarappa, Me.	9-16-33	L	R	5'11	1955	1301	5324	1324	1611	257	95	46	617	717	.303	.412
Griffin, Mike-Michael Joseph-OF 87-89BalAA 90PhiP 91-98BknN	3-20-65	Utica, N.Y.	4-10-08	L	R	5'7	160	1508	5908	1401	1775	316	106	41	719	809	.300	.411
Hines, Paul-Paul A.-OF 76-77ChiN 78-85ProvN 86-87WasN 88-89IndN 90PitN 90BknN 91WasAA	3-1-52	Washington, D.C.	7-10-35	R	R	5'9	173	1471	6207	1073	1864	355	78	56	751	366	.300	.431
Holliday, Bug-James Wear-OF 89CinAA 90-98CinN	2-8-67	St. Louis, Mo.	2-15-10	R	R	5'7	165	920	3604	733	1152	155	70	65	617	359	.320	.456
Jones (Rippy), Charley (Benjamin Wesley) Charles Wesley (Baby)-OF 76-77CinN 77CinN 77-78CinN 81-82SL 83-87CinAA 87NYAA 88KCAA	4-30-50	Alamance Co., N.C.	Deceased	R	R	5'11	202	880	3665	720	1103	171	101	55	582	237	.301	.448
Kelly, King-Michael Joseph-OF, C 78-79CinN 80-86ChiN 87-89 BosN 90, M90BosP 91, M91C-MAA 91BosAA 91BosN 93NYN	12-31-57	Troy, N.Y.	11-8-94	R	R	5'10	170	1443	5901	1367	1813	351	105	69	951	549	.307	.437
Lange, Bill-William Alexander (Little Eva)-OF 93-99ChiN	6-6-71	San Francisco, Cal.	7-23-50	R	R	6'2	190	808	3194	692	1072	142	83	39	577	350	.336	.469
Larkin, Ted-Henry E.-1B, OF 84-89PhiAA 90CleP 91 PhiAA 92-93WasN	1-2-60	Reading, Pa.	1-31-42	R	R	5'9	160	1182	4691	933	1450	263	111	53	836	484	.309	.446
Lyons, Denny-Dennis Patrick Aloysius-3B 85ProvN 86-90PhiAA 91StLAA 92NYN 92-94PitN 95StlN 96-97StLN	3-12-66	Cincinnati, Ohio	1-2-29	R	R	5'10	185	1129	4236	932	1368	237	73	62	755	621	.323	.457
McCarthy, Tommy-Thomas Francis Michael-OF 84BosU 85BosN 86-87PhiN 88-91StLAA 92-95BosN 96 BknN	7-24-64	Boston, Mass.	8-5-22	R	R	5'7	170	1269	5104	1062	1499	194	58	44	757	537	.294	.380
McKean, Ed-Edward John (Mac)-SS 87-88CleAA 89-98CleN 99StLN	6-6-64	Grafton, Ohio	8-16-19	R	R	5'9	160	1655	6842	1213	2079	270	153	66	1124	635	.304	.417
McPhee, Biddy-John Alexander 11-1-59 CinAA 90-99, M01-00	11-1-59	Massena, N.Y.	1-3-42	R	R	5'8	152	2127	8293	1674	2287	309	170	52	1067	981	.276	.373
Nash, Billy-William Mitchell-3B 84 RicAA 85-89BosN 90BosP 91-95BosN 96-98, M96PhiN	6-24-65	Richmond, Va.	11-15-29	R	R	5'8	167	1543	5778	1077	1603	264	91	61	977	804	.277	.386
O'Neill, Tip-James Edward OF 83NYN 84-89StLAA 90ChiP 91StLAA 92CinN	5-25-58	Woodstock, Canada	12-31-15	R	R	6'1	187	1048	4254	871	1389	212	98	52	757	421	.327	.459
Orr, Dave-David L.-1B 83NYN 83-87, M87NYAA 88 BknAA 89ColAA 90BknP	9-29-59	New York, N.Y.	6-3-15	R	R	5'6	160	788	3271	536	1141	197	110	37	627	98	.349	.510
Pfeffer, Fred-Nataniel Frederick (Dandelion)-2B 82 TroyN 83-89ChiN 90ChiP 91 CinN 92-95, M92LouN 96N NYN	3-17-60	Louisville, Ky.	4-10-32	R	R	5'10	168	1667	6507	1090	1677	233	117	95	1019	527	.258	.373
Reilly, Long John-John Good-1B 80CinN 83-89CinAA 90-91CinN	10-5-58	Cincinnati, Ohio	5-31-37	R	R	6'3	178	1135	4658	898	1341	215	138	69	740	156	.288	.438
Richardson, Hardy-Abram Harding (Old True Blue)-2B, OF, 3B 79-85BufN 86-88DetN 89BosN 90BosP 91 BosAA 92WasN 92NYN	1-21-55	Clarksboro, N.J.	1-4-31	R	R	5'9	170	1316	5593	1112	1676	305	124	73	816	377	.300	.438
Rowe, Jack-John Charles-SS, C, OF 79-85BufN 86-88DetN 89PitN 90 90BufP	12-8-56	Hamburg, Pa.	4-26-11	L	R	5'8	170	1034	4366	765	1249	201	89	28	645	224	.286	.392
Start, Joe-Joseph (Old Reliable)-1B 76NYN 77BknN 78ChiN 79-85ProvN 86WasN	10-14-42	New York, N.Y.	3-27-27	L	L	5'9	165	786	3402	590	1020	108	53	7	357	150	.300	.369
Stenzel (Stelzle), Jake-Jacob Charles-OF 90CinN 92-96PitN 97-98BalN 98-99StLN 99CinN 99StlN	6-24-67	Cincinnati, Ohio	1-6-19	R	R	5'10	168	762	2992	662	1028	189	72	33	533	299	.344	.448
Stovey (Stow), Harry-Harry Duffield-OF, 1B 80-82WorN 83PhiAA 90BosP 91-92BknAA 92-93BalN 93BknN	12-20-56	Philadelphia, Pa.	9-20-37	R	R	5'11	180	1482	6072	1488	1866	348	185	121	907	661	.307	.485
Sutton, Ezra-Ezra Ballou-3B, SS 76PhiN 77-88BknN	9-17-50	Palmyra, N.Y.	6-20-07	R	R	5'8	153	1019	4226	734	1215	187	71	21	518	164	.288	.380
Tebeau, Patsy-Oliver Wendell-1B, 3B 87ChiN 90, M90CleP 91-98, M91-98CleN 99-00, M99-00StlN	12-5-64	St. Louis, Mo.	5-15-18	R	R	5'8	163	1159	4555	667	1288	202	57	27	736	319	.283	.370
Tiernan, Mike-Michael Joseph (Silent Mike)-OF 87-99NYN	1-21-67	Trenton, N.J.	11-9-18	L	L	5'11	165	1475	5878	1312	1843	248	159	106	849	747	.311	.464
Tucker, Tommy-Thomas Joseph-1B 87-89BalAA 90-97BosN 97WasN 98BknN 98StLN 93-94N	10-28-63	Holyoke, Mass.	10-22-35	B	R	5'11	165	1686	6461	1083	1888	238	86	42	932	479	.292	.375
Ward, Monte-John Montgomery-SS, 2B, P, C (See Pitchers below)78-82ProvN 83-89, M89 90, M90BknP 91-92BknN 93-94, M93-94NYN	3-3-60	Bellefonte, Pa.	3-4-25	Bats Both 88				1811	7568	1403	2122	232	96	25	867	420	.280	.346
White, Deacon-James Laurie-3B, C, 1B, OF 76ChiN 77BosN 78ChiN 79BufN 81-85BufN-P 86-88DetN 89PitN 90BufN	12-7-47	Caton, N.Y.	7-7-39	L	R	5'11	175	1289	5294	840	1607	205	73	18	756	292	.304	.380
Williamson, Ned-Edward Nagle-3B, SS 78IndN 79-89ChiN 90ChiP	10-24-55	Philadelphia, Pa.	3-3-94	R	R	5'11	210	1192	4523	802	1153	230	83	83	667	506	.255	.384
Wolf, Chicken-William Van Winkle-OF 78IndN 79-89LouN 90ChiP	5-12-62	Louisville, Ky.	5-16-03	R	R	5'9	190	1201	4975	779	1451	214	109	17	625	229	.292	.389
Wright, George-George-SS 76-78BosN 79, M79ProvN 80-81 BosN 82ProvN	1-28-47	Yonkers, N.Y.	8-21-37	R	R	5'9	150	329	1495	264	384	53	20	2	132	43	.257	.323

PITCHERS

All pitchers with at least 150 wins

USE NAMES - GIVEN NAMES (NICKNAMES) / TEAM BY YEAR	BIRTH DATE	BIRTHPLACE	DEATH DATE	B	T	HGT	WGT	W	L	Pct.	G	GS	CG	IP	H	BB	SO	ShO	ERA	ERA NA*
Baldwin, Mark-Marcus Elmore 87-88ChiN 89ColAA 90-93PitN 93NYN	10-29-63	Pittsburgh, Pa.	11-10-29	R	R	6'	190	156	165	.486	347	328	296	2812	2699	1307	1354	14	3.36	none
Bond, Tommy-Thomas Henry 76HarN 77-81BosN 82, M82WorN 84BosU 84IndAA	4-2-56	Granard, Ireland	1-24-41	R	R	5'7	160	192	115	.625	322	314	294	2779	2857	178	860	36	2.15	84
Buffinton, Charlie-Charles G. 82-86BosN 87-89PhiN 90,M90PhiP 91BosAA 92BalN 93HO	6-14-61	Fall River, Mass.	9-23-07	R	R	6'1	180	230	151	.604	414	396	351	3403	3344	856	1700	27	2.96	none
Caruthers, Bob-Robert Lee (Parisian Bob) 84-85StLAA 88-89BknAA 90-91BknN 92STL 93ChiN (sore arm-OF-did not pitch)	1-5-64	Memphis, Tenn.	8-5-11	R	R	5'7	138	217	101	.682	341	310	298	2829	2678	597	900	24	3.16	84-86
Chamberlin, Icebox-Elton P. 86-88LouAA 88-90StLAA 90ColAA 91PhiAA 92-94CinN 96CleN	11-5-67	Buffalo, N.Y.	9-22-29	R	R	5'9	168	157	123	.561	321	301	264	2522	2446	1065	1133	15	3.56	86-87,9*
Clarkson, John-John Gibson 82WorN 84-87ChiN 88-92BosN 92-94CleN	7-1-61	Cambridge, Mass.	2-4-09	R	R	5'10	155	327	176	.650	531	518	485	4536	4295	1191	1978	37	2.84	84
Corcoran, Larry-Lawrence J. 80-85 ChiN 85-86NYN 86WasN 87IndN	8-10-59	Brooklyn, N.Y.	10-14-91	R	R			173	90	.658	277	268	256	2393	2147	496	1103	23	2.27	83-84
Dwyer, Frank-John Francis 88-89ChiN 90ChiP 91C-MAA 92StLN 92-99CinN MO2DetN	3-25-68	Lee, Mass.	2-4-43	R	R	5'9	145	173	141	.551	365	318	270	2809	3301	764	563	12	3.85	none
Galvin, Pud-James Francis (Gentle Jeems, The Little Steam Engine) 79-85, M85BufN 85-86PiaN 87-89PitN 90PitP 91-92PitN 92StLM	12-25-55	St. Louis, Mo.	3-7-02	R	R	5'8	190	361	309	.539	697	682	639	5941	6352	744	1799	56	2.94	81-83
Hecker, Guy-Guy Jackson 82-89LouAA 90, M90PitN	4-3-56	Youngsville, Pa.	12-4-38	R	R	6'	190	174	147	.542	334	320	310	2905	2905	489	1099	15	4.46	92-97
Hutchinson, Bill-William Forrest (Wild Bill) 89-95ChiN 97StLN	12-17-59	New Haven, Conn.	3-19-26	R	R	5'9	175	182	158	.535	373	345	319	3066	3110	1128	1231	21	3.59	none
Keefe, Tim-Timothy John (Sir Timothy) 80-82TroyN 83-84NYAA 85-89NYN 90NYP 91NYN 91-93PhiN	1-1-57	Cambridge, Mass.	4-23-33	R	R	5'10	185	341	224	.604	600	594	552	5051	4442	1224	2542	39	2.65	81-84
Killen, Frank-Frank Bissell 91C-MAA 92WasN 93-98PitN 98-99WasN 99BosN 00ChiN	11-30-70	Pittsburgh, Pa.	12-3-39	L	L	6'1	200	164	111	.596	321	300	253	2511	2730	822	725	13	3.79	none
King (Koenig), Silver-Charles Frederick 86KCN 87-89StLAA 90ChiP 91PitN 92-93NYN 93CinN 94-95VR 96-97WasN	1-11-68	St. Louis, Mo.	5-19-38	R	R	5'10	180	206	152	.575	398	371	329	3190	3105	970	1229	20	3.15	none
Mathews, Bobby-Robert T. 76NYN 77CinN 79,81ProvN 81-82 BosN 83-87PhiAA	11-21-51	Baltimore, Md.	4-17-98	R	R	5'5	145	167	136	.551	323	315	289	2734	3008	336	1199	9	2.95	83-87
McCormick, Jim-James 78IndN 79-84, M79-80CleN 84CinU 85ProvN 85-86ChiN 87PitN	11-3-56	Glasgow, Scotland.	3-10-18	R	R	5'10	226	264	214	.552	492	485	466	4275	4092	749	1704	33	2.49	82-84U
McMahon, Sadie-John Joseph 89-90PhiAA 90B-BAA 91BalAA 92-96BalN 97BknN	9-19-67	Wilmington, Del.	2-20-54	R	R	5'9	185	177	124	.588	321	305	279	2634	2726	945	967	14	3.56	90
Meekin, Jouett-George Jouett 91LouAA 92-93WasN 94-99NYN 99BosN 00PitN	2-21-67	New Albany, Ind.	12-14-44	R	R	6'1	180	156	138	.531	324	308	253	2603	2831	1058	900	9	4.07	none
Morris, Ed-Edward (Cannonball) 84ColAA 85-88PitAA 87-89PitN 90PitP	9-29-62	Brooklyn, N.Y.	4-12-37	B	L	5'7	156	172	125	.579	311	307	297	2678	2468	498	1217	29	3.49	84-86
Mullane, Tony-Anthony John (Count, The Apollo of the Box) 81DetN 82LouAA 83StLAA 85DE 86-89CinN 90-93CinN 93-94BalN 94CleN	1-20-59	Cork, Ireland	4-25-44	B	R	5'10	165	286	213	.573	557	505	469	4545	4203	1409	1817	31	3.46	82-84,86
				Bats Left-82 (Occasionally pitched left-handed)																
Radbourn, Hoss-Charles Gardner 80BufN 81-85ProvN 86-89BosN 90BosP 91CinN	12-11-54	Rochester, N.Y.	2-5-97	R	R	5'9	168	308	191	.617	528	503	489	4535	4335	875	1830	34	2.81	81-83
Stivetts, Jack-John Elmer (Happy Jack) 89-91StLAA 92-98BosN 99ChiN	3-31-68	Ashland, Pa.	4-18-30	R	R	6'2	185	205	128	.616	386	332	278	2887	2905	1155	1223	14	3.77	90
Terry, Adonis-William H. 84-89BknAA 90-91BknN 92BalN 92-94PitN 94-97ChiN	8-7-64	Westfield, Mass.	2-24-15	R	R	5'9	170	205	197	.510	441	407	368	3522	3519	1301	1555	18	3.76	84-87
Ward, Monte-John Montgomery (See Batters above) 78-82ProvN 83-84NYN	3-3-60	Bellefonte, Pa.	3-4-25	L	R	5'9	165	158	102	.608	291	261	244	2462	2317	253	920	24	2.03	81-84
Welch, Mickey-Michael Francis (Smiling Mickey) 80-82TroyN 83-92NYN	7-4-59	Brooklyn, N.Y.	7-30-41	R	R	5'8	160	309	209	.597	565	549	525	4791	4587	1297	1850	41	2.68	81-84
White, Will-William Henry (Whoop-La) 77BosN 78-86CinN 82-86, M84CinAA	10-11-54	Caton, N.Y.	8-31-11	R	R	5'9	175	227	167	.576	403	401	394	3542	3440	496	1041	36	2.06	82-85
Whitney, Jim-James Evans (Long Jim, Grasshopper Jim) 81-85BosN 86KCN 87-88WasN 89IndN 90PhiAA 91DD	11-10-57	Conklin, N.Y.	5-21-91	L	R	6'2	175	191	204	0.484	413	396	377	3496	3567	411	1571	26	3.06	none

10

*Years for which E.R.A. is not available, not included in lifetime E.R.A.

1901-1919
When the Ball Was Dead
and the Bases Alive with the Scurrying of Feet

In an era when leg power dominated and the same lifeless baseball was kept in play throughout the game, the celebrated home run was not the master weapon of the diamond. A study of the final 1901 statistics more than substantiates this fact as the St. Louis Cardinals, with a major league-leading 39 home runs, finished fourth, as compared with the Chicago White Sox, who took the American League crown behind the speed and cunning which accounted for 280 stolen bases, tops in both circuits.

Yet more than the runner, the game belonged to the pitcher. The parks were large and lacked the enclosures which could invite the long ball. The "spitter", which led to an entire array of trick pitches, was legal and a deadly weapon if one could master the art. There were a few, however, whose pitching mastery enabled them to accomplish their tasks on sheer talent alone, sans the spit ball or the trickery other men may have been forced to resort to using. Those who led the list of the seemingly immortals included Cy Young, Walter Johnson, Christy Mathewson, and Grover Cleveland "Pete Alexander, a phenomenal golden-armed quartet which accounted for over 1600 victories in their careers.

In order to combat the mound opposition and survive the disadvantages of their trade, batters were forced to use an entirely different set of tactics than they might employ if playing in the latter part of the twentieth century. Instead of attacking the pitch, the hitter played it defensively and hit, when he could, where the ball was pitched. The players used heavy bats, choking-up and punching or hitting the ball down rather than going for the scalding line-drive shots so frequent in later eras. The result of this style of play made speed a vital factor, and bunting and stealing to squeeze out a run became the prevailing strategy of the times.

Mostly, it was hit and run and go for average, and the man who most typified such execution was Ty Cobb, Detroit's frantic base running demon, who stole 754 bases in the years 1905-1919 while hitting for a .373 average and leading the American League in batting 12 times. Cobb, who used aggressiveness and spikes to accomplish much of his record, was so brilliant a performer that his contemporaries were almost shadowed into obscurity. The point could not be any stronger than as in the case of Shoeless Joe Jackson, who hit a .408 in 1911 and .395 in 1912-only to find himself a frustrated bridesmaid to the fleet-footed Cobb. The

National League's counterpart to Cobb was Honus Wagner who proved nearly as talented as a hitter and far more gracious as a human being. In his years with Pittsburgh, which ran from 1900-1917, Wagner nailed down eight batting titles and almost 700 stolen bases. Wagner also had the satisfaction when he met Cobb on the field for the first and only time during the 1909 World Series to outdo his rival in batting and stolen bases.

More than the individuals, the most important historical event of the age was the birth of the American League. While the older National League circuit had spilled into the twentieth century and had its roots early as 1876, the American League did not strike up its colors until 1901. Mostly because of the leadership and imagination of its chief founder, Ban Johnson, the new league was able to find an equal place in the American limelight. Although peace between the two leagues did not come until 1903-after many battles had been fought and emotions worn thin-baseball found itself with the first true franchise stabilization in history. Except for the American League's switching of Milwaukee to St. Louis in 1902 and Baltimore to New York in 1903, baseball had come upon a suitable geographical mix that would survive for fifty years, or at least as long as the limited scope of railroad travel would permit. Yet before the era could wind itself down, two other events were to take place-both disarming in their emergence. The first occurred in 1914 when the Federal League-a minor circuit-declared itself "major", mostly by using the same tactics of player raiding as Johnson had done in 1901. But whereas the public could withstand two leagues, it could not afford the luxury of all three. The third league lasted through the season of 1915 and left in its wake a string of new ballparks-the most notable being Wrigley Field. To get rid of the Federal League cost a reported $300,000, a figure which was cheap when compared to the holocaust which was to dawn in 1919.

It was in that year when key players on the Chicago White Sox threw away their good names and their careers by throwing the World Series to the underdog Cincinnati Reds. The events surrounding the scandal did not come to light until 1920, and was so staggering a revelation that it looked as though professional baseball would have to close its doors in shame. There was no doubt that it would take a miracle or two to save the game from premature extinction.

1901 A. L.--A Name by Any Other Was Not the Same

The celebration did not equal the event. The bands and fanfare were noticeably absent, and only in the minds of those who fostered the dream was there any clamor at all. What had occurred, for the first time since the collapse of the American Association in 1891, was the unveiling of a second major league circuit. The bosses of the National League welcomed their rivals, the American League, with disdain and fear—elements necessary to give an underdog the impetus to survive.

The new league was first conceived and nurtured in the minds of League President Ban Johnson and White Sox owner Charlie Comiskey. Becoming head of the minor Western League in 1893, Johnson turned the league into the strongest of the minors within two years; this he accomplished by arranging for solid ownership of each of his franchises and by strongly backing his umpires in all disputes, thus assuring the fans that orderly games would be played. By 1896, the wheels were turning in Johnson's head; if the National League should decide to drop any of its 12 franchises, he would be ready to place a team in that territory. As fans continued to come to the firmly controlled games, each year in the late 1890's became a financial success for this regional Midwestern league.

Johnson upgraded his league even more in the century-turning year of 1900. The National League cut back that year to eight franchises, and Johnson moved a team into the abandoned Cleveland area. In addition, he won reluctant consent from the established Cubs; in return, Johnson agreed to abide by the National Agreement which defined his circuit as a minor league. Finally, Johnson conceptually broadened the geographical boundaries of the loop by changing the name from the Western League to the American League. Nevertheless, the league remained a minor circuit in 1900, with all its franchises located in the Midwest and with no pretext of hiring the best baseball talent in the United States.

In 1901, Johnson made his move; with full consent of the team owners, he withdrew from the National Agreement and announced plans to operate independently as a second major league. Expansion into the East erased the regional character of the league; Boston, Philadelphia, Baltimore, and Washington were chosen as sites, the first two being long-time citadels of National League strength. To obtain players, the American League raided the senior loop's rosters for stars as well as everyday players. Large salaries were offered by those financially sound owners Johnson had arranged for his loop. National League contracts were honored, but the new league did not recognize the reserve clause. An incipient players' association found that the new league strengthened its bargaining position; one of its major objectives was to prevent the trading of players to cities to which they did not wish to report—a right which became lost when both leagues came to peaceful terms in 1903.

When the American League's first season opened, each team found itself infused with talent from the older league. Perhaps the brightest star that first year was Nap Lajoie, second baseman for the Philadelphia Athletics, who copped the first American League batting title after jumping over from the rival Phillies. In addition to hitting a prodigious .422, Lajoie also drove in 125 runs and hit 14 home runs to capture the Triple Crown. Connie Mack was on hand to manage his first Athletics' squad and previewed one of his most prominent collegiate finds in 25-year-old Eddie Plank, a 17-game winner fresh from Gettysburg College. Jimmy Collins jumped the Boston National League team to manage and star for the new American League Boston entry and gloated on the arm of his leading pitcher, Cy Young, who came from St. Louis. Young, an 11-year National League veteran, turned in 33 victories to pace the junior circuit. John McGraw played third base while piloting the Baltimore Orioles, and his charges numbered veteran catcher Wilbert Robinson, young catcher Roger Bresnahan, and star hurler Joe McGinnity, a 28-game winner in the older loop in 1900. The new Chicago club got double duty out of Clark Griffith, who managed the club while leading the pitching staff with 24 victories. All of these men, with Johnson and Comiskey, were to eventually earn baseball's accolades by being enshrined in the Baseball Hall of Fame.

The White Sox took the first American League title by four games over a Boston club which suffered a late season pitching collapse. Prophetically, the Philadelphia A's played the best ball in the league during the final two months, giving evidence of better things to come. More important, the new clubs in Boston and Chicago outdrew the established National League teams. Despite litigation pending in the courts and a declared state of war with the old league, the American League was off and running. In fact, there was evidence that the National League would have to divide the spotlight for some time to come.

1901 AMERICAN LEAGUE

NAME	G by Pos	B	AGE	G	AB	R	H	2B	3B	HR	RBI	BB	SO	SB	BA	SA
CHICAGO	**1st 83-53 .610**				**CLARK GRIFFITH**											
TOTALS			30	137	4725	819	1303	173	89	32	656	475		280	.276	.370
Frank Isbell	1B137, 2B2, 3B1, SS1, P1	L	25	137	556	93	143	15	8	3	70	36		52	.257	.329
Sam Mertes	2B132, OF5	R	28	137	545	94	151	16	17	5	98	52		46	.277	.396
Frank Shugart	SS107	B	34	107	415	62	104	9	12	2	47	28		12	.251	.345
Fred Hartman	3B119	R	33	120	473	77	146	23	13	3	89	25		31	.309	.431
Fielder Jones	OF133	L	29	133	521	120	162	16	3	2	65	84		38	.311	.365
Dummy Hoy	OF132	L	39	131	536	113	157	23	11	2	60	86		30	.293	.400
Herm McFarland	OF132	L	31	132	473	83	130	21	9	4	59	75		33	.275	.383
Billy Sullivan	C97, 3B1	R	26	98	367	54	90	15	6	4	56	10		12	.245	.351
Joe Sugden	C42, 1B5	B	30	48	159	22	45	7	1	0	19	13		5	.283	.333
Nixey Callahan (BA)	P27, 3B6, 2B2	R	27	45	118	15	39	7	3	1	19	10		10	.331	.466
2 Jimmy Burke	SS31, 3B11	R	26	42	148	20	39	5	0	0	21	12		11	.264	.297
Clark Griffith	P35	R	31	35	89	21	27	3	1	2	14	23		0	.303	.427
2 Pop Foster	OF9	R	23	12	35	4	10	2	2	1	6	4		0	.286	.543
Dave Brain	2B5	R	24	5	20	2	7	1	0	0	5	1		0	.350	.400
BOSTON	**2nd 79-57 .581 4**				**JIMMY COLLINS**											
TOTALS			28	138	4866	759	1353	183	104	37	632	331		157	.278	.381
Buck Freeman	1B128, 2B1, OF1	L	29	138	489	84	169	22	15	12	114	44		14	.346	.520
Hobe Ferris	2B138, SS1	R	23	138	523	68	131	16	15	3	63	23		13	.250	.350
Freddy Parent	SS138	R	25	138	517	87	158	23	9	4	59	41		16	.306	.408
Jimmy Collins	SB138	R	31	138	563	109	185	42	16	6	94	34		18	.329	.492
Charlie Hemphill	OF136	L	25	136	545	71	142	10	10	3	62	39		11	.261	.332
Chick Stahl	OF131	L	28	131	512	106	159	22	16	6	72	54		29	.311	.439
Tommy Dowd	OF137, 1B2, 3B1	R	32	138	594	104	159	18	7	3	52	38		33	.268	.337
Ossee Schreckengost	C72, 1B4	R	26	86	280	37	85	13	5	0	38	19		6	.304	.386
Lou Criger	C68, 1B4	R	29	76	268	26	62	6	3	0	24	11		7	.231	.276
Charlie Jones	OF10	R	25	10	41	6	6	2	0	0	6	1		2	.146	.195
Larry McLean	1B5	R	19	9	19	4	4	1	0	0	2	0		1	.211	.263
Harry Gleason	3B1	R	26	1	1	1	0	0	0	0	0	0		1	1.000	1.000
Jack Slattery	C1	R	24	1	3	0	1	0	0	0	1	1		0	.333	.333
DETROIT	**3rd 74-61 .548 8.5**				**GEORGE STALLINGS**											
TOTALS			28	136	4676	742	1303	180	80	29	611	380		204	.279	.370
Pop Dillon	1B74	L	27	74	281	40	81	14	6	1	42	15		14	.288	.391
Kid Gleason	2B135	B	34	135	547	82	150	16	12	3	75	41		32	.274	.364
Kid Elberfeld	SS121	R	26	122	436	78	135	21	11	3	76	57		24	.310	.428
Doc Casey	3B127	R	30	128	540	105	153	16	9	2	46	32		34	.283	.357
Ducky Holmes	OF131	L	32	131	537	90	158	28	10	4	62	37		35	.294	.406
Jimmy Barrett	OF135	L	26	135	542	110	159	16	9	3	65	76		26	.293	.378
Doc Nance	OF132	R	24	132	461	72	129	24	5	2	66	51		9	.280	.372
Fritz Buelow	C69	R	25	70	231	28	52	5	5	3	29	11		2	.225	.316
S. McAllister	C35, 1B28, 0F11, 3B10, SS3	B	26	90	306	45	92	9	4	3	57	15		17	.301	.386
Al Shaw	C42, 1B9, 3B2, SS1	R	26	55	171	20	46	7	0	1	23	13		2	.269	.327
Davey Crockett	1B27	L	25	28	102	10	29	2	2	0	14	6		1	.284	.343
1 Harry Lochhead	SS1	R	25	1	4	2	1	0	0	0	0	0		0	.500	.500

NAME	T	AGE	W	L	PCT	SV	G	GS	CG	IP	H	BB	SO	SHO	ERA
		27	83	53	.610	3	137	137	110	1218	1250	312	394	11	2.98
Clark Griffith	R	31	24	7	.774	1	35	30	26	267	275	50	67	5	2.66
Roy Patterson	R	24	20	16	.556	0	41	35	30	312	345	62	127	4	3.88
Nixey Callahan (BA)	R	27	15	7	.682	0	27	22	20	215	195	50	70	1	2.43
Jack Katoll	R	29	13	12	.520	0	27	25	19	208	231	53	59	1	2.81
John Skopec	L	21	6	3	.667	0	9	9	6	68	62	45	24	0	3.18
2 Wiley Piatt	L	26	2	2	.500	1	7	6	4	52	42	14	19	1	2.77
1 Zaza Harvey	L	22	3	6	.333	1	16	9	5	92	91	34	27	0	3.62
Frank Dupee	R	24	0	0	.000	0	1	1	0	0	3	0	0	0	∞
John McAleese	R	23	0	0	.000	0	1	1	0	3	7	1	1	0	9.00
Frank Isbell	R	25	0	0	.000	0	1	1	0	1	2	0	0	0	9.00
		27	79	57	.581	1	138	138	123	1217	1178	294	396	7	3.04
Cy Young	R	34	33	10	.767	0	43	41	38	371	324	37	158	5	1.63
George Winter	R	23	16	10	.615	0	28	28	26	241	234	66	63	1	2.80
Ted Lewis	R	28	16	16	.500	1	39	34	31	316	299	91	103	1	3.53
Fred Mitchell	R	23	6	9	.400	0	17	13	10	109	115	51	34	0	3.80
Nig Cuppy	R	31	4	6	.400	0	13	11	9	93	111	14	22	0	4.16
Win Kellum	L	25	2	3	.400	0	6	6	5	48	61	7	8	0	6.38
Garry Prentiss	R	25	1	1	1.000	0	2	1	1	10	7	6	0	0	1.80
Jake Volz	R	23	1	1	.500	0	1	1	1	7	6	9	5	0	9.00
Deacon Morrissey	R	38	0	1	.000	0	1	0	0	4	5	2	1	0	2.25
1 Frank Foreman	R	38	0	1	.000	0	1	1	1	8	8	2	1	0	9.00
Ben Beville	R	23	0	2	.000	0	2	2	1	9	8	9	1	0	4.00
		25	74*	61	.548	3	136	136	118	1189	1328	313	307	8	3.30
Roscoe Miller	R	24	23	13	.639	1	38	36	35	332	339	98	79	3	2.95
Ed Siever	L	26	18	11	.620	0	38	33	30	289	334	65	85	2	3.24
Joe Yaeger	R	25	12	12	.500	1	26	25	22	200	209	46	38	2	2.61
Jack Cronin	R	27	12	16	.429	1	30	28	21	220	261	42	62	1	3.89
Emil Frisk	R	26	5	4	.556	0	11	7	6	75	94	26	22	0	4.32
Ed High	L	27	2	1	.667	0	4	1	1	18	21	6	4	0	3.50
Frank Owen	R	21	1	4	.200	0	8	5	3	56	70	30	17	0	4.34

* 1 win by forfeit

12

PHILADELPHIA 4th 74-62 .544 9 CONNIE MACK

NAME	G by Pos	B	AGE	G	AB	R	H	2B	3B	HR	RBI	BB	SO	SB	BA	SA
TOTALS			27	137	4882	805	1409	239	87	35	665	301		173	.289	.395
Harry Davis	1B117	R	27	137	496	92	152	28	10	8	76	23		21	.306	.452
Nap Lajoie	2B119, SS12	R	26	131	543	145	229	48	13	14	125	24		27	.422	.635
2 Joe Dolan	SS61, 3B35, 2B1, OF1		28	98	338	50	73	21	2	1	38	26		3	.216	.299
Lave Cross	3B100	R	35	100	420	82	139	31	11	2	73	19		21	.332	.471
Socks Seybold	OF100, 1B14	R	30	114	457	74	152	25	12	8	90	40		14	.334	.492
Dave Fultz	OF106, 2B18, SS9	R	26	132	651	95	164	17	9	0	52	32		36	.292	.355
Matty McIntyre	OF82	L	21	82	308	38	85	12	4	0	46	30		11	.276	.341
Mike Powers	C111, 1B3	R	30	116	431	53	108	26	5	1	47	18		10	.251	.341
Jack Hayden	OF50	L	20	51	211	35	56	6	4	0	17	18		4	.265	.332
1 Phil Geier	OF50, SS2, 3B1	R	25	50	211	42	49	5	2	0	23	24		7	.232	.275
2 Bones Ely	SS45	R	28	45	171	11	37	6	2	0	16	3		6	.216	.275
2 Farmer Steelman	C14, OF12	R	26	27	88	5	23	2	0	0	7	10		4	.261	.275
Harry Smith (RJ)	C9, OF1	R	26	11	34	3	11	1	0	0	3	2		1	.324	.353
2 Harry Lochhead	SS9	R	25	9	34	3	3	0	0	0	2	3		0	.088	.088
Morgan Murphy	C8, 1B1	R	34	9	28	5	6	1	0	0	6	0		1	.214	.250
Fred Ketchum	OF5	L	25	5	22	5	5	0	0	0	2	0		0	.227	.227
2 Tom Leahy	OF2, SS1, C1	R	32	5	15	1	5	1	0	0	1	1		0	.333	.400
Bob Lindemann	OF3	B	20	3	9	0	1	0	0	0	0	0		0	.111	.111
Charlie Carr	1B2	R	24	2	8	0	1	0	0	0	0	0		0	.125	.125
Billy Lauder	3B2	R	27	2	8	1	1	0	0	0	0	0		0	.125	.125
Bob McKinney	2B1, 3B1	L	25	2	8	1	1	0	0	0	0	0		0	.000	.000

NAME	T	AGE	W	L	PCT	SV	G	GS	CG	IP	H	BB	SO	SHO	ERA
		27	74	62	.544	2	137	137	124	1201	1346	374	350	6	4.00
Chick Fraser	R	27	20	15	.571	1	40	37	35	331	344	132	110	2	3.81
Bill Bernhard	R	30	17	11	.607	0	31	27	26	257	287	50	58	1	4.52
Eddie Plank	L	25	17	13	.567	0	33	32	28	261	254	68	90	1	3.31
2 Snake Wiltse	L	29	14	5	.737	0	19	19	18	166	185	35	40	2	3.58
1 Wiley Piatt	L	26	6	12	.333	1	18	18	15	140	176	60	45	0	4.63
1 Dummy Leitner	R	30	0	0	.000	1	1	0	0	2	1	1	0	0	
2 Bock Baker	R	22	0	1	.000	0	1	1	0	6	6	1	0	0	10.50
Pete Loos	R	23	0	1	.000	0	1	1	0	1	2	4	0	0	27.00
John McPherson	R	32	0	1	.000	0	1	1	0	4	7	4	0	0	11.25
Billy Milligan	L	22	0	3	.000	0	6	3	2	33	43	14	5	0	4.36

BALTIMORE 5th 68-65 .511 13.5 JOHN McGRAW

NAME	G by Pos	B	AGE	G	AB	R	H	2B	3B	HR	RBI	BB	SO	SB	BA	SA
TOTALS			27	135	4589	761	1348	179	111	24	633	369		207	.294	.397
Bert Hart	1B58	B	31	58	206	33	64	3	5	0	23	20		7	.311	.374
Jimmy Williams	2B130	R	24	130	501	113	159	26	21	7	96	56		21	.317	.495
Bill Keister	SS112	R	29	115	442	78	145	20	21	2	93	18		24	.328	.482
John McGraw (KJ)	3B69	R	28	73	230	73	81	13	9	0	28	61		25	.352	.487
Cy Seymour	OF133, P1	L	28	135	582	85	167	26	8	1	77	28		33	.303	.373
Jim Jackson	OF96	R	23	99	364	42	91	17	3	2	50	20		11	.250	.330
Mike Donlin	OF74, 1B47	L	23	122	481	108	164	22	14	5	67	53		32	.341	.476
Roger Bresnahan	C69, 3B4, 2B2, P1, 2B1	R	22	86	295	40	79	9	9	1	32	23		10	.268	.369
2 Jack Dunn	3B67, SS19, P9, OF1, 2B1	R	28	96	362	41	90	9	4	0	36	21		10	.249	.296
Steve Brodie	OF83	L	32	84	309	41	96	5	6	2	41	25		10	.311	.385
Wilbert Robinson (RJ)	C67	R	38	71	241	34	72	13	3	0	26	10		9	.299	.378
Harry Howell	P37, OF9, SS6, 1B2, 2B1	R	24	53	188	26	41	10	5	2	26	5		7	.218	.356
Frank Foutz	1B20	R	24	20	72	13	17	4	1	2	14	8		0	.236	.403
George Rohe	1B8, 3B6	R	25	14	36	7	10	2	0	0	4	5		1	.278	.333
Chappie Snodgrass	0F2	R	31	3	10	0	1	0	0	0	1	0		0	.100	.100
Slats Jordan	1B1	L	22	1	3	0	0	0	0	0	0	0		0	.000	.000
Tacks Latimer	C1	R	23	1	4	0	1	0	0	0	0	0		0	.250	.250

NAME	T	AGE	W	L	PCT	SV	G	GS	CG	IP	H	BB	SO	SHO	ERA
		30	68	65*	.511	5	134	134	115	1158	1313	344	271	4	3.73
Joe McGinnity	R	30	26	19	.573	3	48	43	39	382	412	96	75	1	3.56
Harry Howell	R	24	14	21	.400	0	37	34	32	295	333	79	93	1	3.66
2 Frank Foreman	R	38	13	7	.650	1	24	22	18	191	225	58	41	1	3.68
Jerry Nops	L	26	11	10	.524	1	27	23	17	177	192	59	43	1	4.07
2 Jack Dunn	R	28	3	3	.500	0	9	6	6	60	74	21	5	0	3.60
Bill Karns	L	25	1	0	1.000	0	3	1	1	17	30	9	5	0	6.35
Roger Bresnahan	R	22	0	1	.000	0	2	1	0	6	10	4	3	0	6.00
1 Stan Yerkes	R	26	0	1	.000	0	1	1	1	8	12	2	4	0	6.75
Crazy Schmidt	L	35	0	2	.000	0	4	3	1	23	25	16	2	0	1.96

* 1 loss by forfeit

WASHINGTON 6th 61-73 .455 21 JIMMY MANNING

NAME	G by Pos	B	AGE	G	AB	R	H	2B	3B	HR	RBI	BB	SO	SB	BA	SA
TOTALS			29	138	4772	683	1282	191	83	33	561	356		127	.269	.364
Mike Grady	1B59, C30, OF3	R	31	94	347	57	99	17	9	1	56	27		14	.285	.470
John Farrell	2B72, OF62, 3B1	R	24	135	555	100	151	32	11	3	63	52		25	.272	.386
Billy Clingman	SS137	B	31	137	480	66	116	10	7	2	56	42		10	.242	.304
Bill Coughlin	3B137	R	22	137	508	77	141	17	13	6	68	25		15	.278	.398
Sam Dungan	OF104, 1B35	R	34	138	479	54	154	26	12	1	72	40		9	.320	.415
2 Irv Waldron	OF78	L	25	79	332#	54	107	14	3	0	23	22		8	.322	.383
1 Pop Foster	OF102, SS2	R	23	103	392	65	109	16	9	6	54	41		10	.278	.411
Boileryard Clarke	C107, 1B3	R	32	110	422	58	118	15	5	3	54	23		7	.280	.360
Joe Quinn	2B66	R	36	66	266	33	67	10	2	3	34	11		7	.252	.338
Dale Gear	OF34, P24	R	29	58	199	17	47	9	2	0	20	4		2	.236	.302
Win Mercer	P24, OF16, 1B7, SS1, 3B1	R	27	51	140	26	42	7	2	0	16	23		10	.300	.379
Bill Everett	1B33	L	32	33	115	14	22	3	2	0	8	15		7	.191	.252
1 Jack O'Brien	OF11	L	28	11	45	5	8	0	0	0	5	3		2	.178	.178
Charlie Luskey	OF8, C3	R	25	11	41	8	8	3	1	0	3	2		0	.195	.317
Tim Jordan	1B6	L	22	6	20	2	4	0	0	0	2	3		0	.200	.250
Ben Harrison	OF1			1	2	0	0	0	0	0	0	0		0	.000	.000

NAME	T	AGE	W	L	PCT	SV	G	GS	CG	IP	H	BB	SO	SHO	ERA
		26	61	73*	.455	1	138	138	118	1183	1396	284	308	8	4.09
Casey Patten	L	27	17	10	.630	0	32	30	26	254	285	74	109	4	3.93
Watty Lee	L	21	16	16	.500	0	36	33	25	262	328	45	63	2	4.40
Bill Carrick	R	27	14	22	.389	0	42	37	34	324	367	93	70	0	3.75
Win Mercer	R	27	9	13	.409	1	24	22	19	180	217	50	31	1	4.55
Dale Gear	R	29	5	11	.313	0	24	16	14	163	199	22	35	1	4.03

*1 loss by forfeit

#Waldron, also with Milwaukee, league leader in AB with 598

CLEVELAND 7th 55-82 .401 28.5 JIMMY McALEER

NAME	G by Pos	B	AGE	G	AB	R	H	2B	3B	HR	RBI	BB	SO	SB	BA	SA
TOTALS			29	138	4833	666	1311	197	68	12	523	243		125	.271	.348
Candy LaChance	1B133	B	31	133	548	81	166	22	9	1	75	7		11	.303	.381
Erve Beck	2B132	R	22	135	539	78	156	26	8	6	79	23		7	.289	.401
Frank Scheibeck	SS92	R	36	93	329	33	70	11	3	0	38	18		3	.213	.264
Bill Bradley	3B133, P1	R	23	133	516	95	153	28	13	1	55	26		18	.296	.407
2 Jack O'Brien	0F92, 1B35	L	28	92	375	54	106	14	5	0	39	22		13	.283	.347
Ollie Pickering	OF137	L	31	137	547	102	169	25	6	0	40	58		36	.309	.377
Jack McCarthy (KJ)	OF86	L	32	86	343	60	110	14	7	0	32	30		9	.321	.402
Bob Wood	C84, 3B4, OF3, 1B1, 2B1, SS1	R	35	98	346	45	101	23	3	1	49	12		6	.292	.384
2 Zaza Harvey	OF45	L	22	45	170	21	60	5	5	1	24	9		15	.353	.459
1 George Yeager	C25, 1B5, OF3, 2B2, P1	R	27	39	139	13	31	5	0	0	14	4		2	.223	.259
2 Joe Connor	C32, OF4, SS1	R	26	37	121	13	17	3	1	0	6	7		2	.140	.182
Frank Genins	OF26	R	34	26	101	15	23	5	0	0	9	8		3	.228	.277
Danny Shay	SS19	R	24	19	75	4	17	2	2	0	10	2		0	.227	.307
Tom Donovan	OF18, P1	R	28	18	71	9	18	3	1	0	5	0		1	.254	.324
Jim McGuire	SS18	R	26	18	69	4	16	2	0	0	3	0		0	.232	.261
2 Truck Eagan	2B5, 3B1	R	24	5	18	2	3	0	1	0	2	1		0	.167	.278
1 Billy Hallman	SS5	R	34	5	19	2	4	1	0	0	3	2		0	.211	.211
Jimmy McAleer	OF2, 3B1, P1	R	36	3	7	0	1	0	0	0	0	0		0	.143	.143
Charlie Gallagher	OF2	R	29	2	4	0	0	0	0	0	0	0		0	.000	.000
Ed Cermak	OF1	R	19	1	4	0	0	0	0	0	0	0		0	.000	.000
Frank Cross	OF1	R	28	1	5	0	3	0	0	0	0	0		0	.600	.600
Russ Hall	SS1	L	29	1	4	2	2	0	0	0	0	0		0	.500	.500
Harry Hogan	OF1	R	24	1	1	0	0	0	0	0	0	0		0	.000	.000
Paddy Livingston	C1	R	21	1	1	0	0	0	0	0	0	0		0	.000	.000

NAME	T	AGE	W	L	PCT	SV	G	GS	CG	IP	H	BB	SO	SHO	ERA
		29	55+	82	.401	3	138	138	122	1182	1365	464	334	7	4.12
Earl Moore	R	21	16	14	.533	0	31	30	28	251	234	107	99	4	2.90
2 Pete Dowling	L	8	22*	.267		0	33	30	28	256	269	104	99	2	3.87
Ed Scott	R	30	7	6	.538	0	17	16	11	125	149	38	23	0	4.39
Bill Hoffer	R	30	6	7	.462	3	16	10	10	99	113	35	19	0	4.55
Bill Hart	R	35	6	12	.333	0	20	19	16	158	180	57	48	0	3.76
Harry McNeal	R	23	5	6	.455	0	12	10	9	85	120	30	15	0	4.45
Jack Bracken	R	20	4	8	.333	0	12	12	12	100	137	31	18	0	6.21
Dick Braggins	R	21	1	2	.333	0	4	3	2	32	44	15	1	0	4.78
Bill Cristall	L	25	1	4	.200	0	6	6	5	48	54	30	12	1	4.87
1 Gus Weyhing	R	34	0	0	.000	0	1	0	0	11	20	5	0	0	8.18
Bill Bradley	R	23	0	0	.000	0	1	0	0	1	1	0	0	0	0.00
Tom Donovan	R	28	0	0	.000	0	1	0	0	7	14	4	3	0	5.14
Jimmy McAleer	R	36	0	0	.000	0	1	0	0	1	1	1	0	0	0.00
1 Bock Baker	L	22	0	0	.000	0	1	1	0	8	23	6	0	0	5.63

*Dowling, also with Milwaukee, league leader in L with 27

+ 1 win by forfeit

MILWAUKEE 8th 48-89 .350 35.5 HUGH DUFFY

NAME	G by Pos	B	AGE	G	AB	R	H	2B	3B	HR	RBI	BB	SO	SB	BA	SA
TOTALS			26	139	4795	641	1250	192	66	26	513	325		176	.261	.345
John Anderson	1B125, OF13	B	27	138	576	90	190	46	7	8	99	24		35	.330	.476
Billy Gilbert	2B127	R	25	127	492	77	133	14	7	0	43	31		19	.270	.327
Wid Conroy	SS118, 3B12	R	25	131	503	74	129	20	6	5	64	36		21	.256	.350
1 Jimmy Burke	3B64	R	26	64	233	24	48	8	0	0	26	17		6	.206	.240
Bill Hallman	OF139	L	25	139	549	70	135	27	6	2	47	41		12	.246	.328
Hugh Duffy	OF77	R	34	78	286	41	88	14	8	2	45	16		13	.308	.434
1 Irv Waldron	OF62	L	25	62	266#	48	79	8	6	0	29	16		12	.297	.372
Billy Maloney	C72, OF8	R	23	86	290	42	85	3	4	0	22	7		11	.293	.331
Bill Friel	3B61, OF28, 2B9, SS6	L	25	106	376	51	100	13	7	4	35	23		15	.266	.370
George Hogriever	OF54	R	32	54	221	25	52	10	2	0	16	30		7	.235	.299
1 Joe Connor	C30, 2B1, 3B1, OF1	R	26	38	102	10	28	3	1	1	9	6		4	.275	.353
2 Jiggs Donahue	C19, 1B13	L	21	37	108	10	33	4	4	0	16	10		4	.305	.417
1 Tom Leahy	C28, OF2, 2B1	R	32	33	99	18	24	6	2	0	10	11		3	.242	.343
Ed Bruyette	OF21, 2B3, SS1, 3B1	L	23	26	82	7	15	3	0	0	4	12		1	.183	.220
Davy Jones	OF14	L	21	14	52	12	9	1	0	0	2	5		11	.173	.346
George Bone	SS12	B	24	12	43	6	13	2	0	0	6	4		0	.302	.349
2 Phil Geier	OF8, 3B3	R	25	11	39	4	7	1	0	0	6	4		1	.179	.256
Lou Gertenrich	OF1	R	26	2	3	1	1	0	0	0	0	0		0	.333	.333
John Butler	C1	R	21	1	1	0	0	0	0	0	0	0		0	.000	.000
George McBride	SS3	R	20	1	1	0	0	0	0	0	0	0		0	.000	.000

NAME	T	AGE	W	L	PCT	SV	G	GS	CG	IP	H	BB	SO	SHO	ERA
		26	48	89	.350	6	139	139	107	1218	1383	395	376	3	4.06
Bill Reidy	R	27	15	18	.454	1	37	33	28	301	364	62	50	2	4.22
Bert Husting	R	23	9	15	.375	2	34	26	19	217	234	95	67	2	4.24
Ned Garvin	R	27	8	21	.275	2	37	27	22	257	258	90	122	1	3.47
Pink Hawley (IL)	R	28	7	13	.350	0	26	23	17	182	228	41	50	0	4.60
Tully Sparks	R	26	6	17	.260	0	29	26	18	210	228	93	62	0	3.51
1 Pete Dowling	L	3	5*	.375	1	10	4	3	50	71	14	25	0	5.58

*Dowling, also with Cleveland, league leader in L with 27

#Waldron, also with Washington, league leader in AB with 598

1901 N.L. - Breaking Up That Old Monopoly

While the upstart American League was playing its first major league schedule, the established National League had finished its 25th campaign and was established as the bastion of baseball in the United States. Since its founding in 1876, the league had weathered rule changes, shifting franchises, and competition from three rival leagues, establishing its durability and supremacy in the young field of professional baseball. The most vigorous competition had come from the American Association, an innovative organization which was launched in 1882 and which bit the dust financially after the 1891 season. For the greater part of the nineties, the National League reigned supreme over the game, but this domination brought its own troubles. The league expanded from eight to twelve teams in 1892, and some teams like Louisville and Washington spent an entire decade light-years from the first division. In an era dominated on the field by Baltimore and Boston, cooperation and collusion among the owners was the keynote off the field. Late in the era, ownership of two clubs by one group of individuals crept into the loop's structure; Baltimore and Brooklyn came under common management, as did Cleveland with St. Louis and Pittsburgh with Louisville. These abuses did not lead to fixing games, but all the better players in the interlocking ownership generally were concentrated on one team, leaving their counterpart much weaker. In response to such imbalances, the league in 1900 cut down to eight teams, dropping Baltimore, Louisville, Cleveland, and Washington, leaving a circuit of New York, Brooklyn, Boston, Philadelphia, Pittsburgh, Chicago, Cincinnati. and St. Louis - a structure which would stand undisturbed until 1953.

The entry of the American League onto the big league stage in 1901 created more than a second major league. It additionally opened a predicted escape value for the athletes. The National League had always assumed a high-handed stance with the players, and the athletes viewed with satisfaction the bidding war between the new rival and the old monolith. About thirty 1900 regulars jumped over to the junior loop, including stars Nap Lajoie, John McGraw, Jimmy Collins, Joe McGinnity, Clark Griffith, and Cy Young. The new league occupied three of the abandoned National League cities of the 1890's, and new teams were placed in direct competition with the clubs in Boston, Philadelphia, and Chicago.

On the field, the East Coast teams were more severely hurt by the raids than the Western teams. The Pittsburgh Pirates attained first place on June 16, and pulled away from runner-up Philadelphia in September to win the championship by 7 1/2 games. Two of the shining lights of the squad were pirated from Louisville during the days of the interlocking ownership; Fred Clarke managed the team and hit .316 as the left fielder, and Honus Wagner alternated among three positions in the field while batting .353. Deacon Phillippe and Jack Chesbro gave the Bucs two 20-game winners on the mound. The second-place Phillies were hurt by the loss of Lajoie to the American League but still packed dynamite in the bats of Ed Delahanty and Elmer Flick. Champion Brooklyn fell to third place because of a slump in hitting and the defection of pitching ace "Iron Man" Joe McGinnity.

Four baseball immortals topped the batting lists. Jesse Burkett hit .382 to lead the league and bring St. Louis into the first division. Philadelphia's Ed Delahanty and Wee Willie Keeler of Brooklyn followed close on Burkett's heels, while Sam Crawford of Cincinnati hit 16 home runs to lead the circuit. As Brooklyn proudly displayed the league's biggest winner, Wild Bill Donovan, their local rivals, the New York Giants, unveiled the phenomenal arm of Christy Mathewson, a 20-game winner in his first full season.

After the 1901 season, the league owners split into two factions; four owners wanted Al Spalding to assume the league presidency to lead the war against the new league, and four owners supported the incumbent, Nick Young. This deadlock caused a halt in league business during the winter, and resulted in a three-man directorate of John T. Brush, A.H. Soden, and James A. Hart to assume direction of the shaken circuit.

1901 NATIONAL LEAGUE

PITTSBURGH 1st 90-49 .647 FRED CLARKE

NAME	G by Pos	B	AGE	G	AB	R	H	2B	3B	HR	RBI	BB	SO	SB	BA	SA
	TOTALS		29	140	4913	776	1407	182	92	28	636	386		203	.286	.378
Kitty Bransfield	1B139	R	26	139	565	92	165	26	17	0	91	29		28	.292	.398
Claude Ritchey	2B139, SS1	B	27	140	540	66	160	20	4	1	74	47		15	.296	.354
1 Bones Ely	SS64, 3B1	R	38	65	240	18	50	6	3	0	28	6		5	.208	.258
Tommy Leach	3B92, SS4	R	23	95	375	62	112	13	13	1	44	20		16	.299	.411
2 Lefty Davis	OF86	L	26	87	335	87	105	8	11	2	33	58		22	.313	.421
Ginger Beaumont	OF133	L	24	132	555	118	182	14	6	8	72	44		32	.328	.418
Fred Clarke	OF127, SS1, 3B1	L	28	129	527	118	171	24	15	6	60	51		23	.324	.461
Chief Zimmer	C68	R	40	69	236	17	52	7	3	0	21	20		6	.220	.275
Honus Wagner	SS61, OF54, 3B24, 2B1	R	27	140	549	101	194	37	11	6	126	53		48	.353	.494
Jack O'Connor	C59	R	32	61	202	16	39	7	3	0	22	10		2	.193	.257
2 George Yeager	C20, 3B4, 1B1	R	27	26	91	9	24	2	1	0	10	4		1	.264	.308
Ed Poole	P12, OF12, 2B1, 3B1	R	26	26	78	6	16	4	0	1	4	4		1	.205	.295
3 Jimmy Burke	3B14	R	26	14	51	4	10	0	0	0	4	4		1	.196	.196
Lew Carr	SS9, 3B1	R	28	9	28	2	7	1	1	0	4	2		0	.250	.357
Jud Smith	3B6	R	32	6	21	1	3	1	0	0	0	3		0	.143	.190
1 Truck Eagan	SS3	R	24	4	12	0	1	0	0	0	2	0		1	.083	.083
1 Elmer Smith	OF1	L	33	4	4	0	0	0	0	0	0	2		0	.000	.000
1 Jiggs Donahue	C1, OF1	L	21	2	7	1	0	0	0	0	0	0		0	.000	.000
Terry Turner	3B2	R	20	2	7	3	3	0	0	0	1	0		0	.429	.429

NAME	T	AGE	W	L	PCT	SV	G	GS	CG	IP	H	BB	SO	SHO	ERA
		28	90	49	.647	4	140	140	119	1245	1198	244	505	15	2.58
Deacon Phillippe	R	29	22	12	.647	2	37	32	30	296	274	38	103	1	2.22
Jack Chesbro	R	27	21	10	.677	1	36	28	26	288	261	52	129	6	2.37
Jesse Tannehill	L	26	18	10	.643	1	32	30	25	252	240	36	118	4	2.18
Sam Leever (SA)	R	29	14	5	.737	0	21	20	18	176	182	39	82	2	2.86
2 Ed Doheny	L	27	6	2	.750	0	11	10	6	77	68	22	28	1	1.99
Ed Poole	R	26	5	4	.556	0	12	10	8	80	78	30	26	1	3.60
George Merritt	R	21	3	0	1.000	0	3	3	3	24	28	5	5	0	4.88
1 Snake Wiltse	R	29	1	4	.200	0	7	5	3	44	57	13	10	0	4.30
1 Rube Waddell	L	24	0	2	.000	0	2	2	0	8	10	9	4	0	9.00

PHILADELPHIA 2nd 83-57 .593 7.5 BILLY SHETTSLINE

NAME	G by Pos	B	AGE	G	AB	R	H	2B	3B	HR	RBI	BB	SO	SB	BA	SA
	TOTALS		28	140	4793	668	1275	194	58	24	553	430		199	.266	.346
Hugie Jennings	1B80, 2B1, SS1	R	32	81	302	38	83	22	2	1	39	25		13	.274	.371
2 Billy Hallman	2B90, 3B33	R	34	123	445	46	82	13	5	0	38	26		13	.184	.236
Monte Cross	SS139	R	31	139	483	49	95	14	1	1	44	52		24	.197	.236
Harry Wolverton	3B93	R	27	93	379	42	117	15	4	0	43	22		13	.309	.369
Elmer Flick	OF138	L	25	138	542	111	182	31	17	8	88	52		26	.336	.500
Roy Thomas	OF129	L	27	129	479	102	148	5	2	1	28	100		27	.309	.334
Ed Delahanty	OF84, 1B58	R	33	138	538	106	192	38	16	8	108	65		28	.357	.532
Ed McFarland	C74	R	26	74	295	33	84	14	2	1	32	18		11	.285	.356
2 Shad Barry	2B35, 3B16, OF13, SS1	R	22	67	252	35	62	10	0	1	22	15		13	.246	.298
1 Jimmy Slagle	OF48	L	27	48	183	20	37	6	2	1	20	16		5	.202	.273
Klondike Douglass	C41, 1B6, OF2	L	29	51	173	14	56	6	1	0	23	11		10	.324	.370
Al Orth	P35, OF4	R	28	41	128	14	36	6	0	1	15	3		3	.281	.352
Fred Jacklitsch (BG)	C30, 3B1	R	25	33	120	14	30	4	3	0	24	12		2	.250	.333
Doc White	P31, OF1	L	22	27	95	15	26	3	1	1	11	2		11	.274	.358
George Browne	OF8	L	25	8	26	2	5	1	0	0	4	1		2	.192	.231
Bert Conn	2B5		21	5	18	2	4	1	0	0	0	0		0	.222	.278
1 Joe Dolan	2B10		28	10	37	4	3	0	0	0	2	0		0	.081	.081

NAME	T	AGE	W	L	PCT	SV	G	GS	CG	IP	H	BB	SO	SHO	ERA
		26	83	57	.593	2	140	140	128	1247	1221	259	480	15	2.87
Al Orth	R	28	20	12	.625	1	35	33	30	282	250	32	92	6	2.27
Red Donahue	R	28	20	13	.606	1	34	33	33	295	299	59	88	1	2.59
Bill Duggleby	R	28	18	10	.643	1	35	29	26	285	302	41	95	5	2.89
Doc White	L	22	14	13	.518	0	31	27	22	237	241	56	132	0	3.19
Jack Townsend	R	22	9	6	.600	0	19	16	14	144	118	64	72	2	3.44
1 Jack Dunn			0	0		0	5			11	7	1		0	19.80

BROOKLYN 3rd 79-57 .581 9.5 NED HANLON

NAME	G by Pos	B	AGE	G	AB	R	H	2B	3B	HR	RBI	BB	SO	SB	BA	SA
	TOTALS		30	137	4879	744	1399	206	93	32	633	312		178	.287	.387
Joe Kelley	1B115, 3B5	R	29	120	493	77	152	21	12	4	65	40		20	.308	.424
Tom Daly	2B133	B	35	133	520	88	164	38	10	3	90	42		31	.315	.444
Bill Dahlen	SS129, 2B2	R	31	130	513	69	134	17	10	4	82	30		23	.261	.357
2 Charlie Irwin	3B65	R	32	65	242	25	52	13	2	0	20	14		4	.215	.285
Willie Keeler	OF125, 3B10, 2B3	L	29	136	589	124	209	16	15	2	43	21		31	.355	.443
Tom McCreery	OF82, 1B4, SS2	L	26	91	335	47	97	11	14	3	53	32		13	.290	.433
Jimmy Sheckard	OF121, 3B12	L	22	133	558	116	192	31	19	11	104	47		42	.353	.536
Deacon McGuire	C81, 1B3	R	37	85	301	28	89	16	4	0	40	18		4	.296	.375
Duke Farrell	C59, 1B17	R	34	80	284	38	84	10	6	1	31	7		7	.296	.384
2 Cozy Dolan	OF64	L	28	66	253	33	66	11	1	0	29	17		7	.261	.312
Frank Gatins	3B46, SS5		30	50	197	21	45	7	2	1	21	5		6	.228	.299
1 Lefty Davis	OF24, 2B1	L	26	25	91	11	19	2	0	0	7	10		4	.209	.231
John Gochnaur	SS3	R	25	3	11	1	4	0	0	0	2	1		1	.364	.364
Hugh Hearne	C2	R	28	2	5	1	2	0	0	0	3	0		0	.400	.400
1 Farmer Steelman	C1		26	1	3	0	1	0	0	0	1	0		0	.333	.333

NAME	T	AGE	W	L	PCT	SV	G	GS	CG	IP	H	BB	SO	SHO	ERA
		27	79	57	.581	5	137	137	111	1214	1244	435	583	7	3.14
Wild Bill Donovan	R	24	25	15	.625	3	45	38	36	351	324	152	226	2	2.77
Frank Kitson	R	29	19	11	.633	2	38	32	26	281	312	67	127	5	2.98
Jay Hughes	R	27	17	12	.586	0	31	29	24	265	265	102	96	0	3.26
2 Doc Newton	L	23	6	5	.545	0	13	12	9	105	110	30	45	0	2.83
Doc McJames (DD)	R	26	5	6	.455	0	13	12	6	91	104	40	42	0	4.75
Brickyard Kennedy (SA)	R	33	5	3	.375	0	14	8	6	85	80	24	28	0	3.07
Gene McCann	R	25	2	3	.400	0	6	5	3	34	34	16	9	0	3.44
Kid Carsey	R	30	1	0	1.000	0	2	0	0	7	9	3	4	0	10.29
Gene Wright	R	22	0	0		0	1	1	1	6	1	6	1	0	1.00

ST. LOUIS — 4th 76-64 .543 14.5 — PATSY DONOVAN

NAME	G by Pos	B	AGE	G	AB	R	H	2B	3B	HR	RBI	BB	SO	SB	BA	SA
TOTALS			30	142	5039	792	1430	187	94	39	657	314		190	.284	.381
Dan McGann	1B103	B	29	103	426	72	123	14	10	6	56	16		16	.289	.411
Dick Padden	2B115, SS8	R	30	123	489	71	125	17	7	2	62	31		26	.256	.331
Bobby Wallace	SS134	R	27	135	556	69	179	34	16	2	91	20		17	.322	.451
Otto Krueger	3B142	R	24	142	520	77	143	16	12	2	79	50		19	.275	.363
Patsy Donovan	OF129	L	36	142	524	91	154	23	6	1	73	27		24	.294	.366
Snags Heidrick	OF118	L	24	118	502	94	170	24	12	6	67	21		32	.339	.470
Jesse Burkett	OF142	L	32	142	597	139	228	21	17	10	75	59		27	.382	.524
Jack Ryan	C65, 2B9, 1B5, OF3	R	32	83	300	27	59	6	5	0	31	7		5	.197	.250
Art Nichols	C47, OF40	R	29	93	308	50	75	11	3	1	33	10		14	.244	.308
Pop Schriver	C24, 1B19	R	35	53	166	17	45	7	3	1	23	12		2	.271	.367
1 Pete Childs	2B19, OF2, SS1		29	29	79	12	21	1	0	0	8	14		0	.200	.278
Bill Richardson	1B15	R	22	15	52	7	11	2	0	2	7	6		1	.212	.365
Mike Heydon	C13, OF1	L	26	16	43	2	9	1	1	1	6	5		2	.209	.349

NAME	T	AGE	W	L	PCT	SV	G	GS	CG	IP	H	BB	SO	SHO	ERA
		25	76	64	.543	5	142	142	118	1270	1333	332	445	5	3.68
Jack Harper	R	23	23	13	.639	0	39	37	28	309	294	99	128	1	3.61
Jack Powell	R	26	19	19	.500	2	45	37	33	338	351	50	133	2	3.54
Willie Sudhoff	R	26	17	11	.607	2	38	26	25	276	281	92	78	1	3.52
Ed Murphy	R	24	10	9	.526	0	23	21	16	165	201	32	42	0	4.20
2 Stan Yerkes	R	26	3	1	.750	0	4	4	3	35	36	6	15	0	3.18
Mike O'Neill	L	23	2	2	.500	0	5	4	4	41	39	10	16	1	1.32
Cowboy Jones	R	26	2	6	.250	0	10	9	7	76	97	22	25	0	4.50
Farmer Burns	R	25	0	0	—	0	1	0	0	2	1	0	0	0	9.00
2 Chauncey Fisher	R	29	0	0	—	0	1	0	0	3	7	1	0	0	15.00
Bob Wicker	R	23	0	1	.000	0	1	0	0	4	4	1	2	0	4.50
1 Billy Magee	R	25	0	0	—	0	1	1	0	8	4	3	0		4.50
Ted Breitenstein	L	32	0	3	.000	0	3	1	1	15	24	14	3	0	6.60

BOSTON — 5th 69-69 .500 20.5 — FRANK SELEE

NAME	G by Pos	B	AGE	G	AB	R	H	2B	3B	HR	RBI	BB	SO	SB	BA	SA
TOTALS			28	140	4746	530	1180	135	36	28	449	303		158	.249	.310
Fred Tenney	1B113, C2	L	29	113	457	63	127	13	2	1	22	37		15	.278	.322
Gene DeMontreville	2B120, 3B20	R	27	140	570	83	174	14	5	5	72	17		23	.305	.374
Herman Long	SS138	R	35	138	518	55	118	15	8	3	68	25		19	.228	.305
Bobby Lowe	3B111, 2B18	R	32	129	491	47	125	11	1	3	47	17		22	.255	.299
2 Jimmy Slagle	OF66	L	27	66	255	35	69	7	0	0	7	34		14	.271	.298
Billy Hamilton	OF99	L	35	102	349	70	102	11	2	3	38	64		19	.292	.361
Dick Cooley	OF53, 1B10	L	28	63	240	27	62	13	3	0	27	14		5	.258	.338
Mal Kittredge	C113	R	31	114	381	24	96	14	0	2	40	32		2	.252	.304
Pat Moran	C28, 1B13, 3B4, SS3, OF3, 2B1	R	25	52	180	12	38	5	1	2	18	3		3	.211	.283
Kid Nichols	P38, OF7, 1B5	B	31	55	163	16	46	8	7	4	28	8		0	.282	.491
Fred Crolius	OF49		24	49	200	22	48	4	1	1	13	9		6	.240	.285
1 Frank Murphy	OF45	R	25	45	176	13	46	5	3	1	18	4		6	.261	.341
Daff Gammons	OF23, 2B2, 3B1	R	25	28	93	10	18	1	0	0	10	3		5	.194	.215
2 Elmer Smith	OF15	L	33	16	57	5	10	2	1	0	3	6		2	.175	.246
Pat Carney	OF13	L	24	13	55	6	16	2	1	0	6	3		0	.291	.364
Joe Rickert	OF13	R	24	13	60	6	10	1	2	0	1	3		1	.167	.250
1 Shad Barry	OF11	R	22	11	40	3	7	2	0	0	6	2		1	.175	.225
Fred Brown	OF5	R	22	7	14	1	2	0	0	0	1	3		0	.143	.143
George Grossart	OF7		21	7	26	4	3	0	0	0	1	0		5	.115	.115
Billy Lush	OF7	B	27	7	27	2	5	1	1	0	3	3		1	.185	.296
Red Hinton	3B4	R	25	4	13	0	1	0	0	0	0	3		0	.077	.077

NAME	T	AGE	W	L	PCT	SV	G	GS	CG	IP	H	BB	SO	SHO	ERA
		28	69	69	.500	2	140	140	128	1263	1196	349	558	11	2.90
Kid Nichols	R	31	19	16	.543	0	38	34	33	321	306	90	143	4	3.22
Vic Willis	R	25	20	17	.541	2	38	35	33	305	262	78	133	6	2.36
Bill Dinneen	R	25	15	18	.455	0	37	34	31	309	295	77	141	0	2.94
Togie Pittinger	R	29	13	16	.448	0	34	33	27	281	288	76	129	1	3.01
Bob Lawson	R	25	2	2	.500	0	6	4	4	46	45	28	12	0	3.33

CHICAGO — 6th 53-86 .381 37 — TOM LOFTUS

NAME	G by Pos	B	AGE	G	AB	R	H	2B	3B	HR	RBI	BB	SO	SB	BA	SA
TOTALS			27	140	4844	578	1250	153	61	18	481	314		204	.258	.326
Jack Doyle	1B75	R	31	73	278	19	67	10	2	0	39	7		11	.241	.291
Cupid Childs	2B63	L	33	63	237	23	61	9	0	0	21	30		3	.257	.295
Barry McCormick	SS12, 3B3	R	26	115	427	45	100	15	6	1	32	31		12	.234	.304
Fred Raymer	3B82, SS29, 1B5, 2B3	R	25	120	463	41	108	14	2	0	43	11		18	.233	.272
Frank Chance (BW)	OF50, C13, 1B6	R	24	69	241	38	67	12	4	0	36	29		27	.278	.361
Danny Green	OF133	L	24	133	482	82	168	16	12	6	61	40		31	.313	.421
Topsy Hartsel	OF140	L	27	140	558	111	187	25	16	7	54	74		41	.335	.475
Johnny Kling	C69, 1B1, OF1	R	25	74	256	26	70	6	3	0	21	9		8	.273	.320
C. Dexter	1B54, 3B25, OF21, 2B13, C3	R	25	116	460	46	123	9	5	1	66	16		22	.267	.315
2 Mike Kahoe	C63, 1B6	R	27	67	237	21	53	12	2	1	21	8		5	.224	.304
2 Pete Childs	2B60		29	60	210	23	48	5	1	0	14	26		4	.229	.262
Jocko Menefee	OF24, P21, 1B2, 2B1	R	33	48	152	19	39	5	3	0	13	8		4	.257	.329
1 Cozy Dolan	OF41	L	28	43	171	29	45	1	2	0	16	7		3	.263	.292
Jim Delehanty	3B17, 2B1	R	22	17	63	4	12	2	0	0	4	3		5	.190	.222
Bill Gannon	OF15		28	15	61	2	9	0	0	0	0	1		5	.148	.148
Eddie Hickey	3B10	R	22	10	37	4	6	0	0	0	3	2		1	.162	.162
Larry Hoffman	3B5, 2B1	R	22	6	22	2	7	1	0	0	6	0		1	.318	.364
Harry Croft	OF3		25	3	12	1	4	0	0	0	4	0		0	.333	.333
Germany Schaefer	2B1, 3B1	R	24	2	5	0	3	1	0	0	0	2		0	.600	.800

NAME	T	AGE	W	L	PCT	SV	G	GS	CG	IP	H	BB	SO	SHO	ERA
		26	53	86	.381	0	140	140	131	1242	1348	324	586	2	3.33
2 Rube Waddell	L	24	14	14	.500	0	29	28	26	244	239	66	168	0	2.80
Jack Taylor	R	27	13	19	.406	0	33	31	30	276	341	44	60	0	3.36
Long Tom Hughes	R	22	10	23	.303	0	37	35	32	308	309	115	225	1	3.24
Jocko Menefee	R	33	8	12	.400	0	21	20	19	182	201	34	55	0	3.81
Mal Eason	R	22	8	17	.320	0	27	25	23	221	246	60	68	1	3.58
Charlie Ferguson	R	26	0	0	—	0	1	0	0	2	1	2	0	0	0.00
Bert Cunningham	R	34	0	0	.000	0	1	1	1	9	11	3	2	0	5.00

NEW YORK — 7th 52-85 .380 37 — GEORGE DAVIS

NAME	G by Pos	B	AGE	G	AB	R	H	2B	3B	HR	RBI	BB	SO	SB	BA	SA
TOTALS			29	141	4839	544	1225	167	46	19	458	303		133	.253	.318
John Ganzel	1B138	R	27	138	526	42	113	13	3	2	66	20		6	.215	.282
Ray Nelson	2B39	R	25	39	130	12	26	2	0	0	7	10		3	.200	.215
George Davis	SS113, 3B17	R	30	130	495	69	153	21	6	7	65	40		26	.309	.418
Sammy Strang	3B91, 2B37, OF5, SS4	B	24	135	493	55	139	14	6	1	34	59		40	.282	.341
2 Algie McBride	OF65	L	32	68	264	27	74	11	0	2	29	12		3	.280	.345
George Van Haltren	OF135, P1	L	35	133	544	83	186	22	7	1	47	51		25	.342	.414
Kip Selbach	OF125	R	29	125	502	89	145	29	6	1	56	45		8	.289	.376
Jack Warner	C84	R	28	87	291	19	70	6	1	0	20	3		3	.241	.268
Charley Hickman	OF50, SS23, 3B15, P9, 2B7, 1B2	R	25	112	401	43	115	20	6	4	62	15		6	.287	.397
Frank Bowerman	C46, 2B3, SS3, 3B3, 1B1	R	32	56	180	20	39	5	3	0	14	7		3	.217	.278
2 Frank Murphy	2B23, OF12	R	25	35	130	10	21	3	0	0	8	6		2	.162	.185
Broadway Aleck Smith	C25		30	26	78	5	11	0	0	0	6	0		2	.141	.141
Jimmy Jones	OF20, P1	R	24	21	91	10	19	4	3	0	5	4		2	.209	.319
Curt Bernard	OF15, 2B4, SS2, 3B1	R	23	23	76	11	17	0	2	0	6	2		7	.224	.276
Charlie Buelow (KJ)	3B17, 2B2	R	24	22	72	3	8	4	0	0	4	2		0	.111	.167
Jim Miller	2B18	R	20	18	58	3	8	0	0	0	3	6		1	.138	.138
Heinie Smith	2B7, P2	R	29	9	29	5	6	2	1	1	4	1		0	.207	.448
Danny Murphy	2B5	R	24	5	20	0	4	0	0	0	1	0		0	.200	.200
Joe Wall	C2, OF1	L	27	4	8	0	4	0	0	0	1	0		0	.500	.500

NAME	T	AGE	W	L	PCT	SV	G	GS	CG	IP	H	BB	SO	SHO	ERA
		24	52	85	.380	1	141	141	118	1232	1389	377	542	11	3.87
Christy Mathewson	R	20	20	17	.541	0	40	38	36	336	288	97	221	5	2.41
Dummy Taylor	R	26	18	27	.400	0	45	43	37	353	377	112	136	4	3.19
Bill Phyle (ST)	R	26	7	10	.412	1	24	19	16	169	208	54	62	0	4.26
Charlie Hickman	R	25	3	5	.375	0	9	9	6	65	76	26	11	0	4.57
1 Ed Doheny	L	27	2	5	.286	0	10	6	6	74	88	17	36	0	4.50
Roger Denzer	R	29	2	5	.286	0	11	9	3	62	69	5	22	1	3.34
Jake Livingstone	R	21	0	0	—	0	2	0	0	12	26	7	6	0	9.00
Harry Felix	R	31	0	0	—	0	1	0	0	3	0	0	0	0	3.00
Ike Van Zandt	R	25	0	0	—	0	1	0	0	13	16	8	2	0	6.92
George Van Haltren	L	35	0	0	—	0	1	1	0	6	12	6	2	0	3.00
1 Chauncey Fisher	R	29	0	1	.000	0	1	1	1	6	13	2	1	0	15.75
Larry Hesterfer	L	23	0	1	.000	0	1	1	1	6	15	3	2	0	7.50
Jimmy Jones	R	24	0	1	.000	0	1	1	1	3	6	3	0	0	10.80
Heinie Smith	R	29	0	1	.000	0	1	1	1	13	24	5	0	0	8.31
Dummy Deegan	R	26	0	2	.000	0	2	2	2	18	27	4	4	0	4.50
2 Dummy Leitner	R	30	0	2	.000	0	2	2	1	19	39	8	5	0	11.37
Al Maul	R	35	0	2	.000	0	2	1	0	16	21	4	3	0	8.44
Willie Mills	R	23	0	1	.000	0	1	1	1	4	12	3	0	0	9.00
2 Billy Magee	R	25	0	4	.000	0	7	4	2	42	56	11	14	0	6.00

CINCINNATI — 8th 52-87 .374 38 — BID McPHEE

NAME	G by Pos	B	AGE	G	AB	R	H	2B	3B	HR	RBI	BB	SO	SB	BA	SA
TOTALS			27	142	4914	561	1232	173	70	38	476	323		137	.251	.338
Jake Beckley	1B140	R	33	140	590	78	177	39	13	3	79	28		6	.300	.425
Harry Steinfeldt	3B55, 2B50	R	23	105	382	40	95	18	7	6	47	20		10	.249	.380
Maggie Magoon	SS112, 2B15	R	26	127	460	47	116	16	7	1	53	52		15	.252	.324
1 Charlie Irwin	3B67	R	32	67	260	25	62	12	2	0	25	14		13	.238	.300
Sam Crawford	OF126	L	21	131	523	89	175	22	16	16	104	37		12	.335	.530
Johnny Dobbs	OF100, 3B8	L	26	109	435	71	119	17	4	2	27	36		19	.274	.345
Dick Harley	OF133	L	28	133	535	69	146	13	2	4	27	31		37	.273	.327
Bill Bergen	C87	R	28	87	308	15	55	6	4	1	17	8		2	.179	.234
Heinie Peitz	C49, 2B21, 3B6, 1B2	R	30	82	269	24	82	13	5	1	24	23		3	.305	.401
Bill Fox	2B43	B	29	43	159	9	28	2	1	0	7	4		9	.176	.201
Harry Bay	OF40	L	23	41	157	25	33	2	1	2	3	13		4	.210	.261
Tommy Corcoran (IL)	SS30	R	32	31	114	13	24	4	2	0	15	11		7	.184	.254
1 Algie McBride	OF28	L	32	30	123	19	29	7	0	2	18	7		0	.236	.341
Pete O'Brien	2B15	L	26	16	54	1	11	1	0	1	3	2		1	.204	.278
Jerry Hurley	C7	R	26	9	21	1	1	0	0	0	3	0		1	.048	.048
Emil Haberer	3B3, 1B2	R	23	7	30	1	5	1	0	0	2	1		0	.167	.278
Jack Heileman	3B4, 2B1	R	28	5	15	1	2	1	0	0	0	1		0	.133	.200
1 Mike Kahoe	C4	R	27	4	13	0	4	0	0	0	0	0		0	.308	.308
Charlie Krause	2B1	R	21	1	4	0	1	0	0	0	0	0		0	.250	.250

NAME	T	AGE	W	L	PCT	SV	G	GS	CG	IP	H	BB	SO	SHO	ERA
		26	52	87	.374	0	142	142	126	1266	1469	365	542	4	4.17
Noodles Hahn	L	22	22	19	.537	0	42	42	41	375	370	69	239	2	2.71
Bill Phillips	R	32	14	18	.438	0	37	36	29	281	364	67	109	1	4.64
1 Doc Newton	L	23	4	13	.235	0	20	18	17	168	190	59	65	0	4.12
Archie Stimmel	R	28	4	14	.222	0	20	18	14	153	170	44	55	1	4.12
Barney McFadden	R	24	3	4	.429	0	4	4	4	46	54	40	11	0	6.07
Len Swormstedt	R	22	2	1	.667	0	3	3	3	26	19	5	13	0	1.73
Charlie Case	R	21	1	2	.333	0	3	3	3	27	34	6	5	0	4.67
Whitey Guese	R	29	1	4	.200	0	5	5	4	44	62	14	11	0	6.14
Jack Sutthoff	R	29	1	4	.143	0	8	7	6	70	82	39	12	0	5.53
Crese Heismann	L	21	0	0	—	0	3	2	1	14	18	6	9	0	5.79
Doc Parker	R	29	0	1	.000	0	1	1	1	4	7	0	1	0	15.75
Bill Fox	R	29	0	0	—	0	1	0	0	5	4	0	0	0	5.53
Amos Rusie	R	30	0	1	.000	0	3	2	2	22	43	3	6	0	8.59
2 Gus Weyhing	R	34	0	1	.000	0	1	1	1	9	11	2	3	0	3.00
Dick Scott	R	18	0	2	.000	0	2	2	1	21	16	9	7	0	5.14

1902 - A. L. — Checkmate

Midway through its second season, the American League found its Baltimore outpost in the hands of the enemy, making the completion of the loop schedule a muddy issue. Baltimore manager John McGraw was constantly running afoul of League President Ban Johnson. Several times during the 1901 and 1902 seasons he was suspended by Johnson for harassing the league umpires and when the Little Napoleon continued his arbiter-baiting, Johnson dry-docked him indefinitely in July. McGraw decided not to take such treatment lying down and started negotiations which resulted in the Orioles being bought by John T. Brush, Chairman of the National League Executive Committee. With the enemy within its walls, the American League suffered a severe body blow; the new owner released McGraw, Joe McGinnity, Roger Bresnahan, Dan McGann, Cy Seymour, Joe Kelley, and Jack Cronin to sign with the National League clubs, leaving Baltimore with a skeleton crew. When, on July 17, the Orioles could not field a team to meet St. Louis, Johnson used a league regulation to revoke the Baltimore franchise. He planned to operate the team for the rest of the season on league funds, arranged for each team to contribute players to stock the sabotaged team, and appointed local hero Wilbert Robinson to manage the reconstructed squad. The Orioles finished last, but that they finished the schedule at all represented a triumph of American League resiliency and solidarity.

Johnson, however, had more problems in 1902 than McGraw. The Pennsylvania Supreme Court presented the new loop with a courtroom setback by ordering Nap Lajoie, Bill Bernhard, and Chick Fraser to leave the Athletics and rejoin the Phillies, the club they had left the year before. Fraser returned to the National League club, but Johnson found his loophole in the Quaker state law and kept Lajoie and Bernhard by transferring their contracts to Cleveland; whenever the Ohio team visited Philadelphia, Lajoie and Bernhard spent a paid vacation in Atlantic City. Other states involved in the squabble ruled against the reserve clause, and Johnson's jumpers were allowed to remain with their new clubs.

St. Louis replaced Milwaukee in the 1902 circuit, and the new club raided the St. Louis Cardinals, of the old league, for several top players, luring Jesse Burkett, Bobby Wallace, Dick Padden, Snags Heidrick, Jack Harper, and Jack Powell into its fold. St. Louis represented the fourth city in which the two leagues both fielded teams and, in every instance, the new team outdrew the National League team. High salaries continued to induce stars to join American League teams. Besides the St. Louis jumpers, Ed Delahanty, Elmer Flick, and Red Donahue were the top names among those who left the National League for greener American League pastures.

Connie Mack won his first pennant by directing the Athletics to a good second half, which gave them the championship over the new St. Louis Browns. Even with the loss of Lajoie, Mack could field a hard-hitting lineup led by third baseman Lave Cross, and rightfielder Socks Seybold; six .300 hitters dotted the Athletic scorecard, making Lajoie's loss less noticeable. The pitching staff survived the loss of Bernard when Mack purchased lefty Rube Waddell in May from Los Angeles of the California League. Daffy to a fault and colorful to an extreme, the brash Waddell used a blazing fastball to post a 24-7 season mark with a league-leading 210 strikeouts. Steady Eddie Plank developed into a star in his second season by chalking up 20 victories. St. Louis, Boston, and Chicago pursued hotly but could not catch the stretch-running A's. Washington's Ed Delahanty led all batters with a .376 average, while Cy Young of Boston again paced the pitchers with 32 wins.

At the season's end, the Baltimore situation was settled by transferring the franchise to New York, where players for the new squad were pirated from the senior loop. This move, along with the other calamities during the season, convinced the National League the peace was cheaper than war and in January, 1903, the National League decided to sit down and talk to the American League. The senior circuit first proposed a merger, which Johnson wisely refused. After many words and abandoned strategies, the final treaty recognized both leagues as majors, agreed to respect the contracts and reserve clauses of all teams, and allowed the American League to keep practically all the players it had corralled from the National League. When the negotiations were over, the senior circuit was not certain what it had won, but only that it had neutralized the enemy.

And that was a victory.

1902 AMERICAN LEAGUE

NAME	G by Pos	B	AGE	G	AB	R	H	2B	3B	HR	RBI	BB	SO	SB	BA	SA
PHILADELPHIA	1st 83-53 .610															
TOTALS			29	137	4762	775	1369	235	67	38	673	343		201	.287	.389
Harry Davis	1B128, OF5	R	28	132	555	87	171	43	7	6	92	30		31	.308	.443
Danny Murphy	2B76	R	25	76	291	48	91	12	8	1	48	13		12	.313	.419
Monte Cross	SS137	R	32	137	497	72	115	22	2	3	59	32		17	.231	.302
Lave Cross	3B137	R	36	137	558	90	189	37	8	0	108	27		26	.339	.440
Socks Seybold	OF136	R	31	137	523	91	166	27	11	16	97	43		5	.317	.503
Dave Fultz	OF114, 2B16	R	27	129	506	109	153	20	5	1	49	62		44	.302	.368
Topsy Hartsel	OF137	L	28	137	545	109	154	20	12	5	58	87		47	.283	.391
2 Ossee Schreckengost	C71, 1B7, OF1	R	27	79	284	45	92	17	2	2	43	9		3	.324	.419
Mike Powers	C68, 1B3	R	31	71	246	35	65	7	1	2	39	14		3	.264	.325
Louis Castro	2B36, OF3, SS1	R	25	42	143	18	35	8	1	1	15	4		2	.245	.336
Eddie Plank	P36	L	26	36	120	15	35	6	1	0	16	3		4	.292	.358
Rube Waddell (JT)	P33	L	25	34	112	8	32	6	2	1	18	4		1	.286	.402
2 Frank Bonner	2B11	R	32	11	44	2	8	0	0	0	3	0			.182	.182
1 Elmer Flick	OF11	L	26	11	37	15	11	2	1	0	3	6		4	.297	.405
Farmer Steelman	C5, OF5		27	10	32	1	6	1	0	0	6	2		1	.188	.219
1 Nap Lajoie (IN)	2B1	R	27	1	4	0	1	0	0	0	0	0		1	.250	.250

NAME	T	AGE	W	L	PCT	SV	G	GS	CG	IP	H	BB	SO	SHO	ERA
		26	83	53	.610	3	137	137	114	1216	1292	368	455	5	3.29
Rube Waddell (JT)	L	25	24	7	.774	1	33	27	26	276	224	64	210	3	2.05
Eddie Plank	R	26	20	15	.571	0	36	32	31	300	319	61	107	1	3.30
2 Bert Husting	R	24	14	5	.737	0	32	27	17	204	240	91	44	1	3.19
1 Snake Wiltse	L	30	8	8	.500	1	19	17	13	138	182	41	28	0	5.15
Highball Wilson	R	23	7	4	.636	0	13	10	8	96	103	19	18	0	2.44
2 Fred Mitchell	R	24	5	8	.385	1	18	14	9	108	120	59	22	0	3.58
Andy Coakley	R	19	2	1	.667	0	3	3	2	27	25	9	6	0	2.67
1 Bill Berhard (IN)	R	31	1	0	1.000	0	1	1	1	9	7	3	1	0	1.00
1 Bill Duggleby	R	29	1	1	.500	0	2	2	2	17	19	4	4	0	5.29
Ed Kenna	L	24	1	1	.500	0	2	1	1	17	19	11	5	0	5.29
Odie Porter	L	24	0	1	.000	0	2	1	1	8	12	5	2	0	3.38
Tad Quinn	R	20	0	1	.000	0	1	1	1	8	12	1	3	0	4.50
Tom Walker	R	20	0	1	.000	0	1	1	1	8	10	0	2	0	5.63

NAME	G by Pos	B	AGE	G	AB	R	H	2B	3B	HR	RBI	BB	SO	SB	BA	SA
ST. LOUIS	2nd 78-58 .574 5															
TOTALS			28	140	4736	619	1254	208	61	29	520	373		137	.265	.353
John Anderson	1B126, OF3	B	28	126	524	60	149	29	6	4	85	21		15	.284	.385
Dick Padden	2B117	R	31	117	413	54	109	26	3	1	40	30		11	.264	.344
Bobby Wallace	SS131, OF1, P1	R	28	133	495	71	142	33	9	1	63	45		19	.287	.396
Barry McCormick	3B132, SS7, OF1	R	27	139	504	55	124	14	4	3	51	37		10	.246	.308
Charlie Hemphill	OF101, 2B2	L	26	103	416	67	132	14	11	6	58	44		23	.317	.447
Snags Heidrick	OF109, SS1, 3B1, P1	L	25	114	422	59	129	19	10	3	56	34		17	.289	.396
Jesse Burkett	OF137, SS1, 3B1, P1	L	33	137	549	99	168	29	9	5	52	71		22	.306	.418
Joe Sugden	C61, 1B4, P1	R	31	69	208	24	48	7	2	0	15	20		2	.230	.284
Bill Friel	OF33, 2B25, 1B10, 3B8, SS3, C1, P1	L	26	80	267	26	64	9	2	2	20	14		4	.240	.311
2 Mike Kahoe	C53	R	28	55	197	21	48	9	2	2	28	6		4	.244	.340
Jiggs Donahue	C23, 1B5	L	22	29	84	10	21	1	1	1	7	12		1	.250	.321
1 Billy Maloney	OF23, C7	L	24	30	112	8	23	3	0	0	11	6		0	.205	.232
1 Davy Jones	OF15	L	22	15	49	4	11	1	1	0	3	6		5	.224	.286
Jimmy McAleer	OF2	R	37	2	3	0	2	0	0	0	0	0		0	.667	.667

NAME	T	AGE	W	L	PCT	SV	G	GS	CG	IP	H	BB	SO	SHO	ERA
		27	78	58	.574	5	140	140	120	1244	1273	343	348	7	3.34
Red Donahue	R	29	22	11	.667	0	35	34	33	316	322	65	63	2	2.76
Jack Powell	R	27	22	17	.564	0	42	39	36	328	320	93	137	3	3.21
Jack Harper	R	24	17	10	.630	0	29	26	20	222	224	81	74	2	4.14
Willie Sudhoff	R	27	11	13	.458	2	30	25	20	220	213	67	42	0	2.86
2 Charlie Shields	L	22	3	0	1.000	0	4	3	3	30	37	7	6	0	3.30
Bill Reidy	R	28	3	5	.375	0	12	9	7	95	111	13	16	0	4.45
Harry Kane	L	18	0	1	.000	0	1	1	1	23	34	16	7	0	5.48
Jesse Burkett	L	33	0	1	.000	0	1	1	1	4	1	2	1	0	9.00
Bill Friel	R	26	0	0	—	0	1	0	0	4	4	0	0	0	4.50
Snags Heidrick	R	25	0	0	—	0	1	0	0	1	1	0	0	0	0.00
Joe Sugden	R	31	0	0	—	0	1	0	0	1	0	0	0	0	0.00
Bobby Wallace	R	28	0	0	—	0	1	0	0	2	3	0	1	0	0.00

NAME	G by Pos	B	AGE	G	AB	R	H	2B	3B	HR	RBI	BB	SO	SB	BA	SA
BOSTON	3rd 77-60 .582 6.5															
TOTALS			28	138	4875	664	1356	195	95	42	572	275		132	.278	.383
Candy LaChance	1B138	B	32	138	541	60	151	13	4	6	56	18		8	.279	.351
Hobe Ferris	2B134	R	24	134	499	57	122	16	14	8	63	21		11	.244	.381
Freddy Parent	SS138	R	26	138	567	91	156	31	8	3	62	24		16	.275	.374
Jimmy Collins	3B107	R	32	107	425	71	138	21	10	6	61	24		18	.325	.459
Buck Freeman	OF138	L	30	138	569	76	177	37	20	11	121	32		15	.311	.504
Chick Stahl	OF125	L	29	127	507	92	161	25	10	2	58	37		18	.318	.418
Patsy Dougherty	OF102, 3B1	L	25	108	438	77	150	12	6	0	34	42		20	.342	.397
Lou Criger	C80, OF1	R	30	83	266	32	68	16	6	0	28	27		7	.256	.361
Harry Gleason	3B35, OF23, 2B4	R	27	71	240	30	54	5	5	2	25	10		6	.225	.313
Jack Warner	C64	R	29	65	222	19	52	5	7	0	12	13		0	.234	.320
1 Charley Hickman	OF27	R	26	28	108	13	32*	5	2	3	16	3		1	.296	.463
Gary Wilson	2B2	R	23	2	8	1	1	0	0	0	1	0		0	.125	.125

NAME	T	AGE	W	L	PCT	SV	G	GS	CG	IP	H	BB	SO	SHO	ERA
		28	77	60	.562	1	138	138	123	1238	1217	326	431	6	3.02
Cy Young	R	35	32	11	.744	0	45	43	41	385	350	53	160	3	2.15
Bill Dinneen	R	26	21	21	.500	0	42	42	39	371	348	99	136	2	2.94
George Winter (IL)	R	24	11	9	.550	0	20	20	18	168	149	53	51	0	3.90
2 Tully Sparks	R	27	7	9	.467	0	17	15	15	143	151	40	37	1	3.46
1 Garry Prentiss	R	22	2	2	.500	0	7	4	4	55	55	10	9	0	3.60
2 Long Tom Hughes (SA)	R	23	2	4	.333	0	9	8	4	49	51	24	15	0	3.31
Doc Adkins	L	29	1	1	.500	0	3	2	1	20	27	5	3	0	4.05
Nick Altrock	L	25	1	2	.333	1	3	2	1	18	19	7	5	0	2.00
1 Bert Husting	R	24	1	0	1.000	0	1	1	1	8	15	8	4	0	9.00
1 Fred Mitchell	R	24	0	1	.000	0	1	1	0	4	8	5	2	0	11.25
Dave Williams	L	21	0	0	—	0	3	0	0	19	22	11	7	0	5.21
Pep Deininger	L	24	0	0	—	0	2	1	0	12	19	9	2	0	9.75

* Hickman, also with Cleveland, league leader in H with 194

16

CHICAGO 4th 74-60 .552 8 — CLARK GRIFFITH

NAME	G by Pos	B	AGE	G	AB	R	H	2B	3B	HR	RBI	BB	SO	SB	BA	SA
TOTALS			28	138	4654	675	1248	170	50	14	537	411		265	.268	.335
Frank Isbell	1B133, SS4, C1, P1	L	26	137	515	62	130	14	4	4	59	14		38	.252	.318
Tom Daly	2B137	B	36	137	489	57	110	22	3	1	54	55		19	.225	.288
George Davis	SS129, 1B3	B	31	132	480	77	143	27	7	3	93	65		33	.298	.402
Sammy Strang	3B137	B	25	137	536	108	158	18	5	3	46	76		38	.295	.364
Danny Green	OF129	L	25	129	481	77	150	16	11	0	62	53		35	.312	.391
Fielder Jones	OF135	L	30	135	532	98	171	16	5	0	54	57		33	.321	.370
1 S. Mertes	OF120, SS5, C2, 1B1, 2B1, 3B1, P1	R	29	129	497	60	140	23	7	1	79	37		46	.282	.362
Billy Sullivan	C70, 1B2, OF2	R	27	76	263	36	64	12	3	1	26	6		11	.243	.323
Ed McFarland	C69, 1B1	R	27	75	246	29	56	9	2	1	25	19		8	.228	.293
Nixey Callahan	P35, OF23, SS1	R	28	70	218	27	51	7	2	0	13	6		4	.234	.284
1 Herm McFarland	OF7	L	32	7	27	5	5	0	0	0	4	2		1	.185	.185
Ed Hughes	C1	R	21	1	4	0	1	0	0	0	0	0		0	.250	.250

NAME	T	AGE	W	L	PCT	SV	G	GS	CG	IP	H	BB	SO	SHO	ERA
		28	74	60	.552	1	138	138	116	221	1269	331	346	11	3.41
Roy Patterson	R	28	20	12	.625	0	34	30	26	268	262	67	61	2	3.06
Nixey Callahan	R	28	16	14	.533	0	35	31	29	282	287	89	75	2	3.61
Clark Griffith	R	32	15	9	.625	0	28	24	20	213	247	47	51	3	4.18
Wiley Piatt	L	27	12	13	.480	0	32	30	24	246	263	66	96	2	3.51
Ned Garvin	R	28	9	10	.474	1	23	19	16	175	169	43	55	2	2.21
Sam Mertes	R	29	1	0	1.000	0	1	0	0	8	6	0	0	1	1.13
Jim Durham	R	20	1	1	.500	0	3	3	3	20	21	16	3	0	5.85
Frank Isbell	R	26	0	1	.000	0	1	1	0	1	3	1	1	0	9.00
1 Jack Katoll	R	30	0	0	—	0	1	0	0	1	1	0	1	0	0.00
2 Dummy Leitner	R	31	0	0	—	0	1	0	0	4	9	2	0	0	13.50
1 Sam McMackin	L	29	0	0	—	0	1	0	0	2	2	0	0	0	0.00

CLEVELAND 5th 69-67 .507 14 — BILL ARMOUR

NAME	G by Pos	B	AGE	G	AB	R	H	2B	3B	HR	RBI	BB	SO	SB	BA	SA
TOTALS			28	137	4840	686	1401	248	68	33	582	308		140	.289	.389
2 Charley Hickman	1B98, 2B3, P1	R	26	102	427	60	162*	31	10	8	94	12		9	.379	.555
2 Nap Lajoie	2B86	R	27	86	348	81	128	34	5	7	64	19		18	.368	.555
John Gochnaur	SS127	R	26	127	459	45	85	16	4	0	37	38		7	.185	.237
Bill Bradley	3B137	R	24	137	549	106	187	39	12	11	77	27		12	.341	.515
2 Elmer Flick	OF110	L	26	110	427	68	126	20	11	2	61	47		20	.295	.407
2 Harry Bay	OF107	L	24	108	455	71	132	10	5	0	23	36		22	.290	.334
Jack McCarthy	OF95	L	33	95	359	45	102	31	5	0	41	24		12	.284	.398
Harry Bemis	C87, OF2, 2B1	R	28	93	317	42	99	12	7	1	29	19		3	.312	.404
Bob Wood	C52, 1B16, OF2, 2B1, 3B1	R	36	81	258	23	76	18	2	0	40	27		1	.295	.380
Ollie Pickering	OF64, 1B2	R	32	69	293	46	75	5	2	3	26	19		22	.256	.317
1 Frank Bonner	2B34	R	32	34	132	14	37	6	0	0	14	5		1	.280	.326
1 Jack Thoney	2B14, SS11, OF2	R	22	28	105	14	30	7	1	0	11	9		4	.286	.371
Charlie Hemphill	OF19	L	26	25	94	14	25	2	0	0	11	5		4	.266	.287
1 Ossee Schreckengost	1B17	R	27	18	74	5	25	0	0	0	9	0		2	.338	.338
Zaza Harvey (IL)	OF12	L	23	12	46	5	16	2	0	0	5	3		1	.348	.391
3 Hal O'Hagan	1B3	R	32	3	13	2	5	2	0	0	1	0		2	.385	.538
Peaches Graham	2B1	R	25	2	6	0	2	0	0	0	1	1		0	.333	.333
George Starnagle	C1	R	28	1	3	0	0	0	0	0	0	0		0	.000	.000

* Hickman, also with Boston, league leader in H with 194

NAME	T	AGE	W	L	PCT	SV	G	GS	CG	IP	H	BB	SO	SHO	ERA
		25	69	67	.507	4	137	137	116	1204	1199	411	361	16	3.28
2 Bill Bernhard	R	31	17	6	.739	1	27	24	22	217	169	34	57	3	2.20
Earl Moore	R	22	17	17	.500	1	36	34	29	293	304	101	84	4	2.95
Addie Joss	R	22	16	13	.552	1	32	29	28	269	225	75	106	5	2.78
Gene Wright	R	23	7	10	.412	1	21	18	15	148	150	75	52	1	3.95
Gus Dorner	R	25	3	1	.750	0	4	4	4	36	33	13	5	1	1.25
Charlie Smith	R	23	2	1	.667	0	3	3	2	25	21	5	1	1	4.05
Dike Varney	L	21	2	1	.667	0	3	3	0	15	14	12	7	0	6.00
Otto Hess	L	23	2	3	.400	0	7	4	4	44	67	23	13	0	5.93
Ginger Clark	R	23	1	0	1.000	0	1	1	1	6	10	3	1	0	6.00
Jack Katoll	R	25	1	1	.500	0	3	1	1	34	48	16	7	0	6.62
1 Charley Hickman	R	26	0	1	.000	0	1	1	1	6	11	1	0	1	1.59
1 Dummy Leitner	R	31	0	1	.000	0	1	1	1	8	11	1	0	0	4.50
Lou Polchow	R	21	0	1	.000	0	1	1	1	9	11	5	0	0	5.63
Ed Walker	L	27	0	1	.000	0	1	1	1	8	11	3	1	0	3.38
Oscar Streit	L	28	0	7	.000	0	8	7	4	52	72	25	10	0	5.19
Cal Vasbinder	R	21	0	0	.000	0	1	1	1	6	4	2	1	0	9.00

WASHINGTON 6th 61-75 .449 22 — TOM LOFTUS

NAME	G by Pos	B	AGE	G	AB	R	H	2B	3B	HR	RBI	BB	SO	SB	BA	SA
TOTALS			30	138	4734	707	1338	262	66	47	606	329		121	.283	.396
Scoops Carey	1B120	R	31	120	452	46	142	35	11	0	60	20		3	.314	.440
2 Jack Doyle	2B68, 1B7, OF4, C1	R	32	81	315	67	75	15	2	1	20	29		7	.238	.308
Bones Ely	SS105	R	39	105	381	39	100	11	2	1	62	21		3	.262	.310
Bill Coughlin	3B66, SS31, 2B6	R	23	121	487	70	129	16	7	1	46	33		32	.298	.411
Watty Lee	OF95, P13	L	22	109	391	61	100	21	5	4	45	33		8	.256	.366
Jimmy Ryan	OF120	R	39	120	482	92	153	32	6	6	44	43		13	.317	.446
Ed Delahanty	OF111, 1B13	R	34	123	474	103	178	41	15	10	93	62		14	.376	.590
Boileryard Clarke	C87	R	33	87	291	31	78	16	0	6	40	23		1	.268	.385
Bill Keister	OF65, 2B40, 3B14, SS2	R	30	119	483	82	145	33	9	9	90	14		27	.300	.462
13 Lew Drill	C53, OF8, 2B5, 3B1	R	25	71	221	33	58	10	4	1	29	26		5	.262	.357
1 Harry Wolverton	3B59	B	28	59	249	35	62	8	3	1	23	13		8	.249	.317
Jake Atz	2B3	R	23	3	10	1	1	0	0	0	1	0		0	.100	.100
Tim Donahue (DD)	C3	L	32	3	8	0	2	0	0	0	1	0		1	.250	.250
Joe Stanley	OF3	R	21	3	12	2	4	0	0	0	1	0		0	.333	.333

NAME	T	AGE	W	L	PCT	SV	G	GS	CG	IP	H	BB	SO	SHO	ERA
		27	61	75	.449	2	138	138	130	1208	1403	312	300	2	4.36
Al Orth	R	29	19	18	.514	2	38	37	36	324	367	40	76	1	3.97
Casey Patten	L	28	17	17	.500	1	36	34	33	300	331	89	92	1	4.05
Bill Carrick	R	28	12	17	.414	0	31	30	28	258	344	72	36	0	4.85
Jack Townsend	R	23	9	16	.360	0	27	26	22	220	233	89	71	0	4.46
Watty Lee	L	22	4	6	.400	1	13	10	10	98	110	29	24	0	5.05
2 Cy Vorhees	R	27	0	1	.000	0	1	1	1	8	12	2	1	0	4.50

DETROIT 7th 52-83 .385 30.5 — FRANK DWYER

NAME	G by Pos	B	AGE	G	AB	R	H	2B	3B	HR	RBI	BB	SO	SB	BA	SA
TOTALS			29	137	4644	566	1167	141	55	22	488	359		130	.251	.320
1 Pop Dillon	1B66	L	28	66	243	21	50	6	3	0	22	16		2	.206	.255
Kid Gleason	2B118	R	35	118	441	42	109	11	4	1	38	25		17	.247	.297
Kid Elberfeld	SS130	R	27	131	487	70	129	16	7	1	64	55		20	.265	.333
Doc Casey	3B132	R	31	132	520	69	142	18	7	3	55	44		22	.273	.352
Ducky Holmes	OF92	R	33	92	362	50	93	15	4	2	33	28		16	.257	.337
Jimmy Barrett	OF136	L	27	136	509	93	154	19	6	4	44	74		24	.303	.387
Dick Harley	OF125	L	29	125	491	59	138	9	8	2	44	36		20	.281	.344
Deacon McGuire	C70	R	38	73	229	27	52	14	1	2	23	24		0	.227	.323
Fritz Buelow	C63, 1B2	R	26	66	224	23	50	5	2	2	29	9		3	.223	.290
13 Sport McAllister	1B26, OF12, C9, SS6, 3B6, 2B3	B	27	66	229	19	48	5	2	1	32	5		1	.210	.262
Joe Yeager	P19, OF13, 2B12, SS3, 3B1	R	26	50	161	17	39	6	5	1	23	5		0	.242	.360
2 Erve Beck	1B36, OF5	R	23	41	162	23	48	4	0	2	22	4		3	.296	.358
George Mullin	P35, OF4	R	21	40	120	20	39	4	3	0	11	8		1	.325	.408
Pete LePine	OF19, 1B8	L	25	30	96	8	20	3	2	1	19	8		1	.208	.313
1 Harry Arndt	OF10, 1B1	R	23	10	34	4	5	0	1	0	7	6		0	.147	.206
Jack O'Connell	2B6, 1B2			8	22	1	4	0	0	0	0	3		0	.182	.182
Lew Post	OF3		27	3	12	1	1	0	0	0	2	0		0	.083	.083
Lou Schiappacasse	OF2	R	21	2	5	0	0	0	0	0	1	1		0	.000	.000

NAME	T	AGE	W	L	PCT	SV	G	GS	CG	IP	H	BB	SO	SHO	ERA
		25	52	83	.385	4	137	137	116	1191	1267	370	245	9	3.56
Win Mercer	R	28	15	18	.455	1	35	33	28	282	282	80	40	4	3.03
George Mullin	R	21	14	15	.483	0	35	30	25	260	282	95	78	0	3.67
Ed Siever	R	27	8	11	.381	1	25	23	17	188	166	32	36	4	1.91
1 Roscoe Miller	R	25	6	11	.353	1	20	18	15	149	158	57	39	1	3.68
Joe Yeager	R	26	6	12	.333	0	19	15	14	140	171	41	28	0	4.82
Wish Egan	R	21	2	2	.333	0	3	3	2	22	23	6	0	0	2.86
Rube Kisinger	R	25	2	4	.200	0	5	5	5	43	48	14	7	0	3.14
Arch McCarthy	R		1	7	.125	0	10	8	8	72	90	31	10	0	6.13
John Terry		22	0	1	.000	0	1	1	1	8	10	3	0	0	3.60
1 Jack Cronin	R	28	0	0	—	0	4	0	0	17	26	8	5	0	9.53
Ed Fisher	R	25	0	0	—	0	1	0	0	4	4	1	0	0	0.00
2 Sam McMackin	L	29	0	0	—	0	1	0	0	9	7	4	2	0	3.38

BALTIMORE 8th 50-88 .362 34 — JOHN McGRAW 26-31 .456 — WILBERT ROBINSON 24-57 .296

NAME	G by Pos	B	AGE	G	AB	R	H	2B	3B	HR	RBI	BB	SO	SB	BA	SA
TOTALS			28	141	4760	715	1318	202	107	33	598	417		189	.277	.385
1 Dan McGann	1B68	B	30	68	251	42	79	10	7	0	42	19		19	.315	.410
Jimmy Williams	2B104, 3B19, 1B1	R	25	125	498	83	156	27	21	8	83	36		14	.313	.500
Billy Gilbert	SS129	R	26	129	445	74	109	12	3	2	38	45		38	.245	.299
Roger Bresnahan	3B30, C22, OF15	R	23	65	235	30	64	8	6	4	34	21		12	.272	.409
1 Cy Seymour	OF72	L	29	72	270	38	75	8	8	3	41	18		13	.278	.400
2 Herm McFarland	OF61	L	32	61	242	34	78	19	6	3	36	36		10	.322	.488
Kip Selbach	OF127	R	30	128	503	86	161	27	9	3	60	58		22	.320	.427
Wilbert Robinson	C87	R	39	88	336	39	98	14	7	1	57	12		11	.292	.384
Harry Howell	2B26, 3B15, SS11	R	25	96	347	42	93	16	11	2	42	18		7	.268	.395
2 Harry Arndt	OF62, 2B4, 3B2, SS1	R	23	68	248	41	63	7	4	2	28	35		9	.254	.339
1 Joe Kelley	OF48, 3B8, 1B5, SS1	R	30	61	222	50	69	16	7	1	34	34		12	.311	.459
B. Aleck Smith	C27, 1B7, OF4, 2B3, 3B1		31	41	145	10	34	0	4	0	21	8		5	.234	.255
Tom Jones	1B37, 2B1	R	25	37	132	22	45	8	4	0	14	2		1	.283	.384
Jimmy Mathison	3B28, SS1	R	23	29	91	12	24	2	1	0	7	9		2	.264	.308
Andy Oyler	3B20, OF3, SS2, 2B1	R	22	22	97	9	17	1	0	1	6	8		3	.221	.273
1 John McGraw	3B19	L	29	20	63	14	18	3	2	1	3	17		5	.286	.444
2 George Yeager	C11	R	28	11	38	3	7	1	0	0	2	0		0	.184	.211
1 Bill Mellor (NJ)	1B10	R	28	10	36	4	13	3	0	0	5	3		1	.361	.444
1 Jimmy Sheckard	OF4	R	23	4	16	3	4	1	0	0	1	0		0	.250	.313
2 Sport McAllister	2B2, 1B1	B	27	3	11	0	1	0	0	0	1	0		0	.091	.091
2 Jack Thoney (BG)	3B3	R	22	3	11	1	0	0	0	0	0	1		0	.000	.000
2 Pop Dillon	1B2	L	27	2	7	1	2	0	0	0	2	0		0	.286	.571
2 Lew Drill	C1, 1B1	R	25	2	8	1	2	0	0	0	1	1		0	.250	.250
Charlie Burns	C1			1	2	0	0	0	0	0	0	0		0	1.000	1.000
2 Earnie Courtney	3B1	L	27	1	4	3	2	0	0	1	0	1		1	.500	1.000
Slats Jordan	OF1	L	23	1	4	0	0	0	0	0	0	0		0	.000	.000

NAME	T	AGE	W	L	PCT	SV	G	GS	CG	IP	H	BB	SO	SHO	ERA
		28	50	88	.362	0	141	141	119	1210	1531	354	258	3	4.31
1 Joe McGinnity	R	31	13	10	.565	0	25	23	19	199	219	46	39	0	3.35
Harry Howell	R	25	9	14	.391	0	26	23	19	199	243	48	33	1	4.12
1 Long Tom Hughes	R	23	7	6	.538	0	13	13	12	108	120	32	45	1	3.92
1 Snake Wiltse	L	30	7	10	.412	0	19	18	18	164	215	51	37	0	5.10
1 Charlie Shields	L	22	5	11	.313	0	23	15	10	142	201	52	28	1	4.25
2 Jack Cronin	R	30	5	9	.375	0	10	8	8	76	66	24	20	0	2.61
2 Jack Katoll	R	30	3	10	.231	0	15	14	12	123	175	32	25	0	4.02
Ike Butler	R	25	1	6	.154	0	16	14	12	116	168	45	13	0	5.35
Ernie Ross	L	22	1	1	.500	0	2	2	1	17	20	12	2	0	7.41
1 Dad Hale	R	26	1	0	1.000	0	4	1	1	13	21	3	5	0	4.50
Bob Lawson	R	26	0	4	.000	0	5	4	3	31	36	9	6	0	4.85
Frank Foreman	R	39	0	2	.000	0	2	2	2	16	28	6	2	0	6.19
2 Garry Prentiss (DD)	R	26	0	2	.000	0	2	0	0	7	14	5	1	0	10.29
2 Crese Heismann	L	22	0	1	.000	0	2	1	1	16	20	12	2	0	8.44

1902 N. L. — The Worst Laid Plans...

Another year of war with the American League brought an element of battle fatigue to the National League in 1902. A three-man Executive Committee, chaired by John T. Brush, directed the war effort during the season, chalking up its greatest triumph when it purchased the Baltimore American League team and sabotaged it by releasing its better players to sign National League contracts. That victory was short-lived, as the disemboweled Baltimore team was replanted in New York at the season's close by the new league, thus rivaling the Giants in Gotham. To add insult to injury, the new New York club stocked its roster by raiding the National League pantry for players.

A hollow victory was won when the Pennsylvania Supreme Court ruled that Nap Lajoie, Bill Bernhard, and Chick Fraser had to leave the Philadelphia Athletics to return to the rival Phillies, to whom they were bound by the reserve clause. Fraser returned, but Lajoie and Bernhard evaded the court order by joining the Cleveland American team and keeping out of Pennsylvania all season. In addition to not retaining these two, the Phillies lost Elmer Flick, Ed Delahanty, Red Donahue, and Al Orth to further American League raids. Outside of Pennsylvania, state courts generally ruled against the reserve clause and, thus, in favor of the new loop.

The Pittsburgh Pirates managed to avoid any losses to the American League's raiding tactics for the second consecutive year, and the strong Buc squad trounced all the weakened competition in waltzing to a repeat championship by a margin of 27 1/2 games over distant runner-up Brooklyn. The Pirate total of 103 wins topped any team's record in the 27-year history of the league and, after May 4, no team could show its heels to the flying Bucs. League batting champ Ginger Beaumont, manager Fred Clarke, and Honus Wagner all swung hot bats through the year, and Jack Chesbro, Jesse Tannehill, and Deacon Phillippe gave the Bucs three 20-win aces, with Chesbro's 28 wins topping the league's hurlers. In addition, third sacker Tommy Leach led the circuit in home runs with six clouts.

Brooklyn's second-place finish was due in good measure to Willie Keeler's .338 batting and good pitching by Frank Kitson and Wild Bill Donovan. After losing its entire offense and top pitchers to the new league in two years, Philadelphia dropped into seventh place. The New York Giants got off to a dismal start, and even the infusion of Baltimore talent could not stop a basement finish; nevertheless, new manager John McGraw, Joe McGinnity, Roger Bresnahan, and Dan McGann would all serve the Giants well in the years to come.

Peace talks were opened with the American League during the winter with the National League first seeking a merger between the two loops. The American League, united behind Ban Johnson, preferred to retain its own identity, and the peace treaty signed in January, 1903, allowed just that. Both leagues would recognize each other as equals, both would honor each other's reserve lists and contracts, and most of the players currently in the American League were permitted to remain there. The junior loop could follow its plan to invade New York in return for a pledge to leave Pittsburgh to the Pirates. The Giants objected to the treaty's allowance of the American Leagues moving to New York, and Brooklyn took issue with permanently losing the players who had jumped to the rival league, but a reluctant consensus was reached, putting an end to the two-year baseball war and getting down to the sport at hand.

Events followed each other rapidly after the conclusion of the playing season. New raids by the American League stripped Brooklyn of Wee Willie Keeler, Frank Kitson, and Wild Bill Donovan, relieved Pittsburgh of Jesse Tannehill and Jack Chesbro, and took Sam Crawford off Cincinnati's hands. The controlling ownership of the New York Giants was purchased by John T. Brush, and his position as head of the Executive Committee was rendered obsolete by the election of Harry Pulliam of Pittsburgh as President of the National League in December.

1902 NATIONAL LEAGUE

NAME	G by Pos	B	AGE	G	AB	R	H	2B	3B	HR	RBI	BB	SO	SB	BA	SA
PITTSBURGH 1st 103-36 .741			FRED CLARKE													
TOTALS			28	142	4976	775	1410	189	94	19	660	372		228	.286	.374
Kitty Bransfield (KJ)	1B101	R	27	102	412	50	127	21	9	1	69	17		24	.308	.410
Claude Ritchey	2B114, OF1	B	28	115	405	54	112	13	1	2	55	53		10	.277	.328
Wid Conroy	SS95, OF3	R	25	99	365	55	89	10	6	1	47	24		10	.244	.312
Tommy Leach	3B134	R	24	135	514	97	144	21	20	6	85	45		29	.280	.434
Lefty Davis (BN)	OF59	L	27	59	232	52	65	7	3	0	20	35		19	.280	.336
Ginger Beaumont	OF130	L	25	131	544	101	194	21	6	0	67	39		33	.357	.417
Fred Clarke (FJ)	OF113	L	29	113	459	103	145	27	14	2	53	51		29	.316	.449
Harry Smith	C50	R	27	50	185	14	35	4	1	0	12	4		4	.189	.222
Honus Wagner	OF61, SS44, 1B32, 2B1, P1	R	28	136	534	105	176	30	16	3	91	43		43	.330	.463
Jimmy Burke	2B27, OF18, 3B9, SS4	R	27	60	203	24	60	12	2	0	26	17		9	.296	.374
Jack O'Connor	C42, 1B6, OF1	R	33	49	170	13	50	1	2	1	28	3		2	.294	.341
Jesse Tannehill	P26, OF16	B	27	44	148	27	43	6	1	1	17	12		3	.291	.365
Chief Zimmer	C41	R	41	42	142	13	38	4	2	0	17	11		4	.268	.324
Jimmy Sebring	OF19	L	20	19	80	15	26	4	4	0	15	5		2	.325	.475
Eddie Phelps	C13, 1B5	R	23	18	61	5	13	1	0	0	6	4		2	.213	.230
Fred Crolius	OF9	R	25	9	38	4	10	2	1	0	7	0		0	.263	.368
George Merritt	OF2	R	22	2	9	2	3	1	0	0	2	0		0	.333	.444
Lee Fohl	C1	R	25	1	3	0	0	0	0	0	1	0		0	.000	.000
Mike Hopkins	C1	R	29	1	2	0	2	1	0	0	0	0		0	1.000	1.500
Bill Miller	OF1	L	23	1	5	0	1	0	0	0	2	0		0	.200	.200
BROOKLYN 2nd 75-63 .543 27.5			NED HANLON													
TOTALS			29	141	4845	564	1242	147	49	19	476	319		145	.256	.319
Tom McCreery	1B108, OF4	R	27	112	430	49	105	8	4	4	57	29		16	.244	.309
Tim Flood	2B132, OF1	R	25	132	476	43	104	11	4	3	51	23		8	.218	.277
Bill Dahlen	SS138	R	32	136	520	68	139	26	7	2	74	43		29	.267	.356
Charlie Irwin	3B130, SS1	R	33	131	458	59	125	14	0	2	43	39		13	.273	.317
Willie Keeler	OF133	L	30	132	556	84	188	18	7	0	38	21		23	.338	.396
Cozy Dolan	OF141	R	29	141	592	72	166	16	7	1	54	33		24	.280	.336
2 Jimmy Sheckard	OF123	L	23	122	480	84	131	20	10	4	37	57		25	.273	.381
Hugh Hearne	C65	R	29	66	231	22	65	10	0	0	28	16		3	.281	.325
Duke Farrell	C49, 1B24	R	35	74	264	14	64	5	2	0	24	12		6	.242	.277
Ed Wheeler	3B11, 2B10, SS5	R	24	30	96	4	12	0	0	0	5	3		1	.125	.125
Lew Ritter	C16	R	26	16	57	5	12	1	0	0	2	1		2	.211	.228
Rube Ward	OF11	L	23	13	31	4	9	1	0	0	2	2		0	.290	.323
George Hildebrand	OF11	R	23	11	41	3	9	1	0	0	5	3		0	.220	.244
Tacks Latimer	C8	R	24	8	24	0	1	0	0	0	0	0		0	.042	.042
2 Joe Wall	C5	L	28	5	18	0	3	0	0	0	0	3		0	.167	.167
Nig Fuller	C3	R	36	3	9	0	0	0	0	0	0	0		0	.000	.000
Pat Deisel	C1	R	26	1	3	0	2	0	0	0	0	0		0	.667	.667
BOSTON 3rd 73-64 .533 29			AL BUCKENBERGER													
TOTALS			29	142	4728	571	1178	142	39	14	453	398		189	.249	.305
Fred Tenney	1B134	L	30	134	491	88	154	16	3	2	30	73		21	.314	.371
Gene DeMontreville	2B112, SS10	R	28	125	483	50	130	18	5	0	53	12		27	.269	.327
Herman Long	SS107, 2B13	L	36	120	432	41	98	9	0	2	44	31		22	.227	.262
Ed Gremminger	3B140	R	28	140	522	55	134	20	12	1	65	39		7	.257	.347
Pat Carney	OF137, P2	L	25	137	522	75	141	17	4	2	65	42		27	.270	.330
Billy Lush	OF116, 3B1	B	28	120	413	68	92	8	1	2	19	76		30	.223	.262
Dick Cooley	OF127, 1B7	L	29	135	549	73	162	26	8	0	58	34		27	.296	.372
Mal Kittredge	C72	R	32	80	255	18	60	7	0	2	30	24		4	.235	.286
Pat Moran	C71, 1B3, OF1	R	26	80	251	22	60	5	5	1	24	17		6	.239	.311
1 Ernie Courtney	OF39, SS3	R	27	48	165	23	36	3	0	0	17	13		3	.218	.236
2 Charlie Dexter	SS22, 2B19, OF7, 3B1	R	26	48	183	33	47	3	0	1	18	16		16	.257	.290
Fred Brown	OF2	L	23	2	6	1	2	1	0	0	0	0		0	.333	.500
George Grossart (DD) 23																

NAME	T	AGE	W	L	PCT	SV	G	GS	CG	IP	H	BB	SO	SHO	ERA
		29	103	36	.741	3	142	142	131	1265	1142	250	564	21	2.30
Jack Chesbro	R	28	28	6	.824	1	35	33	31	286	242	62	136	8	2.17
Jesse Tannehill	L	27	20	6	.769	0	26	24	23	231	203	25	100	2	1.95
Deacon Phillippe	R	30	20	9	.690	0	31	30	29	272	265	26	122	5	2.05
Ed Doheny (IL)	L	28	16	4	.800	0	22	21	19	188	161	61	88	2	2.54
Sam Leever (SA)	R	30	16	7	.696	2	28	26	23	222	203	31	86	4	2.39
Warry McLaughlin	L	25	3	0	1.000	0	3	3	3	26	27	9	13	0	2.77
Harv Cushman	R	24	0	4	.000	0	4	4	3	26	30	31	12	0	7.27
1 Ed Poole	R	27	0	0	—	0	1	0	0	8	7	3	2	0	1.13
Honus Wagner	R	28	0	0	—	0	1	0	0	5	4	2	5	0	0.00
Frank Kitson	R	27	75	63	.543	3	141	141	131	1256	1113	363	536	14	2.69
Frank Kitson	R	30	19	12	.613	0	31	30	28	260	251	48	107	3	2.84
Wild Bill Donovan	R	25	17	15	.531	1	35	33	30	298	250	111	170	4	2.78
Jay Hughes	R	28	15	11	.577	0	31	30	27	254	228	55	94	0	2.87
Doc Newton	L	24	15	14	.517	2	31	28	26	264	208	87	107	4	2.42
2 Roy Evans	R	28	5	6	.455	0	13	11	11	97	91	33	35	2	2.69
John McMackin	L	24	2	2	.500	0	4	4	4	32	34	11	6	0	3.09
1 Ned Garvin	R	28	1	1	.500	0	2	2	2	18	15	4	7	1	1.00
Gene McCann	R	26	1	2	.333	0	3	3	3	30	32	12	9	0	2.40
Lafe Winham	L	20	0	0	—	0	1	0	0	3	4	2	1	0	0.00
		28	73	64	.533	4	142	142	124	1260	1233	372	523	14	2.61
Togie Pittinger	R	30	27	15	.643	0	46	40	36	389	360	128	174	7	2.52
Vic Willis	R	26	27	19	.587	3	51	46	45	410	372	101	225	4	2.20
John Malarkey (IL)	R	30	9	11	.450	1	21	19	17	170	158	58	39	1	2.90
2 Mal Eason	R	23	9	13	.409	0	27	27	20	214	249	61	51	2	2.90
Fred Klobedanz	L	31	1	0	1.000	0	1	1	1	8	9	2	4	0	1.13
Pat Carney	L	25	1	0	1.000	0	2	1	1	9	5	3	4	0	9.00
Bob Dresser	L	23	0	1	.000	0	1	1	1	9	12	0	8	0	3.00
1 Dad Hale	R	22	0	4	.000	0	8	5	3	40	57	16	11	0	6.08
Sammy Curran	L	27	0	0	—	0	1	0	0	1	1	0	1	0	1.50
Red Long	R	25	0	0	—	0	1	1	1	8	4	3	5	0	1.13

CINCINNATI   4th 70-70 .500 33.5   BID McPHEE 27-37 .422   FRANK BANCROFT 9-7 .563   JOE KELLEY 34-26 .567

NAME	G by Pos	B	AGE	G	AB	R	H	2B	3B	HR	RBI	BB	SO	SB	BA	SA
TOTALS			29	141	4908	632	1383	188	77	18	531	297		131	.282	.362
Jake Beckley	1B129, P1	L	34	129	532	82	176	21	7	5	69	34		16	.331	.425
Heinie Peitz	2B45, C47, 3B6, 1B6	R	31	112	387	54	122	22	5	1	60	24		7	.315	.406
Tommy Corcoran	SS137, 2B1	R	33	137	537	54	135	20	4	0	54	11		23	.251	.304
Harry Steinfeldt	3B129, OF1	R	24	129	479	53	133	20	7	1	49	24		12	.278	.355
Sam Crawford	OF140	L	22	140	555	94	185	16	**23**	3	78	47		15	.333	.461
Dummy Hoy	OF72	L	40	72	279	48	82	16	2	2	20	41		12	.294	.387
1 Johnny Dobbs	OF63	L	27	63	256	39	76	7	3	1	16	19		7	.297	.359
Bill Bergen	C89	R	29	89	322	19	58	8	3	0	36	14		2	.180	.224
2 Cy Seymour	OF61, 3B1, P1	L	29	60	235	28	82	8	2	2	37	12		10	.349	.426
1 Erve Beck	2B32, 1B6, OF6	R	23	48	187	19	57	10	3	1	20	3		2	.305	.406
Maggie Magoon	2B41, SS3	R	27	45	162	29	44	9	2	0	23	13		7	.272	.352
Bill Phillips	P33	R	33	38	114	11	39	1	3	0	11	6		1	.342	.404
2 Joe Kelley	OF20, 2B10, 3B6, SS2	R	30	37	154	24	51	8	2	1	12	15		3	.327	.423
Mike Donlin (JA)	OF32, SS1, P1	L	24	34	143	30	42	4	5	0	9	9		9	.294	.392
2 Billy Maloney	OF18, C7	L	24	27	89	13	22	4	0	1	7	2		8	.247	.348
Jack Morrissey	2B11, OF1	B	25	12	39	5	11	1	1	0	3	4		0	.282	.359
1 Harry Bay	OF3	L	24	6	16	3	6	0	0	0	1	2		1	.375	.375

NAME	T	AGE	W	L	PCT	SV	G	GS	CG	IP	H	BB	SO	SHO	ERA
		27	70	70	.500	1	41	141	130	1239	1228	352	430	9	2.67
Noodles Hahn	L	23	23	12	.657	0	36	36	35	321	282	58	142	6	1.77
Bill Phillips	R	33	16	16	.500	0	33	33	30	269	267	55	85	0	2.51
2 Ed Poole	R	27	12	4	.750	0	16	16	16	138	129	54	55	2	2.15
2 Henry Thielman	R	21	9	15	.375	1	25	23	22	211	201	78	49	0	3.24
Bob Ewing (KJ)	R	29	5	6	.455	0	15	12	10	118	126	47	44	0	2.97
1 Clarence Curry	R	23	3	4	.429	0	10	7	6	65	70	17	20	1	3.74
1 Crese Heismann	L	22	2	1	.667	0	5	3	2	33	33	10	15	0	2.45
Jake Beckley	R	34	0	1	.000	0	1	1	0	4	9	1	2	0	6.75
Martin Glendon	R	25	0	1	.000	0	1	1	0	3	5	4	0	0	12.00
Buck Hooker	R	21	0	1	.000	0	1	1	1	8	11	0	0	0	4.50
Len Swormstedt	R	23	0	2	.000	0	2	2	2	18	22	5	3	0	4.00
Rube Vickers	R	24	0	3	.000	0	3	3	3	21	31	8	6	0	6.00
Archie Stimmel	R	29	0	4	.000	0	3	3	3	26	37	12	7	0	3.46
Mike Donlin (JA)	L	24	0	0	—	0	1	0	0	1	1	0	0	0	9.00
2 Cy Seymour	L	29	0	0	—	0	1	0	0	3	4	3	2	0	9.00

CHICAGO   5th 68-69 .496 34   FRANK SELEE

NAME	G by Pos	B	AGE	G	AB	R	H	2B	3B	HR	RBI	BB	SO	SB	BA	SA
TOTALS			26	141	4802	530	1200	131	40	6	423	353		222	.250	.298
Frank Chance	1B38, C29, OF4	R	25	75	240	39	69	9	4	1	31	35		27	.288	.371
Bobby Lowe	2B117, 3B2	R	33	119	472	41	116	13	3	0	31	11		16	.246	.286
Joe Tinker	SS124, 3B8	R	21	133	494	55	129	19	5	2	54	26		27	.261	.332
Germany Schaefer	3B75, 1B3, OF2, SS1	R	25	81	291	32	57	2	3	0	14	19		12	.196	.223
2 Davy Jones (IL)	OF64	L	22	64	243	41	74	12	3	0	14	38		12	.305	.379
1 Johnny Dobbs	OF59	L	27	59	235	31	71	8	2	0	35	18		3	.302	.353
Jimmy Slagle	OF113	L	28	115	454	64	143	11	4	0	28	53		40	.315	.357
Johnny Kling	C112, SS1	R	26	114	431	49	123	19	3	0	57	29		24	.285	.343
Charlie Dexter	3B39, 1B22, OF10	R	26	69	266	30	60	12	0	2	26	19		13	.226	.293
J. Menefee	P22, OF22, 1B19, 3B2, 2B1	R	34	63	216	24	50	4	1	0	15	15		4	.231	.259
Dakin Miller	OF51	L	25	51	187	17	46	4	1	0	13	7		10	.246	.278
Art Williams	OF24, 1B19	L	24	47	160	17	37	3	0	0	14	15		9	.231	.250
Bunk Congalton	OF45	L	27	45	179	14	40	3	0	1	24	7		3	.223	.257
1 Hal O'Hagen	1B31		32	31	108	10	21	1	3	0	10	11		8	.194	.259
Johnny Evers	2B18, SS8	L	20	25	89	7	20	0	0	0	2	3		1	.225	.225
Fred Clark	1B12	L	28	12	43	1	8	1	0	0	2	4		1	.186	.209
Jim Murray	OF12	R	24	12	47	3	8	0	0	0	1	2		0	.170	.170
Larry Schlafly	OF5, 2B4, 3B2	R	23	10	31	5	10	0	3	0	5	6		2	.323	.516
1 Mike Kahoe	C4, 3B2, SS1	R	28	7	18	0	4	0	0	0	2	0		0	.222	.278
Mike Lynch	OF7		26	7	28	4	4	0	0	0	0	2		0	.143	.143
Mike Jacobs	SS5		24	5	19	1	4	0	0	0	2	0		0	.211	.211
Ed Glenn	SS2			2	7	0	0	0	0	0	0	1		0	.000	.000
2 Jack Hendricks	OF2	L	27	2	7	0	4	0	1	0	0	0		0	.571	.857

2 Sammy Strang 25 B 4-11, Pete Lamer 28 2-9, Chick Pedroes 32 0-6, George Hildebrand 23 R 0-4, Joe Hughes 22 R 0-3, Snapper Kennedy 23 R 0-5

NAME	T	AGE	W	L	PCT	SV	G	GS	CG	IP	H	BB	SO	SHO	ERA
		26	68	69	.496	2	141	141	132	1275	1235	279	437	17	**2.21**
Jack Taylor	R	28	23	11	.676	1	36	33	33	325	271	43	83	7	**1.33**
Jocko Menefee	R	34	12	10	.545	0	22	21	20	197	202	26	60	4	2.42
Pop Williams	R	28	11	16	.407	0	31	31	26	254	259	63	94	1	2.52
Carl Lundgren	R	22	9	9	.500	0	18	18	17	160	158	45	68	1	1.97
Jim St. Vrain	L	19	4	6	.400	0	12	11	10	95	88	25	51	1	2.08
Bob Rhoades	R	22	4	8	.333	1	16	12	12	118	131	42	43	1	3.20
Alex Hardy	L	25	2	2	.500	0	4	4	4	35	29	12	12	1	3.60
1 Mal Eason	R	23	1	1	.500	0	2	2	2	18	21	2	4	0	1.00
Jim Gardner	R	27	1	2	.333	0	3	3	2	25	23	10	6	0	2.88
Deacon Morrissey	R	26	1	3	.250	0	5	5	5	40	40	8	13	0	2.25
Fred Glade	R	26	0	1	.000	0	1	1	1	8	13	3	0	0	9.00

ST. LOUIS   6th 56-78 .418 44.5   PATSY DONOVAN

NAME	G by Pos	B	AGE	G	AB	R	H	2B	3B	HR	RBI	BB	SO	SB	BA	SA
TOTALS			29	140	4751	517	1226	116	37	10	402	273		158	.258	.304
Roy Brashear	1B67, 2B21, OF16, SS3	R	28	110	388	36	107	8	2	1	40	32		9	.276	.314
John Farrell	2B118, SS21	R	25	138	565	68	141	13	5	0	25	43		9	.250	.290
Otto Krueger	SS107, 3B18	R	25	128	467	55	124	15	4	0	46	29		14	.266	.315
Fred Hartman	3B105, SS4, 1B3	R	34	114	416	30	90	10	3	0	52	14		4	.216	.255
Patsy Donovan	OF126	L	37	126	502	68	155	12	4	0	35	28		41	.309	.349
Homer Smoot	OF129	L	24	129	518	58	161	19	4	3	48	23		20	.311	.380
George Barclay	OF137	R	26	137	543	79	163	14	2	3	53	31		30	.300	.350
Jack Ryan	C66, 1B4, 3B4, 2B2, SS1	R	33	76	267	23	48	4	4	0	14	4		2	.180	.225
Art Nichols (JJ)	1B56, C11, OF4	R	30	73	251	36	67	12	0	1	31	21		18	.267	.327
Jack O'Neill	C59	R	29	63	192	13	27	1	1	0	12	13		2	.141	.156
Mike O'Neill	P36, OF1	L	24	51	135	21	43	5	3	2	15	2		0	.319	.444
Jack Calhoun	3B12, 1B5, OF1	R	22	20	64	3	10	2	1	0	8	8		1	.156	.219
Art Weaver	C11		23	11	33	2	6	2	0	0	3	1		0	.182	.242
Doc Hazelton	1B7		24	7	23	0	3	0	0	0	2	2		0	.130	.130
Rudy Kling	SS4	R	32	4	10	1	2	0	0	0	0	4		1	.200	.200
Otto Williams	SS2	R	24	2	5	0	2	0	0	0	2	1		1	.400	.400
John Murphy	3B1		31	1	3	1	2	1	0	0	1	1		0	.667	1.000

NAME	T	AGE	W	L	PCT	SV	G	GS	CG	IP	H	BB	SO	SHO	ERA
		25	56	78	.418	4	140	140	112	1128	**1399**	338	400	7	3.47
Mike O'Neill	L	24	16	15	.516	2	36	32	29	288	297	66	105	2	2.91
Stan Yerkes	R	27	12	21	.364	0	39	37	27	273	341	79	81	1	3.66
Ed Murphy	R	25	10	6	.625	1	23	17	12	164	187	31	37	1	3.24
2 Clarence Curry	R	23	7	5	.583	0	15	12	10	125	125	35	30	2	2.59
Bob Wicker	R	24	5	12	.294	0	22	16	14	152	159	45	78	1	3.20
Wiley Dunham	R	25	2	3	.400	1	7	5	3	38	47	13	15	0	5.68
Aleck Pearson	R	25	2	6	.250	0	11	10	8	82	90	12	24	0	3.95
Bill Popp	R	25	2	6	.250	0	9	7	5	60	87	26	20	0	4.95
Chappie McFarland	R	27	0	1	.000	0	1	1	1	11	11	3	1	0	5.73
Jim Hackett	R	24	0	3	.000	0	4	3	3	30	46	16	7	0	6.30
Joe Adams	L	24	0	0	—	0	1	0	0	7	9	2	0	0	9.00

PHILADELPHIA   7th 56-81 .409 46   BILLY SHETTSLINE

NAME	G by Pos	B	AGE	G	AB	R	H	2B	3B	HR	RBI	BB	SO	SB	BA	SA
TOTALS			27	138	4615	484	1139	110	43	5	389	356		108	.247	.293
Hughie Jennings	1B69, SS5, 2B4	R	33	78	289	31	80	16	3	1	32	14		8	.277	.363
Pete Childs	2B123	L	30	123	403	26	78	5	0	0	25	34		6	.194	.206
Rudy Hulswitt	SS125, 3B3	R	25	128	497	59	135	11	7	0	38	30		12	.272	.322
Billy Hallman	3B72	R	35	73	254	14	63	8	4	0	35	14		9	.248	.311
Shad Barry	OF137, 1B1	R	23	138	543	65	156	20	6	3	58	44		14	.287	.344
Roy Thomas	OF138	L	28	138	500	89	143	4	7	0	24	**107**		17	.286	.322
1 George Browne	OF70	R	26	70	281	41	73	7	1	0	26	16		11	.260	.292
Red Dooin	C84, OF6	R	23	94	333	20	77	7	3	0	35	10		8	.231	.270
Klondike Douglass	1B69, C29, OF10	L	30	109	408	37	95	12	3	0	37	23		6	.233	.277
Henry Krug	OF28, 2B13, SS9, 3B6	R	25	53	198	20	45	3	3	0	14	7		2	.227	.273
Doc White	P36, OF19	L	23	61	179	17	47	3	1	1	15	11		5	.263	.307
Fred Jacklitsch	C29, OF1	R	26	38	114	8	23	4	0	0	8	9		2	.202	.237
2 Harry Wolverton	3B34	B	28	34	136	12	40	3	2	0	16	9		3	.294	.346
Patsy Greene	3B19	R	27	19	65	6	11	1	0	1	2	2		0	.169	.185
Bill Thomas	OF3, 1B1, 2B1	R	24	6	17	1	2	0	0	0	0	1		0	.118	.118
Tom Fleming	OF5		28	5	16	2	6	0	0	0	2	1		0	.375	.375
Bill Clay	OF3	R	27	3	8	1	2	0	0	0	1	0		0	.250	.250
Nap Shea	C3	R	27	3	8	1	1	0	0	0	0	2		0	.125	.125

Howard Berry 29 B 1-4, Tom Maher 27 0-0, Ed Watkins 25 0-3, Frank Mahar 23 0-1

NAME	T	AGE	W	L	PCT	SV	G	GS	CG	IP	H	BB	SO	SHO	ERA
		27	56	81	.409	3	138	138	118	1211	1323	334	504	8	3.50
Doc White	L	23	16	20	.444	1	36	35	34	306	277	72	185	3	2.53
Chick Fraser	R	28	12	13	.480	0	27	26	24	224	238	74	97	3	3.42
2 Bill Duggleby	R	29	11	17	.393	1	33	27	25	259	282	57	60	0	3.37
Ham Iburg	R	28	11	18	.379	0	30	29	20	236	286	62	106	1	3.89
1 Cy Voorhes	R	27	3	5	.375	0	10	8	7	54	63	20	24	1	3.83
2 Billy Magee	R	26	2	4	.333	0	8	7	6	54	61	18	15	0	3.67
Harry Felix	R	32	1	3	.250	0	5	5	5	45	61	11	10	0	5.60
Barney McFadden	R	25	0	1	.000	1	1	1	1	9	14	7	3	0	8.00
Jesse Whiting	R	23	0	1	.000	0	1	1	1	13	6	4	5	0	5.00
Bill Wolff		26	0	1	.000	0	1	1	1	9	11	4	3	0	4.00
Bill Salisbury	R	25	0	0	—	0	1	6	1	15	2	0	1	0	13.50
Henry Fox		28	0	1		0	1	1	0	1	4	1	1	0	18.00

NEW YORK   8th 48-88 .353 53.5   HORACE FOGEL 18-23 .439   HEINE SMITH 5-27 .156   JOHN McGRAW 25-38 .397

NAME	G by Pos	B	AGE	G	AB	R	H	2B	3B	HR	RBI	BB	SO	SB	BA	SA
TOTALS			29	139	4571	401	1088	147	34	8	336	252		187	.238	.290
2 Dan McGann	1B61	B	30	61	226	26	68	6	7	0	21	12		12	.301	.389
Heinie Smith	2B138	R	30	138	511	46	129	19	2	3	33	17		32	.252	.297
Joe Bean	SS48	R	28	48	176	13	39	2	1	0	5	5		9	.222	.244
Billy Lauder	3B121, OF4	R	28	125	482	41	114	20	1	4	44	10		19	.237	.288
Jack Dunn	OF43, SS36, 3B18, P3, 2B1	R	29	100	342	26	72	11	1	0	14	20		13	.211	.249
Steve Brodie	OF109	L	33	109	417	35	117	8	2	3	42	22		11	.281	.332
Jimmy Jones	OF67	R	25	67	249	16	59	11	1	0	19	13		7	.237	.289
Frank Bowerman	C98, 1B3	R	33	105	372	37	94	13	6	0	26	13		5	.253	.320
2 George Browne	OF53	R	26	53	216	30	69	9	5	0	14	9		13	.319	.407
2 R. Bresnahan	OF27, C16, 1B4, SS4, 3B1	R	23	51	178	16	51	9	3	1	22	16		6	.287	.352
1 Jack Doyle	1B49	R	32	50	190	25	57	12	1	1	19	10		10	.300	.389
1 George Yeager	C27, 1B3, OF1	R	28	38	108	6	22	3	2	0	9	11		1	.204	.241
Jim Jackson	OF34	R	24	35	110	14	20	5	1	0	13	15		6	.182	.245
2 John McGraw	SS34	L	29	36	106	13	24	0	0	0	5	26		7	.226	.226
24 Hal O'Hagan	1B18, OF8	R	32	26	84	5	16	2	1	0	8	2		3	.143	.190
George VanHaltren (BN)	OF24	L	36	26	96	14	24	1	2	0	7	17		7	.250	.302
Roy Clark	OF20	L	21	20	76	4	11	1	0	0	5	4		1	.145	.158
Heinie Wagner	SS17	R	21	17	56	4	12	1	0	0	1	5		3	.214	.232
1 Jack Hendricks	OF7	L	27	7	26	3	6	0	0	0	1	3		1	.231	.308
Jim Delahanty	OF7	R	23	7	26	4	6	1	0	0	4	0		0	.231	.269
1 Joe Wall	OF3	L	28	6	20	1	7	0	0	0	1	0		0	.357	.500
Libe Washburn	OF3	L	28	6	9	1	4	0	0	0	1	4		0	.444	.444
Jack Robinson	C3	R	21	4	9	1	0	0	0	0	0	0		0	.000	.000

Jim McDonald R 3-9, John O'Neill 0-8, Jim Callahan 21 R 0-4, Chick Hartley 21 R 0-4

NAME	T	AGE	W	L	PCT	SV	G	GS	CG	IP	H	BB	SO	SHO	ERA
		27	48	88	.353	1	139	139	118	1226	1193	332	501	11	2.82
Christy Mathewson	R	21	14	17	.452	0	34	32	29	277	241	73	159	**8**	2.11
2 Joe McGinnity	R	31	8	8	.500	0	19	16	16	153	122	32	67	1	2.06
1 Roy Evans	R	28	8	12	.400	0	23	17	17	176	186	58	48	0	3.17
2 Dummy Taylor	R	27	7	15	.318	0	26	26	18	201	194	55	87	0	2.28
3 Jack Cronin	R	28	5	6	.455	0	13	12	11	114	105	18	52	0	2.45
1 Tully Sparks	R	27	4	11	.267	1	15	13	11	115	123	40	40	0	3.76
Brickyard Kennedy (IL)	R	34	1	4	.200	0	6	6	4	39	44	16	9	1	3.92
2 Roscoe Miller	R	25	1	8	.111	0	10	9	7	73	77	11	15	0	4.56
John Burke	R	25	0	0	—	0	1	1	0	5	9	5	2	0	5.79
1 Henry Thielman	R	24	1	0	1.000	0	1	1	1	10	9	1	2	0	1.50
Bob Blewett	L	25	0	2	.000	0	5	3	2	28	39	7	8	0	4.82
Jack Dunn	R	29	0	1	.000	0	3	1	1	17	28	12	6	0	3.67
1 Billy Magee	R	26	0	0	—	0	2	1	0	5	2	4	0	0	3.60

1903 The First Embarrassment of a New Peace

The raiding stopped, the polemics ceased, and peace came to the baseball world under a new National Agreement between two equal leagues. The players and managers now concentrated on the ballfield, while the owners concentrated on the turnstiles which clicked at a record pace.

The Pittsburgh Pirates breezed to their third straight National League pennant in an easier race than the final margin of 6 1/2 games would indicate. The heavy-hitting Pirates were never out of the top spot after June 19, staving off threats from New York and Chicago. Honus Wagner took down his second batting crown with a .355 average, while Fred Clarke and Ginger Beaumont, as usual, placed among the league leaders. On the mound, Sam Leever won 25 games and Deacon Phillippe 24 at the head of the pennant column. The Giants rose into second place in the first full year of John McGraw's leadership, Baltimore expatriate Roger Bresnahan swung the stick at a .350 pace, and fellow re-jumper Joe McGinnity teamed up with Christy Mathewson to give the Giants a pair of 30-win aces; the influx of Baltimore talent triggered a rise from sixth to runner-up and an increase in the gate despite fan competition from the new New York Highlanders in the American League.

The success of the new American League club in New York removed any doubts of the major league status of the circuit. Playing in the freshly opened Highlander Park in upper Manhattan, the new club in town got away to a slow start but rallied to finish in the first division; the squad which boasted of Willie Keeler, Jack Chesbro, and Clark Griffith carved for itself a new following out of the Gotham fandom and planted a seed which would bloom into baseball's most successful franchise. At the top of the standings, Boston danced home first with 14 1/2 games to spare, spurred on by Cy Young's 28 wins- tops in the league for the third time. Connie Mack's A's slumped into a distant runner-up spot due to a falloff in hitting.

The two pennant winners became teams of destiny when owners, Barney Dreyfus of Pittsburgh and Henry Killilea of Boston, agreed in August to pit their front-running clubs against each other in the fall in a nine-game series for the "world's" championship. The handshake arrangement between the two magnates set up the first World Series and the first inter-league championship series since the 1890 match of the National League and American Association champs.

A large crowd of 16,242 assembled in Boston on October 1, to witness the first World Series game, a match-up between the legendary Cy Young and Pirate ace Deacon Phillippe. Young's fastballs met a hostile reception as the Bucs belted him for four runs in the top of the first, while Phillippe struck out ten Boston batters on the way to a 7-3 victory. Pittsburgh's Jimmy Seibring spiced the victory with the first home run in the fall classic. After four games, the Bucs had three wins in hand, but Bill Dinneen and Young came back to win two games each as Boston swept the next four to take the first World Series title. Dinneen won three games for the winners, while Chick Stahl and Hobe Ferris led the Boston offense, Phillippe was the victor in all three Pirate victories, as his pitching partner, Sam Leever, was soundly hit in both his appearances.

Before the books on the 1903 season could be closed, two tragic footnotes to baseball would have to be added to the history of the game. The first occurred in January, as a 28-year old Detroit pitcher Win Mercer committed suicide by gas inhalation in San Francisco, thus ending a nine-year major league career. The second tragedy provided the basis for one of baseball's most clouded mysteries. It involved Washington's Ed Delahanty, a superstar who dominated the averages of his time, having won league batting honors with the Phillies in 1899 with a .410 mark and with Washington in 1902 with .376. Delahanty, known to have bouts of drunkenness, reportedly left his team in Detroit to return East to recover from illness. While aboard the New York Central train heading to New York, the train crossed a bridge over Niagara Falls. What happened aboard the train-whether Delahanty lost his balance and fell while searching out the bar car, committed suicide, or got into a brawl and was thrown from the train-is still unknown. The only known fact is that the talented athlete was found below the falls two days later on July 4. His sensational death made newspaper headlines at the time, and his 16-year batting mark of .346 was enough to place him in the Hall of Fame, and fifth lifetime in the history of baseball behind Ty Cobb, Rogers Hornsby, Shoeless Joe Jackson, and Pete Browning.

1903 AMERICAN LEAGUE

BOSTON 1st 91-47 .659 JIMMY COLLINS

NAME	G by Pos	B	AGE	G	AB	R	H	2B	3B	HR	RBI	BB	SO	SB	BA	SA
TOTALS			30	141	4919	707	1336	222	113	48		609	262	141	.272	.392
Candy LaChance	1B141	B	33	141	522	60	134	22	6	1	53	28		12	.257	.328
Hobe Ferris	2B139, SS2	R	25	141	525	69	132	19	7	9	66	25		11	.251	.366
Freddy Parent	SS139	R	27	139	560	83	170	31	17	4	80	13		24	.304	.441
Jimmy Collins	3B130	R	33	130	541	87	160	34	17	5	72	24		22	.296	.449
Buck Freeman	OF141	L	31	141	565	74	161	39	21	13	104	30		4	.285	.497
Chick Stahl (JJ)	OF74	L	30	78	298	60	83	11	6	2	44	28		14	.279	.376
Patsy Dougherty	OF139	L	26	139	590	106	195	19	12	4	59	33		35	.331	.424
Lou Criger	C96	R	31	96	317	41	61	7	10	3	31	26		5	.192	.306
Jack O'Brien	OF71, 3B11, 2B4, SS1	R	30	96	338	44	71	14	4	3	38	21		10	.210	.302
Cy Young	P40	R	36	41	137	21	44	6	3	1	14	4		2	.321	.431
Jack Stahl	C28, OF1	R	24	40	92	14	22	3	5	2	8	4		1	.239	.446
Long Tom Hughes	P33	R	24	33	93	14	26	4	2	1	13	3		1	.280	.398
Duke Farrell (BL)	C17	R	36	17	52	5	21	5	1	0	8	5		1	.404	.538
Broadway Aleck Smith	C10		32	11	33	4	10	1	0	0	1	0		0	.303	.333
Harry Gleason	3B2	R	28	6	13	3	2	1	0	0	2	0		0	.154	.231
George Stone		L	26	2	2	0	0	0	0	0	0	0		0	.000	.000

NAME	T	AGE	W	L	PCT	SV	G	GS	CG	IP	H	BB	SO	SHO	ERA
		28	91	47	.659	3	141	141	123	1255	1142	269	579	20	2.56
Cy Young	R	36	28	9	.757	3	40	35	34	342	294	37	176	7	2.08
Long Tom Hughes	R	24	20	7	.741	0	33	31	25	245	232	60	112	5	2.57
Bill Dinneen	R	27	21	11	.656	1	37	35	32	299	255	66	148	6	2.23
Norwood Gibson	R	26	13	11	.542	0	24	21	17	183	166	65	76	2	3.08
George Winter	R	25	9	8	.529	0	24	18	14	178	182	37	64	0	3.08
1 Nick Altrock (IL)	L	26	0	1	.000	0	1	1	1	8	13	4	3	0	9.00

PHILADELPHIA 2nd 75-60 .556 14.5 CONNIE MACK

NAME	G by Pos	B	AGE	G	AB	R	H	2B	3B	HR	RBI	BB	SO	SB	BA	SA
TOTALS			30	137	4673	597	1236	228	68	31		502	268	157	.264	.362
Harry Davis	1B104, OF2	R	29	101	403	74	120	29	7	5	55	24		24	.298	.436
Danny Murphy	2B133	R	26	133	512	65	141	29	11	4	60	13		17	.275	.381
Monte Cross	SS137, 2B1	R	33	137	470	44	116	21	2	3	45	49		31	.247	.319
Lave Cross	3B136, 1B1	R	37	137	554	61	162	23	5	2	90	10		13	.292	.363
Socks Seybold	OF120, 1B18	R	32	137	531	78	159	43	8	8	84	38		5	.299	.456
Ollie Pickering	OF135	L	33	137	512	93	144	18	6	1	36	53		40	.281	.346
Topsy Hartsel	OF96	L	29	98	373	65	116	19	14	5	26	49		13	.311	.477
Ossee Schreckengost	C77, 1B10	R	28	92	306	26	78	13	4	3	30	11		0	.255	.353
Mike Powers	C66, 1B7	R	32	75	247	19	56	11	1	0	23	5		1	.227	.279
Danny Hoffman	OF62, P1	L	23	74	248	29	61	5	7	2	22	6		7	.246	.347
Bert Daly	2B4, 3B3, SS1	R	22	10	21	2	4	0	2	0	4	1		0	.190	.381
John Kalahan	C1	R	24	1	5	0	0	0	0	0	0	0		0	.000	.000
Ed Hilley	3B1	R	24	1	3	1	1	0	0	0	0	1		0	.333	.333

NAME	T	AGE	W	L	PCT	SV	G	GS	CG	IP	H	BB	SO	SHO	ERA
		24	75	60	.556	1	137	137	112	1207	1124	315	728	10	2.98
Eddie Plank	L	27	23	16	.590	0	43	40	33	336	317	65	176	3	2.38
Rube Waddell	L	26	22	16	.579	0	39	38	34	324	274	85	302	4	2.44
Chief Bender	R	20	17	15	.531	0	36	33	29	270	239	65	127	2	3.07
Weldon Henley	R	22	12	9	.571	0	29	21	13	186	186	67	86	1	3.92
Conny McGeehan	R	20	1	0	1.000	0	3	0	0	9	9	1	4	0	4.50
Lee Fairbank	R	22	0	0	—	0	4	1	1	24	33	12	10	0	4.88
Tad Quinn	R	21	0	0	—	0	2	0	0	9	11	5	1	0	5.00
Danny Hoffman	L	23	0	0	—	0	1	0	0	3	2	1	0	0	3.00
Ed Pinnance	R	23	0	1	.000	1	2	1	0	7	5	2	2	0	2.57
Andy Coakley	R	20	0	3	.000	0	6	3	2	38	48	11	20	0	5.45

CLEVELAND 3rd 77-63 .550 15 BILL ARMOUR

NAME	G by Pos	B	AGE	G	AB	R	H	2B	3B	HR	RBI	BB	SO	SB	BA	SA
TOTALS			28	140	4773	639	1265	231	95	31		550	259	175	.265	.373
Charley Hickman	1B125, 2B7	R	27	130	518	67	171	31	11	12	97	17		15	.330	.502
Nap Lajoie	2B122, 1B1, 3B1	R	27	126	488	90	173	40	13	7	93	24		22	.355	.533
John Gochnaur	SS134	R	27	134	438	48	81	16	4	0	48	48		10	.185	.240
Bill Bradley	3B136	R	25	137	543	103	171	35	22	6	68	25		23	.315	.494
Elmer Flick	OF140	L	27	142	529	84	158	22	16	2	51	51		4	.299	.412
Harry Bay	OF140	L	25	137	579	94	169	15	12	1	35	29		45	.292	.364
1 Jack McCarthy	OF108	L	34	108	415	47	110	20	8	0	43	19		15	.265	.352
Harry Bemis	C74, 1B10, 2B1	R	29	92	314	31	82	20	3	1	41	8		5	.261	.354
Fred Abbott	C71, 1B3	R	28	77	255	26	60	11	3	1	25	7		8	.235	.314
Jack Thoney	OF24, 2B5, 3B2	R	23	32	122	10	25	3	0	1	9	2		7	.205	.254
Billy Clingman	2B11, SS7, 3B3	R	33	21	64	10	18	1	1	0	7	11		2	.281	.328
Jack Hardy	OF5	R	26	5	19	1	3	1	0	0	1	1		1	.158	.211
1 Jack Slattery	1B2	R	26	4	11	1	0	0	0	0	0	0		0	.000	.000
Happy Jack Iott	OF3	R	26	3	10	1	2	0	0	0	0	0		1	.200	.200
Hugh Hill		L	23	1	1	0	0	0	0	0	0	0		0	.000	.000

NAME	T	AGE	W	L	PCT	SV	G	GS	CG	IP	H	BB	SO	SHO	ERA
		25	77	63	.550	2	140	140	125	1244	1161	271	521	20	2.66
Earl Moore	R	23	20	8	.714	1	28	26	26	239	189	56	142	3	1.77
Addie Joss	R	23	18	13	.581	0	33	32	32	293	239	43	126	3	2.15
Bill Bernhard (BG)	R	32	14	6	.700	0	20	19	18	166	151	21	60	3	2.11
2 Red Donahue	R	30	7	9	.438	0	16	15	14	137	142	12	45	4	2.43
Jesse Stovall	R	27	5	1	.833	0	7	5	4	57	44	21	12	2	2.05
Gus Dorner	R	26	3	5	.375	1	12	8	4	74	83	24	28	3	3.28
Ed Killian	L	26	3	5	.375	0	9	8	7	62	61	13	18	3	2.47
1 Gene Wright	R	24	3	9	.250	0	15	12	8	102	122	58	42	0	5.74
2 Bob Rhoades	R	23	2	3	.400	0	5	5	5	41	55	3	21	0	5.27
Martin Glendon	R	26	1	2	.333	0	3	3	2	28	20	7	9	0	0.96
Aleck Pearson	R	26	1	2	.333	0	4	4	2	30	34	3	12	0	3.60
1 Bill Pounds	R	25	0	0	—	0	3	0	0	10	12	3	1	0	10.80
Ed Walker	L	28	0	0	—	0	3	0	0	12	13	10	4	0	5.25

NEW YORK 4th 72-62 .537 17 CLARK GRIFFITH

NAME	G by Pos	B	AGE	G	AB	R	H	2B	3B	HR	RBI	BB	SO	SB	BA	SA
TOTALS			29	136	4565	579	1136	193	62	18	474	332		160	.249	.330
John Ganzel	1B129	R	29	136	476	62	132	25	7	3	71	30		9	.277	.378
Jimmy Williams	2B132	R	26	132	502	60	134	30	12	3	82	39		9	.267	.392
2 Kid Elberfield	SS90	R	28	90	349	49	100	18	5	0	45	22		16	.287	.367
Wid Conroy	3B123, SS4	R	26	126	503	74	137	23	12	1	45	32		33	.272	.372
Willie Keeler	OF128, 3B4	L	31	132	515	98	164	13	7	0	32	32		25	.318	.371
Herm McFarland	OF103	L	33	103	362	41	88	16	9	5	45	46		13	.243	.378
Lefty Davis	OF102, SS1	L	28	104	372	54	88	10	0	0	25	43		11	.237	.263
Monte Beville	C75, 1B3	L	28	82	258	23	50	14	1	0	29	16		4	.194	.256
Dave Fultz	OF77, 3B2	R	28	79	295	39	66	12	1	0	25	25		29	.224	.271
Jack O'Connor (ST)	C63, 1B1	R	34	64	212	13	43	4	1	0	12	8		4	.203	.231
1 Ernie Courtney	SS19, 2B4, 1B1	L	28	25	79	7	21	3	3	1	8	7		1	.266	.418
1 Herman Long	SS22	L	37	22	80	6	15	3	0	0	8	2		3	.188	.225
Jack Zalusky	C6, 1B1	R	24	7	16	2	5	0	0	0	1	1		0	.313	.313
Pat McCauley	C6		33	6	19	0	1	0	0	0	1	0		0	.053	.053
1 Patsy Greene	3B2, SS1	R	28	4	13	1	4	1	0	0	0	0		0	.308	.385
Tim Jordan	1B2	L	24	2	8	2	1	0	0	0	0	0		0	.125	.125
Fred Holmes	1B1	R	25	1	0	0	0	0	0	0	0	0		0	.000	.000

NAME	T	AGE	W	L	PCT	SV	G	GS	CG	IP	H	BB	SO	SHO	ERA
		29	72	62	.537	2	136	136	111	1201	1171	245	463	7	3.08
Jack Chesbro	R	29	21	15	.583	2	40	36	33	325	300	74	147	1	2.77
Jesse Tannehill	L	28	15	15	.500	0	32	31	22	240	258	34	106	2	3.26
Clark Griffith	R	33	14	10	.583	0	25	24	22	213	201	33	69	2	2.70
Harry Howell	R	26	10	7	.588	0	25	15	13	156	140	44	62	0	3.52
Barney Wolfe	R	27	6	9	.400	0	20	16	12	148	143	26	48	1	2.98
2 John Deering	R	24	3	1	.750	0	9	7	6	60	59	18	14	1	3.75
Ambrose Puttmann	L	22	2	0	1.000	0	3	2	1	19	16	4	8	0	0.95
Elmer Bliss	R	28	1	0	1.000	0	1	0	0	5	4	0	2	0	0.00
Doc Adkins	R	30	0	1	.000	0	1	0	0	7	10	5	0	0	7.71
Eddie Quick	L	21	0	1	.000	0	1	1	0	4	5	1	1	0	4.50
Snake Wiltse	L	31	0	3	.000	1	4	3	2	25	35	6	6	0	5.40

DETROIT 5th 65-71 .478 25 WIN MERCER (DD) 0-0 .000 ED BARROW 65-71 .478

NAME	G by Pos	B	AGE	G	AB	R	H	2B	3B	HR	RBI	BB	SO	SB	BA	SA
TOTALS			29	137	4582	567	1229	162	91	12	451	292		128	.268	.351
Charlie Carr	1B135	R	26	135	548	59	154	23	11	2	79	10		10	.281	.374
Heinie Smith	2B93	R	31	93	336	36	75	11	3	1	22	19		12	.223	.283
S. McAllister	SS46, C18, OF5, 3B4, 1B1	B	28	78	265	31	69	8	2	0	22	10		5	.260	.306
Joe Yeager	3B107, SS1, P1	R	27	109	402	36	103	15	6	0	43	18		9	.256	.323
Sam Crawford	OF137	R	23	137	545	49	181	23	25	4	89	25		23	.332	.488
Jimmy Barrett	OF136	L	28	136	513	95	163	13	10	2	31	74		27	.315	.391
Billy Lush	OF101, 3B12, 2B3, SS3	R	29	119	423	71	116	18	14	1	33	70		14	.274	.390
Deacon McGuire	C69, 1B1	R	39	72	248	15	62	12	1	0	21	19		3	.250	.306
2 Herman Long (AJ)	SS38, 2B31	L	37	69	239	21	53	12	0	0	23	10		11	.222	.272
Fritz Buelow	C60, 1B2	R	27	63	192	24	41	3	6	1	13	6		4	.214	.307
George Mullin	P41, OF1	R	22	46	126	11	35	9	1	1	12	2		1	.278	.389
1 Kid Elberfield	SS34, 3B1	R	28	35	132	29	45	5	3	0	19	11		6	.341	.424
1 Doc Gessler	OF28	L	22	29	105	9	25	5	4	0	12	3		1	.238	.362
2 Ernie Courtney	3B13, SS9	L	28	24	74	7	17	0	0	0	6	5		1	.230	.230
John Burns	2B11	R	23	11	37	2	10	0	0	0	3	1		0	.270	.270
John Murphy	SS5		32	5	22	1	4	1	0	0	1	0		0	.182	.227
Simon Nicholls	SS2	L	20	2	8	0	3	0	0	0	0	0		0	.375	.375
2 Patsy Greene	3B1	R	28	1	3	0	0	0	0	0	0	0		0	.000	.000
Sam McMackin (DD)																
Win Mercer (DD)		28														

NAME	T	AGE	W	L	PCT	SV	G	GS	CG	IP	H	BB	SO	SHO	ERA
		26	65	71	.478	3	137	137	123	1196	1169	336	554	15	2.75
George Mullin	R	22	19	14	.576	3	41	36	31	321	284	106	170	6	2.24
Wild Bill Donovan	R	26	17	16	.515	0	35	34	34	307	247	95	187	4	2.29
Frank Kitson	R	31	15	15	.500	0	31	28	28	258	277	38	102	2	2.58
Rube Kisinger	R	26	7	9	.438	0	16	14	13	119	118	27	33	2	2.95
1 John Deering	R	24	3	6	.333	0	10	8	5	61	77	24	14	0	3.84
John Skopec	R	23	2	2	.500	0	6	5	3	39	46	13	14	0	3.46
Mal Eason	R	24	2	4	.333	0	7	6	6	56	60	19	21	1	3.38
Joe Yeager	R	27	0	1	.000	0	1	1	1	9	15	0	1	0	4.00
Alex Jones	L	33	0	2	.000	0	2	2	0	9	19	6	2	0	12.00
Harry Kane	L	19	0	2	.000	0	3	3	2	18	26	8	10	0	8.50

ST. LOUIS 6th 65-74 .468 26.5 JIMMY McALEER

NAME	G by Pos	B	AGE	G	AB	R	H	2B	3B	HR	RBI	BB	SO	SB	BA	SA
TOTALS			28	139	4639	504	1133	166	68	12	408	271		101	.244	.317
John Anderson	1B133, OF7	B	29	138	550	65	156	34	8	2	78	23		16	.284	.385
Bill Friel	2B63, 3B24, OF9	R	27	97	351	46	80	11	8	0	25	23		4	.228	.305
Bobby Wallace	SS135	R	29	136	519	63	127	20	17	1	54	28		11	.245	.355
Hunter Hill	3B86	R	24	86	317	30	77	11	3	0	25	8		2	.243	.297
Charlie Hemphill	OF104	L	27	105	383	36	94	6	3	3	29	23		16	.245	.300
Snags Heidrick	OF119, C1	R	26	120	461	55	129	20	15	1	42	19		19	.280	.395
Jesse Burkett	OF132	L	34	133	514	74	152	20	7	3	40	52		16	.296	.379
Mike Kahoe	C71, OF2	R	29	77	244	26	46	7	5	0	23	11		1	.189	.258
Joe Sudgen	C66, 1B8	B	32	79	243	25	52	4	0	0	22	25		5	.214	.230
1 Barry McCormick	2B28, 3B28, SS4	R	28	61	207	13	45	6	1	1	16	18		5	.217	.271
2 Joe Martin	OF38, 2B6, 3B1	L	27	44	173	18	37	6	4	0	7	6		4	.214	.295
Dick Padden (RJ)	2B29	R	22	29	94	7	19	3	0	0	6	9		5	.202	.234
Benny Bowcock	2B14	R	23	14	50	7	16	3	1	1	10	3		1	.320	.480
Pinky Swander	OF14	L	22	14	51	9	14	2	2	0	6	10		0	.275	.392
Owen Shannon	C8, 1B1	R	23	9	28	1	6	2	0	0	3	1		0	.214	.286
Claude Gouzzie	2B1	R	30	1	1	0	0	0	0	0	0	0		0	.000	.000

NAME	T	AGE	W	L	PCT	SV	G	GS	CG	IP	H	BB	SO	SHO	ERA
		28	65	74	.468	5	139	139	124	1222	1220	237	511	12	2.77
Willie Sudhoff	R	28	21	16	.511	1	38	35	30	294	262	56	104	5	2.27
Jack Powell	R	28	15	19	.441	2	38	34	33	306	294	58	169	4	2.91
Ed Siever	L	28	14	15	.483	0	31	27	24	254	245	39	90	1	2.75
1 Red Donahue	R	30	7	6	.538	1	16	15	14	131	145	22	51	0	2.75
Barney Peity	R	22	3	3	.500	1	7	6	5	49	49	15	20	1	2.39
2 Gene Wright	R	24	2	4	.333	0	8	8	7	61	73	16	37	1	3.69
John Terry		23	1	0	1.000	0	3	1	1	18	21	4	2	0	2.50
2 Roy Evans	R	29	1	4	.200	0	7	4	5	54	66	14	24	0	4.17
1 Bill Reidy	R	29	1	5	.167	0	5	5	5	43	53	7	8	1	3.98
Cy Morgan	R	24	0	2	.000	0	2	1	1	13	12	6	6	0	4.15

CHICAGO 7th 60-77 .438 30.5 NIXEY CALLAHAN

NAME	G by Pos	B	AGE	G	AB	R	H	2B	3B	HR	RBI	BB	SO	SB	BA	SA
TOTALS			29	138	4670	516	1152	176	49	14	436	325		180	.247	.314
Frank Isbell	1B117, 3B19, 2B2, SS1, OF1	L	27	138	546	52	132	25	9	2	59	12		26	.242	.332
2 Maggie Magoon	2B94	R	28	94	334	32	76	11	3	0	25	30		4	.228	.278
Lee Tannehill	SS138	R	22	138	463	48	113	14	3	2	50	25		10	.225	.276
Nixey Callahan	3B102, OF8, P3	R	29	118	439	47	128	26	5	2	56	20		24	.292	.387
Danny Green	OF133	R	26	135	499	75	154	26	7	6	62	47		29	.309	.425
Fiedler Jones	OF136	L	31	136	530	71	152	18	5	0	45	47		21	.287	.340
2 Ducky Holmes	OF82, 3B3	L	34	86	344	53	96	7	5	0	18	25		25	.279	.328
Ed McFarland	C56, 1B1	R	28	61	201	15	42	7	2	1	19	14		3	.209	.279
Bill Hallman	OF57	L	27	63	207	29	43	7	4	0	18	31		11	.208	.280
2 Jack Slattery	C56, 1B5	R	26	63	211	8	46	3	2	0	20	2		2	.218	.251
1 Tom Daly	2B43	B	37	43	150	20	31	11	0	0	19	20		6	.207	.280
Billy Sullivan (IL)	C31	R	28	32	111	10	21	4	0	1	7	5		3	.189	.252
1 Cozy Dolan	1B19, OF4	L	30	27	104	16	27	5	1	0	7	6		5	.260	.327
Pep Clark	3B15	R	20	15	65	7	20	4	2	0	4	5		5	.308	.431

NAME	T	AGE	W	L	PCT	SV	G	GS	CG	IP	H	BB	SO	SHO	ERA
		25	60	77	.438	5	138	138	114	1235	1233	287	391	9	3.02
Doc White	L	24	17	16	.515	0	37	36	29	300	258	69	114	3	2.13
Roy Patterson	R	26	14	15	.483	2	34	30	26	293	275	69	89	2	2.70
Patsy Flaherty	L	27	11	25	.306	0	40	34	29	294	338	50	65	2	3.73
Frank Owen	R	23	8	12	.400	1	26	20	15	167	167	44	66	1	3.50
1 Davey Dunkle	R	30	5	4	.556	1	12	7	6	82	96	31	26	0	4.06
2 Nick Altrock	L	26	4	3	.571	0	8	6	6	71	59	19	19	1	2.15
Nixey Callahan	R	29	1	2	.333	2	4	3	3	28	40	5	12	0	4.50

WASHINGTON 8th 43-94 .314 47.5 TOM LOFTUS

NAME	G by Pos	B	AGE	G	AB	R	H	2B	3B	HR	RBI	BB	SO	SB	BA	SA
TOTALS			29	140	4613	437	1066	172	72	17	372	257		131	.231	.311
Boileryard Clarke	1B88, C37	R	34	126	465	35	111	14	6	2	38	15		12	.239	.308
2 Barry McCormick	2B63		28	63	219	14	47	10	2	0	23	10		3	.215	.279
Charlie Moran (LJ)	SS96, 2B2		24	98	373	41	84	14	5	1	24	33		8	.225	.298
Bill Coughlin	3B119, SS4, 2B2	R	24	125	470	57	118	18	3	1	31	9		30	.251	.309
Watty Lee	OF47, P22	L	23	75	231	17	48	8	4	0	13	18		5	.208	.277
Jimmy Ryan	OF114	R	40	114	430	41	107	26	4	7	46	17		11	.249	.372
Kip Selbach	OF140, 3B1	R	31	140	533	68	134	23	12	3	49	41		20	.251	.356
2 Mal Kittredge	C60	R	33	60	192	8	41	4	1	0	16	10		1	.214	.245
Rabbit Robinson	2B45, OF30, SS24, 3B5	R	21	103	373	41	79	10	8	1	20	33		16	.212	.290
Al Orth	P36, SS7, OF4, 1B2	R	30	55	162	19	49	9	7	0	11	4		3	.302	.444
Lew Drill	C47, 1B3	R	26	51	154	11	39	9	3	0	23	15		4	.253	.351
Scoops Carey (BZ)	1B47	R	32	48	183	8	37	3	2	0	23	4		0	.202	.240
Ed Delahanty (DD)	OF40, 1B1	R	35	43	154	22	52	11	1	1	21	12		3	.338	.436
2 Joe Martin	2B15, 3B13, OF7	R	27	35	119	11	27	4	1	0	7	5		2	.227	.345
Jack Hendricks	OF32	R	28	32	112	10	20	1	3	0	4	13		3	.179	.241
1 Ducky Holmes	OF14, 3B4, 2B2	L	34	21	71	13	16	3	1	0	5	3		10	.225	.338
Gene DeMontreville (BF)	2B11, SS1	R	29	11	40	4	12	2	0	0	3	0		0	.300	.350
Champ Osteen	SS10	L	26	10	40	4	8	0	2	0	4	2		0	.200	.300

NAME	T	AGE	W	L	PCT	SV	G	GS	CG	IP	H	BB	SO	SHO	ERA
		26	43	94	.314	3	140	140	122	1224	1333	306	452	6	3.82
Al Orth	R	30	10	21	.323	2	36	32	30	280	326	62	88	2	4.34
Casey Patten	L	29	10	23	.303	1	36	34	32	300	313	80	133	0	3.60
Watty Lee	L	23	8	13	.381	0	22	20	15	167	169	40	70	2	3.07
Highball Wilson	R	24	8	18	.308	0	30	28	25	242	269	43	56	1	3.31
2 Davey Dunkle	R	30	5	8	.385	0	14	13	10	108	111	33	51	0	4.25
Jack Townsend	R	24	2	11	.154	0	20	13	10	127	145	48	54	0	4.75

PITTSBURGH — 1ST 91-49 .650 — FRED CLARKE

NAME	G by Pos	B	AGE	G	AB	R	H	2B	3B	HR	RBI	BB	SO	SB	BA	SA
TOTALS			27	141	4991	792	1430	208	110	34	650	364		172	.287	.393
Kittty Bransfield	1B127	R	28	127	505	69	134	23	7	2	57	33		13	.265	.350
Claude Ritchey	2B137	B	29	138	506	66	145	28	10	0	59	55		15	.287	.381
Honus Wagner	SS111, OF12, 1B6	R	29	129	512	97	182	30	19	5	101	44		46	.355	.518
Tommy Leach	3B127	R	25	127	507	97	151	16	17	7	87	40		22	.298	.438
Jimmy Sebring	OF124	L	21	124	506	71	140	16	13	4	64	32		20	.277	.383
Ginger Beaumont	OF141	L	26	141	613	137	209	30	6	7	68	44		23	.341	.444
Fred Clarke (XJ)	OF101, SS2	L	30	104	427	88	150	32	15	5	70	41		21	.351	.532
Eddie Phelps	C76, 1B3	R	24	81	273	32	77	7	3	2	31	17		2	.282	.352
Otto Krueger	SS29, OF28, 3B13, 2B3	R	26	80	256	42	63	6	8	1	28	21		5	.246	.344
Harry Smith (RJ)	C60, OF1	R	28	61	212	15	37	3	2	0	19	12		2	.175	.208
Brickyard Kennedy (PJ)	P18	R	34	23	58	7	21	4	3	0	10	2		1	.362	.534
2 Art Weaver	C11, 1B5	R	24	16	48	8	11	0	1	0	3	2		0	.229	.271
Joe Marshall	OF3, SS3, 2B1	R	27	10	23	2	6	1	2	0	2	0		0	.261	.478
George Merritt (BN)	OF7, P1	R	23	9	27	4	4	0	1	0	3	2		1	.148	.222
Fred Carisch	C4	R	21	5	18	4	6	4	0	1	5	0		0	.333	.722
Eude Curtis	OF5	R	20	5	19	2	8	1	0	0	3	1		0	.421	.474
Hans Lobert	3B3, 2B1, SS1	R	21	5	13	1	1	1	0	0	0	1		1	.077	.154
Solly Hofman	OF2	R	20	3	2	1	0	0	0	0	0	0		0	.000	.000
Reddie Grey	OF2	L	28	3	3	1	1	0	0	0	1	1		0	.333	.333
Ernie Diehl	OF1	R	25	1	3	0	1	0	0	0	0	0		0	.333	.333
Lou Gertenrich	OF1	R	28	1	3	0	0	0	0	0	0	0		0	.000	.000

NAME	T	AGE	W	L	PCT	SV	G	GS	CG	IP	H	BB	SO	SHO	ERA
		31	91	49	.650	5	141	141	117	1251	1215	384	454	15	2.91
Sam Leever	R	31	25	7	.781	1	36	34	30	284	255	60	90	7	2.06
Deacon Phillippe	R	31	24	9	.727	2	36	33	31	289	269	29	123	4	2.43
Ed Doheny (IL)	L	29	16	8	.667	2	27	25	22	223	209	89	75	2	3.19
Brickyard Kennedy(PJ)	R	35	9	6	.600	0	18	15	10	125	130	57	39	0	3.80
Bucky Veil	R	21	5	3	.625	0	12	6	4	71	70	36	20	0	3.80
Kaiser Wilhelm	R	29	5	3	.625	0	12	9	7	86	88	25	20	1	3.24
Lafe Winham	L	21	3	1	.750	0	5	4	3	36	33	21	11	1	2.25
Gus Thompson	R	26	2	2	.500	0	5	4	3	42	52	16	22	0	3.56
Cy Falkenberg	R	23	2	5	.286	0	10	6	3	56	65	32	24	0	3.86
George Merritt	R	23	0	0	—	0	1	0	0	4	1	2	2	0	2.25
Lew Moren	R	19	0	1	.000	0	1	1	1	6	9	2	2	0	9.00
Doc Scanlan	R	22	0	1	.000	0	1	1	1	9	5	6	0	0	4.00
Jack Pfiester	L	25	0	1	.000	0	2	2	2	19	26	10	15	0	6.16

NEW YORK — 2nd 84-55 .604 6.5 — JOHN McGRAW

NAME	G by Pos	B	AGE	G	AB	R	H	2B	3B	HR	RBI	BB	SO	SB	BA	SA
TOTALS			30	142	4741	729	1290	181	49	20	570	379		264	.272	.344
Dan McGann	1B129	B	31	129	482	75	130	21	6	3	50	32		36	.270	.357
Billy Gilbert	2B128	R	27	128	413	62	104	9	0	1	40	41		37	.252	.281
Charlie Babb	SS113, 3B8	R	30	121	424	68	105	15	8	0	46	45		22	.248	.321
Billy Lauder	3B108	R	29	108	395	52	111	13	0	0	53	14		19	.281	.314
George Browne	OF141	L	27	141	591	105	185	20	3	3	45	43		27	.313	.372
Roger Bresnahan	OF84, 1B13, C11, 3B4	R	24	113	406	87	142	30	8	4	55	61		34	.350	.493
Sam Mertes	OF137, 1B1, C1	R	30	138	517	100	145	32	14	7	104	61		45	.280	.437
Jack Warner	C85	R	30	89	285	38	81	8	5	0	34	7		5	.284	.347
George Van Haltren (BL)	OF75	L	37	84	280	42	72	6	1	0	28	28		14	.257	.286
Jack Dunn	SS27, 3B25, 2B19, OF1	R	30	78	257	35	62	15	1	0	37	15		12	.241	.307
Frank Bowerman	C55, 1B4, OF1	R	34	64	210	22	58	6	2	1	31	6		5	.276	.338
Christy Mathewson	P45	R	24	45	124	13	28	3	0	1	20	8		1	.226	.274
John McGraw	OF2, 2B2, SS1, 3B1	L	30	12	11	2	3	0	0	0	1	1		1	.273	.273
George Davis (KP)	SS4	R	32	4	15	2	4	0	0	0	1	1		0	.267	.267

NAME	T	AGE	W	L	PCT	SV	G	GS	CG	IP	H	BB	SO	SHO	ERA
		27	84	55	.604	8	142	142	115	1263	1257	371	628	8	2.95
Joe McGinnity	R	32	31	20	.608	2	55	48	44	434	391	109	171	3	2.43
Christy Mathewson	R	22	30	13	.698	2	45	42	37	366	321	100	267	3	2.26
Dummy Taylor	R	28	13	13	.500	0	33	31	18	245	306	89	94	1	4.22
Jack Cronin	R	29	6	4	.600	1	20	11	8	116	130	37	50	0	3.80
Red Ames	R	20	2	0	1.000	0	2	2	1	14	5	8	14	1	1.29
Roscoe Miller	R	26	2	5	.286	0	15	8	6	85	101	24	30	0	4.13
Bill Bartley	R	18	0	1	—	0	1	0	0	3	3	4	2	0	0.00

CHICAGO — 3rd 82-56 .594 8 — FRANK SELEE

NAME	G by Pos	B	AGE	G	AB	R	H	2B	3B	HR	RBI	BB	SO	SB	BA	SA
TOTALS			26	139	4733	695	1300	191	62	9	548	422		259	.275	.347
Frank Chance	1B121, C2	R	26	125	441	83	144	24	10	2	81	78		67	.327	.440
Johnny Evers	2B110, SS11, 3B2	L	21	124	464	70	136	27	7	0	52	19		25	.293	.381
Joe Tinker	SS107, 3B17	R	22	124	460	67	182	21	7	2	70	37		27	.291	.380
Doc Casey	3B112	L	32	112	435	56	126	8	3	1	40	19		11	.290	.329
Dick Harley	OF103	L	30	104	386	72	89	9	1	0	33	45		27	.231	.259
Davy Jones	OF130	L	23	130	497	64	140	18	3	1	62	53		15	.282	.336
Jimmy Slagle	OF139	L	29	139	543	104	162	20	6	0	44	81		33	.298	.357
Johnny Kling	C132	R	27	132	491	67	146	29	13	3	68	22		23	.297	.428
2 Otto Williams	SS26, 2B7, 1B3, 3B1	R	27	38	130	14	29	5	0	0	13	4		8	.223	.262
Tommy Raub	C12, 1B6, OF5, 3B4	R	32	36	84	6	19	3	2	0	7	5		3	.226	.310
Bobby Lowe (BK)	2B22, 1B6, 3B1	R	34	32	105	14	28	5	3	0	15	4		5	.267	.371
2 Jack McCarthy	OF24	L	34	24	101	11	28	5	0	0	14	4		8	.277	.327
1 Johnny Dobbs	OF16	L	28	16	61	8	14	1	1	0	4	7		0	.230	.279
Jim Cook	OF5, 2B2, 1B1	R	23	8	26	3	4	1	0	0	2	2		1	.154	.192
Bill Hanlon	1B8	R	27	8	21	4	2	0	0	0	2	6		1	.095	.095
George Moriarty	3B1	R	17	1	5	1	0	0	0	0	0	0		0	.000	.000
Larry McLean	C1	R	21	1	1	0	0	0	0	0	0	1		1	.000	.000

NAME	T	AGE	W	L	PCT	SV	G	GS	CG	IP	H	BB	SO	SHO	ERA
		28	82	56	.594	6	139	139	117	1240	1182	354	451	6	2.77
Jack Taylor	R	28	21	14	.600	1	37	33	33	312	277	57	83	1	2.45
Jake Weimer	L	29	20	8	.714	0	35	33	27	282	241	104	128	3	2.30
2 Bob Wicker	R	25	20	9	.690	1	32	27	24	247	236	74	110	1	3.02
Carl Lundgren	R	23	11	9	.550	2	27	20	16	193	191	60	67	0	2.94
Jacko Menefee	R	35	8	10	.444	0	20	17	13	147	157	38	39	1	3.00
Alex Hardy	L	26	1	1	.500	0	2	1	1	13	21	7	4	0	6.23
2 Clarence Currie	R	24	1	2	.333	1	6	3	2	33	35	9	9	0	3.00
1 Jack Doscher	L	22	0	1	.000	0	1	1	0	3	6	2	5	0	12.00
Peaches Graham	R	26	0	1	.000	0	1	0	0	5	9	3	4	0	5.40
1 Pop Williams	R	29	0	1	.000	0	1	1	1	5	7	3	4	0	5.40

CINCINNATI — 4th 74-65 .532 16.5 — JOE KELLY

NAME	G by Pos	B	AGE	G	AB	R	H	2B	3B	HR	RBI	BB	SO	SB	BA	SA
TOTALS			31	141	4857	764	1399	228	92	28	652	403		144	.288	.390
Jake Beckley	1B119	L	35	120	459	85	150	29	10	2	81	42		23	.327	.447
2 Tom Daly	2B79	R	37	80	307	42	90	14	9	1	38	16		5	.293	.407
Tommy Corcoran	SS115	R	34	115	459	61	113	18	7	2	73	12		12	.246	.329
Harry Steinfeldt	3B104, SS14	R	25	118	439	71	137	32	12	6	83	47		6	.312	.481
Cozy Dolan	OF93	L	30	93	385	64	111	20	3	0	58	28		11	.288	.356
Cy Seymour	OF135	L	30	135	558	85	191	25	15	7	72	33		25	.342	.478
Mike Donlin	OF118, 1B7	L	25	120	494	110	174	25	18	7	67	56		26	.351	.516
Heinie Peitz	C78, 1B11, 3B9, 2B4	R	32	105	358	45	93	15	3	0	42	37		7	.260	.318
Joe Kelley	OF67, SS12, 2B11, 3B8, 1B6	R	31	105	383	85	121	22	4	3	45	51		18	.316	.418
Bill Bergen	C58	R	30	58	207	21	47	4	2	0	19	7		2	.227	.266
1 Maggie Magoon	2B32, 3B9	R	28	42	139	6	30	6	0	0	9	19		2	.216	.259
Jack Morrissey	2B17, OF8, SS2	B	26	29	89	14	22	1	0	0	9	14		3	.247	.258
Charlie DeArmond	3B11	R	26	11	39	10	11	2	1	0	7	3		1	.282	.385
Pete Cregan	OF6	R	28	6	19	1	2	0	0	0	0	1		0	.105	.105
Emil Haberer	C4	R	25	5	13	1	1	0	0	0	0	2		0	.077	.077
Lee Fohl	C4	R	33	4	14	3	5	1	1	0	2	0		0	.357	.571
Pat Deisel	C1	R	27	2	2	1	0	0	0	0	0	0		0	.000	.000
Harry Wood	OF2	L	22	2	3	0	0	0	0	0	0	1		0	.000	.000
Dan Kerwin	OF2	L	28	2	6	1	4	1	0	0	1	0		1	.667	.833

NAME	T	AGE	W	L	PCT	SV	G	GS	CG	IP	H	BB	SO	SHO	ERA
		29	74	65	.532	1	141	141	126	1230	1277	378	480	11	3.07
Noodles Hahn	L	24	22	12	.647	0	34	34	34	296	297	47	127	5	2.52
Jack Sutthoff	R	30	16	10	.615	0	30	27	21	225	207	79	76	3	2.80
Bob Ewing	R	30	14	13	.519	1	29	28	27	247	254	64	104	1	2.77
Ed Poole	R	28	8	13	.381	0	25	21	18	184	188	77	73	1	3.28
Bill Phillips	R	34	7	6	.538	0	16	13	11	118	134	30	46	1	3.36
Jack Harper	R	25	7	8	.467	0	17	15	13	135	143	70	45	0	4.33
Buck Hooker	R	22	0	0	—	0	1	0	0	2	2	1	0	0	5.40
Jimmy Wiggs	R	26	0	1	.000	0	3	1	0	5	12	12	2	0	5.40
Rip Reagan	R	25	0	2	.000	0	3	2	1	18	40	7	7	0	6.00

BROOKLYN — 5th 70-66 .515 19 — NED HANLON

NAME	G by Pos	B	AGE	G	AB	R	H	2B	3B	HR	RBI	BB	SO	SB	BA	SA
TOTALS			27	139	4534	666	1201	177	56	15	539	522		273	.265	.339
Jack Doyle	1B139	R	33	139	484	66	134	27	6	0	91	54		34	.313	.387
Tim Flood	2B84, SS2, OF1	R	26	89	309	27	77	15	2	0	32	15		14	.249	.311
Bill Dahlen	SS138	R	33	138	474	71	124	17	9	1	64	82		34	.262	.342
Sammy Strang	3B124, OF8, 2B3	B	26	135	508	101	138	21	5	0	38	75		46	.272	.333
Judge McCredie	OF56	R	26	56	213	40	69	5	0	0	20	24		10	.324	.347
2 Johnny Dobbs	OF110	L	28	110	414	61	98	15	7	2	59	48		23	.237	.321
Jimmy Sheckard	OF139	L	24	139	515	99	171	29	9	9	75	75		67	.332	.476
Lew Ritter	C74, OF2	R	27	78	259	26	61	9	6	0	37	19		9	.236	.317
Dutch Jordan	2B54, 3B18, OF4, 1B1	R	23	78	267	27	63	11	1	0	21	9		9	.236	.285
Fred Jacklitsch	C53, 2B1, OF1	R	27	60	176	31	47	8	3	1	21	33		4	.267	.364
2 Doc Gessler	OF43	L	22	49	154	20	38	8	3	0	18	17		9	.247	.383
1 Tom McCreery	OF38	R	28	40	141	13	37	5	2	0	10	20		5	.262	.326
Hugh Hearne	C17, 1B2	R	30	26	57	8	16	3	2	0	4	3		2	.281	.404
Ed Householder	OF12	L	33	12	43	5	9	0	0	0	2	2		3	.209	.209
Henry Thielman	OF5, P4	R	22	9	23	3	5	1	0	1	2	1		0	.217	.391
Hughie Jennings	OF4	R	34	6	17	2	4	1	0	0	1	1		1	.235	.235
Matt Broderick	2B1	R	25	2	2	0	0	0	0	0	0	0		0	.000	.000
Frank McManus	C2	R	27	2	1	0	0	0	0	0	0	0		0	.000	.000
Ed Hug	C1	R	22	1	1	0	0	0	0	0	0	0		0	.000	.000

NAME	T	AGE	W	L	PCT	SV	G	GS	CG	IP	H	BB	SO	SHO	ERA
		28	70	66	.515	4	139	139	118	1221	1276	377	438	11	3.44
Henry Schmidt	R	30	22	13	.629	2	40	36	29	301	321	120	96	5	3.83
Oscar Jones	R	23	19	14	.576	0	38	36	31	322	289	77	95	4	2.94
Ned Garvin	R	29	15	18	.455	2	38	34	30	298	277	84	154	2	1.68
2 Bill Reidy	R	29	6	7	.462	0	15	13	11	104	130	14	21	0	3.46
1 Roy Evans	R	29	5	9	.357	0	11	9	8	110	121	41	42	0	3.27
Grant Thatcher	R	26	3	1	.750	0	4	4	4	28	33	7	9	0	2.89
2 Jack Doscher	L	22	0	0	—	0	3	0	0	7	8	4	4	0	7.71
2 Bill Pounds	R	25	0	0	—	0	1	1	1	7	8	6	2	0	6.00
Rube Vickers	R	25	0	1	.000	0	1	1	1	14	27	9	5	0	10.93
Henry Thielman	R	22	0	3	.000	0	3	3	3	29	31	14	10	0	4.66

BOSTON — 6th 58-80 .420 32 — AL BUCKENBERGER

NAME	G by Pos	B	AGE	G	AB	R	H	2B	3B	HR	RBI	BB	SO	SB	BA	SA
TOTALS			27	140	4682	575	1145	176	47	25	479	398		159	.245	.318
Fred Tenney	1B122	L	31	122	447	79	140	22	3	3	41	70		21	.313	.396
Ed Abbaticcio	2B116, SS17	R	26	136	489	61	111	18	5	1	46	52		23	.227	.290
Harry Aubrey	SS94, 2B1, OF1	R	21	96	325	26	69	8	2	0	27	18		7	.212	.249
Ed Gremminger	3B140	R	29	140	511	57	135	24	9	5	56	31		12	.264	.376
Pat Carney	OF92, P10, 1B1	L	26	110	392	37	94	12	4	1	49	28		10	.240	.298
Charlie Dexter	OF106, SS9, C6	R	27	123	457	82	102	15	1	3	34	61		32	.223	.280
Dick Cooley	OF126, 1B13	L	38	138	553	76	160	26	10	1	70	44		27	.289	.378
Pat Moran	C107, 1B1	R	27	109	389	40	102	18	1	0	54	29		8	.262	.406
Joe Stanley	OF77, SS1, P1	R	22	86	308	40	77	12	5	1	47	18		10	.250	.331
Frank Bonner	2B24, SS22	R	33	48	173	14	38	5	0	1	10	7		2	.220	.266
1 Mal Kittredge	C30	R	33	32	99	10	21	2	0	0	6	11		1	.212	.232
2 Tom McCreery	OF23	R	28	23	83	15	18	2	1	1	10	9		6	.217	.301

NAME	T	AGE	W	L	PCT	SV	G	GS	CG	IP	H	BB	SO	SHO	ERA
		29	58	80	.420	1	140	140	125	1229	1310	480	516	5	3.34
Togie Pittinger	R	31	18	22	.450	1	44	39	35	352	396	143	140	0	3.48
Vic Willis	R	27	12	17	.414	0	33	32	29	278	256	88	125	2	2.98
John Marlarkey	R	31	11	16	.407	0	32	27	25	253	266	96	98	2	3.09
Wiley Piatt	L	28	9	15	.375	0	25	23	18	181	198	61	100	1	3.18
Pat Carney	L	26	4	5	.444	0	10	9	9	78	93	31	29	0	4.04
3 Pop Williams	R	29	4	5	.444	0	10	9	9	83	97	37	20	1	4.12
Joe Stanley	R	22	0	0	—	0	1	0	0	4	4	4	4	0	9.00

PHILADELPHIA — 7th 49-86 .363 39.5 — CHIEF ZIMMER

NAME	G by Pos	B	AGE	G	AB	R	H	2B	3B	HR	RBI	BB	SO	SB	BA	SA
TOTALS			29	139	4781	618	1283	186	62	12	500	338		120	.268	.341
Klondike Douglass	1B97	L	31	105	377	43	96	5	4	1	36	28		6	.255	.297
Kid Gleason	2B102, OF4	R	36	106	412	62	117	19	6	1	49	23		12	.284	.367
Rudy Hulswitt	SS138	R	24	138	519	56	128	22	9	1	58	28		10	.247	.329
Harry Wolverton	3B123	B	29	123	494	72	152	13	12	0	53	18		10	.308	.383
Bill Keister	OF100	R	31	100	400	53	128	27	7	3	63	14		11	.320	.445
Roy Thomas	OF130	L	29	130	477	88	156	11	2	1	27	107		17	.327	.365
Shad Barry	OF107, 1B30, 3B1	R	24	138	550	75	152	24	5	1	60	30		26	.276	.344
Frank Roth	C60, 1B1	R	24	68	220	27	60	11	4	0	22	9		3	.273	.359
John Titus	OF72	L	27	72	280	38	80	15	6	2	34	19		5	.286	.404
Bill Hallman	2B22, 3B19, 1B9, SS3	R	36	63	198	20	42	11	2	0	17	16		2	.212	.288
Red Dooin	C51, 1B1, OF1	R	24	62	188	18	41	5	1	0	14	8		9	.218	.255
Chief Zimmer	C35	R	42	37	118	9	26	3	1	1	19	9		1	.220	.288
Roy Brashear	2B18, 1B2	R	29	20	75	9	17	3	0	0	4	6		2	.227	.267
Dutch Rudolph		L	20	1	1	0	0	0	0	0	0	0		0	.000	.000
John Walsh	3B1	R	24	1	3	0	0	0	0	0	0	0		0	.000	.000

NAME	T	AGE	W	L	PCT	SV	G	GS	CG	IP	H	BB	SO	SHO	ERA
		28	49	86	.363	3	139	139	126	1212	1347	425	381	5	3.97
Bill Duggleby	R	30	13	18	.419	2	36	30	28	264	318	79	57	3	3.75
Chick Fraser	R	29	12	17	.414	1	31	29	26	250	260	97	104	1	4.50
Fred Mitchell	R	25	11	15	.423	0	28	28	24	227	250	102	69	1	4.48
Tully Sparks	R	28	11	15	.423	0	28	28	27	248	248	56	88	0	2.72
2 Pop Williams	R	29	1	1	.500	0	2	2	2	18	21	6	8	0	3.00
Jack McFetridge		33	1	11	.083	0	14	13	11	103	120	49	31	0	4.89
Warry McLaughlin	L	26	0	2	.000	0	3	2	2	23	38	11	3	0	7.04
Fred Burchell	L	23	0	3	.000	0	6	3	2	44	48	14	12	0	2.86
Libe Washburn	L	29	0	4	.000	0	4	4	4	35	44	11	9	0	4.37

ST. LOUIS — 8th 43-94 .314 46.5 — PATSY DONOVAN

NAME	G by Pos	B	AGE	G	AB	R	H	2B	3B	HR	RBI	BB	SO	SB	BA	SA
TOTALS			28	139	4689	505	1176	138	65	8	407	277		171	.251	.313
Jim Hackett	1B89, P7	R	25	99	351	24	80	13	8	0	36	19		2	.228	.311
John Farrell	2B118, OF12	R	26	130	519	83	141	25	8	1	32	48		21	.272	.356
Dave Brain	SS72, 3B46	R	24	119	464	44	107	8	15	4	60	25		21	.231	.319
Jimmy Burke	3B93, 2B15, OF5	R	28	115	431	55	123	13	3	0	42	23		28	.285	.329
Patsy Donovan	OF105	L	38	105	410	63	134	15	3	0	40	25		25	.327	.378
Homer Smoot	OF129	L	25	129	500	67	148	22	8	4	49	32		17	.296	.396
George Barclay	OF107	R	27	108	419	37	104	10	8	0	42	15		12	.248	.310
Jack O'Neill	C74	R	30	75	246	23	58	9	1	0	27	13		11	.236	.280
Jack Ryan	C47, 1B18, SS2	R	34	67	227	18	54	5	1	1	10	10		2	.238	.282
1 Otto Williams	SS52, 2B1	R	25	53	187	10	38	4	2	0	9	9		6	.203	.246
Jack Dunleavy	OF38, P14	L	23	61	193	23	48	3	3	0	10	13		10	.249	.295
Art Nichols	1B25, OF7, C2	R	31	36	120	13	23	2	0	0	9	12		4	.192	.208
Mike O'Neill	P19, OF13	L	25	41	110	12	25	2	2	0	6	8		3	.227	.282
Lee DeMontreville	SS15, 2B4, OF1	R	28	26	70	8	17	3	1	0	7	8		3	.243	.314
1 Art Weaver	C16	R	24	16	49	4	12	0	0	0	5	4		1	.245	.245
Harry Berte	2B3, SS1	R	31	4	15	1	5	0	0	0	1	1		0	.333	.333
John Coveney	C4	R	23	4	14	0	2	0	0	0	0	0		0	.143	.143
Lou Ury	1B2	R	26	2	7	0	1	0	0	0	0	0		0	.143	.143

NAME	T	AGE	W	L	PCT	SV	G	GS	CG	IP	H	BB	SO	SHO	ERA
		25	43	94	.314	2	139	139	111	1182	1353	430	419	4	3.76
Three Finger Brown	R	26	9	13	.409	0	26	24	19	201	231	59	83	1	2.60
Chappie McFarland	R	28	9	18	.333	0	28	26	25	229	253	48	76	1	3.07
Jack Dunleavy	L	23	6	8	.429	0	14	13	9	102	101	57	51	0	4.06
1 Bob Rhoades	R	23	5	8	.385	0	17	13	12	129	154	47	52	1	4.60
Ed Murphy	R	26	4	8	.333	0	15	12	9	106	108	38	16	0	3.31
1 Clarence Currie	R	24	4	12	.250	1	22	16	13	144	155	60	52	1	4.01
Mike O'Neill	L	25	4	13	.235	0	19	17	12	115	184	43	39	0	4.77
Jim Hackett	R	25	1	4	.200	1	7	6	5	48	47	18	21	0	3.75
War Sanders	L	25	1	6	.143	0	8	6	3	40	48	21	9	0	6.08
John Lovett		25	0	0	—	0	3	1	0	5	6	5	3	0	5.40
Larry Milton	R	25	0	1	.000	0	1	0	0	4	3	1	0	0	2.25
Rube Taylor	L	26	0	0	—	0	1	0	0	1	0	0	0	0	0.00
1 Bob Wicker	R	25	0	0	—	0	1	0	0	5	4	3	3	0	0.00
Hal Betts	R	22	0	1	.000	0	1	1	1	9	11	5	2	0	10.00
Pat Hynes	L	18	0	1	.000	0	1	1	1	9	16	6	1	0	4.00
Charley Moran (SA)	R	25	0	1	.000	1	3	2	2	24	30	19	7	0	5.25
Stan Yerkes	R	28	0	0	—	0	1	0	0	5	8	0	3	0	1.80

WORLD SERIES — BOSTON (AL) 5   PITTSBURGH (NL) 3

LINE SCORES

TEAM	1	2	3	4	5	6	7	8	9	10	11	12	R	H	E
Game 1 October 1 at Boston															
PIT(NL)	4	0	1	1	0	0	1	0	0				7	12	2
BOS(AL)	0	0	0	0	0	0	2	0	1				3	6	4
Phillippe								Young							
Game 2 October 2 at Boston															
PIT	0	0	0	0	0	0	0	0	0				0	3	2
BOS	2	0	0	0	0	1	0	0	X				3	9	0
Leever, Veil(2)								Dinneen							
Game 3 October 3 at Boston															
PIT	0	1	2	0	0	0	0	1	0				4	7	0
BOS	0	0	0	1	0	0	0	1	0				2	4	2
Phillippe								Hughes, Young (3)							
Game 4 October 6 at Pittsburgh															
BOS	0	0	0	0	0	1	0	0	3				4	9	1
PIT	1	0	0	0	1	0	3	0	X				5	12	1
Dinneen								Phillippe							
Game 5 October 7 at Pittsburgh															
BOS	0	0	0	0	0	6	4	1	0				11	14	2
PIT	0	0	0	0	0	0	0	2	0				2	6	4
Young								Kennedy, Thompson (8)							
Game 6 October 8 at Pittsburgh															
BOS	0	0	3	0	2	0	1	0	0				6	10	1
PIT	0	0	0	0	0	0	3	0	0				3	10	0
Dinneen								Leever							
Game 7 October 10 at Pittsburgh															
BOS	2	0	0	2	0	2	0	1	0				7	11	4
PIT	0	0	0	1	0	1	0	0	1				3	10	3
Young								Phillippe							
Game 8 October 13 at Boston															
PIT	0	0	0	0	0	0	0	0	0				0	4	3
BOS	0	0	0	2	0	1	0	0	X				3	8	0
Dinneen								Phillippe							

COMPOSITE BATTING

NAME	POS	G	AB	R	H	2B	3B	HR	RBI	BA
Boston (AL)										
Totals		8	282	39	71	4	16	2	34	.252
Collins	3B	8	36	5	9	1	2	0	1	.250
Dougherty	OF	8	34	3	8	0	2	2	5	.235
Stahl	OF	8	33	6	10	1	0	2	5	.303
Freeman	OF	8	32	6	9	0	3	0	4	.281
Parent	SS	8	32	8	9	0	3	0	4	.281
Ferris	2B	8	31	3	9	0	1	0	5	.290
LaChance	1B	8	27	5	6	2	1	0	4	.222
Criger	C	8	26	1	6	0	0	0	4	.231
Young	P	4	15	1	2	0	0	0	3	.133
Dinneen	P	4	12	1	3	0	0	0	0	.250
Farrell	PH	2	2	0	0	0	0	0	1	.000
O'Brien	PH	2	2	0	0	0	0	0	0	.000
Hughes	P	1	1	0	0	0	0	0	0	—
Pittsburgh (NL)										
Totals		8	270	24	64	7	9	1	21	.237
Beaumont	OF	8	34	6	9	0	1	0	1	.265
Clarke	OF	8	34	3	9	2	1	0	2	.265
Leach	3B	8	33	3	9	0	4	0	7	.273
Sebring	OF	8	30	3	11	0	1	1	3	.367
Bransfield	1B	8	29	3	6	0	2	0	3	.207
Wagner	SS	8	27	2	6	1	0	0	3	.222
Ritchey	2B	8	27	2	3	1	0	0	2	.111
Phelps	C	8	26	1	6	2	0	0	1	.231
Phillippe	P	5	18	1	4	0	0	0	1	.222
Leever	P	2	4	0	0	0	0	0	0	.000
Smith	C	1	3	0	0	0	0	0	0	—
Kennedy	P	1	2	0	1	0	0	0	0	.500
Veil	P	1	2	0	0	0	0	0	0	.000
Thompson	P	1	1	0	0	0	0	0	0	.000

COMPOSITE PITCHING

NAME	G	IP	H	BB	SO	W	L	SV	ERA
Boston (AL)									
Totals	8	71	64	14	45	5	3	0	2.15
Dinneen	4	35	29	8	28	3	1	0	2.06
Young	4	34	31	4	17	2	1	0	1.85
Hughes	1	2	4	2	0	0	1	0	9.00
Pittsburgh (NL)									
Totals	8	70	71	14	29	3	5	0	3.73
Phillippe	5	44	38	3	22	3	2	0	2.86
Leever	2	10	13	3	2	0	2	0	5.40
Veil	1	7	6	5	1	0	0	0	1.29
Kennedy	1	7	11	3	3	0	1	0	5.14
Thompson	1	2	3	0	1	0	0	0	4.50

1904 - A. L. — Chesbro and the One That Got Away

Despite his three 20-win seasons since 1901, no one expected Jack Chesbro to have the sort of year he did for the New York Highlanders, turning in a masterful pitching performance and keeping them in the pennant race practically single-handedly. The stocky 30-year-old right-hander won 41 games, a modern baseball record which stands today; he started 51 games and completed all but three of them, a feat of stamina necessitated by the aging of Clark Griffith and the illness of Al Orth.

With Chesbro winning and winning, the Highlanders stayed in the midst of a five-team dogfight for the American League crown. In the final week, it came down to New York and the Boston Pilgrims, and the schedule-maker had shown enough foresight to match these two contenders against each other on the final weekend. The Highlanders took a half-game lead with a victory on October 7, but Boston swept a doubleheader the next day to go back in front by a game-and-a-half. A doubleheader on the tenth would settle it, with New York needing a sweep to cop the title. Jack Chesbro was handed the ball by manager Clark Griffith while Bill Dinneen was given the call for Boston. As the enthusiastic 28,000 New York fans positioned themselves for the dramatics which were to unfold on the last day of the regular season, hopes were high for the Highlanders to win their first American League pennant; after all, New York was starting out with a plus 40-game winner, while all Boston had on the mound was a 22-game winner in Dinneen.

In the third inning Chesbro started the action with a triple to right field. But he was left stranded, and the game went into the fifth inning before New York scored two runs behind three hits and two walks to take a 2-0 lead. In the seventh, with the score still at 2-0, a throwing error to the plate by second baseman Jimmy Williams allowed Boston to tie the game. Then, in the ninth, Chesbro gave a single to Lou Criger who, after a sacrifice and a ground out, found himself on third base. Chesbro's 42nd victory, or at least the thought of it, went the same route as the Highlanders' pennant dreams, as Happy Jack uncorked a wild pitch to allow Criger home with what turned out to be the winning run. Surprisingly enough, New York held on to take the meaningless second game, 1-0, in ten innings.—Boston's tooth and nail struggle for the pennant gave the American League its first repeat championship. Manager Jimmy Collins fielded a lineup which included stars Chick Stahl, Buck Freeman, Freddy Parent, and Collins himself. Boston's long suit, though, was pitching; 37-year-old Cy Young kept rolling along with 26 wins, including a perfect game, and Bill Dinneen and Jesse Tannehill each chipped in with 20-win seasons. The New York club continued its hot work of late 1903 by staying in contention all the way; Chesbro was the main shoulder at the wheel, but Willie Keeler batting and Jack Powell's pitching also merited star acclaim. Chicago, Cleveland, and Philadelphia all had a chance to reach the top as late as September.

Nap Lajoie of Cleveland socked the ball at a .381 clip nailing down his third American League batting crown in four years; Willie Keeler was runner-up with a .343 mark. Of the six .300 hitters in the league, Cleveland fielded three of them¬Lajoie, Elmer Flick, and Bill Bradley. The hitting generally fell off as the league adopted the foul-strike rule, making all fouls before two strikes count as a strike. The National League had held the rule for two years, and this attempt to speed up play represented one of the major changes in the rules of the game of baseball.

Chesbro's 41 victories far and away paced the league in that department; Cy Young, unseated as leading winner for the first time since the league was formed, placed second with 26 wins. While Chesbro was setting a season mark for victories, Philadelphia Rube Waddell blazed his way to a new strikeout record with 349. Addie Joss of Cleveland exhibited enough control to deny the trio at least one major pitching honor with his 1.59 E.R.A.

The American and National Leagues coexisted without incident during the season, but the fall witnessed an unfortunate turn of events. Down the stretch, the Highlanders and Pilgrims both offered to meet the National League champion New York Giants at the conclusion of the season to determine a world's champion. President John T. Brush of the Giants refused the offers, stating that the National League was the premier baseball organization in America and that its prestige should not be jeopardized by contending for a crown with minor leagues. With this snub, Brush declined to play the Series into which the champion owners of 1903 had voluntarily entered. Despite heavy press criticism, Brush remained adamant; later, Giant manager John McGraw admitted the chief responsibility for the decision, owing to his personal coolness towards American League President Ban Johnson. The second World Series went unplayed, and Boston claimed the title for itself by default.

1904 AMERICAN LEAGUE

NAME	G by Pos	B	AGE	G	AB	R	H	2B	3B	HR	RBI	BB	SO	SB	BA	SA
BOSTON 1st 95-59 .617			JIMMY COLLINS													
TOTALS			31	157	5231	608	1294	194	105	26	522	347		101	.247	.340
Candy LaChance	1B157	B	34	157	573	55	130	19	5	1	47	23		7	.227	.283
Hobe Ferris	2B156	R	26	156	563	50	120	23	10	3	63	23		7	.213	.306
Freddy Parent	SS155	R	28	155	591	85	172	22	9	6	77	28		20	.291	.389
Jimmy Collins	3B156	R	34	156	633	85	168	32	13	3	67	27		19	.265	.371
Buck Freeman	OF157	L	32	157	598	64	166	20	19	7	84	32		11	.278	.410
Chick Stahl	OF157	L	31	157	583	84	173	27	22	3	67	64		13	.297	.434
2 Kip Selbach	OF98	R	32	98	376	50	97	19	8	0	30	48		10	.258	.351
Lou Criger	C95	R	32	98	299	34	63	10	5	2	34	27		1	.211	.298
Duke Farrell	C56	R	37	68	198	11	42	9	2	0	15	15		1	.212	.278
1 Patsy Dougherty	OF49	L	27	49	195*	33*	53	5	4	0	4	25		10	.272	.338
1 Bill O'Neill	OF9, SS2	B	24	17	51	7	10	1	0	0	5	2		0	.196	.216
Tom Doran	C11	L	24	12	32	1	4	0	1	0	0	4		1	.125	.188
2 Bob Unglaub	2B3, 3B2, SS1	R	22	9	13	1	2	1	0	0	2	1		0	.154	.231

* Dougherty, also with New York, league leader in AB with 647 and R with 113

NAME	T	AGE	W	L	PCT	SV	G	GS	CG	IP	H	BB	SO	SHO	ERA
		29	95	59	.617	1	157	157	148	1406	1208	233	612	21	2.1
Cy Young	R	37	26	16	.619	1	43	41	40	380	327	29	200	10	1.9
Bill Dinneen	R	28	23	14	.622	0	37	37	37	336	283	63	153	5	2.2
Jesse Tannehill	L	29	21	11	.656	0	33	31	30	282	256	33	116	4	2.0
Norwood Gibson	R	27	17	14	.548	0	33	32	29	273	216	81	112	1	2.2
George Winter	R	26	8	4	.667	0	20	16	12	136	126	27	31	1	2.33

NAME	G by Pos	B	AGE	G	AB	R	H	2B	3B	HR	RBI	BB	SO	SB	BA	SA
NEW YORK 2nd 92-59 .609 1.5			CLARK GRIFFITH													
TOTALS			30	155	5220	598	1354	195	91	27	499	312		163	.259	.347
John Ganzel	1B118, 2B9, SS1	R	30	130	465	50	121	16	10	6	48	24		13	.260	.376
Jimmy Williams	2B146	R	27	146	559	62	147	31	7	2	74	38		14	.263	.354
Kid Elberfield (LJ)	SS122	R	29	122	445	54	114	12	5	2	46	37		16	.256	.319
Wid Conroy	3B110, SS27, OF3	R	28	140	489	58	119	18	12	1	52	43		30	.243	.335
Willie Keeler	OF142	L	32	143	539	76	185	13	10	2	40	35		22	.343	.416
John Anderson	OF112, 1B33	B	30	143	558	62	155	27	12	3	82	23		20	.278	.385
2 Patsy Dougherty	OF106	L	27	106	452*	80*	128	13	10	6	22	19		11	.283	.396
Deacon McGuire	C97, 1B1	R	40	101	322	17	67	12	2	0	20	27		2	.208	.258
Dave Fultz	OF90	R	29	97	339	39	93	17	4	2	32	24		17	.274	.366
Red Kleinow	C62, 3B2, OF1	R	26	68	209	12	43	8	4	0	16	15		4	.206	.282
2 Jack Thoney	3B26, OF10	R	24	36	128	17	24	4	2	0	12	8		9	.188	.250
Champ Osteen	3B17, SS8, 1B4	L	27	28	107	15	21	1	4	2	9	1		0	.196	.336
1 Monte Beville	1B4, C3	L	29	9	22	2	6	2	0	0	2	2		0	.273	.364
1 Bob Unglaub	3B4, SS1	R	22	6	19	2	4	0	0	0	2	0		0	.211	.211
Orth Collins	OF5	L	24	5	17	3	6	1	1	0	1	1		0	.353	.529
2 Frank McManus	C4	R	29	4	7	0	0	0	0	0	0	0		0	.000	.000
Elmer Bliss	OF1	R	29	1	1	0	0	0	0	0	0	0		0	.000	.000

* Dougherty, also with Boston, league leader in AB with 647 and R with 113

NAME	T	AGE	W	L	PCT	SV	G	GS	CG	IP	H	BB	SO	SHO	ERA
		30	92	59	.609	1	155	155	123	1381	1180	311	684	15	2.5
Jack Chesbro	R	30	41	12	.774	0	55	51	48	455	338	88	239	6	1.8
Jack Powell	R	29	23	19	.548	0	47	45	38	390	340	92	202	3	2.4
2 Al Orth	R	31	11	3	.786	0	20	18	11	138	122	19	47	2	2.4
1 Long Tom Hughes	R	25	7	12	.368	0	19	18	12	136	141	48	75	1	3.7
Clarke Griffith	R	34	6	5	.545	1	16	11	8	100	91	16	36	1	2.7
Ambrose Puttmann	L	25	2	2	.500	0	9	3	2	49	40	17	26	1	2.70
Walter Clarkson	R	25	2	3	.400	0	13	4	2	66	63	25	43	0	5.3
1 Barney Wolfe	R	28	0	1	.000	0	7	3	2	34	31	4	8	0	3.1
2 Ned Garvin	R	30	0	2	.000	0	2	0	0	12	14	2	8	0	2.2

NAME	G by Pos	B	AGE	G	AB	R	H	2B	3B	HR	RBI	BB	SO	SB	BA	SA
CHICAGO 3rd 89-65 .578 6			NIXEY CALLAHAN 23-18 .561 FIELDER JONES 66-47 .584													
TOTALS			29	156	5027	600	1217	193	68	14	519	373		216	.242	.316
Jiggs Donahue	1B101	L	24	102	367	47	92	9	8	1	48	25		21	.251	.327
Gus Dundon	2B103, 3B3, SS2	R	29	108	373	40	85	9	3	0	36	30		19	.228	.268
George Davis	SS152	B	33	152	558	74	143	25	14	1	69	43		32	.256	.357
Lee Tannehill	3B153	R	23	153	547	50	125	31	5	0	61	20		14	.229	.303
Danny Green	OF146	L	27	147	536	83	142	16	10	2	62	63		28	.265	.343
Fielder Jones	OF149	L	32	149	547	72	133	14	5	3	42	53		25	.243	.303
Nixey Callahan	OF104, 2B28	R	30	143	482	66	126	23	2	0	54	39		29	.261	.317
Billy Sullivan	C107	R	29	108	371	29	85	18	4	1	44	12		11	.229	.307
Frank Isbell	1B57, 2B27, OF5, SS4	L	28	96	314	27	66	10	3	1	34	16		19	.210	.271
Ducky Holmes	OF63	L	35	68	251	42	55	11	9	1	19	14		13	.311	.438
Ed McFarland	C49	R	29	50	160	22	44	11	3	0	20	17		2	.275	.381
Charlie Jones	OF5	R	28	8	17	2	4	0	1	0	1	1		0	.235	.353
Mike Heydon	C4	L	29	4	10	0	1	1	0	0	1	1		0	.100	.200
13 Fran Huelsman	OF1	R	30	4	7	0	1	1	0	0	0	0		0	.143	.286
Claude Barry	C3	R	24	3	1	0	0	0	0	0	0	0		0	.000	.000

NAME	T	AGE	W	L	PCT	SV	G	GS	CG	IP	H	BB	SO	SHO	ERA
		25	89	65	.578	3	156	156	134	1380	1161	303	550	26	2.3
Nick Altrock	L	27	21	13	.618	0	38	36	31	307	274	48	87	6	2.9
Frank Owen	R	24	21	15	.583	1	37	36	34	315	243	61	103	4	1.9
Frank Smith	R	24	16	10	.615	0	26	23	22	202	157	58	107	4	2.3
Doc White	L	25	16	10	.615	0	30	30	23	228	201	68	115	7	1.7
Roy Patterson	R	23	9	9	.500	1	22	17	14	165	148	24	64	4	2.2
Ed Walsh	R	23	5	5	.500	1	18	8	6	111	90	32	57	1	2.5
1 Patsy Flaherty	R	28	5	2	.333	1	5	5	4	43	36	10	14	0	2.0
Tom Dougherty	R	23	0	0	—	1	2	0	0	2	0	1	0	0	0.0
Elmer Stricklett	R	27	0	0	.000	0	1	1	0	7	12	2	3	0	10.2

CLEVELAND 4th 86-65 .570 7.5 BILL ARMOUR

NAME	G by Pos	B	AGE	G	AB	R	H	2B	3B	HR	RBI	BB	SO	SB	BA	SA
TOTALS			27	154	5152	647	1340	225	90	27	553	307		178	.260	.354
1 Charley Hickman	1B40, 2B45, OF1	R	28	86	337	34	97	22	10	4	45	13		9	.288	.448
Nap Lajoie	2B95, SS44, 1B2	R	29	140	554	92	211	50	14	6	102	27		31	.381	.554
Terry Turner (IL)	SS111	R	23	111	404	41	95	9	6	1	45	11		5	.235	.295
Bill Bradley	3B154	R	26	154	607	95	182	31	8	5	83	26		27	.300	.402
Elmer Flick	OF144, 2B6	L	28	149	575	95	174	31	17	6	56	51		42	.303	.447
Harry Bay	OF132	L	26	132	506	69	122	12	9	3	36	43		38	.241	.318
Billy Lush	OF138	B	30	138	477	76	123	13	8	1	50	72		12	.258	.325
Harry Bemis	C79, 1B13, 2B1	L	30	97	336	35	76	11	6	0	25	8		6	.226	.295
George Stovall	1B38, 2B9, OF3, 3B1	R	26	51	182	18	54	9	1	1	31	2		4	.297	.374
Fred Abbott	C33, 1B7	R	29	41	130	14	22	4	2	0	12	6		2	.169	.231
2 Fritz Buelow	C42	R	28	42	119	11	21	4	1	0	5	11		2	.176	.227
2 Charlie Carr	1B32	R	27	32	120	9	27	5	1	0	7	4		0	.225	.283
Bill Schwartz	1B22, 3B1	R	20	24	86	5	13	2	0	0	9	4		4	.151	.174
Claude Rossman	OF17	L	23	18	62	5	13	5	0	0	6	0		0	.210	.290
Rube Vinson	OF15	R	25	15	49	12	15	1	0	0	2	10		2	.306	.327
Harry Ostdiek	C7	R	23	7	18	1	3	0	1	0	3	3		1	.167	.278
Mike Donovan	SS1	R	22	2	2	0	0	0	0	0	0	0		0	.000	.000

NAME	T	AGE	W	L	PCT	SV	G	GS	CG	IP	H	BB	SO	SHO	ERA
		27	86	65	.570	1	154	154	141	1357	1273	285	627	20	2.22
Bill Bernhard	R	33	21	13	.618	1	38	37	35	321	323	55	137	4	2.13
Red Donahue	R	31	19	14	.576	1	35	32	30	277	281	49	127	6	2.40
Addie Joss (IL)	R	24	14	9	.609	0	25	24	20	192	160	30	83	5	1.59
Earl Moore	R	24	13	11	.542	0	26	24	22	228	186	61	139	1	2.25
Bob Rhoades	R	24	10	9	.526	0	22	19	18	175	175	48	72	0	2.88
Otto Hess	L	25	9	7	.563	0	21	16	15	151	134	31	64	4	1.67
John Hickey	L	22	0	2	.000	0	2	2	1	12	14	11	5	0	7.50

PHILADELPHIA 5th 81-70 .536 12.5 CONNIE MACK

NAME	G by Pos	B	AGE	G	AB	R	H	2B	3B	HR	RBI	BB	SO	SB	BA	SA
TOTALS			31	155	5088	557	1266	197	77	31	486	313		137	.249	.336
Harry Davis	1B102	R	30	102	403	54	124	22	12	10	62	23		10	.308	.511
Danny Murphy	2B150	R	27	149	550	80	158	29	18	2	77	22		22	.287	.444
Monte Cross	SS153	R	34	153	503	33	95	23	4	1	38	46		19	.189	.256
Lave Cross	3B155	R	38	155	607	80	177	29	10	1	71	13		13	.290	.377
Socks Seybold	OF129, 1B13	R	33	143	511	55	144	25	11	3	64	42		12	.282	.391
Ollie Pickering	OF121	R	34	124	455	56	103	10	3	0	30	45		17	.226	.262
Topsy Hartsel	OF147	L	30	147	534	79	135	17	12	2	25	75		19	.253	.341
Ossee Schrechengost	C84, 1B9	R	29	95	311	23	58	9	1	1	21	5		3	.186	.232
Mike Powers	C56, OF1	R	33	57	184	11	35	3	0	0	11	6		3	.190	.207
Danny Hoffman (IL)	OF51	L	24	53	204	31	61	7	5	3	24	5		9	.299	.426
13 Jim Mullin	1B26, 2B5, SS2, OF1	R	20	41	110	9	24	1	0	1	9	5		1	.218	.255
Pete Noonan	C22, 1B10	R	22	39	114	13	23	3	1	2	13	1		1	.202	.298
Lou Bruce	OF25, P2, 2B1, 3B1	L	27	30	101	9	27	3	0	0	8	5		2	.267	.297

NAME	T	AGE	W	L	PCT	SV	G	GS	CG	IP	H	BB	SO	SHO	ERA
		25	81	70	.536	0	155	155	137	1361	1149	366	887	26	2.35
Eddie Plank	L	28	26	17	.605	0	43	43	37	357	309	86	201	7	2.14
Rube Waddell	L	27	26	17	.605	0	46	46	39	383	307	91	349	1	1.62
Weldon Henley	R	23	14	17	.452	0	36	34	31	296	245	76	130	5	2.52
Andy Coakley	R	21	4	4	.500	0	8	8	8	62	50	23	33	2	2.03
Chief Bender	R	21	10	11	.476	0	29	20	18	204	167	59	149	4	2.87
Fred Applegate	R	25	1	2	.333	0	3	3	3	21	29	8	12	0	6.43
Lou Bruce	R	27	0	0	—	0	0	0	0	11	11	2	2	0	4.91
John Barthold	R	23	0	1	.000	0	4	0	0	11	12	8	5	0	4.91
Lee Fairbank	R	23	0	1	.000	0	3	1	1	17	19	13	6	0	6.35

ST. LOUIS 6th 65-87 .428 29 JIMMY McALEER

NAME	G by Pos	B	AGE	G	AB	R	H	2B	3B	HR	RBI	BB	SO	SB	BA	SA
TOTALS			28	156	5291	481	1266	153	53	10	406	322		150	.239	.294
Tom Jones	1B134, 2B23, OF4	R	28	156	625	53	152	15	10	2	68	15		16	.243	.309
Dick Padden	2B132	R	33	132	453	42	108	19	4	0	36	40		23	.238	.298
Bobby Wallace	SS139	R	30	139	550	57	150	28	4	2	69	42		19	.273	.349
2 Charlie Moran	3B81, OF1	R	25	82	272	15	47	3	1	0	14	25		2	.173	.191
Charlie Hemphill	OF108, 2B1	L	28	114	438	47	112	13	2	1	45	35		23	.256	.308
Snags Heidrick	OF130	L	27	133	538	66	147	14	10	1	36	16		35	.273	.342
Jesse Burkett	OF147	L	35	147	576	72	157	15	9	2	27	78		12	.273	.340
Joe Sugden	C79, 1B28	B	33	104	347	25	91	6	3	0	30	28		6	.262	.297
Mike Kahoe	C69	R	30	72	236	9	51	6	1	0	12	8		4	.216	.250
Pat Hynes	OF63, P5	R	19	66	254	23	60	7	3	0	15	3		3	.236	.287
1 Hunter Hill	3B56, OF1	R	25	58	219	19	47	3	0	0	14	6		4	.215	.228
Harry Gleason (PB)	SS20, 3B20, 2B5, OF1	R	29	46	155	10	33	7	1	0	6	4		1	.213	.271
4 Frank Huelsman	OF18	R	30	20	68	6	15	2	1	0	1	6		0	.221	.279
Jack O'Connor	C14	R	35	14	47	4	10	1	0	0	2	2		0	.213	.234
Gene DeMontreville	2B3	R	30	4	9	0	1	0	0	0	0	2		0	.111	.111
Art Bader	OF1	R	17	2	3	0	0	0	0	0	0	0		1	.000	.000
Pinky Swander		L	23	1	1	0	0	0	0	0	0	0		0	.000	.000
Harry Vahrenhorst		R	19	1	1	0	0	0	0	0	0	0		0	.000	.000

NAME	T	AGE	W	L	PCT	SV	G	GS	CG	IP	H	BB	SO	SHO	ERA
		27	65	87	.428	2	156	156	135	1410	1335	333	577	13	2.83
Fred Glade	R	28	18	16	.529	1	35	34	30	289	248	58	156	6	2.27
Barney Pelty	R	23	14	18	.438	1	39	35	31	301	270	77	126	2	2.84
Harry Howell	R	27	13	21	.382	0	34	33	32	300	254	60	122	2	2.19
Ed Siever	L	29	11	15	.423	0	29	24	20	217	235	65	77	2	2.65
Willie Sudhoff	R	29	8	14	.364	0	27	24	20	222	232	54	63	1	3.77
Pat Hynes	L	19	1	0	1.000	0	5	2	1	26	35	7	6	0	6.23
Gene Wright	R	25	0	1	.000	0	1	1	0	4	10	2	3	0	13.50
Cy Morgan	R	25	0	2	.000	0	8	3	2	51	51	10	24	0	3.71

DETROIT 7th 62-90 .408 32 ED BARROW 32-46 .410 BOBBY LOWE 30-44 .405

NAME	G by Pos	B	AGE	G	AB	R	H	2B	3B	HR	RBI	BB	SO	SB	BA	SA
TOTALS			28	162	5321	505	1231	154	69	11	431	344		112	.231	.292
1 Charlie Carr	1B92	R	28	92	360	29	77	13	3	0	40	14		6	.214	.267
2 Bobby Lowe	2B140	R	35	140	506	47	105	14	6	0	40	17		15	.208	.259
Charley O'Leary	SS135	R	21	135	456	39	97	10	3	1	16	21		9	.213	.254
Ed Gremminger	3B83	R	30	83	309	18	66	13	3	1	28	14		3	.214	.285
Sam Crawford	OF150	L	24	150	571	46	141	21	17	2	73	44		20	.247	.354
Jimmy Barrett	OF162	R	29	162	624	83	167	14	9	1	31	79		15	.268	.300
Matty McIntyre	OF152	L	24	152	578	74	146	11	10	2	46	44		11	.253	.317
Bob Wood	C47	R	38	49	175	15	43	6	2	1	17	5		1	.246	.320
R. Robinson	SS30, 3B26, OF20, 2B19	R	22	101	320	30	77	13	6	0	37	29		14	.241	.319
2 Bill Coughlin	3B56	R	25	56	206	22	47	6	0	0	17	5		1	.228	.257
2 Monte Beville	C30, 1B24	R	29	54	174	14	36	5	1	0	13	8		2	.207	.247
George Mullin	OF2	R	23	52	151	14	46	11	2	0	8	10		1	.305	.404
2 Lew Drill	C49, 1B2	R	27	51	160	7	39	6	1	0	13	20		2	.244	.294
1 Fritz Buelow	C42	R	28	42	136	6	15	1	1	0	5	8		2	.110	.132
2 Charley Hickman	1B39	R	28	42	144	18	35	6	6	2	22	11		1	.243	.410
John Burns	2B4	R	24	4	16	3	2	0	0	0	1	1		1	.125	.125
4 Frank Huelsman	OF4	R	30	4	18	1	6	1	0	0	4	1		1	.333	.389
1 Frank McManus	C1	R	28	1	0	0	0	0	0	0	0	0		0	.000	.000

NAME	T	AGE	W	L	PCT	SV	G	GS	CG	IP	H	BB	SO	SHO	ERA
		27	62	90	.408	3	162	162	143	1430	1345	433	556	15	2.77
Wild Bill Donovan	R	27	17	16	.515	0	34	34	30	293	251	94	137	3	2.46
George Mullin	R	23	16	24	.400	1	45	44	42	382	345	131	161	7	2.40
Ed Killian	L	27	15	20	.429	1	40	34	32	332	293	93	124	4	2.44
Frank Kitson	R	32	10	12	.455	1	26	24	19	200	211	38	69	0	3.06
Charlie Jaeger	R	29	2	3	.400	0	8	6	5	49	49	15	13	0	2.57
Jesse Stovall	R	28	2	13	.133	0	22	17	13	147	170	45	41	1	4.41
Cy Ferry	R	25	0	1	.000	0	3	1	1	13	12	11	4	0	6.23
Bugs Raymond	R	22	0	1	.000	0	5	2	1	15	14	6	7	0	3.00

WASHINGTON 8th 38-113 .252 55.5 MAL KITTREDGE 1-16 .059 PATSY DONOVAN 37-97 .276

NAME	G by Pos	B	AGE	G	AB	R	H	2B	3B	HR	RBI	BB	SO	SB	BA	SA
TOTALS			29	157	5149	437	1170	171	57	10	348	283		150	.227	.288
Jake Stahl	1B119, OF23	R	25	142	520	54	136	29	12	3	50	21		25	.262	.381
Barry McCormick	2B113	R	29	113	404	36	88	11	1	0	39	27		9	.218	.250
Joe Cassidy	SS99, OF3, 3B23	R	21	152	581	63	140	12	19	1	33	15		17	.241	.332
2 Hunter Hill	3B71, OF5	R	25	77	290	18	57	6	1	0	17	11		10	.197	.224
Patsy Donovan	OF122	R	39	125	434	32	104	6	0	0	19	24		16	.240	.253
2 Bill O'Neill	OF93, 2B3	B	24	95	365	33	89	10	1	1	16	22		22	.244	.285
5 Frank Huelsman	OF84	R	30	84	303	21	75	19	4	2	30	24		6	.248	.356
Mal Kittredge	C79	R	34	81	265	11	64	7	0	0	24	8		2	.242	.268
Boileryard Clarke	C52, 1B29	R	35	85	275	23	58	8	1	0	17	17		5	.211	.247
1 Bill Coughlin	3B64	R	25	65	265	28	73	15	4	0	17	9		10	.275	.362
1 Charlie Moran	SS61, 3B1	R	25	62	243	27	54	10	0	0	7	22		7	.222	.263
1 Kip Selbach	OF48	R	32	48	178	15	49	8	4	0	14	24		9	.275	.365
1 Lew Drill	C29, OF14	R	27	46	142	17	38	7	2	1	11	21		3	.268	.366
1 Al Orth (IL)	OF18, P10	R	31	31	102	7	22	3	1	0	11	1		2	.216	.265
2 Jim Mullin	2B27	R	20	27	102	10	19	2	2	0	4	4		3	.186	.245
1 Jack Thoney	OF17	R	24	17	70	6	21	3	0	0	6	1		2	.300	.343
Lefty Herring	1B10, OF5	L	24	15	46	3	8	1	0	0	2	7		0	.174	.196
Rabbitt Nill	2B15	R	22	15	48	4	8	1	0	0	3	5		0	.167	.208
Izzy Hoffman	OF9	L	29	10	30	1	3	1	0	0	1	2		0	.100	.133

NAME	T	AGE	W	L	PCT	SV	G	GS	CG	IP	H	BB	SO	SHO	ERA
		26	38	113	.252	3	157	157	137	1360	1487	347	533	7	3.62
Casey Patten	L	30	15	21	.417	2	45	39	37	358	367	79	150	2	3.07
2 Barney Wolfe	R	28	6	9	.400	0	17	16	13	127	131	22	44	2	3.26
Beany Jacobson	L	23	5	23	.179	0	33	30	23	254	276	57	75	1	3.54
Jack Townsend	R	25	5	27	.156	0	36	34	31	291	319	100	143	2	3.59
1 Al Orth (IL)	R	31	3	4	.429	0	10	7	7	74	88	15	23	0	4.74
Davey Dunkle	R	31	2	9	.182	0	12	11	7	94	95	23	23	0	4.99
2 Long Tom Hughes	R	25	2	14	.125	1	16	14	14	124	133	34	48	0	3.48
Del Mason	R	20	0	3	.000	0	3	3	3	33	45	13	16	0	6.00
Highball Wilson	R	25	0	3	.000	0	3	3	3	25	33	4	11	0	4.68

1904 N. L. — One Iron Hand, Two Iron Arms, and Only a Pennant...

Giant fans had been waiting for a pennant for 15 years, and all that was needed, it seemed, was a firm hand at the tiller. The Giants received such a hand, and none in the history of baseball was any firmer. John McGraw joined a last-place Giant squad in 1902, brought it in second the next year, and whipped it home first by a wide margin in 1904. The Little Napoleon had played on championship teams during his days at Baltimore, but the 1904 pennant was his maiden victory as a manager. McGraw built the Giants up by adding new talent; he brought several teammates with him from Baltimore in 1902, and several other key players were enrolled through trades and careful scouting of the minors. Primarily though, McGraw booted his club to the top by insulting, cajoling, and taunting each player to do his best. He was a tough disciplinarian; an icy glare from McGraw could chill any ballplayer and freeze his nerves. As compensation, he insisted that all his men be well paid, since a man good enough to play for him deserved a top salary. McGraw approached the style of the stern platoon sergeant - hated and feared by some, but respected by all.

On the way to their first title since 1889, the Giants started out of the gate fast and sprinted through the summer before pulling away from the pack. Three key additions bolstered the New York lineup, which amassed 106 victories, a new major league record at the time. Mike Donlin came over in mid-season from Cincinnati to add punch to the outfield, and the infield was greatly strengthened by the insertion of rookie Art Devlin at third and the purchase of veteran shortstop Bill Dahlen from Brooklyn. No one Giant performed spectacularly at bat, but solid stick work was consistently turned in by outfielder Sam Mertes, first sacker Dan McGann, and Shortstop Dahlen. The good offense was matched by the best pitching in the league, with the Giants allowing their opponents the smallest sum of runs of any team. An earlier version of the M&M boys made news in the big town; Iron Man Joe McGinnity won 35 games during the year, barely surpassing teammate Christy Mathewson's total of 33. As if these two were not enough, Dummy Taylor developed into a good enough hurler to chalk up 21

victories.

The rest of the teams contented themselves with striving for the leftovers. Chicago caught fire in September and leapfrogged over Pittsburgh and Cincinnati into second place. The Cubs continued assembling parts for future pennant winners, adding Three Finger Brown to the pitching staff to go with their already assembled double play combination of Joe Tinker, Johnny Evers, and Frank Chance. Chicago lived on pitching and defense in 1904, while Cincinnati lived by the bat. The champion Pirates limped home in fourth place, severely hampered by Deacon Phillippe's illness and Fred Clarke's bad leg. The Bucs made the first division in good measure on the strength of Honus Wagner's .349 batting, good for his second straight batting crown.

All the cheers for the Giants turned sour when president John T. Brush announced that his team would not compete against the American League champion at the season's end. Despite fierce press criticism, Brush stood on his decision, attributed overtly to the American League's being an inferior circuit not worthy of playing the National League for a championship. More realistically, however, the true cause of the refusal rested in Brush's ire at having the American League competition in New York and in McGraw's personal antipathy towards junior circuit president Ban Johnson, which resulted from a 1902 dispute between the two men when McGraw was in the American League.

National League president Harry Pulliam supported Brush, stating that the 1903 Series had been a voluntary arrangement, and that no obligatory agreement had ever been reached. But during the off-season, Brush himself seized the opportunity for immortality by proposing that the autumn classic be made an annual and compulsory affair. The proposal was adopted, and the "Brush Rules" governing the Series in playing and financial matters up to the present were used to set the first standards for the annual world's championship.

1904 NATIONAL LEAGUE

Name	G by Pos	B	AGE	G	AB	R	H	2B	3B	HR	RBI	BB	SO	SB	BA	SA
NEW YORK	1st 106-47 .693		JOHN McGRAW													
TOTALS			29	157	5150	744	1347	202	62	31	564	434		283	.262	.344
Dan McGann	1B141	B	32	141	517	81	148	22	6	6	71	36		42	.286	.387
Billy Gilbert	2B146	R	28	146	478	57	121	13	3	1	54	46		33	.253	.299
Bill Dahlen	SS145	R	34	145	523	70	140	26	2	2	80	44		47	.268	.337
Art Devlin	3B130	R	24	130	474	81	133	16	8	1	66	62		33	.281	.354
George Browne	OF149	L	28	150	596	99	169	16	5	4	39	39		24	.284	.347
R. Bresnahan	OF93, 1B10, SS4, 2B1, 3B1	R	28	109	402	81	114	22	7	5	33	58		13	.284	.410
Sam Mertes	OF147, SS1	R	31	148	532	83	147	28	11	4	78	54		47	.276	.393
Jack Warner	C86	L	31	86	287	29	57	5	1	1	15	14		7	.199	.233
Frank Bowerman	C79, 1B9, 2B2, P1	R	35	93	289	38	67	11	4	2	27	16		7	.232	.318
Jack Dunn	3B28, SS10, 2B9, OF7, P1	R	31	64	181	27	56	12	2	1	19	11		11	.309	.414
1 Moose McCormick	OF55	L	23	59	203	28	54	9	5	1	26	13		13	.266	.374
2 Mike Donlin	OF37	L	26	42	132	17	37	7	3	2	14	10		1	.280	.424
24Doc Marshall	C3, OF2, 2B1	R	29	11	17	3	6	1	0	0	2	1		0	.353	.412
Jack McGraw	2B2, SS2			5	12	0	4	0	0	0	0	0		3	.333	.333
Dan Brouthers	1B1	L	46	2	5	0	0	0	0	0	0	0		0	.000	.000
Jim O'Rourke	C1	R	51	1	4	1	1	0	0	0	0	0		0	.250	.250

NAME	T	AGE	W	L	PCT	SV	G	GS	CG	IP	H	BB	SO	SHO	ERA
		26	106	47	.693	15	157	157	127	1397	1151	349	707	21	2.17
Joe McGinnity	R	33	35	8	.814	6	51	44	38	408	307	86	144	9	1.61
Christy Mathewson	R	23	33	12	.733	1	48	46	33	368	306	78	212	4	2.03
Dummy Taylor	R	29	21	15	.583	0	37	36	29	296	231	75	138	5	2.34
Hooks Wiltse	L	24	13	3	.813	3	24	16	14	165	150	61	105	2	2.84
Red Ames	R	21	4	6	.400	2	16	13	11	115	94	38	93	1	2.31
Jack Dunn	R	31	0	0	—	0	1	1	0	4	3	1	0	0	4.50
Frank Bowerman	R	35	0	0	—	0	1	0	0	1	3	1	0	0	9.00
Billy Milligan	L	25	0	1	.000	2	5	1	1	25	36	4	6	0	5.04
2 Claud Elliot	R	24	0	2	.000	0	3	1	1	15	21	3	8	0	3.60

CHICAGO	2nd 93-60 .608 13		FRANK SELEE													
TOTALS			28	156	5210	597	1294	157	62	22	470	298		227	.248	.315
Frank Chance	1B123, C1	R	27	124	451	89	140	16	10	6	49	36		42	.310	.430
Johnny Evers	2B152	R	22	152	532	49	141	14	7	0	47	28		26	.265	.318
Joe Tinker	SS140, OF1	R	23	141	488	55	108	13	4	3	41	21		41	.221	.318
Doc Casey	3B134, C2	L	33	136	548	71	147	20	4	1	43	18		21	.268	.325
Davy Jones	OF97	L	24	98	336	44	82	11	5	3	39	41		14	.244	.333
Jack McCarthy	OF115	L	35	115	432	36	114	14	2	0	51	23		14	.264	.306
Jimmy Slagle	OF120	L	30	120	481	73	125	12	10	1	31	41		28	.260	.333
Johnny Kling	C104, OF10, 1B6	R	28	123	452	41	110	18	0	2	46	16		7	.243	.296
2 Shad Barry	OF30, 1B18, 3B16, SS8, 2B2	R	25	73	263	29	69	7	2	1	26	17		12	.262	.316
O. Williams	OF21, 1B11, SS10, 2B6, 3B6	R	26	57	185	21	37	4	1	0	8	13		9	.200	.232
Bob Wicker	P30, OF20	R	26	50	155	17	34	1	0	0	9	4		4	.219	.226
Jack O'Neill	C49	R	31	51	168	8	36	5	0	1	19	6		1	.214	.262
Harry McChesney	OF22	R	24	22	88	9	23	6	2	0	11	4		2	.261	.375
Wildfire Schulte	OF20	L	21	20	84	16	24	4	3	2	13	2		1	.286	.476
Broadway Aleck Smith	OF6, C1, 3B1		33	10	29	2	6	1	0	0	1	3		1	.207	.241
Solly Hofman	OF6, SS1	R	21	7	26	7	7	0	0	1	4	1		2	.269	.385
George Moriarty	3B2, OF2	R	18	4	13	0	0	0	0	0	0	0		0	.000	.000
Ike Van Zandt	OF3	L	28	3	11	0	0	0	0	0	0	1		0	.000	.000
Bill Carney	OF2	B	30	2	7	0	0	0	0	0	0	0		0	.000	.000
Dutch Rudolph	OF2	L	21	2	3	0	1	0	0	0	0	0		0	.333	.333
Fred Holmes	C1	R	26	1	3	1	1	1	0	0	0	0		0	.333	.667
Tom Stanton	C1	B	29	1	3	0	0	0	0	0	0	0		0	.000	.000

NAME	T	AGE	W	L	PCT	SV	G	GS	CG	IP	H	BB	SO	SHO	ERA
		27	93	60	.608	6	156	156	139	1384	1150	402	618	18	2.30
Jake Weimer	L	30	20	14	.588	0	37	37	31	307	229	97	177	5	1.91
Buttons Briggs	R	28	19	11	.633	3	34	30	28	277	252	77	112	3	2.05
Carl Lundgren	R	24	17	10	.630	1	31	27	25	242	203	77	106	2	2.60
Bob Wicker	R	26	17	8	.680	0	30	27	23	229	201	58	99	4	2.27
Three Finger Brown	R	27	15	10	.600	1	26	23	21	212	155	50	81	4	1.86
1 Frank Corridon	R	23	5	5	.500	0	12	10	9	100	88	37	34	0	3.10
Dango Groth	R	19	0	2	.000	1	3	2	2	16	22	6	9	0	5.63

CINCINNATI	3rd 88-65 .575 18		JOE KELLEY													
TOTALS			25	157	5231	692	1332	189	92	21	561	399		179	.255	.338
Joe Kelley	1B117, OF6, 2B1	R	32	123	449	75	126	21	13	0	63	49		15	.281	.385
Miller Huggins	2B140	B	26	140	491	96	129	12	7	2	30	88		13	.263	.328
Tommy Corcoran	SS150	R	35	150	578	55	133	17	9	2	74	19		19	.230	.301
Harry Steinfeldt (LJ)	3B98	R	26	99	349	35	85	11	6	1	52	29		16	.244	.318
Cozy Dolan	OF102, 1B24	L	31	129	465	84	132	8	10	6	51	39		19	.284	.383
Cy Seymour	OF130	L	31	131	531	71	166	26	13	5	58	29		11	.313	.439
Fred Odwell	OF126, 2B1	R	31	129	468	75	133	22	10	1	58	26		30	.284	.380
Admiral Schlei	C88	R	26	97	291	25	69	8	3	0	32	17		7	.237	.285
Orville Woodruff	3B61, 2B17, SS8, OF1	R	27	87	306	20	58	14	3	0	20	19		9	.190	.255
Heinie Peitz	C64, 1B18, 3B1	R	33	84	272	32	66	13	2	1	30	14		1	.243	.316
1 Mike Donlin (ST)	OF53, 1B6	L	26	60	236	42	84	11	7	1	38	18		21	.356	.475
2 Jimmy Sebring	OF56	L	22	56	222	22	50	9	2	0	24	14		8	.225	.284
Gabby Street	C11	R	21	11	33	1	4	1	0	0	1	1		2	.121	.152
Peaches O'Neill	C5, 1B1	R	24	8	15	0	4	0	0	0	1	1		0	.267	.267

NAME	T	AGE	W	L	PCT	SV	G	GS	CG	IP	H	BB	SO	SHO	ERA
		27	88	65	.575	2	157	157	142	1384	1256	343	502	12	2.35
Jack Harper	R	27	23	8	.742	0	35	35	31	285	262	85	125	6	2.30
Win Kellum	L	28	14	9	.609	2	31	24	22	225	206	46	70	1	2.60
Tom Walker	R	22	15	10	.600	0	24	24	22	217	196	53	64	2	2.20
Noodles Hahn	L	25	16	18	.471	0	35	34	33	298	258	35	98	2	2.06
Bob Ewing	R	31	11	13	.458	0	26	24	22	212	198	58	99	0	2.47
1 Jack Sutthoff	R	31	6	6	.500	0	12	10	8	90	83	43	27	0	2.40
1 Claud Elliott	R	24	3	1	.750	0	9	6	4	58	53	23	19	1	2.95

PITTSBURGH 4th 87-66 .569 19   FRED CLARKE

Name	G by Pos	B	AGE	G	AB	R	H	2B	3B	HR	RBI	BB	SO	SB	BA	SA
TOTALS			27	156	5160	675	1333	164	102	15	522	391		178	.258	.338
Kitty Bransfield	1B139	R	29	139	520	47	116	17	9	0	60	22		11	.223	.290
Claude Ritchey	2B156, SS2	R	30	156	544	79	143	22	12	0	51	59		12	.263	.347
Honus Wagner	SS121, OF8, 1B3, 2B2	R	30	132	490	97	171	44	14	4	75	59		53	.349	.520
Tommy Leach	3B146	R	26	146	579	92	149	15	12	2	56	45		23	.257	.335
1 Jimmy Sebring	OF80	L	22	80	305	28	82	11	7	0	32	17		8	.269	.351
Ginger Beaumont	OF153	L	27	153	615	97	185	12	12	3	54	34		28	.301	.374
Fred Clarke (LJ)	OF70	L	31	72	278	51	85	7	11	0	25	22		11	.306	.410
Eddie Phelps	C91, 1B1	R	25	94	302	29	73	5	3	0	28	15		2	.242	.278
Otto Krueger	OF33, SS32, 3B10	R	27	86	268	34	52	6	2	1	26	29		8	.194	.243
2 Moose McCormick	OF66	L	23	66	238	25	69	10	6	2	23	13		6	.290	.408
Harry Smith	C44, OF3	R	29	47	141	17	35	3	1	0	18	16		5	.248	.284
Fred Carisch	C22, 1B14	R	22	37	125	9	31	3	1	0	4	5		1	.248	.288
Jack Gilbert	OF25		28	25	87	13	21	0	0	0	3	12		3	.241	.241
Bull Smith	OF13	R	23	13	42	2	6	0	1	0	0	1		0	.143	.190
Ernie Diehl	OF7, SS4	R	26	12	37	6	6	0	0	0	4	6		3	.162	.162
Harry Cassady	OF12	L	23	12	44	8	9	0	0	0	3	2		2	.205	.205
Jimmy Archer	C7, OF1	R	21	7	20	1	3	0	0	0	1	0		0	.150	.150
Tom Stankard	SS1, 3B1	R	22	2	2	0	0	0	0	0	0	0		0	.000	.000
1 Bobby Lowe		R	35	1	1	0	0	0	0	0	0	0		0	.000	.000
Jack Rafter	C1	R	29	1	3	0	0	0	0	0	0	0		0	.000	.000

NAME	T	AGE	W	L	PCT	SV	G	GS	CG	IP	H	BB	SO	SHO	ERA
TOTALS		28	87	66	.569	1	156	156	133	1348	1273	379	455	14	2.89
2 Patsy Flaherty	L	28	19	9	.679	0	29	28	28	242	210	59	54	5	2.05
Sam Leever	R	32	18	11	.621	0	34	32	26	253	224	54	63	0	2.17
Mike Lynch	R	29	15	11	.577	0	27	24	24	223	200	91	95	1	2.70
Charlie Case	R	24	10	5	.667	0	18	17	14	141	129	31	49	3	2.94
Deacon Phillippe (IL)	R	32	10	10	.500	1	21	19	17	167	183	26	82	3	3.23
Roscoe Miller	R	27	7	8	.467	0	19	17	11	134	133	39	35	2	3.36
Chick Robitaille	R	25	4	3	.571	0	9	8	6	66	52	13	34	0	1.91
Jack Pfiester	L	26	1	1	.500	0	3	2	1	20	28	9	6	0	7.20
Watty Lee	R	24	1	2	.333	0	5	3	1	23	34	9	5	0	8.61
1 Doc Scanlan	R	22	1	3	.250	0	10	2	2	49	48	20	21	0	4.22
Lew Moren	R	20	0	0	—	0	1	0	0	4	7	4	0	0	9.00
Bucky Veil	R	22	0	0	—	0	1	1	0	5	4	4	1	0	5.40

ST. LOUIS 5th 75-79 .487 31.5   KID NICHOLS

Name	G by Pos	B	AGE	G	AB	R	H	2B	3B	HR	RBI	BB	SO	SB	BA	SA
TOTALS			28	155	5104	602	1292	175	66	24	456	343		199	.253	.327
Jake Beckley	1B142	L	36	142	551	72	179	22	9	1	67	35		17	.325	.403
John Farrell	2B130	R	27	131	509	72	130	23	3	0	20	46		16	.255	.312
Danny Shay	SS97, 2B2	R	27	99	340	45	77	11	1	1	18	39		36	.226	.303
Jimmy Burke	3B118	R	29	118	406	37	92	10	3	0	37	5		17	.227	.266
Spike Shannon	OF123	R	26	134	500	84	140	10	3	1	26	50		34	.280	.318
Homer Smoot	OF137	L	26	137	520	58	146	23	6	3	66	37		23	.281	.365
1 George Barclay	OF103	R	28	103	375	41	75	7	4	1	28	12		14	.200	.248
Mike Grady	C77, 1B11, 2B3, 3B1	R	34	101	323	44	101	15	11	5	43	31		6	.313	.474
Dave Brain	SS59, 3B30, OF19, 2B13, 1B4	R	24	127	488	57	130	24	12	7	72	17		18	.266	.408
Jack Dunleavy	OF44, P7	L	24	51	172	23	40	7	3	1	14	16		8	.233	.326
Dave Zearfoss	C25	R	36	27	80	7	17	2	0	0	9	10		2	.213	.238
Larry McLean	C24	R	22	27	84	5	14	2	1	0	4	4		1	.167	.214
Hugh Hill	OF23	L	24	23	93	13	21	2	1	3	4	4		3	.226	.366
Bill Byers	C16, 1B1	R	26	19	60	3	13	0	0	0	5	1		0	.217	.217
Simmy Murch	2B6, 3B6, SS1	R	23	13	51	3	7	1	0	0	1	1		1	.137	.157
John Butler	C12	R	24	12	37	0	6	1	0	0	1	4		0	.162	.189
1 She Donahue	2B3, SS1	R	27	4	15	1	4	0	0	0	2	0		1	.267	.267
Charlie Swindells	C3	R	25	3	8	0	1	0	0	0	0	0		0	.125	.125

NAME	T	AGE	W	L	PCT	SV	G	GS	CG	IP	H	BB	SO	SHO	ERA
TOTALS		30	75	79	.487	2	155	155	146	1368	1286	319	529	7	2.64
Jack Taylor	R	30	21	19	.565	1	41	39	39	352	297	82	103	2	2.22
Kid Nichols	R	34	21	13	.618	1	36	35	35	317	268	50	134	3	2.02
Chappie McFarland	R	26	14	17	.452	0	32	31	28	270	266	56	111	1	3.20
Mike O'Neill	R	26	10	14	.417	0	25	24	23	220	229	50	68	1	2.09
Joe Corbett (IL)	R	28	5	9	.357	0	14	14	12	109	110	51	68	0	4.38
Jim McGinley	R	25	2	1	.667	0	3	3	3	27	28	6	6	0	2.00
War Sanders	L	26	1	2	.333	0	4	3	1	19	25	1	11	0	4.74
Jack Dunleavy	L	24	1	4	.200	0	7	5	5	53	63	23	28	0	4.42

BROOKLYN 6th 56-97 .366 50   NED HANLON

Name	G by Pos	B	AGE	G	AB	R	H	2B	3B	HR	RBI	BB	SO	SB	BA	SA
TOTALS			28	154	4916	497	1142	159	53	15	390	411		205	.232	.295
Pop Dillon	1B134	R	30	135	511	60	132	18	6	0	31	40		13	.258	.317
Dutch Jordan	2B70, 3B11, 1B4	R	24	87	252	21	45	10	2	0	19	13		7	.179	.234
Charlie Babb	SS151	B	31	151	521	49	138	18	3	0	53	53		34	.265	.311
Dude McCormick (BA)	3B104, 2B1	L	21	105	347	28	64	5	4	0	27	43		22	.184	.222
Harry Lumley	OF150	L	23	150	577	79	161	23	18	9	78	41		30	.279	.428
Johnny Dobbs	OF92, 2B2, SS2	L	29	101	363	36	90	16	2	0	30	28		11	.248	.303
Jimmy Sheckard	OF141, 2B2	L	25	143	507	70	121	23	6	1	46	56		21	.239	.314
Bill Bergen	C93, 1B1	R	31	96	329	17	60	4	2	0	12	9		7	.182	.207
Doc Gessler	OF88, 1B1, 2B1	L	23	104	341	41	99	18	4	2	28	30		13	.290	.384
Sammy Strang (IL)	2B63, 3B61, SS2	R	28	77	271	28	52	11	0	1	9	45		16	.192	.244
Lew Ritter	C57, 2B5, 3B1	R	28	72	214	23	53	4	1	0	19	20		7	.248	.276
Heinie Batch	3B28	R	24	28	94	9	24	1	2	2	7	1		6	.255	.372
Fred Jacklitsch	1B11, 2B8, C5	R	28	26	77	8	18	3	1	0	8	7		3	.234	.299
1 Jack Doyle	1B8	R	24	8	22	2	5	1	0	0	2	6		1	.227	.273
Charlie Loudenslager	2B1		23	1	1	0	0	0	0	0	0	0		0	.000	.000
1 Deacon Van Buren		L	33	1	1	0	1	0	0	0	0	0		0	1.000	1.000

NAME	T	AGE	W	L	PCT	SV	G	GS	CG	IP	H	BB	SO	SHO	ERA
TOTALS		28	56	97	.366	2	154	154	135	1337	1281	414	453	12	2.70
Oscar Jones	R	24	17	25	.405	0	46	41	38	387	387	92	96	0	2.75
Jack Cronin	R	30	12	23	.343	0	40	34	33	307	284	79	110	4	2.70
2 Doc Scanlan	R	23	7	6	.538	0	13	12	11	104	94	40	40	3	2.16
Ed Poole	R	29	7	14	.333	1	25	23	19	178	178	74	67	1	3.39
1 Ned Garvin	R	30	6	14	.300	0	23	22	16	182	141	78	86	2	1.68
Doc Reisling	R	29	3	4	.429	0	7	7	6	51	45	10	19	1	2.12
2 Fred Mitchell	R	26	2	5	.286	0	8	8	8	66	73	23	16	1	3.82
Bull Durham	R	27	1	1	1.000	0	2	1	1	11	10	5	1	0	3.27
Grant Thatcher	R	27	1	1	1.000	0	1	0	0	9	9	2	4	0	4.00
Jack Doscher	L	23	0	1	.000	0	6	1	1	2	0				
Joe Koukalik	R	24	0	1	.000	0	1	1	1	8	10	4	1	2	0	1.13
Bill Reidy	R	30	0	1	.000	0	2	1	1	38	49	6	11	0	4.50

BOSTON 7th 55-98 .359 51   AL BUCKENBERGER

Name	G by Pos	B	AGE	G	AB	R	H	2B	3B	HR	RBI	BB	SO	SB	BA	SA
TOTALS			27	155	5135	491	1217	153	50	24	394	316		143	.237	.300
Fred Tenney	1B144, OF4	L	32	147	533	76	144	17	9	1	37	57		17	.270	.341
Fred Raymer	2B114	R	28	114	419	28	88	12	3	1	27	13		7	.210	.260
Ed Abbaticchio	SS154	R	27	154	579	76	148	18	10	3	54	40		24	.256	.337
Jim Delahanty	3B113, 2B18, OF9, P1	R	25	142	499	56	142	27	8	4	60	27		10	.285	.389
Rip Cannell	OF93	L	24	100	346	32	81	5	1	0	18	23		10	.234	.254
Phil Geier	OF137, 3B7, 2B5, SS1	R	27	149	580	70	141	17	2	1	27	56		18	.243	.284
Dick Cooley	OF116, 1B6	L	31	122	467	41	127	18	7	5	70	24		14	.272	.373
Tom Needham	C77, OF1	R	25	84	269	18	70	12	3	4	19	11		3	.260	.372
Pat Moran	C72, 3B39, 1B12	R	28	113	398	26	90	11	3	4	34	18		10	.226	.299
Pat Carney	OF71, P4, 1B1	R	28	78	279	24	57	5	2	0	11	12		6	.204	.237
2 George Barclay	OF24	R	28	24	93	5	21	3	1	0	10	2		3	.226	.280
Bill Lauterborn	2B20	R	25	20	69	7	19	2	0	0	2	1		1	.275	.304
3 Doc Marshall	C10, OF1	R	29	13	43	3	9	0	1	0	2	2		2	.209	.256
Kid O'Hara	OF8	B	28	8	39	3	6	0	0	0	4	1			.207	.207
Joe Stanley	OF3	B	23	3	8	0	0	0	0	0	0	0		0	.000	.000
Gene McAuliffe	C1	R	32	1	2	0	1	0	0	0	0	0		0	.500	.500
Andy Sullivan	SS1		19	1	1	0	0	0	0	0	0	0		0	.000	.000
Jack White	OF1	R	26	1	5	1	0	0	0	0	0	0		0	.000	.000

NAME	T	AGE	W	L	PCT	SV	G	GS	CG	IP	H	BB	SO	SHO	ERA
TOTALS		28	55	98	.359	0	155	155	136	1348	1405	500	544	13	3.43
Vic Willis	R	28	18	25	.419	0	43	43	39	350	357	109	196	2	2.85
Kaiser Wilhelm	R	30	15	21	.417	0	39	36	30	288	316	74	73	3	3.69
Togie Pittinger	R	32	14	21	.400	0	38	37	35	335	298	144	146	5	2.64
Tom Fisher	R	23	6	15	.286	0	31	21	19	214	257	82	84	2	4.25
Ed McNichol	R	25	2	13	.133	0	17	15	12	122	120	74	39	1	4.28
Joe Stewart	R	25	0	0	—	0	9				1	4	1	0	9.64
Jim Delahanty	R	25	0	0	—	0	1	0	0	6	3	5	1	0	0.00
Pat Carney	L	27	0	3	.000	0	4	4	1	26	40	12	5	0	5.88

PHILADELPHIA 8th 52-100 .342 53.5   HUGH DUFFY

Name	G by Pos	B	AGE	G	AB	R	H	2B	3B	HR	RBI	BB	SO	SB	BA	SA
TOTALS			27	155	5103	571	1268	170	54	23	469	377		159	.248	.316
2 Jack Doyle	1B65, 2B1	R	34	66	236	20	52	10	3	1	22	19		4	.220	.301
Kid Gleason	2B152, 3B1	B	37	153	587	61	161	23	6	0	42	37		17	.274	.334
Rudy Hulswitt	SS113	R	27	113	406	36	99	11	4	1	36	16		8	.244	.298
Harry Wolverton (RJ)	3B102	R	30	102	398	43	106	15	5	0	49	26		18	.266	.329
Sherry Magee	OF94, 1B1	R	19	95	364	51	101	15	12	3	57	14		11	.277	.409
Roy Thomas	OF139	L	30	139	496	92	144	6	6	3	29	102		28	.290	.345
John Titus	OF140	R	28	146	504	60	148	25	5	4	55	46		15	.294	.387
Red Dooin	C96, 1B4, OF3, 3B1	R	25	108	355	41	86	11	4	6	36	8		15	.242	.346
Johnny Lush (DO)	1B62, OF33, P7	L	18	106	369	39	102	22	3	2	42	27		12	.276	.369
Frank Roth	C67, 1B1, 2B1	R	25	81	229	28	59	8	1	1	20	12		8	.258	.314
2 She Donahue	SS29, 3B24, 1B3, 2B2	R	27	58	200	21	43	4	0	0	14	3		7	.215	.235
Bob Hall	3B20, SS15, 1B11	R	25	46	163	11	26	4	0	0	17	14		5	.160	.184
1 Shad Barry	OF25	R	25	35	122	15	25	2	0	0	3	11		2	.205	.221
Hugh Duffy	OF14	R	37	18	46	10	13	1	1	0	5	13		3	.283	.348
2 Deacon Van Buren	OF12	L	33	12	43	2	10	2	0	0	3	3		2	.233	.279
1 Doc Marshall	C7	R	29	7	20	1	2	0	0	0	1	0		0	.100	.100
Jesse Purnell	3B7	R	23	7	19	2	2	0	0	0	1	4		1	.105	.105
Klondike Douglass	1B3	R	32	3	10	0	3	0	0	0	0	1		0	.300	.300
Tom Fleming	OF1	R	30	3	6	0	0	0	0	0	0	0		0	.000	.000
Herman Long	2B1	R	38	1	4	0	1	0	0	0	0	0		0	.250	.250
Butch Rementer	C1	R	26	1	1	0	0	0	0	0	0	0		0	.000	.000

NAME	T	AGE	W	L	PCT	SV	G	GS	CG	IP	H	BB	SO	SHO	ERA
TOTALS		31	52	100	.342	2	155	155	131	1339	1418	425	469	9	3.39
Chick Fraser	R	30	14	24	.368	1	42	36	32	302	287	100	127	2	3.25
Bill Duggleby	R	31	12	14	.462	1	32	27	22	224	265	53	55	2	3.78
Tully Sparks	R	29	7	16	.304	0	26	25	19	201	208	43	67	3	2.64
2 Frank Corridon	R	23	6	5	.545	0	12	11	11	94	88	28	44	1	2.20
2 Jack Sutthoff	R	31	6	13	.316	0	19	18	17	164	172	71	46	0	3.68
1 Fred Mitchell (AJ)	R	26	4	7	.364	0	13	13	11	109	133	25	29	0	3.39
Ralph Caldwell	L	20	2	3	.400	0	6	5	5	41	40	15	30	0	4.17
John McPherson	R	36	1	10	.091	0	15	12	11	128	130	46	32	1	3.66
Tom Barry	R	25	0	1	.000	0	1	1	1	6	6	1	1	0	27.00
1 John Brackinridge	R	23	0	1	.000	0	1	0	0	34	37	16	11	0	5.56
Johnny Lush (DO)	L	18	0	6	.000	0	13			43	52	27	27	0	3.56

1905 — Whitewashing the Elephants

In a pitcher's year which saw only two regular .300 hitters in the American League, the Philadelphia team batting average of .255 was good enough to score a league-leading 617 runs and bring Connie Mack his second championship in four years. The White Elephant's return to the top after two years, and their jump from a 1904 fifth-place finish, came about via Harry Davis' team-leading .284 batting average and the arms of southpaws Rube Waddell and Eddie Plank, who again turned in excellent years but were complemented by the development of Chief Bender and Andy Coakley into reliable starters. The foursome, although mostly accounting for a team E.R.A. of 2.19 and capturing almost every statistical pitching category, had to take a back seat in team earned run honors to the Chicago White Sox, who walked off with the crown on a brilliant 1.99 performance.

Although Chicago's pitching was rich enough to make the race a photo-finish between themselves and the Athletics, the first three months of the campaign saw the struggle for first place between Chicago and the heavy-hitting Cleveland team. The two swapped the top spot through July, while the Athletics paced themselves in a close, third-place berth. Cleveland dropped off after playing-manager, Nap Lajoie, the league's best hitter in 1904, was sidelined in July with blood poisoning, and, on August 2, the Mackmen double-timed ahead of Chicago into first place. With Cleveland fading away, and Chicago's weak hitting catching up with them, the Athletics widened the gap in August and seemingly iced away the crown.

But the White Sox hung tight and started melting away the Athletic's lead until, on September 28, it stood at three percentage points with Chicago coming into Philadelphia for a three-game set. The tired Athletics rallied their forces to take two of the three games to all but finish Chicago - a job which was done by the lowly St. Louis Browns, who beat the hitless wonders twice in the final week to allow the Athletics to walk in with a two-game margin championship.

Chicago consolation came in Ed Walsh, the spit-balling wonder, who opened his major league career by winning eight of eleven decisions while posting a 2.17 E.R.A. The Detroit Tigers moved from seventh to third on the arms of George Mullin, Ed Killian, and Wild Bill Donovan. But a more important event was the arrival of you Ty Cobb, who hit .240 as a part-time outfielder. While the Tigers were moving toward the light of day, the 1904 championship Boston Red Sox pulled a reversal and were neve[r] in the race, as they would up fourth. Despite the addition of hard-hitting Jess[e] Burkett from St. Louis, only Jesse Tannehill provided consistency on the mound fo[r] the Beantowners. Bill Dinneen flattened out at 14-14 after a 23-victory season, an[d] 38-year-old Cy Young posted his worst record since breaking into baseball in 189[0]. Cleveland's Lajoie, the holder of a partial season's .329 average, surrendered th[e] batting title to teammate Elmer Flick, who was joined in the magic .300 circle onl[y] by New York's Willie Keeler. The American League's final individual highlight, o[r] at least one worthy of mention, was Jack Chesbro, who went from his record 41[-] victory 1904 season to a substantial but more realistic 20 wins.

In the National League, John McGraw kept his Giants on top from April 23 on t[o] repeat as champions. Pittsburgh kept within striking distance for most of th[e] summer and made a move to close the gap in August but fell back in the fall, whe[n] they were unable to maintain the momentum picked up during the dog-days of lat[e] summer. The Giants again possessed the most powerful attack in the league[,] featuring Mike Donlin's .356 clouting. Roger Bresnahan hit .302 and handled [a] mound staff which included 32-game winner Christy Mathewson, 20-game aces Re[d] Ames and Joe McGinnity, and solid starters Hooks Wiltse, and Dummy Taylor[.] Pittsburgh received .363 batting from Honus Wagner and good pitching from Sa[m] Leever and returning Deacon Phillippe, but was simply unable to put all the piece[s] together. Wagner himself was unhorsed after two years as batting champion b[y] Cincinnati's Cy Seymour.

After a one-year interruption, the World Series resumed with a dazzling exhibitio[n] of pitching dominance. The rested Giants downed the tired Athletics in five game[s] with each game incredibly being a shutout. Mathewson established himself as a[n] early Series hero by tossing three whitewashings at the Athletics while teammat[e] McGinnity accounted for New York's other shutout. In the phenomenal pitcher'[s] battle, Philadelphia's only three runs of the Series came in Bender's second-gam[e] win. The victory, in addition to avenging the senior circuit's loss in 1903, was a grea[t] personal satisfaction to McGraw, who got the one-upmanship in his long-standin[g] feud with American League President Ban Johnson.

1905 AMERICAN LEAGUE

PHILADELPHIA 1st 92-56 .622 — CONNIE MACK

NAME	G by Pos	B	AGE	G	AB	R	H	2B	3B	HR	RBI	BB	SO	SB	BA	SA
TOTALS			29	152	5107	617	1300	256	51	24	511	376		189	.255	.339
Harry Davis	1B149	R	31	149	602	92	171	47	6	8	83	43		36	.284	.422
Danny Murphy	2B150	R	28	150	533	71	148	36	4	6	71	42		23	.278	.394
Jack Knight	SS81, 3B2	R	19	88	325	28	66	12	1	3	29	9		4	.203	.274
Lave Cross	3B147	R	39	147	583	68	155	26	5	0	77	26		8	.266	.328
Socks Seybold	OF132	R	34	132	488	64	132	36	5	6	59	42		5	.270	.402
Danny Hoffman (HJ)	OF119	L	25	119	454	64	119	10	10	1	35	33		46	.262	.335
Topsy Hartsel	OF147	L	31	148	533	87	147	22	8	0	28	121		36	.276	.347
Ossee Schreckengost	C112, 1B2	R	30	121	416	30	113	19	6	0	45	3		9	.272	.346
Monte Cross	SS76, 2B2	R	35	78	248	28	67	17	2	0	24	19		8	.270	.355
Bris Lord	OF60, 3B1	R	21	66	238	38	57	14	0	0	13	14		3	.239	.298
13Mike Powers	C40	R	34	40	121	8	18	0	0	0	10	3		4	.149	.149
Harry Barton	C13, 1B2, 3B2, OF1	B	30	29	60	5	10	2	1	0	3	3		2	.167	.233

NAME	T	AGE	W	L	PCT	SV	G	GS	CG	IP	H	BB	SO	SHO	ERA
		25	92	56	.622	7	152	152	117	1383	1137	409	895	20	2.19
Rube Waddell (SJ)	L	28	26	11	.703	4	46	34	27	329	231	90	287	7	1.48
Eddie Plank	L	29	25	12	.676	0	41	41	35	347	287	75	210	4	2.26
Andy Coakley	R	22	20	7	.741	0	35	31	21	255	227	73	145	3	1.84
Chief Bender	R	22	16	11	.593	3	35	23	18	229	193	90	142	4	2.83
Weldon Henley	R	24	4	12	.250	0	25	19	13	184	155	67	82	2	2.59
Jimmy Dygert	R	20	1	3	.250	0	6	3	2	35	41	11	24	0	4.37
Joe Myers	R	23	0	0	.—	0	1	1	1	5	3	3	5	0	3.60

CHICAGO 2nd 92-60 .605 2 — FIELDER JONES

NAME	G by Pos	B	AGE	G	AB	R	H	2B	3B	HR	RBI	BB	SO	SB	BA	SA
TOTALS			30	157	5109	613	1212	200	55	11	487	439		194	.237	.304
Jiggs Donahue	1B149	L	25	149	533	71	153	24	2	1	76	44		32	.287	.345
Gus Dundon (CJ)	2B104, SS2	R	30	106	364	30	70	7	3	0	22	23		14	.192	.278
George Davis	SS157	R	34	157	550	74	153	28	3	1	55	60		31	.278	.345
Lee Tannehill	3B142	R	24	142	480	38	96	17	2	0	39	45		8	.200	.244
Danny Green	OF107	L	28	112	379	56	92	13	6	0	44	53		11	.243	.309
Fielder Jones	OF153	L	33	153	568	91	139	17	12	3	38	73		20	.245	.327
Ducky Holmes	OF89	L	36	92	328	42	66	15	2	0	22	19		11	.201	.259
Billy Sullivan	C93, 1B2, 3B1	R	30	99	323	25	65	10	3	2	16	13		14	.201	.269
Nixey Callahan	OF93	R	31	96	345	50	94	18	6	1	43	29		26	.272	.368
Frank Isbell	2B42, OF40, 1B9, SS2	L	29	94	341	55	101	21	11	2	45	15		15	.296	.440
Ed McFarland	C70	R	30	80	250	24	70	13	4	0	31	23		5	.280	.364
George Rohe	3B17, 2B16	R	29	34	113	14	24	1	0	1	12	12		2	.212	.248
Hub Hart	C6	L	27	10	17	2	2	0	0	0	4	3		0	.118	.118

NAME	T	AGE	W	L	PCT	SV	G	GS	CG	IP	H	BB	SO	SHO	ERA
		26	92	60	.605	3	157	157	131	1427	1163	329	613	17	1.99
Frank Owen	R	25	21	13	.611	0	42	38	32	334	276	56	125	3	2.10
Nick Altrock	L	28	21	11	.656	2	38	34	31	316	274	63	97	3	1.88
Frank Smith	R	25	19	13	.594	0	39	31	27	292	215	107	171	4	2.13
Doc White	L	26	18	14	.563	0	36	32	25	260	204	58	120	4	1.77
Ed Walsh	R	24	8	3	.727	1	22	13	9	137	121	29	71	1	2.17
Roy Patterson	R	28	4	5	.444	0	13	9	7	89	73	16	29	1	1.82

DETROIT 3rd 79-74 .516 15.5 — BILL ARMOUR

NAME	G by Pos	B	AGE	G	AB	R	H	2B	3B	HR	RBI	BB	SO	SB	BA	SA
TOTALS			28	153	4968	511	1208	190	54	13	421	375		129	.243	.311
Pinky Lindsay	1B88	R	26	88	329	38	88	14	1	0	31	18		10	.267	.316
Germany Schaefer	2B151, SS3	R	26	153	554	64	135	17	9	2	47	45		19	.244	.318
Charley O'Leary	SS148	R	22	148	512	47	109	13	1	0	33	29		13	.213	.242
Bill Coughlin	3B137	R	26	138	489	48	123	20	6	0	44	34		16	.252	.317
Sam Crawford	OF103, 1B51	L	25	153	575	73	171	40	10	6	75	50		22	.297	.433
Dick Cooley	OF97	L	32	99	377	25	93	11	9	1	32	26		7	.247	.332
Matty McIntyre	OF131	L	25	131	495	59	130	21	5	0	30	48		9	.263	.325
Lew Drill	C70	R	28	71	211	17	55	9	0	0	24	32		7	.261	.303
Bobby Lowe	OF25, 3B22, SS4, 1B1	R	36	60	181	17	35	7	2	0	9	13		3	.193	.254
1 Charley Hickman	OF47, 1B12	R	29	59	213	21	47	12	3	2	20	12		3	.221	.333
Ty Cobb	OF41	L	18	41	150	19	36	6	0	1	15	10		2	.240	.300
2 Jack Warner	C36	R	32	36	119	12	24	2	3	0	7	8		2	.202	.269
2 Tom Doran	C32	L	25	34	94	8	15	3	0	0	4	8		2	.160	.191
Jimmy Barrett	OF18	L	30	20	67	2	17	1	0	0	3	6		0	.254	.269
John Sullivan	C12	R	32	12	31	4	5	0	0	0	0	1		0	.161	.161
Bob Wood	C7	R	39	8	24	1	2	1	0	0	0	1		0	.083	.125
2 Nig Clarke	C2	L	22	3	7	1	3	0	0	1	1	0		0	.429	.857

NAME	T	AGE	W	L	PCT	SV	G	GS	CG	IP	H	BB	SO	SHO	ERA
		28	79	74	.516	2	153	153	124	1348	1226	474	578	16	2.83
Ed Killian	L	28	22	15	.595	2	39	37	33	313	263	102	110	8	2.27
George Mullin	R	24	22	18	.550	0	44	41	35	348	303	138	168	0	2.51
Wild Bill Donvan	R	28	18	14	.563	0	34	32	27	281	236	101	135	5	2.60
Frank Kitson	R	33	11	15	.423	1	33	26	21	226	230	57	78	3	3.46
Jimmy Wiggs (HO)	R	28	3	3	.500	0	7	7	4	41	30	29	37	0	3.29
John Eubank	R	32	2	0	1.000	0	3	2	0	17	13	3	1	0	2.18
Eddie Cicotte	R	21	1	1	.500	0	3	1	1	18	25	5	6	0	3.50
Andy Bruckmiller	R	23	0	0	.—	0	1	0	1	4	1	1	0		27.00
Walt Justis	R	21	0	0	.—	0	1	0	0	1	4	4	1		9.00
George Disch	R	26	0	2	.000	0	8	3	1	48	43	8	14	0	2.62
Gene Ford	R	24	0	2	.000	0	7	1	1	35	51	14	20	0	5.66
Charlie Jackson	R	28	0	2	.000	0	2	1	1	11	14	7	3	0	5.73
Frosty Thomas	R	24	0	2	.000	0	1	0	0	6	10	3	5	0	7.50

NAME	G by Pos	B	AGE	G	AB	R	H	2B	3B	HR	RBI	BB	SO	SB	BA	SA
BOSTON 4th 78-74 .513 16			JIMMY COLLINS													
TOTALS			32	153	5031	583	1177	165	69	29	488	486		131	.234	.311
Moose Grimshaw	1B74	B	29	85	285	39	68	8	2	4	35	21		4	.239	.323
Hobe Ferris	2B140, OF1	R	27	141	523	51	115	24	16	6	59	23		11	.220	.361
Freddy Parent	SS153	R	29	153	602	55	141	16	5	0	33	47		25	.234	.277
Jimmy Collins	3B131	R	35	131	508	66	140	25	5	4	65	37		18	.276	.368
Kip Selbach	OF116	R	33	124	494	71	137	16	6	4	47	67		12	.246	.342
Chick Stahl	OF134	L	32	134	500	61	129	18	4	0	47	50		18	.258	.310
Jesse Burkett	OF149	L	36	149	573	78	147	13	13	4	47	67		13	.257	.346
Lou Criger	C109	R	33	109	313	33	62	6	7	1	36	54		5	.198	.272
Buck Freeman	1B72, OF51, 3B2	L	33	130	455	59	109	20	8	3	49	46		8	.240	.338
Bob Unglaub	3B21, 2B8, 1B2	R	23	43	121	18	27	5	1	0	11	6		2	.223	.281
Charlie Armbruster (RJ)	C35	R	24	35	91	13	18	4	0	0	6	18		3	.198	.242
Art McGovern	C15	R	23	15	44	1	5	1	0	0	1	4		0	.114	.136
John Godwin	OF6, 2B5	R	28	13	37	4	13	1	0	0	10	3		3	.351	.378
Candy LaChance	1B12	B	35	12	41	1	6	1	0	0	5	6		0	.146	.171
Pop Rising	3B4		33	8	18	2	2	1	1	0	2	2		0	.111	.278
Duke Farrell (LJ)	C7	R	38	7	21	2	6	1	0	0	2	1		0	.286	.333
1 Tom Doran	C1	R	25	2	2	0	0	0	0	0	0	0		0	.000	.000
Frank Owens	C1	R	19	1	2	0	0	0	0	0	0	0		0	.000	.000
CLEVELAND 5th 76-78 .494 19			NAP LAJOIE													
TOTALS			28	154	5130	559	1309	211	72	18	482	286		188	.255	.335
Charlie Carr	1B87	R	28	89	306	29	72	12	4	1	31	13		12	.235	.310
Nap Lajoie (LJ)	2B59, 1B5	R	30	65	249	29	82	13	2	2	41	17		11	.329	.422
Terry Turner	SS154	R	24	154	582	48	153	16	14	4	72	14		17	.263	.359
Bill Bradley	3B145	R	27	145	537	63	144	34	6	0	51	27		22	.268	.354
Elmer Flick	OF130, 2B1	L	29	131	496	71	152	29	19	4	64	53		35	.306	.466
Harry Bay	OF143	L	27	143	550	90	164	18	10	0	22	36		36	.298	.367
Jim Jackson	OF105, 3B3	R	27	108	421	58	108	12	4	2	31	34		15	.257	.313
Fritz Buelow	C59, OF8, 1B3, 3B2	R	29	74	236	11	41	4	1	1	18	6		7	.174	.212
George Stovall	1B59, 2B46, OF4	R	27	111	419	41	114	31	3	1	47	13		13	.272	.368
Harry Bemis	C58, 2B4, 1B1	R	31	69	226	27	66	13	3	0	28	13		3	.292	.376
Otto Hess	OF27, P26	L	26	54	175	15	44	8	1	2	13	7		2	.251	.343
13 Nig Clarke	C41	L	22	42	123	11	24	6	1	0	9	11		0	.195	.260
Nick Kahl (IL)	2B31, SS1, OF1	R	26	39	131	16	29	4	1	0	21	4		1	.221	.267
Rube Vinson	OF36	L	26	38	133	12	26	3	1	0	9	7		4	.195	.233
Bunk Congleton	OF12	L	30	12	47	4	17	0	0	0	5	2		3	.362	.362
Jap Barbeau	2B11	R	23	11	37	1	10	1	1	0	2	1		1	.270	.351
Howard Wakefield	C8	R	21	9	25	1	4	0	0	0	1	0		0	.160	.160
Eddie Grant	2B2	L	22	2	8	1	3	0	0	0	0	0		0	.375	.375
Emil Leber	3B2	R	24	2	6	1	0	0	0	0	0	1		0	.000	.000
NEW YORK 6th 71-78 .477 21.5			CLARK GRIFFITH													
TOTALS			30	152	4957	587	1228	163	61	23	480	360		200	.248	.319
Hal Chase	1B122, 2B1, SS1	R	22	126	465	60	116	16	6	3	49	15		22	.249	.323
Jimmy Williams	2B129	R	28	129	470	54	107	20	8	6	62	50		14	.228	.343
Kid Elberfeld	SS108	R	30	111	390	48	102	18	2	0	53	23		18	.262	.318
Joe Yeager	3B90, SS21	R	29	115	401	53	107	16	7	0	42	25		8	.267	.342
Willie Keeler	OF139, 2B12, 3B3	L	33	149	560	81	169	14	4	4	38	43		19	.302	.363
Dave Fultz	OF122	R	30	130	422	49	98	13	3	0	42	39		44	.232	.277
Patsy Dougherty	OF108, 3B1	L	28	116	418	56	110	9	6	3	29	28		17	.263	.330
Red Kleinow (RJ)	C83, 1B3	R	27	88	253	23	56	6	3	1	24	20		7	.221	.281
Wid Conroy	3B48, OF21, SS18, 1B9, 2B3	R	28	102	385	55	105	19	11	2	25	32		25	.273	.395
Deacon McGuire	C71	R	41	72	220	15	50	7	2	0	33	18		3	.219	.268
Eddie Hahn	OF43	L	29	43	160	32	51	5	0	0	11	25		1	.319	.350
1 John Anderson	OF22, 1B3	B	31	32	99	12	23	3	1	0	14	8		9	.232	.283
Jim Cockman	3B13	R	32	13	38	5	4	0	0	0	2	4		2	.105	.105
Frank LaPorte	2B11	R	25	11	40	4	16	1	0	1	12	1		1	.400	.500
2 Mike Powers	1B7, C4	R	34	11	33	3	6	1	0	0	2	1		0	.182	.212
Frank Delahanty (NJ)	1B5, OF3	R	22	9	27	0	6	1	0	0	2	1		0	.222	.259
Joe Connor	C6, 1B2	R	30	8	22	4	5	1	0	0	2	3		1	.227	.273
Rube Oldring	SS8	R	21	8	30	2	9	0	1	1	6	2		4	.300	.467
Fred Curtis	1B2	R	24	2	9	2	2	0	0	0	2	1		1	.222	.333
Phil Cooney	3B1	L	22	1	3	0	0	0	0	0	0	0		0	.000	.000
Jack Doyle	1B1	R	35	1	3	0	0	0	0	0	0	0		0	.000	.000
Fred Jacklitsch	C1	R	29	1	3	1	0	0	0	0	1	1		0	.000	.000
Joe McCarthy	C1	R	23	1	2	0	0	0	0	0	0	0		0	.000	.000
Charlie Fallon		R	24	1	0	0	0	0	0	0	0	0		0	—	—
WASHINGTON 7th 64-87 .424 29.5			JAKE STAHL													
TOTALS			27	156	5009	560	1117	193	68	22	483	298		169	.223	.302
Jake Stahl	1B140	R	26	141	501	66	122	22	12	5	66	28		41	.244	.365
2 Charley Hickman	2B85, 1B69	R	29	88	360	48	112	26	9	2	46	9		3	.311	.450
Joe Cassidy	SS151	R	22	151	576	67	124	16	4	1	43	25		23	.215	.262
Hunter Hill (IL)	3B103	R	26	104	374	37	78	12	1	1	24	32		10	.209	.254
2 John Anderson	OF89, 1B4	B	31	93	400	50	116	21	6	1	38	22		22	.290	.380
Charlie Jones	OF142	R	29	142	544	68	113	18	4	2	41	31		24	.208	.267
Frank Huelsman	OF123	R	31	126	421	48	114	28	8	3	62	31		11	.271	.397
Mike Heydon	C77	R	30	77	203	20	47	7	4	1	26	21		5	.192	.265
Rabbit Nill	3B54, 2B33, SS6	R	23	103	319	46	58	7	3	3	31	33		12	.182	.251
Punch Knoll	OF70, C5, 1B2	R	23	85	244	24	52	10	5	0	29	9		3	.213	.295
Mal Kittredge	C75	R	35	76	238	16	39	8	0	0	14	15		1	.164	.197
Jim Mullin	2B39, 1B7	R	21	50	163	18	31	7	6	0	13	5		5	.190	.307
Joe Stanley	OF27	B	24	28	92	13	24	2	1	1	17	7		4	.261	.337
Harry Cassady	OF9	L	24	9	30	1	4	0	0	0	1	0		1	.133	.133
Claude Rothgeb	OF3	B	25	6	13	2	2	0	0	0	0	0		1	.154	.154
Hughie Tate	OF3	R	25	4	10	1	3	0	1	0	2	0		1	.300	.500
Denny Sullivan	OF3	L	24	3	11	0	0	0	0	0	0	0		0	.000	.000
Shag Shaughnessy	OF1	R	22	1	3	0	0	0	0	0	0	0		0	.000	.000
ST. LOUIS 8th 54-99 .353 40.5			JIMMY McALEER													
TOTALS			30	154	5204	509	1205	153	49	16	415	362		130	.232	.289
Tom Jones	1B135	R	28	135	504	44	122	16	2	0	48	30		5	.242	.282
Ike Rockenfield	2B95	R	28	95	322	40	70	12	0	0	16	46		11	.217	.255
Bobby Wallace	SS156	R	31	156	587	67	159	29	9	1	59	45		13	.271	.356
Harry Gleason	3B144, 2B6	R	30	150	553	55	120	11	5	1	57	34		23	.217	.262
Emil Frisk	OF116	L	30	127	429	58	112	11	6	3	36	42		7	.261	.336
Ben Koehler	OF127, 1B12, 2B6	R	28	142	536	55	127	14	6	2	47	32		22	.237	.297
George Stone	OF154	L	28	154	632	76	187	26	13	7	52	44		26	.296	.411
Joe Sugden	C71, 1B9	B	34	85	266	21	46	4	0	0	23	23		3	.173	.188
Ike Van Zandt	OF74, 1B1, P1	L	29	94	322	31	75	15	1	1	20	7		7	.233	.292
Frank Roth	C29	R	26	31	107	9	25	3	0	0	9	7		6	.234	.262
Tubby Spencer	C34	R	21	35	115	6	27	1	2	0	11	7		2	.235	.278
Charlie Moran	2B21, 3B7	R	26	31	100	11	19	2	0	0	5	6		3	.190	.230
Art Weaver	C28	R	26	28	92	5	11	2	1	0	3	1		0	.120	.163
Charlie Starr	2B16, 3B6	R	26	28	97	7	20	2	1	0	4	3		3	.206	.206
Dick Padden (IL)	2B16	R	34	16	58	5	10	1	0	0	5	6		3	.172	.224
Charlie Gibson	C1	R	25	1	3	0	0	0	0	0	0	0		0	.000	.000
Branch Rickey	C1	L	23	1	1	0	0	0	0	0	0	1		0	.000	.000
Snags Heidrick (VR) 28																

NAME	T	AGE	W	L	PCT	SV	G	GS	CG	IP	H	BB	SO	SHO	ERA
		30	78	74	.513	5	153	153	125	1356	1198	292	652	15	2.84
Jesse Tannehill	L	30	22	10	.688	0	36	31	27	272	238	59	113	6	2.48
Cy Young	R	38	18	19	.486	0	38	34	32	321	248	30	210	5	1.82
Bill Dinneen	R	29	14	14	.500	1	37	29	23	244	235	50	97	2	3.73
George Winter	R	27	14	16	.467	3	35	27	24	264	249	54	119	2	2.97
Norwood Gibson	R	28	4	7	.364	0	23	17	9	134	118	55	67	0	3.69
Ed Hughes	R	24	3	1	.750	0	6	4	2	33	38	9	8	0	4.64
Ed Barry	L	23	1	2	.333	0	7	5	2	41	38	15	18	0	2.85
Joe Harris	R	23	1	2	.333	0	3	3	2	21	18	8	14	0	2.35
Hank Olmsted	R	26	1	2	.333	0	3	3	3	25	18	12	6	0	3.24
		28	76	78	.494	1	154	154	139	1363	1251	334	555	16	2.85
Addie Joss	R	25	20	11	.645	0	33	32	31	286	246	46	132	3	2.01
Bob Rhoades	R	25	17	11	.607	0	28	26	24	235	219	55	61	4	2.83
Earl Moore	R	25	15	15	.500	0	31	30	28	269	232	92	131	3	2.64
Otto Hess	L	26	10	14	.417	0	26	25	22	214	179	72	109	4	3.15
Red Donahue	R	32	6	11	.353	0	20	17	13	138	132	25	45	1	3.39
Bill Bernhard	R	34	6	14	.300	1	22	19	17	174	185	34	56	0	3.36
Hi West	R	20	2	2	.500	0	6	4	4	33	43	10	15	1	4.09
Cy Ferry	R	26	0	0	—	0	1	1	0	2	3	0	2	0	13.50
Jack Halla	L	21	0	0	—	0	3	0	0	13	12	0	4	0	2.77
		29	71	78	.477	9	152	152	88	1354	1235	396	642	10	2.92
Jack Chesbro	R	31	20	15	.571	0	41	38	24	303	262	71	156	1	2.20
Al Orth	R	32	18	18	.500	0	40	37	26	305	273	61	121	4	2.86
1 Jack Powell	R	30	9	13	.409	1	36	23	13	203	214	57	84	1	3.50
Bill Hogg	R	23	9	12	.429	1	39	22	9	205	178	101	125	2	3.20
Clark Griffith	R	35	8	6	.571	3	25	7	4	103	82	15	46	2	1.66
Ambrose Puttmann	L	24	2	7	.222	1	17	9	5	86	79	37	39	0	4.29
Walter Clarkson	R	26	2	2	.500	1	9	4	3	46	40	13	35	0	3.91
Doc Newton	R	27	2	2	.500	0	11	7	2	60	61	24	15	0	2.10
Louis LeRoy	R	26	1	1	.500	0	3	3	2	24	26	1	8	0	3.75
Art Goodwin	R	26	0	0	—	0	1	0	0	1	2	2	0	0	81.00
Wilbur Good	L	19	0	2	.000	0	5	2	0	19	18	14	13	0	4.74
		27	64	87	.424	5	156	156	118	1362	1250	385	539	11	2.87
Long Tom Hughes	R	26	16	16	.500	1	39	35	26	291	239	79	149	5	2.35
Casey Patten	L	31	9	22	.290	0	42	37	29	310	300	86	113	2	3.14
Barney Wolfe	R	29	9	14	.391	2	28	24	17	182	162	37	52	1	2.57
Beany Jacobson (IL)	L	24	8	9	.471	1	22	17	12	144	139	35	50	0	3.31
Jack Townsend	R	26	7	16	.304	0	34	24	22	263	247	84	102	0	2.63
Cy Falkenberg	R	25	4	4	.500	1	12	10	6	75	71	31	35	2	3.84
Harry Hardy	L	29	2	1	.667	0	3	2	2	24	20	6	10	0	1.88
Rick Adams	L	26	2	6	.250	0	11	6	3	63	63	24	25	1	3.67
Moxie Manuel	R	23	0	1	.000	0	1	1	0	10	9	3	6	0	5.40
		28	54	99	.353	3	156	156	109	1385	1245	389	633	10	2.74
Harry Howell	R	28	14	21	.400	0	38	37	36	323	252	101	198	4	1.98
Barney Pelty	R	24	13	14	.481	1	31	28	26	259	222	68	114	1	2.75
Willie Sudhoff	R	30	10	20	.333	0	32	30	23	244	222	78	70	1	2.99
Jim Buchanan	R	28	6	10	.375	2	22	15	14	149	141	54	54	1	3.51
Fred Glade	R	29	7	24	.226	0	32	32	28	275	257	58	127	2	2.81
2 Jack Powell	R	30	2	1	.667	0	3	3	3	28	22	5	12	0	1.61
Cy Morgan	R	26	2	0	.250	0	13	8	5	77	82	37	44	1	3.62
Ike Van Zandt	L	29	1	2	.333	0	1	0	0	2	2	3	0	0	0.00
Harry Ables	L	21	0	0	—	0	6	3	1	31	37	13	11	0	3.77
Jack O'Connor (IL) 38															

NEW YORK — 1st 105-48 .686 — JOHN McGRAW

NAME	G by Pos	B	AGE	G	AB	R	H	2B	3B	HR	RBI	BB	SO	SB	BA	SA
TOTALS			30	155	5094	780	1392	191	88	39	642	517		291	.273	.368
Dan McGann	1B136	B	33	136	491	88	147	23	14	5	75	55		22	.299	.434
Billy Gilbert	2B115	R	29	115	376	45	93	11	3	0	24	41		11	.247	.293
Bill Dahlen	SS147, OF1	R	35	148	520	67	126	20	4	7	81	62		37	.242	.337
Art Devlin	3B153	R	25	153	525	74	129	14	7	2	61	66		59	.246	.310
George Browne	OF127	L	29	127	536	95	157	16	14	4	43	20		26	.293	.397
Mike Donlin	OF150	L	27	150	606	124	216	31	16	7	80	56		33	.356	.495
Sam Mertes	OF150	R	32	150	551	81	154	27	17	5	108	56		52	.279	.417
Roger Bresnahan	C87, OF8	R	26	104	331	58	100	18	3	0	46	50		11	.302	.375
Sammy Strang	2B47, OF38, SS9, 1B1, 3B1	B	28	111	294	51	76	9	4	3	29	58		23	.259	.347
Frank Bowerman	C72, 1B17, 2B1	R	36	98	297	37	80	8	1	3	41	12		6	.269	.333
Boileryard Clarke	1B17, C12	R	36	31	50	2	9	0	0	1	4	4		1	.180	.240
Offa Neal	3B3, 2B1	L	29	4	13	0	0	0	0	0	0	0		0	.000	.000
John McGraw	OF1	L	32	3	0	0	0	0	0	0	0	0		1	.000	.000
Moonlight Graham	OF1	L	28	1	0	0	0	0	0	0	0	0		0	.000	.000
1 Bob Hall	OF1	R	26	1	3	1	1	0	0	0	0	0		0	.333	.333

NAME	T	AGE	W	L	PCT	SV	G	GS	CG	IP	H	BB	SO	SHO	ERA
		27	105	48	.686	15	155	155	117	1370	1160	364	760	17	2.39
Christy Mathewson	R	24	32	8	.800	2	43	37	32	339	252	64	206	8	1.27
Joe McGinnity	R	34	22	16	.579	3	46	38	26	320	289	71	125	2	2.87
Red Ames	R	22	22	8	.733	0	34	31	21	263	220	105	198	2	2.74
Dummy Taylor	R	30	15	9	.625	0	32	28	18	213	200	51	91	4	2.66
Hooks Wiltse	L	25	14	6	.700	4	32	19	18	197	158	61	120	1	2.47
Claud Elliott	R	25	0	1	.000	6	10	2	2	38	41	12	20	0	4.03

PITTSBURGH — 2nd 96-57 .627 9 — FRED CLARKE

NAME	G by Pos	B	AGE	G	AB	R	H	2B	3B	HR	RBI	BB	SO	SB	BA	SA
TOTALS			29	155	5213	692	1385	190	91	22	564	382		202	.266	.350
Del Howard	1B90, OF28, P1	L	27	123	435	56	127	18	5	2	63	27		19	.292	.370
Claude Ritchey	2B153, SS2	B	31	153	533	54	136	29	6	0	52	51		12	.255	.332
Honus Wagner	SS145, OF2	R	31	147	548	114	199	32	14	6	101	54		57	.363	.505
2 Dave Brain	3B78, SS4	R	26	85	307	31	79	17	6	3	46	15		8	.257	.381
Otis Clymer	OF89, 1B1	B	29	96	365	74	108	11	5	0	23	19		23	.296	.353
Ginger Beaumont	OF97	L	28	103	384	60	126	12	8	3	40	22		21	.328	.424
Fred Clarke	OF137	L	32	141	525	95	157	18	15	2	51	55		24	.299	.402
Heinie Peitz	C87, 2B1	R	34	88	278	18	62	10	0	0	27	24		2	.223	.259
Tommy Leach	OF71, 3B58, 2B2, SS2	R	27	131	499	71	128	10	14	2	53	37		17	.257	.345
Bill Clancy	1B52, OF4	R	26	56	227	23	52	11	3	2	34	4		3	.229	.330
George Gibson	C44	R	24	46	135	14	24	2	2	1	14	15		2	.178	.267
Doc Hillebrand	1B16, P10, OF7, C3	R	25	39	110	9	26	3	2	0	7	6		1	.236	.300
Bob Ganley	OF32	L	30	32	127	12	40	1	2	0	7	8		3	.315	.354
Fred Carisch	C30	R	23	32	107	7	22	0	3	0	8	2		1	.206	.262
1 George McBride	3B17, SS8	R	24	27	87	9	19	4	0	0	7	6		2	.218	.264
Steamer Flanagan	OF5	L	24	7	25	5	7	1	1	0	3	1		3	.280	.400
Jim Wallace	OF7	L	23	7	29	3	6	1	0	0	3	3		2	.207	.241
Otto Knabe	3B3	R	23	3	10	0	3	1	0	0	2	3		0	.300	.400
Harry Smith (AJ)	C1	R	30	1	3	0	0	0	0	0	0	1		0	.000	.000

NAME	T	AGE	W	L	PCT	SV	G	GS	CG	IP	H	BB	SO	SHO	ERA
		29	96	57	.627	6	155	155	113	1383	1270	389	512	12	2.86
Deacon Phillippe	R	33	22	13	.629	0	38	33	25	279	235	48	133	5	2.19
Sam Leever	R	33	19	6	.760	1	33	29	20	230	199	54	81	3	2.70
Mike Lynch	L	30	17	8	.680	2	33	22	13	206	191	107	106	0	3.80
Charlie Case	R	25	12	10	.545	1	31	24	18	217	202	66	57	3	2.57
Patsy Flaherty	L	29	9	10	.474	1	27	20	15	188	197	49	44	0	3.49
Chick Robitaille	R	26	8	5	.615	0	17	12	10	120	126	28	32	0	2.93
Lefty Leifield	L	21	5	2	.714	0	8	7	6	56	52	14	10	1	2.89
Doc Hillebrand	R	25	4	2	.667	1	10	6	4	61	43	19	37	0	2.80
Frank Moore	R	27	0	0	—	0	1	0	0	3	2	0	1	0	0.00
Del Howard	R	27	0	0	—	0	1	0	0	6	4	1	0	0	0.00
Ed Kinsella	R	25	0	1	.000	0	3	2	1	17	19	3	11	0	2.65

CHICAGO — 3rd 92-61 .601 13 — FRANK SELEE 37-28 .569 — FRANK CHANCE 55-33 .625

NAME	G by Pos	B	AGE	G	AB	R	H	2B	3B	HR	RBI	BB	SO	SB	BA	SA
TOTALS			28	155	5108	667	1249	157	82	12	522	448		267	.245	.314
Frank Chance	1B115	R	28	118	392	92	124	16	12	2	70	78		38	.316	.434
Johnny Evers (HJ)	2B99	L	23	99	340	44	94	11	2	1	37	27		19	.276	.329
Joe Tinker	SS149	R	24	149	547	70	135	18	8	2	66	34		31	.247	.320
Doc Casey	3B142, SS1	L	34	144	526	66	122	21	10	1	56	41		22	.232	.316
Billy Maloney	OF145	L	27	145	558	78	145	17	14	2	56	43		59	.260	.351
Jimmy Slagle	OF155	L	31	155	568	96	153	19	4	0	37	97		27	.269	.317
Wildfire Schulte	OF123	L	22	123	493	67	135	15	14	1	47	32		16	.274	.367
Johnny King	C106, OF4, 1B1	R	29	111	380	26	83	8	6	1	52	28		13	.218	.279
Solly Hofman	2B59, 1B9, SS9, 3B3, OF3	R	22	86	287	43	68	14	4	1	38	20		15	.237	.324
Jack McCarthy	OF37, 1B6	L	36	59	170	16	47	4	3	0	14	10		8	.276	.335
Jack O'Neill	C50	R	32	53	172	16	34	4	2	0	12	8		6	.198	.244
1 Shad Barry	1B26	R	26	27	104	10	22	2	0	0	10	5		5	.212	.231
Hans Lobert	3B13, OF1	R	23	14	46	7	9	2	0	0	1	3		4	.196	.239

NAME	T	AGE	W	L	PCT	SV	G	GS	CG	IP	H	BB	SO	SHO	ERA
		26	92	61	.601	2	155	155	133	1407	1135	885	627	23	2.04
Three Finger Brown (JJ)	R	28	18	10	.643	0	30	24	24	249	219	44	89	4	2.17
Jake Weimer	L	31	18	12	.600	1	33	30	26	250	212	80	107	2	2.27
Ed Reulbach	R	22	18	14	.562	1	34	29	28	292	208	73	152	5	1.42
Carl Lundgren	R	25	13	5	.722	0	23	19	16	169	132	53	69	3	2.24
Bob Wicker	R	27	13	7	.650	0	22	22	17	178	139	47	86	4	2.02
Buttons Briggs	R	29	8	8	.500	0	20	20	13	168	141	52	68	5	2.14
Big Jeff Pfeffer	R	23	4	5	.444	0	15	11	9	101	84	36	56	0	2.50

PHILADELPHIA — 4th 83-69 .546 21.5 — HUGH DUFFY

NAME	G by Pos	B	AGE	G	AB	R	H	2B	3B	HR	RBI	BB	SO	SB	BA	SA
TOTALS			29	155	5243	708	1362	187	82	16	567	406		180	.260	.336
Kitty Bransfield	1B151	R	30	151	580	55	150	23	9	3	76	27		27	.259	.345
Kid Gleason	2B149	R	38	149	564	117	154	11	8	1	50	45		16	.247	.303
Mickey Doolan	SS135	R	25	136	492	53	125	27	11	1	48	24		17	.254	.360
Ernie Courtney	3B155	L	30	155	601	77	165	14	7	2	77	47		17	.275	.331
John Titus	OF147	L	29	147	548	99	169	36	14	2	89	69		11	.308	.436
Roy Thomas	OF147	L	31	147	562	118	178	11	6	0	31	93		23	.317	.358
Sherry Magee	OF155	R	20	155	603	100	180	24	17	5	98	44		48	.299	.420
Red Dooin	C107, 1B1	R	26	113	380	45	95	13	5	0	36	10		12	.250	.311
Otto Krueger	SS23, OF6, 3B1	R	28	46	114	10	21	1	1	0	12	13		1	.184	.211
Fred Abbott	C34, 1B5	R	30	42	128	9	25	6	1	0	12	6		4	.195	.258
Mike Kahoe	C15	R	31	16	51	2	13	2	0	0	4	1		1	.255	.294
Hugh Duffy	OF8	R	38	15	40	7	12	2	1	0	3	1		0	.300	.400
Red Munson	C8	R	21	9	26	1	3	1	0	0	2	0		1	.115	.154

NAME	T	AGE	W	L	PCT	SV	G	GS	CG	IP	H	BB	SO	SHO	ERA
		31	83	69	.546	5	155	155	119	1399	1303	411	516	12	2.81
Togie Pittinger	R	33	23	15	.605	2	46	37	29	337	311	104	136	4	3.10
Bill Duggleby	R	32	18	17	.514	0	38	36	27	289	270	83	75	1	2.46
Tully Sparks	R	30	14	11	.560	1	34	26	20	260	217	73	98	3	2.18
2 Kid Nichols	R	35	10	6	.625	0	17	16	15	139	129	28	50	1	2.27
Frank Corridon	R	24	10	13	.435	1	35	26	18	212	203	57	79	1	3.48
Jack Sutthoff	R	32	3	4	.429	0	7	6	4	78	82	36	26	1	3.81
Johnny Lush	L	19	2	0	1.000	0	2	2	1	17	12	8	8	0	1.59
King Brady	R	24	1	1	.500	0	2	2	2	13	19	2	3	0	3.46
Ralph Caldwell	L	21	1	1	.500	0	1	7	2	34	44	7	29	0	4.24
Harry Kane	L	21	1	1	.500	0	2	2	2	17	12	8	12	1	1.59
Buck Washer	R	22	0	0	—	0	1	0	0	3	4	5	0	0	6.00

CINCINNATI — 5th 79-74 .516 26 — JOE KELLEY

NAME	G by Pos	B	AGE	G	AB	R	H	2B	3B	HR	RBI	BB	SO	SB	BA	SA
TOTALS			27	155	5205	736	1401	160	101	27	611	434		181	.269	.354
2 Shad Barry	1B23, OF2	R	26	125	494	90	160	11	12	1	56	33		16	.324	.401
Miller Huggins	2B149	B	27	149	564	117	154	11	8	1	38	103		27	.273	.326
Tommy Corcoran	SS151	R	26	151	605	70	150	21	11	2	85	23		28	.248	.329
Harry Steinfeldt	3B103, 1B1, 2B1, OF1	R	27	114	384	49	104	16	9	1	39	30		15	.271	.367
Fred Odwell	OF126	R	32	130	468	79	113	10	9	9	65	26		21	.241	.359
Cy Seymour	OF149	L	32	149	581	95	219	40	21	8	121	51		21	.377	.559
Joe Kelley	OF85, 1B2	R	33	90	321	43	89	7	6	1	37	27		8	.277	.346
Admiral Schlei	C89, 1B6	R	27	99	314	32	71	8	3	1	36	22		4	.226	.280
Al Bridwell	3B43, OF18, 2B7, SS5, 1B1	L	21	82	254	17	64	3	1	0	17	19		8	.252	.272
Jimmy Sebring	OF56	L	23	58	217	31	62	10	5	2	28	14		11	.286	.406
Eddie Phelps	C44	R	26	44	156	18	36	5	3	0	18	12		4	.231	.301
13 Gabby Street	C27	R	22	31	93	8	23	5	1	0	8	6		1	.247	.323
1 Cozy Dolan	1B13, OF9	L	32	22	77	7	18	2	1	0	4	7		2	.234	.286
Cliff Blankenship	1B15	R	25	19	56	8	11	1	1	0	7	4		1	.196	.250
Bill Hinchman	OF12, 3B4, 1B1	R	22	17	51	10	13	4	1	0	10	13		4	.255	.373
Johnny Slagle	OF16	R	30	17	56	9	17	1	2	1	8	7		0	.304	.446
Mike Mowrey	3B7	R	21	7	30	4	10	1	1	0	6	1		0	.267	.300

NAME	T	AGE	W	L	PCT	SV	G	GS	CG	IP	H	BB	SO	SHO	ERA
		27	79	74	.516	2	155	155	119	1366	1409	439	547	10	3.01
Bob Ewing	R	32	20	11	.645	0	40	34	30	312	284	79	164	4	2.51
Orvie Overall	R	24	17	23	.425	0	42	39	32	318	290	147	173	2	2.86
Charlie Chech	R	27	14	14	.500	0	39	25	20	268	300	77	79	1	2.89
Tom Walker	R	23	10	6	.625	0	23	19	12	145	171	44	28	1	3.23
Jack Harper	R	27	9	14	.391	0	26	23	15	179	189	69	70	1	3.87
Noodles Hahn (SA)	L	26	3	3	.625	0	13	6	5	77	85	9	17	1	2.81
Rip Vowinkel	R	20	3	3	.500	0	6	4	4	45	52	10	7	0	4.20
Ollie Johns	L	25	1	0	1.000	0	4	1	1	18	31	4	8	0	3.50
Ernie Baker	R	29	0	0	—	0	1	0	0	1	0	1	0	0	4.50

ST. LOUIS   6th 58-96 .377 47.5   KID NICHOLS 5-9 .357   JIMMY BURKE 34-56 .378   STANLEY ROBISON 19-31 .380

NAME	G by Pos	B	AGE	G	AB	R	H	2B	3B	HR	RBI	BB	SO	SB	BA	SA
TOTALS			28	154	5066	534	1254	140	85	20	446	391		162	.248	.321
Jake Beckley	1B134	L	37	134	514	48	147	20	10	1	57	30		12	.286	.370
Harry Arndt	2B90, OF9, 3B7, SS5	R	26	113	415	40	101	11	6	2	36	24		13	.243	.313
2 George McBride	SS80, 1B1	R	24	81	281	22	61	1	2	2	34	14		10	.217	.256
Jimmy Burke	3B122	R	30	122	431	34	97	9	5	1	30	21		15	.225	.276
Jack Dunleavy (LJ)	OF118, 2B1	L	25	119	435	52	105	8	8	1	25	55		15	.241	.303
Homer Smoot	OF138	L	27	139	534	73	166	21	16	4	58	33		21	.311	.433
Spike Shannon	OF140	B	27	140	544	73	146	16	3	0	41	47		27	.268	.309
Mike Grady	C71, 1B20	R	35	100	311	41	89	20	7	4	41	33		15	.286	.434
Danny Shay (FA)	2B39, SS39	R	26	78	281	30	67	12	1	0	28	35		11	.238	.288
Josh Clarke	OF26, 2B16, SS4	L	26	50	167	31	43	3	2	3	18	27		8	.257	.353
1 Dave Brain	SS29, 3B6, OF6	R	26	44	158	11	36	4	5	1	17	8		4	.228	.335
1 Jack Warner	C41	R	32	41	137	9	35	2	2	1	12	6		1	.255	.321
Tom Leahy	C29	R	36	35	97	3	22	1	3	0	7	8		0	.227	.299
Art Hoelskoetter	3B20, 2B3, P1	R	22	24	83	7	20	2	1	0	5	3		1	.241	.289
Dave Zearfoss	C19	R	37	20	51	2	8	0	1	0	2	4		0	.157	.196
Rube DeGroff	OF15	L	25	15	56	3	14	2	1	0	5	5		1	.250	.321
Jack Himes	OF11	L	26	12	41	3	6	0	0	0	0	1		1	.146	.146
John Farrell	2B7	R	28	7	24	6	4	0	1	0	1	4		1	.167	.250
Simmy Murch	2B2, SS1	R	24	3	9	0	1	0	0	0	0	0		0	.111	.111
Gerry Shea	C2		23	2	6	0	2	0	0	0	0	0		0	.333	.333

NAME	T	AGE	W	L	PCT	SV	G	GS	CG	IP	H	BB	SO	SHO	ERA
		27	58	96	.377	2	154	154	135	1348	1431	367	411	10	3.59
Jake Thielman	R	26	15	16	.484	0	32	29	26	242	265	62	87	0	3.50
Jack Taylor	R	31	15	21	.417	1	37	34	34	309	302	85	102	3	3.44
Chappie McFarland	R	30	9	18	.333	1	31	28	22	250	281	65	85	3	3.82
Buster Brown	R	23	8	11	.421	0	23	21	17	179	172	62	57	3	2.97
Wish Egan	R	24	5	15	.250	0	23	19	18	171	189	39	29	0	3.58
Win Kellum	L	29	3	3	.500	0	11	7	5	74	70	10	19	1	2.92
Bill Campbell	R	31	1	1	.500	0	2	2	1	17	27	7	2	0	7.41
Sandy McDougal	R	31	1	4	.200	0	5	5	4	45	50	12	10	0	3.40
1 Kid Nichols	R	35	1	5	.167	0	7	7	5	52	64	18	16	0	5.37
Art Hoelskoetter	R	22	0	1	.000	0	1	1	1	6	6	5	4	0	1.50
Jim McGinley	R	26	0	1	.000	0	3	1	0	3	5	2	0	0	15.00

BOSTON   7th 51-103 .331 54.5   FRED TENNEY

NAME	G by Pos	B	AGE	G	AB	R	H	2B	3B	HR	RBI	BB	SO	SB	BA	SA
TOTALS			28	156	5190	467	1217	148	52	17	387	302		132	.234	.293
Fred Tenney	1B148, P1	L	33	149	549	84	158	18	3	0	28	67		17	.288	.332
Fred Raymer	2B134, 1B1, OF1	R	29	137	498	26	105	14	2	0	31	8		15	.211	.247
Ed Abbaticchio	SS152, OF1	R	28	153	610	70	170	25	12	3	41	35		30	.279	.374
Harry Wolverton	3B122	R	31	122	463	38	104	15	7	2	55	23		10	.225	.300
2 Cozy Dolan	OF111, 1B2, P2	L	32	112	433	44	119	11	7	3	48	27		21	.275	.353
Rip Cannell	OF154	L	25	154	567	52	140	14	4	0	36	51		17	.247	.286
Jim Delahanty	OF124, P1	R	26	125	461	50	119	11	8	5	55	49		12	.258	.349
Pat Moran	C78	R	29	85	267	22	64	11	5	2	22	8		3	.240	.341
Tom Needham	C77, OF3, 1B2	R	26	83	271	21	59	6	1	2	17	24		3	.218	.269
Bill Lauterborn	3B29, 2B23, SS3, OF2	R	26	67	200	11	37	1	1	0	9	12		1	.185	.200
Bud Sharpe	OF42, C3, 1B1	R	23	46	170	8	31	3	2	0	11	7		0	.182	.224
George Barclay (IL)	OF28	R	29	29	108	5	19	1	0	0	7	2		2	.176	.185
Allie Strobel	3B4, OF1	R	21	5	19	1	2	0	0	0	1	0		0	.105	.105
Dave Murphy	SS2, 3B1		29	3	11	0	2	0	0	0	0	1		0	.182	.182
2 Gabby Street	C3	R	22	3	12	0	2	0	0	0	0	0		1	.167	.167
Bill McCarthy	C1		19	1	3	0	0	0	0	0	0	0		0	.000	.000

NAME	T	AGE	W	L	PCT	SV	G	GS	CG	IP	H	BB	SO	SHO	ERA
		30	51	103	.331	0	156	156	139	1383	1390	433	533	13	3.52
Irv Young	L	27	20	21	.488	0	43	42	41	378	337	71	156	6	2.90
Chick Fraser	R	31	14	21	.400	0	39	37	35	334	320	85	130	2	3.29
Vic Willis	R	29	11	29	.275	0	41	41	36	342	340	107	149	4	3.21
Kaiser Wilhelm	R	31	4	23	.148	0	34	28	23	242	287	75	76	0	4.54
Dick Harley	R	30	2	5	.286	0	9	4	4	66	72	19	19	1	4.64
Jim Delahanty	R	26	0	0	—	0	1	1	0	2	5	1	0	0	4.50
Fred Tenney	L	33	0	0	—	0	1	0	0	2	5	1	0	0	4.50
2 Cozy Dolan	L	32	0	1	.000	0	2	1	1	9	12	1	1	0	9.00
Frank Hershey	R	26	0	1	.000	0	1	0	0	4	7	1	1	0	6.75
Jake Volz	R	27	0	2	.000	0	3	2	0	9	12	8	1	1	10.00

BROOKLYN   8th 48-104 .316 56.5   NED HANLON

NAME	G by Pos	B	AGE	G	AB	R	H	2B	3B	HR	RBI	BB	SO	SB	BA	SA
TOTALS			27	155	5100	506	1255	154	60	29	430	327		186	.246	.317
Doc Gessler	1B107, OF12	L	24	126	431	44	125	17	4	3	46	38		26	.290	.369
Charlie Malay	2B75, OF25, SS1	R	26	102	349	33	88	7	2	1	31	22		13	.252	.292
Phil Lewis	SS118	R	21	118	433	32	110	9	2	3	33	16		16	.254	.305
Heinie Batch	3B145	R	25	145	568	64	143	20	11	5	49	26		21	.252	.352
Harry Lumley	OF129	L	24	130	505	50	148	19	10	7	47	36		22	.293	.412
Johnny Dobbs	OF123	L	30	123	460	29	117	21	4	2	36	31		15	.254	.330
Jimmy Sheckard	OF129	L	26	130	480	58	140	20	11	3	41	61		23	.292	.398
Lew Ritter	C84, OF4, 3B2	R	29	92	311	32	68	10	5	1	28	15		16	.219	.293
Bill Bergen	C76	R	32	79	247	12	47	3	2	0	22	7		4	.190	.219
Charlie Babb	SS36, 1B31, 3B5, 2B2	R	32	76	236	27	44	8	2	0	17	27		10	.186	.237
2 Bob Hall	OF42, 2B7, 1B3	R	26	56	203	21	48	4	1	2	15	11		8	.236	.296
Red Owens	2B43	R	30	43	168	14	36	6	2	1	20	6		1	.214	.292
John Hummel	2B30	R	22	30	109	19	29	3	4	0	7	9		6	.266	.367
Fred Mitchell	P12, 1B7, SS1, OF1	R	27	27	79	4	15	0	0	0	8	4		0	.190	.190
Ed MacGamwell	1B4	L	27	4	15	0	4	0	0	0	0	1		0	.267	.267
Ad Yale	1B4	R	35	4	13	1	1	0	0	0	1	1		0	.077	.077

NAME	T	AGE	W	L	PCT	SV	G	GS	CG	IP	H	BB	SO	SHO	ERA
		26	48	104	.316	3	155	155	125	1347	1416	476	556	7	3.76
Doc Scanlon	R	24	15	11	.577	0	33	28	22	250	220	104	135	2	2.92
Harry McIntire	R	27	8	25	.242	1	40	35	29	309	340	101	135	1	3.70
Elmer Stricklett	R	28	8	19	.296	1	33	28	25	237	259	71	77	1	3.34
Oscar Jones	R	25	8	15	.348	1	29	20	14	174	197	56	66	0	4.66
Mal Eason	R	26	5	21	.192	0	27	24	20	207	230	72	64	3	4.30
Fred Mitchell	R	27	3	7	.300	0	12	10	9	96	107	38	44	0	4.78
Jack Doscher	L	24	1	5	.167	0	12	7	6	71	60	30	33	0	3.17
Doc Reisling	R	30	0	1	.000	0	2	0	0	3	3	4	2	0	3.00

WORLD SERIES — NEW YORK (NL) 4 PHILADELPHIA (AL) 1

LINE SCORES

TEAM	1	2	3	4	5	6	7	8	9	10	11	12	R	H	E

Game 1 October 9 at Philadelphia

	1	2	3	4	5	6	7	8	9	R	H	E
NY(NL)	0	0	0	0	2	0	0	0	1	3	10	1
PHI(AL)	0	0	0	0	0	0	0	0	0	0	4	0

Mathewson   Plank

Game 2 October 10 at New York

	1	2	3	4	5	6	7	8	9	R	H	E
PHI	0	0	1	0	0	0	0	2	0	3	6	2
NY	0	0	0	0	0	0	0	0	0	0	4	2

Bender   McGinnity, Ames (9)

Game 3 October 12 at Philadelphia

	1	2	3	4	5	6	7	8	9	R	H	E
NY	2	0	0	0	5	0	0	0	2	9	8	1
PHI	0	0	0	0	0	0	0	0	0	0	4	5

Mathewson   Coakley

Game 4 October 13 at New York

	1	2	3	4	5	6	7	8	9	R	H	E
PHI	0	0	0	0	0	0	0	0	0	0	5	2
NY	0	0	0	1	0	0	0	0	X	1	4	1

Plank   McGinnity

Game 5 October 14 at New York

	1	2	3	4	5	6	7	8	9	R	H	E
PHI	0	0	0	0	0	0	0	0	0	0	6	0
NY	0	0	0	0	1	0	0	0	X	2	5	1

Bender   Mathewson

COMPOSITE BATTING

NAME	POS	G	AB	R	H	2B	3B	HR	RBI	BA
New York (NL)		5	153	15	31	7	0	0	13	.203
Browne	OF	5	22	4	4	0	0	0	1	.182
Donlin	OF	5	19	4	5	1	0	0	0	.263
McGann	1B	5	17	1	4	2	0	0	4	.235
Gilbert	2B	5	17	1	4	0	0	0	2	.235
Mertes	OF	5	17	2	3	1	0	0	2	.176
Bresnahan	C	5	16	3	5	2	0	0	1	.313
Devlin	3B	5	16	0	4	1	0	0	1	.250
Dahlen	SS	5	15	1	0	0	0	0	1	.000
Mathewson	P	3	8	1	2	0	0	0	0	.250
McGinnity	P	2	5	0	0	0	0	0	0	.000
Strang	PH	1	1	0	0	0	0	0	0	—
Ames	P	1	1	0	0	0	0	0	0	.000
Philadelphia (AL)		5	155	3	25	5	0	0	2	.161
Davis	1B	5	20	0	4	1	0	0	0	.200
Lord	OF	5	20	0	2	1	0	0	0	.100
L. Cross	3B	5	19	0	2	0	0	0	0	.105
Hartsel	OF	5	17	1	5	1	0	0	0	.294
M. Cross	SS	5	17	0	3	0	0	0	0	.176
Murphy	2B	5	16	0	3	0	0	0	0	.188
Seybold	OF	5	16	0	2	1	0	0	0	.125
Schreckengost	C	3	9	2	2	1	0	0	0	.222
Powers	C	3	7	0	1	1	0	0	0	.143
Plank	P	2	6	0	1	0	0	0	0	.167
Bender	P	2	5	0	0	0	0	0	0	.000
Coakley	P	2	2	0	0	0	0	0	0	.000
Hoffman	PH	1	1	0	0	0	0	0	0	.000

COMPOSITE PITCHING

NAME	G	IP	H	BB	SO	W	L	SV	ERA
New York (NL)	5	45	25	5	25	4	1	0	0.00
Mathewson	3	27	14	1	18	3	0	0	0.00
McGinnity	2	17	10	3	6	1	1	0	0.00
Ames	1	1	1	1	1	0	0	0	0.00
Philadelphia (AL)	5	43	31	15	26	1	4	0	1.47
Bender	2	17	9	6	13	1	1	0	1.06
Plank	2	17	14	4	11	0	2	0	1.59
Coakley	1	9	8	5	2	0	1	0	2.00

1906 — West Side, South Side, It's Still Chicago

After 19 years of pennant drought in the National League stronghold of Chicago, victory was finally in sight. Followers of the American League's Chicago team, the White Sox, had tasted success in the first year of the junior league's formation in 1901, and were not as hungry for the pennant. But rooters of the Chicago Cubs, the National League's entry in that city since 1876, had not been able to have a happy winter since the summer of '86.

When the victory rain did come, it came in buckets, and not only on the Cubs, but the White Sox and the entire city of Chicago as well. Indeed, 1906 was a happy and delirious time for the Chicago baseball fan. He could sit back in October with a sporting appetite as satiated as a physical hunger is by a Thanksgiving dinner. After all, the wonderful town had been treated to a full fare of exciting and varied baseball all summer. With both the Cubs and the White Sox fighting for first place, fans turned out in droves for each team, making the Chicago entries tops in attendance in both leagues. As a result, the fans were treated to a double helping of pennant topped by a calorie-rich dessert of World Series.

The New York Giants stayed with the Cubs until June, but fell back when the Bruins shifted into top speed and stayed there all summer. Never running into a slump, the Cubs chalked up an unprecedented 116 victories, wiping out the Giants' 1904 record of 106 wins. A mediocre attack became the bane of opposing pitchers with the pre-season addition of third sacker Harry Steinfeldt, a .327 swinger who gave extra bite to the middle of the batting order. Playing-manager Frank Chance hit over .310 for the fourth straight year, and catcher Johnny Kling shot from .218 the previous year to a robust .312 batting mark. Joe Tinker, Johnny Evers, and Chance made the infield airtight and helped the pitchers allow the lowest total of runs of any team since the turn of the century. Three Finger Brown, in winning 26 games, proved the big reason why the Cubs stayed away from any slumps. Rookie southpaw Jack Pfiester contributed 20 victories, big Ed Reubach 19, Carl Lundgren 17, and Orvie Overall came over from Cincinnati in mid-season to add 12 victories to the Cubs' record win column.

While fans could go to the west side to see the Cubs rolling up victories at a astonishing clip, they could also travel down to the south side to see their "Hitles Wonders", the weak-hitting White Sox, in a dogfight for the American League fla In early August, the White Sox found themselves in fourth place behind the fron running Athletics, New York, and Cleveland. Then, manager Fielder Jones led h charges on a 19 game winning streak, which toppled the A's and installed the Chiso in first place. With the Athletics fading fast, the Sox and New York battled throug September for the first-place plum which the Sox finally grasped in the season's fin week

In their three-game victory margin, the Chisox depended on pitching and defens to carry an attack where only two men hit over .260 as the team itself finished wi the lowest batting average in the league. Frank Owen and funnyman Nick Altroc gave the Sox a pair of 20-win aces, as spitballer Ed Walsh and practicing dentist Do White proved the strongest in the earned run department, with White taking leagu honors with a 1.52 mark. New York and Cleveland flexed the biggest offensiv muscles in the league but had to take a back seat to the Midway weaklings, who mad an art out of defense.

When it came to the World Series, the White Sox upset their crosstown rivals b outpitching them for a six-game victory. Bad fielding by the Cubs gave Altrock a 2 1 triumph over Brown in the curtain raiser, and Walsh and White accounted for thre more notches in the White Sox ledger to down the Cubs for a major surprise. Addin insult to injury, the anemic White Sox attack came alive in games five and six an slashed out with 12-and 14-hit barrages to send starters Reulbach and Brown t early showers before sending the fans to the street, where they could make their wa home in the comfort that would enable them to enter the coming chill of winter in th warmth of victory.

1906 AMERICAN LEAGUE

CHICAGO — 1st 93-58 .616 — FIELDER JONES

NAME	G by Pos	B	AGE	G	AB	R	H	2B	3B	HR	RBI	BB	SO	SB	BA	SA
TOTALS		30		154	4921	570	1132	152	52	6	444	453		214	.230	.286
Jiggs Donahue	1B154	L	26	154	556	70	143	17	6	1	57	48		36	.257	.315
Frank Isbell	2B132, OF14, C1, P1	R	30	143	549	71	153	18	11	0	57	30		37	.279	.352
George Davis	SS129, 2B1	R	35	133	484	63	134	25	6	0	80	41		27	.277	.353
Les Tannehill	3B99, SS17	R	25	116	378	26	69	8	3	0	33	31		7	.183	.220
Bill O'Neill	OF93	B	26	94	330	37	82	4	1	1	21	22		19	.248	.276
Fiedler Jones	OF144	L	34	144	496	77	114	22	4	2	34	83		26	.230	.302
2 Eddie Hahn	OF130	L	30	130	484	80	110	7	5	0	27	69		19	.227	.262
Billy Sullivan	C118	R	31	118	387	37	83	18	4	1	33	22		10	.214	.289
2 Patsy Dougherty	OF74	L	29	75	253	30	59	9	4	1	27	19		11	.233	.312
George Rohe	3B57, 2B5, OF1	R	30	75	225	14	58	5	1	0	25	16		8	.258	.289
Gus Dundon	2B18, SS14	R	31	33	96	7	13	1	0	0	4	11		4	.135	.146
Hub Hart	C15	L	28	17	37	1	6	0	0	0	0	2		0	.162	.162
Frank Roth	C15	R	27	16	51	4	10	1	1	0	1	7		3	.196	.255
Frank Hemphill	OF13	R	28	13	40	0	3	0	0	0	2	9		1	.075	.075
Babe Towne	C12	R	26	13	36	3	10	0	0	0	6	7		0	.278	.278
Ed McFarland	C3	R	31	7	22	3	3	1	0	0	3	3		1	.136	.182
Rube Vinson	OF4	R	27	7	24	2	6	0	0	0	3	2		1	.250	.250
Lee Quillin	SS3	R	24	3	9	1	3	0	0	0	0	0		1	.333	.333

NAME	T	AGE	W	L	PCT	SV	G	GS	CG	IP	H	BB	SO	SHO	ERA
		27	93	58	.616	9	154	154	117	1375	1212	255	543	32	2.13
Frank Owen	R	26	22	13	.629	2	42	36	27	293	289	54	66	7	2.33
Nick Altrock	L	29	20	13	.606	1	38	30	25	288	269	42	99	4	2.06
Doc White	L	27	18	6	.750	0	28	24	20	219	160	38	95	7	1.52
Ed Walsh	R	25	17	13	.567	3	41	31	24	278	215	58	171	10	1.88
Roy Patterson	R	29	10	7	.588	1	21	18	12	142	119	17	45	3	2.09
Frank Smith	R	26	5	5	.500	2	20	13	8	122	124	37	53	1	3.39
Lou Fiene	R	21	1	1	.500	0	6	2	1	31	35	9	12	0	2.90
Frank Isbell	R	30	0	0	—	0	2	1	0	2	1	0	2	0	0.00

NEW YORK — 2nd 90-61 .596 3 — CLARK GRIFFITH

NAME	G by Pos	B	AGE	G	AB	R	H	2B	3B	HR	RBI	BB	SO	SB	BA	SA
TOTALS		27		155	5095	641	1345	166	77	17	528	331		192	.266	.339
Hal Chase	1B150, 2B1	R	23	151	597	84	193	23	10	0	76	13		28	.323	.395
Jimmy Williams	2B139	R	29	139	501	62	139	25	7	3	77	44		9	.277	.373
Kid Elberfeld (JJ)	SS98	R	31	99	346	59	106	12	4	2	31	30		19	.306	.382
Frank LaPorte	3B114, 2B5, OF1	R	26	123	454	60	120	23	9	2	54	22		10	.264	.368
Willie Keeler	OF152	L	34	152	592	96	180	9	3	2	33	40		23	.304	.340
2 Danny Hoffman (KJ)	OF98	L	26	100	320	34	82	10	6	0	23	27		32	.256	.325
Frank Delahanty	OF92	R	23	92	307	37	73	11	8	2	41	16		11	.238	.345
Red Kleinow	C95, 1B1	R	28	96	268	30	59	9	3	0	31	24		8	.220	.276
Wid Conroy	OF97, SS49, 3B2	R	29	148	567	67	139	17	10	4	54	47		32	.245	.332
George Moriarty	3B39, OF15, 1B5, 2B1	R	20	65	197	22	46	7	7	0	23	17		8	.234	.340
Joe Yeager	SS22, 2B13, 3B3	R	30	57	123	20	37	6	1	0	12	13		3	.301	.366
Deacon McGuire	C49, 1B1	R	43	50	144	11	43	5	0	0	14	12		4	.299	.333
Ira Thomas	C42	R	25	44	115	12	23	1	2	0	15	8		2	.200	.243
1 Patsy Dougherty	OF12	L	29	12	52	3	10	2	0	0	4	0		0	.192	.231
1 Eddie Hahn	OF7	L	30	11	22	2	1	0	0	0	1	0		3	.091	.136
John Ganzel (HO) 32																

NAME	T	AGE	W	L	PCT	SV	G	GS	CG	IP	H	BB	SO	SHO	ERA
		30	90*	61	.596	5	155	155	99	1358	1236	351	605	18	2.78
Al Orth	R	33	27	17	.614	0	45	39	36	339	317	66	133	3	2.34
Jack Chesbro	R	32	24	16	.600	1	49	42	24	325	314	75	152	4	2.96
Bill Hogg	R	24	14	13	.519	0	28	25	15	206	171	72	107	3	2.32
Walter Clarkson	R	27	9	4	.692	1	32	16	9	151	135	55	64	3	2.32
Doc Newton	L	28	6	5	.545	0	21	15	6	125	118	33	52	3	3.17
Noodles Hahn	R	27	3	2	.600	0	6	3	3	42	38	6	11	1	3.86
Louis LeRoy	R	27	2	0	1.000	1	11	2	1	45	33	12	28	0	2.20
Slow Joe Doyle	R	24	2	2	.500	0	9	6	3	45	34	13	28	2	2.40
Clark Griffith	R	36	2	0	1.000	2	17	2	1	60	58	15	16	0	3.00
Tom Hughes	R	22	1	0	1.000	0	3	1	1	15	11	1	5	0	4.20
Cy Barger	R	21	0	0	—	0	2	1	0	5	7	3	3	0	10.80

* One win by forfeit

CLEVELAND — 3rd 89-64 .582 5 — NAP LAJOIE

NAME	G by Pos	B	AGE	G	AB	R	H	2B	3B	HR	RBI	BB	SO	SB	BA	SA
TOTALS		28		157	5414	663	1511	240	73	11	548	330		203	.279	.356
Claude Rossman	1B105, OF1	L	25	118	396	49	122	13	2	1	53	17		11	.308	.359
Nap Lajoie	2B130, 3B15, SS7	R	31	152	602	88	214	49	7	0	91	30		20	.355	.460
Terry Turner	SS147	R	25	147	584	85	170	27	7	2	62	35		27	.291	.372
Bill Bradley (BW)	3B82	R	28	82	302	32	83	15	2	2	25	18		13	.275	.358
Bunk Congalton	OF114	L	31	117	419	51	134	13	5	2	50	24		12	.320	.389
Elmer Flick	OF150, 2B8	L	30	157	624	98	194	33	22	1	62	54		39	.311	.439
Jim Jackson	OF105	R	28	105	374	44	80	13	2	0	38	38		25	.214	.259
Harry Bemis	C81	L	32	93	297	28	82	13	5	2	30	12		8	.276	.374
George Stovall	1B55, 3B30, 2B19	R	28	116	443	54	121	19	5	0	37	8		15	.273	.339
Harry Bay (NJ)	OF68	L	28	68	280	47	77	8	3	0	14	26		17	.275	.325
Nig Clarke	C54	L	23	57	179	22	64	12	4	1	21	13		3	.358	.486
Jap Barbeau	3B32, SS6	R	24	42	129	8	25	5	3	0	12	9		5	.194	.279
Fritz Buelow	C33, 1B1	R	34	36	86	7	14	2	0	0	7	9		0	.163	.186
Ben Caffyn	OF29	L	26	30	103	16	20	4	0	0	3	12		2	.194	.233
Joe Birmingham	OF9	R	21	9	37	4	11	2	1	0	6	1		2	.297	.405
Bill Shipke	2B2	R	23	2	3	0	0	0	0	0	0	0		0	.000	.000
2 Mal Kittredge	C1	R	26	1	3	0	0	0	0	0	0	0		0	.000	.000

NAME	T	AGE	W	L	PCT	SV	G	GS	CG	IP	H	BB	SO	SHO	ERA
		28	89	64	.582	5	157	157	133	1413	1197	365	530	27	2.09
Bob Rhoades	R	26	22	10	.688	1	38	34	31	315	259	92	89	7	1.80
Addie Joss	R	26	21	9	.700	1	34	31	28	282	220	43	106	9	1.72
Otto Hess	L	27	20	17	.541	3	43	36	33	334	274	85	167	1	1.83
Bill Bernhard	R	35	16	15	.516	0	31	30	23	255	235	47	85	2	2.54
Harry Eells	R	26	9	4	.444	0	14	8	6	86	77	48	35	1	2.90
Jack Townsend	R	27	3	7	.300	0	17	12	8	93	92	31	31	1	2.90
Glenn Liebhardt	R	23	2	0	1.000	0	2	2	1	18	13	1	9	0	1.50
Earl Moore (HO)	R	26	1	1	.500	0	5	4	2	30	27	18	8	0	3.90

PHILADELPHIA 4th 78-67 .538 12 CONNIE MACK

NAME	G by Pos	B	AGE	G	AB	R	H	2B	3B	HR	RBI	BB	SO	SB	BA	SA
TOTALS			29	149	4883	555	1206	213	49	31		489	385	166	.247	.330
Harry Davis	1B145	R	32	145	551	94	161	40	8	12	96	49		23	.292	.459
Danny Murphy	2B119	R	29	119	448	48	135	24	7	2	60	21		17	.301	.400
Monte Cross	SS134	R	36	134	445	32	89	23	3	0	40	50		22	.200	.265
Jack Knight	3B67, 2B7	R	20	74	253	29	49	7	2	3	20	19		6	.194	.273
Socks Seybold	OF114	R	35	116	411	41	130	21	3	5	59	30		9	.316	.418
Bris Lord	OF115	R	22	115	434	50	101	13	7	1	44	27		12	.233	.302
Topsy Hartsel	OF144	L	32	144	533	96	136	21	9	1	30	88		31	.255	.334
Ossee Schreckengost	C89, 1B4	R	31	98	338	29	96	20	1	1	41	10		5	.284	.358
Harry Armbruster	OF74	L	24	91	265	40	63	6	3	2	24	43		13	.238	.306
Rube Oldring (BN)	3B49, SS3, 2B2, 1B1	R	22	59	174	15	42	10	1	0	19	2		7	.241	.310
Mike Powers	C57, 1B1	R	35	58	185	5	29	1	0	0	7	1		2	.157	.162
Art Brouthers	3B33	R	23	36	144	18	30	5	1	0	14	5		4	.208	.257
Dave Shean	2B22, 3B1	R	28	22	75	7	16	3	2	0	3	5		6	.213	.307
Simon Nicholls	SS12	L	23	12	44	1	8	1	0	0	1	3		0	.182	.205
Claude Berry	C10	R	26	10	30	2	7	0	0	0	2	2		1	.233	.233
Jim Byrnes	C8	R	26	9	23	4	4	0	1	0	0	0		0	.174	.261
1 Danny Hoffman	OF7	L	26	7	22	4	5	0	0	0	0	3		1	.227	.227
Ed Lennox	3B6	R	22	6	17	1	1	1	0	0	1	0		0	.059	.118
Eddie Collins	SS3, 2B1, 3B1	L	19	6	15	2	3	0	0	0	0	0		0	.200	.200
Willy Fetzer	L	22	1	1	0	0	0	0	0	0	0		0	.000	.000
1 Jack Hannifan		B	23	1	1	0	1	0	0	0	0	0		0	1.000	1.000

NAME	T	AGE	W	L	PCT	SV	G	GS	CG	IP	H	BB	SO	SHO	ERA
		25	78	67*	.538	7	149	149	107	1322	1135	425	749	19	2.60
Eddie Plank	L	30	19	5	.792	0	26	25	21	212	173	51	108	5	2.25
Rube Waddell	L	29	16	16	.500	1	43	34	22	273	221	92	196	8	2.21
Chief Bender	R	23	15	10	.600	3	36	27	24	238	208	48	159	0	2.53
Jack Coombs	R	23	10	11	.476	1	23	18	13	173	144	81	90	1	2.50
Jimmy Dygert	R	21	10	13	.435	1	35	25	15	214	175	91	106	4	2.69
Andy Coakley (IL)	R	23	7	8	.467	0	22	16	10	149	144	44	59	0	3.14
Mike Cuningham	R	24	1	0	1.000	0	1	1	1	18	16	9	15	0	3.21
Bill Bartley	R	21	0	1		1	3	0	0	9	10	6	6	0	9.00
Jim Holmes		23	0	1	.000	0	3	1	0	9	15	8	1	0	4.00
Hack Schumann	R	21	0	0	.000	0	4	2	1	18	21	8	9	0	4.00

*One loss by forfeit

ST. LOUIS 5th 76-73 .510 16 JIMMY McALEER

NAME	G by Pos	B	AGE	G	AB	R	H	2B	3B	HR	RBI	BB	SO	SB	BA	SA
TOTALS			28	154	5053	559	1250	145	60	20		456	366	222	.247	.312
Tom Jones	1B143	R	29	144	539	51	136	22	6	0	30	24		27	.252	.315
Pete O'Brien	2B120, 3B20, SS11	L	29	151	524	44	122	9	4	2	57	42		25	.233	.277
Bobby Wallace	SS127	R	32	139	476	64	123	24	7	2	67	58		24	.258	.351
Roy Hartzell	3B103, SS6, 2B2	L	24	113	404	43	86	7	0	0	24	19		21	.213	.230
Harry Niles	OF108, 3B34	R	25	142	541	71	124	14	4	2	31	46		30	.229	.281
Charlie Hemphill	OF154	L	30	154	585	90	169	19	12	4	62	43		33	.289	.383
George Stone	OF154	L	29	154	581	91	208	24	19	6	71	52		35	.358	.496
Jack O'Connor	C57	R	37	61	186	8	37	0	0	0	11	2		5	.199	.199
Ben Koehler	OF52, 2B7, SS1, 3B1	R	29	66	186	27	41	1	1	0	15	24		9	.220	.237
Branch Rickey	C54, OF1	L	24	64	201	22	57	8	3	3	24	16		4	.284	.398
Tubby Spencer	C54	R	21	58	188	15	33	6	1	0	17	7		4	.176	.218
Ike Rockenfield	2B26	R	29	27	89	3	21	4	0	0	8	1		0	.236	.281
Lou Nordyke	1B12	R	29	12	53	4	13	1	0	0	7	10		3	.245	.264
Snags Heidrick (VR) 29																

NAME	T	AGE	W	L	PCT	SV	G	GS	CG	IP	H	BB	SO	SHO	ERA
		28	78	73	.510	5	154	154	133	1358	1132	314	558	17	2.23
Barney Pelty	R	25	17	12	.586	2	34	30	25	261	189	59	92	4	1.59
Harry Howell	R	29	15	13	.536	1	35	33	30	277	233	61	140	6	2.11
Fred Glade	R	30	15	15	.500	0	35	32	28	267	215	59	96	4	2.36
Jack Powell (ST)	R	31	13	14	.481	1	28	26	25	244	196	55	132	3	1.77
Beany Jacobson	L	25	9	9	.500	0	24	15	12	155	146	27	53	0	2.50
Ed Smith	R	27	7	10	.412	1	19	18	15	155	153	53	45	0	3.72

DETROIT 6th 71-78 .477 21 BILL ARMOUR

NAME	G by Pos	B	AGE	G	AB	R	H	2B	3B	HR	RBI	BB	SO	SB	BA	SA
TOTALS			26	151	4927	516	1194	154	64	10		409	333	205	.242	.306
Pinky Lindsay	1B122, 2B17, 3B1	L	27	141	499	59	112	16	2	0	33	45		18	.224	.265
Germany Schaefer	2B114, SS7	R	29	124	446	48	106	14	3	2	42	32		31	.238	.296
Charley O'Leary	SS127	R	23	128	443	34	97	13	2	2	34	17		8	.219	.271
Bill Coughlin	3B147	R	27	147	498	54	117	15	5	2	60	36		31	.235	.297
Sam Crawford	OF116, 1B32	L	26	145	563	65	166	23	16	2	72	38		24	.295	.403
Ty Cobb (IL)	OF96	L	19	98	358	45	113	13	7	1	34	19		23	.316	.399
Matty McIntyre	OF133	L	26	133	493	63	128	19	11	0	39	56		29	.260	.343
Boss Schmidt	C67	B	25	68	216	13	47	4	3	0	10	6		1	.218	.264
Davy Jones	OF84	L	26	84	323	41	84	12	2	0	24	41		21	.260	.310
Freddie Payne	C47, OF17	R	25	72	222	23	60	5	5	0	20	13		4	.270	.338
1 Jack Warner	C49	L	33	50	153	15	37	4	2	0	10	12		4	.242	.294
Bobby Lowe (IL)	SS19, 2B17, 3B5	R	37	41	145	11	30	3	0	1	12	4		3	.207	.248
Sam Thompson	OF8	L	46	8	31	4	7	0	1	0	3	1		0	.226	.290
Frank Scheibeck	2B3	R	41	3	10	1	1	0	0	0	0	2		0	.100	.100
Gus Hetling	3B2	R	20	2	7	0	1	0	0	0	0	0		0	.143	.143

NAME	T	AGE	W	L	PCT	SV	G	GS	CG	IP	H	BB	SO	SHO	ERA
		30	71	78	.477	5	151	151	128	1334	1398	389	469	7	3.06
George Mullin	R	25	21	18	.538	0	40	40	35	330	315	108	123	2	2.78
Ed Siever	L	31	14	10	.583	1	30	25	20	223	240	45	71	1	2.70
Red Donahue	R	33	13	14	.481	0	28	26	24	241	260	54	82	3	2.73
Ed Killian (IL)	L	29	9	6	.600	2	21	16	14	150	165	54	47	0	3.42
Will Bill Donovan	R	29	9	15	.375	0	25	25	22	212	221	72	85	0	3.14
John Eubank	R	33	4	10	.286	2	24	12	7	135	147	35	38	1	3.53
Jimmy Wiggs	R	29	1	1	.500	0	4	1	0	10	11	7	7	0	5.40
Jack Rowan	R	20	1	1	.500	0	1	1	1	9	15	6	0	0	11.00
Ed Willett	R	22	1	3	.000	0	3	3	3	25	24	8	16	0	3.96

WASHINGTON 7th 55-95 .367 37.5 JAKE STAHL

NAME	G by Pos	B	AGE	G	AB	R	H	2B	3B	HR	RBI	BB	SO	SB	BA	SA
TOTALS			29	149	4966	518	1181	144	65	26		433	306	233	.238	.309
Jake Stahl	1B136	R	27	137	482	38	107	9	8	0	51	21		30	.222	.274
Larry Schlafly	2B123	B	27	123	426	60	105	13	8	2	30	50		29	.246	.329
Dave Altizer	SS113, OF2	L	29	115	433	56	111	9	5	1	27	35		37	.256	.307
Lave Cross	3B88	R	40	130	494	55	130	14	6	1	46	28		19	.263	.322
C. Hickman (IL)	OF95, 1B18, 3B5, 2B1	R	30	120	451	53	128	26	4	9	57	14		9	.284	.419
Charlie Jones	OF128, 2B1	L	30	131	497	56	120	11	11	3	42	24		34	.241	.326
John Anderson	OF151	B	32	151	602	82	158	25	4	3	70	19		39	.271	.343
Howard Wakefield	C60	R	22	77	211	17	59	9	2	1	21	7		6	.280	.355
Rabbitt Nill	SS31, 2B25, OF15	R	24	89	315	37	74	8	2	0	15	47		16	.235	.273
Joe Stanley	OF64, P1	R	25	73	221	18	36	0	4	0	9	20		6	.163	.199
Mike Heydon (BG)	C49	L	31	49	145	14	23	7	1	0	10	14		2	.159	.221
2 Jack Warner	C32	L	33	32	103	5	21	4	1	1	9	2		3	.204	.291
1 Mal Kittredge	C27	R	36	27	78	5	14	0	0	0	3	1		0	.179	.179
Otto Williams	SS8, 2B6, 1B2, 3B1	R	28	20	51	3	7	0	0	0	0	0		0	.137	.137
Pat Duff			31	1	1	0	0	0	0	0	0	0		0	.000	.000
Warren Shanabrook	3B1	R	25	1	2	0	0	0	0	0	0	0		0	.000	.000
Joe Cassidy (DD) 23																

NAME	T	AGE	W	L	PCT	SV	G	GS	CG	IP	H	BB	SO	SHO	ERA
		29	55	95	.367	1	151	151	115	1323	1331	451	558	13	3.25
Casey Patten	L	32	19	15	.559	0	38	32	28	283	253	79	96	7	2.16
Cy Falkenberg	R	26	14	19	.424	1	40	36	30	299	277	108	178	2	2.86
Charlie Smith	R	26	9	16	.360	0	33	22	17	235	250	75	105	2	2.91
Long Tom Hughes	R	27	7	17	.292	0	30	24	18	204	230	81	90	1	3.62
Frank Kitson	R	34	6	16	.272	0	30	21	15	197	196	57	59	1	3.65
Con Starkel	R	25	0	1	—	0	1	0	0	3	7	2	1	0	18.00
Joe Stanley	R	25	0	0		0	1	0	0	3	3	1	0	0	12.00
Bob Edmundson	R	27	0	1	.000	0	2	1	1	10	10	2	0	0	4.50
Willy Wilson	R	22	0	1	.000	0	1	1	1	7	3	1	2	0	2.57
Willie Sudhoff	R	31	0	2	.000	0	9	5	0	20	30	9	7	0	4.50
Clyde Goodwin	R	19	0	2	.000	0	2	1	0	20	24	9	12	0	4.50
Harry Hardy	L	30	0	1	.000	0	3	2	1	20	35	12	4	0	5.40
Barney Wolfe	R	30	0	1	.000	0	3	1	0	10	11	5	8	0	4.05

BOSTON 8th 49-105 .318 45.5 JIMMY COLLINS 35-79 .307 CHICK STAHL 14-26 .350

NAME	G by Pos	B	AGE	G	AB	R	H	2B	3B	HR	RBI	BB	SO	SB	BA	SA
TOTALS			28	155	5168	462	1223	160	75	13		408	298	99	.237	.304
Moose Grimshaw (JJ)	1B110	B	30	110	428	46	124	16	12	0	48	23		5	.290	.383
Hobe Ferris	2B126, 3B4	R	28	130	495	47	121	25	13	2	44	10		8	.244	.360
Freddy Parent	SS143, 2B6	R	30	149	600	67	141	14	10	1	49	31		16	.235	.297
Red Morgan	3B88	R	22	88	322	20	66	6	3	1	21	16		7	.215	.264
Jack Hayden (SL)	OF85	R	25	85	322	22	80	6	4	1	14	17		6	.248	.301
Chick Stahl	OF155	L	33	155	595	62	170	24	6	4	51	47		13	.286	.366
Jack Huey	OF94	L	24	94	361	34	88	8	4	0	24	14		10	.244	.288
Charlie Armbruster	C66, 1B1	R	25	72	201	9	29	6	1	0	6	25		1	.144	.184
Buck Freeman	OF65, 1B43, 3B4	L	34	121	392	42	98	20	8	1	30	28		5	.250	.349
J. Godwin (LJ)	3B27, SS14, OF10, 2B3, 1B1	R	29	66	193	11	36	2	1	0	15	6		6	.187	.207
Kip Selbach	OF58	L	34	60	228	15	48	9	2	0	23	18		7	.211	.268
Bob Peterson	C30, 2B3, 1B2, OF1	R	22	39	118	10	24	1	1	1	9	11		3	.203	.254
Bill Carrigan	C35	R	22	37	109	5	23	1	1	0	10	5		1	.211	.211
Jimmy Collins (KJ)	3B32	R	36	37	142	17	39	9	4	1	16	4		1	.275	.415
Jesse Tannehill	P27	L	31	31	79	12	22	2	0	1	6	6		1	.278	.354
Charlie Graham (SA)	C27	R	29	30	90	10	21	1	1	0	12	10		1	.233	.278
Chet Chadbourne	2B11, SS1	L	21	11	43	7	13	1	0	0	3	3		1	.302	.326
Heinie Wagner	2B9	R	25	9	32	3	7	1	0	0	2	2		0	.281	.281
Lou Criger (IL)	C6	R	34	7	17	0	3	0	0	0	1	1		0	.176	.235
Tom Doran	C2	L	26	2	1	0	0	0	0	0	0	0		0	.000	.000

NAME	T	AGE	W	L	PCT	SV	G	GS	CG	IP	H	BB	SO	SHO	ERA
		30	49	105	.318	6	155	155	124	1382	1360	285	549	6	3.41
Jesse Tannehill	L	31	13	11	.542	0	27	26	18	196	207	39	82	2	3.17
Cy Young	R	39	13	21	.382	2	39	34	28	288	288	25	140	0	3.19
Bill Dinneen	R	30	8	19	.296	0	28	27	22	219	209	52	60	1	2.92
George Winter (IL)	R	28	6	18	.250	2	29	22	18	208	215	38	72	1	4.11
Ralph Glaze	R	25	4	6	.400	0	19	10	7	123	110	32	56	0	3.59
Joe Harris	R	24	2	21	.087	2	30	24	20	235	211	67	99	1	3.52
Rube Kroh	L	19	1	0	1.000	0	1	1	1	9	2	4	1	0	1.00
Len Swormstedt	R	31	1	1	.500	0	3	2	1	21	17	0	6	1	1.29
Frank Oberlin	R	30	1	3	.250	0	4	4	4	34	38	13	13	0	3.18
Ed Hughes	R	29	0	0	—	0	2	0	0	5	10	5	3	0	5.40
Norwood Gibson	R	29	0	2	.000	0	2	2	1	19	25	7	3	0	5.21
Ed Barry	L	24	0	3	.000	0	3	3	1	21	23	5	10	0	6.00

CHICAGO — 1st 116-36 .763 — FRANK CHANCE

NAME	G by Pos	B	AGE	G	AB	R	H	2B	3B	HR	RBI	BB	SO	SB	BA	SA
TOTALS			27	154	5018	704	1316	181	71	20	539	448		283	.262	.339
Frank Chance	1B136	R	29	136	474	103	151	24	10	3	71	70		57	.319	.430
Johnny Evers	2B153, 3B1	L	24	154	533	65	136	17	6	1	51	36		49	.255	.315
Joe Tinker	SS147, 3B1	R	25	148	523	75	122	18	4	1	64	43		30	.233	.289
Harry Steinfeldt	3B150, 2B1	R	28	151	539	81	176	27	10	3	83	47		29	.327	.430
Wildfire Schulte	OF146	L	23	146	563	77	158	18	13	7	60	31		25	.281	.396
Jimmy Slagle	OF127	L	32	72	269	35	86	13	8	6	33	63		25	.239	.279
Jimmy Sheckard	OF149	L	27	149	549	90	144	27	10	1	45	67		30	.262	.353
Johnny Kling	C96, OF3	R	30	107	343	45	107	15	8	2	46	23		14	.312	.420
Pat Moran	C61	R	30	70	226	22	57	13	1	0	35	7		6	.252	.319
Solly Hofman	OF23, 1B21, SS9, 2B4, 3B4	R	23	64	195	30	50	2	3	2	20	20		13	.256	.328
2 Doc Gessler	OF21, 1B1	L	25	34	83	8	21	3	0	0	10	12		4	.253	.289
1 Pete Noonan		R	24	5	3	0	1	0	0	0	0	0		0	.333	.333
Tom Walsh	C2	R	21	2	1	0	0	0	0	0	0	0		0	.000	.000
Bull Smith		R	25	1	1	0	0	0	0	0	0	0		0	.000	.000

NAME	T	AGE	W	L	PCT	SV	G	GS	CG	IP	H	BB	SO	SHO	ERA
		27	116	36	.763	10	154	154	125	1379	1018	446	702	30	1.76
Three Finger Brown	R	29	26	6	.813	3	36	32	27	277	198	61	144	9	1.04
Jack Pfiester	L	28	20	8	.714	0	31	29	20	242	173	63	153	4	1.56
Ed Reulbach	R	23	19	4	.826	3	33	24	20	218	129	92	94	6	1.65
Carl Lundgren	R	26	17	6	.739	2	27	24	21	208	160	89	103	5	2.21
2 Orvie Overall	R	25	12	3	.800	1	18	14	13	144	116	51	94	2	1.88
2 Jack Taylor	R	32	12	3	.800	0	17	16	15	147	116	39	34	2	1.84
1 Fred Beebe	R	25	7	1	.875	1	14	6	4	70	56	32	55*	0	2.70
1 Bob Wicker	R	28	3	5	.375	0	8	8	5	72	70	19	25	0	3.00
2 Jack Harper	R	28	0	0	.000	0	1	1	0	1	0	0	0	0	0.00

*Beebe, Also with St. Louis, league leader in SO with 171

NEW YORK — 2nd 96-56 .632 20 — JOHN McGRAW

NAME	G by Pos	B	AGE	G	AB	R	H	2B	3B	HR	RBI	BB	SO	SB	BA	SA
TOTALS			31	152	4768	625	1217	162	53	15	513	563		288	.255	.321
Dan McGann	1B133	B	34	134	451	62	107	14	8	0	37	60		30	.237	.304
Billy Gilbert	2B98	R	30	104	307	44	71	6	1	1	27	42		22	.231	.267
Bill Dahlen	SS143	R	36	143	471	63	113	18	3	1	49	76		16	.240	.297
Art Devlin	3B148	R	26	148	498	76	149	23	8	2	65	74		54	.299	.390
George Browne (IL)	OF121	L	30	122	477	61	126	10	4	0	38	27		32	.264	.302
2 Cy Seymour	OF72	L	33	72	269	35	86	12	3	4	42	18		20	.320	.431
2 Spike Shannon	OF76	B	28	76	287	42	73	5	1	0	25	34		18	.254	.279
Roger Bresnahan	C82, OF40	R	27	124	405	69	114	22	4	0	43	81		25	.281	.356
Sammy Strang	2B57, OF39, SS4, 3B3, 1B1	B	29	113	313	50	100	16	4	4	49	54		21	.319	.435
Frank Bowerman	C67, 1B20	R	37	103	285	23	65	7	3	1	42	15		5	.228	.284
1 Sam Mertes	OF71	R	33	71	253	37	60	9	6	1	33	29		21	.237	.332
1 Doc Marshall	OF16, C13, 1B2	R	31	38	102	8	17	3	2	0	7	7		7	.167	.235
Mike Donlin (BL)	OF29, 1B1	L	28	37	121	15	38	5	1	1	14	11		9	.314	.397
Broadway Aleck Smith	C8, 1B3, OF1	R	35	16	28	0	5	0	0	0	2	1		1	.179	.179
2 Jack Hannifin	SS6, 3B3, 2B1	B	23	10	30	4	6	0	1	0	3	2		1	.200	.267
Frank Burke	OF4	R	26	8	9	2	3	1	1	0	1	1		1	.333	.667
Matty Fitzgerald	C3	R	25	4	6	2	4	0	0	0	2	0		1	.667	.667
John McGraw	3B1	L	33	2	0	0	0	0	0	0	0	0		0	.000	.000

NAME	T	AGE	W	L	PCT	SV	G	GS	CG	IP	H	BB	SO	SHO	ERA
		26	96	56	.632	18	152	152	105	1334	1207	394	639	19	2.49
Joe McGinnity	R	35	27	12	.692	2	45	37	32	340	316	71	105	3	2.25
Christy Mathewson	R	25	22	12	.647	1	38	35	22	267	262	77	128	6	2.97
Dummy Taylor	R	31	17	9	.654	0	31	27	13	213	186	57	91	2	2.20
Hooks Wiltse	L	26	16	11	.593	6	38	24	17	249	227	58	125	4	2.28
Red Ames (KJ)	R	23	12	10	.545	1	31	25	15	203	166	93	156	1	2.66
Cecil Ferguson	R	19	2	1	.667	7	22	1	1	52	43	24	32	1	2.60
Henry Mathewson	R	19	0	1	.000	1	2	1	1	10	7	14	2	0	5.40

PITTSBURGH — 3rd 93-60 .608 23.5 — FRED CLARKE

NAME	G by Pos	B	AGE	G	AB	R	H	2B	3B	HR	RBI	BB	SO	SB	BA	SA
TOTALS			29	154	5030	622	1313	164	67	12	497	424		162	.261	.327
Jim Nelson	1B154	R	21	154	556	82	142	21	12	3	83	53		15	.255	.353
Claude Ritchey	2B151	B	32	152	484	46	130	21	5	1	62	68		6	.269	.339
Honus Wagner	SS137, OF2, 3B1	R	32	143	516	103	175	38	9	2	71	58		53	.339	.459
Tommy Sheehan	3B90	R	28	95	315	28	76	6	3	1	34	18		13	.241	.289
Bob Ganley	OF134	L	31	134	451	63	132	7	6	0	31	41		19	.258	.295
Ginger Beaumont (LJ)	OF78	L	29	80	310	48	82	9	3	2	32	19		1	.265	.332
Fred Clarke	OF110	L	33	118	417	69	129	14	13	1	39	40		18	.309	.412
George Gibson	C81	R	25	81	259	8	46	6	1	0	20	16		1	.178	.208
Tommy Leach	3B65, OF60, SS1	R	28	133	476	66	136	10	7	1	39	33		21	.286	.342
Dutch Meier	OF52, SS17	R	27	43	118	27	32	7	1	4	16	13		4	.256	.326
2 Eddie Phelps	C40	R	27	43	118	9	28	3	1	0	12	9		1	.237	.280
Heinie Peitz	C38	R	35	40	125	13	30	8	0	0	20	13		1	.240	.304
Bill Hallman	OF23	R	30	23	89	12	24	3	1	1	6	15		3	.270	.360
Otis Clymer (BN)	OF11	R	30	11	45	7	11	0	1	0	1	3		1	.244	.289
Otis Abstein	2B3, OF2	R	23	8	20	2	4	0	0	0	3	0		2	.200	.200
Alan Storke	3B2, SS1	R	21	5	12	1	3	1	0	0	1	1		1	.250	.333
Fred Carisch	C4	R	24	4	12	0	1	0	0	0	0	0		1	.083	.083
Harry Smith (IL)	C1	R	31	1	1	0	0	0	0	0	0	0		0	.000	.000

NAME	T	AGE	W	L	PCT	SV	G	GS	CG	IP	H	BB	SO	SHO	ERA
		30	93	60	.608	2	154	154	116	1358	1234	309	532	27	2.21
Vic Willis	R	30	22	13	.629	1	41	36	32	322	295	76	124	6	1.73
Sam Leever	R	34	22	7	.759	0	36	31	25	260	232	48	76	6	2.32
Lefty Leifield	L	22	18	13	.581	1	37	31	24	256	214	68	111	8	1.86
Deacon Phillippe	R	34	15	10	.600	0	33	24	19	219	216	26	90	3	2.42
Mike Lynch	R	31	6	5	.545	0	18	12	7	119	101	31	48	0	2.42
Doc Hillebrand	L	26	3	2	.600	0	7	5	4	53	42	21	32	1	2.21
1 Ed Karger	R	23	2	3	.400	0	6	2	0	28	21	9	8	0	1.93
Howie Camnitz	R	24	1	0	1.000	0	2	1	1	9	6	5	1	0	2.00
Lou Manske	R	21	1	0	1.000	0	2	1	0	12	5	6	6	0	5.63
King Brady	R	25	1	1	.500	0	3	2	1	23	30	4	14	0	2.35
Charlie Case	R	26	1	1	.500	0	2	2	1	11	6	3	5	0	5.73
2 Chappie McFarland	R	31	1	3	.250	0	6	5	2	35	39	7	11	1	2.57
Bert Maxwell	R	19	0	1	.000	0	1	1	0	8	8	2	1	0	5.63
Irish McIlveen	L	25	0	1	.000	0	1	1	0	7	10	2	3	0	7.71

PHILADELPHIA — 4th 71-82 .464 45.5 — HUGH DUFFY

NAME	G by Pos	B	AGE	G	AB	R	H	2B	3B	HR	RBI	BB	SO	SB	BA	SA
TOTALS			28	154	4911	530	1183	197	47	12	444	432		180	.241	.307
Kitty Bransfield	1B139	R	31	140	524	47	144	28	5	1	60	16		12	.275	.353
Kid Gleason	2B135	B	39	135	494	47	112	17	2	0	34	36		17	.227	.269
Mickey Doolan	SS154	R	26	154	535	41	123	19	7	1	55	27		16	.230	.297
Ernie Courtney	3B96, 1B13, OF3, SS1	L	31	116	398	53	94	12	2	0	42	45		6	.236	.276
John Titus	OF142	L	30	145	484	67	129	22	5	1	57	78		12	.267	.339
Roy Thomas	OF142	L	32	142	493	81	125	10	7	0	16	107		22	.254	.302
Sherry Magee	OF154	R	21	154	563	77	159	36	8	6	67	52		55	.282	.407
Red Dooin	C107	R	27	113	351	25	86	19	1	0	32	13		15	.245	.305
Johnny Lush	P37, OF22, 1B1	L	20	76	212	28	56	7	1	0	15	14		6	.264	.307
Paul Sentell	3B33, 2B19, OF2, SS1	R	26	63	192	19	44	5	1	1	14	14		15	.229	.281
Jerry Donovan	C52, OF1, SS1	R	29	61	166	11	33	4	0	0	15	6		2	.199	.223
Joe Ward	3B27, 2B3, SS1	R	21	35	129	12	38	8	6	0	11	5		2	.295	.450
Ches Crist	C6	R	24	6	11	1	0	0	0	0	0	0		0	.000	.000
Harry Houston	C2	R	22	4	0	0	0	0	0	0	0	0		1	.000	.000
Hugh Duffy		R	39	1	1	0	0	0	0	0	0	0		0	.000	.000

NAME	T	AGE	W	L	PCT	SV	G	GS	CG	IP	H	BB	SO	SHO	ERA
		28	71	82	.464	5	154	154	108	1354	1201	436	500	21	2.58
Tully Sparks	R	31	19	16	.543	3	42	37	29	317	244	62	114	6	2.16
Johnny Lush	L	20	18	15	.545	0	37	35	24	281	254	119	151	5	2.37
Bill Duggleby	R	33	13	19	.406	2	42	30	22	280	241	66	83	5	2.25
Lew Richie	R	22	9	11	.450	0	33	22	14	206	170	79	65	3	2.40
Togie Pittinger	R	34	8	10	.444	0	20	16	9	130	128	50	43	2	2.85
Jim McClosky	R	23	3	2	.600	0	9	4	3	41	46	9	6	0	2.85
Harry Kane	L	22	1	3	.250	0	6	3	2	28	28	18	14	0	3.86
Charlie Roy	R	22	0	1	.000	0	7	1	0	18	24	5	6	0	5.00
Kid Nichols	R	36	0	0	.000	0	4	2	1	11	17	13	1	0	9.82
Walter Moser	R	25	0	4	.000	0	6	4	4	43	49	15	17	0	3.63

BROOKLYN — 5th 66-86 .434 50 — PATSY DONOVAN

NAME	G by Pos	B	AGE	G	AB	R	H	2B	3B	HR	RBI	BB	SO	SB	BA	SA
TOTALS			28	153	4897	495	1156	141	68	25	407	388		175	.236	.308
Tim Jordan	1B126	L	27	133	450	67	118	20	8	12	78	59		16	.262	.422
Whitey Alperman	2B104, SS24, 3B1	R	26	128	441	38	111	15	7	3	46	6		13	.252	.338
Phil Lewis	SS155	R	22	138	452	40	110	8	4	0	37	43		14	.243	.279
Doc Casey	3B149	R	35	149	571	71	133	17	8	0	34	52		22	.233	.291
Harry Lumley	OF131	L	25	133	484	72	157	23	12	9	61	48		35	.324	.477
Billy Maloney	OF151	R	28	151	566	71	125	15	7	0	32	49		38	.221	.272
Jack McCarthy	OF86	R	37	91	322	23	98	13	1	0	35	20		9	.304	.351
Bill Bergen	C103	R	33	103	353	9	56	3	3	0	19	7		2	.159	.184
John Hummel	2B50, OF21, 1B15	R	23	97	286	20	57	6	4	1	21	36		10	.199	.259
Lew Ritter	C53, OF9, 1B3, 3B2	R	30	73	226	22	47	1	3	0	15	16		6	.208	.239
Heinie Batch (IL)	OF50, 3B2	R	26	59	203	23	57	7	6	0	11	15		3	.256	.350
1 Doc Gessler	1B9	L	26	9	33	3	8	1	2	0	4	3		3	.242	.394
Patsy Donovan	OF6	R	41	6	21	1	5	0	0	0	0	0		0	.238	.238
Phil Reardon	OF4	R	22	5	14	0	1	0	0	0	0	0		1	.071	.071
John Butler	C1	R	26	1	1	0	0	0	0	0	0	0		0	.000	.000

NAME	T	AGE	W	L	PCT	SV	G	GS	CG	IP	H	BB	SO	SHO	ERA
		27	66	86	.434	11	153	153	119	1349	1255	453	476	22	3.13
Doc Scanlan	R	25	18	13	.581	2	38	33	28	288	230	127	120	6	3.19
Elmer Stricklett	R	29	14	18	.438	5	41	35	28	292	273	77	88	5	2.71
Harry McIntire	R	28	13	21	.382	3	39	31	25	276	254	89	121	4	2.97
Jim Pastorius	L	24	10	14	.417	0	29	24	16	212	225	69	58	3	3.61
Mal Eason	R	27	10	17	.370	1	34	26	18	227	212	74	64	3	3.25
Jesse Whiting	R	27	1	1	.500	0	3	2	2	25	26	6	1	0	2.88
Hub Knolls	R	22	0	0	—	0	2	1	0	13	12	3	3	0	3.86
Jack Doscher (JT)	R	25	0	0	.000	0	2	1	1	14	12	4	10	0	1.29
3 Chappie McFarland	R	31	0	1	.000	0	1	1	0	9	10	5	5	0	8.00

CINCINNATI 6th 64-87 .424 51.5 — NED HANLON

NAME	G by Pos	B	AGE	G	AB	R	H	2B	3B	HR	RBI	BB	SO	SB	BA	SA
TOTALS			29	155	5025	530	1198	140	71	16	454	395		170	.238	.304
Snake Deal	1B65	R	27	65	231	13	48	4	3	0	21	6		15	.208	.251
Miller Huggins	2B146	B	28	146	545	81	159	11	7	0	26	71		41	.292	.338
Tommy Corcoran	SS117	R	37	117	430	29	89	13	1	1	33	19		8	.207	.249
Jim Delahanty	3B105, SS5, OF2	R	27	115	379	63	106	21	4	1	39	45		21	.280	.364
Frank Jude	OF80	R	21	80	308	31	64	6	4	1	31	16		7	.208	.263
1 Cy Seymour	OF79	L	33	79	307	35	79	7	2	4	38	24		9	.257	.332
Joe Kelley	OF122, 1B3, 3B1	R	34	129	465	43	106	19	11	1	53	44		9	.228	.323
Admiral Schlei	C91, 1B21	R	28	116	388	44	95	13	8	4	54	29		7	.245	.351
Hans Lobert	3B35, SS31, 2B10, OF1	R	24	79	268	39	83	5	5	0	19	19		20	.310	.366
1 Shad Barry	1B43, OF30	R	27	73	279	38	80	10	5	1	33	26		11	.287	.369
2 Homer Smoot	OF59	L	28	60	220	11	57	8	1	1	17	13		0	.259	.318
Fred Odwell	OF57	R	33	58	202	20	45	5	4	0	21	15		11	.223	.287
Paddy Livingston	C47	R	26	50	139	8	22	1	4	0	8	12		0	.158	.223
Charlie Carr	1B22	R	29	22	94	9	18	2	3	0	10	2		0	.191	.277
Johnny Siegle (LJ)	OF21	R	31	22	68	4	8	2	2	0	7	3		0	.118	.206
Mike Mowrey	3B15, SS1, 2B1	R	22	21	53	3	17	3	0	0	6	5		2	.321	.377
Bill Hinchman	OF16	R	23	18	54	7	11	1	1	0	1	8		2	.204	.259
Larry McLean	C12	R	24	12	35	3	7	2	0	0	2	4		0	.200	.257
1 Eddie Phelps	C12	R	27	12	40	3	11	0	2	1	5	3		2	.275	.450
Jimmy Barrett	OF4	L	31	5	12	1	0	0	0	0	0	0		0	.000	.000
Eddie Tiemeyer	3B3 P1	R	21	5	11	3	2	0	0	0	0	0		1	.182	.182
Oscar Stanage	C1	R	23	1	1	0	0	0	0	0	0	0		0	.000	.000

ST. LOUIS 7th 52-98 .347 63 — JOHN McCLOSKEY

NAME	G by Pos	B	AGE	G	AB	R	H	2B	3B	HR	RBI	BB	SO	SB	BA	SA
TOTALS			29	154	5075	475	1195	137	69	10	362	361		110	.235	.296
Jake Beckley	1B85	L	38	87	320	29	79	16	6	0	44	13		3	.247	.334
Pug Bennett	2B153	R	32	153	595	66	156	16	7	1	34	56		20	.262	.318
George McBride	SS90	R	25	90	313	24	53	8	2	0	13	17		5	.169	.208
Harry Arndt	3B65, 1B1, OF1	R	27	69	256	30	69	7	9	2	26	19		5	.270	.391
Al Burch	OF91	L	22	91	335	40	89	5	1	0	11	37		15	.266	.287
1 Homer Smoot	OF86	L	28	86	343	41	85	9	10	0	31	11		3	.248	.332
1 Spike Shannon	OF80	R	28	80	302	36	78	4	0	0	25	36		15	.258	.272
Mike Grady	C60, 1B38	R	36	97	280	33	70	11	3	3	27	48		5	.250	.343
Hoelskoetter	3B53, SS16, P12, OF12, 2B1	R	23	94	317	21	71	6	3	0	14	4		2	.224	.262
2 Shad Barry	OF35, 1B21, 3B6	R	27	62	237	26	59	9	1	0	12	15		6	.249	.295
2 Sam Mertes	OF53	R	33	53	191	20	47	7	4	0	19	16		10	.246	.325
Red Murray	OF34, C7	R	22	46	144	18	37	9	7	1	16	9		5	.257	.438
Forrest Crawford	SS39, 3B6	L	25	45	144	8	30	3	1	0	11	7		1	.207	.241
2 Pete Noonan	C23, 1B16	R	24	44	125	8	21	1	3	1	9	11		1	.168	.248
Jack Himes	OF40	L	27	40	155	10	42	5	2	0	14	7		4	.271	.329
2 Doc Marshall	C38	R	31	39	123	6	34	4	1	0	10	6		1	.276	.325
Joe Marshall	OF23, 1B4	R	30	33	95	2	15	1	2	0	7	6		0	.158	.211
Tommy Raub	C22	R	35	24	78	9	22	2	4	0	2	4		2	.282	.410
Bill Phyle	3B21	R	31	22	73	6	13	3	1	0	5	3		0	.178	.247
Joe McCarthy	C15	R	24	15	37	3	9	2	0	0	2	2		0	.243	.297
Tom O'Hara	OF14	R	25	14	53	8	16	1	0	0	0	3		3	.302	.321
Eddie Holly	SS10	R	26	10	34	1	2	1	0	0	0	2		0	.059	.059

Ducky Holmes 22 R 5-27, Eddie Zimmerman 23 R 3-14, Jack Slattery 29 R 2-7, Rube DeGroff 26 L 0-4

BOSTON 8th 49-102 .325 66.5 — FRED TENNEY

NAME	G by Pos	B	AGE	G	AB	R	H	2B	3B	HR	RBI	BB	SO	SB	BA	SA
TOTALS			27	152	4925	408	1115	136	43	16	330	356		93	.226	.281
Fred Tenney	1B143	L	34	143	544	61	154	12	8	1	28	58		17	.283	.340
Allie Strobel	2B93, SS6, OF1	R	22	100	317	28	64	10	3	1	24	29		4	.202	.262
Al Bridwell	SS119, OF1	R	22	120	459	41	104	9	1	0	22	44		6	.227	.251
Dave Brain	3B139	R	27	139	525	43	131	19	5	5	45	29		11	.250	.333
Cozy Dolan	OF144, 2B7, P2, 1B1	L	33	152	549	54	136	20	4	0	39	55		17	.248	.299
Johnny Bates	OF140	R	24	140	504	52	127	21	5	6	54	36		9	.252	.349
Del Howard	OF87, 2B45, SS14, 1B2	L	28	147	545	46	142	19	8	1	54	26		17	.261	.330
Tom Needham	C76, 2B5, 1B2, 3B1, OF1	R	27	83	285	11	54	8	2	1	12	13		3	.189	.242
Sam Brown	C35, OF13, 3B12, 1B3, 2B2	R	28	71	231	12	48	6	1	0	20	13		4	.208	.242
Jack O'Neill	C48, 1B2, OF1	R	33	61	167	14	30	5	1	0	4	12		0	.180	.222
Big Jeff Pfeffer	P35, OF14	R	24	60	158	10	31	3	3	1	11	5		4	.196	.272
Gene Good (AJ)	OF34	R	22	34	119	4	18	0	0	0	0	13		0	.151	.151
Happy Jack Cameron	OF16, P2	R	21	18	61	3	11	0	0	0	1	3		0	.180	.180
Frank Connaughton	SS11, 2B1	R	37	12	44	3	9	0	0	0	1	1		1	.205	.205
Ches Spencer	OF8	R	23	8	27	1	4	1	0	0	0	0		0	.148	.185
Tommy Madden	OF4	L	22	4	15	1	4	0	0	0	0	0		0	.267	.267
Ernie Diehl	OF2, SS1	R	27	3	11	1	5	0	0	0	0	0		0	.455	.636
Jack Schulte	SS2	R	24	2	7	0	0	0	0	0	0	0		0	.000	.000

Ed Abbaticchio (HO) 29

Pitching

Cincinnati

NAME	T	AGE	W	L	PCT	SV	G	GS	CG	IP	H	BB	SO	SHO	ERA
		31	64	87	.424	5	155	155	126	1370	1248	470	567	11	2.69
Jake Weimer	L	32	20	14	.588	0	41	39	31	305	263	99	141	6	2.21
Bob Ewing	R	33	13	14	.481	0	33	32	26	288	248	60	145	2	2.37
Chick Fraser (HO)	R	32	10	20	.333	0	31	28	25	236	221	80	58	2	2.67
2 Bob Wicker	R	28	6	14	.300	0	20	17	14	150	150	46	69	0	2.70
Charley Hall	R	21	4	6	.400	0	9	7	5	95	86	50	49	1	3.32
1 Orvie Overall	R	25	3	5	.375	0	13	10	6	82	77	46	33	0	4.28
Bill Essick	R	25	2	1	.667	0	6	4	3	39	39	16	16	0	3.00
Carl Druhot	R	23	2	2	.500	0	4	3	3	25	27	7	14	0	4.32
1 Gus Dorner	R	29	1	1*	.500	0	2	1	1	15	16	4	5	0	1.20
Leo Hafford	R	22	1	1	.500	0	3	1	1	19	13	11	5	0	0.95
1 Jack Harper (RJ)	R	28	1	4	.200	1	11	5	6	66	59	24	17	0	2.32
Charlie Chech	R	28	1	4	.200	0	5	5	3	37	38	20	10	0	4.14
Eddie Tiemeyer	R	21	0	0	—	0	1	0	0	1	1	1	0	0	0.00
Del Mason	R	22	0	1	.000	0	2	1	1	12	10	6	4	0	4.50

* Dorner, also with Boston, league leader in L with 26

St. Louis

NAME	T	AGE	W	L	PCT	SV	G	GS	CG	IP	H	BB	SO	SHO	ERA
		26	52	98	.347	2	154	154	118	1354	1246	479	559	4	3.04
2 Fred Beebe	R	25	9	9	.500	0	20	19	16	161	115	68	116*	1	3.02
1 Jack Taylor	R	32	8	9	.471	0	17	17	15	133	147	27	51	2	2.15
Buster Brown	R	24	8	16	.333	0	32	24	17	238	208	112	109	0	2.65
2 Carl Druhot	L	23	6	7	.462	0	15	13	12	130	117	46	45	1	2.63
2 Ed Karger	L	23	5	16	.238	1	25	20	17	192	193	43	73	0	2.72
Charlie Rhodes	R	21	3	4	.429	0	9	6	3	45	37	20	32	0	3.40
1 Chappie McFarland	R	31	2	4	.667	—	7	4	3	37	33	8	16	0	1.95
Stony McGlynn	R	34	2	2	.500	0	6	6	6	48	45	15	25	0	2.44
Art Hoelskoetter	R	23	2	4	.333	0	12	3	2	58	53	34	20	0	4.66
Wish Egan	R	25	2	9	.182	0	16	12	7	86	97	27	23	0	4.60
Gus Thompson	R	29	2	11	.154	0	17	12	8	103	111	25	36	0	4.28
Ambrose Puttmann	L	25	1	2	.333	1	4	3	2	19	23	9	12	0	5.21
Art Fromme	R	22	1	2	.333	0	4	2	2	25	19	10	11	1	1.44
Irv Higginbotham	R	24	1	4	.200	0	7	4	4	47	50	11	14	0	3.26
Babe Adams	R	24	0	1	.000	0	3	1	1	6	5	2	1	0	13.50
Jake Thielman	R	27	0	0	—	0	1	0	0	5	5	2	0	0	3.60

* Beebe, also with Chicago, league leader in SO with 171

Boston

NAME	T	AGE	W	L	PCT	SV	G	GS	CG	IP	H	BB	SO	SHO	ERA
		27	49	102	.325	0	152	152	137	1318	1291	436	562	10	3.18
Irv Young	L	28	16	25	.390	0	43	41	37	358	349	83	151	4	2.92
Big Jeff Pfeffer	R	24	13	22	.371	0	35	36	35	302	270	114	158	4	2.95
Vive Lindaman	R	28	12	23	.343	0	39	36	32	307	303	90	115	2	2.43
2 Gus Dorner	R	29	8	25*	.242	0	34	32	29	257	264	103	104	0	3.89
Happy Jack Cameron	R	21	0	0	—	0	2	1	0	6	3	2	0	0	0.00
Bill McCarthy	R	24	0	0	—	0	1	0	0	2	3	0	0	0	9.00
Cozy Dolan	L	33	0	1	.000	0	2	1	1	12	6	7	0	0	4.50
Jim Moroney	L	22	0	3	.000	0	3	3	3	27	28	12	11	0	5.33
Roy Witherup	R	19	0	3	.000	0	6	3	3	46	59	19	14	0	6.26

* Dorner, also with Cincinnati, league leader in L with 26

WORLD SERIES — CHICAGO (AL) 4 CHICAGO (NL) 2

LINE SCORES

TEAM	1 2 3	4 5 6	7 8 9	10 11 12	R	H	E

Game 1 October 9 at West Side Park

TEAM	1 2 3	4 5 6	7 8 9	R	H	E
CHI(AL)	000	011	000	2	4	1
CHI(NL)	000	001	000	1	4	2

Altrock / Brown

Game 2 October 10 at Comiskey Park

TEAM	1 2 3	4 5 6	7 8 9	R	H	E
CHI(NL)	031	001	020	7	10	2
CHI(AL)	000	010	000	1	1	2

Reulbach / White, Owen (4)

Game 3 October 11 at West Side Park

TEAM	1 2 3	4 5 6	7 8 9	R	H	E
CHI(AL)	000	003	000	3	4	1
CHI(NL)	000	000	000	0	2	2

Walsh / Pfiester

Game 4 October 12 at Comiskey Park

TEAM	1 2 3	4 5 6	7 8 9	R	H	E
CHI(NL)	000	000	100	1	7	1
CHI(AL)	000	000	00X	0	2	1

Brown / Altrock

Game 5 October 13 at West Side Park

TEAM	1 2 3	4 5 6	7 8 9	R	H	E
CHI(AL)	102	401	000	8	12	6
CHI(NL)	300	102	000	6	6	0

Walsh, White (7) / Reulbach, Pfiester (3), Overall (4)

Game 6 October 14 at Comiskey Park

TEAM	1 2 3	4 5 6	7 8 9	R	H	E
CHI(NL)	100	010	000	3	7	0
CHI(AL)	340	000	01X	8	14	3

Brown, Overall (2) / White

COMPOSITE BATTING

NAME	POS	G	AB	R	H	2B	3B	HR	RBI	BA
Chicago (AL)										
Totals		6	187	22	37	10	3	0	19	.198
Isbell	2B	6	26	4	8	4	0	0	4	.308
Hahn	OF	6	22	4	6	0	0	0	0	.273
Rohe	3B	6	21	2	7	1	2	0	4	.333
Jones	OF	6	21	4	2	0	0	0	0	.095
Sullivan	C	6	21	0	0	0	0	0	0	.000
Dougherty	OF	6	20	1	2	0	0	0	1	.100
Donahue	1B	6	18	0	6	2	1	0	4	.333
Davis	SS	3	13	4	4	3	0	0	6	.308
Tannehill	SS	3	9	1	1	0	0	0	0	.111
Altrock	P	2	4	0	1	0	0	0	0	.250
Walsh	P	2	4	1	0	0	0	0	0	.000
White	P	3	4	0	1	0	0	0	0	.250
Owen	P	1	2	0	0	0	0	0	0	.000
McFarland	PH	1	1	0	0	0	0	0	0	.000
O'Neill	OF	1	1	0	0	0	0	0	0	.000
Towne	PH	1	1	0	0	0	0	0	0	.000
Chicago (NL)										
Totals		6	184	18	36	9	0	0	11	.196
Schulte	OF	6	26	1	7	3	0	0	3	.269
Hofman	OF	6	23	3	7	1	0	0	2	.304
Chance	1B	6	21	5	5	1	0	0	2	.238
Sheckard	OF	6	21	0	0	0	0	0	0	.000
Steinfeldt	3B	6	20	2	5	0	0	0	2	.250
Evers	2B	6	20	2	3	1	0	0	1	.150
Tinker	SS	6	18	4	3	0	0	0	1	.167
Kling	C	6	17	2	3	1	0	0	0	.176
Brown	P	3	6	0	2	0	0	0	0	.333
Overall	P	2	4	1	1	0	0	0	0	.250
Reulbach	P	2	3	0	0	0	0	0	0	.000
Moran	PH	2	2	0	0	0	0	0	0	.000
Pfiester	P	2	2	0	0	0	0	0	0	.000
Gessler	PH	2	1	0	0	0	0	0	0	.000

COMPOSITE PITCHING

NAME	G	IP	H	BB	SO	W	L	SV	ERA
Chicago (AL)									
	6	54	36	18	28	4	2	1	1.50
Altrock	2	18	11	2	5	1	1	0	1.00
Walsh	2	15	7	6	17	2	0	0	1.20
White	3	15	12	7	4	1	1	1	1.80
Owen	1	6	6	3	2	0	0	0	3.00
Chicago (NL)									
	6	53	37	18	35	2	4	0	3.40
Brown	3	19.2	14	4	12	1	2	0	3.20
Overall	2	12	10	3	8	0	0	0	2.25
Reulbach	2	11	6	8	4	1	0	0	2.45
Pfiester	2	10.1	7	3	11	0	2	0	6.10

1907 — A Peach in the Summer and a Goat in the Fall

The city of Detroit got its start in professional baseball in 1881 as tenants of the National League. The franchise lasted until 1888, a year after the club captured its only pennant. It was not until 1901 that Detroit got another team - this time, as members of the newly established American League. The best the Tigers could do in those six years were two third-place berths. Previously, the championship had been confined to the cities of Chicago, Philadelphia, and Boston. Yet, before the season would be officially closed, the territorial pennant map would see expansion into the future motor city of the world.

One of the key figures in Detroit's new destiny was long-time National Leaguer Hughie Jennings, who took over the reins of the Tigers in the spring and guided them into the hallowed turf of the championship in his first try as manager. Under Jennings' hand, the league watched in surprise as the 1906 sixth-place Tigers rose to the top like cream - a major reason being the maturing of young outfielder Ty Cobb into a star of commanding presence on the field. The 20-year-old Georgia Peach, in his third year with the Tigers, blossomed into a batting terror by socking the ball at a .350 clip to win his first batting championship. The pugnacious right fielder rang fear into the hearts of infielders just as much as pitchers with his league-leading 49 stolen bases, achieved mostly via a style of sliding in high with razor-honed spikes.

With Cobb batting cleanup, Sam Crawford saw enough good pitches in the third slot to bat a rousing .323 - enough to place him second in the league behind Cobb. The duo helped make the Tigers' attack the best in the league, even though the entire team belted only 11 home runs - a credible amount considering it was the era of the dead ball. Veteran Wild Bill Donovan and lefty Ed Killian each won 25 games for the Tigers, while George Mullin chalked up 20 wins but only broke even, as he lost 20 games in a workhorse season of 357 innings.

In reaching for the first American League pennant, Detroit did not have an easy time of it. As of late September, the Tigers were fighting for the flag with Philadelphia, Chicago, and Cleveland, with the issue finally coming down to a crucial series with Philadelphia. On September 27 they knocked off the A's to take over the lead. In the second game of the set, the two nines battled to a 17-inning draw, enabling Detroit to leave with a slim edge which they never relinquished. The late season slump of Rube Waddell, and Chief Bender's sore arm, severely hurt the chances of Philadelphia in the final decisive weeks. Chicago held the best hand of hurlers, aced by 27-game winner Doc White and 24-game winner Ed Walsh but, this time, could not overcome the lack of batting punch in the lineup, while Cleveland could not quite make up for Nap Lajoie's .299 batting average - the worst in his 12-year career.

The National League witnessed the "collapse" of the Cubs to 107 wins, nine less than the previous year but still enough for a 17-game margin over the runner-up Pirates. While four teams threatened in the junior loop, all hands conceded the senior circuit crown to Chicago early in the summer. The heart of the Cubs could be found in the infield in playing-manager Frank Chance, Johnny Evers, Joe Tinker, and forgotten-man Harry Steinfeldt, who covered the diamond with an airtight blanket which smothered many an opponents' rally. In addition to their defensive play Chance and Steinfeldt also supplied the team's offensive power.

The Cubs' pitching department was headed by Orvie Overall, who proved the winningest of five solid starters in a complement which included Three Finger Brown, Carl Lundgren, Jack Pfiester, and Ed Reulbach.

For the second year in a row, the Cubs were favored to win the Series. This time they did not fail, taking four straight from Detroit after an opening game tie called because of darkness. Pfiester, Reulbach, Overall, and Brown all turned in complete game victories in holding the Tigers to only six runs in the five-game set - a pitching success summed up in Crawford's .238 batting average and Cobb's weak .200 mark.

Coupled with the pitching corps spectacular 0.75 E.R.A., was Chicago's superb running game. Led by Jimmy Slagle's six thefts, the Cubs racked up a Series record 18 steals. Slagle, who only managed 28 steals during the regular season, also knocked in four runs - the most RBI's in the Series - and provided the go-ahead run in the Cub's first victory. Steinfeldt's .471 and Ever's .350 hitting, which led the Cubs offense, also aided in bringing Chicago its first world's title.

A tragic footnote to the season occurred in spring training when Chick Stahl, the playing manager of the American League Boston club, violently ended his life on March 28, by drinking carbolic acid. Although it was known that Stahl, only 34, was despondent, the reason for his suicide was never learned.

1907 AMERICAN LEAGUE

NAME	G by Pos	B	AGE	G	AB	R	H	2B	3B	HR	RBI	BB	SO	SB	BA	SA
DETROIT 1st 92-58 .613		HUGHIE JENNINGS														
TOTALS			26	153	5201	696	1382	179	75	11	551	315		192	.266	.335
Claude Rossman	1B153	L	26	153	571	60	158	21	8	0	69	33		20	.277	.342
Red Downs	2B80, OF20, SS1, 3B1	R	23	105	374	28	82	13	5	1	42	13		3	.219	.289
Charley O'Leary	SS138	R	24	139	465	61	112	19	1	0	34	32		11	.241	.286
Bill Coughlin	3B133	R	28	134	519	80	126	10	2	0	46	35		15	.243	.270
Ty Cobb	OF150	L	20	150	605	97	212	29	15	5	119	24		49	.350	.473
Sam Crawford	OF144, 1B2	L	27	144	582	102	188	34	17	4	81	37		18	.323	.460
Davy Jones	OF126	L	27	126	491	101	134	10	6	0	27	60		30	.273	.318
Boss Schmidt	C103	B	26	104	349	32	85	6	6	0	23	5		8	.244	.295
G. Schaefer	2B74, SS18, 3B14, OF1	R	30	109	372	45	96	12	3	1	32	30		21	.258	.315
George Mullin	P46, 1B1	R	26	70	157	16	34	5	3	0	13	12		2	.217	.287
Freddie Payne	C46, OF5	R	26	53	169	17	28	2	2	0	14	7		4	.166	.201
Ed Killian	P41, OF2, 1B1	L	30	46	122	16	39	5	3	0	11	4		3	.320	.410
Matty McIntyre	OF20	L	27	20	81	6	23	1	1	0	9	7		3	.284	.321
Jimmy Archer	C17, 2B1	R	24	18	42	6	5	0	0	0	0	2		0	.119	.119
Bobby Lowe	3B10, OF4, SS2	R	38	17	37	2	9	2	0	0	5	4		2	.243	.297
Tex Erwin	C4	L	21	4	5	0	1	0	0	0	1	1		1	.200	.200
Hughie Jennings	2B1, SS1	R	38	1	4	0	1	1	0	0	0	0		0	.250	.500
Red Killefer	OF1	R	22	1	4	0	0	0	0	0	0	0		0	.000	.000

NAME	T	AGE	W	L	PCT	SV	G	GS	CG	IP	H	BB	SO	SHO	ERA
TOTALS		30	92	58	.613	6	153	153	120	1371	1281	380	512	15	2.33
Wild Bill Donovan	R	30	25	4	.862	1	32	28	27	271	222	82	123	3	2.19
Ed Killian	L	30	25	13	.658	0	41	34	29	314	286	91	96	3	1.78
George Mullin	R	26	20	20	.500	3	46	42	35	357	346	106	146	5	2.60
Ed Siever	L	32	19	10	.655	1	39	33	22	275	256	52	88	3	2.16
John Eubank	R	34	2	3	.400	1	15	8	4	81	88	20	17	1	2.67
Ed Willett	R	23	1	5	.167	0	10	6	1	49	47	20	27	0	3.67
Herm Malloy	R	22	0	1	.000	0	1	1	1	8	13	5	6	0	5.63
Elijah Jones	R	25	0	2	.000	1	4	1	1	16	23	4	9	0	5.06

NAME	G by Pos	B	AGE	G	AB	R	H	2B	3B	HR	RBI	BB	SO	SB	BA	SA
PHILADELPHIA 2nd 88-57 .607 1.5		CONNIE MACK														
TOTALS			31	150	5002	582	1277	220	45	22	485	384		138	.255	.330
Harry Davis	1B149	R	33	149	582	84	155	37	8	8	87	42		20	.266	.399
Danny Murphy	2B122	R	24	124	469	51	127	23	3	2	57	30		11	.271	.345
Simon Nicholls	SS82, 2B28, 3B13	R	24	126	460	75	139	12	2	0	23	24		13	.302	.337
2 Jimmy Collins	3B100	R	37	102	372	39	102	22	1	0	35	24		4	.274	.339
Socks Seybold	OF147	R	36	147	564	58	153	29	4	5	92	40		10	.271	.363
Rube Oldring	OF117	R	23	117	441	48	126	27	8	1	40	7		29	.286	.390
Topsy Hartsel	OF143	L	33	143	507	93	142	23	6	3	29	106		26	.280	.367
Ossee Schreckengost	C99, 1B2	R	32	101	356	30	97	16	3	0	38	17		4	.272	.334
Monte Cross	SS74	R	37	77	248	37	51	9	5	0	18	39		17	.206	.282
Mike Powers	C59	R	36	59	159	9	29	3	0	0	9	7		1	.182	.201
Bris Lord	OF53, P1	R	23	57	170	12	31	3	0	1	11	14		2	.182	.218
1 Jack Knight	3B38	R	21	38	130	9	29	7	1	0	12	10		1	.223	.292
Eddie Collins	SS6	R	20	14	23	0	6	0	1	0	2	0		0	.261	.348
Claude Berry	C8	R	27	8	19	2	4	2	0	0	1	2		2	.211	.316

NAME	T	AGE	W	L	PCT	SV	G	GS	CG	IP	H	BB	SO	SHO	ERA
TOTALS		26	88	57	.607	7	150	150	106	1354	1106	378	789	27	2.35
Eddie Plank	L	31	24	16	.600	0	43	40	33	344	282	85	183	8	2.20
Jimmy Dygert	R	22	20	9	.690	2	42	28	18	262	200	85	151	5	2.34
Rube Waddell	L	30	19	13	.594	0	44	33	20	285	234	73	232	7	2.15
Chief Bender	R	24	16	8	.667	3	33	24	20	219	185	34	112	4	2.05
Jack Coombs (AJ)	R	24	6	9	.400	2	23	17	10	133	109	64	73	2	3.00
Rube Vickers	R	29	2	2	.500	0	10	4	3	50	44	12	21	1	3.42
Charlie Fritz	L	25	1	0	1.000	0	1	1	0	3	0	1	3	0	0.00
George Craig	L	19	0	0	—	0	2	0	0	2	2	3	0	0	9.00
Sam Hope	R	28	0	0	—	0	1	0	0	1	3	0	0	0	9.00
Bris Lord	R	23	0	0	—	0	1	0	0	1	3	0	0	0	0.00
Bill Bartley	R	22	0	2	.000	0	15	3	2	56	44	19	16	0	2.25

NAME	G by Pos	B	AGE	G	AB	R	H	2B	3B	HR	RBI	BB	SO	SB	BA	SA
CHICAGO 3rd 87-64 .576 5.5		FIELDER JONES														
TOTALS			32	157	5079	584	1205	147	34	5	474	421		175	.237	.283
Jiggs Donahue	1B157	L	27	157	609	75	158	16	5	0	68	28		27	.259	.302
Frank Isbell	2B119, OF5, SS1, P1	L	31	125	486	60	118	19	7	0	41	22		22	.243	.311
George Davis	SS131	B	36	132	466	59	111	18	2	1	52	47		15	.238	.292
George Rohe	3B76, 2B39, SS30	R	31	144	494	46	105	11	2	0	51	39		16	.213	.255
Eddie Hahn	OF156	L	31	156	592	87	151	9	7	0	45	84		17	.255	.294
Fielder Jones	OF154	L	35	154	559	72	146	18	1	0	47	67		17	.261	.297
Patsy Dougherty	OF148	L	30	148	533	69	144	17	2	1	59	36		33	.270	.315
Billy Sullivan	C108, 2B1	R	32	112	339	30	59	8	4	0	36	21		6	.174	.221
Ed McFarland	C43	R	32	52	138	11	39	9	1	0	8	12		3	.283	.362
Lee Quillin	3B48	R	25	49	151	17	29	5	0	0	14	10		8	.192	.225
Lee Tannehill (NJ)	3B31, SS2	R	26	33	108	9	26	2	0	0	11	8		3	.241	.259
Hub Hart	C25	L	29	29	70	6	19	1	0	0	7	5		1	.271	.286
Mike Welday	OF15	L	28	35	35	8	8	1	1	0	0	6		0	.229	.314
2 Charley Hickman	OF3	R	31	21	23	1	6	2	0	0	1	4		0	.261	.348
Jake Atz	3B2	R	28	3	7	0	1	0	0	0	0	0		0	.143	.143
2 Charley Armbruster	C1	R	26	1	3	0	0	0	0	0	0	1		0	.000	.000

NAME	T	AGE	W	L	PCT	SV	G	GS	CG	IP	H	BB	SO	SHO	ERA
TOTALS		28	87	64	.576	7	157	157	112	1406	1279	305	604	17	2.22
Doc White	L	27	27	13	.675	2	46	35	24	291	270	38	141	6	2.26
Ed Walsh	R	26	24	18	.571	2	56	46	37	422	341	87	206	5	1.60
Frank Smith	R	27	22	11	.667	0	41	37	29	310	280	111	139	3	2.47
Nick Altrock	L	30	8	12	.400	1	30	21	15	214	210	31	61	1	2.57
Roy Patterson	R	30	4	6	.400	0	19	13	4	96	105	18	27	1	2.63
Frank Owen	R	27	2	3	.400	0	11	4	2	47	43	13	15	0	2.49
Frank Isbell	R	31	0	0	—	1	1	0	0	1	0	0	0	0	0.00
Lou Fiene	R	22	0	1	.000	1	1	1	1	26	30	7	15	0	4.15

CLEVELAND — 4th 85-67 .559 8 — NAP LAJOIE

NAME	G by Pos	B	AGE	G	AB	R	H	2B	3B	HR	RBI	BB	SO	SB	BA	SA
TOTALS			28	158	5068	528	1221	182	68	11	433	335		193	.241	.310
George Stovall	1B122, 3B2	R	29	124	466	38	110	18	7	1	36	18		13	.230	.311
Nap Lajoie	2B128, 1B9	R	32	137	509	53	153	32	6	2	63	30		24	.301	.397
Terry Turner	SS145	R	26	148	524	57	127	20	7	0	46	19		27	.242	.307
Bill Bradley	3B139	R	29	139	498	48	111	20	1	0	34	35		20	.223	.267
Elmer Flick	OF147	L	31	147	549	78	166	17	18	3	58	64		41	.302	.415
Joe Birmingham	OF134, SS3	R	22	138	476	55	112	10	10	1	33	16		22	.235	.305
Bill Hinchman	OF150, 1B4, 2B1	R	24	152	514	62	117	19	9	1	50	47		15	.228	.305
Nig Clarke	C115	L	24	120	390	44	105	19	6	3	33	35		3	.269	.372
Harry Bemis	C51, 1B2	R	33	65	172	12	43	7	0	0	19	7		5	.250	.291
1 Pete O'Brien	2B17, 3B14, SS9	L	30	43	145	9	33	5	2	0	6	7		1	.228	.290
Harry Bay (KJ)	OF31	L	29	34	95	14	17	1	1	0	7	10		7	.179	.211
Howard Wakefield	C11	R	23	26	37	4	5	2	0	0	3	4		0	.135	.189
Pete Lister	1B22	R	25	22	65	5	18	2	0	0	4	3		2	.277	.308
Frank Delahanty	OF15	R	24	15	52	3	9	0	1	0	4	4		2	.173	.212
Harry Hinchman	2B15	B	28	15	51	3	11	3	1	0	9	5		2	.216	.314
2 Rabbit Nill	3B9, SS2	R	25	12	43	5	12	1	0	0	2	3		2	.279	.302
1 Bunk Congalton	OF6	R	32	9	22	2	4	0	0	0	2	4		0	.182	.182

NAME	T	AGE	W	L	PCT	SV	G	GS	CG	IP	H	BB	SO	SHO	ERA
TOTALS		27	85	67	.559	5	158	158	127	1393	1253	362	513	20	2.26
Addie Joss	R	27	27	11	.711	2	42	38	34	339	279	54	127	6	1.83
Glenn Liebhardt	R	24	18	14	.563	1	38	34	27	280	254	85	110	4	2.06
Bob Rhoades	R	27	15	14	.517	1	35	31	23	275	258	84	76	5	2.29
Jake Thielman	R	28	11	8	.579	0	20	18	18	166	151	34	56	3	2.33
Otto Hess (LJ)	L	28	6	6	.500	1	17	14	7	93	84	37	36	0	2.90
2 Walter Clarkson (JJ)	R	28	4	6	.400	0	9	9	7	91	77	29	32	1	1.98
Heinie Berger	R	25	3	3	.500	0	14	7	5	87	74	20	50	1	3.00
1 Earl Moore	R	27	1	1	.500	0	3	2	1	19	18	8	7	0	4.74
Bill Bernhard	R	36	0	4	.000	0	8	4	3	42	58	11	19	0	3.21

NEW YORK — 5th 70-78 .473 21 — CLARK GRIFFITH

NAME	G by Pos	B	AGE	G	AB	R	H	2B	3B	HR	RBI	BB	SO	SB	BA	SA
TOTALS			28	152	5042	604	1257	150	68	15	497	304		206	.250	.315
Hal Chase	1B121, OF4	R	24	125	498	58	138	23	3	2	68	19		32	.287	.357
Jimmy Williams	2B139	R	32	139	504	53	136	17	11	2	63	39		14	.270	.359
Kid Elberfeld	SS118	R	32	120	447	61	121	16	7	0	51	36		22	.271	.336
G. Moriarty	3B91, 1B22, OF9, 2B8, SS1	R	23	126	437	51	121	16	5	0	43	25		28	.277	.338
Willie Keeler	OF107	L	35	107	423	50	99	6	5	0	17	15		7	.234	.272
Danny Hoffman	OF135	L	27	136	517	81	131	10	4	5	46	42		30	.253	.317
Wid Conroy	OF100, SS38	R	30	140	530	58	124	12	11	3	51	30		41	.234	.315
Red Kleinow	C86, 1B1	R	29	90	269	30	71	6	4	0	26	24		5	.264	.316
Frank LaPorte	3B64, OF63, 1B1	R	27	130	470	56	127	20	11	0	48	27		10	.270	.360
Ira Thomas	C66, 1B2	R	26	80	208	20	40	5	4	1	24	10		5	.192	.269
Branch Rickey	OF22, C11, 1B9	L	25	52	137	16	35	1	3	0	15	11		4	.182	.234
Al Orth	P36, OF1	R	34	44	105	11	34	6	0	1	13	4		1	.324	.410
Jack Bell	OF17	R	26	17	52	4	11	2	1	0	3	3		4	.212	.288
Neal Nall	SS11, 2B5	R	26	15	44	5	9	1	1	0	4	1		1	.205	.273
Walter Blair	C7	R	23	7	22	1	4	0	0	0	1	2		0	.182	.182
Baldy Louden	3B3	R	23	4	9	4	1	0	0	0	0	0		0	.111	.111
1 Deacon McGuire	C1	R	43	1	1	0	0	0	0	0	0	0		0	.000	.000

NAME	T	AGE	W	L	PCT	SV	G	GS	CG	IP	H	BB	SO	SHO	ERA
TOTALS		29	70	78	.473	7	152	152	93	1334	1327	428	511	10	3.03
Al Orth	R	34	14	21	.400	1	36	33	21	249	244	53	78	2	2.60
Bill Hogg	R	25	11	8	.579	2	25	21	13	167	173	83	64	0	3.07
Slow Joe Doyle	R	25	11	11	.500	1	29	23	15	194	169	67	94	1	2.64
Jack Chesbro (NJ)	R	33	9	10	.474	0	30	25	17	206	192	46	78	1	2.53
Doc Newton	L	29	7	10	.412	0	19	15	10	133	132	31	70	0	3.18
Tex Neuer	L	30	4	2	.667	0	7	6	6	54	40	19	22	3	2.17
Bobby Keefe	R	25	4	2	.667	2	19	3	0	58	60	20	20	0	2.48
2 Frank Kitson	R	35	3	1	.750	1	12	4	3	61	75	17	14	0	3.10
Tom Hughes	R	23	2	1	.667	0	4	3	2	27	16	11	10	0	2.67
2 Earl Moore	R	28	2	6	.250	1	12	9	3	64	72	30	28	0	3.94
1 Walter Clarkson	L	28	1	1	.500	1	5	2	0	17	19	8	3	0	6.35
Roy Castleton	L	21	1	1	.500	0	3	2	1	16	11	3	3	0	2.81
Lew Brockett	R	26	1	3	.250	0	8	4	1	46	58	26	13	0	6.26
Cy Barger	R	22	0	0	—	0	1	0	0	6	10	1	0	0	3.00
Clark Griffith	R	37	0	0	—	0	4	0	0	8	15	6	5	0	9.00
Ray Fisher	L	23	0	0	—	1	1	1	1	19	33	4	6	0	4.74
Rube Manning	R	24	0	1	.000	0	1	1	1	9	9	7	3	0	3.00

ST. LOUIS — 6th 69-83 .454 24 — JIMMY McALEER

NAME	G by Pos	B	AGE	G	AB	R	H	2B	3B	HR	RBI	BB	SO	SB	BA	SA
TOTALS			29	155	5224	538	1324	154	64	9	433	370		144	.253	.313
Tom Jones	1B155	R	30	155	549	53	137	17	3	0	34	34		24	.250	.291
Harry Niles	2B116, OF1	R	26	120	492	65	142	9	5	2	35	28		19	.289	.339
Bobby Wallace	SS147	R	33	147	538	56	138	19	7	0	70	54		16	.257	.318
Joe Yeager	3B92, 2B17, SS10	R	31	123	436	32	104	21	7	1	44	31		15	.239	.326
Ollie Pickering	OF150	L	31	151	576	63	159	15	10	0	60	35		15	.276	.337
Charlie Hemphill	OF153	L	31	153	603	66	156	20	9	0	38	51		14	.259	.322
George Stone	OF155	L	30	155	596	77	191	14	13	4	59	59		23	.320	.408
Tubby Spencer	C63	R	22	71	230	27	61	11	1	1	25	7		1	.265	.335
Roy Hartzell	3B38, 2B15, SS2, OF2	R	25	60	220	20	52	3	5	0	13	11		7	.236	.295
Jim Stephens	C56	R	23	58	173	15	35	6	3	0	11	15		3	.202	.272
1 Jim Delahanty	3B21, OF4, 2B2	R	31	33	95	8	21	3	0	0	6	5		6	.221	.253
Fritz Buelow	C25	R	31	26	75	9	11	1	0	0	1	7		0	.147	.160
Jack O'Connor	C25	R	38	25	89	2	14	2	0	0	4	0		0	.157	.180
Kid Butler	2B11, 3B5, SS1	R	19	20	59	4	13	2	0	0	6	2		1	.220	.254
Emil Frisk		L	32	4	4	0	1	0	0	0	0	1		0	.250	.250
Jimmy McAleer		R	42	0	0	0	0	0	0	0	0	0		0	.000	.000
Snags Heidrick (VR)			30													

NAME	T	AGE	W	L	PCT	SV	G	GS	CG	IP	H	BB	SO	SHO	ERA
TOTALS		30	69	83	.454	8	155	155	129	1381	1254	352	463	15	2.61
Harry Howell	R	30	16	15	.516	3	42	35	26	316	258	88	118	2	1.94
Jack Powell	R	37	14	16	.467	0	32	31	27	256	229	62	96	4	2.67
Fred Glade	R	31	13	9	.591	0	24	22	18	202	187	45	71	2	2.67
Barney Pelty	R	26	12	21	.364	1	36	34	29	273	234	64	85	5	2.57
2 Bill Dinneen	R	31	7	11	.389	4	24	16	15	155	153	33	38	2	2.44
Bill Bailey	L	19	4	1	.800	0	6	5	3	48	39	15	17	0	2.44
Billy McGill	R	27	1	0	1.000	0	2	2	1	18	22	2	8	0	3.50
1 Cy Morgan	R	28	1	5	.167	0	10	6	4	55	77	17	14	0	6.05
1 Beany Jacobson	L	26	1	5	.167	0	7	6	5	57	55	26	16	0	3.00

BOSTON — 7th 59-90 .396 32.5 — CY YOUNG 3-3 .500 GEORGE HUFF 2-6 .250 BOB UNGLAUB 9-20 .310 DEACON McGUIRE 45-61 .425

NAME	G by Pos	B	AGE	G	AB	R	H	2B	3B	HR	RBI	BB	SO	SB	BA	SA
TOTALS			30	155	5238	466	1223	155	48	18	405	305		124	.234	.292
Bob Unglaub	1B139	R	25	139	544	49	138	17	13	1	62	23		14	.254	.338
Hobe Ferris	2B150	R	29	150	561	41	135	25	2	4	60	10		11	.241	.314
Heinie Wagner (JJ)	SS109, 2B1, 3B1	R	26	131	385	29	82	10	4	2	21	31		20	.213	.275
2 Jack Knight	3B96, SS4	R	21	100	369	28	78	9	3	2	29	19		8	.211	.268
2 Bunk Congalton	OF126	L	32	127	496	44	142	11	8	2	47	20		13	.286	.353
Denny Sullivan	OF143	L	24	144	551	73	135	18	0	1	26	44		16	.245	.283
Jimmy Barrett (KJ)	OF99	L	32	106	390	52	95	11	6	1	28	38		3	.244	.310
Lou Criger	C75	R	35	75	226	12	41	4	0	0	14	19		2	.181	.199
Freddy Parent	OF47, SS43, 3B7, 2B5	R	31	114	409	51	113	19	5	1	26	22		12	.276	.355
Al Shaw	C73, 1B1	R	32	76	198	10	38	1	3	0	7	18		4	.192	.227
Moose Grimshaw	OF23, 1B15, SS2	R	31	64	181	19	37	7	2	0	33	16		6	.204	.265
1 Jimmy Collins	3B39	R	37	39	151	12	44	7	0	0	10	10		4	.291	.338
Jack Hoey	OF21	L	25	39	96	7	21	2	1	0	8	1		2	.219	.260
1 Charles Armbruster	C21	R	26	23	60	2	6	1	0	0	0	8		1	.100	.117
Chet Chadbourne	OF10	L	22	10	31	1	4	0	0	0	3	7		1	.129	.129
Harry Lord	3B10	R	25	10	38	4	6	1	0	0	3	1		1	.158	.184
Tris Speaker	OF4	L	19	7	19	0	3	0	0	0	1	1		0	.158	.158
2 Deacon McGuire	C2	R	43	6	4	1	3	0	0	1	0	0		0	.750	1.500
Buck Freeman	OF3	L	35	6	12	1	2	0	0	0	2	3		0	.167	.417
Bob Peterson	C4	R	23	4	13	1	1	0	0	0	0	0		0	.077	.077
George Whiteman	OF2	R	24	3	11	0	2	0	0	0	1	0		0	.182	.182
Chick Stahl (DD)			34													

NAME	T	AGE	W	L	PCT	SV	G	GS	CG	IP	H	BB	SO	SHO	ERA
TOTALS		30	59	90	.396	8	155	155	100	1414	1222	337	517	17	2.45
Cy Young	R	40	22	15	.595	3	43	37	33	343	286	51	147	6	1.99
George Winter	R	29	9	13	.407	1	35	27	21	257	198	61	88	4	2.07
Ralph Glaze	R	26	9	13	.409	0	32	21	11	182	150	48	68	1	2.32
2 Cy Morgan	R	28	7	6	.538	0	16	13	9	114	77	34	50	2	1.97
Jesse Tannehill	L	32	6	7	.462	1	18	16	10	131	131	20	29	2	2.47
Tex Pruiett	R	24	3	11	.214	3	35	17	6	174	166	59	54	2	3.10
1 Frank Oberlin	R	31	1	4	.200	0	12	4	2	46	48	24	18	0	4.30
2 Beany Jacobson	L	26	1	0	.000	0	2	1	0	9	13	6	1	0	9.00
Ed Barry	L	25	0	1	.000	0	2	2	2	19	12	6	2	0	2.12
Fred Burchell	L	27	0	0	—	0	1	0	0	8	4	2	3	0	2.70
Elmer Steele	R	23	0	1	.000	0	1	1	1	11	11	1	10	0	1.64
1 Bill Dinneen	R	31	0	4	.000	0	5	5	3	33	42	11	8	0	5.18
Rube Kroh	L	20	0	1	.000	0	1	1	1	34	33	8	8	0	2.65
Joe Harris	R	25	0	7	.000	0	12	7	5	59	57	13	24	0	3.05

WASHINGTON — 8th 49-102 .325 43.5 — JOE CANTILLON

NAME	G by Pos	B	AGE	G	AB	R	H	2B	3B	HR	RBI	BB	SO	SB	BA	SA
TOTALS			30	154	5105	505	1243	137	57	12	414	390		223	.243	.300
John Anderson	1B61, OF26	B	33	87	333	33	96	12	4	0	44	34		19	.288	.348
2 Jim Delahanty	2B68, 3B27, OF9, 1B4	R	30	109	404	44	118	18	7	2	54	36		18	.292	.386
Dave Altizer	SS71, 1B50, OF26	L	30	147	540	60	145	15	5	2	42	34		38	.269	.326
Bill Shipke	3B63	R	24	64	189	17	37	3	2	1	9	15		6	.196	.249
Bob Ganley	OF154	L	32	154	605	73	167	10	5	1	35	54		40	.276	.314
Charlie Jones	OF111, 2B5, 1B4, SS2	R	31	121	437	48	116	14	10	0	37	22		26	.265	.343
2 Otis Clymer (NJ)	OF51, 1B5	L	25	63	206	30	65	5	5	1	16	18		18	.316	.403
Jack Warner (RJ)	C64	L	34	72	207	11	53	5	0	0	17	12		3	.256	.280
1 Rabbit Nill	3B32, OF25, 3B1	R	25	66	215	21	47	7	3	0	25	15		6	.219	.279
Mike Heydon	C57	R	32	62	104	14	30	3	0	0	9	25		3	.183	.201
1 Charley Hickman	1B30, OF18, 2B3, P1	R	31	60	198	20	55	9	4	1	23	14		4	.278	.379
Tony Smith	SS51	L	23	51	189	12	26	1	1	0	8	18		3	.187	.209
Clyde Milan	OF47	R	21	48	183	22	51	3	3	0	9	8		8	.279	.328
Nig Perrine	2B24, SS18, OF1	R	22	44	161	13	29	1	1	0	15	13		10	.171	.212
Lave Cross	3B41	R	41	41	161	13	34	8	0	0	10	10		1	.199	.248
2 Pete O'Brien	3B26, SS13, 2B1	L	30	39	154	13	32	5	0	0	12	12		4	.187	.224
Cliff Blankenship (BG)	C22, 1B9	R	27	37	102	6	23	2	0	0	6	3		3	.225	.245
Bill Kay	OF12	L	25	12	30	3	10	0	0	0	7	0		0	.333	.383
Bruno Block	C21	R	22	24	57	3	8	1	0	0	4	5		0	.140	.211
Larry Schlafly	2B24	R	29	24	96	7	13	2	0	0	4	22		7	.135	.176
2 Mike Kahoe	C15	R	33	17	47	3	9	2	0	0	1	0		0	.191	.213
Owen Shannon	C4	R	27	4	7	0	1	0	0	0	0	0		0	.143	.143

NAME	T	AGE	W	L	PCT	SV	G	GS	CG	IP	H	BB	SO	SHO	ERA
TOTALS		28	49	102	.325	4	154	154	106	1352	1381	341	570	12	3.11
Casey Patten	L	33	12	17	.414	0	36	29	20	237	272	63	58	1	3.57
Charlie Smith	R	27	9	20	.310	0	36	31	21	259	254	51	119	3	2.61
Long Tom Hughes	R	28	8	13	.381	3	34	23	18	211	206	47	102	3	3.11
Walter Johnson	R	19	5	9	.357	0	14	12	11	111	98	17	71	2	1.88
Cy Falkenberg	R	27	6	18	.250	1	32	24	17	234	195	77	108	1	2.35
Oscar Graham	R	28	4	10	.286	0	20	14	6	104	116	29	44	0	3.98
Henry Gehring	R	26	3	7	.300	0	15	8	7	87	92	14	31	2	3.31
2 Frank Oberlin	R	31	2	7	.222	0	11	8	3	49	57	12	18	0	4.59
Bull Durham	R	30	0	0	—	0	1	0	0	2	5	2	1	0	12.60
Sam Edmonston	L	23	0	0	—	0	4	1	0	10	4	1	0	0	9.00
1 Charley Hickman	R	31	0	0	—	0	3	2	0	11	13	3	2	0	3.60
Sam Lanford	R	21	0	1	.000	0	1	1	0	6	12	5	4	0	5.14
John McDonald	R	21	0	0	—	0	2	1	0	12	15	3	2	0	9.00
Doc Tonkin	L	25	0	0	—	0	2	1	1	12	15	6	6	0	6.00
1 Frank Kitson	R	35	0	0	.000	0	3	2	1	32	41	9	11	0	3.94

NAME	G by Pos	B	AGE	G	AB	R	H	2B	3B	HR	RBI	BB	SO	SB	BA	SA

CHICAGO 1st 107-45 .704 FRANK CHANCE

	TOTALS		28	156	4892	571	1224	162	48	13	450	435		235	.250	.311
Frank Chance	1B109	R	30	111	382	58	112	19	2	1	50	51		35	.293	.361
Johnny Evers	2B151	L	25	151	508	66	127	18	4	2	51	39		46	.250	.313
Joe Tinker	SS113	R	26	117	402	36	89	11	3	1	36	25		20	.221	.271
Harry Steinfeldt	3B151	R	29	152	542	52	144	25	5	1	70	37		19	.266	.336
Wildfire Schulte (GJ)	OF92	L	24	97	342	44	98	14	7	2	32	22		7	.287	.386
Jimmy Slagle	OF136	L	33	136	489	71	126	6	6	0	32	76		28	.258	.294
Jimmy Sheckard	OF142	L	28	143	484	76	129	14	7	2	36	76		31	.267	.384
Johnny Kling	C98, 1B2	R	31	104	334	44	95	15	8	1	43	27		9	.284	.386
S. Hofman	OF69, SS42, 1B18, 3B4, 2B3	R	24	134	470	67	126	11	3	1	36	41		29	.268	.311
Pat Moran	C59	R	31	68	198	8	45	5	1	1	19	10		5	.227	.278
2 Del Howard	1B33, OF8	L	29	51	148	10	34	2	2	0	13	6		3	.230	.270
1 Newt Randall	OF21	R	27	22	78	6	16	4	2	0	4	8		2	.205	.308
Kid Durbin	P5, OF5	L	20	11	18	2	6	0	0	0	0	1		0	.333	.333
1 Mike Kahoe	C3, 1B1	R	33	5	10	0	4	0	0	0	1	0		0	.400	.400
Heinie Zimmerman	2B4, SS1, OF1	R	20	5	9	0	2	1	0	0	1	0		0	.222	.333
1 Bill Sweeney	SS3	R	21	3	10	1	1	0	0	0	1	1		1	.100	.100
Jack Hardy	C1	R	30	1	4	0	1	0	0	0	0	0		0	.250	.250

NAME		T	AGE	W	L	PCT	SV	G	GS	CG	IP	H	BB	SO	SHO	ERA
			29	107	45	.704	7	156	156	114	1373	1054	402	586	32	1.73
Orvie Overall		R	26	23	8	.742	3	36	31	26	268	201	69	141	8	1.68
Three Finger Brown		R	30	20	6	.769	3	34	27	20	233	180	40	107	6	1.39
Carl Lundgren		R	27	18	7	.720	0	28	25	21	207	130	92	84	7	1.17
Ed Reulbach		R	24	17	4	.810	0	27	22	16	192	147	64	96	4	1.69
Jack Pfiester		L	29	15	9	.625	0	32	22	13	195	143	48	90	3	1.15
Chick Fraser		R	33	8	5	.615	0	22	15	9	138	112	46	41	2	2.28
Jack Taylor		R	33	6	5	.545	0	18	13	8	123	127	33	22	0	3.29
Kid Durbin		L	20	0	1	.000	1	5	1	1	17	14	10	5	0	5.29
Jack Harper (HO) 29																

PITTSBURGH 2nd 91-63 .591 17 FRED CLARKE

	TOTALS	B	28	157	4957	634	1261	133	78	19	485	469		264	.254	.324
Jim Nealon	1B104	B	22	105	381	29	98	10	8	0	47	23		11	.257	.325
Ed Abbaticchio	2B147	R	30	147	496	63	130	14	7	2	82	65		35	.262	.331
Honus Wagner	SS138, 1B4	R	33	142	515	98	180	38	14	6	82	46		61	.350	.513
Alan Storke	3B67, 1B23, 2B7, SS3	R	22	112	357	24	92	6	6	1	39	16		6	.258	.317
Goat Anderson	OF117, 2B5	L	27	127	413	73	85	3	1	1	12	80		27	.206	.225
Tommy Leach	OF111, 3B33, SS6, 2B1	R	29	149	547	102	166	19	12	4	43	40		43	.303	.404
Fred Clarke	OF144	L	34	148	501	97	145	18	13	2	59	68		37	.289	.389
George Gibson	C109, 1B1	R	26	113	382	28	84	8	7	3	35	18		2	.220	.301
Bill Hallman	OF84	L	31	94	302	39	67	6	2	0	15	33		21	.222	.255
Tommy Sheehan (HJ)	3B57, SS10	R	29	75	226	23	62	2	3	0	25	23		10	.274	.310
Eddie Phelps	C35, 1B1	R	28	43	113	11	24	1	0	0	12	9		1	.212	.221
Harry Swacina	1B26	R	25	26	95	9	19	1	1	0	10	4		1	.200	.232
1 Otis Clymer	OF15, 1B1	B	31	22	66	8	15	2	0	0	4	5		4	.227	.258
Harry Smith	C18	R	32	18	38	4	10	1	0	0	1	4		0	.263	.342
Danny Moeller	OF11	R	22	11	42	4	12	1	1	0	3	4		2	.286	.357
Harl Maggart	OF2	L	24	3	6	1	0	0	0	0	0	2		1	.000	.000
Bill McKechnie	3B2, 2B1	B	20	3	8	0	1	0	0	0	0	0		0	.125	.125
Marc Campbell	SS2	L	22	2	4	0	1	0	0	0	1	1		0	.250	.250
Billy Kelsey	C2	R	25	2	5	1	2	0	0	0	0	0		0	.400	.400

			30	91	63	.591	5	157	157	111	1363	1207	368	497	24	2.30
Vic Willis		R	31	22	11	.667	1	39	37	27	293	234	69	107	6	2.33
Lefty Leifield		L	23	20	16	.556	1	40	33	24	286	270	100	112	6	2.33
Sam Leever		R	35	14	9	.609	0	31	24	17	217	182	46	65	5	1.66
Howie Camnitz		R	25	13	8	.619	1	31	19	15	180	135	59	85	4	2.15
Deacon Phillippe		R	35	13	11	.542	2	35	26	17	214	214	36	61	1	2.61
Nick Maddox		R	20	5	1	.833	0	6	6	6	54	32	13	38	1	0.83
2 Bill Duggleby		R	34	2	2	.500	0	9	3	1	40	34	12	4	1	2.70
1 Mike Lynch (IL)		L	32	2	2	.500	0	7	4	2	36	37	22	9	0	2.25
King Brady		R	26	0	0	—	0	1	0	0	2	1	0	0	0	0.00
Connie Walsh		R	25	0	0	—	1	0	0	0	1	1	1	0	0	9.00
2 Harry Wolter		L	22	0	0	—	1	0	0	0	2	3	2	0	0	4.50
Bill Otey		L	20	0	1	.000	0	3	2	1	16	23	4	5	0	4.50
Babe Adams		R	25	0	2	.000	0	4	3	1	22	40	3	11	0	6.95

PHILADELPHIA 3rd 83-64 .565 21.5 BILLY MURRAY

	TOTALS		28	149	4725	514	1113	162	65	12	424	424		154	.236	.305
Kitty Bransfield	1B92	R	32	94	348	25	81	15	2	0	38	14		8	.233	.287
Otto Knabe	2B121, OF5	R	23	129	444	67	113	16	9	1	34	52		18	.255	.338
Mickey Doolan	SS145	R	27	145	509	33	104	19	7	1	47	25		18	.204	.275
E. Courtney	3B75, 1B48, OF4, 2B2, SS2	L	32	130	440	42	107	17	4	2	43	55		6	.243	.314
John Titus	OF142	L	31	145	523	72	144	23	12	3	63	47		9	.275	.382
Roy Thomas	OF121	L	33	121	419	90	102	15	3	1	23	83		11	.243	.301
Sherry Magee	OF139	R	22	140	503	75	165	28	12	4	85	53		46	.328	.455
Red Dooin	C94, 2B1, OF1	R	28	101	313	18	66	8	4	0	14	15		10	.211	.262
Eddie Grant	3B74	L	24	74	268	26	65	4	3	0	19	10		10	.243	.280
Fred Jacklitsch	C58, 1B6, OF1	R	31	73	202	19	43	7	0	0	17	27		7	.213	.248
Ossie Osborn	OF36, 1B1	R	23	56	163	22	45	2	3	0	9	3		4	.276	.325
Kid Gleason	2B26, 1B4, SS4, OF1	B	40	36	126	11	18	3	0	0	6	7		3	.143	.167
Johnny Lush	P8, OF4	L	21	17	40	5	8	1	1	0	5	1		1	.200	.275
Paul Sentell	SS2, OF1	R	27	3	3	0	0	0	0	0	0	0		0	.000	.000

			27	83	64	.565	4	149	149	110	1299	1095	422	499	21	2.43
Tully Sparks		R	32	22	8	.733	1	33	31	25	265	221	51	90	3	2.00
Frank Corridon		R	26	18	14	.563	2	37	32	23	274	228	89	131	3	2.46
Lew Moren		R	23	11	18	.379	1	37	31	21	255	202	101	98	3	2.54
Togie Pittinger		R	35	9	5	.643	0	16	12	8	102	101	35	37	1	3.00
2 Buster Brown		R	25	9	6	.600	0	21	16	13	130	118	56	38	4	2.42
Lew Richie		R	23	6	6	.500	0	25	12	9	117	88	38	40	2	1.77
George McQuillan		R	22	4	0	1.000	0	6	5	5	41	21	11	28	3	0.66
1 Johnny Lush		L	21	3	.375	0	8	8	5	57	48	21	20	2	3.00
Harry Coveleski		L	21	1	0	1.000	0	1	0	0	20	10	3	6	0	0.00
Jim McClosky			24	0	0	—	0	3	0	0	9	15	6	3	0	7.00
1 Bill Duggleby		R	34	0	2	.000	0	5	2	2	29	43	11	8	0	7.45

NEW YORK 4th 82-71 .536 25.5 JOHN McGRAW

	TOTALS		32	155	4874	573	1222	160	48	23	475	516		205	.251	.317
Dan McGann (BA)	1B81	B	35	81	262	29	78	9	1	2	36	29		9	.298	.363
Larry Doyle	2B69	R	21	69	227	16	59	3	0	0	16	20		3	.260	.273
Bill Dahlen	SS143	R	37	143	464	40	96	20	1	0	34	51		11	.207	.254
Art Devlin	3B140, SS3	R	27	143	491	61	136	16	2	1	54	63		38	.277	.324
George Browne	OF121	R	31	127	458	54	119	11	10	5	37	31		15	.260	.360
Cy Seymour	OF126	L	34	131	473	46	139	25	8	3	75	36		21	.294	.400
Spike Shannon	OF155	B	29	155	585	104	155	12	5	1	33	82		33	.265	.308
Roger Bresnahan	C95, 1B6, OF2, 2B1	R	28	110	328	57	83	9	7	4	38	61		11	.253	.360
Sammy Strang	OF70, 2B13, 3B7, 1B5, SS1	B	30	123	306	56	77	20	4	4	30	60		21	.252	.382
Frank Bowerman	C62, 1B29	R	38	96	311	31	81	8	2	0	32	17		11	.260	.299
Tommy Corcoran	2B62	R	38	62	226	21	60	9	2	0	24	7		9	.265	.323
Jack Hannifin	1B29, 3B10, SS9, OF2	B	24	56	149	16	34	7	3	1	15	15		6	.228	.336
Danny Shay	2B13, SS9, OF2	R	30	35	79	10	15	1	1	1	6	12		5	.190	.266
Fred Merkle	1B15	R	18	15	47	0	12	1	0	0	5	1		0	.255	.277
Harry Curtis	C6	R	24	6	9	2	2	0	0	0	1	2		2	.222	.222
Matty Fitzgerald	C6	R	26	7	15	1	2	1	0	0	1	0		0	.133	.200
Monte Pfyl	1B1	R	21	1	0	0	0	0	0	0	0	0		0	.000	.000
Ham Wade	OF1	R		1	1	0	0	0	0	0	0	0		0	.000	.000
Mike Donlin (HO) 29																

			27	82	71	.536	13	155	155	109	1371	1219	369	655	22	2.45
Christy Mathewson		R	26	24	13	.649	2	41	36	31	315	250	53	178	8	2.00
Joe McGinnity		R	36	18	18	.500	4	47	34	23	310	320	58	120	3	3.16
Hooks Wiltse		L	27	13	12	.520	2	33	21	14	190	171	48	79	3	2.18
Dummy Taylor		R	32	11	7	.611	1	28	21	11	171	146	46	56	3	2.42
Red Ames		R	24	10	12	.455	1	39	26	17	233	184	108	146	2	2.16
Cecil Ferguson		R	20	3	1	.750	1	15	5	4	64	63	20	37	0	2.11
2 Mike Lynch		L	32	3	6	.333	1	12	10	7	72	68	30	34	0	3.38
Henry Mathewson		R	20	0	0	—	1	1	0	0	1	1	6	0	0	0.00
Roy Beacher		R	23	0	2	.000	0	2	2	1	14	17	6	5	0	2.57

BROOKLYN 5th 65-83 .439 40 PATSY DONOVAN

	TOTALS		28	153	4895	446	1135	142	63	18	380	336		121	.232	.298
Tim Jordan	1B143	L	28	147	485	43	133	15	8	4	53	74		10	.274	.363
Whitey Alperman	2B115, 3B14, SS12	R	27	141	558	44	130	23	16	2	39	13		5	.233	.342
Phil Lewis	SS136	R	23	136	475	52	118	11	1	0	30	23		16	.248	.276
Doc Casey	3B138	R	36	141	527	55	122	19	3	0	19	34		16	.231	.279
Harry Lumley	OF118	R	26	127	454	47	121	23	11	9	66	31		18	.267	.425
Billy Maloney	OF144	L	29	144	502	55	115	7	10	0	32	31		25	.229	.283
Heinie Batch	OF102, 3B2, 2B1, SS1	R	27	116	388	38	96	10	3	0	31	23		7	.247	.289
Lew Ritter	C89	R	31	93	271	15	55	6	1	0	17	18		5	.203	.232
John Hummel	2B44, OF33, 1B12, SS8	R	24	107	342	41	80	12	3	3	31	26		8	.234	.313
Bill Bergen	C51	R	34	51	138	2	22	3	0	0	14	1		1	.159	.181
2 Al Burch	OF36, 2B1	L	23	40	120	12	35	2	2	0	12	11		5	.292	.342
John Butler	C28, OF1	R	27	30	79	6	10	1	0	0	2	9		0	.127	.139
Jack McCarthy	OF25	L	38	25	91	4	20	2	0	0	8	2		4	.220	.242
Patsy Donovan	OF1	R	42	1	1	0	0	0	0	0	0	0		0	.000	.000
Pat Hurley	C1	R		1	2	0	0	0	0	0	0	1		0	.000	.000
Ed McLane	OF1	R	25	1	2	0	0	0	0	0	0	0		0	.000	.000

			27	65	83	.439	1	153	153	125	1356	1218	463	479	20	2.38
Jim Pastorius		L	25	16	12	.571	0	28	26	20	222	218	77	70	4	2.35
Nap Rucker		L	22	15	13	.536	0	37	30	26	275	242	80	131	4	2.06
Elmer Stricklett		R	30	12	14	.462	0	29	26	23	230	211	65	69	4	2.27
George Bell		R	32	8	16	.333	1	35	27	20	264	222	77	88	3	2.25
Harry McIntire		R	29	7	15	.318	0	28	22	19	200	178	79	49	3	2.38
Doc Scanlan		R	26	6	8	.429	0	17	15	10	107	90	61	59	2	3.20
Weldon Henley		R	26	1	5	.167	0	7	5	5	56	54	21	11	0	3.05
Jesse Whiting		R	28	0	0	—	0	1	0	0	3	3	3	2	0	12.00

CINCINNATI   6th   66-87   .431   41.5   NED HANLON

NAME	G by Pos	B	AGE	G	AB	R	H	2B	3B	HR	RBI	BB	SO	SB	BA	SA
TOTALS			28	156	4966	524	1226	126	90	15	443	372		158	.247	.318
John Ganzel	1B143	R	33	145	531	61	135	20	16	2	64	29		9	.254	.363
Miller Huggins	2B156	B	29	156	561	64	139	12	4	1	31	83		28	.248	.289
Hans Lobert	SS142, 3B5	R	25	148	537	61	132	9	12	1	41	37		30	.246	.313
Mike Mowrey	3B127, SS11	R	23	138	448	43	113	16	6	1	44	35		10	.252	.321
Mike Mitchell	OF146, 1B2	R	27	148	558	64	163	17	12	3	47	37		17	.292	.382
Art Kruger	OF96	R	26	100	317	25	74	10	9	0	28	18		10	.233	.322
Fred Odwell	OF84, 2B1	R	34	94	274	24	74	5	7	0	24	22		10	.270	.339
Larry McLean	C89, 1B13	R	25	113	374	35	108	9	9	0	54	13		4	.289	.361
Admiral Schlei (RJ)	C67, 1B3, OF2	R	29	84	246	28	67	3	2	0	27	28		5	.272	.301
John Kane (JJ)	OF42, 3B25, SS6, 2B2	R	24	79	262	40	65	9	4	3	19	22		20	.248	.347
Lefty Davis	OF70	L	32	73	266	28	61	5	5	1	25	23		9	.229	.297
Dode Paskert	OF16	R	26	16	50	10	14	4	0	1	8	2		2	.280	.420
Mike O'Neill	OF9	L	29	9	29	5	2	0	2	0	2	2		1	.069	.207
Chick Autry	OF7	L	22	7	15	1	3	5	0	0	0	1		0	.200	.200
1 Harry Wolter	OF4	L	22	4	15	1	2	0	0	2	1	0			.133	.133
Bill McCarthy	C3		21	3	8	1	1	0	0	0	0	0			.125	.125
Eddie Tiemeyer		R	22	1	0	1	0	0	0	0	0	0		0	.000	.000
Pete Lamer	C1		33	1	2	0	0	0	0	0	0	0		0	.000	.000

NAME	T	AGE	W	L	PCT	SV	G	GS	CG	IP	H	BB	SO	SHO	ERA
		27	66	87	.431	2	156	156	118	1351	1223	444	481	10	2.41
Andy Coakley	R	24	17	16	.515	1	37	30	21	265	269	79	89	1	2.34
Bob Ewing	R	34	17	19	.472	0	41	37	32	333	279	85	147	2	1.73
Jake Weimer	L	33	11	14	.440	0	29	26	19	209	165	63	67	3	2.41
Roy Hitt	L	23	6	10	.375	0	21	18	14	153	143	56	63	2	3.41
Del Mason	R	23	5	12	.294	0	25	17	13	146	144	55	45	1	3.14
Charley Hall	R	22	4	2	.667	1	8	5	5	68	51	43	25	0	2.51
Bill Campbell	R	33	3	0	1.000	0	3	3	3	31	19	3	4	0	2.14
Fred Smith	R	28	2	7	.222	1	18	9	5	85	90	24	19	0	2.86
Bob Spade	R	29	1	2	.333	0	3	3	3	27	21	9	7	1	1.00
Frank Leary (DD)	R	26	0	1	.000	0	2	1	0	8	7	6	4	0	1.13
Bill Essick	R	26	0	2	.000	0	3	2	2	22	23	8	7	0	2.86
Cotton Minahan	R	24	0	2	.000	0	2	1	1	14	12	13	4	0	1.29

BOSTON   7th   58-90   .392   47   FRED TENNEY

NAME	G by Pos	B	AGE	G	AB	R	H	2B	3B	HR	RBI	BB	SO	SB	BA	SA
TOTALS			28	152	5008	503	1222	142	61	22	395	413		120	.243	.309
Fred Tenney	1B149	L	35	150	554	83	151	18	8	0	26	82		15	.273	.334
Claude Ritchey	2B144	B	33	144	499	45	127	17	4	2	51	50		8	.255	.317
Al Bridwell	SS140	L	23	140	509	49	111	8	2	0	26	61		17	.218	.242
Dave Brain	3B130	R	28	133	509	60	142	24	9	10	56	29		10	.279	.420
Johnny Bates	OF120	L	25	126	447	52	116	18	12	2	49	39		11	.260	.367
Ginger Beaumont	OF149	L	30	150	580	67	187	19	14	4	62	37		25	.322	.424
2 Newt Randall	OF73	R	27	75	258	46	55	6	3	0	15	19		4	.213	.260
Tom Needham	C78, 1B1	R	28	86	260	19	51	6	2	1	19	18		4	.196	.246
Sam Brown	C63, 1B2	R	29	70	208	17	40	6	0	0	14	12		0	.192	.221
2 B. Sweeney	3B23, SS15, OF11, 2B5, 1B1	R	21	58	191	24	50	2	0	0	18	15		8	.262	.272
1 Del Howard	OF45, 2B3	L	29	50	187	20	51	4	2	1	13	11		11	.273	.332
Frank Burke	OF36	R	27	43	129	6	23	0	1	0	8	11		3	.178	.194
Izzy Hoffman	OF19	L	32	19	86	17	24	3	1	0	3	6		2	.279	.337
Jim Ball	C10	R	23	10	36	3	6	2	0	0	3	2		0	.167	.222
Jess Orndorff	C5	B	26	5	17	0	2	0	0	0	0	0		0	.118	.118
Joe Knotts	C3	R	23	3	8	0	0	0	0	0	0	0		0	.000	.000
Oscar Westerberg	SS2	R	24	2	6	0	2	0	0	0	0	1		1	.333	.333
Tom Asmussen	C2		28	2	5	0	0	0	0	0	0	1		0	.000	.000
Bob Brush	1B1	L	32	2	0	0	0	0	0	0	0	0		0	.000	.000
Cozy Dolan (DD)	34															

NAME	T	AGE	W	L	PCT	SV	G	GS	CG	IP	H	BB	SO	SHO	ERA
		28	58	90	.392	2	152	152	121	1339	1324	458	426	9	3.33
Patsy Flaherty	L	31	12	15	.444	0	27	25	23	217	197	59	34	0	2.70
Gus Dorner	R	30	12	16	.429	0	36	31	24	271	253	92	85	2	3.12
Vive Lindaman	R	29	11	15	.423	1	34	28	24	260	252	108	90	2	3.63
Irv Young	L	29	10	23	.303	1	40	32	22	245	287	58	86	3	3.97
Big Jeff Pfeffer (AJ)	R	25	6	8	.429	0	19	16	12	144	129	61	65	1	3.00
Jake Boultes	R	22	5	9	.529	0	24	12	11	140	140	50	49	0	2.70
Frank Barberich	R	25	1	1	.500	0	2	2	1	12	19	5	1	0	6.00
Sammy Frock	R	24	1	2	.333	0	5	3	3	33	28	11	12	1	3.00
Ernie Lindemann	R	24	0	0	—	0	1	1	0	6	6	4	3	0	6.00
Rube Dessau	R	24	0	1	.000	0	1	0	0	9	13	10	1	0	11.00

ST. LOUIS   8th   52-101   .340   55.5   JOHN McCLOSKEY

NAME	G by Pos	B	AGE	G	AB	R	H	2B	3B	HR	RBI	BB	SO	SB	BA	SA
TOTALS			26	156	5008	419	1163	121	51	19	331	312		125	.232	.288
Ed Konetchy	1B91	R	21	91	331	34	83	11	8	3	30	26		13	.251	.360
Pug Bennett	2B83, 3B3	R	33	87	324	20	72	8	2	0	21	21		7	.222	.259
Eddie Holly	SS147, 2B3	R	27	150	545	55	125	18	3	1	40	36		16	.229	.279
Bobby Byrne	3B148, SS1	R	22	149	559	55	143	11	5	0	29	35		21	.256	.293
Shad Barry (KJ)	OF81	R	28	81	294	30	73	5	2	0	19	28		4	.248	.279
Jack Barnett	OF59	R	27	59	206	18	49	8	4	0	12	15		5	.238	.316
Red Murray	OF131	R	23	132	485	46	127	10	10	7	46	24		23	.262	.367
Doc Marshall	C83	R	32	84	268	19	54	8	2	2	18	12		2	.201	.269
Hoelskoetter	2B72, 1B27, OF8, C8, 3B2, P2	R	24	119	397	21	98	6	3	2	28	27		5	.247	.292
Peter Noonan	C70	R	25	74	237	19	53	7	3	1	16	9		3	.224	.291
John Kelly	OF52		28	53	197	12	37	5	0	0	6	13		7	.188	.213
1 Al Burch	OF48	L	23	48	154	18	35	3	1	0	5	17		7	.227	.260
Tom O'Hara	OF47		26	48	173	11	41	2	1	0	5	12		1	.237	.260
Jake Beckley	1B32	L	39	32	115	6	24	3	0	0	7	1		0	.209	.235
3 Harry Wolter	OF9, P3	L	22	16	47	4	16	0	0	0	6	3		1	.340	.340
Buck Hopkins	OF15	L	24	15	44	7	6	3	0	0	3	10		2	.136	.205
Harry Arndt	1B4, 3B3	R	28	11	32	3	6	1	0	0	2	1		0	.188	.219
Al Shaw	OF9	R	26	9	25	2	7	0	0	0	3	1		1	.280	.280
Forrest Crawford (DD)	SS7	R	26	7	22	0	5	0	0	0	3	2		0	.227	.227
Joe Delahanty	OF7	L	31	7	22	3	7	0	0	1	2	0		3	.318	.455
John Baxter	1B6	L	30	6	21	1	4	0	0	0	0	0		0	.190	.190

NAME	T	AGE	W	L	PCT	SV	G	GS	CG	IP	H	BB	SO	SHO	ERA
		26	52	101	.340	2	156	156	127	1366	1212	500	594	19	2.69
Ed Karger	L	24	15	19	.441	2	39	33	29	314	257	65	137	6	2.04
Stony McGlynn	R	35	14	25	.359	1	45	39	33	352	329	112	109	3	2.91
2 Johnny Lush	L	21	7	10	.412	0	20	19	15	144	132	42	71	3	2.50
Fred Beebe	R	26	7	19	.269	0	31	29	24	238	192	109	141	4	2.72
Art Fromme	R	23	5	13	.278	0	23	16	13	146	138	67	67	2	2.90
Bugs Raymond	R	25	2	4	.333	0	8	6	6	65	56	21	34	1	1.66
3 Harry Wolter	R	22	1	2	.333	0	3	3	1	23	27	18	8	0	4.30
1 Buster Brown	R	25	1	6	.143	0	8	6	6	64	57	45	17	0	3.38
Art Hoelskoetter	R	24	0	0	—	0	2	0	0	11	9	10	8	0	5.73
Carl Druhot	L	24	0	1	.000	0	1	1	0	2	3	4	1	0	18.00
Charlie Shields	L	27	0	2	.000	0	3	2	0	7	12	7	1	0	9.00

WORLD SERIES — CHICAGO (NL) 4 DETROIT (AL) 0   One Tie Game

LINE SCORES

TEAM	1	2	3	4	5	6	7	8	9	10	11	12	R	H	E
Game 1 October 8 at Chicago															
DET(AL)	0	0	0	0	0	0	0	3	0	0	0	0	3	9	3
CHI(NL)	0	0	0	1	0	0	0	0	2	0	0	0	3	10	5

Donovan   Overall, Reulbach (10)

TEAM	1	2	3	4	5	6	7	8	9	R	H	E
Game 2 October 9 at Chicago												
DET	0	1	0	0	0	0	0	0	0	1	9	1
CHI	0	1	0	2	0	0	0	0	X	3	9	1

Mullin   Pfiester

TEAM	1	2	3	4	5	6	7	8	9	R	H	E
Game 3 October 10 at Chicago												
DET	0	0	0	0	0	1	0	0	0	1	6	1
CHI	0	1	0	3	1	0	0	0	X	5	10	1

Siever, Killian (5)   Reulbach

TEAM	1	2	3	4	5	6	7	8	9	R	H	E
Game 4 October 11 at Detroit												
CHI	0	0	0	0	2	0	3	0	1	6	7	2
DET	0	0	0	1	0	0	0	0	0	1	5	2

Overall   Donovan

TEAM	1	2	3	4	5	6	7	8	9	R	H	E
Game 5 October 12 at Detroit												
CHI	1	1	0	0	0	0	0	0	0	2	7	1
DET	0	0	0	0	0	0	0	0	0	0	7	2

Brown   Mullin

COMPOSITE BATTING

NAME	POS	G	AB	R	H	2B	3B	HR	RBI	BA
Chicago (NL)										
Totals		5	167	19	43	6	1	0	16	.257
Slagle	OF	5	22	3	6	0	1	0	4	.273
Sheckard	OF	5	21	0	5	2	0	0	4	.238
Evers	2B-SS	5	20	2	7	2	0	0	1	.350
Schulte	OF	5	20	3	5	0	0	0	1	.250
Kling	C	5	19	2	4	0	0	0	1	.211
Steinfeldt	3B	5	17	2	8	1	1	0	2	.471
Chance	1B	5	14	3	3	1	0	0	2	.214
Tinker	SS	5	13	4	2	1	0	0	1	.154
Overall	P	2	5	0	1	0	0	0	2	.200
Reulbach	P	2	5	0	1	0	0	0	0	.200
Howard	1B	2	5	0	1	0	0	0	0	.200
Brown	P	1	5	0	1	0	0	0	0	.200
Pfiester	P	1	2	0	0	0	0	0	0	.000
Zimmerman	2B	1	1	0	0	0	0	0	0	.000
Moran	PH	1	0	0	0	0	0	0	0	—
Detroit (AL)										
Totals		5	172	6	36	4	2	0	6	.209
Crawford	OF	5	21	5	5	1	0	0	3	.238
Schaefer	2B	5	21	3	3	0	0	0	0	.143
Rossman	1B	5	20	1	8	0	0	0	2	.400
Coughlin	3B	5	20	0	5	0	0	0	2	.250
Cobb	OF	5	20	1	4	0	0	0	0	.200
Jones	OF	5	17	1	6	0	0	0	0	.353
O'Leary	SS	5	17	0	1	0	0	0	0	.059
schmidt	C	4	12	0	2	0	0	0	0	.167
Donovan	P	2	8	0	0	0	0	0	0	.000
Mullin	P	2	6	0	0	0	0	0	0	.000
Payne	C	2	4	0	1	0	0	0	1	.250
Archer	C	1	3	0	0	0	0	0	0	.000
Killian	P	1	2	1	1	0	0	0	0	.500
Siever	P	1	1	0	0	0	0	0	0	.000

COMPOSITE PITCHING

NAME	G	IP	H	BB	SO	W	L	SV	ERA
Chicago (NL)									
Totals	5	48	36	9	22	4	0	0	0.75
Overall	2	18	14	4	11	1	0	0	1.00
Reulbach	2	12	6	3	4	1	0	0	0.75
Brown	1	9	7	1	4	1	0	0	0.00
Pfiester	1	9	9	1	3	1	0	0	1.00
Detroit (AL)									
Totals	5	46	43	12	26	0	4	0	2.15
Donovan	2	21	17	5	16	0	1	0	1.71
Mullin	2	17	16	6	8	0	2	0	2.12
Killian	1	4	3	1	1	0	1	0	2.25
Siever	1	4	7	0	1	0	1	0	4.50

1908 — Forty-Five Feet Toward Immortality

Fred Tenney woke up on September 23rd in the throes of a lumbago attack, and 19-year-old substitute Fred Merkle was sent in to take his place at first base. As events turned out, fate would treat Merkle unkindly that day. With 25,000 fans assembled in the Polo Grounds, the second-place Chicago Cubs were playing the leading Giants with only percentage points separating the clubs. A 1-1 tie held fast until the Giants came to bat in the bottom of the ninth. There were two outs: Moose McCormick was on third and young Merkle perched on first after singling to right, (What follows is one account of the many which were offered of what is still known as the greatest goof of all time.) Al Bridwell lashed a Jack Pfiester serve into center field for a clean single, scoring McCormick and apparently ending the game. However, as the crowd started surging onto the field, Merkle, halfway to second, immediately sprinted for the clubhouse without bothering to touch second base, the common practice at the time. With the jubilant New York fans already piling onto the playing field, Cub second baseman Johnny Evers realized that Merkle would be forced out at second for the third out, thereby nullifying the run. Evers called frantically for center fielder Solly Hofman to throw him the ball, but Hofman - unable to clearly see Evers in the crowd - overshot the mark with a heave towards first base. Giant first base coach Joe McGinnity realized what was happening, outwrestled Cub shortstop Joe Tinker for the ball, and with Tinker on his back heaved it toward shortstop. Rube Kroh, a second-line Cub pitcher who was not even in the game, saw a spectator pick up the ball, demanded it, and slugged the customer when he would not cough it up. Kroh retrieved the ball from the now-prone fan, worked his way through the still-unaware crowd, and handed the ball to Evers on second. Umpire Hank O'Day was supposedly watching the whole affair; he called Merkle out and disallowed the run, using darkness as an excuse to call the game a tie. The Giants screamed bloody murder when notified in the clubhouse that their victory was rescinded, but league president Harry Pulliam upheld O'Day's decision. The matter finally went before the Board of Directors who, on October 5, sustained Pulliam's decision. The game grew in proportion when the Cubs and Giants finished the regular season with identical 98-55 records. The tie was rescheduled for October 8, and a record 35,000 spectators crammed into the Polo Grounds and watched Three Finger Brown, in relief, best Christy Mathewson in a 4-2 come-from-behind Chicago victory, which gave the Cubs their third consecutive National League crown.

The Cubs fielded a solid, balanced squad, good in all departments and expected to repeat as champions. The Giants relied on a strong offense led by Mike Donlin and a thin pitching staff aced by Mathewson and Hooks Wiltse to challenge all the way, and the Pirates - eliminated only on the last day of the season - also fielded a balanced squad led by superstar Honus Wagner, the National League batting leader for the sixth time.

The National League held no monopoly on tight races as the Detroit Tigers repeated as champions only by defeating the White Sox on the final day of the season in one of the tightest races ever staged in the American League. Detroit, Cleveland, and Chicago all battled for the top into the final two days of the season, with the Tigers finishing half a game and .004 percentage points ahead of Cleveland. Detroit's victory was blemished somewhat by a rain-out game they did not have to make up. The White Sox did not figure to win the pennant, but got as far as they did because of the iron-man work of spitballer Ed Walsh. Staring regularly with two days rest, relieving between starts, and winning an incredible 40 games over the course of 464 innings, Walsh turned in one of the finest pitching efforts in history. He also took part in the greatest pitching duel ever staged under pressure conditions when , on October 2, against Cleveland, he gave up four hits and struck out 15, only to be victimized 1-0 by the perfect game performance of Addie Joss.

The World Series proved anticlimactic as the favored Cubs disappointed no one in disposing of the Tigers in five games despite Ty Cobb's .368 swinging. Frank Chance, Johnny Evers, and Joe Tinker starred for the Cubs at bat and afield, while Orvie Overall and Three-Finger Brown accounted for all the victories on the mound to end a circus-like season which, oddly enough, would be remembered only for the "bonehead" play of an inexperienced youngster.

1908 AMERICAN LEAGUE

NAME	G by Pos	B	AGE	G	AB	R	H	2B	3B	HR	RBI	BB	SO	SB	BA	SA
DETROIT 1st 90-63 .588 HUGHIE JENNINGS																
TOTALS			27	153	5109	645	1347	199	86	19	520	320		165	.264	.347
Claude Rossman	1B138	L	27	138	524	45	154	33	13	2	71	27		8	.294	.418
Red Downs	2B82, 3B1	R	24	84	289	29	64	10	3	1	35	5		2	.221	.287
Germany Schaefer	SS68, 2B58, 3B29	R	31	153	584	96	151	20	10	3	52	37		40	.259	.342
Bill Coughlin	3B119	R	29	119	405	32	87	5	1	0	23	23		10	.215	.232
Ty Cobb	OF150	L	21	150	581	88	188	36	20	4	108	34		39	.324	.475
Sam Crawford	OF134, 1B17	L	28	152	591	102	184	33	16	7	80	37		15	.311	.457
Matty McIntyre	OF151	L	28	151	569	105	168	24	13	0	28	83		20	.295	.383
Boss Schmidt	C121	B	27	122	419	45	111	14	3	1	38	16		5	.265	.320
Charley O'Leary (IL)	SS64, 2B1	R	25		211	21	53	9	3	0	17	9		4	.251	.322
Davy Jones	OF32	L	28	56	121	17	25	2	1	0	10	13		11	.207	.240
Ian Thomas	C29	R	27	40	101	6	31	1	0	0	8	5		0	.307	.317
Red Killefer	2B16, SS7, 2B4	R	23	28	75	9	16	1	0	0	11	3		4	.213	.227
Donie Bush	SS20	R	20	20	68	13	20	1	1	0	4	7		4	.294	.338
Freddie Payne (BG)	C16, OF2	R	27	20	45	3	3	0	0	0	2	3		1	.067	.067
Clay Perry	3B5	R	26	5	11	0	2	0	0	0	0	0		0	.182	.182

NAME	T	AGE	W	L	PCT	SV	G	GS	CG	IP	H	BB	SO	SHO	ERA
		27	90	63	.588	6	154	154	119	1374	1313	318	553	15	2.40
Ed Summers	R	23	24	12	.667	1	40	32	23	301	271	55	103	5	1.64
Wild Bill Donovan	R	31	18	7	.720	0	29	28	25	243	210	53	141	6	2.07
George Mullin	R	27	17	12	.586	0	39	30	26	291	301	71	121	1	3.09
Ed Willett (NJ)	R	24	15	9	.625	1	30	23	18	197	186	60	77	2	2.28
Ed Killian	L	31	12	10	.545	1	27	23	15	181	170	53	47	0	2.98
2 George Winter	R	30	1	5	.167	1	7	6	5	56	49	7	25	0	1.61
Ed Siever	R	33	2	6	.250	1	11	9	4	62	74	13	23	1	3.48
George Suggs	R	25	1	0	1.000	1	6	1	1	27	32	2	8	0	1.67
Herm Malloy	R	23	0	0	—	0	3	2	2	17	20	4	8	0	3.71

NAME	G by Pos	B	AGE	G	AB	R	H	2B	3B	HR	RBI	BB	SO	SB	BA	SA
CLEVELAND 2nd 90-64 .584 .5 NAP LAJOIE																
TOTALS			28	157	5108	570	1221	188	58	18	458	364		169	.239	.309
George Stovall	1B132, OF5, SS1	R	30	138	534	71	156	29	6	2	45	17		14	.292	.380
Nap Lajoie	2B156, 1B1	R	33	157	581	77	168	32	6	2	74	47		15	.289	.375
George Perring	SS48, 3B41	R	23	89	310	23	67	8	5	0	19	16		0	.216	.274
Bill Bradley	3B116, SS21	R	30	148	548	70	133	24	7	1	46	29		18	.243	.318
Bill Hinchman	OF75, SS51, 1B4	R	25	137	464	55	107	23	8	6	59	38		9	.231	.353
Joe Birmingham (AJ)	OF121, SS1	R	23	122	413	32	88	10	1	2	38	19		15	.213	.257
Josh Clarke	OF131	L	29	131	492	70	119	8	4	1	21	76		37	.242	.280
Nig Clarke	C90	L	25	97	290	34	70	8	6	1	27	30		6	.241	.321
Harry Bemis	C76, 1B2	L	34	91	277	23	62	9	1	0	33	7		14	.224	.264
Charley Hickman	OF28, 1B20, 2B1	R	32	65	197	16	46	6	1	2	16	9		2	.234	.305
Terry Turner (JJ)	OF36, SS17	R	27	60	201	21	48	11	1	0	19	15		18	.239	.303
Wilbur Good	OF42	L	22	46	154	23	43	1	3	1	14	13		7	.279	.344
2 Dave Altizer	OF24, SS3	R	31	29	89	11	19	1	2	0	5	7		7	.213	.270
Rabbit Nill	SS6, OF2, 2B1	R	26	10	23	3	5	0	0	1	0	0		0	.217	.217
Homer Davidson	C5, OF1	R	23	9	4	2	0	0	0	0	0	1		0	.000	.000
Elmer Flick (IL)	OF9	L	32	9	35	4	8	1	1	0	2	3		0	.229	.314
Otto Hess	P4, OF4	L	29	8	14	0	0	0	0	0	0	1		0	.000	.000
Grover Land	C8	R	23	8	16	1	3	0	0	0	2	0		0	.188	.188
2 Denny Sullivan	OF2	L	25	3	6	0	0	0	0	0	0	0		0	.000	.000
Harry Bay		L	30	2	0	0	0	0	0	0	0	0		0	.000	.000
2 Deacon McGuire	1B1	R	44	1	4	0	1	1	0	0	2	0		0	.250	.500

NAME	T	AGE	W	L	PCT	SV	G	GS	CG	IP	H	BB	SO	SHO	ERA
		28	90	64	.584	5	157	157	108	1422	1172	328	548	18	2.02
Addie Joss	R	28	24	11	.686	2	42	35	29	325	232	30	130	9	**1.16**
Bob Rhoades	R	28	18	12	.600	0	37	30	20	270	229	73	62	1	1.77
Glenn Liebhardt	R	25	15	16	.484	0	29	26	19	262	222	81	146	3	2.20
Heinie Berger	R	26	13	8	.619	0	29	24	16	199	152	66	101	0	2.13
Charlie Chech	R	30	11	7	.611	0	27	20	14	166	136	34	51	4	1.73
1 Jake Thielman	R	29	4	3	.571	0	11	8	5	62	59	9	15	0	3.63
1 Cy Falkenberg	R	28	2	5	.286	0	8	7	2	44	52	10	17	0	4.09
Ed Foster	R	23	1	0	1.000	2	6	1	1	21	16	12	11	0	2.14
Jack Ryan	R	23	1	0	1.000	1	8	1	1	36	27	2	7	0	2.25
Bill Lattimore	L	24	1	2	.333	0	4	4	1	24	24	7	5	1	4.50
Otto Hess	L	29	0	0	—	0	4	0	0	7	11	1	2	0	5.14
Walter Clarkson	R	29	0	0	—	0	2	1	0	3	6	2	1	0	12.00
Jack Graney	L	22	0	0	—	0	2	0	0	3	6	1	0	0	6.00

NAME	G by Pos	B	AGE	G	AB	R	H	2B	3B	HR	RBI	BB	SO	SB	BA	SA
CHICAGO 3rd 88-64 .579 1.5 FIELDER JONES																
TOTALS			32	156	5027	535	1127	145	41	3	430	463		209	.224	.271
Jiggs Donahue	1B83	L	28	93	304	22	62	8	2	0	22	25		14	.204	.243
George Davis	2B95, SS23, 1B4	B	37	128	419	41	91	14	1	0	26	41		22	.217	.255
Freddy Parent (KJ)	SS118	R	32	119	391	28	81	7	5	0	35	50		9	.207	.251
Lee Tannehill	3B136, SS5	R	27	141	482	44	104	15	3	0	35	25		6	.216	.259
Eddie Hahn	OF118	L	32	122	447	58	112	12	8	0	21	39		11	.251	.313
Fielder Jones	OF149	L	36	149	529	92	134	11	7	1	50	86		26	.253	.306
Patsy Dougherty	OF138	L	31	138	482	68	134	11	6	0	45	58		47	.278	.326
Billy Sullivan	C137	R	33	137	430	40	82	8	4	0	29	22		15	.191	.228
John Anderson	OF90, 1B9	R	34	123	355	36	93	17	4	0	47	30		21	.262	.315
Frank Isbell	1B65, 2B18	L	32	84	320	31	79	15	3	1	49	19		18	.247	.322
Jake Atz	2B46, SS18, 3B1	R	29	83	206	24	40	3	0	0	27	31		9	.194	.209
Al Shaw	C29	R	33	32	49	4	4	1	0	0	2	2		0	.082	.102
Billy Purtell	3B25	R	22	26	69	3	9	2	0	0	3	2		2	.130	.159
Art Weaver	C15	R	29	15	35	1	7	1	0	0	1	1		0	.200	.229
2 Ossee Schreckengost	C6	R	33	6	16	1	3	0	0	0	0	1		0	.188	.188

NAME	T	AGE	W	L	PCT	SV	G	GS	CG	IP	H	BB	SO	SHO	ERA
		28	88	64	.579	13	156	156	107	1414	1170	284	623	23	2.22
Ed Walsh	R	27	40	15	.727	7	66	49	42	464	343	56	269	11	1.42
Doc White	L	29	18	13	.581	0	41	37	24	296	267	69	126	5	2.55
Frank Smith (JT)	R	28	17	16	.515	1	41	35	24	298	213	73	129	3	2.02
Frank Owen	R	28	6	8	.429	0	25	14	5	140	142	37	48	1	3.41
Nick Altrock	L	31	3	7	.300	0	23	13	8	136	127	16	21	1	2.71
Moxie Manuel	R	26	3	4	.429	1	18	6	3	60	52	25	25	0	3.30
Andy Nelson	R	23	1	0	1.000	0	2	1	0	9	11	4	1	0	2.00
Lou Fiene	R	23	0	1	.000	0	1	1	1	9	7	3	4	0	4.00
Fred Olmstead	R	24	0	0	—	0	1	0	0	2	6	1	1	0	13.50

ST. LOUIS — 4th 83-69 .546 6.5 — JIMMY McALEER

Batting

NAME	G by Pos	B	AGE	G	AB	R	H	2B	3B	HR	RBI	BB	SO	SB	BA	SA
TOTALS			29	155	5152	543	1261	173	56	20	447	343		126	.245	.312
Tom Jones	1B155	R	31	155	549	43	135	14	2	1	50	30		18	.246	.284
Jimmy Williams	2B148	R	31	148	539	63	127	20	7	4	53	55		7	.236	.321
Bobby Wallace	SS137	R	34	137	487	59	123	24	4	1	60	52		5	.253	.324
Hobe Ferris	3B148	R	30	148	555	54	150	26	7	2	74	14		6	.270	.353
Roy Hartzell	OF82, SS18, 3B7, 2B4	L	26	115	422	41	112	5	6	2	32	19		24	.265	.320
Danny Hoffman	OF99	L	28	99	363	41	91	9	7	1	25	23		17	.251	.322
George Stone	OF148	L	31	148	588	89	165	21	8	5	31	55		20	.281	.369
Tubby Spencer	C89	R	23	91	286	19	60	6	1	0	28	17		1	.210	.238
Charlie Jones	OF72	R	32	74	263	37	61	11	2	0	17	14		14	.232	.289
Dode Criss	P9, OF7, 1B1	L	23	64	82	15	28	6	0	0	14	9		1	.341	.415
Al Schweitzer	OF55	R	25	64	182	22	53	4	2	1	14	20		6	.291	.412
Jim Stephens	C45	R	24	47	150	14	30	4	1	0	6	9		0	.200	.240
2 Syd Smith	C25	R	24	27	76	6	14	4	4	0	5	4		2	.184	.342
Snags Heidrick	OF25	L	31	26	93	8	20	2	2	1	6	1		3	.215	.312
1 Bert Blue	C8	R	30	11	25	2	9	1	2	0	1	3		0	.360	.560
Joe Yeager (IL)	2B4, SS1	R	32	10	15	3	5	1	0	0	1	1		2	.333	.400

Pitching

NAME	T	AGE	W	L	PCT	SV	G	GS	CG	IP	H	BB	SO	SHO	ERA
TOTALS		28	83	69	.546	3	155	155	107	1397	1151	387	607	15	2.15
Rube Waddell	L	31	19	14	.576	3	43	36	25	286	223	90	232	5	1.89
Harry Howell	R	31	18	18	.500	0	41	32	27	324	279	70	117	2	1.89
Jack Powell	R	33	16	13	.552	0	33	32	23	256	208	47	85	5	2.11
Bill Dinneen	R	32	14	7	.667	0	27	16	11	167	133	53	39	2	2.10
Barney Pelty	R	27	7	4	.636	0	20	13	7	122	104	32	36	1	1.99
Bill Graham	L	23	6	7	.462	0	21	13	7	117	104	32	47	0	2.31
Bill Bailey	L	20	5	7	.375	0	22	12	7	107	85	50	42	0	3.03
Dode Criss	R	23	0	1	.000	0	9	1	0	18	15	13	9	0	6.50

BOSTON — 5th 75-79 .487 15.5 — DEACON McGUIRE 53-62 .461 / FRED LAKE 22-17 .564

Batting

NAME	G by Pos	B	AGE	G	AB	R	H	2B	3B	HR	RBI	BB	SO	SB	BA	SA
TOTALS			28	155	5047	565	1243	116	88	14	444	289		168	.246	.312
2 Jake Stahl	1B79	R	28	79	258	29	64	9	11	0	23	20		14	.248	.368
Amby McConnell	2B126, SS3	L	25	140	502	77	140	10	6	2	43	38		31	.279	.335
Heinie Wagner	SS153	R	27	153	526	62	130	11	5	1	46	27		20	.247	.293
Harry Lord	3B143	R	26	145	558	61	145	15	6	2	37	22		23	.260	.319
Doc Gessler	OF126	L	27	128	435	55	134	13	14	3	63	51		19	.308	.423
1 Denny Sullivan	OF99	S	25	101	353	33	85	7	7	0	25	14		15	.241	.300
Jack Thoney	OF101	R	28	93	358	46	106	5	9	2	30	13		16	.255	.325
Lou Criger	C84	R	36	84	237	12	45	4	2	0	25	13		1	.190	.224
Gavvy Cravath	OF77, 1B5	R	27	94	277	43	71	10	11	1	34	38		6	.256	.383
1 Bob Unglaub	1B72	R	26	72	266	23	70	11	3	1	25	7		6	.263	.338
1 Frank LaPorte	2B27, 3B12, OF5	R	28	62	156	14	37	1	3	0	15	12		3	.237	.282
Bill Carrigan (IL)	C47, 1B3	R	24	57	149	13	35	5	2	0	14	3		1	.235	.295
Pat Donahue	C32, 1B3	R	24	35	86	8	17	2	0	1	6	9		0	.198	.256
Tris Speaker	OF31	L	20	31	118	12	26	2	3	0	9	4		2	.220	.288
Jim McHale	OF19	R	32	21	67	9	15	2	2	0	7	4		4	.224	.313
Ed McFarland	C13	R	33	19	48	5	10	2	1	0	4	1		0	.208	.292
2 Harry Niles	2B8, SS2	R	27	17	33	4	9	0	0	1	3	6		3	.273	.364
Jack Hoey	OF11	L	26	13	43	5	7	0	0	0	3	0		1	.163	.163
Walter Carlisle	OF3	R	25	3	10	0	1	0	0	0	0	1		1	.100	.100
Jimmy Barrett	OF2	L	33	2	8	0	1	0	0	0	0	1		1	.125	.125
Larry Gardner	3B2	L	22	2	6	0	3	0	0	0	1	0		0	.500	.500
1 Deacon McGuire	C1	R	44	1	1	0	0	0	0	0	0	0		0	.000	.000
Harry Ostdiek	C1	R	27	1	3	0	0	0	0	0	0	0		0	.000	.000

Pitching

NAME	T	AGE	W	L	PCT	SV	G	GS	CG	IP	H	BB	SO	SHO	ERA
TOTALS		29	75	79	.487	7	155	155	102	1381	1200	364	624	12	2.27
Cy Young	R	41	21	11	.656	2	36	33	30	299	230	37	150	3	1.26
Cy Morgan	R	29	13	13	.500	2	30	26	17	205	166	90	99	2	2.46
Eddie Cicotte	R	24	11	12	.478	2	39	24	17	207	198	59	95	2	2.43
Fred Burchell	L	28	10	8	.556	0	31	19	9	180	161	65	94	0	2.95
Elmer Steele	R	24	5	7	.417	0	16	13	9	118	85	13	37	1	1.83
Frank Arellanes	R	26	4	3	.571	0	11	8	6	79	60	18	33	1	1.82
1 George Winter	R	30	4	14	.222	0	22	17	8	148	150	34	55	0	3.04
Ralph Glaze	R	27	2	2	.500	0	10	3	2	35	43	5	13	0	3.34
Tex Pruiett	R	25	2	7	.222	1	13	6	1	59	55	21	28	1	1.98
Doc McMahon	R	21	1	0	1.000	0	1	1	1	9	14	0	3	0	3.00
King Brady	R	27	1	0	1.000	0	1	1	1	9	8	4	3	0	3.00
Smoky Joe Wood	R	18	1	1	.500	0	6	2	1	23	14	16	11	1	2.35
2 Casey Patten	L	34	0	1	.000	0	1	1	0	3	8	1	0	0	15.00
Charlie Hartman	L	19	0	0	—	0	1	0	0	1	2	1	0	0	4.50
1 Jesse Tanehill	L	33	0	0	—	0	1	1	0	5	4	3	2	0	3.60
2 Jake Thielman	R	29	0	0	—	0	1	0	0	1	3	0	0	0	27.00

PHILADELPHIA — 6th 68-85 .444 22 — CONNIE MACK

Batting

NAME	G by Pos	B	AGE	G	AB	R	H	2B	3B	HR	RBI	BB	SO	SB	BA	SA
TOTALS			30	157	5064	487	1131	183	49	21	392	368		116	.223	.291
Harry Davis	1B147	R	34	147	513	65	127	23	9	5	62	61		20	.248	.357
Danny Murphy	OF84, 2B56, 1B2	R	31	142	525	57	139	28	6	4	66	32		16	.265	.364
Simon Nicholls	SS120, 2B23, 3B7	L	25	150	550	58	119	17	3	4	31	35		14	.216	.280
Jimmy Collins	3B115	R	37	115	403	34	94	14	3	0	30	20		5	.217	.263
Jack Coombs	OF47, P26	B	25	78	220	24	56	9	5	1	23	9		6	.255	.355
Rube Oldring (IL)	OF116	R	24	116	464	38	96	14	2	1	39	18		13	.221	.270
Topsy Hartsel	OF129	L	34	129	460	73	112	16	6	4	29	93		15	.243	.330
1 Ossee Schreckengost	C66, 1B1	R	33	71	207	16	46	7	1	0	16	6		1	.222	.266
Eddie Collins	2B47, SS28, OF10	L	21	102	330	39	90	18	7	1	40	16		8	.273	.379
Mike Powers	C60, 1B2	R	37	62	172	8	31	6	1	0	7	5		1	.180	.227
Socks Seybold (JJ)	OF34	R	37	48	130	5	28	2	0	0	3	12		2	.215	.231
1 Syd Smith	C36, 1B6, OF2	R	24	46	128	6	26	8	0	1	10	4		0	.203	.289
Jack Barry	2B20, SS14, 3B3	R	21	40	135	10	30	4	3	0	8	10		5	.222	.296
Frank Manush	3B20, 2B2	R	24	23	77	6	12	2	1	0	2	0		2	.156	.208
Scotty Barr	2B11, 3B4, 1B2, OF2	R	21	19	56	4	8	2	0	0	1	3		0	.143	.179
1 Herbie Moran	OF19	L	24	19	59	4	9	0	0	0	4	6		1	.153	.153
Jack Lapp	C13	L	24	13	35	4	5	0	1	0	1	5		0	.143	.200
Amos Strunk	OF11	L	19	12	34	4	8	1	0	0	0	4		0	.235	.265
Frank Baker	3B9	R	22	9	31	9	9	3	0	0	2	0		0	.290	.387
Jack Fox	OF8	R	23	9	30	2	6	0	0	0	2	0		2	.200	.200
Shag Shaughnessy	OF8	R	25	8	29	2	9	0	0	0	1	2		3	.310	.310
2 Bert Blue	C6	R	30	6	19	2	3	0	0	0	1	0		0	.158	.158
Joe Jackson	OF5	L	18	5	23	0	3	0	0	0	3	0		0	.130	.130
Ben Egan	C2	R	24	2	6	1	1	1	0	0	1	0		0	.167	.333

Pitching

NAME	T	AGE	W	L	PCT	SV	G	GS	CG	IP	H	BB	SO	SHO	ERA
TOTALS		26	68	85	.444	8	157	157	102	1377	1186	409	740	23	2.57
Rube Vickers	R	30	18	19	.486	2	53	34	21	300	264	71	156	6	2.34
Eddie Plank	L	32	14	16	.467	2	34	28	21	245	202	46	135	4	2.17
Jimmy Dygert	R	23	11	15	.423	1	41	28	15	239	184	97	164	5	2.86
Chief Bender	R	25	8	9	.471	1	18	17	14	139	121	21	85	2	1.75
Jack Coombs	R	25	7	5	.583	1	26	18	10	153	130	64	80	4	2.00
Biff Schlitzer	R	23	6	8	.429	0	24	18	11	131	110	45	57	2	3.16
Nick Carter	R	29	2	5	.286	1	14	4	2	61	58	17	17	0	2.95
Harry Krause	L	19	1	1	.500	0	4	2	1	20	20	4	10	0	2.57
Jack Flater	R	24	1	3	.250	0	5	3	3	39	35	12	8	0	2.08
Doc Martin	R	20	0	1	.000	0	2	1	0	9	9	5	2	0	13.50
Gus Salve	L	22	0	1	.000	0	1	1	1	9	9	8	5	0	2.00
Al Kellog	L	21	0	2	.000	0	3	3	0	19	23	9	7	0	5.82
Bert Maxwell	R	21	0	0	—	0	4	0	0	13	23	9	7	1	11.08
Eddie Files	R	25	0	0	—	0	2	0	0	9	8	3	6	0	6.00

WASHINGTON — 7th 67-85 .441 22.5 — JOE CANTILLON

Batting

NAME	G by Pos	B	AGE	G	AB	R	H	2B	3B	HR	RBI	BB	SO	SB	BA	SA
TOTALS			29	155	5040	479	1185	131	74	8	378	368		170	.235	.295
Jerry Freeman	1B154	R	28	154	531	45	134	15	5	1	45	36		6	.252	.305
Jim Delahanty	2B79	R	29	83	287	33	91	11	4	1	30	24		16	.317	.394
George McBride	SS155	R	27	155	518	47	120	10	6	3	34	41		12	.232	.274
Bill Shipke	3B110, SS3	R	25	111	354	40	71	7	8	0	20	38		15	.200	.282
Ollie Pickering	OF98	R	38	113	373	45	84	7	4	2	30	28		13	.225	.282
Clyde Milan	OF122	L	22	130	485	55	116	10	12	1	32	38		23	.239	.315
Bob Ganley	OF150	L	33	150	549	61	131	19	9	1	36	45		30	.239	.311
Gabby Street	C128	R	25	131	394	31	81	12	7	1	32	40		5	.206	.279
Otis Clymer	OF82, 2B13, 3B2	B	32	110	368	32	93	11	4	1	35	20		19	.253	.313
2 Bob Unglaub	3B39, 2B27, 1B4	R	31	72	276	23	85	10	5	0	29	8		8	.308	.380
1 Dave Altizer	2B38, 3B16, 1B4, SS1	L	31	67	205	19	46	1	1	0	18	13		8	.224	.239
Jack Warner (KJ)	C41, 1B1	L	35	51	116	8	28	2	1	0	8	8		7	.241	.276
Eli Cates	P19, 2B3	R	31	40	59	5	11	1	1	0	3	6		0	.186	.237
Bob Edmundson	OF24	R	29	26	80	5	15	4	1	0	2	7		0	.188	.263
Jesse Tannehill (AJ)	P10	B	33	26	43	1	11	1	0	0	3	2		0	.256	.279
Mike Kahoe	C11	R	34	17	27	1	5	1	0	0	1	0		0	.185	.222

Pitching

NAME	T	AGE	W	L	PCT	SV	G	GS	CG	IP	H	BB	SO	SHO	ERA
TOTALS		27	67	85	.441	8	155	155	105	1395	1238	347	649	15	2.34
Long Tom Hughes	R	29	18	15	.545	4	43	31	24	276	224	77	165	3	2.21
Walter Johnson (IL)	R	20	14	14	.500	1	36	30	23	257	196	52	160	6	1.65
Charlie Smith	R	28	8	13	.381	1	26	23	13	184	166	60	83	1	2.40
1 Cy Falkenberg	R	28	6	2	.750	1	17	8	5	85	70	21	34	1	1.91
Bill Burns (BR)	L	28	6	11	.353	0	23	19	11	165	135	18	55	2	1.69
Burt Keeley	R	28	6	11	.353	1	28	15	12	170	173	48	68	1	2.96
Eli Cates	R	31	4	4	.333	0	19	10	7	115	112	32	33	0	2.50
2 Jesse Tannehill (AJ)	L	33	2	4	.333	0	10	9	5	72	77	23	14	0	3.75
Roy Witherup	R	21	2	4	.333	0	6	4	4	48	51	8	31	0	3.00
1 Casey Patten	L	34	1	2	.333	0	1	1	0	18	25	6	6	0	3.50
Henry Gehring	L	27	0	1	.000	0	3	0	0	5	9	2	0	0	14.40

NEW YORK — 8th 51-103 .331 39.5 — CLARK GRIFFITH 24-32 .429 / KID ELBERFELD 27-71 .276

Batting

NAME	G by Pos	B	AGE	G	AB	R	H	2B	3B	HR	RBI	BB	SO	SB	BA	SA
TOTALS			28	155	5036	456	1187	142	51	12	372	288		230	.236	.291
Hal Chase (JT)	1B98, 2B3, OF3, 3B1	R	25	106	404	50	104	11	3	1	36	15		27	.257	.306
1 Harry Niles	2B85, OF7	R	27	96	361	43	90	14	6	4	24	25		18	.249	.355
Neal Ball	SS130, 2B1	R	27	132	446	34	110	16	2	0	38	21		32	.247	.291
Wid Conroy	3B119, 2B12, OF10	R	31	141	531	44	126	23	3	4	39	14		23	.237	.296
Willie Keeler	OF88	L	36	91	323	38	85	3	1	1	14	31		14	.263	.288
Charlie Hemphill	OF142	L	32	142	505	62	150	12	9	0	44	59		42	.297	.356
1 Jake Stahl	OF67, 1B36	R	28	74	234	24	70	18	5	2	42	11		16	.299	.449
Red Kleinow (BG)	C89, 2B2	R	30	96	279	16	47	3	2	1	13	22		5	.168	.204
George Moriarty	1B52, 3B28, OF10, 2B4	R	22	101	348	25	82	12	1	0	27	11		22	.236	.276
Walter Blair	C60, OF9, 1B3	R	24	74	190	17	36	3	3	0	13	11		4	.190	.237
Irish McIlveen	OF44	R	27	44	169	17	36	3	3	0	8	14		6	.213	.266
2 Frank LaPorte	2B26, OF11	R	28	37	125	12	32	1	2	0	15	4		3	.256	.296
Frank Delahanty	OF36	R	25	37	125	12	32	1	2	0	10	10		9	.256	.296
Queenie O'Roarke	OF14, SS11, 2B4, 3B3	R	24	34	108	5	25	1	0	0	3	4		4	.231	.241
Ed Sweeney	C25, 1B1, OF1	R	19	32	144	5	21	0	2	0	4	7		1	.146	.171
Birdie Cree	OF21	R	25	21	78	5	21	3	0	2	4	7		1	.269	.321
Earle Gardner	2B20	R	24	20	75	7	16	2	0	0	7	4		0	.213	.240
Kid Elberfeld (LJ)	SS17	R	33	19	56	11	11	3	0	0	5	6		1	.196	.250
Mike Donovan	3B5	R	26	5	19	2	5	1	0	0	1	0		0	.263	.316

Pitching

NAME	T	AGE	W	L	PCT	SV	G	GS	CG	IP	H	BB	SO	SHO	ERA
TOTALS		29	51	103	.331	6	155	155	90	1363	1286	457	584	11	3.16
Jack Chesbro	R	34	14	20	.412	3	45	31	20	289	271	67	124	3	2.93
Rube Manning	R	25	13	16	.448	2	41	26	19	245	228	86	113	2	2.94
Joe Lake	R	26	9	22	.290	0	38	29	19	269	252	77	110	2	3.18
Doc Newton	L	30	4	6	.400	1	23	13	6	88	78	41	49	1	2.97
Bill Hogg	R	26	4	15	.211	0	24	21	6	152	155	63	72	0	3.02
Pete Wilson	R	23	3	5	.500	0	9	6	4	39	27	33	28	1	3.46
Al Orth	R	35	2	13	.133	0	17	18	13	134	134	30	22	1	3.43
Slow Joe Doyle	R	26	1	6	.500	0	12	4	2	48	42	14	20	1	2.63
Jack Warhop	R	23	1	0	1.000	0	3	3	0	36	40	8	11	0	4.50
Andy O'Connor	R	23	0	1	.000	0	1	1	0	8	15	7	5	0	10.13
Fred Glade (SA)	R	32	0	4	.000	0	5	3	2	30	30	14	11	0	4.22
Harry Billiard	R	24	0	0	—	0	1	0	0	14	13	13	9	0	2.57
Hippo Vaughn (HJ)	L	20	0	1	.000	0	1	1	0	4	2	1	0	0	4.50
Hal Chase	R	25	0	0	—	0	1	0	0	1	0	0	0	0	0.00

CHICAGO   1st 99-55 .643   FRANK CHANCE

NAME	G by Pos	B	AGE	G	AB	R	H	2B	3B	HR	RBI	BB	SO	SB	BA	SA
TOTALS			29	158	5085	625	1267	197	56	19	492	418		212	.249	.321
Frank Chase	1B126	R	31	129	452	65	123	27	4	2	55	37		27	.272	.363
Johnny Evers	2B123	L	26	126	416	83	125	19	6	0	37	66		36	.300	.375
Joe Tinker	SS157	R	27	157	548	67	146	23	14	6	68	32		30	.266	.392
Harry Steinfeldt	3B150	R	30	150	539	63	130	20	6	1	62	36		12	.241	.306
Wildfire Schulte	OF102	L	25	102	386	42	91	20	2	1	43	29		15	.236	.306
Jimmy Slagle	OF101	L	34	104	352	38	78	4	1	0	26	43		17	.222	.239
Jimmy Sheckard	OF115	L	29	115	403	54	93	18	3	2	22	62		18	.231	.305
Johnny Kling	C117, OF6, 1B2	R	32	126	424	51	117	23	5	4	59	21		16	.276	.382
Solly Hofman	OF50, 1B37, 2B22, 3B9	R	25	120	411	55	100	15	5	2	42	33		15	.243	.319
Del Howard	OF81, 1B5	L	30	96	315	42	88	7	3	1	26	23		11	.279	.330
Pat Moran	C45	R	32	50	150	12	39	5	1	0	12	13		6	.260	.307
Heinie Zimmerman	2B20, OF8, 3B1, SS1	R	21	46	113	17	33	4	1	0	9	1		2	.292	.345
Kid Durbin	OF11	L	21	14	28	3	7	1	0	0	0	2		0	.250	.286
2 Doc Marshall	C4, OF3	R	33		20	4	6	0	1	0	3	0		0	.300	.400
Jack Heyden	OF11	R	27	11	45	3	9	2	0	0	2	1		1	.200	.244
Vin Campbell		L	20	1	1	0	0	0	0	0	0	0		0	.000	.000

NAME	T	AGE	W	L	PCT	SV	G	GS	CG	IP	H	BB	SO	SHO	ERA
TOTALS		30	99	55	.643	12	158	158	108	1434	1137	437	668	29	2.14
Three Finger Brown	R	31	29	9	.763	5	44	31	27	312	214	49	123	9	1.47
Ed Reulbach	R	25	24	7	.774	1	46	35	25	298	227	106	133	7	2.02
Orvie Overall (HJ)	R	27	15	11	.577	4	37	27	16	225	165	78	167	4	1.92
Jack Pfiester	L	30	12	10	.545	0	33	29	18	252	204	70	117	3	2.26
Chick Fraser	R	34	11	9	.550	2	26	17	11	163	141	61	66	2	2.36
Carl Lundgren	R	28	6	9	.400	0	23	15	9	139	149	56	38	1	4.21
2 Andy Coakley	R	25	2	0	1.000	0	4	3	2	20	14	6	7	1	0.90
Rube Kroh	L	21	0	0	—	0	2	1	0	12	9	4	11	0	1.50
Bill Mack	L	23	0	0	—	0	1	0	0	6	5	1	2	0	3.00
Carl Spongberg	R	24	0	0	—	0	1	0	0	7	6	4	0	0	9.00

NEW YORK   2nd(Tie) 98-56 .636 1   JOHN McGRAW

NAME	G by Pos	B	AGE	G	AB	R	H	2B	3B	HR	RBI	BB	SO	SB	BA	SA
TOTALS			28	157	5006	652	1339	182	43	20	562	494		181	.267	.333
Fred Tenney	1B156	L	36	156	583	101	149	20	1	2	49	72		17	.256	.304
Larry Doyle	2B102	L	22	104	377	65	116	16	9	0	33	22		17	.308	.398
Al Bridwell	SS147	L	24	147	467	53	133	14	1	0	46	52		20	.285	.319
Art Devlin	3B157	R	28	157	534	59	135	18	4	2	45	62		19	.253	.313
Mike Donlin	OF155	R	30	155	593	71	198	26	13	6	106	23		30	.334	.452
Cy Seymour	OF155	L	35	156	587	60	157	23	2	5	92	30		18	.267	.339
1 Spike Shannon	OF74	R	30	77	268	34	60	2	1	1	21	28		13	.224	.250
Roger Bresnahan	C139	R	29	140	449	70	127	25	3	1	54	83		14	.283	.359
2 Moose McCormick	OF65	L	27	73	252	31	76	16	3	0	32	4		6	.302	.389
Buck Herzog (WJ)	2B42, SS11, 3B3, OF1	R	22	64	160	38	48	6	2	0	11	36		16	.300	.363
Tom Needham	C47	R	29	54	91	8	19	3	0	0	11	12		0	.209	.242
Fred Merkle	1B11, OF5, 2B1, 3B1	R	19	38	41	6	11	2	1	1	7	4		1	.268	.439
2 Shad Barry	OF31	R	29	37	67	5	10	1	1	0	5	9		1	.149	.194
Sammy Strang	2B14, OF5, SS3	B	31	28	53	8	5	0	0	0	2	23		5	.094	.094
2 Dave Brain	2B3, OF3, 3B2, SS1	R	29	11	17	2	3	0	0	0	1	2		1	.176	.176
Fred Snodgrass	C3	R	20	6	4	2	1	0	0	0	0	0		1	.250	.250
Josh Devore	OF2	L	20	5	6	1	1	0	0	0	0	2		1	.167	.167
Steve Evans	OF1	L	23	2	2	0	1	0	0	0	0	0		0	.500	.500
1 Jack Hannifin	OF1	B	25	1	2	0	0	0	0	0	0	0		0	.000	.000
Art Wilson		R	22	1	0	0	0	0	0	0	0	0		0	.000	.000

NAME	T	AGE	W	L	PCT	SV	G	GS	CG	IP	H	BB	SO	SHO	ERA
TOTALS		28	98	56	.636	18	157	157	95	1411	1214	288	656	25	2.14
Christy Mathewson	R	27	37	11	.771	5	56	44	34	391	285	42	259	11	1.43
Hooks Wiltse	L	28	23	14	.622	2	44	38	30	330	266	73	118	7	2.24
Doc Crandall	R	20	12	12	.500	0	32	24	13	215	198	59	77	0	2.93
Joe McGinnity	R	37	11	7	.611	5	37	20	7	186	192	37	55	5	2.27
Dummy Taylor	R	33	8	5	.615	2	27	15	6	128	127	34	50	1	2.32
Red Ames (IL)	R	25	7	4	.636	1	18	15	5	114	96	77	81	0	1.82
Rube Marquard	R	21	0	1	.000	0	1	1	0	5	6	2	2	0	3.60
Bill Malarkey	R	29	0	2	.000	2	15	0	0	35	31	10	12	0	2.57
Roy Beecher	R	24	0	0	—	0	6	1	0	6	11	3	0	0	7.50
Bull Durham	R	31	0	0	—	0	1	0	0	1	2	1	2	0	9.00

PITTSBURGH   2nd(Tie) 98-56 .636 1   FRED CLARKE

NAME	G by Pos	B	AGE	G	AB	R	H	2B	3B	HR	RBI	BB	SO	SB	BA	SA
TOTALS			29	155	5109	585	1263	162	98	25	496	420		186	.247	.332
Harry Swacina	1B50	R	26	53	176	7	38	6	1	0	13	5		4	.216	.261
Ed Abbaticchio	2B144	R	31	146	500	43	125	16	7	1	61	58		22	.250	.316
Honus Wagner	SS151	R	34	151	568	100	201	39	19	10	109	54		53	.354	.542
Tommy Leach	3B150, OF2	R	30	152	583	93	151	24	16	5	41	54		24	.259	.381
Owen Wilson	OF144	L	24	144	529	47	120	8	7	3	43	22		12	.227	.285
2 Roy Thomas	OF101	L	34	102	386	52	99	11	10	1	24	49		11	.256	.345
Fred Clarke	OF151	L	35	151	551	83	146	18	15	2	53	65		24	.265	.363
George Gibson	C140	R	27	143	486	37	111	19	4	2	45	19		4	.228	.296
Alan Storke (RL)	1B49, 3B6, 2B1	R	23	64	202	20	51	5	3	1	12	9		4	.252	.322
Jim Kane	1B40	L	26	55	145	16	35	3	3	0	22	12		5	.241	.303
Danny Moeller	OF27	R	23	36	109	14	21	3	1	0	9	9		4	.193	.239
Eddie Phelps	C20	R	29	34	64	3	15	2	2	0	11	2		0	.234	.328
2 Spike Shannon	OF32	R	30	30	127	10	25	0	2	0	12	9		5	.197	.228
Doc Gill	1B25	R	29	27	76	10	17	0	1	0	14	11		3	.224	.250
1 Beals Becker	OF17	L	21	20	65	4	10	0	1	0	2	2		2	.154	.185
Charlie Starr	2B12, SS5, 3B2	R	29	20	59	8	11	2	0	0	8	13		6	.186	.220
Paddy O'Connor	C4	R	22	12	16	1	3	0	0	0	0	0		0	.188	.188
Hunky Shaw		B	23	1	1	0	0	0	0	0	0	0		0	.000	.000
John Sullivan	C1	R	35	1	1	0	0	0	0	0	0	0		0	.000	.000
Cy Neighbors	OF1	R	27	1	0	0	0	0	0	0	0	0		0	.000	.000

NAME	T	AGE	W	L	PCT	SV	G	GS	CG	IP	H	BB	SO	SHO	ERA
TOTALS		28	98	56	.636	9	155	155	100	1402	1142	406	468	24	2.12
Nick Maddox	R	21	23	8	.742	1	36	32	22	261	209	90	70	4	2.28
Vic Willis	R	32	23	11	.676	0	41	38	25	305	239	69	97	7	2.07
Howie Camnitz	R	26	16	9	.640	2	38	26	17	237	182	69	118	3	1.56
Sam Leever	R	36	15	7	.682	2	38	30	14	193	179	41	28	4	2.10
Lefty Leifield	L	24	15	14	.517	2	34	26	18	219	168	86	87	5	2.10
2 Irv Young	R	30	4	3	.571	1	16	7	3	90	73	21	31	1	2.00
Chick Brandom	R	21	1	0	.000	1	3	1	1	17	13	4	8	0	0.53
Bob Vail	R	26	1	2	.333	0	4	1	0	15	15	7	9	0	6.00
1 Harlan Young	R	24	0	2	.000	0	8	3	0	48	40	10	17	0	2.25
Deacon Phillippe	R	36	0	0	—	0	5	0	0	12	20	3	1	0	11.25
2 Tom McCarthy	R	24	0	0	—	0	2	1	0	6	3	6	1	0	0.00
Doc Hillebrand	L	28	0	0	—	0	1	0	0	1	1	0	1	0	0.00

PHILADELPHIA   4th 83-71 .539 16   BILLY MURRAY

NAME	G by Pos	B	AGE	G	AB	R	H	2B	3B	HR	RBI	BB	SO	SB	BA	SA
TOTALS			28	155	5012	503	1223	194	68	11	400	334		200	.244	.316
Kitty Bransfield	1B143	R	33	144	527	53	160	25	7	3	71	23		30	.304	.395
Otto Knabe	2B151	R	24	151	555	63	121	26	8	0	27	49		27	.218	.294
Mickey Doolan	SS129	R	28	129	445	29	104	25	4	2	49	17		5	.234	.321
Eddie Grant	3B134, SS13	L	25	147	598	69	146	13	8	0	32	35		27	.244	.293
John Titus	OF149	L	32	149	539	75	154	24	5	2	48	53		22	.286	.360
Ossie Osborn	OF152	L	24	152	555	62	148	19	12	4	44	30		16	.267	.355
Sherry Magee	OF142	R	23	143	508	79	144	30	16	2	57	49		40	.283	.417
Red Dooin	C132	R	29	133	435	28	108	17	4	0	41	17		20	.248	.306
Ernie Courtney	3B22, 1B13, 2B5, SS2	L	33	60	160	14	29	3	0	0	6	15		1	.181	.200
Fred Jacklitsch	C30	R	32	37	86	6	19	3	0	0	7	14		3	.221	.256
Wally Clement	OF8	L	26	16	36	0	8	3	0	0	1	0		2	.222	.306
Dave Shean	SS14	R	30	14	48	4	7	2	0	0	2	1		1	.146	.188
1 Moose McCormick	OF5	L	27	11	22	0	2	0	0	0	0	2		0	.091	.091
Charlie Johnson	OF4	R	23	6	16	2	4	0	1	0	2	1		0	.250	.375
1 Roy Thomas	OF6	L	34	6	12	0	2	0	0	0	0	2		0	.167	.167
Kid Gleason	2B1, OF1	B	41	2	1	0	0	0	0	0	0	0		0	.000	.000
Pep Deininger	OF1	L	30	1	0	0	0	0	0	0	0	0		0	.000	.000

NAME	T	AGE	W	L	PCT	SV	G	GS	CG	IP	H	BB	SO	SHO	ERA
TOTALS		27	83	71	.539	6	155	155	116	1393	1167	379	476	22	2.10
George McQuillan	R	23	23	17	.575	2	48	42	32	360	263	91	114	7	1.52
Tully Sparks	R	33	16	15	.516	2	33	31	24	263	251	51	85	2	2.60
Frank Corridon	R	27	14	10	.583	1	27	24	18	208	178	48	50	2	2.51
Lew Moren	L	24	11	14	.440	0	28	16	9	154	146	49	72	4	2.92
Bill Foxen	L	29	7	7	.500	0	22	16	10	147	126	53	52	2	1.96
Lew Richie	R	24	7	10	.412	1	25	15	13	158	125	49	58	2	1.83
Harry Coveleski	L	22	4	1	.800	0	6	5	5	44	29	12	22	2	1.23
Harry Hoch	R	21	1	2	.667	0	5	3	1	26	20	13	4	0	1.00
Earl Moore	R	28	0	0	—	0	3	3	3	26	20	8	16	1	0.00
Buster Brown	R	26	0	0	—	0	1	1	1	7	9	5	3	0	2.57

CINCINNATI   5th 73-81 .474 26   JOHN GANZEL

NAME	G by Pos	B	AGE	G	AB	R	H	2B	3B	HR	RBI	BB	SO	SB	BA	SA
TOTALS			28	155	4879	488	1108	129	77	14	398	372		196	.227	.294
John Ganzel	1B108	R	34	112	388	32	97	16	10	1	53	19		6	.250	.351
Miller Huggins	2B135	B	30	135	498	65	119	14	5	0	23	58		30	.239	.287
Rudy Hulswitt	SS118, 2B1	R	31	119	445	29	104	8	9	5	28	30		7	.228	.285
Hans Lobert	3B99, SS35, OF21	R	26	155	570	71	167	17	18	4	63	46		47	.293	.407
Mike Mitchell	OF118, 1B1	R	28	119	446	41	90	9	6	1	37	46		18	.222	.281
John Kane	OF127, 2B1	R	25	130	455	61	97	11	7	3	23	43		30	.213	.288
Dode Paskert	OF116	R	26	118	395	40	96	14	4	1	36	27		25	.244	.306
Admiral Schlei	C88	R	30	92	300	31	66	6	4	1	22	22		2	.220	.277
Larry McLean	C69, 1B19	R	26	99	309	24	67	9	4	1	28	15		2	.217	.282
Mike Mowrey (KJ)	3B56, SS3, OF3	R	24	77	227	17	50	9	1	0	23	12		5	.220	.269
Bob Bescher	OF32	B	24	32	114	16	31	5	5	0	17	9		10	.272	.404
Dick Hoblitzell	1B29	R	19	29	114	8	29	3	2	0	12	2		2	.254	.316
Dick Bayless	OF19	L	24	19	71	7	16	1	0	0	9	0		0	.225	.282
Dick Egan	2B18	R	24	18	68	8	14	3	1	0	5	2		7	.206	.279
1 Dave Brain (IL)	OF16	R	29	16	55	5	6	1	0	0	1	3		0	.109	.109
Tom Daley	OF13	L	23	14	46	5	5	0	0	0	1	3		1	.109	.109
Bob Coulson	OF6	R	21	8	18	3	6	1	0	0	3	1		0	.333	.500
Bill McGilvray		L	25	2	2	1	0	0	0	0	0	0		0	.000	.000
Bunny Pearce (NJ)	C2	R	23	2	2	0	0	0	0	0	0	0		0	.000	.000

NAME	T	AGE	W	L	PCT	SV	G	GS	CG	IP	H	BB	SO	SHO	ERA
TOTALS		30	73	81	.474	8	155	155	110	1384	1218	415	433	17	2.37
Bob Spade	R	34	17	12	.586	1	35	28	22	249	230	85	74	2	2.75
Bob Ewing	R	35	17	15	.531	3	37	32	23	294	247	57	95	4	2.20
Bill Campbell	L	34	12	13	.480	2	35	24	19	221	203	44	73	2	2.61
Jake Weimer	L	34	7	7	.533	0	15	9	7	117	110	50	36	2	2.38
1 Andy Coakley	R	25	8	18	.308	2	32	28	20	242	219	64	61	4	1.86
Jean Dubuc	R	19	5	6	.455	0	15	9	7	85	62	41	32	1	2.75
Jack Rowan	R	22	3	3	.500	0	7	4	1	49	46	16	24	1	1.84
Marty O'Toole	R	20	1	0	1.000	0	1	1	1	15	15	7	5	0	3.52
Jake Volz	L	27	1	0	.333	0	7	1	1	23	16	12	6	0	3.52
Jack Doscher (BL)	L	27	1	0	.250	0	7	4	3	44	31	22	7	0	1.84
Ralph Savidge	R	23	0	0	—	0	2	1	0	18	18	6	3	0	5.00
1 Tom McCarthy	R	24	0	0	—	0	1	0	0	1	2	1	0	0	9.00
Bill Tozer	R	23	0	0	—	0	1	1	1	11	11	4	1	0	1.64
1 Charlie Rhodes	L	20	0	0	—	0	3	0	0	10	1	0	0	0	3.60

NAME	G by Pos	B	AGE	G	AB	R	H	2B	3B	HR	RBI	BB	SO	SB	BA	SA
BOSTON	6th 63-91 .409 36			JOE KELLEY												
TOTALS			31	156	5131	537	1228	137	43	17	426	414		134	.239	.293
Dan McGann	1B121, 2B9	B	36	135	475	52	114	8	5	2	55	38		9	.240	.291
Claude Ritchey	2B120	B	34	121	421	44	115	10	3	2	36	50		7	.273	.325
Bill Dahlen	SS144	R	38	144	524	50	125	23	2	3	48	35		10	.239	.307
Bill Sweeney	3B123, SS2, 2B1	R	22	127	418	44	102	15	3	0	40	45		17	.244	.294
George Browne	OF138	L	32	138	536	61	122	10	6	1	34	34		13	.228	.274
Ginger Beaumont	OF121	L	31	125	476	66	127	20	6	2	52	42		13	.267	.347
Johnny Bates	OF117	L	26	127	445	48	115	14	6	1	29	35		25	.258	.324
Frank Bowerman (HJ)	C63, 1B11		39	86	254	16	58	8	1	1	25	13		4	.228	.280
Peaches Graham	C62, 2B5	R	31	75	215	22	59	5	0	0	22	23		4	.274	.298
2 Jack Hannifin	3B35, 2B22, SS15, OF7	R	24	74	257	30	53	6	2	2	22	28		7	.206	.268
Joe Kelley	OF38, 1B10	R	36	62	228	25	59	8	2	1	17	27		1	.259	.338
2 Beals Becker	OF43	L	21	43	171	13	47	3	1	0	7	7		5	.275	.304
Harry Smith	C38	R	33	41	130	13	32	2	1	1	16	7		2	.246	.315
Fred Stern	1B18	L	22	19	72	9	20	0	1	0	3	2		1	.278	.306
2 Herbie Moran	OF8	L	24	8	29	3	8	0	0	0	2	1		1	.276	.276
Jim Ball	C6	R	24	6	15	1	1	0	0	0	0	1		0	.067	.067
Tommy Thomas	SS5	R	24	5	13	2	2	0	0	0	1	3		2	.154	.154

NAME	T	AGE	W	L	PCT	SV	G	GS	CG	IP	H	BB	SO	SHO	ERA
		28	63	91	.409	1	156	156	92	1405	1262	423	416	14	2.79
Cecil Ferguson (AJ)	R	21	12	11	.522	1	37	21	13	208	168	84	98	3	2.47
Vive Lindaman	R	30	12	16	.429	1	43	30	21	271	246	70	68	2	2.36
Patsy Flaherty	L	32	12	18	.400	0	31	31	21	244	221	81	50	3	3.25
Gus Dorner	R	31	8	19	.296	0	38	28	14	216	176	77	41	3	3.54
3 Tom McCarthy (BH)	R	24	6	3	.667	0	14	11	7	94	77	28	27	2	1.63
1 Irv Young	L	30	4	8	.333	0	16	11	7	85	94	19	32	1	2.86
Tom Tuckey	R	23	3	3	.500	0	8	8	3	72	60	20	26	1	2.50
Jake Boultes	R	23	3	5	.375	0	17	5	1	75	80	8	28	0	3.00
Bill Chappelle	R	27	4	4	.333	0	13	6	3	70	60	17	23	1	1.80
Al Mattern	L	25	1	3	.250	0	5	3	1	30	30	6	8	1	2.10
2 Harlan Young	R	24	0	1	.000	0	6	2	1	27	29	4	12	0	3.33
Big Jeff Pfeffer (AJ)	R	26	0	0	—	0	4	0	0	10	18	8	3	0	12.60
Chick Maloney	R	22	0	0	—	0	1	0	0	2	3	1	0	0	4.50

NAME	G by Pos	B	AGE	G	AB	R	H	2B	3B	HR	RBI	BB	SO	SB	BA	SA
BROOKLYN	7th 53-101 .344 46			PASTY DONOVAN												
TOTALS			27	154	4897	375	1044	110	60	28	306	323		113	.213	.277
Tim Jordan	1B146	L	29	148	515	58	127	18	5	12	60	59		9	.247	.371
Harry Pattee	2B74	L	26	80	264	19	57	5	2	0	9	25		24	.216	.250
Phil Lewis	SS116	R	24	118	415	22	91	5	6	1	30	13		9	.219	.267
Tommy Sheehan	3B145	R	30	146	468	45	100	18	2	0	29	53		9	.214	.261
Harry Lumley	OF116	L	27	127	440	36	95	13	12	4	39	29		4	.216	.327
Billy Maloney	OF103, C4	L	30	113	359	31	70	5	7	3	17	24		14	.195	.273
Al Burch	OF116	L	24	123	456	45	111	8	4	2	18	33		15	.243	.292
Bill Bergen	C99	R	35	99	302	8	53	8	2	0	15	5		1	.175	.215
John Hummell	OF95, 2B43, SS9, 1B8	R	25	154	594	51	143	11	12	4	41	34		20	.241	.320
W. Alperman (BN)	2B42, 3B9, OF5, SS2	R	28	70	213	17	42	3	1	0	15	9		2	.197	.235
Tommy McMillan	SS29, OF14	R	20	43	147	9	35	3	0	0	3	9		5	.238	.259
Lew Ritter	C37	R	32	38	99	6	19	2	1	0	2	7		0	.192	.232
Joe Dunn	C20	R	23	20	64	3	11	3	0	0	5	0		0	.172	.219
Tom Catterson	OF18	L	23	19	68	5	13	1	1	1	2	5		1	.191	.279
Alex Farmer	C11	R	31	12	30	1	5	1	0	0	1	1		0	.167	.200
Simmy Murch	1B2	R	27	6	11	1	2	1	0	0	0	1		0	.182	.273

NAME	T	AGE	W	L	PCT	SV	G	GS	CG	IP	H	BB	SO	SHO	ERA
		29	53	101	.344	4	154	154	118	1369	1165	444	535	20	2.47
Nap Rucker	L	23	17	19	.472	1	42	37	30	333	265	125	199	6	2.08
Kaiser Wilhelm	R	34	16	22	.571	0	42	36	33	332	266	83	99	6	1.87
Harry McIntire	R	30	11	20	.355	2	40	35	26	288	259	90	108	4	2.69
George Bell	R	33	4	15	.211	1	29	19	12	155	162	45	63	2	3.60
Jim Pastorius	L	26	4	20	.167	0	28	25	16	214	171	74	54	2	2.44
Jim Holmes	R	25	1	4	.200	0	13	1	1	40	37	20	10	0	3.38
Abe Kruger	R	23	0	1	.000	0	2	1	0	6	5	3	2	0	4.50
Pembroke Finlayson	R	19	0	0	—	0	1	0	0	1	0	4	0	0	135.00

NAME	G by Pos	B	AGE	G	AB	R	H	2B	3B	HR	RBI	BB	SO	SB	BA	SA
ST. LOUIS	8th 49-105 .318 50			JOHN McCLOSKEY												
TOTALS			27	154	4959	372	1105	134	57	17	301	282		150	.223	.283
Ed Konetchy	1B154	R	22	154	545	46	135	19	12	5	50	38		16	.248	.354
Billy Gilbert	2B89	R	32	89	276	12	59	7	0	0	10	20		6	.214	.239
Patsy O'Rourke	SS53	R	27	53	164	8	32	4	2	0	16	14		2	.195	.244
Bobby Byrne	3B122, SS4	R	23	127	439	27	84	7	1	0	14	23		5	.191	.212
Red Murray	OF154	R	24	154	593	64	167	19	15	7	62	37		48	.282	.400
Al Shaw	OF91, SS4, 3B1	L	27	107	367	40	97	13	4	1	19	25		9	.264	.330
Joe Delahanty	OF138	L	32	140	499	37	127	14	11	4	44	32		11	.255	.333
Bill Ludwig	C62	R	26	66	187	15	34	2	2	0	8	16		3	.182	.214
Chappie Charles	2B65, SS31, 3B23	R	27	121	454	39	93	14	3	1	17	19		15	.205	.256
1 Shad Barry	OF69, SS2	R	29	74	268	24	61	8	1	0	11	19		9	.228	.265
Art Hoelskoetter	C41, 3B2, 1B1, 2B1	R	25	62	155	10	36	7	1	0	6	6		1	.232	.290
Jack Bliss	C43	R	26	44	136	9	29	4	0	1	5	8		3	.213	.265
Champ Osteen	SS17, 3B12	R	31	29	112	2	22	4	0	0	11	0		0	.196	.232
Tom Reilly	SS29	R	23	29	81	5	14	1	0	1	3	2		4	.173	.222
Wilbur Murdoch	OF16	R	33	27	62	5	16	3	0	0	5	3		4	.258	.306
Walter Morris	SS23	R	28	23	73	1	13	1	1	0	2	0		1	.178	.219
Charley Moran	C16	R	30	21	63	2	11	1	2	0	2	0		0	.175	.254
Ralph McLaurin	OF6	L	23	8	22	2	5	0	0	0	0	0		0	.227	.227
1 Doc Marshall	C6	R	33	6	14	0	1	0	0	0	1	0		0	.071	.071

NAME	T	AGE	W	L	PCT	SV	G	GS	CG	IP	H	BB	SO	SHO	ERA
		26	49	105	.318	4	154	154	97	1368	1217	430	528	13	2.64
Bugs Raymond	R	26	15	25	.375	2	48	37	23	324	236	95	145	5	2.03
Johnny Lush	L	22	11	18	.379	1	38	32	23	251	221	57	93	3	2.12
Fred Beebe	R	27	5	13	.278	0	29	19	12	174	134	66	72	0	2.64
Art Fromme	R	24	5	13	.278	0	20	14	9	116	102	50	62	2	2.72
Ed Karger	R	25	4	9	.308	0	22	15	9	141	148	50	34	1	3.06
Slim Sallee	L	23	3	8	.273	0	25	12	7	129	144	36	39	1	3.14
Irv Higginbotham	R	26	3	8	.273	0	19	11	7	107	113	33	38	1	3.20
2 Charlie Rhodes	R	23	1	2	.333	0	4	4	3	33	23	12	15	0	3.00
Orson Baldwin	R	26	1	3	.250	0	4	4	0	15	16	11	5	0	6.00
Stony McGlynn	R	36	1	6	.143	1	16	6	4	76	76	17	23	0	3.43
Fred Gaiser	R		0	0	—	0	1	1	0	4	3	2	0	0	9.00

WORLD SERIES — CHICAGO (NL) 4 DETROIT (AL) 1

LINE SCORES

TEAM	1	2	3	4	5	6	7	8	9	10	11	12	R	H	E

Game 1   October 10 at Detroit

CHI(NL)	0	0	4	0	0	0	1	0	5				10	14	2
DET(AL)	1	0	0	0	0	3	0	2					6	10	4

Reulbach, **Overall** (7), Killian, **Summers** (3)
Brown (8)

Game 2   October 11 at Chicago

DET	0	0	0	0	0	0	0	1		1	4	1
CHI	0	0	0	0	0	0	6	X		6	7	1

Donovan   Overall

Game 3   October 12 at Chicago

DET	1	0	0	0	0	5	0	2	0		8	11	4
CHI	0	0	0	3	0	0	0	0	0		3	7	2

Mullin   Pfiester, Reulbach (9)

Game 4   October 13 at Detroit

CHI	0	0	2	0	0	0	0	0	1		3	10	0
DET	0	0	0	0	0	0	0	0	0		0	4	1

Brown   Summers, Winter (9)

Game 5   October 14 at Detroit

CHI	1	0	0	0	1	0	0	0	0		2	10	0
DET	0	0	0	0	0	0	0	0	0		0	3	0

Overall   Donovan

COMPOSITE BATTING

NAME	POS	G	AB	R	H	2B	3B	HR	RBI	BA
Chicago (NL)										
Totals		5	164	24	48	4	2	1	20	.293
Sheckard	OF	5	21	2	5	2	0	0	1	.238
Evers	2B	5	20	5	7	1	0	0	2	.350
Chance	1B	5	19	4	8	0	0	0	2	.421
Hofman	OF	5	19	2	6	0	1	0	4	.316
Tinker	SS	5	19	2	5	0	1	4	4	.263
Schulte	OF	5	18	4	7	0	1	0	4	.389
Steinfeldt	3B	5	16	3	4	0	0	0	3	.250
Kling	C	5	16	4	1	0	0	0	2	.250
Overall	P	3	6	0	2	0	0	0	0	.333
Brown	P	2	4	0	0	0	0	0	0	.000
Reulbach	P	2	4	0	0	0	0	0	0	.000
Pfiester	P	1	2	0	0	0	0	0	0	.000
Howard	PH	1	1	0	0	0	0	0	0	.000
Detroit (AL)										
Totals		5	158	15	32	5	0	0	14	.203
Crawford	OF	5	21	2	5	1	0	0	1	.238
Cobb	OF	5	19	3	7	1	0	0	4	.368
Rossman	1B	5	19	3	4	0	0	0	3	.211
O'Leary	SS	5	19	2	3	0	0	0	1	.158
McIntyre	OF	5	18	2	4	1	0	0	0	.222
Schaefer	3B-2B	5	16	0	2	0	0	0	0	.125
Schmidt	C	4	14	0	1	0	0	0	0	.071
Coughlin	3B	3	8	0	1	0	0	0	0	.125
Downs	2B	2	6	1	1	1	0	0	0	.167
Summers	P	2	5	0	1	0	0	0	0	.200
Thomas	C	2	4	0	2	1	0	0	0	.500
Donovan	P	2	3	0	1	0	0	0	0	.333
Mullin	P	1	3	1	1	0	0	0	0	.333
Jones	PH	3	2	1	0	0	0	0	0	.000
Killian	P	1	0	0	0	0	0	0	0	—
Winter	P	1	0	0	0	0	0	0	0	—

COMPOSITE PITCHING

NAME	G	IP	H	BB	SO	W	L	SV	ERA
Chicago (NL)									
Totals	5	45	32	12	26	4	1	0	2.60
Overall	3	18.1	7	7	15	2	0	0	0.98
Brown	2	11	6	1	5	2	0	0	0.00
Pfiester	1	8	10	3	1	0	1	0	7.88
Reulbach	2	7.2	9	1	5	0	0	0	4.70
Detroit (AL)									
Totals	5	44	48	13	26	1	4	0	3.68
Donovan	2	17	17	4	10	0	2	0	4.24
Summers	2	14.2	18	4	7	0	2	0	4.30
Mullin	1	9	7	1	8	1	0	0	0.00
Killian	1	2.1	5	3	1	0	0	0	11.57
Winter	1	1	1	1	0	0	0	0	0.00

1909 Cobb — Everything but the Last Laugh

After winning three straight National League pennants, and coming up on the long end of the 1908 Merkle incident, the Chicago Cubs entered the season confident of an unprecedented fourth consecutive senior circuit title. The Cubs got off to a slow start out of the gate, due largely to the holdout of catcher Johnny Kling and the nervous breakdown of second baseman Johnny Evers, but from May until the season's end, the team played championship ball. Three Finger Brown, Orvie Overall, and Ed Reulbach all pitched effectively, forming the heart of a hill staff that was the heart of the Cubs. The Cubs wound up with 104 victories, five more than the 1908 champions, but had to settle for a disappointing second-place finish. While Chicago played good ball for five months, the Pittsburgh Pirates were consistent winners all year, starting fast and never leaving first place after May 5. Honus Wagner proved the difference as he led the Pirates to the crown afield as well as at bat, winning his fourth consecutive batting crown with a .339 average and knocking in 100 runs to take honors also in that category. Manager Fred Clarke and rookie second baseman Dots Miller also produced well with the bat, contributing to the best offense in the league. Vic Willis and Howie Camnitz chalked up 20-win seasons on the mound for the 110-victory winning Pirates. The rest of the teams trailed badly, with only the Cubs and the New York Giants closer than 30 games to the top.

As a three pennant streak ended in the National League, the same streak was achieved in the American League. The Detroit Tigers overcame a mid-season slump to chalk up their third straight crown. The Mackmen of Philadelphia were expected to be second-division residents, but the rebuilt Athletics held the lead for most of August before the champion Tigers came on with a rush to reclaim the throne. The Tigers flashed strong teeth with Ty Cobb and Sam Crawford filling the center of the lineup. Good claws were evident in a pitching staff aced by 29-victory winner George Mullin and 22-game winner Ed Willett. Outside of Mullin and Willett the only American League pitcher to win 20 games was Frank Smith of the White Sox.

Compared to the Tiger veteran lineup, the Athletics were babes in arms, sporting a new trio of infielders in Eddie Collins, Frank Baker, and Jack Barry. The Athletic pitching staff of Eddie Plank, Chief Bender, Cy Morgan, Harry Krause, and Jack Coombs was the league's best, but the Tiger attack prevailed in the flag chase. Cobb dominated the offensive statistics, pacing the loop in batting average with .377, home runs with 9, and runs batted in with 107. In addition to becoming the second man in modern baseball to capture the Triple Crown, Cobb also took stolen base honors with 76 swipes.

The Series was anticipated as a match between stars Ty Cobb and Honus Wagner, but a Pirate second-line pitcher named Babe Adams stole the spotlight with three complete game victories in leading the Pirates to the championship over the Tigers in seven games. Adams posted a 12-3 mark during regular season as a rookie spot starter and reliever, and manager Clarke fingered him as a surprise opening game pitcher. A victory in game one was repeated in games five and seven to etch Adams' name into the record books. As far as the Wagner-Cobb duel was concerned, the Flying Dutchman bested the Georgia Peach .333-.231 in batting and 6-2 in stolen bases.

Institutions came and passed for the national pastime in 1909. Harry C. Pulliam's six-year reign as National League President came to an end with his nervous breakdown and his suicide by pistol in New York on July 29. On a less morbid note, Forbes Field in Pittsburgh and Shibe Park in Philadelphia opened their gates for the first time, gates which would not be boarded up until 60 years had passed and countless memorable moments in baseball had occurred on their playing fields. Of all the events that were to occur, the one that never came about in the expanse of Forbes Field was a no-hitter, leaving that park the only one in all of baseball history to close its doors without the incident of such notoriety.

1909 AMERICAN LEAGUE

DETROIT — 1st 98-54 .645 — HUGHIE JENNINGS

NAME	G by Pos	B	AGE	G	AB	R	H	2B	3B	HR	RBI	BB	SO	SB	BA	SA
TOTALS			27	158	5095	666	1360	209	58	19	521	397		280	.267	.342
1 Claude Rossman	1B75	L	28	82	287	16	75	8	3	0	39	13		10	.261	.310
1 Germany Schaefer	2B86, OF1	R	32	87	280	26	70	12	0	0	22	14		12	.250	.293
Donie Bush	SS157	B	21	157	532	114	145	18	2	0	33	88		53	.273	.314
George Moriarty	3B106, 1B24	R	23	133	473	43	129	20	4	1	39	24		34	.273	.338
Ty Cobb	OF156	L	22	156	573	116	216	33	10	9	107	48		76	.377	.517
Sam Crawford	OF139, 1B17	L	29	156	589	83	185	35	14	6	97	47		30	.314	.452
Matty McIntyre	OF122	L	29	125	476	65	116	18	9	1	34	54		13	.244	.326
Boss Schmidt	C81, OF1	B	28	84	253	21	53	8	2	1	28	7		7	.209	.269
Oscar Stange	C77	R	26	77	252	17	66	8	6	0	21	11		2	.262	.341
Charley O'Leary	3B54, 2B15, SS4, OF2	R	26	76	261	29	53	10	0	0	13	6		9	.203	.241
Davy Jones	OF57	L	29	69	204	44	57	2	2	0	10	28		12	.279	.309
2 Jim Delahanty	2B46	R	30	46	150	29	38	10	1	0	20	17		9	.253	.333
2 Tom Jones	1B44	R	32	44	153	13	43	9	0	0	18	5		9	.281	.340
1 Red Killefer	2B17, OF1	R	24	23	61	6	17	2	2	1	4	3		2	.279	.428
Heinie Beckendorf	C15	R	25	15	27	1	7	1	0	0	1	2		0	.259	.296
Joe Casey	C3	R	21	3	5	1	0	0	0	0	0	1		0	.000	.000
Del Gainer	1B2	R	22	2	5	0	1	0	0	0	0	0		0	.200	.200
Hughie Jennings	1B2	R	40	2	4	1	2	0	0	0	0	0		2	.500	.500

NAME	T	AGE	W	L	PCT	SV	G	GS	CG	IP	H	BB	SO	SHO	ERA
		27	98	54	.645	14	158	158	117	1420	1254	359	528	17	2.26
George Mullin	R	28	29	8	.763	1	40	35	29	304	258	78	124	3	2.22
Ed Willett	R	25	22	9	.710	1	41	34	25	293	239	76	89	3	2.33
Ed Summers	R	24	19	9	.679	1	35	32	24	282	243	52	107	3	2.23
Ed Killian	L	32	11	9	.550	1	25	19	14	173	150	49	54	3	1.72
Wild Bill Donovan	R	32	8	7	.533	2	21	17	13	140	121	60	76	4	2.31
Ralph Works	R	21	3	1	.750	3	16	4	4	64	62	17	31	0	1.97
Kid Speer	L	23	3	3	.500	2	12	8	4	76	88	13	12	0	2.84
George Suggs	R	26	2	3	.400	1	9	4	2	44	34	10	18	0	2.03
Elijah Jones	R	27	1	1	.500	0	2	2	0	10	10	0	2	0	2.70
Ed Lafitte	R	23	1	0	1.000	1	1	1	1	14	22	2	11	0	3.86
Bill Lelivelt	R	24	0	2	.000	1	4	2	1	20	27	2	4	0	4.50

PHILADELPHIA — 2nd 95-58 .621 3.5 — CONNIE MACK

NAME	G by Pos	B	AGE	G	AB	R	H	2B	3B	HR	RBI	BB	SO	SB	BA	SA
TOTALS			28	153	4905	600	1259	186	87	22	498	403		205	.257	.343
Harry Davis	1B149	R	35	149	530	73	142	22	11	4	75	51		20	.268	.374
Eddie Collins	2B152, SS1	L	22	153	572	104	198	30	10	3	56	62		67	.346	.449
Jack Barry	SS124	R	22	124	409	56	88	11	2	1	23	44		17	.215	.259
Frank Baker	3B146	L	23	148	541	73	165	27	19	4	85	26		20	.305	.447
Danny Murphy	OF149	R	32	149	541	61	152	28	14	5	69	35		19	.281	.412
Rube Oldring	OF89, 1B1	R	25	90	326	39	75	13	7	2	28	20		17	.230	.331
2 Bob Ganley	OF77	L	34	80	274	32	54	4	7	0	9	28		16	.197	.226
Ira Thomas	C84	R	28	84	256	22	57	9	3	0	31	18		4	.223	.281
Topsy Hartsel	OF74	L	35	83	267	30	72	4	4	1	18	48		3	.270	.326
Heinie Heitmuller	OF60	L	26	64	210	36	60	9	8	0	15	18		7	.286	.405
Paddy Livingston	C64	R	29	64	175	15	41	6	4	0	15	15		4	.234	.314
Scotty Barr	OF15, 1B7	R	22	22	51	5	4	1	0	0	1	11		2	.078	.098
Jack Lapp	C19	L	24	21	56	8	19	3	1	0	10	3		1	.339	.464
Simon Nicholls	SS14, 3B5, 1B1	R	26	21	71	10	15	2	1	0	3	3		0	.211	.268
Stuffy McInnis	SS14	R	18	19	46	4	11	0	0	1	4	2		0	.239	.304
Amos Strunk	OF9	L	20	11	35	1	4	0	0	0	2	1		2	.114	.114
Morrie Rath	SS4, 3B2	L	22	7	26	4	7	1	0	0	3	2		1	.269	.308
Joe Jackson	OF4	L	19	5	17	3	5	0	0	0	3	1		0	.294	.294
Ed Larkin	C2	R	24	2	6	0	1	0	0	0	1	1		0	.167	.167
Harry Curry	2B1	R	23	1	4	1	1	0	0	0	0	0		0	.250	.250
Mike Powers (DD)	C1	R	38	1	4	1	1	0	0	0	0	0		0	.250	.250

NAME	T	AGE	W	L	PCT	SV	G	GS	CG	IP	H	BB	SO	SHO	ERA
		27	95	58	.621	5	153	153	111	1388	1069	386	728	27	1.92
Eddie Plank	L	33	19	10	.655	0	34	33	24	275	215	62	132	3	1.70
Chief Bender	R	26	18	8	.692	1	34	29	24	250	196	45	161	5	1.66
Harry Krause	L	20	18	8	.692	1	32	21	16	213	151	49	139	7	1.39
2 Cy Morgan	R	30	16	11	.593	0	28	26	21	229	152	71	81	5	1.65
Jack Coombs	R	26	12	11	.522	1	31	24	19	206	156	73	97	6	2.43
Jimmy Dygert	R	24	8	5	.615	1	32	13	6	137	117	50	79	1	2.43
Rube Vickers	R	31	3	2	.600	1	18	3	1	56	60	19	25	0	3.38
John Kull	L	28	1	0	1.000	0	1	0	0	3	3	5	4	0	3.00
1 Biff Schlitzer	R	24	0	3	.000	0	4	3	0	13	13	7	6	0	5.54
Tommy Atkins	L	21	0	0	—	0	1	1	0	6	6	5	4	0	4.50

BOSTON — 3rd 88-63 .583 9.5 — FRED LAKE

NAME	G by Pos	B	AGE	G	AB	R	H	2B	3B	HR	RBI	BB	SO	SB	BA	SA
TOTALS			26	152	4964	597	1306	151	69	20	474	348		215	.263	.333
Jake Stahl	1B126	R	29	127	435	62	128	19	12	6	60	43		16	.294	.434
Amby McConnell	2B121	L	26	121	453	61	108	14	4	0	36	34		26	.238	.289
Heinie Wagner	SS123, 2B1	R	28	124	430	53	110	16	7	1	49	35		18	.256	.333
Harry Lord	3B134	L	27	136	534	86	166	12	7	0	31	20		36	.311	.360
1 Doc Gessler	OF111, 1B1	L	28	111	386	56	115	26	6	1	46	31		16	.298	.365
Tris Speaker	OF142	L	21	143	544	73	168	26	13	7	77	38		35	.309	.443
Harry Niles	OF117, 3B13, SS9, 2B5	R	28	145	546	64	134	12	5	1	38	39		27	.245	.291
Bill Carrigan	C77, 1B8	R	25	94	280	25	83	13	2	1	36	17		2	.296	.368
Harry Hooper	OF74	L	21	81	255	29	72	3	4	0	12	16		15	.282	.325
Pat Donahue	C58	R	24	64	176	14	42	4	1	2	25	17		2	.239	.307
Harry Wolter	1B17, P10, OF9	L	25	54	110	18	27	7	2	2	10	9		2	.244	.378
Charlie French	2B8, SS23	L	25	51	167	15	42	3	1	0	13	15		8	.251	.281
Tubby Spencer	C26	R	22	28	74	6	12	1	0	0	9	6		2	.162	.176
Larry Gardner	3B8, SS5	L	23	19	37	7	11	1	2	0	5	4		1	.297	.432
Jack Thoney (NJ)	OF10	R	29	13	40	1	5	1	0	0	3	2		2	.125	.150
Tom Madden	C7	R	26	10	17	0	4	0	0	0	2	0		0	.235	.235
Babe Danzig	1B3	R	22	6	13	0	2	0	0	0	2	0		0	.154	.154
Paul Howard	OF6	R	25	6	15	2	3	1	0	0	2	3		0	.200	.267
Steve Yerkes		R	21	2	2	0	1	0	0	0	0	0		0	.500	.500

NAME	T	AGE	W	L	PCT	SV	G	GS	CG	IP	H	BB	SO	SHO	ERA
		25	88	63	.583	19	152	152	75	1358	1214	384	555	11	2.60
Frank Arellanes	R	27	16	12	.571	8	45	26	17	231	192	43	82	1	2.18
Eddie Cicotte	R	25	14	5	.737	0	27	17	10	162	117	56	84	1	1.95
Smoky Joe Wood (KJ)	R	19	11	7	.611	2	24	19	13	159	121	43	88	4	2.21
Charlie Chech	R	31	7	5	.583	0	17	13	6	107	107	27	40	1	2.55
Charley Hall	R	26	4	4	.600	0	11	7	3	60	59	17	27	0	2.55
2 Ed Karger	R	26	3	6	.625	0	12	6	3	68	71	22	17	0	3.18
2 Biff Schlitzer	R	24	5	4	.444	1	13	6	5	76	81	19	24	0	3.93
Ray Collins	L	22	4	3	.571	0	12	8	4	74	70	18	31	2	2.80
Elmer Steele	R	25	3	6	.667	3	16	8	2	76	75	15	32	0	3.93
2 Charlie Smith	R	29	3	0	1.000	0	3	2	2	26	20	8	16	0	2.16
Jack Ryan	R	24	3	3	.500	0	13	6	2	59	65	20	22	0	3.44
Fred Burchell	R	29	3	4	.429	0	10	5	4	52	51	11	12	0	3.46
Harry Wolter	L	24	3	5	.500	1	10	6	0	53	53	28	20	0	3.91
Larry Pape	R	25	2	0	1.000	2	7	4	2	58	46	12	18	1	2.01
1 Cy Morgan	R	30	0	2	.250	1	12	10	5	65	52	31	30	0	2.25
Bill Matthews	R	31	1	0	1.000	0	5	1	0	17	16	10	6	0	3.18
2 Jack Chesbro	R	35	0	1	.000	0	1	1	0	6	7	4	3	0	4.50
Chet Nourse	R	21	0	0	—	0	1	1	0	5	5	5	3	0	7.20
Fred Anderson	R	23	0	0	—	0	1	1	0	8	5	1	5	1	1.13

CHICAGO — 4th 78-74 .513 20 — BILLY SULLIVAN

NAME	G by Pos	B	AGE	G	AB	R	H	2B	3B	HR	RBI	BB	SO	SB	BA	SA
TOTALS			30	159	5017	494	1110	145	56	4	393	441		211	.221	.275
Frank Isbell	1B101, OF9, 2B5	L	33	120	433	33	97	17	6	0	33	23		23	.224	.291
Jake Atz	2B118, OF3, SS1	R	30	119	381	39	90	18	3	0	22	38		14	.236	.299
Freddy Parent	SS98, OF37, 2B1	R	33	136	472	61	123	10	5	0	30	46		32	.261	.303
Lee Tannehill	3B91, SS64	R	28	155	531	39	118	21	5	0	47	31		12	.222	.281
Eddie Hahn (BC)	OF76	L	33	76	287	30	52	6	0	1	16	31		9	.181	.213
Dave Altizer	OF62, 1B45	R	32	116	382	47	89	6	7	1	20	39		27	.233	.293
Patsy Dougherty	OF138	L	32	139	491	71	140	23	13	1	55	51		36	.285	.391
Billy Sullivan	C97	R	34	97	265	11	43	3	0	0	16	17		9	.162	.174
Billy Purtell	3B71, 2B32	R	23	103	361	34	93	9	3	0	40	19		14	.258	.299
Doc White	OF40, P24	L	30	72	192	24	45	1	5	0	7	33		7	.234	.292
Frank Owens	C57	R	23	64	174	12	35	4	1	0	17	8		3	.201	.236
Frank Smith	P51	R	29	53	127	11	22	6	3	0	20	10		0	.173	.268
Willis Cole	OF46	R	27	46	165	17	39	7	3	0	16	16		3	.236	.315
Freddie Payne (NJ)	C27, OF3	R	28	32	82	8	20	2	0	0	12	5		0	.244	.268
Bob Messenger	OF31	B	25	31	112	18	19	1	1	0	0	13		7	.170	.196
Mike Welday	OF20	L	30	29	74	3	14	0	0	0	5	4		2	.189	.189
George Davis	1B17, 2B2	R	38	28	68	5	9	1	0	0	2	10		4	.132	.147
1 Gavvy Cravath	OF18	R	28	19	50	7	9	0	0	1	8	19		1	.180	.240
Barney Reilly	2B11, OF1	R	24	12	25	3	5	0	0	0	3	3		2	.200	.200
Cuke Barrows	OF5	R	25	5	20	1	3	0	0	0	2	0		1	.150	.150
1 Jiggs Donahue	1B2	L	29	2	4	0	0	0	0	0	2	1		0	.000	.000
2 Ham Patterson	1B1	R	31	1	3	2	0	0	0	0	0	1		0	.000	.000

NAME	T	AGE	W	L	PCT	SV	G	GS	CG	IP	H	BB	SO	SHO	ERA
		26	78	74	.513	6	159	159	112	1437	1190	341	671	26	2.04
Frank Smith	R	29	25	17	.595	1	51	40	37	365	278	70	177	7	1.80
Ed Walsh	R	28	15	11	.577	2	31	28	20	230	166	50	127	8	1.41
Jim Scott	R	20	12	12	.500	1	36	29	19	250	194	93	135	4	2.30
Doc White	L	30	11	9	.550	1	24	21	14	178	149	31	77	3	1.72
2 Bill Burns	R	29	7	13	.350	0	22	19	8	174	169	35	52	1	1.97
Fred Olmstead	R	25	3	2	.600	0	6	5	5	55	52	12	21	0	1.80
Rube Suter	R	21	2	3	.400	1	18	7	3	87	72	28	53	1	2.48
Lou Fiene	R	24	2	5	.286	0	13	6	4	72	75	18	24	0	4.13
Frank Owen	R	29	1	1	.500	0	2	1	1	16	19	3	3	0	4.50
1 Nick Altrock	L	32	0	1	.000	1	1	1	1	9	16	1	2	0	5.00

NEW YORK — 5th 74-77 .490 23.5 — GEORGE STALLINGS

NAME	G by Pos	B	AGE	G	AB	R	H	2B	3B	HR	RBI	BB	SO	SB	BA	SA
TOTALS			28	153	4981	591	1234	143	61	16	473	407		187	.248	.311
Hal Chase (IL)	1B118	R	26	118	474	60	134	17	3	4	63	20		25	.283	.357
Frank LaPorte	2B83	R	29	89	309	35	92	19	3	0	31	18		5	.298	.379
Jack Knight	SS78, 1B19, 2B18	R	23	116	360	46	85	8	5	0	40	37		15	.236	.286
Jimmy Austin	3B111, SS23, 2B1	R	29	136	437	37	101	11	5	1	39	32		30	.231	.286
Willie Keeler	OF95	L	37	99	360	44	95	7	5	1	32	24		10	.264	.319
Ray Demmitt	OF109	L	25	123	427	68	105	12	12	4	30	55		16	.246	.358
Clyde Engle	OF134	R	25	135	492	66	137	20	5	3	71	47		18	.278	.358
Red Kleinow	C77	R	31	78	206	24	47	11	4	0	15	25		7	.228	.310
Kid Elberfeld	SS61, 3B43	R	34	106	379	47	90	9	5	0	26	28		23	.237	.288
Birdie Cree	OF77, SS6, 2B4, 3B1	R	26	104	343	48	90	6	3	2	27	30		10	.262	.315
Charlie Hemphill	OF45	L	33	73	181	23	44	5	1	0	10	32		10	.243	.282
Ed Sweeney	C62, 1B3	R	20	67	176	19	47	3	0	0	21	16		3	.267	.284
Walter Blair	C42	R	25	42	110	5	23	2	2	0	11	7		2	.209	.264
Earle Gardner	2B22	R	25	22	85	12	28	4	0	0	15	3		4	.329	.376
George McConnell	1B11, P2	R	31	13	43	4	9	0	1	0	5	1		1	.209	.256
1 Joe Ward	2B7, 1B1	R	24	9	28	3	5	0	0	0	0	1		2	.179	.179
1 Neal Ball	2B8	R	28	8	28	3	5	0	0	0	1	3		2	.207	.310

Bobby Vaughn 24 R 2-14, Irish McIlveen 28 L 0-3, Eddie Tiemeyer 24 R 3-8, Johnny Wanner 23 R 1-8

NAME	T	AGE	W	L	PCT	SV	G	GS	CG	IP	H	BB	SO	SHO	ERA
		26	74	77	.490	14	153	153	94	1332	1223	422	597	18	2.68
Joe Lake	R	27	14	11	.560	2	31	26	17	215	180	59	117	3	1.88
Jack Warhop	R	24	13	15	.464	1	36	23	21	243	197	81	95	3	2.41
Lew Brockett	R	28	10	8	.556	1	26	18	10	152	148	59	70	3	2.37
Jack Quinn (IL)	R	25	9	5	.643	2	23	11	8	119	110	24	36	0	1.97
Slow Joe Doyle	R	27	8	6	.571	0	15	15	8	126	103	37	57	3	2.57
Tom Hughes	R	25	7	8	.467	3	24	15	9	119	109	37	69	2	2.65
Rube Manning	R	26	7	11	.389	2	26	21	11	173	167	48	71	2	3.17
Pete Wilson	L	24	5	6	.455	0	14	13	7	94	82	43	44	1	3.16
Al Orth	R	36	1	0	1.000	0	3	1	0	6	1	1	0	0	12.00
George McConnell	R	31	1	0	.000	0	2	2	1	0	3	3	4	0	2.25
1 Jack Chesbro	R	35	0	3	.000	0	9	4	2	50	70	13	17	0	6.30
Doc Newton	L	31	0	3	.000	0	4	4	1	27	11	11	0	2.86	
Dick Carroll	R	24	0	0	—	0	2	4	1	5	7	1	1	0	3.60
Russ Ford	R	26	0	0	—	0	1	0	3	6	1	1	0	9.00	
Butch Schmidt	L	22	0	0	—	0	5	1	0	10	7	1	2	0	7.20

CLEVELAND — 6th 71-82 .464 27.5 — NAP LAJOIE 57-57 .500 — DEACON McGUIRE 14-25 .359

NAME	G by Pos	B	AGE	G	AB	R	H	2B	3B	HR	RBI	BB	SO	SB	BA	SA
TOTALS			27	155	5044	493	1214	173	81	10	407	283		173	.241	.313
George Stovall	1B145	R	31	145	565	60	139	17	10	2	49	6		25	.246	.322
Nap Lajoie (WJ)	2B120, 1B8	R	34	128	469	56	152	33	7	1	47	35		13	.324	.431
2 Neal Ball	SS95	R	28	95	324	29	83	13	2	1	25	17		17	.256	.318
Bill Bradley	3B87, 2B3, 1B3	R	31	95	334	30	62	6	3	0	22	19		8	.186	.222
Wilbur Good	OF80	L	23	94	318	33	68	6	5	0	17	28		13	.214	.264
Joe Birmingham (EJ)	OF98	R	24	100	343	29	99	10	5	1	38	19		12	.289	.356
Bill Hinchman	OF131, SS6	R	26	139	457	57	118	20	13	2	53	41		22	.258	.372
Ted Easterly	C76	L	24	98	287	32	75	14	10	1	27	13		8	.261	.390
George Perring	3B66, SS11, 2B8	R	24	88	283	26	63	10	9	0	20	19		6	.223	.322
Bris Lord	OF69	R	25	69	249	26	67	7	3	1	25	8		10	.269	.353
Elmer Flick	OF61	L	33	66	235	28	60	10	2	0	15	22		9	.255	.315
Nig Clarke	C44	L	26	55	164	15	45	4	2	0	14	9		1	.274	.323
Terry Turner (JJ)	2B26, SS26	R	28	53	208	25	52	7	4	0	16	14		14	.250	.322
Harry Bemis	C35	R	35	42	123	4	23	2	3	0	13	0		2	.187	.252
Duke Reilley	OF36	L	24	20	62	10	13	0	0	0	4	5			.210	.210
Dolly Stark	SS19	R	24	19	60	4	12	0	0	0	1	6		4	.200	.216
Miles Netzel	3B6, OF2	L	23	10	37	4	7	1	0	0	3	3		1	.189	.216
Bob Higgins	C8	R	22	8	23	0	2	0	0	0	1	2		0	.087	.087

Tom Raftery 27 R 7-32, Josh Clarke 30 L 0-12, Walt Doane 22 L 1-9, Denny Sullivan (IL) 26 L 1-2

NAME	T	AGE	W	L	PCT	SV	G	GS	CG	IP	H	BB	SO	SHO	ERA
		31	71	82	.464	2	155	155	110	1366	1211	349	569	15	2.39
Cy Young	R	42	19	15	.559	0	35	34	30	295	267	59	109	3	2.26
Addie Joss	R	29	14	13	.519	0	33	28	24	243	198	31	67	4	1.70
Heinie Berger	R	27	13	14	.481	1	34	29	19	257	221	58	162	4	2.63
Cy Falkenberg	R	29	10	9	.526	0	24	18	13	165	135	50	82	2	2.91
Bob Rhoades	R	29	5	9	.357	0	20	15	9	133	124	50	46	2	2.91
Jerry Upp	L	25	2	1	.667	0	7	4	2	27	26	12	13	0	1.67
Carl Sitton	R	22	2	2	.500	0	14	5	3	50	50	16	16	0	2.88
Harry Otis (AJ)	L	22	2	2	.500	0	8	5	2	26	26	18	6	0	1.38
Glenn Liebhardt	R	26	2	4	.333	0	12	4	1	52	56	21	19	0	2.94
Harry Ables	L	25	1	1	.500	0	5	3	1	28	26	10	24	0	2.58
Willie Mitchell	L	19	1	1	.333	0	3	1	1	23	17	18	0	1.57	
Red Booles	R	28	1	0	.000	0	4	1	0	23	18	8	6	0	1.96
Walt Doane	L	22	0	1	.000	0	1	1	0	5	10	1	2	0	5.40
Fred Winchell	R	27	0	3	.000	0	5	3	0	14	16	2	7	0	6.43
Lucky Wright	R	29	0	5	.000	0	7	3	0	23	20	8	6	0	3.91

ST. LOUIS — 7th 61-89 .407 36 — JIMMY McALEER

NAME	G by Pos	B	AGE	G	AB	R	H	2B	3B	HR	RBI	BB	SO	SB	BA	SA
TOTALS			30	154	4964	443	1152	116	45	11	352	331		136	.232	.280
1 Tom Jones	1B95, 3B2	R	32	97	337	30	84	9	3	0	29	18		13	.249	.294
Jimmy Williams	2B109	R	32	110	374	32	73	3	6	0	22	29		6	.195	.235
Bobby Wallace	SS87, 3B29	R	35	116	403	36	96	12	1	3	35	38		7	.238	.285
Hobe Ferris	3B114, 2B34	R	31	148	556	36	120	18	5	3	58	12		11	.216	.282
Roy Hartzell	OF85, SS65, 2B1	R	27	152	595	64	161	12	5	0	32	29		14	.271	.308
Danny Hoffman	OF109	L	29	110	387	44	104	6	7	2	26	41		24	.269	.336
George Stone (NJ)	OF81	L	32	93	310	33	89	5	4	1	15	24		8	.287	.339
Lou Criger	C73	R	37	74	212	15	36	1	1	0	9	25		2	.170	.184
Art Griggs	1B49, OF40, 2B8, SS1	R	24	108	364	38	102	17	5	0	43	24		11	.280	.354
John McAleese	OF79, 3B2	R	31	85	267	33	57	7	0	0	12	32		18	.213	.240
Jim Stephens	C72	R	25	79	223	18	49	5	0	3	18	13		5	.220	.283
Bill Bailey	P32, OF2	L	21	38	77	1	22	1	1	0	7	3		1	.286	.325
Dode Criss	P11	L	24	35	48	2	14	6	1	0	7	0		0	.292	.458
Al Schweitzer	OF22	R	26	27	76	7	17	2	0	0	3	5		3	.224	.250
Walt Devoy	OF16, 1B3	R	23	19	69	7	17	3	1	0	3	6		4	.246	.319
Ned Crompton	OF17	L	20	17	63	7	10	2	1	0	2	7		1	.159	.222
1 Ham Patterson	1B6, OF6	R	31	17	49	2	10	1	0	0	5	0		1	.204	.224
Burt Shotton	OF17	L	24	17	61	5	16	0	1	0	5	10		3	.262	.295
Wib Smith	C13, 1B1	L	22	17	42	3	8	1	0	0	2	0		0	.190	.190
Bill Killefer	C11	R	21	11	29	1	4	0	0	0	0	1		0	.138	.138
2 Claude Rossman	OF2	L	28	2	8	1	1	0	0	0	0	0		0	.125	.125

NAME	T	AGE	W	L	PCT	SV	G	GS	CG	IP	H	BB	SO	SHO	ERA
		29	61	89	.407	5	154	154	105	1355	1287	383	620	21	2.88
Jack Powell	R	34	12	16	.429	3	34	27	18	239	221	42	82	4	2.11
Barney Pelty	R	28	11	11	.524	0	27	23	17	199	158	53	88	5	2.31
Rube Waddell	L	32	11	13	.458	1	31	28	16	220	204	57	141	5	2.37
Bill Bailey	L	21	9	12	.429	0	32	20	17	199	174	75	114	1	2.44
Bill Graham (BG)	R	24	8	14	.364	1	34	21	13	187	171	60	82	3	3.13
Bill Dinneen	R	33	6	7	.462	0	17	13	8	112	112	29	26	3	3.46
Harry Howell	R	32	1	1	.500	0	10	3	0	37	42	8	16	0	3.16
Jack Gilligan	R	23	1	2	.333	0	3	3	2	32	32	7	6	0	5.48
Chuck Rose	R	24	1	3	.333	0	5	3	2	35	32	7	6	0	5.40
Dode Criss	R	24	1	5	.167	0	11	6	3	55	53	32	43	0	3.44
Bill McCorry	R	22	0	2	.000	2	2	2	1	15	6	10	0	9.00	
Phil Stremmel	R	29	0	2	.000	0	4	2	0	20	4	6	0	4.50	
Ed Kusel	R	23	0	3	.000	0	3	3	1	24	43	1	2	0	7.13

WASHINGTON — 8th 42-110 .276 56 — JOE CANTILLON

NAME	G by Pos	B	AGE	G	AB	R	H	2B	3B	HR	RBI	BB	SO	SB	BA	SA
TOTALS			28	156	4982	382	1112	148	41	9	306	321		136	.223	.275
2 Jiggs Donahue	1B81	L	29	84	283	13	67	12	1	0	28	22		9	.237	.286
1 Jim Delahanty	2B85	R	30	90	302	18	67	13	5	1	21	23		4	.222	.308
George McBride	SS155	R	28	155	504	38	118	16	0	0	34	36		17	.234	.266
Wid Conroy	3B120, 2B13, OF5, SS1	R	32	139	489	44	119	13	4	1	20	37		24	.244	.319
Jack Lelivelt	OF91	L	23	31	318	25	93	8	6	0	24	19		8	.292	.355
Clyde Milan	OF120	L	23	130	400	33	80	12	4	1	19	31		10	.200	.278
George Browne	OF101	L	33	109	393	40	107	15	5	1	16	17		13	.272	.344
Gabby Street	C137	R	26	137	407	25	86	12	1	0	29	26		2	.211	.246
Bob Unglaub	1B57, OF43, 2B25, 3B4	R	27	130	480	43	127	14	9	3	41	22		15	.265	.350
Otis Clymer (LJ)	OF24, 3B6, C3, 2B3, SS1	B	33	45	138	11	27	5	2	0	6	17		7	.196	.261
2 Red Killefer	OF24, 3B6, C3, 2B3, SS1	R	24	40	121	11	21	1	1	0	5	13		4	.174	.182
Cliff Blankenship	C17, OF4	R	29	39	60	4	15	0	0	0	9	6			.250	.250
2 Germany Schaefer	2B32, 3B1	R	32	32	128	13	31	5	1	0	1	14		2	.242	.250
Jack Slattery	1B11, C5	L	31	32	56	4	12	2	0	0	2	0		1	.214	.250
Warren Miller	OF15	L	23	26	51	5	11	0	0	0	4	3		1	.216	.216
Bill Yohe	3B19	R	30	21	72	5	15	1	0	0	3	3			.208	.236
Jerry Freeman	1B14, OF1	L	24	19	48	2	8	0	0	0	5	1			.167	.208
1 Bob Ganley	OF17	L	34	19	63	5	16	0	0	0	2	5		3	.254	.302
2 Doc Gessler	OF16, 1B1	L	29	17	54	10	13	2	1	0	8	2		1	.241	.315
Speed Kelly	3B10, 2B3, OF1	R	24	17	42	2	10	1	0	1	3	1		1	.143	.238
Jesse Tannehill	OF9, P3	L	34	16	36	2	7	0	0	0	2	2		1	.194	.194

Jack Hardy 32 R 4-24, Bill Shipke 26 R 2-16, Orth Collins 29 L 0-7, Mike Kahoe 35 R 1-8, 2 Gavvy Cravath 28 R 0-5, Tom Crooke 24 R 2-7, Frank Hemphill 31 R 0-3, 2 Jimmy Sebring 27 L 0-0

NAME	T	AGE	W	L	PCT	SV	G	GS	CG	IP	H	BB	SO	SHO	ERA
		27	42	110	.276	2	156	156	99	1375	1288	424	653	11	3.04
Walter Johnson	R	21	13	25	.342	1	40	36	27	297	247	84	164	4	2.21
Bob Groom	R	24	7	26	.212	0	44	31	17	261	218	105	131	6	2.86
Dolly Gray	R	30	5	19	.208	0	36	26	19	218	210	77	87	0	3.59
Long Tom Hughes	R	30	4	7	.364	1	22	13	7	120	113	33	77	2	2.79
Dixie Walker	R	25	3	5	.375	0	14	9	6	31	16	6	25	0	2.50
1 Charlie Smith	R	29	3	12	.200	0	23	15	7	146	140	37	72	1	3.27
Doc Reisling (DE)	R	29	4	4	.333	0	10	6	5	67	70	17	22	2	2.42
1 Bill Burns	L	29	1	0	1.000	0	6	4	1	29	25	7	13	0	1.24
Jesse Tannehill	L	34	1	1	.500	0	3	2	1	20	19	5	8	1	3.43
2 Nick Altrock	L	32	0	3	.250	0	5	2	0	38	55	5	9	0	5.45
Frank Oberlin	R	29	1	4	.200	0	11	4	1	41	41	16	13	0	3.73
Roy Witherup	R	22	1	5	.167	0	12	6	7	68	79	20	26	0	4.24
Bill Forman	R	22	0	0	.000	0	2	1	0	11	7	2	1	0	4.91
Joe Ohl	L	21	0	1	—	0	1	1	0	5	6	2	5	0	2.00
Joe Hovlik	R	24	0	0	—	0	4	1	0	14	13	4	4	0	4.50
Burt Keeley	R	29	0	1	—	0	1	1	0	1	5	1	1	0	11.57
Orth Collins	R	29	0	0	—	0	1	0	0	0	2	1	0	0	0.00

PITTSBURGH 1ST 110-42 .724 — FRED CLARKE

NAME	G by Pos	B	AGE	G	AB	R	H	2B	3B	HR	RBI	BB	SO	SB	BA	SA
TOTALS			28	154	5129	701	1332	218	92	25	585	479		185	.260	.353
Bill Abstein	1B135	R	26	137	512	51	133	20	10	1	70	27		16	.260	.344
Dots Miller	2B150	R	22	151	560	71	156	31	13	3	87	39		14	.279	.396
Honus Wagner	SS136, OF1	R	35	137	495	92	168	39	10	5	100	66		35	.339	.489
1 Jap Barbeau	3B85	R	27	91	350	60	77	16	3	0	25	37		19	.220	.283
Owen Wilson	OF154	L	25	154	569	64	155	22	12	4	59	19		17	.272	.374
Tommy Leach	OF138, 3B13	R	31	151	587	126	153	29	8	6	43	66		27	.261	.368
Fred Clarke	OF152	L	36	152	550	97	158	16	11	3	68	80		31	.287	.373
George Gibson	C150	R	28	150	510	42	135	25	9	2	52	44		9	.265	.361
Ham Hyatt	OF6, 1B2	L	24	48	67	9	20	3	4	0	7	3		1	.299	.463
2 Bobby Byrne	3B46	R	24	46	168	3	43	6	2	0	7	32		8	.256	.315
1 Alan Storke	1B18, 3B14	R	24	37	118	12	30	5	2	0	12	7		1	.254	.331
Ed Abbaticchio	SS18, 2B4, OF1	R	32	36	87	13	20	0	1	0	16	19		2	.230	.264
1 Ward Miller	OF14	L	24	15	56	2	8	0	1	0	4	4		2	.143	.179
Mike Simon	C9	R	26	11	18	2	3	0	0	0	2	1		0	.167	.167
Paddy O'Connor	C3, 3B1	R	29	9	16	1	5	1	0	0	3	0		0	.313	.375
2 Kid Durbin		R	22	1	0	0	0	0	0	0	0	0		0	.000	.000

NAME	T	AGE	W	L	PCT	SV	G	GS	CG	IP	H	BB	SO	SHO	ERA
		30	110	42	.724	11	154	154	93	1402	1174	320	490	21	2.07
Howie Camnitz	R	27	25	6	.806	3	41	30	20	283	207	68	133	6	1.62
Vic Willis	R	33	22	11	.667	1	39	35	24	290	243	83	95	4	2.23
Lefty Leifield	L	25	19	8	.704	0	32	26	13	202	172	54	43	3	2.36
Nick Maddox	R	22	13	8	.619	0	31	27	17	203	173	39	56	4	2.21
Babe Adams	R	27	12	3	.800	2	25	12	7	130	88	23	65	3	1.11
Sam Leever	R	37	8	1	.889	1	19	6	2	70	74	14	23	0	1.78
Deacon Phillippe	R	37	8	3	.727	0	22	13	7	132	121	14	38	1	2.32
Sammy Frock	R	26	2	1	.667	1	8	3	3	36	44	4	11	0	2.50
Chick Brandom	R	22	1	0	1.000	2	13	2	0	41	33	10	21	0	1.10
Bill Powell	R	24	0	1	.000	0	3	1	0	7	7	6	2	0	3.86
Harry Camnitz	R	24	0	0	—	0	1	0	0	4	6	1	1	0	4.50
Gene Moore	L	23	0	0	—	0	1	0	0	2	4	5	2	0	18.00
Jimmy Wacker	L	25	0	0	—	0	1	0	0	2	2	1	0	0	0.00

CHICAGO 2nd 104-49 .680 6.5 — FRANK CHANCE

NAME	G by Pos	B	AGE	G	AB	R	H	2B	3B	HR	RBI	BB	SO	SB	BA	SA
TOTALS			28	155	4999	632	1227	203	60	20	496	420		187	.245	.322
Frank Chance (BS)	1B92	R	32	93	324	53	88	16	4	0	46	30		29	.272	.346
Johnny Evers	2B126	L	27	127	463	88	122	19	6	1	24	73		28	.263	.337
Joe Tinker	SS143	R	28	143	516	56	132	26	11	4	57	17		23	.256	.372
Harry Steinfeldt	3B151	R	31	151	528	73	133	27	6	2	59	57		22	.252	.337
Wildfire Schulte	OF140	L	26	140	538	57	142	16	11	4	60	24		23	.264	.357
Solly Hofman	OF153	R	26	153	527	60	150	21	4	2	58	53		20	.285	.351
Jimmy Sheckard	OF148	L	30	148	525	81	134	29	5	1	43	72		15	.255	.335
Jimmy Archer	C80	R	26	80	261	31	60	9	2	1	30	12		5	.230	.291
Pat Moran	C74	R	33	77	246	18	54	11	1	1	23	16		2	.220	.285
Del Howard	1B57	L	31	69	203	25	40	4	2	1	24	18		6	.197	.251
Heinie Zimmerman	SS12	R	22	65	183	23	50	9	2	0	21	3		7	.273	.344
Joe Stanley	OF16	B	28	22	52	4	7	1	0	0	2	6		0	.135	.154
John Kane	OF8, SS3, 3B3, 2B2	R	26	20	45	6	4	1	0	0	5	2		1	.089	.111
Tom Needham	C7	R	30	13	28	3	4	0	0	0	0	0		0	.143	.143
1 George Browne	OF12	L	33	12	39	7	8	0	1	0	1	5		3	.205	.256
Fred Luderus	1B11	L	23	11	37	8	11	1	1	1	9	3		0	.297	.459
Bill Davidson	OF2	R	25	2	7	2	1	0	0	0	0	1		1	.143	.143
Johnny Kling (HO) 33																

NAME	T	AGE	W	L	PCT	SV	G	GS	CG	IP	H	BB	SO	SHO	ERA
		28	104	49	.680	11	155	155	111	1399	1094	364	680	32	1.75
Three Finger Brown	R	32	27	9	.750	7	50	34	32	343	246	53	172	8	1.31
Orvie Overall	R	28	20	11	.645	3	38	32	23	285	204	80	205	9	1.42
Ed Reulbach	R	26	19	10	.655	0	35	32	23	263	194	82	105	6	1.78
Jack Pfiester	L	31	17	6	.739	0	29	25	13	197	179	49	73	5	2.42
Rube Kroh	L	22	9	4	.692	0	17	13	10	120	97	30	51	2	1.65
1 Irv Higginbotham	R	27	5	2	.714	1	19	6	4	78	64	20	32	0	2.19
Rip Hagerman (PJ)	R	21	4	4	.500	0	13	7	4	79	64	28	32	1	1.82
Ray Brown	R	20	1	0	1.000	0	1	1	1	9	6	3	1	0	2.00
King Cole	R	23	1	0	1.000	0	1	1	1	9	6	3	1	1	1.00
Rudy Schwenk	L	25	1	1	.500	0	3	2	0	4	16	3	3	0	13.50
Carl Lundgren	R	29	0	0	—	0	2	1	0	4	6	4	0	0	4.50
Andy Coakley	R	26	0	1	.000	0	1	1	0	2	7	1	2	0	18.00
2 Pat Ragan	R	23	0	0	—	0	2	0	0	4	4	1	2	0	2.25
Chick Fraser	R	35	0	0	—	0	1	0	0	3	2	4	1	0	0.00

NEW YORK 3rd 92-62 .601 18.5 — JOHN McGRAW

NAME	G by Pos	B	AGE	G	AB	R	H	2B	3B	HR	RBI	BB	SO	SB	BA	SA
TOTALS			28	157	5218	622	1327	173	68	26	510	530		234	.254	.328
Fred Tenney	1B98	L	37	101	375	43	88	8	2	1	23	51		8	.235	.291
Larry Doyle	2B144	R	23	147	570	86	172	27	11	6	49	45		31	.302	.419
Al Bridwell	SS145	L	25	145	476	59	140	11	5	0	55	67		32	.294	.338
Art Devlin	3B143	R	29	143	491	61	130	19	8	0	56	65		26	.265	.336
Red Murray	OF149	R	25	149	570	74	150	15	12	7	91	45		48	.263	.368
Bill O'Hara	OF115	L	25	115	360	48	85	9	3	1	30	41		31	.236	.286
Moose McCormick	OF110	L	28	120	413	68	120	21	8	3	27	49		4	.291	.402
Admiral Schlei	C89	R	31	92	279	25	68	12	0	0	30	40		4	.244	.287
Chief Meyers	C64	R	28	90	220	15	61	10	5	1	30	22		3	.277	.382
Cy Seymour (JJ)	OF74	L	36	80	280	37	87	12	5	1	30	25		14	.311	.400
Fred Merkle	1B70, 2B1	R	20	79	236	15	45	9	1	0	20	16		8	.191	.237
Buck Herzog	OF29, 2B4, 3B4, SS1	R	23	42	130	16	24	2	0	0	8	13		2	.185	.200
Tillie Shafer	3B16, 2B13, OF2	B	20	38	84	11	15	2	1	0	7	14		6	.179	.226
Art Fletcher	SS19, 2B5, 3B5	R	24	29	98	7	21	0	1	0	6	1		0	.214	.235
Fred Snodgrass	OF20, C2, 1B1	R	21	28	70	10	21	5	0	1	6	7		10	.300	.414
Josh Devore (IL)	OF12	L	21	22	28	6	4	1	0	0	1	2		3	.143	.179
Art Wilson	C19	R	23	19	42	4	10	2	1	0	5	4		0	.238	.333
Arlie Latham	2B2	R	49	4	2	1	0	0	0	0	0	1		1	.000	.000
Mike Donlin (HO) 31																

NAME	T	AGE	W	L	PCT	SV	G	GS	CG	IP	H	BB	SO	SHO	ERA
		25	92	61	.601	15	157	157	105	1441	1248	397	695	17	2.27
Christy Mathewson	R	28	25	6	.806	2	37	33	26	275	192	36	149	8	1.14
Hooks Wiltse	L	29	20	11	.645	3	37	30	22	269	228	51	119	4	2.01
Bugs Raymond	R	27	18	12	.600	0	39	30	18	270	239	87	121	2	2.47
Red Ames	R	26	15	10	.600	1	34	26	20	244	217	81	116	2	2.69
Doc Crandall	R	21	6	4	.600	6	30	8	4	122	117	33	55	0	2.69
Rube Marquard	L	22	5	13	.278	1	29	21	8	173	155	73	109	0	2.60
Louis Drucke	R	20	2	1	.667	0	3	2	2	24	20	13	8	0	2.25
Dutch Klawitter	R	20	1	1	.500	1	3	2	1	27	24	13	6	0	2.00
George Daly	R	21	0	3	.000	0	3	3	3	21	31	8	8	0	6.00
Bull Durham	R	32	0	0	—	1	4	0	0	11	15	2	2	0	3.27
Jake Weimer	L	35	0	0	—	0	1	1	0	3	7	0	1	0	9.00
Red Waller	R	28	0	0	—	0	1	0	0	1	3	1	0	0	0.00

CINCINNATI 4th 77-76 .503 33.5 — CLARK GRIFFITH

NAME	G by Pos	B	AGE	G	AB	R	H	2B	3B	HR	RBI	BB	SO	SB	BA	SA
TOTALS			26	157	5088	603	1273	159	72	22	507	478		280	.250	.323
Dick Hoblitzell	1B142	L	20	142	517	59	159	23	11	4	67	44		17	.308	.418
Dick Egan	2B116, SS10	R	25	127	480	59	132	14	3	2	53	37		39	.275	.329
Tom Downey	SS119, C1	R	25	119	416	39	96	9	6	1	32	32		16	.231	.288
Hans Lobert	3B122	R	27	122	425	50	90	13	5	4	52	48		30	.212	.294
Mike Mitchell	OF144, 1B1	R	29	145	523	83	162	17	17	4	86	57		37	.310	.430
Rebel Oakes	OF113	B	25	120	415	55	112	10	5	3	31	40		23	.270	.340
Bob Bescher	OF117	B	25	124	446	73	107	17	6	1	34	56		54	.240	.312
Larry McLean (BK)	C95	R	27	95	324	26	83	12	2	2	36	21		1	.256	.324
Dode Paskert	OF82, 1B6	R	28	104	322	49	81	7	4	0	33	34		23	.252	.298
Miller Huggins	2B31, 3B15	B	31	57	159	18	34	3	1	0	6	28		11	.214	.245
Frank Roth	C54	R	30	56	147	12	35	7	2	0	16	6		5	.238	.313
2 Ward Miller	OF24	L	24	43	113	17	35	3	1	0	4	6		9	.310	.354
1 Mike Mowrey	3B22, SS13	R	25	38	115	10	22	5	0	0	5	20		2	.191	.235
Tommy Clarke	C17	R	21	18	52	5	13	3	2	0	10	6		3	.250	.385
2 Chappie Charles	2B10, SS3	R	28	13	43	3	11	2	0	0	5	4		2	.256	.302
Whitey Ellam	SS9	R	23	10	21	4	4	0	1	1	4	7		1	.190	.429
1 Chick Autry	1B9	L	24	9	33	3	6	2	0	0	4	2		1	.182	.242
1 Kid Durbin		R	22	6	5	1	1	0	0	0	0	1		0	.200	.200
Bill Moriarty	SS6	R	25	6	20	1	4	1	0	0	1	0		2	.200	.250
Emil Haberer	C4	R	31	5	16	1	3	1	0	0	2	0		0	.188	.250
Claire Patterson	OF2	L	21	4	8	0	1	0	0	0	1	0		0	.125	.125
Si Pauxtis	C4	R	23	4	8	2	1	0	0	0	1	0		0	.125	.125
Cozy Dolan	3B3	R	26	3	6	2	1	0	0	0	0	2		0	.167	.167
Doc Johnston	1B3	L	21	3	10	1	0	0	0	0	1	0		0	.000	.000
Swat McCabe	OF3	R	26	3	11	2	6	1	0	0	0	1		1	.545	.636
Mike Konnick	C2	R	20	2	5	0	2	1	0	0	1	0		0	.400	.600
Bunny Pearce	C2	R	24	2	2	0	0	0	0	0	0	0		0	.000	.000
Del Young	OF2	L	23	2	7	0	2	0	0	0	1	1		0	.286	.286
Ezra Midkiff	3B1	R	26	1	2	0	0	0	0	0	0	0		0	.000	.000

NAME	T	AGE	W	L	PCT	SV	G	GS	CG	IP	H	BB	SO	SHO	ERA
		27	77	76	.503	8	157	157	91	1407	1233	510	477	10	2.52
Art Fromme	R	25	19	13	.594	2	37	34	22	279	195	101	126	4	1.90
Harry Gaspar	R	26	18	11	.621	2	44	29	19	260	228	57	65	4	2.01
Jack Rowan	R	23	11	12	.478	0	38	23	14	226	185	104	81	0	2.79
Bob Ewing	R	36	11	12	.478	0	31	29	14	218	195	63	86	2	2.44
Bill Campbell	L	35	7	11	.389	2	30	15	7	148	162	39	37	0	2.68
Bob Spade (HO)	R	31	5	5	.500	0	14	13	8	98	91	39	31	0	2.85
Jean Dubuc (IL)	R	20	3	5	.375	1	19	5	2	71	72	46	19	0	3.68
Tom Cantwell	R	20	1	0	1.000	0	6	1	1	22	16	7	7	0	1.64
Roy Castleton	L	23	1	1	.500	0	4	1	1	14	14	6	5	0	1.93
1 Ed Karger	L	26	1	3	.250	0	9	5	1	34	26	30	8	0	4.50
1 Pat Ragan	R	23	0	1	.000	0	7	3	2	23	16	8	7	0	3.38
Jack Bushelman	R	23	0	0	—	0	1	1	1	7	4	3	2	0	6.00
Clark Griffith	R	39	0	1	.000	0	2	0	0	6	11	2	3	0	6.00
Chet Carmichael	R	21	0	0	—	0	2	0	0	7	9	3	2	0	0.00
2 Bill Chappelle	R	28	0	0	—	0	1	0	0	5	8	3	2	0	2.25
Ralph Savidge	R	30	0	0	—	0	2	0	0	4	10	3	2	0	22.50

PHILADELPHIA 5th 74-79 .484 36.5 — BILLY MURRAY

NAME	G by Pos	B	AGE	G	AB	R	H	2B	3B	HR	RBI	BB	SO	SB	BA	SA
TOTALS			28	153	5036	515	1228	185	53	12	417	370		185	.244	.309
Kitty Bransfield	1B138	R	34	140	527	47	154	27	6	1	59	18		17	.292	.372
Otto Knabe	2B110, OF1	R	25	114	402	40	94	13	3	0	34	35		9	.234	.281
Mickey Doolan	SS147	R	29	147	493	39	106	12	10	1	35	37		10	.215	.290
Eddie Grant	3B154	R	26	154	631	75	170	18	4	1	37	35		28	.269	.315
John Titus	OF149	L	33	149	522	60	146	22	6	3	46	66		23	.280	.350
2 Johnny Bates	OF73	L	27	77	266	43	78	11	1	1	15	28		22	.293	.353
Sherry Magee	OF143	R	24	143	522	60	141	33	14	2	66	44		37	.270	.398
Red Dooin	C140	R	30	141	468	42	105	14	1	2	38	21		14	.224	.271
2 Joe Ward	2B48, SS8, 1B5, OF2	R	24	74	184	21	49	8	2	0	23	9		7	.266	.332
Ossie Osborn	OF54	L	25	55	168	12	31	4	2	0	19	12		6	.185	.217
Pep Deininger	OF45, 2B1	L	31	55	169	22	44	9	0	0	16	11		5	.260	.314
1 Dave Sheen	2B14, 1B11, OF3, SS1	R	31	38	112	14	26	2	1	0	4	14		3	.232	.286
Marty Martel	C12	R	26	24	41	1	11	3	1	0	7	4		0	.268	.390
Fred Jacklitsch	C11, 2B1	R	33	20	32	6	10	1	1	0	1	10		1	.313	.406
1 Wally Clement		L	27	3	3	0	0	0	0	0	0	0		0	.000	.000
2 Charlie Starr			30	3	3	0	0	0	0	0	0	0		0	.000	.000
Ben Froelich	C1	R	21	3	1	0	0	0	0	0	0	0		0	.000	.000
Ed McDonough	C1	R	22	1	1	0	0	0	0	0	0	0		0	.000	.000

NAME	T	AGE	W	L	PCT	SV	G	GS	CG	IP	H	BB	SO	SHO	ERA
		28	74	79	.484	6	154	154	89	1391	1190	472	612	17	2.44
Earl Moore	R	29	18	12	.600	0	38	34	24	300	238	108	173	4	2.10
Lew Moren	R	25	16	15	.516	1	40	31	19	258	226	93	110	2	2.65
George McQuillan (IL)	R	24	13	16	.448	2	41	28	16	248	202	54	96	4	2.14
Frank Corridon	R	28	11	7	.611	0	27	19	11	171	147	61	69	3	2.11
Harry Covaleski	L	23	6	10	.375	1	24	17	8	122	109	49	56	2	2.73
Tully Sparks	R	34	6	11	.353	2	24	16	6	122	126	32	40	1	3.36
Bill Foxen	L	30	3	7	.300	0	18	7	5	83	65	32	37	1	3.36
1 Lew Richie	R	25	1	1	.500	1	11	1	0	45	40	18	11	0	3.00
1 Buster Brown	R	27	0	0	—	0	7	1	1	22	16	10	10	0	3.24
Frank Scanlan	L	19	0	0	—	0	1	0	0	11	8	5	5	0	1.64
Ben Van Dyke	R	21	0	0	—	0	1	0	0	7	4	1	3	0	3.68

BROOKLYN — 6th 55-98 .359 55.5 — HARRY LUMLEY

NAME	G by Pos	B	AGE	G	AB	R	H	2B	3B	HR	RBI	BB	SO	SB	BA	SA
TOTALS			27	155	5056	442	1157	176	59	16	370	330		141	.229	.296
Tim Jordan	1B95	L	30	103	330	47	90	20	3	3	36	59		13	.273	.379
Whitey Alperman	2B108	R	29	111	420	35	104	19	12	1	41	2		7	.248	.357
Tommy McMillan	SS105, 2B2, 3B1	R	21	108	373	18	79	15	1	0	24	20		11	.212	.257
Ed Lennox	3B121	R	25	126	435	33	114	18	9	2	44	47		11	.262	.359
Harry Lumley (SJ)	OF52	L	28	55	172	13	43	8	3	0	14	16		1	.250	.331
Al Burch	OF151, 1B1	L	25	152	601	80	163	20	6	1	30	51		38	.271	.329
2 Wally Clement	OF88	L	27	92	340	35	87	8	4	0	17	18		11	.256	.303
Bill Bergen	C112	R	36	112	346	16	48	1	1	1	15	10		4	.139	.156
John Hummel	1B54, 2B38, SS36, OF5	R	26	146	542	54	152	15	9	4	52	22		16	.280	.363
P. McElveen	3B37, OF13, SS10, 1B5, 2B5	R	27	81	258	22	51	8	1	3	25	14		6	.198	.271
Joe Kustus	OF50	R	26	53	173	12	25	5	0	1	11	11		9	.145	.191
Doc Marshall	C49, OF1	R	34	50	149	7	30	7	1	0	10	6		1	.201	.262
George Hunter	OF23, P16	B	22	44	123	8	28	7	0	0	8	9		1	.228	.285
Zack Wheat	OF26	L	21	26	102	15	31	7	3	0	4	6		1	.304	.431
1 Jimmy Sebring	OF25	L	27	25	81	11	8	1	1	0	5	11		3	.099	.136
Red Downey	OF19	L	20	19	78	7	20	1	0	0	8	2		4	.256	.269
Joe Dunn	C7	R	24	9	25	1	4	1	0	0	2	0		0	.160	.200
Tom Catterson	OF6	L	24	9	18	0	4	0	0	0	1	3		0	.222	.222
Lee Meyer	SS7		21	7	23	1	3	0	0	0	0	2		0	.130	.130
Hy Myers	OF6	R	20	6	22	1	5	1	0	0	6	2		1	.227	.273
Harry Redmond	2B5	R	21	6	6	1	0	0	0	0	0	0		0	.000	.000

NAME	T	AGE	W	L	PCT	SV	G	GS	CG	IP	H	BB	SO	SHO	ERA
Totals		29	55	98	.359	3	155	155	126	1384	1277	528	594	18	3.10
George Bell	R	34	16	15	.516	1	33	30	29	256	236	73	95	6	2.71
Nap Rucker	L	24	13	19	.406	1	38	33	28	309	245	101	201	6	2.24
Doc Scanlan	R	28	8	7	.533	0	19	17	12	141	125	65	72	2	2.94
Harry McIntire	R	31	7	17	.292	1	32	26	20	228	200	91	84	2	3.63
George Hunter	R	22	4	10	.286	0	16	13	10	104		38	43	0	2.47
Kaiser Wilhelm	R	35	3	13	.188	0	22	17	14	163	176	59	45	1	3.10
Eddie Dent	R	21	2	4	.333	0	6	4	2	42	47	15	11	0	4.29
Elmer Knetzer	R	23	1	3	.250	0	5	4	3	36	33	22	7	0	3.00
Jim Pastorius	L	27	1	9	.100	0	12	9	5	80	91	58	23	1	5.74
Sam Fletcher	R	28	0	1	.000	0	1	1	1	9	13	2	5	0	8.00
Pembroke Finlayson	R	20	0	0	—	0	1	0	0	7	7	4	2	0	5.14

ST. LOUIS — 7st 54-98 .355 56 — ROGER BRESNAHAN

NAME	G by Pos	B	AGE	G	AB	R	H	2B	3B	HR	RBI	BB	SO	SB	BA	SA
TOTALS			27	154	5108	583	1242	148	56	15	479	568		161	.243	.303
Ed Konetchy	1B152	R	23	152	576	88	165	23	14	4	80	65		25	.286	.396
1 Chappie Charles	2B71, SS28, 3B2	R	28	99	339	33	80	7	3	0	29	31		7	.236	.274
Rudy Hulswitt	SS65, 2B12	R	32	82	289	21	81	8	3	0	29	19		7	.280	.329
Bobby Byrne	3B105	R	24	105	421	61	90	13	6	1	33	46		21	.214	.280
Steve Evans	OF141, 1B2	L	24	143	498	67	129	17	6	2	56	66		14	.259	.329
Al Shaw	OF92	L	28	114	331	45	82	12	7	2	34	55		15	.248	.344
Rube Ellis	OF145	L	23	149	575	76	154	10	9	3	46	56		16	.268	.332
Eddie Phelps	C82	R	30	100	306	43	76	13	1	0	22	39		7	.248	.297
Joe Delahanty	OF63, 2B48	R	33	123	411	28	88	16	4	2	54	42		10	.214	.287
Roger Bresnahan	C59, 2B9, 3B1	R	30	72	234	27	57	4	1	0	23	46		11	.244	.269
Alan Storke	SS44, 2B4, 1B1	R	24	48	174	11	49	5	0	0	10	12		5	.282	.310
2 Jap Barbeau	3B46	R	27	47	175	23	44	3	0	0	5	28		14	.251	.280
Jack Bliss	C32	R	27	35	113	12	25	2	1	1	8	12		2	.221	.283
Howard Murphy	OF19	L	27	25	60	3	12	0	0	0	3	4		1	.200	.200
Champ Osteen	SS16	L	32	16	45	6	9	1	0	0	7	7		1	.200	.222
Billy Gilbert	2B12	R	33	12	29	4	5	1	0	0	4	4		1	.172	.172
2 Mike Mowrey	2B7, 3B2	R	25	12	29	3	7	1	0	0	4	0		1	.241	.276
Bob James	OF6		24	6	21	1	6	0	0	0	0	4		0	.286	.286
Tom Reilly	SS5	R	24	5	7	0	2	0	1	0	2	0		0	.286	.571
Charlie Enright	SS2	L	21	3	7	1	1	0	0	0	1	2		0	.143	.143
Connie Blank	C1	R	16	1	2	0	0	0	0	0	0	0		0	.000	.000

NAME	T	AGE	W	L	PCT	SV	G	GS	CG	IP	H	BB	SO	SHO	ERA
Totals		23	54	98	.355	4	154	154	84	1380	1368	483	435	5	3.41
Fred Beebe	R	28	15	21	.417	1	44	34	18	288	256	104	105	1	2.81
Johnny Lush	L	23	11	18	.379	0	34	28	21	221	215	69	66	2	3.14
Slim Sallee	L	24	11	11	.476	0	32	27	12	219	223	59	55	1	2.42
Bob Harmon	R	21	6	11	.353	0	21	17	10	159	155	65	48	0	3.68
Eddie Higgins	R	23	3	5	.500	0	16	5	5	66	68	17	15	0	4.50
Charlie Rhodes	R	24	3	5	.357	0	12	10	4	61	55	33	25	0	3.98
Les Backman	R	23	3	11	.214	0	21	15	8	128	146	39	35	0	4.15
1 Irv Higginbotham	R	27	1	0	1.000	0	3	1	1	11	5	2	7	0	1.64
1 Forrest More	L	22	1	10	.091	0	15	10	3	81	85	21	26	0	3.78
John Raleigh	R	23	1	0	.000	0	23	1	0	64	79	20	24	0	3.52
Steve Melter	R	24	1	2	.000	0	7	3	1	29	28	30	14	0	6.21
Grover Lowdermilk	R	24	0	2	.000	0	2	1	0	7	7	4	2	1	36.00
Harry Sullivan	L	21	0	1	.000	0	3	2	1	11	9	2	5	0	0.00
Joe Bernard	R	27	0	0	—	0	1	1	1	2	2	1	2	0	0.00

BOSTON — 8th 45-108 .294 65.5 — FRANK BOWERMAN 22-54 .290 HARRY SMITH 23-54 .299

NAME	G by Pos	B	AGE	G	AB	R	H	2B	3B	HR	RBI	BB	SO	SB	BA	SA
TOTALS			28	155	5017	427	1121	124	43	15	338	400		135	.223	.274
Fred Stem	1B68	L	23	73	245	13	51	2	3	0	11	12		5	.208	.241
2 Dave Shean	2B72	R	31	75	267	32	66	11	4	1	29	17		14	.247	.330
Jack Coffey	SS73	R	22	73	257	21	48	4	4	0	20	11		2	.187	.233
Bill Sweeney	3B112, SS26	R	22	152	493	44	120	19	3	1	36	37		25	.243	.300
Beals Becker	OF152	L	22	152	562	60	138	15	6	4	24	47		21	.246	.326
Ginger Beaumont	OF111	L	32	123	407	35	107	11	4	0	60	35		12	.263	.310
Roy Thomas	OF71	L	35	83	281	36	74	9	4	0	11	47		5	.263	.302
Peaches Graham	C76, OF6, SS1, 3B1	R	32	92	267	27	64	6	3	0	17	24		7	.240	.285
Fred Beck	OF57, 1B33	L	22	96	334	20	66	4	6	3	27	17		5	.198	.272
Bill Dahlen	SS46, 2B6, 3B2	R	39	69	197	22	46	6	1	2	16	29		4	.234	.305
2 Chick Autry	1B61, OF4	L	24	65	199	16	39	4	0	0	13	21		5	.196	.216
1 Johnny Bates	OF60	L	27	63	236	27	68	15	3	1	23	20		15	.288	.394
1 Charlie Starr	2B54, SS6, 3B3	R	30	61	216	16	48	2	3	0	6	31		7	.222	.259
Harry Smith (KJ)	C31	R	34	43	148	6	33	2	0	0	9	1		2	.223	.236
Gus Getz	3B36, 2B2, SS2	R	19	40	99	6	21	2	0	0	4	5		3	.212	.232
Frank Bowerman	C27	R	39	33	87	4	15	1	0	0	3	8		1	.172	.184
Claude Ritchey	2B25	B	35	30	41	1	4	1	0	0	0	5		0	.098	.098
Al Shaw	C13	R	24	13	41	1	4	1	0	0	1	4		1	.143	.167
Bill Rariden	C13	R	21	13	42	1	6	1	0	0	1	4		0	.130	.130
Hosea Siner	3B5, 2B1, SS1	R	24	10	23	1	3	0	0	0	1	0		0	.130	.130
Herbie Moran	OF8	L	25	8	31	8	7	1	0	0	0	5		0	.226	.258
Ernie Diehl	OF1	R	31	4	1	2	1	0	0	0	0	0		0	.500	.750
Bill Dam	OF1	L	24	2	1	0	1	0	0	0	1	0		0	.500	1.000

NAME	T	AGE	W	L	PCT	SV	G	GS	CG	IP	H	BB	SO	SHO	ERA
Totals		26	45	108	.294	6	155	155	98	1371	1329	543	414	13	3.20
Al Mattern	L	26	16	20	.444	3	47	32	24	316	322	108	98	2	2.85
2 Lew Richie	R	25	7	7	.500	2	25	19	13	132	118	44	42	2	2.32
Kirby White	R	25	6	13	.316	0	23	19	11	148	134	80	53	1	3.22
Cecil Ferguson	R	22	5	23	.179	0	36	30	19	227	235	83	87	3	3.72
Cliff Curtis	R	27	5	4	.444	0	10	9	8	83	53	30	22	2	1.41
2 Buster Brown	R	27	4	10	.286	0	18	17	8	123	108	56	32	2	3.15
1 Bill Chappelle	R	28	1	1	.500	0	5	3	2	29	31	11	8	0	1.86
Gus Dorner	R	32	1	3	.333	1	5	2	2	25	17	7	7	0	2.52
Vive Lindaman	R	31	1	6	.143	0	15	6	6	66	75	28	13	1	4.64
Chick Evans	R	19	0	3	.000	0	4	3	1	22	25	14	11	0	4.50
2 Forrest More	R	27	0	4	.000	0	10	4	3	49	47	20	10	0	4.41
Tom McCarthy	R	25	0	0	.000	0	8	7	3	46	47	28	11	0	3.52
Tom Tuckey	L	24	0	0	.000	0	17	10	4	91	104	22	16	0	4.25
Cush Cooney	R	26	0	0	—	0	1	0	0	6	4	2	3	0	1.50
Jake Boultes	R	24	0	1	.000	0	1	0	0	4	4	1	0	1	6.75

WORLD SERIES — PITTSBURGH (NL) 4   DETROIT (AL) 3

LINE SCORES

TEAM	1	2	3	4	5	6	7	8	9	10	11	12	R	H	E
Game 1 October 8 at Pittsburgh															
DET (AL)	1	0	0	0	0	0	0	0	0				1	6	4
PIT (NL)	0	0	0	1	2	1	0	0	X				4	5	0

Mullin / **Adams**

TEAM	1	2	3	4	5	6	7	8	9				R	H	E
Game 2 October 9 at Pittsburgh															
DET	0	2	3	0	0	0	0	0	0				7	9	3
PIT	2	0	0	0	0	0	0	0	0				2	5	1

Donovan / Camnitz, Willis (3)

TEAM	1	2	3	4	5	6	7	8	9				R	H	E
Game 3 October 9 at Detroit															
PIT	5	1	0	0	0	0	0	0	2				8	10	3
DET	0	0	0	0	4	0	2	0					6	10	5

Maddox / Summers, Willett (1), Works (8)

TEAM	1	2	3	4	5	6	7	8	9				R	H	E
Game 4 October 12 at Detroit															
PIT	0	0	0	0	0	0	0	0	0				0	5	6
DET	0	2	0	3	0	0	0	0	X				5	8	0

Leifield, Phillippe (5) / **Mullin**

TEAM	1	2	3	4	5	6	7	8	9				R	H	E
Game 5 October 13 at Pittsburgh															
DET	1	0	0	1	0	0	0	1	0				4	6	1
PIT	1	1	1	0	0	0	4	1	X				8	10	2

Summers, Willett (8) / **Adams**

TEAM	1	2	3	4	5	6	7	8	9				R	H	E
Game 6 October 14 at Detroit															
PIT	3	0	0	0	0	0	0	0	1				4	7	3
DET	1	0	0	2	1	1	0	0	X				5	10	3

Willis, Camnitz (6), Phillippe (7) / **Mullin**

TEAM	1	2	3	4	5	6	7	8	9				R	H	E
Game 7 October 16 at Detroit															
PIT	0	2	0	2	0	3	0	1	0				8	7	0
DET	0	0	0	0	0	0	0	0	0				0	6	3

Adams / Donovan, Mullin (4)

COMPOSITE BATTING

NAME	POS	G	AB	R	H	2B	3B	HR	RBI	BA
Pittsburgh (NL)										
Totals		7	223	34	50	13	1	2	25	.224
Miller	2B	7	28	2	7	1	0	0	4	.250
Abstein	1B	7	26	3	6	2	0	0	2	.231
Wilson	OF	7	26	2	4	1	0	0	1	.154
Leach	OF-3B	7	25	8	9	4	0	0	2	.360
Gibson	C	7	25	2	6	2	0	0	2	.240
Wagner	SS	7	24	4	8	2	0	0	6	.333
Byrne	3B	7	24	5	6	1	0	0	0	.250
Clarke	OF	7	19	7	4	0	0	2	7	.211
Adams	P	3	9	0	0	0	0	0	0	.000
Willis	P	2	4	0	0	0	0	0	0	.000
Hyatt	OF	4	4	1	0	0	0	0	1	.000
Maddox	P	1	4	0	0	0	0	0	0	.000
O'Connor	PH	1	1	0	0	0	0	0	0	.000
Abbaticchio	PH	2	1	0	0	0	0	0	0	.000
Camnitz	P	2	1	0	0	0	0	0	0	.000
Leifield	P	1	1	0	0	0	0	0	0	.000
Phillippe	P	2	1	0	0	0	0	0	0	.000
Detroit (AL)										
Totals		7	233	28	55	16	0	2	26	.236
D. Jones	OF	7	30	6	7	0	0	1	1	.233
Crawford	OF-1B	7	28	4	7	3	0	1	2	.250
Delahanty	2B	7	26	2	9	4	0	0	4	.346
Cobb	OF	7	26	3	6	3	0	0	6	.231
T. Jones	1B	7	24	3	6	1	0	0	2	.250
Bush	SS	7	23	5	6	1	0	0	4	.261
Moriarty	3B	7	22	4	6	1	0	0	1	.273
Schmidt	C	6	18	0	4	2	0	0	4	.222
Mullin	P	4	16	1	3	0	0	0	0	.188
Stanage	C	2	4	0	0	0	0	0	0	.000
Donovan	P	2	4	0	0	0	0	0	0	.000
McIntyre	OF	2	3	0	0	0	0	0	0	.000
Summers	P	2	3	0	0	0	0	0	0	.000
O'Leary	3B	2	2	0	0	0	0	0	0	.000
Willett	P	2	2	0	0	0	0	0	0	.000
Works	P	1	0	0	0	0	0	0	0	—

COMPOSITE PITCHING

NAME	G	IP	H	BB	SO	W	L	SV	ERA
Pittsburgh (NL)									
Totals	7	61	55	20	22	4	3	0	2.80
Adams	3	27	18	6	11	3	0	0	1.33
Willis	2	11.1	10	8	3	1	0	0	3.97
Maddox	1	9	10	2	4	1	0	0	1.00
Phillippe	2	6	2	1	0	0	0	0	0.00
Leifield	1	4	7	1	0	0	1	0	11.25
Camnitz	2	3.2	8	2	2	0	1	0	9.82
Detroit (AL)									
Totals	7	61	50	20	34	3	4	0	3.10
Mullin	4	32	23	8	20	2	1	0	2.25
Donovan	2	12	7	8	7	1	1	0	3.00
Summers	2	7.1	13	4	4	0	2	0	8.60
Willett	2	7.2	10	1	0	0	0	0	9.00
Works	1	2	4	0	0	0	0	0	9.00

1910 The Day It All Became "Official"

U.S. President William H. Taft opened the 1910 baseball season by throwing out the first ball. His actions served to mark baseball as the "official" national pastime and advanced the state of the political art into the twentieth century. Those in attendance at the game, including Vice President James Sherman, hailed the unprecedented event. Washington's pitcher, Walter Johnson, responded to the turnout of the robust chief executive by turning in a one-hit performance and blanking the Philadelphia Athletics, 1-0. Taft's presence, although getting the season off on a respected high note, was not an omen of prosperity, either for the Senators who finished last, or for a season whose attendance would be cut by poor early season weather and pennant races which were virtually over by July 1.

The Philadelphia Athletics recovered from that opening day whitewash by playing winning ball all year. Three-time champion Detroit stayed in the running for a fourth crown until the Athletics pulled away from the field in June and July. Philadelphia's attack boasted of three .300 hitters in Eddie Collins, Danny Murphy and Rube Oldring but, as usual, the pitching staff was the spearhead of the team. Jack Coombs won 31 games in developing into a star hurler and pitched 46 consecutive scoreless innings at one stage in the season. Chief Bender notched 23 victories, and Eddie Plank and Cy Morgan were also consistent winners for the American League's first 100-victory team. Detroit's offense remained strong, but the Tiger's pitching fell apart, prompting a fall into third place behind the surprising New York Yankees. Pittsburgh's 1909 National League pennant victory turned out only to be an interlude in the reign of the Chicago Cubs as kingpins in the senior loop. Finishing 13 games ahead of the field, the Cubs easily won their fourth pennant in five years, never leaving first after May. As usual, the Cub infield was airtight with Tinker, Evers, and Chance on duty, and outfielders Sol Hofman and Wildfire Schulte supplying much of the drive in the attack. Three Finger Brown lodged his usual 25 victories, but the key mound development turned out to b King Cole, who became an unexpected 20-game winner in his first full season. The Giant came in second, running into hot and cold streaks all year; Christy Mathewson provide a rare element of consistency in winning 27 games. Pittsburgh's collapse could be trace to their pitching. Although Babe Adams registered 18 victories, Howie Camnitz fell o from 24 to 12 victories. Vic Willis, who won 23 games in 1909 for the Bucs, spent th season with St. Louis where he compiled a dismal 9-12 mark.

Connie Mack led his Athletics into the World Series against the Cubs with grea confidence in his pitching staff, a confidence which was amply awarded by five complet games in five contests. Jack Coombs hurled three complete game victories, while Chie Bender won one and lost on while pitching two complete gams. Using only two pitcher the Athletics used a full lineup to rack up a .316 team batting mark, with Eddie Collin and Frank Baker logging .400 averages. The Chicago batters were held to a collectiv .222 winning only a ten-inning fourth-game from Connie Mack's White Elephants.

During the season both leagues introduced a new "jack¬rabbit" ball. Although mod estly boosting run and home run production, it was inevitable that the "livelier" ba would drastically alter baseball's playing style before the century was much older.

1910 AMERICAN LEAGUE

Batting

NAME	G by Pos	B	AGE	G	AB	R	H	2B	3B	HR	RBI	BB	SO	SB	BA	SA
PHILADELPHIA 1st 102-48 .680 CONNIE MACK																
TOTALS			28	155	5167	672	1376	194	106	19	541	409		207	.266	.356
Harry Davis	1B169	R	36	139	492	61	122	19	4	1	41	53		17	.248	.309
Eddie Collins	2B153	L	23	153	583	81	188	16	15	3	81	49		81	.322	.417
Jack Barry	SS145	R	23	145	487	64	126	19	5	3	60	52		14	.259	.337
Frank Baker	3B146	L	24	146	561	83	159	25	15	2	74	34		21	.283	.392
Danny Murphy	OF151	R	33	151	560	70	168	28	18	4	64	31		18	.300	.436
Rube Oldring	OF134	R	26	134	546	79	168	27	14	4	57	23		17	.308	.430
Topsy Hartsel	OF83	L	36	90	285	45	63	10	3	0	22	58		11	.221	.277
Jack Lapp	C63	L	25	71	192	18	45	4	3	0	17	20			.234	.286
2 Bris Lord	OF71	R	26	72	288	55	80	16	12	1	20	23		6	.278	.427
Ira Thomas	C60	R	29	60	180	14	50	8	2	1	19	6		2	.278	.361
Eddie Plank	P38	L	34	38	86	6	11	2	0	0	8	2		0	.128	.151
Stuffy McInnis	SS17, 2B5, 3B4, OF1	R	19	38	73	10	22	2	4	0	12	7		3	.301	.438
Paddy Livingston	C37	R	30	37	120	11	25	4	3	0	9	6		2	.208	.292
Ben Houser (SJ)	1B26	L	26	34	69	9	13	3	2	0	7	7		0	.188	.290
Heinie Heitmuller	OF28	L	27	31	111	11	27	2	2	0	7	7		6	.243	.297
1 Morris Rath	3B11, 2B3	R	23	18	26	3	4	0	0	0	1	5		0	.154	.154
Amos Strunk	OF14	L	21	16	48	9	16	0	1	0	2	3		4	.333	.375
24 Pat Donahue	C14	R	26	15	37	2	6	0	0	0	4	3		1	.162	.162
Earle Mack	C1	R	20	1	4	0	2	0	1	0	0	0		0	.500	1.000
Claude Derrick	SS1	R	24	1	1	0	0	0	0	0	0	0		0	.000	.000
NEW YORK 2nd 88-63 .583 14.5 GEORGE STALLINGS 78-59 .569 HAL CHASE 10-4 .714																
TOTALS			28	156	5050	629	1252	163	75	20	492	464		289	.248	.322
Hal Chase	1B130	R	27	130	524	67	152	20	5	3	73	16		40	.290	.365
Frank LaPorte	2B79, OF24, 3B15	R	30	124	432	43	114	14	6	2	67	33		16	.264	.338
Jack Knight	SS79, 1B23, 2B7, 3B4, OF1	R	24	117	414	58	129	25	4	3	45	34		23	.312	.413
Jimmy Austin	3B133	B	30	133	432	46	94	11	4	2	36	47		23	.218	.275
Harry Wolter	OF130	L	25	135	479	42	128	15	9	4	42	66		38	.267	.361
Charlie Hemphill	OF94	L	34	102	351	45	84	9	4	0	21	55		19	.239	.288
Birdie Cree	OF134	R	27	134	467	58	134	19	16	4	73	40		28	.287	.422
Ed Sweeney	C78	R	21	78	215	25	43	4	4	0	13	17		12	.200	.256
Bert Daniels	OF85, 3B6, 1B4	R	27	95	356	68	90	13	8	1	17	41		41	.253	.343
Earle Gardner	2B70	R	26	86	271	36	66	4	2	1	24	21		10	.244	.284
Roxy Roach	SS58, OF9	R	25	70	220	27	47	5	2	0	20	29		15	.214	.273
Fred Mitchell	C68	R	32	68	196	16	45	7	2	0	18	9		6	.230	.286
Eddie Foster	SS22	R	23	30	83	5	11	2	0	0	1	8		2	.133	.157
Lou Criger (IL)	C27	R	38	27	69	3	13	2	0	0	4	10		0	.188	.217
Walter Blair	C6	R	26	6	22	2	5	0	1	0	2	0		0	.227	.318
Les Channell (BL)	OF6	L	24	6	19	3	6	0	0	0	3	2		2	.316	.316
1 Red Kleinow (SA)	C5	R	32	6	12	1	5	0	0	0	2	1		2	.417	.417
1 Clyde Engle	OF3	R	26	5	13	0	3	0	0	0	0	0		1	.231	.231
Joe Walsh	C1	R	23	3	0	0	0	0	0	0	0	2		0	.000	.000
Tommy Madden		L	26	1	1	0	0	0	0	0	0	0		0	.000	.000
Larry McClure	OF1	R	25	1	1	0	0	0	0	0	0	0		0	.000	.000
Lew Brockett (HO) 29																
Bill Hogg (DD) 29																
DETROIT 3rd 86-68 .558 18 HUGHIE JENNINGS																
TOTALS			28	155	5048	679	1319	192	73	26	548	459		249	.261	.344
Tom Jones	1B135	R	33	135	432	32	110	13	4	0	45	35		22	.255	.303
Jim Delahanty	2B106	R	31	106	378	67	111	16	3	2	45	43		15	.294	.368
Donie Bush	SS141, 3B1	B	24	142	496	90	130	13	4	3	34	78		49	.262	.323
George Moriarty	3B134	R	24	136	490	53	123	24	4	2	60	33		33	.251	.324
Sam Crawford	OF153, 1B1	L	30	154	588	83	170	26	19	5	120	37		20	.289	.423
Ty Cobb	OF137	L	23	140	508	106	194	35	13	8	91	64		65	.382	.549
Davy Jones	OF101	L	30	101	377	77	100	6	6	0	24	51		25	.265	.313
Oscar Stanage	C84	R	27	88	284	24	57	7	4	2	25	20		1	.207	.284
Matty McIntyre	OF77	L	30	83	305	40	72	15	5	0	25	39		4	.236	.318
Boss Schmidt	C66	B	29	71	197	22	51	7	7	1	23	2		2	.259	.381
Charley O'Leary	2B38, SS16, 3B6	R	27	65	211	23	51	7	1	0	9	9		7	.242	.284
Hack Simmons	1B22, 3B1	R	25	42	110	12	25	3	1	0	9	10		1	.227	.273
Chick Lathers	3B13, 2B7, SS4	L	21	41	82	4	19	2	0	0	3	8		0	.232	.256
Joe Casey	C22	R	22	23	62	3	12	3	0	0	2	1		1	.194	.242
Jay Kirke	2B7, OF1	L	22	9	25	3	5	0	1	0	2	0		1	.200	.240
1 Heinie Beckendorf	C2	R	26	3	13	0	3	0	0	0	0	1		0	.231	.231

Pitching

NAME	T	AGE	W	L	PCT	SV	G	GS	CG	IP	H	BB	SO	SHO	ERA
PHILADELPHIA TOTALS		27	102	48	.680	8	155	155	123	1422	1103	480	789	24	1.78
Jack Coombs	R	27	31	9	.775	2	45	38	35	353	248	115	224	13	1.30
Chief Bender	R	27	23	5	.821	1	30	28	25	250	182	47	155	3	1.58
Cy Morgan	R	31	18	12	.600	0	36	34	23	291	214	117	134	3	1.55
Eddie Plank	L	34	16	10	.615	2	38	32	22	250	218	55	123	1	2.02
Harry Krause	L	21	6	6	.500	0	16	11	9	112	99	42	60	2	2.89
Jimmy Dygert	R	25	4	4	.400	1	19	8	6	99	81	49	59	1	2.55
Tommy Atkins	L	22	3	2	.600	2	15	3	2	57	53	23	29	0	2.68
Lefty Russell	L	19	1	0	1.000	0	1	1	1	9	8	2	5	1	.93
NEW YORK TOTALS		25	88	63	.583	10	156	156	110	1411	1238	364	654	14	2.59
Russ Ford	R	27	26	6	.813	1	36	33	29	300	194	70	209	8	1.65
Jack Quinn	R	26	18	12	.600	0	35	31	20	237	214	58	82	0	2.43
Jack Warhop	R	25	14	14	.500	2	37	27	20	254	219	79	75	0	2.87
Hippo Vaughn	L	22	13	11	.542	2	30	25	18	222	190	58	107	5	1.83
Tom Hughes	R	26	7	9	.438	1	23	15	11	152	153	37	64	0	3.49
Ray Fisher	R	22	5	3	.625	1	17	7	3	91	95	18	42	0	2.93
Rube Manning	R	27	2	4	.333	0	16	9	4	75	80	25	25	0	3.72
John Frill	L	31	2	2	.500	1	10	5	3	48	55	5	27	1	4.50
Ray Caldwell	R	22	1	0	1.000	2	6	2	1	19	19	9	17	0	3.79
1 Slow Joe Doyle	R	28	0	3		2	5	3	2	12	19	5	6	0	8.25
DETROIT TOTALS		27	86	68	.558	5	155	155	108	1375	1257	460	532	17	2.84
George Mullin	R	29	21	12	.636	0	38	32	27	289	260	102	98	5	2.87
Wild Bill Donovan	R	33	18	7	.720	0	26	23	20	209	184	61	107	3	2.41
Ed Willett	R	26	16	11	.593	0	37	25	18	224	175	74	65	4	2.37
Ed Summers	R	25	12	12	.500	1	28	15	7	130	123	41	63	3	2.53
Sailor Stroud	R	25	5	9	.357	1	28	15	7	130	123	41	63	3	3.26
Ed Killian	L	33	4	3	.571	0	11	9	5	74	75	27	20	1	3.04
Hub Pernoll	L	22	4	3	.571	0	11	5	4	55	54	14	20	2	2.94
Ralph Works	R	22	3	6	.333	1	18	10	5	86	73	39	36	0	3.56
Frank Browning	R	27	2	2	.500	2	11	6	2	42	51	10	16	0	3.00
Art Loudell	R	28	1	1	.500	0	5	2	1	21	23	14	12	0	3.43
Marv Peasley	L	20	0	1	.000	0	1	1	0	10	13	11	4	0	8.10
Bill Lelivelt	R	25	0	0	.000	0	1	1	0	6	4	2	1	0	1.00
Dave Skeels	R	18	0	0	.000	0	1	1	0	6	4	2	0	0	12.00

BOSTON — 4th 81-72 .529 22.5 — PATSY DONOVAN

NAME	G by Pos	B	AGE	G	AB	R	H	2B	3B	HR	RBI	BB	SO	SB	BA	SA
TOTALS			25	158	5205	637	1350	175	87	43	527	430		194	.259	.351
Jake Stahl	1B142	R	30	144	531	68	144	19	16	10	77	42		22	.271	.424
Larry Gardner	2B113	L	24	113	413	58	117	12	10	2	36	41		8	.283	.375
Heinie Wagner	SS140	R	29	142	491	61	134	26	7	1	52	44		26	.273	.360
Harry Lord	3B70, SS11	L	28	77	288	26	72	5	5	1	32	14		17	.250	.313
Harry Hooper	OF155	L	22	155	584	81	156	9	10	2	27	62		40	.267	.327
Tris Speaker	OF140	L	22	141	538	92	183	20	14	7	65	52		35	.340	.468
Duffy Lewis	OF149	R	21	151	541	64	153	29	7	8	68	32		10	.283	.393
Bill Carrigan	C110	R	26	114	342	36	85	11	1	3	53	23		10	.249	.313
2 Clyde Engle	3B51, 2B27, OF15, SS7	R	26	106	363	59	96	18	7	2	38	31		12	.264	.369
2 Red Kleinow (SA)	C49	R	32	50	147	9	22	1	0	1	8	20		3	.150	.177
2 Billy Purtell	3B41, SS8	R	24	49	168	15	35	1	2	1	15	18		2	.208	.256
Hugh Bradley	1B21, C3, OF1	R	25	32	83	8	14	6	2	0	7	5		2	.169	.289
1 Harry Niles	OF15	R	29	18	57	6	12	3	0	1	3	4		1	.211	.316
Tom Madden	C12	L	27	14	35	4	13	3	0	0	4	3		0	.371	.457
1 Amby McConnell	2B10	L	27	12	36	6	6	0	0	0	1	5		4	.167	.167
1 Charlie French	2B8	R	26	9	40	4	8	1	0	0	3	1		0	.200	.225

Dutch Lerchen 21 R 0-15, Hap Myers (IL) 23 R 2-6, 1 Pat Donahue 26 R 0-4, Ed Hearn 22 R 0-2, Ralph Pond 20 1-4, Doc Moskiman 30 R 1-9, Jack Thoney (JJ) 29

NAME	T	AGE	W	L	PCT	SV	G	GS	CG	IP	H	BB	SO	SHO	ERA
		26	81	72	.529	9	158	158	100	1429	1236	414	670	12	2.46
Eddie Cicotte	R	26	15	11	.577	9	36	30	20	250	213	86	104	3	2.74
Ray Collins	L	23	13	11	.542	0	35	26	18	245	205	41	109	4	1.62
Charley Hall	R	25	11	9	.550	5	35	16	13	189	142	73	95	0	1.91
Charlie Smith	R	30	12	6	.667	0	24	18	11	156	141	35	53	0	2.30
Smoky Joe Wood	R	20	12	13	.480	0	35	17	14	199	155	56	145	3	1.68
Ed Karger	L	27	11	7	.611	1	27	25	16	183	162	53	81	1	3.20
Frank Arellanes	R	28	4	6	.400	0	28	13	2	100	106	24	33	0	2.88
Ben Hunt	R	22	2	4	.333	0	7	7	3	47	45	20	19	0	4.02
2 Frank Smith	R	30	1	2	.333	0	4	3	2	28	22	11	8	0	4.82
Frank Barberich	R	28	0	0	—	0	2	0	0	5	7	2	0	0	7.20
Louis LeRoy	R	31	0	0	—	0	1	0	0	4	7	2	3	0	11.25
Chris Mahoney	R	25	0	1	.000	0	2	1	0	11	16	5	6	0	3.27
Marty McHale (SA)	R	23	0	1	.000	0	2	1	0	14	15	6	14	0	4.50

CLEVELAND — 5th 71-81 .467 32 — DEACON McGUIRE

NAME	G by Pos	B	AGE	G	AB	R	H	2B	3B	HR	RBI	BB	SO	SB	BA	SA
TOTALS			29	161	5359	548	1310	185	63	9	460	366		189	.244	.308
George Stovall	1B132, 2B2	R	32	142	521	48	136	19	4	0	52	14		16	.261	.313
Nap Lajoie	2B149, 1B10, SS4	R	35	159	592	94	227	53	8	4	76	60		27	.383	.520
Terry Turner	SS94, 3B46, 2B9	R	29	150	574	71	132	14	6	0	33	53		31	.230	.275
Bill Bradley	3B61	R	32	61	214	12	42	9	0	0	12	10		6	.196	.210
Jack Graney	OF114	L	24	116	454	62	107	13	9	1	31	37		18	.236	.311
Joe Birmingham	OF103, 3B1	R	25	104	364	41	84	11	2	0	35	23		18	.231	.272
13 Art Kruger	OF62	R	29	62	223	19	38	6	3	0	14	20		12	.170	.224
Ted Easterly	C66, OF30	L	25	110	363	34	111	16	6	0	55	21		10	.306	.383
2 Harry Niles	OF56, SS7, 3B5	R	29	70	240	25	51	6	4	1	18	15		9	.213	.283
Harry Bemis (BG)	C46	L	36	61	167	12	36	5	1	1	16	5		3	.216	.275
1 Bris Lord	OF55	R	26	56	201	23	44	5	6	0	17	12		4	.219	.303
Neal Ball	SS27, 2B6, OF6, 3B3	R	29	53	119	12	25	3	1	0	12	9		4	.210	.252
George Perring	3B33, 1B4	R	25	39	122	14	27	6	3	0	7	2		1	.221	.320
Grover Land	C33	R	25	34	111	4	23	0	0	0	7	2		1	.207	.207
2 Morrie Rath	2B22, SS1	L	24	24	67	5	13	3	0	0	10	12		4	.194	.239
Elmer Flick	OF18	L	34	24	68	5	18	2	1	1	7	10		1	.265	.368
Nig Clarke (IL)	C17	L	27	21	58	4	9	2	0	0	4	8		0	.155	.190
Joe Jackson	OF20	L	20	20	75	15	29	2	5	0	11	8		4	.387	.587

Cotton Knaupp 20 R 14-59, Ed Hohnhorst 25 L 20-62, Art Thomason 21 L 9-57, Roger Peckinpaugh 19 R 9-45, ,Dave Callahan 21 L 8-44, Syd Smith 26 R 9-27
Jack Adams 19 B 3-13, Herman Bronkie 25 R 2-9, Simon Nicholls 27 L 0-0, 3 Pat Donahue 25 R 0-4, Deacon McGuire 46 R 1-3, Jim Rutherford 23 L 1-2

NAME	T	AGE	W	L	PCT	SV	G	GS	CG	IP	H	BB	SO	SHO	ERA
		27	71	81	.467	14	161	161	92	1462	1386	487	614	13	2.89
Cy Falkenberg	R	30	14	13	.519	4	37	29	18	257	246	75	107	3	2.94
Willie Mitchell	L	20	12	8	.600	1	35	18	11	184	155	55	102	1	2.59
Specs Harkness	R	22	9	7	.563	3	26	16	6	136	132	55	60	1	3.04
Cy Young	R	43	7	10	.412	0	21	20	14	163	149	27	58	1	2.54
George Kahler	R	20	6	4	.600	0	12	6	3	95	80	46	38	2	1.61
Elmer Koestner	R	24	5	10	.333	4	27	13	8	145	145	63	44	1	3.04
1 Fred Link	L	24	5	6	.455	1	22	13	6	123	115	49	52	1	3.29
Addie Joss (SA)	R	30	5	5	.500	0	13	8	2	107	96	18	49	1	2.27
Heinie Berger	R	28	4	4	.500	0	13	8	2	65	57	32	24	0	3.05
Harry Fanwell	R	23	2	9	.182	1	17	11	5	92	87	38	30	1	3.62
Fred Blanding	R	22	2	2	.500	0	5	4	3	45	43	12	25	1	2.80
Walt Doane	L	23	0	0	—	0	6	0	0	18	31	8	7	0	5.50
Casey Kirsch	R	22	0	0	—	0	2	0	1	3	5	1	5	0	6.00
Ben DeMott	R	21	0	3	.000	0	6	4	1	28	45	8	13	0	5.46

CHICAGO — 6th 68-85 .444 35.5 — HUGH DUFFY

NAME	G by Pos	B	AGE	G	AB	R	H	2B	3B	HR	RBI	BB	SO	SB	BA	SA
TOTALS			28	156	5028	456	1062	115	58	7	351	403		183	.211	.261
Chick Gandil	1B74, OF2	R	22	77	275	21	53	7	3	2	21	24		12	.193	.262
Rollie Zeider	2B87, SS45, 3B4	R	26	136	498	57	108	9	2	0	31	62		49	.217	.243
Lena Blackburne	SS74	R	23	75	242	16	42	3	1	0	10	19		4	.174	.194
1 Billy Purtell	3B102	R	24	102	368	21	86	5	3	1	36	21		5	.234	.272
Shano Collins	OF65, 1B27	R	21	65	222	29	62	10	8	1	24	25		10	.197	.289
Paul Meloan	OF65	L	21	65	222	29	54	6	6	0	23	17		4	.243	.324
Patsy Dougherty	OF121	L	33	127	443	45	110	8	4	1	43	41		22	.248	.300
Freddie Payne	C78, OF2	R	29	91	257	17	56	5	4	0	19	11		6	.218	.268
Freddy Parent (BG)	OF62, 2B11, SS4, 3B1	R	34	81	258	23	46	6	1	1	16	29		14	.178	.221
Lee Tannehill (JJ)	SS38, 1B23, 3B6	R	29	67	230	17	51	10	0	1	21	11		3	.222	.278
Doc White	P33, OF14	L	31	56	126	14	25	1	2	0	8	14		2	.198	.238
Bruno Block	C47	R	25	55	152	12	32	1	1	0	9	13		3	.211	.230
2 Charlie French	OF16, 2B28	R	26	45	170	17	28	1	1	0	4	10		5	.165	.182
Billy Sullivan (JJ)	C45	R	35	45	142	10	26	4	1	0	6	7		0	.183	.225
2 Harry Lord	3B44	R	26	44	165	26	49	6	3	0	10	14		17	.297	.370
Charlie Mullen	1B37, OF2	R	21	41	123	15	24	2	1	0	13	4		4	.195	.228
2 Amby McConnell (IL)	2B32	R	27	32	119	13	33	2	3	0	5	7		4	.277	.345
2 George Browne	OF29	L	34	30	112	17	27	4	1	0	4	12		5	.241	.295
Dutch Zwilling	OF27	L	21	27	87	7	16	5	0	0	5	11		1	.184	.241
Felix Chouinerd	OF23, 2B1	R	22	24	82	6	16	3	2	0	9	8		4	.195	.280
Willis Cole	OF22	R	28	22	80	6	14	2	1	0	2	4		0	.175	.225
Eddie Hahn	OF14	L	25	14	53	2	6	2	0	0	1	7		0	.113	.151
Red Kelly	OF9	R	26	9	26	7	6	0	1	0	4	1		0	.156	.200
Bob Messenger	OF5	B	26	9	26	7	6	0	1	0	4	1		0	.231	.308
Cuke Barrows	OF6	R	26	6	20	0	4	0	0	0	1	3		0	.200	.200
Red Bowser	OF1		28	1	2	0	0	0	0	0	0	0		0	.000	.000

NAME	T	AGE	W	L	PCT	SV	G	GS	CG	IP	H	BB	SO	SHO	ERA
		28	68	85	.444	10	156	156	103	1430	1130	381	785	23	2.01
Ed Walsh	R	29	18	20	.474	6	45	36	33	370	242	61	258	7	1.27
Doc White	L	31	15	13	.536	1	33	29	20	246	219	50	111	2	2.57
Fred Olmstead	R	26	10	12	.455	1	32	20	14	174	174	50	68	4	1.95
Frank Lange	R	26	9	4	.692	0	23	15	6	131	93	54	98	1	1.66
Jim Scott	R	21	8	18	.308	2	41	23	14	230	182	86	135	2	2.43
1 Frank Smith	R	30	4	9	.308	0	19	15	9	129	91	40	50	2	2.03
Irv Young	L	32	4	8	.333	0	27	17	7	136	122	39	64	4	2.71
1 Bill Burns	L	30	0	0	—	0	1	0	0	1	0	1	0	0	0.00
Chief Chouneau	R	21	0	1	.000	0	1	1	0	5	7	0	1	0	3.60

WASHINGTON — 7th 66-85 .437 36.5 — JIMMY McALEER

NAME	G by Pos	B	AGE	G	AB	R	H	2B	3B	HR	RBI	BB	SO	SB	BA	SA
TOTALS			29	157	4983	498	1175	145	46	9	393	449		192	.236	.289
Bob Unglaub	1B124	R	28	124	431	29	101	9	4	0	44	21		21	.234	.274
Red Killefer	2B88, OF12	R	25	106	345	35	79	7	1	0	24	29		17	.229	.284
George McBride	SS154	R	29	154	514	54	118	19	4	1	55	61		11	.230	.288
Kid Elberfeld	3B113, 2B10, SS3	R	35	127	455	53	114	9	2	2	42	35		19	.251	.292
Doc Gessler	OF144	L	29	145	487	58	126	17	11	2	50	62		18	.259	.351
Clyde Milan	OF142	L	24	154	531	89	148	17	6	0	16	71		44	.279	.333
Jack Lelivelt	OF89, 1B7	R	24	110	347	40	92	10	3	0	33	40		20	.265	.311
Gabby Street	C86	R	27	89	257	13	52	6	0	1	16	23		1	.202	.237
Wid Conroy	3B48, OF46, 2B5	R	33	105	351	36	89	11	3	1	27	30		11	.254	.311
Germany Schaefer	2B35, OF26, 3B2	R	33	74	229	27	63	6	3	0	14	25		17	.275	.345
2 Heinie Beckendorf	C36	R	20	37	97	8	15	1	0	0	10	5		0	.155	.165
Eddie Ainsmith	C30	R	20	33	104	4	20	1	2	0	9	6		0	.192	.240
John Henry	C18, 1B10	R	24	28	87	2	13	1	1	0	5	2		2	.149	.184
Bill Cunningham	2B22	R	24	22	74	3	22	5	1	0	14	12		4	.297	.392
Doc Ralston	OF22	R	24	22	73	4	15	1	0	0	3	3		2	.205	.219
Jock Somerlott	1B16	R	25	17	63	6	14	0	0	0	3	2		2	.222	.222
Tom Crooke	1B5	R	25	8	21	1	4	1	0	0	1	1		0	.190	.238
2 George Browne	OF5	L	34	7	22	1	4	0	0	0	0	1		0	.182	.182
Jack Hardy	C4, OF1	L	33	7	8	1	2	0	0	0	0	1		0	.250	.250

NAME	T	AGE	W	L	PCT	SV	G	GS	CG	IP	H	BB	SO	SHO	ERA
		27	66	85	.437	5	157	157	119	1376	1223	374	675	19	2.45
Walter Johnson	R	22	25	17	.595	2	45	42	38	374	269	76	313	8	1.35
Bob Groom	R	23	12	17	.414	0	34	30	22	258	255	77	98	3	2.75
Dixie Walker	R	23	11	11	.500	0	29	26	16	199	167	68	85	3	3.30
Doc Reisling (IL)	R	35	9	10	.474	2	30	20	13	191	185	44	57	2	2.54
Dolly Gray	L	31	8	19	.296	0	34	29	21	229	216	64	84	3	2.63
Frank Oberlin	R	34	1	6	.143	0	8	6	6	57	50	23	18	0	3.00
Bill Forman	R	23	0	0	—	0	1	0	0	1	2	0	1	0	9.00
Joe Hovlik	R	25	0	0	—	0	3	0	0	7	10	3	5	0	13.50
Dutch Hinrichs	R	21	0	1	.000	0	3	0	0	7	10	3	5	0	2.57
Bill Otey	L	23	0	1	.000	0	6	1	1	35	40	6	12	0	3.35
Ed Moyer	R	24	0	3	.000	0	6	3	2	25	22	13	3	0	3.24

Jimmy Sebring (DD) 27

ST. LOUIS — 8th 47-107 .305 57 — JACK O'CONNOR

NAME	G by Pos	B	AGE	G	AB	R	H	2B	3B	HR	RBI	BB	SO	SB	BA	SA
TOTALS			28	158	5077	454	1115	131	60	12	347	415		169	.220	.276
Pat Newnam	1B103	R	29	103	384	45	83	3	8	2	26	29		16	.216	.281
Frank Truesdale	2B123	R	26	123	415	39	91	7	2	1	25	48		29	.219	.253
Bobby Wallace	SS98, 3B40	R	36	138	508	47	131	19	7	0	37	49		12	.258	.323
Roy Hartzell	3B89, SS38, OF23	R	27	151	542	52	118	13	5	2	30	49		18	.218	.271
Al Schweitzer	OF109	R	27	113	379	37	87	11	2	2	27	34		16	.230	.285
Danny Hoffman	OF106	L	30	106	380	20	90	11	5	0	27	34		16	.237	.292
George Stone	OF107	L	33	152	562	60	144	17	12	0	40	48		20	.256	.329
Jim Stephens	C96	R	26	99	299	24	72	3	7	0	23	16		2	.241	.298
Art Griggs	OF49, 2B41, 1B17, SS3, 3B3	R	25	123	416	28	98	22	5	2	30	25		11	.236	.327
Bill Killefer	C73	R	22	74	193	14	24	2	0	0	7	12		0	.124	.155
Dode Criss	1B12, P6	R	25	70	91	11	21	4	1	0	4	3		5	.231	.352
Red Corriden	SS14, 3B12	R	22	26	84	19	13	1	0	0	4	13		5	.155	.226
Hub Northen	OF26	R	23	26	96	6	19	1	0	0	16	5		2	.198	.308
Bill Abstein	1B23	R	27	25	87	1	13	2	0	0	3	5		1	.149	.172
Red Fisher	OF19	R	22	22	56	5	12	2	0	0	3	1		1	.214	.286
Sled Allen	C12, 1B1	R	23	23	84	6	10	1	0	0	2	1		5	.130	.174
Ray Demmitt	OF19	L	26	19	43	2	10	0	1	0	5	4		1	.174	.209
Joe McDonald	3B10	R	22	10	32	4	5	1	0	0	3	1		1	.156	.156

Bert Graham 24 B 3-26, Tommy Mee 20 R 3-19, Joe Crisp 24 R 0-1, Ray Jansen 21 R 4-5, Jack O'Connor 41 R 0-0

NAME	T	AGE	W	L	PCT	SV	G	GS	CG	IP	H	BB	SO	SHO	ERA
		27	47	107	.305	4	158	158	100	1391	1356	532	557	9	3.09
Joe Lake	R	28	11	18	.379	2	35	29	24	261	243	71	141	2	2.21
Jack Powell	R	35	7	11	.389	0	21	18	9	129	121	28	52	3	2.30
Red Nelson	R	24	5	1	.833	0	9	6	5	60	57	14	30	1	2.55
Barney Pelty	R	29	5	10	.333	0	27	19	12	165	157	70	48	3	3.49
Roy Mitchell	R	24	4	3	.667	0	8	6	5	52	43	12	23	0	2.60
Farmer Ray	R	23	4	10	.286	0	21	16	11	141	146	49	35	0	3.57
Rube Waddell	L	33	3	1	.750	0	10	5	2	33	34	11	16	0	3.55
Bill Bailey	L	22	3	18	.143	1	34	20	13	192	186	97	90	2	3.29
Dode Criss	R	25	2	1	.667	0	19	2	1	30	26	9	12	9	1.42
Ed Kinsella	R	30	1	3	.250	0	10	5	2	50	62	16	10	0	3.78
2 Bob Spade	R	32	1	3	.250	0	7	4	3	35	34	18	9	0	4.37
Mark Hall	R	23	1	2	.333	0	5	5	3	46	50	31	25	0	4.30
Bill Crouch	R	23	0	0	—	0	1	0	0	2	2	2	1	0	12.00
Harry Howell	L	33	0	2	.000	0	6	1	0	17	24	13	5	0	4.24
2 Fred Link	R	24	0	0	—	0	1	0	0	1	1	1	0	0	0.00
Phil Stremmel	R	26	0	3	.000	0	6	3	2	31	36	17	7	0	3.72
Ray Boyd	R	23	0	1	.000	0	3	1	0	16	15	12	4	0	4.50
Jack Gilligan	L	23	0	2	.000	0	4	1	0	22	13	4	3	0	3.69
Alex Malloy	R	23	0	3	.000	0	4	3	1	34	47	17	12	0	2.55
Bill Graham	L	25	0	8	.000	0	12	9	4	93	46	13	14	0	3.56

CHICAGO — 1ST 104-50 .675 — FRANK CHANCE

NAME	G by Pos	B	AGE	G	AB	R	H	2B	3B	HR	RBI	BB	SO	SB	BA	SA
TOTALS			29	154	4977	711	1333	219	84	34	586	542	501	173	.268	.366
Frank Chance	1B87	R	33	88	295	54	88	12	8	0	36	37	15	16	.298	.393
Johnny Evers (BL)	2B125	L	28	125	433	87	114	11	7	0	28	108	18	28	.263	.321
Joe Tinker	SS131	R	29	133	473	48	136	25	9	3	69	24	35	20	.288	.397
Harry Steinfeldt	3B128	R	32	129	448	70	113	21	1	2	58	36	29	10	.252	.317
Wildfire Schulte	OF150	R	27	151	559	93	168	29	15	10	68	39	57	22	.301	.460
Solly Hofman	OF110,1B24,3B1	R	27	136	477	83	155	24	16	3	86	65	34	29	.325	.461
Jimmy Sheckard	OF143	L	31	144	507	82	130	27	6	5	51	83	53	22	.256	.363
Johnny Kling	C86	R	34	91	297	31	80	17	2	2	32	37	27	3	.269	.360
H. Zimmerman	2B33,SS26,3B22,OF4,1B1	R	23	99	335	35	95	16	6	3	38	20	36	7	.284	.394
Jimmy Archer	C49,1B40	R	27	98	313	36	81	17	6	2	41	14	49	6	.259	.371
Ginger Beaumont	OF56	L	33	76	172	30	46	5	1	2	22	28	14	4	.267	.343
John Kane	OF18,2B6,3B4,SS2	R	27	32	62	11	15	0	0	1	5	12	9	0	.242	.290
Tom Needham	C27,1B1	R	31	31	76	9	14	3	1	0	10	10	10	1	.184	.250
1 Fred Luderus	1B17	L	24	24	54	5	11	1	1	0	3	4	3	0	.204	.259
1 Doc Miller		L	27	1	1	0	0	0	0	0	0	0	0	0	.000	.000

NAME	T	AGE	W	L	PCT	SV	G	GS	CG	IP	H	BB	SO	SHO	ERA
TOTALS		29	104	50	.675	13	154	154	99	1379	1171	474	609	25	2.51
Three Finger Brown	R	33	25	13	.658	7	46	31	27	295	256	64	143	6	1.80
King Cole	R	24	20	4	.833	1	33	29	21	240	174	130	114	4	1.80
Harry McIntire	R	32	13	9	.591	0	28	19	10	176	152	50	65	2	3.07
Orvie Overall (SA)	R	29	12	6	.667	1	23	21	11	145	106	54	92	4	2.66
Ed Reulbach (IL)	R	27	12	8	.600	0	24	23	13	173	161	49	55	1	3.12
2 Lew Richie	R	26	11	4	.733	4	27	8	8	130	117	51	53	3	2.70
Jack Pfiester	L	32	6	3	.667	0	14	13	5	100	82	26	34	2	1.80
Rube Kroh (ST)	L	23	3	1	.750	0	6	4	1	34	33	15	16	0	4.50
Big Jeff Pfeffer	R	28	1	0	1.000	0	13	1	1	41	43	16	11	0	3.29
Orlie Weaver	R	22	1	2	.333	0	7	2	2	32	34	15	22	0	3.66
Al Carson	R	27	0	0	—	0	2	0	0	7	6	1	2	0	3.86
2 Bill Foxen	L	31	0	0	—	0	2	0	0	5	7	3	2	0	9.00

NEW YORK — 2nd 91-63 .591 13 — JOHN McGRAW

NAME	G by Pos	B	AGE	G	AB	R	H	2B	3B	HR	RBI	BB	SO	SB	BA	SA
TOTALS			26	155	5061	715	1391	204	83	31	621	562	489	282	.275	.366
Fred Merkle	1B144	R	21	144	506	75	148	35	14	4	70	44	59	23	.292	.441
Larry Doyle	2B151	L	24	151	575	97	164	21	14	8	59	72	46	39	.285	.412
Al Bridwell	SS141	L	26	142	492	74	136	15	7	0	48	73	23	14	.276	.335
Art Devlin	3B147	R	30	147	493	71	128	17	5	2	67	62	32	28	.260	.327
Red Murray	OF148	R	26	149	553	78	153	27	8	4	87	52	51	57	.277	.376
Fred Snodgrass	OF101,1B9,3B1,C1	R	22	123	396	69	127	22	8	2	44	71	52	33	.321	.432
Josh Devore	OF130	L	22	133	490	92	149	11	10	2	27	46	67	43	.304	.380
Chief Meyers	C117	R	29	127	365	25	104	18	0	1	62	40	18	5	.285	.342
Beals Becker	OF45,1B1	R	23	80	126	18	36	2	4	3	24	14	25	11	.286	.437
Cy Seymour	OF76	L	37	79	287	32	76	9	4	1	40	23	15	4	.265	.334
Admiral Schlei	C49	R	32	55	99	10	19	2	1	0	8	14	10	4	.192	.232
Art Fletcher	SS22,2B11,3B11	R	25	51	125	12	28	2	1	0	13	4	9	2	.224	.256
Doc Crandall	P42,SS1	R	22	45	73	10	25	2	4	1	13	5	7	0	.342	.521
Tillie Shafer	3B8,2B2,SS2	R	21	29	21	5	4	1	0	0	1	0	6	0	.190	.238
Art Wilson	C25,1B1	R	24	26	52	10	14	4	1	0	5	9	6	2	.269	.385
Wilie Keeler	OF2	R	38	19	10	5	3	0	0	0	3	0	3	1	.300	.300
Hank Gowdy	1B5	R	20	7	14	1	3	1	0	0	2	2	3	1	.214	.286
1 Elmer Zacher	OF1	R	29	1	0	0	0	0	0	0	0	0	0	0	.000	.000
Mike Donlin (VR) 32																
Fred Tenney (CJ) 38																

NAME	T	AGE	W	L	PCT	SV	G	GS	CG	IP	H	BB	SO	SHO	ERA
TOTALS		26	91	63	.591	10	155	155	96	1392	1290	397	717	9	2.68
Christy Mathewson	R	29	27	9	.750	0	38	35	27	318	292	60	184	2	1.90
Doc Crandall	R	22	17	4	.810	5	42	18	13	208	194	43	73	2	2.55
Hooks Wiltse	L	30	14	12	.538	2	36	30	18	235	232	52	88	2	2.72
Red Ames	R	27	12	11	.522	0	33	23	13	190	161	63	94	3	2.22
Louis Drucke	R	21	12	10	.545	0	34	27	15	215	174	82	151	0	2.47
Rube Marquard	R	23	4	4	.500	0	13	8	2	71	65	40	52	0	4.44
Bugs Raymond	R	26	4	11	.267	0	19	11	6	99	106	49	55	0	3.82
Walt Dickson	R	31	1	0	1.000	0	12	1	0	30	31	9	9	0	5.40
Dutch Klawitter	R	21	0	0	—	0	1	0	0	1	2	2	0	0	9.00
Ed Hendricks	L	25	0	1	.000	1	4	1	1	12	12	4	2	0	3.75
Dick Rudolph	R	21	0	1	.000	0	3	1	1	12	14	2	9	0	7.50

PITTSBURGH — 3rd 86-67 .562 17.5 — FRED CLARKE

NAME	G by Pos	B	AGE	G	AB	R	H	2B	3B	HR	RBI	BB	SO	SB	BA	SA
TOTALS			28	154	5125	655	1364	214	83	33	543	437	524	148	.266	.360
Jack Flynn (KJ)	1B93	R	26	96	332	32	91	10	2	6	52	30	47	6	.274	.370
Dots Miller	2B117,SS2	R	23	120	444	45	101	13	10	1	48	33	41	11	.227	.309
Honus Wagner	SS138,1B11,2B2	R	36	150	556	90	178	34	8	4	81	59	47	24	.320	.432
Bobby Byrne	3B148	R	25	148	602	101	178	43	12	2	52	66	27	36	.296	.417
Owen Wilson	OF146	L	26	146	536	59	148	14	13	4	50	21	68	8	.276	.373
Tommy Leach	OF131,SS2,2B1	R	32	135	529	83	143	24	5	4	52	38	62	18	.270	.357
Fred Clarke	OF118	L	37	123	429	57	113	23	9	2	63	53	23	12	.263	.373
George Gibson	C143	R	29	143	482	53	125	22	6	3	44	47	31	7	.259	.349
Vin Campbell	OF74	L	22	97	282	42	92	9	5	4	21	26	23	17	.326	.436
Ham Hyatt	1B38,OF4	L	25	74	175	19	46	5	6	1	30	8	14	5	.263	.377
Bill McKechnie	2B36,SS14,3B8,1B4	B	23	71	212	23	46	1	2	0	12	11	23	4	.217	.241
Mike Simon	C14	R	27	22	50	3	10	0	1	0	5	1	2	1	.200	.240
Jack Kading	1B8	R	25	8	23	5	7	2	1	0	4	4	5	0	.304	.478
Paddy O'Connor	C1	R	30	6	4	0	1	0	0	0	0	0	1	0	.250	.250
2 Bud Sharpe	1B4	R	28	4	16	2	3	0	1	0	1	0	2	0	.188	.313
Alex McCarthy	SS3	R	22	3	12	1	1	0	1	0	1	0	4	0	.083	.250
1 Ed Abbaticchio	SS1	R	33	3	3	0	0	0	0	0	0	0	0	0	.000	.000
Max Carey	OF2	B	20	2	6	2	3	1	0	0	2	2	1	0	.500	.833

NAME	T	AGE	W	L	PCT	SV	G	GS	CG	IP	H	BB	SO	SHO	ERA
TOTALS		30	86	67	.562	12	154	154	73	1376	1254	392	479	13	2.83
Babe Adams	R	28	18	9	.667	0	34	30	16	245	217	60	101	3	2.24
Lefty Leifield	L	26	15	12	.556	2	40	30	13	218	197	67	64	3	2.65
Deacon Phillippe	R	38	14	2	.875	4	31	9	5	122	111	9	30	1	2.29
Howie Camnitz	R	28	12	13	.480	2	38	31	16	260	246	61	120	1	3.22
2 Kirby White	R	26	10	9	.526	2	30	21	7	153	142	75	42	3	3.47
Sam Leever	R	38	6	5	.545	2	26	8	4	111	104	25	33	0	2.76
Bill Powell	R	25	4	6	.400	0	12	9	4	75	65	34	23	2	2.40
Lefty Webb	L	25	2	1	.667	0	7	3	2	29	29	9	6	0	5.67
Gene Moore	R	24	2	1	.667	0	4	1	0	17	19	7	9	0	3.18
Nick Maddox	R	23	2	3	.400	0	20	7	2	87	73	28	29	0	3.41
Jack Ferry	R	23	1	2	.333	0	6	3	2	26	8	12	0	2.32	
Skip Dowd	R	21	0	0	—	0	1	0	0	3	1	1	0	0	0.00
Jack Mercer	R	21	0	0	—	0	1	0	0	2	1	0	0	0	0.00
1 Sammy Frock	R	27	0	1	.000	0	3	1	0	13	11	4	1	0	4.50
Elmer Steele	R	26	0	3	.000	0	3	3	2	24	19	3	7	0	2.25

PHILADELPHIA — 4th 78-75 .510 25.5 — RED DOOIN

NAME	G by Pos	B	AGE	G	AB	R	H	2B	3B	HR	RBI	BB	SO	SB	BA	SA
TOTALS			29	157	5171	674	1319	223	71	22	565	506	559	199	.255	.338
Kitty Bransfield	1B110	R	35	123	427	39	102	17	4	5	52	30	47	10	.239	.319
Otto Knabe	2B136	R	26	137	510	73	133	18	6	1	44	47	42	15	.261	.325
Mickey Doolan	SS148	R	30	148	536	58	141	26	6	2	57	35	56	16	.263	.354
Eddie Grant	3B152	R	27	152	579	70	155	15	5	1	67	39	54	20	.268	.316
John Titus	OF142	L	34	143	535	91	129	26	5	3	35	93	44	20	.241	.325
Johnny Bates	OF131	L	28	135	498	91	152	26	11	3	61	61	49	31	.305	.420
Sherry Magee	OF154	R	25	154	519	110	172	39	17	6	123	94	36	49	.331	.507
Red Dooin (BN)	C91,OF3	R	31	103	331	30	80	13	4	0	30	22	17	10	.242	.305
Jimmy Walsh	OF27,2B26,SS9,3B5	R	24	88	242	28	60	8	3	3	31	25	38	5	.248	.343
Pat Moran	C56	R	34	68	199	13	47	7	1	0	11	17	16	6	.236	.281
Joe Ward	1B32,SS1,3B1	R	25	48	124	11	18	2	1	0	13	3	11	1	.145	.177
Fred Jacklitsch	C13,1B2,2B1,3B1	R	34	25	51	7	10	3	0	0	2	9	5	0	.196	.255
Roy Thomas	OF20	L	36	23	71	7	13	0	2	0	4	7	5	4	.183	.239
2 Fred Luderus	1B19	L	24	21	68	10	20	5	2	0	14	5	9	2	.294	.426
Ed McDonough	C4	R	23	5	9	1	1	0	0	0	0	0	3	0	.111	.111
John Castle	OF2	R	31	4	4	1	1	0	0	0	0	0	1	1	.250	.250
Harry Cheek	C2		31	1	4	0	2	1	0	0	0	0	0	0	.500	.750

NAME	T	AGE	W	L	PCT	SV	G	GS	CG	IP	H	BB	SO	SHO	ERA
TOTALS		27	78	75	.510	9	157	157	84	1411	1297	547	657	17	3.05
Earl Moore	R	30	22	15	.595	0	46	35	19	283	228	121	185	6	2.58
Bob Ewing	R	37	16	14	.533	0	34	32	20	255	235	86	102	4	3.00
Lew Moren	R	26	13	14	.481	1	34	26	12	205	207	82	74	1	3.56
George McQuillan	R	25	9	6	.600	1	24	17	13	152	109	50	71	3	1.60
Eddie Stack	R	22	6	7	.462	0	20	16	7	117	115	34	48	1	4.00
1 Bill Foxen	L	31	5	5	.500	0	16	9	5	78	73	40	33	0	2.54
Ad Brennan	L	22	3	0	1.000	0	19	5	2	73	72	28	28	0	2.34
Lou Schettler	R	24	2	6	.250	1	27	7	3	107	96	51	62	0	3.20
George Chalmers	R	22	1	1	.500	0	4	3	3	11	11	12		0	5.32
Jim Moroney	L	26	1	2	.333	1	12	2	1	42	43	11	13	0	2.14
Bill Culp	R	23	0	0	—	0	1	0	0	7	8	4	4	0	7.71
Patsy Flaherty	L	34	0	0	—	0	1	0	0	4	10	13	3	0	4.50
Bert Humphries	R	29	0	0	—	2	5	0	0	13	13	3	9	0	6.00
Barney Slaughter	R	25	0	1	.000	0	7	1	0	27	33	11	11	0	6.34
Charlie Girard	R	25	0	1	.000	0	7	1	0	15	22	2	4	0	6.00
Tully Sparks	R	35	0	0	—	0	2	0	0						

CINCINNATI — 5th 75-79 .487 28 — CLARK GRIFFITH

NAME	G by Pos	B	AGE	G	AB	R	H	2B	3B	HR	RBI	BB	SO	SB	BA	SA
TOTALS			26	156	5121	620	1326	150	79	23	526	529	515	310	.259	.333
Dick Hoblitzell	1B148,2B7	L	21	155	611	85	170	24	13	4	70	47	32	28	.278	.380
Dick Egan	2B131,SS3	R	26	135	474	70	116	11	5	0	46	53	38	41	.245	.289
2 Tommy McMillan	SS82	R	22	82	248	20	46	0	3	0	13	31	23	7	.185	.210
Hans Lobert (XJ)	3B90	R	28	93	314	43	97	16	3	6	40	30	9	41	.309	.395
Mike Mitchell	OF149,1B7	R	30	156	583	79	167	16	18	5	88	59	56	35	.286	.401
Dode Paskert	OF139,1B2	R	28	144	506	63	152	21	5	2	46	70	60	51	.300	.374
Bob Bescher	OF150	R	26	150	589	95	147	20	10	4	48	81	75	70	.250	.338
Larry McLean	C119	R	28	127	423	27	126	14	7	2	71	26	23	4	.298	.378
Tom Downey	SS68,3B41	R	26	111	378	43	102	9	3	2	32	34	28	12	.270	.325
Ward Miller	OF26	L	25	81	126	21	30	6	0	0	10	22	13	10	.238	.286
Tommy Clarke	C56	R	22	64	151	19	42	6	5	1	20	19	17	1	.278	.404
Frank Roth	C4,OF1	R	31	26	29	3	7	2	0	0	2	7	6	1	.241	.310
Art Phelan	3B8,2B5,OF3,SS1	R	22	23	42	7	9	0	0	0	4	7	6	5	.214	.214
Orville Woodruff	3B17,2B4	R	33	21	61	6	9	1	0	0	5	5	9	0	.148	.164
Mickey Corcoran	2B14	R	27	14	46	3	10	3	0	0	5	1	6	0	.217	.283
Swat McCabe	OF9	L	28	13	35	3	9	1	0	0	1	3	9	0	.257	.286
Jim Doyle	3B3,OF1	R	28	7	13	1	2	2	0	0	1	0	2	0	.154	.308
Chappie Charles	SS4	R	29	4	15	1	2	0	0	0	0	3	4	1	.133	.267
Dave Altizer		L	33	4	10	3	6	0	0	0	0	5	0	3	.600	.600
George Wheeler		R	22	2	5	1	1	0	0	0	0	0	0	0	.000	.000
Bob Meinke	SS2	R	23	2	4	0	0	0	0	0	0	0	1	0	.000	.000
Rabbit Robinson	3B2	R	28	2	4	1	1	0	0	0	0	1	0	0	.250	.250
Joe Burns (IL)		L	21	1	1	1	1	0	0	0	0	0	0	0	1.000	1.000
Ned Crompton	OF1	R	27	1	4	0	0	0	0	0	0	0	1	0	.000	.000
Clark Griffith		R	40	1	1	0	0	0	0	0	0	0	0	0	.000	.000
Mike Konnick	SS1	R	21	1	1	0	0	0	0	0	0	0	0	0	.000	.000

NAME	T	AGE	W	L	PCT	SV	G	GS	CG	IP	H	BB	SO	SHO	ERA
TOTALS		28	75	79	.487	11	156	156	86	1387	1334	528	497	16	3.08
George Suggs	R	28	19	11	.633	3	35	30	23	266	248	48	91	2	2.40
Harry Gaspar	R	27	15	17	.469	7	48	31	16	275	257	75	74	4	2.59
Jack Rowan	R	24	14	13	.519	1	42	30	18	261	242	105	108	4	2.93
Fred Beebe	R	29	12	15	.444	0	35	26	11	214	193	94	93	2	3.07
2 Bill Burns	L	30	8	13	.381	0	31	21	13	179	183	49	57	2	3.48
Art Fromme (IL)	R	26	3	4	.429	0	11	5	1	49	44	39	10	0	2.94
Rube Benton	L	20	1	1	.500	0	12	2	0	38	44	23	15	0	4.74
Harry Coveleski	L	24	1	1	.500	0	7	4	1	39	35	42	27	0	5.31
Roy Castleton	L	24	1	2	.333	0	7	2	1	14	15	6	5	0	3.21
1 Bob Spade	R	32	1	2	.333	0	5	3	1	17	35	9	1	0	6.89
2 Slow Joe Doyle	R	28	0	0	—	0	3	1	0	17	16	11	10	0	4.76
Tom Cantwell	R	21	0	1	.000	0	2	1	0	11	16	17	11	0	6.54
Walt Slagle	R	31	0	0	—	0	1	0	0	4	9	9	2	0	9.00
Mysterious Walker	R	26	0	0	—	0	4	3	1	24		3	4	1	0	3.00

NAME	G by Pos	B	AGE	G	AB	R	H	2B	3B	HR	RBI	BB	SO	SB	BA	SA
BROOKLYN 6th 64-90 .416 40				**BILL DAHLEN**												
TOTALS			27	156	5125	497	1174	166	73	25	408	434	706	151	229	.305
Jake Daubert	1B144	L	26	144	552	67	146	15	15	8	50	47	53	23	.264	.389
John Hummel	2B153	R	27	153	578	67	141	21	13	5	74	57	81	21	.244	.351
Tony Smith	SS101, 3B6	R	26	106	321	31	58	10	1	1	16	69	53	9	.181	.227
Ed Lennox	3B100	R	26	110	367	19	95	19	4	3	32	36	39	7	.259	.357
Jack Dalton	OF72	R	25	77	273	33	62	9	4	1	21	26	30	5	.227	.300
Bill Davidson	OF131	R	26	136	509	48	121	13	7	0	34	24	54	27	.238	.291
Zack Wheat	OF156	L	22	156	606	78	172	36	15	2	55	47	80	16	.284	.403
Bill Bergen	C89	R	37	89	249	11	40	2	1	0	14	6	39	0	.161	.177
Al Burch	OF70, 1B18	L	26	103	352	41	83	8	3	1	20	22	30	13	.236	.284
Tex Erwin	C68	L	24	81	202	15	38	3	1	1	10	24	12	1	.188	.228
Pryor McElveen	3B54, SS6, 2B3, C1	R	28	74	213	19	48	8	3	1	26	22	47	6	.225	.300
Hap Smith	OF16	L	26	35	76	6	18	2	0	0	5	4	14	4	.237	.263
Otto Miller	C28	R	21	31	66	5	11	3	0	0	2	2	19	1	.167	.212
Dolly Stark	SS30	R	25	30	103	7	17	3	0	0	8	7	19	2	.165	.194
Bob Coulson	OF25	R	23	25	89	14	22	3	4	1	13	6	14	9	.247	.404
1 Tommy McMillan	SS23	R	22	23	74	2	13	1	0	0	2	6	10	4	.176	.189
Harry Lumley	OF4	L	29	8	21	3	3	0	0	0	0	3	6	0	.143	.143
Tim Jordan (KJ)		L	31	5	5	1	1	0	0	1	3	0	2	0	.200	.800
Bill Dahlen		R	40	3	2	0	0	0	0	0	0	0	1	0	.000	.000
George Hunter	OF1	B	23	1	0	0	0	0	0	0	0	0	0	0	—	—

NAME	T	AGE	W	L	PCT	SV	G	GS	CG	IP	H	BB	SO	SHO	ERA
		29	64	90	.416	5	156	156	103	1420	1331	545	555	15	3.07
Nap Rucker	L	25	17	18	.486	0	41	39	27	320	293	84	147	6	2.59
Cy Barger	R	25	15	15	.500	1	35	30	25	272	267	107	87	2	2.88
George Bell	R	35	10	27	.270	1	44	36	25	310	267	82	102	4	2.64
Doc Scanlan	R	29	9	11	.450	2	34	25	14	217	175	116	103	0	2.61
Elmer Knetzer	R	24	7	5	.583	0	20	15	10	133	122	60	56	3	3.18
Kaiser Wilhelm	R	36	3	7	.300	0	15	5	0	68	88	18	17	0	4.76
Rube Dessau	R	27	2	3	.400	0	9	0	0	51	67	29	24	0	5.82
Fred Miller	L	24	1	1	.500	0	6	2	2	21	25	13	2	0	4.71
George Crable	L	25	0	0	—	0	2	1	1	7	5	5	3	0	5.14
Frank Schneiberg	R	30	0	0	—	1	0	0	1	5	4	4	0	0	63.00
Sandy Burk	R	23	0	3	.000	0	4	3	1	19	17	27	14	0	6.16

NAME	G by Pos	B	AGE	G	AB	R	H	2B	3B	HR	RBI	BB	SO	SB	BA	SA
ST. LOUIS 7st 63-90 .412 40.5				**ROGER BRESNAHAN**												
TOTALS			27	153	4912	637	1217	167	70	15	527	655	581	179	.248	.319
Ed Konetchy	1B144, P1	R	24	144	520	87	157	23	16	3	78	78	59	18	.302	.425
Miller Huggins	2B151	B	32	151	547	101	145	15	6	1	36	116	46	34	.265	.320
Arnold Hauser	SS117, 3B1	R	21	119	375	37	77	7	2	2	36	49	39	15	.205	.251
Mike Mowrey	3B141	R	26	143	489	69	138	24	6	2	70	67	38	21	.282	.368
Steve Evans	OF141, 1B10	L	26	150	506	73	122	21	8	2	73	78	63	10	.241	.326
Rebel Oakes	OF127	L	26	131	468	50	118	14	6	0	43	38	38	16	.252	.308
Rube Ellis	OF141	L	24	150	550	87	142	18	8	4	54	62	70	25	.258	.342
Ed Phelps	C80	R	31	93	270	25	71	4	2	0	37	36	29	0	.263	.293
Roger Bresnahan	C77, OF2, P1	R	31	88	234	35	65	15	3	0	27	55	17	13	.278	.368
Rudy Hulswitt	SS30, 3B2	R	33	63	133	9	33	7	2	0	14	13	10	5	.248	.331
2 Elmer Zacher	OF36, 2B1	R	29	47	132	7	28	5	1	0	10	10	19	3	.212	.265
Frank Betcher	SS12, 3B7, 2B6, OF2	B	22	35	89	7	18	2	0	0	6	7	14	1	.202	.225
Ody Abbott	OF21	R	23	22	70	2	13	2	1	0	6	6	20	3	.186	.243
Jack Bliss	C13	R	28	16	33	2	2	0	0	0	3	4	8	0	.061	.061
Bill O'Hara	OF4, 1B1, P1	L	27	9	20	1	3	0	0	0	2	1	3	1	.150	.150
Jap Barbeau	3B6, 2B1	R	28	7	21	4	4	0	1	0	3	2	3	3	.190	.286
Billy Kelly	C1	R	24	2	2	1	0	0	0	0	0	0	1	0	.000	.000
Ernie Lush	OF1	R	25	1	4	0	0	0	0	0	0	1	0	0	.000	.000
Alan Storke (DD) 25																

NAME	T	AGE	W	L	PCT	SV	G	GS	CG	IP	H	BB	SO	SHO	ERA
		26	63	90	.412	14	153	153	83	1337	1396	541	466	4	3.78
Johnny Lush	L	24	14	13	.519	1	36	25	13	225	235	70	54	1	3.20
Bob Harmon	R	22	13	15	.464	2	43	33	15	236	227	133	87	0	4.46
Vic Willis	R	34	9	12	.429	3	33	23	12	212	224	61	67	1	3.35
Slim Sallee (ST)	L	25	7	8	.467	2	18	13	9	115	112	24	46	1	2.97
Les Backman	R	22	6	7	.462	2	26	11	6	116	117	53	41	0	3.03
Frank Corridon	R	29	6	14	.300	3	30	18	9	156	168	55	51	0	3.81
Bill Steele	R	24	4	4	.500	1	9	8	8	72	71	24	25	0	3.25
Roy Golden	R	21	2	3	.400	0	7	6	3	43	44	33	31	0	4.39
Cy Alberts	R	28	1	2	.333	0	4	3	2	28	35	20	10	0	6.11
Bunny Hearn	L	19	1	3	.250	0	5	4	2	39	49	16	14	0	5.08
John Raleigh	R	23	0	0	—	0	5	1	0	8	8	2	2	0	9.00
Charlie Pickett	R	27	0	0	—	0	2	0	0	6	7	2	2	0	1.50
Harry Patton		26	0	0	—	0	1	0	0	4	4	1	0	0	2.25
Ed Konetchy	R	24	0	0	—	0	1	0	0	4	4	1	0	0	4.50
Roger Bresnahan	R	31	0	0	—	0	1	0	0	3	6	1	0	0	0.00
Bill O'Hara	L	27	0	0	—	0	1	0	0	1	0	0	0	0	0.00
Bill Chambers	R	21	0	0	—	0	1	0	0	2	5	0	0	0	4.50
Rube Geyer	R	26	0	1	.000	0	4	0	0	4	5	3	5	0	4.50
Eddie Higgins	R	22	0	1	.000	0	2	0	0	10	15	7	1	0	4.50
Elmer Rieger	R	21	0	1	.000	0	3	1	0	21	26	7	9	0	6.25
Ed Zmich	L	25	0	5	.000	0	9	6	2	36	38	29	19	0	6.25

NAME	G by Pos	B	AGE	G	AB	R	H	2B	3B	HR	RBI	BB	SO	SB	BA	SA
BOSTON 8th 53-100 .346 50.5				**FRED LAKE**												
TOTALS			28	157	5123	495	1260	173	49	31	421	359	540	152	.246	.317
1 Bud Sharpe	1B113	R	28	115	439	30	105	14	3	0	29	14	31	4	.239	.304
Dave Shean	2B148	R	32	150	543	50	130	12	7	3	36	42	45	16	.239	.304
Bill Sweeney	SS110, 3B21, OF2	R	24	150	499	43	133	22	4	5	46	61	28	25	.267	.397
Buck Herzog	3B105	R	24	106	380	51	95	20	4	3	32	30	34	11	.250	.342
Doc Miller	OF130	L	27	130	482	48	138	27	4	3	61	19	55	8	.286	.378
Fred Beck	OF134, 1B19	L	23	154	571	52	157	32	9	10	64	19	55	8	.275	.415
Bill Collins	OF151	B	28	151	584	67	141	6	7	3	40	43	48	36	.241	.291
Peaches Graham	C87, 3B2, 1B1, OF1	R	33	110	291	31	82	13	2	0	21	33	15	5	.282	.340
Harry Smith	C38	R	35	70	147	8	35	4	0	1	15	5	14	5	.238	.286
Gus Getz	3B22, 2B13, OF8, SS4	R	20	54	144	14	28	0	1	0	7	6	10	2	.194	.208
2 Ed Abbaticchio	SS46, 2B1	R	33	52	178	20	44	4	2	0	10	12	16	2	.247	.292
Bill Rariden	C49	R	22	49	137	15	31	5	1	1	14	12	22	1	.226	.299
Wilbur Good	OF23	L	24	23	86	15	29	5	4	0	11	6	13	5	.337	.488
Herbie Moran	OF20	L	26	20	67	11	8	0	3	0	3	13	14	6	.119	.119
Pete Burg	3B12, SS1	R	28	13	46	7	15	0	1	0	10	7	12	5	.326	.370
Rube Sellers	OF9	R	29	12	32	3	5	0	0	0	2	6	5	1	.156	.156
Marty Martel	1B10	R	27	10	31	0	4	0	0	0	1	2	4	0	.129	.129
Cush Cooney	OF2	R	27	8	12	2	3	1	0	0	1	2	0	0	.250	.250
Fred Liese		L	24	5	4	0	0	0	0	0	0	0	0	0	.000	.000
Fred Lake		R	43	3	1	0	0	0	0	0	0	0	0	0	.000	.000
Rowdy Elliott	C1	R	19	3	2	0	0	0	0	0	0	0	0	0	.000	.000
2 Art Kruger		R	29	3	4	0	0	0	0	0	0	1	0	0	.000	.000
Jimmy Riley		R	29	1	1	0	0	0	0	0	0	1	1	0	.000	.000

NAME	T	AGE	W	L	PCT	SV	G	GS	CG	IP	H	BB	SO	SHO	ERA
		25	53	100	.346	9	157	157	74	1390	1328	599	531	12	3.22
Al Mattern	L	27	16	19	.457	1	51	37	17	305	288	121	94	6	2.98
2 Sammy Frock	R	27	11	19	.367	2	45	29	15	255	245	91	170	2	3.21
Buster Brown	R	28	9	23	.281	2	46	29	16	263	251	94	88	1	2.67
Cecil Ferguson	R	23	8	7	.533	0	26	14	10	123	110	58	40	1	3.80
Cliff Curtis	R	28	6	24	.200	2	43	37	12	251	251	124	85	2	3.55
Billy Burke	L	20	1	0	1.000	0	19	1	0	64	68	29	22	0	4.08
Chick Evans	R	20	1	1	.500	2	13	1	0	31	28	27	12	0	5.23
1 Kirby White	R	26	1	2	.333	0	3	3	0	26	15	12	6	0	1.38
Ralph Good	R	24	0	0	—	0	1	0	0	9	4	2	0	0	2.00
Lefty Tyler	L	20	0	0	—	0	2	1	1	11	11	6	6	0	2.46
Jiggs Parson	R	24	0	2	.000	0	10	4	0	35	35	26	7	0	3.86
1 Lew Richie	R	26	0	3	.000	0	4	2	0	16	20	9	7	0	2.81

WORLD SERIES — PHILADELPHIA (AL) 4 CHICAGO (NL) 1

LINE SCORES

TEAM	1	2	3	4	5	6	7	8	9	10	11	12	R	H	E
Game 1 October 17 at Philadelphia															
CHI(NL)	0	0	0	0	0	0	0	0	1				1	3	1
PHI(AL)	0	2	1	0	0	0	0	0	X				4	7	2

Overall, McIntyre (4)   Bender

Game 2 October 18 at Philadelphia															
CHI	1	0	0	0	0	0	1	0	1				3	8	3
PHI	0	0	2	0	1	0	6	0	X				9	14	4

Brown, Richie (8)   Coombs

Game 3 October 20 at Chicago															
PHI	1	2	5	0	0	0	4	0	0				12	15	1
CHI	1	2	0	0	0	0	0	2	0				5	6	5

Coombs   Reulbach, McIntyre (3)
          Pfiester

Game 4 October 22 at Chicago															
PHI	0	0	1	2	0	0	0	0	0	0			3	11	3
CHI	1	0	0	1	0	0	0	0	1	1			4	9	1

Bender   Cole, Brown (9)

Game 5 October 23 at Chicago															
PHI	1	0	0	0	1	0	0	5	0				7	9	1
CHI	0	1	0	0	0	0	0	1	0				2	9	2

Coombs   Brown

COMPOSITE BATTING

NAME	POS	G	AB	R	H	2B	3B	HR	RBI	BA
Philadelphia (AL)										
Totals		5	177	35	56	19	1	1	30	.316
Baker	3B	5	22	6	9	3	0	0	4	.409
Lord	OF	5	22	3	4	2	0	0	1	.182
Collins	2B	5	21	5	9	4	0	0	3	.429
Murphy	OF	5	20	6	7	3	0	1	9	.350
Strunk	1B	4	18	2	5	1	1	0	2	.278
Davis	1B	5	17	5	6	3	0	0	2	.353
Barry	SS	5	17	4	4	2	0	0	3	.235
Coombs	P	3	13	0	5	1	0	0	3	.385
Thomas	C	4	12	2	3	0	0	0	1	.250
Bender	P	2	6	1	2	0	0	0	1	.333
Hartsel	OF	1	5	2	1	0	0	0	0	.200
Lapp	C	1	4	0	1	0	0	0	1	.250
Chicago (NL)										
Totals		5	158	15	35	11	0	0	13	.222
Steinfeldt	3B	5	20	2	2	1	0	0	0	.100
Tinker	SS	5	18	2	6	2	0	0	0	.333
Chance	1B	5	17	1	6	1	0	0	4	.353
Schulte	OF	5	17	3	6	3	0	0	2	.353
Zimmerman	2B	5	17	0	4	1	0	0	2	.235
Hofman	OF	5	15	2	4	0	0	0	4	.267
Sheckard	OF	5	14	5	4	2	0	0	1	.286
Kling	C	5	13	0	1	0	0	0	0	.077
Archer	1B-C	3	11	1	2	1	0	0	0	.182
Brown	P	3	7	0	0	0	0	0	0	.000
Beaumont	PH	3	2	1	0	0	0	0	0	.000
Cole	P	1	2	0	0	0	0	0	0	.000
Pfiester	P	1	2	0	0	0	0	0	0	.000
McIntire	P	2	1	0	0	0	0	0	0	.000
Needham	PH	1	1	0	0	0	0	0	0	.000
Overall	P	1	1	0	0	0	0	0	0	.000
Kane	PR	1	0	0	0	0	0	0	0	—
Reulbach	P	1	0	0	0	0	0	0	0	—
Richie	P	1	0	0	0	0	0	0	0	—

COMPOSITE PITCHING

NAME	G	IP	H	BB	SO	W	L	SV	ERA
Philadelphia (AL)									
Totals	5	45.2	35	18	31	4	1	0	2.76
Coombs	3	27	23	14	17	3	0	0	3.33
Bender	2	18.2	12	4	14	1	1	0	1.93
Chicago (NL)									
Totals	5	44	56	17	24	1	4	0	4.70
Brown	3	18	23	7	14	1	2	0	5.50
Cole	1	8	10	3	5	0	0	0	3.38
Pfiester	1	6.2	9	1	4	0	1	0	6.75
McIntire	2	5.1	4	3	3	0	1	0	6.75
Overall	1	3	6	1	1	0	0	0	9.00
Reulbach	1	2	3	2	0	0	0	0	9.00
Richie	1	1	1	0	0	0	0	0	0.00

1911 The Fire Fighters of Philadelphia

It seemed that Fate would frown on the New York Giants in 1911 when the Polo Grounds caught fire on April 14, and was extensively damaged. The orphaned Giants were taken into Highlander Park by the Yankees, but this was hardly an auspicious manner in which to begin a season. Despite the spring mishap, John McGraw's men stayed close to the pace-setting Chicago Cubs during the summer before taking off in August and leaving the pack behind. The Giants' hot streak dated from the time utility man Art Fletcher was given the shortstop job, and Buck Herzog was reacquired from Boston to fill the third base slot. Staying free of injuries, the Giants passed the Cubs on August 24, and wrapped up the pennant with 20 victories in their final 24 games. The injury-plagued Cubs could not match the Giant pace and had to settle for a second-place finish, 7 1/2 games back. Perhaps aiding the Giants most of all down the stretch was moving back into the rebuilt Polo Grounds in September.

The Giants victory could be found in Rube Marquard who, after two years of mediocrity, fulfilled the promise that had prompted McGraw to shell out $11,000 to purchase his contract in 1908. The left-handed hurler developed into the league's top southpaw, winning 24 games and leading the league in strikeouts. He formed a counterpoint to righty Christy Mathewson, giving McGraw the top pitching duo in baseball. Larry Doyle, Art Fletcher, and Chief Meyers posted .300 averages for the Giants, and Fred Merkle provided power and run production for the offense.

Honus Wagner took his eighth and last batting crown with a .334 mark, and Wildfire Schulte of Chicago won the home run title with a tremendous total of 21 circuit blasts, the best power mark since 1899. Eight pitchers chalked up 20 victories, with rookie Grover "Pete" Alexander of the Phillies leading the way with 28.

The American League race was a two-team affair as the Philadelphia Athletics and Detroit Tigers ran away from the rest of the field. Philadelphia started slowly, while Detroit began the year as a hot team. The Athletics righted themselves and played winning ball from May on to stay hot on Detroit's tail throughout the summer. Both teams possessed high octane offenses, but Connie Mack's pitching staff gave the Athletics the edge. Behind ace pitchers Jack Coombs and Eddie Plank, Philadelphia passed the Tigers on August 4, and did not stop until they had the pennant won by 13 1/2 games. The Athletic infield of Stuffy McInnis, Eddie Collins, Jack Barry, and Frank Baker became known as the $100,000 infield, and a team batting mark of .296 enabled the strong pitching staff to win 101 games.

Ty Cobb and Sam Crawford formed the most feared batting tandem in the league, but mediocre pitching negated their efforts and failed to give Detroit the balance to overhaul the Athletics. Cobb won his fifth consecutive batting title with a career-high .420 mark, although rookie outfielder Joe Jackson of the Cleveland Indians threatened him all the way with a .408 average - the highest runner-up average ever recorded in baseball. Philadelphia's Frank Baker led all batters with 11 homers, and teammate Jack Coombs led in wins with 28.

The Athletics' pitchers continued to handcuff batters in the World Series as they held the Giants to a .175 batting average and 13 runs in a six-game Series won by the Mackmen. Bender, Coombs, and Plank all pitched complete game victories, but the star of the Series was Athletic third baseman Frank Baker. Besides hitting .375, his home run in the second game beat Rube Marquard, and another homer in the ninth inning of the third game of Christy Mathewson tied the score. The third baseman's power performance was substantial enough to have the press immediately dub him as Home Run Baker - one of the early heroes of Series play.

1911 AMERICAN LEAGUE

NAME	G by Pos	B	AGE	G	AB	R	H	2B	3B	HR	RBI	BB	SO	SB	BA	SA
PHILADELPHIA	1st 101-50 .669		CONNIE MACK													
	TOTALS		27	152	5199	861	1540	233	93	35	692	424		226	.296	.397
Stuffy McInnis	1B97, SS24	R	20	126	468	76	150	20	10	3	77	25		23	.321	.425
Eddie Collins	2B132	L	24	132	493	92	180	22	13	3	73	62		38	.365	.481
Jack Barry	SS127	R	24	127	442	73	117	18	7	1	63	38		30	.265	.344
Frank Baker	3B148	L	25	148	592	96	198	38	4	11	115	40		38	.334	.468
Danny Murphy	OF136, 2B4	R	34	141	508	104	167	27	11	6	66	50		22	.329	.461
Rube Oldring	OF119	R	27	121	495	84	147	11	14	3	59	21		21	.297	.394
Bris Lord	OF132	R	27	134	574	92	178	36	11	3	55	35		15	.310	.427
Ira Thomas	C103	R	30	103	297	33	81	14	3	0	39	23		4	.273	.340
Amos Strunk	OF62, 1B2	L	22	74	215	42	55	7	2	1	21	35		13	.256	.321
Jack Lapp	C57, 1B4	L	26	68	167	35	59	10	3	1	26	24		4	.353	.467
Harry Davis	1B53	R	37	57	183	27	36	9	1	1	22	24		2	.197	.273
Jack Coombs	P47	R	28	52	141	31	45	6	1	2	23	8		5	.319	.418
Claude Derrick	2B20, SS6, 1B3, 3B2	R	25	36	100	14	23	1	2	0	5	7		7	.230	.280
Paddy Livingston (NJ)	C26	R	31	27	71	9	17	4	0	0	8	7		1	.239	.296
Topsy Hartsel	OF10	L	37	25	38	8	9	2	0	0	1	8		0	.237	.289
Chester Emerson	OF7	L	21	7	18	2	4	0	0	0	0	6		1	.222	.222
1 Willie Hogan	OF6	R	26	7	19	1	2	1	0	0	2	0		0	.105	.158
Earle Mack	3B2	L	21	2	4	0	0	0	0	0	0	0		0	.000	.000
DETROIT	2nd 89-65 .578 13.5		HUGHIE JENNINGS													
	TOTALS		27	154	5294	831	1544	230	96	30	657	471		276	.292	.388
Jim Delahanty	1B72, 2B59, 3B12	R	32	144	542	83	184	30	14	3	94	56		15	.339	.463
Charley O'Leary	2B67, 3B6	R	25	74	256	29	68	8	2	0	25	21		10	.266	.313
Donie Bush	SS150	B	23	150	561	126	130	18	2	1	36	98		42	.232	.287
George Moriarty	3B129, 1B1	R	25	130	478	51	116	20	4	1	60	27		28	.243	.308
Sam Crawford	OF146	L	31	146	574	109	217	36	14	7	115	61		37	.378	.526
Ty Cobb	OF146	L	24	146	591	147	248	47	24	8	127	44		83	.420	.621
Davy Jones	OF92	L	31	98	341	78	93	10	0	0	19	41		25	.273	.302
Oscar Stanage	C141	R	28	141	503	45	133	13	7	3	51	20		3	.264	.336
Delos Drake	OF83, 1B2	R	24	95	315	37	88	9	9	1	36	17		20	.279	.375
Del Gainer (BW)	1B69	R	24	70	248	32	75	11	4	2	25	20		10	.302	.403
George Mullin (IL)	P30	R	30	40	98	4	28	7	2	0	5	10		1	.286	.398
Biff Schaller	OF16, 1B1	L	21	40	60	8	8	0	1	1	7	4		1	.133	.217
Chick Lathers	2B9, 3B8, SS4, 1B3	L	22	29	45	5	10	1	0	0	4	5		0	.222	.244
Boss Schmidt (AJ)	C9, OF1	B	30	28	46	4	13	2	1	0	2	0		0	.283	.370
Paddy Baumann	2B23, OF3	R	25	26	94	8	24	2	4	0	11	6		1	.255	.362
Joe Casey	C12, OF3	R	23	15	33	2	5	0	0	0	3	3		0	.152	.152
Guy Tutweiler	2B6, OF3	L	21	13	32	3	6	2	0	0	3	2		1	.188	.250
Jack Ness	1B12	R	25	12	39	6	6	0	0	0	2	2		0	.154	.154
Squanto Wilson	C5	B	22	5	16	2	3	0	0	0	0	2		0	.188	.188
CLEVELAND	3rd 80-73 .523 22		DEACON McGUIRE 6-11 .353 GEORGE STOVALL 74-62 .544													
	TOTALS		28	156	5314	691	1500	238	81	20	579	354		209	.282	.369
George Stovall	1B118, 2B2	R	33	126	458	48	124	17	7	0	79	21		11	.271	.338
Neal Ball	2B95, 3B17, SS1	R	30	116	412	45	122	14	9	6	47	27		21	.296	.396
Ivy Olson	SS139, 3B1	R	25	140	545	89	142	20	8	1	50	34		20	.261	.332
Terry Turner	3B94, 2B14, SS10	R	30	117	417	59	105	16	9	0	28	34		29	.252	.333
Joe Jackson	OF147	L	21	147	571	126	233	45	19	7	83	56		41	.408	.590
Joe Birmingham	OF101, 3B16	R	26	125	447	55	136	18	5	2	51	15		16	.304	.380
Jack Graney	OF142	L	25	146	527	84	142	25	5	1	45	66		21	.269	.342
Gus Fisher	C58, 1B1	R	25	70	203	20	53	6	3	0	12	7		6	.261	.320
Ted Easterly	OF54, C23	L	26	99	287	34	93	19	5	1	37	8		6	.324	.436
Nap Lajoie (XJ)	1B41, 2B37	R	36	90	315	36	115	20	1	2	60	26		13	.365	.454
Syd Smith	C48, 1B1, 3B1	R	27	58	154	8	46	8	1	1	21	11		0	.299	.383
Hank Butcher	OF34		24	38	133	21	32	7	3	1	11	11		9	.241	.361
Grover Land	C34, 1B1	R	26	35	107	5	15	1	2	0	10	3		2	.140	.187
Art Griggs (JJ)	2B11, OF4, 3B3, 1B1	R	26	27	68	7	17	3	2	1	7	5		1	.250	.397
Bill Lindsay	3B15, 2B1	L	30	19	66	6	16	2	0	0	5	1		2	.242	.273
Cotton Knaupp	SS13	L	21	13	39	2	4	1	0	0	0	2		1	.103	.128
Jack Mills	3B7	L	21	13	17	5	5	0	0	0	1	1		1	.294	.294
Steve O'Neill	C9	R	19	9	27	1	4	1	0	0	1	4		0	.148	.185
Dave Callahan	OF3	L	22	5	12	1	4	1	0	1	0	1		0	.333	.500
Tim Hendryx	3B2	R	20	2	4	0	1	0	0	0	0	0		0	.250	.250
Jack Adams	C2	R	20	2	5	0	1	0	0	0	0	0		0	.200	.200
Herman Bronkie	3B2	R	26	2	6	0	1	0	0	0	0	0		0	.167	.167
Simon Nichols (DD) 28																

NAME		T	AGE	W	L	PCT	SV	G	GS	CG	IP	H	BB	SO	SHO	ERA
			29	101	50	.669	15	152	152	97	1376	1343	487	739	13	3.01
Jack Coombs		R	28	28	12	.700	3	47	40	26	337	360	119	185	1	3.53
Eddie Plank		L	35	22	8	.733	5	40	30	24	257	237	77	149	6	2.10
Chief Bender		R	28	17	5	.773	4	31	24	16	216	198	58	114	2	2.17
Cy Morgan		R	32	15	7	.682	1	38	30	15	250	217	113	136	2	2.70
Harry Krause		L	22	11	8	.579	2	27	19	12	169	155	47	85	1	3.04
Dave Danforth		L	21	5	2	.714	0	14	2	1	34	29	17	21	0	3.71
Elmer Leonard		R	22	2	2	.500	0	5	1	1	19	26	10	10	0	2.84
Doc Martin		R	23	1	2	.333	0	11	3	1	38	40	17	21	0	4.50
Boardwalk Brown		R	26	0	1	.000	0	3	1	1	12	12	2	6	0	4.50
Howard Armstrong		R	21	0	1	.000	0	1	0	0	3	3	1	0	0	0.00
Lefty Russell		L	20	0	2	.000	0	7	2	0	32	45	18	7	0	7.60
Lep Long		R	22	0	0	—	0	4	0	0	8	15	5	4	0	4.50
Allan Collamore		R	24	0	0	—	0	2	0	0	2	6	3	1	0	36.00
			27	89	65	.578	8	154	154	108	1388	1514	460	538	8	3.73
George Mullin (IL)		R	30	18	10	.643	0	30	29	25	234	245	61	87	2	3.08
Ed Willett		R	27	13	14	.481	2	38	27	15	231	261	80	86	2	3.66
Ralph Works		R	23	11	5	.688	1	30	15	9	167	173	67	68	3	3.92
Ed Lafitte		R	25	11	8	.579	1	29	20	15	172	205	52	63	0	3.92
Edgar Summers		R	26	11	11	.500	2	30	20	13	179	189	51	65	0	3.67
Wild Bill Donovan		R	34	10	9	.526	1	20	19	15	168	160	64	81	1	3.32
Bill Covington		R	24	7	1	.875	1	17	6	5	84	94	33	29	0	4.07
Jack Lively		R	26	7	5	.583	0	18	14	10	114	143	34	45	0	4.58
Clarence Mitchell		L	20	1	0	1.000	0	5	1	0	14	20	7	4	0	8.35
Wiley Taylor		R	23	0	0	—	0	3	2	1	19	18	10	9	0	3.79
Pug Cavet		L		0	0	—	0	1	1	0	4	6	1	1	0	4.50
			24	80	73	.523	10	156	156	93	1382	1376	550	673	6	3.37
Vean Gregg		L	26	23	7	.767	0	34	26	22	244	172	86	125	5	1.81
Gene Krapp		R	24	12	8	.600	3	34	26	14	215	182	136	130	1	3.53
George Kahler		R	21	9	8	.529	2	30	17	10	154	153	66	97	0	3.28
Cy Falkenberg		R	31	8	5	.615	1	15	13	7	107	117	24	46	0	3.28
Fred Blanding		R	23	7	11	.389	2	29	16	11	178	190	60	80	0	3.68
Willie Mitchell		L	21	7	14	.333	1	30	22	9	177	190	60	78	0	3.76
Bill James		R	24	3	4	.429	0	8	6	4	52	58	32	21	0	4.84
1 Cy Young		R	44	3	4	.429	0	7	7	4	46	54	13	20	0	3.92
Earl Yingling		L	22	2	1	.667	0	4	3	1	22	20	9	6	0	4.50
Specs Harkness		R	23	2	2	.500	0	12	6	3	52	62	21	25	0	4.33
Hi West		R	26	2	4	.333	1	13	8	3	65	84	18	17	0	3.74
Pat Page		L	28	1	0	1.000	0	2	1	1	16	21	7	6	0	4.50
Jim Baskette		R	23	1	2	.333	0	4	2	2	21	19	7	8	0	3.43
Josh Swindell		R	27	1	1	.500	0	2	2	1	17	19	4	6	0	2.12
Bugs Reisigl		R	23	0	1	.000	0	1	1	0	13	13	3	6	0	6.23
Ben DeMott		R	22	0	1	.000	1	1	0	0	4	10	2	2	0	11.25
Addie Joss (DD) 31																

CHICAGO — 4th 77-74 .510 24 — HUGH DUFFY

NAME	G by Pos	B	AGE	G	AB	R	H	2B	3B	HR	RBI	BB	SO	SB	BA	SA
TOTALS			30	154	5210	717	1399	179	92	20	593	385		201	.269	.350
Shano Collins	1B97, 2B3, OF3	R	25	106	370	48	97	16	12	4	48	20		14	.262	.403
Amby McConnell (LJ)	2B103	L	28	104	396	45	111	11	5	1	34	23		7	.280	.341
Lee Tannehill	SS102, 2B27, 3B8, 1B5	R	30	141	516	60	131	17	6	0	49	32		0	.254	.310
Harry Lord	3B138	R	27	141	561	103	180	18	18	3	61	32		43	.321	.433
Matty McIntyre	OF146	L	31	146	569	102	184	19	11	1	52	64		17	.323	.401
Ping Bodie	OF128, 2B16	R	23	145	551	75	159	27	13	4	97	49		14	.289	.407
Nixey Callahan	OF114	R	37	120	466	64	131	13	5	3	60	15		45	.281	.350
Billy Sullivan	C89	R	36	89	256	26	55	9	3	0	31	16		1	.215	.273
Patsy Dougherty	OF56	L	34	76	211	39	61	10	9	0	32	26		19	.289	.422
Rollie Zeider	1B29, SS17, 3B10, 2B9	R	27	73	217	39	55	3	0	2	21	29		28	.253	.295
Freddie Payne	C56	R	30	66	133	14	27	2	1	1	19	8		6	.203	.256
Frank Lange	P29	R	27	54	73	7	22	6	2	0	16	7		2	.301	.421
Ray Corhan (PB)	SS43	R	23	43	131	14	28	6	2	0	8	15		2	.214	.290
Bruno Block	C38	R	26	39	115	11	35	6	1	1	18	6		0	.304	.400
Charlie Mullen	1B20	R	22	20	59	7	12	2	1	0	5	5		1	.203	.271
Felix Chouinard	2B4, OF4	R	23	14	17	3	3	0	0	0	0	0		0	.176	.176
Cuke Barrows	OF13	R	27	13	46	5	9	2	0	0	4	7		2	.196	.239
Bob Messenger	OF4	B	27	13	17	4	2	0	1	0	0	3		0	.118	.235
Tex Jones	1B9	R	25	9	31	4	6	1	0	0	4	3		1	.194	.226
Ralph Kreitz	C7	R	25	7	17	0	4	1	0	0	1	1		0	.235	.294

Freddy Parent 35 R 4-9, Marty Berghammer 25 L 0-5, Jimmy Johnston 21 R 0-2, Wally Mayer 20 R 0-3, 1 Paul Meloan 22 L 1-3, Lena Blackburne (KJ) 24

NAME	T	AGE	W	L	PCT	SV	G	GS	CG	IP	H	BB	SO	SHO	ERA
		28	77	74	.510	19	154	154	86	1366	1349	384	752	17	3.02
Ed Walsh	R	30	27	18	.600	7	56	37	33	369	327	72	255	5	2.22
Jim Scott	R	22	14	11	.560	2	39	26	14	202	195	81	128	3	2.63
Doc White	L	32	10	14	.417	3	34	29	16	214	219	35	72	4	2.99
Frank Lange	R	27	8	8	.500	0	29	22	8	162	151	77	104	1	3.22
Fred Olmstead	R	27	6	6	.500	2	25	11	7	118	146	30	45	1	4.19
Irv Young	L	33	5	6	.455	2	24	11	2	93	99	25	40	1	4.36
Joe Benz	R	23	3	2	.600	0	9	2		56	52	13	28	0	2.25
Joe Hovlik	R	26	2	0	1.000	1	12	3	1	47	47	0	24	1	3.06
Jesse Baker	L	23	2	7	.222	1	22	8	3	94	101	30	51	0	3.93
George Mogridge	L	22	0	2	.000	0	4	1	0	13	12	1	5	0	5.38

BOSTON — 5th 78-75 .510 24 — PATSY DONOVAN

NAME	G by Pos	B	AGE	G	AB	R	H	2B	3B	HR	RBI	BB	SO	SB	BA	SA
TOTALS			25	153	5024	680	1379	203	66	35	559	506		190	.274	.362
Clyde Engle	1B65, 3B51, 2B13, OF10	R	27	146	514	58	139	13	3	2	48	51		24	.270	.319
Heinie Wagner	2B40, SS32	R	30	80	261	34	67	13	8	1	38	29		15	.257	.379
Steve Yerkes	SS116, 2B14, 3B11	R	23	142	502	70	140	24	3	1	57	52		14	.279	.345
Larry Gardner	3B72, 2B62	L	23	138	492	80	140	17	8	4	44	64		27	.285	.376
Harry Hooper	OF130	L	23	130	524	93	163	20	6	4	45	73		38	.311	.395
Tris Speaker	OF138	L	23	141	500	88	167	34	13	8	70	59		25	.334	.502
Duffy Lewis	OF125	R	22	130	469	64	144	32	4	7	86	25		11	.307	.437
Bill Carrigan (BH)	C62, 1B6	R	27	72	232	29	67	6	1	1	30	26		5	.289	.336
Rip Williams (BL)	1B57, C38	R	29	95	284	36	68	8	5	0	31	24		9	.239	.303
Les Nunamaker	C59	R	22	62	183	18	47	8	3	0	19	12		1	.257	.311
Joe Riggert	OF38	R	24	50	146	19	31	4	4	2	13	12		5	.212	.336
Olaf Hendriksen	OF25	L	23	47	93	17	34	2	1	0	8	14		4	.366	.409
Billy Purtell	3B16, 2B3, SS3, OF1	R	25	27	82	5	23	5	3	0	7	1		1	.280	.415
Jack Thoney		R	30	26	20	5	5	0	0	0	2	0		1	.250	.250
Jack Lewis	2B18	R	27	18	59	7	16	0	0	0	6	7		2	.271	.271
2 Hap Myers	1B12	R	24	13	38	3	14	2	0	0	4	4		4	.368	.421
Hugh Bradley (BL)	1B12	R	26	12	41	9	13	2	0	1	4	2		1	.317	.439
Hal Janvrin	3B5, 1B4	R	18	9	27	2	4	1	0	0	1	3		0	.148	.185

Walt Lonergan 25 R 7-26, 1 Red Kleinow 33 R 3-14, Hy Gunning 22 L 1-9, 1 Tom Madden 28 R 3-15, Les Wilson 25 L 0-7, Swede Carlstrom 24 R 1-6, Tony Tonneman 29 R 1-5, Tracey Baker 19 R 0-0, Joe Giannini 22 L 1-2

NAME	T	AGE	W	L	PCT	SV	G	GS	CG	IP	H	BB	SO	SHO	ERA
		25	78	75	.510	16	153	153	87	1364	1314	475	713	10	2.73
Smoky Joe Wood	R	21	23	17	.575	5	44	33	25	277	226	76	231	5	2.02
Larry Pape	R	27	11	8	.579	2	27	19	10	176	167	63	49	1	2.46
Ray Collins	L	24	11	12	.478	2	31	24	14	204	189	46	88	0	2.39
Eddie Cicotte	R	27	11	15	.423	0	35	25	16	221	236	73	106	1	2.81
Charley Hall	R	26	8	7	.533	5	32	10	6	147	149	72	83	0	3.74
Buck O'Brien	R	29	5	1	.833	0	6	5	5	48	30	21	31	2	0.38
Ed Karger	L	28	5	8	.385	1	25	18	6	131	134	42	57	1	3.37
Jack Killilay	R	23	4	2	.600	1	14	7	1	61	65	36	28	0	3.54
2 Judge Nagel	R	31	3	1	.500	0	14	5	1	27	27	6	12	0	3.33
1 Walter Moser	R	30	0	1	.000	0	6	3	1	25	37	11	11	0	3.96
Jack Bushelman	R	25	0	1	.000	0	8	1		17	16	8	10	5	3.00
Casey Hageman	R	24	0	2	.000	0	2	2	1	17	16	5	8	0	2.10
Marty McHale	R	24	0	0	—	0	4	1	0	9	19	3	3	0	9.00
Blaine Thomas	R	22	0	1	.000	0	3	1	0	5	7	3	0	0	0.00
1 Charlie Smith	R	31	0	0	—	0	2	2		9	2	1	0	0	9.00
1 Frank Smith	R	31	0	0	—	0	3	1		6	3	1	1	0	18.00

NEW YORK — 6th 76-76 .500 25.5 — HAL CHASE

NAME	G by Pos	B	AGE	G	AB	R	H	2B	3B	HR	RBI	BB	SO	SB	BA	SA
TOTALS			27	153	5056	686	1375	190	96	25	577	493		270	.272	.362
Hal Chase	1B124, OF7, 2B2, SS1	R	28	133	527	82	166	32	7	3	62	21		36	.315	.419
Earle Gardner	2B101	R	27	102	357	36	94	13	2	0	39	20		14	.263	.311
Jack Knight	SS82, 1B27, 2B21, 3B1	R	26	132	470	69	126	16	7	3	62	42		18	.268	.351
Roy Hartzell	3B124, SS12, OF8	L	29	144	527	67	156	17	11	3	91	63		22	.296	.387
Harry Wolter	OF113, 1B2	L	26	122	434	78	132	17	15	4	36	62		28	.304	.440
Bert Daniels	OF120	R	28	131	462	74	132	16	9	2	31	48		40	.286	.372
Birdie Cree	OF137, SS4, 2B1	R	28	137	520	90	181	30	22	4	88	56		48	.348	.513
Walter Blair	C84, 1B1	R	27	85	222	18	43	9	2	0	26	16		2	.194	.252
Ed Sweeney	C83	R	22	83	229	17	53	6	5	0	18	14		8	.231	.301
Otie Johnson (AJ)	SS47, 3B4	R	27	71	209	21	49	9	6	3	36	39		12	.234	.378
Charlie Hemphill (IL)	OF56	L	35	69	201	32	57	4	1	1	15	37		9	.284	.338
Bob Williams	C20	R		17	47	3	9	2	0	0	8	5		1	.191	.234
Cozy Dolan	3B19	R	28	19	69	19	21	1	2	0	6	8		12	.304	.377
Justin Fitzgerald	OF9	L	20	16	37	6	10	1	0	0	4	4		4	.270	.297
Stubby Magner	SS6, 2B5	R	23	13	33	3	7	0	0	0	4	4		1	.212	.212
Roxey Roach	SS8, 2B5	R	26	13	40	4	10	2	1	0	2	6		0	.250	.350
Ed Wilkinson	OF3, 2B1	R	21	10	13	2	3	0	0	0	1	0		0	.231	.231
Guy Zinn	OF8	L	24	9	27	5	4	2	0	0	1	2		0	.148	.296
Johnnie Priest	2B5, 3B2	R	20	7	21	2	3	0	0	0	1	2		3	.143	.143

Bill Bailey 29 L 1-9, Gene Elliott 22 L 1-13, Mike Handiboe 23 L 1-15, Harry Curry 25 R 2-11, Joe Walsh R 24 2-9

NAME	T	AGE	W	L	PCT	SV	G	GS	CG	IP	H	BB	SO	SHO	ERA
		26	76	76	.500	9	153	153	91	1361	1404	406	667	5	3.54
Russ Ford	R	28	22	11	.667	1	37	33	26	281	251	76	158	0	2.28
Ray Caldwell	R	23	14	14	.500	3	41	26	19	255	240	79	145	1	3.35
Jack Warhop	R	26	12	13	.480	1	31	25	17	210	239	44	71	1	4.16
Ray Fisher	R	23	10	11	.476	1	29	22	8	172	178	55	99	3	3.24
Jack Quinn	R	27	7	10	.412	3	40	16	7	175	203	41	71	0	3.75
Hippo Vaughn (IL)	L	23	8	10	.444	0	26	19	11	146	158	54	74	0	4.38
Lew Brockett	R	30	3	4	.429	0	16	8	2	75	73	39	25	0	4.68
Harry Ables	L	27	0	0	—	0	3	2	0	11	16	7	6	0	9.82
Red Hoff	L	20	0	1	.000	0	5	1	0	21	21	7	10	0	2.14
Ed Klepfer	R	23	0	0	—	0	2	0	0	4	5	2	4	0	6.75

WASHINGTON — 7th 64-90 .416 38.5 — JIMMY McALEER

NAME	G by Pos	B	AGE	G	AB	R	H	2B	3B	HR	RBI	BB	SO	SB	BA	SA
TOTALS			28	154	5062	624	1307	159	53	16	493	466		215	.258	.320
Germany Schaefer	1B108, OF7	R	34	125	440	74	147	14	7	0	45	57		22	.334	.398
Bill Cunningham	2B93	R	25	94	331	34	63	10	5	3	37	19		9	.190	.278
George McBride	SS154	R	30	154	557	58	131	11	4	0	59	52		15	.235	.269
Wid Conroy	3B85, OF15, 2B1	R	34	106	349	40	81	11	4	2	28	20		12	.232	.304
Doc Gessler	OF126, 1B1	L	30	128	450	65	127	19	5	4	78	74		29	.282	.373
Clyde Milan	OF154	L	25	154	616	109	194	24	8	3	35	74		58	.315	.394
Tilly Walker	OF94	R	23	99	356	44	99	6	4	2	39	15		12	.278	.334
Gabby Street	C71	R	28	72	216	16	48	7	1	0	14	14		4	.222	.264
1 Kid Elberfeld	2B66, 3B54	R	36	127	404	58	110	19	4	0	47	65		24	.272	.339
John Henry	C51, 1B30	R	21	82	261	24	53	5	0	0	21	25		8	.203	.222
Jack Lelivelt	OF49, 1B7	R	25	72	225	29	72	12	4	0	22	22		7	.320	.409
Eddie Ainsmith	C49	R	21	61	149	12	33	2	3	0	14	10		5	.221	.275
Dixie Walker	P32	R	24	34	66	6	20	2	0	0	5	3		0	.303	.333
1 Ray Morgan	3B25	R	22	25	89	11	19	2	0	0	5	4		2	.213	.236
2 Warren Miller	OF9	L	25	21	34	3	5	0	0	0	4	5		0	.147	.147
Tommy Long	OF13	R	21	14	48	1	11	3	0	0	5	1		4	.229	.292
Jock Somerlott	1B12	R	28	13	40	2	7	0	0	0	2	0		2	.175	.175
Bull Smith		R	30	2	1	0	0	0	0	0	0	0		0	.000	.000

NAME	T	AGE	W	L	PCT	SV	G	GS	CG	IP	H	BB	SO	SHO	ERA
		27	64	90	.416	6	154	154	106	1354	1471	410	628	13	3.52
Walter Johnson	R	23	25	13	.658	1	40	37	36	323	292	70	207	6	1.89
Bob Groom	R	26	13	17	.433	2	37	32	20	255	280	67	135	2	3.82
Long Tom Hughes	R	32	10	17	.370	2	34	27	17	223	251	77	86	2	3.47
Dixie Walker	R	24	8	14	.364	1	32	24	15	186	205	50	65	2	3.38
Charlie Becker	L	20	3	5	.375	0	11	6	5	71	80	23	31	1	4.06
Carl Cashion	R	20	3	4	.400	0	11	9	5	71	67	47	26	0	4.19
Dolly Gray	L	32	2	13	.133	0	28	15	6	121	160	40	42	0	5.06
Bill Otey	L	24	1	4	.200	0	12	2	0	18	68	15	16	0	6.30
Fred Sherry	R	22	0	0	—	0	2	0	0	52	63	19	20	0	4.33
Walt Herrell		22	0	1	.000	0	1	1	0	5	2			0	18.00

ST. LOUIS — 8th 45-107 .296 56.5 — BOBBY WALLACE

NAME	G by Pos	B	AGE	G	AB	R	H	2B	3B	HR	RBI	BB	SO	SB	BA	SA
TOTALS			27	152	5005	567	1192	187	63	17	473	460		125	.238	.311
Jack Black	1B54	R	21	54	186	13	28	4	0	0	7	10		4	.154	.172
Frank LaPorte	2B133, 3B3	R	31	136	507	71	159	37	12	2	82	34		4	.314	.446
Bobby Wallace	SS124, 2B1	R	37	125	410	35	95	12	2	0	31	46		8	.232	.271
Jimmy Austin	3B148	R	31	148	541	84	141	25	11	2	45	69		26	.261	.359
Al Schweitzer	OF68	R	28	76	237	31	51	11	4	0	34	43		12	.215	.295
Burt Shotton	OF139	L	26	139	572	85	146	11	8	0	36	51		26	.255	.302
2 Willie Hogan	OF117, 1B5	R	26	123	443	53	115	17	8	2	62	43		18	.260	.348
Nig Clarke	C73, 1B4	L	28	82	256	22	55	10	1	0	18	26		2	.215	.262
Jim Stephens	C66	R	27	70	212	11	49	5	5	0	17	17		1	.231	.302
2 Paul Meloan	OF22	L	22	64	206	30	54	11	2	3	19	14		15	.262	.379
Dode Criss	1B14, P4	L	26	58	83	10	21	3	1	2	15	11		0	.253	.386
Ed Hallinan	SS34, 2B15, 3B3	R	22	52	169	13	35	3	1	0	14	14		4	.207	.237
Jim Murray	OF25	R	33	31	102	8	19	3	1	0	11	5		0	.186	.324
Pete Compton	OF28	L	21	28	107	9	29	4	3	0	8	4		2	.271	.308
Paul Krichell	C25	R	28	28	82	6	19	3	0	0	8	4		2	.232	.268
Joe Kutina	1B26	R	26	26	101	12	26	3	2	3	16	7		2	.257	.446
Danny Hoffman	OF23	L	31	24	81	11	17	3	2	0	5	13		3	.210	.296
Pat Newnam	1B20	L	30	20	62	11	12	4	0	0	5	6		4	.194	.258
Dave Rowan	1B18	L	28	18	65	9	25	1	0	0	11	4		0	.385	.431
1 Hap Myers	1B11	R	24	11	37	4	11	2	0	0	7	4		1	.297	.324
Gus Williams	OF7	L	23	9	26	1	7	0	1	0	1	3		1	.269	.385

Allie Moulton 25 R 1-15, Clyde Southwick 24 L 3-12, Al Clancy 22 R 0-5, Red Gust 23 R 0-12, Joe Crisp 25 R 1-1, Elmer Duggen 26 L 0-4, Frank Truesdale 27 B 0-0

NAME	T	AGE	W	L	PCT	SV	G	GS	CG	IP	H	BB	SO	SHO	ERA
		27	45	107	.296	3	152	152	92	1342	1465	463	383	8	3.83
Joe Lake	R	29	10	15	.400	2	30	25	14	215	245	40	69	2	3.30
Jack Powell	R	38	8	19	.296	1	31	27	18	208	224	44	52	1	3.29
Barney Pelty	R	30	7	13	.350	1	28	22	18	207	197	69	59	1	2.83
Earl Hamilton	L	19	5	12	.294	1	32	17	10	177	190	69	55	1	3.97
Roy Mitchell	R	26	4	8	.333	0	28	12	8	134	134	45	40	1	3.83
Red Nelson	R	25	3	9	.250	1	16	13	6	81	103	44	24	0	5.22
Lefty George	R	24	1	10	.231	0	17	11	6	126	136	51	23	1	4.19
Elmer Brown	R	27	2	1	.667	0	5	3	1	36	39	22	11	0	6.75
Mack Alison	R	24	2	0	.667	0	3	2	2	26	24	5	2	0	2.08
Ed Hawk	R	23	1	4	.200	0	4	4	3	38	38	14	14	0	3.31
Howie Gregory	R	25	1	3	.250	0	7	3	1	37	11	4	1	0	5.14
2 Walter Moser	R	30	0	2	.000	0	8	2	1	18	24	10	9	0	24.00
Dode Criss	R	26	0	1	.000	0	4	1	0	18	24	10	9	0	8.50
Curly Brown	L	22	0	9	.000	0	19	12	7	102	130	49	32	0	2.74
George Curry	R	32	0	3	.000	0	3	2	1	19	24	10	9	0	7.32
Bill Bailey	L	22	0	0	—	0	3	3	3	12	18	16	8	0	4.50
Bill Harper	R	22	0	0	—	0	2	1		11	8	8	2	0	6.75
Jeff Pfeffer	R	23	0	0	—	0	1	1		11				0	7.20
1 Joe Willis	L	21	0	1	.000	0	1	1		14				0	5.14

NEW YORK — 1ST 99-54 .647 — JOHN McGRAW

NAME	G by Pos	B	AGE	G	AB	R	H	2B	3B	HR	RBI	BB	SO	SB	BA	SA
TOTALS			26	154	5006	756	1399	225	103	41	651	530	506	347	.279	.390
Fred Merkle	1B148	R	22	149	541	80	153	24	10	12	84	43	60	49	.283	.431
Larry Doyle	2B148	L	25	143	526	102	163	25	25	13	77	71	39	38	.310	.527
1 Al Bridwell	SS76	L	27	76	263	28	71	10	1	0	31	33	10	8	.270	.316
Art Devlin	3B79, 1B6, 2B6, SS6	R	31	95	260	42	71	16	2	0	25	42	19	6	.273	.350
Red Murray	OF131	R	27	140	488	70	142	27	15	3	78	43	37	48	.291	.426
Fred Snodgrass	OF149, 1B1, 2B1	R	23	151	534	83	157	27	10	1	77	72	59	51	.294	.388
Josh Devore	OF149	L	23	149	565	96	158	19	10	3	50	81	69	61	.280	.365
Chief Meyers	C128	R	30	133	391	48	130	18	9	4	61	25	33	7	.332	.432
Art Fletcher	SS74, 3B21, 2B13	R	26	112	326	73	104	17	8	1	37	30	27	20	.319	.429
Beals Becker	OF55	L	24	88	172	28	45	11	1	1	20	26	22	19	.262	.355
2 Buck Herzog	3B65, 2B3, SS1	R	25	69	247	37	66	14	4	1	26	14	19	22	.267	.368
Art Wilson	C64	R	25	66	109	17	33	9	1	1	17	19	12	6	.303	.431
Doc Crandall	P41, SS6, 2B3	R	23	61	113	12	27	1	4	2	21	8	16	2	.239	.372
1 Mike Donlin	OF3	L	33	12	12	3	4	0	0	1	1	1	0	2	.333	.583
Grover Hartley	C10	R	23	11	18	1	4	2	0	0	1	1	1	1	.222	.333
Gene Paulette	1B7, SS1, 3B1	R	20	10	12	1	2	0	0	0	1	0	1	0	.167	.167
George Burns	OF6	R	21	6	17	2	1	0	0	0	0	0	0	0	.059	.059
1 Hank Gowdy	1B2	R	21	4	4	1	1	1	0	0	0	2	0	0	.250	.500
Admiral Schlei		R		1	1	0	0	0	0	0	0	0	1	0	.000	.000

NAME	T	AGE	W	L	PCT	SV	G	GS	CG	IP	H	BB	SO	SHO	ERA
		27	99	54	.647	13	154	154	95	1368	1267	369	771	19	2.69
Christy Mathewson	R	30	26	13	.667	3	45	37	29	307	303	38	141	5	1.99
Rube Marquard	L	24	24	7	.774	0	45	33	22	278	221	106	237	5	2.49
Doc Crandall	R	23	15	5	.750	5	41	15	9	199	199	51	94	2	2.63
Hooks Wiltse	L	31	12	9	.571	0	30	24	11	187	177	39	92	4	3.28
Red Ames	R	28	11	10	.524	2	34	13	13	205	170	54	118	1	2.68
Bugs Raymond	R	29	6	4	.600	0	17	9	4	82	73	33	31	1	3.30
Louis Drucke	R	22	4	4	.500	0	15	10	4	76	83	41	42	0	4.02
Bert Maxwell	R	24	1	2	.333	0	4	3	3	31	37	7	8	0	2.90
Charlie Faust	R	30	0	0	—	0	2	0	0	2	2	0	0	0	4.50
Dick Rudolph	R	22	0	0	—	0	1	1	0	8	10	3	5	0	9.00

CHICAGO — 2nd 92-62 .597 7.5 — FRANK CHANCE

NAME	G by Pos	B	AGE	G	AB	R	H	2B	3B	HR	RBI	BB	SO	SB	BA	SA
TOTALS			27	157	5130	757	1335	218	101	54	626	585	617	214	.260	.374
Vic Saier	1B73	R	20	86	259	42	67	15	1	5	37	25	37	11	.259	.336
Heinie Zimmerman	2B108, 3B20, 1B11	R	24	143	535	80	164	22	17	9	85	25	50	23	.307	.462
Joe Tinker	SS143	R	30	144	536	61	149	24	12	4	69	39	31	30	.278	.390
Jim Doyle	3B127	R	29	130	472	69	133	23	12	5	62	40	54	19	.282	.413
Wildfire Schulte	OF154	R	28	154	577	105	173	30	21	21	107	76	68	23	.300	.534
Solly Hofman	OF107, 1B36	R	28	143	512	66	129	17	2	2	70	60	60	23	.252	.305
Jimmy Sheckard	OF156	L	32	156	539	121	149	26	11	4	50	147	58	32	.276	.388
Jimmy Archer	C102, 1B10, 2B1	R	28	116	387	41	98	18	5	4	41	18	43	5	.253	.357
2 Wilbur Good	OF40	L	25	58	145	27	39	5	4	2	21	11	19	10	.269	.400
Dave Shean	2B23, SS19, 3B1	R	33	58	145	19	28	5	4	2	15	8	15	4	.193	.221
Johnny Evers (IL)	2B33, 3B11	L	29	46	155	29	35	4	3	0	7	34	10	6	.226	.290
2 Peaches Graham	C28	R	34	36	71	6	17	3	0	0	8	11	8	2	.239	.282
Frank Chance (NJ)	1B29	R	34	31	87	23	21	6	3	1	17	25	13	9	.241	.414
1 Al Kaiser	OF23	R	24	27	84	16	21	0	5	0	7	7	12	6	.250	.369
1 Johnny Kling	C25	R	35	27	80	8	14	3	2	1	5	8	14	0	.175	.300
Tom Needham	C23	R	32	27	62	4	12	2	0	0	5	9	14	2	.194	.226
2 Bill Collins	OF4	B	25	7	5	2	1	1	0	0	0	1	3	0	.200	.400
2 Kitty Bransfield	1B3	R	36	3	10	0	4	2	0	0	0	2	0	0	.400	.600

NAME	T	AGE	W	L	PCT	SV	G	GS	CG	IP	H	BB	SO	SHO	ERA
		28	92	62	.597	16	157	157	85	1411	1270	525	582	12	2.90
Three Finger Brown	R	34	21	11	.656	13	53	27	21	270	267	55	129	0	2.80
King Cole	R	25	18	7	.720	0	33	27	13	221	188	99	101	2	3.13
Ed Reulbach	R	28	16	9	.640	0	33	29	15	222	191	103	79	2	2.96
Lew Richie	R	27	15	11	.577	1	36	29	18	253	213	103	78	4	2.31
Harry McIntire	R	33	11	7	.611	0	25	17	9	149	147	33	56	1	4.11
2 Charlie Smith	R	31	3	2	.600	0	7	5	3	38	31	7	11	1	1.42
1 Orlie Weaver	R	23	3	2	.600	0	6	3	1	44	29	17	20	1	2.04
Larry Cheney	R	25	1	0	1.000	0	3	1	0	10	8	3	11	0	0.90
Fred Toney	R	22	1	1	.500	0	18	4	1	67	55	35	27	0	2.42
Bill Foxen	L	32	1	1	.500	0	3	1	0	13	12	12	6	0	2.08
Reggie Richter	R	24	1	3	.250	0	22	5	0	55	62	20	34	0	3.11
2 Cliff Curtis	R	29	1	2	.333	0	4	1	0	7	7	5	4	0	3.86
Cy Slapnicka	R	25	0	0	—	0	1	1	0	24	21	7	10	0	3.38
Jack Pfiester	L	33	0	4	.000	0	5	3	0	34	34	18	15	0	3.97
1 Hank Griffin	R	24	0	0	—	0	1	1	0	1	3	1	0	0	18.00
Ernie Ovitz	R	25	0	0	—	0	2	0	0	4	9	1	0	0	4.50
2 Jack Rowan	R	25	0	0	—	0	1	0	0	1	1	2	1	0	4.50
Orvie Overall (VR) 30															

PITTSBURGH — 3rd 85-69 .552 14.5 — FRED CLARKE

NAME	G by Pos	B	AGE	G	AB	R	H	2B	3B	HR	RBI	BB	SO	SB	BA	SA
TOTALS			29	155	5137	744	1345	206	106	48	633	525	583	160	.262	.371
Newt Hunter	1B61	R	31	65	209	35	53	10	6	2	24	25	43	9	.254	.388
Dots Miller	2B129	R	24	137	470	82	126	17	8	6	78	51	48	21	.268	.377
Honus Wagner	SS101, 1B28, OF1	R	37	130	473	87	158	23	16	9	89	67	34	20	.334	.507
Bobby Byrne	3B152	R	26	153	598	96	155	24	17	2	52	67	41	23	.259	.366
Owen Wilson	OF146	L	27	148	544	72	163	34	12	12	107	41	55	10	.300	.472
Max Carey	OF122	B	21	129	427	77	110	15	10	3	43	44	75	27	.258	.375
Fred Clarke	OF101	L	38	110	392	73	127	23	13	5	49	53	27	10	.324	.492
George Gibson	C98	R	30	111	311	32	65	12	2	0	19	29	16	3	.209	.260
Tommy Leach	OF89, SS13, 3B1	R	33	108	386	60	92	12	6	3	43	46	50	19	.238	.324
Bill McKechnie	1B57, 2B17, SS12, 3B6	B	24	104	321	40	73	8	7	2	37	28	18	9	.227	.315
Mike Simon	C68	R	28	71	215	19	49	4	3	0	22	10	14	1	.228	.274
Alex McCarthy	SS33, 2B11, 3B1, OF1	R	23	50	150	18	36	5	1	2	31	14	24	4	.240	.327
Vin Campbell (VR)	OF21	L	23	42	93	12	29	3	1	0	10	8	7	1	.312	.366
Jack Flynn	1B13, OF1	R	27	33	59	5	12	0	1	0	3	9	8	0	.203	.237
Brown Keen	1B1	R	18	6	7	0	0	0	0	0	0	1	4	0	.000	.000
Billy Kelly	C1	R	25	6	8	0	1	0	0	0	0	0	1	0	.125	.125
Jerry Dorsey	OF1	R	25	2	7	0	0	0	0	0	0	0	5	0	.000	.000
Mickey Keliher	1B2	L	21	2	7	0	0	0	0	0	0	0	0	0	.000	.000
John Shovlin		L	20	3	1	0	0	0	0	0	0	0	0	0	.000	.000

NAME	T	AGE	W	L	PCT	SV	G	GS	CG	IP	H	BB	SO	SHO	ERA
		26	85	69	.552	11	155	155	91	1380	1249	375	605	13	2.84
Babe Adams	R	29	22	12	.647	0	40	37	24	293	253	42	133	6	2.84
Howie Camnitz	R	29	20	15	.571	0	40	33	18	268	245	84	133	1	3.14
Lefty Leifield	L	27	16	16	.500	1	42	37	26	318	301	82	111	2	2.63
1 Elmer Steele	R	27	9	9	.500	2	31	16	7	166	153	31	52	2	2.60
Jack Ferry	R	24	6	4	.600	3	26	8	4	86	83	27	32	1	3.11
1 Judge Nagle	R	31	4	5	.444	0	8	3	1	27	33	6	11	0	3.66
Claude Hendrix	R	22	4	6	.400	1	22	12	6	119	85	53	57	1	2.73
Marty O'Toole (SA)	R	23	3	2	.600	0	5	3	3	38	23	20	34	0	2.37
Harry Gardner	R	24	1	1	.500	2	13	3	2	42	39	20	24	0	4.50
Hank Robinson	R	23	0	1	.000	0	2	0	0	13	13	5	8	0	2.77
Kirby White	R	27	0	1	.000	0	3	1	0	9	5	2	1	0	9.00
Deacon Phillippe	R	39	0	0	—	0	2	0	0	5	5	1	6	0	7.50
Dick Cottrell	L	22	0	1	.000	0	1	0	0	5	4	4	6	0	9.00
Sherry Smith	L	20	0	0	—	0	1	1	0	1	1	1	1	0	36.00

PHILADELPHIA — 4th 79-73 .520 19.5 — RED DOOIN

NAME	G by Pos	B	AGE	G	AB	R	H	2B	3B	HR	RBI	BB	SO	SB	BA	SA
TOTALS			28	153	5044	658	1307	214	56	60	564	490	588	153	.259	.359
Fred Luderus	1B146	L	28	146	551	69	166	24	11	16	99	40	76	6	.301	.472
Otto Knabe	2B142	R	27	142	528	99	125	15	6	1	42	94	35	2	.237	.294
Mickey Doolan	SS145	R	31	146	512	51	122	23	6	1	49	44	65	14	.238	.313
Hans Lobert	3B147	R	29	147	541	94	154	20	9	4	72	66	31	40	.285	.405
John Titus (BL)	OF60	L	35	76	236	35	67	14	1	8	26	32	16	5	.284	.453
Dode Paskert	OF153	R	29	153	560	96	153	18	5	4	47	70	70	28	.273	.345
Sherry Magee (SL)	OF120	R	26	121	445	72	128	32	5	15	94	49	33	22	.288	.483
Red Dooin (BL)	C74	R	32	74	247	18	81	15	1	1	16	14	12	6	.328	.409
J. Walsh	OF48, 2B14, SS9, 3B7, C4, 1B1	R	25	94	289	29	78	20	1	1	31	21	30	5	.270	.370
2 Fred Beck	OF61	L	24	66	210	26	59	8	3	3	25	17	21	3	.281	.390
Pat Moran	C32	R	35	34	103	2	19	3	0	0	8	3	13	0	.184	.214
2 Tom Madden (RJ)	C22	R	28	28	76	4	21	1	1	0	4	4	0	13	0	.276	.316
Harry Welchonce	OF17	R	27	26	66	9	14	4	0	0	3	7	10	0	.212	.273
1 Kitty Bransfield	1B8	R	36	23	43	4	11	1	1	0	2	3	5	1	.256	.326
Clarence Lehr	OF5, 2B4, SS4	L	25	23	27	2	4	0	0	0	2	0	7	0	.148	.148
Roy Thomas	OF11	L	37	21	30	5	5	2	0	0	2	6	0	1	.167	.233
Dick Cotter	C17	R	21	20	46	2	13	0	0	0	5	5	7	1	.283	.283
Tubby Spencer	C11	R	27	11	32	2	5	1	0	1	3	2	4	0	.156	.281
Bill Killefer	C6	R	23	6	16	3	3	0	0	0	1	0	3	0	.188	.188
Paddy Mayes	OF2	L	26	5	5	1	0	0	0	0	0	1	2	0	.000	.000
2 Red Kleinow	C4	R	33	4	4	0	1	0	0	0	0	1	0	0	.250	.250
Hughie Miller		R	24	3	4	0	0	0	0	0	0	0	0	0	.000	.000
John Quinn	C1	R	25	2	4	0	0	0	0	0	0	0	2	0	.000	.000

NAME	T	AGE	W	L	PCT	SV	G	GS	CG	IP	H	BB	SO	SHO	ERA
		27	79	73	.520	10	153	153	90	1373	1285	598	697	20	3.30
Pete Alexander	R	24	28	13	.683	3	48	37	31	367	285	129	227	7	2.57
Earl Moore	R	31	15	19	.441	1	42	36	21	308	265	164	174	5	2.63
George Chalmers	R	23	13	10	.565	4	38	22	11	209	196	101	101	3	3.10
Eddie Stack	R	23	5	5	.500	0	13	10	5	78	67	41	36	1	3.57
2 Bill Burns	L	31	4	7	.364	1	21	14	8	121	132	26	47	3	3.42
Ad Brennan	R	23	3	1	.750	0	5	3	1	23	22	12	12	0	3.52
1 Bert Humphries	R	30	3	1	.750	1	11	5	2	41	56	10	13	0	4.17
Fred Beebe	R	30	3	4	.429	0	9	8	3	48	52	24	20	0	4.50
3 Jack Rowan	R	25	3	4	.429	0	12	6	2	45	59	20	17	0	4.70
3 Cliff Curtis	R	29	2	1	.667	0	8	5	3	45	45	15	13	1	2.60
Bert Hall	R	22	0	1	.000	0	7	1	0	18	19	13	8	0	4.00
Buck Stanley	R	21	0	1	.000	0	4	0	0	11	14	9	5	0	6.54
Jimmy Walsh	R	25	0	1	.000	0	3	1	0	7	7	7	1	0	12.00
Bob Ewing	R	38	0	1	.000	1	3	3	0	24	29	14	12	0	7.88
Toots Shultz	R	22	0	0	—	0	3	2	0	25	30	15	9	0	9.36
Jake Smith	R	22	0	0	—	0	2	0	0	4	3	2	1	0	9.00
Troy Puckett	R	21	0	0	—	0	2	0	0	2	4	2	1	0	13.50

ST. LOUIS — 5th 75-74 .503 22 — ROGER BRESNAHAN

NAME	G by Pos	B	AGE	G	AB	R	H	2B	3B	HR	RBI	BB	SO	SB	BA	SA
TOTALS			27	158	5132	671	1295	199	85	27	567	592	650	175	.252	.340
Ed Konetchy	1B158	R	25	158	571	90	165	38	13	6	88	81	63	27	.289	.433
Miller Huggins	2B136	B	33	138	509	106	133	19	2	0	24	96	52	31	.261	.312
Arnold Hauser	SS134, 3B2	R	22	136	515	61	124	11	8	3	46	27	67	24	.241	.311
Mike Mowrey	3B134, SS1	R	27	137	471	59	126	29	7	0	61	59	46	15	.268	.359
Steve Evans	OF150	L	26	154	547	74	161	24	13	5	71	46	52	13	.294	.413
Rebel Oakes	OF151	R	24	152	551	69	145	13	6	2	59	41	35	25	.263	.319
Rube Ellis	OF148	L	25	155	555	69	139	20	10	3	66	46	64	9	.250	.339
Jack Bliss	C84, SS1	R	29	97	258	36	59	6	4	1	27	42	25	5	.229	.295
Roger Bresnahan	C77, 2B2	R	32	81	227	22	63	17	4	3	41	45	19	4	.278	.463
Wally Smith	3B26, SS25, 2B8, OF1	R	23	81	194	23	42	6	5	2	19	21	33	5	.216	.330
Otto McIver	OF17	R	26	30	62	11	14	2	1	1	9	4	9	1	.226	.339
Denny Wilie	OF15	L	20	28	51	10	12	3	1	0	3	8	11	3	.235	.333
Lee Magee	2B18, SS3	B	22	69	69	9	18	1	1	0	4	4	6	1	.261	.304
Ivy Wingo	C18	L	20	25	57	4	12	2	0	0	6	3	4	2	.211	.246
Jim Clark	OF8	R	23	14	18	2	3	0	1	0	3	4	2	1	.167	.278
Hap Morse	SS2, OF2	L	22	10	6	0	0	0	0	0	0	0	3	0	.000	.000
Dan McGeehan	2B3	R	26	4	9	1	2	0	0	0	1	2	1	0	.222	.222
Ed Conwell	3B1	R	21	2	4	0	0	0	0	0	0	0	1	0	.000	.000
Frank Gilhooley	OF1	L	19	1	0	0	0	0	0	0	0	0	0	0	.000	.000
Milt Reed		L	20	1	2	0	0	0	0	0	0	0	0	0	.000	.000

NAME	T	AGE	W	L	PCT	SV	G	GS	CG	IP	H	BB	SO	SHO	ERA
		24	75	74	.503	10	158	158	88	1402	1296	701	561	6	3.68
Bob Harmon	R	23	23	16	.590	4	51	41	28	348	290	181	144	2	3.13
Bill Steele	R	25	18	19	.486	3	43	34	23	287	287	113	115	1	3.74
Slim Sallee	L	26	15	9	.625	3	36	30	18	245	234	64	74	1	2.76
Rube Geyer	R	22	9	7	.563	0	29	11	7	149	141	56	46	1	3.26
Roy Golden	R	22	4	9	.308	0	30	25	6	149	127	129	81	0	5.01
Lou Lowdermilk	L	24	3	4	.429	0	16	3	3	65	72	29	20	0	3.46
Ed Zmich	L	26	1	0	1.000	0	4	0	0	8	4	4	2	0	2.08
Harry Camnitz	R	26	1	0	1.000	0	1	0	0	4	3	1	0	0	0.00
Gene Woodburn	R	24	1	5	.167	0	11	6	1	38	22	40	23	0	5.45
Grover Lowdermilk	R	26	0	1	.000	0	11	2	1	33	37	33	15	1	7.36
2 Joe Willis	R	21	0	1	.000	0	9	1	0	13	14	5	6	0	4.20
George Zachert	R	26	0	0	—	0	1	0	0	7	11	4	6	0	11.57
Gene Dale	R	22	0	0	—	0	2	0	0	15	13	16	13	0	6.60
Jack McAdams	R	24	0	0	—	0	3	1	0	9	16	5	3	0	3.60
Jack Reis	R	20	0	0	—	0	1	0	0	1	1	0	1	0	1.00
Bunny Hearn	L	20	0	0	—	0	2	0	0	10	9	4	3	0	12.00
Roy Radebough	R	30	0	0	—	0	1	0	0	10	10	3	2	0	2.70
Pete Standridge	R	20	0	0	—	0	1	0	0	4	9	2	0	0	9.00

CINCINNATI — 6th 70-83 .458 29 — CLARK GRIFFITH

NAME	G by Pos	B	AGE	G	AB	R	H	2B	3B	HR	RBI	BB	SO	SB	BA	SA
TOTALS			26	159	5291	682	1379	180	105	21	595	578	594	290	.261	.346
Dick Hoblitzell	1B158	L	22	158	622	81	180	19	13	11	91	42	44	32	.289	.415
Dick Egan	2B152	R	27	153	558	80	139	11	5	1	56	59	50	37	.249	.292
Tom Downey	SS93, 2B6, 3B5, 1B2, OF1	R	27	111	360	50	94	16	7	0	36	44	38	10	.261	.344
Eddie Grant	3B122, SS11	L	28	136	458	49	102	12	7	1	53	51	47	28	.223	.286
Mike Mitchell	OF140	R	31	136	529	74	154	22	22	2	84	44	34	35	.291	.427
Johnny Bates	OF147	R	29	148	518	89	151	24	13	1	61	103	59	33	.292	.394
Bob Bescher	OF153	B	27	153	599	106	165	32	10	1	45	102	78	81	.275	.367
Larry McLean	C98	R	29	107	328	24	94	7	2	4	34	20	18	1	.287	.320
Tommy Clarke (XJ)	C81, 1B	R	23	86	203	20	49	6	7	1	25	25	22	4	.241	.355
Jimmy Esmond	SS44, 3B14, 2B2	R	21	73	198	27	54	4	6	1	11	17	30	7	.273	.369
Armando Marsans	OF34, 1B3, 3B1	R	24	58	138	17	36	2	2	0	11	15	11	11	.261	.304
1 Fred Beck	OF16, 1B6, OF1	L	24	41	87	7	16	1	2	2	20	1	13	2	.184	.310
Dave Altizer	SS23, 1B1, 2B1, OF1	R	34	37	75	8	17	4	1	0	4	9	5	2	.227	.307
Hank Severeid	C22	R	20	37	56	5	17	6	1	0	10	3	6	0	.304	.446
Rafael Almeida	3B27, 2B1, SS1	R	24	36	96	9	30	5	1	0	15	9	16	3	.313	.385
Mike Balenti	SS2, OF1	R	24	8	8	2	2	0	0	0	0	0	1	3	.250	.250
Danny Mahoney		R	22	1	0	0	0	0	0	0	0	0	0	0	.000	.000
1 Hub Northen		L	24	1	0	0	0	0	0	0	0	0	0	0	.000	.000

NAME	T	AGE	W	L	PCT	SV	G	GS	CG	IP	H	BB	SO	SHO	ERA
		28	70	83	.458	12	159	159	77	1425	1410	476	557	4	3.26
George Suggs	R	28	15	13	.536	0	36	29	17	261	258	79	91	1	3.00
Bobby Keefe	R	29	12	13	.480	3	39	26	15	234	196	76	105	0	2.69
Art Fromme	R	27	10	11	.476	0	38	26	11	234	190	79	107	1	3.46
2 Frank Smith	R	31	10	14	.417	1	34	18	10	176	198	55	67	0	3.99
Harry Gaspar	R	28	10	17	.370	4	44	32	11	254	272	69	76	2	3.29
2 Bert Humphries	R	30	7	7	.571	0	14	7	3	65	62	18	16	0	2.35
Ray Boyd	R	24	3	2	.600	1	7	4	3	44	34	19	20	0	2.66
Rube Benton	L	21	3	3	.500	0	6	6	5	45	44	23	28	0	2.00
George McQuillan(ST)	R	24	2	6	.250	0	19	5	2	77	92	31	28	0	4.68
1 Bill Burns	L	31	1	0	1.000	1	6	3	0	18	17	3	5	0	3.00
Jack Compton	R	29	0	1	.000	1	6	3	0	10	19	15	6	0	3.96
Barney Schreiber	L	29	0	0	—	1	3	0	0	10	19	2	5	0	5.40
Herb Juul	L	25	0	0	—	1	1	0	0	4	3	4	2	0	4.50
Jesse Tannehill	L	36	0	0	—	1	0	0	0	5	8	1	0	0	6.75

Lew Moren (AJ) 27

BROOKLYN — 7th 64-86 .427 33.5 — BILL DAHLEN

NAME	G by Pos	B	AGE	G	AB	R	H	2B	3B	HR	RBI	BB	SO	SB	BA	SA
TOTALS			27	154	5059	539	1198	151	71	28	465	425	683	184	.237	.311
Jake Daubert	1B149	L	27	154	573	89	176	17	8	5	45	51	56	32	.307	.391
John Hummel	2B127, 1B4, SS2	R	28	137	477	54	129	21	11	5	58	67	66	16	.270	.392
Bert Tooley	SS114	R	24	119	433	55	89	11	3	1	29	53	63	18	.206	.252
Eddie Zimmerman	3B122	R	28	122	417	31	77	10	7	3	36	34	37	9	.185	.264
Bob Coulson	OF145	R	24	146	521	52	122	23	7	0	50	42	78	32	.234	.305
Zack Wheat	OF136	L	23	140	534	55	153	26	13	5	76	29	58	21	.287	.412
Bill Bergen	C84	R	38	84	227	8	30	3	1	0	14	14	42	2	.132	.154
Tex Erwin	C74	L	25	91	218	30	59	13	2	7	34	31	23	5	.271	.445
Dolly Stark	SS34, 2B18, 3B3	R	26	70	193	25	57	4	1	0	19	20	24	6	.295	.326
Cy Barger	P30, OF11, 1B1	R	26	57	145	16	33	1	1	0	9	5	20	2	.228	.248
Al Burch	OF43, 2B3	L	27	54	167	18	38	2	3	0	7	15	22	3	.228	.275
Red Smith	3B28	R	21	28	111	10	29	6	1	0	19	5	13	5	.261	.333
Otto Miller	C22	R	22	25	66	7	13	2	2	0	8	0	4	2	.197	.306
Jud Daley	OF16	L	27	19	65	8	15	2	1	0	7	2	8	2	.231	.292
2 Hub Northen	OF19	L	24	19	76	16	24	3	2	0	1	14	9	4	.316	.395
Pryor McElveen	2B5, SS1	R	29	16	31	1	6	0	0	0	5	0	3	0	.194	.194
Hy Myers	OF13	R	22	13	43	2	7	1	0	0	3	1	8	1	.163	.186
Tony Smith	SS10, 2B3	R	27	13	40	3	6	1	0	0	2	3	6	2	.150	.175

George Browne 35 L 4-12, Al Humphrey 25 L 5-27, Larry LeJeune 25 R 3-19, Bob Higgins 24 R 3-10, Bill Dahlen 41 R 0-3

NAME	T	AGE	W	L	PCT	SV	G	GS	CG	IP	H	BB	SO	SHO	ERA
		28	64	86	.427	10	154	154	81	1372	1310	566	533	13	3.39
Nap Rucker	L	28	22	18	.550	4	48	33	23	316	255	110	190	5	2.72
Elmer Knetzer	R	25	11	12	.478	0	35	20	11	204	202	93	66	3	3.49
Cy Barger	R	26	11	15	.423	0	30	30	21	217	224	71	60	1	3.53
George Bell	R	36	6	7	.455	0	19	12	6	101	123	28	28	2	4.28
Bill Schardt	R	25	5	5	.250	4	39	22	10	195	190	91	77	1	3.60
Pat Ragan	R	25	4	3	.571	1	22	7	5	94	81	31	39	1	2.11
Doc Scanlan	R	30	3	10	.231	1	22	15	3	114	101	69	45	0	3.64
Eddie Dent	R	23	2	1	.667	0	5	3	2	32	30	13	8	0	3.65
Sandy Burk	R	24	1	3	.250	0	13	7	1	58	54	47	15	0	5.12
Walt Miller	R	26	0	1	.000	0	3	2	0	11	16	6	0	0	6.55
Jack Ryan	R	26	0	1	.000	0	3	1	0	9	9	4	1	0	3.00
Raleigh Aitchison	L	23	0	1	.000	0	1	1	0	1	1	0	0	0	0.00
2 Elmer Steele	R	27	0	0	—	0	5	2	0	23	24	5	9	0	3.13

BOSTON — 8th 44-107 .291 54 — FRED TENNEY

NAME	G by Pos	B	AGE	G	AB	R	H	2B	3B	HR	RBI	BB	SO	SB	BA	SA
TOTALS			27	156	5308	699	1417	249	54	37	594	554	577	169	.267	.355
Fred Tenney	1B93, OF2	L	39	102	369	52	97	13	4	1	36	50	17	5	.263	.328
Bill Sweeney	2B136	R	25	137	523	92	164	33	6	3	63	77	26	33	.314	.417
1 Buck Herzog	SS74, 3B4	R	25	76	294	53	91	19	5	4	41	33	21	26	.310	.459
S. Ingerton	3B58, OF43, 1B17, 2B11, SS4	R	25	136	521	63	130	24	4	5	61	39	68	15	.250	.340
Doc Miller	OF146	R	28	146	577	69	192	36	4	3	91	43	43	32	.333	.442
2 Mike Donlin	OF56	L	33	56	222	33	70	16	1	2	34	22	17	7	.315	.423
2 Al Kaiser	OF58	R	24	65	197	20	40	5	2	2	15	10	26	4	.203	.279
2 Johnny Kling	C71, 3B1	R	35	75	241	32	54	8	1	2	24	30	29	0	.224	.290
Bill Rariden	C65, 3B3, 2B1	R	23	70	246	22	56	9	0	0	21	21	18	3	.228	.264
Harry Spratt	SS26, 2B5, 3B4, OF4	L	23	62	154	22	37	4	4	2	13	13	25	1	.240	.357
Ed McDonald	3B53, SS1	R	24	54	175	28	36	7	3	1	21	40	39	11	.206	.297
2 Al Bridwell	SS51	L	27	51	182	29	53	5	0	0	10	33	8	2	.291	.319
1 Wilbur Good	OF43	L	25	45	165	21	44	9	4	2	15	12	22	3	.267	.358
George Jackson	OF39	R	29	39	147	28	51	11	2	0	25	12	21	12	.347	.449
Patsy Flaherty	OF19, P4	R	35	38	94	9	27	3	2	2	20	8	11	2	.287	.426
2 Peaches Graham	C26	R	34	33	88	7	24	6	1	0	12	14	5	2	.273	.364
1 Hank Gowdy	1B26, C1	R	21	29	97	9	28	4	2	0	16	4	19	2	.289	.371
2 Hank Clarke	OF30	R	32	32	120	16	28	7	3	1	4	29	22	6	.233	.367
Art Butler	3B14, 2B4, SS1	R	23	27	68	11	12	2	0	0	2	9	6	0	.176	.206
Bill Jones	OF18	L	24	24	51	6	11	2	1	0	3	15	7	1	.216	.294
Ben Houser	1B20	L	27	20	71	11	18	1	0	1	9	8	6	2	.254	.310
Jay Kirke	OF14, 1B3, 2B1, SS1, 3B1	L	23	20	89	9	32	5	5	0	12	2	6	3	.360	.528
Harry Steinfeldt (BG)	3B19	R	33	19	63	5	16	4	0	1	8	6	3	1	.254	.365
Bill Collins	OF15, 3B1	B	29	17	44	8	6	1	1	0	8	1	8	0	.136	.205
Herman Young	3B5, SS3	R	25	9	25	2	6	0	1	0	0	3	2	0	.240	.240
Bert Weeden		L	28	1	0	0	0	0	0	0	0	0	0	0	.000	.000

NAME	T	AGE	W	L	PCT	SV	G	GS	CG	IP	H	BB	SO	SHO	ERA
		26	44	107	.291	7	156	156	73	1374	1570	672	486	5	5.08
Buster Brown	R	29	8	18	.309	2	42	25	13	241	258	116	76	0	4.29
Big Jeff Pfeffer (AJ)	R	29	7	5	.583	2	26	6	4	97	116	57	24	1	4.73
Lefty Tyler	L	21	7	10	.412	0	28	20	10	165	150	109	90	1	5.08
Hub Perdue (AJ)	R	29	6	10	.375	1	24	19	9	137	180	41	40	0	5.00
2 Cy Young	R	44	4	5	.444	0	11	11	8	80	83	15	35	2	3.71
Al Mattern	R	24	4	15	.211	0	33	21	11	186	228	63	51	0	4.99
Ed Donnelly	R	31	3	2	.600	0	5	4	4	37	33	9	16	1	2.43
2 Orlie Weaver	R	23	3	12	.200	0	27	17	4	121	140	84	50	0	6.47
Cecil Ferguson	R	24	1	0	.250	0	6	3	0	24	40	12	4	0	9.75
1 Cliff Curtis	R	29	1	8	.111	1	12	9	5	77	79	34	23	0	4.44
Jiggs Parson	R	25	0	1	.000	0	2	1	0	25	36	15	7	0	6.48
Sammy Frock	R	28	0	1	.000	0	1	1	0	16	29	5	8	0	5.63
Billy Burke	L	21	0	0	—	0	2	1	0	3	6	5	1	0	21.00
Patsy Flaherty (BA)	R	35	0	2	.000	0	4	1	1	14	21	6	2	0	7.07
Brad Hogg	R	22	0	0	—	1	3	2	1	26	33	14	8	0	6.58
Bill McTigue	L	20	0	0	—	0	3	1	0	37	37	49	23	0	7.05
2 Hank Griffin	R	24	0	0	—	0	15	6	1	93	96	34	30	0	5.20
Fuller Thompson	R	22	0	0	—	0	3	0	0	5	2	0	0	0	3.60

WORLD SERIES — PHILADELPHIA (AL) 4 NEW YORK (NL) 2

LINE SCORES

TEAM	1 2 3	4 5 6	7 8 9	10 11 12	R	H	E

Game 1   October 14 at New York

| PHIA(L) | 010 | 000 | 000 | | 1 | 6 | 2 |
| NY(NL) | 000 | 100 | 10X | | 2 | 5 | 0 |

Bender — Mathewson

Game 2   October 16 at Philadelphia

| NY | 010 | 000 | 000 | | 1 | 5 | 3 |
| PHI | 100 | 002 | 00X | | 3 | 4 | 0 |

Marquard, Crandall (8) — Plank

Game 3   October 17 at New York

| PHI | 000 | 000 | 001 | 0 | 2 | 3 9 2 |
| NY | 001 | 000 | 000 | 0 | 1 | 2 3 5 |

Coombs — Mathewson

Game 4   October 24 at Philadelphia

| NY | 200 | 000 | 000 | | 2 | 7 | 3 |
| PHI | 000 | 310 | 00X | | 4 | 11 | 1 |

Mathewson, Wiltse (8) — Bender

Game 5   October 25 at New York

| PHI | 003 | 000 | 0100 | | 3 | 7 | 1 |
| NY | 000 | 000 | 1021 | | 4 | 9 | 2 |

Coombs, Plank (10) — Marquard, Ames (4), Crandall (8)

Game 6   October 26 at Philadelphia

| NY | 100 | 000 | 001 | | 2 | 4 | 3 |
| PHI | 013 | 401 | 70X | | 13 | 13 | 5 |

Ames, Wiltse (5), Marquard (7) — Bender

COMPOSITE BATTING

NAME	POS	G	AB	R	H	2B	3B	HR	RBI	BA
Philadelphia (AL)										
Totals		6	205	27	50	15	0	3	21	.244
Lord	OF	6	27	2	5	2	0	0	1	.185
Oldring	OF	6	25	2	5	2	0	1	3	.200
Baker	3B	6	24	7	9	2	0	2	5	.375
Davis	1B	6	24	3	5	1	0	0	5	.208
Murphy	OF	6	23	4	7	3	0	0	3	.304
Collins	2B	6	21	4	6	1	0	0	1	.286
Barry	SS	6	19	2	7	4	0	0	2	.368
Thomas	C	4	12	1	1	0	0	0	1	.083
Bender	P	3	11	0	1	0	0	0	0	.091
Coombs	P	2	8	1	2	0	0	0	2	.250
Lapp	C	2	8	0	2	0	0	0	1	.250
Plank	P	2	2	0	0	0	0	0	0	.000
McInnis	1B	1	0	0	0	0	0	0	0	—
Strunk	PH	1	1	0	0	0	0	0	0	.000
New York (NL)										
Totals		6	189	13	33	11	1	0	10	.175
Devore	OF	6	24	1	4	1	0	0	3	.167
Doyle	2B	6	23	3	7	3	0	0	1	.304
Fletcher	SS	6	23	1	3	1	0	0	1	.130
Herzog	3B	6	21	3	4	2	0	0	0	.190
Murray	OF	6	21	0	0	0	0	0	0	.000
Meyers	C	6	20	2	6	2	0	0	3	.300
Merkle	1B	6	20	1	3	1	0	0	5	.150
Snodgrass	OF	6	19	1	2	0	0	0	1	.105
Mathewson	P	3	7	0	2	0	0	0	1	.286
Becker	PH	3	3	0	0	0	0	0	0	.000
Crandall	P	3	2	1	1	1	0	0	1	.500
Ames	P	3	2	0	0	0	0	0	0	.000
Marquard	P	2	2	0	0	0	0	0	0	.000
Wiltse	P	2	1	0	0	0	0	0	0	.000
Wilson	C	1	1	0	0	0	0	0	0	.000

COMPOSITE PITCHING

NAME	G	IP	H	BB	SO	W	L	SV	ERA
Philadelphia (AL)									
Totals	6	55.2	33	14	44	4	2	0	1.29
Bender	3	26	16	8	20	2	1	0	1.04
Coombs	2	20	11	6	16	1	0	0	1.35
Plank	2	9.2	6	0	8	1	1	0	1.86
New York (NL)									
Totals	6	54	50	4	31	2	4	0	2.83
Mathewson	3	27	25	2	13	1	2	0	2.00
Marquard	2	11.2	9	1	8	0	1	0	1.54
Ames	2	8	6	1	6	0	1	0	2.25
Crandall	2	4	2	0	2	1	0	0	0.00
Wiltse	2	3.1	8	0	2	0	0	0	18.90

1912 All for One and All to Sixth

Ty Cobb, who had been the heart of a Tiger team that finished near the top for five years, all too often displayed an extreme battling attitude on the field. Finally, on May 15, Cobb's anger and aggressiveness caught up with him. During a game in New York, Cobb went into the grandstands after a heckler and handed him a sound thrashing before park police could break it up. American League President Ban Johnson suspended Cobb indefinitely, and the entire roster of the Detroit club supported Cobb by refusing to take the field unless the suspension was lifted. Johnson was adamant and so were the Tigers. The strike was on. On May 18, Detroit manager Hughie Jennings was forced to field a pickup team of collegians, sandlotters, and aging coaches against the Philadelphia Athletics; the A's laughed themselves to a 23-2 victory over the one-day major leaguers. Another such game was to be played on May 20, but Connie Mack graciously allowed it to be postponed. The Tiger players finally rescinded and took the field on May 21. Cobb was reinstated on May 26, but poor morale and weak pitching tumbled the Tigers into a sixth-place finish.

While tempers were flaming in Detroit, clear heads and a new field boss were prevailing in Boston, where the fifth-place 1911 Red Sox moved to a new American League record for victories - 105 - and their third junior circuit pennant. Under new manager Jake Stahl, the Sox played steady ball all year and avoided any prolonged slumps in finishing 14 games ahead of the pack. An excellent attack centered around outfielders Tris Speaker and Duffy Lewis, and the arm of Smoky Joe Wood, who proved to be the team star. Wood, a ripe 22-year-old veteran of four years, used a smoking fastball to win 34 games against 5 losses and finish second in strikeouts only to the whiff master himself, Walter Johnson. The Red Sox victory was even more pleasant in light of the fact that Fenway Park opened its gates in April for the first time, and by October it had an American League pennant flying high over its freshly painted enclosures.

Another 1911 second division club, the Washington Senators, also surprised experts by rushing into second place. Streaks of 17 and 10 wins punctuated the season, and Walter Johnson's 32 victories and Clyde Milan's 88 stolen bases were high points of manager Clark Griffith's first year at the helm of the Nats. The Philadelphia Athletics got off to their usual slow start but could not come back any farther than third place; injuries and weakened pitching relegated the White Elephants to an also-ran role.

Whereas the Giants had won the National League crown with a late-season rush in 1911, they repeated in 1912 by rushing out to an early lead and never giving it up. A slump in July and August took some wind out of the sails of what appeared to be a record-breaking season but could not even threaten New York's perch on top. Rube Marquard won a record 19 consecutive games on the way to 26 victories, while Christy Mathewson brought home his 23 wins on schedule. A burly rookie spitballer, Jeff Tesreau, joined these two as a mound ace for John McGraw by winning 17 games and leading the league in E.R.A. Fred Merkle and Larry Doyle sparked the best offense in the league.

Good pitching enabled the Pirates to finish second, but the aging and ailing Cubs limped home in third. Frank Chance no longer played, Three Finger Brown was on the downhill side of his career, and Solly Hofman was traded off, signifying the breakup of the champion Cubs at the turn of the decade.—The Series lasted eight games, due to a tie game before Boston defeated the Giants for the championship. In a pitcher's series, Joe Wood played the star's role, winning three games and losing one.

One face during the season was noticeable absent. Cy Young, after 22 years of pitching and 511 victories, announced his retirement in the spring, thus ending one of baseball's legendary careers and certainly taking with him a winning statistic that would never again be equaled.

1912 AMERICAN LEAGUE

NAME	G by Pos	B	AGE	G	AB	R	H	2B	3B	HR	RBI	BB	SO	SB	BA	SA
BOSTON	1st 105-47 .691		JAKE STAHL													
TOTALS			27	154	5071	800	1404	269	84	29	654	565		185	.277	.380
Jake Stahl	1B92	R	32	95	326	40	98	21	6	3	60	31		13	.301	.429
Steve Yerkes	2B131	R	24	131	523	73	132	22	6	0	42	41		4	.252	.317
Heinie Wagner	SS144	R	31	144	504	75	138	25	6	2	68	62		21	.274	.359
Larry Gardner	3B143	L	26	143	517	88	163	24	18	3	86	56		25	.315	.449
Harry Hooper	OF147	R	24	147	590	98	143	20	12	2	53	66		29	.242	.327
Tris Speaker	OF153	L	24	153	580	136	222	53	12	10	90	82		52	.383	.567
Duffy Lewis	OF154	R	23	154	581	85	165	36	9	6	109	52		4	.284	.408
Bill Carrigan	C87	R	28	87	266	24	70	7	1	0	24	38		7	.263	.297
Clyde Engle	1B25, 2B15, 3B11, SS2, OF1	R	28	57	171	32	40	5	3	0	18	28		12	.234	.298
Hick Cady (NJ)	C43, 1B4	R	26	47	135	19	35	13	2	0	9	10		0	.259	.385
Smoky Joe Wood	P43	R	22	43	124	17	36	13	1	1	13	11		0	.290	.435
Hugh Bradley	1B40	R	27	40	137	16	26	11	1	1	19	15		3	.190	.307
Olaf Henricksen	OF10	L	24	37	56	20	18	3	1	0	4	8		1	.321	.411
Les Nunamaker	C35	R	23	35	103	15	26	5	2	0	6	6		2	.252	.340
2 Neal Ball	2B17	R	32	18	45	10	9	2	0	0	6	3		5	.200	.244
Marty Krug	SS9, 2B4	R	23	16	39	6	12	2	1	0	7	5		2	.308	.410
Pinch Thomas	C12	L	24	12	30	4	9	0	0	0	5	2		1	.290	.300

NAME	T	AGE	W	L	PCT	SV	G	GS	CG	IP	H	BB	SO	SHO	ERA
		25	105	47	.691	8	154	154	110	1362	1243	385	712	18	2.76
Smoky Joe Wood	R	22	34	5	.872	1	43	38	35	344	267	82	258	10	1.91
Hugh Bedient	R	22	20	9	.690	3	41	28	19	231	206	55	122	0	2.92
Buck O'Brien	R	30	19	13	.594	1	37	34	26	276	237	90	115	2	2.57
Charley Hall	R	27	15	8	.652	2	34	20	10	191	178	70	83	2	3.02
Ray Collins (KJ)	L	25	14	8	.636	0	27	24	17	199	192	42	82	4	2.54
Jack Bushelman	R	26	1	0	1.000	0	3	0	0	9	8	5	5	0	4.50
Larry Pape	R	28	1	1	.500	1	13	2	1	49	74	16	17	0	4.96
1 Eddie Cicotte	R	28	1	3	.250	0	9	6	2	46	58	15	20	0	5.67
Ben Van Dyke	L	24	0	1	—	0	3	1	0	14	13	7	8	0	3.21
Casey Hageman	R	25	0	0	—	0	2	1	0	1	5	3	1	0	36.00
Doug Smith	L	19	0	0	—	0	1	0	0	3	4	1	1	0	3.00

NAME	G by Pos	B	AGE	G	AB	R	H	2B	3B	HR	RBI	BB	SO	SB	BA	SA
WASHINGTON	2nd 91-61 .599 14		CLARK GRIFFITH													
TOTALS			26	154	5074	698	1298	202	86	20	575	472		274	.256	.341
Chick Gandil	1B117	R	24	117	443	59	135	20	15	2	81	27		21	.305	.431
Ray Morgan	2B75, SS4, 3B1	R	23	80	273	40	65	10	1	1	30	29		11	.238	.337
George McBride	SS152	R	31	152	521	56	118	13	7	1	50	38		17	.226	.284
Eddie Foster	3B154	R	25	154	618	98	176	34	9	2	70	53		27	.285	.379
Danny Moeller	OF132	B	27	132	519	90	143	26	10	6	46	52		30	.276	.399
Clyde Milan	OF154	L	26	154	601	105	184	19	11	1	79	63		88	.306	.379
Howard Shanks	OF113	R	21	115	399	52	92	14	7	1	48	40		21	.231	.308
John Henry (KJ)	C63	R	22	63	191	23	37	4	1	0	9	31		10	.194	.225
Eddie Ainsmith	C58	R	22	60	186	22	42	7	2	0	22	14		4	.226	.285
Germany Schaefer	OF19, 1B15, 2B15, P1	R	35	60	166	21	41	7	3	0	19	23		11	.247	.325
Rip Williams	C45	R	30	57	157	14	50	11	4	0	22	7		2	.318	.439
Walter Johnson	P50	R	24	55	144	16	38	6	4	2	20	7		2	.264	.403
2 Frank LaPorte	2B37	R	32	39	136	13	42	9	1	0	17	12		3	.309	.390
Tilly Walker	OF31, 2B1	R	24	36	110	22	30	2	1	0	9	8		11	.273	.309
Jack Knight	2B27, 1B5	R	26	32	93	10	15	2	1	0	9	16		4	.161	.204
Jack Flynn	1B20	R	28	20	71	9	12	4	1	0	5	7		2	.169	.254
Duke Kenworthy	OF10	B	25	12	38	6	9	1	0	0	2	2		3	.237	.263
Bill Cunningham	2B7	R	26	7	27	5	5	1	0	1	8	3		2	.185	.333
Roy Moran	OF5	R	27	5	13	1	2	0	0	0	0	8		3	.154	.154
Roxey Roach	SS2	R	27	2	2	1	1	0	0	1	1	0		0	.500	2.000
Joe Agler		L	25	1	1	0	0	0	0	0	0	0		0	.000	.000
Dave Howard		R	23	1	0	0	0	0	0	0	0	0		0	.000	.000
Tommy Long		R	22	1	1	0	0	0	0	0	0	0		0	.000	.000
Jack Ryan	3B1	R	43	1	4	0	0	0	0	0	0	0		0	.000	.000

NAME	T	AGE	W	L	PCT	SV	G	GS	CG	IP	H	BB	SO	SHO	ERA
		25	91	61	.599	9	154	154	99	1376	1219	525	828	11	2.69
Walter Johnson	R	24	33	12	.733	3	50	37	34	368	259	76	303	7	1.39
Bob Groom	R	27	24	13	.649	1	43	40	29	316	287	94	179	2	2.62
Long Tom Hughes	R	33	13	10	.565	1	31	26	11	196	201	78	108	1	2.94
Carl Cashion	R	21	10	6	.625	1	26	17	13	170	150	103	84	1	3.18
2 Hippo Vaughn	L	24	4	3	.571	0	12	8	4	81	75	43	49	0	2.89
Dixie Walker	R	25	3	4	.429	0	9	8	5	60	72	18	29	0	5.25
Joe Engel	R	19	2	5	.286	0	17	10	2	75	70	50	29	0	3.96
2 Barney Pelty	R	31	1	6	.143	0	11	4	1	44	40	10	15	0	3.28
Paul Musser	R	23	1	1	.500	1	7	2	0	21	16	16	10	0	2.57
Jerry Akers	R	24	0	0	.000	1	5	1	0	20	24	15	11	0	4.95
Charlie Becker	R	21	0	0	.000	0	4	0	0	9	8	6	5	0	3.00
Joe Boehling	L	21	0	0	.000	0	4	0	0	5	4	6	2	0	7.20
Bert Gallia	R	20	0	0	.000	0	3	0	0	5	7	4	3	0	3.60
Lefty Schegg	R	22	0	0	.000	0	2	1	0	5	7	4	3	0	3.60
Nick Altrock	L	35	0	0	.000	0	1	0	0	1	4	0	0	0	18.00
Clark Griffith	R	42	0	0	.000	0	1	0	0	1	0	0	0	0	0.00
Herb Herring	R	20	0	0	—	0	1	0	0	1	1	0	0	0	∞
1 Steve White	R	27	0	0	—	0	1	0	0	1	0	1	0	0	0.00
Germany Schaefer	R	34	0	0	—	0	1	0	0	0	0	0	0	0	0.00

NAME	G by Pos	B	AGE	G	AB	R	H	2B	3B	HR	RBI	BB	SO	SB	BA	SA
PHILADELPHIA	3rd 90-62 .592 15		CONNIE MACK													
TOTALS			27	153	5111	780	1442	204	108	22	620	485		258	.282	.377
Stuffy McInnis	1B153	R	21	153	568	83	186	25	13	3	101	49		27	.327	.433
Eddie Collins	2B153	L	25	153	543	137	189	25	11	0	64	101		63	.348	.435
Jack Barry	SS139	R	25	139	483	76	126	19	9	0	55	47		22	.261	.337
Frank Baker	3B149	L	26	149	577	116	200	40	21	10	130	50		40	.347	.541
Bris Lord	OF96	R	28	96	378	63	90	12	9	0	25	34		15	.238	.317
Rube Oldring	OF97	R	28	98	395	61	119	14	5	1	24	10		17	.301	.370
Amos Strunk	OF118	L	23	120	412	58	119	13	12	3	63	47		29	.289	.400
Jack Lapp	C82	L	27	90	281	26	82	15	6	1	34	19		3	.292	.399
Harl Maggert	OF61	L	29	72	242	39	62	8	6	1	13	36		10	.256	.351
Ben Egan	C46	R	28	48	138	9	24	3	4	0	13	6		3	.174	.254
Ira Thomas	C46	R	31	46	139	14	30	4	2	1	13	8		3	.216	.295
Danny Murphy	OF36	R	35	36	130	27	42	6	2	2	20	16		8	.323	.446
Eddie Murphy	OF33	L	20	33	142	24	45	4	0	0	6	11		7	.317	.359
Jimmy Walsh	OF30	L	26	31	107	11	27	8	2	0	15	12		7	.252	.364
Claude Derrick	SS18	L	26	21	58	7	14	0	1	0	7	5		1	.241	.276
Howard Fahey	3B2, 2B1, SS1	R	20	5	8	0	0	0	0	0	0	0		0	.000	.000
Joe Mathes	3B4	B	20	4	14	0	2	0	0	0	1	0		0	.143	.143
Chester Emerson		L	22	1	0	0	0	0	0	0	0	0		0	.000	.000

NAME	T	AGE	W	L	PCT	SV	G	GS	CG	IP	H	BB	SO	SHO	ERA
		27	90	62	.592	13	153	153	100	1357	1273	518	601	11	3.32
Eddie Plank	L	36	26	6	.813	2	37	30	24	260	234	83	110	5	2.21
Jack Coombs	R	29	21	10	.677	3	40	32	23	262	227	94	120	1	3.29
Chief Bender	R	29	13	8	.619	2	27	19	12	171	169	33	90	1	2.74
Boardwalk Brown	R	27	13	11	.542	1	34	24	16	199	204	87	64	3	3.66
Duke Houck	R	20	8	8	.500	1	30	17	12	181	148	74	75	0	2.93
Cy Morgan	R	33	3	8	.283	0	16	14	5	94	75	51	47	0	3.74
Stan Coveleski	R	22	2	1	.667	0	5	2	2	21	18	4	9	1	3.43
2 Roy Crabb	L	21	2	4	.333	0	7	7	3	43	48	17	12	0	3.77
Roger Salmon	R	21	1	0	1.000	0	5	7	4	5	9	0	2	0	9.00
Herb Pennock	L	18	1	2	.333	2	17	2	1	50	48	30	38	0	4.50
1 Harry Krause	L	23	0	2	.000	0	4	5	1	6	10	2	3	0	14.40
Lefty Russell	R	21	0	0	.000	0	5	2	2	17	18	14	9	0	7.42
Hardin Barry	R	21	0	0	—	0	1	0	0	13	18	4	3	0	7.62
Dave Danforth	L	22	0	0	—	0	3	0	0	20	26	12	8	0	4.05
Doc Martin	R	24	0	0	—	0	1	0	0	4	5	4	2	0	11.25
Bullet Joe Bush	R	19	0	0	—	0	1	1	1	8	14	4	3	0	7.88
Slim Harrell	R	21	0	0	—	0	2	1	0	3	4	1	0	0	0.00

NAME	G by Pos	B	AGE	G	AB	R	H	2B	3B	HR	RBI	BB	SO	SB	BA	SA	NAME	T	AGE	W	L	PCT	SV	G	GS	CG	IP	H	BB	SO	SHO	ERA

CHICAGO 4th 78-76 .506 28 NIXEY CALLAHAN

NAME	G by Pos	B	AGE	G	AB	R	H	2B	3B	HR	RBI	BB	SO	SB	BA	SA
TOTALS			27	158	5181	640	1321	174	80	17	537	423		205	.255	.329
Rollie Zeider	1B66, 3B56, SS1	R	28	129	420	57	103	12	10	1	42	50		47	.245	.329
Morrie Rath	2B157	L	25	157	591	104	161	10	2	1	19	95		30	.272	.301
Buck Weaver	SS147	L	21	147	523	55	117	21	8	1	43	9		12	.224	.300
Harry Lord	3B106, OF45	L	30	151	570	71	152	19	12	5	54	52		28	.267	.368
Shano Collins	OF105, 1B46	R	26	153	575	75	168	34	10	2	81	29		26	.292	.397
Ping Bodie	OF130	R	24	137	472	58	139	24	7	5	72	43		12	.294	.407
Nixey Callahan	OF107	R	38	111	408	45	111	9	7	1	52	12		19	.272	.336
Walt Kuhn	C75	R	25	75	178	16	36	7	0	0	10	20		5	.202	.242
Chick Mattick	OF78	R	25	88	285	45	74	7	9	1	35	27		15	.260	.358
Bruno Block	C46	R	27	46	136	8	35	5	6	0	26	7		1	.257	.382
Matty McIntyre	OF45	L	32	45	84	10	14	0	0	0	10	14		3	.167	.167
Billy Sullivan (SJ)	C39	R	37	39	91	9	19	2	1	0	15	9		0	.209	.253
Jack Fournier	1B17	L	22	35	73	5	14	5	2	0	2	4		1	.192	.315
Babe Borton	1B30	L	23	31	105	15	39	3	1	0	17	8		1	.371	.419
2 Ted Easterly	C10, OF1	L	27	30	55	5	20	2	0	0	14	2		1	.364	.400
Ray Schalk	C23	R	19	23	63	7	18	2	0	0	8	3		2	.286	.317
Ernie Johnson	SS16	L	24	18	42	7	11	0	1	0	5	1		0	.262	.310
Cuke Barrows	OF3	R	28	8	13	0	3	0	0	0	2	2		1	.231	.231
Wally Mayer	C6	R	21	7	9	1	0	0	0	0	0	0		0	.000	.000

Lena Blackburne (ST) 25 R 0-1, Mutz Ens 25 L 0-6, Lee Tannehill (BA) 31 R 0-3, Denny Berran 24 L 1-4, Polly McLarry 21 L 0-2, Kid Gleason 45 B 1-2, 1 Harold Paddock 25 L 0-1, Polly Wolfe 23 L 0-1

NAME	T	AGE	W	L	PCT	SV	G	GS	CG	IP	H	BB	SO	SHO	ERA
		28	78	76	.506	15	158	158	84	1412	1397	426	697	14	3.06
Ed Walsh	R	31	27	17	.614	10	62	41	32	393	332	94	254	6	2.15
Joe Benz	R	26	12	18	.400	0	41	31	11	238	230	70	96	3	2.92
Frank Lange	R	28	10	10	.500	3	31	20	11	165	165	68	96	2	3.28
2 Eddie Cicotte	R	28	9	7	.563	0	20	18	13	152	159	37	70	1	2.84
Doc White	R	33	8	9	.471	0	32	19	7	172	172	47	57	1	3.24
Rube Peters	R	27	5	6	.455	0	28	11	4	109	134	33	39	0	4.11
George Mogridge	L	23	3	4	.429	2	17	8	2	65	69	15	31	0	3.99
Jim Scott (IL)	R	23	3	2	.500	0	6	4	2	38	36	15	23	1	2.13
Harry Smith	R	22	1	0	1.000	0	1	1	1	10	8	1	1	0	1.80
Wiley Taylor	R	24	1	1	.500	0	3	3	0	20	21	14	4	0	4.95
Phil Douglas	R	22	0	1	.000	0	1	1	0	12	21	6	7	0	7.50
1 Roy Crabb	R	21	0	1	.000	0	1	1	0	9	6	4	3	0	1.00
Walt Johnson	R	19	0	0	—	0	4	0	0	14	11	10	8	0	3.21
Rip Jordan (BL)	R	22	0	0	—	0	3	0	0	10	13	0	0	0	6.30
Ralph Bell	L	21	0	0	—	0	3	0	0	6	8	5	0	0	9.00
Flame Delhi	R	19	0	0	—	0	1	0	0	6	8	4	1	0	9.00
Fred Lamline	R	24	0	0	—	0	1	0	0	2	7	2	1	0	31.50

CLEVELAND 5th 75-78 .490 30.5 HARRY DAVIS 54-71 .432 JOE BIRMINGHAM 21-7 .750

NAME	G by Pos	B	AGE	G	AB	R	H	2B	3B	HR	RBI	BB	SO	SB	BA	SA
TOTALS			26	155	5134	680	1403	218	77	10	561	407		194	.273	.352
Art Griggs	1B71	R	27	89	273	29	83	16	7	0	39	33		10	.304	.414
Nap Lajoie (XJ)	2B97, 1B20	R	37	117	448	66	165	34	4	0	90	28		18	.368	.462
Roger Peckinpaugh	SS67	R	21	69	236	18	50	4	1	1	22	16		11	.212	.250
Terry Turner	3B103	R	31	103	370	54	114	14	4	0	33	31		19	.308	.368
Joe Jackson	OF150	L	22	152	572	121	226	44	26	3	90	54		35	.395	.579
Joe Birmingham	OF96, 1B9	R	27	107	369	49	94	19	3	0	45	26		15	.255	.322
Buddy Ryan	OF90	L	26	93	328	53	89	12	9	1	31	30		12	.271	.372
Steve O'Neill (BG)	C67	R	20	68	215	17	49	4	0	0	14	12		2	.228	.247
Ivy Olson	SS56, 3B35, 2B21, OF3	R	26	123	467	68	118	13	1	0	33	21		16	.253	.285
Jack Graney (JJ)	OF75	L	26	78	264	44	64	13	2	0	20	50		9	.242	.307
1 Ted Easterly	C51	L	27	63	186	17	55	4	0	1	21	7		3	.296	.333
Doc Johnston	1B41	L	24	43	164	22	46	7	4	1	11	11		8	.280	.390
1 Neal Ball (BG)	2B37	R	31	37	132	12	30	4	1	0	14	9		7	.227	.273
Ray Chapman	SS31	R	21	31	109	29	34	6	3	0	19	10		10	.312	.422
Hank Butcher	OF20	R	25	24	82	9	16	4	1	1	10	6		3	.195	.305
Fred Carisch	C23	R	30	24	69	9	19	3	1	0	5	1		3	.275	.348
Tim Hendryx	OF22	R	21	23	70	9	17	2	4	1	9	6		2	.243	.429
Bill Hunter	OF16	L	21	21	55	6	9	3	2	0	2	10		4	.640	.200
Jack Adams	C20	B	21	20	54	5	11	2	1	0	6	6		0	.204	.278

Paddy Livingston 32 B 11-47, Art Hauger 18 L 1-18, Ed Hohnhorst 27 L 11-54, Howard Baker 24 R 5-30, Ken Nash 23 B 4-24, Herman Bronkie 27 R 0-16
Jack Kibble 20 B 0-8, Moxie Meixel 24 L 1-2, Lou Nagelson 25 R 0-3, Harry Davis 38 R 0-5, Hack Eibel 18 L 0-3, Harvey Grubb 21 R 0-0

NAME	T	AGE	W	L	PCT	SV	G	GS	CG	IP	H	BB	SO	SHO	ERA
		24	75	78	.490	8	155	155	96	1353	1367	523	622	7	3.30
Vean Gregg	L	27	20	13	.606	2	37	34	26	271	242	90	184	1	2.59
Fred Blanding	R	24	18	14	.563	2	39	31	24	262	259	79	75	1	2.92
George Kahler	R	22	12	19	.387	1	41	32	17	246	263	121	104	3	3.70
Bill Steen	R	24	9	8	.529	0	26	16	6	143	163	45	61	1	3.78
Jim Baskette	R	24	6	3	.667	0	29	11	7	116	109	46	51	1	3.18
Willie Mitchell	L	22	5	8	.385	2	29	15	9	164	149	56	94	0	2.80
Gene Krapp	R	25	2	5	.286	0	9	7	4	59	57	42	22	0	4.57
Bert Brenner	R	24	1	1	—	0	1	1	1	13	14	4	3	0	2.77
Lefty James	L	23	0	1	.000	0	3	1	0	6	4	1	6	0	7.50
2 Harry Krause	R	23	0	1	.000	0	2	1	0	10	19	5	4	0	10.80
Lefty George	L	25	0	0	—	0	11	5	2	44	69	18	18	0	4.91
Bill James	R	24	0	0	—	0	3	0	0	14	15	9	5	0	4.50
Roy Walker	R	19	0	0	—	0	1	0	0	3	1	0	0	0	0.00
Jim Neher	R	23	0	0	—	0	1	0	0	1	0	1	0	0	0.00
Ernie Wolf	R	23	0	0	—	0	1	0	0	6	8	4	1	0	6.00

DETROIT 6th 69-84 .451 36.5 HUGHIE JENNINGS

NAME	G by Pos	B	AGE	G	AB	R	H	2B	3B	HR	RBI	BB	SO	SB	BA	SA
TOTALS			27	154	5141	720	1375	189	86	19	569	530		270	.267	.349
George Moriarty	1B71, 3B33	R	26	105	375	38	93	23	4	0	54	26		27	.248	.315
Baldy Louden	2B86, 3B26, SS5	R	28	121	403	57	99	12	4	1	36	58		28	.241	.298
Donie Bush	SS144	B	24	144	511	107	118	14	8	2	38	117		35	.231	.301
Charlie Deal	3B41	R	20	41	142	13	32	4	2	0	11	9		4	.225	.282
Sam Crawford	OF149	L	32	149	581	81	189	30	21	4	109	42		41	.325	.470
Ty Cobb	OF140	L	25	140	553	119	227	30	23	7	83	43		61	.410	.586
Davy Jones	OF81	L	32	97	316	54	93	5	2	0	24	38		16	.294	.323
Oscar Stanage	C119	R	29	119	394	35	103	9	4	0	41	34		3	.261	.305
Jim Delahanty	2B44, OF33	R	33	78	266	34	76	14	4	0	41	42		9	.286	.346
Ossie Vitt	OF27, 3B24, 2B15	R	22	73	273	39	67	4	4	0	19	18		17	.245	.289
Del Gainer	1B50	R	25	51	179	28	43	5	6	0	20	18		14	.240	.335
Red Corriden	3B25, 2B7, SS3	R	24	38	138	22	28	6	0	0	5	15		4	.203	.246
George Mullin	P30	R	31	38	90	13	25	5	1	0	12	17		0	.278	.356
Eddie Onslow	1B35	L	19	35	128	11	29	1	2	1	13	3		2	.227	.289
Jack Onslow	C31	R	23	31	69	7	11	1	0	0	4	10		1	.159	.174
Brad Kocher	C23	R	24	24	63	5	13	3	1	0	9	4		0	.203	.286
Bobby Veach	OF22	L	24	23	79	8	27	1	0	0	15	5		2	.342	.430
Paddy Baumann	3B6, 2B5, OF1	R	26	13	42	4	7	1	0	0	7	6		3	.167	.194
Hank Perry	OF7	R	25	13	36	3	6	1	1	0	2	1		2	.167	.194

Al Bashang 23 B 1-12, Red McDermott 23 R 4-15, Charley O'Leary 29 R 2-10, Jack Smith 17 R 0-0, Ed Irwin 30 R 2-3, Hughie Jennings 43 R 0-1, Bill Leinhauser 18 R 0-4,
Billy Maharg 31 R 0-1, Jim McGarr 23 R 0-4, Dan McGarvey 24 R 0-3, Deacon McGuire 48 R 1-2, Vince Maney 25 R 0-4, Ollie O'Mara 21 R 0-4, Joe Sugden 41 B 1-4, Hap Ward 26 R 0-2

NAME	T	AGE	W	L	PCT	SV	G	GS	CG	IP	H	BB	SO	SHO	ERA
		27	69	84	.451	6	154	154	104	1358	1424	517	506	7	3.78
Jean Dubuc	R	23	17	10	.630	3	37	26	23	250	217	109	97	2	2.77
Ed Willett	R	28	17	15	.531	0	37	31	24	284	281	84	89	1	3.29
George Mullin	R	31	12	17	.414	0	30	29	22	226	214	92	88	2	3.54
2 Joe Lake	R	30	9	12	.429	2	26	14	12	163	190	39	86	0	3.10
1 Ralph Works	R	25	5	10	.333	1	27	16	9	157	185	66	64	1	4.24
Bill Covington	L	25	4	3	.429	0	14	9	2	63	58	30	19	1	4.14
Ed Summers	R	27	2	1	.667	0	3	3	1	17	16	3	5	0	4.72
Wild Bill Donovan	R	35	1	0	1.000	0	3	1	0	10	5	2	6	0	0.90
George Boehler	R	20	1	2	.333	0	4	4	1	31	49	14	13	0	6.68
Willie Jensen	R	22	1	1	.500	0	4	4	1	25	30	14	4	0	5.40
Bill Burns	L	32	1	4	.200	0	6	5	2	39	52	9	6	0	5.31
Hooks Dauss	R	23	0	0	—	0	2	2	2	17	11	9	7	0	3.18
Pat McGehee	R	23	0	0	—	0	2	2	1	18	26	7	1	0	5.00
Allan Traverse	R	20	0	1	.000	0	1	1	1	8	26	7	1	0	15.75
Bun Troy	R	23	0	1	.000	0	1	1	0	7	8	3	1	0	5.14
Harry Moran	L	23	0	0	—	0	5	2	1	15	19	12	3	0	4.80
Charlie Wheatley	R	19	0	4	.000	0	5	5	2	35	45	17	14	0	6.17
Hub Pernoll	L	24	0	1	.000	0	1	1	1	9	4	3	3	0	6.00
Ed Lafitte (ST)	R	26	0	1	.000	0	3	0	0	6	9	3	1	0	6.00
Alex Remneas	R	26	0	1	.000	0	1	1	0	4	8	5	0	0	22.50

ST. LOUIS 7th 53-101 .344 53 BOBBY WALLACE 12-27 .308 GEORGE STOVALL 41-74 .357

NAME	G by Pos	B	AGE	G	AB	R	H	2B	3B	HR	RBI	BB	SO	SB	BA	SA
TOTALS			29	157	5081	556	1263	166	71	19	468	449		176	.249	.320
George Stovall	1B94	R	34	115	398	35	101	17	5	0	45	14		1	.254	.322
Del Pratt	2B121, SS21, OF8, 3B1	R	24	151	570	74	172	26	15	5	69	36		24	.302	.426
Bobby Wallace	SS86, 3B10, 2B2	R	38	99	323	39	78	14	5	0	31	43		3	.241	.316
Jimmy Austin	3B149	R	32	149	536	57	135	14	8	2	44	58		28	.252	.319
Pete Compton	OF72	L	22	100	268	26	75	6	4	2	30	22		11	.280	.354
Burt Shotton	OF154	L	27	154	580	87	168	15	8	2	40	86		35	.290	.353
Willie Hogan	OF99	R	27	107	360	32	77	10	2	1	36	34		7	.214	.283
Jim Stephens	C66	R	28	74	205	13	51	7	5	0	22	7		3	.249	.332
1 Frank LaPorte	2B39, OF32	R	32	80	266	32	83	11	4	1	38	20		7	.312	.395
Joe Kutina	1B51, OF1	R	27	65	205	18	42	9	3	1	18	13		0	.205	.293
Gus Williams	OF62	R	24	64	216	32	63	13	7	2	32	27		18	.292	.444
Paul Krichell	C57	R	29	57	167	19	35	6	0	0	19	8		2	.217	.255
Walt Alexander	C37	R	21	37	91	11	27	4	0	0	6	13		1	.297	.385
Heinie Jantzen	OF31	R	22	31	119	10	22	0	1	0	4	1		3	.185	.227
Ed Hallinan	SS26	R	23	28	86	11	19	2	0	0	1	5		3	.221	.244
John Daley	SS17	B	25	17	52	7	9	1	0	0	4	4		4	.173	.231

Bunny Brief 19 R 13-42, Eddie Miller 23 R 9-46, Bill Brown 18 L 4-20, George Alton 21 R 4-17, Frank Crossin 21 R 5-22, Charlie Snell 18 R 4-19, Harry Smoyer 22 R 3-14,
Doc Shanley 22 R 0-8, Phil Ketter 28 2-6, Tom Tennant 29 L 0-2, Lou Criger 40 R 0-1, Charlie Miller 20 0-2, Fred Walden 22 R 0-0

NAME	T	AGE	W	L	PCT	SV	G	GS	CG	IP	H	BB	SO	SHO	ERA
		26	53	101	.344	7	157	157	89	1370	1433	442	547	8	3.71
George Baumgardner	R	20	11	14	.440	0	30	27	19	218	222	79	102	2	3.38
Earl Hamilton	L	20	11	14	.440	2	41	26	17	250	228	86	139	1	3.24
Jack Powell	R	37	9	16	.360	0	32	27	21	235	248	52	67	0	3.11
Mack Allison	R	25	6	17	.261	1	31	20	11	169	171	49	43	1	3.62
Elmer Brown	R	28	5	12	.385	1	23	13	2	120	122	42	45	1	3.00
Roy Mitchell	R	27	5	4	.429	0	17	7	5	62	81	17	22	0	4.65
2 Joe Lake	R	30	2	7	.222	0	11	6	4	57	70	16	28	0	4.42
Willie Adams	R	21	3	4	.400	0	13	5	0	46	50	19	16	0	4.50
Carl Weilman	L	23	4	4	.333	1	9	6	5	48	42	13	24	1	2.81
Curly Brown	L	23	1	3	.250	0	16	4	2	65	69	35	28	1	4.84
1 Barney Pelty	R	31	1	5	.167	0	6	5	0	43	50	15	10	0	5.56
Buddy Napier	R	22	0	0	—	0	7	2	0	25	33	15	10	0	5.40
1 Red Nelson	R	26	0	0	—	0	4	0	0	11	12	4	4	0	7.00
Bill Bailey	L	24	0	1	.000	0	1	1	1	15	10	2	9	0	9.00
1 John Frill	R	33	0	0	—	0	4	1	0	16	11	2	2	0	22.50
Fred Spencer	R	27	0	0	—	0	1	0	0	3	4	2	0	0	5.40

NEW YORK 8th 50-102 .329 55 HARRY WOLVERTON

NAME	G by Pos	B	AGE	G	AB	R	H	2B	3B	HR	RBI	BB	SO	SB	BA	SA
TOTALS			26	153	5095	632	1320	168	79	18	502	463		247	.259	.334
Hal Chase	1B121, 2B8	L	29	131	522	61	143	21	9	4	58	17		33	.274	.372
Hack Simmons	2B88, 1B13, SS6	R	27	101	405	46	96	17	2	0	41	33		19	.239	.292
Jack Martin	SS64, 3B4, 2B1	R	25	69	231	30	52	6	4	0	19	37		14	.225	.290
2 Harold Paddock	3B41, 2B2, OF1	L	25	45	156	26	45	5	3	1	14	23		9	.288	.378
Guy Zinn	OF106	L	25	106	401	56	105	15	10	6	55	50		17	.262	.394
Roy Hartzell	OF55, 3B56, SS10, 2B2	L	30	123	416	50	113	10	11	3	48	54		20	.272	.356
Bert Daniels	OF131	R	29	133	496	72	136	25	11	2	41	51		37	.274	.381
Ed Sweeney	C108	R	23	110	351	37	94	12	1	0	30	27		6	.268	.308
Dutch Sterrett	OF37, 1B17, C10, 2B1	R	22	66	230	30	61	4	7	1	32	11		5	.265	.357
Birdie Cree (BW)	OF50	R	29	50	190	25	63	11	6	0	22	20		12	.332	.453
Earle Gardner	2B43	R	28	43	160	14	45	3	0	0	26	5		11	.281	.313
George McConnell	P23, 1B2	R	34	42	91	11	27	4	0	0	12	15		1	.297	.385
Tommy McMillan	SS41	R	24	41	149	24	34	7	2	0	12	15		18	.228	.295
Russ Ford	P36, 2B2, OF2	R	29	40	112	13	27	6	3	0	8	6		3	.241	.348
Bill Strumpf	SS26, 2B8, 3B4, 1B1, OF1	R	20	40	129	8	31	4	0	0	10	6		5	.240	.271
Jack Lelivelt	OF36	L	26	36	149	12	54	5	2	1	24	6		4	.362	.537
Harry Wolverton	3B7	L	38	33	50	6	15	3	0	0	7	6		1	.300	.360
Gabby Street	C28	R	30	28	66	2	12	1	0	0	4	2		0	.182	.216
Pat Maloney	OF20	R	24	22	79	9	17	5	0	0	2	3		3	.215	.228

Ezra Midkiff 29 L 21-86, Bob Williams 18 R 6-44, 1 Cozy Dolan 29 L 12-60, Curt Coleman 25 L 9-37, Harry Wolter (RJ) 27 L 11-32, John Dowd 21 R 6-31,
Klondike Smith 25 L 5-27, Benny Kauff 22 L 3-11, Gus Fisher 26 L 1-10, Bill Otis 22 L 1-20, Jack Little 21 R 3-12, Johnnie Priest 21 R 1-2,
George Batten 20 R 0-3, Homer Thompson 21 R 0-0

NAME	T	AGE	W	L	PCT	SV	G	GS	CG	IP	H	BB	SO	SHO	ERA
		27	50	102	.329	3	153	153	109	1335	1448	436	637	5	4.13
Russ Ford	R	29	13	21	.382	0	36	35	32	292	317	79	112	0	3.55
Jack Warhop	R	27	10	19	.345	3	39	22	16	258	256	59	110	2	2.86
George McConnell	R	34	8	12	.400	0	23	19	17	177	172	52	91	0	2.75
Ray Caldwell	R	24	8	16	.333	0	28	26	14	183	196	67	95	3	4.47
Jack Quinn	R	28	6	8	.417	0	18	11	7	103	139	23	47	0	5.77
Ray Fisher	R	24	2	8	.200	0	13	9	6	90	107	32	47	0	5.90
1 Hippo Vaughn	L	24	2	8	.200	0	15	10	6	83	66	37	46	1	5.14
Al Schultz	R	22	1	1	.500	0	7	1	1	17	15	11	10	0	6.35
George Davis	R	22	1	4	.200	0	10	5	4	54	61	28	22	0	6.50
Red Hoff	L	21	0	1	.000	0	7	2	1	28	43	13	15	0	6.75
Carl Thompson	R	22	0	0	—	0	2	1	1	11	8	6	2	0	6.00
Ray Keating	R	18	0	2	.000	0	3	3	1	36	38	18	21	0	5.75
George Shears	L	22	0	1	.000	0	4	0	0	15	14	11	9	0	5.40

NEW YORK — 1ST 103-48 .682 — JOHN McGRAW

NAME	G by Pos	B	AGE	G	AB	R	H	2B	3B	HR	RBI	BB	SO	SB	BA	SA
TOTALS			26	154	5067	823	1451	231	89	47	702	522	497	319	.286	.393
Fred Merkle	1B129	R	23	129	479	82	148	22	6	11	84	42	70	37	.309	.449
Larry Doyle	2B143	L	26	143	558	98	184	33	8	10	90	56	20	36	.330	.471
Art Fletcher	SS126,2B2,3B1	R	27	129	419	64	118	17	9	1	57	16	29	16	.282	.372
Buck Herzog	3B140	R	26	140	482	72	127	20	9	2	47	57	34	17	.263	.355
Red Murray	OF143	R	28	143	549	83	152	26	20	3	92	27	45	38	.277	.413
Beals Becker	OF117	L	25	125	402	66	106	18	8	6	58	54	35	30	.264	.393
Fred Snodgrass	OF116,1B28,2B1	R	24	146	535	91	144	24	9	3	69	70	65	43	.269	.364
Chief Meyers	C122	R	31	126	371	60	133	16	5	6	54	47	20	8	.358	.477
Josh Devore	OF96	L	24	106	327	66	90	14	6	2	37	51	43	27	.275	.373
Tillie Shafer	SS31,2B20,3B7	B	23	78	163	48	47	4	1	0	23	30	19	22	.288	.387
Art Wilson	C61	R	26	65	121	17	35	6	0	3	19	13	14	2	.289	.413
Doc Crandall	P37,2B2,1B1	R	24	50	80	9	25	6	2	0	19	6	7	0	.313	.438
Moose McCormick	OF6,1B1	L	31	42	39	4	13	4	1	0	8	6	9	1	.333	.487
George Burns	OF23	R	22	29	51	11	15	4	0	0	8	8	9	7	.294	.373
Heinie Groh (JJ)	2B12,SS7,3B6	R	22	27	48	8	13	2	1	0	3	8	7	6	.271	.354
Grover Hartley	C25	R	23	25	34	3	8	2	1	0	7	8	4	2	.235	.353
Dave Robertson	1B1	L	22	3	2	1	1	0	0	0	1	0	1	1	.500	.500

NAME	T	AGE	W	L	PCT	SV	G	GS	CG	IP	H	BB	SO	SHO	ERA
		27	103	48	.682	15	154	154	93	1370	1352	338	652	8	2.58
Rube Marquard	L	25	26	11	.703	5	43	38	22	295	286	80	175	1	2.57
Christy Mathewson	R	31	23	12	.657	4	43	34	27	310	311	34	134	0	2.12
Jeff Tesreau	R	24	17	7	.708	1	36	28	19	243	177	106	119	3	1.96
Doc Crandall	R	24	13	7	.650	2	37	10	7	162	181	35	60	0	3.61
Red Ames	R	29	11	5	.688	2	33	22	9	179	194	35	83	2	2.46
Hooks Wiltse	L	32	9	6	.600	3	28	17	5	134	140	28	58	0	3.16
Lore Bader	R	24	2	0	1.000	0	3	1	1	11	9	6	3	0	0.90
LaRue Kirby	R	22	1	0	1.000	0	1	1	1	11	13	6	2	0	5.73
Al Demaree	R	27	1	0	1.000	0	2	1	1	16	17	2	11	1	1.69
Louis Drucke	R	23	0	0	—	0	2	0	0	2	5	1	0	0	13.50
Ted Goulait	R	22	0	0	—	0	1	1	1	7	11	4	6	0	6.43
Ernie Shore	R	21	0	0		1	1	0	0	1	8	1	1	0	27.00

PITTSBURGH — 2nd 93-58 .616 10 — FRED CLARKE

NAME	G by Pos	B	AGE	G	AB	R	H	2B	3B	HR	RBI	BB	SO	SB	BA	SA
TOTALS			28	152	5252	751	1493	222	129	39	657	420	514	177	.284	.398
Dots Miller	1B147	R	25	148	567	74	156	33	12	4	87	37	45	18	.275	.397
Alex McCarthy	2B105,3B4	R	24	111	401	53	111	12	4	1	41	30	36	8	.277	.334
Honus Wagner	SS143	R	38	145	558	91	181	35	20	7	102	59	38	26	.324	.496
Bobby Byrne	2B130	R	27	130	528	99	152	31	11	3	35	54	40	20	.288	.405
Mike Donlin	OF62	L	34	77	244	27	77	9	2	2	35	20	16	8	.316	.443
Owen Wilson	OF152	L	28	152	583	80	175	19	36	11	95	35	67	16	.300	.513
Max Carey	OF150	B	22	150	587	114	177	23	8	5	66	61	78	45	.302	.394
George Gibson	C94	R	31	95	300	23	72	14	3	2	35	20	16	0	.240	.327
Billy Kelly	C39	R	26	48	132	20	42	3	2	1	12	6	16	8	.318	.394
Claude Hendrix	P39	R	23	46	121	25	39	10	6	1	15	3	18	1	.322	.529
Ham Hyatt	OF15,1B3	R	27	46	97	13	28	3	1	0	22	6	8	2	.289	.340
Art Butler	2B43	R	24	43	154	19	42	4	2	1	17	15	11	2	.273	.344
Mike Simon	2B43	L	24	42	113	10	34	2	1	0	11	5	9	1	.301	.336
Eddie Mensor	OF32	B	26	39	99	19	26	3	2	0	5	23	12	10	.263	.333
Jim Viox	3B10,SS8,OF3,2B1	R	21	33	70	8	13	2	3	1	7	3	5	2	.186	.343
1 Tommy Leach	OF24	R	34	28	97	24	29	4	2	0	19	12	9	6	.299	.381
Bill McKechnie	3B15,SS4,2B3,1B2	B	25	24	73	8	18	0	1	0	4	2	1	2	.247	.274
2 Solly Hofman	OF15	L	29	17	53	7	15	4	1	0	2	5	6	0	.283	.396
Stump Edington	OF14	L	20	15	53	4	16	0	2	0	2	3	1	0	.302	.377
Wally Rehg	OF2	R	23	8	9	1	0	0	0	0	0	2	1	0	.000	.000
Stan Gray	1B4	L	23	6	20	4	5	0	1	0	2	0	3	0	.250	.350

Ovid Nicholson 23 L 5-11, Ona Dodd 25 R 0-9, Mickey Keliher 22 L 0-0, Rivington Bisland 22 R 0-1, Earl Blackburn 19 R 0-0, Ralph Capron 23 L 0-0

NAME	T	AGE	W	L	PCT	SV	G	GS	CG	IP	H	BB	SO	SHO	ERA
		26	93	58	.616	2	152	152	94	1385	1268	497	664	18	2.85
Claude Hendrix	R	23	24	9	.727	1	39	32	25	289	256	105	176	4	2.58
Howie Camnitz	R	30	22	12	.647	2	41	32	22	277	256	82	121	2	2.83
Marty O'Toole	R	24	15	17	.469	0	37	36	17	275	237	159	150	6	2.72
Hank Robinson	L	24	12	7	.626	2	33	16	11	175	146	30	79	0	2.26
Babe Adams	R	30	11	8	.579	0	28	20	11	170	169	35	63	2	2.91
Wilbur Cooper	L	20	3	0	1.000	0	4	3	3	38	32	15	30	2	1.66
Jack Ferry	R	25	3	0	1.000	0	6	4	3	39	33	23	10	1	3.00
2 King Cole	R	26	2	2	.500	0	12	5	2	49	61	18	11	0	6.43
Ed Warner	L	23	1	1	.500	0	11	3	1	45	40	18	13	1	3.60
1 Lefty Leifield	L	28	1	2	.333	0	6	1	1	24	29	10	8	0	4.12
Sherry Smith	L	21	0	0	—	0	4	0	1	6	4	6	1	0	6.75
Harry Gardner	R	25	0	0	—	0	1	0	0	3	1	0	0	0	0.00

CHICAGO — 3rd 91-59 .552 11.5 — FRANK CHANCE

NAME	G by Pos	B	AGE	G	AB	R	H	2B	3B	HR	RBI	BB	SO	SB	BA	SA
TOTALS			29	152	5048	756	1398	245	91	43	639	560	615	164	.277	.387
Vic Saier	1B120	L	21	122	451	74	130	25	14	2	61	34	65	11	.288	.419
Johnny Evers	2B143	L	30	143	478	73	163	23	11	1	63	74	16	16	.341	.441
Joe Tinker	SS142	R	31	142	550	80	155	24	7	5	75	38	21	25	.282	.351
Heinie Zimmerman	3B121,1B22	R	25	145	557	95	207	41	14	14	99	38	60	23	.372	.571
Wildfire Schulte	OF139	L	29	139	553	90	146	27	11	13	64	53	70	17	.264	.423
2 Tommy Leach	OF73,3B4	R	34	82	265	50	64	10	3	2	32	50	20	14	.242	.325
Jimmy Sheckard	OF146	L	33	146	523	85	128	22	10	3	47	122	81	15	.245	.342
Jimmy Archer	C118	R	29	120	385	35	109	20	3	5	58	22	36	7	.283	.384
Ward Miller	OF64	L	27	86	241	45	74	11	4	0	22	26	18	11	.307	.386
2 Red Downs	2B16,SS9,3B5	R	28	43	95	9	25	4	3	1	14	9	17	5	.263	.400
Wilbur Good	OF10	L	26	39	35	7	5	0	0	0	3	3	5	1	.143	.143
1 Solly Hofman (IL)	OF27,1B9	R	29	36	125	28	34	11	0	0	18	22	13	5	.272	.360
Tom Needham	C32	R	33	33	90	12	16	5	0	0	10	7	13	3	.178	.233
Cy Williams	OF22	L	24	28	62	3	15	1	1	0	1	6	14	2	.242	.290
Ed Lennox	3B24	R	22	28	81	13	19	4	1	1	16	12	10	1	.235	.346
Dick Cotter	C24	R	22	26	54	6	15	0	2	0	1	6	13	0	.278	.352
2 Tom Downey	SS5,3B3,2B1	R	28	13	22	4	4	0	0	0	1	2	4	1	.182	.273

Charlie Moore 27 R 2-9, Frank Chance 35 R 1-5, Mike Hechinger 22 R 0-3, Harry Chapman 24 R 1-4, George Yantz 25 R 1-1

NAME	T	AGE	W	L	PCT	SV	G	GS	CG	IP	H	BB	SO	SHO	ERA
		30	91	59	.607	9	152	152	80	1359	1307	493	554	15	3.42
Larry Cheney	R	26	26	10	.722	0	42	37	28	303	262	111	140	4	2.85
Lew Richie	R	28	16	8	.667	0	39	27	15	238	222	74	69	4	2.95
Jimmy Lavender	R	28	16	13	.552	3	42	31	15	252	240	89	109	3	3.03
Ed Reulbach	R	29	10	6	.625	4	39	19	8	169	161	60	75	0	3.78
2 Lefty Leifield	L	28	7	2	.778	0	13	9	4	71	68	21	23	1	2.41
Charlie Smith	R	32	7	4	.636	1	20	5	1	94	92	31	47	0	4.21
Three Finger Brown	R	35	5	6	.455	0	15	8	5	89	92	20	34	2	2.63
Jim Moroney	R	28	1	1	.500	1	10	3	1	24	25	17	5	0	4.50
Fred Toney	R	23	1	2	.333	0	9	2	0	24	21	11	9	0	5.25
1 King Cole	R	26	1	2	.333	0	9	3	0	19	36	8	9	0	10.89
Harry McIntire	R	34	1	3	.333	0	4	3	2	24	22	6	9	0	3.75
Len Madden	R	21	0	1	.000	0	2	1	0	12	16	9	5	0	3.00
Grover Lowdermilk	R	27	0	0	—	0	2	1	1	13	17	14	8	0	9.69
Rudy Sommers	L	24	0	1	.000	0	3	0	0	3	4	2	0	0	3.00
George Pierce	L	24	0	0	—	0	3	0	0	15	15	12	9	0	5.40
Dick Cottrell	L	23	0	0	—	0	2	0	0	4	8	1	1	0	9.00
Bill Powell	R	27	0	0	—	0	2	0	0	2	2	1	0	0	9.00
Joe Vernon	R	22	0	0	—	0	4	0	0	4	6	1	0	0	11.25

Orvie Overall (VR) 31

CINCINNATI — 4th 75-78 .490 29 — HANK O'DAY

NAME	G by Pos	B	AGE	G	AB	R	H	2B	3B	HR	RBI	BB	SO	SB	BA	SA
TOTALS			27	155	5115	656	1310	183	89	21	565	479	492	248	.256	.339
Dick Hoblitzell	1B147	L	23	148	558	73	164	32	12	2	85	48	28	23	.294	.405
Dick Egan	2B149	R	28	149	507	69	125	14	5	0	52	56	26	24	.247	.294
Jimmy Esmond	SS74	R	22	82	231	24	45	5	3	1	40	20	31	11	.195	.255
Art Phelan	3B127,2B3	R	24	130	461	56	112	9	11	3	54	46	37	25	.243	.330
Mike Mitchell	OF144	R	32	147	552	60	156	14	13	4	78	41	43	23	.283	.377
Armando Marsans	OF98,1B6	R	25	110	416	59	132	19	7	1	38	20	17	35	.317	.404
Bob Bescher	OF143	B	28	145	548	120	154	29	11	4	38	83	61	67	.281	.396
Larry McLean	C98	R	30	102	333	17	81	15	1	1	27	16	15	1	.243	.303
Eddie Grant	SS56,3B15	L	29	96	255	37	61	6	1	2	20	18	27	11	.239	.294
Johnny Bates	OF65	L	30	81	239	45	69	12	7	1	29	47	16	10	.289	.410
Tommy Clarke	C63	R	24	72	146	19	41	7	2	0	22	28	14	9	.281	.356
Tex McDonald	SS42	R	23	61	140	16	36	3	4	1	15	13	24	5	.257	.357
Hank Severeid	C20,1B7,OF6	R	21	50	114	10	27	0	3	0	13	8	11	0	.237	.289
Pete Knisely	OF13,2B3,1B1	R	28	21	67	10	22	7	3	0	4	5	8	0	.328	.522
Rafael Almeida	3B16	R	25	16	59	6	13	4	3	0	10	5	8	0	.220	.390
Andy Kyle	OF7	L	24	9	21	3	7	1	0	0	4	4	2	0	.333	.381
2 Earl Blackburn	C1	R	19	1	5	0	0	0	0	0	0	0	1	0	.000	.000

NAME	T	AGE	W	L	PCT	SV	G	GS	CG	IP	H	BB	SO	SHO	ERA
		28	75	78	.490	10	155	155	82	1378	1455	452	561	13	3.42
George Suggs	R	30	19	16	.543	2	42	36	25	303	320	56	104	5	2.94
Rube Benton	L	22	18	21	.462	2	50	39	22	302	316	118	162	2	3.10
Art Fromme	R	28	16	18	.471	0	43	37	23	296	285	88	120	3	2.74
Bert Humpries	R	31	9	11	.450	2	30	15	9	159	162	36	58	1	3.22
Jim Bagby	R	22	0	0	—	1	4	0	0	17	17	9	10	0	3.18
Frank Gregory	R	23	2	0	1.000	0	4	2	1	16	19	7	4	0	4.50
2 John Frill	R	33	1	0	1.000	0	2	1	0	15	22	7	5	0	7.11
Howard McGraner	L	22	1	0	1.000	0	2	1	1	9	7	3	6	0	4.50
Ed Donalds	R	27	1	0	1.000	0	4	1	0	4	7	0	1	0	4.50
Gene Packard	L	24	1	0	1.000	0	3	1	0	8	8	2	4	0	3.00
Frank Smith	R	32	1	0	.500	0	7	3	1	23	34	15	5	0	6.26
2 Ralph Works	R	24	1	1	.500	0	7	1	1	10	4	5	5	0	2.70
Frank Harter	R	25	1	2	.333	0	6	5	3	35	35	11	12	0	3.11
Bobby Keefe	R	30	1	3	.250	0	17	6	0	69	78	33	29	0	5.22
Harry Gaspar	R	29	1	3	.250	0	7	2	0	37	38	16	13	1	4.14
Dixie Davis	R	21	0	0	—	0	2	1	0	15	15	12	10	0	2.66
Gene Moore	L	26	0	1	.000	0	5	2	0	16	11	3	4	0	3.00
Sam Fletcher	R	31	0	0	—	0	3	1	0	10	15	11	3	0	11.70
Ben Taylor	R	33	0	0	—	0	2	0	0	3	2	3	2	0	3.00
Bill Cramer	R	21	0	0	—	0	2	0	0	2	8	2	0	0	0.00
Bill Doak	R	21	0	0	—	0	2	0	0	4	4	0	2	0	0.00
Hanson Horsey	R	22	0	0	—	0	2	0	0	4	14	3	0	0	22.50
Bill Prough	R	24	0	0	—	0	2	0	0	3	7	1	0	0	6.00
Chuck Thompkins	R	22	0	0	—	0	3	0	0	3	5	1	0	0	0.00

PHILADELPHIA — 5th 73-79 .480 30.5 — RED DOOIN

NAME	G by Pos	B	AGE	G	AB	R	H	2B	3B	HR	RBI	BB	SO	SB	BA	SA
TOTALS			30	152	5077	670	1354	244	68	43	570	464	615	159	.267	.368
Fred Luderus	1B146	L	26	148	572	77	147	31	5	10	69	44	65	8	.257	.381
Otto Knabe	2B123	R	28	126	426	56	108	14	0	0	46	55	20	16	.282	.326
Mickey Doolan	SS146	R	32	146	532	47	137	26	6	1	62	34	59	6	.258	.335
Hans Lobert	3B64	R	30	65	257	37	84	12	5	2	33	19	13	13	.327	.436
Gavvy Cravath	OF113	R	31	130	436	63	124	30	9	11	70	47	77	6	.284	.470
Dode Paskert	OF141,2B2,3B1	R	30	145	540	102	170	37	5	2	43	67	46	36	.315	.413
Sherry Magee	OF124,1B6	R	27	132	464	79	142	25	9	6	66	55	54	30	.306	.438
Bill Killefer	C85	R	24	85	268	18	60	6	1	0	21	4	14	6	.224	.280
Red Dooin	C58	R	33	69	184	20	43	9	0	0	22	5	12	8	.234	.283
2 Doc Miller	OF40	L	29	67	177	24	51	12	5	0	21	9	13	5	.288	.412
1 Tom Downey	2B46,SS1,3B3	R	28	54	171	27	50	6	3	1	23	21	20	3	.292	.380
Jimmy Walsh	2B31,3B12,C5	R	26	51	150	16	40	6	3	2	19	8	20	3	.267	.387
1 John Titus	OF42	L	36	45	157	43	43	9	5	3	22	33	14	6	.274	.452
John Dodge	3B23,2B5,SS1	R	23	30	92	3	11	1	0	0	4	3	11	2	.120	.130
Peaches Graham	C19	R	35	24	59	6	17	1	0	1	6	4	8	1	.288	.356
Jack Boyle	3B6,SS2	L	23	22	15	2	5	4	1	0	0	1	7	1	.333	.733
Pat Moran	C13	R	36	13	28	8	14	2	2	0	4	5	1	0	.500	.714
2 Cozy Dolan	3B11	R	29	28	50	8	14	2	2	0	7	3	10	3	.280	.400
George Mangus	OF5	L	22	10	25	2	9	0	0	0	3	4	2	0	.360	.360
Bill Brinker	3B2,OF2	R	28	19	9	1	2	0	0	0	1	0	4	0	.222	.278
George Browne	3B1	R	36	6	5	1	1	0	0	0	0	0	1	0	.200	.200

Gene Steinbrenner 19 R 2-9, Jim Savage 28 B 0-3, Mike Loan 17 R 1-2

NAME	T	AGE	W	L	PCT	SV	G	GS	CG	IP	H	BB	SO	SHO	ERA
		25	73	79	.480	9	152	152	82	1355	1381	515	616	10	3.25
Pete Alexander	R	25	19	17	.528	3	46	34	26	310	289	105	195	3	2.82
Tom Seaton	R	24	16	12	.571	2	44	27	16	255	246	106	118	2	3.28
Ad Brennan	L	24	11	9	.550	2	27	19	13	174	185	49	78	1	3.57
Eppa Rixey	L	21	10	10	.500	0	23	20	10	162	147	54	59	3	2.50
Earl Moore	R	33	9	14	.391	0	31	24	10	182	186	77	79	1	3.31
George Chalmers	R	24	3	4	.429	0	12	8	3	58	64	37	22	0	3.26
2 Red Nelson	R	30	1	0	1.000	0	2	1	1	19	25	6	5	0	3.79
1 Cliff Curtis	R	29	1	5	.167	0	10	8	1	59	75	35	20	0	3.24
Toots Schultz	R	23	1	4	.200	0	12	4	1	59	75	35	20	0	4.58
Erskine Mayer	R	22	1	1	.500	0	4	1	0	21	27	7	5	0	6.43
Rube Marshall	R	22	0	0	—	0	14	4	0	46	50	10	10	0	2.55
Happy Finneran	R	21	0	0	—	0	3	1	0	14	19	11	10	0	3.21
Huck Wallace	L	29	0	0	—	0	1	0	0	2	4	1	0	0	4.50
Hank Ritter	R	18	0	0	—	0	1	0	0	1	2	0	0	0	4.50
Frank Nicholson	R	22	0	0	—	0	3	0	0	3	5	1	0	0	6.75

ST. LOUIS 6th 63-90 .412 36 ROGER BRENAHAN

NAME	G by Pos	B	AGE	G	AB	R	H	2B	3B	HR	RBI	BB	SO	SB	BA	SA
TOTALS			26	153	5092	659	1366	190	77	27	561	508	620	193	.268	.352
Ed Konetchy	1B142, OF1	R	26	143	538	81	169	26	13	8	82	62	66	25	.314	.455
Miller Huggins	2B114	B	34	120	431	82	131	16	4	0	29	87	31	35	.304	.357
Arnold Hauser	SS132	R	23	133	479	73	124	14	7	1	42	39	69	26	.259	.324
Mike Mowrey	3B108	R	28	114	408	59	104	13	8	2	50	46	29	19	.255	.341
Steve Evans	OF134	R	27	135	491	59	139	23	9	6	72	36	51	11	.283	.403
Rebel Oakes	OF136	L	28	136	495	57	139	19	5	3	58	31	24	26	.281	.358
Lee Magee	OF85, 2B23, 1B6, SS1	B	23	128	468	60	133	13	8	0	40	39	29	16	.290	.354
Ivy Wingo	C92	L	21	100	310	38	82	18	8	2	44	23	45	3	.265	.394
Rube Ellis	OF76	L	26	109	305	47	82	18	2	4	33	34	36	6	.269	.380
Wally Smith	3B32, SS22, 1B6	R	24	75	219	22	56	5	5	0	26	29	27	4	.256	.324
Jack Bliss	C41	R	30	49	114	11	28	3	1	0	18	19	14	1	.246	.289
Roger Bresnahan (IL)	C28	R	33	48	108	8	36	7	2	1	15	14	9	4	.333	.463
Denny Willie	OF16	L	21	30	48	2	11	0	1	0	6	7	9	0	.229	.271
Bad News Galloway	2B16, SS1	B	24	21	54	4	10	2	0	0	4	5	8	2	.185	.222
Frank Gilhooley	OF11	L	20	13	49	5	11	0	0	0	2	3	8	0	.224	.224
Elmer Miller	OF11	R	25	12	37	5	7	1	0	0	3	4	9	1	.189	.216
Possum Whitted	3B12	R	22	12	46	7	12	3	0	0	7	3	5	1	.261	.326
Frank Snyder	C11	R	18	11	18	2	2	0	0	0	0	2	7	1	.111	.111
John Kelleher	3B3	R	18	8	12	0	4	1	0	0	1	0	2	0	.333	.417
Ted Cather	OF5	R	23	5	19	4	8	1	1	0	2	0	4	1	.421	.579

Roy Rolling 25 R 3-15, Jim Clark 24 R 0-1, Ed Burns 24 R 0-1, John Mercer 20 L 0-1, Mike Murphy 23 R 0-1

NAME	T	AGE	W	L	PCT	SV	G	GS	CG	IP	H	BB	SO	SHO	ERA
		25	63	90	.412	12	153	153	62	1353	1466	560	487	6	3.85
Bob Harmon	R	24	18	18	.500	0	43	34	15	268	284	116	73	3	3.93
Slim Sallee	L	27	16	17	.485	6	48	32	20	294	289	72	108	3	2.60
Bill Steele	R	26	9	13	.409	2	40	25	7	194	245	66	67	0	4.69
Rube Geyer	R	28	7	14	.333	0	41	18	6	181	191	84	61	0	3.28
Joe Willis	L	22	4	9	.308	2	31	17	4	130	143	62	55	0	4.43
Dan Griner	R	24	3	4	.429	0	12	7	2	54	59	15	20	0	3.17
Phil Redding	R	22	2	1	.667	0	3	3	2	25	31	11	9	0	5.04
Pol Perritt	R	20	1	1	.500	0	6	3	1	31	25	10	13	0	3.19
Lou Lowdermilk	L	25	1	1	.500	1	4	1	1	15	14	9	2	0	3.00
2 Sandy Burk	R	25	1	3	.250	1	12	4	2	45	37	12	17	0	2.40
Gene Woodburn	R	25	1	4	.200	0	20	5	1	48	60	42	25	0	5.63
Gene Dale	R	23	0	5	.000	0	19	3	1	62	76	51	37	0	6.53
Wheezer Dell	R	26	0	0	—	0	3	0	0	2	3	0	1	0	13.50
Roland Howell	R	20	0	0	—	0	3	0	0	2	5	5	0	0	22.50
Bob Ewing	R	39	0	0	—	0	1	0	1	2	1	1	0	0	0.00
George Zackert	L	27	0	0	—	0	1	0	1	0	1	0	0	0	18.00

BROOKLYN 7th 58-95 .379 46 BILL DAHLEN

NAME	G by Pos	B	AGE	G	AB	R	H	2B	3B	HR	RBI	BB	SO	SB	BA	SA
TOTALS			26	153	5141	651	1377	220	73	32	561	490	584	179	.268	.358
Jake Daubert	1B143	L	28	145	559	81	172	19	16	3	66	48	45	29	.308	.415
George Cutshaw	2B91, 3B5, SS1	R	25	102	357	41	100	14	4	0	28	31	16	16	.280	.342
Bert Tooley	SS76	R	25	77	265	34	62	6	5	2	37	19	21	12	.234	.317
Red Smith	3B125	R	22	128	486	75	139	28	6	4	57	54	51	22	.286	.393
Hub Northen	OF102	L	25	118	412	54	116	26	6	3	46	41	46	8	.282	.396
Herbie Moran	OF129	R	28	130	508	77	140	18	10	1	40	69	38	26	.276	.356
Zack Wheat (NJ)	OF122	L	24	123	453	70	138	28	7	8	65	39	40	16	.305	.450
Otto Miller	C94	R	23	98	316	35	88	18	1	1	31	18	50	11	.278	.351
John Hummel	2B58, OF44, 1B11	R	29	122	411	55	116	21	7	5	54	49	55	7	.282	.404
Bobby Fisher	SS74, 2B1, 3B1	R	25	82	257	27	60	10	3	0	26	14	32	7	.233	.296
Jud Daley	OF55	L	28	61	199	22	51	9	1	1	13	24	17	2	.256	.327
Tex Erwin	C41	R	26	59	133	14	28	3	0	2	14	18	16	1	.211	.278
Eddie Phelps	C32	R	33	52	111	8	32	4	0	0	23	16	15	1	.288	.378
Enos Kirkpatrick	3B29, SS3	R	27	32	94	13	18	1	1	0	6	9	15	5	.191	.223
Casey Stengel	OF17	L	21	17	57	9	18	1	0	1	13	15	9	5	.316	.386
1 Red Downs	2B9	R	28	9	8	2	8	1	0	0	3	1	5	3	.250	.344
Dolly Stark	SS7	R	27	8	22	2	4	0	0	0	2	1	3	2	.182	.182
Bob Higgins	C1	R	25	1	2	0	0	0	0	0	0	0	0	0	.000	.000

NAME	T	AGE	W	L	PCT	SV	G	GS	CG	IP	H	BB	SO	SHO	ERA
		26	58	95	.379	8	153	153	71	1357	1399	510	553	10	3.64
Nap Rucker	L	27	18	21	.462	4	45	34	23	298	272	72	151	6	2.21
Eddie Stack	R	24	7	5	.583	1	28	17	4	142	139	55	45	0	3.36
Elmer Knetzer	R	26	7	9	.438	0	33	16	4	140	135	70	61	1	4.56
Pat Ragan	R	26	7	18	.280	1	36	26	12	208	211	65	101	1	3.63
Earl Yingling	L	23	6	11	.353	0	25	16	12	163	186	56	51	1	3.59
Maury Kent	R	26	5	5	.500	0	20	9	2	93	107	46	24	1	4.84
2 Cliff Curtis	R	30	4	7	.364	1	19	9	3	80	72	37	22	0	3.94
Frank Allen	L	23	3	9	.250	0	20	15	5	109	119	57	58	1	3.63
Cy Barger	R	27	1	9	.100	0	16	11	6	94	120	42	30	0	5.46
Bill Schardt	R	26	0	1	.000	1	7	0	0	21	25	6	7	0	4.28
1 Sandy Burk	R	25	0	0	—	0	2	0	0	8	9	3	2	0	3.38
Eddie Dent	R	24	0	0	—	0	1	0	0	4	1	1	0	0	36.00

BOSTON 8th 52-101 .340 52 JOHNNY KLING

NAME	G by Pos	B	AGE	G	AB	R	H	2B	3B	HR	RBI	BB	SO	SB	BA	SA
TOTALS			28	155	5361	693	1465	227	68	35	605	454	691	137	.273	.361
Ben Houser	1B83	L	28	108	332	38	95	17	3	8	52	22	29	1	.286	.428
Bill Sweeney	2B153	R	26	153	593	84	204	31	13	1	100	68	34	27	.344	.445
Frank O'Rourke	SS59	R	20	61	196	11	24	3	1	0	16	11	50	1	.122	.148
Ed McDonald	3B118	R	25	121	459	70	119	23	6	2	34	70	91	22	.259	.349
2 John Titus	OF96	R	36	96	345	56	112	23	6	2	48	49	20	5	.325	.443
Vin Campbell	OF144	R	24	145	624	102	185	32	9	3	48	32	44	19	.296	.319
George Jackson	OF107	R	30	110	397	55	104	13	5	4	48	38	72	22	.262	.350
Johnny Kling	C74	R	36	81	252	26	80	10	3	2	30	15	30	3	.317	.405
Art Devlin	1B69, SS26, 3B26, OF1	R	32	124	436	59	126	18	8	0	54	51	37	11	.289	.367
Jay Kirke	OF71, 3B32, 1B1	L	24	103	359	53	115	11	4	4	62	9	46	7	.320	.407
Bill Rariden	C73	R	24	79	247	27	55	3	1	1	14	18	35	3	.223	.255
1 Doc Miller	OF50	L	27	51	201	26	47	8	1	2	24	14	17	6	.234	.313
Hank Gowdy	C22, 1B7	R	22	44	96	16	26	6	1	3	10	16	13	3	.271	.448
Al Bridwell (FJ)	SS31	L	20	31	106	6	25	5	1	0	14	7	6	2	.236	.302
Harry Spratt	SS23	L	24	27	89	6	23	3	2	3	15	7	11	2	.258	.438
Rabbit Maranville	SS26	R	20	26	86	8	18	2	0	0	8	9	14	1	.209	.233
Al Kaiser	OF4	R	25	4	13	0	0	0	0	0	0	0	3	0	.000	.000
Joe Schultz	2B4	R	18	4	12	1	3	1	0	0	4	0	0	0	.250	.333
Dave Sheen	SS4	R	18	4	10	1	3	0	0	0	2	0	0	0	.300	.300
Bill Jones		L	25	3	2	1	0	0	0	0	0	0	0	0	.500	.500
Gil Whitehouse	C2	B	18	2	6	0	0	0	0	0	0	0	3	0	.000	.000
Mike Gonz	C1	R	21	4	1	0	0	0	0	0	0	0	1	0	.000	.000
Art Schvino	3B1	B	22	1	2	0	1	0	0	0	0	0	0	0	.500	.500

NAME	T	AGE	W	L	PCT	SV	G	GS	CG	IP	H	BB	SO	SHO	ERA
		30	52	101	.340	5	155	155	92	1391	1544	521	542	4	4.17
Hub Perdue	R	30	13	16	.448	3	37	30	20	249	295	54	101	1	3.80
Otto Hess	L	33	12	17	.414	0	33	31	21	256	270	90	80	0	3.76
Lefty Tyler	L	22	12	22	.353	0	42	31	18	256	262	126	144	0	4.19
Ed Donnelly	R	32	5	10	.333	0	37	18	10	184	225	72	67	0	4.36
Buster Brown	R	30	4	15	.211	0	31	21	13	168	146	66	68	4	4.00
Walt Dickson	R	33	3	19	.136	1	36	20	9	189	233	61	47	1	3.86
Bill McTigue	L	21	2	0	1.000	0	10	1	1	35	39	18	17	0	5.40
Brad Hogg	R	23	1	1	.500	1	10	1	0	31	37	16	12	0	6.97
Al Mattern	R	29	0	1	.000	0	2	1	0	10	11	3	0	0	7.50
Hank Griffin	R	25	0	0	—	0	3	0	0	2	3	3	0	0	22.50
Rube Kroh	L	25	0	0	—	0	2	0	0	8	6	1	0	0	6.00
2 Steve White	R	27	0	0	—	0	3	0	0	6	8	1	0	0	6.00
King Brady	R	31	0	0	—	0	1	0	0	3	3	0	0	0	18.00
Bill Brady	R	22	0	0	—	0	1	0	0	2	2	1	0	0	0.00

WORLD SERIES — BOSTON (AL) 4 NEW YORK (NL) 3 (One Tie)

LINE SCORES

TEAM	1	2	3	4	5	6	7	8	9	10	11	12	R	H	E

Game 1 October 8 at New York
BOS(AL) 000 001 300 4 6 1
NY(NL) 002 000 001 3 8 1
Wood   Tesreau, Crandall (8)

Game 2 October 9 at Boston
NY 010 100 030 10 6 11 5
BOS 300 010 010 10 6 10 1
Mathewson Collins, Hall, Bedient (11) Game called by darkness

Game 3 October 10 at Boston
NY 010 010 000 2 7 1
BOS 000 000 001 1 7 0
Marquard O'Brien, Bedient (9)

Game 4 October 11 at New York
BOS 010 100 001 3 8 1
NY 000 000 010 1 9 1
Wood Tesreau, Ames (8)

Game 5 October 12 at Boston
NY 000 000 100 1 3 1
BOS 002 000 00X 2 5 1
Mathewson Bedient

Game 6 October 14 at New York
BOS 020 000 000 2 7 2
NY 500 000 00X 5 11 2
O'Brien,Collins (2), Marquard

Game 7 October 15 at Boston
NY 610 000 2 1 0 11 16 4
BOS 010 000 2 1 0 4 9 3
Tesreau Wood, Hall (2)

Game 8 October 16 at Boston
NY 001 000 000 1 2 9 2
BOS 000 000 100 2 3 8 5
Mathewson Bedient, Wood (8)

COMPOSITE BATTING

NAME	POS	G	AB	R	H	2B	3B	HR	RBI	BA
Boston (AL)										
Totals		8	273	25	60	14	6	1	21	.220
Stahl	1B	8	32	3	8	2	0	0	2	.250
Yerkes	2B	8	32	3	8	0	2	0	4	.250
Lewis	OF	8	32	4	6	3	0	0	2	.188
Hooper	OF	8	31	3	9	2	1	0	2	.290
Speaker	OF	8	30	4	9	1	2	0	2	.300
Wagner	SS	8	30	1	5	1	0	0	0	.167
Gardner	3B	8	28	4	5	2	1	1	4	.179
Cady	C	7	22	3	3	0	0	0	1	.136
Wood	P	4	7	1	2	0	0	0	0	.286
Carrigan	C	2	7	0	0	0	0	0	0	.000
Bedient	P	4	6	0	0	0	0	0	0	.000
Collins	P	2	5	0	0	0	0	0	0	.000
Hall	P	2	4	0	3	1	0	0	0	.750
Engle	PH	3	3	1	1	0	0	0	2	.333
O'Brien	P	2	2	0	0	0	0	0	0	.000
Hendriksen	PH-PR	2	1	0	1	0	0	0	1	1.000
Ball	PH	1	1	0	0	0	0	0	0	.000
New York (NL)										
Totals		8	274	31	74	14	4	1	25	.270
Merkle	1B	8	33	5	9	2	1	0	3	.273
Doyle	2B	8	33	5	8	1	0	1	2	.242
Snodgrass	OF	8	33	2	7	2	0	0	0	.212
Murray	OF	8	31	5	10	2	0	0	5	.323
Herzog	3B	8	30	6	12	4	1	0	4	.400
Meyers	C	8	28	2	10	0	1	0	3	.357
Fletcher	SS	8	28	1	5	1	0	0	3	.179
Davore	OF	7	24	4	6	0	0	0	0	.250
Mathewson	P	3	12	0	2	0	0	0	0	.167
Tesreau	P	3	8	0	3	0	0	0	0	.375
McCormick	PH	2	4	1	1	0	0	0	0	.250
Becker	OF	2	4	1	0	0	0	0	0	.000
Marquard	P	2	4	0	0	0	0	0	0	.000
Wilson	C	2	1	0	1	0	0	0	0	1.000
Crandall	P	1	1	0	0	0	0	0	0	.000
Shafer	SS	3	0	0	0	0	0	0	0	—
Ames	P	1	1	0	0	0	0	0	0	.000

COMPOSITE PITCHING

NAME	G	IP	H	BB	SO	W	L	SV	ERA
Boston (AL)									
Totals	8	74	74	22	39	4	3	0	2.80
Wood	4	22	27	3	21	3	1	0	3.68
Bedient	2	18	10	7	7	1	0	0	1.00
Collins	2	14.1	14	0	6	0	0	0	1.88
Hall	2	10.2	11	9	1	0	0	0	3.38
O'Brien	2	9	12	3	4	0	2	0	5.00
New York (NL)									
Totals	8	73.2	60	19	36	3	4	0	1.71
Mathewson	3	28.2	23	5	10	0	2	0	1.25
Tesreau	3	23	19	11	15	1	2	0	3.13
Marquard	2	18	14	2	9	2	0	0	0.50
Crandall	1	2	1	0	2	0	0	0	0.00
Ames	1	2	3	1	0	0	0	0	4.50

1913 Offenses and Defenses Along the Eastern Front

A pennant race was nary in sight as the Athletics and Giants ran away and hid from their competitors. Connie Mack's Athletics quickly squelched any suspense in the American League chase by moving out into first place in late April and never relinquishing the position. The Athletic pitching suffered from the loss of Jack Coombs to illness, but Mack covered himself by using veterans Eddie Plank and Chief Bender in double duty as starters and as relievers for young starters Broadwalk Brown, Joe Bush, and Duke Houck. For a change, the Athletic offense carried the main responsibility for victory. Stuffy McInnis, Eddie Collins, and Frank Baker all hit .320 or better, and Baker won his third consecutive homer title with a total of 12. These three, along with shortstop Jack Barry, had earned the respect of fans as the class infield of their era.

Washington again captured second place, due to good pitching, and the batting duo of Nap Lajoie and Joe Jackson propelled Cleveland into third place. Boston fell from first in 1912 to a distant fourth place, costing Manager Jake Stahl his job in mid-season, less than a year after winning the World Series. More than the Red Sox hitters' inability to match their 1912 run production, the big blow to Boston was Joe Wood's broken hand, which limited him to eleven victories. Detroit went through the season without the confrontation which troubled them in 1912, but were again relegated to a dismal sixth-place finish because of poor pitching.

The National League race also revealed no surprises as the New York Giants recovered from a slow start to coast to a third consecutive pennant. A pitching staff led by three 20-game winners, screwballer Christy Mathewson, fastballer Rube Marquard, and spitballer Jeff Tesreau, allowed the lowest total of runs in the league. Infielders Larry Doyle and Art Fletcher acted as sparkplugs for a Giant attack which was third in the loop in run production.

The Philadelphia Phillies surprised all by finishing in second place, 12½ games out. Young pitchers Tom Seaton and Grover "Pete" Alexander excelled in 20-game winning seasons, and Gavvy Cravath led the attack with a .341 mark and a league-pacing 19 home runs.

The Cubs finished third in a year of rebuilding under the new managership of second baseman Johnny Evers. Former manager Frank Chance was released before the season began, pitcher Ed Reulbach was traded to Brooklyn, and shortstop Joe Tinker and pitching ace Three Finger Brown were dispatched to Cincinnati. All things considered, Evers' feat of bringing the Cubs home third was an admirable achievement. His two former cohorts, Chance and Tinker, did not fare as well in their new managerial roles. Chance managed the New York Yankees and Tinker the Reds, with both clubs finishing a poor seventh. Brooklyn finished sixth with batting champ Jack Daubert, a rookie outfielder named Casey Stengel, and a new home in Ebbets Field.

John McGraw again had no luck in the World Series as Mack's Athletics defeated McGraw's Giants in five games. The Giant pitchers shaped up better on paper, but Bender, Plank, and Bush all pitched complete game victories for the Mackmen. Frank Baker and Eddie Collins were Series stars with .400 batting marks.

The end of the season was marked by the announcement that the Federal League, an independent minor circuit, planned to expand to major league status by raiding the rosters of the National and American League teams. The Federals showed their serious intentions by signing Joe Tinker and Three Finger Brown to contracts soon after the season's end. It seemed that baseball would have to contend with its own war, much as would Europe, also preparing to protect itself against a more ominous intruder.

1913 AMERICAN LEAGUE

NAME	G by Pos	B	AGE	G	AB	R	H	2B	3B	HR	RBI	BB	SO	SB	BA	SA
PHILADELPHIA	**1st 96-57 .627**															
TOTALS			25	153	5044	794	1412	223	80	33	660	534	547	221	.280	.375
Stuffy McInnis	1B148	R	22	148	543	79	177	30	4	4	90	45	31	16	.326	.418
Eddie Collins	2B148	L	26	148	534	125	184	23	13	3	73	85	37	54	.345	.453
Jack Barry	SS134	R	26	134	455	62	125	20	6	3	85	44	32	15	.275	.365
Frank Baker	3B149	L	27	149	565	116	190	34	9	12	117	63	31	34	.336	.492
Eddie Murphy	OF135	L	21	136	508	105	150	14	7	1	30	70	44	21	.295	.356
Jimmy Walsh	OF88	L	27	94	303	56	77	16	5	0	27	38	40	15	.254	.340
Rube Oldring	OF136, SS5	R	29	136	538	101	152	27	9	5	71	34	37	40	.283	.394
Jack Lapp	C77, 1B1	L	28	81	238	23	54	4	4	1	20	37	26	1	.227	.290
Amos Strunk	OF80	L	24	93	292	30	89	11	12	0	46	29	23	14	.305	.425
Wally Schang	C71	B	23	76	207	32	55	16	3	3	30	34	44	4	.266	.415
Tom Daley	OF38	L	28	59	141	13	36	2	1	0	11	13	28	4	.255	.284
Danny Murphy	OF9	R	36	40	59	3	19	5	1	0	6	4	3	0	.322	.441
Bill Orr	SS16, 1B3, 2B2, 3B2	R	22	27	67	6	13	1	1	0	7	4	10	1	.194	.239
Ira Thomas	C21	R	32	21	53	3	15	4	1	0	6	4	0	0	.283	.396
Harry Davis	1B6	R	39	7	17	2	6	2	0	0	4	1	4	0	.353	.471
George Brickley	OF4	R	18	5	12	0	2	0	1	0	0	0	4	0	.167	.333
Harry Fritz	3B5	R	22	5	13	1	0	0	0	0	0	0	2	1	.000	.000
2 Doc Lavan	SS5	R	22	5	14	1	1	0	1	0	1	0	1	0	.071	.214
Wickey McAvoy 18 R 1-9, Press Cruthers 22 R 3-12, Joe Giebel 21 R 1-3, Monte Pfeiffer 23 R 0-3																
WASHINGTON	**2nd 90-64 .584 6.5**															
TOTALS			26	155	5074	596	1281	156	80	20	484	440	595	291	.252	.327
Chick Gandil	1B145	R	25	148	550	61	175	25	8	1	72	36	33	22	.318	.398
Ray Morgan	2B133, SS4	R	24	137	481	58	131	19	8	0	57	68	63	19	.272	.345
George McBride	SS150	R	32	150	499	52	107	18	7	1	52	43	46	12	.214	.285
Eddie Foster (IL)	3B105	R	26	106	409	56	101	11	5	1	41	36	31	25	.247	.306
Danny Moeller	OF153	B	28	153	589	88	139	15	10	5	42	72	103	62	.236	.321
Clyde Milan	OF154	L	27	154	579	92	173	18	9	3	54	58	25	75	.299	.377
Howard Shanks	OF109	R	22	109	390	38	99	11	5	1	37	15	40	23	.254	.315
John Henry	C96	R	23	96	273	26	61	8	4	1	26	30	43	5	.223	.293
Eddie Ainsmith	C79, P1	R	23	79	229	26	49	4	4	2	20	12	41	17	.214	.293
Frank LaPorte	3B46, 2B13, OF12	R	33	79	242	25	61	5	4	1	18	17	16	10	.252	.306
Rip Williams	C18, 1B8, OF5	R	31	65	106	9	30	6	2	0	12	9	16	3	.283	.406
G. Schaefer	2B17, 1B5, 3B2, OF1, P1	B	36	52	100	17	32	1	1	1	7	15	12	6	.320	.350
Joe Gedeon	OF14, 3B8, 2B2, SS1, P1	R	19	27	71	3	13	1	2	0	6	1	6	3	.183	.296
Jack Calvo	OF12	L	29	16	33	5	8	0	0	0	2	1	4	0	.242	.333
Merito Acosta	OF7	L	17	9	20	3	6	0	1	1	4	2	2	3	.300	.400
Ben Spencer	OF8	L	23	8	21	2	6	1	1	0	2	2	4	0	.286	.429
Carl Cashion (AJ)	P4, OF3	R	22	7	12	1	3	0	0	0	2	1	1	0	.250	.250
Bill Morley	2B1	R	23	2	3	0	0	0	0	0	0	1	0	0	.000	.000
Jack Ryan	C1	R	44	1	1	0	0	0	0	0	0	0	0	0	.000	.000
CLEVELAND	**3rd 86-66 .566 9.5**															
TOTALS			25	155	5030	631	1348	205	74	16	527	420	557	420	.268	.348
Doc Johnston	1B133	L	25	133	530	74	135	19	12	2	39	35	65	19	.255	.347
Nap Lajoie	2B126	R	37	137	465	66	156	25	2	1	68	33	17	17	.335	.404
Ray Chapman	SS138	R	22	140	508	78	131	19	7	3	39	46	51	29	.258	.341
Ivy Olson	3B73, 1B22, 2B1	R	27	104	370	47	92	13	3	0	32	22	28	7	.249	.300
Joe Jackson	OF148	L	23	148	528	109	197	39	17	7	71	80	26	26	.373	.551
Nemo Leibold	OF72	L	21	84	286	37	74	11	6	0	12	21	43	16	.259	.339
Jack Graney	OF148	L	27	148	517	56	138	18	12	3	68	48	55	27	.267	.366
Fred Carisch	C70	R	31	81	222	11	48	4	2	0	26	21	19	6	.216	.252
Terry Turner	3B71, 2B25, SS21	R	32	120	388	60	96	13	4	0	44	55	35	13	.247	.302
Steve O'Neill	C78	R	21	78	234	19	69	13	3	0	29	10	24	5	.295	.376
Buddy Ryan	OF67, 1B1	R	27	73	243	26	72	6	1	0	32	11	13	9	.296	.329
Joe Birmingham (BF)	OF37	R	28	47	131	16	37	9	1	0	15	8	22	7	.282	.366
2 Jack Lelivelt		L	27	23	23	0	9	2	0	0	1	1	1	0	.391	.478
Ray Bates	3B12, OF2	R	23	20	30	4	5	0	2	0	4	3	9	3	.167	.300
Grover Land (JJ)	C17	R	28	17	47	3	11	1	0	0	9	4	1	1	.234	.255
George Dunlop	SS4, 3B3	R	24	7	17	3	4	1	0	0	0	0	5	0	.235	.294
1 Johnny Beall		L	31	6	6	0	1	0	0	0	1	0	1	0	.167	.167
Larry Kopf	2B3, 3B1	B	22	5	9	1	2	0	0	0	0	1	2	0	.222	.222
Ernie Krueger	C4	L	23	5	9	1	0	0	0	0	0	2	2	0	.000	.000
Eddie Edmonson	1B1, OF1	R	23	3	11	0	0	0	0	0	0	0	0	0	.000	.000
George Young 23 L 0-2, Johnny Bassler 18 L 0-2, Josh Billings 21 R 0-3, 1 Roger Peckinpaugh 22 R 0-0, Billy Southworth 20 L 0-0, Josh Swindell 29 R 0-0																

NAME	T	AGE	W	L	PCT	SV	G	GS	CG	IP	H	BB	SO	SHO	ERA
		25	96	57	.627	21	153	153	69	1351	1200	532	630	15	3.20
Chief Bender	R	30	21	10	.677	12	48	21	16	237	208	59	135	2	2.21
Boardwalk Brown	R	28	17	11	.607	1	43	35	11	235	200	87	70	3	2.85
Eddie Plank	L	37	18	10	.643	4	41	30	18	243	211	57	151	7	2.59
Duke Houck	R	21	14	6	.700	0	41	19	4	176	147	122	71	1	4.15
Bullet Joe Bush	R	20	14	6	.700	3	39	16	5	200	199	66	81	1	3.83
Bob Shawkey	R	22	8	5	.615	0	18	15	8	111	92	50	52	1	2.35
Herb Pennock	L	19	2	1	.667	0	14	3	1	33	30	22	17	0	5.18
Weldon Wyckoff	R	21	2	4	.333	0	17	7	3	62	56	46	31	0	4.36
Bill Taff	R	23	1	0	1.000	1	7	1	0	18	22	5	9	0	6.50
Pat Bohen	R	22	0	1	.000	0	1	1	1	8	3	2	5	0	1.13
Charlie Boardman	L	20	0	2	.000	0	2	2	1	9	10	6	4	0	2.00
Dave Morey	R	24	0	0	—	0	2	0	0	4	2	2	1	0	4.50
Jack Coombs (IL)	R	30	0	0	—	0	2	2	0	5	5	6	0	0	10.80
Dick Cottrell	L	24	0	0	—	0	2	1	1	10	15	2	3	0	5.40
		25	90	64	.584	22	155	155	80	1396	1177	465	757	23	2.72
Walter Johnson	R	25	36	7	.837	3	47	36	30	346	232	38	243	11	1.14
Joe Boehling	L	22	17	7	.708	4	38	25	18	235	197	82	110	3	2.14
Bob Groom	R	28	16	16	.500	0	37	36	18	264	258	81	156	4	3.24
Joe Engel	R	20	8	9	.471	2	36	23	6	165	124	85	70	2	3.05
Long Tom Hughes	R	32	4	12	.250	7	36	13	4	130	129	61	59	0	4.29
2 George Mullin	R	32	3	5	.375	0	12	9	3	57	69	25	14	0	5.05
Doc Ayres	R	22	2	1	.333	1	4	2	1	18	12	4	17	1	1.50
Slim Love	L	22	1	0	1.000	1	5	1	0	17	14	6	5	0	1.59
Jack Bentley	L	18	1	0	1.000	1	3	1	0	11	5	2	5	0	0.00
Carl Cashion (AJ)	R	22	1	1	.500	0	4	3	0	9	7	14	3	0	6.00
Bert Gallia	R	21	1	5	.167	3	31	4	0	96	85	46	46	0	4.13
Jim Shaw	R	19	0	1	.000	0	2	1	0	13	8	7	14	0	2.08
Harry Harper	L	18	0	0	—	0	4	0	0	13	10	5	9	0	3.47
Nick Altrock	L	36	0	0	—	0	3	0	0	9	7	4	2	0	5.00
John Wilson	L	23	0	0	—	0	3	0	0	4	4	3	1	0	4.50
Tom Drohan	R	25	0	0	—	0	2	0	0	1	4	1	1	0	9.00
Mutt Williams	R	23	0	0	—	0	1	0	0	4	4	2	1	0	4.50
Eddie Ainsmith	R	23	0	0	—	0	1	0	0	2	0	0	0	0	54.00
Rex Dawson	R	24	0	0	—	0	1	0	0	1	1	0	0	0	0.00
Clark Griffith	R	43	0	0	—	0	1	0	0	1	0	0	1	0	0.00
Doc Hedgpeth	L	24	0	0	—	0	1	0	0	1	1	1	0	0	0.00
Germany Schaefer	R	36	0	0	—	0	1	0	0	1	1	0	0	0	54.00
Joe Gedeon	R	20	0	0	—	0	1	0	0	0	0	1	0	0	0.00
		26	86	66	.566	4	155	155	95	1387	1278	502	689	18	2.52
Cy Falkenberg	R	33	23	10	.700	0	39	36	23	276	238	88	166	6	2.22
Vean Gregg	L	28	20	13	.606	4	44	34	23	286	258	124	166	3	2.23
Fred Blanding	R	25	15	10	.600	0	41	22	14	235	234	72	63	3	2.55
Willie Mitchell	L	23	14	8	.636	0	34	22	14	217	153	88	141	4	1.74
George Kahler	R	23	5	11	.313	0	22	15	5	118	118	32	43	0	3.15
Bill Steen (BW)	R	25	4	5	.444	1	23	13	8	128	113	49	57	2	2.46
Nick Cullop	L	25	3	7	.300	0	11	8	4	98	105	35	30	0	4.41
Lefty James	L	24	2	1	.500	2	4	4	3	39	42	9	18	0	3.00
Jim Baskette	R	25	0	0	—	0	6	0	0	14	14	2	6	0	5.40
Lynn Brenton	R	23	0	0	—	0	2	0	0	7	4	6	3	0	9.00
Lee Dashner	R	26	0	0	—	0	2	0	0	4	4	2	1	0	4.50
Luke Glavenich	R	20	0	1	.000	0	1	0	0	3	3	1	1	0	9.00
Dave Gregg	R	22	0	0	—	0	1	0	0	1	2	1	0	0	18.00

BOSTON — 4th 79-71 .527 15.5 — JACK STAHL 39-41 .488 — BILL CARRIGAN 40-30 .571

NAME	G by Pos	B	AGE	G	AB	R	H	2B	3B	HR	RBI	BB	SO	SB	BA	SA
TOTALS			26	151	4965	630	1334	220	101	17	531	466	534	189	.269	.364
Clyde Engle	1B133, OF2	R	29	143	498	75	144	17	12	2	50	53	41	28	.289	.384
Steve Yerkes	2B129	R	25	136	483	67	129	29	6	1	48	50	32	11	.267	.358
Heinie Wagner (SA)	SS105, 2B4	R	25	110	365	43	83	14	8	2	34	40	29	9	.227	.326
Larry Gardner	3B130	L	27	131	473	64	133	17	10	0	63	47	34	18	.281	.359
Harry Hooper	OF147	L	25	148	586	100	169	29	12	4	40	60	51	26	.288	.397
Tris Speaker	OF139	L	25	141	520	94	189	35	22	3	71	65	22	46	.363	.533
Duffy Lewis	OF142	R	24	149	524	54	164	31	12	0	90	30	55	12	.298	.397
Bill Carrigan	C81	R	29	85	256	17	62	15	5	0	28	27	26	6	.242	.340
Hal Janvrin	SS48,3B19, 2B8, 1B6	R	20	86	276	18	57	5	1	3	25	23	27	17	.207	.264
Hick Cady	C38	R	27	39	96	10	24	5	2	0	6	5	14	1	.250	.344
Pinch Thomas	C30	L	25	37	91	6	26	1	2	1	15	2	11	1	.286	.374
Olaf Henriksen (IL)	OF7	L	25	30	40	8	15	1	0	0	2	7	5	3	.375	.400
Wally Rehg	OF27	R	24	30	101	13	28	3	2	0	9	2	7	4	.277	.347
Les Nunamaker	C27	R	24	29	65	9	14	5	2	0	9	4	8	2	.215	.354
Neal Ball	2B10, SS8, 3B1	R	33	21	58	9	10	2	0	0	4	9	13	3	.172	.207
Bill Mundy	1B14	L	24	15	47	4	12	0	0	0	4	4	12	0	.255	.255
Wally Snell	C1	R	24	2	4	1	3	0	0	0	0	0	0	1	.275	.375
Jack Stahl		R	33	2	2	0	0	0	0	0	0	0	1	0	.000	.000

NAME	T	AGE	W	L	PCT	SV	G	GS	CG	IP	H	BB	SO	SHO	ERA
TOTALS		25	79	71	.527	15	151	151	87	1358	1323	442	710	12	2.93
Ray Collins	L	26	19	8	.704	0	30	30	19	247	242	37	88	3	2.63
Hugh Bedient	R	23	15	14	.517	5	43	28	19	259	255	67	122	1	2.78
Dutch Leonard	R	21	14	16	.467	1	42	28	14	259	245	94	144	3	2.39
Smoky Joe Wood (BH)	R	23	11	5	.688	3	23	18	12	146	120	61	123	1	2.29
Earl Moseley	R	25	9	5	.643	0	24	15	7	121	105	49	62	3	3.12
Charley Hall	R	28	4	4	.500	5	21	10	2	105	97	46	48	0	3.43
1 Buck O'Brien	R	31	4	9	.308	0	15	12	6	90	103	35	54	0	3.70
Rube Foster	R	25	3	4	.429	1	19	8	4	68	64	28	36	1	3.18
Fred Anderson	R	27	0	6	.000	0	10	8	4	57	84	21	32	0	6.00
Paul Maloy	R	21	0	0	—	0	2	0	0	2	2	1	0	0	9.00
Harry Hooper	R	25	0	0	—	0	1	0	0	1	1	1	0	0	0.00
Esty Chaney	R	22	0	0	—	0	1	0	0	1	1	2	0	0	9.00
Duffy Lewis	R	24	0	0	—	0	1	0	0	1	3	0	1	0	18.00

CHICAGO — 5th 78-74 .513 17.5 — NIXEY CALLAHAN

NAME	G by Pos	B	AGE	G	AB	R	H	2B	3B	HR	RBI	BB	SO	SB	BA	SA
TOTALS			25	153	4822	486	1139	157	66	23	410	398	550	156	.236	.310
2 Hal Chase	1B102	L	30	104	363	49	110	11	10	2	39	16	41	9	.286	.383
Morris Rath	2B86	R	26	90	295	37	59	2	0	0	12	46	22	22	.200	.207
Buck Weaver	SS151	R	22	151	533	51	145	17	8	4	52	15	60	20	.272	.356
Harry Lord	3B150	L	31	150	547	62	154	18	12	1	42	45	39	24	.263	.346
Shano Collins	OF147	R	27	148	535	53	128	26	9	1	47	32	60	22	.239	.327
Ping Bodie	OF119	R	25	127	406	39	107	14	8	8	48	35	57	5	.264	.397
Chick Mattick	0F63	R	26	68	207	15	39	8	1	0	11	18	16	3	.188	.237
Ray Schalk	C125	R	20	128	401	38	98	15	5	1	38	27	36	14	.244	.314
Joe Berger	2B69, SS4, 3B1	R	26	77	223	27	48	6	2	2	20	36	28	5	.215	.287
Jack Fournier	1B29, OF23	L	23	68	171	20	40	8	5	1	23	21	23	7	.234	.357
Larry Chappell	OF59	L	23	60	208	20	48	8	1	0	15	18	22	7	.231	.279
Ted Easterly	C19	L	28	60	97	3	23	1	0	0	8	4	9	2	.237	.247
Biff Schaller	OF32	L	23	34	96	12	21	3	0	1	4	20	16	5	.219	.250
1 Babe Borton	1B26	L	24	28	80	9	22	5	0	0	13	23	5	0	.275	.338
Walt Kuhn	C24	R	26	26	50	5	8	1	0	0	5	5	13	0	.160	.180
2 Johnny Beall	OF17	L	31	17	60	10	16	0	1	2	3	0	6	0	.267	.400
1 Rollie Zeider	3B6, 1B3, 2B1	R	29	13	20	4	7	0	0	0	2	4	1	3	.350	.350

Jim Breton 21 R 5-30, Davy Jones 33 L 6-21, Edd Roush 20 L 1-10, Nixey Callahan 39 R 2-9, Don Rader 19 L 1-3, Tom Daley 21 R 0-3, Billy Meyer 20 R 1-1

NAME	T	AGE	W	L	PCT	SV	G	GS	CG	IP	H	BB	SO	SHO	ERA
TOTALS		27	78	74	.513	9	153	153	86	1360	1189	438	602	17	2.33
Reb Russell	L	24	22	16	.579	4	51	36	25	316	249	79	122	8	1.91
Jim Scott	R	24	20	20	.500	1	48	38	27	312	252	86	158	4	1.91
Eddie Cicotte	R	29	18	12	.600	1	41	30	18	268	224	73	121	3	1.58
Ed Walsh (SA)	R	32	1	1	.727	0	16	14	7	98	91	39	34	1	2.57
Joe Benz	R	27	7	10	.412	2	33	17	7	151	146	59	79	1	2.74
Doc White	L	34	4	4	.333	0	19	8	2	103	106	39	39	0	3.50
Frank Lange	R	29	1	3	.250	0	12	3	0	41	46	20	20	0	4.83
Frank Miller	R	27	0	1	.000	1	2	0	0	2	4	3	2	0	22.50
Pop Boy Smith	R	21	0	0	.000	0	15	2	0	32	31	11	13	0	3.38
2 Buck O'Brien	R	31	0	3	.000	0	6	3	0	18	21	13	4	0	4.00
Bill Lathrop	R	21	0	0	—	0	4	0	0	17	16	12	9	0	4.24
Jim Scoggins	L	21	0	0	—	0	1	0	0	1	0	1	0	0	0.00
Bob Smith	R	22	0	0	—	0	1	0	0	3	3	1	1	0	13.50
Lena Blackburne (ST) 26															

DETROIT — 6th 66-87 .431 30 — HUGHIE JENNINGS

NAME	G by Pos	B	AGE	G	AB	R	H	2B	3B	HR	RBI	BB	SO	SB	BA	SA
TOTALS			27	153	5064	624	1344	180	101	24	519	496	501	218	.265	.355
Del Gainer	1B102	R	26	104	363	47	97	16	8	2	25	30	45	10	.267	.372
Ossie Vitt	2B78, 3B17, OF2	R	23	99	359	45	86	11	3	2	33	31	18	5	.240	.304
Donnie Bush	SS152	R	25	152	593	98	149	19	10	1	40	80	32	44	.251	.326
George Moriarty	3B93, OF7	R	27	102	347	29	83	5	2	0	30	24	25	33	.239	.265
Sam Crawford	OF140, 1B13	L	33	153	610	78	193	32	23	9	83	52	28	13	.316	.489
Ty Cobb	OF118, 2B1	L	26	122	428	70	167	18	16	4	67	58	31	52	.390	.535
Bobby Veach	OF136	L	25	139	494	54	133	22	10	0	64	53	31	22	.269	.354
Oscar Stanage	C77	R	30	80	241	19	54	13	2	0	21	21	35	5	.224	.295
Hugh High	OF50	L	25	80	183	18	42	6	1	0	16	28	24	6	.230	.273
Baldy Louden	2B32, 3B26, SS6, OF5	R	29	72	191	28	46	4	5	0	23	24	22	6	.241	.314
Jean Dubuc	P36, OF3	R	24	68	135	17	36	5	3	2	11	2	17	1	.267	.393
Red McKee	C61	R	22	67	187	16	53	3	4	1	20	21	21	7	.283	.358
Paddy Baumann	2B48	R	27	49	191	31	57	7	4	1	22	16	18	4	.298	.393
Henri Rondeau	C14, 1B6	R	26	35	70	5	13	2	0	0	5	14	16	1	.186	.214
Ed Willett	P34	R	29	35	92	8	26	4	1	1	13	3	23	0	.283	.380
Frank Gibson	C19, OF1	R	22	20	57	8	8	1	0	0	2	3	9	2	.140	.158
Eddie Onslow	1B17	L	20	17	55	7	14	1	0	0	8	5	9	1	.255	.273
1 Charlie Deal	3B15	R	21	16	50	3	11	0	2	0	5	1	7	2	.220	.300
Guy Tutweiler	3B14	L	24	14	47	4	10	0	1	0	7	4	12	2	.213	.255
Let Hennessey	2B9	R	19	12	22	2	3	0	0	0	0	3	6	1	.136	.136
Wally Pipp	1B10	L	20	12	31	3	5	0	0	0	3	1	8	0	.161	.161

Al Platte 23 L 2-18, Joe Burns 24 L 5-13, Pepper Peploski 21 R 2-4, Ray Powell 24 L 0-0, Steve Partenheimer 21 R 0-2

NAME	T	AGE	W	L	PCT	SV	G	GS	CG	IP	H	BB	SO	SHO	ERA
TOTALS		25	66	87	.431	5	153	153	90	1360	1359	504	468	4	3.41
Jean Dubuc	R	24	16	14	.533	0	36	28	22	243	228	91	73	1	2.89
Hooks Dauss	R	23	13	12	.520	1	33	29	22	225	188	82	107	2	2.48
Ed Willett	R	29	13	14	.481	0	34	30	19	242	237	89	59	0	3.09
Mark Hall (NJ)	R	25	9	12	.429	0	30	21	8	165	154	79	69	1	3.27
Joe Lake	R	31	8	7	.533	1	28	12	6	137	149	24	35	0	3.28
Ralph Comstock	R	22	5		.286	1	10	7	1	60	90	16	37	0	5.40
Will House	R	22	1	2	.333	0	19	2	0	54	64	17	16	0	5.17
Dutch Klawitter	R	24	1	2	.333	0	8	5	1	32	39	15	10	0	5.06
Lefty Williams	L	20	1	3	.250	1	5	4	3	29	34	4	9	0	4.97
Carl Zamloch	R	23	1	6	.143	1	17	5	3	70	66	23	28	0	2.71
1 George Mullin	R	32	1	6	.143	0	7	7	4	52	53	18	16	0	2.77
George Boehler	R	21	0	1	.000	0	8	1	1	6	10	9	3	0	6.75
Lou North	R	22	0	1	.000	0	6	1	0	10	9	3	5	0	15.00
Erwin Renfer	R	22	0	0	—	0	5	1	0	13	11	6	3	1	6.00
Al Clauss	L	22	0	0	—	0	5	1	0	13	11	12	1	0	4.84
Heinie Elder	L	22	0	1	.000	0	4	1	0	11	9	7	2	0	9.00
Burt Grover (BH)	R	23	0	0	—	0	2	1	0	11	9	7	2	0	3.28
Charlie Harding	R	21	0	0	—	0	1	0	0	2	3	1	1	0	9.00
Lefty Lorenzen	L	20	0	0	—	0	1	0	0	2	4	3	0	0	18.00
Ed Lafitte (ST) 27															

NEW YORK — 7th 57-94 .377 38 — FRANK CHANCE

NAME	G by Pos	B	AGE	G	AB	R	H	2B	3B	HR	RBI	BB	SO	SB	BA	SA
TOTALS			27	153	4880	529	1157	154	45	9	430	534	617	203	.237	.293
Jack Knight	1B50, 2B21	R	27	70	250	24	59	10	0	0	24	25	27	7	.236	.276
Roy Hartzel	2B81, OF30, 3B21, SS4	L	31	141	490	60	127	18	1	0	38	67	40	14	.259	.300
2 Roger Peckinpaugh	SS93	R	22	95	340	35	91	10	7	1	32	24	47	19	.268	.347
Ezra Midkiff	3B76, SS4, 2B2	L	30	83	284	22	56	9	1	0	14	12	33	9	.197	.236
Bert Daniels	OF87	R	30	93	320	52	69	13	5	0	22	44	36	27	.216	.288
Harry Wolter	OF121	L	28	126	425	53	108	13	6	4	43	60	50	13	.254	.339
Birdie Cree	OF144	R	30	145	534	51	145	25	6	1	63	50	51	22	.272	.346
Ed Sweeney	C112, 1B1	R	24	117	351	35	93	10	2	2	40	37	41	11	.265	.322
Ray Caldwell	P27, OF3	R	25	55	97	10	28	3	0	1	11	3	15	3	.289	.361
Fritz Maisel	3B51	R	23	51	187	30	48	4	3	0	12	34	20	25	.257	.310
2 Rollie Zeider	SS23, 2B19, 1B4, 3B2	R	29	49	159	15	37	2	0	0	12	25	9	5	.233	.245
2 Bill McKechnie	2B27, SS7, 3B2	R	26	44	112	7	15	0	0	0	8	8	17	2	.134	.134
Ray Fisher	P43	R	25	43	79	5	22	2	0	0	3	1	15	1	.278	.304
1 Hal Chase	1B29, 2B5, OF5	R	30	39	146	15	31	4	2	0	9	11	5	5	.212	.281
Dick Gossett	C38	L	22	39	105	9	17	2	0	0	9	11	18	1	.162	.181
2 Bebe Borton	1B33	L	24	33	108	8	14	1	0	0	11	18	19	1	.130	.167
Harry Williams	OF26	R	21	27	82	18	21	1	1	0	12	15	10	6	.256	.354
Frank Gilhooley	OF24	L	21	24	65	7	19	1	0	1	0	14	4	9	.341	.388
Claud Derrick	SS14, 3B4, 2B1	R	23	20	65	7	19	1	0	1	5	2	2	4	.292	.354
Dutch Sterrett	1B6, C1, OF1	R	23	21	35	0	6	1	0	0	3	1	5	1	.171	.171
Doc Cook	OF20	L	27	20	72	9	19	2	0	0	1	6	12	4	.264	.319

Bill Holden 23 R 16-53, 1 Jack Lelivelt 27 L 6-28, Joe Smith 19 R 5-32, Bill Stumpf 21 R 6-29, Frank Chance 36 R 5-24, George Whiteman 30 R 11-32, Ralph Young 24 B 1-15, Bob Williams 19 R 3-19, Luke Boone 23 R 4-12, Bill Reynolds 28 R 0-5, Dan Costello 21 L 1-2, Harry Hanson 17 R 0-2

NAME	T	AGE	W	L	PCT	SV	G	GS	CG	IP	H	BB	SO	SHO	ERA
TOTALS		27	57	94	.377	6	153	153	78	1344	1318	455	530	8	3.27
Ray Fisher	R	25	11	17	.393	0	43	31	15	246	244	71	92	1	3.19
Russ Ford	R	30	11	17	.379	3	33	28	16	237	244	58	72	1	2.66
Ray Caldwell	R	25	9	8	.529	1	27	16	15	164	131	60	87	2	2.43
Al Schulz	L	24	8	14	.364	0	38	22	9	193	197	69	77	0	3.73
Ray Keating	R	19	6	12	.333	0	28	21	9	151	147	51	83	2	3.22
George McConnell	R	35	5	15	.250	2	35	20	9	180	162	60	72	0	3.20
Jack Warhop (SA)	R	28	4	4	.500	0	15	7	1	62	69	33	11	1	3.77
Marty McHale	R	26	2	4	.333	0	7	4	1	49	49	10	11	1	2.94
Cy Pieh	R	26	1	0	1.000	0	9	1	0	22	17	6	6	0	4.50
George Clark	R	22	0	0	—	0	11	0	0	19	12	19	5	0	9.00
Ed Klepfer	R	25	0	0	—	0	8	1	0	25	38	12	10	0	7.56
Red Hoff	L	22	0	0	—	0	2	0	0	4	1	2	0	0	0.00
Jim Hanley	L	27	0	0	—	0	1	0	0	6	3	4	2	0	6.75

ST. LOUIS — 8th 57-96 .373 39 — GEORGE STOVALL 50-84 .373 — JIMMY AUSTIN 2-6 .250 — BRANCH RICKEY 5-6 .455

NAME	G by Pos	B	AGE	G	AB	R	H	2B	3B	HR	RBI	BB	SO	SB	BA	SA
TOTALS			27	155	5031	528	1193	179	73	18	422	459	769	209	.237	.312
George Stovall	1B76	R	35	89	303	34	87	14	3	1	24	6	25	7	.287	.363
Del Pratt	2B146, 1B9	R	25	155	592	60	175	31	13	2	87	43	57	37	.296	.402
Mike Balenti	SS56, OF8	R	26	70	211	17	38	2	4	1	17	32	50	5	.180	.227
Jimmy Austin	3B142	B	33	149	489	56	130	18	6	2	42	46	51	26	.266	.339
Gus Williams	OF143	R	25	147	538	72	147	21	16	5	53	59	87	31	.273	.400
Burt Shotton	OF146	L	27	147	549	105	163	23	7	2	39	99	63	43	.297	.373
Johnny Johnston	OF106	R	23	109	380	37	85	14	4	2	27	45	51	11	.224	.290
Sam Agnew	C103	R	26	104	307	27	64	9	5	2	24	21	49	11	.208	.290
Bunny Brief	1B62, OF8	R	20	84	258	24	56	11	6	1	26	22	45	3	.217	.318
Pete Compton	OF21	L	23	61	100	14	18	1	2	0	17	13	13	2	.180	.330
Bobby Wallace (BH)	SS38, 3B7	R	39	53	147	11	31	5	0	0	14	16	16	1	.211	.245
Bill McAllester	C37	R	24	47	85	3	13	4	2	0	6	4	15	2	.153	.200
1 Doc Lavan	SS46	R	22	46	149	8	21	1	0	1	6	10	46	3	.141	.168
Walt Alexander	C43	R	24	43	110	5	15	2	0	0	3	11	29	1	.136	.173
Tilly Walker	OF23	R	25	23	85	7	24	2	0	2	11	2	9	1	.294	.365
Dee Walsh	SS22, 3B1	R	20	23	60	7	9	0	3	0	5	4	8	1	.150	.183
Sam Covington	1B16	L	18	20	60	3	9	1	1	0	6	1	3	2	.150	.183
Rivington Bisland	SS12	R	23	12	31	3	5	0	0	0	3	1	9	0	.161	.161

George Maisel 21 R 3-18, Buzzy Wares 27 R 10-35, Tod Sloan 22 L 7-26, Ernie Walker 22 L 3-14, Frank Crossin 22 R 1-4, Charlie Flannigan 21 R 0-3, Fred Graf 24 R 2-5, Walt Meinert 22 L 3-8, Luther Bonin 25 L 0-1, George Tomer 17 L 0-1

NAME	T	AGE	W	L	PCT	SV	G	GS	CG	IP	H	BB	SO	SHO	ERA
TOTALS		24	57	96	.373	4	155	155	101	1382	1369	454	476	14	3.06
Earl Hamilton	L	21	13	12	.520	0	31	24	19	217	197	83	101	3	2.57
Roy Mitchell	R	28	13	16	.448	1	33	27	21	245	265	47	59	4	3.02
George Baumgardner	R	21	10	19	.345	2	38	31	22	253	267	84	78	2	3.13
Carl Weilman	L	23	10	20	.333	0	39	27	14	252	262	60	79	2	3.39
Walt Leverenz	R	24	7	17	.261	1	30	27	14	203	159	89	87	2	2.57
Dwight Stone	R	22	5	0	.250	0	18	7	3	91	94	46	37	1	3.56
Hal Schwenk	L	22	1	0	1.000	0	1	1	1	11	12	4	3	0	2.52
Curly Brown	R	26	1	1	.500	0	7	1	1	14	12	4	3	0	2.57
Mack Allison	R	26	0	3	.250	0	11	4	1	51	52	13	12	0	4.78
Wiley Taylor	R	22	0	1	.000	0	4	1	0	9	6	10	5	0	10.00
Willie Adams	R	22	0	0	—	0	5	0	0	4	3	1	1	0	0.00
Jack Powell	R	21	0	1	.000	0	4	1	0	11	16	2	6	0	4.50
Pete Schmidt	R	22	0	0	—	0	1								

NEW YORK — 1st 101-51 .664 — JOHN McGRAW

NAME	G by Pos	B	AGE	G	AB	R	H	2B	3B	HR	RBI	BB	SO	SB	BA	SA
TOTALS			27	156	5218	684	1477	226	70	31	580	444	501	296	.273	.361
Fred Merkle	1B153	R	24	153	563	78	147	30	12	3	69	41	60	35	.261	.373
Larry Doyle	2B130	L	27	132	482	67	135	25	6	5	73	59	29	38	.280	.388
Art Fletcher	SS136	R	28	136	538	76	160	20	9	4	71	24	35	32	.297	.390
Buck Herzog	3B84 2B2	R	27	96	290	46	83	15	3	3	31	22	12	23	.286	.390
Red Murray	OF147	R	29	147	520	70	139	21	3	2	59	34	28	35	.267	.331
Fred Snodgrass	OF133 1B3 2B1	R	25	141	457	65	133	21	6	3	49	53	44	27	.291	.383
George Burns	OF150	R	23	150	605	81	173	37	4	2	54	58	74	40	.286	.370
Chief Meyers	C116	R	32	120	378	37	118	18	5	3	47	37	22	7	.312	.410
Tillie Shafer	3B79 2B25 SS17 OF15	B	24	138	508	74	146	17	12	5	52	61	55	32	.287	.398
Moose McCormick	OF15	L	32	57	80	9	22	2	3	0	15	5	13	0	.275	.375
Art Wilson	C49 1B2	R	27	54	79	5	15	0	1	0	8	11	11	1	.190	.215
13Doc Crandall	P35 2B2	R	25	46	47	7	15	4	1	0	4	3	8	0	.319	.447
2 Larry McLean	C28	R	31	30	75	3	24	4	0	0	9	4	4	1	.320	.373
Cladue Cooper	OF15	L	20	27	30	11	9	4	0	0	4	4	6	3	.300	.433
2 Eddie Grant	3B5 2B3 SS1	R	30	27	20	8	4	1	0	0	1	2	1	2	.200	.250
Grover Hartley	C21 1B1	R	24	23	19	4	6	0	0	0	0	1	2	1	.316	.316
Jim Thorpe	OF9	R	26	19	35	6	5	0	0	1	2	1	9	2	.143	.229
1 Josh Devore	OF8	R	25	16	21	4	4	0	1	0	1	3	4	6	.190	.286
Milt Stock	SS1	R	19	17	17	2	3	1	0	0	1	0	2	1	.176	.235
1 Heinie Groh	3B2 SS1	R	23	4	2	0	0	0	0	0	0	0	1	0	.000	.000
Joe Evers		R	21	1	0	0	0	0	0	0	0	0	0	0	.000	.000
Howard Merritt	OF1	R	18	1	0	0	0	0	0	0	0	0	0	0	.000	.000

NAME	T	AGE	W	L	PCT	SV	G	GS	CG	IP	H	BB	SO	SHO	ERA
		28	101	51	.664	17	156	156	82	1420	1276	315	651	12	2.43
Christy Mathewson	R	32	25	11	.694	2	40	35	25	306	291	21	93	4	2.06
Rube Marquard	R	26	23	10	.697	3	42	33	20	288	248	49	151	4	2.50
Jeff Tesreau	R	25	22	13	.629	0	41	38	17	282	222	119	167	1	2.17
Al Demaree	R	28	13	4	.765	2	31	24	11	200	176	38	76	2	2.21
2 Art Fromme	R	29	11	6	.647	0	26	12	3	112	112	29	50	0	4.01
13Doc Crandall	R	25	4	4	.500	6	35	3	2	98	102	24	42	0	2.84
1 Red Ames	R	30	2	1	.667	1	7	4	2	42	35	8	30	0	2.57
Bunny Hearn	L	22	1	1	.500	0	2	1	1	13	13	7	8	0	2.77
Rube Schauer	R	22	0	1	.000	0	1	2	0	14	9	7	7	0	7.50
Hooks Wiltse	L	33	0	0	—	3	17	2	0	58	53	8	25	0	1.55
Ferdie Schupp	L	22	0	0	—	0	5	1	0	12	10	3	2	0	0.75

PHILADELPHIA — 2nd 88-63 .583 12.5 — RED DOOIN

NAME	G by Pos	B	AGE	G	AB	R	H	2B	3B	HR	RBI	BB	SO	SB	BA	SA
TOTALS			29	159	5400	693	1433	257	78	73	597	383	578	156	.265	.382
Fred Luderus	1B155	R	27	155	588	67	154	32	7	18	86	34	51	5	.262	.432
Otto Knabe	2B148	R	29	148	571	70	150	25	7	2	53	45	26	14	.263	.342
Mickey Doolan	SS148 2B3	R	33	151	518	32	113	12	6	1	43	24	68	17	.218	.270
Hans Lobert	3B145 SS3 2B1	R	31	150	573	98	172	28	11	7	55	42	34	41	.300	.424
Gavvy Cravath	OF141	R	32	147	525	78	179	34	14	19	128	55	63	10	.341	.568
Dode Paskert	OF120	R	31	124	454	83	119	21	9	4	29	65	69	12	.262	.374
Sherry Magee	OF123 1B4	R	28	138	470	92	144	36	6	11	70	38	36	23	.306	.479
Bill Killefer	C118 1B1	R	25	120	360	25	88	14	3	0	24	4	17	2	.244	.300
2 Beals Becker	OF77 1B1	L	26	88	306	53	99	19	10	9	44	22	30	11	.324	.539
Doc Miller	OF12	L	30	69	87	9	30	6	0	0	11	6	6	2	.345	.414
1 Cozy Dolan	OF12 SS10 2B9 3B4 1B1	R	30	55	126	15	33	4	0	0	8	1	21	9	.262	.294
Red Dooin	C50	R	34	55	129	6	33	4	1	0	13	3	9	1	.256	.302
Dan Howley	C22	R	27	26	32	4	4	2	0	0	2	4	3	1	.125	.188
Jimmy Walsh	2B6 SS3 3B1 OF1	R	27	26	30	3	10	4	0	0	5	1	5	1	.333	.467
3 Josh Devore	OF14	L	25	23	39	6	11	1	0	0	5	4	7	0	.282	.308
2 Bobby Byrne	3B15	R	28	19	58	9	13	1	0	1	4	5	5	2	.224	.293

Ed Burns 25 R 6-30, Milt Reed 22 L 6-24, Vem Duncan 23 L 5-12, 1 John Dodge 24 R 1-3,Ralph Capron 24 L 0-1, Pat Moran 37 R 0-1

NAME	T	AGE	W	L	PCT	SV	G	GS	CG	IP	H	BB	SO	SHO	ERA
		25	88	63	.583	11	159	159	77	1455	1407	512	667	20	3.16
Tom Seaton	R	25	27	12	.692	1	52	35	21	322	262	136	168	5	2.60
Pete Alexander	R	26	22	8	.733	2	47	36	23	306	288	75	159	9	2.79
Ad Brennan	L	31	14	12	.538	1	40	24	12	207	204	46	94	1	2.39
Eppa Rixey	R	22	9	5	.643	2	35	19	9	156	148	56	75	1	3.11
Erskine Mayer	R	23	9	9	.500	1	39	19	7	171	172	46	51	2	3.11
2 Howie Camnitz	R	31	3	3	.500	1	9	5	1	49	49	23	21	0	3.67
George Chalmers	R	25	3	10	.231	1	26	15	4	116	133	51	46	0	4.81
1 Earl Moore	R	33	1	3	.250	1	12	5	0	52	50	40	24	0	5.02
Rube Marshall	R	22	0	1	.000	1	14	1	0	45	54	22	18	0	4.60
Doc Imlay	R	24	0	0	—	0	3	0	0	14	14	7	7	0	7.07
Happy Finneran	R	24	0	0	—	0	3	0	0	5	12	2	0	0	7.20
1 Red Nelson	R	27	0	0	—	0	3	0	0	8	9	4	3	0	2.25
Jim Haislip	R	21	0	0	—	0	3	1	0	3	4	3	0	0	6.00
Ray Hartranft	L	22	0	0	—	0	1	0	0	3	5	4	1	0	9.00

CHICAGO — 3rd 88-65 .575 13.5 — JOHNNY EVERS

NAME	G by Pos	B	AGE	G	AB	R	H	2B	3B	HR	RBI	BB	SO	SB	BA	SA
TOTALS			29	154	5010	720	1286	194	96	59	617	553	634	181	.257	.369
Vic Saier	1B148	L	23	148	588	67	154	14	21	14	92	62	62	26	.288	.477
Johnny Evers	2B135	L	31	135	444	81	126	20	5	3	49	50	14	11	.284	.372
Al Bridwell	SS135	L	29	135	405	35	97	6	6	1	37	74	28	12	.240	.291
Heinie Zimmerman	3B125	R	26	127	447	69	140	28	12	9	95	41	40	18	.313	.490
Wildfire Schulte	OF129	L	30	131	495	85	138	28	6	9	68	39	68	21	.279	.414
Tommy Leach	OF119 3B2	R	35	130	454	99	131	23	10	6	37	77	44	21	.289	.423
1 Mike Mitchell	OF33	R	33	81	278	37	72	11	6	4	33	32	33	15	.259	.385
Jimmy Archer	C108 1B8	R	30	110	367	38	98	14	7	2	44	19	27	4	.267	.360
Art Phelan	2B46 3B38 SS1	R	25	90	259	41	65	11	6	2	35	29	25	8	.251	.363
Ward Miller	OF63	L	28	80	203	23	48	5	7	1	16	34	33	13	.236	.345
Roger Bresnahan	C58	R	34	68	161	20	37	5	2	1	21	21	17	1	.230	.304
Wilbur Good	OF26	L	27	49	91	11	23	7	2	1	12	11	16	5	.253	.363
Cy Williams	OF44	L	25	49	156	17	35	3	3	4	32	5	26	5	.224	.359
Red Corriden	SS36 2B2 3B1	R	25	45	97	13	17	3	0	2	9	9	14	4	.175	.268
1 Otis Clymer	OF26	R	37	30	105	16	24	5	1	0	7	14	18	9	.229	.295
Tom Needham	C14	R	34	20	42	5	10	4	1	0	11	4	8	0	.238	.381
Tuffy Stewart	OF1	R	25	9	8	1	1	1	0	0	1	2	1	0	.125	.250

Bubbles Hargrave 20 R 1-3, Milo Allison 22 L 2-6, 1 Mike Hechinger 23 R 0-2, Chick Keating 21 R 1-5, Pete Knisely 29 R 0-2
Fritz Mollowitz 23 R 3-7,Ed McDonald 26 R 0-0

NAME	T	AGE	W	L	PCT	SV	G	GS	CG	IP	H	BB	SO	SHO	ERA
		29	88	65	.575	15	154	154	89	1372	1330	478	556	12	3.13
Larry Cheney	R	27	21	14	.600	11	54	36	25	305	271	98	136	2	2.57
Bert Humphries	R	32	16	4	.800	1	28	20	13	181	169	24	61	2	2.69
George Pierce	L	25	13	5	.722	0	25	21	14	163	137	59	73	3	2.32
Jimmy Lavender	R	29	10	14	.417	2	40	24	10	204	206	98	91	0	3.66
Charlie Smith	R	33	7	9	.438	0	20	17	8	138	138	34	47	1	2.55
Hippo Vaughn	L	25	5	1	.833	0	7	6	5	56	37	26	36	2	1.45
2 Eddie Stack	R	25	4	2	.667	1	11	7	3	51	56	15	28	1	4.24
Orvie Overall	R	32	4	5	.444	0	11	6	0	68	73	26	30	1	3.31
Fred Toney	R	24	2	2	.500	0	7	5	2	39	52	22	12	0	6.00
Lew Richie	R	29	2	4	.333	0	16	5	1	65	77	30	15	0	5.82
Doc Watson	L	28	1	0	1.000	0	3	1	0	9	8	6	1	0	1.00
Zip Zabel	R	22	1	0	1.000	0	7	1	0	5	3	1	0	0	0.00
1 Earl Moore	R	33	1	1	.500	0	7	2	0	28	34	12	10	0	4.50
1 Ed Reulbach	R	30	1	3	.250	0	10	3	1	39	41	21	10	0	4.38
Lefty Leifield	L	29	0	0	—	0	6	1	0	21	28	5	4	0	5.57

PITTSBURGH — 4th 78-71 .523 21.5 — FRED CLARKE

NAME	G by Pos	B	AGE	G	AB	R	H	2B	3B	HR	RBI	BB	SO	SB	BA	SA
TOTALS			29	155	5252	673	1383	210	86	35	570	391	545	181	.263	.356
Dots Miller	1B150 SS3	R	26	154	580	75	158	24	20	7	90	37	52	20	.272	.419
Jim Viox	2B124 SS10 OF2	R	22	137	492	86	156	32	8	2	65	64	28	14	.317	.427
Honus Wagner	SS105	R	39	114	413	51	124	18	4	3	56	26	40	21	.300	.385
1 Bobby Byrne	3B110	R	28	113	448	54	121	22	0	1	47	29	28	10	.270	.326
Owen Wilson	OF155	R	29	155	580	71	154	12	14	10	73	32	62	9	.266	.386
2 Mike Mitchell	OF54	R	33	54	199	25	54	8	2	1	16	14	15	8	.271	.372
Max Carey	OF154	R	23	154	620	99	172	23	10	5	49	55	67	61	.277	.371
Mike Simon	C92	R	30	92	255	23	63	6	2	1	17	10	15	3	.247	.298
Art Butler	2B27 SS24 3B2 OF2	R	25	82	214	40	60	9	3	0	20	32	14	9	.280	.350
Ham Hyatt	1B5 OF5	L	28	63	81	8	27	6	2	4	16	3	8	0	.333	.605
George Gibson (BN)	C48	R	32	48	118	6	33	4	2	0	12	10	8	2	.280	.347
Billy Kelly	C40	R	27	48	82	11	22	2	2	0	9	2	12	0	.268	.341
Eddie Mensor	OF18 2B1 SS1	B	27	44	56	9	10	1	0	0	1	8	13	2	.179	.196
Babe Adams	P43	R	31	43	114	13	33	6	2	0	13	1	16	0	.289	.377
Fred Kommers	OF40	R	27	40	155	14	36	5	4	0	22	10	29	1	.232	.316
2 Cozy Dolan	OF35	R	30	35	133	22	27	5	9	1	15	14	14	14	.203	.271
Alex McCarthy	SS12 3B12 2B6	R	25	31	74	7	15	0	7	0	10	7	1	1	.203	.270
Everett Booe	OF22	L	23	29	80	9	16	2	0	0	7	6	6	2	.200	.250
Solly Hofman	OF24	R	30	28	83	11	19	5	0	0	7	8	6	5	.229	.337
Bob Coleman	C24	R	23	24	50	3	9	2	0	0	9	2	9	0	.180	.220
Roy Wood	OF8 1B1	R	20	14	35	4	10	4	0	0	2	1	6	2	.286	.400
Fred Clarke	OF2	L	40	13	6	0	1	0	0	0	0	5	1	0	.077	.154

Gil Britton 21 R 0-12, Jake Kafora 24 R 0-1, Mike Donlin (VR) 35

NAME	T	AGE	W	L	PCT	SV	G	GS	CG	IP	H	BB	SO	SHO	ERA
		26	78	71	.523	7	155	155	74	1400	1344	434	590	9	2.90
Babe Adams	R	31	21	10	.677	0	43	37	24	314	271	49	144	4	2.15
Hank Robinson	L	25	14	9	.609	0	43	22	8	196	184	41	50	1	2.39
Claude Hendrix	R	24	14	15	.483	2	42	25	17	241	216	89	138	2	3.84
George McQuillan	R	28	8	6	.571	1	25	16	7	142	144	35	59	0	3.42
Marty O'Toole (IL)	R	25	4	8	.429	1	26	16	7	145	148	55	58	0	3.29
1 Howie Camnitz	R	31	6	17	.261	2	36	22	5	192	203	84	64	1	3.75
Wilbur Cooper	L	21	3	0	.625	0	30	2	5	93	98	45	39	1	3.29
Bill Luhrsen	R	29	3	1	.750	0	3	2	0	29	25	16	11	0	2.48
Jack Ferry	R	26	1	0	1.000	0	15	13	5	9	0				5.40
Joe Conzelman	R	27	1	0	1.000	0	2	1	15	13	5	2	0		1.20
Jack Schenberg	R	25	0	1	.000	0	1	1	0	6	10	2	1	0	6.00
Eddie Eayrs	L	22	0	0	—	0	1	0	0	4	2	3	0	0	2.25
Bernie Duffy	R	19	0	0	—	0	2	1	0	3	18	3	8	0	5.72
Al Mamaux	R	19	0	0	—	0	1	0	0	3	2	1	2	0	3.00

BOSTON — 5th 69-82 .457 31.5 — GEORGE STALLINGS

NAME	G by Pos	B	AGE	G	AB	R	H	2B	3B	HR	RBI	BB	SO	SB	BA	SA
TOTALS			27	154	5145	641	1318	191	60	32	533	488	641	177	.256	.335
Hap Myers	1B135	R	27	140	524	74	143	20	1	2	50	38	48	57	.273	.326
Bill Sweeney	2B137	R	27	139	502	65	129	17	6	0	47	66	50	18	.257	.315
Rabbit Maranville	SS143	R	21	143	571	68	141	13	8	2	48	68	62	25	.247	.308
Art Devlin	3B69	R	33	73	210	19	48	7	5	0	12	29	17	8	.229	.310
John Titus	OF75	L	37	87	269	33	80	14	2	5	38	35	22	4	.297	.420
Les Mann	OF120	R	20	120	407	54	103	24	4	3	51	18	73	7	.253	.369
Joey Connolly	OF124	L	29	126	429	77	156	22	11	5	57	66	47	18	.281	.410
Bill Rariden	C87	R	25	95	246	31	58	9	2	3	30	30	21	5	.236	.325
Fred Smith	3B59 2B14 SS11 OF4	R	26	92	285	35	65	9	3	0	27	29	55	7	.228	.281
Bert Whaling	C77	R	25	79	211	22	53	5	1	0	25	10	32	3	.242	.299
Bris Lord	OF62	R	29	73	235	22	59	12	1	6	26	24	22	7	.251	.387
2 Tex McDonald	3B31 2B6 OF1	L	24	62	145	24	52	4	4	0	18	15	17	4	.359	.441
Cy Seymour	OF18	L	40	39	73	2	13	2	0	0	10	7	12	0	.178	.205
Tommy Griffith	OF35	L	23	37	127	16	32	4	1	2	15	9	28	1	.252	.323
Guy Zinn	OF35	L	26	36	138	15	41	6	2	1	15	4	23	3	.297	.406
Otto Hess	P29	L	34	35	83	9	26	4	1	0	11	7	15	0	.313	.410
Butch Schmidt	1B22	L	26	17	38	3	12	2	0	0	14	2	5	1	.308	.423
Jay Kirke	OF13	L	25	17	38	3	9	1	0	0	4	1	6	0	.237	.289
Wilson Collins	OF9	L	23	14	9	3	3	0	0	0	0	3	0	0	.333	.333

Drummond Brown 28 R 11-34, 2 Otis Clymer 37 B 12-37, 2 Charlie Deal 21 R 11-36, Joe Schultz 19 R 4-18,Bill Calhoun 23 L 1-13, Oscar Dugey 25 R 2-8, Fred Mitchell 35 R 1-3,
Rex DeVogt 25 R 0-6, Hank Gowdy 23 R 3-5, George Jackson 31 R 3-10, Art Bues (IL) 25 R 0-1, Jeff McCleskey 21 L 0-3, Walt Tragesser 26 R 0-0, 1 Bill McKechnie 26 B 0-4, Bill McTigue 22 R 0-0
Ben Houser (KJ) 29

NAME	T	AGE	W	L	PCT	SV	G	GS	CG	IP	H	BB	SO	SHO	ERA
		28	69	82	.457	3	154	154	105	1373	1343	419	597	13	3.19
Hub Perdue	R	31	16	13	.552	1	38	32	16	212	201	39	91	3	3.27
Lefty Tyler	L	23	16	13	.485	2	38	34	28	290	245	108	143	4	2.79
Dick Rudolph	R	24	14	13	.519	0	33	22	17	249	258	59	109	2	2.93
Otto Hess	L	34	7	17	.292	0	29	27	19	218	231	70	80	2	3.84
Walt Dickson	R	34	6	7	.462	0	19	15	8	128	118	45	47	0	3.23
Bill James	R	21	6	10	.375	0	24	14	10	136	134	57	73	1	2.78
Jack Quinn	R	29	4	3	.571	0	8	7	2	56	55	7	33	1	2.43
Lefty Gervais	L	22	1	0	1.000	0	5	2	1	16	18	4	1	0	5.63
Gene Cocreham	R	28	0	1	.000	0	3	1	0	13	4	3	0	0	7.88
Win Noyes	R	24	0	0	—	0	11	0	0	21	22	6	5	0	4.72
Paul Strand	L	19	0	0	—	0	7	0	0	17	22	12	6	0	2.12
Buster Brown	R	31	0	0	—	0	2	0	0	13	10	3	3	0	4.84
George Davis	R	23	0	0	—	0	8	1	0	8	7	3	5	0	4.50

BROOKLYN 6th 65-84 .436 34.5 — BILL DAHLEN

NAME	G by Pos	B	AGE	G	AB	R	H	2B	3B	HR	RBI	BB	SO	SB	BA	SA
TOTALS			26	152	5165	595	1394	193	86	39	502	361	555	188	.270	.363
Jake Daubert	1B138	L	29	152	508	76	178	17	7	2	52	44	40	25	.350	.423
George Cutshaw	2B147	R	26	147	592	72	158	23	13	7	80	39	22	39	.267	.385
Bobby Fisher	SS131	R	26	132	474	42	124	11	10	4	54	10	43	16	.262	.352
Red Smith	3B151	R	23	151	540	70	160	40	10	6	76	45	67	22	.296	.441
Herbie Moran	OF129	L	27	132	515	71	137	15	5	0	26	45	29	21	.266	.315
Casey Stengel	OF119	L	22	124	438	60	119	16	8	7	43	56	58	19	.272	.393
Zack Wheat	OF135	L	25	138	535	64	161	28	10	7	58	25	45	17	.301	.430
Otto Miller	C103 1B	R	24	104	320	26	87	11	7	0	26	10	31	7	.272	.350
John Hummel	OF28 SS17 1B6 2B3	R	30	67	198	20	48	7	7	2	24	13	23	4	.242	.379
Bill Fischer	C51	L	22	62	165	16	44	9	4	1	12	10	5	0	.267	.388
Enos Kirkpatrick	SS10 1B8 2B6 3B4	R	28	48	89	13	22	4	1	1	5	3	18	5	.247	.348
Earl Yingling	P26	L	24	40	60	11	23	1	0	0	5	9	8	0	.383	.400
Benny Meyer	OF27 C1	R	28	38	87	12	17	0	1	1	10	14	14	3	.195	.253
Leo Callahan	OF8	L	24	33	41	6	7	3	1	0	3	4	5	0	.171	.293
Bill Collins	OF27	B	31	32	95	8	18	1	0	0	4	8	11	2	.189	.200
Tex Erwin (BA)	C13	R	27	20	31	6	8	1	0	0	3	4	5	0	.258	.290
Eddie Phelps	C4	R	34	15	18	0	4	0	0	0	0	1	2	0	.222	.222
2 Mark Hechinger	C4	R	23	9	11	1	2	1	0	0	0	0	2	0	.182	.273
Lew McCarty	C9	R	24	9	26	1	6	0	0	0	2	2	1	0	.231	.231
Al Scheer	OF6	L	24	6	22	3	5	0	0	0	0	2	4	1	.227	.227
Ray Mowe	SS2	R	27	5	9	0	1	0	0	0	0	0	1	0	.111	.111

NAME	T	AGE	W	L	PCT	SV	G	GS	CG	IP	H	BB	SO	SHO	ERA
TOTALS		27	65	84	.436	7	152	152	70	1373	1287	439	548	9	3.13
Pat Ragan	R	27	15	18	.455	0	44	32	14	265	284	64	109	4	3.77
Nap Rucker	L	28	14	15	.483	2	41	33	16	260	236	67	111	4	2.87
Earl Yingling	L	24	8	8	.500	0	26	13	8	147	158	10	40	2	2.57
Cliff Curtis	R	30	8	9	.471	2	30	16	5	152	145	55	57	0	3.26
2 Ed Reulbach	R	30	7	6	.538	0	15	12	8	110	77	34	46	2	2.05
Bull Wagner	R	25	6	3	.667	0	11	9	7	71	77	30	110	0	5.45
1 Eddie Stack	R	25	4	4	.500	0	23	9	4	87	79	32	34	1	2.38
Frank Allen	L	24	4	18	.182	2	34	25	11	175	144	81	82	0	2.83
Mysterious Walker	R	29	1	3	.250	0	11	8	3	58	44	35	35	0	3.57
Jeff Pfeffer	R	25	1	1	.000	1	5	2	1	24	28	13	13	0	3.38
Maury Kent	R	27	0	0	—	0	7				5	2	1	0	2.57
Elmer Brown	R	29	0	0	—	0	3	1	0	13	6	10	6	0	2.08
Bill Hall	R	19	0	0	—	0	3	0	0	5	5	3	0		5.40
Elmer Knetzer (HO) 27															

CINCINNATI 7th 64-89 .418 37.5 — JOE TINKER

NAME	G by Pos	B	AGE	G	AB	R	H	2B	3B	HR	RBI	BB	SO	SB	BA	SA
TOTALS			28	156	5132	607	1339	170	96	27	541	438	579	226	.261	.347
Dick Hoblitzell	1B134	R	24	137	502	59	143	23	7	3	62	35	26	18	.285	.376
2 Heinie Groh	2B113 SS4	R	23	117	397	51	112	19	5	3	48	38	36	24	.282	.378
Joe Tinker	SS101 3B9	R	32	110	382	47	121	20	13	1	57	20	26	13	.317	.445
2 John Dodge	3B91	R	24	94	323	35	78	8	8	4	45	10	34	11	.241	.353
Johnny Bates	OF111	L	31	131	407	63	113	13	7	6	51	67	30	21	.278	.369
Armando Marsans	OF94 1B22 3B2 SS1	R	26	118	435	49	129	7	6	0	38	17	25	37	.297	.340
Bob Bescher	OF138	R	29	141	511	86	132	22	11	1	37	94	68	38	.258	.350
Tommy Clarke	C100	R	25	114	330	29	87	11	8	1	38	39	40	2	.264	.355
Johnny Kling	C63	R	37	80	209	20	57	7	6	0	23	14	14	2	.273	.364
Marty Berghammer	SS53 2B13	R	25	74	188	25	41	4	1	3	13	10	29	16	.218	.298
2 Josh Devore	OF57	R	25	66	217	30	58	6	4	3	14	21	27	17	.267	.373
Dick Egan	2B38 SS17 3B2	R	29	60	195	15	55	7	3	0	22	15	13	6	.282	.349
Rafael Almeida	3B37 OF3 SS2 2B1	R	26	50	130	14	34	4	2	1	21	11	16	4	.262	.392
2 Jimmy Sheckard	OF38	L	34	47	116	16	22	1	3	0	7	27	16	6	.190	.250
1 Beals Becker	OF28	L	26	30	108	11	32	5	3	0	14	6	12	0	.296	.398
1 Eddie Grant	3B26	L	30	27	94	12	20	1	0	0	9	11	10	7	.213	.223
Al Wickland	OF24	L	25	26	79	7	17	5	5	0	8	15	12	3	.215	.405
Earl Blackburn	C12	R	20	17	27	1	7	0	0	0	3	2	5	2	.259	.259
1 Tex McDonald	SS1	R	24	7	21	1	6	0	0	0	2	2	4	0	.286	.286

Hank Severeid 22 R 0-6, Bill Hobbs 20 R 0-4, Karl Meister 22 R 2-7, Harry Chapman 25 R 1-2, Bert Niehoff 29 R 0-8, Mark Stewart 23 L 0-1

NAME	T	AGE	W	L	PCT	SV	G	GS	CG	IP	H	BB	SO	SHO	ERA
TOTALS		28	64	89	.418	10	156	156	71	1380	1398	456	522	10	3.46
Chief Johnson	R	27	14	16	.467	0	44	31	13	269	251	86	107	3	3.01
Rube Benton (JJ)	L	23	11	11	.611	0	23	22	9	144	140	60	68	1	3.50
Three Finger Brown	R	36	11	12	.478	6	39	16	11	173	174	44	41	1	2.92
2 Red Ames	R	30	11	13	.458	2	31	24	12	187	185	70	80	1	2.89
George Suggs	R	31	8	15	.348	2	36	22	9	199	220	35	73	2	4.03
Gene Packard	L	25	7	11	.389	0	39	21	9	191	208	64	73	2	2.97
Frank Harter	R	26	1	1	.500	0	17	2	0	47	47	19	10	0	3.83
1 Art Fromme	R	29	1	4	.200	0	9	7	2	56	55	21	24	0	4.18
Chick Smith	L	20	0	1	.000	0	5	1	0	18	15	11	11	0	3.50
Ralph Works	R	25	0	0	—	0	9	0	0	15	15	8	4	0	7.80
Dick Robertson	R	21	0	0	—	0	1	0	0	10	13	9	1	0	7.20
Bill Powell	R	28	0	0	—	0	1	1	1	2		2	0		54.00
Harry McIntire	R	35	0	0	—	0	1	1	0	3		5		0	27.00
Cy Morgan	R	34	0	0	—	0	1	0	0	5	1	2		0	18.00
Jack Rowan	R	25	0	0	—	0	5	5	5	39	37	9	21	0	3.00
Ernie Herbert	R	26	0	0	—	0	6	0	0	17	12	5	5	0	2.12
2 Red Nelson	R	27	0	0	—	0	2	0	0	4	6	3		0	31.50
Hal Betts	R	32	0	0	—	0	1	0	0	2	1	1		0	9.00
Frank Harrington	R	24	0	0	—	0	4	0	0	4	6	1		0	9.00
Joe McManus	R	25	0	0	—	0	1	0	0	2	1	1		0	18.00

ST. LOUIS 8th 51-99 .340 49 — MILLER HUGGINS

NAME	G by Pos	B	AGE	G	AB	R	H	2B	3B	HR	RBI	BB	SO	SB	BA	SA
TOTALS			27	153	4952	523	1221	152	72	14	427	450	573	171	.247	.315
Ed Konetchy	1B139 P1	R	27	139	502	74	137	18	17	7	68	53	41	25	.273	.418
Miller Huggins	2B112	R	35	120	381	73	109	12	0	0	27	94	49	23	.286	.318
Charley O'Leary	SS102 2B15	R	31	120	404	32	88	15	5	0	31	20	34	3	.218	.280
Mike Mowrey	3B130	R	29	131	461	61	116	18	4	0	33	53	40	21	.252	.318
Steve Evans	OF74 1B1	R	28	97	245	49	61	15	6	1	31	20	28	5	.249	.371
Rebel Oakes	OF144	R	29	146	537	59	156	14	5	0	49	43	32	22	.291	.355
Lee Magee	OF107 2B21 1B6 SS2	B	24	136	529	53	140	13	7	2	31	34	30	23	.265	.327
Ivy Wingo	C79 1B5 OF1	L	22	111	305	25	78	5	8	2	35	17	41	18	.256	.344
P.Whitted	OF40 SS37 3B21 2B7 1B2	R	23	122	402	44	89	10	5	0	38	31	44	9	.221	.271
Ted Cather	OF57 1B1 P1	R	24	67	183	16	39	8	4	0	12	9	24	7	.213	.301
1 Jimmy Sheckard	OF46	L	34	52	136	18	27	2	1	0	17	41	25	5	.199	.228
1 Larry McLean	C42	R	31	48	152	7	41	9	0	0	12	6	9	0	.270	.329
Pete Hildebrand	C22 OF1	R	28	26	55	3	9	2	0	0	1	1	10	1	.164	.200
Skipper Roberts	C16	R	25	26	41	4	6	2	0	0	3	3	13	1	.146	.195
Arnold Hauser	SS8 2B4	R	24	22	45	3	13	0	3	0	9	2	4	0	.289	.422
Finners Quinlan	OF12	L	25	13	50	1	8	0	1	0	9	5	9	1	.160	.160
Zinn Beck	SS5 3B5	R	27	10	30	4	5	1	0	0	4	4	10	1	.167	.200
Wes Callahan	SS6	R	24	7	14	0	4	0	0	0	1	2	1	0	.286	.286
Frank Snyder	C7	R	19	7	21	1	4	0	0	0	2	2	4	0	.190	.286

Chuck Miller 23 L 2-12, Heinie Peitz 42 R 1-4, 2 Doc Crandall 25 R 0-2, Al Cabrera 32 0-2, John Vann 23 R 0-1, Jimmy Whelan 23 R 0-1

NAME	T	AGE	W	L	PCT	SV	G	GS	CG	IP	H	BB	SO	SHO	ERA
TOTALS		25	51	99	.340	11	152	152	70	1349	1423	476	464	6	4.24
Slim Sallee	L	28	18	15	.545	5	49	29	17	273	254	59	105	3	2.70
Dan Griner	R	25	10	22	.313	0	34	34	18	225	279	66	79	1	5.08
Bob Harmon	R	25	8	21	.276	2	42	37	17	273	291	99	66	1	3.92
Pol Perritt	R	21	6	14	.300	0	36	21	8	175	205	64	64	0	5.25
Bill Steele	R	27	4	4	.500	0			2	54	58	18	10	0	5.00
Bill Doak	R	22	2	4	.200	1	15	12	5	93	79	39	51	1	3.10
Ed Konetchy	R	26	1	2	.333	1	19	7	0	70	81	33	29	0	5.14
Sandy Burk	R	24	1	5	.167	0	30			4	2			0	5.27
Rube Geyer	R	29	1	5	.167	1	30	25	8	15				0	4.50
Harry Trekell	R	22	1	0	.000	1	7	1	1	30	25	8	15	0	4.50
Walt Marbet	R	22	1	0	.000	1								0	18.00
Ben Hunt	L	24	1	0	.000	1					6	6	3	0	3.38
Dick Niehaus	L	20	0	3	.000	0	3	2		24	20	13	4	0	4.13
Bill Hopper	R	21	0	3	.000	0	3	2		24	20	8	4	0	3.75
Joe Willis	L	23	0	0	—	0	10	9	1	11	6		7	0	54.00
Ted Cather	R	24	0	0	—	0	1	1		2	1	0			6.00
Phil Redding	R	23	0	0	—	0					2	1	1	0	

WORLD SERIES — PHILADELPHIA (AL) 4 NEW YORK (NL) 1

LINE SCORES

TEAM	1	2	3	4	5	6	7	8	9	10	11	12	R	H	E

Game 1 October 7 at New York

													R	H	E
PHI (AL)	0	0	0	3	2	0	0	1	0				6	11	1
NY(NL)	0	0	1	0	3	0	0	0	0				4	11	0

Bender / Marquard, Crandall (6), Tesreau (8)

Game 2 October 8 at Philadelphia

													R	H	E
NY	0	0	0	0	0	0	0	0	3	0			3	7	2
PHI	0	0	0	0	0	0	0	0	0	0			0	8	2

Mathewson / Plank

Game 3 October 9 at New York

										R	H	E
PHI	3	0	2	0	0	0	2	1	0	8	12	1
NY	0	0	0	0	1	0	1	0	0	2	5	1

Bush / Tesreau, Crandall (7)

Game 4 October 10 at Philadelphia

										R	H	E
NY	0	0	0	0	0	0	3	2	0	5	8	2
PHI	0	1	0	3	2	0	0	0	X	6	9	0

Bender / Demaree, Marquard (5)

Game 5 October 11 at New York

										R	H	E
PHI	1	0	2	0	0	0	0	0	0	3	6	1
NY	0	0	0	0	1	0	0	0	X	1	2	2

Plank / Mathewson

COMPOSITE BATTING

Philadelphia (AL)

NAME	POS	G	AB	R	H	2B	3B	HR	RBI	BA
Totals		5	174	23	46	4	4	2	21	.204
Oldring	OF	5	22	5	6	0	0	0	1	.273
E.Murphy	OF	5	22	5	5	0	0	0	0	.227
Baker	3B	5	20	2	9	0	0	1	7	.450
Barry	SS	5	20	3	6	3	0	0	3	.300
Collins	2B	5	19	5	8	0	0	0	3	.421
McInnis	1B	5	17	1	2	1	0	0	2	.118
Strunk	OF	5	17	3	2	0	0	0	0	.118
Schang	C	4	14	2	5	0	0	1	6	.357
Bender	P	2	8	0	0	0	0	0	0	.000
Plank	P	2	7	0	1	0	0	0	1	.143
Bush	P	1	4	0	1	0	0	0	0	.250
Lapp	C	1	4	0	1	0	0	0	0	.250

New York (NL)

NAME	POS	G	AB	R	H	2B	3B	HR	RBI	BA
Totals		5	164	15	33	3	1	1	15	.201
Doyle	2B	5	20	1	3	0	0	0	2	.150
Burns	OF	5	19	2	3	0	0	0	0	.158
Shafer	OF -3B	5	19	2	3	1	1	0	0	.158
Herzog	3B	5	19	1	1	0	0	0	0	.053
Fletcher	SS	5	18	1	5	0	0	0	4	.278
Murray	OF	5	16	2	4	0	0	0	0	.250
Merkle	1B	4	13	3	3	0	0	1	3	.231
McLean	C	5	12	0	6	0	0	0	1	.500
Mathewson	P	2	5	1	3	0	0	0	0	.600
Crandall	P	2	4	1	0	0	0	0	0	.000
Meyers	C	1	4	0	0	0	0	0	0	.000
Snodgrass	1B-OF	3	3	0	1	0	0	0	0	.333
Wilson	C	2	3	0	0	0	0	0	0	.000
McCormick	PH	2	2	0	1	0	0	0	0	.500
Wiltse	1B	2	2	0	0	0	0	0	0	.000
Tesreau	P	2	2	0	0	0	0	0	0	.000
Marquard	P	2	1	0	0	0	0	0	0	.000
Grant	PH-PR	2	1	0	0	0	0	0	0	.000
Demaree	P	1	1	0	0	0	0	0	0	.000
Cooper	PR	2	0	0	0	0	0	0	0	—

COMPOSITE PITCHING

Philadelphia (AL)

NAME	G	IP	H	BB	SO	W	L	SV	ERA
Totals	5	46	33	8	19	4	1	0	2.15
Plank	2	19	9	3	7	1	1	0	0.95
Bender	2	18	19	1	9	2	0	0	4.00
Bush	1	9	5	4	3	1	0	0	1.00

New York (NL)

NAME	G	IP	H	BB	SO	W	L	SV	ERA
Totals	5	45	46	7	16	1	4	0	3.80
Mathewson	2	19	14	2	7	1	1	0	0.95
Marquard	2	9	10	3	3	0	1	0	7.00
Tesreau	2	8.1	11	1	4	0	1	0	6.48
Crandall	2	4.2	7	1	0	0	1	0	3.86
Demaree	1	4	7	1	0	0	1	0	4.50

1914 The Miracle in Boston

Europe had broken out into war in the summer, and the world of baseball had its first war between leagues since the American League was formed in 1901. The Federal League set up shop as a third major league and proceeded to raid both established leagues for players. The National League lost more players to the Feds than the American, but the National was compensated by one of the most exciting pennant races in its history.

John McGraw led his Giants out to a substantial lead in June, apparently on the way to a fourth straight pennant. Though Rube Marquard was losing more than he was winning, Christy Mathewson and Jeff Tesreau were piling up enough victories to keep the Giants on top, despite slumps by Red Murray and Larry Doyle.

The Boston Braves, mired in last place as late as July 18, were a club made up of castoffs who had finished fifth the previous year. Then, suddenly, around mid-July the Braves caught fire and started moving up. Behind the direction of dapper manager George Stallings, the Braves moved into fourth place on July 21, and kept going until reaching second place August 12. Bill James, Dick Rudolph, and Lefty Tyler assumed practically all the Brave pitching chores during the drive, and all three were consistent winners. Joey Connolly represented the only .300 hitter on the club, but ex-Cub Johnny Evers and shortstop Rabbit Maranville provided solid infielding around second base in addition to clutch stick work. The Braves poked their heads into the clouds of first place on September 2, and passed the slumping Giants for keeps on September 8, capping a drive of 34 wins in 44 tries. The Braves, so recently doormats, kept winning until the season's end, finishing 10½ games over the faded Giants and writing the greatest comeback story in baseball's annals.

The American League race exhibited none of the drama of the pennant chase--the Philadelphia Athletics were expected to win, and they did so quite handily. Connie Mack's machine ground out 749 runs, tops in the league, as Stuffy McInnis, Eddie Collins, and

Frank Baker provided teeth for the Philadelphia attack. With Jack Coombs again out with illness, Chief Bender and Eddie Plank provided the mound savvy and were helped by young hurlers, Bob Shawkey and Joe Bush.

The Red Sox came in second, relying on good pitching to keep the team in contention. Manager Bill Carrigan had "The Grey Eagle," Tris Speaker, as the heart of his lineup, and Ray Collins and Dutch Leonard developed into top starters. Joe Wood could not return to his form of 1912, as he again won only nine games. A more historical note out of Boston occurred in September, when the Red Sox purchased a promising young pitcher named Babe Ruth from Providence of the International League.

The World Series promised to be an easy Athletic win, but the momentum which swept the Braves on to their pennant crested and broke over the back of Philadelphia. Boston won the first game behind Dick Rudolph, 7-1, and the upset materialized as the Braves swept the next 3 games to shut the Mackmen out of the win column. The Boston staff of Rudolph, James, and Tyler held the Athletics to a .172 batting average, while Boston's hot hitters included Johnny Evers at .438 and catcher Hank Gowdy at .545.

The Series marked the end of the line for the 1914 edition of Connie Mack's Athletics. Mack could not meet the salary demands of star players who were being wooed by the Federal League, so he began selling most of his top players to other teams in the circuit to keep the American League intact. Breaking up the perennially tough Athletics spelled disaster to Mack's dynasty, and the Tall Tactician would have to rebuild his team over the course of a dozen years before they could return to the status of contenders.

1914 AMERICAN LEAGUE

PHILADELPHIA 1st 99-53 .651 — CONNIE MACK

NAME	G by Pos	B	AGE	G	AB	R	H	2B	3B	HR	RBI	BB	SO	SB	BA	SA
TOTALS			26	157	5126	749	1392	165	80	29	627	545	517	231	.272	.352
Stuffy McInnis	1B149	R	23	149	576	74	181	12	8	1	95	19	27	25	.314	.368
Eddie Collins	2B152	L	27	152	526	122	181	23	14	2	85	97	31	58	.344	.452
Jack Barry	SS140	R	27	140	467	57	113	12	0	0	42	53	34	22	.242	.268
Frank Baker	3B149	L	28	150	570	84	182	23	10	9	89	53	37	19	.319	.442
Eddie Murphy	OF148	L	22	148	573	101	156	12	9	3	43	87	46	36	.272	.340
Amos Strunk	OF120	L	25	122	404	58	111	15	3	2	45	57	38	25	.275	.342
Rube Oldring	OF117	R	30	119	466	68	129	21	7	3	49	18	35	14	.277	.371
Wally Schang	C100	B	24	107	307	44	88	11	8	3	45	32	33	7	.287	.404
Jack Lapp	C67	R	29	69	199	22	46	7	2	0	19	31	14	1	.231	.286
2 Jimmy Walsh	OF56 1B3 3B3 SS1	L	28	67	216	35	51	11	6	3	36	30	27	6	.236	.384
Larry Kopf	SS13 3B8 2B5	B	23	35	69	8	13	2	2	0	12	8	14	6	.188	.275
1 Tom Daley	OF24	L	29	29	86	17	22	1	3	0	7	12	14	4	.256	.337
Chick Davies	OF10 P1	L	22	19	46	6	11	3	1	0	5	5	13	1	.239	.348
Shag Thompson	OF8	R	21	16	29	3	5	0	1	0	2	7	8	1	.172	.241
Bill Orr	SS6 3B1	R	23	10	24	3	4	1	1	0	1	2	5	1	.167	.292
Wickey McAvoy	C8	R	19	8	16	1	2	0	1	0	0	4	4	0	.125	.250
Harry Davis	1B1	R	40	5	7	0	3	0	0	0	2	1	0	0	.429	.429
Press Cruthers	2B4	R	23	4	15	1	3	0	1	0	0	0	4	0	.200	.333
Dean Sturgis	C1	R	21	4	4	1	1	0	0	0	0	1	2	0	.250	.250
Sam Crane	SS2	R	19	2	6	0	0	0	0	0	0	0	3	0	.000	.000
Earle Mack	1B2	L	24	2	2	0	0	0	0	0	0	1	0	1	.000	.000
Ferdie Moore	1B2	R	18	2	4	1	2	0	1	0	0	1	0	2	.500	.500

Toots Coyne 19 0-2, Ben Rochefort 17 L 1-2, Charlie Sweeney 24 0-1, Ira Thomas 33 R 0-3

NAME	T	AGE	W	L	PCT	SV	G	GS	CG	IP	H	BB	SO	SHO	ERA
		25	99	53	.651	13	157	157	88	1404	1264	521	720	24	2.78
Chief Bender	R	31	17	3	.850	0	28	23	14	179	159	55	107	7	2.26
Bullet Joe Bush	R	21	17	12	.586	2	38	23	14	206	184	81	109	2	3.06
Bob Shawkey	R	23	16	8	.667	2	38	30	18	237	223	75	89	5	2.73
Eddie Plank	L	38	15	7	.683	2	34	23	11	185	178	42	110	4	2.87
Herb Pennock	L	20	11	4	.733	2	28	14	8	152	136	65	90	3	2.78
Weldon Wyckoff	R	22	11	8	.579	2	32	20	11	185	153	103	86	0	3.42
Rube Bressler	L	19	10	3	.769	2	29	10	8	148	112	56	96	1	1.76
Chick Davies	L	22	1	0	1.000	0	1	1	1	9	8	3	4	0	1.00
1 Boardwalk Brown	R	29	1	6	.143	0	15	7	2	66	64	26	20	0	4.09
Jack Coombs	R	31	0	1	.000	0	2	2	0	8	8	3	1	0	4.50
Willie Jensen	R	24	0	1	.000	0	1	1	0	9	7	2	1	0	2.00
1 Duke Houck	R	22	0	0	—	0	3	0	0	11	14	6	4	0	3.27
Charlie Boardman	R	21	0	0	—	0	2	0	0	7	10	4	2	0	5.14
Fred Worden	R	19	0	0	—	0	1	0	0	2	8	0	1	0	18.00

BOSTON 2nd 91-62 .595 8.5 — BILL CARRIGAN

NAME	G by Pos	B	AGE	G	AB	R	H	2B	3B	HR	RBI	BB	SO	SB	BA	SA
TOTALS			25	159	5117	589	1278	226	85	18	513	490	549	177	.250	.338
2 Dick Hoblitzell	1B68	L	29	68	229	31	73	10	3	0	33	16	21	12	.319	.389
1 Steve Yerkes	2B91	R	26	92	293	23	64	17	2	1	23	14	23	5	.218	.300
Everett Scott	SS143	R	21	144	539	66	129	15	6	2	37	32	43	9	.239	.301
Larry Gardner	3B153	L	28	155	553	50	143	23	19	3	68	35	39	16	.259	.385
Harry Hooper	OF140	L	26	141	530	85	137	23	15	1	41	58	47	19	.258	.364
Tris Speaker	OF156 1B1 P1	L	26	158	571	101	193	46	18	4	90	77	25	42	.338	.503
Duffy Lewis	OF142	R	25	146	510	53	142	39	6	2	79	57	41	22	.278	.398
Bill Carrigan	C78	R	30	81	178	18	45	5	1	1	22	40	18	1	.253	.309
Hal Janvrin	2B57 1B56 SS20 3B6	R	21	143	492	65	117	18	6	1	36	38	50	29	.238	.305
Wally Rehg	OF42	R	25	84	151	14	33	4	2	0	11	18	11	5	.219	.272
Pinch Thomas	C61 1B1	L	26	63	130	9	25	1	0	0	5	18	17	1	.192	.200
Hick Cady	C58	R	28	61	159	14	41	6	1	0	8	12	22	2	.258	.308
Olaf Hendriksen	OF61	L	26	61	95	16	25	2	1	1	5	22	12	5	.263	.337
1 Clyde Engle	1B29 2B5 3B2	R	30	55	134	14	26	2	0	0	9	14	11	4	.194	.209
2 Del Gainer (JJ)	1B18 2B11	R	27	38	84	11	20	9	2	2	13	8	14	2	.238	.464
Bill Swanson	2B6 3B3 SS1	B	25	11	20	0	4	2	0	0	0	3	4	0	.200	.300
Larry Pratt	C5	R	26	5	4	0	0	0	0	0	0	0	0	0	.000	.000
1 Les Nunamaker	C2 1B1	B	25	4	5	0	1	0	0	0	0	1	0	0	.200	.200
Squanto Wilson	1B1	B	25	1	0	0	0	0	0	0	0	0	0	0	—	—

Hienie Wagner (IL) 32

NAME	T	AGE	W	L	PCT	SV	G	GS	CG	IP	H	BB	SO	SHO	ERA
		25	91	62	.595	11	159	159	87	1434	1212	397	605	24	2.35
Ray Collins	L	27	20	13	.606	0	39	36	16	272	252	56	72	6	2.48
Dutch Leonard	L	22	19	5	.792	4	36	25	17	225	139	59	175	7	0.96
Rube Foster (KJ)	R	26	14	8	.636	0	32	27	17	212	164	52	90	5	1.65
Smoky Joe Wood	R	24	9	3	.750	1	18	14	11	113	94	34	67	1	2.63
Ernie Shore	R	23	9	4	.692	2	21	16	9	142	103	35	52	1	1.96
Hugh Bedient	R	24	8	12	.400	3	42	16	7	177	185	45	70	1	3.61
2 Vean Gregg	L	29	4	4	.500	0	13	9	3	76	78	41	26	0	3.56
1 Rankin Johnson	R	26	4	9	.308	0	16	13	4	99	92	34	24	2	3.10
Babe Ruth	L	19	2	1	.667	0	4	3	1	23	21	7	3	0	3.91
2 Guy Cooper	R	21	1	1	.500	0	9	1	0	22	23	9	5	0	5.32
1 Fritz Coumbe	L	24	1	2	.333	1	17	5	1	62	49	16	17	0	1.45
Ed Kelly	R	25	0	0	—	0	3	0	0	7	9	1	4	0	0.00
Matt Zeiser	R	25	0	0	—	0	2	0	0	10	9	5	1	0	1.80
Tris Speaker	L	26	0	0	—	0	1	0	0	2	3	0	0	0	9.00

WASHINGTON 3rd 81-73 .526 19 — CLARK GRIFFITH

NAME	G by Pos	B	AGE	G	AB	R	H	2B	3B	HR	RBI	BB	SO	SB	BA	SA
TOTALS			28	157	5108	572	1245	176	81	18	470	470	640	220	.244	.320
Chick Gandil	1B145	R	26	145	526	48	136	24	10	3	75	44	44	30	.259	.359
Ray Morgan	2B146	R	25	147	491	50	126	22	8	1	49	62	34	24	.257	.340
George McBride	SS156	R	33	156	503	49	102	12	4	0	24	43	70	12	.203	.243
Eddie Foster	3B156	R	27	156	616	82	172	16	10	2	50	60	47	31	.282	.351
Danny Moeller	OF150	R	29	151	571	83	143	19	10	1	45	71	89	26	.250	.364
Clyde Milan (JJ)	OF113	L	28	115	437	63	129	19	11	3	39	32	26	38	.295	.396
Howard Shanks	OF139	R	23	143	500	44	112	22	10	4	64	29	51	18	.224	.332
John Henry	C91	R	24	91	261	22	44	7	4	0	20	37	47	7	.169	.226
Rip Williams	C44 1B8 OF1	R	32	81	169	17	47	6	4	1	22	13	19	2	.278	.379
Eddie Ainsmith (BW)	C51	R	24	58	151	11	34	7	0	1	13	9	28	8	.225	.272
2 Mike Mitchell	OF53	R	34	55	193	20	55	5	3	1	20	22	19	9	.285	.358
Wally Smith	2B12 1B7 SS7 3B5 OF1	R	26	45	97	11	19	4	1	0	8	3	12	1	.196	.258
Merito Acosta	OF18	L	18	38	74	10	19	2	2	0	4	11	18	3	.257	.338
Germany Schaefer	2B3 OF3	R	37	25	29	6	7	1	0	0	2	5	4	4	.241	.276
Charlie Pick	OF7	L	26	10	23	0	9	0	0	0	1	4	4	1	.391	.391
Joe Gedeon	OF3	R	20	3	2	0	0	0	0	0	0	0	0	0	.000	.000
Doug Neff	SS3	R	23	3	2	0	0	0	0	0	0	0	0	0	.000	.000
Irish Meusel	OF1	R	21	2	1	0	0	0	0	0	0	0	0	0	.000	.000
Tom Wilson	C1	B	24	1	1	0	0	0	0	0	0	0	0	0	.000	.000

NAME	T	AGE	W	L	PCT	SV	G	GS	CG	IP	H	BB	SO	SHO	ERA
		22	81	73	.526	16	157	157	75	1421	1170	520	784	24	2.54
Walter Johnson	R	26	28	18	.635	1	51	40	33	372	287	74	225	9	1.72
Jim Shaw	R	20	15	17	.469	4	48	31	15	257	198	137	164	6	2.70
Joe Boehling	L	23	12	8	.600	1	27	24	14	196	180	76	91	2	3.03
Doc Ayres	R	23	12	16	.429	2	49	32	8	265	221	54	148	3	2.55
Joe Engel	R	21	7	5	.583	2	35	15	1	124	108	75	41	0	2.98
Jack Bentley	L	19	5	7	.417	4	30	11	3	125	110	53	55	2	2.38
Harry Harper	L	19	2	1	.667	0	23	3	1	57	45	35	50	0	3.47
Carl Cashion	R	23	0	1	.000	0	2	1	0	5	4	3	0	1	10.80
Mutt Williams	R	21	0	0	—	0	5	0	0	7	5	4	3	0	5.14
Bert Gallia	R	22	0	0	—	0	6	0	0	3	4	4	0	0	4.50
Jin Stevens	R	24	0	0	—	0	3	0	0	6	3	2	0	0	9.00
Nick Altrock	L	37	0	0	—	0	1	0	0	1	1	0	0	0	0.00
Frank Barron	L	23	0	0	—	0	1	1	0	7	5	4	1	0	0.00
Clark Griffith	R	44	0	0	—	0	1	0	0	1	1	0	0	0	0.00

DETROIT — 4th 80-73 .523 19.5 — HUGHIE JENNINGS

NAME	G by Pos	B	AGE	G	AB	R	H	2B	3B	HR	RBI	BB	SO	SB	BA	SA
TOTALS			26	157	5102	615	1318	195	84	25	513	557	537	211	.258	.344
George Burns	1B137	R	21	137	478	55	139	22	5	5	57	32	56	23	.291	.389
Marty Kavanagh	2B115 1B4	R	23	127	439	60	109	21	6	4	35	41	42	16	.248	.351
Conie Bush	SS157	B	26	157	596	97	150	18	4	0	32	112	54	35	.252	.295
George Moriarty (BG)	3B126 1B3	R	28	130	465	56	118	19	5	1	40	39	27	34	.254	.323
Sam Crawford	OF157	L	34	157	582	74	183	22	26	8	104	69	31	25	.314	.483
Ty Cobb (BR)	OF96	R	27	97	345	69	127	22	11	2	57	57	22	35	.368	.513
Bobby Veach	OF145	L	26	149	531	56	146	19	14	1	72	50	29	20	.275	.369
Oscar Stanage	C122	R	31	122	400	16	77	8	4	0	25	24	58	2	.193	.233
Hugh High	OF53	L	26	80	184	25	49	5	3	0	17	26	11	7	.266	.326
Jean Dubuc	P36	R	25	70	124	9	28	8	1	1	11	7	11	1	.226	.331
Harry Heilmann	OF29 1B16 2B6	R	19	67	182	25	41	8	1	2	18	22	29	1	.225	.313
Ossie Vitt (BW)	2B36 3B16 OF2 SS1	R	24	66	195	35	49	7	0	0	8	31	8	10	.251	.287
Del Baker	C38	R	22	43	70	4	15	2	1	0	1	6	9		.214	.271
Red McKee	C27	R	23	32	64	7	12	1	1	0	8	14	16	1	.188	.234
Billy Purtell	3B16 2B1 SS1	R	28	26	76	4	13	4	0	1	3	2	7	1	.171	.224

Paddy Baumann 28 R 0-11, 1 Ray Demmitt 30 L 0-0, 1 Del Gainer 27 R 0-0, Fred McMullin 22 R 0-1

NAME	T	AGE	W	L	PCT	SV	G	GS	CG	IP	H	BB	SO	SHO	ERA
TOTALS		25	80	73	.523	13	157	157	81	1412	1285	498	567	14	2.86
Harry Covelski	L	28	22	12	.647	2	44	36	23	303	251	100	124	5	2.49
Hooks Dauss	R	24	18	15	.545	4	45	35	22	302	286	87	150	3	2.86
Jean Dubuc	R	25	13	14	.481	1	36	27	15	224	216	76	70	2	3.46
Pug Cavet	L	24	7	7	.500	2	31	14	6	151	129	44	51	1	2.45
Alex Martin	R	30	6	6	.500	3	32	12	5	138	131	59	55	1	2.67
Ross Reynolds	R	26	5	3	.625	1	26	7	3	78	62	39	31	1	2.08
Mark Hall	R	26	4	6	.400	2	25	8	1	90	88	27	18	0	2.70
George Boehler	R	22	2	3	.400	0	18	6	2	63	54	48	37	0	3.57
Red Oldham	L	20	2	4	.333	0	9	7	3	45	42	8	23	0	3.40
Ed McCreery	R	24	1	0	1.000	0	3	1	0	4	6	3	4	0	11.25
Johnny Williams(IL)	R	24	0	3	.000	0	4	3	1	11	17	5	4	0	6.54
Lefty Williams	L	21	0	0	—	0	1	1	0	1	3	2	0	0	0.00

ST. LOUIS — 5th 71-82 .464 28.5 — BRANCH RICKEY

NAME	G by Pos	B	AGE	G	AB	R	H	2B	3B	HR	RBI	BB	SO	SB	BA	SA
TOTALS			27	159	5101	523	1241	185	75	17	430	423	863	233	.243	.319
John Leary	1B130 C15	R	23	144	533	35	141	28	7	0	45	10	71	9	.265	.343
Del Pratt	2B1562 OF5 SS1	R	26	158	584	85	165	34	13	5	65	50	45	37	.283	.411
Doc Lavan	SS73	R	23	74	239	21	63	7	4	1	21	17	39	6	.264	.339
Jimmy Austin	3B127	B	34	130	466	55	111	16	4	0	30	40	59	20	.238	.290
Gus Williams	OF141	L	26	143	499	51	126	19	6	4	47	36	120	35	.253	.339
Burt Shotton	OF152	L	29	154	515	63	156	19	9	0	38	64	66	40	.269	.333
Tilly Walker	OF145	R	26	151	517	67	154	24	16	6	78	51	72	29	.298	.441
Sam Agnew	C113	R	27	113	311	22	66	5	4	0	16	24	63	10	.212	.254
Ivon Howard	3B33 1B28 OF2 SS1	B	31	81	209	21	51	6	2	0	20	28	42	14	.244	.292
Buzzy Wares	SS68 2B8	R	28	81	215	20	45	10	1	0	23	28	35	10	.209	.265
Ernie Walker	OF36	L	23	71	131	19	39	5	3	1	14	13	26	6	.298	.405
Frank Crossin	C41	R	23	43	90	5	11	1	1	0	5	10	10	3	.122	.156
Eddie Miller	1B8 2B5 OF5 3B2	R	25	34	58	8	8	0	1	0	6	3	12	2	.138	.172
Bill Rumler	C9 OF6	R	23	33	46	2	8	1	0	0	6	3	12		.174	.196
Bobby Wallace (FR)	SS19 3B2	R	40	26	73	3	16	2	1	0	5	5	13	1	.219	.274
Joe Jenkins	C9	R	19	32	0	4	1	1	0	1	0	1		.125	.219
Tim Bowden	OF4	L	22	7	9	0	2	0	0	0	0	0	2		.222	.222
Bob Clemens	OF5	R	27	13	1	3	0	1	0	3	2	1		.231	.385
Dick Kauffman	1B6	R	26	7	15	1	4	1	0	0	2	0	3		.267	.333
Dee Walsh	SS7	R	24	7	23	1	2	0	0	0	0	1	4		.087	.087

George Hale 19 R 2-11, 1 Jack Erzenroth 28 R 1-6, Ed Hemmingway 21 B 0-5, Dutch Bold 19 R 0-1, Branch Rickey 32 L 0-2, Bob Messenger 30 B 0-2, Duitch Schrick 24 R 0-0

NAME	T	AGE	W	L	PCT	SV	G	GS	CG	IP	H	BB	SO	SHO	ERA
TOTALS		25	71	82	.464	9	159	159	80	1411	1309	540	553	15	2.84
Carl Weilman	L	24	18	13	.581	0	44	36	20	299	260	84	119	3	2.08
Earl Hamilton	L	22	17	18	.486	2	44	35	20	302	265	100	111	5	2.50
Bill James	R	27	15	14	.517	0	44	35	19	284	269	109	109	3	2.85
George Baumgardner	R	22	14	13	.519	3	45	18	9	184	152	84	93	3	2.79
Roy Mitchell	R	29	4	5	.444	2	28	9	4	103	134	38	38	0	4.37
Wiley Taylor	R	26	2	5	.286	0	16	8	2	50	41	25	21	1	3.42
Walt Leverenz	L	25	1	12	.077	0	27	16	5	111	107	63	41	0	3.81
Harry Hoch	R	27	0	2	.000	0	15	2	1	54	55	27	13	0	3.00
Grover Baichley	R	24	0	0	—	0	7			9			3	0	5.14
Ernie Manning	R	23	0	0	—	0	10			11			3	0	3.60
Allan Sothoron	R	21	0	0	—	0	6			6		4	3	0	6.00

CHICAGO — 6th(tie) 70-84 .455 30 — NIXEY CALLAHAN

NAME	G by Pos	B	AGE	G	AB	R	H	2B	3B	HR	RBI	BB	SO	SB	BA	SA
TOTALS			26	157	5040	487	1205	161	71	19	390	408	609	167	.239	.311
Jack Fournier	1B97 OF6	R	24	109	379	44	118	14	9	6	44	31	44	10	.311	.443
Lena Blackburne	2B143	R	27	144	474	52	105	10	5	1	35	66	58	25	.222	.290
Buck Weaver	SS134	R	23	136	541	64	133	20	9	2	28	20	40	14	.246	.327
Jim Breton	3B79	R	22	81	231	21	49	7	2	0	24	24	42	9	.212	.260
Shano Collins	OF154	R	28	154	598	61	164	34	9	3	65	27	49	30	.274	.376
Ping Bodie	OF95	R	26	107	327	21	75	9	5	3	29	21	35	12	.229	.315
2 Ray Demmitt	OF142	L	30	146	515	63	133	13	12	2	46	61	48	12	.258	.342
Ray Schalk	C124	R	21	135	392	30	106	13	2	0	36	38	24	24	.270	.314
Tom Daly	OF23 3B5 C4 1B2	R	22	61	133	13	31	2	0	0	8	7	13	3	.233	.248
1 Hal Chase	1B58	R	31	58	206	27	55	10	5	0	20	23	19	9	.267	.364
Scotty Alcock	3B48 2B1	R	28	54	156	12	27	4	2	0	7	7	14	4	.173	.224
Joe Berger	SS27 2B12 3B7	R	27	47	148	11	23	3	1	0	3	13	9	2	.155	.189
Wally Mayer	C33 3B1	R	23	39	85	7	14	3	1	0	5	14	23	1	.165	.224
Braggo Roth	OF34	R	21	34	126	14	37	4	6	1	10	8	25	3	.294	.444
Larry Chappell	OF9	L	24	21	39	3	9	0	0	0	1	1	11		.231	.231
Harry Lord (JT)	3B19 OF1	L	32	21	69	8	13	1	1	1	3	5	3	2	.188	.275
Walt Kuhn	C16	R	27	17	40	4	11	2	0	0	0	8	11	2	.275	.300
Howard Baker	3B15	R	26	15	47	4	13	1	1	0	5	3	8	2	.277	.340
Carl Manda	2B7	R	27	9	15	2	4	0	0	0	1	3	1		.267	.267
Polly Wolfe	OF8	L	25	9	14	1	3	0	0	0	0	1	3	1	.214	.214

Cecil Coombs 26 R 4-23, Charlie Kavanagh 23 R 1-5, Delos Brown 21 R 0-1, Irv Porter 26 B 1-4, Hank Schreiber 22 R 0-2, Billy Sullivan 39 R 0-0

NAME	T	AGE	W	L	PCT	SV	G	GS	CG	IP	H	BB	SO	SHO	ERA
TOTALS		27	70	84	.455	15	157	157	74	1399	1207	401	660	17	2.48
Jim Scott	R	25	14	18	.438	2	43	33	12	253	228	75	138	2	2.84
Joe Benz	R	28	14	19	.424	3	48	35	16	283	245	66	142	4	2.26
Eddie Cicotte	R	30	11	16	.407	3	45	30	15	269	220	72	122	4	2.04
Red Faber	R	25	10	9	.526	4	40	19	11	181	154	64	88	2	2.68
Mellie Wolfgang	R	24	9	5	.643	2	24	11	9	119	96	32	50	2	1.89
Reb Russell	L	25	8	12	.400	1	38	23	8	167	168	33	79	1	2.91
Ed Walsh	R	33	2	3	.400	0	6	5	3	45	32	20	15	1	2.90
Hi Jasper	R	22	1	0	1.000	0	16	0	0	32	22	20	19	0	3.38
Bill Lathrop	R	22	1	2	.333	0	19	1	0	48	41	19	7	0	2.63

NEW YORK — 6th(tie) 70-84 .455 30 — FRANK CHANCE 60-74 .448 / ROGER PECKINPAUGH 10-10 .500

NAME	G by Pos	B	AGE	G	AB	R	H	2B	3B	HR	RBI	BB	SO	SB	BA	SA
TOTALS			26	157	4994	536	1144	149	52	12	416	577	711	251	.229	.287
Charlie Mullen	1B93	R	25	93	323	33	84	8	0	0	44	33	55	11	.260	.285
Luke Boone	2B90 3B9	R	24	106	370	43	82	8	2	0	21	31	41	10	.222	.254
Roger Peckinpaugh	SS157	R	23	157	570	62	127	14	6	3	51	51	73	23	.223	.284
Fritz Maisel	3B148	R	24	149	548	79	131	23	9	2	47	76	69	74	.239	.325
Doc Cook	OF126	L	28	131	469	59	133	11	3	1	40	44	60	26	.283	.326
Birdie Cree	OF76	R	31	77	275	45	85	18	5	0	40	30	24	9	.309	.411
Roy Hartzell	OF128 2B5	L	32	137	481	55	112	15	9	1	32	68	38	22	.233	.308
Ed Sweeney	C78	R	25	87	258	25	55	8	1	1	22	30	30	19	.213	.264
2 Les Nunamaker	C70 1B5	R	25	87	257	19	68	10	3	2	29	22	34	11	.265	.350
Frank Truesdale	2B67 3B4	R	30	77	217	23	46	4	0	0	13	39	35	11	.212	.230
2 Tom Daley	OF57	L	29	67	191	36	48	6	4	0	9	38	13	8	.251	.325
Ray Caldwell	P31 1B6	R	26	59	113	9	22	4	0	0	10	7	24	2	.195	.230
Harry Williams	1B58	R	24	59	178	29	29	5	2	1	17	26	26	2	.163	.224
1 Bill Holden	OF45	R	24	55	165	12	30	3	2	0	12	16	26	6	.182	.224
1 Jimmy Walsh	OF41	L	28	43	136	13	26	1	3	1	11	29	21	6	.191	.265
Dick Gossett	C9	R	23	9	21	3	3	0	0	0	1	5	5		.143	.143
Angel Aragon	OF1	R	23	6	7	1	1	0	0	0	0		4		.143	.143
Jay Rogers	C4	R	24	5	8	0	0	0	0	0	1	2			.000	.000
Harry Kingman	1B1	L	22	4	4	0	0	0	0	0	0	1			.000	.000
Charlie Meara	OF3	L	23	4	7	1	2	0	0	0	0	3			.286	.286
Bill Reynolds	C1	R	29	4	5	0	2	0	0	0	0	3			.400	.400

Joe Harris 23 R 0-1, Pi Schwert 21 R 0-6, Alex Burr 20 R 0-0, Frank Chance 37 R 0-0 , Frank Gilhooley 22 L 2-3, Les Channell 28 L 1-1

NAME	T	AGE	W	L	PCT	SV	G	GS	CG	IP	H	BB	SO	SHO	ERA
TOTALS		27	70	84	.455	7	157	157	97	1397	1277	390	563	9	2.82
Ray Caldwell	R	26	17	9	.654	2	31	23	22	213	153	51	92	5	1.94
Ray Fisher	R	26	10	12	.455	1	29	26	17	209	177	61	86	2	2.28
King Cole	R	28	11	9	.550	0	33	15	8	187	172	45	83	2	3.29
Jack Warhop	R	29	8	15	.348	0	37	23	15	217	182	44	56	0	2.37
Ray Keating	R	20	7	11	.389	1	34	25	13	210	198	67	109	0	2.96
Marty McHale	R	27	7	16	.304	2	31	23	12	191	195	33	75	0	2.97
2 Boardwalk Brown	R	29	5	5	.500	1	20	14	8	122	123	42	57	0	3.25
Cy Pieh	R	27	4	4	.500	0	18	4	1	62	68	29	24	0	5.08
1 Al Schulz	R	25	1	3	.250	0	4	1	1	28	27	10	18	0	4.82
1 Guy Cooper	R	21	0	0	—	0	1	0	0	3	3	3	1	0	9.00

CLEVELAND — 8th 51-102 .333 48.5 — JOE BIRMINGHAM

NAME	G by Pos	B	AGE	G	AB	R	H	2B	3B	HR	RBI	BB	SO	SB	BA	SA
TOTALS			27	157	5157	538	1262	178	70	10	438	450	685	167	.245	.312
Doc Johnston	1B89 OF2	R	26	103	340	43	83	15	4	0	23	28	46	14	.244	.294
Nap Lajoie	2B80 1B4	R	39	121	419	37	108	14	3	0	50	32	15	14	.258	.305
Ray Chapman (NJ)	SS72 2B33	R	23	106	375	59	103	16	10	2	42	48	45	24	.275	.387
Terry Turner	3B103 2B17	R	33	120	428	43	105	14	9	1	33	44	36	17	.245	.327
Joe Jackson	OF119	L	26	122	453	61	153	22	13	3	53	41	34	22	.338	.464
Nemo Leibold	OF107	L	22	114	402	46	106	13	3	0	32	54	56	12	.264	.311
Jack Graney	OF127	L	28	130	460	63	122	17	10	1	39	67	46	20	.265	.352
Steve O'Neill	C81 1B1	R	22	86	269	28	68	12	2	0	20	15	35	1	.253	.312
Ivy Olson	SS31 2B23 3B19 OF6 1B3	R	28	89	310	22	75	6	2	1	20	13	24	15	.242	.284
Roy Wood	OF41 1B20	R	21	94	224	42	56	6	3	1	15	13	26	6	.236	.355
Jay Kirke	OF42 1B18	R	26	67	242	18	66	10	2	1	25	7	30	5	.273	.343
Johnny Bassler	C25 3B1 OF1	L	19	43	100	5	26	3	1	0	8	13	13	3	.182	.221
Bill Wambsganss	SS36 2B4	R	20	43	143	12	31	6	0	0	12	8	24	2	.217	.287
Fred Carisch	C38	R	32	40	102	8	22	2	3	0	11	7	13		.216	.284
Jack Lelivelt	OF12 1B1	R	28	32	64	6	21	4	1	0	2	3	10	2	.328	.438
Ben Egan	C30	R	30	24	88	6	14	3	2	0	3		20		.159	.250
Larry Pezold	3B20 OF1	R	29	23	71	4	16	0	1	0	5	1	13	2	.225	.254
Joe Birmingham	OF14	R	29	19	47	2	6	1	0	0	2	0	6		.128	.128
Rivington Bisland	SS15 3B1	R	24	18	57	9	6	1	0	0	2	2	5		.105	.123
Walter Barbare (JJ)	3B14 SS1	R	23	16	57	6	4	1	0	0	4	3	4	5	.308	.423
Elmer Smith	OF13	L	21	13	53	16	7	1	0	0	2	11	1		.321	.377

Josh Billings (JJ) 22 R 2-8, Bruce Hartford 22 R 4-22, Frank Mills 19 L 1-8, Tinsley Ginn 22 L 0-1, Al Cypert 24 R 0-1, George Dunlop 25 R 0-3 Tom Reilly 29 R 0-1

NAME	T	AGE	W	L	PCT	SV	G	GS	CG	IP	H	BB	SO	SHO	ERA
TOTALS		25	51	102	.333	2	157	157	69	1392	1365	666	688	9	3.20
Willie Mitchell	L	24	13	17	.433	0	39	32	16	257	207	124	179	3	3.19
Bill Steen (BW)	R	26	9	14	.391	0	30	22	13	201	201	68	97	1	2.60
Rip Hagerman	R	26	9	15	.375	0	37	26	12	198	189	118	112	3	3.06
1 Vean Gregg	L	29	8	7	.727	0	17	12	6	97	88	48	56	0	3.06
Allan Collamore	R	27	3	7	.300	0	28	6	3	105	100	49	32	0	3.26
Fred Blanding	R	26	3	9	.250	1	22	10	2	73	74	45	27	1	4.44
Abe Bowman	R	21	2	7	.222	0	22	10	2	73	74	45	27	1	4.44
Al Tedrow	L	22	1	2	.333	0	4	3	1	22	19	14	4	0	1.22
Paul Carter	R	22	1	1	.250	0	5	1		35	35	9		0	2.88
2 Fritz Coumbe	L	24	1	5	.167	0	14	5	2	55	59	16	22	0	3.28
Guy Morton	R	21	1	13	.071	1	25	13	5	128	116	55	80	0	3.02
Harley Dillinger	R	19	1	0	1.000	0	11	2	1	34	41	25	11	0	4.50
Lloyd Bishop	L	24	0	1	.000	0	5	1	1	14	7	11	3	0	5.63
Heorge Kahler	R	24	0	1	—	0	8	1		14	17	7	3	0	3.86
1 Nick Cullop	R	25	0	0	—	0	17	6	1	51	44	32	16	0	3.18
Lefty James	L	25	0	0	—	0	3	3						0	2.08
George Beck	R	24	0	0	—	0	1		3	35	9	9		0	2.08
Omer Benn	R	24	0	0	—	0	1	1		5	3	5		0	3.00
Sad Sam Jones	R	21	0	0	—	0	1			3		3		0	3.00

BOSTON 1ST 94-59 .614 GEORGE STALLINGS

NAME	G by Pos	B	AGE	G	AB	R	H	2B	3B	HR	RBI	BB	SO	SB	BA	SA
TOTALS			25	158	5206	657	1307	213	60	35	572	502	617	139	.251	.335
Butch Schmidt	1B147	L	27	147	537	67	153	17	9	1	71	43	55	14	.285	.356
Johnny Evers	2B139	L	32	139	491	81	137	20	3	1	40	87	26	12	.279	.338
Rabbit Maranville	SS156	R	22	156	586	74	144	23	6	4	78	45	56	28	.246	.326
Charlie Deal	3B74 SS1	R	22	79	257	17	54	13	2	0	23	20	23	4	.210	.276
Larry Gilbert	OF60	L	22	72	224	32	60	6	1	5	25	26	34	3	.268	.371
Les Mann	OF123	R	21	126	389	44	96	16	11	4	40	24	50	9	.247	.375
Joey Connolly	OF118	L	30	120	399	64	122	28	10	9	65	49	36	12	.306	.494
Hank Gowdy	C115 1B9	R	24	128	366	42	89	17	6	3	46	48	40	14	.243	.347
2 P. Whitted	OF38 2B15 3B5 1B4 SS3	R	24	66	218	36	57	11	4	2	31	18	18	10	.261	.376
2 Red Smith	3B60	R	24	60	207	30	65	17	1	3	37	28	24	2	.314	.449
Bert Whaling	C59	R	26	60	172	18	36	7	0	0	12	21	28	2	.209	.250
Oscar Dugey	OF17 2B16 3B1	R	26	58	109	17	21	2	0	1	10	10	15	5	.193	.239
2 Josh Devore	OF42	L	26	51	128	22	29	4	0	1	5	18	14	2	.227	.273
2 Ted Cather	OF48	R	25	50	145	19	43	11	2	0	27	7	28	7	.297	.400
2 Herbie Moran	OF41	L	30	41	154	24	41	3	1	0	4	17	11	4	.266	.299
Jim Murray	OF32	R	36	39	112	10	26	4	2	0	12	6	24	2	.232	.304
1 Jack Martin	3B27 1B1 2B1	R	27	33	85	10	18	2	0	0	5	6	7	0	.212	.235
Otto Hess	P14 1B5	L	35	31	47	5	11	1	0	1	6	1	11	0	.234	.319
Wilson Collins	OF19	L	24	27	35	5	9	0	0	0	1	2	8	0	.257	.257
Tommy Griffith	OF14	R	24	16	48	3	5	0	0	0	1	2	6	0	.104	.104
Clancy Tyler	C6	R	22	6	19	2	2	0	0	0	2	1	5	0	.105	.105
Clarence Kraft	1B1	R	27	3	3	0	1	0	0	0	0	0	1	0	.333	.333
Billy Martin	SS1	R	20	1											.000	.000

NAME	T	AGE	W	L	PCT	SV	G	GS	CG	IP	H	BB	SO	SHO	ERA
		24	94	59	.614	5	158	158	104	1421	1272	477	606	19	2.74
Dick Rudolph	R	25	26	10	.722	1	42	36	31	336	288	61	138	6	2.36
Bill James	R	22	26	7	.788	2	46	37	30	332	261	118	156	4	1.90
Lefty Tyler	L	24	16	14	.533	2	38	34	21	271	247	101	140	5	2.09
Paul Strand (SA)	L	20	6	2	.750	0	16	3	1	55	47	23	13	0	2.45
Dick Crutcher	R	24	5	6	.455	0	33	15	5	159	169	66	48	1	3.46
Otto Hess	L	35	5	6	.455	1	14	11	7	89	89	33	24	1	3.03
George Davis	R	24	3	3	.500	0	9	6	4	56	42	26	26	1	3.38
Gene Cocreham	R	29	3	4	.429	0	15	3	1	45	48	27	15	0	4.80
Tom Hughes	R	30	2	1	1.000	0	7	4	4	17	14	4	11	0	2.65
1 Hub Perdue	R	32	2	5	.286	0	9	9	2	51	60	11	13	0	5.82
Dolf Luque	R	23	0	1	.000	0	2	1	1	9	5	4	1	0	4.00
Dick Cottrell	R	25	0	1	.000	0	1	1	0	1	2	3	1	0	9.00
Buster Brown (DD) 32															

NEW YORK 2nd 84-70 .545 10.5 JOHN McGRAW

NAME	G by Pos	B	AGE	G	AB	R	H	2B	3B	HR	RBI	BB	SO	SB	BA	SA
TOTALS			27	156	5146	672	1363	222	59	30	566	447	479	239	.265	.348
Fred Merkle	1B146	R	25	146	512	71	132	25	7	7	63	52	80	23	.258	.375
Larry Doyle	2B145	L	28	145	539	87	140	19	8	5	63	58	25	17	.260	.353
Art Fletcher	SS135	R	29	135	514	62	147	26	8	2	79	22	37	15	.286	.379
Milt Stock	3B113 SS1	R	20	115	365	52	96	17	1	3	41	34	21	11	.263	.340
Fred Snodgrass	OF96 1B14 2B1 3B1	R	26	113	392	54	103	20	4	0	44	37	43	25	.263	.334
Bob Bescher	OF126	B	30	135	512	82	138	23	4	6	35	45	48	36	.270	.365
George Burns	OF154	R	24	154	561	100	170	35	5	1	60	89	53	62	.303	.417
Chief Meyers	C126	R	33	134	381	33	109	13	5	1	55	34	25	4	.286	.354
Eddie Grant	3B52 SS21 2B16	L	31	88	282	34	78	7	1	0	29	23	21	11	.277	.309
Red Murray	OF49	R	30	86	139	19	31	6	3	0	23	9	11		.223	.309
Dave Robertson	OF71	L	24	82	256	25	68	12	3	2	32	10	26	9	.266	.359
Larry McLean	C74	R	32	79	154	8	40	6	0	0	14	4	9	4	.260	.299
Sandy Piez	OF4	R	25	37	8	9	3	0	1	0	3	0	1	4	.375	.625
Mike Donlin		L	36	35	31	1	5	1	1	1	3	5	3	0	.161	.355
Jim Thorpe	OF4	R	27	30	31	5	6	1	0	0	2	0	4	1	.194	.226
Elmer Johnson	C11	R	30	11	12	0	2	1	0	0	1	0	0	0	.167	.250
Ben Dyer	SS6 2B1	R	21	7	4	1	1	0	0	0	0	0	1	1	.250	.250
Harry Smith	C4	R	24	5	7	0	3	0	0	0	2	3	1	1	.429	.429
Des Beatty	SS1 3B1	R	21	2	3	0	0	0	0	0	0	0	0	0	.000	.000
Fred Brainard	2B2	L	21	2	5	1	1	0	0	0	0	0	1	0	.200	.200
Walter Holke	1B2	L	21	2	6	0	2	0	0	0	0	0	0	0	.333	.333

NAME	T	AGE	W	L	PCT	SV	G	GS	CG	IP	H	BB	SO	SHO	ERA
		30	84	70	.545	9	156	156	88	1391	1298	367	563	20	2.94
Jeff Tesreau	R	26	26	10	.722	1	42	41	26	322	238	128	189	8	2.38
Christy Mathewson	R	33	24	13	.649	2	41	35	29	312	314	23	80	5	3.00
Rube Marquard	L	27	12	22	.353	2	39	33	15	268	261	47	92	4	3.06
Al Demaree	R	29	10	17	.370	0	38	29	13	224	219	77	89	2	3.09
Art Fromme	R	30	9	5	.643	2	38	12	3	138	142	44	57	1	3.20
Hank Ritter	R	20	1	0	1.000	0	1	0	0	8	4	4	0	1	1.13
Hooks Wiltse	L	34	1	1	.500	1	20	0	0	38	41	12	19	0	2.84
2 Marty O'Toole	R	26	1	1	.500	0	10	5	2	34	34	12	13	0	4.24
Eric Erickson	R	22	0	1	.000	0	1	1	0	5	3	3	0	0	0.00
Ferdie Schupp	L	23	0	0	—	0	1	0	0	17	19	9	9	0	5.82
Rube Schauer	R	23	0	0	—	0	6	0	0	22	16	8	6	0	3.28
Al Huenke	R	23	0	0	—	0	1	0	0	2	2	0	1	0	4.50

ST. LOUIS 3rd 81-72 .529 13 MILLER HUGGINS

NAME	G by Pos	B	AGE	G	AB	R	H	2B	3B	HR	RBI	BB	SO	SB	BA	SA
TOTALS			27	157	5046	558	1249	203	65	33	461	445	618	204	.248	.333
Dots Miller	1B98 SS53 2B5	R	27	155	573	67	166	27	10	4	88	34	52	16	.290	.393
Miller Huggins	2B147	B	36	148	509	85	134	17	4	1	24	105	63	32	.263	.318
Art Butler (SJ)	SS84 OF1	R	26	86	274	29	55	12	3	1	24	39	23	14	.201	.277
Zinn Beck	3B122 SS16	R	28	137	457	42	106	15	11	3	45	28	32	14	.232	.333
Owen Wilson	OF154	R	30	154	580	64	150	27	12	9	73	32	66	14	.259	.393
Lee Magee	OF102 1B40 2B6	B	25	142	529	79	150	23	4	2	40	42	24	36	.284	.353
Cozy Dolan	OF97 3B29	R	31	126	421	76	101	16	3	4	32	55	74	42	.240	.321
Frank Snyder	C98	R	20	100	326	19	75	15	4	1	25	13	28	1	.230	.310
Walton Cruise	OF81	L	24	95	256	20	58	9	3	4	28	25	42	3	.227	.332
Ivy Wingo	C70	L	23	80	237	24	71	8	5	4	26	18	17	15	.300	.426
Lee Dressen	1B38	R	24	46	103	16	24	2	1	0	7	11	20	2	.233	.272
1 Ted Cather	OF28	R	25	39	99	11	27	7	0	0	13	3	15	4	.273	.343
Chuck Miller	OF19	R	24	36	36	4	7	1	0	0	2	3	9	2	.194	.222
2 Joe Riggert	OF30	R	27	34	89	9	19	5	2	0	8	5	14	4	.213	.315
Ken Nash	SS10 2B6 SS3	B	25	24	51	4	14	3	1	0	6	6	10	0	.275	.373
1 Possum Whitted	3B11 OF3 2B1	R	24	20	31	3	4	1	0	0	1	0	6	0	.129	.161
Jack Roche	C9	R	23	12	9	1	6	2	1	0	3	0	1	1	.667	1.111
Paddy O'Connor	C7	R	34	10	9	0	0	0	0	0	0	2	2	0	.000	.000
Bruno Betzel	2B4 3B1	R	19	7	9	2	0	0	0	0	0	1	1	0	.000	.000
Rolla Daringer	SS1	L	24	2	4										.500	.750
Arnold Hauser (IL) 25																

NAME	T	AGE	W	L	PCT	SV	G	GS	CG	IP	H	BB	SO	SHO	ERA
		27	81	72	.529	12	157	157	83	1425	1279	422	531	16	2.38
Bill Doak	R	23	19	6	.760	1	36	33	16	256	193	87	118	7	1.72
Slim Sallee	L	29	18	17	.514	6	46	29	18	282	252	72	105	3	2.11
Pol Perritt	R	22	16	13	.552	2	41	32	18	286	248	93	115	3	2.36
Dan Griner	R	26	9	13	.409	2	37	17	11	179	163	57	74	2	2.51
2 Hub Perdue	R	32	8	5	.500	0	22	19	12	153	160	35	43	0	2.83
Hank Robinson	L	26	7	8	.467	0	26	16	6	126	128	32	30	1	3.00
1 Bill Steele	R	28	2	2	.500	0	17	2	0	53	55	7	16	0	2.72
Dick Niehaus	L	21	1	0	1.000	0	3	1	1	17	18	8	6	0	3.18
1 Casey Hageman	R	27	1	4	.200	0	12	7	1	55	43	20	21	0	2.46
Steamboat Williams	R	22	0	1	.000	0	5	1	0	11	13	6	2	0	6.55
Bill Hopper	R	22	0	0	—	0	3	0	0	6	5	1	0	0	3.60

CHICAGO 4th 78-76 .506 16.5 HENRY F. O'DAY

NAME	G by Pos	B	AGE	G	AB	R	H	2B	3B	HR	RBI	BB	SO	SB	BA	SA
TOTALS			29	156	5050	605	1229	199	74	42	502	501	577	164	.243	.337
Vic Saier	1B153	L	23	153	537	87	129	24	8	18	72	94	61	19	.240	.415
Bill Sweeney	2B134	R	28	134	463	45	101	14	5	1	38	53	15	18	.218	.276
Red Corriden	SS96 3B8 2B3	R	26	107	318	42	73	9	5	3	29	35	33	13	.230	.318
Heinie Zimmerman	3B119 SS15 2B12	R	27	146	564	75	167	36	12	4	87	20	46	17	.296	.428
Wilbur Good	OF154	L	28	154	580	70	158	24	7	2	43	59	74	31	.272	.348
Tommy Leach	OF137 3B16	R	36	153	597	80	152	24	9	7	46	79	50	16	.263	.373
Wildfire Schulte	OF134	R	31	137	465	54	112	22	7	5	61	39	55	16	.241	.351
Roger Bresnahan	C85 2B14 OF1	R	35	101	248	42	69	10	4	0	24	49	20	14	.278	.351
Jimmy Archer (EJ)	C76	R	31	79	248	17	64	9	2	0	19	9	9	1	.258	.310
Cy Williams	OF27	L	26	55	94	12	19	2	2	0	5	13	13	0	.202	.266
Jimmy Johnston	OF28 2B4	R	24	50	101	9	23	3	2	1	8	4	9	3	.228	.327
Pete Knisely	OF16	R	30	37	69	5	9	0	1	0	5	5	6	0	.130	.159
2 Claud Derrick	SS28	R	28	28	96	5	21	3	1	0	13	5	13	2	.219	.271
Art Phelan	3B7 2B3 SS2	R	26	25	46	5	13	2	1	0	3	4	3	0	.283	.370
Bubbles Hargrave	C16	R	21	23	36	3	8	2	0	0	2	0	4	2	.222	.278
Chick Keating	SS16	R	22	20	30	3	3	0	1	0	0	6	6	0	.100	.167
Bobby Fisher	SS15	R	27	15	50	5	15	2	0	0	5	3	4	1	.300	.420
Art Bues	3B12	R	26	14	45	3	10	1	1	0	4	5	6	1	.222	.289
1 Fritz Mollwitz	1B4 OF1	R	24	13	20	0	3	0	0	0	1	0	3	1	.150	.150

2 Johnny Bates 32 L 1-8, Tom Needham 35 R 2-17, Tuffy Stewart 30 L 0-1, Milo Allison 23 L 1-1, Herman Bronkie 29 R 1-1, Earl Tyree 24 R 0-4

NAME	T	AGE	W	L	PCT	SV	G	GS	CG	IP	H	BB	SO	SHO	ERA
		28	78	76	.506	11	156	156	70	1389	1169	528	651	14	2.71
Hippo Vaughn	L	26	21	13	.618	1	42	35	23	294	236	109	165	4	2.05
Larry Cheney	R	28	20	18	.526	5	50	40	21	311	239	140	157	6	2.55
Jimmy Lavender	R	30	11	11	.500	0	37	28	11	214	191	87	157	2	3.07
Bert Humphries	R	33	10	11	.476	0	34	21	8	171	162	37	62	2	2.68
George Pierce	L	26	8	12	.333	1	30	17	4	141	122	65	78	0	3.51
Zip Zabel	R	23	4	4	.500	3	29	7	2	128	104	45	50	0	2.18
2 Casey Hageman	R	27	1	2	.667	1	16	1	0	47	44	12	17	0	3.45
Charlie Smith	R	34	2	4	.333	0	16	5	1	54	49	15	17	0	3.83
George McConnell	R	36	1	0	1.000	0	3	1	0	8	7	3	3	0	1.29
Eddie Stack	R		0	0	—	0	4			16	13	11	9	0	5.06
1 Elmer Koestner	R	28	0	0	—	0	4	0	0	6	4	6	0		3.00

BROOKLYN 5th 75-79 .487 19.5 WILBERT ROBINSON

NAME	G by Pos	B	AGE	G	AB	R	H	2B	3B	HR	RBI	BB	SO	SB	BA	SA
TOTALS			26	154	5152	622	1386	172	90	31	529	376	559	173	.269	.355
Jake Daubert	1B126	L	30	126	474	89	156	17	7	6	45	30	34	25	.329	.432
George Cutshaw	2B153	R	27	153	583	69	150	22	12	2	78	30	32	34	.257	.346
Dick Egan	SS83 3B10 OF3 2B2 1B1	R	30	106	337	30	76	10	3	1	31	22	25	8	.226	.282
1 Red Smith	3B90	R	24	90	330	39	81	10	8	4	48	30	26	1	.245	.361
Casey Stengel	OF121	L	23	126	412	55	130	13	10	4	60	56	55	19	.316	.425
Jack Dalton	OF116	R	29	124	442	65	141	13	8	1	45	53	39	19	.319	.391
Zack Wheat	OF144	L	26	145	533	66	170	26	9	9	89	47	50	20	.319	.452
Lew McCarty	C84	R	25	90	284	20	72	14	2	1	30	14	22	1	.254	.327
John Hummel	1B36 OF19 2B1 SS1	R	31	73	208	25	55	8	9	0	20	16	25	5	.264	.389
Hy Myers	OF60	R	25	70	227	35	65	10	2	1	17	7	24	2	.286	.379
Ollie O'Mara (BL)	SS63	R	23	67	247	41	65	10	2	1	7	16	26	14	.263	.332
Gus Getz	3B55	R	25	55	210	13	52	5	3	0	22	2	15	9	.248	.295
Otto Miller	C50	R	25	54	169	17	39	6	1	0	9	7	20	0	.231	.278
Bill Fischer	C30	L	23	43	165	9	38	7	0	0	8	8	12	1	.230	.315
Kid Elberfeld	SS18 2B1	R	39	30	62	7	14	1	0	0	5	6	4	0	.226	.242
1 Joe Riggert	OF20	R	27	21		6		1	3	2		4	20	1	.193	.349
1 Tex Erwin	C4	R	25		11	0	5								.455	.455

NAME	T	AGE	W	L	PCT	SV	G	GS	CG	IP	H	BB	SO	SHO	ERA
		27	75	79	.487	11	154	154	80	1368	1282	466	605	11	2.82
Jeff Pfeffer	R	26	23	12	.657	4	43	34	27	315	264	91	135	3	1.97
Raleigh Aitchison	L	26	12	7	.632	0	26	17	8	172	156	60	87	3	2.67
Pat Ragan	R	28	10	15	.400	3	38	25	14	208	214	85	106	1	2.99
Ed Reulbach	R	31	11	18	.379	3	44	29	14	256	228	83	119	3	2.64
1 Frank Allen	L	25	8	14	.364	0	36	21	10	171	165	57	68	1	3.11
Nap Rucker	L	29	7	6	.538	0	16	16	5	104	113	27	35	0	3.38
Elmer Brown	R	30	7	2	.500	0	11	5	1	37	33	23	22	0	3.89
Johnny Enzmann	R	24	1	0	1.000	0	1	1	0	8	3	5	0		4.74
Charlie Schmutz	R	23	1	3	.250	0	18	5	1	57	51	19	13	0	3.33
2 Bill Steele	R	28	0	1	.000	0	3	1	0	16	17	7	7	0	5.63
Bull Wagner	R	26	0	1	.000	0	4	0	0	12	14	4	1	0	6.75

PHILADELPHIA — 6th 74-80 .481 20.5 — RED DOOIN

NAME	G by Pos	B	AGE	G	AB	R	H	2B	3B	HR	RBI	BB	SO	SB	BA	SA
TOTALS			29	154	5110	651	1345	211	52	62	564	472	570	145	.263	.362
Fred Luderus	1B121	L	28	121	443	55	110	16	5	12	55	33	31	2	.248	.388
2 Bobby Byrne	2B101 3B22	R	29	126	467	61	127	12	1	0	26	45	44	9	.272	.302
Jack Martin	SS83	R	30	83	292	26	74	5	3	0	21	27	29	6	.253	.291
Hans Lobert	3B133 SS2	R	32	135	505	83	139	24	5	1	52	49	32	31	.275	.349
Gavvy Cravath	OF143	R	33	149	499	76	149	27	8	19	100	83	72	14	.299	.499
Dode Paskert	OF128 SS4	R	32	132	451	59	119	25	6	3	44	56	68	23	.264	.361
Beals Becker	OF126	L	27	138	514	76	167	25	5	9	66	37	59	16	.325	.446
Bill Killefer	C90	R	26	98	299	27	70	10	1	0	27	8	17	3	.234	.274
Sherry Magee	OF67 SS39 1B32 2B8	R	29	146	544	96	171	39	11	15	103	55	42	25	.314	.509
Ed Burns	C55	R	26	70	139	8	36	3	4	0	16	20	42	5	.259	.338
Hal Irelan	2B44 SS3 1B2 3B2	B	23	67	165	16	39	8	0	1	16	21	22	2	.236	.315
Red Doolan	C40	R	35	53	118	10	21	2	0	1	8	4	14	4	.178	.220
Milt Reed	SS22 2B11 3B1	R	23	44	107	10	22	2	1	0	2	10	13	4	.206	.243
1 Josh Devore	OF9	L	26	30	53	5	16	2	0	0	7	4	5	2	.302	.340
Dummy Murphy	SS9	R	27	9	26	1	4	1	0	0	3	0	4	1	.154	.192
Pat Hilly	OF4	R	27	8	10	2	3	0	0	0	1	1	5	0	.300	.300
Fred Mollenkamp	1B3		24	3	8	0	1	0	0	0	0	2	0	0	.125	.125
Frank Fletcher		R	23	1	1	0	0	0	0	0	0	0	1	0	.000	.000
Pat Moran	C1	R	38	1	1	0	0	0	0	0	0	0	1	0	.000	.000
George McAvoy		L	30	1	1	0	0	0	0	0	0	0	0	0	—	—

NAME	T	AGE	W	L	PCT	SV	G	GS	CG	IP	H	BB	SO	SHO	ERA
		24	74	80	.481	7	154	154	85	1379	1403	452	650	14	3.06
Pete Alexander	R	27	27	15	.643	1	46	39	32	355	327	76	214	6	2.38
Erskine Mayer	R	24	21	19	.525	2	48	38	24	321	308	91	116	4	2.58
Ben Tincup	R	21	7	10	.412	2	28	17	9	155	165	62	108	3	2.61
Rube Marshall	R	23	6	7	.462	1	27	17	7	134	144	50	49	0	3.76
Joe Oeschger	R	22	4	8	.333	1	32	12	5	124	129	54	47	0	3.77
Stan Baumgartner	L	29	3	2	.600	0	15	4	2	60	60	16	24	1	3.30
Eddie Matteson	R	29	3	2	.600	0	15	8	5	58	58	23	28	0	3.10
Eppa Rixey	R	23	2	11	.154	0	24	15	2	103	124	45	41	0	4.37
Elmer Jacobs	R	21	1	3	.250	0	14	7	1	51	65	20	17	0	4.76
George Chalmers	R	26	0	3	.000	0	3	2	1	18	23	15	6	0	5.50

PITTSBURGH — 7th 60-93 .448 25.5 — FRED CLARKE

NAME	G by Pos	B	AGE	G	AB	R	H	2B	3B	HR	RBI	BB	SO	SB	BA	SA
TOTALS			29	158	5145	503	1197	148	79	18	437	416	608	147	.233	.303
Ed Konetchy	1B154	R	28	154	563	56	140	28	9	4	51	32	48	20	.249	.343
Jim Viox	2B138 SS2 OF2	R	23	143	506	52	140	18	5	1	57	63	33	9	.265	.326
Honus Wagner	SS132 3B17 1B1	R	40	150	552	60	139	15	9	1	50	51	51	23	.252	.317
Mike Mowrey	3B78	R	30	79	284	24	72	7	5	1	25	22	20	8	.254	.324
1 Mike Mitchell	OF76	R	34	76	273	31	64	11	7	2	23	16	16	5	.234	.333
Joe Kelly	OF138	R	27	141	508	47	113	19	9	1	48	39	59	21	.222	.301
Max Carey	OF154	R	24	156	593	76	144	25	17	1	31	59	56	38	.243	.347
George Gibson	C101	R	33	102	274	19	78	9	5	0	30	27	27	4	.285	.354
Ham Hyatt	1B7 C1	L	29	74	79	2	17	3	1	1	15	7	14	1	.215	.316
Bob Coleman	C72	R	23	73	150	11	40	4	1	1	14	15	32	3	.267	.327
Alex McCarthy	3B36 2B10 SS6	R	26	57	173	14	26	0	1	1	14	6	17	2	.150	.179
Joe Leonard	3B38 SS1	L	19	53	126	17	25	2	2	0	4	12	21	4	.198	.246
Zip Collins	OF49	L	22	49	182	14	44	2	0	1	8	10	8	3	.242	.253
Eddie Mensor	OF25	R	28	44	89	15	18	2	1	1	6	22	13	2	.202	.281
Barney Kelly	OF7	L	30	32	44	4	10	2	1	0	3	2	9	1	.227	.318
Dan Costello	OF20	L	22	21	64	7	19	1	0	0	5	8	16	2	.297	.313
Jake Kafora	C17	R	25	21	23	1	3	0	0	0	0	0	6	0	.130	.130
Wally Gerber	SS17	R	22	17	54	5	13	1	1	0	5	2	10	1	.241	.296
Ike McAuley	SS5 3B3 2B2	R	22	15	24	3	3	0	0	0	0	0	8	0	.125	.125

Paddy Siglin 22 R 6-39, Bobby Schang 27 R 8-35, Fritz Scheeren 23 R 9-31, Clarence Berger 19 L 1-13, Syd Smith 30 R 3-11
Pete Falsey 23 L 0-1, Bill Wagner 20 R 0-1, Fred Clarke 41 L 0-2, Sam Brenegan 23 L 0-0, Pat Killhullen 23 R 0-1, Ralph Schaefer 20 0-0

NAME	T	AGE	W	L	PCT	SV	G	GS	CG	IP	H	BB	SO	SHO	ERA
		26	69	85	.448	11	158	158	86	1405	1272	392	488	10	2.68
Wilbur Cooper	L	22	16	15	.516	0	40	34	19	267	246	79	102	0	2.12
Babe Adams	R	32	13	16	.448	1	40	35	19	283	253	39	91	3	2.51
George McQuillan	R	29	13	17	.433	4	45	28	15	259	248	60	96	0	2.99
Bob Harmon	R	26	13	17	.433	0	37	30	19	245	226	55	61	2	2.53
Al Mamaux	R	20	5	2	.714	0	13	6	4	63	41	24	30	2	1.71
Joe Conzelman	R	28	5	6	.455	2	33	9	4	101	88	40	39	1	2.94
Erv Kantlehner	L	21	3	2	.600	0	21	5	3	67	51	39	26	2	3.09
1 Marty O'Toole	R	26	1	8	.111	1	19	9	1	92	92	47	36	0	4.70
Herb Kelly	L	22	0	0	.000	0	5	2	2	26	24	7	6	0	2.43
Pat Bohen	R	23	0	0	—	0	1	1	0	4	2	2	0	0	18.00
Dixie McArthur	R	22	0	0	—	0	1	0	0	1	1	1	0	0	0.00

CINCINNATI — 8th 60-94 .390 34.5 — BUCK HERZOG

NAME	G by Pos	B	AGE	G	AB	R	H	2B	3B	HR	RBI	BB	SO	SB	BA	SA
TOTALS			27	157	4491	530	1178	142	64	16	432	441	627	224	.236	.300
1 Dick Hoblitzell	1B75	R	25	78	248	31	52	8	7	0	26	26	26	7	.210	.298
Heinie Groh	2B134 SS2	R	24	139	455	59	131	18	4	2	32	64	29	24	.288	.358
Buck Herzog	SS137 SS2	R	28	138	498	54	140	14	8	1	40	42	27	46	.281	.347
Bert Niehoff	3B134 2B3	R	30	142	484	46	117	16	9	4	49	38	77	20	.242	.337
1 Herbie Moran	OF107	L	30	107	395	43	93	10	5	1	35	41	29	25	.235	.294
Bert Daniels	OF71	R	31	71	269	29	59	9	7	0	19	19	40	14	.219	.305
George Twombly	OF68	R	22	68	240	22	56	6	5	0	19	14	27	12	.233	.275
Tommy Clarke	C108	R	26	113	313	30	82	13	7	2	35	31	30	6	.262	.367
Mike Gonzales	C83	R	23	95	176	19	41	6	0	0	10	13	16	2	.233	.267
Doc Miller	OF47	L	31	93	192	8	49	7	2	0	33	16	18	4	.255	.313
Marty Berghammer	SS33 2B13	R	22	77	112	6	25	2	0	0	6	10	18	4	.223	.295
Bill Kellogg	1B38 2B11 OF2 3B1	R	30	71	126	14	22	0	1	0	7	14	28	7	.175	.190
1 Johnny Bates	OF57	L	32	67	163	36	40	7	5	2	15	29	18	4	.245	.387
Earl Yingling	P34 OF13	R	25	61	120	9	23	2	0	1	11	9	15	3	.192	.233
Maury Uhler	OF36	R	27	46	56	12	12	2	0	0	3	5	11	4	.214	.250
Red Killefer	OF35 2B5 3B1	R	29	42	141	16	39	6	1	0	12	20	18	11	.277	.333
Fritz Von Kolnitz	3B20 OF11 C2 1B1	R	21	41	104	8	23	2	0	0	6	6	16	4	.221	.240
1 Armando Marsans	OF36	R	27	36	124	6	37	3	0	0	22	14	6	13	.298	.323
Johnny Rawlings	3B10 2B7 SS6	R	21	33	60	10	13	1	0	0	6	3	9	2	.217	.233
2 Fritz Mollwitz	1B32	R	24	32	111	12	18	2	0	0	5	3	9	2	.162	.180
Tiny Graham	1B25	R	21	25	61	5	14	1	0	0	3	3	10	1	.230	.246
Harry LaRoss	OF20	R	26	22	48	7	11	1	0	0	5	2	10	4	.229	.250

Howie Lohr 22 R 10-47, Tex Erwin 28 L 11-35, 2 Bill Holden 24 R 6-28, Norm Glockson 20 R 0-12, Kid McLaughlin 26 L 0-2,
1Claude Derrick 28 R 2-6, Ed Kippert 35 R 0-2

NAME	T	AGE	W	L	PCT	SV	G	GS	CG	IP	H	BB	SO	SHO	ERA
		25	60	94	.390	15	157	157	74	1387	1259	489	607	15	2.94
Rube Benton	R	24	17	18	.437	2	41	35	16	271	223	95	121	4	2.96
Red Ames	R	31	15	23	.395	6	47	29	18	297	274	94	128	4	2.64
Phil Douglas	R	24	11	18	.379	1	45	25	13	239	186	92	121	0	2.56
Earl Yingling	L	25	8	13	.381	0	34	27	9	198	207	54	80	3	3.45
Pete Schneider	R	21	5	13	.278	1	29	15	11	144	143	56	62	1	2.81
1 Dave Davenport	R	24	2	2	.500	2	10	4	3	56	38	30	22	1	2.50
King Lear	R	23	1	2	.333	1	17	4	3	56	55	19	20	1	3.05
Jack Rowan	R	28	1	3	.250	2	12	2	0	39	38	10	16	0	3.46
Paul Fittery	R	26	0	0	.000	0	8	4	2	44	41	12	21	0	3.07
Pete Fahrer	R	24	0	0	—	0	5	0	0	8	4	4	2	0	1.13
2 Elmer Koestner	R	28	0	0	—	0	5	1	0	18	18	9	6	0	4.50
Karl Adams	R	28	0	0	—	0	8	0	0	14	5	5	2	0	9.00
Bob Ingersoll	R	31	0	0	—	0	4	0	0	15	5	5	2	0	3.00
Pat Griffin	R	21	0	0	—	0	1	0	0	4	6	2	1	0	6.00
1 Chief Johnson	R	28	0	0	—	0	1	0	0	4	6	2	1	0	6.75

WORLD SERIES — BOSTON (NL) 4 PHILADELPHIA (AL) 0

LINE SCORES

TEAM	1	2	3	4	5	6	7	8	9	10	11	12	R	H	E

Game 1 October 9 at Philadelphia

													R	H	E
BOS(NL)	0	2	0	0	1	3	0	1	0				7	11	2
PHI(AL)	0	1	0	0	0	0	0	1					5	0

Rudolph   Bender, Wycoff (6)

Game 2 October 10 at Philadelphia

													R	H	E
BOS	0	0	0	0	0	0	0	0	1				1	7	1
PHI	0	0	0	0	0	0	0	0	0				0	2	1

James   Plank

Game 3 October 12 at Boston

													R	H	E
PHI	1	0	0	1	0	0	0	0	0	2	0	0	4	8	2
BOS	0	1	0	1	0	0	0	0	0	2	0	1	5	9	1

Bush   Tyler, James (10)

Game 4 October 13 at Boston

													R	H	E
PHI	0	0	0	0	1	0	0	0	0				1	7	0
BOS	0	0	0	1	2	0	0	0	X				3	6	0

Shawkey, Pennock (6)   Rudolph

COMPOSITE BATTING

NAME	POS	G	AB	R	H	2B	3B	HR	RBI	BA
Boston (NL) Totals		4	135	16	33	6	2	1	14	.244
Schmidt	1B	4	17	2	5	0	0	0	2	.294
Evers	2B	4	16	2	7	0	0	0	2	.438
Deal	3B	4	16	1	2	2	0	0	0	.125
Whitted	OF	4	14	2	3	0	1	0	2	.214
Maranville	SS	4	13	1	4	0	0	0	3	.308
Moran	OF	3	13	2	1	1	0	0	0	.077
Gowdy	C	4	11	3	6	3	1	1	3	.545
Connolly	OF	3	9	1	1	0	0	0	0	.111
Mann	OF	3	7	1	2	0	0	0	1	.286
Rudolph	P	2	6	1	2	0	0	0	0	.333
Cather	OF	2	5	0	0	0	0	0	0	.000
James	P	2	4	0	0	0	0	0	0	.000
Tyler	P	2	4	0	0	0	0	0	0	.000
Devore	PH	1	1	0	0	0	0	0	0	.000
Gilbert	PH	1	0	0	0	0	0	0	0	—
Philadelphia (AL) Totals		4	128	6	22	9	0	0	5	.172
Baker	3B	4	16	0	4	2	0	0	2	.250
Murphy	OF	4	16	2	3	2	0	0	0	.188
Oldring	OF	4	15	0	1	0	0	0	0	.067
Collins	2B	4	14	0	3	0	0	0	1	.214
McInnis	1B	4	14	2	2	0	0	0	0	.143
Barry	SS	4	14	1	1	0	0	0	1	.071
Schang	C	4	12	1	2	0	0	0	0	.167
Strunk	OF	2	7	0	2	0	0	0	0	.286
Walsh	OF	3	6	0	2	0	0	0	0	.333
Bush	P	1	5	0	0	0	0	0	0	.000
Shawkey	P	1	2	0	1	0	0	0	0	.500
Bender	P	1	2	0	0	0	0	0	0	.000
Plank	P	1	2	0	0	0	0	0	0	.000
Wycoff	P	1	1	0	1	0	0	0	0	1.000
Lapp	C	1	1	0	0	0	0	0	0	.000
Pennock	P	1	1	0	0	0	0	0	0	.000

COMPOSITE PITCHING

NAME	G	IP	H	BB	SO	W	L	SV	ERA
Boston (NL) Totals	4	39	22	13	28	4	0	0	1.15
Rudolph	2	18	12	4	15	2	0	0	0.50
James	2	11	8	4	9	2	0	0	0.00
Tyler	1	10	8	3	4	0	0	0	3.60
Philadelphia (AL) Totals	4	37	33	15	18	0	4	0	3.41
Bush	1	11	9	4	4	0	1	0	3.27
Plank	1	9	7	4	6	0	1	0	1.00
Bender	1	5.1	8	2	3	0	1	0	10.13
Shawkey	1	5	4	2	3	0	0	0	3.60
Wycoff	1	3.2	3	1	4	0	0	0	2.45
Pennock	1	3	2	1	3	0	0	0	0.00

1914 F. L. — Gilmore's Green Glory

Like the new leagues of the present era, the Federal League was born with high hopes and plenty of money. When Chicago businessman James A. Gilmore became president of the minor Federal League in 1913, he planned to turn the sectional midwest loop into a national major league. Using broad strokes and rosy colors, Gilmore painted a picture of baseball as a profitable financial venture and lined up backing for most of the eight franchises in his loop. Leading industrialists, such as Phil Ball, Charles Weeghman, and Robert Ward, backed franchises with visions of sizeable profits and free advertising from their nationally-known clubs.

With a bankroll intact, confidence soaring, and the reality of risk neatly tucked away in the unknown and optimistic future, Gilmore proclaimed the Federal League as a third major league in 1914 and stated that his loop would not honor the "monopolistic" reserve clause set up by the baseball establishment. Big money was freely waved around, and the first major catch for the Feds was star shortstop Joe Tinker, signed to manage and play for the Chicago Whales. Other established players followed Tinker on the golden brick road into the new league. Some older players past their prime cashed in one last big paycheck by signing with the Feds; Three Finger Brown and Solly Hofman of the old Cub champions, George Mullin of the Tiger triple pennant winners, Danny Murphy of Connie Mack's Athletics, and veteran National Leaguers, Howie Camnitz and Al Bridwell, brought along their names but little of their former skills. Some younger veterans joined the loop, among them star-hurler Tom Seaton, the Phillies' double-play tandem of Otto Knabe and Mickey Doolan, outfielder Rebel Oakes, and pitchers Doc Crandall, Russ Ford, Bob Groom, Cy Falkenburg, and Claude Hendrix. Star first-sacker Hal Chase, always amenable to a well-greased palm, jumped the White Sox in mid-season to join with the Feds. Minor leaguers, major league rejects, and youngsters filled the remainder of the berths. Overtures were made to superstars Ty Cobb, Tris Speaker, and Walter Johnson, but they stayed put when their salaries were boosted by sweating American League moguls.

The 1914 season opened with franchises bucking the established competition in Brooklyn, Chicago, St. Louis, and Pittsburgh, and with teams in the minor AAA cities of Baltimore, Buffalo, Kansas City, and Indianapolis. New parks were constructed in all eight cities and were ready for the openers. Chicago's entry played in what was eventually called Wrigley Field.

As the season progressed, attendance was not far behind the established loops, but all three circuits suffered from having the paying public spread thinly among three markets. The Fed's gate was boosted by a spirited pennant race in which almost every team, atone time or another, contended. Indianapolis and Chicago raced neck and neck into the final week, with Chicago losing a slight lead over the Hoosiers by dropping a doubleheader to the Kansas City Packers on October 6, which allowed the Indianians to finally grab the brass ring.

A 24-year-old bon vivant on the order of Joe Namath paced the Hoosiers and became the league's top star. Outfielder Benny Kauff led the loop in batting and stolen bases and lived in a style befitting a champ, which included, among other indulgences, diamond rings and silk underwear. Frank LaPorte provided solid batting behind Kauff, and Cy Falkenberg paced the Indianapolis Hurlers with 25 victories. Bill McKechnie and Edd Roush were other youngsters on the flag-winners who would make names for themselves in future campaigns. The runner-up Chicago Whales fielded Joe Tinker, Dutch Zwilling (a star slugger who would later flop in the National League), and Max Flack (a .247 hitter who would later play 10 years in the senior circuit). Other league stars included established hurlers, Hendrix and Seaton, the ever-ready Hal Chase, ex-Cardinal Steve Evans, and Senator reject Duke Kenworthy.

As the year closed, the Feds continued to wave hefty contracts under star noses. Although it was a tactic that would eventually harm all the owners, the money was welcomed by the players themselves who, long frustrated by a closed market, found it profitable.

1914 FEDERAL LEAGUE

INDIANAPOLIS — 1st 88-65 .575 — BILL PHILLIPS

NAME	G by Pos	B	AGE	G	AB	R	H	2B	3B	HR	RBI	BB	SO	SB	BA	SA
TOTALS			27	157	5176	762	1474	230	90	33	629	470		273	.285	.383
Charlie Carr	1B115	R	37	115	441	44	129	11	10	3	69	26		19	.293	.383
Frank LaPorte	2B132	R	34	133	505	86	157	27	12	4	107	36		15	.311	.436
Jimmy Esmond	SS151	R	24	151	542	74	160	23	15	2	49	40		25	.295	.404
Bill McKechnie	3B149	B	27	149	571	107	174	22	6	2	38	53		47	.305	.375
Benny Kauff	OF154	L	24	154	571	120	211	44	13	8	95	72		75	.370	.534
Vin Campbell	OF132	L	26	134	544	92	173	23	11	7	44	37		26	.318	.439
Al Scheer	OF102, 2B4, SS1	L	25	120	363	63	111	23	6	3	45	49		9	.306	.427
Bill Rariden	C130	R	26	131	396	44	93	15	5	0	47	61		12	.235	.298
Edd Roush	OF43, 1B2	L	21	74	166	26	54	8	4	1	30	6		12	.325	.440
Al Kaiser (IL)	OF50, 1B8	R	27	59	187	22	43	10	0	1	16	17		6	.230	.299
George Mullin	P36	R	33	43	77	11	24	5	3	0	21	11		0	.312	.455
Carl Vandagrift	2B28, 3B12, SS5	R	31	43	136	25	34	4	0	0	9	9		7	.250	.279
Biddy Dolan	1B31	R	32	32	103	13	23	4	2	1	15	12		5	.223	.330
Hack Warren	C23	L	30	26	50	5	12	0	0	0	5	5		2	.240	.240
George Textor	C21	B	27	22	57	2	10	0	0	0	4	2		0	.175	.175
1 Everett Booe	OF5, SS3	L	24	20	31	5	7	1	0	0	6	7		4	.226	.258
Frank Rooney	1B9	R	29	12	35	1	7	0	1	1	8	1		2	.200	.343

NAME	T	AGE	W	L	PCT	SV	G	GS	CG	IP	H	BB	SO	SHO	ERA
		28	88	65	.575	9	157	157	104	1398	1352	476	664	16	3.06
Cy Falkenberg	R	34	25	16	.610	3	49	43	33	377	332	89	236	9	2.22
Earl Moseley	R	26	19	18	.514	1	43	38	29	317	303	123	205	4	3.47
George Kaiserling	R	21	17	10	.630	0	37	33	20	275	288	72	75	1	3.11
George Mullin	R	33	14	10	.583	2	36	20	11	203	202	91	74	1	2.70
Harry Billiard	R	28	8	7	.533	2	32	16	5	126	117	63	45	0	3.71
Charlie Whitehouse	L	20	2	0	1.000	0	8	2	2	26	34	5	10	0	4.50
2 Ed Henderson	L	29	1	0	1.000	0	2	1	1	10	8	4	1	0	4.50
Katsey Keifer	L	20	1	0	1.000	0	1	1	1	9	6	2	2	0	2.00
Frank Harter	R	27	1	2	.333	0	6	1	1	25	33	7	8	0	3.96
Ralph McConnaughey	R	26	0	2	.000	0	7	2	1	26	23	16	7	0	4.85
Clarence Woods	R	23	0	0	—	1	2	0	0	2	1	2	1	0	4.50
Fred Ostendorf	L	21	0	0	—	0	1	0	0	2	5	2	0	0	22.50

CHICAGO — 2nd 87-67 .565 1.5 — JOE TINKER

NAME	G by Pos	B	AGE	G	AB	R	H	2B	3B	HR	RBI	BB	SO	SB	BA	SA
TOTALS			26	157	5098	621	1314	227	50	51	544	520		171	.258	.352
Fred Beck	1B157	R	27	157	555	51	155	23	4	11	77	44		9	.279	.395
Jack Farrell	2B155, SS3	B	22	156	524	58	123	23	4	0	35	52		12	.235	.294
Joe Tinker (BR)	SS125	R	33	127	440	53	114	22	7	2	46	38		24	.259	.355
Rollie Zeider	3B117, SS1	R	30	120	456	59	120	15	2	1	36	44		35	.263	.311
Al Wickland	OF157	R	26	157	536	74	148	31	10	6	68	81		17	.276	.405
Dutch Zwilling	OF154	L	25	154	592	91	185	38	8	15	95	46		21	.313	.480
Max Falck	OF133	R	24	134	502	66	124	15	3	2	39	51		13	.247	.301
Art Wilson	C132	R	28	137	440	78	128	31	8	10	64	70		13	.291	.466
Harry Fritz	3B46, SS9, 2B1	R	23	65	174	16	37	5	1	0	13	18		2	.213	.253
Austin Walsh	OF30	L	22	57	121	14	29	6	1	1	10	4		0	.240	.331
Jim Stanley	SS40, 3B3, 2B1, OF1	B	25	54	98	13	19	3	0	0	4	19		2	.194	.224
Bruno Block	C33	R	29	43	100	8	19	4	1	0	13	11		1	.190	.250
Bill Jackson	OF6, 1B4	L	33	26	25	2	1	0	0	0	1	3		0	.040	.040
Count Clemens	C8	R	27	13	27	4	4	0	0	0	2	3		0	.148	.148
Leo Kavanagh	SS5	R	19	5	11	0	3	0	0	0	1	1		0	.273	.273
2 Skipper Roberts		L	26	4	3	0	1	0	0	0	1	1		0	.333	.333
Jack Kading		R	29	3	3	0	0	0	0	0	0	0		0	.000	.000
Jimmy Smith	SS3	R	19	3	6	1	3	1	0	0	1	0		0	.500	.667

NAME	T	AGE	W	L	PCT	SV	G	GS	CG	IP	H	BB	SO	SHO	ERA
		26	87	67	.565	8	157	157	93	1420	1204	393	650	17	2.44
Claude Hendrix	R	25	29	10	.744	5	49	37	34	362	262	77	189	6	1.69
Erv Lange	R	26	12	11	.522	2	36	22	10	190	162	55	87	2	2.23
Max Fiske	R	25	12	12	.500	0	38	22	7	198	161	59	87	0	3.14
2 Rankin Johnson	R	26	9	5	.643	0	16	14	12	120	88	29	60	2	1.58
1 Doc Watson	L	29	9	8	.529	1	26	18	10	172	145	49	69	3	2.04
Ad Brennan	L	26	5	5	.500	0	16	11	5	86	84	21	31	1	3.56
Tom McGuire	R	22	5	6	.455	0	24	12	7	131	143	57	37	0	3.71
Mike Prendergast	L	25	5	9	.357	0	30	19	7	136	131	40	71	1	2.38
Dave Black	R	22	1	0	1.000	0	8	1	1	25	28	4	19	0	6.12
Babe Sherman	R	24	0	1	.000	0	1	1	0	1	0	2	0	0	0.00

BALTIMORE — 3rd 84-70 .545 4.5 — OTTO KNABE

NAME	G by Pos	B	AGE	G	AB	R	H	2B	3B	HR	RBI	BB	SO	SB	BA	SA
TOTALS			30	160	5120	645	1374	222	67	32	551	487		152	.268	.357
Harry Swacina	1B158	R	32	158	617	70	173	26	8	0	90	14		15	.280	.348
Otto Knabe	2B114	R	30	146	470	45	107	25	3	2	42	53		10	.228	.306
Mickey Doolan	SS145	R	34	144	486	58	119	25	6	1	53	40		34	.245	.327
Jimmy Walsh	3B113, 2B1, SS1, OF1	R	28	120	428	54	132	25	4	10	65	22		18	.308	.456
Benny Meyer	OF132, SS4	R	29	143	500	76	152	18	10	5	40	71		23	.304	.410
Vern Duncan	OF148, OF8, 2B1	L	24	157	557	99	160	20	8	2	53	67		13	.287	.363
Hack Simmons	OF73, 2B26, 1B4, SS2, 3B1	R	29	114	352	50	95	16	5	1	38	32		9	.270	.352
Fred Jacklitsch	C118	R	38	122	337	40	93	21	4	2	48	52		7	.276	.380
Harvey Russell	C47, SS1, OF1	L	27	81	168	18	39	3	2	0	13	18		2	.232	.274
Guy Zinn (BL)	OF57	L	27	61	225	30	63	10	6	3	25	16		6	.280	.418
3 Johnny Bates	OF59	L	32	59	190	24	58	6	3	1	29	38		6	.305	.384
E. Kirkpatrick (BL)	3B36, SS11, OF3, 1B1	R	29	55	174	22	44	7	2	2	16	18		10	.253	.351
1 Medric Boucher	C7, 1B1, OF1	R	28	16	16	2	5	1	1	0	2	1		0	.313	.500
2 Fred Kommers	OF12	L	28	16	42	5	9	1	0	1	1	7		0	.214	.310
2 Doc Kerr	C13, 1B1	B	32	14	34	4	9	1	1	0	1	1		1	.265	.353
Frank Lobert	3B7, 2B1	R	30	11	30	3	6	0	1	0	2	0		0	.200	.267
Jack McCandless	OF8	R	23	11	31	5	8	0	1	0	1	3		0	.258	.323
3 Felix Chouinard	OF2	R	27	5	9	3	4	0	0	0	1	0		0	.444	.444

NAME	T	AGE	W	L	PCT	SV	G	GS	CG	IP	H	BB	SO	SHO	ERA
		30	84	70	.545	13	160	160	88	1392	1389	392	732	15	3.13
Jack Quinn	R	30	26	14	.650	1	46	42	27	343	335	65	164	4	3.48
George Suggs	R	31	24	14	.632	4	46	38	26	319	322	57	132	6	2.91
Kaiser Wilhelm	R	40	12	17	.414	5	47	27	11	244	263	81	113	1	4.02
Frank Smith	R	34	10	8	.556	2	39	22	9	175	180	47	83	1	2.98
Bill Bailey	L	26	7	9	.438	0	19	18	10	129	106	68	131	1	3.07
Snipe Conley	R	20	4	6	.400	1	35	11	4	125	112	47	86	2	2.52
Ducky Yount	R	28	1	1	.500	0	13	1	1	41	44	19	19	0	4.18
Jack Ridgway	R	24	0	1	.000	0	4	1	0	9	20	3	2	0	11.00
Vern Hughes	L	21	0	0	—	0	3	0	0	3	0	0	0	0	3.00
John Allen	R	23	0	0	—	0	1	0	0	2	2	2	1	0	18.00

BUFFALO 4th 80-71 .530 7 — LARRY SCHLAFLY

NAME	G by Pos	B	AGE	G	AB	R	H	2B	3B	HR	RBI	BB	SO	SB	BA	SA
TOTALS			29	155	5064	620	1264	177	74	38	508	430		228	.250	.336
Joe Agler	1B76, OF54	L	27	135	463	82	126	17	6	0	20	77		21	.282	.335
Tom Downey	2B129, SS16, 3B5	R	30	151	541	69	118	20	3	2	42	40		35	.218	.277
Baldy Louden	SS115	R	30	126	431	73	135	11	4	6	63	52		35	.313	.399
Fred Smith	3B127, SS19, 1B1	R	27	145	473	48	104	12	10	2	45	49		24	.220	.300
2 Tex McDonald	OF61, 2B10	L	25	69	250	32	74	13	6	3	32	20		11	.296	.432
Charlie Hanford	OF155	R	32	155	597	83	174	28	13	13	90	32		37	.291	.447
1 Frank Delahanty	OF78	R	31	79	274	29	55	4	7	2	27	23		21	.201	.288
Walter Blair	C128	R	30	128	378	22	92	11	2	0	33	32		6	.243	.283
Del Young	OF41	L	28	80	174	17	48	5	5	4	22	3		0	.276	.431
2 Hal Chase	1B73	R	31	75	291	43	103	19	9	3	48	6		10	.354	.512
2 Everett Booe	OF58, SS8, 3B2, 2B1	L	24	76	241	29	54	9	2	0	14	21		8	.224	.278
Art LaVigne	C34, 1B3	R	29	51	90	10	14	2	0	0	4	7		0	.156	.178
Larry Schlafly	2B23, 1B7, 3B1, OF1, C1	R	35	51	127	16	33	7	1	2	19	12		3	.260	.378
Nick Allen	C26	R	25	32	63	3	15	1	0	0	4	3		4	.238	.254
2 Clyde Engle	3B23, OF9	R	30	32	110	12	28	4	1	0	12	11		5	.255	.309
Luther Bonin	OF20	R	26	20	76	6	14	4	1	0	4	7		3	.184	.263
Bill Collins	OF15	B	32	21	47	6	7	2	2	0	2	3		0	.149	.277
Del Wertz	SS1	R	25	3	1	0	0	0	0	0	0	0		0	.000	.000
Ned Pettigrew		R	32	2	2	0	0	0	0	0	0	0		0	.000	.000
Jack Snyder	C1	R	27	1	2	0	0	0	0	0	0	0		1	.000	.000

NAME	T	AGE	W	L	PCT	SV	G	GS	CG	IP	H	BB	SO	SHO	ERA
		28	80	71	.530	16	155	155	89	1387	1249	505	662	15	3.16
Russ Ford	R	28	21	6	.778	6	35	26	19	247	190	41	123	5	1.82
Gene Krapp	R	27	16	14	.533	2	36	29	18	253	198	115	106	1	2.49
Fred Anderson	R	28	13	15	.464	0	37	28	21	260	243	64	144	2	3.08
Earl Moore	R	34	11	15	.423	2	36	27	14	195	184	99	96	2	4.29
Harry Moran	L	25	10	7	.588	2	34	16	7	154	159	53	73	2	4.27
2 Al Schulz	L	25	9	12	.429	2	27	23	10	171	160	77	87	0	3.37
Joe Houser	R	22	0	1	.000	0	7	2	0	23	21	20	6	0	5.48
Eddie Porray	R	25	0	1	.000		3	3	0	10	18	7		0	4.50
Bob Smith	R	23	0	0	—	3	15	1	0	37	39	16	13	0	3.40
Dan Woodman	R	20	0	0	—	1	13	0	0	34	30	11	13	0	2.39
Biff Schlitzer	R	29	0	0	—	3	3	0	0	3	7	2	1	0	18.00

BROOKLYN 5th 77-77 .500 11.5 — BILL BRADLEY

NAME	G by Pos	B	AGE	G	AB	R	H	2B	3B	HR	RBI	BB	SO	SB	BA	SA
TOTALS			29	157	5221	662	1402	225	85	42	573	404		220	.269	.368
Hap Myers	1B88	R	27	92	305	61	67	10	5	1	29	44		43	.220	.295
Solly Hofman	2B108, 1B22, OF21, SS1	R	31	147	515	65	148	25	12	5	83	54		34	.287	.412
Eddie Gagnier	SS88, 3B6	R	32	94	337	22	63	12	2	0	25	13		8	.187	.234
Tex Wisterzil	3B149	R	26	149	534	54	137	18	10	0	66	34		17	.257	.328
Steve Evans	OF112, 1B27	L	29	154	513	99	147	41	15	12	96	50		18	.348	.456
Al Shaw	OF102	L	33	112	376	81	122	27	7	5	49	44		24	.324	.473
Claude Cooper	OF101	L	22	113	399	56	96	14	11	2	25	26		25	.241	.346
Grover Land	C97	R	29	102	335	24	92	6	2	0	29	12		7	.275	.304
George Anderson	OF92	L	24	98	364	58	115	13	3	3	24	31		16	.316	.393
Al Halt	SS71, 2B3, OF1	R	23	80	261	26	61	6	2	3	25	13		11	.234	.307
Jim Delahanty	2B55, 1B5	R	35	74	214	28	62	13	5	0	15	25		4	.290	.397
Frank Owens	C58	R	28	58	184	15	51	7	3	2	20	9		2	.277	.380
Danny Murphy	OF46	R	37	50	161	16	50	9	0	4	32	17		4	.311	.441
Art Griggs	1B27, OF46	R	29	40	112	10	32	6	1	1	15	5		1	.286	.384
2 Felix Chouinard	OF21	R	27	32	79	7	20	1	2	0	8	4		3	.253	.316
Art Watson	C18	R	27	22	46	7	13	4	1	1	3	1		0	.283	.478
Bill Bradley		R	36	7	6	1	3	1	0	0	3	0		0	.500	.667
Rinaldo Williams	3B4	L	20	4	15	1	4	2	0	0	0	0		0	.267	.400

NAME	T	AGE	W	L	PCT	SV	G	GS	CG	IP	H	BB	SO	SHO	ERA
		26	77	77	.500	9	157	157	91	1386	1375	559	636	11	3.33
Tom Seaton	R	26	25	14	.641	2	44	38	26	303	299	102	172	5	3.03
Ed Lafitte	R	28	18	15	.545	2	42	33	23	291	260	127	137	0	2.63
Happy Finnernan	R	23	12	11	.522	1	27	23	13	185	153	60	54	2	3.19
Bill Chappelle (JJ)	R	33	4	2	.667	0	16	6	4	74	71	29	31	0	3.16
Jim Bluejacket	R	26	4	5	.444	1	17	7	3	67	77	19	29	1	3.76
Don Marion	R	24	3	2	.600	0	17	9	4	89	97	38	41	0	3.94
Bert Maxwell	R	27	3	4	.429	1	12	8	6	71	76	24	19	1	3.29
Rube Peters	R	29	2	2	.500	0	11	3	1	38	52	16	13	0	3.79
2 Three Finger Brown	R	37	2	5	.286	0	9	8	5	58	63	18	32	0	4.19
2 Duke Houck	R	22	2	6	.250	0	17	9	3	92	95	43	45	0	3.13
Rudy Sommers	L	23	2	7	.222	2	23	8	2	82	88	34	40	0	4.06
Fin Wilson	L	25	2	7	.222	0	2	1	1	7	7	11	4	0	7.71
Herold Juul	R	21	0	3	.000	0	9	3	0	29	26	31	16	0	6.21
Esty Chaney	R	23	0	0	—	0	4	0	0	4	7	2	1	0	6.75
John McGraw	R	24	0	0	—	0	1	0	0	3	4	5	0	0	0.00
Joe Vernon	R	24	0	0	—	0	1	0	1	3	4	1	0	0	12.00

KANSAS CITY 6th 67-84 .444 20 — GEORGE STOVALL

NAME	G by Pos	B	AGE	G	AB	R	H	2B	3B	HR	RBI	BB	SO	SB	BA	SA
TOTALS			28	154	5127	644	1369	226	77	39	557	399		171	.267	.364
George Stovall	1B116, 3B1	R	36	122	448	50	121	20	5	7	75	23		8	.270	.364
Duke Kenworthy	2B145	B	27	146	545	93	173	40	14	15	91	36		37	.317	.525
Pep Goodwin	SS67, 3B40, 1B1	L	22	112	374	38	88	15	6	1	32	27		4	.235	.316
George Perring	3B101, 1B41, SS1, P1	R	29	144	496	68	138	28	10	2	69	59		7	.278	.387
Grover Gilmore	OF132	L	25	139	530	91	152	25	5	1	32	37		23	.287	.358
Art Kruger	OF120	R	33	122	441	45	114	24	7	4	47	23		11	.259	.372
Chet Chadbourne	OF146	L	29	147	581	92	161	22	8	1	37	69		42	.277	.348
Ted Easterly	C128	L	29	134	436	58	146	20	12	1	67	31		10	.335	.443
Cad Coles	OF39, 1B3	L	28	78	194	17	49	7	3	1	25	5		6	.253	.335
Cliff Daringer	SS24, 3B19, 2B14	R	29	64	160	12	42	2	1	0	16	11		9	.263	.288
2 Johnny Rawlings	SS61	R	21	61	196	18	41	3	0	0	15	22		6	.209	.224
Fred Potts	OF31	L	27	41	102	14	27	4	0	1	9	25		7	.265	.333
Drummond Brown	C23, 1B2	R	29	31	58	4	11	3	0	0	5	7		1	.190	.241
2 Jack Enzenroth	C24	R	28	26	67	7	12	4	1	0	5	5		0	.176	.269
Walt Tappan	SS8, 3B6, 2B1	R	23	18	39	1	8	1	0	1	4	1		1	.205	.308

NAME	T	AGE	W	L	PCT	SV	G	GS	CG	IP	H	BB	SO	SHO	ERA
		26	67	84	.444	12	154	154	82	1361	1387	445	600	10	3.41
Gene Packard	L	26	20	14	.588	5	42	34	24	302	282	88	154	4	2.89
2 Nick Cullop	L	26	14	19	.424	1	44	36	22	296	256	87	149	4	2.34
2 Chief Johnson	R	28	9	10	.474	0	20	19	12	134	157	33	78	2	3.16
Dwight Stone	R	27	6	14	.364	0	39	22	6	187	205	77	88	0	4.09
Ben Harris	R	24	7	7	.500	1	31	14	5	154	179	41	40	0	4.09
Pete Henning	R	26	5	10	.333	2	28	14	7	138	153	58	45	0	4.83
Dan Adams	R	25	4	9	.308	3	36	14	6	136	141	52	37	0	3.51
George Hogan	R	28	0	0	.000	0	4	1	0	13	12	7	1	0	4.15
George Perring	R		0	0	—	0	1	0	0	1	2	1	0	0	9.00
Harry Swan	R	26	0	0	—	0	1	0	0	1	0	1	1	0	0.00

PITTSBURGH 7th 64-86 .427 22.5 — DOC GESSLER 3-8 .273 / REBEL OAKES 61-78 .439

NAME	G by Pos	B	AGE	G	AB	R	H	2B	3B	HR	RBI	BB	SO	SB	BA	SA
TOTALS			30	154	5114	605	1339	180	90	34	520	410		153	.262	.352
Hugh Bradley	1B118	R	29	118	427	41	131	20	6	0	61	27		7	.307	.382
Jack Lewis	2B115, SS1	R	30	117	394	32	92	14	5	1	48	17		9	.234	.302
Eddie Holly	SS94, 2B1, OF2	R	34	100	350	28	86	16	5	2	38	17		14	.246	.294
Ed Lennox	3B123	R	30	124	430	71	134	25	10	11	84	71		19	.312	.493
Jim Savage	OF93, 3B29, SS11, 2B3	R	30	132	479	81	136	19	9	1	26	67		17	.284	.347
Rebel Oakes	OF145	L	30	145	571	92	178	18	10	5	75	35		28	.312	.415
Davy Jones	OF93	L	34	97	352	58	96	9	8	2	24	42		15	.273	.361
Claude Berry	C122	R	34	124	411	35	98	18	9	2	36	26		6	.238	.341
Cy Rheam	1B43, 3B13, 2B11, OF1	R	20	73	214	15	45	5	3	0	20	9		6	.210	.262
Mike Menoskey	OF41	L	19	68	140	26	37	4	1	2	9	16		5	.264	.350
1 Tex McDonald	OF29, 2B27, SS5	L	26	57	223	27	71	16	7	3	29	13		9	.318	.493
13 Skipper Roberts	C23, OF1	L	26	52	94	12	22	4	2	1	8	2		3	.234	.351
1 Doc Kerr	C18	B	32	32	71	3	17	4	2	1	7	10		0	.239	.394
2 Frank Delahanty	OF36, 2B4	R	31	41	159	25	38	4	4	1	7	11		7	.239	.333
2 Steve Yerkes	SS39	R	26	39	142	18	48	9	5	1	25	11		2	.338	.493
Ralph Mattis	OF24	R	23	36	85	14	21	4	1	0	8	9		2	.247	.318
Bob Coulson	OF18	R	27	18	64	7	13	1	0	0	3	7		2	.203	.219
1 Felix Chouinard	2B4, OF3, SS1	R	27	9	30	2	9	1	0	1	3	0		1	.300	.433
Jim Scott	SS8	R	25	8	24	2	6	1	0	0	1	5		1	.250	.292
Red Madden	C1	L	21	2	2	0	1	0	0	0	0	0		0	.500	.500
2 Medric Boucher		R	28	1	1	0	0	0	0	0	0	0		0	.000	.000

NAME	T	AGE	W	L	PCT	SV	G	GS	CG	IP	H	BB	SO	SHO	ERA
		29	64	86	.427	6	154	154	97	1370	1416	444	510	9	3.56
Elmer Knetzer	R	28	20	12	.625	1	37	30	20	272	257	88	146	3	2.88
Howie Camnitz	R	32	14	19	.424	1	36	34	20	262	256	90	82	1	3.23
Cy Barger	R	29	10	16	.385	1	33	26	18	228	252	63	70	1	4.34
Walt Dickson	R	35	9	19	.321	1	40	32	19	257	262	74	63	3	3.15
George LeClair	R	27	5	2	.714	0	22	7	5	103	99	25	49	1	4.02
Mysterious Walker	R	30	4	16	.200	0	34	21	12	169	197	74	79	0	4.32
2 Frank Allen	L		0	1	1.000	0	1	1	1	7	9	0	3	0	5.14
Willie Adams	R	23	1	1	.500	2	15	6	1	55	70	22	14	0	3.76
1 Ed Henderson	L	29	0	1	.000	0	6	1	1	16	14	8	4	0	3.94

ST. LOUIS 8th 62-89 .411 25 — THREE FINGER BROWN 50-63 .442 / FIELDER JONES 12-26 .316

NAME	G by Pos	B	AGE	G	AB	R	H	2B	3B	HR	RBI	BB	SO	SB	BA	SA
TOTALS			27	154	5078	565	1254	193	65	26	480	503		113	.247	.326
Hughie Miller	1B130	R	27	132	490	51	109	20	9	0	46	27		4	.222	.284
Doc Crandall	2B63, P27, SS1, OF1	R	26	118	278	40	86	16	5	2	41	58		3	.309	.424
Al Bridwell	SS103, 2B11	L	30	117	381	46	90	6	5	1	33	71		9	.236	.284
Allie Boucher	3B147	R	32	147	516	62	119	26	4	2	49	52		13	.231	.308
Jack Tobin	OF132	L	22	137	530	80	143	24	11	7	35	51		20	.270	.396
Ward Miller	OF111	L	29	121	402	49	110	17	7	4	50	59		18	.294	.400
Delos Drake	OF116, 1B18	R	27	138	514	51	129	18	8	3	42	31		17	.251	.355
Mike Simon	C78	R	31	93	276	21	57	11	2	0	21	18		2	.207	.261
John Misse	2B50, SS48, 3B2	R	29	99	306	28	60	8	1	0	22	36		3	.196	.229
Grover Hartley	C32, 2B13, 1B9, 3B3, OF2	R	25	86	213	24	61	15	2	1	25	12		4	.286	.390
1 Fred Kommers	OF67	L	28	76	244	33	75	9	8	3	41	24		7	.307	.447
Harry Chapman	C51, 1B1, 2B1, OF1	R	26	64	181	16	38	2	1	0	14	13		2	.210	.232
LaRue Kirby	OF50	B	24	52	195	21	48	6	3	2	18	14		5	.246	.338
Joe Mathes (JJ)	2B23	R	22	26	85	10	25	3	0	0	6	9		1	.294	.329
Manuel Cueto (SC)	3B10, SS5, 2B2	R	22	19	43	2	4	0	0	0	2	5		0	.093	.093
2 Armando Marsans (SC)	2B7, SS2	R	27	9	40	5	14	0	2	0	3	1		4	.350	.450
Fielder Jones		L	42	5	15	1	5	2	0	0	0	1		0	.333	.333

NAME	T	AGE	W	L	PCT	SV	G	GS	CG	IP	H	BB	SO	SHO	ERA
		29	62	89	.411	6	154	154	97	1367	1418	409	661	9	3.59
Doc Crandall	R	26	13	9	.591	0	27	21	18	196	194	52	84	1	3.54
Bob Groom	R	29	13	20	.394	1	42	34	23	281	281	75	167	1	3.24
1 Three Finger Brown	R	37	12	6	.667	0	26	18	13	175	172	43	81	2	3.29
2 Dave Davenport	R	24	8	13	.381	4	33	26	15	216	204	80	142	2	3.46
Hank Keupper	L	27	8	20	.286	0	42	25	12	213	256	49	70	1	4.27
Ed Willett	R	30	4	16	.200	0	27	22	14	175	208	56	73	0	4.22
2 Doc Watson	R	29	3	4	.429	0	9	7	4	56	41	24	18	2	1.93
Ernie Herbert	R	27	1	1	.500	0	18	1	0	50	56	27	24	0	3.78
Ted Welch	R	21	0	0	—	0	3	0	0	6	3	2	0	0	6.00

1915 F. L. - A Short Life

The Federal League began its second year in the courts and ended it as a mere footnote in the history of the national pastime. An antitrust suit against organized baseball was filed in January in the United States District Court in Chicago. The presiding judge in the suit was Kenesaw M. Landis, later to become baseball's first commissioner. Litigation continued through the spring and summer, as he baseball wars resumed both on the field and on the dotted line.

Two plums were plucked for the Feds when star hurlers, Eddie Plank and Chief Bender, were induced to leave Connie Mack's Athletics. Two veteran National League pitchers who had seen better years-Ed Reulbach and Hooks Wiltse-also joined the new loop, as did young hitters, Ed Konetchy and Lee Magee. Several lesser lights came along with the "names" to strengthen the Federal playing ranks this second time around.

As the curtain rose on the playing season, 1914 champion Indianapolis no longer graced the circuit. The Hoosier franchise had been transferred to Newark, New Jersey, for economic reasons. Another close race evolved, with Chicago, St. Louis, and Pittsburgh racing head-and-head down the stretch. The Chicago Whales, managed by Joe Tinker, received offensive firepower from Dutch Zwilling and the pair of McConnell and 38-year-old Three Finger Brown. St. Louis was paced by star hurlers, Eddie Plank, Doc Crandall, and Dave Davenport, and Pittsburgh's shining light was first-sacker Ed Konetchy.

Going into the final day of the season, one game separated the three contenders. After a doubleheader split between Chicago and Pittsburgh and a St. Louis victory, the smoke cleared on a .001 pennant-winning margin for Chicago over St. Louis. Pittsburgh, incredibly enough, finished third, one-half game and .004 percentage points behind. Chicago had played two fewer games than St. Louis, due to rainouts. Under today's practices, the race would not have ended here. Nevertheless, the exciting finish marked the second straight attractive race for the Feds.—Individual heroics spiced the play throughout. Bennie Kauff, sold to Brooklyn by the defunct Indianapolis club, again paced the league's batters with a .342 mark and led in stolen bases. In the pitching ranks, 6'3" George McConnell won 25 games for Chicago to lead the circuit.

As the season went on, Judge Landis urged the parties before the bench to discuss an amicable settlement. Finally, due to mounting losses and the possible U.S. entry into the Great War, the Feds were forced to sue for peace. The treaty was signed on December 21, with several key arrangements. Charles Weeghman, owner of the Chicago club, was permitted to purchase the Chicago Cubs, and St. Louis' Phil Ball was to buy the Browns. All Federal players, except the Chicago and St. Louis squads, were to be sold to the highest bidder, and all remaining contracts continued as the responsibility of the Federal League owners. Several Federal owners were to be reimbursed for their losses and long-term leases on ball parks.

Out of the debris came the beginning-as well as the end-of certain careers. Several players who made the debut in the Federal League went on to successful careers in the established circuits. They included Bennie Kauff (for whom the New York Giants paid a record $35,000), Edd Roush, Jack Tobin, Howard Ehmke, and Max Flack. Among those who saw the last of full-time playing activity in what had been described as "the outlaw league" were Joe Tinker, Three Finger Brown, George Mullin, Al Bridwell, Howie Camnitz and Hooks Wiltse.

The Peace settlement made no provision for the Baltimore owners, who were simply left out in the cold. The jilted owners responded with an antitrust suit, which resulted in Justice Oliver Wendell Holmes' edict in 1922 "that baseball is exempt from antitrust regulations due to its peculiar nature." And, as history would bear witness, the effects of the edict and the Federal League were not at all short-range.

1915 FEDERAL LEAGUE

NAME	G by Pos	B	AGE	G	AB	R	H	2B	3B	HR	RBI	BB	SO	SB	BA	SA
CHICAGO 1st 86-66 .566			JOE TINKER													
TOTALS			26	155	5133	641	1320	185	77	50	558	444		161	.257	.352
Fred Beck	1B117	L	28	121	373	35	83	9	3	5	38	24		4	.223	.303
Rollie Zeider	2B83, 3B30, SS21	R	31	130	493	65	115	24	2	0	34	43		16	.233	.290
Harry Fritz	3B70, 2B6, SS1	R	24	79	236	27	59	8	4	3	26	13		4	.250	.356
1 Jimmy Smith	SS92, 2B1	B	20	95	318	32	69	11	4	4	30	14		4	.217	.314
Max Flack	OF138	L	25	141	523	88	164	20	14	3	45	40		37	.314	.423
Dutch Zwilling	OF148, 1B3	L	26	150	548	65	157	32	7	13	94	67		24	.286	.442
Les Mann	OF130, SS1	R	22	135	468	75	143	14	19	4	58	36		18	.306	.442
Art Wilson	C87	R	29	96	269	44	82	11	2	7	31	65		8	.305	.439
Bill Fischer	C80	L	24	105	292	30	96	15	4	4	50	24		5	.329	.449
Charlie Hanford	OF43	R	33	77	179	27	43	4	5	0	22	12		10	.240	.318
Jack Farrell	2B70, SS1	B	23	70	222	27	48	10	1	0	14	25		8	.216	.270
Bill Jackson	1B36, OF1	L	34	50	98	15	16	1	0	1	12	14		3	.163	.204
24 Tex Wisterzil	3B48	R	27	49	164	15	40	4	1	0	14	8		2	.244	.280
Three Finger Brown	P35, OF1	R	38	36	82	10	24	2	1	0	6	3		0	.293	.341
Joe Tinker	SS16, 2B5, 3B4	R	34	30	69	7	19	2	1	0	9	13		3	.275	.333
1 Al Wickland	OF24	L	27	30	86	11	21	2	2	1	5	13		3	.244	.349
Joe Weiss	1B29	R	21	29	85	6	19	1	2	0	11	3		0	.224	.282
2 Mickey Doolan	SS24	R	35	24	86	9	23	1	1	0	9	2		5	.267	.302
Arnold Hauser (IL)	SS16, 3B6	R	26	23	54	6	11	1	0	0	4	5		2	.204	.222
Charlie Pechous	3B18	R	18	18	51	4	9	3	0	0	4	4		1	.176	.235
Count Clemens	C9, 2B2	R	28	11	22	3	3	1	0	0	3	1		0	.136	.182
ST. LOUIS 2nd 87-67 .565 0			FIELDER JONES													
TOTALS			27	159	5145	634	1344	193	81	23	547	576		195	.261	.352
Babe Borton	1B159	L	26	159	549	97	157	20	14	3	83	92		17	.286	.390
Bobby Vaughn	2B127, SS12, 3B8	R	30	144	521	69	146	19	9	0	32	58		24	.280	.351
Ernie Johnson	SS152	R	27	152	512	58	123	18	10	7	67	46		32	.240	.355
Charlie Deal	3B65	R	23	65	223	21	72	12	4	1	27	12		10	.323	.426
Jack Tobin	OF158	L	23	158	623	91	186	29	14	6	51	68		31	.299	.403
Delos Drake	OF97, 1B1	R	28	102	343	32	91	23	4	1	41	23		6	.265	.364
Ward Miller	OF154	L	30	154	536	80	164	19	9	1	63	79		33	.306	.381
Grover Hartley	C113, 1B1	R	26	117	395	47	107	20	6	1	50	42		10	.271	.359
Doc Crandall	P51	R	27	84	141	18	40	2	2	1	19	27		4	.284	.348
Al Bridwell	2B42, 3B15, 1B1	L	31	65	175	20	40	3	2	0	9	25		6	.229	.269
Harry Chapman	C53	R	27	62	186	19	37	6	3	1	29	22		4	.199	.280
LaRue Kirby	OF52, P1	R	25	61	178	15	38	7	2	0	16	17		3	.213	.275
Art Kores	3B60	R	28	60	201	18	47	3	4	0	22	21		6	.234	.313
Armando Marsans	OF35	R	28	36	124	16	22	3	0	0	6	14		5	.177	.202
2 Jimmy Walsh	3B9	R	29	17	31	5	6	1	0	0	1	3		1	.194	.226
3 Tex Wisterzil	3B8	R	27	8	24	1	5	1	0	0	4	2		2	.208	.250
Fielder Jones	OF3	L	43	7	6	1	0	0	0	0	0	0		0	.000	.000
Hughie Miller	1B6	R	28	7	6	0	3	1	0	0	3	0		0	.500	.667
1 Pete Compton	OF2	L	25	2	8	0	2	0	0	0	3	0		0	.250	.250
PITTSBURGH 3rd 86-67 .562 .5			REBEL OAKES													
TOTALS			30	156	5040	592	1318	180	80	20	507	448		224	.262	.341
Ed Konetchy	1B152	R	29	152	578	79	179	31	18	10	93	41		27	.310	.478
Steve Yerkes	2B114, SS8	R	27	121	434	44	125	17	8	1	49	30		17	.288	.371
Marty Berghammer	SS132	L	27	132	469	96	114	10	6	0	33	83		26	.243	.290
Mike Mowrey	3B151	R	31	151	521	56	147	27	5	1	49	66		40	.282	.359
Barney Kelly	OF148	L	31	148	524	68	154	12	17	4	50	35		38	.294	.405
Rebel Oakes	OF153	R	31	153	580	55	161	24	5	0	82	37		21	.278	.336
2 Al Wickland	OF109	L	27	110	389	63	117	12	8	1	30	52		23	.301	.380
Claude Berry	C99	R	35	100	292	32	56	11	1	0	26	29		7	.192	.247
Jack Lewis	2B45, SS11, OF6, 1B5, 3B1	R	31	82	231	24	61	6	5	0	26	8		7	.264	.333
Paddy O'Connor	C66	R	35	70	219	15	50	10	1	0	16	14		4	.228	.283
Ed Lennox	3B3	R	31	55	53	1	16	3	1	1	9	7		0	.302	.453
Cy Rheam	OF22, 1B1	R	21	34	69	10	12	0	0	1	5	1		4	.174	.217
1 Hugh Bradley	OF15	R	30	26	66	3	8	1	0	0	6	4		2	.273	.364
Eddie Holly	SS11, 3B3	R	35	16	42	8	11	2	0	0	5	5		3	.262	.310
Mike Menosky	OF9	L	20	17	21	3	2	0	0	0	1	2		2	.095	.095
Frank Delahanty	OF11	R	32	14	42	3	10	1	0	0	3	1		0	.238	.262
Davy Jones	OF13	L	35	14	49	6	16	2	0	0	4	6		1	.327	.367
Jim Savage	OF3, 3B1	B	31	14	21	0	3	0	0	0	1	1		0	.143	.143
Orie Kerlin	C3	B	24	3	1	0	0	0	0	0	0	0		0	.000	.000

NAME	T	AGE	W	L	PCT	SV	G	GS	CG	IP	H	BB	SO	SHO	ERA
		30	86	66	.566	10	155	155	97	1398	1232	402	576	21	2.64
George McConnell	R	37	25	10	.714	1	44	35	23	303	262	89	151	4	2.20
Three Finger Brown	R	38	17	8	.680	4	35	25	17	236	189	64	95	3	2.10
Claude Hendrix	R	26	16	15	.516	4	40	31	26	285	256	84	107	5	3.00
Mike Prendergast	L	26	14	12	.538	0	42	30	16	254	220	67	95	3	2.48
1 Dave Black	L	23	6	7	.462	0	25	10	2	121	104	33	43	0	2.45
2 Bill Bailey	L	27	3	1	.750	0	5	5	3	33	23	10	24	3	2.18
Ad Brennan	L	27	3	9	.250	0	19	13	7	106	117	30	40	2	3.74
1 Rankin Johnson	R	27	2	4	.333	1	11	6	3	57	58	23	19	0	4.42
Henry Rasmussen	R	20	0	0	—	0	2	0	0	2	3	2	2	0	13.50
		30	87	67	.565	9	159	159	94	1426	1267	396	698	24	2.73
Dave Davenport	R	25	22	18	.550	1	55	46	30	393	300	96	229	10	2.20
Eddie Plank	L	39	21	11	.656	3	42	31	23	268	212	54	147	6	2.08
Doc Crandall	R	27	21	15	.583	1	51	33	22	313	307	77	117	4	2.59
Bob Groom	R	30	11	11	.500	2	37	26	11	209	200	73	111	4	3.27
Doc Watson	L	30	9	9	.500	0	33	20	6	136	132	58	45	0	3.97
Ed Willett	R	31	3	4	.400	2	17	2	1	53	61	18	19	0	4.58
Ernie Herbert	R	28	1	0	1.000	0	11	1	1	48	48	18	23	0	3.38
LaRue Kirby	R	25	0	0	—	0	1	0	0	7	7	2	7	0	5.14
	L	28	86	67	.562	12	156	156	88	1382	1273	441	517	16	2.79
Frank Allen	R	26	23	13	.639	0	41	37	24	283	230	100	127	6	2.51
Elmer Knetzer	R	29	18	14	.563	3	41	33	22	279	256	89	120	3	2.58
Clint Rogge	R	25	17	11	.607	0	37	31	17	254	240	93	93	5	2.55
Cy Barger	R	30	9	8	.529	6	34	13	8	153	130	47	41	1	2.29
Walt Dickson	R	36	7	5	.583	0	27	11	4	97	115	33	36	0	4.18
Bunny Hearn	L	24	6	11	.353	0	29	17	8	176	187	37	49	1	3.38
2 Ralph Comstock	R	24	3	3	.500	2	12	7	3	53	44	7	18	0	3.23
Sandy Burk (DE)	R	28	2	0	1.000	0	2	1	1	18	8	11	9	0	1.00
1 George LeClair	R	28	1	2	.333	1	14	3	1	46	43	13	10	0	3.33
Howie Camnitz	R	33	0	0	—	0	4	2	0	20	19	11	6	0	4.50
Al Braithwood	L	23	0	0	—	0	2	0	0	3	0	2	0	0	0.00
Johnny Miljus	R	20	0	0	—	0	1	0	0	1	1	0	0	0	0.00

KANSAS CITY 4th 81-71 .529 5.5 — GEORGE STOVALL

NAME	G by Pos	B	AGE	G	AB	R	H	2B	3B	HR	RBI	BB	SO	SB	BA	SA
TOTALS			30	153	4937	547	1206	200	66	28	483	368		144	.244	.329
George Stovall	1B129	R	37	130	481	48	112	21	3	0	43	29		8	.233	.289
Duke Kenworthy	2B108, OF7	B	28	122	396	59	118	30	7	3	52	28		20	.298	.432
Johnny Rawlings	SS120	R	22	120	398	40	85	9	2	2	24	27		17	.214	.261
George Perring	3B102, 1B31, 2B31, SS1	R	30	153	553	67	143	23	7	7	68	57		10	.259	.364
Grover Gilmore	OF119	L	26	119	411	53	117	22	15	1	47	26		19	.285	.418
Chet Chadbourne	OF152	L	30	152	587	75	133	16	9	1	35	62		29	.227	.290
Al Shaw	OF124	L	34	132	448	67	126	22	10	6	67	46		15	.281	.415
Ted Easterly	C88	L	30	110	309	32	84	12	5	3	32	21		2	.272	.372
Pep Goodwin	SS42, 2B23	L	23	81	229	22	54	5	1	0	16	15		6	.236	.266
Art Kruger	OF66	R	34	80	240	24	57	9	2	2	26	12		5	.238	.317
Drummond Brown	C65, 1B1	R	30	77	227	13	55	10	1	1	26	12		3	.242	.308
Bill Bradley	3B61	R	37	66	203	16	39	10	1	0	9	9		6	.192	.251
Jack Enzenroth	C8	R	29	14	19	3	3	0	0	0	1	3		0	.158	.158

NAME	T	AGE	W	L	PCT	SV	G	GS	CG	IP	H	BB	SO	SHO	ERA
		28	81	72	.529	11	153	153	95	1359	1210	390	526	16	2.82
Nick Cullop	R	28	22	11	.667	2	44	36	22	302	278	67	111	3	2.44
Gene Packard	L	27	20	12	.625	2	42	31	21	282	250	74	108	5	2.68
Chief Johnson	R	29	17	17	.500	2	46	34	19	281	253	71	118	4	2.75
Alex Main	R	31	13	14	.481	3	35	28	18	230	181	75	91	2	2.54
Pete Henning	R	27	9	15	.375	2	40	20	15	207	181	76	73	1	3.17
Babe Blackburn	R	20	0	1	.000	0	7	2	0	16	19	13	7	0	8.44
Dan Adams	R	28	0	2	.000	0	11	2	0	35	41	13	16	0	4.63
Joe Gingras	R	21	0	0	—	0	2	0	0	4	6	1	2	0	6.75
Ben Harris	R	25	0	0	—	0	1	0	0	1	0	1	0	0	0.00

NEWARK 5th 80-72 .526 6 — BILL PHILLIPS 26-27 .491 / BILL McKECHNIE 54-45 .546

NAME	G by Pos	B	AGE	G	AB	R	H	2B	3B	HR	RBI	BB	SO	SB	BA	SA
TOTALS			28	155	5097	585	1283	210	80	17	487	438		184	.252	.334
Emil Huhn	1B101, C16	R	23	124	415	34	94	18	1	4	41	28		13	.227	.282
Frank LaPorte	2B146	R	35	148	469	67	132	28	10	2	56	48		14	.253	.351
Jimmy Esmond	SS155	R	27	155	569	79	147	20	10	5	62	59		18	.258	.355
Bill McKechnie	3B117, OF1	B	28	126	448	49	115	22	5	1	43	41		28	.257	.335
Vin Campbell	OF126	L	27	127	525	78	163	18	10	1	44	29		24	.310	.389
Edd Roush	OF144	L	22	145	551	73	164	20	11	3	60	38		28	.298	.390
Al Scheer	OF155	L	26	155	546	75	146	25	14	2	60	65		31	.267	.375
Bill Rariden	C142	R	27	142	444	49	120	30	7	0	40	60		8	.270	.369
Germany Schaefer	OF17, 1B13, 3B9, 2B2	R	38	59	154	26	33	5	3	0	8	25		3	.214	.286
Rupert Mills	1B37	R	22	41	134	12	27	5	1	0	16	6		6	.201	.254
Johnny Strands	3B12, 2B9, OF2	R	29	35	75	7	14	3	1	1	11	6		1	.187	.293
Gil Whitehouse	OF28, C1, P1	B	21	35	120	16	27	6	2	0	9	6		3	.225	.308
Ted Reed	3B20	R	24	20	77	5	20	1	2	0	4	2		1	.260	.325
3 Hugh Bradley	1B8	R	30	12	33	0	5	0	0	0	2	2		2	.152	.152
2 Larry Pratt	C3	R	27	5	4	2	2	2	0	0	0	3		2	.500	1.000
Hack Warren	1B1, C1	L	31	5	3	0	1	0	0	0	0	0		0	.333	.333
George Textor	C3	B	28	3	6	1	2	0	0	0	0	0		0	.333	.333

NAME	T	AGE	W	L	PCT	SV	G	GS	CG	IP	H	BB	SO	SHO	ERA
		29	80	72	.526	7	155	155	100	1407	1308	453	581	16	2.60
Ed Reulbach	R	32	21	10	.677	1	33	30	23	270	233	69	117	4	2.23
George Kaiserling	R	27	15	15	.500	2	41	29	16	261	246	73	75	5	2.24
Herb Moseley	R	27	15	15	.500	1	38	32	22	268	222	99	142	5	1.91
Harry Moran	R	26	13	9	.591	0	34	23	13	206	193	66	87	2	2.53
1 Cy Falkenberg	R	35	9	11	.450	1	25	21	14	172	175	47	76	0	3.24
Charlie Whitehouse	L	21	2	2	.500	0	11	3	1	40	46	17	18	0	4.28
George Mullin	R	34	2	2	.500	0	5	4	3	32	41	16	14	0	5.91
2 Tom Seaton	R	27	2	6	.250	1	12	10	7	75	61	21	28	0	2.28
Chick Brandom	R	28	1	1	.500	0	16	1	1	50	55	15	15	0	3.42
Harry Billiard	R	29	0	1	.000	1	14	2	0	28	32	28	7	0	5.79
Fred Trautman	R	33	0	0	—	0	1	0	0	3	4	1	2	0	6.00
Gil Whitehouse	R	21	0	0	—	0	1	0	1	1	0	1	0	0	0.00

BUFFALO 6th 74-78 .487 12 — LARRY SCHLAFLY 13-28 .317 / WALTER BLAIR 1-1 .500 / HARRY LORD 60-49 .550

NAME	G by Pos	B	AGE	G	AB	R	H	2B	3B	HR	RBI	BB	SO	SB	BA	SA
TOTALS			30	153	5065	574	1261	193	68	40	506	420		184	.249	.338
Hal Chase	1B143, OF1	R	32	145	566	85	161	33	10	17	89	20		23	.284	.468
Baldy Louden	2B88, SS27, 3B19	R	31	141	469	67	132	18	5	4	48	64		30	.281	.367
Roxey Roach	SS92	R	30	92	346	35	93	20	3	2	31	17		11	.269	.361
Harry Lord	3B92, OF1	R	33	97	359	50	97	12	6	1	21	21		15	.270	.345
Jack Dalton	OF119	R	30	132	437	68	128	17	3	2	46	50		28	.293	.359
Clyde Engle	OF100, 2B21, 3B17, 1B1	R	31	141	501	56	131	22	8	3	71	34		24	.261	.355
2 Benny Meyer	OF88	R	30	93	333	37	77	8	6	1	29	40		9	.231	.300
Walter Blair	C97	R	31	98	290	23	65	15	3	2	20	18		4	.224	.317
Solly Hofman	OF82, 1B11, 3B4, 2B2, SS1	R	32	109	346	29	81	10	6	0	27	30		12	.234	.298
Tom Downey	2B48, 3B35, SS2, 1B1	R	31	92	282	24	56	9	1	1	19	26		11	.199	.248
Tex McDonald	OF65	R	26	87	251	31	68	9	6	6	39	27		5	.271	.426
Nick Allen	C80	R	26	84	215	14	44	7	1	0	17	18		4	.205	.247
1 Fred Smith	SS32, 3B1	R	28	35	114	8	27	2	4	0	11	13		2	.237	.325
1 Joe Agler	OF20, 1B1	L	28	25	73	11	13	1	2	0	2	20		2	.178	.247
2 Art Watson	C6, OF1	L	31	22	30	6	14	1	0	1	13	0		0	.467	.600
Del Young	OF3	L	29	12	15	0	2	0	0	0	0	1		1	.133	.133
2 Eddie Gagnier	2B1	R	33	1	2	0	0	0	0	0	0	0		0	.000	.000

NAME	T	AGE	W	L	PCT	SV	G	GS	CG	IP	H	BB	SO	SHO	ERA
		26	74	78	.487	11	153	153	79	1360	1271	553	594	14	3.38
Al Schulz	L	26	21	14	.600	0	42	38	25	310	264	149	160	5	3.08
Fred Anderson	R	29	19	13	.594	0	36	28	14	240	192	72	142	5	2.51
Hugh Bedient	R	25	16	18	.471	10	53	30	16	269	284	69	106	2	3.18
Gene Krapp	R	28	9	19	.321	0	38	30	14	231	188	123	91	3	3.51
Russ Ford	R	32	9	5	.357	0	21	15	7	127	140	48	34	0	4.54
Rube Marshall	R	29	2	1	.667	0	21	4	2	59	62	33	21	0	3.97
2 Ed Lafitte	R	29	2	2	.500	1	14	5	1	50	53	22	17	0	3.42
Howard Ehmke	R	21	0	0	.000	0	18	2	0	54	69	25	18	0	5.50
Dan Woodman	R	21	0	0	—	0	5	1	0	15	14	9	1	0	4.20
2 George LeClair	R	28	0	0	—	0	1	0	0	3	4	1	2	0	6.00
Bob Smith	R	24	0	0	—	0	1	0	1	5	2	3	0	0	18.00

BROOKLYN 7th 70-82 .461 16 — LEE MAGEE 53-64 .453 / JOHN GANZEL 17-18 .486

NAME	G by Pos	B	AGE	G	AB	R	H	2B	3B	HR	RBI	BB	SO	SB	BA	SA
TOTALS			27	153	5035	647	1348	205	75	36	561	473		249	.268	.360
Hap Myers	1B107	R	28	118	341	61	98	9	1	1	36	32		28	.287	.328
Lee Magee	2B115, 1B2	B	26	121	452	87	146	19	10	4	49	22		34	.323	.436
2 Fred Smith	SS94, 3B15	R	28	130	385	41	95	16	6	5	58	25		21	.247	.358
Al Halt	3B111, SS40	L	24	151	524	41	131	22	7	3	64	39		20	.250	.336
George Anderson	OF134	L	25	136	458	55	135	23	9	2	39	52		20	.264	.356
Benny Kauff	OF136	L	25	136	483	92	165	23	11	12	83	85		55	.342	.509
Claude Cooper	OF121, 1B32	L	25	136	522	75	155	26	12	2	63	77		31	.294	.400
Grover Land	C81	R	30	96	290	25	75	13	2	0	22	6		3	.259	.317
1 Steve Evans	OF61, 1B1	L	30	63	216	44	64	14*	4	3	30	35		7	.296	.440
Mike Simon	C45	R	32	47	142	7	25	5	1	0	12	9		1	.176	.225
Ty Helfrich	2B34, OF1	R	24	43	104	12	25	6	0	0	5	15		2	.240	.298
2 Hugh Bradley	1B26, OF7, C1	R	30	37	126	7	31	3	2	0	18	4		6	.246	.302
1 Tex Wisterzil	3B31	R	27	36	106	13	33	3	3	0	21	21		8	.311	.396
2 Harry Smith	C19, OF1	R	25	28	65	5	13	0	0	1	4	7		2	.200	.246
Art Griggs	1B5, OF1	R	30	27	38	4	11	1	0	0	2	5		0	.289	.395
Dave Howard	2B12, OF2, SS1, 3B1	R	26	24	36	5	8	1	0	0	1	1		0	.222	.250
1 Eddie Gagnier	SS13, 2B6	R	32	33	50	8	13	1	0	0	2	2		2	.260	.280
1 Larry Pratt	C17	R	27	20	49	5	9	1	0	1	2	2		2	.184	.265
Jim Delahanty	2B4	R	36	17	25	0	6	1	0	0	2	3		1	.240	.280
Milt Reed	SS10	L	24	10	31	2	9	1	1	0	8	2		2	.290	.387
1 Art Watson	C7	L	31	9	19	4	5	3	0	1	3	0		0	.263	.579
Tiny Tesch	2B3	B	25	8	7	2	2	1	0	0	0	2		0	.286	.429
Danny Murphy	2B1, OF1	R	38	5	12	0	2	0	0	0	0	0		0	.167	.167
Felix Chouinard	OF2	L	28	4	4	1	2	0	0	0	0	1		0	.500	.500
Dick Wright	C3	R	28	4	5	0	0	0	0	0	0	0		0	.000	.000
Frank Kane	OF2	L	20	3	10	2	2	0	1	0	1	0		2	.200	.400

NAME	T	AGE	W	L	PCT	SV	G	GS	CG	IP	H	BB	SO	SHO	ERA
		28	70	82	.461	16	153	153	78	1356	1299	536	467	10	3.37
Don Marion	R	25	12	9	.571	0	35	25	15	208	193	64	46	2	3.20
1 Tom Seaton	R	27	12	11	.522	3	32	25	13	189	199	99	86	0	4.57
Jim Bluejacket (LJ)	R	27	10	11	.476	0	24	21	10	163	155	75	48	2	3.15
Happy Finneran	R	24	10	12	.455	2	37	24	12	215	197	87	68	1	2.80
Bill Upham	R	27	6	8	.429	5	33	11	4	121	129	40	46	2	3.05
1 Ed Lafitte	R	29	6	9	.400	1	17	16	7	118	126	57	34	0	3.97
2 Frank Smith	R	35	5	2	.714	0	15	5	4	63	69	18	24	1	3.14
2 Cy Falkenberg	R	35	4	3	.500	0	7	7	5	48	31	12	20	1	1.50
Hooks Wiltse	L	35	3	5	.375	1	18	3	1	59	49	7	17	0	2.29
Mysterious Walker	R	31	4	3	.333	1	13	7	2	66	61	22	28	0	3.68
Fin Wilson	L	26	1	8	.111	4	19	11	5	102	85	53	47	0	3.79
Bill Herring	R	21	0	1	.000	0	3	0	0	5	2	3	0	0	15.00

*Evans, also with Baltimore, league leader in 2B with 34

BALTIMORE 8th 47-107 .305 40 — OTTO KNABE

NAME	G by Pos	B	AGE	G	AB	R	H	2B	3B	HR	RBI	BB	SO	SB	BA	SA
TOTALS			29	154	5060	550	1235	196	53	36	465	470		128	.244	.325
Harry Swacina	1B75, 2B1	R	33	85	301	24	74	13	1	1	38	9		9	.246	.306
Otto Knabe	2B94, OF1	R	31	100	319	38	80	16	6	5	21	35		7	.251	.323
1 Mickey Doolan	SS119	R	35	119	404	41	75	13	7	2	21	24		10	.186	.257
Jimmy Walsh	3B106	R	29	100	401	43	121	20	1	9	60	21		12	.302	.424
2 Steve Evans	OF88, 1B4	L	30	88	340	50	107	20*	6	1	37	28		8	.315	.418
Vern Duncan	OF124, 3B21, 2B1	L	25	146	531	68	142	18	4	2	43	54		19	.267	.328
Jack McCandless	OF105	L	24	117	406	47	87	6	7	5	34	41		9	.214	.300
Frank Owens	C99	R	29	99	334	32	84	14	7	3	28	17		4	.251	.362
Guy Zinn	OF88	L	28	102	312	30	84	18	3	5	43	35		2	.269	.394
2 Joe Agler	1B58, OF4, 2B3	L	28	68	171	22	41	4	2	0	14	34		15	.240	.310
Enos Kirkpatrick	3B28, 2B21, 1B5, SS5	R	30	68	171	22	41	8	2	0	19	24		12	.240	.310
Harvey Russell	C21	L	28	53	73	5	19	1	2	0	11	14		1	.260	.329
Fred Jacklitsch	C45, SS1	R	39	49	135	20	32	9	2	1	13	31		2	.237	.348
John Gallagher	2B37, SS35, 3B1	R	23	40	126	11	25	4	0	0	4	9		1	.198	.230
Hack Simmons	2B13, OF13	R	30	39	88	8	18	7	1	1	14	10		1	.205	.341
1 Benny Meyer	OF34	L	28	35	120	20	29	2	0	0	9	8		6	.242	.258
2 Jimmy Smith	SS33	B	20	33	108	9	19	1	1	1	11	11		3	.176	.231
Ken Crawford	1B14, OF4	L	28	23	82	4	20	7	0	1	7	1		0	.244	.293
Jim Hickman	OF20	R	23	20	81	7	17	4	1	1	7	4		5	.210	.321
Karl Kolseth	1B6	R	23	6	23	1	6	1	0	0	1	0		0	.261	.391
Doc Kerr	C2, 1B1	R	33	6	9	1	3	0	0	0	1	0		0	.333	.333
Wally Reincker	3B3	R	27	4	8	0	1	1	0	0	0	1		0	.125	.125
Charlie Eakle	2B2		27	2	7	0	2	0	0	0	1	0		0	.286	.429
Ed Forsyth	3B1	R	28	1	3	0	0	0	0	0	0	0		0	.000	.000
Charlie Maisel	C1	R	21	1		0	0	0	0	0	0	0		0	.000	.000
Charlie Miller		R	37	1		0	0	0	0	0	0	0		0	.000	.000

NAME	T	AGE	W	L	PCT	SV	G	GS	CG	IP	H	BB	SO	SHO	ERA
		29	47	107	.305	7	154	154	85	1360	1455	466	570	5	3.96
George Suggs	R	32	11	17	.393	3	35	25	12	233	288	68	71	0	4.13
Jack Quinn	R	31	9	22	.290	1	44	31	21	274	289	63	118	0	3.45
2 Rankin Johnson	R	27	7	11	.389	2	23	19	12	151	143	58	62	2	3.34
1 Bill Bailey	R	26	6	19	.240	0	36	23	11	190	179	115	98	2	4.64
1 Frank Smith	R	35	4	4	.500	0	17	9	2	89	108	31	37	0	4.65
Chief Bender	R	32	4	16	.200	1	26	23	15	178	198	37	89	0	3.99
Charlie Young	R	22	3	2	.400	0	9	5	1	35	39	21	13	0	5.91
Larry Douglas	R	25	1	0	1.000	0	3	3	2	15	10	5	3	0	3.00
2 Dave Black	R	23	1	3	.250	0	4			34	32	15	10	0	3.71
2 George LeClair	R	28	1	8	.111	1	20	9	6	84	76	22	30	1	2.46
Tommy Vereker	R	21	0	0	—	0	1	0	0	3	2	1	0	0	15.00
Kaiser Wilhelm	R	41	0	0	.000	0	1	0	0	1	0	1	0	0	0.00

*Evans, also with Brooklyn, league leader in 2B with 34

1915 The White Elephant Crumbles

It was much like yesterday's victor reentering the arena without the armor or weapons that brought glory a time before.

The Athletics entered the season with the American League championship but without the players that won it. Financial pressures had caused manager Connie Mack to sell most of his high-salaried veteran players for whom the rival Federal League had created a bull market. Ace pitchers Eddie Plank and Chief Bender had signed with the Federal League and Eddie Murphy went to the Chicago White Sox during the winter. Jack Coombs was released by Mack and picked up by Brooklyn. In addition to these divestment's, Frank Baker decided to pack baseball in to devote full time to his farm. Mack, nevertheless, felt he could defend the championship with the good young talent he had held in reserve behind his veterans. The kids, however, fell on their faces at bat and on the mound, and the A's fell deep into the second division from the very start. On the way to 109 losses, the worst record in the Athletics' 15-year history, Mack continued unloading during the season, sending Bob Shawkey to the Yankees and Jack Barry and Herb Pennock to the Red Sox.

Barry played in his third World Series in as many years as the Boston Red Sox edged the fast-closing Detroit Tigers for first place. The Tigers held the top spot for most of the first half, but a slump enabled the Bosox to take over the lead which they never relinquished. Tris Speaker and Duffy Lewis starred with the bat for Boston, and deep pitching gave the Red Sox an edge over the rest of the circuit. Five starters won 14 or more games: righties Rube Foster, Ernie Shore, and Joe Wood, and lefties Dutch Leonard and Babe Ruth. In addition, rookie submarine pitcher Carl Mays provided the best relief work in the league. Ruth won 18 games in his first full season, while unveiling a glimpse of things to come as he led the champions in home runs with four blasts in 92 times at bat. Detroit finished 2½ games out with Ty Cobb, Sam Crawford, and Bobby Veach leading the attack. Cobb won his ninth consecutive batting title with a .369 mark, while setting a modern stolen base record with 96 thefts.

While the Athletics were plummeting into the depths of the American League basement, the cross-town rival Philadelphia Phillies shot from a fifth-place finish the previous year into the National League pennant. Rookie manager Pat Moran led his team to eight wins in a row to start the year, and a first-half challenge from the Cubs faded after June to leave the Phillies alone at the top. The two team stars were 31-game winner Grover "Pete" Alexander and league homer-champ Gavvy Cravath, but a strong supporting cast included 21-game winner Erskine Mayer, first baseman Fred Luderus, and slick-fielding rookie shortstop Dave "Beauty" Bancroft. Boston again made a late season rush, but injuries to Bill James and Johnny Evers limited their rise to second place this time around. New manager Wilbert Robinson led a Brooklyn team without stars into a surprising third-place finish. The New York Giants fell with a thud into last place; Larry Doyle and Jeff Tesreau continued to star but Christy Mathewson, Rube Marquard, and Fred Snodgrass--among others--had bad years to cut the heart out of the Giants.

By the time the World Series was over, Boston again claimed the championship. This time, however, it belonged to the Red Sox, who won it in a slightly less impressive way than the Braves. Alexander held Boston to one run in winning the first game of the Series for the Phillies, but the Red Sox pitchers took over to win the next four games by holding Philadelphia to a Series .182 batting average.

The Federal League ended its existence at the end of the season, putting an end to the three league setup and the two years of financial hardship on practically all teams, thus again allowing baseball to relax. The settlement with the Federal League cost $300,000. It was indeed an expensive page in baseball's history.

1915 AMERICAN LEAGUE

NAME	G by Pos	B	AGE	G	AB	R	H	2B	3B	HR	RBI	BB	SO	SB	BA	SA
BOSTON	1st 101-50 .669		**BILL CARRIGAN**													
	TOTALS		27	155	5024	668	1308	202	76	14	575	527	476	118	.260	.339
Dick Hoblitzell	1B117	L	26	124	399	54	113	15	12	2	61	38	26	9	.283	.396
Heinie Wagner	2B79,3B1,OF1	R	34	84	267	38	64	11	2	0	29	37	34	8	.240	.296
Everett Scott	SS100	R	22	100	359	25	72	11	0	0	28	17	21	4	.201	.231
Larry Gardner(JJ)	3B127	L	29	127	430	51	111	14	6	1	55	39	24	11	.258	.326
Harry Hooper	OF147	L	27	149	566	90	133	20	13	2	51	89	36	22	.235	.327
Tris Speaker	OF150	L	27	150	547	108	176	25	12	0	69	81	14	29	.322	.411
Duffy Lewis	OF152	R	26	152	557	69	162	31	7	2	76	45	63	14	.291	.382
Pinch Thomas	C82	L	27	86	203	21	48	4	4	0	21	13	20	3	.236	.296
Hal Janvrin	SS64,3B20,2B8	R	22	99	316	41	85	9	1	0	37	14	27	8	.269	.304
Del Gainer	1B56,OF6	R	28	82	200	30	59	5	8	1	29	21	31	7	.295	.415
2 Jack Barry	2B78	R	28	78	248	30	65	13	2	0	26	24	11	6	.262	.331
Hick Cady	C77	R	29	78	205	25	57	10	2	0	17	19	25	0	.278	.346
Olaf Henriksen	OF25	L	27	73	92	9	18	2	2	0	13	18	7	1	.196	.261
Bill Carrigan	C44	R	31	46	95	10	19	3	0	0	7	16	12	0	.200	.232
Babe Ruth	P32	L	20	42	92	16	29	10	1	4	21	9	23	0	.315	.576
Rube Foster	P37	R	27	40	83	10	23	7	0	1	9	6	18	0	.277	.398
Mike McNally	3B18,2B5	R	21	23	53	7	8	0	1	0	0	3	7	0	.151	.189
2 Bill Rodgers	2B6	R	27	11	6	2	0	0	0	0	0	3	2	0	.000	.000
Chick Shorten	OF5	L	23	6	14	1	3	1	0	0	0	0	2	0	.214	.286
Pat Haley	C4	R	24	5	7	2	1	1	0	0	1	0	1	0	.143	.286
Wally Rehg	OF1	R	26	5	5	2	1	0	0	0	0	0	1	1	.200	.200
DETROIT	2nd 100-54 .649 2.5		**HUGHIE JENNINGS**													
	TOTALS		27	156	5128	778	1372	207	94	23	647	681	527	241	.268	.358
George Burns	1B104	R	22	105	392	49	99	18	3	5	50	22	51	9	.253	.352
Ralph Young	2B119	B	26	123	378	44	92	6	5	0	31	53	46	3	.243	.286
Donie Bush	SS155	B	27	155	561	99	128	12	8	1	44	118	44	35	.228	.283
Ossie Vitt	3B151,2B2	R	25	152	560	116	140	18	13	1	48	80	22	26	.250	.334
Sam Crawford	OF156	L	35	156	612	81	183	31	19	5	112	66	29	24	.299	.436
Ty Cobb	OF156	L	28	156	563	144	208	31	13	3	99	118	43	96	.369	.487
Bobby Veach	OF152	L	27	152	569	81	178	40	10	3	112	68	43	16	.313	.434
Oscar Stanage	C100	R	32	100	300	27	67	9	2	1	31	20	41	5	.223	.277
Marty Kavanagh	1B44,2B42,SS2,OF2	R	24	113	332	55	98	14	13	3	49	42	44	8	.295	.443
Del Baker	C61	R	23	68	134	16	33	3	3	0	15	15	15	3	.246	.313
Jean Dubuc	P39	R	26	60	112	7	23	2	1	0	14	8	15	0	.205	.241
Red McKee	C35	L	25	55	106	10	29	5	0	1	17	13	16	1	.274	.349
1 Baby Doll Jacobson	1B10,OF7	R	24	37	65	5	14	6	2	0	4	5	14	1	.215	.369
George Moriarty	3B12,1B1,2B1,OF1	R	30	31	38	2	8	1	0	0	0	5	7	1	.211	.237
Frank Fuller	2B9,SS1	B	22	14	32	6	5	0	0	0	2	9	7	2	.156	.156
John Peters	C1	R	21	1	3	0	0	0	0	0	0	0	1	0	.000	.000
Marc Hall(DD)27																
CHICAGO	3rd 93-61 .604 9.5		**PANTS ROWLAND**													
	TOTALS		25	155	4918	717	1269	163	102	25	598	583	575	233	.258	.348
Jack Fournier	1B65,OF57	L	25	126	422	86	136	20	18	5	77	64	37	21	.322	.491
Eddie Collins	2B155	L	28	155	521	118	173	22	10	4	77	119	27	46	.332	.436
Buck Weaver	SS148	R	24	148	563	83	151	18	11	3	49	32	58	24	.268	.363
Lena Blackburne	3B83,SS9	B	28	96	283	33	61	5	1	0	25	35	34	13	.216	.240
2 Eddie Murphy	OF70	L	23	70	273	51	86	11	5	0	26	39	12	20	.315	.388
Happy Felsch	OF118	R	23	121	427	65	106	18	11	3	53	51	59	16	.248	.363
Shano Collins	OF104,1B47	R	29	153	576	73	148	24	17	2	85	28	50	33	.257	.368
Ray Schalk	C134	R	22	135	413	46	110	14	4	1	54	62	21	15	.266	.327
1 Braggo Roth	3B35,OF30	R	22	70	240	44	60	6	10	3*	35	29	50	12	.250	.396
Bunny Brief	1B46	R	22	48	154	13	33	6	2	2	17	16	28	8	.214	.318
1 Joe Jackson	OF46	L	25	46	162	21	43	4	5	2	36	24	12	6	.265	.389
Finners Quinlan	OF32	L	27	42	114	11	22	3	0	0	7	4	11	3	.193	.219
2 Nemo Leibold	OF22	L	22	36	74	10	17	1	0	0	11	15	11	1	.230	.243
Tom Daly	C19,1B1	R	23	29	47	5	9	1	0	0	3	5	9	0	.191	.213
Pete Johns	3B28	R	27	28	100	7	21	2	1	0	11	8	11	2	.210	.250
Wally Mayer	C20	R	24	22	54	3	12	3	1	0	5	5	8	0	.222	.315
Jim Breton	3B14,2B1,SS1	B	23	16	36	3	5	1	0	0	1	5	9	2	.139	.167
Ray Demmitt	OF3	L	31	9	6	3	0	0	0	0	0	2	1	0	.000	.000
1 Howard Baker		R	27	2	2	0	0	0	0	0	0	0	0	0	.000	.000
Larry Chappell		R	25	1	1	1	0	0	0	0	0	0	0	0	.000	.000
Charlie Jackson		L	21	1	1	0	0	0	0	0	0	0	0	0	.000	.000

NAME	T	AGE	W	L	PCT	SV	G	GS	CG	IP	H	BB	SO	SHO	ERA
		25	101	50	.669	16	155	155	82	1397	1164	446	634	16	2.39
Rube Foster	R	27	20	8	.714	1	37	33	22	255	217	86	82	5	2.12
Ernie Shore	R	24	19	8	.704	0	38	32	17	247	207	66	102	4	1.64
Babe Ruth	L	20	18	6	.750	0	32	28	16	218	166	85	112	1	2.44
Smoky Joe Wood	R	25	14	5	.737	4	25	16	10	157	120	44	63	3	1.49
Dutch Leonard	L	23	14	7	.667	1	32	21	10	183	130	67	116	2	2.36
Vean Gregg(SA)	L	30	5	3	.625	3	19	9	3	75	71	32	43	1	3.36
Ray Collins	L	28	5	7	.417	1	25	9	2	105	101	31	43	0	4.28
Carl Mays	R	23	6	5	.400	6	38	6	2	132	119	21	65	0	2.59
1 Ralph Comstock	R	24	2	0	1.000	0	9	10	2	1	2	1	0	0	2.00
2 Herb Pennock	L	21	0	0	—	0	5	1	0	14	23	10	7	0	9.64
Guy Cooper	R	22	0	0	—	0	1	0	0	2	0	2	0	0	0.00
		25	100	54	.649	21	156	156	86	1413	1259	489	550	9	2.86
Harry Coveleski	L	29	23	13	.639	4	50	38	20	313	271	87	150	1	2.44
Hooks Dauss	R	25	23	13	.639	3	46	35	27	310	261	112	132	1	3.21
Jean Dubuc	R	26	17	12	.586	2	39	33	22	258	231	88	74	5	3.10
Bernie Boland	R	23	13	6	.684	3	45	18	8	203	167	75	72	1	3.10
2 Bill James	R	28	7	3	.700	0	11	9	3	67	57	33	24	1	2.42
2 Bill Steen	R	27	5	1	.833	4	20	7	3	79	83	22	28	0	2.73
2 Grover Lowdermilk	R	30	4	1	.800	0	7	5	0	28	17	24	18	0	4.18
Pug Cavet	L	25	4	3	.571	1	17	7	2	71	83	22	26	4	4.06
Red Oldham	L	21	3	0	1.000	4	17	2	1	58	52	17	17	0	2.79
George Boehler	R	23	1	2	.333	0	8	0	0	15	19	4	7	0	1.80
Ross Reynolds	R	27	0	1	.000	0	11	1	0	17	15	2	6	0	6.54
Razor Ledbetter	R	20	0	0	—	1	1	0	0	1	1	0	0	0	0.00
		27	93	61	.604	9	155	155	92	1401	1242	350	635	17	2.43
Jim Scott	R	26	24	11	.686	2	48	35	23	299	256	78	120	7	2.04
Red Faber	R	26	24	13	.649	2	50	32	22	300	264	99	182	3	2.55
Joe Benz	R	29	15	11	.577	0	39	28	17	238	209	43	81	2	2.12
Eddie Cicotte	R	31	13	12	.520	3	39	26	15	223	216	48	106	1	3.02
Reb Russell	L	26	11	11	.500	2	41	25	10	229	215	47	90	3	2.59
Ed Walsh	R	34	3	0	1.000	0	3	3	2	27	19	7	12	1	1.33
Mellie Wolfgang	R	25	2	0	.500	0	17	2	0	54	39	12	21	0	1.83
1 Ed Klepfer	R	27	1	0	1.000	0	3	2	1	13	11	5	3	0	2.77
Hi Jasper	R	34	0	1	.000	0	3	2	1	16	8	9	15	0	4.50
Dixie Davis	R	24	0	0	—	0	2	0	0	3	2	2	0	0	3.00
Walt Johnson	R	22	0	0	—	0	1	0	0	3	3	0	0	0	9.00

* Roth, also with Cleveland, League Leader in HR with 7

WASHINGTON   4th 85-68 .556 17   CLARK GRIFFITH

NAME	G by Pos	B	AGE	G	AB	R	H	2B	3B	HR	RBI	BB	SO	SB	BA	SA
TOTALS			27	155	5029	571	1225	152	79	12	465	458	541	186	.244	.312
Chick Gandil	1B134	R	27	136	485	53	141	20	15	2	64	29	33	20	.291	.406
Ray Morgan (ST)	2B57,SS23B2	R	26	62	193	21	45	5	4	0	21	30	15	6	.233	.301
George McBride	SS146	R	34	146	476	54	97	8	4	1	30	29	60	10	.204	.252
Eddie Foster	3B79,2B75	R	28	154	618	75	170	25	10	0	52	48	30	20	.275	.348
Danny Moeller	0F116	B	30	118	438	65	99	11	10	2	23	59	63	32	.226	.311
Clyde Milan	0F151	L	29	153	573	83	165	13	7	2	66	53	32	40	.288	.348
Howard Shanks	0F80,3B49,2B10	R	24	141	492	52	123	19	8	0	47	30	42	12	.250	.321
John Henry	C94	R	25	95	277	20	61	9	2	1	22	36	28	10	.220	.278
Rip Williams	C40,1B15,3B1	R	33	91	197	14	48	3	4	0	31	18	20	4	.244	.325
Merito Acosta	0F53	L	19	72	163	20	34	4	1	0	18	28	15	8	.209	.245
Tom Connolly	3B24,0F19,SS4	L	22	50	141	14	26	3	2	0	7	14	19	5	.184	.234
Eddie Ainsmith (KJ)	C42	R	25	47	120	13	24	4	2	0	6	10	18	7	.200	.267
Doug Neff	3B12,2B10,SS7	R	23	30	60	1	10	1	0	0	4	4	6	1	.167	.183
Jim Shaw	P25	R	21	25	43	2	10	2	0	0	3	3	20	0	.233	.279
Turner Barber	0F19	L	21	20	53	9	16	1	1	0	6	6	7	0	.302	.358
Charlie Jamieson	0F17	L	22	17	68	9	19	3	2	0	7	6	9	0	.279	.382
Manny Kopp	0F9	R	23	16	32	2	8	0	0	0	0	5	7	1	.250	.250
Henri Rondeau	0F11	L	28	14	40	3	7	0	0	0	4	4	3	1	.175	.175
Joe Judge	1B10,0F2	L	21	12	41	7	17	0	0	0	9	4	6	2	.415	.463
Sam Mayer	0F9,1B1,P1	R	22	11	29	5	7	0	0	1	4	4	2	1	.241	.345
Horace Milan	0F10	L	21	11	27	6	11	1	1	0	7	8	7	2	.407	.519
Carl Sawyer	2B6,SS4	B	24	10	32	8	8	1	0	0	3	4	5	2	.250	.251
Charlie Pick		L	27	3	2	0	0	0	0	0	0	0	0	0	.000	.000

NAME	T	AGE	W	L	PCT	SV	G	GS	CG	IP	H	BB	SO	SHO	ERA
TOTALS		23	85	68	.556	14	155	155	87	1394	1161	455	715	19	2.30
Walter Johnson	R	27	27	13	.675	5	47	39	35	337	258	56	203	7	1.55
Bert Gallia	R	23	16	10	.615	1	43	29	14	260	220	64	130	3	2.28
Doc Ayres	R	24	16	9	.625	2	40	16	8	211	178	38	96	2	2.22
Joe Boehling	L	24	12	13	.480	0	40	32	14	229	217	119	108	2	3.22
Harry Harper	L	20	5	4	.556	1	19	10	5	86	66	40	54	2	1.78
Jim Shaw	R	21	5	12	.294	2	25	18	7	133	102	76	78	1	2.50
George Dumont	R	19	2	1	.667	0	3	3	40	23	12	18		2	2.03
Sam Rice	R	25	1	0	1.000	0	1	1		18	13	9	9	0	2.00
Joe Engel	R	22	1	3	.250	0	11	3	0	34	30	19	9	0	3.18
Bill Hopper	R	23	0	1	.000	1	13	0	0	31	39	16	8	0	4.64
Jack Bentley	L	20	0	2	.000	0	2	0	0	11	8	3	0	0	0.82
Nick Altrock	L	38	0	0	—	0	3	0	0	3	7	1	2	0	9.00
Sam Mayer	R	22	0	0	—	0	2	0	0	0	2	0	0	0	0.00

NEW YORK   5th 69-83 .454 32.5   WILD BILL DONOVAN

NAME	G by Pos	B	AGE	G	AB	R	H	2B	3B	HR	RBI	BB	SO	SB	BA	SA
TOTALS			27	154	4982	583	1162	167	50	31	459	570	668	198	.233	.305
Wally Pipp	1B134	L	22	136	479	59	118	20	13	4	60	66	81	14	.246	.367
Luke Boone	2B115,SS12,3B3	R	25	130	431	44	88	12	2	5	43	41	53	14	.204	.276
Roger Peckinpaugh	SS142	R	24	142	540	67	119	18	7	5	44	49	72	19	.220	.317
Fritz Maisel	3B134	R	25	135	530	77	149	16	6	4	46	48	35	51	.281	.357
Doc Cook	0F131	L	29	132	416	70	129	16	5	2	33	62	43	29	.271	.338
Hugh High	0F117	L	27	119	427	51	110	19	7	1	43	62	47	22	.258	.342
Roy Hartzell	0F107,3B49,1B2	R	33	119	387	39	97	11	2	3	60	57	37	7	.251	.313
Les Nunamaker	C77,1B2	R	26	87	249	24	56	6	3	0	17	23	24	1	.225	.273
Paddy Baumann	2B43,3B19	R	29	76	219	30	64	13	1	2	28	28	32	9	.292	.388
Birdie Cree	0F53	R	32	74	196	23	42	8	2	0	15	36	22	7	.214	.276
Ray Caldwell	P36	R	27	72	144	27	35	4	1	4	20	9	32	4	.243	.368
Ed Sweeney	C53	R	26	53	137	12	26	2	0	0	5	25	12	3	.190	.204
Charlie Mullen	1B27	R	26	40	90	11	24	1	0	0	7	10	12	1	.267	.278
Elmer Miller	0F26	R	28	26	83	4	12	1	0	0	3	4	14	0	.145	.157
2 Walt Alexander	C24	R	24	25	68	7	17	4	0	1	5	13	16	1	.250	.353
Tim Hendryx	0F12	R	24	13	40	4	8	2	0	0	1	4	2	0	.200	.250
1 Ed Barney	0F10	L	25	11	36	1	7	0	0	0	8	3	6	1	.194	.194
Tim Daley	0F2	L	30	10	4	0	0	0	0	0	1	2	1	0	.250	.250
Ernie Krueger	C8	R	24	10	29	3	5	1	0	0	0	0	5	0	.172	.207
Skeeter Shelton	0F10	R	27	10	40	1	1	0	0	0	0	2	10	0	.025	.025

Pi Schwert 22 R 5-18, Gene Layden 21 L 2-7, Roxy Walters 21 R 1-3, Frank Gilhooley 23 L 0-4

NAME	T	AGE	W	L	PCT	SV	G	GS	CG	IP	H	BB	SO	SHO	ERA
TOTALS		28	69	83	.454	2	154	154	100	1383	1272	517	559	11	3.09
Ray Caldwell	L	27	19	16	.543	0	36	35	31	305	266	107	130	3	2.89
Ray Fisher	R	27	18	11	.621	0	30	28	19	248	219	62	97	4	2.10
Jack Warhop	R	30	7	9	.438	0	21	19	12	143	164	52	34	0	3.96
Cy Pieh	R	28	4	5	.444	1	21	8	3	94	78	39	46	2	2.87
2 Bob Shawkey	R	24	4	7	.364	0	16	9	5	86	78	35	31	0	3.24
Boardwalk Brown	R	30	3	6	.333	0	19	10	5	97	95	47	34	0	4.08
Ray Keating	R	21	3	6	.333	0	11	10	8	79	66	45	37	1	3.65
Marty McHale	R	28	3	7	.300	0	13	11	6	78	86	19	25	0	4.27
Cliff Markle	R	21	2	0	1.000	0	3	2	2	23	15	6	12	0	0.39
King Cole	R	29	2	1	.400	1	10	6	2	51	41	22	19	0	3.18
George Mogridge	R	26	2	3	.400	0	6	3	1	41	33	11	11	1	1.76
Dan Tipple	R	25	1	1	.500	0	3	2	2	19	14	11	14	0	2.84
Allen Russell	R	21	1	2	.333	0	5	3	1	27	21	21	21	0	2.67
Dick Cottrell	R	26	0	1	.000	0	3	1	0	21	29	7	7	0	3.43
Will Bill Donovan	R	38	0	3	.000	0	4	3	1	34	35	10	17	0	3.60
2 Dazzy Vance	R	24	0	3	.000	0	9	7	6	28	26	16	18	0	3.54
Neal Brady	R	18	0	0	—	0	2	1	0	9	7	6	5	0	3.00

ST. LOUIS   6th 63-91 .409 39.5   BRANCH RICKEY

NAME	G by Pos	B	AGE	G	AB	R	H	2B	3B	HR	RBI	BB	SO	SB	BA	SA
TOTALS			27	159	5112	521	1255	166	65	19	439	472	765	202	.246	.315
John Leary	1B53,C11	R	24	75	227	19	55	10	0	5	15	5	36	2	.242	.286
Del Pratt	2B158	R	27	159	602	61	175	31	11	3	78	26	43	30	.291	.394
Doc Lavan	SS157	R	24	157	514	44	112	17	7	1	48	42	83	13	.218	.284
Jimmy Austin	3B141	B	35	141	477	61	127	6	6	1	30	64	60	18	.266	.310
Dee Walsh	0F45,3B2,2B1,SS1,P1	B	23	59	163	13	33	5	0	0	6	14	25	6	.220	.233
Tilly Walker	0F139	R	27	144	510	53	137	20	7	5	49	36	77	20	.269	.365
Burt Shotton	0F154	L	30	156	559	93	158	18	11	3	30	118	62	43	.283	.360
Sam Agnew	C102	R	28	104	295	18	60	4	2	0	19	12	36	5	.203	.231
Ivon Howard	1B48,3B23,0F17,SS2,2B1	B	32	113	324	43	90	10	7	2	43	43	48	29	.278	.370
George Sisler	1B37,0F29,P15	L	22	81	274	28	78	10	2	3	29	7	27	10	.285	.369
Hank Severeid	C64	R	24	80	203	12	45	6	1	1	22	16	25	2	.222	.276
Ernie Walker	0F33	L	24	50	109	15	23	4	2	0	9	23	32	5	.211	.284
Gus Williams	0F35	L	27	45	119	15	24	2	2	1	11	6	16	11	.202	.277
Dick Kauffman (AJ)	1B32,0F1	R	27	37	124	9	32	8	0	0	14	5	27	0	.258	.355
2 Baby Doll Jacobson	0F32	R	24	34	115	13	24	6	1	1	9	10	26	3	.209	.304
Billy Lee	0F15,3B1	R	21	18	59	2	11	1	0	0	4	6	15	1	.186	.203
Muddy Ruel	C6	R	24	10	4	0	0	0	0	0	0	0	1	0	.000	.000

Bobby Wallace 41 R 3-13, George O'Brien 25 R 2-9, Pat Parker 22 R 1-6, Bill Dalrymple 24 0-2, Ray Schmandt 19 R 0-4, Walt Alexander 24 R 0-1, Chris Burkam 22 L 0-1, Shorty Dee 25 R 0-3

NAME	T	AGE	W	L	PCT	SV	G	GS	CG	IP	H	BB	SO	SHO	ERA
TOTALS		25	63	91	.409	5	159	159	76	1403	1256	612	566	6	3.07
Carl Weilman	L	25	18	18	.500	4	47	31	19	290	240	83	125	3	2.34
Earl Hamilton	L	23	9	17	.346	0	35	27	13	204	203	69	63	1	2.87
1 Grover Lowdermilk	R	30	9	19	.321	0	38	29	14	222	183	133	130	1	3.12
1 Bill James	R	28	6	10	.375	1	34	23	8	170	155	92	58	0	3.60
Ernie Koob	R	22	5	6	.455	0	28	13	6	134	119	50	37	0	2.35
George Sisler	R	22	4	4	.500	0	15	8	6	70	62	38	41	0	2.83
Tim McCabe	R	20	3	1	.750	0	7	4	4	42	25	9	17	1	2.36
Jim Park	R	22	2	0	1.000	0	3	3	1	23	18	9	5	0	1.17
Red Hoff	R	24	2	2	.500	0	11	3	2	44	26	24	23	0	1.23
Parson Perryman	R	26	2	3	.400	0	24	3	0	50	52	16	19	0	3.96
Pete Sims	R	24	1	0	1.000	0	3	2	0	6	4	4	0		4.50
Walt Leverenz	R	26	1	3	.333	0	5	4	1	28	28	12	5	0	3.00
Tom Phillips	R	26	1	3	.250	0	5	4	1	28	28	12	5	0	3.00
Allan Sothoron	R	22	1	0	1.000	0	3	1	0	12	12	9	0		6.75
George Baumgardner	R	23	0	2	.000	0	7	1	0	22	29	11	6	0	4.50
Harry Hoch	R	28	0	3	.000	0	12	3	1	40	40	23	13	0	7.20
Rollin Cook	R	24	0	3	.000	0	5	3	0	14	16	9	7	0	7.07
Alex Remneas	R	29	0	0	—	0	3	2	0	6	4	3	1	0	3.00
Johnny Tillman	R	21	0	1	.000	0	1	1	0	10	6	1	6	0	0.90

Carl East 20 R 0-0, Rip Mckay 23 R 0-0, Scott Perry 24 R 0-0, Dee Walsh 25 R 0-0

CLEVELAND   7th 57-95 .375 44.5   JOE BIRMINGHAM 12-16 .429, LEE FOHL 45-79 .363

NAME	G by Pos	B	AGE	G	AB	R	H	2B	3B	HR	RBI	BB	SO	SB	BA	SA
TOTALS			25	154	5030	539	1102	169	79	20	456	490	681	138	.241	.317
Jay Kirke	1B87	L	27	87	339	35	105	19	7	2	46	14	21	5	.310	.395
Bill Wambsganss	2B78,3B35	R	21	121	375	30	73	4	4	0	21	36	50	8	.195	.227
Ray Chapman	SS154	R	24	154	570	101	154	14	17	3	67	70	82	36	.270	.370
Walter Barbere	3B68,1B51	R	23	77	246	15	47	3	1	0	11	10	27	6	.191	.211
Elmer Smith	0F123	R	22	144	476	37	118	23	12	4	67	36	75	10	.248	.366
1 Nemo Leibold	0F53	L	23	57	203	32	53	5	4	0	14	29	13	6	.256	.319
Jack Graney	0F115	L	29	116	404	42	105	20	7	1	56	59	29	12	.260	.351
Steve O'Neill	C115	R	23	121	386	32	91	14	2	2	34	26	41	2	.236	.298
1 Joe Jackson	0F49,1B27	L	25	82	299	42	99	16	9	3	45	28	11	10	.331	.475
Terry Turner	2B51,3B20	R	34	75	262	35	66	14	1	0	14	29	13	12	.252	.313
Billy Southworth	0F44	L	22	60	177	25	39	2	5	0	8	36	12	2	.220	.328
Denny Wilie	0F35	L	24	45	131	14	33	4	1	2	10	26	18	2	.252	.344
Ben Egan	C40	R	31	42	120	4	13	3	0	0	6	8	14	0	.108	.133
Joe Evans	3B30,2B2	R	20	42	109	17	28	4	2	0	11	22	6	6	.257	.330
2 Braggo Roth	0F39	R	22	39	144	23	43	4	7	4	20	22	22	14	.299	.507
Jack Hammond	2B19	R	24	35	84	9	18	2	1	0	4	1	19	0	.214	.262
Roy Wood	1B21,0F2	R	22	33	78	5	15	2	0	0	3	2	13	1	.192	.244
Pete Shields	1B23	R	23	23	72	4	15	6	0	0	6	4	5	3	.208	.292

1 Bill Rodgers 27 L 14-45, Jim Eschen 23 R 10-42, Tex Hoffman 21 L 2-13, Ben Paschal 19 R 1-9, Josh Billings 23 R 4-21, Homer Haworth 21 L 1-7, Lee Gooch 25 R 1-2

NAME	T	AGE	W	L	PCT	SV	G	GS	CG	IP	H	BB	SO	SHO	ERA
TOTALS		24	57	95	.375	12	154	154	62	1372	1287	518	610	11	3.13
Guy Morton	R	22	16	15	.516	1	34	27	15	240	189	60	134	6	2.14
Willie Mitchell	L	25	11	14	.440	1	36	30	12	236	210	84	149	1	2.82
Rip Hagerman	R	27	6	13	.316	0	29	22	7	151	156	77	69	0	3.52
Roy Walker	R	25	5	9	.357	1	25	15	4	131	122	65	57	0	3.98
Fritz Coumbe	L	25	4	7	.364	2	30	12	4	114	123	31	47	3	3.47
Oscar Harstad	R	23	3	6	.333	1	32	7	4	82	81	35	35	0	3.40
Sad Sam Jones	R	22	3	8	.273	5	48	9	2	146	131	63	42	0	3.64
Clarence Garrett	R	24	2	2	.500	0	4	4	3	19	6	5	2	0	3.35
Lynn Brenton	R	25	2	3	.400	0	11	5	1	51	60	20	18	1	3.35
Allan Collamore	R	25	2	5	.286	0	11	6	5	64	52	20	15	2	2.39
Paul Carter	R	21	2	3	.333	1	10	3	3	42	44	18	14	0	3.21
1 Bill Steen	R	27	1	4	.200	0	9	7	2	43	47	11	13	0	5.00
2 Ed Klepfer	R	27	1	6	.143	0	7	2	2	45	47	11	13	0	4.26
Abe Bowman	R	24	0	1	.000	0	1	1	0	7	10	6	3	0	9.00
Herb Hill	R	23	0	0	—	0	1	0	0	1	2	1	0	0	27.00

* Roth, also with Chicago, league leader in HR with 7

PHILADELPHIA   8th 43-109 .283 58.5   CONNIE MACK

NAME	G by Pos	B	AGE	G	AB	R	H	2B	3B	HR	RBI	BB	SO	SB	BA	SA
TOTALS			26	154	5081	545	1204	183	72	16	440	436	634	127	.237	.311
Stuffy McInnis	1B119	R	24	119	456	44	143	14	4	0	49	14	17	8	.314	.395
Nap Lajoie	2B110,SS10,1B5,3B2	R	40	129	490	40	137	24	5	1	61	11	16	10	.280	.355
Larry Kopf	SS74,3B42,2B2	B	24	118	386	39	87	10	2	1	33	41	45	2	.225	.269
Wally Schang	3B43,0F41,C26	B	25	116	359	64	89	9	11	1	44	66	47	18	.248	.343
Jimmy Walsh	0F109,3B21,1B1	R	29	117	417	48	86	15	6	1	20	57	64	22	.206	.278
Amos Strunk	0F111,1B19	L	26	132	485	76	144	28	16	1	45	56	45	17	.297	.427
Rube Oldring	0F96,3B8	R	31	107	418	49	101	23	4	2	42	20	11	14	.242	.363
Jack Lapp	C89,1B12	L	30	112	312	26	85	16	2	1	31	30	29	5	.272	.375
Lew Malone	2B43,3B12,0F4,SS2	R	18	60	201	17	41	4	4	1	17	21	40	7	.204	.279
Wickey McAvoy	C64	R	20	68	184	20	35	7	2	0	6	11	32	0	.190	.250
1 Eddie Murphy	0F58,3B6	R	23	68	260	37	60	9	4	0	29	28	22	13	.231	.273
Chick Davies	0F32,P4	R	23	57	134	20	29	6	0	1	11	14	31	2	.182	.265
1 Jack Barry	SS54	R	28	48	194	16	43	6	4	0	15	16	30	6	.222	.273
Tom Healy	3B117,SS1	R	19	23	77	11	17	3	0	0	4	4	21	2	.221	.234
Shag Thompson	0F7	R	22	17	33	4	11	0	0	0	1	0	3	0	.333	.394
Harry Damrau	3B16	R	23	16	39	2	7	1	0	0	4	1	10	1	.196	.214
Bill Bankston	0F8	L	22	11	36	6	5	0	0	0	1	1	3	1	.139	.306
Socks Seibold	SS7	R	19	10	16	2	3	0	0	0	0	0	6	0	.115	.154
Sam Crane	SS6,2B1	R	20	8	23	4	2	0	0	0	0	2	4	0	.087	.174
Cy Perkins	C5	R	19	6	20	0	4	0	0	0	2	0	5	0	.200	.250
Sam McConnell	3B5	L	20	6	11	1	2	1	0	0	0	3	2	0	.182	.273

Harry Davis 41 R 1-3, Owen Conway 24 1-15, Buck Danner 24 R 3-12, Bill Haeffner 20 R 1-4, Henry Bostock 20 R 0-7, Ralph Edwards 22 R 0-5, Fred Lear 21 R 0-2, Bunny Corcoran 20 0-4, Ira Thomas 34 R 0-0, Frank Baker 29 (HO)

NAME	T	AGE	W	L	PCT	SV	G	GS	CG	IP	H	BB	SO	SHO	ERA
TOTALS		22	43	109	.283	2	154	154	78	1348	1358	827	588	6	4.33
Weldon Wyckoff	R	23	10	22	.313	1	43	34	20	276	238	165	157	1	3.52
1 Bob Shawkey	R	24	6	6	.500	0	17	13	7	100	103	38	56	1	4.05
Bullet Joe Bush	R	22	5	15	.250	0	25	18	8	146	137	89	89	0	4.13
Tom Knowlson	R	20	4	7	.364	0	18	9	7	99	60	24	23	0	3.47
Tom Sheehan	R	21	4	8	.333	0	18	8	2	102	121	38	22	1	4.15
Rube Bressler	R	21	4	17	.190	0	22	20	7	178	183	118	69	1	5.21
1 Herb Pennock	L	21	3	6	.333	0	11	9	3	44	46	29	24	1	5.32
Bill Morrisette	R	21	2	1	.667	0	3								5.50
Cap Crowell	R	22	2	2	.500	0	10	8		54	56	47	15	0	5.50
Joe Sherman	R	21	1	0	1.000	0									0.00
Elmer Myers	R	21	1	0	1.000	0	1	1	1	9	5	5	12	1	0.00
Chick Davies	R	23	1	1	.333	0	4	2	0	15	20	12	9	0	5.40
Bill Meehan	R	21	1	0		0	1								11.25
Tink Turner	R	25	0	1	.000	0									22.50
Carl Ray	R	21	0	1	.000	0									5.14
Jack Harper	R	21	0	1											3.00
Jack Richardson	R	21	0	2											2.63
Harry Eccles	R	21	0	1							65				6.86
Bud Davis	R	24	0	2							14	23	13		6.75
Bruno Haas	L	24	0								4				3.43
Harry Weaver	R														3.00
Dana Fillingim	R	21					1				39	42	15		3.43
Jack Nabors	R	27	0	5			14			58	35	18		5.50

Walter Ancker 22 R 0-0, Squiz Pillion 21 L 0-0, Bob Cone 21 L 0-0, Bob Pepper 20 R 0-0

PHILADELPHIA — 1ST 90-62 .592 — PAT MORAN

Batting

NAME	G by Pos	B	AGE	G	AB	R	H	2B	3B	HR	RBI	BB	SO	SB	BA	SA
TOTALS			28	153	4916	589	1216	202	39	58	486	460	600	121	.247	.340
Fred Luderus	1B141	L	28	141	499	55	157	36	7	7	62	42	36	9	.315	.457
Bert Niehoff	2B148	R	31	148	529	61	126	27	4	2	49	30	63	21	.238	.308
Dave Bancroft	SS153	B	24	153	563	85	143	18	2	7	30	77	62	15	.254	.330
Bobby Byrne	3B105	R	30	105	387	50	81	6	4	0	21	39	28	4	.209	.245
Gavvy Cravath	0F150	R	34	150	522	89	149	31	7	24	115	86	77	11	.285	.510
Dode Paskert	0F92,1B5	R	33	109	328	51	80	17	4	3	43	29	47	9	.244	.348
Possum Whitted	OF119,1B7	R	25	128	464	46	126	17	3	1	43	29	47	3	.271	.339
Bill Killefer	C105	R	27	105	320	26	76	9	2	0	24	18	14	5	.238	.278
Beals Becker	OF98	L	28	112	338	38	83	16	4	11	38	26	48	12	.246	.414
Milt Stock	3B55,SS4	R	21	69	227	37	59	7	3	1	15	22	26	6	.260	.330
Ed Burns	C67	R	27	67	174	11	42	5	0	0	16	20	12	1	.241	.270
Oscar Dugey	2B14	R	27	42	39	4	6	1	0	0	0	7	5	2	.154	.179
Bud Weiser	OF20	R	24	37	64	6	9	2	0	0	8	7	12	2	.141	.172
Jack Adams	C23,1B1	B	24	24	27	1	3	0	0	0	2	2	3	0	.111	.111

Pitching

NAME	T	AGE	W	L	PCT	SV	G	GS	CG	IP	H	BB	SO	SHO	ERA
TOTALS		26	90	62	.592	8	153	153	98	1374	1161	342	652	20	2.17
Pete Alexander	R	28	31	10	.756	3	49	42	36	376	253	64	241	12	1.22
Erskine Mayer	R	25	21	15	.583	2	43	33	20	275	240	59	114	2	2.36
Al Demaree	R	28	14	11	.560	1	32	26	13	210	201	58	69	3	3.04
Eppa Rixey	L	24	11	12	.478	1	29	22	10	177	163	64	88	2	2.39
George Chalmers	R	27	8	9	.471	1	26	20	13	170	159	45	82	1	2.49
2 George McQuillan	R	30	4	3	.571	0	9	8	5	64	60	11	13	0	2.11
Joe Oeschger	R	23	1	0	1.000	0	8	1	1	24	21	9	8	0	3.38
Stan Baumgartner	L	22	0	0	.000	0	10	1	0	48	33	23	27	0	2.44
Ben Tincup	R	22	0	0	—	0	10	0	0	31	26	9	10	0	2.03

BOSTON — 2nd 83-69 .546 7 — GEORGE STALLINGS

Batting

NAME	G by Pos	B	AGE	G	AB	R	H	2B	3B	HR	RBI	BB	SO	SB	BA	SA
TOTALS			28	157	5070	582	1219	231	57	17	496	549	620	121	.240	.319
Butch Schmidt	1B127	L	28	127	458	46	115	26	7	2	60	36	59	3	.251	.352
Johnny Evers (NJ)	2B83	L	33	83	278	38	73	4	1	1	22	50	16	7	.263	.295
Rabbit Maranville	SS149	R	23	149	509	51	124	23	6	2	43	45	65	18	.244	.324
Red Smith	3B157	R	25	157	549	66	145	34	4	2	65	67	49	16	.264	.360
Herbie Moran	0F123	L	31	130	419	59	84	13	5	0	21	66	41	16	.200	.255
Sherry Magee	0F134,1B22	R	30	156	571	72	160	34	12	2	87	54	39	15	.280	.392
Joey Connolly	0F93	L	31	104	305	48	91	14	8	0	23	39	35	13	.298	.397
Hank Gowdy	C118	R	25	118	316	27	78	15	3	2	30	41	34	10	.247	.332
Ed Fitzpatrick	2B71,0F29	R	25	105	303	54	67	19	3	0	24	43	36	13	.221	.304
2 Dick Egan	0F24,2B22,SS10,1B9,3B4	R	31	83	209	20	57	9	1	0	21	28	18	3	.259	.309
Bert Whaling	C72	R	27	72	190	10	42	6	2	0	13	8	38	0	.221	.274
Larry Gilbert	0F27	L	23	45	106	11	16	4	0	0	4	11	13	4	.151	.189
Ted Cather	0F40	R	26	40	102	10	21	3	1	2	18	15	19	2	.206	.314
2 Pete Compton	0F35	L	25	35	116	10	28	7	1	1	12	8	11	4	.241	.345
Paul Strand	P6,0F5	R	21	24	22	3	2	0	0	0	2	0	4	0	.091	.091
2 Fred Snodgrass	0F18,1B5	R	27	23	79	10	22	2	0	0	9	7	9	0	.278	.304
Walt Tragesser	C7	R	28	7	7	0	0	0	0	0	0	0	2	0	.000	.000
2 Zip Collins	0F5	L	23	5	14	3	4	1	1	0	2	1	3	1	.286	.500
Joe Shannon	0F4,2B1	R	18	5	10	3	2	0	0	0	1	0	3	0	.200	.200
Earl Blackburn	C3	R	22	3	6	0	1	0	0	0	0	0	1	0	.167	.167
Fletcher Low	3B1	R	22	1	4	1	1	0	0	0	1	0	0	0	.250	.250
Red Shannon	2B1	B	18	1	1	0	0	0	0	0	0	0	0	0	.000	.000

Pitching

NAME	T	AGE	W	L	PCT	SV	G	GS	CG	IP	H	BB	SO	SHO	ERA
TOTALS		28	83	69	.546	13	157	157	95	1406	1257	366	630	17	2.57
Dick Rudolph	R	26	22	19	.537	1	44	43	30	341	304	64	147	3	2.38
Tom Hughes	R	31	16	14	.533	9	50	25	17	280	208	58	171	4	2.12
2 Pat Ragan	R	29	15	12	.556	0	33	26	13	227	208	59	81	3	2.46
Lefty Tyler	L	25	10	9	.526	0	32	24	15	205	182	84	99	1	2.85
Bill James (SJ)	R	23	5	4	.556	0	13	9	4	68	68	22	23	0	3.04
Art Nehf	L	22	5	4	.556	0	12	10	6	78	60	21	39	4	2.54
Jesse Barnes	R	22	4	0	1.000	0	9	3	2	45	41	10	16	0	1.40
George Davis	R	25	3	3	.500	0	15	9	4	73	85	19	26	0	3.82
Dick Crutcher	R	25	2	2	.500	2	14	4	1	44	50	16	17	0	4.29
Paul Strand (IL)	L	21	1	1	.500	1	6	2	2	23	26	3	13	0	2.35
Otto Hess	L	36	0	1	.000	1	4	1	1	14	16	6	5	0	3.86
Dolf Luque	R	24	0	0	—	0	2	1	0	5	6	4	3	0	3.60
Gene Cocreham	R	30	0	0	—	0	1	0	0	2	3	1	0	0	4.50

BROOKLYN — 3rd 80-72 .526 10 — WILBERT ROBINSON

Batting

NAME	G by Pos	B	AGE	G	AB	R	H	2B	3B	HR	RBI	BB	SO	SB	BA	SA
TOTALS			26	154	5120	536	1268	165	75	14	449	313	496	131	.248	.317
Jake Daubert	1B150	L	31	150	544	62	164	21	8	2	47	57	48	11	.301	.381
George Cutshaw	2B154	R	28	154	566	68	139	18	9	0	62	34	35	28	.246	.309
Ollie O'Mara	SS149	R	24	149	577	59	141	26	3	0	31	51	40	11	.244	.300
Gus Getz	3B128,SS2	R	25	130	477	39	123	10	5	2	46	8	14	19	.258	.312
Casey Stengel	OF129	L	24	132	459	52	109	20	12	3	50	34	46	5	.237	.353
Hy Myers	OF153	R	26	153	603	69	156	21	7	2	46	17	51	19	.259	.383
Zack Wheat	OF144	L	27	146	528	64	136	15	12	5	66	52	42	21	.258	.360
Otto Miller	C84	R	26	84	254	20	57	4	6	0	25	6	28	3	.224	.287
Lew McCarty	C84	R	26	84	276	19	66	9	4	0	19	7	23	7	.239	.301
1 Joe Schultz	3B55,SS1	R	21	56	120	13	35	3	2	0	4	10	18	3	.292	.350
John Hummel	OF20,1B11,SS1	R	32	53	100	6	23	2	3	0	8	6	11	1	.230	.310
Jack Coombs	P29	R	32	29	75	8	21	1	1	0	5	2	17	0	.280	.320
Bill Zimmerman	OF18	R	28	22	57	3	16	2	0	0	7	4	8	1	.281	.316
Red Smyth	OF9	L	24	19	22	3	3	1	0	0	3	4	2	1	.136	.182
2 Ivy Olson	2B10,SS7,3B1,0F1	R	29	18	26	2	2	0	1	0	3	1	0	0	.077	.154
Al Nixon	OF14	R	29	14	26	3	6	1	0	0	2	2	4	1	.231	.269
Mack Wheat	C8	R	22	8	14	0	1	0	0	0	0	0	5	0	.071	.071
1 Dick Egan	3B1	R	31	3	3	0	0	0	0	0	0	0	0	0	.000	.000
John Karst (BN)	3B1	L	21	1	0	0	0	0	0	0	0	0	0	0	.000	.000

Pitching

NAME	T	AGE	W	L	PCT	SV	G	GS	CG	IP	H	BB	SO	SHO	ERA
TOTALS		27	80	72	.526	8	154	154	87	1390	1252	473	499	16	2.65
Jeff Pfeffer	R	27	19	14	.576	3	40	34	26	292	243	76	84	6	2.10
Jack Coombs	R	32	15	10	.600	0	29	24	17	196	166	91	56	2	2.57
Sherry Smith	L	24	14	8	.636	2	29	20	11	174	169	42	52	2	2.59
Wheezer Dell	R	29	11	10	.524	1	40	24	12	215	166	100	94	4	2.34
Nap Rucker	L	30	9	4	.692	1	19	15	7	123	134	28	38	1	2.41
2 Phil Douglas	R	25	5	5	.500	0	20	13	5	117	104	17	63	1	2.61
Ed Appleton	R	23	4	10	.286	0	34	10	5	138	133	66	50	0	3.33
2 Rube Marquard	L	28	2	2	.500	1	6	3	0	25	29	5	13	0	6.12
1 Pat Ragan	R	29	1	0	1.000	0	3	0	0	20	11	8	7	0	0.90
Duster Mails	L	20	0	1	.000	0	2	1	0	6	8	6	3	0	3.60
Leon Cadore	R	24	0	2	.000	0	7	2	1	21	28	8	12	0	5.57
2 Larry Cheney	R	29	0	2	.000	0	5	4	1	27	16	17	11	0	1.67
Raleigh Aitchison	R	27	0	4	.000	0	7	5	2	33	36	6	14	0	4.91
Elmer Brown	R	31	0	0	—	0	1	0	0	2	4	1	1	0	9.00
Charlie Schmutz	R	24	0	0	—	0	1	0	0	4	7	1	1	0	6.75

CHICAGO — 4th 73-80 .477 17.5 — ROGER BRESNAHAN

Batting

NAME	G by Pos	B	AGE	G	AB	R	H	2B	3B	HR	RBI	BB	SO	SB	BA	SA
TOTALS			29	156	5114	570	1246	212	66	53	485	393	639	166	.244	.342
Vic Saier	1B139	L	24	144	497	74	131	35	11	11	64	64	62	29	.264	.445
Heinie Zimmerman	2B100,3B36,SS4	R	28	139	520	65	138	28	11	3	62	21	33	19	.265	.379
Bobby Fisher	SS147	R	28	147	566	68	153	22	5	5	53	30	51	9	.287	.370
Art Phelan	3B110,2B24	R	27	133	448	41	98	16	7	3	35	55	42	12	.219	.306
Wilbur Good	OF125	L	29	128	446	66	126	18	9	2	27	34	65	19	.253	.337
Cy Williams	OF149	R	27	151	518	59	133	20	6	13	64	26	49	15	.257	.398
Wildfire Schulte	OF147	L	32	151	550	66	137	20	6	12	62	49	68	19	.249	.373
Jimmy Archer	C88	R	32	97	309	21	75	11	5	1	27	11	38	5	.243	.320
Roger Bresnahan	C68	R	36	77	221	19	45	8	1	1	19	29	23	19	.204	.262
Polly McLarry	1B25,2B20	L	24	68	127	16	25	3	0	1	12	14	20	2	.197	.244
Pete Knisely	OF34,2B9	R	31	64	134	12	33	9	0	0	17	15	18	1	.246	.313
2 Red Murray	OF39,2B1	R	31	51	144	20	43	6	1	0	11	8	8	6	.299	.354
2 Alex McCarthy	2B12,3B12,SS1	R	27	23	72	4	19	3	0	1	6	5	7	2	.264	.347
Bubbles Hargrave	C9	R	22	15	19	2	3	0	1	0	2	1	5	0	.158	.263
Eddie Mulligan	SS10,3B1	R	20	11	22	1	8	1	0	0	2	5	1	2	.364	.409
2 Joe Schultz	2B2	R	21	7	8	1	2	0	0	0	1	0	1	0	.250	.250
Red Corriden	3B1,0F1	R	27	6	3	1	0	0	0	0	0	2	1	0	.000	.000
John Fluhrer	OF2	R	21	6	6	0	2	0	0	0	0	1	0	1	.333	.333
Chick Keating	SS2	R	23	4	3	0	0	0	0	0	0	0	1	0	.000	.000
Bob O'Farrell	C2	R	18	3	3	0	1	0	0	0	0	0	0	0	.333	.333
Jack Wallace	C2	R	22	2	7	1	2	0	0	0	0	0	2	0	.286	.286

Pitching

NAME	T	AGE	W	L	PCT	SV	G	GS	CG	IP	H	BB	SO	SHO	ERA
TOTALS		27	73	80	.477	8	156	156	71	1399	1272	480	657	18	3.11
Hippo Vaughn	L	27	20	12	.625	1	41	34	18	270	240	77	148	4	2.87
George Pierce	L	27	13	9	.591	0	36	20	8	176	158	77	96	2	3.32
Jimmy Lavender	R	31	10	16	.385	4	41	24	13	220	178	67	117	1	2.58
1 Larry Cheney	R	29	9	9	.471	0	25	18	6	131	120	55	68	2	3.57
Bert Humphries	R	34	8	13	.381	3	31	22	10	172	183	23	45	4	3.20
Zip Zabel	R	24	7	10	.412	0	36	17	8	163	124	84	60	3	3.20
Pete Standridge	R	24	4	1	.800	0	29	3	2	112	120	36	42	0	3.62
Brad Hogg	R	26	1	0	1.000	0	2	1	1	13	12	6	0	1	2.08
3 Phil Douglas	R	25	1	1	.500	0	4	2	1	25	17	7	18	1	1.16
Karl Adams	R	23	1	9	.100	0	26	12	3	107	105	43	57	0	4.71
Ed Schorr	R	23	0	0	—	0	6	0	0	6	9	5	3	0	7.50
Bob Wright	R	23	0	1	.000	0	3	1	0	9	7	3	1	0	2.25

PITTSBURGH — 5th 73-81 .474 18 — FRED CLARKE

Batting

NAME	G by Pos	B	AGE	G	AB	R	H	2B	3B	HR	RBI	BB	SO	SB	BA	SA
TOTALS			29	156	5113	557	1259	197	91	24	464	419	656	182	.246	.334
Doc Johnston	1B147	L	27	147	543	71	144	19	12	5	64	38	40	26	.265	.372
Jim Viox	2B135,3B13,OF2	R	24	150	503	56	129	17	8	2	49	75	31	12	.256	.334
Honus Wagner	SS131,3B12,1B10	R	41	156	566	68	155	32	17	6	78	39	64	22	.274	.422
Doug Baird	3B120,OF20,2B3	R	23	145	512	49	112	26	12	1	53	37	88	29	.219	.322
Bill Hinchman	OF156	R	32	158	577	72	177	33	14	5	77	48	75	17	.307	.438
1 Zip Collins	OF101	R	23	106	354	51	104	8	5	3	23	24	38	6	.294	.353
Max Carey	OF139	R	25	140	564	76	143	26	5	3	27	57	58	36	.254	.333
George Gibson	C120	R	34	120	351	28	88	15	6	1	30	31	25	5	.251	.336
Dan Costello	OF17	L	22	71	125	16	27	4	1	0	11	7	23	7	.216	.264
Wally Gerber	SS23,3B23,2B2	R	23	56	144	8	28	2	0	0	7	9	16	6	.194	.208
1 Bobby Schang	C44	R	28	56	125	13	23	6	3	0	14	14	32	2	.184	.280
2 Ed Barney	OF26	L	25	32	99	16	27	1	2	0	5	11	12	7	.273	.323
Leo Murphy	C34	R	26	34	41	4	4	0	0	0	3	4	12	0	.098	.098
1 Alex McCarthy	2B9,SS5,3B4,1B1	R	27	21	49	3	10	0	1	0	3	5	10	1	.204	.245
Larry Lejeune	OF18	R	29	18	65	4	11	0	1	0	2	1	6	1	.169	.200
Paddy Siglin	2B1	R	23	6	7	1	2	0	0	0	1	1	0	1	.286	.286
Ike McAuley	SS5	R	21	5	15	0	2	1	0	0	1	0	6	0	.133	.200
Bill Wagner	C3	R	21	5	5	0	0	0	0	0	0	0	2	0	.000	.000
Fritz Scheeren	OF1	R	24	4	3	0	1	0	0	0	1	0	2	0	.200	.200
Pat Duncan	OF1	R	21	3	5	0	1	0	0	0	2	0	3	0	.200	.200
Fred Clarke	OF1	L	42	1	2	0	1	0	0	0	1	0	0	0	.500	.500
Harry Daubert	OF1	R	23	1	1	0	0	0	0	0	0	0	0	0	.000	.000
Syd Smith	C1	R	31	1	0	0	0	0	0	0	0	0	0	0	.000	.000

Pitching

NAME	T	AGE	W	L	PCT	SV	G	GS	CG	IP	H	BB	SO	SHO	ERA
TOTALS		26	73	81	.474	11	156	156	91	1380	1229	384	544	18	2.60
Al Mamaux	R	21	21	8	.724	0	38	31	17	252	182	96	152	8	2.03
Bob Harmon	R	27	16	17	.485	1	37	32	25	270	242	62	86	5	2.50
Babe Adams	R	33	14	14	.500	2	40	30	17	245	229	34	62	2	2.87
1 George McQuillan(SA)	R	30	8	10	.444	1	30	20	9	149	160	39	56	0	2.84
Erv Kantlehner	L	22	5	12	.294	3	29	18	10	163	135	58	64	1	2.26
Wilbur Cooper	L	23	5	16	.238	3	38	21	11	186	180	52	71	1	3.29
Carmen Hill	R	19	2	1	.667	0	8	4	2	47	42	13	24	1	1.15
Joe Conzelman	R	29	1	0	1.000	0	18	1	0	47	41	20	22	0	3.45
Herb Kelly	R	23	1	1	.500	1	5	1	1	11	10	4	6	0	4.09
1 Dazzy Vance	R	24	0	3	.000	0	9	3	0	28	26	16	18	0	9.00
Phil Slattery	L	22	0	0	—	0	3	0	0	8	5	1	1	0	0.00

ST. LOUIS   6th 72-81 .471 18.5   MILLER HUGGINS

NAME	G by Pos	B	AGE	G	AB	R	H	2B	3B	HR	RBI	BB	SO	SB	BA	SA
TOTALS			28	157	5106	590	1297	159	92	20	483	457	658	162	.254	.333
Dots Miller	1B83,2B55,3B9,SS3	R	28	150	553	73	146	17	10	2	72	43	48	27	.264	.342
Miller Huggins	2B107	B	37	107	353	57	85	5	2	2	24	74	68	13	.241	.283
Art Butler	SS130	R	27	130	469	73	119	12	5	1	31	47	34	26	.254	.307
Bruno Betzel	3B105,2B3,SS2	R	20	117	367	42	92	12	4	0	27	18	48	10	.251	.305
Tommy Long	OF140	R	25	140	507	61	149	21	25	2	61	31	50	19	.294	.446
Owen Wilson	OF107	L	31	107	348	33	96	13	6	3	39	19	43	8	.276	.374
Bob Bescher	OF130	B	31	130	486	71	128	15	7	4	34	52	53	27	.263	.348
Frank Snyder	C144	R	21	144	473	41	141	22	7	2	55	39	49	3	.298	.387
Cozy Dolan	OF98	R	32	111	322	53	90	14	9	2	38	34	37	17	.280	.398
Ham Hyatt	1B81,OF25	L	30	106	295	23	79	8	9	2	46	28	24	3	.268	.398
Zinn Beck	3B62,SS4,2B2	R	29	70	223	21	52	9	4	0	15	12	31	3	.233	.309
Mike Gonzalez	C31,1B8	R	24	51	97	12	22	2	2	0	10	8	9	3	.227	.289
Jack Roche	C4	R	24	46	39	2	8	0	1	0	6	4	8	1	.205	.256
Rogers Hornsby	SS18	R	19	18	57	5	14	2	0	0	4	2	6	0	.246	.281
Rolla Daringer	SS10	L	25	10	23	3	2	0	0	0	0	0	5	0	.087	.087
Harry Glenn	C5	L	25	6	16	1	5	0	0	0	1	3	0	0	.313	.313
Jack Smith	OF4	L	25	4	16	2	3	0	1	0	1	1	5	0	.188	.313
Don Brown	OF1	R	22	1	2	0	1	0	0	0	0	2	1	0	.500	.500

NAME	T	AGE	W	L	PCT	SV	G	GS	CG	IP	H	BB	SO	SHO	ERA
		27	72	81	.471	9	157	157	79	1401	1320	402	538	12	2.88
Bill Doak	R	27	16	18	.471	1	38	36	19	276	263	85	124	3	2.46
Lee Meadows	R	20	13	11	.542	0	39	26	14	244	232	88	104	1	2.99
Slim Sallee	L	30	13	17	.433	3	46	33	17	275	245	57	91	2	2.85
2 Red Ames	R	32	9	3	.750	1	15	14	8	113	93	32	48	2	2.47
Hank Robinson	L	27	7	8	.467	0	32	15	6	143	128	35	57	1	2.45
Hub Perdue	R	33	6	12	.333	1	31	13	5	115	141	19	29	1	4.23
Dan Griner	R	27	5	11	.313	3	37	18	9	150	137	46	46	2	2.82
Dick Niehaus	R	22	1	0	1.000	0	6	2	0	45	48	22	21	0	4.00
Charlie Boardman	R	22	1	0	1.000	0	3	1	1	19	12	15	7	0	1.42
Fred Lamline	R	23	0	0	—	0	4	0	0	19	21	3	11	0	2.84

CINCINNATI   7th 71-83 .461 20   BUCK HERZOG

NAME	G by Pos	B	AGE	G	AB	R	H	2B	3B	HR	RBI	BB	SO	SB	BA	SA
TOTALS			27	160	5231	516	1323	194	84	15	425	360	512	156	.253	.331
Fritz Mollwitz	1B153	R	25	153	525	36	136	21	3	1	51	15	49	19	.259	.316
3 Bill Rodgers	2B56,SS6,3B1,OF1	L	27	72	213	20	51	13	4	0	12	11	29	4	.239	.338
Buck Herzog	SS153,1B2	R	29	155	562	59	143	14	10	1	42	34	21	9	.254	.316
Heinie Groh	3B131,2B29	R	25	160	587	72	170	32	9	3	50	50	33	12	.290	.390
Tommy Griffith	OF160	L	25	160	583	59	179	31	16	4	85	41	34	6	.307	.436
Red Killefer	OF153,1B2	R	30	155	555	75	151	25	11	1	41	38	23	12	.272	.342
Tommy Leach	OF96	R	37	107	335	42	75	7	5	0	17	56	38	20	.224	.275
Ivy Wingo	C97,OF1	L	24	119	339	26	75	11	6	3	29	13	33	10	.221	.316
Tommy Clarke	C72	R	27	96	226	23	65	7	2	0	21	33	22	7	.288	.336
Joe Wagner	2B46,SS12,3B2	R	26	75	197	17	35	5	2	0	13	8	35	4	.178	.223
Ken Williams	OF62	L	25	71	219	22	53	10	4	0	16	15	20	4	.242	.324
1 Ivy Olson	2B37,3B15,1B7	R	29	63	207	18	48	5	4	0	14	12	15	10	.232	.295
F. Von Kolnitz	3B18,SS6,1B3,C2,OF1	R	22	50	78	6	15	4	1	0	6	7	11	1	.192	.269
George Twombly	OF46	L	23	46	66	5	13	0	1	0	5	8	9	5	.197	.227
Johnny Beall	OF10	L	33	10	34	3	8	1	0	0	3	5	10	0	.235	.265
1 Red Dooin	C10	R	36	10	31	2	10	0	0	0	5	3	3	1	.323	.323

NAME	T	AGE	W	L	PCT	SV	G	GS	CG	IP	H	BB	SO	SHO	ERA
		26	71	83	.461	12	160	160	80	1432	1304	497	572	19	2.84
Gene Dale	R	26	18	17	.514	3	49	35	20	297	256	107	104	4	2.45
Fred Toney	R	27	15	6	.714	2	36	23	18	223	160	73	108	6	1.57
Pete Schneider	R	22	13	19	.406	2	48	35	16	276	254	104	108	5	2.48
1 Rube Benton	L	25	9	13	.409	4	35	21	6	176	165	67	83	2	3.32
King Lear	R	24	6	10	.375	0	40	15	9	168	169	45	46	0	3.00
Limb McKenry	R	26	5	5	.500	0	21	11	5	110	94	39	37	0	2.94
Lefty George	L	28	2	2	.500	0	5	3	2	28	24	8	11	1	3.86
1 Red Ames	R	32	2	4	.333	1	17	7	4	68	82	24	26	1	4.50
1 Phil Douglas	R	25	1	5	.167	0	8	7	0	47	53	23	29	0	5.36
Curly Brown	R	26	0	2	.000	0	7	3	0	27	26	6	13	0	4.67
Ray Callahan	L	23	0	0	—	0	3	0	0	6	12	1	4	0	9.00
Harry McCluskey	R	23	0	0	—	0	3	0	0	5	4	0	2	0	5.40
Al Cochran	R	24	0	1	.000	0	1	0	0	5	5	0	1	0	9.00

NEW YORK   8th 69-83 .454 21   JOHN McGRAW

NAME	G by Pos	B	AGE	G	AB	R	H	2B	3B	HR	RBI	BB	SO	SB	BA	SA
TOTALS			28	155	5218	582	1312	195	68	24	501	315	547	155	.251	.329
Fred Merkle	1B111,OF29	R	26	140	505	52	151	25	3	4	62	36	39	20	.299	.384
Larry Doyle	2B147	L	29	150	591	86	189	40	10	4	70	32	28	22	.320	.442
Art Fletcher	SS149	R	30	149	562	59	143	17	7	3	74	6	36	22	.254	.319
Hans Lobert (KJ)	3B106	R	33	106	386	46	97	18	4	0	38	25	24	14	.251	.319
Dave Robertson	OF138	L	25	141	544	72	160	17	10	3	58	22	52	22	.294	.379
1 Fred Snodgrass	OF75	R	27	80	252	36	49	9	0	0	20	35	33	11	.194	.230
George Burns	OF155	R	25	155	622	83	169	27	14	3	51	56	57	27	.272	.375
Chief Meyers	C110	R	34	110	289	24	67	10	5	1	26	26	18	4	.232	.311
Fred Brainard	1B45,3B16,SS9,2B1,OF1	R	23	91	249	31	50	7	2	1	21	21	44	6	.201	.257
Eddie Grant	3B55,2B9,1B1,SS1	L	32	87	192	18	40	2	1	0	10	9	20	5	.208	.229
2 Red Dooin	C46	R	36	46	124	9	27	2	2	0	9	3	15	0	.218	.266
1 Red Murray	OF34	R	31	45	127	12	28	1	2	3	11	7	15	2	.220	.331
Charlie Babington	OF12,1B1	R	20	28	33	5	8	3	1	0	2	0	4	1	.242	.394
1 Harry Smith	C18	R	25	21	32	1	4	0	1	0	3	6	12	0	.125	.188
Lew Wendell	C18	B	23	20	36	0	8	1	1	0	5	2	9	1	.222	.306
Marty Becker	OF16	B	21	17	52	5	13	2	0	0	4	1	9	0	.250	.288
George Kelly	1B9,OF4	R	19	17	38	2	6	0	0	0	4	1	9	0	.158	.237
Jim Thorpe	OF15	B	28	17	52	8	12	3	1	0	1	2	16	4	.231	.327
Larry McLean (ST)	C12	R	33	13	33	0	5	0	0	0	4	1	4	0	.152	.152
2 Bobby Schang	C6	R	28	12	21	1	3	0	0	1	5	4	3	1	.143	.143
Merwin Jacobson	OF5	L	21	8	24	0	2	0	0	0	0	1	5	0	.083	.083
Ben Dyer	3B6,SS1	R	22	9	19	4	4	0	0	0	4	4	3	0	.211	.316
Brad Kocher	C3	R	27	4	11	3	5	0	1	0	2	0	1	0	.455	.636
2 Howard Baker	3B1	R	27	1	3	0	0	0	0	0	0	0	0	0	.000	.000

NAME	T	AGE	W	L	PCT	SV	G	GS	CG	IP	H	BB	SO	SHO	ERA
		26	69	83	.454	9	155	155	78	1385	1350	325	637	15	3.11
Jeff Tesreau	R	27	19	16	.543	3	43	39	24	306	235	75	176	8	2.29
Pol Perritt	R	23	12	18	.400	0	35	29	16	220	226	59	91	4	2.66
Sailor Stroud	R	30	11	9	.550	1	32	22	8	184	194	35	62	0	2.79
1 Rube Marquard	L	28	9	8	.529	2	27	21	10	169	178	33	79	2	3.73
Christy Mathewson	R	34	8	14	.364	0	27	24	11	186	199	20	57	1	3.58
2 Rube Benton	L	25	4	4	.444	1	10	6	3	61	57	9	26	0	2.80
Hank Ritter	R	21	2	1	.667	2	22	1	0	58	66	15	35	0	4.65
Rube Schauer	R	24	2	8	.200	0	32	6	1	105	101	35	65	0	3.57
Ferdie Schupp	L	24	1	0	1.000	0	23	1	0	55	57	29	28	0	5.07
Fred Herbert	R	28	1	1	.500	0	2	1	1	17	12	4	6	0	1.06
Art Fromme	R	31	0	1	.000	0	4	1	0	12	15	2	4	0	6.00
Emilio Palermo	L	22	0	2	.000	0	3	2	1	12	10	9	8	0	3.00

WORLD SERIES — BOSTON (AL) 4   PHILADELPHIA(NL) 1

LINE SCORES

```
Game 1  October 8 at Philadelphia
                                      R  H  E
BOS(AL) 0 0 0  0 0 0  0 1 0          1  8  1
PHI(NL) 0 0 0  1 0 0  0 2 X          3  5  1
        Shore                Alexander

Game 2  October 9 at Philadelphia
BOS     1 0 0  0 0 0  0 0 1          2 10  0
PHI     0 0 0  0 1 0  0 0 0          1  3  1
        Fester               Mayer

Game 3  October 11 at Boston
PHI     0 0 1  0 0 0  0 0 0          1  3  0
BOS     0 0 1  0 0 0  0 0 1          2  6  1
        Alexander            Leonard

Game 4  October 12 at Boston
PHI     0 0 0  0 0 0  0 1 0          1  7  0
BOS     0 0 1  0 0 1  0 0 X          2  8  1
        Chalmers             Shore

Game 5  October 13 at Philadelphia
BOS     0 1 1  0 0 0  0 2 1          5 10  1
PHI     2 0 0  2 0 0  0 0 0          4  9  1
        Fester               Mayer, Rixey (3)
```

COMPOSITE BATTING

Boston (AL)

NAME	POS	G	AB	R	H	2B	3B	HR	RBI	BA
Totals		5	159	12	42	2	2	3	11	.264
Hooper	OF	5	20	4	7	0	0	2	3	.350
Lewis	OF	5	18	1	8	1	0	1	5	.444
Scott	SS	5	18	0	1	0	0	0	0	.056
Speaker	OF	5	17	2	5	0	1	0	0	.294
Gardner	3B	5	17	2	4	0	1	0	0	.235
Barry	2B	5	17	1	3	0	0	0	1	.176
Hoblitzell	1B	5	16	1	5	0	0	0	1	.313
Foster	P	2	8	0	4	1	0	0	1	.500
Cady	C	4	6	0	2	0	0	0	0	.333
Shore	P	2	5	0	1	0	0	0	0	.200
Thomas	C	2	5	0	1	0	0	0	0	.200
Gainer	1B	3	3	1	1	0	0	0	0	.333
Leonard	P	1	3	0	0	0	0	0	0	.000
Henriksen	PH	2	2	0	0	0	0	0	0	.000
Carrigan	C	1	2	0	0	0	0	0	0	.000
Janvrin	SS	1	1	0	0	0	0	0	0	.000
Ruth	PH	1	1	0	0	0	0	0	0	.000

Philadelphia (NL)

NAME	POS	G	AB	R	H	2B	3B	HR	RBI	BA
Totals		5	148	10	27	4	1	1	9	.182
Paskert	OF	5	19	2	3	0	0	0	0	.158
Bancroft	SS	5	17	2	5	0	0	0	1	.294
Stock	3B	5	17	1	2	1	0	0	0	.118
Luderus	1B	5	16	1	7	2	0	1	6	.438
Burns	C	5	16	1	3	0	0	0	0	.188
Cravath	OF	5	16	2	2	1	1	0	0	.125
Niehoff	2B	5	16	1	1	0	0	0	1	.063
Whitted	OF,1B	5	15	0	1	0	0	0	1	.067
Alexander	P	2	5	0	1	0	0	0	0	.200
Mayer	P	2	4	0	0	0	0	0	0	.000
Chalmers	P	1	3	0	1	0	0	0	0	.333
Rixey	P	1	2	0	1	0	0	0	0	.500
Byrne	PH	1	1	0	0	0	0	0	0	.000
Killefer	PH	1	1	0	0	0	0	0	0	.000
Becker	OF	2	0	0	0	0	0	0	0	—
Dugey	PR	2	0	0	0	0	0	0	0	—

COMPOSITE PITCHING

Boston (AL)

NAME	G	IP	H	BB	SO	W	L	SV	ERA
Totals	5	44	27	10	25	4	1	0	1.84
Foster	2	18	12	2	13	2	0	0	2.00
Shore	2	17	12	8	6	1	1	0	2.12
Leonard	1	9	3	0	6	1	0	0	1.00

Philadelphia (NL)

NAME	G	IP	H	BB	SO	W	L	SV	ERA
Totals	5	43.2	42	11	25	1	4	0	2.30
Alexander	2	17.2	14	4	10	1	1	0	1.53
Mayer	2	11.1	16	4	9	0	1	0	2.38
Chalmers	1	8	8	3	6	0	1	0	2.25
Rixey	1	6.2	4	2	0	0	1	0	4.05

1916 Streaking to Nowhere

Of the 86 games won by the Giants, half were won in an unusual manner. In fact, the entire season included the sublime and ridiculous for Giant rooters. After losing eight straight games at home and unable to get going, the Giants took to the road and won 17 straight. But their brief fling at glory quickly waned, prompting manager John McGraw to quickly rebuild the team. He got rid of Bill McKechnie, Fred Merkle, and Larry Doyle. His one-time ace, Christy Mathewson, went to Cincinnati to manage, while Buck Herzog, the Reds' manager, came to New York as a utility infielder. McGraw also acquired Heinie Zimmerman from the Cubs to bolster the infield.

New blood seemed to be the answer as the Giants entered September and made a frantic dash down the stretch, winning a record 26 in a row at home and almost pulling off the impossible, before falling to Boston on the 30th and winding up seven games out in fourth place. Other streaks, which mostly added up to zero, included Washington's 16 in a row on the road, the Browns' 14 in a row, and the Athletics' 20 in a row—the last of which came on the downside and accounted for an experiment of young players by Connie Mack which did not work and cost him 117 losses, the most ever in the American League to that time. Individual streaks were made by Zack Wheat of the Dodgers and Sherry Magee of the Braves. Wheat hit in 29 straight games, and Magee handled 170 chances in left field before making a miscue.

Close races in both leagues helped offset bad weather and the costly financial burden of the Federal League settlement. In the National League, Brooklyn survived a tough race to win their first pennant by a scant margin. Philadelphia and Boston were alive going into the last week, but were forced to play in a pair of double headers and took turns eliminating each other. The Phillies, although dethroned, again produced the most prolific hurler of the year in Grover "Pete" Alexander, who registered 16 shutouts, 33 victories, and a low 1.55 E.R.A. Third-place Boston was unable to overcome injuries which took their toll on Sherry Magee, Tom Hughes and Johnny Evers, the first two suffering broken bones and Evers an attack of neuritis in his throwing arm. Before the season started, Frank Chance had his choice of 50 players with which to form a club. As a result of the Federal League settlement, he had the roster of the disbanded Chicago Federal League team in addition to his own Cubs and still could do no better than fifth place. One bright spot came from the last-place Cardinals: Roger Hornsby played his first full year and hit .313.

In the American League, the Red Sox proved the most adept at musical chairs and won their second pennant in a row. Before the season started, they sold Tris Speaker to Cleveland, after Speaker and the Red Sox owners could not agree on Speaker's 1916 contract. Speaker's roommate and friend, pitcher Smoky Joe Wood, then held out for the entire year until he was also dealt to Cleveland. Luckily, Tilly Walker handled Speaker's post adequately, and a young lefthander, Babe Ruth, blossomed to win 23 games and post the lowest E.R.A. in the league with 1.75.

Detroit's Ty Cobb, although managing to lead the league with 68 stolen bases, lost the batting title for the first time in ten years, losing it to Speaker, who hit .386 to the Georgia Peach's .371.

The World Series was a case of Red Sox pitching and defense against Brooklyn's superiority with the bat. The former proved more meaningful, and Boston decisively beat Brooklyn four games to one.

1916 AMERICAN LEAGUE

NAME	G by Pos	B	AGE	G	AB	R	H	2B	3B	HR	RBI	BB	SO	SB	BA	SA
BOSTON	**1st 91-63 .591**				**BILL CARRIGAN**											
	TOTALS		27	156	5017	548	1245	196	56	14	454	464	482	129	.248	.318
Dick Hoblitzell	1B126	R	27	130	417	57	108	17	1	0	39	47	28	10	.259	.305
Jack Barry	2B94	R	29	94	330	28	67	6	1	0	20	17	24	8	.203	.227
Everett Scott	SS121,2B1,3B1	R	23	123	366	37	85	19	2	0	27	23	24	8	.232	.295
Larry Gardner	3B147	L	30	148	493	47	152	19	7	2	62	48	27	12	.308	.387
Harry Hooper	OF151	L	28	151	575	75	156	20	11	1	37	80	35	27	.271	.350
Tilly Walker	OF128	R	28	128	467	68	124	29	11	3	46	23	45	14	.266	.394
Duffy Lewis	OF151	R	27	152	563	56	151	29	5	1	56	33	56	16	.268	.343
Pinch Thomas	C90	L	28	99	216	21	57	10	1	1	21	33	13	4	.264	.333
Hal Janvrin	SS59,2B39,1B4,3B3	R	23	117	310	26	69	11	4	0	26	32	32	6	.223	.284
Mike McNally	2B35,3B14,SS7,OF1	R	22	87	135	28	23	0	0	0	9	10	19	9	.170	.170
Hick Cady	C63,1B3	R	30	78	162	5	31	6	3	0	13	15	16	0	.191	.265
Olaf Henriksen	OF31	L	28	68	99	13	20	2	2	0	11	19	15	2	.202	.263
Babe Ruth	P44	L	21	67	136	18	37	5	3	3	15	10	23	0	.272	.419
Del Gainer	1B48,2B2	R	29	56	142	14	36	6	0	3	18	10	24	5	.254	.359
Chick Shorten	OF33	L	24	53	112	14	33	2	1	0	11	10	6	1	.295	.330
Sam Agnew	C38	R	29	40	67	4	14	2	1	0	7	6	4	0	.209	.269
Bill Carrigan	C27	R	32	33	63	7	17	2	1	0	11	11	3	2	.270	.333
2 Jimmy Walsh	OF6,3B2	L	30	13	16	5	2	0	0	0	2	4	2	3	.125	.125
Heinie Wagner	3B4,2B1,SS1	R	35	6	8	2	4	1	0	0	3	0	2	2	.500	.625
1 Pat Haley		R	25	1	1	0	0	0	0	0	0	1	0	0	.000	.000
CHICAGO	**2nd 89-65 .578 2**				**PANTS ROWLAND**											
	TOTALS		26	155	5081	601	1277	194	100	17	484	447	591	197	.251	.339
Jack Fournier	1B85,OF1	R	26	105	313	36	75	13	9	3	44	36	40	19	.240	.367
Eddie Collins	2B155	L	29	155	545	87	168	14	17	0	52	86	36	40	.308	.396
Zeb Terry	SS93	R	25	94	269	20	51	8	4	0	17	33	36	4	.190	.249
Buck Weaver	3B85,SS66	R	25	151	582	78	132	27	6	3	38	30	48	22	.227	.309
Shano Collins	OF136,1B4	R	30	143	527	74	128	28	12	0	42	59	51	16	.243	.342
Happy Felsch	OF141	R	24	146	546	73	164	24	12	7	70	31	67	13	.300	.427
Joe Jackson	OF155	L	26	155	592	91	202	40	21	3	78	46	25	24	.341	.495
Ray Schalk	C124	R	23	129	410	36	95	12	9	0	41	41	31	30	.232	.305
Jack Ness	1B69	R	30	75	258	32	69	7	5	1	34	9	32	4	.267	.345
Fred McMullin (JJ)	3B63,SS2,2B1	R	24	68	187	8	48	3	0	0	10	19	30	9	.257	.273
Eddie Murphy	OF24,2B1	L	24	51	105	14	22	5	1	0	4	9	5	3	.210	.276
Nemo Leibold	OF24	L	24	45	82	5	20	1	2	0	13	7	7	7	.244	.305
Jack Lapp	C34	L	31	40	101	6	21	0	1	0	7	8	10	1	.208	.228
Byrd Lynn	C13	R	27	31	40	4	9	1	0	0	3	4	7	2	.225	.250
Fritz Von Kolnitz	3B13	R	23	24	44	1	10	3	0	0	7	2	6	0	.227	.295
Ziggy Hasbrouck	1B7	R	22	9	8	1	1	0	0	0	0	1	2	1	.125	.125
Cy Wright	SS8	R	22	8	18	0	0	0	0	0	0	0	5	0	.000	.000
George Moriarty	1B1,3B1	R	30	7	5	1	1	0	0	0	2	0	0	0	.200	.200
Ted Jourdan		L	20	3	2	0	0	0	0	0	0	1	1	0	.000	.000
Ray Shook		R	25	1	0	0	0	0	0	0	0	0	0	0	.000	.000
Joe Fautsch		R	27	1	1	0	0	0	0	0	0	0	0	0	.000	.000
DETROIT	**3rd 87-67 .565 4**				**HUGHIE JENNINGS**											
	TOTALS		28	155	5193	673	1371	202	96	17	560	545	529	190	.264	.350
George Burns	1B124	R	23	135	479	60	137	22	6	4	73	22	30	12	.286	.382
Ralph Young	2B146,SS6,3B1	B	27	153	528	60	139	16	6	1	45	62	43	20	.263	.322
Donie Bush	SS144	B	28	145	550	73	124	5	9	0	34	75	42	19	.225	.267
Ossie Vitt	3B151,SS2	R	26	153	597	88	135	17	12	0	42	75	28	18	.226	.295
Harry Heilmann	OF77,1B30,2B9	R	21	136	451	57	127	30	11	2	73	42	40	9	.282	.410
Ty Cobb	OF143,1B1	L	29	145	542	113	201	31	10	5	68	78	39	68	.371	.493
Bobby Veach	OF150	L	28	150	566	92	173	33	15	3	91	52	41	24	.306	.433
Oscar Stanage	C94	R	33	94	291	16	69	17	3	0	30	17	48	3	.237	.316
Sam Crawford	OF79,1B2	L	36	100	322	41	92	11	13	0	42	37	10	10	.286	.401
Del Baker	C59	R	24	61	98	15	15	4	0	0	6	11	8	2	.153	.194
1 Marty Kavanagh	OF11,2B2,3B2	R	25	58	78	6	11	4	0	0	3	5	9	15	.141	.192
George Harper (BL)	OF14	L	24	44	56	4	9	1	0	0	3	5	6	1	.161	.179
Red McKee	C26	L	25	32	76	3	16	1	2	0	4	6	11	0	.211	.276
Frank Fuller	2B8,SS1	L	23	20	10	2	1	0	0	0	1	1	4	3	.100	.100
Tubby Spencer	C19	R	32	19	54	7	20	1	1	1	10	6	6	2	.370	.481
Jack Dalton	OF4	L	31	19	11	1	2	0	0	0	0	0	5	0	.182	.182
George Maisel	3B3	R	24	7	5	2	0	0	0	0	0	0	0	0	.000	.000
Ben Dyer	SS4	R	23	4	14	4	4	1	0	0	2	0	0	0	.286	.357
Bert Ellison	3B2	R	19	2	7	0	1	0	0	0	0	0	0	0	.143	.143
Billy Sullivan	C1	R	41	1	0	0	0	0	0	0	0	0	0	0	.000	.000

NAME	T	AGE	W	L	PCT	SV	G	GS	CG	IP	H	BB	SO	SHO	ERA
		26	91	63	.591	16	156	156	76	1411	1221	463	584	23	2.47
Babe Ruth	L	21	23	12	.657	1	44	40	23	324	230	118	170	9	1.75
Dutch Leonard	L	24	18	11	.621	5	48	34	17	274	244	66	144	6	2.36
Carl Mays	R	24	18	13	.581	3	44	25	14	245	208	74	76	2	2.39
Ernie Shore	R	25	17	10	.630	1	38	27	10	226	221	49	62	3	2.63
Rube Foster	R	28	13	8	.619	3	33	20	9	182	173	86	53	3	3.07
Vean Gregg	L	31	2	5	.286	0	21	7	3	78	71	30	41	0	3.00
Sad Sam Jones	R	23	0	1	.000	1	12	0	0	27	25	10	7	0	3.67
1 Marty McHale	R	29	0	1	.000	0	2	1	0	6	7	4	1	0	3.00
Herb Pennock	L	22	0	2	.000	1	9	2	0	27	23	8	12	0	3.00
2 Weldon Wyckoff(SA)	R	24	0	0	—	1	8	0	0	23	19	18	18	0	4.70
Smoky Joe Wood (HO) 26															

NAME	T	AGE	W	L	PCT	SV	G	GS	CG	IP	H	BB	SO	SHO	ERA
		29	89	65	.578	16	155	155	73	1412	1189	405	644	18	2.36
Reb Russell	L	27	17	11	.607	4	56	26	16	264	207	42	112	5	2.42
Eddie Cicotte	R	32	15	7	.682	4	44	20	11	187	138	70	91	2	1.78
Red Faber	R	27	16	9	.640	2	35	25	15	205	167	61	87	3	2.02
Lefty Williams	L	23	13	7	.650	1	43	25	10	224	220	65	138	2	2.89
Joe Benz	R	30	9	5	.643	0	28	16	6	142	108	32	57	4	2.03
Jim Scott	R	27	9	14	.391	2	32	20	8	165	155	53	71	1	2.73
Dave Danforth	L	26	6	5	.545	2	28	8	1	94	87	37	49	0	3.26
Mellie Wolfgang	R	26	4	6	.400	1	27	14	6	127	103	42	36	1	1.98
Ed Walsh	R	35	0	1	.000	0	2	1	0	3	4	3	3	0	9.00

NAME	T	AGE	W	L	PCT	SV	G	GS	CG	IP	H	BB	SO	SHO	ERA
		26	87	67	.565	12	155	155	81	1410	1254	578	531	9	2.97
Harry Coveleski	L	30	21	11	.656	2	44	39	22	324	278	63	108	3	1.97
Hooks Dauss	R	26	19	12	.613	4	39	29	18	239	220	90	95	1	3.20
Bernie Boland	R	24	10	3	.769	1	46	9	5	130	111	73	69	1	3.95
Jean Dubuc	R	27	10	10	.500	1	36	16	8	170	134	84	40	1	2.96
2 Willie Mitchell	L	26	7	5	.583	0	23	17	7	128	119	48	60	2	3.03
George Cunningham	R	21	7	10	.412	2	35	14	5	150	146	74	68	0	2.76
Bill James	R	29	7	12	.368	2	30	20	8	152	141	79	61	0	3.67
Howard Ehmke	R	22	3	1	.750	0	5	4	3	37	34	15	15	0	3.16
2 Earl Hamilton	L	24	2	2	.500	0	7	5	3	37	34	22	7	1	2.68
George Boehler	R	24	1	1	.500	0	5	2	1	13	12	9	8	0	4.85
1 Grover Lowdermilk	R	31	1	1	.500	0	4	1	1	15	5	5	1	0	0.00
Bill McTigue	L	25	0	1	.000	0	3	0	0	5	5	6	1	0	5.40
Eric Erickson	R	24	0	0	—	0	9	1	0	16	13	8	7	0	2.81
Deacon Jones	R	22	0	0	—	0	3	0	0	5	5	2	1	0	2.57

NEW YORK — 4th 80-74 .519 11 — WILD BILL DONOVAN

NAME	G by Pos	B	AGE	G	AB	R	H	2B	3B	HR	RBI	BB	SO	SB	BA	SA
TOTALS			26	156	5200	575	1277	194	59	35	492	516	632	179	.246	.326
Wally Pipp	1B148	L	23	151	545	70	143	20	14	12	93	54	82	16	.262	.417
Joe Gedeon	2B122	R	22	122	435	50	92	14	4	0	27	40	61	14	.211	.262
Roger Peckinpaugh	SS146	R	25	146	552	65	141	22	8	4	58	62	50	18	.255	.346
Frank Baker	3B96	L	30	100	360	46	97	23	2	10	52	36	30	15	.269	.428
Frank Gilhooley (BN)	OF57	L	24	58	223	46	62	5	3	1	10	37	17	6	.278	.341
Lee Magee 2	OF128, 2B12	B	27	131	510	57	131	18	4	3	45	50	31	29	.257	.325
Hugh High	OF109	L	28	115	377	44	99	13	4	1	28	47	44	13	.263	.346
Les Nunamaker	C79	R	27	91	260	25	77	14	7	0	28	34	21	4	.296	.404
Paddy Baumann	OF28, 3B26, 2B9	R	30	79	237	35	68	5	3	1	25	19	16	10	.287	.346
Roxy Walters	C65	R	23	66	203	13	54	9	3	0	23	14	42	2	.266	.340
Charlie Mullen	2B20, 1B17, OF6	R	27	59	146	11	39	9	1	0	18	9	13	7	.267	.342
Fritz Maisel	OF26, 3B11, 2B4	R	26	53	138	16	36	5	0	0	7	20	18	4	.228	.259
Luke Boone	3B25, SS12, 2B7	R	26	46	124	14	23	4	0	1	8	8	10	7	.185	.242
Ray Caldwell	P21, OF3	L	28	45	93	6	19	2	0	0	4	2	17	1	.204	.226
Elmer Miller	OF42	R	29	43	152	12	34	3	2	1	18	11	18	8	.224	.289
2 Rube Oldring	OF43	R	32	43	158	17	37	8	0	1	12	12	13	6	.234	.304
Walt Alexander	C27	R	25	36	78	8	20	6	1	0	3	13	20	1	.256	.359
Roy Hartzell	OF28	L	34	33	64	12	12	1	0	0	7	9	3	1	.188	.203
Tim Hendrix	OF15	R	25	15	62	10	18	7	1	0	5	8	6	4	.290	.435
Angel Aragon	3B8, OF3	R	25	13	27	1	5	0	0	0	3	2	2	1	.185	.185

1 Solly Hoffman 33 R 8-27, Doc Cook 30 L 1-10, Germany Schaefer 39 R 0-0

NAME	T	AGE	W	L	PCT	SV	G	GS	CG	IP	H	BB	SO	SHO	ERA
		26	80	74	.519	18	156	156	83	1428	1249	476	616	10	2.77
Bob Shawkey	R	25	24	14	.632	9	53	27	21	277	204	81	122	4	2.21
Nick Cullop	R	28	13	6	.684	1	28	22	9	167	151	32	77	0	2.05
Ray Fisher	R	28	10	8	.556	3	31	21	9	179	191	51	56	1	3.17
Allen Russell	R	22	6	10	.375	5	34	19	8	171	138	75	104	1	3.21
George Mogridge	L	27	6	12	.333	0	31	19	7	195	174	45	66	1	2.31
Urban Shocker	R	25	5	3	.625	0	12	9	4	82	67	32	43	1	2.63
Ray Keating	R	22	5	6	.455	0	14	11	6	91	91	37	35	0	3.07
Ray Caldwell	R	28	5	12	.294	0	21	18	14	166	142	65	76	1	2.98
Cliff Markle	R	22	4	3	.571	0	11	7	3	46	41	31	14	1	4.50
Slim Love	L	25	2	0	1.000	0	20	1	0	48	46	23	21	0	4.88
Jesse Buckles	L	26	0	0	—	0	2	0	0	4	3	1	0	0	2.25
Mike Cantwell	L	22	0	0	—	0	1	0	0	1	1	0	2	0	0.00
Wild Bill Donovan	R	39	0	0	—	0	1	0	0	1	1	0	0	0	0.00
King Cole (DD) 29															

ST. LOUIS — 5th 79-75 .513 12 — FIELDER JONES

NAME	G by Pos	B	AGE	G	AB	R	H	2B	3B	HR	RBI	BB	SO	SB	BA	SA
TOTALS			28	155	5159	591	1262	181	50	14	499	627	610	234	.245	.308
George Sisler	1B139, OF3, P3	L	23	151	580	83	177	21	11	4	76	40	37	34	.305	.400
Del Pratt	2B158	R	28	158	596	64	159	35	12	5	103	54	56	26	.267	.391
Doc Lavan	SS106	R	25	110	343	32	81	13	1	0	19	32	38	7	.236	.280
Jimmy Austin	3B124	R	36	129	411	55	85	15	6	1	28	74	59	19	.207	.280
Ward Miller	OF135, 2B1	R	31	146	485	72	129	17	5	1	50	72	76	25	.266	.328
Armando Marsans	OF150	R	29	151	525	51	134	12	1	1	60	57	41	46	.254	.288
Burt Shotton	OF157	R	31	156	614	97	174	23	6	1	36	110	65	41	.283	.345
Hank Severeid	C89, 1B1, 3B1	R	25	100	293	23	80	8	2	0	34	26	17	3	.273	.314
Grover Hartley	C75	R	27	89	222	19	50	8	0	0	12	30	24	4	.225	.261
Jack Tobin	OF41	L	24	77	150	16	32	4	1	0	10	12	13	7	.213	.253
Ernie Johnson	SS60, 3B12	R	28	74	236	29	54	9	3	0	19	30	23	13	.229	.292
Babe Borton	1B22	L	27	66	98	10	22	1	2	1	12	19	13	1	.224	.306
Bill Rumler	C9	R	25	27	37	6	12	3	0	0	10	3	7	0	.324	.405
1 Charlie Deal	3B22, 2B1	R	24	23	74	7	10	1	0	0	10	6	8	4	.135	.149
Harry Chapman	C14	R	28	18	31	2	3	0	0	0	0	2	5	0	.097	.097
Bobby Wallace	3B9, SS5	R	42	16	18	1	5	0	0	0	2	0	1	0	.278	.278

Billy Lee 22 R 2-11, Gene Paulette 25 R 2-4, George Hale 21 R 0-1, Verne Clemons 24 L 1-7, Ray Kennedy 21 R 0-1

NAME	T	AGE	W	L	PCT	SV	G	GS	CG	IP	H	BB	SO	SHO	ERA
		28	79	75	.513	12	158	158	71	1444	1292	478	505	9	2.58
Carl Weilman	L	26	17	18	.486	2	46	31	19	276	237	76	91	1	2.15
Eddie Plank	L	40	16	15	.500	4	37	26	17	236	203	67	88	3	2.33
Bob Groom	R	31	14	9	.609	3	41	26	6	217	174	98	92	1	2.57
Dave Davenport	R	26	12	11	.522	1	59	31	13	291	267	100	129	1	2.85
Ernie Koob (IL)	R	23	11	8	.579	2	33	20	10	167	153	56	26	2	2.53
13 Earl Hamilton	L	24	5	7	.417	0	23	13	2	95	101	30	25	0	3.32
Tim McCabe	R	21	2	0	1.000	1	13	0	0	26	29	7	7	0	3.12
George Baumgardner	R	24	1	0	1.000	0	4	2	0	8	12	5	4	0	7.88
George Sisler	L	23	1	2	.333	0	3	2	1	27	18	6	12	1	1.00
Jim Park	R	23	1	4	.200	1	26	6	1	79	69	25	26	0	2.62
Bill Fincher	R	22	0	1	.000	0	12	0	0	21	22	7	5	0	2.14
Doc Crandall	R	28	0	0	—	0	2	0	0	7	7	1	0	0	36.00

CLEVELAND — 6th 77-88 .500 14 — LEE FOHL

NAME	G by Pos	B	AGE	G	AB	R	H	2B	3B	HR	RBI	BB	SO	SB	BA	SA
TOTALS			27	157	5064	630	1264	233	66	16	533	522	605	160	.250	.331
Chick Gandil	1B145	R	28	146	533	51	138	26	9	0	72	36	48	13	.259	.341
Ivon Howard	2B65, 1B7	R	33	81	246	20	46	11	5	0	23	30	34	9	.187	.272
Bill Wambsganss	SS106, 2B24, 3B5	R	22	136	475	57	117	14	4	0	45	41	40	13	.246	.293
Terry Turner	3B77, 2B42	R	35	124	428	52	112	15	3	0	38	40	29	15	.262	.311
Braggo Roth	OF112	R	23	125	409	50	117	19	7	4	72	38	48	29	.286	.396
Tris Speaker	OF151	L	28	151	546	102	211	41	8	2	79	82	20	35	.386	.502
Jack Graney	OF154	L	30	155	589	106	142	41	14	5	54	102	72	10	.241	.384
Steve O'Neill	C128	R	24	130	378	30	89	23	0	0	29	24	33	2	.235	.296
Ray Chapman (KJ)	SS52, 3B36, 2B16	R	25	109	346	50	80	15	9	0	27	50	46	21	.231	.289
1 Elmer Smith	OF57	L	23	79	213	25	59	15	3	3	40	18	35	3	.277	.418
Joe Evans	3B28	R	21	33	82	4	12	1	0	0	7	7	12	4	.146	.159
Tom Daly	C25, OF1	R	24	31	73	3	16	1	1	0	8	1	2	0	.219	.260
2 Danny Moeller	OF8, 2B1	R	31	25	30	5	2	0	0	0	1	0	0	0	.067	.067
Josh Billings	C12	R	24	22	31	2	5	0	0	0	1	2	11	0	.161	.161
Bob Coleman	C12	R	25	19	28	3	6	2	0	0	4	7	6	0	.214	.286
2 Marty Kavanagh	2B9, 1B1, 3B1	R	24	19	44	4	11	2	1	1	10	2	5	0	.250	.409
Hank DeBerry	C14	R	21	15	33	7	9	4	0	0	4	0	6	0	.273	.394
Milo Allison	OF5	L	25	14	18	10	5	0	0	0	1	1	1	1	.278	.278
Walter Barbare	3B12	R	25	14	13	4	3	1	1	0	1	0	3	0	.229	.250
Clyde Engle	3B7, 1B2, OF1	R	32	11	26	1	4	0	0	0	1	1	5	0	.154	.154

Dutch Bergman 25 R 3-14, Lou Guisto 21 R 3-19, 1 Larry Chappell 26 L 0-2, 1 Joe Leonard 22 L 0-2, Howie Lohr 24 R 1-17, Jack Bradley 22 R 0-3, Ollie Welf 27 R 0-0

NAME	T	AGE	W	L	PCT	SV	G	GS	CG	IP	H	BB	SO	SHO	ERA
		27	77	77	.500	16	157	157	65	1416	1383	467	537	9	2.99
Stan Coveleski	R	26	16	14	.533	3	45	27	11	232	247	58	76	1	3.41
Jim Bagby	R	26	16	16	.500	5	48	27	14	279	253	67	88	3	2.55
Guy Morton (LJ)	R	23	12	6	.667	2	27	18	9	150	139	42	88	0	2.88
Fritz Coumbe	L	26	7	5	.583	0	29	13	7	120	121	27	39	2	2.03
Fred Beebe	R	35	6	3	.667	2	20	12	5	101	92	37	32	1	2.41
Ed Klepfer	R	28	6	7	.462	2	31	13	4	143	136	46	62	1	2.52
Al Gould	R	23	6	7	.417	1	30	9	6	107	101	40	41	1	2.52
Otis Lambeth	R	26	3	3	.500	1	15	9	3	74	69	38	28	2	2.92
2 Joe Boehling	L	25	3	4	.429	0	12	9	3	61	63	23	18	0	2.66
Pop Boy Smith	R	24	1	2	.333	0	5	3	0	46	55	19	24	0	5.11
1 Willie Mitchell	L	26	1	5	.167	2	12	6	1	44	55	19	24	0	5.11
1 Grover Lowdermilk	R	31	1	5	.167	0	10	9	2	51	52	45	28	0	5.82
2 Marty McHale	R	29	0	0	—	0	2	1	0	11	10	6	2	0	5.73
Ken Penner	R	20	0	0	—	0	2	0	0	3	3	3	1	0	4.15
Rip Hagerman	R	28	0	0	—	0	2	0	0	4	5	2	1	0	11.25
Shorty DesJardien	R	22	0	0	—	0	1	0	0	1	0	1	1	0	18.00
Red Gunkel	R	22	0	0	—	0	1	0	0	1	0	1	0	0	0.00

WASHINGTON — 7th 76-77 .497 14.5 — CLARK GRIFFITH

NAME	G by Pos	B	AGE	G	AB	R	H	2B	3B	HR	RBI	BB	SO	SB	BA	SA
TOTALS			28	159	5113	534	1239	170	60	12	468	535	597	185	.242	.306
Joe Judge (IL)	1B103	L	22	103	336	42	74	10	8	0	28	54	44	18	.220	.298
Ray Morgan	2B82, SS9, 1B3, 3B1	R	27	99	315	41	84	12	4	1	29	59	29	14	.267	.340
George McBride	SS139	R	35	139	466	36	106	15	4	1	36	23	58	8	.227	.283
Eddie Foster	3B84, 2B72	R	28	152	606	75	153	18	9	1	44	68	26	23	.252	.317
1 Danny Moeller	OF65	R	31	78	240	30	59	8	1	3	23	30	55	12	.246	.300
Clyde Milan	OF149	L	30	150	565	58	154	14	3	1	45	56	31	34	.273	.313
Howard Shanks	OF88, 3B31, SS8, 1B7	R	26	145	471	51	119	15	7	1	48	41	34	23	.253	.321
John Henry	C116	R	26	117	305	28	76	12	3	0	46	49	40	12	.249	.308
Rip Williams	1B34, C23, 3B1	R	34	76	202	16	54	10	2	0	20	15	19	5	.267	.337
Charlie Jamieson	OF41, 1B4, P1	L	23	64	145	16	36	4	0	0	13	18	18	5	.248	.276
Sam Rice	OF46, P5	L	26	58	197	26	59	8	3	1	17	15	13	4	.299	.386
Eddie Ainsmith	C46	R	26	51	100	11	17	4	0	0	8	14	13	1	.170	.210
Henri Rondeau	C48	R	29	50	162	20	36	5	3	1	28	18	18	7	.222	.309
2 Elmer Smith	OF45	L	23	45	168	12	36	10	3	2	27	18	28	4	.214	.345
2 Joe Leonard	3B42	R	21	44	168	20	46	7	0	0	14	22	23	4	.274	.315
Patsy Gharrity	C18, 1B15	R	24	39	92	8	21	5	1	0	9	8	18	1	.228	.304
Carl Sawyer	2B6, SS5, 3B1	B	25	16	31	3	6	1	0	0	2	4	4	5	.194	.226
Turner Barber	OF9	L	22	15	33	3	7	0	1	0	5	2	3	1	.212	.364
Mike Menosky	OF9	L	21	10	37	5	6	1	1	0	3	1	10	1	.162	.243
Merito Acosta	OF4	L	20	7	7	0	1	0	0	0	0	0	3	0	.143	.143

NAME	T	AGE	W	L	PCT	SV	G	GS	CG	IP	H	BB	SO	SHO	ERA
		24	76	77	.497	1	159	159	84	1432	1271	490	706	11	2.66
Walter Johnson	R	28	25	20	.556	1	48	38	36	371	290	82	228	3	1.89
Bert Gallia	R	24	17	13	.567	3	49	31	13	284	278	99	120	1	2.76
Harry Harper	L	21	15	10	.600	0	36	34	12	250	209	101	149	2	2.45
1 Joe Boehling	L	25	8	10	.444	1	27	19	7	140	134	54	52	2	3.09
Doc Ayres	R	25	5	9	.357	2	43	17	7	157	173	52	69	0	3.78
Jim Shaw	R	22	3	8	.273	1	26	9	5	106	86	50	44	2	2.63
George Dumont	R	20	3	4	.429	1	17	5	2	53	37	17	21	0	3.06
Claude Thomas	R	26	1	1	.333	0	7	4	1	28	27	13	3	1	4.18
Sam Rice	R	26	1	0	1.000	0	5	1	0	21	18	10	3	0	9.00
Molly Craft	R	20	0	1	.000	0	6	1	0	22	25	6	3	0	3.27
Marv Goodwin	R	25	0	0	—	0	3	0	0	5	4	5	9	0	9.00
Jack Bentley	L	21	0	0	—	0	1	0	0	1	1	0	0	0	0.00
Charley Jamieson	L	23	0	0	—	0	1	0	0	3	3	1	0	0	0.00

PHILADELPHIA — 8th 36-117 .235 54.5 — CONNIE MACK

NAME	G by Pos	B	AGE	G	AB	R	H	2B	3B	HR	RBI	BB	SO	SB	BA	SA
TOTALS			27	154	5010	447	1212	169	65	19	380	406	631	151	.242	.313
Stuffy McInnis	1B140	R	25	140	512	42	151	25	3	1	60	25	19	7	.295	.361
Nap Lajoie	2B105, 1B5, OF2	R	41	113	426	33	105	14	4	2	35	14	26	15	.246	.316
Whitey Witt	SS142	L	20	143	563	64	138	16	15	2	36	55	71	19	.245	.337
Charlie Pick	3B108, OF8	R	28	121	398	29	96	10	3	0	20	40	24	25	.241	.291
1 Jimmy Walsh	OF113, 1B1	L	30	114	390	42	91	13	6	1	27	54	36	27	.233	.305
Amos Strunk	OF143, 1B7	L	27	150	544	71	172	30	9	3	49	66	59	21	.316	.421
Wally Schang	OF61, C36	B	26	110	338	41	90	15	8	7	38	48	44	14	.266	.420
Billy Meyer	C48	R	23	50	138	12	32	2	2	1	12	8	11	3	.232	.297
Lee McElwee	3B30, SS1	R	22	54	155	9	41	3	0	0	10	8	17	0	.265	.284
Lee King	OF22, SS11, 3B5, 2B2	R	22	42	144	13	27	2	0	0	8	7	15	4	.188	.222
Otis Lawrey	2B29, OF5	L	22	41	123	10	25	0	0	0	4	9	21	4	.203	.203
1 Rube Oldring	OF40	R	32	40	146	10	36	8	0	0	14	14	9	1	.247	.342
Val Picinich	C37	R	19	40	118	8	23	3	1	0	5	11	18	1	.195	.237
2 Pat Haley	C33	R	25	34	108	6	25	3	0	0	6	6	19	0	.231	.278
Bill Stellbauer	OF14	R	22	25	48	2	13	2	0	0	7	2	21	1	.271	.354
Roy Grover	2B20	R	24	20	77	8	21	7	0	0	6	10	12	0	.273	.338
Les Lanning	OF9, P6	R	24	20	41	4	8	1	0	0	3	6	10	0	.182	.242
Harland Rowe	3B7, OF1	R	20	17	41	4	9	1	0	0	3	2	6	0	.139	.167
Shag Thompson	OF12	R	23	14	43	6	10	2	0	0	4	1	4	0	.238	.405
Don Brown	OF12	R	24	14	27	3	3	0	0	0	1	2	9	0	.111	.111
Mike Murphy	C12	R	22	13	36	2	4	0	0	0	1	4	6	0	.111	.111
Ralph Mitterling	OF12	R	26	13	39	1	6	1	0	0	3	1	10	0	.154	.154
Charlie Grimm	OF7	L	17	13	44	5	4	0	0	0	0	1	10	0	.091	.091

Doc Carroll 24 R 2-22, Buck Thrasher 26 L 9-29, Tom Healy 20 R 6-23, Lew Malone 19 R 0-4, Harry Davis 42 R 0-0, Bill Johnson 23 L 4-15, Sam Crane 21 R 1-4, Moxie Divis 22 1-6

NAME	T	AGE	W	L	PCT	SV	G	GS	CG	IP	H	BB	SO	SHO	ERA
		24	36	117	.235	3	154	154	94	1344	1311	715	575	11	3.84
Bullet Joe Bush	R	22	15	24	.385	0	40	33	25	287	222	130	157	8	2.57
Elmer Myers	R	22	14	23	.378	1	44	35	31	315	280	168	182	2	3.66
Rube Parnham	R	21	2	1	.667	0	4	3	2	25	27	13	8	0	0.36
Jing Johnson	R	21	2	9	.182	0	12	12	8	84	90	39	25	0	3.75
Socks Seibold	R	20	1	2	.333	0	3	2	1	22	22	9	5	1	4.09
Tom Sheehan	R	22	1	16	.063	0	38	17	8	188	197	94	54	0	3.69
Jack Nabors	R	28	1	18	.048	0	40	30	11	213	206	95	74	0	3.46
1 Weldon Wyckoff	L	21	1	0	1.000	0	3	1	0	9	14	5	0	0	5.57
Carl Ray	R	27	1	1	.500	0	3	1	0	9	14	5	1	0	5.00
Mike Driscoll	L	21	1	0	1.000	0	1	1	0	9	9	5	5	0	5.40
Rube Bressler	L	21	1	4	.200	0	23	6	5	75	70	38	27	0	6.60
Les Lanning	R	24	1	1	.500	0	6	3	2	25	16	16	9	0	8.25
George Hesselbacher	R	21	0	3	.000	0	5	4	1	24	37	22	6	0	7.50
Cap Crowell	R	20	0	1	.000	0	4	1	0	14	14	4	5	0	4.50
Marsh Williams	L	23	0	3	.000	1	3	3	1	51	71	31	17	0	7.94
Harry Weaver	R	23	0	2	.000	0	3	2	0	13	14	6	9	0	10.13
Axel Lindstrom	R	20	0	1	.000	0	1	1	0	4	6	6	0	0	4.50
Bill Morrisette	R	22	0	1	.000	0	4	1	0	16	16	16	9	0	6.75
Jack Richardson	R	23	0	0	—	0	1	0	0	1	1	3	1	0	27.00
Doc Whittaker	R	22	0	0	—	0	2	0	0	4	6	6	0	0	4.50

BROOKLYN 1ST 94-60 .610 — WILBERT ROBINSON

NAME	G by Pos	B	AGE	G	AB	R	H	2B	3B	HR	RBI	BB	SO	SB	BA	SA
TOTALS			29	156	5234	585	1366	195	80	28	493	355	550	187	.261	.345
Jake Daubert	1B126	L	32	127	478	75	151	16	7	3	33	38	39	21	.316	.397
George Cutshaw	2B154	R	29	154	581	58	151	16	7	3	63	25	32	27	.260	.320
Ivy Olson	SS103, 2B3, 1B1	R	30	108	351	29	89	13	4	1	38	21	27	14	.254	.322
Mike Mowrey	3B144	R	32	144	495	57	121	22	6	0	60	50	60	16	.244	.313
Jimmy Johnston	OF106	R	26	118	425	58	107	13	8	1	26	35	38	22	.252	.327
Hy Myers	OF106	R	27	113	412	54	108	12	14	3	36	21	35	17	.262	.381
Zack Wheat	OF149	L	28	149	568	76	177	32	13	9	73	43	49	19	.312	.461
Chief Meyers	C74	R	35	80	239	21	59	10	3	0	21	26	15	2	.247	.314
Casey Stengel	OF121	L	25	127	462	66	129	27	8	8	53	33	51	11	.279	.424
Otto Miller	C69	R	27	73	216	16	55	9	2	1	17	7	29	6	.255	.329
Ollie O'Mara	SS51	R	25	72	193	18	39	5	2	0	15	12	20	10	.202	.249
1 Lew McCarty	C27, 1B17	R	27	55	150	17	47	6	1	0	13	14	16	4	.313	.367
Jeff Pfeffer	P41, OF4	R	28	43	122	5	34	2	2	0	12	4	32	2	.279	.328
Gus Getz	3B20, SS7, 1B3	R	26	40	96	9	21	1	2	0	8	0	5	9	.219	.271
2 Fred Merkle	1B15, OF4	R	27	23	69	6	16	1	0	0	2	7	4	2	.232	.246
Jim Hickman	OF3	R	24	9	5	3	1	0	0	0	0	2	0	1	.200	.200
Hack Miller	OF3	R	24	3	3	0	1	0	1	0	1	1	1	0	.333	1.000
Bunny Fabrique	SS2	B	28	2	2	0	0	0	0	0	0	0	0	1	.000	.000

John Kelleher 22 R 0-3, Red Smyth 25 L 0-5, Mack Wheat 23 R 0-2, Artie Dede 20 R 0-1, Al Nixon 30 R 2-2

NAME	T	AGE	W	L	PCT	SV	G	GS	CG	IP	H	BB	SO	SHO	ERA
		29	94	60	.610	9	156	156	96	1427	1201	372	634	22	2.12
Jeff Pfeffer	R	28	25	11	.694	1	41	36	30	329	274	63	128	6	1.91
Larry Cheney	R	30	18	12	.600	0	41	32	15	253	178	105	166	5	1.92
Sherry Smith	L	25	14	10	.583	1	36	25	15	219	193	45	97	4	2.34
Rube Marquard	L	29	13	6	.684	5	36	21	15	205	169	38	107	1	1.58
Jack Coombs	R	33	13	8	.619	0	27	19	10	159	136	44	47	3	2.66
Wheezer Dell	R	30	8	9	.471	2	32	16	9	155	143	43	76	2	2.26
Nap Rucker	L	31	2	1	.667	0	9	1	1	37	34	7	14	0	1.70
Ed Appleton	R	24	1	2	.333	1	14	8	1	47	48	14	10	3	3.06
Duster Mails	L	21	0	1	.000	0	11	0	0	17	15	9	13	0	3.71
Leon Cadore	R	25	0	0	—	0	1	0	0	6	10	1	2	0	4.50

PHILADELPHIA 2nd 91-62 .595 2.5 — PAT MORAN

NAME	G by Pos	B	AGE	G	AB	R	H	2B	3B	HR	RBI	BB	SO	SB	BA	SA
TOTALS			29	154	4985	581	1244	223	53	42	486	399	571	149	.250	.341
Fred Luderus	1B146	L	30	146	508	52	143	26	3	5	53	41	32	8	.281	.374
Bert Niehoff	2B146, 3B1	R	32	146	548	65	133	42	4	4	61	37	57	20	.243	.356
Dave Bancroft	SS142	B	25	142	477	53	101	10	0	3	33	74	57	15	.212	.252
Milt Stock	3B117, SS15	R	22	132	509	61	143	25	6	1	43	27	33	21	.281	.360
Gavvy Cravath	OF130	R	35	137	448	70	127	21	8	11	70	64	89	9	.283	.440
Dode Paskert	OF146, SS1	R	34	149	555	82	155	30	7	8	46	54	76	22	.279	.402
Possum Whitted	OF136, 1B16	R	26	147	526	68	148	20	12	6	68	19	46	29	.281	.399
Bill Killefer	C91	R	28	97	286	22	62	5	4	3	27	8	14	2	.217	.294
Ed Burns	C75, SS1, OF1	R	28	78	219	14	51	8	1	0	14	16	18	3	.233	.279
Wilbur Good	OF46	L	30	75	136	25	34	4	3	1	15	8	13	7	.250	.346
Claude Cooper	OF29, 1B1	L	24	26	104	9	20	2	0	0	11	7	15	1	.192	.212
Bobby Byrne	3B40	R	31	48	141	22	33	10	1	0	9	14	7	6	.234	.319
Oscar Dugey	2B12	R	28	41	50	9	11	3	0	0	1	9	8	3	.220	.280
Jack Adams (HJ)	C11	B	25	11	13	2	3	0	0	0	1	0	3	0	.231	.231
Bud Weiser	OF4	L	22	4	10	1	3	1	0	0	1	0	1	0	.300	.400
Bob Gandy	OF1	L	24	2	2	0	0	0	0	0	0	0	1	0	.000	.000
Billy Maharg	OF1	R	35	1	1	0	0	0	0	0	0	0	0	0	.000	.000
Ben Tincup		L	23	1	1	0	0	0	0	0	0	0	0	0	.000	.000

NAME	T	AGE	W	L	PCT	SV	G	GS	CG	IP	H	BB	SO	SHO	ERA
		29	91	62	.595	9	154	154	97	1382	1238	295	601	24	2.36
Pete Alexander	R	29	33	12	.733	3	48	45	38	389	323	50	167	16	1.55
Eppa Rixey	L	25	22	10	.688	0	38	33	20	287	239	74	134	3	1.85
Al Demaree	R	31	19	14	.576	1	39	35	25	285	252	48	130	3	2.62
Erskine Mayer	R	26	7	7	.500	0	28	16	7	140	148	33	62	2	3.15
Chief Bender	R	33	7	7	.500	3	27	13	4	123	137	34	43	0	3.73
Joe Oeschger	R	24	1	1	.000	0	14	0	0	30	18	14	17	0	2.40
George Chalmers	R	28	1	4	.200	0	12	8	2	54	49	19	21	0	3.17
George McQuillan	R	31	1	7	.125	2	21	3	1	62	58	15	22	0	2.76
Gary Fortune	R	20	1	0	.000	0	1	1	0	5	2	4	3	0	3.60
2 Erv Kantlehner	L	23	0	0	—	0	3	0	0	4	7	3	2	0	9.00
Stan Baumgartner	L	23	0	0	—	0	1	0	0	4	5	1	0	0	2.25

BOSTON 3rd 89-63 .586 4 — GEORGE STALLINGS

NAME	G by Pos	B	AGE	G	AB	R	H	2B	3B	HR	RBI	BB	SO	SB	BA	SA
TOTALS			28	158	5075	542	1181	166	73	22	472	437	646	141	.233	.307
Ed Konetchy	1B158	R	30	158	566	76	147	29	13	3	70	43	46	13	.260	.373
Johnny Evers (AJ)	2B71	L	34	71	241	33	52	4	1	0	15	40	19	5	.216	.241
Tabbit Maranville	SS155	R	24	155	604	79	142	16	13	4	38	50	69	32	.235	.325
Red Smith	3B150	R	26	150	569	48	132	16	10	3	60	53	55	13	.259	.348
Joe Wilhoit	OF108	R	30	116	383	44	88	13	4	2	38	27	45	18	.230	.300
Fred Snodgrass	OF110	R	28	112	382	33	95	13	5	1	32	34	54	14	.249	.317
Sherry Magee	OF120, 1B2, SS1	R	31	120	419	44	101	17	5	3	54	44	52	10	.241	.327
Hank Gowdy	C116	R	26	118	349	32	88	12	1	1	34	24	33	4	.252	.301
Zip Collins	OF78	R	24	93	268	39	56	1	6	1	18	18	42	4	.209	.269
Dick Egan	2B53, SS12, 3B8	R	32	83	238	23	53	8	3	0	16	19	21	2	.223	.282
Ed Fitzpatrick	2B46, OF28	R	26	83	216	17	46	8	0	1	18	15	26	5	.213	.264
Joey Connolly	OF31	L	32	62	110	11	25	5	2	0	12	14	13	5	.227	.309
Earl Blackburn	C44	R	23	47	110	12	30	4	4	0	7	9	21	2	.273	.382
Walt Tragesser	C29	R	29	41	54	3	11	1	0	0	4	5	10	0	.204	.222
Lefty Tyler	P34	L	26	39	93	10	19	3	1	3	20	9	15	0	.204	.355
1 Pete Compton	OF30	L	26	34	98	13	20	2	0	0	9	7	7	5	.204	.224
2 Larry Chappell	OF14	R	26	20	53	4	12	1	0	0	9	2	4	1	.226	.283
Fred Bailey	OF2	L	20	6	10	0	1	0	0	0	1	0	3	0	.100	.100
Art Rico	C4	R	20	4	4	0	0	0	0	0	0	0	0	0	.000	.000
Joe Mathes	2B2	B	25	2	0	0	0	0	0	0	0	0	0	0	—	—

NAME	T	AGE	W	L	PCT	SV	G	GS	CG	IP	H	BB	SO	SHO	ERA
		28	89	63	.586	11	158	158	97	1416	1206	325	644	21	2.19
Dick Rudolph	R	27	19	12	.613	3	41	38	27	312	266	38	133	5	2.16
Lefty Tyler	L	26	17	10	.630	1	34	28	21	249	200	58	117	6	2.02
Tom Hughes	R	32	16	3	.842	5	40	13	7	161	121	51	97	1	2.35
Pat Ragan	R	30	9	9	.500	0	28	23	14	182	143	47	94	3	2.08
Frank Allen	L	27	8	2	.800	1	19	14	7	113	102	31	63	2	2.07
Art Nehf	L	23	7	5	.583	0	22	13	6	121	110	20	36	1	2.01
Ed Reulbach	R	33	7	6	.538	0	21	11	6	109	99	41	47	0	2.48
Jesse Barnes	R	23	6	14	.300	1	33	18	9	163	154	37	55	3	2.37
1 Elmer Knetzer	R	30	0	2	.000	1	5	2	0	11	2	2	0	0	7.20
Bill James (SJ) 24															

NEW YORK 4th 86-66 .566 7 — JOHN McGRAW

NAME	G by Pos	B	AGE	G	AB	R	H	2B	3B	HR	RBI	BB	SO	SB	BA	SA
TOTALS			28	155	5152	597	1305	188	74	42	500	356	558	206	.253	.343
1 Fred Markle	1B112	R	27	112	401	45	95	19	3	7	44	33	46	17	.237	.352
1 Larry Doyle	2B113	L	30	113	441	55	118	24	10	2	47	23	41	17	.268	.381
Art Fletcher	SS133	R	31	133	500	53	143	23	8	3	66	13	36	15	.286	.382
1 Bill McKechnie	3B71	R	29	71	260	22	64	9	1	0	17	7	20	7	.246	.288
Dave Robertson	OF144	L	26	150	587	88	180	18	8	12	69	14	56	21	.307	.426
Benny Kauff	OF154	L	26	154	552	71	146	22	15	9	74	68	65	40	.264	.408
George Burns	OF155	R	26	155	623	105	174	24	8	5	41	63	47	37	.279	.368
Bill Rariden	C119	R	28	120	351	23	78	9	3	1	29	55	32	4	.222	.274
2 Buck Herzog	2B44, 3B27, SS9	R	30	77	280	40	73	10	4	0	25	22	24	19	.261	.325
George Kelly	1B13, OF12, 3B1	R	20	49	76	4	12	2	1	0	3	6	24	1	.158	.211
Hans Lobert (KJ)	3B20	R	34	48	76	6	17	3	2	0	11	5	8	2	.224	.316
2 Heinie Zimmerman	3B40	R	29	40	151	22	41	4	0	0	19*	7	10	9	.272	.298
1 Edd Roush	OF15	L	23	39	69	4	13	0	1	0	5	4	9	4	.188	.217
Walter Holke	1B34	B	23	34	111	16	39	4	2	0	13	6	16	10	.351	.423
Brad Kocher	C30	R	27	34	65	1	7	2	0	2	0	7	10	0	.108	.138
2 Lew McCarty	C24	R	27	25	68	6	27	3	4	0	9	7	9	0	.397	.559
1 Herb Hunter	3B6, 1B2	L	20	21	28	3	7	0	0	0	4	0	5	0	.250	.357
2 Mickey Doolan	SS16, 2B2	R	36	18	51	4	12	3	1	1	3	2	4	1	.235	.392
Red Dooin	C37	R	37	15	17	1	3	0	0	0	4	0	3	0	.118	.118

Fred Brainard 24 R 0-7, 2 Red Killefer 31 R 1-1, Lew Wendell 24 R 0-2, Duke Kelleher 22 0-0, Joe Rodriguez 21 R 0-0, Heinie Stafford 24 R 0-1

Zimmerman, also with Chicago, league leader in RBI with 83

NAME	T	AGE	W	L	PCT	SV	G	GS	CG	IP	H	BB	SO	SHO	ERA
		27	86	66	.566	12	155	155	88	1397	1267	310	638	22	2.60
Pol Perritt	R	24	18	11	.621	2	40	29	17	251	243	56	115	5	2.62
Rube Benton	L	26	16	8	.667	2	40	29	15	239	210	58	115	3	2.86
Jeff Tesreau	R	28	14	14	.500	2	40	32	23	268	249	65	113	5	2.92
Ferdie Schupp	L	25	9	3	.750	0	30	11	8	140	79	37	86	4	0.90
2 Slim Sallee	L	31	9	4	.692	0	15	11	7	112	96	10	35	2	1.37
Fred Anderson	R	30	9	13	.409	2	38	27	13	188	206	38	98	2	3.40
George Smith	R	24	3	0	1.000	0	3	1	0	21	14	6	9	0	2.57
Sailor Stroud	R	31	3	1	.600	1	14	4	0	47	47	9	16	0	2.68
1 Christy Mathewson	R	35	3	4	.429	2	12	6	4	66	59	7	16	1	2.32
Hank Ritter	R	22	1	0	1.000	0	5	0	0	5	3	0	0	0	0.00
Rube Schauer	R	25	1	4	.200	0	19	3	1	44	44	16	24	0	2.93
Emilio Palmero	L	21	0	0	—	0	3	1	0	16	17	8	10	0	7.88

CHICAGO 5th 67-86 .438 26.5 — JOE TINKER

NAME	G by Pos	B	AGE	G	AB	R	H	2B	3B	HR	RBI	BB	SO	SB	BA	SA
TOTALS			28	156	5179	520	1237	194	56	46	456	399	662	133	.239	.325
Vic Saier	1B147	L	25	147	498	60	126	25	3	7	50	79	68	20	.253	.357
2 Otto Knabe	2B42, SS1, 3B1, OF1	R	32	51	145	17	40	8	0	0	7	9	18	3	.276	.331
Chuck Wortman	SS69	R	24	69	234	17	47	4	2	2	16	18	22	4	.201	.261
1 Heinie Zimmerman	3B75, 2B14, SS4	R	29	107	398	54	116	25	5	6	64*	16	33	15	.291	.425
Max Flack	OF136	L	26	141	466	65	117	16	14	3	20	42	43	24	.258	.320
Cy Williams	OF116	L	28	118	405	55	113	19	9	12	66	51	64	6	.279	.459
Les Mann	OF115	R	23	127	445	46	113	13	9	2	29	19	31	11	.272	.361
Jimmy Archer	C65, 3B1	R	33	77	205	11	45	6	2	1	30	12	24	3	.220	.283
R. Zeider	3B55, 2B33, OF7, SS5, 1B2	R	32	98	345	29	81	11	2	1	22	26	26	9	.235	.287
1 Wildfire Schulte	OF65	L	33	72	230	31	68	11	1	5	27	20	35	9	.296	.417
1 Bill Fischer	C56	R	25	65	179	15	35	9	2	1	14	11	12	2	.196	.285
Eddie Mulligan	SS58	R	21	58	189	13	29	3	1	0	9	8	30	1	.153	.212
Joe Kelly	OF46	R	29	54	169	18	43	7	1	2	15	9	16	10	.254	.343
Steve Yerkes	2B41	R	28	44	137	12	36	7	0	0	10	9	7	1	.263	.358
1 Alex McCarthy	2B34, SS3	R	28	37	107	10	26	2	3	0	6	11	7	1	.243	.318
2 Art Wilson	C34	R	30	35	53	4	22	1	0	6	5	6	14	1	.193	.237
Dutch Zwilling	OF10	L	27	35	53	4	6	1	0	0	4	3	13	0	.113	.189
2 Fritz Mollwitz	1B19, OF6	R	26	33	71	1	19	7	1	0	11	0	11	4	.268	.296
2 Mickey Doolan	SS24	R	36	28	70	4	15	2	1	0	9	4	20	0	.214	.271
Rowdy Elliott	C18	R	25	22	69	5	10	1	0	0	4	3	21	1	.145	.188
Charlie Pechous	3B22	R	19	22	59	6	9	2	1	0	4	6	9	1	.153	.220
Earl Smith	OF7	R	25	14	27	2	7	2	0	1	4	2	3	0	.259	.370

2 Larry Doyle 30 L 15-38, Joe Tinker 35 R 1-10, Nick Allen 21 R 1-16, 2 Solly Hofman 33 R 5-16, Merwin Jacobson 22 L 3-13, 2 Charlie Deal 24 R 2-8,
2 Herb Hunter 20 L 0-4, Marty Shay 20 R 2-7, John O'Connor 24 R 0-0, Bob O'Farrell 19 R 0-1, Eddie Sicking 19 R 0-1, Count Clemens 29 R 0-15

Zimmerman, also with New York, league leader in RBI with 83

NAME	T	AGE	W	L	PCT	SV	G	GS	CG	IP	H	BB	SO	SHO	ERA
		30	67	86	.438	13	156	156	72	1417	1265	365	616	11	2.65
Hippo Vaughn	L	28	17	15	.531	1	44	35	21	294	269	67	144	4	2.20
Gene Packard	L	28	10	6	.625	5	37	16	5	155	154	38	36	2	2.79
Jimmy Lavender	R	32	10	16	.417	2	36	25	9	188	163	62	91	4	2.82
Claude Hendrix	R	27	8	16	.333	2	36	24	15	218	193	67	117	3	2.68
Tom Seaton	R	28	6	6	.500	1	31	12	4	121	108	43	45	0	3.27
Mike Pendergast	R	27	6	11	.353	2	35	10	4	152	127	23	56	2	2.31
George McConnell	R	38	4	12	.250	0	28	21	8	171	137	35	82	1	2.58
Scott Perry	R	25	1	2	.667	0	4	3	2	28	30	3	10	1	2.57
Paul Carter	R	22	2	2	.500	0	8	5	2	36	26	17	14	0	2.75
Three Finger Brown	R	39	2	3	.400	0	12	3	2	48	52	9	21	0	3.94
George Pierce	L	28	0	0	—	0	4	4	0	4	6	1	0	0	2.25

PITTSBURGH 6th 65-89 .422 29   NIXEY CALLAHAN

NAME	G by Pos	B	AGE	G	AB	R	H	2B	3B	HR	RBI	BB	SO	SB	BA	SA
TOTALS			27	157	5181	484	1246	147	91	20	406	372	618	173	.240	.316
Doc Johnston	1B110	L	28	114	404	33	86	10	10	0	39	20	42	17	.213	.287
Jack Farmer	2B31,OF15,SS4,3B1	R	23	55	166	10	45	6	4	0	14	7	24	1	.271	.355
Honus Wagner (HJ)	SS92,1B24,2B4	R	42	123	432	45	124	15	9	1	39	34	36	11	.287	.370
Doug Baird	3B80,2B29,OF16	R	24	128	430	41	93	10	7	1	28	24	49	20	.216	.279
Bill Hinchman	OF124,1B31	R	33	152	555	64	175	18	16	4	76	54	61	10	.315	.427
Max Carey	OF154	B	26	154	599	90	158	23	11	7	42	59	58	63	.264	.374
2 Wildfire Schulte	OF48	L	33	55	177	12	45	5	3	0	14	17	19	5	.254	.316
Walter Schmidt	C57	R	29	64	184	16	35	1	2	0	15	10	13	3	.190	.250
Joe Schultz	2B24,3B24,OF6,SS1	R	22	77	204	18	53	8	2	0	22	7	14	6	.260	.319
Dan Costello	OF41	L	24	60	159	11	38	1	3	0	8	6	23	3	.239	.283
1 Art Wilson	C39	R	30	53	133	11	33	5	2	1	12	13	27	4	.258	.352
2 Alex McCarthy	SS39,2B7,3B5	R	28	50	146	11	29	3	0	0	3	15	10	3	.199	.219
Ed Barney	OF40	L	26	45	137	16	27	4	0	0	9	23	15	8	.197	.226
Hooks Warner	3B42,2B1	L	22	44	168	12	40	1	1	2	14	6	19	6	.238	.292
Carson Bigbee	2B23,OF19,3B1	L	21	43	164	17	41	3	6	0	3	7	14	8	.250	.341
Jim Viox	2B25,3B11	R	25	43	132	12	33	7	0	1	17	17	11	2	.250	.326
1 Bill Fischer	C35	L	25	42	113	11	29	7	1	1	6	10	3	1	.257	.363
Jimmy Smith	SS27,3B6	B	21	36	96	4	18	1	1	0	5	6	22	0	.188	.219
George Gibson	C29	R	35	33	84	4	17	2	2	0	4	3	7	0	.202	.274
1 Otto Knabe	2B28	R	32	28	89	4	17	3	1	0	9	6	6	1	.191	.247
Bill Wagner	C15	R	22	19	38	2	9	0	2	0	2	5	8	0	.237	.342
Ray O'Brien	OF14	L	23	16	57	5	12	3	2	0	3	1	14	0	.211	.333

Jesse Altenburg 23 L 6-14, Lee King 23 R 2-18, Frank Symkal 26 R 3-10, Pete Compton 26 L 1-16, Ike McAuley 24 R 2-8, Paddy Siglin 24 R 1-4, Bill Batsch 24 R 0-0, Wilbur Fisher 21 L 0-1, Billy Gleason 21 R 0-2, Newt Halliday 20 R 0-1, Gene Madden 26 L 0-1

NAME	T	AGE	W	L	PCT	SV	G	GS	CG	IP	H	BB	SO	SHO	ERA
		26	65	89	.422	7	157	157	88	1420	1277	443	596	10	2.76
Al Mamaux	R	22	21	15	.583	2	45	37	26	310	264	136	163	1	2.53
Wilbur Cooper	L	24	12	11	.522	2	42	23	16	246	189	74	111	2	1.87
Bob Harmon	R	28	8	11	.421	0	31	17	10	173	175	39	62	2	2.81
Frank Miller	R	30	7	10	.412	1	30	20	10	173	135	49	88	2	2.29
Elmer Jacobs	R	23	6	10	.375	0	34	17	8	153	151	38	46	0	2.94
1 Erv Kantlehner	R	23	5	15	.250	2	34	21	7	165	151	57	49	2	3.16
Burleigh Grimes	R	22	2	3	.400	0	6	5	4	46	40	10	20	0	2.35
Bill Evans	R	23	2	5	.286	0	13	7	3	63	57	16	21	0	3.00
Babe Adams	R	34	2	9	.182	0	16	10	4	72	91	12	22	1	5.75
Paul Carpenter	R	21	0	0	—	0	5	0	0	8	4	5	0	0	1.13
Carmen Hill	R	20	0	0	—	0	2	0	0	6	11	5	5	0	9.00
Jack Scott	R	24	0	0	—	1	1	0	0	5	3	4	2	0	10.80

CINCINNATI 7th(tie) 60-93 .392 33.5   BUCK HERZOG 34-49 .410   IVY WINGO 1-1 .500   CHRISTY MATHEWSON 25-43 .368

NAME	G by Pos	B	AGE	G	AB	R	H	2B	3B	HR	RBI	BB	SO	SB	BA	SA
TOTALS			28	155	5254	505	1336	187	88	14	422	362	573	157	.254	.331
Hal Chase	1B98,OF25,2B16	R	28	155	542	66	184	29	12	4	82	19	48	22	.339	.459
Baldy Louden	2B108,SS23	R	32	134	439	38	96	16	4	1	32	54	54	12	.219	.280
1 Buck Herzog	SS65,3B12,OF1	R	30	73	281	30	75	14	2	1	24	21	12	15	.267	.342
Heinie Groh	3B110,2B33,SS5	R	26	149	553	85	149	24	14	2	28	84	34	13	.269	.374
Tommy Griffith	OF155	R	26	155	595	50	158	28	7	2	61	36	37	16	.266	.346
2 Edd Roush	OF69	L	23	69	272	34	78	7	14	0	15	13	19	15	.287	.415
Greasy Neale	OF153	L	24	85	530	53	139	13	5	0	20	19	79	17	.262	.364
Ivy Wingo	C107	R	25	119	347	30	85	8	11	2	40	25	27	4	.245	.349
Tommy Clarke	C51	R	28	78	177	10	42	10	1	0	17	24	20	8	.237	.305
1 Red Killefer	OF68	R	31	70	234	29	57	9	1	1	18	21	8	7	.244	.303
1 Fritz Mollwitz	1B54	R	26	65	183	12	41	4	4	0	16	5	12	6	.224	.290
Bobby Fisher	SS29,2B6,OF1	R	29	61	136	9	37	4	3	0	11	8	14	7	.272	.346
Clarence Mitchell	P29,1B9,OF3	L	25	56	117	11	28	2	1	0	11	4	6	1	.239	.274
Frank Emmer	SS29,OF2,2B1,3B1	R	20	42	89	8	13	3	1	0	2	7	27	1	.146	.202
Emil Huhn	C18,1B14,OF1	R	24	37	94	4	24	3	2	0	3	2	11	0	.255	.300
2 Bill McKechnie	3B35	B	20	37	130	4	36	3	0	0	10	3	12	4	.277	.300
Larry Kopf	SS11	R	25	11	40	2	11	2	0	0	5	1	4	1	.275	.325
Paul Smith	OF10	L	28	10	44	5	10	0	1	0	1	1	8	3	.227	.273

Ken Williams (JJ) 26 L 3-27, Johnny Beall 34 L 7-21, Bill Hobbs 23 R 2-11, Bill Rodgers 28 L 0-4, George Twombly 24 R 0-5

NAME	T	AGE	W	L	PCT	SV	G	GS	CG	IP	H	BB	SO	SHO	ERA
		27	60	93	.392	6	155	155	86	1408	1356	458	569	7	3.10
Fred Toney	R	27	14	17	.452	1	41	38	21	300	247	78	146	3	2.28
Clarence Mitchell	L	25	11	10	.524	0	29	24	17	195	211	45	52	1	3.14
Pete Schneider	R	23	10	19	.345	1	44	31	16	274	259	82	117	3	2.69
Al Schulz	L	27	10	19	.296	2	44	22	10	215	208	93	95	0	3.14
Earl Moseley	R	28	7	10	.412	1	31	15	7	150	145	69	60	0	3.90
2 Elmer Knetzer	R	30	5	12	.294	1	36	16	12	171	161	45	70	0	2.89
Gene Dale (ST)	R	27	5	7	.429	0	17	5	2	70	80	33	23	0	5.14
2 Christy Mathewson	R	35	1	0	1.000	0	1	1	1	9	15	1	3	0	8.00
Limb McKenry	R	27	1	1	.500	0	6	1	0	15	14	8	2	0	4.20
Jim Bluejacket	R	28	0	0	—	0	3	0	0	7	12	3	1	0	7.71
Twink Twining	R	22	0	0	—	0	1	0	0	2	4	1	0	0	13.50

ST. LOUIS 7th(tie) 60-93 .392 33.5   MILLER HUGGINS

NAME	G by Pos	B	AGE	G	AB	R	H	2B	3B	HR	RBI	BB	SO	SB	BA	SA
TOTALS			26	153	5030	476	1223	155	74	25	413	335	651	182	.243	.318
Dots Miller	1B93,2B38,SS21,3B1	R	29	143	505	47	120	22	7	1	46	40	49	18	.238	.315
Bruno Betzel	2B113,3B33,OF7	R	21	130	419	40	119	15	11	1	37	39	77	22	.284	.313
Roy Corhan	SS84	R	28	92	295	30	62	6	9	0	18	20	31	15	.210	.251
Rogers Hornsby	3B83,SS45,1B15,2B1	R	20	139	495	63	155	17	15	6	65	40	63	17	.313	.444
Tommy Long	OF106	R	26	119	403	37	118	11	10	1	33	10	43	21	.293	.377
Jack Smith	OF120	L	21	130	357	43	87	6	5	6	34	20	50	24	.244	.353
Bob Bescher	OF151	B	32	151	561	78	132	24	8	4	43	60	50	39	.235	.339
Mike Gonzalez	C93,1B13	R	25	118	331	33	79	15	4	0	29	28	18	5	.239	.308
Frank Snyder	C72,1B46,SS1	R	29	120	406	23	105	12	4	0	39	18	31	7	.259	.308
Owen Wilson	OF113	L	32	120	355	30	85	8	2	3	32	20	46	4	.239	.299
Art Butler	OF15,2B8,3B2,SS2	R	28	86	110	9	23	5	0	0	7	7	12	3	.209	.255
Zinn Beck (KJ)	3B52,1B1,2B1	R	30	62	184	8	41	7	1	0	10	14	21	3	.223	.272
Tony Brottem	C15,OF2	R	25	26	33	3	6	1	0	0	4	3	10	1	.182	.212
Miller Huggins	2B7	B	38	18	9	2	3	0	0	0	2	0	3	0	.333	.333
Sammy Bohne	SS14	R	19	14	38	3	9	0	0	0	1	0	4	6	.237	.237
Stuffy Stewart	2B8	R	22	9	17	0	3	0	0	0	1	0	3	0	.176	.176
Walton Cruise	OF2	L	26	3	3	0	2	0	0	0	0	0	1	0	.667	.667

Jack Roche (ST) 25

NAME	T	AGE	W	L	PCT	SV	G	GS	CG	IP	H	BB	SO	SHO	ERA
		26	60	93	.392	15	153	153	58	1355	1331	445	529	11	3.14
Bill Doak	R	25	12	8	.600	0	29	26	11	192	177	55	82	3	2.63
Lee Meadows	R	21	12	23	.343	2	51	36	11	289	261	119	120	1	2.58
Red Ames	R	33	11	16	.407	8	45	25	10	228	225	57	98	2	4.20
Steamboat Williams	R	24	6	7	.462	1	36	8	5	105	121	27	25	0	4.20
1 Slim Sallee	L	31	5	5	.500	1	16	7	4	70	75	23	28	2	3.47
Hi Jasper	R	35	5	6	.455	1	21	9	2	107	97	42	37	0	3.28
Bob Steele	L	22	5	15	.250	0	29	21	7	148	156	42	67	1	3.41
Milt Watson	R	26	4	6	.400	0	18	13	5	103	109	33	27	2	3.06
Joe Lotz	R	25	0	3	.000	0	12	3	1	40	31	17	18	0	4.28
Charley Hall	R	31	0	4	.000	1	10	5	2	43	45	14	15	0	5.44
Murphy Currie	R	22	0	0	—	0	6	0	0	14	7	9	8	0	1.93
Dan Griner	R	28	0	0	—	1	4	0	0	11	15	3	3	0	4.09
Cy Warmoth	L	23	0	0	—	0	5	1	0	5	12	4	1	0	14.40

WORLD SERIES — BOSTON (AL) 4 BROOKLYN (NL) 1

LINE SCORES

TEAM	1	2	3	4	5	6	7	8	9	10	11	12	13	14	R	H	E

Game 1 October 7 at Boston

															R	H	E
BKN(NL)	0	0	0	1	0	0	0	0	4						5	10	4
BOS(AL)	0	0	1	0	1	0	3	1	X						6	8	1

Marquard, Pfeffer (8)   Shore, Mays (9)

Game 2 October 9 at Boston (14 Innings)

	1	2	3	4	5	6	7	8	9	10	11	12	13	14	R	H	E
BKN	1	0	0	0	0	0	0	0	0	0	0	0	0	0	1	6	2
BOS	0	0	1	0	0	0	0	0	0	0	0	0	0	1	2	7	1

Smith   Ruth

Game 3 October 10 at Brooklyn

	1	2	3	4	5	6	7	8	9	R	H	E
BOS	0	0	0	0	0	2	0	1	0	3	7	1
BKN	0	0	1	1	2	0	0	0	X	4	10	0

Mays, Foster (6)   Coombs, Pfeffer (7)

Game 4 October 11 at Brooklyn

	1	2	3	4	5	6	7	8	9	R	H	E
BOS	0	3	0	1	1	0	1	0	0	6	10	1
BKN	2	0	0	0	0	0	0	0	0	2	5	4

Leonard   Marquard, Cheney (5), Rucker (8)

Game 5 October 12 at Boston

	1	2	3	4	5	6	7	8	9	R	H	E
BKN	0	1	0	0	0	0	0	0	0	1	3	3
BOS	0	1	2	0	1	0	0	0	X	4	7	2

Pfeffer, Dell (8)   Shore

COMPOSITE BATTING

NAME	POS	G	AB	R	H	2B	3B	HR	RBI	BA
Boston (AL)										
Totals		5	164	21	39	7	6	2	18	.238
Janvrin	2B	5	23	2	5	3	0	0	1	.217
Hooper	OF	5	21	6	7	1	0	0	1	.333
Lewis	OF	5	17	3	6	1	0	0	1	.353
Hoblitzell	1B	5	17	3	4	1	1	0	2	.235
Gardner	3B	5	17	2	3	0	0	2	6	.176
Scott	SS	5	16	1	2	0	1	0	1	.125
Walker	OF	3	11	3	3	0	1	0	1	.273
Shorten	OF	2	7	0	4	0	0	0	2	.571
Thomas	C	2	7	0	1	0	1	0	0	.143
Shore	P	2	7	0	0	0	0	0	0	.000
Ruth	P	1	5	0	0	0	0	0	0	.000
Cady	C	2	4	1	1	0	0	0	0	.250
Carrigan	C	1	3	0	2	0	0	0	0	.667
Walsh	OF	1	3	0	0	0	0	0	0	.000
Leonard	P	1	3	0	0	0	0	0	0	.000
Gainer	PH	2	1	0	1	0	0	0	1	1.000
Mays	P	2	1	0	0	0	0	0	0	.000
Foster	P	1	1	0	0	0	0	0	0	.000
Henriksen	PH	1	1	0	0	0	0	0	0	—
McNally	PR	1	0	1	0	0	0	0	0	—
Brooklyn (NL)										
Totals		5	170	13	34	2	5	1	11	.200
Myers	OF	5	22	2	4	0	0	1	3	.182
Wheat	OF	5	19	2	4	0	1	0	1	.211
Cutshaw	2B	5	19	2	2	0	0	0	2	.105
Mowrey	3B	5	17	2	3	0	0	0	1	.176
Daubert	1B	4	17	1	3	0	1	0	0	.176
Olson	SS	5	16	1	4	0	0	0	0	.250
Stengel	OF	4	11	2	4	0	0	0	0	.364
Johnston	OF	3	10	1	3	0	0	0	0	.300
Meyers	C	3	10	0	2	0	0	0	0	.200
Miller	C	2	8	0	1	0	0	0	0	.125
Smith	P	1	5	0	1	0	0	0	0	.200
Pfeffer	P	4	4	0	1	0	0	0	0	.250
Merkle	1B	1	3	0	1	0	0	0	0	.333
Coombs	P	1	3	0	1	0	0	0	0	.333
Marquard	P	2	3	0	0	0	0	0	0	.000
Getz	PH	1	1	0	0	0	0	0	0	.000
O'Mara	PH	1	1	0	0	0	0	0	0	.000
Cheney	P	1	0	0	0	0	0	0	0	—
Dell	P	1	0	0	0	0	0	0	0	—
Rucker	P	1	0	0	0	0	0	0	0	—

COMPOSITE PITCHING

NAME	G	IP	H	BB	SO	W	L	SV	ERA
Boston (AL)									
Totals	5	49	34	14	19	4	1	1	1.47
Shore	2	17.2	12	4	9	2	0	0	1.53
Ruth	1	14	6	3	4	1	0	0	0.64
Leonard	1	9	5	4	3	1	0	0	1.00
Mays	2	5.1	8	3	2	0	1	1	5.06
Foster	1	3	3	0	1	0	0	0	0.00
Brooklyn (NL)									
Totals	5	47.1	39	18	25	1	4	1	3.04
Smith	1	13.1	7	6	2	0	1	0	1.35
Marquard	2	11	12	6	9	0	2	0	6.55
Pfeffer	3	10.2	7	4	5	0	1	1	1.69
Coombs	1	6.1	7	1	1	1	0	0	4.26
Cheney	1	3	4	1	5	0	0	0	3.00
Rucker	1	2	1	0	3	0	0	0	0.00
Dell	1	1	1	0	0	0	0	0	0.00

1917 Little Napoleon Returns to the Front

The genius of John McGraw, who was aptly dubbed "Little Napoleon" lay in his ability to motivate his players. But his rebuilding of the Giants into pennant winners in 1917 underscored his administrative ability. Two years before, the Giants had fallen into the basement, and 1916 had proved to be a year of streaks and slumps. This year, the Gotham club reached the top of the heap to stay on June 27, and won easily over the second-place Phillies by ten games. McGraw completely revised his infield, using young Walter Holke at first, three-time Giant Buck Herzog at second, and heavy-hitting ex-Cub Heinie Zimmerman at third--to go along with holdover shortstop Art Fletcher. Federal League standout Benny Kauff starred in center field, and right fielder Dave Robertson hit 12 home runs to form, with Zimmemman, the power punch of the Giants. McGraw needed new starting pitchers and found able arms in lefties Ferdie Schupp, Slim Sallee, and Rube Benton and righty Pol Perritt.

The Phillies were done in by a mid-season-batting slump which affected the entire lineup. Grover "Pete" Alexander had 30 victories for the third time in as many years, and Gavvy Cravath again led the batting attack for the Phils. Johnny Evers was purchased from Boston to fill the keystone slot, but age had taken its toll on the old Cub star and he could manage to hit only .224. Third-place St. Louis had the league's worst pitching, but its second best hitter in young Rogers Hornsby. Cincinnati also held a batting ace in Edd Roush, another Federal League discovery, who won the batting crown with a .341 mark. In the second division, Brooklyn fell from the pennant the year before into a dismal seventh place finish. The failure of the pitching staff, Jake Daubert's average, and Zack Wheat's inability to contribute the extra base hits he did in 1916 were chiefly responsible for Brooklyn's sudden turnaround. Boston also was expected to contend but was fortunate to barely beat out Brooklyn for sixth place.

The Chicago White Sox capped a three-year rise under manager Pants Rowland by winning the American League title over the Red Sox by nine games. Boston and Chicago kept trading the first and second slots until the White Sox staked a permanent claim on the lead on August 18. Good pitching and hitting made the Chisox the class of the league. Outfielders Happy Felsch and Joe Jackson were .300 hitters, and pitcher Eddie Cicotte led the way in wins with 28 and E.R.A. with 1.53. Rookie Swede Risberg came through at shortstop with a good glove that tied together the inner defense, permitting Buck Weaver to play regularly at third base.

The Red Sox entered their title defense under a new manager, Jack Barry, but a record almost identical to their 1916 winning season could only net them a runner-up position. The hitting fell off from recent years, but young pitchers Babe Ruth and Carl Mays both logged 20-win seasons.

Ty Cobb returned to the batting throne for the tenth time in 11 seasons after a one-year sabbatical, and his .383 mark easily led young runner-up George Sisler and third-placer Tris Speaker, both of whom hit over .350.

When the World Series dawned on October 6, McGraw found himself in the fall classic for the fifth time. His fortunes had not improved since his first visit to the Series in 1905, when he came out a winner. Eddie Cicotte took a close 2-1 opening game win en route to a six-game White Sox Series victory. Red Faber won the other three games for the White Sox by hurling complete victories and winning once in relief. Veteran Eddie Collins led the White Sox in batting, but New York's Dave Robertson paced all hitters with a .500 average for the Series.

Four future Hall of Famers hung up their spikes in 1917. Sam Crawford was reduced to a pinch hitter for Detroit, and he ended a career as one of the early American League's top sluggers. Eddie Plank wound up his 17-year career with 325 victories, all but 21 of which were earned in the American League--the crafty southpaw providing ace pitching on Connie Mack's early pennant winners. Johnny Evers hit a paltry .214 for the Braves and Phillies and that prompted the 35-year-old second baseman to pack it in. Finally, Honus Wagner ended his 21-year career, at age 43, as a part-time first sacker for Pittsburgh--the all-time great shortstop retiring with eight National League batting crowns to his credit.

1917 AMERICAN LEAGUE

NAME	G by Pos	B	AGE	G	AB	R	H	2B	3B	HR	RBI	BB	SO	SB	BA	SA
CHICAGO	**1st 100-54 .649**										**PANTS ROWLAND**					
	TOTALS		26	156	5057	657	1281	152	81	18	535	522	479	219	.253	.326
Chick Gandil	1B149	R	29	149	553	53	151	9	7	0	57	30	36	16	.273	.315
Eddie Collins	2B156	L	30	156	564	91	163	18	12	0	67	89	16	53	.289	.363
Swede Risberg	SS146	R	22	149	474	59	96	20	8	1	45	59	65	16	.203	.285
Buck Weaver	3B107,SS10	B	26	118	447	64	127	16	5	3	32	27	29	19	.284	.362
Nemo Leibold	OF122	L	25	125	428	59	101	12	6	0	29	74	34	27	.236	.292
Happy Felsch	OF152	R	25	152	575	75	177	17	10	6	102	33	52	26	.308	.403
Joe Jackson	OF145	L	27	146	538	91	162	20	17	5	75	57	25	13	.301	.429
Ray Schalk	C139	R	24	140	424	48	96	12	5	2	51	59	27	19	.226	.292
Shano Collins	OF73	R	31	82	252	38	59	13	3	1	14	10	27	14	.234	.321
Fred McMullin	3B52,SS2	R	25	59	194	35	46	2	1	0	12	27	17	9	.237	.258
Eddie Murphy	OF9	L	25	53	51	9	16	2	1	0	16	5	1	4	.314	.392
Byrd Lynn	C29	R	28	35	72	7	16	2	0	0	5	7	11	1	.222	.250
Ted Jourdan	1B14	L	21	17	34	2	5	0	1	0	2	4	3	0	.147	.206
Joe Jenkins	C	R	26	10	9	0	1	0	0	0	2	0	5	0	.111	.111
Ziggy Hasbrouck	2B1	R	23	2	1	1	0	0	0	0	0	0	0	0	.000	.000
Zeb Terry	SS1	R	26	2	1	0	0	0	0	0	0	2	0	0	.000	.000
2 Bobby Byrne	2B1	R	32	1	1	0	0	0	0	0	0	0	0	0	.000	.000
Jack Fournier		L	27	1	1	0	0	0	0	0	0	0	1	0	.000	.000

NAME	T	AGE	W	L	PCT	SV	G	GS	CG	IP	H	BB	SO	SHO	ERA
		28	100	54	.649	23	156	156	79	1424	1236	413	517	21	2.16
Eddie Cicotte	R	33	28	12	.700	4	49	35	29	347	246	70	150	7	1.53
Lefty Williams	L	24	17	8	.680	1	45	29	8	230	221	81	85	1	2.97
Red Faber	R	28	16	13	.552	3	41	29	17	248	224	85	84	3	1.92
Red Russell	L	28	15	5	.750	4	35	24	11	189	170	32	54	5	1.95
Dave Danforth	L	27	11	6	.647	11	50	9	1	173	155	74	79	1	2.65
Joe Benz	R	31	7	3	.700	0	19	13	7	95	76	23	25	2	2.46
Jim Scott (MS)	R	28	6	7	.462	0	24	17	6	125	126	42	37	2	1.87
Mellie Wolfgang (JJ)	R	27	0	0	—	0	5	0	0	18	18	6	3	0	5.00

NAME	G by Pos	B	AGE	G	AB	R	H	2B	3B	HR	RBI	BB	SO	SB	BA	SA
BOSTON	**2nd 90-62 .592 9**										**JACK BARRY**					
	TOTALS		29	157	5048	556	1243	198	64	14	476	466	473	105	.246	.319
Dick Hoblitzell	1B118	L	28	120	420	49	108	19	7	1	47	46	22	12	.257	.343
Jack Barry	2B116	R	30	116	388	45	83	9	0	2	30	47	27	12	.214	.253
Everett Scott	SS157	R	24	157	528	40	127	24	7	0	50	20	46	12	.241	.313
Larry Gardner	3B146	L	31	146	501	53	133	23	7	1	61	54	37	16	.265	.345
Harry Hooper	OF151	L	29	151	559	89	143	21	11	3	45	80	40	21	.256	.349
Tilly Walker	OF96	R	28	106	337	41	83	18	7	2	37	25	38	6	.246	.359
Duffy Lewis	OF150	R	28	150	553	55	167	29	4	1	65	29	54	8	.302	.392
Sam Agnew	C85	R	30	85	260	17	54	6	2	0	16	19	30	2	.208	.246
Pinch Thomas	C77	L	29	83	202	24	48	7	0	0	24	27	9	2	.238	.272
Chick Shorten	0F43	L	25	69	168	12	30	4	2	0	16	10	10	2	.179	.226
Jimmy Walsh	0F47	R	31	57	185	25	49	6	3	0	12	25	14	6	.265	.330
Hal Janvrin	2B38,SS10,1B1	R	24	55	127	21	25	3	0	0	8	11	13	2	.197	.220
Del Gainer	1B50	R	30	52	172	28	53	10	2	2	19	15	21	1	.308	.424
Babe Ruth	P41	L	22	52	123	14	40	6	3	2	12	12	18	0	.325	.472
Mike McNally	3B14,SS9,2B6	R	23	42	50	9	15	1	0	0	2	6	3	3	.300	.320
Hick Cady	C14	R	31	17	46	4	7	1	1	0	2	1	6	0	.152	.217
Olaf Henriksen		L	29	15	12	1	1	0	0	0	1	3	4	0	.083	.083
Jimmy Cooney	2B10,SS1	R	26	22	11	36	4	8	1	0	0	3	6	2	.222	.250
Wally Mayer	C4	R	26	4	12	2	2	0	0	0	0	5	2	0	.167	.167

NAME	T	AGE	W	L	PCT	SV	G	GS	CG	IP	H	BB	SO	SHO	ERA
		26	90	62	.592	6	157	157	115	1421	1197	413	509	15	2.20
Babe Ruth	L	22	24	13	.649	2	41	38	35	326	244	108	128	6	2.01
Carl Mays	R	25	22	9	.710	0	35	33	27	289	230	74	91	2	1.74
Dutch Leonard	L	25	16	17	.485	1	37	36	26	294	257	72	144	4	2.17
Ernie Shore	R	26	13	10	.565	1	29	27	14	227	201	55	57	1	2.22
Rube Foster (AJ)	R	29	8	7	.533	0	17	16	9	125	108	53	34	1	2.52
Herb Pennock	L	23	5	5	.500	1	24	5	4	101	90	23	35	1	3.30
Lore Bader (BJ)	R	29	2	0	1.000	0	15	1	0	38	48	18	14	0	2.37
Sad Sam Jones	R	24	0	1	.000	0	9	1	0	16	15	6	5	0	4.50
Weldon Wyckoff	R	25	0	0	—	0	1	0	0	5	4	1	1	0	1.80

NAME	G by Pos	B	AGE	G	AB	R	H	2B	3B	HR	RBI	BB	SO	SB	BA	SA
CLEVELAND	**3rd 88-66 .571 12**										**LEE FOHL**					
	TOTALS		25	156	4994	584	1224	218	64	13	475	594	596	210	.245	.322
Joe Harris	1B95,OF5,3B1	R	26	112	369	40	112	22	4	0	65	55	32	11	.304	.385
Bill Wambsganss	2B138,1B2	R	23	141	499	52	127	17	6	0	43	37	42	16	.255	.313
Ray Chapman	SS156	R	26	156	563	98	170	28	13	2	36	61	65	52	.302	.409
Joe Evans	3B127	R	22	132	385	36	73	4	5	2	33	44	44	12	.190	.242
Braggo Roth	OF135	R	24	145	495	69	141	30	9	1	62	52	73	51	.285	.388
Tris Speaker	OF142	L	29	142	523	90	184	42	11	2	60	67	14	30	.352	.486
Jack Graney	OF145	L	31	146	535	87	122	29	7	3	35	94	49	16	.228	.325
Steve O'Neill	C127	R	25	129	370	21	68	10	2	0	29	41	55	2	.184	.222
Lou Guisto (MS)	1B59	R	22	73	200	9	37	4	2	0	29	25	18	3	.185	.225
Terry Turner	3B40,2B23,SS1	R	36	69	180	16	37	7	0	0	15	14	18	4	.206	.244
Josh Billings	C48	R	25	66	129	8	23	3	2	0	9	8	21	2	.178	.233
2 Elmer Smith	OF40	L	24	64	161	21	42	5	1	3	22	13	18	6	.261	.360
Milo Allison	OF11	R	26	32	35	4	5	0	0	0	0	3	5	1	.143	.143
Ivon Howard	3B6,2B4,OF4	B	34	27	39	7	4	0	0	0	3	5	1	1	.103	.103
Hank DeBerry	C9	R	22	25	33	3	9	2	0	0	1	2	7	0	.273	.333
1 Ray Miller	1B4	L	29	19	21	1	4	1	0	0	8	3	6	0	.190	.238
Marty Kavanagh	OF2	R	26	14	14	1	4	0	0	0	1	0	0	0	.000	.000
Ford Eunick	3B1	R	25	1	2	0	0	0	0	0	0	0	0	0	.000	.000

NAME	T	AGE	W	L	PCT	SV	G	GS	CG	IP	H	BB	SO	SHO	ERA
		26	88	66	.571	20	156	156	74	1413	1270	438	451	19	2.52
Jim Bagby	R	27	23	13	.639	6	49	37	26	321	277	73	83	7	1.96
Stan Coveleski	R	27	19	14	.576	4	45	36	25	298	202	94	133	9	1.81
Ed Klepfer	R	29	14	4	.778	1	41	27	9	213	208	55	66	1	2.37
Guy Morton	R	24	10	10	.500	2	35	18	6	161	158	59	62	1	2.74
Fritz Coumbe	L	27	8	6	.571	4	34	10	4	134	119	35	30	1	2.15
Otis Lambeth	R	27	7	6	.538	2	26	10	2	97	97	30	27	0	3.15
Al Gould	R	24	4	4	.500	0	27	7	1	90	95	52	24	0	3.64
Red Torkelson	R	23	2	1	.667	0	4	3	0	22	33	13	10	0	7.77
Joe Boehling	L	26	1	6	.143	0	12	7	1	46	50	16	11	0	4.70
Pop Boy Smith	R	25	0	0	.000	0	9	0	0	14	14	3	3	0	8.00
Smoky Joe Wood (SA)	R	27	0	0	.000	1	5	1	0	16	17	7	2	0	3.38
George Dickerson	R	24	0	0	—	0	1	0	0	6	4	1	3	0	0.00

DETROIT 4th 78-75 .510 21.5 — HUGHIE JENNINGS

NAME	G by Pos	B	AGE	G	AB	R	H	2B	3B	HR	RBI	BB	SO	SB	BA	SA
TOTALS			28	154	5093	639	1317	204	76	26	535	483	476	163	.259	.344
George Burns	1B104	R	24	119	407	42	92	14	10	1	40	15	33	3	.226	.317
Ralph Young	2B141	B	28	141	503	64	116	18	2	1	35	61	35	8	.231	.280
Donie Bush	SS147	B	29	147	581	112	163	18	3	0	24	80	40	34	.281	.322
Ossie Vitt	3B140	R	27	140	512	65	130	13	6	0	47	56	15	18	.254	.303
Harry Heilmann	OF123, 1B27	R	22	150	556	57	156	22	11	5	86	41	54	11	.281	.387
Ty Cobb	OF152	L	30	152	588	107	225	44	24	6	102	61	34	55	.383	.570
Bobby Veach	OF154	L	29	154	571	79	182	31	12	8	103	61	44	21	.319	.457
Oscar Stanage	C95	R	34	99	297	19	61	14	1	0	30	20	35	3	.205	.259
Tubby Spencer	C62	R	33	70	192	13	46	8	3	0	22	15	15	0	.240	.313
Sam Crawford	1B15,OF3	L	37	61	104	6	18	4	2	0	12	4	6	0	.173	.269
George Harper	OF31	L	25	47	117	6	24	3	0	0	12	11	15	2	.205	.231
Bob Jones	2B18, 3B8	R	27	46	77	16	12	1	2	0	2	4	8	3	.156	.221
Ben Dyer	SS14, 3B8	R	24	30	67	6	14	5	0	0	0	2	17	1	.209	.284
Archie Yelle	C24	R	25	25	51	4	7	1	0	0	5	4	2		.137	.157
Fred Nicholson	OF3	R	22	13	14	4	4	1	0	1	1	2	0		.286	.357
Bert Ellison	1B9	R	20	9	29	2	5	1	2	1	4	6	3	0	.172	.448
Ira Flagstead	OF2	R	23	4	4	0	0	0	0	0	0	0	1	0	.000	.000
2 Tony DeFate	2B1	R	22	3	2	1	0	0	0	0	0	0	1	0	.173	.269
Frank Walker		R	22	2	2	0	0	0	0	0	0	0	0	1	.000	.000

NAME	T	AGE	W	L	PCT	SV	G	GS	CG	IP	H	BB	SO	SHO	ERA
		26	78	75	.510	15	154	154	78	1396	1209	504	516	20	2.56
Hooks Dauss	R	27	17	14	.548	2	37	31	22	271	243	87	102	6	2.42
Bernie Boland	R	25	16	11	.593	6	43	28	13	238	192	95	89	3	2.68
Bill James	R	30	13	10	.565	1	34	23	10	198	163	96	62	2	2.09
Willie Mitchell	L	27	12	8	.600	0	30	22	12	185	172	46	80	5	2.19
Howard Ehmke	R	23	10	15	.400	2	35	25	13	206	174	88	90	4	2.97
Deacon Jones	R	24	4	4	.500	0	24	6	2	77	69	26	28	0	2.92
Harry Coveleski	L	31	4	6	.400	1	16	11	2	69	70	14	15	0	2.61
George Cunningham	R	22	2	7	.222	4	44	8	4	139	113	51	49	0	2.91
Johnny Couch	R	26	0	0	—	0	3	0	0	13	13	1	1	0	2.77

WASHINGTON 5th 74-79 .484 25.5 — CLARK GRIFFITH

NAME	G by Pos	B	AGE	G	AB	R	H	2B	3B	HR	RBI	BB	SO	SB	BA	SA
TOTALS			28	157	5142	543	1238	173	70	4	462	500	574	166	.241	.304
Joe Judge	1B100	L	23	102	393	62	112	15	15	2	30	50	40	17	.285	.415
Ray Morgan	2B95, 3B3	R	28	101	338	32	90	9	1	1	33	40	29	7	.266	.308
Howard Shanks	SS90, OF26, 1B2	R	26	126	430	45	87	15	5	0	28	33	37	15	.202	.260
Eddie Foster	3B86, 2B57	R	30	143	554	66	130	16	8	0	43	46	23	11	.235	.292
Sam Rice	OF155	L	27	155	586	77	177	25	7	0	69	50	41	35	.302	.369
Clyde Milan	OF153	L	31	155	579	60	170	15	4	0	48	58	26	20	.294	.333
Mike Menosky	OF94	L	22	114	322	46	83	12	10	1	34	45	55	22	.258	.366
Eddie Ainsmith	C119	R	27	125	350	38	67	17	4	0	42	40	48	16	.191	.263
Joe Leonard	3B67, 1B20, SS1, OF1	L	22	99	297	30	57	6	7	0	23	45	40	6	.192	.259
Patsy Gharrity	1B46, C5, OF1	R	25	76	176	15	50	5	0	0	18	14	18	7	.284	.313
John Henry	C59	R	27	65	163	10	31	6	0	0	18	24	16	1	.190	.227
George McBride	SS41, 3B6, 2B2	R	36	50	141	6	27	3	0	0	9	10	17	1	.191	.213
1 Elmer Smith	OF29	L	24	35	117	8	26	4	3	0	17	5	14	1	.222	.308
Sam Crane	SS32	R	22	32	95	6	17	2	0	0	4	4	14	0	.179	.200
Horace Milan	OF23	R	23	31	73	8	21	3	1	0	9	4	9	4	.288	.356
Charlie Jamieson	OF9,P1	R	24	20	35	4	6	2	0	0	2	6	5	0	.171	.229
Bill Murray	2B6, SS1	B	23	8	21	2	3	1	0	0	4	2	1	1	.143	.238

NAME	T	AGE	W	L	PCT	SV	G	GS	CG	IP	H	BB	SO	SHO	ERA
		24	74	79	.484	7	157	157	84	1413	1217	537	637	20	2.75
Walter Johnson	R	29	23	16	.590	1	47	34	30	326	248	68	188	8	2.21
Jim Shaw	R	23	15	14	.517	1	47	31	15	266	233	123	118	2	3.21
Doc Ayres	R	26	11	10	.524	1	40	15	12	208	192	59	78	3	2.16
Harry Harper	L	22	11	12	.478	0	31	31	10	179	145	106	99	4	3.02
Bert Gallia	R	25	9	13	.409	1	42	23	9	208	191	93	84	1	2.99
George Dumont	R	21	5	14	.263	1	37	23	8	205	171	76	65	2	2.55
Molly Craft	R	21	0	0	—	1	8	0	0	14	17	8	2	0	3.86
Doc Waldbauer	R	25	0	0	—	1	2	0	0	5	10	2	2	0	7.20
1 Charlie Jamieson	L	24	0	0	—	1	2	1	0	2	10	2	1	0	45.00

NEW YORK 6th 71-82 .464 28.5 — WILD BILL DONOVAN

NAME	G by Pos	B	AGE	G	AB	R	H	2B	3B	HR	RBI	BB	SO	SB	BA	SA
TOTALS			27	155	5136	524	1226	172	52	27	445	496	535	136	.239	.308
Wally Pipp	1B155	R	24	155	587	82	143	29	12	9	70	60	66	11	.244	.380
Fritz Maisel	2B100,3B7	R	27	113	404	46	80	4	9	0	20	36	18	29	.198	.228
Roger Peckinpaugh	SS148	R	26	148	543	63	141	24	7	0	41	64	46	17	.260	.330
Frank Baker	3B146	L	31	146	553	57	156	24	2	6	71	48	27	18	.282	.365
Elmer Miller	OF112	R	30	114	379	43	95	11	3	3	35	40	44	11	.251	.319
Tim Hendryx	OF107	R	26	125	393	49	98	14	7	5	44	62	45	6	.249	.359
Hugh High	OF100	L	29	103	365	37	86	11	6	1	19	48	31	8	.236	.307
Les Nunamaker	C91	R	28	104	310	22	81	9	2	0	33	21	25	5	.261	.303
Ray Caldwell	P32,OF8	L	29	63	124	12	32	6	1	2	12	16	16	2	.258	.371
Roxy Walters	C57	R	24	61	171	16	45	2	0	0	14	9	22	2	.263	.275
Frank Gilhooley (AJ-BC)	OF46	L	25	54	165	14	40	6	1	0	8	30	13	6	.242	.291
1 Lee Magee	OF50	R	27	58	173	17	38	4	1	0	8	13	18	3	.220	.254
Paddy Baumann	2B18,OF7,3B1	R	31	49	110	10	24	2	1	0	8	7	13	4	.218	.255
Joe Gedeon	2B31	R	23	33	117	15	28	7	0	0	8	7	13	4	.239	.299
2 Armando Marsans (BL)	OF25	R	30	25	88	10	20	4	0	0	15	8	3	6	.227	.273
Walt Alexander (RJ)	C20	R	26	20	51	1	7	2	1	0	4	4	11	1	.137	.216
Angel Aragon	OF6,3B4,SS2	R	26	14	45	2	3	1	0	0	2	2	4	0	.067	.089
Chick Fewster	2B11	R	21	11	36	2	8	0	0	0	1	5	5	1	.222	.222
Bill Lamar	OF11	L	20	11	41	2	10	0	0	0	3	0	2	1	.244	.244
Sammy Vick	OF10	R	22	10	36	4	10	3	0	0	2	1	6	2	.278	.361
Aaron Ward	SS7	R	20	8	26	0	3	0	0	0	1	1	5	0	.115	.115
Muddy Ruel	C6	R	21	6	17	1	2	0	0	0	1	2	2	1	.118	.118
Howie Camp	OF5	L	24	5	21	4	6	0	0	0	2	0	2	0	.286	.333

Rube Oldring (VR) 33

NAME	T	AGE	W	L	PCT	SV	G	GS	CG	IP	H	BB	SO	SHO	ERA
		27	71	82	.464	6	155	155	87	1411	1280	427	571	9	2.66
Bob Shawkey	R	27	13	15	.464	0	32	26	16	236	207	72	97	2	2.44
Ray Caldwell	R	29	13	16	.448	1	32	29	21	236	199	76	102	1	2.86
George Mogridge	L	28	9	11	.450	0	29	25	15	196	185	39	46	1	2.98
Urban Shocker	R	26	8	5	.615	1	26	13	7	145	124	46	68	0	2.61
Ray Fisher	R	29	8	9	.471	0	23	18	12	144	126	43	64	3	2.19
Allen Russell	R	23	7	8	.467	2	25	10	6	104	89	39	55	0	2.25
Slim Love	L	26	6	5	.545	1	33	9	2	130	115	57	82	0	2.35
Nick Cullop	L	29	5	9	.357	0	30	18	5	146	161	31	27	2	3.33
Ed Monroe	R	24	1	0	1.000	1	9	1	1	29	35	6	12	0	3.41
Neal Brady	R	20	1	0	1.000	0	1	1	0	9	6	3	4	0	2.00
Bob McGraw	R	22	0	1	.000		2			11	9	3		0	0.82
Jack Enright	R	21	0	1	.000		1	1	1	1		3	5	2	5.40
Bill Piercy	R	21	0	1	.000		1	1	1	1		3	9	2	3.00
Hank Thormahlen	R	20	0	1			1	1	0	8	6	2	1	0	2.25
Walt Smallwood	R	24	0	0	—		2			1	1	1	1	0	0.00

ST. LOUIS 7th 57-97 .370 43 — FIELDER JONES

NAME	G by Pos	B	AGE	G	AB	R	H	2B	3B	HR	RBI	BB	SO	SB	BA	SA
TOTALS			28	155	5090	511	1249	183	63	15	425	405	540	157	.245	.315
George Sisler	1B133,2B2	L	24	135	539	60	190	30	9	2	52	30	19	37	.353	.453
Del Pratt	2B119,1B4	R	29	123	540	40	111	22	8	1	53	33	36	18	.247	.338
Doc Lavan (AJ)	SS110,2B7	R	26	118	355	19	85	8	5	0	30	19	34	5	.239	.290
Jimmy Austin	3B121,SS6	B	37	125	455	61	109	18	8	0	19	50	46	13	.240	.314
Tod Sloan	OF77	R	26	109	313	32	72	6	2	2	25	28	34	8	.230	.281
Baby Doll Jacobson	OF131,1B11	R	26	148	529	53	131	23	7	4	55	31	67	10	.248	.340
Burt Shotton	OF107	L	32	118	398	47	89	7	1	0	20	62	47	16	.224	.259
Hank Severeid	C139,1B1	R	26	143	501	45	133	23	4	1	57	28	20	6	.265	.333
Ernie Johnson	SS39,2B18,3B14	L	29	80	199	28	49	6	2	2	20	12	16	13	.246	.327
Bill Rumler	OF9	R	26	78	88	7	23	3	4	1	16	8	9	2	.261	.420
1 Armando Marsans	OF67,3B5,2B1	R	30	75	257	31	59	12	0	0	20	20	6	11	.230	.276
Earl Smith	OF51	R	26	52	199	31	56	7	0	0	10	15	21	5	.281	.387
Ward Miller	OF25	L	32	43	82	13	17	1	1	1	8	16	15	7	.207	.280
George Hale	C28	R	22	38	61	4	12	2	1	0	8	10	12	0	.197	.262
2 Lee Magee	3B20,2B6,1B5,OF1	B	28	36	112	11	19	1	0	0	4	6	6	3	.170	.179
Grover Hartley (JT)	C4,SS1,3B1	R	28	19	13	2	3	0	0	0	0	2	1	0	.231	.231
Ray Demmitt	OF14	L	33	14	53	6	15	1	2	0	7	0	8	1	.283	.377
Wally Gerber	SS12,2B2	R	25	14	39	2	12	1	1	0	3	2	3	1	.308	.385
1 Gene Paulette	1B5,2B3,3B1	R	26	14	11	1	2	0	0	0	0	3	1	1	.182	.182
Duke Kenworthy	2B4	B	30	5	10	1	1	0	0	0	0	1	1	1	.100	.100

Scrappy Moore 24 R 1-8, Ed Murray 21 R 0-1, Ott Neu 22 R 0-0, Tom Richardson 23 R 0-1, Ivan Bigler 24 R 0-0

NAME	T	AGE	W	L	PCT	SV	G	GS	CG	IP	H	BB	SO	SHO	ERA
		27	57	97	.370	12	155	155	65	1385	1320	537	429	12	3.20
Dave Davenport	R	27	17	17	.500	2	47	39	19	281	273	105	100	3	3.07
Allan Sothoron	R	24	14	19	.424	4	48	33	17	277	259	96	85	3	2.83
Bob Groom	R	32	8	19	.296	3	38	28	11	233	193	95	82	4	2.94
Ernie Koob	L	24	6	14	.300	1	39	18	3	134	139	57	47	1	3.90
Eddie Plank	L	41	5	6	.455	1	20	13	8	131	105	38	26	1	1.79
Tom Rogers	R	25	3	6	.333	0	24	8	3	109	112	44	27	0	3.88
Grover Lowdermilk	R	32	2	1	.667	0	3	2	2	19	16	4	9	1	1.42
Jim Park	R	24	1	1	.500	0	13	0	0	27	12	9	6	0	6.75
Carl Weilman (IL)	R	27	1	2	.333	0	5	3	3	19	19	6	9	0	1.89
Speed Martin	R	23	0	1	.000	0	9	2	0	16	20	5	5	0	5.63
Earl Hamilton	L	25	0	9	.000	1	27	8	2	83	86	41	19	0	3.14
Rasty Wright	R	21	0	0	—	0	16	1	0	40	48	10	5	0	5.40
Vince Molyneaux (JT)	R	28	0	0	—	2	3	0	0	22	18	20	4	0	4.91
Tim McCabe (IL)	R	22	0	1	.000	0	1	0	0	1	3	4	1	0	27.00
Kewpie Pennington	R	20	0	0	—	0	1	0	0	1	0	1	0	0	0.00

PHILADELPHIA 8th 55-98 .359 44.5 — CONNIE MACK

NAME	G by Pos	B	AGE	G	AB	R	H	2B	3B	HR	RBI	BB	SO	SB	BA	SA
TOTALS			26	154	5111	527	1296	177	62	17	457	435	519	112	.254	.322
Stuffy McInnis	1B150	R	26	150	567	50	172	19	4	0	44	33	19	18	.303	.351
Roy Grover	2B139	R	25	141	482	45	108	15	7	0	34	43	53	12	.224	.284
Whitey Witt	SS111, OF7,3B6	R	21	128	452	62	114	13	4	0	28	65	45	12	.252	.299
Ray Bates	3B124	R	27	127	485	47	115	20	7	2	66	21	39	12	.237	.320
2 Charlie Jamieson	OF83	L	24	85	345	41	92	6	0	0	27	37	36	8	.267	.296
Amos Strunk	OF146	L	28	148	540	83	152	26	7	1	45	68	37	16	.281	.361
Ping Bodie	OF145, 1B1	R	29	148	557	50	162	28	11	7	74	53	40	13	.291	.418
Wally Schang	C79, 3B12, OF7	B	27	118	316	41	90	14	9	3	36	29	46	6	.285	.415
Billy Meyer	C55	R	24	62	162	9	38	5	1	0	9	7	14	0	.235	.284
Bill Johnson	OF30	R	24	48	109	7	19	2	2	1	8	8	14	4	.174	.257
Joe Dugan	SS39, 2B2	R	20	43	134	9	26	8	0	0	16	3	16	2	.194	.254
Pat Haley	C34	R	26	41	98	7	27	2	1	0	11	4	12	2	.276	.316
Otis Lawry	2B17, OF1	L	23	30	55	7	9	0	0	0	1	4	9	2	.164	.182
Buck Thrasher	OF22	L	27	23	77	5	18	2	1	0	3	3	12	0	.234	.286
Pug Griffin	1B3	L	21	18	25	4	5	1	0	0	2	0	3	0	.200	.360
Lee Gooch	OF16	R	27	17	59	4	17	2	0	0	5	8	9	0	.288	.373
Eddie Palmer	3B13, SS1	R	24	16	52	7	11	2	0	0	5	7	7	1	.212	.231
Ralph Sharman	OF10	L	22	15	59	7	13	1	1	0	7	3	14	1	.297	.405
Red Shannon	SS10	B	20	11	35	8	10	0	0	0	7	6	9	2	.286	.286
Wickey McAvoy	C8	R	22	10	24	1	6	1	0	0	2	0	5	0	.250	.417
Cy Perkins	C6	R	21	6	18	1	3	0	0	0	0	2	1	0	.167	.167
Gene Bailey		R	23	5	12	1	1	0	0	0	1	1	6	1	.083	.083

Pat French 23 R 0-2, Windy Bradshaw 21 L 0-4, Val Picinich 20 R 2-6, Harry Davis 43 R 0-1

NAME	T	AGE	W	L	PCT	SV	G	GS	CG	IP	H	BB	SO	SHO	ERA
		26	55	98	.359	6	154	154	80	1366	1310	562	516	8	3.27
Bullet Joe Bush	R	24	11	17	.393	1	37	31	17	233	207	111	121	4	2.47
Win Noyes	R	28	10	10	.500	1	27	24	11	156	157	64	64	1	2.95
Jing Johnson	R	22	9	12	.429	0	34	23	13	191	184	56	55	0	2.78
Elmer Myers	R	23	9	16	.360	3	38	23	13	202	221	79	88	2	4.41
Rube Schauer	R	26	7	16	.304	0	33	21	10	215	209	69	62	0	3.14
Socks Seibold	R	21	4	16	.200	1	33	15	9	160	141	85	55	1	3.94
Rollie Naylor	R	25	2	2	.500	0	5	5	3	33	30	11	11	0	1.64
Cy Falkenberg	R	37	2	6	.250	0	15	8	4	81	86	26	35	0	3.33
Dave Keefe	R	20	1	0	1.000	0	2	1	1	13	6	6	3	0	1.80
Rube Parnham	R	23	0	1	.000	0	2	1	1	12	9	4	4	0	4.09
Walt Johnson	R	21	0	1	.000	0	4	1	0	14	16	15	8	0	7.07
Walter Anderson	L	19	0	0	—	0	14	2	0	39	32	21	10	0	3.00
Jack Nabors	R	22	0	0	—	0	1	0	0	1	3	2	0	0	9.00
Eddie Bacon	R	22	0	0	—	0	1	0	0	1	1	0	0	0	6.00
Red Hill	L	24	0	0	—	0	1	0	1	5	11	6	0	0	6.00

NEW YORK 1ST 98-56 .636 — JOHN McGRAW

NAME	G by Pos	B	AGE	G	AB	R	H	2B	3B	HR	RBI	BB	SO	SB	BA	SA
TOTALS			28	158	5211	635	1360	170	71	39	537	373	533	162	.261	.343
Walter Holke	1B153	B	24	153	527	55	146	12	7	2	55	34	54	13	.277	.338
Buck Herzog	2B113	R	31	114	417	69	98	10	8	2	31	31	36	12	.235	.312
Art Fletcher	SS151	R	32	151	557	70	145	24	5	4	56	23	28	12	.260	.343
Heinie Zimmerman	3B149, 2B5	R	30	150	585	61	174	22	9	5	102	16	43	13	.297	.391
Dave Robertson	OF140	L	27	142	532	64	138	16	9	12	54	10	47	17	.259	.391
Benny Kauff	OF153	R	27	153	559	89	172	22	4	5	68	59	54	30	.308	.388
George Burns	OF152	R	27	152	597	103	180	25	13	5	45	75	55	40	.302	.412
Bill Rariden	C100	R	29	101	266	20	72	10	1	0	25	42	17	3	.271	.316
Lew McCarty	C54	R	28	56	162	15	40	3	2	2	19	14	6	1	.247	.327
Hans Lobert	3B21	R	35	50	52	4	10	1	0	1	5	5	5	2	.192	.269
Jimmy Smith	2B29, SS7	B	22	36	96	12	22	5	1	0	2	9	18	6	.229	.302
George Gibson	C35	R	36	35	82	1	14	3	0	0	5	7	2	1	.171	.207
3 Joe Wilhoit	OF11	L	31	34	50	9	17	2	2	0	8	8	5	0	.340	.460
1 Pete Kilduff	2B21, SS5, 3B1	R	24	31	78	12	16	3	0	1	12	4	11	2	.205	.282
2 Jim Thorpe	OF18	R	30	26	57	12	11	3	2	0	4	8	10	1	.193	.316
Red Murray	OF11,C1	R	33	22	22	1	1	1	0	0	3	4	3	0	.045	.091
Al Baird	2B7, SS3	R	22	20	24	1	7	0	0	0	4	2	2	2	.292	.292
Jack Onslow	C9	R	28	9	8	1	2	1	0	0	0	0	1	0	.250	.375
1 Ernie Krueger	C6	R	26	8	10	0	0	0	0	0	0	0	4	0	.000	.000
Ed Hemingway	3B7	B	24	7	25	3	8	1	1	0	1	2	1	1	.320	.440
Joe Rodriguez	1B7	R	22	7	20	2	4	0	1	0	2	2	3	0	.200	.300
Ross Youngs	OF7	L	20	7	26	5	9	2	3	0	1	1	5	1	.346	.654

NAME	T	AGE	W	L	PCT	SV	G	GS	CG	IP	H	BB	SO	SHO	ERA
		29	98	56	.631	14	158	158	92	1427	1221	327	551	17	2.27
Ferdie Schupp	L	26	21	7	.750	0	36	32	25	272	202	70	147	6	1.95
Slim Sallee	L	32	18	7	.720	0	34	24	18	216	199	34	54	1	2.17
Pol Perritt	R	25	17	7	.708	0	35	26	14	215	186	45	72	5	1.88
Rube Benton	R	27	15	9	.625	3	35	25	14	215	190	41	70	3	2.72
Jeff Tesreau	R	29	13	8	.619	2	33	20	11	184	168	58	85	1	3.08
Fred Anderson	R	31	8	8	.500	3	38	18	8	162	122	34	69	1	1.44
2 Al Demaree	R	32	4	5	.444	0	15	11	7	78	70	17	23	0	2.65
1 George Kelly	R	21	1	0	1.000	0	1	0	0	5	4	1	2	0	0.00
Jim Middleton	R	28	1	1	.500	1	13	0	0	36	35	8	9	0	2.75
Ad Swigler	R	21	0	1	.000	0	1	1	0	6	7	8	4	0	6.00
George Smith	R	25	0	3	.000	0	14	1	1	38	38	11	16	0	2.84

PHILADELPHIA 2nd 87-65 .572 10 — PAT MORAN

NAME	G by Pos	B	AGE	G	AB	R	H	2B	3B	HR	RBI	BB	SO	SB	BA	SA
TOTALS			31	154	5084	578	1262	225	60	38	526	435	533	109	.248	.339
Fred Luderus	1B154	L	31	154	522	57	136	24	4	5	72	65	35	5	.261	.351
Bart Niehoff	2B96, 1B7, 3B6	R	33	114	361	30	92	17	4	2	42	23	29	8	.255	.341
Dave Bancroft	SS120, 2B3, OF2	B	26	127	478	56	116	22	5	4	43	44	42	14	.243	.335
Milt Stock	3B133, SS19	R	23	150	564	76	149	27	6	3	53	51	34	25	.264	.349
Gavvy Cravath	OF139	R	36	140	503	70	141	29	16	12	83	70	57	6	.280	.473
Dode Paskert	OF138	R	35	141	546	78	137	27	11	4	43	62	63	19	.251	.363
Possum Whitted	OF141, 1B10, 2B1	R	27	149	553	69	155	24	9	4	70	30	56	10	.280	.373
Bill Killefer	C120	R	29	125	409	28	112	12	0	0	31	15	21	4	.274	.330
2 Wildfire Schulte	OF42	L	34	64	149	21	32	10	0	1	15	16	22	4	.215	.302
2 Johnny Evers (AJ)	2B49, 3B7	R	35	56	183	20	41	5	1	1	12	30	13	8	.224	.279
Oscar Dugey	2B15, OF4	R	29	44	72	12	14	4	1	0	9	4	9	2	.194	.278
Jack Adams	C38, 1B1	R	26	43	107	4	22	4	1	1	7	0	20	0	.206	.290
Claude Cooper	OF12	R	25	24	29	5	3	1	0	0	1	5	4	0	.103	.138
Ed Burns	C15	R	29	20	49	2	10	1	0	0	6	1	5	2	.204	.224
Patsy McGaffigan	SS17, OF1	R	28	19	60	5	10	1	0	0	6	0	7	1	.167	.183
1 Bobby Byrne	3B4	R	32	13	14	1	5	0	0	0	0	0	3	0	.357	.357
Harry Pearce	SS4	R	27	7	16	2	4	1	0	0	0	0	4	0	.250	.438

NAME	T	AGE	W	L	PCT	SV	G	GS	CG	IP	H	BB	SO	SHO	ERA
		29	87	65	.572	5	154	154	103	1389	1258	327	617	22	2.46
Pete Alexander	R	30	30	13	.698	0	45	44	35	388	336	58	201	8	1.86
Eppa Rixey	L	26	16	21	.432	1	39	36	23	281	249	67	121	4	2.27
Joe Oeschger	R	25	15	14	.517	1	42	30	18	262	241	72	123	5	2.75
Erskine Mayer	R	27	11	6	.647	0	28	18	11	160	160	33	64	1	2.76
Chief Bender	R	34	8	2	.800	2	20	10	8	113	84	26	43	1	1.67
Jimmy Lavender	R	33	6	8	.429	1	28	14	7	129	119	44	52	0	3.56
Paul Fittery	L	29	1	1	.500	0	17	2	1	56	69	27	13	0	4.50
Stan Baumgartner (VR) 24															

ST. LOUIS 3rd 82-70 .539 15 — MILLER HUGGINS

NAME	G by Pos	B	AGE	G	AB	R	H	2B	3B	HR	RBI	BB	SO	SB	BA	SA
TOTALS			25	154	5083	571	1271	159	93	26	436	359	652	159	.250	.333
2 Gene Paulette	1B93	R	26	95	332	32	88	21	7	0	34	16	16	9	.265	.370
Dots Miller	2B92, 1B46, SS11	R	30	148	544	61	135	15	9	2	45	33	52	14	.248	.320
Rogers Hornsby	SS144	R	21	145	523	86	171	24	17	8	66	45	34	17	.327	.484
2 Doug Baird	3B103, OF2	R	25	104	364	38	92	19	12	0	24	23	52	18	.253	.371
Tommy Long	OF137	L	27	144	530	49	123	12	14	3	41	37	44	21	.232	.325
Jack Smith	OF128	L	22	137	462	64	137	16	11	3	34	38	65	25	.297	.398
Walton Cruise	OF152	L	27	153	529	70	156	20	10	5	59	38	73	16	.295	.399
Frank Snyder	C94	R	23	115	313	18	74	9	2	1	33	27	43	4	.236	.288
Bruno Betzel	2B75, OF23, 3B4	R	22	106	328	24	71	4	3	1	17	20	47	9	.216	.256
Mike Gonzalez	C68, 1B18, OF1	R	26	106	290	20	76	8	1	1	28	22	24	12	.262	.307
Fred Smith	3B51, 2B2, SS1	R	30	56	165	11	30	0	2	1	17	17	22	4	.182	.224
Bob Bescher	OF32	R	33	42	110	10	17	1	1	1	8	20	13	3	.155	.209
2 Red Smyth	OF23	L	26	38	72	5	15	0	2	0	4	4	9	3	.208	.264
1 Tony DeFate	3B5, 2B1	R	22	14	14	0	2	0	0	0	1	0	5	0	.143	.143
Stuffy Stewart	OF7, 2B2	R	23	13	9	4	0	0	0	0	0	0	4	0	.000	.000
Bobby Wallace	3B5, SS2	R	43	8	10	0	1	0	0	0	2	0	1	0	.100	.100
John Brock	C4	R	20	7	15	4	6	1	0	0	2	2	2	2	.400	.467
Paddy Livingston	C6	R	37	7	20	0	4	0	0	0	2	0	1	2	.200	.200
Ike McAuley	SS3	R	25	7	7	0	2	0	0	0	1	0	1	0	.286	.286
Jack Roche	C1	R	26	7	7	0	0	0	0	0	0	0	0	0	.000	.000

NAME	T	AGE	W	L	PCT	SV	G	GS	CG	IP	H	BB	SO	SHO	ERA
		26	82	70	.539	10	154	154	66	1392	1257	421	502	16	3.03
Bill Doak	R	26	16	20	.444	2	44	37	16	281	257	85	111	3	3.11
Lee Meadows	R	22	15	9	.625	2	43	37	18	265	253	90	100	4	3.09
Red Ames	R	34	15	10	.600	3	43	19	10	209	189	57	62	2	2.71
Milt Watson	R	27	10	13	.435	0	41	20	5	161	149	51	45	3	3.52
Oscar Horstman	R	26	9	4	.692	1	35	11	4	138	111	54	50	1	3.46
2 Gene Packard	R	29	9	6	.600	0	34	11	6	153	138	25	44	0	2.47
Marv Goodwin	R	26	6	4	.600	0	14	12	6	85	70	19	38	3	2.22
George Pierce	R	29	1	1	.500	0	10	7	3	42	33	19	23	0	3.60
1 Bob Steele	R	23	1	3	.250	0	12	6	1	42	33	19	23	0	3.21
Jakie May	L	21	0	0	—	0	3	0	0	29	29	11	18	0	3.41
Lou North	R	26	0	0	—	0	5	0	0	14	14	4	4	0	4.09
Bruce Hitt	L	19	0	0	—	0	2	0	0	4	7	1	1	0	9.00
Tim Murchison	L	20	0	1	.000	0	1	0	0	2	2	2	1	0	0.00

CINCINNATI 4th 78-76 .506 20 — CHRISTY MATHEWSON

NAME	G by Pos	B	AGE	G	AB	R	H	2B	3B	HR	RBI	BB	SO	SB	BA	SA
TOTALS			29	157	5251	601	1385	196	100	26	513	312	477	153	.264	.354
Hal Chase	1B151	R	34	154	602	71	167	28	15	4	86	15	49	21	.277	.394
Dave Shean	2B131	R	39	131	442	36	93	9	2	5	35	22	39	10	.210	.267
Larry Kopf	SS145	B	26	148	573	81	146	19	8	2	26	28	48	17	.255	.326
Heinie Groh	3B154, 2B2	R	27	156	599	91	182	39	11	6	53	71	30	15	.304	.411
Tommy Griffith	OF100	L	27	115	363	45	98	18	7	1	45	19	23	5	.270	.366
Edd Roush	OF134	L	24	136	522	82	178	19	14	4	67	27	24	21	.341	.454
Greasy Neale	OF119	R	25	121	385	40	113	14	9	3	30	24	36	25	.294	.400
Ivy Wingo	C120	L	26	121	399	37	106	16	11	2	39	25	13	9	.266	.376
1 Jim Thorpe	OF69	R	30	77	251	29	62	2	8	4	36	6	35	11	.247	.367
Tommy Clark	C29	R	29	58	110	11	32	3	3	1	13	11	12	2	.291	.400
Manuel Cueto	OF38, 2B6, C5	R	25	56	140	10	28	3	0	1	11	16	17	4	.200	.243
Bill McKechnie (BH)	2B26, SS13, 3B4	R	30	48	134	11	34	3	1	0	15	7	7	5	.254	.291
Clarence Mitchell	P32, 1B6, OF5	L	26	47	90	13	25	3	0	0	5	5	5	0	.278	.311
2 Sherry Magee	OF41, 1B2	R	32	45	137	17	44	8	4	0	23	16	7	4	.321	.438
Emil Huhn	C15	R	25	23	52	2	10	1	2	0	1	2	5	1	.196	.294
Dutch Ruether	P7	L	23	19	24	1	5	2	0	0	1	3	6	1	.208	.292
Harry Smith	C7	R	27	17	17	0	2	0	0	0	1	1	0	0	.118	.118
Gus Getz	2B4, 3B3	R	27	7	14	2	4	0	0	0	2	0	3	0	.286	.286

NAME	T	AGE	W	L	PCT	SV	G	GS	CG	IP	H	BB	SO	SHO	ERA
		25	78	76	.506	6	157	157	94	1405	1363	404	492	11	2.66
Fred Toney	R	28	24	16	.600	1	43	42	31	340	300	77	123	7	2.20
Pete Schneider	R	24	20	19	.513	0	46	42	25	342	316	119	142	0	1.97
Mike Regan	R	29	11	10	.524	0	32	26	16	216	228	41	50	1	2.71
Hod Eller	R	22	10	5	.667	1	31	11	7	152	131	37	77	1	2.37
Clarence Mitchell	L	26	9	15	.375	1	32	20	10	159	166	34	37	2	3.23
Jimmy Ring	R	22	3	9	.300	2	24	7	3	88	90	35	33	0	4.40
Dutch Reuther	L	23	1	2	.333	0	7	4	0	36	43	14	12	0	3.50
Roy Sanders	R	24	1	0	1.000	0	2	1	0	14	12	16	3	0	4.50
Joe Engel	R	24	1	1	.500	1	8	1	1	28	12	6	2	0	5.63
Ellmer Knetzer	R	31	0	0	—	1	11	0	0	27	28	12	7	0	3.00
2 Scott Perry	R	26	0	0	—	0	3	1	0	13	17	8	4	0	6.92
Rube Bressler	R	22	0	0	—	0	9	0	0	9	15	5	2	0	6.00
Herman Pillette	R	20	0	0	—	0	1	0	0	2	3	0	1	0	18.00

CHICAGO 5th 74-80 .481 24 — FRED MITCHELL

NAME	G by Pos	B	AGE	G	AB	R	H	2B	3B	HR	RBI	BB	SO	SB	BA	SA
TOTALS			28	157	5135	552	1229	194	67	17	458	415	599	127	.239	.313
2 Fred Merkle	1B140, OF6	R	28	146	549	65	146	30	9	3	57	42	60	13	.266	.370
Larry Doyle	2B128	L	31	135	476	48	121	19	5	6	61	48	28	5	.254	.353
Chuck Wortman	SS65, 2B1, 3B1	R	25	75	190	24	33	4	1	0	9	18	23	6	.174	.205
Charlie Deal	3B130	R	25	135	449	46	114	15	3	0	47	19	18	10	.254	.292
Max Flack	OF117	L	27	131	447	65	111	18	7	0	21	51	34	17	.248	.320
Cy Williams	OF136	L	29	138	468	63	113	22	4	5	42	38	78	8	.241	.338
Les Mann	OF116	R	24	117	444	63	121	19	10	1	44	27	46	14	.273	.367
Art Wilson	C75	R	31	81	211	17	45	9	2	2	25	32	36	1	.213	.303
Harry Wolter	OF97, 1B1	L	32	117	353	44	88	15	7	0	28	38	40	7	.249	.331
Rollie Zeider	SS48, 3B23, 2B24, 1B1, OF1	R	33	108	354	36	86	14	2	0	27	28	30	17	.243	.294
Rowdy Elliott	C73	R	26	85	223	18	56	8	5	0	28	11	11	4	.251	.332
2 Pete Kilduff	SS51, 2B5	R	24	56	202	23	56	9	5	0	15	12	19	11	.277	.371
Pickles Dillhoefer	C37	R	23	42	95	3	12	1	0	0	8	2	9	1	.126	.158
1 Dutch Ruether	P10, 1B5	L	23	31	44	3	12	1	3	0	11	8	11	0	.273	.432
Morrie Schick	OF12	R	25	14	34	3	5	0	0	0	3	3	10	0	.147	.147
Paddy Driscoll	2B8, 3B2, SS1	R	22	13	41	2	10	0	0	0	1	2	9	1	.244	.244
Charlie Pechous	3B7, SS5	R	20	13	41	2	10	0	0	0	1	2	9	1	.244	.244
1 Harry Wolfe	OF2, SS1	R	24	9	5	1	2	0	0	0	1	0	5	0	.400	.400
Turner Barber	OF7	L	23	7	28	4	6	1	1	0	0	2	1	0	.214	.250
Roy Leslie	1B6	R	24	7	19	1	4	0	0	0	1	2	1	0	.211	.211
Vic Saier (BL)	1B6	L	26	6	21	5	5	1	0	2	0	1	0	1	.238	.286
Herb Hunter	2B1, 3B1	R	24	4	8	0	0	0	0	0	0	0	3	0	.000	.000
Bill Marriott	OF1	L	24	2	6	0	0	0	0	0	0	0	1	0	.000	.000

Bob O'Farrell 20 R 3-8, Jimmy Archer (VR) 34 R 0-2, Earl Blackburn 24 R 0-2

NAME	T	AGE	W	L	PCT	SV	G	GS	CG	IP	H	BB	SO	SHO	ERA
		27	74	80	.481	9	157	157	79	1404	1303	374	654	15	2.62
Hippo Vaughn	L	29	23	13	.639	0	41	38	27	296	255	91	195	5	2.01
Phil Douglas	R	25	14	20	.412	1	51	37	20	293	269	50	151	5	2.55
Claude Hendrix	R	28	10	12	.455	1	40	21	13	215	202	72	81	1	2.60
Vic Aldridge	R	23	6	6	.500	2	30	6	1	107	100	37	44	1	3.11
Tom Seaton	R	29	5	4	.556	1	16	9	3	75	60	23	27	1	2.52
Paul Carter	R	23	5	8	.385	2	23	13	6	113	115	19	34	0	3.27
1 Al Demaree	R	32	3	3	.357	1	24	18	6	141	125	37	43	1	2.55
Mike Pendergast	R	28	3	6	.333	1	35	8	1	99	112	21	43	0	3.36
1 Dutch Ruether	R	23	2	0	1.000	0	10	4	1	36	37	12	23	0	2.50
Harry Weaver	R	25	1	1	.500	0	4	1	0	20	17	7	8	1	2.70
Roy Walker	R	24	0	0	—	0	3	0	0	7	8	5	4	0	3.86
1 Gene Packard	L	29	0	0	—	0	2	0	0	2	0	1	0	0	9.00

NAME	G by Pos	B	AGE	G	AB	R	H	2B	3B	HR	RBI	BB	SO	SB	BA	SA
BOSTON 6th 72-81 .471 25.5	**GEORGE STALLINGS**		28	157	5201	536	1280	169	75	22	452	427	587	155	.246	.320
TOTALS																
Ed Konetchy (BL)	1B129	R	31	130	474	56	129	19	4	2	54	36	40	16	.272	.380
Johnny Rawlings	2B96, SS17, 3B1, OF1	R	24	122	371	37	95	9	4	2	31	38	32	12	.256	.318
Rabbit Maranville	SS142	R	25	142	561	69	146	19	13	3	43	40	47	27	.260	.357
Red Smith	3B147	R	27	147	505	60	149	31	6	2	62	53	61	16	.295	.392
Wally Rehg	OF86	R	28	86	341	48	92	12	6	1	31	24	32	6	.270	.349
Ray Powell	OF88	L	28	88	357	42	97	10	4	4	30	24	54	12	.272	.356
Joe Kelly	OF116	R	30	116	445	41	99	9	8	3	36	26	45	21	.222	.299
Walt Tragesser	C98	R	30	98	297	23	66	10	2	0	25	15	36	5	.222	.273
1 Sherry Magee	OF65, 1B2	R	32	72	246	24	63	8	4	1	29	13	23	7	.256	.333
Ed Fitzpatrick	2B22, OF19, 3B15	R	27	63	178	20	45	8	4	0	17	12	22	4	.253	.343
Lefty Tyler	P32, 1B11	L	27	61	134	8	31	4	0	1	11	17	19	2	.231	.261
1 Joe Wilhoit	OF52	L	31	54	186	20	51	5	0	1	10	17	15	5	.274	.317
Fred Bailey	OF27	R	21	50	110	9	21	2	1	1	5	9	25	3	.191	.255
Hank Gowdy (MS)	C49	R	27	49	154	12	33	7	0	0	14	15	13	2	.214	.260
George Twombly	OF29, 1B1	R	25	32	102	8	19	1	1	0	9	18	5	4	.186	.216
Mike Massey	2B25	B	23	31	91	12	18	0	0	0	2	15	15		.198	.198
2 Chief Meyers	C24	R	36	25	68	5	17	4	0	0	4	4	0	2	.250	.426
1 Johnny Evers	2B24	L	35	24	83	5	16	0	0	0	0	13	8	1	.193	.193
Sam Covington	1B17	L	22	17	66	8	13	2	0	1	10	5	5	1	.197	.273

Art Rico 21 R 4-14, Zip Collins 25 L 4-27, Larry Chappell 27 L 0-2, Hank Schreiber 26 R 2-7, Fred Jacklitsch 41 R 0-0

NAME	T	AGE	W	L	PCT	SV	G	GS	CG	IP	H	BB	SO	SHO	ERA
		27	72	81	.471	3	157	157	105	1425	1309	371	593	19	2.77
Art Nehf	L	24	17	8	.680	0	38	23	17	233	197	39	101	5	2.16
Lefty Tyler	L	27	14	12	.538	1	32	28	22	239	203	86	98	4	2.52
Dick Rudolph	R	28	13	13	.500	0	32	30	22	243	252	54	96	5	3.41
Jesse Barnes	R	24	13	21	.382	1	50	33	27	295	261	50	107	2	2.68
Pat Ragan	R	31	6	9	.400	1	30	13	5	148	138	35	61	1	2.92
Tom Hughes (XJ)	R	33	5	3	.625	0	11	8	6	74	54	30	40	2	1.95
Frank Allen	L	28	3	11	.214	0	29	14	2	112	124	47	56	0	3.94
Jack Scott	R	25	1	2	.333	0	7	3	3	40	36	5	21	0	1.80
Ed Reulbach	R	34	0	1	.000	0	5	2	0	22	21	15	9	0	2.86
Ed Walsh	R	36	0	1	.000	0	4	3	1	18	22	9	4	0	3.50
Cal Crum	R	27	0	1	—	0	1	1	1	1	1	1	0	0	0.00
Bill James (SJ) 25															
1 Scott Perry (JT) 26															

NAME	G by Pos	B	AGE	G	AB	R	H	2B	3B	HR	RBI	BB	SO	SB	BA	SA
BROOKLYN 7th 70-81 .464 26.5	**WILBERT ROBINSON**		29	156	5251	511	1299	159	78	25	429	334	527	130	.247	.322
TOTALS																
Jake Daubert	1B125	L	33	125	468	59	122	4	4	2	30	51	30	11	.261	.299
George Cutshaw	2B134	R	30	135	487	42	126	17	7	4	49	21	26	22	.259	.347
Ivy Olson	SS133, 3B6	R	31	139	580	64	156	18	5	2	38	14	34	6	.269	.328
Mike Mowrey	3B80, 2B2	R	33	83	271	20	58	9	5	0	25	29	25	7	.214	.284
Casey Stengel	OF150	L	26	150	549	69	141	23	12	6	73	60	62	18	.257	.375
Jim Hickman	OF101	R	25	114	370	46	81	15	4	6	36	17	66	14	.219	.330
Zack Wheat	OF98	L	29	109	362	38	113	15	11	1	41	20	18	5	.312	.423
Otto Miller	C91	R	28	92	274	19	63	5	4	1	17	14	29	5	.230	.288
Hy Myers (SJ)	OF66, 1B22, 2B19, 3B15	R	28	120	471	37	126	15	10	1	41	18	25	5	.268	.348
J. Johnston (XJ)92	1B14, SS4, 2B3, 3B3	R	27	103	330	33	89	10	4	0	25	23	28	16	.270	.324
Frank O'Rourke	3B58	R	25	64	198	18	47	7	1	0	15	14	25	11	.237	.283
1 Chief Meyers	C44	R	36	47	132	8	28	3	0	1	3	13	7	4	.212	.235
2 Ernie Krueger	C23	R	26	31	81	10	22	2	1	1	6	5	7	1	.272	.383
1 Red Smyth	3B4, OF2	L	26	29	24	5	3	0	0	0	1	4	6	0	.125	.125
Mack Wheat	C18, OF9	R	24	29	60	2	8	1	0	0	3	1	12	1	.133	.150
Bunny Fabrique	SS21	B	29	25	88	8	18	3	0	0	3	8	9	0	.205	.273

Jack Snyder 30 R 3-11, Bill Leard 31 R 0-3, 1 Fred Merkle 28 R 1-8, Lew Malone 20 R 0-0

NAME	T	AGE	W	L	PCT	SV	G	GS	CG	IP	H	BB	SO	SHO	ERA
		30	70	81	.464	9	156	156	99	1421	1288	405	582	7	2.78
Rube Marquard	L	30	19	12	.613	0	37	29	14	233	200	60	117	2	2.55
Leon Cadore	R	26	13	13	.500	3	37	30	21	264	231	63	115	1	2.45
Sherry Smith	L	26	12	12	.500	3	38	23	15	211	210	51	58	0	3.33
Jeff Pfeffer	R	29	11	15	.423	0	30	30	24	266	225	66	115	3	2.23
Larry Cheney	R	31	8	12	.400	2	35	24	14	210	185	73	102	1	2.36
Jack Coombs	R	34	7	11	.389	0	31	14	9	141	147	49	34	0	3.96
Jack Russell	L	22	0	1	.000	0	5	1	1	16	12	6	1	0	4.50
Johnny Miljus	R	22	0	1	.000	0	4	1	1	15	14	8	9	0	0.60
Wheezer Dell	R	31	0	4	.000	1	17	4	0	58	55	25	28	0	3.72
Paul Wachter	R	29	0	0	—	0	2	0	0	9	4	3	0	0	10.50
Rich Durning	L	24	0	0	—	0	1	0	0	1	0	1	0	0	0.00
Duster Mails (MS) 21															

NAME	G by Pos	B	AGE	G	AB	R	H	2B	3B	HR	RBI	BB	SO	SB	BA	SA
PITTSBURGH 8th 51-103 .331 47	**NIXEY CALLAHAN 20-40 .333 HONUS WAGNER 1-4 .200 HUGO BEZDEK 30-59 .337**		28	157	5169	464	1230	160	61	9	396	399	580	150	.238	.298
TOTALS																
Honus Wagner (HO)	1B47, 3B18, 2B2, SS1	R	43	74	230	15	61	7	1	0	24	24	17	5	.265	.304
Jake Pitler	2B106, OF3	R	23	109	382	39	89	8	5	0	23	30	24	6	.233	.280
Chuck Ward	SS122, 2B8, 3B5	R	22	125	423	25	100	12	3	0	43	32	43	5	.236	.279
Tony Boeckel	3B62	R	24	64	219	24	58	11	4	0	23	8	31	6	.265	.324
Lee King	OF102	R	24	111	381	32	95	14	5	1	35	15	58	5	.249	.320
Max Carey	OF153	B	27	155	588	82	174	21	12	1	51	58	38	46	.296	.378
Carson Bigbee	OF107, 2B16, SS2	L	22	133	469	46	112	11	6	0	21	37	16	19	.239	.288
Bill Fischer	C69, 1B2	L	26	95	245	25	70	9	2	3	25	17	19	11	.286	.376
Walter Schmidt	C61	R	30	72	183	9	45	7	0	0	17	11	11	4	.246	.284
Bill Hinchman (BL)	OF48, 1B20	R	34	69	244	27	46	5	5	2	29	33	27	5	.189	.275
Bill Wagner	C37, 1B12	R	23	53	151	15	31	7	2	0	9	11	22	1	.205	.278
Alex McCarthy	3B26, 2B13, SS9	R	29	49	151	15	33	4	0	0	8	11	13	1	.219	.245
1 Doug Baird	3B41, 2B2	R	25	43	135	17	35	6	1	0	18	20	19	8	.259	.319
Charlie Jackson	OF36	L	23	41	121	7	29	3	2	0	1	10	22	4	.240	.298
Adam Debus	SS21, 3B18	R	24	38	115	9	30	5	4	0	7	7	14	2	.261	.328
Fritz Mollwitz	1B36, 2B1	R	27	36	140	16	36	4	0	0	12	8	8	4	.257	.300
Bunny Brief	1B34	R	24	36	115	15	25	5	2	1	15	21	25	4	.217	.330
1 Wildfire Schulte	OF28	L	34	30	103	11	22	5	1	0	7	10	14	5	.214	.282
Buster Caton	SS14	R	20	14	57	6	12	1	1	0	4	1	6	0	.211	.298
Don Flinn	OF12	R	24	14	37	1	11	1	0	1	1	6	1	2	.297	.378
Bill Gleason	2B13	R	22	13	42	3	7	1	0	0	5	1	7	1	.167	.190

Jesse Altenburg 24 L 3-17, Red Smith 25 R 3-21, 2 Joe Wilhoit 31 L 2-10, 2 George Kelly 21 R 2-23, 2 Ray Miller 29 L 4-27, Billy Webb 22 R 3-15, Fred Blackwell 21 L 2-10, Hooks Warner 23 L 1-5, Ben Shaw 24 R 0-2, 2 Harry Wolfe 24 R 0-5, Arch Reilly 25 R 0-0

NAME	T	AGE	W	L	PCT	SV	G	GS	CG	IP	H	BB	SO	SHO	ERA
		25	51	103	.331	6	157	157	84	1418	1318	432	509	17	3.01
Wilbur Cooper	L	25	17	11	.607	1	40	34	23	298	276	54	99	7	2.36
Frank Miller	R	31	10	19	.345	2	38	28	14	224	216	60	92	5	3.16
Hal Carlson	R	25	7	11	.389	1	34	17	9	161	140	49	68	1	2.91
Elmer Jacobs	R	24	6	19	.240	2	38	25	10	207	214	76	58	1	2.81
2 Bob Steele	L	23	5	11	.313	1	27	19	13	180	158	53	82	1	2.75
Burleigh Grimes	R	23	3	16	.158	0	37	17	8	194	186	70	72	1	3.53
Al Mamaux (ST)	R	23	2	11	.154	0	16	13	5	86	92	50	22	0	5.23
Elmer Ponder	R	24	1	1	.500	0	3	2	1	21	12	6	11	1	1.71
Bill Evans (IL)	R	24	0	4	.000	0	8	2	1	27	24	14	5	0	3.33

WORLD SERIES — CHICAGO (AL) 4   NEW YORK (NL) 2

LINE SCORES

TEAM	1	2	3	4	5	6	7	8	9	10	11	12	R	H	E
Game 1 October 6 at Chicago															
NY (NL)	0	0	0		0	1	0		0	0	0		1	7	1
CHI (AL)	0	0	1		1	0	0		0	0	X		2	7	1
Sallee								**Cicotte**							
Game 2 October 7 at Chicago															
NY	0	2	0		0	0	0		0	0	0		2	8	1
CHI	0	2	0		5	0	0		0	0	X		7	14	1

Schupp, **Anderson** (2)   **Faber**
Perritt (4), Tesreau (8)

Game 3 October 10 at New York															
CHI	0	0	0		0	0	0		0	0	0		0	5	3
NY	0	0	0		2	0	0		0	0	X		2	8	2
Cicotte								**Benton**							

Game 4 October 11 at New York															
CHI	0	0	0		0	0	0		0	0	0		0	7	0
NY	0	0	0		1	1	0		1	2	X		5	10	1

Faber, Danforth (8)   **Schupp**

Game 5 October 13 at Chicago															
NY	2	0	0		2	0	0		1	0	0		5	12	3
CHI	0	0	1		0	0	1		3	3	X		8	14	6

Sallee, Perritt (8)   Russell, Cicotte (1), Williams (7), **Faber** (8)

Game 6 October 15 at New York															
CHI	0	0	0		3	0	0		0	0	1		4	7	1
NY	0	0	0		0	2	0		0	0	0		2	6	3

Faber   **Benton**, Perritt (6)

COMPOSITE BATTING

NAME	POS	G	AB	R	H	2B	3B	HR	RBI	BA
Chicago (AL)										
Totals		6	197	21	54	6	0	1	18	.274
McMullin	3B	6	24	1	3	1	0	0	2	.125
Jackson	OF	6	23	4	7	0	0	0	2	.304
Gandil	1B	6	23	1	6	0	0	0	5	.261
E. Collins	2B	6	22	4	9	1	0	0	1	.409
Felsch	OF	6	22	4	6	1	0	1	3	.273
Weaver	SS	6	21	3	7	1	0	0	1	.333
J. Collins	OF	6	21	2	6	1	0	0	0	.286
Schalk	C	6	19	1	5	0	0	0	2	.263
Faber	P	4	7	0	1	0	0	0	0	.143
Cicotte	P	3	7	0	1	0	0	0	0	.143
Leibold	OF	2	5	1	2	0	0	0	0	.400
Risberg	PH	2	2	0	1	0	0	0	1	.500
Lynn	PH	1	1	0	0	0	0	0	0	.000
Danforth	P	1	0	0	0	0	0	0	0	—
Russell	P	1	0	0	0	0	0	0	0	—
Williams	P	1	0	0	0	0	0	0	0	—
New York (NL)										
Totals		6	199	17	51	5	4	2	16	.256
Fletcher	SS	6	25	2	5	1	0	0	0	.200
Kauff	OF	6	25	2	4	1	0	2	5	.160
Zimmerman	3B	6	25	1	3	0	1	0	0	.120
Herzog	2B	6	24	1	6	0	1	0	2	.250
Robertson	OF	6	22	3	11	1	1	0	1	.500
Burns	OF	6	22	3	5	0	0	0	2	.227
Holke	1B	6	21	2	6	2	0	0	1	.286
Rariden	C	5	13	2	5	0	0	0	0	.385
Sallee	P	2	6	0	1	0	0	0	0	.167
McCarty	C	3	5	1	2	0	0	0	0	.400
Schupp	P	2	4	0	1	0	0	0	0	.250
Benton	P	2	3	0	0	0	0	0	0	.000
Perritt	P	3	2	0	2	0	0	0	1	1.000
Wilhoit	PH	2	2	0	0	0	0	0	0	.000
Thorpe	OF	1	1	0	0	0	0	0	0	—
Anderson	P	1	1	0	0	0	0	0	0	—
Tesreau	P	1	0	0	0	0	0	0	0	—

COMPOSITE PITCHING

NAME	G	IP	H	BB	SO	W	L	SV	ERA
Chicago (AL)									
Totals	6	52	51	6	27	4	2	0	2.77
Faber	4	27	21	3	9	3	1	0	2.33
Cicotte	3	23	23	2	13	1	1	0	1.95
Williams	1	2	0	3	0	0	0	0	9.00
Danforth	1	1	3	0	2	0	0	0	18.00
Russell	1	0	2	1	0	0	0	0	∞
New York (NL)									
Totals	6	51	54	11	28	2	4	0	3.00
Sallee	2	15.1	20	4	4	0	2	0	5.28
Benton	2	14	9	1	8	1	1	0	0.00
Schupp	2	10.1	11	2	9	1	0	0	1.74
Perritt	3	8.1	9	3	3	0	0	0	2.16
Anderson	1	2	5	0	3	0	1	0	18.00
Tesreau	1	1	0	1	1	0	0	0	0.00

1918 The "Non-Essential" Season

With America entering full force into World War I, baseball could not continue unscathed. Many players were taken by the draft, some enlisted in the armed forces, and others went to work in war industries. In June, Provost Marshall General Crowder issued a "work-or-fight" order, forcing all draft-age men into either the military or essential industries. Baseball was ruled "non-essential", and a schedule curtailed to September 2, could be completed only in a period of grace granted by Secretary of War Baker. Labor Day marked the end of the war-shortened race--any further play could only be carried on by teams of the old and very young. Even before September, many players and managers were drafted or left their teams, making it a season of scrambling for players and make-shift teams.

The Boston Red Sox won the American League pennant by 2½ games over Cleveland. Despite losing playing-manager Jack Barry and left fielder Duffy Lewis to the military, Boston's good fortunes lay in having Babe Ruth. The baby faced strong man filled in for Lewis and responded by hitting 11 home runs and batting .300, while still finding time to win 13 games on the mound. Carl Mays gathered 21 wins to his credit, and Boston manager Ed Barrow was able to obtain Stuffy McInnis, Amos Strunk, Wally Schang, and Joe Bush from the Athletics to plug up other holes. The Indians were hurt by the suspension of star Tris Speaker for the balance of the season for his assaulting umpire Tom Connelly in a home play dispute in a game at Philadelphia on August 28. Speaker and pitcher-turned-outfielder Joe Wood proved to be the big bats for the Indians. The White Sox were hard hit by the war and fell to sixth; Red Faber and Swede Risberg were drafted, and Joe Jackson, Happy Felsch, and Lefty Williams all left to do war work.

Ty Cobb collected his eleventh batting title, while Ruth's power performance was enough to help him garner his first home run crown by tying Tilly Walker of Philadelphia. Ruth also came through in the clutch by batting in 66 runs, good enough for a third-place tie with Joe Wood of Cleveland. Walter Johnson continued to dominate the pitching statistics by leading in wins, E.R.A., strikeouts, and tying in shutouts with Carl Mays of

Boston.

Despite the fall of the White Sox, the Chicago Cubs upheld the Windy City's honor by waltzing into the National League pennant by 10½ games. The Cubs had purchased star pitcher Grover "Pete" Alexander from the Phillies during the winter, but he was drafted after only three games. Nevertheless, the Cubs were mostly a blend of veterans who played solid ball all year. Rookie Charlie Hollocher hit .316 and played good shortstop, and ex-Giant Fred Merkle also provided heavy stick work. Pitchers, Hippo Vaughn, Lefty Tyler, and Claude Hendrix all won consistently, enabling the Cubs to coast in first.

The runner-up Giants felt the pinch of the war more than the Cubs. Benny Kauff hit .315 in 67 games and was then drafted. Pitcher Rube Benton enlisted, and Jeff Tesreau and Walter Holke left for the war industries. In addition, Ferdie Schupp and Heinie Zimmerman had off-years, leaving rookie outfielder Ross Youngs the only true bright spot by season's end.

Secretary of War Baker permitted the World Series to go on, and the Red Sox beat the Cubs four games to two. Babe Ruth pitched a shutout in game one and extended his record scoreless innings' streak in Series play to 29 2/3 innings before the Cubs scored against him in the fourth game. This record would stand until broken by Whitey Ford of the Yankees in 1961. In addition to Ruth, Mays also took two games in what was marked as a pitcher's Series, as both teams collected a grand total of 19 runs--the lowest Series run total since the classic pitcher's confrontation of 1905, which produced five shutouts in five games and only 18 runs.

1918 AMERICAN LEAGUE

NAME	G by Pos	B	AGE	G	AB	R	H	2B	3B	HR	RBI	BB	SO	SB	BA	SA
BOSTON	**1st 75-51 .595**				ED BARROW											
	TOTALS		29	126	3982	473	990	159	54	15	390	406	324	110	.249	.327
Stuffy McInnis (MS)	1B94 3B23	R	27	117	423	40	115	11	5	0	56	19	10	10	.272	.322
Dave Shean	2B115	R	40	115	425	58	112	16	3	0	34	40	25	11	.264	.315
Everett Scott	SS126	R	25	126	443	40	98	11	5	0	43	12	16	11	.221	.269
Fred Thomas (MS)	3B41 SS1	R	25	44	144	19	37	2	1	1	11	15	20	4	.257	.306
Harry Hooper	OF126	L	30	126	474	81	137	26	13	1	44	75	25	24	.289	.405
Amos Strunk	OF113	L	29	114	413	50	106	18	9	0	35	36	13	20	.257	.344
Babe Ruth	OF59 P20 1B13	L	23	95	317	50	95	18	11	11	66	58	58	6	.300	.555
Sam Agnew	C72	R	31	72	199	11	33	8	0	0	6	11	26	0	.166	.206
Wally Schang	C57 OF16 3B5 SS1	B	28	88	225	36	55	7	1	0	20	46	35	4	.244	.284
George Whiteman	OF69	R	35	71	214	24	57	14	0	1	28	20	9	9	.266	.346
Carl Mays	P35	R	26	38	104	10	30	3	3	0	5	9	15	1	.288	.375
Bullet Joe Bush	P36	R	25	36	98	8	27	3	2	0	14	6	11	0	.276	.347
Wally Mayer (MS)	C23	R	27	26	49	7	11	4	0	0	5	7	7	0	.224	.306
George Cochran	3B23 SS1		29	25	63	8	8	0	0	0	3	11	7	3	.127	.127
Dick Hobitzell (MS)	1B19	L	29	25	69	4	11	1	0	0	4	8	3	1	.159	.174
Jack Stansbury	3B18 OF2	R	32	20	47	3	6	1	0	0	2	6	3	0	.128	.149
2 Jack Coffey	3B14 2B1	R	31	15	44	5	7	1	0	1	2	3	2	1	.159	.250
Frank Truesdale	2B10	B	34	15	36	6	10	1	0	0	2	4	5	1	.278	.306
Walter Barbara	3B11 SS1	R	26	13	29	2	5	3	0	0	2	0	1	1	.172	.276
Hack Miller	OF10	R	24	12	29	2	8	2	0	0	4	0	2	0	.276	.345

Heinie Wagner 36 R 1-8 ,Eusebio Gonzales 25 R 1-2 ,Red Bluhm 24 R 0-1, Jack Barry (MS) 31, Jimmy Cooney (MS) 23, Del Gainer (MS)31,Hal Janvrin (MS) 25, Duffy Lewis (MS) 30, Mike McNally (MS) 24, Chick Shorten (MS) 26 Jimmy Walsh (MS) 22

NAME		T	AGE	W	L	PCT	SV	G	GS	CG	IP	H	BB	SO	SHO	ERA
			25	75	51	.595	2	126	126	105	1120	931	380	392	25	2.31
Carl Mays		R	26	21	13	.618	0	35	33	30	293	230	81	114	8	2.21
Sad Sam Jones		R	25	16	5	.762	0	24	21	16	184	151	70	44	5	2.25
Bullet Joe Bush		R	25	15	15	.500	2	36	31	26	273	241	91	125	7	2.11
Babe Ruth		L	23	13	7	.650	0	20	19	18	166	125	49	40	1	2.22
Dutch Leonard (MS)		L	26	8	6	.571	0	16	16	12	126	119	53	47	3	2.71
Vince Molyneaux		R	29	1	0	1.000	1	6	0	0	11	3	8	1	0	3.27
Lore Bader		R	30	1	3	.250	0	5	4	2	27	26	12	10	1	3.33
Dick McCabe		R	22	0	1	.000	0	3	1	0	10	13	2	3	0	2.70
Jean Dubuc		R	29	0	1	.000	0	2	1	1	11	11	5	1	0	4.09
Walt Kinney		L	24	0	0	—	0	5	0	0	15	5	8	4	0	1.80
Bill Pertica		R	19	0	0	—	0	1	0	0	3	3	0	1	0	3.00
Weldon Wycoff		R	26	0	0	—	0	1	0	0	2	4	1	2	0	0.00

Herb Pennock (MS) 24
Paul Musser (MS) 29

NAME	G by Pos	B	AGE	G	AB	R	H	2B	3B	HR	RBI	BB	SO	SB	BA	SA
CLEVELAND	**2nd 73-54 .575 2.5**				LEE FOHL											
	TOTALS		28	129	4166	510	1084	176	67	9	423	492	386	165	.260	.341
Doc Johnson	1B73	L	30	74	273	30	62	12	2	0	25	26	19	12	.227	.286
Bill Wambsganss	2B87	R	24	87	315	34	93	15	2	0	40	21	21	16	.295	.356
Ray Chapman	SS128 OF1	R	27	128	446	84	119	19	8	1	32	84	46	30	.267	.352
Joe Evans (MS)	3B74	R	23	79	243	38	64	9	7	1	22	30	29	7	.263	.358
Braggo Roth	OF106	R	25	106	375	53	106	21	12	1	59	53	41	35	.283	.411
Tris Speaker	OF127	L	30	127	471	73	150	33	11	0	61	64	9	27	.318	.435
Smoky Joe Wood	OF95 2B19 1B4	R	28	119	422	41	125	22	4	5	66	36	38	8	.296	.403
Steve O'Neill	C113	R	26	114	359	34	87	8	7	1	35	48	22	5	.242	.312
Terry Turner	3B46 2B26 SS1	R	37	74	233	24	58	7	2	0	23	22	15	6	.249	.296
Jack Graney	OF45	L	32	70	177	29	42	7	4	0	9	29	13	3	.237	.322
Eddie Miller	1B22 OF4	R	29	32	96	9	22	4	3	0	3	12	10	2	.229	.333
Pinch Thomas	C24	R	30	32	73	2	18	0	1	0	5	6	6	0	.247	.274
Rip Williams	1B21 C1	R	36	28	71	5	17	2	2	0	7	9	6	2	.239	.324
Al Halt	3B14 2B4 SS4 1B2	R	27	26	69	9	12	2	0	0	1	9	12	4	.174	.203
Bob Bescher	OF17	B	34	25	60	12	20	2	1	0	6	17	5	3	.333	.400
1 Marty Kavanagh	1B12	R	27	13	38	4	8	2	0	0	6	7	7	1	.211	.263
Jack Farmer	3B5	R	25	7	9	1	2	0	0	0	1	0	3	2	.222	.222
1 Gus Getz	OF3	R	28	6	15	2	2	1	0	0	4	0	4	1	.133	.200
Josh Billings (MS)	C1	R	26	2	3	0	1	0	0	0	0	1	0	0	.333	.333

Eddie Onslow 25 L 1-6, John Peters 24 R 0-1, Germany Schaefer 41 R 0-5, Hank DeBerry (MS) 23,Lou Guisto (MS) 24, Joe Harris (MS) 27, Elmer Smith (MS) 25

NAME		T	AGE	W	L	PCT	SV	G	GS	CG	IP	H	BB	SO	SHO	ERA
			27	73	54	.575	13	129	129	80	1161	1126	343	364	6	2.64
Stan Coveleski		R	28	22	13	.629	1	38	33	25	311	261	76	87	2	1.82
Jim Bagby		R	28	17	16	.515	6	45	31	23	271	274	78	57	2	2.69
Guy Morton (MS)		R	25	14	8	.636	0	30	28	13	215	189	77	123	1	2.64
Fritz Coumbe		L	28	13	7	.650	3	30	17	11	150	146	52	41	1	3.06
Johnny Enzmann		R	28	5	7	.417	2	30	14	8	137	130	29	38	0	2.36
Bob Groom		R	33	2	2	.500	0	14	5	0	43	70	18	8	0	7.12
George McQuillan		R	33	0	1	.000	1	5	1	0	23	25	4	7	0	2.35
Otis Lambeth (MS)		R	28	0	0	—	0	7	0	1	10	6	3	6	0	6.43
2 Ad Brennan		L	30	0	0	—	0	3	3	0	3	3	4	0	0	3.00
Roy Wilkinson		R	25	0	0	—	0	1	1	0	1	1	0	0	0	0.00

Ed Klepfer (MS) 30
Red Torkelson (MS) 24

NAME	G by Pos	B	AGE	G	AB	R	H	2B	3B	HR	RBI	BB	SO	SB	BA	SA
WASHINGTON	**3rd 72-56 .563 4**				CLARK GRIFFITH											
	TOTALS		30	130	4472	461	1144	156	48	5	404	376	361	137	.256	.316
Joe Judge	1B130	L	24	130	502	56	131	23	7	1	46	49	32	20	.261	.341
Ray Morgan	2B80 OF2	R	29	88	300	25	70	11	1	0	30	36	14	4	.233	.277
Doc Lavan	SS117 OF1	R	27	117	464	44	129	17	2	0	45	14	21	12	.278	.323
Eddie Foster	3B127 2B2	R	31	129	519	70	147	13	3	0	29	41	20	12	.283	.320
Wildfire Schulte	OF75	R	35	93	267	35	77	14	3	0	44	47	36	5	.288	.363
Clyde Milan	OF124	L	32	128	503	56	146	16	5	0	56	36	14	26	.290	.346
Burt Shotton	OF122	L	33	126	505	68	132	16	7	0	21	67	28	25	.261	.321
Eddie Ainsmith (MS)	C89	R	28	96	292	22	62	10	9	0	20	29	44	6	.212	.308
Howard Shanks	OF64 2B48 3B3	R	27	120	436	42	112	19	4	1	56	31	21	23	.257	.326
Walter Johnson	P39 OF4	R	30	65	150	10	40	4	4	1	18	9	18	2	.267	.367
Val Picinich (MS)	C46	R	21	47	148	13	34	3	2	1	12	9	25	0	.230	.297
George McBride	SS14 2B2	R	37	18	53	2	7	0	0	0	1	6	5	1	.132	.132
Joe Casey	C8	R	30	9	17	3	4	0	0	0	2	2	4	0	.235	.235
Sam Rice (MS)	OF6	L	28	7	23	3	8	1	0	0	2	3	0	1	.348	.391
Patsy Gharrity (VR)		R	26	4	8	1	2	0	1	0	2	2	1	0	.250	.500
1 Merito Acosta		L	22	4	5	1	0	0	0	0	0	0	0	1	.000	.000

Bob Berman 19 R 0-0, Joe Leonard (MS) 23, Mike Menosky (MS) 23, Horace Milan (MS) 24

NAME		T	AGE	W	L	PCT	SV	G	GS	CG	IP	H	BB	SO	SHO	ERA
			26	72	56	.563	8	130	130	75	1227	1021	395	505	20	2.14
Walter Johnson		R	30	23	13	.639	3	39	29	29	325	241	70	162	8	1.27
Jim Shaw		R	24	16	12	.571	1	41	30	14	241	201	90	129	4	2.43
Harry Harper		L	23	11	10	.524	1	35	32	14	244	182	104	78	3	2.18
Doc Ayres		R	27	11	12	.478	3	40	24	11	220	215	63	67	4	2.82
Eddie Matteson		R	33	5	3	.625	0	14	6	2	68	57	15	17	0	1.72
Ed Hovlik		R	26	2	1	.667	0	8	2	1	28	25	10	10	1	1.29
Ing Hansen		L	19	1	0	1.000	0	5	0	0	9	10	3	2	0	3.00
Nellie Reese		L	19	1	0	1.000	0	4	0	0	5	5	3	0	0	0.00
George Dumont		R	22	1	1	.500	1	4	1	1	14	18	6	12	0	5.14
Earl Yingling (MS)		L	29	1	2	.333	0	5	2	2	38	30	12	15	0	2.13
Nick Altrock		R	41	2	0	.000	0	5	3	1	24	24	6	5	0	3.00
Molly Craft (MS)		R	22	0	1	—	0	1	0	0	5	5	1	0	0	1.29
1 Ad Brennan		L	30	0	0	—	0	1	0	0	3	5	7	5	0	5.40
Garland Buckeye		L	20	0	0	—	0	1	0	0	2	3	6	2	0	18.00

NEW YORK   4th   60-63   .488   13.5   MILLER HUGGINS

NAME	G by Pos	B	AGE	G	AB	R	H	2B	3B	HR	RBI	BB	SO	SB	BA	SA
TOTALS			28	126	4224	491	1085	160	45	20	406	367	370	88	.257	.330
Wally Pipp (MS)	1B91	L	25	91	349	48	106	15	9	2	44	22	34	11	.304	.415
Del Pratt	2B126	R	30	126	477	65	131	19	7	2	55	35	26	12	.275	.356
Roger Peckinpaugh	SS122	R	27	122	446	59	103	15	3	0	43	43	41	12	.231	.278
Frank Baker	3B126	L	32	126	504	65	154	24	5	6	62	38	13	8	.306	.409
Frank Gilhooley	OF111	L	26	112	427	58	118	13	5	1	23	53	24	7	.276	.337
Elmer Miller	OF62	R	31	67	202	18	49	9	2	1	22	19	17	2	.243	.322
Ping Bodie	OF90	R	30	91	324	36	83	12	6	3	46	27	24	6	.256	.358
Truck Hannah	C88	R	29	90	250	24	55	6	0	2	21	51	25	5	.220	.268
Ray Caldwell	P24, OF19	L	30	65	151	13	44	10	0	1	18	13	23	2	.291	.377
Roxy Walters	C50, OF9	R	25	64	191	18	38	5	1	0	12	9	18	3	.199	.236
Ham Hyatt	OF25, 1B5	L	33	53	131	15	30	8	0	2	10	8	8	1	.229	.336
Armando Marsans	OF36	R	31	37	123	13	29	5	1	0	9	5	3	3	.236	.293
Bill Lamar (MS)	OF27	L	21	28	110	12	25	3	0	0	2	6	2	2	.227	.255
Jack Fournier	1B27	L	28	27	100	9	35	6	1	0	12	7	7	7	.350	.430
John Hummel	OF15, 1B3, 2B1	R	35	22	61	9	18	1	2	0	4	11	8	3	.295	.377
Aaron Ward (MS)	SS11, 2B4, OF4	R	21	20	32	2	4	1	0	0	1	2	7	1	.125	.156
Zinn Beck	1B5	R	32	11	8	0	0	0	0	0	1	0	1	0	.000	.000
Hugh High	OF4	L	30	7	10	1	0	0	0	0	0	1	1	0	.000	.000
Chick Fewster	2B2	R	22	5	2	1	1	0	0	0	0	0	0	0	.500	.500
Muddy Ruel	C2	R	22	3	6	0	2	0	0	0	0	0	2	1	.333	.333
Sammy Vick (MS)	OF1	R	23	2	3	1	2	0	0	0	1	0	0	0	.667	.667
Paddy O'Connor	C1	R	38	1	3	0	1	0	0	0	0	0	0	0	.333	.333
Howie Camp (MS) 25																

NAME	T	AGE	W	L	PCT	SV	G	GS	CG	IP	H	BB	SO	SHO	ERA
TOTALS		26	60	63	.488	11	126	126	59	1148	1103	463	369	9	3.03
George Mogridge	L	29	16	13	.552	6	45	19	13	230	232	43	62	1	2.27
Slim Love	L	27	13	12	.520	1	38	29	13	229	207	116	95	1	3.07
Ray Caldwell	R	30	9	8	.529	1	24	21	14	177	173	62	59	1	3.05
Allen Russell	R	24	8	11	.421	3	27	18	7	141	139	73	54	2	3.26
Hank Thormahlen	L	21	7	3	.700	0	16	12	5	113	85	52	22	3	2.47
Ray Keating	R	24	2	2	.500	0	15	6	1	48	39	30	16	0	3.94
Hank Robinson	L	30	2	4	.333	0	11	8	1	48	47	16	14	0	3.00
2 Happy Finneran	R	27	2	6	.250	0	23	13	4	114	134	35	34	0	3.79
Bob Shawkey (MS)	R	27	1	1	.500	0	3	2	1	16	7	10	3	1	1.13
Bob McGraw (MS)	R	23	0	1	.000	0	1	1	0	9	4	1	0	0	∞
Roy Sanders	R	24	0	2	.000	0	6	2	0	26	28	16	8	0	4.15
Dazzy Vance	R	27	0	0	—	0	2	1	0	9	2	0	0	0	18.00
Walter Bernhardt	R	25	0	0	—	0	1	0	0	1	0	0	1	0	0.00
Alex Ferguson (MS)	R	21	0	0	—	0	1	0	0	2	2	1	0	0	0.00
Ed Monroe (MS)	R	25	0	0	—	0	1	0	0	2	2	1	0	0	4.50
Neal Brady (MS) 21															
Ray Fisher (MS) 30															
Ernie Shore (MS) 27															
Walt Smallwood (MS) 25															

ST. LOUIS   5th   58-64   .475   15   FIELDER JONES 22-24 .478   JIMMY AUSTIN 7-9 .438   JIMMY BURKE 29-31 .483

NAME	G by Pos	B	AGE	G	AB	R	H	2B	3B	HR	RBI	BB	SO	SB	BA	SA
TOTALS			28	123	4019	426	1040	152	40	5	360	397	340	138	.259	.320
George Sisler	1B114, P2	L	25	114	452	69	154	21	9	2	41	40	17	45	.341	.440
Joe Gedeon	2B123	R	24	123	441	39	94	14	3	1	41	27	29	7	.213	.265
Jimmy Austin	SS57, 3B48	R	38	110	367	42	97	14	4	0	20	53	32	18	.264	.324
Fritz Maisel	3B79, OF1	R	28	90	284	43	66	4	2	0	16	46	17	11	.232	.261
Ray Demmitt	OF114	L	34	116	405	45	114	23	5	1	61	38	35	10	.281	.370
Jack Tobin	OF122	L	26	122	480	59	133	19	5	0	36	48	26	13	.277	.338
Earl Smith	OF81	R	27	89	286	28	77	10	5	0	32	13	16	13	.269	.339
Les Nunamaker	C81, 1B1, OF1	R	29	85	274	22	71	9	2	0	28	28	16	6	.259	.307
Tim Hendryx	OF65	R	27	88	219	22	61	14	3	0	33	37	35	5	.279	.370
Wally Gerber (MS)	SS56	R	26	56	171	10	41	4	0	0	10	19	11	2	.240	.263
Hank Severeid	C42	R	27	51	133	8	34	4	0	0	11	18	4	4	.256	.286
Pete Johns	1B10, SS4, 3B4, OF4, 2B2	R	30	46	89	5	16	1	1	0	11	4	6	0	.180	.213
Ernie Johnson	SS11, 3B1	L	30	29	34	7	9	1	0	0	1	3	2	4	.265	.294
George Hale	C11	R	23	12	30	0	4	1	0	0	1	1	5	0	.133	.167
Ken Williams (MS)		R													.000	.000
Baby Doll Jacobson (MS) 27, Bill Rumler (MS) 27, Tod Sloan (MS) 27																

NAME	T	AGE	W	L	PCT	SV	G	GS	CG	IP	H	BB	SO	SHO	ERA
TOTALS		26	58	64	.475	7	123	123	67	1111	993	402	346	7	2.75
Allan Sothoron	R	25	13	12	.520	0	29	24	14	209	152	67	71	2	1.94
Dave Davenport	R	28	10	11	.476	1	31	22	12	180	182	69	60	2	3.25
Rasty Wright	R	22	8	2	.800	0	18	13	6	111	99	18	25	1	2.51
Tom Rogers	R	23	8	10	.444	2	29	16	11	154	148	49	29	0	3.27
Bert Gallia	R	26	7	6	.538	0	19	17	10	124	126	61	48	1	3.48
Urban Shocker (MS)	R	27	6	5	.545	2	14	9	7	95	69	40	33	0	1.80
Duke Houck	R	26	2	4	.333	2	27	2	0	72	58	29	29	0	2.38
Lefty Leifield	L	34	2	6	.250	0	15	6	3	67	61	19	9	1	2.55
Grover Lowdermilk	R	33	2	6	.250	0	13	11	4	80	74	38	25	0	3.15
Bugs Bennett	R	26	0	2	.000	0	4	2	0	10	12	7	0	0	3.60
George Sisler	L	25	0	0	—	0	2	1	0	8	10	4	4	0	4.50
Tim McCabe	R	23	0	0	—	0	1	0	0	2	1	0	1	0	18.00
Ernie Koob (MS) 25															

CHICAGO   6th   57-67   .460   17   PANTS ROWLAND

NAME	G by Pos	B	AGE	G	AB	R	H	2B	3B	HR	RBI	BB	SO	SB	BA	SA
TOTALS			28	124	4132	457	1057	136	54	9	375	375	358	116	.256	.321
Chick Gandil	1B114	R	30	114	439	49	119	18	4	0	55	27	19	9	.271	.330
Eddie Collins (MS)	2B96	L	31	97	330	51	91	8	2	2	30	73	13	22	.276	.330
Buck Weaver	SS98, 3B11, 2B1	B	27	112	420	37	126	12	5	0	29	11	24	20	.300	.352
Fred McMullin	3B69, 2B9, OF3	R	26	70	235	32	65	7	0	1	16	25	26	7	.277	.319
Eddie Murphy	OF63, 2B8	R	26	91	286	36	85	9	0	0	23	42	18	6	.297	.350
Shano Collins	OF92, 1B5, 2B1	R	32	103	365	30	100	18	11	1	56	17	19	7	.274	.392
Nemo Leibold	OF114	L	26	116	440	57	110	14	6	1	31	63	32	13	.250	.316
Ray Schalk	C106	R	25	108	333	35	73	6	3	0	22	36	22	12	.219	.255
Risberg (MS)	SS30, 3B24, 2B12, 1B7, OF3	R	23	82	273	36	70	12	3	1	27	23	32	5	.256	.333
Happy Felsch (WW)	OF53	R	26	53	206	16	52	7	1	0	20	15	13	6	.252	.325
Wilbur Good	OF35	L	32	35	148	24	37	9	4	0	11	11	16	1	.250	.365
Otto Jacobs	C21	R	29	29	73	4	15	3	0	0	3	5	0	2	.205	.274
Babe Pinelli	3B24	R	22	24	78	7	18	1	1	1	7	7	8	3	.231	.308
Joe Jackson (HO-WW)	OF17	L	28	17	65	9	23	2	2	1	20	8	1	3	.354	.492
Johnny Mostil	2B9	R	22	10	33	4	9	2	0	0	4	1	6	1	.273	.455
Al DeVormer (MS)	C6, OF1	R	26	8	19	2	5	2	0	0	0	0	4	0	.263	.368
Ted Jourdan (MS)	1B2	L	22	7	10	1	1	0	0	0	1	0	1	0	.100	.100
Byrd Lynn	C4	R	29	5	8	0	2	0	0	0	2	1	1	0	.250	.250
Kid Wilson		L	22	4	1	2	0	0	0	0	0	0	0	0	.000	.000
Pat Hardgrove (MS)		R	22	2	2	0	0	0	0	0	0	0	1	0	.000	.000
Joe Jenkins (MS) 27																

NAME	T	AGE	W	L	PCT	SV	G	GS	CG	IP	H	BB	SO	SHO	ERA
TOTALS		28	57	67	.460	6	124	124	76	1126	1092	300	349	10	2.69
Eddie Cicotte	R	34	12	19	.387	2	38	30	24	266	275	40	104	1	2.64
Frank Shellenback	R	19	10	12	.455	1	28	20	10	183	180	74	47	3	2.66
Joe Benz	R	32	7	8	.467	0	29	17	10	154	156	28	30	1	2.51
Lefty Williams (WW)	L	25	6	4	.600	1	15	14	7	106	76	47	30	2	2.72
Reb Russell	L	29	6	5	.545	0	19	14	10	125	117	33	38	2	2.59
Dave Danforth	R	28	6	15	.286	2	39	13	5	139	148	40	48	0	3.43
Red Faber (MS)	R	29	5	1	.833	0	11	9	5	81	70	23	26	1	1.22
Jack Quinn	R	34	5	1	.833	0	6	5	5	51	38	7	22	0	2.29
Mellie Wolfgang	R	28	0	1	.000	0	4	0	0	8	12	3	1	0	5.63
1 Roy Mitchell	R	33	0	1	.000	2	2	0	0	18	20	3	3	0	7.50
Ed Corey (BN)	R	23	0	0	—	0	1	0	0	2	1	0	0	0	4.50
Jim Scott (MS) 30															
Tom McGuire (MS) 26															

DETROIT   7th   55-71   .437   20   HUGHIE JENNINGS

NAME	G by Pos	B	AGE	G	AB	R	H	2B	3B	HR	RBI	BB	SO	SB	BA	SA
TOTALS			29	128	4262	473	1063	141	56	13	393	452	380	123	.249	.318
Harry Heilmann (MS)	OF40, 1B37, 2B2	R	23	79	286	34	79	10	6	5	39	35	10	13	.276	.406
Ralph Young	2B91	B	29	91	298	31	56	7	1	0	21	54	17	15	.188	.218
Donie Bush	SS198	R	30	128	500	74	117	10	3	0	22	79	31	9	.234	.266
Ossie Vitt	3B66, 2B9, OF3	R	28	81	267	29	64	5	2	0	17	32	6	5	.240	.273
George Harper	OF64	R	26	69	227	19	55	5	2	0	16	18	14	3	.242	.282
Ty Cobb	OF93, 1B13, 3B2, P2, 2B1	L	31	111	421	83	161	19	14	3	64	41	21	34	.382	.515
Bobby Veach	OF127, P1	L	30	127	499	59	139	21	13	3	78	35	23	21	.279	.391
Archie Yelle	C52	R	26	56	144	7	25	3	0	0	7	9	15	0	.174	.194
Bob Jones	3B63, 1B6	L	28	74	287	43	79	14	4	0	21	17	16	7	.275	.352
Tubby Spencer	C48, 1B1	R	34	66	155	11	34	8	1	0	8	19	18	1	.219	.284
Frank Walker	OF45	R	23	55	167	10	33	10	3	1	20	7	29	3	.198	.311
Oscar Stanage (BG)	C47, 1B5	R	35	54	186	9	47	4	0	1	14	11	18	2	.253	.290
Lee Dressen	1B28	L	28	31	107	10	19	1	2	0	3	21	10	2	.178	.224
Art Griggs	1B25	R	33	28	99	11	36	8	0	0	16	10	5	2	.364	.444
1 Jack Coffey	2B22	R	31	22	67	7	14	0	2	0	4	8	5	2	.209	.269
Ben Dyer (MS)	1B2, OF2, P2, 2B1	R	25	18	18	1	5	0	0	0	2	0	8	0	.278	.278
3 Marty Kavanagh	1B12	R	27	13	44	2	12	3	0	0	9	1	6	0	.273	.341
Bert Ellison (MS)	OF4, 2B3	R	21	7	23	1	6	1	0	0	2	1	1	0	.261	.304
Harry Curry	2B5	R	32	5	20	1	5	1	0	0	0	1	0	0	.250	.250
Joe Cobb (MS)		R	23	2	0	0	0	0	0	0	0	0	0	0	—	—
Hughie Jennings	1B1	R	49	1	0	0	0	0	0	0	0	0	0	0	—	—
Ira Flagstead (MS) 24																
Fred Nicholson (MS) 23																

NAME	T	AGE	W	L	PCT	SV	G	GS	CG	IP	H	BB	SO	SHO	ERA
TOTALS		26	55	71	.437	8	128	128	74	1161	1130	437	371	8	3.40
Bernie Boland	R	26	14	10	.583	0	29	25	14	204	176	67	63	4	2.65
Hooks Dauss	R	28	13	16	.448	3	33	26	21	250	243	58	73	1	2.99
Rudy Kallio	R	25	8	13	.381	0	30	22	10	181	178	76	70	2	3.63
George Cunningham	R	23	6	7	.462	1	27	14	10	140	131	38	39	0	3.15
Bill James (MS)	R	31	6	11	.353	0	19	18	8	122	127	68	42	1	3.76
Eric Erickson	R	26	4	5	.444	1	12	9	8	94	81	29	48	2	2.49
Deacon Jones	R	24	2	2	.500	2	21	4	1	67	60	38	12	0	3.09
Wild Bill Donovan	R	41	1	1	.500	0	3	2	2	14	10	5	3	0	1.50
1 Happy Finneran	R	33	1	2	.333	1	5	2	1	14	22	8	2	0	9.64
Charley Hall	R	33	0	1	.000	0	3	1	0	13	14	6	2	0	6.92
Harry Coveleski	L	32	0	1	.000	0	3	1	1	14	17	16	3	0	3.86
Willie Mitchell (MS)	L	28	0	1	.000	0	3	1	0	9	10	7	1	0	9.00
Bill Bailey	L	30	0	2	.000	0	4	1	0	38	53	26	13	0	5.92
Herb Hall	R	25	0	0	—	0	2	1	0	12	7	1	0	0	15.00
Ty Cobb	R	31	0	0	—	0	2	0	0	4	4	0	0	0	4.50
Ben Dyer (MS)	R	25	0	0	—	0	2	0	0	6	12	7	1	0	4.50
Bobby Veach	R	30	0	0	—	0	1	0	0	2	4	0	0	0	4.50
Johnny Couch (MS) 27															
Howard Ehmke (MS) 24															

PHILADELPHIA   8th   52-76   .406   24   CONNIE MACK

NAME	G by Pos	B	AGE	G	AB	R	H	2B	3B	HR	RBI	BB	SO	SB	BA	SA
TOTALS			25	130	4278	412	1039	124	44	22	356	343	485	83	.243	.308
George Burns	1B128, OF2	R	25	130	505	61	178	22	9	6	70	23	25	8	.352	.467
Jimmy Dykes (MS)	2B56, 3B1	R	21	59	186	13	35	3	0	0	13	19	32	5	.188	.237
Joe Dugan	SS85, 2B35	R	21	120	406	25	79	13	3	1	34	16	55	4	.195	.259
Larry Gardner	3B127	L	32	127	463	50	132	22	6	1	52	43	22	9	.285	.365
Charlie Jamieson	OF102, P5	L	25	110	416	50	84	11	2	0	11	54	30	11	.202	.238
Tilly Walker	OF109	R	31	114	414	56	122	20	0	11	48	41	44	8	.295	.423
Manny Kopp (MS)	OF96	B	26	96	363	60	85	7	7	0	18	42	55	22	.234	.292
Wickey McAvoy	C74, 1B1, OF1, P1	R	23	83	271	14	66	5	3	0	32	13	23	5	.244	.284
Red Shannon	SS45, 2B26	B	22	72	225	23	54	6	5	0	16	42	52	5	.240	.311
Cy Perkins	C60	R	22	68	218	9	41	4	1	1	14	8	15	1	.188	.229
2 Merito Acosta	OF45	L	22	49	169	23	24	1	2	0	6	11	8	10	.140	.158
Rube Oldring	OF30, 2B2, 3B2	R	34	49	133	5	31	2	1	0	11	8	10	0	.233	.263
Claude Davidson	2B15, OF8, 3B1	L	21	31	81	4	15	1	0	0	5	8	13	0	.185	.198
Jake Munch	1B2, OF2	R	27	22	30	3	8	0	0	0	3	1	2	0	.267	.333
Frank Fahey	OF5, P3	R	22	10	17	2	4	0	0	0	1	0	3	0	.176	.235
Gene Bailey (MS) 24, Ray Bates (MS) 25, Pat Haley (MS) 27, Otis Lawry (MS) 24, Whitey Witt (MS) 22																

NAME	T	AGE	W	L	PCT	SV	G	GS	CG	IP	H	BB	SO	SHO	ERA
TOTALS		27	52	76	.406	7	130	130	80	1156	1105	479	279	12	3.22
Scott Perry	R	27	21	19	.525	1	44	36	30	332	295	111	81	3	1.98
Vean Gregg	L	33	8	14	.364	2	30	25	17	199	180	67	63	3	3.12
Mule Watson	R	21	6	10	.375	0	21	19	11	142	139	44	30	3	3.36
Willie Adams	R	27	3	6	.333	0	32	14	7	169	164	97	39	0	4.42
Elmer Myers (MS)	R	24	4	8	.333	1	18	15	5	95	101	42	17	1	4.64
Bob Geary (MS)	R	27	3	5	.375	3	16	7	6	87	94	31	22	2	2.69
Charlie Jamieson	L	25	2	1	.667	0	5	3	2	23	24	13	2	0	4.30
Tom Zachary (MS)	L	22	1	0	1.000	0	1	1	1	9	5	5	3	0	5.63
Roy Johnson	R	24	1	5	.167	0	10	8	3	50	47	27	14	0	3.42
Bill Pierson	R	19	0	1	.000	0	8	1	0	22	20	20	6	0	3.27
Vic Keen	R	19	0	1	.000	0	1	1	0	8	9	3	3	0	3.38
Frank Fahey	R	22	0	0	—	0	3	0	0	5	5	14	1	0	6.00
Red Shea	R	19	0	0	—	0	3	0	0	9	14	2	2	0	4.00
Chick Holmes	R	19	0	0	—	0	2	0	0	4	2	2	0	0	13.50
Lou Bauer	R	19	0	0	—	0	1	0	0	2	1	2	1	0	∞
Wickey McAvoy	R	23	0	0	—	0	1	0	0	1	0	1	0	0	0.00
Walter Anderson (MS) 20, Jing Johnson (MS) 23, Dave Keefe (MS) 21, Rollie Naylor (MS) 26, Win Noyes (MS) 29, Socks Seibold (MS) 22															

CHICAGO 1ST 84-45 .651 FRED MITCHELL

NAME	G by Pos	B	AGE	G	AB	R	H	2B	3B	HR	RBI	BB	SO	SB	BA	SA
TOTALS			29	131	4325	538	1147	164	53	21	438	358	343	159	.265	.342
Fred Merkle	1B129	R	29	129	482	55	143	25	5	3	65	35	36	21	.297	.388
Rollie Zeider	2B79, 1B1, 3B1	R	34	82	251	31	56	3	2	0	26	23	20	16	.223	.251
Charlie Hollocher	SS131	L	22	131	509	72	161	23	6	2	38	47	30	26	.316	.397
Charlie Deal	3B118	R	26	119	414	43	99	9	3	2	34	21	13	11	.239	.290
Max Flack	OF121	L	28	123	478	74	123	17	10	4	41	56	19	17	.257	.360
Dode Paskert	OF121, 3B6	R	36	127	461	69	132	24	4	3	59	53	49	20	.286	.371
Les Mann	OF129	R	25	129	489	69	141	27	7	2	55	38	45	21	.288	.384
Bill Killefer	C104	R	30	104	331	30	77	10	3	0	22	17	10	5	.233	.281
Turner Barber	OF27, 1B4	L	24	55	123	11	29	3	2	0	10	9	16	3	.236	.293
Bob O'Farrell	C45	R	21	52	113	9	32	7	3	1	14	10	15	0	.283	.425
Pete Kilduff	2B30	R	25	30	93	7	19	2	2	0	13	7	7	1	.204	.269
Charlie Pick	2B20, 3B8	L	30	29	89	13	29	4	1	0	12	14	4	7	.326	.393
Bill McCabe	2B13, OF4	L	25	29	45	9	8	0	1	0	5	4	7	2	.178	.222
Chuck Wortman	2B8, SS4	R	26	17	17	4	2	0	0	1	3	1	2	3	.118	.294
Rowdy Elliott (MS)	C5	R	27	5	10	0	0	0	0	0	0	2	1	0	.000	.000
Fred Lear		R	24	2	1	0	0	0	0	0	0	0	1	0	.000	.000
Tommy Clarke	C1	R	30	1	0	0	0	0	0	0	0	0	0	0	.000	.000
Tom Daly	C1	R	26	1	1	0	0	0	0	0	0	0	0	0	.000	.000

Paddy Driscoll (MS) 23, Bill Marriott (MS) 25, Morrie Schick (MS) 26

NAME	T	AGE	W	L	PCT	SV	G	GS	CG	IP	H	BB	SO	SHO	ERA
		28	84	45	.651	8	131	131	92	1197	1050	296	472	23	2.18
Hippo Vaughn	L	30	22	10	.688	0	35	33	27	290	216	76	148	8	1.74
Claude Hendrix	R	29	20	7	.741	1	32	27	15	233	229	54	86	3	2.78
Lefty Tyler	L	28	19	8	.704	1	33	30	22	269	218	67	102	8	2.01
Phil Douglas	R	28	10	9	.526	2	25	19	11	157	145	31	51	2	2.12
Speed Martin	R	24	5	2	.714	1	9	5	4	54	47	14	16	1	1.83
Paul Carter	R	24	3	2	.600	2	21	4	1	73	78	19	13	0	2.71
Pete Alexander (MS)	R	31	2	1	.667	0	3	3	3	26	19	3	15	0	1.73
Harry Weaver (MS)	R	26	2	2	.500	1	8	3	1	33	27	7	9	1	2.18
Roy Walker	R	25	1	3	.250	1	13	7	2	43	50	15	20	0	2.72
Vic Aldridge (MS)	R	24	0	1	.000	0	2	1	0	12	11	6	10	0	1.50
Buddy Napier	R	28	0	0	—	0	1	0	0	7	10	4	2	0	5.14

NEW YORK 2nd 71-53 .573 10.5 JOHN McGRAW

NAME	G by Pos	B	AGE	G	AB	R	H	2B	3B	HR	RBI	BB	SO	SB	BA	SA
TOTALS			29	124	4164	480	1081	150	53	13	400	271	365	130	.260	.330
Walter Holke (WW)	1B88	B	25	88	326	38	82	17	4	1	27	10	26	10	.252	.337
Larry Doyle (IL)	2B73	L	32	75	257	38	67	7	4	3	36	37	10	10	.261	.354
Art Fletcher	SS124	R	33	124	468	51	123	20	2	0	47	18	26	12	.263	.314
Heinie Zimmerman	3B100, 1B19	R	31	121	463	43	126	19	10	1	56	13	23	14	.272	.363
Ross Youngs	OF120	L	21	124	474	70	143	16	8	1	25	48	49	10	.302	.376
Benny Kauff (MS)	OF67	L	28	67	270	41	85	19	4	2	39	16	30	9	.315	.437
George Burns	OF119	R	28	119	465	80	135	22	6	4	51	43	37	40	.290	.384
Lew McCarty	C75	R	29	86	257	16	69	7	3	0	24	17	13	2	.268	.319
Bill Rariden	C63	R	30	69	183	15	41	5	1	0	17	15	15	1	.224	.262
Joe Wilhoit	OF55	L	32	64	135	13	37	3	3	0	15	17	14	4	.274	.341
Jim Thorpe	OF44	R	31	58	113	15	28	4	4	1	11	4	18	3	.248	.381
Joe Rodriguez	2B40, 1B8, 3B2	R	23	50	125	15	20	0	2	0	4	5	12	3	.160	.192
Eddie Sicking (MS)	3B24, 2B18, SS2	R	21	46	132	9	33	4	0	0	12	6	11	2	.250	.280
Pete Compton	OF19	L	28	21	60	5	13	0	1	0	5	5	4	2	.217	.250
Jay Kirke	1B16	L	30	17	56	1	14	1	0	0	3	1	3	0	.250	.268
2 Bert Niehoff (BL)	2B7	R	34	7	23	3	6	0	0	0	1	0	4	0	.261	.261
George Gibson	C4	R	37	4	2	0	1	0	0	0	0	0	2	0	.500	1.000

Al Baird (MS) 23
George Kelly (MS) 22
Dave Robertson (WW) 28

NAME	T	AGE	W	L	PCT	SV	G	GS	CG	IP	H	BB	SO	SHO	ERA
		30	71	53	.573	11	124	124	74	1112	1002	228	330	18	2.64
Pol Perritt	R	26	19	13	.581	0	35	31	19	233	212	38	60	6	2.74
Red Causey	R	24	11	6	.647	2	29	18	10	158	143	42	48	2	2.79
Al Demaree	R	33	8	6	.571	1	26	14	8	142	143	25	39	2	2.47
Slim Sallee	L	33	8	8	.500	2	18	16	12	132	122	12	33	1	2.25
Jesse Barnes (MS)	R	25	6	1	.857	0	9	9	4	55	53	13	12	2	1.60
2 Fred Toney	R	29	6	2	.750	*1	11	9	7	85	55	7	19	1	1.69
Fred Anderson (MS)	R	32	4	2	.667	3	18	4	2	71	62	17	24	1	2.66
Jeff Tesreau (WW)	R	30	4	4	.500	0	12	9	3	74	61	21	31	1	2.31
2 Bob Steele	R	24	3	5	.375	1	12	7	5	66	56	11	24	1	2.59
2 George Smith	R	26	2	3	.400	1	5	2	1	27	26	6	4	0	4.00
Rube Benton (MS)	L	28	1	2	.333	0	3	3	2	24	17	3	9	0	1.88
Ferdie Schupp (AJ)	L	27	0	1	.000	0	7	4	1	33	42	27	22	0	7.64
Jack Ogden	R	20	0	0	—	0	5	0	0	9	8	3	1	0	3.00
Waite Hoyt	R	18	0	0	—	0	1	0	0	2	2	3	3	0	0.00
George Ross	L	26	0	0	—	0	1	1	0	2	2	1	0	0	0.00

* Toney, also with Cincinnati, tied for league lead in SV with 3

CINCINNATI 3rd 68-60 .531 15.5 CHRISTY MATHEWSON 61-57 .517 HEINIE GROH 7-3 .700

NAME	G by Pos	B	AGE	G	AB	R	H	2B	3B	HR	RBI	BB	SO	SB	BA	SA
TOTALS			29	129	4265	538	1185	165	84	15	447	304	303	128	.278	.366
Hal Chase (ST)	1B67, OF2	R	35	74	259	30	78	12	6	2	38	13	15	5	.301	.417
Lee Magee	2B114, 3B3	B	29	119	459	62	133	22	13	0	28	28	19	29	.290	.394
Lena Blackburne	SS125	R	31	125	435	35	99	8	10	1	45	25	30	6	.228	.299
Heinie Groh	3B126	R	28	126	493	88	158	28	3	1	37	84	24	11	.320	.396
Tommy Griffith	OF118	L	28	118	427	47	113	10	4	2	48	39	30	10	.265	.321
Edd Roush	OF113	L	25	113	435	61	145	18	10	5	62	22	10	24	.333	.455
Greasy Neale	OF102	L	26	107	371	59	100	11	11	1	42	24	38	23	.270	.367
Ivy Wingo	C93, OF5	L	27	100	323	36	82	15	6	0	31	19	18	6	.254	.337
Sherry Magee	1B66, OF38, 2B6	R	33	115	400	46	119	15	13	0	76	37	18	14	.298	.415
Manuel Cueto	OF19, 2B10, SS9, C6	R	26	48	108	14	32	5	1	0	14	19	5	4	.296	.361
Nick Allen (MS)	C31	R	29	37	96	6	25	2	2	0	5	4	7	0	.260	.323
Pete Schneider	P33	R	23	36	83	11	24	3	2	1	7	0	12	0	.289	.410
Harry Smith	C6, OF1	R	28	13	27	4	5	1	2	0	4	3	6	1	.185	.370
3 Jimmy Archer	C7, 1B1	R	35	9	26	3	7	1	0	0	2	1	3	0	.269	.308

Pat Duncan (MS) 24
Larry Kopf (WW) 27
Morrie Rath (MS) 31

NAME	T	AGE	W	L	PCT	SV	G	GS	CG	IP	H	BB	SO	SHO	ERA
		26	68	60	.531	6	129	129	84	1143	1136	381	321	14	3.00
Hod Eller	R	23	16	12	.571	2	37	22	14	218	205	59	84	0	2.35
Pete Schneider	R	25	10	15	.400	0	33	30	17	218	213	117	51	2	3.51
Jimmy Ring	R	23	9	5	.643	0	21	18	13	142	130	48	26	4	2.45
Rube Bressler (MS)	L	23	8	5	.615	0	17	13	10	128	124	39	37	0	2.46
Dolf Luque	R	27	6	3	.667	0	12	10	9	83	84	32	26	1	3.80
1 Fred Toney	R	29	6	10	.375	*2	21	19	9	137	148	31	32	1	2.89
Mike Regan	R	30	5	5	.500	2	22	6	4	80	77	29	15	3	3.26
2 Ray Mitchell	R	33	4	0	1.000	0	5	3	3	36	27	5	5	0	0.75
Snipe Conley	R	24	2	0	1.000	0	5	1	1	14	17	5	2	0	5.14
1 George Smith	R	26	2	3	.400	0	10	6	4	55	71	11	19	1	4.09
Larry Jacobus	R	23	1	0	1.000	0	1	1	0	17	25	1	8	0	5.82
Dutch Ruether (MS)	L	24	1	0	1.000	0	2	1	0	10	10	3	10	0	2.70
Jesse Haines	R	25	0	0	—	0	1	0	0	5	5	1	2	0	1.80

*Toney, also with New York, tied for league lead in SV with 3

PITTSBURGH 4th 65-60 .520 17 HUGO BEZDEK

NAME	G by Pos	B	AGE	G	AB	R	H	2B	3B	HR	RBI	BB	SO	SB	BA	SA
TOTALS			27	126	4091	466	1016	107	72	15	391	371	285	200	.248	.321
Fritz Mollwitz	1B119	R	28	119	434	43	116	12	7	0	45	23	24	23	.269	.329
George Cutshaw	2B126	R	31	126	463	56	132	16	10	5	68	27	18	25	.285	.395
Buster Caton (MS)	SS79	R	21	80	303	37	71	5	7	0	17	32	16	12	.234	.297
Bill McKechnie	3B126	R	31	126	435	34	111	13	9	2	43	24	22	12	.255	.340
Billy Southworth	OF64	L	25	64	246	37	84	15	7	2	43	26	9	19	.341	.443
Max Carey	OF126	L	28	126	468	70	128	14	6	3	48	62	25	58	.274	.348
Carson Bigbee	OF92	L	23	92	310	47	79	11	3	1	19	42	10	19	.255	.319
Walter Schmidt	C104	R	31	105	323	31	77	6	3	0	27	17	19	7	.238	.276
Bill Hinchman	OF40, 1B3	R	35	50	111	10	26	5	2	0	13	15	8	1	.234	.315
Casey Stengel (MS)	OF27	L	27	39	122	18	30	4	1	1	12	16	14	11	.246	.320
Lee King (MS)	OF36	R	25	36	112	9	26	3	3	0	11	11	15	3	.232	.321
Tommy Leach	OF23, SS3	R	40	30	72	14	14	2	3	0	5	19	5	2	.194	.306
Luke Boone	SS26, 2B1	R	28	28	91	7	18	3	0	0	3	8	6	1	.198	.231
Whitey Eilam	SS26	R	32	26	77	9	10	1	1	0	2	17	17	2	.130	.169
1 Jimmy Archer	C21, 1B1	R	35	24	58	4	9	1	2	0	1	1	6	0	.155	.241
Ben Shaw (MS)	1B9, C5	R	25	21	36	5	7	1	0	0	2	2	2	0	.194	.222
Red Smith	C10	R	26	15	24	1	4	1	0	0	3	4	3	0	.167	.208
Fred Blackwell (MS)	C8	L	22	8	13	1	2	0	0	0	4	3	4	0	.154	.154
2 Gus Getz	3B2	R	28	7	10	0	2	0	0	0	0	0	0	0	.200	.200
Jake Pitler	2B1	R	24	2	1	0	0	0	0	0	0	0	1	0	.000	.000

Tony Boeckel (MS) 25
Adam Debus (MS) 25
Charlie Jackson (MS) 25
Ray Miller (MS) 30, Hooks Warner (MS) 24, Billy Webb (MS) 22

NAME	T	AGE	W	L	PCT	SV	G	GS	CG	IP	H	BB	SO	SHO	ERA
		28	65	60	.520	7	126	126	85	1140	1005	299	367	10	2.48
Wilbur Cooper	L	26	19	14	.576	3	38	29	26	273	219	65	117	3	2.11
Frank Miller	R	32	11	8	.579	2	29	23	14	170	152	37	47	2	2.38
2 Erskine Mayer	R	28	9	3	.750	0	15	14	11	123	122	27	25	1	2.62
Roy Sanders	R	25	7	9	.438	1	28	14	6	156	135	52	55	1	3.26
Earl Hamilton (MS)	L	26	6	0	1.000	0	6	6	6	54	47	13	20	1	0.83
Ralph Comstock	R	27	5	6	.455	1	15	8	6	81	78	14	44	0	3.00
1 Bob Steele	L	24	2	3	.400	1	10	4	2	49	44	17	21	1	3.31
Carmen Hill	R	22	2	4	.333	0	6	4	3	44	24	17	15	0	1.23
Bob Harmon	R	30	2	7	.222	0	16	9	5	82	76	12	7	0	2.63
Babe Adams	R	36	1	1	.500	0	3	2	2	23	15	4	6	0	1.17
Cy Slapnicka	R	32	1	4	.200	1	7	6	4	49	50	22	3	0	4.78
1 Elmer Jacobs	R	25	0	1	.000	0	4	2	0	31	34	14	2	0	5.87
Hal Carlson (MS)	R	26	0	0	—	0	3	0	0	12	12	5	5	0	3.75

Bill Evans (MS) 25
Elmer Ponder (MS) 25

BROOKLYN 5th 57-69 .452 25.5 WILBERT ROBINSON

NAME	G by Pos	B	AGE	G	AB	R	H	2B	3B	HR	RBI	BB	SO	SB	BA	SA
TOTALS			30	126	4212	360	1052	121	62	10	303	212	326	113	.250	.315
Jake Daubert	1B105	L	34	108	396	50	122	12	15	2	47	27	18	10	.308	.429
Mickey Doolan	2B91	R	38	92	308	14	55	8	2	0	18	22	24	8	.179	.218
Ivy Olson	SS126	R	32	126	506	63	121	16	4	1	17	27	18	21	.239	.292
Ollie O'Mara	3B121	R	27	121	430	37	104	8	4	1	24	7	18	11	.242	.291
Jimmy Johnston	OF96, 1B21, 3B4, 2B1	R	28	123	484	54	136	16	8	1	27	33	31	22	.281	.347
Hy Myers	OF107	L	29	107	440	36	104	19	8	4	40	20	26	17	.236	.348
Zack Wheat	OF105	L	30	105	409	39	137	15	6	0	51	16	17	9	.335	.386
Otto Miller	C62, 1B1	R	29	75	228	8	44	6	1	0	8	9	20	1	.193	.228
Mack Wheat	C38, OF7	R	25	57	157	11	34	7	1	3	8	24	2	2	.217	.293
Jim Hickman (MS)	OF46	R	26	53	167	14	39	4	7	1	16	8	31	5	.234	.359
Jack Coombs	P27, OF13	R	35	46	113	6	19	3	0	0	8	7	13	1	.168	.230
Ray Schmandt (MS)	2B34	R	22	34	114	11	35	5	4	0	18	7	7	1	.307	.421
Ernie Krueger (MS)	C23	R	27	30	84	4	25	4	0	1	7	4	9	2	.287	.379
2 Jimmy Archer	C7	R	35	9	22	3	6	1	0	0	0	0	5	0	.273	.364
Al Nixon	OF4	R	32	6	11	1	5	1	0	0	1	2	1	0	.455	.455
Frank O'Rourke	2B2, OF1	R	24	6	12	0	2	0	0	0	3	1	6	0	.167	.167
Al Bashang	OF3	B	29	2	1	0	0	0	0	0	0	1	0	0	.000	.000
Red Sheridan	2B2	R	21	2	4	0	1	0	0	0	1	0	0	0	.250	.250
Chuck Ward (MS)	3B2	R	23	2	6	0	2	0	0	0	0	0	3	0	.333	.333

Lew Malone (MS) 21

NAME	T	AGE	W	L	PCT	SV	G	GS	CG	IP	H	BB	SO	SHO	ERA
		30	57	69	.452	2	126	126	85	1131	1024	320	395	17	2.81
Burleigh Grimes	R	24	19	9	.679	1	40	30	19	270	210	76	113	7	2.13
Larry Cheney	R	32	11	13	.458	1	32	21	15	201	177	74	83	0	3.00
Rube Marquard	L	31	9	18	.333	0	34	29	19	239	231	59	89	4	2.64
Jack Coombs	R	35	8	14	.364	0	27	20	16	189	191	49	44	2	3.81
3 George Smith	R	26	4	1	.800	0	5	4	4	50	43	5	18	0	2.34
Dick Robertson	R	26	3	6	.333	0	13	9	7	87	87	28	18	1	2.59
Leon Cadore (MS)	R	27	1	0	1.000	0	3	2	2	17	6	7	3	1	0.53
Jeff Pfeffer (IL)	R	30	1	0	1.000	0	1	1	1	9	1	3	1	1	1.00
Dan Griner	R	30	1	6	.167	0	11	6	3	54	47	15	22	1	2.17
Al Mamaux	R	24	0	1	.000	0	4	2	1	14	2	4	6	0	6.75
Harry Heitmann (MS)	R	21	0	1	.000	0	1	1	0	0	4	0	0	0	108.00
Clarence Mitchell (MS)	L	27	0	1	.000	0	1	1	0	0	4	0	0	0	108.00
Rich Durning	R	25	0	0	—	0	2	1	0	8	11	3	3	0	13.50
Jake Hehl	R	18	0	0	—	0	1	0	0	2	2	0	0	0	0.00
Lefty Hermann	R	25	0	0	—	0	1	0	0	4	5	5	1	0	4.50
Norman Plitt	R	25	0	0	—	0	1	0	0	2	4	0	0	0	18.00
Jack Russell (MS)	L	23	0	0	—	0	1	0	0						

Johnny Miljus (MS) 23
Sherry Smith (MS) 27
Duster Mails (MS) 22

NAME	G by Pos	B	AGE	G	AB	R	H	2B	3B	HR	RBI	BB	SO	SB	BA	SA
PHILADELPHIA 6th 55-68 .447 26					**PAT MORAN**											
TOTALS			29	125	4192	429	1022	158	28	25	376	346	400	97	.244	.313
Fred Luderus	1B125	L	32	125	468	54	135	23	2	5	67	42	33	4	.288	.378
Patsy Mc Gaffigan (MS)	2B53 SS1	R	29	54	192	17	39	3	2	1	8	16	23	3	.203	.255
Dave Bancroft	SS125	B	27	125	499	69	132	19	4	0	26	54	35	11	.265	.319
Milt Stock	3B123	R	24	123	481	62	132	14	1	1	42	35	22	20	.274	.314
Gavvy Cravath	OF118	R	37	121	426	43	99	27	5	8	54	54	46	7	.232	.357
Cy Williams	OF91	L	30	94	351	49	97	14	1	6	39	27	30	6	.276	.383
Irish Meusel	OF120 2B4	R	25	124	473	47	132	25	6	4	62	30	21	18	.279	.381
Jack Adams	C76	B	27	84	227	10	40	4	0	0	12	10	26	5	.176	.194
Ed Burns	C68	R	30	68	184	10	38	1	1	0	9	20	9	1	.207	.223
Justin Fitzgerald	OF57	L	27	66	133	21	39	8	0	1	6	13	6	3	.293	.353
Harry Pearce	2B46 SS2 1B1 3B1	R	25	118	164	16	40	3	2	0	18	9	31	5	.244	.287
Ed Hemingway	2B25 3B3 1B1	B	25	33	108	7	23	4	0	1	12	7	9	4	.213	.269
Possum Whitted	OF22 1B1	R	28	24	86	7	21	4	0	0	3	4	10	4	.244	.291
Pickles Dillhoefer (MS)	C6	R	24	8	11	0	1	0	0	0	0	1	1	2	.091	.091

Mickey Devine 26 R 1-8, Ty Pickup 20 R 1-1, Cladue Cooper (MS) 25

NAME	T	AGE	W	L	PCT	SV	G	GS	CG	IP	H	BB	SO	SHO	ERA
		27	55	68	.447	6	125	125	78	1140	1086	369	312	10	3.15
Brad Hogg	R	29	13	13	.500	1	29	25	17	228	201	61	81	3	2.53
Mike Pendergast	L	29	13	14	.481	1	33	30	20	252	257	46	41	0	2.89
2 Elmer Jacobs	R	25	9	5	.643	0	18	14	12	123	91	42	33	3	2.41
1 Erskine Mayer	R	28	7	4	.636	0	13	13	17	104	108	16	16	0	3.12
Joe Oeschger	R	26	6	18	.250	3	30	23	13	184	159	83	60	2	3.03
Milt Wilson	R	28	5	7	.417	0	23	11	6	113	126	39	34	0	3.42
Alex Main	R	34	2	2	.500	0	8	4	1	35	30	16	14	1	4.63
Ben Tincup	R	25	0	1	.000	0	8	1	0	17	24	6	6	0	7.41
Dixie Davis (MS)	R	27	0	2	.000	0	17	5	2	47	43	30	18	0	3.06
Gary Fortune	R	23	0	2	.000	0	5	2	1	31	41	19	10	0	8.13
Frank Woodward (MS)	R	24	0	0	—	0	2	0	0	6	6	4	4	0	6.00

Stan Baumgartner (VR) 25
Eppa Rixey (MS) 27

NAME	G by Pos	B	AGE	G	AB	R	H	2B	3B	HR	RBI	BB	SO	SB	BA	SA
BOSTON 7th 53-71 .427 28.5					**GEORGE STALLINGS**											
TOTALS			30	124	4162	424	1014	107	59	13	353	350	438	83	.244	.307
Ed Konetchy	1B112 OF6 P1	R	32	119	437	33	103	15	5	2	56	32	35	5	.236	.307
Buck Herzog	2B99 1B2 SS7	R	32	118	473	57	108	12	6	0	26	29	28	10	.228	.279
Johnny Rawlings	SS71 2B20 OF18	R	25	111	410	32	85	9	2	0	21	30	31	10	.207	.239
Red Smith	3B119	R	28	119	429	55	128	20	3	2	65	45	47	8	.298	.373
Al Wickland	OF95	L	30	95	332	55	87	7	13	4	32	53	39	12	.262	.398
Ray Powell (MS)	OF53	L	29	53	188	31	40	7	5	0	20	29	30	4	.213	.303
Roy Massey	OF45 1B4 SS1 3B1	R	27	66	203	20	59	6	2	0	18	23	20	1	.291	.340
Art Wilson	C85	R	32	89	280	15	69	8	2	0	19	24	31	5	.246	.289
Joe Kelly (MS)	OF45	R	31	47	155	20	36	2	4	0	15	6	12	12	.232	.297
John Henry	C38	R	28	43	102	6	21	2	0	0	4	10	15	0	.206	.225
Wally Rehg (MS)	OF38	R	29	40	133	6	32	5	1	1	12	5	14	3	.241	.316
Bob Taggert	OF35	L	24	35	146	19	48	1	4	0	4	9	9	4	.329	.390
Jimmy Smith	SS9 2B7 OF6 3B5	B	23	34	102	8	23	3	4	1	14	3	13	1	.225	.363
Zeb Terry	SS27	R	27	28	105	17	32	2	2	0	8	8	14	1	.305	.362
Chet Chadbourne	OF27	L	33	27	104	9	27	2	1	0	6	5	5	5	.260	.298
Rip Conway (MS)	2B5 3B1	L	22	14	24	4	4	0	0	0	2	4	1	1	.167	.167
Doc Crandall	P5 OF3	R	30	14	28	1	8	0	0	0	2	4	3	0	.286	.286
Bill Wagner	C13	R	24	14	47	2	10	0	0	1	7	4	5	0	.213	.277
Rabbit Maranville (MS)	SS11	R	26	11	38	3	12	0	1	0	3	4	0	0	.316	.368
Buzz Murphy	OF9	R	23	9	32	6	12	2	3	1	9	3	5	0	.375	.719
Walt Tragresser (MS)	C7	R	31	7	1	0	0	0	0	0	0	0	0	0	.000	.000
Fred Bailey (MS)		R														

Sam Covington (MS) 23 L 1-3, Tom Miller 20 L 0-2, Doc Bass 19 L 1-1, Hank Gowdy (MS) 28, Art Rico (MS) 21, Hank Schreiber (MS) 26, Ed Fitzpatrick (MS) 28

NAME	T	AGE	W	L	PCT	SV	G	GS	CG	IP	H	BB	SO	SHO	ERA
		28	53	71	.427	0	124	124	96	1117	1111	277	340	13	2.90
Art Nehf	L	25	15	15	.500	0	32	31	28	284	274	76	96	2	2.69
Dick Rudolph (HO)	R	29	9	10	.474	0	21	20	15	154	144	30	48	3	2.57
Pat Ragan	R	32	8	17	.320	2	30	25	15	206	212	54	68	2	3.23
Dana Fillingim (MS)	R	24	7	6	.538	0	14	13	10	113	99	28	29	4	2.23
Bunny Hearn	L	27	5	6	.455	0	17	13	9	126	119	29	30	1	2.50
Jake Northrop	R	30	5	1	.833	0	7	4	4	40	26	3	4	1	1.35
Hugh McQuillan	R	22	1	0	1.000	0	1	1	1	9	7	5	1	0	3.00
Bill Upham	R	30	1	1	.500	0	3	2	2	21	28	1	8	0	5.14
Doc Crandall	R	30	1	2	.333	0	5	3	3	34	39	4	4	0	2.38
Lefty George	L	31	1	5	.167	0	9	5	4	54	56	21	22	0	2.33
Cal Crum	R	28	0	1	.000	0	1	1	1	6	3	0	0	0	18.00
Ed Konetchy	R	32	0	1	.000	0	1	1	0	8	14	2	3	0	6.75
Tom Hughes	R	34	0	2	.000	0	3	1	1	18	17	6	4	0	3.50
Hugh Canavan (MS)	L	21	0	4	.000	0	11	3	3	47	70	15	18	0	6.32

Bill James (MS) 26

NAME	G by Pos	B	AGE	G	AB	R	H	2B	3B	HR	RBI	BB	SO	SB	BA	SA
ST. LOUIS 8th 51-78 .395 33					**JACK HENDRICKS**											
TOTALS			25	131	4369	454	1066	147	64	27	388	329	461	119	.244	.325
Gene Paulette	1B97 SS12 2B7 OF6 3B2 C1 P1	R	27	125	461	33	126	15	3	0	52	27	16	11	.273	.319
Bobby Fisher	2B63	R	31	63	246	36	78	11	3	2	20	15	11	7	.317	.411
Rogers Hornsby	SS109 OF2	R	22	115	416	51	117	19	11	5	60	40	43	8	.281	.416
Doug Baird (MS)	3B81 SS1 OF1	B	26	82	316	41	78	8	2	2	25	23	42	25	.247	.354
Walton Cruise (MS)	OF65	L	28	70	240	34	65	5	4	6	39	30	26	2	.271	.400
Cliff Heathcote	OF88	L	20	88	348	37	90	12	3	4	32	20	40	12	.259	.345
Austin McHenry	OF80	R	22	80	272	32	71	6	12	6	29	21	24	8	.261	.360
Mike Gonzalez	C100 OF5 1B2	R	27	117	349	33	81	14	3	3	20	30	34	14	.232	.338
Bruno Betzel	3B34 OF21 2B10	R	23	76	230	18	51	6	7	0	13	12	16	8	.222	.309
Charlie Grimm	1B42 OF2 3B1	L	19	50	141	11	31	7	0	0	12	6	15	2	.220	.270
Jack Smith (MS)	OF42	L	23	42	166	24	35	2	1	0	4	7	21	5	.211	.235
Red Smyth	OF25 2B11	R	27	40	113	19	24	1	2	0	4	16	11	3	.212	.257
Frank Snyder (MS)	C27 1B3	R	24	30	112	5	28	7	1	0	10	6	13	4	.250	.330
George Anderson	OF35	L	28	35	132	20	39	4	5	0	6	15	7	0	.295	.402
Bobby Wallace	2B17 1B3 3B1	R	44	32	98	3	15	1	0	0	4	5	1	1	.153	.163
John Brock	C18 OF1	R	21	27	52	9	11	2	0	0	4	5	10	1	.212	.250
1 Bert Niehoff	2B22	R	34	22	84	5	15	2	0	0	5	2	10	2	.179	.202
Johnny Beall	OF18	L	36	19	49	2	11	1	0	0	6	3	6	0	.224	.245
Herman Bronkie	3B18	R	33	18	68	7	15	3	0	1	7	2	4	0	.221	.309
2 Marty Kavanagh	OF8 2B4	R	27	12	44	6	8	1	1	0	1	2	3	1	.182	.273
Dutch Distel	2B5 SS2 OF1	R	22	8	17	3	3	1	1	0	1	2	3	0	.143	.143
Chick Mattick	OF3	R	31	8	14	0	2	0	0	0	0	2	2	0	.143	.143
Bob Larmore	SS2	R	21	4	7	0	2	0	0	0	0	0	3	0	.286	.286
Dick Wheeler	OF2	R	20	3	6	0	0	0	0	0	0	0	3	0	.000	.000

Tony Brottem (MS) 27 R 0-4, Ted Menze 20 R 0-3, Dots Miller (MS) 31

NAME	T	AGE	W	L	PCT	SV	G	GS	CG	IP	H	BB	SO	SHO	ERA
		26	51	78	.395	5	131	131	72	1193	1148	352	361	3	2.96
Gene Packard	L	30	12	12	.500	2	30	23	10	182	184	33	46	1	3.51
Red Ames	R	35	9	14	.391	1	27	25	17	207	192	52	68	0	2.30
Bill Doak	R	27	9	15	.375	1	31	23	16	165	176	56	49	0	3.60
Lee Meadows	R	23	8	14	.364	1	30	23	12	165	176	56	74	1	2.43
Bill Sherdel	L	21	6	12	.333	0	35	16	9	182	174	49	40	1	2.72
Jakie May (MS)	R	22	5	6	.455	0	29	15	6	153	149	69	61	0	3.82
Rankin Johnson	R	30	1	1	.500	0	6	1	0	23	20	7	4	0	2.74
Oscar Tuero	R	25	1	2	.333	0	11	3	2	44	32	10	13	0	1.02
Oscar Horstmann (MS)	R	27	0	1	.000	0	3	2	0	23	29	14	6	0	5.48
Earl Howard	R	25	0	0	—	0	1	0	0	2	0	2	0	0	0.00
Gene Paulette	R	26	0	0	—	0	1	0	0	1	.1	0	0	0	0.00

Marv Goodwin (MS)
Lou North (MS) 27
Bruce Hitt (MS) 20

WORLD SERIES — BOSTON (AL) 4　CHICAGO (NL) 2

LINE SCORES

TEAM	1	2	3		4	5	6		7	8	9		10	11	12		R	H	E
Game 1 September 5 at Chicago																			
BOS(AL)	0	0	0		1	0	0		0	0	0						1	5	0
CHI(NL)	0	0	0		0	0	0		0	0	0						0	6	0

Ruth　　　　　Vaughn

Game 2　September 6 at Chicago																			
BOS	0	0	0		0	0	0		0	0	1						1	6	1
CHI	0	3	0		0	0	0		0	0	X						3	7	1

Bush　　　　　Tyler

Game 3　September 7 at Chicago																			
BOS	0	0	0		2	0	0		0	0	0						2	7	0
CHI	0	0	0		0	1	0		0	0	0						1	7	1

Mays　　　　　Vaughn

Game 4　September 9 at Boston																			
CHI	0	0	0		0	0	0		2	0	0						2	7	1
BOS	0	0	2		0	0	0		1	X	0						3	4	0

Tyler, **Douglas** (8)　　　**Ruth**, Bush (9)

Game 5　September 10 at Boston																			
CHI	0	0	1		0	0	0		0	2	0						3	7	0
BOS	0	0	0		0	0	0		0	0	0						0	5	0

Vaughn　　　　　Jones

Game 6　September 11 at Boston																			
CHI	0	0	0		1	0	0		0	0	0						1	3	2
BOS	0	0	2		0	0	0		0	0	X						2	5	0

Tyler, Hendrix (8)　　　**Mays**

COMPOSITE BATTING

NAME	POS	G	AB	R	H	2B	3B	HR	RBI	BA
Boston (AL)										
Totals		6	172	9	32	2	3	0	6	.186
Strunk	OF	6	23	1	4	1	1	0	0	.174
Scott	SS	6	21	0	2	0	0	0	1	.095
McInnis	1B	6	20	2	5	0	0	0	1	.250
Whiteman	OF	6	20	2	5	0	1	0	1	.250
Hooper	OF	6	20	0	4	0	0	0	0	.200
Shean	2B	6	19	2	4	1	0	0	0	.211
Thomas	3B	6	16	0	2	0	0	0	0	.125
Schang	C	5	9	1	4	0	0	0	0	.444
Agnew	C	6	9	0	0	0	0	0	0	.000
Ruth	P-OF	3	5	0	1	0	1	0	2	.200
Mays	P	2	5	1	1	0	0	0	0	.200
Bush	P	2	2	0	0	0	0	0	0	.000
Dubuc	PH	1	1	0	0	0	0	0	0	.000
Miller	PH	1	1	0	0	0	0	0	0	.000
Jones	P	1	1	0	0	0	0	0	0	.000
Chicago (NL)										
Totals		6	176	10	37	5	0	0	10	.210
Mann	OF	6	22	0	5	2	0	0	2	.227
Hollocher	SS	6	21	2	4	1	0	1	1	.190
Paskert	OF	6	21	0	4	1	0	0	1	.190
Flack	OF	6	19	2	5	0	0	0	0	.263
Pick	2B	6	18	2	7	1	0	0	0	.389
Merkle	1B	6	18	1	5	0	0	0	1	.278
Deal	3B	6	17	0	3	0	0	0	0	.176
Killefer	C	6	17	2	2	1	0	0	2	.118
Vaughn	PO	3	10	0	0	0	0	0	0	.000
Tyler	P	3	5	1	1	0	0	0	2	.200
O'Farrell	C	3	3	0	0	0	0	0	0	.000
Barber	PH	2	2	0	0	0	0	0	0	.000
Hendrix	P	2	2	0	2	0	0	0	1	1.000
Wortman	2B	2	1	0	0	0	0	0	0	.000
McCabe	PR-PH	2	1	0	0	0	0	0	0	.000
Zeider	3B	2	0	0	0	0	0	0	0	—
Douglas	P	2	0	0	0	0	0	0	0	—

COMPOSITE PITCHING

NAME	G	IP	H	BB	SO	W	L	SV	ERA
Boston (AL)									
Totals		6	53	37	18	14	4	2	0	1.70
Mays	2	18	10	3	5	2	0	0	1.00
Ruth	2	17	13	7	4	2	0	0	1.06
Bush	2	9	7	3	0	0	1	1	3.00
Jones	1	9	7	5	5	0	1	0	3.00
Chicago (NL)									
Totals		6	52	32	16	21	2	4	0	1.04
Vaughn	3	27	17	5	17	1	2	0	1.00
Tyler	3	23	14	11	4	1	1	0	1.17
Douglas	1	1	1	0	0	0	1	0	0.00
Hendrix	1	1	0	0	0	0	0	0	0.00

1919 Prelude to Disaster

After war had shortened the 1918 baseball season, peace and the national pastime each staged comebacks in this year of the armistice. A nation of baseball fans turned out at the ball parks in swarms in individual pursuit of a "return to normalcy", and interest in the game surpassed any level since the Federal League conflict. The highest number of fans since 1912 attended the World Series between the favored Chicago White Sox and the lightly-held Cincinnati Reds, and this nightcap to the season, experimentally lengthened to nine games, showed the Reds easily downing the Sox five games to three. The educated opinion on the Series outcome postulated that Chicago had been tired out by a rigorous pennant race, while Cincinnati had saved its strength by climbing its pennant early.

The shiny Series cup concealed the corruption within. The public did not yet know that seven White Sox players had agreed to throw the Series in return for $100,000 from gambling interests. The average fan could not realize that Joe Jackson's .375 batting average only camouflaged his intentional failings in clutch situations, and the man in the bleachers did not suspect that star Sox pitchers, Eddie Cicotte and Lefty Williams, were being shelled from the mound because of lack of effort to fire the ball. Had the public known of the sordid deal, they would have better appreciated the gutty performance of pitcher Dickie Kerr, who won two games despite the treason of half the team behind him in the field. But the public did not know and would not until September of the following year. There were only some unsupported rumors about White Sox' dishonesty, thus making the 1919 World Series a simple upset victory and a fitting end to a good season.

Fate would have been kinder if it had not allowed the White Sox to edge out the Cleveland Indians for the American League flag. But Joe Jackson and Happy Felsch, both Series throwers, and Eddie Collins, not involved in the fix, provided too much talent to keep Chicago away from the pennant. The trio sparked the league's best offense, while Eddie Cicotte and Lefty Williams proved a pair of aces on the hill. Freshman manager Kid Gleason led his charges into first place on July 10, and strong challenges by the Indians and the New York Yankees could not budge the Sox from that top spot the rest of the way. Regardless of the World Series fix, the Sox had to honestly fight down to the wire to win by a 3½ game final bulge over the Indians for the pennant.

The Cincinnati Reds became a part of baseball's notoriety by winning the National League pennant over the New York Giants, whom they caught in August and then turned away in two crucial series late in the season. The Reds, in winning their first senior circuit title, piled up a final nine-game margin, sparked by the batting of Edd Roush and Heinie Groh and the pitching of Slim Sallee, Hod Eller, and Dutch Reuther. Although the stirring Series win seemingly capped a glorious Cincinnati season, in retrospect one overlooks that the Reds won--remembering only that the White Sox threw it all away.

For the runner-up Giants, their season was brightened by Jesse Barnes, who returned from the military to lead the circuit with his 25 wins. Another war-time returnee, Grover "Pete" Alexander, posted a 16-11 mark with a league-leading 1.72 E.R.A.--a fine performance, especially when coupled with teammate Hippo Vaughn's 21 wins and 1.79 E.R.A., but not enough to help Chicago repeat as league champions.

The year, in addition to bringing later disaster, also ushered in a legend which would eventually restore the faith of the game. A free-swinging young slugger by the name of Babe Ruth became the sensation of baseball by developing into the greatest power hitter in history. The pitcher turned-outfielder set a new season's home run record by clouting 29 circuit-blasts, eclipsing Ned Williamson's mark of 27 set in 1884 for Chicago. The lusty Ruth also found time to pitch 17 games for the Red Sox. It was a herculean feat, yet not enough to prevent the Beantowners from falling from the top in 1918 to a sixth-place finish. Boston's fall from glory was attributed in large measure to star pitcher Carl Mays' jumping of the team and subsequent sale to the Yankees--a deal which triggered a severe internal squabble within the American League. Boston owner Harry Frazee's troubles due to a deserting star and second-division finish did not end there. He found himself pinched for funds and restocked his empty coffers by selling the fabulous Ruth to the Yankees during the winter for $125,000, thus enabling New York to begin the greatest dynasty in the history of baseball.

1919 AMERICAN LEAGUE

NAME	G by Pos	B	AGE	G	AB	R	H	2B	3B	HR	RBI	BB	SO	SB	BA	SA
CHICAGO 1st 88-52 .629 KID GLEASON																
TOTALS			28	140	4675	668	1343	218	70	25	571	427	358	150	.287	.380
Chick Gandil	1B115	R	31	115	411	54	128	24	7	1	60	20	20	10	.290	.383
Eddie Collins	2B140	L	32	140	518	87	165	19	7	4	80	68	27	33	.319	.450
Swede Risberg	SS97 1B22	R	24	119	414	48	106	19	6	2	38	35	38	19	.256	.345
Buck Weaver	3B97 SS43	B	28	140	571	89	169	33	9	3	75	11	21	22	.296	.401
Nemo Leibold	OF122	L	27	122	434	81	131	18	2	0	26	72	30	17	.302	.353
Happy Felsch	OF135	R	27	135	502	68	138	34	11	7	86	40	35	19	.275	.428
Joe Jackson	OF139	L	29	139	516	79	181	31	14	7	96	60	10	9	.351	.506
Ray Schalk	C129	R	26	131	394	57	111	9	3	0	34	51	25	11	.282	.320
Shano Collins	OF46 1B8	R	33	63	179	21	50	6	3	1	16	7	11	3	.279	.363
Fred McMullin	3B46 2B5	R	27	60	170	31	50	8	4	0	19	11	18	4	.294	.388
Eddie Murphy	OF6	L	27	30	35	8	17	4	0	0	5	7	0	4	.486	.600
Byrd Lynn	C28	L	30	29	66	4	15	4	0	0	4	4	9	0	.227	.288
Joe Jenkins	C4	R	28	11	19	0	3	1	0	0	1	1	1	1	.158	.211
Harvey McClellan	3B3 SS2	R	24	7	12	2	4	0	0	0	1	1	1	0	.333	.333
CLEVELAND 2nd 84-55 .604 3.5 LEE FOHL 44-34 .564 TRIS SPEAKER 40-21 .656																
TOTALS			29	139	4565	634	1268	254	71	25	547	498	367	113	.278	.381
Doc Johnston	1B98	L	31	102	331	42	101	17	3	1	33	25	18	21	.305	.384
Bill Wambsganss	2B139	R	25	139	526	60	146	17	6	2	60	32	24	18	.278	.344
Ray Chapman	SS115	R	28	115	433	75	130	23	10	3	53	31	38	18	.300	.420
Larry Gardner	3B139	L	33	139	524	67	157	29	7	2	79	39	29	7	.300	.382
Elmer Smith	OF111	R	26	114	395	60	110	24	6	9	54	41	30	15	.278	.438
Tris Speaker	OF134	L	31	134	494	83	146	38	12	2	63	73	12	15	.296	.433
Jack Graney	OF125	L	33	128	461	79	108	22	8	1	30	105	39	7	.234	.323
Steve O'Neill	C123	R	27	125	398	46	115	35	7	2	47	48	21	4	.289	.427
Smoky Joe Wood	OF64 P1	R	29	72	192	30	49	10	5	1	27	32	21	3	.255	.375
Joe Harris	1B46 SS4	R	28	62	184	30	69	16	1	1	46	33	21	3	.375	.489
PinchThomas	C21	L	31	34	46	2	5	0	0	0	2	4	3	0	.109	.109
Harry Lunte	SS24	R	26	26	77	2	15	2	0	0	2	1	7	0	.195	.221
Les Nunamaker	C16	R	30	26	56	6	14	1	1	0	7	2	6	0	.250	.304
Charlie Jamieson	P4 OF3	R	26	26	17	3	6	2	1	0	2	0	2	1	.353	.588
Joe Evans	SS6	R	24	21	14	9	1	0	0	0	0	2	1	1	.071	.071
NEW YORK 3rd 80-59 .576 7.5 MILLER HUGGINS																
TOTALS			28	141	4475	582	1275	193	49	45	499	386	479	101	.267	.356
Wally Pipp	1B138	L	26	138	523	74	144	23	10	7	50	39	42	9	.275	.398
Del Pratt	2B140	R	31	140	527	69	154	27	7	4	56	36	24	22	.292	.393
Roger Peckinpaugh	SS121	R	28	122	453	89	138	20	2	7	33	59	37	10	.305	.404
Frank Baker	3B141	L	33	141	567	70	166	22	1	10	83	44	18	13	.293	.388
Sammy Vick	OF100	R	24	106	407	59	101	15	9	2	27	20	55	4	.248	.344
Ping Bodie	OF134	R	31	134	475	45	132	27	8	6	59	36	46	15	.278	.406
Duffy Lewis	OF141	R	30	141	559	67	152	23	4	7	89	17	42	4	.272	.365
Muddy Ruel	C81	R	23	81	233	18	56	6	0	0	31	34	26	4	.240	.266
Chick Fewster	OF41 SS23 2B4 3B2	R	23	81	244	38	69	9	3	1	15	34	36	8	.283	.357
Truck Hannah	C73 1B1	R	30	75	227	14	54	8	3	1	20	22	19	0	.238	.313
Aaron Ward	1B5 3B3 SS2 2B1	R	22	27	34	5	7	2	0	0	2	5	6	0	.206	.265
Al Wickland	OF15	L	31	26	46	2	7	1	0	0	1	2	10	0	.152	.174
Lefty O'Doul	P3 OF1	L	22	19	16	2	4	0	0	0	1	1	2	1	.250	.250
George Halas	OF6	B	24	12	22	0	2	0	0	0	0	0	8	0	.091	.091
1 Bill Lamar	OF3 1B1	L	22	11	16	1	3	1	0	0	0	0	2	1	.188	.250
Frank Gleich	OF4	L	25	5	4	0	1	0	0	0	0	1	0	0	.250	.250
Fred Hofmann	C1	R	25	1	1	0	0	0	0	0	0	0	0	0	.000	.000
Frank Kane		R	24	1	1	0	0	0	0	0	0	0	0	0	.000	.000
Curt Walker		L	22	1	1	0	0	0	0	0	0	0	0	0	.000	.000

NAME	T	AGE	W	L	PCT	SV	G	GS	CG	IP	H	BB	SO	SHO	ERA
		30	88	52	.629	2	140	140	87	1266	1245	342	468	14	3.04
Eddie Cicotte	R	35	29	7	.806	1	40	35	29	307	256	49	110	5	1.82
Lefty Williams	L	26	23	11	.676	0	41	40	27	297	265	58	125	5	2.64
Dickie Kerr	R	25	13	8	.619	0	39	17	10	212	208	64	79	1	2.89
Red Faber (SA)	R	30	11	9	.550	0	25	20	9	162	185	45	45	0	3.83
2 Grover Lowdermilk	R	34	5	5	.500	0	20	11	5	97	95	43	43	0	2.78
3 Bill James	R	32	3	1	.750	0	5	5	3	39	39	14	11	2	2.54
Roy Wilkinson	R	26	1	1	.500	0	4	1	1	22	21	10	5	1	2.05
Dave Danforth	L	29	1	2	.333	1	15	1	0	42	58	20	17	0	7.71
Frank Shellenback	R	20	1	3	.250	0	8	4	2	35	40	16	10	0	5.14
2 Erskine Mayer	R	29	1	3	.250	0	6	2	0	24	30	11	9	0	8.25
John Sullivan	L	25	0	1	.000	0	4	2	1	15	24	8	9	0	4.20
Charlie Robertson	R	23	0	0	.000	0	1	1	0	2	1	1	0	0	9.00
Joe Benz	R	33	0	0	—	0	1	0	0	2	2	0	0	0	0.00
Tom McGuire	R	27	0	0	—	0	3	0	0	3	5	3	0	0	9.00
Win Noyes	R	30	0	0	—	0	1	0	0	6	10	0	4	0	7.50
3 Pat Ragan	R	33	0	0	—	0	1	1	0	1	1	0	0	0	0.00
Reb Russell (SA)	L	30	0	0	—	0	1	0	0	1	1	1	0	0	0.00
		27	84	55	.604	9	139	139	80	1255	1242	362	432	10	2.92
Stan Coveleski	R	29	29	12	.667	3	43	34	24	296	286	60	118	4	2.52
Jim Bagby	R	29	17	11	.607	3	35	32	21	241	258	44	61	0	2.80
George Uhle	R	20	10	5	.667	0	26	12	7	127	129	43	50	1	2.91
Guy Morton	R	26	10	9	.526	0	26	20	9	147	128	47	64	3	2.82
Elmer Myers	R	25	8	7	.533	0	23	15	6	135	134	43	38	1	3.73
2 Ray Caldwell	R	31	5	1	.833	0	6	6	4	53	33	19	24	1	1.70
Hi Jasper	R	38	4	5	.444	0	12	10	5	83	83	28	25	0	3.58
Tom Phillips	R	30	3	2	.600	0	22	3	2	55	55	34	18	0	2.95
Johnny Enzmann	R	29	2	2	.500	1	14	4	2	55	67	8	13	0	2.29
Fritz Coumbe	L	29	1	1	.500	1	8	2	0	24	32	9	7	0	5.25
Tony Faeth	R	25	0	0	—	0	6	0	0	18	13	10	7	0	0.50
Ed Klepfer	R	31	0	0	—	0	5	0	0	7	12	6	7	0	7.71
Charlie Jamieson	L	26	0	0	—	0	4	1	0	13	12	8	0	0	5.54
Joe Engel	R	26	0	0	—	0	1	0	0	0	0	3	0	0	∞
Smoky Joe Wood	R	29	0	0	—	0	1	0	0	1	0	0	0	0	0.00
		28	80	59	.576	7	141	141	85	1303	1143	433	500	14	2.78
Bob Shawkey	R	28	20	11	.645	4	41	27	22	261	218	92	122	3	2.27
Jack Quinn	R	35	15	15	.500	0	38	31	18	264	242	65	97	4	2.63
Hank Thormahlen	L	22	13	9	.591	1	30	25	13	189	155	61	62	2	2.62
George Mogridge	L	30	10	7	.588	0	35	18	13	187	159	46	58	3	2.50
2 Carl Mays	R	27	9	3	.750	0	13	13	12	120	96	37	54	1	1.65
Ernie Shore	R	28	5	8	.385	0	20	13	3	95	105	44	24	0	4.17
1 Allen Russell	R	25	4	5	.444	2*	23	9	4	91	89	32	50	1	3.46
Luke Nelson	R	25	3	0	1.000	0	9	0	0	24	22	11	11	0	3.00
1 Bob McGraw (MS)	R	24	1	0	1.000	0	16	1	0	30	23	6	7	0	3.38
Pete Schneider	R	26	0	0	—	0	7	4	0	29	19	22	11	0	3.41
Lefty O'Doul	L	22	0	0	—	0	3	0	0	5	7	4	2	0	3.60
Walt Smallwood (MS)	R	26	0	0	—	0	6	0	0	22	20	9	6	0	4.91

*Russell, also with Boston, league leader in SV with 6

DETROIT — 4th 80-60 .571 8 — HUGHIE JENNINGS

NAME	G by Pos	B	AGE	G	AB	R	H	2B	3B	HR	RBI	BB	SO	SB	BA	SA
TOTALS			29	140	4665	620	1319	222	84	23	544	429	427	121	.283	.381
Harry Heilmann	1B140	R	24	140	537	74	172	30	15	8	93	37	41	7	.320	.477
Ralph Young	2B121, SS4	B	30	125	456	63	96	13	5	1	25	53	32	8	.211	.268
Donie Bush	SS129	B	31	129	509	82	124	11	6	0	26	75	36	22	.244	.289
Bob Jones	3B127	L	29	127	439	37	114	18	9	1	57	34	39	11	.260	.335
Ira Flagstead	OF83	R	25	97	287	43	95	22	3	5	41	35	39	6	.331	.481
Ty Cobb	OF123	L	32	124	497	92	**191**	36	13	1	70	38	22	28	**.384**	.515
Bobby Veach	OF138	L	31	139	538	87	**191**	**45**	17	3	101	33	33	19	.355	.519
Eddie Ainsmith	C106	R	29	114	364	42	99	17	12	3	32	45	30	9	.272	.409
Chick Shorten	OF75	R	27	95	270	37	85	9	3	0	22	22	13	5	.315	.370
Bert Ellison	2B25, OF10, SS1	R	22	56	134	18	29	4	1	0	11	13	24	4	.216	.246
Ben Dyer	3B23, SS11,OF1	R	26	44	85	11	21	4	0	0	15	8	19	0	.247	.294
Oscar Stanage	C36, 1B1	R	36	38	120	9	29	4	1	1	15	7	12	1	.242	.317
Archie Yelle	C5	R	27	5	4	1	0	0	0	0	0	0	1	0	.000	.000
1 Snooks Dowd		R	21	2	1	0	0	0	0	0	0	0	1	0	.000	—

NAME	T	AGE	W	L	PCT	SV	G	GS	CG	IP	H	BB	SO	SHO	ERA
TOTALS		27	80	60	.571	5	140	140	85	1256	1254	431	428	10	3.30
Hooks Dauss	R	29	21	9	.700	0	34	32	22	256	262	63	73	2	3.55
Howard Ehmke	R	25	17	10	.630	0	33	31	20	249	255	107	79	2	3.18
Dutch Leonard	L	27	14	13	.519	0	29	28	18	217	212	65	102	4	2.78
Bernie Boland	R	27	14	16	.467	1	35	30	18	243	222	80	71	1	3.04
Slim Love	L	28	5	4	.556	2	22	8	4	90	92	40	46	0	3.00
2 Doc Ayres	R	28	5	3	.625	0	24	5	3	94	88	28	32	1	2.68
1 Bill James	R	32	3	5	.375	0	9	12	5	62	64	16	9	0	6.00
George Cunningham	R	32	1	1	.500	1	17	0	0	48	54	15	11	0	4.88
Willie Mitchell	L	29	1	2	.333	0	3	2	0	15	17	10	4	0	5.14
1 Eric Erickson	R	26	0	2	.000	0	3	2	0	15	17	10	4	0	6.60
Rudy Kallio	R	26	0	0	—	1	12	1	0	12	21	8	3	0	5.73

ST. LOUIS — 5th 67-72 .482 20.5 — JIMMY BURKE

NAME	G by Pos	B	AGE	G	AB	R	H	2B	3B	HR	RBI	BB	SO	SB	BA	SA
TOTALS			30	140	4671	535	1234	187	73	31	460	391	443	74	.264	.355
George Sisler	1B131	L	26	132	511	96	180	31	15	10	83	27	20	28	.352	.530
Joe Gedeon	2B118	R	25	120	437	57	111	13	4	0	27	50	35	4	.254	.302
Wally Gerber	SS140	R	27	140	462	46	105	14	6	1	37	49	36	1	.227	.290
Jimmy Austin	3B98	B	39	106	396	54	94	9	9	1	21	42	31	8	.237	.313
Earl Smith (JJ)	OF68	R	28	88	252	21	63	12	5	1	36	18	27	1	.250	.349
Baby Doll Jacobson	OF105, 1B8	R	28	128	455	70	147	31	8	4	51	24	47	9	.323	.453
Jack Tobin	OF123	L	27	127	486	54	159	22	7	6	57	36	24	8	.327	.438
Hank Severeid	C103	R	28	112	351	16	87	12	2	0	36	21	13	2	.248	.293
Ray Demmitt	OF49	L	35	79	202	19	48	11	2	1	19	14	27	3	.238	.327
Herman Bronkie	3B34, 2B16, 1B2	R	34	67	196	23	50	14	2	0	14	23	23	2	.255	.327
Ken Williams (JJ)	OF63	L	29	65	227	32	68	10	5	6	35	26	25	7	.300	.467
Josh Billings	C27, 1B1	R	27	38	76	9	15	1	1	0	3	1	12	0	.197	.237
Wally Mayer	C25	R	28	30	62	2	14	4	1	0	5	8	11	0	.226	.323
Tod Sloan	OF20	L	28	27	63	9	15	1	3	0	6	1	3	3	.238	.349
Joe Schepner	3B13	R	23	14	48	2	10	4	0	0	6	1	5	1	.208	.292
Pat Collins	C5	R	22	10	20	2	3	1	0	0	1	4	2	0	.150	.200
John Shovlin	2B9	R	28	9	35	4	7	0	0	0	1	5	2	0	.200	.200
Gene Robertson	SS2	L	20	5	7	1	1	0	0	0	0	1	0	0	.143	.143

NAME	T	AGE	W	L	PCT	SV	G	GS	CG	IP	H	BB	SO	SHO	ERA
TOTALS		29	67	72	.482	6	140	140	77	1256	1255	421	415	14	3.13
Allan Sothoron	R	28	20	13	.606	3	40	30	21	270	256	87	106	3	2.20
Urban Shocker	R	26	13	11	.542	0	30	25	13	211	193	55	86	5	2.69
Bert Gallia	R	27	12	14	.462	2	34	25	14	222	220	92	83	1	3.61
Carl Weilman (XJ)	R	29	10	6	.625	0	20	20	12	148	133	45	44	2	2.07
Lefty Leifield	L	35	4	6	.400	0	19	9	6	92	96	25	18	2	2.93
Ernie Koob	L	26	2	3	.400	0	25	4	0	66	77	23	11	0	4.64
Dave Davenport	R	29	2	11	.154	1	24	16	5	123	135	41	37	0	3.95
Elam Vangilder	R	23	1	1	1.000	0	3	1	1	13	15	3	6	0	2.08
Bill Bayne	L	20	1	1	.500	0	2	1	1	12	16	6	0	0	5.25
1 Tom Rogers	R	24	0	1	.000	0	2	0	1	7	0	1	0	0	27.00
Rolla Mapel	R	29	0	3	.000	0	4	3	2	20	17	17	2	0	4.50
Rasty Wright	R	23	0	5	.000	0	24	5	2	63	79	20	14	0	5.57
1 Grover Lowdermilk	R	34	0	0	—	0	7	0	0	12	6	1	0	0	0.75
Hal Haid	R	21	0	0	—	0	2	0	0	5	3	1	0	0	18.00

BOSTON — 6th 66-71 .482 20.5 — ED BARROW

NAME	G by Pos	B	AGE	G	AB	R	H	2B	3B	HR	RBI	BB	SO	SB	BA	SA
TOTALS			26	138	4548	565	1188	181	49	33	494	471	411	108	.261	.344
Stuffy McInnis	1B118	R	28	120	440	32	134	12	5	1	58	23	11	8	.305	.361
2 Red Shannon	2B79	B	22	80	290	36	75	11	7	0	17	17	42+	5	.259	.345
Everett Scott	SS138	R	26	138	507	41	141	19	0	0	38	19	26	8	.278	.316
Ossie Vitt	3B133	R	29	133	469	64	114	10	3	0	40	44	11	5	.243	.277
Harry Hooper	OF128	L	31	128	491	76	131	25	6	3	49	79	28	23	.267	.360
2 Braggo Roth	OF55	R	26	63	227	38	59	13	3	0	23	32	35	9	.256	.330
Babe Ruth	OF111, P17, 1B4	L	24	130	432	**103**	139	34	12	**29**	**114**	101	58	7	.322	**.657**
Wally Schang	C103	B	24	113	330	43	101	16	3	0	55	71	42	15	.306	.373
1 Amos Strunk	OF48	L	30	48	184	27	50	11	3	0	17	13	13	3	.272	.364
2 Bill Lamar	OF36	L	22	48	148	18	43	5	1	0	14	5	9	3	.291	.338
Roxy Walters	C47	R	26	48	135	5	26	2	0	0	9	7	15	1	.193	.207
Frank Gilhooley	OF33	L	27	48	112	14	27	4	0	0	1	12	8	2	.241	.277
Del Gainer	1B21, OF18	R	31	47	118	9	28	6	2	0	13	13	15	5	.237	.322
Mike McNally	SS11, 3B11, 2B3	R	25	33	42	10	11	4	0	0	1	2	4	2	.262	.357
Jack Barry	2B31	R	32	31	108	13	26	5	1	0	2	5	5	2	.241	.306
Dave Shean	2B29	R	41	29	100	4	14	0	0	0	3	4	7	1	.140	.140
Joe Wilhoit	OF5	L	33	6	18	7	6	0	0	0	2	5	2	1	.333	.333
Norm McNeil	C5	R	26	5	9	0	3	0	0	0	1	1	0	0	.333	.333
Dick Hoblitzell (MS) 30																

NAME	T	AGE	W	L	PCT	SV	G	GS	CG	IP	H	BB	SO	SHO	ERA
TOTALS		26	66	71	.482	7	138	138	86	1222	1251	420	380	**15**	3.30
Herb Pennock	L	25	16	8	.667	0	32	26	16	219	223	48	70	5	2.71
Sad Sam Jones	R	26	12	20	.375	0	35	31	21	245	258	95	67	5	3.75
2 Allen Russell	R	25	9	4	.692	4*	21	11	9	120	105	39	63	1	2.55
Babe Ruth	L	24	8	5	.615	2	17	15	12	133	148	58	30	0	2.98
1 Ray Caldwell	R	31	7	4	.636	0	18	12	6	86	90	22	33	1	3.96
1 Carl Mays	R	27	7	11	.389	1	21	16	11	145	131	40	53	2	2.48
Waite Hoyt	R	19	4	6	.400	0	13	11	6	105	99	22	28	1	3.26
2 Bill James	R	32	3	5	.375	0	13	7	4	73	74	39	12	0	4.07
2 Bob McGraw	R	24	0	2	.000	0	10	1	0	27	33	17	6	0	6.67
Paul Musser (MS)	R	30	0	2	.000	0	5	4	1	20	26	8	14	0	4.05
George Dumont	R	23	0	4	.000	0	5	3	1	35	45	19	12	0	4.37
Bullet Joe Bush (SA)	R	26	0	0	—	0	3	2	0	9	11	4	3	0	5.00
George Winn	R	22	0	0	—	0	5	0	0	12	16	3	3	0	7.20

*Russell, also with New York, league leader in SV with 6
+Shannon, also with Philadelphia, league leader in SO with 70

WASHINGTON — 7th 56-84 .400 32 — CLARK GRIFFITH

NAME	G by Pos	B	AGE	G	AB	R	H	2B	3B	HR	RBI	BB	SO	SB	BA	SA
TOTALS			27	142	4757	533	1238	177	63	24	459	416	511	142	.260	.339
Joe Judge	1B133	L	25	135	521	83	150	33	12	2	31	81	35	23	.288	.409
1 Hal Janvrin	2B56, SS2	R	26	61	208	17	37	4	1	1	13	19	17	8	.178	.221
Howard Shanks	SS94, 2B34, OF6	R	28	135	491	33	122	8	7	1	54	25	48	13	.248	.299
Eddie Foster	3B115	R	32	120	478	57	126	12	5	0	26	33	21	20	.264	.310
Sam Rice	OF141	L	29	141	557	80	179	23	9	3	71	42	26	26	.321	.411
Clyde Milan (IL)	OF86	L	33	88	321	43	92	12	6	0	37	40	16	11	.287	.361
Mike Menosky	OF103	L	24	116	342	62	98	15	3	6	39	44	46	13	.287	.401
Val Picinich	C69	R	22	80	212	18	52	12	3	3	22	17	43	6	.274	.401
Patsy Gharrity	C60, OF33, 1B7	R	27	111	347	35	94	19	4	2	43	25	39	4	.271	.366
Buzz Murphy	OF73	R	24	79	252	19	66	7	4	0	28	19	32	5	.262	.321
Joe Leonard	2B28, 3B25, 1B4, OF1	R	24	71	198	26	51	8	3	2	20	20	28	3	.258	.359
Sam Agnew	C36	R	32	42	98	6	23	7	0	0	10	10	8	1	.235	.306
Frank Ellerbe	SS28	R	23	28	105	13	29	4	1	0	16	2	15	5	.276	.333
2 Roy Grover	2B24	R	27	24	75	6	14	0	0	0	7	6	10	2	.187	.187
George McBride	SS15	R	38	15	40	3	8	1	1	0	4	3	3	0	.200	.275
Bucky Harris	2B8	R	22	8	28	0	6	2	0	0	4	1	3	0	.214	.286
Ike Davis	SS4	R	24	8	14	0	0	0	0	0	0	0	0	0	.000	.000
Claude Davidson	3B2	R	22	7	7	1	3	0	0	0	0	0	0	0	.429	.429
Jesse Baker	SS1	R	22	2	1	0	0	0	0	0	0	0	0	0	.000	.000
Frank Kelliher		L	20	1	1	0	0	0	0	0	0	0	0	0	.000	.000
Danny Silva	3B1	R	22	1	4	0	1	0	0	0	0	0	0	0	.250	.250
George Twombly	OF1	R	27	1	4	0	0	0	0	0	0	1	0	0	.000	.000

NAME	T	AGE	W	L	PCT	SV	G	GS	CG	IP	H	BB	SO	SHO	ERA
TOTALS		25	56	84	.400	8	142	142	69	1274	1237	451	**536**	12	3.01
Walter Johnson	R	31	20	14	.588	2	39	29	27	290	235	51	**147**	7	**1.49**
Jim Shaw	R	26	17	17	.485	4	45	38	23	307	274	101	128	3	2.73
Harry Harper	L	24	6	21	.222	0	35	30	8	208	220	97	87	0	3.72
2 Eric Erickson	R	27	6	10	.375	0	20	15	7	132	130	63	86	1	3.95
Harry Courtney	L	25	2	0	1.000	0	4	3	2	26	25	19	6	1	2.77
Al Schacht	R	25	2	0	1.000	0	12	1	1	15	14	4	4	0	2.40
Ed Gill	R	23	1	1	.500	0	16	2	0	37	38	21	7	0	4.86
Tom Zachary (MS)	R	23	1	5	.167	0	7	7	0	62	68	20	19	0	2.90
1 Doc Ayres	R	28	1	6	.143	0	11	5	0	44	52	17	12	0	2.86
Charlie Whitehouse	R	25	0	1	.000	0	11	0	0	13	16	9	5	0	4.50
Bill Snyder	R	21	0	0	—	0	6	1	0	16	6	3	5	0	1.13
Dick Robertson	R	27	0	2	.000	0	12	0	0	17	24	10	1	0	2.25
1 Harry Thompson	R	29	0	3	.000	0	12	3	0	43	48	8	10	0	3.56
Molly Craft	R	23	0	1	.000	0	12	0	0	49	59	18	17	0	3.86
Ed Hovlik	R	27	0	0	—	0	2	0	0	6	12	5	1	0	12.00
Clarence Fisher	L	22	0	0	—	0	4	0	0	3	4	0	0	0	13.50
Nick Altrock	L	42	0	0	—	0	1	0	0	4	4	0	0	0	0.00
Rip Jordan	R	29	0	1	.000	0	1	0	0	4	6	2	1	0	11.25

PHILADELPHIA — 8th 36-104 .257 52 — CONNIE MACK

NAME	G by Pos	B	AGE	G	AB	R	H	2B	3B	HR	RBI	BB	SO	SB	BA	SA
TOTALS			25	140	4730	459	1156	175	71	35	396	349	**565**	103	.244	.334
George Burns	1B86, OF34	R	25	126	470	63	139	29	9	8	57	19	18	5	.296	.447
1 Red Shannon	2B37	B	22	39	155	14	42	7	4	0	14	12	28*	4	.271	.342
Joe Dugan	SS98, 2B4, 3B2	R	22	104	387	25	105	17	2	1	30	11	30	9	.271	.333
Fred Thomas	3B124	R	26	124	443	42	96	11	10	2	23	43	52	12	.212	.294
Manny Kopp	OF65	R	27	75	235	34	53	2	4	1	12	42	43	16	.226	.281
Tilly Walker	OF115	R	31	125	456	47	133	30	6	10	64	26	41	8	.292	.450
Whitey Witt	OF59, 2B56, 3B4	L	23	122	460	56	123	15	6	0	33	46	26	11	.267	.326
Cy Perkins	C87, SS8	R	23	101	305	22	77	12	7	2	29	27	22	2	.252	.357
Dick Burrus	1B38, OF10	L	21	70	194	17	50	3	4	0	8	9	25	2	.258	.314
Wickey McAvoy	C57	R	24	62	170	10	24	5	2	0	11	14	21	1	.141	.194
2 Amos Strunk	OF52	L	30	60	194	15	41	6	0	0	13	23	15	3	.211	.284
Walt Kinney	P43, OF1	L	25	57	88	11	25	6	0	1	11	10	15	0	.284	.386
1 Braggo Roth	OF48	R	26	48	195	33	63	13	8	5	29	15	21	11	.323	.549
Terry Turner	SS19, 2B17, 3B1	R	38	38	127	4	21	1	0	0	6	5	7	2	.189	.213
1 Roy Grover	2B12, 3B3	R	27	22	56	8	13	1	0	0	1	7	11	0	.232	.250
Jimmy Dykes	2B16	R	22	17	49	4	9	1	0	0	2	7	9	1	.184	.204
Chick Galloway	SS17	R	22	17	49	4	7	1	0	0	2	6	9	0	.143	.143
Ivy Griffin	1B17	L	22	17	68	5	20	2	0	0	6	3	10	0	.294	.382
Frank Welch	OF15	R	21	15	47	5	14	2	0	1	7	1	10	0	.305	.424
Al Elliott	OF6	R	25	15	29	2	4	0	0	0	1	2	5	0	.138	.182
Art Ewoldt	3B9	R	25	9	32	2	7	1	0	0	5	2	7	0	.219	.250
Lena Styles	C8	R	19	9	23	1	6	0	0	0	2	1	8	0	.261	.318
Johnny Walker	C3	R	22	9	9	1	1	0	0	0	0	1	1	0	.111	.111
Lew Groh	3B1	R	35	2	1	0	0	0	0	0	0	0	0	0	.000	.000
Ray Haley (MS) 28, Otis Lawrey (MS) 25																

NAME	T	AGE	W	L	PCT	SV	G	GS	CG	IP	H	BB	SO	SHO	ERA
TOTALS		26	36	104	.257	2	140	140	72	1239	1371	503	417	1	4.26
Jing Johnson	R	24	9	15	.375	0	34	25	12	202	222	62	67	0	3.61
Walt Kinney	L	25	9	15	.375	1	43	21	13	203	199	91	97	0	3.64
Rollie Naylor	R	27	5	18	.217	0	31	23	17	205	210	64	68	0	3.34
2 Tom Rogers	R	24	4	12	.250	0	23	18	7	140	152	60	37	1	4.31
Scott Perry	R	28	4	17	.190	1	25	21	12	184	193	72	38	0	3.57
Socks Seibold	R	23	3	3	.400	0	14	4	1	46	58	26	19	0	5.28
Walter Anderson	L	21	1	0	1.000	0	3	3	0	14	13	8	10	0	3.86
Jimmy Zinn	R	24	1	3	.250	0	5	3	2	26	38	10	9	0	6.23
1 Win Noyes	R	30	1	5	.167	0	10	4	2	49	66	15	20	0	5.69
2 Harry Thompson	R	29	0	1	.000	0	12	0	0	16	16	3	1	0	6.75
Mule Watson	R	22	0	4	.000	0	11	5	1	45	68	14	18	0	7.07
Danny Boone	R	24	0	1	.000	0	15	0	0	15	24	10	1	0	6.60
Charlie Eckert	R	21	0	2	.000	0	16	1	0	17	17	3	6	0	3.94
Dave Keefe	R	23	0	1	.000	0	17	2	0	21	11	9	8	0	4.00
Ray Roberts	R	23	0	2	.000	0	4	1	0	13	14	2	5	0	7.71
Bob Hasty	R	23	0	1	.000	0	7	1	0	11	11	8	6	0	5.25
Pat Martin	L	24	0	1	.000	0	2	1	0	11	11	8	6	0	4.09
Lefty York	R	26	0	2	.000	0	3	1	0	6	12	11	4	0	27.00
Bob Geary	R	28	0	0	—	0	3	1	0	12	32	18	9	0	4.78
Bill Grevell	R	21	0	0	—	0	2	1	0	8	15	6	2	0	14.25
Mike Kircher	R	21	0	0	—	0	4	0	0	4	4	1	2	0	7.88
Bill Pierson	L	20	0	0	—	0	2	1	0	7	11	5	3	0	3.38
Willie Adams	R	28	0	0	—	0	1	0	0	2	5	1	2	0	3.60

+Shannon, also with Boston, league leader in SO with 70

CINCINNATI 1st 96-44 .686 · PAT MORAN

NAME	G by Pos	B	AGE	G	AB	R	H	2B	3B	HR	RBI	BB	SO	SB	BA	SA
TOTALS			29	140	4577	578	1204	135	83	20	489	405	368	143	.263	.342
Jake Daubert	1B140	L	35	140	537	79	148	10	12	2	44	35	23	11	.276	.350
Morrie Rath	2B138	L	32	138	537	77	142	13	1	2	29	64	24	17	.264	.298
Larry Kopf	SS135	B	28	135	503	51	136	18	5	0	58	28	27	18	.270	.326
Heinie Groh	3B121	R	29	122	448	79	139	17	11	5	63	56	26	21	.310	.431
Greasy Neale	OF138	L	27	139	500	57	121	10	12	1	54	47	51	28	.242	.316
Edd Roush	OF138	L	26	133	504	73	162	19	12	4	71	42	19	20	.321	.431
Rube Bressler	OF48, P13	R	24	61	165	22	34	4	2	1	17	23	15	2	.206	.309
Ivy Wingo	C75	L	28	76	245	30	67	12	6	0	27	23	19	4	.273	.371
Bill Rariden	C70	R	31	74	218	16	47	6	3	1	24	17	19	4	.216	.284
Sherry Magee (IL)	OF47, 2B1, 3B1	R	34	56	163	11	35	6	1	0	21	26	19	4	.215	.264
Hod Eller	P38	R	24	38	93	10	26	3	3	1	13	0	16	0	.280	.409
Pat Duncan (MS)	OF27	R	25	31	90	9	22	3	3	2	17	8	7	2	.244	.411
Manuel Cueto	OF25, 3B1	R	27	29	88	10	22	2	0	0	4	10	4	5	.250	.273
Jimmy Smith	3B6, SS5, 2B4, OF4	B	24	28	40	9	11	3	1	0	10	4	8	1	.275	.525
Hank Schreiber	3B17, SS2	R	27	19	58	5	13	4	0	0	4	0	12	0	.224	.293
Nick Allen	C12	R	30	15	25	7	8	0	1	0	5	2	6	0	.320	.400
Charlie See	OF4	L	22	8	14	1	4	0	0	0	1	1	0	0	.286	.286
Wally Rehg	OF5	R	30	5	12	1	2	0	0	0	3	1	0	0	.167	.167
2 Billy Zitzmann	OF1	R	21	2	1	0	0	0	0	0	0	0	0	0	.000	.000

NAME	T	AGE	W	L	PCT	SV	G	GS	CG	IP	H	BB	SO	SHO	ERA
TOTALS		28	96	44	.686	9	140	140	89	1274	1104	298	407	23	2.23
Slim Sallee	L	34	21	7	.750	0	29	28	22	228	221	20	24	4	2.05
Hod Eller	R	24	20	9	.690	0	38	30	16	248	216	50	137	7	2.40
Dutch Ruether	L	25	19	6	.760	0	33	29	20	243	195	83	78	3	1.81
Ray Fisher	R	31	14	5	.737	0	26	20	12	174	141	38	41	5	2.17
Jimmy Ring	R	24	10	9	.526	3	32	18	12	183	150	51	61	2	2.26
Dolf Luque	R	28	9	3	.750	3	30	9	6	106	89	36	40	2	2.63
Rube Bressler	L	24	2	4	.333	0	13	4	1	42	37	8	13	0	3.43
Ed Gerner	L	21	1	0	1.000	0	5	1	0	17	22	3	2	0	3.18
Roy Mitchell	R	34	0	1	.000	0	7	1	0	31	32	9	10	0	2.32
Mike Regan	R	31	0	0	—	0	1	0	0	2	1	0	1	0	0.00

NEW YORK 2nd 87-53 .621 9 JOHN McGRAW

NAME	G by Pos	B	AGE	G	AB	R	H	2B	3B	HR	RBI	BB	SO	SB	BA	SA
TOTALS			29	140	4664	605	1254	204	64	40	505	328	407	157	.269	.366
Hal Chase (DU)	1B107	R	36	110	408	58	116	17	7	5	45	17	40	16	.284	.397
Larry Doyle	2B100	L	33	113	381	61	110	14	10	7	52	31	17	12	.289	.433
Art Fletcher	SS127	R	34	127	488	54	135	20	5	3	54	9	28	6	.277	.357
Heinie Zimmerman (DU)	3B123	R	32	123	444	56	113	20	6	4	58	21	30	8	.255	.354
Ross Youngs	OF130	L	22	130	489	73	152	31	7	2	43	51	47	24	.311	.415
Benny Kauff	OF134	L	29	135	491	73	136	27	7	10	67	39	45	21	.277	.422
George Burns	OF139	R	29	139	534	86	162	30	9	2	46	82	37	40	.303	.404
Lew McCarty	C59	R	30	85	210	17	59	5	4	2	21	18	15	2	.281	.371
Mike Gonzalez	C52, 1B4	R	28	58	158	18	30	6	0	0	8	20	9	3	.190	.228
Frankie Frisch	2B29, 3B28, SS1	B	20	53	190	21	43	3	2	2	24	4	14	15	.226	.295
Al Baird	2B24, SS9, 3B5	R	24	38	83	8	20	1	0	0	5	5	9	3	.241	.253
George Kelly	1B32	R	23	32	107	12	31	6	2	1	14	3	15	1	.290	.411
2 Frank Snyder	C31	R	25	32	92	7	21	6	0	0	11	8	9	1	.228	.293
Jigger Statz	OF18, 2B5	R	21	21	60	7	18	2	1	0	6	3	8	2	.300	.367
Earl Smith	C14, 2B1	L	22	21	36	5	9	2	1	0	8	3	3	1	.250	.361
Lee King	OF7	R	26	21	20	5	2	1	0	0	1	1	6	0	.100	.150
1 Eddie Sicking	SS6	R	22	6	15	2	5	0	0	0	3	0	0	0	.333	.333
Jimmy Cooney	SS4, 2B1	R	24	5	14	3	3	0	0	0	1	0	0	0	.214	.214
Chick Bowen	OF2	R	21	3	5	0	1	0	0	0	1	1	2	0	.200	.200
Bob Kinsella	OF3	L	20	3	9	1	2	0	0	0	0	0	0	3	.222	.222
1 Jim Thorpe	OF2	R	29	2	3	0	1	0	0	0	1	0	0	0	.333	.333
1 Dave Robertson	OF2	L	29	2	3	0	1	0	0	0	0	0	0	0	.333	.333

NAME	T	AGE	W	L	PCT	SV	G	GS	CG	IP	H	BB	SO	SHO	ERA
TOTALS		28	87	53	.621	13	140	140	72	1256	1153	305	340	11	2.70
Jesse Barnes	R	26	25	9	.735	1	38	34	23	296	263	35	92	4	2.40
Rube Benton	L	29	17	11	.607	3	35	28	11	209	181	52	53	1	2.63
Fred Toney	R	30	13	6	.684	1	24	20	14	181	157	35	40	4	1.84
2 Art Nehf	L	26	9	2	.818	0	13	12	9	102	70	19	24	2	1.50
1 Red Causey	R	25	9	3	.750	0	19	16	6	105	99	38	25	0	3.69
Jean Dubuc	R	30	6	4	.600	3	36	5	1	132	119	37	32	0	2.66
2 Phil Douglas	R	29	2	4	.333	0	8	6	4	51	53	6	21	0	2.12
2 Pat Ragan	R	33	1	0	1.000	0	7	1	1	23	19	14	7	0	1.57
Pol Perritt	R	27	1	1	.500	1	11	3	0	19	27	12	2	0	7.11
Bill Hubbell	R	22	1	1	.500	0	2	2	1	18	19	2	3	0	2.00
Jesse Winters	R	25	1	2	.333	3	16	2	0	28	39	13	6	0	5.46
Rosy Ryan	R	21	1	2	.333	0	4	3	1	20	20	9	7	0	3.15
1 Ferdie Schupp (AJ)	L	28	1	3	.250	1	9	4	0	32	32	18	17	0	5.63
2 Joe Oeschger	R	27	0	1	.000	0	5	1	0	8	12	2	3	0	4.50
Colonel Snover	L	24	0	1	.000	0	1	0	0	9	7	3	4	0	1.00
Bob Steele	L	25	0	1	.000	0	3	3	2	10	6	0	0		6.00
1 George Smith	R	27	0	2	.000	0	11	1	0	19	18	4	0		5.73
Johnny Jones	R	26	0	0	—	0	1	0	0	7	9	3	3	0	5.14
Virgil Barnes	R	22	0	0	—	0	2	2	1	1	6	1	1	0	18.00

CHICAGO 3rd 75-65 .536 21 FRED MITCHELL

NAME	G by Pos	B	AGE	G	AB	R	H	2B	3B	HR	RBI	BB	SO	SB	BA	SA
TOTALS			28	140	4581	454	1174	166	58	21	387	298	359	150	.256	.332
Fred Merkle	1B132	R	30	133	498	52	133	20	6	3	62	33	35	20	.267	.349
1 Charlie Pick	2B71, 3B3	L	25	75	269	27	65	8	6	0	18	14	12	17	.242	.316
Charlie Hollocher	SS115	R	23	115	430	51	116	14	5	3	26	44	19	6	.270	.347
Charlie Deal	3B116	R	27	116	405	37	117	23	5	2	52	12	12	11	.289	.385
Max Flack	OF116	L	29	116	469	71	138	20	4	6	35	34	13	16	.294	.392
Dode Paskert	OF80	R	37	88	270	21	53	11	3	2	29	28	33	7	.196	.281
1 Les Mann	OF78	R	26	80	299	30	68	8	8	1	22	11	29	12	.227	.318
Bill Killefer	C100	R	31	103	315	17	90	10	2	0	22	15	8	5	.286	.330
2 Lee Magee	OF44, SS13, 3B10, 2B	B	30	79	267	36	78	12	4	1	17	18	16	14	.292	.378
Turner Barber	OF68	L	25	76	230	26	72	9	4	0	21	14	17	7	.313	.387
2 Buck Herzog	2B52	R	33	52	193	15	53	4	4	0	17	10	7	12	.275	.337
Bob O'Farrell	C38	R	22	49	125	11	27	4	2	0	9	7	10	2	.216	.280
Fred Lear	1B9, 2B9, SS3	R	25	40	76	8	17	3	1	1	11	8	11	2	.224	.329
Bill McCabe	OF19, SS4, 3B1	R	26	33	84	8	13	3	1	0	5	9	15	3	.155	.214
1 Pete Kilduff	3B14, 2B8, SS7	R	26	31	88	5	24	4	2	0	8	10	5	1	.273	.364
2 Dave Robertson	OF25	L	29	27	96	8	20	2	0	1	10	1	10	3	.208	.260
Tom Daly	C18	R	27	25	50	4	11	0	1	0	1	2	5	0	.220	.260
Barney Friberg	OF7	R	19	8	20	0	4	1	0	0	1	0	3	0	.200	.250
Hal Reilly	OF1	R	25	1	3	0	0	0	0	0	0	1	0	0	.000	.000

NAME	T	AGE	W	L	PCT	SV	G	GS	CG	IP	H	BB	SO	SHO	ERA
TOTALS		28	75	65	.536	5	140	140	80	1265	1127	294	495	21	2.21
Hippo Vaughn	L	31	21	14	.714	1	38	37	25	307	264	62	141	4	1.79
Pete Alexander	R	32	16	11	.593	1	30	27	20	235	180	38	121	9	1.72
1 Phil Douglas	R	29	10	6	.625	0	25	19	8	162	133	34	63	4	2.00
Claude Hendrix	R	30	10	14	.417	0	33	25	15	206	208	42	69	2	2.62
Speed Martin	R	25	8	8	.500	2	35	14	7	164	158	52	54	2	2.47
Paul Carter	R	25	5	4	.556	1	28	7	2	85	81	28	17	0	2.65
Sweetbreads Bailey	R	24	3	5	.375	0	21	5	0	71	75	20	19	0	3.17
Lefty Tyler (SJ)	L	29	2	2	.500	0	6	5	3	30	20	13	9	0	2.10
Harry Weaver	R	27	0	1	.000	0	3	1	0	9	12	0	0		12.00
Joel Newkirk	R	23	0	0	—	0	1	0	0	2	2	3	1	0	13.50

PITTSBURGH 4th 71-68 .511 24.5 HUGO BEZDEK

NAME	G by Pos	B	AGE	G	AB	R	H	2B	3B	HR	RBI	BB	SO	SB	BA	SA
TOTALS			28	139	4538	472	1132	130	82	17	394	344	381	196	.249	.325
Vic Saier	1B51	L	27	58	166	19	37	3	3	2	17	18	13	5	.223	.313
George Cutshaw	2B139	R	32	139	512	49	124	15	8	3	51	30	22	36	.242	.320
Zeb Terry	SS127	R	28	129	472	46	107	12	6	0	27	31	26	12	.227	.278
Walter Barbare	3B80, 2B1	R	27	85	293	34	80	11	5	1	34	18	18	11	.273	.355
1 Casey Stengel	OF87	L	28	89	321	38	94	10	10	4	43	35	35	12	.293	.424
Carson Bigbee	OF124	L	24	125	478	61	132	11	4	2	27	37	26	31	.276	.328
Billy Southworth	OF121	L	26	121	453	56	127	14	14	3	61	32	22	23	.280	.400
Walter Schmidt	C85	R	32	85	267	23	67	9	2	0	29	23	9	5	.251	.300
Max Carey (IL)	OF63	B	29	66	244	41	75	10	2	0	9	25	24	18	.307	.365
1 Fritz Mollwitz	1B52, OF2	R	29	56	168	11	29	2	4	0	12	15	18	4	.173	.232
1 Tony Boeckel	3B45	R	26	45	152	18	38	9	2	0	16	18	20	11	.250	.336
Cliff Lee	C28, OF6	R	22	42	112	5	22	2	4	0	2	6	5	2	.196	.286
Buster Caton	SS17, 3B11, OF1	R	22	39	102	13	18	1	2	0	5	12	10	2	.176	.225
2 Possum Whitted	1B33, 3B2, OF1	R	29	35	131	15	51	7	7	0	21	6	4	7	.389	.550
Wilbur Cooper	P35	L	27	35	101	9	29	2	2	0	7	4	9	5	.287	.347
Fred Nicholson	OF17, 1B1	R	24	30	66	8	18	2	1	0	6	6	11	2	.273	.409
Fred Blackwell	C22	R	23	24	65	3	14	3	0	0	4	3	9	0	.215	.262
Ed Sweeney	C15	R	30	17	42	0	4	1	0	0	0	6	5	1	.095	.119
Charlie Grimm	1B11	L	20	12	44	4	14	1	3	0	4	1	2	1	.318	.477
Billy Zitzmann	OF8	R	21	11	26	5	5	1	0	0	2	0	6	2	.192	.231
Hooks Warner	3B3	R	25	3	8	0	1	0	0	0	2	3	1	0	.125	.125

Adam Debus (MS) 26, Bill McKechnie (VR) 32

NAME	T	AGE	W	L	PCT	SV	G	GS	CG	IP	H	BB	SO	SHO	ERA
TOTALS		30	71	68	.511	4	139	139	92	1249	1113	263	391	16	2.88
Wilbur Cooper	L	27	19	13	.594	1	35	32	27	287	229	74	106	4	2.67
Babe Adams	R	37	17	10	.630	1	34	29	23	263	213	23	92	6	1.98
Frank Miller	R	33	13	12	.520	0	32	26	16	202	170	34	59	3	3.03
Hal Carlson	R	27	8	10	.444	0	22	14	7	141	114	39	49	1	2.23
Earl Hamilton	L	27	8	11	.421	1	28	19	10	160	167	49	39	1	3.32
1 Erskine Mayer	R	29	5	3	.625	1	18	10	6	88	100	12	20	0	4.50
John Wisner	R	19	1	0	1.000	0	4	1	1	19	12	7	4	0	0.95
Bill Evans	R	26	0	4	.000	0	7	3	2	37	41	18	15	0	5.59
Elmer Ponder (MS)	R	26	0	5	.000	0	6	4	0	47	55	6	6	0	4.02
Carmel Hill	R	23	0	0	—	0	4	0	0	5	12	1	1	0	9.00

BROOKLYN 5th 69-71 .493 27 WILBERT ROBINSON

NAME	G by Pos	B	AGE	G	AB	R	H	2B	3B	HR	RBI	BB	SO	SB	BA	SA
TOTALS			29	141	4844	525	1272	167	66	25	452	258	405	112	.263	.340
Ed Konetchy	1B132	R	33	132	486	46	145	24	9	1	47	29	39	14	.298	.391
Jimmy Johnston	2B87, OF14, 1B2, SS1	R	29	117	405	56	114	11	4	1	23	29	26	11	.281	.336
Ivy Olson	SS140	R	33	140	590	73	164	14	9	1	38	30	12	26	.278	.337
Lew Malone	3B47, 2B2, SS2	L	22	51	162	9	33	7	3	0	11	6	18	1	.204	.284
Tommy Griffith	OF125	L	29	125	484	65	136	18	4	6	57	23	32	8	.281	.372
Hy Myers	OF131	R	30	133	512	69	157	23	14	5	73	23	34	13	.307	.436
Zack Wheat	OF137	L	31	137	536	70	159	23	11	5	62	33	27	15	.297	.409
Ernie Krueger	C66	R	28	80	226	24	56	7	4	5	36	19	25	4	.248	.381
Jim Hickman	OF29	R	27	57	104	16	20	3	1	0	11	6	17	2	.192	.240
Otto Miller	C51	R	30	51	164	18	37	5	0	0	5	7	14	2	.226	.256
Ray Schmandt	2B18, 1B12, 3B6	R	27	47	127	8	21	4	0	0	10	4	13	0	.165	.197
1 Lee Magee	2B36, 3B9	B	30	45	181	16	43	7	2	0	7	5	6	5	.238	.298
Chuck Ward (LJ)	3B45	R	24	45	150	7	35	1	2	0	8	1	14	0	.233	.287
Mack Wheat	C38	R	26	41	112	5	23	3	0	0	8	2	22	1	.205	.232
2 Pete Kilduff	3B26, 2B1	R	26	32	73	9	22	6	2	0	8	12	11	5	.301	.370
3 Doug Baird	3B17	R	27	20	60	6	11	0	1	0	8	5	10	3	.183	.217
Horace Allen	OF2	L	20	4	4	2	0	0	0	0	0	2	1	0	.000	.000
Tom Fitzsimmons	3B4	R	29	4	11	1	1	0	0	0	2	2	1	0	.091	.091
Ollie O'Mara	3B2	R	18	2	7	1	4	0	0	0	0	0	0	0	.000	.000

NAME	T	AGE	W	L	PCT	SV	G	GS	CG	IP	H	BB	SO	SHO	ERA
TOTALS		27	69	71	.493	1	141	141	98	1281	1256	292	476	12	2.73
Jeff Pfeffer	R	31	17	13	.567	0	30	30	26	267	270	49	92	4	2.66
Leon Cadore	R	28	14	12	.538	0	35	27	16	251	228	39	94	3	2.37
Burleigh Grimes (JJ)	R	25	10	11	.476	0	25	21	13	181	179	60	82	1	3.48
Al Mamaux	R	25	10	12	.455	0	30	22	16	199	174	66	80	2	2.67
Clarence Mitchell	L	28	7	5	.583	0	23	11	9	109	123	23	43	0	3.06
Sherry Smith	L	28	7	7	.500	0	30	19	13	173	181	29	40	2	2.24
Rube Marquard (BL)	L	32	3	3	.500	0	7	4	3	59	54	10	29	0	2.29
1 Larry Cheney	R	33	1	3	.250	1	9	3	1	39	45	14	14	0	4.15
Lafayette Henion	R	20	0	0	—	0	1	0	0	3	2	2	2	0	6.00

BOSTON — 6th 57-82 .410 38.5 — GEORGE STALLINGS

NAME	G by Pos	B	AGE	G	AB	R	H	2B	3B	HR	RBI	BB	SO	SB	BA	SA
TOTALS			29	140	4746	465	1201	142	62	24	399	355	481	145	.253	.324
Walter Holke	1B136	B	26	140	518	48	151	14	6	0	48	21	25	19	.292	.342
1 Buck Herzog	2B70, 1B1	R	33	73	275	27	77	8	5	1	25	13	11	16	.280	.356
2 Rabbit Maranville	SS131	R	27	131	480	44	128	18	10	5	43	36	23	12	.267	.377
Tony Boeckel	3B93	R	26	95	365	42	91	11	5	1	26	35	13	10	.249	.315
Ray Powell	OF122	L	30	123	470	51	111	12	12	2	33	41	79	6	.236	.326
Joe Riggert	OF61	R	32	63	240	34	68	8	5	4	17	25	30	9	.283	.408
2 Walton Cruise	OF66	L	29	73	241	23	52	7	0	1	21	17	29	8	.216	.257
Hank Gowdy (MS)	C74, 1B1	R	29	78	219	18	61	8	1	1	22	19	16	5	.279	.338
Red Smith	OF48, 3B23	R	29	87	241	24	59	6	0	1	24	40	22	6	.245	.282
Johnny Rawlings	2B58, OF12, SS5	R	26	77	275	30	70	8	2	1	16	16	20	10	.255	.309
Art Wilson	C64, 1B1	R	33	71	191	14	49	8	1	0	16	25	19	2	.257	.309
Jim Thorpe	OF38, 1B2	R	32	60	156	16	51	7	3	1	25	6	30	7	.327	.429
2 Les Mann	OF40	R	26	40	145	15	41	6	4	3	20	9	14	7	.283	.441
2 Charlie Pick	2B21, 3B5, OF3, 1B2	L	31	34	114	12	29	1	1	1	7	5	4	2	.254	.307
1 Lena Blackburne	3B24, 1B1, 2B1, SS1	R	32	31	80	5	21	3	1	0	4	6	7	3	.263	.325
1 Walt Tragresser	C14	R	32	20	40	3	7	2	0	0	3	2	10	1	.175	.225
Joe Kelly	OF16	R	32	32	64	5	9	1	0	0	3	0	11	2	.141	.156
Dizzy Nutter	OF12	L	25	18	52	4	11	0	0	0	3	4	5	1	.212	.212
Dixie Carroll	OF13	L	25	15	49	10	13	3	1	0	7	1	5	1	.256	.367
Mickey O'Neil	C11	R	21	11	28	5	6	0	0	0	1	1	7	0	.214	.214
Hod Ford	SS8, 3B2	R	21	21	28	4	6	0	1	0	3	2	6	0	.214	.286
Lloyd Christenbury	OF7	L	25	7	31	5	9	1	0	0	4	2	1	0	.290	.323

Tom Miller 21 L 2-6, Gene Bailey 25 R 2-6, Lee King 25 R 0-1, Sam White 26 L 0-1, Art Rico (DD) 22

NAME	T	AGE	W	L	PCT	SV	G	GS	CG	IP	H	BB	SO	SHO	ERA
		27	57	82	.410	9	140	140	79	1271	1313	337	374	5	3.17
Dick Rudolph	R	30	13	18	.419	2	37	32	24	282	274	54	76	2	2.17
1 Art Nehf	L	26	8	9	.471	0	22	19	13	169	151	40	53	1	3.09
Ray Keating	R	25	7	11	.389	0	24	14	9	136	129	45	48	1	2.98
Al Demaree	R	34	6	6	.500	3	25	13	6	128	147	35	34	0	3.80
Jack Scott	R	25	6	6	.500	1	19	12	7	104	109	39	44	0	3.12
Dana Fillingim	R	25	5	13	.316	2	32	18	9	186	185	39	50	0	3.39
3 Joe Oeschger	R	27	4	2	.667	0	7	7	4	57	63	21	16	1	2.53
2 Red Causey	R	25	4	5	.444	0	10	10	3	69	81	20	14	0	4.57
Hugh McQuillan	R	23	2	3	.400	1	16	7	2	60	66	14	13	0	3.45
Jake Northrop	R	31	1	5	.167	0	11	3	2	37	43	10	9	0	4.62
2 Larry Cheney	R	33	0	2	.000	0	8	2	0	33	35	15	13	0	3.55
1 Pat Ragan	R	33	0	2	.000	0	4	3	1	13	16	3	3	0	6.92
Bill James	R	27	0	0	—	0	1	0	0	5	6	2	1	0	3.60

ST. LOUIS — 7th 54-83 .394 40.5 — BRANCH RICKEY

NAME	G by Pos	B	AGE	G	AB	R	H	2B	3B	HR	RBI	BB	SO	SB	BA	SA
TOTALS			26	138	4588	463	1175	163	52	18	398	304	418	148	.256	.326
Dots Miller	1B68, 2B28	R	32	101	346	38	80	10	4	1	24	13	23	6	.231	.292
Milt Stock	2B77, 3B58	R	25	135	492	56	151	16	4	0	52	49	21	17	.307	.356
Doc Lavan	SS99	R	28	100	356	25	86	12	2	1	25	11	30	4	.242	.295
Rogers Hornsby	3B72, SS37, 2B25, 1B5	R	23	138	512	68	163	15	9	8	71	48	41	17	.318	.430
Jack Smith	OF111	L	24	119	408	47	91	16	3	0	15	24	29	30	.223	.277
Cliff Heathcote	OF101, 1B2	L	21	114	401	53	112	13	4	1	29	20	41	26	.279	.339
Austin McHenry	OF103	R	23	110	371	41	106	19	11	4	47	19	57	7	.286	.404
Verne Clemons	C75	R	27	88	239	14	63	13	2	2	22	26	13	4	.264	.360
Joe Schultz	OF49, 2B5	R	25	88	229	24	58	9	1	2	21	11	7	4	.253	.328
Burt Shotton	OF67	L	34	85	270	35	77	13	5	1	20	22	25	17	.285	.381
1 Frank Snyder	C48, 1B1	R	25	50	154	7	28	4	2	0	14	5	13	2	.182	.234
Pickles Dillhoefer	C39	R	25	45	108	11	23	3	2	0	12	8	6	5	.213	.278
1 Gene Paulette	1B35, SS3	R	28	43	144	11	31	6	0	0	11	9	6	4	.215	.257
2 Fritz Mollwitz	1B25	R	29	25	83	7	19	3	0	0	5	7	3	2	.229	.265
2 Doug Baird	3B8, 2B1, OF1	R	27	16	33	4	7	1	0	0	4	2	3	2	.212	.273
Roy Leslie	1B9	R	24	12	24	2	5	1	0	0	4	4	3	0	.208	.250
1 Walton Cruise	OF5, 1B2	L	29	21	0	2	1	0	0	0	1	0	6	0	.095	.143
Sam Fishburne	1B1, 2B1	R	26	9	6	0	2	0	0	0	2	0	1	0	.333	.500
2 Hal Janvrin	2B2, SS1, 3B1	R	26	9	14	1	3	0	0	0	2	2	0		.214	.286

Bobby Fisher 32 R 3-11, Wally Kimmick 22 R 0-1, 2 Mike Pasquariello 20 R 0-1

NAME	T	AGE	W	L	PCT	SV	G	GS	CG	IP	H	BB	SO	SHO	ERA
		26	54	83	.394	8	138	138	55	1217	1146	415	414	6	3.23
Bill Doak	R	28	13	14	.481	0	31	29	13	203	182	55	69	3	3.10
Marv Goodwin	R	28	11	9	.550	0	33	17	7	179	163	33	48	0	2.51
Oscar Tuero	R	26	5	7	.417	4	45	16	4	155	137	42	45	0	3.19
Bill Sherdel	L	22	5	9	.357	1	36	11	7	137	137	42	52	0	3.48
2 Ferdie Schupp	L	28	4	4	.500	0	10	10	6	70	55	30	37	0	3.73
1 Lee Meadows	R	24	4	10	.286	0	22	12	3	92	100	30	28	1	3.03
1 Red Ames	R	36	3	5	.375	1	23	6	1	70	88	25	19	0	4.89
2 Frank Woodward	R	25	3	5	.375	1	17	6	2	72	65	28	18	0	2.63
2 Elmer Jacobs	R	26	3	6	.333	1	17	8	4	85	81	25	31	1	2.54
Jakie May	L	23	3	12	.200	0	28	19	8	126	99	87	58	1	3.21
Oscar Horstmann	R	28	2	3	.400	0	6	3	1	15	14	3	5	0	3.00
Bill Bolden	R	26	1	0	.000	0	3	1	0	12	17	4	4	0	5.25
Roy Parker	R	23	0	0	—	0	2	0	0	7	6	1	0	0	31.50
Willis Koenigsmark	R	23	0	0	—	0	1	0	0	2	1	0	0		∞
Art Reinhart	L	20	0	0	—	0	1	0	0	0	0	0	0	0	0.00

PHILADELPHIA — 8th 47-90 .343 47.5 — JACK COOMBS 18-44 .290 — GAVVY CRAVATH 29-46 .387

NAME	G by Pos	B	AGE	G	AB	R	H	2B	3B	HR	RBI	BB	SO	SB	BA	SA
TOTALS			29	138	4746	510	1191	208	50	42	436	323	469	114	.251	.342
Fred Luderus	1B138	R	33	138	509	60	149	30	6	5	49	54	48	6	.293	.405
2 Gene Paulette	2B53, OF10, 1B1	R	28	67	243	20	63	8	3	1	31	19	10	6	.259	.329
Dave Bancroft (JJ)	SS88	B	28	92	335	45	91	13	7	0	25	31	30	8	.272	.352
2 Lena Blackburne	3B72, 1B1, 2B1, SS1	R	28	72	291	32	58	10	5	2	19	10	22	2	.199	.289
Leo Callahan	OF58	L	28	81	235	26	54	14	4	1	9	29	19	5	.230	.336
Cy Williams	OF108	L	31	109	435	54	121	21	1	9	39	30	43	9	.278	.393
Irish Meusel	OF128	R	26	135	521	65	159	26	7	5	59	15	13	24	.305	.411
Jack Adams	C73	B	28	78	232	14	54	7	2	1	17	6	27	4	.233	.293
Gavvy Cravath	OF56	R	38	83	214	34	73	18	5	12	45	35	21	8	.341	.640
1 Possum Whitted	OF47, 2B20, 1B2	R	29	78	289	32	72	14	1	3	32	14	20	7	.249	.336
Harry Pearce	2B43, SS23, 3B2	R	29	68	244	24	43	3	3	0	9	8	21	6	.180	.217
1 Doug Baird	3B66	R	27	66	242	33	61	13	3	2	30	22	28	13	.252	.355
2 Eddie Sicking	SS35, 2B21	R	22	61	185	16	40	4	1	0	15	8	17	4	.216	.238
2 Walt Tragresser	C34	R	32	35	114	7	27	7	0	0	9	8	31	4	.237	.298
Hick Cady	C29	B	32	34	98	6	21	6	0	1	19	4	8	1	.214	.306
Nig Clarke	C22	L	36	26	62	4	15	3	0	0	2	4	5	1	.242	.290
Bevo LeBourveau	OF17	L	25	17	63	4	17	2	0	0	4	3	5	2	.270	.270

Bert Yeabsley 25 R 0-0, Doc Wallace 25 R 1-4, John Cavanaugh 19 R 0-1, Mike Pasquariello 20 R 1-1, Lou Raymond 24 R 1-2, 2 Casey Stengel (ST) 28, Stan Baumgartner (VR) 26

NAME	T	AGE	W	L	PCT	SV	G	GS	CG	IP	H	BB	SO	SHO	ERA
		27	47	90	.343	2	138	138	93	1243	1391	408	397	6	4.17
2 Lee Meadows	R	28	8	10	.444	0	18	17	15	149	128	49	88	3	2.48
Gene Packard	L	31	6	8	.429	1	21	16	10	164	167	30	24	1	4.16
1 Frank Woodward	R	25	6	9	.400	0	17	12	6	101	109	35	27	0	4.72
1 Elmer Jacobs	R	26	6	10	.375	0	17	15	13	129	150	44	37	0	3.84
Eppa Rixey (MS)	L	28	6	12	.333	0	23	18	11	154	160	50	63	1	3.97
2 George Smith	R	30	5	11	.313	0	31	19	11	185	194	46	42	1	3.21
Brad Hogg	R	29	5	12	.294	0	22	19	13	150	163	55	48	0	4.44
Milt Watson	R	29	2	4	.333	0	8	7	3	47	51	19	12	0	5.17
3 Larry Cheney	R	33	2	5	.286	0	9	6	5	57	69	28	25	0	4.58
Mike Cantwell	L	25	1	3	.250	0	5	4	2	27	36	9	6	0	5.67
1 Joe Oeschger	R	27	0	1	.000	0	5	4	2	38	52	16	5	0	5.92
Mike Prendergast	L	30	0	1	.000	0	5	1	0	15	20	10	5	0	8.40
Pat Murray	L	21	0	0	—	0	8	1	1	34	50	12	11	0	6.35
2 Red Ames	R	36	0	2	.000	0	4	2	0	16	26	3	4	0	6.19
Rags Faircloth	R	26	0	0	—	0	2	0	0	4	6	3	0	0	9.00
Lefty Weinert	L	17	0	0	—	0	4	0	0	4	11	2	0	0	18.00

WORLD SERIES — CINCINNATI (NL) 5 CHICAGO (AL) 3

LINE SCORES

TEAM	1	2	3	4	5	6	7	8	9	10	11	12	R	H	E

Game 1   October 1 at Cincinnati
CHI (AL) 0 1 0 0 0 0 0 0 0   1 6 1
CIN (NL) 1 0 0 5 0 0 2 1 X   9 14 1
Cicotte, Wilkinson (4), Ruether
Lowdermilk (8)

Game 2   October 2 at Cincinnati
CHI 0 0 0 0 0 0 2 0 0   2 10 1
CIN 0 0 0 3 0 1 0 0 X   4 4 2
Williams   Sallee

Game 3   October 3 at Chicago
CIN 0 0 0 0 0 0 0 0 0   0 3 1
CHI 0 2 0 1 0 0 0 0 X   3 7 0
Fisher, Luque (8)   Kerr

Game 4   October 4 at Chicago
CIN 0 0 0 0 2 0 0 0 0   2 5 2
CHI 0 0 0 0 0 0 0 0 0   0 3 2
Ring   Cicotte

Game 5   October 6 at Chicago
CIN 0 0 0 0 0 4 0 0 1   5 4 0
CHI 0 0 0 0 0 0 0 3 3
Eller   Williams, Mayer (9)

Game 6   October 7 at Cincinnati
CHI 0 0 0 0 1 3 0 0 0 1   5 10 3
CIN 0 0 2 2 0 0 0 0 0 0   4 11 0
Kerr   Ruether, Ring (6)

Game 7   October 8 at Cincinnati
CHI 1 0 1 0 2 0 0 0 0   4 10 1
CIN 0 0 0 0 0 1 0 0 0   1 7 4
Cicotte   Sallee, Fisher (5), Luque (6)

Game 8   October 9 at Chicago
CIN 4 1 0 0 1 3 0 1 0   10 16 2
CHI 0 0 1 0 0 0 0 4 0   5 10 1
Eller   Williams, James (1), Wilkinson (6)

COMPOSITE BATTING

Cincinnati (NL)

NAME	POS	G	AB	R	H	2B	3B	HR	RBI	BA
		8	251	35	64	10	7	0	34	.255
Rath	2B	8	31	5	7	1	0	0	2	.226
Daubert	1B	8	29	4	7	0	1	0	1	.241
Groh	3B	8	29	6	5	2	0	0	2	.172
Neale	OF	8	28	3	10	1	1	0	4	.357
Roush	OF	8	28	6	6	2	1	0	7	.214
Kopf	SS	8	27	3	6	0	2	0	3	.222
Duncan	OF	8	26	3	7	2	0	0	8	.269
Rariden	C	5	19	0	4	0	0	0	0	.211
Wingo	C	3	7	1	4	0	0	0	1	.571
Eller	P	2	7	2	2	1	0	0	0	.286
Ruether	P	3	6	2	4	1	2	0	4	.667
Ring	P	2	5	0	0	0	0	0	0	.000
Sallee	P	2	4	0	0	0	0	0	0	.000
Magee	PH	2	2	0	1	0	0	0	0	.500
Fisher	P	2	2	0	1	0	0	0	0	.500
Luque	P	2	2	0	0	0	0	0	0	.000
Smith	PR	1	0	0	0	0	0	0	0	—

Chicago (AL)

NAME	POS	G	AB	R	H	2B	3B	HR	RBI	BA
		8	263	20	59	10	3	1	17	.224
Weaver	3B	8	34	4	11	4	1	0	0	.324
Jackson	OF	8	32	5	12	3	0	1	6	.375
E. Collins	2B	8	31	2	7	1	0	0	1	.226
Gandil	1B	8	30	1	7	0	1	0	5	.233
Felsch	OF	8	26	2	5	0	0	0	3	.192
Risberg	SS	8	25	3	2	0	0	0	0	.080
Schalk	C	8	23	1	7	0	0	0	2	.304
Leibold	OF	5	18	0	1	0	0	0	0	.056
S. Collins	OF	4	16	2	4	0	0	0	1	.250
Cicotte	P	3	8	0	0	0	0	0	0	.000
Kerr	P	2	6	1	1	0	0	0	0	.167
Williams	P	3	5	0	1	0	0	0	0	.200
McMullin	PH	2	2	0	1	0	0	0	0	.500
Murphy	PH	2	2	0	0	0	0	0	0	.000
Wilkinson	P	2	2	0	0	0	0	0	0	.000
Lynn	C	1	1	0	0	0	0	0	0	.000
Lowdermilk	P	1	0	0	0	0	0	0	0	—
Mayer	P	1	1	0	0	0	0	0	0	

COMPOSITE PITCHING

Cincinnati (NL)

NAME	G	IP	H	BB	SO	W	L	SV	ERA
	8	72	59	15	30	5	3	0	1.62
Eller	2	18	13	2	15	2	0	0	2.00
Ring	2	14	7	6	4	1	1	0	0.64
Ruether	2	14	12	4	1	1	0	0	2.57
Sallee	2	13.1	19	1	2	1	1	0	1.35
Fisher	2	7.2	7	2	2	0	1	0	2.35
Luque	2	5	1	0	6	0	0	0	0.00

Chicago (AL)

NAME	G	IP	H	BB	SO	W	L	SV	ERA
	8	71	64	25	22	3	5	0	3.42
Cicotte	3	21.2	19	5	7	1	2	0	2.91
Kerr	2	19	14	3	6	2	0	0	1.42
Williams	3	16.1	12	8	4	0	3	0	6.61
Wilkinson	2	7.1	9	4	3	0	0	0	1.23
James	1	4.2	3	2	0	0	0	0	5.79
Mayer	1	1	0	1	0	0	0	0	0.00
Lowdermilk	1	1	2	2	0	0	0	0	9.00

USE NAME - GIVEN NAMES (NICKNAMES)	TEAM BY YEAR	BIRTH DATE	BIRTH PLACE	DEATH DATE	B	T	HGT	WGT	G	AB	R	H	2B	3B	HR	RBI	BB	SO	SB	BA	SA
Abbaticchio,Ed-Edward James	97-98PhiN 03-05BosN 06HO 07-10PitN 10BosN	04-15-77	Latrobe, Pa.	01-06-57	R	R	5'11	170	850	3032	356	772	99	44	11	324	289		142	.255	.327
Abbott (Winbigler), Fred-Harry Frederick	03-04CleA 05PhiN	10-22-74	Versailles, Ohio	06-11-35	R	R	5'10	180	160	513	48	107	21	6	1	49	19		14	.209	.279
Abbott, Ody-Ody Cleon (Toby)	10StlN	09-05-86	New Eagle, Pa	04-13-33	R	R	6'2	180	22	70	2	13	2	1	0	6	6	20	3	.186	.243
Abstein, Bill-William Henry (Big Bill)	06,09PitN 10StlA	02-02-83	St. Louis, Mo.	04-08-40	R	R	6'2	185	170	619	54	150	22	10	1	76	29		21	.242	.315
Acosta, Merito-Balmadero Pedro	13-16,18WasA 18PhiA	06-02-96	Bauto, Cuba	11-16-63	L	L	5'7	140	175	435	56	111	9	7	0	37	63	46	17	.255	.308
Adams, Jack-John Bertram	10-12CleA 15-19PhiN	06-21-91	Wharton, Tex	06-24-40	B	R	6'1	185	267	678	37	137	17	4	2	45	23		9	.202	.248
Agler, Joe-Joseph Abram	12WasA14-15BuffF 15BalF	06-12-87	Coshocton, Ohio	04-26-71	L	L	5'11	185	233	751	121	185	22	10	0	36	131		38	.246	.302
Agnew, Sam-Samuel Lester	13-15StlA 16-18BosA 19WasA	04-12-87	Farmington, Mo.	07-19-51	R	R	5'11	185	560	1537	105	314	41	14	2	98	103	216	29	.204	.253
Ainsmith (Anshmedt), Eddie-Edward Wilbur	10-18WasA 19-21DetA 21-23StlN 23BknN 24NYN	02-04-90	Cambridge, Mass.	09-06-81	R	R	5'11	180	1068	3048	299	707	108	54	22	317	263		86	.232	.324
Aiton, George-George Wilson (Bill)	12StlL	12-29-90	Kingman, Kans.	08-16-76	B	R	5'11	175	8	17	1	4	0	0	0	1	4		0	.235	.235
Alcock, Scotty-John Forbes	14ChiA	11-29-85	Wooster, Ohio	01-30-73	R	R	5'9	160	54	156	12	27	4	2	0	7	7	14	4	.173	.224
Alexander, Walt-Walter Ernest	12-13, 15StlA 15-17NYA	03-05-91	Marietta, Ga.	12-29-78	R	R	5'10	165	162	405	26	76	18	3	1	24	43	83	5	.188	.254
Allen, Bob (see Al Elliott)																					
Allen, Horace-Horace Tanner (Pug)	19BknN	06-11-99	DeLand, Fla.	07-05-81	L	R	6'	187	4	7	0	0	0	0	0	0	0	2	0	.000	.000
Allen, Nick-Artemus Ward	14-15BuffF 16ChiN 18-20ConN	06-11-99	Norton, Kans.	10-16-39	R	R	6'2	200	216	500	41	116	13	5	0	36	33		8	.232	.278
Allen, Sled-Fletcher Manson	10StL	08-23-86	West Plains, Mo.	10-16-59	R	R	6'1	180	14	23	3	3	1	0	0	1	1		0	.130	.174
Allison, Milo-Milo Henry (Pete)	13-14ChiN 16-17CleA	10-16-90	Elk Rapids, Mich.	06-18-57	L	R	6'	163	49	60	15	13	0	0	0	0	15	9	4	.217	.217
Almeida, Rafael-Rafael D.	11-13CinN	06-30-87	Havana, Cuba	05-18-69	R	R	5'9	164	102	285	32	77	13	6	3	46	25	40	7	.270	.389
Alperman, Whitey-Charles (Augustus)	06-09BknN	11-11-79	Etna, Pa.	12-25-42	R	R	5'10	180	450	1632	134	387	60	36	7	141	30		27	.237	.331
Altenburg, Jesse-Jesse Howard (Chip)	16-17PitN	01-02-93	Ashley, Mich.	03-12-73	L	R	5'8	158	19	31	3	9	1	1	0	3	1	5	0	.290	.387
Altizer, Dave-David Tildon (Filipino)	06-08WasA 08CleA 09ChiA 10-11CinN	11-06-76	Pearl, Ill.	05-14-64	L	R	5'10	160	514	1734	204	433	36	21	4	116	140		119	.250	.302
Anderson (Jendrus), George-George Andrew Jendrus	14-15BknF 18StlN	09-26-89	Cleveland, Ohio	05-28-62	L	R	5'8	160	269	1007	148	289	40	17	5	69	98		36	.287	.379
Anderson, Goat-Edward John	07PitN	01-13-80	Cleveland, Ohio	03-15-23	L	R			127	413	73	85	3	1	1	12	80		27	.206	.225
Anderson, John-John Joseph (Honest John)	94-98BknN 98WasN 98StlN 01MilA 02-03StlA 04-05NYA 05-07WasA 08ChiA	12-14-73	Sarpsborg, Norway	07-23-49	B	R	6'2	180	1620	6343	866	1852	326	126	48	976	310		347	.292	.406
Aragon, Angel-Angel (Valdez) (Bing, Pete)	14,16-17NYA	08-02-90	Havana, Cuba	01-24-52	R	R	5'5	150	33	79	4	9	1	0	0	5	5	6	2	.114	.127
Archer, Jimmy-James Patrick	04PitN 07DetA 09-17ChiN 18PhiN 18BknN 18CinN	05-13-83	Dublin, Ireland	03-29-58	R	R	5'10	176	846	2645	247	660	106	34	16	296	124		36	.250	.333
Armbruster, Charlie-Charles Anthony	05-07BosA 07ChiA	08-30-80	Cincinnati, Ohio	10-07-64	R	R	5'9	180	131	355	24	53	11	1	0	12	52		6	.149	.186
Armbruster, Harry-Henry George (Buster, Army)	06PhiA	03-20-82	Liverpool, Ohio	12-10-53	L	L	5'10	190	91	265	40	63	6	3	2	24	43		13	.238	.306
Arndt, Harry-Harry John	02DetA 02BalA 05-07StlN	02-12-79	South Bend, Ind.	03-25-21	R	R		165	271	985	118	244	26	20	6	99	85		27	.248	.333
Asmussen, Tom-Thomas William	07BosN	09-26-78	Chicago, Ill.	08-21-63		R			2	5	0	0	0	0	0	0	0		0	.000	.000
Atz, Jake-Jacob Henry	02WasA 07-09ChiA	07-01-79	Washington, D.C.	05-22-45	R	R	5'11	160	208	604	64	132	21	3	0	49	69		23	.219	.263
Aubrey, Harry-Harry Herbert	03BosN	07-05-81	St. Joseph, Mo.	09-18-53	R	R	5'7	130	96	325	26	69	8	2	0	27	18		7	.212	.249
Austin, Jimmy-James Philip (Pepper)	09-10NYA 11-23, 25-26,29,M13 18,23StlA	12-08-79	Swansea, Wales	03-06-65	B	R	5'7	155	1580	5388	661	1328	174	76	13	390	593		245	.246	.314
Autry, Chick-William Askew	07,09CinN 09BosN	01-02-85	Humboldt, Tenn.	01-16-76	L	L	5'11	168	81	257	22	50	6	0	0	17	24		6	.195	.218
Babb, Charlie-Charles Amos	03NYN 04-05BknN	02-20-73	Milwaukie, Ore.	03-19-54	R	R	5'10	165	348	1181	144	287	41	13	0	116	125		66	.243	.300
Babington, Charlie-Charles Percy	15NYN	05-04-95	Cranston, R.I.	03-22-57	R	R	6'	170	28	33	5	8	3	0	0	2	0	4	1	.242	.394
Bader, Art-Arthur Herman	04StlA	09-21-86	St. Louis, Mo.	04-05-57	R	R	5'10	170	2	3	0	0	0	0	0	0	0	1	0	.000	.000
Bailey, Bill-Harry Lewis	11NYA	11-19-81	Shawnee, Ohio	10-27-67	R	R	5'10	170	5	9	1	1	0	0	0	0	0		0	.111	.111
Bailey, Fred-Frederick Middleton (Penny)	16-18BosN	08-16-95	Mt. Hope, W.Va.	08-16-72	L	L	5'11	150	60	124	10	23	2	1	1	6	9	29	5	.185	.242
Baird, Al-Albert Wells	17NYN 18MS 19NYN	06-02-95	Cleburne, Tex.	11-27-76	R	R	5'9	160	48	107	9	27	1	0	0	9	7	11	3	.252	.262
Baird, Doug-Howard Douglas	15-17PitN 17-18StlN 19PhiN 19StlN 19-20BknN 20NYN	09-27-91	St.Charles, Mo.	06-13-67	R	R	5'9	148	617	2106	230	492	86	45	6	191	157	295	118	.234	.326
Baker, Del-Delmer David	14-16,M33,38-42DetA M60BosA	05-03-92	Sherwood, Ore.	09-11-73	R	R	5'11	176	172	302	27	63	9	4	0	22	32	32	5	.209	.265
Baker, Frank-John Franklin (Home Run)	08-14PhiA 15HO 16-19, 21-22NYA 20VR	03-13-86	Trappe, Md.	06-28-63	L	R	5'11	173	1575	5985	887	1838	311	103	96	987	473		235	.307	.442
Baker, Howard-Howard Francis	12CleA 14-15ChiA 15NYN	03-01-88	Bridgeport, Conn.	01-16-64	R	R	5'11	175	29	82	5	18	1	1	0	7	8	10	0	.220	.256
Baker (Silverman), Jesse (Michael)-Myron Jesse	19WasA	03-04-95	Cleveland, Ohio	07-29-76	R	R	5'4	140	1	0	0	0	0	0	0	0	0		0	—	—
Baker, Tracy-Trace Lee	11BosA	11-07-91	Pendelton, Ore.	03-14-75	R	R	6'1	180	1	0	0	0	0	0	0	0	0		0	—	—
Balenti, Mike-Michael Richard	11CinN 13StlA	07-03-86	Calumet, Okla.	08-04-55	R	R	6'1	175	78	219	19	40	2	4	0	11	7	33	6	.183	.228
Ball, Jim-James Chandler	07-08BosA	02-22-84	Hartford, Md.	04-07-63	R	R	5'11	175	16	51	4	7	2	0	0	3	3		0	.137	.176
Ball, Neal-Cornelius	07-09NYA 09-12CleA 12-13BosA	04-22-81	Grand Haven, Mich.	10-15-57	R	R	5'7	145	496	1609	161	404	56	17	4	151	99		92	.251	.314
Bankston, Bill-Wilborn Everett	15PhiA	05-25-93	Barnesville, Ga.	02-26-70	R	R	5'11	180	11	36	6	5	1	1	1	2	2	5	1	.139	.306
Barbeau, Jap-William Joseph	05-06CleA 09PhiN 09-10StlN	06-10-82	New York, NY	09-10-69	R	R	5'5	140	198	712	96	160	25	8	0	46	78		39	.225	.282
Barclay, George-George Oliver (Deerfoot)	02-04StlN 04-05BosN	05-16-76	Millville, Pa.	04-02-09	R	R	5'10	162	401	1538	167	382	35	15	4	140	62		61	.248	.298
Barnett, Jack-John Jeirus		12-15-79	Ventura, Cal.	09-03-23	R	R			59	206	18	49	8	4	0	12	15		5	.238	.316
Barney, Ed-Edmund J.	15NYA 15-16PitN	01-23-90	Amery, Wis.	10-04-67	L	R	5'9	178	88	272	33	61	5	2	0	22	37	33	17	.224	.257
Barr, Scotty-Hyder Edward	08-09PhiN	10-06-86	Bristol, Tenn.	12-02-34	R	R	6'	175	41	107	9	12	3	0	0	2	14		0	.112	.140
Barrett, Jimmy-James Erigena	99-00CinN 01-05DetA 06CinN 07-08BosA	03-28-75	Athol, Mass.	10-24-21	L	L	5'7	170	866	3304	581	962	82	48	16	255	440		145	.291	.360
Barrows, Cuke-Roland	09-12ChiA	10-20-83	Gray, Me.	02-10-55	R	L	5'8	158	32	99	6	19	2	1	0	9	12		3	.192	.242
Barry, Jack-John Joseph	08-15PhiA 15-17,M17BosA 18MS 19BosA	04-26-87	Meriden, Conn.	04-23-61	R	R	5'9	158	1222	4146	533	1009	142	38	10	429	396		153	.243	.303
Barry, Shad-John C.	99WasN 00-01BosN 01-04PhiN 04-05ChiN 05-06CinN 06-08StlN 08NYN	10-27-78	Newburgh, N.Y.	11-27-36	R	R			1100	4007	515	1075	130	48	10	391	279		143	.268	.332
Barton, Harry-Harry Lamb	05PhiA	01-20-75	Chester, Pa.	01-25-55	B	R	5'6	150	29	60	5	10	2	1	0	3	3		2	.167	.233
Bashang (Baschang), Al-Albert C.	12DetA 18BknN	08-22-88	Cincinnati, Ohio	06-23-67	L	R	5'8	150	7	17	3	2	0	0	0	0	3		0	.118	.118
Bass, Doc-William Capers	12BosN	12-04-98	Macon, Ga.	01-12-70	L	L	5'10	165	2	1	1	1	0	0	0	0	0		0	1.000	1.000
Batch, Heinie-Emil (Ace)	04-07BknN	01-21-80	Brooklyn, N.Y.	08-23-26	R	R	5'7	170	348	1253	134	315	38	22	7	98	65		37	.251	.334
Bates, Johnny-John William	06-09BosN 09-10PhiN 11-14CinN 14ChiN 14BalF	01-10-82	Steubenville, Ohio	02-10-49	L	L	5'7	168	1163	3921	572	1088	167	73	25	417	504		187	.277	.376
Bates, Ray-Raymond	13CleA 17PhiA 18MS	02-08-90	Paterson, N.J.	08-15-70	R	R	6'	168	147	515	51	120	20	9	2	70	24	48	15	.233	.318
Batsch, Bill-William McKinley	16PitN	05-18-92	Mingo Junction, Ohio	12-31-63	R	R	5'10	168	1	0	0	0	0	0	0	0	0		0	—	—
Batten, George-George Burnett	12NYA	10-07-91	Haddonfield, N.J.	08-04-72	R	R	5'11	165	1	3	0	0	0	0	0	0	0		0	.000	.080
Baumann, Paddy-Charles John	11-14DetA 15-17NYA	12-20-85	Indianapolis, Ind.	11-20-69	R	R	5'9	160	295	904	118	248	30	13	4	101	81		30	.274	.350
Baxter, John-John Morris (Moose)	07StlN	07-27-76	Chippewa Falls, Wis.	08-07-26	L	L	6'2	200	6	21	1	4	0	0	0	0	0		0	.190	.190
Bay, Harry-Harry Elbert (Deerfoot)	01-02CinN 02-08CleA	01-17-78	Pontiac, Ill.	03-20-52	L	L	5'8	138	673	2638	413	720	65	42	5	141	195		169	.273	.335
Bayless, Dick-Harry Owen	08CinN	09-06-83	Joplin, Mo.	12-16-20	L	R	5'9	178	19	71	7	16	1	0	1	3	6		0	.225	.282
Beall, Johnny-John Woolf	13CleA 13ChiA 15-16CinN 18StlN	03-12-82	Beltsville, Md.	06-13-26	L	R	6'	180	58	170	18	43	4	1	3	17	11	25	2	.253	.341
Bean, Joe-Joseph William	02NYN	03-18-74	Boston, Mass.	02-15-61	R	R	5'8	138	48	176	13	39	7	1	0	5	5		9	.222	.244
Beatty, Des-Desmond Aloysius (Desperate)	14NYN	04-07-93	Baltimore, Md.	10-06-69	R	R	5'8	158	2	4	0	0	0	0	0	0	0		0	.000	.000
Beaumont, Ginger-Clarence Howeth	99-06PitN 07-09BosN 10ChiN	07-23-76	Rochester, Wis.	04-10-56	L	R	5'8	190	1463	5647	953	1754	182	82	39	617	425		243	.311	.393
Beck, Erve-Ervin Thomas (Dutch)	99BknN 01CleA 02CinN 02DetA		Toledo, Ohio	12-23-16	R	R	5'10	180	232	912	122	265	42	11	9	123	30		12	.291	.390
Beck, Fred-Frederick Thomas (Liz)	09-10BosN 11CinN 11PhiN 14-15ChiF	11-17-86	Havana, Ill.	03-12-62	R	R	6'1	180	635	2130	191	536	77	27	34	251	122		31	.252	.361
Beck, Zinn-Zinn Bertram	13-16StlN 18NYN	09-30-85	Steubenville, Ohio	03-19-81	R	R	5'10	180	290	902	75	204	32	16	3	73	58	95	21	.226	.307
Beckendorf, Heinie-Henry Ward	09-10DetA 10WasA	06-15-84	New York, N.Y.	09-15-49	R	R	5'9	174	55	137	9	25	2	0	0	13	8		0	.182	.197
Becker, Beals-David Beals	08PitN 08-09BosN 10-12NYN 13CinN 13-15PhiN	07-05-86	El Dorado, Kans.	08-16-43	L	L	5'11	176	876	2764	367	763	114	43	45	292	241		129	.276	.397
Becker, Marty-Martin Henry	15NYN	12-25-93	Tiffin, Ohio	09-25-57	B	R	5'9	168	17	52	5	13	2	0	0	3	2	9	3	.250	.288
Beckley, Jake-Jacob Peter (Eagle Eye)	88-89PitN 90PitP 91-96PitN 96-97StlN 97-03CinN 04-07StlN	08-04-67	Hannibal, Mo.	06-25-18	L	L	5'10	200	2383	9476	1601	2930	455	246	87	1574	616		335	.309	.437
Bell (Baerwald), Jack (Rudolph Fred)-John	07NYN	01-01-81	Wausau, Wis.	07-28-55	R	R	5'8	158	17	52	4	11	2	1	0	3	3		4	.212	.288
Bemis, Harry-Harry Parker	02-10CleA	02-01-74	Farmington, N.H.	05-23-47	R	R	5'6	155	703	2229	214	569	92	29	5	234	79		49	.255	.329
Bennett, Pug-Justin Titus	06-07StlN	09-12-74	Ponca, Neb.	12-16-35	R	R	5'11	165	240	919	86	228	21	14	1	55	77		27	.248	.297
Bergen, Bill-William Aloysius	01-03CinN 04-11BknN	06-13-73	N. Brookfield, Mass.	12-19-43	R	R	6'	184	947	3028	138	516	45	21	2	193	88		23	.170	.201
Berger, Clarence-Clarence Edward	14PitN	11-01-94	East Cleveland, Ohio	06-30-59	L	R	6'	185	6	13	2	1	0	0	0	0	2	4	0	.077	.077
Berger, Joe-Joseph August (Fats)	13-14ChiA	12-20-86	St. Louis, Mo.	03-06-56	R	R	5'10	170	124	371	38	71	9	3	2	23	49	37	7	.191	.248
Berghammer, Marty-Martin Andrew (Pepper)	11ChiA 13-14CinN 15PitF	06-18-88	Elliott, Pa.	12-21-57	R	R	5'11	155	285	774	136	180	16	7	1	52	103		46	.233	.275
Bergman, Dutch-Alfred Henry	16CleA	09-27-90	Peru, Ind.	06-20-61	R	R	5'7	155	8	14	2	3	0	0	0	0	5		1	.214	.214
Berman, Bob-Robert Leon	18WasA	01-24-99	New York, N.Y.	08-02-88	R	R	5'9	160	2	4	0	1	0	0	0	0	0		0	.250	.250
Bernard, Curt-Curtis Henry	00-01NYN	02-18-78	Parkersburg, W.Va.	04-10-55	L	R	5'10	150	42	146	20	34	7	2	0	14	13		5	.233	.274
Berran, Denny-Dennis Martin	12ChiA	10-08-87	Merrimac, Mass.	04-28-43	L	L			2	4	1	1	0	0	0	0	0		0	.250	.250
Berry, Claude-Claude Elzy (Admiral)	04ChiA 06-07PhiA 14-15PitF	02-04-80	Losantville, Ind.	02-01-74	R	R	5'7	165	245	753	72	165	31	11	3	65	60		14	.219	.288
Berry, Howard-Joseph Howard Sr. (Hodge)	02PhiN	09-10-72	Wheeling, W.Va.	03-13-61	B	R	5'9	172	1	4	1	1	0	0	0	0	1		1	.250	.250
Berte, Harry-Harry Thomas	03StlN	05-10-72	Covington, Ky.	05-06-52	R	R	5'10	160	4	15	1	5	0	0	0	3	1		1	.333	.333

USE NAME - GIVEN NAMES (NICKNAMES)	TEAM BY YEAR	BIRTH DATE	BIRTH PLACE	DEATH DATE	B	T	HGT	WGT	G	AB	R	H	2B	3B	HR	RBI	BB	SO	SB	BA	SA
Bescher, Bob-Robert Henry	08-13CinN 14NYN 15-17StLN 18CleA	02-25-84	London, Ohio	11-29-42	B	L	6'1	200	1228	4536	749	1171	190	74	28	345	619		428	.258	.351
Betcher (Bettger), Frank-Franklin Lyle	10StLN	02-15-88	Philadelphia, Pa.	11-27-81	R	R	5'11	173	35	89	7	18	2	0	0	6	7	14	1	.202	.225
Betzel, Bruno-Christian Frederick Albert John Henry David	14-18StLN	12-06-94	Chattanooga, Ohio	02-07-65	R	R	5'9	158	448	1444	135	333	37	25	2	94	90	189	49	.231	.295
Beville, Monte-Henry Monte	03-04NYA 04DetA	02-24-75	Dublin, Ind.	01-24-55	L	R	5'11	180	145	454	39	92	21	2	0	44	26		6	.203	.258
Bigler, Ivan-Ivan Edward	17StLA	12-13-92	Bradford, Ohio	04-01-75	R	R	5'9	150	1	0	0	0	0	0	0	0	0	0	0	—	—
Billings, Josh-John Augustus	13-18CleA 19-23StLA	11-30-91	Grantville, Kans.	12-30-81	R	R	5'11	165	240	488	44	106	9	5	1	29	23	73	5	.217	.262
Birmingham, Joe-Joseph Lee (Dode)	06-14,M12-15CleA	08-06-84	Elmira, N.Y.	04-24-46	R	R	6'	185	771	2627	283	667	89	28	6	265	129		108	.254	.316
Bisland, Rivington-Rivington Martin	12PitN 13StLA 14CleA	02-17-90	New York, N.Y.	01-11-73	R	R	5'9	155	31	102	12	12	1	0	0	5	8	7	2	.118	.127
Black (Haddow), John-Jack Falconer	11StLA	02-23-90	Covington, Ky.	03-20-62	R	R	6'1	185	54	186	13	28	4	0	0	7	10		4	.151	.172
Blackburn, Earl-Earl Stuart	12PitN12-13CinN 15-16BosN 17ChiN	11-01-92	Leesville, Ohio	08-03-66	R	R	5'11	180	71	145	13	38	4	4	0	10	14	27	4	.262	.345
Blackburne, Lena-Russell Aubrey (Slats) (See P20-45)	10ChiA 11KJ 12ChiA 18CinN 18BosN 19PhiN 27,29,M28-29ChiA	10-23-86	Clifton Heights, Pa.	02-29-68	R	R	5'11	160	548	1807	174	387	39	23	4	139	162		54	.214	.268
Blackwell, Fred-Frederick William (Blacky)	17-19PitN	09-07-95	Bowling Green, Ky.	12-08-75	L	R	5'10	160	35	88	5	18	3	0	0	10	6	16	0	.205	.239
Blair, Walter-Walter Allen (Heavy)	07-11NYA 14-15,M15BufF	10-13-83	Landrus, Pa.	08-20-48	R	R	6'	185	442	1255	90	272	42	11	3	106	86		18	.217	.275
Blank, Coonie-Frank Ignatz	09StLN	10-18-92	St. Louis, Mo.	12-08-61	R	R	5'11		1	3	0	0	0	0	0	0	0		0	.000	.000
Blankenship, Cliff-Clifford Douglas	05CinN 07,09WasN	04-10-80	Columbus, Ga.	04-26-56	R	R	5'10	165	95	218	16	49	3	1	0	22	7		6	.225	.248
Bliss, Elmer-Elmer Ward (See P01-19)	03-04NYA		Penfield, Pa.	03-18-62	L	R	6'	180	2	4	0	0	0	0	0	0	0		0	.000	.000
Bliss, Jack-John Joseph Albert	08-12StLN	01-09-82	Vancouver, Wash.	10-23-68	R	R	5'10	160	241	654	70	143	15	6	3	61	85		13	.219	.274
Block (Blochowitz), Bruno-James John	07WasA 10-12ChiA 14ChiF	03-13-85	Wisconsin Rapids, Wis.	08-06-37	R	R	5'8	185	207	560	42	129	18	10	1	68	39		5	.230	.304
Blue, Bert-Bird Wayne	08StLA 08PhiA	12-09-77	Bettsville, Ohio	09-02-29	R	R	6'3	200	17	44	4	12	1	2	1	2	3		0	.273	.364
Bluhm, Red-Harvey Fred	18BosA	06-27-94	Cleveland, Ohio	05-07-52	R	R	5'11	165	1	1	0	0	0	0	0	0	0		0	.000	.000
Bodie, (Pezzolo), Ping (Francesco Stephano)-Frank Stephan (The Rockefeller of Telegraph Hill)	11-14ChiA 17PhiA 18-21NYA	10-08-87	San Francisco, Cal.	12-07-61	R	R	5'8	195	1049	3670	392	1011	169	72	43	516	312		83	.275	.396
Bold, Dutch-Charles Dickens	14StLN	10-27-94	Karlskrona, Sweden	07-29-78	R	R	6'2	185	2	1	0	0	0	0	0	0	0		0	.000	.000
Bone, George-George Drummond	01MilA	08-08-76	New Haven, Conn.	05-26-18	B	R	5'7	152	12	43	6	13	2	0	0	6	4		0	.302	.349
Bonin, Luther-Ernest Luther	13StLA 14BufF	01-13-88	Greenhill, Ind.	01-03-66	R	R	5'9	178	21	77	6	14	4	1	0	4	7		3	.182	.260
Bonner, Frank-Frank J. (The Human Flea)	94-95BalN 95StLN 96BknN 99WasN 02CleA 02PhiA 03BosN	08-20-69	Lowell, Mass.	12-31-05	R	R	5'7	170	240	941	114	239	44	7	4	115	55		32	.254	.328
Booe, Everett-Everett Little	13PitN 14IndF 14BufF	09-28-90	Mocksville, N.C.	05-21-69	L	R	5'8	165	125	352	43	77	10	4	0	22	34		14	.219	.270
Boone, Luke-Luke Joseph (Danny)	13-16NYA 18PitN	05-06-90	Pittsburgh, Pa.	07-24-82	R	R	5'10	168	314	1028	102	215	27	4	6	76	91	111	32	.209	.264
Borton, Babe-William Baker	12-13ChiA 13NYA 15StLF 16StLA	08-14-88	Marion, Ill.	07-29-54	L	L	6'	178	317	940	139	254	30	17	5	136	160		21	.270	.354
Bostick (Lipschitz), Henry-Henry Landers	15-17StLA	01-12-95	Boston, Mass.	09-16-68	R	R			2	7	1	0	0	0	0	0	0		0	.000	.000
Boucher, Allie-Alexander Francis (Bo)	14StLF	11-13-81	Franklin, Mass.	06-23-74	R	R	5'8	156	147	516	62	119	26	4	2	49	52		13	.231	.308
Boucher, Medric-Medric Charles Francis (Bush)	14BalF 14PitF	03-12-86	St. Louis, Mo.	03-12-74	R	R	5'10	165	17	17	2	5	1	1	0	2	1		0	.294	.471
Bowcock, Benny-Benjamin James	03StLA	10-28-79	Fall River, Mass.	06-16-61	R	R	5'7	150	14	50	7	16	3	1	0	10	3		1	.320	.480
Bowden, Tim-David Timon	14StLA	08-15-91	McDonough, Ga.	10-25-49	R	R	5'10	175	7	9	0	2	0	0	0	2	1	6	0	.222	.222
Bowen, Chick-Emmons Joseph	19NYN	07-26-97	New Haven, Conn.	08-09-48	R	R	5'7	165	2	3	1	1	0	0	0	0	1		0	.333	.333
Bowerman, Frank-Frank Eugene (Mike)	95-98BalN 98-99PitN 00-07NYN 08-09,M09BosN	12-05-68	Romeo, Mich.	11-30-48	R	R	6'1	195	1040	3383	345	861	100	38	13	392	129		86	.255	.318
Bowser, Red-James Harvey	10ChiA	09-20-81	Greensburg, Pa.	05-22-43	R	R			1	2	0	0	0	0	0	0	0		0	.000	.000
Boyle, Jack-John Bellow	12PitN	07-09-89	Morris, Ill.	04-03-71	R	R	5'11	165	15	25	4	7	1	0	0	2	1	5	0	.280	.320
Bradley, Bill-William Joseph	99-00ChiN 01-10CleA 14,M14BknF 15KCF	02-13-78	Cleveland, Ohio	03-11-54	R	R	6'	185	1460	5452	761	1484	273	84	34	552	290		193	.272	.372
Bradley, Hugh-Hugh Frederick (Corns)	10-12BosA 14-15PitF 15BknF 16NewkF	05-23-85	Grafton, Mass.	01-26-49	R	R	5'11	175	277	913	84	238	46	12	2	117	59		23	.261	.344
Bradley, Jack-John Thomas	16CleA	09-20-93	Denver, Colo.	03-18-69	R	R	5'11	175	2	3	0	0	0	0	0	0	0	1	0	.000	.000
Bradshaw, Windy-Dallas Carl (Rabbit)	17PhiA	11-23-95	Wolf Creek, Ill.	12-11-39	L	R	5'7	145	2	4	0	0	0	0	0	0	0		0	.000	.000
Brady, Fred (See Larry Kopf)																					
Brain, Dave-David Leonard	01ChiA 03-05StLN 05PitN 06-07BosN 08CinN 08NYN	01-24-79	Hereford, England	05-25-59	R	R	5'10	170	679	2543	254	641	97	52	27	303	134		73	.252	.363
Brainard, Fred-Frederick F.	14-16NYN	02-17-92	Champaign, Ill.	04-17-59	R	R	6'	176	95	261	32	51	7	2	1	21	22	44	6	.195	.249
Bransfield, Kitty-William Edward	98BosN 01-04PitN 05-11PhiN 11CinN	01-07-75	Worcester, Mass.	05-01-47	R	R	5'11	207	1330	4997	530	1350	225	77	14	637	221		175	.270	.354
Brashear, Roy-Roy Parks	02StLN 03PhiN	01-03-74	Ashtabula, Ohio	04-20-51	R	R	5'11	200	133	465	45	125	11	2	1	44	38		11	.269	.308
Brenegan, Sam-Olaf Selmer	14PitN	09-01-90	Galesville, Wis.	04-20-56	L	R	6'2	185	1	0	0	0	0	0	0	0	0	0	0	—	—
Bresnahan, Roger-Roger Philip (The Duke of Tralee)	97WasN 00ChiN 01-02BalA 02-08NYN 09-12,M09-12StLN 13-15,M15ChiN	06-11-79	Toledo, Ohio	12-04-44	R	R	5'9	200	1445	4481	682	1252	218	71	26	530	714		212	.279	.377
Breton, Jim-John Frederick	13-15ChiA	07-15-91	Chicago, Ill.	05-30-73	R	R	5'10	176	107	297	25	59	9	3	0	27	30	56	11	.199	.249
Brickley, George-George Vincent 20-21 played in N.F.L.	13-15ChiA	07-19-94	Everett, Mass.	02-23-47	R	R	5'10	180	5	12	0	2	1	0	0	3	1		1	.167	.333
Bridwell, Al-Albert Henry	05CinN 06-07BosN 08-11NYN 11-12BosN 13CinN 14-15StLF	01-04-84	Friendship, Ohio	01-23-69	L	R	5'9	150	1251	4169	457	1064	95	32	2	348	559		136	.255	.295
Brief (Grzeszkowki), Bunny (Antony John)-Anthony Vincent	12-13StLA 15ChiA 17PitN	07-03-92	Remus, Mich.	02-11-63	R	R	6'1	185	183	569	61	127	25	9	5	59	59		17	.223	.235
Brinker, Bill-William Hutchinson (Dode)	12PhiN	08-30-83	Warrensburg, Mo.	02-05-65	B	R	6'1	190	9	18	1	4	0	0	0	2	3		0	.222	.278
Britton, Gil-Stephen Gilbert	13PhiN	09-21-91	Parsons, Kans.	06-20-83	R	R	5'10	160	3	12	0	0	0	0	0	0	0		0	.000	.000
Brock, John-John Roy	17-18StLN	10-16-96	Hamilton, Ill.	10-27-51	R	R	5'8	165	34	67	13	17	3	0	0	5	8	3	12	.254	.299
Broderick, Matt-Matthew Thomas	03BknN	12-01-77	Lattimer Mines, Pa.	02-26-40	R	R	5'6	135	2	2	0	0	0	0	0	0	0		0	.000	.000
Brodie, Steve-Water Scott	90-91BosN 92-93StLN 93-96BalN 97-98PitN 98-99BalN 01BalA 02NYN	09-11-68	Warrenton, Va.	10-30-35	L	R	5'9	176	1439	5686	853	1749	193	89	25	901	420		310	.308	.386
Bronkie, Herman-Herman Charles (Dutch)	10-12CleA 14ChiN 18StLN 19StLA	03-30-85	S. Manchester, Conn.	05-27-68	R	R	5'9	165	121	360	40	87	14	9	0	34	33		3	.242	.317
Brothers, Art-Arthur Henry	06PhiA	11-25-82	Montgomery, Ala.	09-28-59	R	R	6'1		36	144	18	30	5	1	0	14	5		4	.208	.257
Brouthers, Dan-Dennsin Joseph (Big Dan)	79-80TroyN 81-85BufN 86-88DetN 89BosN 90BosP 91BosAA 92-93BknN 94-95BalN 95LouN 96PhiN 04NYN	05-08-58	Sylvan Lake, N.Y.	08-02-32	L	L	6'2	207	1665	6682	1513	2288	446	212	106	1296	840	239	261	.342	.520
Brown, Bill-William Verna	12StLA	07-08-93	Coleman, Tex.	05-13-65	L	L	5'8	185	9	20	0	4	0	0	0	1	0		0	.200	.200
Brown, Delos-Delos Hight	10-04-92	Anna, Ill.	12-21-64	R	R	5'9	160	1	1	0	0	0	0	0	0	0		0	.250	.250
Brown, Don-James Donaldson (Moose)	15StLN 16PhiA	03-31-93	Laurel, Md.	Deceased	R	R	6'	178	15	44	6	11	2	1	1	5	6	10	0	.250	.409
Brown, Drummond-Drummond Nicol	13BosN 14-15KCF	01-31-85	Los Angeles, Cal.	01-27-27	R	R	6'	180	123	319	20	77	14	1	2	33	21		4	.241	.310
Brown, Fred-Fred Herbert	01-02BknN	04-12-79	Ossipee, N.H.	02-03-55	R	R	5'10	180	9	20	4	4	1	0	0	2	0		0	.200	.250
Brown, Sam-Samuel Wakefield	06-07BosN	05-21-78	Webster, Pa.	11-08-31	R	R			141	439	29	88	12	1	0	34	25		4	.200	.232
Browne, George-George Edward	01-02PhiN 02-07NYN 08BosN 09CinN 09-10WasN 10ChiA 11BknN 12PhiN	01-12-76	Richmond, Va.	12-09-20	L	R	5'10	160	1102	4300	614	1176	119	55	18	303	259		190	.273	.339
Bruce, Lou-Louis R.	04PhiA	01-16-77	St. Regis, N.Y.	02-09-68	L	R	5'5	145	30	101	9	27	3	0	0	8	5		2	.267	.297
Brush, Bob-Robert	07BknN	03-08-83	Osage, Iowa	04-02-44	R	R	5'10		2	2	0	0	0	0	0	0	0		0	.000	.000
Bruyette, Ed-Edward T.	08-31-77	Manawa, Wis.	08-05-40	R	R	5'10	170	26	82	7	15	3	0	0	4	12		1	.183	.220
Buelow, Charlie-Charles John	01MilA	08-31-77	Dubuque, Iowa	03-04-51	R	R			22	72	3	8	0	0	0	4	2		0	.111	.167
Buelow, Fritz-Frederick William Alexander	99-00StLN 01-04DetA 04-06CleA 07StLA	02-13-76	Berlin, Germany	12-27-33	R	R	5'10	170	430	1331	125	256	25	18	6	112	69		20	.192	.252
Bues, Art-Arthur Frederick	13BosN 14ChiN	03-03-88	Milwaukee, Wis.	11-07-54	R	R	5'11	184	16	46	3	10	1	1	0	5	5	7	1	.217	.283
Burch, Al-Albert William	06-07StLN 07-11BknN	10-07-83	Albany, N.Y.	10-05-26	L	R	5'8	160	611	2185	254	554	48	20	4	103	186		96	.254	.299
Burg, Pete-Joseph Peter	10BosN	06-04-82	Chicago, Ill.	04-28-69	R	R	5'10	143	19	46	7	15	0	1	0	10	7	12	5	.326	.370
Burkam, Chris-Chauncey DePew	15StLA	10-13-92	Benton Harbor, Mich.	05-09-64	R	R	5'11	175	1	1	0	0	0	0	0	0	0		0	.000	.000
Burke, Frank-Frank Aloysius	06NYN 07BosN	02-16-80	Carbon Co., Pa.	09-17-46		R			51	138	8	26	1	1	0	9	12		4	.188	.217
Burke, Jimmy-James Timothy (Sunset Jimmy)	98CleN 99MilA 01MilA 01ChiA 01-02PitN 03-05,M05StLN M18-20StLA	10-12-74	St. Louis, Mo.	03-26-42	R	R	5'7	160	550	1947	200	475	58	13	1	187	112		87	.244	.289
Burkett, Jesse-Jesse Cail (The Crab) (See P01-19)	90NYN 91-98CleN 99-01StLN 02-04StLA 05BosA	12-04-68	Wheeling, W.Va.	05-27-53	L	L	5'8	155	2063	8389	1708	2872	314	185	75	952	1029		392	.342	.451
Burns, Charlie-Charles Brittingham (C.B.)	02BalA	05-15-79	Bayview, Md.	06-06-68	R	R	6'	175	1	1	0	1	0	0	0	0	0		0	1.000	1.000
Burns, Ed-Edward James	12StLN 13-18PhiN	10-31-87	San Francisco,Cal.	05-30-42	R	R	5'11	200	321	796	48	183	21	6	0	65	83	59	14	.230	.271
Burns, George-George Joseph	11-21NYN 22-24CinN 25PhiN	11-24-89	Utica, N.Y.	08-15-66	R	R	5'7	160	1853	7241	1188	2077	362	108	41	611	872	565	383	.287	.384
Burns, Joe-Joseph Francis	10CinN 13DetA	03-26-89	Ipswich, Mass.	07-12-87	L	L	5'11	170	5	14	0	6	0	0	0	1	2	4	1	.429	.429
Burns, John-John Joseph	03-04DetA	05-13-80	Avoca, Pa.	06-24-57	R	R	5'10	160	15	53	5	12	0	0	0	4	0		1	.226	.226
Burr, Alex-Alexander Thompson	14NYA	11-01-93	Chicago, Ill.	10-12-18	R	R	6'2	190	1	0	0	0	0	0	0	0	0		0	—	—
Bush, Donie-Owen Joseph (Ownie)	08-21DetA 21-23,M23WasA M27-29PhiN M30-31ChiA M33CinN	10-08-87	Indianapolis, Ind.	03-28-72	B	R	5'6	140	1945	7206	1280	1803	186	74	9	436	1158		405	.250	.300
Butcher, Hank-Henry Joseph	11-12CleA	07-12-86	Chicago, Ill.	12-28-79	R	R	5'10	180	62	215	30	48	11	4	2	21	17		10	.223	.340
Butler (Bouthillier), Art-Arthur Edward	11BosN 12-13PitN 14-16StLN	12-19-87	Fall River, Mass.	10-07-84	R	R	5'8	165	454	1289	181	311	44	13	0	101	146	100	54	.241	.318
Butler, John-John Albert (01 played as Fred King)	01MilA 04-StLN 06-07BknN	12-17-79	Boston, Mass.	02-02-50	R	R	5'7	170	44	119	6	16	1	0	0	3	13		4	.134	.152
Butler, Kid-Willis Everett	07StLA	08-09-87	Franklin, Pa.	02-22-64	R	R	5'11	155	20	59	4	13	2	0	0	1	0		1	.220	.254
Byers, Bill-James William (Big Bill)	04StLN	10-03-77	Bridgeton, Ind.	09-08-48	L	R	5'7	210	19	60	3	13	1	0	0	4	1		0	.217	.217

USE NAME - GIVEN NAMES (NICKNAMES)	TEAM BY YEAR	BIRTH DATE	BIRTH PLACE	DEATH DATE	B	T	HGT	WGT	G	AB	R	H	2B	3B	HR	RBI	BB	SO	SB	BA	SA
Byrne, Bobby-Robert Matthew	07-09StLN 09-13PitN 13-17PhiN 17ChiA	12-31-84	St. Louis, Mo.	12-31-64	R	R	5'7	145	1283	4831	667	1225	186	60	10	329	456		176	.254	.323
Byrnes,Jim-James Joseph	06PhiA	01-05-80	San Francisco, Cal.	07-31-41	R	R	5'9	150	9	23	2	4	0	1	0	0	0		0	.174	.261
Cabrera, Al-Alfredo A.	13StLN	05-11-81	Canary Islands	- -64		R			1	2	0	0	0	0	0	0	0		0	.000	.000
Cady (Bergland), Hick-Forrest LeRoy	12-17BosA 19PhiN	01-26-86	Bishop Hill, Ill.	03-03-46	R	R	6'2	179	354	901	83	216	47	11	1	74	66	91	4	.240	.320
Caffyn, Ben-Benjamin Thomas	06CleA	02-10-80	Peoria, Ill.	11-22-42	L	L	5'10	175	30	103	16	20	4	0	0	3	12		2	.194	.233
Caldwell, Ray-Raymond Benjamin (Slim) (See P01-19)	10-18NYA 19BosA 19-21CleA	04-26-88	Corydon, Pa.	08-17-67	L	R	6'2	190	582	1164	137	289	46	8	8	114	78	158	23	.248	.322
Calhoun, Bill-William Davitte (Mary)	13BosN	06-23-90	Rockmart, Ga.	01-28-55	L	L	6'	180	6	13	0	1	0	0	0	0	0	3	0	.077	.077
Calhoun, Jack-John Charles (Red)	02StLN	12-14-79	Pittsburgh, Pa.	02-27-47	R	R	6'	185	20	64	3	10	2	1	0	8	8		1	.156	.219
Callahan, Dave-David Joseph	10-11CleA	07-20-88	Seneca, Ill.	10-28-69	L	R	5'10	165	18	56	7	12	1	1	0	2	5		5	.214	.268
Callahan(Callaghan), Jim-James Timothy (Red)	02NYN	01-12-81	Collier Twp., Pa.	03-09-68	R	R	5'9	145	1	4	0	0	0	0	0	0	0		0	.000	.000
Callahan, Leo-Leo David	13BknN 19PhiN	08-09-90	Jamaica Plain, Mass.	05-02-82	L	L	5'8	142	114	276	32	61	17	5	1	12	33	24	5	.221	.330
Callahan, Nixey-James Joseph (See P01-19)	94PhiN 97-00ChiN 01-05,11-13,M03-04,M12-14,M16-17ChiA	03-18-74	Fitchburg, Mass.	10-04-34	R	R	5'10	180	922	3296	440	906	137	46	11	394	159		185	.275	.354
Callahan, Wes-Wesley LeRoy	13StLN	07-03-88	Lyons, Ind.	09-13-53	R	R	5'7	155	7	14	0	4	0	0	0	1	2	2	1	.286	.286
Calvo (Del Calvo), Jack-Jacinto [Gonzalez]	13,20WasA	06-11-94	Havana, Cuba	06-15-65	L	L	5'11	185	33	56	10	9	0	1	1	4	3	6	0	.161	.250
Cameron, Happy Jack-John Stanley	06BosN	09-22-84	Sydney, Canada	07-12-63	R	R	5'10	170	18	61	3	11	0	0	0	4	2		0	.180	.180
Camp, Howie-Howard Lee (Red)	17NYA 18MS	07-01-93	Munford, Ala.	05-08-60	L	R	5'9	165	5	21	3	6	1	0	0	0	1	2	0	.286	.333
Campbell, Marc-Marc Thaddeus (Hutch)	07PitN	11-29-84	Punxsutawney, Pa.	02-13-46	R	R	5'10	155	2	4	0	1	0	0	0	1	1		0	.250	.250
Campbell, Vin-Arthur Vincent	08ChiN 10-11PitN 12BosN 13VR 14IndF 15NwkF	01-30-88	St. Louis, Mo.	11-16-69	L	R	6'	185	546	2069	326	642	85	36	15	167	132		92	.310	.408
Cannell, Rip-Virgin Virt	04-05BosN	01-23-80	South Bridgton, Me.	08-26-48	L	L	5'10	182	254	913	84	221	19	5	0	54	74		27	.242	.274
Capron, Ralph-Ralph Earl (Cape) 20 played in N.F.L	12PitN 13PhiN	06-16-89	Minneapolis, Minn.	09-19-80	L	L	5'11	165	3	1	1	0	0	0	0	0	0		0	.000	.000
Carey, Scoops-George C.	95BalN 98LouN 02-03WasA	12-04-70	Pittsburgh, Pa.	12-17-16	R	R	5'11	175	299	1150	114	316	60	20	1	159	52		6	.275	.364
Carisch, Fred-Frederick Behlmer	03-06PitN 12-14CleA 23DetA	11-14-81	Fountain City, Wis.	04-19-77	R	R	5'10	174	225	655	43	149	17	9	1	57	46		16	.227	.285
Carlisle, Walter-Walter (Rosy)	08BosA	07-06-82	Yeadon, England	05-27-45	B	R	5'9	154	3	10	0	1	0	0	0	0	1		1	.100	.100
Carlstrom, Swede-Albin Oscar	11BosA	10-26-86	Elizabeth, N.J.	04-28-35	R	R	5'11	175	2	6	0	1	0	0	0	0	0		0	.167	.167
Carney, Bill-William John	04ChiN	03-25-74	St. Paul, Minn.	07-01-38	B	R	5'10	175	2	7	0	0	0	0	0	0	1		0	.000	.000
Carney, Pat-Patrick Joseph (Doc) (See P01-19)	01-04BosN	08-07-76	Holyoke, Mass.	01-09-53	L	L	6'	200	338	1248	142	308	36	11	3	131	85		43	.247	.300
Carr, Charlie-Charles Carbitt	98WasN 01PhiA 03-04DetA 04-05CleA 06CinN 14IndF	12-27-76	Coatesville, Pa.	11-25-32	R	R	6'2	195	507	1948	185	492	68	32	6	240	71		48	.253	.330
Carr, Lew-Lewis Smith	01PitN	08-15-72	Union Springs, N.Y.	06-15-54	R	R	6'2	200	9	28	2	7	1	1	0	4	2		0	.250	.357
Carrigan, Bill-William Francis (Rough)	06,08-16,M13-16,27-29BosA	10-22-83	Lewiston, Me.	07-08-69	R	R	5'8	175	706	1970	194	506	67	14	6	235	206		37	.257	.314
Carroll, Dixie-Dorsey Lee	19BosN	05-19-91	Paducah, Ky.	10-13-84	L	R	5'11	165	15	49	10	13	3	1	0	7	7	1	5	.265	.367
Carroll, Doc-Ralph Arthur (Red)	16PhiA	12-28-91	Worcester, Mass.	06-27-83	R	R	6'	170	10	22	1	2	0	0	0	0	0	8	0	.091	.091
Casey, Doc-James Patrick	98-99WasN 99-00,06-07BknN 01-02DetA 03-05ChiN	03-15-71	Lawrence, Mass.	12-31-36	L	R	5'6	157	1116	4340	585	1120	136	52	9	354	270		194	.258	.320
Casey, Joe-Joseph Felix	09-11DetA 18WasA	08-15-87	Boston, Mass.	06-02-66	R	R	5'9	180	50	117	9	21	3	0	0	7	8		1	.179	.205
Cassady, Harry-Delbert Harry (Cassaday)	04PitN 05WasA	07-20-80	Bellflower, Ill.	04-19-69	L	L	5'8	145	21	74	9	13	0	0	0	4	2		2	.176	.176
Cassidy, Joe-Joseph Phillip	04-05WasA	02-08-83	Chester, Pa.	03-25-06	R	R			303	1157	130	264	28	23	2	76	40		40	.228	.297
Castle, John-John Francis	10PhiN	06-01-79	Honey Brook, Pa.	04-13-29		R	5'10		4	4	1	1	0	0	0	0	0		0	.250	.250
Castro, Louis-Louis Manuel (Jud)	02PhiA	11-25-76	Colombia	09-24-41	R	R	5'7		42	143	18	35	8	1	1	15	4		2	.245	.336
Caton, Buster-James Howard (Howdy)	17-20PitN	07-16-96	Zanesville, Ohio	01-08-48	R	R	5'6	165	231	814	85	184	18	16	0	53	83	52	18	.226	.287
Catterson, Tom-Thomas Henry	08-09BknN	08-25-84	Warwick, R.I.	02-05-20	L	L	5'10	170	28	86	5	17	1	1	1	3	8		0	.198	.267
Cavanaugh, John-John Joseph	19PhiN	06-05-00	Scranton, Pa.	01-14-61	R	R	5'9	160	1	1	0	0	0	0	0	0	0		0	.000	.000
Cermak, Ed-Edward Hugo	01CleA	03-10-82	Cleveland, Ohio	11-22-11	R	R	5'11	170	1	4	0	0	0	0	0	0	0		0	.000	.000
Chadbourne, Chet-Chester James (Pop)	06-07BosA 14-15KCF 18BosN	10-28-84	Parkman, Me.	06-21-43	R	R	5'9	170	347	1353	183	345	41	18	2	82	146		78	.255	.304
Chance, Frank-Frank Leroy (Husk, The Peerless Leader)	98-12,M05-12ChiN 13-14,M13-14NYA M23BosA	09-09-76	Fresno, Cal.	09-15-24	R	R	6'	190	1287	4296	797	1273	200	79	20	597	554		401	.296	.394
Channell, Les-Lester Clark (Goat, Gint)	10,14NYA	03-03-86	Crestline, Ohio	05-08-54	L	L	6'	180	7	20	3	7	1	0	0	3	2		2	.350	.400
Chapman, Harry-Harry E.	12ChiN 13CinN 14-15StLF 16StLA	10-26-87	Severance, Kans.	10-21-18	R	R	5'11	160	147	404	38	80	8	5	1	44	37		7	.198	.250
Chapman, Ray-Raymond Johnson	12-20CleA	01-15-91	Beaver Dam, Ky.	08-17-20	R	R	5'10	170	1050	3785	671	1053	162	81	17	364	452		233	.278	.377
Chappell, Larry-LaVerne Ashford	13-15ChiA 16CleA 16-17BosN	02-19-90	McClusky, Ill.	11-08-18	L	L	6'2	186	109	305	27	69	9	2	0	26	25	42	9	.226	.269
Charles (Achenbach), Chappie (Charles Shuh)-Raymond	08-09StLN 09-10CinN	03-25-81	Phillipsburg, N.J.	08-04-59	R	R	5'11	175	237	851	76	186	23	7	1	51	54		24	.219	.264
Chase, Hal-Harold Homer (Prince Hal)	05-13 M10-11NYA 13-14ChiA 14-15BufF 16-18CinN 19NYN 19DU	02-13-83	Los Gatos, Cal.	05-18-47	R	L	6'	175	1917	7416	980	2156	324	124	57	941	276		363	.291	.391
Cheek, Harry-Harry G.	10PhiN	03-01-79	Sedalia, Mo.	06-25-56	R				2	4	1	2	1	0	0	0	0		0	.500	.750
Childs, Cupid-Clarence Lemuel	88PhiN 90SyraN 91-98CleN 99StLN 00-01ChiN	08-08-67	Calvert Co., Md.	11-08-12	L	R	5'8	185	1463	5624	1218	1757	200	102	20	743	991		285	.312	.395
Childs, Pete-Pierre Peter	01StLN 01ChiN 02PhiN	11-15-71	Philadelphia, Pa.	02-15-22	R	R			212	692	60	147	11	1	0	47	74		10	.212	.231
Chouinard, Felix-Felix George	10-11ChiA 14PitF 14BknF 14BalF 15BknF	10-05-88	Chicago, Ill.	04-28-55	R	R	5'7	150	88	221	22	54	5	4	1	23	12		8	.244	.317
Clancy, Al-Albert Harrison	11StLA	04-12-79	Santa Fe, N.M.	10-17-51	R	R	5'10	175	3	5	0	0	0	0	0	0	0		0	.000	.000
Clancy, Bill-William Edward	05PitN	04-12-79	Redfield, N.Y.	02-10-48	R	R	6'2	180	56	227	23	52	11	3	2	34	4		3	.229	.282
Clark, Fred-Alfred Robert (Dad)	02ChiN	07-16-73	San Francisco, Cal.	07-26-56	L	L	5'11	170	12	43	1	8	1	0	0	2	4		1	.186	.209
Clark, Jim-James Francis	11-12StLN	12-26-87	Brooklyn, N.Y.	03-20-69	R	R	5'11	175	16	19	2	3	0	1	0	3	5	5	2	.158	.263
Clark, Pep-Harry	03ChiA	03-18-83	Union City, Ohio	06-08-65	R	R	5'7	175	15	65	7	20	3	1	0	9	2		5	.308	.431
Clark, Roy-Roy Elliott (Pepper)	02NYN	05-11-74	New Haven, Conn.	11-01-25	L	R	5'8	170	21	76	4	11	1	0	0	3	1		5	.145	.158
Clarke, Boileryard-William Jones	93-98BalN 99-00BosN 01-04WasA 05NYN	10-18-68	New York, N.Y.	07-29-59	R	R	5'11	170	941	3314	395	860	112	33	20	429	176		50	.260	.323
Clarke, Fred-Fred Clifford (Cap)	94-99,M97-99LouN 00-11,13-15,M00-15PitN	10-03-72	Winterset, Iowa	08-14-40	L	R	5'10	165	2246	8584	1622	2678	361	220	67	1015	874		509	.312	.429
Clarke, Josh-Joshua Baldwin (Pepper)	98LouN 05StLN 08-09CleA 11BosN	03-08-79	Winfield, Kans.	07-02-62	L	R	5'10	180	223	809	118	193	18	9	1	43	135		51	.239	.302
Clarke, Nig-Jay Justin	05CleA 05DetA 05-10CleA 11StLA 19PhiN 20PitN	12-15-82	Amherstburg, Canada	06-15-49	L	R	5'8	165	506	1536	157	390	64	20	6	127	138		16	.254	.333
Clarke, Tommy-Thomas Aloysius	09-17CinN 18CinN	05-09-88	New York, N.Y.	08-14-45	R	R	5'11	175	700	1708	166	453	66	37	6	191	216		42	.265	.358
Clay, Bill-Frederick C.	02PhiN	11-23-74	Baltimore, Md.	10-12-17	R	L		175	3	8	1	2	0	0	0	1	0		0	.250	.250
Clemens, Bob-Robert Baxter	14StLA	08-09-86	Odessa, Mo.	04-05-64	R	R	5'9	163	7	13	1	3	0	1	0	3	2	1	0	.231	.385
Clemens (Ulatowski), Count-Clement Lambert	14-15ChiF 16CinN	11-21-86	Chicago, Ill.	11-02-67	R	R	5'11	176	34	64	7	7	1	0	0	5	4		1	.109	.125
Clement, Wally-Wallace Oakes	08-09PhiN 09BknN	07-21-81	Auburn, Me.	11-01-53	L	L	5'11	175	111	379	35	95	11	4	0	18	18		13	.251	.301
Clingman, Billy-William Frederick	90CinN 91CinAA 95PitN 96-99LouN 00ChiN 01WasA 03CleA	11-21-69	Cincinnati, Ohio	05-14-58	B	R	5'11	150	817	2870	406	709	87	33	8	300	303		96	.247	.309
Clymer, Otis-Otis Edgar (Gump)	05-07PitN 07-09WasA 13ChiN 13BosN	01-27-76	Pine Grove, Pa.	02-27-26	B	R	6'	170	385	1330	182	355	42	19	2	98	99		83	.267	.332
Cobb (Serafin), Joe-Joseph Stanley	18DetA	01-24-95	Hudson, Pa.	12-24-47	R	R	5'9	170	1	0	0	0	0	0	0	0	0		0	—	—
Cobb, Ty-Tyrus Raymond (The Georgia Peach)	05-26,M21-26DetA 27-28PhiA	12-18-86	Narrows, Ga.	07-17-61	L	R	6'1	175	3034	11436	2246	4189	723	298	117	1939	1249		892	.366	.512
Cochran, George-George Leslie	18BosA	02-12-89	Rusk, Tex.	05-21-60	R	R			25	63	8	8	0	0	0	3	11	7	3	.127	.127
Cockman, Jim-James	05NYA	04-26-73	Guelph, Canada	09-28-47	R	R	5'6	145	13	38	5	4	0	0	0	2	4		2	.105	.105
Coffey, Jack-John Francis	09BosN 18DetA18BosA	01-28-87	New York, N.Y.	02-14-66	R	R	5'11	178	110	368	33	69	5	6	1	26	22		6	.188	.242
Cole, Willis-Willis Russell	09-10ChiA	01-06-82	Milton Junction, Wis.	10-11-65	R	R	5'8	170	68	245	23	53	9	4	0	18	20		3	.216	.286
Coleman, Bob-Robert Hunter	13-14PitN 16CleA M43-45BosN	09-26-90	Huntingburg, Ind.	07-16-59	R	R	6'2	190	116	228	19	55	8	1	1	27	29	46	3	.241	.298
Coleman, Curt-Curtis Hancock	12NYA	02-18-87	Salem, Ore.	07-01-80	R	R	5'11	180	12	37	4	9	3	0	0	4	7		0	.243	.351
Coles, Cad-Cadwallader	14KCF	01-17-86	Rock Hill, S.C.	06-30-42	L	R	6'	174	78	194	17	49	7	3	1	15	5		3	.253	.361
Collins, Bill-William Shirley	10-11BosN 11ChiN 13BknN 14BufF	03-27-82	Chestertown, Ind.	06-26-61	B	R	6'	175	228	775	91	173	11	10	3	54	54		42	.223	.275
Collins, Eddie-Edward Trowbridge Sr. (Cocky) (Played as Eddie Sullivan 06)	06-14PhiA 15-26,M25-26ChiA 27-30PhiA	05-02-87	Millerton, N.Y.	03-25-51	L	R	5'9	175	2826	9951	1821	3315	438	187	47	1300	1503		743	.333	.429
Collins, Jimmy-James Joseph	95BosN 95LouN 96-00BosN 01-07,M01-06BosA 07-08PhiA	01-16-70	Buffalo, N.Y.	03-06-43	R	R	5'9	175	1720	6792	1057	1999	351	117	65	983	426		192	.294	.409
Collins, Orth-Orth Stein (Buck)	04NYA 09WasA	04-27-80	Lafayette, Ind.	12-13-49	L	R	6'	150	13	24	3	6	0	0	0	1	1		0	.250	.375
Collins, Shano-John Francis	10-20ChiA 21-25,M31-32BosA	12-04-85	Charlestown, Mass.	09-10-55	R	R	6'	185	1799	6386	747	1687	309	133	22	705	331		225	.264	.365
Collins, Wilson-Cyril Wilson	13-14BosN	05-07-89	Pulaski, Tenn.	02-28-41	R	R	5'9	165	43	38	8	10	0	0	0	5	2	9	0	.263	.263
Collins, Zip-John Edgar	14-15PitN 15-17BosN 21PhiA	05-04-92	Brooklyn, N.Y.	12-19-83	L	L	5'11	158	286	916	124	232	17	14	2	63	58	100	15	.253	.309
Compton,Pete-Anna Sebastian (Bash)	11-13StLA 15StLF 15-16BosN 16PitN18NYN	09-28-89	San Marcos, Tex.	02-03-78	R	R	5'11	170	287	773	78	186	24	8	5	80	65		26	.241	.312
Congalton, Bunk-William Millar (Buck)	02ChiN 05-07CleA 07BosA	01-24-75	Guelph, Canada	08-19-37	L	L	5'11	190	310	1163	115	337	27	13	5	128	57		31	.290	.348
Conn, Bert-Albert Thomas (See P01-19)	98,00-01PhiN	09-22-79	Philadelphia, Pa.	11-02-44	R	R	5'9	165	7	5	0	0	0	0	0	0	0		0	.000	.000
Connaughton, Frank-Frank Henry	94BosN 96NYN 06BosN	01-01-69	Clinton, Mass.	12-02-42	R	R	5'9	165	144	525	89	146	13	4	4	77	44		21	.278	.354
Connolly, Joey-Joseph Francis Aloysius	13-16BosN	02-01-84	North Smithfield, R.I.	09-01-43	L	R	5'7	165	412	1241	202	358	65	31	14	157	168	131	48	.288	.425
Connolly, Tom-Thomas Francis (Blackie), (Ham)	15WasA	12-30-92	Boston, Mass.	05-14-66	L	R	5'11	175	50	141	14	26	5	0	0	7	14	19	5	.184	.234

USE NAME - GIVEN NAMES (NICKNAMES)	TEAM BY YEAR	BIRTH DATE	BIRTH PLACE	DEATH DATE	B	T	HGT	WGT	G	AB	R	H	2B	3B	HR	RBI	BB	SO	SB	BA	SA
Connor, Joe-Joseph Francis	95StLN 00BosN 01MilA 01Cle A 05NYA	12-08-74	Waterbury, Conn.	11-08-57	R	R	6'2	185	92	271	29	54	7	2	1	22	18		8	.199	.251
Conroy, Wid-William Edward	01MilA 02PitN 03-08NYA 09-11WasA	04-05-77	Philadelphia, Pa.	12-06-59	R	R	5'9	158	1377	5061	605	1257	176	82	22	452	345		262	.248	.329
Conway, Owen-Owen Sylvester	15PhiA	10-23-90	New York, N.Y.	03-13-42		R			4	15	2	1	0	0	0	0	0	3	0	.067	.067
Conway, Rip-Richard Daniel	18BosN	04-18-96	White Bear Lake, Minn.	12-02-72	L	R	5'6	160	14	24	4	4	0	0	0	2	2	4	1	.167	.167
Conwell, Ed-Edward James (Irish)	11StLN	01-29-90	Chicago, Ill.	05-01-26	R	R	5'11	155	1	1	0	0	0	0	0	0	0	1	0	.000	.000
Cook, Doc-Luther Almus	13-16NYA	06-24-86	Witt, Tex.	06-30-73	L	R	6'	170	286	1028	138	282	29	9	3	75	116	109	56	.274	.329
Cook, Jim-James Fitchie	03CinN	11-10-79	Dundee, Ill.	06-17-49	R	R	5'9	163	8	26	3	4	1	0	0	2	2		1	.154	.192
Cooley, Dick-Duff Gordon (Sir Richard)	93-96StLN 96-99PhiN 00PitN 01-04BosN 05DetA	03-29-73	Leavenworth, Kans.	03-14-73	L	L	5'11	158	1311	5361	846	1582	179	106	26	558	365		233	.295	.383
Coombs, Cecil-Cecil Lysander	14ChiA	03-18-88	Moweaqua, Ill.	11-25-75	R	R	5'9	160	7	23	1	4	1	0	0	1	1	7	0	.174	.217
Cooney, Cush-William Ambrose	09-10BosN	04-07-83	Boston, Mass.	11-06-28	R				13	22	2	6	0	0	0	0	0		0	.273	.273
Cooney(Cohen), Phil-Philip Clarence	05NYA	09-14-82	New York, N.Y.	10-06-57	R	R	5'8	155	1	3	0	0	0	0	0	0	0		0	.000	.000
Cooper, Claude-Claude William	13NYN 14-15BknF 16-17PhiN 18MS	04-01-92	Troup, Tex.	01-21-74	L	L	5'9	158	373	1089	156	283	47	23	4	104	119		6	.260	.356
Corcoran, Bunny-Arthur Andrew 20-23 played in the N.F.L.	15PhiA	11-23-94	Roxbury, Mass.	07-27-58	R	R	5'11	175	1	4	0	0	0	0	0	0	0		0	.000	.000
Corcoran, Mickey-Michael Joseph	01CinN	08-26-82	Buffalo, N.Y.	12-09-50	R	R	5'8	165	14	46	3	10	3	0	0	7	5	9	0	.217	.283
Corcoran, Tommy-Thomas William (Tommy the Cork)	90PhiP 91PhiAA 92-96BknN 97-06CinN 07NYN	01-04-69	New Haven, Conn.	06-25-60	R	R	5'10	164	2199	8776	1179	2248	288	151	34	1135	382		415	.256	.335
Corhan, Roy-Roy George (Irish)	11CinN 16StLN	10-21-87	Indianapolis, Ind.	11-24-58	R	R	5'9	165	135	426	44	90	12	5	0	26	35		17	.211	.263
Corriden, Red-John Michael Sr.	10StLA 12DetA 13-15ChiN M50ChiA	09-04-87	Logansport, Ind.	09-28-59	R	R	5'9	165	222	640	97	131	21	5	6	47	74		26	.205	.281
Costello, Dan-Daniel Francis (Dashing Dan)	13NYA14-16PitN	09-09-91	Jessup, Pa.	03-26-36	R	R	5'11	175	154	350	35	85	6	4	0	24	21	62	12	.243	.283
Costello, J.A. (See Ken Nash)																					
Cotter, Dick-Richard Raphael	11PhiN 12CinN	10-12-89	Manchester, N.H.	04-04-45	R	R	5'11	172	46	100	8	28	4	2	0	15	11	20	2	.280	.320
Coughlin, Bill-William Paul (Scranton Bill)	99WasN 01-04WasA 04-08DetA	07-12-78	Scranton, Pa.	05-07-43	R	R	5'9	180	1047	3855	484	972	133	39	15	380	203		162	.252	.319
Coulson, Bob-Robert Joseph	08CinN 10-11BknN 14PitF	06-17-87	Courtney, Pa.	09-11-53	R	R	5'10	175	197	692	76	163	28	12	1	67	58		43	.236	.315
Courtney, Ernie-Edward Ernest	02BosN 02BalA 03NYA 03DetA 05-08PhiN	01-20-75	Des Moines, Iowa	02-29-20	L	R	5'8	168	558	1921	226	471	52	17	5	200	188		35	.245	.298
Coveney, John-John Patrick	03StLN		South Natick, Mass.	03-28-61	R	R	5'9	165	4	14	0	2	0	0	0	0	0		0	.143	.143
Covington, Sam-Clarence Calvert	13StLA 17-18BosN	11-18-94	Denison, Tex.	01-04-63	R	L	6'1	190	40	129	11	23	2	1	1	14	9	11	4	.178	.233
Coyne, Toots-Martin Albert	14PhiA	10-20-94	St. Louis, Mo.	09-18-39	R				1	2	0	0	0	0	0	0	0	2	0	.000	.000
Crandall, Doc-James Otis (Otey) (See P01-19)	08-13NYN 13StLN 13NYN 14-15StLF 16StLA 18BosN	10-08-87	Wadena, Ind	08-17-51	R	R	5'10	180	500	887	109	253	35	19	9	126	118		7	.285	.398
Crane, Sam-Samuel Byren (Red)	14-16PhiA 17WasA 20-21CinN 22BknN	09-13-94	Harrisburg, Pa.	11-12-55	R	R	5'11	154	174	495	51	103	19	2	0	30	29	46	7	.208	.255
Cravath, Gavvy-Clifford Carlton (Cactus)	08BosA 09ChiA 09WasA 12-20,M19-20PhiN	03-23-81	Poway, Cal.	05-23-63	R	R	5'10	186	1219	3950	575	1134	232	83	119	719	561		89	.287	.478
Crawford, Forrest-Forrest A.	06-07StLN	05-10-81	Rockdale, Tex.	03-29-08	L	R			52	167	8	35	3	1	0	14	9		1	.210	.240
Crawford, Ken-Kenneth Daniel	15BalF	10-31-94	South Bend, Ind.	11-11-76	L	R	5'9	145	23	82	4	20	2	1	0	7	1		0	.244	.293
Crawford, Sam-Samuel Earl (Wahoo Sam)	99-02CinN 03-17DetA	04-18-80	Wahoo, Neb.	06-15-68	L	L	6'	190	2517	9579	1392	2964	455	312	97	1524	760		367	.309	.452
Cree, Birdie-William Franklin	08-15NYA	10-22-82	Khedive, Pa.	11-08-42	R	R	5'6	150	742	2603	345	761	117	62	11	332	269		132	.292	.398
Cregan, Pete-Peter James (Peekskill Pete)	99NYN 03CinN	04-13-75	Kingston, N.Y.	05-18-45	R	R	5'7	150	7	21	0	2	0	0	0	0	1		0	.095	.095
Criger, Lou-Louis	96-98CleN 99-00StLN 01-08BosA 09StLA 10NYA 12 StLA	02-03-72	Elkhart, Ind.	05-14-34	R	R	5'10	150	1012	3199	337	706	87	49	11	342	309		58	.221	.298
Crisp, Joe-Joseph Shelby	10-11StLA	07-08-85	Higginsville, Mo.	02-05-39	R	R	6'4	200	2	2	0	1	0	0	0	0	0		0	.500	.500
Criss, Dode-Dode (See P01-19)	08-11StLA	03-12-85	Sherman, Miss.	09-08-55	L	R	6'2	200	227	304	38	84	19	4	3	47	31		3	.276	.395
Crist, Ches-Chester Arthur (Squack)	06PhiN	02-10-82	Cozadale, Ohio	01-07-57	R	R	5'11	165	6	11	1	0	0	0	0	0	0		0	.000	.000
Crockett, Davey-David Solomon	01DetA	10-05-75	Roanoke, Va.	02-23-61	L	R	6'1	175	28	102	10	29	2	2	0	14	6		1	.284	.343
Croft, Harry-Henry T.	99LouN 99PhiN 01CinN	08-01-75	Chicago, Ill.	12-11-33					7	21	1	5	0	0	0	4	1		0	.238	.238
Crolius, Fred-Frederick Joseph	01BosN 02PitN	12-16-76	Jersey City, N.J.	08-25-60					58	238	26	58	6	3	1	20	9		6	.244	.298
Crompton, Ned-Edward	09StLA 10CinN	02-13-89	Cheshire, England	09-28-50	L	R	5'10	175	22	65	7	10	2	1	0	2	7		1	.154	.215
Crooke, Tom-Thomas Aloysius	09-10WasA	07-26-84	Washington, D.C.	04-05-29	R	R	6'	180	11	28	3	6	2	0	0	3	3		1	.214	.286
Cross, Frank-Frank Atwell (Mickey)	01CleA	01-20-73	Cleveland, Ohio	11-02-32	R		5'9	161	1	5	0	3	0	0	0	0	0		0	.600	.600
Cross, Lave-Lafayette Napoleon	87-88LouAA 89PhiAA 90PhiP 91PhiAA 92-97PhiN 98StLN 99,M99CleN 99-00StLN 00BknN 01-05PhiA 06-07WasA 02-07PhiA	05-12-66	Milwaukee, Wis.	09-06-27	R	R	5'8	155	2265	9065	1349	2645	402	134	47	1368	464		307	.292	.381
Cross, Monte-Montford Montgomery	92BalN 94-95PitN 96-97StLN 98-01PhiN 02-07PhiA	08-31-69	Philadelphia, Pa.	06-21-34	R	R	5'9	150	1679	5813	718	1376	234	68	30	621	616		316	.237	.316
Crossin, Frank-Frank Patrick	12-14StLA	06-15-91	Avondale, Pa.	12-06-65	R	R	5'10	160	55	116	8	17	1	1	0	7	12	11	4	.147	.172
Cruise, Walton-Walton Edwin	14,16-19StLN 19-24BosN	05-06-90	Childersburg, Ala.	01-09-75	L	R	6'	175	736	2321	293	644	83	39	30	272	238	250	49	.277	.386
Cruthers, Press-Charles Preston	13-14PhiA	09-08-90	Marshallton, Del.	12-27-76	R	R	5'9	152	7	27	6	1	1	0	0	0	4	0	0	.222	.333
Cueto, Manuel-Manuel (Potato)	14StLF 17-19CinN	02-28-92	Guanajay, Cuba	06-29-42	R	R	5'4	160	150	379	36	86	10	1	1	31	50		13	.227	.266
Cunningham, Bill-William James	10-12WasA 06BosN	06-09-86	Schenectady, N.Y.	02-21-46	R	R	5'9	170	123	432	42	90	16	6	4	59	34		16	.208	.301
Cunningham, George-George Harold (See P01-19)	16-19,21DetA	07-13-94	Sturgeon Lake, Minn.	03-10-72	R	R	5'11	185	162	210	27	47	6	3	1	13	36	67	4	.224	.295
Curry, Harry-James L.	09PhiA 11NYA 18DetA	03-10-86	Camden, N.J.	08-02-38	R	R	5'11	160	10	35	5	8	1	0	0	1	0		0	.229	.257
Curtis, Fred-Frederick Marion	05NYA	10-30-80	Beaver Lake, Mich.	04-05-39	R	R	6'1		2	9	1	2	0	0	0	0	0		0	.222	.333
Curtis, Eude-Eugene Holmes	03-PitN	05-05-83	Bethany, W.Va.	01-01-19	R	R	6'3	220	5	19	2	8	1	0	0	3	1		0	.421	.474
Curtis, Harry-Harry Albert	07NYN	02-19-83	Portland, Me.	08-01-51	R	R	5'10	170	5	9	0	2	0	0	0	1	2		2	.222	.222
Cutshaw, Goerge-George William (Clancy)	12-17BknN 18-21PitN 22-23DetA	07-29-86	Wilmington, Ill.	08-22-73	R	R	5'9	160	1516	5621	629	1487	195	89	25	653	300	242	271	.265	.344
Cypert, Al-Alfred Boyd (Cy)	14CinN	08-07-89	Little Rock, Ark.	01-09-73	R	R	5'10	150	1	2	0	0	0	0	0	0	1	0	0	.000	.000
Dahlen, Bill-William Frederick (Bad Bill)	91-98ChiN 99-03BknN 04-07NYN 08-09BosN 10-11,M10-13BknN	01-05-70	Nelliston, N.Y.	12-05-50	R	R	5'9	180	2442	9019	1594	2478	403	166	84	1233	1064		587	.275	.384
Daley, John-John Francis	12StLA	05-25-87	Pittsburgh, Pa.	08-31-88	R	R	5'7	155	17	52	7	9	1	0	0	3	9		4	.173	.231
Daley, Jud-Judson Lawrence	08CinN 13-14PhiA 14-15NYA	03-14-84	S. Coventry, Conn.	01-26-67	L	R	5'8	170	82	305	30	66	11	2	1	20	26	25	4	.250	.318
Daley, Tom-Thomas Francis (Pete)	15StLA	11-13-84	Du Bois, Pa.	12-02-34	L	R	5'5	168	179	472	73	113	9	8	0	29	68		18	.239	.292
Dalrymple, Bill-William Dunn	14StLF 16DetA	02-07-91	Baltimore, Md.	07-14-67	R				2	2	0	0	0	0	0	0	0		0	.000	.000
Dalton, Jack-Talbot Percy	10,14BknN 15BufF 16DetA	07-03-84	Henderson, Tenn.	Deceased	R	R	5'10	187	345	1163	167	333	39	15	4	112	129		52	.286	.356
Daly, Bert-Albert Joseph	03PhiA	04-08-81	Bayonne, N.J.	09-03-52	R	R	5'9	170	10	21	2	4	0	2	0	4	1		0	.190	.381
Daly, Tom-Thomas Daniel (Kid)	13-15ChiA 16CleA 18-21ChiN	12-12-91	St. John, Canada	11-07-46	R	R	5'11	170	243	540	49	129	13	3	0	55	25	43	5	.239	.281
Daly, Tom-Thomas Peter (Tido)	87-88ChiN 89WasN 90-96,90-01BknN 02-03CinN 03CinN	02-07-66	Philadelphia, Pa.	10-29-38	B	R	5'7	170	1560	5671	1030	1588	261	103	49	811	687		403	.280	.388
Dam, Bill-Elbridge Rust (Arbie)	09BosN	04-04-85	Cambridge, Mass.	06-22-30	L	L			2	1	1	1	0	0	0	0	1		0	.500	.500
Damrau, Harry-Harry Robert	15PhiA	09-11-90	Newburgh, N.Y.	08-21-57	R	R	5'10	178	16	56	4	11	4	0	0	3	5	17	1	.196	.214
Daniels, Bert-Bernard Elmer	10-13NYA 14CinN	10-31-82	Danville, Ill.	06-06-58	R	R	5'9	180	523	1903	295	486	76	40	5	130	203		159	.255	.345
Danner, Buck-Henry Frederick	15BosA	06-08-91	Dedham, Mass.	09-21-49	R	R	5'6	135	3	12	1	3	0	0	0	0	1		1	.250	.250
Danzig, Babe-Harold Paul	09BosA	04-30-87	Binghamton, N.Y.	07-14-31	R	R	6'2	205	6	13	0	2	0	0	0	0	0		0	.154	.154
Daringer, Cliff-Clifford Clarence (Shanty)	14KCF	04-10-85	Hayden, Ind.	12-26-71	L	R	5'7	155	64	160	12	42	7	0	0	16	11		9	.263	.288
Daringer, Rolla-Rolla Harrison	14-15StLN	11-15-89	Hayden, Ind.	05-23-74	L	R	5'9	155	12	27	4	4	1	0	0	0	2		0	.148	.185
Daubert, Harry-Harry J. (Jake)	15PhiN	06-19-92	Columbus, Ohio	01-08-44	R	R	6'	160	1	1	0	0	0	0	0	0	0	1	0	.000	.000
Daubert, Jake-Jacob Ellsworth	10-18BknN 19-24CinN	04-07-84	Shamokin, Pa.	10-09-24	L	L	5'10	160	2014	7673	1117	2326	250	165	56	722	623	489	251	.303	.401
Davidson, Bill-William Simpson	09ChiN 10-11BknN	05-10-84	Lafayette, Ind.	05-23-54	R	R	5'10	170	225	808	83	190	16	11	1	60	41	76	46	.235	.306
Davidson, Claude-Claude Boucher (Davey)	18PhiA	10-13-96	Boston, Mass.	04-18-56	L	R	5'11	155	33	88	5	18	1	0	0	4	6	10	0	.205	.216
Davidson, Homer-Homer Hurd (Divvy)	08CleA	10-14-84	Cleveland, Ohio	07-26-48	R	R	5'10	155	9	30	1	0	0	0	0	0	1		0	.000	.000
Davies, Chick-Lloyd Garrison (See P20-45)	14-15PhiA 25-26NYN	03-06-92	Peabody, Mass.	09-05-73	L	R	5'8	145	117	202	24	39	11	0	0	17	22	50	3	.193	.272
Davis, George-George Stacey	90-92PhiN 93-01,03,M95,00-01NYN 02,04-09ChiA	08-23-70	Cohoes, N.Y.	10-17-40	B	R	5'9	180	2378	9027	1546	2683	442	167	73	1432	870		632	.297	.407
Davis, Harry-Harry H. (Jasper)	95-96NYN 96-98PhiN 98LouN 98-99WasN 01-11PhiA 12,M12CleA 13-17PhiA	07-10-73	Philadelphia, Pa.	08-11-47	R	R	5'10	180	1745	6619	986	1835	364	143	74	952	525		312	.277	.409
Davis, Lefty-Alphonzo DeFord	01BknN 01-02PitN 03NYA 07CinN	02-04-75	Nashville, Tenn.	02-04-19	L	L	5'10	170	348	1296	232	338	32	19	3	110	167		65	.261	.327
Deal, Charlie-Charles Albert	12-13DetA 13-14BosN 15StLF 16StLA 16-21CinN	10-30-91	Wilkinsburg, Pa.	09-16-79	R	R	5'10	170	850	2930	295	732	104	34	11	318	135		65	.257	.327
Deal, Snake-John Wesley	06CinN	01-21-79	Lancaster, Pa.	05-09-44	R	R	6'	164	65	231	13	48	4	3	0	21	6		15	.208	.251
DeArmond, Charlie-Charles Hommer (Hummer)	03CinN	12-17-33	Okeana, Ohio	05-13-77	R	R	5'10	165	11	39	10	11	0	0	0	3	3		1	.282	.308
Debus, Adam-Adam Joseph	17PitN 18-19MS	10-07-92	Chicago, Ill.		R	R	5'10	170	38	131	9	30	5	1	0	7	14		2	.229	.328
Dede, Artie-Arthur Richard	16BknN	07-12-95	Brooklyn, N.Y.	09-06-71	R	R	5'9	155	1	3	0	0	0	0	0	0	0		0	.000	.000
Dee, Shorty-Maurice Leo	15StLA	10-04-89	Halifax, Canada	08-12-71	R	R	5'6	155	17	56	4	7	1	0	0	4	2		1	.125	.125
DeFate, Tony-Clyde Herbert	17StLN 17DetA	02-22-95	Kansas City, Mo.	09-03-63	R	R	5'8	158	17	61	1	2	0	0	0	1	1		0	.033	.033
DeGroff, Rube-Edward Arthur	05-06StLN	09-02-79	Hyde Park, N.Y.	12-17-55	L	L	5'11		16	60	4	14	2	1	0	6	1		1	.233	.300
Deininger, Pep-Otto Charles (See P01-19)	02BosA 08-09PhiN	10-10-77	Wasseralfingen, Germ.	09-25-50	L	L	5'8	180	58	175	22	46	3	2	0	16	11		5	.263	.331
Deisel, Pat-Edward	02BknN 03CinN	04-29-76	Ripley, Ohio	07-17-48	R	R	5'10	180	3	3	1	2	0	0	0	0	1		0	.667	.667

USE NAME - GIVEN NAMES (NICKNAMES)	TEAM BY YEAR	BIRTH DATE	BIRTH PLACE	DEATH DATE	B	T	HGT	WGT	G	AB	R	H	2B	3B	HR	RBI	BB	SO	SB	BA	SA
Delahanty, Ed-Edward James (Big Ed)	88-89PhiN 90CleP 91-01PhiN 02-03WasA	10-30-67	Cleveland, Ohio	07-02-03	R	R	6'1	170	1828	7493	1596	2593	522	182	100	1464	741		478	.346	.504
Delahanty, Frank-Frank George (Pudgie)	05-06,08NYA 07CleA 14BufF 14-15PitF	12-29-82	Cleveland, Ohio	07-22-66	R	R	5'9	160	287	986	109	223	22	22	5	94	66		50	.226	.308
Delahanty, Jim-James Christopher	01ChiN 02NYN 04-05BosN 06CinN 07StLA	06-20-79	Cleveland, Ohio	10-17-53	R	R	5'10	170	1186	4091	520	1159	191	60	18	489	378		151	.283	.373
	07-09WasA 09-12DetA 14-15BknF																				
Delahanty, Joe-Joseph Nicholas	07-09StLN	10-18-75	Cleveland, Ohio	01-29-36	L	R	5'9	168	270	932	68	222	30	15	4	100	74		24	.238	.315
Demmitt, Ray-Charles Raymond	09NYA 10StLA 14DetA 14-15ChiA 17-19StLA	02-02-84	Illiopolis, Ill.	02-19-56	L	R	5'8	170	498	1631	205	419	61	33	8	165	172		42	.257	.349
DeMontreville, Gene-Eugene Napoleon	94PitN 95-97WasN 98-99BalN 99ChiN	09-10-73	St. Paul, Minn.	02-18-35	R	R	5'8	165	913	3589	535	1106	129	32	17	497	174		235	.308	.376
	00BknN 01-02BosN 03WasA04StLA																				
DeMontreville, Lee-Leon	03StLN	09-23-74	Washington Co., Minn.	03-22-62	R	R	5'7	140	26	70	8	17	3	1	0	7	8		3	.243	.314
Derrick, Claude-Claude Lester (Deek)	10-12PhiA 13NYA 14CinN 14ChiN	06-11-86	Burton, Ga.	07-15-74	R	R	6'	175	110	326	35	79	6	4	1	33	22		13	.242	.294
Devlin, Art-Arthur McArthur	04-11NYN 12-13BosN	10-16-79	Washington, D.C.	09-18-48	R	R	6'	175	1313	4412	603	1185	164	57	10	505	576		285	.269	.338
DeVogt, Rex-Rex Eugene	13BosN	01-04-88	Clare, Mich.	11-09-35	R	R	5'10	170	3	6	0	0	0	0	0			3	0	.000	.000
Devore, Josh-Joshua M.	08-13NYN 13CinN 13-14PhiN 14BosN	11-13-87	Murray City, Ohio	10-06-54	L	L	5'8	175	601	1874	331	520	58	31	1	149	222		160	.277	.359
Devoy, Wally-Walter Joseph	09StLA	03-14-86	St. Louis, Mo.	12-17-53	R	R	5'11	165	19	69	7	17	3	1	0	8	3		4	.246	.319
Dexter, Charlie-Charles Dana	96-99LouN 00-02ChiN 02-03BosN	06-15-76	Evansville, Ind.	06-09-34	R	R	5'7	155	763	2867	429	756	91	23	16	346	198		182	.264	.328
Diehl, Ernie-Ernest Guy	03-04PitN 06,09BosN	10-02-77	Cincinnati, Ohio	11-06-58	R	R	6'1	190	17	55	8	14	1	1	0	4	6		3	.255	.309
Dillon, Pop-Frank Edward	99-00PiN 01-02DetA 02BalA 04BknN	10-17-73	Normal, Ill.	09-12-31	L	R	6'1	185	312	1180	146	298	44	16	1	116	78		31	.253	.319
Distel, Dutch-George Adam	18StLN	04-15-96	Madison, Ind.	02-12-67	R	R	5'9	165	8	17	3	3	1	0	0	1	2		0	.176	.353
Divis, Moxie-Edward George	16PhiA	01-16-94	Cleveland, Ohio	12-19-55			5'6		3	6	0	1	0	0	0	0	0	2	0	.167	.167
Dobbs, Johnny-John Gordon	01-02CinN 02-03ChiN 03-05BknN	06-03-75	Chattanooga, Tenn.	09-09-34	L	R	5'9	170	582	2224	305	585	85	23	7	207	187		78	.263	.331
Dodd, Ona-Ona Melvin	12PitN	10-14-86	Springtown, Tex.	12-17-56	R	R	5'8	150	5	9	0	0	0	0	0				0	.000	.000
Dodge, John-John Lewis	12-13PhiN 13CinN	04-27-89	Bolivar, Tenn.	06-19-16	R	R	5'11	165	127	418	38	90	9	8	4	48	16	45	13	.215	.304
Dolan, Biddy-Leon Mark	14IndF	07-09-81	Onalaska, Wis.	07-15-50	R	R	6'		32	103	13	23	4	2	1	15	12		5	.223	.330
Dolan (Alberts), Cozy (James)-Alvin James	09CinN 11-12NYA 12-13PhiN 13PitN	12-06-82	Oshkosh, Wis.	12-10-58	R	R	5'10	180	378	1187	210	299	43	21	6	111	121		102	.252	.339
	14-15StLN 22NYN																				
Dolan, Cozy-Patrick Henry (See P01-19)	95-96BosN 00-01CinN 01-02BknN	12-03-72	Cambridge, Mass.	03-29-07	L	L	5'10	160	830	3173	428	856	99	37	10	315	227		114	.270	.334
	03ChiA 03-05CinN 05-06BosN																				
Dolan, Joe-Joseph	96-97LouN 99-01PhiN 01PhiA	02-24-73	Baltimore, Md.	03-24-38	R	R	5'10	155	319	1148	140	247	37	10	6	122	72		30	.215	.280
Donahue, Jiggs-John Augustus	00-01PitN 01MilA 02StLA 04-09ChiA 09WasA	07-13-79	Springfield, Ohio	07-19-13	L	L	6'1	178	812	2858	320	731	91	30	4	327	215		145	.256	.313
Donahue, Pat-Patrick William	08-10BosA 10PhiA 10CleA 10PhiA	11-03-84	Springfield, Ohio	01-31-66	R	R	6'	175	118	307	24	65	6	1	3	35	29		3	.212	.267
Donahue, She-Charles Michael	04StLN 04PhiN	06-29-77	Oswego, N.Y.	08-28-47	R	R	5'9		62	215	22	47	4	1	0	16	3		10	.219	.237
Donahue, Tim-Timothy Cornelius	91BosAA 95-00ChiN 02WasA	06-08-70	Raynham, Mass.	06-12-02	R	R	5'11	180	454	1493	197	360	56	11	2	163	142		55	.241	.297
Donlin, Mike-Michael Joseph (Turkey Mike)	99-00StLN 01BalA 02-04CinN	05-30-78	Peoria, Ill.	09-24-33	L	L	5'9	170	1050	3859	670	1287	174	98	51	543	312		210	.334	.469
	04-06NYN 07HO 08NYN 09-10VR 11NYN 11BosN																				
Donovan, Jerry-Jeremiah Francis	12PitN 13VR 14NYN 06PhiN	09-03-76	Lock Haven, Pa.	06-27-38	R	R			61	166	11	33	4	0	0	15	6		2	.199	.223
Donovan, Mike-Michael Berchman	04CleA 08NYN	10-18-81	Brooklyn, N.Y.	02-03-38	R	R	5'8	155	7	21	2	5	1	0	0	2	0		0	.238	.286
Donovan, Patsy-Patrick Joseph	90BosN 90BknN 91LouAA 91WasA 92WasN	03-16-65	Queenstown, Ireland	12-25-53	L	L	5'11	175	1817	7450	1324	2266	213	72	16	737	453		528	.304	.384
	92-99,M97,99PitN 00-03,M01-03StLN 04,M04WasA 06-07,M06-08BknN																				
	M10-11BosA																				
Donovan, Tom-Thomas Joseph	01CleA	01-01-73	Troy, N.Y.	03-25-33	R	R	6'2	168	18	71	9	18	3	1	0	5	0		1	.254	.324
Dooin, Red-Charles Sebastian	02-14,M10-14PhiN 15CinN 15-16NYN	06-12-79	Cincinnati, Ohio	05-14-52	R	R	5'9	165	1290	4004	333	961	139	31	10	344	155		133	.240	.298
Doolan (Doolittle), Mickey-Michael Joseph	05-13PhiN 14-15BalF 15ChiF	05-07-80	Ashland, Pa.	11-01-51	R	R	5'10	170	1727	5968	513	1377	246	81	15	554	370		178	.231	.307
	16ChiN 16NYN 18BknN																				
Doran, Tom-Thomas J.	04-05BosA 05DetA 06BosA	02-02-80	Westchester Co., N.Y.	06-22-10	L	L	5'11	152	50	131	10	19	3	1	0	4	12		3	.145	.183
Dorsey, Jerry-Jeremiah Edward	11PitN	08-19-85	Oakland, Cal.	Deceased	L	L	5'11	175	2	6	0	0	0	0	0	0	0	1	0	.000	.000
Dougherty, Patsy-Patrick Henry	02-04BosA 04-06NYA 06-11ChiA	10-27-76	Andover, N.Y.	04-30-40	L	R	6'2	190	1233	4558	677	1294	138	78	17	413	378		261	.284	.360
Douglass, Klondike-William Bigham	96-97StLN 98-04PhiN	05-10-72	Boston, Pa.	12-13-53	R	R	6'	200	746	2797	371	775	83	30	10	275	227		93	.277	.339
Dowd (O'Dowd), John-John Leo	12NYA	01-03-91	S. Weymouth, Mass.	01-31-81	R	R	5'8	170	10	31	1	6	1	0	0	0	6		0	.194	.226
Dowd, Snooks-Raymond Bernard 25-26 played in A.B.L.	19DetA 19PhiA 26BknN	12-20-97	Springfield, Mass.	04-04-62	R	R	5'8	163	16	26	4	3	0	0	0	6	0	5	2	.115	.115
Dowd, Tommy-Thomas Jefferson (Buttermilk Tommy)	91BosAA 91WasAA	04-20-69	Holyoke, Mass.	07-02-33	R	R	5'8	173	1313	5478	904	1491	160	87	23	501	369		384	.272	.346
	92WasN 93-97,M96-97StLN 97PhiN 98StLN 99CleN 01BosA																				
Downey, Red-Alexander Cummings	09BknN	02-06-89	Aurora, Ind.	07-10-49	L	L	5'11	174	19	78	7	20	1	0	0	8	2		4	.256	.269
Downey, Tom-Thomas Edward	09-11CinN 12PhiN 12ChiN 14-15BufF	01-01-84	Lewistown, Me.	08-03-61	R	R	6'	178	651	2170	256	520	69	25	7	188	198		87	.240	.304
Downs, Red-Jerome Willis (Jerry)	07-08DetA 12BknN 12ChiN	08-23-83	Neola, Iowa	10-19-39	R	R	5'11	170	241	790	68	179	30	11	3	94	28		13	.227	.304
Doyle, Jack-John Joseph (Dirty Jack)	89-90ColAA 91-92CleN 92-95,M95NYN	10-25-69	Killorgin, Ireland	12-31-58	R	R	5'9	155	1542	6013	997	1814	305	66	25	968	437		558	.302	.387
	96-97BalN 98,M98WasN 98-00NYN 01ChiN																				
	02NYN 02WasA 03-04BknN 04PhiN 05NYA																				
Doyle, Jim-James Francis	10CinN 11ChiN	12-25-81	Detroit, Mich.	02-01-12	R	R	5'10	168	137	485	70	135	25	12	6	63	40	56	19	.278	.410
Doyle, Larry-Lawrence Joseph (Laughing Larry)	07-16NYN 16-17ChiN 18-20NYN	07-31-85	Caseyville, Ill.	03-01-74	L	R	5'10	165	1766	6509	960	1887	299	123	74	793	625		298	.290	.408
Drake, Delos-Delos Daniel	11DetA 14-15StLF	12-23-86	Girard, Ohio	10-03-65	R	R	5'11	170	335	1172	120	308	50	21	5	119	71		43	.263	.354
Dressen, Lee-Leo August	14StlN 18DetA	07-23-89	Ellinwood, Kans.	06-30-31	L	L	6'	165	77	210	26	43	3	4	0	10	32	30	4	.206	.248
Drill, Lew-Lewis L.	02WasA 02BalA 02-04WasA 04-05DetA	05-09-77	Browerville, Minn.	07-04-69	R	R	5'6	186	292	896	87	231	41	10	2	100	114		21	.258	.333
Driscoll, Paddy-John Leo 20-29 played in N.F.L.	17ChiN 18MS	01-11-95	Evanston, Ill.	06-28-68	R	R	5'8	155	13	28	2	3	1	0	0	3	2	6	2	.107	.143
21-22,56-57 Head Coach in N.F.L.																					
Duff, Pat-Patrick Henry	06WasA	05-06-75	Providence, R.I.	09-11-25	R	R	5'10		1	1	0	0	0	0	0				0	.000	.000
Duffy, Hugh-Hugh	88-89ChiN 90ChiP 91BosA 92-00BosN 01,M01MilA	11-26-66	Cranston, R.I.	10-19-54	R	R	5'7	168	1733	7024	1555	2313	310	118	109	1304	662		599	.329	.453
	04-06,M04-06PhiN M10-11ChiA M21-22BosA																				
Dugey, Oscar-Oscar Joseph	13-14BosN 15-17PhiN 20BosN	10-25-87	Palestine, Tex.	01-01-66	R	R	5'8	160	195	278	45	54	10	1	1	20	31	38	17	.194	.248
Duggan, Elmer-James Elmer (Mer)	05BosN	06-01-85	Whiteland, Ind.	12-05-51	L	L	5'10	165	1	4	1	0	0	0	0				0	.000	.000
Duncan, Vern-Vernon Van Duke (Frank)	13PhiN 14-15BalF	01-06-90	Clayton, N.C.	01-01-54	L	R	5'9	155	311	1100	170	307	39	12	4	97	121		32	.279	.347
Dundon, Gus-Augustus Joseph	04-06ChiA	07-10-74	Columbus, Ohio	09-01-40	R	R	5'10	165	247	833	77	168	17	6	0	62	64		37	.202	.236
Dungan, Sam-Samuel Morrison	92-94ChiN 94LouN 00ChiN 01WasA	07-29-66	Ferndale, Cal.	03-16-39	L	R	5'11	180	393	1521	213	467	74	26	3	196	116		40	.307	.396
Dunleavy, Jack-John Francis (See P01-19)	03-05StLN	09-14-79	Harrison, N.J.	04-11-44	L	L	5'6	167	231	800	98	193	18	14	2	49	84		33	.241	.306
Dunlop, George-George Henry	13-14CleA	07-19-88	Meriden, Conn.	12-12-71	R	R	5'10	170	8	20	3	4	0	0	0	0	1		0	.200	.200
Dunn, Jack-John Joseph (See P01-19)	97-00BknN 00-01PitN 01BalA 02-04NYN	10-06-72	Meadville, Pa.	10-22-28	R	R	5'9		488	1612	196	398	55	10	1	164	83		57	.247	.301
Dunn, Joe-Joseph Edward	08-09BknN	03-11-85	Springfield, Mass.	03-19-44	R	R	5'9	160	30	89	4	15	4	0	0	7	0		0	.169	.213
Durbin, Kid-Blaine Alphonsus	07-08ChiN 09CinN 09PitN	09-10-86	Lamar, Mo.	09-11-43	L	L	5'8	155	32	51	6	14	1	0	0	0	4		0	.275	.294
Dyer, Ben-Benjamin Franklin	14-15NYN 16-19DetA	12-13-93	Chicago, Ill.	08-07-59	R	R	5'10	170	105	207	27	49	10	1	0	18	15	47	4	.237	.295
Eagan, Truck-Charles Eugene	01PitN 01CleA	08-10-76	San Francisco, Cal.	03-19-49	R	R	5'11	190	9	30	2	4	1	0	0				1	.133	.200
Eakle, Charlie-Charles Emory	15BalF	09-27-87	Baltimore, Md.	06-15-59					2	7	0	2	1	0	0		0		1	.286	.429
Easterly, Ted-Theodore Harrison	09-12CleA12-13ChiA 14-15KCF	04-20-85	Lincoln, Neb.	07-06-51	L	R	5'8	165	704	2020	215	607	88	38	7	261	107		42	.300	.382
Edington, Stump-Jacob Frank	12PitN	04-07-91	Koleen, Ind.	11-29-69	L	L	5'7	180	15	53	4	16	0	2	0	12	3		1	.302	.377
Edmonson, Eddie-Earl Edward (Axel)	13CleA	11-20-89	Paris, Ky.	05-10-71	L	R	6'	175	2	5	0	0	0	0	0	0	0		0	.000	.000
Edmundson, Bob-Robert E.	06,08WasA	04-30-79	Hopewell, Pa.	08-14-31	R	R	5'11	185	29	83	6	16	1	0	0	5	6		0	.193	.265
Edwards, Ralph-Ralph Strunk	15PhiA	12-14-82	Brewster, N.Y.	01-05-49	R	R	5'9	165	2	3	0	0	0	0	0		0		0	.000	.000
Egan, Ben-Arthur Augustus	08,12ChiN 14-15CleA	11-20-83	Augusta, N.Y.	02-18-68	R	R	6'2	190	121	352	21	58	9	5	0	30	18		3	.165	.227
Egan, Dick-Richard Joseph	08-13CinN 14-15BknN 15-16BosN	06-23-84	Portland, Ore.	07-07-47	R	R	5'11	165	937	3080	374	767	87	29	4	292	291		167	.249	.300
Elberfeld, Kid-Norman Arthur (The Tabasco Kid)	98PhiN 99CinN 01-03DetA	04-13-75	Pomeroy, Ohio	01-13-44	R	R	5'6	135	1293	4561	647	1234	166	58	10	535	427		209	.271	.339
	03-09,M08NYA 10-11WasA 14BknN																				
Ellam, Whitey-Roy (Slippery)	09CinN 18PitN	02-08-86	W. Conshohocken, Pa.	10-28-48	R	R	5'10	203	36	98	13	14	1	2	1	6	24		3	.143	.204
Elliott, Al-Alvah Charles	19PhiA	10-13-94	Muscoda, Wis.	12-18-75	R	R	5'9	175	9	22	3	3	0	0	0	3	0	7	0	.136	.136
(played as Bob Allen) 22-24 played in N.F.L.																					
Elliott, Gene-Eugene Birminghouse	11NYA	08-28-89	Fayette Co., Pa.	01-05-76			5'7	150	5	13	1	1	0	0	0		2		0	.077	.154
Elliott, Rowdy-Harold Bell	10BosN 16-18ChiN 20BknN	07-08-90	Kokomo, Ind.	02-12-34	R	R	5'9	160	157	402	36	97	15	5	1	44	19	23	5	.241	.311
Ellis, Rube-George William	09-12StLN	11-17-85	Downey, Cal.	03-13-38	L	L	6'	170	555	1985	279	517	66	29	14	199	216		56	.260	.344
Ellison, Bert-Herbert Spencer (Babe)	09-12StLN	08-11-15	Ola, Ark.	04-20-55	R	R	5'11	170	135	348	32	75	13	4	1	39	30	55	9	.216	.284
Ely, Bones-William Frederick	84BufN 86LouAA 90SyrAA 91BknN	06-07-63	North Girard, Pa.	01-10-52	R	R	6'1	155	1339	5124	649	1330	146	70	24	652	256		164	.259	.328
	93-95StLN 96-01PitN 01PhiA 02WasA																				
Emerson, Chester-Chester Arthur (Chuck)	11-12PhiA	10-27-89	Stow, Me.	07-02-71	L	R	5'9	170	8	19	2	4	1	0	0	0	1		1	.211	.263
Engle, Clyde-Arthur Clyde (Hack)	09-10NYA 10-14BosA 14-15BufF 16CleA	03-19-84	Dayton, Ohio	12-26-39	R	R	5'10	190	831	2822	373	748	101	39	12	318	271		128	.265	.341
Ens, Mutz-Anton	12ChiA	03-24-87	St. Louis, Mo.	06-28-50	L	L	6'1	185	3	4	1	0	0	0	0	1	0		0	.000	.000
Enwright, Charlie-Charles Michael (Massey)	09StLN	10-06-87	Sacramento, Cal.	01-19-17	R	R	5'10		3	7	1	1	0	0	0	4	0		0	.143	.143
Enzenroth, Jack-Clarence Herman	14StLA 14-15KCF	11-04-85	Mineral Point, Wis.	02-21-44	R	R	5'10	164	43	92	10	16	4	0	0	8	13		0	.174	.239
Erwin, Tex-Ross Emil	07DetA 10-14BknN 14CleA	05-02-85	Forney, Tex.	04-05-53	R	R	6'	185	276	635	70	150	23	3	11	70	82	61	10	.236	.334
Eschen, Jim-James Godrich	15CleA	08-21-91	Brooklyn, N.Y.	09-27-60	R	R	5'11	160	42	111	10	13	1	2	0	3	10		3	.238	.262
Esmond, Jimmy-James Joseph	11-12CinN 14IndF 15NwkF	10-08-89	Albany, N.Y.	06-26-48	R	R	5'10	167	461	1540	204	406	52	34	9	162	136		61	.264	.358
Eunick, Ferd-Fernandes Bowen (Dutch)	15PhiA	04-24-92	Baltimore, Md.	12-09-59	R	R	5'6	160	1	2	0	0	0	0	0	0	0		0	.000	.000
Evans, Steve-Louis Richard	08NYN 09-13StLN 14-15KbnF 15BalF	02-17-85	Cleveland, Ohio	12-28-43	L	L	5'10	175	978	3359	478	963	175	67	32	466	359		96	.287	.407
Everett, Bill-William Lee (Big William)	95-00ChiN 01WasA	12-13-68	Fort Wayne, Ind.	01-19-38	L	R	6'	188	697	2839	535	909	82	39	11	341	212		199	.320	.338

USE NAME - GIVEN NAMES (NICKNAMES)	TEAM BY YEAR	BIRTH DATE	BIRTH PLACE	DEATH DATE	B	T	HGT	WGT	G	AB	R	H	2B	3B	HR	RBI	BB	SO	SB	BA	SA
Evers, Joe-Joseph Francis	13NYN	09-10-91	Troy, N.Y.	01-04-49	L	R	5'9	135	1	0	0	0	0	0	0	0	0		0	.000	.000
Evers, Johnny-John Joseph (Crab, The Trojan)	02-13,M13ChiN 14-17BosN 17PhiN M21ChiN 22,M24ChiA 29BosN	07-21-81	Troy, N.Y.	03-28-47	L	R	5'9	125	1782	6134	919	1658	216	70	12	538	779		324	.270	.334
Ewoldt, Art-Arthur Lee (Sheriff)	19PhiA	01-08-94	Paullina, Iowa	12-08-77	R	R	5'10	165	9	32	2	7	1	0	0	2	1	5	0	.219	.250
Fabrique, Bunny-Albert LaVerne	16-17BknN	12-23-87	Clinton, Mich.	01-10-60	B	R	5'8	150	27	90	8	18	3	0	1	3	8	10	0	.200	.267
Fahey, Frank-Francis Raymond	18PhiA	01-22-96	Milford, Mass.	03-19-54	R	R	6'1	190	10	17	2	3	1	0	0	1	0	3	0	.176	.235
Fahey, Howard-Howard Simpson (Cap. Kid)	12PhiA	06-24-92	Medford, Mass.	10-24-71	R	R	5'7	145	5	8	0	0	0	0	0	0	0		0	.000	.000
Fallon, Charlie-Charles Augustus	05NYA	03-07-81	New York, N.Y.	06-10-60	R	R	5'6		1	0	0	0	0	0	0	0	0		0	.000	.000
Falsey, Pete-Peter James	14PitN	04-24-91	New Haven, Conn.	05-23-76	L	L	5'6	132	3	1	0	0	0	0	0	0	0	1	0	.000	.000
Farmer, Alex-Alexander Johnson	08BknN	05-09-77	New York, N.Y.	03-05-20	R	R	6'	175	12	30	1	5	1	0	0	2	1		0	.167	.200
Farmer, Jack-Floyd Haskell	16PitN 18CleA	07-14-92	Granville, Tenn.	05-21-70	R	R	6'	180	62	175	11	47	6	4	0	15	7	27	3	.269	.349
Farrell, Duke-Charles Andrew	88-89ChiN 90ChiP 92BosAA 92PitN 93WasN 94-96NYN 96-99WasN 99-02BknN 03-05BosA	08-31-66	Oakdale, Mass.	02-15-25	B	R	6'1	200	1566	5623	826	1575	211	123	51	912	477		150	.280	.389
Farrell, Jack-John Joseph	14-15ChiF	06-16-92	Chicago, Ill.	03-24-18	B	R	5'8	145	226	746	85	171	33	5	0	49	77		20	.229	.287
Farrell, John-John Sebastian	01WasA 02-05StLN	12-04-76	Covington, Ky.	05-13-21	R	R	5'10	160	541	2172	329	567	93	28	4	141	193		68	.261	.335
Fautsch, Joe-Joseph Roamon	16ChiA	02-28-87	Minneapolis, Minn.	03-16-71	R	R	5'10	162	1	1	0	0	0	0	0	0	0	0	0	.000	.000
Felsch, Happy-Oscar Emil	15-20ChiA 20DL	08-22-91	Milwaukee, Wis.	08-17-64	R	R	5'10	170	749	2812	385	825	135	64	38	446	207	251	88	.293	.427
Ferris, Hobe-Albert Sayles	01-07BosA 08-09StLA	12-07-77	Providence, R.I.	03-18-38	R	R	5'8	170	1286	4800	473	1146	192	89	39	550	161		89	.239	.340
Fetzer, Willy-William McKinnon	06PhiN	06-24-84	Concord, N.C.	05-03-59	L	R	5'10	180	1	1	0	0	0	0	0	0	0		0	.000	.000
Fischer, Bill-William Charles	13-14BknN 15ChiF 16ChiN 16-17PitN	03-02-91	New York, N.Y.	09-04-45	R	R	6'	174	412	1099	109	301	50	15	10	115	90		20	.274	.374
Fishburn, Sam-Samuel E.	19StLN	05-15-93	Haverhill, Mass.	04-11-65	R	R	5'9	157	9	6	0	2	1	0	0	2	0	0	0	.333	.500
Fisher, Bobby-Robert Taylor	12-13BknN 14-15ChiN 16CinN 18-19StLN	11-03-86	Nashville, Tenn.	08-04-63	R	R	5'11	170	503	1742	189	480	61	26	11	170	80	157	48	.276	.359
Fisher, Gus-Augustus Harris	11CleA 12NYA	10-21-85	Pottsboro, Tex.	04-08-72	R	R	5'10	175	74	213	21	54	6	3	0	12	7		6	.254	.310
Fisher, Red-John Gustave	10StLA	06-22-87	Pittsburgh, Pa.	02-01-40	L	R	5'9	176	23	72	5	9	2	1	0	3	8		5	.125	.181
Fisher, Wilbur-Wilbur McCullough	16PitN	07-18-94	Green Bottom, W.Va.	10-24-60	R	R	6'3	190	1	1	0	0	0	0	0	0	0		0	.000	.000
Fitzgerald, Justin-Justin Howard	11NYA 18PhiN	06-26-91	San Mateo, Cal.	01-18-45	R	R	5'8	160	82	170	27	49	9	0	0	12	17		7	.288	.341
Fitzgerald, Matty-Matthew William	06-07NYN	08-31-80	Albany, N.Y.	09-22-49	R	R	6'	185	11	21	3	6	1	0	0	3	0	1	1	.286	.333
Fitzpatrick, Ed-Edward Henry	15-17BosN 18MS	12-09-89	Lewiston, Pa.	10-23-65	R	R	5'11	170	251	697	91	158	35	7	1	59	70	84	22	.227	.301
Fitzsimmons, Tom-Thomas William	04-06-90		Oakland, Cal.	12-20-71	R	R	6'1	190	4	4	1	0	0	0	0	0	0	2	0	.000	.000
Flack, Max-Max John	14-15ChiF 16-22ChiN 22-25StLN	02-05-90	Belleville, Ill.	07-31-75	L	L	5'7	148	1411	5252	783	1461	212	72	35	391	474		200	.278	.366
Flanagan, Steamer-James Paul	05PitN	04-20-81	Kingston, Pa.	04-21-47	L	L	6'1	185	7	25	7	7	1	1	0	3	1		3	.280	.400
Flannigan, Charlie-Charles Joseph	13StLA	12-13-91	Oakland, Cal.	01-08-30	R	R	6'	175	4	3	0	0	0	0	0	0	0	0	0	.000	.000
Fleming, Tom-Thomas Vincent (Sleuth)	99NYN 02,04PhiN	11-20-73	Philadelphia, Pa.	12-26-57	L	L	5'11	155	28	92	11	24	0	2	0	6	2		1	.261	.272
Fletcher, Art-Arthur Nichol	09-20NYN 20PhiN 21VR 22,M23-26PhiN M29NYN	01-05-85	Collinsville, Ill.	02-06-50	R	R	5'10	170	1529	5541	684	1534	238	77	32	675	203		159	.277	.365
Fletcher, Frank-Oliver Frank	14PhiN	03-06-91	Hildreth, Ill.	10-07-74	R	R	5'9	161	1	1	0	0	0	0	0	0	0	1	0	.000	.000
Flick, Elmer-Elmer Harrison	98-01PhiN 02PhiA 02-10CleA	01-11-76	Bedford, Ohio	01-09-71	L	R	5'9	168	1483	5597	948	1765	268	169	48	756	597		341	.315	.449
Flinn, Don-Don Raphael	17PitN	11-17-92	Bluffdale, Tex.	03-09-59	R	R	6'1	185	14	37	1	11	1	1	0	1	1	6	1	.297	.324
Flood, Tim-Thomas Timothy	99StLN 02-03BknN	03-13-77	Montgomery City, Mo.	06-15-29	R	R	5'9	160	231	816	70	190	26	6	3	86	42		23	.233	.293
Fluhrer, John-John Lester	15ChiN	01-03-94	Adrian, Mich.	07-17-46	R	R	5'9	165	6	6	0	2	0	0	0	0	0	0	1	.333	.333
Flynn, Jack-John Anthony	10-11PitN 12WasA	09-07-83	Providence, R.I.	03-23-35	R	R	6'	175	149	462	46	115	14	4	6	60	46		8	.249	.335
Fohl, Lee-Leo Alexander	02PitN 03CinN M15-19CleA M21-23StLA M24-26BosA	11-28-76	Lowell, Ohio	10-30-65	R	R	5'10	175	5	17	3	5	1	1	0	3	0		0	.294	.471
Foley, Pat (See Willie Greene)																					
Forsyth, Ed-Edward James	15BalF	04-30-87	Kingston, N.Y.	06-22-56	R	R	5'10	155	1	3	0	0	0	0	0	0	0	1	0	.000	.000
Foster, Eddie-Edward Cunningham (Kid)	10NYA 12-19WasA 20-22BosA 22-23StLA	02-13-87	Chicago, Ill.	01-15-37	R	R	5'6	145	1499	5652	732	1490	191	71	6	446	446		198	.264	.326
Foster, Pop-Clarence Francis	98-00NYN 01WasA 01PhiA	04-08-78	New Haven, Conn.	04-16-44	R	R	5'8		261	922	146	263	37	19	10	137	76		17	.285	.399
Foutz, Frank-Frank Hayes	10BalA	04-08-77	Baltimore, Md.	12-25-61	R	R	5'11	165	20	72	13	17	4	1	2	14	8		9	.236	.403
Fox, Bill-William Henry	97WasN 01CinN	01-15-72	Sturbridge, Mass.	05-07-46	R	R	5'8	160	47	173	13	32	2	1	0	7	5		9	.185	.208
Fox, Jack-John Paul	08PhiA	05-21-85	Reading, Pa.	06-28-63	R	R	5'10	185	9	30	2	6	0	0	0	0	0		2	.200	.200
Freeman, Buck-John Frank	91WasAA 98-99WasN 00BosN 01-07BosA	10-30-71	Catasauqua, Pa.	06-25-49	L	L	5'9	165	1126	4211	583	1238	202	130	82	713	272		93	.294	.462
Freeman, Jerry-Frank Ellsworth (Buck)	08-09WasA	12-26-79	Placerville, Cal.	09-30-52	L	R	6'2	200	173	579	47	142	15	6	1	48	40		9	.245	.297
French, Charlie-Charles Calvin	09-10BosA 10ChiA	10-12-83	Indianapolis, Ind.	03-30-62	R	R	5'6	140	105	377	36	78	5	2	0	20	26		13	.207	.231
French, Pat-Frank Alexander	17PhiA	09-22-93	Dover, N.H.	07-13-69	R	R	6'1	180	3	2	0	0	0	0	0	0	0	0	0	.000	.000
Friel, Bill-William Edward	01MilA 02-03StLA	04-01-76	Renovo, Pa.	12-24-59	R	R	5'10	165	283	994	123	244	33	17	6	80	60		23	.245	.331
Frisk, Emil-John Emil (See P01-19)	99CinN 01DetA 05,07StLA	10-15-74	Kalkaska, Mich.	01-27-22	L	R	6'1	190	160	506	73	135	15	6	4	45	48		7	.267	.344
Fritz, Harry-Harry Koch (Dutchman)	13PhiA 14-15ChiF	09-30-90	Philadelphia, Pa.	11-04-74	R	R	5'8	170	149	423	44	96	13	5	3	39	33		6	.227	.303
Froelich, Ben-William Palmer	09PhiN	11-12-87	Pittsburgh, Pa.	09-01-16	R	R			1	1	0	0	0	0	0	0	0		0	.000	.000
Fuller, Frank-Frank Edward (Rabbit)	15-16DetA 23BosA	01-01-93	Detroit, Mich.	10-29-65	L	R	5'7	150	40	63	11	11	0	0	0	3	11	12	6	.175	.175
Fuller, Nig-Charles F.	02BknN	03-30-79	Toledo, Ohio	11-12-47	R	R	5'11	165	3	9	0	0	0	0	0	0	0		0	.000	.000
Fultz, Dave-David Lewis	98-99PhiN 99BalN 01-02PhiA 03-05NYA	05-29-75	Staunton, Va.	10-29-59	R	R	5'11	170	644	2393	369	651	86	26	3	223	201		190	.272	.333
Gagnier, Eddie-Edward John	14-15BknF 15BufF	09-13-46	Paris, France	09-13-46	R	R	5'9		115	389	30	76	13	2	0	29	23		10	.195	.239
Gainer, Del-Dellos Clinton (Sheriff)	09,11-14DetA 14-17,19BosA 18MS 22StLN	11-10-86	Montrose, W.Va.	01-29-47	R	R	6'	180	546	1608	218	438	75	36	14	185	149		54	.272	.390
Gallagher, Charlie-Charles William (Shorty)	01CleA		Detroit, Mich.	06-23-24			5'8		2	4	0	0	0	0	0	0	0		0	.000	.000
Gallagher, John-John Carroll	15BlaF	02-18-92	Pittsburgh, Pa.	03-30-52	R	R	5'10	156	40	126	11	25	4	0	0	4	5		1	.198	.230
Galloway, Bad News-James Cato	12StLN	09-16-87	Iredell, Tex.	05-03-50	B	R	6'3	187	21	54	4	10	0	4	5	8	2		2	.185	.222
Gammons, Daff-John Ashley	01BosN	03-17-76	New Bedford, Mass.	09-24-63	R	R	5'11	170	28	93	10	18	0	1	0	10	3		5	.194	.215
Gandil, Chick-Charles Arnold	10ChiA 12-15WasA 16CleA 17-19ChiA 20HO-DL	01-19-88	St. Paul, Minn.	12-13-70	R	R	6'1	190	1147	4245	449	1176	173	78	11	557	273		153	.277	.362
Gandy, Bob-Robert Brinkley (String)	16PhiN	08-25-93	Jacksonville, Fla.	06-19-45	L	R	6'3	180	1	2	0	0	0	0	0	0	0		0	.000	.000
Ganley, Bob-Robert Stephen	05-06PitN 07-09WasA 09PhiA	04-23-75	Lowell, Mass.	10-10-45	L	L	5'7	155	572	2129	246	540	44	24	2	123	177		112	.254	.300
Gannon, Bill-William Patrick	01ChiN	03-17-73	New Haven, Conn.	04-26-27	R	R	5'9	170	15	61	2	9	0	0	0		5		5	.148	.148
Ganzel, John-John Henry	98PitN 00ChiN 01NYN 03-04NYA 05-06HO 07-08,M08CinN M15BknF	04-07-74	Kalamazoo, Mich.	01-14-59	R	R	6'	195	747	2718	281	682	104	50	18	336	136		46	.251	.346
Gardner, Earle-Earle McClurkin	08-12NYA	01-24-84	Sparta, Ill.	03-02-43	R	R	5'11	160	273	948	105	249	26	5	1	108	50		39	.263	.304
Gardner, Larry-William Lawrence	08-17BosA 18PhiA 19-24CleA	05-13-86	Enosburg Falls, Vt.	03-11-76	L	R	5'8	165	1922	6684	866	1931	300	129	27	929	654		165	.289	.385
Gatins, Frank-Frank Anthony	98WasN 01BknN	03-06-71	Johnstown, Pa.	11-08-11	R	R	5'9		66	253	26	59	9	2	1	26	8		6	.233	.296
Gear, Dale-Dale Dudley (See P01-19)	96-97CleN 01WasA	02-02-72	Lone Elm, Kans.	09-23-51	R	R	5'11	165	69	238	25	57	11	3	0	25	8		4	.239	.311
Gedeon, Joe-Elmer Joseph	13-14WasA 16-17NYA 18-20StLA 20DL	12-05-93	Sacramento, Cal.	05-19-41	R	R	6'	167	581	2109	259	515	82	19	2	171	180	181	33	.244	.304
Geier, Phil-Louis Phillip (Little Phil)	96-97PhiN 00CinN 01PhiA 01MilA 04BosN	11-03-75	Washington, D.C.	09-25-67	R	R	5'7	145	349	1312	199	330	30	12	2	102	154		54	.252	.297
Genins, Frank-C.Frank (Frenchy)	92CinN 92StLN 95PitN 01CleA 01MilA 03PitN	11-02-66	St. Louis, Mo.	09-30-22	R				147	511	74	116	19	0	2	44	43		27	.227	.276
Gertenrich, Lou-Louis Wilhelm	03DetA 03-06BknN 06ChiN 08-09BosN 09-11WasA M14PitF	05-04-75	Chicago, Ill.	10-20-33	R	R	5'8	175	3	6	1	1	0	0	0	0	0	0	0	.167	.167
Gessler, Doc-Henry Homer	12-23-80		Greensburg, Pa.	12-24-24	L	L	5'10	180	880	2959	369	831	127	49	14	363	333		142	.281	.371
Getz, Gus-Gustave (Gee-Gee)	09-10BosN 14-16BknN 17CinN 18CleA 18PitN	08-03-89	Pittsburgh, Pa.	05-28-69	R	R	5'11	165	339	1114	85	265	22	9	2	93	24	46	41	.238	.279
Giannini, Joe-Joseph Francis	11BosA	09-08-88	Drytown, Cal.	09-26-42	R	R	5'8	155	1	2	0	1	0	0	0	0	0		0	.500	.500
Gibson, Charlie-Charles Ellsworth	05StLA	11-17-79	Sharon, Pa.	11-22-54	R	R	5'8	160	12	15	1	2	0	0	0	0	2		0	.133	.133
Gibson, George-George C. (Moon)	05-16PitN 17-18NYN M20-22PitN M25ChiN M32-34PitN	07-22-80	London, Canada	01-25-67	R	R	5'11	190	1213	3776	295	893	142	49	15	345	286		40	.236	.312
Giebel, Joe-Joseph Henry	13PhiA	11-30-91	Washington, D.C.	03-17-81	R	R	5'10	175	1	3	0	1	0	0	0	0	0	0	0	.333	.333
Gilbert, Billy-William Oliver	01MilA 02BalA 03-06NYN 08-09StLN	06-21-76	Tully Town, Pa.	08-08-27	R	R	5'4	153	850	2816	375	695	72	17	5	237	270		167	.247	.290
Gilbert, Jack-John Robert (Jackrabbit)	98WasN 98NYN 04PhiN	06-21-76	Rhinecliff, N.Y.	07-07-41					28	96	13	23	0	0	0		4	13	5	.240	.240
Gilbert, Larry-Lawrence William	14-15BosN	12-02-91	New Orleans, La.	02-17-65	L	L	5'9	158	117	330	43	76	10	1	5	29	37	47	7	.230	.312
Gilhooley, Frank-Frank Patrick (Flash)	11-12StLN 13-18NYA 19BosA	06-10-92	Toledo, Ohio	07-11-59	L	R	5'8	155	312	1068	141	289	30	10	2	58	140	80	37	.271	.323
Gill, Doc-Warren Darst	08PitN		Ladoga, Ind.	11-26-52	R	R	6'1	175	27	76	10	17	5	0	0	14	11		3	.224	.250
Gilmore, Grover-Ernest Grover	14-15KCF	11-01-88	Chicago, Ill.	11-25-19	L	L	5'9	170	258	941	144	269	47	20	2	79	63		42	.286	.385
Ginn, Tinsley-Tinsley Rucker	14CleA		Royston, Ga.	08-30-31	R	R	5'9	180	2	5	1	1	0	0	0	0	0	1	0	.200	.200
Gleason, Harry-Harry Gilbert	01-03BosA 04-05StLA	03-28-75	Camden, N.J.	10-21-61	R	R	5'8	150	274	944	88	206	24	11	3	90	48		31	.218	.276
Gleason, Kid-William J. (See P01-19)	88-91PhiN 92-94StLN 94-95BalN 96-00NYN 01-02DetA 03-08PhiN 12,M19-23ChiA	10-26-66	Camden, N.J.	01-02-33	B	R	5'7	158	1969	7445	1017	1951	216	85	15	823	500		332	.262	.320
Glenn, Ed-Edward D.	98WasN 98NYN 02ChiN	10-??-75	Cincinnati, Ohio	12-06-11	R	R			5	15	1	1	0	0	0		0	4	1	.067	.067
Glenn, Harry-Harry Melville (Husky)	15StLN	06-09-90	Shelburn, Ind.	10-12-18	R	R	5'9	185	6	16	1	5	0	0	0	0	2		1	.313	.313
Glockson, Norm-Norman Stanley (Tango) 22 played in N.F.L.	14CinN	06-15-94	Blue Island, Ill.	08-05-55	R	R	6'2	200	7	12	0	0	0	0	0	0	0	6	0	.000	.000

USE NAME - GIVEN NAMES (NICKNAMES)	TEAM BY YEAR	BIRTH DATE	BIRTH PLACE	DEATH DATE	B	T	HGT	WGT	G	AB	R	H	2B	3B	HR	RBI	BB	SO	SB	BA	SA
Gochnaur, John-John Peter	01BknN 02-03CleA	09-12-75	Altoona, Pa.	09-27-25	R	R	5'9	160	264	908	94	170	32	8	0	87	87		18	.187	.240
Godwin, John-John Henry (Bunny)	05-06BosA	03-10-77	East Liverpool, Ohio	05-05-56	R	R	6'	190	79	230	15	49	3	1	0	25	9		9	.213	.235
Gonzalez, Eusebio-Eusebio Miguel [Lopez] (Papo)	18BosA	07-13-92	Havana, Cuba	02-14-76	R	R	5'10	165	2	2	1	1	0	1	0	0	0		0	.500	1.500
Gooch Lee-Lee Currin	15CleA 17PhiA	02-23-90	Oxford, N.C.	05-18-66	R	R	6'	190	19	61	4	18	2	0	1	8	4	10	0	.295	.377
Good, Gene-Eugene Joseph	06BosN	12-13-83	Roxbury, Mass.	08-06-47	L	R	5'6	130	2	3	0	0	0	0	0	0	0	2	0	.000	.000
Good, Wilbur-Wilbur David (Lefty) (See P01-19)	05NYA 08-09CleA 10-11BosN 11-15ChiN 16PhiN 18ChiA	09-28-85	Punxsutawney, Pa.	12-30-63	L	L	5'11	180	750	2634	324	609	84	44	9	187	190		104	.258	.342
Goodwin, Pep-Claire Vernon	14-15KCF	12-19-91	Pocatello, Idaho	02-15-72	L	R	5'10	160	193	603	60	142	20	7	1	48	42		10	.235	.297
Gossett, Dick-John Star	13-14NYA	08-21-90	Dennison, Ohio	10-06-62	R	R	5'11	185	48	126	12	20	2	0	0	10	15	27	1	.159	.175
Gouzzie, Claude-Claude	03StLA	??-??-73	France	09-21-07	R	R	5'9	170	1	0	0	0	0	0	0	0	0		0	.000	.000
Gowdy, Hank-Henry Morgan (Harry)	10-11NYN 11-17BosN 18MS 19-23BosN 23-25NYN 29-30BosN	08-24-89	Columbus, Ohio	08-01-66	R	R	6'2	182	1050	2735	270	738	122	27	21	322	311	247	59	.270	.327
Grady, Mike-Michael William (Mich)	94-97PhiN 97StLN 98-00NYN 01WasA 04-06StLN	12-23-69	Kennett Square, Pa.	12-03-43	R	R	5'11	190	914	2991	487	885	155	68	35	459	311		111	.296	.428
Graf, Fred-Frederick Gottleib	13StLA	08-25-89	Canton, Ohio	10-04-79	R	R	5'10	164	4	5	1	2	1	0	0	2	3	3	0	.400	.600
Graham, Bert-Albert	10StLA	04-03-86	Tilton, Ill.	06-19-71	B	R	6'1	187	8	26	1	3	2	1	0	5	1		0	.115	.269
Graham, Charlie-Charles Henry	06BosA	04-25-78	Santa Clara, Cal.	08-29-48	R	R	5'11	180	30	90	10	21	1	0	1	12	10		1	.233	.278
Graham, Moonlight-Archibald Wright	05NYN	11-09-76	Fayetteville, N.C.	08-25-65	L	R	5'10	170	1	0	0	0	0	0	0	0	0		0		
Graham, Peaches-George Frederick (See P01-19)	02CleA 03ChiN 08-11BosN 11ChiN 12PhiN	03-23-77	Aledo, Ill.	07-25-39	R	R	5'9	180	373	999	99	265	34	6	1	85	114		21	.265	.314
Graham, Tiny-Dawson Francis	14CinN	12-09-92	Nashville, Tenn.	12-29-62	R	R	6'2	185	25	61	5	14	1	0	0	3	3	10	1	.230	.246
Graney, Jack-John Gladstone (Mickey) (See P01-19)	08,10-22CleA	12-09-92	St. Thomas, Canada	04-20-78	L	L	5'9	180	1403	4705	706	1178	219	79	18	420	713		148	.250	.342
Grant, Eddie-Edward Leslie (Harvard Eddie)	05CleA 07-10PhiN 11-13CinN 13-15NYN	05-21-83	Franklin, Mass.	10-05-18	L	R	5'11	170	990	3385	399	844	79	30	5	277	233		153	.249	.295
Gray, Stan-Stanley Oscar (Dolly)	12PitN	12-10-88	Ladonia, Tex.	10-11-64	R	R	6'1	184	6	20	4	5	0	1	0	2	0		0	.250	.350
Green, Danny-Edward Joseph	98-01ChiN 02-05ChiA	11-06-76	Burlington, N.J.	11-09-14	L	R			923	3481	551	1024	123	65	29	422	315		192	.294	.392
Greene, Patsy-Patrick Joseph (Played as Pat Foley 02)	02PhiN 03NYA 03DetA	03-20-75	Providence, R.I.	10-20-34	R	R	5'8	150	24	81	7	15	2	0	0	1	2		2	.185	.210
Gremminger, Ed-Lorenzo Edward (Battleship)	95CleN 02-03BosN 04DetA	03-30-74	Canton, Ohio	05-26-42	R	R	6'1	200	382	1422	140	357	58	24	7	164	89		23	.251	.340
Grey (Gray), Reddie-Romer Carl	03PitN	04-08-75	Zanesville, Ohio	11-08-34	L	L	5'11	175	1	3	1	1	0	0	0	0	0		0	.333	.333
Griffin, Pug-Francis Arthur	17PhiA 20NYN	04-24-96	Lincoln, Neb.	10-12-51	R	R	5'11	187	23	29	4	6	1	0	1	3	2	11	1	.207	.345
Griffith, Tommy-Thomas Herman	13-14BosN 15-18CinN 19-25BknN 25ChiN	10-26-89	Prospect, Ohio	04-13-67	L	R	5'10	175	1401	4947	589	1383	208	72	52	619	351	262	70	.280	.382
Griggs, Art-Arthur Carle	09-10StLA 11-12CleA 14-15BknF 18CleA	01-10-83	Topeka, Kans.	12-19-38	R	R	5'11	185	442	1370	127	379	73	20	5	152	105		36	.277	.370
Grimshaw, Moose-Myron Frederick	05-07BosA	11-30-75	St. Johnsville, N.Y.	12-11-36	R	R	6'1	173	259	894	104	229	31	16	4	116	60		15	.256	.340
Groh, Heinie-Henry Knight	12-13NYN 13-21,M18CinN 22-26NYN 27PitN	09-18-89	Rochester, N.Y.	08-22-68	R	R	5'8	158	1676	6074	920	1774	308	87	26	566	696	345	180	.292	.384
Groh, Lew-Lewis Carl (Silver)	19PhiA	10-16-83	Rochester, N.Y.	10-20-60	R	R			2	4	0	0	0	0	0	0	0	2	0	.000	.000
Grossart, George-George Albert	01BosN	04-11-80	Meadville, Pa.	04-18-02	R	R			7	26	4	3	0	0	0	1	0		0	.115	.115
Grover, Roy-Roy Arthur	16-17,19PhiA 19WasA	01-17-92	Snohomish, Wash.	02-07-78	R	R	5'8	150	207	690	67	156	17	9	0	50	60	79	19	.226	.277
Grubb, Harvey-Harvey Harrison	12CleA	09-18-90	Lexington, N.C.	01-25-70	R	R	6'	189	1	0	0	0	0	0	0	0	0		0		
Gunning, Hy-Hyland	11BosA	06-08-88	Maplewood, N.J.	03-28-75	R	R	6'1	189	4	9	0	1	0	0	0	2	1		0	.111	.111
Gust, Red-Ernest Herman Frank	11StLA	01-24-88	Bay City, Mich.	10-26-45	R	R	6'	170	3	12	0	0	0	0	0	0	0		0	.000	.000
Haberer, Emil-Emil Karl	01,03,09CinN	02-02-78	Cincinnati, Ohio	10-19-51	R	R	6'1	204	16	47	4	7	1	1	0	3	5		0	.149	.213
Hackett, Jim-James Joseph (Sunny Jim) (See P01-19)	02-03StLN	10-01-77	Jacksonville, Ill.	03-28-61	R	R	6'2	185	105	372	26	86	14	8	0	40	21		3	.231	.312
Hahn, Eddie-William Edgar	05-06NYA 06-10ChiA	08-27-75	Nevada, Ohio	11-29-41	L	R		160	553	2045	291	484	42	20	1	122	258		59	.237	.278
Halas, George-George Stanley 20-29 played in N.F.L. 20-29,33-42,46-55,58-68 head coach in N.F.L.	19NYA	02-02-95	Chicago, Ill.	10-31-83	B	R	6'	182	12	22	0	2	0	0	0	0	0	8	0	.091	.091
Hale, George-George Wagner (Ducky)	14, 16-18StLA	11-01-45	Dexter, Kans.	11-01-45	R	R	5'10	160	60	103	5	18	3	1	0	9	11	21	0	.175	.243
Haley, Pat-Raymond Timothy	15-16BosA 16-17PhiA 18-19MS	01-23-91	Danbury, Iowa	11-08-73	R	R	5'11	180	81	214	17	53	8	1	0	15	11	32	2	.248	.294
Hall, Bob-Robert Prill	04PhiN 05NYN 05BknN	12-20-78	Baltimore, Md.	12-01-50	R	R	5'10	158	103	369	33	75	8	1	2	32	25		13	.203	.247
Hall, Russ-Robert Russell	98StLN 01CleA	09-29-71	Shelbyville, Ky.	07-01-37	L	L	5'10	170	40	147	15	38	1	0	0	10	7		1	.259	.279
Halliday, Newt-Newton Schurz	16PitN	06-18-96	Chicago, Ill.	04-06-18	R	R	6'1	175	1	1	0	0	0	0	0	0	0	1	0	.000	.000
Hallinan, Ed-Edward S.	11-12StLA	08-23-88	San Francisco, Cal.	08-24-40	R	R	5'9	168	80	255	24	54	5	1	0	15	19		7	.212	.239
Hallman, Bill-William Harry	01MilA 03ChiA 06-07PhiN	03-15-76	Philadelphia, Pa.	04-23-50	L	L	5'8	165	319	1147	150	269	43	13	3	86	120		47	.235	.303
Hallman, Billy-William Wilson	88-89PhiN 90PhiP 91PhiA 92-97PhiN 97,M97StLN 98BknN 01CleA 01-03PhiN	03-31-67	Pittsburgh, Pa.	09-11-20	R	R	5'8	160	1501	5999	943	1664	243	86	20	769	425		205	.277	.357
Halt, Al-Alva William	14-15BknF 18CleA	11-23-90	Sandusky, Ohio	01-22-73	L	R	6'	180	257	854	76	204	30	9	6	90	61		35	.239	.316
Hamilton, Billy-William Robert (Sliding Billy)	88-89KCAA 90-95PhiN 96-01BosN	02-16-66	Newark, N.J.	12-15-40	L	L	5'6	165	1582	6262	1690	2157	225	94	40	736	1187		937	.344	.430
Hammond, Jack-Walter Charles (Wobby)	15,22CleA 22PitN	02-26-91	Amsterdam, N.Y.	03-04-42	R	R	5'11	170	45	99	13	22	2	1	0	2	4	19	0	.222	.263
Handiboe, Mike-Aloysius James (Coalyard Mike)	11NYA	02-17-88	Washington, D.C.	01-31-53	L	L	5'10	155	5	15	0	1	0	0	0	0	2		0	.067	.067
Hanford, Charlie-Charles Joseph	14BufF 15ChiF	06-03-82	Tunstall, England	07-19-63	R	R	5'6	145	232	776	110	217	32	18	13	112	44		47	.280	.418
Hanlon, Bill-William Joseph (Big Bill)	03ChiN	06-24-76	Los Angeles, Cal.	11-23-05	R	R	6'	175	8	21	4	2	0	0	0	2	6		1	.095	.095
Hannah, Truck-James Harrison	18-20NYA	06-05-89	Larimore, N.D.	04-27-82	R	R	6'1	190	244	736	62	173	25	4	5	66	97	79	2	.235	.300
Hannifin, Jack-John Joseph	06PhiA 06-08NYN 08BosN	02-25-83	Holyoke, Mass.	07-27-45	B	R	5'10	160	142	439	50	94	13	6	3	40	45		14	.214	.282
Hanson, Harry-Harry Francis	13NYA	01-17-96	Elgin, Ill.	10-05-66	R	R	5'11		1	2	0	0	0	0	0	0	0		0	.000	.000
Hardy, Jack-John Doolittle	03CleA 07ChiN 09-10WasA	06-23-77	Cleveland, Ohio	10-20-21	R	R	6'	185	23	55	5	10	1	0	0	5	2		1	.182	.200
Hardgrove, Pat-William Henry	18ChiA	05-10-95	Palmyra Ct. H., Kans.	01-26-73	R	R	5'10	158	2	2	0	0	0	0	0	0	0		0	.000	.000
Harley, Dick-Richard Joseph	97-98StLN 99CleN 00-01CinN 02DetA 03ChiN	09-25-72	Blue Bell, Pa.	04-03-52	L	R	5'10	165	743	2881	388	756	59	28	10	236	223		135	.262	.313
Harrison, Ben	01WasA			Deceased	R	R			1	2	0	0	0	0	0	0	1		0	.000	.000
Hart, Hub-James Henry	05-07ChiA	02-02-78	Everett, Mass.	10-10-60	R	L	5'11	170	56	124	9	27	1	0	0	11	10		1	.218	.226
Hart, Bert-James Burton	01BalA	06-28-70	Long Tree Lake, Minn.	01-29-21	B		6'3	200	58	206	33	64	3	5	0	23	20		7	.311	.374
Hartford, Bruce-Bruce Daniel	14CleA	05-14-92	Chicago, Ill.	05-25-75	R	R	6'	190	8	22	5	4	1	0	0	0	4		0	.182	.227
Hartley, Chick-Walter Scott	02NYN	08-22-80	Philadelphia, Pa.	07-18-48	R	R	5'8	180	1	4	0	0	0	0	0	0	0		0	.000	.000
Hartley, Grover-Grover Allen (Slick)	11-13NYN 14-15StLF 16-17StLA 24-26NYN 27BosA 28DP 29-30CleA 34StLA	07-02-88	Osgood, Ind.	10-19-64	R	R	5'11	175	566	1321	135	352	61	11	3	144	135		29	.266	.336
Hartman, Fred-Frederick Orrin (Dutch)	94PitN 97StLN 98-99NYN 01ChiA 02StLA	04-25-68	Pittsburgh, Pa.	11-11-38	R	R	5'8	170	583	2246	298	620	75	46	10	332	118		87	.276	.384
Hartsel, Topsy-Tully Frederick	98-99LouN 00CinN 01ChiN 02-11PhiA	06-26-74	Polk, Ohio	10-14-44	L	L	5'5	155	1351	4834	824	1334	183	92	31	341	837		247	.276	.371
Hartzell, Roy-Roy Allen	06-10StLA 11-16NYA	07-06-81	Golden, Colo.	11-06-61	L	R	5'8	155	1288	4548	503	1146	112	55	12	397	455		182	.252	.309
Harvey, Zaza-Ervin King (Silent) (See P01-19)	00ChiN 01ChiA 01-02CleA	04-05-79	Saratoga, Cal.	06-03-54	L	L	6'	190	76	259	37	86	10	6	1	32	14		17	.332	.429
Hasbrook(Hasbrouck), Ziggy-Robert Lyndon	16-17ChiA	11-21-93	Grundy Center, Iowa	02-09-76	R	R	6'1	180	11	9	2	1	0	0	0	0	1		0	.111	.111
Hauger, Art-John Arthur	12CleA	11-18-93	Delhi, Ohio	08-02-44	L	R	5'11	168	15	18	0	1	0	0	0	0	1		0	.056	.056
Hauser, Arnold-Arnold George (Pee-Wee)	10-13StLN 14IL 15ChiF	09-25-88	Chicago, Ill.	05-22-66	R	R	5'6	145	433	1468	180	349	33	20	6	137	121		68	.238	.300
Haworth, Homer-Homer Howard (Cully)	15CleA	08-27-93	Newburg, Ore.	01-28-53	R	R	5'10	165	7	7	0	1	0	0	0	1	2		0	.143	.143
Hayden, Jack-John Francis	01PhiA 06BosA 08ChiN	10-21-80	Bryn Mawr, Pa.	08-03-42	L	L	5'9	170	147	578	60	145	14	8	1	33	36		11	.251	.308
Hazleton, Doc-Willard Carpenter	02StLN	08-28-76	Stafford, Vt.	03-10-41	R				7	23	1	3	0	0	0	0	2		0	.130	.130
Healy, Tom-Thomas Fitzgerald	15-16PhiA	10-30-95	Altoona, Pa	01-15-74	R	R	6'	172	29	100	15	23	2	1	0	7	7	6	1	.230	.270
Hearn (Hearne), Ed-Edmund	10BosA	09-17-87	Ventura, Cal.	09-08-52	R	R	5'9	160	2	2	0	0	0	0	0	0	0		0	.000	.000
Hearne, Hugh-Hugh Joseph (Hughie)	01-03BknN	04-18-73	Troy, N.Y.	09-22-32	R	R	5'8	182	94	293	31	83	13	2	0	35	19		5	.283	.341
Hechinger, Mike-Michael Vincent	12-13ChiN 13BknN	02-14-90	Chicago, Ill.	08-13-67	R	R	6'	175	13	16	1	2	1	0	0	2	1		0	.125	.188
Heidrick, Snags-R. Emmett	98CleN 99-01StLN 02-04,08StLA 05-07VR	07-09-76	Queenstown, Pa.	01-20-16	L	R	6'	185	758	3049	470	915	109	74	16	342	146		181	.300	.400
Heileman, Jack-John George	01CinN	08-10-72	Cincinnati, Ohio	07-19-40	R	R	5'10	155	5	15	1	2	0	0	0	1	0		0	.133	.200
Heitmuller, Heinie-William Frederick	09-10PhiA	05-25-83	San Francisco, Cal.	10-08-12	R	R	6'2	215	95	321	47	87	11	10	0	22	35		13	.271	.368
Helfrich, Ty-Emory Wilbur	15BknF	10-09-90	Pleasantville, N.J.	03-18-55	R	R	5'10	178	43	104	12	25	6	0	0	5	15		2	.240	.404
Hemingway, Ed-Edson Marshall	14StLA 17NYN 18BosN	05-08-93	Sheridan, Mich.	07-05-69	R	R	5'11	165	43	138	10	31	5	0	0	13	10	11	1	.225	.290
Hemphill, Charlie-Charles Judson (Eagle Eye)	99StLN 99CleN 01BosA 02CleA 02-04,06-07,09WasA 08-11NYA	04-20-76	Greenville, Mich.	06-22-53	L	L	5'9	160	1240	4539	581	1230	118	69	22	421	435		209	.271	.342
Hemphill, Frank-Frank Vernon	06ChiA 09WasA	05-13-78	Greenville, Mich.	11-16-50	R	R	5'11	165	14	43	0	3	0	0	0	2	9		1	.070	.070
Hendricks, Jack-John Charles	02NYN 02ChiN 03WasA M18StLN M24-29CinN	04-09-75	Joliet, Ill.	05-13-43	R	R			42	145	11	30	3	0	0	4	15		5	.207	.283
Hendryx, Tim-Timothy Green	11-12CleA 15-17NYA 18StLA 20-21BosA	01-31-91	Le Roy, Ill.	08-04-57	R	R	5'9	170	414	1288	152	355	68	22	9	191	185		26	.276	.377
Hennessey, Let-Lester Baan	13DetA	12-12-93	Lynn, Mass.	11-20-76	R	R	6'	190	12	22	3	3	0	1	0	1	1		0	.136	.136
Henriksen, Olaf-Olaf (Swede)	11-17BosA	04-26-88	Kirkerup, Denmark	10-17-62	L	L	5'7	158	311	487	84	131	12	7	1	48	97		15	.269	.329
Henry, John-John Park (Bull)	10-17WasA 18BosN	12-26-89	Amherst, Mass.	11-24-41	R	R	6'	190	683	1920	161	397	54	15	2	171	244		56	.207	.254
Herring(Harrington), Lefty-Silas Clarke	99WasN 04WasA	03-04-80	Philadelphia, Pa.	02-11-65	L	L	5'11	160	17	47	4	9	1	2	0		8		0	.191	.213

USE NAME - GIVEN NAMES (NICKNAMES)	TEAM BY YEAR	BIRTH DATE	BIRTH PLACE	DEATH DATE	B	T	HGT	WGT	G	AB	R	H	2B	3B	HR	RBI	BB	SO	SB	BA	SA
Herzog, Buck-Charles Lincoln	08-09NYN 10-11BosN 11-13NYN 14-16,M14-16CinN 16-17NYN 18-19BosN 19-20ChiN 21DU		Baltimore, Md.	09-04-53	R	R	5'11	160	1493	5284	705	1370	191	75	20	445	427		312	.259	.335
Hetling, Gus-Augustus Julius	06DetA	11-21-85	St. Louis, Mo.	10-13-62	R	R	5'10	165	2	7	0	1	0	0	0				0	.143	.143
Heydon, Mike-Michael Edward (Ed)	98BalN 99WasN 01StLN 04ChiA 05-07WasA	07-15-74	Mo.	10-13-13	L	R	6'		214	619	52	111	19	6	2	53	70		12	.179	.239
Hickey, Eddie-Edward A.	01ChiN	08-18-72	Cleveland, Ohio	03-25-41	R	R			10	37	4	6	0	0	0	3	2		1	.162	.162
Hickman, Charley-Charles Taylor (Piano Legs) (See P01-19)	97-99BosN 00-01NYN 02BosA 02-04CleA 04-05DetA 05-07WasA 07ChiA 08CleA	03-04-76	Taylortown, Pa.	04-19-34	R	R	5'9	185	1074	3968	480	1199	212	87	58	614	153		76	.302	.443
Hickman, Jim-David James	15BalF 16-19BknN	05-19-92	Johnson City, Tenn.	12-30-58	R	R	5'7	170	253	727	84	158	26	13	8	70	37	114	27	.217	.322
Higgins, Bob-Robert Stone	09CleA 11-12BknN	09-23-86	Fayetteville, Tenn.	05-25-41	R	R	5'8	176	13	35	1	5	0	0	0	2	1	1	1	.143	.143
High, Hugh-Hugh Jenken (Bunny, Lefty)	13-14DetA 15-18NYA	10-24-87	Pottstown, Pa.	11-16-62	L	L	5'7	145	504	1546	176	386	54	21	3	123	212	168	56	.250	.318
Hildebrand, George-George Albert	02BknN	09-06-78	San Francisco, Cal.	05-30-60	R	R	5'8	170	11	41	3	9	1	0	0	5	3		0	.220	.244
Hildebrand, Pete-Palmer Marion	13StlN	12-23-84	Schauck, Ohio	01-25-60	R	R	5'11	180	26	55	3	9	1	0	0		1		1	.164	.200
Hildebrand, George-George Albert	02ChiN	09-06-78	San Francisco, Cal.	05-30-60	R	R	5'8	170	1	4	1	0	0	0	0	0	0		0	.000	.000
Hill, Hugh-Hugh Ellis	03CleA 04StLN	07-21-79	Ringgold, Ga.	09-06-58	L	R	5'11	168	24	94	13	21	2	1	3	4	2		3	.223	.362
Hill, Hunter-Hunter Benjamin	03-04StLA 04-05WasA	06-21-79	Austin, Tex.	02-22-59	R	R			325	1200	104	259	32	5	1	80	57		26	.216	.293
Hill, Doc-Homer Hiller Henry (See P01-19)	05-06,08PhiA	10-10-79	Freeport, Ill.	01-23-74	R	L	5'8	165	47	131	10	31	4	2	0	10	7		1	.237	.298
Hilley, Ed-Edward Garfield (Whitey)	03PhiA	06-17-79	Cleveland, Ohio	11-14-56	R	R	5'10	170	1	3	1	1	0	0	0		1		0	.333	.333
Hilly (Hilgerink), Pat-William Edward	14PhiN	02-24-87	Fostoria, Ohio	07-25-53	R	R	5'11	180	8	10	2	3	0	0	0	1	1	5	0	.300	.300
Himes, Jack-John Herby	05-06StLN	09-22-78	Bryan, Ohio	12-16-49	L	R	6'2	225	52	196	13	48	5	2	0	14	8		4	.245	.291
Hinchman, Bill-William White	05-06CinN 07-09CleA 15-18,20PhiN	04-04-83	Philadelphia, Pa.	02-20-63	R	R	5'11	190	908	3043	364	793	128	69	20	369	298		85	.261	.368
Hinchman, Harry-Harry Sibley	07CleA	08-04-78	Philadelphia, Pa.	01-19-33	B	R	5'11	165	15	51	3	11	3	1	0	9	5		2	.216	.314
Hinton, Red-John Robert	01BosN	06-20-76	Pittsburgh, Pa.	07-19-20	R	R	6'	205	4	13	0	1	0	0	0	0	2		0	.077	.077
Hobbs, Bill-William Lee	13,16CinN	05-07-93	Grant's Lick, Ky.	01-05-45	R	R	5'9	155	10	15	1	2	1	0	0	1	2	3	1	.133	.200
Hoblitzell, Dick-Richard Carleton	08-14CinN 14-18BosA 19-20MS	10-26-88	Waverly, W.Va.	11-14-62	L	L	6'	172	1314	4706	591	1310	194	88	27	593	407		173	.278	.374
Hoelskoetter, Art-Arthur William (Holley, Hoss) (See P01-19) (Played as Art Hostetter 07-08)	05-08StlN	09-30-82	St. Louis, Mo.	08-03-54	R	R	6'2		300	952	59	225	21	8	2	53	40		9	.236	.282
Hoey, Jack-John Bernard	06-08BosA	11-10-81	Watertown, Mass.	11-14-47	L	L	5'9	185	146	508	39	116	10	5	0	35	15		13	.232	.272
Hoffman, Danny-Daniel John	03-06PhiA 06-07NYA 08-11StLA	03-02-80	Canton, Conn.	03-14-22	L	L	5'9	175	828	2976	359	761	71	53	14	235	226		185	.256	.329
Hoffman, Izzy-Harry C.	04WasA 07BosN	01-05-75	Bridgeport, N.J.	11-13-42	L	L	5'9	160	29	116	18	27	4	1	0	4	8		2	.233	.284
Hoffman, Larry-Lawrence Charles	01CinN	07-18-78	Chicago, Ill.	12-29-48	R	R	5'8	175	6	22	2	7	0	0	0	6	0		1	.318	.364
Hoffman, Tex-Edward Adolph (Dutch)	15CleA	11-30-93	San Antonio, Tex.	05-19-47	R	R	5'9	195	9	13	1	2	0	0	0	2	1	5	0	.154	.154
Hofman, Solly-Arthur Frederick (Circus Solly)	03PitN 04-12ChiN 12-13PitN 14BknN 15BufF 16NYA 16ChiN	10-29-82	St. Louis, Mo.	03-10-56	R	R	6'	160	1194	4072	554	1095	162	60	19	495	421		208	.269	.352
Hogan, Harry-Harry Sweet	01CleA	11-01-76	Syracuse, N.Y.	01-25-34					1	4	0	0	0	0	0	0	0		0	.000	.000
Hogan, Willie-William Henry (Happy)	11PhiA 11-12StLA	09-14-84	North San Juan, Cal.	09-28-74	R	R	5'10	175	237	822	86	194	28	10	3	100	77		35	.236	.305
Hogriever, George-George C.	95CinN 01MilA	03-17-69	Cincinnati, Ohio	01-26-61	R	R	5'10	160	121	458	86	118	18	9	2	50	66		47	.258	.349
Hohnhurst, Ed-Edward Hicks	10,12CleA	01-31-85	Covington, Ky.	03-28-16	L	L	6'1	175	31	116	13	31	4	1	0	8	8		6	.267	.319
Holden, Bill-William Paul	13-14NYA 14CinN	09-07-89	Birmingham, Ala.	09-14-71	R	R	6'	170	79	246	20	52	3	6	0	21	27	36	2	.211	.260
Holly(Ruthlavy), Eddie-Edward William	06-07StLN 14-15PitF	07-06-79	Chicago, Ill.	11-27-73	R	R	5'10	165	276	971	92	224	29	7	1	78	63		33	.231	.276
Holmes, Ducky-Howard Elbert	06StLN	07-08-83	Dayton, Ohio	09-18-45	R	R	5'10	160	9	27	2	5	0	0	0	2	2		0	.185	.185
Holmes, Ducky-James William	95-97LouN 97NYN 98StLN 98-99BalN 01-02DetA 03WasA 03-05ChiA	01-28-69	Des Moines, Iowa	08-06-32	L	R	5'6	170	931	3586	545	1017	143	59	17	374	236		244	.284	.371
Holmes, Fred-Frederick Clarence	03NYA 04ChiN	07-01-78	Chicago, Ill.	02-13-56	R	R	5'7	145	2	3	1	1	0	0	0	0	1		0	.333	.667
Hooper, Harry-Harry Bartholomew	09-20BosA 21-25ChiA	08-24-87	Bell Station, Cal.	12-17-74	L	R	5'10	168	2308	8784	1429	2466	389	160	75	817	1136		375	.281	.387
Hopkins, Mike-Michael Joseph (Skinner)	02PitN	11-01-72	Glasgow, Scotland	02-05-72	R	R	5'8	160	1	2	0	2	0	0	0				0	1.000	1.500
Hopkins, Buck-John Winton (Sis)	07StLN	01-03-83	Grafton, Va.	10-02-29	L	L	5'10	165	15	44	7	6	3	0	0	3	10		2	.136	.205
Householder, Ed-Edward H.	03BknN	10-12-69	Pittsburgh, Pa.	07-03-24	L	L	5'9	180	12	43	5	9	0	0	0	9	2		3	.209	.209
Houser, Ben-Benjamin Franklin	10PhiA 11-12BosN 13KJ	11-30-83	Shenandoah, Pa.	01-15-52	L	L	6'1	185	162	472	58	126	21	5	9	68	37		3	.267	.390
Howard, Dave-David Austin (Del)	12WasA 15BknF	05-01-89	Washington, D.C.	01-26-56	R	R	5'11	165	25	36	6	8	1	0	0	1	1		0	.222	.250
Howard, Del-George Elmer	05PitN 06-07BosN 07-09ChiN	12-24-77	Kenney, Ill.	12-24-56	L	R	6'	180	536	1833	199	482	54	22	6	193	111		67	.263	.326
Howard, Ivon-Ivan Chester	14-15StLA 16-17CleA	10-12-82	Kenney, Ill.	03-30-67	B	R	5'10	170	302	818	91	191	27	14	2	86	104	129	53	.233	.304
Howard, Paul-Paul Joseph (Del)	09BosA	05-20-84	Boston, Mass.	08-29-68	R	R	5'8	170	6	15	2	3	0	0	0	2	3		0	.200	.267
Howell, Harry-Harry Taylor (Handsome Harry) (See P01-19)	98BknN 99BalN 00BknN 01-02BalA 03NY 04-10StLA	11-14-76	Brooklyn, N.Y.	05-22-56	R	R	5'9		457	1395	143	301	59	26	10	130	64		20	.216	.317
Howley, Dan-Daniel Philip (Dapper Dan)	13PhiN M27-29StLA M30-32CinN	10-16-85	East Weymouth, Mass.	03-10-44	R	R	6'	167	26	32	5	4	3	0	0	2	4	4	3	.125	.188
Hoy, Dummy-William Ellsworth	88-89WasN 90BufP 91StLA 92-93WasN 94-97CinN 98-99LouN 01ChiA 02CinN	05-23-62	Houcktown, Ohio	12-15-61	L	R	5'6	160	1795	7098	1424	2067	237	118	40	726	1004		607	.291	.375
Huelsman, Frank-Frank Elmer	97StLN 04ChiA 04DetA 04ChiA 04StLA 04-05WasA	06-05-74	St. Louis, Mo.	06-09-59	R	R	6'2	210	240	824	76	213	52	13	5	97	62		18	.258	.371
Hug, Edward Ambrose	03BknN	07-14-80	Fayetteville, Ohio	05-11-53	R	R			1	0	0	0	0	0	0	0	0	0	0	—	—
Huggins, Miller-Miller James (Hug, The Mighty Mite)	04-09CinN 10-16, M13-17StLN, M18-29NYA	03-27-78	Cincinnati, Ohio	09-25-29	B	R	5'6	140	1585	5557	947	1474	146	50	9	318	1002		324	.265	.314
Hughes, Ed-Edward J. (See P01-19)	02ChiN, 05-06BosA	10-05-80	Chicago, Ill.	10-14-27	R	R	6'1	180	9	21	2	4	0	0	0	2	0		0	.190	.190
Hughes, Joe-Joseph Thompson	02-21-80	Pardo, Oh.	03-13-51		R	R	5'10	165	1	3	0	0	0	0	0	0	0		0	.000	.000
Huhn, Emil-Emil Hugo (Hap)	15NwkF 16-17CinN	02-21-80	North Vernon, Ind.	03-13-51	R	R	6'	180	184	560	40	128	22	5	1	47	32		14	.229	.291
Hulswitt, Rudy-Rudolph Edward	99LouN 02-04PhiN 08CinN 09-10StLN	02-23-77	Newport, Ky.	01-16-50	R	R	5'11	165	644	2230	208	564	64	32	3	203	136		49	.253	.314
Hummel, John-John Edwin (Silent John)	05-15BknN 18NYA	04-04-83	Bloomsburg, Pa.	05-18-59	R	R	5'11	180	1161	3906	421	991	128	84	29	394	346		117	.254	.352
Humphrey, Al-Alfred	11BknN	02-28-86	Ashtabula, Ohio	05-13-61	L	R	5'11	180	8	27	4	5	0	0	0	3	0	7	0	.185	.185
Hunter, Bill-William Ellsworth	12CleA	07-08-86	Buffalo, N.Y.	04-10-34	L	L	5'7	155	21	55	6	9	2	0	0	2	6		0	.164	.200
Hunter, George-George Henry (See P01-19)	09-10BknN	07-08-86	Buffalo, N.Y.	01-11-68	B	L	5'8	165	45	123	8	28	7	0	0	13	5		9	.228	.285
Hunter, Herb-Herbert Harrison	16NYN 16-17ChiN 20BosA 21StlN	12-25-95	Boston, Mass.	07-25-70	R	R	6'	180	39	49	8	8	1	0	0	4	3	6	0	.163	.224
Hunter, Newt-Frederick Creighton	11PitN	01-05-80	Chillicothe, Ohio	10-26-63	R	R	6'	180	65	209	35	53	10	5	1	24	25	43	9	.254	.388
Hurley, Jerry-Jeremiah	01CinN	04-??-75	New York, N.Y.	12-27-19	R	R			9	21	1	1	0	0	0				1	.048	.048
Hurley, Pat-Patrick	07BknN				R	R			1	2	0	0	0	0	0	0	0		0	.000	.000
Huston, Harry-Harry Emanuel Kress	06PhiN	10-14-83	Bellefontaine, Ohio	10-13-69	R	R	5'9	168	2	1	0	0	0	0	0	0	0		0	.000	.000
Hyatt, Ham-Robert Hamilton	09-10,12-14PitN 15StLN 18NYA	11-01-84	Buncombe Co., N.C.	09-11-63	L	R	6'1	185	464	925	85	247	36	23	10	146	63		11	.267	.388
Hynes, Pat-Patrick Joseph (See P01-19)	03StLN 04StLA	03-12-85	St. Louis, Mo.	03-12-07	L				67	257	23	60	7	3	0	15	3		3	.233	.284
Ingerton, Scotty-William John	11BosN	01-08-89	Rapid City, S.D.	06-15-56	R	R	6'1	172	136	521	53	130	24	4	5	61	39	68	6	.250	.340
Iott (Hoyot), Happy Jack-Frederick Bidds (Biddo)	03CleA	01-07-76	Houlton, Me.	02-17-41	R	R	5'10	175	3	10	1	2	0	0	0	0	2		1	.200	.200
Irelan, Hal-Harold (Grump)	14PhiN	08-05-90	Burnettsville, Ind.	07-16-44	B	R	5'7	165	67	165	16	39	4	3	0	16	21	22	4	.236	.303
Irwin, Charlie-Charles Edwin	93-95ChiN 96-01CinN 01-02BknN	02-15-69	Clinton, Ill.	09-21-25	R	R	5'10	170	990	3683	554	991	144	47	16	488	286		191	.269	.347
Irwin, Ed-Edward Edward	12DetA	??-??-82	Philadelphia, Pa.	02-05-16	R	R			1	3	0	2	1	0	0				0	.667	2.000
Isbell, Frank-William Frank (Bald Eagle) (See P01-19)	98StLN 01-09ChiA	08-21-75	Delavan, N.Y.	07-14-41	L	R	5'11	190	1119	4217	500	1056	156	62	13	455	190		253	.250	.327
Jacklitsch, Fred-Frederick Lawrence	00-02PhiN 03-04BknN 05NYA 07-10PhiN 14-15BalF 17BosN	05-24-76	Brooklyn, N.Y.	07-18-37	R	R	5'9	180	490	1344	160	327	64	12	5	153	201		35	.243	.320
Jackson, Bill-William Riley	14-15ChiF	04-04-81	Pittsburgh, Pa.	09-26-58	L	L	6'	150	76	123	17	17	1	0	0	13	17		3	.138	.171
Jackson, Charlie-Charles Herbert (Lefty)	15ChiA 17PitN 18MS	02-07-94	Granite City, Ill.	05-27-68	L	L	5'9	150	42	122	7	29	3	2	0	1	10	23	4	.238	.295
Jackson, George-George Christopher (Hickory)	11-13BosN	01-02-82	Springfield, Mo.	11-25-72	R	R	6'	180	152	554	85	158	24	7	4	73	50	95	34	.285	.375
Jackson, Jim-James Benner	01BalA 02NYN 05-06CleA	11-28-77	Philadelphia, Pa.	10-09-55	R	R	6'1	180	347	1269	158	299	47	10	4	132	107		57	.236	.298
Jackson, Joe-Joseph Jefferson (Shoeless Joe)	08-09PhiA 10-15CleA 15-20ChiA 20DL	07-16-89	Brandon Mills, S.C.	12-05-51	L	R	6'1	200	1330	4981	873	1774	307	168	54	785	519		202	.356	.518
Jacobs, Mike-Morris Elmore	02ChiN	12-??-77	Louisville, Ky.	03-21-49					2	9	1	2	0	0	0	0	1		0	.211	.211
Jacobs, Otto-Otto Albert	18ChiA	04-19-89	Chicago, Ill.	11-19-55	R	R	5'9	180	29	73	4	15	3	1	0	5	3	8	0	.205	.274
James, Bob-Barton Hulon (Jesse)	09StLN	07-07-84	Coopertown, Tenn.	01-02-59	R	R	5'11	185	6	21	1	6	0	0	0	4	0		0	.286	.286
Jansen, Ray-Raymond William	10StLA	01-06-89	St. Louis, Mo.	03-19-34	R	R	5'11	165	1	5	1	4	0	0	0	2			0	.800	.800
Jantzen, Heinie-Walter Charles	12StlA	04-09-90	Chicago, Ill.	04-01-48	R	R	5'11	170	31	119	10	22	5	1	0	11	5		3	.185	.227
Janvrin, Hal-Harold Chandler (Childe Harold)	11,13-17BosA 18MS 19WasA 19-21StLN 21-22BknN	08-27-92	Haverhill, Mass.	03-02-62	R	R	5'11	168	756	2221	250	515	68	18	6	210	171		79	.232	.287
Jenkins, Joe-Joseph Daniel	14StLA 17ChiA 18MS 19CleA	10-12-90	Shelbyville, Tenn.	06-21-74	R	R	5'11	170	40	60	7	8	1	0	0	5		17	3	.133	.200
Jennings, Hughie-Hugh Ambrose (Ee-Yah)	91LouAA 92-93LouN 93-99BalN 99-00BknN 01-02PhiN 03BknN 07,09,12,18,M07-20DetA	04-02-69	Pittston, Pa.	02-01-28	R	R	5'8	165	1274	4884	996	1530	227	88	18	840	347		372	.313	.407
Johns, Pete-William R.	15ChiA 18StLA	01-17-88	Cleveland, Ohio	08-09-64	R	R	5'11	165	74	189	12	37	3	2	0	22	12	17	2	.196	.233
Johnson, Bill-William Lawrence	16-17PhiN	10-18-92	Chicago, Ill.	11-05-50	R	R	5'9	180	52	124	8	23	3	0	1	5	7	18	4	.185	.266
Johnson, Charlie-Charles Cleveland (Home Run)	08PhiN	03-12-85	Slatington, Pa.	08-28-40	L	L	5'9	150	6	16	2	4	0	0	0	2	1		0	.250	.375

USE NAME - GIVEN NAMES (NICKNAMES)	TEAM BY YEAR	BIRTH DATE	BIRTH PLACE	DEATH DATE	B	T	HGT	WGT	G	AB	R	H	2B	3B	HR	RBI	BB	SO	SB	BA	SA
Johnson, Elmer-Elmer Ellsworth (Hickory)	14NYN	06-12-84	Beard, Ind.	10-31-66	R	R	5'9	185	11	12	0	2	1	0	0		0	1	3	0	.167	.250
Johnson, Ote-Otis L. (Home Run)	11NYA	11-05-83	Fowler, Ind.	11-09-15	R	R	5'9	185	71	209	21	49	9	6	3		36	39		12	.234	.378
Johnson, Walter-Walter Perry (The Big Train, Barney) (See P01-19)	11WasA 07-27,M29-32WasA M33-35CleA	11-06-87	Humboldt, Kans.	12-10-46	R	R	6'1	200	937	2329	242	549	94	41	24		256	113		13	.236	.342
Johnston, Doc-Wheeler Roger	09CinN 12-14CleA 15-16PitN 18-21CleA 22PhiA	09-09-87	Chattanooga, Tenn.	02-17-61	L	L	6'	170	1055	3774	478	992	154	68	14		379	264		139	.263	.351
Johnston, Johnny-John Thomas	13StLA	03-28-90	Longview, Tex.	03-07-40	L	R	5'11	172	109	380	37	85	14	4	2		27	45	51	11	.224	.297
Jones, Bill-William Dennis (Midget)	11-12BosN	04-08-87	Hartland, Canada	10-10-46	R	R	5'6	157	27	53	6	12	2	1	0		5	15	8	1	.226	.302
Jones, Charlie-Charles Claude (Casey)	01BosA 04ChiA 05-07WasA 08StLA	06-02-76	Butler, Pa.	04-02-47	R	R	6'1	165	483	1799	217	420	56	28	5		144	93		100	.233	.304
Jones, Davy-David Jefferson (Kangaroo)	01MilA 02StLA 02-04DetA 06-12DetA 13ChiA 14-15PitF	06-30-80	Cambria, Wis.	03-30-72	R	R	5'10	165	1085	3772	643	1020	98	40	9		289	478		207	.270	.325
Jones, Fielder-Fielder Allison	96-00BknN 01-08,M04-08ChiA 14-15,M14-15StLF M16-18StLA	08-13-71	Shinglehouse, Pa.	03-13-34	L	R	5'11	180	1787	6761	1181	1929	200	76	22		633	817		359	.285	.348
Jones, Jimmy-James Tilford (Sheriff)	97LouN 01-02NYN	12-25-76	London, Ky.	05-06-53	R	R	5'10	150	90	344	28	79	16	4	0		24	18		9	.230	.299
Jones, Tex-William Roderick	11ChiA	08-04-85	Marion, Kans.	02-26-38	R	R	6'1	190	9	31	4	6	1	0	0		4	3		1	.194	.226
Jones, Tom-Thomas	02BalA 04-09StLA 09-10DetA	01-22-77	Honesdale, Pa.	06-19-23	R	R	6'1	190	1058	3847	341	964	123	34	3		336	193		135	.251	.303
Jordan, Dutch-Adolf Otto	03-04BknN	01-05-80	Pittsburgh, Pa.	12-23-72	R	R	5'10	185	165	519	48	108	21	3	0		40	32		16	.208	.260
Jordan, Slats-Clarence Veasey	01-02BalA	09-27-78	Baltimore, Md.	12-07-53	L	L	6'1	190	2	7	0	0	0	0	0		0	0		0	.000	.000
Jordan, Tim-Timothy Joseph (Hoboken)	01WasA 01-02BalA 03NYA 06-10BknN	02-14-79	New York, N.Y.	09-13-49	L	L	6'1	170	542	1820	220	474	74	24	32		232	254		48	.260	.380
Joyce, Mike (See Mike O'Neill-see P01-19)																					
Jude, Frank-Frank	06CinN	11-11-84	Libby, Minn.	05-04-61	R	R	5'7	150	80	308	31	64	6	4	1		31	16		7	.208	.263
Kading, Jack-John Frederick	10PitN 14ChiF	11-27-84	Waukesha, Wis.	06-02-64	R	R	6'3	190	11	26	5	7	2	1	0		4	4		0	.269	.423
Kafora, Jake-Frank Jacob (Tomatoes)	13-14PitN	10-16-88	Chicago, Ill.	03-23-28	R	R	6'	180	22	24	3	3	0	0	0		3	3	7	0	.125	.125
Kahl, Nick-Nicholas Alexander	05CleA	04-10-79	Coulterville, Ill.	07-13-59	R	R	5'9	185	39	131	16	29	4	1	0		21	4		1	.221	.267
Kahoe, Mike-Michael Joseph	95,99-01CinN 01-02ChiN 02-04StLA 05PhiN 07ChiN 07-09WasA	09-03-73	Yellow Springs, Ohio	05-14-49	R	R	6'	190	410	1311	103	278	44	14	4		105	39		21	.212	.276
Kaiser, Al-Alfred Edward (Deerfoot)	11CinN 11-12BosN 14IndF	08-03-86	Cincinnati, Ohio	04-11-69	R	R	5'10	180	155	481	58	104	15	7	3		38	34		16	.216	.295
Kalahan, John-John Joseph	05StLA	09-30-78	Philadelphia, Pa.	06-20-52	R	R	6'	165	1	5	0	0	0	0	0		0	0		0	.000	.000
Kane, Frank-Francis Thomas (Sugar)	15BknF 19NYA	03-05-95	Whitman, Mass.	09-09-62	R	R	5'11	175	4	11	2	2	0	1	0		2	1		0	.182	.364
Kane, Jim-James Joseph (Shamus)	08PitN	11-27-81	Scranton, Pa.	10-02-47	L	L	6'2	225	55	145	16	35	3	3	0		22	12		5	.241	.303
Kane, John-John Francis	07-08CinN 09-10ChiN	09-24-82	Pittsburg, Kans.	01-28-34	R	R	5'6	138	261	824	118	181	21	11	7		59	76		53	.220	.297
Karst, John-John Gottlieb (King)	15BknN	10-15-93	Philadelphia, Pa.	05-21-76	R	R	5'11	175	1	0	0	0	0	0	0		0	0		0	——	——
Kauff, Benny-Benjamin Michael (The Ty Cobb of the Feds)	12NYA 14IndF 15BknF 16-20NYN 21DL	01-05-90	Pomeroy, Ohio	11-17-61	L	L	5'8	157	859	3094	521	961	169	57	49		454	367		234	.311	.450
Kauffman, Dick-Howard Richard	14-15StLA	06-22-88	East Lewisburg, Pa.	04-16-48	R	R	6'3	190	44	139	10	36	9	2	0		16	5	30	0	.259	.353
Kavanagh, Charlie-Charles Hugh (Silk)	14ChiA	06-09-91	Chicago, Ill.	09-06-73	R	R	5'10	170	5	5	0	1	0	0	0		0	2		0	.200	.200
Kavanagh, Leo-Leo Daniel	14ChiF	08-09-94	Chicago, Ill.	08-10-50	R	R	5'9	180	5	11	0	3	0	0	0		1	0		0	.273	.273
Kavanagh, Marty-Martin Joseph	14-16DetA 16-18CleA 18StLN 18DetA	06-13-91	Harrison, N.J.	07-28-60	L	R	5'9	187	369	1033	138	257	47	20	9		122	118	122	26	.249	.359
Kay, Bill-Walter Brocton (King Bill)	07WasA	02-05-78	New Castle, Va.	12-03-45	L	R	6'2	180	25	60	8	20	1	1	0		7	0		1	.333	.383
Keating, Chick-Walter Francis	13-15ChiN 26PhiN	08-08-91	Philadelphia, Pa.	07-13-59	R	R	5'9	155	30	45	5	4	1	1	0		0	6	13	1	.089	.156
Keeler, (O')Kelleher), Willie-William Henry (Wee Willie)	92-93NYN 93BknN 94-98BalN 99-02BknN 03-09NYA 10NYN	03-03-72	Brooklyn, N.Y.	01-01-23	L	L	5'4	140	2125	8570	1720	2955	234	155	34		810	524		519	.345	.420
Keen, Brown-William Brown (Rebel, Buster)	12WasA	08-16-92	Ogelthorpe, Ga.	07-16-47	R	R	6'	181	6	7	0	0	0	0	0		0	0		0	.000	.000
Keister, Bill-William Hoffman (Wagon Tongue)	96BalN 98BosN 99BalN 00StLN 01BalA 02WasA 03PhiN	08-17-71	Baltimore, Md.	08-19-24	R	R	5'5	168	621	2435	401	759	133	63	17		399	90		134	.312	.439
Keliher, Mickey-Maurice Michael	11-12PitN	01-11-90	Washington, D.C.	09-07-30	L	L	6'	175	4	7	1	0	0	0	0		0	0		0	.000	.000
Kelleher, Duke-Albert Aloysius	09-30-93	New York, N.Y.	09-28-47	R	5'7			1	0	0	0	0	0	0		0	0		0	——	——
Kelley, Joe-Joseph James	91BosN 92PitN 92-98BalN 99-01BknN 02BalA 02-06,M02-05CinN 08,M08BosN	12-09-71	Cambridge, Mass.	08-14-43	R	R	5'11	190	1836	6989	1425	2245	353	189	66		1194	911		458	.321	.454
Kelliher, Frank-Francis Mortimer (Yucca)	19WasA	05-23-99	Somerville, Mass.	03-04-56	L	L	5'11	180	1	1	0	0	0	0	0		0	0		0	.000	.000
Kellogg, Bill-William Dearstyne	14CinN	05-25-84	Albany, N.Y.	12-12-71	R	R	5'10	153	71	126	14	22	0	1	0		7	14	28	7	.175	.190
Kelly, Barney (See Bob Taggert)																					
Kelly, Billy-William Joseph	10StLA 11-13PitN	05-01-86	Baltimore, Md.	06-03-40	R	R	6'	183	104	224	32	65	5	4	1		20	5	30	9	.290	.362
Kelly, Joe-Joseph Henry	14PitN 16ChiN 17-19BosN	09-23-86	Weir City, Kans.	08-16-77	R	R	5'9	172	376	1341	131	300	38	22	6		117	80	143	66	.224	.298
Kelly, John-John Benedict	07StLN	03-13-79	Clifton Heights, Pa.	03-19-44			5'9	165	52	197	12	37	5	0	0		6	13		7	.188	.213
Kelly, Red-Albert Michael	10ChiA	11-15-84	Union, Ill.	02-04-61	R	R	5'11	165	14	45	6	7	1	0	0		0	6		1	.156	.200
Kelly, Speed-Robert Brown	09WasA	08-19-84	Bryan, Ohio	05-06-49	R	R	6'2	185	17	42	3	6	2	1	0		1	3		1	.143	.236
Kelsey, Billy-George William	07PitN	08-24-81	Covington, Ohio	04-25-68	R	R	5'10	160	2	5	1	2	0	0	0		1	1		0	.400	.400
Kennedy, Ray-Raymond Lincoln	16StLA	05-19-95	Pittsburgh, Pa.	01-18-69	R	R	5'9	165	1	1	0	0	0	0	0		0	0		0	.000	.000
Kennedy, Snapper-Sherman Montgomery	02ChiN	11-01-78	Conneaut, Ohio	08-15-45	B	R	5'10	165	1	5	0	0	0	0	0		0	0		0	.000	.000
Kenworthy, Duke-William Jennings (Iron Duke)	12WasA 14-15KCF 17StLA	07-04-86	Cambridge, Ohio	09-21-50	B	R	5'7	165	285	989	159	301	71	21	18		146	67		61	.304	.473
Kerlin, Orie-Orie Milton (Cy)	15PitF	01-23-91	Summerfield, Ill.	10-29-74	L	R	5'7	150	3	1	0	0	0	0	0		0	0		0	.000	.000
Kerr, Doc-John Jonas	14PitF 14-15BalF	01-17-82	Delroy, Ohio	06-09-37	R	R	5'10	190	59	111	8	28	5	3	0		8	12		1	.252	.306
Kerwin, (Kervin), Dan-Daniel Patrick	03CinN	09-09-74	Philadelphia, Pa.	07-13-60	L	L	5'9	164	2	6	1	4	1	0	0		1	2		0	.667	.833
Ketchum, Fred-Frederick L.	99LouN 01PhiA	07-27-75	Elmira, N.Y.	03-12-68	L	R	5'8	157	20	83	18	24	1	0	0		0	0		4	.289	.301
Ketter, (Ketterer), Phil-Philip	12StLA	04-13-84	St. Louis, Mo.	04-09-65	R	R			2	0	0	0	0	0	0		0	0		0	——	——
Kibble, Jack-John Wesley (Happy)	12CleA	01-02-92	Seatonville, Ill.	12-13-69	B	R	5'9	154	5	8	1	2	0	0	0		0	0		0	.333	.333
Kilhullen, Pat-Joseph Isadore	14PitN	08-10-90	Carbondale, Pa.	10-25-22	R	R	5'9	175	1	2	0	0	0	0	0		1	0		0	.000	.000
Killefer, Bill-William Lavier (Reindeer Bill)	09-10StLA 11-17PhiN 18-21,M21-25ChiN M30-33StLA	10-10-87	Bloomingdale, Mich.	07-02-60	R	R	5'10	180	1035	3150	237	751	86	21	4		240	113		39	.238	.286
Killefer, Red-Wade Hampton (Lollypop)	07-09DetA 09-10WasA 14-16CinN 16NYN	04-13-85	Bloomingdale, Mich.	09-04-58	R	R	5'9	175	467	1537	181	381	61	16	3		116	128		57	.248	.304
King, Fred (See John Butler)																					
King, Lee-Edward Lee	16PhiA 19BosN	01-24-84	New Britain, Conn.	09-07-38	R	R	5'10	150	44	145	13	27	1	2	0		8	7	15	4	.186	.221
Kingman, Harry-Henry Lees	14NYA	04-03-92	Tientsin, China	12-27-82	L	L	6'1	165	4	3	0	0	0	0	0		0	0	0	0	.000	.000
Kinsella, Bob-Robert Francis (Red)	19-20NYN	01-05-99	Springfield, Ill.	12-30-51	L	R	5'9	165	4	12	1	3	0	0	0		1	0	5	1	.250	.250
Kippert, Ed-Edward August	14CinN	01-23-79	Detroit, Mich.	03-03-60	R	R	5'10	180	2	2	0	0	0	0	0		0	0		0	.000	.000
Kirby, LaRue-LaRue (See P01-19)	12NYN 14-15StLF	12-30-89	Eureka, Mich.	06-10-61	B	R	6'	185	116	378	37	87	14	5	2		34	31		8	.230	.310
Kirke, Jay-Judson Fabian	10DetA 11-13BosN 14-15CleA 18NYN	06-16-88	Fleischmanns, N.Y.	08-31-68	L	R	6'1	195	320	1148	122	346	49	13	7		148	35		21	.301	.385
Kirkpatrick, Enos-Enos Claire	12-13BknN 14-15BalF	12-09-84	Pittsburgh, Pa.	04-14-64	R	R	5'11	185	203	528	70	125	20	9	4		64	70		22	.237	.314
Kittredge, (Kittredge), Mal-Malachi Jeddidah	90-97ChiN 98-99LouN 99WasN 01-03BosN 03-06,M04WasA 06CleA	10-12-69	Clinton, Mass.	06-23-28	R	R	5'10	170	1212	4005	376	882	110	31	17		390	314		65	.220	.276
Kleinow, Red-John Peter (Doc, Jack)	04-10NYA 10-11BosA 11PhiN	07-20-77	Milwaukee, Wis.	10-09-29	R	R	5'10	165	584	1665	146	354	45	20	3		13	153		42	.213	.269
Kling, Johnny-John (Noisy)	00-08ChiN 09HO 10-11ChiN 11-12,M12BosN 13CinN	11-13-75	Kansas City, Mo.	01-31-47	R	R	5'9	160	1260	4241	474	1149	176	64	20		513	281		121	.271	.357
Kling, Rudy-Rudolph A.	02StLN	03-14-37	St. Louis, Mo.		R	R	5'10	178	4	10	1	2	0	0	0		0	0		1	.200	.200
Knabe, Otto-Franz Otto (Frank, Dutch)	05PitN 07-13PhiN 14-15,M14-15BalF 16PitN 16ChiN	06-12-84	Carrick, Pa.	05-17-61	R	R	5'8	175	1275	4469	572	1103	177	50	8		365	485		143	.247	.314
Knaupp, Cotton-Henry Antone	10-11CleA	08-13-89	San Antonio, Tex.	07-06-67	R	R	5'9	165	31	98	5	18	4	1	0		11	8		4	.184	.245
Knight, Jack-John Wesley (Schoolboy)	05-07PhiA 07BosA 09-11NYA 12WasA 13NYN	10-06-85	Philadelphia, Pa.	12-19-65	R	R	6'2	180	767	2664	301	636	96	24	14		270	211		86	.239	.309
Knisely, Pete-Peter Cole	12CinN 13-15ChiN	08-11-83	Waynesburg, Pa.	07-01-48	R	R	5'9	185	124	272	27	64	16	4	0		29	24	30	4	.235	.324
Knoll, Punch-Charles Elmer	05WasA	10-07-81	Evansville, Ind.	02-08-60	R	R	5'7	170	85	244	24	52	10	5	0		29	9		3	.213	.295
Knotts, Joe-Joseph Steven	07BosN	03-03-84	Greensboro, N.C.	09-15-50	R	R	5'9	170	3	3	0	0	0	0	0		0	0		0	.000	.000
Kocher, Brad-Bradley Wilson	12DetA 15-16NYN	01-16-88	White Haven, Pa.	02-13-65	R	R	5'11	188	62	139	9	25	5	2	0		12	6		0	.180	.245
Koehler, Ben-Bernard James	05-06StLA	09-17-76	Schoerndorn, Germany	05-21-61	R	R	5'10	175	208	722	82	168	15	7	2		62	56		31	.233	.292
Kolseth, Karl-Karl Dickey (Koley)	14BalF 15BalF	12-25-92	Cambridge, Mass.	03-03-56	L	R	6'	182	6	23	1	6	1	0	0		1	1		0	.261	.391
Kommers, Fred-Fred Raymond (Bugs)	13PitN, 14StLF 14BalF	03-31-86	Chicago, Ill.	06-14-43	L	R	6'	175	132	441	52	120	15	12	4		64	41		8	.272	.388
Konetchy, Ed-Edward Joseph (Big Ed)	07-13StLN 14PitN 15PitF 16-18BosN 19-21BknN 21PhiN	09-03-85	LaCrosse, Wis.	05-27-47	R	R	6'2	195	2084	7649	971	2146	344	181	74		992	689		255	.281	.402
Konnick, Mike-Michael Aloysius	09-10CinN	07-09-71	Glen Lyon, Pa.	07-09-72	R	R	5'9	180	3	4	0	1	0	0	0		1	0		0	.250	.375
Kopf, Larry-William Lorenz (Played as Fred Brady 13)	13CleA 14-15PhiA 16-17CinN 18MS 19-21CinN 22-23BosN	11-03-90	Bristol, Conn.	10-15-86	B	R	5'9	160	850	3009	348	749	83	30	5		266	242	214	72	.249	.301
Kopp, Manny-Merlin Henry	15WasA 18-19PhiA	01-02-92	Toledo, Ohio	05-06-60	B	R	5'6	158	187	630	96	146	9	11	2		30	89	105	39	.232	.286
Kores, Art-Arthur Emil (Dutch)	15StLF	07-22-86	Milwaukee, Wis.	03-26-74	R	R	5'9	167	60	201	18	47	9	2	0		22	21		6	.234	.313
Kraft, Clarence-Clarence Otto (Big Boy)	14BosN	06-09-87	Evansville, Ind.	03-26-58	R	R	6'	190	3	3	0	1	0	0	0		1	1		0	.333	.333
Krause, Charlie-Charles Fredrick	01CinN	10-02-73	Detroit, Mich.		R	R	5'6		1	4	1	1	0	0	0		0	0		0	.250	.250
Kreitz, Ralph-Ralph Wesley (Red)	11ChiA	01-13-85	Plum Creek, Neb.	07-20-41	R	R	5'9	175	7	4	0	1	0	0	0		0	0		0	.250	.250
Krichell, Paul-Paul Bernard	11-12StLA	12-19-82	New York, N.Y.	06-04-57	R	R	5'7	150	85	243	25	54	9	2	0		16	23		4	.222	.276
Krueger, Ernie-Ernest George	13CleA 15NYA 17NYN 17-21BknN 25CinN	12-27-90	Chicago, Ill.	04-22-76	R	R	5'10	185	318	836	87	220	33	14	11		93	64	85	12	.263	.376

USE NAME - GIVEN NAMES (NICKNAMES)	TEAM BY YEAR	BIRTH DATE	BIRTH PLACE	DEATH DATE	B	T	HGT	WGT	G	AB	R	H	2B	3B	HR	RBI	BB	SO	SB	BA	SA
Krueger, Otto-Arthur William ('Oom Paul)	99CleN 00-02StLN 03-04PhiN 05PhiN	09-17-76	Chicago, Ill.	02-20-61	R	R	5'7	165	507	1704	230	427	40	33	5		196	160		48	.251	.322
Krug, Henry-Henry Charles	02PhiN	12-04-76	San Francisco, Cal.	01-14-08	R	R			53	198	20	45	3	3	0		14	7		2	.227	.273
Kruger, Art-Arthur Theodore	07CinN 10CleA 10BosN 10CleA 10KCF	03-16-81	San Antonio, Tex.	11-28-49	R	R	6'	185	365	1222	133	283	49	21	6		115	73		38	.232	.321
Kuhn, Walt-Charles Walter (Red)	12-14ChiA	02-02-87	Fresno, Cal.	06-14-35	R	R	5'7	162	118	268	25	55	9	0	0		15	41		8	.205	.239
Kustus, Joe-Joseph J. (Jul)	09BknN	09-05-82	Detroit, Mich.	04-27-16	R	R	5'10		53	173	12	25	1	1	0		11	11		9	.145	.191
Kutina, Joe-Joseph Peter	11-12StLA	01-16-85	Chicago, Ill.	04-13-45	R	R	6'2	205	93	306	30	68	15	5	4		33	15		2	.222	.333
Kyle, Andy-Andrew Ewing	12CinN	10-29-89	Toronto, Canada	09-06-71	L	L	5'8	160	9	21	3	7	0	1	0		4	4	2	0	.333	.381
LaChance, Candy-George Joseph	93-98BknN 99BalN 01CleA 02-05BosA	02-14-70	Putnam, Conn.	08-18-32	L	R	6'1	183	1261	4934	681	1382	199	89	39		690	219		210	.280	.380
Lajoie, Nap-Napoleon (Larry)	96-00PhiN 01-02PhiA 02-14, M05-09CleA 15-16PhiA	09-05-74	Woonsocket, R.I.	02-07-59	R	R	6'1	195	2480	9593	1504	3245	661	163	83		1599	516		383	.338	.467
Lake, Fred-Frederick Lovett	91BosN 94LouN 97BosN 98PiN M08-09BosA	10-16-66	Cornwallis, Canada	11-24-31	R	R	5'10	170	48	123	12	29	7	0	1		16	17		4	.236	.317
	10, M10BosN																				
Lamer(Lamers), Pete-Pierre	02CinN 07CinN	12-27-73	New York, N.Y.	10-24-31		R	5'10	170	3	11	2	2	0	0	0		0	0		0	.182	.182
Land, Grover-Grover Cleveland	08,10-11,13CleA 14-15BknF	09-22-84	Frankfort, Ky.	07-22-58	R	R	6'	190	292	906	62	219	26	5	2		79	27		14	.242	.288
Lanning, Les-Lester Alfred	16PhiN	05-13-95	Harvard, Ill.	06-13-62	L	L	5'9	155	19	33	5	6	2	0	0		1	10	9	0	.182	.242
LaPorte, Frank-Frank Breyfogle (Pot)	05-08NYA 08BosA 08-10NYA 11-12StLA	02-06-80	Uhrichsville, Ohio	09-25-39	R	R	5'8	175	1193	4212	501	1185	198	80	14		560	288		101	.281	.376
	12-13WasA 14IndF 15NwkF																				
Lapp, Jack-John Walker	08-15PhiA 16ChiA	09-10-84	Frazer, Pa.	02-06-20	L	R	5'8	175	565	1581	168	416	59	26	5		166	177		16	.263	.343
Larkin, Ed-Edward Francis	09PhiA	07-01-85	Wyalusing, Pa.	03-28-34	R	R	5'8		2	6	0	1	0	0	0		1	1		0	.167	.167
Larmore, Bob-Robert McCahan (Red)	18StLN	12-06-96	Anderson, Ind.	01-15-64	R	R	5'10	185	4	7	0	2	0	0	0		0	0	2	0	.286	.286
LaRoss, Harry-Harry Raymond (Spike)	14CinN	01-02-88	Easton, Pa.	03-22-54	R	R	5'11	170	22	48	7	11	1	0	0		5	2	10	4	.229	.250
Latham, Arlie-Walter Arlington (The Freshest Man on Earth)	80BufN 83-89StLAA	03-15-60	West Lebanon, N.H.	11-29-52	R	R	5'8	150	1621	6815	1470	1851	249	86	27		641	589		791	.272	.345
	90ChiP 90-95CinN 96,M96StLN 99WasN 09NYN										*For Latham, Stolen Bases include the years 86-09*										
Lathers, Chick-Charles Ten Eyck	10-11DetA	10-22-88	Dearborn, Mich.	07-26-71	L	R	6'	180	70	127	9	29	3	0	0		7	13		0	.228	.252
Latimer, Tacks-Clifford Wesley	98NYN 99LouN 00PitN 01BalA 02BknN	11-30-77	Loveland, Ohio	04-24-36	R	R	6'	180	27	86	5	19	3	0	0		2	1		1	.221	.256
Lauder, Billy-William	98-99PhiN 01PhiA 02-03NYN	02-23-74	New York, N.Y.	05-20-33	R	R	5'10	160	481	1823	207	476	64	14	6		254	77		60	.261	.321
Lauterborn, Bill-William Bernard	04-05BosN	06-09-79	Hornell, N.Y.	04-19-65	R	R	5'6	140	87	269	18	56	3	1	0		11	13		2	.208	.227
Lavan(Laven), Doc-John Leonard	13StLA 13PhiA 14-17StLA 18WasA 19-24StLN	10-28-90	Grand Rapids, Mich.	05-30-52	R	R	5'8	151	1162	3891	338	954	134	45	7		377	209	376	71	.245	.308
LaVigne, Art-Arthur David	14BufF	01-26-85	Worcester, Mass.	07-18-50	R	R	5'10	162	51	90	10	14	2	0	0		4	7		0	.156	.178
Lawry, Otis-Otis Carrol (Rabbit)	16-17PhiA 19-19MS	11-01-93	Fairfield, Me.	10-23-65	L	R	5'8	153	71	178	17	34	1	0	0		5	11	30	5	.191	.197
Layden, Gene-Eugene Francis	15NYA	03-14-94	Pittsburgh, Pa.	12-12-84	L	L	5'9	160	3	7	2	2	0	0	0		0	0		0	.286	.286
Leach, Tommy-Thomas William (Tommy the Wee)	98-99LouN 00-12PitN	11-04-77	French Creek, N.Y.	09-29-69	R	R	5'6	150	2147	7954	1352	2144	277	170	62		810	820		364	.270	.371
	12-14ChiN 15CinN 18PitN																				
Leahy, Tom-Thomas Joseph	97PitN 97-98WasN 09MilA 01PhiA 05StLN	06-02-69	New Haven, Conn.	06-12-51	R	R	5'11	168	131	411	55	106	15	10	0		42	44		17	.258	.343
Lear, Fred-Frederick Francis (King)	15PhiA 18-19ChiN 20NYN	04-07-94	New York, N.Y.	10-13-55	R	R	6'	180	75	166	16	39	3	2	2		18	17	28	4	.235	.313
Leard, Bill-William Wallace (Wild Bill)	17BknN	10-14-85	Oneida, N.Y.	01-15-70	R	R	5'10	155	3	3	0	0	0	0	0		0	0		0	.000	.000
Leary, John-John Louis (Jack)	14-15StLA	05-02-91	Waltham, Mass.	08-18-61	R	R	5'11	170	219	760	54	196	38	7	0		60	15	107	11	.258	.326
Leber, Emil-Emil Bohmiel	05CleA	05-15-81	Cleveland, Ohio	11-06-24	R	R	5'11	170	2	6	1	0	0	0	0		0	0		0	.000	.000
Lee, Billy-William Joseph	15-16StLN	01-09-94	Bayonne, N.J.	01-06-84	R	R	5'9	165	25	70	3	13	0	0	0		4	7		1	.186	.200
Lee, Watty-Wyatt Arnold (Indian) (See P01-19)	01-03WasA 04PhiN	12-12-79	Lynch Station, Va.	03-06-36	L	L	5'10	180	235	763	94	185	35	13	4		70	58		13	.242	.338
Lehr, Clarence-Clarence Emanuel (King)	11PhiN	05-16-86	Escanaba, Mich.	01-31-48	R	R	5'11	165	23	27	2	4	0	0	0		2	0	7	0	.148	.148
Leibold, Nemo-Harry Loran	13-15CleA 15-20ChiA 21-23BosA 23-25WasA	02-17-92	Butler, Ind.	02-04-77	L	L	5'6	157	1258	4167	638	1109	145	48	5		283	571	335	133	.266	.327
Leinhauser, Bill-William Charles	12DetA	11-04-93	Philadelphia, Pa.	04-14-78	R	R	5'10	150	1	4	0	0	0	0	0		0	0		0	.000	.000
LeJeune, Larry-Sheldon Aldenbert	11BknN 15PitN	07-22-85	Chicago, Ill.	04-21-52	R	R	6'	185	24	84	6	14	0	1	0		4	4	15	6	.167	.190
Lelivelt, Jack-John Frank	09-11WasA 12-13NYA 13-14CleA	11-14-85	Chicago, Ill.	01-20-41	L	L	5'11	175	381	1154	114	347	43	22	2		126	89		46	.301	.381
Lennox, Ed-James Edgar (Eggie)	06PhiA 09-10BknN 12ChiN 14-15PitF	11-03-83	Camden, N.J.	10-26-39	R	R	5'11	175	448	1383	138	379	70	25	18		185	174		38	.274	.400
Leonard, Joe-Joseph Howard	14PitN 16CleA 16-17WasA 18MS 19-20WasA	11-15-94	West Chicago, Ill.	05-01-20	L	R	5'7	156	269	791	94	179	23	12	2		61	99	113	17	.226	.293
LePine, Pete-Louis Joseph	02DetA	09-05-76	Montreal, Canada	12-03-49	L	L	5'10	142	30	96	9	20	3	2	1		19	8		1	.208	.271
Lerchen, Dutch-Bertram Roe	10BosA	04-04-89	Detroit, Mich.	01-07-62	R	R	5'9	165	6	15	1	0	0	0	0		0	0		0	.000	.000
Lewis, Duffy-George Edward	10-17BosA 18MS 19-20NYA 21WasA	04-18-88	San Francisco, Cal.	06-17-79	R	R	5'10	165	1459	5351	612	1518	289	68	38		793	352		113	.284	.384
Lewis, Jack-John David	11BknN 14-15PitF	02-14-84	Pittsburgh, Pa.	02-25-56	R	R	5'8	158	217	684	63	169	20	10	1		80	32		18	.247	.310
Lewis, Phil-Philip	05-08BknN	10-07-83	Pittsburgh, Pa.	08-08-59	R	R	6'	195	508	1775	146	429	33	13	4		130	95		55	.242	.282
Liese, Fred-Frederick Richard	10BosN	10-07-85	Wis.	06-30-67	L	L	5'8	150	5	4	0	0	0	0	0		0	1	2	0	.000	.000
Lindemann, Bob-John Frederick Mann	01PhiA	06-05-81	Philadelphia, Pa.	12-19-51	B	R	6'	175	3	9	0	1	0	0	0		0	0		0	.111	.111
Lindsay, Bill-William Gibbons	11CleA	02-24-81	Madison, N.C.	07-14-63	R	R	5'10	165	19	66	6	16	2	0	0		5	1		2	.242	.273
Lindsay, Pinky-Christian Haller (The Crab)	05-06CleA	07-24-78	Beaver Co., Pa.	01-25-41	R	R	6'	190	229	828	97	200	30	3	0		64	63		28	.242	.285
Lister, Pete-Morris Elmer	07CleA	07-21-81	Savanna, Ill.	03-27-47	R	R	6'	190	22	65	5	18	2	0	0		4	3		2	.277	.308
Little, Jack-William Arthur	12NYA	03-12-91	Mart, Tex.	07-27-61	R	R	5'11	175	3	12	2	3	0	0	0		0	1		1	.250	.250
Livingston, Paddy-Patrick Joseph	01CleA 06CinN 09-11PhiA 12CleA 17StLN	01-14-80	Cleveland, Ohio	09-19-77	R	R	5'8	197	205	574	48	120	17	12	0		45	41		9	.209	.280
Loan, Mike-William Joseph	12PhiN	09-27-94	Philadelphia, Pa.	11-21-66	R	R	5'8	185	1	2	1	1	0	0	0		1	0	0	0	.500	.500
Lobert, Frank-Frank John	14BalF	11-26-83	Williamsport, Pa.	05-29-32	R	R	6'	180	11	30	3	6	0	1	0		2	0		0	.200	.233
Lobert, Hans-John Bernard	03PitN 05ChiN 06-10CinN 11-14PhiN 15-17NYN M38-42PhiN	10-18-81	Wilmington, Del.	09-14-68	R	R	5'9	170	1317	4563	640	1252	159	82	32		482	395		316	.274	.366
Lochhead, Harry-Robert Henry	99CleN 01DetA 01PhiA	03-29-76	Stockton, Cal.	08-22-09	R	R	5'11	172	156	585	56	127	8	1	1		45	24		21	.217	.239
Lohr, Howie-Howard Sylvester	14CinN 16CleA	06-03-92	Philadelphia, Pa.	06-09-77	R	R	6'	165	21	54	6	11	1	1	0		8	0	9	3	.204	.259
Lonergen, Walt-Walter E.	11BosA	09-22-85	Boston, Mass.	01-23-58	R	R	5'7	156	10	26	2	7	0	0	0		1	1		1	.269	.269
Long, Herman-Herman C. (Germany, Dutch)	89KCAA 90-02BosN 03NYA 03DetA 04PhiA	04-13-66	Chicago, Ill.	09-17-09	L	R	5'8	160	1870	7657	1456	2142	317	97	92		1054	612		554	.280	.383
Long, Tommy-Thomas Augustus	11-12WasA 15-17StLN	06-01-90	Coffeyville, Ala.	06-15-72	R	R	5'10	165	418	1489	148	401	47	49	6		140	79		65	.269	.379
Lord, Bris-Bristol Robotham (The Human Eyeball)	05-07PhiA 09-10CleA 10-12PhiA 13BosN	09-21-83	Upland, Pa.	11-13-64	R	R	5'9	185	741	2767	381	707	119	49	13		236	175		74	.256	.348
Lord, Harry-Harry Donald	07-10BosA 10-14ChiA 15,M15BufF	03-08-82	Porter, Me.	08-09-48	L	R	5'10	165	972	3689	506	1024	107	70	14		294	226		206	.278	.356
Louden, Baldy-William P. Jr.	07NYA 12-13DetA 14-15BufF 16CinN	08-27-83	Pittsburgh, Pa.	12-08-35	R	R	5'11	175	598	1942	267	507	61	22	12		202	254		112	.261	.344
Loudenslager, Charlie-Charles Edward	04BknN	05-21-81	Baltimore, Md.	10-31-33	L	R	5'9	186	1	2	0	0	0	0	0		0	0		0	.000	.000
Low, Fletcher-Fletcher	15BosN	04-07-93	Essex, Mass.	06-06-73	R	R	5'10	175	1	4	1	1	0	0	1		0	0		0	.250	.750
Lowe, Bobby-Robert Lincoln (Link)	90-01BosN 02-03ChiN 04PitN 04-07,M04DetA	07-10-68	Pittsburgh, Pa.	12-08-51	R	R	5'10	155	1814	7020	1129	1925	230	85	71		982	473		310	.274	.362
Luderus, Fred-Frederick William	09-10ChiN 10-20PhiN	09-12-85	Milwaukee, Wis.	01-04-61	L	R	5'11	185	1346	4851	570	1344	251	54	84		642	414		55	.277	.403
Ludwig, Bill-William Lawrence	08StLN	05-27-82	Louisville, Ky.	09-05-47	R	R			66	187	15	34	2	2	0		8	16		3	.182	.214
Lumley, Harry-Harry Garfield (Judge)	04-10, M09BknN	09-29-80	Forest City, Pa.	05-22-38	L	L	5'10	183	730	2653	300	728	109	66	38		305	204		110	.274	.408
Lunte, Harry-Harry August	19-20CleA	09-15-92	St. Louis, Mo.	07-27-65	R	R	5'11	165	49	148	8	29	2	0	0		9	6	13	0	.196	.209
Lush, Billy-William Lucas	95-97WasN 01-02BosN 03DetA 04CleA	11-10-73	Bridgeport, Conn.	08-28-51	B	R	5'8	165	497	1717	291	427	49	35	4		152	291		79	.249	.332
Lush, Ernie-Ernest Benjamin	10StLN	10-31-84	Birdsboro, Conn.	02-26-37	R	L			1	1	0	0	0	0	0		0	1	1	0	.000	.000
Lush, Johnny-John Charles (See P01-19)	04-07PhiN 07-10StLN	10-08-85	Williamsport, Pa.	11-18-46	L	L	5'9	165	369	993	107	252	40	11	2		94	69		28	.254	.322
Luskey, Charlie-Charles Melton	01WasA	04-06-76	Washington, D.C.	12-20-62	R	R	5'7	170	11	41	8	8	3	1	0		3	2		0	.195	.317
Lynch, Mike-Michael Joseph	02ChiN	09-10-75	St. Paul, Minn.	04-02-47	R	R	5'10	155	7	28	4	4	0	0	0		0	2		0	.143	.143
Lynn, Byrd-Byrd	16-20ChiA	03-13-89	Unionville, Ill.	02-05-40	R	R	5'11	165	116	211	15	50	9	1	0		15	18	31	3	.237	.289
MacGamwell, Ed-Edward M.	05BknN		Buffalo, N.Y.	05-26-24	L	L			4	15	0	4	0	0	0		0	0		0	.267	.267
Mack (McGillicuddy), Earle-Earle Thaddeus	10-11,14PhiA	02-01-90	Spencer, Mass.	02-05-67	L	R	5'8	140	5	16	0	2	0	0	0		0	0		0	.125	.250
Madden, Gene-Eugene	14PitF	06-05-90	Elm Grove, W.Va	04-06-49	L	R	5'10	155	1	0	0	0	0	0	0		0	0		0	.000	.000
Madden, Red-Francis A.	16PitN	10-17-92	Pittsburgh, Pa.	04-30-52					2	2	0	1	0	0	0		0	0		0	.500	.500
Madden, Tom-Thomas Francis (Bunny)	09-11BosA 11PhiN	09-14-82	Boston, Mass.	01-20-54	R	R	5'10	190	56	143	16	41	4	1	0		11	13		2	.287	.327
Madden, Tommy-Thomas Joseph	06BosN 10NYA	07-31-83	Philadelphia, Pa.	06-26-36	L	R	5'11	160	5	16	1	4	0	0	0		2	0		0	.250	.250
Magee (Hoernschemeyer), Lee-Leopold Christopher	11-14StLN 15-17NYA 17StLA 18CinN 19BknN 19CinN 20DL	06-04-89	Cincinnati, Ohio	03-14-66	B	R	5'11	165	1014	3739	467	1029	133	54	12		277	265		186	.275	.349
Magee, Sherry-Sherwood Robert	04-14PhiN 15-17BosN 17-19CinN	08-06-84	Clarendon, Pa.	03-13-29	R	R	5'11	180	2085	7441	1112	2169	425	166	83		1177	737		441	.291	.427
Maggert, Harl-Harl Vestin	07PitN 12PhiA	02-13-83	Cromwell, Ind.	01-07-63	L	R	5'8	155	75	248	40	62	8	6	1		13	38		11	.250	.343
Magner, Stubby-Edmund Burke	11NYA	02-10-88	Kalamazoo, Mich.	09-06-56	R	R	5'3	135	13	33	3	7	0	0	0		1	5		2	.212	.212
Magoon, Maggie-George Henry (Topsy)	98BknN 99BalN 99ChiN 01-03CinN 03CinN	03-27-75	St. Albans, Me.	12-06-43	R	R	5'9	165	521	1836	197	441	60	16	2		201	194		49	.240	.294
Mahar, Frank-Frank Edward	02PhiN	12-04-78	Natick, Mass.	12-05-61	R	R	5'10		1	1	0	0	0	0	0		0	0		0	.000	.000
Maharg, Billy-William Joseph	12DetA 16PhiN	03-19-81	Philadelphia, Pa.	11-20-53	R	R	5'5	150	2	3	0	0	0	0	0		0	0		0	.000	.000
Maher, Tom-Thomas Francis	02PhiN	??-??-75	N.Y.	08-25-29		R			1	0	0	0	0	0	0		0	0		0	—	—
Mahoney, Danny-Daniel Joseph	11CinN	09-06-88	Haverhill, Mass.	09-28-60	R	R	5'6	145	1	1	0	0	0	0	0		0	0		0	.000	.000
Maisel, Charlie-Charles Lewis	05BalF	04-21-94	Catonsville, Md.	08-25-53	R	R	6'		1	0	1	0	0	0	0		0	0		0	—	—
Maisel, Fritz-Frederick Charles (Flash)	13-17NYA 18StLA	12-23-89	Catonsville, Md.	04-22-67	R	R	5'7	170	591	2111	295	510	56	24	6		148	260	177	194	.242	.299
Malay, Charlie-Charles Francis	05BknN	06-13-79	Brooklyn, N.Y.	09-18-49	B	R	5'11	175	102	349	33	88	7	2	1		31	22		13	.252	.292

USE NAME - GIVEN NAMES (NICKNAMES)	TEAM BY YEAR	BIRTH DATE	BIRTH PLACE	DEATH DATE	B	T	HGT	WGT	G	AB	R	H	2B	3B	HR	RBI	BB	SO	SB	BA	SA
Malone, Lew-Lewis Aloysius	15-16PhiA 17BknN 18MS 19BknN	03-13-97	Baltimore, Md.	02-17-72	R	R	5'11	175	133	367	28	74	11	7	1	28	28	60	8	.202	.278
Maloney, Bill-William Alphonse	01MilA 02StLA 02CinN 05ChiN 06-08BknN	06-05-78	Lewiston, Me.	09-02-60	L	R	5'10	177	696	2476	294	585	54	42	6	177	162		155	.236	.299
Maloney, Pat-Patrick William	12NYA	01-19-88	Grosvenordale, Conn.	06-27-29	R	R	6'	150	22	79	9	17	1	0	0	4	6		3	.215	.228
Manda, Carl-Carl Alan	14ChiA	11-16-86	Little River, Kans.	03-09-83	R	R	5'10	170	9	15	2	4	0	0	0	1	3	3	1	.267	.267
Maney, Vince-Stephen Vincent	12DetA	10-14-86	Batavia, N.Y.	03-13-52	R	R	6'	175	1	2	0	0	0	0	0	0	0		0	.000	.000
Mangus, George-George Graham	12PhiN	05-22-90	Red Creek, N.Y.	08-10-33	L	R	5'11	165	10	25	2	5	3	0	0	3	1	6	0	.200	.320
Mann, Les-Leslie	13-14BosN 15ChiF 16-19ChiN 19-20BosN 21-23StLN 23CinN 24-27BosN 27-28NYN	11-18-92	Lincoln, Neb.	01-14-62	R	R	5'9	172	1498	4714	678	1331	205	106	44	503	324		192	.282	.399
Manush, Frank-Frank Henry Benjamin	08PhiA		Tuscumbia, Ala.	01-05-65	R	R	5'10	175	23	77	6	12	2	1	0	2	2		2	.156	.208
Marsans, Armando-Armando	11-14CinN 14-15StLF 16-17StLA 17-18NYA	10-03-86	Matanzas, Cuba	09-03-60	R	R	5'10	157	655	2273	267	612	67	19	2	221	173		171	.269	.318
Marshall, Doc-William Riddle	04PhiN 04NYN 04BosN 04,06NYN 06-08StLN 08ChiN 09BknN	09-22-75	Butler, Pa.	12-11-59	R	R	6'1	185	261	756	51	159	23	8	2	54	34		15	.210	.270
Marshall, Joe-Joseph Hanley (Home Run Joe)	03PitN 06StLN	02-19-76	Audubon, Minn.	09-11-31	R	R	5'8	170	43	118	4	21	2	4	0	9	6		0	.178	.263
Martel, Marty-Leon Alphonse (Doc)	09PhiN 10BosN	06-29-83	Weymouth, Mass.	10-11-47	R	R	6'	185	34	72	1	15	3	1	0	8	6		0	.208	.278
Martin, Billy-William Lloyd	14BosN	02-13-94	Washington, D.C.	09-14-49	R	R	5'8	170	1	3	0	0	0	0	0	0	0	0	0	.000	.000
Martin, Jack-John Christopher	12NYA 14BosN 14PhiN	04-19-87	Plainfield, N.J.	07-04-80	R	R	5'7	150	185	608	66	144	13	4	0	43	70		20	.237	.271
Martin, Joe-Joseph Samuel (Silent Joe)	03WasA 03StLA	01-01-76	Hollidaysburg, Pa.	05-25-64	L	L	5'9	155	79	292	29	64	10	9	0	14	11		2	.219	.315
Massey, Mike-William Herbert	17BosN	09-28-93	Galveston, Tex.	10-17-71	B	R	5'11	168	31	91	12	18	0	0	0	2	15	15	2	.198	.198
Massey, Roy-Roy Hardee (Red)	18BosN	10-09-90	Sevierville, Tenn.	06-23-54	L	R	5'11	170	66	203	22	59	6	2	0	18	23	20	1	.291	.340
Mathes, Joe-Joseph John	12PhiA 14StLF 16BosN	07-28-91	Milwaukee, Wis.	12-21-78	B	R	6'	180	32	99	10	27	3	0	0	6	3		1	.273	.303
Mathison, Jimmy-James Michael Ignatius	02BalA	11-11-78	Baltimore, Md.	07-04-11	R				29	91	12	24	2	1	0	7	9		2	.264	.308
Mattick, Chick-Walter Joseph	12-13ChiA 18StLN	03-12-87	St. Louis, Mo.	11-05-68	R	R	5'10	180	164	506	60	115	15	10	1	47	47		18	.227	.302
Mattis, Ralph-Ralph (Matty)	14PitF	08-24-90	Roxborough, Pa.	09-13-60	R	R	5'11	172	36	85	14	21	4	1	0	8	9		2	.247	.318
Maul, Al-Albert Joseph (Smiling Al) (See P01-19)	84PhiU 87PhiN 88-89PitN 90PitP 91PitN 93-97WasN 97-98BalN 99BknN 00PhiN 01NYN	10-09-65	Philadelphia, Pa.	05-03-58	R	R	6'	180	401	1350	191	328	44	30	7	179	182		46	.243	.336
Mayer (Erskine), Sam-Samuel Frankel (Craven)	15WasA	02-28-93	Atlanta, Ga.	07-01-62	R	L	5'8	155	11	29	5	7	0	0	1	4	4	2	1	.241	.345
Mayer, Wally-Walter A. (Kid)	11-12,14-15ChiA 17-18BosA 19StLA	08-08-90	Cincinnati, Ohio	11-18-51	R	R	5'11	168	129	274	22	53	14	3	0	20	42		1	.193	.266
Mayes, Paddy-Adair Bushyhead	11PhiN	03-17-85	Locust Grove, Okla.	05-28-63	L	R	5'11	160	5	5	1	0	0	0	0	0	0	2	0	.000	.000
McAleer, Jimmy-James Robert	89CleN 90CleP 91-98CleN 01,M01CleA 02,07,M02-09StLA M10-11WasA	07-10-64	Youngstown, Ohio	04-29-31	R	R	6'	175	1017	3972	614	1031	114	38	13	469	365		262	.260	.317
McAleese, John-John James (See P01-19)	01ChiA 09StLA	08-22-77	Sharon, Pa.	11-15-50	R	R	5'8		86	268	33	57	7	0	0	12	32		18	.213	.239
McAllester, Bill-William Lusk	13StLA	12-29-88	Chattanooga, Tenn.	03-03-70	R	R	5'11	170	47	85	3	13	4	0	0	6	11	12	2	.153	.200
McAllister, Sport-Lewis William (See P01-19)	96-99CleN 01-02DetA 02BalA 02-03DetA	07-23-74	Austin, Miss.	07-17-62	B	R	5'11	180	416	1441	154	357	35	18	5	164	67		33	.248	.307
McAuley, Ike-James Earl	14-16PitN 17StLN 25ChiN	08-19-91	Wichita, Kans.	04-06-28	R	R	5'9	150	64	179	14	44	8	2	0	13	11	28	1	.246	.313
McAuliffe, Gene-Eugene Leo	04BosN	08-27-82	Randolph, Mass.	04-29-53	R	R	6'1	180	1	2	0	1	0	0	0	0	0		0	.500	.500
McAvoy, George-George Robert	14PhiN	03-12-84	East Liverpool, Ohio	08-19-52	L	R			1	1	0	0	0	0	0	0	0		0	.000	.000
McAvoy, Wickey-James Eugene	13-15, 17-19PhiA	10-20-94	Rochester, N.Y.	07-06-73	R	R	5'11	172	235	674	38	134	18	8	1	53	38	87	6	.199	.254
McBride, Algie-Algernon Griggs	96ChiN 98-01CinN 01NYN	05-23-69	Washington, D.C.	01-10-56	L	L	5'9	152	401	1581	256	463	58	26	12	179	132		37	.293	.385
McBride, George-George Florian	01MilA 05PitN 05-06StLN 08-20,M21WasA	11-20-80	Milwaukee, Wis.	07-02-73	R	R	5'11	170	1656	5518	516	1201	140	47	7	447	419		133	.218	.264
McCabe, William Francis	18-20ChiN 20BknN	10-28-92	Chicago, Ill.	09-02-66	R	R	5'9	180	106	199	28	32	3	2	0	13	15	28	3	.161	.196
McCabe, Swat-James Arthur	09-10CinN		Towanda, Pa.	12-09-44	L	R	5'10		16	46	5	15	2	0	0	5	1		1	.326	.370
McCandless, Jack-Scott Cook	14-15BalF	05-05-91	Pittsburgh, Pa.	08-17-61	R	R	6'	170	128	437	52	95	6	8	5	35	44		9	.217	.302
McCarthy, Alex-Alexander George	10-15PitN 15-16ChiN 16-17PitN	05-12-88	Chicago, Ill.	03-12-78	R	R	5'9	150	432	1335	136	306	34	11	5	122	104	133	23	.229	.282
McCarthy, Bill-William John	05BosN 06CinN	02-14-86	Boston, Mass.	02-24-28	R				4	11	1	1	0	0	0	0	0		0	.091	.091
McCarthy, Jack-John Arthur	93-94CinN 98-99PitN 00ChiN 01-03CleA 03-05ChiN 06-07BknN	03-26-69	Gilbertville, Mass.	09-11-31	L	L	5'9	155	1091	4196	549	1206	169	68	8	475	268		152	.287	.369
McCarthy, Joe-Joseph Nicodemus	05NYA 06StLN	12-25-81	Syracuse, N.Y.	01-12-37	R	R			16	39	2	9	2	0	0	2	2		0	.231	.282
McCarty, Lew-George Lewis	13-16BknN 16-20NYN 20-21StLN	11-17-88	Milton, Pa.	06-09-30	R	R	5'11	192	532	1479	113	393	47	20	5	137	102	107	20	.266	.335
McCauley, Pat-Patrick F.	93StLN 96WasN 03NYA	06-10-70	Ware, Mass.	01-23-17	R	R	5'10	156	37	119	14	23	3	0	2	12	7		3	.193	.269
McChesney, Harry-Harry Vincent (Pud)	04ChiN	06-01-80	Pittsburgh, Pa.	08-11-60	R	R	5'9	165	22	88	9	23	6	2	0	11	4		2	.261	.375
McCleskey, Jeff-Jefferson Lamar	13BosN	11-16-91	Americus, Ga.	05-11-71	R	R	5'11	160	2	3	0	0	0	0	0	0	1		0	.000	.000
McClure, Larry-Lawrence Ledwith	10NYA	10-08-84	Wayne, W.Va.	09-01-49	R	R	5'6	130	1	1	0	0	0	0	0	0	0		0	.000	.000
McConnell, Amby-Ambrose Moses	08-10BosA 10-11ChiA	04-29-83	North Pownal, Vt.	05-20-42	L	R	5'7	150	409	1506	202	398	30	22	3	119	107		72	.264	.319
McConnell, Sam-Samuel Faulkner	15PhiN	04-08-95	Maysville, Ky.	05-27-81	L	R	5'6	150	6	11	1	2	1	0	0	0	1	3	0	.182	.273
McCormick, Barry-William J.	95LouN 96-01ChiN 02-03StLA 03-04WasA	12-25-74	Cincinnati, Ohio	01-28-56	R	R	5'9		987	3637	432	865	112	43	15	417	280		136	.238	.305
McCormick, Dude-Michael J.	04BknN	05-??-83	Scotland	11-19-53	L	R	5'3	155	105	347	28	64	5	4	0	27	43		22	.184	.222
McCormick, Moose-Harry Elwood	04NYN 04PitN 08PhiN 08-09,12-13NYN	02-28-81	Philadelphia, Pa.	07-09-62	L	L	5'11	180	418	1247	165	356	62	26	6	133	92		30	.285	.391
McCredie, Judge-Walter Henry	03BknN	11-09-76	Manchester, Iowa	07-29-34	L	R	6'2	195	56	213	40	69	5	0	0	20	24		10	.324	.347
McCreery-Tom-Thomas Livingston	95-97LouN 97-98NYN 98-00PitN 01-03BknN 03BosN	10-19-74	Beaver, Pa.	07-03-41	B	R	5'11	180	796	2965	468	859	100	77	26	387	308		118	.290	.402
McDermott, Red-Frank A. (Irish)	12DetA	11-11-88	Philadelphia, Pa.	09-11-64	R	R	5'6	150	5	15	2	4	1	0	0	0	0		1	.267	.333
McDonald, Ed-Edward Cyril	11-12BosN 13ChiN	10-28-86	Albany, N.Y.	03-11-46	R	R	6'	180	176	634	98	154	30	9	3	55	110	130	33	.244	.334
McDonald, Jim-James	02NYN		Philadelphia, Pa.	Deceased	R	R	6'	180	2	9	0	3	0	0	0	0	0		0	.333	.333
McDonald, Joe-Malcolm Joseph (Tex)	10StLA	04-09-88	Galveston, Tex.	05-30-63	R	R	5'11	175	10	32	4	5	0	0	0	1	1		0	.156	.156
McDonald (Crabtree), Tex-Charles C.	12-13CinN 13BosN 14PitF 14-15BufF	01-31-89	Farmersville, Tex.	03-31-43	L	R	5'10	160	357	1019	131	304	45	27	13	135	88		34	.298	.434
McDonnough, Ed-Edward Sebastian	09-10PhiN	09-11-86	Elgin, Ill.	09-02-26	R	R	6'	160	6	10	1	1	0	0	0	0	0		0	.100	.100
McElveen, Pryor-Pryor Mynatt (Humpy)	09-11BknN	11-05-81	Atlanta, Ga.	10-27-51	B	R	5'10	168	171	502	42	105	16	4	4	56	36		12	.209	.281
McElwee, Lee-Leland Stanford	16PhiA	05-23-94	La Mesa, Cal.	02-08-57	R	R	5'10	160	54	155	9	41	9	0	0	10	8	17	0	.265	.284
McFarland, Ed-Edward William	93CleN 96-97StLN 97-01PhiN 02-07ChiA 08BosA	08-03-74	Cleveland, Ohio	11-28-59	R	R	5'10	180	886	3001	396	819	147	50	13	384	254		72	.273	.368
McFarland, Herm-Hermas Walter	96LouN 98CinN 01-02ChiA 02BalA 03NYA	03-11-70	Des Moines, Iowa	09-21-35	L	R	5'6	150	348	1266	202	338	61	28	13	167	175		66	.267	.390
McGaffigan, Patsy-Mark Andrew	17-18PhiN	09-12-28	Carlyle, Ill.	12-22-40	R	R	5'8	140	73	252	22	49	4	2	1	14	16	30	4	.194	.238
McGann, Dan-Dennis Lawrence (Cap)	96BosN 98BalN 99BknN 99WasN 00-01StLN 02BalA 02-07NYN 08BosN	07-15-71	Shelbyville, Ky.	12-13-10	B	R	6'1	190	1436	5227	844	1491	183	100	42	727	429		282	.285	.383
McGarr, Jim-James Vincent (Reds)	12DetA	11-08-88	Philadelphia, Pa.	07-21-81	R	R	5'9	170	1	4	0	0	0	0	0	0	0		0	.000	.000
McGarvey, Dan-Daniel Francis	12DetA	12-02-87	Philadelphia, Pa.	03-07-47	R				1	3	0	0	0	0	0	0	0		0	.000	.000
McGeehan, Dan-Daniel DeSales	11StLN	06-07-85	Jeddo, Pa.	07-12-55	R	R	5'6	135	3	9	0	2	0	0	0	1	0		0	.222	.222
McGilvray, Bill-William Alexander (Big Bill)	08CinN	04-29-83	Portland, Ore.	05-23-52	L	L	6'	160	2	9	0	2	0	0	0	0	0		0	.222	.222
McGovern, Art-Arthur John	05BosA	02-27-82	St. John, Canada	11-14-15	R	R	5'10	160	15	44	1	5	1	0	0	1	4		0	.114	.136
McGraw, John-John Joseph (Muggsy, Little Napoleon)	91BalA 92-99,M99BalN 00StLN 01-02,M01-02BalA 02-06,M02-32NYN	04-07-73	Truxton, N.Y.	02-25-34	L	R	5'7	155	1093	3928	1021	1312	124	72	13	462	836		441	.334	.412
McGuire, Deacon-James Thomas	84TolA 85DetN 86-88PhiN 88DetN 88CleA 90RocA 91WasA 92-99,M98WasN 99-01BknN 02-03DetA 04-07NYA 07-08,M07-08BosA 08,10,M09-11CleA 12DetA	11-18-63	Youngstown, Ohio	10-31-36	R	R	6'1	185	1777	6239	770	1737	298	75	45	850	515		137	.278	.372

For D. McGuire, Stolen Bases include the years, 86-12

USE NAME - GIVEN NAMES (NICKNAMES)	TEAM BY YEAR	BIRTH DATE	BIRTH PLACE	DEATH DATE	B	T	HGT	WGT	G	AB	R	H	2B	3B	HR	RBI	BB	SO	SB	BA	SA
McGuire, Jim-James A.	01CleA	02-04-75	Dunkirk, N.Y.	01-26-17	R				18	69	4	16	2	0	0	3	0		0	.232	.261
McHale, Jim-James Bernard	08PhiN	08-17-79	Miners Mills, Pa.	10-18-60	R	R	5'11	170													
McIlveen, Irish-Henry Cooke (See P01-19)	06PitN 08-09NYA	07-27-80	Belfast, Ireland	10-18-60	L	L	5'11	180	53	177	18	38	3	3	0	8	15		6	.215	.266
McInnis, Stuffy-John Phalen (Jack)	09-17PhiA 18-21BosA 22CleA 23-24BosN 25-26PitN 27,M27PhiN	09-19-90	Gloucester, Mass.	02-16-60	R	R	5'9	162	2128	7822	872	2406	312	101	20	1060	380		172	.308	.381
McIntyre, Matty-Matthew Martin	01PhiA 04-10DetA 11-12ChiA	06-12-80	Stonington, Conn.	04-02-20	L	L	5'11	175	1068	3958	562	1066	140	69	4	319	439		120	.269	.343
McIver, Otto-Edward Otto	11StLN	07-26-84	Greenville, Tex.	05-04-54	B	L	5'11	175	30	62	11	14	2	1	1	9	9	14	0	.226	.339
McKechnie, Bill-William Boyd (Deacon)	07,10-12PitN 13BosN 13NYA 14IndF 15,M15NwkF 16NYN 16-17CinN 18PitN 19VR M20-21StLN M22-26PitN M28-29StLN M30-37BosN M38-46CinN	08-07-86	Wilkinsburg, Pa.	10-29-65	B	R	5'10	160	844	2841	319	716	84	33	8	240	188		127	.252	.313
McKee, Red-Raymond Ellis	13-16DetA	07-20-90	Shawnee, Ohio	08-05-72	L	R	5'11	180	186	433	38	110	10	7	2	49	54	64	9	.254	.323
McKinney, Bob-Robert Francis	01PhiA	10-04-75	McSherrystown, Pa.	08-19-46	R	R	5'7	165	2	2	0	0	0	0	0	0	0		0	.000	.000
McLane, Ed-Edward Cameron	07PhiA	09-15-84	Weston, Mass.	08-21-75	R	R	5'10	179	1	2	0	0	0	0	0	0	0		0	.000	.000
McLarry, Polly-Howard Zell	12ChiA 15CinN	03-25-91	Leonard, Tex.	11-04-71	R	R	6'	185	70	129	16	25	3	1	0	12	14		2	.194	.240
McLaughlin, Kid-James Anson (Sunshine)	14CinN	04-12-88	Randolph, N.Y.	11-17-34	L	R	5'9	158	3	2	1	0	0	0	0	0	1		0	.000	.000
McLaurin, Ralph-Ralph Edgar	08StLN	05-23-85	Kissimmee, Fla.	02-11-43					8	22	3	5	0	0	0	0	0		0	.227	.227
McLean, Larry-John Bannerman	01BosA 03ChiN 04StLN 06-12CinN 13StLN 13-15NYN	07-18-81	Fredericton, Canada	03-14-21	R	R	6'5	228	862	2647	183	694	90	26	6	298	136		20	.262	.323
McManus, Frank-Francis E.	99WasN 03BknN 04DetA 04NYA	09-21-75	Lawrence, Mass.	09-01-23	R	R	5'7	150	14	35	3	8	0	0	0	2	2		3	.229	.257
McMillan, Tommy-Thomas Law (Rebel)	08-10BknN 10CinN 12NYA	04-18-88	Pittston, Pa.	07-15-66	R	R	5'5	130	297	991	73	207	21	4	0	54	81		45	.209	.238

USE NAME - GIVEN NAMES (NICKNAMES)	TEAM BY YEAR	BIRTH DATE	BIRTH PLACE	DEATH DATE	B	T	HGT	WGT	G	AB	R	H	2B	3B	HR	RBI	BB	SO	SB	BA	SA
McMullin, Fred-Fred Drury	14DetA 16-20ChiA 20DL	10-13-91	Scammon, Kans.	11-20-52	R	R	5'11	170	304	914	120	234	21	9	1	70	91	105	30	.256	.302
McNeil, Norm-Norman Francis	19BosA	10-22-92	Chicago, Ill.	04-11-42	R	R	5'11	180	5	9	0	3	0	0	0	1	1	0	0	.333	.333
Meara, Charlie-Charles Edward (Goggy)	14NYA	04-16-91	New York, N.Y.	02-08-62	L	R	5'10	160	4	7	2	2	0	0	0	1	2	2	0	.286	.286
Mee, Tommy-Thomas William (Judge)	10StlA	03-18-90	Chicago, Ill.	05-16-81	R	R	5'8	165	8	19	1	3	2	0	0	1	0	0	0	.158	.263
Meier, Dutch-Arthur Ernst	06PitN	03-30-79	St. Louis, Mo.	03-23-48	R	R	6'	180	82	273	32	70	11	4	0	16	13		4	.256	.326
Meinert, Walt-Walter Henry	13StlA	12-11-90	New York, N.Y.	11-09-58	L	L	5'7	150	4	8	1	3	0	0	0	1	3	0		.375	.375
Meinke, Bob-Robert Bernard	10CinN	06-25-87	Chicago, Ill.	12-29-52	R	R	5'10	135	2	1	0	0	0	0	0	0	0	0	0	.000	.000
Meister, Karl-Karl Daniel (Dutch)	13CinN	05-15-91	Marietta, Ohio	08-15-67	R	R	6'	178	4	7	1	2	1	0	0	2	0	4	0	.286	.429
Meixell, Moxie-Merton Merrill	12CleA	10-08-87	Lake Crystal, Minn.	08-17-82	L	R	5'10	168	2	2	0	1	0	0	0	0	0		0	.500	.500
Mellor, Bill-William Harpin	02BalA	06-06-74	Camden, N.J.	11-04-40	R	R	6'	190	10	36	4	13	3	0	0	5	3		1	.361	.444
Meloan, Paul-Paul B. (Molly)	10-11ChiA 11StlA	08-23-88	Paynesville, Mo.	02-11-50	R	R	5'10	175	130	431	53	109	17	8	3	38	32		11	.253	.350
Menefee, Jocko-John (See P01-19)	92PitN 93-94LouN 94-95PitN 98NYN 00-03ChiN	01-15-68	Rowlesburg, W. Va.	03-11-53	R	R	6'	165	219	676	74	151	15	7	0	57	52		14	.223	.266
Mensor, Eddie-Edward E. (Midget)	12-14PitN	11-07-85	Woodville, Ore.	04-20-70	B	R	5'6	145	127	244	43	54	6	3	1	8	53	38	14	.221	.283
Menze, Ted-Theodore Charles	18StlN	11-04-97	St. Louis, Mo.	12-23-69	R	R	5'9	172	1	3	0	0	0	0	0	0	0	0	0	.000	.000
Mercer, John-John Locke	12StlN	06-22-92	Taylortown, La.	12-21-82	L	L	5'10	155	1	1	0	0	0	0	0	0	0	0	0	.000	.000
Mercer, Win-George Barclay (See P01-19)	94-99WasN 00NYN 01WasA 02DetA	06-20-74	Chester, W.Va.	01-12-03	R	R	5'7	140	561	1739	276	509	35	23	7	197	141		88	.293	.351
Merkle, Fred-Carl Frederick Rudolf	07-16NYN 16-17BknN 17-20ChiN 25-26NYA	12-20-88	Watertown, Wis.	03-02-56	R	R	6'1	190	1638	5782	720	1580	290	81	60	733	545		272	.273	.383
Merritt, Goerge-George Washington (See P01-19)	01-03PitN	04-14-80	Patterson, N.J.	02-21-38		R	6'	160	15	47	8	10	1	0	0	5	2		1	.213	.319
Merritt, Howard-John Howard (Lefty)	13NYN	10-06-94	Plantersville, Miss.	11-03-55	R	L	5'11	170	1	0	0	0	0	0	0	0	0	0	0		
Mertes, Sam-Samuel Blair (Sandow, Bus)	96PhiN 98-00ChiN 01-02ChiA 03-06NYN 06StlN	08-06-72	San Francisco, Cal.	03-12-45	R	R	5'10	185	1183	4393	696	1230	191	109	40	721	422		395	.280	.400
Messenger, Bob-Charles Walter	09-11ChiA 14StlA	03-19-84	Bangor, Me.	07-10-51	B	R	5'9	165	54	157	29	27	1	4	0	4	20		10	.172	.217
Meyer, Benny-Bernhard (Earache)	13BknN 14-15BalF 15BufF 25PhiN	01-21-85	Hematite, Mo.	02-06-74	L	R	5'9	170	310	1041	146	276	29	17	7	84	158		46	.265	.346
Meyer, Billy-William Adam	13ChiA 16-17PhiA M48-52PitN	01-14-93	Knoxville, Tenn.	03-31-57	R	R	5'9	170	113	301	15	71	7	3	0	21	15	25	3	.236	.289
Meyer, Lee-Leo	09BknN	03-29-88	Iowa City, Iowa	09-02-88	R				7	23	1	3	0	0	0	0	2		0	.130	.130
Meyers, Chief-John Tortes	09-15NYN 16-17BknN 17BosN	07-29-80	Riverside, Cal.	07-25-71	R	R	5'11	194	992	2834	276	826	120	41	14	363	274		44	.291	.378
Midkiff, Exra-Ezra Millington (Salt Rock)	09CinN 12-13NYA	11-13-82	Salt Rock, W.Va.	03-21-57	L	R	5'10	180	105	372	31	77	10	4	0	23	19		13	.207	.239
Milan, Clyde-Jesse Clyde (Deerfoot)	07-22,M22WasA WasA	03-25-87	Linden, Tenn.	03-03-53	L	R	5'9	180	1981	7359	1004	2099	240	105	17	617	685		495	.285	.353
Milan, Horace-Horace Robert	15,17WasA 18MS	04-07-94	Linden, Tenn.	06-29-55	R	R	5'9	175	42	100	14	32	4	2	0	16	12	16	6	.320	.400
Miller, Bill-William Alexander	02PitN	05-23-79	Bad Schwalbach, Ger.	09-08-57	L	L	6'2	170	1	5	0	1	0	0	0	1	0		0	.200	.200
Miller, Charlie-Charles Elmer	12StlA	01-04-92	Warrensburg, Mo.	04-23-72	R				1	2	0	0	0	0	0	0	0		0	.000	.000
Miller, Charlie-Charlie Hess	15BalF	12-30-77	Conestoga, Pa.	01-13-51	R	R	6'	190	1	1	0	0	0	0	0	0	0		0	.000	.000
Miller, Chuck-Charles Marion	13-14StlN	09-18-89	Woodville, Ohio	06-16-61	L	L	5'7	150	40	48	4	9	0	0	0	3	3	11	2	.188	.208
Miller, Dakin-Dakin Evans (Dusty)	02CinN	09-03-76	Malvern, Iowa	04-19-50	R	R	5'10	170	51	187	17	46	4	1	0	16	10		10	.246	.278
Miller, Doc-Roy Oscar	10ChiN 10-12BosN 12-13PhiN 14CinN	02-04-83	Chatham, Canada	07-31-38	L	L	5'10	170	557	1717	184	507	96	15	12	235	121	149	64	.295	.390
Miller, Dots-John Barney	09-13PitN 14-17StlN 18MS 19StlN 20-21PhiN	08-09-86	Kearny, N.J.	09-05-23	R	R	5'11	170	1589	5805	711	1526	232	108	32	715	319		177	.263	.357
Miller, Eddie-Edwin Collins	12,14StlA 18CleA	11-24-88	Annville, Pa.	04-17-80	R	R	6'	180	79	200	21	39	5	4	0	12	18		4	.195	.260
Miller, Elmer-Elmer	12StlN 15-18,21-22NYA 22ChiA	11-28-44	Evansville, Ind.	07-28-86	R	R	5'11	175	413	1414	170	343	43	20	16	151	113	140	29	.243	.335
Miller, Hughie-Hugh Stanley (Cotton)	11PhiN 14-15StlF	12-22-86	St. Louis, Mo.	12-24-45	R	R	6'1	175	140	496	51	112	21	5	0	49	27		4	.226	.288
Miller, Jim-James McCurdy (Rabbit)	01NYN	10-02-80	Pittsburgh, Pa.	02-07-37	R	R	5'4	143	18	58	3	8	0	0	0	3	6		1	.138	.138
Miller, Otto-Lowell Otto (Moonie)	10-22BknN	06-01-89	Minden, Neb.	03-29-62	R	R	6'	196	927	2836	229	695	97	33	5	231	104	301	40	.245	.308
Miller, Ray-Raymond Peter	17CleA 17PitN 18MS	02-12-88	Pittsburgh, Pa.	04-07-27	L	L	5'10	168	25	48	2	8	1	0	0	2	10	6	0	.167	.208
Miller, Tom-Thomas Royall	18-19BosN	07-05-97	Powhatan Ct. House, Va.	08-13-80	R	R	5'11	180	9	8	2	2	0	0	0	0	1		1	.250	.250
Miller, Ward-Ward Taylor (Windy)	09PitN 09-10CinN 12-13ChiN 14StlF 16-17StlA	07-05-84	Mt. Carroll, Ill.	09-04-58	L	R	5'11	177	769	2244	322	623	79	35	8	221	318		128	.278	.355
Miller, Warren-Warren Lemuel (Gitz)	09,11WasA	07-14-85	Philadelphia, Pa.	08-12-56	L	L	5'10	160	47	85	8	16	0	0	0	5	4		0	.188	.188
Mills, Frank-Frank LeMoyne	14CleA	05-13-95	Knoxville, Ohio	08-31-83	L	R	6'	180	4	8	0	1	0	0	0	0	1	2	0	.125	.125
Mills, Jack-Abbott Paige	11CleA	10-23-89	S. Williamstown, Mass.	06-03-73	R	R	6'	165	13	17	5	5	0	0	0	0	1	1		.294	.294
Mills, Rupert-Rupert Frank	15NwkF	10-12-92	Newark, N.J.	07-20-29	R	R	6'2	185	41	134	12	27	5	1	0	16	6		6	.201	.254
Misse, John-John Beverly	14StlF	05-30-85	Highland, Kans.	03-18-70	R	R	5'9	150	99	306	28	60	8	1	0	22	38		3	.196	.229
Mitchell (Yapp), Fred-Frederick Francis (See P01-19)	01-02BosA 02PhiA 03-04PhiN 04-05BknN 10NYA 13BosN M17-20ChiN M21-23BosN	06-05-78	Cambridge, Mass.	10-13-70	R	R	5'9	185	202	572	55	120	16	7	0	52	22		8	.210	.262
Mitchell, Mike-Michael Francis	07-12CinN 13ChiN 13-14PitN 14WasA 16PhiA	12-12-79	Springfield, Ohio	07-16-61	R	R	6'1	185	1123	4094	514	1137	130	104	27	514	368		202	.278	.380
Mitterling, Ralph-Ralph (Sarge)	16PhiA	04-19-90	Freeburg, Pa.	01-22-56	R	R	5'8	165	13	39	1	6	0	0	0	2	3	6	0	.154	.154
Moeller, Danny-Danny Edward	07-08PitN 12-16WasA 16CleA	03-23-85	DeWitt, Iowa	04-14-51	R	R	5'11	185	704	2538	379	618	83	43	15	192	302		171	.243	.328
Mollenkamp, Fred-Frederick Henry	14PhiN	03-15-90	Cincinnati, Ohio	11-01-48			6'2	195	3	4	0	0	0	0	0	2	0	0	.125	.125
Mollwitz, Fritz-Frederick August (Zip)	13-14ChiN 14-16CinN 16ChiN 17-19PitN 19StlN	06-16-90	Coburg, Germany	10-03-67	R	R	6'2	170	534	1740	138	420	50	19	1	158	83	132	70	.241	.294
Moore, Charley-Charles Wesley	12ChiN	12-01-84	Jackson Co., Ind.	07-29-70	R	R	5'10	160	5	9	2	2	0	0	0	0	0		0	.222	.444
Moore, Ferdie-Ferdinand De Paige	14PhiN	02-22-96	Camden, N.J.	05-06-47			6'		2	4	1	2	0	0	0	1	0		0	.500	.500
Moore, Scrappy-William Allen	17StlA	12-16-92	St. Louis, Mo.	10-13-64	R	R	5'8	153	4	8	1	1	0	0	0	1	0		1	.125	.125
Moran, Charley-Charles Barthell (Uncle Charley) (See P01-19)	03,08StlN	02-22-78	Nashville, Tenn.	06-14-49	R	R	5'5	180	25	77	4	17	1	1	0	2	2		1	.221	.286
Moran, Charles-Charles Vincent	03-04WasA 04-05StlA	03-26-79	Washington, D.C.	04-11-34		R			270	970	89	201	28	6	1	50	91		20	.207	.252
Moran, Herbie-John Herbert	08PhiA 08-10BosN 12-13BknN 14CinN 14-15BosN	02-16-84	Costello, Pa.	09-21-54	L	R	5'6	150	595	2177	300	527	60	26	2	135	264		103	.242	.296
Moran, Pat-Patrick Joseph	01-05BosN 06-09ChiN 10-14,M15-18PhiN M19-23CinN	02-07-76	Fitchburg, Mass.	03-07-24	R	R	5'10	180	818	2634	198	618	102	24	18	262	142		55	.235	.312
Moran, Roy-Roy Ellis (Deedle)	12WasA	09-17-84	Vincennes, Ind.	07-18-66	R	R	5'8	155	5	13	1	2	0	0	0	0	8		3	.154	.154
Morgan, Ray-Raymond Caryll	11-18WasA	06-14-89	Baltimore, Md.	02-15-40	R	R	5'8	155	739	2480	278	630	90	33	4	254	320		87	.254	.322
Morgan, Red-James Edward	06BosA	10-06-83	Council Bluffs, Iowa	03-25-81	R	R	5'10	180	88	307	20	66	6	3	1	21	16		7	.215	.264
Moriarty, Bill-William Joseph	09CinN	08-??-83	Chicago, Ill.	12-25-16	R	R	6'2	190	6	20	1	4	1	0	0	1	0		0	.200	.250
Moriarty, George-George Joseph	03-04ChiN 06-08NYA 09-15DetA 16ChiA M27-28DetA	07-07-85	Chicago, Ill.	04-08-64	R	R	6'1	185	1071	3671	372	920	147	32	5	376	234		248	.251	.312
Morley, (Jennings) Bill-William Morley	13WasA	01-23-90	Holland, Mich.	05-14-85			5'11	170	2	5	0	0	0	0	0	0	0		0	.000	.000
Morris, Walter-John Walter	08StlN	01-31-80	Rockwell, Tex.	08-02-61	R	R	5'11		23	73	1	13	2	1	0	12	18		1	.178	.219
Morrissey, Jack-John Albert (King)	02-03CinN	05-02-76	Lansing, Mich.	10-30-36	B	R	5'10	170	41	128	19	33	2	1	0	12	18		3	.258	.289
Morse, Hap-Peter Raymond	11StlN	12-06-86	St. Paul, Minn.	06-19-74	R	R	5'8	160	4	8	0	0	0	0	0	0	2		0	.000	.000
Moskiman, Doc-William Bankhead	10BosA	12-20-79	Oakland, Cal.	01-11-53	R	R	6'	170	5	9	1	1	0	0	0	1	2		0	.111	.111
Moulton, Allie-Albert Theodore	11StlA	01-16-86	Medway, Mass.	07-10-68	R	R	5'6	155	9	15	4	1	0	0	0	0	0		0	.067	.067
Mowe, Ray-Raymond Benjamin	13BknN	07-12-89	Rochester, Ind.	08-14-68	L	R	5'7	160	13	9	0	1	0	0	0	0	1		0	.111	.111
Mowrey, Mike-Harry Harlan	05-09CinN 09-13StlN 14PitN 14-16FedL 16-19BosN	04-20-84	Brown's Mill, Pa.	03-20-47	R	R	5'8	160	1275	4290	485	1099	184	53	7	461	469		167	.256	.329
Mullen, Charlie-Charles George	02-13DetA 13WasA 14-16NYA	03-15-89	Seattle, Wash.	06-06-63	R	R	5'10	155	253	741	77	183	22	3	6	87	61		28	.247	.285
Mullin, George-George Joseph (Wabash Geroge) (See P01-19)	02-13DetA 13WasA 14IndF 15NwkF	07-04-80	Toledo, Ohio	01-07-44	R	R	5'11	188	615	1531	163	401	70	23	3	137	122		18	.262	.344
Mullin, Jim-James Henry	04PhiA 04WasA 04PhiA 05WasA	10-16-83	New York, N.Y.	01-24-25	R	R	5'10	173	118	375	37	74	10	8	1	26	14		12	.197	.275
Munch, Jake-Jacob Ferdinand	18PhiA	11-16-90	Morton, Pa.	06-08-66	L	L	6'2	170	22	30	3	8	1	0	0	0	0	5	0	.267	.333
Mundy, Bill-William Edward	13BosA	06-28-89	Salineville, Ohio	09-23-58	R	R	5'10	154	15	47	4	12	0	0	0	4	5	2	0	.255	.255
Munson, Red-Clarence Hanford	05PhiN	07-31-83	Cincinnati, Ohio	02-19-57	R	R	5'11		9	26	1	3	1	0	0	1	3		0	.115	.154
Murch, Simmy-Simeon Augustus	04-05StlN 08BknN	11-21-80	Castine, Me.	06-06-39	R	R	6'2	230	22	71	4	10	2	0	0	2	2		0	.141	.169
Murdoch, Wilbur-Wilbur Edwin	08StlN	03-14-75	Avon, N.Y.	10-29-41	R				27	62	5	16	3	0	0	5	3		4	.258	.306
Murphy, Buzz-Robert Sylvester (Buzz)	18BosN 19WasA	04-26-95	Denver, Colo.	05-11-38	L	L	5'9	155	88	284	25	78	9	7	1	37	22	37	5	.275	.366
Murphy, Danny-Daniel Francis	00-01NYN 02-13PhiA 14-15BknF 16-17BosN	08-11-76	Philadelphia, Pa.	11-22-55	R	R	5'9	175	1491	5379	707	1559	285	103	44	702	335		193	.290	.406
Murphy, Dave-David Francis (Dirty)	05BosN	05-04-76	Adams, Mass.	04-08-40	R				3	11	0	2	0	0	0	0	0		0	.182	.182
Murphy, Dummy-Herbert Courtland	14PhiN	12-18-86	Olney, Ill.	10-10-62	R	R	5'10	165	9	26	1	4	1	0	0	1	0		0	.154	.192
Murphy, Eddie-John Edward (Honest Eddie)	12-15PhiA 15-21ChiA 26PitN	10-02-91	Hancock, N.Y.	02-21-69	L	R	5'10	155	760	2373	411	680	66	32	4	195	294		111	.287	.346
Murphy, Frank-Francis Patrick	01BosN 01NYN	04-06-76	North Tarrytown, N.Y.	11-04-12	R	R			80	306	23	67	8	3	1	26	10		8	.219	.275
Murphy, Howard-Howard	09StlN	01-02-82	Birmingham, Ala.	10-05-26	L	R	5'8	160	25	60	3	12	3	0	0	3	2		1	.200	.200
Murphy, John-John Patrick	02StlN 03DetA	??-??-71	New Haven, Conn.	04-20-49			5'7	160		25			3	0	0		0		0	.240	.320
Murphy, Leo-Leo Joseph (Red)	15PitN	01-07-89	Terre Haute, Ind.	08-12-60	R	R	6'1	180	34	41	4	4	0	0	0	4	3	12	0	.098	.098
Murphy, Mike-Michael Jerome	12StlN 16PhiA	08-19-88	Forestville, Pa.	10-27-52	R	R	5'9	170	15	28	0	3	0	0	0	2	1	3	0	.107	.107

USE NAME - GIVEN NAMES (NICKNAMES)	TEAM BY YEAR	BIRTH DATE	BIRTH PLACE	DEATH DATE	B	T	HGT	WGT	G	AB	R	H	2B	3B	HR	RBI	BB	SO	SB	BA	SA
Murphy, Morg-Morgan Edward	90BosP 91BosAA 92-95CinN 96-97StLN 98PitN 98,00PhiN 01PhiA	02-14-67	E. Providence, R.I.	10-03-38	R	R	5'8	160	562	1973	251	446	59	13	10	227	157		55	.226	.284
Murray, Bill-William Allenwood (Dasher)	17WasA	09-06-93	Vinalhaven, Me.	09-14-43	B	R	5'10	175	8	21	2	3	0	1	0	4	2	2	1	.143	.238
Murray, Ed-Edward Francis	17StLA	05-08-95	Mystic, Conn.	11-08-70	R	R	5'6	145	1	1	0	0	0	0	0	0	0	1	0	.000	.000
Murray, Jim-James Oscar	02ChiN 11StLA 14BosN	01-16-78	Galveston, Tex.	04-25-45	R	L	5'10	180	82	261	21	53	9	2	3	24	13		2	.203	.287
Murray, Red-John Joseph (Jack)	06-08StLN 09-15NYN 15ChiN 17NYN	03-04-84	Arnot, Pa.	12-04-58	R	R	5'10	190	1264	4334	555	1170	168	96	37	579	299		321	.270	.379
Myers, Hap-Ralph Edward	10BosA 11BosA 13BosN 14-15BknF	04-08-87	San Francisco, Cal.	06-30-67	R	R	6'3	175	377	1251	203	335	42	7	4	116	119		132	.268	.322
Myers, Hy-Henry Harrison	09,11,14-22BknN 23-25StLN 25CinN 25StLN	04-27-89	East Livecpool, Ohio	05-01-65	R	R	5'9	175	1310	4910	555	1380	179	100	32	559	195	360	107	.281	.378
Nagelsen (Nageleisen), Lou-Louis Marcellus	12CleA	06-29-87	Piqua, Ohio	10-21-65	R	R	6'2	180	2	3	0	0	0	0	0	0	0		0	.000	.000
Nance (Cooper), Doc-William Gideon (Kid)	97-98LouN 01DetA	08-02-76	Fort Worth, Tex.	05-28-58	R	R	5'7	165	188	657	110	183	34	7	7	99	83		14	.279	.384
Nash, Ken-Kenneth Leland (played as J.A. Costello part of 1912)	12CleA 14StLN	07-14-88	S. Weymouth, Mas.	02-16-77	B	R	5'8	140	36	75	6	18	3	1	0	6	9		0	.240	.307
Neal, Offa-Theophilus Fountain	05NYN	06-05-76	Logan, Ill.	04-11-50	L	R	6'	185	4	13	0	0	0	0	0	0	0		0	.000	.000
Neale, Greasy-Alfred Earle 41-50 head coach in N.F.L.	16-20CinN 21PhiN 21-22CinN 23VR 24CinN	11-05-91	Parkersburg, W.Va.	11-02-73	L	R	6'	170	768	2661	321	688	71	50	8	200	201	281	139	.259	.332
Nealon, Jim-James Joseph	06-07PitN	12-15-84	Sacramento, Cal.	04-02-10	R	R	6'1		259	937	111	240	31	20	3	130	76		26	.256	.342
Needham, Tom-Thomas Joseph (Deerfoot)	04-07BosN 08NYN 09-14ChiN	04-17-79	Ireland	12-14-26	R	R	5'10	180	523	1491	113	311	50	10	8	117	109		20	.209	.272
Neff, Doug-Douglas Williams	14-15WasA	10-08-91	Harrisonburg, Va.	05-23-32	R	R	5'9	140	33	62	1	10	1	0	0	4	4	6	1	.161	.177
Neighbors, Cy-Fleming Cecil	08PitN	09-23-80	Fayetteville, Mo.	05-20-64	R		5'10	178	1	0	0	0	0	0	0	0	0		0	.000	—
Nelson (Kellogg), Ray (Raymond Nelson)-Raymond (Kell)	01NYN		Holyoke, Mass.	01-08-61	R	R	5'9	150	39	130	12	26	2	0	0	7	10		3	.200	.215
Ness, Jack-John Charles	11DetA 16ChiA	11-11-85	Chicago, Ill.	12-03-57	R	R	6'2	165	87	297	38	75	7	5	1	36	11		4	.253	.320
Netzel, Milo-Miles Albion	09CleA	05-12-86	Eldred, Pa.	03-18-38	L	L			10	37	2	7	1	0	0	3	3		1	.189	.216
Neu, Otto-Otto Adam	17StLA	09-24-94	Springfield, Ohio	09-19-32	R	R	5'11	170	1	0	0	0	0	0	0	0	0		0	—	—
Newnam, Pat-Robert Albert	10-11StLA	12-10-80	Hemstead, Tex.	06-20-38	L	R	6'	180	123	446	66	95	7	8	2	31	41		20	.213	.278
Nicholls, Simon-Simon Burdette	03DetA 06-09PhiA 10CleA	07-18-82	Germantown, Md.	03-12-11	R	R	5'11	165	314	1133	144	284	32	6	4	58	65		27	.251	.300
Nichols (Meikle), Art-Arthur Francis	98-00ChiN 01-03StLN	07-14-71	Manchester, N.H.	08-09-45	R	R	5'10	175	241	793	112	194	28	3	2	89	50		51	.245	.295
Nicholson, Ovid-Ovid Edward	12PitN	12-30-88	Salem, Ind.	03-24-68	L	R	5'9	155	6	11	2	5	0	0	0	3	1	2	0	.455	.455
Niehoff, Bert-John Albert	13-14CinN 15-17PhiN 18StLN 18NYN	05-13-84	Louisville, Colo.	12-08-74	R	R	5'10	170	581	2037	210	489	104	19	12	207	131	242	71	.240	.327
Niles, Harry-Herbert Clyde	06-07StLA 08NYA 08-10BosA 10CleA	09-10-80	Buchanan, Mich.	04-18-53	R	R	5'8	175	298	2270	278	562	58	24	12	152	163		107	.248	.310
Nill, Rabbit-George Charles	04-07WasA 07-08CleA	07-14-81	Fort Wayne, Ind.	05-24-62	R	R	5'7	160	295	963	116	204	23	9	3	77	103		36	.212	.264
Noonan, Pete-Peter John	04PhiA 06CinN 06-07StLN	11-24-81	W. Stockbridge, Mass.	02-11-65	R	R	6'	180	163	479	40	98	11	7	4	38	21		5	.205	.282
Nordyke, Lou-Louis Ellis	06StLA	08-07-76	Brighton, Iowa	09-27-45	R	R	6'	185	25	53	4	13	1	0	0	7	10		3	.245	.264
Northen, Hub-Hubbard Edwin	10StLA 11CinN 11-12BknN	08-16-86	Atlanta, Tex.	10-01-47	L	L	5'8	175	164	584	76	159	29	8	3	63	60		14	.272	.365
Nunamaker, Les-Leslie Grant	11-14BosA 14-17NYA 18StLA 19-22CleA	01-25-89	Malcolm, Neb.	11-14-38	R	R	6'2	190	715	1990	194	533	75	30	2	215	176		36	.268	.339
Nutter, Dizzy-Everett Clarence	19BosN	08-27-93	Roseville, Ohio	07-25-58	L	R	5'10	160	18	52	4	11	0	0	0	3	4	5	1	.212	.212
Oakes, Rebel-Ennis Telfair	09CinN 10-13StLN 14-15,M14-15PitF	12-17-83	Lisbon, La.	03-01-48	L	R	5'9	170	985	3617	427	1009	112	42	15	397	265		163	.279	.346
O'Brien, George-George Joseph	15StLA	11-04-89	Cleveland, Ohio	03-24-66	R	R	6'	185	3	9	1	2	0	0	0	0	1	2	0	.222	.222
O'Brien, Jack-John Joseph	99WasN 01WasA 01CleA 03BosA	06-05-73	Watervliet, N.Y.	06-10-33	L	R	6'1	165	321	1217	166	313	38	14	9	133	77		44	.257	.334
O'Brien, Pete-Peter J.	01CinN 06StLN 07CleA 07WasA	06-17-77	Binghamton, N.Y.	01-31-17	R	R	5'7	170	249	857	60	191	18	7	3	78	63		30	.223	.271
O'Brien, Ray-Raymond Joseph	16PitN	10-31-92	St. Louis, Mo.	03-31-42	L	L	5'9	170	16	57	5	12	3	2	0	3	1	14	0	.211	.333
O'Connell, Jack-John Joseph	91BalAA 02DetA		Lawrence, Mass.	05-14-08	R	R	5'9	170	16	51	3	9	1	1	0	7	6		2	.176	.196
O'Connor, Jack-John Joseph (Peach Pie)	87-88CinAA 89-91ColAA 92-98CleN 99-00StLN 00-02PitN 03NYA 04,06-07,10,M10StLA	06-02-69	St. Louis, Mo.	11-14-37	R	R	5'10	170	1434	5346	693	1430	201	66	18	738	301		215	.267	.340
O'Connor, John-John Charles (Bucky)	16ChiN	12-01-91	Cahirciveen, Ireland	05-30-82	R	R	5'9		1	0	0	0	0	0	0	0	0		0	—	—
O'Connor, Paddy-Patrick Francis	08-10PitN 14StLN 15PitF 18NYA	08-04-79	County Kerry, Ireland	08-17-50	R	R	5'8	168	108	267	17	60	11	1	0	21	17		4	.225	.258
Odwell, Fred-Frederick William (Fritz)	04-07CinN	09-25-72	Downsville, N.Y.	08-19-48	R	R	5'9	160	411	1412	198	365	42	30	10	168	89		72	.258	.352
O'Hagan, Hal-Patrick Henry	92WasN 02ChiN 02NYN 02CleA 02NYN	09-30-69	Washington, D.C.	01-14-13	R	R	6'	173	61	209	18	39	5	4	0	19	13		13	.187	.249
O'Hara, Bill-William Alexander	09NYN 10StLN	08-14-83	Toronto, Canada	06-13-31	L	R	5'10	165	124	380	49	88	9	3	1	32	42		31	.232	.270
O'Hara, Kid-James Francis	04BosN	12-19-75	Wilkes-Barre, Pa.	12-01-54	B	R	5'7	152	8	29	3	6	0	0	0	0	4		1	.207	.207
O'Hara, Tom-Thomas Francis	06-07StLN	12-19-75	Waverly, N.Y.	06-08-54					62	226	19	57	3	1	0	5	15		4	.252	.274
Oldring, Rube-Reuben Henry	05NYA 06-16PhiA 16NYA 17VR 18PhiA	05-30-84	New York, N.Y.	09-09-61	R	R	5'10	186	1237	4690	616	1268	205	75	28	471	206		197	.270	.364
O'Leary, Charley-Charles Timothy	04-12DetA 13StLN 34StLN	10-15-75	Chicago, Ill.	01-06-41	R	R	5'7	165	954	3230	317	731	104	18	3	213	164		74	.226	.272
Olson, Ivy-Ivan Massie	11-15CleA 15-24BknN	10-14-85	Kansas City, Mo.	09-01-65	R	R	5'11	175	1572	6111	730	1575	191	69	13	446	285		156	.258	.318
O'Mara, Ollie-Oliver Edward	12DetA 14-16,18-19BknN	03-08-91	St. Louis, Mo.	10-24-89	R	R	5'8	140	412	1478	166	341	49	8	2	77	86	105	46	.231	.279
O'Neill, Bill-William John	04BosA 04WasA 06ChiA	01-22-80	St. John, Canada	07-20-20	B	R	5'11	175	206	746	77	181	15	2	2	42	46		41	.243	.276
O'Neill, Jack-John Joseph	02-03StLN 04-05ChiN 06BosN	01-10-73	Maam, Ireland	06-29-35	R	R	5'10	165	303	945	74	185	24	5	1	74	52		20	.196	.235
O'Neill, John-John J.	99,02NYN		New York, N.Y.	Deceased	R				4	15	0	0	0	0	0	0	0		0	.000	.000
O'Neill, Mike-Michael Joyce (See P01-19) (Played as Mike Joyce 01)	01-14StLN 07CinN		Maam, Ireland	08-12-59	L	L	5'11	185	137	380	50	97	14	9	2	41	20		4	.255	.355
O'Neill, Peaches-Philip Bernard	04CinN	08-02-55	Anderson, Ind.	08-12-55	R	R	5'11	165	15	45	0	4	0	0	0	2	4		0	.267	.267
O'Neill, Steve-Stephen Francis	11-23CleA 24BosA 25NYA 27-28StLA M35-37CleA M43-48DetA M50-51BosA M52-54PhiN	07-06-91	Minooka, Pa.	01-26-62	R	R	5'10	175	1586	4795	448	1259	248	34	13	537	592		30	.263	.337
Onslow, Eddie-Edward Joseph	12-13DetA 18CleA 27WasA	02-17-93	Meadville, Pa.	05-08-81	L	L	6'1	170	63	207	23	48	3	2	1	22	9		4	.232	.280
Onslow, Jack-John James	12DetA 17NYN M49-50ChiA	10-13-88	Scottdale, Pa.	12-22-60	R	R	5'11	180	40	77	4	13	0	1	0	4	10		1	.169	.195
Orndorff, Jess-Jesse Walworth Thayer	07BosN	08-30-91	Chicago, Ill.	09-28-60	B	R	6'	168	5	17	0	2	0	0	0	0	1		0	.118	.118
O'Rourke, Jim-James Henry (Orator Jim)	76-78BosN 79ProvN 80BosN 81-84,M81-84BufN 85-89NYN 90NYP 91-92NYN 93,M93WasN 04NYN	08-24-52	Bridgeport, Conn.	01-08-19	R	R	5'8	185	1762	7368	1439	2300	385	139	51	1010	481	349	211	.312	.423
							For Jim O'Rourke, Stolen Bases includes the years 86-04														
O'Rourke, Patsy-Joseph Leo Sr.	08StLN	04-13-81	Philadelphia, Pa.	04-18-56	R	R	5'7	160	53	164	8	32	4	2	0	16	14		2	.195	.244
O'Rourke, Qieenie-James Stephen	08NYA	12-26-83	Bridgeport, Conn.	12-22-55	R	R	5'7	150	34	108	5	25	1	0	0	3	4		4	.231	.241
Orr, Billy-William John	13-14PhiA	04-22-91	San Francisco, Cal.	03-10-67	R	R	5'11	168	37	91	9	17	2	2	0	8	6	15	2	.186	.221
Orth, Al-Albert Lewis (The Curveless Wonder) (See P01-19)	95-01PhiN 02-04WasA 04-09NYA	09-05-72	Tipton, Ind.	10-08-48	L	R	6'	200	603	1683	184	461	60	30	12	184	51		39	.274	.384
Osborn, Ossie-Wilfred Pearl (Green, Fred)	07-09PhiN	11-28-83	Nevada, Ohio	09-02-54	L	R	5'9	178	266	907	98	228	25	16	2	72	45		26	.251	.321
Ostdiek, Harry-Harry Girard	04CleA 08BosA	04-12-81	Ottumwa, Iowa	05-06-56	R	R	5'11	165	8	21	1	3	0	1	0	3	3		1	.143	.238
Osteen, Champ-James Champlin	03WasA 04NYA 08-09StLN	02-24-77	Hendersonville, N.C.	12-14-62	R	R	5'8	150	83	304	27	60	6	6	2	31	10		1	.197	.276
Otis, Bill-Paul Franklin	12NYA	12-24-89	Scituate, Mass.	12-15-90	R	R	5'10	150	4	20	1	1	0	0	0	2	3		0	.050	.050
Owens, Frank-Frank Walter (Yip)	05BosA 09ChiA 14BknF 15BalF	06-01-86	Toronto, Canada	07-02-58	R	R	6'	170	222	694	59	170	25	11	5	65	34		9	.245	.334
Owens, Red-Thomas Llewellyn	99PhiN 05BknN	11-01-74	Pottsville, Pa.	08-21-52	R	R	5'10	175	51	189	14	37	6	2	1	21	8		1	.196	.265
Oyler, Andy-Andrew Paul (Pepper)	02BalA	05-05-80	Newville, Pa.	10-24-70	R	R	5'8	138	27	77	9	17	1	0	0	6	8		3	.221	.273
Padden, Dick-Richard Joseph (Brains)	96-98PitN 99WasN 01StLN 02-05StLA	09-17-70	Wheeling, W. Va.	10-31-22	R	R	5'10	165	873	3160	421	811	116	46	11	334	224		131	.257	.333
Paddock, Harold-Delmar Harold	12ChiA 12NYA	06-06-87	Volga, S.D.	02-06-52	L	R	5'9	165	46	157	26	45	5	3	0	19	23		9	.287	.376
Palmer, Eddie-Edwin Henry (Baldy)	17PhiA	06-01-93	Petty, Tex.	01-09-83	R	R	5'9	175	16	52	7	11	0	0	0	5	7	7	1	.212	.212
Parent, Freddy-Frederick Alfred	99StLN 01-07BosA 08-11ChiA	11-25-75	Biddeford, Me.	11-02-72	R	R	5'7	154	1327	4984	633	1306	180	74	20	471	333		184	.262	.340
Parker, Pat-Clarence Perkins	15StLA	12-22-93	Somerville, Mass.	03-21-67	R	R	5'7	160	3	6	0	1	0	0	0	1	0	3	0	.167	.167
Partenheimer, Steve-Harold Philip	13DetA	08-30-91	Greenfield, Mass.	06-16-71	R	R	5'8	145	2	2	0	0	0	0	0	0	0		0	.000	.000
Paskert, Dode-George Henry	07-10CinN 11-17PhiN 18-20CinN 21CinN	08-28-81	Cleveland, Ohio	02-12-59	R	R	5'11	165	1716	6017	868	1613	279	77	42	577	715		293	.268	.361
Pasquariello, Mike-Michael John (Toney)	19PhiN 19StLN	11-07-98	Philadelphia, Pa.	04-05-65	R	R	6'2	190	2	2	0	1	0	0	0	0	0		0	.500	.500
Pattee, Harry-Harry Ernest	08BknN	01-17-82	Charlestown, Mass.	07-17-71	L	R	5'8	150	80	264	19	57	9	0	0	9	25		24	.216	.250
Patterson, Claire-Lorenzo Clare	09CinN	10-05-87	Arkansas City, Kans.	03-28-13	L	R	6'	180	4	8	0	1	0	0	0	0	0		0	.125	.125
Patterson, Ham-Hamilton	09StLA 09CinN	11-25-45	Belleville, Ill.	11-25-45	R	R	6'2	185	18	52	4	10	1	0	0	1	0		1	.192	.212
Paulette, Gene-Eugene Edward	11NYN 16-17StLA 17-19StLN 19-20PhiN 21DL	05-26-91	Centralia, Ill.	02-08-66	R	R	6'	150	500	1780	160	478	66	19	2	165	108	69	43	.269	.330
Pauxtis, Si-Simon Francis	09CinN	07-20-85	Pittston, Pa.	03-13-61	R	R	6'	175	4	8	1	1	0	0	0	0	0		0	.125	.125
Payne, Freddie-Frederick Thomas (Doc)	06-08DetA 09-11ChiA	09-02-80	Camden, N.Y.	01-16-54	R	R	5'10	162	334	908	82	194	16	12	1	86	47		21	.214	.261
Pearce, Bunny-William Charles	08-09CinN	03-17-85	Corning, Ohio	05-22-33	R	R	6'1	185	4	4	0	0	0	0	0	0	0		0	.000	.000
Pearce, Harry-Harry James	17-19PhiN	07-12-89	Philadelphia, Pa.	01-08-42	R	R	5'9	158	135	424	42	88	9	5	0	29	17	62	11	.208	.274
Pechous, Charlie-Charles Edward	15ChiF 16-17ChiN	10-05-96	Chicago, Ill.	09-13-80	R	R	6'	165	53	161	11	29	9	1	0	10	13		0	.180	.217
Peckinpaugh, Roger-Roger Thorpe	10,12-13CleA 13-21,M14NYA 22-26WasA 27ChiA M28-33,41CleA	02-05-91	Wooster, Ohio	11-17-77	R	R	5'10	165	2012	7233	1006	1876	256	75	48	739	814		207	.259	.336
Pedroes (Pedro), Chick-Charles P.	02ChiN	10-27-69	Chicago, Ill.	08-06-27					2	6	0	0	0	0	0	0	0		0	.000	.000
Peitz, Heinie-Henry Clement	92-95StLN 96-04CinN 05-06PitN 13StLN	11-28-70	St. Louis, Mo.	10-23-43	R	R	5'11	165	1230	4114	542	1128	192	65	16	560	409		94	.274	.364

USE NAME - GIVEN NAMES (NICKNAMES)	TEAM BY YEAR	BIRTH DATE	BIRTH PLACE	DEATH DATE	B	T	HGT	WGT	G	AB	R	H	2B	3B	HR	RBI	BB	SO	SB	BA	SA
Peploski, Pepper-Joseph Aloysius	13DetA	09-12-91	Brooklyn, N.Y.	07-13-72	R	R	5'8	155	2	4	1	2	0	0	0	0	0		0	.500	.500
Perrine, Nig-John Grover	07WasA	01-14-85	Clinton, Wis.	08-13-48	R	R	5'9	160	44	146	13	25	4	1	0	15	13		10	.171	.212
Perring, George-George Wilson	08-10CleA 14-15KCF	08-13-84	Sharon, Wis.	08-20-60	R	R	6'	190	513	1764	198	438	75	34	9	183	154		26	.248	.345
Perry, Clay-Clayton Shields	08DetA	12-18-81	Rice Lake, Wis.	01-16-54	R	R	5'10	175	5	11	0	2	0	0	0	0	0		0	.182	.182
Perry, Hank-William Henry (Socks)	12DetA	07-28-96	Howell, Mich.	07-18-56	L	R	5'11	195	13	36	3	6	1	0	0	0	3		3	.167	.194
Peterson, Bob-Robert Andrew	06-07BosA	06-16-84	Philadelphia, Pa.	11-27-62	R	R	6'1	160	43	131	11	25	1	1	1	9	11		1	.191	.237
Pettigrew, Ned-Jim Ned	14BufF	08-25-81	Honey Grove, Tex.	08-20-52	R	R	5'10	175	2	2	0	0	0	0	0	0	0		0	.000	.000
Pezold, Larry-Lorenz Johannes	14CleA	06-22-93	New Orleans, La.	10-22-57	R	R	5'9	175	23	71	4	16	0	1	0	5	9	6	2	.225	.254
Pfeiffer, Monte Montague	10-07-90	New York, N.Y.	09-27-41	R	R	5'4	147	1	3	0	0	0	0	0	0	1		0	.000	.000
Pfyl, Monte-Meinhard Charles	07NYN 09-13DO	05-11-86	St. Louis, Mo.	10-18-45	R	R	6'3	190	1	0	0	0	0	0	0	0	0		0	—	—
Phelan, Art-Arthur Thomas (Dugan)	10,12CinN 13-15ChiN	08-14-87	Niantic, Ill.	12-27-64	R	R	5'8	160	401	1256	150	297	38	25	8	131	141	113	50	.236	.326
Phelps, Eddie-Edward Jaykill (Yaller)	02-04,06-08PitN 05-06CinN 09-10StLN 12-13BknN	03-03-79	Albany, N.Y.	01-31-42	R	R	5'10	185	629	1832	186	460	45	20	3	205	163		31	.251	.302
Phyle, Bill-William Joseph (See P01-19)	98-99ChiN 01NYN 06StLN	06-25-75	Duluth, Minn.	08-07-53		R			61	182	17	32	5	1	0		8	9	2	.176	.214
Pick, Charlie-Charles Thomas	14-15WasA 16PhiA 18-19ChiN 19-20CinN	04-10-88	Brookneal, Va.	06-26-54	L	R	5'10	160	367	1278	115	333	39	17	3	86	102	60	64	.261	.325
Pickering, Ollie-Oliver Daniel	96-97LouN 97CleN 01-02CleA 03-04PhiA 07StLA 08WasA	04-09-70	Olney, Ill.	01-20-52	L	R	5'11	170	885	3347	500	910	97	39	9	287	286		198	.272	.332
Pickup, Ty-Clarence William	18PhiN	10-29-97	Philadelphia, Pa.	08-02-74	R	R	6'	180	1	1	0	1	0	0	0	0	0		0	1.000	1.000
Piez, Sandy-Charles William	14NYN	10-13-88	New York, N.Y.	12-29-30	R	R	5'10	170	35	8	9	3	0	1	0	3	0	1	4	.375	.625
Pitler, Jake-Jacob Albert	17-18PitN	04-22-94	New York, N.Y.	02-03-68	R	R	5'8	150	111	383	40	89	8	5	0	23	31	24	8	.232	.279
Platte, Al-Alfred Joseph	13DetA	04-13-90	Grand Rapids, Mich.	08-29-76	L	L	5'11	165	7	18	1	2	1	0	0	0	1	1	0	.111	.167
Pond, Ralph-Raph Benjamin	10BosA	05-04-90	Eau Claire, Wis.	09-08-47		R	5'9		1	4	0	1	0	0	0	0	0		0	.250	.250
Porter, Irv-Irving Marble	14ChiA	05-17-88	Lynn, Mass.	02-20-71	R	R	5'9	155	1	4	0	1	0	0	0	0	0		0	.250	.250
Post, Lew-Lewis George	02DetA	04-12-75	Woodland, Mich.	08-21-44	R	R			3	12	2	1	0	0	0	1	0		0	.083	.083
Potts, Fred-John Frederick	14KCF	02-06-87	Tipp City, Ohio	09-05-62	L	R	5'7	165	41	102	14	27	4	0	1	9	25		7	.265	.333
Powers, Mike-Michael Riley (Doc)	98-99LouN 99WasN 01-05PhiA 05NYA 05-09PhiA	09-22-70	Pittsfield, Mass.	04-26-09	R	R	5'7	165	643	2079	184	453	72	13	4	199	72		27	.218	.271
Pratt, Del-Derrill Burnham	12-17StLA 18-20NYA 21-22BosA 23-24DetA	01-10-88	Walhalla, S.C.	09-30-77	R	R	5'11	175	1835	6826	856	1996	392	117	43	966	513		246	.292	.403
Pratt, Larry-Lester John	14BosA 15BknF 15NwkF	10-08-87	Gibson City, Ill.	01-08-69	R	R	6'	183	30	57	7	11	3	0	1	2	5		4	.193	.298
Priest, Johnnie-John Gooding	11-12NYA	06-23-91	St. Joseph, Mo.	11-04-79	R	R	5'10	170	9	23	3	4	0	0	0	2	4		1	.174	.174
Purnell, Jesse-Jesse Rhoades (Scrappy)	04PhiN	05-11-81	Glenside, Pa.	07-04-66	L	R	5'5	140	7	19	2	2	0	0	0		1	4	1	.105	.105
Purtell, Billy-William Patrick	08-10ChiA 10-11BosA 14DetA	01-06-86	Columbus, Ohio	03-17-62	R	R	5'9	165	333	1124	82	259	26	11	2	104	63		24	.230	.278
Quillin, Lee-Leon Abner	06-07ChiA	05-05-82	North Branch, Minn.	05-14-65	R	R	5'10	165	53	160	18	32	5	0	0	14	10		9	.200	.231
Quinlan, Finners-Thomas Finners	13StLN 15ChiA	10-21-87	Scranton, Pa.	02-17-66	L	L	5'8	154	55	164	12	30	3	0	0	8	5	20	3	.183	.201
Quinn, Joe-Joseph J. (Uncle Joe)	84StLU 85-86StLN 88-89BosN 90BosP 91-92BosN 93-96,M95StLN 96-98BalN 98StLN 99,M99CleN 00StLN 00CinN 01NwkA	12-25-64	Sydney, Australia	11-12-40	R	R	5'7	158	1759	6841	887	1799	226	69	30	794	364		278	.263	.329
												For Joe Quinn, Stolen Bases includes the years, 86-01										
Quinn, John-John Edward (Pit)	11PhiN	09-12-85	Framingham, Mass.	04-09-56	R	R	6'2	185	1	2	0	0	0	0	0	0	0		0	.000	.000
Rafter, Jack-John Cornelius	04PitN	02-20-75	Troy, N.Y.	01-05-43	R	R	5'8	165	1	3	0	0	0	0	0	0	0		0	.000	.000
Raftery (Rafferty), Tom-Thomas Francis	09CleA	10-05-81	Boston, Mass.	12-31-54	R	R	5'10	175	8	32	6	7	2	1	0		4		1	.219	.344
Ralston, Doc-Samuel Beryl	10WasA	08-03-85	Pierpont, Ohio	08-29-50	R	R	6'	185	22	73	4	15	1	0	0	3	3		2	.205	.219
Randall, Newt-Newton John	07ChiN 07BosN	02-03-80	New Lowell, Canada	05-03-55	R	R	5'10	180	97	336	22	71	10	5	0	19	27		6	.211	.271
Rariden, Bill-William Angel (Bedford Bill)	09-13BosN 14IndF 15NwkF 16-18NYN 19-20CinN	02-04-88	Bedford, Ind.	08-28-42	R	R	5'10	168	982	2877	272	682	105	24	7	272	340		47	.237	.308
Rath, Morrie-Morris Charles	09-10PhiA 10CleA 12-13ChiA 18MS 19-20CinN	12-25-86	Mobeetie, Tex.	11-18-45	L	R	5'8	160	563	2048	291	521	36	7	4	92	258		82	.254	.285
Raub, Tommy-Thomas Jefferson	03ChiN 15StLN	12-01-70	Raubsville, Pa.	02-15-49	R	R	5'10	155	60	162	15	41	5	6	0	9	9		5	.253	.358
Raymer, Fred-Frederick Charles	01ChiN 04-05BosN	11-12-75	Leavenworth, Kans.	06-12-57	R	R	5'11	185	371	1380	95	301	40	7	1	101	32		50	.218	.259
Raymond (Raymond Jack), Lou-Louis Anthony	19PhiN	12-11-94	Buffalo, N.Y.	05-02-79	R	R	5'10	187	1	2	0	1	0	0	0	0	0		0	.500	.500
Reardon, Phil-Philip Michael	06BknN	10-03-83	Brooklyn, N.Y.	09-28-20	R	R	5'9	160	5	14	0	1	0	0	0	0	0		0	.071	.071
Redmond, Harry-Harry John	09BknN	09-13-87	Cleveland, Ohio	07-10-60	R	R	5'8	170	6	19	3	0	0	0	0	1	0		0	.000	.000
Reed, Milt-Milton D. Jr.	11StLN 13-14PhiN 15BknF	07-04-90	Atlanta, Ga.	07-27-38	L	R	5'9	150	68	163	16	37	4	2	0	10	13		7	.227	.276
Reed, Ted-Ralph Edwin	15NwkF	10-18-90	Beaver, Pa.	02-06-59	R	R	5'11	190	20	77	5	20	1	2	0	4	2		1	.260	.325
Rehg, Wally-Walter Phillip	12PitN 13-15BosA 17-18BosA 19CinN	08-31-88	Summerfield, Ill.	04-05-46	R	R	5'8	160	258	752	85	188	24	11	2	66	52	66	26	.250	.319
Reilley, Duke-Alexander Aloysius (Midget)	09CleA	08-25-84	Chicago, Ill.	03-04-68	R	R	5'4	148	20	62	10	13	0	0	0	0	4		5	.210	.210
Reilly, Arch-Archer Edwin	17PitN	08-17-91	Alton, Ill.	11-29-63	R	R	5'10	163	1	0	0	0	0	0	0	0	0		0	—	—
Reilly, Barney-Bernard Eugene	09ChiA	02-07-85	Brockton, Mass.	11-15-34	R	R	6'1	175	12	25	3	5	0	0	0	3	3		2	.200	.200
Reilly, Hal-Harold John	19CinN	04-01-94	Oshkosh, Wis.	12-24-57	R	R	6'1	180	1	3	0	0	0	0	0	0	0		0	.000	.000
Reilly, Tom-Thomas Henry	08-09StLN 14CleA	08-03-84	St. Louis, Mo.	10-19-18	R	R	5'10		35	89	5	16	1	1	0	5	9		4	.180	.247
Reinecker (Smith), Wally-Walter Joseph	15BalF	04-21-90	Pittsburgh, Pa.	04-18-57	R	R	5'6	150	3	8	0	1	0	0	0	0	0		0	.125	.125
Rementer, Butch-Willis J. H.	04PhiN	03-14-78	Philadelphia, Pa.	09-23-22	R	R	5'7	180	1	2	0	0	0	0	0	0	0		0	.000	.000
Reynolds, Bill-William Dee	13-14NYA	08-14-84	Eastland, Tex.	06-05-24	R	R	6'	190	9	10	0	2	0	0	0	0	5		0	.200	.200
Rheam, Cy-Kenneth Johnston	14-15PitF	09-28-93	Pittsburgh, Pa.	10-23-47	R	R	6'	175	107	283	25	57	5	3	1	25	10		10	.201	.251
Richardson, Bill-William Henry (Jumbo)	01StLN	09-24-78	Salem, Ind.	11-06-49	R	R	5'11	200	15	52	7	11	2	0	0	7	6		1	.212	.365
Richardson, Tom-Thomas Mitchell	17StLA	08-07-83	Louisville, Ill.	11-15-39	R	R	6'	190	1	1	0	0	0	0	0	0	0		0	.000	.000
Rickert, Joe-Joseph Francis (Diamond Joe)	98PitN 01BosN	12-12-76	London, Ohio	10-15-43	R	R	5'10	165	15	66	6	11	2	0	0		3		1	.167	.242
Rickey, Branch-Wesley Branch (The Mahatma)	05-06StLA 07NYA 14,M13-15StLA M19-25StLN	12-20-81	Flat, Ohio	12-09-65	L	R	5'9	175	119	343	38	82	9	6	3	39	27		8	.239	.327
Rico, Art-Arthur Ramon	16-17BosN 18MS	07-23-95	Roxbury, Mass.	01-03-19	R	R	5'9	185	17	18	1	4	1	0	0	2	0		0	.222	.278
Riggert, Joe-Joseph Aloysius	11BosA 14BknN 14StLN 19BosN	12-11-86	Janesville, Wis.	12-10-73	R	R	5'9	170	174	558	68	134	18	14	8	44	46		20	.240	.366
Riley, Jimmy-James Joseph	10BosN	11-10-86	Buffalo, N.Y.	03-25-49	R	R	6'	165	6	14	1	0	0	0	0	0	3	3	0	.000	.000
Risberg, Swede-Charles August	17-20ChiA 20DL	10-13-94	San Francisco, Cal.	10-13-75	R	R	6'	165	476	1619	196	394	72	27	6	175	148	180	52	.243	.332
Rising, Pop-Percival Sumner		01-02-72	Industry, Pa.	01-28-38		R			8	18	2	2	1	1	0	2	2		0	.111	.278
Ritchey, Claude-Claude Cassius (Little All Right)	97CinN 98-99LouN 00-06PitN 07-09BosN	10-05-73	Emlenton, Pa.	11-08-51	B	R	5'6	167	1671	5929	711	1636	217	67	18	673	607		149	.276	.344
Ritter, Lew-Lewis Elmer (Old Dog)	02-08BknN	09-07-75	Liverpool, Pa.	05-27-52	R	R	5'9	190	462	1437	129	315	33	17	1	120	96		55	.219	.268
Roach, Roxey-Rudolph Charles	10-11NYA 12WasA 15BufF	11-28-82	Anita, Pa.	12-26-47	R	R	5'11	160	177	608	67	151	31	6	3	54	52		26	.248	.334
Roberts, Skipper-Clarence Ashley	13StLN 14PitF 14ChiF 14PitF	05-17-92	Wardner, Idaho	12-24-63	L	R	5'10	175	82	138	16	29	6	2	1	12	6		4	.210	.304
Robertson, Dave-Davis Aydelotte	12,14-17NYN 18MS 19NYN 19-21ChiN 21PitN 22NYN	09-25-89	Portsmouth, Va.	11-05-70	L	L	6'	186	804	2830	366	812	117	44	47	364	113	262	94	.287	.409
Robinson, Jack-John W. (Bridgeport)	02NYN	07-15-80	Portland, Me.	07-22-21	R	R			4	9	0	0	0	0	0	0	0		0	.000	.000
Robinson, Rabbit-William Clyde (Tug)	03WasA 04DetA 10CinN	03-05-82	Wellsburg, W. Va.	04-19-15	R	R	5'5	148	200	700	71	156	23	14	1	58	63		30	.223	.300
Robinson, Wilbert-Wilbert (Uncle Robbie)	86-90PhiAA 90-91BalAA 92-98BalN 00StLN 01-02,M02BalAA M14-31BknN	06-02-63	Bolton, Mass.	08-08-34	R	R	5'8	215	1361	5046	637	1399	211	54	18	740	286		227	.277	.351
Roche, Jack-John Joseph (Red)	14-15StLN 16ST 17StLN	12-01-91	Los Angeles, Cal.	03-31-83	R	R	6'1	178	59	49	3	14	2	2	0	5	4	9	2	.286	.408
Rochefort (Gilbert), Ben (Bennett Harold Rochefort)-Bennett Harold	14PhiA	08-15-96	Camden, N.J.	04-02-81	L	R	6'2	185	2	2	0	1	0	0	0	0	0		0	.500	.500
Rockenfield, Ike-Issac Broc	05-06StLA	11-03-76	Omaha, Neb.	02-17-58	R	R	5'7	150	122	411	43	91	6	5	0	24	47		11	.221	.260
Rodgers, Bill-Wilbur Kincaid (Raw Meat Bill)	15CleA 15BosA 15-16CinN	11-03-87	Pleasant Ridge, Ohio	12-24-78	L	R	5'8	160	102	268	30	65	15	4	0	19	22	40	11	.243	.328
Rodriguez, Joe-Jose (El Hombre Goma)	16-18NYN	02-23-94	Havana, Cuba	03-23-48	R	R	6'	170	58	145	17	24	0	3	0	17	14	4	8	.166	.207
Rogers, Jay-Jay Lewis	14NYA	08-03-88	Sandusky, N.Y.	07-01-64	R	R	5'11	178	5	0	0	0	0	0	0	0	0		0	.000	.000
Rohe, George-George Anthony (Whitey)	01BalA 05-07ChiA	09-15-75	Cincinnati, Ohio	06-10-57	R	R	5'9	165	267	868	81	197	33	9	3	92	72		9	.227	.306
Rolling, Ray-Raymond Copeland	12StLN	09-08-86	Martinsburg, Mo.	08-25-66	R	R	5'10	160	5	15	0	3	0	0	0	0	5		0	.200	.200
Rondeau, Henri-Henri Joseph	13DetA 15-16WasA	05-05-87	Danielson, Conn.	05-28-43	R	R	5'10	175	99	272	28	56	7	3	1	37	36	37	9	.206	.265
Rooney (Rovny), Frank-Frank	14IndF	10-12-84	Polebrady, Austria-Hungary	04-06-77					12	35	1	7	1	0	0	2	2		3	.200	.343
Rossman, Claude-Claud R.	04,06CleA 07-09DetA 09BosA	06-17-81	Philmont, N.Y.	01-16-28	L	L	6'	188	511	1848	175	523	80	26	3	238	90		49	.283	.359
Roth, Braggo-Robert Frank	14-15ChiA 15-18CleA 19PhiN 19BosA 20WasA 21NYA	08-28-92	Burlington, Wis.	09-11-36	R	R	5'7	170	811	2831	427	804	138	73	30	422	335	389	189	.284	.416
Roth, Frank-Francis (Germany)	03-04PhiN 05StLA 06ChiA 07BosN	08-28-92	Chicago, Ill.	03-27-55	R	R	5'8	160	282	783	83	196	32	8	1	75	36		19	.250	.315
Rothgeb, Claude-Claude James	05WasA	01-01-80	Milford, Ill.	07-06-44	R	R	6'	190	6	13	2	2	0	0	0	0	4		0	.154	.154
Rowan (Drohan), Dave-David	11StLA	12-06-82	Elora, Canada	07-30-55	L	L	5'11	175	18	65	7	25	1	0	0	11	4		0	.385	.431
Rowe, Harland-Harland Stimson (Hypie)	16PhiA	04-20-96	Springvale, Me.	05-26-65	R	R	6'1	170	17	36	2	5	3	0	0	2	3	8	0	.139	.194
Rudolph, Dutch-John Herman	03PhiN 04CinN	07-10-82	Natrona, Pa.	04-17-67	R	R	6'1	160	11	4	0	1	0	0	0	1	0		0	.250	.250
Rumler, Bill-William George	14,16-17StLA 18MS	03-27-91	Milford, Neb.	05-26-66	R	R	6'1	190	138	171	15	43	7	4	1	32	14	28	4	.251	.357
Russell, Harvey-Harvey Holmes	14-15BalF	01-10-87	Marshall, Va.	01-08-80	L	R	5'9	163	134	241	23	58	4	0	1	24	32		3	.241	.290
Rutherford, Jim-James Hollis	10CleA	09-26-86	Stillwater, Minn.	09-18-56	L	R	5'11	180	2	4	0	2	0	0	0	0	0		0	.500	.500

USE NAME - GIVEN NAMES (NICKNAMES)	TEAM BY YEAR	BIRTH DATE	BIRTH PLACE	DEATH DATE	B	T	HGT	WGT	G	AB	R	H	2B	3B	HR	RBI	BB	SO	SB	BA	SA
Ryan, Buddy-John Budd	12-13CleA		Near Denver, Colo.	07-09-56	L	R	5'9	172	166	571	79	161	18	10	1		63	41		13	.282	.354
Ryan, Jack-John Bernard	89-91LouAA 94-96BosN 98BknN 99BalN 01-03StLN 12-13WasA	11-12-68	Haverhill, Mass.	08-21-52	R	R	5'10	165	616	2199	245	479	71	30	4		193	85		26	.218	.283
Ryan, Jimmy-James Edward (Pony)	85-89ChiN 90ChiP 91-00ChiN 02-03WasA	02-11-63	Clinton, Mass.	10-26-23	R	L	5'9	162	2008	8165	1640	2524	439	153	118		1093	803		434	.309	.444
For Jimmy Ryan, Stolen Bases includes the years 86-03																						
Saier, Vic-Victor Sylvester	11-17ChiN 19PitN	05-04-91	Lansing, Mich.	05-14-67	L	R	5'11	185	864	2947	454	774	142	61	55	395	378	369	121	.263	.408
Savage, Jim-James Harold	12PhiN 14-15PitF	08-29-83	Southington, Conn.	06-26-40	B	R	5'5	150	148	503	82	139	9	9	1	26	69		17	.276	.336
Sawyer, Carl-Carl Everett (Huck)	15-16WasA	10-19-90	Seattle, Wash.	01-18-57	R	R	5'11	160		63	11	14	2	0	0	5	8	9	5	.222	.254
Schefer, Germany-William Herman	01-02ChiN 05-09DetA 09-14WasA 15NwkF 16NYA 18CleA	04-02-77	Chicago, Ill.	05-16-19	R	R	5'9	175	1143	3783	497	972	117	48	9	308	333		201	.257	.320
Schalk, Ray-Raymond William (Cracker)	12-28,M27-28ChiA 29NYN	08-12-92	Harvel, Ill.	05-19-70	R	R	5'9	165	1760	5306	579	1345	199	49	11	594	638		176	.253	.316
Schaller, Biff-Walter	11DetA 13ChiA	09-23-89	Chicago, Ill.	10-09-39	L	R	5'11	168	74	156	20	29	3	1	1	11	24		6	.186	.237
Schang, Bobby-Robert Martin	14-15PitN 15NYN 27StLN	12-07-86	Wales Center, N.Y.	08-29-66	R	R	5'7	165	82	186	14	35	7	4	0	6	18	47	3	.188	.269
Scheer, Al-Allen George	13BknN 14IndF 15NwkF	10-27-88	Groveport, Ohio	05-06-59	L	R	5'9	165	281	931	141	262	48	20	5	105	116		41	.281	.392
Scheeren, Fritz-Frederick (Dutch)	14-15PitN		Kokomo, Ind.	06-17-73	R	R	6'	180	15	34	4	9	0	1	1	2	1	6	1	.265	.412
Scheibeck, Frank-Frank S.	87CleAA 88DetN 90TolAA 94PitN 94-95,99WasN 01CleA 06DetA	06-28-65	Detroit, Mich.	10-22-56	R	R	5'7	145	389	1401	214	327	37	18	2	146	182		93	.233	.290
Schepner, Joe-Joseph Maurice (Gentleman Joe)	19StLA	08-10-95	Aliquippa, Pa.	07-25-59	R	R	5'10	170	14	48	2	10	4	0	0	6	1	5	0	.208	.292
Schiappacasse, Lou-Louis Joseph (Shippy)	02StLA	03-29-81	Ann Arbor, Mich.	09-20-10	R	R	5'7	145	2	5	0	0	0	0	0		1	1	0	.000	.000
Schick, Morrie-Maurice Francis	17ChiN 18MS	04-17-92	Chicago, Ill.	10-25-79	R	R	5'11	170	14	34	3	5	0	0	0	3	3	10	0	.147	.147
Schirick, Dutch-Harry Ernest	14StLA	06-15-90	Ruby, N.Y.	11-12-68	R	R	5'8	160	1	0	0	0	0	0	0	0	0	1	2	—	—
Schlafly, Larry-Harry Fenton	02ChiN 06-07WasA 14M,14-15BufF	09-19-78	Port Washington, Ohio	06-29-19	R	R	5'11	185	208	658	91	158	20	12	5	28	90		41	.240	.330
Schlei, Admiral-George Henry	04-08CinN 09-11NYN	01-24-78	Cincinnati, Ohio	10-24-58	R	R	5'10	185	636	1918	195	455	52	21	6	209	172		38	.237	.296
Schmidt, Boss-Charles	06-11DetA	09-12-80	Coal Hill, Ark.	11-14-32	B	R	5'11	200	477	1480	137	360	41	22	3	124	36		23	.243	.307
Schmidt, Butch-Charles John (See P01-19)	09NYA 13-15BosN	07-19-86	Baltimore, Md.	09-04-52	L	L	6'	175	297	1075	119	292	45	18	4	145	81		18	.272	.358
Schreckengost(Schrecongost), Ossee-Ossee Freeman	97LouN 98CleN 99StLN 99CleN 99StLN 01BosA 02CleA 02-08PhiA 08ChiA	04-11-75	New Bethlehem, Pa.	07-09-14	R	R	5'10	180	892	3048	304	830	130	34	9	338	102		45	.272	.346
Schreiber, Hank-Henry Walter	14ChiA 17BosN 18MS 19NYN 21NYN 26ChiN	07-12-91	Cleveland, Ohio	02-21-68	R	R	5'11	165	36	91	10	18	5	0	0	6	1	16	0	.198	.253
Schriver, Pop-William Frederick	86BknAA 88-90PhiN 91-94ChiN 95NYN 97CinN 98-00PitN 01StLN	07-11-65	Brooklyn, N.Y.	12-27-32	R	R	5'11	175	796	2705	362	715	112	40	16	375	223		54	.264	.353
Schulte, Jack-John Herman Frank	06BknN	11-15-81	Cincinnati, Ohio	08-17-75	R	R	5'9	180	2	7	0	0	0	0	0		0	0	0	.000	.000
Schulte, Wildfire-Frank M.	04-16ChiN 16-17PitN 17PhiN 18WasA	09-17-82	Cohocton, N.Y.	10-02-49	L	R	5'10	170	1805	6531	906	1766	288	124	93	792	545		233	.270	.395
Schwartz, Bill-William Charles (Blab)	04CleA	04-22-84	Cleveland, Ohio	08-29-61	R	R	6'2	185	24	86	5	13	2	0	0		4		4	.151	.174
Schweitzer, Al-Albert Casper (Cheese)	08-11StLA	12-23-82	Cincinnati, Ohio	01-27-69	R	R	5'6	170	280	874	97	208	28	8	3	87	104		47	.238	.299
Schwert, Pi-Pius Louis	14-15NYA	11-22-92	Angola, N.Y.	03-11-41	R	R	5'11	160	12	24	6	5	3	0	0	6	3	9	0	.208	.333
Schwind, Art-Arthur Edwin	12BknN		Fort Wayne, Ind.	01-13-68	B	R	5'8	150	1	2	0	1	0	0	0	0	0		0	.500	.500
Scott, Jim-James Walter	14PitF	09-22-88	Shenandoah, Pa.	05-12-72	R	R	5'9	185	8	24	2	6	1	0	0		1	5	1	.250	.292
Sebring, Jimmy-James Dennison	02-04PitN 04-05CinN 09BknN 09NYA	03-25-82	Liberty, Pa.	12-22-09	L	R	6'	180	363	1411	178	368	51	32	6	168	93		52	.261	.355
Selbach, Kip-Albert Karl	94-98WasN 99CinN 00-01NYN 02BalA 03-04WasA 04-06BosA	03-24-72	Columbus, Ohio	02-17-56	R	R	5'7	190	1608	6140	1067	1816	291	154	44	779	783		335	.296	.415
Sellers, Rube-Oliver	10BknN	03-07-81	Duquesne, Pa.	01-14-52	R	R	5'10	180	12	32	3	5	0	0	0	2	6	5	1	.156	.156
Sentell, Paul-Leopold Theodore	06-07PhiN	08-27-79	New Orleans, La.	04-27-23	R	R	5'9	176	66	195	19	44	5	1	1	14	15		15	.226	.277
Seybold, Socks-Ralph Orlando	99CinN 01-08PhiA	11-23-70	Washingtonville, Ohio	12-22-21	R	R	5'11	190	996	3701	479	1083	213	55	51	556	293		64	.293	.421
Seymour, Cy-James Bentley (See P01-19)	96-00NYN 01-02BalA 02-06CinN 06-10NYN 13BosN	12-09-72	Albany, N.Y.	09-20-19	L	L	6'	200	1522	5657	738	1720	232	97	52	799	354		218	.304	.407
Shafer, Ralph-Ralph Newton	14PitN	03-17-94	Cincinnati, Ohio	02-05-50			5'11		1	0	0	0	0	0	0		0		0	—	—
Shafer, Tillie-Arthur Joseph	09-10,12-13NYN	03-22-89	Los Angeles, Cal.	01-10-62	B	R	5'10	165	283	776	138	212	24	14	5	83	105		60	.273	.360
Shanabrook, Warren-Warren Hilton	06WasA	11-30-80	Massillon, Ohio	03-10-64	R	R	5'11	170	2	2	0	0	0	0	0	0	0		0	.000	.000
Shanks, Howard-Howard Samuel (Hank)	12-22WasA 23-24BosA 24NYA	07-21-90	Chicago, Ill.	07-30-41	R	R	5'11	170	1664	5699	604	1440	212	97	25	620	415		184	.253	.337
Shanley, Doc-Harry Root	12StLA	01-30-90	Granbury, Tex.	12-13-34	R	R	5'11	174	5	8	1	0	0	0	0		1	2		0	.000	.000
Shannon, Joe-Joseph Aloysius		02-11-97	Jersey City, N.J.	07-28-55	R	R	5'11	170	5	10	3	2	0	0	0		1	0	0	.200	.200
Shannon, Owen-Owen Dennis Ignatius	03StLN 07WasA	12-22-79	Omaha, Neb.	04-10-18	R	R			13	35	1	7	2	0	0	1	3		0	.200	.257
Shannon, Red-Maurice Joseph	15BosN 17-19PhiA 19BosA 20WasA 20-21PhiA 26BknN	02-11-97	Jersey City, N.J.	04-12-70	B	R	5'11	170	310	1070	124	277	38	22	0	91	109	178	21	.259	.336
Shannon, Spike-William Porter	04-06StLN 06-08NYN 08PitN	02-07-78	Pittsburgh, Pa.	05-16-40	B	R	5'11	180	694	2613	383	677	49	15	3	183	286		145	.259	.293
Sharman, Ralph-Ralph Edward (Bally)	17PhiA	04-24-95	Cleveland, Ohio	05-24-18	R	R	5'11	176	13	37	2	11	2	1	0		1		1	.297	.405
Sharpe, Bud-Bayard Heston	05,10BosN 10PitN	08-06-81	West Chester, Pa.	05-31-16	R	R	6'1	175	165	625	40	139	17	6	0	41	21		4	.222	.269
Shaughnessy, Shag-Francis Joseph	05WasA 08PhiA	04-08-83	Amboy, Ill.	05-15-69	R	R	6'1	165		32	2	9	0	0	0		1	2		3	.281	.281
Shaw, Al-Albert Simpson	07-09StLN 14BknF 15KCF	03-01-81	Toledo, Ohio	12-30-74	L	R	5'8	165	474	1547	235	434	74	28	14	170	173		64	.281	.392
Shaw, Al-Alfred (Shoddy)	01DetA 07BosA 08ChiA 09BosN	10-03-74	Burslem, England	03-25-58	R	R	5'8	160	180	459	31	92	9	3	1	32	35		6	.200	.240
Shaw, Ben-Benjamin Nathaniel	17-18PitN	06-18-93	La Center, Ky.	03-16-59	R	R	5'11	190	23	38	5	7	1	0	1	2	2		0	.184	.211
Shaw, Hunky-Royal N.	08PitN	09-29-84	Yakima, Wash.	07-03-69	R	R	5'8	165	1	1	0	0	0	0	0		0		0	.000	.000
Shay, Danny-Daniel Charles (Shea)	04-05StLN 07NYN	11-08-76	Springfield, Ohio	12-01-27	R	R	5'10		231	775	89	186	26	5	2	62	88		52	.240	.294
Shea, Gerry-Gerald Joseph	05StLN	10-26-81	St. Louis, Mo.	05-04-64	R	R	5'7	160	2	6	0	2	0	0	0		0		0	.333	.333
Shea, Nap-Napoleon Edward	02PitN	05-23-74	Ware, Mass.	07-08-68	R	R	5'5	155	3	8	1	1	0	0	0		0	1	0	.125	.125
Shean, Dave-David William	06PhiA 08-09PhiN 09-10BosN 11CinN 12BosN 17-18BosA 18-19BosA	05-23-78	Ware, Mass.	05-22-63	R	R	5'11	175	630	2167	225	495	59	23	6	166	155		66	.228	.285
Sheckard, Jimmy-Samuel James Tilden	97-98BknN 99BalN 00-01BknN 02BalA 02-05BknN 06-12ChiN 13StLN 13CinN	11-23-78	Upper Chanceford, Pa.	01-15-47	L	R	5'9	175	2121	7603	1296	2097	356	138	56	813	1135		475	.276	.381
Sheehan, Tommy-Thomas Patrick	00NYN 06-07PitN 08BknN	11-05-77	Sacramento, Cal.	05-22-59	R	R	5'8	160	317	1011	96	238	26	8	1	88	94		32	.236	.280
Shelton, Skeeter-Andrew Kempler	15NYA	06-29-88	Huntington, W.Va.	01-09-54	R	R	5'11	175	10	40	1	1	0	0	0	0	2	10	0	.025	.025
Sheridan, Red-Eugene Anthony (Gene)	18,20BknN	11-14-96	Brooklyn, N.Y.	11-25-75	R	R	5'10	160	5	6	0	1	0	0	0		0	1	1	.167	.167
Shields, Pete-Frank LeRoy	15CleA	09-21-91	Swiftwater, Miss.	02-11-61	R	R	6'	175	23	72	4	15	6	0	0	3	6	14	3	.208	.292
Shipke (Shipkrethaver), Bill-William Martin (Skipper Bill)	06CleA 07-09WasA	11-18-82	St. Louis, Mo.	09-10-40	R	R	5'7	145	186	552	59	110	11	10	1	29	55		21	.199	.261
Shook, Ray-Raymond Curtis	16ChiA	11-18-90	Perry, Ohio	09-16-70	R	R	5'7	155	1	0	0	0	0	0	0		0		0	—	—
Shotton, Burt-Burton Edwin (Barney)	09,11-17StLA 18WasA 19-23StLN M28-33PhiN M34CinN M47,48-50BknN	10-18-84	Brownhelm, Ohio	07-29-62	L	R	5'11	175	1387	4945	747	1338	154	65	9	290	713		294	.271	.333
Shovlin, John-John Joseph	11PitN 19-20StLA	02-12-76	Drifton, Pa.	02-12-70	R	R	5'7	163	18	43	7	9	0	0	0	3	5	3	0	.209	.209
Shugart, Frank-Frank Harry (Shugarts)	90ChiP 91-93PitN 93-94StLN 95LouN 97PhiN 01ChiA	12-10-66	Luthersburg, Pa.	09-09-44	B	R	5'8	170	742	2987	483	802	111	80	21	384	218		132	.268	.380
Sicking, Eddie-Edward Joseph	16ChiN 18-19NYN 19PhiN 20NYN 20CinN 27PitN	03-30-97	St. Bernard, Ohio	08-30-78	R	R	5'9	165	203	597	51	135	13	2	0	59	39	43	14	.226	.255
Siegle, Johnny-John Herbert	05-06CinN	07-08-74	Urbana, Ohio	02-12-68	R	R	5'10	165	39	124	13	25	3	4	1	15	10		0	.202	.315
Siglin, Paddy-Wesley Peter	14-16PitN		Aurelia, Iowa	08-05-56	R	R	5'9	160	23	50	5	9	0	0	0	2	5	10	2	.180	.180
Silva, Danny-Daniel James	19WasA	10-05-96	Everett, Mass.	04-04-74	R	R	6'	170	4	4	0	1	0	0	0		0		0	.250	.250
Simmons, Heck-George Washington	10DetA 12NYA 14-15BalF	01-29-85	Brooklyn, N.Y.	04-26-42	R	R	5'8	180	305	951	115	234	43	9	2	102	85		28	.246	.317
Simon, Mike-Michael Edward	09-13PitN 14StLF 15BknF	04-13-83	Hayden, Ind.	06-10-63	R	R	5'11	188	378	1069	85	241	28	10	1	90	54		9	.225	.262
Siner, Hosea-Hosea John	09BknN	03-07-85	Shelburn, Ind.	06-11-48	R	R	5'10	185	10	23	1	3	0	0	0	1	0		0	.130	.130
Slagle, Jimmy-James Franklin (Rabbit, Shorty)	99WasN 00-01PhiN 01BosN 02-08ChiN	07-11-73	Worthville, Pa.	05-10-56	L	R	5'7	145	1298	4989	779	1348	128	55	2	344	619		273	.270	.319
Slattery, Jack-John Terrence	01BosA 03CleA 03ChiA 06StLN 09WasA M28BosN	01-06-77	Boston, Mass.	07-17-49	R	R	6'2	190	103	288	14	61	5	2	0	27	6		3	.212	.243
Sloan, Tod-Yale Yeastman	13,17StLA 18MS 19StLA	12-24-90	Madisonville, Tenn.	09-12-56	L	R	6'	175	143	402	43	94	8	5	2	33	41	46	3	.234	.294
Smith, Broadway Aleck-Alexander Benjamin	97-99BknN 99BalN 00BknN 01NYN 02BalA 03BosA 04CinN 06NYN	??-??-71	New York, N.Y.	07-09-19	R				283	948	108	251	32	11	1	130	26		38	.265	.325
Smith, Bull-Lewis Oscar	04PitN 06CinN 11WasA	08-20-80	Plum, W.Va.	05-01-28	R	R	6'	180	15	43	2	6	0	1	0		5		0	.140	.186
Smith, Elmer-Elmer Ellsworth (Mike) (See P01-19)	86-89CinAA 92-97PitN 98-00CinN 00NYN 01PitN 01BknN	03-23-68	Pittsburgh, Pa.	11-03-45	L	L	5'11	178	1233	4675	931	1462	202	131	37	661	636		243	.313	.436
Smith, Fred-Fred Vincent	13BknN 14-15BufF 15BknF 17StLN	07-29-86	Cleveland, Ohio	05-28-61	R	R	5'11	185	438	1422	143	321	39	25	8	158	133		58	.226	.302
Smith, Hap-Henry Joseph	10BknN	07-09-86	Coquille, Ore.	02-26-61	L	R	6'	185	35	76	6	18	2	0	0	8	14	14	4	.237	.263
Smith, Harry-Harry Thomas	01PhiA 02-07PitN 08-10,M09BosN	10-31-74	Yorkshire, England	02-17-33	R	R	5'8	165	343	1004	83	214	22	7	2	89	55		23	.213	.263
Smith, Harry-James Harry	14-15NYN 15BknF 17-18CinN	05-15-90	Brooklyn, N.Y.	04-01-22	R	R	5'10	180	75	148	10	27	1	1	0	14	21	26	4	.182	.250
Smith, Heinie-George Henry	97-98LouN 99PitN 01-02,M02NYN		Pittsburgh, Pa.	06-25-39	R	R	5'9	160	309	1120	117	269	43	7	3	91	51		54	.240	.299
Smith (Coffey), Jack-John Joseph	12DetA	08-08-94	Oswayo, Pa.	12-04-62	R	R	5'9		1	0	0	0	0	0	0		0		0	—	—
Smith, Jimmy-James Lawrence	14-15ChiF 15BalF 16PitN 17NYN 18BosN 19CinN 21-22PhiN	05-15-95	Pittsburgh, Pa.	01-01-74	B	R	5'10	152	370	1127	119	247	32	15	12	101	63		18	.219	.306

Bats Right 14

USE NAME - GIVEN NAMES (NICKNAMES)	TEAM BY YEAR	BIRTH DATE	BIRTH PLACE	DEATH DATE	B	T	HGT	WGT	G	AB	R	H	2B	3B	HR	RBI	BB	SO	SB	BA	SA
Smith (Persico), Joe-Salvatore Joseph	13NYA	12-29-93	New York, N.Y.	01-12-74	R	R	5'8	190	13	32	1	5	0	0	0	2	1	14	1	.156	.156
Smith, Jud-Grant Judson	93CinN 93StLN 96PitN 98WasN 01PitN	01-13-69	Green Oak, Mich.	12-07-47	R	R	6'	185	102	344	49	90	11	5	4	37	37		14	.279	.375
Smith, Klondike-Armstrong Frederick	12NYA	01-04-87	London, England	11-15-59	L	L	5'9	165	7	27	0	5	1	0	0	0	1		1	.185	.222
Smith, Paul-Paul Stoner	16CinN	05-07-88	Mt. Zion, Ill.	07-03-58	R	R	6'1	190	10	44	5	10	0	1	0	1	1	8	3	.227	.273
Smith, Red-James Carlisle	11-14BknN 14-19BosN	04-06-90	Greenville, S.C.	10-10-66	R	R	5'11	165	1117	3907	477	1087	208	49	27	514	420	415	117	.278	.377
Smith, Red-Willard Jehu	17-18PitN	04-11-92	Logansport, Ind.	07-17-72	R	R	5'8	165	26	45	2	7	0	0	0	5	6	4	1	.156	.200
Smith, Syd-Sydney A.	08PhiA 08StLA 10-11CleA 14-15PitN	08-31-83	Smithville, S.C.	06-05-61	R	R	5'10	190	146	397	24	98	21	5	2	40	22		2	.247	.340
Smith, Tony-Anthony (Irish)	07WasA 10-11BknN	05-14-84	Chicago, Ill.	02-27-64	R	R	5'9	150	170	500	46	90	12	2	1	26	95		13	.180	.218
Smith, Wally-Wallace Henry	11-12StLN 14WasA	03-13-88	Philadelphia, Pa.	06-10-30	R	R	5'11	180	201	510	56	117	15	11	2	53	53	72	12	.229	.314
Smith, Wib-Wilbur Floyd	09StLN	08-30-86	Evart. Mich.	11-18-59	R	R	5'10	165	17	42	3	8	0	0	0	2	3		0	.190	.190
Smoot, Homer-Homer Vernon (Doc)	02-06StLN 06CinN	03-23-78	Galestown, Md.	03-25-28	L	R	6'	190	680	2635	308	763	102	45	15	269	149		84	.290	.380
Smoyer (Smowery), Harry-Henry Neitz (Hennie)	12StLA	04-24-90	Fredericksburg, Pa.	02-28-58	R	R	5'6		6	14	1	3	0	0	0	0	0		1	.214	.214
Smykal (Smeikal), Frank-Frank John	16PhiN	10-13-89	Chicago, Ill.	08-11-50	R	R	5'7	150	6	10	1	3	0	0	0	2	3	1	1	.300	.300
Smyth, Red-James Daniel	15-17BknN 17-18StLN	01-30-91	Holly Springs, Miss.	04-14-58	L	R	5'9	152	128	236	32	45	2	4	1	12	28	31	7	.191	.233
Snell(Schnell), Charlie-Charles Anthony	12StLA	11-29-93	Hampstead, Md.	04-04-88	R	R	5'11	170	8	19	0	4	1	0	0	0	3		0	.211	.263
Snell, Wally-Walter Henry (Doc)	13BosA	05-19-89	West Bridgewater, Mass.	07-23-80	R	R	5'10	178	5	8	1	3	0	0	0	0	1		0	.375	.375
Snodgrass, Fred-Fred Carlisle (Snow)	08-15NYN 15-16BosN	10-19-87	Ventura, Cal.	04-05-74	R	R	5'11	175	923	3101	453	852	143	42	11	351	386		215	.275	.359
Snodgrass, Chappie-Amzie Beal	01BalA	03-18-70	Springfield, Ohio	09-09-51	R	R	6'1	165	3	10	0	1	0	0	0		1		0	.100	.100
Snyder, Jack-John William	14BufF 17BknN	10-06-86	Lincoln, Pa.	12-13-81	R	R	5'9	170	8	11	1	3	0	0	0		1		0	.273	.273
Somerlott, Jock-John Wesley	10-11WasA	10-26-82	Flint, Ind.	04-21-65	R	R	6'	170	29	103	9	21	0	0	0	4	3		4	.204	.204
Southwick, Clyde-Clyde Aubra	11StLA	11-03-86	Maxwell, Iowa	10-14-61	L	R	6'	180	4	12	3	3	0	0	0	0	1		0	.250	.250
Speaker, Tris-Tristram E. (The Grey Eagle)	07-15BosA 16-26,M19-26CleA 27WasA 28PhiA	04-04-88	Hubbard, Tex.	12-08-58	L	L	5'11	193	2789	10197	1882	3514	792	223	117	1527	1381		433	.345	.500
Spencer, Ben-Lloyd Benjamin	13WasA	05-15-90	Patapsco, Md.	09-01-70	L	L	5'8	160	8	21	2	6	1	1	0	2	4		0	.286	.429
Spencer, Ches-Chester Arthur	06BosN	03-04-83	South Webster, Ohio	11-10-38	R	R	6'	180	8	27	1	4	1	0	0	0	0		0	.148	.185
Spencer, Tubby-Edward Russell	05-08StLA 09BosA 11PhiN 16-18DetA	01-26-84	Oil City, Pa.	02-01-45	R	R	5'10	215	449	1326	106	298	43	10	3	133	87		13	.225	.279
Spratt, Harry-Henry Lee (Jack)	11-12BosN	07-10-87	Broadford, Pa.	07-03-69	R	R	5'8	175	89	243	28	60	7	6	5	28	20	36	3	.247	.387
Stafford, Heinie-Henry Alexander	16NYN	11-01-91	Orleans, Vt.	01-29-72	R	R	5'7	160	1	1	0	0	0	0	0	0	0		0	.000	.000
Stahl, Chick-Charles Sylvester	97-00BosN 01-06,M06BosA	01-10-73	Avilla, Ind.	03-28-07	L	L	5'10	160	1303	5062	856	1552	218	117	36	622	470		173	.307	.417
Stahl, Jake-Garland	03BosA 04-06,M05-06WasA 08NYA 08-10BosA 11VR 12-13,M12-13BosA	04-13-79	Elkhart, Ind.	09-18-22	R	R	6'2	195	981	3421	405	891	149	87	31	437	221		178	.260	.382
Stanage, Oscar-Oscar Harland	06CinN 09-20,25DetA	03-17-83	Tulare, Cal.	11-11-64	R	R	5'11	190	1094	3503	248	819	123	34	8	321	219		30	.234	.295
Stankard, Tom-Thomas Francis	04PitN	03-20-82	Waltham, Mass.	06-13-58	R	R	6'1	190	2	2	0	0	0	0	0	0	0		0	.000	.000
Stanley, Jim-James Francis	14ChiF	05-07-89	Chicago, Ill.	06-30-35	R	R	5'6	148	54	98	13	19	3	0	0	4	19		2	.194	.224
Stanley, Joe-Joseph Bernard	97WasN 02WasA 03-04BosN 05-06WasA 09ChiN	04-02-81	Washington, D.C.	09-13-67	B	R	5'9	150	216	694	77	148	15	10	2	76	51		20	.213	.272
Stansbury, Jack-John James	12-06-85	Phillipsburg, N.J.	12-26-70	R	R	5'9	165	20	47	3	6	1	0	0	2	6	3	0	.128	.149		
Stanton, Tom-Thomas Patrick	04ChiN	10-25-74	St. Louis, Mo.	01-17-57	R	R	5'10	175	1	3	0	0	0	0	0	0	0		0	.000	.000
Stark, Dolly-Monroe Randolph	09CleA 10-12BknN	01-19-85	Ripley, Miss.	12-01-24	R	R	5'9	160	127	378	38	90	7	1	0	30	34		14	.238	.262
Starnagle (Steuernagel), George-George Henry	02CleA		Belleville, Ill.	02-15-46	R	R	5'11	155	1	3	0	0	0	0	0	0	0		0	.000	.000
Starr, Charlie-Charles Watkin	05StLA 08PitN 09BosN 09PhiN	08-30-78	Pike Co.,Ohio	10-18-37	L	R	5'10	165	108	375	33	79	4	3	0	20	51		13	.211	.237
Steelman, Farmer-Morris James	99LouN 00-01BknN 01-02PhiN	06-29-75	Millville, N.J.	09-16-44		R	5'11		43	142	8	31	3	1	0	15	14		6	.218	.254
Steinbrenner, Gene-Eugene Gass	12PhiN	11-17-92	Pittsburgh, Pa.	04-25-70	R	R	5'9		3	9	0	2	1	0	0	1	0	3	0	.222	.333
Steinfeldt, Harry-Harry M.	98-05CinN 06-10ChiN 11BosN	09-29-77	St. Louis, Mo.	08-17-14	R	R	5'10	180	1645	5898	762	1575	282	91	27	762	471		189	.267	.359
Stellbauer, Bill-William Jennings	16PhiA	03-20-94	Bremond, Tex.	02-16-74	R	R	5'10	175	25	48	2	13	2	1	0	5	6	7	2	.271	.354
Stem, Fred-Frederick Boothe	08-09BosN	09-22-85	Oxford, N.C.	09-05-64	L	R	6'2	180	92	317	22	71	2	4	0	14	14		6	.224	.256
Stengel, Casey-Charles Dillon (The Old Professor)	12-17BknN 18-19PitN 19-21PhiN 21-23NYN 24-25BosN M34-36BknN M38-43BosN M49-60NYA M62-65NYN	07-30-90	Kansas City, Mo.	09-29-75	L	L	5'11	175	1277	4288	575	1219	182	89	60	535	437	453	131	.284	.410
Stephens, Jim-James Walter (Little Nemo)	07-12StLA	12-10-83	Salineville, Ohio	01-02-65	R	R	5'6	157	427	1262	95	286	30	21	3	97	77		14	.227	.291
Sterrett, Dutch-Charles Hurlbut	12-13NYA	10-01-89	Milroy, Pa.	12-09-65	R	R	5'11	165	87	265	30	67	4	7	1	35	12		9	.253	.332
Stewart, Mark-Mark (Big Slick)	13CinN	10-14-89	Whitlock, Tenn.	01-17-32	L	R	6'1	180	1	1	0	0	0	0	0	0	0		0	.000	.000
Stewart, Tuffy-Charles Eugene	13PitN	07-31-83	Chicago, Ill.	11-18-34	L	L	5'10	167	11	9	1	1	0	0	0	2	2	5	1	.111	.222
Stone, George-George Robert	03BosA 05-10StLA	09-03-76	Lost Nation, Iowa	01-03-45	L	L	5'7	175	848	3271	426	984	107	69	23	268	282		132	.301	.397
Storke, Alan-Alan Marshall	06-09PitN 09StLN	09-27-84	Auburn, N.Y.	03-18-10	R	R	6'1		266	863	68	225	22	11	2	74	45		17	.261	.319
Stovall, George-George Thomas (Firebrand)	04-11,M11CleA 12-13,M12-13StLA 14-15,M14-15KCF	11-23-77	Leeds, Mo.	11-05-51	R	R	6'2	180	1409	5218	545	1375	231	59	15	563	171		145	.264	.339
Strands, Johnny-John Lawrence	15NwkF	12-05-85	Chicago, Ill.	01-19-57	R	R	5'10	165	35	75	7	14	3	0	0	11	6		1	.187	.293
Strang (Nicklin), Sammy (Samuel Strang)-Samuel Nicklin (The Dixie Thrush)	96LouN 00ChiN 01NYN 02ChiA 02ChiN 03-04BknN 05-08NYN	12-16-76	Chattanooga, Tenn.	03-13-32	B	R	5'8	160	901	2925	479	787	112	28	16	253	464		219	.269	.343
Street, Gabby-Charles Evard (Old Sarge)	04-05CinN 05BosN 05CinN 08-11WasA 12NYA 31,M29-33StLN M38StLA	09-30-82	Huntsville, Ala.	02-06-51	R	R	5'10	180	503	1501	98	312	44	11	2	105	119		17	.208	.256
Strobal, Allie-Albert Irving	05-06BosN	06-11-84	Boston, Mass.	02-10-55	R	R	6'	180	105	336	29	66	10	3	1	26	29		2	.196	.253
Strunk, Amos-Amos Aaron	08-17PhiA 18-19BosA 19-20PhiA 20-24ChiA 24PhiA	01-22-89	Philadelphia, Pa.	07-22-79	L	L	5'11	175	1507	4994	695	1415	212	96	15	528	573		185	.283	.373
Stumpf, Bill-William Frederick	12-13NYA	03-21-92	Baltimore, Md.	02-14-66	R	R	6'	175	52	158	13	37	1	0	0	11	9		5	.234	.241
Sturgis, Dean-Dean Donnell	14PhiA	12-01-92	Beloit, Kans.	08-04-50	R	R	6'1	180	4	4	1	1	0	0	0	0	0	2	0	.250	.250
Sugden, Joe-Joseph	93-97PitN 98StLN 99CleN 01ChiA 02-05StLA 12DetA	07-31-70	Philadelphia, Pa.	06-28-59	R	R	5'10	180	822	2703	295	695	72	24	3	283	220		49	.257	.305
Sullivan, Andy-Andrew Raymond	04BosN	08-30-84	Southborough, Mass.	02-14-20		R			1	1	0	0	0	0	0	0	0		0	.000	.000
Sullivan, Billy-William Joseph Sr.	99-00BosN 01-12,14,M09CliiA 16DetA	01-28-65	Oakland, Wis.	01-28-65	R	R	5'9	155	1143	3651	363	775	118	33	20	378	170		99	.212	.279
Sullivan, Denny-Dennis William	05WasA 07-08BosA 08-09CleA	09-28-82	Hillsboro, Wis.	06-02-56	L	R	5'10		254	923	106	221	25	7	1	51	59		31	.239	.285
Sullivan, Eddie (See Eddie Collins)																					
Sullivan, John-John Eugene	05DetA 08PitN	02-16-73	Chicago, Ill.	06-05-24	R	R	5'10	170	13	32	4	5	0	0	0	4	4		0	.156	.156
Swacina, Harry-Harry Joseph (Swats)	07-08PitN 14-15BalF	08-22-81	St. Louis, Mo.	06-21-44	R	R	6'2	190	322	1189	110	304	46	11	3	151	32		29	.256	.315
Swander, Pinky-Edward Ottis	03-04StLA	07-04-80	Portsmouth, Ohio	10-24-44	L	L	5'9	180	15	52	9	14	2	2	0	6	10		0	.269	.385
Swanson, Bill-William Andrew	14BosA	10-12-88	New York, N.Y.	10-14-54	B	R	5'7	140	11	20	0	4	2	0	0	3	4		0	.200	.300
Sweeney, Bill-William John	07ChiN 07-13BosN 14ChiN	03-06-86	Covington, Ky.	05-26-48	R	R	5'10	175	1039	3692	442	1004	153	40	11	389	423		172	.272	.344
Sweeney, Charlie-Charles Francis (Buck)	14PhiA	04-16-90	Pittsburgh, Pa.	03-13-55			5'8		1	0	0	0	0	0	0	0	0		0	.000	.000
Sweeney, Ed-Edward Francis (Jeff)	08-15NYA 19PitN	07-19-88	Chicago, Ill.	07-04-47	R	R	6'1	200	644	1841	174	427	48	13	5	151	181		63	.232	.277
Swindells, Charlie-Charles Jay	04StLN	10-26-78	Rockford, Ill.	07-22-40	R	R	5'11	180	3	8	0	1	0	0	0	0	0		0	.125	.125
Taggert, Bob-Robert John (played as Barney Kelly 14-15)	14PitN 15PitF 18BosN	02-01-84	Bloomfield, N.J.	04-10-61	L	R	5'11	180	215	714	91	212	15	22	4	57	46		42	.297	.396
Tannehill, Jesse-Jesse Niles (See P01-19)	94CinN 97-02PitN 03NYA 04-08BosA 08-09WasA 11ChiN	07-14-74	Dayton, Ky.	09-22-56	B	L	5'8	150	505	1409	191	361	59	23	6	143	105		19	.256	.344
Tannehill, Lee-Lee Ford	03-12ChiA	10-26-80	Dayton, Ky.	02-16-38	R	R	5'11	170	1089	3778	331	833	135	27	3	346	229		63	.220	.273
Tappan, Walt-Walter Van Dorn (Tap)	14KCF	10-08-90	Carlinville, Ill.	12-19-67	R	R	5'8	158	18	39	1	8	0	0	0	3	1		1	.205	.308
Tate, Hughie-Hugh Henry	05WasA	08-07-56	Everett, Pa.	08-07-56	R	R	5'11	190	4	10	1	3	0	0	0	0	1		0	.300	.500
Tennant, Tom-Thomas Francis	12StLA	07-03-82	Monroe, Wis.	02-15-55	L	L	5'11	165	2	2	0	0	0	0	0	0	0		0	.000	.000
Tenney, Fred-Frederick	94-07,M05-07BosN 08-09NYN 11,M11BosN	11-26-71	Georgetown, Mass.	07-03-52	L	L	5'9	155	1980	7587	1271	2239	264	80	22	688	874		285	.295	.360
Tesch, Tiny-Albert John	15BknF	01-27-90	Jersey City, N.J.	08-03-47	B	R	5'11	190	8	7	2	2	1	0	0	2	0		0	.286	.429
Textor, George-George Brnhardt (Tex)	14IndF 15NwkF 02PhiN	12-27-86	Newport, Ky.	03-11-54	B	R	5'10	174	25	63	3	12	1	0	0	4	5		0	.190	.190
Thomas, Bill-William Miskey	12PhiN	12-08-77	Norristown, Pa.	01-14-50	R	R	5'10	190	6	17	1	2	0	0	0	2	0		0	.118	.118
Thomas, Fred-Frederick Harvey	18BosA 19-20PhiA 20WasA	12-19-92	Milwaukee, Wis.	01-15-86	R	R	5'10	160	247	859	88	193	19	14	4	45	84	90	24	.225	.293
Thomas, Ira-Ira Felix	06-07NYA 08DetA 09-15PhiA	01-22-81	Ballston Spa, N.Y.	10-11-58	R	R	6'	190	481	1352	124	327	46	17	3	155	82		20	.242	.308
Thomas, Pinch-Chester David (Goat)	12-17BosA 18-21CleA	01-24-88	Camp Point, Ill.	12-24-53	R	R	5'9	173	408	1035	88	245	28	17	3	102	110		12	.237	.284
Thomas, Roy-Roy Allen	99-08PhiN 08PitN 09BosN 11PhiN	03-24-74	Norristown, Pa.	11-20-59	L	L	5'11	150	1472	5292	1008	1539	99	54	7	299	1042		251	.291	.304
Thomas, Tommy-William Walter	08BosN	04-28-84	Foot-of-Ten, Pa.	06-06-50	R	R	5'8	156	13	13	2	2	0	0	0	0	1		2	.154	.154
Thomason, Art-Arthur Wilson (Sillie)	10CleA	02-12-89	Liberty, Mo.	05-02-44	L	R	5'11	170	16	57	6	9	1	0	0	1	2		1	.158	.193
Thompson, Homer-Homer Thomas	12NYA	06-01-91	Spring City, Tenn.	09-12-57	R	R	5'9	160	1	0	1	0	0	0	0	0	0		0	—	—
Thompson, Sam-Samuel Luther (Big Sam)	85-88DetN 89-98PhiN 06DetA	03-05-60	Danville, Ind.	11-07-22	L	L	6'3	207	1406	5972	1259	1984	326	156	128	1299	450		235	.332	.503
								For Sam Thompson, Stolen Bases includes the years 86-06													
Thompson, Shag-James Alfred	14-16PhiA	04-29-93	Black Mountain, N.C.	01-07-90	L	R	5'8	165	48	79	12	16	2	1	0	4	18	20	2	.203	.253
Thoney (Thoeny), Jack-John (Bullet Jack)	02CleA 02BalA 03CleA 04WasA 04NYA 08-09,11BosA	12-08-79	Fort Thomas, Ky.	10-24-48	R	R	5'10	175	264	912	126	216	23	12	3	73	36		42	.237	.298
Thorpe, Jim-James Francis 20-26, 28 played in N.F.L.	13-15NYN 17CinN 17-19NYN 19BosN	05-22-87	Prague, Okla.	03-28-53	R	R	6'1	200	289	698	91	176	20	18	7	82	27	122	29	.252	.362
					Bats Both 15																

USE NAME - GIVEN NAMES (NICKNAMES)	TEAM BY YEAR	BIRTH DATE	BIRTH PLACE	DEATH DATE	B	T	HGT	WGT	G	AB	R	H	2B	3B	HR	RBI	BB	SO	SB	BA	SA
Thrasher, Buck-Frank Edward	16-17PhiA	08-06-89	Watkinsville, Ga.	06-12-38	L	R	6'	182	30	106	9	27	4	2	0	6	5	13	0	.255	.330
Tiemeyer, Eddie-Edward Carl	06-07CinN 09NYA	05-09-85	Cincinnati, Ohio	09-27-46	R	R	5'11	185	9	19	5	5	1	0	0	3	0		0	.263	.316
Tinker, Joe-Joseph Bert	02-12ChiN 13,M13CinN 14-15,M14-15ChiF 16,M16CinN	07-27-80	Muscotah, Kans.	07-27-48	R	R	5'9	175	1803	6438	777	1690	264	114	31	782	416		341	.263	.353
Titus, John-John Franklin (Silent John)	03-12PhiN 12-13BosN	02-21-76	St. Clair, Pa.	01-08-43	L	R	5'9	166	1402	4960	738	1401	253	72	38	561	620		140	.282	.385
Tomer, George-George Clarence	13StLA	11-26-95	Perry, Iowa	12-15-84	L	R	6'	180	1	0	0	0	0	0	0	0	0	1	0	.000	.000
Tonneman, Tony-Charles Richard	11BosA	09-10-81	Chicago, Ill.	08-04-51	R	R	5'10	175	2	5	0	1	1	0	0	3	1		0	.200	.400
Tooley, Bert-Albert R.	11-12BknN	08-30-86	Howell, Mich.	08-17-76	R	R	5'10	155	196	698	89	151	17	8	3	66	72	84	30	.216	.277
Towne, Babe-Jay King	06ChiA	03-12-80	Coon Rapids, Iowa	10-29-38	R	R	5'10	190	13	36	3	10	0	0	0	6	7		0	.278	.278
Tragesser, Walt-Walter Joseph	13,15-19BosN 19-20PhiN	06-14-87	Lafayette, Ind.	12-14-70	R	R	6'	175	272	689	54	148	31	3	6	66	35	125	14	.215	.295
Truesdale, Frank-Frank Day	10-11StLA 14NYA 18BosA	03-31-84	St. Louis, Mo.	08-27-43	B	R	5'8	145	216	668	69	147	12	2	1	40	91		41	.220	.249
Turner, Terry-Terrence Lamont (Cotton Top)	01PitN 04-18CleA 19PhiA	02-28-81	Sandy Lake, Pa.	07-18-60	R	R	5'8	150	1665	5917	698	1497	207	77	8	528	435		256	.253	.336
Tutwiler, Guy-Guy Isbel (King Tut)	11,13DetA	07-17-89	Coalburg, Ala.	08-15-60	L	R	6'	175	27	79	7	16	2	1	0	10	6		2	.203	.253
Twombly, George-George Frederick (Silent George)	14-16CinN 17BosN	06-04-92	Jamaica Plain, Mass.	02-17-75	R	R	5'8	150	150	417	35	88	1	7	0	33	41	41	21	.211	.247
Tyler, Clancy-Frederick Franklin	14BosN	12-16-91	Derry, N.H.	10-14-45	R	R	5'10	180	6	19	2	2	0	0	0	2	1	5	0	.105	.105
Tyree, Earl-Earl Carlton	14ChiN	03-04-90	Huntsville, Ill.	05-17-54	R	R	5'8	160	1	4	1	0	0	0	0	0	0		0	.000	.000
Uhler, Maury-Maurice William	14CinN	12-14-86	Pikesville, Md.	05-04-18	R	R	5'11	165	46	56	12	12	2	0	0	3	5	11	4	.214	.250
Unglaub, Bob-Robert Alexander	04NYA 04-05,07-08,M07BosA 08-10WasA	07-31-81	Baltimore, Md.	11-29-16	R	R	5'11	178	595	2150	188	554	67	35	5	215	88		66	.258	.328
Ury, Lou-Louis Newton	03StLN	04-??-77	Fort Scott, Kans.	03-14-18	R	R	6'		2	7	0	1	0	0	0	0	0		0	.143	.143
Vahrenhorst, Harry-Harry Henry (Dutch)	04StLA	02-13-85	St. Louis, Mo.	10-10-43	R	R	6'1	175	1	1	0	0	0	0	0	0	0		0	.000	.000
Van Buren, Deacon-Edward Eugene	04BknN 04PhiN	12-14-70	La Salle Co., Ill.	06-29-57	L	R	5'10	175	13	44	2	11	2	0	0	3	3		2	.250	.295
Vandagrift, Carl-Carl William	14IndF	04-22-83	Centralia, Ill.	10-09-20	R	R	5'8	155	43	136	25	34	4	0	0	9	9		7	.250	.279
Van Haltren, George-George Edward Martin (See P01-19)	87-89ChiN 90BknP	03-30-66	St. Louis, Mo.	09-29-45	L	L	5'11	170	1979	8007	1650	2558	293	159	69	1014	868		564	.319	.422
	91,M91BalAA 92,M92BalN 92-93PitN 94-03NYN																				
Vann, John-John Silas	13StLN	06-07-90	Fairland, Okla.	06-10-58	R	R		186	1	0	0	0	0	0	0	0	0	1	0	.000	.000
Van Zandt, Ike-Charles Isaac	01NYN 04ChiN 05StLA	02-??-76	Brooklyn, N.Y.	09-14-08	L	L			100	339	32	76	15	1	1	20	7		7	.224	.283
Vaughn, Bobby-Robert	09NYA 15StLF	06-04-85	Stamford, N.Y.	04-11-65	R	R	5'9	150	149	535	70	148	19	9	0	32	59		25	.277	.346
Veach, Bobby-Robert Hayes	12-23DetA 24-25BosA 25NYA 25WasA	06-29-88	St. Charles, Ky.	08-07-45	L	R	5'11	160	1821	6659	953	2064	393	147	64	1166	571		195	.310	.442
Vick, Sammy-Samuel Bruce	17-20NYA 21BosA	04-12-95	Batesville, Miss.	08-17-86	R	R	5'10	163	213	641	90	159	28	11	2	50	51	91	12	.248	.335
Vinson, Rube-Ernest Augustus	04-05CleA 06ChiA	03-20-79	Dover, Del.	10-12-51	L	R	5'9	168	60	206	26	47	4	1	0	14	19		7	.228	.257
Viox, Jim-James Henry	12-16PitN	12-30-90	Lockland, Ohio	01-06-69	R	R	5'7	150	506	1703	214	465	76	24	7	191	222	108	39	.273	.358
Vitt, Ossie-Oscar Joseph	12-18DetA 19-21BosA M38-40CleA	01-04-90	San Francisco, Cal.	01-31-63	R	R	5'10	150	1062	3760	560	894	106	48	4	294	455		114	.238	.295
Von Kolnitz, Fritz-Alfred Holmes	14-15CinN 16ChiA	05-20-93	Charleston, S.C.	03-18-48	R	R	5'10	175	115	226	15	48	9	1	0	19	15	33	5	.212	.261
Wade, Ham-Abraham Lincoln	07NYN	12-20-80	Spring City, Pa.	07-21-68	R	R	5'8	155	1	0	0	0	0	0	0	0	0		0	---	---
Wagner, Bill-William Joseph	14-17PitN 18BosN	01-02-94	Jessup, Iowa	01-11-51	R	R	6'	187	93	242	19	50	7	4	1	18	21	37	1	.207	.281
Wagner, Heinie-Charles F.	02NYN 06-13BosA 14IL 15-16,18,M30BosA	09-23-80	New York, N.Y.	03-20-43	R	R	5'9	183	983	3333	402	834	128	47	10	343	310		144	.250	.326
Wagner, Honus-John Peter (The Flying Dutchman)	97-99LouN 00-17,M17PitN	02-24-74	Chartiers, Pa.	12-06-55	R	R	5'11	200	2791	10439	1739	3420	643	252	101	1732	963		720	.328	.467
Wagner, Joe-Joseph Bernard	15CinN	04-24-89	New York, N.Y.	11-15-48	R	R	5'11	165	75	197	17	35	3	2	0	13	8	35	4	.178	.223
Wakefield, Howard-Howard John	05CleA 06WasA 07CleA	04-02-84	Bucyrus, Ohio	04-16-41	R	R	6'1	205	112	273	24	68	11	2	1	25	10		6	.249	.315
Walden, Fred-Thomas Fred	12StLA	06-25-90	Fayette, Mo.	09-27-55	R	R			1	0	0	0	0	0	0	0	0		0	---	---
Waldron, Irv-Irving J. (Wally, Torpedo Boat)	01MilA 01WasA	01-21-76	Queens, N.Y.	07-22-44	L	R	5'6	155	141	598	102	186	22	9	0	52	38		20	.311	.378
Walker, Ernie-Ernest Robert	13-15StLA	09-17-90	Blossburg, Ala.	04-01-65	L	R	6'	165	128	254	34	65	9	5	1	25	36	63	11	.256	.343
Walker, Tilly-Clarence William	11-12WasA 13-15StLA 16-17BosA 18-23PhiA	09-04-87	Telford, Tenn.	09-20-59	R	R	5'11	175	1421	5067	696	1423	244	71	118	679	415		130	.281	.427
Wall, Joe-Joseph Francis (Gummy)	01-02NYN 02BknN	07-24-73	Brooklyn, N.Y.	07-17-36	L	L			15	40	2	12	2	0	0	1	5		0	.300	.350
Wallace, Bobby-Rhoderick John (Rhody) (See P01-19)	94-98CleN 99-01StLN	11-04-73	Pittsburgh, Pa.	11-03-60	R	R	5'8	170	2385	8629	1056	2308	395	149	35	1121	774		209	.267	.360
	02-16,M11-12StLA 17-18StLN M37CinN																				
Wallace, Doc-Frederick Renshaw	19PhiN	09-20-93	Church Hill, Md.	12-31-64	R	R	5'6	135	2	4	0	1	0	0	0	0	0	1	0	.250	.250
Wallace, Jack-Clarence Eugene	15CinN	08-06-90	Winnfield, La.	10-15-60	R	R	5'11	175	2	7	1	2	0	0	0	0	0	2	0	.286	.286
Wallace, Jim-James Leo	05PitN	11-14-81	Boston, Mass.	05-16-53	L	L	5'9	150	7	29	3	6	1	0	0	3	3		2	.207	.241
Walsh, Austin-Austin Edward	14ChiF	09-01-91	Cambridge, Mass.	01-26-55	L	L	5'11	175	57	121	14	29	6	1	1	10	4		0	.240	.331
Walsh, Dee-Leo Thomas	13-15StLA	03-28-90	St. Louis, Mo.	07-14-71	B	R	5'9	165	89	226	22	44	5	1	0	12	22	40	10	.195	.226
Walsh, Jimmy-James Charles	12-13PhiA 14NYA 14-16PhiA 16-17BosA 18MS	09-22-85	Kallila, Ireland	07-03-62	L	R	5'10	170	536	1770	235	409	70	31	6	150	249		92	.231	.316
Walsh, Jimmy-James Timothy (Runt)	10-13PhiN 14-15BalF 15StLF	03-25-86	Lima, Ohio	01-21-47	R	R	5'9	174	502	1571	178	447	84	14	25	212	101		45	.285	.404
Walsh, Joe-Joseph Francis	10-11NYA	10-14-86	Minersville, Pa.	01-06-67	R	R	6'2	170	5	12	2	2	1	0	0	2	0		0	.167	.250
Walsh, John-John Thomas	03PhiN	03-25-79	Wilkes-Barre, Pa.	04-25-47	R	R	5'8	162	1	4	0	0	0	0	0	0	0		0	.000	.000
Walsh, Tom-Thomas Joseph	06ChiN	02-28-85	Davenport, Iowa	03-16-63	R	R	5'11	170	2	1	0	0	0	0	0	0	0		0	.000	.000
Wanner, Johnny-Clarence Curtis	09NYA	11-29-85	Geneseo, Ill.	05-28-19	R	R	5'11	190	3	8	0	1	0	0	0	0	0		1	.125	.125
Ward, Chuck-Charles William	17PitN 18-22BknN	07-30-94	St. Louis, Mo.	04-04-69	R	R	6'2	180	236	769	52	175	20	6	0	72	51	67	7	.228	.269
Ward, Hap-Harry Nichols	12DetA	11-15-85	Leesburg, N.J.	09-13-79	R	R	5'6		1	2	0	0	0	0	0	0	0		0	.000	.000
Ward, Joe-Joseph Aloysius	06PhiN 09NYA 09-10PhiN	09-02-84	Philadelphia, Pa.	08-11-34	R	R			166	465	47	110	18	9	0	47	18		12	.237	.314
Ward, Rube-John Andrew	02BknN	02-06-79	New Lexington, Ohio	01-17-45			5'7	152	13	31	4	9	1	0	0	2	2		0	.290	.323
Wares, Buzzy-Clyde Ellsworth	13-14StLA	03-23-86	Vandalia, Mich.	05-26-64	R	R	5'10	150	91	250	25	55	12	1	0	24	29	38	12	.220	.276
Warner, Hooks-Hoke Hayden	16-17PitN 18MS 19PitN 21StLN	05-22-94	Del Rio, Tex.	02-19-47	L	R	5'10	170	67	219	16	50	2	1	2	19	11	22	7	.228	.274
Warner, Jack-John Joseph	95BosN 95-96LouN 96-01NYN 02BosA 03-04NYN	08-15-72	New York, N.Y.	12-21-43	R	R	5'10	165	1066	3474	340	866	80	35	6	304	181		83	.249	.298
	05StLN 05-06DetA 06-08WasA																				
Warren, Hack-William Hackney (Hughie)	14IndF 15NwkF	02-11-84	Cairo, Ill.	01-28-60	R	R	5'8	165	31	53	5	13	2	0	0	6	5		2	.245	.283
Washburn, Libe-Libeus	02NYN 03PhiN	06-16-74	Lyme, N.H.	03-22-40	B	L	5'10	180	14	27	2	7	0	0	0	1	3		1	.259	.259
Watkins, Ed-James Edward	02PhiN	06-21-77	Philadelphia, Pa.	03-29-33					1	0	0	0	0	0	0	0	0		0	.000	.000
Watson, Art-Arthur Stanhope (Watty)	14-15BknF 15BufF	11-11-84	Jefferson, Ind.	05-09-50	L	R	5'11	170	53	95	17	32	5	4	1	17	4		0	.337	.537
Weaver, Art-Arthur Coggshall	02-03StLN 03PitN 05StLA 08ChiA	04-07-79	Wichita, Kans.	03-23-17	R	R	6'1	160	86	257	20	47	5	2	0	15	9		1	.183	.218
Weaver, Buck-George Daniel	12-20ChiA 20DL	08-18-90	Stowe, Pa.	01-31-56	B	R	5'11	170	1254	4809	623	1308	198	69	21	420	183		172	.272	.355
					Bats Right 12-16																
Webb, Billy-William Joseph	17PitN 18MS	06-25-95	Chicago, Ill.	01-12-43	R	R	5'10	160	5	15	1	3	0	0	0	0	0		0	.200	.200
Weeden, Bert-Charles Albert	11BosN	12-21-82	Northwood, N.H.	01-07-39	L	R	6'	200	1	1	0	0	0	0	0	0	0		0	.000	.000
Weiser, Bud-Harry Budson	15-16PhiN	01-08-91	Shamokin, Pa.	07-31-61	R	R	5'11	165	41	74	7	12	3	0	0	9	7	15	2	.162	.203
Weiss, Joe-Joseph Harold	15ChiF	01-27-94	Chicago, Ill.	07-07-67	R	R	6'	175	29	85	6	19	1	2	0	11	3		0	.224	.282
Welchonce, Harry-Harry Monroe	11PhiN	11-20-83	North Point, Pa.	02-26-77	L	R	5'11	170	26	66	9	14	4	0	0	6	7	8	0	.212	.273
Welday, Mike-Lyndon Earl	07,09ChiA	12-13-78	Conway, Iowa	05-28-42	L	L	5'8	165	53	109	9	22	1	1	0	5	10		2	.202	.229
Welf, Ollie-Oliver Henry	16CleA	01-17-89	Cleveland, Ohio	06-15-67	R	L	5'9	160	1	0	0	0	0	0	0	0	0		0	---	---
Wertz, Del-Dwight Lyman Moody	14BufF	10-11-88	Canton, Ohio	05-26-58	R	R	5'6	150	3	0	1	0	0	0	0	0	0		0	---	---
Westerberg, Oscar-Oscar William	07BosN	07-08-82	Alameda, Cal.	04-17-09	B	R	6'	185	2	6	0	2	0	0	0	1	1		0	.333	.333
Whaling, Bert-Albert James (Moose)	13-15BosN	06-22-88	Los Angeles, Cal.	01-21-65	R	R	6'	185	211	573	50	129	21	4	0	50	39	98	5	.225	.276
Wheat, Mack-McKinley Davis (Buck)	15-19BosN 20-21PhiN	06-09-93	Polo, Mo.	08-14-79	R	R	5'11	167	225	602	34	123	23	5	4	59	39	102	7	.204	.279
Wheat, Zack-Zachariah Davis	09-26BknN 27PhiA	05-23-88	Hamilton, Mo.	03-11-72	L	R	5'10	170	2410	9106	1289	2884	476	172	132	1248	650		205	.317	.450
Wheeler (Maynard), Dick (Richard Wheeler)-Richard	18StLN	01-14-98	Keene, N.H.	02-12-62	R	R	5'11	185	3	6	0	0	0	0	0	0	0		0	.000	.000
Wheeler, Ed-Edward Leroy	02BknN	06-15-78	Sherman, Mich.	08-15-60	B	R	5'10	160	30	96	9	12	0	0	0	5	3		1	.125	.125
Wheeler, George-George Harrison (Heavy)	10CinN	11-10-81	Shelburn, Ind.	06-14-18	R	R	5'9	180	3	3	0	0	0	0	0	0	0		0	.000	.000
Whelan, Jimmy-James Francis	13StLN	05-11-90	Kansas City, Kans.	11-29-29	R	R	5'8	165	1	0	0	0	0	0	0	0	0		0	---	---
White, Doc-Guy Harris (See P01-19)	01-02PhiN 03-13ChiA	04-09-79	Washington, D.C.	02-19-69	L	L	6'1	165	547	1279	147	277	22	13	2	76	147		32	.217	.259
White, Jack-John Wallace (Doc)	04BosN	01-19-78	Traders Point, Ind.	09-30-63	R	R	5'6		1	5	1	0	0	0	0	0	0		0	.000	.000
White, Sam-Samuel Lambeth	19BosN	08-23-92	Kinsley, England	11-11-29	L	R	6'	185	1	1	0	0	0	0	0	0	0		0	.000	.000
Whitehouse, Gil-Gilbert Arthur	12BosN 15NwkF	10-15-93	Somerville, Mass.	02-14-26	B	R	5'10	170	37	126	6	27	6	0	0	9	6		3	.214	.294
Whiteman, George-George (Lucky)	07BosA 17NYA 18BosA	12-23-82	Peoria, Ill.	02-10-47	R	R	5'7	160	85	257	32	70	13	2	1	27	17		11	.272	.358
Whitted, Possum-George Bostic	12-14StLN 14BosN 15-19PhiN 19-21PitN 22BknN	02-04-90	Durham, N.C.	10-16-62	R	R	5'8	168	1024	3628	440	978	145	60	23	451	215	310	116	.270	.362
Wickland, Al-Albert	13CinN 14-15ChiF 15PitF 18BosN 19NYA	01-27-88	Chicago, Ill.	03-14-80	L	L	5'7	155	444	1468	212	397	58	38	12	144	207		58	.270	.386
Wilhoit, Joe-Joseph William	16-17BosN 17PitN 17-18NYN 19BosA	12-20-85	Hiawatha, Kans.	09-25-30	L	R	6'2	175	283	782	93	201	23	9	3	73	75	82	28	.257	.321
Wilie, Denny-Denney Earnest	11-12StLN 15CleA	09-22-90	Mt. Calm, Tex.	06-20-66	L	L	5'8	155	103	230	26	56	7	3	0	19	41	38	5	.243	.326

USE NAME - GIVEN NAMES (NICKNAMES)	TEAM BY YEAR	BIRTH DATE	BIRTH PLACE	DEATH DATE	B	T	HGT	WGT	G	AB	R	H	2B	3B	HR	RBI	BB	SO	SB	BA	SA
Wilkinson, Ed-Edward Henry	11NYA	06-20-90	Jacksonville, Ore.	04-09-18	R	R	6'	170	10	13	2	3	0	0	0	1	0		0	.231	.231
Williams, Art-Arthur Franklin	02ChiN	08-26-77	Somerville, Mass.	05-16-41	L	R			47	160	17	37	3	0	0	14	15		9	.231	.250
Williams, Bob-Robert Elias	11-13NYA	04-27-94	Monday, Ohio	08-06-62	R	R	6'	190	46	110	10	18	3	0	0	11	15		1	.164	.191
Williams, Gus-August Joseph (Gloomy Gus)	11-15StLA	05-07-88	Omaha, Neb.	04-16-64	L	L	6'	185	403	1398	171	367	58	31	12	143	128		95	.263	.374
Williams, Harry-Harry Peters	13-14NYA	06-23-90	Omaha, Neb.	12-21-63	R	R	6'2	200	86	260	27	50	8	3	2	29	41	36	9	.192	.269
Williams, Jimmy-James Thomas (Buttons)	99-00PitN 01-02BalA 03-07NYA 08-09StLA	12-20-76	St. Louis, Mo.	01-16-65	R	R	5'9	175	1457	5483	775	1507	243	138	49	796	474		159	.275	.396
Williams, Otto-Otto George	02-03StLN 03-04ChiN 06WasA	11-02-77	Newark, N.J.	03-19-37	R	R	5'8	165	170	558	48	113	13	3	0	34	29		24	.203	.237
Williams, Rinaldo-Rinaldo Louis	14BknF	12-18-93	Santa Cruz, Cal.	04-24-66	L	R			4	15	1	4	2	0	0	0	0		0	.267	.400
Williams, Rip-Alva Mitchel (Buff)	11BosA 12-16WasA 18CleA	01-31-82	Carthage, Ill.	07-23-33	R	R	5'11	180	493	1186	111	314	51	23	2	145	95		27	.265	.352
Wilson Art-Arthur Earl (Dutch)	08-13NYN 14-15ChiF 16-17ChiN 18-20BosN 21CleA	12-11-85	Macon, Ill.	06-12-60	R	R	5'8	170	812	2056	237	536	96	22	24	226	292		50	.261	.364
Wilson, Gary-James Garrett	02BosA	01-12-79	Baltimore, Md.	05-01-69	R	R	5'7	168	2	8	0	1	0	0	0	1	0		0	.125	.125
Wilson, Les-Lester Wilbur (Tug)	11BosA	07-18-85	St. Louis, Mich.	04-04-69	L	R	5'11	170	5	7	0	0	0	0	0	0	2		0	.000	.000
Wilson, Owen-John Owen (Chief)	08-13PitN 14-16StLN	08-21-83	Austin, Tex.	02-22-54	L	R	6'2	185	1280	4624	520	1246	157	114	59	571	241		98	.269	.391
Wilson, Squanto-George Frank	11DetA 14BosA	03-29-89	Old Town, Me.	03-26-67	R	R	5'9	170	6	16	2	3	0	0	0	0	2		0	.188	.188
Wilson, Tom-Thomas G. (Slats)	14WasA	06-03-90	Fleming, Kans.	03-07-53	B	R	6'1	160	1	1	0	0	0	0	0	0	0	0	0	.000	.000
Wingo, Ivy-Ivey Brown	11-14StLN 15-26,29,M16CinN	07-08-90	Gainesville, Ga.	03-01-41	L	R	5'10	160	1326	4001	363	1039	147	81	25	455	264	285	87	.260	.356
Wisterzil, Tex-George John	14-15BknF 15ChiF 15StLF 15ChiF	03-07-88	Detroit, Mich.	06-27-64	R	R	5'9	150	242	828	83	215	26	14	0	105	65		29	.260	.325
Wolfe, Harry-Harold (Whitey)	17ChiN 17PhiN	11-24-92	Cleveland, Ohio	07-28-71	R	R	5'8	160	12	10	1	2	0	0	0	1	2	5	0	.200	.200
Wolfe, Polly-Roy Chamberlain	12,14ChiA	09-01-88	Knoxville, Ill.	11-21-38	L	R	5'10	170	10	29	0	6	0	0	0	0	3		1	.207	.207
Wolter, Harry-Harry Meiggs (See P01-19)	07CinN 07PitN 07StLN 09BosN 10-13NYA 17ChiN	07-11-84	Monterey, Cal.	07-06-70	L	R	5'10	175	587	1905	286	514	69	42	12	167	268		94	.270	.369
Wolverton, Harry-Harry Sterling	98-00ChiN 00-01PhiN 02WasA 02-04PhiN 05BosN 12,M12NYA	12-06-73	Mt. Vernon, Ohio	02-04-37	B	R	5'11	205	779	2993	345	834	94	52	7	352	166		81	.279	.352
Wood, Bob-Robert Lynn	98-00CinN 01-02CleA 04-05DetA	07-28-65	Thorn Hill, Ohio	05-22-43	R	R	5'8	153	379	1232	146	347	70	15	2	168	89		14	.282	.368
Wood, Harry-Harold Austin	03CinN	02-10-81	Waterville, Me.	05-18-55	R	R	5'10	155	2	3	0	0	0	0	0	0	1		0	.000	.000
Wood, Smoky Joe-Howard Ellsworth (See P01-19)	08-15BosA 16HO 17-22CleA	10-25-89	Kansas City, Mo.	07-27-85	R	R	5'11	180	695	1952	267	553	118	30	24	325	208		23	.283	.411
Wood, Roy-Roy Winton (Woody)	13PitN 14-15CleA	08-29-92	Monticello, Ark.	04-06-74	R	R	6'	175	119	333	33	77	12	4	1	20	16	47	7	.231	.300
Woodruff, Orville-Orville Francis (Sam)	04,10CinN	12-27-76	Chilo, Ohio	07-22-37	R	R	5'9	160	108	367	26	67	15	3	0	22	26		11	.183	.240
Wortman, Chuck-William Lewis	16-18ChiN	01-05-92	Baltimore, Md.	08-19-77	R	R	5'7	150	161	441	45	82	8	3	3	28	37	47	13	.186	.238
Wright, Cy-Ceylon	16ChiA	08-16-93	Minneapolis, Minn.	11-07-47	L	R	5'9	150	8	18	0	0	0	0	0	0	1	7	0	.000	.000
Wright, Dick-Willard James	15BknF	05-05-90	Worcester, N.Y.	01-24-52	R	R	5'10	170	4	5	0	0	0	0	0	0	0		0	.000	.000
Yale, Ad-William M.	05BknN	04-17-70	Bristol, Conn.	04-27-48	R	R			4	13	1	1	0	0	0	1	1		0	.077	.077
Yantz, George-George Webb	12ChiN	07-27-86	Louisville, Ky.	02-26-67	R	R	5'6	168	1	1	0	1	0	0	0	0	0		0	1.000	1.000
Yeabsley, Bert-Robert Watkins	19PhiN	12-17-93	Philadelphia, Pa.	02-08-61	R	R	5'9	175	3	0	0	0	0	0	0	0	1	0	0		
Yeager, George-George J.	96-99BosN 01CleA 01PitN 02NYN 02BalN	06-05-74	Cincinnati, Ohio	07-05-40	R	R	5'10	190	211	694	89	164	25	6	5	73	45		9	.236	.311
Yeager, Joe-Joseph Francis (Little Joe) (See P01-19)	98-00BknN 01-03DetA 05-06NYA 07-08StLA	08-28-75	Philadelphia, Pa.	07-02-37	R	R	5'10	160	572	1844	203	467	77	29	4	201	110		37	.253	.333
Yelle, Archie-Archie Joseph	17-19DetA	06-11-92	Saginaw, Mich.	05-02-83	R	R	5'10	170	86	199	12	32	4	0	0	7	15	19	2	.161	.181
Yerkes, Steve-Stephen Douglas	09,11-14BosA 14-15PitF 16ChiN	05-15-88	Hatboro, Pa.	01-31-71	R	R	5'8	180	707	2516	307	675	124	32	6	254	207		54	.268	.350
Yohe, Bill-William Clyde	09WasA	09-02-78	Mount Erie, Ill.	12-24-38	R	R	5'8	180	21	72	6	15	2	0	0	4	3		2	.208	.236
Young, Del-Delmer John	09CinN 14-15BufF	10-24-85	Macon City, Mo.	12-17-59	L	R	5'11	195	94	196	17	52	5	5	4	23	5		1	.265	.403
Young, George-Goerge Joseph	13CleA	04-01-90	Brooklyn, N.Y.	03-13-50	L	R	5'10	180	2	2	0	0	0	0	0	0	0		0	.000	.000
Young, Herman-Herman John	11BosN	04-14-86	Roxbury, Mass.	12-13-66	R	R	5'8	155	9	25	2	6	0	0	0	0	3		0	.240	.240
Young, Ralph-Ralph Stuart (Pep)	13NYA 15-21DetA 22PhiA	09-19-88	Philadelphia, Pa.	01-24-65	B	R	5'9	165	1022	3643	480	898	108	30	4	254	495	235	92	.247	.296
Zacher, Elmer-Elmer Henry (Silver)	10NYN 10StLN	09-17-80	Buffalo, N.Y.	12-20-44	R	R	5'9	190	48	132	7	28	5	1	0	10	10	19	3	.212	.265
Zalusky, Jack-John Francis	03NYA	06-22-79	Minneapolis, Minn.	08-11-35	R	R	5'11	172	7	16	2	5	0	0	0	1	1		0	.313	.313
Zearfoss, Dave-David William Tilden	96-98NYN 04-05StLN	01-01-68	Schenectady, N.Y.	09-12-45	R	R	5'9		72	201	15	42	3	3	0	17	19		1	.209	.254
Zeider, Rollie-Rollie Hubert (Bunions)	10-13ChiA 13NYA 14-15ChiF 16-18ChiN	11-16-83	Auburn, Ind.	09-12-67	R	R	5'10	162	938	3213	392	768	93	22	5	253	334		223	.239	.286
Zimmer, Chief-Charles Louis	84DetN 86NYAA 87-88CleAA 89-99CleN 99LouN 00-02PitN 03,M03PhiN	11-23-60	Marietta, Ohio	08-22-49	R	R	6'	190	1277	4528	622	1227	221	80	26	625	390		158	.271	.372
														For Zimmer, Stolen Bases includes the years, 86-03							
Zimmerman, Bill-William Frederick	15BknN	01-20-87	Kengen, Germany	10-04-52	R	R	5'8	172	22	57	3	16	2	0	0	7	4	8	1	.281	.316
Zimmerman, Eddie-Edward Desmond	06StLN 11BknN	01-04-83	Oceanic, N.J.	05-06-45	R	R	5'9	160	127	431	31	80	10	7	3	37	34		9	.186	.262
Zimmerman, Heinie-Henry	07-16ChiN 16-19NYN 19DU	02-09-87	New York, N.Y.	03-14-69	R	R	5'11	176	1456	5304	695	1566	275	105	58	796	242		175	.295	.419
Zinn, Guy-Guy	11-12NYA 13BosN 14-15BalF	02-13-87	Holbrook, W.Va.	10-06-49	L	R	5'10	170	314	1103	136	297	51	23	15	139	109		28	.269	.398
Zwilling, Dutch-Edward Harrison	10ChiA 14-15ChiF 16ChiN	11-02-88	St. Louis, Mo.	03-27-78	L	L	5'6	160	366	1280	167	364	76	15	29	202	128		46	.284	.435

USE NAMES - GIVEN NAMES (NICKNAMES)	TEAM BY YEAR	BIRTH DATE	BIRTHPLACE	DEATH DATE	B	T	HGT	WGT	W	L	Pct.	SV	G	GS	CG	IP	H	BB	SO	ShO	ERA
Ables, Harry-Harry Terrell (Hal, Hans)	05StLA 09CleA 11NYA	10-04-83	Terrell, Tex.	02-08-51	R	L	6'2	200	1	5	.167	0	14	8	4	72	79	30	41	0	4.00
Adams, Babe-Charles Benjamin	06StLN 07,09-16,18-26PitN	05-18-82	Tipton, Ind.	07-27-68	R	R	5'11	185	194	140	.581	15	482	354	206	2995	2841	430	1036	44	2.76
Adams, Dan-Daniel Leslie (Rube)	14-15KCF	06-19-87	St. Louis, Mo.	10-06-64	R	R	5'11	165	4	11	.267	3	47	16	6	171	182	65	54	0	3.74
Adams, Joe-Joseph Edward (Wagon Tongue)	02StLN	10-28-77	Cowden, Ill.	10-08-52	R	L	6'	190	0	0	—	0	1	0	0	4	9	2	0	0	9.00
Adams, Karl-Karl Tutwiler (Rebel)	14CinN 15ChiN	08-11-91	Columbus, Ga.	09-17-67	R	R	6'2	170	0	9	.100	0	30	12	3	115	119	48	62	0	5.01
Adams, Rick-Reuben Alexander	05WasA	12-24-78	Paris, Tex.	03-10-55	L	L	6'	165	2	6	.250	0	11	6	3	63	63	24	25	1	3.57
Adams, Willie-James Irvin	12-13StLA 14PitF 18-19PhiA	06-18-37	Clearfield, Pa.		R	R	6'4	180	9	16	.360	2	65	21	8	284	303	144	74	0	4.37
Adkins, Doc-Merle Theron (Babe)	02BosA 03NYA	08-05-72	Troy, Wis.	09-12-55	R	R	5'11	220	1	2	.333	1	6	3	1	27	40	12	3	0	5.00
Aitchison, Raleigh-Raleigh Leonidas (Redskin)	11,14-15BknN	12-05-87	Tyndall, S.D.	09-26-58	R	L	5'11	175	12	12	.500	1	34	22	10	206	193	67	101	3	3.01
Akers, Jerry-Albert Earl	12WasA	11-01-87	Shelbyville, Ind.	05-15-79	R	R	5'11	175	0	0	—	1	20	24	15	11	0	4.95				
Alberts, Cy-Frederick Joseph	10StLN	01-14-82	Grand Rapids, Mich.	08-27-17	R	R	6'	230	0	2	.333	0	4	3	2	28	35	20	6	0	6.11
Alexander, Pete-Grover Cleveland	11-17PhiN 18-26ChiN 26-29StLN 30PhiN	02-26-87	Elba, Neb.	11-04-50	R	R	6'1	185	373	208	.642	32	696	600	439	5190	4868	951	2199	90	2.56
Allen, Frank-Frank Leon (Lefty)	12-14BknN 14-15PhiN 16-17BosN	08-26-88	Newbern, Ala.	07-30-33	R	L	5'8	175	50	67	.427	3	180	127	60	970	893	373	457	10	2.93
Allen, John-John Marshall	14BalF	10-27-90	Berkeley Springs, W.Va.	09-24-67	R	R	6'1	170	0	0	—	0	1	0	0	2	2	2	2	0	18.00
Allison, Mack-Mack Pendleton	11-13StLA	01-23-87	Owensboro, Ky.	03-13-64	R	R	6'1	185	9	21	.300	1	45	27	16	246	247	67	57	1	3.18
Altrock, Nick-Nicholas	98LouN 02-03BosA 03-09ChiA 09,12-15,18-19,24,29,31,33WasA	09-15-76	Cincinnati, Ohio	01-20-65	B	L	5'10	197	82	72	.532	11	218	161	128	1515	1455	272	425	16	2.67
Ames, Red-Leon Kessling (Kalamity)	03-13NYN 13-15CinN 15-19StLN 19PhiN	08-02-82	Warren, Ohio	10-08-36	B	R	5'10	185	183	167	.523	36	533	370	209	3195	2896	1034	1662	26	2.63
Ancker, Walter-Walter (Liver, Gee)	15PhiA	04-10-93	New York, N.Y.	02-13-54	R	R	6'1	190	0	0	—	0	4	1	0	18	19	17	4	0	3.50
Anderson, Fred-John Fred (Spitball)	09,13BosA 14-15BufF 16-18NYN	12-11-85	Calahan, N.C.	11-08-57	R	R	6'2	180	53	57	.482	8	178	114	62	986	912	247	514	11	2.86
Anderson, Walter-Walter Carl (Lefty)	17PhiA 18MS	09-25-97	Grand Rapids, Mich.	01-06-90	L	L	6'2	160	1	0	1.000	0	17	2	1	53	45	29	20	0	3.23
Anderson, Wingo-Wingo Charlie	10CinN	08-13-86	Lillian, Tex.	12-19-50	R	L	5'10	150	0	0	—	0	7	2	0	17	16	17	11	0	4.76
Applegate, Fred-Frederick Romaine (Snitz)	04PhiA	05-09-79	Bradford, Pa.	04-21-68	R	R	6'2	180	1	2	.333	0	3	3	3	21	29	8	12	0	6.43
Appleton, Ed-Edward Samuel (Whitey, Roastie, Big Ed)	15-16BknN	02-29-92	Arlington, Tex.	01-27-32	R	R	6'2	185	5	12	.294	1	48	13	6	185	182	84	64	0	3.26
Arellanes, Frank-Frank Julian	08-10BosA	01-28-82	Santa Cruz, Cal.	12-13-18	R	R	5'11	175	24	21	.533	8	74	49	25	410	358	85	148	2	2.28
Armstrong, Howard-Howard Elmer	11PhiA	12-02-89	East Claridon, O.	03-08-26	R	R	5'9	165	0	1	.000	0	3	3	1	0	0	0.00				
Atkins, Tommy-Francis Montgomery	09-10PhiA	12-09-87	Ponca, Neb.	05-07-56	L	L	5'10	165	3	2	.600	2	16	4	2	63	59	28	33	0	2.86
Ayers, Doc-Yancey Wyatt	13-19WasA 19-21DetA	05-20-91	Snake Creek, Va.	05-26-68	R	R	6'1	185	70	80	.467	13	299	139	59	1429	1357	379	622	16	2.84
Backman, Les-Lester John	09-10StLN	03-20-88	Cleves, Ohio	11-08-75	R	R	6'	175	9	18	.333	2	47	26	14	244	263	92	76	0	3.61
Bacon, Eddie-Edgar Suter	17PhiA	04-08-95	Frankfort, Ky.	10-02-63					0	0	—	0	6	5	7	0	0	6.00			
Bader, Lore-Lore Verne (King)	12NYN 17-18BosA 19BosA	04-27-88	Bader, Ill.	06-02-73	L	R	6'	175	5	3	.625	0	21	8	3	75	83	36	27	1	2.52
Bagby, Jim-James Charles Jacob Sr. (Sarge)	12CinN 16-22CleA 23PitN	10-05-89	Barnett, Ga.	07-28-54	R	R	6'1	180	127	87	.593	28	316	209	132	1828	1884	458	450	15	3.10
Baichley, Grover-Grover Cleveland	14StLA	12-10-89	Toledo, Ill.	06-28-56	R	R	5'8	165	0	0	—	0	4	0	0	7	9	3	3	0	5.14
Bailey, Bill-William F.	07-12StLA 14-15BalF 15ChiF 18DetA 21-22StLN	04-12-88	Fort Smith, Ark.	11-02-26	L	L	5'11	165	37	78	.322	1	203	117	71	1086	1035	527	570	8	3.56
Baker, Bock-Charles	01CleA 01PhiA	07-17-78	Troy, N.Y.	08-17-40		L	5'9	180	0	2	.000	0	2	2	1	14	29	12	1	0	7.71
Baker, Ernie-Ernest Gould	05CleA	08-08-75	Concord, Mich.	10-25-45	R	R	5'10	160	0	0	—	0	1	0	0	4	7	0	1	0	4.50
Baker, Jesse-Jesse Ormand	11CleA	06-03-88	Anderson I., Wash.	09-26-72	L	L	5'11	188	2	7	.222	1	22	8	3	94	101	30	51	0	3.93
Baldwin, Orson-Orson F.	08BosA	11-03-81	Carson City, Mich.	02-16-42	R	R		185	1	3	.250	0	4	4	1	15	16	11	5	0	6.00
Barberich, Frank-Frank Frederick	07BosN 10BosA	02-03-82	Queens, N.Y.	05-01-65	R	R	5'10	175	1	1	.500	0	2	1	1	17	26	7	1	0	6.35
Barger, Cy-Enos Bolivar	06-07NYA 10-12BknN 14-15PitF	05-18-85	Jamestown, Ky.	09-23-64	L	R	6'	160	46	63	.422	8	151	111	78	975	1010	334	297	5	3.56
Barron, Frank-Frank John	14WasA	08-06-90	St. Mary's, W.Va.	09-18-64	L	L	6'1	175	0	0	—	0	1	1	0	1	1	0	1	0	0.00
Barry, Ed-Edward (Jumbo)	05-07BosA	10-16-81	Madison, Wis.	06-19-20	R	L	6'3	185	1	6	.143	0	12	10	6	79	74	25	34	0	3.53
Barry, Hardin-Hardin (Finn)	12PhiA	03-26-91	Susanville, Cal.	11-05-69	R	R	6'	195	0	0	—	0	3	0	0	13	18	4	3	0	7.62
Barry, Tom-Thomas Arthur	04PhiN	04-10-79	St. Louis, Mo.	06-04-46		R	5'9	155	0	1	.000	0	1	1	1	6	1	1	0	27.00		
Barthold, John-John Francis (Hans)	04-14-82	Philadelphia, Pa.	11-04-46	B	R	5'11	197	0	1	.000	0	4	1	0	11	12	8	5	0	4.91		
Bartley, Bill-William Jackson	03NYN 06-07PhiA	08-08-85	Cincinnati, Ohio	05-17-65	R	R	5'11	190	0	0	—	0	19	3	2	68	57	29	24	0	3.04
Baskette, Jim-James Blain (Big Jim)	11-13CleA	12-10-87	Athens, Tenn.	07-30-42	R	R	6'	185	9	6	.600	0	35	14	9	142	138	57	59	1	3.30
Bauer, Lou-Louis Walter (Kid)	18PhiA	11-30-98	Egg Harbor C., N.J.	02-04-79	R	R	6'	175	0	0	—	0	1	0	0	0	0	2	0	0	∞
Baumgardner, George-George Washington	12-16StLA	07-22-91	Barboursville, W.Va.	12-13-70	L	R	5'11	178	36	48	.429	4	124	78	51	685	682	263	283	7	3.22
Beck, George-Ernest George Bernard (Eaglebeak)	14CleA	02-21-90	South Bend, Ind.	10-29-73	R	R	5'10	162	0	0	—	0	1	0	0	1	0	0	0	0	0.00
Becker, Charlie-Charles Schlggel (Buck)	11-12WasA	10-14-90	Washington, D.C.	07-30-28	L	L	6'2	180	3	5	.375	0	15	5	4	80	88	29	36	1	3.94
Bedient, Hugh-Hugh Carpenter	12-14BosA 15BufF	10-23-89	Gerry, N.Y.	07-21-65	R	R	6'1	185	59	53	.527	21	179	102	61	936	930	236	420	4	3.09
Beebe, Fred-Frederick Leonard	06ChiN 06-09StLN 10CinN 11PhiN 16CleA	12-31-80	Lincoln, Neb.	10-30-57	R	R	6'1	190	63	85	.426	4	202	153	93	1294	1090	534	634	9	2.86
Beecher, Roy-LeRoy (Colonel)	07-08NYN	05-10-84	Swanton, Ohio	10-11-52	L	R	6'2	180	0	2	.000	1	4	2	2	20	28	9	5	0	4.05
Bell, George-George Glenn (Farmer)	07-11BknN	11-02-74	Greenwood, N.Y.	12-25-41	R	R	6'	195	43	79	.352	4	160	124	92	1086	1010	305	376	17	2.85
Bell, Ralph-Ralph Albert	12ChiA	11-16-90	Kahoka, Mo.	10-18-59	L	L	5'11	170	0	0	—	0	3	0	0	8	8	5	0	0	9.00
Bender, Chief-Charles Albert	03-14PhiA 15BalF 16-17PhiN 25ChiA	05-05-83	Crow Wing Co., Minn.	05-22-54	R	R	6'2	185	210	128	.621	36	459	334	257	3017	2645	712	1711	40	2.46
Benn, Omer-Henry Omer	14CleA	01-25-90	Viola, Wis.	06-04-67	R	R	6'		0	0	—	0	2	1	0	7	0	1	0		
Benton, Rube-John Cleave	10-15CinN * 15-21NYN 22DE 23-25CinN	06-27-90	Clinton, N.C.	12-12-37	R	L	6'1	190	156	145	.518	21	437	311	145	2518	2472	712	950	23	3.09
* - pitched in 1 game for PitN-game protested and all records ordered thrown out by N.L. president																					
Benz, Joe-Joseph Louis (Blitzen, Butcher Boy)	11-19ChiA	01-21-86	New Alsace, Ind.	04-22-57	R	R	6'2	190	74	76	.493	5	250	163	76	1359	1224	334	538	17	2.42
Berger, Heinie-Charles Carl	07-10CleA	01-07-82	LaSalle, Ill.	02-10-54	R	R	5'9		32	29	.532	1	90	68	42	608	504	176	337	5	2.56
Bernard, Joe-Joseph Carl	09StLN	03-24-82	Springfield, Ill.	09-22-60	R	R	6'	175	0	0	—	0	1	0	0	1	1	2	2	0	0.00
Bernhard, Bill-William Henry (Strawberry Bill)	99-00PhiN 01-02PhiA 02-07CleA	03-16-71	Clarence, N.Y.	03-30-49	B	R	6'4	225	112	82	.577	5	231	200	175	1792	1860	365	545	14	3.04
Bernhardt, Walter-Walter Jacob	18NYA	05-20-93	Pleasant Valley, Pa.	07-26-58	R	R			0	0	—	0	1	0	0	1	0	0	0	0	0.00
Betts, Hal-Harold Matthew (Chubby)	03StLN 13CinN	06-14-81	Alliance, Ohio	05-22-46	R	R	5'10	200	0	1	.000	0	2	1	1	12	12	8	2	0	8.25
Beville, Ben-Clarence Benjamin (Candy)	01BosA	08-28-77	Colusa,Cal.	01-05-37	R	R	5'9	190	0	2	.000	0	2	2	1	9	8	9	1	0	4.00
Billiard, Harry-Harry Pree (Pre)	08NYA 14IndF 15NwkF	11-11-83	Monroe, Ind.	06-03-23	R	R	6'	190	1	8	.500	3	51	18	5	168	162	104	61	0	3.96
Bishop, Lloyd-Lloyd Clifton	14CleA	04-25-90	Conway Sprs., Kans.	06-18-68	R	R	6'	175	0	1	.000	0	8	1	0	14	13	3	1	0	5.63
Black, Dave-David Edward	14-15ChiF 15BalF 23BosA	04-17-92	Perkins Co., Neb.	10-27-36	L	L	6'2	175	8	10	.444	0	43	15	4	181	166	52	72	0	3.18
Blackburn, Babe-Foster Edwin (Charlie)	15KCF 21CleA	01-06-95	Chicago, Ill.	03-09-84	R	R	6'1	200	1	3	.000	0	2	0	0	17	19	14	7	0	7.94
Blanding, Fred-Frederick James (Fritz)	10-14CleA	02-08-88	Redlands, Cal.	07-16-50	R	R	6'	185	45	46	.495	4	144	86	58	814	859	277	278	5	3.13
Blewett, Bob-Robert Lawrence	02NYN	06-28-77	Fond du Lac, Wis.	03-17-58	L	L	5'11	170	0	2	.000	0	5	2	2	28	39	7	8	0	4.82
Bliss, Elmer-Elmer Ward (See B01-19)	03NYA	03-09-75	Penfield, Pa.	03-18-62	L	R	6'	190	1	0	1.000	0	5	4	0	2	0.00					
Bluejacket (Smith), Jim-James	14-15BknF 16CinN	07-08-87	Adair, Okla.	03-26-47	R	R	6'2	200	14	17	.452	1	44	30	13	237	244	97	78	3	3.46
Boardman, Charlie-Charles Louis	13-14PhiA 15StLN	03-27-93	Seneca Falls, N.Y.	08-10-68	L	L	6'2	194	1	2	.333	0	7	3	2	36	32	25	13	0	4.75
Boehler, George-George Henry	12-16DetA 20-21StLA 23PitN 26BknN	01-03-92	Lawrenceburg, Ind.	06-23-58	R	R	6'2	180	7	13	.350	0	60	18	7	201	231	134	91	0	4.75
Boehling, Joe-John Joseph	12-16WasA 16-17,20CleA	03-20-91	Richmond, Va.	09-08-41	L	L	5'11	168	53	49	.520	5	162	118	57	924	861	386	396	9	3.07
Bohen, Pat-Leo Ignatius	13PhiA 14PitN	09-30-90	Oakland, Iowa	04-08-42	R	R	5'10	160	0	1	.000	0	2	1	1	9	5	4	3	0	3.00
Boland, Bernie-Bernard Anthony	15-20DetA 21StLA	01-21-92	Rochester, N.Y.	09-12-73	R	R	5'8	168	68	52	.567	10	210	119	59	1063	925	432	364	10	3.24
Bolden, Bill-William Horace (Big Bill)	19StLN	05-09-93	Dandridge, Tenn.	12-08-66	R	R	6'4	200	1	2	.333	0	7	3	1	28	34	20	12	0	3.86
Booles, Red-Seabron Jesse	09CleA	07-14-80	Bernice, La.	03-16-55	L	R	5'10	150	0	0	—	0	4	0	0	13	23	7	4	0	1.96
Boultes, Jake-Jacob John	07-09BosN	08-06-84	St. Louis, Mo.	12-24-55	R	R	6'3		8	14	.364	0	42	17	12	223	229	58	78	0	2.95
Bowman, Abe-Alvah Edson	14-15CleA	01-25-93	Greenup, Ill.	10-11-79	R	R	6'1	190	2	8	.200	1	24	11	2	74	75	48	27	1	4.74
Boyd, Ray-Raymond C.	10StLA 11CinN	02-11-87	Hortonville, Ind.	02-11-20	R	R	5'10	160	3	4	.429	1	10	6	4	58	50	24	26	0	3.10
Bracken, Jack-John James	01CleA	04-14-81	Cleveland, Ohio	07-16-54	R	R	5'11	175	4	8	.333	0	12	12	12	100	137	31	18	0	6.21
Brackenridge, John-John Givler	04PhiN	12-24-80	Harrisburg, Pa.	03-20-53	R	R	6'		0	1	.000	0	7	1	0	34	37	16	11	0	5.56
Brady, Bill-William Aloysius	12BosN	08-18-89	New York, N.Y.	04-10-56	R	R	6'2	180	0	0	—	0	1	0	0	4	6	1	0	0	4.50
Brady, King-James Ward	05PhiN 06-07PitN 08BosA 12BosN	05-28-81	Elmer, N.J.	08-21-47	R	R	6'	190	3	2	.600	0	9	5	4	50	64	10	20	1	3.10
Braggins, Dick-Richard Realf	01CleA	12-25-79	Mercer, Pa.	08-16-63	R	R	5'11	170	0	2	.333	1	4	4	15	1	0	4.78				
Braithwood, Al-Alfred	15PitF	02-15-92	Braceville, Ill.	11-24-60	R	L	6'1	145	0	0	—	0	3	0	0	7	6	4	1	0	0.00
Brandom, Chick-Chester Milton	08-09PitN 15NwkF	03-31-87	Coldwater, Kans.	10-07-58	R	R	5'10	170	3	1	.750	2	32	4	2	108	101	29	44	0	2.08
Breitenstein, Theo-Theodore P.	91StLAA 92-96StLN 97-00CinN 01StLN	06-01-69	St. Louis, Mo.	05-03-35	L	L	5'9	150	165	170	.496	3	379	341	300	2965	3091	1203	889	12	4.04

USE NAMES - GIVEN NAMES (NICKNAMES)	TEAM BY YEAR	BIRTH DATE	BIRTHPLACE	DEATH DATE	B	T	HGT	WGT	W	L	Pct.	SV	G	GS	CG	IP	H	BB	SO	ShO	ERA
Brennan, Ad-Addison Foster	10-13PhiN 14-15ChiF 18WasA 18CleA	07-18-87	La Harpe, Kans.	01-07-62	L	L	5'11	170	39	36	.520	3	129	76	40	677	694	194	283	5	3.11
Brenner, Bert-Delbert Henry (Dutch)	12CleA	07-18-87	Minneapolis, Minn.	04-11-71	R	R	6'	175	1	0	1.000	0	2	1	1	13	14	4	3	0	2.77
Bressler, Rube-Raymond Bloom (See B20-45)	14-15PhiA 17-20CinN	10-23-94	Coder, Pa.	11-07-66	L	R	6'	187	26	31	.456	2	107	52	27	540	511	242	229	3	3.40
Briggs, Buttons-Herbert Theodore	96-98,04-05ChiN	07-08-75	Poughkeepsie, N.Y.	02-08-11	R	R	6'1	180	45	47	.489	4	106	97	84	856	879	332	338	3	3.41
Brockett, Lew-Lewis Albert (King)	07,09NYA 10HO 11NYA	07-23-80	Brownsville, Ill.	09-19-60	R	R	5'10	168	14	15	.483	1	50	30	13	273	279	124	108	3	3.66
Brown, Boardwalk-Carroll William	11-14PhiA 14-15NYA	02-20-89	Woodbury, N.J.	02-08-77	R	R	6'2	195	39	40	.494	3	133	91	43	731	694	291	251	6	3.47
Brown, Buster-Charles Edward (Yank)	05-07StLN 07-09PhiN 09-13BosN	08-31-81	Boone, Iowa	02-09-14	R	R	6'	180	51	105	.327	4	234	165	107	1451	1368	631	501	10	3.21
Brown, Curly-Charles Roy (Lefty)	11-13StLA 15CinN	12-09-88	Spring Hill, Kans.	06-10-68	L	L	5'10	165	2	8	.200	0	28	11	5	129	129	50	52	1	4.19
Brown, Elmer-Elmer Young (Shook)	11-12StLN 13-15BknN	08-25-83	Southport, Ind.	01-23-55	L	R	5'11	172	9	11	.450	1	43	22	4	188	181	92	79	2	3.49
Brown, Ray-Paul Percival	09CleN	01-31-89	Chicago, Ill.	05-29-55	R	R	6'1	172	1	0	1.000	0	1	1	1	9	5	4	2	0	2.00
Brown, Three Finger-Mordecai Peter Centennial (Miner)	03StLN 04-12ChiN 13CinN 14,M14StLF 14BknF 15ChiF 16ChiN	10-19-76	Nyesville, Ind.	02-14-48	B	R	5'10	175	239	127	.653	49	481	332	271	3171	2708	673	1375	55	2.06
Browning, Frank-Frank	10DetA	10-29-82	Falmouth, Ky.	05-19-48	R	R	5'5	145	2	2	.500	2	11	6	2	42	51	10	16	0	3.00
Bruckmiller, Andy-Andrew	05DetA	01-01-82	Pittsburgh, Pa.	01-12-70	R	R	5'11	175	0	0	—	0	1	0	0	3	1	0	0	0	∞
Buchanan, Jim-James Forrest	05StLA	07-01-76	Chatham Hill, Va.	06-15-49	R	R	5'10	165	6	10	.375	2	22	15	12	141	149	27	54	1	3.51
Buckles, Jess-Jesse Robert (Jim)	16NYA	05-20-90	Lordsburg, Cal.	08-02-75	L	L	6'2	205	0	0	—	0	2	0	0	4	3	1	2	0	2.25
Burchell, Fred-Frederick Duff	03PhiN 07-09BosA	07-14-79	Perth Amboy, N.J.	11-20-51	R	L	5'11	190	13	16	.448	0	49	28	12	286	268	92	124	0	2.93
Burk, Sandy-Charles Sanford	10-12BknN 12-13StLN 15PitF	04-22-87	Columbus, Ohio	10-11-34	R	R	5'8	155	5	11	.313	2	52	23	5	218	206	133	86	0	4.25
Burke, Billy-William Ignatius	10-11BosN	07-11-89	Clinton, Mass.	02-09-67	L	L	5'10	165	1	1	.500	0	21	7	1	67	74	34	23	0	4.84
Burke, John-John Patrick	02NYN	01-27-77	Hazelton, Pa.	08-04-50	R	R			0	1	.000	0	2	1	1	14	21	3	3	0	5.79
Burkett, Jesse-Jesse Cail (The Crab) (See B01-19)	90NYN 94CleN 02StLA	12-04-68	Wheeling, W.Va.	05-27-53	L	L	5'8	155	1	12	.077	0	23	12	6	123	144	94	84	0	5.56
Burns, Bill-William Thomas (Sleepy Bill)	08-09WasA 09-10ChiA 10-11CinN 11PhiN 12DetA	01-27-80	San Saba, Tex.	06-06-53	B	L	6'2	195	28	49	.364	2	116	85	43	726	713	148	235	10	2.69
Burns, Farmer-James Joseph (Slab)	01StLN		Ashtabula, Ohio	Deceased		R	5'7	168	0	0	—	0	1	0	0	2	1	0	0		9.00
Bushelman, Jack-John Francis	09CinN 11-12BosA	08-29-85	Cincinnati, Ohio	10-26-55	R	R	6'2	175	2	2	.333	1	7	2	2	27	24	19	13	0	3.33
Butler, Ike-Isaac Burr	02BalA		Langston, Mich.	03-17-48		R	6'	175	2	11	.154	0	16	14	12	116	168	45	13	0	5.35
Caldwell, Ralph-Ralph Grant (Lefty)	04-05PhiN	01-18-84	Philadelphia, Pa.	08-05-69	L	L	5'9	155	3	4	.429	1	13	7	6	75	84	22	59	0	4.20
Caldwell, Ray-Raymond Benjamin (Slim) (See B01-19)	10-18NYA 19BosA 19-21CleA	04-26-88	Corydon, Pa.	08-17-67	R	R	6'2	190	133	120	.526	14	343	260	185	2242	2089	737	1005	20	3.22
Callahan, Nixey-James Joseph (See B01-19)	94PhiN 97-00ChiN 01-03,M03-04,12-14ChiA M16-17PitN	03-18-74	Fitchburg, Mass.	10-04-34	R	R	5'10	180	100	75	.571	2	195	177	169	1602	1748	437	445	11	3.39
Callahan, Ray-Raymond James (Pat)	15CinN	08-29-91	Ashland, Wis.	01-23-73	L	L	5'10	170	0	0	—	0	3	0	0	6	12	1	4	0	9.00
Camnitz, Harry-Henry Richardson	09PitN 11StLN	10-26-84	McKinney, Ky.	01-06-51	R	R	6'1	168	1	0	1.000	0	3	0	0	6	6	2	3	0	3.00
Camnitz, Howie-Samuel Howard (Red)	04,06-12PitN 13PhiN 14-15PitF	08-22-81	Covington, Ky.	03-02-60	L	R	5'9	169	133	105	.559	15	326	237	137	2086	1852	656	915	20	2.75
Campbell, Bill-William James	05StLN 07-09CinN	11-05-73	Pittsburgh, Pa.	10-06-57	L	L	5'10	165	23	25	.479	4	70	44	31	407	411	93	116	2	2.81
Canavan, Hugh-Hugh Edward (Hugo)	18BosN	05-13-97	Worcester, Mass.	09-04-67	L	L	5'8	160	0	4	.000	0	11	3	3	47	70	15	18	0	6.32
Cantwell, Mike-Michael Joseph	16NYA 19-20PhiN	06-15-94	Washington, D.C.	01-05-53	R	R	6'1	168	1	6	.143	0	11	4	2	52	61	26	14	0	4.67
Cantwell, Tom-Thomas Aloysius	09-10CinN	12-23-88	Washington, D.C.	04-01-68	R	L	6'1	175	1	0	1.000	0	8	1	1	23	18	10	7	0	2.35
Carmichael, Chet-Chester Keller	09CinN	01-09-88	Muncie, Ind.	08-23-60	R	R	5'11	200	0	0	—	0	2	0	0	7	9	3	2	0	0.00
Carney, Pat-Patrick Joseph (Doc) (See B01-19)	02-04BosN	08-07-76	Holyoke, Mass.	01-09-53	L	L	6'	200	4	9	.308	0	16	13	10	109	139	46	37	0	4.71
Carpenter, Paul-Paul Calvin	16PitN	08-12-94	Granville, Ohio	03-14-68	R	R	5'11	165	0	0	—	0	5	0	0	8	8	4	5	0	1.13
Carrick, Bill-William Martin (Doughnut Bill, Wee Willie)	98-00NYN 01-02WasA	09-05-73	Erie, Pa.	03-07-32	R	R	5'10	150	64	86	.427	0	167	155	138	1326	1650	400	239	4	4.13
Carroll, Dick-Richard Thomas (Shadow)	09NYA	07-21-84	Cleveland, Ohio	11-22-45	R	R	6'1	190	2	1	.667	0	2	1	0	5	7	1	1	0	3.60
Carsey, Kid-Wilfred	91WasAA 92-97PhiN 97-98StLN 99CleN 99WasN 99NYN 01BknN	10-22-70	New York, N.Y.	03-29-60	R	R	5'7	168	117	134	.466	3	294	256	218	2222	2780	796	484	4	4.95
Carson, Al-Albert James (Soldier)	10ChiN	08-22-82	Chicago, Ill.	11-26-62	R	R	5'10	162	0	0	—	0	2	0	0	7	6	1	2	0	3.86
Carter, Nick-Conrad Powell	08PhiA	05-19-79	Oatlands, Va.	11-23-61	L	R	5'8	140	2	5	.286	1	14	4	2	61	58	17	17	0	2.95
Carter, Paul-Paul Warren (Nick)	14-15CleA16-20ChiN 21DU	05-01-94	Lake Park, Ga.	09-11-84	L	R	6'3	175	20	27	.426	8	127	43	16	480	510	142	115	0	3.32
Case, Charlie-Charles Emmett	01CinN 04-06PitN	09-07-79	Smith's Landing, Ohio	04-16-64	R	R	6'	170	24	18	.571	1	54	46	36	396	373	108	114	6	2.93
Cashion, Carl-Jay Carl	11-14WasA	06-06-91	Mecklenburg, N.C.	11-17-35	R	R	6'2	200	13	11	.542	0	43	30	18	255	228	170	114	3	3.71
Castleton, Roy-Royal Eugene	07NYA 09-10CinN	07-26-85	Salt Lake City, Utah	06-24-67	L	L	5'11	167	3	4	.429	0	11	5	2	44	40	15	13	0	2.66
Cates, Eli-Eli Eldo	08WasA	01-26-77	Greens Fork, Ind.	05-29-64	R	R	5'9	175	4	8	.333	0	19	10	7	115	112	32	33	0	2.50
Cavet, Pug-Tillar H.	11,14-15DetA	12-26-89	McGregor, Tex.	08-04-66	L	L	6'3	176	11	10	.524	3	49	22	8	226	218	67	78	1	2.99
Chalmers, George-George W. (Dut)	10-16PhiN	06-07-88	Aberdeen, Scotland	08-05-60	R	R	6'1	189	29	41	.414	6	121	78	36	647	645	279	290	3	3.41
Chambers, Bill-William Christopher	10StLN	09-13-88	Cameron, W.Va.	03-27-62	R	R	6'	185	0	0	—	0	1	0	0	1	1	0	0	0	0.00
Chaney, Estey-Estey Clyon	13BosA 14BknF	01-29-91	Hadley, Pa.	02-05-52	R	R	5'11	170	0	0	—	0	2	0	0	5	8	4	1	0	7.20
Chappelle, Bill-William Hogan (Big Bill)	08-09BosN 09CinN 14BknF	03-22-81	Waterloo, N.Y.	12-31-44	R	R	6'2	206	7	7	.500	0	35	15	9	177	167	59	62	1	2.39
Chech, Charlie-Charles William	05-06CinN 08CleA 09BosA	04-27-78	Madison, Wis.	01-31-38	R	R	5'11	190	33	31	.516	3	94	63	45	607	602	162	187	6	2.52
Cheney, Larry-Laurence Russell	11-15ChiN 15-19BknN 19BosN 19PhiN	05-02-86	Belleville, Kans.	01-06-69	R	R	6'1	185	116	100	.537	19	313	225	132	1880	1605	733	926	20	2.70
Chesbro, Jack-John Dwight (Happy Jack)	99-02PitN 03-09NYA 09BosA	06-05-74	N. Adams, Mass.	11-06-31	R	R	5'9	180	198	130	.604	7	392	332	260	2898	2642	690	1265	33	2.68
Chouneau (Cadreau), Chief-William	10ChiA	09-02-88	Cloquet, Minn.	09-17-46	R	R	5'9	150	0	1	.000	0	5	2	1	5	7	0	1	0	3.60
Cicotte, Eddie-Edward Victor (Dash, Knuckles)	05DetA 08-12BosA 12-20ChiA 20DL	06-19-84	Springwells, Mich.	05-05-69	R	R	5'9	175	209	149	.584	23	502	362	248	3227	2897	827	1376	35	2.37
Clark, George-George Myron	13NYA	05-19-91	Smithland, Iowa	11-14-40	R	L	6'	190	0	1	.000	0	11	1	0	19	22	19	5	0	9.00
Clark, Ginger-Harvey Daniel	02CleN	03-07-79	Wooster, Ohio	05-10-43	R	R	5'11	165	1	0	1.000	0	1	0	0	6	10	3	1	0	6.00
Clarkson, Walter-Walter Hamilton	04-07NYA 07-08CleA	11-03-78	Cambridge, Mass.	10-10-46	R	R	5'10	150	18	16	.529	3	78	37	23	374	340	132	178	4	3.18
Clauss, Al-Albert Stanley (Lefty)	13DetA	06-24-91	New Haven, Conn.	09-13-52	L	L	5'10	178	0	2	.000	0	5	1	0	13	11	12	1	0	4.85
Coakley, Andy-Andrew James (Played as Jack McAllister 02)	02-06PhiA 07-08CinN 08-09ChiN 11NYA	11-20-82	Providence, R.I.	09-27-63	L	R	6'	165	60	59	.504	3	150	124	88	1073	1023	314	428	11	2.36
Cochran, Al-Alvah Jackson (Goat)	15CinN	01-31-91	Concord, Ga.	05-23-47	R	R	5'9	175	0	0	—	0	2	0	0	5	1	0	0	0	9.00
Cocreham, Gene-Eugene	13-15BosN	11-14-84	Luling, Tex.	12-27-45	R	R	6'3	192	3	5	.375	2	17	4	1	55	64	31	18	0	5.24
Cole, King-Leonard Leslie	09-12ChiN 12PitN 14-15NYA	04-15-86	Toledo, Iowa	01-06-16	R	R	6'1	170	55	27	.671	2	129	86	47	731	657	331	298	9	3.12
Collamore, Allan-Allan Edward	11PhiA 14-15DetA	06-05-87	Worcester, Mass.	08-08-80	R	R	6'	170	5	12	.294	0	40	14	8	171	158	74	48	2	3.32
Collins, Ray-Ray Williston	09-15BosA	02-11-87	Colchester, Vt.	01-09-70	L	L	6'1	185	86	62	.581	3	199	151	90	1346	1251	271	513	19	2.50
Compton, Jack-Harry Leroy	11CinN	03-09-82	Lancaster, Ohio	07-04-74	R	R	5'9	157	0	1	.000	1	2	0	0	25	19	15	6	0	3.96
Comstock, Ralph-Ralph Remick (Commy)	13DetA 15BosA 15PitF 18PhiN	11-24-90	Sylvania, Ohio	09-13-66	R	R	5'10	168	11	14	.440	6	40	22	10	203	222	39	100	0	3.72
Cone, Bob-Robert Earl (Ike)	15PhiN	02-27-94	Galveston, Tex.	05-24-55	R	R	6'2	172	0	0	—	0	1	0	0	1	5	0	0	0	27.00
Conley, Snipe-James Patrick	14-15BalF 18CinN	04-25-94	Cressona, Pa.	01-07-78	R	R	5'11	175	7	10	.412	2	65	17	8	225	226	84	128	2	3.36
Conn, Bert-Albert Thomas (See B01-19)	98,00PhiN	09-22-79	Philadelphia, Pa.	11-02-44		R	6'	178	0	3	.000	0	5	2	1	24	42	18	5	0	7.88
Conzelman, Joe-Joseph Harrison	13-15PitN	07-14-85	Bristol, Conn.	04-17-79	R	R	5'9	170	6	8	.429	2	54	12	5	163	142	65	70	1	2.93
Cook, Rollin-Rollin Edward	15StLA	10-05-90	Toledo, Ohio	08-11-75	R	R	5'9	152	0	0	—	0	14	0	0	14	16	9	7	0	7.07
Coombs, Jack-John Wesley (Colby Jack)	06-14PhiA 15-18BknN M19PhiN 20DetA	11-18-82	LeGrand, Iowa	04-15-57	B	R	6'	185	158	111	.587	13	355	268	188	2320	2034	841	1052	35	2.78
Cooper, Guy-Guy Evans (Rebel)	14NYA 14-15BosA	01-08-93	Rome, Ga.	08-02-51	R	R	6'1	185	1	1	.500	0	11	1	0	27	26	13	8	0	5.25
Cooper, Wilbur-Arley Wilbur	12-24PitN 25-26ChiN 26DetA	02-24-92	Bearsville, W.Va.	08-07-73	R	L	5'11	175	216	178	.548	14	517	407	279	3482	3415	853	1252	36	2.89
Corbett, Joe-Joseph Aloysius	95WasN 96-97BalN 04StLN	12-04-75	San Francisco, Cal.	05-02-45	R	R	5'10	175	32	21	.604	1	62	57	52	482	497	192	248	1	3.42
Corey (Cohen), Ike(Abraham Simon)-Edward Norman	18ChiA	07-13-94	Chicago, Ill.	09-17-70	R	R		170	0	0	—	0	2	0	0	4	4	2	0	0	4.50
Corridon, Frank-Francis Joseph (Fiddler)	04ChiN 04-05,07-09PhiN 10StLN	11-25-80	Newport, R.I.	02-21-41	B	R	6'	170	70	68	.507	7	180	140	99	1216	1100	375	458	10	2.81
Cottrell, Dick-Ensign Stover	11PitN 12ChiN 13PhiA 14BosN 15NYA	08-29-88	Hoosick Falls, N.Y.	02-27-47	R	R	5'9	173	2	0	1.000	0	37	2	1	87	78	34	12	0	4.86
Coumbe, Fritz-Frederick Nicholas	14BosA 14-19CleA 20-21CinN	12-13-89	Antrim, Pa.	03-21-78	L	L	5'10	152	38	38	.500	12	193	70	32	762	773	217	212	5	2.80
Coveleski (Kowalewski), Harry-Harry Frank (The Giant Killer)	07-09PhiN 10CinN 14-18DetA	04-23-86	Shamokin, Pa.		B	L	5'11	180	82	55	.599	9	198	151	83	1248	1070	376	511	13	2.39
Covington, Bill-William Wilkes (Tex)	11-12ChiA	08-29-88	Henryville, Tenn.	12-10-31	R	R	6'1	175	10	5	.667	2	31	15	7	147	152	63	48	1	4.10
Crabb, Roy-James Roy	12ChiA 12PhiA	08-23-90	Monticello, Iowa	03-03-40	R	R	5'11	160	2	5	.286	1	8	7	6	52	54	21	15	0	3.29
Crable, George-George Elmer	10BknN	01-09-85	Brooklyn, N.Y.	Deceased	L	L	6'1	190	0	0	—	0	1	0	0	1	2	0	0	0	5.14
Craft, Molly-Maurice Montague	16-19WasA	11-28-95	Portsmouth, Va.	10-25-78	R	R	6'2	165	1	0	.000	0	29	3	1	81	93	33	33	0	3.56
Craig, George-George McCarthy (Lefty)	07PhiA	11-15-87	Philadelphia, Pa.	04-23-11		L			0	0	—	0	2	0	0	5	9	2	1	0	9.00
Cramer, Bill-William Wendell	12CinN	05-22-91	Bedford, Ind.	09-11-66	R	R	6'	175	0	0	—	0	1	0	0	2	0	0	2	0	0.00
Crandall, Doc-James Otis (Otey) (See B01-19)	08-13NYN 13StLN 13NYN 14-15StLF 16StLA 18BosN	10-08-87	Wadena, Ind.	08-17-51	R	R	5'10	180	102	62	.622	25	302	135	91	1548	1538	379	606	2	2.92
Criss, Dode-Dode (See B01-19)	08-11StLA	03-12-85	Sherman, Miss.	09-08-55	L	R	6'2	200	3	9	.250	0	30	9	3	110	104	64	70	0	4.42

USE NAMES - GIVEN NAMES (NICKNAMES)	TEAM BY YEAR	BIRTH DATE	BIRTHPLACE	DEATH DATE	B	T	HGT	WGT	W	L	Pct.	SV	G	GS	CG	IP	H	BB	SO	ShO	ERA
Cristall, Bill-William Arthur (Lefty)	01CleA	09-12-75	Odessa, Russia	01-28-39	L	L	5'7	145	1	4	.200		6	6	5	48	54	30	12	1	4.88
Cronin, Jack-John J.	95BknN 98PitN 99CinN 01-02DetA 02BalA 02-03NYN 04BknN	05-26-74	Staten Island, N.Y.	07-13-29	R	R	6'	200	42	58	.420	4	128	102	88	924	973	235	318	6	3.40
Crouch, Bill-William Henry (Skip)	10StlA	12-03-86	Kiamensi, Del.	12-22-45	L	L	6'1	210	0	0	—		1	1	1	8	6	7	2	0	3.38
Crowell, Cap-Minot Joy	15-16PhiA	09-05-92	Roxbury, Mass.	09-30-62	R	R	6'1	178	2	11	.154	0	19	14	5	94	99	81	30	0	5.17
Crum, Cal-Clarence Newton	17-18BosN	07-25-89	Cooks Mills, Ill.	12-07-45	R	R	6'1	175	0	1	.000	0	2	1	0	3	7	4	0	0	12.00
Crutcher, Dick-Richard Luther	14-15BosN	11-25-89	Frankfort, Ky.	06-19-52	R	R	5'9	148	7	8	.467	2	47	19	6	203	219	82	65	1	3.64
Cullop, Nick-Norman Andrew	13-14CleA 14-15KCF 16-17NYA 21StlA	09-17-87	Chilhowie, Va.	04-15-61	R	L	5'11	172	57	55	.509	4	174	121	62	1024	973	259	400	9	2.73
Culp, Bill-William Edward	10PhiN	06-11-87	Bellaire, Ohio	09-03-69	R	R	6'1	165	0	0	—	1	4	0	0	7	8	4	4	0	7.71
Cunningham, Bert-Ellsworth Elmer	87BknAA 88-89BalAA 90PhiP 90BufP 91BalAA 95-99LouN 00-01CleA	11-25-66	Wilmington, Del.	05-14-52	R	R	5'6	187	145	168	.463	2	314	310	286	2727	3063	1064	718	4	4.22
Cunningham, George-George Harold (See B01-19)	16-19DetA	07-13-94	Sturgeon Lake, Minn.	03-10-72	R	R	5'11	185	16	25	.390	8	123	36	19	477	444	167	167	0	3.13
Cunningham, Mike-Mody	06DetA	06-14-82	Lancaster, S.C.	12-10-69	R	R	5'10	175	0	0	—	0	3	1	1	28	29	9	15	0	3.21
Cuppy (Koppe), Nig-George Joseph	92-98CleN 99StlN 00BosN 01BosA	07-03-69	Logansport, Ind.	07-27-22	R	R	5'7	160	161	100	.617	5	302	262	224	2284	2520	609	504	9	3.49
Curran, Sammy-Simon Francis		10-30-74	Dorchester, Mass.	05-19-36	L				0	0	—	0	1	0	0	6	6	0	3	0	1.50
Currie, Clarence-Clarence Franklin	02CinN 02-03StlN 03CinN	12-30-78	Windsor, Canada	07-15-41	R	R	5'10	170	15	23	.395	2	53	38	31	371	385	121	111	3	3.39
Currie, Murphy-Archibald Murphy	16StlN	08-31-93	Fayetteville, N.C.	06-22-39	R	R	5'11	165	0	0	—	0	4	0	0	14	7	9	8	0	1.93
Curry, George-George James (Soldier Boy)	11StlA	12-21-88	Bridgeport, Conn.	10-05-63	R	R	6'	185	0	3	.000	0	3	3	0	16	19	24	2	0	7.31
Curtis, Cliff-Clifton Garfield	09-11BosN 11ChiN 11-12PhiN 12-13BknN	07-03-81	Delaware, Ohio	04-23-43	R	R	6'2	180	28	61	.315	6	136	94	38	745	707	317	236	5	3.31
Cushman, Harv-Harvey Barnes	02PitN	07-05-77	Rockland, Me.	12-27-20					0	4	.000	0	4	4	3	26	30	31	12	0	7.27
Dale, Gene-Emmett Eugene	11-12StlN 15-16CinN	06-16-89	St. Louis, Mo.	03-20-58	R	R	6'3	190	21	28	.429	3	90	45	23	444	425	207	177	4	3.59
Daley, George-George Joseph (Pecks)	09NYN	07-28-87	Buffalo, N.Y.	12-12-57	R	R	5'10	175	0	3	.000	0	3	3	3	21	31	8	8	0	6.00
Dashner, Lee-Lee Claire (Lefty)	13CleA	04-25-87	Renault, Ill.	12-16-59	B	L	5'11	192	0	0	—	0	1	0	0	2	0	0	2	0	4.50
Dauss(Daus), Hooks-George August	12-26DetA	09-22-89	Indianapolis, Ind.	07-27-63	R	R	5'10	168	221	182	.548	41	538	388	245	3391	3407	1064	1201	22	3.30
Davenport, Dave-David W. (Big Dave)	14CinN 14-15StLF 16-19StLA	02-20-90	Alexandria, La.	10-16-54	R	R	6'6	220	75	85	.469	12	259	186	95	1538	1399	521	719	18	2.93
Davis, Bud-John Wilbur (Country)	15PhiA	12-07-95	Merry Point, Va.	05-26-67	L	R	6'	207	0	2	.000	0	18	2	2	67	65	59	18	0	4.03
Davis, George-George Allen (Iron)	13-15BosN	03-09-90	Lancaster, N.Y.	06-04-61	B	R	5'10	175	7	10	.412	0	36	22	13	191	195	78	77	1	4.48
Dawson, Rex-Rexford Paul	13WasA	02-10-89	Skagit Co., Wash.	10-20-58	R	R	6'	185	0	0	—	0	1	0	0	1	0	0	0	0	0.00
Deegan, Dummy-William Joseph	01NYN	11-16-74	Bronx, N.Y.	05-17-57					0	2	.000	0	2	1	1	17	27	6	8	0	6.35
Deering, John-John Thomas	03DetA 03NYA	06-25-79	Lynn, Mass.	02-15-43	R	R	6'	180	6	7	.462	0	19	15	11	121	136	42	28	1	3.79
Deininger, Pep-Otto Charles (See B01-19)	02BosA	10-10-77	Wasseralfingen, Ger.	09-25-50	L	L	5'8	180	0	0	—	0	1	0	0	12	19	9	2	0	9.75
Delhi, Flame-Lee William	12ChiA	11-05-92	Harqua Hala, Ariz.	05-09-66	R	R	6'2	198	0	0	—	0	1	0	0	3	7	3	2	0	9.00
Dell, Wheezer-William George	12StlN 15-17BknN	06-11-86	Tuscarora, Nev.	08-24-66	R	R	6'4	200	19	23	.452	3	92	44	21	430	367	171	198	6	2.55
Demaree, Al-Albert Wentworth	12-14NYN 15-16PhiN 17ChiN 17-18NYN 19BosN	09-08-84	Quincy, Ill.	04-30-62	R	R	6'	170	80	72	.526	3	232	172	84	1425	1350	337	514	14	2.77
DeMott, Ben-Benyew Harrison	10-11CleA	04-02-89	Green Village, N.J.	07-05-63	R	R	6'	192	0	4	.000	0	7	5	1	32	55	10	15	0	6.19
Dent, Eddie-Elliott Estill	09,11-12BknN	12-08-87	Baltimore, Md.	11-25-74	R	R	6'1	190	4	5	.444	2	12	8	5	75	81	26	21	0	4.44
Denzer, Roger-Roger (Peaceful Valley)	97ChiN 01NYN	10-05-71	Le Sueur, Minn.	09-18-49	L	R	6'	180	5	11	.313	2	23	19	11	157	194	39	39	1	4.41
DesJardien, Shorty-Paul Raymond 20,22 played in N.F.L.	16CleA	08-24-93	Coffeyville, Kans.	03-07-56	R	R	6'4	205	0	0	—	0	1	0	0	1	1	1	0	0	18.00
Dessau, Rube-Frank Rolland	07BosN 10BknN	03-29-83	New Galilee, Pa.	05-06-52	B	R	5'11	175	2	4	.333	1	21	2	1	60	80	39	25	0	6.60
Dickerson, George-George Clark	17CleA	12-01-92	Renner, Tex.	07-09-38	R	R	6'1	170	0	0	—	0	1	0	0	1	0	0	1	0	0.00
Dickson, Walt-Walter Raleigh (Hickory)	10NYN 12-13BosN 14-15PitF	12-03-78	New Summerfield, Tex.	12-09-18	R	R	6'1	185	26	50	.342	0	134	79	40	701	759	222	202	4	3.59
Dillinger, Harley-Harley Hugh (Hoke, Lefty)	14CleA	10-30-94	Pomeroy, Ohio	01-08-59	R	L	5'11	175	0	1	.000	0	11	2	1	34	41	25	11	0	4.50
Dinneen (Dineen), Bill-William Henry (Big Bill)	98-99WasN 00-01BosN 02-07BosA 07-09StlA	04-05-76	Syracuse, N.Y.	01-13-55	R	R	6'1	190	173	177	.494	6	391	353	306	3075	2957	829	1127	24	3.01
	Bats left part of 00																				
Disch, George-George Charles	05DetA	03-15-79	Lincoln, Neb.	08-25-50	R	R	5'11		0	2	.000	0	3	1	1	48	43	8	14	0	2.63
Doak, Bill-William Leopold (Spittin' Bill)	12CinN 13-24StlN 24BknN 25-26VR 27-28BknN 29StlN	01-28-91	Pittsburgh, Pa.	11-26-54	R	R	6'	165	169	157	.518	16	453	369	162	2782	2676	851	1014	36	2.98
Doane, Walt-Walter Rudolph	09-10CleA	03-12-87	Bellevue, Idaho	10-19-35	L	L	6'	165	0	1	.000	0	7	1	0	23	41	9	9	0	5.48
Doheny, Ed-Edwin Richard	95-01NYN 01-03PitN	11-24-73	Northfield, Vt.	12-29-16	L	L	5'10	165	79	82	.491	2	183	168	140	1393	1412	665	567	6	3.75
Dolan, Cozy-Patrick Henry (See B01-19)	95-96,05-06BosN	12-03-72	Cambridge, Mass.	03-29-07	L	L	5'10	160	12	13	.480	1	35	26	21	255	289	101	66	3	3.45
Donahue, Red-Francis Rostell	93NYN 95-97StlN 98-01PhiN 02-03StlA 03-05CleA 06DetA	01-23-73	Waterbury, Conn.	08-25-13	R	R	6'	187	167	169	.497	4	367	339	311	2966	3376	689	787	25	3.61
Donalds, Ed-Edward Alexander (Skipper, Erston)	12CinN	06-22-85	Bidwell, Ohio	07-03-50	R	R	5'11	180	1	0	1.000	0	1	0	0	4	7	0	1	0	4.50
Donnelly (O'Donnell), Ed-Edward		07-29-79	Hampton, N.Y.	11-28-57	R	R	6'1	205	2	3	.400	0	42	22	14	221	258	81	83	1	4.03
Donovan, Wild Bill-William Edward (Smiling Bill)	98WasN 99-02BknN 03-12DetA 15-16,M15-17NYA 18DetA M21PhiN	10-13-76	Lawrence, Mass.	12-09-23	B	R	5'11	190	187	138	.575	9	378	327	289	2968	2631	1059	1552	35	2.69
Dorner, Gus-Augustus	02-03CleA 06CinN 06-09BosN	08-18-76	Chambersburg, Pa.	05-04-56	R	R	5'10	176	36	69	.343	2	131	106	76	894	842	330	275	8	3.33
Doscher, Jack-John Henry Jr.	03ChiN 03-06BknN 08CinN	07-27-80	Troy, N.Y.	05-27-71	L	L	6'1	205	2	11	.154	0	27	13	10	145	118	68	61	0	2.86
Dougherty, Tom-Thomas James (Sugar Boy)	04BknN	03-19-80	Chicago, Ill.	11-06-53	L	R	5'11	195	0	0	—	0	2	0	0	3	2	3	1	0	0.00
Douglas, Larry-Howard Lawrence	15BalF	06-05-90	Jellico, Tenn.	11-04-49	R	R	6'3	175	1	0	1.000	0	2	0	0	3	1	1	1	0	3.00
Douglas, Phil-Phillip Brooks (Shufflin' Phil)	12ChiA 14-15CinN 15BknN 15-19ChiN 19-22NYN 22DL	06-17-90	Cedartown, Ga.	08-01-52	R	R	6'5	210	94	93	.503	8	299	200	95	1708	1626	411	683	20	2.80
Dowd, Skip-James Joseph		02-16-89	Holyoke, Mass.	12-20-60	R	R	5'11	160	0	0	—	0	1	0	0	3	4	2	1	0	0.00
Dowling, Pete-Henry Peter	97-99LouN 01MilA 01CleA		St. Louis, Mo.	06-30-05	L	L	5'11	165	38	65	.369	0	117	102	92	908	984	339	299	2	3.87
Doyle, Slow Joe-Judd Bruce	06-10NYA 10CinN	09-15-81	Clay Center, Kans.	11-21-47	L	L	5'8	150	22	22	.500	1	75	50	29	437	383	147	209	7	2.84
Dresser, Bob-Robert Nicholson	02BosN	10-04-78	Newton, Mass.	07-27-24	L	L			0	1	.000	0	1	1	1	9	12	9	3	0	3.00
Driscoll, Mike-Michael Columbus	16PhiA	10-19-92	North Abington, Mass.	03-21-53	R	R	5'11	160	0	1	.000	0	3	1	0	5	6	2	0	0	5.40
Drohan, Tom-Thomas F.	13WasA	08-26-87	Fall River, Mass.	09-17-26	R	R	5'10	175	0	0	—	0	2	0	0	2	5	0	2	0	9.00
Drucke, Louis-Louis Frank	09-12NYN	12-03-88	Waco, Tex.	09-22-55	R	R	6'1	188	18	15	.545	2	53	40	21	317	282	137	201	0	2.90
Druhot, Carl-Carl A.	06CinN 06-07StlN	09-01-82	Ohio	02-05-18	L	L	5'7	150	8	10	.444	0	20	17	13	157	147	57	60	1	3.10
Dubuc, Jean-Jean Joseph Octave (Chauncey)	08-09CinN 12-16DetA 18BosA 19NYN	09-15-88	St. Johnsbury, Vt.	08-28-58	R	R	5'10	185	87	76	.540	12	256	150	101	1444	1290	577	438	12	3.04
Duffy, Bernie-Bernard Allen	13PitN	08-18-93	Vinson, Okla.	02-09-62	R	R	5'11	180	0	0	—	0	3	0	0	11	18	3	8	0	5.73
Duggleby, Bill-William James (Frosty Bill)	98,01PhiN 02-07PhiN 07PitN	03-17-74	Utica, N.Y.	08-30-44	R				93	105	.470	6	241	192	159	1741	1844	424	453	17	3.18
Dumont, George-George Henry (Pea Soup)	15-18WasA 19BosA	11-13-95	Minneapolis, Minn.	10-13-56	R	R	5'10	160	10	23	.303	2	77	35	14	347	294	130	128	4	2.85
Dunham, Wiley-Henry Houston	02StlN	01-30-77	Piketon, Ohio	01-16-34			6'1	180	2	3	.400	1	7	5	3	38	47	13	15	0	5.68
Dunkle, Davey-Edward Parks	97-98PhiN 99WasN 03ChiA 03-04WasA	08-19-72	Philipsburg, Pa.	11-19-41	B	R	6'2	220	18	30	.375	3	61	47	36	420	503	162	139	0	5.04
Dunleavy, Jack-John Francis (See B01-19)	03-04StlN		Harrison, N.J.	04-11-44	L	L	5'6	167	1	2	.368	0	21	18	14	157	164	80	79	0	4.18
Dunn, Jack-John Joseph (See B01-19)	97-00BknN 00-01PhiN 01BalA 02,04NYN	10-06-72	Meadville, Pa.	10-22-28	R	R	5'9		63	59	.516	3	142	118	103	1077	1217	334	171	3	4.11
Dupee, Frank-Frank Oliver	01ChiA	04-29-77	Monkton, Vt.	08-14-56	R	R	6'1	200	0	0	—	0	1	0	0	2	0	0	0	0	∞
Durham (Staub), Bull (Louis Raphael)-Louis Staub (Judge, Whitey)	04BknN 07WasA 08-09NYN	06-28-77	New Oxford, Pa.	06-26-60	R	R	5'10		1	0	1.000	0	9	2	1	29	37	12	6	0	5.28
Durham, Jim-James Garfield	02CleA	10-07-81	Douglass, Kans.	05-07-49	R	R	6'	175	1	1	.500	0	3	3	1	20	21	16	3	0	5.85
Durning, Rich-Richard Knott	17-18BknN	10-10-92	Louisville, Ky.	09-23-48	L	L	6'2	178	0	0	—	0	3	0	0	3	4	0	0	0	9.00
Dygert, Jimmy-James Henry (Sunny Jim)	05-10PhiA	07-05-84	Utica, N.Y.	02-08-36	R	R	5'10	158	54	49	.524	6	175	105	62	986	798	383	583	16	2.95
Eason, Mal-Malcolm Wayne (Kid)	00-02ChiN 02BosN 03DetA 05-06BknN	03-13-79	Brookville, Pa.	04-16-70	R	R	6'	175	36	73	.330	5	125	114	90	952	1027	291	274	10	3.41
East, Carl-Carlton William (See B20-45)	15StlA	08-27-94	Marietta, Ga.	01-15-53	L	R	6'2	170	0	0	—	0	1	0	0	3	6	4	0	0	18.00
Eccles, Harry-Harry Josiah (Bugs)	15PhiA	07-09-93	Kennedy, N.Y.	06-02-55	L	L	5'11	185	0	1	.000	0	5	1	0	18	16	8	13	0	6.86
Edmonston, Sam-Samuel Sherwood	07WasA	08-30-83	Washington, D.C.	04-12-79	L	L	5'11	180	0	0	—	0	1	0	0	3	8	0	0	0	9.00
Eells, Harry-Harry Archibald	06CleA	02-14-80	Danbury, Iowa	12-07-40	R	R	5'10	170	4	5	.444	0	14	8	6	86	77	48	35	1	2.62
Egan, Wish-Aloysius Jerome	02DetA 05-06StlN	06-16-81	Evart, Mich.	04-13-51	R	R	6'3	185	8	26	.235	0	42	34	17	279	309	72	52	0	3.84
Elder, Heinie-Henry Knox	13DetA	08-23-90	Seattle, Wash.	11-13-58	L	L	6'2	200	0	0	—	0	3	1	0	9	11	6	5	0	9.00
Eller, Hod-Horace Owen	17-21CinN	07-18-94	Muncie, Ind.	07-18-61	R	R	5'11	185	61	40	.604	5	160	89	52	862	806	213	381	10	2.62
Elliott, Claud-Claud Judson (Chaucer, Old Pardee)	04CinN 04-05NYN	11-17-79	Pardeeville, Wis.	06-21-23	R	R	6'	190	3	4	.429	0	22	9	7	111	115	38	47	1	3.38
Engel, Joe-Joseph William	12-15WasA 17CinN 19CleA 20WasA	03-12-93	Washington, D.C.	06-12-69	R	R	6'2	193	18	23	.439	4	102	52	10	408	344	242	151	2	3.38
Enright, John-John Percy	17NYA	11-29-95	Fort Worth, Tex.	08-18-75	R	R	5'11	177	0	0	—	0	5	0	0	7	3	1	0	0	5.40
Enzmann, Johnny-John (Gentleman John)	14BknN 18-19CleA 20PhiN	03-04-90	Brooklyn, N.Y.	03-14-84	R	R	5'10	165	10	12	.455	2	67	21	11	270	297	61	91	0	2.83
Essick, Bill-William Earl (Vinegar Bill)	06-07CinN	12-18-80	Grand Ridge, Ill.	10-11-51	R	R	5'10	175	3	3	.500	0	11	6	2	61	62	24	23	0	4.05
Eubank, John-John Franklin (Honest John)	05-07DetA	09-09-72	Servia, Ind.	11-03-58	R	R	6'2	215	8	13	.381	2	42	22	11	233	248	58	56	2	3.13
Evans, Bill-William James	16-17PitN 18MS 19PitN	02-10-93	Reidsville, N.C.	12-21-46	R	R	6'	175	2	13	.133	0	28	12	6	127	122	48	41	0	3.83

USE NAMES - GIVEN NAMES (NICKNAMES)	TEAM BY YEAR	BIRTH DATE	BIRTHPLACE	DEATH DATE	B	T	HGT	WGT	W	L	Pct.	SV	G	GS	CG	IP	H	BB	SO	ShO	ERA
Evans, Chick-Charles	09-10BosN	10-15-89	Franklin, Vt.	09-02-16	R	R			3	4	.200	2	17	4	1	53	53	41	23	0	4.92
Evans, Roy-Leroy	97StLN 97LouN 98-99WasN 02NYN 02-03BknN	03-19-74	Knoxville, Tenn.	08-15-15	R	R	6'	180	30	42	.417	2	84	68	57	614	673	233	211	2	3.66
	03StLA																				
Ewing, Bob-George Lemuel (Long Bob)	02-09CinN 10-11PhiN 12StLN	04-24-73	New Hampshire, Ohio	06-20-47	R	R	6'5	175	124	119	.510	4	291	264	205	2302	2097	614	998	19	2.49
Fahrer, Pete-Clarence Willie	14CinN	03-10-90	Holgate, Ohio	06-10-67	L	R	6'	190	0	0	—	0	5	0	0	8	8	4	2	0	1.13
Fairbank, Lee-James Lee (Smoky)	03-04PhiN	03-17-81	Deansboro, N.Y.	12-27-55	R	R	5'11	185	0	1	.000	0	7	2	2	41	52	16	16	0	5.49
Faircloth, Rags-James Lamar	19PhiN	08-19-92	Kenton, Tenn.	10-05-53	R	R	5'11	160	0	0	—	0	2	1	0	5	5	0	0	0	9.00
Falkenberg, Cy-Frederick Peter	03PitN 05-08WasA 08-11, 13ClaA 14IndF 15NwkF 15BknF 17PhiA	12-17-79	Chicago, Ill.	04-15-61	R	R	6'5	180	128	126	.504	13	330	266	180	2276	2090	690	1164	27	2.68
Fanwell, Harry-Harry Clayton	10ClaA	10-16-86	Patapsco, Md.	07-15-65	R	R	6'	175	2	9	.182	1	17	11	5	92	87	38	30	1	3.62
Faust, Charlie-Charles Victor (Victory)	11NYN	10-09-80	Marion, Kans.	06-18-15	R	R	6'2	170	0	0	—	0	2	0	0	2	2	0	0	0	4.50
Felix, Harry-Harry	01NYN 02PhiN	??-??-70	Brooklyn, N.Y.	10-17-61	R	R	5'7	160	1	3	.250	0	10	5	3	47	64	11	10	0	5.36
Ferguson, Cecil-George Cecil	06-07NYN 08-11BosN	08-19-86	Ellsworth, Ind.	09-05-43	R	R	6'	165	29	46	.387	8	142	74	47	698	659	281	298	8	3.34
Ferguson, Charlie-Charles Augustus	01ChiN	05-10-75	Okemos, Mich.	05-17-31		R	5'11		0	0	—	0	1	0	0	2	1	2	0	0	0.00
Ferry, Cy-Alfred Joseph	04DetA 05ClaA	09-27-78	Hudson, N.Y.	09-27-38	R	R	6'1	170	0	1	.000	0	4	2	1	15	15	11	6	0	7.20
Ferry, Jack-John Francis	10-13PitN	04-07-87	Pittsfield, Mass.	08-29-54	R	R	5'11	175	10	6	.625	4	47	14	7	161	146	60	56	2	3.02
Fiene, Lou-Louis Henry (Big Finn)	06-09ChiA	12-29-84	Fort Dodge, Iowa	12-22-64	R	R	6'	175	3	8	.273	1	26	10	7	138	149	35	54	0	3.85
Files, Eddie-Charles Edward	08PhiA	05-19-83	Portland, Me.	05-10-54	R	R			0	0	—	0	2	0	0	9	8	3	6	0	6.00
Fincher, Bill-William Allen	16StLA	05-26-94	Atlanta, Ga.	05-08-46	R	R	6'1	180	0	1	.000	0	4	1	0	21	22	7	5	0	2.14
Finlayson, Pembroke-Pembroke	08-09BknN	07-31-88	Cheraw, S.C.	03-06-12	R	R	5'6	140	0	0	—	0	7	7	8	2	0	11.57			
Finneran, Happy-Joseph Ignatius (Smokey Joe)	12-13PhiN 14-15BknF 18DetA 18NYA	10-29-90	East Orange, N.J.	02-03-42	R	R	5'10	169	25	33	.431	5	109	66	29	569	568	202	168	3	3.31
Fisher, Chauncey-Chauncey Burr (Peach)	93-94ClaN 94,96CinN 97BknN 01NYN 01StLN	01-08-72	Anderson, Ind.	04-27-39	R	R	5'11	175	19	29	.396	3	65	44	36	436	583	140	80	3	5.37
Fisher, Ed-Edward Fredrick	02DetA	10-31-76	Wayne, Mich.	07-24-51	R	R	6'2	200	0	0	—	0	1	0	0	4	4	1	0	0	0.00
Fisher, Ray-Ray Lyle (Pick)	10-17NYA 18MS 19-20CinN	10-04-87	Middlebury, Vt.	11-03-82	R	R	5'11	180	98	95	.508	8	279	207	110	1755	1667	481	680	20	2.82
Fisher, Tom-Thomas Chalmers (Red)	04BosN	11-01-80	Anderson, Ind.	09-03-72	R	R	5'11	175	6	15	.286	0	31	21	19	214	257	82	84	2	4.25
Fiske, Max-Maximilian Patrick (Ski)	14ChiF	10-12-88	Chicago, Ill.	05-25-28	R	R	6'	210	12	12	.500	2	38	22	7	198	161	59	87	0	3.14
Fittery, Paul-Paul Clarence	14CinN 17PhiN	10-12-88	Lebanon, Pa.	01-28-74	B	L	5'8	168	1	3	.250	0	25	6	3	100	110	39	34	0	3.87
Flaherty, Patsy-Patrick Joseph	99LouN 00PhiN 03-04ChiA 04-05PitN 07-08BosN 10PhiN 11BosN	06-29-76	Mansfield, Pa.	01-23-68	L	L	5'8	165	66	85	.437	1	173	150	125	1303	1292	331	271	7	3.10
Flater, Jack-John William	08PhiA	09-22-83	Sandymount, Md.	03-20-70	R	R	5'10	175	1	3	.250	0	5	3	3	39	35	12	8	0	2.08
Fletcher, Sam-Samuel Scott	09BknN 12CinN	02-21-81	Bedford, Pa.	Deceased		R	6'2	210	0	1	.000	0	3	1	1	19	28	13	8	0	9.95
Ford, Gene-Eugene Wyman	05DetA	04-16-81	Milton, Canada	08-23-73	R	R	6'	170	0	0	—	0	6	1	0	15	23	15	2	0	10.69
Ford, Russ-Russell William	09-13NYA 14-15BufF	04-25-83	Brandon, Canada	01-24-60	R	R	5'11	175	98	71	.580	11	199	170	129	1487	1340	376	710	14	2.59
Foreman, Frank-Francis Isaiah (Monkey)	84ChiU 84KCU 85-89BalAA 90-98CinN 91WasAA 92WasN 92BalN 93NYN 95-96ChiN 01BosA 01-02BalA	05-01-63	Baltimore, Md.	11-19-57	R	R	6'	160	100	93	.518	4	230	206	170	1728	1863	661	591	8	3.95
Forman, Bill-William Orange	09-10WasA	10-10-86	Venango, Pa.	10-02-58	B	R	5'11	180	0	2	.000	0	3	2	1	12	9	7	2	0	5.25
Foster, Ed-Eddy Lee (Slim)	08ClaA	??-??-85	Ga.	03-01-29	R	R	6'1		1	0	1.000	2	6	1	1	21	16	12	11	0	2.14
Foster, Rube-George	01-05BosA	01-05-88	Lehigh, Okla.	03-01-76	R	R	5'8	160	58	35	.624	5	138	104	61	842	726	305	295	15	2.36
Fox (Fuchs), Henry-Henry H.	02PhiN	11-18-73	Scranton, Pa.	06-06-27					0	0	—	1	1	0	0	1	0	0	1	0	18.00
Foxen, Bill-William Aloysius	08-10PhiN 10-11ChiN	05-31-79	Tenafly, N.J.	04-17-37	L	L	5'11	165	16	20	.444	0	61	33	20	326	283	140	130	3	2.57
Fraser, Chick-Charles Carrollton	96-98LouN 98ClaN 99-00PhiN 01PhiA 02-04PhiN 05BosN 06CinN 07-09PhiN	08-26-73	Chicago, Ill.	05-08-40	R	R	5'10	188	176	208	.458	7	433	388	342	3355	3460	1332	1098	22	3.68
Frill, John-John Edmond	10NYA 12StLA 12CinN	04-03-79	Reading, Pa.	09-29-18	R	L	5'10	170	3	2	.600	1	16	10	3	67	90	7	33	1	5.91
Frisk, Emil-John Emil (See B01-19)	99CinN 01DetA	10-15-74	Kalkaska, Mich.	01-27-22	L	R	6'1	190	8	10	.444	0	20	16	15	143	175	43	39	0	4.15
Fritz, Charlie-Charles Cornelius	07BosN 09-10PitN 10-11BosN	06-13-82	Mobile, Ala.	07-30-43	L				0	1	.000	0	1	1	0	3	0	3	1	0	3.00
Frock, Sammy-Samuel William	06-08StLN 09-13CinN 13-15NYN	12-23-82	Baltimore, Md.	11-03-25	R	R	6'	168	14	24	.368	3	63	38	22	342	348	113	202	3	3.24
Fromme, Art-Arthur Henry		09-03-83	Quincy, Ill.	08-24-56	R	R	6'	178	80	90	.471	2	252	167	90	1437	1297	530	638	14	2.91
Gaiser, Fred-Frederick Jacob	08StLN	08-31-85	Stuttgart, Germany	10-09-18		R	6'		0	0	—	0	1	0	0	2	4	3	2	0	9.00
Gallia, Bert-Melvin Allys	12-17WasA 18-20StLA 20PhiN	10-14-91	Beeville, Tex.	03-19-76	R	R	6'	165	64	68	.485	12	242	135	61	1278	1210	494	550	7	3.13
Gardner, Harry-Harry Ray	11-12PitN	06-01-87	Quincy, Mich.	08-02-61	R	R	6'2	180	1	1	.500	2	14	3	2	42	42	21	24	0	4.50
Gardner, Jim-James Anderson	95,97-99PitN 02ChiN	10-04-74	Pittsburgh, Pa.	04-24-05	R	R			25	23	.521	0	59	49	37	422	468	130	115	1	3.86
Garrett, Clarence-Clarence Raymond (Laz)	15ClaA	03-06-91	Reader, W.Va.	02-11-77	R	R	6'5	185	2	2	.500	0	4	4	2	23	19	6	5	0	2.35
Garvin, Ned-Virgil Lee	96PhiN 99-00ChiN 01MilA 02ChiA 02-04BknN 04NYA	01-01-74	Navasota, Tex.	06-16-08	R	R	6'3	160	59	97	.378	5	181	158	134	1400	1320	413	612	13	2.72
Gaspar, Harry-Harry Lambert	09-12CinN	04-28-83	Kingsley, Iowa	05-14-40	R	R	6'	180	44	48	.478	13	143	98	48	826	795	217	228	11	2.69
Gear, Dale-Dale Dudley (See B01-19)	96ClaN 01WasA	02-02-72	Lone Elm, Kans.	09-23-51	R	R	5'11	165	5	13	.278	0	27	18	16	186	234	28	41	1	4.21
Geary, Bob-Robert Norton (Speed)	18-19PhiA 21CinN	05-10-91	Cincinnati, Ohio	01-30-80	R	R	5'11	168	4	9	.308	3	35	10	7	148	164	51	41	2	3.47
Gehring, Henry-Henry	07-08WasA	04-24-81	St. Paul, Minn.	04-18-12	R	R			3	8	.273	0	18	10	8	92	101	16	31	2	3.91
George, Lefty-Thomas Edward	11StLA 12ClaA 15CinN 18BosN	08-13-86	Pittsburgh, Pa.	05-13-55	L	L	6'	155	6	22	.214	9	52	26	14	242	285	98	74	2	3.87
Gerner, Ed-Edwin Frederick (Lefty)	19CinN	07-22-97	Philadelphia, Pa.	05-15-70	L	L	5'8	175	1	0	1.000	0	5	1	0	17	22	3	2	0	3.18
Gervais, Lefty-Lucien Edward	13BosN	07-06-90	Grover, Wis.	10-19-50	L	L	5'10	165	0	1	.000	0	5	2	1	16	18	4	1	0	5.63
Geyer, Rube-Jacob Bowman (Jake)	10-13StLN	03-26-84	Allegheny, Pa.	10-12-62	R	R	5'10	170	17	26	.395	1	104	33	15	413	420	181	133	1	3.66
Gibson, Norwood-Norwood Ringold	03-06BosA	03-11-77	Peoria, Ill.	07-07-59	R	R	5'10	150	32	32	.500	0	85	72	56	609	525	208	258	3	2.93
Gill, Ed-Edward James	19WasA	08-07-95	Somerville, Mass.	10-10-95	R	R	5'11	180	1	1	.500	0	16	2	0	37	38	21	7	0	4.86
Gilligan(Gilgen), Jack-John Peter	09-10StLA	10-18-84	Chicago, Ill.	11-19-80	B	R	6'	190	1	5	.167	0	12	8	5	62	65	37	14	0	4.35
Gingras, Joe-Joseph Elzead John	15KCF	01-10-94	New York, N.Y.	09-06-47	R	R	6'2	188	0	2	.000	0	2	0	0	4	6	1	2	0	6.75
Girard, Charlie-Charles August	10PhiN	12-16-84	Brooklyn, N.Y.	08-06-36	R	R	5'10	175	0	2	.000	0	2	1	0	27	33	12	11	0	6.33
Glade, Fred-Frederick Monroe	02ChiN 04-07StLA 08NYA	01-25-76	Dubuque, Iowa	11-21-34	R	R	6'1	200	53	69	.434	1	132	126	107	1073	950	237	464	14	2.62
Glavenich, Luke-Luke Frank	13ClaA	01-17-93	Jackson, Cal.	05-22-35	R	R	5'9	189	0	1	.000	0	1	0	0	3	3	1	0	0	9.00
Glaze, Ralph-Daniel Ralph	06-08BosA	03-13-81	Denver, Colo.	10-31-68	R	R	5'9	165	15	21	.4170	0	61	34	20	340	303	85	137	1	2.89
Gleason, Kid-William J. (See B01-19)	89-91PhiN 92-94StLN 94-95BalN M19-23ChiA	10-26-66	Camden, N.J.	01-02-33	B	R	5'7	158	136	129	.513	6	299	266	240	2389	2552	906	744	11	3.79
Glendon, Martin-Martin J. (Buns)	02CinN 03ClaA	02-08-77	Milwaukee, Wis.	11-06-50	R	R	6'	165	1	3	.250	0	4	4	3	31	25	11	9	0	2.03
Golden, Roy-Roy Kramer	10-11StLN	07-12-88	Madisonville, Ohio	10-04-61	R	R	6'1	195	6	12	.333	0	37	31	9	192	171	162	112	0	4.88
Good, Ralph-Ralph Nelson	10BosN	04-25-86	Monticello, Me.	11-24-65	R	R	6'	165	0	1	.000	0	2	1	0	9	4	6	4	0	4.50
Good, Wilbur-Wilbur David (Lefty) (See B01-19)	05NYA	09-28-85	Punxsutawney, Pa.	12-30-63	L	L	5'6	165	0	2	.000	0	2	2	0	19	18	14	13	0	4.74
Goodwin, Art-Arthur Ingram	05NYA	02-27-77	Whitley Twp., Pa.	06-19-43	R	R	5'8	195	0	0	—	0	1	2	2	0	0	81.00			
Goodwin, Clyde-Clyde Samuel	06WasA	11-12-86	Shade, Ohio	10-12-63	R	R	5'11	145	0	2	.000	0	4	3	1	22	20	13	9	0	4.50
Goodwin, Marv-Marvin Mardo	16WasA 17StLN 18MS 19-22StLN 25CinN	01-16-91	Gordonsville, Va.	10-21-25	R	R	6'	175	21	25	.457	2	102	48	19	447	467	100	121	3	3.30
Goulait, Ted-Theodore Lee (Snooze)	12NYN	08-12-89	St. Clair, Mich.	07-15-36	R	R	5'9	172	0	1	.000	0	1	1	1	7	11	4	6	0	6.43
Gould, Al-Albert Frank (Pudgy)	16-17ClaA	01-20-93	Muscatine, Iowa	08-08-82	R	R	5'6	160	9	11	.450	1	57	16	7	201	196	92	65	1	3.04
Graham(Grahame), Bill-William James	08-10StLA	07-22-84	Owosso, Mich.	02-15-36	R	R	6'		14	29	.326	1	64	40	21	347	321	105	141	3	2.90
Graham, Oscar-Oscar Marion	07WasA	07-20-73	Plattsmouth, Neb.	10-15-31	L	L	6'	180	4	10	.286	0	20	14	6	104	116	29	44	0	3.98
Graham, Peaches-George Frederick (See B01-19)	03ChiN	03-23-77	Aledo, Ill.	07-25-39	R	R	5'9	180	0	1	.000	0	2	0	0	4	4	1	0	0	5.40
Graney, Jack-John Gladstone (Mickey) (See B01-19)	08ClaA	06-10-86	St. Thomas, Canada	04-19-78	L	L	5'9	180	0	0	—	0	3	1	0	8	6	6	1	0	6.00
Gray, Dolly-William Denton	09-11WasA	12-04-78	Houghton, Mich.	04-03-56	L	L	6'2	160	15	51	.227	3	98	70	46	568	586	181	213	3	3.52
Gregg, Dave-David Charles (Highpockets)	13ClaA	03-14-91	Chehalis, Wash.	11-12-65	R	R	6'3	185	0	0	—	0	1	0	0	1	1	9	0	18.00	
Gregg, Vean-Sylveanus Augustus	11-14ClaA 14-16BosA 18PhiA 25WasA	04-13-85	Chehalis, Wash.	07-29-64	L	L	6'1	185	92	64	.590	12	240	161	105	1400	1248	556	722	14	2.69
Gregory, Frank-Frank Ernst	12CinN	07-25-90	Spring Valley, Wis.	11-05-55	R	R	5'11	185	0	0	—	0	1	1	0	16	19	7	4	1	4.50
Gregory, Howie-Howard Watterson	11StLA	11-18-86	Hannibal, Mo.	05-30-70	L	R	6'	175	1	3	.250	0	7	7	4	11	4	1	0	5.14	
Grevell, Bill-William Joseph Jr.	19PhiA	03-05-98	Williamstown, N.J.	06-21-23	R	R	5'11	170	0	1	.000	0	2	2	1	12	15	18	3	0	14.25
Griffin, Hank-James Linton (Pepper)	11ChiN 11-12BosN	07-11-86	Whitehouse, Tex.	11-30-51	L	R	6'	170	1	4	.200	0	19	7	1	86	100	40	31	0	5.76
Griffin, Pat-Patrick Richard	14CinN	05-06-93	Niles, Ohio	06-07-27	R	R	6'2	190	0	0	—	0	1	0	0	2	3	1	1	0	9.00
Griffith, Clark-Clark Calvin (The Old Fox)	91StLAA 91BosAA 93-00ChiN 01-02,M01-02ChiA 03-07,M03-08NYA 09-10,M09-11CinN 12-14,M12-20WasA	11-20-69	Clear Creek, Mo.	10-27-55	R	R	5'6	156	235	143	.622	9	453	372	337	3388	3670	774	955	22	3.31
Griner, Dan-Donald Dexter (Rusty)	12-16StLN 18BknN	03-07-88	Centerville, Tenn.	06-03-50	L	R	6'1	200	28	55	.337	6	135	82	43	673	700	202	244	6	3.49
Groom, Bob-Robert	09-13WasA 14-15StLF 16-17StLA 18ClaA	09-12-84	Belleville, Ill.	02-19-48	R	R	6'2	175	120	150	.444	12	367	288	157	2337	2216	783	1159	22	3.10
Groth, Dango-Ernest John	04ChiN	12-24-84	Cedarburg, Wis.	05-23-50	R	R	5'11	170	0	2	.000	0	3	3	2	16	22	6	9	0	5.63
Grover, Burt-Charles Byrd (Bugs)	13DetA	06-20-90	Gallipolis, Ohio	05-24-71	L	R	6'1	185	0	0	—	0	1	0	0	11	9	7	5	0	3.27
Guese, Whitey-Theodore	01CinN	01-24-72	New Bremen, Ohio	04-08-51	R	R	6'	200	1	4	.200	0	5	5	4	44	62	14	11	0	6.14
Gunkel, Red-Woodward William	16ClaA	04-15-94	Sheffield, Ill.	04-19-54	B	R	5'8	158	0	0	—	0	1	0	0	2	1	0	0	0	0.00

USE NAMES - GIVEN NAMES (NICKNAMES)	TEAM BY YEAR	BIRTH DATE	BIRTHPLACE	DEATH DATE	B	T	HGT	WGT	W	L	Pct.	SV	G	GS	CG	IP	H	BB	SO	ShO	ERA
Haas, Bruno-Bruno Philip (Boon)	15PhiA	05-05-91	Worcester, Mass.	06-05-52	B	L	5'10	180	0	2	.000	0	6	2	1	14	23	28	7	0	12.21
Hackett, Jim-James Joseph (Sunny Jim) (See B01-19)	02-03StLN	10-01-77	Jacksonville, Ill.	03-28-61	R	R	6'2	185	1	7	.125	0	11	9	8	78	93	34	28	0	4.73
Hafford, Leo-Leo Edgar	06CinN	09-17-83	Somerville, Mass.	10-01-11	R	R	6'	170	1	1	.500	0	3	1	1	19	13	11	5	0	0.95
Hageman, Casey-Kurt Moritz	11-12BosA 14StLN 14ChiN	04-01-87	Mt. Oliver, Pa.	04-01-64	R	R	5'10	186	3	7	.300	0	32	11	3	120	108	40	47	0	3.08
Hagerman, Rip-Zerah Zequiel	09ChiN 14-16Clea	06-20-88	Lyndon, Kans.	01-29-30	R	R	6'2	200	19	32	.385	0	81	55	23	432	414	225	214	4	3.08
Hahn, Noodles-Frank George	99-05CinN 06NYA	04-29-79	Nashville, Tenn.	02-06-60	L	L	5'9	160	130	94	.580	0	242	230	211	2021	1906	380	912	25	2.55
Haislip, Jim-James Clifton (Slim)	13PhiA	08-04-91	Farmersville, Tex.	11-22-70	R	R	6'3	186	0	0	—	0	3	4	3	0	0	6	0	6.00
Hale, Dad-Ray Luther	02BosN 02BalA	02-18-80	Allegan, Mich.	02-01-46	R	R	5'10	180	0	5	.000	0	11	7	4	54	78	22	17	0	5.67
Hall, Bert-Herbert Ernest	11PhiN	10-15-88	Portland, Ore.	07-18-48	R	R	5'10	185	0	1	.000	0	7	1	0	18	19	13	8	0	4.00
Hall, Bill-William Bernard (Beanie)	13BknN	02-22-94	Charleston, W.Va.	08-15-47	R	R	6'2	210	0	0	—	0	3	0	0	5	4	5	3	0	5.40
Hall (Clolo), Charley (Carlos)-Charles Louis (Sea Lion)	06-07CinN 09-13BosA 16StLN 18DetA	07-27-84	Ventura, Cal.	12-06-43	R	R	6'1	187	53	45	.541	20	188	82	50	911	821	391	427	3	3.08
Hall, Herb-Herbert Silas (Iron Duke)	18DetA	06-05-93	Steeleville, Ill.	07-03-70	B	R	6'4	220	0	0	—	0	3	0	0	6	12	7	1	0	15.00
Hall, Mark-Marcus	10StLA 13-14DetA	08-12-87	Joplin, Mo.	02-24-15	R	R	6'1	190	14	25	.359	0	63	36	14	301	292	137	112	1	3.26
Halla, Jack-John Arthur	05Clea	08-12-87	St. Louis, Mo.	09-30-47	L	L	5'11	175	0	0	—	0	3	0	0	13	12	0	4	0	2.77
Hamilton, Earl-Earl Andrew	11-16StLA 16DetA 16-17StLA 18-23PitN 24PhiN	07-19-91	Gibson City, Ill.	11-17-68	L	L	5'8	160	117	147	.443	13	410	262	140	2342	2319	773	790	17	3.16
Hanley, Jim-James Patrick	13NYA	10-13-85	Providence, R.I.	05-01-61	R	R	5'11	165	0	0	—	0	1	0	0	4	5	4	2	0	6.75
Hansen, Ing-Roy Inglof	18WasA	03-06-98	Beloit, Wis.	02-09-77	R	R	6'	165	1	0	1.000	0	5	0	0	9	10	3	2	0	3.00
Harding, Charlie-Charles Harold (Slim)	13DetA	01-03-91	Nashville, Tenn.	10-30-71	R	R	6'2	172	0	0	—	0	1	0	0	2	3	1	0	0	4.50
Hardy, Alex-David Alexander (Dooney)	02-03ChiN	??-??-77	Toronto, Canada	04-22-40	R	R	5'10	175	3	3	.500	0	7	7	5	48	50	19	16	1	4.31
Hardy, Harry-Harry	05-06WasA	11-05-75	Steubenville, Ohio	09-04-43	L	L	5'6	155	2	4	.333	0	8	5	4	44	55	18	14	0	5.11
Harkness, Specs-Frederick Harvey	10-11Clea	12-13-87	Los Angeles, Cal.	05-16-52	R	R	5'11	180	11	9	.550	3	38	22	9	188	194	76	85	1	3.40
Harley, Dick-Henry Risk	05BosN	08-18-74	Springfield, Ohio	05-16-61	R	R			5	2	.286	0	9	4	4	66	72	19	19	1	4.64
Harmon, Bob-Robert Greene (Hickory Bob)	09-13StLN 14-16,18PitN	10-15-87	Liberal, Mo.	11-27-61	B	R	6'	187	107	133	.446	12	321	240	143	2054	1966	762	634	15	3.33
Harper, Bill-William Homer (Blue Sleeve)	11StLA	06-14-89	Bertrand, Mo.	06-17-51	B	R	6'1	180	0	0	—	0	2	0	0	8	4	4	6	0	6.75
Harper, Harry-Harry Clayton	13-19WasA 20BosA 21NYA 23BknN	04-24-95	Hackensack, N.J.	04-23-63	L	L	6'2	165	59	76	.437	2	219	170	65	1257	1100	582	623	12	2.86
Harper, Jack-Charles William	99Clea N 00-01StLN 02StLA 03-06CinN 06ChiN 07HO	04-02-78	Franklin, Pa.	09-30-50	R	R	6'	178	81	62	.566	1	158	148	115	1208	1198	438	466	10	3.58
Harper, Jack-John Wesley	15PhiN	08-05-93	Hendricks, W.Va.	06-18-27	R	R	5'11	180	0	1	.000	0	3	0	0	9	5	1	3	0	3.00
Harrell, Slim-Oscar Martin	12PhiA	07-31-90	Grandview, Tex.	04-30-71	R	R	6'3	180	0	0	—	0	3	4	0	1	4	0	1	0	0.00
Harrington, Frank-Andrew Francis	13CinN	11-13-88	Wakefield, Mass.	11-12-38	R	R	6'	193	0	0	—	0	1	0	0	4	6	1	1	0	9.00
Harris, Ben-Benjamin Franklin	14-15KCF	12-17-89	Donelson, Tex.	04-29-27	R	R	6'1	195	7	7	.500	1	32	14	5	156	180	41	40	0	4.04
Harris, Joe-Joseph White	05-07BosA	02-01-82	Melrose, Mas.	04-12-66	R	R	6'1	198	3	30	.091	2	45	32	26	317	284	88	137	1	3.35
Harstad, Oscar-Oscar Theander	15Clea	05-24-92	Parkland, Wash.	11-14-85	R	R	6'	174	3	6	.333	1	32	7	4	82	81	35	35	0	3.40
Hart, Bill-William Franklin (The Bond Hill Boy)	86-87PhiAA 92BknN 95PitN 96-97StLN 98PitN 01Clea	07-19-65	Louisville, Ky.	09-19-36	R	R	5'10	163	65	110	.371	3	206	190	162	1583	1819	704	431	5	4.60
Harter, Frank-Franklin Pierce (Chief)	12-13CinN 14IndF	09-19-86	Keyesport, Ill.	04-14-59	R	R	5'11	165	3	5	.375	1	29	6	2	101	105	37	30	0	3.65
Hartman, Charlie-Charles Otto	08BosA	08-10-88	Los Angeles, Cal.	10-22-60		L			0	0	—	0	1	0	0	2	1	2	1	0	4.50
Hartranft, Ray-Raymond Joseph (Rube)	13PhiN	09-19-90	Quakertown, Pa.	02-10-55	L	L	6'1	195	0	0	—	0	1	0	0	3	1	1	0	0	9.00
Harvey, Zaza-Ervin King (Silent) (See B01-19)	00ChiN 01Clea	01-05-79	Saratoga, Cal.	06-03-54	L	L	6'	190	3	6	.333	1	17	9	5	96	94	35	27	0	3.47
Hawk, Ed-Edward	11StLA	02-22-88	Exeter, Mo.	03-26-36	L	R	5'11	175	1	4	.200	0	5	4	4	38	38	8	14	0	3.32
Hawley, Pink-Emerson Pink	92-94StLN 95-97PitN 98-99CinN 00NYN 01MilA	12-05-72	Beaver Dam, Wis.	09-19-38	L	R	5'10	185	165	177	.482	3	393	344	297	3011	3334	973	869	11	3.97
Hearn, Bunny-Charles Bunn	10-11StLN 13NYN 15PitF 18,20BosN	05-21-91	Chapel Hill, N.C.	10-19-59	L	L	5'11	190	13	24	.351	0	66	40	24	400	429	100	111	2	3.56
Hedgpeth, Doc-Harry Malcolm	13WasA	09-04-88	Fayetteville, N.C.	07-30-66	L	L	6'1	190	0	0	—	0	1	0	0	1	1	1	0	0	0.00
Hehl, Jake-Herman Charles	18BknN	12-10-99	Brooklyn, N.Y.	07-04-61	R	R	5'11	180	0	0	—	0	1	0	0	1	0	0	0	0	0.00
Heismann, Crese-Christian Ernest	01-02CinN 02BalA	04-16-80	Cincinnati, Ohio	11-19-51	R	L	6'2	175	2	5	.286	0	11	8	5	63	71	28	23	0	4.71
Heitmann, Harry-Harry Anton	18BknN	10-06-96	Albany, N.Y.	12-15-58	R	R	6'1	205	0	1	.000	0	1	1	0	1	4	0	0	0	108.00
Henderson (Ball), Ed (Eugene J.)-Edward J.	14PitF 14IndF	12-25-84	Newark, N.J.	01-15-64	L	L	5'9	168	1	1	.500	0	8	2	2	26	22	12	5	0	4.15
Hendricks, Ed-Edward (Big Ed)	10NYN	06-20-85	Zeeland, Mich.	11-28-30	L	L	6'3	200	0	1	.000	1	4	1	1	12	12	4	2	0	3.75
Hendrix, Claude-Claude Raymond	11-13PitN 14-15ChiF 16-20ChiN 21DU	04-13-89	Olathe, Kans.	03-22-44	R	R	6'	195	144	116	.554	17	360	257	184	2372	2123	697	1092	27	2.65
Henion, Lafayette-Lafayette Marion	19BknN	06-07-99	San Diego, Cal.	07-22-55	R	R	5'11	154	0	0	—	0	1	0	0	3	2	2	0	0	6.00
Henley, Weldon-Weldon	03-05PhiA 07BknN	10-25-80	Jasper, Ga.	11-16-60	R	R	6'	175	31	42	.425	0	97	81	62	722	640	231	309	8	2.94
Henning, Pete-Ernest Herman	14-15KCF	12-28-87	Crown Point, Ind.	11-04-39	R	R	6'1	185	14	25	.359	4	68	34	22	345	334	134	118	1	3.83
Herbert, Ernie-Earn Albert (Tex)	13CinN 14-15StLF	01-30-87	Hale, Mo.	01-13-68	R	R	5'10	165	2	1	.667	1	35	2	1	115	116	50	52	0	3.37
Herbert (Kemman), Fred (Herbert Frederick)-Frederick	15NYN	03-04-87	LaGrange, Ill.	05-29-63	R	R	6'	185	1	1	.500	0	2	1	1	17	12	4	6	0	1.06
Herrmann, Lefty-Martin John	18BknN	01-10-93	Oldenburg, Ind.	09-11-56	L	L	5'10	150	0	0	—	0	1	0	0	1	1	1	0	0	0.00
Herrell, Walt-Walter William (Reds)	11WasA	02-19-89	Rockville, Md.	01-23-49					0	0	—	0	1	0	0	2	5	2	0	0	18.00
Herring, Bill-William Francis (Smoke)	15BknF	10-31-93	New York, N.Y.	09-10-62	R	R	6'3	185	0	0	—	0	2	0	0	3	5	3	3	0	15.00
Herring, Herb-Herbert Lee	12WasA	07-22-91	Danville, Ark.	04-22-64	R	R	5'11	178	0	0	—	0	1	0	0	1	1	1	0	0	0.00
Hershey, Frank-Frank	05BosN	09-13-78	Gorham, N.Y.	12-15-49	R	R	6'	175	0	1	.000	0	1	0	4	1	1	6	1	0	6.75
Hess, Otto-Otto C.	02,04-08Clea 12-15BosN	10-10-78	Berne, Switzerland	02-25-26	L	L	6'1	170	71	88	.447	5	198	165	129	1418	1355	448	580	18	2.98
Hesselbacher, George-George Edward	16PhiA	01-18-95	Philadelphia, Pa.	02-18-80	R	R	6'2	175	0	4	.000	0	6	4	2	26	37	22	6	0	7.27
Hesterfer, Larry-Lawrence	01NYN	05-13-78	Newark, N.J.	04-22-43	R	L	5'8	160	0	1	.000	0	1	1	1	6	15	3	2	0	7.50
Hickey, John-John William	04Clea	11-03-81	Minneapolis, Minn.	12-28-41	R	R	5'10	170	0	2	.000	0	2	2	1	12	14	11	5	0	7.50
Hickman, Charley-Charles Taylor (Piano Legs) (See B01-19)	97-99BosN 01NYN 02Clea 07WasA	03-04-76	Taylortown, Pa.	04-19-34	R	R	5'9	185	12	8	.600	4	30	22	15	185	175	94	37	3	4.24
Higginbotham, Irv-Irving Clinton	06,08-09StLN 09ChiN	04-26-82	Homer, Neb.	06-12-59	R	R	6'1	196	10	14	.417	1	48	24	16	243	232	66	86	1	2.81
Higgins, Eddie-Thomas Edward (Irish, Doc)	09-10StLN	03-18-88	Nevada, Ill.	02-14-59	R	R	6'	175	3	4	.429	0	18	5	5	76	83	24	16	0	4.50
High, Ed-Edward Thomas (Lefty)	01DetA	10-26-73	Baltimore, Md.	02-10-26		L			2	1	.667	0	4	1	1	18	21	6	4	0	3.50
Hill, Herb-Herbert Lee	15Clea	08-19-91	Hutchins, Tex.	09-01-70	R	R	5'11	175	0	0	—	0	1	0	0	1	0	1	0	0	0.00
Hill, Red-Clifford Joseph	17PhiA	02-20-93	Marshall, Tex.	08-11-38	B	L			0	0	—	0	1	0	0	3	1	1	0	0	6.00
Hillebrand, Doc-Homer Hiller Henry (See B01-19)	05-06,08PitN	10-10-79	Freeport, Ill.	01-23-74	R	L	5'8	165	7	4	.636	1	18	11	8	115	86	40	70	1	2.50
Hinrichs, Dutch-William Louis	10WasA	04-27-89	Orange, Cal.	08-18-72	R	R	6'3	195	0	0	—	0	3	0	0	7	10	3	5	0	2.57
Hitt, Bruce-Bruce Smith	17StLN 18MS	03-14-98	Comanche, Tex.	11-10-73	R	R	6'1	190	0	0	—	0	2	0	0	4	7	1	1	0	9.00
Hitt, Roy-Roy Wesley (Rhino)	07CinN	06-22-84	Carleton, Neb.	02-08-56	R	R	5'10	200	6	10	.375	0	21	18	14	153	143	56	63	2	3.41
Hoch, Harry-Harry Keller	08PhiN 14-15StLA	01-09-87	Woodside, Del.	10-27-81	R	R	5'10	165	2	6	.250	0	30	8	4	120	127	66	26	0	4.35
Hoelskoetter, Art-Arthur William (Holley, Hoss) (See B01-19) (Played as Art Hostetter 07)	05-07StLN	09-30-82	St. Louis, Mo.	08-03-54	R	R	6'2		2	5	.286	0	15	4	3	75	68	49	32	0	4.56
Hoff, Red-Chester Cornelius	11-13NYA 15StLA	05-08-91	Ossining, N.Y.	09-17-98	L	L	5'9	162	2	4	.333	0	23	5	2	84	67	38	49	0	2.46
Hoffer, Bill-William Leopold (Wizard)	95-98BalN 98-99PitN 01Clea	07-21-59	Cedar Rapids, Ia.	02-21-59	R	R	5'9	155	95	45	.679	3	161	142	125	1254	1333	453	314	10	3.75
Hogan, George-George Augustine	14KCF	09-25-85	Marion, Ohio	02-22-22	R	R	5'11	160	0	1	.000	0	4	1	0	13	12	7	7	0	4.15
Hogg, Bill-William Johnston (Buffalo Bill)	05-08NYA	09-11-81	Port Huron, Mich.	12-08-09	R	R	6'	200	38	49	.437	1	116	89	43	730	677	319	368	5	3.06
Hogg, Brad-Carter Bradley	11-12BosN 15ChiN 18-19PhiN	08-26-89	Buena Vista, Ga.	04-02-35	L	R	6'	185	20	29	.408	3	71	50	33	448	446	152	149	4	3.70
Holmes, Chick-Elwood Marter	18PhiA	03-22-96	Beverly, N.J.	04-15-54		R			0	0	—	0	1	0	0	4	1	0	0	0	13.50
Holmes, Jim-James Scott	06PhiA 08BknN	08-02-82	Lawrenceburg, Ky.	03-10-60					1	5	.167	0	16	2	1	49	47	28	11	0	3.49
Hooker, Cy-William Edward (Buck)	02-03CinN	08-28-80	Richmond, Va.	07-02-29	R	R	5'6		0	0	—	0	1	0	0	10	13	2	0	0	3.60
Hope, Sam-Samuel Everett	07PhiA	12-04-78	Brooklyn, N.Y.	06-30-46	R	R	5'10		0	0	—	0	1	0	0	4	3	3	1	0	9.00
Hooper, Bill-William Booth (Bird Dog)	13-14PhiN 15WasA	08-26-91	Jackson, Tenn.	01-14-65	R	R	6'	175	0	4	.000	1	19	3	2	60	65	29	12	0	4.20
Horsey, Hanson-Hanson Galena	12CinN	11-26-89	Galena, Md.	12-01-49	R	R	5'11	154	0	0	—	0	1	0	0	4	9	1	2	0	22.50
Horstmann, Oscar-Oscar Theodore	17-19StLN	06-02-91	Alma, Mo.	05-11-77	R	R	5'11	165	9	7	.563	0	50	15	4	176	154	80	61	1	3.68
Houck, Duke-Byron Simon	12-14PhiA 14BknF 18StLA	08-28-91	Prosper, Minn.	06-17-69	R	R	6'	175	26	24	.520	3	118	50	19	532	462	274	224	1	3.30
House, Will-Willard Edwin	13DetA	10-03-90	Cabool, Mo.	11-16-23	R	R	6'		0	2	.000	0	19	2	0	54	64	17	16	0	5.17
Houser, Joe-Joseph William	14BufF	07-03-91	Steubenville, Ohio	01-03-53	L	L	5'9	160	1	0	—	0	2	0	0	23	21	20	6	0	5.48
Hovlik, Ed-Edward Charles (Hick)	18-19WasA	08-20-91	Cleveland, Ohio	03-19-55	R	R	6'	180	2	1	.667	0	11	2	1	34	37	19	13	0	3.18
Hovlik, Joe-Joseph (Brick)	09-10WasA 11ChiA	08-16-84	Czechoslovakia	11-03-51	R	R	5'10	185	2	0	1.000	0	16	3	1	55	66	23	25	1	3.60
Howard, Earl-Earl Nycum	18StLN	05-25-93	Everett, Pa.	04-04-37	R	R	6'1	160	0	0	—	0	1	0	0	3	1	0	0	0	0.00

USE NAMES - GIVEN NAMES (NICKNAMES)	TEAM BY YEAR	BIRTH DATE	BIRTHPLACE	DEATH DATE	B	T	HGT	WGT	W	L	Pct.	SV	G	GS	CG	IP	H	BB	SO	ShO	ERA
Howell, Harry-Harry Taylor (Handsome Harry) (See B01-19)	98BknN 99BalN 00BknN 09-02BalA 03NYA 04-10StLA	11-14-76	Brooklyn, N.Y.	05-22-56	R	R	5'9		132	141	.484	5	340	282	244	2567	2435	677	986	20	2.74
Howell, Roland-Roland Boatner (Billiken)	12StLN	01-03-92	Napolenville, La.	03-31-73	R	R	6'4	210	0	0	—	0	3	0	0	2	5	5	0	0	22.50
Huenke, Al-Albert Alfred	14NYN	06-26-91	New Bremen, Ohio	09-20-74	R	R	6'	175	0	0	—	0	1	0	0	2	2	5	0	0	4.50
Hughes, Ed-Edward J. (See B01-19)	05-06BosA	10-05-80	Chicago, Ill.	10-14-27	R	R	6'	190	3	1	.750	0	8	4	2	43	53	12	11	0	4.81
Hughes, Jay-James Jay	98BalN 99,01-02BknN	01-22-74	Sacramento, Cal.	06-02-24	R	R	6'1	190	81	39	.675	0	134	128	111	1089	1006	372	368	8	3.00
Hughes, Long Tom-Thomas James	00-01ChiN 02BalA 02-03BosA 04NYA 05-09,11-13WasA	11-29-78	Chicago, Ill.	02-08-56	R	R	6'1	175	129	174	.426	20	399	314	227	2644	2610	853	1368	24	3.09
Hughes, Tom-Thomas L.	06-07,09-10NYA 14-18BosN	01-28-84	Coal Creek, Colo.	11-01-61	R	R	6'2	175	56	40	.583	18	160	85	55	863	703	235	476	9	2.56
Hughes, Vern-Vernon Alexander (Lefty)	14BalF	04-15-93	Etna, Pa.	04-26-61	L	L	5'10	155	0	0	—	0	3	0	0	5	3	0	0	0	3.00
Humphries, Bert-Albert	10-11PhiN 11-12CinN 13-15ChiN	09-26-80	California, Pa.	09-21-45	R	R	5'11	182	50	43	.538	9	153	90	45	797	807	151	258	9	2.78
Hunt, Ben-Benjamin Franklin (Highpockets)	10BosA 13StLN	11-10-88	Eufaula, Okla.	09-27-27	L	L	6'5	190	2	5	.286	0	9	8	3	55	51	29	25	0	3.93
Hunter, George-George Henry (See B01-19)	10BosA	07-08-86	Buffalo, N.Y.	01-11-68	B	L	5'8	165	4	10	.286	0	16	13	10	113	104	38	43	0	2.47
Husting, Bert-Berthold Juneau (Pete)	00PitN 01MilA 02BosA 02PhiA	03-06-78	Mayville, Wis.	09-03-48	R	R	5'10	185	23	21	.523	2	69	54	37	437	499	199	122	1	4.16
Hynes, Pat-Patrick Joseph (See B01-19)	03StLN 04StLA	03-12-85	St. Louis, Mo.	03-12-07	L				1	1	.500	0	6	3	2	35	45	13	7	0	5.66
Iburg, Ham-Herman Edward	02PhiN	10-30-73	San Francisco, Cal.	02-11-45	R	R	5'11	165	11	18	.379	0	30	29	20	236	286	62	106	1	3.89
Imlay, Doc-Harry Miller	13PhiN	11-21-89	Allentown, N.J.	10-07-48	R	R	6'	168	0	0	—	0	9	0	0	14	19	7	7	0	7.07
Ingersoll, Bob-Robert Randolph	14CinN	01-08-83	Rapid City, S.D.	01-13-27	R	R	5'11	175	0	0	—	0	4	0	0	6	5	5	2	0	3.00
Isbell, Frank-William Frank (Bald Eagle) (See B01-19)	98ChiN 01-02,06-07ChiA	08-21-75	Delevan, N.Y.	07-15-41	L	R	5'11	190	4	7	.364	1	17	10	7	85	92	43	19	0	3.60
Jackson, Charlie-Charles Bernard	05DetA	11-23-57	Versailles, Ohio		R				0	2	.000	0	2	2	1	11	14	7	3	0	5.73
Jacobs, Elmer-William Elmer	14PhiN 16-18PitN 18-19PhiN 19-20StLN 24-25ChiN 27ChiA	08-10-92	Salem, Mo.	02-10-58	R	R	6'	165	50	81	.382	7	250	133	65	1189	1223	423	336	1	3.55
Jacobson, Beany-Albin Leonard	04-05WasA 06-07StLA 07BosA	06-05-81	Pt. Washington, Wis.	01-31-33	L	L	6'	170	23	46	.333	4	88	70	53	612	618	148	195	1	3.19
Jacobus, Larry-Stuart Louis	18CinN	12-13-94	Cincinnati, Ohio	08-19-65	B	R	6'2	186	0	1	.000	0	5	0	0	17	25	1	8	0	5.82
Jaeger, Charlie-Charles Thomas	04DetA	04-17-75	Ottawa, Ill.	09-27-42	R	R	6'1	195	2	3	.400	0	8	6	5	49	49	15	13	0	2.57
James, Bill-William Henry (Big Bill)	11-12CleA 14-15StLA 15-19DetA 19BosA 19ChiA	01-20-87	Detroit, Mich.	05-25-42	B	R	6'4	195	65	70	.481	2	203	147	67	1180	1108	576	408	3	3.21
James, Bill-William Lawrence (Seattle Bill)	13-15BosN 16-17SJ 18MS 19BosN	03-12-92	Iowa Hill, Cal.	03-10-71	L	R	6'3	196	37	21	.638	2	84	60	44	541	469	199	253	5	2.28
James, Lefty-William A.	12-14CleA	07-01-89	Glen Roy, Ohio	05-03-33	R	L	5'11	175	2	6	.250	1	31	11	5	96	94	45	36	0	3.38
Jamieson, Charlie-Charles Devine (The Jersey Comet) (See B20-45)	16WasA 17-18PhiA 19,22CleA	02-07-93	Paterson, N.J.	10-27-69	L	L	5'9	165	2	1	.667	1	13	3	1	48	55	30	7	0	6.19
Jasper, Hi-Harry W.	14-15ChiA 16StLN 19CleA	11-15-80	St. Louis, Mo.	05-22-37	R	R	5'11	180	10	12	.455	1	52	21	8	238	210	99	96	0	3.48
Jensen, Willie-William Christian	12DetA 14PhiA	11-17-89	Philadelphia, Pa.	03-27-17	R	R	5'11	170	1	2	.333	0	5	5	2	34	37	16	5	0	4.50
Johns, Ollie-Oliver Tracy	05CinN	08-21-79	Trenton, Ohio	06-17-61	L	L	6'	180	1	0	1.000	0	4	1	1	18	31	4	8	0	3.50
Johnson, Chief-George Howard (Murphy, Big Murph)	13-14CinN 14-15KCF	03-30-86	Winnebago, Neb.	06-12-22	R	R	5'11	190	40	43	.482	2	111	85	44	688	667	192	304	9	2.95
Johnson, Jing-Russell Conwell	16-17PhiA 18MS 19,27-28PhiA	10-09-94	Parker Ford, Pa.	12-06-50	R	R	5'9	172	24	38	.387	0	101	64	36	548	559	179	171	0	3.33
Johnson, Rankin-Adam Rankin Sr. (Tex)	14BosA 14-15ChiF 15BalF18StLN	02-04-88	Burnet, Tex.	07-02-72	R	R	6'1	185	23	30	.434	2	72	53	31	450	401	151	169	6	2.92
Johnson, Roy-Roy (Hardrock)	18PhiA 14ChiN	10-01-93	Madill, Okla.	01-10-86	R	R	6'	185	1	5	.167	0	10	8	3	50	47	27	14	0	3.42
Johnson, Walt-Ellis Walter	12,15CinN 17PhiA	10-01-93	Minneapolis, Minn.	11-14-65	R	R	6'1	185	0	2	.000	0	9	2	0	30	29	15	19	0	5.40
Johnson, Walter-Walter Perry (Barney, The Big Train) (See B01-19)	07-27WasA M29-32WasA M33-35CleA	11-06-87	Humboldt, Kans.	12-10-46	R	R	6'1	200	417	279	.599	36	802	667	532	5923	4918	1355	3509	110	2.17
Jones, Alex-Alexander H.	89PitN 92LouN 92WasN 94PhiN 03DetA	12-25-69	Pittsburgh, Pa.	04-04-41	L	L	5'8	135	9	16	.360	0	26	24	18	201	199	77	65	1	3.72
Jones, Cowboy-Albert Edward (Bronco)	98CleN 99-01StLN	08-23-74	Golden, Colo.	02-08-58	L	L	5'10	160	25	35	.417	0	70	66	52	526	618	155	147	3	3.61
Jones, Deacon-Carroll Elmer	16-18DetA	12-20-93	Arcadia, Kans.	12-28-52	R	R	6'1	174	6	6	.500	2	46	10	3	151	136	69	45	0	2.98
Jones, Elijah-Elijah Albert (Bumpus)	07,09DetA	01-27-82	Oxford, Mich.	04-29-43	R	R	5'7		1	3	.250	1	6	3	1	26	33	4	11	0	4.15
Jones, Oscar-Oscar Lafayette (Flip Flap)	03-05BknN	10-22-79	Carter Co., Mo.	03-16-53	R	R	5'7	163	44	54	.449	1	113	97	83	875	904	225	257	4	3.20
Jordan, Rip-Raymond Willis (Lanky)	12ChiA 19WasA	09-28-89	Portland, Me.	06-05-60	L	R	6'	172	0	0	—	0	4	1	0	14	19	2	2	0	7.71
Joss, Addie-Adrian (See Mike O'Neill)	02-10CleA 10IL	04-12-80	Woodland, Wis.	04-14-11	R	R	6'3	185	159	95	.626	6	287	261	235	2336	1895	370	926	45	1.88
Joyce, Mike (See Mike O'Neill)																					
Justis, Walt-Walter Newton (Smoke)	05DetA	08-17-83	Moores Hill, Ind.	10-04-41	R	R	5'8	195	0	0	—	0	2	0	0	3	4	6	0	0	9.00
Juul, Herold-Earl Herold	14BknF	05-21-93	Chicago, Ill.	01-04-42	R	R	5'9	150	0	3	.000	0	9	3	0	29	26	31	16	0	6.21
Juul, Herb-Herbert Victor	11CinN	02-02-86	Chicago, Ill.	11-14-28	L	L	5'11	150	0	0	—	0	1	0	0	4	3	4	2	0	4.50
Kahler, George-George Runnells (Krum)	10-14CleA	09-06-89	Athens, Ohio	02-07-24	R	R	6'	183	32	43	.427	3	109	77	41	627	631	272	285	5	3.17
Kaiserling, George-George P. (Shiny)	14IndF 15NwkF	05-12-93	Steubenville, Ohio	03-02-18	R	R	6'	180	32	25	.561	2	78	62	36	536	534	145	150	6	2.69
Kallio, Rudy-Rudolph	18-19DetA 25BosA	12-13-92	Portland, Ore.	04-06-79	R	R	5'10	160	9	17	.346	1	49	27	10	222	234	93	75	2	4.18
Kane (Cohen), Harry-Harry (Klondike)	02StLA 03DetA 05-06PhiN	07-27-83	Hamburg, Ark.	09-15-32	L	L			2	7	.222	0	15	9	7	86	100	50	43	1	4.81
Kantlehner, Erv-Erving Leslie	14-16PitN 16PhiN	07-31-92	San Jose, Cal.	02-03-90	L	L	6'	190	13	29	.310	5	89	44	20	399	344	157	141	5	2.84
Karger, Ed-Edwin (Loose)	06PitN 06-08StLN 09CinN 09-11BosA	05-06-83	San Angelo, Tex.	09-09-57	L	L	5'11	175	48	68	.414	3	165	123	81	1091	1012	314	415	9	2.79
Karns, Bill-William Arthur	01BalA	12-08-75	Richmond, Iowa	11-15-41	R				1	0	1.000	0	1	1	0	9	5	6	0	0	6.35
Katoll, Jack-John (Big Jack, Katy)	98-99ChiN 01-02ChiA 02BalA	06-24-72	Germany	08-18-55	R	R	6'4	200	17	24	.415	1	47	41	35	361	432	80	90	0	3.32
Keating, Ray-Raymond Herbert	12-16,18NYA 19BosN	07-21-93	Bridgeport, Conn.	12-29-63	R	R	5'11	185	30	51	.370	1	130	93	49	751	706	293	349	4	3.30
Keefe, Bobby-Robert Francis	07NYA 11-12CinN	06-16-82	Folsom, Cal.	12-06-64	R	R	5'11	155	17	18	.486	7	75	35	15	361	334	129	154	0	3.14
Keeley, Burt-Burton Elwood (Speed)	08-09WasA	11-02-79	Wilmington, Ill.	05-03-52	R	R	5'9	170	6	11	.353	1	30	15	12	177	185	49	68	1	3.31
Keifer, Katsey-Sherman Carl	14IndF	09-03-91	California, Pa.	02-19-27	B	L			1	0	1.000	1	9	6	2	9	6	2	2	0	2.00
Kellogg, Al-Albert Clement (Lefty)	08PhiA	09-09-86	Providence, R.I.	07-21-53	L		6'3	208	0	2	.000	0	3	3	2	17	20	9	8	0	5.82
Kellum, Win-Winford Ansley	01BosA 04CinN 05StLN	04-11-76	Waterford, Canada	08-10-51	B	L	5'8	160	19	15	.559	2	48	37	32	347	337	63	97	2	3.19
Kelly, Ed-Edward Leo	14BosA	12-10-86	Pawtucket, R.I.	11-04-28	R	R	5'11	173	0	0	—	0	3	1	1	2	1	1	4	0	0.00
Kelly, Herb-Herbert Barrett (Moke)	14-15PhiN	05-18-73	Mobile, Ala.		L	L	5'9	160	1	3	.250	0	10	3	2	37	34	11	12	0	2.92
Kenna, Ed-Edward Benninghaus (The Pitching Poet)	02PhiA	10-17-77	Charleston, W.Va.	03-22-12	R	R	6'	180	1	1	.500	0	2	1	1	17	19	11	5	0	5.29
Kennedy, Brickyard-William Park	92-01BknN 02NYN 03PitN	10-07-67	Ballaire, Ohio	09-23-15	R	R	5'11	160	182	163	.528	9	405	353	293	3021	3276	1201	797	12	3.96
Kent, Maury-Maurice Allen	12-13BknN	09-17-85	Marshalltown, Iowa	11-19-66	R	R	6'	168	5	5	.500	0	23	9	2	100	112	49	25	1	4.68
Keupper, Hank-Henry John	14StLF	06-24-87	Staunton, Ill.	08-14-60	L	L	6'	180	8	20	.286	0	42	25	12	213	256	49	70	1	4.27
Killian, Ed-Edwin Henry (Twilight Ed)	03CleA 04-10DetA	11-12-76	Racine, Wis.	07-18-28	L	L	5'11	170	101	81	.555	6	213	180	149	1599	1463	482	516	22	2.38
Killilay, Jack-John William	05DetA	05-24-87	Leavenworth, Kans.	10-21-68	R	R	5'11	165	4	3	.571	1	14	7	1	61	65	36	28	0	3.54
Kinney, Walt-Walter William	18BosA 19-20,23PhiA	09-09-93	Denison, Tex.	07-01-71	L	L	6'2	186	11	20	.355	1	63	30	18	291	274	136	129	1	3.59
Kinsella, Ed-Edward William (Rube)	05PitN 10StLA	01-15-80	Lexington, Ill.	01-17-76	R	R	6'1	175	1	4	.200	0	13	7	4	67	81	19	21	0	3.49
Kirby, LaRue-LaRue (See B01-19)	12NYN 15StLF	12-30-89	Eureka, Mich.	06-10-61	B	R		185	1	0	1.000	0	4	1	1	18	20	8	9	0	5.50
Kirsch, Casey-Harry Louis	10CleA	10-17-87	Philadelphia, Pa.	12-25-25	R	R	5'11	170	0	0	—	0	3	1	0	5	5	1	5	0	6.00
Kissinger, Rube-Charles Samuel	02-03DetA	12-13-76	Adrian, Mich.	07-17-41	L	L	6'	190	8	13	.381	0	21	19	18	162	166	41	40	2	3.00
Kitson, Frank-Frank R.	98-99BalN 00-02BknN 03-05DetA 06-07WasA 07NYA	04-11-72	Hopkins, Mich.	04-14-30	L	R	5'10	165	126	118	.516	4	304	249	212	2223	2333	492	731	18	3.17
Klawitter, Dutch-Albert Hermann	09-10NYN 13DetA	03-29-89	Wilkes-Barre, Pa.	02-02-50	R	R	5'11	187	2	3	.400	0	15	6	3	60	65	30	16	0	4.20
Klepfer, Ed-Edward Lloyd (Big Ed)	11-13NYA 15ChiA 15-17CleA 18MS 19CleA	03-17-88	Summerville, Pa.	08-09-50	R	R	6'	185	22	18	.550	3	98	50	16	448	457	137	165	2	2.81
Klobedanz, Fred-Frederick Augustus (Duke)	96-99,02BosN	06-13-71	Waterbury, Conn.	04-12-40	L	L	5'11	190	53	25	.679	0	89	85	69	702	742	266	181	2	4.12
Knetzer, Elmer-Elmer Ellsworth (Baron)	09-12BknN 13HO 14-15PitF 16BosN 16-17CinN	07-22-85	Carrick, Pa.	10-03-75	R	R	5'10	180	69	69	.500	2	220	134	82	1267	1206	481	535	13	3.15
Knolls, Hub-Oscar Edward	06BknN	12-18-83	Valparaiso, Ind.	07-01-46	R	R	6'2	190	0	0	—	0	2	0	0	7	13	2	3	0	3.86
Knowlson, Tom-Thomas Herbert (Doc)	15PhiN	04-23-95	Pittsburgh, Pa.	04-11-43	B	R	5'10	165	4	7	.364	0	10	8	8	101	99	60	24	0	3.48
Koenigsmark, Willis-Willis Thomas	19StLN	02-27-96	Waterloo, Ill.	07-01-72	R	R	6'4	180	0	0	—	0	1	0	0	1	0	0	0	0	∞
Koestner, Elmer-Elmer Joseph (Bob)	10CleA 14ChiN 14CinN	11-30-85	Piper City, Ill.	10-27-59	R	R	6'1	175	5	10	.333	0	36	14	8	170	169	76	56	1	3.18
Koob, Ernie-Ernest Gerald	15-17StLA 18MS 18StLA	09-11-92	Keeler, Mich.	11-12-41	L	L	5'10	160	24	31	.436	3	125	55	19	501	488	186	121	3	3.13
Koukalik, Joe-Joseph	04BknN	03-03-80	Chicago, Ill.	01-02-47	R	R			1	0	1.000	0	1	1	1	8	10	4	1	0	1.13
Krapp, Gene-Eugene Hamlet (Rubber Arm)	11-12CleA 14-15BufF	05-12-87	Rochester, N.Y.	04-13-23	R	R	5'5	168	39	46	.459	2	117	92	50	758	625	416	351	3	3.23
Krause, Harry-Harry William (Hal)	08-12PhiA	07-12-88	San Francisco, Cal.	10-23-40	B	L	5'10	165	36	26	.581	4	85	57	39	525	446	146	298	10	2.50
Kroh, Rube-Floyd Myron	06-07BosA 08-10ChiN 12BosN	08-25-86	Friendship, N.Y.	03-17-44	B	L	6'2	185	13	9	.591	4	36	25	13	215	182	67	92	3	2.30
Kruger, Abe-Abraham	08BknN	02-14-85	Morris Run, Pa.	07-04-62	R	R	6'2	190	0	1	.000	0	5	2	0	14	20	5	0	0	4.50
Kull(Kalinowsky), John-John A.	09PhiA	06-24-81	Shenandoah, Pa.	03-30-36	L	L	6'2	187	1	0	1.000	0	3	0	0	5	3	4	0	0	3.00
Kusel, Ed-Edward Daniel	09StLA	02-15-86	Cleveland, Ohio	10-20-48	R	R	6'	165	0	3	.000	0	3	2	1	24	43	1	2	0	7.13
Lafitte, Ed-Edward Francis (Jean)	09,11-12DetA 13ST 14-15BknF 15BufF	04-07-86	New Orleans, La.	04-12-71	R	R	6'2	188	37	35	.514	5	106	75	47	647	668	262	262	1	3.34

USE NAMES - GIVEN NAMES (NICKNAMES)	TEAM BY YEAR	BIRTH DATE	BIRTHPLACE	DEATH DATE	B	T	HGT	WGT	W	L	Pct.	SV	G	GS	CG	IP	H	BB	SO	ShO	ERA
Lake, Joe-Joseph Henry	08-09NYA 10-12StLA 12-13DetA	12-06-81	Brooklyn, N.Y.	06-30-50	R	R	6'	185	63	92	.406	7	199	139	96	1317	1329	332	594	8	2.85
Lambeth, Otis-Otis Samuel	16-18CleA	05-13-90	Berlin, Kans.	06-05-76	R	R	6'	175	10	9	.526	3	43	19	5	178	176	74	58	0	3.19
Lamline(Lamlein), Fred-Frederick Arthur (Dutch, Punk)	12ChiA 15StLN	08-14-87	Port Huron, Mich.	09-20-70	R	R	5'11	171	0	0	—	0	5	0	0	21	28	5	12	0	5.57
Lanford, Sam-Lewis Grover	07WasA	01-08-86	Woodruff, S.C.	09-14-70	L	R	5'5	155	0	0	—	0	2	1	0	7	10	5	2	0	5.14
Lange, Erv-Erwin Henry	14ChiF	08-12-87	Forest Park, Ill.	04-24-71	R	R	5'10	145	12	11	.522	2	36	22	10	190	162	55	87	2	2.23
Lange, Frank-Frank Herman (Seagan)	10-13ChiA	10-28-83	Columbus, Wis.	12-26-45	R	R	5'11	160	28	25	.528	3	95	60	25	499	455	219	318	4	2.96
Lathrop, Bill-William George	13-14ChiA	08-12-91	Hanover, Wis.	11-20-58	R	R	6'2	184	1	2	.333	0	25	1	0	65	57	31	16	0	3.05
Lattimore, Bill-William Hershel (Slothful Bill, Tex)	08CleA	05-25-84	Roxton, Tex.	10-30-19	L	L	5'9	165	1	2	.333	0	4	4	1	24	24	7	5	1	4.50
Lavender, Jimmy-James Sanford	12-16ChiN 17PhiN	03-26-84	Barnesville, Ga.	01-12-60	R	R	5'11	165	63	76	.453	12	224	142	65	1207	1097	447	547	10	3.09
Lawson, Bob-Robert Baker	01BosN 02BalA	03-23-75	Lynchburg, Va.	10-28-52	R	R	5'10	170	2	4	.333	0	9	6	5	59	66	31	17	0	3.66
Lear, King-Charles Bernard	14-15CinN	01-23-91	Greencastle, Pa.	10-31-76	R	R	6'	175	7	12	.368	1	57	19	12	224	224	64	66	1	3.01
Leary, Frank-Francis Patrick	07CinN	02-26-81	Wayland, Mass.	10-04-07		R	5'10	190	0	1	.000	0	2	1	0	8	7	6	4	0	1.13
LeClaire, George-George Lewis (Frenchy)	14-15PitF 15BufF 15BalF	10-18-86	Milton, Vt.	10-10-18	R	R	5'9	170	7	12	.368	2	55	19	12	236	222	61	91	2	3.36
Ledbetter, Razor-Ralph Overton	15DetA	12-08-94	Rutherford College, N.C.	02-01-69	R	R	6'3	190	0	0	—	0	1	0	0	1	1	0	0	0	0.00
Lee, Watty-Wyatt Arnold	01-03WasA 04PitN	12-25-79	Lynch Station, Va.	03-06-36	L	L	5'10	171	29	37	.439	1	76	66	51	550	649	114	162	4	4.29
Leever, Sam-Samuel (The Goshen Schoolmaster)	98-10PitN	12-23-71	Goshen, Ohio	05-19-53	R	R	5'10	175	194	101	.658	13	388	299	241	2661	2449	587	847	38	2.47
Leifield, Lefty-Albert Peter	05-12PitN 12-13ChiN 18-20StLA	09-05-83	Trenton, Ill.	10-10-70	L	L	6'1	165	124	96	.564	7	296	216	138	1838	1673	554	616	32	2.47
Leitner, Dummy-George Michael	01PhiA 01NYN 02CleA 02ChiA	06-19-71	Parkton, Md.	02-20-60	L	R	5'7	120	0	3	.000	0	5	3	2	32	48	8	4	0	5.34
Lelivelt, Bill-William John	09-10DetA	10-21-84	Chicago, Ill.	02-14-68	R	R	6'	195	0	3	.000	1	5	3	2	29	33	5	6	0	3.41
Leonard, Dutch-Hubert Benjamin	13-18BosA 19-21DetA 22VR 23ST 24-25DetA	04-16-92	Birmingham, Ohio	07-11-52	L	L	5'10	185	138	111	.554	14	330	272	152	2190	2019	661	1158	33	2.77
Leonard, Elmer-Elmer Ellsworth (Tiny)	11PhiA	11-12-88	Napa, Cal.	05-27-81	R	R	6'3	210	2	2	.500	0	5	1	1	19	26	10	10	0	2.84
LeRoy, Louis-Louis Paul (Chief)	05-06NYA 10BosA	02-18-79	Omro, Wis.	10-10-44	R	R	5'10	180	3	1	.750	0	15	5	3	73	66	15	39	0	3.21
Leverenz, Walt-Walter Fred (Tiny, Lefty)	13-15StLA	07-21-88	Chicago, Ill.	03-19-73	L	L	5'10	175	8	31	.205	1	62	44	19	323	277	160	131	2	3.15
Lewis, Ted-Edward Morgan (Parson)	96-00BosN 01BosA	12-25-72	Machynlleth, Wales	05-23-36	R	R	5'10	158	92	63	.594	4	183	153	136	1405	1379	511	378	7	3.53
Liebhardt, Glenn-Glenn John	06-09CleA	03-10-83	Milton, Ind.	07-13-56	R	R	5'10	175	37	34	.521	7	91	66	49	612	543	183	280	7	2.18
Lindaman, Vive-Vivan Alexander	06-09BosN	10-28-77	Charles City, Iowa	02-13-27	R	R	6'1	200	36	60	.375	1	131	100	82	904	876	296	286	7	2.92
Lindemann, Ernie-Ernest	07BosN	06-10-83	New York, N.Y.	12-27-51	R	R	5'10	180	0	0	—	0	1	1	0	6	6	4	3	0	6.00
Lindstrom, Axel-Axel Olaf	16PhiA	08-26-95	Gustavsburg, Sweden	06-24-40	R	R	5'10	180	0	0	—	0	1	0	0	1	2	0	1	0	4.50
Link, Fred-Frederick Theodore (Laddie)	10CleA 10StLA	03-11-86	Columbus, Ohio	05-22-39	L	L	6'	170	5	7	.417	1	25	16	6	140	139	62	57	1	3.41
Lively, Jack-Henry Everett	11DetA	05-29-85	Joppa, Ala.	12-05-67	R	R	5'9	185	7	5	.583	2	18	14	10	114	143	34	45	0	4.58
Livingstone, Jake-Jacob M.	01NYN	01-01-80	St. Petersburg, Russia	03-22-49					0	0	—	0	2	0	0	12	26	7	6	0	9.00
Long, Les-Lester	11PhiN	12-12-88	Summit, N.J.	10-21-58	R	R	5'10	153	0	0	—	0	4	0	0	8	15	5	4	0	4.50
Long, Red-Nelson	02BosN	09-28-76	Burlington, Canada	08-11-29	R	R	6'1	190	0	0	—	0	1	1	1	4	2	1	0	1.13
Loos, Pete-Ivan	01PhiA	03-23-78	Philadelphia, Pa.	02-23-56		R	5'9		0	1	.000	0	1	1	0	7	8	4	5	0	27.00
Lorenzen, Lefty-Adolph Andreas	13DetA	01-12-93	Davenport, Iowa	03-05-63	L	L	5'10	164	0	0	—	0	2	0	0	2	4	3	0	0	18.00
Lotz, Joe-Joseph Peter (Smokey)	16StLN	01-02-91	Remsen, Iowa	01-01-71	R	R	5'9	175	0	3	.000	0	12	3	1	40	31	17	18	0	4.28
Loudell (Laudel), Art-Arthur	10DetA	04-10-82	Latham, Mo.	02-19-61	R	R	5'11	173	1	1	.500	0	5	2	1	21	23	14	12	0	3.43
Love, Slim-Edward Haughton	13WasA 16-18NYA 19-20DetA	08-01-90	Love, Miss.	11-30-42	L	L	6'7	205	27	21	.563	5	119	48	19	518	480	246	251	1	3.04
Lovett, John-John	03StLN	05-06-78	Monday, Ohio	12-05-37					0	0	—	0	3	1	0	5	5	3	0	0	5.40
Lowdermilk, Grover-Grover Cleveland	09,11StLN 12ChiN 15StLA 15-16DetA 18CleA 17-19StLA 19-20ChiA	01-15-85	Sandborn, Ind.	03-31-68	R	R	6'4	190	23	40	.365	0	122	73	30	590	534	376	296	3	3.81
Lowdermilk, Lou-Louis Bailey	11-12StLN	02-23-87	Sandborn, Ind.	12-27-75	R	L	6'1	180	4	5	.444	1	20	4	4	80	86	38	22	0	3.38
Luhrsen, Bill-William Ferdinand (Wild Bill)	13PitN	04-14-84	Buckley, Ill.	08-15-73	R	R	5'9	165	3	1	.750	0	5	3	2	29	25	16	11	0	2.48
Lundbom, Jack-John Frederick	02CleA	03-10-77	Manistee, Mich.	10-31-49	R	R	6'2	187	1	1	.500	0	8	3	1	34	48	16	7	0	4.50
Lundgren, Carl-Carl Leonard	02-09ChiN	02-16-80	Marengo, Ill.	08-21-34	R	R	5'11	175	91	56	.619	6	179	149	125	1322	1129	476	535	19	2.42
Lush, Johnny-John Charles (See B01-19)	04-07PhiN 07-10StLN	10-08-85	Williamsport, Pa.	11-18-46	L	L	5'9	165	66	85	.437	2	182	155	105	1239	1169	413	490	16	2.68
Lynch, Mike-Michael Joseph	04-07PitN 07NYN	06-28-75	Holyoke, Mass.	04-02-27	R	L	6'2	170	43	32	.573	3	97	72	53	656	597	281	292	1	3.05
Mack, Bill-William Francis	08ChiN	02-12-85	Elmira, N.Y.	09-30-71	L	L	6'1	155	0	2	.000	0	2	2	0	6	5	1	2	0	3.00
Madden, Len-Leonard Joseph (Lefty)	12ChiN	02-10-89	Toledo, Ohio	09-09-49	L	L	6'2	175	1	0	1.000	0	6	2	0	12	16	9	5	0	3.00
Maddox, Nick-Nicholas	07-10PitN	11-09-86	Govanstown, Md.	11-27-54	R	R	6'	175	43	20	.683	1	93	72	47	605	487	170	193	9	2.29
Magee, Billy-William J.	97-99LouN 99PhiN 99WasN 01StLN 01-02NYN 02PhiN	07-06-75	St. John, Canada	Deceased	R	R	5'10	154	30	50	.375	0	106	89	69	742	837	350	161	5	4.94
Mahoney, Chris-Christopher John (Steve)	10BosA	06-11-85	Milton, Mass.	07-15-54	R	R	5'9	165	0	1	.000	1	2	1	0	11	16	5	6	0	3.27
Main, Alex-Miles Grant	14DetA 15KCF 18PhiN	05-13-84	Montrose, Mich.	12-29-65	R	R	6'5	195	21	22	.488	6	75	44	24	403	342	150	160	4	2.77
Malarkey, Bill-William John	08NYN	11-26-78	Port Byron, Ill.	12-12-56	R	L	5'10	185	0	2	.000	0	15	0	0	35	31	10	12	0	2.57
Malarkey, John-John S.	94-96WasN 99ChiN 02-03BosN	05-10-72	Springfield, Ohio	10-29-49	R	R	5'11	155	22	38	.367	3	80	59	51	566	629	227	179	3	3.64
Malloy, Alex-Archibald Alexander (Lick)	10StLA	10-31-86	Laurinburg, N.C.	03-01-61	R	R	6'2	180	0	6	.000	0	7	6	4	53	47	17	27	0	2.55
Malloy, Herm-John Herman (Tug)	07-08DetA	06-01-85	Massillon, Ohio	05-09-42	R	R	6'		0	3	.000	0	4	3	3	25	33	9	14	0	4.32
Maloney, Chic-Charles Michael	08BosN	05-22-86	Cambridge, Mass.	01-17-67	R	R	5'8	155	0	0	—	0	1	0	0	2	3	1	0	0	4.50
Maloy, Paul-Paul Augustus (Biff)	13BosA	06-04-92	Bascom, Ohio	03-18-76	R	R	6'	185	0	0	—	0	2	0	0	2	1	4	0	0	9.00
Mamaux, Al-Albert Leon	13-17PitN 18-23BknN 24NYA	05-30-94	Pittsburgh, Pa.	12-31-62	R	R	6'	168	76	67	.531	10	254	138	78	1294	1138	511	625	15	2.89
Manning, Ernie-Ernest Devon (Ed)	14StLA	04-28-73	Florala, Ala.	04-28-73	L	R	6'	175	0	0	—	0	4	0	0	10	11	3	3	0	3.60
Manning, Rube-Walter S. (Speedy)	07-10NYA	04-29-83	Chambersburg, Pa.	04-23-30	R	R	6'	180	22	32	.407	4	84	57	35	502	483	162	212	4	3.14
Manske, Lou-Louis Hugo	06PitN	07-04-84	Milwaukee, Wis.	04-27-63	L	L	6'		0	1	.000	0	2	1	0	8	12	5	6	0	5.63
Manuel, Moxie-Mark Garfield	05WasA 08ChiA	10-16-81	Metropolis, Ill.	04-26-24	R	R	5'11	170	3	5	.375	1	21	7	4	70	61	28	28	0	3.60
Mapel, Rolla-Rolla Hamilton (Lefty)	19StLA	03-09-90	Lee's Summit, Mo.	04-06-66	R	L	5'11	165	0	2	.000	0	3	2	2	20	17	17	2	0	4.50
Marbet, Walt-Walter William	13StLN	09-13-90	Plymouth Co., Iowa	09-24-56	R	R	6'1	175	0	1	.000	0	3	1	0	9	4	1	0	0	18.00
Marion, Don-Donald George (Dan, Rube)	14-15BknF	07-31-89	Bowling Green, Ohio	01-19-33	R	R	6'1	187	15	11	.577	0	52	34	19	297	290	102	87	2	3.42
Marquard, Rube-Richard William	08-15NYN 15-20BknN 21CinN 22-25BosN	10-09-86	Cleveland, Ohio	06-01-80	B	L	6'3	180	201	177	.532	19	536	406	197	3307	3233	858	1593	30	3.08
Marshall, Rube-Roy DeVerne	12-14PhiN 15BufF	06-11-80	Salineville, Ohio	07-19-90	R	R	5'11	170	8	10	.444	2	64	23	9	241	272	106	90	0	4.18
Martin, Doc-Harold Winthrop	08,11-12PhiA	03-23-87	Roxbury, Mass.	04-15-35	R	R	5'11	165	1	3	.250	0	14	4	1	44	47	25	27	0	5.52
Mason, Del-Adelbert William	04WasA 06-07CinN	10-29-83	Newfane, N.Y.	12-31-62	R	R	6'	160	5	16	.238	2	32	21	16	191	199	74	65	1	3.72
Mathewson, Christy-Christopher (Big Six)	00-16NYN 16,M16-18CinN	08-12-80	Factoryville, Pa.	10-07-25	R	R	6'2	195	374	188	.665	28	635	551	434	4780	4218	844	2502	79	2.13
Mathewson, Henry-Henry	06-07NYN	12-24-86	Factoryville, Pa.	07-01-17	R	R	6'3	175	0	1	.000	0	3	1	1	11	8	14	2	0	4.91
Mattern, Al-Alonzo Albert	08-12BosN	06-16-83	West Rush, N.Y.	11-06-58	L	L	5'10	165	36	59	.379	4	138	94	53	843	878	299	254	9	3.37
Matteson, Eddie-Henry Edson	14PhiN	09-07-84	Guys Mills, Pa.	09-01-43	R	R	5'10	160	3	5	.615	0	29	4	4	126	115	38	45	0	2.36
Matthews, Bill-William Calvin	09BosN	01-12-78	Mahanoy City, Pa.	01-23-46	R				1	0	1.000	0	3	1	0	17	16	10	6	0	3.18
Maul, Al-Albert Joseph (Smiling Al) (See B01-19)	84PhiU 87PhiN 88-89PhiN 90PitP 91PitN 93-97WasN 97-98BalN 99BknN 00PhiN 01NYN	10-09-65	Philadelphia, Pa.	05-03-58	R	R	6'	175	85	78	.521	1	187	167	143	1433	1659	518	346	4	4.42
Maxwell, Bert-James Albert	06PitN 08PhiA 11NYN 14BknF	10-17-86	Texarkana, Ark.	12-10-61	B	R	6'	180	4	7	.364	1	21	12	9	123	144	42	35	1	4.17
Mayer (Erskine), Erskine (Jacob)-Erskine Jacob	12-18PhiN 19ChiN 18-19PitN 19ChiA	01-16-90	Atlanta, Ga.	03-10-57	R	R	5'11	168	91	70	.565	4	245	164	93	1427	1415	345	482	12	2.96
McAdams, Jack-George Decalve	11StLN	05-21-37	Bryant, Ark.	05-21-37	R	R	6'1		0	0	—	0	6	0	0	10	7	5	4	0	3.60
McAleese, John-John James (See B01-19)	01ChiA	08-22-77	Sharon, Pa.	11-15-50	R	R	5'8		0	0	—	0	1	0	0	3	7	1	1	0	9.00
McAllister, Jack (See Andy Coakley)																				
McAllister, Sport-Lewis William (See B01-19)	96-99CleN	07-23-74	Austin, Miss.	07-17-62	B	R	5'11	180	1	7	.364	0	17	11	10	113	140	44	21	0	5.34
McArthur, Dixie-Oland Alexander	14PitN	02-01-92	Vernon, Ala.	05-31-86	R	R	6'	185	0	0	—	0	1	0	0	1	1	1	0	0	9.00
McCabe, Dick-Richard James	18BosA 22ChiA	02-21-96	Mamaroneck, N.Y.	04-11-50	R	R	5'10	159	1	1	.500	0	6	1	0	13	17	2	4	0	3.46
McCabe, Tim-Timothy J.	15-18StLA	05-18-94	Graniteville, Mo.	04-12-77	R	R	5'10	165	5	1	.833	2	22	4	4	71	60	21	26	1	3.55
McCann, Gene-Henry Eugene (Mike)	01-02BknN	06-13-76	Baltimore, Md.	04-26-43	R	R	5'10	185	3	5	.375	0	9	7	5	64	66	28	18	0	3.60
McCarthy, Arch-Archibald Joseph	02DetA		Ypsilanti, Mich.	Deceased	R	R	6'	160	1	7	.125	1	10	8	6	72	90	31	10	0	6.13
McCarthy, Bill-William Thomas	06BosN	04-11-82	Ashland, Mass.	05-29-39	R	R	6'1	170	0	0	—	0	1	0	0	2	5	0	0	0	9.00
McCarthy, Tom-Thomas Patrick	08CinN 08PitN 08-09BosN	05-22-84	Fort Wayne, Ind.	03-28-33		R	5'7	170	6	9	.400	2	25	20	10	150	133	65	42	2	2.34
McClosky, Jim-James John	06-07PhiN	08-20-82	Wyoming, Pa.	06-05-19		R	5'9	175	3	2	.600	0	12	4	3	50	61	15	9	0	3.60
McCluskey, Harry-Harry Robert (Lefty)	15CinN	03-29-92	Clay Center, Ohio		L	L	5'11	173	0	0	—	0	4	0	0	7	9	5	1	0	5.40
McConnaughey, Ralph-Ralph Jennison	14IndF	08-05-89	Homer City, Pa.	06-04-66	R	R	5'8	166	0	2	.000	0	7	2	1	26	23	16	7	0	4.85
McConnell, George-George Neely	09,12-13NYA 14ChiN 15ChiF 16ChiN	09-16-77	Shelbyville, Tenn.	05-10-64	R	R	6'3	190	42	51	.452	3	133	98	59	842	739	242	403	5	2.60
McCorry, Bill-William Charles	09StLA	09-07-87	Saranac Lake, N.Y.	03-22-73	L	R	5'9	157	0	2	.000	0	5	1	1	15	29	6	10	0	9.00

USE NAMES - GIVEN NAMES (NICKNAMES)	TEAM BY YEAR	BIRTH DATE	BIRTHPLACE	DEATH DATE	B	T	HGT	WGT	W	L	Pct.	SV	G	GS	CG	IP	H	BB	SO	ShO	ERA
McCreery, Ed-Esley Porterfield (Big Ed)	14DetA	12-24-89	Floence, Colo.	10-19-60	R	R	6'1	190	1	0	1.000	0	3	1	0	4	6	3	4	0	11.25
McDonald (McDonnell), John-John Joseph	07WasA	01-27-83	Throop, Pa.	04-09-50	R	R	6'1	170	0	0	—	0	6	12	2	3	0	9.00
McDougal, Sandy-John Auchanbolt	95BknN 05StLN	05-21-74	Buffalo, N.Y.	10-02-10	R	R	5'10	155	1	4	.200	0	6	5	5	48	55	17	12	0	3.94
McFadden, Barney-Bernard Joseph	01CinN 02PhiN	03-20-77	Eckley, Pa.	04-28-24	R	R	6'1	195	3	5	.375	0	9	6	5	55	68	47	14	0	6.38
McFarland, Chappie-Charles Amos	02-06StLN 06PitN 06BknN	03-13-75	White Hall, Ill.	12-14-24	R		6'1		35	59	.372	2	106	96	81	841	893	192	307	6	3.35
McFetridge, Jack-John Reed	90,03PhiN	08-25-69	Philadelphia, Pa.	01-10-17			6'	175	2	11	.154	0	15	14	12	112	125	51	35	0	4.58
McGeehan, Conny-Cornelius Bernard	03PhiA	08-25-82	Drifton, Pa.	07-04-07	R				1	0	1.000	0	3	0	0	10	9	1	4	0	4.50
McGehee, Pat-Patrick Henry	12DetA	07-02-88	Meadville, Miss.	12-30-46	R		6'2	180	0	0	—	0	1	1	0	0	1	1	0	0	0.00
McGill, Billy-William Jacob (Parson)	07StLA	06-29-80	Galva, Kans.	08-07-59	R	R	6'2	185	1	0	1.000	0	2	2	1	18	22	2	8	0	3.50
McGinley, Jim-James William	04-05StLN	10-02-78	Groveland, Mass.	09-20-61	R	R	5'9	165	2	2	.500	0	4	4	3	30	33	8	6	0	3.30
McGinnity (McGinty), Joe-Joseph Jerome (Iron Man)	99BalN 00BknN 01-02BalA 02-08NYN	03-20-71	Cornwall, Ill.	11-14-29	R	R	5'11	206	247	147	.635	25	465	381	314	3441	3276	812	1068	32	2.65
McGlynn, Stony-Ulysses Simpson Grant	06-08StLN	05-26-72	Lancaster, Pa.	08-26-41	R	R	5'11	185	17	33	.340	2	67	51	43	476	448	144	157	3	2.95
McGraner, Howard-Howard (Muck)	12CinN	09-11-89	Luhrig, Ohio	10-22-52	L	L	5'7	155	1	0	1.000	0	4	0	0	19	22	7	5	0	7.11
McGraw, Jim-John Roy Elmer	14BknF	12-08-90	Intercourse, Pa.	04-27-67	R	R	5'9	160	0	0	—	0	1	0	0	2	0	0	2	0	0.00
McGuire, Tom-Thomas Patrick (Elmer)	14ChiF 18MS 19ChiA	01-21-92	Chicago, Ill.	12-07-59	R	R	6'	175	5	6	.455	0	25	12	7	134	148	60	37	0	3.83
McHale, Marty-Martin Joseph	10-11BosA 13-15NYA 16BosA 16CleA	10-30-86	Stoneham, Mass.	05-07-79	R	R	5'11	174	12	30	.286	2	64	44	23	358	381	81	131	1	3.57
McIlveen, Irish-Henry Cooke (See B01-19)	06PitN	07-27-80	Belfast, N. Ireland	10-18-60	L	L	5'11	180	0	1	.000	0	2	1	0	7	10	2	3	0	7.71
McIntire, Harry-John Reid (Rocks)	05-09BknN 10-12ChiN 13CinN	01-11-78	Detroit, Mich.	01-09-49	R	R	5'11	180	71	117	.378	7	237	188	140	1651	1555	539	626	17	3.22
McJames (James), Doc-James McCutchen	95-97WasN 98BalN 99,01BknN	08-27-74	Williamsburg Co., S.C.	09-23-01		R			76	77	.497	4	178	162	137	1361	1414	563	593	6	3.43
McKay, Rip-Reeve Stewart	15StLA	11-16-81	Morgan, Tex.	01-18-46	R	R	6'1	168	0	0	—	0	1	0	0	1	1	0	0	0	9.00
McKenry, Limb-Frank Gordon (Big Pete)	15-16CinN	08-13-88	Piney Flats, Tenn.	11-01-56	R	R	6'4	205	6	6	.500	0	27	12	5	125	108	47	39	0	3.10
McLaughlin, Warry-Warren A.	00PhiN 02PitN 03PhiN	01-27-77	N. Plainfield, N.J.	10-22-23		L			3	2	.600	0	7	5	5	55	69	26	17	0	4.75
McMackin, John-John Weaver (Spartanburg John)	02BknN	03-06-78	Spartanburg, S.C.	09-25-56	R	L	5'11	165	2	2	.500	0	4	4	3	32	34	11	6	0	3.09
McMackin, Sam-Samuel	02ChiA 02DetA	11-??-72	Cleveland, Ohio	02-11-03	R	L			0	0	—	0	2	1	1	11	10	4	4	0	2.45
McMahon, Doc-Henry John	08BosA	12-19-86	Woburn, Mass.	12-11-29	R				1	0	1.000	0	1	1	1	9	14	0	3	0	3.00
McManus, Joe-Joab Logan	13CinN	09-07-87	Palmyra, Ill.	12-23-55	R	R	6'1	185	0	0	—	0	1	0	0	2	3	4	1	0	18.00
McNeal, Harry-John Harley	01CleA	08-11-77	Iberia, Ohio	01-11-45	R	R	6'3	175	5	6	.455	0	12	10	9	85	120	30	15	0	4.45
McNichol, Ed-Edwin Briggs	04BosN	01-10-79	Martins Ferry, Ohio	11-01-52	R	R	5'5	170	2	13	.133	0	17	15	12	122	120	0.74	39	1	4.28
McPherson, John-John Jacob	01PhiA 04PhiN	03-09-69	Easton, Pa.	09-30-41	R				1	11	.083	0	16	13	11	132	137	50	32	1	3.89
McQuillan, George-George Watt	07-10PhiN 11CinN 13-15PhiN 15-16PhiN 18CleA	05-01-85	Brooklyn, N.Y.	03-30-40	R	R	5'11	175	85	89	.489	14	273	173	105	1577	1382	401	590	17	2.38
McTigue, Bill-William Patrick (Pud, Lefty)	11-13BosN 16DetA	06-03-91	Nashville, Tenn.	05-08-20	L	L	6'1	170	2	6	.250	0	27	9	1	77	81	72	41	0	6.19
Meehan, Bill-William Thomas	15PhiA	09-04-89	Osceola, Pa.	10-08-82	R	R	5'9	155	0	1	.000	0	1	1	0	4	7	3	4	0	11.25
Melter, Steve-Stephen Blasius	09StLN	01-02-86	Cherokee, Iowa	01-28-62	R	R	6'2	180	0	1	.000	0	3	1	0	64	79	20	24	0	3.52
Menefee, Jocko-John	92PitN 93-94LouN 94-95PitN 98NYN 00-03ChiN (See B01-19)	01-15-68	Rowlesburg, W. Va.	03-11-53	R	R	6'	165	56	69	.448	0	139	125	111	1110	1290	273	293	7	3.82
Mercer, Jack-Harry Vernon	10PitN	03-10-89	Zanesville, Ohio	06-25-45					0	0	—	0	1	0	0	1	0	2	1	0	0.00
Mercer, Win-George Barclay (See B01-19)	94-99WasN 00NYN 01WasA 02DetA	06-20-74	Chester, W.Va.	01-12-03	R	R	5'7	140	135	164	.452	9	330	298	252	2466	3057	752	525	11	3.98
Merritt, George-George Washington (See B01-19)	01-03PhiN	04-14-80	Paterson, N.J.	02-21-38	R	R	6'		3	0	1.000	0	4	3	3	28	32	6	5	0	4.50
Miller, Frank-Frank Lee (Bullet)	13ChiA 16-19PitN 22-23BosN	03-13-86	Salem, Mich.	02-19-74	R	R	6'	188	52	66	.441	4	163	127	68	1010	944	254	359	14	3.01
Miller, Fred-Frederick Holman (Speedy)	10BknN	02-02-88	Fairfield, Ind.	05-02-53	L	L	6'2	190	1	1	.500	0	6	2	0	21	25	13	2	0	4.71
Miller, Roscoe-Roscoe Clyde (Roxy, Rubberlegs)	01-02DetA 02-03NYN 04PitN	12-02-76	Croydon, Ind.	04-18-13	R	R	6'2	190	39	45	.464	5	102	88	74	772	808	229	198	6	3.45
Miller, Walt-Walter W.	11BknN	10-19-83	Spiceland, Ind.	03-01-56	R	R	5'11	180	0	1	.000	0	3	2	0	11	16	6	0	0	6.55
Milligan, Billy-William Joseph	01PhiA 04NYN	08-19-78	Buffalo, N.Y.	10-14-28	R	L	5'7		0	4	.000	2	11	4	3	58	79	18	11	0	4.81
Mills, Willie-William Grant (Wee Willie)	01NYN	08-15-77	Schenevus, N.Y.	07-05-14	R	R	5'7	150	2	2	.500	0	2	2	2	16	21	4	3	0	8.44
Milton, Larry-Samuel Lawrence (Tug)	03StLN	05-04-78	Owensboro, Ky.	05-15-42	R	R	6'		0	1	.000	0	4	3	1	0	3	1	0	0	2.25
Minahan, Cotton-Edmund Joseph	07CinN	12-10-82	Springfield, Ohio	05-20-58	R	R		190	0	0	—	0	2	2	1	14	12	13	4	0	1.29
Mitchell (Yapp), Fred-Frederick Francis (See B01-19)	01-02BosA 02PhiA 03-04PhiN 04-05BknN M17-20ChiN M21-23BosN	06-05-78	Cambridge, Mass.	10-13-70	R	R	5'9	185	31	52	.373	1	97	86	71	719	806	303	216	2	4.09
Mitchell, Roy-Albert Roy	10-14StLA 18CinA 18-19CinN	04-19-85	Belton, Tex.	09-08-59	R	R	5'9	170	32	37	.464	5	122	67	47	675	734	177	204	7	3.43
Mitchell, Willie-William	09-16CleA 16-19DetA	12-01-89	Pleasant Grove, Miss.	11-23-73	R	L	6'	176	84	92	.477	3	275	190	94	1632	1464	605	921	16	2.86
Molyneaux, Vince-Vincent Leo	17StLN 18BosA	08-17-88	Lewiston, N.Y.	05-04-50	R	R	6'	180	1	0	1.000	0	13	0	0	33	21	28	5	0	4.36
Monroe, Ed-Edward Oliver (Peck)	17-18NYA	02-22-93	Louisville, Ky.	04-29-69	R	R	6'5	187	1	0	1.000	0	10	1	1	31	36	8	13	0	3.48
Moore, Earl-Earl Alonzo (Crossfire, Big Ebbie)	01-07CleA 07NYA 08-13PhiN 13ChiN 14BufF	07-29-79	Pickerington, Ohio	11-28-61	R	R	6'	190	164	153	.517	7	387	324	230	2767	2467	1102	1397	34	2.78
Moore, Frank-Frank Jonah	05PitN	09-11-77	Dover, Ohio	05-20-64	B	R	6'4	200	0	1	.000	0	1	0	0	3	2	0	1	0	0.00
Moore, Gene-Eugene Sr. (Blue Goose)	09-10PitN 12CinN	11-09-85	Lancaster, Tex.	08-31-38	L	L	6'2	185	2	2	.500	0	10	3	0	34	40	21	17	0	4.76
Moran, Charley-Charles Barthell (Uncle Charley)	03StLN	02-22-78	Nashville, Tenn.	06-14-49	R	R	5'5	180	0	1	.000	0	3	2	2	24	30	19	7	0	5.25
Moran, Harry-Harry Edwin (Lefty)	12DetA 15BufF 15NwkF	04-02-89	Slater, W.Va.	11-28-62	L	L	6'1	165	23	17	.575	4	73	41	21	375	371	131	163	4	3.34
More, Forrest-Forrest Theodore	09StLN 09BosN	01-29-83	Hayden, Ind	09-30-81	R	R	6'	180	2	10	.167	0	25	6	4	99	95	40	27	0	4.73
Moren, Lew-Lewis Howard (Hicks)	03-04PitN 07-10PhiN 11AJ	08-20-81	Pittsburgh, Pa.	11-02-66	R	R	5'11	150	48	57	.457	3	141	105	62	882	797	331	356	10	2.95
Morey, Dave-David Beale	13PhiA	02-25-89	Malden, Mass.	01-04-86	L	R	6'	185	0	0	—	0	4	2	1	4	2	2	4	0	4.50
Morgan, Cy-Harry Richard	03-05,07StLA 07-09BosA 09-12PhiA 13CinN	11-10-78	Pomeroy, Ohio	06-28-62	R	R	6'	175	77	79	.494	5	210	172	107	1445	1180	578	667	15	2.51
Moroney, Jim-James Francis	06BosN 10PhiN 12CinN	12-04-83	Boston, Mass.	02-26-29	L	L	6'1		2	6	.250	3	25	8	5	93	96	40	29	0	3.68
Morrissey, Deacon-Michael Joseph (Frank)	01BosA 02ChiN	05-03-76	Baltimore, Md.	02-22-39		R	5'4	140	1	3	.250	0	6	5	5	44	45	10	14	0	2.25
Morton, Guy-Guy Sr. (The Alabama Blossom)	14-24CleA	06-01-93	Vernon, Ala.	10-18-34	R	R	6'2	175	97	86	.530	6	316	184	80	1629	1520	583	830	19	3.13
Moseley, Earl-Earl Victor (Vic)	13BosA 14IndF 15NwkF 16CinN	09-07-87	Middleburg, Ohio	07-01-63	R	R	5'9	168	50	48	.510	3	136	100	65	856	775	340	469	12	3.01
Moser, Walter-Walter Frederick	06PhiN 11BosA 11StLA	02-27-81	Concord, N. C.	12-10-46	R	R	5'9		0	7	.000	0	14	9	5	71	97	30	30	0	4.56
Moyer, Ed-Charles Edward	10WasA	08-15-85	Andover, Ohio	11-18-62		R			0	3	.000	0	6	3	2	25	22	13	3	0	3.24
Mullin, George-George Joseph (Wabash George) (See B01-19)	02-13DetA 13WasA 14IndF 15NwkF	07-04-80	Toledo, Ohio	01-07-44	R	R	5'11	188	229	192	.544	11	488	428	353	3687	3518	1238	1482	34	2.82
Murphy, Ed-Edward James	98PhiN 01-03StLN	01-12-77	Auburn, N.Y.	01-29-35		R	6'1	185	25	26	.490	1	68	53	39	465	537	111	103	1	3.64
Murray, Pat-Patrick Joseph	19PhiN	07-18-97	Scottsville, N.Y.	11-05-83	R	L	6'	175	0	2	.000	0	3	2	1	34	50	12	11	0	6.35
Musser, Paul-Paul	12WasA 18MS 19BosA	06-24-89	Millheim, Pa.	07-07-73	R	R	6'	175	1	2	.333	1	12	6	1	41	42	24	24	0	3.29
Myers, Elmer-Elmer Glenn	15-18PhiA 19-20CleA 20-22BosA	03-02-94	York Springs, Pa.	07-29-76	R	R	6'2	185	55	72	.433	4	185	127	78	1102	1148	440	428	8	4.06
Myers, Joe-Joseph William	05PhiA	03-18-82	Wilmington, Del.	02-11-56	R	R	5'11	205	0	0	—	0	1	1	1	5	3	5	1	0	3.60
Nabors, Jack-Herman John	15-17PhiA	11-19-87	Montevallo, Ala.	10-29-23	R	R	6'3	185	1	25	.038	1	52	37	13	270	266	131	94	0	3.87
Nagle, Judge-Walter Harold (Lucky)	11PitN 11PhiA	03-10-80	Santa Rosa, Cal.	05-26-71	R	R	6'	176	5	3	.625	1	9	8	5	54	60	12	23	0	3.50
Neher, Jim-James Gilmore	12CleA	02-05-89	Rochester, N.Y.	11-11-51	R	R	5'11	185	0	0	—	0	1	0	0	1	0	0	0	0	—
Nelson, Andy-Andrew Anthony	08ChiA	13-30-84	St. Paul, Minn.	Deceased	L		6'2		1	0	1.000	0	1	1	0	6	4	4	1	0	2.00
Nelson, Luke-Luther Martin	19NYA	12-04-93	Cable, Ill.	11-14-85	R	R	6'	180	1	0	1.000	0	3	1	0	24	22	11	11	0	3.00
Nelson (Horazdovsky), Red-Albert Francis	10-12StLA 12-13PhiN 13CinN	05-19-86	Cleveland, Ohio	10-26-56	R	R	5'11	190	10	13	.435	2	39	24	13	188	221	85	68	0	4.55
Neuer, Tex-John S.	07NYA	06-08-77	Hazelton, Pa.	01-14-66		L			4	2	.667	0	7	6	6	54	40	19	22	3	2.17
Newton, Doc-Eustace James	00-01CinN 01-02BknN 05-09NYA	10-26-77	Mt. Carmel, Ind.	05-14-31	L	L	6'	185	53	72	.424	3	177	139	99	1200	1179	416	502	8	3.23
Nichols, Kid-Charles Augustus	90-01BosN 04-05,M04-05StLN 05-06PhiN	09-14-69	Madison, Wis.	04-11-53	B	R	5'10	175	361	208	.634	16	620	561	531	5062	4917	1268	1869	48	2.95
Nicholson, Frank-Frank Collins	12PhiN	08-29-89	Berlin, Pa.	11-10-72	R	R	6'2	175	0	0	—	0	4	0	0	8	8	2	1	0	6.75
Niehaus, Dick-Richard J.	13-15StLN 20CleA	10-24-92	Covington, Ky.	03-12-57	L	L	5'11	165	4	5	.444	0	45	9	3	126	128	59	43	0	3.79
Nops, Jerry-Jeremiah Henry	96PhiN 96-99BalN 00BknN 01BalA	06-23-75	Toledo, Ohio	03-26-37	L	L	5'8	168	72	44	.621	4	136	122	99	989	1083	281	294	7	3.69
Northrop, Jake-George Howard	18-19BosN	03-05-88	Monroeton, Pa.	11-06-45	R	R	5'11	170	6	6	.500	0	18	7	6	77	69	13	13	1	2.92
Nourse, Chet-Chester Linwood	09BosA	08-07-87	Ipswich, Mass.	04-20-58	R	R	6'3		0	0	—	0	1	1	0	5	5	3	0	0	7.20
Noyes, Win-Winfield Charles	13BosN 17PhiA 18MS 19PhiA 19ChiA	06-16-89	Pleasanton, Neb.	04-08-69	R	R	6'	180	11	15	.423	1	49	29	14	247	254	98	93	1	3.75
Oberlin, Frank-Frank Rufus (Flossie)	06-07BosA 07,09-10WasA	03-29-76	Elsie, Mich.	01-06-52	R	R	6'	165	6	24	.200	4	44	26	16	227	236	88	80	0	3.77
O'Brien, Buck-Thomas Joseph	11-13BosA 13ChiA	05-10-82	Brockton, Mass.	07-25-59	R	R	5'10	185	28	26	.519	4	64	54	37	433	391	159	204	4	2.62
O'Connor, Andy-Andrew James	08NYA	09-14-84	Roxbury, Mass.	09-26-80	R	R	6'	160	0	1	.000	0	1	1	0	8	15	7	1	0	4.50
Ohl (von Ohl), Joe-Joseph Earl	09WasA	09-07-77	Jobstown, N.J.	12-18-51	R	R	6'1	170	0	0	—	0	1	0	0	2	4	2	0	0	2.00
Olmstead, Fred-Frederic William (Omy)	08-11ChiA	07-03-83	Sac Bay, Mich.	10-22-36	R	R	6'	180	19	20	.487	6	69	37	26	359	378	93	135	5	2.73
Olmsted, Hank-Henry Theodore	05BosA	01-12-79	Saginaw Bay, Mich.	01-06-69	R	R	5'8	147	1	2	.333	0	3	3	2	25	18	12	6	0	3.24
O'Neill, Mike-Michael Joyce (Played as Mike Joyce 01) (See B01-19)	01-04StLN	09-07-77	Galaway, Ireland	08-12-59	L	L	5'11	185	32	44	.421	1	85	77	68	664	739	169	228	4	2.86

USE NAMES - GIVEN NAMES (NICKNAMES)	TEAM BY YEAR	BIRTH DATE	BIRTHPLACE	DEATH DATE	B	T	HGT	WGT	W	L	Pct.	SV	G	GS	CG	IP	H	BB	SO	ShO	ERA
Orth, Al-Albert Lewis (The Curveless Wonder) (See B01-19)	95-01PhiN 02-04WasA 04-09NYA	09-05-72	Tipton, Ind.	10-08-48	L	R	6'	200	203	183	.526	8	440	394	324	3355	3564	661	948	29	3.37
Ostendorf, Fred-Frederick K.	14IndF	08-05-92	Baltimore, Md.	03-02-65	L	L	6'	169	0	0	—	0	1	0	0	2	5	2	0	0	22.50
Otey, Bill-William Tilford (Steamboat Bill)	07PittN 10-11WasA	12-16-86	Dayton, Ohio	04-23-31	L	L	6'2	181	1	6	.143	0	24	5	2	101	131	25	33	0	4.99
Otis, Harry-Harry George (Cannonball)	09CleA	10-05-86	W. New York, N.J.	01-29-76	R	L	6'	180	2	2	.500	0	5	3	0	26	26	18	6	0	1.38
O'Toole, Marty-Martin James	08CinN 11-14PitN 14NYN	11-27-87	Framingham, Mass.	02-18-49	R	R	5'11	175	27	36	.429	2	99	84	56	599	554	300	296	6	3.29
Overall, Orvie-Orval	05-06CinN 06-10ChiN 11-12VR 13ChiN	02-02-81	Farmersville, Cal.	07-14-47	B	R	6'2	214	106	72	.596	12	218	182	133	1535	1232	551	935	30	2.23
Ovitz, Ernie-Ernest Gayhart	11ChiN	10-07-85	Mineral Point, Wis.	09-11-80	R	R	5'8	156	0	0	—	0	1	0	0	2	3	3	0	0	4.50
Owen, Frank-Frank Malcolm (Yip)	01DetA 03-09ChiA	12-23-79	Ypsilanti, Mich.	11-24-42	R	R	5'11	180	83	69	.546	4	194	155	119	1368	1249	298	443	16	2.55
Packard, Gene-Eugene Milo	12-13CinN 14-15KCF 16-17ChiN 17-18StLN	07-13-87	Colorado Spr., Colo.	05-19-59	L	L	5'10	155	85	69	.552	17	248	153	86	1410	1393	356	488	15	3.01
Paige, Pat-George Lynn (Piggy)	11CleA	05-05-83	Paw Paw, Mich.	06-08-39	L	R	5'11	175	0	0	1.000	0	2	1	1	16	21	7	6	0	4.50
Pape, Larry-Laurence Albert	09,11-12BosA	07-21-83	Norwood, Ohio	07-21-18	R	R	5'11	175	14	9	.609	5	51	24	13	283	287	91	84	2	2.80
Park, Jim-James	15-17StLA	11-10-92	Richmond, Ky.	12-17-70	R	R	6'2	175	4	5	.444	0	42	9	2	122	114	46	40	0	3.02
Parker, Doc-Harley Park	93,95-96ChiN 01CinN	06-14-72	Theresa, N.Y.	03-03-41	R	R	6'2	200	5	9	.357	1	18	14	13	134	196	39	24	1	5.91
Parker, Roy-Roy William (Spots)	19StLN	02-29-96	Union, Mo.	05-17-54	R	R	6'3	200	0	0	—	0	2	0	0	2	6	1	0	0	31.50
Parnham, Rube-James Arthur	16-17PhiA	02-01-94	Heidelberg, Pa.	11-25-63	R	R	6'3	185	2	2	.500	0	6	5	2	36	39	22	12	0	1.50
Parson, Jiggs-William Edwin	10-11BosN	12-27-85	Parker, S.D.	05-19-67	R	R	6'2	180	3	9	.250	0	17	4	0	60	71	41	14	0	4.95
Pastorius, Jim-James Washington	06-09BknN	07-12-81	Pittsburgh, Pa.	05-10-41	L	L	5'9	165	31	55	.360	1	97	84	57	728	705	278	205	10	3.11
Patten, Casey-Case Lyman (Pat)	01-08WasA 08BosA	05-07-74	Westport, N.Y.	05-31-35	B	L	6'	175	107	126	.459	4	270	239	206	2063	2154	557	757	17	3.36
Patterson, Roy-Roy Lewis (The Boy Wonder)	01-07ChiA	12-17-76	Stoddard, Wis.	04-14-53	R	R	6'	185	81	70	.536	3	184	152	119	1365	1327	273	442	17	2.75
Patton, Harry-Harry Claude	10StLN	06-29-84	Gillespie, Ill.	06-09-30					0	0	—	0	1	0	0	4	4	2	2	0	2.25
Pearson, Aleck-Alexander Franklin	02StLN 03CleA	03-09-77	Greensboro, Pa.	10-30-66	R	R	5'10	160	3	8	.273	0	15	13	10	112	124	25	36	0	3.86
Peasley, Marv-Marvin Warren	10DetA	07-16-89	Jonesport, Me.	12-27-48	L	L	6'1	175	0	0	1.000	0	2	1	0	10	13	11	4	0	8.10
Pelty(Peltheimer), Barney-Barney (The Yiddish Curver)	03-12StLA 12WasA	09-10-80	Farmington, Mo.	05-24-39	R	R	5'9	175	91	118	.435	6	266	217	173	1918	1663	532	693	22	2.62
Pennington, Kewpie-George Louis	17StLA	09-24-96	New York, N.Y.	05-03-53	R	R	5'8	170	0	0	—	0	1	0	0	1	1	0	0	0	0.00
Pepper, Bob-Robert Ernest	15PhiA	05-03-95	Rooston, Pa.	04-08-68	R	R	6'2	178	0	0	—	0	1	0	0	5	6	2	1	0	1.80
Perdue, Hub-Herbert Rodney (The Gallatin Squash)	11-14BosN 14-15StLN	06-07-82	Bethpage, Tenn.	10-31-68	R	R	5'10	192	51	64	.443	7	161	122	64	917	1037	199	317	5	3.86
Pernoll, Hub-Henry Huston	10,12DetA	03-14-88	Applegate, Ore.	02-18-44	R	L	5'8	175	4	3	.571	0	14	5	4	64	63	18	28	0	3.38
Perritt, Pol-William Dayton	12-14StLN 15-21NYN 21DetA	08-30-91	Arcadia, La.	10-15-47	R	R	6'	175	92	78	.541	8	256	177	93	1470	1416	390	543	23	2.89
Perry, Scott-Herbert Scott	15StLA 16ChiN 17BosN 17CinN 18-21PhiA	04-17-91	Dennison, Tex.	10-27-59	L	R	6'1	190	41	68	.376	4	132	104	69	893	927	284	231	5	3.07
Perryman, Parson-Emmett Key	15StLA	10-24-88	Everette Sprs., Ga.	09-12-66	R	R	6'4	195	2	3	.400	2	24	3	0	50	52	16	19	0	3.96
Peters, Rube-Oscar Casper	12ChiA 14BknF	03-15-85	Grantfork, Ill.	02-07-65	R	R	6'1	195	7	8	.467	0	39	14	5	147	186	49	52	0	4.04
Pfeffer, Big Jeff-Francis Xavier	05ChiN 06-08BosN 10ChiN 11BosN	03-31-82	Champaign, Ill.	12-19-54	R	R	6'1	185	31	40	.437	2	112	70	59	695	660	292	317	6	3.30
Pfeffer, Jeff-Edward Joseph	11StLA 13-21BknN 21-24StLN 24PitN	03-04-88	Seymour, Ill.	08-15-72	R	R	6'3	210	158	112	.585	10	347	279	194	2407	2320	592	836	28	2.77
Pfiester (Hagenbush), Jack-John Albert (Jack the Giant Killer)	03-04PitN 06-11ChiN	05-24-78	Cincinnati, Ohio	09-03-53	R	L	6'	170	72	44	.621	10	149	128	75	1059	869	293	503	17	2.04
Phillippe, Deacon-Charles Louis	99LouN 00-13PitN	05-23-72	Rural Retreat, Va.	03-30-52	L	R	6'1	180	189	109	.634	12	372	289	242	2608	2518	363	929	27	2.58
Phillips, Bill-William Corcoran (Whoa Bill, Silver Bill)	90PitN 95,99-03CinN 14IndF M15NwkF	11-09-68	Allenport, Pa.	10-25-41	R	R	5'11	180	69	74	.483	3	176	152	120	1295	1477	363	374	6	4.09
Phyle, Bill-William Joseph (See B01-19)	98-99CinN 01NYN		Duluth, Minn.	08-07-53	L	R			11	19	.367	2	37	31	28	276	324	89	76	2	3.95
Piatt, Wiley-Wiley Harlan (Iron Man)	98-00PhiN 01PhiA 01-02ChiA 03BosN	07-13-74	Blue Creek, Ohio	09-20-46	L	L	5'10	175	85	80	.515	2	182	170	139	1391	1481	455	517	12	3.60
Pickett, Charlie-Charles Albert	10StLN	03-01-83	Delaware, Ohio	05-20-69	R	R	6'1	175	0	0	—	0	2	0	0	7	2	2	2	0	1.50
Pieh, Cy-Edwin John	13-15NYA	09-29-86	Waunakee, Wis.	09-12-45	R	R	6'2	190	9	9	.500	1	43	12	4	166	156	75	76	2	3.89
Pierce, George-George Thomas	12-16ChiN 17StLN	01-10-88	Shabbona, Ill.	10-11-35	L	L	5'10	175	35	27	.565	1	103	60	26	509	445	217	260	5	3.11
Pierson, Bill-William Morris (Wild Bill)	18-19,24PhiA	06-14-99	Atlantic City, N.J.	02-20-59	R	R	6'2	180	0	1	.000	1	11	2	0	33	32	31	10	0	3.27
Pillion, Squiz-Cecil Randolph	15PhiA	04-13-94	Hartford, Conn.	09-30-62	L	L	6'	178	0	0	—	0	5	0	0	5	10	2	0	0	7.20
Pinnance, Ed-Elijah Edward (Peanuts)	03PhiA	10-22-79	Walpole I., Canada	12-12-44	R	R	6'1	180	0	0	—	0	2	1	0	7	5	2	2	0	2.57
Pittinger, Togie-Charles Reno (Horse Race, King)	00-04BosN 05-07PhiN	01-12-72	Greencastle, Pa.	01-14-09	L	R	6'2	175	114	113	.502	3	262	227	187	2040	2017	734	832	20	3.10
Plank, Eddie-Edward Stewart (Gettysburg Eddie)	01-14PhiA 15StLF 16-17StLA	08-31-75	Gettysburg, Pa.	02-24-26	L	L	5'11	175	325	193	.627	25	622	529	410	4506	3956	1072	2246	69	2.34
Polchow, Lou-Louis William	02CleA	03-14-81	Mankato, Minn.	08-15-12			5'9		0	1	.000	0	1	1	1	8	9	4	2	0	5.63
Poole, Ed-Edward Isaih (Pee Wee)	00-02PitN 02-03CinN 04BknN	09-07-74	Canton, Ohio	03-11-19	R	R	6'	175	33	35	.485	1	80	70	61	595	584	238	226	5	3.04
Popp, Bill-William Peter	02StLN	06-07-77	St. Louis, Mo.	09-07-09	R	R	5'10	170	0	6	.000	0	9	7	5	60	87	26	20	0	4.95
Porray, Eddie-Edmund Joseph	14BufF	12-05-88	on ship-Atlantic O.	07-13-54	R	R	5'11	170	0	1	.000	0	2	0	0	10	18	7	0	0	4.50
Porter, Odie-Odie Oscar	02PhiA	07-24-77	Borden, Ind.	05-02-03	L				0	1	.000	0	1	1	1	8	12	5	2	0	3.38
Pounds, Bill-Jeared Wells	03CleA 03BknN	03-11-78	Paterson, N.J.	07-07-36	R	R	5'11	178	0	0	—	0	2	0	0	11	16	2	4	0	8.18
Powell, Bill-William Burris	09-10PitN 12ChiN 13CinN	05-08-85	Taylor Co., W.Va.	09-28-67	R	R	6'2	182	4	8	.333	0	17	11	4	84	76	43	25	2	2.97
Powell, Jack-John Joseph (Red)	97-98CleN 99-01StLN 02-03StLA 04-05NYA 05-12StLA	07-09-74	Bloomington, Ill.	10-17-44	R	R	5'11	195	248	255	.493	14	577	516	424	4389	4319	1021	1621	46	2.97
Powell, Jack-Jack-Reginald Bertrand	13StLA	08-17-91	Holcomb, Mo.	03-11-30	R	R	6'2		0	0	—	0	2	0	0	2	1	2	0	0	0.00
Prendergast, Mike-Michael Thomas	14-15ChiF 16-17ChiN 18-19PhiN	12-15-88	Arlington, Ill.	11-18-67	R	R	5'10	165	41	53	.436	4	180	98	48	908	867	207	311	6	2.74
Prentiss (Wilson), Garry-George Pepper (Kitten) (Played as George Wilson 01)	01-02BosA 02BalA	06-10-76	Wilmington, Del.	09-08-02	B	R	5'11	175	3	4	.429	0	11	7	4	58	76	21	10	0	5.28
Prough, Bill-Herschel Clinton	12CinN	11-28-87	Markle, Ind.	12-29-36	R	R	6'3	185	0	0	—	0	1	0	0	3	7	1	1	0	6.00
Pruiett, Tex-Charles LeRoy	07-08BosA	04-10-83	Osgood, Ind.	03-06-53	L	R	5'8	176	5	18	.217	1	48	23	7	233	221	80	82	3	2.82
Puckett, Troy-Troy Levi	11PhiN	12-10-89	Winchester, Ind.	04-13-71	R	R	6'2	186	0	0	—	0	4	2	1	2	1	0	1	0	13.50
Puttmann, Ambrose-Ambrose Nicholas	03-05NYA 06StLN	09-09-80	Cincinnati, Ohio	06-21-36	L	L	6'4	185	7	11	.389	1	33	18	8	173	158	67	85	1	3.59
Quick, Eddie-Edwin S.	03NYA	12-??-81	Baltimore, Md.	06-19-13	L		5'11		0	1	.000	0	1	1	0	4	5	1	1	0	4.50
Quinn, Tad-Clarence Carr	02-03PhiA	09-25-81	Torrington, Conn.	08-06-46	R	R	6'1	210	0	0	—	0	1	1	1	17	23	7	4	0	4.76
Radebaugh, Roy-Roy	11StLN	02-22-81	Champaign, Ill.	01-17-45	R	R	5'7	160	0	0	—	0	2	1	0	10	6	4	1	0	2.70
Ragan, Pat-Don Carlos Patrick	09CinN 09ChiN 11-15BknN 15-19BosN 19NYN 19ChiA 23PhiN	11-15-85	Blanchard, Iowa	09-04-56	R	R	5'10	185	76	104	.422	4	283	181	93	1610	1555	470	680	12	2.99
Raleigh, John-John Austin	09-10StLN	04-21-87	Elkhorn, Wis.	08-24-55	R	L	5'9	165	1	10	.091	0	18	11	3	86	93	21	28	0	4.08
Rasmussen, Henry-Henry Florian (Hans)	51ChiF	04-18-95	Chicago, Ill.	01-01-49	R	R	6'6	220	0	0	—	0	2	0	0	2	3	2	0	0	13.50
Ray, Carl-Carl Grady	15-16PhiA	01-31-89	Danbury, N.C.	04-02-70	L	L	5'11	170	0	2	.000	0	16	0	0	16	20	20	11	0	5.06
Ray, Farmer-Robert Henry	10StLA	09-17-86	Fort Lyon, Colo.	03-11-63	L	R	5'11	160	4	10	.286	0	21	16	11	141	146	49	35	0	3.57
Raymond, Bugs-Arthur Lawrence	04DetA 07-08StLN 09-11NYN	02-24-82	Chicago, Ill.	09-07-12	R	R	5'10	180	45	57	.441	2	136	95	58	855	724	282	401	9	2.48
Reagan (Ragan), Rip-Arthur Edgar	03CinN	06-05-78	Lincoln, Ill.	06-08-53	R	R	5'11	170	0	0	—	0	3	2	2	18	40	7	7	0	6.00
Redding, Phil-Philip Hayden	12-13StLN	01-25-90	Crystal Sprs., Miss.	03-31-29	L	R	5'11	190	2	1	.667	0	4	3	2	28	33	12	10	0	5.14
Rees, Nellie-Stanley Milton	18WasA	02-25-99	Cynthiana, Ky.	08-30-37	L	L	6'3	190	1	0	1.000	0	2	1	0	3	4	1	0	0	6.00
Regan, Mike-Michael John	17-19CinN	11-19-87	Phoenix, N.Y.	05-22-61	R	R	5'11	165	16	15	.516	2	55	30	20	298	306	70	66	4	2.84
Reidy, Bill-William Joseph (Wee Willie)	96NYN 99BknN 01MilA 02-03StLA 03-04BknN	10-09-73	Cleveland, Ohio	10-14-15	R	R	5'8	155	25	39	.391	3	79	66	55	601	740	106	109	3	4.18
Reis, Jack-Harrie Crane	11StLN	06-14-91	Carthage, Ohio	07-20-39	R	R	5'10	175	0	0	—	0	3	0	0	5	8	4	4	0	1.00
Reisigl, Bugs-Jacob	11CleA	12-12-87	Brooklyn, N.Y.	02-24-57	R	R	5'10	175	0	1	.000	0	3	1	1	13	13	3	6	0	6.23
Reisling, Doc-Frank Carl	04-05BknN 06-08DE 09-10WasA	07-25-74	Martins Ferry, Ohio	03-04-55	R	R	5'10	180	14	19	.424	1	49	33	25	312	303	75	100	4	2.45
Remneas, Alex-Alexander Norman	12DetA 15StLA	02-21-86	Minneapolis, Minn.	08-27-75	R	R	6'	180	0	1	.000	0	6	2	0	16	13	9	6	0	6.75
Renfer, Erwin-Erwin Arthur	13DetA	12-11-91	Elgin, Ill.	10-26-57	R	R	6'	180	0	1	.000	0	2	1	0	6	5	3	1	0	6.00
Reulbach, Ed-Edward Marvin (Big Ed)	05-13ChiN 13-14BknN 15NwkF 16-17BosN	12-01-82	Detroit, Mich.	07-17-61	R	R	6'1	190	182	106	.632	13	399	300	200	2633	2117	892	1137	40	2.28
Reynolds, Ross-Ross Ernest (Doc)	14-15DetA	08-20-87	Barksdale, Tex.	06-23-70	R	R	6'2	175	5	4	.556	0	30	9	3	89	79	44	33	1	2.63
Rhoads, Bob-Barton Emory (Dusty)	02ChiN 03StLN 03-09CleA	10-04-79	Wooster, Ohio	02-12-67	R	R	6'1	215	98	84	.538	3	218	185	154	1691	1664	494	522	21	2.61
Rhodes, Charlie-Charles Anderson	06StLN 08CinN 08-09StLN	04-07-85	Caney, Kans.	10-26-18	R	R	5'7	160	7	11	.389	0	26	20	10	143	116	67	76	0	3.46
Rice, Sam-Edgar Charles (See B20-45)	15-16WasA	02-20-90	Morocco, Ind.	10-13-74	L	R	5'9	150	1	1	.500	0	9	3	1	39	31	19	12	0	2.54
Richardson, Jack-John William	15-16PhiA	10-03-92	Central City, Ill.	01-18-70	B	R	6'3	197	0	1	.000	0	4	2	0	21	26	12	6	0	3.60
Richie, Lew-Elwood Lewis	06-09PhiN 09-10BosN 10-13ChiN	08-23-83	Ambler, Pa.	08-15-36	R	R	5'8	165	74	65	.532	9	241	137	87	1360	1190	495	438	20	2.54
Richter, Reggie-Emil Henry	11ChiN	09-14-88	Dusseldorf, Germany	08-03-34	R	R	6'2	180	1	3	.250	0	22	5	0	55	62	20	34	0	3.11
Ridgway, Jack-Jacob A.	14BalF	07-23-89	Philadelphia, Pa.	02-23-28	L	L	5'11	174	0	1	.000	0	1	1	0	6	6	2	0	0	11.00
Rieger, Elmer-Elmer Jay	10StLN	02-25-89	Perris, Cal.	10-21-59	R	R	6'	175	0	2	.000	0	13	1	0	21	26	7	9	0	4.50
Ritter, Hank-William Herbert	12PhiN 14-16NYN	10-12-93	McCoysville, Pa.	09-03-64	R	R	6'	180	4	1	.800	2	29	1	0	77	78	24	43	0	3.97

USE NAMES - GIVEN NAMES (NICKNAMES)	TEAM BY YEAR	BIRTH DATE	BIRTHPLACE	DEATH DATE	B	T	HGT	WGT	W	L	Pct.	SV	G	GS	CG	IP	H	BB	SO	ShO	ERA
Roberts, Ray-Raymond	19PhiA	08-24-95	Cruger, Miss.	01-30-62	L	R	5'11	180	0	2	.000	0	3	2	0	14	21	3	2	0	7.71
Roberston, Dick-Preston James	13CinN 18BknN 19WasA	09-16-91	Rockville, Md.	10-02-44	R	R	5'9	160	3	9	.250	0	22	14	8	125	125	46	26	1	2.88
Robinson (Roberson), Hank-John Henry (Rube)	11-13PitN 14-15StLN 18NYA	08-16-87	Floyd, Ark.	07-03-65	R	L	6'1	175	42	37	.532	2	150	72	32	701	646	159	238	3	2.53
Robitaille, Chick-Joseph Anthony	04-05PitN	03-02-79	Whitehall, N.Y.	07-30-47	R	R	5'8	150	12	8	.600	0	26	20	18	186	178	41	66	0	2.56
Rogers, Tom-Thomas Andrew (Shotgun)	17-19StLA 19PhiA 21NYA	03-07-95	Scottville, Ky.	03-07-36	R	R	6'1	195	15	30	.333	3	83	42	21	415	431	162	94	1	3.95
Rogge, Clint-Francis Clinton	15PitF 21CinN	07-19-89	Memphis, Mich.	01-06-69	R	R	5'10	185	18	13	.581	0	43	34	17	289	283	102	105	5	2.74
Rose, Chuck-Charles Alfred	09StLA	09-01-85	Macon, Mo.	08-04-61	L	L	5'8	150	1	2	.333	0	3	3	3	25	32	7	6	0	5.40
Ross, Ernie-Ernest Bertram (Curly)	02BalA	03-31-80	Toronto, Canada	03-28-50	L	L	5'8	150	1	1	.500	0	2	2	2	17	20	12	2	0	7.41
Ross, George-George Sidney	18NYN	06-27-92	Kentfield, Cal.	04-22-35	L	L	5'10	175	0	0	—	1	1	0	0	2	2	3	2	0	0.00
Rowan, Jack-John Albert	06DetA 08-10, 13-14CinN 11PhiN 11ChiN	06-16-86	New Castle, Pa.	09-29-66	R	R	6'1	210	32	40	.444	3	119	74	44	671	623	272	267	5	3.07
Roy, Charlie-Robert Charles	06PhiN	02-22-84	Beaulieu, Minn.	02-10-50	R	R	5'10	190	0	1	.000	0	7	1	0	18	24	5	6	0	5.000
Rucker, Nap-George	07-16BknN	09-30-84	Crabapple, Ga.	12-19-70	R	L	5'11	200	134	134	.500	14	336	274	186	2375	2089	701	1217	38	2.42
Rudolph, Dick-Richard (Baldy)	10-11NYN 13-20BosN 21DP 22-23,27BosN	08-25-88	New York, N.Y.	10-20-49	R	R	5'9	160	121	108	.528	8	279	240	172	2048	1971	402	786	27	2.66
Rusie, Amos-Amos Wilson (The Hoosier Thunderbolt)	89IndN 90-95NYN 96HO 97-98NYN 99-00HO 01CinN	05-30-71	Mooresville, Ind.	12-06-42	R	R	6'1	200	248	170	.593	5	462	427	392	3769	3384	1704	1934	30	3.08
Russell, Lefty-Clarence Dixon	10-12PhiN	07-08-90	Baltimore, Md.	01-22-62	L	L	6'1	195	1	4	.200	0	13	5	3	58	71	34	21	1	6.36
Russell, Reb-Ewell Albert (See B20-45)	13-19ChiA	12-13-89	Jackson, Miss.	09-30-73	L	L	5'11	185	79	60	.568	15	241	148	80	1290	1127	267	495	24	2.34
Ruth, Babe-George Herman (The Sultan of Swat, The Bambino) (See B20-21,30,33NYA)	14-19BosA 20-21,30,33NYA	02-06-95	Baltimore, Md.	08-16-48	L	L	6'2	195	93	44	.679	5	163	147	107	1221	974	441	488	17	2.28
Ryan, Jack-Jack (Gulfport)	08CleA 09BosA 11BknN	09-19-84	Lawrenceville, Ill.	10-16-49	R	R	5'10	165	4	4	.500	1	24	10	3	101	101	26	30	0	2.94
St. Vrain, Jim-James Marcellin	02CinN	06-06-83	Ralls Co., Mo.	06-12-37	R	L	5'9	175	4	6	.400	0	12	11	10	95	88	25	51	1	2.08
Salisbury, Bill-William Ansil (Solly)	02PhiN	11-12-76	Algona, Iowa	01-17-52	R	R	6'	180	0	0	—	0	2	1	0	6	15	2	0	0	13.50
Sallee, Slim-Harry Franklin (Scatter)	08-16StLN 16-18NYN 19-20CinN 20-21NYN	02-03-85	Higginsport, Ohio	03-23-50	L	L	6'3	180	173	143	.547	36	475	305	188	2819	2726	572	835	25	2.57
Salmon, Roger-Roger Elliott	12ChiN	05-11-91	Newark, N.J.	06-17-74	L	L	6'2	170	1	0	1.000	0	2	1	0	5	7	4	5	0	9.00
Salve, Gus-Augustus William	08PhiA	12-29-85	Boston, Mass.	05-29-71	L	L	6'	190	0	1	.000	0	1	1	1	9	8	5	5	0	2.00
Sanders, Roy-Roy Garvin (Butch, Pep)	17CinN 18PitN	08-01-92	Stafford, Kans.	01-17-50	R	R	6'	195	7	10	.412	1	30	16	7	170	147	68	58	1	2.75
Sanders, Roy-Roy Lee (Simon)	18NYA 20StLA	06-10-94	Pittsburg, Kans.	07-08-63	R	R	6'	185	1	3	.250	0	14	3	0	43	48	33	10	0	4.60
Sanders, War-Warren Williams	03-04StLN	08-02-77	Maynardville, Tenn.	08-03-62	R	L	5'10	160	2	8	.200	0	12	9	4	59	73	22	20	0	5.64
Savidge, Ralph-Ralph Austin (The Human Whipcord)	08-09CinN	02-03-79	Jerseytown, Pa.	07-22-59	R	R	6'2	210	0	1	.000	0	5	1	1	25	28	11	9	0	5.76
Scanlan, Doc-William Dennis	03-04PitN 04-07BknN 08IL 09-11BknN	03-07-81	Syracuse, N.Y.	05-29-49	L	R	5'8	180	67	70	.489	5	181	149	102	1252	1061	608	584	15	3.00
Scanlan, Frank-Frank Aloysius (Dreamy)	09PhiN	04-28-90	Syracuse, N.Y.	04-09-69	R	R	6'1	175	0	0	—	1	6	0	0	11	8	5	5	0	1.64
Schardt, Bill-Wilbur (Big Bill)	11-12BknN	01-20-86	Cleveland, Ohio	07-26-64	R	R	6'4	210	5	16	.238	1	46	22	10	216	215	97	84	1	3.67
Schauer, Rube-Alexander John	13-16NYN 17PhiA	03-19-91	Kamenka, Russia	04-15-57	R	R	6'2	192	10	29	.256	7	83	32	16	400	384	137	164	0	3.55
Schegg (Price), Lefty-Gilbert Eugene	12WasA	08-29-89	Leesville, Ohio	02-27-63	L	L	5'11	180	0	0	—	0	2	1	0	5	7	4	3	0	3.60
Scheneberg, Jack-John Bluford	13PitN 20StLA	11-20-87	Guyandotte, W.Va.	09-26-50	R	R	6'	180	0	1	.000	0	2	1	0	8	17	3	1	0	11.25
Schettler, Lou-Louis Martin	10PhiN	06-12-86	Pittsburgh, Pa.	05-01-60	R	R	5'11	180	2	6	.250	1	27	7	3	107	96	51	62	0	3.20
Schlitzer, Biff-Victor Joseph	08-09PhiA 09BosA 14BufF	12-04-84	Rochester, N.Y.	01-04-48	R	R	5'11	175	10	16	.385	1	44	29	16	223	211	73	88	2	3.51
Schmidt, Butch-Charles John (See B01-19)	09NYA	07-19-86	Baltimore, Md.	09-04-52	L	L	6'	175	0	0	—	0	1	0	0	5	10	1	2	0	7.20
Schmidt, Henry-Henry Martin	03BknN	06-26-73	Brownsville, Tex.	04-23-26	R	R	5'8	150	22	13	.629	2	40	36	29	301	321	120	96	5	3.83
Schmidt, Pete-Friedrich Christoph Herman	13StLA	07-30-90	Lowden, Iowa	03-11-73	R	R	6'	175	0	0	—	1	1	0	0	2	2	4	0	0	4.50
Schmit, Crazy-Frederic M. (Germany)	90PitN 92-93BalN 93NYN 99CleN 01BalA	12-13-66	Chicago, Ill.	10-05-40	L	L	5'10	165	7	36	.163	0	54	48	37	361	464	185	93	1	5.46
Schmutz, Charlie-Charles Otto (King)	14-15BknN	01-01-91	San Diego, Cal.	06-27-62	R	R	6'3	195	1	3	.250	0	19	5	1	61	64	14	22	0	3.54
Schneiberg, Frank-Frank Fred	10BknN	03-12-80	Milwaukee, Wis.	05-18-48	R	R	6'1	165	0	0	—	0	1	0	0	1	5	4	0	0	63.00
Schneider, Pete-Peter Joseph	14-18CinN 19NYA	08-20-92	Los Angeles, Cal.	06-01-57	R	R	6'1	190	58	86	.403	4	207	157	85	1283	1204	500	491	11	2.621
Schorr, Ed-Edward Walter	15CinN	02-16-92	Bremen, Ohio	09-12-69	R	R	6'1	180	0	0	—	0	5	0	0	6	3	5	3	0	7.50
Schreiber, Barney-David Henry	11CinN	05-08-82	Waverly, Ohio	10-06-64	L	L	6'	185	0	0	—	0	3	0	0	10	19	2	5	0	5.40
Schultz, Al-Albert Christopher (Heinie, Lefty)	12-14NYA 14-15BufF 16CinN	05-12-89	Toledo, Ohio	12-13-31	R	L	6'1	182	48	63	.432	4	160	114	56	933	867	409	445	5	3.32
Schumann, Hack-Charles J.	06PhiA	08-13-84	Buffalo, N.Y.	03-25-46	R	R	6'2	230	0	2	.000	0	4	2	1	18	21	8	9	0	4.00
Schupp, Ferdie-Ferdinand Maurice	13-19NYN 19-21StLN 21BknN 22ChiA	01-16-91	Louisville, Ky.	12-16-71	R	L	5'10	150	61	39	.610	6	216	121	62	1054	938	464	553	11	3.32
Schwenck, Rudy-Rudolph Christian	09ChiN	04-06-84	Louisville, Ky.	11-27-41	L	L	5'6	175	1	1	.500	0	3	2	0	16	16	3	3	0	13.50
Schwenk, Hal-Harold Edward (Lefty)	13StLA	08-23-90	Schuylkill Haven, Pa.	09-04-55	L	L	6'	185	1	0	1.000	0	3	1	1	11	12	4	3	0	3.27
Scoggins, Jim-Lynn James (Lefty)	13ChiA	07-09-91	Kileen, Tex.	08-16-23	L	L	5'11	165	0	0	—	0	1	1	1	7	4	1	0	0	0.00
Scott, Dick-Amos Richard	01CinN	02-05-83	Bethel, Ohio	01-18-11	R	R	6'	180	1	2	.333	0	3	2	2	21	26	9	7	0	5.14
Scott, Ed-Phillip Edwin	00CinN 01CleA	08-12-70	Walbridge, Ohio	11-01-33	R	R	6'3		24	26	.480	1	60	52	43	448	529	104	115	0	3.98
Scott, Jim-James (Death Valley Jim)	09-17ChiA 18MS	04-23-88	Deadwood, S.D.	04-07-57	R	R	6'1	215	109	113	.491	12	317	225	125	1871	1624	609	945	26	2.32
Seaton, Tom-Thomas Gordon	12-13PhiN 14-15BknF 15NwkF 16-17ChiN	08-30-87	Blair, Neb.	04-10-40	R	R	6'	175	93	65	.589	5	231	154	90	1340	1235	530	644	15	3.14
Seymour, Cy-James Bentley (See B01-19)	96-00NYN 02CinN	12-09-72	Albany, N.Y.	09-20-19	L	L	6'	200	63	54	.538	1	140	123	105	1033	953	661	584	6	3.76
Shaw, Jim-James Aloysius (Grunting Jim)	13-21WasA	08-13-93	Pittsburgh, Pa.	01-27-62	R	R	6'	180	82	99	.453	16	287	195	96	1599	1446	688	767	17	3.07
Shears, George-George Penfield	12NYA	04-13-90	Marshall, Mo.	11-12-78	R	L	6'3	180	0	0	—	0	2	0	0	15	24	11	9	0	5.40
Shellenback, Frank-Frank Victor	18-19ChiA	12-16-98	Joplin, Mo.	08-17-69	R	R	6'2	192	11	15	.423	1	36	24	12	218	220	90	57	3	3.05
Sherman, Babe-Lester Daniel (Dan, The Connecticut Moistballer)	14ChiF	09-16-85	Hubbardsville, N.Y.	05-09-90	R	R	5'6	145	0	0	—	0	1	0	0	2	0	0	0	0	0.00
Sherman, Joe-Joel Powers	15PhiN	11-04-90	Yarmouth, Mass.	12-21-87	R	R	6'	165	1	0	1.000	0	1	1	1	15	15	1	5	0	2.40
Sherry, Fred-Scheuerholz), Fred-Fred Peter	11WasA	06-13-89	Honesdale, Pa.	07-27-75	R	R	6'	170	0	4	.000	0	10	3	2	52	63	19	20	0	4.33
Shields, Charlie-Charles Jessamine	02BalA 02StLA 07StLN	12-10-79	Jackson, Tenn.	08-27-53	L	L	5'8		8	14	.364	1	30	21	13	179	250	46	35	1	4.27
Shore, Ernie-Ernest Grady	12NYN 14-17 BosA 18MS 19-20NYA	03-24-91	East Bend, N.C.	09-24-80	R	R	6'4	195	65	42	.607	6	161	120	55	982	906	271	310	9	2.47
Shultz, Toots-Wallace Luther	11-12PhiN	10-10-88	Homestead, Pa.	01-30-59	R	R	5'10	175	1	7	.125	1	27	7	3	84	105	50	29	0	6.00
Siever, Ed-Edward Tilden	01-02DetA 03-04StLA 06-08DetA	04-02-75	Goddard, Kans.	02-04-20	L	L	6'	190	86	80	.518	3	203	174	136	1508	1550	311	470	14	2.60
Sims, Pete-Clarence	15StLA	05-24-91	Crown City, Ohio	12-02-68	R	R	5'11	165	0	0	—	0	2	0	0	6	6	4	4	0	4.50
Sincock, Bert-Herbert Sylvester	09-08-87	09-08-87	Barkerville, Can.	08-01-46	L	L	5'10	165	0	0	—	0	1	0	0	5	3	0	1	0	3.60
Sisler, George-George Harold (Gorgeous George) (See B20-45)	15-16,18,20,25-26StLA M24-26StLA, 28BosN	03-24-93	Manchester, Ohio	03-26-73	L	L	5'11	170	5	6	.455	2	24	12	9	111	91	52	63	1	2.35
Sitton, Carl-Charles Vetter	09CleA	09-22-81	Pendelton, S.C.	09-11-31	R	R	5'10	170	2	2	.500	0	14	5	3	50	50	16	16	0	2.88
Skeels, Dave-David	10DetA	12-29-91	Addy, Wash.	12-02-26	R	R	6'1	187	0	0	—	0	1	1	0	6	9	4	2	0	12.00
Skopec, John-John S. (Buckshot)	01ChiA 03DetA	05-08-80	Chicago, Ill.	10-20-12	R	L	5'10	190	8	5	.615	0	15	14	9	107	108	58	38	0	3.28
Slagle, Walt-Walter Jennings	10CinN	12-15-78	Kenton, Ohio	06-14-74	R	R	6'	165	0	0	—	0	1	0	0	1	3	3	0	0	9.00
Slapnicka, Cy-Cyril Charles	11ChiN 18PitN	03-23-86	Cedar Rapids, Iowa	10-20-79	B	R	5'10	165	1	6	.143	1	10	8	5	73	71	29	13	0	4.32
Slattery, Phil-Philip Ryan	15PitN	02-25-93	Harper, Iowa	03-12-68	R	L	5'11	160	0	0	—	0	3	0	0	8	5	1	1	0	0.00
Slaughter, Barney-Byron Atkins	10PhiN	10-06-84	Smyrna, Del.	05-17-61	R	R	5'11	160	0	1	.000	0	3	1	0	18	21	11	7	0	5.50
Smallwood, Walt-Walter Clayton	17NYA 18MS 19NYA	04-24-93	Dayton, Md.	04-29-67	R	R	6'2	190	0	0	—	0	3	1	0	21	21	10	7	0	4.50
Smith, Bob-Robert Ashley (played as Bob Brown 14)	13ChiA 14-15BufF	07-20-90	Woodbury, Vt.	12-27-65	R	R	5'11	160	3	1	.750	0	17	1	0	40	43	21	14	0	4.27
Smith, Charlie-Charles Edwin	02CleA 06-09WasA 09-11BosA 11-14ChiN	07-20-80	Cleveland, Ohio	01-03-29	R	R	6'1	185	65	87	.428	1	212	148	86	1351	1309	353	570	10	2.81
Smith, Chick-John William	13CinN	12-02-92	Dayton, Ky.	10-11-35	L	L	5'8	165	0	1	.000	0	19	0	0	18	15	11	11	0	3.50
Smith, Doug-Douglass Weldon	12BosA	05-25-93	Millers Falls, Mass.	09-18-73	L	L	6'	168	0	0	—	0	1	1	0	3	5	1	3	0	3.00
Smith, Ed-Rhesa Edward	06StLA	02-21-79	Mentone, Ind.	03-20-55	R	R	5'11	170	7	10	.412	1	19	18	13	155	153	53	45	0	3.72
Smith, Elmer-Elmer Ellsworth (Mike) (See B01-19)	86-89CinAA 92,94PitN 98CinN	03-23-68	Pittsburgh, Pa.	11-03-45	L	L	5'11	178	76	58	.567	0	150	137	123	1219	1175	438	526	9	3.24
Smith (Schmidt), Frank-Frank Elmer (Piano Mover)	04-10ChiA 10-11BosA 11-12CinN 14-15BalF 15BknF	10-28-79	Pittsburgh, Pa.	11-03-52	R	R	5'10	194	138	113	.550	2	354	255	184	2275	1975	676	1051	27	2.59
Smith, Fred-Frederick C.	07CinN	11-24-78	New Diggings, Wis.	02-04-64	R	R	5'10	186	2	7	.222	1	18	9	5	85	90	24	19	0	2.86
Smith, Harry-Harrison Morton	12ChiA	02-20-89	Union, Neb.	07-26-64	R	R	5'9	168	0	1	.000	0	1	1	0	3	2	1	0	0	1.80
Smith (Schmidt), Jake-Jacob John	11PhiN	06-10-87	Dravosburg, Pa.	11-07-48	B	L	6'4	200	0	0	—	0	1	0	0	1	1	1	0	0	0.00
Smith, Pop Boy-Clarence Ossie	13ChiA 16-17CleA	05-23-92	Newport, Tenn.	02-16-24	R	R	6'1	176	1	5	.167	0	26	5	0	67	70	26	20	0	4.16
Snover, Colonel-Colonel Lester (Bosco)	19NYN	05-16-95	Hallstead, Pa.	04-30-69	R	R	6'	200	1	1	.500	0	3	2	1	22	19	7	3	1	5.00
Sommers, Rudy-Rudolph	12ChiN 14BknDP 26-27BosA	10-30-87	Cincinnati, Ohio	03-18-49	B	L	5'11	185	2	8	.200	1	36	11	3	101	113	53	44	0	4.81
Spade, Bob-Robert	07-10CinN 10StLA	01-04-78	Akron, Ohio	09-07-24	R	R	5'10	190	25	24	.510	2	62	52	36	426	411	159	121	4	2.96
Sparks, Tully-Thomas Frank	97PhiN 99PitN 01MilA 02NYN 02BosA 03-10PhiN	12-12-74	Etna, Georgia	07-15-37	R	R	5'10	160	120	137	.467	8	313	269	202	2337	2231	629	778	19	2.79

USE NAMES - GIVEN NAMES (NICKNAMES)	TEAM BY YEAR	BIRTH DATE	BIRTHPLACE	DEATH DATE	B	T	HGT	WGT	W	L	Pct.	SV	G	GS	CG	IP	H	BB	SO	ShO	ERA
Speer, Kid-George Nathan	09DetA	06-16-86	Corning, Mo.	01-13-46	L	L	5'9	152	3	3	.500	2	12	8	4	76	88	13	12	0	2.84
Spencer, Fred-Fred Calvin (Hack)	12StLA	04-25-85	St. Cloud, Minn.	02-05-69	R	R	5'7	170	0	0	—	0	1	0	0	2	2	0	0	0	9.00
Spongberg, Carl-Carl Gustave	08ChiN	05-21-84	Idaho Falls, Idaho	07-21-38	R	R	6'2	208	0	0	—	0	1	0	0	7	9	6	4	0	9.00
Stack, Eddie-William Edward (Smoke)	10-11PhiN 12-13BknN 13-14ChiN	10-24-87	Chicago, Ill.	08-28-58	R	R	6'	180	26	24	.520	2	102	60	23	491	469	188	200	4	3.52
Standridge, Pete-Alfred Peter	11StLN 15ChiN	04-25-91	Black Diamond, Wash.	08-02-63	R	R	6'	180	4	1	.800	0	31	3	2	117	130	40	45	0	3.85
Stanley, Buck-John Leonard	11PhiN	11-13-89	Washington, D.C.	08-13-40	L	L	5'10	160	0	1	.000	0	4	0	0	11	14	9	5	0	6.55
Starkel, Con-Conrad	06WasA	11-16-80	Red Oak, Iowa	01-19-33	R	R	6'	200	0	0	—	0	3	1	2	7	2	1	1	0	18.00
Steele, Bill-William Mitchell (Big Bill)	10-14StLN 14BknN	10-05-85	Milford, Pa.	10-19-49	R	R	6'2	196	37	43	.463	7	129	79	40	677	733	235	236	1	4.02
Steele, Bob-Robert Wesley	16-17StLN 17-18PitN 18-19PhiN	03-29-94	Cassburn, Canada	01-27-62	B	L	5'10	175	16	38	.296	3	91	57	28	488	450	144	217	4	3.04
Steele, Elmer-Elmer Rae	07-09BosA 10-11PitN 11BknN	05-17-84	Muitzeskill, N.Y.	03-09-66	R	R	5'11	200	18	22	.450	5	75	43	20	418	367	68	147	3	2.41
Steen, Bill-William John	12-15ClnN 15DetA	11-11-87	Pittsburgh, Pa.	03-13-79	R	R	6'	180	28	34	.452	5	108	65	32	597	611	199	265	4	3.05
Stevens, Jim-James Arthur (Steve)	14WasA	08-25-89	Williamsburg, Md.	09-25-66	R	R	5'11	180	0	0	—	0	2	0	0	3	4	2	0	0	9.00
Stewart, Joe-Joseph Lawrence (Ace)	04BosN	03-11-79	Monroe, N.C.	02-09-13	R	R	5'10	175	0	0	—	0	2	0	0	9	12	4	1	0	10.00
Stimmel, Archie-Archibald May (Lumbago)	00-02CinN	05-30-73	Woodsboro, Md.	08-18-58	R	R	6'	175	5	19	.208	0	26	22	18	192	225	60	64	1	4.22
Stone, Dwight-Dwight Ely	13StLA 14KCF	08-02-86	Holt Co., Neb.	06-03-76	R	R	6'1	170	10	20	.333	0	57	29	9	278	299	123	125	1	4.08
Stovall, Jesse-Jesse Cramer (Scout)	03ClnA 04DetA	07-24-75	Leeds, Mo.	07-12-55	L	R	6'	175	7	14	.333	0	28	23	19	204	214	66	53	3	3.75
Strand, Paul-Paul Edward (See B20-45)	13-15BosN	12-19-93	Carbonado, Wash.	07-02-74	R	L	6'	190	7	3	.700	1	29	5	3	95	95	38	52	0	2.37
Streit, Oscar-Oscar William	99BosN 02ClnA	07-07-73	Florence, Ala.	10-10-35	L	L	6'5	190	1	7	.125	0	10	8	5	67	87	40	10	0	5.51
Stremmel, Phil-Philip	09-10StLA	04-16-80	Zanesville, Ohio	12-26-47	R	R	6'	175	0	4	.000	0	7	4	4	47	51	20	13	0	4.02
Stricklett, Elmer-Elmer Griffin	04ChiA 05-07BknN	08-29-76	Glasco, Kans.	06-07-64	R	R	5'6	140	34	52	.395	6	104	90	78	766	755	215	237	10	2.84
Stroud, Sailor-Ralph Vivian	10DetA 15-16NYN	05-15-85	Ironia, N.J.	04-11-70	R	R	6'	160	19	20	.487	3	70	40	15	361	364	85	141	3	2.94
Sudhoff, Willie-John William (Wee Willie)	97-98StLN 99ClnN 99-01StLA 02-05StLA 06WasA	09-17-74	St. Louis, Mo.	05-25-17	R	R	5'7	165	100	136	.424	6	279	240	200	2082	2171	607	518	10	3.60
Suggs, George-George Franklin	08-09DetA 10-13CinN 14-15BalF	07-07-82	Kinston, N.C.	04-04-49	R	R	5'7	168	99	89	.527	17	245	185	115	1652	1722	355	588	16	3.11
Sullivan, Harry-Harry Andrew	09StLN	04-22-88	Rockford, Ill.	09-22-19	L	L			0	0	—	0	2	1	0	1	4	2	1	0	36.00
Sullivan, John-John Jeremiah (Lefty)	19ChiA	05-31-94	Chicago, Ill.	07-07-58	L	L	5'11	165	0	1	.000	0	4	2	1	15	24	8	9	0	4.20
Summers, Ed-Oron Edgar (Kickapoo, Chief)	08-12DetA	12-05-84	Ladoga, Ind.	05-12-53	B	R	6'2	180	68	45	.602	5	138	112	79	999	930	221	362	9	2.42
Suter, Rube-Harry Richard	09ChiA	09-15-87	Independence, Mo.	07-24-71	L	L	5'10	190	2	3	.400	0	18	7	3	87	72	28	53	1	2.48
Sutthoff, Jack-John Gerhard (Sunny Jack)	98WasN 99StLN 01,03-04CinN 04-05PhiN	06-29-73	Cincinnati, Ohio	08-03-42	R	R	5'9	175	33	42	.440	1	88	68	56	653	664	287	196	4	3.56
Swan, Harry-Harry Gordon (Ducky)	14KCF	08-11-87	Lancaster, Pa.	05-08-46	R	R	5'10	165	0	0	—	0	1	0	1	0	1	1	1	0	0.00
Swigler, Ad-Adam William (Doc)	17NYN	09-21-95	Philadelphia, Pa.	02-05-75	R	R	5'10	180	0	1	.000	0	1	1	0	6	7	8	4	0	6.00
Swindell, Josh-Joshua Ernest	11,13ClnA	07-05-83	Rose Hill, Kans.	03-19-69	R	R	6'	180	0	1	.000	0	4	1	1	17	19	4	6	0	2.12
Swormstedt, Len-Leonard Jordan	01-02ClnN 06BosA	10-06-78	Cincinnati, Ohio	07-19-64	R	R	5'11	165	3	4	.429	0	8	7	7	65	58	10	22	0	2.22
Taff, Bill-John Gallatin	13PhiA	06-03-90	Austin, Tex.	05-15-61	R	R	6'	170	0	1	.000	1	2	1	0	18	22	5	9	0	6.50
Tannehill, Jesse-Jesse Niles (See B01-19)	94CinN 97-02PitN 03NYA 04-08BosA 08-09WasA 11CinN	07-14-74	Dayton, Ky.	09-22-56	B	L	5'8	150	194	119	.620	8	357	318	263	2751	2787	477	940	34	2.78
Bats Left 03																					
Taylor, Ben-Benjamin Harrison	12CinN	04-02-89	Paoli, Ind.	11-03-46	R	R	5'11	163	0	0	—	0	2	0	0	6	9	3	2	0	3.00
Taylor, Dummy-Luther Haden	00-01NYN 02ClnA 02-08NYN	02-21-75	Oskaloosa, Kans.	08-22-58	R	R	6'1	160	115	106	.520	3	274	237	160	1916	1877	551	767	21	2.75
Taylor, Rube-Edgar Ruben	03StLN	03-23-77	Palestine,Tex.	01-30-12	L	L			0	0	—	0	3	0	0	3	0	1	0	0	0.00
Taylor, Jack-John William (Brakeman Jack)	98-03ChiN 04-06StLN 06-07ChiN	01-24-74	Straightville, Ohio	03-04-38	R	R	5'10	170	151	140	.519	5	310	286	278	2617	2502	582	657	19	2.67
Taylor, Wiley-Philip Wiley	11DetA 12ChiA 13-14StLA	03-18-88	Wamego, Kans.	07-08-54	R	R	6'1	175	3	10	.231	0	27	17	4	121	113	65	45	1	4.09
Tedrow, Al-Allen Seymour	14ClnA	12-14-91	Westerville, Ohio	01-23-58	R	L	6'	180	1	2	.333	0	4	3	1	22	19	14	4	1	1.23
Terry, John-John Burchard	02DetA 03StLA	11-01-79	Waterbury, Conn.	04-27-33					1	1	.500	0	4	2	2	23	29	5	2	0	2.74
Tesreau, Jeff-Charles Monroe	12-18NYN	03-05-88	Ironton, Mo.	09-24-46	R	R	6'2	218	115	72	.615	9	247	207	123	1679	1350	572	880	27	2.43
Thatcher, Grant-Ulysses Grant	03-04BknN	02-23-77	Maytown, Pa.	03-17-36	R	R	5'10	180	4	1	.800	0	5	4	4	37	42	9	13	0	3.16
Thielman, Henry-Henry Joseph	02NYN 02CinN 03BknN	10-03-80	St. Cloud, Minn.	09-02-42	R	R	5'11	175	9	19	.321	0	31	28	25	246	240	98	64	0	3.37
Thielman, Jake-John Peter	05-06StLN 07-08ClnA 08BosA	05-20-79	St. Cloud, Minn.	01-28-28	R	R	6'	175	31	28	.525	0	65	56	49	475	483	107	158	3	3.16
Thomas, Blaine-Blaine M. (Baldy)	11BosA	08-??-88	Glendora, Cal.	08-21-15	R	R	5'10	165	0	0	—	0	2	0	0	5	3	7	0	0	0.00
Thomas, Claude-Claude Alfred (Lefty)	16WasA	05-15-90	Stanberry, Mo.	03-06-46	L	L	6'1	180	1	2	.333	0	7	4	1	28	27	12	7	1	4.18
Thomas, Frosty-Forrest	05DetA	05-23-81	Faucett, Mo.	03-18-70	R	R	6'	185	0	2	.000	0	2	1	0	6	10	3	5	0	7.50
Thompson, Carl-Thomas Carl	12NYA	11-07-89	Spring City, Tenn.	01-16-63	R	R	5'9	170	0	0	—	0	7	2	1	33	43	13	15	0	6.00
Thompson, Fuller-Fuller Weidner	11BosN	05-01-89	Los Angeles, Cal.	02-19-72	R	R	5'11	164	0	0	—	0	3	0	0	5	5	2	0	0	3.60
Thompson, Gus-John Gustav	03PitN 06StLN	06-22-77	Humboldt, Iowa	03-28-58	R	R	6'2	185	4	13	.235	0	22	16	11	146	163	41	58	0	4.07
Thompson, Harry-Harold	19WasA 19PhiA	09-09-89	Nanticoke, Pa.	02-14-51	L	L	5'8	150	0	4	.000	1	15	2	0	55	64	11	11	0	4.25
Thormahlen, Hank-Herbert Ehler (Lefty)	17-20NYA 21BosA 25BknN	07-05-96	Jersey City, N.J.	02-06-55	L	L	6'	180	30	29	.508	2	104	63	26	565	550	203	148	5	3.33
Tift, Ray-Raymond Frank	07NYA	06-21-84	Fitchburg, Mass.	03-29-45		L	5'10	155	0	1		0	4	1	0	19	33	4	6	0	4.74
Tillman, Johnny-John Lawrence	15StLA	10-06-93	Bridgeport, Conn.	04-07-64	B	R	5'11	170	0	0	—	0	2	1	0	10	6	4	6	0	0.90
Tincup, Ben-Austin Ben	14-16,18PhiN 28ChiN	04-14-93	Adair, Okla.	07-05-80	R	R	6'1	180	7	11	.389	2	48	18	9	212	229	78	127	3	3.10
Tipple, Dan-Daniel E. (Big Dan, Rusty)	15NYA	02-13-90	Rockford, Ill.	03-26-60	R	R	6'	176	1	1	.500	0	3	2	2	19	14	14	14	0	2.84
Tompkins, Chuck-Charles Herbert	12CinN	09-20-89	Prescott, Ark.	09-20-75	R	R	6'	185	0	0	—	0	1	0	0	3	5	0	1	0	0.00
Toney, Fred-Fred Alexandra	11-13ChiN 15-18CinN 18-22NYN 23StLN	12-11-88	Nashville, Tenn.	03-11-53	R	R	6'2	215	137	102	.573	12	336	271	158	2206	2037	583	718	28	2.69
Tonkin, Doc-Harry Glenville	07WasA	08-11-81	Concord, N.H.	05-30-59	L	L	5'9	165	0	0	—	0	3	0	0	5	6	3	0	0	6.00
Torkelson, Red-Chester LeRoy	17ClnA 18MS	03-19-94	Chicago, Ill.	09-22-64	R	R	6'	175	2	1	.667	0	4	3	0	22	33	13	10	0	7.77
Townsend, Jack-John Jr. (Happy)	01PhiN 02-05WasA 06ClnA	04-09-79	Townsend, Del.	12-21-63	R	R	6'	190	34	84	.288	0	153	125	107	1138	1154	416	473	5	2.88
Tozer, Bill-William Louis	08CinN	07-03-82	St. Louis, Mo.	02-23-55	R	R	6'	200	0	1	.000	0	4	0	0	11	11	4	5	0	1.64
Trautman, Fred-Frederick Orlando	15NwkF	03-24-92	Bucyrus, Ohio	02-15-64	R	R	6'	175	0	0	—	0	3	0	0	3	4	1	2	0	6.00
Travers, Allan-Aloysius Joseph	12DetA	05-07-92	Philadelphia, Pa.	04-19-68	R	R	6'1	180	0	1	.000	0	1	1	1	8	26	7	1	0	15.75
Trekell, Harry-Harry Roy	13StLN	11-18-92	Buda, Ill.	11-04-65	R	R	6'1	170	0	1	.000	0	7	1	1	30	25	8	15	0	4.50
Troy, Bun-Robert Gustave	12DetA	08-27-88	Bad Wurzach, Germany	10-07-18	R	R	6'4	195	0	1	.000	0	1	1	0	7	9	3	1	0	5.14
Tuckey, Tom-Thomas Henry (Tabasco Tom)	08-09BosN	10-07-84	Union City, Conn.	11-07-50		L	6'	190	3	12	.200	0	25	18	7	163	164	42	42	1	3.48
Tuero (Monzon), Oscar-Oscar Monzon [Tuero]	18-20StLN	12-17-92	Havana, Cuba	10-21-60	R	R	5'8	158	6	9	.400	4	58	19	6	200	174	53	58	0	2.88
Turner, Tink-Thomas Lovatt	15PhiA	02-20-90	Swarthmore, Pa.	02-25-62	R	R	6'1	190	0	1		0	1	1	0	2	5	3	0	0	22.50
Twining, Twink-Howard Earle (Doc)	16CinN	05-30-94	Horsham, Pa.	06-14-73	R	R	6'	168	0	0	—	0	2	0	0	4	1	0	0	0	13.50
Tyler, Lefty-George Albert	10-17BosN 18-21ChiN	12-14-89	Derry, N.H.	09-29-53	L	L	5'10	175	127	118	.518	7	323	267	182	2228	1990	829	1003	31	2.95
Upham, Bill-William Lawrence	15BknF 18BosN	04-04-88	Akron, Ohio	09-14-59	R	R	6'	178	7	9	.438	5	36	13	6	142	157	41	54	2	3.36
Upp, Jerry-George Henry	09ClnA	12-10-83	Sandusky, Ohio	06-30-37	L				2	1	.667	0	4	2	2	27	26	12	13	0	1.67
Vail, Bob-Robert Garfield (Doc)	08PitN	09-24-81	Linneus, Me.	03-22-42	R	R	5'10	165	1	2	.333	0	4	1	0	15	15	7	9	0	6.00
Van Dyke, Ben-Benjamin Harrison	09PhiN 12BosA	08-15-88	Clintonville, Pa.	10-22-73	R	L	6'1	150	0	0	—	0	5	1	0	21	20	11	13	0	3.43
Van Haltren, George-George Edward Martin (See B01-19)	87-88ChiN 90BknP 91,M91BalAA 92,M92BalN 95-96,00-01NYN	03-30-66	St. Louis, Mo.	09-29-45	L	L	5'11	170	41	29	.586	4	93	68	65	690	810	244	281	5	4.05
Varney(de Varney), Dike-Lawrence Delano	02ClnA	08-09-90	Dover, N.H.	04-23-50	L	L	5'7	165	2	1	.667	0	5	3	1	15	14	12	7	0	6.00
Vasbinder, Cal-Moses Calhoun	02ClnA	07-19-80	Scio, ohio	12-22-50	R	R	6'2		0	0	—	0	2	0	0	5	5	3	2	0	9.00
Vaughn, Hippo-James Leslie	08,10-11NYA 12WasA 13-21ChiN	04-09-88	Weatherford, Tex.	05-29-66	B	L	6'4	215	178	137	.565	6	390	331	216	2731	2461	817	1416	41	2.49
Veil, Bucky-Frederick William	03-04PitN	08-02-81	Tyrone, Pa.	04-16-31	R	R	5'8	165	5	3	.625	0	13	7	4	76	74	40	21	0	3.91
Vereker, Tommy-John James	15BalF	12-02-93	Baltimore, Md.	04-02-74			5'10	185	0	0	—	0	3	0	0	3	3	2	1	0	15.00
Vernon, Joe-Joseph Henry	12ChiN 14BknF	11-25-89	Mansfield, Mass.	03-13-55	R	R	5'11	160	0	0	—	0	7	1	0	7	8	11	1	0	11.57
Vickers, Rube-Harry Porter	02CinN 03BknN 07-09PhiA	05-17-78	St. Mary's, Canada	12-09-58	R	R	6'2	225	23	27	.460	3	88	45	29	441	426	119	213	7	3.04
Volz, Jake-Jacob Phillip (Silent Jake)	01BosA 05BosN 08CinN	04-04-78	San Antonio, Tex.	08-11-62	R	R	5'10	175	2	4	.333	0	11	7	2	39	34	29	12	0	6.00
Vorhees, Cy-Henry Bert	02PhiN 02WasA	09-30-74	Lodi, Ohio	02-08-10		R	6'3	200	3	4	.429	0	11	6	4	62	73	22	25	1	3.92
Vowinkel, Rip-John Henry	05CinN	11-18-84	Oswego, N.Y.	07-13-66	R	R	5'10	195	3	3	.500	0	6	4	3	45	52	10	7	0	4.20
Wachtel, Paul-Paul Horine	17BknN	04-30-88	Myersville, Md.	12-15-64	R	R	5'11	175	0	0	—	0	2	0	0	4	6	2	2	0	10.50
Wacker, Jimmy-Charles James	09PitN	12-08-83	Jeffersonville, Ind.	08-07-48	L	L	5'9	175	0	0	—	0	1	0	0	2	1	0	0	0	4.50
Waddell, Rube-George Edward	97,99LouN 00-01PitN 01ClnN 02-07PhiA 08-10StLA	10-13-76	Bradford, Pa.	04-01-14	R	L	6'1	196	195	140	.582	12	407	340	261	2962	2460	803	2316	50	2.16
Wagner, Bull-William George	13-14BknN	12-25-87	Lilley, Mich.	10-20-67	R	R	6'	225	4	3	.571	2	24	1	0	83	91	42	15	0	5.64
Waldbauer, Doc-Albert Charles	17WasA	02-22-92	Richmond, Va.	07-16-69	R	R	6'2	190	0	0	—	0	2	0	0	5	10	2	2	0	7.20
Walker, Dixie-Ewart Gladstone	09-12WasA	06-01-87	Brownsville, Pa.	11-14-65	L	R	6'1	192	25	30	.455	1	74	92	40	481	475	142	204	5	3.52

USE NAMES - GIVEN NAMES (NICKNAMES)	TEAM BY YEAR	BIRTH DATE	BIRTHPLACE	DEATH DATE	B	T	HGT	WGT	W	L	Pct.	SV	G	GS	CG	IP	H	BB	SO	ShO	ERA
Walker, Ed-Edward Harrison	02-03CleA	08-11-74	Cambois, England	09-29-47	L	L	6'5	242	0	1	.000	0	4	4	1	20	24	13	5	0	4.50
Walker, Mysterious-Frederick Mitchell	10CinN 12CleA 13BknN 14PitF 15KnF	03-21-84	Utica, Neb.	02-01-58	R	R	5'10	185	7	23	.233	1	60	36	17	296	306	135	143	0	4.01
Walker, Tom-Thomas William	02PhiA 04-05CinN	08-01-81	Philadelphia, Pa.	07-10-44	R	R	5'11	170	25	17	.595	0	48	44	35	370	377	97	94	3	2.70
Wallace, Bobby-Rhoderick John (Rhody)　(See B01-19)	94-96CleN 02,M11-12StLA M37CinN	11-04-73	Pittsburgh, Pa.	11-03-60	R	R	5'8	170	24	21	.533	1	57	48	38	402	469	158	120	3	3.89
Wallace, Huck-Harry Clinton (Lefty)	12PhiN	07-27-82	Richmond, Ind.	07-06-51	L	L	5'6	160	0	0	—	0	4	0	0	5	7	4	4	0	0.00
Waller, Red-John Francis	09NYN	06-16-83	Washington, D.C.	02-09-15	R	R	6'	175	0	0	—	0	1	0	0	1	1	0	0	0	0.00
Walsh, Connie-Cornelius Robert	07PitN	04-23-82	St. Louis, Mo.	04-05-53	R				0	0	—	0	1	0	0	1	1	1	0	0	9.00
Walsh, Ed-Edward Augustine (Big Ed)	04-16ChiA 17BosN	05-14-81	Plains, Pa.	05-26-59	R	R	6'1	193	194	128	.602	40	430	315	250	2965	2346	617	1736	57	1.82
Warhop (Wauhop), Jack-John Milton (Chief, Crab)	08-15NYA	07-04-84	Hinton, W.Va.	10-04-60	R	R	5'9	168	69	91	.431	10	221	150	105	1423	1366	400	463	4	3.09
Warner, Ed-Edward Emory	12PitN	06-20-89	Fitchburg, Mass.	02-05-54	R	L	5'10	165	1	1	.500	0	11	3	1	45	40	18	13	1	3.60
Washer, Buck-William	05PhiN	10-11-82	Akron, Ohio	12-08-55	R	R	5'10	175	0	0	—	0	1	0	0	3	4	5	0	0	6.00
Watson, Doc-Charles John	13ChiN 14ChiF 14-15StLF	01-30-85	Carroll Co., Ohio	12-30-49	L	L	6'	180	22	21	.512	1	69	46	21	373	326	137	133	5	2.70
Watson, Milt-Milton Robert (Mule)	16-17StLN 18-19PhiN	01-10-90	Flovilla, Ga.	04-10-62	R	R	6'1	180	21	30	.412	0	90	48	19	424	435	139	113	5	3.57
Weaver, Harry-Harry Abraham	15-16PhiA 17-19CinN	02-26-92	Clarendon, Pa.	05-30-83	R	R	5'11	173	3	6	.333	1	19	8	4	82	82	31	21	2	3.62
Weaver, Orlie-Orville Forest (Buck)	10-11ChiN 11BosN	06-04-88	Newport, Tenn.	12-28-70	R	R	6'3	180	7	15	.318	0	40	22	7	197	203	116	92	1	5.03
Webb, Lefty-Cleon Earl	10PitN	03-01-85	Mt.Gilead, Ohio	01-12-58	B	L	5'11	165	2	1	.667	0	7	3	2	27	29	9	6	0	5.67
Weilman (Weilenmann), Carl-Carl Woolworth (Zeke)	12-17StLA 18IL 19-20StLA	11-29-89	Hamilton, Ohio	05-25-24	L	L	6'5	187	85	94	.475	9	240	179	105	1521	1394	418	536	15	2.67
Weimer, Jake-Jacob (Tornado Jake)	03-05CinN 06-08CinN 09NYN	11-29-73	Ottumwa, Iowa	06-17-28	L	L	5'11	175	97	69	.584	2	191	180	143	1473	1227	493	657	21	2.23
Welch, Ted-Floyd John	14StLF	06-13-88	Coyville, Kans.	01-07-43	R	R	5'9	160	0	0	—	0	3	0	0	6	6	3	2	0	6.00
West, Hi-James Hiram	05,11CleA	08-08-84	Roseville, Ill.	05-24-63	R	R	6'	185	4	6	.400	1	19	12	7	98	127	28	32	1	3.86
Weyhing, Gus-August	87-88PhiAA 90BknP 91PhiAA 92-95PhiN 95PitN 95-96LouN 97VR 98-99WasN 00StLN 00BknN 01CleA 01CinN	09-29-66	Louisville, Ky.	09-04-55	R	R	5'10	145	266	229	.537	4	538	503	448	4324	4562	1566	1665	28	3.89
Wheatley, Charlie-Charles D.	12DetA	06-27-93	Rosedale, Kans.	12-10-82	R	R	5'11	174	0	4	.000	0	5	5	2	35	45	17	14	0	6.17
White, Doc-Guy Harris (See B01-19)	01-02PhiN 03-13ChiA	04-09-79	Washington, D.C.	02-19-69	L	L	6'1	190	190	154	.552	8	427	362	262	3050	2743	670	1384	45	2.38
White, Kirby-Oliver Kirby (Redbuck)	09-10BosN 10-11PitN	01-03-84	Hillsboro, Ohio	04-22-43	L	R	6'	190	17	25	.405	2	58	44	21	330	294	168	102	4	3.25
White, Steve-Stephen Vincent	12WasA 12BosN	12-21-84	Dorchester, Mass.	01-29-75	R	R	5'10	190	0	0	—	0	7	11	5	3	0	5	14	0	5.14
Whitehouse, Charlie-Charles Evis (Lefty)	14IndF 15NwkF 19WasA	01-25-94	Charleston, Ill.	07-09-60	B	L	6'	152	4	3	.571	0	25	6	3	78	93	28	33	0	4.50
Whitehouse, Gil-Gilbert Arthur	15NwkF	10-15-93	Somerville, Mass.	02-14-26	B	R	5'10	170	0	0	—	0	1	0	0	1	0	1	0	0	0.00
Whiting, Jesse-Jesse Way	02PhiN 06-07BknN	05-30-79	Phieldphia, Pa.	10-28-37	R	R	5'10	155	1	2	.333	1	5	3	3	37	42	15	9	1	4.14
Whittaker, Doc-William Elton	16PhiA	06-11-94	Chelsea, Mass.	08-07-65	R	R	5'9	165	0	0	—	0	1	0	0	2	3	2	0	0	4.50
Wicker, Bob-Robert Kitridge	01-03StLN 03-06ChiN 06CinN	05-25-78	Bedford, Ind.	01-22-55	R	R	6'1	195	64	55	.538	1	138	117	97	1036	963	293	472	10	2.73
Wiggs, Jimmy-James Alvin (Big Jim)	03CinN 05-06DetA	11-20-63	Trondheim, Norway	01-20-63	R	R	6'4	200	4	5	.444	0	13	9	4	56	53	38	46	0	3.86
Wilhelm, Kaiser-Irvin Key	03PitN 04-05BosN 08-10BknN 14-15BalF 21,M21-22PhiN	01-26-74	Wooster, Ohio	05-22-36	R	R	6'	162	58	106	.354	1	216	158	118	1432	1495	418	444	12	3.44
Willett, Ed-Robert Edgar	06-13DetA 14-15StLF	03-07-84	Norfolk, Va.	05-10-34	R	R	6'	183	103	99	.510	6	274	203	138	1773	1719	565	600	12	3.08
Williams, Dave-David Owen	02BosA	02-07-81	Scranton, Pa.	04-25-18	R	L	5'11	167	0	0	—	0	19	22	11	7	0	5	21	0	5.21
Williams, Johnny-John Brodie (Honolulu Johnny)	14DetA	07-16-89	Honolulu, Hawaii	09-08-63	R	R	6'	180	0	3	.000	0	4	3	1	11	17	5	4	0	6.55
Williams, Lefty-Claud Preston	13-14DetA 16-20ChiA 20DL	03-09-93	Aurora, Mo.	11-04-59	R	L	5'9	160	81	47	.633	4	189	151	81	1186	1121	347	515	10	3.13
Williams, Marsh-Marshall McDiarmid (Cap)	16PhiA	02-21-93	Faison, N.C.	02-22-35	R	R	6'2	175	0	6	.000	0	10	4	3	51	71	31	17	0	7.94
Williams, Mutt-David Carter	13-14WasA	07-31-92	Ozark, Ark.	03-30-62	R	R	6'2	185	0	0	—	0	11	9	6	4	4	0	0	0	4.91
Williams, Pop-Walter Merrill	98WasN 02-03ChiN 03PhiN 03BosN	05-19-74	Bowdoinham, Me.	08-04-59	R	R	5'11	190	16	25	.390	0	46	46	40	377	418	113	127	2	3.20
Williams, Steamboat-Rees Gephardt	14,16StLN	06-29-79	Cascade, Mont.	06-29-72	L	R	5'11	170	6	8	.429	1	41	14	4	116	134	33	27	0	4.42
Willis, Joe-Joseph Denk	11StLA 11-13StLN	04-09-90	Coal Grove, Ohio	12-04-66	R	R	6'1	185	4	10	.286	3	41	20	5	161	173	80	66	0	4.61
Willis, Vic-Victor Gazaway (The Delaware Peach)	98-05BosN 06-09PitN 10StLN	04-12-76	Iron Hall, Md.	08-03-47	R	R	6'3	205	248	203	.550	13	513	471	388	3997	3621	1212	1652	50	2.63
Wilson, Fin-Finis Elbert	14-15KnF	12-09-88	East Fork, Ky.	03-09-59	L	L	6'1	185	1	9	.100	0	20	12	6	109	92	64	51	0	4.05
Wilson, George (See George Prentiss)																					
Wilson, Highball-Howard Paul	99CleN 02PhiA 03-04WasA	08-09-78	Philadelphia, Pa.	10-16-34	R	R	5'9	164	15	26	.366	0	47	42	37	371	417	71	86	1	3.30
Wilson, John-John Nicodemus (Lefty)	13WasA	06-15-90	Boonsboro, Md.	09-23-54	R	L	6'1	185	0	0	—	0	3	0	0	4	4	3	1	0	4.50
Wilson, Pete-Alec Peter	08-09NYA	10-09-84	Springfield, Mass.	06-05-57	L		5'10	150	8	9	.471	2	20	19	11	133	109	76	72	2	3.25
Wilson, Willy-Howard William	06WasA	10-28-85	Columbus, Ohio	10-28-21	R	R			0	1	.000	0	1	1	1	7	3	2	1	0	2.57
Wiltse, Hooks-George LeRoy	04-14NYN 15BknF	09-07-79	Hamilton, N.Y.	01-21-59	R	L	6'	185	138	90	.605	34	357	226	154	2111	1892	498	965	27	2.47
Wiltse, Snake-George DeWitt	01PitN 01-02PhiA 02BalA 03NYA	12-05-71	Bouckville, N.Y.	08-25-28	R	L			30	29	.508	2	68	62	54	537	674	146	121	2	4.59
Winchell (Cook), Fred-Frederick Russell	09ClaA	01-23-82	Arlington, Mass.	08-08-58	R		5'8		0	3	.000	1	4	3	0	14	16	2	7	0	6.43
Winham, Lafe-Lafayette Sharkey	02BknN 03PitN	10-23-81	Brooklyn, N.Y.	09-12-51	L	L	5'11	200	3	1	.750	0	6	4	3	39	37	23	23	1	2.08
Winter, George-George Lovington (Sassafras)	01-08BosA 08DetA	04-27-78	New Providence, Pa.	05-26-51	R	R	5'8	155	80	100	.444	7	220	181	146	1656	1552	377	568	9	2.87
Witherup, Roy-Foster LeRoy	06BosN 08-09WasA	07-26-86	N. Washington, Pa.	12-23-41	R	R	6'	185	3	12	.250	0	26	17	12	162	189	47	71	0	4.44
Wolf, Ernie-Ernest Adolf	12CleA	02-02-89	Newark, N.J.	05-23-64	R	R	5'11	174	0	0	—	0	6	8	4	1	9	6	0	0	6.00
Wolfe, Barney-Wilbert Otto	03-04NYA 04-06WasA	01-09-76	Allentown, Pa.	02-27-53	R	R	6'1		21	36	.368	2	76	62	46	510	484	99	160	4	2.96
Wolff, Bill-William Franklyn	02PhiN	01-14-76	Pa.	Deceased			5'9		0	1	.000	0	1	1	1	9	11	4	3	0	4.00
Wolfgang, Mellie-Meldon John (Red)	14-18ChiA	03-20-90	Albany, N.Y.	06-30-47	R	R	5'9	160	15	14	.517	3	77	27	15	326	268	95	111	3	2.18
Wolter, Harry-Harry Meiggs (See B01-19)	07PitN 07StLN 09BosA	07-11-84	Monterey, Cal.	07-07-70	L	L	5'10	175	4	5	.444	1	14	9	1	78	83	48	28	0	4.04
Wood, Smoky Joe-Howard Ellsworth (See B01-19)	08-15BosA 16HO 17,19-20CleA	07-25-85	Kansas City, Mo.	07-27-85	R	R	5'11	180	115	57	.669	18	225	158	121	1436	1138	421	989	28	2.03
Woodburn, Gene-Eugene Stewart	11-12StLN	08-20-86	Bellaire, Ohio	01-18-61	R	R	6'	175	2	9	.182	0	31	11	2	86	82	82	48	0	5.55
Woodman, Dan-Daniel Courtney (Cocoa)	14-15BufF	07-08-93	Danvers, Mass.	12-14-62	R	R	5'8	160	0	0	—	0	18	1	0	49	44	20	14	0	2.94
Woods, Clarence-Clarence Cofield	14IndF	01-06-87	Ohio Co., Ind.	07-02-69	R	R	6'5	230	0	0	—	0	2	0	0	2	1	2	1	0	4.50
Woodward, Frank-Frank Russell	18-19PhiN 19StLN 21-22WasA 23ChiA	05-17-94	New Haven, Conn.	06-11-61	R	R	5'10	175	9	15	.375	1	42	21	8	194	199	74	55	0	4.22
Worden, Fred-Frederick Bamford	14PhiA	09-04-94	St. Louis, Mo.	11-09-41	R	R			0	0	—	0	1	0	0	2	8	0	1	0	18.00
Works, Ralph-Ralph Talmadge (Judge, Big Fellow)	09-12DetA 12-13CinN	03-16-88	Payson, Ill.	08-10-41	R	R	6'2	185	23	24	.489	6	99	48	28	499	512	202	208	4	3.79
Wright, Bob-Robert Cassius	15ChiN	12-13-91	Greensburg, Ind.	07-30-93	R	R	6'1	175	0	0	—	0	2	0	0	4	6	0	3	0	2.25
Wright, Gene-Clarence Eugene (Big Gene)	01BknN 02-03CleA 03-04StLA	12-11-78	Cleveland, Ohio	10-29-30	R	R	6'2	190	13	22	.371	0	46	40	31	324	361	152	140	2	4.50
Wright, Lucky-William Simmons (William the Red, Deacon)	09CleA	02-21-80	Waterville, Ohio	07-07-41	R	R	6'	180	0	5	.000	0	5	4	3	20	8	6	0	3.91
Wyckoff, Weldon-John Weldon	13-16PhiA 16-18BosA	02-19-92	Williamsport, Pa.	05-08-61	R	R	5'11	175	23	35	.397	4	109	63	35	574	494	357	299	1	3.55
Yeager, Joe-Joseph Francis (Little Joe) (See B01-19)	98-00BknN 01-03DetA	08-28-75	Philadelphia, Pa.	07-02-37	R	R	5'10	160	35	48	.422	3	94	80	73	705	805	188	145	3	3.74
Yerkes, Stan-Stanley Lewis (Yank)	01BalA 01-03StLN	11-28-74	Cheltenham, Pa.	07-28-40	R	R	5'10	165	15	24	.385	0	45	43	32	320	396	87	103	1	3.66
Yingling, Earl-Earl Hershey (Chink)	11CleA 12-13BknN 14CinN 18WasA	10-29-88	Chillicothe, Ohio	10-02-62	L	L	5'11	180	25	35	.417	0	94	61	31	568	611	141	192	5	3.22
Young, Charlie-Charles	15BalF	01-12-93	Philadelphia, Pa.	05-12-52	R	R	5'10	165	2	3	.400	0	9	5	1	35	39	21	13	0	5.91
Young, Cy-Denton True	90-98CleN 99-00StLN 01-08,M07BosA 09-11CleA 11BosN	03-29-67	Gilmore, Ohio	11-04-55	R	R	6'2	210	511	315	.619	18	906	816	750	7357	7092	1217	2803	77	2.63
Young, Harlan-Harlan Edward (Cy the Third)	08PitN 08BosN	08-28-83	Portland, Ind.	03-26-75	R	R	6'2	190	0	3	.000	0	14	5	1	76	69	14	29	0	2.61
Young, Irv-Irving Melrose (Young Cy, Cy the Second)	05-08BosN 08PitN 10-11ChiA	07-21-77	Columbia Falls, Me.	01-14-35	L	L	5'10	180	63	94	.401	4	209	161	119	1385	1361	316	560	20	3.11
Yount, Ducky-Herbert Macon (Hub)	14BalF	12-07-85	Newton, N.C.	05-07-70	R	R	6'5	190	1	1	.500	0	13	1	1	41	44	19	19	0	4.17
Zabel, Zip-George Washington	13-15ChiN	02-18-91	Wetmore, Kans.	05-31-70	R	R	5'11	185	12	14	.462	3	66	25	10	296	231	130	110	3	2.71
Zackert, George-George Carl (Zeke)	11-12StLN	12-24-84	Horton, Vt.	02-18-77	L	L	6'	177	0	2	.000	0	8	3	1	19	7	6	6	0	12.38
Zamloch, Carl-Carl Eugene	13DetA	10-06-89	Oakland, Cal.	08-19-63	R	R	6'1	176	1	6	.143	1	17	5	3	70	66	23	28	0	2.44
Zeiser, Matt-Mathias John	14BosA	09-25-88	Chicago, Ill.	06-10-42	R	R	5'10	170	0	0	—	0	2	0	0	10	9	8	0	0	1.80
Zmich, Ed-Edward Albert (Ike)	10-11StLN	10-01-84	Cleveland, Ohio	08-20-50	L	L	6'	180	1	5	.167	0	13	6	2	49	46	37	23	0	5.14

1920-1945
Then There Was Ruth, the Yankees, and the Things You Could Count On

The era of baseball marked by the greatest stability the game has ever known, was ushered in by the ouster of eight Chicago White Sox players. Their exile from the diamonds of professional baseball came as a result of their throwing the 1919 World Series to the Cincinnati Reds. The man responsible for the punishment was Judge Kennesaw Mountain Landis, baseball's first commissioner.

Landis was appointed in 1920, the year the scandal broke. Although his stern actions helped restore the public's confidence, it served only half a measure in preserving the good name of the sport. What the public needed most was a hero of fantasy proportions-a knight who could enter the hallowed grounds of major league baseball and destroy the evil with one stab of his mighty lance, someone to cleanse the tarnished name while setting the turnstiles into a frenzied motion. But a knight did not come. Instead, it was a king. They dubbed him the Sultan of Swat and he honored the sobriquet by belting home runs at an unprecedented clip.

The Sultan, the Bambino, the Babe, was George Herman Ruth, who came from the Boston Red Sox to the New York Yankees in 1920 for the tidy sum of $125,000. Ruth's life style and power not only renewed the public's enthusiasm, but set an entirely new strategy in motion. Aided by a livelier ball, Ruth hit 54 home runs during his first season in New York, an unthinkable amount when compared to the 29 he poled the year before, which had then set the all-time single season's mark.

Along with Ruth came the New York Yankees, who had lingered in the depths of the second division for most of their existence in the American League. It wasn't until 1921 that they collected their first pennant in the beginning of what was to be the most successful dynasty in baseball history. Yet beyond the Yankees and Ruth himself, was the influence of the home run ball. Its affects produced a profound change in the style of the game. The emphasis, especially in the American League where power hitters abounded, moved away from bunting and stealing, mostly because of such men as Lou Gehrig, Joe DiMaggio, Hank Greenberg, Jimmie Foxx, Al Simmons, and Ted Williams, a marvelous collection of super heroes who accounted for over 2500 home runs.

The advent of power hitting did more than alter the face of the game. With its coming was the imbalance that is inevitable with such a drastic change. Those who paid the heaviest price were baseball's minority breed, the pitcher. Once a feared and revered figure, he became the object of many a cannon blast. At the same time as baseball had cleansed its ranks of those who soiled the good name of the game, it also saw fit to sanitize the batter-pitcher relationship. The spitball, the most famous of all trick pitches,

was abolished in 1920, although a few pitchers were still allowed to use it. To further complicate the pitcher's life, new balls were introduced into play sooner to give the batter an advantage he had never enjoyed. Following these demoralizing blows to the mound corps came the new stadiums, built between 1909 and 1923 in such places as Detroit, St. Louis, Brooklyn, and New York. All of these stadiums were enclosed with distances to tempt the most mediocre of power hitters.

The combination of the livelier ball and easier home run barriers gave the pitcher an entirely different set of strategies. Instead of finding all batters choking up and waiting to punch the ball where they could, the pitcher was faced with some players starting to swing up and go for the long ball, as well as trying to pull nearly everything that was offered across the plate. To say the least, it was not a happy time for those trying to eke out a living atop a mound of dirt. To add insult to injury, men such as Dale Alexander and Zeke Bonura, who would have been denied entrance to the major leagues during earlier days, suddenly found themselves in major league uniforms because of their ability to merely hit a baseball.

With the pitcher reduced to a more subdued role and the sudden infusion of power, baseball emerged into the more rampant pace of the twentieth century. More accurately, it joined the exaggerated motion of the Roaring Twenties. As baseball began churning out its greatest stars, attendance swelled and salaries began to spiral to add to the growing aura of the sport, while at the same time lifting the average ballplayer to first class citizenry. Of course, no one equaled the money which Ruth earned. In his heyday he made $80,000 a season-a staggering amount considering low taxes and depression. But while Ruth's salary symbolized the emergence of the Yankees as a structure of power and money, it by no means typified the economics of the times. The chemistry of Ruth and the Yankees was simply that perfect mixture which nature seems to produce once in every century.

Although not as dramatic and as sudden in coming as Ruth, was another occurrence that was to have a more lasting effect on the game of baseball. In the 1920's, Branch Rickey, general manager of the St. Louis Cardinals, established a string of farm clubs where young and inexpensively signed St. Louis talent could be nurtured. Rickey, in effect, had created St. Louis' own minor league system, and it was successful enough to not only produce Stan Musial, one of the greatest players the National League was to ever have, but also to give the Cardinals a dynasty that was nearly as successful as the Yankees. Rickey later made the same contribution to the Brooklyn Dodgers-an influence that soon changed the way all ball clubs acquired most of their new players.

123

1920 Here Come De Judge

The cheers and heroics of the 1920 season were overshadowed by the sordid and the tragic, and off-the-field developments elicited more interest from the public than did the actual playing; indeed, courtroom revelations made it debatable whether baseball contests deserved any serious following at all. Rumors had drifted about since the past autumn that some members of the Chicago White Sox had been bought by gamblers to throw the 1919 World Series and in September a Chicago grand jury hung baseball's dirty laundry out for an airing. Confessions from Ed Cicotte and Joe Jackson confirmed that Cicotte, Jackson, Lefty Williams, Chick Gandil, Swede Risberg, Fred McMullin, and Happy Felsch had, indeed, agreed to dump the Series in return for $100,000 from New York gambling interests, of which only $20,000 was delivered and that Buck Weaver had, at least, concealed his knowledge of the fix. The shock wave hit the National Pastime with many repercussions. The most immediate result was the suspension of the soiled Sox by Chicago owner Charles Comiskey, thus ruining his club's pennant chances for 1920 in a close title race with the Cleveland Indians. Another revelation stemming from the grand jury was that three National League players, Hal Chase, Heinie Zimmerman, and Lee Magee, had been unofficially barred after the 1919 season, without publicity, for throwing games; indeed, Chase was exposed as a go-between in the Series fix.

A less immediate result of the scandal was the reorganization of baseball's government. The office of Commissioner was created and Judge Kenesaw M. Landis of Chicago was appointed to fill it at a salary of $42.500 yearly. To take the position, Landis demanded and received strong discretionary powers. He proved uncompromising and despotic, but provided a stern paternal image for the game.

Tragedy descended onto the ball field August 16, at the Polo Grounds in New York. Yankee pitcher Carl Mays had a reputation for brushing batters back, but a fast ball that eluded him skulled Cleveland's Ray Chapman, leaving him a limp figure in the dust. Without regaining consciousness, Chapman died the next day—the first and only fatality of major league baseball.

Cleveland's morale sunk to zero after shortstop Chapman's death, but Manager Tris Speaker proved magnificent at rallying his men together. A close fight with the White Sox and Yankees was won in September by the Indians when shortstop Joe Sewell and pitcher Walter "Duster" Mails were recalled and chipped in with key performances. The Sox stayed close all year, despite dissension between "honest" and "crooked" players, and

might have won it again, to the embarrassment of all baseball, had not stars Jackson, Weaver, Felsch, Cicotte, and Williams been exposed by the grand jury and thrown off the team with only two weeks remaining in the season.

The disgrace of the Black Sox scandal was softened by the unprecedented power of Babe Ruth's bat, aided by a much livelier ball. In 1919, the New York Yankees shelled out $177,500 to the money-poor Red Sox for Ruth and Carl Mays—obtaining Mays during that season and Ruth in the winter. Mays, despite the Chapman tragedy, led New York pitchers in 1920 with 26 wins, while Ruth, now a full-time outfielder, found the Polo Grounds cozy enough to clout 54 round-trippers, an outrageous total that surpassed any one team's total output—setting a homer record which few expected ever to be equaled. But the new infusion of talent could not better the Yankees' third-place 1919 finish. Their one consolation was a closer pennant loss and the optimism that they would dominate the future.

Bothered by a bad knee, Ty Cobb gave up his batting title to young George Sisler of St. Louis. Prophetically though, Cobb's remaining nine years, which would be good enough to be desired by any ball player, would never again produce a batting title.

Brooklyn won the National League pennant behind good pitching aced by spitballer Burleigh Grimes. Wilbert Robinson's Dodgers beat out the Giants by seven games for the top spot, but dropped the Series to the Indians in another five-of-nine classic. Cleveland needed only seven games to claim the crown.

Led by Stan Coveleski's three route-going victory pitching performances, Bill Wambsganss' unassisted triple play—the only one in Series history, and Elmer Smith's grand slam—the first in Series history, the door on baseball's greatest season of extremes was finally closed.

1920 AMERICAN LEAGUE

NAME	G by Pos	B	AGE	G	AB	R	H	2B	3B	HR	RBI	BB	SO	SB	BA	SA
CLEVELAND 1st 98-56 .636				TRIS SPEAKER												
TOTALS			29	154	5196	857	1574	300	95	35	758	576	379	73	.303	.417
Doc Johnston	1B147	L	32	147	535	68	156	24	10	2	71	28	32	13	.292	.385
Bill Wambsganss	2B153	R	26	153	565	83	138	16	11	1	55	54	26	9	.244	.317
Ray Chapman (KB)	SS111	R	29	111	435	97	132	27	8	3	49	52	38	13	.303	.423
Larry Gardner	3B154	L	34	154	597	72	185	31	11	3	118	53	25	3	.310	.414
Elmer Smith	OF129	L	27	129	456	82	144	37	10	12	103	53	35	6	.316	.520
Tris Speaker	OF149	L	32	150	552	137	214	50	11	8	107	97	13	10	.388	.562
Charlie Jamieson	OF98, 1B4	L	27	108	370	69	118	17	7	1	40	41	26	2	.319	.411
Steve O'Neill	C148	R	28	149	489	63	157	39	5	3	55	69	39	3	.321	.440
Jack Graney	OF47	L	34	62	152	31	45	11	1	0	13	27	21	4	.296	.382
Smoky Joe Wood	OF54, P1	R	30	61	137	25	37	11	2	1	30	25	16	1	.270	.401
Joe Evans	OF43, SS6	R	25	56	172	32	60	9	9	0	23	15	3	6	.349	.506
2 George Burns	1B12	R	27	44	56	7	15	4	1	0	13	4	3	1	.268	.375
Les Nunamaker	C17, 1B6	R	31	34	54	10	18	3	3	0	14	4	5	1	.333	.500
Harry Lunte	SS21, 2B3	R	27	23	71	6	14	0	0	0	1	5	6	0	.197	.197
Joe Sewell	SS22	L	21	22	70	14	23	4	1	0	12	9	4	1	.329	.414
Pinch Thomas	C7	L	32	9	9	2	3	1	0	0	0	3	1	0	.333	.444
Joe Harris (DO) 29																

NAME	T	AGE	W	L	PCT	SV	G	GS	CG	IP	H	BB	SO	SHO	ERA
		28	98	56	.636	7	154	154	93	1376	1448	401	466	10	3.41
Jim Bagby	R	30	31	12	.721	0	48	39	30	340	338	79	73	3	2.89
Stan Coveleski	R	30	24	14	.632	2	41	37	26	315	284	65	133	3	2.48
Ray Caldwell	R	32	20	10	.667	0	34	33	20	238	286	63	80	0	3.86
Guy Morton	R	27	8	6	.571	1	29	17	5	137	140	57	72	1	4.47
Duster Mails	L	25	7	0	1.000	0	9	8	6	63	54	18	25	2	1.85
George Uhle	R	21	4	5	.444	1	27	6	2	85	98	29	27	0	5.19
1 Elmer Myers	R	26	2	4	.333	1	16	7	2	71	93	23	16	0	4.82
Dick Niehaus	L	27	1	2	.333	2	19	3	0	40	42	16	12	0	3.60
Bob Clark	R	22	1	2	.333	0	11	2	2	42	59	13	8	1	3.43
Joe Boehling	L	29	0	1	.000	0	3	2	0	13	16	10	4	0	4.85
Tony Faeth	R	26	0	0	—	0	13	0	0	25	31	20	14	0	4.32
Tim Murchison	L	23	0	0	—	0	2	0	0	5	3	4	0	0	0.00
Goerge Ellison	R	23	0	0	—	0	1	0	0	1	0	2	1	0	0.00
Smoky Joe Wood	R	30	0	0	—	0	1	1	0	2	4	2	1	0	22.50

NAME	G by Pos	B	AGE	G	AB	R	H	2B	3B	HR	RBI	BB	SO	SB	BA	SA
CHICAGO 2nd 96-58 .623 2				KID GLEASON												
TOTALS			29	154	5330	794	1569	267	94	37	702	473	355	111	.294	.401
Shano Collins	1B117, OF12	R	34	133	495	70	150	21	10	1	63	23	24	12	.303	.392
Eddie Collins	2B153	L	33	153	602	117	224	38	13	3	76	69	19	19	.372	.493
Swede Risberg (DL)	SS124	R	25	126	458	53	122	21	10	2	65	31	45	12	.266	.369
Buck Weaver (DL)	3B126, SS25	B	29	151	629	102	208	34	8	2	74	28	23	19	.331	.420
Nemo Leibold (BH)	OF108	L	28	108	413	61	91	16	3	1	28	55	30	7	.220	.281
Happy Felsch (DL)	OF142	R	28	142	556	88	188	40	15	14	115	37	25	8	.338	.540
Joe Jackson (DL)	OF145	L	30	146	570	105	218	42	20	12	121	56	14	9	.382	.589
Ray Schalk	C151	R	27	151	485	64	131	25	5	1	61	68	19	10	.270	.348
Eddie Murphy	OF19, 3B3	L	28	58	118	22	40	2	1	0	19	12	4	1	.339	.373
2 Amos Strunk	OF49	L	31	51	183	32	42	7	1	1	14	28	15	1	.230	.295
Ted Jourdan	1B40	L	24	48	150	16	36	6	1	0	8	17	17	3	.240	.293
Fred McMullin (DL)	3B29, 2B3, SS1	R	28	46	127	14	25	1	4	0	13	9	13	1	.197	.268
Byrd Lynn	C14	R	31	16	25	0	8	2	1	0	3	1	3	0	.320	.480
Harvey McClellan	SS4, 3B2	R	25	10	18	4	6	1	1	0	5	4	1	2	.333	.500
Bibb Falk	OF4	L	21	7	17	1	5	1	1	0	2	0	5	0	.294	.471
Bubber Jonnard	C1	R	22	2	1	0	0	0	0	0	0	0	0	1	.000	.000
Chick Gandil (HO-DL) 32																

NAME	T	AGE	W	L	PCT	SV	G	GS	CG	IP	H	BB	SO	SHO	ERA
		29	96	58	.632	10	154	154	112	1386	1467	405	438	8	3.59
Red Faber	R	31	23	13	.639	1	40	39	28	319	332	88	108	1	2.99
Lefty Williams (DL)	L	27	22	14	.611	0	39	38	26	299	302	90	128	0	3.91
Dickie Kerr	L	26	21	9	.700	5	45	27	20	254	266	72	72	3	3.37
Eddie Cicotte (DL)	R	36	21	10	.677	2	37	35	28	303	316	74	87	4	3.27
Roy Wilkinson	R	27	7	9	.437	2	34	12	9	145	162	48	30	0	4.03
George Payne	R	31	1	1	.500	0	12	0	0	30	39	9	7	0	5.40
Shovel Hodge	R	26	1	1	.500	0	4	2	1	20	15	12	5	0	2.25
Joe Kiefer	R	20	0	1	.000	0	2	1	0	5	7	5	1	0	14.40
Spencer Heath	R	26	0	0	—	0	4	0	0	7	19	2	0	0	15.43
Grover Lowdermilk	R	35	0	0	—	0	1	0	0	5	9	5	0	0	7.20

NAME	G by Pos	B	AGE	G	AB	R	H	2B	3B	HR	RBI	BB	SO	SB	BA	SA
NEW YORK 3rd 95-59 .617 3				MILLER HUGGINS												
TOTALS			28	154	5176	838	1448	268	71	115	747	539	626	64	.280	.426
Wally Pipp	1B153	L	27	153	610	109	171	30	14	11	76	48	54	4	.280	.430
Del Pratt	2B154	R	32	154	574	84	180	37	8	4	97	50	24	12	.314	.427
Roger Peckinpaugh	SS137	R	29	139	534	109	144	26	6	8	54	72	47	8	.270	.386
Aaron Ward	3B114, SS12	R	23	127	496	62	127	18	7	11	54	33	84	7	.256	.387
Babe Ruth	OF139, 1B2, P1	L	25	142	458	158	172	36	9	54	137	150	80	14	.376	.847
Ping Bodie	OF129	R	32	129	471	63	139	26	12	7	79	40	30	6	.295	.446
Duffy Lewis (KJ)	OF99	R	31	107	365	34	99	14	1	4	61	24	32	2	.271	.332
Muddy Ruel	C80	R	24	82	261	30	70	14	1	1	15	15	18	4	.268	.341
Bob Meusel	OF64, 3B45, 1B2	R	23	119	460	75	151	40	7	11	83	20	72	4	.328	.517
Truck Hannah	C78	R	31	79	259	24	64	11	1	2	25	24	35	2	.247	.320
Sammy Vick	OF33	R	25	51	118	21	26	7	1	0	11	14	20	1	.220	.297
Frank Gleich	OF15	L	26	24	41	6	5	0	0	0	3	6	10	0	.122	.122
Chick Fewster	SS5, 2B2	R	24	21	61	8	6	1	0	0	1	7	2	0	.286	.333
Fred Hofmann	C14	R	26	15	24	3	7	0	0	0	5	3	2	0	.292	.292
Joe Lucey	2B1, SS1	R	23	3	4	0	0	0	0	0	0	0	0	0	.000	.000
Ray French	SS1	R	25	2	5	0	0	0	0	0	0	0	2	0	.000	.000
Tom Connelly		L	21	1	1	0	0	0	0	0	0	0	0	0	.000	.000
Frank Baker (VR) 34																

NAME	T	AGE	W	L	PCT	SV	G	GS	CG	IP	H	BB	SO	SHO	ERA
		28	95	59	.617	11	154	154	88	1368	1414	420	480	16	3.31
Carl Mays	R	28	26	11	.703	2	45	37	26	312	310	84	92	6	3.06
Bob Shawkey	R	29	20	13	.606	2	38	31	20	268	246	85	126	5	2.45
Jack Quinn	R	36	18	10	.643	3	41	31	16	253	271	48	101	2	3.20
Rip Collins	R	24	14	8	.636	1	36	20	12	187	171	79	66	3	3.18
Hank Thormahlen	L	23	9	6	.600	1	29	14	5	143	178	43	35	0	4.16
George Mogridge	L	31	5	9	.357	1	26	15	7	125	146	36	35	0	4.32
Ernie Shore	R	29	2	2	.500	1	14	5	2	44	61	21	12	0	4.90
Babe Ruth	L	25	1	0	1.000	0	1	1	0	4	3	2	0	0	4.50
Bob McGraw	R	25	0	0	—	0	15	0	0	27	24	20	11	0	4.67
Lefty O'Doul	L	23	0	0	—	0	2	0	0	4	4	2	1	0	4.50

ST. LOUIS — 4th 76-77 .497 21.5 — JIMMY BURKE

NAME	G by Pos	B	AGE	G	AB	R	H	2B	3B	HR	RBI	BB	SO	SB	BA	SA
TOTALS			29	154	5358	797	1651	279	83	50	708	427	339	120	.308	.419
George Sisler	1B154, P1	L	27	154	631	137	257	49	18	19	122	46	19	42	.407	.632
Joe Gedeon	2B153	R	26	153	606	95	177	33	6	0	61	55	36	1	.292	.366
Wally Gerber	SS154	R	28	154	584	70	163	26	2	3	60	58	32	4	.279	.341
Jimmy Austin	3B75	B	40	83	280	38	76	11	3	1	32	31	15	2	.271	.343
Jack Tobin	OF147	L	26	147	593	94	202	34	10	4	62	39	23	21	.341	.452
Baby Doll Jacobson	OF154, 1B1	R	29	154	609	97	216	34	14	9	122	46	37	11	.355	.501
Ken Williams	OF138	L	30	141	521	90	160	34	13	10	72	41	26	18	.307	.477
Hank Severeid	C117	R	29	123	422	46	117	14	5	2	49	33	11	5	.277	.348
Earl Smith	3B70, OF15	B	29	103	353	45	108	21	8	3	55	13	18	11	.306	.436
Josh Billings	C40	R	28	66	155	19	43	5	2	0	11	11	10	1	.277	.335
Pat Collins	C7	R	23	23	28	5	6	1	0	0	6	3	5	0	.214	.250
Frank Thompson	3B14, 2B2	R	24	22	53	7	9	0	0	0	5	13	10	1	.170	.170
Lyman Lamb	OF7	R	25	9	24	4	9	2	0	1	4	0	7	2	.375	.458
John Shovlin	SS5	R	29	7	7	2	2	0	0	0	0	0	0	0	.286	.286
Dutch Wetzel	OF5	R	26	6	19	5	9	1	1	0	5	4	1	0	.474	.632
Billy Mullen	SS1	R	23	1	1	0	0	0	0	0	0	0	0	0	.000	.000
Dud Lee	SS1		20	1	2	2	2	0	0	0	1	0	0	1	1.000	1.000

Johnnie Heving 24 R 0-1, Marty McManus 20 R 1-3, Earl Pruess 25 R 0-0, Paul Speraw 26 R 0-2

NAME	T	AGE	W	L	PCT	SV	G	GS	CG	IP	H	BB	SO	SHO	ERA
		26	76	77	.497	14	154	154	84	1379	1481	578	444	9	4.03
Urban Shocker	R	29	20	10	.667	5	38	28	22	246	224	70	107	5	2.71
Dixie Davis	R	29	18	12	.600	0	38	31	22	269	250	149	85	0	3.18
Carl Weilman	L	30	9	13	.409	2	30	24	13	183	201	61	45	1	4.47
Allan Sothoron	R	27	8	15	.348	2	36	26	12	218	263	89	81	1	4.71
Bill Burwell	R	25	6	4	.600	4	33	2	0	113	133	42	30	0	3.66
Bill Bayne	L	21	5	6	.455	0	18	13	6	100	102	41	38	1	3.69
Elan Vangilder	R	24	3	8	.273	0	24	13	4	105	131	40	25	0	5.49
Adrian Lynch	R	23	2	0	1.000	0	5	3	1	22	23	17	8	0	4.91
Ray Richmond	R	24	2	0	1.000	0	17	1	0	18	19	9	4	0	6.35
Joe DeBerry	R	23	2	4	.333	0	10	7	3	55	65	20	12	1	4.90
Roy Sanders	R	28	1	1	.500	0	8	1	0	17	17	7	2	0	5.29
George Boehler	R	28	1	1	.000	0	3	1	0	7	10	4	2	0	7.71
1 Bert Gallia	R	28	0	1	.000	0	2	1	0	4	8	3	0	0	5.40
Hod Leverette	R	31	0	2	.000	0	3	2	0	10	9	12	0	0	5.40
Lefty Leifield	L	36	0	0	---	0	4	0	0	17	13	3	0	0	7.00
Jack Scheneberg	R	32	0	0	---	0	1	0	0	2	7	1	0	0	27.00
Goerge Sisler	L	27	0	0	---	0	1	0	0	1	0	1	2	0	0.00

BOSTON — 5th 72-81 .471 25.5 — ED BARROW

NAME	G by Pos	B	AGE	G	AB	R	H	2B	3B	HR	RBI	BB	SO	SB	BA	SA
TOTALS			28	154	5199	650	1397	216	71	22	575	533	429	98	.269	.350
Stuffy McInnis	1B148	R	29	148	559	50	166	21	3	2	71	18	19	6	.297	.356
Mike McNally	2B76, SS8, 1B6	R	26	93	312	42	80	5	1	0	23	31	24	13	.256	.279
Everett Scott	SS154	R	27	154	569	41	153	21	12	4	61	21	15	4	.269	.369
Eddie Foster	3B88, 2B21	R	33	117	386	48	100	17	6	0	41	42	17	10	.259	.334
Mike Menosky	OF141	L	25	141	532	80	158	24	9	3	64	65	52	23	.297	.393
Jim Hendryx	OF98	R	29	99	363	54	119	21	5	0	73	42	27	7	.328	.413
Harry Hooper	OF139	L	32	139	536	91	167	30	17	7	53	88	27	16	.312	.470
Roxy Walters	C85, 1B2	R	27	88	258	25	51	11	1	0	28	30	21	2	.198	.248
Wally Schang	C73, OF40	B	30	122	387	58	118	30	7	4	51	64	37	7	.305	.450
Ossie Vitt	3B64, 2B21	R	30	87	296	50	65	10	4	1	28	43	10	5	.220	.291
Benn Karr	P26	L	26	57	75	8	21	5	0	1	15	6	18	0	.280	.387
Cliff Brady	2B53	R	23	53	180	16	41	5	1	0	12	13	12	2	.228	.267
2 Gene Bailey	OF40	L	26	46	135	14	31	2	0	0	5	9	15	2	.230	.244
Hack Eibel	OF5, P3, 1B1	L	26	29	43	4	8	2	0	0	6	3	6	1	.186	.233
Hob Hiller	3B6. SS5. 2B2. OF1	R	27	17	29	4	5	1	1	0	2	5	7	0	.172	.276
Ben Paschal	OF7	R	24	9	29	5	10	0	0	0	5	5	2	1	.357	.357
Mickey Devine	C5	R	28	8	12	1	2	0	0	0	0	0	1	2	.167	.167
Bert Chaplin	C2	L	24	6	5	2	1	1	0	0	1	4	0	0	.200	.400
Herb Hunter	OF4	R	24	4	12	1	1	0	0	0	0	0	1	1	.083	.083
George Orme	OF3	R	28	4	3	1	1	0	0	0	0	0	0	0	.333	.333

Paddy Smith 26 L 0-2, 2 Jigger Statz 22 R 0-3, Ray Grimes 26 R 1-4, Dick Hoblitzell (MS) 31

NAME	T	AGE	W	L	PCT	SV	G	GS	CG	IP	H	BB	SO	SHO	ERA
		25	72	81	.471	6	154	154	91	1395	1481	461	481	11	3.83
Herb Pennock	L	26	16	13	.552	2	37	31	19	242	244	61	68	4	3.68
Bullet Joe Bush	R	27	15	15	.500	1	35	32	18	244	287	94	88	0	4.24
Sad Sam Jones	R	27	13	16	.448	0	37	33	20	274	302	79	86	3	3.94
2 Elmer Myers	R	26	9	1	.900	0	12	10	9	97	90	24	34	1	2.13
Waite Hoyt	R	20	6	6	.500	1	22	11	6	121	123	47	45	2	4.39
Allen Russell	R	26	5	6	.455	1	16	10	7	108	100	38	53	0	3.00
Harry Harper	L	25	5	14	.263	0	27	22	11	163	163	66	71	1	3.03
Benn Karr	R	26	3	8	.273	1	26	2	0	92	109	24	21	0	4.80
Gary Fourtune	R	25	0	2	.000	0	14	3	1	42	46	23	10	0	5.79
Hack Eibel	L	26	0	0	---	0	3	0	0	10	10	3	5	0	3.60
Hal Deviney	R	29	0	0	---	0	1	1	0	3	7	2	0	0	15.00

WASHINGTON — 6th 68-84 .447 29 — CLARK GRIFFITH

NAME	G by Pos	B	AGE	G	AB	R	H	2B	3B	HR	RBI	BB	SO	SB	BA	SA
TOTALS			27	153	5251	723	1526	233	81	36	620	433	543	161	.291	.386
Joe Judge	1B124	R	26	124	493	103	164	19	15	5	51	65	34	12	.333	.462
Bucky Harris	2B135	R	23	137	506	76	152	26	4	1	68	41	36	16	.300	.381
Jim O'Neill	SS80, 2B2	R	27	86	294	27	85	17	7	1	40	13	30	7	.289	.405
Frank Ellerbe	3B75, SS19, OF1	R	24	101	336	38	98	14	2	0	36	19	23	5	.292	.345
Braggo Roth	OF128	R	27	138	468	80	136	23	8	9	92	75	57	24	.291	.432
Sam Rice	OF153	L	30	153	624	83	211	29	9	3	80	39	23	63	.338	.428
Clyde Milan	OF123	L	34	126	506	70	163	22	5	3	41	28	12	10	.322	.403
Patsy Gharrity	C120, 1B7, OF1	R	28	131	428	51	105	18	3	3	44	37	52	6	.245	.350
H. Shanks	3B63, OF35, 1B14, 2B5, SS1	R	29	128	444	56	119	16	7	4	37	29	43	11	.268	.363
1 Red Shannon	SS31, 2B16, 3B15	B	23	62	222	30	64	8	7	0	30	22	32	2	.288	.387
Val Picinich	C45	R	23	48	133	14	27	6	2	3	14	9	33	0	.203	.346
Frank Brower	OF20, 1B9, 3B1	L	27	36	119	21	37	7	2	1	13	9	11	1	.311	.429
Jack Calvo	OF10	L	36	17	23	5	1	0	1	0	2	2	2	0	.043	.130
Ricardo Torres	1B7, C5	R	27	16	30	8	10	1	0	0	3	1	4	0	.333	.367
Frank O'Rourke	SS13, 3B1	R	28	14	54	8	16	1	0	0	5	2	3	0	.296	.315
George McBride	SS13	R	39	13	41	6	9	1	0	0	3	2	3	0	.220	.244
Doc Prothro	SS2, 3B2	R	26	6	13	2	5	0	0	0	2	0	4	0	.385	.385
Bobby LaMotte	SS1, 3B1	R	22	4	3	0	0	0	0	0	0	1	1	0	.000	.000
Bill Hollahan	3B3	R	23	3	4	1	1	0	0	0	0	1	2	1	.250	.250
2 Fred Thomas	3B2	R	27	3	7	0	1	0	0	0	0	0	1	0	.143	.143
Ed Johnson		L	21	2	4	0	1	0	0	0	0	0	2	0	.250	.250

Elmer Bowman 23 R 0-1, Allie Watt 20 R 1-1, Joe Leonard (DD) 25 L 0-0

NAME	T	AGE	W	L	PCT	SV	G	GS	CG	IP	H	BB	SO	SHO	ERA
		26	68	84	.447	10	153	153	80	1367	1521	520	418	10	4.17
Tom Zachary	L	26	15	16	.484	2	44	30	18	263	289	78	53	3	3.76
Eric Erickson	R	28	12	16	.429	1	39	28	12	239	231	128	87	0	3.84
Jim Shaw	R	26	11	18	.378	1	38	32	17	236	285	87	88	0	4.28
Walter Johnson (LJ-SA)	R	32	8	10	.444	3	21	15	12	144	135	27	78	4	3.13
Harry Courtney	L	21	8	11	.421	0	37	24	10	188	223	77	48	1	4.74
Al Schacht	R	26	6	4	.600	1	22	11	5	99	130	30	19	1	4.45
Jose Acosta	R	29	5	4	.556	1	17	5	4	83	92	26	19	1	4.01
Bill Snyder	R	22	2	1	.667	1	16	4	1	54	59	28	17	0	4.17
Harry Biemiller	R	22	1	0	1.000	0	5	2	1	21	15	13	10	0	4.76
Clarence Fisher	R	21	0	1	.000	0	2	0	0	4	5	6	0	0	9.00
Duke Shirey	R	22	0	1	.000	0	2	1	0	12	17	6	4	0	6.75
Gus Bono	R	25	0	2	.000	0	4	1	0	12	17	6	4	0	9.00
Leon Carlson	R	25	0	0	---	0	3	2	0	13	13	8	3	0	3.75
Joe Gleason	R	24	0	0	---	0	3	0	0	8	14	6	2	0	13.50
Jerry Conway	L	19	0	0	---	0	1	0	0	2	1	1	0	0	0.00
Joe Engel	R	27	0	0	---	0	1	0	0	1	0	5	1	0	18.00

DETROIT — 7th 61-93 .396 37 — HUGHIE JENNINGS

NAME	G by Pos	B	AGE	G	AB	R	H	2B	3B	HR	RBI	BB	SO	SB	BA	SA
TOTALS			29	155	5215	652	1408	228	72	30	560	479	391	76	.270	.359
Harry Heilmann	1B122, OF21	R	25	145	543	66	168	28	5	9	89	39	32	3	.309	.429
Ralph Young	2B150	B	31	150	594	84	173	21	6	0	33	85	30	6	.291	.347
Donie Bush	SS140	B	32	141	506	85	133	18	5	1	33	73	32	15	.263	.324
Babe Pinelli	3B74, SS18, 2B1	R	24	102	284	33	65	9	3	0	21	28	16	6	.229	.282
Chick Shorten	OF99	R	28	116	364	35	105	9	4	1	40	28	14	2	.288	.354
Ty Cobb (KJ)	OF112	L	33	112	428	86	143	28	8	2	63	58	28	15	.334	.451
Bobby Veach	OF154	L	32	154	612	92	188	34	15	11	113	36	22	11	.307	.474
Oscar Stanage	C77	R	37	78	238	12	55	17	0	0	14	16	21	0	.231	.303
Ira Flagstead	OF82	R	26	110	311	40	73	13	5	3	35	37	27	3	.235	.338
Bob Jones	3B67, 2B5, SS1	L	30	81	265	36	66	4	3	1	18	22	13	3	.249	.306
Sammy Hale	3B16, OF4, 2B1	R	23	76	116	13	34	3	3	1	14	5	15	2	.293	.397
Eddie Ainsmith	C61	R	30	69	186	19	43	5	3	1	19	14	19	4	.231	.306
Bert Ellison	1B38, OF4, 3B1	R	23	61	155	11	34	7	2	0	21	8	26	4	.219	.290
Clyde Manion	C30	R	25	32	80	4	22	4	1	0	8	4	7	0	.275	.350
Larry Woodall	C15	R	25	18	49	4	12	2	0	0	2	6	0	0	.245	.265
Clarence Huber	3B11	R	24	11	42	4	9	0	0	0	3	6	6	0	.214	.310
Dave Claire	SS3	R	22	3	7	1	1	0	0	0	0	0	0	0	.143	.143

NAME	T	AGE	W	L	PCT	SV	G	GS	CG	IP	H	BB	SO	SHO	ERA
		27	61	93	.396	7	155	155	76	1385	1487	561	483	7	4.04
Howard Ehmke	R	27	15	18	.455	3	38	33	23	268	250	124	98	1	3.29
Hooks Dauss	R	30	13	21	.382	0	38	32	18	270	308	84	82	0	3.56
Dutch Leonard	L	28	10	17	.370	0	28	27	10	191	192	63	76	3	4.34
Red Oldham	L	26	8	13	.381	1	39	23	11	215	248	91	62	1	3.85
Doc Ayres	R	29	7	14	.333	1	46	22	9	209	217	62	103	2	3.88
Allen Conkwright	R	23	2	1	.667	1	5	3	0	29	16	4	7	0	7.10
John Bogart	R	19	2	1	.667	0	2	2	1	24	16	8	5	0	3.00
Roy Crumpler	R	25	1	0	1.000	0	2	3	1	13	17	11	2	0	5.54
Bill Morrisette	R	25	1	1	.500	0	8	3	1	27	25	19	15	0	4.33
Mutt Wilson	R	23	1	1	.500	0	2	3	1	13	12	5	4	0	3.46
Frank Okrie	L	23	1	1	.333	0	11	1	0	41	44	18	9	0	5.27
Ernie Alten	L	25	1	0	1.000	0	14	1	0	23	40	9	4	0	9.00
Harry Baumgartner	R	27	0	0	---	0	3	1	0	18	18	6	7	0	4.00
Bernie Boland	R	28	0	0	---	0	2	1	0	8	18	6	4	0	7.94
John Glaiser	R	25	0	1	.000	0	9	1	0	17	23	8	3	0	6.35
Red Cox	R	25	0	0	---	0	5	0	0	5	9	5	1	0	5.40
Jack Coombs	R	37	0	0	---	0	2	0	0	6	7	2	1	0	3.00
Cy Fried	L	22	0	0	---	0	1	0	0	4	6	3	0	0	16.20
Slim Love	L	29	0	1	.000	0	1	0	0	4	8	4	2	0	8.31
Lou Vedder	R	23	0	0	---	0	1	0	0	1	0	1	1	0	0.00

PHILADELPHIA — 8th 48-106 .312 50 — CONNIE MACK

NAME	G by Pos	B	AGE	G	AB	R	H	2B	3B	HR	RBI	BB	SO	SB	BA	SA
TOTALS			25	156	5258	557	1326	219	49	44	470	356	594	51	.252	.338
Ivy Griffin	1B126, 2B2	L	23	129	543	46	111	15	1	0	20	15	49	3	.238	.274
Jimmy Dykes	2B108, 3B36	R	23	142	546	81	140	25	4	8	35	52	73	6	.256	.361
Chick Galloway	SS84, 2B4, 3B3	R	23	98	298	28	60	9	3	0	18	22	22	2	.201	.252
1 Fred Thomas	3B61, SS12	R	27	76	255	27	59	6	3	1	11	26	17	6	.231	.290
1 Amos Strunk	OF54	L	31	58	202	23	60	9	0	1	20	21	9	0	.297	.371
Frank Welch	OF97	R	22	100	360	43	93	17	5	4	40	26	41	2	.258	.367
Tilly Walker	OF149	R	32	149	585	79	157	23	7	17	82	40	59	9	.268	.419
Cy Perkins	C146, 2B1	R	24	148	492	40	128	24	6	5	52	28	35	5	.260	.364
Joe Dugan	3B59, 2B32, SS32	R	23	123	491	65	158	40	5	3	60	19	51	5	.322	.442
Dick Burrus	1B31, OF2	L	22	71	135	11	25	8	0	0	18	12	22	1	.185	.244
Glen Myatt	C21	L	22	70	196	14	49	8	3	0	18	12	22	1	.250	.321
Whitey Witt	OF50, 2B11, SS2	L	24	65	218	29	70	11	3	1	25	27	16	2	.321	.413
Lyle Bigbee	OF12, P12	L	26	37	70	4	13	1	1	0	8	4	10	1	.186	.243
2 Red Shannon	SS24	B	23	25	88	4	15	1	0	0	3	4	12	1	.170	.205
Lena Styles	C9, 1B7	R	24	24	50	5	13	6	0	0	7	5	6	0	.260	.360
Frank Walker	OF24	R	25	24	91	10	21	7	0	0	10	5	14	0	.231	.297
1 George Burns	OF13	L	27	22	60	1	14	3	0	0	5	3	3	1	.233	.333
Paul Johnson	OF18	R	23	18	72	6	15	0	0	0	5	4	1	0	.208	.208
Charlie High	OF17	L	21	17	65	7	20	2	1	0	5	4	8	0	.308	.415
Emmett McCann	SS11	R	18	13	34	4	9	1	0	0	3	3	6	0	.265	.353
Bill Kelly	1B2	R	22	9	13	0	3	0	0	0	1	0	5	0	.231	.308
Johnny Walker	C6	R	23	9	22	0	5	0	0	0	1	0	1	0	.227	.273

Ted Kearns 20 R 0-1, Ed Wingo 24 R 1-4

NAME	T	AGE	W	L	PCT	SV	G	GS	CG	IP	H	BB	SO	SHO	ERA
		24	48	106	.312	2	156	156	81	1380	1612	461	423	5	3.92
Scott Perry	R	29	11	25	.306	1	42	34	20	264	310	65	79	1	3.62
Rollie Naylor	R	29	10	23	.303	0	42	36	20	251	306	86	90	0	4.47
Slim Harriss	R	23	9	14	.391	0	31	25	11	192	226	57	60	0	4.08
Eddie Rommel	R	22	7	7	.500	1	33	12	8	174	165	43	43	2	2.84
Dave Keefe	R	22	6	7	.462	0	31	13	7	130	129	30	41	1	2.97
Walt Kinney	L	26	4	4	.333	0	10	8	5	61	59	28	19	1	3.10
Bob Hasty	R	24	3	4	.250	0	19	4	1	72	82	40	19	0	5.00
Pat Martin	L	28	1	2	.200	0	8	5	2	32	48	25	14	0	6.19
Roy Moore	L	21	1	13	.071	0	24	16	7	133	161	64	45	0	4.67
John Slappey	R	21	0	0	---	0	3	1	0	6	15	4	1	0	7.50
Bill Knowlton	R	25	0	0	---	0	3	1	0	12	15	4	4	0	4.50
Fred Heimach	R	19	0	1	.000	0	5	1	0	13	13	1	0	0	14.40
Lyle Bigbee	L	26	0	0	---	0	12	0	0	45	66	25	12	0	8.00
Charlie Eckert	R	22	0	0	---	0	4	0	0	13	19	8	4	0	4.50
Bill Shanner	R	25	0	0	---	0	1	0	0	1	1	0	1	0	6.75

BROOKLYN — 1ST 93-61 .604 — WILBERT ROBINSON

NAME	G by Pos	B	AGE	G	AB	R	H	2B	3B	HR	RBI	BB	SO	SB	BA	SA
TOTALS			30	155	5399	660	1493	205	99	28	566	359	391	70	.277	.367
Ed Konetchy	1B130	R	34	131	497	62	153	22	5	3	63	33	18	3	.308	.431
Pete Kilduff	2B134,3B5	R	27	141	478	62	130	26	8	0	58	54	43	2	.272	.360
Ivy Olson	SS125,2B21	R	34	143	637	71	162	13	11	1	46	20	19	4	.254	.314
Jimmy Johnston	3B146,OF7,SS3	R	30	155	635	87	185	17	12	1	52	43	23	19	.291	.361
Tommy Griffith	OF92	L	30	93	334	41	87	9	4	2	30	15	18	3	.260	.329
Hy Myers	OF152,3B2	R	31	154	582	83	177	36	22	4	80	35	54	3	.304	.462
Zack Wheat	OF148	L	32	148	583	89	191	26	13	9	73	48	21	8	.328	.463
Otto Miller	C89	R	31	90	301	16	87	9	2	0	33	9	18	0	.289	.332
Bernie Neis	OF83	R	24	95	249	38	63	11	2	2	22	26	35	9	.253	.337
Clarence Mitchell	P19,1B11,OF4	L	29	55	107	9	25	2	2	0	11	8	9	1	.234	.290
Ernie Krueger	C46	R	29	52	146	21	42	4	2	1	17	16	13	2	.288	.363
Burleigh Grimes	P40	R	26	43	111	9	34	8	3	0	16	8	21	2	.306	.432
Rowdy Elliott	C39	R	29	41	112	13	27	4	0	1	13	3	6	0	.241	.304
2 Billy McCabe	SS13,OF6,2B4,3B3	B	29	41	68	10	10	0	0	0	3	2	6	1	.147	.147
Ray Schmandt	1B20	R	24	28	63	7	15	2	1	0	4	0	1	0	.238	.302
Bill Lamar	OF12	L	23	24	44	5	12	4	0	0	4	0	1	0	.273	.364
Chuck Ward (IL)	SS19	R	25	19	71	7	11	1	0	0	4	3	3	1	.155	.169
Zack Taylor	C9	R	21	9	13	3	5	2	0	0	5	0	2	0	.385	.538
1 Wally Hood	OF5	R	25	7	14	4	2	1	0	0	1	4	4	2	.143	.214
1 Doug Baird	3B2	R	28	6	6	1	2	0	0	0	1	2	1	0	.333	.333
Jack Sheehan	SS2,3B1	B	27	3	5	0	2	1	0	0	1	0	1	0	.400	.600
Red Sheridan	SS3	R	23	3	2	0	0	0	0	0	0	0	1	0	.000	.000

NAME	T	AGE	W	L	PCT	SV	G	GS	CG	IP	H	BB	SO	SHO	ERA
		29	93	61	.604	10	155	155	89	1427	1381	327	553	17	2.62
Burleigh Grimes	R	26	23	11	.676	10	40	33	25	304	271	67	131	5	2.22
Jeff Pfeffer	R	32	16	9	.640	0	30	28	20	215	225	45	80	2	3.01
Leon Cadore	R	29	15	14	.517	0	35	30	16	254	256	56	79	4	2.62
Al Mamaux	R	26	12	8	.600	4	41	17	9	191	172	63	101	2	2.68
Sherry Smith	L	29	11	9	.550	3	33	13	6	184	134	27	33	2	1.85
Rube Marquard	L	33	10	7	.588	0	28	26	10	190	181	35	89	1	3.22
Clarence Mitchell	L	29	5	2	.714	1	19	7	3	79	85	23	18	1	3.08
Johnny Miljus	R	25	1	0	1.000	9	9	0	0	23	24	9	10	0	3.13
George Mohart	R	28	0	1	.000	0	13	1	0	36	33	7	13	0	1.75

NEW YORK — 2nd 86-68 .558 7 — JOHN McGRAW

NAME	G by Pos	B	AGE	G	AB	R	H	2B	3B	HR	RBI	BB	SO	SB	BA	SA
TOTALS			27	155	5309	682	1427	210	76	46	590	432	545	131	.269	.363
George Kelly	1B156	R	24	155	590	69	157	22	11	11	94	41	92	6	.266	.431
Larry Doyle	2B133	L	34	137	471	48	134	21	2	4	50	47	28	11	.285	.363
2 Dave Bancroft	SS108	B	29	109	442	79	132	29	7	0	31	33	32	7	.299	.396
Frankie Frisch (IL)	3B109,SS2	B	21	110	440	57	123	10	10	4	77	20	18	34	.280	.375
Ross Youngs	OF153	L	23	153	581	92	204	27	14	6	78	75	55	18	.351	.477
Lee King	OF84	R	27	93	261	32	72	11	4	7	42	21	38	3	.276	.429
George Burns	OF154	R	30	154	581	115	181	35	9	6	46	76	48	22	.287	.397
Frank Snyder	C84	R	26	87	264	26	66	13	4	3	27	17	18	2	.250	.364
Earl Smith	C82	L	23	91	262	20	77	7	1	3	30	18	16	5	.294	.340
Benny Kauff	OF51	L	30	55	157	31	43	12	3	3	26	25	14	3	.274	.209
1 Eddie Sicking	3B28,2B15,SS3	R	23	46	134	11	23	3	1	0	9	10	10	6	.172	.209
Vern Spencer	OF40	R	26	45	140	15	28	2	3	0	19	11	17	4	.200	.257
1 Art Fletcher	SS41	R	35	41	171	21	44	7	2	0	24	1	15	1	.257	.322
1 Lew McCarty	C5	R	31	36	38	2	5	0	0	0	4	2	2	0	.132	.132
Fred Lear	3B24,2B1	R	26	31	87	12	22	0	1	1	7	8	15	0	.253	.310
Roy Grimes	2B21	R	26	26	57	5	9	1	0	0	3	3	8	1	.158	.175
Al Lefevre	SS9,2B6,3B1	L	21	17	27	5	4	0	1	0	0	0	13	0	.148	.222
1 Jigger Statz	OF21	R	22	16	30	4	4	0	1	0	5	2	9	0	.133	.200
Mike Gonzalez	C8	R	29	11	13	1	3	0	0	0	0	3	1	1	.231	.231
Curt Walker	OF4	R	23	8	14	0	1	0	0	0	1	0	3	0	.071	.071
1 Doug Baird	3B4	R	28	7	8	0	1	0	0	0	1	0	1	0	.125	.125
Pug Griffin	OF2	R	24	5	4	0	1	0	0	0	1	0	2	0	.250	.250
Alex Gaston	C3	R	27	4	10	2	1	0	0	0	1	0	3	0	.100	.100
Eddie Brown	OF2	R	28	3	8	1	1	0	0	0	1	0	0	0	.125	.125
Bob Kinsella	OF1	L	21	1	3	0	1	0	0	0	1	0	2	0	.333	.333

NAME	T	AGE	W	L	PCT	SV	G	GS	CG	IP	H	BB	SO	SHO	ERA
		29	86	68	.558	9	155	155	86	1409	1379	297	380	18	2.80
Fred Toney	R	21	21	11	.656	1	42	37	17	278	266	57	81	4	2.65
Art Nehf	L	27	21	12	.636	0	40	33	22	281	273	45	79	5	3.08
Jesse Barnes	R	27	20	15	.571	0	43	34	23	293	271	56	63	2	2.65
Phil Douglas	R	30	14	10	.583	2	46	21	10	226	225	55	71	3	2.71
Rube Benton	L	30	9	16	.360	2	33	25	12	193	222	31	52	4	3.03
2 Slim Sallee	L	35	1	0	1.000	0	5	1	0	17	16	0	2	0	1.59
1 Bill Hubbell	R	23	0	1	.000	2	14	0	0	36	28	15	8	0	2.10
Rosy Ryan	R	22	0	0	—	0	3	1	1	15	14	4	5	0	4.80
Virgil Barnes	R	23	0	1	.000	0	1	0	0	7	9	1	2	0	3.86
Tom Grubbs	R	26	0	0	—	0	1	0	0	5	4	2	0	0	7.20
Jesse Winters	R	26	0	0	—	0	21	0	0	46	37	28	14	0	3.52
Pol Perritt	R	28	0	0	—	0	8	0	0	15	9	4	3	0	1.80
Claude Davenport	R	22	0	0	—	0	1	0	0	2	2	1	0	0	4.50
Jean Dubuc (DL) 31															

CINCINNATI — 3rd 82-71 .536 10.5 — PAT MORAN

NAME	G by Pos	B	AGE	G	AB	R	H	2B	3B	HR	RBI	BB	SO	SB	BA	SA
TOTALS			30	154	5176	639	1432	169	76	18	546	382	367	158	.277	.349
Jake Daubert	1B140	L	36	142	553	97	168	28	13	4	48	47	29	11	.304	.423
Morrie Rath	2B126,3B1,OF1	B	33	129	506	61	135	7	4	2	28	38	24	10	.267	.308
Larry Kopf	SS123,2B2,3B2,OF1	B	29	126	458	56	112	15	6	0	59	35	24	14	.245	.303
Heinie Groh	3B144,SS1	R	30	145	550	86	164	28	12	0	49	60	29	16	.298	.393
Greasy Neale	OF150	L	28	150	530	55	135	10	7	3	46	45	48	29	.255	.317
Edd Roush	OF139,1B11,2B1	L	27	149	579	81	196	22	16	4	90	42	22	36	.339	.453
Pat Duncan	OF154	R	26	154	576	75	170	26	11	2	83	42	42	18	.295	.372
Ivy Wingo	C107,2B2	L	29	108	364	32	96	11	5	2	38	19	13	6	.264	.338
Sam Crane	SS25,3B10,2B4,OF3	R	25	54	144	20	31	4	0	0	9	7	9	5	.215	.243
Charlie See	OF17,P1	L	23	47	82	9	25	4	0	0	15	1	7	3	.305	.354
Nick Allen	C36	R	32	39	85	10	23	3	1	0	4	6	11	0	.271	.329
Bill Rariden	C37	R	32	39	101	9	25	3	0	0	10	5	0	2	.248	.277
2 Eddie Sicking	2B25,SS9,3B2	R	23	37	122	12	33	3	0	0	17	13	5	2	.268	.293
Rube Bressler	P10,OF3,1B2	R	25	21	30	4	8	1	0	0	3	1	4	1	.267	.300

NAME	T	AGE	W	L	PCT	SV	G	GS	CG	IP	H	BB	SO	SHO	ERA
		29	82	71	.536	9	154	154	90	1391	1327	393	435	12	2.90
Jimmy Ring	R	25	17	16	.515	1	42	33	18	267	268	92	73	1	3.55
Dutch Ruether	L	26	16	12	.571	3	37	33	23	266	235	96	99	5	2.47
Dolf Luque	R	29	13	9	.591	1	37	23	10	208	168	60	72	1	2.51
Hod Eller	R	25	13	12	.520	0	35	23	15	210	208	52	76	2	2.96
Ray Fisher	R	32	10	11	.476	1	33	21	10	201	189	50	56	1	2.73
1 Slim Sallee	L	35	5	8	.455	2	21	12	6	116	129	16	13	0	3.34
Buddy Napier	R	30	4	2	.667	0	9	5	4	49	47	7	17	1	1.29
Rube Bressler (BN)	R	25	2	0	1.000	0	10	2	1	20	24	2	4	1	1.80
Lynn Brenton	R	30	2	1	.667	1	5	1	1	18	17	4	13	0	5.00
Fritz Coumbe	L	30	0	1	.000	0	15	1	2	7	0	4.80			
Dazzy Swartz	R	23	0	0	—	0	1	1	1	12	17	2	2	0	4.50
George Lowe	R	25	0	0	—	0	1	0	0	2	1	1	0	0	0.00
Charlie See	L	23	0	0	—	0	1	0	0	6	4	3	0	0	6.00
Jack Theis	R	28	0	0	—	0	1	0	0	3	5	0	0	0	0.00

PITTSBURGH — 4th 79-75 .513 10.5 — GEORGE GIBSON

NAME	G by Pos	B	AGE	G	AB	R	H	2B	3B	HR	RBI	BB	SO	SB	BA	SA
TOTALS			27	155	5219	530	1342	162	90	16	449	374	405	181	.257	.332
Charlie Grimm	1B148	L	21	149	533	38	121	13	7	2	54	30	40	7	.227	.289
George Cutshaw	2B129	R	33	131	488	56	123	16	8	0	47	23	10	17	.252	.318
Buster Caton	SS96	R	23	98	332	29	83	11	5	0	27	33	19	4	.250	.331
Possum Whitted	3B125,1B10,OF1	R	30	134	494	53	129	11	12	1	74	35	36	11	.261	.338
Billy Southworth	OF142	L	27	146	546	64	155	17	13	2	53	52	20	23	.284	.374
Max Carey	OF129	B	30	130	485	74	140	18	4	1	35	59	31	52	.289	.348
Carson Bigbee	OF133	L	25	137	550	78	154	19	15	4	32	45	28	31	.280	.391
Walter Schmidt	C92	R	33	94	310	22	86	8	4	0	29	24	15	0	.277	.329
Fred Nicholson	OF58	R	25	99	247	33	89	16	4	4	30	18	31	9	.360	.530
Walter Barbare (BJ)	SS34,2B12,3B5	R	28	57	186	19	51	5	2	0	12	9	11	5	.274	.323
Bill Haeffner	C52	R	25	54	175	8	34	4	1	0	14	8	14	1	.194	.229
Bill McKechnie	3B20,SS10,2B6,1B1	B	33	40	133	13	29	3	1	1	13	4	7	7	.218	.278
Cliff Lee	C19,OF2	R	23	37	76	9	18	2	2	0	8	4	14	0	.237	.316
Bill Hinchman		R	37	18	16	0	3	0	0	0	1	1	3	0	.188	.188
Pie Traynor	SS17	R	21	17	52	6	11	3	1	0	2	3	6	1	.212	.308
Clyde Barnhart	3B12	R	24	12	46	5	15	4	2	0	5	1	2	1	.326	.500
Cotton Tierney	2B10,SS2	R	26	12	46	4	11	5	0	0	8	3	4	1	.239	.348
Homer Summa	OF6	R	21	10	22	1	7	1	1	0	3	1	1	0	.318	.455
Nig Clark	C3	L	37	3	7	0	0	0	0	0	0	0	2	0	.000	.000
2 Wally Hood		R	25	2	1	1	0	0	0	0	0	0	1	0	.000	.000

NAME	T	AGE	W	L	PCT	SV	G	GS	CG	IP	H	BB	SO	SHO	ERA
		28	79	75	.513	10	155	155	92	1416	1389	280	444	17	2.89
Wilbur Cooper	L	28	24	15	.615	2	44	37	28	327	307	52	114	3	2.39
Babe Adams	R	38	17	13	.567	2	35	33	19	263	240	18	84	8	2.16
Hal Carlson	R	28	14	13	.519	3	39	31	16	247	262	63	62	3	3.36
Elmer Ponder	R	27	11	15	.423	0	33	23	13	196	182	40	62	2	2.62
Earl Hamilton	L	28	10	13	.435	3	39	23	12	230	223	69	74	0	3.25
Johnny Morrison	R	24	1	0	1.000	0	2	1	1	7	4	1	3	0	1.29
Jimmy Zinn	R	25	1	1	.500	0	6	1	1	32	32	5	18	0	3.48
John Wisner	R	20	1	3	.250	0	17	2	1	45	46	10	13	0	3.40
Johnny Meador	R	27	0	2	.000	0	12	2	0	36	48	7	5	0	4.25
Sheriff Blake	R	20	0	0	—	0	3	0	0	13	21	6	7	0	8.31
2 Mule Watson	R	23	0	0	—	0	1	0	0	11	15	7	1	0	9.00
Whitey Glazner	R	25	0	0	—	0	2	0	0	9	2	1	9	0	3.00

CHICAGO — 5th(Tie) 75-79 .487 18 — FRED MITCHELL

NAME	G by Pos	B	AGE	G	AB	R	H	2B	3B	HR	RBI	BB	SO	SB	BA	SA
TOTALS			29	154	5117	619	1350	223	67	34	535	428	421	115	.264	.354
Fred Merkle	1B85,OF1	R	31	92	333	33	94	20	4	3	38	24	32	3	.283	.397
Zeb Terry	SS70,2B63	R	29	133	496	56	139	26	9	0	52	44	22	12	.280	.369
Charlie Hollocher (IL)	SS80	L	24	80	332	56	96	17	2	0	22	41	15	20	.289	.389
Charlie Deal	3B128	R	28	129	450	48	108	10	5	3	39	20	14	5	.240	.304
Max Flack	OF132	L	30	123	520	85	157	30	6	4	49	52	15	13	.302	.406
Dode Paskert	OF137	R	38	139	487	59	136	22	10	5	71	64	58	16	.279	.396
Dave Robertson	OF134	L	30	134	500	68	150	29	11	10	75	40	44	17	.300	.462
Bob O'Farrell	C86	R	23	94	270	29	67	11	4	3	19	34	23	1	.248	.362
Turner Barber	1B69,OF17,2B2	L	26	94	340	27	90	10	5	2	50	9	26	5	.265	.324
Buck Herzog	2B59,3B28,1B1	R	34	91	355	39	66	9	2	0	19	20	21	3	.193	.236
Babe Twombly	OF45,2B2	L	24	78	183	25	43	1	1	0	14	17	20	5	.235	.284
Bill Killefer (BG)	C61	R	32	96	191	16	42	7	1	0	16	8	5	2	.220	.267
Barney Friberg	2B24,3B5	R	20	50	114	11	24	5	1	0	7	6	20	2	.211	.272
Tom Daly	C29	L	29	44	90	9	28	4	2	0	13	2	6	1	.311	.378
Bill Marriott	2B14	R	27	14	43	7	12	4	0	0	3	6	5	1	.279	.465
Hal Leathers	SS6,2B3	R	26	12	43	3	7	1	0	0	1	3	4	1	.304	.478
1 Bill McCabe		B	27	3	2	1	0	0	0	0	0	0	1	0	.000	.000
Sumpter Clarke	3B1	R	22	2	3	0	1	0	0	0	0	0	0	0	.333	.333
Lee Magee (DL)																

NAME	T	AGE	W	L	PCT	SV	G	GS	CG	IP	H	BB	SO	SHO	ERA
		29	75	79	.487	9	154	154	95	1389	1459	382	508	13	3.27
Pete Alexander	R	33	27	14	.659	5	46	40	33	363	335	69	173	7	1.91
Hippo Vaughn	L	32	19	16	.543	0	40	38	24	301	301	81	131	4	2.54
Lefty Tyler	L	30	11	12	.478	0	27	27	18	193	193	57	57	2	3.31
Claude Hendrix	R	31	9	9	.429	0	27	23	12	204	216	54	72	0	3.57
Speed Martin	R	26	4	15	.211	2	35	13	6	136	165	50	44	0	4.83
Paul Carter	R	26	3	6	.333	2	31	8	2	106	131	36	14	0	4.67
Chippy Gaw	R	26	1	1	.500	0	7	3	1	16	13	6	4	0	4.85
Sweetbreads Bailey	R	25	1	2	.333	0	21	1	0	37	55	11	8	0	7.06
Joel Newkirk	R	24	0	1	.000	0	2	0	0	9	6	2	5	0	5.14
Virgil Cheeves	R	19	0	0	—	0	2	0	0	18	16	7	3	0	3.50
Percy Jones	R	20	0	0	—	0	2	0	0	7	15	3	0	0	11.57
Joe Jaeger	R	25	0	0	—	0	1	0	0	2	6	2	1	0	12.00
Ted Turner	R	28	0	0	—	0	1	0	0	2	9	2	1	0	18.00

ST. LOUIS — 5th(tie) 75-79 .487 18 — BRANCH RICKEY

NAME	G by Pos	B	AGE	G	AB	R	H	2B	3B	HR	RBI	BB	SO	SB	BA	SA
TOTALS			27	155	5495	675	1589	238	96	32	600	373	484	126	.289	.385
Jack Foumier	1B138	L	30	141	530	77	162	33	14	3	61	42	42	26	.306	.438
Rogers Hornsby	2B149	R	24	149	589	96	218	44	20	9	94	60	50	12	.370	.559
Doc Lavan	SS138	R	29	142	516	52	149	21	10	1	63	19	38	11	.289	.374
Milt Stock	3B155	R	26	155	639	85	204	28	6	0	76	40	27	15	.319	.382
Joe Schultz	OF80	R	26	99	320	38	84	5	5	0	32	21	11	5	.263	.309
Cliff Heathcote	OF129	L	22	133	489	55	139	18	8	3	56	25	31	21	.284	.372
Austin McHenry	OF133	R	24	137	504	66	142	19	11	10	62	25	73	8	.282	.423
Verne Clemons	C103	R	28	112	338	17	95	10	6	1	36	30	12	1	.281	.355
Jack Smith	OF83	L	25	91	313	53	104	22	5	1	28	25	23	14	.332	.444
Hal Janvrin	SS27, 1B25, OF20, 2B6	R	27	87	270	33	74	8	4	1	28	17	19	5	.274	.344
Pickles Dillhoefer	C74	R	26	76	224	26	59	8	3	0	13	13	7	2	.263	.326
Burt Shotton	OF51	L	35	62	180	28	41	5	0	1	12	18	14	5	.228	.272
Mike Knode	OF9, 2B4, SS2, 3B2	L	24	42	65	11	15	1	1	0	12	5	6	0	.231	.277
Tim Griesenbeck	C3	R	22	5	3	1	1	0	0	0	0	0	0	0	.333	.333
2 Lew McCarty	C3	R	31	5	7	0	2	0	0	0	0	0	5	0	.286	.286
Heinie Mueller	OF4	L	20	4	22	0	7	1	0	0	1	2	4	1	.318	.364
George Gilham	C1	L	20	3	0	0	0	0	0	0	0	0	0	0	.000	.—
Ed Hock	OF1	L	21	1	0	0	0	0	0	0	0	0	0	0	.000	.000
Bill Schindler	C1	R	23	1	0	0	0	0	0	0	0	0	0	0	.000	.000

NAME	T	AGE	W	L	PCT	SV	G	GS	CG	IP	H	BB	SO	SHO	ERA
TOTALS		27	75	79	.487	12	155	155	72	1427	1488	479	529	9	3.43
Bill Doak	R	29	20	12	.625	0	39	37	20	270	256	80	90	5	2.53
Ferdie Schupp	L	29	16	13	.552	0	38	37	17	251	246	127	119	0	3.51
Jesse Haines	R	26	13	20	.394	2	47	37	19	302	303	80	120	4	2.98
Bill Sherdel	L	23	11	10	.524	6	43	7	4	170	183	40	74	0	3.28
Elmer Jacobs	R	27	4	8	.333	1	23	9	1	78	91	33	21	0	5.19
Lou North	R	29	3	2	.600	1	24	6	3	88	90	32	37	0	3.27
Marv Goodwin	R	29	3	8	.273	1	32	12	3	116	153	28	23	0	4.97
Mike Kitcher	R	22	2	1	.667	1	37	50	5	5				0	5.19
George Lyons	R	22	2	1	.667		7	2	1	23	21	9	5	0	3.13
Jakie May	L	24	1	4	.200	0	16	5	3	71	65	37	33	0	3.04
Hal Kime	R	22	0	0	—	0	4	0	0	7	9	2	1	0	2.57
Bob Glenn	R	26	0	0	—	0	2	0	0	2	2	0	0	0	0.00
Walt Schultz	R	20	0	0	—	0	2	0	0	6	10	2	0	0	6.00
George Scott	R	24	0	0	—	0	2	0	0	6	4	3	1	0	4.50
Oscar Tuero	R	27	0	0	—	0	1	0	0	1	5	1	0	0	36.00

BOSTON — 7th 62-90 .408 30 — GEORGE STALLINGS

NAME	G by Pos	B	AGE	G	AB	R	H	2B	3B	HR	RBI	BB	SO	SB	BA	SA
TOTALS			28	153	5218	523	1358	168	86	23	456	385	488	88	.260	.339
Walter Holke	1B143	B	27	144	551	53	162	15	11	3	64	28	31	4	.294	.377
Charlie Pick	2B94	L	32	95	383	34	105	16	6	2	28	23	11	10	.274	.363
Rabbit Maranville	SS133	R	28	134	493	48	131	19	15	1	43	28	24	14	.266	.371
Tony Boeckel	3B149, SS3, 2B1	R	27	153	582	70	156	28	5	3	62	38	50	18	.268	.349
Walton Cruise	OF82	L	30	91	288	40	80	7	5	1	21	31	26	5	.278	.347
Ray Powell	OF147	L	31	149	609	69	137	12	12	6	29	44	83	10	.225	.314
Les Mann	OF110	R	27	115	424	48	117	9	7	8	32	38	42	4	.276	.351
Mickey O'Neil	C105, 2B1	R	22	112	304	19	86	14	4	0	28	21	20	4	.283	.326
Hod Ford	2B59, SS18, 1B4	R	25	87	257	16	62	12	5	1	30	18	25	3	.241	.339
Eddie Eayers	OF63, P7	L	29	87	244	31	80	5	4	2	24	30	18	4	.328	.377
John Sullivan	OF66, 1B6	R	30	81	250	36	74	14	4	1	28	29	29	3	.296	.396
Hank Gowdy	C74	R	30	80	214	14	52	11	2	0	18	20	15	6	.243	.313
L. Christenbury	OF14, SS7, 2B6, 3B2	L	26	65	106	17	22	2	2	0	14	13	12	0	.208	.264
Art Wilson	3B6, C2	R	34	16	19	0	1	0	0	0	0	1	1	0	.053	.053
1 Gene Bailey	OF8	R	26	13	24	2	2	0	0	0	0	3	3	0	.083	.083
Oscar Dugey		R	32	5	0	2	0	0	0	0	0	0	0	0	.000	.000
1 Johnny Rawlings	2B1	R	27	5	3	0	0	0	0	0	0	0	1	0	.000	.000
Red Torphy	1B3	R	28	3	15	1	3	2	0	0	2	0	1	0	.200	.333
Tom Whelan	1B1	R	26	1	1	0	0	0	0	0	0	0	0	0	.000	.000

NAME	T	AGE	W	L	PCT	SV	G	GS	CG	IP	H	BB	SO	SHO	ERA
TOTALS		27	62	90	.408	6	153	153	93	1386	1464	415	368	13	3.54
Joe Oeschger	R	28	15	13	.536	0	38	30	20	299	294	99	80	5	3.46
Dana Fillingim	R	26	12	21	.364	0	37	31	22	272	292	79	66	2	3.11
Hugh McQuillan	R	24	11	15	.423	5	38	26	17	226	230	70	53	1	3.55
Jack Scott	R	28	10	21	.323	1	44	33	22	291	308	85	94	3	3.53
13 Mule Watson	R	23	5	4	.556	0	13	10	4	75	79	17	16	2	3.60
Dick Rudolph	R	31	4	8	.333	0	18	11	3	89	104	24	24	0	4.04
Leo Townsend	L	29	2	2	.500	0	7	1	1	24	18	2	0	0	1.50
Johnny Jones	R	24	1	1	.500	0	3	1	0	10	16	5	6	0	6.30
Al Pierotti	R	24	1	1	.500	0	6	2	2	25	23	9	12	0	2.88
Eddie Eayrs	L	29	1	2	.333	0	7	3	0	26	36	12	7	0	5.54
Bunny Hearn	L	29	0	3	.000	0	11	4	2	43	54	11	9	0	5.65
Ira Townsend	R	26	0	0	—	0	4	1	0	7	10	2	1	0	1.29

PHILADELPHIA — 8th 62-91 .405 30.5 — GAVVY CRAVATH

NAME	G by Pos	B	AGE	G	AB	R	H	2B	3B	HR	RBI	BB	SO	SB	BA	SA
TOTALS			30	253	5264	565	1385	229	54	64	483	283	531	100	.263	.364
Gene Paulette	1B139, SS2	R	29	143	562	59	162	16	6	1	36	33	16	9	.288	.364
2 Johnny Rawlings	2B97	R	27	98	384	39	90	19	2	3	30	22	25	9	.234	.368
2 Art Fletcher	SS101	R	35	102	379	36	112	25	7	4	38	15	28	4	.296	.430
Ralph Miller	3B91, 1B3, SS2, OF1	R	24	97	338	28	74	14	1	0	28	11	32	3	.219	.266
Casey Stengel	OF118	L	29	129	445	53	130	25	6	9	50	28	35	7	.292	.436
Cy Williams	OF147	L	32	148	590	88	192	36	10	15	72	32	45	18	.325	.497
Irish Meusel	OF129, 1B3	R	27	138	518	75	160	27	8	14	69	32	27	17	.309	.473
Mark Wheat	C74	R	27	78	230	15	52	10	3	3	20	8	35	3	.226	.335
Dots Miller	2B59, 3B17, SS12, 1B9, OF1	R	29	88	343	41	87	12	2	1	27	16	17	13	.254	.309
Bevo LeBourveau	OF72	L	23	84	261	29	67	7	2	3	13	11	36	5	.257	.345
Russ Wrightstone	3B56, SS2, 2B1	L	27	76	206	23	54	6	1	3	17	10	25	3	.262	.345
Walt Tragesser	C52	R	33	62	176	17	37	11	1	6	26	4	36	4	.210	.386
Frank Withrow	C48	R	29	48	132	8	24	4	1	0	12	8	26	0	.182	.227
Gavvy Cravath	OF5	R	39	46	45	2	13	5	0	1	11	9	12	0	.289	.467
1 Dave Bancroft	SS42	B	39	42	171	23	51	7	2	0	5	9	12	1	.298	.363
Fred Luderus	1B7	L	34	16	32	1	5	2	0	0	4	3	6	0	.156	.219
Walt Walsh		R	23	2	0	0	0	0	0	0	0	0	0	0		

NAME	T	AGE	W	L	PCT	SV	G	GS	CG	IP	H	BB	SO	SHO	ERA
TOTALS		27	62	91	.405	11	153	153	77	1381	1480	444	419	8	3.63
Lee Meadows	R	25	16	14	.533	0	35	33	19	247	249	90	95	3	2.84
George Smith	R	28	13	18	.419	2	43	28	10	251	265	51	51	2	3.44
Eppa Rixey	L	29	11	22	.333	2	41	34	25	284	288	69	109	1	3.48
2 Bill Hubbell	R	23	9	9	.500	2	24	18	9	150	176	42	26	1	3.84
Red Causey	R	26	7	14	.333	1	35	26	11	181	203	79	30	1	4.33
Johnny Enzmann	R	30	2	3	.400	0	16	2	1	59	79	16	35	0	3.82
2 Bert Gallia	R	28	2	6	.250	2	18	5	1	72	79	29	35	0	4.50
Huck Betts	R	23	1	1	.500	0	27	4	1	88	86	33	18	0	3.58
Lefty Weinert	L	18	1	1	.500	0	10	2	0	22	27	19	10	0	6.14
Mike Cantwell	L	26	0	3	.000	0	5	1	0	23	25	15	8	0	3.91
Jimmie Keenan	L	22	0	0	—	0	1	0	0	3	1	2	1	0	3.00
Stan Baumgartner (VR) 27															

WORLD SERIES — CLEVELAND (AL) 5 BROOKLYN (NL) 2

LINE SCORES

TEAM	1	2	3	4	5	6	7	8	9	10	11	12	R	H	E
Game 1 October 5 at Brooklyn															
CLE (AL)	0	2	0	1	0	0	0	0	0				3	5	0
BKN (NL)	0	0	0	0	0	1	0	0	X				1	5	1

Coveleski | Marquard, Mamaux (7), Cadore (9)

TEAM	1	2	3	4	5	6	7	8	9	R	H	E
Game 2 October 6 at Brooklyn												
CLE	0 0 0	0 0 0	0 0 0							0	7	1
BKN	1 0 1	0 1 0	0 0 X							3	7	0

Bagby, Uhle (7) | Grimes

Game 3 October 7 at Brooklyn												
CLE	0 0 0	1 0 0	0 0 0							1	3	1
BKN	2 0 0	0 0 0	0 0 X							2	6	1

Caldwell, Mails (1), Uhle (8) | S. Smith

Game 4 October 9 at Cleveland												
BKN	0 0 0	1 0 0	0 0 0							1	5	1
CLE	2 0 2	0 0 1	0 0 X							5	12	2

Cadore, Mamaux (2), Marquard (3), Pfeffer (6) | Coveleski

Game 5 October 10 at Cleveland												
BKN	0 0 0	0 0 0	0 0 1							1	13	1
CLE	4 0 0	3 1 0	0 0 X							8	12	2

Grimes, Mitchell (4) | Bagby

Game 6 October 11 at Cleveland												
BKN	0 0 0	0 0 0	0 0 1							0	3	0
CLE	0 0 0	0 0 1	0 0 X							1	7	3

S. Smith | Mails

Game 7 October 12 at Cleveland												
BKN	0 0 0	0 0 0	0 0 0							0	5	2
CLE	0 0 0	1 1 0	1 0 X							3	7	3

Grimes, Mamaux (8) | Coveleski

COMPOSITE BATTING

NAME	POS	G	AB	R	H	2B	3B	HR	RBI	BA
Cleveland (AL)										
Totals		7	217	21	53	9	2	2	17	.244
Wambsganss	2B	7	26	3	4	0	0	0	1	.154
Speaker	OF	7	25	6	8	2	1	0	1	.320
Gardner	3B	7	24	1	5	1	0	0	2	.208
Sewell	SS	7	23	0	4	0	0	0	0	.174
O'Neill	C	7	21	1	7	3	0	0	2	.333
Jamieson	OF	6	15	2	5	1	0	0	1	.333
E. Smith	OF	5	13	1	4	1	0	1	5	.308
Evans	OF	4	13	0	4	0	0	0	0	.308
D. Johnston	1B	5	11	3	3	0	0	0	0	.273
Burns	1B	5	10	1	3	1	0	0	2	.300
Wood	OF	4	10	2	2	1	0	0	0	.200
Coveleski	P	3	10	2	1	0	0	0	0	.100
Bagby	P	2	6	1	2	0	0	0	3	.333
Mails	P	2	5	0	0	0	0	0	0	.000
Graney	OF	3	3	0	0	0	0	0	0	.000
Nunamaker	C	2	4	0	2	0	0	0	0	.500
Uhle	P	2	0	0	0	0	0	0	0	.—
Caldwell	P	1	0	0	0	0	0	0	0	.—
Lunte	2B	1	1	0	0	0	0	0	0	.000
Thomas	C	1	0	0	0	0	0	0	0	.—
Brooklyn (NL)										
Totals		7	215	8	44	5	1	0	1	.205
Wheat	OF	7	27	2	9	2	0	0	2	.333
Myers	OF	7	26	0	6	0	0	0	1	.231
Olson	SS	7	25	2	8	1	0	0	0	.320
Konetchy	1B	7	23	0	4	1	0	0	1	.174
Griffith	OF	7	21	1	4	2	0	0	0	.190
Kilduff	2B	7	21	0	2	0	0	0	0	.095
J. Johnston	3B	4	14	2	3	0	0	0	0	.214
Miller	C	6	14	0	2	0	0	0	0	.143
Sheehan	3B	3	11	0	2	0	0	0	0	.182
Grimes	P	3	6	1	2	0	0	0	0	.333
Krueger	C	2	6	0	1	0	0	0	0	.167
S. Smith	P	2	5	0	0	0	0	0	0	.000
Neis	OF	3	4	0	0	0	0	0	0	.000
Mitchell	P	2	3	0	1	0	0	0	0	.333
Lamar	PH	3	3	0	0	0	0	0	0	.000
Mamaux	P	3	2	0	0	0	0	0	0	.000
Marquard	P	2	1	0	0	0	0	0	0	.000
Pfeffer	P	1	1	0	0	0	0	0	0	.000
Schmandt	PH	1	1	0	0	0	0	0	0	.000

McCabe PR 0-0, Cadore P 0-0

COMPOSITE PITCHING

NAME	G	IP	H	BB	SO	W	L	SV	ERA
Cleveland (AL)									
Totals	7	61	44	10	20	5	2	0	0.89
Coveleski	3	27	15	2	8	3	0	0	0.67
Mails	2	15.2	6	6	6	1	0	0	0.00
Bagby	2	15	20	3		1	1	0	1.80
Uhle	2	3	1	0	3	0	0	0	0.00
Caldwell	1	.1	2	1	0	0	0	1	27.00
Brooklyn (NL)									
Totals	7	59	53	21	21	2	5	0	2.75
Grimes	3	19.1	23	9	4	1	2	0	4.19
S. Smith	2	17	10	3	3	1	1	0	0.53
Marquard	2	9	7	3	6	0	1	0	3.00
Mitchell	1	4.2	3	1	0	0	0	0	0.00
Mamaux	3	4	2	0	5	0	0	0	4.50
Pfeffer	1	3	4	1	0	1	0	0	3.00
Cadore	2	2	4	1	1	0	0	0	9.00

1921 The Year They Took the Series Underground

In 1906, the city of Chicago had enjoyed the privilege of monopolizing the World Series. This happened when the Cubs and White Sox both managed to win their respective flags at the same time. In 1921, the city of New York duplicated the achievement and even added an oddity to the feat. New York made full use of its underground railroad system to provide baseball with the first subway World Series.

New York had the Giants and Dodgers. But, since both were in the National League, it meant that only the Yankees had to be included if such an historic occasion was to occur. The Yankees had never before won a pennant, but thanks to the bat of Babe Ruth, a Cleveland team hurt by injuries to Tris Speaker and Steve O'Neill, and running out of gas down the backstretch, the American League occupants in New York racked up their first pennant in late September.

It was an exciting enough race to attract fan interest, but those who came out to the ball park did so more to see Ruth than the Yankees. The Sultan of Swat became the talk of the baseball world by popping home runs at an unprecedented rate, chalking up 59 clouts in his ledger by the time the season ended. Ruth grew into the biggest drawing card in sports' history, bringing fans out in droves at home and on the road and, in good measure, overcoming the effect of the 1919 World Series scandal on the game's public image. In addition to his 59 homers, Ruth also amassed 170 runs batted in, tops in the majors, while swinging the wood to a .378 tune, a performance that perhaps is regarded as the most outstanding set of statistics ever aggregated in a single season. But all in all, Ruth was denied the Triple Crown, as he finished third in hitting. And for all of his future greatness, it was destined that this achievement of batting would never be his.

Ruth's supporting cast on the attack included Bob Meusel, A.L. runnerup in homers and third in runs batted in, and clutch-hitting first baseman Wally Pipp. The unheralded Yankee pitching staff turned in the best performance in the league—Carl Mays racked up 27 victories, and newly-acquired Waite Hoyt and Bob Shawkey won 19 and 18 games apiece. Despite these assets, the Yankees could not shake the pre-season favorite Indians until September, and the final margin of victory was only 4 1/2 games.

Joining the Yankees in the Subway Series were the Giants as John McGraw led his team to the top of the National League for the seventh time during his 19-year tenure in New York. The Pittsburgh Pirates used good pitching to remain ahead of the pack going into August, but a five-game series sweep in late August by McGraw's boys turned the tide against the Bucs. Good baseball down the stretch enabled the heavy-hitting Giants to overtake slumping Pittsburgh in September and win the crown by four games. George Kelly led the league with 23 home runs and drove in 122 runs for the Giants, and Frankie Frisch and Ross Youngs spiced high batting averages with 100 RBI's each. Dave Bancroft hit .318 while playing standout ball at shortstop, and Emil "Irish" Meusel hit .329 after joining the team in mid-season from Philadelphia.

The anticipated best of nine Subway Series got off to a surprising start when Carl Mays and Waite Hoyt threw shutouts to give the Yankees a two game lead. But the Yankees could only win one of the next three games before a bad arm prevented Ruth from making any further appearances. The Giants then proceeded to take the next three games and the world championship. Ruth managed only one homer, but he alone of the Yankees' batters was able to hit .300, a mark attained by five Giants.

After the Series, Ruth and Bob Meusel took part in a barnstorming tour, which Judge Landis had ruled unallowed. Landis backed up his tough stance with fines, which covered the players' Series shares, and suspensions of the two until May 20 of the following season. And all in one motion, baseball knew it had an uncompromising boss and a traveling hero.

1921 AMERICAN LEAGUE

NAME	G by Pos	B	AGE	G	AB	R	H	2B	3B	HR	RBI	BB	SO	SB	BA	SA
NEW YORK 1st 98-55 .641	MILLER HUGGINS		28	153	5249	948	1576	285	87	134	861	588	567	89	.300	.464
TOTALS																
Wally Pipp	1B153	L	28	153	588	96	174	35	9	8	97	45	28	17	.296	.427
Aaron Ward	2B123, 3B33	R	24	153	556	77	170	30	10	5	75	42	68	6	.306	.423
Roger Peckinpaugh	SS149	R	30	149	577	128	166	25	7	8	71	84	44	0	.288	.397
Frank Baker	3B83	L	35	94	330	46	97	16	2	9	71	26	12	8	.294	.436
Bob Meusel	OF147	R	24	149	598	104	190	40	16	24	135	34	88	17	.318	.559
Elmer Miller	OF56	R	34	56	242	41	72	9	8	4	36	19	16	2	.298	.450
Babe Ruth	OF152, 1B2, P2	L	26	152	540	177	204	44	16	59	171	145	81	17	.378	.846
Wally Schang	C132	B	31	134	424	77	134	30	5	6	55	78	35	7	.316	.453
Mike McNally	3B48, 2B16	R	27	71	215	36	56	4	2	1	24	14	15	5	.260	.312
Chick Fewster	OF43, 2B16	R	25	66	207	44	58	19	0	1	19	28	43	4	.280	.386
Carl Mays	P49	R	29	51	143	18	49	5	1	2	22	4	7	0	.343	.434
Braggo Roth	OF37	R	28	43	152	29	43	9	2	2	10	19	20	1	.283	.408
Chicken Hawks	OF15	L	25	41	73	16	21	2	3	2	15	5	12	0	.288	.479
Bob Shawkey (LJ)	P38	R	30	38	90	13	27	2	1	1	11	2	13	0	.300	.378
Ping Bodie	OF25	R	33	31	87	5	15	2	2	0	12	8	8	0	.172	.241
Fred Hofmann	C18, 1B1	R	27	23	62	7	11	1	1	1	5	8	13	0	.177	.274
Al DeVormer	C17	R	29	22	49	6	17	4	0	0	7	2	4	2	.347	.429
Johnny Mitchell	SS7, 2B5	B	26	13	42	4	11	1	0	0	2	4	4	1	.262	.286
Tom Connelly	OF3	R	23	9	5	1	1	0	0	0	0	1	1	0	.200	.200
Frank Gleich (IL) 27																

NAME	T	AGE	W	L	PCT	SV	G	GS	CG	IP	H	BB	SO	SHO	ERA
		28	98	55	.641	15	153	153	92	1374	1461	470	481	7	3.79
Carl Mays	R	29	27	9	.750	7	49	38	30	337	332	76	70	1	3.04
Waite Hoyt	R	21	19	13	.594	3	43	32	21	282	301	81	102	1	3.10
Bob Shawkey (LJ)	R	30	18	12	.600	2	38	31	18	245	245	86	126	3	4.08
Rip Collins	R	25	11	5	.688	0	28	16	7	137	158	78	64	1	5.45
Jack Quinn	R	37	8	7	.533	0	33	13	6	129	158	32	44	0	3.49
Bill Piercy	R	25	5	4	.556	0	14	10	5	82	82	28	35	1	2.86
Harry Harper (BG)	L	26	4	3	.571	0	8	7	4	53	52	25	22	0	3.74
Alex Ferguson	R	24	3	1	.750	1	17	4	1	56	64	27	9	0	5.95
Babe Ruth	L	26	2	0	1.000	0	2	1	0	9	14	9	2	0	9.00
Tom Sheehan	R	27	1	0	1.000	1	12	1	0	33	43	19	7	0	5.45
Tom Rogers	R	29	1	0	1.000	1	5	0	0	11	12	9	0	0	7.36

NAME	G by Pos	B	AGE	G	AB	R	H	2B	3B	HR	RBI	BB	SO	SB	BA	SA
CLEVELAND 2nd 94-60 .610 4.5	TRIS SPEAKER		29	154	5383	925	1656	355	90	42	845	614	376	58	.308	.430
TOTALS																
Doc Johnston	1B116	L	33	118	384	53	114	20	7	2	44	29	15	2	.297	.401
Bill Wambsganss (BA)	2B103, 3B2	R	27	107	410	80	117	28	5	2	46	44	27	13	.285	.393
Joe Sewell	SS154	R	22	154	572	101	182	36	12	4	91	80	17	7	.318	.444
Larry Gardner	3B152	L	35	153	586	101	187	32	14	3	115	65	16	3	.319	.437
Elmer Smith	OF127	L	28	129	431	98	125	28	9	16	84	46	54	6	.290	.508
Tris Speaker	OF128	L	33	132	506	107	183	52	14	3	74	68	16	2	.362	.538
Charlie Jamieson	OF137	L	28	140	536	94	166	33	10	1	45	67	27	8	.310	.414
Steve O'Neill (BG)	C105	R	29	106	335	39	108	22	1	1	50	57	22	0	.322	.403
George Burns	1B73	R	28	84	244	52	88	21	4	0	41	13	13	2	.361	.480
Jack Graney	OF32	L	35	68	107	19	32	3	0	2	18	20	9	1	.299	.383
Smoky Joe Wood	OF64	R	31	66	194	32	71	16	5	4	60	25	17	2	.366	.562
Riggs Stephenson	2B54, 3B2	R	23	65	206	45	68	17	2	2	34	23	15	4	.330	.461
Joe Evans	OF47	R	26	57	153	36	51	11	0	0	21	19	5	4	.333	.405
Les Nunamaker (BL)	C46	R	32	46	131	16	47	7	2	0	24	11	8	1	.359	.443
Ginger Shinault	C20	R	28	22	39	5	11	1	0	0	3	6	5	1	.379	.414
Pinch Thomas	C19	L	33	21	35	1	9	3	0	0	4	10	2	0	.257	.343
Tex Jeanes	OF4	R	20	4	2	2	1	0	0	0	1	0	0	0	.500	.500
Luke Sewell	C3	R	20	3	6	0	0	0	0	0	0	1	0	3	.000	.000
Lou Guisto	1B1	R	26	2	1	0	0	0	0	0	0	1	0	1	.000	.000
Art Wilson	C2	R	35	2	1	0	0	0	0	0	0	0	0	0	.000	.000

NAME	T	AGE	W	L	PCT	SV	G	GS	CG	IP	H	BB	SO	SHO	ERA
		29	94	60	.610	14	154	154	81	1378	1534	431	475	11	3.90
Stan Coveleski	R	31	23	13	.639	2	43	40	29	316	341	84	99	2	3.36
George Uhle	R	22	16	13	.552	2	41	28	13	238	288	63	63	2	4.01
Duster Mails	L	26	14	8	.636	2	34	24	10	194	210	89	87	2	3.94
Jim Bagby	R	31	14	12	.538	4	40	26	12	192	238	44	37	0	4.69
3 Allan Sothoron	R	28	12	4	.750	0	22	16	10	145	144	58	61	2	3.23
Guy Morton	R	28	8	3	.727	0	30	6	2	108	98	32	45	2	2.75
Ray Caldwell	R	33	6	6	.500	4	37	13	5	147	159	49	76	1	4.90
Ted Odenwald	L	19	1	0	1.000	0	10	0	0	17	16	4	4	0	1.59
Bernie Henderson	R	22	0	1	.000	0	3	1	0	5	5	1	0	0	9.00
Bob Clark	R	23	0	0	—	0	5	0	0	23	6	2	0	0	15.00
Jesse Petty	L	26	0	0	—	0	4	0	0	9	10	0	0	0	4.00
Joe Harris (DO) 30															

NAME	G by Pos	B	AGE	G	AB	R	H	2B	3B	HR	RBI	BB	SO	SB	BA	SA
ST. LOUIS 3rd 81-73 .526 17.5	LEE FOHL		27	154	5442	835	1655	246	106	67	720	413	407	92	.304	.425
TOTALS																
George Sisler	1B138	L	28	138	582	125	216	38	18	12	104	34	27	35	.371	.560
Marty McManus	2B96, 3B13, 1B10, SS2	R	21	121	412	49	107	19	8	3	64	27	30	5	.260	.367
Wally Gerber (BH)	SS113	R	29	114	436	55	121	12	9	2	48	34	19	3	.278	.360
2 Frank Ellerbe	3B105	R	25	105	430	65	124	20	12	2	48	22	42	1	.288	.405
Jack Tobin	OF150	L	29	150	671	132	236	31	18	8	59	35	22	7	.352	.487
Baby Doll Jacobson	OF141, 1B11	R	30	151	599	90	211	38	14	5	90	42	30	8	.352	.487
Ken Williams	OF145	L	31	146	547	115	190	31	7	24	117	74	42	20	.347	.561
Hank Severeid	C126	R	30	143	472	60	153	23	7	2	78	42	9	7	.324	.415
Dud Lee	SS31, 2B30, 3B3	L	21	72	180	18	30	4	2	0	11	14	34	1	.167	.211
Dutch Wetzel	OF27	R	27	61	119	16	25	2	0	2	10	9	20	0	.210	.277
Pat Collins	C31	R	24	58	111	9	27	3	0	1	10	16	17	1	.243	.369
Lyman Lamb	3B23, 2B7, OF6	R	26	45	134	18	34	9	2	1	17	4	12	0	.254	.373
Jimmy Austin (BA)	SS14, 2B6, 3B2	R	41	27	66	8	18	2	1	0	8	7	6	2	.273	.333
Billy Gleason	2B25	R	26	26	74	6	19	0	1	0	8	6	6	0	.257	.284
1 Earl Smith	3B13, OF4	R	30	25	78	7	26	2	2	0	14	3	4	0	.333	.513
Josh Billings	C12	R	29	20	46	2	10	0	0	0	4	2	3	0	.217	.217
Billy Mullen	3B2	R	24	4	5	0	0	0	0	0	0	0	0	0	.000	.000
Jim Riley	2B4	L	26	4	11	0	0	0	0	0	0	0	5	0	.000	.000
Luke Stuart	2B3	R	29	3	3	0	1	0	1	0	2	0	1	0	.333	1.333

NAME	T	AGE	W	L	PCT	SV	G	GS	CG	IP	H	BB	SO	SHO	ERA
		26	81	73	.526	9	154	154	79	1381	1543	557	478	9	4.61
Urban Shocker	R	30	27	12	.692	4	47	39	31	327	345	86	132	4	3.55
Dixie Davis	R	30	16	16	.500	0	40	36	20	265	279	123	100	2	4.45
Bill Bayne	L	22	11	5	.688	3	47	14	7	164	167	80	82	1	4.72
Elam VanGilder	R	25	11	12	.478	0	31	21	10	180	196	67	48	1	3.95
Ray Kolp	R	26	9	8	.533	0	37	18	5	167	208	51	43	1	4.96
Emilio Palmero	L	26	4	7	.364	0	24	9	4	90	109	49	26	0	5.00
Bill Burwell	R	26	4	3	.333	2	33	3	1	84	102	29	17	0	5.14
1 Allan Sothoron	R	28	1	2	.333	0	5	4	2	38	33	8	9	0	5.14
Bernie Boland	R	29	1	4	.200	0	8	6	0	28	34	28	6	0	9.00
Joe DeBerry	R	24	0	1	.000	0	3	1	0	12	15	10	1	0	6.75
Ray Richmond	R	25	0	0	—	0	2	1	0	15	23	14	7	0	11.40
Nick Cullop	L	33	0	2	.000	0	1	1	0	12	18	6	9	0	8.25
George Boehler	R	29	0	0	—	0	1	0	0	6	11	4	6	0	0.00
Dutch Henry	L	19	0	0	—	0	1	0	0	4	4	1	0	0	4.50
2 Bugs Bennett	R	26	0	0	—	0	1	0	0	6	11	6	1	0	13.50

WASHINGTON 4th 80-73 .523 18 — GEORGE McBRIDE

NAME	G by Pos	B	AGE	G	AB	R	H	2B	3B	HR	RBI	BB	SO	SB	BA	SA
TOTALS			29	154	5294	704	1468	240	96	42	609	462	470	111	.277	.383
Joe Judge	1B152	L	27	153	622	87	187	26	11	7	72	68	35	21	.301	.412
Bucky Harris	2B154	R	24	154	584	82	169	22	8	0	54	54	39	29	.289	.354
Frank O'Rourke	SS122	R	29	123	444	51	104	17	8	3	54	26	56	6	.234	.329
Howard Shanks	3B154	R	30	154	562	81	170	25	19	7	69	57	38	11	.302	.452
Clyde Milan	OF98	L	35	112	406	55	117	19	11	1	40	37	13	4	.288	.397
Sam Rice	OF141	L	31	141	561	83	185	39	13	4	79	38	10	25	.330	.467
Bing Miller	OF109	R	26	114	420	57	121	28	8	9	71	25	50	3	.288	.457
Patsy Gharrity	C115	R	29	121	387	62	120	19	8	7	55	45	44	1	.310	.455
Frank Brower	OF47, 1B4	L	28	83	203	31	53	12	3	1	35	18	7	1	.261	.365
2 Earl Smith	OF43, 3B1	B	30	59	180	20	39	5	2	2	12	10	19	1	.217	.300
Val Picinich	C45	R	29	45	141	10	39	9	0	0	12	16	21	0	.277	.340
Duffy Lewis	OF27	R	32	27	102	11	19	4	1	0	14	8	10	1	.186	.245
2 Donie Bush	SS21	B	33	23	84	15	18	1	0	0	2	12	4	2	.214	.226
Bobby LaMotte	SS12	R	23	16	41	5	8	0	0	0	2	5	0	0	.195	.195
Goose Goslin	OF14	L	20	14	50	8	13	1	1	1	6	5	5	0	.260	.380
1 Frank Ellerbe	3B1	R	25	10	10	1	2	0	1	0	2	0	3	0	.200	.400
1 Tony Brottem	C4	R	30	4	7	1	1	0	0	0	0	0	2	0	.143	.143
George Foss	3B2	R	24	4	7	0	0	0	0	0	0	0	1	0	.000	.000
Ricardo Torres	C2	R	28	2	3	1	1	0	0	0	0	0	1	0	.333	.333

NAME	T	AGE	W	L	PCT	SV	G	GS	CG	IP	H	BB	SO	SHO	ERA
TOTALS		28	80	73	.523	10	154	154	80	1384	1568	442	452	8	3.97
George Mogridge	L	32	18	14	.563	0	38	36	21	288	301	66	101	4	3.00
Tom Zachary	L	25	18	16	.529	1	39	30	17	250	314	59	53	1	3.96
Walter Johnson	R	33	17	14	.548	1	35	32	25	264	265	92	143	1	3.51
Eric Erickson	R	29	8	10	.444	0	32	22	9	179	181	65	71	2	3.62
Al Schacht	R	27	6	6	.500	2	29	5	2	83	110	27	15	0	4.88
Harry Courtney	L	22	6	9	.400	1	30	15	3	133	159	71	26	0	5.62
Jose Acosta	R	30	5	4	.556	3	30	5	3	116	148	36	30	0	4.35
Jim Shaw	R	27	1	0	1.000	2	15	5	0	40	59	17	4	0	7.43
Tom Phillips	R	32	1	0	1.000	0	1	1	1	9	9	3	2	0	2.00
Nemo Gaines (ML)	L	23	0	0	—	0	4	0	0	5	5	2	1	0	0.00
Frank Woodward	R	27	0	0	—	0	1	0	0	11	11	3	4	0	5.73
Red Bird	L	31	0	0	—	0	1	0	0	5	5	1	2	0	5.40
Ralph Miller	L	22	0	0	—	0	1	0	0	1	0	1	0	0	0.00
Vance Mcilree	R	23	0	0	—	0	1	0	0	1	0	1	0	0	9.00

BOSTON 5th 75-79 .487 23.5 — HUGH DUFFY

NAME	G by Pos	B	AGE	G	AB	R	H	2B	3B	HR	RBI	BB	SO	SB	BA	SA
TOTALS			30	154	5206	668	1440	248	69	17	584	428	329	83	.277	.361
Stuffy McInnis	1B152	R	30	152	584	72	179	31	10	0	74	21	9	2	.307	.394
Del Pratt	2B134	R	33	135	521	80	169	36	10	5	100	44	10	5	.324	.461
Everett Scott	SS154	R	28	154	576	65	151	21	9	1	60	27	21	5	.262	.335
Eddie Foster	3B94, 2B22	R	34	120	412	51	117	18	6	0	30	57	15	13	.284	.357
Shano Collins	OF138, 1B3	R	35	141	542	63	155	29	12	4	65	18	38	15	.286	.406
Nemo Leibold	OF117	L	29	123	467	88	143	26	6	0	30	41	27	13	.306	.388
Mike Menosky	OF133	L	26	133	477	77	143	18	5	1	43	60	45	12	.300	.377
Muddy Ruel	C109	R	25	113	358	41	99	21	1	1	43	41	15	2	.277	.349
Ossie Vitt	3B71, OF3, 1B2	R	31	78	232	29	44	11	1	0	12	45	13	1	.190	.246
Roxy Walters	C45	R	28	54	169	27	34	4	0	1	13	10	11	3	.201	.237
Bullet Joe Bush	P37, OF4	R	28	51	120	19	39	5	4	0	14	3	14	2	.325	.433
Tim Hendryx (BG)	OF41	R	30	49	137	10	33	8	2	0	21	24	13	1	.241	.328
Sammy Vick	OF14, C1	R	26	44	77	5	20	3	1	0	9	1	10	0	.260	.325
Pinky Pittinger	OF27, 3B3, SS2, 2B1	R	22	40	91	6	18	1	0	0	5	4	13	3	.198	.209
Ernie Neitzke	OF8, P2	R	26	11	25	3	6	1	0	0	4	4	4	0	.240	.240
Jack Perrin	OF4	L	27	4	13	3	3	0	0	0	1	0	3	0	.231	.231
Bert Chaplin	C1	L	27	3	2	0	0	0	0	0	0	0	1	0	.000	.000
Hob Hiller		R	28	3	2	0	0	0	0	0	0	0	0	0	.000	.000

NAME	T	AGE	W	L	PCT	SV	G	GS	CG	IP	H	BB	SO	SHO	ERA
TOTALS		27	75	79	.487	5	154	154	88	1364	1521	452	446	9	3.99
Sad Sam Jones	R	28	23	16	.590	1	40	38	25	299	318	78	98	5	3.22
Bullet Joe Bush	R	28	16	9	.640	1	37	32	21	254	244	93	96	3	3.51
Herb Pennock	L	27	13	14	.481	0	32	31	15	223	268	59	91	1	4.04
Benn Karr	R	28	8	7	.533	0	26	7	5	118	123	38	37	0	3.66
Elmer Myers	R	27	8	12	.400	0	30	20	11	172	217	53	40	0	4.87
Allen Russell	R	27	6	11	.353	3	39	14	7	173	204	77	60	0	4.11
Hank Thormahlen	L	24	1	7	.125	0	23	9	1	96	101	34	17	0	4.50
Curt Fullerton	R	22	1	1	.500	0	5	2	1	15	22	10	4	0	9.00
2 Allan Sothoron	R	28	0	2	.000	2	2	0	0	6	15	5	2	0	13.50
Ernie Neitzke	R	26	0	0	—	0	2	0	0	7	8	4	1	0	6.43
Sam Dodge	L	31	0	0	—	0	1	0	0	1	0	0	0	0	9.00

DETROIT 6th 71-82 .464 27 — TY COBB

NAME	G by Pos	B	AGE	G	AB	R	H	2B	3B	HR	RBI	BB	SO	SB	BA	SA
TOTALS			29	154	5461	883	1724	268	100	58	800	582	376	95	.316	.433
Lu Blue	1B152	B	24	153	585	103	180	33	11	5	75	103	47	13	.308	.427
Ralph Young	2B106	R	32	107	401	70	120	29	4	0	29	69	23	11	.299	.334
1 Donnie Bush	SS81, 2B23	R	33	104	402	72	113	6	5	0	27	45	23	8	.281	.321
Bob Jones	3B141	L	31	141	554	82	168	23	9	1	72	37	24	8	.303	.383
Harry Heilmann	OF145, 1B4	R	26	149	602	114	237	43	14	19	139	53	37	2	.394	.606
Ty Cobb	OF121	L	34	128	507	124	197	37	16	12	101	56	19	22	.389	.596
Bobby Veach	OF149	L	33	150	612	110	207	43	13	16	128	48	31	14	.338	.529
Johnny Bassler	C115	L	26	119	388	37	119	18	5	0	56	58	16	2	.307	.379
Chick Shorten	OF52, C1	L	29	92	217	33	59	11	3	0	23	20	11	2	.272	.350
Ira Flagstead	SS55, OF12, 2B8, 3B1	R	27	85	259	40	79	15	1	0	31	21	21	7	.305	.371
Joe Sargent	2B24, 3B23, SS19	R	27	66	178	21	45	8	4	1	22	24	26	2	.253	.388
Larry Woodall	C24	R	26	46	80	10	29	4	1	0	14	6	7	1	.363	.438
1 Eddie Ainsmith	C34	R	31	35	98	6	27	5	2	0	12	13	7	1	.276	.367
Howard Ehmke	P30	R	27	30	74	9	21	3	1	0	9	1	7	0	.284	.351
Herm Merritt	SS17	R	24	20	46	3	17	1	2	0	6	1	5	1	.370	.478
Clyde Manion	C4	R	24	12	40	4	8	0	0	0	7	2	2	0	.200	.200
Sammy Hale		R	24	9	2	2	0	0	0	0	0	0	1	0	.000	.000
Sammy Barnes	2B2	L	21	7	11	2	2	1	0	0	0	0	2	0	.182	.273
Jackie Tavener	SS2	R	23	6	4	1	0	0	0	0	0	0	1	0	.000	.000
George Cunningham	OF1	R	26	1	0	0	0	0	0	0	0	0	0	0	—	—
Clarence Huber	3B1	R	25	1	0	0	0	0	0	0	0	0	0	0	—	—

NAME	T	AGE	W	L	PCT	SV	G	GS	CG	IP	H	BB	SO	SHO	ERA
TOTALS		28	71	82	.464	17	154	154	73	1386	1634	495	452	4	4.40
Howard Ehmke	R	27	13	14	.481	0	30	22	13	196	220	81	68	1	4.55
Dutch Leonard	L	29	11	13	.458	1	36	32	16	245	273	63	120	1	3.75
Red Oldham	R	27	11	14	.440	1	40	28	12	229	258	81	67	1	4.25
Hooks Dauss	R	31	10	15	.400	1	32	28	16	233	275	81	68	0	4.33
Bert Cole	R	25	7	4	.636	1	20	11	7	110	134	36	22	1	4.25
Suds Sutherland	R	27	6	2	.750	0	13	8	3	58	80	18	18	0	4.97
Jim Middleton	R	32	6	11	.353	7	38	10	2	122	144	44	31	0	5.01
Slicker Parks	R	25	3	2	.600	0	10	1	0	25	33	16	10	0	5.76
Carl Holling	R	24	3	7	.300	4	35	11	4	136	162	58	38	0	4.30
2 Pol Perritt	R	29	1	0	1.000	0	2	0	0	13	18	7	3	0	4.85
Lefty Stewart	L	20	0	0	—	1	3	0	0	9	20	5	4	0	12.00
Jim Walsh	L	26	0	0	—	0	3	0	0	4	2	1	3	0	2.25
Doc Ayres	R	30	0	0	—	0	1	0	0	3	9	4	0	0	9.00
Danny Boone	R	26	0	0	—	0	1	0	0	1	0	1	1	0	0.00

CHICAGO 7th 62-92 .403 36.5 — KID GLEASON

NAME	G by Pos	B	AGE	G	AB	R	H	2B	3B	HR	RBI	BB	SO	SB	BA	SA
TOTALS			29	154	5329	683	1509	242	82	35	608	445	474	97	.283	.379
Earl Sheely	1B154	R	28	154	563	68	171	25	6	11	95	57	34	4	.304	.428
Eddie Colins	2B136	L	34	139	526	79	177	20	10	2	58	66	11	12	.337	.424
Ernie Johnson	SS141	L	33	142	613	93	181	28	7	1	51	29	24	22	.295	.369
Eddie Mulligan	3B152, SS1	R	26	152	609	92	153	21	12	1	45	32	53	13	.251	.330
Harry Hooper (BH)	OF108	L	33	108	419	74	137	26	5	8	58	55	21	13	.327	.470
Amos Strunk	OF111	L	32	121	401	68	133	19	10	3	69	38	27	7	.332	.451
Bibb Falk	OF149	L	22	152	585	62	167	31	11	5	82	37	69	4	.285	.402
Ray Schalk	C128	R	28	128	416	32	105	24	4	0	47	40	36	3	.252	.329
Johnny Mostil	OF91, 2B1	R	25	100	326	43	98	21	7	3	42	28	35	10	.301	.436
Harvey McClellan	2B20, SS15, OF15, 3B5	R	26	63	196	20	35	4	1	1	14	14	18	2	.179	.224
Yam Yaryan	C34	R	28	45	102	11	31	8	2	0	15	9	16	0	.304	.442
George Lees	C16	R	26	20	42	3	9	2	0	0	5	4	6	0	.214	.262
Fred Bratchi	OF5	R	29	16	28	0	8	1	0	0	3	0	2	0	.286	.321
Red Ostergard		R	25	12	11	2	4	0	0	0	0	2	5	0	.364	.364
Elmer Leifer	3B1, OF1	R	28	9	10	0	3	0	0	0	1	0	3	0	.300	.300
Eddie Murphy		L	29	6	5	1	1	0	0	0	0	2	0	0	.200	.200
Frank Pratt		L	23	1	1	0	0	0	0	0	0	0	0	0	.000	.000

NAME	T	AGE	W	L	PCT	SV	G	GS	CG	IP	H	BB	SO	SHO	ERA
TOTALS		28	62	92	.403	9	154	154	86	1365	1603	549	392	7	4.94
Red Faber	R	32	25	15	.625	1	43	39	32	331	293	87	124	4	2.48
Dickie Kerr	L	27	19	17	.528	1	44	37	25	309	357	96	80	3	4.72
Shovel Hodge	R	27	6	8	.429	2	36	11	6	143	191	54	35	0	6.54
Roy Wilkinson	R	28	4	20	.174	3	36	22	11	198	259	78	50	0	5.14
Doug McWeeny	R	24	3	6	.333	2	27	9	4	98	127	45	46	0	6.06
Jack Russell	L	25	2	5	.286	0	11	8	4	66	82	35	15	0	5.32
Dominick Mulrennan	R	26	2	8	.200	0	12	10	3	56	84	36	10	0	7.24
Cy Twombly	L	24	1	2	.333	0	7	4	0	28	26	25	7	0	5.79
Jack Wieneke	L	27	1	1	.500	0	10	3	0	25	39	17	10	0	8.28
Sarge Connally	R	22	0	1	.000	0	13	2	0	35	41	32	9	0	6.54
Lum Davenport	R	21	0	3	.000	0	13	2	0	32	35	41	32	0	6.94
Lee Thompson	L	23	0	3	.000	0	4	2	0	21	32	4	8	0	8.14
1 Bugs Bennett	R	29	0	3	.000	0	13	2	0	18	19	16	2	0	6.00
Russ Pence	R	21	0	0	—	0	1	0	0	2	2	2	2	0	9.00
Hod Fenner	R	23	0	0	—	0	1	0	0	7	14	3	1	0	7.71
John Michaelson	R	27	0	0	—	0	1	0	0	1	3	1	0	0	9.00
Babe Blackburn	R	26	0	0	—	0	1	0	0	1	0	1	0	0	0.00

PHILADELPHIA 8th 53-100 .346 45 — CONNIE MACK

NAME	G by Pos	B	AGE	G	AB	R	H	2B	3B	HR	RBI	BB	SO	SB	BA	SA
TOTALS			24	155	5465	657	1497	256	64	82	601	424	561	68	.274	.389
Johnny Walker	1B99, C7	R	24	111	423	41	109	14	5	2	45	9	29	5	.258	.329
Jimmy Dykes	2B155	R	24	155	613	88	168	32	13	16	77	60	75	6	.274	.447
Chick Galloway	SS110, 3B20, 2B1	R	24	131	465	42	123	28	5	3	47	29	43	12	.265	.366
Joe Dugan	3B119	R	24	119	461	54	136	22	6	10	58	24	45	5	.295	.434
Whitey Witt	OF154	L	25	154	629	100	198	31	11	4	45	77	52	16	.315	.418
Frank Welch	OF104	R	23	115	403	48	115	16	4	7	45	34	43	6	.285	.412
Tilly Walker	OF142	R	33	142	556	89	169	32	5	23	101	73	41	3	.304	.504
Cy Perkins	C141	R	25	141	538	58	155	31	4	12	73	32	32	5	.288	.428
Frank Brazill	1B36, 3B9	L	21	66	177	17	48	3	1	0	19	23	21	2	.271	.299
Emmett McCann	SS32, 3B9, 2B2, 1B1, C1	R	19	52	157	15	35	5	0	0	15	4	6	2	.223	.255
Paul Johnson	OF32	R	24	48	127	17	40	6	2	1	10	9	17	0	.315	.417
Glenn Myatt	C27	R	23	44	69	6	14	2	0	0	5	3	16	0	.203	.232
Ivy Griffin	1B28	L	24	39	103	14	33	4	2	0	13	5	6	1	.320	.398
Zip Collins	OF21	R	29	21	71	14	20	5	1	0	5	6	5	1	.282	.380
Frank Walker	OF19	R	26	19	66	6	15	3	1	0	5	8	11	1	.227	.333
Bill Barrett	SS7, P4, 3B2, 1B1	R	21	14	30	3	7	0	0	0	2	6	3	0	.233	.267
Frank Callaway	SS14	R	23	14	50	7	12	2	0	0	3	1	2	1	.240	.300
Ben Mallonee	OF6	R	27	6	24	2	6	1	0	0	3	1	4	0	.250	.292
Lena Styles	C2	R	21	3	5	1	1	0	0	0	1	0	2	0	.200	.200
Elmer Yoter		R	21	3	4	0	0	0	0	0	0	0	0	0	.000	.000
Dot Fulghum	SS1	R	20	2	1	0	0	0	0	0	0	0	1	0	.000	.000
Red Shannon		B	24	1	0	0	0	0	0	0	0	0	0	0	—	—

NAME	T	AGE	W	L	PCT	SV	G	GS	CG	IP	H	BB	SO	SHO	ERA
TOTALS		24	53	100	.346	7	155	155	75	1403	1645	548	431	2	4.61
Eddie Rommel	R	23	16	23	.410	3	46	32	20	285	312	87	71	0	3.95
Slim Harriss	R	24	11	16	.407	2	39	28	14	228	258	73	92	0	4.27
Roy Moore	L	22	10	10	.500	0	29	26	12	192	206	122	64	0	4.50
Bob Hasty	R	25	5	16	.238	0	35	22	9	179	238	40	46	0	4.88
Scott Perry	R	30	3	6	.333	1	12	8	5	70	77	24	19	0	4.11
Rollie Naylor	R	24	3	13	.188	2	32	19	6	169	214	55	39	0	4.84
Dave Keefe	R	24	2	9	.182	1	44	12	1	173	214	64	68	0	4.68
Bill Barrett	R	21	1	1	1.000	0	4	2	2	18	26	9	5	0	7.20
Fred Heimach	L	20	1	1	1.000	0	6	2	1	22	26	5	7	0	1.00
Harvey Freeman	R	23	1	4	.200	2	18	4	2	51	65	35	5	0	7.24
Arlas Taylor	L	25	0	1	.000	0	4	1	0	12	20	16	1	0	22.50
Jim Sullivan	R	27	0	2	.000	0	2	2	1	17	20	7	8	0	3.18
Lefty Wolf	L	21	0	0	—	0	1	0	0	15	16	12	2	0	7.20
Bill Bishop	R	20	0	0	—	0	1	0	0	8	10	4	9	0	9.00
Ray Miner	L	24	0	0	—	0	2	0	0	3	5	1	3	0	36.00

Batting

NAME	G by Pos	B	AGE	G	AB	R	H	2B	3B	HR	RBI	BB	SO	SB	BA	SA
NEW YORK 1ST 94-59 .614														JOHN McGRAW		
TOTALS			27	153	5278	840	1575	237	93	75	748	469	390	137	.298	.421
George Kelly	1B149	R	25	149	587	95	181	42	9	23	122	40	73	4	.308	.528
2 Johnny Rawlings	2B86, SS1	R	28	86	307	40	82	8	1	0	30	18	19	4	.267	.309
Dave Bancroft	SS153	B	30	153	606	121	193	26	15	6	67	66	23	17	.318	.441
Frankie Frisch	3B93, 2B61	R	22	153	618	121	211	31	17	8	100	42	28	49	.341	.485
Ross Youngs	OF137	L	24	141	504	90	165	24	16	3	102	71	47	21	.327	.456
George Burns	OF149, 3B1	R	31	149	605	111	181	28	9	4	61	80	24	19	.299	.395
2 Irish Meusel	OF62	R	28	62	243	37	80	12	6	2	36	15	12	5	.329	.453
Frank Snyder	C101	R	27	108	309	36	99	13	2	8	45	27	24	3	.320	.453
Earl Smith	C78	L	24	89	229	35	77	8	4	10	51	27	8	4	.336	.537
Eddie Brown	OF30	L	29	70	128	16	36	6	2	0	12	4	11	1	.281	.359
1 Curt Walker	OF58	L	24	64	192	30	55	13	5	3	35	15	8	4	.286	.453
1 Goldie Rapp	3B56	R	27	58	181	21	39	9	1	0	15	15	13	3	.215	.276
Bill Cunningham	OF20	R	26	40	76	10	21	2	1	1	2	3	3	0	.276	.368
1 Lee King	OF35, 1B1	R	28	39	94	17	21	4	2	0	7	13	6	0	.223	.309
Bill Patterson	3B14, SS7	R	24	23	35	5	14	0	0	1	5	2	5	0	.400	.486
Alex Gaston	C11	R	28	20	22	1	5	1	1	0	3	1	9	0	.227	.364
1 John Monroe	2B8, SS1	R	22	19	21	4	3	0	0	1	3	3	6	0	.143	.286
2 Casey Stengel	OF8	L	30	18	22	4	5	1	0	0	2	1	5	0	.227	.273
Mike Gonzalez	1B6, C2	R	30	13	24	3	9	1	0	0	1	0	1	0	.375	.417
Howard Berry	2B7	R	26	9	6	0	2	0	0	1	0	2	1	0	.333	.667
Hank Schreiber	2B2, SS2, 3B1	R	29	4	6	2	2	0	0	0	1	0	1	0	.333	.333
Joe Connolly	OF1	R	25	2	4	0	0	0	0	0	0	1	1	0	.000	.000
Wally Kopf	3B2	R	21	2	3	0	1	0	0	0	1	0	1	0	.333	.333
Bud Heine	2B1	L	20	1	2	0	0	0	0	0	0	0	0	0	.000	.000
1 Butch Henline		R	26	1	1	0	0	0	0	0	0	0	0	0	—	—
Jim Mahady	2B1	R	20	1	0	0	0	0	0	0	0	0	0	0	—	—
Benny Kauff (DL) 31																
PITTSBURGH 2nd 90-63 .588 4														GEORGE GIBSON		
TOTALS			29	154	5379	692	1533	231	104	37	623	341	371	134	.285	.387
Charlie Grimm	1B150	L	22	151	562	62	154	21	17	7	71	31	38	6	.274	.409
George Cutshaw	2B84	R	34	98	350	46	119	18	4	0	53	11	11	14	.340	.414
Rabbit Maranville	SS153	R	29	153	612	90	180	25	12	1	70	47	38	25	.294	.379
Clyde Barnhart	3B118	R	26	124	449	66	116	15	13	3	62	32	36	3	.258	.370
Possum Whitted	OF102, 1B7	R	31	108	403	60	114	23	7	6	63	26	21	5	.283	.427
Max Carey	OF139	B	31	140	521	85	161	34	4	7	56	70	30	37	.309	.430
Carson Bigbee	OF146	L	26	147	632	100	204	23	17	3	42	41	19	21	.323	.427
Walter Schmidt	C111	R	34	114	393	30	111	9	3	0	38	12	13	10	.282	.321
Cotton Tierney	2B72, 3B32, OF4, SS3	R	27	117	442	49	132	22	8	3	52	24	31	4	.299	.405
2 Dave Robertson	OF58	L	31	60	230	29	74	18	3	6	48	12	16	4	.322	.504
2 Tony Brottem	C29	R	30	30	91	6	22	2	0	0	9	3	11	0	.242	.264
Ray Rohwmer	OF10	L	26	30	40	6	10	3	2	0	6	4	8	0	.250	.425
Johnny Mokan	OFf5	R	25	19	52	7	14	3	2	0	9	5	3	0	.269	.404
Bill Skiff	C13	R	25	16	45	7	13	2	0	0	11	0	4	1	.289	.333
Johnny Gooch	C13	B	26	13	38	2	9	0	0	0	3	3	1	1	.237	.237
Pie Traynor	3B3, SS1	R	22	7	19	0	5	0	0	0	2	1	2	1	.263	.263
Mike Wilson	C5	R	24	5	4	0	0	0	0	0	0	0	0	0	.000	.000
Kiki Cuyler	OF1	R	22	3	3	0	0	0	0	0	0	0	0	0	.000	.000
Bill Warwick	C1	R	23	1	1	0	0	0	0	0	0	0	0	0	.000	.000
ST. LOUIS 3rd 87-66 .569 7														BRANCH RICKEY		
TOTALS			27	154	5309	809	1635	260	88	83	733	382	452	94	.308	.437
Jack Fournier	1B149	L	31	149	574	103	197	27	9	16	86	56	43	20	.343	.505
Rogers Hornsby	2B142, OF6, SS3, 3B3, 1B1	R	25	154	592	131	235	44	18	21	126	60	48	13	.397	.639
Doc Lavan	SS150	R	30	150	560	58	145	23	11	2	82	23	30	7	.259	.350
Milt Stock	3B149	R	27	149	587	96	180	27	6	3	84	48	26	11	.307	.388
Jack Smith	OF103	L	26	116	411	66	135	22	9	7	33	21	24	11	.328	.477
Les Mann	OF79	R	28	97	256	57	84	12	7	7	30	23	28	5	.328	.512
Austin McHenry	OF152	R	25	152	574	92	201	37	8	17	102	38	49	10	.350	.531
Verne Clemons	C109	R	29	117	341	29	109	16	2	2	48	33	17	0	.320	.396
Joe Schultz	OF67, 3B3, 1B2	R	27	92	275	37	85	20	3	6	45	15	11	4	.309	.469
Pickles Dillhoefer	C69	R	27	76	162	19	39	4	0	0	15	11	7	2	.241	.315
Cliff Heathcote (BP)	OF51	L	23	62	156	18	38	6	2	0	9	10	9	7	.244	.308
Heinie Mueller	OF54	L	21	55	176	25	62	10	6	1	34	11	22	2	.352	.494
Burt Shotton	OF11	L	36	38	48	9	12	1	1	1	7	10	3	0	.250	.375
2 Eddie Ainsmith	C23, 1B1	R	31	27	62	5	18	0	1	0	5	3	4	0	.290	.323
Specs Toporcer	2B12, SS2	R	22	22	53	4	14	1	0	0	2	3	4	1	.264	.283
1 Hal Janvrin	1B9, 3B1	R	28	18	32	5	9	1	0	0	5	1	0	1	.281	.313
Herb Hunter	1B1	R	25	9	7	3	0	0	0	0	0	0	0	0	.000	.000
Charlie Niebergall	C3	R	22	5	6	1	1	0	0	0	1	0	1	0	.167	.167
Walt Irwin		R	23	4	1	1	0	0	0	0	0	0	1	0	.000	.000
Reuben Ewing	SS1	R	21	3	1	0	0	0	0	0	0	0	1	0	.000	.000
Howie Jones	OF1	L	24	3	2	0	0	0	0	0	0	0	0	0	.000	.000
George Gilham		R	21	1	1	0	0	0	0	0	0	0	0	0	.000	.000
Lew McCarty		R	32	1	1	0	0	0	0	0	0	0	1	0	.000	.000
BOSTON 4th 79-74 .516 15														FRED MITCHELL		
TOTALS			28	153	5385	721	1561	209	100	61	630	377	470	94	.290	.400
Walter Holke	1B150	R	28	150	579	60	151	15	10	3	63	41	41	8	.261	.337
Hod Ford	2B119, SS33	R	23	152	555	50	155	29	5	3	61	36	49	2	.279	.360
Walter Barbare	SS121, 3B18, 2B2	R	29	134	550	66	166	22	7	0	49	24	28	11	.302	.367
Tony Boeckel	3B153	R	28	153	592	93	185	20	13	10	84	52	41	20	.313	.441
Billy Southworth	OF141	L	28	141	569	86	175	25	15	7	79	36	13	22	.308	.441
Ray Powell	OF149	L	32	149	624	114	191	25	18	12	74	58	85	6	.306	.462
Walton Cruise	OF102, 1B2	L	31	108	344	47	119	16	7	8	55	48	24	10	.346	.503
Mickey O'Neil	C95	R	23	98	277	26	69	9	4	2	29	23	21	2	.249	.332
Fred Nicholson	OF59, 1B4, 2B2	R	26	83	245	36	80	11	7	5	41	17	29	5	.327	.490
Hank Gowdy	C53	R	31	64	164	17	49	7	2	2	17	16	11	2	.299	.402
Frank Gibson	C41	B	30	83	125	14	33	5	4	2	13	3	17	0	.264	.416
Lloyd Christenbury	2B32, SS2, 3B2	L	27	63	125	34	44	6	2	3	16	21	7	3	.352	.504
Al Nixon	OF45	L	35	62	138	25	33	6	1	1	9	7	11	3	.239	.348
Jack Scott	P47	L	29	51	88	14	30	5	1	1	12	5	7	1	.341	.455
John Sullivan		R	31	5	5	0	0	0	0	0	0	0	1	0	.000	.000
BROOKLYN 5th 77-75 .507 16.5														WILBERT ROBINSON		
TOTALS			31	152	5263	667	1476	209	85	59	584	325	400	91	.280	.386
Ray Schmandt	1B92	R	25	95	350	42	107	15	5	5	43	11	22	3	.306	.366
Pete Kilduff	2B105, 3B1	R	28	107	372	45	107	15	10	3	45	31	36	6	.288	.406
Ivy Olson	SS133, 2B20	R	35	151	652	88	174	22	10	3	35	28	26	4	.267	.345
Jimmy Johnston	3B150, SS3	R	31	152	624	104	203	41	14	5	56	45	26	28	.325	.460
Tommy Griffith	OF124	L	31	129	455	66	142	21	6	12	71	36	13	2	.312	.464
Hy Myers	OF124, 2B21, 3B1	L	32	144	549	51	158	14	4	4	68	22	51	8	.288	.350
Zack Wheat	OF148	L	33	148	568	91	182	31	10	14	85	44	19	11	.320	.484
Otto Miller	C91	R	32	91	286	22	67	8	6	1	27	9	26	2	.234	.315
Bernie Neis	OF77, 2B1	B	25	102	230	34	59	5	4	4	34	25	41	9	.257	.365
Ernie Krueger	C52	L	30	65	163	18	43	11	4	3	21	14	12	2	.264	.436
Wally Hood	OF20	R	26	56	65	16	17	1	2	1	4	9	14	2	.262	.385
1 Ed Konetchy	1B54	R	35	55	197	25	53	6	5	3	23	19	21	3	.269	.396
Dutch Ruether	P36	L	27	49	97	12	34	5	2	1	14	7	6	3	.351	.505
2 Hal Janvrin	SS17, 2B10, 1B8, 3B5, OF1	R	28	44	92	8	18	4	0	0	14	7	6	3	.196	.239
Zack Taylor	C30	R	22	30	102	6	23	6	0	0	8	4	5	1	.196	.235
Chuck Ward (XJ)	SS12	R	26	12	28	1	2	1	0	0	1	1	1	0	.071	.107
2 Eddie Eayrs		L	30	6	6	0	1	0	0	0	2	0	0	0	.167	.167
Jack Sheehan	2B2, SS1, 3B1	R	28	5	12	2	0	0	0	0	0	0	1	0	.000	.000
Bill Lamar	OF1	L	24	3	3	1	1	0	0	0	0	1	0	0	.333	.333

Pitching

NAME	T	AGE	W	L	PCT	SV	G	GS	CG	IP	H	BB	SO	SHO	ERA
		30	94	59	.614	18	153	153	71	1372	1497	295	357	9	3.56
Art Nehf	L	28	20	10	.667	1	41	34	18	261	266	55	67	2	3.62
Fred Toney	R	32	18	11	.621	3	42	32	16	249	274	65	63	1	3.61
Jesse Barnes	R	28	15	9	.625	6	42	31	15	259	298	44	56	1	3.10
Phil Douglas	R	31	15	10	.600	2	40	27	13	222	266	55	55	3	4.21
Rosy Ryan	R	23	7	10	.412	3	36	16	5	147	140	32	58	0	3.74
Slim Sallee	L	36	6	4	.600	2	37	0	0	96	115	14	23	0	3.65
Rube Benton (DE)	L	31	5	2	.714	0	18	9	3	72	72	17	11	1	2.87
Red Shea	R	22	5	2	.714	0	1	3	2	32	32	2	10	0	3.09
1 Pol Perritt	R	29	2	0	1.000	0	5	1	0	12	12	2	5	0	3.75
2 Red Causey	R	27	1	1	.500	0	7	1	0	15	15	6	1	0	2.40
Walt Zink	R	22	0	0	—	0	2	0	0	4	4	3	1	0	2.25
Claude Jonnard	R	23	0	0	—	0	4	0	0	4	4	0	7	0	0.00
		29	90	63	.588	10	154	154	88	1416	1448	322	500	10	3.16
Wilbur Cooper	L	29	22	14	.611	0	38	38	29	327	341	80	134	2	3.25
Whitey Glazner	R	27	14	5	.737	1	36	25	15	234	214	58	88	0	2.77
Babe Adams	R	39	14	5	.737	2	25	20	11	160	155	18	55	2	2.64
Earl Hamilton	L	29	13	15	.464	0	35	30	12	225	237	58	59	2	3.36
Johnny Morrison	R	25	9	7	.563	0	21	17	11	144	131	33	52	3	2.88
Jimmy Zinn	R	26	7	6	.538	4	32	9	5	127	159	30	49	1	3.68
Chief Yellowhorse (GJ)	R	23	5	3	.625	1	10	4	1	48	45	13	19	0	3.00
Hal Carlson	R	29	4	8	.333	4	31	10	3	110	121	23	37	0	4.26
1 Elmer Ponder	R	28	2	0	1.000	0	8	1	1	25	19	3	3	0	2.16
Lyle Bigbee	R	26	0	0	—	0	5	0	0	8	4	4	1	0	1.13
Bill Hughes	R	24	0	0	—	0	1	0	0	2	3	1	2	0	4.50
Phil Morrison	R	26	0	0	—	0	1	0	0	1	0	1	0	0	0.00
Drew Rader	R	20	0	0	—	0	1	0	0	2	1	0	1	0	0.00
Rip Wheeler	R	23	0	0	—	0	3	0	0	3	6	1	0	0	9.00
		28	87	66	.569	16	154	154	70	1372	1486	399	464	10	3.62
Jesse Haines	R	27	18	12	.600	0	37	29	13	244	261	56	84	2	3.50
Bill Doak	R	30	15	6	.714	1	32	29	13	209	224	37	83	1	2.58
Bill Pertica	R	22	14	10	.583	2	28	31	15	208	212	70	67	2	3.38
Roy Walker	R	28	11	12	.478	3	28	23	11	171	194	53	25	0	4.21
2 Jeff Pfeffer	R	33	9	3	.750	0	18	13	7	99	115	28	22	1	4.27
Bill Sherdel	L	24	9	8	.529	1	28	8	5	144	137	38	57	1	3.19
Lou North	R	30	4	4	.500	7	40	0	0	86	81	32	28	0	3.56
1 Ferdie Schupp	L	30	2	0	1.000	1	9	4	1	37	42	21	22	0	4.13
Bill Bailey	L	33	2	5	.286	0	19	6	3	74	95	22	20	1	4.26
Tink Riviere	R	21	1	0	1.000	0	18	2	0	38	45	20	15	0	6.16
Marv Goodwin	R	29	1	2	.333	1	14	4	1	36	47	9	7	0	3.75
Jakie May	L	25	1	3	.250	0	8	5	1	21	29	12	5	0	4.71
Mike Kircher	R	23	0	1	.000	3	3	0	0	3	4	1	2	0	9.00
		26	79	74	.516	12	153	153	74	1385	1488	420	382	11	3.90
Joe Oeschger	R	29	20	14	.588	0	46	36	19	299	303	97	68	3	3.52
Dana Fillingim	R	27	15	10	.600	1	44	23	11	240	249	56	54	3	3.45
Jack Scott	R	29	15	13	.536	3	47	28	16	234	258	57	83	2	3.69
Mule Watson	R	24	14	13	.519	2	44	31	15	259	269	57	48	1	3.86
Hugh McQuillan	R	25	13	17	.433	5	45	31	13	250	284	90	94	2	4.00
Cy Morgan	L	25	1	1	.500	1	17	0	0	37	37	17	8	0	6.60
Garland Braxton	L	21	1	3	.250	0	17	2	0	37	44	17	16	0	4.87
Johnny Cooney	L	20	0	1	.000	0	21	19	10	9	6	3	0	3.86
Al Pierotti	R	25	0	0	—	0	2	0	0	3	3	1	3	0	18.00
Leo Townsend (SA)	L	30	0	0	—	0	1	0	0	1	2	2	0	0	36.00
Ira Townsend	R	27	0	0	—	0	4	0	0	7	11	4	0	0	6.43
1 Eddie Eayrs	R	30	0	0	—	0	5	0	0	9	9	1	6	0	16.20
Dick Rudolph (DP) 33															
		28	77	75	.507	12	152	152	82	1363	1556	361	471	8	3.70
Burleigh Grimes	R	27	22	13	.629	0	37	35	30	302	313	76	136	2	2.84
Leon Cadore	R	30	13	14	.481	0	35	23	12	212	243	46	79	1	4.16
Clarence Mitchell	L	30	11	9	.550	2	37	18	13	190	206	46	39	3	3.89
Dutch Ruether	L	27	10	13	.435	2	36	27	12	211	247	67	78	1	4.27
Sherry Smith	L	30	7	11	.389	4	35	17	9	175	232	34	36	0	3.91
Johnny Miljus	R	26	3	5	.667	1	28	9	3	94	115	37	37	0	4.21
Al Mamaux	R	27	3	3	.500	1	12	1	0	43	36	13	21	0	3.14
2 Ferdie Schupp	L	30	3	4	.429	2	20	7	1	61	75	27	26	0	4.57
Ray Gordinier	R	29	1	0	1.000	2	3	0	0	12	10	8	4	0	5.25
1 Jeff Pfeffer	R	33	1	0	.167	0	1	0	0	1	3	0	0	0	4.50
2 Sweetbreads Bailey	R	26	0	0	—	0	24	0	0	24	35	7	6	0	5.25
George Mohart	R	29	0	0	—	0	2	0	0	1	1	1	1	0	3.86

NAME	G by Pos	B	AGE	G	AB	R	H	2B	3B	HR	RBI	BB	SO	SB	BA	SA
CINCINNATI 6th 70-83 .458 24	**PAT MORAN**															
TOTALS			28	153	5112	618	1421	221	94	20	560	375	308	117	.278	.370
Jake Daubert	1B136	L	37	136	516	69	158	18	12	2	64	24	16	12	.308	.399
Sammy Bohne	2B102, 3B53	B	24	153	613	98	175	28	16	3	44	54	38	26	.285	.398
Larry Kopf	SS93, 2B4, 3B3, OF1	B	30	107	367	36	80	8	3	1	25	43	20	3	.218	.264
Heinie Groh (HO)	3B97	R	31	97	357	54	118	19	6	1	48	36	17	22	.331	.417
Rube Bressler	OF85, 1B6	R	26	109	323	41	99	18	6	1	54	39	20	5	.307	.409
Edd Roush	OF108	L	28	112	418	68	147	27	12	4	71	31	8	19	.352	.502
Pat Duncan	OF145	R	27	145	532	57	164	27	10	2	60	44	33	3	.308	.408
Ivy Wingo	C92, OF1	L	30	95	295	20	79	7	6	3	38	21	14	3	.268	.363
Bubbles Hargrave	C73	R	28	93	263	28	76	17	8	1	38	12	15	4	.289	.430
Lew Fonseca	2B50, 1B16, OF16	R	22	82	297	38	82	10	3	1	41	8	13	2	.276	.340
Sam Crane	SS63, 3B2, OF1	R	26	73	215	20	50	10	2	0	16	14	14	2	.233	.298
2 Greasy Neale	OF60	L	29	63	241	39	58	10	5	0	12	22	16	4	.241	.324
Charlie See	OF30	L	24	37	106	11	26	5	1	1	7	5	3	3	.245	.340
Dode Paskert	OF24	R	39	27	92	8	16	1	1	0	4	4	8	0	.174	.207
Denny Williams	OF1	L	24	10	7	0	0	0	0	0	0	0	2	0	.000	.000
Astyanax Douglass	C4	L	23	4	7	1	1	0	0	0	0	0	1	0	.143	.143
Wally Kimmick	3B2	R	24	3	6	0	1	0	0	0	1	0	1	0	.167	.167
Kenny Hogan	OF1	L	18	1	2	0	0	0	0	0	0	0	1	0	.000	.000

NAME		T	AGE	W	L	PCT	SV	G	GS	CG	IP	H	BB	SO	SHO	ERA
			29	70	83	.458	9	153	153	83	1363	1500	305	408	7	3.46
Eppa Rixey		L	30	19	18	.514	1	40	36	21	301	324	66	76	2	2.78
Rube Marquard		L	34	17	14	.548	0	39	35	18	266	291	50	88	3	3.38
Dolf Luque		R	30	17	19	.472	3	41	36	25	304	318	64	102	3	3.38
Pete Donohue		R	20	7	6	.538	1	21	11	7	118	117	26	44	0	3.36
Fritz Coumbe		L	31	3	4	.429	1	28	6	3	87	89	21	12	0	3.20
Hod Eller		R	26	2	2	.500	1	10	5	3	34	46	15	7	0	5.03
Cliff Markle		R	27	2	6	.250	0	10	6	5	67	75	20	23	0	3.76
Bob Geary		R	30	1	1	.500	0	6	3	1	29	38	2	10	0	4.35
Clint Rogge		R	31	1	2	.333	0	6	3	0	35	43	9	12	0	4.11
Lynn Brenton		R	31	1	8	.111	1	17	9	2	60	80	17	19	0	4.05
Alan Clarke		L	25	0	1	.000	1	7	1	1	5	7	2	1	0	5.40
Buddy Napier		R	31	0	2	.000	1	22	6	1	57	72	13	14	0	5.53
Ray Fisher (DL) 33																

NAME	G by Pos	B	AGE	G	AB	R	H	2B	3B	HR	RBI	BB	SO	SB	BA	SA
CHICAGO 7th 64-89 .418 30	**JOHNNY EVERS** 41-55 .427	**BILL KILLEFER** 23-34 .404														
TOTALS			28	153	5321	668	1553	234	56	37	609	343	374	70	.292	.378
Ray Grimes	1B147	R	27	147	530	91	170	38	6	6	79	70	55	5	.321	.449
Zeb Terry	2B122	R	30	123	488	59	134	18	1	2	45	27	19	1	.275	.328
Charlie Hollocher	SS137	L	25	140	558	71	161	28	8	3	37	43	13	5	.289	.384
Charlie Deal	3B113	R	29	115	422	52	122	19	4	0	66	13	9	3	.289	.393
Max Flack	OF130	L	31	133	572	80	172	31	4	6	37	32	15	17	.301	.400
George Michael	OF108	R	29	111	393	54	122	7	2	0	43	11	13	17	.310	.338
Turner Barber	OF123	L	27	127	452	73	141	14	4	1	54	41	24	5	.314	.369
Bob O'Farrell	C90	R	24	96	260	32	65	12	7	4	32	18	14	2	.250	.396
J. Kelleher 3B37, 2B27, 1B11, SS11, OF1		R	27	95	301	31	93	11	7	4	47	16	16	2	.309	.432
Babe Twombly	OF45	L	25	87	175	22	66	8	1	1	18	11	10	4	.377	.451
2 John Sullivan	OF66	R	31	76	240	28	79	14	4	4	41	19	26	3	.329	.471
Tom Daly	C47	R	29	51	143	12	34	7	1	0	22	8	8	1	.238	.301
Bill Killefer	C42	R	33	45	133	11	43	1	0	0	16	4	4	3	.323	.331
Pete Alexander	P31	R	34	31	95	8	29	3	1	1	14	2	13	0	.305	.389
Bill Marriott	2B6, SS1, 3B1, OF1	L	31	30	38	3	12	1	1	0	7	4	1	0	.316	.395
1 Dave Robertson	OF7	L	31	22	36	7	8	0	0	0	14	1	3	0	.222	.306
Hooks Warner	3B10	L	27	14	38	4	8	1	0	0	2	1	1	1	.211	.237
Carter Elliott	SS10	R	27	12	28	5	7	2	0	0	5	3	0	1	.250	.321
Red Thomas	OF8	R	23	8	30	5	8	3	0	0	2	0	5	2	.267	.367
Kettle Wirts	C5	R	23	7	11	0	2	0	0	0	1	0	3	0	.182	.182
Joe Klugman	2B5	R	24	6	21	6	6	0	0	0	2	4	5	0	.286	.286

NAME		T	AGE	W	L	PCT	SV	G	GS	CG	IP	H	BB	SO	SHO	ERA
			27	64	89	.418	7	153	153	73	1363	1605	409	441	7	4.39
Pete Alexander		R	34	15	13	.536	1	31	30	21	252	286	33	77	3	3.39
Virgil Cheeves		R	20	11	12	.478	0	37	26	13	163	192	47	39	1	4.64
Speed Martin		R	27	11	15	.423	1	37	28	13	217	245	68	86	1	4.36
Buck Freeman		R	27	9	7	.474	3	38	20	6	177	189	70	42	0	4.12
Lefty York		R	28	5	9	.357	1	40	11	4	139	170	63	57	1	4.73
Lefty Tyler		L	31	3	2	.600	0	10	6	4	50	59	14	8	0	3.24
Percy Jones		L	21	3	5	.375	0	32	3	1	99	116	39	46	0	4.55
2 Elmer Ponder		R	28	3	6	.333	0	16	11	5	89	117	17	31	0	4.75
Hippo Vaughn		L	33	3	11	.214	0	17	14	7	109	153	31	30	0	6.03
Tony Kaufmann		R	20	1	0	1.000	1	3	13	12	3	4	0	0	0	4.15
George Stueland		R	22	0	1	.000	2	1	0	1	11	11	7	4	0	5.73
Ollie Hanson		R	25	0	2	.000	0	5	4	1	9	9	6	2	0	7.00
Vic Keen		R	22	0	3	.000	0	5	5	1	25	29	9	9	0	4.68
1 Sweetbreads Bailey		R	26	0	0	—	1	3	0	0	5	6	2	2	0	3.60
Oscar Fuhr		L	27	0	0	—	0	1	0	1	4	11	0	2	0	9.00
Claude Hendrix (DO) 32																

NAME	G by Pos	B	AGE	G	AB	R	H	2B	3B	HR	RBI	BB	SO	SB	BA	SA
PHILADELPHIA 8th 51-103 .331 43.5	**WILD BILL DONOVAN** 25-62 .287	**KAISER WILHELM** 23-34 .404														
TOTALS			28	154	5329	617	1512	238	50	88	573	294	615	66	.284	.397
2 Ed Konetchy	1B71	R	35	72	268	38	86	17	4	8	59	21	17	3	.321	.504
Jimmy Smith	2B66	R	26	67	247	31	57	8	4	1	22	11	28	2	.231	.320
Frank Parkinson	SS106, 3B1	R	26	108	391	36	99	20	2	5	32	13	81	3	.253	.353
Russ Wrightstone	3B54, OF37, 2B4	L	28	119	372	59	110	13	4	9	51	10	28	4	.296	.425
Bevo LeBourveau	OF76	L	24	93	281	42	83	12	5	6	35	29	51	4	.295	.438
Cy Williams	OF146	L	33	146	562	67	180	21	6	18	75	30	32	5	.320	.488
1 Irish Meusel	OF84	R	28	84	343	59	121	21	7	12	55	18	17	8	.353	.560
Frank Bruggy	C86, 1B2	R	30	96	277	28	86	11	2	8	28	23	37	6	.310	.419
Cliff Lee	1B48, OF27, C2	R	24	88	286	31	88	14	4	9	29	13	34	3	.308	.427
Dots Miller	3B41, 1B38, 2B6	R	34	86	320	37	95	11	3	4	23	15	27	3	.297	.350
Lee King	OF57	R	28	64	216	25	58	19	4	4	32	8	37	1	.269	.449
1 Johnny Rawlings	2B60	R	28	60	254	20	74	14	2	1	16	8	12	4	.291	.374
Ralph Miller	SS46, 3B10	R	25	57	204	19	62	10	0	3	26	6	10	3	.304	.397
John Peters	C44	R	27	55	155	7	45	4	3	0	23	6	13	4	.290	.374
2 Goldie Rapp	3B50, 2B1	B	27	52	202	28	56	7	1	1	10	14	8	6	.275	.337
2 John Monroe	2B28, 3B9	R	22	41	133	13	38	4	2	1	8	11	9	2	.286	.368
2 Butch Henline	C32	R	26	33	111	8	34	2	0	4	6	2	6	1	.306	.324
1 Casey Stengel (LJ)	OF15	L	30	24	59	7	18	3	1	0	4	6	7	1	.305	.390
1 Greasy Neale	OF16	L	29	22	57	7	12	1	0	1	1	9	5	3	.211	.228
2 Curt Walker	OF21	L	24	21	77	11	26	2	1	0	8	5	5	0	.338	.390
Lance Richbourg	2B4	L	23	10	5	2	1	1	0	0	0	0	3	1	.200	.400
Mack Wheat	C9	L	28	10	27	1	5	2	0	0	1	1	6	0	.185	.333
Don Rader	SS9	L	27	9	32	4	9	1	0	0	3	5	5	0	.281	.344
Art Fletcher (VR) 36, Gene Paulette (DL) 30																

NAME		T	AGE	W	L	PCT	SV	G	GS	CG	IP	H	BB	SO	SHO	ERA
			25	51	103	.331	8	154	154	82	1349	1665	371	333	5	4.48
Lee Meadows		R	26	11	16	.407	0	28	27	15	194	226	62	52	2	4.31
Jimmy Ring		R	26	10	19	.345	1	34	30	21	246	258	88	88	0	4.25
Bill Hubbell		R	24	8	16	.360	2	36	30	15	220	269	38	43	1	4.34
Jesse Winters		R	27	5	10	.333	0	18	14	10	114	142	38	22	0	3.64
George Smith		R	29	4	20	.167	1	39	28	12	221	303	52	45	1	4.76
1 Red Causey		R	27	3	3	.500	0	7	4	4	51	58	11	8	0	2.82
Stan Baumgartner		L	28	3	6	.333	0	22	7	2	67	103	22	13	0	6.98
Huck Betts		R	24	3	7	.300	4	32	2	1	101	141	14	28	0	4.46
Lefty Weinert		L	19	1	0	1.000	0	8	0	0	12	8	5	2	0	1.50
Jimmie Keenan		L	23	1	2	.333	0	15	2	0	32	48	15	7	0	6.75
Duke Sedgwick		R	23	1	2	.250	0	16	5	1	71	81	32	21	0	4.94
Petie Behan		R	33	0	1	.000	0	2	2	1	11	17	1	3	0	5.73
Kaiser Wilhelm		R	47	0	0	—	0	4	0	0	8	11	3	1	0	3.38

WORLD SERIES — NEW YORK (NL) 5   NEW YORK (AL) 3

LINE SCORES

TEAM	1	2	3	4	5	6	7	8	9	10	11	12	R	H	E
Game 1 October 5 at Polo Grounds															
NY(AL)	1	0	0		0	1	1		0	0	0		3	7	0
NY(NL)	0	0	0		0	0	0		0	5	0		0	5	0
		Mays				Douglas, Barnes (1)									
Game 2 October 6 at Polo Grounds															
NY(NL)	0	0	0		0	0	0		0	0	0		0	2	3
NY(AL)	0	0	0		1	0	0		0	2	X		3	3	0
		Nehf				Hoyt									
Game 3 October 7 at Polo Grounds															
NY(AL)	0	0	4		0	0	0		0	1	0		5	8	0
NY(NL)	0	0	4		0	0	0		8	1	X		13	20	0
		Shawkey, Quinn (3), Collins (7), Rogers (7)				Toney, Barnes (3)									
Game 4 October 9 at Polo Grounds															
NY(NL)	0	0	0		0	0	0		0	3	1		4	9	1
NY(AL)	0	0	0		0	1	0		0	0	1		2	7	1
		Douglas				Mays									
Game 5 October 10 at Polo Grounds															
NY(AL)	0	0	1		2	0	0		0	0	0		3	6	1
NY(NL)	1	0	0		0	0	0		0	0	0		1	10	1
		Hoyt				Nehf									
Game 6 October 11 at Polo Grounds															
NY(NL)	0	3	0		4	0	1		0	0	0		8	13	0
NY(AL)	3	2	0		0	0	0		0	0	0		5	7	2
		Toney, Barnes (1)				Harper, Shawkey (2), Piercy (9)									
Game 7 October 12 at Polo Grounds															
NY(AL)	0	1	0		0	0	0		0	0	0		1	8	1
NY(NL)	0	0	0		1	0	0		1	0	X		2	6	0
		Mays				Douglas									
Game 8 October 13 at Polo Grounds															
NY(NL)	1	0	0		0	0	0		0	0	0		1	6	0
NY(AL)	0	0	0		0	0	0		0	0	0		0	4	1
		Nehf				Hoyt									

COMPOSITE BATTING

NAME	POS	G	AB	R	H	2B	3B	HR	RBI	BA
New York (NL)										
Totals		8	264	29	71	13	4	2	28	.269
Burns	OF	8	33	2	11	4	1	0	2	.333
Bancroft	SS	8	33	3	5	1	0	0	3	.152
Rawlings	2B	8	30	2	10	3	0	0	4	.333
Frisch	3B	8	30	5	9	0	1	0	1	.300
Kelly	1B	8	30	3	7	1	0	0	4	.233
I. Meusel	OF	8	29	4	10	2	1	1	7	.345
Youngs	OF	8	25	3	7	1	1	0	4	.280
Snyder	C	7	22	4	8	1	0	1	3	.364
Barnes	P	3	9	3	4	0	0	0	0	.444
Nehf	P	3	9	0	0	0	0	0	0	.000
Douglas	P	3	7	0	0	0	0	0	0	.000
Smith	C	3	7	0	0	0	0	0	0	.000
Toney	P	2	0	0	0	0	0	0	0	—
New York (AL)										
Totals		8	241	22	50	7	1	2	20	.207
Miller	OF	8	31	3	5	1	0	2	0	.161
B. Meusel	OF	8	30	3	6	2	0	0	3	.200
Peckinpaugh	SS	8	28	2	5	1	0	0	1	.179
Ward	2B	8	26	1	6	0	0	0	4	.231
Pipp	1B	8	26	1	4	1	0	0	4	.154
Schang	C	7	21	1	6	1	1	0	1	.286
McNally	3B	7	20	3	4	1	0	0	1	.200
Ruth	OF	6	16	3	5	0	0	1	4	.313
Fewster	OF	4	10	3	2	0	0	0	2	.200
Hoyt	P	3	9	0	2	0	0	0	0	.222
Mays	P	3	9	0	1	0	0	0	0	.111
Baker	3B	4	8	0	2	1	0	0	0	.250
Shawkey	P	2	4	1	2	0	0	0	0	.500
Quinn	P	2	2	0	0	0	0	0	0	.000
DeVormer	C	2	2	0	0	0	0	0	0	.000
Collins	P	1	1	0	0	0	0	0	0	—
Harper	P	1	0	0	0	0	0	0	0	—
Piercy	P	1	0	0	0	0	0	0	0	—
Rogers	P	1	0	0	0	0	0	0	0	—

COMPOSITE PITCHING

NAME	G	IP	H	BB	SO	W	L	SV	ERA
New York (NL)									
Totals	8	71	50	27	44	5	3	0	2.53
Nehf	3	26	13	13	8	1	2	0	1.38
Douglas	3	26	20	5	17	2	1	0	2.07
Barnes	3	16.1	10	6	18	2	0	0	1.65
Toney	2	2.2	7	3	1	0	0	0	23.63
New York (AL)									
Totals	8	70	71	22	38	3	5	0	3.09
Hoyt	3	27	18	11	18	2	1	0	0.00
Mays	3	26	20	0	9	1	2	0	1.73
Shawkey	2	9	13	6	5	0	1	0	7.00
Quinn	1	3.2	8	2	2	0	1	0	9.82
Harper	1	1.1	4	0	1	0	0	0	20.25
Rogers	1	1.1	3	0	1	0	0	0	6.75
Piercy	1	1	2	2	0	0	1	0	0.00
Collins	1	0.2	4	1	0	0	0	0	54.00

1922 It's a Bird, It's a plane, It's . . .

The fact that both pennant winners would repeat their 1921 championships paled into insignificance in face of the continuing trend to more home runs—a trend that would surely change the complexion of the national game. As the Roaring Twenties were reaching full stride, baseball too, hypoed its activity by spicing the 1922 season with 1,055 homers, a remarkable feat in comparison to five years before when both leagues combined for only 339 ciruit clouts. Although the new slightly more lively ball introduced in 1909 started a slow rise in thc home run totals, it was the outlawing of the spitball and other trick pitches in 1920 combined with the introduction of a really lively ball in 1920 (American League) and 1921 (National League) which was responsible for launching a skyrocketing acceleration in home run production in both leagues. Babe Ruth drew national attention to the majestic circuit clout. After watching Ruth's following and salary grow, an instantaneous chain reaction was set in motion, with the result that hitters concentrated more on hitting the long ball than on going for averages. If anything, the ball player found that the home run was the way to instant success and the knowledge that someone, somewhere, would have remembered him for being a colossus of strength, if only for a fleeting moment. Such was the effect of the new weapon that by the time the cheering subsided and the season closed, both leagues found their total earned run average had climbed to over four runs a game, a statistical embarrassment symptomatic of pitching's subservience to hitting in the lively post-war era.

Ironically, the man who altered baseball for all time was not in uniform for the start of the fireworks. Commissioner Landis had suspended Ruth and teammate Bob Meusel for barnstorming after the 1921 World Series, and not until May 20 were the two Yankee sluggers permitted to suit up. Although New York managed to stay on top of the American League, even before the return of the two outfielders, the charging St. Louis Browns edged past the Yankees to take a slight lead in July. The Brownies were winning consistently with good pitching and the best attack in the league by holding a hand of four eventual 100-RBI men in Marty McManus, Baby Doll Jacobson, Ken Williams, and George Sisler, who also won his second batting crown with a torrid .420 average. Yet, while the Browns were winning, so were the Yankees. And when both teams got together in St. Louis in mid-August, the Yankees were able to make the better of it to retake the top spot. Both teams stayed hot during the Indian summer, but

the Yankees never relinquished their slight lead and finished in front with a paper-thin margin of one game. Nevertheless, the Browns' 93 wins made their 1922 edition the best club in the history of the franchise—a franchise which would end in 1953.

The National League race was dominated by the New York Giants, who led all year and held a seven-game margin at the finish. Irish Meusel, George Kelly, and Ross Youngs led a team attack which finished with a .304 batting average, and veteran Casey Stengel hit .368 after being installed in center field in mid-season. Ace pitcher Phil Douglas was 11-4 when he was barred in mid-season after writing a foolish letter implying that he would welcome a bribe to throw games, but his slack was taken up by Art Nehf, Rosie Ryan, Jesse Barnes, and free-agent signee Jack Scott, who recovered from a sore arm to win eight games after Douglas' ouster. Cincinnati threatened with its pitching, and the Cards and Pirates boasted of strong offenses, but none of them could overtake the Giants after New York's early-season getaway. Rogers Hornsby of St. Louis, singlehandedly kept the Cardinals in the first division by hitting .401, belting 42 home runs, and driving 152 runs across the plate, a performance which earned him the National League's first Triple Crown since Hugh Duffy turned the trick for Boston in 1894.

The Yankees came into the World Series with high hopes but flopped miserably, dropping four games while managing only a second-game tie. The Giant pitchers shut off the Yankee attack by holding Babe Ruth to a pitiful .118 mark. In comparison, Heinie Groh and Frankie Frisch of the Giants both posted .470 plus averages. The Series return to the best four-of-seven format also marked the first appearance of radio microphones at the fall classic.

1922 AMERICAN LEAGUE

NAME	G by Pos	B	AGE	G	AB	R	H	2B	3B	HR	RBI	BB	SO	SB	BA	SA
NEW YORK	1st 94-60 .610			MILLER HUGGINS												
	TOTALS		29	154	5245	758	1504	220	75	95	674	497	532	62	.287	.412
Wally Pipp	1B152	L	29	152	577	96	190	32	10	9	90	56	32	7	.329	.466
Aaron Ward	2B152, 3B2	R	25	154	558	69	149	19	5	7	68	45	64	7	.267	.357
Everett Scott	SS154	R	29	154	557	64	150	23	5	3	45	23	22	4	.269	.345
2 Joe Dugan	3B60	R	25	60	252	44	72	9	1	3	25	13	21	1	.286	.365
Bob Meusel (SL)	OF121	R	25	121	473	61	151	26	11	16	84	40	58	13	.319	.522
Whitey Witt	OF138	L	26	140	528	98	157	11	6	4	40	89	29	5	.297	.364
Babe Ruth (SL)	OF110, 1B1	B	27	110	406	94	128	24	8	35	99	84	80	2	.315	.672
Wally Schang	C119	B	32	124	408	46	130	21	7	1	53	53	36	12	.319	.412
Frank Baker (JJ)	3B60	L	36	69	234	30	65	12	3	7	36	15	14	1	.278	.444
Mike McNally	3B34, 2B9, SS4, 1B1	R	28	52	143	20	36	2	2	0	18	16	14	2	.252	.294
1 Elmer Miller	OF51	R	35	51	172	31	46	7	2	3	18	11	12	2	.267	.384
1 Chick Fewster	OF38, 2B2	R	26	44	132	20	32	4	1	1	9	16	23	1	.242	.311
Bullet Joe Bush (RJ)	P39	R	29	39	95	15	31	6	2	0	12	3	11	0	.326	.432
Fred Hofmann	C28	R	28	37	91	13	27	5	3	2	10	9	12	0	.297	.484
Norm McMillan	OF23, 3B5	R	26	33	78	7	20	1	2	0	11	6	10	4	.256	.321
Camp Skinner	OF4	L	25	27	33	1	6	0	0	0	0	0	0	0	.182	.182
Al DeVormer	C17, 1B1	R	30	24	59	8	12	4	1	0	11	1	6	0	.203	.305
2 Elmer Smith	OF10	L	29	21	27	1	5	0	0	1	5	3	5	0	.185	.296
1 Johnny Mitchell	SS4	B	27	4	4	1	0	0	0	0	0	0	1	0	.000	.000

NAME	T	AGE	W	L	PCT	SV	G	GS	CG	IP	H	BB	SO	SHO	ERA
		27	94	60	.610	14	154	154	98	1394	1402	423	458	7	3.39
Bullet Joe Bush	R	29	26	7	.788	3	39	30	20	255	240	85	92	0	3.32
Bob Shawkey	R	31	20	12	.625	1	39	33	19	300	286	98	130	3	2.91
Waite Hoyt	R	22	19	12	.613	0	37	31	17	265	271	76	95	3	3.43
Sad Sam Jones	R	29	13	13	.500	8	45	28	21	260	270	76	81	0	3.67
Carl Mays	R	30	12	14	.462	2	34	29	21	240	257	50	41	1	3.60
George Murray	R	23	4	2	.667	0	22	3	0	57	53	26	14	0	3.95
Lefty O'Doul	L	25	0	0	—	0	6	0	0	16	24	12	5	0	3.38
Clem Llewellyn	R	26	0	0	—	0	1	0	0	1	1	0	0	0	0.00

NAME	G by Pos	B	AGE	G	AB	R	H	2B	3B	HR	RBI	BB	SO	SB	BA	SA
ST. LOUIS	2nd 93-61 .604 1			LEE FOHL												
	TOTALS		29	154	5416	867	1693	291	94	98	785	473	381	135	.313	.455
George Sisler	1B141	L	29	142	586	134	246	42	18	8	105	49	14	51	.420	.594
Marty McManus	2B153, 1B1	R	22	154	606	88	189	34	11	11	109	38	41	9	.312	.495
Wally Gerber	SS152	R	30	153	604	81	161	22	8	1	51	52	34	6	.267	.334
Frank Ellerbe (BK)	3B91	R	26	91	342	42	84	16	3	1	33	25	37	1	.246	.319
Jack Tobin	OF145	L	30	146	625	122	207	34	8	13	66	56	22	7	.331	.474
Baby Doll Jacobson	OF137, 1B7	R	31	145	555	88	176	22	16	9	102	46	36	19	.317	.463
Ken Williams	OF153	L	32	153	585	128	194	34	11	39	155	74	31	37	.332	.627
Hank Severeid	C134	R	31	137	517	49	166	27	7	3	78	28	12	1	.321	.427
Pat Collins	C27, 1B5	R	25	63	127	14	39	6	0	8	23	21	21	0	.307	.543
Chick Shorten	OF31	L	30	55	131	22	36	12	5	2	16	16	8	0	.275	.489
Elam Vangilder	P43	R	26	45	93	16	32	10	2	2	11	5	11	0	.344	.559
2 Eddie Foster	3B37	R	35	37	144	29	44	4	0	0	12	20	8	3	.306	.333
Herman Bronkie	3B18	R	37	23	64	7	18	4	1	0	2	6	7	0	.281	.375
Gene Robertson	3B7, SS6, 2B1	B	23	18	27	2	8	2	1	0	1	1	1	1	.296	.444
Jimmy Austin	3B11, 2B2	B	42	15	31	6	9	3	1	0	1	3	2	0	.290	.452
Cedric Durst	OF6	L	25	15	12	5	4	1	0	0	0	0	1	0	.333	.417
Josh Billings	C3	R	30	5	7	0	3	1	0	0	0	0	0	0	.429	.571

NAME	T	AGE	W	L	PCT	SV	G	GS	CG	IP	H	BB	SO	SHO	ERA
		27	93	61	.604	22	154	154	79	1392	1412	419	534	8	3.38
Urban Shocker	R	31	24	17	.585	3	48	38	29	348	365	57	149	2	3.93
Elam Vangilder	R	26	19	13	.594	4	43	30	19	245	248	48	63	3	3.42
Ray Kolp	R	27	14	4	.778	0	32	18	9	170	199	36	54	1	3.92
Dixie Davis	R	31	11	6	.647	0	25	25	7	174	162	87	65	2	4.00
Rasty Wright	R	26	9	7	.563	5	31	16	5	154	148	50	44	0	2.92
Hub Pruett	L	21	7	7	.500	7	39	8	4	120	99	59	70	0	2.32
Dave Danforth	L	32	5	2	.714	1	20	10	3	80	93	38	48	0	3.27
Bill Bayne	L	23	4	5	.444	2	26	9	3	93	86	27	38	0	4.55
Dutch Henry	L	20	0	0	—	0	4	0	0	5	7	5	2	0	5.40
Heinie Meine	R	26	0	0	—	0	1	0	0	4	5	2	0	0	4.50

NAME	G by Pos	B	AGE	G	AB	R	H	2B	3B	HR	RBI	BB	SO	SB	BA	SA
DETROIT	3rd 79-75 .513 15			TY COBB												
	TOTALS		30	155	5377	828	1641	250	87	54	735	530	378	78	.305	.414
Lu Blue	1B144	B	35	145	584	131	175	31	9	6	45	82	48	8	.300	.141
George Cutshaw	2B132	R	35	132	499	57	133	14	8	2	61	20	13	11	.267	.339
Topper Rigney	SS155	R	25	155	536	68	161	17	7	2	63	68	44	17	.300	.369
Bob Jones	3B119	L	32	124	455	65	117	10	6	3	44	36	18	4	.257	.325
Harry Heilmann (BC)	OF115, 1B5	R	27	118	455	92	162	27	10	21	92	58	28	8	.356	.598
Ty Cobb	OF134	L	35	137	526	99	211	42	16	4	99	55	24	9	.401	.565
Bobby Veach	OF154	L	34	155	618	96	202	34	13	9	126	42	27	9	.327	.468
Johnny Bassler	C117	L	27	121	372	41	120	14	0	0	41	62	12	2	.323	.360
Dan Clark	2B38, OF5, 3B1	L	28	83	185	31	54	11	3	2	26	15	11	1	.292	.432
Fred Haney	3B44, 1B11, SS2	R	24	81	213	41	75	7	4	0	25	32	14	3	.352	.423
Larry Woodall	C39	R	27	50	125	19	43	2	2	0	18	8	11	0	.344	.392
Ira Flagstead	OF31	R	28	44	91	21	28	5	3	0	11	18	11	3	.308	.527
Bob Fothergill	OF39	R	24	42	152	20	49	12	4	0	29	8	6	1	.322	.454
Clyde Manion	C21, 1B1	R	25	42	69	9	19	4	1	0	6	4	2	0	.275	.362
Chick Gagnon	SS1, 3B1	R	24	9	16	2	4	0	0	0	2	0	1	0	.250	.250
Johnny Mohardt	OF3	R	24	5	1	2	1	0	0	0	0	0	0	0	1.000	1.000

NAME	T	AGE	W	L	PCT	SV	G	GS	CG	IP	H	BB	SO	SHO	ERA
		26	79	75	.513	15	155	155	67	1391	1554	473	461	7	4.27
Herman Pillette	R	25	19	12	.613	1	40	37	18	275	270	95	71	4	2.84
Howard Ehmke	R	28	17	17	.500	1	45	29	16	280	299	101	108	1	4.21
Hooks Dauss	R	32	13	13	.500	4	39	25	12	219	251	59	72	1	4.19
Red Oldham	L	28	10	13	.435	3	43	28	9	212	256	59	72	0	4.67
Syl Johnson (BH)	R	21	7	3	.700	1	29	8	3	97	99	30	29	0	3.71
Ole Olsen	R	27	7	6	.538	3	37	15	5	137	147	40	52	0	4.54
Lil Stoner	R	23	4	4	.500	0	17	7	2	63	76	35	18	0	7.00
Carl Holling	R	25	1	1	.500	1	9	1	0	9	21	5	2	0	16.00
Bert Cole	L	26	1	6	.143	0	23	5	2	79	105	39	21	1	4.90
2 Roy Moore	R	23	0	0	—	2	4	0	0	20	29	10	9	0	5.85
Ken Holloway	R	24	0	0	—	0	2	1	0	3	4	1	1	0	0.00
Dutch Leonard (VR)															

132

CLEVELAND   4th 77-76   .506 16   TRIS SPEAKER

NAME	G by Pos	B	AGE	G	AB	R	H	2B	3B	HR	RBI	BB	SO	SB	BA	SA
TOTALS			30	155	5293	768	1544	320	73	32	698	554	331	89	.292	.398
Stuffy McInnis	1B140, C1	R	31	142	537	58	164	28	7	1	78	15	5	1	.305	.389
Bill Wambsganss	SB124, SS16, C1	R	28	143	538	89	141	22	6	0	47	60	26	17	.262	.325
Joe Sewell	SS139, 2B12	L	23	153	558	80	167	28	7	2	83	73	20	10	.299	.385
Larry Gardner	3B128	L	36	137	470	74	134	31	3	2	68	49	21	9	.285	.377
Smoky Joe Wood	OF140, 1B1	R	32	142	505	74	150	33	8	8	92	50	63	5	.297	.442
Tris Speaker	OF110	L	34	131	426	85	161	48	8	11	71	77	11	8	.378	.606
Charlie Jamieson	OF144, P2	L	29	145	567	87	183	29	11	3	57	54	22	15	.323	.429
Steve O'Neill	C130	R	30	133	392	33	122	27	4	2	65	73	25	2	.311	.416
Riggs Stephenson	3B33, 2B24, OF3	R	24	86	233	47	79	24	5	2	32	27	18	3	.339	.511
Joe Evans	OF49	R	27	75	145	35	39	6	2	0	22	8	4	11	.269	.338
Luke Sewell	C38	R	21	41	87	14	23	5	0	0	10	5	8	1	.264	.322
Jack Graney	OF13	L	36	37	58	6	9	0	0	0	2	9	12	0	.155	.155
Lou Guisto	1B24	R	27	35	84	7	21	10	1	0	9	2	7	0	.250	.393
Les Nunamaker	C15	R	33	25	43	8	13	2	0	0	7	4	3	0	.302	.349
Pat McNulty	OF22	L	23	22	59	10	16	2	1	0	5	9	5	4	.271	.339
Ginger Shinault	C11	R	29	13	15	1	2	1	0	0	0	0	2	0	.133	.200
Homer Summa	OF12	L	23	12	46	9	16	3	3	1	6	1	1	1	.348	.609
Joe Connolly	OF12	R	26	12	45	6	11	2	1	0	6	5	8	1	.244	.333
Ike Kahdot	3B2	R	22	4	2	0	0	0	0	0	0	0	1	0	.000	.000
Bill Doran	3B2	R	22	3	2	0	1	0	0	0	0	0	0	0	.500	.500
Joe Rabbitt	OF1	L	22	2	3	1	1	0	0	0	0	0	0	0	.333	.333
Chick Sorrells	SS1	R	25	2	1	0	0	0	0	0	0	0	1	0	.000	.000
1 Jack Hammond	2B1	R	31	1	4	1	1	0	0	0	0	0	0	0	.250	.250
Uke Clanton	1B1	L	24	1	1	0	0	0	0	0	0	0	0	1	.000	.000

NAME	T	AGE	W	L	PCT	SV	G	GS	CG	IP	H	BB	SO	SHO	ERA
		28	78	76	.506	7	155	155	76	1379	1605	464	489	14	4.60
George Uhle	R	23	22	16	.579	3	50	40	23	287	328	89	82	5	4.08
Stan Coveleski	R	32	17	14	.548	0	35	33	21	277	292	64	98	5	3.31
Guy Morton	R	29	14	9	.609	0	38	23	13	203	218	85	102	3	3.99
Jim Bagby	R	32	4	5	.444	1	25	10	4	98	134	39	25	0	6.34
Jim Lindsey	R	24	4	5	.444	0	29	5	0	84	105	24	29	0	6.00
Duster Mails	L	27	4	7	.364	0	26	13	4	104	122	40	54	1	5.28
Danny Boone	R	27	4	6	.400	0	11	10	4	75	87	19	9	2	4.08
Jim Joe Edwards	L	27	3	8	.273	0	25	7	0	88	113	40	44	0	4.70
Dewey Metivier	R	24	2	0	1.000	0	2	2	2	18	18	3	1	0	4.50
2 Sherry Smith	L	31	1	0	1.000	0	2	1	1	16	18	3	4	0	3.38
Phil Bedgood	R	24	1	0	1.000	0	1	1	1	9	7	4	5	0	4.00
George Winn	R	24	1	2	.333	0	8	3	1	34	44	5	7	0	4.50
Allan Sothoron	R	29	1	3	.250	0	6	4	2	25	26	14	8	0	6.48
John Middleton	R	21	0	1	.000	0	1	1	0	7	8	8	2	0	7.71
Dave Keefe	R	25	0	0	—	0	18	1	0	36	47	12	11	0	6.25
Charlie Jamieson	L	29	0	0	—	0	2	0	0	6	7	4	2	0	3.00
Joe Shaute	L	22	0	0	—	0	2	0	0	4	7	3	3	0	18.00
Logan Drake	R	22	0	0	—	0	1	0	0	3	4	2	1	0	3.00
George Edmondson	R	26	0	0	—	0	2	0	0	2	4	1	0	0	9.00
Nellie Pott	R	22	0	0	—	0	2	0	0	2	7	1	0	0	31.50
Ted Odenwald	L	20	0	0	—	0	1	0	0	1	6	2	2	0	54.00
Doc Hamann	R	21	0	0	—	0	1	0	0	0	3	3	0	0	□
Tex Jeanes	R	21	0	0	—	0	1	0	0	1	0	1	0	0	0.00

CHICAGO   5th 77-77   .500 17   KID GLEASON

NAME	G by Pos	B	AGE	G	AB	R	H	2B	3B	HR	RBI	BB	SO	SB	BA	SA
TOTALS			30	155	5267	691	1463	243	62	45	635	482	463	106	.278	.373
Earl Sheely	1B149	R	29	149	526	72	167	37	4	6	80	60	27	4	.317	.437
Eddie Collins	1B154	L	35	154	598	92	194	20	12	1	69	73	16	20	.324	.403
Ernie Johnson	SS141	L	34	145	603	85	153	17	3	0	56	40	30	21	.254	.292
Eddie Mulligan	3B86, SS7	R	27	103	372	39	87	14	8	0	31	22	32	7	.234	.315
Harry Hooper	OF149	R	34	152	602	111	183	35	8	11	80	68	33	16	.304	.444
Johnny Mostil	OF123	R	26	132	458	74	139	28	14	7	70	38	39	14	.303	.472
Bibb Falk	OF129	L	23	131	483	58	144	27	1	12	59	27	55	2	.298	.433
Ray Schalk	C142	R	29	142	442	57	124	22	3	4	60	67	36	12	.281	.371
Amos Strunk	OF75, 1B9	L	33	92	311	36	90	11	4	0	23	33	28	9	.289	.350
Harvey McClellan	3B71, SS8, 2B2, OF1	R	27	91	301	28	68	17	3	2	28	16	32	3	.226	.322
Yam Yaryan	C25	R	29	36	71	9	14	2	0	2	9	6	10	1	.197	.310
Roy Graham	C3	R	27	5	3	0	0	0	0	0	0	0	0	0	.000	.000
John Jenkins	2B1, SS1	R	25	5	3	0	0	0	0	0	1	0	2	0	.000	.000
Hal Bubser		R	26	3	3	0	0	0	0	0	0	0	2	0	.000	.000
Jimmie Long	C2	R	24	3	0	0	0	0	0	0	0	0	0	0	.000	—
Johnny Evers	2B1	L	40	3	0	0	0	0	0	0	1	2	0	0	.000	—
Elmer Pence	OF1	R	21	1	0	0	0	0	0	0	0	0	0	0	.000	—
Augie Swentor	C1	R		1	0	0	0	0	0	0	0	0	1	0	.000	—

NAME	T	AGE	W	L	PCT	SV	G	GS	CG	IP	H	BB	SO	SHO	ERA
		27	77	77	.500	8	155	155	86	1407	1472	529	484	13	3.93
Red Faber	R	33	21	17	.553	2	43	38	31	353	334	83	148	4	2.80
Charlie Robertson	R	26	14	15	.483	0	37	34	21	272	294	89	83	3	6.36
Dixie Leverett	R	28	13	10	.565	2	33	27	16	225	224	79	60	4	3.32
Ted Blankenship	R	21	8	10	.444	1	24	15	7	128	124	47	42	0	3.80
Shovel Hodge	R	28	7	6	.538	1	35	8	2	139	154	65	37	0	4.14
2 Harry Courtney	L	28	5	6	.455	0	18	11	5	88	100	37	28	0	4.91
Ferdie Schupp	L	31	3	3	.500	0	18	12	3	74	79	66	38	1	6.08
Frank Mack	R	22	2	2	.500	0	8	4	1	34	36	16	11	1	3.71
Lum Davenport	L	22	1	1	.500	0	9	1	0	17	14	13	9	0	10.59
Larry Duff	R	25	1	1	.500	0	3	1	0	13	16	3	7	0	4.85
Dick McCabe	R	26	1	0	1.000	0	3	0	0	3	4	3	1	0	6.00
Roy Wilkinson	R	29	0	1	.000	1	11	4	0	14	24	6	3	0	9.00
Doug McWeeny (ST)	R	25	0	1	.000	0	4	1	0	11	13	7	5	0	5.73
Jack Russell	R	24	0	1	.000	1	4	1	0	7	7	4	3	0	6.43
Jose Acosta	R	31	0	2	.000	0	5	1	0	15	25	6	6	0	8.40
Homer Blankenship	R	19	0	0	—	0	4	0	0	13	21	5	3	0	4.85
Emmett Bowles	R	23	0	0	—	0	1	0	0	1	2	1	0	0	27.00
Ernie Cox	R	28	0	0	—	0	1	0	0	1	1	2	0	0	18.00
Dickie Kerr (HO) 28															

WASHINGTON   6th 69-85   .448 25   CLYDE MILAN

NAME	G by Pos	B	AGE	G	AB	R	H	2B	3B	HR	RBI	BB	SO	SB	BA	SA
TOTALS			28	154	5201	650	1395	229	76	45	575	458	442	97	.268	.367
Joe Judge	1B148	L	28	148	591	84	174	32	15	10	81	50	20	5	.294	.450
Bucky Harris	1B154	R	25	154	602	95	162	24	8	2	40	52	38	25	.269	.346
Roger Peckinpaugh	SS147	R	31	147	520	62	132	14	4	2	48	55	36	11	.254	.308
Bobby LaMotte	3B62, SS	R	24	68	214	22	54	10	2	1	23	15	21	6	.252	.332
Frank Brower	OF121, 1B7	L	29	139	471	61	138	20	6	9	71	52	25	8	.293	.418
Sam Rice	OF154	L	32	154	633	91	187	37	13	6	69	48	13	20	.295	.423
Goose Goslin (BW)	OF92	R	21	101	358	44	116	19	7	3	53	25	26	4	.324	.441
Patsy Gharrity (JJ)	C87	R	30	96	273	40	70	16	6	5	45	36	30	1	.256	.414
Howard Shanks	3B54, OF27	R	31	84	272	35	77	10	9	1	32	25	25	6	.283	.397
Val Picinich	C76	R	26	76	210	16	48	12	2	0	19	23	33	1	.229	.305
Earl Smith	OF49, 3B1	B	31	65	205	22	53	12	2	1	23	8	17	4	.259	.351
Clyde Milan	OF11	L	36	42	74	8	17	5	0	0	5	2	2	0	.230	.297
Donie Bush (IJ)	3B37, 2B1	B	34	41	134	17	32	4	1	0	7	21	7	1	.239	.284
Ed Goebel	OF15	R	27	37	59	13	16	1	0	1	3	8	16	1	.271	.339
Tom Zachary	P32	L	26	32	71	4	21	2	1	1	14	3	20	1	.296	.394
Ossie Bluege	3B17, SS2	R	21	19	61	5	12	1	0	0	2	7	7	1	.197	.213
Pete Lapan	C11	R	31	11	34	7	11	1	0	1	6	3	4	1	.324	.441
Ricardo Torres	C3	R	29	4	4	0	0	0	0	0	0	0	0	0	.000	.000
George McNamara	OF3	R	21	3	3	3	3	0	0	0	1	1	2	0	.273	.273

NAME	T	AGE	W	L	PCT	SV	G	GS	CG	IP	H	BB	SO	SHO	ERA
		29	69	85	.448	10	154	154	84	1362	1485	500	422	11	3.81
George Mogridge	L	33	18	13	.581	0	34	32	18	252	300	72	61	3	3.57
Walter Johnson	R	34	15	16	.484	4	41	31	23	280	283	99	105	4	2.99
Tom Zachary	L	26	15	10	.600	1	32	25	13	185	190	43	37	1	3.11
Ray Francis	L	29	7	18	.280	2	39	26	15	225	265	66	64	2	4.28
Jim Brillheart	L	18	4	6	.400	1	31	10	3	120	120	72	47	0	3.60
Eric Erickson	R	30	4	12	.250	2	30	17	6	142	144	73	61	0	4.94
Tom Phillips	R	33	3	7	.300	0	17	7	2	70	72	22	19	1	4.89
Joe Gleason	R	26	2	2	.500	0	8	5	3	41	53	18	12	0	4.61
Cy Warmoth	L	29	1	0	1.000	0	5	0	0	19	15	9	8	0	1.42
1 Harry Courtney	L	23	0	0	—	0	5	0	0	10	11	9	4	0	3.60
Lucas Turk	R	24	0	1	—	0	2	1	0	12	16	5	1	0	6.75
Chief Youngblood	R	22	0	1	.000	0	2	2	0	4	9	7	0	0	15.75
Slim McGrew	R	22	0	0	—	0	1	0	0	3	1	1	0	0	9.00
Frank Woodward	R	28	0	0	—	0	1	0	0	2	3	3	2	0	13.50

PHILADELPHIA   7th 65-89   .422 29   CONNIE MACK

NAME	G by Pos	B	AGE	G	AB	R	H	2B	3B	HR	RBI	BB	SO	SB	BA	SA
TOTALS			27	155	5241	705	1409	229	63	111	631	437	591	60	.269	.400
Joe Hauser	1B94	L	23	111	368	61	119	21	5	9	43	30	37	1	.323	.481
Ralph Young	2B120	B	33	125	470	62	105	19	2	1	35	55	21	8	.223	.279
Chick Galloway	SS155	R	25	155	571	83	185	26	9	6	69	39	38	10	.324	.433
Jimmy Dykes	3B140, 2B5	R	25	145	501	66	138	29	7	12	68	55	98	6	.275	.421
Frank Welch	OF104	R	24	114	375	43	97	17	3	11	49	40	43	3	.259	.408
Bing Miller	OF139	R	27	143	535	90	180	29	12	21	90	24	42	10	.336	.553
Tilly Walker	OF148	R	34	153	565	111	160	31	4	37	99	61	64	4	.283	.549
Cy Perkins	C141	R	26	148	505	58	135	20	6	6	69	40	30	1	.267	.366
Beauty McGowan	OF82	L	20	99	300	36	69	10	5	1	20	40	46	6	.230	.307
Doc Johnston	1B65	L	34	71	260	41	65	11	7	1	29	24	15	7	.250	.358
Frank Bruggy (JJ)	C31	L	31	53	111	10	31	7	0	0	9	6	11	1	.279	.342
Heinie Scheer	2B29, 3B10	R	21	51	135	10	23	3	0	4	12	3	25	1	.170	.281
Frank Callaway (KJ)	2B11, 3B5, SS4	R	24	29	48	5	13	0	2	0	4	0	13	0	.271	.354
Ollie Fuhrman	C4	R	25	6	6	1	2	1	0	0	0	0	0	0	.333	.500
Frank Brazill	3B2	L	22	6	13	0	1	0	0	0	1	0	1	0	.077	.077
Frank McCue	3B2	B	20	2	5	0	0	0	0	0	0	0	0	0	.000	.000
Johnny Berger	C2	R	20	2	1	0	1	0	0	0	0	0	0	0	1.000	1.000

NAME	T	AGE	W	L	PCT	SV	G	GS	CG	IP	H	BB	SO	SHO	ERA
		25	65	89	.422	6	155	155	73	1363	1573	469	373	4	4.59
Eddie Rommel	R	24	27	13	.675	2	51	33	22	294	294	63	54	3	3.28
Rollie Naylor	R	30	10	15	.400	0	35	26	11	171	212	51	37	0	4.74
Bob Hasty	R	25	9	14	.391	0	28	26	14	192	225	41	33	1	4.27
Slim Harriss	R	25	9	20	.310	3	47	32	13	230	262	94	102	0	5.01
Fred Heimach	L	21	7	11	.389	1	37	19	7	172	220	63	47	0	5.02
Rube Yarrison	R	26	1	2	.333	0	18	1	1	34	50	12	10	0	8.21
Otto Rettig	R	28	1	2	.333	0	4	1	1	18	18	12	1	0	5.00
Curly Ogden	R	21	1	4	.200	0	15	6	1	72	59	33	20	0	3.12
Gus Ketchum	R	25	0	1	.000	0	16	1	0	19	14	9	4	0	5.63
Jim Sullivan	R	28	0	2	.000	0	20	2	1	51	76	25	15	0	5.47
Charlie Eckert	R	23	0	3	.000	0	16	0	0	50	61	23	15	0	4.68
1 Roy Moore	L	23	0	3	.000	0	15	6	0	51	65	32	29	0	7.59
Red Schillings	R	22	0	0	—	0	6	0	0	8	10	11	4	0	6.75
Harry O'Neill	R	29	0	0	—	0	1	0	0	1	0	1	0	0	3.00

BOSTON   8th 61-93   .396 50   HUGH DUFFY

NAME	G by Pos	B	AGE	G	AB	R	H	2B	3B	HR	RBI	BB	SO	SB	BA	SA
TOTALS			29	154	5288	598	1392	250	55	45	510	366	455	60	.263	.357
George Burns	1B140	R	29	147	558	71	171	32	5	12	73	20	28	8	.306	.446
Del Pratt	2B154	R	34	154	607	73	183	44	7	6	86	53	20	7	.301	.427
2 Johnny Mitchell	SS58	B	27	59	203	20	51	4	1	1	8	16	17	1	.251	.296
Joe Dugan	3B63, SS20	R	25	84	341	45	98	22	3	3	38	9	28	2	.287	.396
Shano Collins	OF117, 1B1	R	36	135	472	33	128	24	7	1	52	7	16	7	.271	.358
Joe Harris	OF83, 1B21	R	31	119	408	53	129	30	9	6	54	30	15	2	.316	.478
Mike Menosky	OF103	L	27	126	406	61	115	16	5	3	32	40	33	9	.283	.369
Muddy Ruel	C112	R	26	116	361	34	92	15	1	0	28	41	26	4	.255	.302
Nemo Leibold	OF71	L	30	81	271	42	70	8	1	1	18	41	14	1	.258	.306
1 Elmer Smith	OF59	L	29	73	231	43	66	13	6	6	32	25	21	0	.286	.472
Frank O'Rourke	SS48, 3B19	R	30	67	216	28	57	14	3	1	17	20	28	6	.264	.370
Pinky Pittinger	3B31, SS29	R	23	66	186	16	48	3	0	0	7	9	10	2	.258	.274
Benn Karr	P41	R	28	66	98	7	21	2	0	0	4	4	7	1	.214	.235
1 Eddie Foster	3B28, SS2, C2	R	35	48	109	11	23	1	0	0	3	9	10	1	.211	.239
2 Elmer Miller	OF35	R	32	44	147	16	28	3	4	1	16	5	10	3	.190	.327
Roxy Walters	C36	R	29	38	98	4	19	4	0	0	4	9	11	0	.194	.214
Bert Chaplin	C21	R	28	21	69	8	13	1	1	0	4	2	9	0	.188	.232
2 Chick Fewster	3B23	R	26	23	83	8	24	4	1	0	9	6	10	3	.289	.361
Chick Maynard	SS12	R	25	12	24	1	3	0	0	0	0	1	4	0	.125	.125
Dick Reichle	OF6	R	25	6	24	3	6	1	0	0	1	0	5	0	.250	.292
Jabber Lynch	C3	R	25	3	2	1	1	0	0	0	0	0	1	0	.500	.500

NAME	T	AGE	W	L	PCT	SV	G	GS	CG	IP	H	BB	SO	SHO	ERA
		28	61	93	.396	6	154	154	71	1373	1508	503	359	10	4.30
Rip Collins	R	26	14	11	.560	2	32	29	15	211	219	103	69	3	3.75
Jack Quinn	R	38	13	15	.464	0	40	33	16	256	263	59	67	4	3.48
Herb Pennock	L	28	10	17	.370	1	32	26	15	202	230	74	59	1	4.32
Alex Ferguson	R	25	9	16	.360	2	39	27	10	198	201	62	44	1	4.32
Allen Russell	R	28	5	6	.462	2	34	11	1	126	152	57	34	0	5.00
Benn Karr	R	28	5	12	.294	1	41	13	7	183	212	45	41	0	4.47
Bill Piercy (SL)	R	26	3	9	.250	0	19	11	8	124	140	35	17	0	4.69
Curt Fullerton	R	23	0	1	.000	0	31	3	0	64	70	35	17	0	5.48
Elmer Myers	R	28	0	1	.000	0	5	1	0	6	10	3	1	0	16.50
Sam Dodge	R	32	0	0	—	0	3	0	0	11	3	3	0	0	4.50

Batting

NAME	G by Pos	B	AGE	G	AB	R	H	2B	3B	HR	RBI	BB	SO	SB	BA	SA
NEW YORK 1ST 93-61 .604											**JOHN McGRAW**					
TOTALS			28	156	5455	852	1661	253	90	89	756	448	421	116	.304	.428
George Kelly	1B151	R	26	151	592	96	194	33	8	17	107	30	65	12	.328	.497
Frankie Frisch	2B85, 3B53, SS1	B	23	132	514	101	168	16	13	5	51	47	13	31	.327	.438
Dave Bancroft	SS156	B	31	156	651	117	209	41	5	4	60	79	27	16	.321	.418
Heinie Groh	3B110	R	32	115	426	63	113	21	3	3	51	53	21	5	.265	.350
Ross Youngs	OF147	L	25	149	559	105	185	34	10	7	86	55	50	17	.331	.465
Casey Stengel	OF77	L	31	84	250	48	92	8	10	7	48	21	17	4	.368	.564
Irish Meusel	OF154	R	29	154	617	100	204	28	17	16	132	35	33	12	.331	.509
Frank Snyder	C97	R	28	104	318	34	109	21	5	5	51	23	25	1	.343	.487
Earl Smith	C75	L	25	90	234	29	65	11	4	9	39	37	12	1	.278	.474
Johnny Rawlings	2B77, 3B5	R	29	88	308	46	87	13	8	1	30	23	15	7	.282	.386
Bill Cunningham	OF71, 3B1	R	27	85	229	37	75	15	2	2	33	7	9	4	.328	.437
Ralph Shinners (PB)	OF37	R	26	56	135	16	34	4	2	0	15	5	22	5	.252	.311
Dave Robertson	OF8	L	31	42	47	5	13	2	0	1	3	3	7	0	.277	.383
2 Lee King	1B5, OF5	R	29	20	34	6	6	3	0	0	2	5	2	1	.176	.265
Alex Gaston	C13	R	29	16	26	1	5	0	0	0	1	0	6	0	.192	.192
Howard Berry		B	27	6	0	0	0	0	0	0	0	0	0	0	—	—
Freddie Maguire	2B3	R	23	5	12	4	4	0	0	0	1	0	1	0	.333	.333
Mahlon Higbee	OF3	R	20	3	10	2	4	0	0	1	5	0	1	0	.400	.700
Travis Jackson	SS3	R	18	3	8	1	0	0	0	0	0	0	2	0	.000	.000
Waddy MacPhee	3B2	R	22	2	7	2	2	0	1	0	1	0	1	0	.286	.571
Ike Boone		L	25	2	2	0	1	0	0	0	0	0	0	0	.500	.500
Cozy Dolan		R	39	1	0	0	0	0	0	0	0	0	0	0	—	—
CINCINNATI 2nd 86-68 .558 7											**PAT MORAN**					
TOTALS			29	156	5282	766	1562	226	99	45	686	436	381	130	.298	.402
Jack Daubert	1B156	L	38	156	610	114	205	15	22	12	66	56	21	14	.336	.492
Sammy Bohne	2B85, SS22	R	25	112	383	53	105	14	5	3	51	39	18	13	.274	.360
Ike Caveney	SS118	R	27	118	394	41	94	12	9	3	54	29	33	6	.239	.338
Babe Pinelli	3B156	R	26	156	547	77	167	19	7	1	72	48	37	17	.305	.351
George Harper	OF109	L	30	128	430	67	146	22	8	2	68	35	22	11	.340	.442
George burns	OF156	R	32	156	631	104	180	26	10	1	53	78	38	30	.285	.353
Pat Duncan	OF151	R	28	151	607	94	199	44	12	8	94	40	31	12	.328	.479
Bubbles Hargrave	C87	R	29	98	320	49	101	22	10	7	57	26	18	7	.316	.513
Lew Fonseca	2B71	R	23	81	291	55	105	20	3	4	45	14	18	7	.361	.491
Ivy Wingo	C78	L	31	80	260	24	74	13	3	3	45	23	11	1	.285	.392
Rube Bressler	1B3, OF2	L	27	52	83	7	15	0	2	0	8	4	4	1	.283	.358
Edd Roush (HO)	OF43	L	29	49	165	29	58	7	4	1	24	19	5	5	.352	.461
Wally Kimmick	SS30, 2B3, 3B1	R	25	39	89	11	22	2	1	0	12	3	12	0	.247	.292
Greasy Neale	OF16	L	30	25	43	11	10	2	1	0	2	6	3	0	.233	.326
Red Lutz	C1	R	23	1	1	0	1	0	0	0	0	0	0	0	1.000	2.000
PITTSBURGH (Tie) 3rd 85-69 .552 8											**GEORGE GIBSON 32-33 .492 BILL McKECHNIE 53-36 .596**					
TOTALS			27	155	5521	865	1698	239	110	52	777	423	326	145	.308	.419
Charlie Grimm	1B154	L	23	154	593	64	173	28	13	0	76	43	15	6	.292	.383
Cotton Tierney	2B105, OF2, SS1, 3B1	R	28	122	441	58	152	26	14	7	86	22	40	7	.345	.515
Rabbit Maranville	SS138, 2B18	R	30	155	672	115	198	26	15	0	63	61	43	24	.295	.378
Pie Traynor	3B124, SS18	R	23	142	571	89	161	17	12	4	81	27	28	17	.282	.375
Reb Russell	OF60	L	33	60	220	51	81	14	8	12	75	14	18	4	.368	.668
Max Carey	OF155	B	32	155	629	140	207	28	12	10	70	80	26	51	.329	.459
Carson Bigbee	OF150	L	27	150	614	113	215	29	15	5	99	56	13	24	.350	.471
Johnny Gooch	C103	B	24	105	353	45	116	15	3	1	42	39	15	1	.329	.397
Clyde Barnhart	OF26, 3B30	R	26	75	209	30	69	7	5	1	38	25	7	3	.330	.426
Ray Rohwer	OF30	L	27	53	129	19	38	7	3	3	29	10	17	1	.295	.457
Jewel Ens	2B29, 3B3, 1B2, SS1	R	32	47	142	18	42	7	3	0	17	7	9	3	.296	.387
Walter Schmidt (HO)	C40	R	35	40	152	21	50	11	0	0	22	1	5	2	.329	.414
Walter Mueller	OF31	R	27	32	122	21	33	5	1	2	18	5	7	1	.270	.377
1 Johnny Mokan	OF23	R	26	31	89	9	23	3	1	0	9	4	9	1	.258	.315
Jim Mattox	C21	L	25	29	51	11	15	1	1	0	3	1	3	0	.294	.353
Bubber Jonnard	C10	R	22	10	21	4	5	0	1	0	2	4	0	0	.238	.333
2 Jack Hammond	2B4	R	31	9	11	3	3	0	0	0	1	0	0	0	.273	.273
Stuffy Steward	2B3	R	28	3	13	3	2	0	0	0	0	1	0	1	.154	.154
Jake Miller	OF3	R	26	3	11	1	1	0	0	0	0	0	3	0	.091	.091

Kiki Cuyler 23 R 0-0, Grover Lovelace 23 R 0-1, Art Merewether 19 R 0-1, Tom McNamara 26 R 0-1

NAME	G by Pos	B	AGE	G	AB	R	H	2B	3B	HR	RBI	BB	SO	SB	BA	SA
ST. LOUIS (Tie) 3rd 85-69 .552 8											**BRANCH RICKEY**					
TOTALS			28	154	5425	863	1634	280	88	107	787	447	425	73	.301	.444
Jack Fournier	1B109, P1	L	32	128	404	64	119	23	9	10	61	40	21	6	.295	.470
Rogers Hornsby	2B154	R	26	154	623	141	250	46	14	42	152	65	50	17	.401	.722
Specs Toporcer	SS91, 3B6, 2B1, OF1	R	23	116	352	56	114	25	4	1	36	24	18	2	.324	.455
Milt Stock	3B149, SS1	R	28	151	581	89	177	33	9	5	79	42	29	7	.305	.418
2 Max Flack	OF66	L	32	66	267	46	78	12	1	2	21	31	11	3	.292	.367
Jack Smith	OF138	L	27	143	510	117	158	23	12	8	46	50	30	18	.310	.449
Joe Schultz	OF89	R	28	112	344	50	108	13	4	2	64	19	10	3	.314	.392
Eddie Ainsmith	C116	R	32	119	379	46	111	14	4	3	59	28	43	2	.293	.454
Doc Lavan	SS82, 3B5	R	31	89	264	24	60	8	1	0	27	16	13	0	.227	.265
Les Mann	OF57	R	29	84	147	42	51	14	1	2	20	16	12	0	.347	.497
Verne Clemons	C63	R	30	71	160	9	41	4	0	0	15	18	5	1	.256	.281
Austin McHenry (IL)	OF61	R	26	64	238	31	72	18	3	5	43	14	27	2	.303	.466
Heinie Mueller	OF44	L	22	61	159	20	43	7	2	3	26	14	18	2	.270	.396
Del Gainer	1B26, OF10	L	34	43	97	19	26	7	4	2	23	14	6	0	.268	.485
Jim Bottomley	1B34	L	22	37	151	29	49	8	5	5	35	6	13	3	.325	.543
Ray Blades	OF29, SS4, 3B1	R	25	37	130	27	39	2	4	3	21	25	21	3	.300	.446
1 Cliff Heathcote	OF32	L	24	34	98	11	24	5	2	0	14	9	4	2	.245	.337
Burt Shotton	OF3	L	37	34	30	5	6	1	0	0	2	6	1	0	.200	.233
Harry McCurdy	C9, 1B2	L	22	13	27	3	8	2	0	0	3	5	1	0	.296	.519
Ernie Vick	C3	R	21	3	6	1	2	0	0	0	2	0	2	0	.330	.667
Howard Freigau (DD)	SS2, 3B1	R	19	3	1	0	0	0	0	0	0	0	0	0	.000	.000

Pickles Dillhoefer (DD) 27

NAME	G by Pos	B	AGE	G	AB	R	H	2B	3B	HR	RBI	BB	SO	SB	BA	SA
CHICAGO 5th 80-74 .519 13											**BILL KILLEFER**					
TOTALS			26	156	5335	771	1564	248	71	42	667	525	447	97	.293	.390
Ray Grimes	1B138	R	28	138	509	99	180	45	12	14	99	75	33	7	.354	.572
Zeb Terry	2B125, SS4, 3B3	R	30	131	496	56	142	24	2	0	67	34	16	2	.286	.343
Charlie Hollocher	SS152	L	26	152	592	90	201	37	8	3	69	58	5	19	.340	.444
Marty Krug	3B104, 2B23, SS1	R	33	127	450	67	124	23	4	4	60	43	43	7	.276	.371
Barney Friberg	OF74, 1B6, 3B5, 2B3	R	22	97	296	51	92	8	2	0	23	37	37	8	.311	.351
Jigger Statz (BH)	OF110	B	24	110	462	77	137	19	5	1	34	41	31	16	.297	.366
Hack Miller	OF116	R	28	122	466	61	164	28	5	12	78	16	39	1	.352	.511
Bob O'Farrell	C125	R	25	128	392	68	127	18	8	4	60	79	34	5	.324	.441
Turner Barber	OF47, 1B16	R	28	84	226	35	70	7	4	0	29	8	4	7	.310	.376
2 Cliff Heathcote	OF60	L	22	76	243	37	68	8	7	1	34	18	15	5	.280	.383
Marty Callaghan	OF53	L	22	74	175	31	45	7	4	0	20	17	17	2	.257	.343
John Kelleher	3B46, SS7, 1B4	R	28	63	193	23	50	7	1	0	20	15	14	5	.259	.306
George Maisel	OF26	R	30	38	84	9	18	1	0	0	4	6	4	4	.190	.226
Gabby Hartnett	C27	R	21	31	72	4	14	1	1	0	4	6	8	0	.194	.236
Kettle Wirts	C27	R	24	31	58	7	10	2	1	0	6	12	15	0	.172	.259
1 Max Flack	OF15	L	32	17	54	7	12	1	0	2	5	2	6	2	.222	.241
Sparky Adams	2B11	R	27	11	40	5	10	1	0	0	1	5	1	1	.250	.295
Howie Fitzgerald	OF6	L	20	10	24	3	8	1	0	0	1	4	4	0	.333	.375
George Grantham	3B5	L	22	7	23	3	4	0	1	0	2	3	6	1	.174	.304
Butch Weis		L	21	3	2	1	1	0	0	0	0	0	0	0	.500	.500
Walt Golvin	1B2	L	24	3	2	0	0	0	0	0	0	0	1	0	.000	.000

Joe Klugman 27 R 0-2, Harvey Cotter 22 L 1-1

Pitching

NAME	T	AGE	W	L	PCT	SV	G	GS	CG	IP	H	BB	SO	SHO	ERA
		28	93	61	.604	15	156	156	76	1396	1454	393	388	7	3.45
Art Nehf	L	29	19	13	.594	1	37	35	20	268	286	64	60	3	3.29
Rosy Ryan	R	24	17	12	.586	3	46	22	12	192	194	74	75	1	3.00
Jesse Barnes	R	29	13	8	.619	0	37	29	14	213	236	38	52	2	3.51
Phil Douglas (DL)	R	32	11	4	.733	0	23	21	9	158	154	35	33	1	2.62
2 Jack Scott	R	30	8	2	.800	2	17	10	5	80	83	23	37	0	4.39
Claude Jonnard	R	24	6	1	.857	5	13	0	0	96	96	28	44	0	3.84
2 Hugh McQuillan (HO)	R	26	6	5	.545	1	15	13	5	94	111	34	24	0	3.83
Fred Toney (HO)	R	33	5	6	.455	0	13	12	6	86	91	31	10	0	4.19
Red Causey	R	28	4	3	.571	1	24	2	1	71	69	34	13	0	3.17
Carmen Hill	R	26	2	1	.667	0	8	4	0	28	33	5	6	0	4.82
Virgil Barnes	R	25	1	0	1.000	2	22	2	1	52	46	11	16	0	3.46
Clint Blume	R	23	1	0	1.000	0	1	1	1	9	7	1	2	0	1.00
Mike Cvengros	L	21	0	1	.000	0	1	1	1	9	6	3	3	0	4.00
Fred Johnson	R	28	0	2	.000	0	2	2	2	18	20	1	8	0	4.00
Red Shea	R	23	0	0	.000	0	11	2	0	23	22	11	5	0	4.70
		27	86	68	.558	3	156	156	88	1386	1481	326	357	8	3.53
Eppa Rixey	L	31	25	13	.658	0	40	38	26	313	337	45	80	2	3.54
Pete Donohue (AJ)	R	21	18	9	.667	1	33	30	18	242	257	43	66	2	3.12
Johnny Couch	R	31	16	9	.640	1	43	33	18	264	301	56	45	2	3.89
Dolf Luque	R	31	13	23	.361	0	39	33	18	261	266	72	79	0	3.31
Cactus Keck	R	23	7	6	.538	1	27	15	5	131	138	29	27	1	3.37
Cliff Markle	R	28	4	5	.444	0	25	3	2	76	75	33	34	1	3.79
Johnny Gillespie	R	22	3	3	.500	0	31	4	1	78	84	29	21	0	4.50
Karl Schnell	R	22	0	0	—	0	10	0	0	20	21	18	5	0	2.70
1 Jack Scott (AJ)	R	30	0	1	.000	0	1	0	0	1	2	1	0	0	9.00
		30	85	69	.552	7	155	155	88	1387	1613	358	490	15	3.98
Wilbur Cooper	L	30	23	14	.662	0	41	36	27	295	330	61	129	4	3.18
Johnny Morrison	R	26	17	11	.607	1	45	33	20	286	315	87	104	5	3.43
Earl Hamilton	L	30	11	7	.611	2	33	14	9	160	183	40	34	1	3.99
Whitey Glazner	R	28	11	12	.478	1	34	26	10	193	238	52	71	1	4.38
Hal Carlson	R	30	9	12	.429	2	39	18	6	145	193	58	64	0	5.71
Babe Adams	R	40	8	11	.421	0	27	19	12	171	191	15	39	4	3.58
Myrl Brown	R	27	3	1	.750	0	7	5	2	35	42	13	9	0	5.91
Chief Yellowhorse	R	24	3	1	.750	0	28	4	2	78	92	20	24	0	4.50
Bonnie Hollingsworth	R	26	0	0	—	0	9	0	0	14	17	8	7	0	7.71
Jimmy Zinn	R	27	0	0	—	0	3	0	0	10	11	2	3	0	1.80
Rip Wheeler	R	24	0	0	—	0	2	0	0	2	2	0	3	0	0.00
		29	85	69	.552	12	154	154	60	1362	1609	447	465	8	4.44
Jeff Pfeffer	R	34	19	12	.617	2	44	32	19	261	286	58	83	1	3.58
Bill Sherdel	L	25	17	13	.567	2	47	31	15	242	298	62	79	3	3.87
Jesse Haines	R	28	11	9	.550	0	29	26	11	183	207	45	62	2	3.84
Bill Doak	R	31	11	13	.458	2	37	29	8	180	222	69	73	2	5.55
Lou North	R	30	10	3	.769	4	53	10	4	150	164	64	84	0	4.44
Bill Pertica	R	23	8	8	.500	0	34	15	2	117	153	65	30	0	5.92
Epp Sell	R	25	4	2	.667	0	7	5	0	33	47	6	5	0	6.82
Clyde Barfoot	R	30	4	5	.444	2	42	2	1	118	139	30	19	0	4.19
Roy Walker	R	29	1	2	.333	0	12	0	0	32	34	15	14	0	4.78
Bill Bailey	L	34	1	2	.333	0	12	0	0	32	38	23	11	0	5.35
Eddie Dyer	L	22	0	0	—	0	12	0	0	4	7	0	3	0	2.25
Marv Goodwin	R	31	0	0	—	0	1	0	0	4	1	0	2	0	2.25
Johnny Stuart	R	21	0	0	—	0	2	0	0	9	12	2	4	0	9.00
Jack Knight	R	27	0	0	—	0	1	0	0	1	4	1	0	0	9.00
Jack Fournier	L	29	0	0	—	0	1	0	0	1	0	0	0	0	0.00
Sid Benton	R	27	0	0	—	0	1	0	0	1	2	1	0	0	9.00
		25	80	74	.519	12	156	156	74	1398	1579	475	402	8	4.34
Pete Alexander	R	35	16	13	.552	1	33	31	20	246	283	34	48	1	3.62
Vic Aldridge	R	22	16	15	.516	0	36	34	20	258	287	56	66	2	3.52
Virgil Cheeves	R	21	12	11	.522	2	39	22	9	183	195	76	40	1	4.09
George Stueland	R	23	9	4	.692	0	35	11	4	113	129	49	44	0	5.81
Tiny Osborne	R	29	9	5	.643	3	41	14	7	184	183	95	81	1	4.50
Percy Jones	L	22	8	9	.471	1	44	24	7	162	197	68	45	2	4.78
Tony Kaufmann	R	21	7	13	.350	2	37	14	4	153	161	57	45	1	4.06
Speed Martin	R	28	1	0	1.000	0	6	1	0	10	22	2	2	0	7.50
Fred Fussel	L	26	1	1	.500	0	7	1	2	19	24	8	4	0	4.74
Vic Keen	R	23	1	2	.333	1	7	2	1	35	36	10	11	0	3.86
Buck Freeman	R	28	0	1	.000	1	11	1	0	26	47	10	10	0	8.66
Ed Morris	R	22	0	0	—	0	5	1	0	12	6	4	5	0	8.25
Uel Eubanks	R	19	0	0	—	0	1	0	0	1	1	0	1	0	22.50

BROOKLYN 6th 75-78 .494 17 — WILBERT ROBINSON

NAME	G by Pos	B	AGE	G	AB	R	H	2B	3B	HR	RBI	BB	SO	SB	BA	SA
TOTALS			30	155	5413	743	1569	235	76	56	674	339	318	79	.290	.392
Ray Schmandt	1B110	R	26	110	396	54	106	17	3	2	44	21	28	6	.268	.341
Ivy Olson	2B85, SS51	R	36	136	551	63	150	26	6	1	47	25	10	8	.272	.347
Jimmy Johnston	2B62, SS50, 3B26	R	32	138	567	110	181	20	7	4	49	28	17	18	.319	.400
Andy High	3B130, SS22, 2B1	L	24	153	579	82	164	27	10	6	65	59	26	9	.283	.396
Tommy Griffith	OF82	L	32	99	329	44	104	17	8	4	49	23	10	7	.316	.453
Hy Myers	OF152, 2B1	L	33	153	618	82	196	29	9	6	89	13	26	9	.317	.408
Zack Wheat	OF152	L	34	152	600	92	201	29	12	16	112	45	22	9	.335	.503
Hank DeBerry	C81	R	27	85	259	29	78	10	1	3	35	20	9	4	.301	.382
Bert Griffith	OF77, 1B6	R	26	106	325	45	100	22	8	2	35	5	11	5	.308	.443
Dutch Ruether	P35	L	28	67	125	12	26	6	1	2	20	12	11	0	.208	.320
Bernie Neis	OF27	B	26	61	70	15	16	4	1	1	9	13	8	3	.229	.357
Otto Miller	C57	R	33	59	180	20	47	11	1	1	23	6	13	0	.261	.350
Clarence Mitchell (NJ)	1B42, P5	L	31	56	155	21	45	6	3	3	28	19	6	0	.290	.426
Bernie Hungling	C36	R	26	39	102	9	23	1	2	1	13	6	20	1	.225	.304
Chuck Ward (IL)	SS31, 3B2	R	27	33	91	12	25	5	1	0	14	5	8	1	.275	.352
Hal Janvrin	2B15, SS4, 3B2, 1B1, OF1	R	29	30	57	7	17	3	1	0	4	4	4	0	.298	.386
Sam Post	1B8	L	25	9	25	3	7	0	0	0	4	1	4	1	.280	.280
Zack Taylor	C6	R	23	7	14	0	3	0	0	0	2	1	1	0	.214	.214
Sam Crane	SS3	R	27	8	8	1	2	1	0	0	0	0	1	0	.250	.375
Wally Hood		R	27	2	0	2	0	0	0	0	0	0	0	0	—	—
Possum Whitted		R	32	1	1	0	0	0	0	0	0	0	0	0	.000	.000

NAME	T	AGE	W	L	PCT	SV	G	GS	CG	IP	H	BB	SO	SHO	ERA
TOTALS	L	29	76	78	.494	8	155	155	82	1383	1568	490	499	12	4.04
Dutch Ruether	L	28	21	12	.636	0	35	35	26	267	290	92	89	2	3.54
Dazzy Vance	R	31	18	12	.600	0	36	31	16	246	259	94	134	5	3.70
Burleigh Grimes	R	28	17	14	.548	1	35	34	18	256	318	84	99	1	4.75
Leon Cadore	R	31	8	15	.348	0	29	21	13	190	224	57	49	0	4.36
Harry Shriver	R	25	4	6	.400	0	25	13	4	108	114	48	38	2	3.00
1 Sherry Smith	L	31	4	8	.333	2	28	8	3	109	128	35	15	1	4.55
Art Decatur	R	28	3	4	.429	1	37	3	1	88	87	29	31	0	2.76
Al Mamaux	R	28	1	4	.200	3	37	5	1	88	97	33	35	0	3.68
Clarence Mitchell (NJ)	L	31	0	3	.000	0	5	3	0	13	28	7	1	0	13.85
Ray Gordinier	R	30	0	0	—	0	5	0	0	11	13	8	5	0	9.00
Jim Murray	L	21	0	0	—	1	4	0	0	6	8	3	3	0	4.50
Paul Schreiber	R	19	0	0	—	0	1	0	0	2	1	0	0	0	0.00

PHILADELPHIA 7th 57-96 .373 35.5 — KAISER WILHELM

NAME	G by Pos	B	AGE	G	AB	R	H	2B	3B	HR	RBI	BB	SO	SB	BA	SA
TOTALS			28	154	5459	738	1537	268	55	116	685	450	611	48	.282	.415
Roy Leslie	1B139	R	27	141	513	44	139	23	2	6	50	37	49	3	.271	.359
Frank Parkinson	2B139	R	25	145	545	86	150	18	6	15	70	55	93	3	.275	.413
Art Fletcher	SS106	R	37	110	396	46	111	20	5	7	53	21	14	3	.280	.409
Goldie Rapp	3B117, SS2	B	28	119	502	58	127	26	3	0	38	32	39	6	.253	.317
Curt Walker	OF147	R	25	148	581	102	196	36	11	12	89	56	46	11	.337	.499
Cy Williams	OF150	L	34	151	584	98	180	30	6	26	92	74	49	11	.308	.514
Cliff Lee	OF89, 1B18, 3B1	R	25	122	422	65	136	29	6	27	77	32	43	2	.322	.540
Butch Henline	C119	R	27	125	430	57	136	20	4	14	64	36	33	2	.316	.479
Russ Wrightstone	3B40, SS35, 1B2	L	29	99	331	56	101	18	6	5	33	28	17	4	.305	.441
Bevo LeBourveau	OF42	L	25	74	167	24	45	8	3	2	20	24	29	3	.269	.389
John Peters	C39	R	28	55	143	15	35	9	1	4	24	9	18	0	.245	.406
2 Johnny Mokan	OF37, 3B2	R	26	47	151	20	38	7	1	3	27	16	25	1	.252	.371
Jimmy Smith	SS23, 2B13, 3B1	B	27	38	114	13	25	1	0	1	6	5	9	1	.219	.254
Lee Meadows	P33	R	27	33	86	8	27	4	0	0	5	1	25	0	.314	.360
1 Lee King	OF15	R	29	19	53	8	12	5	1	2	13	8	6	0	.226	.472
Frank Withrow	C8	R	31	10	21	3	7	2	0	0	3	3	5	0	.333	.429
Stan Benton	2B5	L	26	6	19	1	4	1	0	0	3	2	1	0	.211	.263

NAME	T	AGE	W	L	PCT	SV	G	GS	CG	IP	H	BB	SO	SHO	ERA
TOTALS		26	57	96	.373	5	154	154	73	1372	1692	460	394	6	4.64
Jimmy Ring	R	27	12	18	.400	1	40	33	17	249	292	103	116	0	4.59
Lee Meadows	R	27	12	18	.400	0	33	33	19	237	264	71	62	2	4.02
Lefty Weinert	L	20	8	11	.421	1	34	22	10	167	189	70	58	0	3.39
Bill Hubbell	R	25	7	15	.318	1	35	26	11	189	257	41	33	1	5.00
Jesse Winters	R	28	6	6	.500	2	34	9	4	138	176	56	29	0	5.35
George Smith	R	30	5	14	.263	0	42	16	6	194	250	35	44	1	4.78
Petie Behan	R	34	4	2	.667	0	7	5	3	47	49	14	13	1	2.49
Huck Betts	R	25	1	0	1.000	0	7	0	0	15	23	8	4	0	9.60
Stan Baumgartner	L	29	1	1	.500	0	7	0	0	10	18	5	2	0	6.30
John Singleton	R	25	1	10	.091	0	22	9	3	93	127	38	27	1	5.90
Letron Pinto	R	23	0	1	.000	0	9	0	0	25	31	14	4	0	5.04
Tom Sullivan	L	26	0	0	—	0	3	0	0	8	16	5	2	0	11.25

BOSTON 8th 53-100 .346 39.5 — FRED MITCHELL

NAME	G by Pos	B	AGE	G	AB	R	H	2B	3B	HR	RBI	BB	SO	SB	BA	SA
TOTALS			30	154	5161	596	1355	162	73	32	509	387	451	67	.263	.341
Walter Holke (LJ)	1B105	B	29	105	395	35	115	9	4	0	46	14	23	6	.291	.334
Larry Kopf	2B78, SS33, 3B13	B	31	126	466	59	124	6	3	1	37	45	22	8	.266	.298
Hod Ford	SS115, 2B28	R	24	143	515	58	140	23	9	2	60	30	36	2	.272	.363
Tony Boeckel	3B106	R	29	119	402	61	116	19	6	4	47	35	32	14	.289	.410
Walton Cruise	OF100, 1B2	L	32	104	352	51	98	15	10	4	46	44	20	4	.278	.412
Ray Powell	OF136	L	33	142	550	82	163	22	11	6	37	59	66	3	.296	.409
Al Nixon	OF79	R	36	86	318	35	84	14	4	2	22	9	19	6	.264	.352
Mickey O'Neil	C79	R	24	83	251	18	56	5	2	0	26	14	11	4	.223	.259
Walter Barbare	2B45, 3B38, 1B14	R	30	106	373	38	86	5	4	0	40	21	22	2	.231	.265
Hank Gowdy	C72, 1B1	R	32	92	221	23	70	11	1	1	27	24	13	2	.317	.389
Fred Nicholson	OF63	R	27	78	222	31	56	4	5	2	19	23	24	1	.252	.342
Lloyd Christenbury	OF32, 2B5, 3B2	L	28	71	152	22	38	5	2	1	13	18	11	2	.250	.329
Frank Gibson	C29, 1B20	R	31	66	164	15	49	7	2	3	20	10	27	4	.299	.421
Billy Southworth (LJ)	OF41	L	29	43	158	27	51	4	4	4	18	18	1	4	.323	.475
Bunny Roser	OF32	L	20	32	113	13	27	3	4	0	16	10	19	2	.239	.336
Snake Henry	1B18	L	26	18	66	5	13	4	1	0	5	2	8	2	.197	.288
Gil Gallagher	SS6	B	25	7	22	1	1	0	0	0	2	1	7	0	.045	.091

NAME	T	AGE	W	L	PCT	SV	G	GS	CG	IP	H	BB	SO	SHO	ERA
TOTALS		28	53	100	.346	6	154	154	63	1348	1565	489	360	7	4.37
Frank Miller	R	36	11	13	.458	1	31	23	14	200	213	60	65	2	3.51
Rube Marquard	L	35	11	15	.423	1	39	25	7	198	255	66	57	0	5.09
Mule Watson	R	25	8	14	.364	1	41	27	8	201	262	59	53	1	4.70
Joe Oeschger	R	30	6	21	.222	1	46	23	10	196	234	81	51	1	5.05
Dana Fillingim (SA)	R	28	5	9	.357	2	25	12	5	117	143	37	25	1	4.54
1 Hugh McQuillan	R	26	5	10	.333	0	28	17	7	136	154	56	33	0	4.24
Tim McNamaara	R	23	3	4	.429	0	24	5	4	71	55	26	16	2	2.41
Harry Hulihan	R	23	2	3	.400	0	7	6	2	40	40	26	16	0	3.15
Garland Braxton (IL)	L	22	1	2	.333	0	25	5	2	67	75	24	15	0	3.36
Johnny Cooney	L	21	1	2	.333	0	4	3	1	25	19	6	7	0	2.16
Gene Lansing	R	24	0	1	.000	0	15	1	0	41	46	22	14	0	5.93
Joe Mathews	L	23	0	1	.000	0	1	0	0	10	5	6	0	0	3.60
Al Yeargin	R	20	0	1	.000	0	1	1	1	3	5	2	1	0	1.29
Joe Genewich	R	25	0	2	.000	0	6	2	1	23	29	11	4	0	7.04
Dick Rudolph	R	33	0	2	.000	0	3	1	1	16	22	5	3	0	5.06
Cy Morgan	R	26	0	0	—	0	1	0	0	1	2	1	0	0	36.00

WORLD SERIES — NEW YORK (NL) 4 NEW YORK (AL) 0 (one tie game)

LINE SCORES

TEAM	1	2	3	4	5	6	7	8	9	10 11 12	R	H	E
Game 1 October 4 at Polo Grounds													
NY (AL)	0	0	0	0	0	1	1	0	0		2	7	0
NY (NL)	0	0	0	0	0	0	3	0	X		3	11	3
Bush, Hoyt (8) Nehf, Ryan (8)													
Game 2 October 5 at Polo Grounds													
NY (NL)	3	0	0	0	0	0	0	0	0	0	3	8	1
NY (AL)	1	0	0	1	0	0	0	1	0	0	3	8	0
J. Barnes Shawkey Stopped by darkness													
Game 3 October 6 at Polo Grounds													
NY (AL)	0	0	0	0	0	0	0	0	0		0	4	1
NY (NL)	0	0	2	0	0	0	1	0	X		3	12	1
Hoyt, Jones (8) Scott													
Game 4 October 7 at Polo Grounds													
NY (NL)	0	0	0	4	0	0	0	0	0		4	9	1
NY (AL)	2	0	0	0	0	0	1	0	0		3	8	0
McQuillan Mays, Jones (8)													
Game 5 October 8 at Polo Grounds													
NY (AL)	0	0	0	0	1	0	1	0	0		3	5	0
NY (NL)	0	2	0	0	0	0	0	3	X		5	10	0
Bush Nehf													

COMPOSITE BATTING

NAME	POS	G	AB	R	H	2B	3B	HR	RBI	BA
New York (NL)										
Totals		5	162	18	50	2	1	1	18	.309
I. Meusel	OF	5	20	3	5	0	0	1	7	.250
Groh	3B	5	19	4	9	0	0	0	0	.474
Bancroft	SS	5	19	4	4	0	0	0	2	.211
Kelly	1B	5	18	0	5	0	0	0	2	.278
Frisch	2B	5	17	3	8	1	0	0	2	.471
Youngs	OF	5	16	2	6	0	0	0	0	.375
Snyder	C	5	15	1	5	0	0	0	0	.333
Cunningham	OF	4	10	0	2	0	0	0	2	.200
E. Smith	C	4	7	0	1	0	0	0	0	.143
Stengel	OF	2	5	0	2	0	0	0	0	.400
J. Scott	P	1	4	1	1	0	0	0	0	.250
McQuillan	P	1	4	0	1	1	0	0	0	.250
J. Barnes	P	1	4	0	0	0	0	0	0	.000
Nehf	P	2	3	0	0	0	0	0	0	.000
King	OF	1	2	0	1	0	0	0	1	1.000
Ryan	P	1	1	0	0	0	0	0	0	.000
New York (AL)										
Totals		5	158	11	32	6	2	11		.203
Pipp	1B	5	21	0	6	1	0	0	3	.286
B. Meusel	OF	5	20	2	6	1	0	0	2	.300
Dugan	3B	5	20	4	5	1	0	0	0	.250
Witt	OF	5	18	1	4	1	1	0	0	.222
Ruth	OF	5	17	1	2	1	0	0	1	.118
Schang	C	5	16	0	3	1	0	0	0	.188
E. Scott	SS	5	14	0	2	0	0	0	0	.143
Ward	2B	5	13	3	2	0	0	2	3	.154
Bush	P	2	5	0	1	0	0	0	0	.167
Shawkey	P	1	4	0	0	0	0	0	0	.000
Hoyt	P	2	4	0	2	0	0	0	0	.500
Elmer Smith	PH	1	2	0	0	0	0	0	0	.000
Mays	P	1	2	0	0	0	0	0	0	.000
McMillan	OF	1	1	0	0	0	0	0	0	.000
Baker	PH	1	1	0	0	0	0	0	0	.000
McNally	2B	1	0	0	0	0	0	0	0	—
Jones	P	2	0	0	0	0	0	0	0	—

COMPOSITE PITCHING

NAME	G	IP	H	BB	SO	W	L	SV	ERA
New York (NL)									
Totals	5	46	32	8	20	4	0	0	1.76
Nehf	2	16	11	3	6	2	0		2.25
J. Barnes	1	10	8	2	6	0	0	0	1.80
J. Scott	1	9	4	1	2	1	0	0	0.00
McQuillan	1	9	8	2	4	1	0	0	3.00
Ryan	1	2	1	0	2	1	0	0	0.00
New York (AL)									
Totals	5	43	50	12	15	0	4	0	3.35
Bush	2	15	21	5	6	0	2	0	4.80
Shawkey	1	10	8	2	4	0	0	0	2.70
Hoyt	2	8	11	2	4	0	1	0	1.13
Mays	1	8	9	2	1	0	1	0	4.50
Jones	2	2	1	0	0	0	0	0	0.00

1923 The Haunting Eviction

New York owned the baseball world. If there was any doubt to the claim, the final standings of 1921 and 1922 could easily back it up. During both previous seasons, the Giants and Yankees had won their league flags, and 1923 seemed to pose no problem for either of the clubs. But when problems from without are not present, the strife seems to manifest from within. Such was the case when an overabundance of success or jealousy of others' good fortunes caused the Giants to inform Yankee owner Colonel Jacob Ruppert that his American Leaguers were no longer welcome tenants in the Polo Grounds.

This decision sent the Colonel out to build Yankee Stadium—a 62,000-seat palace within ¼ mile of the National League park. With the most attractive stadium in the country, an exciting club, and a super drawing card in slugger Babe Ruth, the Yankees enjoyed a banner year at the gate and won a third consecutive American League pennant on the field. Although the Bambino swatted 41 homers into the friendly seats of the stadium, drove home 131 runs, and batted a robust .393, the Yankee long suits were pitching and defense. A trade with Boston brought lefty Herb Pennock into the starting rotation with Joe Bush, Sam Jones, Bob Shawkey, and Waite Hoyt to form the class hill staff of the loop. A solid infield cut off many opponent's runs, and the attack led by Ruth, Bob Meusel, and Wally Pipp provided enough Yankee runs for a final 16-game pennant margin.

Detroit and Cleveland, both possessors of .300 team batting averages, were the distant runner-ups to the New Yorkers. The Tigers fielded a Hall of Fame outfield in batting leader Harry Heilmann, manager Ty Cobb, and rookie Heinie Manush, while Tris Speaker both managed the Indians and provided the sock with his .380 batting average and 130 runs batted in. Both clubs, though, lacked the pitching to finish closer to the top. The fall of 1922's contending St. Louis Browns into the second division was insured by the eye ailment which sidelined star first-sacker George Sisler for the entire campaign.

With their hometown rivals unfurling a championship and a new stadium, the Giants felt obligated to match the upstarts. To begin the promotional campaign, the Polo Grounds were embellished and enlarged to a capacity of 54,000 seats. To further woo spectators into their den, the Giants won their third straight championship in a close race with the Cincinnati Reds. While no slugger on the order of Ruth graced the Jints' lineup, Frankie Frisch starred in his own manner with a .348 batting mark and blazing speed afield and on the bases. While Ross Youngs belted only three homers, he hit .336 and covered right field more gracefully than the Babe. George Kelly provided solid batting, and Giant Irish Meusel enjoyed a better year than brother Yankee Bob. Dave Bancroft, as usual, played an air-tight shortstop, but his late-season bout with pneumonia gave rookie Travis Jackson an extended trial in his slot. The pitching staff flashed no aces, but enough numbers to get by, as Jack Scott and reliever Rosie Ryan led the staff with 16 victories apiece.

Cincinnati boasted of the loop's top pitching with 20-game winners Dolf Luque, Eppa Rixey, and Pete Donohue, but lacked enough hitters like Edd Roush to overtake New York. Second-division clubs held the league batting stars, as Rogers Hornsby of the Cardinals won his fourth straight batting title, and Cy Williams the home run title to give his last-place Philadelphia Phillies' teammates something to cheer about.

For the third straight October, the World Series was played in New York, but this time in two parks. Casey Stengel won the opener in Yankee Stadium for the Giants with a ninth-inning inside-the-park home run and gave Art Nehf a 1-0 victory in game three with another circuit blast. But the Nationals won no other games, as the Yankees' attack found the Giants' pitchers easy marks. A six-game Series victory, spiced with three Ruth homers, marked the Yankees emergence from the underdog role in New York—a part which they had reluctantly held since their birth in 1903.

1923 AMERICAN LEAGUE

NEW YORK — 1st 98-54 .645 — MILLER HUGGINS

NAME	G by Pos	B	AGE	G	AB	R	H	2B	3B	HR	RBI	BB	SO	SB	BA	SA
TOTALS			29	152	5347	823	1554	231	79	105	770	521	516	69	.291	.422
Wally Pipp	1B144	L	30	144	569	79	173	19	8	6	108	36	28	6	.304	.397
Aaron Ward	2B152	R	26	152	567	79	161	26	11	10	82	56	65	8	.284	.422
Everett Scott	SS152	R	30	152	533	48	131	16	4	6	60	13	19	1	.246	.325
Joe Dugan	3B146	R	26	146	644	111	182	30	7	7	67	25	41	4	.283	.384
Babe Ruth	OF148, 1B4	L	28	152	522	151	205	45	13	41	131	170	93	17	.393	.764
Whitey Witt	OF144	L	27	146	596	113	187	18	10	6	56	67	42	2	.314	.408
Bob Meusel	OF121	R	26	132	460	59	144	29	10	9	91	31	52	13	.313	.478
Wally Schang (GJ)	C81	B	33	84	272	39	75	8	2	2	29	27	17	3	.276	.342
Fred Hofmann	C70	R	29	72	238	24	69	10	4	3	26	18	27	2	.290	.403
Elmer Smith	OF47	L	30		183	30	56	6	2	7	35	21	21	3	.306	.475
Harvey Hendrick	OF12	L	25	37	66	9	18	3	1	3	12	2	3	3	.273	.485
Mike McNally	SS13, 3B7, 2B5	R	29	30	38	5	8	0	0	0	1	3	4	1	.211	.211
Hinkey Haines	OF14	R	24	28	25	9	4	2	0	0	3	4	5	3	.160	.240
Benny Bengough	C19	R	24	19	53	1	7	2	0	0	3	4	2	0	.132	.170
2 Ernie Johnson	SS15, 3B1	R	35	19	38	6	17	1	1	1	8	2	1	0	.447	.605
Lou Gehrig	1B9	L	20	13	26	6	11	4	1	1	9	2	5	0	.423	.769
Mike Gazella	SS4, 2B2, 3B2	R	27	13	13	2	1	0	0	0	1	2	3	0	.077	.077

NAME	T	AGE	W	L	PCT	SV	G	GS	CG	IP	H	BB	SO	SHO	ERA
		29	98	54	.645	10	152	152	102	1381	1365	491	506	9	3.62
Sad Sam Jones	R	30	21	8	.724	4	39	27	18	243	239	69	68	3	3.63
Herb Pennock	R	29	19	6	.760	3	35	27	21	238	235	68	93	1	3.14
Bullet Joe Bush	R	30	19	15	.559	0	37	30	23	276	263	117	125	3	3.42
Waite Hoyt	R	23	17	9	.654	1	37	28	19	239	227	66	60	1	3.01
Bob Shawkey	R	32	16	11	.593	1	36	31	17	259	232	102	125	1	3.51
Carl Mays	R	31	5	2	.714	0	23	7	2	81	119	32	16	0	6.22
George Pipgras	R	23	1	3	.250	0	8	2	2	33	34	25	12	0	6.00
Oscar Roettger	R	23	0	0	—	1	5	0	0	12	16	12	7	0	8.25

DETROIT — 2nd 83-71 .539 16 — TY COBB

NAME	G by Pos	B	AGE	G	AB	R	H	2B	3B	HR	RBI	BB	SO	SB	BA	SA
TOTALS			29	155	5266	831	1579	270	69	41	739	596	385	87	.300	.401
Lu Blue	1B129	B	26	129	504	100	143	27	7	1	46	96	40	9	.284	.371
Fred Haney	2B69, 3B55, SS16	R	25	142	503	85	142	13	4	4	67	45	23	12	.282	.348
Topper Rigney	SS129	R	26	129	470	63	148	24	11	1	74	55	35	7	.315	.419
Bob Jones	3B97	L	33	100	372	51	93	15	4	1	40	29	13	7	.250	.320
Harry Heilmann	OF130, 1B12	R	28	144	524	121	211	44	11	18	115	74	40	8	.403	.632
Ty Cobb	OF141	L	36	145	556	103	189	40	7	6	88	66	14	9	.340	.469
Heinie Manush	OF79	L	21	109	308	59	103	20	5	4	54	20	21	3	.334	.471
Johnny Bassler	C128	L	28	135	383	45	114	12	3	0	49	76	13	2	.298	.345
Bobby Veach	OF85	L	35	114	293	45	94	13	3	2	39	29	21	10	.321	.406
Bob Fothergill	OF68	R	25	101	241	34	76	18	2	1	49	12	19	4	.315	.419
Del Pratt	2B60, 1B17, 3B12	R	35	101	297	43	92	18	3	0	40	25	9	2	.310	.391
Larry Woodall	C60	R	28	71	148	20	41	12	2	1	19	22	9	2	.277	.405
George Cutshaw (IL)	2B43, 3B2	R	36	45	143	15	32	1	2	0	13	9	5	2	.224	.259
Clyde Manion	C3, 1B1	R	26	23	22	0	3	0	0	0	2	2	2	0	.136	.136
John Kerr	SS15	B	24	19	42	4	9	1	0	0	1	4	5	0	.214	.238
Les Burke	3B2, 2B1	L	20	7	10	2	1	0	0	0	2	0	1	0	.100	.100
Fred Carisch	C2	R	41	2	0	0	0	0	0	0	0	0	0	0	.000	.000
1 Ira Flagstead		R	29	1	1	0	0	0	0	0	0	0	0	0	.000	.000

NAME	T	AGE	W	L	PCT	SV	G	GS	CG	IP	H	BB	SO	SHO	ERA
		27	83	71	.539	12	155	155	61	1374	1502	449	447	9	4.09
Hooks Dauss	R	33	21	13	.618	5	50	39	22	316	331	78	105	4	3.62
Herman Pillette	R	26	14	19	.424	1	47	37	14	250	280	83	64	0	3.85
Bert Cole	R	27	13	5	.722	5	52	13	5	163	183	61	32	1	4.14
Syl Johnson	R	22	12	7	.632	0	37	18	7	176	181	47	93	1	3.99
Ken Holloway	R	25	11	10	.524	1	42	24	7	194	232	75	55	1	4.45
Ray Francis	L	30	5	8	.385	1	33	6	0	79	95	28	27	0	4.45
Rip Collins	R	27	3	7	.300	0	17	13	3	92	104	22	25	1	4.88
Earl Whitehill	L	23	2	0	1.000	0	8	3	2	33	22	15	19	1	2.73
Ole Olsen	R	28	1	1	.500	0	17	2	1	41	42	17	12	0	6.37
Rufe Clarke	R	23	1	1	.500	0	5	0	0	6	6	6	2	0	4.50
Ed Wells	L	23	0	0	—	0	5	0	0	11	11	6	6	0	5.40
Roy Moore	R	24	0	0	—	0	3	0	0	12	15	11	7	0	3.00
Dutch Leonard (ST) 31															

CLEVELAND — 3rd 82-71 .536 16.5 — TRIS SPEAKER

NAME	G by Pos	B	AGE	G	AB	R	H	2B	3B	HR	RBI	BB	SO	SB	BA	SA
TOTALS			28	153	5290	888	1594	301	75	59	807	633	384	86	.301	.420
Frank Brower	1B112, OF2	L	29	126	397	77	113	25	8	16	66	62	32	6	.285	.509
Bill Wambsganss	2B88, 3B4, SS2	R	29	101	345	59	100	20	4	1	59	43	15	12	.290	.380
Joe Sewell	SS151	L	24	153	553	98	195	41	10	3	109	98	12	9	.353	.479
Rube Lutzke	3B143	R	25	143	511	71	131	20	3	3	65	59	57	0	.256	.337
Homer Summa	OF136	L	24	137	525	92	172	27	6	3	69	33	20	9	.328	.419
Tris Speaker	OF152	L	35	150	574	133	218	59	11	17	130	93	15	8	.380	.610
Charlie Jamieson	OF152	L	30	152	644	130	222	36	12	2	51	80	37	19	.345	.447
Steve O'Neill	C111	R	31	113	330	31	82	12	0	0	50	64	34	0	.248	.285
Glenn Myatt	C69	L	25	92	220	36	63	7	6	3	40	16	18	0	.286	.414
Riggs Stephenson	2B66, OF3, 3B1	R	25	91	301	48	96	20	6	5	65	15	25	6	.319	.475
George Uhle	P54	R	24	58	144	23	52	10	3	0	22	7	10	2	.361	.472
Joe Connolly	OF39	R	27	52	109	25	33	10	1	3	15	3	3	1	.303	.495
Larry Gardner	3B19	L	37	52	79	4	20	5	1	0	12	12	7	0	.253	.342
Lou Guisto	1B40	L	28	40	144	17	26	5	0	0	18	15	15	1	.181	.215
Ray Knode	1B21	L	22	22	38	7	11	0	0	2	9	2	8	1	.289	.447
Luke Sewell	C7	R	22	10	10	2	2	0	1	0	1	2	1	0	.200	.400
Wally Shaner	OF2, 3B1	R	23	3	4	1	1	0	0	0	1	0	0	0	.250	.250
Tom Gulley	OF1	L	23	2	3	1	1	0	0	0	1	0	0	0	.333	.667
Jackie Gallagher	OF1	L	21	3	1	1	1	0	0	0	0	0	0	0	1.000	1.000
Sumpter Clarke	OF1	R	25	1	3	0	0	0	0	0	0	0	0	0	.000	.000
Kenny Hogan		L	20	1												

NAME	T	AGE	W	L	PCT	SV	G	GS	CG	IP	H	BB	SO	SHO	ERA
		28	82	71	.536	11	153	153	77	1375	1517	466	407	10	3.91
George Uhle	R	24	26	16	.619	5	54	44	29	358	378	102	109	1	3.77
Stan Coveleski (IL)	R	33	13	14	.481	2	33	31	17	228	251	42	54	5	2.76
Joe Shaute	L	23	10	8	.556	0	33	16	7	172	176	53	61	0	3.52
Jim Joe Edwards	L	28	10	10	.500	1	38	21	8	179	200	75	68	1	3.73
Sherry Smith	L	32	9	6	.600	1	30	16	10	124	129	37	23	1	3.27
Guy Morton	R	30	9	6	.600	1	32	14	3	128	133	56	54	2	4.29
Dewey Metivier	R	25	4	2	.667	1	26	5	1	73	111	38	9	0	6.53
Danny Boone (SA)	R	28	4	6	.400	0	27	4	2	70	93	31	15	0	6.04
Jim Sullivan	R	29	1	0	1.000	0	5	1	0	10	5	4	1	0	14.40
Phil Bedgood	R	25	0	0	—	0	2	0	0	19	16	14	7	0	5.21
Logan Drake	R	23	0	0	—	0	4	1	0	4	5	2	0	0	4.50
Emil Levsen	R	25	0	0	—	0	1	0	0					0	0.00
George Edmondson	R	27	0	0	—	0	4	0	0	4	8	4	1	0	11.25
Johnson Fry	R	21	0	0	—	0	1	0	0	4	8	4	1	0	11.25
George Winn	L	25	0	0	—	0	1	0	0					0	0.00

WASHINGTON   4th 75-78 .490 23.5   DONIE BUSH

NAME	G by Pos	B	AGE	G	AB	R	H	2B	3B	HR	RBI	BB	SO	SB	BA	SA
TOTALS			28	155	5244	720	1436	224	93	26	628	532	448	102	.274	.367
Joe Judge (KJ)	1B112	L	29	113	405	56	127	24	6	2	63	58	20	11	.314	.417
Bucky Harris	2B144, SS11	R	26	145	532	60	150	21	13	2	70	50	29	3	.282	.382
Roger Peckinpaugh	SS154	R	32	154	568	73	150	18	4	2	62	64	30	10	.264	.320
Ossie Bluege (KJ)	3B107, 2B	R	22	109	379	48	93	15	7	2	42	48	53	5	.245	.338
Sam Rice	OF147	L	33	148	595	117	188	35	18	3	75	57	12	20	.316	.450
2 Nemo Leibold	OF84	L	31	95	315	68	96	13	4	1	22	53	16	7	.305	.381
Goose Goslin	OF149	L	22	150	600	86	180	29	18	9	99	40	53	7	.300	.453
Muddy Ruel	C133	R	27	136	449	63	142	24	3	0	54	55	21	4	.316	.383
Joe Evans	OF72, 3B21, 1B5	R	28	106	372	42	98	15	3	0	38	27	18	6	.263	.320
Patsy Gharrity	C35, 1B33	R	31	93	251	26	52	9	4	3	33	22	27	6	.207	.311
Pinky Hargrave	3B8, C5, OF1	R	27	33	59	4	17	2	0	0	8	2	6	0	.288	.322
Rip Wade	OF19	L	25	33	69	8	16	2	2	0	14	5	10	0	.232	.406
Jim O'Neill	2B8, 3B6, OF1	R	30	23	33	6	9	1	0	0	3	1	3	0	.273	.303
Pep Conroy (IL)	3B10, 1B6, OF1	R	24	18	60	6	8	2	2	0	2	4	9	0	.133	.233
Showboat Fisher	OF5	L	24	13	23	4	6	2	0	0	2	4	3	0	.261	.348
Donie Bush	3B6, 2B1	B	35	10	22	6	9	0	0	0	0	1	0	0	.409	.409
Bobby Murray	3B10	L	28	10	39	2	7	1	0	0	2	1	4	1	.179	.205
Doc Prothro	3B6	R	29	6	8	2	2	0	0	0	3	1	3	0	.250	.500
Carr Smith	OF4	R	22	5	9	0	1	0	0	0	1	0	0	0	.111	.222
Jim Riley	1B2	L	28	2	3	1	0	0	0	0	0	0	2	0	.000	.000
Pete Lapan		L	28	3	2	2	0	0	0	0	0	0	0	0	.000	.000
Jake Propst		L	28	1	1	0	0	0	0	0	0	0	0	0	.000	.000

NAME	T	AGE	W	L	PCT	SV	G	GS	CG	IP	H	BB	SO	SHO	ERA
TOTALS		30	75	78	.490	16	155	155	71	1375	1531	559	474	8	3.99
Walter Johnson	R	35	17	12	.586	4	43	35	18	262	267	69	130	3	3.54
George Mogridge	L	34	13	13	.500	1	33	28	18	211	228	56	62	3	3.11
Allen Russell	R	29	10	7	.588	9	52	6	4	181	177	77	67	0	3.03
Tom Zachary	L	27	10	16	.385	0	35	29	10	204	270	63	40	0	4.50
Paul Zahniser	R	26	9	10	.474	0	33	21	10	177	201	76	52	1	3.86
Cy Warmoth	R	30	7	5	.583	0	21	13	3	105	103	76	45	0	4.28
Firpo Marberry	R	24	4	0	1.000	0	11	4	2	45	42	17	18	0	2.80
Bonnie Hollingsworth	R	27	3	7	.300	0	11	8	1	73	72	50	26	0	4.07
Monroe Mitchell	R	21	2	4	.333	0	10	6	3	42	57	22	8	1	6.43
Jim Brillheart	L	19	0	1	.000	0	12	0	0	18	27	12	8	0	7.00
Skipper Friday	R	25	0	1	.000	0	7	2	1	30	35	22	9	0	6.90
Duke Sedgwick	R	25	0	1	.000	0	5	2	1	16	27	6	4	0	7.88
Clay Roe	L	19	0	1	.000	0	1	1	0	6	6	2	0	0	0.00
Slim McGrew	R	23	0	0	—	0	3	0	0	5	11	1	1	0	12.60
Squire Potter	R	21	0	0	—	0	1	0	0	3	11	4	1	0	21.00
Fred Schemanske	R	20	0	0	—	0	1	0	0	1	3	0	0	0	27.00
Ted Wingfield	R	23	0	0	—	0	1	0	0	1	1	0	0	0	0.00

ST. LOUIS   5th 74-78 .487 24   LEE FOHL 52-49 .515   JIMMY AUSTIN 22-29 .431

NAME	G by Pos	B	AGE	G	AB	R	H	2B	3B	HR	RBI	BB	SO	SB	BA	SA
TOTALS			29	154	5298	688	1489	248	62	82	613	422	423	64	.281	.398
2 Dutch Schliebner	1B127	R	32	127	444	50	122	19	6	4	52	39	60	3	.275	.372
Marty McManus	2B133, 1B20	R	23	154	582	86	180	35	10	15	94	49	50	14	.309	.481
Wally Gerber	SS154	R	31	154	605	85	170	26	3	1	62	54	50	4	.281	.339
Homer Ezzell	3B73, 2B8	R	27	88	275	31	68	6	0	0	14	15	20	4	.247	.269
Jack Tobin	OF151	L	31	151	637	91	202	32	15	13	73	42	13	8	.317	.476
Baby Doll Jacobson	OF146	R	32	147	592	76	183	29	6	8	81	29	27	8	.309	.419
Ken Williams	OF145	L	33	147	555	106	198	37	12	29	91	79	32	18	.357	.623
Hank Severeid	C116	R	32	122	432	50	133	27	6	3	51	31	11	3	.308	.419
Pat Collins	C47	R	26	85	181	9	32	8	0	3	30	15	45	0	.177	.271
Gene Robertson (VR)	3B74, 2B1	R	24	78	251	36	62	10	1	0	17	21	7	4	.247	.295
Cedric Durst	OF10, 1B8	L	26	45	85	12	18	2	0	5	11	8	14	0	.212	.412
Eddie Foster	2B20, 3B7	R	36	27	100	9	18	2	0	0	4	7	7	0	.180	.200
Bill Whaley	OF13	L	24	23	50	5	12	2	1	0	1	4	2	0	.240	.320
Frank Ellerbe	3B14	R	27	18	49	6	9	0	0	0	1	1	5	0	.184	.184
Johnny Schulte	1B1, C1	R	26	7	3	1	0	0	0	0	0	0	0	0	.000	.000
Herschel Bennett	OF1	L	26	5	4	0	0	0	0	0	0	0	1	0	.000	.000
Josh Billings	C4	R	31	4	9	0	0	0	0	0	0	0	2	0	.000	.000
Harry Rice		L	22	4	3	0	0	0	0	0	0	0	0	0	.000	.000
Jimmy Austin	C1	B	43	1	0	0	0	0	0	0	0	0	0	0	—	—
Bill Mizeur		L	26	1	1	0	0	0	0	0	0	0	0	0	.000	.000

Syl Simon 25 R 0-1, Chick Shorten (VR) 31, George Sisler (IJ) 30

NAME	T	AGE	W	L	PCT	SV	G	GS	CG	IP	H	BB	SO	SHO	ERA
TOTALS		28	74	78	.487	10	154	154	84	1373	1430	528	488	10	3.93
Urban Shocker	R	32	20	12	.625	5	43	35	25	277	292	49	109	3	3.41
Dave Danforth	R	33	16	14	.533	1	38	29	16	226	221	87	96	1	3.94
Elam Vangilder	R	27	16	17	.485	1	41	35	20	282	276	120	74	4	3.06
Rasty Wright	R	27	7	4	.636	0	20	8	4	83	107	34	26	0	6.40
Ray Kolp	R	28	5	12	.294	1	34	17	11	171	178	54	44	1	3.90
Dixie Davis	R	32	4	6	.400	0	19	17	5	109	106	63	36	1	3.64
Hub Pruett (BA)	L	22	4	7	.364	2	32	8	3	104	109	64	59	0	4.33
Bill Bayne	L	24	2	2	.500	0	19	2	0	46	49	31	15	0	4.50
Charlie Root	R	24	0	4	.000	0	27	2	0	60	68	18	27	0	5.70
George Grant	R	20	0	0	—	0	9	0	0	15	3	2	0	0	5.00
1 Sloppy Thurston	R	24	0	0	—	0	2	1	0	4	8	1	0	0	6.75
Jumbo Jim Elliott	L	22	0	0	—	0	1	1	0	1	3	0	0	0	27.00

PHILADELPHIA   6th 69-83 .454 29   CONNIE MACK

NAME	G by Pos	B	AGE	G	AB	R	H	2B	3B	HR	RBI	BB	SO	SB	BA	SA
TOTALS			25	153	5196	661	1407	229	65	52	577	445	517	72	.273	.370
Joe Hauser	1B146	L	24	146	537	93	165	21	10	16	94	69	52	6	.307	.473
Jimmy Dykes	2B102, SS20, 3B2	R	26	124	416	50	105	28	1	4	43	35	40	6	.252	.353
Chick Galloway	SS134	R	26	134	504	64	140	18	9	2	62	37	30	12	.278	.361
Sammy Hale	3B107	R	26	115	434	68	125	22	8	3	51	17	31	8	.288	.396
Frank Welch	OF117	R	25	125	421	56	125	19	9	4	55	48	40	1	.297	.413
Wid Matthews	OF127	L	26	129	485	52	133	11	6	1	25	67	46	16	.274	.328
Bing Miller	OF119	R	28	123	458	68	137	25	4	12	64	27	34	9	.299	.450
Cy Perkins	C137	R	27	143	500	53	135	34	5	2	65	65	30	1	.270	.370
Beauty McGowan	OF79	L	22	95	287	41	73	9	1	1	19	36	25	4	.254	.303
Heinie Scheer	2B61	R	22	69	210	26	50	8	1	2	21	17	41	3	.238	.314
Fred Heimach	P40, 1B6	L	22	63	118	14	30	4	1	1	11	4	18	0	.254	.331
Harry Riconda	3B47, SS2	R	26	55	175	23	46	11	4	0	12	12	18	4	.263	.371
Frank Bruggy	C34, 1B5	R	32	54	105	4	22	3	0	1	6	4	9	1	.210	.267
Tilly Walker	OF26	R	35	52	109	12	30	5	2	2	16	14	11	1	.275	.413
Walt French	OF10	L	23	16	39	7	9	3	0	0	2	5	7	0	.231	.308
Chuck Rowland	C4	R	23	5	6	0	0	0	0	0	0	0	0	0	.000	.000
Doc Wood	SS3	R	23	3	4	0	1	0	0	0	0	0	0	0	.333	.333
John Jones	OF1	R	23	2	4	0	1	0	0	0	0	0	1	0	.250	.250

NAME	T	AGE	W	L	PCT	SV	G	GS	CG	IP	H	BB	SO	SHO	ERA
TOTALS		26	69	83	.454	12	153	153	65	1365	1465	550	400	7	4.08
Eddie Rommel	R	25	18	19	.486	5	56	31	19	298	306	108	76	3	3.27
Bob Hasty	R	27	13	15	.464	1	44	36	10	243	274	72	56	1	4.45
Rollie Naylor (LJ)	R	31	12	7	.632	0	26	20	9	143	149	59	27	2	3.46
Slim Harriss	R	26	10	16	.385	6	40	28	9	209	221	95	89	0	4.00
Fred Heimach	L	22	6	12	.333	0	40	19	10	208	238	69	63	0	4.33
2 Rube Walberg	L	26	4	8	.333	0	26	10	4	115	122	60	38	0	5.32
Roy Meeker	R	22	3	0	1.000	0	5	2	2	25	24	13	12	0	3.60
Denny Burns	R	25	2	1	.667	0	4	3	2	27	21	7	8	0	2.00
Curly Ogden	R	22	1	2	.333	0	18	2	0	46	63	32	14	0	5.67
Al Kellett	R	21	0	1	.000	0	5	0	0	10	11	8	1	0	6.30
Walt Kinney	L	29	0	1	.000	0	1	0	0	12	11	9	8	0	7.50
Hank Hulvey	R	25	0	1	.000	0	1	0	0	7	10	2	2	0	7.71
Harry O'Neill	R	30	0	0	—	0	1	0	0	0	0	0	0	0	0.00
Chuck Wolfe	R	26	0	0	—	0				*10	6	8	1	0	3.60
Ren Kelly	R	23	0	0	—	0	7	0	0	7	4	1	0	0	2.57
Doc Ozmer	R	22	0	0	—	0	1	1	0	2	1	1	0	0	4.50

CHICAGO   7th 69-85 .448 30   KID GLEASON

NAME	G by Pos	B	AGE	G	AB	R	H	2B	3B	HR	RBI	BB	SO	SB	BA	SA
TOTALS			29	156	5246	692	1463	254	57	42	604	532	458	191	.279	.373
Earl Sheely	1B156	R	30	156	570	74	169	25	3	4	88	79	30	5	.296	.372
Eddie Collins	2B142	L	36	145	505	89	182	22	5	5	67	84	8	49	.360	.453
Harvey McClellan	SS139, 2B2	R	28	141	550	67	129	29	3	1	41	27	44	14	.235	.304
Willie Kamm	3B149	R	23	149	544	75	159	39	9	6	87	62	82	17	.292	.430
Harry Hooper	OF143	L	35	145	576	87	166	32	4	10	65	68	22	18	.288	.410
Johnny Mostil	OF143, 3B6, SS1	R	27	153	546	91	159	37	15	3	64	62	51	41	.291	.430
Bibb Falk	OF80	L	24	87	274	44	84	18	6	5	38	25	12	4	.307	.471
Ray Schalk	C121	R	30	123	382	42	87	12	2	1	44	39	28	6	.228	.277
Roy Elsh	OF57	R	32	81	209	28	52	7	2	0	24	16	23	15	.249	.301
Amos Strunk	OF4, 1B3	L	34	54	54	7	17	0	0	0	8	8	5	1	.315	.315
2 Sloppy Thurston	P44	R	24	54	79	10	25	5	1	0	4	2	6	0	.316	.405
Bill Barrett	OF40, 3B1	R	23	44	162	17	44	7	2	2	23	9	24	12	.272	.377
Roy Graham	C33	R	28	36	82	3	16	2	0	0	9	10	3	0	.195	.220
John Happenny	2B20, SS8	R	22	32	86	7	19	5	0	0	3	3	13	0	.221	.279
Buck Crouse	C22	L	25	22	70	6	18	2	1	1	7	3	4	0	.257	.357
Maurice Archdeacon	OF20	L	25	22	87	23	35	5	1	0	4	6	8	2	.402	.483
1 Ernie Johnson	SS12	R	35	12	53	5	10	2	0	0	1	3	5	2	.189	.226
Lou Rosenberg	2B2	R	19	3	4	0	1	0	0	0	0	0	0	1	.250	.250
Leo Taylor		R	22	1	0	0	0	0	0	0	0	0	0	0	—	—
Charlie Dorman	C1		25	1	2	0	1	0	0	0	0	0	0	0	.500	.500
Shine Cortazzo		R	18	1	1	0	0	0	0	0	0	0	0	0	.000	.000
Roxy Snipes		L	26	1	1	0	0	0	0	0	0	0	0	0	.000	.000

NAME	T	AGE	W	L	PCT	SV	G	GS	CG	IP	H	BB	SO	SHO	ERA
TOTALS		26	69	85	.448	11	156	156	74	1402	1512	534	467	5	4.03
Red Faber	R	34	14	11	.560	0	32	31	15	232	233	62	91	2	3.41
Charlie Robertson	R	27	13	18	.419	0	38	34	18	255	262	104	91	1	3.81
Mike Cvengros	L	22	13	13	.480	3	40	26	14	214	216	107	86	0	4.42
Dixie Leverett	R	29	10	13	.435	3	38	24	9	193	212	64	64	0	4.06
Ted Blankenship	R	22	9	14	.391	4	44	23	9	209	219	100	57	1	4.27
2 Sloppy Thurston	R	24	7	8	.467	4	44	12	8	192	223	36	55	0	3.05
Ted Lyons	R	22	2	1	.667	0	9	1	0	23	30	15	6	0	6.26
Homer Blankenship	R	20	1	1	.500	0	4	0	0	5	9	1	1	0	3.60
Claral Gillenwater	R	23	1	3	.250	0	9	3	1	28	26	21	11	0	5.57
Frank Mack	R	29	0	1	.000	0	11	0	0	23	23	11	6	0	4.30
Frank Woodward	R	29	0	1	.000	0	2	1	1	2	4	2	1	0	13.50
2 Leon Cadore	R	32	0	0	—	0	1	0	0	1	3	1	0	0	27.00
Paul Castner	L	26	0	0	—	0	6	0	0	10	14	5	0	0	6.30
Sarge Connally	R	24	0	0	—	0	7	1	0	9	7	12	3	0	6.00
Lum Davenport	R	23	0	0	—	0	4	0	0	7	4	1	0	0	6.75
Red Proctor	R	22	0	0	—	0	4	0	0	4	11	2	0	0	13.50
Slim Embry	R	21	0	0	—	0	1	0	0	4	6	4	1	0	9.00

Dickie Kerr (SL) 29
Doug McWeeny (ST) 26

BOSTON   8th 61-91 .401 37   FRANK CHANCE

NAME	G by Pos	B	AGE	G	AB	R	H	2B	3B	HR	RBI	BB	SO	SB	BA	SA
TOTALS			29	154	5181	584	1354	253	54	34	525	391	480	80	.261	.351
George Burns	1B146	R	30	146	551	91	181	47	5	7	82	45	33	9	.328	.470
Chick Fewster	2B49, SS7, 3B1	R	27	90	284	32	67	10	1	0	15	39	35	7	.236	.278
Johnny Mitchell	SS87, 2B5	B	28	92	347	40	78	15	4	0	19	34	18	7	.225	.291
Howard Shanks	3B83, 2B37, OF6, SS2	R	32	131	464	38	118	19	5	3	57	19	37	6	.254	.336
2 Ira Flagstead	OF102	R	29	109	382	55	119	23	4	8	53	37	26	4	.312	.455
Dick Reichle	OF93, 1B2	R	26	122	361	40	93	17	3	1	39	22	34	3	.258	.330
Joe Harris	OF132, 1B9	R	32	142	483	82	162	28	11	13	76	52	27	5	.335	.520
Val Picinich	C81	R	26	87	268	33	74	21	1	2	31	46	32	3	.276	.384
Norm McMillan	3B67, 2B34, SS28	R	27	131	459	37	116	24	5	0	42	28	44	13	.253	.327
Shano Collins	OF89	R	37	97	342	41	79	10	5	0	18	11	29	7	.231	.289
Mike Menosky	OF49	L	28	84	188	22	43	8	4	0	25	22	19	3	.229	.314
Al DeVormer	C55, 1B2	R	31	74	209	20	54	7	3	0	18	6	21	3	.258	.321
Pinky Pittinger	2B42, SS10, 3B3	R	24	60	177	15	38	5	0	0	15	5	10	3	.215	.243
Roxy Walters	C36, 2B1	R	30	40	104	9	26	4	0	0	9	5	7	0	.250	.288
1 Nemo Leibold	OF10	L	31	12	18	1	2	1	0	0	1	1	0	0	.111	.111
John Donahue	OF9	L	29	10	36	5	10	4	0	0	1	0	6	0	.278	.389
Camp Skinner	OF2	L	26	5	21	3	5	1	0	0	1	2	5	0	.238	.333
Frank Fuller	2B6	L	30	6	21	3	5	0	0	0	1	2	1	1	.238	.238
Ike Boone	OF4	L	26	15	14	0	0	0	0	0	0	0	0	0	.267	.400

NAME	T	AGE	W	L	PCT	SV	G	GS	CG	IP	H	BB	SO	SHO	ERA
TOTALS		28	61	91	.401	11	154	154	78	1372	1534	520	412	3	4.20
Howard Ehmke	R	29	20	17	.541	3	43	39	28	317	318	119	121	2	3.78
Jack Quinn	R	39	13	17	.433	7	42	28	16	243	302	53	71	1	3.89
Alex Ferguson	R	26	9	13	.409	0	34	27	11	198	229	67	72	0	4.05
Bill Piercy	R	27	8	13	.320	0	30	24	11	187	193	73	51	0	3.42
George Murray	R	24	7	11	.389	0	39	18	5	178	190	87	40	0	4.90
Curt Fullerton	R	24	2	15	.118	1	36	16	7	142	167	71	37	0	5.13
Les Howe	R	27	1	0	1.000	0	12	2	0	30	23	7	7	0	2.40
Lefty O'Doul	L	26	1	1	.500	0	23	0	0	53	69	31	10	0	5.43
Clarence Blethen	R	29	0	0	—	0	6	0	0	12	9	7	2	0	7.00
Carl Stimson	R	28	0	0	—	0	4	0	0	4	12	5	1	0	22.50
Dave Black	R	31	0	0	—	0	2	0	0	5	9	4	0	0	9.00

NEW YORK 1st 95-58 .621 JOHN McGRAW

NAME	G by Pos	B	AGE	G	AB	R	H	2B	3B	HR	RBI	BB	SO	SB	BA	SA
TOTALS			27	153	5452	854	1610	248	76	85	790	487	406	106	.295	.415
George Kelly	1B145	R	27	145	560	82	172	23	5	16	103	47	64	14	.307	.452
Frankie Frisch	2B135, 3B17	B	24	151	641	116	223	32	10	12	111	46	12	29	.348	.485
Dave Bancroft (IL)	SS96, 2B11	B	32	107	444	80	135	33	3	1	31	62	23	9	.304	.399
Heinie Groh	3B118	R	33	123	465	91	135	22	5	4	48	60	22	3	.290	.385
Ross Youngs	OF152	L	26	152	596	121	200	33	12	3	87	73	36	13	.336	.446
Jimmy O'Connell	OF64, 1B8	L	22	87	252	42	63	9	2	6	39	34	32	7	.250	.373
Irish Meusel	OF145	R	30	146	595	102	177	22	14	19	125	38	16	8	.297	.477
Frank Snyder	C112	R	29	120	402	37	103	13	6	5	63	24	29	5	.256	.356
Travis Jackson	SS60, 3B31, 2B1	R	19	96	327	45	90	12	7	4	37	22	40	3	.275	.391
Bill Cunningham	OF68, 2B4	R	28	79	203	22	55	7	1	5	27	10	9	5	.271	.389
Casey Stengel	OF57	L	32	75	218	39	74	11	5	5	43	20	18	6	.339	.505
2 Hank Gowdy	C43	R	33	53	122	13	40	6	3	1	18	21	9	2	.328	.451
Jack Bentley	P31	L	28	52	89	9	38	6	2	1	14	3	4	0	.427	.573
Freddie Maguire	2B16, 3B1	R	24	41	30	11	6	1	0	0	2	2	4	1	.200	.233
Jack Scott (LJ)	P40	L	31	40	79	12	25	4	0	1	10	3	5	1	.316	.405
Ralph Shinners	OF6	R	27	33	13	5	2	1	0	0	0	2	1	0	.154	.231
1 Earl Smith	C12	L	26	24	34	2	7	1	1	1	4	4	1	0	.206	.382
Alex Gaston	C21	R	30	22	39	3	8	2	0	1	5	0	6	0	.205	.333
Bill Terry	1B2	L	24	3	7	1	1	0	0	0	0	0	0	0	.143	.143
Hack Wilson	OF3	R	23	3	10	0	2	0	0	0	0	0	1	0	.200	.200
Mose Solomon	OF2	L	22	2	8	0	3	1	0	0	1	0	1	0	.375	.500

NAME	T	AGE	W	L	PCT	SV	G	GS	CG	IP	H	BB	SO	SHO	ERA
		27	95	58	.621	18	153	153	62	1378	1440	424	453	10	3.90
Rosy Ryan	R	25	16	5	.762	4	45	15	7	173	169	46	58	0	3.49
Jack Scott (LJ)	R	31	16	7	.696	1	40	25	9	220	223	65	79	3	3.89
Hugh McQuillan	R	27	15	14	.517	0	38	32	15	230	224	66	75	5	3.40
Jack Bentley	L	28	13	8	.619	3	31	26	12	183	198	67	80	1	4.48
Art Nehf	L	30	13	10	.565	2	34	27	7	196	219	49	50	1	4.50
2 Mule Watson	R	26	8	5	.615	0	17	15	8	108	117	21	26	0	3.42
Claude Jonnard	R	25	4	3	.571	5	45	1	1	96	105	35	45	0	3.28
1 Jesse Barnes	R	30	3	1	.750	1	12	4	1	36	48	13	12	0	6.25
Clint Blume	R	24	2	0	1.000	0	12	1	0	24	22	20	2	0	3.75
Fred Johnson	R	29	2	0	1.000	0	3	1	1	17	11	7	5	0	4.24
Virgil Barnes	R	26	2	3	.400	1	22	2	0	53	59	19	6	0	3.91
Dinty Gearin	L	25	1	1	.500	0	6	2	1	24	23	10	9	0	3.38
Walter Huntzinger	R	24	0	1	.000	0	2	1	0	8	9	1	2	0	7.88
Red Lucas	R	21	0	0	—	0	3	0	0	5	4	1	1	0	0.00
1 Rube Walberg	L	26	0	0	—	0	2	0	0	5	4	1	1	0	1.80

CINCINNATI 2nd 91-63 .591 4.5 PAT MORAN

NAME	G by Pos	B	AGE	G	AB	R	H	2B	3B	HR	RBI	BB	SO	SB	BA	SA
TOTALS			30	154	5278	708	1506	237	95	45	645	439	367	96	.285	.392
Jake Daubert	1B121	L	39	125	500	63	146	27	10	2	54	40	20	11	.292	.398
Sammy Bohne	2B96, 3B35, SS9, 1B1	R	26	139	539	77	136	18	10	3	47	48	37	16	.252	.340
Ike Caveney	SS138	R	28	138	488	58	135	21	9	4	63	26	41	5	.277	.381
Babe Pinelli (JJ)	3B116	R	27	117	423	44	117	14	5	0	51	27	29	10	.277	.333
George Burns	OF154	R	33	154	614	99	168	27	13	3	45	101	46	10	.274	.375
Edd Roush	OF137	L	30	138	527	88	185	41	18	6	88	46	16	10	.351	.531
Pat Duncan	OF146	R	29	147	566	92	185	26	8	7	83	30	27	15	.327	.438
Bubbles Hargrave	C109	R	30	118	378	54	126	23	9	10	78	44	22	4	.333	.521
Lew Fonseca	2B45, 1B14	R	24	65	237	33	66	11	4	3	28	9	16	4	.278	.397
George Harper	OF29	L	31	61	125	14	32	4	2	3	16	11	9	0	.256	.392
Ivy Wingo	C57	L	32	61	171	10	45	9	2	1	24	9	11	1	.263	.357
Rube Bressler	1B22, OF6	R	28	54	119	25	33	3	1	0	18	20	4	3	.277	.319
Rube Benton	P33	L	36	33	80	5	23	3	0	0	4	1	12	0	.288	.325
Wally Kimmick	2B17, 3B4, SS1	R	26	29	80	11	18	2	1	0	6	5	15	3	.225	.275
Boob Fowler	SS10	L	22	11	33	9	11	0	1	1	6	1	9	1	.333	.485
Eddie Pick	OF4	R	24	9	8	2	3	0	0	0	2	3	3	0	.375	.375
2 Les Mann		R	30	8	1	1	0	0	0	0	0	0	0	0	.000	.000
Gus Sandberg	C5	R	28	7	17	1	3	1	0	0	1	1	1	0	.176	.235
Ed Hock		L	24	2	0	0	0	0	0	0	0	0	0	0	—	—
Greasy Neale (VR) 31																

NAME	T	AGE	W	L	PCT	SV	G	GS	CG	IP	H	BB	SO	SHO	ERA
		28	91	63	.591	9	154	154	88	1391	1465	359	450	11	3.21
Dolf Luque	R	32	27	8	.771	2	41	37	28	322	279	88	151	6	1.93
Eppa Rixey	L	32	20	15	.571	1	42	37	23	309	334	65	97	3	2.80
Pete Donohue	R	22	21	15	.583	1	42	36	19	274	304	68	84	2	3.38
Rube Benton	L	33	14	10	.583	1	33	26	15	219	243	57	59	0	3.66
Bill Harris	R	23	3	2	.600	2	12	7	6	70	79	18	18	0	5.14
Cactus Keck	R	24	3	6	.333	2	35	6	1	87	84	32	16	0	3.72
1 Johnny Couch	R	32	2	7	.222	0	19	8	1	69	98	15	14	0	6.00
Herb McQuaid	R	24	1	0	1.000	0	12	1	0	34	31	10	9	0	2.38
George Abrams	R	25	0	0	—	0	3	0	0	5	10	3	1	0	9.00
Haddie Gill	L	24	0	0	—	0	1	0	0	1	1	1	0	0	0.00
Karl Schnell	R	23	0	0	—	0	2	1	0	2	2	0	1	0	36.00

PITTSBURGH 3rd 87-67 .565 8.5 BILL McKECHNIE

NAME	G by Pos	B	AGE	G	AB	R	H	2B	3B	HR	RBI	BB	SO	SB	BA	SA
TOTALS			30	154	5405	786	1592	224	111	49	701	407	362	154	.295	.404
Charlie Grimm	1B152	L	24	152	563	78	194	29	13	7	99	41	43	6	.345	.480
Johnny Rawlings	2B119	R	30	119	461	53	131	18	4	1	45	25	29	9	.284	.347
Rabbit Maranville	SS141	R	31	141	581	78	161	19	9	1	41	42	34	14	.277	.346
Pie Traynor	3B152, SS1	R	24	153	616	108	208	19	19	12	101	34	19	28	.338	.489
Clyde Barnhart	OF92	R	27	114	327	60	106	25	13	9	72	47	21	5	.324	.563
Max Carey	OF153	B	33	153	610	120	188	32	19	6	63	73	28	51	.308	.452
Carson Bigbee	OF122	L	28	123	499	79	149	19	7	0	54	43	15	10	.299	.363
Walter Schmidt	C96	R	36	97	335	39	83	7	2	0	37	22	12	10	.248	.281
Reb Russell	OF76	R	34	94	291	49	84	18	7	9	58	20	21	3	.289	.491
Johnny Gooch	C66	R	25	66	202	16	56	10	2	1	20	17	13	2	.277	.361
Walter Mueller	OF26	R	28	40	111	11	34	4	4	0	20	4	6	2	.306	.414
1 Cotton Tierney	2B29	R	29	29	120	22	35	5	2	2	23	2	10	2	.292	.417
Spencer Adams	2B11, SS6	L	25	25	56	11	14	0	1	0	4	6	6	2	.250	.286
Jim Mattox	C8	R	26	22	32	4	6	1	0	1	1	5	0	1	.188	.281
Jewel Ens	1B4, 3B3	R	33	12	29	3	8	1	0	0	5	0	3	2	.276	.379
Kiki Cuyler	OF11	R	24	11	40	4	10	1	1	0	2	5	3	2	.250	.325
Frank Luce	OF5	R	26	9	12	2	6	0	0	0	3	2	2	1	.500	.500
Eddie Moore	SS6	R	24	6	26	6	7	1	0	0	1	0	4	1	.269	.308
Eppie Barnes	1B1	R	22	2	2	0	1	0	0	0	0	0	1	0	.500	.500

NAME	T	AGE	W	L	PCT	SV	G	GS	CG	IP	H	BB	SO	SHO	ERA
		30	87	67	.565	9	154	154	92	1376	1513	402	414	5	3.87
Johnny Morrison	R	27	25	13	.658	2	42	37	27	302	287	110	114	2	3.49
Wilbur Cooper	L	31	17	19	.472	0	39	38	26	295	331	71	77	1	3.57
2 Lee Meadows	R	28	16	10	.615	0	31	25	17	227	250	44	66	1	3.01
Babe Adams	R	41	13	7	.650	1	26	22	11	159	196	25	38	0	4.42
Earl Hamilton	L	31	9	8	.438	1	28	15	5	141	148	42	42	0	3.77
Jim Bagby	R	33	3	2	.600	3	21	6	2	69	95	25	16	0	5.22
Ray Steineder	R	28	2	0	1.000	0	15	2	1	55	58	18	23	0	4.75
1 Whitey Glazner	R	29	2	1	.667	1	7	4	1	30	29	11	8	1	3.30
Earl Kunz	R	24	1	2	.333	1	21	2	1	46	48	24	12	0	5.48
George Boehler	R	31	1	3	.250	0	10	3	1	28	33	26	12	0	6.11
Arnie Stone	L	30	1	0	1.000	0	9	0	0	12	19	4	2	0	8.25
Hal Carlson	R	31	0	4	.000	0	4	0	0	13	19	2	4	0	4.85

CHICAGO 4th 83-71 .539 12.5 BILL KILLEFER

NAME	G by Pos	B	AGE	G	AB	R	H	2B	3B	HR	RBI	BB	SO	SB	BA	SA
TOTALS			26	154	5259	756	1516	243	52	90	675	455	485	181	.288	.406
Ray Grimes (XJ)	1B62	R	29	64	216	32	71	7	2	2	36	24	17	5	.329	.407
George Grantham	2B150	L	23	152	570	81	160	36	8	8	70	71	92	43	.281	.414
Sparky Adams	SS79, OF1	R	28	95	311	40	90	12	4	0	35	26	10	20	.289	.367
Barney Friberg	3B146	R	23	146	547	91	174	27	11	12	88	45	49	13	.318	.473
Cliff Heathcote	OF112	L	25	117	393	48	98	14	3	1	27	25	22	32	.249	.308
Jigger Statz	OF154	R	25	154	655	110	209	33	8	10	70	56	42	29	.319	.440
Hack Miller	OF129	R	29	135	485	74	146	24	2	20	88	27	39	6	.301	.482
Bob O'Farrell	C124	R	26	131	452	73	144	25	4	12	84	67	38	10	.319	.471
Gabby Hartnett	C39, 1B31	R	22	85	231	28	62	12	2	8	39	25	22	4	.268	.442
Charlie Hollocher (IL)	SS65	R	27	66	260	46	89	14	2	1	28	26	5	9	.342	.423
John Kelleher	1B22, SS14, 3B11, 2B6	R	29	66	193	27	59	10	0	6	21	14	9	2	.306	.451
Marty Callaghan	OF38	L	23	61	129	18	29	1	3	0	14	8	18	2	.225	.279
Allen Elliott	1B52	R	25	53	168	21	42	8	2	2	29	2	12	3	.250	.357
Otto Vogel	OF24, 3B1	R	23	41	81	10	17	0	1	1	8	9	7	11	.210	.272
Denver Grigsby	OF22	L	22	24	72	8	21	5	2	0	5	5	9	1	.292	.417
Butch Weis	OF6	R	22	22	26	2	6	1	0	0	2	5	6	0	.231	.269
Kettle Wirts	C3	R	25	5	1	1	0	0	0	0	0	1	0	0	.200	.200

Bob Barrett 24 R 1-3, Pete Turgeon 26 R 1-6, Tony Murray 19 R 1-4

NAME	T	AGE	W	L	PCT	SV	G	GS	CG	IP	H	BB	SO	SHO	ERA
		26	83	71	.539	11	154	154	80	1367	1419	435	408	8	3.82
Pete Alexander	R	36	22	12	.647	2	39	36	26	305	308	30	72	3	3.19
Vic Aldridge	R	29	16	9	.640	0	30	30	15	217	209	67	64	2	3.48
Tony Kaufmann	R	22	14	10	.583	3	33	24	18	206	209	67	72	2	3.10
Vic Keen	R	24	12	8	.600	1	35	17	10	177	169	57	46	0	3.00
Tiny Osborne	R	30	8	15	.348	1	37	25	8	180	174	89	69	1	4.55
Virgil Cheeves	R	22	3	4	.429	0	19	8	0	71	89	37	13	0	6.21
Nick Dumovich	L	21	3	5	.375	1	28	8	1	94	118	45	23	0	4.60
Fred Fussell	L	27	3	5	.375	3	28	2	1	76	90	31	38	0	5.57
Phil Collins	R	21	1	0	1.000	0	5	0	1	5	8	1	2	0	3.60
Rip Wheeler	R	25	1	2	.333	0	3	1	1	24	28	5	5	0	4.88
George Stueland	R	24	0	0	1.000	0	8	1	1	22	11	5	2	0	5.63
Guy Bush	R	21	0	0	—	0	1	0	0	1	0	1	0	0	0.00
Ed Stauffer	R	25	0	0	—	0	1	1	0	4	7	1	0	0	13.50

ST. LOUIS 5th 79-74 .516 16 BRANCH RICKEY

NAME	G by Pos	B	AGE	G	AB	R	H	2B	3B	HR	RBI	BB	SO	SB	BA	SA
TOTALS			27	154	5526	746	1582	274	76	63	676	438	446	89	.286	.398
Jim Bottomley	1B130	L	23	134	523	79	194	34	5	8	94	45	44	4	.371	.535
Rogers Hornsby (IL)	2B96, 1B10	R	27	107	424	89	163	32	10	17	83	55	29	3	.384	.627
H. Freigau	SS87, 2B16, 1B9, 3B1, OF1	R	20	113	358	30	94	18	1	1	35	25	36	5	.263	.327
Milt Stock	3B150, 2B1	R	29	151	603	63	174	33	4	2	96	40	21	9	.289	.363
Max Flack	OF121	L	33	128	505	82	147	16	9	3	28	41	16	7	.291	.376
Hy Myers	OF87	L	34	96	330	29	99	18	2	2	48	12	19	5	.300	.385
Jack Smith	OF109	L	28	124	407	98	126	16	6	5	41	27	20	32	.310	.415
1 Eddie Ainsmith	C80	R	33	82	263	22	56	11	6	3	34	22	19	4	.213	.335
Ray Blades	OF83, 3B4	R	26	98	317	48	78	21	5	5	44	37	46	4	.246	.391
Specs Toporcer	2B52, SS33, 1B1, 3B1	R	24	97	303	45	77	11	3	3	35	41	14	4	.254	.340
Heinie Mueller	OF74	R	23	78	265	39	91	16	4	3	41	18	16	4	.343	.528
Harry McCurdy	C58	L	23	67	185	17	49	11	2	0	15	11	11	3	.265	.346
Verne Clemons	C41	R	31	57	130	6	37	9	1	0	13	10	11	0	.285	.369
Doc Lavan	SS40, 3B4, 1B3, 2B1	R	32	50	111	10	22	6	0	1	12	9	7	0	.198	.279
Bill Sherdel	P39	L	26	45	83	13	28	2	0	1	9	7	8	0	.337	.398
2 Les Mann	OF26	R	30	38	89	20	33	5	2	5	11	9	5	1	.371	.640
Eddie Dyer	OF8, P4	L	22	35	45	17	12	3	2	0	5	5	6	1	.267	.467
Les Bell	SS15	R	21	15	51	5	19	2	1	0	5	1	9	1	.373	.451
Jake Flowers	SS7, 2B2, 3B2	R	21	13	32	0	3	1	0	0	1	2	6	0	.094	.125
Charlie Niebergall	C7	R	24	9	28	4	3	1	0	0	1	0	6	0	.107	.143
Taylor Douthit	OF7	R	22	7	27	4	5	1	0	0	3	4	0	1	.185	.333
Jimmy Hudgens	1B3, 2B1	L	20	6	12	1	3	1	0	0	2	4	0	0	.250	.333
Tige Stone	OF4, P1	R	23	4	1	0	1	0	0	0	0	3	1	0	1.000	1.000

George Kopshaw 27 R 1-5, Joe Schultz 29 R 2-7, Speed Walker 25 R 2-7, Burt Shotton 38 L 0-0

NAME	T	AGE	W	L	PCT	SV	G	GS	CG	IP	H	BB	SO	SHO	ERA
		30	79	74	.516	7	154	154	77	1398	1539	456	398	9	3.87
Jesse Haines	R	29	20	13	.606	0	37	36	23	266	283	75	73	1	3.11
Bill Sherdel	R	26	15	13	.536	2	39	26	14	225	270	59	78	0	4.32
Fred Toney	R	34	11	12	.478	0	29	28	16	197	211	61	48	1	3.84
Johnny Stuart	R	22	10	8	.556	3	37	10	7	150	139	70	55	1	4.26
Jeff Pfeffer	R	35	8	9	.471	0	26	18	7	152	171	40	32	1	4.03
Bill Doak	R	32	8	13	.381	0	30	26	7	185	199	69	53	3	3.26
Clyde Barfoot	R	31	3	3	.500	1	34	3	0	101	112	27	23	1	3.74
Lou North	R	32	4	4	.429	1	34	3	0	72	90	31	24	0	5.13
Eddie Dyer	L	23	2	1	.667	0	22	2	0	30	35	7	7	1	4.09
Epp Sell	R	26	0	0	—	0	5	1	0	15	16	8	2	0	6.00
Fred Wigington	R	25	0	0	—	0	3	0	0	8	11	5	2	0	3.38
Tige Stone	R	21	0	0	—	0	2	0	0	2	2	0	1	0	12.00
Bill Pertica	R	24	0	0	—	0	2	1	0	2	2	3	2	0	4.50

BROOKLYN — 6th 76-78 .494 19.5 — WILBERT ROBINSON

NAME	G by Pos	B	AGE	G	AB	R	H	2B	3B	HR	RBI	BB	SO	SB	BA	SA
TOTALS			29	155	5476	753	1559	214	81	62	674	425	382	71	.285	.387
Jack Fournier	1B133	L	33	133	515	91	181	30	13	22	102	43	28	11	.351	.588
Jimmy Johnston	2B84, SS52, 3B14	R	33	151	625	111	203	29	11	4	60	53	15	16	.325	.426
Moe Berg	2B1	R	21	49	129	9	24	3	2	0	6	2	5	1	.186	.240
Andy High	3B80, SS45, 2B5	L	25	123	426	51	115	23	9	3	37	47	13	4	.270	.387
Tommy Griffith	OF127	L	33	131	481	70	141	21	9	8	66	50	19	8	.293	.424
Bernie Neis	OF111	B	27	126	445	78	122	17	4	5	37	36	38	9	.274	.364
Gene Bailey	OF100, 1B5	R	29	127	411	71	109	11	7	1	42	43	34	9	.265	.333
Zack Taylor	C84	R	24	96	337	29	97	11	6	0	46	19	19	0	.288	.368
Zack Wheat (IL)	OF87	L	35	98	349	63	131	13	5	8	65	23	12	3	.375	.510
Ivy Olson	2B72, 3B4, SS2, 1B2	R	37	82	292	33	76	11	1	1	35	14	10	5	.260	.315
Bert Griffith	OF62	R	27	79	248	23	73	8	4	2	37	13	16	1	.294	.383
Hank DeBerry	C60	R	28	78	235	21	67	11	6	1	48	20	12	2	.285	.396
Bill McCarren	3B66, OF1	R	27	69	216	28	53	10	1	3	27	22	39	0	.245	.343
Ray French	SS30	R	28	43	73	14	16	1	1	0	7	4	7	0	.219	.274
Charlie Hargreaves	C15	R	26	20	57	5	16	0	0	0	4	1	2	0	.281	.281
1 Dutch Schliebner	1B19	R	32	19	76	11	19	4	0	0	4	5	7	1	.250	.303
Turner Barber	OF12	L	29	13	46	3	10	2	0	0	8	2	2	0	.217	.261
Billy Mullen	3B4	R	27	4	11	1	3	0	0	0	0	0	0	0	.273	.273
Stuffy Stewart	2B3	R	29	4	11	3	4	1	0	1	1	1	1	1	.364	.727
2 Eddie Ainsmith	C2	R	33	2	10	0	2	0	0	0	2	0	1	0	.200	.200
Bernie Hungling	C1	R	27	4	0	0	0	0	0	0	0	0	0	0	.000	.000

NAME	T	AGE	W	L	PCT	SV	G	GS	CG	IP	H	BB	SO	SHO	ERA
		28	76	78	.494	5	155	155	94	1397	1503	476	548	8	3.74
Burleigh Grimes	R	29	21	18	.538	0	39	38	33	327	356	100	119	2	3.58
Dazzy Vance	R	32	18	15	.545	0	37	35	21	280	263	100	197	3	3.50
Dutch Ruether	L	29	15	14	.517	0	34	34	20	275	308	86	87	0	4.22
Leo Dickerman	R	26	8	12	.400	0	35	20	7	160	180	72	58	1	3.71
1 Leon Cadore	R	32	4	1	.800	0	8	4	3	36	39	13	5	0	3.25
Dutch Henry	L	21	4	6	.400	0	17	9	5	94	105	28	28	2	3.93
Art Decatur	R	23	3	3	.500	3	36	5	2	98	101	32	25	0	2.57
George Smith	R	31	3	6	.333	1	25	9	3	91	99	28	15	0	3.66
Harry Harper	L	28	0	1	.000	0	1	1	0	8	3	4	3	0	13.50
Al Mamaux	R	29	0	2	.000	0	5	1	0	13	20	6	5	0	8.31
Paul Schreiber	R	20	0	0	—	0	9	0	0	15	16	8	4	0	4.20
Harry Shriver	R	26	0	0	—	0	7	0	0	8	13	6	0	0	6.75

BOSTON — 7th 54-100 .351 41.5 — FRED MITCHELL

NAME	G by Pos	B	AGE	G	AB	R	H	2B	3B	HR	RBI	BB	SO	SB	BA	SA
TOTALS			29	155	5329	636	1455	213	58	32	569	429	404	57	.273	.353
Stuffy McInnis	1B154	R	32	154	607	70	191	23	9	2	95	26	12	7	.315	.392
Hod Ford	2B95, SS19	R	25	111	380	27	103	16	7	2	50	31	30	1	.271	.366
Bob Smith	SS101, 2B8	R	28	115	375	30	94	16	3	0	40	17	35	4	.251	.309
Tony Boeckel	3B147, SS1	R	30	148	568	72	169	32	4	7	79	51	31	11	.298	.405
Billy Southworth	OF151, 2B2	L	30	153	611	95	195	29	16	6	78	61	23	14	.319	.448
Ray Powell	OF84	L	34	97	338	57	102	20	4	4	38	45	36	1	.302	.420
Gus Felix	OF123, 2B5, 3B4	R	28	139	506	64	138	17	2	6	44	51	65	8	.273	.350
Mickey O'Neil	C95	R	25	96	306	29	65	7	4	0	20	17	14	3	.212	.261
Al Nixon	OF80	R	37	88	321	53	88	12	4	0	19	24	14	2	.274	.336
2 Earl Smith	C54	R	26	72	191	22	55	15	1	3	19	24	10	4	.288	.424
Art Conlon	2B36, SS6, 3B4	R	25	59	147	23	32	3	0	0	17	11	11	0	.218	.238
Bill Bagwell	OF22	L	28	56	93	8	27	4	2	2	10	6	12	0	.290	.441
Johnny Cooney	P23, OF11, 1B1	L	22	42	66	7	25	1	0	0	3	4	2	0	.379	.394
Frank Gibson	C20	B	32	41	50	13	15	1	0	0	5	2	7	0	.300	.320
Larry Kopf	SS37, 2B4	B	32	39	138	15	38	3	1	0	10	13	6	3	.275	.312
Al Hermann	2B15, 3B5, 1B4	R	24	31	93	2	22	4	0	0	11	0	7	3	.237	.280
1 Hank Gowdy	C15	R	33	23	48	5	6	1	1	0	5	15	5	1	.125	.188
Walton Cruise	OF9	L	33	21	38	4	8	2	0	0	3	2	1	1	.211	.263
Bob Emmerich	OF8	R	25	13	24	4	2	0	0	0	0	2	3	1	.083	.083
Snake Henry		L	27	9	9	1	1	0	0	0	0	0	0	0	.111	.111

Ernie Padgett 24 R 2-11, Dee Cousineau 24 R 2-2

NAME	T	AGE	W	L	PCT	SV	G	GS	CG	IP	H	BB	SO	SHO	ERA
		28	54	100	.351	7	155	155	54	1393	1662	394	351	13	4.22
Joe Genewich	R	26	13	14	.481	1	43	24	12	227	272	46	54	1	3.73
Rube Marquard	L	36	11	14	.440	0	38	29	11	239	265	65	78	3	3.73
2 Jesse Barnes	R	30	10	14	.417	2	31	23	12	195	204	43	41	5	2.77
Larry Benton	R	25	5	9	.357	0	35	9	1	128	141	57	42	0	4.99
Joe Oeschger	R	31	5	15	.250	2	44	19	6	166	227	54	33	1	5.69
Johnny Cooney	L	22	3	5	.375	0	23	9	7	98	92	22	23	2	3.31
Tim McNamara	R	24	3	13	.188	0	32	16	3	139	185	29	32	0	4.92
1 Mule Watson	R	26	1	2	.333	1	4	1	1	9	12	1	3	0	7.00
Dick Rudolph	R	34	1	2	.333	0	4	1	1	29	27	10	3	1	3.79
Dana Fillingim	R	29	1	9	.100	0	35	12	1	100	141	36	27	0	5.22
Frank Miller	R	37	0	0	.000	1	8	6	0	39	54	11	6	0	4.62

PHILADELPHIA — 8th 50-104 .325 45.5 — ART FLETCHER

NAME	G by Pos	B	AGE	G	AB	R	H	2B	3B	HR	RBI	BB	SO	SB	BA	SA
TOTALS			28	155	5491	748	1528	259	39	112	677	414	556	70	.278	.401
Walter Holke	1B146, P1	B	30	147	562	64	175	31	4	7	70	16	37	7	.311	.418
2 Cotton Tierney	2B114, OF5, 3B2	R	29	121	480	68	152	31	1	11	65	24	42	4	.317	.454
Heinie Sand	SS120, 3B11	R	25	132	470	85	107	16	5	4	32	82	56	7	.228	.309
Russ Wrightstone	3B72, SS21, 2B9	L	30	119	392	59	107	21	7	7	57	21	19	5	.273	.416
Curt Walker	OF137, 1B1	L	26	140	527	66	148	25	5	6	66	45	31	12	.281	.378
Cy Williams	OF135	L	35	136	535	98	157	22	3	41	114	59	57	11	.293	.576
Johnny Mokan	OF105, 3B1	R	27	113	400	76	125	23	3	10	48	53	31	6	.313	.460
Butch Henline	C96, OF1	R	28	111	330	45	107	14	3	7	46	37	33	7	.324	.448
Cliff Lee	OF83, 1B16	R	26	107	355	54	114	20	4	11	47	20	39	3	.321	.493
Jimmie Wilson	C69, OF2	R	22	85	252	27	66	9	0	1	25	4	17	2	.262	.310
Frank Parkinson	2B37, SS15, 3B11	R	28	67	219	21	53	12	0	3	28	13	31	4	.242	.338
Clarence Mitchell	P29	L	32	53	78	10	21	3	2	1	9	4	11	0	.269	.397
Freddy Leach	OF26	L	25	52	104	5	27	4	0	1	16	3	14	1	.260	.327
Goldie Rapp	3B45	B	29	47	179	27	47	5	0	1	10	14	14	1	.263	.307
Carl Lord	3B14	R	23	17	47	3	11	2	0	0	2	3	2	0	.234	.277
Mickey O'Brien	C9	R	28	15	21	3	7	2	0	0	3	1	3	0	.333	.429
Andy Woehr	3B13	R	27	13	41	3	14	2	0	0	3	1	9	0	.341	.390
Lenny Metz	2B6, SS6	R	23	12	37	4	8	0	0	0	3	1	5	0	.216	.216
Tod Dennehey	OF9	R	24	7	24	4	7	2	0	0	2	1	4	0	.292	.375

Dixie Parker 28 L 1-5, Joe Bennett 22 R 0-0

NAME	T	AGE	W	L	PCT	SV	G	GS	CG	IP	H	BB	SO	SHO	ERA
		28	50	104	.325	8	155	155	68	1376	1801	549	384	3	5.34
Jimmy Ring	R	28	18	16	.529	0	39	36	23	304	336	115	112	0	3.88
Clarence Mitchell	L	32	9	10	.474	0	29	19	8	139	170	46	41	1	4.73
2 Whitey Glazner	R	29	7	14	.333	1	28	23	12	161	195	63	51	2	4.70
Lefty Weinert	L	21	4	17	.190	1	38	20	8	156	207	81	46	0	5.42
Petie Behan	R	35	3	12	.200	2	31	17	5	131	182	57	27	0	5.50
Huck Betts	R	26	2	4	.333	1	19	4	3	84	100	14	18	0	3.11
2 Johnny Couch	R	32	2	4	.333	0	11	7	2	65	91	21	18	0	5.26
Ralph Head	R	29	2	9	.182	0	35	13	5	132	185	57	24	0	6.68
1 Lee Meadows	R	28	1	3	.250	1	8	5	0	20	40	15	10	0	13.05
Bill Hubbell	R	26	1	6	.143	0	22	5	1	55	102	17	8	0	8.35
Jesse Winters	R	30	1	6	.143	1	19	6	1	78	116	39	23	0	7.38
Jim Bishop	R	25	0	3	.000	1	15	0	0	33	48	11	5	0	6.27
Broadway Jones	L	24	0	1	—	0	2	0	0	4	7	1	0	0	9.00
Jim Grant	L	28	0	0	—	0	2	0	0	4	10	4	0	0	13.50
Art Gardiner	R	23	0	0	—	0	1	0	0	.1	1	0	0	0	0.00
Walter Holke	L	30	0	0	—	0	1	0	0	1					27.00
Red Miller	R	26	0	0	—	0	2	0	0	6	7	1	0	0	6.00
Pat Ragan	R	37	0	0	—	0	1	0	0	6					6.00

WORLD SERIES — NEW YORK (AL) 4 NEW YORK (NL) 2

LINE SCORES

TEAM	1 2 3	4 5 6	7 8 9	10 11 12	R	H	E
Game 1	October 10 at Yankee Stadium						
NY (NL)	0 0 4	0 0 0	0 0 1		5	8	0
NY (AL)	1 2 0	0 0 0	1 0 0		4	12	1

Watson, **Ryan** (3) — Hoyt, **Bush** (3)

Game 2	October 11 at Polo Grounds						
NY (AL)	0 1 0	2 1 0	0 0 0		4	10	0
NY (NL)	0 0 1	0 0 1	0 0 0		2	9	2

Pennock — McQuillan, Bentley (4)

Game 3	October 12 at Yankee Stadium						
NY (NL)	0 0 0	0 0 0	1 0 0		1	4	0
NY (AL)	0 0 0	0 0 0	0 0 0		0	6	1

Nehf — Jones, Bush (9)

Game 4	October 13 at Polo Grounds						
NY (AL)	0 6 1	1 0 0	0 0 0		8	13	1
NY (NL)	0 0 0	0 3 1	0 0 0		4	13	1

Shawkey, Pennock (8) — **J. Scott**, Ryan (2), McQuillan (2), Jonnard (8), Barnes (9)

Game 5	October 14 at Yankee Stadium						
NY (NL)	0 0 0	1 0 0	0 0 0		1	3	2
NY (AL)	3 4 0	1 0 0	0 0 X		8	14	0

Bentley, J. Scott (2), Barnes (4), Jonnard (8) — **Bush**

Game 6	October 15 at Polo Grounds						
NY (AL)	1 0 0	0 0 0	0 5 0		6	5	0
NY (NL)	1 0 0	1 1 1	0 0 0		4	10	1

Pennock, Jones (8) — **Nehf**, Ryan (8)

COMPOSITE BATTING

NAME	POS	G	AB	R	H	2B	3B	HR	RBI	BA
New York (AL)										
Totals		6	205	30	60	8	4	5	29	.293
B. Meusel	OF	6	26	1	7	1	0	0	8	.269
Dugan	3B	6	25	5	7	2	1	1	5	.280
Witt	OF	6	25	1	6	0	0	0	0	.240
Ward	2B	6	24	4	10	0	0	1	2	.417
Scott	SS	6	22	2	7	1	0	0	0	.318
Schang	C	6	22	3	7	0	0	0	0	.318
Pipp	1B	6	20	2	5	0	0	0	2	.250
Ruth	OF-1B	6	19	8	7	1	1	3	3	.368
Bush	P	4	7	2	3	1	0	0	1	.429
Pennock	P	3	6	0	0	0	0	0	0	.000
Shawkey	P	1	3	0	1	0	0	0	1	.333
Jones	P	2	2	0	0	0	0	0	0	.000
Haines	OF	1	1	0	0	0	0	0	0	.000
Hendrick	PH	1	1	0	0	0	0	0	0	.000
Hofmann	PH	2	1	0	0	0	0	0	0	.000
Hoyt	P	1	1	0	0	0	0	0	0	.000
Johnson	SS	1	0	0	0	0	0	0	0	—
New York (NL)										
Totals		6	201	17	47	2	3	5	17	.234
Frisch	2B	6	25	2	10	1	2	0	1	.400
I. Meusel	OF	6	25	3	7	0	1	1	2	.280
Bancroft	SS	6	24	1	2	0	0	0	0	.083
Youngs	OF	6	23	2	8	0	0	0	3	.348
Groh	3B	6	22	3	4	0	0	0	2	.182
Kelly	1B	6	22	4	4	0	0	0	2	.182
Snyder	C	5	17	1	2	0	0	0	0	.118
Stengel	OF	6	12	3	5	0	0	2	4	.417
Cunningham	OF	4	7	0	1	0	0	0	0	.143
Nehf	P	2	6	0	1	0	0	0	1	.167
Bentley	P	3	5	0	3	0	0	1	0	.600
Gowdy	C	3	4	0	0	0	0	0	0	.000
McQuillan	P	3	3	0	0	0	0	0	0	.000
Ryan	P	4	2	0	0	0	0	0	0	.000
Barnes	P	2	2	0	0	0	0	0	0	.000
Jackson	PH	2	2	0	0	0	0	0	0	.000
O'Connell	PH	2	1	0	0	0	0	0	0	.000
J. Scott	P	2	0	0	0	0	0	0	0	—
Gearin	PR	1	0	0	0	0	0	0	0	—
Jonnard	PR	2	0	0	0	0	0	0	0	—
Maguire	PR	2	0	0	0	0	0	0	0	—
Watson	P	1	0	0	0	0	0	0	0	—

COMPOSITE PITCHING

NAME	G	IP	H	BB	SO	W	L	SV	ERA
New York (AL)									
Totals	6	54	47	12	18	4	2		2.83
Pennock	3	17.1	19	1	8	2	0	1	3.63
Bush	3	16.2	7	4	5	1	1	0	1.08
Jones	2	10	5	2	3	0	1	1	0.90
Shawkey	1	7.2	12	4	2	1	0	0	3.52
Hoyt	1	2.1	4	1	0	0	0	0	15.43
New York (NL)									
Totals	6	53	60	20	22	2	4	0	4.25
Nehf	2	16.1	10	6	7	1	0	0	2.76
Ryan	3	9.1	11	3	1	1	0	0	0.96
McQuillan	2	9	12	4	3	0	1	0	5.00
Bentley	2	6.2	10	4	1	0	1	0	9.45
Barnes	2	4.2	4	1	0	0	0	0	0.00
J. Scott	2	3	9	1	2	0	0	0	12.00
Jonnard	2	2	1	1	1	0	0	0	0.00
Watson	1	1	3	1	1	0	1	0	13.50

1924 New York—Seven Flags in Four Years

When the season opened, the odds were greatly in favor of New York City taking another pennant, if not the Series. The odds makers were well aware that no city, let alone a team, had ever been able to put four straight flags together. But no city ever had the advantage of New York. The Yankees and Giants were coming off the 1923 season with three consecutive pennants. Each had the talent to repeat and each virtually had the same team. If the Giants failed, there was always the Yankees and Babe Ruth.

In fact, the Yankees looked a cinch to repeat. Yet they, as the Giants, were in for a surprise-only one of which was to survive the unexpected. Manager John McGraw sized up his National League competition among Cincinnati, Chicago, and Pittsburgh. Little thought was given to the Brooklyn club, which had finished sixth in 1923.

Cincinnati had injury problems and never threatened. Chicago did threaten until their ace hurler, Grover "Pete" Alexander, broke his wrist in mid-August. But it was Pittsburgh, expected, and the Dodgers, unexpected, who proved to be a hindrance in the end. The Dodgers were greatly strengthened by manager Wilbert Robinson's shifting men at key positions and moving them from the bench to the starting lineup, as well as the remarkable pitching of Burleigh Grimes and Dazzy Vance, who fashioned 50 victories. Vance took league honors with 28 wins and a 2.16 E.R.A.

While the Dodgers, Giants, and Pirates were fighting to decide the pennant, baseball's most prolific hitter since Ty Cobb was trying to put some self-respect into the St. Louis lineup. Although the final results would be more remembered for the individual rather than the team, Rogers Hornsby was on his way to a fifth straight batting title with an average of .424, the highest ever recorded in the twentieth century.

By the time the dust of the last week settled, McGraw had won his fourth and unprecedented pennant by 1½ games over the Dodgers and three over Pittsburgh. The Yankees were not as fortunate. Their loss of the pennant by two games could be traced to the decline of the pitching staff which, except for Herb Pennock, fell off badly from their previous form. It could also be traced to Carl Mays, a temperamental on-again, off-again pitcher. The Yankees released Mays and Cincinnati picked him up. Mays, who had the misfortune to kill Ray Chapman with a pitched ball in 1920, went on to win 20 games.

Most of all, though, the Yankees' relegation to second place was a direct result of the Washington Senators who, for the first time in their history, found themselves winners. They became winners by surviving the Yankees with Ruth and his league-leading 46 homers and .378 batting average, as well as third place Detroit with five regulars over .300. The fact that Washington had survived to win the pennant could be credited to their masterful veteran Walter Johnson. He proved the mainstay of a corps of young moundsmen with his League-leading 23 wins and 2.72 E.R.A. Johnson's performance (adding up to 373 lifetime wins at the year's end) was not much different than the artistry he had provided Washington for 18 years. The difference this time was that he was not alone in his contribution: Goose Goslin hit .344, Sam Rice .334, and Joe Judge, .324. And George Mogridge and Tom Zachary combined for 31 wins.

The World Series, Johnson's first and McGraw's last, saw Johnson lose his first two starts. Then, in the ninth inning of the seventh and final game, Johnson entered as a reliever and held off the Giants until the 12th frame, when Earl McNeely made him a winner with a grounder that took a freak hop over Fred Lindstrom's head.

1924 AMERICAN LEAGUE

NAME	G by Pos	B	AGE	G	AB	R	H	2B	3B	HR	RBI	BB	SO	SB	BA	SA
WASHINGTON 1st 92-62 .597																
BUCKY HARRIS TOTALS			28	156	5304	755	1558	255	88	22	688	513	392	117	.294	.387
Joe Judge	1B140	L	30	140	516	71	167	38	9	3	79	53	21	13	.324	.450
Bucky Harris	2B143	R	27	143	544	88	146	28	9	1	58	56	41	19	.268	.358
Roger Peckinpaugh	SS155	R	33	155	523	72	142	20	5	2	73	72	45	11	.272	.340
Ossie Bluege	3B102, 2B10, SS4	R	23	117	402	59	113	15	4	2	49	39	36	7	.281	.353
Sam Rice	OF154	L	34	154	646	106	216	38	14	1	76	46	24	24	.334	.441
Nemo Leibold	OF70	L	32	84	246	41	72	6	4	0	20	42	10	6	.293	.350
Goose Goslin	OF154	L	23	154	579	100	199	30	17	12	129	68	29	16	.344	.516
Muddy Ruel	C147	R	28	149	501	50	142	20	2	0	57	62	20	7	.283	.331
Wid Matthews	OF44	L	27	53	169	25	51	10	4	0	13	11	4	3	.302	.408
Doc Prothro	3B45	R	30	46	159	17	53	11	5	0	24	15	11	4	.333	.465
Earl McNeely	OF42	R	26	43	179	31	59	5	6	0	15	5	21	3	.330	.425
Walter Johnson	P38	R	36	39	113	18	32	9	0	1	14	3	11	0	.283	.389
Tom Zachary	P33	L	28	33	72	7	22	1	0	0	8	5	8	0	.306	.319
Mule Shirley	1B25, C1	L	23	30	77	12	18	2	2	0	16	3	7	0	.234	.312
Tommy Taylor	3B16, 2B2, OF1	R	31	26	73	11	19	3	1	0	10	2	8	2	.260	.329
Pinky Hargrave	C8	R	28	24	33	3	5	1	1	0	5	1	4	0	.152	.242
Bennie Tate	C14	L	22	21	43	2	13	2	0	0	7	1	2	0	.302	.349
Showboat Fisher	OF11	L	25	15	41	7	9	1	0	0	6	6	6	2	.220	.244
Lance Richbourg	OF7	L	26	15	32	3	9	2	1	0	1	2	6	0	.281	.406
Ralph Miller	2B3	R	28	9	15	1	2	0	0	0	0	1	1	1	.133	.133
Bert Griffith	OF2	R	28	6	8	1	1	0	0	0	0	0	1	0	.125	.125
Carr Smith	OF4	R	23	5	10	1	2	0	0	0	0	0	3	0	.200	.200
2 Wade Lefler	OF1	L	28	5	8	0	5	3	0	0	6	0	0	0	.625	1.000

Chick Gagnon 26 R 1-5, Carl East 30 L 2-6, Patsy Gharrity (DE) 32

NAME	T	AGE	W	L	PCT	SV	G	GS	CG	IP	H	BB	SO	SHO	ERA
		29	92	62	.597	25	156	156	74	1383	1329	505	469	13	3.34
Walter Johnson	R	36	23	7	.767	0	38	38	20	278	233	77	158	6	2.72
George Mogridge	L	35	16	11	.593	0	30	30	13	213	217	61	48	2	3.76
Tom Zachary	L	28	15	9	.625	2	33	27	13	203	198	53	45	1	2.75
Firpo Marberry	R	25	11	12	.478	15	50	14	6	195	190	70	68	0	3.09
2 Curly Ogden	R	23	9	5	.643	0	16	16	9	108	83	51	23	3	2.58
Joe Martina	R	34	6	8	.429	0	24	14	8	125	129	56	57	0	4.68
Allen Russell	R	30	5	1	.833	8	37	0	0	82	83	45	17	0	4.39
Paul Zahniser	R	27	5	7	.417	0	24	14	5	92	98	49	28	1	4.40
By Speece	R	27	2	1	.667	0	21	1	0	54	60	27	15	0	2.87
Slim McGraw	R	24	0	1	.000	0	6	2	0	23	25	12	8	0	5.09
1 Ted Wingfield	R	24	0	0	—	0	4	0	0	7	9	4	2	0	2.57
Nick Altrock	L	47	0	0	—	0	1	0	0	2	4	0	0	0	0.00

NAME	G by Pos	B	AGE	G	AB	R	H	2B	3B	HR	RBI	BB	SO	SB	BA	SA
NEW YORK 2nd 89-63 .586 2																
MILLER HUGGINS TOTALS			29	153	5240	798	1516	218	86	98	734	478	420	69	.289	.426
Wally Pipp	1B153	L	31	153	589	88	174	30	19	9	113	51	36	12	.295	.457
Aaron Ward (LJ)	2B120, SS1	R	27	120	400	42	101	13	10	8	66	40	45	1	.253	.395
Everett Scott	SS153	R	31	153	548	56	137	12	6	4	64	21	15	3	.250	.316
Joe Dugan	3B148, 2B2	R	27	148	610	105	184	31	7	3	56	34	25	1	.302	.390
Babe Ruth	OF152	L	29	153	529	143	200	39	7	46	121	142	81	9	.378	.739
Whitey Witt	OF143	L	28	147	600	88	178	1	36	45	20	9	297	.362	.297	.362
Bob Meusel	OF143, 3B2	R	27	143	579	93	188	40	11	12	120	32	43	26	.325	.494
Wally Schang	C106	B	34	114	356	46	104	19	7	5	52	48	43	2	.292	.427
Ernie Johnson (JJ)	2B27, SS9, 3B2	L	36	64	119	24	42	4	8	3	12	11	7	1	.353	.597
Fred Hofmann	C54	R	30	62	166	17	29	1	1	1	11	12	15	2	.175	.241
Bullet Joe Bush	P39	R	31	60	124	13	42	9	3	1	14	7	6	0	.339	.484
Mike McNally (JJ)	2B25, 3B13, SS6	R	30	49	69	11	17	0	0	0	2	5	6	3	.246	.246
Harvey Hendrick	OF17	L	26	40	76	7	20	0	0	1	11	2	7	1	.263	.303
Bob Shawkey	P38	R	33	38	69	12	22	4	1	1	15	7	5	0	.319	.449
Earle Combs (BN)	OF11	L	25	24	35	10	14	5	0	0	4	2	0	0	.400	.543
Shags Horan	OF13	L	28	22	31	4	9	1	0	0	7	1	5	0	.290	.323
Benny Bengough	C11	R	25	11	16	4	5	1	1	0	3	2	0	0	.313	.500
Lou Gehrig	1B2, OF1	L	21	10	12	2	6	1	0	0	5	1	3	0	.500	.583
Ben Paschal	OF4	R	28	4	12	2	3	1	0	0	3	1	0	0	.250	.333

Martin Autry 21 R 0-0, Mack Hillis 22 R 0-1

NAME	T	AGE	W	L	PCT	SV	G	GS	CG	IP	H	BB	SO	SHO	ERA
		30	89	63	.586	13	153	153	76	1359	1483	522	487	13	3.86
Herb Pennock	L	30	21	9	.700	3	40	34	25	286	302	64	101	4	2.83
Waite Hoyt	R	24	18	13	.581	4	46	32	14	247	295	76	71	2	3.79
Bullet Joe Bush	R	31	17	16	.515	1	39	31	19	252	262	109	80	3	3.57
Bob Shawkey	R	33	16	11	.593	0	38	25	10	208	226	74	114	1	4.11
Sad Sam Jones	R	31	9	6	.600	3	36	21	8	179	187	76	53	3	3.62
Milt Gaston	R	28	5	3	.625	1	29	2	0	86	92	44	24	0	4.50
Walter Beall	R	24	1	0	1.000	0	4	2	0	23	19	17	18	0	3.52
Al Mamaux	R	30	1	1	.500	0	14	2	0	38	44	20	12	0	5.68
George Pipgras	R	24	1	0	1.000	0	3	1	0	15	20	18	4	0	9.00
Cliff Markle	R	30	0	3	.000	0	7	3	0	23	29	20	7	0	10.20
Ben Shields	L	21	0	0	—	0	2	0	0	6	2	3	2	0	27.00
Oscar Roettger	R	24	0	0	—	0	1	0	0	1	3	2	0	0	0.00

NAME	G by Pos	B	AGE	G	AB	R	H	2B	3B	HR	RBI	BB	SO	SB	BA	SA
DETROIT 3rd 86-68 .558 6																
TY COBB TOTALS			29	156	5389	849	1604	315	76	35	758	607	400	100	.298	.404
Lu Blue	1B108	B	27	108	395	81	123	26	7	2	50	64	26	9	.311	.428
Del Pratt	2B63, 1B51, 3B4	R	36	121	429	56	130	32	3	1	77	31	10	6	.303	.399
Topper Rigney	SS146	R	27	147	499	81	144	29	9	4	93	102	39	11	.289	.407
Bob Jones	3B106	L	34	110	393	52	107	27	4	0	47	20	20	1	.272	.361
Harry Heilmann	OF147, 1B4	R	29	153	570	107	197	45	16	10	113	78	41	13	.346	.533
Ty Cobb	OF155	L	37	155	625	115	211	38	10	4	79	85	18	23	.338	.450
Heinie Manush	OF106, 1B1	L	22	120	422	83	122	24	8	9	68	27	30	14	.289	.448
Johnny Bassler	C121	L	29	124	379	43	131	20	3	1	68	62	11	2	.346	.422
Fred Haney	3B59, SS4, 2B3	R	26	86	256	54	79	11	1	1	30	39	13	7	.309	.371
Al Wingo	OF43	L	26	78	150	21	43	12	2	1	26	21	13	2	.287	.413
Les Burke	2B58, SS6	L	21	72	241	30	61	10	4	0	17	22	20	2	.253	.328
Larry Woodall	C62	R	29	67	165	23	51	9	2	0	24	21	5	0	.309	.388
Bob Fothergill	OF45	R	26	54	166	28	50	8	3	0	15	5	13	2	.301	.386
Frank O'Rourke	2B40, SS7	R	30	52	147	18	43	7	6	0	19	6	7	7	.293	.422
John Kerr	3B3, OF2	R	25	17	11	3	3	0	0	0	1	0	0	0	.273	.273
Clyde Manion	C3, 1B1	R	27	11	11	0	3	1	0	0	1	2	1	0	.273	.364
Charlie Gehringer	2B5	L	21	5	13	2	6	0	0	0	1	2	1	1	.462	.462

NAME	T	AGE	W	L	PCT	SV	G	GS	CG	IP	H	BB	SO	SHO	ERA
		27	86	68	.558	20	156	156	60	1391	1582	465	439	5	4.20
Earl Whitehill	L	24	17	9	.654	0	35	32	16	233	260	79	65	2	3.86
Ken Holloway	R	26	14	6	.700	3	49	13	5	181	209	61	46	0	4.08
Rip Collins	R	28	14	7	.667	3	34	30	11	216	199	63	75	1	3.21
Hooks Dauss	R	34	12	11	.522	6	40	10	5	131	155	40	44	0	4.60
Lil Stoner	R	25	11	11	.500	0	35	25	10	216	271	65	65	1	4.71
Ed Wells	L	24	6	8	.429	4	29	15	5	102	117	42	33	0	4.06
Syl Johnson	R	23	5	4	.556	3	29	9	2	104	117	42	55	0	4.93
Dutch Leonard	L	32	3	2	.600	1	8	7	3	49	65	16	25	0	4.78
Bert Cole	R	28	1	3	.250	2	17	2	1	108	134	35	16	1	4.75
Herman Pillette (SA)	R	27	1	1	.500	1	19	3	1	38	46	14	13	0	4.74
Willie Ludolph	R	24	0	0	—	0	4	0	0	6	6	8	4	0	4.50
Rufe Clarke	R	24	0	0	—	0	2	0	0	5	5	3	1	0	3.60
Ken Jones	R	21	0	0	—	0	2	0	0	2	1	1	0	0	4.50

ST. LOUIS — 4th 74-78 .487 17 — GEORGE SISLER

NAME	G by Pos	B	AGE	G	AB	R	H	2B	3B	HR	RBI	BB	SO	SB	BA	SA
TOTALS			30	153	5236	769	1543	265	62	67	679	465	349	85	.295	.407
George Sisler	1B151	L	31	151	636	94	194	27	10	9	74	31	29	19	.305	.421
Marty McManus	2B119	R	24	123	442	71	147	23	5	5	80	55	40	13	.333	.441
Wally Gerber	SS147	R	32	148	496	61	135	20	4	0	55	43	34	4	.272	.329
Gene Robertson	3B110, 2B2	L	25	121	439	70	140	26	4	4	52	36	14	3	.319	.424
Jack Tobin	OF131	L	32	136	569	87	170	30	8	2	48	50	12	6	.299	.390
Baby Doll Jacobson	OF152	R	33	152	579	103	184	41	12	19	84	69	17	20	.324	.533
Ken Williams (NJ)	OF108	L	34	114	398	78	129	21	4	18	84	69	17	20	.324	.533
Hank Severeid	C130	R	33	137	432	37	133	23	2	4	48	36	15	1	.308	.398
Joe Evans	OF49	R	29	77	209	30	53	3	3	0	19	24	12	1	.254	.297
Norm McMillan	2B37, 3B17, SS7, 1B2	R	28	76	201	25	56	12	2	0	27	12	17	6	.279	.358
Harry Rice	3B15, 2B4, 1B2, SS2, OF2	L	23	44	93	19	26	7	0	0	15	7	5	1	.280	.355
Herschel Bennett (BA)	OF21	L	27	41	94	16	31	4	3	1	11	3	6	1	.330	.468
Pat Collins	C20	R	27	32	54	9	17	2	0	1	11	11	14	0	.315	.407
Tony Rego	C23	R	26	24	59	5	13	1	0	0	5	1	3	0	.220	.237
Syl Simon	3B6, SS5	R	26	23	32	5	8	1	1	0	6	3	5	0	.250	.344
1 Frank Ellerbe	3B21	R	28	21	61	7	12	3	0	0	2	2	3	0	.197	.246
Ellie Ellmore	OF3	L	24	7	17	2	3	3	0	0	0	1	3	0	.176	.353
Pat Burke	3B1	R	23	1	3	0	0	0	0	0	1	0	0	0	.000	.000
Bill Mizeur		L	27	1	1	0	0	0	0	0	0	0	0	0	.000	.000

NAME	T	AGE	W	L	PCT	SV	G	GS	CG	IP	H	BB	SO	SHO	ERA
		28	74	78	.487	7	153	153	66	1353	1511	517	386	11	4.58
Urban Shocker	R	33	16	13	.552	1	40	33	17	246	270	52	88	4	4.21
Dave Danforth	L	34	15	12	.556	4	41	27	12	220	246	69	65	1	4.50
Ernie Wingard	L	23	13	12	.520	1	36	26	14	218	215	85	23	0	3.51
Dixie Davis	R	33	11	13	.458	0	29	24	11	160	159	72	45	5	4.11
Ray Kolp	R	29	5	7	.417	0	25	12	5	97	131	25	29	1	5.66
Elam Vangilder	R	28	5	10	.333	1	43	18	5	145	183	55	49	0	5.77
George Lyons	R	33	3	2	.600	0	26	6	2	78	97	45	25	0	5.19
Hub Pruett	L	23	3	4	.429	0	33	1	0	65	64	42	27	0	4.57
Ollie Voigt	R	25	1	0	1.000	0	8	1	0	16	21	13	4	0	5.63
George Grant	R	21	1	2	.333	0	22	2	0	51	69	25	11	0	6.35
Bill Bayne	L	25	1	3	.250	0	22	3	0	51	47	29	20	0	4.41
Bill Lasley	R	21	0	0	—	0	2	0	0	4	7	2	0	0	6.75
Ed Barnhart	R	19	0	0	—	0	1	0	0	1	0	1	1	0	0.00
Boom-Boom Beck	R	19	0	0	—	0	1	0	0	2	1	0	0	0	0.00

PHILADELPHIA — 5th 71-81 .467 20 — CONNIE MACK

NAME	G by Pos	B	AGE	G	AB	R	H	2B	3B	HR	RBI	BB	SO	SB	BA	SA
TOTALS			27	152	5184	685	1459	251	59	63	608	374	482	79	.281	.389
Joe Hauser	1B146	L	25	149	562	97	162	31	8	27	115	56	52	7	.288	.516
Max Bishop	2B80	L	24	91	294	52	75	13	2	2	21	54	30	4	.255	.333
Chick Galloway	SS129	R	27	129	464	41	128	16	4	2	48	23	23	11	.276	.341
Harry Riconda	3B73, SS2, C1	R	27	83	281	34	71	16	3	1	21	27	43	3	.253	.342
Bing Miller	OF94, 1B7	R	29	113	398	62	136	22	4	6	62	12	24	11	.342	.462
Al Simmons	OF152	R	22	152	594	69	183	31	9	8	102	30	60	16	.308	.431
Bill Lamar	OF87	L	27	87	367	68	121	22	5	7	48	18	21	8	.330	.474
Cy Perkins	C128	R	28	128	392	31	95	19	4	0	32	31	20	3	.242	.311
Jimmy Dykes	2B77, 3B27, SS4	R	27	110	410	68	128	26	6	3	50	38	59	1	.312	.427
Frank Welch	OF74	R	26	94	293	47	85	13	2	5	31	35	27	2	.290	.399
Sammy Hale	3B55, OF5, SS1, C1	L	27	80	261	41	83	14	2	2	17	17	19	3	.318	.410
Fred Heimach	P40	L	23	58	90	14	29	3	2	0	12	3	8	1	.322	.400
Frank Bruggy	C44	R	33	50	113	9	30	6	0	0	8	8	15	4	.265	.319
Paul Strand	OF44	R	30	47	167	15	38	9	4	0	13	4	9	3	.228	.329
2 Amos Strunk	OF8	L	35	30	42	5	6	0	0	0	1	7	4	0	.143	.143
John Chapman	SS19	R	24	19	71	7	20	4	1	0	6	3	3	0	.282	.366
Charlie Gibson	C12	R	24	12	15	1	2	0	0	0	1	0	0	0	.133	.133
Ed Sherling	OF3	R	26	4	2	1	1	1	0	0	0	0	0	0	.500	1.000
Joe Greene		R	26	1	1	0	0	0	0	0	0	0	0	0	.000	.000

NAME	T	AGE	W	L	PCT	SV	G	GS	CG	IP	H	BB	SO	SHO	ERA
		26	71	81	.467	10	152	152	68	1345	1527	597	371	8	4.39
Eddie Rommel	R	26	18	15	.545	1	43	34	21	278	302	94	72	3	3.95
Fred Heimach	L	23	14	12	.538	0	40	26	10	198	243	60	60	0	4.73
Stan Baumgartner	L	31	13	6	.684	1	36	16	12	181	181	73	45	1	0.29
Sam Gray	R	28	5	7	.533	2	34	19	8	152	169	89	54	2	3.97
Denny Burns	R	26	6	8	.429	1	37	17	7	154	191	68	26	0	5.08
Slim Harriss	R	27	6	10	.375	2	36	12	4	123	138	62	45	1	4.68
Roy Meeker	R	26	5	12	.294	0	30	14	5	146	166	81	37	1	4.68
Bob Hasty	R	26	1	3	.250	0	18	4	0	53	70	30	15	0	5.60
1 Curly Ogden	R	23	0	3	.000	0	5	1	0	13	14	7	4	0	4.85
Rollie Naylor	R	32	0	5	.000	0	10	7	1	38	53	20	10	0	6.39
Rube Walberg	L	27	0	0	—	0	6	2	0	7	10	10	3	0	12.86
Bill Pierson	R	25	0	0	—	0	1	0	0	3	3	0	0	0	3.00

CLEVELAND — 6th 67-86 .438 24.5 — TRIS SPEAKER

NAME	G by Pos	B	AGE	G	AB	R	H	2B	3B	HR	RBI	BB	SO	SB	BA	SA
TOTALS			27	153	5332	755	1580	306	59	41	676	492	371	84	.296	.399
George Burns	1B127	R	31	129	462	64	143	37	5	4	66	29	27	14	.310	.437
Chick Fewster	2B94, 3B5	R	28	101	322	36	86	12	2	0	36	24	36	12	.267	.317
Joe Sewell	SS153	L	25	153	594	99	188	45	5	4	104	67	13	3	.316	.429
Rube Lutzke	3B103, 2B3	R	26	106	341	37	83	18	3	0	42	38	46	4	.243	.314
Homer Summa	OF95	R	25	111	390	55	113	21	6	2	38	11	16	4	.290	.390
Tris Speaker	OF128	L	36	135	486	94	167	36	9	9	65	72	13	5	.344	.510
Charlie Jamieson	OF143	R	31	143	594	98	213	34	8	3	53	47	15	21	.359	.458
Glenn Myatt	C95	R	26	105	342	55	117	22	7	8	73	33	12	6	.342	.518
Pat McNulty	OF75	R	25	101	291	46	78	13	5	0	26	33	22	10	.268	.347
Riggs Stephenson (LJ)	2B58, OF7	R	26	71	240	33	89	20	4	4	44	27	10	1	.371	.504
Frank Brower	1B26, P4, OF3	L	31	66	107	16	30	10	1	3	20	27	9	1	.280	.477
Luke Sewell	C57	R	23	63	165	27	48	9	1	0	17	22	13	1	.291	.358
George Uhle	P28	R	25	59	107	10	33	6	1	1	19	4	8	0	.308	.411
2 Frank Ellerbe	3B39, 2B2	R	28	46	120	7	31	1	3	1	14	1	9	0	.258	.342
Sumpter Clarke	OF33	R	26	45	104	17	24	6	1	0	11	6	12	0	.231	.308
Larry Gardner	3B8, 2B6	R	38	38	50	3	10	0	0	0	4	5	1	0	.200	.200
Roxy Walters	C25, 2B7	R	31	32	74	10	19	2	0	0	5	10	6	0	.257	.284
Elmer Yoter	3B19	R	24	19	66	3	18	1	1	0	7	5	8	0	.273	.318
Ray Knode	1B10	L	23	11	37	6	9	1	0	0	4	3	4	2	.243	.270
Tom Gulley	OF5	L	24	8	20	4	3	0	0	1	2	1	1	0	.150	.250
Joe Wyatt	OF4	R	24	4	11	1	2	0	0	0	1	0	0	0	.182	.182
Freddie Spurgeon	2B3	R	22	3	8	0	1	0	0	0	0	0	1	0	.125	.250
Kenny Hogan		L	21	1	1	0	0	0	0	0	0	0	0	0	.000	.000

NAME	T	AGE	W	L	PCT	SV	G	GS	CG	IP	H	BB	SO	SHO	ERA
		27	67	86	.438	7	153	153	87	1349	1603	503	312	7	4.40
Joe Shaute	L	24	20	17	.543	2	46	34	21	283	317	83	68	2	3.75
Stan Coveleski	R	34	15	16	.484	0	33	33	18	240	286	73	58	2	4.05
Sherry Smith	L	33	12	14	.462	1	39	27	20	248	267	42	31	2	3.01
George Uhle	R	25	9	15	.375	1	28	25	15	196	238	75	57	0	4.78
Jim Joe Edwards (KJ)	L	29	4	3	.571	0	10	7	5	57	64	34	15	1	2.84
Bud Messenger	R	26	2	0	1.000	0	5	2	1	25	28	14	4	0	4.32
Emil Levsen	R	21	1	1	.500	0	4	1	1	16	22	4	3	0	4.50
Carl Yowell	R	21	1	1	.500	0	4	2	0	20	24	21	7	0	6.67
Joe Dawson	R	27	1	2	.333	0	4	4	0	30	24	17	7	0	6.75
Watty Clark	L	22	1	3	.250	0	12	1	0	25	36	7	4	0	6.92
Dewey Metivier	R	26	1	5	.167	0	26	6	1	76	110	34	14	0	5.33
Guy Morton	R	31	0	0	.000	0	10	0	0	12	13	6	0	0	6.75
Logan Drake	R	24	0	1	.000	0	11	0	0	18	16	10	8	0	10.64
Jake Miller	L	26	0	1	.000	0	2	1	1	12	13	5	4	0	9.00
Bob Kuhn	R	24	0	1	.000	0	5	0	0	4				0	27.00
Luther Roy	R	21	0	5	.000	0	16	5	2	49	62	31	14	0	7.71
Virgil Cheeves	R	23	0	0	—	0	17			17		7	1	0	7.94
George Edmondson	R	28	0	0	—	0	5			10		5		0	9.00
Frank Brower	R	31	0	0	—	0	4	0	0	10	7	4	0	0	0.90
Jim Lindsay	R	26	0	0	—	0	3	0	0	3	6	3	0	0	21.00
Frank Wayenberg	R	25	0	0	—	0	4	0	0	5	11	5	1	0	5.14
Bob Fitzke	R	23	0	0	—	0	4	1	0	5	3	1	0	0	4.50

BOSTON — 7th 67-87 .435 25 — LEE FOHL

NAME	G by Pos	B	AGE	G	AB	R	H	2B	3B	HR	RBI	BB	SO	SB	BA	SA
TOTALS			31	157	5344	737	1481	302	63	30	666	604	418	79	.277	.374
Joe Harris	1B128, OF3	R	33	133	491	82	148	36	9	3	77	81	25	6	.301	.430
Bill Wambsganss	2B156	R	30	156	636	93	174	41	5	0	49	54	33	14	.274	.354
Dud Lee	SS90	L	24	94	288	36	73	9	4	0	29	40	17	8	.253	.313
Danny Clark	3B94	L	30	104	325	36	90	23	2	3	54	51	19	4	.277	.385
Ike Boone	OF124	R	27	128	486	71	162	30	4	13	96	55	32	2	.333	.492
Ira Flagstead	OF144	R	30	149	560	106	171	35	7	5	43	77	41	10	.305	.420
Bobby Veach	OF130	L	36	142	519	77	153	35	9	5	99	47	18	5	.295	.426
Steve O'Neill	C92	R	32	106	307	29	73	15	1	0	38	63	23	0	.238	.293
Homer Ezzell	3B63, SS21, C1	R	28	89	273	33	75	8	4	0	32	13	20	12	.275	.333
Shano Collins	OF56, 1B12	R	38	89	240	37	70	16	5	0	28	18	17	4	.292	.400
H. Shanks	SS38, 3B22, OF4, 1B2, 2B2	R	33	72	193	22	50	16	3	0	25	21	12	1	.259	.373
Val Picinich	C52	R	27	69	161	25	44	6	3	1	24	29	19	5	.273	.366
Phil Todt	1B18, OF4, 1B2	L	22	52	103	17	27	8	2	1	14	6	9	0	.262	.408
Johnnie Heving	C29	R	28	45	109	15	31	5	1	0	11	10	7	0	.284	.349
Chappie Geygan	SS32	R	21	33	82	7	21	5	2	0	4	4	16	0	.256	.366
Denny Williams	OF19	L	27	25	85	17	31	3	0	0	10	6	5	3	.365	.400
Joe Connolly	OF3	R	28	14	10	1	1	0	0	0	2	2	1	0	.100	.100

NAME	T	AGE	W	L	PCT	SV	G	GS	CG	IP	H	BB	SO	SHO	ERA
		28	67	87	.435	16	157	157	73	1391	1563	523	414	8	4.35
Howard Ehmke	R	30	19	17	.528	4	45	36	26	315	324	81	119	4	3.46
Alex Ferguson	R	27	14	17	.452	2	41	32	15	238	259	108	78	0	3.78
Jack Quinn	R	40	12	13	.480	7	44	25	13	229	241	52	64	2	3.26
Curt Fullerton	R	25	7	12	.368	2	33	20	9	152	166	73	33	0	4.32
Bill Piercy	R	28	5	7	.417	0	23	18	3	121	156	66	20	0	5.95
Buster Ross	L	21	4	3	.571	1	30	2	1	93	109	30	16	1	3.48
Oscar Fuhr	L	30	4	6	.333	0	23	10	4	80	100	39	30	1	5.96
George Murray	R	25	2	9	.182	0	28	7	0	80	97	32	27	0	6.75
Les Howe	R	28	1	0	1.000	0	7	1	0	7	11	2	3	0	7.71
Clarence Winters	R	25	0	1	.000	0	2	2	0	6	4	7	3	0	20.57
1 Ted Wingfield	R	24	0	0	—	0	3	2	0	26	23	8	4	0	2.42
Hoge Workman	R	24	0	0	—	0	11	0	0	16	25	11	7	0	8.50
Red Ruffing	R	20	0	0	—	0	8	0	0	23	29	9	10	0	6.65
John Woods	R	26	0	0	—	0	1	0	0	1	0	0	1	0	0.00
Charley Jamerson	L	24	0	0	—	0	1	0	0	1				0	18.00
Al Kellett	R	22	0	0	—	0	2	0	0					0	☐

CHICAGO — 8th 66-87 .431 25.5 — JOHNNY EVERS

NAME	G by Pos	B	AGE	G	AB	R	H	2B	3B	HR	RBI	BB	SO	SB	BA	SA
TOTALS			29	154	5255	793	1512	254	58	41	710	604	418	138	.288	.382
Earl Sheely	1B146	R	31	146	535	84	171	34	3	3	103	95	28	7	.320	.411
Eddie Collins	2B150	L	37	152	556	108	194	27	7	6	86	89	16	42	.349	.455
Bill Barrett	SS77, OF27, 3B8	R	24	119	406	52	110	18	5	2	56	30	38	15	.271	.355
Willie Kamm	3B145	R	24	147	528	58	134	28	6	6	93	64	59	9	.254	.364
Harry Hooper	OF123	L	36	130	476	107	156	27	8	10	62	65	26	16	.328	.481
Johnny Mostil	OF105	R	28	118	385	75	125	22	5	4	49	45	41	7	.325	.439
Bibb Falk	OF134	L	25	138	526	77	185	37	8	6	99	47	21	6	.352	.487
Buck Crouse	C90	L	27	94	305	30	79	10	1	1	44	8	32	2	.259	.308
Maurice Archdeacon	OF77	R	26	95	288	59	92	9	3	0	25	40	30	11	.319	.372
Roy Elsh	OF38, 1B2	R	33	60	147	21	45	9	1	0	11	10	14	6	.306	.381
Ray Schalk	C56	R	31	57	153	15	30	4	2	1	11	21	10	1	.196	.268
Ray French	SS28, 2B3	R	29	37	112	13	20	0	0	0	11	10	13	0	.179	.214
H. McClellan (IL)	SS21, 2B7, 3B1, OF1	R	29	32	85	9	15	3	0	0	7	8	5	3	.176	.212
Ray Morehart	SS27, 2B2	L	24	31	100	10	20	4	2	0	8	17	7	3	.200	.280
Johnny Grabowski	C19	R	24	20	56	10	14	3	0	0	6	3	4	0	.250	.304
Bud Clancy	1B8	R	23	13	35	5	9	1	0	0	6	2	3	1	.257	.286
Ike Davis	SS10	R	23	29	10	33	5	8	1	0	3	5	4	0	.242	.333
Joe Burns	C6	R	24	8	19	1	2	0	0	0	1	0	1	0	.105	.105
Bill Black	2B1	R	24	5	10	2	2	0	0	0	0	2	0	0	.200	.200
Kettle Wirts	C5	R	26	6	12	1	1	0	0	0	0	0	2	0	.083	.083
Wally Dashiell	SS1	R	21												.000	.000
Frank Naleway	SS1														.000	.000
Bernie de Viveiros	SS1	R	23												.000	.000
1 Amos Strunck		L	35													

NAME	T	AGE	W	L	PCT	SV	G	GS	CG	IP	H	BB	SO	SHO	ERA
		26	66	87	.431	11	154	154	76	1367	1635	512	360	1	4.75
Sloppy Thurston	R	25	20	14	.588	1	38	36	28	291	330	60	37	1	3.80
Ted Lyons	R	23	12	11	.522	3	41	22	12	216	279	72	52	0	4.88
Red Faber (AJ)	R	35	9	11	.450	0	21	20	9	161	173	58	47	0	3.86
Ted Blankenship (ST)	R	23	7	6	.538	1	25	17	7	125	167	38	36	0	5.18
Sarge Connally	R	25	7	13	.350	6	44	13	6	160	177	68	55	0	4.05
Charlie Robertson (SA)	R	28	4	10	.286	0	17	14	5	97	108	54	29	0	5.01
Mike Cvengros	L	23	3	12	.200	0	26	15	2	106	119	67	36	0	5.86
Dixie Leverett	R	30	2	3	.400	0	21	11	4	99	123	41	29	0	5.82
Doug McWeeny	R	27	1	3	.250	0	5	2	2	43	47	17	18	0	4.60
Leo Mangum	R	28	1	2	.200	0	13	7	1	47	69	25	12	0	7.09
Happy Foreman	L	26	0	0	—	0	3	0	0	4	6	3	2	0	2.25
Milt Steengrafe	R	26	0	0	—	0	6	0	0	4	15	4	3	0	12.00
Bob Barnes	L	22	0	0	—	0	5	0	0	14	0	1	0	0	18.00
Lum Davenport	R	22	0	0	—	0	1	0	0	1	0	1	0	0	9.00
John Dobb	L	22	0	0	—	0	1	0	0	1	4	1	1	0	9.00
Bob Lawrence	R	24	0	0	—	0	1	0	0					0	9.00
Webb Schultz	R	26	0	0	—	0	1	0	0					0	9.00
Dickie Kerr (SL) 30															

NEW YORK — 1ST 93-60 .608 — JOHN McGRAW

NAME	G by Pos	B	AGE	G	AB	R	H	2B	3B	HR	RBI	BB	SO	SB	BA	SA
TOTALS			28	154	5445	857	1634	269	81	95	781	467	479	82	.300	.432
George Kelly	1B125, OF14, 2B5, 3B1	R	28	154	571	91	185	37	9	21	136	38	52	7	.324	.531
Frankie Frisch	2B143, SS10, 3B2	R	25	145	603	121	198	33	15	7	69	56	24	22	.328	.468
Travis Jackson	SS151	R	20	151	596	81	180	26	8	11	76	21	56	6	.302	.428
Heinie Groh	3B145	R	34	145	559	82	157	32	3	2	48	27	18	6	.281	.360
Ross Youngs	OF132, 2B1	L	27	133	526	112	187	33	12	10	74	77	31	11	.355	.521
Hack Wilson	OF103	R	24	107	383	62	113	19	12	10	57	44	46	4	.295	.486
Irish Meusel	OF138	R	31	139	549	75	170	26	9	6	102	33	18	11	.310	.423
Frank Snyder	C110	R	30	118	354	37	107	18	3	5	53	30	43	3	.302	.412
Billy Southworth	OF75	L	31	94	281	40	72	13	0	3	36	32	16	1	.256	.335
Hank Gowdy	C78	R	34	87	191	25	62	9	1	4	37	26	11	1	.325	.445
Bill Terry	1B42	L	25	77	163	26	39	7	2	5	24	17	18	1	.239	.399
Fred Lindstrom	2B23, 3B11	R	18	52	79	19	20	3	1	0	4	6	10	3	.253	.316
Jimmy O'Connell (DL)	OF29, 2B1	L	22	52	104	24	33	4	2	2	18	11	16	2	.317	.452
Art Nehf	P30, OF1	L	31	33	57	11	13	1	0	5	13	6	4	1	.228	.509
Eddie Ainsmith	C9	R	34	10	5	0	3	0	0	0	0	0	6	0	.600	.600
Grover Hartley	C3	R	35	4	7	1	2	1	0	0	1	1	0	1	.286	.429
Buddy Crump	OF1	L	22	1	4	0	0	0	0	0	0	0	1	0	.000	.000

NAME	T	AGE	W	L	PCT	SV	G	GS	CG	IP	H	BB	SO	SHO	ERA
		26	93	60	.608	21	154	154	71	1379	1464	392	406	4	3.62
Jack Bentley	L	29	16	5	.762	1	28	24	13	188	196	56	60	1	3.78
Virgil Barnes	R	27	16	10	.615	3	35	29	15	229	239	57	59	1	3.07
Art Nehf	L	31	14	4	.778	2	30	20	11	172	167	42	72	0	3.66
Hugh McQuillan	R	28	14	8	.636	3	27	23	14	184	179	43	49	1	2.69
Rosy Ryan	R	26	8	6	.571	5	37	9	2	125	137	37	36	0	4.25
Mule Watson	R	27	7	4	.636	0	22	16	6	100	122	24	18	1	3.78
Wayland Dean	R	22	6	12	.333	0	26	20	6	126	139	45	39	0	5.00
Harry Baldwin	R	24	3	1	.750	0	10	2	1	34	42	11	5	0	4.23
Claude Jonnard	R	26	3	5	.375	2	34	3	1	90	80	24	40	0	2.40
1 Joe Oeschger	R	32	2	0	1.000	0	10	2	1	29	35	14	10	0	3.10
Ernie Maun	R	23	2	1	.667	1	22	0	0	35	46	10	5	0	5.91
Walter Huntzinger	R	25	1	1	.500	1	12	2	0	32	41	9	6	0	4.50
1 Dinty Gearin	L	26	1	2	.333	0	6	3	2	29	30	16	4	0	2.48
Leon Cadore	R	33	0	0	—	0	2	0	0	4	2	3	2	0	0.00
Kent Greenfield	R	22	0	1	.000	0	3	1	1	9	9	1	1	0	15.00
Jack Scott (LJ) 32															

BROOKLYN — 2nd 92-62 .597 1.5 — WILBERT ROBINSON

NAME	G by Pos	B	AGE	G	AB	R	H	2B	3B	HR	RBI	BB	SO	SB	BA	SA
TOTALS			31	154	5339	717	1534	227	54	72	662	447	357	34	.287	.391
Jack Fournier	1B153	L	34	154	563	93	188	25	4	27	116	83	46	7	.334	.536
Andy High	2B133, SS17, 3B1	L	26	144	582	98	191	26	13	6	61	57	16	3	.328	.448
Johnny Mitchell	SS64	B	29	64	243	42	64	10	0	1	16	37	22	3	.263	.317
Milt Stock	3B142	R	30	142	561	66	136	14	4	2	52	26	32	3	.242	.292
Tommy Griffith	OF139	L	34	140	482	43	121	19	5	3	67	34	19	0	.251	.330
Eddie Brown	OF114	R	32	114	455	56	140	30	4	5	78	26	15	3	.308	.424
Zack Wheat	OF139	L	36	141	566	92	212	41	8	14	97	49	18	3	.375	.549
Zack Taylor	C93	R	25	99	345	36	100	9	4	1	39	14	14	0	.290	.348
Jimmy Johnston	SS63, 3B10, 1B4, OF1	R	34	86	315	51	94	11	2	2	29	27	10	5	.298	.365
Bernie Neis	OF62	B	28	80	211	43	64	8	3	4	26	27	17	4	.303	.427
Hank DeBerry	C63	R	29	77	218	20	53	10	3	3	26	20	21	0	.243	.358
Dick Loftus	OF29, 1B1	L	23	46	81	18	22	6	0	0	8	7	2	1	.272	.346
Burleigh Grimes	P38	R	30	40	124	11	37	3	0	0	7	5	13	1	.298	.323
Joe Klugman	2B28, SS1	R	29	31	79	7	13	2	1	0	3	2	9	0	.165	.215
Gene Bailey	OF17	R	30	18	46	7	11	3	0	1	4	7	6	1	.239	.370
Charlie Hargreaves	C9	R	27	15	27	4	11	2	0	0	5	1	1	0	.407	.481
Binky Jones	SS10	R	24	10	37	0	4	1	0	0	2	0	3	1	.108	.135
Ivy Olson	SS8, 2B2	R	34	13	27	0	6	1	0	0	0	3	1	0	.222	.259
Fred Johnston	2B1, 3B1	R	24	4	4	1	1	0	0	0	0	0	1	0	.250	.250

NAME	T	AGE	W	L	PCT	SV	G	GS	CG	IP	H	BB	SO	SHO	ERA
		30	92	62	.597	5	154	154	97	1376	1432	403	638	10	3.64
Dazzy Vance	R	33	28	6	.824	0	35	34	30	309	238	77	262	3	2.16
Burleigh Grimes	R	30	22	13	.629	1	38	36	30	311	351	91	135	1	3.82
2 Bill Doak	R	33	11	5	.688	0	21	16	8	149	130	35	32	2	3.08
Art Decatur	R	30	10	9	.526	1	31	10	3	126	156	27	38	0	4.14
Dutch Ruether	L	30	8	13	.381	3	30	21	13	168	190	45	63	2	3.93
2 Tiny Osborne	R	31	6	5	.545	0	21	13	6	104	123	54	52	0	5.11
Rube Ehrhardt	R	29	5	3	.625	0	15	9	6	84	71	17	13	2	2.25
Bonnie Hollingsworth	R	28	1	0	1.000	1	9			8	10	7		0	6.00
Dutch Henry	L	22	1	2	.333	0	16	4	0	46	69	15	11	0	5.67
Nelson Greene	L	24	0	1	.000	0	4	1	0	9	14	7	3	0	4.00
Rube Watson	R	28	0	2	.000	0	8	2	0	11	12	3	2	0	6.55
Jim Roberts	R	28	0	3	.000	0	11	5	0	25	41	8	10	0	7.56
1 Leo Dickerman	R	27	0	0	—	0	7	2	0	20	20	16	9	0	5.40
Tex Wilson	L	22	0	0	—	0	2	0	0	7	11	5	1	0	13.50
Tom Long	L	26	0	1	—	0	1	0	0	2	2	0	1	0	9.00

PITTSBURGH — 3rd 90-63 .588 3 — BILL McKECHNIE

NAME	G by Pos	B	AGE	G	AB	R	H	2B	3B	HR	RBI	BB	SO	SB	BA	SA
TOTALS			28	153	5288	724	1517	222	122	43	658	366	396	181	.287	.399
Charlie Grimm	1B151	L	25	151	542	53	156	25	12	2	63	37	22	3	.288	.389
Rabbit Maranville	2B152	R	32	152	594	62	158	33	20	2	71	35	53	18	.266	.399
Glenn Wright	SS153	R	23	153	616	80	177	28	18	7	111	27	52	14	.287	.425
Pie Traynor	3B141	R	25	142	545	86	160	26	13	5	82	37	26	24	.294	.417
Clyde Barnhart	OF88	R	28	102	344	49	95	6	11	3	51	30	17	5	.276	.384
Max Carey	OF149	B	34	149	599	113	178	30	9	7	55	58	17	49	.297	.412
Kiki Cuyler	OF114	R	25	117	466	94	165	27	16	9	85	30	62	32	.354	.539
Johnny Gooch	C69	B	26	70	224	26	65	6	9	0	25	16	12	1	.290	.362
Carson Bigbee	OF75	L	29	89	282	42	74	4	1	0	15	26	12	15	.262	.284
Eddie Moore	OF35, 3B13, 2B4	R	25	72	209	47	75	8	4	2	13	27	12	6	.359	.464
Walter Schmidt (RJ)	C57	R	37	58	177	16	43	3	2	1	20	13	5	6	.243	.299
2 Earl Smith	C35	L	27	39	111	12	41	10	1	4	21	13	4	2	.369	.586
Wilbur Cooper	P38	L	32	58	104	11	36	5	2	0	15	5	8	2	.346	.433
Walter Mueller	OF15	R	29	30	50	6	13	1	1	0	8	4	4	1	.260	.320
Cliff Knox	C6	R	22	6	18	1	4	0	0	0	2	0	1	0	.222	.222
Jewel Ens	1B5	R	34	5	10	2	3	0	0	0	0	0	3	0	.300	.300
Johnny Rawlings		R	31	3	3	0	1	0	0	0	0	0	0	0	.333	.333
Eppie Barnes	1B1	L	23	2	5	0	0	0	0	0	0	0	0	0	.000	.000

NAME	T	AGE	W	L	PCT	SV	G	GS	CG	IP	H	BB	SO	SHO	ERA
		30	90	63	.588	5	153	153	85	1382	1387	323	364	15	3.27
Wilbur Cooper	L	32	20	14	.588	1	38	35	25	269	296	40	62	4	3.28
Ray Kremer	R	31	18	10	.643	1	41	30	17	259	262	51	64	4	3.20
Emil Yde	L	24	16	3	.842	0	33	22	14	194	171	62	53	4	2.83
Lee Meadows	R	29	13	12	.520	0	36	30	15	229	240	51	61	3	3.26
Johnny Morrison	R	28	11	16	.407	2	41	25	10	238	213	73	85	0	3.74
2 Jeff Pfeffer	R	36	3	3	.625	0	15	4	1	59	68	17	19	0	3.05
Arnie Stone	R	31	4	2	.667	0	26	2	1	64	57	15	7	0	2.95
Babe Adams (SA)	R	42	3	1	.750	0	9	3	2	40	31	3	5	0	1.13
Del Lundgren	R	24	0	1	.000	0	8	1	0	17	25	3	4	0	6.35
1 Ray Steineder	R	29	0	1	.000	0	5	0	0	3	3	4	1	0	12.00
Don Songer	L	25	0	0	—	0	1	1	0	1	2	1	0	0	7.00
Buckshot May	R	24	0	0	—	0	1	0	0	1	2	1	0	0	0.00
Fred Sale	R	22	0	0	—	0	1	0	0	1	1	1	0	0	0.00

CINCINNATI — 4th 83-70 .542 10 — PAT MORAN (DD) 48 0-0 .000   JACK HENDRICKS 83-70 .542

NAME	G by Pos	B	AGE	G	AB	R	H	2B	3B	HR	RBI	BB	SO	SB	BA	SA
TOTALS			30	153	5301	649	1539	236	111	36	586	349	334	103	.290	.397
Jake Daubert	1B102	L	40	102	405	47	114	14	9	1	31	28	17	5	.281	.368
Hughie Critz	2B96, SS1	R	23	102	413	67	133	15	14	3	35	19	18	19	.322	.450
Ike Caveney (BT)	SS90, 2B5	R	29	95	337	36	92	19	1	4	32	14	21	2	.273	.371
Babe Pinelli	3B143	R	28	144	510	61	156	16	7	0	70	32	32	23	.306	.365
2 Curt Walker	OF109	L	27	109	397	55	119	21	10	4	46	44	15	7	.300	.433
Edd Roush	OF119	L	31	121	483	67	168	23	21	3	72	22	11	17	.348	.501
George Burns	OF90	R	34	93	336	43	86	19	2	2	33	29	21	3	.256	.342
Bubbles Hargrave	C91	R	31	98	312	42	94	19	10	3	33	30	20	2	.301	.455
Rube Bressler	1B50, OF49	L	29	115	383	41	133	14	13	4	49	22	20	9	.347	.483
Sammy Bohne	2B48, SS40, 3B12	R	27	100	349	42	89	15	9	4	46	18	24	9	.255	.384
Pat Duncan	OF83	R	30	96	319	34	86	21	6	2	37	20	23	1	.270	.392
Ivy Wingo	C65, 1B1	L	33	66	192	21	55	5	4	1	23	14	8	1	.286	.370
Boob Fowler	SS32, 2B4, 3B2	R	29	59	129	20	43	6	1	0	9	5	15	2	.333	.395
Chick Shorten	OF15	L	32	41	69	7	19	3	0	0	6	4	2	0	.275	.319
Carl Mays	P37	R	32	38	83	9	24	6	2	1	12	4	12	0	.289	.446
1 George Harper	OF22	L	32	28	74	7	20	3	0	0	3	13	5	1	.270	.311
Gus Sandberg	C24	R	29	24	52	1	9	0	0	0	3	2	7	0	.173	.173
Lew Fonseca (JJ)	2B10, 1B6	R	25	20	57	5	13	2	1	0	9	4	4	1	.228	.298
Ed Hock	OF2	L	25	16	10	7	1	0	0	0	0	0	2	0	.100	.100
2 Cliff Lee	OF1	R	27	6	6	1	2	1	0	0	2	0	2	0	.333	.333
Greasy Neale	OF2	L	32	5	3	0	0	0	0	0	0	0	1	0	.000	.000
Eddie Pick	OF1	R	25	3	2	0	0	0	0	0	0	0	0	0	.000	.000
Jim Begley	2B2	R	21	2	5	1	1	0	0	0	0	0	2	0	.200	.200
Jack Blott	C1	R	21	1	0	0	0	0	0	0	0	0	0	0	.000	.000

NAME	T	AGE	W	L	PCT	SV	G	GS	CG	IP	H	BB	SO	SHO	ERA
		30	83	70	.542	9	153	153	77	1378	1408	293	451	14	3.12
Carl Mays	R	32	20	9	.690	0	37	27	15	226	238	36	63	2	3.15
Pete Donohue	R	23	16	9	.640	0	35	31	16	222	248	36	72	3	3.61
Eppa Rixey	L	33	15	14	.517	1	35	29	15	238	219	47	57	4	2.76
Dolf Luque	R	33	10	15	.400	0	31	28	13	219	229	53	86	2	3.16
Tom Sheehan	R	30	9	11	.450	1	39	14	8	167	170	54	52	2	3.23
Rube Benton	L	34	7	9	.438	1	32	19	6	163	166	24	42	1	2.76
Pedro Dibut	R	31	3	0	1.000	0	9	2	2	37	24	12	15	0	2.19
Jakie May	L	28	3	3	.500	6	38	2	1	99	104	29	59	0	3.00
Bill Harris	R	24	0	0	—	0	3	0	0	7	10	2	5	0	9.00

CHICAGO — 5th 81-72 .529 12 — BILL KILLEFER

NAME	G by Pos	B	AGE	G	AB	R	H	2B	3B	HR	RBI	BB	SO	SB	BA	SA
TOTALS			26	154	5134	698	1419	207	59	66	634	469	521	137	.276	.378
Harvey Cotter	1B90	L	24	98	310	39	81	16	4	4	33	36	31	3	.261	.377
George Grantham	2B118, 3B6	R	24	127	469	85	148	19	6	12	60	55	63	21	.316	.458
Sparky Adams	SS88, 2B19	R	29	117	418	68	117	11	5	1	27	40	20	15	.280	.337
Barney Friberg	3B142	R	24	142	495	67	138	19	3	9	82	66	53	19	.279	.360
Cliff Heathcote	OF111	L	26	113	392	66	121	19	7	0	30	28	28	26	.309	.393
Jigger Statz	OF131, 2B1	R	26	135	549	69	152	22	5	3	49	50	13	13	.277	.352
Denver Grigsby	OF121	L	23	124	411	59	123	18	4	3	48	31	47	10	.299	.375
Gabby Hartnett	C105	R	23	111	354	56	106	17	7	16	67	39	37	10	.299	.523
Charlie Hollocher (HO)	SS71	L	28	76	286	28	70	12	4	2	21	18	7	4	.245	.336
Bob O'Farrell	C57	R	27	71	183	25	44	6	4	2	28	30	13	2	.240	.344
Otto Vogel	OF53, 3B2	R	24	70	172	28	46	11	2	1	24	10	26	4	.267	.372
Bob Barrett	2B25, 1B10, 3B8	R	25	54	133	12	32	3	3	5	21	7	29	1	.241	.414
Hack Miller	OF32	R	30	53	131	11	44	8	1	4	25	4	11	1	.336	.504
Ray Grimes	1B50	R	30	51	177	33	53	6	5	3	34	28	15	4	.299	.475
Butch Weis	OF36	L	23	37	133	19	37	8	1	0	23	15	14	4	.278	.353
Tony Kaufmann	P34	R	23	35	76	6	24	5	0	1	14	3	10	0	.316	.421
Allen Elliott	1B10	R	26	10	14	0	2	0	0	0	0	2	1	0	.143	.143
Ralph Michaels	SS4	R	22	8	11	0	4	0	0	0	2	0	1	0	.364	.364
Howie Fitzgerald	OF5	L	27	7	19	1	3	0	0	0	0	2	5	0	.158	.158
John Churry	C3	R	23	6	7	0	1	0	0	0	0	0	2	0	.143	.286
Ted Kearns	1B4	R	24	4	16	0	4	1	0	0	4	0	2	0	.250	.375

NAME	T	AGE	W	L	PCT	SV	G	GS	CG	IP	H	BB	SO	SHO	ERA
		27	81	72	.529	6	154	154	85	1381	1459	438	416	4	3.83
Tony Kaufman	R	23	16	11	.593	0	34	26	16	208	218	66	79	3	4.02
Vic Aldridge	R	30	15	12	.556	0	32	32	20	244	260	80	74	0	3.50
Vic Keen	R	25	15	14	.517	0	40	28	15	235	242	80	75	0	3.79
Pete Alexander (BW)	R	37	12	5	.706	0	21	20	12	169	183	25	33	0	3.04
Elmer Jacobs	R	31	11	12	.478	1	38	22	13	190	181	72	50	1	3.74
Sheriff Blake	R	24	6	6	.500	1	29	11	4	108	123	44	42	0	4.59
Rip Wheeler	R	26	3	6	.333	0	29	4	0	101	103	21	16	0	3.92
Guy Bush	R	22	2	5	.286	0	18	5	4	81	91	24	36	0	4.00
George Milstead	L	21	1	1	.500	0	13	2	1	30	41	13	6	0	6.00
Ray Pierce	R	27	0	0	—	0	6	0	0	7	7	4	2	0	7.71
1 Tiny Osborne	R	31	0	0	—	0	2	0	0	3	3	1	0	0	3.00
Herb Brett	R	24	0	1	—	0	1	0	0	6	7	1	1	0	5.40

ST. LOUIS — 6th 65-89 .422 28.5 — BRANCH RICKEY

NAME	G by Pos	B	AGE	G	AB	R	H	2B	3B	HR	RBI	BB	SO	SB	BA	SA
	TOTALS		27	154	5349	740	1552	270	87	67	672	382	418	86	.290	.411
Jim Bottomley	1B133, 2B1	L	24	137	528	87	167	31	12	14	111	35	35	5	.316	.500
Rogers Hornsby	2B143	R	28	143	536	121	227	43	14	25	94	89	32	5	.424	.696
Jimmy Cooney	SS99, 3B7, 2B1	R	29	110	383	44	113	20	8	5	57	20	20	12	.295	.397
Howard Freigau	3B98, SS2	R	21	98	376	35	101	17	6	2	39	19	24	10	.269	.362
Jack Smith	OF114	L	29	124	459	91	130	18	6	2	33	33	27	24	.283	.362
Wattie Holm	OF64, C19, 3B4	R	23	92	293	40	86	10	4	0	23	8	16	1	.294	.355
Ray Blades	OF109, 2B7, 3B7	R	27	131	456	86	142	21	13	11	68	35	38	7	.311	.487
Mike Gonzalez	C119	R	33	120	402	34	119	27	1	3	53	24	22	1	.296	.391
Heinie Mueller	OF53, 1B27	L	24	92	296	39	78	12	6	2	37	19	16	8	.264	.365
Specs Toporcer	3B33, SS25, 2B3	R	25	70	198	30	62	10	3	1	24	11	14	2	.313	.409
Max Flack	OF52	L	34	67	209	31	55	11	3	2	21	21	5	3	.263	.373
Taylor Douthit	OF50	R	23	53	173	24	48	13	1	0	13	16	19	4	.277	.364
Eddie Dyer	P29, OF1	L	23	50	76	8	18	2	3	0	8	3	8	1	.237	.342
Hy Myers	OF22, 3B12, 2B3	R	35	43	124	12	26	5	1	1	15	3	10	1	.210	.290
Charlie Niebergall	C34	R	25	40	58	6	17	6	0	0	7	3	9	0	.293	.397
Verne Clemons	C17	R	32	25	56	3	18	3	0	0	6	2	3	0	.321	.375
Chick Hafey	OF24	R	21	24	91	10	23	5	2	2	22	4	8	1	.253	.418
Tommy Thevenow	SS23	R	20	23	89	4	18	4	1	0	7	1	6	1	.202	.270
Les Bell	SS17	R	22	17	57	5	14	3	2	1	5	3	7	0	.246	.421
Ernie Vick	C16	R	23	16	23	2	8	1	0	0	5	3	3	0	.348	.391
1 Joe Schultz	OF2	R	30	12	12	0	2	0	0	0	0	0	0	0	.167	.167

Ed Clough 17 L 1-14, Joe Bratcher 25 0-1, Doc Lavan 33 R 0-6, Ray Sheperdson 27 R 0-6

NAME	T	AGE	W	L	PCT	SV	G	GS	CG	IP	H	BB	SO	SHO	ERA
		28	65	89	.422	6	154	154	79	1365	1528	486	393	7	4.15
Allan Sothoron	R	31	10	16	.385	0	29	28	16	197	209	84	62	4	3.56
Johnny Stuart	R	23	9	11	.450	0	28	22	13	159	167	60	54	0	4.75
Bill Sherdel	L	27	8	9	.471	1	35	10	6	169	188	38	57	0	3.41
Eddie Dyer	L	24	8	11	.421	0	29	15	7	137	174	51	23	1	4.60
Jesse Haines	R	30	8	19	.296	0	35	31	16	223	275	66	69	1	4.40
2 Leo Dickerman	R	27	5	4	.636	0	18	13	8	120	108	51	28	1	2.40
1 Jeff Pfeffer	R	36	4	5	.444	0	16	12	3	78	102	30	20	0	5.31
	R	26	3	2	.600	0	28	10	5	113	124	29	29	0	4.94
Hi Bell	R	33	2	1	.667	3	11	1	0	22	25	14	7	0	3.27
1 Bill Doak	R	33	2	1	.667	3	11	0	0	22	30	11	4	0	4.50
Flint Rhem	R	23	2	2	.500	0	6	3	3	32	31	17	20	0	1.80
Art Delaney	R	29	1	0	1.000	0	8	1	1	20	19	6	2	0	4.36
Jesse Fowler	L	25	1	1	.500	0	13	3	1	18	22	18	5	0	4.50
Pea Ridge Day	R	24	1	1	.500	0	12	1	0	12	10	3	4	0	3.00
Vince Shields	R	23	1	1	.500	0	5	1	0	15	15	9	6	0	6.60
1 Lou North	R	33	0	0	—	0	4	0	0	8	8	4	0	0	5.63
Jack Berly	R	21	0	0	—	0	4	0	0	4	4	1	0	0	9.00
Bob Vines	R	27	0	0	—	0	2	0	0	1	23	0	0	0	9.00

PHILADELPHIA — 7th 55-96 .364 37 — ART FLETCHER

NAME	G by Pos	B	AGE	G	AB	R	H	2B	3B	HR	RBI	BB	SO	SB	BA	SA
	TOTALS		29	152	5306	676	1459	256	56	94	615	382	452	57	.275	.397
Walter Holke	1B148	B	31	152	563	60	169	23	6	6	64	25	33	3	.300	.394
Hod Ford	2B145	R	26	145	530	58	144	27	6	3	53	27	40	1	.272	.358
Heinie Sand	SS137	R	26	137	539	79	132	21	6	6	40	52	57	5	.245	.340
Russ Wrightstone	3B97, 2B9, SS5, OF1	L	31	118	388	55	119	24	4	7	58	27	15	5	.307	.443
2 George Harper	OF109	L	32	109	411	68	121	26	6	16	55	38	23	10	.294	.504
Cy Williams	OF145	L	36	148	558	101	183	31	11	24	93	67	49	7	.328	.552
Johnny Moken	OF94	R	28	96	366	50	95	15	1	7	44	30	27	7	.260	.363
Butch Henline	C83, OF2	R	29	115	289	41	82	18	4	5	37	28	15	1	.284	.426
Jimmie Wilson	C82, 1B2, OF1	R	23	95	280	32	78	16	3	6	39	17	12	5	.279	.421
2 Joe Schultz	OF76	R	30	88	284	35	80	15	1	5	29	20	18	6	.282	.394
Clarence Mitchell	P30	L	33	69	102	7	26	3	0	0	13	2	7	1	.255	.284
Frank Parkinson	3B28, SS21, 2B10	R	29	62	156	14	33	7	0	1	19	14	28	3	.212	.276
Andy Woehr	3B44, 2B1	R	28	50	152	11	33	4	5	0	17	5	8	2	.217	.309
Hal Carlson	P38	R	30	39	76	6	21	1	0	2	8	2	8	0	.276	.368
Fritz Henrich	OF32	L	25	36	90	4	19	4	0	0	4	2	12	0	.211	.256
1 Curt Walker	OF20	L	27	24	71	11	21	6	1	4	8	7	4	0	.296	.451
1 Cliff Lee	OF13, 1B4	R	27	21	56	4	14	3	2	1	7	5	4	0	.250	.429
Lew Wendell	C17	R	32	21	32	3	8	2	0	1	2	2	3	5	.250	.281
Freddy Leach	OF7	L	26	8	28	6	13	2	1	2	7	1	1	0	.464	.821
Lenny Metz	SS6	R	24	7	7	1	2	0	0	0	1	1	0	0	.286	.286
Spoke Emery	OF1	R	27	5	3	3	2	0	0	0	0	0	0	0	.667	.667

NAME	T	AGE	W	L	PCT	SV	G	GS	CG	IP	H	BB	SO	SHO	ERA
		31	55	96	.364	10	152	152	59	1355	1689	469	349	7	4.87
Bill Hubbell	R	27	10	9	.526	2	36	22	9	179	233	45	30	2	4.83
Jimmy Ring	R	29	10	12	.455	0	32	31	16	215	236	108	72	1	3.98
Hal Carlson	R	32	8	17	.320	2	38	23	12	204	267	55	66	1	4.85
Huck Betts	R	27	7	10	.412	2	37	9	2	144	160	42	46	0	4.31
Whitey Glazner	R	31	7	16	.304	0	35	24	8	157	210	63	46	2	5.85
Clarence Mitchell	R	33	5	13	.316	1	30	26	9	165	223	58	41	1	5.62
2 Johnny Couch	R	33	4	8	.333	3	37	7	3	137	170	39	36	0	4.73
2 Joe Oeschger	R	32	2	7	.222	0	19	8	0	65	88	16	23	0	4.43
2 Ray Steineder	L	29	1	1	.500	0	9	0	0	29	29	16	8	0	4.34
Lefty Weinert	L	22	1	1	.500	0	8	0	0	15	10	11	7	0	2.40
Jim Bishop	R	26	1	1	.500	0	7	1	0	24	7	3	5	0	3.00
Earl Hamilton	L	32	0	1	.000	0	6	0	0	6	9	2	2	0	10.50
Bert Lewis	R	28	0	0	—	0	12	0	0	18	23	7	3	0	6.00
Lerton Pinto	L	27	0	0	—	0	3	0	0	6	9	5	0	0	9.00

BOSTON — 8th 53-100 .346 40 — DAVE BANCROFT

NAME	G by Pos	B	AGE	G	AB	R	H	2B	3B	HR	RBI	BB	SO	SB	BA	SA
	TOTALS		30	154	5283	520	1355	194	52	25	459	354	451	74	.256	.327
Stuffy McInnis	1B146	R	33	146	581	57	169	23	7	1	59	15	6	9	.291	.360
Cotton Tierney	2B115, 3B22	R	30	136	505	38	131	16	1	6	58	22	37	11	.259	.331
Bob Smith	SS80, 3B23	R	29	106	347	32	79	12	3	2	38	15	26	5	.228	.297
Ernie Padgett	3B113, 2B29	R	25	116	408	42	104	25	9	1	46	37	56	4	.255	.347
Casey Stengel	OF126	L	33	131	461	57	129	20	6	5	39	45	39	13	.280	.382
Frank Wilson	OF55	L	23	81	216	20	51	7	0	1	15	23	22	3	.237	.284
Bill Cunningham	OF109	R	29	114	437	44	119	15	8	1	40	8	22	7	.272	.350
Mickey O'Neil	C106	R	26	106	362	32	89	4	1	0	22	14	27	4	.246	.262
Frank Gibson	C46, 1B10, 3B2	R	33	90	229	25	71	15	6	1	30	10	23	1	.310	.441
Dave Bancroft (IL)	SS79	B	33	79	319	49	89	11	1	2	21	37	24	4	.279	.339
Ray Powell	OF46	L	35	74	188	21	49	9	1	1	15	21	28	1	.261	.335
Gus Felix	OF51	R	29	59	204	25	43	7	1	1	10	18	16	5	.254	.285
Johnny Cooney	P34, OF16, 1B1	L	23	55	130	10	33	2	1	0	4	9	5	0	.254	.323
1 Earl Smith	C13	R	27	33	59	1	16	3	0	0	9	5	5	0	.271	.322
Les Mann	OF28	R	31	32	102	13	28	7	4	0	10	8	10	1	.275	.422
Herb Thomas	OF32	R	22	32	127	12	28	4	1	1	8	4	9	5	.220	.291
Ed Sperber	OF17	L	29	24	59	8	17	1	2	1	12	10	9	3	.288	.373
Marty Shay	2B19, SS1	R	28	19	68	4	16	3	1	0	2	1	5	1	.235	.309

Walton Cruise 34 L 4-9, Hunter Lane 23 R 1-15, Eddie Phillips 23 R 0-3, Dee Cousineau 25 R 0-2, Al Hermann 25 R 0-1, John Kelleher 30 R 0-1, 1 Wade Lefier 28 L 0-1, Tony Boeckel (DD) 31

NAME	T	AGE	W	L	PCT	SV	G	GS	CG	IP	H	BB	SO	SHO	ERA
		26	53	100	.346	4	154	154	66	1379	1607	402	364	10	4.46
Jesse Barnes	R	31	15	20	.429	0	37	32	21	268	292	53	49	4	3.22
Joe Genewich	R	27	10	19	.345	4	34	27	11	200	258	65	43	2	5.22
Johnny Cooney	L	23	8	9	.471	2	34	19	12	181	176	50	67	2	3.18
Tim McNamara	R	25	8	12	.400	3	35	21	6	179	242	31	35	2	5.18
Larry Benton	R	26	5	7	.417	1	30	13	4	128	129	64	41	0	4.15
Dutch Stryker	R	28	3	8	.273	0	20	10	2	73	90	22	22	0	6.04
Rube Marquard (IL)	L	37	1	2	.333	0	6	6	1	36	33	13	10	0	3.00
2 Lou North	R	33	1	2	.333	0	9	1	1	35	45	19	11	0	5.40
Red Lucas	R	22	1	0	.200	0	27	4	1	84	112	18	30	0	5.14
Al Yeargin	L	22	1	11	.083	0	32	12	6	141	162	42	34	0	5.11
Ike Kamp	L	23	0	1	.000	0	7	1	0	7	9	8	3	0	5.14
2 Dinty Gearin	L	26	0	1	.000	0	4	0	0	10	9	6	3	0	3.82
Kyle Graham	R	24	0	4	.000	0	5	4	1	33	33	11	15	0	3.82
Joe Muich	R	20	0	0	—	0	4	0	0	9	19	5	1	0	11.00
Joe Batchelder (IL)	R	25	0	0	—	0	5	0	0	9	4	2	3	0	3.60

WORLD SERIES — WASHINGTON (AL) 4 NEW YORK (NL) 3

LINE SCORES

TEAM	1	2	3		4	5	6		7	8	9		10	11	12		R	H	E

Game 1 October 4 at Washington
```
                                                     NY (NL)
0    1 0 1   0 0 0   0 0 0      0 2 4      14  1
WAS  0 0 0   0 0 1   0 0 1      0 0 1      3  10  1
  Nehf                  Johnson
```

Game 2 October 5 at Washington
```
                                                     NY
0    0 0 0   0 0 1   0 0 0         3  6  0
WAS  2 0 0   1 0 0   0 0 1         4  6  1
  Bentley          Zachary, Marberry (9)
```

Game 3 October 6 at New York
```
WAS  0 0 0   2 0 0   0 1 1      4  9  2
NY   0 2 1   1 0 1   0 1 X      6  12  0
  Marberry, Russell (4),   McQuillan, Ryan (4),
  Martina (7), Speece (8)   Jonnard (9), Watson (9)
```

Game 4 October 7 at New York
```
WAS  0 0 3   0 2 0   0 2 0      7  13  3
NY   1 0 0   0 0 1   0 1 1      4  6  1
  Mogridge, Marberry (8)   Barnes, Baldwin (6),
                           Dean (8)
```

Game 5 October 8 at New York
```
WAS  0 0 0   1 0 0   1 0 0      2  9  1
NY   0 0 1   0 2 0   0 3 X      6  13  0
  Johnson          Bentley, McQuillan (8)
```

Game 6 October 9 at Washington
```
                                                     NY
1    0 0 0   0 0 0   0 0 0      1  7  1
WAS  0 0 0   0 0 2   0 0 X      2  4  0
  Nehf, Ryan (8)          Zachary
```

Game 7 October 10 at Washington
```
NY   0 0 0   0 0 3   0 0 0      0 0 0      3  8  3
WAS  0 0 0   1 0 0   0 2 0      0 0 1      4  10  4
  Barnes, Nehf (8), McQuillan (9),   Ogden, Mogridge (1),
  Bentley (11)                       Marberry (8), Johnson (9)
```

COMPOSITE BATTING

NAME	POS	G	AB	R	H	2B	3B	HR	RBI	BA
Washington (AL)										
Totals		7	248	26	61	9		5	24	.246
Harris	2B	7	33	5	11	0	0	2	7	.333
Goslin	OF	7	32	4	11	0	0	3	7	.344
Rice	OF	7	29	2	6	0	0	0	1	.207
McNeely	OF	7	27	4	6	3	0	0	1	.222
Judge	1B	7	26	4	10	1	0	0	0	.385
Bluege	3B-SS	7	26	2	5	0	0	0	0	.192
Ruel	C	7	21	2	2	1	0	0	0	.095
Peckinpaugh	SS	4	12	1	5	2	0	0	4	.417
Miller	3B	4	11	0	2	0	0	0	2	.182
Johnson	P	3	9	0	1	0	0	0	1	.111
Leibold	OF	3	6	1	1	1	0	0	0	.167
Mogridge	P	2	5	0	0	0	0	0	0	.000
Zachary	P	2	5	0	0	0	0	0	0	.000
Shirley	PH	3	2	1	1	0	0	0	0	.500
Marberry	P	4	2	0	0	0	0	0	0	.000
Taylor	3B	2	2	0	0	0	0	0	0	.000
Tate	PH	3	2	0	0	0	0	0	1	—
Martina	P	1	0	0	0	0	0	0	0	—
Ogden	P	2	0	0	0	0	0	0	0	—
Russell	P	1	0	0	0	0	0	0	0	—
Speece	P	1	0	0	0	0	0	0	0	—
New York (NL)										
Totals		7	253	27	66	9	2	4	22	.261
Kelly	OF-2B-1B	7	31	7	9	0	0	1	4	.290
Lindstrom	3B	7	30	1	10	2	0	0	4	.333
Frisch	2B-3B	7	30	1	10	4	1	0	0	.333
Wilson	OF	7	30	3	7	1	0	0	3	.233
Gowdy	C	7	27	4	7	0	0	0	1	.259
Youngs	OF	7	27	3	5	1	0	0	2	.185
Jackson	SS	7	27	3	2	0	0	0	1	.074
Terry	1B	5	14	3	6	1	0	1	1	.429
Meusel	OF	4	13	0	2	1	0	0	2	.154
Nehf	P	3	7	1	3	0	0	0	2	.429
Bentley	P	5	9	2	1	1	0	1	4	.286
Barnes	P	2	5	0	0	0	0	0	0	.000
Ryan	P	2	2	1	1	0	0	0	0	.500
McQuillan	P	3	2	0	2	0	0	0	1	1.000
Groh	PH	1	1	1	1	0	0	0	0	1.000
Southworth	OF	1	1	0	0	0	0	0	0	.000
Snyder	PH	1	1	0	0	0	0	0	0	.000
Baldwin	P	2	0	0	0	0	0	0	0	—

Dean P 0-0, Jonnard P 0-0, Watson P 0-0

COMPOSITE PITCHING

NAME	G	IP	H	BB	SO	W	L	SV	ERA
Washington (AL)									
Totals	7	67	66	25	40	4	3	2	2.15
Johnson	3	24	30	11	20	1	2	0	2.25
Zachary	2	17.2	13	3	3	2	0	0	2.04
Mogridge	2	12	7	6	5	1	0	0	2.25
Marberry	4	8	9	4	10	0	1	2	1.13
Russell	1	3	4	0	0	0	0	0	3.00
Martina	1	3	3	0	1	0	0	0	0.00
Speece	1	1	0	0	1	0	0	0	9.00
Ogden	2								0.00
New York (NL)									
Totals	7	66.2	61	29	34	3	4	2	3.24
Nehf	3	19.2	15	9	7	1	1	0	1.83
Bentley	3	17	18	8	10	1	2	0	3.71
Barnes	2	12.2	15	1	9	0	1	0	5.68
McQuillan	3	7	2	4	3	1	0	1	2.57
Ryan	2	5.2	7	4	3	0	0	1	3.18
Baldwin	1	2	1	6	0	0	0	0	0.00
Dean	1	2	3	0	2	0	0	0	4.50
Watson	1	.2	0	1	0	0	0	0	0.00
Jonnard	1	0	0	0	0	0	0	0	0.00

1925 The Abdominal Disaster That Ached a Dynasty

The world, or at least that part of it which included baseball in its territorial domain, was in for the greatest disillusionment since the 1919 World Series scandal. Oddly enough, the man most responsible for restoring the faith of the nation in the national game also became the catalyst for destroying that faith again. This time, though, it was not the shock of immorality, but that baseball's superstar was human after all.

Babe Ruth's popular image rested not only on his home run hitting, but also upon his prodigious appetites: for soda pop, for hot dogs, for alcohol, for steak, for women, for the night life, for the good life, for life itself. The Babe touched all bases, even off the diamond, and a winter of burning the candle at both ends inevitably caught up with him when he keeled over on April 8, as the Yankees were in the final stages of spring training. The press bellowed over Ruth's "bellyache" as the Bambino returned to New York for surgery to remove an intestinal abscess—an operation which would lay the slugger up until June. The Yankees had just missed out on a fourth straight pennant in 1924 and expected to return to the top once again. The absence of Ruth and the onslaughts of age, however, sapped the Bronx Bombers of their strength and desire, and the Yanks limped home a weak seventh. Even after his return, Ruth performed at less-than-peak efficiency, and a miserable season came to an early end for the Babe when manager Miller Huggins suspended him in September and slapped him with a record $5,000 fine for insubordination and constant breaking of club training rules. Out of the rubble, though, rose a new Yankee powerhouse. Lou Gehrig took over first base from Wally Pipp, Earle Combs established himself in center field, and shortstop Mark Koenig joined the team late in the year.

With the Yankees out of competition, the Senators and Athletics battled it out for the pennant, and the veteran Washington team pulled away from Connie Mack's young squad when the A's went into a 12-game tailspin in August. The Senators boasted of the league's best pitching in what was a hitters year, as they posted a league-low 3.67 E.R.A. Thirty-seven-year-old Walter Johnson squeezed enough fastballs out of his right arm to win 20 games, while 35-year-old Stan Coveleski came over from Cleveland to notch 20 victories and 33-year-old Dutch Reuther chalked up 18 victories after being picked up on waivers from the National League. And when the aged starting staff ran into trouble, it fell back for help onto big Firpo Marberry, one of the first of baseballs great relief specialists, who posted a league-leading 15 saves. Twenty-eight-year-old Bucky Harris was the boy manager of the squad, and he and Roger Peckinpaugh held the defense together with their play at second base and shortstop.

The New York Giants dropped out of the first place slot after four straight National League pennants, giving way to a young Pittsburgh Pirate team. The Bucs defeated the Giants with a hard-hitting lineup, led by Max Carey and Kiki Cuyler, and a deep pitching staff which held no stars, but five solid starters. Rogers Hornsby proved to be the hitting story of the year, winning the Triple Crown by hitting .403, swatting 39 homers, and driving 143 runs across the plate. In addition, the Cardinal second baseman succeeded Branch Rickey as manager after a slow start and brought the team up to a fourth place finish.

In the World Series, the Pirates became the first team in history to come back from a 3-1 deficit in games to win the championship. Although the Senators got stellar performances from Walter Johnson, Goose Goslin, Joe Harris, and Sam Rice, star shortstop Roger Peckinpaugh committed eight errors during the Series to keep the Bucs in the fray. The decisive seventh game was played in a steady downpour and was decided on Cuyler's double in the eighth inning, which scored the winning runs to defeat Walter Johnson and the Senators, 9 to 7.

1925 AMERICAN LEAGUE

NAME	G by Pos	B	AGE	G	AB	R	H	2B	3B	HR	RBI	BB	SO	SB	BA	SA
WASHINGTON 1st 96-55 .597	**BUCKY HARRIS**		30	152	5206	829	1577	251	72	56	747	533	427	140	.303	.411
TOTALS																
Joe Judge	1B109	L	31	112	376	65	118	31	5	8	66	55	21	7	.314	.487
Bucky Harris	2B144	R	28	144	551	91	158	30	3	1	66	55	21	14	.287	.358
Roger Peckinpaugh	SSA24, 1B1	R	34	126	422	67	124	16	4	4	64	49	23	13	.294	.379
Ossie Bluege	3B44, SS4	R	24	145	522	77	150	27	4	4	79	59	56	16	.287	.377
Sam Rice	OF152	L	35	152	649	111	227	31	13	1	87	37	10	26	.350	.442
Earl McNeely	OF112, 1B1	R	27	122	385	76	110	14	2	3	37	48	54	14	.286	.356
Goose Goslin	OF150	L	24	150	601	116	201	34	20	18	113	53	50	26	.334	.547
Muddy Ruel	C126, 1B1	R	29	127	393	55	122	9	2	0	54	63	16	4	.310	.346
2 Joe Harris	1B57, OF41	R	34	100	300	60	97	21	9	12	59	51	28	5	.323	.573
Nemo Leibold	OF26, 3B1	L	33	56	84	14	23	1	1	0	7	15	8	1	.274	.310
Dutch Ruether	P30, 1B1	L	31	55	108	18	36	3	2	1	15	10	8	0	.333	.444
2 Hank Severeid	C35	R	34	50	110	11	39	8	1	0	14	13	6	0	.355	.445
Spencer Adams	2B15, SS8, 3B3	L	27	39	55	11	15	4	1	0	4	5	4	1	.273	.382
Walter Johnson	P30	R	37	36	97	12	42	6	1	2	20	3	6	0	.433	.577
2 Everett Scott	SS30, 3B2	R	32	33	103	10	28	6	1	0	18	4	4	1	.272	.350
3 Bobby Veach	OF11	L	37	18	37	4	9	3	0	0	8	3	3	0	.243	.324
Bennie Tate	C14	L	23	16	27	0	13	3	0	0	7	2	2	0	.481	.593
Tex Jeanes	OF13	R	24	15	19	2	5	1	0	1	4	3	2	1	.263	.474
Mule Shirley	1B9	L	24	14	23	2	3	1	0	0	2	1	7	0	.130	.174
Mike McNally	3B7, SS2, 2B1	R	31	12	21	1	3	0	0	0	0	1	4	0	.143	.143

Wid Matthews 28 L 4-9, Stuffy Stewart 31 R 6-17, 1 Pinky Hargrave 23 R 3-6, Buddy Myer 21 2-8, Tubby McGee 26 R 0-3, Roy Carlyle 26 L 0-1, Patsy Gharrity (DE) 23

NAME	T	AGE	W	L	PCT	SV	G	GS	CG	IP	H	BB	SO	SHO	ERA
		32	96	55	.636	21	152	152	69	1358	1426	543	464	10	3.67
Stan Coveleski	R	35	20	5	.800	0	32	32	15	241	230	73	58	3	2.84
Walter Johnson	R	37	20	7	.741	0	30	29	16	229	211	78	108	3	3.07
Dutch Ruether	L	31	18	7	.720	0	30	29	16	223	241	105	68	1	3.87
Tom Zachary	L	29	12	15	.444	2	38	33	11	218	247	74	58	1	3.84
Firpo Marberry	R	26	8	6	.571	15	55	0	0	93	84	45	53	0	3.48
3 Alex Ferguson	R	28	5	1	.833	0	7	6	3	55	52	23	24	0	3.27
1 George Mogridge	L	36	4	3	.571	0	10	8	3	53	56	18	13	0	3.40
Curly Ogden	R	24	3	1	.750	0	17	4	2	42	45	18	6	1	4.50
Vean Gregg	L	40	2	2	.500	2	26	5	1	74	87	38	18	0	4.14
Allen Russell	R	31	2	4	.333	2	32	2	0	69	85	37	25	0	5.74
Win Ballou	R	27	1	1	.500	0	10	1	1	28	38	13	13	0	4.50
Harry Kelley	R	19	1	1	.500	0	6	1	0	16	30	12	7	0	9.00
Lefty Thomas	L	21	0	2	.000	0	2	2	1	13	14	7	10	0	2.08
Jim Lyle	R	24	0	0	—	0	1	0	0	3	5	1	3	0	6.00
Spence Pumpelly	R	32	0	0	—	0	1	0	0	1	1	1	0	0	9.00

NAME	G by Pos	B	AGE	G	AB	R	H	2B	3B	HR	RBI	BB	SO	SB	BA	SA
PHILADELPHIA 2nd 88-64 .579 8.5	**CONNIE MACK**		27	153	5399	831	1659	298	79	76	767	453	432	67	.307	.434
TOTALS																
Jim Poole	1B123	L	30	133	480	65	143	29	8	5	67	27	37	5	.298	.423
Max Bishop	2B104	L	25	105	368	66	103	18	4	4	27	87	37	5	.280	.383
Chuck Galloway	SS148	R	28	149	481	52	116	11	4	3	71	59	28	16	.241	.299
Sammy Hale	3B96, 2B1	R	28	110	391	62	150	37	4	1	63	17	27	7	.384	.540
Bing Miller	OF115, 1B12	R	30	124	474	78	151	29	10	10	81	19	14	11	.319	.485
Al Simmons	OF153	R	23	153	658	122	253	43	12	24	129	35	41	7	.384	.596
Bill Lamar	OF131	L	28	138	568	85	202	39	8	3	77	21	17	2	.356	.468
Mickey Cochrane	C133	L	22	134	420	69	139	21	5	6	55	44	19	7	.331	.448
Jimmy Dykes	3B64, 2B58, SS2	R	28	122	465	93	150	32	11	5	55	46	49	9	.323	.471
Frank Welch	OF57	R	27	85	202	40	56	5	4	4	41	29	14	2	.277	.401
Walt French	OF19	L	25	67	100	20	37	9	0	0	14	1	9	1	.370	.460
Cy Perkins	C58, 3B1	R	29	65	140	21	43	10	0	1	18	26	6	0	.307	.400
Bill Bagwell	OF4	L	30	36	50	4	15	2	1	0	10	2	2	0	.300	.380
Red Holt	1B25	R	30	27	88	13	24	7	0	1	8	12	9	0	.273	.386
Red Smith	SS16, 3B2	L	25	20	14	1	4	0	0	0	1	2	5	0	.286	.286
Charlie Berry	C4	R	22	10	14	1	3	1	0	0	3	0	2	0	.214	.286
Jimmie Foxx	C1	R	17	10	9	2	6	1	0	0	0	1	0	1	.667	.778
Carl Husta	SS6	R	23	6	22	2	3	0	0	0	0	2	3	0	.136	.136
Jim Keesey	1B2	R	22	5	5	1	2	0	0	0	3	0	0	0	.400	.400
1 Doc Gautreau	2B4	R	23	4	7	0	0	0	0	0	0	0	3	0	.000	.000
Charlie Engle	SS1	R	21	1	0	0	0	0	0	0	0	0	0	0	—	—

Joe Hauser (BK) 26

NAME	T	AGE	W	L	PCT	SV	G	GS	CG	IP	H	BB	SO	SHO	ERA
		30	88	64	.579	18	153	153	61	1373	1468	544	495	8	3.89
Eddie Rommel	R	27	21	10	.677	3	52	28	14	261	285	95	67	1	3.69
Slim Harris	R	28	19	12	.613	1	46	33	15	252	263	95	95	2	3.50
Sam Gray (BG)	R	27	16	8	.667	3	32	28	14	196	199	63	80	4	3.40
Lefty Grove	L	25	10	12	.455	1	45	18	5	197	207	131	116	0	4.75
Rube Walberg	L	28	8	14	.364	7	53	20	7	192	197	77	82	0	3.98
Stan Baumgartner	L	32	6	3	.667	3	37	12	2	113	120	35	18	1	3.58
2 Jack Quinn	R	41	5	3	.625	0	18	13	4	100	119	16	19	0	3.87
Tom Glass	R	27	1	0	1.000	0	2	0	0	5	8	0	2	0	5.40
Art Stokes	R	28	1	1	.500	0	12	0	0	24	24	10	7	0	4.12
Fred Heimach (SJ)	L	24	0	1	.000	0	10	0	0	20	24	9	6	0	4.05
Elbert Andrews	R	23	0	0	—	0	3	0	0	8	12	11	0	0	10.13
Lefty Willis	L	19	0	0	—	0	1	1	0	5	9	2	3	0	10.80

NAME	G by Pos	B	AGE	G	AB	R	H	2B	3B	HR	RBI	BB	SO	SB	BA	SA
ST. LOUIS 3rd 82-71 .536 15	**GEORGE SISLER**		30	154	5440	900	1620	304	68	110	798	498	375	85	.298	.439
TOTALS																
George Sisler	1B150, P1	L	32	150	649	100	224	21	15	12	105	27	24	11	.345	.479
Marty McManus	2B154, OF1	R	25	154	587	108	169	44	8	13	90	73	69	5	.288	.457
Bobby LaMotte	SS93, 3B3	R	27	97	356	61	97	20	4	2	51	34	22	5	.272	.388
Gene Robertson	3B154, SS1	L	26	154	582	97	158	26	5	14	76	81	30	10	.271	.405
Harry Rice	OF85, 1B3, 2B1, 3B1, C1	L	24	154	354	87	127	25	8	11	47	54	15	8	.359	.568
Baby Doll Jacobson	OF139	R	34	142	540	103	184	30	9	15	76	45	26	3	.341	.513
Ken Williams (PB)	OF102	L	35	102	411	83	136	31	5	25	105	37	14	10	.331	.613
Leo Dixon	C75	R	30	76	205	27	46	11	1	1	19	24	42	3	.224	.302
Herschel Bennett	OF73	L	28	93	298	46	83	11	6	2	37	18	16	4	.279	.376
Jack Tobin	OF39, 1B3	L	33	77	193	25	58	11	0	2	27	9	5	8	.301	.389
Wally Gerber (BL)	SS71	R	33	72	246	29	67	13	1	0	19	26	15	1	.272	.333
2 Pinky Hargrave	C82	R	29	67	193	25	54	64	15	2	43	13	13	2	.284	.476
Bullet Joe Bush	P33, OF1	R	32	57	102	10	26	12	0	2	18	6	18	0	.255	.431
Joe Evans	OF47	R	30	37	79	27	50	12	0	0	20	16	6	6	.314	.390
1 Hank Severeid	C31	R	34	34	109	15	40	9	0	1	21	11	2	0	.367	.477
Tony Rego	C19	R	27	20	32	5	13	2	1	0	5	1	3	0	.406	.531
Johnny Austin	3B1	B	45	1	1	0	0	0	0	0	0	0	0	0	.000	.000

NAME	T	AGE	W	L	PCT	SV	G	GS	CG	IP	H	BB	SO	SHO	ERA
		30	82	71	.536	10	154	154	67	1393	1598	675	419	7	4.85
Milt Gaston	R	29	15	14	.517	1	42	29	14	239	284	101	84	0	4.41
Bullet Joe Bush	R	32	14	14	.500	0	33	30	15	214	239	91	63	2	4.96
Elam Vangilder	R	29	14	8	.636	6	52	16	4	193	225	92	61	1	4.71
Dixie Davis	R	34	12	7	.632	0	35	22	9	180	192	106	58	0	4.60
Joe Giard	L	26	10	5	.667	0	30	21	9	161	179	87	43	4	5.03
Ernie Wingard	L	24	9	10	.474	0	32	18	8	153	184	77	20	0	5.06
Dave Danforth	L	35	7	9	.438	2	38	15	5	159	172	61	53	0	4.36
2 George Mogridge (AJ)	L	36	1	1	.500	0	7	2	1	15	17	5	8	0	5.40
Ed Stauffer	R	27	0	1	.000	0	3	1	0	30	34	21	13	0	5.40
George Grant	R	22	0	2	.000	0	12	0	0	16	26	8	7	0	6.19
Chet Falk	L	20	0	0	—	0	13	0	0	25	38	17	7	0	8.28
Brad Springer	L	21	0	0	—	0	2	0	0	3	1	3	1	0	3.00
George Blaeholder	R	21	0	0	—	0	2	0	0	2	6	1	1	0	31.50
George Sisler	L	32	0	0	—	0	1	0	0	1	1	1	0	0	0.00

DETROIT — 4th 81-73 .526 16.5 — TY COBB

NAME	G by Pos	B	AGE	G	AB	R	H	2B	3B	HR	RBI	BB	SO	SB	BA	SA
TOTALS			28	156	5371	903	1621	277	84	50	797	640	386	97	.302	.412
Lu Blue	1B148	B	28	150	532	91	163	18	9	3	94	83	29	19	.306	.391
Frank O'Rourke	2B118,3B6	R	33	124	482	88	141	40	7	5	57	32	37	5	.293	.436
Jackie Tavener	SS134	L	27	134	453	45	111	11	11	0	47	39	60	5	.245	.318
Fred Haney	3B107	R	27	114	398	84	111	15	3	0	40	66	29	11	.279	.332
Harry Heilmann	OF148	R	30	150	573	97	225	40	11	13	133	67	27	6	.393	.569
Ty Cobb	OF105,P1	L	38	121	415	97	157	31	12	12	102	65	12	13	.378	.598
Al Wingo	OF122	L	27	130	440	104	163	34	10	5	68	69	31	14	.370	.527
John Bassler	C118	L	30	121	344	40	96	19	3	0	52	74	6	1	.279	.352
Heinie Manush	OF73	L	23	99	277	46	84	14	3	5	47	24	21	8	.303	.430
Les Burke	2B52	R	22	77	180	32	52	6	3	0	24	17	8	4	.289	.356
Larry Woodall	C75	R	30	75	171	20	35	4	1	0	13	24	8	1	.205	.240
Bob Fothergill	OF59	R	28	71	204	38	72	14	0	2	18	21	15	2	.353	.451
Topper Rigney	SS51,3B4	R	28	62	146	21	36	5	2	2	18	21	15	2	.247	.349
Johnny Neun	1B13	B	24	60	75	15	20	3	3	0	4	9	12	2	.267	.387
Bob Jones	3B46	L	35	50	148	18	35	6	0	0	15	9	5	1	.236	.277
Jack Warner	3B10	R	21	10	39	7	13	0	0	0	2	3	6	0	.333	.333
Charlie Gehringer	2B6	L	22	8	18	3	3	0	0	0	0	2	0	0	.167	.167
Oscar Stanage	C3	R	42	3	5	0	1	0	0	0	0	0	1	0	.200	.200
Andy Harrington		R	22	1	1	0	0	0	0	0	0	0	0	0	.000	.000

NAME	T	AGE	W	L	PCT	SV	G	GS	CG	IP	H	BB	SO	SHO	ERA
		28	81	73	.526	18	156	156	66	1384	1582	556	419	2	4.61
Hooks Dauss	R	35	16	11	.593	1	35	30	16	228	238	85	58	1	3.16
Ken Hollaway	R	27	13	4	.765	2	35	14	6	158	170	67	29	0	4.61
Earl Whitehill	L	25	11	11	.500	2	35	33	15	239	267	88	83	1	4.67
Dutch Leonard (SA)	L	33	11	4	.733	0	18	18	9	126	143	43	65	0	4.50
Lil Stoner	R	26	10	9	.526	1	34	18	8	152	166	53	51	0	4.26
Rip Collins	R	29	11	9	.550	1	27	18	9	149	149	52	33	0	4.56
Ed Wells	L	25	6	9	.400	1	35	14	5	134	190	62	45	0	6.18
Jess Doyle	R	27	4	7	.364	8	45	3	0	118	158	50	31	0	5.95
Ownie Carroll	R	22	2	2	.500	0	10	4	1	41	46	28	12	0	3.73
1 Bert Cole	L	29	2	3	.400	1	14	2	1	34	44	15	7	0	5.82
Syl Johnson (BY)	R	24	0	0	.000	0	6	0	0	13	11	10	5	0	3.46
Ty Cobb	L	38	0	0	—	0	1	0	0	1	0	0	0	0	0.00
Bill Moore	R	22	0	0	—	0	1	0	0	0	3	0	0	0	0.00

CHICAGO — 5th 79-75 .513 18.5 — EDDIE COLLINS

NAME	G by Pos	B	AGE	G	AB	R	H	2B	3B	HR	RBI	BB	SO	SB	BA	SA
TOTALS			30	154	5224	811	1482	299	59	38	738	662	405	131	.284	.385
Earl Sheely	1B153	L	32	153	600	93	189	43	3	9	111	68	23	3	.315	.442
Eddie Collins (LJ)	2B116	L	38	118	425	80	147	26	3	3	80	87	8	19	.346	.442
Ike Davis	SS144	R	30	146	562	105	135	31	9	0	61	71	58	19	.240	.327
Willie Kamm	3B152	R	25	152	509	82	142	32	4	6	83	90	36	11	.279	.393
Harry Hooper	OF124	L	37	127	442	62	117	23	5	6	55	54	21	5	.265	.380
Johnny Mostil	OF153	R	29	153	605	135	181	36	16	2	50	90	52	43	.299	.421
Bibb Falk	OF154	L	26	154	602	80	181	35	9	4	99	51	25	4	.301	.409
Ray Schalk	C125	R	32	125	343	44	94	18	1	0	52	57	27	11	.274	.332
Bill Barrett	2B41,OF27,SS4,3B4	R	25	81	245	44	89	23	3	3	40	24	27	5	.363	.518
Spence Harris	OF27	L	28	56	92	12	26	2	0	1	13	14	13	1	.283	.337
Buck Crouse	C48	R	28	54	131	18	46	7	0	2	25	12	4	1	.351	.450
Sloppy Thurston	P36	R	26	44	84	2	24	1	2	0	13	5	13	0	.286	.417
Roy Elsh	OF16,1B3	R	34	32	48	6	9	4	0	0	4	5	1	2	.188	.208
Johnny Grabowski	C21	R	25	21	46	5	14	1	1	0	10	2	4	1	.304	.435
John Kane	SS8,2B6	L	27	14	56	6	10	0	0	0	5	3	0	3	.179	.196
Maurice Archdeacon	OF1	L	27	10	9	2	1	0	0	0	0	1	1	0	.111	.111
1 George Bishoff	C4	L	24	7	11	1	1	0	0	0	0	1	5	0	.091	.091
Bud Clancy		L	24	4	3	0	0	0	0	0	0	0	0	0	.000	.000
Jule Mallonee	OF1	L	25	3	1	0	0	0	0	0	0	0	1	0	.000	.000
Leo Tankersley	C1	R	24	3	3	0	0	0	0	0	0	0	1	0	.000	.000

NAME	T	AGE	W	L	PCT	SV	G	GS	CG	IP	H	BB	SO	SHO	ERA
		27	79	75	.513	4	154	154	71	1369	1583	493	375	12	4.34
Ted Lyons	R	24	21	11	.656	3	43	32	19	263	274	83	45	5	3.25
Ted Blankenship	R	24	17	8	.680	1	40	23	16	222	218	69	81	3	3.16
Red Faber	R	36	12	11	.522	0	34	32	16	238	266	59	71	1	3.78
Sloppy Thurston	R	26	10	14	.417	1	36	25	9	175	250	47	35	0	6.17
Charlie Robertson	R	29	8	12	.400	0	24	23	6	137	181	47	27	2	5.26
Sarge Connally	R	26	6	7	.462	8	40	2	0	108	126	62	46	0	4.75
Mike Cvengros	L	24	3	9	.250	0	22	11	4	105	109	55	32	0	4.29
2 Jim Joe Edwards	L	30	2	3	.333	0	9	4	1	45	46	23	20	1	4.00
Leo Mangum	R	29	1	0	1.000	0	7	0	0	15	25	6	6	0	7.80
Dickie Kerr	L	31	0	0	—	0	12	0	0	37	45	18	4	0	5.11
Frank Mack	R	25	0	0	—	0	2	0	0	13	24	13	6	0	9.69
Ken Ash	R	23	0	0	—	0	2	0	0	9	9	2	0	0	9.00
Jake Freeze	R	25	0	0	—	0	2	0	0	4	8	1	1	0	2.25
Tink Riviere	R	25	0	0	—	0	2	0	0	6	7	1	1	0	31.50
Chief Bender	R	42	0	0	—	0	1	0	0	1	1	0	0	0	18.00

CLEVELAND — 6th 70-84 .455 27.5 — TRIS SPEAKER

NAME	G by Pos	B	AGE	G	AB	R	H	2B	3B	HR	RBI	BB	SO	SB	BA	SA
TOTALS			28	155	5436	782	1613	285	58	52	697	520	379	90	.297	.399
George Burns	1B126	R	32	127	488	69	164	41	4	1	79	24	24	16	.336	.473
Chick Fewster	2B86,3B10,OF1	R	29	93	294	39	73	16	1	1	38	36	25	4	.248	.320
Joe Sewell	SS153,2B3	L	26	155	608	78	204	37	7	1	98	64	4	7	.336	.424
Rube Lutzke	3B69,2B10	R	27	81	238	31	52	9	0	1	16	26	29	2	.218	.269
Pat McNulty	OF111	L	26	118	373	70	117	18	2	6	43	47	23	7	.314	.421
Tris Speaker (EJ)	OF109	L	37	117	429	79	167	35	5	12	87	70	12	5	.389	.578
Charlie Jamieson	OF135	L	32	138	557	109	165	24	5	4	42	72	26	14	.296	.379
Glenn Myatt	C98,OF1	L	27	106	358	51	97	15	9	11	54	29	24	2	.271	.455
Freddie Spurgeon	3B56,2B46,SS3	R	23	107	376	50	108	9	3	0	32	15	21	8	.287	.327
Cliff Lee	OF70	R	28	77	230	43	74	15	6	4	42	21	33	6	.322	.491
Homer Summa	OF54,3B2	L	26	75	224	28	74	10	1	0	25	13	6	3	.330	.384
Luke Sewell	C66,OF2	R	24	74	220	30	51	10	2	0	18	33	18	6	.232	.295
George Uhle	P29	R	26	55	101	10	29	3	3	0	13	7	7	0	.287	.376
Ray Knode (BZ)	1B34	L	24	45	108	13	27	5	0	0	11	10	4	3	.250	.296
Joe Klugman	2B29,1B4,3B2	R	25	38	85	12	28	9	2	0	12	8	4	1	.329	.482
Johnny Hodapp	3B37	R	19	37	130	12	31	5	1	0	14	11	7	2	.238	.292
Sherry Smith	P31	L	34	31	92	9	28	3	1	1	15	6	13	1	.304	.391
Harvey Hendrick	1B3	L	27	25	28	2	8	1	2	0	9	3	5	0	.286	.464
Riggs Stephenson	OF16	R	27	19	54	8	16	3	1	1	9	7	3	1	.296	.444
Fred Eichrodt	OF13	R	22	15	52	4	12	3	1	0	4	2	7	0	.231	.327
Roxy Walters	C5	R	32	12	20	1	4	1	0	0	5	2	3	0	.200	.200

Chuck Tolson 26 R 3-12, Gene Bedford 28 B 0-3, Frank McCrea 28 R 1-5, Dutch Ussat 21 R 0-1

NAME	T	AGE	W	L	PCT	SV	G	GS	CG	IP	H	BB	SO	SHO	ERA
		28	70	84	.455	9	155	155	93	1372	1604	493	345	6	4.49
Garland Buckeye	L	27	13	8	.619	0	30	18	11	153	161	58	49	1	3.65
George Uhle	R	26	13	11	.542	0	29	26	17	211	218	78	68	1	4.09
Benn Karr	R	31	11	12	.478	0	32	24	12	198	248	80	41	1	4.77
Sherry Smith	L	34	11	14	.440	1	31	30	22	237	296	48	30	1	4.86
Jake Miller	L	27	10	13	.435	2	32	22	13	190	207	62	51	0	3.32
Joe Shaute	L	25	4	12	.250	0	26	17	10	131	160	44	34	1	5.43
By Speece	R	28	3	5	.375	1	28	3	3	90	106	28	26	0	4.30
Carl Yowell	L	22	3	4	.400	0	12	4	1	36	40	17	12	0	4.50
Ray Benge	R	23	1	0	1.000	0	2	1	1	12	9	3	3	1	1.50
2 Bert Cole	L	29	1	1	.500	1	13	2	0	44	55	25	9	0	6.14
Emil Levsen	R	27	1	1	.500	0	3	2	2	26	30	16	9	0	5.62
1 Jim Joe Edwards	R	30	0	3	—	0	13	3	1	36	60	23	12	0	8.25
Luther Roy	R	22	0	0	—	0	6	1	0	14	11	1	1	0	3.60

NEW YORK — 7th 69-85 .448 28.5 — MILLER HUGGINS

NAME	G by Pos	B	AGE	G	AB	R	H	2B	3B	HR	RBI	BB	SO	SB	BA	SA
TOTALS			29	156	5353	706	1471	247	74	110	638	470	482	67	.275	.410
Lou Gehrig	1B114,OF6	L	22	126	437	73	129	23	10	20	68	46	49	6	.295	.531
Aaron Ward	2B113,3B10	R	28	125	439	41	108	22	3	4	38	49	49	3	.246	.337
Pee Wee Wanninger	SS111,3B3,2B1	L	23	117	403	35	95	13	6	1	22	11	34	3	.236	.305
Joe Dugan	3B96	R	28	102	404	50	118	19	4	0	31	19	20	2	.292	.359
Babe Ruth (IL)	OF98	L	30	98	359	61	104	12	2	25	66	59	68	2	.290	.543
Earle Combs	OF150	L	26	150	593	117	203	36	13	3	61	65	43	12	.342	.462
Bob Meusel	OF131,3B27	R	28	156	624	101	181	34	12	33	138	54	55	10	.290	.542
Benny Bengough	C94	R	26	95	283	17	73	14	2	0	23	19	9	0	.258	.322
Ben Paschal	OF66	R	29	89	247	49	89	16	5	12	56	22	29	14	.360	.611
Ernie Johnson	2B34,SS28,3B2	R	37	76	170	30	48	5	1	5	17	8	10	6	.282	.412
Wally Schang	C58	B	35	73	167	17	40	5	1	5	24	17	9	3	.240	.335
Howard Shanks	3B26,2B21,OF4	L	34	66	155	15	40	3	1	1	18	20	15	1	.258	.310
Wally Pipp (PB)	1B47	L	32	62	178	19	41	6	3	0	24	13	12	3	.230	.348
2 Bobby Veach	OF33	L	37	56	116	13	41	10	2	0	15	8	0	1	.353	.474
Waite Hoyt	P46	R	25	46	79	5	24	2	3	0	8	2	10	0	.304	.405
Steve O'Neill	C31	R	35	35	91	7	26	5	0	1	13	10	3	0	.286	.374
Whitey Witt	OF10	L	29	31	40	9	8	2	1	0	9	4	2	1	.200	.300
Frank Koenig	SS28	B	22	28	110	14	23	6	1	0	4	5	4	0	.209	.282
1 Everett Scott	SS18	R	32	22	60	3	13	0	0	0	4	1	4	0	.217	.217

Roy Luebbe 24 B 0-15, Fred Merkle 36 R 5-13, Fred Hofmann 31 R 0-2, Leo Durocher 19 R 0-1, Heinie Odom 24, B 1-1

NAME	T	AGE	W	L	PCT	SV	G	GS	CG	IP	H	BB	SO	SHO	ERA
		29	69	85	.448	13	156	156	80	1388	1560	505	492	8	4.33
Herb Pennock	L	31	16	17	.485	2	47	31	21	277	267	71	88	2	2.96
Sad Sam Jones	R	32	15	21	.417	2	43	31	14	247	267	104	92	1	4.63
Urban Shocker	R	34	12	12	.500	2	41	30	15	244	278	58	74	2	3.65
Waite Hoyt	R	25	11	14	.440	6	46	30	17	243	283	78	86	1	4.00
Bob Shawkey	R	34	6	14	.300	3	19	9	6	186	209	67	81	1	4.11
2 Alex Ferguson	R	28	4	2	.667	1	21	6	2	54	83	42	20	0	7.83
Ben Shields	L	22	2	0	1.000	0	7	1	0	25	28	20	5	0	4.88
Garland Braxton	L	25	1	1	.500	0	19	1	0	26	26	11	5	0	6.63
Hank Johnson	R	19	1	1	.250	0	24	4	2	37	37	25	18	0	6.85
Walter Beall	R	25	0	0	—	0	9	1	1	19	11	19	8	0	13.09
1 Ray Francis	L	32	0	0	—	0	6	0	0	9	7	3	1	0	7.20
Charlie Caldwell	R	23	0	0	—	0	3	0	0	5	7	3	0	0	15.00
Jim Marquis	R	24	0	0	—	0	2	1	0	12	5	6	0	0	10.29

BOSTON — 8th 47-105 .309 49.5 — LEE FOHL

NAME	G by Pos	B	AGE	G	AB	R	H	2B	3B	HR	RBI	BB	SO	SB	BA	SA
TOTALS			28	152	5166	639	1375	257	64	41	591	513	422	42	.266	.364
Phil Todt	1B140	L	23	141	544	62	151	29	13	11	75	44	29	3	.278	.439
Bill Wambsganss	2B103,1B6	R	31	111	360	50	83	12	4	1	41	52	21	3	.231	.294
Dud Lee	SS84	R	25	84	255	22	57	7	3	0	19	34	19	2	.224	.275
Doc Prothro	3B108,SS3	R	31	119	415	44	130	23	3	0	51	52	21	9	.313	.383
Ike Boone	OF118	L	28	133	476	79	157	34	5	9	68	60	19	1	.330	.479
Ira Flagstead	OF144	R	31	148	572	84	160	38	2	6	61	63	30	5	.280	.385
2 Roy Carlyle	OF67	L	24	93	276	36	90	20	2	7	49	16	29	1	.326	.496
Val Picinich	C74,1B2	R	28	90	251	31	64	21	0	1	25	33	21	2	.255	.351
Tex Vache	OF53	R	36	110	252	41	79	15	7	3	44	21	33	2	.313	.464
Denny Williams	OF52	L	28	68	218	28	50	13	3	0	13	17	11	2	.229	.261
Homer Ezzell	3B47,2B9	R	29	58	186	40	53	6	4	0	17	16	19	3	.285	.360
Billy Rogell	2B49,SS8	B	20	58	169	12	33	5	1	0	17	11	17	0	.195	.237
Johnnie Heving	C34	R	29	45	119	14	20	7	0	0	6	12	7	0	.168	.227
Bud Connolly	SS34,3B2	R	24	43	107	12	28	7	1	0	11	23	9	0	.262	.346
2 George Bischoff	C40	R	30	41	133	13	37	4	1	1	16	6	11	1	.278	.383
Jack Rothrock	SS22	B	20	22	55	4	19	5	3	0	7	5	4	0	.345	.509
Si Rosenthal	OF17	L	21	19	72	6	19	5	2	0	1	3	3	1	.264	.389
Al Stokes	C17	R	25	17	57	2	12	0	0	0	5	5	6	0	.212	.250
Tom Jenkins	OF15	R	27	15	64	9	19	5	0	0	5	4	8	0	.297	.359
Herb Welch	SS13	R	26	14	46	2	13	0	0	0	4	3	7	1	.283	.348
Mike Herrara	2B10	R	27	10	39	2	15	1	0	0	7	4	2	1	.385	.385
Turkey Gross	SS9	R	23	9	32	1	3	0	0	0	2	1	6	0	.094	.094
1 Joe Harris	1B6	R	34	8	19	4	3	1	0	0	3	1	2	0	.158	.368

Chappie Geygan 22 2-11, Shano Collins 39 R 1-3, 1 Bobby Veach 37 L 1-5

NAME	T	AGE	W	L	PCT	SV	G	GS	CG	IP	H	BB	SO	SHO	ERA
		28	47	105	.309	6	152	152	68	1327	1615	510	310	6	4.96
Ted Wingfield	R	25	12	19	.387	2	41	27	18	254	267	92	30	2	3.97
Howard Ehmke	R	31	9	20	.310	1	34	31	22	261	285	95	95	0	3.69
Red Ruffing	R	21	9	18	.333	1	37	27	13	217	253	75	64	3	5.02
1 Jack Quinn	R	41	7	8	.467	0	19	15	8	105	140	26	24	0	4.37
Paul Zahniser	R	28	5	12	.294	1	37	21	7	177	232	89	30	1	5.14
Buster Ross	L	23	3	8	.273	3	33	8	0	94	119	40	15	0	6.22
Rudy Kallio	R	33	1	6	.143	0	13	7	2	72	93	37	13	0	7.58
Hal Neubauer	R	23	1	0	1.000	0	7	0	0	11	18	14	2	0	12.60
Joe Lucey	R	28	0	1	.000	0	9	1	0	11	18	14	2	0	9.00
2 Ray Francis	L	32	0	2	.000	0	5	4	0	13	44	13	4	0	7.71
2 Alex Ferguson	R	28	0	2	.000	0	5	4	0	16	22	5	5	0	10.69
Joe Kiefer	R	25	0	2	.000	0	4	4	0	16	22	6	5	0	6.00
Curt Fullerton	R	26	0	3	.000	0	5	3	1	23	22	9	3	0	3.13
Oscar Fuhr	L	31	0	6	.000	0	39	5	1	91	138	30	27	0	6.63
Bob Adams	R	23	0	0	—	0	6	0	0	10	3	1	1	0	7.50

PITTSBURGH 1ST 95-58 .621 BILL McKECHNIE

NAME	G by Pos	B	AGE	G	AB	R	H	2B	3B	HR	RBI	BB	SO	SB	BA	SA
TOTALS			28	153	5372	912	1651	316	105	78	820	499	363	159	.307	.449
George Grantham	1B102	L	25	114	359	74	117	24	6	8	52	50	29	14	.326	.493
Eddie Moore	2B122, OF15, 3B3	R	26	142	547	106	163	29	8	6	77	73	26	19	.298	.413
Glenn Wright	SS153, 3B1	R	24	153	614	97	189	32	10	18	121	31	32	3	.308	.480
Pie Traynor	3B150, SS1	R	26	150	591	114	189	39	14	6	106	52	19	15	.320	.464
Kiki Cuyler	OF153	L	26	153	617	144	220	43	26	18	102	58	56	41	.357	.598
Max Carey	OF130	B	35	133	542	109	186	39	13	5	44	66	19	46	.343	.491
Clyde Barnhart	OF138	R	29	142	539	85	175	32	11	4	114	59	25	9	.325	.447
Earl Smith	C96	L	28	109	329	34	103	22	3	6	64	31	13	4	.313	.471
Johnny Gooch	C76	B	27	79	215	24	64	8	4	0	30	20	16	1	.298	.372
Carson Bigbee	OF42	L	30	66	126	31	30	7	0	0	8	7	8	2	.238	.294
Stuffy McInnis	1B46	R	34	59	155	19	57	10	4	0	24	17	1	1	.368	.484
Johnny Rawlings	2B29	R	32	36	110	17	31	7	0	2	13	8	8	1	.282	.400
1 Al Niehaus	1B15	R	26	17	64	7	14	8	0	0	7	1	5	0	.219	.344
Roy Spencer	C11	R	25	14	28	1	6	1	0	0	1	1	5	1	.214	.250
Fresco Thompson	2B12	R	23	14	37	4	9	2	1	0	8	4	1	2	.243	.351
Mule Haas	OF2	L	21	4	3	1	0	0	0	0	0	0	0	1	.000	.000
Jewel Ens	1B3	R	35	3	5	1	4	1	0	0	1	0	0	0	.800	.800

NAME	T	AGE	W	L	PCT	SV	G	GS	CG	IP	H	BB	SO	SHO	ERA
TOTALS		32	95	58	.621	13	153	153	77	1355	1526	387	386	2	3.87
Lee Meadows	R	32	19	10	.655	1	35	31	20	255	272	67	87	1	3.67
Ray Kremer	R	32	17	8	.680	1	40	27	14	215	232	47	62	0	3.68
Johnny Morrison	R	29	17	14	.548	4	44	26	10	211	245	60	60	0	3.88
Emil Yde	L	25	17	9	.654	3	33	28	13	207	254	75	41	0	4.13
Vic Aldridge	R	31	15	7	.682	0	33	26	14	213	218	74	88	1	3.63
Babe Adams	R	43	6	5	.545	3	33	10	3	101	129	17	18	0	5.44
Red Oldham	L	31	3	2	.600	1	22	7	1	53	66	18	10	0	3.91
2 Tom Sheehan	R	31	1	1	.500	2	23	0	0	57	63	13	13	0	2.68
Bud Culloton	R	28	0	1	.000	0	9	1	0	21	19	1	3	0	2.57
Don Songer	R	26	0	1	.000	0	12	1	0	21	19	1	3	0	2.25
Lou Koupal	R	26	0	0	—	0	6	0	0	9	14	7	0	0	9.00

NEW YORK 2nd 86-66 .566 8.5 JOHN McGRAW

NAME	G by Pos	B	AGE	G	AB	R	H	2B	3B	HR	RBI	BB	SO	SB	BA	SA
TOTALS			27	152	5327	736	1507	239	61	114	682	411	494	79	.283	.415
Bill Terry	1B126	L	26	133	489	75	156	31	6	11	70	42	52	4	.319	.474
George Kelly	2B108, 1B25, OF17	R	29	147	586	87	181	29	3	20	99	35	54	5	.309	.471
Travis Jackson (KJ)	SS110	R	21	112	411	51	117	15	2	9	59	24	43	8	.285	.397
Fred Lindstrom (BG)	3B96, 2B1, SS1	R	19	104	356	43	102	15	12	4	33	22	20	5	.287	.430
Ross Youngs	OF127, 2B3	L	28	130	500	82	132	24	6	6	53	66	51	17	.264	.372
Billy Southworth	OF119	L	32	123	473	79	138	19	5	6	44	51	11	6	.292	.391
Irish Meusel	OF126	R	32	135	516	82	169	35	8	21	111	26	19	5	.328	.548
Frank Snyder	C96	R	31	107	325	21	78	9	1	5	51	20	49	0	.240	.375
Frankie Frisch (HJ)	3B46, 2B42, SS39	B	26	120	502	89	166	26	6	11	48	32	14	21	.331	.472
Jack Bentley	P28, OF3, 1B1	L	30	64	99	10	30	5	2	3	18	9	11	0	.303	.485
Hack Wilson	OF50	R	25	62	180	28	43	7	4	6	30	21	33	5	.239	.422
Hank Gowdy	C41	R	35	47	114	14	37	4	3	3	19	12	7	0	.325	.491
Grover Hartley	C37, 1B8	R	36	46	95	9	30	1	1	0	8	3	2	2	.316	.347
Frank Walter	OF21	R	30	39	81	12	18	1	0	1	5	9	11	1	.222	.272
Doc Farrell	SS13, 3B7, 2B1	R	23	27	56	6	12	1	0	0	4	6	6	0	.214	.232
Heinie Groh (KJ)	3B16, 2B2	R	35	25	65	7	15	4	0	0	4	6	3	0	.231	.292
Mickey Devine	C11, 3B1	R	33	21	33	6	9	3	0	0	4	6	3	0	.273	.364
Pip Koehler	OF3	R	23	12	2	1	0	0	0	0	0	0	0	0	.000	.000
Hugh McMullen	C5	B	23	5	15	1	2	1	0	0	0	0	3	0	.133	.200
Earl Webb		L	27	4	3	0	0	0	0	0	0	0	0	0	.000	.000
Al Moore	OF2	R	22	2	8	0	1	0	0	0	0	0	1	2	.125	.125
Blackie Carter	OF1	R	22	2	4	0	0	0	0	0	0	0	0	0	.000	.000

NAME	T	AGE	W	L	PCT	SV	G	GS	CG	IP	H	BB	SO	SHO	ERA
TOTALS		28	86	66	.566	8	152	152	80	1354	1532	408	446	6	3.94
Virgil Barnes	R	28	15	11	.577	2	32	27	17	222	242	53	53	1	3.53
Jack Scott	R	33	14	15	.483	3	36	28	18	240	251	55	87	2	3.15
Kent Greenfield	R	23	12	8	.600	0	29	20	12	172	195	64	66	0	3.87
Jack Bentley	L	30	11	9	.550	0	28	22	11	157	200	59	47	0	5.04
Art Nehf	L	32	11	9	.550	1	29	20	8	155	193	50	63	1	3.77
Wayland Dean	R	23	10	7	.588	1	33	14	6	151	169	50	53	1	4.65
Freddie Fitzsimmons	R	23	6	3	.667	0	10	8	6	75	70	18	17	1	2.64
Walter Huntzinger	R	26	5	1	.833	0	26	1	0	64	68	17	19	0	3.52
Hugh McQuillan	R	29	2	3	.400	1	14	11	2	70	95	23	23	0	6.04
John Wisner	R	25	0	0	—	0	25	0	0	40	33	14	13	0	3.83
Chick Davies	R	33	0	0	—	1	2	1	0	7	13	4	5	0	6.43
Harry Baldwin	R	25	0	0	—	0	1	1	0	1	1	1	0	0	9.00

CINCINNATI 3rd 80-73 .523 15 JACK HENDRICKS

NAME	G by Pos	B	AGE	G	AB	R	H	2B	3B	HR	RBI	BB	SO	SB	BA	SA
TOTALS			29	153	5233	690	1490	221	90	44	624	409	327	108	.285	.387
2 Walter Holke	1B65	B	32	65	232	24	65	8	4	1	20	17	12	1	.280	.362
Hughie Critz	2B144	R	24	144	541	74	150	14	8	2	51	34	17	13	.277	.344
Ike Caveney	SS111	R	30	115	358	38	89	9	5	2	47	28	31	2	.249	.318
Babe Pinelli	3B109, SS17	R	29	130	492	68	139	33	6	2	49	22	28	8	.283	.394
Curt Walker	OF141	L	28	145	509	86	162	22	16	6	71	57	31	14	.318	.460
Edd Roush	OF134	L	32	134	540	91	183	28	16	8	83	35	14	22	.339	.483
Billy Zitzmann	OF89, SS1	R	27	104	301	53	76	13	9	0	21	35	22	11	.252	.316
Bubbles Hargrave	C84	R	32	87	273	28	82	13	6	2	33	25	23	4	.300	.414
Rube Bressler (NJ)	1B52, OF38	L	30	97	319	43	111	17	6	4	61	40	16	9	.348	.476
Elmer Smith	OF80	L	32	96	284	47	77	13	7	8	46	28	20	6	.271	.451
Chuck Dressen	3B47, 2B5, OF4	R	26	76	215	35	59	8	2	3	19	12	4	5	.274	.372
Sammy Bohne	SS49, 2B10, OF4, 1B2, 3B2	B	28	73	214	24	55	9	1	2	24	14	14	9	.257	.336
Ivy Wingo	C55	L	34	55	146	6	30	7	0	0	12	11	8	1	.205	.253
2 Al Niehaus	1B45	R	26	51	147	16	44	10	2	0	14	13	10	1	.299	.395
Pete Donohue	P42	R	24	43	109	13	32	3	1	1	12	4	9	0	.294	.367
Ernie Krueger	C30	L	34	37	88	7	27	4	0	1	7	6	8	1	.307	.386
2 Joe Schultz	OF15, 2B1	L	31	33	62	6	20	3	1	0	13	3	1	3	.323	.403
Astyanax Douglass	C7	L	27	7	17	1	3	0	0	0	1	1	3	0	.176	.176

Frank Bruggy 34 R 3-14, Boob Fowler 24 L 2-5, Jimmy Hudgens 22 L 3-7, Ollie Klee 25 L 0-1, 2 Hy Myers 36 R 1-6, Tom Sullivan 18 R 0-1, Jake Daubert (DD) 40

NAME	T	AGE	W	L	PCT	SV	G	GS	CG	IP	H	BB	SO	SHO	ERA
TOTALS		30	80	73	.523	12	153	153	92	1375	1447	324	437	11	3.38
Eppa Rixey	L	34	21	11	.656	1	39	36	22	287	302	47	69	2	2.89
Pete Donohue	R	24	21	14	.600	2	42	38	27	301	310	49	78	3	3.08
Dolf Luque	R	34	16	18	.471	0	36	36	22	291	263	78	140	4	2.63
Rube Benton	R	35	9	10	.474	1	33	16	6	147	182	34	36	1	4.04
Jackie May	L	29	9	9	.471	2	36	12	7	137	146	45	74	1	3.88
Carl Mays (SA)	R	33	3	5	.375	2	12	5	3	52	60	13	10	0	3.29
Neal Brady	R	28	1	3	.250	1	20	3	2	64	73	20	12	0	4.64
1 Tom Sheehan	R	31	1	0	1.000	1	3	1	1	29	37	12	5	0	8.07
Harry Biemiller	R	27	0	1	.000	2	23	1	0	47	45	21	9	0	4.02
Marv Goodwin	R	34	0	2	.000	0	4	3	2	21	26	5	4	0	4.71
Pedro Dibut	R	32	0	0	—	0	1	0	0	3				0	

ST. LOUIS 4th 77-76 .503 18 BRANCH RICKEY 13-25 .342 ROGERS HORNSBY 64-51 .557

NAME	G by Pos	B	AGE	G	AB	R	H	2B	3B	HR	RBI	BB	SO	SB	BA	SA
TOTALS			27	153	5329	828	1592	292	80	109	752	446	414	70	.299	.445
Jim Bottomley	1B153	L	25	153	619	92	227	44	12	21	128	47	36	3	.367	.578
Rogers Hornsby	2B136	R	29	138	504	133	203	41	10	39	143	83	39	5	.403	.756
Specs Toporcer	SS66, 2B7	R	26	83	268	38	76	11	2	1	18	41	9	1	.284	.384
Les Bell	3B153, SS1	R	23	153	586	80	167	29	9	11	88	43	47	4	.285	.422
Chick Hafey	OF88	R	22	93	358	36	108	25	2	5	57	10	29	3	.302	.425
Heinie Mueller (BF)	OF72	R	25	78	243	33	76	16	4	1	26	17	11	9	.313	.424
Ray Blades	OF114, 3B1	R	28	122	462	112	150	37	8	12	57	69	47	6	.342	.535
2 Bob O'Farrell	C92	R	28	94	317	37	88	13	2	3	32	46	26	0	.278	.360
Jack Smith	OF64	L	30	80	243	53	61	11	4	4	31	19	13	20	.251	.379
Max Flack	OF59	L	35	59	241	23	60	7	8	0	28	21	9	5	.249	.344
Ralph Shinners	OF66	R	29	74	251	39	74	11	2	0	36	12	19	8	.295	.430
Jimmy Cooney	SS37, 2B15, OF1	R	30	54	187	27	51	11	2	0	18	4	5	1	.273	.353
Tommy Thevenow	SS50	R	21	50	175	17	47	7	2	0	17	12	7	12	.269	.331
Walter Schmidt	C31	R	38	37	87	9	22	3	1	0	8	4	3	1	.253	.299
Taylor Douthit	OF21	R	24	30	73	13	20	3	1	1	8	8	2	6	.274	.384
Art Reinhart	P20	L	26	28	67	9	22	2	1	0	7	2	10	2	.328	.388
1 Mike Gonzalez	C22	R	34	22	71	9	22	3	0	0	4	6	2	1	.310	.352
Ernie Vick	C9	R	24	14	32	3	6	2	0	0	3	3	1	0	.188	.313
Wattie Holm	OF13	R	23	14	58	10	12	1	1	0	2	3	6	1	.207	.259
Bill Warwick	C13	R	27	13	41	8	12	1	2	1	6	5	5	0	.293	.488
1 Howard Freigau	SS7, 2B1	R	23	9	26	4	4	0	0	0	0	0	2	1	.154	.154
13 Hy Myers		R	36	2	1	1	1	0	0	0	0	0	0	0	1.000	1.000

NAME	T	AGE	W	L	PCT	SV	G	GS	CG	IP	H	BB	SO	SHO	ERA
TOTALS		27	77	76	.503	7	153	153	82	1336	1480	470	428	8	4.36
Bill Sherdel	L	28	15	6	.714	1	32	21	17	200	216	42	53	2	3.11
Jesse Haines	R	31	13	14	.481	0	29	25	15	207	234	52	63	0	4.57
Art Reinhart	L	26	11	5	.688	0	20	16	15	145	149	47	24	1	3.04
Allan Sothoron	R	32	10	10	.500	0	28	22	8	156	173	63	67	2	4.04
Flint Rhem	R	24	8	13	.381	1	34	24	8	170	204	58	66	1	4.92
Duster Mails (SJ)	L	30	7	7	.500	0	21	16	9	131	145	58	49	0	4.60
Eddie Dyer (SA)	L	25	4	3	.571	3	27	5	3	82	93	24	25	0	4.17
Leo Dickerman	R	28	4	11	.267	1	29	18	7	131	135	79	40	2	5.56
Johnny Stuart	R	24	2	2	.500	0	11	1	1	47	52	24	14	0	6.13
Pea Ridge Day	R	26	1	4	.333	1	17	4	1	40	53	7	13	0	6.30
Wild Bill Hallahan	L	22	1	0	1.000	0	6	0	0	15	14	11	8	0	3.60
Ed Clough	L	18	0	0	—	0	10	1	0	11	15	3	0	0	8.10
Gil Paulsen	R	22	0	0	—	0	1	0	0	6	13	5	1	0	0.00

BOSTON 5th 70-83 .468 25 DAVE BANCROFT

NAME	G by Pos	B	AGE	G	AB	R	H	2B	3B	HR	RBI	BB	SO	SB	BA	SA
TOTALS			28	153	5365	708	1567	260	70	41	643	405	380	77	.292	.390
Dick Burrus	1B151	L	27	152	588	82	200	41	4	5	87	51	29	8	.340	.426
2 Doc Gautreau	2B68	R	24	80	279	45	73	3	0	0	23	35	13	11	.262	.330
Dave Bancroft	SS125	B	34	128	479	75	153	29	8	2	49	64	22	7	.319	.426
Bill Marriott	3B89, OF1	L	32	103	370	37	99	11	1	1	40	28	26	3	.268	.305
Jim Welsh	OF116, 2B3	L	23	122	484	69	151	25	8	4	63	29	24	7	.312	.440
Gus Felix	OF114	R	30	121	459	60	141	25	7	2	66	30	34	5	.307	.405
Bernie Neis	OF87	B	29	106	355	47	101	25	4	5	45	38	19	6	.285	.434
Frank Gibson	C86, 1B2	B	34	104	316	36	88	23	5	2	50	15	28	3	.278	.402
Dave Harris	OF90	R	25	92	340	49	90	8	7	5	36	27	44	6	.265	.374
Ernie Padgett	2B47, SS18, 3B7	R	26	88	256	31	78	9	7	0	29	14	14	3	.305	.395
Mickey O'Neill	C69	R	27	70	222	29	57	6	3	0	30	21	16	1	.257	.356
2 Andy High	3B60, 2B1	L	27	60	219	31	63	11	4	1	28	24	2	3	.288	.402
Les Mann	OF57	R	32	60	184	27	63	11	4	2	23	5	11	6	.342	.478
Bob Smith	SS21, 2B15, P13, OF1	R	30	58	174	17	49	9	4	0	23	5	6	2	.282	.379
Johnny Cooney	P31, 1B3, OF1	L	24	54	103	17	33	7	0	0	13	6	6	1	.320	.388
Oscar Siemer	C16	L	23	16	46	5	14	1	0	0	2	6	4	0	.304	.413
Casey Stengel	OF1	L	34	12	13	0	1	0	0	0	2	4	5	1	.077	.077
Frank Wilson	OF10	R	24	12	31	3	6	1	0	0	0	4	8	0	.194	.226
Hod Kibbie	2B8, SS3	R	21	11	41	5	11	0	1	0	4	6	5	0	.268	.317
Shanty Hogan	OF5	R	19	9	21	2	6	1	0	0	2	1	3	0	.286	.429
Red Lucas	2B6	L	23	6	20	1	3	0	0	0	2	0	4	0	.150	.150
Abie Hood	2B5	R	23	6	13	2	4	1	0	0	1	0	0	0	.268	.524
Herb Thomas	2B5	R	23	5	17	2	4	1	0	0	1	0	0	0	.235	.353

Ed Sperber 30 L 0-2, Dee Cousineau 26 R 0-0

NAME	T	AGE	W	L	PCT	SV	G	GS	CG	IP	H	BB	SO	SHO	ERA
TOTALS		28	70	83	.458	4	153	153	77	1367	1567	458	351	5	4.39
Larry Benton	R	27	14	7	.667	1	31	21	16	183	170	70	49	2	3.10
Johnny Cooney	L	24	14	14	.500	0	31	29	20	246	267	50	65	2	3.48
Joe Genewich	R	28	12	10	.545	0	34	21	10	169	185	41	34	0	4.40
Jesse Barnes	R	32	11	16	.407	0	32	28	17	216	253	63	55	0	4.54
Kyle Graham	R	25	7	12	.368	1	34	23	5	157	177	62	32	0	4.41
Bob Smith	R	30	5	3	.625	0	13	10	6	93	110	36	19	0	4.45
Ike Kamp	L	24	3	4	.333	0	24	4	1	58	68	35	12	0	5.12
Rube Marquard	L	38	2	8	.200	0	26	8	1	72	105	27	19	0	5.75
Rosy Ryan	R	27	2	8	.200	2	37	7	1	123	152	52	48	0	6.29
Bill Vargus	L	25	1	1	.500	1	11	2	1	36	45	13	5	0	4.00
Joe Batchelder	R	27	0	0	—	0	7	0	1	10	11	2	0	0	5.14
Bill Anderson	R	29	0	0	—	0	4	0	0	9	7	10	1	2	9.00
Foster Edwards	R	21	0	0	—	0	6	1	0	8	16	5	1	0	9.00
Tim McNamara	R	26	0	0	—	0	1	0	0	1	6	3	0	0	81.00
Joe Ogrodowski	R	18	0	0	—	0	1	0	0	1	6	3	0	0	54.00

NAME	G by Pos	B	AGE	G	AB	R	H	2B	3B	HR	RBI	BB	SO	SB	BA	SA
BROOKLYN	**6th(Tie)** 68-85 .444 27															
TOTALS			31	153	5468	786	1617	250	80	64	722	437	383	37	.296	.406
Jack Fournier	1B145	L	35	145	545	99	191	21	16	22	130	86	39	4	.350	.569
Milt Stock	2B141, 3B5	R	31	146	615	98	202	28	9	1	62	38	28	8	.328	.408
Johnny Mitchell	SS90	B	30	97	336	45	84	8	3	0	18	28	19	2	.250	.292
Jimmy Johnston	3B81, OF20, 1B8, SS2	R	35	123	431	63	128	23	2	3	43	45	15	7	.297	.355
Dick Cox	OF111	R	29	122	434	68	143	23	10	7	64	37	29	4	.329	.477
Eddie Brown	OF153	R	33	153	618	88	189	39	11	9	99	22	18	6	.306	.429
Zack Wheat	OF149	L	37	150	616	125	221	42	14	14	103	45	22	3	.359	.541
Zack Taylor	C96	R	26	109	352	33	109	16	4	3	44	17	19	0	.310	.403
Cotton Tierney	3B61, 1B1, 2B1	R	31	93	265	27	68	14	4	2	39	12	23	0	.257	.362
Hank DeBerry	C55	R	30	67	193	26	50	11	4	2	24	16	8	2	.259	.342
Hod Ford (HO)	SS66	R	27	66	216	32	59	11	0	1	15	26	15	0	.273	.338
Dick Loftus	OF38	L	24	51	131	16	31	6	0	0	13	5	6	2	.237	.282
Charlie Hargreaves	C18, 1B2	L	28	45	83	9	23	3	0	0	13	6	1	1	.277	.337
1 Andy High	SS14	B	27	44	115	11	23	4	1	0	6	14	5	0	.200	.252
Chuck Corgan	2B14	R	22	14	47	4	8	1	1	0	3	2	9	0	.170	.234
1 Tommy Griffith	OF2	L	35	7	4	2	0	0	0	0	0	0	2	0	.000	.000
Roy Hutson	OF4	L	23	7	8	1	0	0	0	0	1	1	1	0	.000	.000
2 Bob Barrett		R	26	1	1	0	0	0	0	0	0	0	0	0	.000	.000
Jerry Standaert		R	23	1	0	0	0	0	0	0	0	0	0	0	.000	.000
PHILADELPHIA	**6th(Tie)** 68-85 .444 27															
TOTALS			29	153	5412	812	1598	288	58	100	731	456	542	48	.295	.425
Chicken Hawks	1B90	L	29	105	320	52	103	15	5	5	45	32	33	3	.322	.447
2 Barney Friberg	2B77, 3B14, C1, P1	R	25	91	304	41	82	12	1	5	22	39	35	1	.270	.365
Heinie Sand	SS143	R	27	148	496	69	138	30	7	3	55	64	65	1	.278	.385
Clarence Huber	3B120	R	29	124	436	46	124	28	5	5	54	17	33	3	.284	.406
Cy Williams	OF96	L	37	107	314	78	104	11	5	13	60	53	34	4	.331	.522
George Harper	OF126	L	33	132	495	86	173	25	7	18	97	28	32	10	.349	.558
George Burns	OF88	R	35	88	349	65	102	29	4	3	22	33	20	4	.292	.390
Jimmie Wilson	C89, OF1	R	24	108	335	42	110	19	3	4	54	32	25	5	.328	.430
Lew Fonseca	2B69, 1B55	R	26	126	467	78	149	30	5	7	60	21	42	6	.319	.460
Butch Henline	C68, OF1	R	30	93	263	43	80	12	5	8	48	24	16	3	.304	.479
R.Wrightstone	OF45, SS12, 3B11, 2B10, 1B6	L	32	92	286	48	99	18	5	14	61	19	18	0	.346	.591
Johnny Mokan	OF68	R	29	75	209	30	69	11	2	6	42	27	9	3	.330	.488
Wally Kimmick	SS28, 3B21, 2B13	R	28	70	141	16	43	3	2	1	10	22	26	1	.305	.376
Freddy Leach	OF65	L	27	65	292	47	91	15	4	5	28	5	21	1	.312	.442
Clarence Mitchell	P32, 1B2	L	34	52	92	7	18	2	0	0	13	5	9	2	.196	.217
1 Walter Holke	1B23	B	32	39	86	11	21	5	0	1	17	3	6	0	.244	.337
1 Joe Schultz	OF20	R	31	24	64	10	22	6	0	0	8	4	1	1	.344	.438
Lew Wendell	C9	R	33	18	26	0	2	0	0	0	3	1	3	0	.077	.077
Lenny Metz	SS9, 2B2	R	25	11	14	1	0	0	0	0	1	0	0	0	.000	.000
George Durning	OF4	L	27	5	14	3	5	0	0	0	1	0	1	0	.357	.357
Benny Meyer	2B1	R	40	1	1	0	0	0	0	0	1	0	0	0	1.000	2.000
CHICAGO	**8th** 68-86 .442 27.5															
TOTALS			28	154	5353	723	1473	254	70	86	660	397	470	94	.275	.397
Charlie Grimm	1B139	L	26	141	519	73	159	29	5	10	76	38	25	4	.306	.439
Sparky Adams	2B144, SS5	R	31	149	627	95	180	29	2	8	48	44	15	26	.287	.368
Rabbit Maranville (BL)	SS74	R	33	75	266	37	62	10	3	0	23	29	20	6	.233	.293
2 Howard Freigau	3B96, SS17, 1B7	R	22	117	476	77	146	22	10	8	71	30	31	10	.307	.445
Cliff Heathcote	OF99	L	27	109	380	57	100	14	5	5	39	39	26	15	.263	.366
Mandy Brooks	OF89	R	27	90	349	55	98	25	7	14	72	19	28	10	.281	.513
Art Jahn	OF58	R	29	58	226	30	68	10	8	0	37	11	20	2	.301	.416
Gabby Hartnett	C110	R	24	117	398	61	115	28	3	24	67	36	77	1	.289	.555
2 Tommy Griffith	OF60	L	35	76	235	38	67	12	1	7	27	21	11	2	.285	.434
2 Mike Gonzalez	C50, 1B9	R	34	70	197	26	52	13	1	3	18	13	15	2	.264	.386
Butch Weis (IL)	OF47	L	24	67	180	16	48	5	3	2	25	23	22	2	.267	.361
Pinky Pittinger	SS24, 3B24	R	28	59	173	21	54	7	2	0	15	12	7	5	.312	.376
Denver Grigsby (BC)	OF39	L	24	51	137	20	35	5	0	0	20	19	12	1	.255	.292
2 Barney Friberg	3B26, OF12, 1B6, SS2	R	25	44	152	12	39	5	3	1	16	14	22	0	.257	.349
Jigger Statz	OF37	R	27	38	148	21	38	9	4	1	16	11	12	0	.257	.378
Ike McAuley	SS37	R	33	37	125	10	35	7	2	0	11	11	12	1	.280	.368
Hack Miller	OF21	R	31	24	86	10	24	3	2	2	9	2	6	0	.279	.430
Ralph Michaels	3B15, 1B1, 2B1, SS1	R	23	22	50	10	14	1	0	0	6	6	9	1	.280	.300
1 Bob O'Farrell	C3	R	28	17	22	2	4	1	0	3	2	5	1	0	.182	.273
1 Red Barrett	3B6, 2B4	R	26	14	32	1	10	1	0	0	7	1	4	1	.313	.344
Alex Metzler	OF9	L	22	9	38	7	7	0	0	0	3	1	4	0	.184	.237
Joe Munson	OF9	R	25	9	35	5	13	3	1	0	9	1	1	1	.371	.514

Chink Taylor 27 R 0-6, Gale Staley 26 R 11-26, John Churry 24 R 3-6, Ted Kearns 25 R 1-2, Mel Kerr 22 L 0-0

NAME	T	AGE	W	L	PCT	SV	G	GS	CG	IP	H	BB	SO	SHO	ERA
(Brooklyn pitching)		28	68	85	.444	4	153	153	82	1351	1608	477	518	4	4.77
Dazzy Vance	R	24	22	9	.710	0	31	31	26	265	247	66	221	4	3.53
Burleigh Grimes	R	31	12	19	.387	0	33	31	19	247	305	102	73	0	5.03
Rube Ehrhardt	R	30	10	14	.417	1	36	25	12	208	239	62	47	0	5.02
Jesse Petty	L	30	9	9	.500	0	28	21	7	153	188	47	59	0	4.88
Tiny Osborne	R	32	8	15	.348	1	41	22	10	175	210	75	59	0	4.94
2 Bill Hubbell	R	28	3	6	.667	1	33	5	3	87	120	24	16	0	5.28
Nelson Greene	L	25	2	0	1.000	0	11	0	0	22	45	7	4	0	10.64
Guy Cantrell	R	21	1	0	1.000	0	14	3	1	36	42	14	13	0	3.00
Joe Oeschger	R	33	1	2	.333	0	21	3	1	37	60	19	6	0	6.08
Andy Rush	R	25	0	1	.000	0	3	2	1	9	13	6	4	0	9.00
Jumbo Jim Elliott	L	24	0	2	.000	0	8	1	0	11	17	9	3	0	8.18
Bob McGraw	R	30	0	2	.000	0	3	2	1	20	14	13	3	0	3.15
Lloyd Brown	L	20	0	0	.000	0	17	5	1	63	79	25	23	0	4.14
Hank Thormahlen	L	28	0	3	.000	0	4	2	0	16	22	9	7	0	3.94
Jim Roberts	R	29	0	0	—	0	1	0	0	1	3	0	0	0	18.00
1 Art Decatur	R	31	0	0	—	1	1								
Bill Doak (VR) 34															
(Philadelphia pitching)		30	68	85	.444	9	153	153	69	1351	1753	444	371	8	5.02
Jimmy Ring	R	30	14	16	.467	0	38	37	21	270	325	119	93	1	4.37
Hal Carlson	R	33	13	14	.481	0	35	32	18	234	281	52	80	4	4.23
Clarence Mitchell	L	34	10	17	.370	1	32	26	12	199	245	51	46	1	5.29
Jack Knight	R	30	7	6	.538	3	33	11	4	105	161	36	19	0	6.86
Ray Pierce	L	28	5	4	.556	0	23	8	4	90	134	24	18	0	5.50
Johnny Couch	R	34	5	6	.455	2	34	7	2	94	112	31	11	1	5.46
Huck Betts	R	28	4	5	.444	1	35	7	1	97	146	38	28	0	5.57
2 Art Decatur	R	31	4	13	.235	2	25	15	4	128	170	35	31	0	5.27
Dutch Ulrich	R	25	3	3	.500	0	21	4	2	65	73	12	29	1	3.05
Claude Willoughby	R	26	2	1	.667	0	5	3	2	26	26	11	6	0	1.96
Dana Fillingim	R	31	1	0	1.000	0	5	1	0	9	19	6	2	0	10.00
Skinny O'Neal	R	26	0	0	—	0	11	0	0	20	35	12	6	0	9.45
Roy Crumpler	L	28	0	0	—	0	3	0	0	4	3	3	0	0	7.20
Bob Vines	R	28	0	0	—	0	3	0	0	4	8	2	0	0	11.25
1 Bill Hubbell	R	28	0	0	—	0	5	0	0	9	15	4	3	0	0.00
2 Barney Friberg	R	25	0	0	—	0	1	0	0	4	4	1	1	0	4.50
(Chicago pitching)		28	68	86	.442	10	154	154	75	1374	1579	488	436	5	4.41
Pete Alexander	R	38	15	11	.577	0	32	30	20	236	270	29	63	1	3.39
Tony Kaufmann	R	24	13	13	.500	2	32	23	14	196	221	77	49	2	4.50
Wilbur Cooper	L	33	12	14	.462	0	32	26	13	212	249	61	41	0	4.29
Sheriff Blake	R	25	10	18	.357	2	36	31	14	231	260	114	93	0	4.87
Percy Jones	L	25	6	6	.500	0	28	13	6	124	123	71	60	1	4.65
Guy Bush	R	23	6	13	.316	4	42	15	5	182	213	52	76	0	4.30
Elmer Jacobs	R	32	2	3	.400	1	18	4	1	56	63	22	19	1	5.14
Vic Keen	R	26	2	6	.250	1	30	8	1	83	125	41	19	0	6.29
Herb Brett	R	25	1	1	.500	0	10	1	0	17	12	3	6	0	3.71
George Milstead	L	22	1	1	.500	0	21	1	1	26	8	7	0	3.00
Jumbo Brown	R	18	0	0	—	0	2	0	0	6	5	4	2	0	3.00
George Stueland	R	26	0	0	—	0	4	1	0	3	3	2	2	0	9.00
Bob Osborn	R	22	0	0	—	0	2	0	0	6	6	0	0	0	0.00
1 Barney Friberg	R	25	0	0	—	0	4	4	3	1	1	0	0	4.50

Managers: WILBERT ROBINSON (Brooklyn); ART FLETCHER (Philadelphia); BILL KILLEFER 33-42 .440 / RABBIT MARANVILLE 23-30 .434 / GEORGE GIBSON 12-14 .462 (Chicago)

WORLD SERIES — PITTSBURGH (NL) 4 WASHINGTON (AL) 3

LINE SCORES

TEAM	1	2	3	4	5	6	7	8	9	10	11	12	R	H	E
Game 1 October 7 at Pittsburgh															
WAS (AL)	0	1	0	0	2	0	0	0	1				4	8	1
PIT (NL)	0	0	0	0	1	0	0	0	0				1	5	0
Johnson						Meadows, Morrison (9)									
Game 2 October 8 at Pittsburgh															
WAS	0	1	0	0	0	0	0	0	1				2	8	2
PIT	0	0	0	1	0	0	0	2	X				3	7	0
Coveleski						Aldridge									
Game 3 October 10 at Washington															
PIT	0	1	0	1	0	1	0	0	0				3	8	3
WAS	0	0	1	0	0	1	0	2	X				4	10	1
Kremer						Ferguson, Marberry (8)									
Game 4 October 11 at Washington															
PIT	0	0	0	0	0	0	0	0	0				0	6	1
WAS	0	0	4	0	0	0	0	0	X				4	12	0
Yde, Morrison (3), Adams (8)					Johnson										
Game 5 October 12 at Washington															
PIT	0	0	2	0	0	0	2	1	1				6	13	0
WAS	1	0	0	1	0	0	1	0	0				3	8	1
Aldridge					Coveleski, Ballou (7), Zachary (8), Marberry (9)										
Game 6 October 13 at Pittsburgh															
WAS	1	1	0	0	0	0	0	0	0				2	6	2
PIT	0	0	0	1	2	0	0	0	X				3	7	1
Ferguson, Ballou (8)					Kremer										
Game 7 October 15 at Pittsburgh															
WAS	4	0	0	2	0	0	0	1	0				7	7	2
PIT	0	3	0	1	0	2	3	X					9	15	2
Johnson					Aldridge, Morrison (1), Kremer (5), Oldham (9)										

COMPOSITE BATTING

NAME	POS	G	AB	R	H	2B	3B	HR	RBI	BA
Pittsburgh (NL)										
Totals		7	230	25	61	12	2	4	25	.265
Barnhart	OF	7	28	1	7	1	0	0	5	.250
Wright	SS	7	27	3	5	1	0	1	5	.185
Traynor	3B	7	26	2	9	0	2	1	4	.346
Cuyler	OF	7	26	3	7	3	0	1	6	.269
Moore	2B	7	26	7	6	1	0	0	2	.231
Carey	OF	7	24	6	11	4	0	0	2	.458
Smith	C	6	20	0	7	1	0	0	0	.350
Grantham	1B	5	15	0	2	0	0	0	0	.133
McInnis	1B	4	14	0	4	0	0	0	1	.286
Kremer	P	3	7	0	1	0	0	0	0	.143
Aldridge	P	3	7	0	0	0	0	0	0	.000
Bigbee	PH	4	3	1	1	0	0	0	0	.333
Gooch	C	3	2	0	1	0	0	0	0	.500
Morrison	P	3	2	1	1	0	0	0	0	.500
Yde	P	2	1	1	0	0	0	0	0	.000
Meadows	P	1	1	0	0	0	0	0	0	.000
Adams	2B	1	1	0	0	0	0	0	0	—
Oldham	P	1	1	0	0	0	0	0	0	.000
Washington (AL)										
Totals		7	225	26	59	8	0	8	25	.262
Rice	OF	7	33	5	12	0	0	0	3	.364
Goslin	OF	7	26	6	8	1	0	3	6	.308
J. Harris	OF	7	25	5	11	2	0	3	6	.440
Peckinpaugh	SS	7	24	5	6	1	0	0	2	.250
Judge	1B	7	23	2	4	1	0	0	3	.174
B. Harris	2B	7	23	2	2	0	0	0	1	.087
Ruel	C	7	19	0	6	1	0	0	0	.316
Bluege	3B	5	18	2	5	1	0	0	1	.278
Johnson	P	3	11	0	1	0	0	0	0	.091
Myer	3B	3	8	0	2	0	0	0	0	.250
Ferguson	P	2	5	0	0	0	0	0	0	.000
Severeid	C	2	3	0	1	0	0	0	0	.333
Leibold	PH	2	2	0	1	0	0	0	0	.500
Coveleski	P	2	2	0	0	0	0	0	0	.000
Adams	2B	2	1	0	0	0	0	0	0	.000
Veach	PH	2	1	0	0	0	0	0	0	.000
Ruether	PH	1	1	0	0	0	0	0	0	.000
McNeely	OF	4	0	2	0	0	0	0	0	—
Ballou	P	2	0	0	0	0	0	0	0	—
Marberry	P	2	0	0	0	0	0	0	0	—
Zachary	P	1	0	0	0	0	0	0	0	—

COMPOSITE PITCHING

NAME	G	IP	H	BB	SO	W	L	SV	ERA
Pittsburgh (NL)									
Totals	7	61	59	17	32	4	3	1	3.69
Kremer	3	21	17	4	9	2	1	0	3.00
Aldridge	3	18.1	18	9	7	2	0	0	4.42
Morrison	3	9.1	11	1	7	0	0	0	2.89
Meadows	1	8	6	4	5	0	0	0	3.38
Yde	1	2.1	3	3	1	0	1	0	11.57
Adams	1	1	3	0	2	0	0	0	0.00
Oldham	1	1	0	0	2	0	0	1	0.00
Washington (AL)									
Totals	7	60	61	17	32	3	4	1	2.85
Johnson	3	26	26	4	15	2	1	0	2.08
Coveleski	2	14.1	16	5	3	0	2	0	3.77
Ferguson	2	14	13	6	11	1	1	0	3.21
Marberry	2	2.1	1	2	1	0	0	1	0.00
Ballou	2	1.2	0	1	0	0	0	0	0.00
Zachary	1	1.2	5	1	0	0	0	0	10.80

1926 The Spoils of Temperament

To say that the Cardinals were overdue would be an understatement. St. Louis had never seen a National League pennant flying over the city, and the last championship St. Louis team was the Browns in the American Association in 1888. Rogers Hornsby ended the drought by squeezing his Cards home two games ahead of the Cincinnati Reds. The Rajah took over the reins of the club from Branch Rickey in 1925 with the Cards in the basement and brought them up to a fourth-place finish.

Hornsby's managerial Midas touch continued to glint as his team edged into first place in early September to beat the Reds in head-on competition and lock up the 1926 crown. Hornsby, the batter, fell off from his spectacular 1925 Triple Crown performance but still managed to hit .317 and drive 93 Cards across the plate. Additional offensive fire power was generated by Sunny Jim Bottomley and Les Bell, who along with Hornsby, accounted for 313 runs batted in. Catcher Bob O'Farrell and shortstop Tommy Thevenow glued together the St. Louis defense, which often bailed out starters Flint Rhem, Bill Sherdel, and Jesse Haines. The Reds came close with a good attack which featured the first catcher ever to win a major league batting crown in Bubbles Hargrave, while the Pirates fell off to a close third, despite a .336 season from rookie outfielder Paul Waner.

The Yankees seemed to have the American League pennant ready to hoist but had to fight off three late-season challengers before claiming the flag. With a ten-game lead in mid-August, the Yankees were expected to waltz home, but Cleveland, Philadelphia, and Washington made New York work for their return to the top. The Indians, led by Tris Speaker, came to within four games shortly after Labor Day before the Yankees stiffened.

The Athletics relied on a deep and talented pitching staff, led by Lefty Grove, to finish a strong third, and the Senators had to recover from a poor start to reach fourth place. Washington continued to torment opposing pitchers, but the Senators' trio of Walter Johnson, Stan Coveleski, and Dutch Reuther all fell off in their hurling, as age seemingly caught up with all three simultaneously, to end the team's brief dominance of glory. The Yankees blended established stars like Babe Ruth, Bob Meusel, and Joe Dugan, along with a brigade of younger talent in Lou Gehrig, Earle Combs, Mark Koenig and rookie Tony Lazzeri to field a lineup which was the scourge of the league. No new names appeared in the pitching ledger, but Herb Pennock, Urban Shocker, and Waite Hoyt all had enough left to win consistently.

Although Ruth swatted four homers for the Yankees in the World Series, the 1926 fall classic is best remembered for the dramatic seventh and final game won by the Cardinals. St. Louis' Jesse Haines had been staked to a 3-1 lead in the fourth inning. In the seventh frame the score stood at 3-2 with three Yankees on base, young slugger Tony Lazzeri at bat, and two out. Hornsby, sensing disaster, stopped the action and waved 39-year old Grover "Pete" Alexander into the fray.

In the twilight of a brilliant career, "Old Pete" had pitched his second complete game victory of the Series only the day before, and legend has it that he was sleeping off the affects of a celebration bender in the bullpen when Hornsby called him. Nonetheless, the veteran hiked up his trousers, strode to the mound, and dramatically fanned Lazzeri to end the threat. No Yankee reached base against Alexander until Ruth walked with two down in the ninth. With slugger Meusel at bat and Gehrig on deck, Ruth astonished everyone in the park—except the Cardinals—by lighting out for second. Bob O'Farrell had plenty of time to gun the ball down to Hornsby, who slapped the tag on the Babe to bring the first world's championship to St. Louis.

The final postscript to the season proved that talent and a championship were not enough to gain lasting security. Hornsby, superb as a ball player, was equally difficult as a human being—so much so that his confrontations with Cardinal owner, Sam Breadon, found him traded to the Giants for Frankie Frisch when the 1927 season rolled around.

1926 AMERICAN LEAGUE

NAME	G by Pos	B	AGE	G	AB	R	H	2B	3B	HR	RBI	BB	SO	SB	BA	SA
NEW YORK	1st 91-63 .591				MILLER HUGGINS											
TOTALS			27	155	5221	847	1508	262	75	121	794	642	580	79	.289	.437
Lou Gehrig	1B155	L	23	155	572	135	179	47	20	16	112	105	73	6	.313	.549
Tony Lazzeri	2B149, SS5, 3B1	R	22	155	589	79	162	28	14	18	114	54	96	16	.275	.462
Mark Koenig	SS141	B	23	147	617	93	167	26	8	5	62	43	37	4	.271	.363
Joe Dugan	3B122	R	29	123	434	39	125	19	5	1	64	25	16	2	.288	.362
Babe Ruth	OF149, 1B2	L	31	152	495	139	184	30	5	47	146	144	76	11	.372	.737
Earle Combs	OF145	L	27	145	606	113	181	31	12	8	55	47	23	8	.299	.429
Bob Meusel (BF)	OF107	R	29	108	413	73	130	22	3	12	81	37	32	16	.315	.470
Pat Collins	C100	R	29	102	290	41	83	11	3	7	35	73	56	1	.286	.417
Ben Paschal	OF76	R	30	96	258	46	74	12	3	7	32	26	35	7	.287	.438
Mike Gazella	3B45, SS11	R	30	66	168	21	39	6	0	0	20	25	24	2	.232	.268
2 Hank Severeid	C40	R	35	41	127	13	34	8	1	0	13	13	4	1	.268	.346
Benny Bengough (SJ)	C35	R	27	36	84	9	32	6	0	0	14	7	4	1	.381	.452
2 Roy Carlyle	OF16	L	25	35	53	3	20	5	1	0	11	4	9	0	.377	.509
Spencer Adams	2B4, 3B1	L	28	28	25	7	3	1	0	0	1	3	7	1	.120	.160
Aaron Ward	2B4, 3B1	R	29	22	31	5	10	2	0	0	3	2	6	0	.323	.387
2 Dutch Ruether	P5	L	32	13	21	2	2	0	0	0	0	0	1	0	.095	.095
Bill Skiff	C6	R	30	6	11	0	1	0	0	0	0	0	1	0	.091	.091
Nick Cullop		R	25	2	2	0	1	0	0	0	0	0	1	0	.500	.500
Honey Barnes	C1	R	26	1	0	0	0	0	0	0	0	1	0	0	.000	.000
Kiddo Davis	OF1	R	24	1	0	0	0	0	0	0	0	0	0	0	.000	.000
Fred Merkle	1B1	R	37	1	2	0	0	0	0	0	0	0	0	0	.000	.000
CLEVELAND	2nd 88-66 .571 3				TRIS SPEAKER											
TOTALS			29	154	5293	738	1529	333	49	27	643	455	331	88	.289	.386
George Burns	1B151	R	33	151	603	97	216	64	3	4	114	28	33	13	.358	.494
Freddie Spurgeon	2B149	R	24	149	614	101	181	31	3	0	49	27	36	7	.295	.355
Joe Sewell	SS154	L	27	154	578	91	187	41	5	4	85	65	7	17	.324	.433
Rube Lutzke	3B142	R	28	142	475	42	124	28	6	0	59	34	35	6	.261	.345
Homer Summa	OF154	L	27	154	581	74	179	31	6	4	76	47	9	15	.308	.403
Tris Speaker	OF149	L	38	150	539	96	164	52	8	7	86	94	15	6	.304	.469
Charlie Jamieson	OF143	L	33	143	555	89	166	33	7	2	45	53	22	9	.299	.395
Luke Sewell	C125	R	25	126	433	41	103	16	4	0	46	36	27	1	.238	.293
Glenn Myatt	C35	L	28	56	117	14	29	5	2	0	13	13	13	1	.248	.325
Pat McNulty	OF9	L	27	48	56	3	14	2	1	0	6	5	9	0	.250	.321
Fred Eichrodt	OF27	R	23	37	80	14	25	7	1	0	7	2	11	1	.313	.425
Ernie Padgett	3B29, SS2	R	27	36	62	7	13	0	1	0	6	8	3	1	.210	.242
Ray Knode	1B11	L	25	31	24	6	8	1	1	0	2	2	3	0	.333	.458
Cliff Lee	OF9, C3	L	29	21	40	4	7	1	0	1	2	6	8	0	.175	.275
Guy Lacy	2B11, 3B2	L	29	13	24	2	4	0	0	1	2	2	2	0	.167	.292
Martin Autry (IL)	C3	R	23	3	7	1	1	0	0	0	1	0	1	0	.143	.143
Johnny Hodapp (BL)	3B3	R	20	3	5	0	1	0	0	0	0	0	1	0	.200	.200
PHILADELPHIA	3rd 83-67 .553 6				CONNIE MACK											
TOTALS			27	154	5046	677	1359	259	65	61	619	523	449	56	.269	.383
Jim Poole	1B101, OF1	L	31	112	361	49	106	23	5	8	63	23	25	4	.294	.452
Max Bishop	2B119	L	26	122	400	77	106	22	0	0	33	116	41	4	.265	.325
Chick Galloway	SS133	R	29	133	408	37	98	13	6	0	49	31	20	8	.240	.301
Sammy Hale	3B77, OF1	R	29	111	327	49	92	22	9	4	43	13	36	1	.281	.440
Walt French	OF98	L	26	112	397	51	121	18	7	0	36	18	24	2	.305	.393
Al Simmons	OF147	R	24	147	581	90	199	53	10	19	109	48	49	10	.343	.566
Bill Lamar	OF107	L	29	116	419	62	119	17	6	5	50	18	15	4	.284	.389
Mickey Cochrane	C115	L	23	120	370	50	101	8	9	8	47	56	15	5	.273	.408
Jimmy Dykes	3B77, 2B44, SS1	R	29	124	429	54	123	32	5	1	44	49	34	6	.287	.392
Joe Hauser	1B65	R	27	91	229	31	44	10	0	8	36	39	34	1	.192	.341
Frank Welch	OF49	R	28	75	174	26	49	8	1	4	23	26	9	2	.282	.408
Cy Perkins	C55	R	30	63	148	14	43	6	0	0	19	18	7	0	.291	.331
Bill Wambsganss	SS15, 2B8	R	32	54	54	11	19	3	0	0	1	8	8	1	.352	.407
1 Bing Miller	OF34, 1B1	R	31	38	110	13	52	8	0	0	13	11	6	4	.292	.436
Jimmie Foxx	C12, OF3	R	18	26	32	8	10	2	1	0	5	1	6	1	.313	.438
Alex Metzler	OF17	L	23	20	67	8	16	3	0	0	12	7	5	1	.239	.284
Dave Barbee	OF10	R	21	19	47	7	8	1	1	1	5	2	4	0	.170	.298
Charlie Engle	SS16	R	22	19	57	7	6	0	0	0	0	6	10	6	.105	.105
Frank Sigafoos	SS12	R	22	13	43	4	11	0	0	0	3	0	6	0	.256	.256
2 Tom Jenkins	OF6	L	28	6	23	3	4	1	0	0	0	2	1	0	.174	.261

NAME	T	AGE	W	L	PCT	SV	G	GS	CG	IP	H	BB	SO	SHO	ERA
		30	91	63	.591	20	155	155	64	1372	1442	478	486	4	3.86
Herb Pennock	L	32	23	11	.676	2	40	33	19	266	294	43	78	1	3.62
Urban Shocker	R	35	19	11	.633	2	41	33	19	258	272	71	59	0	3.38
Waite Hoyt	R	26	16	12	.571	4	40	27	12	218	224	62	79	1	3.85
Sad Sam Jones	R	33	9	8	.529	5	39	23	6	161	186	80	69	1	4.98
Bob Shawkey (BF)	R	35	8	7	.522	3	29	10	3	104	102	37	63	1	3.63
Myles Thomas	R	28	6	6	.500	0	33	13	3	140	140	65	38	0	4.24
Garland Braxton	L	26	5	1	.833	2	37	1	0	67	71	19	30	0	2.69
2 Dutch Ruether	L	32	2	3	.400	1	5	5	1	36	32	18	8	0	3.50
Walter Beall	R	26	2	4	.333	1	20	9	1	82	71	68	56	0	3.51
Herb McQuaid	R	27	1	0	1.000	0	17	1	0	38	48	13	6	0	6.16
Hank Johnson	R	20	0	0	—	1	1	0	0	1	2	2	0	0	18.00
		29	88	66	.571	4	154	154	96	1374	1412	450	381	11	3.40
George Uhle	R	27	27	11	.711	1	39	36	32	318	300	118	159	3	2.83
Emil Levsen	R	28	16	13	.552	0	33	31	18	237	235	85	53	2	3.42
Joe Shaute	L	26	14	10	.583	1	34	25	15	207	215	65	47	1	3.52
Sherry Smith	L	35	11	10	.524	0	27	24	16	188	214	31	25	1	3.73
Jake Miller (SA)	L	28	7	4	.636	1	18	11	5	83	99	18	24	3	3.26
Garland Buckeye	L	28	6	9	.400	0	32	18	5	166	160	69	36	1	3.09
Benn Karr	R	32	5	6	.455	1	30	7	4	113	137	41	23	0	5.01
Ray Benge	R	24	1	0	1.000	0	8	0	0	12	15	4	3	0	3.75
Willis Hudlin	R	20	1	3	.250	0	8	2	1	32	25	13	6	0	2.81
Norm Lehr	R	25	0	0	—	0	4	0	0	15	11	4	4	0	3.00
By Speece	R	29	0	0	—	0	2	0	0	3	1	2	1	0	0.00
		31	83	67	.553	16	150	150	62	1346	1362	451	571	10	3.00
Lefty Grove	L	26	13	13	.500	6	45	33	20	258	227	101	194	1	2.51
2 Howard Ehmke	R	32	12	4	.750	0	20	18	10	147	125	50	55	1	2.82
Rube Walberg	L	29	12	10	.545	2	40	19	5	151	168	60	72	2	2.80
Eddie Rommel	R	28	11	11	.500	0	37	26	12	219	225	54	52	3	3.08
Sam Gray	R	28	11	12	.478	0	38	18	5	151	164	50	82	0	3.64
Jack Quinn	R	42	10	11	.476	1	31	21	8	164	191	36	58	3	3.40
Joe Pate	L	34	9	0	1.000	4	47	0	0	113	109	51	24	0	2.71
1 Slim Harriss	R	29	3	5	.375	0	12	10	2	57	66	22	13	0	4.10
1 Fred Heimach	L	25	1	0	1.000	0	3	2	1	32	28	5	8	0	2.81
Stan Baumgartner	L	33	1	1	.500	0	10	1	0	28	28	10	0	0	4.10
Lefty Willis	L	20	0	0	—	1	13	1	0	32	31	12	13	0	1.41

WASHINGTON — 4th 81-69 .540 8 — BUCKY HARRIS

NAME	G by Pos	B	AGE	G	AB	R	H	2B	3B	HR	RBI	BB	SO	SB	BA	SA
TOTALS			29	152	5223	802	1525	244	97	43	721	555	369	122	.292	.401
Joe Judge	1B128	L	32	134	453	70	132	25	11	7	92	53	25	7	.291	.442
Bucky Harris	2B141	R	29	141	537	94	152	39	9	1	63	58	41	16	.283	.395
Buddy Myer	SS117,3B8	L	22	132	434	66	132	18	6	1	62	45	19	10	.304	.380
Ossie Bluege	3B134,SS8	R	25	139	487	69	132	19	8	3	65	70	46	12	.271	.361
Sam Rice	OF152	L	36	152	641	98	216	32	14	3	76	42	20	25	.337	.445
Earl McNeely	OF120	R	28	124	442	84	134	20	12	0	48	44	28	18	.303	.403
Goose Goslin	OF147	L	25	147	567	105	201	26	15	17	108	63	38	8	.354	.543
Muddy Ruel	C117	R	30	117	368	42	110	22	4	1	53	61	14	7	.299	.389
Joe Harris	1B36,OF35	R	35	92	257	43	79	13	9	5	55	37	9	2	.307	.486
Stuffy Stewart	2B25,3B1	R	32	62	63	27	17	6	1	0	9	6	6	8	.270	.397
Bennie Tate	C45	L	24	59	142	17	38	5	2	1	13	15	1	0	.268	.352
Roger Peckinpaugh	SS46,1B1	R	35	57	147	19	35	4	1	1	14	28	12	3	.238	.299
1 Dutch Ruether	P23	L	32	47	92	6	23	2	0	1	11	6	10	0	.250	.304
1 Jack Tobin	OF7	L	34	27	33	5	7	0	1	0	3	0	0	0	.212	.273
1 Hank Severeid	C16	R	35	22	34	2	7	1	0	0	4	3	2	0	.206	.235
Tex Jeanes	OF14	R	25	21	30	6	7	2	0	0	3	3	0	0	.233	.300
Danny Taylor	OF12	R	25	21	50	10	15	0	0	1	5	5	7	1	.300	.400
Bobby Reeves	3B16,2B1,SS1	R	22	20	49	4	11	0	1	0	7	6	9	1	.224	.265
Russ Ennis	C1	R	29	1	0	0	0	0	0	0	0	0	0	0	—	—
Patsy Gharrity (DE) 34																

NAME	T	AGE	W	L	PCT	SV	G	GS	CG	IP	H	BB	SO	SHO	ERA
		30	81	69	.540	26	152	152	65	1349	1489	566	418	5	4.34
Walter Johnson	R	38	15	16	.484	0	33	33	22	262	259	73	125	2	3.61
Stan Coveleski	R	36	14	11	.560	1	36	34	11	245	272	81	50	3	3.12
1 Dutch Ruether	L	32	12	7	.667	0	23	23	9	169	214	66	48	0	4.85
Firpo Marberry	R	27	12	7	.611	22	64	5	3	138	120	66	43	0	3.00
General Crowder	R	27	7	4	.636	1	19	12	6	100	97	60	26	0	3.96
George Murray	R	27	6	3	.667	0	12	12	5	81	89	37	28	0	5.67
Curly Ogden	R	26	3	3	.500	0	9	4	1	96	114	45	21	0	4.31
Bill Morrell	R	26	3	3	.500	1	26	2	1	70	83	29	16	0	5.27
Alex Ferguson	R	29	3	4	.429	1	19	4	0	48	69	18	11	0	7.69
Dick Jones	R	24	2	1	.667	0	4	3	1	21	20	11	3	0	4.29
Emilio Palmero	L	31	2	2	.500	0	7	3	0	17	22	15	6	0	4.77
1 Bullet Joe Bush	R	33	1	8	.111	0	12	11	3	71	83	35	27	0	6.72
Harry Kelley	R	20	0	0	—	0	7	1	0	10	17	8	6	0	8.10
Lefty Thomas	L	22	0	0	—	0	6	0	0	8	10	3	5	0	5.00
Jimmie Uchrinscko	R	25	0	0	—	0	1	0	0	8	13	8	0	0	10.12
Bump Hadley	R	21	0	0	—	0	1	0	0	3	6	2	0	0	12.00
Pat Loftus	R	28	0	0	—	0	1	0	0	1	3	2	1	0	9.00

CHICAGO — 5th 81-72 .529 9.5 — EDDIE COLLINS

NAME	G by Pos	B	AGE	G	AB	R	H	2B	3B	HR	RBI	BB	SO	SB	BA	SA
TOTALS			29	155	5220	730	1508	314	60	32	666	556	381	124	.289	.390
Earl Sheely	1B144	R	33	145	525	77	157	40	2	6	89	75	13	3	.299	.417
Eddie Collins (LJ)	2B101	L	39	106	375	66	129	32	4	1	62	62	8	13	.344	.459
Bill Hunnefield	SS98,3B17,2B15	R	27	131	470	81	129	26	4	3	48	37	28	24	.274	.366
Willie Kamm	3B142	R	26	143	480	63	141	24	10	0	62	77	24	14	.294	.385
Bill Barrett	OF102,1B2	R	26	111	368	46	113	31	4	6	61	25	26	9	.307	.462
Johnny Mostil	OF147	R	30	148	600	120	197	41	15	4	42	79	55	35	.328	.467
Bibb Falk	OF155	L	27	155	606	86	195	43	4	8	108	66	22	9	.345	.477
Ray Schalk	C80	R	33	82	226	26	60	9	1	0	32	27	11	5	.265	.314
Spence Harris	OF63	L	25	80	222	36	56	11	3	2	27	20	15	8	.252	.356
Ray Morehart	2B48	L	26	73	192	27	61	10	3	0	21	11	15	3	.318	.401
Buck Crouse	C45	L	29	49	135	10	32	4	1	0	17	14	7	0	.237	.281
Johnny Grabowski	C38,1B1	R	26	48	122	6	32	1	1	1	11	4	15	0	.262	.311
Harry McCurdy	C25,1B8	L	26	44	86	16	28	7	2	1	11	6	10	0	.326	.488
Moe Berg	SS31,2B2,3B1	R	24	41	113	4	25	6	0	0	7	6	9	0	.221	.274
1 Everett Scott	SS39	R	33	40	143	15	36	10	1	0	13	9	8	1	.252	.336
Tom Gulley	OF12	R	26	16	35	5	8	1	0	0	8	5	2	0	.229	.371
Bud Clancy	1B10	L	22	12	38	3	13	2	2	0	7	1	3	0	.342	.500
Pid Purdy	OF9	L	24	11	33	5	6	2	1	0	6	2	1	0	.182	.303
Pat Veltman	SS1	R	20	5	4	1	1	0	0	0	1	1	0	0	.250	.250

NAME	T	AGE	W	L	PCT	SV	G	GS	CG	IP	H	BB	SO	SHO	ERA
		28	81	72	.529	12	155	155	85	1380	1426	506	458	11	3.74
Ted Lyons	R	28	18	16	.529	2	39	31	24	284	268	106	51	3	3.02
Red Faber	R	37	15	9	.625	0	27	25	13	185	203	57	65	1	3.55
Tommy Thomas	R	26	15	12	.556	2	44	32	13	249	225	110	127	2	3.80
Ted Blankenship (BG)	R	25	13	10	.565	1	29	26	15	209	217	65	66	1	3.62
Sarge Connally	R	27	6	5	.545	3	31	8	5	108	128	35	47	0	3.17
Sloppy Thurston	R	27	6	8	.429	3	31	13	6	134	164	36	35	1	5.04
Jim Joe Edwards	L	31	6	9	.400	1	32	16	8	142	140	63	41	3	4.18
Dixie Leverett	R	32	1	1	.500	0	6	3	1	24	31	7	12	0	6.00
Milt Steengrafe	R	28	1	1	.500	0	13	1	0	38	43	19	10	0	4.03
Les Cox	R	20	1	0	.000	0	2	0	0	5	6	5	3	0	5.40
Pryor McBee	L	25	0	0	.000	0	1	0	0	1	3	1	0	0	9.00

DETROIT — 6th 79-75 .513 12 — TY COBB

NAME	G by Pos	B	AGE	G	AB	R	H	2B	3B	HR	RBI	BB	SO	SB	BA	SA
TOTALS			29	157	5315	793	1547	281	90	36	717	599	423	88	.291	.398
Lu Blue	1B109,OF1	B	29	128	429	92	123	24	14	1	52	90	18	13	.287	.415
Charlie Gehringer	2B112,3B6	R	23	123	459	62	127	19	17	1	48	30	42	9	.277	.399
Jackie Tavener	SS156	R	26	156	532	65	141	22	14	1	58	52	53	8	.265	.365
Jack Warner	3B95,SS3	R	22	100	311	41	78	8	1	0	34	38	24	8	.251	.315
Harry Heilmann	OF134	R	31	141	502	90	184	41	8	9	103	67	19	6	.367	.534
Heinie Manush	OF120	L	24	136	498	95	188	35	8	14	86	31	28	11	.378	.564
Bob Fothergill	OF103	R	28	110	387	63	142	31	7	3	73	33	23	4	.367	.508
Clyde Manion	C74	R	29	75	176	15	35	4	0	0	14	24	16	1	.199	.222
Frank O'Rourke	3B60,2B41,SS10	R	34	111	363	43	88	16	1	1	41	35	33	8	.242	.300
Al Wingo	OF74,3B2	L	28	108	298	45	84	19	0	1	45	52	32	4	.282	.356
Johnny Neun	1B49	B	25	97	242	47	72	14	4	0	15	27	26	4	.298	.388
Ty Cobb	OF55	L	39	79	233	48	79	18	5	4	62	26	2	9	.339	.511
Larry Woodall	C59	R	31	67	146	18	34	5	0	0	15	15	2	0	.233	.267
Johnny Bassler (BN)	C63	L	31	66	174	20	53	8	1	0	22	45	6	0	.305	.362
Les Burke	2B15,3B7,SS1	L	23	38	75	9	17	1	0	0	4	7	3	1	.227	.240
Ray Hayworth	C8	R	22	12	11	1	3	0	0	0	0	0	1	0	.273	.273
Billy Mullen	3B9	R	30	11	13	2	1	0	0	0	0	5	1	1	.077	.077

NAME	T	AGE	W	L	PCT	SV	G	GS	CG	IP	H	BB	SO	SHO	ERA
		28	79	75	.513	18	157	157	57	1395	1570	555	469	10	4.41
Earl Whitehill	L	26	16	13	.552	0	36	34	13	252	271	79	109	0	4.00
Hooks Dauss	R	36	12	6	.667	9	34	5	0	124	135	49	27	0	4.21
Sam Gibson	R	26	12	9	.571	2	35	24	16	199	199	75	61	2	3.49
Ed Wells	L	26	12	10	.545	0	36	26	9	178	201	76	58	4	4.15
Rip Collins	R	30	8	8	.500	1	30	13	5	122	128	44	44	3	2.73
Lil Stoner	R	27	7	10	.412	0	32	22	7	160	179	63	57	0	5.46
Augie Johns	L	26	6	4	.600	1	35	14	3	113	117	69	40	1	5.34
Ken Hollaway	R	28	4	4	.400	2	36	12	3	139	192	42	43	0	5.12
George Smith	R	24	1	2	.333	0	23	1	0	44	55	33	15	0	6.95
Clyde Barfoot	R	34	1	2	.333	2	11	1	0	31	42	9	7	0	4.94
Rudy Kneisch	R	27	0	1	.000	0	2	1	1	17	18	6	4	0	2.65
2 Wilbur Cooper	L	34	0	4	.000	0	8	3	0	14	27	9	2	0	10.93
Jess Doyle	R	28	0	0	—	1	2	0	0	4	6	1	2	0	4.50

ST. LOUIS — 7th 62-92 .403 29 — GEORGE SISLER

NAME	G by Pos	B	AGE	G	AB	R	H	2B	3B	HR	RBI	BB	SO	SB	BA	SA
TOTALS			31	155	5259	682	1449	253	78	72	608	437	465	63	.276	.394
George Sisler	1B149,P1	L	33	150	613	78	178	21	12	7	71	30	30	12	.289	.398
Oscar Melillo (AJ)	2B88,3B11	R	26	99	385	54	98	18	5	1	30	32	31	6	.255	.335
Wally Gerber	SS129	R	34	131	411	37	111	8	0	0	42	40	29	0	.270	.290
Marty McManus	3B84,2B61,1B4	R	26	149	549	102	156	30	10	9	68	55	62	5	.284	.424
2 Bing Miller	OF94	R	31	94	353	60	117	27	5	4	50	22	7	3	.331	.470
Harry Rice	OF133,3B7,2B4,SS2	L	25	148	578	86	181	27	10	9	59	63	40	10	.313	.441
Ken Williams	OF92,2B1	L	36	108	347	55	97	15	7	17	74	39	23	5	.280	.510
Wally Shang	C82,OF3	B	36	103	285	36	96	19	5	8	50	52	20	5	.330	.516
Pinky Hargrave	C58	R	30	92	235	20	66	16	3	7	37	10	38	3	.281	.464
Herschel Bennett	OF50	L	29	80	225	33	60	14	2	1	26	22	21	2	.267	.360
Cedric Durst	OF57,1B4	L	29	80	219	32	52	7	5	3	16	22	19	5	.237	.356
Gene Robertson	3B55,SS10,2B3	L	27	78	247	12	62	12	6	1	19	17	10	5	.251	.360
1 Baby Doll Jacobson	OF50	R	35	50	182	18	52	15	1	2	21	9	14	1	.286	.412
Bobby LaMotte	SS30,3B1	R	28	36	79	11	16	4	3	0	9	11	6	0	.202	.329
Leo Dixon (BW)	C33	R	31	33	89	7	17	3	1	0	8	11	14	1	.191	.247
Jimmy Austin	3B1	B	46	15	2	1	1	0	0	0	1	0	0	1	.500	1.000

NAME	T	AGE	W	L	PCT	SV	G	GS	CG	IP	H	BB	SO	SHO	ERA
		28	62	92	.403	9	155	155	64	1368	1549	654	337	5	4.66
Tom Zachary	L	30	14	15	.483	0	34	31	18	247	264	97	53	3	3.61
Win Ballou	R	28	11	10	.500	2	43	13	5	154	186	71	59	0	4.79
Milt Gaston	R	30	10	18	.357	0	32	28	14	214	227	101	39	1	4.33
Elam Vangilder	R	30	9	11	.450	1	42	19	8	181	196	98	40	1	5.17
Ernie Wingard	L	25	5	8	.385	3	39	16	7	169	188	76	30	0	3.57
Chet Falk	L	21	4	4	.500	0	18	8	3	74	95	27	7	0	5.35
Dixie Davis	R	35	3	8	.273	1	27	7	2	83	93	40	39	0	4.66
Joe Giard	L	27	3	10	.231	0	22	16	2	90	113	67	18	0	7.00
Ernie Nevers	R	23	2	4	.333	0	11	7	1	75	82	24	16	0	4.44
Charlie Robertson	R	30	1	2	.333	0	8	7	1	28	38	21	13	0	8.36
Claude Jonnard	R	28	0	0	.000	1	12	3	0	36	46	24	13	0	6.00
Stew Bolen	L	23	0	0	—	0	1	0	0	15	21	6	7	0	5.98
George Sisler	R	33	0	0	—	0	1	1	0	8	9	1	0	0	0.00

BOSTON — 8th 46-107 .301 44.5 — LEE FOHL

NAME	G by Pos	B	AGE	G	AB	R	H	2B	3B	HR	RBI	BB	SO	SB	BA	SA
TOTALS			29	154	5185	562	1325	249	54	32	521	465	450	52	.256	.343
Phil Todt	1B154	L	24	154	599	56	153	19	12	7	69	40	38	3	.255	.362
Bill Regan	2B106	R	27	108	403	40	106	21	3	4	34	23	37	6	.263	.360
Topper Rigney	SS146	R	28	148	525	71	142	32	6	4	53	108	31	4	.270	.377
Fred Haney	3B137	R	28	138	462	47	102	15	7	0	52	74	28	13	.221	.284
2 Baby Doll Jacobson	OF98	R	35	98	394	44	120	36	1	6	69	22	22	4	.305	.447
Ira Flagstead (ST)	OF98	R	32	98	415	65	124	31	7	3	31	36	22	4	.299	.429
Si Rosenthal	OF67	L	22	104	285	34	76	12	3	4	34	19	18	4	.267	.372
Alex Gaston	C98	R	33	98	301	37	67	5	3	0	21	21	28	3	.223	.259
Mike Herrara	2B48,3B16,SS4	R	28	74	237	20	61	14	1	0	19	15	13	0	.257	.325
Fred Bratchi	OF37	R	34	72	167	12	46	12	1	0	19	14	15	0	.275	.347
Wally Shaner	OF48	R	26	69	191	20	54	12	2	0	21	17	13	1	.283	.366
George Bischoff	C46	R	31	59	127	6	33	11	2	0	19	15	16	1	.260	.378
2 Jack Tobin	OF51	L	34	51	209	26	57	9	0	1	14	16	3	6	.273	.330
1 Roy Carlyle	OF23	L	25	45	164	27	47	6	2	2	16	4	18	0	.287	.384
Howie Fitzgerald	OF23	L	24	31	97	11	25	2	0	0	5	1	7	1	.258	.278
Al Stokes	C29	R	26	30	86	7	14	3	0	0	8	8	28	0	.163	.267
1 Tom Jenkins	OF13	L	28	21	50	3	9	1	0	0	1	1	6	0	.180	.240
Jack Rothrock	SS2	B	21	15	17	3	5	0	0	0	0	0	0	0	.294	.353
Emmett McCann	SS1,3B1	R	24	6	3	0	0	0	0	0	0	1	0	0	.000	.000
Bill Moore	C5	L	24	5	3	0	0	0	0	0	0	0	0	0	.167	.167
Chappie Geygan	3B3	R	23	4	10	0	3	0	0	0	0	1	0	0	.300	.300
Boob Fowler	3B2	R	25	2	1	0	0	0	0	0	0	0	1	0	.125	.125
Dud Lee	SS2	L	26	4	7	1	1	0	0	0	0	1	1	0	.143	.143
Sam Langford	OF2	L	26	4	1	1	1	0	0	0	0	0	0	0	.000	.000

NAME	T	AGE	W	L	PCT	SV	G	GS	CG	IP	H	BB	SO	SHO	ERA
		25	46	107	.301	5	154	154	53	1362	1520	546	336	6	4.72
Ted Wingfield	R	26	11	16	.407	3	43	20	9	191	220	50	30	1	4.43
Hal Wiltse	L	22	8	15	.348	0	37	29	9	196	201	99	59	1	4.22
2 Slim Harriss	R	29	6	10	.375	2	21	18	6	113	135	33	34	1	4.46
Red Ruffing	R	22	6	15	.286	2	37	22	6	166	169	68	58	0	4.39
Paul Zahniser	R	29	6	18	.250	0	30	24	7	172	213	69	35	1	4.97
Tony Welzer	R	27	4	3	.571	0	40	5	1	141	167	57	30	1	4.79
1 Howard Ehmke	R	32	3	10	.231	0	14	14	7	97	115	45	38	1	5.47
2 Fred Heimach	L	25	2	9	.182	0	20	13	6	102	119	42	17	0	5.65
Danny MacFayden	R	21	0	1	.000	0	5	1	0	13	10	7	1	0	4.85
Buster Ross	L	23	0	0	.000	0	17	2	0	29	35	24	10	0	8.07
Del Lundgren	R	26	0	2	.000	0	11	3	0	35	34	10	8	0	4.80
Joe Kiefer	R	26	0	2	.000	0	5	3	0	30	29	16	4	0	4.80
Jack Russell	R	20	0	5	.000	0	36	5	1	98	94	24	17	0	3.58
Happy Foreman	L	28	0	0	.000	0	6	0	0	7	3	5	3	0	3.86
Bill Clowers	R	27	0	0	—	0	1	0	0	6	0	0	0	0	0.00
Rudy Sommers	L	38	0	0	—	0	1	0	0	2	6	2	1	0	13.50

ST. LOUIS — 1ST 89-65 .578 — ROGERS HORNSBY

NAME	G by Pos	B	AGE	G	AB	R	H	2B	3B	HR	RBI	BB	SO	SB	BA	SA
TOTALS			27	156	5381	817	1541	259	82	90	756	478	518	83	.286	.415
Jim Bottomley	1B154	L	26	154	603	98	180	40	14	19	120	58	52	4	.299	.506
Rogers Hornsby	2B134	R	30	134	527	96	167	34	5	11	93	61	39	3	.317	.463
Tommy Thevenow	SS156	R	22	156	563	64	144	15	5	2	63	27	26	8	.256	.311
Les Bell	3B155	R	24	155	581	85	189	33	14	17	100	54	62	5	.325	.518
2 Billy Southworth	OF99	L	33	99	391	76	124	22	6	11	69	26	9	13	.317	.488
Taylor Douthit	OF138	R	25	139	530	96	163	20	4	3	52	55	46	23	.308	.377
Ray Blades (KJ)	OF105	R	29	107	416	81	127	17	12	8	43	62	57	6	.305	.462
Bob O'Farrell	C146	R	29	147	492	63	144	30	9	7	68	61	44	1	.293	.431
Chick Hafey	OF54	R	23	78	225	30	61	19	2	4	38	11	36	2	.271	.427
Specs Toporcer	2B27, SS5, 3B1	L	27	64	88	13	22	3	2	0	9	8	9	1	.250	.330
Wattie Holm	OF39	R	24	55	144	18	41	5	1	0	21	18	14	3	.285	.333
1 Heinie Mueller	OF51	L	26	52	191	36	51	7	5	3	28	11	6	8	.267	.403
Jake Flowers	2B11, 1B3, SS1	R	24	40	74	13	20	1	0	3	9	5	9	1	.270	.405
Art Reinhart	P27	L	27	40	63	7	20	2	2	0	11	1	3	1	.317	.413
Ernie Vick	C23	R	25	24	51	6	10	2	0	0	4	3	4	0	.196	.235
Bill Warwick	C9	R	28	9	14	0	5	0	0	0	2	0	2	0	.357	.357
1 Jack Smith		L	31	1	1	0	0	0	0	0	0	0	0	0	.000	.000

NAME	T	AGE	W	L	PCT	SV	G	GS	CG	IP	H	BB	SO	SHO	ERA
		29	89	65	.578	6	156	156	90	1399	1423	397	365	10	3.67
Flint Rhem	R	25	20	7	.741	0	34	34	20	258	241	75	72	1	3.21
Bill Sherdel	L	29	16	12	.571	0	34	29	17	235	255	49	59	3	3.49
Jesse Haines	R	32	13	4	.765	1	33	20	14	183	186	48	46	3	3.25
Art Reinhart	L	27	10	5	.667	0	27	11	9	143	159	47	26	0	4.22
Vic Keen	R	27	10	9	.526	0	26	21	12	152	179	42	29	1	4.56
2 Pete Alexander (SA-ST)	R	39	9	7	.563	2	23	16	11	148	136	24	35	2	2.92
Hi Bell	R	28	6	6	.500	0	27	8	3	85	82	17	27	0	3.18
Allan Sothoron	R	33	3	3	.500	0	15	4	1	43	37	16	19	0	4.19
Eddie Dyer	L	26	1	0	1.000	0	9	1	0	14	14	4	0	0	12.00
Wild Bill Hallahan	L	23	1	4	.200	0	19	3	0	57	45	32	28	0	3.63
Duster Mails	L	31	0	1	.000	0	2	1	0	1	2	1	1	0	0.00
Syl Johnson (BT, BR)	R	25	0	3	.000	1	19	6	1	49	54	15	10	0	4.22
1 Walter Huntzinger	R	27	0	4	.000	0	9	4	2	34	35	14	9	0	4.24
Ed Clough	L	19	0	0	—	0	1	0	0	2	5	3	0	0	22.50

CINCINNATI — 2nd 87-67 .565 — 2 — JACK HENDRICKS

NAME	G by Pos	B	AGE	G	AB	R	H	2B	3B	HR	RBI	BB	SO	SB	BA	SA
TOTALS			30	157	5320	747	1541	242	120	35	692	454	333	51	.290	.400
Wally Pipp	1B155	L	33	155	574	72	167	22	15	6	99	49	26	8	.291	.414
Hughie Critz	2B155	R	25	155	607	96	164	24	14	3	79	39	25	7	.270	.371
Frank Emmer	SS79	R	30	80	224	22	44	7	6	0	18	13	30	1	.196	.281
Chuck Dressen	3B123, SS1, OF1	R	27	127	474	76	126	27	11	4	48	49	31	6	.266	.395
Curt Walker	OF152	L	29	155	571	83	175	24	20	6	78	60	31	3	.306	.450
Edd Roush	OF143, 1B1	L	33	144	563	95	182	37	10	7	79	38	17	8	.323	.462
Cuckoo Christensen	OF93	L	26	114	329	41	115	15	7	0	41	40	18	8	.350	.438
Bubbles Hargrave	C93	R	33	105	326	42	115	22	8	6	62	25	17	2	.353	.525
Val Picinich	C86	R	29	89	240	33	63	16	1	2	31	29	22	4	.263	.363
Rube Bressler (IL)	OF80, 1B4	R	31	86	297	58	106	15	9	1	51	37	20	3	.357	.478
Babe Pinelli	3B40, SS27, 2B3	R	30	71	207	26	46	7	4	0	24	15	5	2	.222	.290
Red Lucas	P39, 2B1	L	24	66	76	15	23	4	4	0	14	10	13	0	.303	.461
Hod Ford	SS57	R	28	57	197	14	55	6	1	0	18	14	12	1	.279	.320
Billy Zitzmann	OF31	R	28	53	94	21	23	2	1	0	3	6	7	3	.245	.287
Pete Donohue	P47	R	25	47	106	8	33	5	2	0	14	5	8	0	.311	.396
Dolf Luque	P34	R	35	34	78	8	27	5	0	0	8	5	4	0	.346	.410
1 Sammy Bohne	SS20	R	29	25	54	8	11	0	2	0	5	4	8	1	.204	.278
Ethan Allen	OF9	R	22	18	13	3	4	1	0	0	0	3	0	0	.308	.385
Jimmy Hudgens	1B6	L	23	17	20	2	5	1	0	0	1	1	0	0	.250	.300
Ivy Wingo	C7	L	35	7	10	0	2	0	0	0	1	0	1	0	.200	.200
Howard Carter	2B3, SS1	R	21	5	1	0	0	0	0	0	0	0	0	0	.000	.000

2 Everett Scott (LJ) 33 4-6, Doc Prothro 32 R 1-5, Clyde Sukeforth 24 L 0-1

NAME	T	AGE	W	L	PCT	SV	G	GS	CG	IP	H	BB	SO	SHO	ERA
		31	87	67	.565	8	157	157	88	1409	1449	324	424	14	3.42
Pete Donohue	R	25	20	14	.588	2	47	36	17	286	298	39	73	5	3.37
Carl Mays	R	34	19	12	.613	1	39	33	24	281	286	53	58	3	3.14
Eppa Rixey	L	35	14	8	.636	0	37	29	14	233	231	58	61	3	3.40
Jakie May	L	30	13	9	.591	3	45	15	9	168	175	44	103	1	3.21
Dolf Luque	R	35	13	16	.448	0	34	31	16	234	231	77	83	1	3.42
Red Lucas	R	24	8	5	.615	2	39	11	7	154	161	30	34	1	3.68
2 Art Nehf	L	33	0	1	.000	0	7	1	0	17	25	5	4	0	3.71
Roy Meeker	L	25	0	0	—	0	7	0	0	21	24	9	5	0	6.43
Pea Ridge Day	R	27	0	0	—	0	9	0	0	7	13	2	2	0	7.71
Mul Holland	R	23	0	0	—	0	3	0	0	7	3	5	0	0	1.29
Rufe Meadows	R	18	0	0	—	0	1	0	0	1	0	1	0	0	0.00
Brad Springer	L	22	0	0	—	0	1	0	0	5	6	5	0	0	9.00
Marv Goodwin (DD) 35															

PITTSBURGH — 3rd 84-69 .549 4.5 — BILL McKECHNIE

NAME	G by Pos	B	AGE	G	AB	R	H	2B	3B	HR	RBI	BB	SO	SB	BA	SA
TOTALS			28	157	5312	769	1514	243	106	44	707	434	350	91	.285	.396
George Grantham	1B132	R	26	141	449	66	143	27	13	8	70	60	42	6	.318	.490
Hal Rhyne	2B66, SS44, 3B1	R	27	109	366	46	92	14	3	2	39	35	21	1	.251	.322
Glenn Wright	SS116	R	25	119	458	73	141	15	15	8	77	19	26	6	.308	.454
Pie Traynor	3B148, SS3	R	27	152	574	83	182	25	17	3	92	38	14	8	.317	.436
Paul Waner	OF139	L	23	144	536	101	180	35	22	8	79	66	19	11	.336	.528
1 Max Carey	OF82	B	36	86	324	46	72	6	5	0	28	30	14	10	.222	.296
Kiki Cuyler	OF157	R	27	157	614	113	197	31	15	8	92	50	66	35	.321	.458
Earl Smith	C98	L	29	105	292	36	101	17	2	2	46	28	7	1	.346	.438
Johnny Gooch	C80	B	28	86	218	19	59	15	1	1	42	20	14	1	.271	.362
Clyde Barnhart	OF61	R	30	76	203	26	39	3	0	0	10	23	13	1	.192	.207
Johnny Rawlings	2B59	R	33	63	181	27	42	6	0	0	20	14	10	3	.232	.265
Stuffy McInnis	1B40	R	35	47	127	12	38	6	1	0	13	7	3	1	.299	.362
1 Eddie Moore	2B24, 3B9, SS1	R	27	43	132	19	30	8	1	0	19	12	6	3	.227	.303
Carson Bigbee	OF21	L	31	42	68	15	15	3	1	2	4	3	0	2	.221	.382
Joe Cronin	2B27, SS7	R	19	38	83	9	22	2	2	0	11	6	15	0	.265	.337
Roy Spencer	C12	R	26	28	43	5	17	3	0	0	4	1	0	0	.395	.465
Fred Brickell	OF14	L	19	24	55	11	19	3	1	0	4	3	6	0	.345	.436
Walter Mueller	OF15	R	31	19	58	8	15	0	1	0	3	0	2	0	.242	.274
Eddie Murphy	OF3	L	34	16	17	3	2	0	0	0	2	3	0	0	.118	.118
Adam Comorosky	OF6	R	21	8	15	2	4	1	0	0	1	0	1	1	.267	.467

NAME	T	AGE	W	L	PCT	SV	G	GS	CG	IP	H	BB	SO	SHO	ERA
		32	84	69	.549	18	157	157	83	1379	1422	455	387	12	3.67
Ray Kremer	R	33	20	6	.769	5	37	26	18	231	221	51	74	5	2.61
Lee Meadows	R	31	20	9	.690	0	36	31	15	227	254	52	54	1	3.96
Vic Aldridge	R	32	10	13	.435	1	30	26	12	190	204	73	61	1	4.07
Emil Yde	L	26	8	7	.533	0	37	22	12	187	181	81	34	1	3.66
Don Songer	L	27	7	8	.467	2	35	14	5	126	118	52	27	1	3.14
2 Bullet Joe Bush	R	33	6	6	.500	3	19	11	9	111	97	35	38	2	3.00
Johnny Morrison (ST)	R	30	6	8	.429	2	26	13	6	122	119	44	39	2	3.39
Carmen Hill	R	30	3	3	.500	0	6	6	4	40	42	9	8	1	3.38
Red Oldham	R	32	2	2	.500	2	17	2	0	42	56	18	16	0	5.57
Babe Adams	R	44	3	4	.400	3	19	0	0	37	51	8	7	0	6.08
Tom Sheehan	R	32	0	2	.000	0	9	4	1	49	62	25	8	0	6.68
Lou Koupal	R	27	0	2	.000	0	6	1	0	20	22	8	7	0	3.15
Roy Mahaffey	R	22	0	0	—	0	4	0	0	5	3	1	0	0	6.75
Bud Culloton	R	29	0	0	—	0	4	0	0	8	13	5	2	0	7.88
Chet Nichols	R	28	0	0	—	0	3	0	0	13	15	5	2	0	7.88

CHICAGO — 4th 82-72 .532 7 — JOE McCARTHY

NAME	G by Pos	B	AGE	G	AB	R	H	2B	3B	HR	RBI	BB	SO	SB	BA	SA
TOTALS			28	155	5229	682	1453	291	49	66	630	445	447	85	.278	.390
Charlie Grimm	!B147	L	27	147	524	58	145	30	6	8	82	49	25	3	.277	.403
Sparky Adams	2B136, 3B19, SS2	R	31	154	624	95	193	35	3	0	39	52	27	27	.309	.375
Jimmy Cooney	SS141	R	31	141	513	52	129	18	5	1	47	23	10	11	.251	.313
Howard Freigau	3B135, SS2, OF1	R	23	140	508	51	137	27	4	3	51	43	42	6	.270	.368
Cliff Heathcote	OF133	L	28	139	510	98	141	33	3	10	53	64	30	18	.276	.424
Hack Wilson	OF140	R	26	142	529	97	170	36	8	21	109	69	61	10	.321	.539
Riggs Stephenson	OF74	R	28	82	281	40	95	15	3	3	44	31	16	2	.338	.456
Gabby Hartnett	C88	R	25	93	284	35	78	25	3	8	41	32	37	0	.275	.468
Mike Gonzalez	C78	R	35	80	253	24	63	13	1	0	23	13	17	3	.249	.336
Pete Scott	OF59, 3B1	R	28	77	189	34	54	13	1	3	34	22	31	3	.286	.413
Joe Kelly	OF39	L	26	65	176	16	59	15	3	0	32	7	11	0	.335	.455
Chuck Tolson	1B13	R	27	57	80	4	25	6	1	1	8	5	8	0	.313	.450
Joe Munson	OF28	R	26	33	101	17	26	2	2	3	15	8	4	0	.257	.406
Clyde Beck	2B30	R	26	30	81	10	16	0	0	1	4	7	15	0	.198	.235
Mandy Brooks	OF18	R	28	26	48	7	9	1	0	1	6	5	6	0	.188	.271
Red Shannon	SS13	B	29	19	51	9	17	5	0	0	4	3	3	0	.333	.431
Hank Schreiber	SS3, 3B3, 2B1	R	34	16	18	2	1	1	0	0	1	1	1	0	.056	.111

John Churry 25 R 0-4, Joe Graves L 20 0-5, Ralph Michaels 24 R 0-0

NAME	T	AGE	W	L	PCT	SV	G	GS	CG	IP	H	BB	SO	SHO	ERA
		26	82	72	.532	14	155	155	77	1378	1407	486	508	13	3.26
Charlie Root	R	27	18	17	.514	2	42	32	21	271	267	62	127	2	2.82
Guy Bush	R	24	13	9	.591	2	35	15	7	157	149	42	32	2	2.87
Percy Jones	L	26	12	7	.632	2	30	12	10	160	151	90	80	2	3.09
Sheriff Blake	R	26	11	12	.478	1	39	27	11	198	204	92	95	4	3.59
Tony Kaufmann	R	25	9	7	.563	2	26	22	14	170	169	44	52	1	3.02
Bob Osborn	R	23	6	5	.545	1	31	15	6	136	157	58	43	0	3.64
Bill Piercy	R	30	6	5	.545	0	19	5	1	90	96	37	31	0	4.50
1 Pete Alexander	R	39	3	3	.500	0	7	7	5	52	55	7	12	0	3.46
Wilbur Cooper	L	34	2	1	.667	0	8	3	3	55	65	21	18	2	4.42
Pete Scott	R	28	1	0	1.000	0	—	—	—	—	—	—	—	—	—
George Milstead	L	23	1	5	.167	2	18	4	0	55	63	24	14	0	3.60
Johnny Welch	R	19	0	0	—	0	3	0	0	6	1	1	3	0	2.25

NEW YORK — 5th 74-77 .490 13.5 — JOHN McGRAW

NAME	G by Pos	B	AGE	G	AB	R	H	2B	3B	HR	RBI	BB	SO	SB	BA	SA
TOTALS			27	151	5167	663	1435	214	58	73	617	339	420	94	.278	.384
George Kelly	1B114, 2B18	R	30	136	499	70	151	24	4	13	80	36	52	4	.303	.445
Frankie Frisch	2B127, 3B7	B	27	135	545	75	171	29	4	5	44	33	16	23	.314	.409
Travis Jackson	SS108, OF1	R	22	111	385	64	124	24	8	8	51	20	26	3	.322	.496
Fred Lindstrom	3B138, OF1	R	20	140	543	90	164	19	9	9	76	39	21	11	.302	.420
Ross Youngs (IL)	OF94	R	29	95	372	62	114	12	5	4	43	37	19	21	.306	.398
Ty Tyson	OF92	R	34	97	335	40	98	16	1	3	35	15	29	6	.293	.373
Irish Meusel	OF112	R	33	129	449	51	131	25	10	6	65	16	18	5	.292	.432
Paul Florence	C76	B	26	76	188	19	43	4	2	1	14	23	12	2	.229	.314
Bill Terry	1B38, OF14	L	27	98	225	26	65	12	5	5	43	22	17	3	.289	.453
2 Heinie Mueller	OF82	R	26	85	305	36	76	6	2	4	29	21	17	7	.249	.321
Doc Farrell	SS53, 2B3	R	24	67	171	19	49	10	1	2	23	12	17	4	.287	.392
Hugh McMullen	C56	B	24	57	91	5	17	2	0	0	8	5	8	1	.187	.209
Frank Snyder (BH)	C55	R	32	55	148	10	32	7	2	0	16	13	13	0	.216	.365
Jack Scott	P50	L	34	51	83	4	28	4	2	1	13	3	6	0	.337	.470
2 Jimmy Johnston	OF14	R	36	37	69	11	16	0	1	0	5	6	5	0	.232	.232
1 Billy Southworth	OF29	L	33	36	116	23	38	6	1	5	30	7	1	1	.328	.526
Mel Ott	0F10	L	17	35	60	7	23	2	0	0	4	1	9	1	.383	.417
Andy Cohen	2B10, SS10, 3B2	R	21	32	35	4	9	0	3	0	7	2	5	0	.257	.314
Al Moore	OF20	R	23	28	81	12	18	5	2	0	10	5	7	1	.222	.272
Grover Hartley	C13	R	37	13	42	3	2	0	0	0	3	2	0	0	.048	.048
Heinie Groh	3B7	R	36	12	35	2	8	0	0	0	2	2	3	0	.229	.286
Jack Cummings	C6	R	22	7	16	3	5	1	0	0	1	1	1	0	.313	.500
Blackie Carter	OF4	R	23	5	17	4	4	1	0	0	2	0	1	0	.235	.471

Mike Smith 21 1-7, Joe Connell 24 L 0-1, Pete Cote 23 R 0-1, Scottie Slayback 24 R 0-8, Fresco Thompson 24 R 5-8, Jim Boyle 22 R 0-0, Sam Hamby R 28 0-3

NAME	T	AGE	W	L	PCT	SV	G	GS	CG	IP	H	BB	SO	SHO	ERA
		29	74	77	.490	15	151	151	61	1342	1370	427	419	4	3.77
Freddie Fitzsimmons	R	24	14	10	.583	0	37	26	12	219	224	58	48	0	2.88
Kent Greenfield	R	24	13	10	.520	1	39	26	8	223	206	82	74	1	3.96
Jack Scott	R	34	13	15	.464	5	50	22	13	226	242	53	82	0	4.34
Hugh McQuillan	R	30	11	10	.524	0	33	22	12	167	171	42	47	1	3.72
Jimmy Ring	R	31	11	10	.524	2	39	23	5	183	207	74	76	0	4.57
Virgil Barnes (JJ)	R	29	9	13	.381	1	31	25	9	185	183	56	54	2	2.87
John Wisner	R	28	2	2	.500	0	5	3	1	33	40	13	9	0	3.54
Chick Davies	L	34	2	4	.333	6	38	1	0	89	96	35	27	0	3.94
Joe Poetz	R	26	0	1	—	0	6	0	0	9	8	7	3	0	3.38
1 Art Nehf	L	33	0	1	—	0	6	0	0	6	7	4	4	0	9.00
Ned Porter	L	21	0	0	—	0	2	0	0	4	6	2	0	0	4.50
2 Jack Bentley	L	31	0	0	—	0	3	0	0	5	6	2	1	0	9.00
Al Smith	R	22	0	0	—	0	1	0	0	3	5	1	2	0	9.00

BROOKLYN 6th 71-82 .464 17.5 — WILBERT ROBINSON

NAME	G by Pos	B	AGE	G	AB	R	H	2B	3B	HR	RBI	BB	SO	SB	BA	SA
TOTALS			31	155	5130	623	1348	246	62	40	568	475	464	76	.263	.358
Babe Herman	1B101, OF35	L	23	137	496	64	158	35	11	11	81	44	53	8	.319	.500
Chick Fewster	2B103	R	30	105	337	53	82	16	3	2	24	45	49	9	.243	.326
Johnny Butler	SS102, 3B42, 2B8	R	33	147	501	54	135	27	5	1	68	54	44	6	.269	.349
Bill Marriott	3B104	L	33	109	360	39	96	13	9	3	42	17	20	12	.267	.378
Dick Cox	OF117	R	30	124	398	53	118	17	4	1	45	46	20	6	.296	.367
Gus Felix	OF125	R	31	134	432	64	121	21	7	3	53	51	32	9	.280	.382
Zack Wheat	OF102	L	38	111	411	68	119	31	2	5	35	21	14	4	.290	.411
Mickey O'Neil	C74	R	38	75	201	19	42	5	3	0	20	23	8	3	.209	.264
Merwin Jacobson	OF86	L	32	110	288	41	71	9	2	0	23	36	24	5	.247	.292
Jack Fournier	1B64	R	36	87	243	39	69	9	2	11	48	30	16	0	.284	.473
Charlie Hargreaves	C70	R	29	85	208	14	52	13	2	2	23	19	10	1	.250	.361
Rabbit Maranville	SS60, 2B18	R	34	78	234	32	55	8	5	0	24	26	24	7	.235	.312
Jerry Standaert	2B21, 3B14, SS6	R	24	66	113	13	39	8	2	0	14	5	7	0	.345	.451
Whitey Witt	OF22	L	30	63	85	13	22	1	1	0	3	12	6	1	.259	.294
Hank DeBerry	C37	R	31	48	115	6	33	11	0	0	13	8	5	0	.287	.383
2 Sammy Bohne	2B31, 3B15	R	29	47	125	4	25	3	2	1	11	12	9	1	.200	.280
2 Max Carey	OF27	B	36	27	100	18	26	3	1	0	7	8	5	0	.260	.310
Moose Clabaugh	OF2	L	24	11	14	2	1	1	0	0	1	0	0	0	.071	.143

Milt Stock 32 R 0-8, Snooks Dowd 28 R 0-8

NAME	T	AGE	W	L	PCT	SV	G	GS	CG	IP	H	BB	SO	SHO	ERA
TOTALS		32	71	82	.464	9	155	155	83	1362	1440	472	517	5	3.82
Jesse Petty	L	31	17	17	.500	0	38	33	23	276	246	79	101	1	2.84
Burleigh Grimes	R	32	12	13	.480	0	30	29	18	225	238	88	64	1	3.72
Doug McWeeny	R	29	11	13	.458	1	42	24	10	216	213	84	96	1	3.04
Jesse Barnes	R	33	10	11	.476	1	34	24	10	158	204	35	29	1	5.24
Dazzy Vance	R	35	9	10	.474	1	24	22	12	169	172	58	140	1	3.89
Bob McGraw	R	31	9	13	.409	1	33	21	10	174	197	67	49	0	4.60
Rube Ehrhardt	R	31	3	5	.286	0	44	1	0	97	101	35	25	0	3.90
George Boehler	R	34	1	0	1.000	0	10	1	0	35	42	23	10	0	4.37
Leon Williams	L	20	0	0	—	0	8	0	0	16	2	3	0		5.63
Dutch Stryker	R	30	0	0	—	0	2	0	0	2	1	1	0		27.00
Ray Moss	R	24	0	0	—	0	1	0	0	3	1	0	0		9.00

Bill Doak (VR) 35

BOSTON 7th 66-86 .434 22 — DAVE BANCROFT

NAME	G by Pos	B	AGE	G	AB	R	H	2B	3B	HR	RBI	BB	SO	SB	BA	SA
TOTALS			28	153	5216	624	1444	209	62	16	560	426	348	81	.277	.350
Dick Burrus	1B128	L	28	131	486	59	131	21	1	3	61	37	16	4	.270	.335
Doc Gautreau	2B74	R	24	79	266	36	71	9	4	0	8	35	24	17	.267	.331
Dave Bancroft	SS123, 3B2	B	35	127	453	70	141	18	6	3	44	64	29	3	.311	.384
Andy High	3B81, 2B49	L	28	130	476	55	141	17	10	2	66	39	9	4	.296	.387
Jim Welsh	OF129	L	23	134	490	69	136	18	11	3	57	33	28	6	.278	.378
2 Jack Smith	OF83	L	31	96	322	46	100	15	2	2	25	28	12	11	.311	.388
Eddie Brown	OF153	R	33	153	612	71	201	31	8	2	84	23	20	5	.328	.415
Zack Taylor	C123	R	27	125	432	36	110	22	3	0	42	28	27	1	.255	.319
Eddie Taylor	3B62, SS33	R	24	92	272	37	73	8	2	0	33	38	26	4	.268	.313
Frank Wilson	OF56	L	25	87	236	22	56	11	3	0	23	20	21	3	.237	.309
Johnny Cooney	1B31, P19, OF1	L	25	64	126	17	38	3	2	0	18	13	7	6	.302	.357
2 Eddie Moore	2B39, SS14, 3B1	R	26	54	184	17	49	3	2	0	15	16	12	6	.266	.304
Les Mann	OF46	R	33	50	129	23	39	8	2	1	20	9	9	5	.302	.419
Bob Smith	P33	R	31	40	84	10	25	6	2	0	13	2	4	0	.298	.417
Oscar Siemer	C30	R	24	31	73	3	15	1	0	0	5	2	4	0	.205	.219
Bernie Neis	OF23	B	30	30	93	16	20	5	2	0	8	8	10	4	.215	.312
Frank Gibson	C13	R	35	24	47	3	16	4	0	0	7	4	6	2	.340	.426
1 Jimmy Johnston	3B14, 2B2, OF1	R	36	23	57	7	14	1	1	0	5	10	3	2	.246	.316
Shanty Hogan	C4	R	20	14	14	1	4	1	0	0	5	0	0	0	.286	.500
Harry Riconda	3B4	R	29	4	12	1	2	0	0	0	0	0	0	0	.167	.167
Sid Womack	C1	R	30	4	2	0	0	0	0	0	0	1	0	0	.000	.000

NAME	T	AGE	W	L	PCT	SV	G	GS	CG	IP	H	BB	SO	SHO	ERA
TOTALS		28	66	86	.434	9	153	153	60	1365	1536	455	408	9	4.01
Larry Benton	R	28	14	14	.500	1	43	27	12	232	244	81	103	1	3.84
Johnny Wertz	R	28	11	9	.550	0	32	23	7	189	212	47	65	1	3.29
Bob Smith	R	31	10	13	.435	1	33	23	14	201	199	75	44	4	3.76
Joe Genewich	R	29	8	16	.333	2	37	26	12	216	239	63	59	2	3.88
George Mogridge	L	37	6	10	.375	3	39	10	2	142	173	36	46	0	4.50
Hal Goldsmith	R	27	5	7	.417	0	19	15	5	101	135	28	16	0	4.37
Bunny Hearn	L	22	4	3	.571	0	34	12	3	117	121	56	40	0	4.23
Johnny Cooney	L	25	3	3	.500	0	19	8	3	83	106	29	23	1	4.01
Kyle Graham	R	26	3	3	.500	0	15	4	1	36	54	19	7	0	8.00
Foster Edwards	R	22	2	0	1.000	0	3	1	0	25	20	13	4	0	0.72
Rosy Ryan	R	28	2	0	—	0	7	2	0	19	29	7	1	0	7.58
Bill Vargus	L	26	0	0	—	0	4	0	0	4	6	4	1	0	3.00

PHILADELPHIA 8th 58-93 .384 29.5 — ART FLETCHER

NAME	G by Pos	B	AGE	G	AB	R	H	2B	3B	HR	RBI	BB	SO	SB	BA	SA
TOTALS			31	152	5254	687	1479	244	50	75	632	422	479	47	.281	.390
1 Jack Bentley	1B56, P7	L	31	75	240	19	62	12	3	2	27	5	4	0	.258	.358
Barney Friberg	2B144	R	26	144	478	38	128	21	3	1	51	57	77	2	.268	.331
Heinie Sand	SS149	R	28	149	567	99	154	30	5	4	37	66	56	2	.272	.363
Clarence Huber	3B115	R	30	118	376	45	92	17	7	1	34	42	29	9	.245	.335
Cy Williams	OF93	L	38	107	336	63	116	13	4	18	53	38	35	2	.345	.568
Freddy Leach	OF123	L	28	129	492	73	162	29	7	11	71	16	33	6	.329	.484
Johnny Mokan	OF123	R	30	127	456	68	138	23	5	6	62	41	31	4	.303	.414
Jimmie Wilson	C79	R	25	90	279	40	85	10	2	4	32	25	20	3	.305	.398
R. Wrightstone	1B53, 3B37, 2B13, OF5	L	33	112	368	55	113	23	1	7	57	27	11	5	.307	.432
Butch Henline	C77, 1B4, OF2	R	31	99	283	32	80	14	1	2	30	25	18	1	.283	.360
Al Nixon	OF88	R	40	93	311	38	91	18	2	4	41	13	20	5	.293	.402
Wayland Dean	P33	R	24	63	102	11	27	4	0	3	19	5	26	0	.265	.392
George Harper	OF55	L	34	56	194	32	61	6	5	7	38	16	7	6	.314	.505
Ray Grimes	1B28	R	32	32	101	13	30	5	0	0	15	6	13	0	.297	.347
Wally Kimmick	1B5, SS4, 3B4, 2B1	R	29	20	28	0	6	1	0	0	2	3	7	0	.214	.357
Bubber Jonnard	C15	R	26	19	34	3	4	1	0	0	3	0	4	0	.118	.147
Bob Rice	3B15, 2B2, SS2	R	27	19	54	3	8	0	1	0	10	3	4	0	.148	.185
Dick Attreau	1B17	L	29	17	61	9	14	1	1	0	1	1	4	1	.230	.279
Ed Cotter	3B8, SS5	R	21	17	26	3	8	1	0	0	1	4	1	1	.308	.385
Denny Sothern	OF13	R	22	14	53	5	13	1	0	3	10	4	10	0	.245	.434
George Stutz	SS5	R	33	6	8	0	0	0	0	0	0	0	0	0	.000	.000

Joe Buskey 23 R 0-8, Lee Dunham 24 L 1-4, Chick Keating 34 R 0-2, Lew Wendell 34 R 0-4

NAME	T	AGE	W	L	PCT	SV	G	GS	CG	IP	H	BB	SO	SHO	ERA
TOTALS		28	58	93	.384	5	152	152	68	1334	1699	454	331	5	5.03
Hal Carlson	R	34	17	12	.586	0	35	34	20	267	293	47	55	3	3.24
Clarence Mitchell	L	35	9	14	.391	1	38	25	12	179	232	55	52	0	4.58
Claude Willoughby	R	27	8	12	.400	1	47	18	6	168	218	71	37	0	5.95
Dutch Ulrich	R	26	8	13	.381	1	45	16	8	148	178	37	52	1	4.07
Wayland Dean	R	24	8	16	.333	0	33	26	15	204	245	89	52	1	4.90
Jack Knight	R	31	3	12	.200	2	35	15	5	143	206	48	29	0	6.61
Ed Baecht	R	19	2	0	1.000	0	7	1	0	56	73	28	14	0	6.11
Ray Pierce	L	29	2	7	.222	0	37	7	1	85	128	35	18	0	5.61
Ernie Maun	R	25	1	4	.200	0	14	5	0	38	57	18	9	0	6.39
Rusty Yarnall	R	23	0	1	.000	0	1	0	0	1	3	1	0	0	18.00
1 Jack Bentley	L	31	0	0	—	0	7	3	0	25	37	10	7	0	8.28
Lefty Taber	L	26	0	0	—	0	6	0	0	8	5	0	7	0	7.88
Mike Kelly	R	17	0	0	—	0	4	0	0	7	9	4	2	0	9.00
Art Decatur	R	32	0	0	—	0	2	1	0	3	6	4	0	0	6.00
Pete Rambo	R	19	0	0	—	0	1	0	0	4	6	4	1	0	13.50

WORLD SERIES — ST. LOUIS (NL) 4 NEW YORK (AL) 3

LINE SCORES

TEAM	1	2	3	4	5	6	7	8	9	10	11	12	R	H	E

Game 1 — October 2 at New York
| STL (NL) | 0 | 0 | 0 | 0 | 0 | 0 | 0 | 0 | 0 | | | | 1 | 3 | 1 |
| NY (AL) | 1 | 0 | 0 | 0 | 0 | 1 | 0 | 0 | X | | | | 2 | 6 | 0 |

Sherdel, Haines (8) Pennock

Game 2 — October 3 at New York
| STL | 0 | 0 | 2 | 0 | 0 | 0 | 3 | 0 | 1 | | | | 6 | 12 | 1 |
| NY | 0 | 2 | 0 | 0 | 0 | 0 | 0 | 0 | 0 | | | | 2 | 4 | 0 |

Alexander Shocker, Shawkey (8), Jones (9)

Game 3 — October 5 at St. Louis
| NY | 0 | 0 | 0 | 0 | 0 | 0 | 0 | 0 | 0 | | | | 0 | 5 | 1 |
| STL | 0 | 0 | 0 | 3 | 1 | 0 | 0 | 0 | X | | | | 4 | 8 | 0 |

Reuther, Shawkey (5), Thomas (8) Haines

Game 4 — October 6 at St. Louis
| NY | 1 | 0 | 1 | 1 | 4 | 2 | 1 | 0 | 0 | | | | 10 | 14 | 1 |
| STL | 1 | 0 | 0 | 0 | 0 | 0 | 0 | 0 | 1 | | | | 5 | 14 | 0 |

Hoyt Rhem, Reinhart (5), H. Bell (5), Hallahan (7), Keen (9)

Game 5 — October 7 at St. Louis
| NY | 0 | 0 | 0 | 0 | 1 | 0 | 0 | 1 | 1 | 0 | | | 3 | 9 | 1 |
| STL | 0 | 0 | 0 | 1 | 0 | 0 | 1 | 0 | 0 | 0 | | | 2 | 7 | 1 |

Pennock Sherdel

Game 6 — October 9 the New York
| STL | 3 | 0 | 0 | 0 | 1 | 0 | 5 | 0 | 1 | | | | 10 | 13 | 2 |
| NY | 0 | 0 | 0 | 1 | 0 | 0 | 1 | 0 | 0 | | | | 2 | 8 | 1 |

Alexander Shawkey, Shocker (7), Thomas (8)

Game 7 — October 10 at New York
| STL | 0 | 0 | 0 | 3 | 0 | 0 | 0 | 0 | 0 | | | | 3 | 8 | 0 |
| NY | 0 | 0 | 1 | 0 | 0 | 1 | 0 | 0 | 0 | | | | 2 | 8 | 3 |

Haines, Alexander (7) Hoyt, Pennock (7)

COMPOSITE BATTING

NAME	POS	G	AB	R	H	2B	3B	HR	RBI	BA
St. Louis (NL) Totals		7	239	31	65	12	1	4	30	.272
Bottomley	1B	7	29	4	10	3	0	1	5	.345
Southworth	OF	7	29	6	10	1	1	1	4	.345
Hornsby	2B	7	28	2	7	1	0	0	4	.250
L. Bell	3B	7	27	4	7	1	0	1	6	.259
Hafey	OF	7	27	2	5	2	0	0	0	.185
Thevenow	SS	7	24	5	10	1	0	1	4	.417
O'Farrell	C	7	23	2	7	1	0	0	2	.304
Holm	OF	5	16	1	2	1	0	0	1	.125
Douthit	OF	4	15	3	4	2	0	0	1	.267
Alexander	P	3	7	1	0	0	0	0	0	.000
Haines	P	3	5	1	3	0	0	1	2	.600
Sherdel	P	2	5	0	0	0	0	0	0	.000
Flowers	PH	3	3	0	0	0	0	0	0	.000
Rhem	P	1	1	0	0	0	0	0	0	.000
H. Bell	P	1	0	0	0	0	0	0	0	—
Hallahan	P	1	0	0	0	0	0	0	0	—
Keen	P	1	0	0	0	0	0	0	0	—
Reinhart	P	1	0	0	0	0	0	0	0	—
Toporcer	PH	1	0	0	0	0	0	0	0	—
New York (AL) Totals		7	223	21	54	10	1	4	20	.242
Koenig	SS	7	32	2	4	1	0	0	2	.125
Combs	OF	7	28	3	10	2	0	0	2	.357
Lazzeri	2B	7	26	2	5	1	0	0	3	.192
Dugan	3B	7	24	2	8	2	0	0	2	.333
Gehrig	1B	7	23	1	8	2	0	0	4	.348
Severeid	C	4	22	1	6	1	0	0	0	.273
Meusel	OF	7	21	3	5	1	0	1	4	.238
Ruth	OF	7	20	6	6	0	0	4	5	.300
Pennock	P	2	7	1	1	0	0	0	1	.143
Hoyt	P	2	6	0	0	0	0	0	0	.000
Paschal	PH	5	4	1	1	0	0	0	2	.250
Reuther	P	3	4	0	0	0	0	0	0	.000
Collins	C	2	3	0	0	0	0	0	0	.000
Shawkey	P	3	2	0	0	0	0	0	0	.000
Shocker	P	2	2	0	0	0	0	0	0	.000
Adams	PR	2	0	0	0	0	0	0	0	—
Gazella	3B	1	0	0	0	0	0	0	0	—
Jones	P	2	0	0	0	0	0	0	0	—
Thomas	P	2	0	0	0	0	0	0	0	—

COMPOSITE PITCHING

NAME	G	IP	H	BB	SO	W	L	SV	ERA
St. Louis (NL) Totals	7	63	54	31	31	4	3	1	2.71
Alexander	3	20.1	12	4	17	2	0	1	1.33
Sherdel	2	17	15	8	3	0	2	0	2.12
Haines	3	16.2	13	9	5	2	0	0	1.08
Rhem	1	4	7	2	3	0	0	0	6.75
H. Bell	1	2	4	1	1	0	0	0	9.00
Hallahan	1	2	2	3	1	0	0	0	4.50
Keen	1	1	0	0	0	0	0	0	0.00
Reinhart	1	1	4	0	0	0	1	0	—
New York (AL) Totals	7	63	65	11	30	3	4	0	2.86
Pennock	3	22	13	4	8	2	0	0	1.23
Hoyt	2	15	19	1	10	1	1	0	1.20
Shawkey	3	10	8	2	7	0	1	0	5.40
Shocker	2	7.2	13	0	3	0	1	0	5.87
Roether	1	4.1	7	3	0	1	0	0	4.16
Thomas	1	3	1	0	1	1	0	0	3.00
Jones	1	1	2	1	0	0	1	0	9.00

1927 The Finest Crop

By the time 1927 drew to a close, the Yankees owned every offensive statistic the American League could offer, with the exception of doubles and stolen bases. In fact, New York's attack was so devastating that by season's end it was unanimous that the junior circuit had experienced the strongest team ever to take the field. The results of the barrage was such that the pennant race became a pennant chase with the Yankees easily repeating as league champions.

Such was the attack that the Bronx Bombers did not leave first place for even one day as they finished with a 19-game lead over Philadelphia, the biggest winning margin in loop history. The Yankees chalked up 110 victories and a .714 percentage, both new American League records, and manager Miller Huggins had the best offense and best pitching in the League at his fingertips. Although Babe Ruth set a new single season's record for home runs by belting 60 circuit clouts, surprisingly little commotion was raised over this now-revered feat, simply because it was expected that the Bambino would knock even more homers next year. Young Lou Gehrig hit 47 round-trippers, joining the 32-year-old Ruth to form the most feared batting twosome in history. Tony Lazzeri and Bob Meusel joined this duo as 100-RBI men, and Earle Combs hit .356 in the leadoff slot. Thirty-year-old Wilcy Moore surfaced from the minors for the first time and won 19 games, posted the lowest E.R.A. in the league, and became the first sensational relief pitcher in a long chain of Yankee firemen. Connie Mack's Philadelphia Athletics climbed into second place as Al Simmons, Mickey Cochrane, Jimmie Foxx, and Lefty Grove showed the efficiency of Mack's rebuilding program. Ty Cobb also aided the team after his dismissal as Detroit manager and hit .357, enough to give him fifth place league batting honors.

In contrast to the Yankee runaway, the Pittsburgh Pirates clinched the National League pennant on the final day of the season. The Bucs were the early season leaders, but the Chicago Cubs took the lead throughout August behind Hack Wilson's hitting and Charlie Root's pitching. The Cubs, however, faded as summer waned, and the Bucs seized first place on September 1 by beating Chicago 4 to 3 at Forbes Field. The Pirates stayed ahead the rest of the way, pursued hotly by the rallying Cardinals and the Giants. Paul Waner spearheaded the Pirates by brandishing a .380 cutlass and driving in 131 runs. Lloyd Waner, Pie Traynor, and Glenn Wright also starred with the stick for Pittsburgh, and when Kiki Cuyler was benched after a midseason run-in with Manager Donie Bush, Clyde Barnhart stepped in with a .319 stick. Carmen Hill led the Pirate pitchers with 22 wins, while Lee Meadows and Ray Kremer each chipped in with 19 victories.

The World Series itself did nothing to dispel the Yankee might of the regular season. In fact, as more and more time separates that final season's stanza from the rest of history, the events of the Series are more attributed to the chilling display of power which took place before the cry of "play ball" was heard. Legend has it that the Pirates watched the Yankees destroy the baseball in batting practice the day before the World Series opener and were beaten before they began. But oddly enough, even though the Yankees swept the Series in four games, the Pirates outhit them in the first game, and only Ruth—in the last two games—hit the kind of blows the Bucs supposedly expected the entire lineup to deliver.

The season's end brought three departures from the major league stage of longtime leading characters. Ban Johnson resigned as American League President after heading that organization since before its inception as a major league in 1901. August Herrmann, who had been Chairman of the National Commission which governed baseball prior to the appointment of Judge Landis in 1920, resigned as Cincinnati President, and Washington's Walter Johnson left the game with 417 wins, 3,509 strikeouts, and a 2.16 E.R.A., all remarkable achievements in light of the fact that the Senators finished in the second division for ten of Johnson's 21 years.

1927 AMERICAN LEAGUE

NAME	G by Pos	B	AGE	G	AB	R	H	2B	3B	HR	RBI	BB	SO	SB	BA	SA
NEW YORK	1st 110-44 .714															
TOTALS	MILLER HUGGINS		28	155	5347	975	1644	291	103	158	908	635	605	90	.307	.489
Lou Gehrig	1B155	L	24	155	584	149	218	52	18	47	175	109	84	10	.373	.765
Tony Lazzeri	2B113, SS38, 3B9	R	23	153	570	92	176	29	8	18	102	69	82	22	.309	.482
Mark Koenig	SS122	B	24	123	526	99	150	20	11	3	62	25	21	3	.285	.382
Joe Dugan	3B111	R	30	112	387	44	104	24	3	2	43	27	37	1	.269	.362
Babe Ruth	OF151	L	32	151	540	158	192	29	8	60	164	138	89	7	.356	.772
Earle Combs	OF152	L	28	152	648	137	231	36	23	6	64	62	31	15	.356	.511
Bob Meusel	OF131	R	30	135	516	75	174	47	9	8	103	45	58	24	.337	.510
Pat Collins	C89	R	30	92	251	38	69	9	3	7	36	54	24	0	.275	.418
Ray Morehart	2B53	L	27	73	195	45	50	7	2	1	20	29	18	4	.256	.328
Johnny Grabowski	C68	R	27	70	195	29	54	2	4	0	25	20	15	0	.277	.328
Cedric Durst	OF36, 1B2	L	30	65	129	18	32	4	3	0	25	6	7	0	.248	.326
Mike Gazella	3B44, SS6	R	31	54	115	17	32	8	4	0	9	23	16	4	.278	.417
Ben Paschal	OF27	R	31	50	82	16	26	9	2	2	16	4	10	0	.317	.549
Julie Wera	3B19	R	25	38	42	7	10	3	0	1	8	1	5	0	.239	.381
Benny Bengough	C30	R	28	31	85	6	21	3	3	0	10	4	4	0	.247	.353
PHILADELPHIA	2nd 91-63 .591 19		31	155	5296	841	1606	281	70	56	767	551	326	101	.303	.414
TOTALS	CONNIE MACK															
Jimmy Dykes	1B82,3B25,2B5,SS5,OF5,P2	R	30	121	417	61	135	33	6	3	60	44	23	2	.324	.453
Max Bishop	2B106	L	27	117	372	80	103	15	1	0	22	105	28	8	.277	.323
Joe Boley	SS114	R	30	118	370	49	115	18	8	1	52	26	14	8	.311	.411
Sammy Hale	3B128	R	30	131	501	77	157	24	8	5	81	32	32	11	.313	.423
Ty Cobb	OF126	L	40	134	490	104	175	32	7	5	94	67	12	22	.357	.482
Al Simmons (IL)	OF105	R	25	106	406	86	159	36	11	15	108	31	30	10	.392	.645
Walt French	OF94	L	27	109	326	49	99	10	5	0	41	16	14	9	.304	.365
Mickey Cochrane	C123	L	24	126	432	80	146	20	6	12	80	50	7	9	.338	.495
Eddie Collins	2B56, SS1	L	40	95	225	50	76	12	1	1	15	60	9	6	.338	.413
Zack Wheat	OF62	L	39	88	247	34	80	12	1	1	38	18	5	2	.324	.393
Bill Lamar (ST)	OF79	L	30	84	324	48	97	20	4	2	47	16	10	4	.299	.426
Chick Galloway	SS61, 3B7	R	30	77	181	15	48	10	4	0	22	18	9	1	.265	.365
Jimmie Foxx	1B32, C5	R	19	61	130	23	42	6	5	3	20	14	11	2	.323	.515
Cy Perkins	C54, 1B1	R	31	59	137	11	35	7	2	1	15	12	8	0	.255	.358
Jim Poole	1B31	L	32	38	99	4	22	2	0	0	10	9	6	0	.222	.242
Dud Branom	1B26	L	29	30	94	8	22	1	0	0	13	2	5	2	.234	.245
3 Baby Doll Jacobson	OF14	R	36	17	35	3	8	3	0	1	5	0	3	0	.229	.400
Charlie Bates	OF9	R	19	9	38	5	9	2	2	0	2	3	5	3	.237	.395
Rusty Saunders	OF4	R	21	5	15	2	2	1	0	0	2	3	2	0	.133	.200
Joe Mellana	3B2	R	22	4	7	1	2	0	0	0	1	1	1	0	.286	.286
WASHINGTON	3rd 85-69 .552 25		30	157	5389	782	1549	268	87	29	696	498	359	133	.287	.386
TOTALS	BUCKY HARRIS															
Joe Judge	1B136	L	33	137	522	68	161	29	11	2	71	45	22	10	.308	.418
Bucky Harris	2B128	R	30	128	475	98	127	20	3	1	55	66	33	18	.267	.328
Bobby Reeves	SS96, 3B12, 2B2	R	23	112	380	37	97	11	5	1	39	21	53	3	.255	.318
Ossie Bluege	3B146	R	26	146	503	71	138	21	10	1	66	57	47	15	.274	.362
Sam Rice	OF139	L	36	142	603	98	179	33	14	2	65	36	11	19	.297	.408
Tris Speaker	OF120, 1B1	L	39	141	523	71	171	43	6	2	73	55	8	9	.327	.444
Goose Goslin	OF148	L	26	148	581	96	194	37	15	13	120	50	28	21	.334	.516
Muddy Ruel	C128	R	31	131	428	61	132	16	5	1	52	63	18	9	.308	.376
Earl McNeely	OF47, 1B4	R	29	73	185	40	51	10	4	0	16	11	13	11	.276	.373
Bennie Tate	C39	L	25	61	131	12	41	5	1	1	24	8	4	0	.313	.389
Stuffy Stewart	2B37, 3B2	R	33	56	129	24	31	6	2	0	4	8	15	12	.240	.318
2 Topper Rigney	SS32, 3B6	R	30	45	132	20	36	5	4	0	13	22	10	1	.273	.371
Sloppy Thurston	P29	R	28	42	92	11	29	4	2	1	17	5	10	1	.315	.467
Sammy West (PB)	OF18	L	22	38	67	9	16	4	1	0	6	8	8	1	.239	.358
Ollie Tucker	OF5	L	25	20	24	1	5	2	0	0	8	4	2	0	.208	.292
1 Nick Cullop	OF5, 1B1	R	26	15	23	2	5	2	0	0	1	1	6	0	.217	.304
1 Buddy Myer	SS15	L	23	15	51	7	11	0	0	0	7	8	3	3	.216	.235
Babe Ganzel	OF13	R	26	13	48	7	21	4	2	1	13	7	3	0	.438	.667
Grant Gillis	SS10	R	26	10	36	8	8	3	1	0	2	2	0	0	.222	.361
Jackie Hayes	SS8, 3B1	R	20	10	29	2	7	0	0	0	1	1	2	0	.241	.241
Johnny Berger	C9	R	25	9	15	1	4	1	0	0	1	2	3	0	.267	.333
Eddie Onslow	1B5	L	34	9	18	1	4	1	0	0	1	0	0	0	.222	.278
1 Mickey O'Neil	C4	R	29	6	6	0	0	0	0	0	0	1	1	0	.000	.000
Red Barnes	OF3	L	23	3	11	5	4	1	0	0	0	1	2	0	.364	.455
Buddy Deer	2B1	R	21	1	1	0	0	0	0	0	0	0	0	0	.000	.000
Lefty Atkinson		L	23	1	0	0	0	0	0	0	0	0	0	0	.000	.000
Patsy Gharrity (DE)34																

NAME	T	AGE	W	L	PCT	SV	G	GS	CG	IP	H	BB	SO	SHO	ERA
		31	110	44	.714	20	155	155	82	1390	1403	409	431	11	3.20
Waite Hoyt	R	26	22	7	.759	1	36	32	23	256	242	54	86	3	2.64
Wilcy Moore	R	30	19	7	.731	13	50	12	6	213	185	59	75	1	2.28
Herb Pennock	L	33	19	8	.704	2	34	26	18	210	225	48	51	1	3.00
Urban Shocker	R	36	18	6	.750	0	31	27	13	200	207	41	35	2	2.84
Dutch Ruether	L	33	13	6	.684	0	27	26	12	184	202	52	45	3	3.38
George Pipgras	R	27	10	3	.769	0	29	21	9	166	148	77	81	1	4.12
Myles Thomas	R	29	7	4	.636	0	21	9	1	89	111	43	25	0	4.85
Bob Shawkey	R	36	2	3	.400	4	19	2	0	44	44	16	23	0	2.86
Joe Giard	L	28	0	0	—	0	16	0	0	27	38	19	10	0	8.00
Walter Beall	R	27	0	0	—	0	1	0	0	1	1	0	0	0	9.00
		31	91	63	.591	25	155	155	66	1390	1467	442	553	8	3.95
Lefty Grove	L	27	20	13	.606	9	51	28	14	262	251	79	174	1	3.20
Rube Walberg	L	30	17	12	.586	4	46	33	15	249	257	91	136	0	3.98
Jack Quinn	R	43	15	10	.600	1	34	26	11	207	211	37	43	3	3.17
Howard Ehmke	R	33	12	10	.545	0	30	27	10	190	200	60	68	1	4.21
Eddie Rommel	R	29	11	3	.786	1	30	17	8	147	166	48	33	2	4.35
Sam Gray	R	29	8	6	.571	3	37	13	3	133	153	51	49	1	4.53
Jing Johnson	R	32	4	2	.667	0	17	3	2	52	42	16	16	0	3.46
Lefty Willis	R	21	3	1	.750	0	15	2	1	27	32	11	7	0	5.67
Ike Powers	R	21	1	1	.500	0	11	1	0	26	26	7	3	0	4.50
2 Guy Cantrell	R	23	0	2	.000	0	2	2	1	18	25	7	7	0	5.00
Joe Pate	L	35	0	0	—	6	32	0	0	54	67	21	14	0	5.17
Neal Baker	R	23	0	0	—	0	5	2	0	17	27	7	3	0	5.82
Jimmy Dykes	R	30	0	0	—	1	2	0	0	2	2	1	0	0	4.50
Buzz Wetzel	R	32	0	0	—	0	2	0	0	5	8	5	0	0	7.20
Carroll Yerkes	L	24	0	0	—	0	1	0	0	1	1	0	0	0	0.00
		28	85	69	.552	23	157	157	62	1408	1444	491	497	10	3.95
Hod Lisenbee	R	28	18	9	.667	0	39	34	17	242	221	78	105	4	3.57
Bump Hadley	R	22	14	6	.700	0	30	27	13	199	177	86	60	0	2.85
Sloppy Thurston	R	28	13	13	.500	0	29	28	13	205	254	60	38	2	4.48
Firpo Marberry	R	28	10	7	.588	9	56	10	2	155	177	68	74	0	4.64
Garland Braxton	L	17	10	9	.526	13	59	2	0	156	144	33	96	0	2.94
Walter Johnson (BL)	R	39	5	6	.455	0	18	15	7	108	113	26	48	1	5.08
1 General Crowder	R	28	4	7	.364	0	15	11	4	67	58	42	32	2	4.57
2 Tom Zachary	L	31	4	7	.364	0	15	14	5	110	126	30	13	1	3.68
Bobby Burke	L	20	3	2	.600	0	35	6	1	99	91	32	20	0	4.00
Stan Coveleski	R	37	2	1	.667	0	5	4	0	14	13	8	3	0	3.21
Paul Hopkins	R	22	1	0	1.000	0	2	1	0	9	13	6	5	0	5.00
George Murray	R	28	1	1	.500	0	7	3	0	18	18	15	5	0	7.00
Dick Coffman	R	20	0	1	—	0	5	2	0	16	20	2	5	0	3.37
Dick Jones	R	25	0	0	—	0	3	1	0	9	4	1	0	0	24.00
Clay Van Alstyne	R	27	0	0	—	0	2	0	0	1	1	1	1	0	3.00
Ralph Judd	R	16	0	0	—	0	3	0	0	4	8	1	0	0	6.75

DETROIT — 4th 82-71 .536 27.5 — GEORGE MORIARTY

NAME	G by Pos	B	AGE	G	AB	R	H	2B	3B	HR	RBI	BB	SO	SB	BA	SA
TOTALS			28	156	5299	845	1533	282	100	51	755	587	420	141	.289	.409
Lu Blue	1B104	B	30	112	365	71	95	17	9	1	42	71	28	13	.260	.364
Charlie Gehringer	2B121	L	24	133	508	110	161	29	11	4	61	52	31	17	.317	.441
Jackie Tavener	SS114	L	29	116	419	60	115	22	9	5	59	36	38	20	.274	.406
Jack Warner	3B138	R	23	139	559	78	149	22	9	1	45	47	45	15	.267	.343
Harry Heilmann	OF135	R	32	141	505	106	201	50	9	14	120	72	16	11	.398	.616
Heinie Manush	OF150	L	25	152	593	102	177	31	18	6	80	47	29	12	.298	.442
Bob Fothergill	OF137	R	29	143	527	93	189	38	9	9	114	47	31	9	.359	.516
Larry Woodall	C86	R	32	88	246	28	69	8	6	0	39	37	9	9	.280	.362
Marty McManus	SS39, 2B35, 3B22, 1B6	R	27	108	369	60	99	19	7	9	69	34	38	8	.268	.431
Johnny Bassler	C67	L	32	81	200	19	57	7	0	0	24	45	9	1	.285	.320
Johnny Neun	1B53	B	26	79	204	38	66	9	4	0	27	35	13	22	.324	.407
Al Wingo	OF34	R	29	75	137	15	32	8	2	0	20	25	14	1	.234	.321
Art Ruble	OF43	L	24	56	91	16	15	4	2	0	11	14	15	2	.165	.253
Merv Shea	C31	R	26	34	85	5	15	6	3	0	9	7	15	0	.176	.318
Bernie deViveiros	SS14, 3B1	R	26	24	22	4	5	1	0	0	2	2	8	1	.227	.273
Cyde Manion		R	30	1	0	0	0	0	0	0	0	0	0	0	—	—

NAME	T	AGE	W	L	PCT	SV	G	GS	CG	IP	H	BB	SO	SHO	ERA
TOTALS		27	82	71	.536	17	156	156	75	1393	1542	577	421	5	4.13
Earl Whitehill	L	27	16	14	.533	3	41	31	17	236	238	105	95	3	3.36
Rip Collins	R	31	13	7	.650	0	30	25	10	173	207	59	37	1	4.68
Ken Hollaway	R	29	11	6	.478	6	36	23	11	183	210	61	36	1	4.09
Sam Gibson	R	27	11	12	.478	0	33	26	11	190	201	86	76	0	3.70
Ownie Carroll	R	24	10	6	.625	0	31	15	8	172	186	73	41	0	3.98
Lil Stoner	R	28	10	13	.435	5	38	24	13	215	251	77	63	0	3.98
Haskell Billings	R	19	5	4	.556	0	10	9	5	67	64	39	18	0	4.84
George Smith	R	25	4	1	.800	0	29	0	0	71	62	50	32	0	3.93
Don Hankins	R	25	2	1	.667	2	20	1	0	42	67	13	10	0	6.43
Ed Wells	L	27	0	1	.000	1	8	1	0	20	28	5	5	0	6.75
Jess Doyle	R	29	0	0	—	0	7	0	0	12	16	5	5	0	8.25
Jim Walkup	L	31	0	0	—	0	2	0	0	2	3	0	0	0	4.50
Augie Johns	L	27	0	0	—	0	1	1	0	1	1	1	1	0	9.00
Rufus Smith	L	22	0	0	—	0	1	0	0	8	3	2	0	0	3.38

CHICAGO — 5th 70-83 .458 39.5 — RAY SCHALK

NAME	G by Pos	B	AGE	G	AB	R	H	2B	3B	HR	RBI	BB	SO	SB	BA	SA
TOTALS			28	153	5157	662	1433	285	61	36	610	493	389	90	.278	.378
Bud Clancy	1B123	L	26	130	464	46	139	21	2	3	53	24	24	4	.300	.373
Aaron Ward	2B138, 3B6	R	30	145	463	75	125	25	8	5	56	63	56	6	.270	.391
Bill Hunnefield	SS78, 2B17, 3B1	B	28	112	365	45	104	25	1	2	36	25	24	13	.285	.375
Willie Kamm	3B146	R	27	148	540	85	146	32	13	0	59	70	18	7	.270	.378
Bill Barrett	OF147	R	27	147	556	62	159	35	9	4	83	52	46	20	.286	.403
Alex Metzler	OF134	L	24	134	543	87	173	29	11	3	61	61	39	15	.319	.429
Bibb Falk	OF145	L	28	145	535	76	175	35	6	8	83	52	19	5	.327	.465
Harry McCurdy	C82	L	27	86	262	34	75	19	3	1	27	32	24	6	.286	.393
Buck Crouse	C81	L	30	85	222	22	53	11	0	0	20	21	10	4	.239	.288
Roger Peckinpaugh	SS60	R	36	68	217	23	64	6	3	0	23	21	6	2	.295	.350
2 Bernie Neis	OF21	B	31	45	76	9	22	5	0	0	11	10	9	1	.289	.355
Earl Sheely	1B36	R	34	45	129	11	27	3	0	2	16	20	5	1	.209	.279
Sarge Connally	P43	R	28	43	67	5	22	1	0	0	6	2	10	0	.328	.343
Moe Berg (RL)	2B10, C10, SS6, 3B3	R	25	35	69	4	17	4	0	0	4	10	4	0	.246	.304
Ike Boone (IL)	OF11	L	30	29	53	10	12	4	0	1	11	3	4	0	.226	.358
Ray Flaskamper	SS25	B	25	26	95	12	21	5	0	0	6	3	8	0	.221	.274
Ray Schalk	C15	R	34	16	26	2	6	2	0	0	2	2	1	0	.231	.308
Carl Reynolds	OF13	R	24	14	42	5	9	3	0	1	7	5	7	1	.214	.357
Johnny Mostil (IL)	OF6	R	31	13	16	3	2	0	0	0	1	0	1	1	.125	.125
Kid Wilson	OF2	L	31	7	10	1	1	0	0	0	1	0	2	1	.100	.100
Jim Battle	3B84, SS2	R	26	6	8	1	3	0	1	0	0	0	3	0	.375	.625
Randy Moore	OF4	R	22	6	15	0	0	0	0	0	0	1	0	0	.000	.000
Bobby Way	2B1	R	21	5	3	1	1	0	0	0	0	1	0	1	.333	.333
Lena Blackburne		R	40	1	1	0	1	0	0	0	0	1	0	0	1.000	1.000

NAME	T	AGE	W	L	PCT	SV	G	GS	CG	IP	H	BB	SO	SHO	ERA
TOTALS		30	70	83	.458	8	153	153	85	1367	1467	440	365	10	3.91
Ted Lyons	R	26	22	14	.611	2	39	34	30	308	291	67	71	2	2.84
Tommy Thomas	R	27	19	16	.543	1	40	36	24	308	271	94	107	3	2.97
Ted Blankenship	R	26	12	17	.414	0	37	34	11	237	280	74	51	3	5.05
Sarge Connally	R	28	12	15	.400	5	43	18	11	198	217	83	58	1	4.09
Red Faber (SA)	R	38	4	7	.364	0	18	15	6	111	131	41	30	0	4.54
Elmer Jacobs	R	34	4	4	.333	0	25	3	2	74	105	37	22	1	4.63
Bert Cole	L	31	1	4	.200	0	27	2	0	67	79	19	12	0	4.70
Frank Stewart	R	20	0	1	.000	0	1	1	0	9	9	6	1	0	9.00
Charlie Barnabe	L	27	0	5	.000	0	17	5	1	61	86	20	5	0	5.31
Joe Brown	R	26	0	0	—	0	1	0	0	2	1	0	0	0	

CLEVELAND — 6th 66-87 .431 43.5 — JACK McCALLISTER

NAME	G by Pos	B	AGE	G	AB	R	H	2B	3B	HR	RBI	BB	SO	SB	BA	SA
TOTALS			28	153	5202	668	1471	321	52	26	616	381	366	64	.283	.379
George Burns	1B139	R	34	140	549	84	175	51	2	3	78	42	27	13	.319	.435
Lew Fonseca	2B96, 1B13	R	28	112	428	60	133	26	7	2	40	12	17	12	.311	.404
Joe Sewell	SS153	R	28	153	569	83	180	48	5	1	92	51	7	3	.316	.424
Rube Lutzke	3B98	R	29	100	311	35	78	12	3	0	41	22	29	2	.251	.309
Homer Summa	OF145	R	28	145	574	72	164	41	7	4	74	32	18	6	.286	.402
Fred Eichrodt	OF81	R	24	85	267	24	59	9	2	0	25	16	25	2	.221	.307
Charlie Jamieson	OF127	L	34	127	489	73	151	23	6	0	36	64	14	7	.309	.380
Luke Sewell	C126	R	26	128	470	52	138	27	4	0	53	20	23	4	.294	.377
Johnny Hodapp	3B67, 1B4	R	21	79	240	25	73	15	3	5	40	14	23	2	.304	.454
Freddie Spurgeon	2B52	R	25	57	179	30	45	6	1	2	19	18	14	8	.251	.313
Glenn Myatt	C26	L	29	55	94	15	23	6	0	2	8	12	7	1	.245	.340
Joe Shaute	P45	L	27	45	83	7	27	5	1	0	6	2	13	0	.325	.410
2 Nick Cullop	OF20, P1	R	26	32	68	9	16	2	3	1	8	9	19	0	.235	.397
1 Baby Doll Jacobson	OF31	R	36	32	103	13	26	5	0	0	13	6	4	0	.252	.301
1 Bernie Neis	OF29	B	31	32	96	17	29	9	0	4	18	10	9	0	.302	.521
Johnny Gill	OF17	L	27	21	60	8	13	3	0	1	4	7	13	1	.217	.317
Sam Langford	OF20	R	27	20	67	10	18	5	0	0	7	5	7	0	.269	.388
Pat McNulty	OF12	L	27	19	41	3	13	1	0	0	4	4	3	1	.317	.341
Johnny Burnett	2B2	R	22	7	8	0	2	0	0	0	0	3	1	0	.000	.000
Martin Autry	C14	R	24	16	43	5	11	4	1	0	7	0	4	0	.256	.395
Carl Lind	2B11, SS1	R	23	12	37	2	5	1	0	0	1	5	7	1	.135	.135
Ernie Padgett	2B4	R	28	7	7	1	2	0	0	0	0	1	0	0	.286	.286
George Garken	OF5	R	23	6	14	1	3	0	0	0	2	1	3	0	.214	.214
Dutch Ussat	3B4	R	23	4	16	4	3	0	1	0	0	2	1	0	.188	.313

NAME	T	AGE	W	L	PCT	SV	G	GS	CG	IP	H	BB	SO	SHO	ERA
TOTALS		28	66	87	.431	8	153	153	72	1353	1542	508	366	5	4.27
Willis Hudlin	R	21	18	12	.600	0	43	30	18	265	291	83	65	1	4.01
Jake Miller	L	29	10	8	.556	0	34	23	11	185	189	48	53	0	3.21
Garland Buckeye	L	29	10	17	.370	1	35	25	13	205	231	74	38	2	3.95
Joe Shaute	L	27	9	16	.360	2	45	28	14	230	255	75	63	0	4.23
George Uhle (SA)	R	28	8	9	.471	1	25	22	10	153	187	59	69	1	4.36
George Grant	R	24	4	6	.400	1	25	3	2	75	85	40	19	0	4.44
Benn Karr	R	33	3	3	.500	2	22	5	1	77	92	32	17	0	5.02
Emil Levsen (AJ)	R	29	3	7	.300	0	25	13	2	80	96	37	15	1	5.52
Sherry Smith	L	36	1	1	.200	1	11	2	1	38	53	14	8	0	5.44
Hal McKain	R	20	1	1	.000	0	11	1	0	11	18	4	5	0	4.09
Jumbo Brown (NJ)	R	20	0	2	.000	0	9	1	0	19	19	26	8	0	6.16
Willie Underhill	R	22	0	2	.000	0	4	0	0	8	12	11	4	0	10.13
Hap Collard	R	28	0	0	—	0	5	0	0	5	8	3	2	0	5.40
2 Nick Cullop	R	26	0	0	—	0	1	0	0	3	3	0	0	0	9.00
Wes Farrell	R	19	0	0	—	0	1	0	0	3	2	0	0	0	27.00

ST. LOUIS — 7th 59-94 .386 50.5 — DAN HOWLEY

NAME	G by Pos	B	AGE	G	AB	R	H	2B	3B	HR	RBI	BB	SO	SB	BA	SA
TOTALS			32	155	5220	724	1440	262	59	55	657	443	420	91	.276	.380
George Sisler	1B149	L	34	149	614	87	201	32	8	5	97	24	15	27	.327	.430
Oscar Melillo	2B101	R	27	107	356	45	80	18	2	0	26	25	28	3	.225	.287
Wally Gerber	SS141, 3B1	R	35	142	438	44	98	13	9	0	45	35	25	2	.224	.295
Frank O'Rourke	3B120, 2B16, 1B3	R	32	140	538	85	144	25	3	1	39	64	43	19	.268	.331
Harry Rice	OF130, 3B7	R	26	137	520	90	149	26	9	7	68	50	21	6	.287	.412
Bing Miller	OF126	R	32	143	492	83	160	32	7	5	75	30	26	9	.325	.469
Ken Williams	OF113	L	37	131	421	70	136	23	6	17	74	57	30	9	.323	.527
Wally Schang	C75	B	37	97	263	40	84	15	2	5	42	41	33	3	.319	.449
Herschel Bennett	OF55	L	30	93	256	40	68	12	2	3	30	14	21	6	.266	.363
Spencer Adams	2B54, 3B28	R	29	88	259	32	69	11	3	0	29	24	33	1	.266	.332
Steve O'Neill	C60	R	35	74	191	14	44	7	0	1	22	20	6	0	.230	.283
Fred Schulte (BW-CN)	OF49	R	26	60	189	32	60	16	5	3	34	20	14	5	.317	.503
Otto Miller	SS35, 3B11	R	26	51	76	8	17	5	0	0	8	5	0	2	.224	.289
Leo Dixon	C35	R	32	36	103	6	20	3	1	0	12	7	6	0	.194	.243
Red Kress	SS7	R	22	7	23	3	7	2	1	1	3	3	3	0	.304	.609
Guy Sturdy	1B5	L	27	5	21	5	9	1	0	0	5	7	0	1	.429	.476

NAME	T	AGE	W	L	PCT	SV	G	GS	CG	IP	H	BB	SO	SHO	ERA
TOTALS		29	59	94	.386	8	155	155	80	1353	1592	604	385	4	4.95
Milt Gaston	R	31	13	17	.433	1	37	30	21	254	275	100	77	0	5.00
Elam Vangilder	R	31	10	12	.455	1	44	23	12	203	245	102	62	3	4.79
Lefty Stewart	L	26	8	11	.421	2	27	19	11	156	187	43	43	0	4.27
Sad Sam Jones	R	34	8	14	.364	0	30	26	11	190	211	102	72	0	4.31
Win Ballou	R	29	5	6	.455	0	21	11	4	90	105	46	17	0	4.80
1 Tom Zachary	L	31	4	6	.400	0	13	12	6	78	110	27	13	0	4.38
2 General Crowder	R	28	5	3	.375	3	21	8	2	74	71	42	30	1	4.99
Ernie Nevers	R	24	3	8	.273	2	27	5	2	95	105	35	22	0	4.92
Ernie Wingard	L	26	2	13	.133	0	38	17	7	156	213	79	28	0	6.58
Boom Boom Beck	R	22	1	0	1.000	0	1	1	0	11	15	5	6	0	5.72
Chet Falk	R	22	1	0	1.000	0	16	5	2	65	81	25	10	2	5.62
Jiggs Wright	R	26	1	0	1.000	0	4	1	0	12	8	4	4	0	4.50
Stew Bolen	L	24	0	1	.000	0	14	1	0	14	18	14	5	0	8.10
George Blaeholder	R	23	0	0	—	0	1	0	0	5	8	2	0	0	5.00

BOSTON — 8th 51-103 .331 59 — BILL CARRIGAN

NAME	G by Pos	B	AGE	G	AB	R	H	2B	3B	HR	RBI	BB	SO	SB	BA	SA
TOTALS			28	154	5207	597	1348	271	78	28	550	430	456	82	.259	.357
Phil Todt	1B139	R	28	140	516	55	122	22	6	6	52	28	23	6	.236	.337
Bill Regan	2B121	R	28	129	468	43	128	37	10	2	66	26	51	0	.274	.408
2 Buddy Myer	SS101, 3B14, OF10, 2B1	L	23	133	469	59	135	22	11	2	47	48	15	9	.288	.394
Billy Rogell	3B53, 2B2, OF2	B	22	82	207	35	55	14	4	2	28	24	35	3	.266	.420
Jack Tobin	OF93	L	35	111	374	52	116	18	3	2	40	36	9	5	.310	.390
Ira Flagstead	OF129	R	33	131	466	63	133	26	4	8	69	57	25	12	.285	.401
Wally Shaner	OF108, 1B1	R	27	122	406	54	111	33	6	3	49	21	35	11	.273	.406
Grover Hartley	C86	R	38	103	244	23	67	11	0	1	30	7	10	2	.275	.332
Jack Rothrock	SS40, 2B36, 3B20, 1B13	R	23	117	428	61	111	24	8	1	36	24	46	5	.259	.360
Cleo Carlyle	OF83	L	24	95	278	31	65	12	8	1	28	36	40	4	.234	.345
Fred Hofmann	C81	R	33	87	217	20	59	19	1	0	24	21	26	2	.272	.359
Red Rollings	3B44, 1B10, 2B2	L	23	84	184	19	49	4	1	0	9	12	10	3	.266	.299
1 Fred Haney	3B34, OF1	R	29	47	116	23	32	3	1	0	12	25	14	4	.276	.405
1 Baby Doll Jacobson	OF39	R	36	45	155	11	38	4	0	0	24	5	12	1	.245	.342
Bill Moore	C42	L	21	45	69	7	15	2	0	0	4	13	8	0	.217	.246
Arlie Tarbert	OF27	R	22	33	69	5	13	1	0	0	4	3	12	0	.188	.203
1 Pee Wee Wanninger	SS15	R	24	18	64	4	5	1	0	0	0	4	6	0	.078	.094
Frank Welch	OF6	R	29	15	28	2	5	1	0	0	4	0	3	0	.179	.250
1 Topper Rigney	3B4, SS1	R	30	6	9	1	1	0	0	0	0	3	4	0	.111	.167
Marty Karow	SS3, 3B2	R	22	6	10	0	2	0	0	0	0	1	1	0	.200	.200
Elmer Eggert	2B1	R	23	1	0	0	0	0	0	0	0	0	0	0	—	—
John Freeman	OF3	R	26	4	4	0	0	0	0	0	0	0	2	0	.000	.000
Fred Bratchi		R	35	2	1	0	0	0	0	0	0	0	1	0	.000	.000

NAME	T	AGE	W	L	PCT	SV	G	GS	CG	IP	H	BB	SO	SHO	ERA
TOTALS		25	51	103	.331	7	154	154	63	1376	1603	558	381	6	4.68
Slim Harriss	R	30	14	21	.400	1	44	27	11	218	253	66	77	1	4.17
Hal Wiltse	L	23	10	18	.357	1	36	29	13	219	276	76	47	1	5.09
Tony Welzer	R	28	6	11	.353	1	37	19	8	182	214	71	56	0	4.45
Danny MacFayden	R	22	5	8	.385	2	34	16	6	160	176	59	42	1	4.27
Del Lundgren	R	27	5	12	.294	0	30	17	5	136	160	87	39	2	6.29
Red Ruffing	R	23	5	13	.278	0	34	15	4	147	172	40	25	1	4.10
Jack Russell	R	21	4	9	.308	0	34	5	4	123	16	7	6	0	3.13
Herb Bradley	R	24	1	1	.500	0	12	2	1	35	16	7	6	0	3.13
Ted Wingfield	R	27	1	7	.125	0	20	6	2	75	105	27	11	0	5.04
Frank Bennett	R	22	0	1	.000	0	6	2	0	12	11	6	3	0	3.00
John Wilson	R	24	0	0	—	0	2	1	0	25	31	13	8	0	3.60
Rudy Sommers	L	39	0	0	—	0	1	0	0	18	14	2	0		8.36
Bob Cremins	L	21	0	0	—	0	4	0	0	5	8	14	2	0	5.40
Frank Bushey	R	20	0	0	—	0	2	1	0	7	2	2	0	0	9.00

Batting

NAME	G by Pos	B	AGE	G	AB	R	H	2B	3B	HR	RBI	BB	SO	SB	BA	SA
PITTSBURGH 1ST 94-60 .610		DONIE BUSH														
TOTALS			28		5397	817	1648	258	78	54	759	437	355	65	.305	.412
Joe Harris	1B116, OF3	R	36	129	411	57	134	27	9	5	73	48	19	0	.326	.472
George Grantham	2B124, 1B29	L	27	151	531	96	162	33	11	8	66	74	39	9	.305	.454
Glenn Wright	SS143	R	26	143	570	78	160	26	4	9	105	39	46	4	.281	.388
Pie Traynor	3B143, SS9	R	28	149	573	93	196	32	9	5	106	22	11	11	.342	.455
Paul Waner	OF143, 1B14	L	24	155	623	113	237	40	17	9	131	60	14	5	.380	.543
Lloyd Waner	OF150, 2B1	L	21	150	629	133	223	17	6	2	27	37	23	14	.355	.410
Clyde Barnhart	OF94	R	31	108	360	66	115	25	5	3	54	37	19	2	.319	.442
Johnny Gooch	C91	B	29	101	291	22	75	17	2	2	48	19	21	0	.258	.351
Kiki Cuyler	OF73	L	28	85	285	60	88	13	7	3	31	37	36	20	.309	.435
Earl Smith (ST)	C61	L	30	66	189	16	51	3	1	5	25	11	11	0	.270	.376
Hal Rhyne (IL)	2B45, 3B10, SS7	R	28	62	168	21	46	5	0	0	17	14	9	0	.274	.304
Roy Spencer	C34	R	27	38	92	9	26	3	1	0	13	3	3	0	.283	.337
Fred Brickell	OF3	L	20	32	21	6	6	1	0	1	4	1	0	0	.286	.476
Adam Comorosky	OF16	R	22	18	61	5	14	1	0	0	4	3	1	0	.230	.246
Heinie Groh	3B12	R	37	14	35	2	10	1	0	0	3	2	3	0	.286	.314
Joe Cronin	2B7, SS4, 1B1	R	20	12	22	2	5	1	0	0	3	2	3	0	.227	.273
Herman Layne	OF2	R	26	11	6	3	0	0	0	0	0	0	0	0	.000	.000
Eddie Sicking	2B5	R	30	6	7	1	1	1	0	0	3	1	0	0	.143	.286
Dick Bartell	SS1	R	19	1	2	0	0	0	0	0	0	0	2	0	.000	.000
ST. LOUIS 2nd 92-61 .601 1.5		BOB O'FARRELL														
TOTALS			27	153	5207	754	1450	264	79	84	700	484	511	110	.278	.408
Jim Bottomley	1B152	L	27	152	574	95	174	31	15	19	124	74	49	8	.303	.509
Frankie Frisch	2B153, SS1	B	28	153	617	112	208	31	11	10	78	43	10	48	.337	.472
Heinie Schuble (RL)	SS65	R	20	65	218	29	56	6	2	4	28	7	27	0	.257	.358
Les Bell	3B100, SS10	R	25	115	390	48	101	26	6	9	65	34	63	5	.259	.426
Wattie Holm	OF97, 3B9	R	25	110	419	55	120	27	8	3	66	24	29	9	.286	.411
Taylor Douthit	OF125	R	26	130	488	81	128	29	6	5	50	52	45	6	.262	.377
Chick Hafey (IL)	OF94	R	24	103	346	62	114	26	5	18	63	36	41	12	.329	.590
Frank Snyder	C62	R	33	64	194	7	50	5	0	1	30	9	18	0	.258	.299
Billy Southworth	OF83	L	34	92	306	52	92	15	5	2	39	23	7	10	.301	.402
Specs Toporcer	3B54, SS27, 2B2, 1B1	R	28	86	290	37	72	13	4	0	19	27	16	5	.248	.321
Johnny Schulte	C59	R	30	64	156	35	45	8	2	9	32	47	19	1	.288	.538
Ray Blades (KJ)	OF50	R	30	61	180	33	57	8	5	2	29	28	22	3	.317	.450
Bob O'Farrell (SA)	C53	R	30	61	178	19	47	10	1	0	18	22	22	1	.264	.331
Tommy Thevenow (BN)	SS59	R	23	59	191	23	37	6	1	0	4	14	8	2	.194	.236
Danny Clark	OF9	L	33	58	72	8	17	2	2	0	13	8	7	0	.236	.319
Ernie Orsatti	OF26	L	24	27	92	15	29	7	3	0	12	11	12	2	.315	.457
Rabbit Maranville	SS9	R	35	9	29	0	7	1	0	0	0	2	2	0	.241	.276
Wally Roettger	OF3	R	24	5	1	0	0	0	0	0	0	0	0	0	.000	.000
Bobby Schang	C3	R	40	3	5	0	1	0	0	0	0	0	0	0	.200	.200
Homer Peel	OF1	R	24	2	2	0	0	0	0	0	0	0	1	0	.000	.000
NEW YORK 3rd 92-62 .597 2		JOHN McGRAW (IL) 70-52 .574		ROGERS HORNSBY 22-10 .688												
TOTALS			28	155	5372	817	1594	251	62	109	765	461	462	73	.297	.427
Bill Terry	1B150	L	28	150	580	101	189	32	13	20	121	46	53	1	.326	.529
Rogers Hornsby	2B155	R	31	155	568	133	205	32	9	26	125	86	38	9	.361	.586
Travis Jackson (IL)	SS124, 3B2	R	23	127	469	67	149	29	4	14	98	32	30	8	.318	.484
Fred Lindstrom	3B87, OF51	R	21	138	562	107	172	36	8	7	58	40	40	10	.306	.436
George Harper	OF142	L	35	145	483	85	160	19	6	16	87	84	27	1	.331	.495
Edd Roush	OF138	L	34	140	570	83	173	27	4	7	58	26	15	18	.304	.402
Heinie Mueller	OF56, 1B1	R	27	84	190	33	55	6	3	3	19	25	12	2	.289	.379
2 Zack Taylor	C81	R	28	83	258	18	60	7	3	0	21	17	20	2	.233	.283
Andy Reese	3B64, OF16, 1B1	R	23	97	355	43	94	14	2	4	21	13	52	5	.265	.349
Mel Ott	OF32	L	18	82	163	23	46	7	3	1	19	13	9	2	.282	.380
Al DeVormer	C54, 1B3	R	36	68	141	14	35	3	1	2	21	11	11	1	.248	.326
Jack Cummings	C34	R	23	43	80	8	29	6	1	2	14	5	10	0	.363	.538
Ty Tyson	OF41	R	35	43	159	24	42	7	2	1	17	10	19	5	.264	.352
1 Doc Farrell	SS36, 3B2	R	25	42	142	13	55	10	1	3	34	12	11	0	.387	.535
2 Les Mann	OF22	R	34	29	67	13	22	4	1	2	10	8	7	2	.328	.507
Sam Hamby	C19	R	29	21	52	6	10	0	1	0	5	7	5	0	.192	.231
2 Mickey O'Neil	C16	R	29	16	38	2	5	0	0	0	1	1	5	0	.132	.132
2 Herb Thomas	OF3, SS1	R	25	13	17	2	3	1	0	0	1	1	2	0	.176	.353
Tex Jeanes	OF6, P1	R	26	11	20	5	6	0	0	0	2	2	0	1	.300	.300
Buck Jordan		L	20	5	5	0	1	0	0	0	0	0	0	0	.200	.200
Joe Klinger	OF1	R	24	3	5	0	2	0	0	0	1	0	1	0	.400	.400
Red Smith	C1	R	23	1	1	0	0	0	0	0	0	0	0	0	.000	.000
Ross Youngs (IL) 30																
CHICAGO 4th 85-68 .556 8.5		JOE McCARTHY														
TOTALS			28	153	5303	750	1505	266	63	74	692	481	492	65	.284	.400
Charlie Grimm	1B147	L	28	147	543	68	169	29	6	2	74	45	21	3	.311	.398
Clyde Beck	2B99, 3B17, SS1	R	27	117	391	44	101	20	5	2	44	43	37	0	.258	.350
Woody English	SS84, 3B1	R	20	87	334	46	97	14	4	1	28	16	26	1	.290	.365
Sparky Adams	2B60, 3B53, SS40	R	32	146	647	100	189	17	4	0	49	42	26	26	.292	.340
Earl Webb	OF86	R	29	102	332	58	100	18	4	14	52	48	43	3	.301	.506
Hack Wilson	OF146	R	27	146	551	119	175	30	12	30	129	71	70	13	.318	.579
Riggs Stephenson	OF146, 3B6	R	29	152	579	101	199	46	9	7	82	65	28	8	.344	.491
Gabby Hartnett	C125	R	26	127	449	56	132	32	5	10	80	44	42	2	.294	.454
Cliff Heathcote	OF57	L	29	83	228	28	67	12	4	2	25	20	16	6	.294	.408
Pete Scott	OF36	R	29	71	156	28	49	18	1	0	21	19	18	1	.314	.442
Eddie Pick	3B49, 2B1, OF1	R	28	54	181	23	31	5	2	1	15	20	26	0	.171	.254
Mike Gonzalez	C36	R	36	39	108	15	26	4	1	0	15	15	10	8	.241	.324
Chuck Tolson	1B8	R	28	39	54	6	16	0	2	0	17	4	9	0	.296	.481
1 Jimmy Cooney	SS33	R	32	33	132	16	32	2	0	0	6	8	7	1	.242	.258
Howard Freigau	3B30	R	24	30	86	12	20	5	0	0	4	9	10	0	.233	.291
Elmer Yoter	3B11	R	27	13	27	2	6	1	1	0	5	4	4	0	.222	.333
2 Fred Haney		R	29	4	3	0	0	0	0	0	0	0	0	0	.000	.000
Harry Wilke	3B3	R	26	3	9	0	0	0	0	0	0	0	0	0	.000	.000
John Churry	C1	R	26	1	0	0	0	0	0	0	0	0	0	0	.000	.000
Tommy Sewell		L	21	1	1	0	0	0	0	0	0	0	0	01.000	1.000	
CINCINNATI 5th 75-78 .490 18.5		JACK HENDRICKS														
TOTALS			29	153	5185	643	1439	222	77	29	575	402	332	62	.278	.367
Wally Pipp	1B114	L	34	122	443	49	115	19	6	2	41	32	11	2	.260	.343
Hughie Critz (HO)	2B113	R	26	115	396	50	110	16	8	4	49	16	18	7	.278	.374
Hod Ford	SS104, 2B12	R	29	115	409	45	112	16	2	1	46	33	34	0	.274	.330
Chuck Dressen	3B142, SS2	R	28	144	548	78	160	36	10	2	55	71	32	7	.292	.405
Curt Walker	OF141	L	30	146	527	60	154	16	10	6	80	47	19	6	.292	.395
Ethan Allen	OF98	R	23	111	359	54	106	26	4	2	20	14	23	12	.295	.407
Rube Bressler	OF120	R	32	124	467	43	136	18	4	3	77	32	22	4	.291	.375
Bubbles Hargrave	C92	R	34	102	305	36	94	18	3	0	35	31	18	0	.308	.387
Billy Zitzmann	OF60, SS8, 3B3	R	29	88	232	47	66	10	4	0	24	20	18	9	.284	.362
Red Lucas	P37, 2B5, SS3, OF1	L	25	80	150	14	47	5	2	0	28	12	10	0	.313	.373
Val Picinich	C61	R	30	65	173	16	44	8	3	0	12	24	15	1	.254	.335
George Kelly	1B49, 2B13, OF2	R	31	61	222	27	60	16	4	5	21	11	23	1	.270	.446
Cuckoo Christensen	OF50	L	27	57	185	25	47	6	0	0	16	20	16	4	.254	.286
Clyde Sukeforth	C24	L	25	58	58	10	11	2	0	0	8	4	3	2	.190	.224
Pinky Pittinger	2B20, SS9, 3B2	R	28	31	84	11	23	3	0	0	10	2	5	0	.274	.369
Babe Pinelli	3B15, SS9, 2B5	R	31	30	76	11	15	7	3	0	8	6	7	2	.197	.263
2 Pee Wee Wanninger	SS28	L	24	29	93	14	23	2	2	0	8	6	9	1	.247	.312
Pid Purdy	OF16	L	23	18	62	15	22	4	1	0	12	4	1	1	.355	.565
Jack White	2B3, SS2	R	21	5	4	1	0	0	0	0	0	0	0	0	.000	.000
Ray Wolf	1B1	R	22	1	1	0	0	0	0	0	0	0	0	0	.000	.000

Pitching

NAME	T	AGE	W	L	PCT	SV	G	GS	CG	IP	H	BB	SO	SHO	ERA
		31	94	60	.610	10	156	156	90	1385	1400	418	435	10	3.66
Carmen Hill	R	31	22	11	.667	3	43	31	22	278	260	80	95	2	3.24
Ray Kremer	R	34	19	8	.704	2	35	28	18	226	205	53	63	3	2.47
Lee Meadows	R	32	19	10	.655	0	40	38	25	299	315	66	84	2	3.40
Vic Aldridge	R	33	15	10	.600	1	35	34	17	239	248	74	86	1	4.25
Johnny Miljus	R	32	8	3	.727	0	19	6	3	76	62	17	24	2	1.89
Johnny Morrison (ST)	R	31	3	2	.600	3	21	2	1	46	63	21	21	0	4.17
Joe Dawson	R	30	3	7	.300	0	20	7	4	81	80	32	17	0	4.44
Mike Cvengros	L	26	2	1	.667	1	23	4	0	54	55	24	21	0	3.33
Roy Mahaffey	R	23	1	0	1.000	0	2	1	0	9	9	9	4	0	8.00
1 Bullet Joe Bush	R	34	1	2	.333	0	5	3	0	7	9	6	1	0	12.86
Emil Yde	L	27	1	3	.250	0	9	2	0	30	45	15	9	0	9.60
Chet Nichols	R	29	0	3	.000	0	8	0	0	28	34	17	9	0	5.79
1 Don Songer	L	28	0	0	—	0	5	0	0	5	10	4	1	0	10.80
Red Peery	L	20	0	0	—	0	1	0	0	1	0	1	0	0	0.00
		31	92	61	.601	11	153	153	89	1367	1416	363	394	14	3.57
Jesse Haines	R	31	24	10	.706	1	38	36	25	301	273	77	89	6	2.72
Pete Alexander	R	40	21	10	.677	3	37	30	22	268	261	38	48	2	2.52
Bill Sherdel	L	30	17	12	.586	6	39	28	18	232	241	48	59	0	3.53
Flint Rhem	R	26	10	12	.455	0	27	26	9	169	189	54	51	2	4.42
Fred Frankhouse	R	23	5	1	.833	0	6	5	5	50	41	16	20	1	2.70
Art Reinhart	L	28	5	2	.714	1	21	9	4	82	82	36	15	2	4.17
2 Bob McGraw	R	32	4	5	.444	0	18	12	4	94	121	30	37	1	5.07
Carlisle Littlejohn	R	25	3	1	.750	0	14	2	1	42	47	14	16	0	4.50
Vic Keen	R	28	2	1	.667	0	21	0	0	34	39	8	12	0	4.76
Hi Bell (JJ)	R	29	1	3	.250	0	25	1	0	57	71	22	31	0	3.95
Jimmy Ring	R	32	0	4	.000	0	13	3	1	33	39	17	13	0	6.55
Syl Johnson	R	26	0	0	—	1	3	0	0	6	5	2	1	0	6.00
Eddie Dyer	L	27	0	0	—	0	2	1	0	2	5	2	1	0	18.00
3 Tony Kaufman	R	26	0	0	—	0	1	0	0	1	4	1	0	0	81.00
		28	92	62	.597	16	155	155	65	1382	1520	453	442	7	3.97
Burleigh Grimes	R	33	19	8	.704	2	39	34	15	260	274	87	102	2	3.53
Freddie Fitzsimmons	R	25	17	10	.630	3	42	31	14	245	260	67	78	1	3.71
Virgil Barnes	R	30	14	11	.560	2	35	29	12	229	251	51	66	2	3.97
2 Larry Benton	R	29	13	5	.722*	2	29	23	8	173	183	54	65	1	3.95
Dutch Henry	L	25	11	6	.647	4	45	15	7	164	184	31	40	1	4.22
1 Hugh McQuillan	R	31	5	4	.556	0	11	9	5	58	73	22	17	0	4.50
2 Don Songer	L	28	3	5	.375	1	22	1	0	50	48	31	9	0	2.88
Bill Clarkson	R	28	3	9	.250	2	26	7	2	87	92	52	28	0	4.34
1 Kent Greenfield	R	25	2	2	.500	0	12	1	0	20	39	13	4	0	9.45
Jim Faulkner	L	27	1	0	1.000	0	3	1	0	13	13	5	2	0	3.60
2 Norman Plitt	R	34	1	0	1.000	0	3	0	0	7	6	1	0	0	3.86
Mul Holland	R	24	1	0	1.000	0	2	0	0	2	3	0	0	0	0.00
Ben Cantwell	R	25	1	1	.500	0	5	2	1	20	24	8	4	0	4.05
2 Bullet Joe Bush	R	34	1	1	.500	0	3	2	1	12	18	5	6	0	7.50
Fay Thomas	R	23	0	0	—	0	6	0	0	16	19	4	11	0	3.38
Jack Bentley	L	32	0	0	—	0	10	0	0	10	7	10	3	0	2.70
Hank Boney	R	23	0	0	—	0	4	0	0	8	4	5	0	0	2.25
Virgil Cheeves	R	26	0	0	—	0	1	0	0	4	6	4	1	0	4.50
Bill Walker	L	23	0	0	—	0	1	0	0	1	6	5	1	0	9.00
Tex Jeanes	R	26	0	0	—	0	1	0	0	1	3	1	0	0	9.00
Art Johnson	L	30	0	0	—	0	1	0	0	2	4	1	1	0	9.00
Ned Porter	R	22	0	0	—	0	2	0	0	3	1	0	0	0	0.00

*Benton, also with Boston, league leader in PCT with .708

		27	85	68	.556	5	153	153	75	1385	1439	514	465	11	3.65
Charlie Root	R	28	26	15	.634	2	48	36	21	309	296	117	145	4	3.76
Sheriff Blake	R	27	13	14	.481	0	32	27	13	224	238	82	64	2	3.29
2 Hal Carlson	R	35	12	8	.600	0	27	22	15	184	201	27	27	2	3.18
Guy Bush	R	25	10	10	.500	2	36	22	9	193	177	79	62	1	3.03
Percy Jones (EJ)	L	27	7	8	.467	0	30	11	5	113	123	72	37	1	4.06
Bob Osborn	R	24	5	5	.500	0	24	12	2	108	125	48	45	0	4.17
Jim Brillheart	L	23	4	2	.667	0	32	12	4	129	140	38	36	0	4.12
Luther Roy	R	24	3	1	.750	0	11	0	0	20	14	11	5	0	2.25
1 Tony Kaufman	R	26	3	3	.500	0	9	6	3	53	75	19	21	0	6.45
2 Art Nehf	L	34	1	1	.500	2	26	2	1	26	26	9	12	1	1.38
Lefty Weinert	L	25	1	1	.500	0	20	1	0	38	41	21	6	5	4.50
2 Wayland Dean	R	25	0	0	—	0	2	0	0	4	6	1	1	0	9.00
Hank Grampp	R	23	0	0	—	0	3	0	0	9	14	3	0	0	9.00
Johnny Welch	R	21	0	0	—	0	1	0	0	3	1	0	0	0	9.00

		31	75	78	.490	12	153	153	87	1368	1472	316	407	12	3.54
Red Lucas	R	25	18	11	.621	2	37	23	19	240	231	39	51	4	3.37
Jakie May	L	31	15	12	.556	1	44	28	17	236	242	70	121	2	3.51
Dolf Luque	R	36	13	12	.520	2	34	27	17	231	225	56	76	2	3.19
Eppa Rixey	L	36	12	10	.545	1	34	29	11	220	240	43	42	1	3.48
Pete Donohue	R	26	6	16	.273	1	33	24	12	191	253	32	48	1	4.10
Ray Kolp	R	32	3	3	.500	3	24	5	2	82	86	29	28	1	3.07
1 Art Nehf	L	34	3	5	.375	4	21	5	1	45	59	14	21	0	5.60
Carl Mays (GJ)	R	35	3	7	.300	1	14	9	6	82	89	10	17	0	3.51
Pete Appleton	R	23	2	1	.667	0	12	2	0	30	29	17	3	1	1.80
Jim Beckman	R	22	0	1	.000	0	4	1	0	12	18	6	0	0	6.00

BROOKLYN 6th 65-88 .425 28.5 — WILBERT ROBINSON

NAME	G by Pos	B	AGE	G	AB	R	H	2B	3B	HR	RBI	BB	SO	SB	BA	SA
TOTALS			30	154	5193	541	1314	195	74	39	499	368	494	106	.253	.342
Babe Herman	1B105, OF1	L	24	130	412	65	112	26	9	14	73	39	41	4	.272	.481
Jay Partridge	2B140	L	24	146	572	72	149	17	6	7	40	20	36	9	.260	.348
John Butler	SS90, 3B96	R	34	149	521	39	124	13	6	2	38	14	22	1	.238	.298
Bob Barrett	3B96	R	28	99	355	29	92	10	2	5	38	14	22	1	.259	.341
Max Carey	OF141	B	37	144	538	70	143	30	10	1	54	64	18	32	.266	.364
Jigger Statz	OF122, 3B96	R	29	130	507	64	139	24	7	1	21	26	43	10	.274	.355
Gus Felix	OF119	R	32	130	445	43	118	21	8	0	57	39	47	6	.265	.348
Hank DeBerry	C67	R	32	68	201	15	47	3	1	2	21	17	8	1	.234	.284
Harvey Hendrick	OF64, 1B53, 2B1	L	29	128	458	55	142	18	11	4	50	24	40	29	.310	.424
Jake Flowers	SS65, 2B1	R	25	67	231	26	54	5	5	2	20	21	25	3	.234	.325
Butch Henline	C60	R	32	67	177	12	47	10	3	1	18	17	10	1	.266	.373
Charlie Hargreaves	C44	R	30	46	133	9	38	3	1	0	11	14	7	1	.286	.323
Irish Meusel	OF17	R	34	42	74	7	18	3	1	1	7	11	5	0	.243	.351
Overton Tremper	OF18	R	21	26	60	4	14	0	0	0	4	0	2	0	.233	.233
Chuck Corgan (IL)	2B13, SS3	R	27	26	57	3	15	1	0	0	1	4	1	0	.263	.281
Merwin Jacobson	OF3	L	33	11	6	4	0	0	0	0	1	0	1	0	.000	.000
Bill Marriott	3B2	L	34	6	9	0	1	0	1	0	1	2	2	1	.111	.333
Oscar Roettger	OF1	R	27	5	4	0	0	0	0	0	0	1	1	0	.000	.000
Chick Fewster		R	31	4	1	0	0	0	0	0	0	0	0	0	.000	.000

NAME	T	AGE	W	L	PCT	SV	G	GS	CG	IP	H	BB	SO	SHO	ERA
		32	65	88	.425	10	154	154	74	1375	1382	418	574	7	3.36
Dazzy Vance	R	36	16	15	.516	1	34	32	25	273	242	69	184	2	2.70
Jesse Petty	L	32	13	18	.419	1	42	33	19	272	263	53	101	2	2.98
Bill Doak	R	36	11	8	.579	0	27	20	6	145	153	40	32	1	3.48
Watty Clark	L	25	7	2	.778	2	27	3	1	74	74	19	32	0	2.31
Jumbo Jim Elliott	L	26	6	13	.316	3	30	21	12	188	188	60	99	2	3.30
Doug McWeeney	R	30	4	8	.333	1	34	6	2	96	90	37	22	0	3.57
Rube Ehrhardt	R	32	3	7	.300	2	46	3	2	96	164	70	73	0	3.56
Ray Moss	R	34	2	6	.250	0	19	6	1	62	73	36	9	0	4.93
1 Norman Plitt	R	34	2	10	.167	0	18	10	2	79	106	25	14	0	5.70
Jesse Barnes	R	35	1	0	1.000	0	1	1	0	8	11	1	1	0	3.38
1 Bob McGraw	R	32	0	1	.000	0	1	1	0	4	5	2	2	0	9.00
1 Guy Cantrell	R	23	0	0	—	0	1	0	0	10	10	6	5	0	2.70

BOSTON 7th 60-94 .390 34 — DAVE BANCROFT

NAME	G by Pos	B	AGE	G	AB	R	H	2B	3B	HR	RBI	BB	SO	SB	BA	SA
TOTALS			29	155	5370	651	1498	216	61	37	582	346	363	100	.279	.363
Jack Fournier	1B102	L	37	122	374	55	106	18	2	10	53	44	16	4	.283	.422
Doc Gautreau	2B57	R	25	87	236	38	58	12	2	0	20	25	20	11	.246	.314
Dave Bancroft	SS104, 3B1	L	36	111	375	44	91	13	4	1	31	43	36	5	.243	.307
Andy High	3B89, 2B8, SS2	L	29	115	384	59	116	15	9	4	46	26	11	4	.302	.419
Lance Richbourg	OF110	L	29	115	450	57	139	12	4	2	34	22	30	24	.309	.389
Jim Walsh	OF129, 1B1	L	24	131	497	72	143	26	7	9	54	23	27	11	.288	.423
Eddie Brown	OF150, 1B1	R	35	155	558	64	171	35	6	4	75	28	20	1	.306	.401
Shanty Hogan	C61	R	21	71	229	24	66	17	1	3	32	9	23	2	.288	.410
2 Eddie Moore	3B52, 2B38, OF16, SS1	R	28	112	411	53	124	14	4	1	32	39	17	5	.302	.363
Doc Farrell	SS57, 2B40, 3B18	R	25	110	424	44	124	13	2	1	58	14	21	4	.292	.340
Jack Smith	OF48	L	32	84	183	27	58	6	4	1	24	16	12	8	.317	.410
Dick Burrus	1B61	R	29	72	220	22	70	8	3	0	32	17	10	3	.318	.382
Frank Gibson	C47	B	36	60	167	7	37	12	2	0	19	3	6	1	.222	.251
Luke Urban	C34	R	30	35	111	11	32	5	0	0	13	6	3	0	.288	.333
1 Zack Taylor	C27	R	28	30	96	8	23	2	1	1	14	8	5	0	.240	.313
1 Les Mann	OF24	R	24	29	66	8	17	2	1	0	6	3	9	2	.258	.333
1 Herb Thomas	2B17, SS2	R	24	24	74	11	17	6	1	0	6	3	9	2	.230	.338
Earl Clark	OF13	R	19	13	44	6	12	1	0	0	3	2	4	0	.273	.295
Dinny McNamara	OF3	L	21	11	9	3	0	0	0	0	0	0	0	0	.000	.000
Johnny Cooney (SA)		R	26	10	1	3	0	0	0	0	0	0	0	0	.000	.000
Sid Graves	OF5	R	25	7	20	5	5	1	1	0	2	0	1	1	.250	.400

NAME	T	AGE	W	L	PCT	SV	G	GS	CG	IP	H	BB	SO	SHO	ERA
		29	60	94	.390	11	155	155	52	1390	1602	468	402	3	4.22
Joe Genewich	R	30	11	8	.579	1	40	19	7	181	199	54	38	0	3.83
2 Kent Greenfield	R	25	11	14	.440	0	27	26	11	190	203	59	59	1	3.84
Bob Smith	R	32	10	18	.357	3	41	32	16	261	297	75	81	1	3.76
Charlie Robertson	R	31	7	17	.292	0	28	22	6	154	188	46	49	0	4.73
George Mogridge	L	38	6	4	.600	5	20	7	3	49	48	15	26	0	3.67
1 Larry Benton	R	29	4	2	.667*	1	11	10	3	60	72	27	23	0	4.50
Johnny Wertz	R	29	4	10	.286	1	42	15	4	164	204	52	39	0	4.55
2 Hugh McQuillan	R	31	3	5	.375	0	13	11	2	78	109	24	17	0	5.54
Foster Edwards	R	23	2	8	.200	0	29	11	1	92	95	45	37	0	4.99
Guy Morrison	R	31	1	2	.333	0	11	3	1	34	40	15	6	0	4.50
Hal Goldsmith	R	28	1	3	.250	1	22	5	1	72	83	26	13	0	3.50
Art Mills	R	24	0	1	.000	0	15	0	0	38	41	18	7	0	3.79
Bunny Hearn	L	23	0	0	.000	0	13	1	0	16	16	9	5	0	4.15
Jack Knight	R	32	0	0	.000	0	3	0	0	3	6	2	0	0	15.00
Dick Rudolph	R	38	0	0	.000	0	1	0	0	1	1	0	0	0	0.00

*Benton, also with New York, League leader with .708

PHILADELPHIA 8th 51-103 .331 43 — STUFFY McINNIS

NAME	G by Pos	B	AGE	G	AB	R	H	2B	3B	HR	RBI	BB	SO	SB	BA	SA
TOTALS			31	155	5317	678	1487	216	46	57	617	434	482	68	.280	.370
Russ Wrightstone	1B136, 2B1, 3B1	L	34	141	533	62	163	24	5	6	75	48	20	9	.306	.403
Fresco Thompson	2B153	R	25	141	597	78	181	32	14	1	70	34	36	19	.303	.409
Heinie Sand	SS86, 3B58	R	29	141	535	87	160	22	8	1	49	68	59	5	.299	.376
Barney Friberg	3B103, 2B5	R	27	111	335	31	78	8	2	1	26	41	36	1	.233	.278
Cy Williams	OF130	L	39	131	492	86	135	18	2	30	98	61	57	0	.274	.502
Freddy Leach	OF139	L	30	140	536	69	164	30	4	12	83	21	32	2	.306	.444
Dick Spalding	OF113	L	33	115	442	68	131	16	3	0	25	38	40	5	.296	.346
Jimmie Wilson	C124	R	26	128	443	50	122	15	2	2	45	34	15	13	.275	.332
Jack Scott	P48	L	35	83	114	6	33	6	0	1	17	9	9	0	.289	.368
2 Jimmy Cooney (JJ)	SS74	R	32	76	259	33	70	12	1	0	15	13	9	4	.270	.324
Johnny Mokan	OF63	R	31	74	213	22	61	13	2	0	33	25	21	5	.286	.366
Al Nixon	OF44	R	41	54	154	18	48	7	0	0	18	5	5	1	.312	.357
Bubber Jonnard	C41	R	27	53	143	18	42	6	0	0	14	7	7	0	.294	.336
Dick Attreau	1B26	L	30	44	83	17	17	1	1	1	11	14	18	1	.205	.277
Harry O'Donnell	C12	R	33	16	16	1	1	0	0	0	2	2	2	0	.063	.063
Bill Hohman	OF6	R	23	7	18	1	5	0	0	0	2	1	2	0	.278	.278
Henry Baldwin	SS3, 3B2	R	33	6	16	1	5	0	0	0	1	2	3	0	.313	.313
Bill Deitrick	SS5	R	25	5	6	1	1	0	0	0	0	0	0	0	.167	.167
Stuffy McInnis	1B1	R	36	1	0	0	0	0	0	0	0	0	0	0	.000	.000

NAME	T	AGE	W	L	PCT	SV	G	GS	CG	IP	H	BB	SO	SHO	ERA
		29	51	103	.331	6	155	155	81	1357	1710	462	377	5	5.35
Jack Scott	R	35	9	21	.300	1	48	25	17	233	304	69	69	1	5.10
Dutch Ulrich	R	27	8	11	.421	1	32	18	14	193	201	40	42	1	3.17
Alex Ferguson	R	30	8	16	.333	0	31	31	16	227	280	65	73	0	4.84
Hub Pruett	L	26	7	17	.292	1	31	28	12	186	238	89	90	1	6.05
Clarence Mitchell	L	36	6	3	.667	0	13	12	8	95	89	28	17	1	4.07
1 Hal Carlson	R	35	4	5	.444	1	11	9	4	64	80	18	13	0	5.20
Art Decatur	R	33	3	5	.375	0	29	3	0	95	130	20	27	0	7.39
Claude Willoughby	R	28	3	7	.300	2	35	6	1	98	126	53	14	1	6.52
Les Sweetland	L	25	2	10	.167	0	21	13	6	104	147	53	21	0	6.14
Russ Miller	R	27	1	5	.500	0	2	1	1	5	21	3	4	0	5.40
1 Wayland Dean	R	25	0	0	.000	0	3	0	0	3	6	2	1	0	12.00
Lefty Taber	L	27	0	1	.000	0	1	1	0	6	8	5	0	0	21.00
Ed Baecht	R	20	0	1	.000	0	1	1	0	6	12	2	0	0	12.00
Augie Walsh	R	22	0	1	.000	1	11	1	0	12	15	12	5	0	10.42
2 Tony Kaufmann	R	26	0	3	.000	0	5	1	0	19	37	8	4	0	9.00
Skinny O'Neal	R	28	0	0	—	0	1	0	0	3	9	2	2	0	9.00

WORLD SERIES — NEW YORK (AL) 4 PITTSBURGH (NL) 0

LINE SCORES

TEAM	1 2 3	4 5 6	7 8 9	10 11 12	R	H	E
Game 1 October 5 at Pittsburgh							
NY (AL)	1 0 3	0 1 0	0 0 0		5	6	1
PIT (NL)	1 0 1	0 1 0	0 1 0		4	9	2

Hoyt, Moore (8) — Kremer, Miljus (6)

TEAM	1 2 3	4 5 6	7 8 9	10 11 12	R	H	E
Game 2 October 6 at Pittsburgh							
NY	0 0 3	0 0 0	0 3 0		6	11	0
PIT	1 0 0	0 0 0	0 1 0		2	7	2

Pipgras — Aldridge, Cvengros (8), Dawson (9)

TEAM	1 2 3	4 5 6	7 8 9	10 11 12	R	H	E
Game 3 October 7 at New York							
PIT	0 0 0	0 0 0	0 1 0		1	3	1
NY	2 0 0	0 0 0	0 0 X		8	9	0

Meadows, Cvengros (7) — Pennock

TEAM	1 2 3	4 5 6	7 8 9	10 11 12	R	H	E
Game 4 October 8 New York							
PIT	1 0 0	0 0 0	2 0 0		3	10	1
NY	1 0 0	0 2 0	0 0 1		4	12	2

Hill, Miljus (7) — Moore

COMPOSITE BATTING

NAME	POS	G	AB	R	H	2B	3B	HR	RBI	BA
New York (AL) Totals		4	136	23	38	6	2	2	19	.279
Koenig	SS	4	18	5	9	2	0	0	2	.500
Meusel	OF	4	17	1	2	0	0	0	1	.188
Combs	OF	4	16	6	5	0	0	0	0	.313
Ruth	OF	4	15	4	6	0	0	2	7	.400
Lazzeri	2B	4	15	1	4	1	0	0	2	.267
Dugan	3B	4	15	2	3	0	0	0	0	.200
Gehrig	1B	4	13	2	4	2	2	0	4	.308
Collins	C	2	5	0	3	1	0	0	0	.600
Moore	P	2	5	0	1	0	0	0	0	.200
Bengough	C	2	4	1	0	0	0	0	0	.000
Pennock	P	1	4	1	0	0	0	0	0	.000
Pipgras	P	1	3	0	1	0	0	0	0	.333
Hoyt	P	1	3	0	0	0	0	0	0	.000
Grabowski	C	1	2	0	0	0	0	0	0	.000
Durst	PH	1	1	0	0	0	0	0	0	.000
Pittsburgh (NL) Totals		4	130	10	29	6	1	0	10	.223
Barnhart	OF	4	16	0	5	1	0	0	4	.313
L. Waner	OF	4	15	5	6	1	1	0	0	.400
P. Waner	OF	4	15	0	5	0	0	0	3	.333
Harris	1B	4	15	0	3	0	0	0	1	.200
Traynor	3B	4	15	1	3	0	0	0	2	.200
Wright	SS	4	13	1	2	0	0	0	0	.154
Grantham	2B	3	11	0	4	1	0	0	0	.364
Smith	C	3	8	0	0	0	0	0	0	.000
Gooch	C	3	5	0	0	0	0	0	0	.000
Rhyne	2B	1	4	0	0	0	0	0	0	.000
Kremer	P	2	3	0	1	0	0	0	0	.500
Brickell	PH	2	2	1	0	0	0	0	0	.000
Aldridge	P	2	2	0	0	0	0	0	0	.000
Meadows	P	2	2	0	0	0	0	0	0	.000
Miljus	P	2	2	0	0	0	0	0	0	.000
Spencer	C	1	1	0	0	0	0	0	0	.000
Groh	PH	1	1	0	0	0	0	0	0	.000
Hill	P	1	1	0	0	0	0	0	0	.000
Yde	PR	1	0	0	0	0	0	0	0	—
Cvengros	P	2	0	0	0	0	0	0	0	—
Dawson	P	1	0	0	0	0	0	0	0	—

COMPOSITE PITCHING

NAME	G	IP	H	BB	SO	W	L	SV	ERA
New York (AL) Totals	4	36	29	4	7	4	0	1	2.00
Moore	2	10.2	11	2	1	1	0	1	0.84
Pennock	1	9	3	0	1	1	0	0	1.00
Pipgras	1	9	7	3	1	1	0	0	2.00
Hoyt	1	7.1	8	1	2	1	0	0	4.91
Pittsburgh (NL) Totals	4	34.2	38	13	25	0	4	0	5.19
Aldridge	2	7.1	10	4	4	0	1	0	7.36
Miljus	2	6.2	4	4	6	0	1	0	1.35
Meadows	1	6.1	7	1	6	0	1	0	9.95
Hill	1	6	9	1	6	0	0	0	4.50
Kremer	1	5	5	1	3	0	1	0	3.60
Cvengros	2	2.1	3	0	2	0	0	0	3.86
Dawson	1	1	0	0	0	0	0	0	0.00

1928 That Near Eclipse Over the Bronx

Connie Mack's Athletics had not won a pennant since the Tall Tactician dismantled his powerhouse squad after the 1914 Series, but his rebuilt A's came extremely close in what proved to be the two team dog fight of 1928. The Yankees had bludgeoned their opposition into oblivion in 1927, and the first three months of the new season promised to be another Bronx runaway. Such was not the case, as a comfortable Yankee lead started to wilt under the heat of the Athletics' 25-8 record in July. The lead continued to melt off the Yankees' margin as the White Elephants stayed hot through August and then, with Al Simmons swinging a torrid bat and Lefty Grove pitching great ball, the Mackmen pulled even with the Yankees on September 7, and actually climbed into first with a win the next day. On the following day, Sunday, September 9, the Athletics came to the Bronx to face Babe Ruth, Lou Gehrig, and company in a doubleheader. The largest baseball crowd in history, 85,264, piled into Yankee Stadium to see the pivotal point in the pennant race, and left the park with full hearts as the Yankees captured both games, 3-0 and 7-3, to retake the league lead. The Athletics remained close on New York's heels, but they could never reach the top again as the Bronx Bombers clinched the flag on September 28, two days before the end of the season.

Both squads had star-studded rosters. The Yankees, with Ruth and Gehrig one-two in the league in home runs, were also one-two-three in the league in RBI's with Ruth, Gehrig, and Bob Meusel. Although Earle Combs and Tony Lazzeri added more fire to the best attack in the league, New York's pitching was not up to 1927 standards. But Waite Hoyt continued to win 20 games, and George Pipgras broke that barrier for the first time and led the pitchers with 24 wins. As Al Simmons, Jimmie Foxx, Mickey Cochrane, Bing Miller, Ty Cobb, and Max Bishop made the Athletic lineup a nightmare for pitchers, Grove provided the nightmare for batters as he tied Pipgras for the league lead in wins and led the circuit in strikeouts with 183.

Goose Goslin of the Senators, Heinie Manush of St. Louis, and Buddy Myer of Boston were the only American Leaguers to break the Yankees' and A's monopoly on the offensive statistical categories. Goslin won the batting crown with .379, Manush had the most hits with 241, and Myer was the best of the base stealers with 30.

The Giants won 25 games in September, but fell short of the National League pennant by finishing two games behind the champion St. Louis Cardinals. The steady Cards weathered the New York storm and clinched the flag on September 29. Sunny Jim Bottomley led the Cardinal's offense, pacing the loop in homers and runs batted in, and Chick Hafey and Frankie Frisch also chipped in with solid batting. Bill Sherdel and Jess Haines gave St. Louis two 20-game aces on the hill, enough to make new manger Bill McKechnie's first season a pleasant one. The New York lineup sported top hitters, Bill Terry, Freddy Lindstrom, and Mel Ott, and Larry Benton and Fat Freddy Fitzsimmons led a solid pitching staff with 20-win seasons.

The batting title went to Rogers Hornsby of Boston, who was playing with his third team in three years. Jim Bottomley was alone at the top with 136 RBI's, but shared the league lead with 31 home runs with Hack Wilson.

The Giants' Benton and Pittsburgh's spitballing Burleigh Grimes won 25 games apiece to pace the league's pitchers, as Brooklyn's Dazzy Vance used a blazing fast ball to win the E.R.A. title with a 2.09 mark.

The Series aped the 1927 Classic in that the Yankees again blasted their opposition out of the park in four games. The awesome duo of Ruth & Gehrig told the whole story, as Ruth hit .625 with three home runs, and Gehrig hit .545 with four homers. Game four best exemplified Yankee thunder as Ruth collected his entire Series output with three homers, and Gehrig hit his fourth round-tripper. Hoyt worked through the barrage and gave up 11 hits in the 7-3 contest enroute to his second victory and the clincher in what turned out to be the revenge for the Cardinal's 1926 Series win.

The year also saw several well-known ships pass in the night. Leo Durocher joined the Yankees as a utility infielder just in time to see Ty Cobb and Tris Speaker end their illustrious careers as outfielders on Connie Mack's near-miss Athletics.

1928 AMERICAN LEAGUE

NAME	G by Pos	B	AGE	G	AB	R	H	2B	3B	HR	RBI	BB	SO	SB	BA	SA
NEW YORK 1st 101-53 .656	**MILLER HUGGINS**															
TOTALS			28	154	5337	894	1578	269	79	133	817	562	544	51	.296	.450
Lou Gehrig	1B154	L	25	154	562	139	210	47	13	27	142	95	69	4	.374	.648
Tony Lazzeri (SJ)	2B110	R	24	116	404	62	134	30	11	10	82	43	50	15	.332	.535
Mark Koenig	SS125	L	25	132	533	89	170	19	10	4	63	32	19	3	.319	.415
Joe Dugan (KJ)	3B91	R	31	94	312	33	86	15	0	6	34	16	15	1	.276	.381
Babe Ruth	OF154	L	33	154	536	163	173	29	8	54	142	135	87	4	.323	.709
Earle Combs	OF149	L	29	149	626	118	194	33	21	7	56	77	33	10	.310	.463
Bob Meusel (NJ)	OF131	R	31	131	518	77	154	45	5	11	113	39	56	6	.297	.467
Johnny Grabowski	C75	R	28	75	202	21	48	7	1	1	21	10	21	0	.238	.297
Leo Durocher	2B66, SS29	B	22	102	296	46	80	8	6	0	31	22	52	1	.270	.338
Gene Robertson	3B70, 2B3	L	29	83	251	29	73	9	0	1	36	14	6	2	.291	.339
Cedric Burst	OF33, 1B3	L	31	74	135	18	34	2	1	2	10	7	9	1	.252	.326
Pat Collins	C70	R	31	70	136	18	30	5	0	6	14	35	16	0	.221	.390
Ben Paschal	OF25	R	32	65	79	12	25	6	1	1	15	8	11	1	.316	.456
Benny Bengough (HJ)	C58	R	29	58	161	12	43	3	1	0	9	7	8	2	.267	.298
Mike Gazella	3B16, 2B4, SS3	R	32	32	56	11	13	0	0	0	2	6	7	1	.232	.232
Bill Dickey	C10	L	21	10	15	1	3	1	1	0	2	0	2	0	.200	.400
2 George Burns	1B2	R	35	4	4	1	2	0	0	0	0	0	0	0	.500	.500
PHILADELPHIA 2nd 98-55 .641 2.5	**CONNIE MACK**															
TOTALS			30	153	5226	829	1540	323	75	89	759	533	442	59	.295	.436
Joe Hauser	1B88	L	29	95	300	61	78	19	5	16	59	52	45	4	.260	.517
Max Bishop	2B125	L	28	126	472	104	149	27	5	6	50	97	36	9	.316	.432
Joe Boley	SS132	R	31	132	425	49	112	20	3	0	49	32	11	5	.264	.325
Sammy Hale	3B79	R	31	88	314	38	97	20	9	4	58	9	21	2	.309	.468
Ty Cobb	OF85	L	41	95	353	54	114	27	4	1	40	34	16	5	.323	.431
Bing Miller	OF133	R	33	139	510	76	168	34	7	8	85	27	24	10	.329	.471
Al Simmons (IL)	OF114	R	26	119	464	78	163	33	9	15	107	31	30	4	.351	.558
Mickey Cochrane	C130	L	25	131	468	92	137	26	12	10	57	76	25	7	.293	.464
Jimmie Foxx	3B60, 1B30, C19	R	20	118	400	85	131	29	10	13	79	60	43	3	.328	.548
Mule Haas	OF82	L	24	91	332	41	93	21	4	6	39	23	20	2	.280	.422
Jimmy Dykes	2B32,SS27,3B20,1B8,OF1	R	31	85	242	39	67	11	0	5	30	27	21	2	.277	.384
Tris Speaker	OF50	L	40	64	191	28	51	22	2	3	29	10	5	2	.267	.450
Ossie Orwoll	1B34, P27	L	27	64	170	28	52	13	2	0	22	16	24	3	.306	.406
Walt French	OF20	L	28	49	74	9	19	4	0	0	7	2	5	1	.257	.311
Eddie Collins	2B2, SS1	L	41	36	33	3	10	3	0	0	7	4	0	2	.303	.394
Joe Hassler	SS28	R	23	28	34	5	9	2	0	0	3	2	4	0	.265	.324
Cy Perkins	C19	R	32	19	29	1	5	0	0	0	1	1	1	0	.172	.172
ST. LOUIS 3rd 82-72 .532 19	**DAN HOWLEY**															
TOTALS			29	154	5217	722	1431	276	76	63	707	548	479	76	.274	.393
Lu Blue	1B154	B	31	154	549	116	154	32	11	14	80	105	43	12	.281	.455
Otis Brannan	2B135	L	29	135	483	68	118	18	3	0	66	60	19	3	.244	.356
Red Kress	SS150	R	25	150	560	78	153	26	10	3	81	48	70	5	.273	.371
Frank O'Rourke (BG)	3B96, SS2	R	36	99	391	54	103	24	3	1	62	21	19	10	.263	.348
Earl McNeely	OF120	R	30	127	496	66	157	27	7	0	44	37	39	8	.236	.319
Fred Schulte	OF143	R	27	146	556	90	159	44	6	7	85	51	60	6	.286	.424
Heinie Manush	OF154	L	26	154	638	104	241	47	20	13	108	39	14	17	.378	.575
Wally Schang	C82	B	38	91	245	41	70	10	5	3	39	68	26	8	.286	.404
Clyde Manion	C71	R	31	76	243	25	55	5	1	2	31	15	18	3	.226	.280
Larry Bettencourt	3B41, OF2, C1	R	22	67	159	30	45	9	4	4	24	22	19	2	.283	.465
Guy Sturdy	1B1	R	28	54	45	3	10	1	0	2	8	8	12	1	.222	.311
Oscar Melillo	2B28, 3B19	R	28	51	132	9	25	3	0	0	9	6	14	0	.189	.250
Beauty McGowen	OF47	R	26	47	168	35	61	13	4	2	18	16	15	2	.363	.524
Ollie Sax	3B9	R	23	16	17	4	3	1	0	0	1	2	4	0	.176	.176
Billy Mullen (KJ)	3B6	R	32	15	18	2	7	1	0	0	2	3	4	0	.389	.444
Steve O'Neill (JJ)	C10	R	36	10	24	4	7	1	0	0	5	6	1	0	.292	.333
Fred Bennett	OF1	R	26	9	8	2	2	0	0	0	0	2	2	0	.250	.250
1 Wally Gerber	SS6	R	36	6	18	1	5	1	0	0	0	0	5	0	.278	.333
2 Frank Wilson	OF1	R	27	6	5	1	0	0	0	0	0	0	3	0	.000	.000
Ike Danning	C2	R	23	2	4	1	2	0	0	0	0	0	1	2	.500	.500

NAME	T	AGE	W	L	PCT	SV	G	GS	CG	IP	H	BB	SO	SHO	ERA
		29	101	53	.656	21	154	154	82	1375	1466	452	487	13	3.74
George Pipgras	R	28	24	13	.649	3	46	38	22	301	314	103	139	4	3.38
Waite Hoyt	R	28	23	7	.767	8	42	31	19	273	279	60	67	3	3.36
Herb Pennock (IL)	L	34	17	6	.739	3	28	24	18	211	215	40	53	5	2.56
Hank Johnson	R	22	14	9	.609	0	31	22	10	199	188	104	110	1	4.30
Al Shealy	R	28	8	6	.571	2	23	12	3	96	124	42	39	0	5.06
Stan Coveleski	R	38	5	1	.833	0	12	8	2	58	72	20	5	0	5.74
Wilcy Moore (SA)	R	31	4	4	.500	2	35	2	0	60	71	31	18	0	4.20
2 Tom Zachary	L	32	3	3	.500	1	7	6	3	46	54	15	7	0	3.91
Fred Heimach	L	27	2	3	.400	0	13	9	5	68	66	16	25	0	3.31
Myles Thomas	R	30	1	0	1.000	0	12	1	0	32	33	9	10	0	3.38
Archie Campbell	R	24	1	0	1.000	2	13	1	0	24	30	11	9	0	5.25
Rosy Ryan	R	30	0	0	—	0	3	0	0	6	17	1	5	0	16.50
Urban Shocker (IL-DD)	R	37	0	0	—	0	1	0	0	2	3	0	0	0	0.00
		32	98	55	.641	16	153	153	81	1368	1349	424	607	15	3.36
Lefty Grove	L	28	24	8	.750	4	39	31	24	262	228	64	183	4	2.57
Jack Quinn	R	44	18	7	.720	1	31	28	18	211	239	34	43	4	2.90
Rube Walberg	L	31	17	12	.586	1	38	30	14	236	236	64	112	3	3.55
Eddie Rommel	R	30	13	5	.722	4	43	11	6	174	177	26	37	0	3.05
Howard Ehmke	R	34	9	8	.529	0	23	18	5	139	135	44	34	1	3.63
George Earnshaw	R	28	7	7	.500	1	26	22	7	158	143	100	117	3	3.82
Ossie Orwoll	L	27	6	5	.545	2	27	8	3	106	110	50	53	0	4.58
Bullet Joe Bush	R	35	2	1	.667	1	11	2	1	35	39	18	15	0	5.14
Ike Powers	R	22	1	0	1.000	2	9	0	0	12	8	10	4	0	4.50
Bill Shores	R	24	1	1	.500	0	3	2	1	14	13	7	5	0	3.21
Carroll Yerkes	L	25	0	1	.000	0	2	1	1	9	7	2	1	0	2.00
Jing Johnson	R	33	0	0	—	0	3	0	0	11	13	5	3	0	4.91
Art Daney	R	23	0	0	—	1	1	0	0	1	0	0	0	0	0.00
		26	82	72	.532	15	154	154	80	1374	1487	454	456	6	4.17
General Crowder	R	29	21	5	.808	2	41	31	19	244	238	91	99	1	3.69
Sam Gray	R	30	20	12	.625	3	35	31	21	263	256	86	102	3	3.19
Jack Ogden	R	30	15	16	.484	2	38	31	18	243	257	80	67	1	4.15
George Blaeholder	R	24	10	15	.400	2	38	26	9	214	235	52	87	1	4.37
Lefty Stewart	L	27	9	17	.438	3	29	17	7	143	173	32	25	1	4.65
Dick Coffman	R	21	4	4	.444	1	29	7	3	86	122	37	25	0	6.07
Boom-Boom Beck	R	23	2	3	.400	0	16	4	2	49	52	20	17	0	4.41
2 Hal Wiltse	L	24	2	5	.286	0	26	5	0	72	93	35	23	0	5.25
Ernie Nevers	R	25	1	0	1.000	0	6	0	0	9	9	2	1	0	3.00
Ed Strelecki	R	20	0	0	—	1	22	0	0	50	49	17	8	0	4.32
Jiggs Wright	R	27	0	0	—	0	3	1	0	3	2	1	0	0	13.50

WASHINGTON — 4th 75-79 .487 26 — BUCKY HARRIS

NAME	G by Pos	B	AGE	G	AB	R	H	2B	3B	HR	RBI	BB	SO	SB	BA	SA
TOTALS			27	155	5320	718	1510	277	93	40	681	481	390	110	.284	.393
Joe Judge	1B149	L	34	153	542	78	166	31	10	3	93	80	19	16	.306	.417
Bucky Harris	2B96, 3B1, 0F1	R	31	99	358	34	73	11	5	0	28	27	26	5	.204	.263
Bobby Reeves	SS66, 2B22, 3B8, 0F1	R	24	102	353	44	107	16	8	3	42	24	47	4	.303	.419
Ossie Bluege	3B144	R	27	148	518	78	154	33	7	2	75	46	27	18	.297	.400
Sam Rice	0F147	L	38	148	616	95	202	32	15	2	55	49	15	16	.328	.418
Red Barnes	0F104	L	24	114	417	82	126	22	15	6	51	55	38	7	.302	.470
Goose Goslin	0F125	L	27	135	456	80	173	36	10	17	102	48	19	16	.379	.614
Muddy Ruel	C101, 1B2	R	32	108	350	31	90	18	2	0	55	44	14	12	.257	.320
Sammy West	0F116	L	23	125	378	59	114	30	7	3	40	20	23	5	.302	.442
Joe Cronin	SS63	R	21	63	227	23	55	10	4	0	25	22	27	3	.243	.322
Jackie Hayes	2B41, SS15, 3B2	R	24	60	210	30	54	7	3	0	22	5	10	3	.257	.319
Bennie Tate	C30	L	26	57	122	10	30	6	0	0	15	10	4	1	.246	.295
Ed Kenna	C34	R	30	41	118	14	35	4	2	1	20	14	8	1	.297	.390
Grant Gillis	SS16, 2B5, 3B3	R	27	24	87	13	22	5	1	0	10	4	5	0	.253	.333
1 George Sisler	1B5, 0F5	L	35	20	49	1	12	1	0	0	2	1	2	0	.245	.265
Dick Spaulding	0F11	L	34	16	23	1	8	0	0	0	0	0	4	0	.348	.348
Harley Boss	1B5	L	19	12	12	1	3	0	0	0	2	3	1	0	.250	.250
Babe Ganzel	0F7	R	27	10	26	2	2	1	0	0	4	1	4	0	.077	.115
Pelham Ballenger	3B3	R	34	3	9	0	1	0	0	0	0	0	1	0	.111	.111

Al Bool 30 R 1-7, Ed Crowley 21 R 0-1, Hugh McMullen 26 B 0-1, Patsy Gharrity (DE) 36

NAME	T	AGE	W	L	PCT	SV	G	GS	CG	IP	H	BB	SO	SHO	ERA
TOTALS		28	75	79	.487	10	155	155	77	1384	1420	466	462	15	3.88
Sad Sam Jones	R	35	17	7	.708	0	30	27	19	225	209	78	663	4	2.84
Garland Braxton	L	28	13	11	.542	6	38	24	15	218	177	44	94	2	2.52
Firpo Marberry	R	29	13	13	.500	3	48	11	7	161	160	42	76	1	3.86
Bump Hadley	R	23	12	13	.480	0	33	31	16	232	236	100	80	3	3.53
Milt Gaston	R	32	6	12	.333	0	28	22	8	149	179	53	45	3	5.50
1 Tom Zachary	L	32	6	9	.400	0	20	14	5	103	130	40	19	1	5.42
Lloyd Brown	L	23	4	4	.500	2	17	10	2	107	112	40	38	0	4.04
Bobby Burke	L	21	2	4	.333	0	26	7	2	85	87	51	27	1	3.92
Hod Lisenbee	R	29	2	6	.250	0	16	9	3	77	102	32	13	0	6.08
Clay Van Alstyne	R	28	0	0	—	0	4	0	0	21	26	13	5	0	5.57
Jim Weaver	R	24	0	0	—	0	2	0	0	6	6	2	1	0	1.50

CHICAGO — 5th 72-82 .468 29 — RAY SCHALK 32-42 .432 — LENA BLACKBURNE 40-40 .500

NAME	G by Pos	B	AGE	G	AB	R	H	2B	3B	HR	RBI	BB	SO	SB	BA	SA
TOTALS			28	155	5207	656	1405	231	77	24	592	469	488	144	.270	.358
Bud Clancy	1B128	L	27	130	487	64	132	19	11	2	37	42	25	4	.271	.368
Bill Hunnefield	2B83, SS3, 3B1	R	29	94	333	42	98	8	3	2	24	26	24	16	.294	.354
Bill Cissell	SS123	R	24	125	443	66	115	22	3	1	60	29	41	18	.260	.330
Willie Kamm	3B155	R	28	155	552	70	170	30	12	1	84	73	22	17	.308	.411
Alex Metzler	0F134	L	25	139	464	71	141	18	14	3	55	77	30	16	.304	.422
Johnny Mostil	0F131	R	32	133	503	69	136	19	8	0	51	66	54	23	.270	.340
Bibb Falk	0F78	L	29	98	286	42	83	18	4	1	37	25	16	5	.290	.392
Moe Berg	C73	R	26	76	224	25	55	16	0	0	29	14	25	2	.246	.317
Buck Redfern	2B45, SS33, 3B1	R	26	86	261	22	61	6	3	0	35	12	19	8	.234	.280
Carl Reynolds	0F74	R	25	84	291	51	94	21	11	2	36	17	13	15	.323	.491
Buck Crouse	C76	L	31	78	218	17	55	5	2	2	20	19	14	3	.252	.321
Bill Barrett	0F37, 2B25	R	28	76	235	34	65	11	2	3	26	14	30	3	.277	.379
Harry McCurdy	C34	L	28	49	103	12	27	10	0	2	13	8	15	1	.262	.417
Art Shires	1B32	L	20	33	123	20	42	6	1	1	11	13	10	0	.341	.431
George Blackerby	0F20	R	24	30	83	8	21	0	0	0	12	4	10	2	.253	.253
Randy Moore	0F16	L	23	24	61	6	13	4	1	0	5	3	5	0	.213	.311
Karl Swanson	2B21	R	27	22	64	2	9	1	0	0	6	4	7	3	.141	.156
Johnny Mann	3B3	R	30	6	6	0	2	0	0	0	1	0	1	0	.333	.333
Ray Schalk	C1	R	35	2	1	0	1	0	0	0	0	0	0	1	1.000	1.000

NAME	T	AGE	W	L	PCT	SV	G	GS	CG	IP	H	BB	SO	SHO	ERA
TOTALS		29	72	82	.468	11	155	155	88	1378	1516	501	418	6	3.98
Tommy Thomas	R	28	17	16	.515	2	36	32	24	283	277	76	129	3	3.08
Ted Lyons	R	27	15	14	.517	6	39	27	21	240	276	68	60	0	3.98
Red Faber	R	39	13	9	.591	0	27	27	16	201	223	68	43	2	3.76
Grady Adkins	R	31	10	16	.385	1	36	27	14	225	233	89	54	0	3.72
Ted Blankenship	R	27	9	11	.450	0	27	22	8	158	186	80	36	0	4.61
Ed Walsh	R	23	7		.364	0	14	10	3	78	86	42	32	0	4.96
Sarge Connally	R	29	2	5	.286	2	28	5	1	74	89	29	28	0	4.87
George Cox	R	23	1	2	.333	0	26	2	0	89	110	39	22	0	5.26
Bob Weiland	L	22	1	0	1.000	0	1	1	1	9	7	5	9	1	0.00
Charlie Barnabe	L	21	0	0	—	0	7	2	0	10	17	0	3	0	6.30
John Goodell	L	21	0	0	—	0	2	0	0	3	6	2	0	0	18.00
Rudy Leopold	R	22	0	0	—	0	1	0	0	2	1	0	0	0	4.50
Al Williamson	R	28	0	0	—	0	1	2	1	2	0	0	0	0	0.00
Roy Wilson	R		0	0	—	0	1	0	0	1	0	0	2	0	0.00
Dan Dugan	L	21	0	0	—	0	1	0	0	.1	0	1	0	0	0.00

DETROIT — 6th 68-86 .442 33 — GEORGE MORIARTY

NAME	G by Pos	B	AGE	G	AB	R	H	2B	3B	HR	RBI	BB	SO	SB	BA	SA
TOTALS			29	154	5292	744	1476	265	97	62	686	469	438	113	.279	.401
Bill Sweeney	1B75, OF3	R	24	89	309	47	78	15	5	0	19	15	28	12	.252	.333
Charlie Gehringer	2B154	L	25	154	603	108	193	29	16	6	74	69	22	15	.320	.451
Jackie Tavener	SS131	L	30	132	473	59	123	24	15	5	52	33	51	15	.260	.406
Marty McManus	3B92, 1B45, SS1	R	28	139	500	78	144	37	5	8	73	51	32	11	.288	.430
Harry Heilmann	OF126, 1B25	R	33	151	558	83	183	38	10	14	107	57	45	7	.328	.507
Harry Rice	OF129, 3B2	L	27	131	510	87	154	21	12	6	81	44	27	20	.302	.425
Bob Fothergill	OF90	R	30	111	347	49	110	28	10	3	63	24	19	8	.317	.481
Pinky Hargrave	C88	B	32	121	321	38	88	13	5	10	63	32	28	4	.274	.439
Al Wingo	OF71	L	30	87	242	30	69	13	2	2	30	40	17	2	.285	.380
Jack Warner	3B52, SS7	R	24	75	206	33	44	4	4	0	13	16	15	4	.214	.272
Larry Woodall	C62	R	33	65	186	19	39	5	1	0	13	24	10	3	.210	.247
C. Galloway (PB)	SS22, 3B21, 1B1, OF1	R	31	53	148	17	39	5	2	1	17	15	3	7	.264	.345
Paul Easterling	OF34	R	22	43	114	17	37	7	1	3	12	8	24	2	.325	.482
Merv Shea	C30	R	27	39	85	8	20	2	3	0	9	9	11	2	.235	.329
Johnny Neun (IL)	1B25	B	27	36	108	15	23	5	0	1	5	7	10	2	.213	.259
John Stone	OF26	L	22	26	113	20	40	10	3	2	21	5	9	1	.354	.549

NAME	T	AGE	W	L	PCT	SV	G	GS	CG	IP	H	BB	SO	SHO	ERA
TOTALS		27	68	86	.442	16	154	154	65	1372	1481	567	451	5	4.32
Ownie Carroll	R	25	16	12	.571	2	34	28	19	231	219	87	51	2	3.27
Elam Vangilder	R	32	11	10	.524	2	38	11	7	156	163	68	43	0	3.92
Earl Whitehill	L	28	11	16	.407	0	31	30	12	196	214	78	93	1	4.32
Vic Sorrell	R	27	8	11	.421	0	29	23	7	171	182	83	67	0	4.79
Haskell Billings	R	20	5	10	.333	0	21	16	3	111	118	59	48	1	5.11
Sam Gibson	R	28	5	8	.385	0	20	18	5	120	155	52	29	1	5.40
Lil Stoner	R	29	5	8	.385	4	36	11	4	128	151	42	29	0	4.36
Ken Holloway	R	30	4	8	.333	2	30	11	5	120	137	32	32	0	4.35
Phil Page	L	22	1	0	1.000	0	3	2	2	22	21	10	3	0	2.45
George Smith	R	26	1	1	.500	3	39	2	0	106	103	50	54	0	4.42
Charlie Sullivan	R	25	0	2	.000	0	3	2	0	12	18	6	2	0	6.75

CLEVELAND — 7th 62-92 .403 39 — ROGER PECKINPAUGH

NAME	G by Pos	B	AGE	G	AB	R	H	2B	3B	HR	RBI	BB	SO	SB	BA	SA
TOTALS			28	155	5386	674	1536	299	61	34	611	377	426	50	.285	.382
Lew Fonseca (BL)	1B56, 3B15, SS4, 2B1	R	29	75	263	38	86	19	4	3	36	13	17	4	.327	.464
Carl Lind	2B154	R	24	154	650	102	191	42	4	1	54	36	48	8	.294	.371
Joe Sewell	SS137, 3B19	R	29	155	588	79	190	40	4	3	70	58	9	7	.323	.418
Johnny Hodapp	3B101, 1B13	R	23	126	449	51	145	31	6	2	73	20	20	2	.323	.432
Homer Summa	OF132	L	29	134	504	60	143	26	3	3	57	20	15	4	.284	.365
Sam Langford	OF107	L	30	110	427	50	118	17	8	4	50	21	35	3	.276	.374
Charlie Jamieson	OF111	L	35	112	433	63	133	18	4	1	37	56	20	3	.307	.374
Luke Sewell	C118	R	27	122	411	52	111	16	9	3	52	26	27	3	.270	.375
1 George Burns	1B53	R	35	82	209	29	52	12	1	5	30	17	11	2	.249	.388
Eddie Morgan	1B36, 0F21, 3B14	R	24	76	265	42	83	24	6	4	54	21	17	5	.313	.494
Glenn Myatt	C30	L	30	58	125	9	36	7	2	1	15	13	13	0	.288	.400
George Uhle (SA)	P31	R	29	55	98	9	28	3	2	1	17	8	4	0	.286	.388
Luther Harvel	OF39	R	22	40	136	12	30	6	1	0	12	4	17	1	.221	.279
George Gerken	OF22	R	22	38	115	16	26	7	2	0	9	12	22	3	.226	.322
Ed Montague	SS15, 3B9	R	24	32	51	12	12	0	3	0	3	6	7	3	.235	.275
Red Dorman	OF24	R	27	25	77	12	28	6	0	1	11	9	6	1	.364	.442
Martin Autry	C18	R	25	22	60	6	18	6	1	1	9	1	7	1	.300	.483
Bruce Caldwell	OF10, 1B1	L	26	18	27	2	6	1	1	0	3	2	2	1	.222	.333
Ollie Tucker	OF14	R	24	14	47	5	6	0	0	0	2	2	6	0	.128	.191
Jonah Goldman	SS7	R	21	7	21	1	5	1	0	0	0	0	0	0	.238	.286
Aaron Ward	3B3, SS2, 2B1	R	31	6	9	1	1	0	0	0	0	1	2	0	.111	.111
Al Van Camp	1B5	L	24	5	17	0	4	1	0	0	2	0	1	1	.235	.294
Cecil Bolton	1B4	L	24	4	13	1	2	1	0	0	2	2	1	0	.154	.462
Johnny Burnett	SS2	L	23	3	10	3	5	0	0	0	0	0	1	0	.500	.500

Johnny Gill 23 L 0-2, Art Reinholz 25 R 1-3, 1 Frank Wilson 27 L 0-1, Grover Hartley (DP) 39

NAME	T	AGE	W	L	PCT	SV	G	GS	CG	IP	H	BB	SO	SHO	ERA
TOTALS		26	62	92	.403	15	155	155	70	1378	1615	511	416	4	4.47
Willis Hudlin	R	22	14	14	.500	7	42	26	10	220	231	90	62	0	4.05
Joe Shaute	L	28	13	11	.433	2	36	32	21	254	295	68	81	1	4.04
George Uhle (SA)	R	29	12	17	.414	3	31	28	18	214	252	48	74	2	4.08
George Grant	R	25	10	8	.556	0	28	18	6	155	196	76	39	1	5.05
Jake Miller	L	30	8	9	.471	0	25	23	7	158	203	43	37	0	4.44
Bill Bayne	L	29	2	5	.286	3	37	6	3	109	128	43	39	0	5.13
Willie Underhill	R	23	1	2	.333	0	11	3	1	28	30	16	0	0	4.50
2 Johnny Miljus	R	33	1	4	.200	1	11	4	1	51	46	20	19	0	2.65
1 Garland Buckeye	L	30	1	1	.167	0	9	4	0	35	58	5	6	0	6.69
Jumbo Brown	R	21	1	0	1.000	0	2	2	1	11	14	12	2	0	6.60
Clint Brown	R	24	0	1	.000	0	2	1	0	9	15	12	0	0	4.91
Les Barnhart	R	23	0	0	—	0	9	0	0	13	4	1	7	0	7.00
Jim Moore	R	24	0	0	—	0	1	1	0	3	4	5	1	0	2.00
Mel Harder	R	18	0	0	—	1	23	1	0	49	64	32	15	0	6.61
Wes Ferrell	R	20	0	0	—	0	2	1	0	16	15	5	4	0	2.25
Emil Levsen	R	30	0	0	—	0	11	0	0	41	39	31	7	0	5.49
Hap Collard	R	29	0	0	—	0	3	1	0	4	4	1	2	0	2.25

BOSTON — 8th 57-96 .373 43.5 — BILL CARRIGAN

NAME	G by Pos	B	AGE	G	AB	R	H	2B	3B	HR	RBI	BB	SO	SB	BA	SA
TOTALS			29	154	5132	589	1356	260	62	38	544	389	512	99	.264	.361
Phil Todt	1B144	L	26	144	539	61	136	31	8	12	73	26	47	6	.252	.406
Bill Regan	2B137, 0F1	R	29	138	511	53	135	30	6	7	75	21	40	9	.264	.387
2 Wally Gerber	SS103	R	36	104	300	21	64	6	1	0	28	32	31	6	.213	.240
Buddy Myer	3B144	L	24	147	536	78	168	26	6	1	44	53	28	30	.313	.394
Doug Taitt	OF139, P1	L	25	143	482	51	144	28	14	3	61	36	32	13	.299	.434
Ira Flagstead	OF135	R	34	140	510	84	148	41	4	1	39	60	23	12	.290	.392
Ken Williams	OF127	L	38	133	462	59	140	25	1	8	67	37	15	4	.303	.413
Fred Hofmann	C71	R	34	78	199	14	45	9	1	0	16	11	25	0	.226	.276
Jack Rothrock	OF53, 3B17, 1B16, SS13, 2B2, C1, P1	B	23	117	344	52	92	9	4	3	22	33	40	12	.267	.343
Billy Rogell	SS67, 2B22, 0F6, 3B3	B	23	102	296	33	69	10	4	0	29	22	47	2	.233	.294
Johnnie Heving	C62	R	32	82	158	11	41	7	2	0	11	10	10	1	.259	.329
Charlie Berry	C63	R	25	80	177	18	46	7	3	0	18	11	19	1	.260	.350
Red Ruffing	P42	R	24	60	121	12	38	13	1	2	19	4	39	1	.314	.488
Red Rollings	1B5, 2B4, OF4, 3B1	L	24	50	48	7	11	3	0	0	3	5	6	0	.276	.379
Carl Sumner	OF10	L	31	19	16	29	6	8	1	0	2	3	2	1	.222	.379
Denny Williams	OF6	L	25	16	18	4	5	2	0	0	1	3	3	0	.176	.275
George Loepp	OF6	R	23	15	16	9	0	3	0	0	1	1	0	1	.188	.250
Casper Asbjornson	C8	R	19	6	16	0	3	1	0	0	0	0	1	0	.176	.235
Arlie Tarbert	OF8	R	24	3	5	1	0	0	0	0	0	0	1	0	—	—
Paul Hinson		R	24	3	3	1	1	0	0	0	0	0	0	0	.333	.333
Freddie Moncewicz	SS2	R	24	3	2	0	0	0	0	0	0	0	0	0	.000	.000

NAME	T	AGE	W	L	PCT	SV	G	GS	CG	IP	H	BB	SO	SHO	ERA
TOTALS		25	57	96	.373	9	154	154	69	1352	1492	452	407	5	4.39
Ed Morris	R	28	19	15	.559	5	47	29	20	258	255	80	104	0	3.52
Jack Russell	R	22	11	14	.440	2	36	26	10	201	233	41	27	2	3.85
Red Ruffing	R	24	10	25	.286	2	42	34	25	289	303	96	118	1	3.90
Danny MacFayden	R	23	9	15	.375	0	33	28	9	195	215	78	61	0	4.75
Slim Harriss	R	31	8	11	.421	1	27	15	6	128	141	33	37	1	4.64
Pat Simmons	L	19	0	2	.000	1	31	3	0	69	69	38	16	0	4.04
1 Hal Wiltse	L	24	0	0	—	0	2	1	0	12	16	1	5	0	9.00
Herb Bradley	R	25	0	3	.000	0	9	5	0	47	66	14	14	1	7.28
Marty Griffin	R	26	0	4	.000	0	10	3	0	38	42	17	9	0	4.97
Merle Settlemire	L	25	0	6	.000	0	30	9	0	82	116	34	12	0	5.49
Cliff Garrison	R	21	0	0	—	0	6	2	0	16	22	6	0	0	7.88
Steve Slayton	R	26	0	0	—	0	3	0	0	6	5	3	1	0	3.86
John Wilson	R	23	0	0	—	0	4	1	0	13	16	4	1	0	9.00
Jack Rothrock	R	23	0	0	—	0	1	0	0	5	6	0	1	0	0.00
Frank Bennett	R	23	0	0	—	0	2	1	0	4	8	3	1	0	18.00
John Shea	R	23	0	0	—	0	1	0	0	1	2	1	0	0	27.00
Doug Taitt	L	25	0	0	—	0	1	0	0	1	4	1	0	0	27.00

ST. LOUIS — 1ST 95-59 .617 — BILL McKECHNIE

NAME	G by Pos	B	AGE	G	AB	R	H	2B	3B	HR	RBI	BB	SO	SB	BA	SA
TOTALS			28	154	5357	807	1505	292	70	113	749	568	438	82	.281	.425
Jim Bottomley	1B148	L	28	149	576	123	187	42	20	31	136	71	54	10	.325	.628
Frankie Frisch	2B139	B	29	141	547	107	164	29	9	10	86	64	17	29	.300	.441
Rabbit Maranville	SS112, 2B2	R	36	112	366	40	88	14	10	1	34	36	27	3	.240	.342
Wattie Holm	3B83, OF7	R	26	102	386	61	107	24	6	3	47	32	17	1	.277	.394
2 George Harper	OF84	L	30	99	272	41	83	8	2	17	58	51	15	2	.305	.537
Taylor Douthit	OF154	R	27	154	648	111	191	35	3	3	43	48	36	11	.295	.372
Chick Hafey	OF133	R	25	138	520	101	175	46	6	27	111	40	53	8	.337	.604
2 Jimmie Wilson	C120	R	27	120	411	45	106	26	2	2	50	45	24	9	.258	.345
Andy High	3B73, 2B19	L	30	111	368	58	105	14	3	6	37	30	10	2	.285	.389
Tommy Thevenow	SS64, 3B3, 1B1	R	24	69	171	11	35	8	3	0	13	20	12	0	.205	.287
Wally Roettger (BL)	OF66	R	25	68	262	27	89	17	4	6	44	10	22	2	.341	.506
Ray Blades	OF19	R	31	51	85	9	20	7	1	1	19	20	26	0	.235	.376
Pepper Martin	OF4	R	24	39	13	11	4	0	0	0	0	1	2	2	.308	.308
Pete Alexander	P34	R	41	34	86	13	25	2	0	1	11	4	8	0	.291	.349
Ernie Orsatti	OF17, 1B5	L	25	27	69	10	21	6	0	3	15	10	11	0	.304	.522
2 Earl Smith	C18	R	31	24	58	3	13	2	0	0	7	5	4	0	.224	.259
1 Bob O'Farrell	C14	R	31	16	52	6	11	1	0	0	4	13	9	2	.212	.231
Gus Mancuso	C11	R	22	11	38	2	7	0	1	0	3	0	5	0	.184	.237
Howie Williamson		R	23	10	9	0	2	0	0	0	0	0	4	0	.222	.222
Specs Toporcer	1B1, 2B1	L	29	8	14	0	0	0	0	0	0	1	3	0	.000	.000
1 Spud Davis	C2	R	23	2	5	1	1	0	0	0	1	1	0	0	.200	.200

NAME	T	AGE	W	L	PCT	SV	G	GS	CG	IP	H	BB	SO	SHO	ERA
		31	95	59	.617	21	154	154	83	1415	1470	399	422	4	3.38
Bill Sherdel	L	31	21	10	.677	5	38	27	20	249	251	56	72	2	2.86
Jesse Haines	R	34	20	8	.714	0	33	28	20	240	238	72	77	1	3.19
Pete Alexander	R	41	16	9	.640	2	34	31	18	244	262	37	59	1	3.36
Flint Rhem	R	27	11	8	.579	3	28	22	9	170	199	71	47	0	4.13
Syl Johnson	R	27	8	4	.667	3	34	6	2	120	117	33	66	0	3.90
2 Clarence Mitchell	L	37	8	9	.471	0	18	9	9	150	149	38	31	1	3.30
Art Reinhart	L	29	4	6	.400	2	23	9	3	75	80	27	12	1	2.88
Fred Frankhouse	R	24	3	2	.600	1	21	10	1	84	91	36	29	0	3.96
Hal Haid	R	30	2	2	.500	5	27	0	0	47	39	11	21	0	2.30
Carlisle Littlejohn	R	26	2	1	.667	0	12	2	1	32	36	14	6	0	3.66
Tony Kaufmann	R	27	0	0	—	0	4	1	0	5	8	4	2	0	9.00

NEW YORK — 2nd 93-61 .604 2 — JOHN McGRAW

NAME	G by Pos	B	AGE	G	AB	R	H	2B	3B	HR	RBI	BB	SO	SB	BA	SA
TOTALS			26	155	5459	807	1600	276	59	118	758	444	376	62	.293	.430
Bill Terry	1B149	L	29	149	568	100	185	36	11	17	101	64	36	7	.326	.518
Andy Cohen	2B126, SS3, 3B1	R	23	129	504	64	138	24	7	9	59	31	17	3	.274	.403
Travis Jackson	SS149	R	24	150	537	73	145	35	6	14	77	56	46	8	.270	.436
Fred Lindstrom	3B153	R	22	153	646	99	231	39	9	14	107	25	21	15	.358	.511
Mel Ott	OF115, 2B5, 3B1	L	19	124	435	69	140	26	4	18	77	52	36	3	.322	.524
Jim Welsh	OF117	L	25	124	476	77	146	22	5	9	54	29	30	4	.307	.431
Lefty O'Doul	OF94	L	31	114	354	67	113	19	4	8	46	30	8	9	.319	.463
Shanty Hogan	C124	R	22	131	411	48	137	25	2	10	71	42	25	0	.333	.457
Andy Reese	OF64, 2B26, 1B6, SS6, 3B6	R	24	109	406	61	125	18	4	6	44	13	24	7	.308	.416
Les Mann	OF68	R	35	82	193	29	51	7	1	2	25	18	9	2	.264	.342
2 Bob O'Farrell	C63	R	31	75	133	23	26	6	0	2	20	34	16	2	.195	.286
Edd Roush (MJ)	OF39	L	35	46	163	20	41	5	3	2	13	14	9	1	.252	.356
Jack Cummings	C4	R	24	33	27	4	9	2	0	2	9	3	4	0	.333	.630
2 Russ Wrightstone	1B2	L	35	30	25	3	4	0	0	1	5	3	2	1	.160	.280
1 George Harper	OF18	L	36	19	57	11	13	1	0	2	7	10	4	1	.228	.351
Chick Fullis		R	24	11	5	1	0	0	0	0	0	0	1	0	.000	.000
1 Art Jahn	OF8	R	32	10	29	7	8	1	0	1	7	2	5	0	.276	.414
Ray Foley		R	22	2	1	1	0	0	0	0	0	0	1	0	.000	.000
Bill Haeffner	C2	R	33	2	1	0	0	0	0	0	0	0	0	0	.000	.000
1 Al Spohrer	C3	R	25	2	2	0	0	0	0	0	0	0	1	0	.000	.000
Joe Price	OF1	R	31	1	1	0	0	0	0	0	0	0	1	0	.000	.000
Pat Veltman	OF1	R	22	1	3	0	1	0	0	0	0	0	0	0	.333	1.000

NAME	T	AGE	W	L	PCT	SV	G	GS	CG	IP	H	BB	SO	SHO	ERA
		29	93	61	.604	16	155	155	79	1395	1454	405	399	7	3.66
Larry Benton	R	30	25	9	.735	4	42	36	28	310	299	71	90	2	2.73
Freddie Fitzsimmons	R	26	20	9	.690	1	40	32	16	261	264	65	67	1	3.69
2 Joe Genewich	R	31	11	4	.733	2	26	18	10	158	136	64	37	2	3.19
Carl Hubbell	L	25	10	6	.625	1	20	14	8	124	117	21	37	1	2.83
Jim Faulkner	L	28	9	8	.529	2	38	8	3	117	131	41	32	0	3.54
Jack Scott	R	36	4	1	.800	1	16	3	3	50	59	11	17	0	3.60
Vic Aldridge (HO)	R	34	4	7	.364	2	22	16	3	119	133	45	33	0	4.84
1 Virgil Barnes	R	31	3	3	.500	0	10	9	3	55	71	18	11	1	5.07
Dutch Henry (HJ-ST)	L	26	3	6	.333	1	17	8	1	64	82	25	23	0	3.80
Bill Walker	L	24	3	6	.333	1	22	8	1	76	79	31	39	0	4.74
1 Ben Cantwell	R	26	1	0	1.000	1	7	1	0	18	20	4	0	0	4.50
Tiny Chaplin	R	22	0	2	.000	0	12	1	0	24	27	8	5	0	4.50
1 Bill Clarkson	R	29	0	0	—	0	4	0	0	6	10	1	3	0	7.50
Chet Nichols	R	30	0	0	—	0	3	0	0	3	11	3	1	0	21.00
2 Garland Buckeye	L	30	0	0	—	0	4	0	0	4	9	2	3	0	13.50
Leo Mangum	R	32	0	0	—	0	1	0	0	3	5	1	0	0	15.00

CHICAGO — 3rd 91-63 .591 4 — JOE McCARTHY

NAME	G by Pos	B	AGE	G	AB	R	H	2B	3B	HR	RBI	BB	SO	SB	BA	SA
TOTALS			29	154	5260	714	1460	251	64	92	665	508	517	83	.278	.402
Charlie Grimm	1B147	L	29	147	547	67	161	25	5	5	62	39	20	7	.294	.386
Freddie Maguire	2B138	R	29	140	574	67	160	24	5	1	41	25	38	6	.279	.350
Woody English	SS114, 3B2	R	21	116	475	68	142	22	4	2	34	30	28	4	.299	.375
Clyde Beck	3B87, SS47, 2B1	R	28	131	483	72	124	18	4	3	52	58	58	3	.257	.329
Kiki Cuyler	OF127	R	29	133	499	92	142	25	9	17	79	51	61	37	.285	.473
Hack Wilson	OF143	R	28	145	520	89	163	32	9	31	120	77	94	4	.313	.588
Riggs Stephenson	OF135	R	30	137	512	75	166	36	9	8	90	68	29	8	.324	.477
Gabby Hartnett	C118	R	27	120	388	61	117	26	9	14	57	65	32	3	.302	.523
Cliff Heathcote	OF39	L	30	67	137	26	39	8	0	3	18	17	12	6	.285	.409
Johnny Butler	3B59, SS2	R	35	62	174	17	47	7	0	0	16	19	7	2	.270	.310
Earl Webb	OF31	L	30	62	140	22	35	7	3	3	23	14	17	0	.250	.407
Mike Gonzalez	C45	R	37	49	158	12	43	9	2	1	21	12	7	2	.272	.373
Norm McMillan	2B19, 3B18	R	32	49	123	11	27	2	2	1	12	13	19	0	.220	.293
Joe Kelly	1B10	L	28	32	52	3	11	1	0	1	7	1	3	0	.212	.288
Johnny Moore		R	26	4	4	0	0	0	0	0	0	0	0	0	.000	.000
Ray Jacobs		R	26	2	2	0	0	0	0	0	0	0	1	0	.000	.000
Elmer Yoter	3B1	R	28	2	4	0	0	0	0	0	0	0	1	0	—	—

NAME	T	AGE	W	L	PCT	SV	G	GS	CG	IP	H	BB	SO	SHO	ERA
		30	91	63	.591	14	154	154	75	1381	1383	508	531	12	3.39
Pat Malone	R	25	18	13	.581	2	42	25	16	251	218	99	155	2	2.83
Sheriff Blake	R	28	17	11	.607	1	34	29	16	241	209	101	78	4	2.46
Guy Bush	R	26	15	6	.714	2	42	24	9	204	229	86	61	2	3.84
Charlie Root	R	29	14	18	.438	2	40	30	13	237	214	73	122	1	3.57
Art Nehf	L	35	13	7	.650	0	31	21	10	177	190	52	40	2	2.64
Percy Jones	L	28	10	6	.625	3	39	19	9	154	167	56	41	1	4.03
Hal Carlson (IL)	R	36	3	2	.600	4	20	4	2	56	74	15	11	0	5.95
Lefty Weinert	L	26	1	0	1.000	0	10	1	0	17	24	9	8	0	5.29
Ed Holley	R	28	0	0	—	0	13	1	0	31	31	16	10	0	3.77
Ben Tincup	R	35	0	0	—	0	2	0	0	9	14	1	3	0	7.00
Johnny Welch	R	21	0	0	—	0	3	0	0	4	13	0	2	0	15.75

PITTSBURGH — 4th 85-67 .559 9 — DONIE BUSH

NAME	G by Pos	B	AGE	G	AB	R	H	2B	3B	HR	RBI	BB	SO	SB	BA	SA
TOTALS			27	152	5371	837	1659	246	100	52	768	435	352	64	.309	.421
George Grantham	1B119, 2B1, 3B1	L	28	124	440	93	142	24	9	10	85	59	37	9	.323	.486
Sparky Adams	2B107, SS27, OF1	R	33	135	539	91	149	14	6	0	38	64	18	8	.276	.325
Glenn Wright (BY)	SS101, 1B1, OF1	R	27	108	407	63	126	20	8	8	66	21	53	3	.310	.457
Pie Traynor	3B144	R	29	144	569	91	192	38	12	3	124	28	10	12	.337	.462
Paul Waner	OF131, 1B24	L	25	152	602	142	223	50	19	6	86	77	16	6	.370	.547
Lloyd Waner	OF152	L	22	152	659	121	221	22	14	5	61	40	13	6	.335	.434
Fred Brickell	OF50	L	21	81	202	34	65	4	4	3	41	20	18	5	.322	.426
2 Charlie Hargreaves	C77	R	31	99	260	15	74	8	2	1	32	12	9	1	.285	.342
Dick Bartell	2B39, SS27, 3B1	R	20	72	233	27	71	8	4	1	36	21	18	4	.305	.386
Clyde Barnhart	OF48, 3B1	R	33	61	196	18	58	6	2	4	30	11	9	3	.296	.408
Pete Scott (CN)	OF42, 1B8	R	30	60	177	33	55	10	4	5	33	18	14	1	.311	.497
Adam Comorosky (AJ)	OF49	R	23	51	176	22	52	6	3	2	34	15	6	1	.295	.398
Rollie Hemsley	C49	R	21	50	133	14	36	2	0	3	18	4	10	1	.271	.331
Burleigh Grimes	P48	R	34	48	131	17	42	8	1	0	16	4	15	1	.321	.397
1 Earl Smith	C28	R	31	32	85	8	21	6	0	0	11	11	7	0	.247	.388
1 Johnny Gooch	C31	R	30	31	80	7	19	2	1	0	5	3	4	0	.238	.288
Eddie Mulligan	3B6, 2B4	R	33	27	43	4	10	2	0	0	5	3	6	0	.233	.279
1 Joe Harris	1B6	L	37	16	23	2	9	2	1	0	2	4	2	0	.391	.565
Mack Hillis	2B8, 3B1	R	26	11	36	6	9	2	3	1	7	2	6	1	.250	.556
Cobe Jones	SS1	B	22	5	2	0	1	0	0	0	0	2	0	0	.500	.500
John O'Connell	C1	R	24	1	2	0	0	0	0	0	0	0	0	0	.000	.000
Bill Windle	1B1	L	23	1	1	1	1	1	0	0	0	0	0	0	1.000	2.000

NAME	T	AGE	W	L	PCT	SV	G	GS	CG	IP	H	BB	SO	SHO	ERA
		31	85	67	.559	11	152	152	82	1354	1422	446	385	8	3.95
Burleigh Grimes	R	34	25	14	.641	3	48	37	28	331	311	77	97	4	2.99
Carmen Hill	R	32	16	10	.615	2	35	31	16	237	229	81	73	1	3.53
Ray Kremer	R	35	15	13	.536	0	34	31	17	219	253	68	61	1	4.64
Fred Fussell	L	32	9	8	.471	1	28	20	9	160	183	41	43	2	3.60
Erv Brame	R	26	7	4	.636	0	24	11	6	96	110	44	22	0	5.06
Joe Dawson	R	31	7	7	.500	3	31	7	1	129	116	56	36	0	3.28
1 Johnny Miljus	R	33	5	7	.417	1	21	10	3	70	90	33	26	0	5.27
Bill Burwell	R	33	1	0	1.000		4	1	0	21	18	8	2	0	5.14
Lee Meadows (SA)	R	33	1	1	.500	0	4	2	1	10	18	5	3	0	8.10
Homer Blankenship	R	25	0	0	—	0	5	2	1	22	27	9	6	0	5.73
Walt Tauscher	R	26	0	0	—	0	17	0	0	29	28	12	7	0	4.97
Les Bartholomew	L	25	0	0	—	0	3	0	0	23	31	9	6	0	7.04
Glenn Spencer	R	22	0	0	—	0	4	0	0	6	4	1	2	0	1.50
Elmer Tutwiler	R	22	0	0	—	0	3	0	1	4	10	3	0	0	4.50

CINCINNATI — 5th 78-74 .513 16 — JACK HENDRICKS

NAME	G by Pos	B	AGE	G	AB	R	H	2B	3B	HR	RBI	BB	SO	SB	BA	SA
TOTALS			29	153	5184	648	1449	229	67	32	588	386	330	83	.280	.368
George Kelly	1B99, OF13	R	32	116	402	46	119	33	7	3	58	28	35	2	.296	.435
Hughie Critz	2B153	R	27	153	641	95	190	21	11	5	52	37	24	18	.296	.387
Hod Ford	SS149	R	30	149	506	49	122	17	4	0	54	47	31	1	.241	.291
Chuck Dressen	3B135	R	24	135	498	72	145	26	3	1	59	43	22	10	.291	.361
Curt Walker (FS)	OF122	L	31	123	427	64	119	15	12	6	73	49	14	9	.279	.412
Ethan Allen	OF98	L	24	129	485	55	148	30	7	1	62	27	29	6	.305	.402
Billy Zitzmann	OF78, 3B1	R	30	101	266	53	79	9	3	3	33	13	22	3	.297	.387
Val Picinich	C93	R	31	96	324	29	98	15	1	7	35	20	25	1	.302	.420
Wally Pipp	1B72	L	35	95	272	30	77	11	3	2	35	25	13	1	.283	.368
Marty Callaghan	OF69	R	28	81	238	29	69	11	4	0	24	27	10	1	.290	.370
Pid Purdy (BY)	OF61	L	24	70	223	32	69	11	2	0	23	20	13	1	.309	.368
Bubbles Hargrave	C57	R	35	65	190	19	56	12	0	3	23	14	14	2	.295	.389
Joe Stripp	OF21, 3B17, SS1	R	25	44	149	18	40	7	3	1	17	8	10	2	.268	.403
Pinky Pittinger	SS12, 3B4, 2B3	R	29	40	38	12	9	1	0	0	2	2	7	0	.237	.289
Red Lucas (BN)	P27	L	26	39	73	8	23	6	1	0	7	4	3	0	.315	.370
Clyde Sukeforth	C26	R	26	33	53	5	7	2	1	0	3	6	4	0	.132	.208
Jack White	2B1	B	22	3	5	1	1	0	0	0	0	0	1	0	.000	.000

NAME	T	AGE	W	L	PCT	SV	G	GS	CG	IP	H	BB	SO	SHO	ERA
		31	78	74	.513	11	153	153	68	1372	1516	410	355	11	3.94
Eppa Rixey	L	37	19	18	.514	2	43	37	17	291	317	67	58	3	3.43
Ray Kolp	R	33	13	10	.565	3	44	23	12	209	219	55	61	1	3.19
Red Lucas (BA)	R	26	13	9	.591	1	27	19	13	167	164	42	35	4	3.40
Dolf Luque	R	37	11	10	.524	1	33	29	11	234	254	84	72	1	3.58
Pete Donohue	R	27	7	11	.389	0	23	18	8	150	180	32	37	0	4.74
Carl Mays	R	36	4	1	.800	1	14	6	4	63	67	22	10	1	3.86
Ken Ash	R	26	3	4	.429	0	13	3	0	83	101	22	20	0	6.50
Pete Appleton	R	24	3	4	.429	0	17	3	0	77	91	25	35	0	6.50
Jakie May (IL)	L	32	3	5	.375	0	21	11	1	79	99	35	39	1	4.44
Jim Joe Edwards	L	33	2	2	.500	0	13	4	3	43	20	11	10	0	7.59
Jim Beckman	R	23	1	0	1.000	0	2	0	0	15	19	9	4	0	6.00
Si Johnson	R	21	0	0	—	0	4	0	0	9	12	5	4	0	4.50
Harlan Pyle	R	22	0	0	—	0	1	0	0	2	6	0	1	0	27.00

BROOKLYN 6th 77-76 .503 17.5 — WILBERT ROBINSON

NAME	G by Pos	B	AGE	G	AB	R	H	2B	3B	HR	RBI	BB	SO	SB	BA	SA
TOTALS			32	155	5243	665	1393	229	70	66	621	557	510	81	.266	.374
Del Bissonette	1B155	L	28	155	587	90	188	30	13	25	106	70	75	5	.320	.543
Jake Flowers	2B94, SS6	R	26	103	339	51	93	11	6	2	44	47	30	10	.274	.360
Dave Bancroft	SS149	B	37	149	515	47	127	19	5	0	51	59	20	7	.247	.303
Harvey Hendrick	3B91, OF17	L	30	126	425	83	135	15	10	11	59	54	34	16	.318	.478
Babe Herman	OF127	L	25	134	486	64	165	37	6	12	91	38	36	1	.340	.514
Max Carey	OF95	R	38	108	296	41	73	11	0	2	19	47	24	18	.247	.304
Rube Bressler	OF137	R	33	145	501	78	148	29	13	4	70	80	33	2	.295	.429
Hank DeBerry	C80	R	33	82	258	19	65	9	2	0	23	18	15	3	.252	.298
Harry Riconda	2B53, 3B21, SS16	R	31	92	281	22	63	15	4	3	35	20	28	6	.224	.338
Jigger Statz	OF52, 2B1	R	30	77	171	28	40	8	1	0	16	18	12	3	.234	.287
Ty Tyson	OF55	R	36	59	210	25	57	11	1	1	21	10	14	3	.271	.348
Butch Henline	C45	R	33	55	132	12	28	3	1	2	8	17	8	2	.212	.295
2 Joe Harris	OF16	R	37	55	89	8	21	6	1	1	8	14	4	0	.236	.360
2 Johnny Gooch	C38	B	30	42	101	9	32	1	2	0	12	7	9	0	.317	.366
Wally Gilbert	3B39	R	27	39	153	26	31	4	0	0	3	14	8	2	.203	.229
Jay Partridge	2B18, 3B2	L	25	37	73	18	18	0	1	0	12	13	6	2	.247	.274
1 Charlie Hargreaves	C20	R	31	20	61	3	12	2	0	0	5	6	6	1	.197	.230
1 Howard Freigau	3B10, SS1	R	25	17	34	6	7	2	0	0	3	1	3	0	.206	.265
Overton Tremper	OF9	R	22	10	31	1	6	2	1	0	1	0	1	0	.194	.323
Max West	OF6	R	23	7	21	4	6	1	1	0	1	4	1	0	.286	.429
Al Lopez	C3	R	19	3	12	0	0	0	0	0	0	0	0	0	.000	.000
Chuck Corgan (DD) 25																

NAME	T	AGE	W	L	PCT	SV	G	GS	CG	IP	H	BB	SO	SHO	ERA
		31	77	76	.503	15	155	155	75	1396	1378	468	551	16	3.25
Dazzy Vance	R	37	22	10	.688	2	38	32	24	280	226	72	200	4	2.09
Jesse Petty	L	33	15	15	.500	1	40	31	15	234	264	56	74	4	4.04
Doug McWeeny	L	31	14	14	.500	1	42	32	12	244	218	114	79	4	3.17
Watty Clark	L	26	12	9	.571	2	40	19	10	195	193	50	85	2	2.68
Jumbo Jim Elliott	R	27	9	14	.391	1	41	21	7	192	194	64	74	2	3.89
Bill Doak	R	37	3	8	.273	3	28	12	4	99	104	35	12	1	3.27
Rube Ehrhardt	R	31	3	3	.250	2	28	2	1	54	74	27	12	0	4.67
Lou Koupal	R	29	1	0	1.000	1	17	1	0	37	43	15	10	0	2.43
Ray Moss	R	26	0	3	.000	1	22	5	1	60	62	35	5	1	4.95

BOSTON 7th 50-103 .327 44.5 — JACK SLATTERY 11-20 .355 ROGERS HORNSBY 39-83 .320

NAME	G by Pos	B	AGE	G	AB	R	H	2B	3B	HR	RBI	BB	SO	SB	BA	SA
TOTALS			31	153	5228	631	1439	241	41	52	577	477	377	60	.275	.367
2 George Sisler	1B118, P1	L	35	118	491	71	167	26	4	4	68	30	15	11	.340	.434
Rogers Hornsby	2B140	R	32	140	486	99	188	42	7	21	94	107	41	5	.387	.632
Doc Farrell	SS132, 2B1	R	26	134	483	36	104	14	2	3	43	26	26	3	.215	.271
Les Bell	3B153	R	26	153	591	58	164	36	7	10	91	40	45	1	.277	.413
Lance Richbourg	OF148	L	30	148	612	105	206	26	12	2	52	42	39	11	.337	.428
Jack Smith	OF65	L	33	96	254	30	71	9	2	1	32	21	14	6	.280	.343
Eddie Brown	OF129, 1B1	R	36	142	523	45	140	28	2	4	59	24	22	6	.268	.340
Zack Taylor	C124	R	29	125	399	36	100	15	1	2	30	33	29	2	.251	.308
Eddie Moore	OF54, 2B1	R	29	68	215	27	51	9	0	2	18	19	12	7	.237	.307
Dick Burrus	1B32	L	30	64	137	15	37	6	0	3	19	19	8	1	.270	.380
2 Howard Freigau	SS14, 2B11	R	25	52	109	11	28	8	1	1	17	9	14	1	.257	.376
2 Al Spohrer	C48	R	25	51	124	15	27	3	0	0	9	5	11	1	.218	.242
Heinie Mueller	OF41	L	28	42	151	25	34	9	1	0	19	17	9	1	.225	.258
Earl Clark	OF27	R	20	28	112	18	34	9	1	0	10	4	8	0	.304	.402
Doc Gautreau	2B4, SS1	R	26	23	18	3	5	0	1	0	1	4	3	1	.278	.389
Jimmy Cooney	SS11, 2B4	R	33	18	51	2	7	0	0	0	3	2	1	0	.137	.137
Luke Urban	C10	R	31	15	17	0	3	0	0	0	0	2	0	1	.176	.176
Dinny McNamara	OF3	L	22	9	4	1	1	0	0	0	0	0	2	0	.250	.250
Charlie Fitzberger		L	24	7	7	0	2	0	0	0	0	3	0	0	.286	.286
Dave Harris	OF6	R	28	7	17	2	2	1	0	0	3	2	6	0	.118	.176
Bill Cronin	C3	R	25	3	2	1	0	0	0	0	0	1	0	0	.000	.000
Earl Williams	C1	R	25	3	2	0	0	0	0	0	0	0	0	0	.000	.000

NAME	T	AGE	W	L	PCT	SV	G	GS	CG	IP	H	BB	SO	SHO	ERA
		28	50	103	.327	6	153	153	54	1360	1596	524	343	1	4.83
Bob Smith	R	33	13	17	.433	2	38	26	14	244	274	74	59	0	3.87
Ed Brandt	L	23	9	21	.300	0	38	32	12	253	234	109	84	1	5.08
Art Delaney	R	33	9	17	.346	2	39	22	8	192	197	56	45	0	3.80
2 Ben Cantwell	R	26	3	3	.500	0	22	10	3	90	112	36	18	0	5.10
Johnny Cooney	L	27	3	7	.300	0	24	5	2	90	106	31	18	0	4.30
1 Joe Genewich	R	31	3	7	.300	0	13	11	4	81	88	18	15	0	4.11
Kent Greenfield	R	26	3	11	.214	0	32	20	5	144	173	60	30	0	5.31
2 Virgil Barnes	R	31	2	7	.222	0	16	10	1	60	86	26	7	0	5.85
Foster Edwards	R	24	2	1	.667	0	21	3	2	49	67	23	17	0	5.69
Charlie Robertson	R	32	1	5	.286	1	13	7	3	59	73	16	17	0	5.34
Bunny Hearn	L	24	1	0	1.000	0	9	0	0	10	6	9	8	0	6.30
Emilio Palmero	L	33	1	0	1.000	0	7	1	0	7	14	2	0	0	5.14
2 Bill Clarkson	R	29	0	0	.000	0	19	2	0	35	53	22	8	0	6.69
Johnny Wertz	R	30	0	0	.000	0	18	1	0	31	38	5	0	0	10.50
Bonnie Hollingsworth	R	32	0	0	.000	0	20	0	0	30	13	10	5	0	5.32
Clay Touchstone	R	25	0	—	—	0	8	1	0	4	5	2	1	0	4.50
Hal Goldsmith	R	29	0	0	—	0	8	0	0	14	11	1	1	0	3.38
Art Mills	R	25	0	0	—	0	4	0	0	17	8	0	0	0	12.38
Ray Boggs	L	23	0	0	—	0	4	0	0	5	2	7	0	0	5.40
Guy Morrison	R	32	0	0	—	0	4	1	0	4	3	0	1	0	12.00
2 George Sisler	L	35	0	0	—	0	1	0	0	0	0	0	0	0	0.00

PHILADELPHIA 8th 43-109 .283 51 — BURT SHOTTON

NAME	G by Pos	B	AGE	G	AB	R	H	2B	3B	HR	RBI	BB	SO	SB	BA	SA
TOTALS			27	152	5234	660	1396	257	47	85	606	503	510	53	.267	.382
Don Hurst	1B104	L	22	107	396	73	113	24	3	19	64	68	40	3	.285	.508
Fresco Thompson	2B152	R	26	152	634	99	182	34	11	3	50	42	27	19	.287	.390
Heinie Sand	SS137	R	30	141	426	38	90	26	1	0	38	60	47	1	.211	.277
Pinky Whitney	3B149	R	23	151	585	73	176	35	4	10	103	36	30	3	.301	.426
Chuck Klein	OF63	L	23	64	253	41	91	14	4	11	34	14	22	0	.360	.577
Denny Sothern	OF136	R	24	141	579	82	165	27	5	5	38	34	53	17	.285	.375
Freddy Leach	OF120, 1B25	L	30	145	588	83	179	26	11	13	96	30	30	4	.304	.469
Walt Lerian	C74	R	25	96	239	28	65	16	2	2	25	24	29	1	.272	.381
Cy Williams	OF69	L	40	99	238	31	61	9	0	12	37	54	34	0	.256	.445
2 Spud Davis	C49	R	23	67	163	16	46	2	0	3	18	15	11	0	.282	.350
Johnny Schulte	C34	R	23	51	113	14	28	2	2	4	17	15	11	0	.248	.407
Bill Deitrick (BL)	OF21, SS8	L	26	52	100	13	20	6	0	0	7	10	17	1	.200	.260
Barney Friberg	SS31, 3B5, 2B3, OF3, 1B2	R	28	52	94	11	19	3	0	1	7	12	16	0	.202	.266
2 Art Jahn	OF29	R	32	36	94	8	21	4	0	0	11	4	11	0	.223	.266
1 Russ Wrightstone	OF26, 1B4	L	35	33	91	7	19	5	1	1	11	14	5	0	.209	.319
Al Nixon	OF20	R	42	25	64	7	15	2	0	0	7	6	4	1	.234	.266
Bill Kelly	1B23	R	29	23	71	6	12	1	0	5	7	20	0		.169	.211
1 Jimmie Wilson	C20	R	27	21	70	11	21	4	1	0	13	9	8	3	.300	.386
Harvey MacDonald	OF2	L	30	13	16	0	4	0	0	0	0	0	2	0	.250	.250
Dutch Ulrich (IL) 28																

NAME	T	AGE	W	L	PCT	SV	G	GS	CG	IP	H	BB	SO	SHO	ERA
		29	43	109	.283	11	152	152	42	1356	1660	675	404	4	5.54
Ray Benge	R	26	8	18	.308	1	40	28	12	202	219	88	68	1	4.54
Bob McGraw	R	33	7	8	.467	1	39	3	0	132	150	56	28	0	4.64
Claude Willoughby	R	29	6	5	.545	1	35	13	5	131	180	83	26	1	5.29
Alex Ferguson	R	31	5	10	.333	2	34	19	5	135	168	52	51	1	5.88
Augie Walsh	R	23	4	9	.308	2	38	11	2	122	160	40	38	0	6.20
Jimmy Ring	R	33	4	17	.190	1	35	25	4	173	214	103	72	0	6.40
Les Sweetland	L	26	3	15	.167	2	37	18	5	135	163	97	23	0	6.60
Hub Pruett	L	27	2	4	.333	0	13	9	4	71	78	49	35	0	4.56
Ed Baecht	R	21	1	1	.500	0	12	3	1	24	37	9	10	0	6.00
Earl Caldwell	R	23	1	4	.200	0	5	5	1	35	46	17	6	1	5.66
Marty Walker	L	29	0	1	.000	0	4	1	0	3	2	3	0	0	
Russ Miller	R	28	0	12	.000	1	33	12	1	108	137	34	19	0	5.42
Ed Lennon	R	30	0	0	—	0	5	0	0	12	19	10	6	0	9.00
1 Clarence Mitchell	L	37	0	0	—	0	6	1	0	13	2	0	0	0	9.00
June Green	R	28	0	0	—	0	3	1	0	5	10	6	0	0	9.00

WORLD SERIES — NEW YORK (AL) 4 ST. LOUIS (NL) 0

LINE SCORES

TEAM	1	2	3	4	5	6	7	8	9	10	11	12	R	H	E
Game 1 October 4 at New York															
STL (NL)	0	0	0	0	0	0	1	0	0				1	3	1
NY (AL)	1	0	0	2	0	0	0	1	X				4	7	0

Sherdel, Johnson (8)   **Hoyt**

TEAM	1	2	3	4	5	6	7	8	9	R	H	E
Game 2 October 5 at New York												
STL	0	3	0	0	0	0	0	0	0	3	4	1
NY	3	1	4	0	0	0	1	0	X	9	8	2

Alexander, Mitchell (3)   **Pipgras**

TEAM	1	2	3	4	5	6	7	8	9	R	H	E
Game 3 October 7 at St. Louis												
NY	0	1	0	2	0	3	1	0	0	7	7	2
STL	2	0	0	0	1	0	0	0	0	3	9	3

Zachary   Haines, Johnson (7), Rhem (8)

TEAM	1	2	3	4	5	6	7	8	9	R	H	E
Game 4 October 9 at St. Louis												
NY	0	0	0	1	0	0	4	2	0	7	15	2
STL	0	0	1	1	0	0	0	0	1	3	11	0

Hoyt   Sherdel, Alexander (7)

COMPOSITE BATTING

NAME	POS	G	AB	R	H	2B	3B	HR	RBI	BA
New York (AL)										
Totals		4	134	27	37	7	0	9	25	.276
Koenig	SS	4	19	1	3	0	0	0	0	.158
Ruth	OF	4	16	9	10	3	0	3	4	.625
Meusel	OF	4	15	5	3	1	0	1	3	.200
Bengough	C	4	13	1	3	0	0	0	1	.231
Lazzeri	2B	4	12	2	3	1	0	0	2	.250
Gehrig	1B	4	11	5	6	1	0	4	9	.545
Paschal	OF	3	10	0	2	0	0	0	0	.200
Durst	OF	4	8	3	3	0	0	1	2	.375
Robertson	3B	3	8	1	1	0	0	0	2	.125
Hoyt	P	2	7	0	1	0	0	0	0	.143
Dugan	3B	2	6	0	1	0	0	0	1	.167
Zachary	P	1	4	0	0	0	0	0	0	.000
Durocher	2B	4	2	0	0	0	0	0	1	.000
Pipgras	P	1	2	0	0	0	0	0	1	.000
Collins	C	1	1	0	1	1	0	0	0	1.000
Combs	PH	1	1	0	0	0	0	0	1	.000
St. Louis (NL)										
Totals		4	131	10	27	5	1	1	9	.207
High	3B	4	17	1	5	2	0	0	0	.294
Hafey	OF	4	15	0	3	0	0	0	0	.200
Bottomley	1B	4	14	1	3	0	1	1	3	.214
Maranville	SS	4	13	2	4	1	0	0	0	.308
Frisch	2B	4	13	1	3	0	0	0	0	.231
Douthit	OF	3	11	1	1	0	0	0	0	.091
Wilson	C	3	11	1	1	0	0	0	0	.091
Harper	OF	3	9	1	1	0	0	0	0	.111
Orsatti	OF	4	7	1	2	1	0	0	0	.286
Holm	OF	3	6	0	1	0	0	0	0	.167
Sherdel	P	2	5	0	0	0	0	0	0	.000
Smith	C	1	4	0	3	0	0	0	0	.750
Haines	P	2	4	0	0	0	0	0	0	.000
Mitchell	P	1	2	0	0	0	0	0	0	.000
Alexander	P	2	2	0	0	0	0	0	0	.000
Blades	PH	1	1	0	0	0	0	0	0	.000
Johnson	P	2	0	0	0	0	0	0	0	—
Martin	PR	1	0	1	0	0	0	0	0	—
Rhem	P	1	0	0	0	0	0	0	0	—
Thevenow	SS	1	0	0	0	0	0	0	0	—

COMPOSITE PITCHING

NAME	G	IP	H	BB	SO	W	L	SV	ERA
New York (AL)									
Totals	4	36	27	11	29	4	0	0	2.00
Hoyt	2	18	14	6	14	2	0	0	1.50
Pipgras	1	9	4	4	8	1	0	0	2.00
Zachary	1	9	9	1	7	1	0	0	3.00
St. Louis (NL)									
Totals	4	34	37	13	12	0	4	0	6.00
Sherdel	2	13.1	15	3	3	0	2	0	4.73
Haines	1	6	6	3	3	0	1	0	4.50
Mitchell	1	5.2	2	2	2	0	0	0	1.59
Alexander	2	5	10	4	2	0	1	0	19.80
Johnson	2	2	4	1	1	0	0	0	4.50
Rhem	1	2	1	0	1	0	0	0	0.00

1929 The Return from Exile

When Connie Mack dismantled his 1914 American League champions, he could not have foreseen the long wait he would have before returning to the throne. It took 15 years of wandering in the bush for the White Elephants and 104 victories in 1929 before Mack and his Athletics could claim dear superiority over the rest of the loop. Mack had slowly pieced together the elements of his current machine by plucking them one by one from the minor league ranks. Lefty Grove and George Earnshaw provided Mack with a pair of 20-win stoppers. Behind the two aces, four additional hurlers won in double figures, led by Rube Walberg's 18 victories. Al Simmons and Jimmie Foxx formed the heart of the lineup, as both hit over .350, swatted over 30 homers, and knocked in over 115 runs, and Bing Miller, Mule Haas, Mickey Cochrane, and Jimmy Dykes complemented the pair by each hitting over .310.

The Yankees were forced to rebuild in places and could not keep pace with the Athletics. Miller Huggins experimented on the left side of the infield, giving Leo Durocher a lot of time at shortstop, while coming up with a gem in rookie catcher Bill Dickey. Good years from Babe Ruth, Lou Gehrig, and Tony Lazzeri could carry the club no closer than a distant second, as Waite Hoyt and Herb Pennock fell off in their pitching and Bob Meusel no longer could provide the slugging threat of former years. To cap a poor season with tragedy, manager Miller Huggins took ill and died in September.

While the Athletics were reclaiming a crown they had held years ago, the Chicago Cubs were also picking up a scepter for the first time in 11 years. Joe McCarthy's squad had finished third in 1928, and additional punch was infused into the lineup by trading for Rogers Hornsby from Boston. Playing with his fourth club in as many years, the Rajah sparkled for the Bruins by hitting .380, belting 39 round-trippers, and propelling 149 runs across the plate. Hornsby was helped by the all-star outfield of Kiki Cuyler, Hack Wilson, and Riggs Stephenson, all of whom hit over .340 and together accounted for 371 RBI's. Even with star catcher Gabby Hartnett sidelined for most of the season with a sore arm, the Cubs managed an easy victory as Charlie Root, Guy Bush, and Pat Malone led a pitching staff which trailed only the Giants in team E.R.A.

Connie Mack surprised everyone by naming 35-year-old Howard Ehmke, who appeared in only 11 games all year, as his opening game pitcher in the World Series. In passing up his ace, Lefty Grove, Mack came out smelling like a rose, as Ehmke used a variety of slow stuff to fan a record 13 Cubs and win the opener 3-1 over Charlie Root. George Earnshaw hurled the next two games, winning the first with relief help from Grove and losing the second. The Cubs appeared to be on the edge of evening the Series with an 8-0 lead in the seventh inning of game four. But lightning then struck, and Mackmen electrified the Philadelphia crowd by scoring an incredible 10 runs, greatly aided by Cub centerfielder Hack Wilson's losing two fly balls in the sun. The fans expected to see the A's quickly finish off a disheartened Cub squad in game five, but such did not prove to be the case as Cub pitcher Pat Malone held a 2-0 edge going into the last of the ninth with one out. But then, quick as another lightning bolt, Max Bishop singled and Haas homered to knot the score. After another out, Simmons belted a double to reignite the pandemonium. Bing Miller then capped the comeback, the season, and the pandemonium by doubling Simmons across the plate to once again make Mack and the White elephants the toast of Philadelphia.

1929 AMERICAN LEAGUE

NAME	G by Pos	B	AGE	G	AB	R	H	2B	3B	HR	RBI	BB	SO	SB	BA	SA
PHILADELPHIA	**1st 104-46 .693**			**CONNIE MACK**												
TOTALS			29	151	5204	901	1539	288	76	122	845	543	440	63	.296	.451
Jimmie Foxx	1B142, 3B7	R	21	149	517	123	183	23	9	33	117	103	70	9	.354	.625
Max Bishop	2B129	R	29	129	475	102	110	19	6	3	36	128	44	1	.232	.316
Joe Boley	SS88, 3B1	R	32	91	303	36	76	17	6	2	47	24	16	1	.251	.366
Sammy Hale	3B89, 2B1	R	32	101	379	51	105	14	3	1	40	12	18	6	.277	.338
Bing Miller	OF145	R	34	147	556	84	186	32	16	8	93	40	25	24	.335	.493
Mule Haas	OF139	L	25	139	578	115	181	41	9	16	82	34	38	5	.313	.498
Al Simmons	OF142	R	27	143	581	114	212	41	9	34	157	31	38	4	.365	.642
Mickey Cochrane	C135	L	26	135	514	113	170	37	8	7	95	69	8	7	.331	.475
Jimmy Dykes	SS60, 3B45, 2B12	R	32	119	401	76	131	34	6	13	79	51	25	8	.327	.539
Walt French	OF10	L	29	45	45	7	12	1	0	1	9	2	3	0	.267	.356
Cy Perkins	C38	R	33	38	76	4	16	4	0	0	9	5	4	0	.211	.263
Homer Summa	OF24	L	30	37	81	12	22	4	0	0	10	2	1	1	.272	.321
Ossie Orwoll	P12, OF9	L	28	30	51	6	13	2	1	0	6	2	11	0	.255	.333
2 George Burns	1B19	R	36	29	49	5	13	5	0	1	11	2	3	1	.265	.429
Jim Cronin	2B10, SS9, 3B4	B	23	25	56	7	13	2	1	0	4	5	7	1	.232	.304
Bevo LeBourveau	OF3	L	32	12	16	1	5	0	1	0	2	5	1	0	.313	.438
Eddie Collins		L	42	9	7	0	0	0	0	0	0	2	0	0	.000	.000
Bud Morse	2B8	L	24	8	27	1	2	0	0	0	0	0	0	0	.074	.074
Joe Hassler	SS2	R	24	4	4	1	0	0	0	0	0	0	0	0	.000	.000
Eric McNair	SS4	R	20	4	8	2	4	1	0	0	3	0	1	1	.500	.625
Cloy Mattox	C3	R	26	3	6	0	1	0	0	0	0	1	1	0	.167	.167
Doc Cramer	OF1	L	23	2	6	0	0	0	0	0	0	0	2	0	.000	.000
Rudy Miller	3B2	R	28	2	4	1	1	0	0	0	0	1	3	0	.250	.250
NEW YORK	**2nd 88-66 .571 18**			**MILLER HUGGINS (DD) 50 82-61 .573 ART FLETCHER 6-5 .545**												
TOTALS			27	154	5379	899	1587	262	74	142	828	554	518	51	.295	.450
Lou Gehrig	1B154	L	26	154	553	127	166	33	9	35	126	122	68	4	.300	.582
Tony Lazzeri	2B129	R	25	147	545	101	193	37	11	18	106	69	45	9	.354	.561
Leo Durocher	SS93, 2B12	R	23	106	341	53	84	4	5	0	32	34	33	4	.246	.287
1 Gene Robertson	3B77	L	30	90	309	45	92	15	6	0	35	28	6	3	.298	.385
Babe Ruth	OF133	L	34	135	499	121	172	26	6	46	154	72	60	5	.345	.697
Earl Combs	OF141	L	30	142	586	119	202	33	15	3	65	69	32	11	.345	.468
Bob Meusel	OF96	R	32	100	391	46	102	15	3	10	57	17	42	1	.261	.391
Bill Dickey	C127	L	22	130	447	60	145	30	6	10	65	14	16	4	.324	.485
Mark Koenig	SS61, 3B37, 2B1	B	26	116	373	44	109	27	5	3	41	23	17	1	.292	.416
Cedric Durst	OF72, 1B1	L	32	92	202	32	52	3	3	4	31	15	25	3	.257	.361
Lyn Lary	3B55, SS14, 2B2	R	23	80	236	48	73	9	2	5	26	24	15	4	.309	.428
Sammy Byrd	OF54	R	22	62	170	32	53	12	0	5	28	28	18	1	.312	.471
Ben Paschal	OF20	R	33	42	72	13	15	3	0	2	11	6	3	1	.208	.333
Benny Bengough (AJ)	C23	R	30	23	62	5	12	2	1	0	7	0	2	0	.194	.258
Johnny Grabowski	C22	R	29	22	59	4	12	1	0	0	3	4	1	0	.203	.220
Art Jorgens	C15	R	24	18	34	6	11	3	0	0	4	6	7	0	.324	.412
1 George Burns		R	36	9	9	0	0	0	0	0	0	0	0	0	.000	.000
Julie Wera	3B4	R	27	5	12	1	5	0	0	0	2	1	1	0	.417	.417
Liz Funk		L	24	1	0	0	0	0	0	0	0	0	0	0	—	—
CLEVELAND	**3rd 81-71 .533 24**			**ROGER PECKINPAUGH**												
TOTALS			28	152	5187	717	1525	294	79	62	684	453	363	75	.294	.417
Lew Fonseca	1B147	R	30	148	566	97	209	44	15	6	103	50	23	19	.369	.532
Johnny Hodapp	2B72	R	4	90	294	30	96	12	7	4	51	15	14	3	.327	.456
Jackie Tavener	SS89	L	31	92	250	25	53	9	4	2	26	24	28	1	.212	.304
Joe Sewell	3B152	R	30	152	578	90	182	38	3	7	73	48	4	6	.315	.427
Bibb Falk	OF121	L	26	130	430	66	133	30	7	13	94	42	14	4	.309	.502
Earl Averill	OF152	L	27	152	603	110	199	43	13	18	97	64	53	13	.330	.534
Charlie Jamieson	OF93	L	36	102	364	56	106	22	1	0	26	50	12	2	.291	.357
Luke Sewell	C123	R	28	124	406	41	96	16	3	1	39	29	26	1	.236	.298
Eddie Morgan	OF81	L	25	93	318	60	101	19	10	3	38	37	24	4	.318	.469
Ray Gardner	SS82	R	27	82	256	28	67	3	2	1	24	29	16	10	.262	.301
Dick Porter	OF30, 2B22	L	27	71	192	26	63	16	5	1	24	17	14	3	.328	.479
Carl Lind	2B64, 3B1	R	25	66	225	19	54	8	1	0	12	13	17	4	.240	.284
Glenn Myatt	C41	L	31	59	129	14	30	4	1	1	17	7	5	0	.233	.326
Joe Hauser	1B8	L	30	37	48	4	12	1	1	3	9	4	8	0	.250	.500
Grover Hartley	C13	R	40	24	59	2	9	0	1	0	2	3	0	0	.273	.339
Johnny Burnett	SS10, 2B4	L	24	19	33	2	5	1	0	0	2	1	2	1	.152	.182
Dan Jessee		L	28	4	11	2	4	1	1	0	2	0	2	0	.250	.455

NAME	T	AGE	W	L	PCT	SV	G	GS	CG	IP	H	BB	SO	SHO	ERA
		31	104	46	.693	24	151	151	72	1357	1371	487	573	8	3.44
George Earnshaw	R	29	24	8	.750	1	44	33	13	255	233	125	149	2	3.29
Lefty Grove	L	29	20	6	.769	4	42	37	21	275	278	81	170	2	2.82
Rube Walberg	L	32	18	11	.621	4	40	33	20	268	256	99	94	3	3.59
Eddie Rommel	R	31	12	2	.857	4	32	6	4	114	135	34	25	0	2.84
Jack Quinn	R	45	11	9	.550	2	35	18	7	161	182	39	41	0	3.97
Bill Shores	R	25	11	6	.647	7	39	13	5	153	150	59	49	1	3.60
Howard Ehmke	R	35	7	2	.778	0	11	8	2	55	48	15	20	0	3.27
Carroll Yerkes	R	26	1	0	1.000	0	19	2	1	37	47	13	11	0	4.62
Bill Breckinridge	R	21	0	0	—	0	3	1	0	10	16	2	0	0	8.10
Ossie Orwoll	L	28	0	2	.000	1	12	0	0	30	32	6	12	0	4.80
		30	88	66	.571	18	154	154	64	1373	1475	485	484	12	4.18
George Pipgras	R	29	18	12	.600	0	39	33	13	225	229	95	125	3	4.24
Ed Wells	L	29	13	9	.591	0	31	23	10	193	179	81	78	3	4.42
Tom Zachary	L	33	12	0	1.000	2	26	11	7	120	131	30	35	2	2.47
Fred Heimach	L	28	11	6	.647	4	35	10	3	135	141	29	24	3	4.00
Waite Hoyt	R	29	10	9	.526	1	30	25	12	202	219	69	57	0	4.23
Herb Pennock	L	35	9	11	.450	2	27	23	8	158	205	28	49	1	4.90
Wilcy Moore	R	32	6	4	.600	8	41	0	0	62	64	19	21	0	4.06
Roy Sherid	R	22	6	6	.500	1	33	15	9	160	165	55	51	0	3.49
Hank Johnson (XJ)	R	23	3	3	.500	2	8	2	0	43	37	39	24	0	5.02
Bots Nekola	L	22	0	0	—	0	9	1	0	19	21	15	2	0	4.28
1 Myles Thomas	R	31	0	2	.000	1	7	1	0	15	27	9	3	0	10.80
Gordon Rhodes	R	21	0	0	.000	0	10	4	0	43	57	16	13	0	4.81
		29	81	71	.533	10	152	152	80	1352	1570	488	389	8	4.05
Wes Farrell	R	21	21	10	.677	5	43	25	18	243	256	109	100	1	3.59
Willis Hudlin	R	23	17	15	.531	1	40	33	22	280	299	73	60	2	3.34
Jake Miller	L	31	14	12	.538	0	29	29	14	206	227	60	58	2	3.58
Johnny Miljus	R	34	8	8	.500	2	34	15	4	128	174	64	42	0	5.20
Joe Shaute (SA)	R	29	8	8	.500	0	26	24	8	162	211	52	43	0	4.28
Ken Hollwway (HJ)	R	31	6	5	.545	0	25	11	6	119	118	37	32	2	3.02
Jimmy Zinn	R	34	4	6	.400	2	18	11	6	105	150	33	29	1	5.06
Milt Shoffner	L	23	2	3	.400	0	11	3	1	45	46	22	15	0	5.00
Mel Harder	R	19	1	0	1.000	0	11	0	0	18	24	5	4	0	5.50
Jim Moore	R	25	0	0	—	0	4	0	0	10	9	2	1	0	4.50
George Grant	R	26	0	2	.000	0	12	0	0	24	41	23	5	0	10.50
Clint Brown	R	25	0	0	.000	0	3	1	1	16	18	6	1	0	3.38

NAME	G by Pos	B	AGE	G	AB	R	H	2B	3B	HR	RBI	BB	SO	SB	BA	SA
ST. LOUIS 4th 79-73 .520 26	**DAN HOWLEY**															
TOTALS			30	154	5174	733	1426	276	63	46	672	589	431	72	.276	.380
Lu Blue	1B151	B	32	151	573	111	168	40	10	6	61	126	32	12	.293	.429
Oscar Melillo	2B141	R	29	141	494	57	146	17	10	5	67	29	30	11	.296	.401
Red Kress	SS146	R	24	147	557	82	170	38	4	9	107	52	54	5	.305	.436
Frank O'Rourke	3B151, 2B3, SS2	R	37	154	585	81	147	23	9	2	62	41	28	14	.251	.332
Beauty McGowan	OF117	L	27	125	441	62	112	26	6	2	51	61	34	5	.254	.354
Fred Schulte	OF116	R	28	121	446	63	137	24	5	3	71	59	44	8	.307	.404
Heinie Manush	OF141	L	27	142	574	85	204	45	10	6	81	43	24	9	.355	.500
Wally Schang	C85	B	39	94	249	43	59	10	5	5	36	74	22	1	.237	.378
Earl McNeely	OF62	R	31	69	230	27	56	8	1	1	18	7	13	2	.243	.300
Rick Ferrell	C45	R	23	64	144	21	33	6	1	0	20	32	10	1	.229	.285
Red Badgro	OF37	R	26	54	148	27	42	12	0	1	18	11	15	1	.284	.385
Clyde Manion	C34	R	32	35	111	16	27	2	0	0	11	15	3	1	.243	.261
Otis Brannan	2B19	L	29	33	51	4	15	1	0	1	8	4	4	2	.294	.373
Tom Jenkins	OF3	L	31	21	22	1	4	0	1	0	4	0	8	0	.182	.273
Len Dondero	3B10, 2B5	R	25	19	31	2	6	0	0	1	8	4	6	0	.194	.290
Ed Roetz	SS8, 1B5, 2B2 3B1	R	23	16	45	7	11	4	1	0	5	4	6	1	.244	.378
Jimmy Austin	3B1	B	49	1	1	0	0	0	0	0	0	0	0	0	.000	.000
WASHINGTON 5th 71-81 .467 34	**WALTER JOHNSON**															
TOTALS			29	153	5237	730	1445	244	66	48	656	556	400	86	.276	.375
Joe Judge	1B142	L	35	143	543	83	171	35	8	6	71	73	33	12	.315	.442
Buddy Myer	2B88, 3B53	L	25	141	563	80	169	29	10	3	82	63	33	18	.300	.403
Joe Cronin	SS143, 2B1	R	22	145	492	72	139	29	8	8	60	85	37	5	.283	.423
Jackie Hayes	3B63, 2B56, SS9	R	22	142	424	52	117	20	3	2	57	24	29	4	.276	.351
Sam Rice	OF147	L	39	150	616	119	199	39	10	1	62	55	9	16	.323	.424
Sammy West	OF139	L	34	142	510	60	136	16	8	3	75	45	41	9	.267	.347
Goose Goslin	OF142	L	28	145	552	82	159	28	7	18	91	66	33	10	.288	.462
Bennie Tate	C74	L	27	81	265	26	78	12	3	0	30	16	8	2	.294	.362
Red Barnes	OF30	L	25	72	130	16	26	5	2	1	15	13	12	1	.200	.292
Muddy Ruel	C63	R	33	69	188	16	46	4	2	0	20	31	7	0	.245	.287
Ossie Bluege (KJ)	3B34, 2B14, SS10	R	28	64	220	35	65	6	0	5	31	19	15	6	.295	.391
Roy Spencer	C41	R	29	50	116	18	18	4	0	1	9	8	15	0	.155	.216
Charlie Gooch	1B7, 3B7, SS1	R	27	39	57	6	16	2	1	0	5	7	8	0	.281	.351
Harley Boss	1B18	L	20	28	66	9	18	2	1	0	6	2	6	0	.273	.333
Stuffy Stewart	2B3	R	35	22	6	10	0	0	0	0	0	2	2	1	.000	.000
2 Ira Flagstead	OF11	R	35	18	39	5	7	1	0	0	9	4	5	1	.179	.205
Spence Harris	OF4	L	28	6	14	1	3	1	0	0	1	0	3	0	.214	.286
Pastsy Gharrity		R	37	3	2	0	0	0	0	0	0	1	2	0	.000	.000
Nick Altrock	OF1	B	52	1	1	0	1	0	0	0	0	0	0	0	1.000	1.000
Doc Land	OF1	R	24	1	3	0	0	0	0	0	0	0	1	0	.000	.000
DETROIT 6th 70-84 .455 36	**BUCKY HARRIS**															
TOTALS			28	155	5592	926	1671	339	97	110	851	521	496	95	.299	.453
Dale Alexander	1B155	R	26	155	626	110	215	43	15	25	137	56	63	5	.343	.580
Charlie Gehringer	2B154	L	26	155	634	131	215	45	19	13	106	64	19	27	.339	.532
Heinie Schuble	SS86, 3B2	R	22	92	258	35	60	11	7	2	28	19	23	3	.233	.353
Marty McManus	3B150, SS9	R	29	154	599	99	168	38	8	18	90	60	52	16	.280	.451
Harry Heilmann	OF113, 1B1	R	34	125	453	86	156	41	7	15	120	50	39	5	.344	.565
Harry Rice	OF127, 3B3	L	28	148	536	97	163	33	7	6	69	61	23	6	.304	.425
Roy Johnson	OF146	R	26	148	640	128	201	45	14	10	69	67	60	20	.314	.475
Eddie Phillips	C63	R	28	68	221	24	52	13	1	2	23	16	20	0	.235	.330
Bob Fothergill	OF59	R	31	115	277	42	98	24	9	6	62	11	11	3	.354	.570
Pinky Hargrave	C48	B	33	76	185	26	61	12	0	3	26	20	24	1	.330	.443
Yats Wuestling	SS52, 2B1, 3B1	R	25	54	150	13	30	4	1	0	16	9	24	1	.200	.240
John Stone	OF36	L	23	51	150	23	39	11	2	2	15	11	13	1	.260	.400
Merv Shea	C50	R	28	50	162	23	47	6	0	3	24	19	18	2	.290	.383
George Uhle	P32	R	30	40	108	18	37	1	1	0	13	6	6	0	.343	.370
Bill Akers	SS24	R	24	24	83	15	22	4	1	1	9	10	9	2	.265	.373
Ray Hayworth	C14	R	25	14	43	5	11	0	0	0	4	3	8	0	.256	.256
1 Frank Sigafoos	3B6, SS5	R	25	14	23	3	4	1	0	0	2	5	4	1	.174	.217
Nolen Richardson	SS13	R	26	13	21	2	4	0	0	0	2	2	1	1	.190	.190
Bucky Harris	2B4, SS1	R	32	7	11	3	1	0	0	0	0	2	0	1	.091	.091
Larry Woodall		R	34	1	1	0	0	0	0	0	0	0	0	0	.000	.000
CHICAGO 7th 59-93 .388 46	**LENA BLACKBURNE**															
TOTALS			26	152	5248	627	1406	240	74	37	558	425	436	112	.268	.363
Art Shires	1B88, 2B2	L	21	100	353	41	110	20	7	3	41	32	20	4	.312	.433
John Kerr	2B122	R	30	127	419	50	108	20	4	1	39	31	24	9	.258	.332
Bill Cissell	SS152	R	25	152	618	83	173	27	12	5	82	28	53	26	.280	.387
Willie Kamm	3B145	R	29	147	523	72	140	33	6	3	63	75	23	12	.268	.371
Carl Reynolds	OF130	R	26	131	517	87	164	24	12	11	67	20	37	19	.317	.474
Dutch Hoffman	OF89	L	25	107	337	27	87	16	5	3	37	24	24	6	.258	.362
Alex Metzler	OF141	L	26	146	568	80	156	23	13	2	49	80	45	11	.275	.371
Moe Berg	C106	R	27	107	352	32	101	7	0	0	47	17	16	5	.287	.307
Bud Clancy	1B74	L	28	92	290	36	82	14	6	3	45	16	19	3	.283	.403
Johnny Watwood	OF77	R	23	85	278	33	84	12	6	2	28	22	21	6	.302	.410
Bill Hunnefield	2B26, 3B4, SS2	B	30	47	127	13	23	5	0	0	9	7	3	7	.181	.220
2 Doug Taitt	OF30	L	26	47	124	11	21	7	0	0	12	8	13	0	.169	.226
Buck Crouse	C40	L	32	45	107	11	29	7	0	2	12	5	7	2	.271	.393
Martin Autry	C30	R	26	43	96	7	20	6	0	1	12	1	8	0	.208	.302
Buck Redfern	2B11, 3B5, SS4	R	27	21	46	0	6	0	0	0	3	3	3	1	.130	.130
Johnny Mostil (BN)	OF11	R	33	12	35	4	8	3	0	0	6	2	1	1	.229	.314
2 Frank Sigafoos	2B6	R	25	7	3	1	1	0	0	0	1	2	1	0	.333	.333
1 Bill Barrett		R	29	3	1	0	0	0	0	0	0	0	0	0	.000	.000
Karl Swanson		L	28	3	1	0	0	0	0	0	0	0	0	0	.000	.000
BOSTON 8th 58-96 .377 48	**BILL CARRIGAN**															
TOTALS			28	155	5160	605	1377	285	69	28	561	413	494	86	.267	.365
Phil Todt	1B153	L	27	153	534	49	140	38	10	6	63	31	28	6	.262	.393
Bill Regan	2B91, 3B10, 1B1	R	30	104	371	38	107	27	7	1	54	22	38	7	.288	.407
Hal Rhyne	SS114,3B1, 0F1	R	30	120	346	41	87	24	5	0	38	25	14	4	.251	.350
Bobby Reeves	3B132, 2B2, 1B1	R	25	140	460	66	114	23	4	2	28	60	57	7	.248	.311
2 Bill Barrett	OF109, 3B1	R	29	111	370	57	100	23	4	3	35	51	38	11	.270	.378
Jack Rothrock	OF128	B	24	143	473	70	142	19	7	6	59	43	47	23	.300	.408
Russ Scarritt	OF145	R	26	151	540	69	159	26	17	1	72	34	38	13	.294	.411
Charlie Berry	C72	R	26	77	207	19	50	11	4	1	21	15	29	2	.242	.348
Elliot Bigelow	OF58	L	30	100	211	23	60	16	0	1	26	23	18	1	.284	.374
Bill Narleski	SS51, 2B28, 3B10	R	29	96	260	30	72	16	1	0	25	21	22	4	.277	.346
Johnnie Heving	C55	R	33	76	188	26	60	4	3	0	23	8	7	1	.319	.372
Ken Williams	OF36, 1B2	L	39	74	139	21	48	14	2	3	22	15	7	1	.345	.540
Bob Barrett	3B34, 1B4, 2B2, 0F1	R	39	68	126	15	34	10	0	0	19	10	6	3	.270	.349
Wally Gerber	SS30, 2B22	R	37	61	91	6	15	3	1	0	5	8	12	1	.165	.220
Red Ruffing	P35, OF2	R	25	60	114	9	35	9	0	2	17	2	13	0	.307	.439
Alex Gaston	C49	R	36	55	116	14	26	5	2	2	10	6	8	1	.224	.353
Grant Gillis	2B25	R	28	28	73	5	18	4	0	0	11	6	3	0	.247	.301
1 Doug Taitt	OF21	L	26	26	65	6	18	4	0	0	5	5	7	3	.277	.338
Jerry Standaert	1B10	R	27	19	18	1	3	2	0	0	4	3	2	0	.167	.278
Casper Asbjornson	C15	R	27	17	29	1	3	0	0	0	1	1	9	0	.103	.103
1 Ira Flagstead	OF13	R	35	16	36	9	11	2	0	0	3	5	1	1	.306	.361
Joe Cicero	OF7	R	18	10	32	6	10	4	0	0	4	0	6	0	.313	.500
Ed Connolly	C5	R	20	5	7	0	0	0	0	0	0	1	1	0	.000	.000
Jack Ryan	OF2	R	24	3	1	0	0	0	0	0	0	0	0	0	.000	.000
Denny Williams (DD)	29															

NAME	T	AGE	W	L	PCT	SV	G	GS	CG	IP	H	BB	SO	SHO	ERA
		28	79	73	.520	10	154	154	83	1371	1474	462	415	15	4.08
Sam Gray	R	31	18	15	.545	1	43	37	23	305	336	96	109	4	3.72
General Crowder	R	30	17	15	.531	4	40	34	19	267	233	93	79	4	3.91
George Blaeholder	R	25	14	15	.483	2	42	24	15	222	237	61	72	4	4.18
Rip Collins	R	33	11	6	.647	1	26	20	10	155	162	73	47	1	4.00
Lefty Stewart	L	28	9	6	.600	0	23	18	8	150	137	49	47	1	3.24
Jack Ogden	R	31	4	8	.333	0	34	14	7	131	154	44	32	0	4.94
Chad Kimsey	R	22	3	6	.333	1	24	3	1	64	88	19	13	0	5.07
Fred Stiely	L	28	1	1	1.000	0	1	1	1	9	11	3	2	0	0.00
Dick Coffman	R	22	1	1	.500	2	7	3	1	53	61	14	11	1	5.94
Ed Strelecki	R	21	1	1	.500	0	7	0	0	11	12	6	2	0	4.91
2 Paul Hopkins	R	24	0	0	—	0	2	0	0	2	2	1	0	0	0.00
Herb Cobb	R	24	0	0	—	0	1	0	0	1	3	1	0	0	36.00
Oscar Estrada	L	25	0	0	—	0	1	0	0	1	1	1	0	0	0.00
		27	71	81	.467	17	153	153	62	1354	1429	496	494	3	4.34
Firpo Marberry	R	30	19	12	.613	11	49	26	16	250	233	69	121	0	3.06
Garland Braxton	R	29	10	11	.476	4	37	20	9	182	219	51	59	0	4.85
Sad Sam Jones	R	36	9	9	.500	0	24	24	8	154	156	49	36	1	3.91
Lloyd Brown	L	24	8	7	.533	0	40	15	7	168	186	69	48	1	4.18
2 Myles Thomas	R	31	8	8	.467	2	22	14	7	125	139	48	33	0	3.53
Bobby Burke	L	22	6	8	.429	0	37	17	4	141	154	55	51	0	4.79
Bump Hadley	R	24	6	16	.273	0	37	27	7	195	196	85	98	1	5.63
Ad Liska (SA)	R	22	3	9	.250	0	24	10	4	94	87	42	33	0	4.79
Walter Beall	R	29	1	0	1.000	0	3	0	0	7	7	8	3	0	3.86
Paul McCullough	R	30	0	0	—	0	3	0	0	7	6	2	0	0	9.00
Don Savidge	R	20	0	0	—	0	3	0	0	6	12	2	2	0	9.00
Ed Wineapple	L	23	0	1	.000	0	1	1	0	3	6	4	1	0	4.50
1 Paul Hopkins	R	24	0	1	.000	0	7	0	0	16	15	9	5	0	2.25
Archie Campbell	R	25	0	1	.000	0	4	0	0	4	10	5	1	0	15.75
		28	70	84	.455	9	155	155	82	1390	1641	646	467	5	4.96
George Uhle	R	30	15	11	.577	0	32	30	23	249	283	58	100	1	4.08
Vic Sorrell	R	28	14	15	.483	1	36	31	13	226	270	106	81	1	5.18
Earl Whitehill	L	29	14	15	.483	1	38	28	18	245	267	96	103	1	4.63
Ownie Carroll	R	26	9	17	.346	1	34	26	12	202	249	86	54	0	4.63
Emil Yde	L	29	7	3	.700	0	29	6	4	87	100	63	23	1	5.27
George Smith	R	27	3	2	.600	0	14	2	1	36	42	36	13	0	5.75
Lil Stoner	R	30	3	3	.500	4	24	3	1	53	57	31	12	0	5.26
Art Herring	R	23	2	1	.667	0	4	2	2	32	38	19	15	0	4.78
Chief Hogsett	L	25	2	1	.333	0	4	2	1	29	34	9	9	1	2.79
Kyle Graham	R	29	1	3	.250	1	13	6	2	52	70	33	7	0	5.53
Augie Prudhomme	R	26	1	6	.143	1	34	6	2	94	119	53	26	0	6.22
Haskell Billings (XJ)	R	21	0	1	.000	0	3	1	0	19	27	9	1	0	5.21
Elam Vangilder	R	33	0	1	.000	0	1	1	0	11	16	7	3	0	6.54
Whit Wyatt	R	21	0	1	.000	0	3	0	0	30	18	14	6	0	6.84
Frank Barnes	L	29	0	1	.000	0	5	0	0	5	10	3	0	0	7.20
Phil Page	L	23	0	2	.000	0	5	2	0	25	29	19	6	0	8.28
		28	59	93	.388	7	152	152	78	1358	1481	505	328	5	4.41
Tommy Thomas	R	29	14	18	.438	1	36	31	24	260	270	60	62	2	3.19
Ted Lyons	R	28	14	20	.412	2	37	31	21	259	276	76	57	1	4.10
Red Faber	R	40	13	13	.500	0	31	31	15	234	241	61	68	1	3.88
Hal McKain	R	22	6	9	.400	1	34	10	4	158	158	85	33	1	3.65
Ed Walsh	R	24	6	11	.353	0	24	20	7	129	156	64	31	0	5.65
Grady Adkins	R	32	2	11	.154	0	31	15	5	138	168	67	24	0	5.35
Bob Weiland	L	23	2	4	.333	1	15	9	1	62	62	43	25	0	5.81
Dan Dugan	L	22	1	4	.200	1	19	2	0	65	77	19	15	0	6.65
2 Dutch Henry	L	27	1	0	1.000	0	2	1	1	15	20	7	2	0	6.00
Sarge Connally	R	30	0	0	—	1	11	0	0	11	13	8	3	0	4.91
Lena Blackburne	R	42	0	0	—	0	1	0	0	.1	0	0	0	0	0.00
Jerry Byrne	R	22	0	1	.000	0	3	1	0	11	11	6	1	0	7.71
Ted Blankenship (HO)	R	28	0	2	.000	0	3	1	0	18	28	9	7	0	9.00
		26	58	96	.377	5	155	155	84	1366	1537	496	416	9	4.43
Ed Morris	R	29	14	14	.500	1	33	26	17	208	227	95	73	2	4.45
Milt Gaston	R	33	12	19	.387	2	39	28	20	244	265	81	83	1	3.73
Danny MacFayden	R	24	10	18	.357	0	32	27	14	221	225	81	61	4	3.62
Red Ruffing	R	25	9	22	.290	1	35	32	18	244	280	118	109	1	4.87
Jack Russell	R	23	8	18	.250	0	35	28	13	227	263	40	37	0	3.92
Bill Bayne	L	30	5	5	.500	0	27	6	2	84	111	29	26	0	6.75
Ed Carroll	R	21	1	0	1.000	0	24	0	0	67	77	20	13	0	5.56
Ed Durham	R	21	1	0	1.000	0	34	34	14	6	9	1	1	0	9.41
Ray Dobens	L	22	0	0	—	0	11	1	0	28	32	9	4	0	3.86
Hod Lisenbee	R	30	0	0	—	0	9	0	0	4	2	0	0	0	5.00
Herb Bradley	R	26	0	0	—	0	3	0	0	7	6	3	2	0	6.75
Pat Simmons	R	20	0	0	—	0	2	0	0	7	6	3	2	0	0.00

CHICAGO — 1ST 98-54 .645 — JOE McCARTHY

NAME	G by Pos	B	AGE	G	AB	R	H	2B	3B	HR	RBI	BB	SO	SB	BA	SA
TOTALS			30	156	5471	982	1655	310	46	139	933	589	567	103	.303	.452
Charlie Grimm (BW)	1B120	L	30	120	463	66	138	28	3	10	91	42	25	3	.298	.436
Rogers Hornsby	2B156	R	33	156	602	156	229	47	8	39	149	87	65	2	.380	.679
Woody English	SS144	R	22	144	608	131	168	29	3	1	52	68	50	13	.276	.339
Norm McMillan	3B120	R	33	124	495	77	134	35	5	5	55	36	43	13	.271	.392
Kiki Cuyler	OF129	R	30	139	509	111	183	29	7	15	102	66	56	43	.360	.532
Hack Wilson	OF150	R	29	150	574	135	198	30	5	39	159	78	83	3	.345	.618
Riggs Stephenson	OF130	R	31	136	495	91	179	36	6	17	110	67	21	10	.362	.562
2 Zack Taylor	C64	R	30	64	215	29	59	16	3	1	31	19	18	0	.274	.391
Cliff Heathcote	OF52	L	31	82	224	45	70	17	0	2	31	25	17	9	.313	.415
Mike Gonzalez	C60	R	38	60	167	15	40	3	0	0	18	18	14	1	.240	.257
Clyde Beck	3B33, SS14	R	27	54	190	28	40	7	0	0	9	19	24	3	.211	.247
Johnny Moore	OF15	L	27	37	63	13	18	1	0	2	8	4	6	0	.286	.397
Chuck Tolson	1B31	R	30	32	109	13	28	5	0	1	19	9	16	0	.257	.330
Johnny Schulte	C30	R	32	31	69	6	18	3	0	0	9	7	11	0	.261	.304
Earl Grace	C27	L	22	27	80	7	20	1	0	2	17	9	7	0	.250	.338
Footsie Blair	3B8, 1B7, 2B2	R	28	26	72	10	23	5	0	1	9	3	4	1	.319	.431
Gabby Hartnett (SA)	C1	R	28	25	22	2	6	2	1	1	9	5	5	1	.273	.591
Tom Angley	C5	R	24	5	16	1	4	1	0	0	6	2	2	0	.250	.313
Danny Taylor	OF1	R	28	3	0	0	0	0	0	0	0	0	1	0	.000	.000

NAME	T	AGE	W	L	PCT	SV	G	GS	CG	IP	H	BB	SO	SHO	ERA
TOTALS		30	98	54	.645	21	156	156	79	1399	1542	564	548	14	4.16
Pat Malone	R	26	22	10	.688	2	40	30	19	267	283	102	166	5	3.57
Charlie Root	R	30	19	6	.760	5	43	31	19	272	286	83	124	4	3.47
Guy Bush	R	27	18	7	.720	8	50	30	18	271	277	107	82	2	3.55
Sheriff Blake	R	29	14	13	.519	1	35	29	13	218	244	130	70	1	4.29
Hal Carlson (IL)	R	37	11	5	.688	2	31	13	6	112	131	31	35	2	5.14
Art Nehf	L	36	8	5	.615	1	32	14	4	121	148	39	27	0	5.58
Mike Cvengros	L	28	5	4	.556	2	32	4	0	64	82	29	23	0	4.64
Trader Horne	R	30	1	1	.500	0	11	1	0	23	24	21	6	0	5.09
Bob Osborne	R	26	0	0	—	0	3	1	0	9	8	2	1	0	3.00
Claude Jonnard	R	32	0	1	.000	0	12	2	0	28	41	11	11	0	7.39
Ken Penner	R	33	0	1	.000	0	5	0	0	13	14	6	3	0	2.77
Hank Grampp	R	25	0	0	—	0	1	0	0	2	4	3	1	0	27.00

PITTSBURGH — 2nd 88-65 .575 10.5 — DONIE BUSH 67-51 .568 — JEWEL ENS 21-14 .600

NAME	G by Pos	B	AGE	G	AB	R	H	2B	3B	HR	RBI	BB	SO	SB	BA	SA
TOTALS			27	154	5490	904	1663	285	116	60	828	503	351	94	.303	.430
Earl Sheely	1B139	R	36	139	485	63	142	22	4	6	88	75	24	6	.293	.392
George Grantham	2B76, OF19, 1B12	L	29	110	349	85	107	23	10	12	90	93	38	10	.307	.533
Dick Bartell	SS74, 2B70	R	21	143	610	101	184	40	13	2	57	40	29	11	.302	.420
Pie Traynor	3B130	R	30	130	540	94	192	27	12	4	108	30	7	13	.356	.472
Paul Waner	OF143, 1B7	L	26	151	596	131	200	43	15	15	100	89	24	15	.336	.534
Lloyd Waner	OF151	L	23	151	662	134	234	28	20	5	74	37	20	6	.353	.479
Adam Comorosky	OF121	R	24	127	473	86	152	26	11	6	97	40	22	19	.321	.461
Charlie Hargreaves	C101	R	32	102	328	33	88	12	5	1	44	16	12	1	.268	.345
Rollie Hemsley	C80	R	22	88	235	31	68	13	7	0	37	11	22	1	.289	.404
Sparky Adams	SS30, 2B20, 3B15, OF2	R	34	74	196	37	51	8	1	0	11	15	5	3	.260	.311
Fred Brickell	OF27	L	22	60	118	13	37	4	2	0	17	17	12	3	.314	.381
Erv Brame	P37	R	27	59	116	9	36	8	1	4	25	2	7	0	.310	.500
Stu Clarke	SS41, 3B15, 2B1	R	23	57	178	20	47	5	7	2	21	19	21	3	.264	.404
Burleigh Grimes	P33	R	35	33	91	11	26	3	0	0	12	4	10	0	.286	.385
3 Ira Flagstead	OF9	R	35	26	50	8	14	2	1	0	6	4	2	1	.280	.360
Cobe Jones	SS15	B	23	25	63	6	16	5	1	0	4	1	5	1	.254	.365
Bob Linton	C8	R	27	17	18	0	2	0	0	0	1	1	2	0	.111	.111
Jim Mosolf	OF3	L	23	8	13	3	6	1	1	0	2	1	1	0	.462	.692
Harry Riconda	SS4	R	32	8	15	3	7	2	0	0	2	0	0	0	.467	.600
Jim Stroner	3B2	R	28	6	8	0	3	1	0	0	1	0	1	0	.375	.500
Mel Ingram		R	24	3	0	1	0	0	0	0	0	0	0	0	—	—
John O'Connell	C2	R	25	3	7	1	1	0	0	0	1	0	1	0	.143	.286
Ben Sankey	SS2	R	21	2	7	1	1	0	0	0	0	1	1	0	.143	.143
Bill Windle	1B2	L	24	2	7	1	0	0	0	0	0	0	1	0	.000	.000

NAME	T	AGE	W	L	PCT	SV	G	GS	CG	IP	H	BB	SO	SHO	ERA
TOTALS		31	88	65	.575	13	154	154	79	1379	1530	439	409	5	4.36
Ray Kremer	R	36	18	10	.643	0	34	27	14	222	226	60	66	0	4.26
Burleigh Grimes	R	35	17	7	.708	2	33	29	18	233	245	70	62	2	3.13
Erv Brame	R	27	16	11	.593	0	37	28	19	230	250	71	68	1	4.54
Jesse Petty	L	34	11	10	.524	0	36	25	12	184	197	42	58	1	3.72
Steve Swetonic	R	25	8	10	.444	2	41	12	3	144	172	50	35	0	4.81
Larry French	L	21	7	5	.583	1	30	13	6	123	130	62	49	0	4.90
Heinie Meine	R	33	7	6	.538	1	22	13	7	108	120	34	19	1	4.50
Fred Fussell	L	33	2	2	.500	1	21	3	0	40	68	8	18	0	8.55
1 Carmen Hill	R	33	2	3	.400	0	27	3	0	79	94	35	28	0	3.99
Leon Chagnon	R	26	0	0	—	0	1	0	0	7	11	1	4	0	9.00
Ralph Erickson	R	25	0	0	—	0	1	0	0	1	2	1	0	0	27.00
Lee Meadows	R	34	0	0	—	0	1	1	0	4	9	2	1	0	9.00
Joe Dawson	R	32	0	1	.000	0	9	0	0	13	3	2	7	0	8.00

NEW YORK — 3rd 84-67 .556 13.5 — JOHN McGRAW

NAME	G by Pos	B	AGE	G	AB	R	H	2B	3B	HR	RBI	BB	SO	SB	BA	SA
TOTALS			27	152	5388	897	1594	251	47	136	829	482	405	85	.296	.436
Bill Terry	1B149, OF1	L	30	150	607	103	226	39	5	14	117	48	35	10	.372	.522
Andy Cohen	2B94, SS1, 3B1	R	24	101	347	40	102	12	2	5	47	11	15	3	.294	.383
Travis Jackson	SS149	R	25	149	551	92	162	21	12	21	90	64	56	10	.294	.490
Fred Lindstrom	3B128	R	23	130	549	99	175	26	6	15	91	30	28	10	.319	.464
Mel Ott	OF149, 2B1	L	20	150	545	138	179	37	2	42	151	113	38	6	.328	.635
Edd Roush (LJ)	OF107	R	36	115	450	76	146	19	7	8	52	15	14	10	.324	.451
Freddy Leach	OF95	L	31	113	411	74	150	22	6	8	47	17	14	10	.290	.431
Shanty Hogan	C93	R	23	102	317	19	95	13	0	5	45	25	22	1	.300	.388
Bob O'Farrell	C84	R	32	91	248	35	76	14	3	4	42	28	30	3	.306	.435
Chick Fullis	OF78	R	25	86	274	67	79	11	1	7	29	30	26	7	.288	.412
Pat Crawford	1B7, 3B1	L	27	65	57	13	17	3	0	3	24	11	5	1	.298	.509
2 Doc Farrell	3B28, 2B25, SS4	R	27	63	178	18	38	6	0	0	16	9	7	1	.213	.247
Andy Reese (IL)	2B44, OF8, 3B4	R	25	58	209	36	55	11	3	0	21	15	19	8	.263	.344
Tony Kaufmann	OF16	R	28	39	32	18	1	0	0	0	1	6	4	3	.031	.031
1 Jim Welsh	OF35	L	26	38	129	25	32	7	0	1	8	9	9	3	.248	.349
Doc Marshall	2B5	R	23	5	15	6	6	2	0	0	4	0	0	3	.400	.533
Ray Schalk	C5	R	36	5	5	0	0	0	0	0	0	1	0	0	.000	.000
1 Jack Cummings	C1	R	25	3	3	0	1	0	0	0	0	0	1	0	.333	.333
Buck Jordan	1B1	L	22	2	2	1	1	0	0	0	1	0	0	0	.500	.500
Pat Veltman	C1	R	23	2	1	1	0	0	0	0	0	0	0	0	.000	.000
Sam Leslie	OF1	L	23	1	0	0	0	0	0	0	0	0	0	0	—	—

NAME	T	AGE	W	L	PCT	SV	G	GS	CG	IP	H	BB	SO	SHO	ERA
TOTALS		30	84	67	.556	13	152	152	68	1372	1536	387	431	9	3.97
Carl Hubbell	L	26	18	11	.621	1	39	35	19	268	273	67	106	1	3.69
Freddie Fitzsimmons	R	27	15	11	.577	1	37	30	16	222	242	66	55	4	4.09
Bill Walker	L	25	14	7	.667	0	29	23	13	178	188	57	65	1	3.08
Larry Benton	R	31	11	17	.393	3	39	31	14	237	276	61	63	3	4.14
Carl Mays	R	37	7	2	.778	4	37	8	1	123	140	31	32	0	4.32
Jack Scott	R	37	7	6	.538	1	30	6	2	92	89	27	40	0	3.52
1 Dutch Henry	L	27	5	6	.455	1	27	9	4	101	129	31	27	0	3.83
Ralph Judd	R	27	3	0	1.000	0	18	0	0	51	79	11	21	0	2.65
Joe Genewich (SJ)	R	32	3	7	.300	1	21	9	1	85	133	30	19	0	6.78
Roy Parmelee	R	22	1	0	1.000	0	2	1	0	7	13	1	9	0	9.00
Ray Lucas	R	20	0	0	—	1	3	0	0	8	3	1	1	0	0.00
Jim Tennant	R	21	0	0	—	0	2	0	0	1	1	0	1	0	9.00

ST. LOUIS — 4th 78-74 .513 20 — BILLY SOUTHWORTH 43-45 .489 — GABBY STREET 1-0 1.000 — BILL McKECHNIE 34-29 .540

NAME	G by Pos	B	AGE	G	AB	R	H	2B	3B	HR	RBI	BB	SO	SB	BA	SA
TOTALS			27	154	5364	831	1569	310	84	100	779	490	455	72	.293	.438
Jim Bottomley	1B145	L	29	146	560	108	176	31	12	29	137	70	54	3	.314	.568
Frankie Frisch	2B121, 3B13, SS1	B	30	138	527	93	176	40	12	5	74	53	12	24	.334	.484
Charlie Gelbert	SS146	R	23	146	512	60	134	29	8	3	65	51	46	8	.262	.367
Andy High	3B123, 2B22	L	31	129	603	95	178	32	4	10	63	38	15	7	.295	.411
Ernie Orsatti	OF77, 1B10	L	26	113	346	64	115	21	7	3	39	33	43	7	.332	.460
Taylor Douthit	OF150	R	28	150	613	128	206	42	7	9	62	79	49	8	.336	.471
Chick Hafey	OF130	R	26	134	517	101	175	47	9	29	125	45	42	7	.338	.632
Jimmie Wilson	C119	R	28	120	394	59	128	27	4	4	71	43	19	4	.325	.464
Wally Roettger	OF69	R	26	79	269	27	68	11	3	4	42	13	27	0	.253	.349
Wattie Holm	OF44, 3B1	R	27	64	176	21	41	5	6	0	14	12	8	1	.233	.330
Earl Smith	C50	L	32	57	145	9	50	8	0	1	22	18	6	0	.345	.421
Carey Selph (FJ)	SS9, 2B7, 3B3	R	27	25	51	8	12	1	1	0	7	6	4	1	.235	.294
Eddie Delker	SS5, 2B7, 3B3	B	23	22	40	5	6	0	1	0	3	2	12	0	.150	.200
Billy Southworth	OF5	L	36	19	32	1	6	2	0	0	3	2	4	0	.188	.250
Bubber Jonnard	C18	R	29	18	31	1	3	0	0	0	3	0	6	0	.097	.097
Johnny Butler	3B9, SS6	R	26	17	55	5	9	1	1	0	5	4	5	0	.164	.218
Fred Haney	3B6	R	31	9	26	4	3	1	1	0	2	1	2	0	.115	.231

NAME	T	AGE	W	L	PCT	SV	G	GS	CG	IP	H	BB	SO	SHO	ERA
TOTALS		32	78	74	.513	8	154	154	83	1360	1604	474	453	6	4.66
Syl Johnson	R	28	13	7	.650	3	42	19	12	182	186	56	80	3	3.61
Jesse Haines	R	35	13	10	.565	0	28	25	12	180	230	73	59	0	5.70
Bill Sherdel	L	32	10	15	.400	0	33	22	11	196	278	58	69	1	5.92
Pete Alexander (ST)	R	42	9	8	.529	0	22	19	8	132	149	23	33	0	3.89
Hal Haid	R	31	9	9	.500	4	38	14	8	155	171	66	41	0	4.06
Clarence Mitchell	L	38	8	11	.421	0	25	22	16	173	221	60	39	0	4.27
Fred Frankhouse	R	25	7	2	.778	1	30	10	6	133	149	43	37	0	4.13
Wild Bill Hallahan	L	26	4	6	.400	0	20	12	5	94	94	60	52	0	4.40
Al Grabowski	R	27	3	2	.600	0	8	4	1	50	44	8	22	2	2.52
Jim Lindsey	R	31	1	1	.500	0	2	1	0	16	20	2	8	0	5.63
Bill Doak	R	38	1	2	.333	0	4	3	0	9	9	4	3	0	12.00
2 Carmen Hill	R	33	0	0	—	0	9	0	0	9	14	5	1	0	8.00
Hal Goldsmith	R	30	0	0	—	0	4	0	0	10	14	7	2	0	6.75
Mul Holland	R	26	0	0	—	0	6	0	0	14	13	1	5	0	9.64
Hi Bell (IL)	R	31	0	0	.000	0	3	0	0	13	19	4	6	0	6.92

PHILADELPHIA — 5th 71-82 .464 27.5 — BURT SHOTTON

NAME	G by Pos	B	AGE	G	AB	R	H	2B	3B	HR	RBI	BB	SO	SB	BA	SA
TOTALS			26	154	5484	897	1693	305	51	153	841	573	470	59	.309	.467
Don Hurst	1B154	L	23	154	589	100	179	29	4	31	125	80	36	10	.304	.525
Fresco Thompson	2B148	R	27	148	623	115	202	41	3	4	53	75	34	16	.324	.419
Tommy Thevenow (BJ)	SS90	R	25	90	317	30	72	11	0	0	35	25	3	2	.227	.262
Pinky Whitney	3B154	R	24	154	612	89	200	43	14	8	115	61	35	7	.327	.482
Chuck Klein	OF149	L	24	149	616	126	219	45	6	43	145	54	61	5	.356	.657
Denny Sothern	OF71	R	25	76	294	52	90	21	3	2	24	26	14	13	.306	.449
Lefty O'Doul	OF154	L	32	154	638	152	254	35	6	32	122	76	19	2	.398	.622
Walt Lerian (DD)	C103	R	26	105	273	28	61	13	2	7	25	53	37	0	.223	.363
Barney Friberg	SS73, OF40, 2B8, 1B2	R	29	128	455	74	137	21	10	3	55	49	54	1	.301	.437
Spud Davis	C89	R	24	98	263	31	90	18	0	7	48	19	17	1	.342	.490
Cy Williams	OF11	L	41	66	65	11	19	2	0	5	21	22	9	0	.292	.554
Homer Peel	OF39, 1B1	R	26	53	156	16	42	12	1	0	19	12	7	1	.269	.359
Les Sweetland	P43	R	27	53	89	14	26	2	0	0	12	3	18	0	.292	.315
Elmer Miller	P8, OF4	L	25	31	38	9	9	3	0	0	4	4	8	0	.237	.342
June Green	OF5	L	30	21	19	1	4	0	0	0	4	0	9	0	.211	.263
George Susce	C11	R	21	17	17	1	5	1	0	0	3	2	4	0	.294	.647
Tripp Sigman	OF10	L	30	29	17	4	9	1	0	1	7	6	1	0	.517	.759
Joe O'Rourke		R	24	3	1	0	0	0	0	0	0	0	0	0	.000	.000
Terry Lyons	1B1	R	20	1	0	0	0	0	0	0	0	0	0	0	—	—
Dutch Ulrich (DD)	28															

NAME	T	AGE	W	L	PCT	SV	G	GS	CG	IP	H	BB	SO	SHO	ERA
TOTALS		28	71	82	.464	24	154	154	45	1348	1743	616	369	5	6.13
Claude Willoughby	R	30	15	14	.517	4	49	35	14	243	288	108	50	1	5.00
Les Sweetland	R	27	13	11	.542	2	43	26	10	204	255	87	47	2	5.12
Ray Benge	R	27	11	15	.423	4	38	26	9	199	255	77	78	2	6.29
Phil Collins	R	27	9	7	.563	5	43	11	3	153	172	83	61	0	5.77
Bob McGraw	R	34	5	5	.500	4	41	4	0	86	113	43	22	0	5.76
2 Lou Koupal	R	26	5	5	.500	2	15	11	3	87	106	29	18	0	4.76
Harry Smythe	L	24	4	6	.400	1	19	9	2	69	94	15	12	0	5.22
1 Luther Roy	R	26	3	6	.333	0	21	11	1	89	137	37	16	0	8.39
Hal Elliott	R	30	3	7	.300	2	40	8	2	114	146	59	32	0	6.08
Sam Dailey	R	25	2	3	.500	0	7	3	1	51	74	23	18	0	7.59
1 Alex Ferguson	R	32	1	2	.333	1	3	1	0	13	19	10	3	0	11.77
June Green	R	29	0	0	—	0	1	0	0	14	33	9	4	0	19.29
Jim Holloway	R	23	0	0	—	0	5	1	0	15	21	9	0	0	12.60
Elmer Miller	L	26	0	0	—	0	11	1	0	29	44	21	9	0	11.45
John Milligan	L	25	0	0	.000	0	1	0	0	10	29	10	2	0	16.20

BROOKLYN 6th 70-83 .458 28.5 WILBERT ROBINSON

NAME	G by Pos	B	AGE	G	AB	R	H	2B	3B	HR	RBI	BB	SO	SB	BA	SA
TOTALS			31	153	5273	755	1535	282	69	99	705	504	454	80	.291	.427
Del Bissonette (IL)	1B113	L	29	116	431	68	121	28	10	12	75	46	58	2	.281	.476
Eddie Moore	2B74, SS36, OF2, 3B1	R	30	111	402	48	119	18	6	0	48	44	16	3	.296	.371
Dave Bancroft	SS102	B	38	104	358	35	99	11	3	1	44	29	11	7	.277	.332
Wally Gilbert	3B142	L	28	143	569	88	173	31	4	3	58	42	29	5	.304	.388
Babe Herman	OF141, 1B2	L	26	146	569	105	217	42	13	21	113	55	45	21	.381	.612
Johnny Frederick	OF143	L	27	148	628	127	206	52	6	24	75	34	63	6	.328	.545
Rube Bressler	OF122	L	34	136	456	72	145	22	8	9	77	67	27	4	.318	.461
Val Picinich	C85	R	32	93	273	28	71	16	4	6	31	34	24	3	.260	.407
Harvey Hendrick	OF42, 1B39, 3B7, SS4	L	31	110	384	69	136	25	6	14	82	31	20	14	.354	.500
Billy Rhiel	2B47, 3B7, SS2	R	28	76	205	27	57	9	4	4	25	19	25	0	.278	.420
Hank DeBerry	C68	R	34	68	210	13	55	11	1	1	25	17	15	1	.262	.338
Jake Flowers (IL)	2B39	R	27	46	130	16	26	6	0	1	16	22	6	9	.200	.269
Butch Henline	C21	R	34	27	62	5	15	2	0	1	7	9	9	2	.242	.323
Glenn Wright (AJ)	SS3	R	28	24	25	4	5	0	0	1	6	3	6	0	.200	.320
Max Carey	OF4	L	39	19	23	2	7	0	0	0	1	3	2	0	.304	.304
Jack Warner	SS17	L	25	17	62	3	17	2	0	4	7	6	3	3	.274	.306
Nick Cullop (BG)	OF11, 1B1	R	30	13	41	7	8	2	1	1	5	8	7	0	.195	.415

Max West 24 R 2-8, 1 Johnny Gooch 31 B 0-1

NAME	T	AGE	W	L	PCT	SV	G	GS	CG	IP	H	BB	SO	SHO	ERA
		30	70	83	.458	16	153	153	59	1358	1553	549	549	8	4.92
Watty Clark	L	27	16	19	.457	1	41	39	19	279	295	71	140	3	3.74
Dazzy Vance	R	38	14	13	.519	0	31	27	17	231	244	47	126	1	3.90
Johnny Morrison	R	33	13	7	.650	0	39	10	4	137	150	61	57	0	4.47
Ray Moss	R	71	6	6	.647	0	35	20	7	182	214	81	59	2	5.04
Clise Dudley	R	25	6	14	.300	0	35	20	8	157	202	64	33	1	5.68
Doug McWeeny	R	32	4	10	.286	1	36	22	4	146	167	93	59	0	6.10
Cy Moore	R	24	3	3	.500	2	9	4	0	68	87	31	17	0	5.56
Win Ballou	R	31	2	3	.400	0	25	2	0	58	69	38	20	0	6.67
Jumbo Jim Elliott	R	28	1	2	.333	0	6	3	0	19	21	16	7	0	6.63
2 Kent Greenfield	R	27	0	0	—	0	9	0	0	13	13	3	1	0	8.00
Joe Bradshaw	R	31	0	0	—	0	4	0	0	4	3	4	1	0	4.50
2 Luther Roy	R	26	0	0	—	0	1	0	0	4	4	1	0	0	4.50
Clarence Blethen	R	35	0	0	—	0	2	0	0	4	7	1	0	0	9.00
1 Lou Koupal	R	30	0	1	.000	0	18	3	0	40	49	25	17	0	5.40
Jimmy Pattison	L	20	0	1	.000	0	6	0	0	12	9	4	5	0	4.50
2 Alex Ferguson	R	32	0	0	.000	0	3	2	0	2	7	1	1	0	22.50
Bobo Newsom	R	21	0	0	.000	0	3	2	0	9	15	5	6	0	11.00

CINCINNATI 7th 66-88 .429 33 JACK HENDRICKS

NAME	G by Pos	B	AGE	G	AB	R	H	2B	3B	HR	RBI	BB	SO	SB	BA	SA
TOTALS			29	155	5269	686	1478	258	79	34	618	412	347	134	.281	.379
George Kelly	1B147	R	33	147	577	73	169	45	9	5	103	33	61	7	.293	.428
Hughie Critz (KJ)	2B106, SS1	R	28	107	425	55	105	17	9	1	50	27	21	9	.247	.336
Hod Ford	SS108, 2B42	R	31	148	529	60	146	14	6	3	50	41	25	4	.276	.342
Chuck Dressen	3B98, 2B8	R	30	110	401	49	98	23	3	1	36	41	21	8	.244	.322
Curt Walker	OF138	L	32	141	492	76	154	28	15	7	83	85	17	17	.313	.474
Ethan Allen	OF137	R	25	143	538	69	157	27	11	6	64	20	21	21	.292	.416
Ever Swanson	OF142	R	26	148	574	100	172	35	12	4	43	41	47	33	.300	.423
2 Johnny Gooch	C86	B	31	92	287	22	86	13	5	0	34	24	10	4	.300	.380
Clyde Sukeforth	C76	L	27	84	237	30	84	16	2	1	33	17	6	8	.354	.451
Pid Purdy	OF42	L	27	82	181	22	49	7	5	1	16	19	8	2	.271	.381
Pinky Pittinger	SS50, 3B8, 2B4	R	30	77	210	31	62	11	0	0	27	5	4	8	.295	.348
Red Lucas	P32	L	27	76	140	15	41	6	0	0	13	13	15	1	.293	.336
Joe Stripp	3B55, 2B2	R	26	64	187	24	40	3	2	3	20	24	15	4	.214	.299
Billy Zitzmann	OF22, 1B5	R	31	47	84	18	19	3	0	0	6	9	10	4	.226	.262
Pete Donohue	P32	R	28	32	60	1	20	0	0	0	13	1	4	0	.333	.333
Leo Dixon	C14	R	34	14	30	0	5	2	0	0	2	3	7	0	.167	.233
Wally Shaner	1B8, OF2	R	29	13	28	5	9	0	0	1	4	4	5	1	.321	.429

Estel Crabtree 25 L 0-1, Hugh McMullen 27 B 0-1, Ivy Wingo 38 L 0-1

NAME	T	AGE	W	L	PCT	SV	G	GS	CG	IP	H	BB	SO	SHO	ERA
		32	66	88	.429	8	155	155	75	1369	1558	413	347	5	4.41
Red Lucas	R	27	19	12	.613	0	32	32	28	270	267	58	72	2	3.60
Eppa Rixey	L	38	10	13	.435	1	35	24	11	201	235	60	37	0	4.16
Pete Donohue	R	28	10	13	.435	0	27	17	8	178	243	51	30	0	5.41
Jakie May	L	33	10	14	.417	3	41	24	10	199	219	75	92	0	4.61
Ray Kolp	R	34	8	10	.444	0	30	16	4	145	151	39	27	1	4.03
Dolf Luque	R	38	5	16	.238	0	32	22	8	176	213	56	43	1	4.50
Ken Ash	R	27	5	1	.167	2	29	7	2	82	91	30	26	0	4.83
Marv Gudat	L	23	1	1	.500	0	7	2	2	27	29	4	0	0	3.33
Rube Ehrhardt	R	34	1	2	.333	1	24	1	1	49	58	22	9	1	4.78
Benny Frey	R	23	1	2	.333	0	3	3	2	24	29	8	1	0	4.13
Dutch Kemner	R	30	0	0	—	0	9	0	0	15	19	8	10	0	7.80
Si Johnson	R	22	0	1	—	0	1	0	0	2	1	0	0	0	4.50
Paul Zahniser	R	32	0	0	—	0	1	1	0	2	7	1	0	0	27.00

BOSTON 8th 56-98 .364 43 JUDGE FUCHS

NAME	G by Pos	B	AGE	G	AB	R	H	2B	3B	HR	RBI	BB	SO	SB	BA	SA
TOTALS			30	154	5291	657	1481	252	77	33	598	408	432	65	.280	.375
George Sisler	1B154	L	36	154	629	67	205	40	8	2	79	33	17	6	.326	.424
Freddie Maguire	2B138, SS1	R	30	138	496	54	125	26	8	0	41	19	40	8	.252	.337
Rabbit Maranville	SS145, 2B1	R	37	146	560	87	159	26	10	0	55	47	33	13	.284	.366
Les Bell	3B127, 2B1, SS1	R	27	139	483	58	144	23	5	9	72	50	42	4	.298	.422
Lance Richbourg	OF134	L	31	139	557	76	170	24	13	3	56	42	26	7	.305	.411
Earl Clark	OF74	R	21	84	279	43	88	13	5	1	36	15	38	5	.315	.394
George Harper	OF130	L	37	136	457	65	133	25	5	10	68	69	27	5	.291	.433
Al Spohrer	C109	R	26	114	342	42	93	21	8	2	48	26	35	1	.272	.398
Joe Dugan	3B24, SS5, 2B2, OF2	R	32	60	125	14	38	10	0	0	15	8	8	0	.304	.384
2 Jim Welsh	OF51	L	26	53	186	24	54	8	7	2	16	13	9	1	.290	.441
Bernie James	2B32, OF1	B	23	49	101	12	31	3	2	0	9	13	3	3	.307	.376
Heinie Mueller	OF24	L	29	46	93	10	19	2	1	0	11	12	12	2	.204	.247
Johnny Cooney	OF16, P14	R	28	41	72	10	23	4	1	0	6	3	3	1	.319	.403
Lou Legett	C28	R	28	39	81	7	13	2	0	0	6	3	18	0	.160	.185
1 Zack Taylor	C31	R	30	34	101	8	25	7	0	0	10	7	9	0	.248	.317
Socks Seibold	P33	R	33	33	70	6	20	7	0	0	9	6	6	0	.286	.514
Phil Voyles	OF20	L	29	20	68	9	16	0	2	0	14	6	8	0	.235	.292
Jack Smith	OF9	L	34	19	20	2	5	0	0	0	0	6	2	2	.250	.250
Buzz Boyle	OF17	L	21	17	57	8	15	2	1	1	2	6	11	2	.263	.386
Red Barron	OF6	R	29	10	21	3	4	1	0	0	1	1	4	1	.190	.238
Bill Dunlap	OF9	R	20	10	29	6	12	0	1	1	4	4	1	0	.414	.586
Hank Gowdy	C9	R	39	10	16	1	7	0	0	0	5	2	1	0	.438	.438
2 Gene Robertson	3B6, SS1	L	30	8	28	1	8	0	0	0	6	1	0	1	.286	.286
Pat Collins	C6	R	32	7	5	1	0	0	0	0	0	2	3	0	.000	.000
Bill Cronin	C6	R	26	6	9	0	1	0	0	0	0	0	1	0	.111	.111
Henry Peploski	3B2	L	23	3	5	0	1	0	0	0	2	0	0	0	.200	.200

1 Doc Farrell 27 R 1-8, Jack Cummings 25 R 1-6, Al Weston 23 R 0-3, Johnny Evers 47 L 0-0

NAME	T	AGE	W	L	PCT	SV	G	GS	CG	IP	H	BB	SO	SHO	ERA
		30	56	98	.364	12	154	154	78	1353	1604	530	366	4	5.12
Socks Seibold	R	33	12	17	.414	1	33	27	16	206	228	80	54	1	4.72
Bob Smith	R	34	11	17	.393	3	34	29	19	231	256	71	65	1	4.68
Ed Brandt	L	24	8	13	.381	2	26	21	13	168	196	83	50	0	5.52
Percy Jones	L	29	7	15	.318	0	35	22	11	188	219	84	69	1	4.64
Bruce Cunningham	R	23	4	6	.400	1	17	9	7	92	100	32	22	0	4.50
Ben Cantwell	R	27	4	13	.235	2	27	20	8	157	171	52	25	0	4.47
Art Delaney	R	34	3	5	.375	0	24	12	3	98	135	30	28	0	6.12
Dixie Leverett	R	35	3	7	.300	1	24	12	3	98	135	30	28	0	6.34
Bunny Hearn	L	25	2	0	1.000	0	10	1	0	18	18	9	12	0	4.50
Johnny Cooney	R	28	2	3	.400	3	14	2	1	45	57	22	11	0	5.00
1 Kent Greenfield	R	27	0	0	—	0	16	0	0	33	15	7	0	10.69
Johnny Wertz	R	31	0	0	—	1	4	0	0	6	4	1	0	10.50
Clay Touchstone	R	26	0	0	—	0	1	0	0	3	6	1	0	15.00
Red Peery	L	22	0	1	—	0	4	4	1	14	53	9	3	0	5.11
Bill Clarkson	R	30	0	1	.000	0	7	2	1	16	4	1	0	10.29

WORLD SERIES — PHILADELPHIA (AL) 4 CHICAGO (NL) 1

LINE SCORES

TEAM	1	2	3	4	5	6	7	8	9	10	11	12	R	H	E
Game 1 October 8 at Chicago															
PHI (AL)	0	0	0		0	0	0		1	0	2		3	6	1
CHI (NL)	0	0	0		0	0	0		0	0	1		1	8	2

Ehmke   Root, Bush (8)

Game 2 October 9 at Chicago															
PHI	0	0	3		3	0	0		1	2	0		9	12	0
CHI	0	0	0		0	3	0		0	0	0		3	11	1

Earnshaw, Grove (5)   Malone, Blake (4), Carlson (6), Nehf (9)

Game 3 October 11 at Philadelphia															
CHI	0	0	0		0	0	3		0	0	0		3	6	1
PHI	0	0	0		0	1	0		0	0	0		1	9	1

Bush   Earnshaw

Game 4 October 12 at Philadelphia															
CHI	0	0	0		2	0	5		1	0	0		8	10	2
PHI	0	0	0		0	0	0		10	0	X		10	15	2

Root, Nehf (7), Blake (7), Malone (7), Carlson (8)   Quinn, Walberg (6), Rommel (7), Grove (8)

Game 5 October 14 at Philadelphia															
CHI	0	0	0		2	0	0		0	0	0		2	8	1
PHI	0	0	0		0	0	0		0	0	3		3	6	0

Malone   Ehmke, Walberg (4)

COMPOSITE BATTING

Philadelphia (AL)

NAME	POS	G	AB	R	H	2B	3B	HR	RBI	BA
Totals		5	171	26	48	5	0	6	26	.281
Haas	OF	5	21	3	5	0	0	2	6	.238
Bishop	2B	5	21	4	4	0	0	0	1	.190
Foxx	1B	5	20	5	7	1	0	2	5	.350
Simmons	OF	5	20	6	6	1	0	2	5	.300
Dykes	3B	5	19	2	8	1	0	0	4	.421
Miller	OF	5	19	1	7	1	0	0	4	.368
Boley	SS	5	17	1	4	0	0	0	1	.235
Cochrane	C	5	15	5	6	1	0	0	0	.400
Ehmke	P	2	5	1	1	0	0	0	0	.200
Earnshaw	P	2	5	1	0	0	0	0	0	.000
Grove	P	2	5	0	0	0	0	0	0	.000
Burns	PH	1	2	0	0	0	0	0	0	.000
Quinn	P	1	2	0	0	0	0	0	0	.000
Walberg	P	2	2	0	0	0	0	0	0	.000
French	PH	1	1	0	0	0	0	0	0	.000
Summa	PH	1	1	0	0	0	0	0	0	.000
Rommel	P	1	0	0	0	0	0	0	0	—

Chicago (NL)

NAME	POS	G	AB	R	H	2B	3B	HR	RBI	BA
Totals		5	173	17	43	6	2	1	15	.249
Hornsby	2B	5	21	4	5	1	1	0	1	.238
English	SS	5	21	1	4	2	0	0	1	.190
Cuyler	OF	5	20	4	6	1	0	0	0	.300
McMillan	3B	5	20	0	2	0	0	0	0	.100
Stephenson	OF	5	19	3	6	1	0	0	3	.316
Grimm	1B	5	18	2	7	0	0	0	4	.389
Wilson	OF	5	17	2	8	0	1	0	5	.471
Taylor	C	5	17	0	3	1	0	0	0	.176
Root	P	2	5	0	0	0	0	0	0	.000
Malone	P	3	4	0	1	0	0	0	0	.250
Hartnett	PH	3	3	0	0	0	0	0	0	.000
Bush	P	2	3	0	0	0	0	0	0	.000
Blake	P	2	1	0	1	0	0	0	0	1.000
Gonzalez	C	2	1	0	0	0	0	0	0	.000
Blair	PH	1	1	0	0	0	0	0	0	.000
Heathcote	PH	1	1	0	0	0	0	0	0	.000
Tolson	PH	1	1	0	0	0	0	0	0	.000
Carlson	P	2	0	0	0	0	0	0	0	—
Nehf	P	2	0	0	0	0	0	0	0	—

COMPOSITE PITCHING

Philadelphia (AL)

NAME	G	IP	H	BB	SO	W	L	SV	ERA
Totals	5	45	43	13	50	4	1	2	2.40
Earnshaw	2	13.2	14	6	17	1	0	0	2.63
Ehmke	2	12.2	14	3	13	1	0	0	1.42
Grove	2	6.1	3	1	10	0	0	2	0.00
Walberg	2	6.1	8	1	8	1	0	0	0.00
Quinn	1	5	7	2	2	0	0	0	9.00
Rommel	1	1	2	1	0	1	0	0	9.00

Chicago (NL)

NAME	G	IP	H	BB	SO	W	L	SV	ERA
Totals	5	43.2	48	13	27	1	4	0	4.33
Root	2	13.1	12	3	8	0	1	0	4.73
Malone	3	13	12	7	11	0	2	0	4.15
Bush	2	11	12	2	4	1	0	0	0.82
Carlson	2	4	7	1	3	0	0	0	6.75
Blake	2	1.1	4	0	1	0	1	0	13.50
Nehf	2	1	1	0	0	0	0	0	18.00

1930 The Guns of Summer

The barrage began in the spring, reached a deafening crescendo during the heat of summer, and subsided in the cool sanity of autumn. Never before had such an offensive been staged, and never again would the cannon fire of baseball bats strike so often and so effectively. With the depression in full bloom and pocketbooks near empty, baseball juiced up the ball to liven the attendance and the action. For the batters, it was a vision of heaven on earth. And for the pitchers, it was the fright and embarrassment that open season had been declared on them. Even the spitball, once the wet tool of a crafty artisan, was now gone. All that remained were frantic batting averages and over-inflated earned run averages.

Although all clubs enjoyed the glory of the hitter, and all suffered the agony of the pitcher, none matched the extremes of the Philadelphia Phillies. They rapped out hits at a .315 batting clip as five .300 hitters filled the lineup. Outfielders Lefty O'Doul and powerful Chuck Klein, led the attack with plus .380 averages. Yet, instead of moving towards the top of the heap, the Phils dropped three slots into the National League basement on the dismal arms of a pitching staff which posted a monstrous 6.71 earned run average.

Beyond the Phillies, the proof of the shambles was as great. One team since 1937 has posted a team .300 batting average. In 1930, nine clubs reached that high plateau. The entire National League compiled a .303 average while American League swingers settled for a more reasonable .288 rate. The New York Giants boosted the senior circuit tally with a club .319 mark, tops in the majors, with first sacker Bill Terry hitting .401, the last National Leaguer to scale that sacred peak. Another stellar individual performance was delivered by the Cubs' Hack Wilson. The stumpy outfielder staged the first race on Babe Ruth's home run record by launching 56 circuit blasts and, in the process, driving in an all-time high of 190 runs. Of all clubs in the majors, only

Washington managed to get a team E.R.A. below 4.00 from its pitching staff, as the bulk of hurlers merely stuck fingers in crumbling dams trying to hold back floods of runs.

In the National League, the mayhem was greater. Even with Wilson's fantastic season and the return of tomato-face Gabby Hartnett to full-time action, the Cubs failed to repeat as champions, though a foot injury to Rogers Hornsby understandably slowed them down. The pennant, instead, went to the St. Louis Cardinals, led by new manager Gabby Street. All eight St. Louis starters hit over .300, but Frankie Frisch and bespectacled Chick Hafey stood out for their excellence. Wild Bill Hallahan climbed out of a rut of mediocrity to win 15 games on the mound, and the mid-season acquisition of aging spitballer Burleigh Grimes helped Street immensely. With hitting stars legion, Brooklyn's Dazzy Vance shined as the only hurler in the loop to post an E.R.A. under 3.00.

The Athletics' Lefty Grove filled the same slot as Vance in the American League, but did it in more spectacular fashion by winning 28 games and tallying up a 2.54 E.R.A. to combine with George Earnshaw to give Connie Mack the only pair of 20-win aces in the majors. With Al Simmons, Double-X Jimmie Foxx, and Mickey Cochrane swinging the timber, Mack's eighth pennant came easily. Only Washington, sparked by shortstop Joe Cronin, provided any competition for the A's.

When the World Series rolled around, the loud guns of summer quieted to an almost unrecognizable whimper as the Cardinals managed a robust .200 rate, while the Mackmen compiled a stirring .197 mark. The difference between the clubs proved to be the hurling of Grove and Earnshaw. It was a difference good enough for a six-game Philadelphia triumph and the last world's championship that Connie Mack would ever claim.

1930 AMERICAN LEAGUE

PHILADELPHIA 1st 102-52 .662 CONNIE MACK

NAME	G by Pos	B	AGE	G	AB	R	H	2B	3B	HR	RBI	BB	SO	SB	BA	SA
TOTALS			28	154	5345	951	1573	319	74	125	895	599	531	50	.294	.452
Jimmie Foxx	1B153	R	22	153	562	127	188	33	13	37	156	93	66	7	.335	.637
Max Bishop	2B127	L	30	130	441	117	111	27	6	10	38	128	60	3	.252	.408
Joe Boley	SS120	R	33	121	420	41	116	22	2	4	55	32	26	0	.276	.367
Jimmy Dykes	3B123, OF1	R	33	125	435	69	131	28	4	6	73	74	53	3	.301	.425
Bing Miller	OF154	R	35	154	585	89	177	38	7	9	100	47	22	13	.303	.438
Mule Haas	OF131	L	26	132	532	91	159	33	7	2	68	43	33	2	.299	.398
Al Simmons	OF136	R	28	138	554	152	211	41	16	36	165	39	34	9	.381	.708
Mickey Cochrane	C130	L	27	130	487	110	174	42	5	10	85	55	18	5	.357	.526
Eric McNair	SS31, 3B29, 2B5, OF1	R	21	78	237	27	63	12	2	0	34	9	19	5	.266	.333
Dib Williams	2B39, SS19, 3B11	R	20	67	191	24	50	10	3	3	22	15	19	2	.262	.393
Wally Schang	C36	B	40	45	92	16	16	4	1	1	9	17	15	1	.174	.272
Doc Cramer	OF21, SS1	L	24	30	82	12	19	1	1	0	6	2	8	0	.232	.268
Homer Summa	OF15	R	31	25	54	10	15	2	1	1	5	4	1	0	.278	.407
Spence Harris	OF13	R	29	22	49	4	9	1	0	0	5	5	2	0	.184	.204
Cy Perkins	C19, 1B1	R	34	20	38	1	6	2	0	0	4	2	3	0	.153	.211
2 Jimmy Moore	OF13	R	27	15	50	10	19	3	0	2	12	2	4	1	.380	.506
Pinky Higgins	3B5, 2B2, SS1	R	21	14	24	1	6	2	0	0	0	4	5	0	.250	.333
Jim Keesey	1B3	R	27	11	12	2	3	1	0	0	2	1	2	0	.250	.333
Eddie Collins		L	43	3	2	1	1	0	0	0	0	0	0	0	.500	.500

NAME	T	AGE	W	L	PCT	SV	G	GS	CG	IP	H	BB	SO	SHO	ERA
		32	102	52	.662	21	154	154	72	1371	1457	488	672	8	4.28
Lefty Grove	L	30	28	5	.848	9	50	32	22	291	273	60	209	2	2.54
George Earnshaw	R	30	22	13	.629	2	49	39	20	296	299	139	193	3	4.44
Rube Walberg	L	33	13	12	.520	1	38	30	12	205	207	85	100	2	4.70
Bill Shores	R	26	12	4	.750	0	31	19	7	159	169	70	48	1	4.19
Eddie Rommel	R	32	9	4	.692	3	35	9	5	130	142	27	35	0	4.29
Roy Mahaffey	R	26	9	5	.643	0	33	17	6	153	186	53	38	0	5.00
Jack Quinn	R	46	9	7	.563	6	35	6	0	90	109	22	28	0	4.40
Glenn Liebhardt	R	19	0	1	.000	0	5	0	0	9	14	8	2	0	11.00
Howard Ehmke	R	36	0	1	.000	0	3	1	0	10	22	2	4	0	11.70
Charlie Perkins	L	24	0	0	—	0	8	1	0	24	25	15	15	0	6.37
Al Mahon	L	20	0	0	—	0	3	0	0	4	11	7	0	0	24.75

WASHINGTON 2nd 94-60 .610 8 WALTER JOHNSON

NAME	G by Pos	B	AGE	G	AB	R	H	2B	3B	HR	RBI	BB	SO	SB	BA	SA
TOTALS			29	154	5370	892	1620	300	98	57	819	537	438	101	.302	.426
Joe Judge	1B117	L	36	126	442	83	144	29	11	10	80	60	29	3	.326	.509
Buddy Myer	2B134, OF2	L	26	138	541	97	164	18	8	2	61	58	31	14	.303	.377
Joe Cronin	SS154	R	23	154	587	127	203	41	9	13	126	72	84	17	.346	.513
Ossie Bluege	3B134	R	29	134	476	64	138	27	7	3	69	51	40	15	.290	.395
Sam Rice	OF145	L	40	147	593	121	207	35	13	1	47	55	14	13	.349	.457
Sammy West (EJ)	OF118	L	25	120	411	75	135	22	10	6	67	37	34	5	.328	.474
2 Heinie Manush	OF86	L	28	88	356	74	129	28	8	7	65	26	17	4	.362	.559
Roy Spencer	C93	R	30	93	321	32	82	11	4	0	36	18	27	3	.255	.315
2 Dave Harris	OF59	R	30	73	205	40	65	19	8	4	44	28	35	6	.317	.546
Muddy Ruel	C60	R	34	66	198	18	50	3	4	0	26	24	13	1	.253	.308
Jackie Hayes	2B29, 3B9, 1B8	R	23	51	166	25	47	7	2	1	20	7	8	2	.283	.367
George Loepp	OF48	B	28	50	134	23	37	7	1	0	14	7	13	2	.276	.343
1 Goose Goslin	OF47	L	29	47	188	34	51	11	5	7	38	19	19	3	.271	.495
2 Art Shires	1B21	L	22	38	84	11	31	5	0	1	19	5	5	1	.369	.464
Firpo Marberry	P33	R	31	33	73	9	24	4	0	0	14	4	7	0	.329	.384
Joe Kuhel	1B16	L	24	18	63	9	18	3	3	0	17	5	6	1	.286	.429
Jim McLeod	3B10, SS7	R	21	18	34	3	9	1	0	0	1	1	5	0	.265	.294
1 Bennie Tate	C9	L	28	14	20	1	5	0	0	0	2	0	1	0	.250	.250
1 Red Barnes		R	28	12	12	1	2	1	0	0	0	0	3	0	.167	.250
2 Pinky Hargrave	C9	B	34	10	31	3	6	2	2	1	4	3	1	0	.194	.484
2 Bill Barrett	OF1	R	30	6	4	0	0	0	0	0	0	1	2	0	.000	.000
Ray Treadaway	3B4	R	22	6	19	1	4	2	0	0	1	0	3	0	.211	.316

Harley Boss 21 0-3, Jake Powell 21 R 0-4, Patsy Gharrity 38 R 0-1

NAME	T	AGE	W	L	PCT	SV	G	GS	CG	IP	H	BB	SO	SHO	ERA
		28	94	60	.610	14	154	154	78	1369	1367	504	524	4	3.96
Lloyd Brown	L	25	16	12	.571	0	38	22	10	197	220	65	59	1	4.25
Firpo Marberry	R	31	15	5	.750	1	33	22	9	185	190	53	56	2	4.09
Sad Sam Jones (SA)	R	37	15	7	.682	0	25	25	14	183	195	61	60	0	4.09
2 General Crowder	R	31	15	9	.625	1	27	25	20	202	191	69	65	0	3.61
Bump Hadley	R	25	15	11	.577	2	42	34	15	260	242	105	162	0	3.74
Ad Liska	R	23	9	7	.563	1	32	16	7	151	140	71	40	1	3.28
1 Garland Braxton	L	30	3	2	.600	5	15	0	0	27	22	9	7	0	3.33
Bobby Burke	L	23	3	4	.429	3	24	4	2	74	62	29	35	0	3.65
Myles Thomas	R	32	2	2	.500	0	12	2	0	34	49	15	12	0	8.21
Carl Fischer	L	24	1	1	.500	0	8	4	1	33	37	18	21	0	4.91
Harry Child	R	25	0	0	—	0	1	0	0	10	10	5	5	0	6.30
Carlos Moore	R	23	0	0	—	0	4	0	0	12	9	4	2	0	2.25

NEW YORK 3rd 86-68 .558 16 BOB SHAWKEY

NAME	G by Pos	B	AGE	G	AB	R	H	2B	3B	HR	RBI	BB	SO	SB	BA	SA
TOTALS			27	154	5448	1062	1683	298	110	152	986	644	569	91	.309	.488
Lou Gehrig	1B153	L	27	154	581	143	220	42	17	41	174	101	63	12	.379	.721
Tony Lazzeri	2B77, 3B60, SS8, 1B1, OF1	R	26	143	571	109	173	34	15	9	121	60	62	4	.303	.462
Lynn Lary	SS113	R	24	117	464	93	134	20	8	3	52	45	40	14	.289	.386
Ben Chapman	3B91, 2B45	R	21	138	513	74	162	31	10	10	81	43	58	14	.316	.474
Babe Ruth	OF144, P1	L	35	145	518	150	186	28	9	49	153	136	61	10	.359	.732
2 Harry Rice	OF87, 1B6, 3B1	L	29	100	346	62	103	17	5	7	74	31	21	3	.298	.436
Earle Combs	OF135	L	31	137	532	129	183	30	22	7	82	74	26	16	.344	.523
Bill Dickey	C101	L	23	109	366	55	124	25	7	5	65	21	14	7	.339	.486
Sammy Byrd	OF85	R	23	92	218	46	62	12	6	3	31	30	18	5	.284	.440
Dusty Cooke	OF73	L	23	92	216	43	55	12	3	6	29	32	61	4	.255	.421
Jimmy Reese	2B48, 3B5	L	28	77	188	44	65	14	2	3	18	11	8	1	.346	.489
2 Red Ruffing	P34	R	26	52	99	15	37	6	4	2	21	7	7	0	.374	.596
Bubbles Hargrave	C34	R	37	45	108	11	30	7	0	0	12	10	9	0	.278	.435
Benny Bengough	C44	R	31	40	102	10	24	4	0	0	12	3	12	1	.235	.314
2 Yats Wuestling	SS21, 3B3	R	26	25	58	6	15	3	0	0	5	0	6	0	.190	.224
1 Mark Koenig	SS19	B	27	21	74	9	17	5	0	0	6	5	9	0	.230	.297
Art Jorgens	C16	R	25	16	30	7	7	0	0	0	2	1	1	0	.367	.467
1 Cedric Durst	OF8	L	33	8	19	0	3	1	0	0	5	0	1	0	.158	.211
Bill Werber	SS3, 3B1	R	22	4	14	5	4	0	0	0	0	0	1	0	.286	.286
Bill Karlon	OF1	R	21	2	1	0	0	0	0	0	0	0	0	0	.000	.000

NAME	T	AGE	W	L	PCT	SV	G	GS	CG	IP	H	BB	SO	SHO	ERA
		28	86	68	.558	15	154	154	65	1368	1586	524	572	7	4.88
2 Red Ruffing	R	26	15	5	.750	1	34	25	12	198	220	62	117	2	4.25
George Pipgras	R	30	15	15	.500	4	30	30	15	222	230	70	111	3	4.11
Hank Johnson	R	24	14	11	.560	2	44	15	7	175	177	104	115	1	4.68
Ed Wells	L	30	12	3	.800	0	27	21	7	151	185	49	46	0	5.18
Roy Sherid	R	23	12	13	.480	4	37	21	8	184	214	87	59	0	5.23
Herb Pennock	L	36	11	7	.611	2	35	19	11	156	194	20	46	1	4.33
1 Waite Hoyt	R	30	2	2	.500	0	8	7	2	48	64	9	10	0	4.50
Lefty Gomez	L	21	2	5	.286	1	15	6	2	60	66	28	22	0	5.55
Babe Ruth	L	35	1	0	1.000	0	1	1	1	9	11	2	3	0	3.00
1 Tom Zachary	L	34	1	1	.500	0	3	0	0	17	18	9	1	0	6.35
Lou McEvoy	R	28	1	3	.250	3	28	1	0	52	64	29	14	0	6.75
2 Ownie Carroll	R	27	0	0	—	0	10	1	0	33	49	18	8	0	6.54
Frank Barnes	R	30	0	1	.000	0	2	2	0	12	13	13	2	0	8.25
Sam Gibson	R	30	0	1	.000	0	1	0	0	2	2	0	1	0	15.00
2 Ken Hollaway	R	32	0	0	—	0	16	0	0	34	52	8	11	0	5.29
Bill Henderson	R	28	0	0	—	0	2	0	0	7	4	4	2	0	4.50
Gordon Rhodes	R	22	0	0	—	0	4	3	0	20	25	5	4	0	9.00
Foster Edwards	R	26	0	0	—	0	1	0	0	2	6	0	0	0	18.00

CLEVELAND — 4th 81-73 .526 21 — ROGER PECKINPAUGH

NAME	G by Pos	B	AGE	G	AB	R	H	2B	3B	HR	RBI	BB	SO	SB	BA	SA
TOTALS			28	154	5439	890	1654	358	59	72	830	490	461	51	.304	.431
Eddie Morgan	1B129, OF19	R	26	150	584	122	204	47	11	26	136	62	66	8	.349	.601
Johnny Hodapp	2B154	R	24	154	635	111	225	51	8	9	121	32	29	6	.354	.502
Jonah Goldman	SS93, 3B20	R	23	111	306	52	74	18	0	1	44	28	25	3	.242	.310
Joe Sewell	3B97	L	31	109	353	44	102	17	6	0	48	42	3	1	.289	.371
Dick Porter (PB)	OF118	L	28	119	480	100	168	43	8	6	57	55	31	3	.350	.498
Earl Averill	OF134	L	28	139	534	102	181	33	8	19	119	56	48	10	.339	.537
Charlie Jamieson	OF95	L	37	103	366	64	110	22	1	1	52	36	20	5	.301	.374
Luke Sewell (BG)	C76	R	29	76	292	40	75	21	2	1	43	14	9	5	.257	.353
Glenn Myatt	C71	R	32	86	265	30	78	23	2	2	37	18	17	2	.294	.419
Bob Seeds	OF70	R	23	85	277	37	79	11	3	3	32	12	22	1	.285	.379
Bibb Falk	OF42	L	31	82	191	34	62	12	1	4	36	23	8	2	.325	.461
Ed Montague	SS46, 3B13	R	24	58	179	37	47	5	2	1	16	37	38	1	.263	.330
Johnny Burnett	3B27, SS19	L	25	54	170	28	53	13	0	0	20	17	8	2	.312	.388
Wes Ferrell	P43	R	22	53	118	19	35	8	3	0	14	12	15	0	.297	.415
Lew Fonseca (BA)	1B28, 3B6	R	31	40	129	20	36	9	2	0	17	7	7	1	.279	.380
Ray Gardner	SS22	R	28	33	13	7	1	0	0	0	1	0	1	0	.077	.077
Carl Lind	SS22, 2B1	R	26	24	69	8	17	3	0	0	6	3	7	0	.246	.390
Joe Sprinz	C17	R	27	17	45	5	8	1	0	0	2	4	4	0	.178	.200
Joe Vosmik	OF5	R	20	9	26	1	6	2	0	0	4	1	1	0	.231	.308

Ralph Winegarner 20 R 10-22, George Detore 23 R 2-12, Grover Hartley 41 R 3-4

NAME	T	AGE	W	L	PCT	SV	G	GS	CG	IP	H	BB	SO	SHO	ERA
TOTALS		25	81	73	.526	14	154	154	69	1360	1663	528	441	5	4.88
Wes Ferrell	R	22	25	13	.658	3	43	35	25	297	299	106	143	1	3.30
Willis Hudlin	R	24	13	16	.448	1	37	33	13	271	255	76	60	1	4.56
Mel Harder	R	20	11	10	.524	2	36	19	7	175	205	68	44	0	4.22
Clint Brown	R	26	11	13	.458	1	35	31	16	214	271	51	54	3	4.01
Pete Appleton	R	26	8	7	.533	1	39	7	2	119	122	53	45	0	4.01
Jake Miller	L	32	4	4	.500	0	24	9	1	88	147	38	31	0	7.16
Belve Bean	R	25	3	3	.500	2	24	4	1	74	99	32	19	0	5.47
Milt Shoffner	L	24	3	4	.429	0	24	10	1	85	129	50	17	0	7.94
Les Barnhart	R	25	1	0	1.000	0	8	0	0	12	8	4	1	0	6.75
1 Ken Hollaway	R	32	1	1	.500	2	12	2	0	30	49	14	8	0	8.40
Roxie Lawson	R	24	1	2	.333	0	7	4	2	34	46	12	10	0	6.09
Sal Gliatto	R	28	0	0	—	2	8	0	0	15	21	9	7	0	6.60
Joe Shaute (SA)	L	30	0	0	—	0	5				8	4	2	0	14.40

DETROIT — 5th 75-79 .487 27 — BUCKY HARRIS

NAME	G by Pos	B	AGE	G	AB	R	H	2B	3B	HR	RBI	BB	SO	SB	BA	SA
TOTALS			26	154	5297	783	1504	298	90	82	728	461	508	98	.284	.421
Dale Alexander	1B154	R	27	154	602	86	196	38	9	20	135	42	56	6	.326	.507
Charlie Gehringer	2B154	R	27	154	610	144	201	47	15	16	98	69	17	19	.330	.534
2 Mark Koenig	SS70, 3B2, P2, OF1	B	27	126	367	37	64	9	2	1	16	20	15	2	.240	.300
Marty McManus	3B130, SS3, 1B1	R	30	132	484	74	155	40	4	9	89	59	28	23	.320	.475
Roy Johnson	OF118	R	27	125	462	84	127	30	13	2	35	40	46	17	.275	.409
Liz Funk	OF129	L	25	140	527	74	145	26	11	4	65	39	39	6	.275	.455
John Stone	OF108	L	24	126	422	60	132	29	11	3	56	32	49	6	.313	.455
Ray Hayworth	C76	R	26	77	227	24	63	15	4	0	22	20	19	0	.278	.379
Bill Akers (JJ)	SS49, 3B26	R	25	85	233	36	65	8	5	9	40	36	34	5	.278	.472
George Uhle	P33	R	31	59	117	15	36	4	2	2	21	8	13	0	.308	.427
Pinky Hargrave	C40	B	34	55	137	18	39	8	0	5	18	20	12	2	.285	.453
Bob Fothergill	OF38	R	32	55	143	14	37	9	2	2	14	6	10	1	.259	.406
Bill Rogell	SS33, 3B13, OF1	R	25	54	144	20	24	4	2	0	9	15	23	1	.167	.222
Gene Desautels	C42	R	23	42	126	13	24	4	2	0	9	5	16	0	.190	.254
1 Harry Rice	OF35	L	29	37	128	16	39	6	0	2	24	19	8	0	.305	.398
Paul Easterling	OF25	R	24	29	79	7	16	4	1	0	14	6	18	0	.203	.316
Jimmy Shevlin	1B25	L	20	28	14	4	2	0	0	0	2	3	0	0	.143	.143
Frank Doljack	OF20	R	22	20	74	10	19	5	1	3	17	2	11	0	.257	.473
1 Tony Rensa	C18	R	28	20	37	6	10	2	1	1	5	8	4	0	.270	.459
Tom Hughes	OF16	L	22	17	59	8	22	5	0	0	3	6	4	1	.373	.508

Johnny Watson 22 L 3-12, 1 Yats Wuestling 26 R 0-9, Hughie Wise 24 R 2-6, Hank Greenberg 19 R 0-1

NAME	T	AGE	W	L	PCT	SV	G	GS	CG	IP	H	BB	SO	SHO	ERA
TOTALS		27	75	79	.487	17	154	154	68	1352	1507	570	574	3	4.70
Earl Whitehill	L	30	17	13	.567	1	34	31	16	221	248	80	109	0	4.24
Vic Sorrell	R	29	16	11	.593	1	35	30	14	233	245	106	97	2	3.86
George Uhle	R	31	12	12	.500	3	33	29	18	239	239	75	117	1	3.65
Chief Hogsett	L	26	8	8	.529	1	33	17	4	146	174	63	54	0	5.42
2 Waite Hoyt	R	30	9	8	.529	4	26	20	8	136	176	47	25	0	4.76
Whit Wyatt (SA)	R	22	4	5	.444	2	21	7	2	86	76	35	68	0	3.56
Tommy Bridges	R	23	3	4	.600	0	8	5	2	38	28	23	17	0	4.03
Art Herring	R	24	3	3	.500	2	23	6	1	78	97	36	16	0	5.31
Charlie Sullivan	R	27	1	5	.167	5	40	3	2	94	112	53	38	0	6.51
Guy Cantrell	R	26	1	5	.167	0	16	2	1	35	38	20	20	0	5.66
Phil Page	L	24	0	1	.000	0	12	0	0	12	23	9	2	0	9.75
2 Mark Koenig	R	27	0	1	.000	2	1	0	0	11	20	9	4	0	11.00
1 Ownie Carroll	R	27	0	5	.000	0	6	5	0	30	30	9	4	0	10.80
Joe Samuels	R	25	0	0	—	0	2	0	0	6	11	5	1	0	16.50

ST. LOUIS — 6th 64-90 .416 38 — BILL KILLEFER

NAME	G by Pos	B	AGE	G	AB	R	H	2B	3B	HR	RBI	BB	SO	SB	BA	SA
TOTALS			29	154	5278	751	1415	289	67	75	691	497	550	93	.268	.391
Lu Blue	1B111	B	33	117	425	85	100	27	5	4	42	81	44	12	.235	.351
Oscar Melillo	2B148	R	30	149	574	62	147	30	10	5	59	23	44	15	.256	.394
Red Kress	SS123, 3B31	R	25	154	614	94	192	43	8	16	112	50	56	3	.313	.487
Frank O'Rourke	3B84, SS23, 1B3	R	38	115	400	52	107	15	4	1	41	35	30	11	.268	.333
Ted Gullic	OF82, 1B9	R	23	92	308	39	77	7	5	4	44	27	43	4	.250	.344
Fred Schulte	OF98, 1B5	R	29	113	392	59	109	23	5	6	62	41	44	12	.278	.434
Goose Goslin	OF101	L	29	101	396	81	129	25	7	30	100	48	35	14	.326	.652
Rick Ferrell	C101	R	24	101	314	43	84	18	4	1	41	46	10	1	.268	.360
Red Badgro	OF61	L	27	89	234	30	56	18	3	1	27	13	27	3	.239	.355
Earl McNeely	OF38, 1B27	R	32	76	235	33	64	19	1	0	20	22	14	8	.272	.362
Sammy Hale	3B47	R	33	62	190	21	52	8	1	2	25	8	18	1	.274	.358
Chad Kimsey	P42	R	23	60	70	14	24	4	1	2	14	5	16	1	.343	.514
Clyde Manion	C56	R	33	57	148	12	32	1	0	1	11	24	17	0	.216	.243
2 Alex Metzler	OF56	L	27	56	209	30	54	6	3	1	23	21	12	5	.258	.330
1 Heinie Manush	OF48	L	29	49	198	26	65	16	4	2	29	5	7	3	.328	.480
Bernie Hungling	C10	R	34	10	31	4	10	2	0	0	5	2	5	0	.323	.387
Jack Burns	1B8	L	23	8	30	5	9	3	0	0	5	3	5	0	.300	.400
Jim Levey	SS8	B	23	8	37	7	9	3	0	0	3	2	5	0	.243	.297
Lin Storti	2B6	R	23	7	28	5	9	2	0	0	3	5	6	0	.321	.429

Jack Crouch 26 R 2-14, Joe Hassler 25 R 2-8, Tom Jenkins 32 L 2-8

NAME	T	AGE	W	L	PCT	SV	G	GS	CG	IP	H	BB	SO	SHO	ERA
TOTALS		27	64	90	.416	10	154	154	68	1372	1639	449	470	5	5.07
Lefty Stewart	L	29	20	12	.625	0	35	33	23	271	281	70	79	1	3.45
George Blaeholder	R	26	11	13	.458	4	37	23	10	191	235	46	70	1	4.62
Rip Collins	R	34	9	7	.563	2	35	20	6	172	168	63	75	1	4.35
Dick Coffman	R	23	8	18	.308	1	38	20	12	196	250	69	54	1	5.14
Chad Kimsey	R	23	6	10	.375	4	42	4	1	113	139	45	32	0	6.37
Sam Gray	R	32	4	15	.211	0	27	24	7	168	215	52	51	0	6.26
Rollie Stiles	R	23	3	6	.333	0	27	7	1	102	136	41	25	0	5.91
1 General Crowder	R	31	3	7	.300	1	13	10	5	77	85	27	42	1	4.67
Herm Holshouser	R	23	0	1	.000	1	25	1	0	62	103	28	17	0	7.84
Fred Stiely	L	29	0	2	.000	0	4	2	1	19	27	8	5	0	8.53

Jack Ogden (VR) 32

CHICAGO — 7th 62-92 .403 40 — DONIE BUSH

NAME	G by Pos	B	AGE	G	AB	R	H	2B	3B	HR	RBI	BB	SO	SB	BA	SA
TOTALS			27	154	5419	729	1496	256	90	63	675	389	479	74	.276	.391
Johnny Watwood	1B62, OF43	L	24	133	427	75	129	25	4	2	51	52	35	5	.302	.393
Bill Cissell	1B106, 3B24, SS10	R	26	141	561	82	152	28	9	2	48	28	32	16	.271	.364
Greg Mulleavy	SS73	R	24	77	289	27	76	14	5	0	28	20	23	5	.263	.346
Willie Kamm (HO)	3B105	R	30	111	331	49	89	21	5	4	47	51	20	5	.269	.396
Smead Jolley	OF151	L	28	152	616	76	193	38	12	16	114	28	52	3	.313	.492
2 Red Barnes	OF72	L	26	85	266	48	66	12	7	1	31	26	20	4	.248	.357
Carl Reynolds	OF132	R	27	138	563	103	202	25	18	22	104	20	39	16	.359	.584
2 Bennie Tate	C70	R	28	72	230	26	73	11	2	0	27	18	10	2	.317	.383
John Kerr	2B51, SS19	R	31	70	266	37	77	11	6	3	27	21	23	4	.289	.410
Bud Clancy (JJ)	1B60	L	29	68	234	28	57	8	3	3	27	12	18	3	.244	.342
Ted Lyons	P42	R	29	57	122	20	38	6	3	1	15	2	18	0	.311	.434
1 Alex Metzler	OF27	L	27	56	76	12	14	4	0	0	5	11	6	0	.184	.237
2 Bob Fothergill	OF30	R	32	51	131	10	40	9	0	0	24	4	8	0	.305	.374
Buck Crouse	C38	L	33	42	118	14	30	8	1	0	15	17	10	1	.254	.339
Irv Jeffries	3B20, SS13	R	24	40	97	14	23	3	0	2	11	3	7	2	.237	.330
1 Art Shires	1B33	L	22	37	128	14	33	5	1	1	18	6	6	2	.258	.336
Martin Autry	C29	R	27	34	71	9	18	1	0	0	5	4	9	2	.254	.296
1 Dave Harris	OF23, 2B1	R	30	34	86	16	21	3	1	1	13	7	22	0	.244	.465
Bill Hunnefield	SS22, 1B1	B	31	31	81	11	22	2	0	1	10	6	13	2	.272	.333
Blondy Ryan	3B23, SS2, 2B1	R	24	28	93	7	14	2	0	1	4	3	6	0	.241	.333
Johnny Riddle	C25	R	24	25	58	7	14	3	0	0	4	3	6	0	.241	.328
Ernie Smith	SS21	R	30	24	79	5	19	3	0	0	3	0	5	1	.241	.278
Moe Berg (KJ)	C20	R	28	20	61	4	7	3	0	0	7	1	5	0	.115	.164
1 Jimmy Moore	OF9	R	27	16	39	4	8	2	0	0	3	2	6	0	.205	.256

Luke Appling 23 R 8-26, Bruce Campbell 20 L 5-10, Joe Klinger 27 R 3-8, Butch Henline 35 R 1-8, Hugh Willingham 24 R 1-4

NAME	T	AGE	W	L	PCT	SV	G	GS	CG	IP	H	BB	SO	SHO	ERA
TOTALS		29	62	92	.403	10	154	154	67	1361	1629	407	471	2	4.71
Ted Lyons	R	29	22	15	.595	1	42	36	29	298	331	57	69	1	3.77
Pat Caraway	L	24	10	10	.500	1	38	21	9	193	194	57	83	1	3.87
Red Faber	R	41	8	13	.381	1	29	26	10	169	188	49	62	0	4.21
Hal McKain	R	23	6	4	.600	1	35	10	3	89	108	42	52	0	5.56
Tommy Thomas	R	30	5	13	.278	0	34	27	7	169	229	44	59	0	5.22
2 Garland Braxton	L	30	4	10	.286	1	19	10	2	91	127	33	44	0	6.43
Jim Moore	R	25	2	1	.667	1	9	5	2	40	42	12	11	0	3.60
Ted Blankenship	R	29	2	1	.667	0	7	1	0	15	23	7	2	0	9.00
Dutch Henry	L	28	2	17	.105	0	35	16	4	155	211	48	35	0	4.88
Ed Walsh	R	25	1	4	.200	1	37	4	4	104	131	30	37	0	5.36
Bob Weiland	L	24	0	4	.000	0	14	3	0	38	38	21	15	0	6.54
Biggs Wehde	R	23	0	0	—	0	3	0	0	7	7	3	1	0	10.50

BOSTON — 8th 52-102 .338 50 — HEINIE WAGNER

NAME	G by Pos	B	AGE	G	AB	R	H	2B	3B	HR	RBI	BB	SO	SB	BA	SA
TOTALS			29	154	5286	612	1393	257	68	47	533	358	552	42	.264	.365
Phil Todt	1B104	L	28	111	383	49	103	22	5	11	62	24	33	4	.269	.439
Bill Regan	2B127, 3B2	R	31	134	507	54	135	35	10	3	53	25	60	4	.266	.393
Hal Rhyne	SS107	R	31	107	296	34	60	8	0	0	23	25	19	1	.203	.264
Otto Miller	3B83, 2B15	L	31	110	370	49	106	30	6	3	46	21	21	2	.286	.373
Earl Webb	OF116	L	32	127	449	61	145	30	6	16	66	44	56	2	.323	.523
Tom Oliver	OF154	R	27	154	646	86	189	34	2	0	46	42	25	6	.293	.351
Russ Scarritt	OF110	L	27	113	447	48	129	17	8	2	48	12	49	4	.289	.376
Charlie Berry	C85	R	27	88	256	31	74	6	3	5	35	16	22	2	.289	.441
2 Cedric Durst	OF75	L	33	102	302	29	74	19	5	1	24	17	24	3	.245	.351
Bobby Reeves (JJ)	3B62, SS15, 2B11	R	26	92	272	41	59	7	4	2	18	50	36	6	.217	.294
Bill Sweeney	1B56, 3B1	R	26	88	243	32	75	13	0	4	30	5	19	5	.309	.412
Johnnie Heving	C71	R	34	75	220	15	61	8	0	0	17	11	14	2	.277	.327
Rabbit Warstler	SS54	R	27	54	162	16	30	2	1	2	13	20	21	0	.185	.253
Jack Rothrock (BL)	OF9, 3B1	R	25	45	65	4	18	3	0	0	4	2	6	1	.277	.354
Bill Narleski	SS19, 3B14, 2B5	R	30	39	98	11	23	9	0	0	7	4	13	0	.235	.327
Ed Connolly	C26	R	21	27	48	1	9	2	0	0	2	4	10	0	.188	.229
Charlie Small	OF1	R	24	18	18	4	3	0	0	0	4	2	4	0	.167	.222
Joe Cicero	OF5, 3B2	R	19	18	30	5	5	0	0	0	4	1	5	1	.167	.333

1 Bill Barrett 30 R 3-18, Jim Galvin 22 R 0-2, Tom Winsett 20 L 0-1

NAME	T	AGE	W	L	PCT	SV	G	GS	CG	IP	H	BB	SO	SHO	ERA
TOTALS		28	52	102	.338	5	154	154	78	1360	1505	488	356	4	4.76
Milt Gaston	R	34	13	20	.394	2	38	34	20	273	272	98	99	2	3.92
Danny MacFayden	R	24	11	14	.440	2	36	33	18	269	293	93	76	1	4.21
Hod Lisenbee	R	31	10	17	.370	0	37	31	15	237	254	86	47	0	4.40
Jack Russell	R	24	9	20	.310	0	35	30	15	230	302	53	35	0	5.44
Ed Morris (SJ)	R	30	4	9	.308	0	18	9	3	95	67	38	28	0	4.16
Ed Durham	R	22	4	15	.211	1	33	12	6	140	144	43	71	1	4.69
George Smith	R	28	1	2	.333	0	27	2	0	74	92	49	21	0	6.81
Frank Bushey	R	23	1	0	1.000	0	11	0	0	30	34	15	4	0	6.30
Frank Mulroney	R	27	0	1	.000	0	4	1	0	7	11	8	0	0	3.00
1 Red Ruffing	R	26	0	3	.000	0	4	3	0	24	26	6	14	0	6.38
Ben Shields	L	27	0	0	—	0	3	0	0	10	16	6	1	0	9.00
Bill Bayne	L	31	0	0	—	0	3	0	0	4	2	1	1	0	4.50
Bob Kline	R	20	0	0	—	0	1	0	0	1	1	0	1	0	9.00

ST. LOUIS — 1ST 92-62 .597 — GABBY STREET

NAME	G by Pos	B	AGE	G	AB	R	H	2B	3B	HR	RBI	BB	SO	SB	BA	SA
TOTALS			29	154	5512	1004	1732	373	89	104	942	479	496	72	.314	.471
Jim Bottomley	1B124	L	30	131	487	92	148	33	7	15	97	44	36	5	.304	.493
Frankie Frisch	2B123, 3B10	B	31	133	540	121	187	46	9	10	114	55	16	3	.346	.520
Charlie Gelbert	SS139	R	24	139	513	92	156	39	11	3	72	43	41	6	.304	.441
Sparky Adams	3B104, 2B25, SS7	R	35	137	570	98	179	36	9	0	55	45	27	5	.314	.409
George Watkins	OF89, 1B13, 2B1	L	30	119	391	85	146	32	7	17	87	24	49	5	.373	.621
Taylor Douthit	OF154	R	29	154	664	109	201	41	10	7	93	60	38	4	.303	.426
Chick Hafey	OF116	R	27	120	446	108	150	39	12	26	107	46	51	12	.336	.652
Jimmie Wilson	C99	R	29	107	362	54	115	25	7	1	58	28	17	8	.318	.434
Showboat Fisher	OF67	R	31	92	254	49	95	18	6	8	61	25	21	4	.374	.587
Gus Mancuso	C61	R	24	76	227	39	83	17	2	7	59	18	16	1	.366	.551
Andy High	3B48, 2B3	L	32	72	215	34	60	12	2	2	29	23	6	1	.279	.381
Ernie Orsatti	1B22, OF11	L	27	48	131	24	42	8	4	1	15	12	18	1	.321	.466
Ray Blades	OF32	R	33	45	101	26	40	6	2	4	25	21	15	1	.396	.614
Homer Peel	OF21	R	27	26	73	9	12	2	0	0	10	3	4	0	.164	.192
1 Doc Farrell	SS15, 2B6, 1B1	R	28	23	81	3	13	1	1	0	6	4	2	1	.123	.262
George Puccinelli	OF3	R	23	11	16	5	9	1	0	3	8	0	1	0	.563	1.188
Earl Smith	C6	L	33	8	10	0	0	0	0	0	0	3	1	0	.000	.000
Pepper Martin		R	26	6	1	5	0	0	0	0	0	0	0	0	.000	.000

NAME	T	AGE	W	L	PCT	SV	G	GS	CG	IP	H	BB	SO	SHO	ERA
TOTALS		31	92	62	.597	21	154	154	63	1380	1595	477	641	5	4.40
Wild Bill Hallahan	L	27	15	9	.625	2	35	32	13	237	233	126	177	2	4.67
2 Burleigh Grimes	R	36	13	6	.684	0	22	19	10	152	174	43	58	1	3.02
Jesse Haines	R	36	13	8	.619	1	29	24	14	182	215	54	68	0	4.30
Flint Rhem	R	29	12	8	.600	0	26	19	9	140	173	37	47	0	4.44
Syl Johnson	R	29	12	10	.545	2	32	24	9	188	215	38	92	2	4.64
Jim Lindsey	R	32	7	5	.583	3	39	6	3	106	131	46	50	0	4.42
Al Grabowski	R	28	4	4	.500	1	33	4	1	106	121	50	45	0	4.84
Hi Bell	R	32	4	3	.571	3	39	9	2	115	143	23	42	0	3.91
Hal Haid	R	32	3	2	.600	2	20	0	0	33	38	14	13	0	4.09
1 Bill Sherdel	L	33	3	2	.600	0	13	7	1	64	86	13	29	0	4.64
1 Fred Frankhouse	R	26	2	3	.400	0	8	1	0	20	31	11	4	0	7.20
Dizzy Dean	R	19	1	0	1.000	0	1	1	1	9	3	3	5	0	1.00
1 Clarence Mitchell	L	39	1	0	1.000	1	1	0	0	15	12	3	6	0	6.00
Carmen Hill	R	34	0	1	.000	0	2	1	0	15	15	4	2	0	7.20
Tony Kaufmann	R	29	0	1	.000	0	2	1	0	10	15	4	2	0	8.10

CHICAGO — 2nd 90-64 .584 2 — JOE McCARTHY 86-64 .573   ROGERS HORNSBY 4-0 1.000

NAME	G by Pos	B	AGE	G	AB	R	H	2B	3B	HR	RBI	BB	SO	SB	BA	SA
TOTALS			29	156	5581	998	1722	305	72	171	941	588	635	70	.309	.481
Charlie Grimm	1B113	L	31	114	429	58	124	27	6	6	66	41	26	1	.289	.403
Footsie Blair	2B115, 3B13	L	29	134	578	97	158	24	12	6	59	20	58	9	.273	.388
Woody English	3B83, SS78	R	23	156	638	152	214	36	17	14	59	100	72	3	.335	.511
Les Bell (AJ)	3B70, 1B2	R	28	74	248	35	69	15	4	5	47	24	27	1	.278	.431
Kiki Cuyler	OF156	R	31	156	642	155	228	50	17	13	134	72	49	37	.355	.547
Hack Wilson	OF155	R	30	155	585	146	208	35	6	56	191	105	84	3	.356	.723
Riggs Stephenson	OF80	R	32	109	341	56	125	21	1	5	68	32	20	2	.367	.478
Gabby Hartnett	C136	R	29	141	508	84	172	31	3	37	122	55	62	0	.339	.630
Clyde Beck	SS57, 2B24, 3B2	R	30	83	244	32	52	7	0	6	34	36	32	2	.213	.316
Danny Taylor	OF52	R	29	74	219	43	62	14	3	2	37	27	34	6	.283	.402
Cliff Heathcote	OF35	L	32	70	150	30	39	10	1	9	18	18	15	4	.260	.520
Guy Bush	P46	R	28	46	78	7	22	0	1	0	7	6	19	0	.282	.308
2 Doc Farrell	SS38, 2B1	R	28	46	113	21	33	6	0	1	16	9	5	0	.292	.372
Pat Malone	P45	R	27	45	105	12	26	0	4	0	10	7	19	0	.248	.362
Rogers Hornsby (FJ)	2B25	R	34	42	104	15	32	5	1	2	18	12	12	0	.308	.433
2 George Kelly	1B39	R	34	39	166	22	55	6	1	3	19	7	16	0	.331	.434
Zack Taylor	C28	R	31	32	95	12	22	2	1	1	11	2	12	0	.232	.305
Chuck Tolson	1B5	R	31	13	20	6	6	1	0	0	6	5	6	1	.300	.350

NAME	T	AGE	W	L	PCT	SV	G	GS	CG	IP	H	BB	SO	SHO	ERA
TOTALS		28	90	64	.584	12	156	156	67	1404	1642	528	601	6	4.80
Pat Malone	R	27	20	9	.690	4	45	35	22	272	290	96	142	2	3.94
Charlie Root	R	31	16	14	.533	3	37	30	15	220	247	63	124	4	4.34
Guy Bush	R	28	15	10	.600	3	46	25	11	225	291	86	75	0	6.20
Bud Teachout	L	26	11	4	.733	0	40	16	6	153	178	48	59	0	4.06
Bob Osborn	R	27	10	6	.625	1	35	13	3	127	147	53	42	0	4.96
Sheriff Blake	R	30	10	14	.417	0	34	24	7	187	213	99	80	0	4.81
Hal Carlson (DD)	R	38	4	2	.667	0	8	6	3	52	68	14	14	0	5.02
Lynn Nelson	R	25	3	2	.600	0	37	3	0	81	97	28	29	0	5.11
2 Jesse Petty	L	35	1	3	.250	0	9	3	0	39	51	6	18	0	3.00
Al Shealy	R	30	0	0	—	0	24	0	0	27	37	14	14	0	8.00
Mal Moss	L	25	0	0	—	1	12	1	0	19	18	14	4	0	6.16
Bill McAfee	R	22	0	0	—	0	3	0	0	5	5	3	1	0	0.00
Lon Warneke	R	21	0	0	—	0	1	0	0	2	5	0	5	0	45.00

NEW YORK — 3rd 84-67 .565 5 — JOHN McGRAW

NAME	G by Pos	B	AGE	G	AB	R	H	2B	3B	HR	RBI	BB	SO	SB	BA	SA
TOTALS			27	154	5553	959	1769	264	83	143	880	422	382	59	.319	.473
Bill Terry	1B154	L	31	154	633	139	254	39	15	23	129	57	33	8	.401	.619
2 Hughie Critz	2B124	R	29	124	534	93	148	17	11	4	50	24	26	7	.265	.357
Travis Jackson (IL)	SS115	R	26	116	431	70	146	28	8	13	82	32	25	6	.339	.529
Fred Lindstrom	3B148	R	24	148	609	127	231	39	7	22	106	48	33	15	.379	.575
Mel Ott	OF146	R	21	148	521	122	182	34	5	25	119	103	35	9	.349	.578
Wally Roettger	OF114	R	27	121	420	51	119	15	5	5	51	25	29	1	.283	.379
Freddy Leach	OF124	L	32	126	544	90	178	19	13	13	71	22	25	2	.327	.482
Shanty Hogan	C96	R	24	122	389	60	132	26	2	13	75	21	24	2	.339	.517
Bob O'Farrell	C69	R	33	94	249	37	75	16	4	4	54	31	21	1	.301	.446
Doc Marshall	SS45, 2B17, 3B5	R	24	78	223	33	69	5	3	0	21	13	9	5	.309	.359
2 Ethan Allen	OF62	R	26	76	238	48	73	9	2	7	31	12	23	5	.307	.450
Andy Reese	OF32, 3B10, 1B1	R	28	67	172	26	47	4	2	4	25	10	12	1	.273	.390
2 Pat Crawford	2B18, 1B1	L	28	25	76	11	21	3	2	3	17	7	2	0	.276	.487
Chick Fullis	OF2	R	26	13	6	2	0	0	0	0	0	0	1	0	1.000	.000
Dave Bancroft	SS8	R	39	10	17	0	1	1	0	0	0	2	1	0	.059	.118
Harry Rosenberg	OF3	R	22	9	5	1	0	0	0	0	1	0	4	0	.000	.000
Francis Healy	C1	R	20	7	2	2	0	0	0	0	0	0	1	0	.000	.000
Jo-Jo Moore	OF1	L	21	3	5	1	1	0	0	0	0	0	1	0	.200	.200
Sam Leslie		L	24	2	2	0	1	0	0	0	0	0	1	0	.500	.500

NAME	T	AGE	W	L	PCT	SV	G	GS	CG	IP	H	BB	SO	SHO	ERA
TOTALS		29	87	67	.565	19	154	154	64	1363	1546	439	522	6	4.60
Freddie Fitzsimmons	R	28	19	7	.731	1	41	29	17	224	230	59	76	1	4.26
Carl Hubbell	L	27	17	12	.586	2	37	32	17	242	263	58	117	3	3.87
Bill Walker	L	26	17	15	.531	1	39	34	13	245	258	88	105	2	3.93
2 Clarence Mitchell	L	39	10	3	.769	0	24	16	5	129	151	36	40	0	4.88
Joe Heving	R	29	7	5	.583	6	41	2	0	90	109	27	37	0	5.20
2 Pete Donohue	R	29	7	6	.538	1	18	11	4	87	135	18	26	0	6.10
Hub Pruett	L	29	5	4	.556	3	45	8	1	136	152	63	49	0	4.76
Joe Genewich	R	33	2	5	.286	1	18	9	3	61	71	20	13	0	5.61
Tiny Chaplin	R	24	2	6	.250	1	19	8	3	73	89	16	20	0	5.18
1 Larry Benton	R	32	1	3	.250	1	8	4	1	30	42	14	16	0	7.80
Roy Parmelee	R	23	1	0	1.000	0	11	1	0	21	18	26	19	0	9.43
Ray Lucas	R	21	0	0	—	0	6	0	0	10	9	10	1	0	7.20
Ralph Judd	R	28	0	0	—	0	2	0	0	8	13	3	0	0	5.63
Bill Morrell	R	30	0	0	—	0	2	0	0	8	6	1	3	0	1.13

BROOKLYN — 4th 86-68 .558 6 — WILBERT ROBINSON

NAME	G by Pos	B	AGE	G	AB	R	H	2B	3B	HR	RBI	BB	SO	SB	BA	SA
TOTALS			29	154	5433	871	1654	303	73	122	836	481	541	53	.304	.454
Del Bissonette	1B146	L	30	146	572	102	192	33	13	16	113	58	66	4	.336	.523
Neal Finn	2B81	R	28	87	273	42	76	13	0	3	30	26	18	2	.278	.359
Glenn Wright	SS134	R	29	135	532	83	171	28	12	22	126	32	70	2	.321	.543
Wally Gilbert	3B150	L	29	150	623	92	183	34	5	3	67	47	33	7	.294	.379
Babe Herman	OF153	L	27	153	614	143	241	48	11	35	130	66	66	18	.393	.678
Johnny Frederick	OF142	L	28	142	616	120	206	44	11	17	76	46	34	1	.334	.524
Rube Bressler	OF90, 1B7	L	35	109	335	53	100	12	8	3	52	51	19	4	.299	.409
Al Lopez	C126	R	21	128	421	60	130	20	4	6	57	33	35	3	.309	.418
Jake Flowers	2B65, OF1	R	28	89	253	37	81	18	3	2	50	21	18	5	.320	.439
Eddie Moore	2B23, OF23, SS17,3B1	R	31	76	196	24	55	13	1	1	20	21	7	1	.281	.372
Harvey Hendrick	OF42, 1B7	L	32	68	167	29	43	10	1	5	28	20	19	2	.257	.419
Ike Boone	OF27	L	33	40	101	13	30	9	1	3	13	14	8	0	.297	.495
Hank DeBerry	C35	R	35	35	95	11	28	3	0	0	14	4	10	0	.295	.326
Gordon Slade	SS21	R	25	25	37	8	8	2	0	1	2	3	5	0	.216	.351
Val Picinich	C22	R	33	23	46	4	10	3	0	0	3	8	5	1	.217	.283
Hal Lee	OF12	L	25	22	37	5	6	0	0	1	4	4	5	1	.162	.243
Jack Warner	3B6	R	26	21	25	4	8	1	0	0	2	0	2	7	.320	.360

NAME	T	AGE	W	L	PCT	SV	G	GS	CG	IP	H	BB	SO	SHO	ERA
TOTALS		31	86	68	.558	15	154	154	74	1372	1480	394	526	13	4.03
Dazzy Vance	R	39	17	15	.531	0	35	31	20	259	241	55	173	4	2.61
Ray Phelps	R	26	14	7	.667	0	36	24	11	180	198	52	64	2	4.10
Dolf Luque	R	39	14	8	.636	2	31	24	16	199	221	58	62	2	4.30
Watty Clark	L	28	13	13	.500	6	44	24	9	200	209	38	81	1	4.19
Jumbo Jim Elliott	L	29	10	7	.588	1	35	21	6	198	204	70	59	2	3.95
Ray Moss	R	28	9	6	.600	1	36	11	5	118	127	55	30	0	5.11
Sloppy Thurston	R	31	6	4	.600	1	24	11	5	106	110	17	26	2	3.40
Clise Dudley	R	26	2	4	.333	1	21	7	2	67	103	27	18	0	6.31
Johnny Morrison	R	34	2	2	.333	1	16	0	0	35	47	16	11	0	5.40
Fred Heimach	L	29	0	2	.000	1	9			7	14	3	1	0	5.14
Jim Faulkner	L	30	0	0	—	0	3	0	0	2	3	1	0	0	81.00
Bobo Newsom	R	22	0	0	—	0	1	0	0	2	9	2	1	0	0.00
Cy Moore	R	25	0	0	—	0	2	0	0	2	1	0	0	0	0.00

PITTSBURGH — 5th 80-74 .519 12 — JEWEL ENS

NAME	G by Pos	B	AGE	G	AB	R	H	2B	3B	HR	RBI	BB	SO	SB	BA	SA
TOTALS			27	154	5346	891	1622	285	119	86	844	494	449	76	.303	.449
Gus Suhr	1B151	L	24	151	542	99	155	24	16	17	107	80	56	11	.286	.480
George Grantham	2B141, 1B4	R	30	146	552	120	179	34	14	18	99	81	66	5	.342	.534
Dick Bartell	SS126	R	22	129	475	69	152	32	13	4	75	39	34	8	.320	.467
Pie Traynor	3B130	R	31	130	497	90	182	22	11	9	119	48	19	7	.366	.509
Paul Waner	OF143	L	27	145	589	117	217	32	18	8	77	57	18	18	.368	.525
Lloyd Waner (IL)	OF65	L	24	68	260	32	94	8	3	1	36	5	3	2	.362	.427
Adam Comorosky	OF152	R	25	152	590	117	208	47	23	12	119	51	33	14	.313	.529
Rollie Hemsley	C98	R	23	104	324	45	82	19	6	2	45	22	21	5	.253	.367
Al Bool	C65	R	32	78	216	56	56	12	4	7	46	25	29	0	.259	.449
1 Fred Brickell	OF61	L	23	68	219	65	65	9	3	1	14	15	20	3	.297	.379
Charlie Engle	3B24, SS23, 2B10	R	26	67	216	57	57	10	1	0	15	22	20	1	.264	.319
Erv Brame	P32	R	28	50	116	41	41	5	0	3	22	0	2	0	.353	.474
Ira Flagstead	OF40	R	36	44	156	39	39	7	4	2	21	17	9	1	.250	.385
Jim Mosolf	OF12, P1	L	24	40	51	17	17	2	1	0	9	4	9	4	.333	.412
2 Denny Sothern	OF13	R	26	17	51	9	9	4	0	1	4	2	2	0	.176	.314
Ben Sankey	SS6, 2B4	R	22	17	51	9	9	3	0	0	5	5	10	0	.167	.167
Charlie Hargreaves	C11	R	33	11	31	7	7	1	0	0	2	0	1	0	.226	.258
Gus Dugas	OF9	L	23	9	9	2	9	3	0	0	1	1	1	0	.290	.355
Stu Clark (NJ)	2B2	R	24	4	9	4	4	1	0	0	2	0	0	0	.444	.667
Howdy Groskloss	SS1	R	24	2	1	1	1	0	0	0	0	1	0	0	.333	.333

NAME	T	AGE	W	L	PCT	SV	G	GS	CG	IP	H	BB	SO	SHO	ERA
TOTALS		28	80	74	.519	13	154	154	80	1361	1730	438	393	5	5.24
Ray Kremer	R	37	20	12	.625	0	39	33	18	276	366	63	58	1	5.02
Erv Brame	R	28	17	8	.680	0	32	28	22	236	291	56	55	0	4.69
Larry French	R	22	17	18	.486	1	42	35	21	275	325	89	90	3	4.35
Glenn Spencer	R	24	8	9	.471	4	41	11	5	157	185	63	60	0	5.39
Steve Swetonic (IL)	R	26	6	6	.500	5	23	6	3	97	107	27	35	1	4.45
Heinie Meine (IL)	R	34	6	8	.429	1	20	16	4	117	168	44	18	0	6.15
Spades Wood	L	21	4	3	.571	0	7	5	2	58	61	32	23	0	5.12
Ralph Erickson	R	28	1	0	1.000	0	7	0	0	14	21	10	2	0	7.07
1 Jesse Petty	L	35	1	6	.143	1	10	7	0	41	67	13	16	0	8.34
Percy Jones	L	30	0	2	.000	0	9	2	0	19	26	11	3	0	6.63
Leon Chagnon	R	27	0	0	—	0	8	0	0	42	92	23	27	0	6.82
Lil Stoner	R	31	0	0	—	0	6	0	0	6	7	3	1	0	4.50
Andy Bednar	R	24	0	0	—	0	1	0	0	2	2	1	1	0	36.00
Marty Lang	L	24	0	0	—	0	1	0	0	1	5	2	1	0	45.00
Bernie Walter	L	21	0	0	—	0	2	0	0	1	3	1	0	0	27.00
Jim Mosolf	R	24	0	0	—	0	1	0	0	1	2	1	0	0	0.00

BOSTON 6th 70-84 .455 22 BILL McKECHNIE

NAME	G by Pos	B	AGE	G	AB	R	H	2B	3B	HR	RBI	BB	SO	SB	BA	SA
TOTALS			29	154	5356	693	1503	246	78	66	631	332	397	69	.281	.393
George Sisler	1B107	L	37	116	431	54	133	15	7	3	67	23	15	7	.309	.397
Freddie Maguire	2B146	R	31	146	516	54	138	21	5	0	52	20	22	4	.267	.328
Rabbit Maranville	SS138, 3B4	R	38	142	558	85	157	26	8	2	43	48	23	9	.281	.367
Buster Chatham	3B92, SS17	R	28	112	404	48	108	20	11	5	56	37	41	8	.267	.408
Lance Richbourg	OF128	L	32	130	529	81	161	23	8	1	54	19	31	13	.304	.395
Jim Welsh	OF110	L	27	113	422	51	116	21	9	3	56	29	23	5	.275	.389
Wally Berger	OF145	R	24	151	555	98	172	27	14	38	119	54	69	3	.310	.614
Al Spohrer	C108	R	27	112	356	44	113	22	8	2	37	22	24	3	.317	.441
Randy Moore	OF34, 3B13	L	25	83	191	24	55	9	0	2	34	10	13	3	.288	.366
Earl Clark	OF63	R	22	82	233	29	69	11	3	3	28	7	22	3	.296	.408
Johnny Neun	1B55	B	29	81	212	39	69	12	2	2	23	21	18	9	.325	.429
Bill Cronin	C64	R	27	66	178	19	45	9	1	0	17	4	8	0	.253	.315
Red Rollings	3B28, 2B10	L	26	52	123	10	29	6	0	0	10	9	5	2	.236	.285
Gene Robertson	3B17	L	31	21	59	7	11	1	0	0	7	5	3	0	.186	.203
Billy Rhiel	3B13, 2B2	R	29	20	47	3	8	4	0	0	4	2	5	0	.170	.255
Bill Dunlap	OF7	R	21	16	29	3	2	1	0	0	0	0	6	0	.069	.103
Hank Gowdy	C15	R	40	16	25	0	5	1	0	0	2	3	1	0	.200	.240
Bernie James	2B7	R	24	8	11	1	2	1	0	0	1	0	1	0	.182	.273
Buzz Boyle	OF1	L	22	1	1	0	0	0	0	0	0	0	0	0	.000	.000
Owen Kahn		R	25	1	0	1	0	0	0	0	0	0	0	0	—	—

NAME	T	AGE	W	L	PCT	SV	G	GS	CG	IP	H	BB	SO	SHO	ERA
		30	70	84	.455	11	154	154	71	1361	1624	475	424	6	4.91
Socks Seibold	R	34	15	16	.484	2	36	33	20	251	288	85	70	1	4.12
2 Tom Zachary	R	34	11	5	.688	0	24	22	10	151	192	50	57	1	4.59
Bob Smith	R	35	10	14	.417	5	38	24	14	220	247	85	84	2	4.25
Ben Cantwell	R	28	9	15	.375	2	31	21	10	173	213	45	43	0	4.89
2 Fred Frankhouse	R	26	7	6	.538	0	27	11	3	111	138	43	30	1	5.59
2 Bill Sherdel	L	33	6	5	.545	1	21	14	7	119	131	30	26	0	4.76
Bruce Cunningham	R	24	5	6	.455	0	36	6	2	107	121	41	28	0	5.47
Ed Brandt	L	25	4	11	.267	1	41	13	4	147	168	59	65	1	5.02
1 Burleigh Grimes	R	36	3	5	.375	0	11	9	1	49	72	22	15	0	7.35
Ken Jones	R	27	0	1	.000	0	8	1	0	20	28	4	4	0	5.85
Bob Brown	R	19	0	0	—	0	3	0	0	6	11	6	1	0	10.50
Johnny Cooney	L	29	0	0	—	0	2	0	0	7	16	3	1	0	18.00

CINCINNATI 7th 59-95 .383 33 DAN HOWLEY

NAME	G by Pos	B	AGE	G	AB	R	H	2B	3B	HR	RBI	BB	SO	SB	BA	SA
TOTALS			30	154	5245	665	1475	265	67	74	625	445	489	48	.281	.400
Joe Stripp	1B75, 3B48	R	27	130	464	74	142	37	6	3	64	51	37	15	.306	.431
Hod Ford	SS74, 2B66	R	32	132	424	36	98	16	7	1	34	24	28	1	.231	.309
Leo Durocher	SS103, 2B13	R	24	119	354	31	86	15	3	3	32	20	45	0	.243	.328
Tony Cuccinello	3B109, 2B15, SS4	R	22	125	443	64	138	22	5	10	78	47	44	5	.312	.451
Harry Heilmann	OF106, 1B19	R	35	142	459	79	153	43	6	19	91	64	50	2	.333	.577
Bob Meusel	OF112	R	33	113	443	62	128	30	8	10	62	26	63	9	.289	.460
Curt Walker	OF120	L	33	134	472	74	145	26	11	8	51	64	30	4	.307	.460
Clyde Sukeforth	C82	R	28	94	296	30	84	19	1	1	19	17	12	1	.284	.345
Evar Swanson	OF71	R	27	95	301	43	93	15	3	2	22	11	17	4	.309	.399
Johnny Gooch	C79	B	32	82	276	29	67	10	3	2	30	27	15	0	.243	.322
Red Lucas	P33	L	28	80	113	18	38	4	1	1	19	17	4	0	.336	.442
Marty Callaghan	OF54	L	30	79	225	28	62	9	2	0	16	19	25	1	.276	.333
2 Pat Crawford	2B54, 1B13	L	28	76	224	24	65	7	1	3	26	23	10	2	.290	.371
1 George Kelly	1B50	R	34	51	188	18	54	10	1	5	35	7	20	1	.287	.431
Benny Frey	P44	R	24	44	88	7	25	4	1	0	5	4	18	0	.284	.352
Chuck Dressen	3B10, 2B3	R	31	33	19	0	4	0	0	0	1	3	1	0	.211	.211
1 Hughie Critz	2B28	R	29	28	104	15	24	3	2	0	11	6	6	1	.231	.298
1 Ethan Allen	OF15	R	26	21	46	10	10	1	0	3	7	5	2	1	.217	.435
Nick Cullop	OF5	R	31	7	22	2	4	0	0	1	5	1	9	0	.182	.318
Lena Styles	C5, 1B1	R	30	7	12	2	3	0	1	0	1	1	2	0	.250	.417
Harry Riconda		R	33	1	1	0	0	0	0	0	0	0	0	0	.000	.000

NAME	T	AGE	W	L	PCT	SV	G	GS	CG	IP	H	BB	SO	SHO	ERA
		30	59	95	.383	11	154	154	61	1335	1650	394	361	6	5.08
Red Lucas	R	28	14	16	.467	1	33	28	18	211	270	44	53	1	5.37
Benny Frey	R	24	11	18	.379	1	44	28	14	245	295	62	43	2	4.70
Eppa Rixey	L	39	9	13	.409	0	32	21	5	164	207	47	37	0	5.10
Ray Kolp	R	35	7	12	.368	3	37	19	5	168	180	34	40	2	4.23
2 Larry Benton	R	32	7	12	.368	1	35	22	9	178	246	45	47	0	5.11
Si Johnson	R	23	3	7	.300	0	35	6	3	78	86	31	47	0	4.96
Jakie May	L	34	3	11	.214	0	26	18	5	112	147	41	44	1	5.79
Ken Ash	R	28	2	2	.500	0	16	1	1	39	37	16	15	0	3.46
Archie Campbell	R	26	2	4	.333	4	23	3	1	58	71	31	19	0	5.43
1 Pete Donohue	R	29	1	3	.250	0	14	2	0	34	53	13	4	0	6.35
3 Ownie Carroll	R	27	0	1	.000	0	3	1	0	14	17	3	4	0	4.50
Al Eckert	L	24	0	1	.000	0	2	1	0	5	7	4	1	0	7.20
Biff Wysong	R	25	0	1	.000	0	2	1	0	2	6	3	1	0	22.50
Doug McWeeny	R	33	0	2	.000	0	8	1	0	28	20	10	0	7.27

PHILADELPHIA 8th 52-102 .338 40 BURT SHOTTON

NAME	G by Pos	B	AGE	G	AB	R	H	2B	3B	HR	RBI	BB	SO	SB	BA	SA
TOTALS			27	156	5667	944	1783	345	44	126	884	450	459	34	.315	.458
Don Hurst	1B96, OF7	L	24	119	391	78	128	19	3	17	78	46	22	6	.327	.522
Fresco Thompson	2B112	R	28	122	478	77	135	34	4	4	46	35	29	1	.282	.395
Tommy Thevenow	SS156	R	26	156	573	57	164	21	1	0	78	23	26	1	.286	.326
Pinky Whitney	3B148	R	25	149	606	87	207	41	5	8	117	40	41	3	.342	.465
Chuck Klein	OF156	L	25	156	648	158	250	59	8	40	170	54	50	4	.386	.687
1 Denny Sothern	OF84	R	26	90	347	66	97	16	5	2	36	22	37	6	.280	.403
Lefty O'Doul	OF131	L	33	140	528	122	202	37	7	22	97	63	21	3	.383	.604
Spud Davis	C96	R	25	106	359	41	103	16	1	14	65	17	20	1	.313	.495
Barney Friberg	2B44, OF35, SS12, 3B8	R	30	105	331	62	113	21	4	4	42	47	35	1	.341	.447
Monk Sherlock	1B70, 2B5, OF5, C41	R	25	92	299	51	97	18	2	0	38	27	28	0	.324	.398
Harry McCurdy	C41	R	30	80	148	23	49	6	2	1	25	15	12	0	.331	.419
2 Tony Rensa	C49	R	28	54	172	31	49	11	2	3	31	10	18	0	.285	.424
2 Fred Brickell	OF53	L	23	53	240	33	59	12	6	0	17	13	21	1	.246	.346
Tripp Sigman	OF19	L	31	52	100	15	27	4	1	1	15	9		0	.270	.450
Cy Williams	OF3	L	42	31	17	1	8	2	0	0	2	4	0	0	.471	.588
Jim Spotte	C2	R	21	3	2	1	0	0	0	0	0	0	1	0	.000	.000
Walt Lerian (DD) 27																

NAME	T	AGE	W	L	PCT	SV	G	GS	CG	IP	H	BB	SO	SHO	ERA
		28	52	102	.338	7	156	156	54	1373	1993	543	384	2	6.71
Phil Collins	R	28	16	11	.593	3	47	25	17	239	287	86	87	1	4.78
Ray Benge	R	28	11	15	.423	1	38	29	14	226	305	81	70	0	5.69
Les Sweetland	L	28	7	15	.318	0	34	25	8	167	271	60	36	0	7.71
Hal Elliott	R	31	6	11	.353	0	48	11	2	117	191	58	37	0	7.69
Hap Collard	R	31	6	12	.333	0	30	15	4	127	188	39	25	0	6.80
Claude Willoughby	R	31	4	17	.190	1	41	24	5	153	241	68	38	1	7.59
Chet Nichols (HO)	R	32	1	2	.333	0	16	5	1	60	76	16	15	0	6.75
John Milligan	R	26	1	2	.333	0	9	2	1	28	26	21	7	0	3.21
Harry Smythe	L	25	0	3	.000	2	25	3	0	50	84	31	9	0	7.74
Pete Alexander	R	43	0	3	.000	0	9	3	0	22	40	6	6	0	9.00
Lou Koupal	R	31	0	4	.000	0	13	4	1	37	52	17	11	0	8.51
Snipe Hansen	L	23	0	7	.000	0	22	9	1	84	123	38	15	0	6.75
Buz Phillips	R	26	0	0	—	0	14	1	0	44	68	18	9	0	7.98
By Speece	R	33	0	0	—	0	11	0	0	20	41	4	9	0	13.05

WORLD SERIES — PHILADELPHIA (AL) 4 ST. LOUIS (NL) 2

LINE SCORES

TEAM	1	2	3	4	5	6	7	8	9	10	11	12	R	H	E

Game 1 October 1 at Philadelphia

													R	H	E
STL (NL)	0	0	2	0	0	0	0	0	0				2	9	0
PHI (AL)	0	1	0	1	0	1	1	1	X				5	5	0

Grimes / Grove

Game 2 October 2 at Philadelphia

													R	H	E
STL	0	1	0	0	0	0	0	0	0				1	6	2
PHI	2	0	2	2	0	0	0	0	X				6	7	2

Rhem, Lindsey (4), Johnson (7) / Earnshaw

Game 3 October 4 at St. Louis

													R	H	E
PHI	0	0	0	0	0	0	0	0	0				0	7	0
STL	0	0	0	1	1	0	2	1	X				5	10	0

Walberg, Shores (5), Quinn (7) / Hallahan

Game 4 October 5 at St. Louis

													R	H	E
PHI	1	0	0	0	0	0	0	0	0				1	4	1
STL	0	0	1	2	0	0	0	0	X				3	5	1

Grove / Haines

Game 5 October 6 at St. Louis

													R	H	E
PHI	0	0	0	0	0	0	0	0	2				2	5	0
STL	0	0	0	0	0	0	0	0	0				0	3	1

Earnshaw, Grove (8) / Grimes

Game 6 October 8 at Philadelphia

													R	H	E
STL	0	0	0	0	0	0	0	0	1				1	5	1
PHI	2	0	1	2	1	1	0	0	X				7	7	0

Hallahan, Johnson (3), Landsey (6), Bell (8) / Earnshaw

COMPOSITE BATTING

Philadelphia (AL)

NAME	POS	G	AB	R	H	2B	3B	HR	RBI	BA
Totals		6	178	21	35	10	2	6	21	.197
Simmons	OF	6	22	4	8	2	0	2	4	.364
Foxx	1B	6	21	3	7	2	1	1	3	.333
Miller	OF	6	21	0	3	2	0	0	3	.143
Boley	SS	6	21	1	2	0	0	0	1	.095
Dykes	3B	6	18	2	4	1	0	1	5	.222
Cochrane	C	6	18	5	4	1	0	2	4	.222
Bishop	2B	6	18	5	4	0	0	0	0	.222
Haas	OF	6	18	1	2	0	1	0	1	.111
Earnshaw	P	3	9	0	0	0	0	0	0	.000
Grove	P	3	6	0	0	0	0	0	0	.000
Moore	OF	3	3	0	1	0	0	0	0	.333
Walberg	P	1	2	0	0	0	0	0	0	.000
McNair	PH	1	1	0	0	0	0	0	0	.000
Quinn	P	1	0	0	0	0	0	0	0	—
Shores	P	1	0	0	0	0	0	0	0	—

St. Louis (NL)

NAME	POS	G	AB	R	H	2B	3B	HR	RBI	BA
Totals		6	190	12	38	10	1	2	11	.200
Frisch	2B	6	24	0	5	2	0	0	0	.208
Douthit	OF	6	24	1	2	0	0	0	2	.083
Hafey	OF	6	22	6	6	5	0	0	2	.273
Bottomley	1B	6	22	1	1	1	0	0	0	.045
Adams	3B	6	21	0	3	0	0	0	1	.143
Gelbert	SS	6	17	2	6	0	0	1	2	.353
Wilson	C	4	15	0	4	1	0	0	2	.267
Watkins	OF	6	12	2	2	0	0	1	1	.167
Blades	OF	5	9	2	1	0	0	0	0	.111
Mancuso	C	2	7	1	2	0	0	0	0	.286
Grimes	P	2	5	0	2	0	0	0	0	.400
Haines	P	1	2	0	1	0	0	0	0	.500
Fisher	PH	2	2	0	1	0	0	0	1	.500
High	3B	2	2	1	1	0	0	0	0	.500
Hallahan	P	2	2	0	1	0	0	0	0	.500
Lindsey	P	2	1	0	1	0	0	0	0	1.000
Orsatti	PH	1	1	0	0	0	0	0	0	.000
Puccinelli	PH	1	1	0	0	0	0	0	0	.000
Rhem	P	1	1	0	0	0	0	0	0	.000
Bell	P	1	0	0	0	0	0	0	0	—
Johnson	P	1	0	0	0	0	0	0	0	—

COMPOSITE PITCHING

Philadelphia (AL)

NAME	G	IP	H	BB	SO	W	L	SV	ERA
Totals	6	52	38	11	33	4	2	0	1.73
Earnshaw	3	25	13	7	19	2	0	0	0.72
Grove	3	19	15	3	10	2	1	0	1.42
Walberg	1	4.2	4	1	3	0	1	0	3.86
Quinn	1	2	3	1	0	0	0	0	4.50
Shores	1	1.1	3	0	0	0	0	0	13.50

St. Louis (NL)

NAME	G	IP	H	BB	SO	W	L	SV	ERA
Totals	6	51	35	24	32	2	4	0	3.35
Grimes	2	17	10	6	13	0	2	0	3.71
Hallahan	2	11	9	8	8	1	1	0	1.64
Haines	1	9	4	4	2	1	0	0	1.00
Johnson	2	5	4	3	4	0	0	0	7.20
Lindsey	2	4.2	1	2	3	0	1	0	1.93
Rhem	1	3.1	7	2	3	0	1	0	10.80
Bell	1	1	0	0	0	0	0	0	0.00

1931 Adding Pepper to the Wounds

Cornelias Alexander McGillicuddy, more commonly know as Connie Mack, first broke in as a catcher with Washington in the National League in 1886. His playing career lasted until 1896 and was ordinary. But his managerial career, which began with Pittsburgh in 1894, was an event which would place his name high on the list whenever baseball history was discussed.

Mack's stay with Pittsburgh until 1896 was not the reason he would be remembered. Rather, it was the seed which led to his taking over the Philadelphia Athletics as owner and manager when the American League started in 1901. Now, thirty years later and still serving in the same dual capacity, Mack was on the threshold of an unprecedented event—three world championships in as many years. His courage and imagination had inspired him to lead other Athletics clubs to titles eight times before, only to tear his teams apart and almost start anew. In many instances the reason seemed to be economics, but it is almost certain that a strong pioneering spirit accompanied the moves.

The season of 1931 proved a cakewalk for Mack, finishing a strong 13 games ahead of the Yankees and climaxing three years of winning over 100 games. In winning the pennant, the A's put two streaks together which devastated their rivals. The first was a 17-game stint in May, and the other came in July and lasted for 13 games. Mack's mainstay was MVP Lefty Grove, his pitching ace who compiled an amazing set of statistics—and probably one of the greatest records ever to stand. Grove won 31 and lost 4 for an amazing .886 percentage. He was low with a 2.05 E.R.A. and at one time reeled off 16 victories in a row. Grove's 1929-31 record of 79-15 was also unnerving.

The Cardinals had an easy time with the National League, winning by a full 13 games behind the MVP leadership of second baseman Frankie Frisch.

Statistics in both leagues came closer to the norm, as some of the unnecessary juice was taken out of the baseballs. Chuck Klein of the Phillies, for instance, drove in 121 runs and won the title, while a year before he knocked in 170 runs and proved a poor second to Hack Wilson's 190.

In the World Series of 1929, Mack's forces had no trouble with the Cubs, easily winning four games to one. In 1930 the Cardinals also proved to be no problem, the Series going six games before Mack could claim victory. 1931 seemed to be the easiest Series in the last three years. The Cardinals were back and not that much stronger, and the Athletics were said to be the best team Mack had ever fielded, making them an odds-on choice to win their third straight title.

If the years had taught Mack anything, it was not to be overconfident. He wasn't. But what he did not take into account until it was too late was St. Louis' brash, young center fielder, Pepper Martin, whose career up to the Series deserved no special mention. Yet, suddenly Martin seemed blessed by divinity. After Grove brought Mack victory in the first game, Martin and Bill Hallahan beat the A's in the second game, 2-0. Martin contributed two hits in the third-game victory, and denied George Earnshaw a no-hitter in the Series evener by collecting the only two Cardinal hits.

In the fifth game, Martin got three hits and drove in four runs in a 5-1 victory. Grove evened matters in the sixth game, 8-1, but Martin, who wound up the Series with a .500 average, fittingly snuffed the final A's surge in the ninth inning of the finale with a two-out, two-on catch of Max Bishop's smoking line drive, which gave St. Louis a 4-2 win and the championship-an event Mack would never again witness from the dugout.

1931 AMERICAN LEAGUE

NAME	G by Pos	B	AGE	G	AB	R	H	2B	3B	HR	RBI	BB	SO	SB	BA	SA
PHILADELPHIA	**1st 107-45 .704**										**CONNIE MACK**					
	TOTALS		28	153	5377	858	1544	311	64	118	798	526	543	27	.287	.435
Jimmie Foxx	1B112, 3B20, OF1	R	23	139	515	93	150	32	10	30	120	73	84	4	.291	.567
Max Bishop	2B130	L	31	130	497	115	146	30	4	5	37	112	51	3	.294	.400
Dib Williams	SS72, 2B10, OF1	R	21	86	294	41	79	12	2	6	40	19	21	2	.269	.384
Jimmy Dykes	3B87, SS15	R	34	101	355	48	97	28	2	3	46	49	47	1	.273	.389
Bing Miller	OF137	R	36	137	534	75	150	43	5	8	77	36	16	5	.281	.425
Mule Haas (BW)	OF102	L	27	102	440	82	142	29	7	8	56	30	29	0	.323	.475
Al Simmons	1B128	R	29	128	513	105	200	37	13	22	128	47	45	3	.390	.641
Mickey Cochrane	C117	L	28	122	459	87	160	31	6	17	89	56	21	2	.349	.553
Eric McNair	3B47, 2B16, SS13	R	22	79	280	41	76	10	1	5	33	11	19	1	.271	.368
Joe Boley	SS62, 2B1	L	34	67	224	26	51	9	3	0	20	15	13	1	.228	.295
Doc Cramer (BG)	OF55	L	25	65	223	37	58	8	2	2	20	11	15	2	.260	.341
Phil Todt	1B52	L	29	62	197	23	48	14	2	5	44	8	22	1	.244	.411
Jimmy Moore	OF36	R	28	49	143	18	32	5	1	2	21	11	13	0	.223	.315
Johnnie Heving	C40	R	35	42	113	8	27	3	2	1	12	6	8	0	.239	.327
Joe Palmisano	C16, 2B1	R	28	19	44	5	10	2	0	0	4	6	3	0	.227	.273
Lou Finney	OF8	L	20	9	24	7	9	0	1	0	3	6	1	0	.375	.458

NAME	T	AGE	W	L	PCT	SV	G	GS	CG	IP	H	BB	SO	SHO	ERA
		30	107	45	.704	16	153	153	97	1366	1342	457	574	12	3.47
Lefty Grove		31	31	4	.886	5	41	30	27	289	249	62	175	4	2.05
George Earnshaw	R	31	21	7	.750	6	43	30	23	282	255	75	152	3	3.67
Rube Walberg	L	34	20	12	.625	3	44	35	19	291	298	109	106	0	3.74
Roy Mafaffey	R	27	15	4	.789	2	30	20	8	162	161	82	59	0	4.22
2 Waite Hoyt	R	31	10	5	.667	0	16	14	9	111	130	37	30	2	4.22
Eddie Rommel	R	33	7	5	.583	2	25	10	8	118	136	27	18	1	2.97
Hank McDonald	R	20	2	4	.333	0	19	10	1	70	62	41	23	1	3.73
Lew Krausse	R	19	1	0	1.000	0	3	1	1	11	6	6	1	0	4.09
Jim Peterson	R	22	0	1	.000	0	6	1	1	13	18	4	7	0	6.23
Bill Shores	R	27	0	3	.000	0	6	2	0	16	26	10	2	0	5.06
Sol Carter	R	22	0	0	—	0	2	0	0	2	1	4	1	0	22.50

NAME	G by Pos	B	AGE	G	AB	R	H	2B	3B	HR	RBI	BB	SO	SB	BA	SA
NEW YORK	**2nd 94-59 .614 13.5**										**JOE McCARTHY**					
	TOTALS		28	155	5608	1067	1667	277	78	155	990	748	554	139	.297	.457
Lou Gehrig	1B154, OF1	L	28	155	619	163	211	31	15	46	184	117	56	17	.341	.662
Tony Lazzeri	2B90, 3B39	R	27	135	484	67	129	27	7	8	83	79	80	18	.267	.401
Lyn Lary	SS155	R	25	155	610	100	171	25	9	10	107	88	54	13	.280	.416
Joe Sewell	3B121, 2B1	L	32	130	484	102	146	22	1	6	64	62	8	1	.302	.388
Babe Ruth	OF142, 1B1	L	36	145	534	149	199	31	3	46	163	128	51	5	.373	.700
Earle Combs	OF129	L	32	138	563	120	179	31	13	5	58	68	34	11	.318	.446
Ben Chapman	OF137, 2B11	R	22	149	600	120	189	28	11	17	122	75	77	61	.315	.483
Bill Dickey	C125	L	24	130	477	65	156	17	10	6	78	39	20	2	.327	.442
Sammy Byrd	OF88	R	24	115	248	51	67	18	2	3	32	29	26	5	.270	.395
Jimmy Reese	2B61	L	29	65	245	41	59	10	2	3	26	17	10	2	.241	.335
Red Ruffing	P37, OF1	R	27	48	109	14	36	8	1	3	12	1	13	0	.330	.505
Art Jorgens	C40	R	26	46	100	12	27	1	2	0	14	9	3	0	.270	.320
Myril Hoag	OF23, 3B1	R	23	44	28	6	4	2	0	0	3	1	8	0	.143	.214
Dusty Cooke (SJ)	OF11	L	24	27	39	10	13	1	0	1	6	8	11	4	.333	.436
Cy Perkins	C16	R	35	16	47	3	12	1	0	0	7	4	2	0	.255	.277
Dixie Walker	OF2	L	20	2	10	1	3	2	0	0	1	0	4	0	.300	.500
Red Rolfe	SS1	L	22	1	1	0	0	0	0	0	0	0	0	0	—	—

NAME	T	AGE	W	L	PCT	SV	G	GS	CG	IP	H	BB	SO	SHO	ERA
		28	94	59	.614	17	155	155	78	1410	1461	543	686	4	4.20
Lefty Gomez	L	22	21	9	.700	3	40	26	17	243	206	85	150	0	2.63
Red Ruffing	R	27	16	14	.533	2	37	30	19	237	240	87	132	1	4.40
Hank Johnson	R	25	13	8	.619	4	40	23	8	196	176	102	106	0	4.73
Herb Pennock	L	37	11	6	.647	0	25	25	12	189	247	30	65	1	4.28
Ed Wells	L	31	9	5	.643	2	27	10	6	117	130	37	34	0	4.31
George Pipgras	R	31	7	6	.538	3	36	14	6	138	134	58	59	0	3.78
Gordon Rhodes	R	23	6	3	.667	0	18	11	4	87	82	52	36	0	3.41
Roy Sherid	R	24	5	5	.500	2	17	8	3	74	94	24	39	0	5.70
Ivy Andrews	R	24	2	1	.667	0	7	3	1	34	36	8	10	0	4.23
Jim Weaver	R	27	2	1	.667	0	17	5	2	58	66	29	28	0	5.27
Lefty Weinert	L	29	2	2	.500	0	17	0	0	25	31	19	24	0	6.12
Lou McEvoy	R	29	0	0	—	1	6	0	0	12	19	12	3	0	12.75

NAME	G by Pos	B	AGE	G	AB	R	H	2B	3B	HR	RBI	BB	SO	SB	BA	SA
WASHINGTON	**3rd 92-62 .597 16**										**WALTER JOHNSON**					
	TOTALS		29	156	5576	843	1588	308	93	49	788	481	459	72	.285	.400
Joe Kuhel	1B139	L	25	139	524	70	141	34	8	8	85	47	45	7	.269	.410
Buddy Myer	2B137	L	27	139	591	114	173	30	11	4	56	58	42	11	.293	.406
Joe Cronin	SS155	R	24	156	611	103	187	44	13	12	126	81	52	10	.306	.480
Ossie Bluege	3B152, SS1	R	30	152	570	82	155	25	7	8	98	50	39	16	.272	.382
Sam Rice	OF105	L	41	120	413	81	128	21	8	0	42	35	11	6	.310	.400
Sammy West	OF127	L	26	132	526	77	175	43	13	9	91	30	37	6	.333	.481
Heinie Manush	OF143	L	29	146	616	110	189	41	11	6	70	36	27	5	.307	.428
Roy Spencer	C145	R	31	145	483	48	133	16	3	1	60	35	21	0	.275	.327
Dave Harris	OF60	R	31	77	231	49	72	14	8	5	50	49	38	7	.312	.506
Harry Rice	OF42	L	30	47	162	32	43	5	6	0	15	12	10	2	.265	.370
Pinky Hargrave	C25	B	25	40	80	6	26	8	0	1	19	9	12	1	.325	.463
Jackie Hayes	2B19, 3B8, SS3	R	24	38	108	11	24	2	0	0	8	6	4	1	.222	.259
Joe Judge (IL)	1B15	L	37	35	74	11	21	3	0	0	9	8	4	0	.284	.324
Cliff Bolton	C13	L	24	23	43	3	11	1	0	0	6	1	3	0	.256	.326
Buck Jordan	1B7	L	24	9	18	3	4	2	0	0	1	0	3	0	.222	.333
Johnny Gill	OF8	L	26	8	15	2	4	0	0	0	1	0	1	0	.267	.400
Bill Andrus	3B2	R	23	3	7	0	0	0	0	0	0	0	1	0	.000	.000
Babe Phelps		L	23	3	3	0	1	0	0	0	0	0	0	0	.333	.333
Nick Altrock		B	54	1	0	0	0	0	0	0	0	0	0	0	—	—

NAME	T	AGE	W	L	PCT	SV	G	GS	CG	IP	H	BB	SO	SHO	ERA
		29	92	62	.597	24	156	156	60	1394	1434	498	582	6	3.76
General Crowder	R	32	18	11	.621	2	44	26	13	234	255	72	85	1	3.89
Firpo Marberry	R	32	16	4	.800	7	45	25	11	249	211	63	88	1	3.45
Lloyd Brown	L	26	15	14	.517	2	42	32	15	259	256	79	79	1	3.20
Carl Fischer	L	25	13	9	.591	3	46	23	7	191	207	80	96	0	4.38
Bump Hadley	R	26	11	10	.524	8	55	11	2	180	145	92	124	0	3.05
Sad Sam Jones	R	38	9	10	.474	1	25	24	8	148	185	47	58	1	4.32
Bobby Burke	L	24	8	3	.727	2	30	13	3	129	124	50	38	1	4.26
Walt Tauscher	R	29	1	0	1.000	0	6	0	0	12	24	4	5	0	7.50
Monty Weaver	R	25	1	0	1.000	0	3	1	1	10	11	6	6	0	4.50
Ad Liska (SA)	R	24	0	1	.000	0	10	0	0	4	9	1	2	0	6.75
Walt Masters	R	24	0	1	—	1	3	0	0	9	7	4	1	0	2.00

CLEVELAND — 4th 78-76 .506 30 — ROGER PECKINPAUGH

NAME	G by Pos	B	AGE	G	AB	R	H	2B	3B	HR	RBI	BB	SO	SB	BA	SA
TOTALS		28	155	5445	885	1612	321	69	71	812	555	433	63		.296	.419
Eddie Morgan	1B117, 3B3	R	27	131	462	87	162	33	4	11	86	83	46	4	.351	.511
Johnny Hodapp	2B121	R	25	122	468	71	138	19	4	2	56	27	23	1	.295	.365
Ed Montague	SS64	R	25	64	193	27	55	8	3	1	26	21	22	3	.285	.373
2 Willie Kamm	3B114	R	31	114	410	68	121	31	5	0	66	64	13	3	.295	.395
Dick Porter	OF109, 2B1	L	29	114	414	82	129	24	3	1	38	56	36	6	.312	.391
Earl Averill	OF155	L	29	155	627	140	209	36	10	32	143	68	38	9	.333	.576
Joe Vosmik	OF147	R	21	149	591	80	189	36	14	7	117	38	30	7	.320	.464
Luke Sewell	C105	R	30	108	375	45	103	30	4	1	53	36	17	1	.275	.384
Johnny Burnett	SS63, 2B35, 3B21, OF1	L	29	111	427	85	128	25	5	1	53	39	25	5	.300	.389
Bibb Falk	OF33	L	32	79	161	30	49	13	4	2	28	17	13	1	.304	.435
Glenn Myatt	C58	L	33	65	195	21	48	14	2	1	29	21	13	2	.246	.354
Wes Ferrell	P40	R	23	48	116	24	37	6	1	9	30	10	21	0	.319	.621
Bob Seeds	OF33, 1B2	R	24	48	134	26	41	4	1	1	10	11	11	1	.306	.373
George Detore	3B13, SS10, 2B3	R	24	30	56	3	15	6	0	0	7	8	2	0	.268	.375
Jonah Goldman	SS30	R	24	30	62	0	8	1	0	0	3	4	6	1	.129	.145
Charlie Jamieson	OF7	L	38	28	43	7	13	2	1	0	4	5	1	1	.302	.395
1 Lew Fonseca	1B26	R	32	26	108	21	40	9	1	1	14	8	7	3	.370	.500
Odell Hale	3B15, 2B10, SS1	R	22	25	92	14	26	2	4	1	5	8	2	3	.283	.424
1 Bill Hunnefield	SS21, 2B1	B	32	21	71	13	17	4	1	0	4	9	7	3	.239	.324
Bruce Connatser	1B12	R	28	12	49	5	14	3	0	0	4	3	0	0	.286	.347
Moe Berg	C8	R	29	10	13	1	1	0	0	0	0	1	1	0	.077	.154
Joe Sprinz	C1	R	28	1	3	0	0	0	0	0	0	0	0	0	.000	.000

NAME	T	AGE	W	L	PCT	SV	G	GS	CG	IP	H	BB	SO	SHO	ERA
		26	78	76	.506	9	155	155	76	1355	1577	561	470	6	4.63
Wes Ferrell	R	23	22	12	.647	3	40	35	27	276	276	130	123	2	3.75
Willis Hudlin	R	25	15	14	.517	4	44	34	15	254	313	88	83	1	4.61
Mel Harder	R	21	13	14	.481	1	40	24	9	194	229	72	63	0	4.36
Clint Brown	R	27	11	15	.423	0	39	33	12	233	284	55	50	1	4.72
Sarge Connally	R	32	5	5	.500	1	17	9	5	86	87	50	37	0	4.19
Pete Jablonowski	R	27	4	4	.500	0	29	4	3	80	100	29	25	0	4.62
Oral Hilderbrand	R	24	2	1	.667	0	5	2	2	27	25	13	6	0	4.33
Jake Miller (AJ)	R	33	2	1	.667	0	10	5	1	41	45	19	17	1	4.39
Milt Shoffner	L	25	2	3	.400	0	12	4	1	41	55	26	12	0	7.24
Fay Thomas	R	27	2	4	.333	0	16	2	1	49	63	32	25	0	5.14
Belve Bean	R	26	0	1	.000	0	4	0	0	7	11	4	3	0	6.43
Howard Craighead	R	23	0	0	—	0	4	0	0	8	2	2	0	0	6.00
2 Pete Donohue	R	30	0	0	—	0	2	0	0	5	5	4	0	0	9.00
Roxie Lawson	R	25	0	2	.000	0	17	3	0	56	72	36	20	0	7.55

ST. LOUIS — 5th 63-91 .409 45 — BILL KILLEFER

NAME	G by Pos	B	AGE	G	AB	R	H	2B	3B	HR	RBI	BB	SO	SB	BA	SA
TOTALS		27	154	5374	721	1455	287	62	76	666	488	580	73	.271	.390
Jack Burns	1B143	L	23	144	580	75	148	27	7	4	70	42	58	19	.255	.347
Oscar Melillo	2B151	R	31	151	617	88	189	34	11	2	75	37	29	7	.306	.407
Jim Levey	SS139	R	24	139	498	53	104	19	2	5	38	33	83	13	.209	.285
Red Kress	3B84, OF40, SS38, 1B10	R	26	150	605	87	188	46	8	16	114	46	48	3	.311	.493
Tom Jenkins	OF58	L	33	81	232	20	61	7	2	3	25	17	25	1	.263	.352
Fred Schulte	OF134	R	30	134	553	100	168	32	7	9	65	56	49	6	.304	.436
Goose Goslin	OF151	L	30	151	591	114	194	42	10	24	105	80	41	9	.328	.555
Rick Ferrell	C108	R	25	117	386	47	118	30	4	3	57	56	12	2	.306	.427
Lin Storti	3B67, 2B7	B	24	86	273	32	60	15	4	3	26	15	50	4	.220	.337
Larry Bettencourt	OF58	R	25	74	206	27	53	9	2	3	26	31	35	4	.257	.364
Earl McNeely	OF36	R	33	49	102	12	23	4	0	0	15	9	5	4	.225	.265
Ed Grimes	3B22, 2B4, SS3	R	25	43	57	9	15	1	2	0	5	9	3	1	.263	.351
Benny Bengough	C37	R	32	40	140	6	35	4	1	0	12	4	4	0	.250	.293
Russ Young	C16	R	28	16	34	2	4	0	0	1	2	2	4	0	.118	.206
Frank Waddey	OF7	L	25	14	22	3	6	1	0	0	2	2	3	0	.273	.318
Buck Stanton	OF1	L	25	13	15	3	3	2	0	0	0	0	4	0	.200	.333
Jack Crouch	C7	R	28	8	12	0	0	0	0	0	0	0	4	0	.000	.000
Frank O'Rourke	SS2, 1B1	R	39	8	9	0	2	0	0	0	0	0	3	0	.222	.222
Nap Kloza	OF3	R	28	1	7	0	1	0	0	0	0	1	1	0	.143	.143

NAME	T	AGE	W	L	PCT	SV	G	GS	CG	IP	H	BB	SO	SHO	ERA
		26	63	91	.409	10	154	154	65	1362	1623	448	436	4	4.76
Lefty Stewart	L	30	14	17	.452	0	36	33	20	258	287	85	89	1	4.40
George Blaeholder	R	27	11	15	.423	0	35	32	13	226	280	56	79	1	4.54
Sam Gray	R	33	11	24	.314	2	43	37	13	258	323	54	80	0	5.09
Dick Coffman	R	24	9	13	.409	1	32	17	11	169	159	51	39	2	3.89
Wally Hebert	L	23	6	7	.462	0	23	13	5	103	128	43	26	0	5.07
Rip Collins	R	25	5	5	.500	0	17	14	2	107	130	38	34	0	3.79
Chad Kimsey	R	24	4	6	.400	7	42	1	0	94	121	27	27	0	4.40
Rollie Stiles	R	24	3	1	.750	0	34	2	0	81	112	60	32	0	7.22
Bob Cooney	R	23	0	3	.000	0	5	4	1	39	46	20	13	0	4.15
2 Garland Braxton	L	31	0	0	—	0	11	0	0	18	27	10	7	0	10.50
Fred Stiely	L	30	0	0	—	0	4	0	0	7	7	3	2	0	6.43
Jess Doyle	R	33	0	0	—	0	1	0	0	3	1	0	1	0	27.00

BOSTON — 6th 62-90 .408 45 — SHANO COLLINS

NAME	G by Pos	B	AGE	G	AB	R	H	2B	3B	HR	RBI	BB	SO	SB	BA	SA
TOTALS		29	153	5379	625	1409	289	34	37	572	405	565	43	.262	.349
Bill Sweeney	1B124	R	27	131	498	48	147	30	3	1	58	20	30	5	.295	.373
Rabbit Warstler	2B42, SS19	R	27	66	181	20	44	5	3	0	10	15	27	2	.243	.304
Hal Rhyne	SS147	R	32	147	565	75	154	34	3	0	51	57	41	3	.273	.343
Otto Miller	3B75, 2B6	R	30	107	389	38	106	12	1	0	43	15	20	1	.272	.308
Earl Webb	OF151	L	33	151	589	96	196	67	3	14	103	70	51	2	.333	.528
Tom Oliver	OF148	R	28	148	586	52	162	35	5	0	70	25	17	4	.276	.353
J. Rothrock	OF79, 2B23, 1B8, 3B2, SS1	B	26	133	475	81	132	32	3	4	42	47	48	13	.278	.381
Charlie Berry	C102	R	28	111	357	41	101	16	2	6	49	29	38	1	.283	.389
Urban Pickering	3B74, 2B16	R	32	103	341	48	86	13	4	9	52	32	53	3	.252	.393
Al VanCamp	OF59, 1B25	R	27	101	324	34	89	15	4	0	33	20	24	3	.275	.346
Tom Winsett	OF8	L	21	64	76	6	15	1	0	1	7	4	21	0	.197	.250
Ed Connolly	C41	R	22	42	93	3	7	1	0	0	3	5	18	0	.075	.086
Bobby Reeves (BH)	2B29, P1	R	27	36	84	11	14	2	2	0	1	14	16	0	.167	.238
1 Muddy Ruel	C30	R	35	33	86	6	25	5	0	0	6	9	6	0	.291	.361
Ollie Marquardt	2B13	R	28	17	39	4	7	1	0	0	2	2	5	0	.179	.205
2 Marty McManus	3B11, 2B7	R	31	17	62	8	18	4	0	1	9	8	1	1	.290	.403
Gene Rye	OF10	L	24	17	39	3	7	0	0	0	1	2	5	0	.179	.179
Marv Olson	2B15	R	28	15	53	8	10	1	0	0	3	5	3	1	.189	.208
Russ Scarritt	OF9	L	28	10	39	2	6	1	0	0	1	2	2	0	.154	.179

George Stumpf 20 L 7-28, Howie Storie 20 R 2-17, Pat Creeden 25 L 0-8, Jack Smith 24 B 2-15, Johnny Lucas 28 R 0-2, Bill McWilliams 20 R 0-0, Bill Marshall 19 R 0-0

NAME	T	AGE	W	L	PCT	SV	G	GS	CG	IP	H	BB	SO	SHO	ERA
		28	62	90	.408	10	153	153	61	1367	1559	473	365	5	4.60
Danny MacFayden	R	26	16	12	.571	0	35	32	17	231	263	79	74	1	4.01
Wilcy Moore	R	34	11	13	.458	10	53	14	3	185	195	55	37	1	3.89
Jack Russell	R	25	10	18	.357	0	36	31	13	232	298	65	45	0	5.16
Ed Durham	R	23	8	10	.444	0	38	15	7	165	175	50	53	2	4.26
Bob Kline (IL)	R	21	5	5	.500	0	28	10	3	98	110	35	25	0	4.41
Ed Morris	R	31	5	7	.417	0	37	14	3	131	131	74	46	0	4.74
Hod Lisenbee	R	32	5	12	.294	0	41	17	6	165	190	49	42	0	5.18
Milt Gaston (SA)	R	35	2	13	.133	0	23	18	4	119	137	41	33	0	4.46
Jim Brillheart	L	27	0	0	—	0	11	0	2	20	27	15	7	0	5.40
Jud McLaughlin	R	19	0	0	—	0	2	0	0	8	8	3	0	0	12.00
Walter Murphy	R	23	0	0	—	0	2	0	0	4	4	1	0	0	9.00
Bobby Reeves (BH)	R	27	0	0	—	0	1	0	0	7	6	1	0	0	3.86

DETROIT — 7th 61-93 .396 47 — BUCKY HARRIS

NAME	G by Pos	B	AGE	G	AB	R	H	2B	3B	HR	RBI	BB	SO	SB	BA	SA
TOTALS		28	154	5430	651	1456	292	69	43	599	480	468	117	.268	.371
Dale Alexander	1B126, OF4	R	28	135	517	75	168	47	3	3	87	64	35	5	.325	.445
Charlie Gehringer (AJ)	2B78, 1B9	L	28	101	383	67	119	24	5	4	53	29	15	13	.311	.431
Billy Rogell	SS48	B	28	48	185	21	56	12	3	2	24	24	17	8	.303	.432
1 Marty McManus	3B79, 2B21, 1B1	R	31	107	362	39	98	17	3	3	53	49	22	7	.271	.359
Roy Johnson	OF150	R	28	151	621	107	173	37	19	8	55	72	51	33	.279	.438
Hub Walker	OF66	L	24	90	252	27	72	13	1	0	16	23	25	10	.286	.345
John Stone	OF147	L	25	147	584	86	191	28	11	10	76	56	48	13	.327	.464
Ray Hayworth	C88	R	27	88	273	28	70	10	3	0	25	19	27	0	.256	.315
Mark Koenig	2B55, SS35, P3	B	28	106	364	33	92	24	4	1	39	14	12	8	.253	.349
Marv Owen	SS37, 3B37, 1B27, 2B4	R	25	105	377	35	84	11	6	3	39	29	38	2	.223	.308
Frank Doljack	OF54	R	23	63	187	20	52	13	3	4	20	15	17	3	.278	.444
Gee Walker	OF44	R	23	59	189	20	56	17	2	1	28	14	21	10	.296	.423
George Uhle	P29	R	32	53	90	8	22	6	0	2	7	8	8	0	.244	.378
Johnny Grabowski	C39	R	31	40	136	9	32	7	1	1	14	6	19	0	.235	.324
Nolen Richardson	3B38	R	28	38	148	13	40	9	2	0	16	6	3	2	.270	.358
Wally Schang	C30	B	41	30	76	9	14	2	0	0	2	14	11	1	.184	.211
Bill Akers	SS21, 2B2	R	26	29	66	5	13	2	0	0	3	7	6	0	.197	.288
Lou Brower	SS20, 2B2	R	31	24	62	3	10	1	0	0	3	5	1	0	.161	.177
2 Muddy Ruel	C14	R	35	14	50	1	6	1	0	0	2	5	4	0	.120	.140
George Quellich	OF13	R	25	13	54	6	12	5	0	1	11	3	4	1	.222	.370
Joe Dugan	3B5	R	34	17	17	1	4	1	0	0	0	0	3	0	.235	.235
Bucky Harris	2B3	R	34	8	9	1	1	0	0	0	0	1	1	0	.111	.250
Gene Desautels	C3	R	24	3	11	1	1	0	0	0	1	0	1	0	.091	.091
Ivey Shiver	OF2	R	24	2	9	2	1	0	0	0	0	3	0	0	.111	.111

NAME	T	AGE	W	L	PCT	SV	G	GS	CG	IP	H	BB	SO	SHO	ERA
		28	61	93	.396	6	154	154	86	1392	1549	597	511	5	4.56
Vic Sorrell	R	30	13	14	.481	1	35	32	19	247	267	114	99	1	4.12
Earl Whitehill	L	31	13	16	.448	0	34	34	22	272	287	118	81	0	4.07
George Uhle	R	32	11	12	.478	2	29	18	15	193	190	49	63	1	3.50
Tommy Bridges	R	24	8	16	.333	0	35	23	8	173	182	108	105	1	5.00
Art Herring	R	25	7	13	.350	1	35	16	7	165	186	67	64	0	4.31
Charlie Sullivan	R	28	3	2	.600	0	14	4	1	99	109	46	28	0	4.73
1 Waite Hoyt	R	31	3	8	.273	0	16	12	5	92	124	32	10	0	5.87
Chief Hogsett	R	27	3	9	.250	2	22	12	5	112	150	33	47	0	5.97
Orlin Collier	R	24	0	1	.000	0	2	0	0	10	17	7	3	0	8.10
Whit Wyatt (SA)	R	23	0	2	.000	0	4	1	1	21	30	12	8	0	8.57
Mark Koenig	R	28	0	0	—	0	3	0	0	14	7	11	3	0	6.43

CHICAGO — 8th 56-97 .366 51.5 — DONIE BUSH

NAME	G by Pos	B	AGE	G	AB	R	H	2B	3B	HR	RBI	BB	SO	SB	BA	SA
TOTALS		28	156	5481	704	1423	238	69	27	649	483	445	94	.260	.343
Lu Blue	1B155	B	34	155	589	119	179	23	15	1	62	127	60	13	.304	.399
John Kerr	2B117, SS1	R	32	128	444	51	119	24	5	1	50	35	22	1	.268	.329
Bill Cissell	SS83, 2B23, 3B1	R	27	109	409	42	90	13	5	1	46	16	26	18	.220	.284
Billy Sullivan	3B83, OF2, 1B3	L	20	92	363	48	100	14	5	2	33	20	14	4	.275	.364
Carl Reynolds	OF109	R	28	118	462	71	134	24	14	6	77	24	26	17	.290	.442
Johnny Watwood	OF102, 1B4	L	25	128	367	51	104	16	6	1	47	56	30	9	.283	.368
2 Lew Fonseca	OF95, 2B21, 1B2, 3B1	R	32	121	465	65	139	26	5	2	71	32	22	4	.299	.389
Bennie Tate	C85	L	29	89	273	29	73	12	3	0	22	26	10	1	.267	.333
Bob Fothergill	OF74	R	33	108	312	25	89	9	4	3	56	17	17	2	.282	.365
Luke Appling	SS76, 2B1	R	24	96	297	36	69	13	4	1	28	29	27	2	.232	.313
Frank Grube	C81	R	26	88	265	29	58	13	2	1	24	22	22	2	.219	.294
Irv Jeffries	3B61, 2B6, SS5	R	25	79	223	29	50	10	2	0	16	14	9	3	.224	.296
Mel Simons	OF59	R	31	68	189	24	52	9	0	0	12	12	17	1	.275	.323
Smead Jolley	OF23	L	29	54	110	5	33	11	0	3	28	4	9	0	.300	.482
Fred Eichrodt	OF32	R	28	34	117	9	25	5	1	0	5	4	3	4	.214	.282
Bill Norman	OF17	R	20	24	55	7	10	2	0	0	6	4	10	0	.182	.218
1 Willie Kamm	3B18	R	31	18	59	1	15	4	0	0	9	7	6	1	.254	.322
Butch Henline	C4	R	36	11	15	2	1	0	0	0	2	1	0	0	.067	.133
Hank Garrity	C7	R	23	9	14	0	3	0	0	0	2	1	2	1	.214	.286
Bruce Campbell	OF4	R	21	9	17	5	7	2	1	0	3	3	2	0	.412	.882

NAME	T	AGE	W	L	PCT	SV	G	GS	CG	IP	H	BB	SO	SHO	ERA
		29	56	97	.366	10	156	156	54	1387	1611	588	420	6	5.05
Vic Frasier	R	26	13	15	.464	4	46	29	13	254	258	127	87	2	4.46
Pat Caraway	L	25	10	24	.294	2	51	32	11	220	268	101	55	1	6.22
Red Faber	R	42	10	14	.417	1	44	19	5	184	210	57	49	1	3.82
Tommy Thomas	R	31	10	14	.417	2	42	36	11	242	296	69	71	2	4.80
Hal McKain (AJ)	R	24	9	4	.400	0	27	4	5	112	134	57	39	0	5.71
Ted Lyons (SA)	R	30	4	6	.400	0	22	12	7	101	117	33	16	0	4.01
Bob Weiland	L	25	2	7	.222	0	15	6	3	75	75	46	28	0	5.16
Biggs Wehde	R	24	1	1	.500	0	10	0	0	16	19	10	6	0	6.75
Grant Bowler	R	23	0	1	.000	0	13	3	1	35	40	24	15	0	5.40
Lou Garland	R	24	0	1	.000	0	7	2	0	17	30	15	9	0	10.06
Jim Moore	R	27	0	0	—	0	33	4	0	84	93	27	15	0	4.93
1 Garland Braxton	L	31	0	3	.000	0	17	3	0	47	71	23	28	0	6.89

ST. LOUIS — 1ST 101-53 .656 — GABBY STREET

NAME	G by Pos	B	AGE	G	AB	R	H	2B	3B	HR	RBI	BB	SO	SB	BA	SA
TOTALS			29	154	5435	815	1554	353	74	60	751	432	475	114	.286	.411
Jim Bottomley	1B93	L	31	108	382	73	133	34	5	9	75	34	24	3	.348	.534
Frankie Frisch	2B129	B	32	131	518	96	161	24	4	4	82	45	13	28	.311	.396
Charlie Gelbert	SS130	R	25	131	447	61	129	29	5	1	62	54	31	7	.289	.383
Sparky Adams	3B138, SS6	R	36	143	608	97	178	46	5	1	40	42	24	16	.293	.390
George Watkins	OF129	L	31	131	503	93	145	30	13	13	51	31	66	15	.288	.477
Pepper Martin	OF110	R	27	123	413	68	124	32	8	7	75	30	40	16	.300	.467
Chick Hafey	OF118	R	28	122	450	94	157	35	8	16	95	39	43	11	.349	.569
Jimmie Wilson	C110	R	30	115	383	45	105	20	2	0	51	28	15	5	.274	.337
Ripper Collins	1B68, OF3	B	27	89	279	34	84	20	10	4	59	18	24	1	.301	.487
Ernie Orsatti	OF45, 1B1	L	28	70	158	27	46	16	6	0	19	14	16	1	.291	.468
Gus Mancuso	C56	R	25	67	187	13	49	16	1	1	23	18	13	2	.262	.374
Andy High	3B23, 2B19	L	33	63	130	20	35	6	1	0	19	24	4	0	.267	.328
2 Jake Flowers	SS24, 2B21, 3B1	R	29	45	137	19	34	11	1	2	19	9	6	7	.248	.387
2 Wally Roettger	OF42	R	28	45	151	16	43	12	2	0	17	9	14	0	.285	.391
1 Taylor Douthit	OF36	R	30	36	133	24	44	11	2	1	21	11	9	1	.331	.466
Ray Blades	OF20	R	34	35	67	10	19	4	0	1	5	10	7	1	.284	.388
Mike Gonzalez	C12	R	40	15	19	1	2	0	0	0	3	0	3	0	.105	.105
Joe Benes	SS6, 2B2, 3B1	R	30	10	12	1	2	0	0	0	0	2	1	0	.167	.167
Joel Hunt	OF1	R	25	4	1	2	0	0	0	0	0	0	1	0	.000	.000
Ray Cunningham	3B3	R	26	3	4	0	0	0	0	0	0	1	0	0	.000	.000
Eddie Delker	3B1	R	25	1	2	0	1	1	0	0	2	0	0	0	.500	1.000
Gabby Street	C1	R	48	1	1	0	0	0	0	0	0	0	0	0	.000	.000

NAME	T	AGE	W	L	PCT	SV	G	GS	CG	IP	H	BB	SO	SHO	ERA
		31	101	53	.656	20	154	154	80	1385	1470	449	626	17	3.45
Wild Bill Hallahan	L	28	19	9	.679	4	37	34	16	249	242	112	159	3	3.29
Paul Derringer	R	24	18	8	.692	2	35	23	15	212	225	65	134	4	3.35
Burleigh Grimes	R	37	17	9	.654	0	29	28	17	212	240	59	67	3	3.65
Jesse Haines	R	37	12	3	.800	1	19	17	8	122	134	28	27	2	3.02
Syl Johnson	R	30	11	9	.550	2	32	16	7	186	186	29	82	2	3.00
Flint Rhem	R	30	11	10	.524	1	33	26	10	207	214	60	72	2	3.57
Allyn Stout	R	26	6	0	1.000	3	30	3	1	73	87	34	40	0	4.19
Jim Lindsey	R	33	6	4	.600	7	35	2	1	75	77	45	32	1	5.00
Tony Kaufmann	R	30	1	1	.500	1	15	1	0	49	65	17	13	0	6.06

NEW YORK — 2nd 87-65 .572 13 — JOHN McGRAW

NAME	G by Pos	B	AGE	G	AB	R	H	2B	3B	HR	RBI	BB	SO	SB	BA	SA
TOTALS			28	153	5372	768	1554	251	64	101	727	383	395	83	.289	.416
Bill Terry	1B153	L	32	153	611	121	213	43	20	9	112	47	36	8	.349	.529
Hughie Critz (AJ)	2B54	R	30	66	238	33	69	7	2	4	17	8	17	4	.290	.387
Travis Jackson	SS145	R	27	145	555	65	172	26	10	5	71	36	23	13	.310	.420
Johnny Vergez	3B152	R	24	152	565	67	157	24	2	13	81	29	65	11	.278	.396
Fred Lindstrom (BF)	OF73, 2B4	R	25	78	303	38	91	12	6	5	36	26	12	5	.300	.429
Mel Ott	OF137	L	22	138	497	104	145	23	8	29	115	80	44	10	.292	.545
Freddy Leach	OF125	L	33	129	515	75	159	30	5	6	61	29	9	4	.309	.421
Shanty Hogan	C113	R	25	123	396	42	119	17	1	12	65	29	29	1	.301	.439
Ethan Allen	OF77	R	27	94	298	58	98	18	2	5	43	15	15	6	.329	.453
Chick Fullis	OF68, 2B9	R	27	89	302	61	99	15	2	3	28	23	13	13	.328	.421
Bob O'Farrell	C80	R	34	85	174	11	39	8	3	1	19	21	23	0	.224	.322
Doc Marshall	2B47, SS11, 3B3	R	25	68	194	15	39	6	2	0	10	8	8	1	.201	.253
3 Bill Hunnefield	2B56, SS5	B	32	64	196	23	53	5	0	1	17	9	16	3	.270	.311
Sam Leslie	1B6	R	25	53	53	11	16	4	0	3	5	1	2	3	.302	.547
Freddie Fitzsimmons	P35	R	29	35	92	16	21	3	1	4	18	7	18	0	.228	.413
Francis Healy	C4	R	21	6	7	1	1	0	0	0	0	0	0	0	.143	.143
Jo-Jo Moore	OF1	L	22	4	8	0	2	1	0	0	3	0	1	0	.250	.375
Gil English	3B3	R	21	3	8	0	0	0	0	0	0	0	1	0	.000	.000

NAME	T	AGE	W	L	PCT	SV	G	GS	CG	IP	H	BB	SO	SHO	ERA
		30	87	65	.572	12	153	153	90	1360	1341	422	570	17	3.30
Freddie Fitzsimmons	R	29	18	11	.621	0	35	33	19	254	242	62	78	4	3.05
Bill Walker	L	27	16	9	.640	3	37	28	19	239	222	64	121	6	2.26
Carl Hubbell	L	28	14	12	.538	3	36	30	21	248	211	67	156	4	2.65
Clarence Mitchell	L	40	13	11	.542	0	27	25	13	190	221	52	39	0	4.07
Jim Mooney	L	24	7	1	.875	0	10	6	2	72	71	16	38	2	2.00
Jack Berly	R	28	7	8	.467	0	27	1	4	111	114	51	45	1	3.89
Bill Morrell	R	31	5	3	.625	1	20	7	2	66	83	27	16	0	1.36
Tiny Chaplin	R	25	3	0	1.000	1	16	3	1	42	39	16	7	0	3.21
Roy Parmelee	R	24	2	0	.500	0	13	5	4	59	47	33	30	0	3.66
Hal Schumacher	R	20	1	1	.500	1	8	2	1	18	31	14	11	0	11.00
Joe Heving	R	30	1	6	.143	0	22	0	0	42	48	11	26	0	4.93
1 Pete Donohue	R	30	0	1	.000	0	4	1	0	11	14	4	4	0	5.73
Emil Planeta	R	22	0	0	.000	0	2	0	0	5	7	4	0	0	10.80
Ray Lucas	R	22	0	0	—	0	1	0	0	2	1	1	0	0	4.50

CHICAGO — 3rd 84-70 .545 17 — ROGERS HORNSBY

NAME	G by Pos	B	AGE	G	AB	R	H	2B	3B	HR	RBI	BB	SO	SB	BA	SA
TOTALS			28	156	5451	828	1578	340	67	84	766	577	641	49	.289	.423
Charlie Grimm	1B144	L	32	146	531	65	176	33	11	4	66	53	29	1	.331	.458
Rogers Hornsby	2B69, 3B26	R	25	100	357	64	118	37	1	16	90	56	23	1	.331	.574
Woody English	SS138, 3B18	R	24	156	634	117	202	38	8	2	53	68	80	12	.319	.413
Les Bell	3B70	R	29	75	252	30	71	17	1	4	32	19	22	0	.282	.405
Kiki Cuyler	OF153	R	32	154	613	110	202	37	12	9	88	72	54	13	.330	.473
Hack Wilson	OF103	R	31	112	395	66	103	22	4	13	61	63	69	1	.261	.435
Riggs Stephenson (BN)	OF66	R	33	80	263	34	84	14	4	1	52	37	14	1	.319	.414
Gabby Hartnett	C105	R	30	116	380	53	107	32	1	8	70	52	48	3	.282	.434
Bill Jurges	3B54, 2B33, SS3	R	23	88	293	34	59	15	5	0	23	25	41	2	.201	.287
Danny Taylor	OF67	R	30	88	270	48	81	13	6	5	41	31	46	4	.300	.448
Footsie Blair	2B44, 1B23, 3B1	L	23	66	240	31	62	19	5	3	29	14	26	1	.258	.417
Vince Barton	OF81	L	23	66	239	45	57	10	1	13	50	21	40	1	.238	.452
2 Rollie Hemsley	C53	R	24	66	204	28	63	17	4	3	31	17	30	4	.309	.475
Johnny Moore	OF22	R	29	39	104	19	25	3	1	2	16	7	5	1	.240	.346
Billy Herman	2B25	R	21	25	98	14	32	7	0	0	16	13	6	2	.327	.398
Jimmy Adair	SS18	R	24	18	76	9	21	3	1	0	3	1	8	1	.276	.342
Zack Taylor	C5	R	32	8	4	0	1	0	0	0	0	2	1	0	.250	.250
1 Earl Grace	C2	L	24	7	9	2	1	0	0	0	1	4	1	0	.111	.111
Mike Kreevich	OF4	R	23	5	12	0	2	0	0	0	0	0	6	1	.167	.167

NAME	T	AGE	W	L	PCT	SV	G	GS	CG	IP	H	BB	SO	SHO	ERA
		29	84	70	.545	8	156	156	80	1386	1448	524	541	8	3.97
Charlie Root	R	32	17	14	.548	2	39	31	19	251	240	71	131	3	3.48
Guy Bush	R	29	16	8	.667	2	39	24	14	180	190	66	54	1	4.50
Pat Malone	R	28	16	9	.640	0	36	30	12	228	229	88	112	2	3.91
Bob Smith	R	36	15	12	.556	2	36	29	18	240	239	62	63	2	3.23
Les Sweetland	L	29	5	7	.533	0	26	14	9	130	156	61	32	0	5.05
Jakie May (CN)	L	35	5	5	.500	2	31	4	1	79	81	43	38	0	3.87
John Welch	R	24	6	3	.667	0	8	3	1	34	39	10	7	0	3.71
Ed Baecht	R	24	2	4	.333	0	22	6	2	67	64	32	34	0	3.76
Lon Warneke	R	22	2	4	.333	0	20	7	3	64	67	37	27	0	3.23
Bud Teachout	R	27	1	2	.333	0	27	3	1	61	79	28	14	0	5.75
1 Sheriff Blake	R	31	0	4	.000	0	13	4	1	50	64	26	29	0	5.22

BROOKLYN — 4th 79-73 .520 21 — WILBERT ROBINSON

NAME	G by Pos	B	AGE	G	AB	R	H	2B	3B	HR	RBI	BB	SO	SB	BA	SA
TOTALS			29	153	5309	681	1464	240	77	71	633	409	512	45	.276	.390
Del Bissonette	1B152	L	31	152	587	90	170	19	14	12	87	59	53	4	.290	.431
Neal Finn	2B112	R	29	118	413	46	113	22	2	0	45	21	42	2	.274	.337
Gordon Slade	SS82, 3B2	R	26	85	272	27	65	13	2	1	29	23	28	2	.239	.313
Wally Gilbert	3B145	R	30	145	552	60	147	25	6	0	46	39	38	3	.266	.333
Babe Herman	OF150	L	28	151	610	93	191	43	16	18	97	50	65	17	.313	.525
Johnny Frederick	OF145	R	29	146	611	81	165	34	8	17	51	24	50	2	.270	.435
Lefty O'Doul	OF132	L	34	134	512	85	172	32	11	7	75	48	16	5	.336	.482
Al Lopez	C105	R	22	111	360	38	97	13	4	0	40	28	33	1	.269	.328
Glenn Wright	SS75	R	30	77	268	36	76	9	4	9	32	14	35	1	.284	.448
Fresco Thompson	2B43, SS10, 3B5	R	29	74	181	26	48	6	1	1	21	23	16	5	.265	.326
Ernie Lombardi	C50	R	23	73	182	20	54	7	1	4	23	12	12	1	.297	.412
Rube Bressler	OF35, 1B1	R	36	67	153	22	43	4	5	0	26	11	10	0	.281	.373
Val Picinich	C15	R	34	24	45	5	12	4	0	1	4	4	9	1	.267	.422
1 Jake Flowers	2B6, SS1	R	29	22	31	3	7	0	0	0	1	7	4	1	.226	.226
Denny Sothern	OF10	R	27	19	31	10	5	1	0	0	0	4	8	0	.161	.194
Jack Warner (JJ)	SS2, 3B1	R	27	16	10	2	5	0	0	0	1	0	0	0	.500	.500
Ike Boone		L	34	6	5	0	1	0	0	0	0	1	2	0	.200	.200
Bobby Reis	3B6	R	22	6	9	3	2	0	0	0	1	0	2	0	.294	.294
Max Rosenfeld	OF3	R	28	3	9	0	2	1	0	0	1	0	1	0	.222	.333
Alta Cohen	OF1	L	22	3	1	0	2	0	0	0	0	0	2	0	.667	.667
1 Harvey Hendrick		L	33	1	0	0	0	0	0	0	0	0	0	0	.000	.000

NAME	T	AGE	W	L	PCT	SV	G	GS	CG	IP	H	BB	SO	SHO	ERA
		33	79	73	.520	18	153	153	64	1356	1520	351	546	9	3.84
Watty Clark	L	29	14	10	.583	1	34	28	16	233	243	52	96	3	3.21
Joe Shaute	L	31	11	8	.579	0	25	19	6	129	162	32	50	0	4.81
Dazzy Vance	R	40	11	13	.458	0	30	29	12	219	221	53	150	2	3.37
Fred Heimach	R	30	9	7	.563	1	31	10	7	135	145	23	43	1	3.47
Sloppy Thurston	R	32	9	9	.500	2	24	17	11	143	175	39	23	0	4.54
Dolf Luque	R	40	7	6	.538	0	19	15	5	103	122	27	25	0	5.01
Ray Phelps	R	27	7	9	.438	0	28	26	3	149	184	44	50	2	5.01
Jack Quinn	R	47	5	4	.556	15	39	1	0	64	65	24	25	0	2.67
Van Lingle Mungo	R	20	3	1	.750	0	5	4	2	31	33	12	18	1	2.32
Pea Ridge Day	R	32	2	2	.500	2	22	4	1	57	75	13	30	0	4.19
Cy Moore	R	26	2	3	.333	0	23	1	1	62	62	13	35	0	3.77
Earl Mattingly	R	26	0	0	—	0	14			14	15	10	6	0	0.00
Phil Gallivan	R	24	0	1	.000	0	5	1	0	15	13	7	5	0	5.40
1 Ray Moss	R	29	0	0	—	0	1	0	0	1	1	0	0	0	0.00

PITTSBURGH — 5th 75-79 .487 26 — JEWEL ENS

NAME	G by Pos	B	AGE	G	AB	R	H	2B	3B	HR	RBI	BB	SO	SB	BA	SA
TOTALS			27	155	5636	636	1425	243	70	41	597	493	454	59	.266	.360
George Grantham	1B78, 2B51	R	31	127	465	91	142	26	6	10	46	71	50	5	.305	.452
Tony Piet	2B44, SS1	R	24	44	167	22	50	12	4	0	24	13	24	10	.299	.419
Tommy Thevenow	SS132	R	27	120	404	35	86	12	1	0	38	28	22	0	.213	.248
Pie Traynor	3B155	R	32	155	615	81	183	37	15	2	103	54	28	6	.298	.416
Paul Waner	OF138, 1B21	L	28	150	559	88	180	35	10	6	70	73	21	6	.322	.453
Lloyd Waner	OF153, 2B1	L	25	154	681	90	214	25	13	4	57	39	16	7	.314	.407
Adam Comorosky	OF90	R	26	99	350	37	85	12	1	1	48	34	28	11	.243	.291
Eddie Phillips	C103	R	30	108	353	30	82	18	3	7	44	41	49	1	.232	.360
Gus Suhr	1B76	L	25	87	270	26	57	13	4	4	32	38	25	4	.211	.333
Woody Jensen	OF67	L	23	73	267	43	65	5	4	3	17	10	18	4	.243	.326
Ben Sankey	SS49, 2B2, 3B2	R	23	57	132	14	30	2	5	0	14	14	10	2	.227	.318
Howdy Groskloss	2B39, SS3	R	25	53	161	13	45	7	2	0	20	11	16	1	.280	.348
Erv Brame	P26	R	29	48	95	6	26	4	1	0	15	4	16	0	.274	.337
2 Earl Grace	C45	L	24	47	150	18	42	5	1	2	20	13	5	0	.280	.353
Jim Mosolf	OF4	L	25	39	44	7	11	1	0	1	6	8	6	0	.250	.341
Fred Bennett	OF21	R	29	32	89	6	25	4	0	1	8	11	6	0	.281	.371
Bill Regan	2B28	R	32	28	104	8	21	8	0	1	10	5	19	2	.202	.308
Hal Finney	C8	R	26	10	13	3	1	0	0	0	1	3	1	0	.308	.346
1 Rollie Hemsley	C9	R	24	10	35	3	6	3	0	0	3	1	6	1	.171	.257
Pete McClanahan		R	24	7	4	2	2	0	0	0	0	1	0	0	.500	.500
Bill Steinecke	C1	R	24	3	4	0	0	0	0	0	0	1	0	0	.000	.000

NAME	T	AGE	W	L	PCT	SV	G	GS	CG	IP	H	BB	SO	SHO	ERA
		29	75	79	.487	5	155	155	89	1390	1489	442	345	9	3.66
Heinie Meine	R	35	19	13	.594	0	36	35	22	284	278	87	58	3	2.98
Larry French	L	23	15	13	.536	1	39	33	20	276	301	70	73	1	3.26
Glenn Spencer	R	25	11	12	.478	3	38	18	11	187	180	65	51	1	3.42
Ray Kremer	R	38	11	15	.423	0	30	30	15	230	246	65	58	1	3.33
Erv Brame	R	29	9	13	.409	0	26	21	15	180	211	45	33	2	4.20
Bob Osborn	R	28	6	1	.857	0	27	2	0	65	85	20	9	0	4.98
Bill Harris	R	31	2	2	.500	0	11	3	1	30	31	16	10	1	0.87
Spades Wood	R	22	2	6	.250	0	15	10	2	64	69	46	33	0	6.05
Steve Swetonic (SA)	R	27	0	2	.000	0	14	0	0	28	28	16	8	0	3.86
Claude Willoughby	R	32	0	0	—	0	2	1	0	26	32	12	4	0	6.23
George Grant	R	28	0	0	—	0	17	2	1	28	17	6		0	7.41
Andy Bednar	R	22	0	0	—	0	2	0	0	4	10	0	0	0	11.25
Gus Dugas (BJ) 24															

PHILADELPHIA 6th 68-88 .429 35   BURT SHOTTON

NAME	G by Pos	B	AGE	G	AB	R	H	2B	3B	HR	RBI	BB	SO	SB	BA	SA
TOTALS			26	155	5375	684	1502	299	52	81	649	437	492	42	.279	.400
Don Hurst	1B135	L	25	137	489	63	149	37	5	11	91	64	28	8	.305	.468
Les Mallon	2B97, 1B5, SS3, 3B3	R	25	122	375	41	116	19	2	1	45	29	40	5	.309	.379
Dick Bartell	SS133, 3B2	R	23	135	554	88	160	43	7	0	34	27	38	6	.289	.392
Pinky Whitney	3B128	R	26	130	501	64	144	36	5	9	74	30	38	6	.287	.433
Buzz Arlett	OF94, 1B13	B	32	121	418	65	131	26	7	18	72	45	39	3	.313	.538
Fred Brickell	OF122	L	24	130	514	77	130	14	5	1	34	42	49	7	.253	.305
Chuck Klein	OF148	L	26	148	594	121	200	34	10	31	121	59	49	7	.337	.584
Spud Davis	C114	R	26	120	393	30	128	32	1	4	51	36	28	0	.326	.443
Barney Friberg	2B64, 3B25, 1B5, SS3	R	31	103	353	33	92	19	5	1	26	33	25	1	.261	.351
Fred Koster	OF41	L	25	76	151	21	34	2	2	0	8	14	21	4	.225	.265
Harry McCurdy	C45	L	31	66	150	21	43	9	0	1	25	23	16	2	.287	.367
Hal Lee	OF38	R	26	44	151	13	29	10	0	2	12	10	18	0	.221	.344
Doug Taitt	OF38	L	28	38	151	13	34	4	2	1	15	4	14	0	.225	.298
Hugh Willingham	SS8, 3B2, 2B2, OF1	R	26	23	35	5	9	2	1	0	3	2	9	0	.257	.457
Tony Rensa	C17	R	29	19	29	2	3	1	0	0	2	6	2	0	.103	.138
Bobby Stevens	SS10	L	24	12	35	3	12	0	0	0	4	2	2	0	.343	.343
Gene Connell	C6	R	25	6	12	1	3	0	0	0	1	0	3	0	.250	.250

NAME	T	AGE	W	L	PCT	SV	G	GS	CG	IP	H	BB	SO	SHO	ERA
TOTALS		28	66	88	.429	16	155	155	60	1360	1603	511	499	6	4.58
Jumbo Jim Elliott	L	30	19	14	.576	5	52	30	12	249	286	83	99	2	4.27
Ray Benge	R	29	14	18	.438	2	38	31	16	247	251	61	117	2	3.17
Phil Collins	R	29	12	16	.429	4	42	27	16	240	268	83	73	2	3.86
Clise Dudley	R	27	8	14	.364	0	30	24	8	179	206	56	50	0	3.52
Frank Watt	R	28	5	5	.500	2	38	5	2	123	147	49	25	0	4.83
2 Sheriff Blake	R	31	4	5	.444	1	14	9	1	71	90	35	31	0	5.58
Stew Bolen	L	28	3	12	.200	0	28	16	2	99	117	63	55	0	6.36
Ben Shields	R	28	1	0	1.000	0	4	1	0	6	9	7	0	0	16.20
Bob Adams	R	24	0	1	.000	0	6	0	0	14	1	3	0	0	9.00
Chet Nichols	R	33	0	1	.000	0	4	0	0	6	11	1	1	0	9.00
Hal Elliott	R	32	0	2	.000	2	16	4	0	33	46	19	8	0	9.55
Ed Failenstein	R	22	0	0	—	0	24	0	0	42	56	26	15	0	7.07
Dutch Schesler	R	31	0	0		0	17	0	0	38	65	18	14	0	7.34
Lil Stoner	R	32	0	0	—	0	7	1	0	14	22	5	2	0	6.43
John Milligan	R	27	0	0		0	3	0	0	4	1	4	6	0	3.38
Hal Wiltse	L	27	0	0		0	1	0	0	1	3	1	0	0	9.00

BOSTON 7th 64-90 .416 37   BILL McKECHNIE

NAME	G by Pos	B	AGE	G	AB	R	H	2B	3B	HR	RBI	BB	SO	SB	BA	SA
TOTALS			30	156	5296	533	1367	221	59	34	490	368	430	46	.258	.341
Earl Sheely	1B143	R	38	147	538	30	147	15	2	1	77	34	21	0	.273	.314
Freddie Maguire	2B148	R	32	148	492	36	.112	18	2	0	26	16	26	3	.228	.272
Rabbit Maranville	SS137, 2B11	R	39	145	562	69	146	22	5	0	33	56	34	9	.260	.317
Billy Urbanski	3B68, SS19	R	28	82	303	22	72	13	4	0	17	10	32	3	.238	.307
Wes Schulmerich	OF87	R	29	95	327	36	101	17	7	2	43	28	30	0	.309	.422
Wally Berger	OF156, 1B1	R	25	156	617	94	199	44	8	19	84	55	70	13	.323	.512
Red Worthington	OF124	R	25	128	491	47	143	25	10	4	44	26	38	1	.291	.407
Al Spohrer	C111	R	28	114	350	23	84	17	5	0	27	22	27	2	.240	.317
Lance Richbourg	OF71	L	33	97	286	32	82	11	6	2	29	19	14	9	.287	.388
Randy Moore	OF29, 3B22, 2B1	L	26	83	192	19	50	8	1	3	34	13	3	1	.260	.359
Johnny Neun	1B36	B	30	79	104	17	23	1	3	0	11	11	14	2	.221	.288
Bill Cronin	C50	R	28	51	107	8	22	6	1	0	10	7	5	0	.206	.280
Al Bool	C37	L	30	49	85	5	16	1	0	0	6	9	13	0	.188	.200
Bill Dreesen	3B47	R	26	48	180	38	40	10	4	1	10	23	23	1	.222	.339
Buster Chatham	SS6, 3B6	R	29	17	44	4	10	1	0	1	3	6	6	0	.227	.318
Earl Clark	OF14	R	23	16	50	8	11	2	0	0	4	7	4	1	.220	.260
Charlie Wilson	3B14	R	26	16	58	7	11	4	0	1	11	3	5	0	.190	.310
2 Bill Hunnefield	3B5, 2B4	B	32	11	21	2	6	0	0	0	1	2	1	0	.286	.286
Bucky Walters	3B6, 2B3	R	22	9	38	2	8	2	0	0	1	1	6	0	.211	.263
John Scalzi		R	24	2	1	0	0	0	0	0	0	0	1	0	.000	.000
Pat Veltman		R	25	1	1	0	0	0	0	0	0	0	0	0	.000	.000

NAME	T	AGE	W	L	PCT	SV	G	GS	CG	IP	H	BB	SO	SHO	ERA
TOTALS		30	64	90	.416	9	156	156	78	1380	1465	406	419	12	3.90
Ed Brandt	L	26	18	11	.621	2	33	29	23	250	228	77	112	3	2.92
Tom Zachary	L	35	11	15	.423	2	33	28	16	229	243	53	64	3	3.10
Socks Seibold	R	35	10	18	.357	0	33	29	10	206	226	65	50	3	4.67
Fred Frankhouse	R	27	8	8	.500	1	26	15	6	127	125	43	50	0	4.04
Ben Cantwell	R	29	7	9	.438	2	33	16	9	156	160	34	32	2	3.63
Bill Sheidel	R	34	6	10	.375	0	27	14	8	138	163	35	34	0	4.24
Bruce Cunninghaam	R	25	3	12	.200	1	33	16	6	137	157	54	32	1	4.47
2 Ray Moss	R	29	3		.250	1	12	5	0	45	56	16	14	0	4.60
Bill McAfee	R	23	0	1	.000	0	18	1	0	30	39	10	9	0	6.30
Bob Brown	R	20	0	1	.000	0	1	0	0	6	9	3	2	0	9.00
Hal Haid	R	33	0	2	.000	1	27	0	0	56	59	16	20	0	4.50

CINCINNATI 8th 58-96 .377 43   DAN HOWLEY

NAME	G by Pos	B	AGE	G	AB	R	H	2B	3B	HR	RBI	BB	SO	SB	BA	SA
TOTALS			30	154	5343	592	1439	241	70	21	562	403	463	24	.269	.352
2 Harvey Hendrick	1B137	R	33	137	530	74	167	32	9	1	75	53	40	3	.315	.415
Tony Cuccinello	2B154	R	23	154	575	67	181	39	11	2	93	54	28	1	.315	.431
Leo Durocher	SS120	R	25	121	361	26	82	11	5	1	29	18	32	0	.227	.294
Joe Stripp	3B96, 1B9	R	27	105	426	71	138	26	2	3	42	21	31	5	.324	.415
Estel Crabtree	OF101, 3B4, 1B2	L	27	117	443	70	119	12	6	4	37	23	33	3	.269	.377
2 Taylor Douthit	OF95	R	30	95	374	42	98	9	1	0	24	42	24	4	.262	.291
Edd Roush	OF88	L	38	101	376	46	102	12	5	1	41	17	5	0	.271	.338
Clyde Sukeforth	C106	R	29	112	351	22	90	15	4	0	25	38	13	0	.256	.322
Nick Cullop	OF83	R	32	104	334	29	88	23	7	8	48	22	86	1	.263	.446
Red Lucas	P29	R	29	97	153	15	43	4	0	0	17	12	9	0	.281	.307
Cliff Heathcote	OF59	L	33	90	252	24	65	15	6	0	28	32	16	3	.258	.365
Hod Ford	SS73, 2B3, 3B1	R	33	84	175	18	40	8	1	0	13	13	13	0	.229	.286
Clyde Beck	3B38, SS6	R	31	53	136	17	21	4	2	0	19	21	14	1	.154	.213
Casper Asbjornson (BG)	C31	R	22	45	118	13	36	7	1	0	22	7	23	0	.305	.381
1 Wally Roettger	OF44	R	29	49	185	25	65	11	4	1	20	7	9	1	.351	.470
Lena Styles	C31	R	31	34	87	7	21	3	0	0	5	8	7	0	.241	.276
Frank Sigafoos	3B15, SS2	R	27	21	65	6	11	2	0	0	8	0	6	0	.169	.200
Mickey Heath (BA)	1B7	L	27	7	26	2	7	0	0	0	3	2	5	0	.269	.269
Chuck Dressen	3B4	R	32	5	15	0	1	0	0	0	0	1	0	0	.067	.067
Gene Moore	OF3	L	21	4	14	2	2	1	0	0	1	0	2	0	.143	.214
Ray Fitzgerald		R	26	1	1	0	0	0	0	0	0	0	0	0	.000	.000
Harry Heilmann (IL) 36																

NAME	T	AGE	W	L	PCT	SV	G	GS	CG	IP	H	BB	SO	SHO	ERA
TOTALS		31	58	96	.377	6	154	154	70	1345	1545	399	317	7	4.22
Red Lucas	R	29	14	13	.519	0	29	29	24	238	261	39	56	3	3.59
Si Johnson	R	24	11	19	.367	0	42	33	14	262	273	74	95	0	3.78
Larry Benton	R	33	10	15	.400	2	38	23	12	204	240	53	35	2	3.35
Benny Frey	R	24	8	12	.400	2	34	17	7	134	166	36	19	1	4.90
Eppa Rixey	L	40	4	7	.364	0	22	17	4	127	143	30	22	0	3.90
Jack Ogden	R	33	4	8	.333	1	22	9	3	89	79	32	24	1	2.93
Ray Kolp	R	36	4	9	.308	1	30	10	2	107	135	39	24	0	4.96
Ownie Carroll	R	28	3	9	.250	0	29	12	4	107	135	51	24	0	5.55
Al Eckert	L	25	0	1	.000	0	14	1	0	19	26	9	5	0	9.00
Whitey Hilcher	R	22	0	1		0	9	3	0	9	9	6	2	0	3.00
Biff Wysong	L	26	0	2	.000	0	12	2	0	22	25	23	5	0	7.77
Ed Strelecki	R	23	0	0		0	13	0	0	24	37	9	3	0	9.38

WORLD SERIES — ST. LOUIS (NL) 4   PHILADELPHIA (AL) 3

LINE SCORES

TEAM	1	2	3	4	5	6	7	8	9	10	11	12	R	H	E

Game 1 October 1 at St. Louis

	1	2	3	4	5	6	7	8	9	R	H	E
PHI (AL)	0	0	4	0	0	0	2	0	0	6	11	0
STL (NL)	2	0	0	0	0	0	0	0	0	2	12	0

Grove | Derringer, Johnson (8)

Game 2 October 2 at St. Louis

	1	2	3	4	5	6	7	8	9	R	H	E
PHI	0	0	0	0	0	0	0	0	0	0	3	0
STL	0	1	0	0	0	0	1	0	X	2	6	1

Earnshaw | Hallahan

Game 3 October 5 at Philadelphia

	1	2	3	4	5	6	7	8	9	R	H	E
STL	0	2	0	2	0	0	0	0	1	5	12	0
PHI	0	0	0	0	0	0	0	0	2	2	2	0

Grimes | Grove, Mahaffey (9)

Game 4 October 6 at Philadelphia

	1	2	3	4	5	6	7	8	9	R	H	E
STL	0	0	0	0	0	0	0	0	0	0	2	1
PHI	1	0	0	0	0	2	0	0	X	3	10	0

Johnson, Lindsey (6), Derringer (8) | Earnshaw

Game 5 October 7 at Philadelphia

	1	2	3	4	5	6	7	8	9	R	H	E
STL	1	0	0	0	0	2	0	1	1	5	12	0
PHI	0	0	0	0	0	0	1	0	0	1	9	0

Hallahan | Hoyt, Walberg (7), Rommel (9)

Game 6 October 9 at St. Louis

	1	2	3	4	5	6	7	8	9	R	H	E
PHI	0	0	0	0	4	0	4	0	0	8	8	1
STL	0	0	0	0	0	1	0	0	0	1	5	2

Grove | Derringer, Johnson (5), Lindsey (7), Rhem (9)

Game 7 October 10 at St. Louis

	1	2	3	4	5	6	7	8	9	R	H	E
PHI	0	0	0	0	0	0	0	0	2	2	7	1
STL	2	0	2	0	0	0	0	0	X	4	5	0

Earnshaw, Walberg (8) | Grimes, Hallahan (9)

COMPOSITE BATTING

NAME	POS	G	AB	R	H	2B	3B	HR	RBI	BA
St. Louis (NL)										
Totals		7	229	19	54	11	0	2	17	.236
Frisch	2B	7	27	2	7	2	0	0	1	.259
Bottomley	1B	7	25	2	4	1	0	0	2	.160
Martin	OF	7	24	5	12	4	0	1	5	.500
Hafey	OF	6	24	1	4	0	0	0	0	.167
Gelbert	SS	7	23	0	6	1	0	0	3	.261
Wilson	C	7	23	0	5	0	0	0	0	.217
High	3B	4	15	3	4	0	0	0	0	.267
Watkins	OF	5	14	4	4	1	0	1	2	.286
Roettger	OF	3	14	1	4	1	0	0	0	.286
Flowers	3B	5	11	1	1	1	0	0	0	.091
Grimes	P	3	7	0	2	0	0	0	2	.286
Hallahan	P	3	6	0	0	0	0	0	0	.000
Adams	3B	2	4	1	1	0	0	0	0	.250
Orsatti	OF	1	3	0	0	0	0	0	0	.000
Blades	PH	2	2	0	0	0	0	0	0	.000
Collins	PH	2	2	0	0	0	0	0	0	.000
Derringer	P	3	2	0	0	0	0	0	0	.000
Johnson	C	2	2	0	0	0	0	0	0	.000
Mancuso	C	2	1	0	0	0	0	0	0	.000
Lindsey	P	2	1	0	0	0	0	0	0	—
Rhem	P	1	0	0	0	0	0	0	0	—
Philadelphia (AL)										
Totals		7	227	22	50	5	0	3	20	.220
Simmons	OF	7	27	4	9	2	0	2	8	.333
Bishop	2B	7	27	4	4	0	0	0	0	.148
Miller	OF	7	26	3	7	1	0	0	1	.269
Williams	SS	7	25	2	8	1	0	0	1	.320
Cochrane	C	7	25	2	4	0	0	0	1	.160
Foxx	1B	7	23	3	8	0	0	1	3	.348
Haas	OF	7	23	1	3	1	0	0	2	.130
Dykes	3B	7	22	2	5	0	0	0	1	.227
Grove	P	3	10	0	0	0	0	0	0	.000
Earnshaw	P	3	8	0	0	0	0	0	0	.000
Moore	OF	2	3	0	1	0	0	0	0	.333
McNair	2B	2	2	0	0	0	0	0	0	.000
Cramer	PH	2	2	0	1	0	0	0	0	.500
Hoyt	P	1	2	0	0	0	0	0	0	.000
Boley	PH	1	1	0	0	0	0	0	0	.000
Hoving	PH	1	1	0	0	0	0	0	0	.000
Walberg	P	3	1	0	0	0	0	0	0	—
Mahaffey	P	1	1	0	0	0	0	0	0	.000

Rommel P 0-0, Todt PH 0-0

COMPOSITE PITCHING

NAME	G	IP	H	BB	SO	W	L	SV	ERA
St. Louis (NL)									
Totals	7	62	50	28	46	4	3	1	2.32
Hallahan	3	18.1	12	8	12	2	0	1	0.49
Grimes	2	17.2	9	9	11	2	0	0	2.04
Derringer	3	12.2	14	7	14	0	2	0	4.26
Johnson	3	9	10	1	6	0	1	0	3.00
Lindsey	2	3.1	4	3	2	0	0	0	5.40
Rhem	1	1	1	1	1	0	0	0	0.00
Philadelphia (AL)									
Totals	7	61	54	9	41	3	4	0	2.66
Grove	3	26	28	2	16	2	1	0	2.42
Earnshaw	3	24	12	4	20	1	2	0	1.88
Hoyt	1	6	7	0	1	0	1	0	4.50
Walberg	2	3	3	2	4	0	0	0	3.00
Mahaffey	1	1	1	1	0	0	0	0	9.00
Rommel	1	1	3	0	1	0	0	0	9.00

1932 Start with Hornsby and End with Ruth

With his Chicago Cubs in first place on August 2, a funny thing happened to manager Rogers Hornsby; he was bounced. Despite the lofty perch of his charges, Hornsby felt the axe after a severe disagreement in policy matters with president William Veeck, the father of baseball's daring promotion genius, Bill Veeck. When first baseman Charley Grimm was handed the reins, the press wondered if the Cubs could maintain their slight lead over the Pittsburgh Pirates.

As it turned out, the Bruins rallied under Jolly Cholly's leadership to stay out in front and wind up first by four games. Riggs Stephenson knocked in 85 runs in providing heart for the lineup, and player Grimm aided his managerial cause by driving 80 Cubs home. Billy Herman steadied the infield with his keystone play, and Gabby Hartnett tied all the loose ends together with his brainy receiving. A sore spot was eased late in the year when ex-Yankee Mark Koenig was brought to play shortstop after Billy Jurges had been shot in the hand by a girl in Chicago. Rookie Lou Warneke proved to be the league pitching sensation by posting an E. R. A. of 2.37 to go with 22 victories, as Guy Bush, Pat Malone, and Charlie Root provided veteran pitching talent to complement the rookie s performance.

Pittsburgh used the batting of Paul Waner, Lloyd Waner, Pie Traynor, and rookie Arky Vaughan to take second honors after a slow start. Brooklyn moved a notch up to third on the bat of Lefty O'Doul's .368 league-leading average, while Philadelphia could only manage fourth—despite the League's best offense led by Chuck Klein and Don Hurst. New York fell to sixth as manager John McGraw resigned early in the season for health reasons after 30 years at the helm. The defending champion Cardinals, despite 18 wins from rookie pitcher Dizzy Dean, collapsed into sixth place, due to age and the failure of several key personnel to perform at their previous year's level.

In the American League, the New York Yankees returned to the top after three years of Philadelphia Athletics' monopoly of the pennant penthouse. The Yankees' 107 wins were good enough for a 13-game bulge over the Mackmen, as Joe McCarthy won his first junior circuit pennant in an easy fashion. The schedule, which called for the Yankees to play the better teams in the first half and the weaker western teams as the major fare after June, gave way to an early Yankee lead and little doubt over the final outcome.

In New York's victory, Babe Ruth, at the ripe age of 37, still managed 41 homers, and Lou Gehrig rode the crest wave of his career with a .349 average and 151 Rbl's. Tony Lazzeri and Ben Chapman each sent over 100 Yankees across the plate, and young Frankie Crosetti filled the shortstop slot and went to his first World Series. Lefty Gomez and Red Ruffing provided a left-right pitching combination unmatched in the League while supported by Johnny Allen, who was 17-4 in his maiden season.

Although relegated to runner-ups, Philadelphia unseated Cubs Yankees as the home run powerhouse of the league, directly as the result of Jimmie Foxx—who took the home run crown from the head of Ruth for the first time since 1925 by launching 58 clouts into the atmosphere. Foxx's 169 RBI's also paced the league, and his .364 average barely trailed Dale Alexander's for the batting crown. Al Simmons and Mickey Cochrane also contributed standout offensive years, but the Athletics' pitching fell off badly from its championship performances, as even Lefty Grove, with a 25-10 record, was not anywhere near his 1931 mark of 31-4. The Senators closely followed the A's in third on the strength of the batting of Heinie Manush and Joe Cronin and the pitching of General Crowder's league-leading 26 wins.

For the third time in six years, the Yankees swept the Series in four games. The Yankees' attack completely destroyed the Cubs as Gehrig hit three home runs and Ruth and Lazzeri each contributed a pair. One of Ruth's home runs came in the third game and was a blast which became permanently lodged in baseball's folklore. There were bad feelings between the two teams, and Ruth supposedly responded to the Cubs' heckling by pointing to the center field bleachers with an 0-2 count and calling his home run shot. Charley Root, the pitcher who served up the legendary blast, went to his grave denying that Ruth ever called the home run which, ironically enough, turned out to be the Babe's final World Series round-tripper.

1932 AMERICAN LEAGUE

NAME	G by Pos	B	AGE	G	AB	R	H	2B	3B	HR	RBI	BB	SO	SB	BA	SA
NEW YORK	**1st 107-47 .695**			**JOE McCARTHY**												
	TOTALS		28	156	5477	1002	1564	279	82	160	955	766	527	77	.286	.454
Lou Gehrig	1B156	L	29	156	596	138	208	42	9	34	151	108	38	4	.349	.621
Tony Lazzeri	2B134, 3B5	R	28	142	510	79	153	28	16	15	113	82	64	11	.300	.506
Frankie Crosetti	SS84, 3B33, 2B1	R	21	116	398	47	96	20	9	5	57	51	51	3	.241	.374
Joe Sewell	3B123	L	33	125	503	95	137	21	3	11	68	56	3	0	.272	.392
Babe Ruth	OF128, 1B1	L	37	133	457	120	156	13	5	41	137	130	62	2	.341	.661
Earle Combs	OF139	L	33	144	591	143	190	32	10	9	65	81	16	3	.321	.455
Ben Chapman	OF150	R	23	151	581	101	174	41	15	10	107	71	55	38	.299	.473
Bill Dickey (SL)	C108	L	25	108	423	66	131	20	4	15	84	34	13	2	.310	.482
Sammy Byrd	OF91	R	25	105	209	49	62	12	1	8	30	30	20	1	.297	.478
Lyn Lary	SS80, 1B5, 2B2, 3B2, OF1	R	26	91	280	56	65	14	4	3	39	52	28	9	.232	.343
Art Jorgens	C56	R	27	56	151	13	33	7	1	2	19	14	11	0	.219	.318
Red Ruffing	P35	R	28	55	124	20	38	6	1	3	19	6	10	0	.306	.444
Myril Hoag	OF35, 1B1	R	24	46	54	18	20	5	0	1	7	7	13	1	.370	.519
Doc Farrell	2B16, SS5, 1B2, 3B1	R	30	26	63	4	11	1	1	0	4	2	8	0	.175	.222
Jack Saltzgaver	2B16	L	27	20	47	10	6	2	1	0	5	10	10	1	.128	.213
Eddie Phillips	C9	R	31	9	31	4	9	1	0	2	4	2	3	1	.290	.516
Joe Glenn	C5	R	23	6	16	0	2	0	0	0	0	1	0	5	.125	.125
Roy Schalk	2B3	R	23	3	12	3	3	1	0	0	0	2	2	0	.250	.333
Dusty Cooke (BL)		L	25	3	0	1	0	0	0	0	0	0	0	0	—	—
PHILADELPHIA	**2nd 94-60 .610 13**			**CONNIE MACK**												
	TOTALS		30	154	5537	981	1606	303	52	172	923	647	640	38	.290	.457
Jimmie Foxx	1B141, 3B13	R	24	154	585	151	213	33	9	58	169	116	96	3	.364	.749
Max Bishop	2B106	L	32	114	409	89	104	24	2	5	37	110	43	2	.254	.359
Eric McNair	SS133	R	23	135	554	87	158	47	3	18	95	26	49	2	.285	.478
Jimmy Dykes	3B141, SS10, 2B1	R	35	153	558	71	148	29	5	7	90	77	65	8	.265	.373
Doc Cramer (BC)	OF86	L	26	92	384	73	129	27	6	3	46	17	27	3	.336	.461
Mule Haas	OF137	L	28	143	558	91	170	28	5	6	65	62	49	1	.305	.405
Al Simmons	OF154	R	30	154	670	144	216	28	9	35	151	47	76	4	.322	.548
Mickey Cochrane	C137, OF1	L	29	139	518	118	152	35	4	23	112	100	22	0	.293	.510
Bing Miller	OF84	R	37	95	305	40	90	17	4	7	58	20	11	7	.295	.446
Dib Williams	2B53, SS3	R	32	62	215	30	54	10	1	4	24	22	23	0	.251	.363
Lefty Grove	P44	L	32	44	107	10	18	1	0	4	12	5	51	0	.168	.290
George Earnshaw	P36	R	32	36	91	10	26	4	1	0	9	0	12	0	.286	.352
Johnnie Heving	C28	R	36	33	77	14	21	6	1	0	10	7	6	0	.273	.377
Ed Coleman (BN)	OF16	L	30	26	73	13	25	7	0	1	13	1	6	1	.342	.507
Oscar Roettger	1B15	R	32	26	60	7	14	1	0	0	6	5	4	0	.233	.250
Ed Madjeski	C8	R	23	17	35	4	8	0	0	0	3	1	4	0	.229	.229
1 Joe Boley	SS10	R	35	10	34	2	7	2	0	0	4	1	4	0	.206	.265
Al Reiss	SS6	R	33	9	5	0	1	0	0	0	1	1	1	0	.200	.200
John Jones	OF1	L	31	4	6	0	1	0	0	0	0	0	3	0	.167	.167
Ed Cihocki		R	25	1	4	0	0	0	0	0	0	0	1	0	.000	.000
WASHINGTON	**3rd 93-61 .604 14**			**WALTER JOHNSON**												
	TOTALS		31	154	5515	840	1565	303	100	61	776	505	442	70	.284	.408
Joe Kuhel	1B85	L	26	101	347	52	101	21	5	4	52	32	19	5	.291	.415
Buddy Myer	2B139	L	28	143	577	120	161	38	16	5	52	69	33	12	.279	.426
Joe Cronin	SS141	R	25	143	557	95	177	43	18	6	116	66	45	7	.318	.492
Ossie Bluege	3B149	R	31	149	507	64	131	22	4	5	64	84	41	9	.258	.345
Carl Reynolds (BJ)	OF95	R	29	102	406	53	124	28	7	9	63	14	19	8	.305	.475
Sammy West	OF143	L	27	146	554	88	159	27	12	6	83	48	57	4	.287	.412
Heinie Manush	OF146	L	30	149	625	121	214	41	14	14	116	36	29	7	.342	.520
Roy Spencer	C98	R	32	102	317	28	78	9	0	1	41	24	17	0	.246	.284
Sam Rice	OF69	L	42	106	288	58	93	16	7	1	34	32	6	7	.323	.438
Joe Judge	1B78	L	38	82	291	45	75	16	3	2	39	37	19	3	.258	.364
Dave Harris	OF34	R	32	81	156	26	51	7	4	6	29	19	34	4	.327	.538
Moe Berg	C75	R	30	75	195	16	46	8	1	1	26	8	13	1	.236	.303
John Kerr	2B17, SS14, 3B8	R	33	51	132	14	36	6	1	0	15	13	3	3	.273	.333
Monty Weaver	P43	R	24	44	94	13	27	6	1	0	7	3	16	0	.287	.372
Howie Maple	C41	R	28	44	41	6	10	0	1	0	7	7	7	0	.244	.293
Wes Kingdon	3B8, SS4	R	28	18	34	10	11	3	1	0	3	5	2	0	.324	.471
Jim McLeod	SS1	R	23	7	9	1	0	0	0	0	0	1	0	0	—	—
Danny Musser	3B1	L	26	4	2	0	1	0	0	0	0	0	0	0	.500	.500

NAME	T	AGE	W	L	PCT	SV	G	GS	CG	IP	H	BB	SO	SHO	ERA
		29	107	47	.695	15	156	156	95	1409	1425	561	780	11	3.98
Lefty Gomez	L	23	24	7	.774	1	37	31	21	265	266	105	176	1	4.21
Red Ruffing	R	28	18	7	.720	2	35	29	22	259	219	115	190	3	3.09
Johnny Allen	R	27	17	4	.810	4	43	21	13	192	162	76	109	3	3.70
George Pipgras	R	32	16	9	.640	0	32	27	14	219	235	87	111	2	4.19
Herb Pennock	L	38	9	5	.643	0	22	21	9	147	191	38	54	1	4.59
2 Danny MacFayden	R	27	7	5	.583	1	17	15	8	121	137	37	33	0	3.94
Jumbo Brown	R	25	5	2	.714	1	19	3	3	56	58	30	31	1	4.50
Ed Wells	L	32	3	3	.500	2	22	0	0	32	38	12	13	0	4.22
2 Wilcy Moore	R	35	2	0	1.000	4	10	1	0	25	27	6	8	0	2.52
1 Ivy Andrews	R	25	2	1	.667	0	4	1	1	25	29	9	7	0	1.80
Hank Johnson (IL)	R	26	2	2	.500	0	5	4	2	31	34	15	27	0	4.93
Charlie Devens	R	22	1	0	1.000	0	1	1	1	9	6	7	4	0	2.00
1 Gordon Rhodes	R	24	1	2	.333	0	10	2	1	24	25	21	5	0	7.88
Johnny Murphy	R	23	0	0	—	0	2	0	0	3	7	3	2	0	18.00
		29	94	60	.610	10	154	154	94	1386	1477	511	595	10	4.45
Lefty Grove	L	32	25	10	.714	7	44	30	27	292	269	79	188	4	2.84
George Earnshaw	R	32	19	13	.594	0	36	33	20	245	262	94	109	1	4.78
Rube Walberg	L	35	17	10	.630	1	41	34	19	272	305	103	96	3	4.73
Roy Mahaffey	R	28	13	13	.500	0	37	28	13	223	245	96	106	0	5.09
Tony Freitas	L	24	12	5	.706	0	23	18	10	150	150	48	31	1	3.84
Lew Krausse	R	20	4	1	.800	0	20	3	2	57	64	24	16	1	4.58
Sugar Cain	R	25	3	4	.429	0	10	6	3	45	42	28	24	0	5.00
Eddie Rommel	R	34	1	2	.333	2	17	0	0	65	84	18	16	0	5.54
Joe Bowman	R	22	1	0	1.000	0	7	0	0	11	14	6	4	0	8.18
Jim McKeithan	R	25	0	1	.000	0	4	0	0	13	18	5	0	0	6.93
Jimmie DeShong	R	22	0	0	—	0	6	0	0	10	17	9	5	0	11.70
Irv Stein	R	21	0	0	—	0	1	0	0	3	7	1	0	0	12.00
		29	93	61	.604	22	154	154	66	1384	1463	526	437	10	4.16
General Crowder	R	33	26	13	.667	1	50	39	21	327	319	77	103	3	3.33
Monty Weaver	R	24	22	10	.688	2	43	30	13	234	236	112	83	1	4.08
Lloyd Brown	L	27	15	12	.556	5	46	24	10	203	239	55	53	2	4.44
Firpo Marberry	R	33	8	4	.667	13	54	15	8	198	202	72	66	1	4.00
2 Tommy Thomas	R	32	8	7	.533	0	18	14	7	117	114	46	36	1	3.95
Bill McAfee	R	24	6	1	.857	0	8	5	2	41	47	22	10	0	3.95
1 Carl Fischer	L	26	3	2	.600	1	7	5	1	51	57	31	23	1	4.94
Bobby Burke	L	25	3	6	.333	0	22	10	2	91	98	44	32	0	5.14
Frank Ragland	R	28	1	0	1.000	0	12	1	0	38	54	21	11	0	7.34
2 Dick Coffman	R	25	0	0	.143	0	9	2	0	76	92	31	17	1	4.85
Bob Friedrich	R	25	0	0		0	1	0	0	6	9	2	0	0	11.25
Bud Thomas	R	21	0	0		0	1	0	0	4	6	1	0	0	0.00
Ed Edelen	R	20	0	1	.000	0	2	0	0	3	6	3	2	0	27.00

172

CLEVELAND — 4th 87-65 .572 19 — ROGER PECKINPAUGH

NAME	G by Pos	B	AGE	G	AB	R	H	2B	3B	HR	RBI	BB	SO	SB	BA	SA
TOTALS			27	153	5412	845	1544	310	74	78	778	556	454	52	.285	.413
Eddie Morgan	1B142	R	28	144	532	96	156	32	7	4	68	94	44	7	.293	.402
2 Bill Cissel	2B129, SS6	R	28	131	541	78	173	35	6	6	93	28	25	18	.320	.440
Johnny Burnett	SS103, 2B26	L	27	129	512	81	152	23	5	4	53	46	27	2	.297	.383
Willie Kamm	3B148	R	32	148	524	76	150	34	9	3	83	75	36	6	.286	.403
Dick Porter	OF145	L	30	146	621	106	191	42	8	4	60	64	43	5	.308	.424
Earl Averill	OF153	L	30	153	631	116	198	37	14	32	124	75	40	5	.314	.569
Joe Vosmik	OF153	R	22	153	621	106	194	39	12	10	97	58	42	2	.312	.442
Luke Sewell	C84	R	31	87	300	36	76	20	2	2	52	38	24	4	.253	.353
Glenn Myatt	C65	L	34	82	252	45	62	12	1	8	46	28	21	2	.246	.397
Ed Montague	SS57, 3B11	R	26	66	192	29	47	5	1	0	24	21	24	3	.245	.281
Bruce Connatser	1B14	R	29	23	60	8	14	3	1	0	4	4	8	1	.233	.317
Charlie Jamieson (CJ)	OF2	L	39	16	16	0	1	1	0	0	0	2	3	0	.063	.125
Mike Powers	OF8	L	26	14	33	4	6	4	0	0	5	2	2	0	.182	.303
Frankie Pytlak	C12	R	23	12	29	5	7	1	1	0	4	3	2	0	.241	.345
1 Johnny Hodapp	2B7	R	26	7	16	2	2	1	0	0	0	0	2	0	.125	.188
1 Bob Seeds	OF1	R	25	2	1	0	0	0	0	0	0	0	0	0	.000	.000

Boze Berger 22 R 0-1, 2 Joe Boley 35 R 1-4

NAME	T	AGE	W	L	PCT	SV	G	GS	CG	IP	H	BB	SO	SHO	ERA
		26	87	65	.572	8	153	153	93	1377	1506	446	439	6	4.12
Wes Ferrell	R	24	23	13	.639	1	38	34	26	288	299	104	105	3	3.65
Clint Brown	R	28	15	12	.556	1	37	32	21	268	298	50	59	1	4.07
Mel Harder	R	22	15	13	.536	0	39	32	17	255	277	68	90	1	3.74
Willis Hudlin	R	26	12	8	.600	2	33	21	11	182	204	59	65	0	4.70
Sarge Connally	R	33	8	6	.571	0	35	7	4	112	119	42	32	1	4.34
Oral Hildebrand	R	25	8	6	.571	0	27	15	7	129	124	62	49	0	3.70
2 Jack Russell	R	26	5	7	.375	0	18	16	6	113	146	27	23	0	4.70
Ralph Winegarner	R	22	1	0	1.000	0	5	1	1	17	13	5	10	0	1.06
Monte Pearson	R	23	0	0	—	0	8	0	0	8	10	11	5	0	10.13
1 Pete Appleton	R	28	0	0	—	0	4	0	0	5	11	3	1	0	16.20
Leo Moon	L	33	0	0	—	0	6	0	0	6	11	7	1	0	10.50

DETROIT — 5th 76-75 .503 29.5 — BUCKY HARRIS

NAME	G by Pos	B	AGE	G	AB	R	H	2B	3B	HR	RBI	BB	SO	SB	BA	SA
TOTALS			27	153	5409	799	1479	291	80	80	742	486	523	105	.273	.401
Harry Davis	1B141	L	22	141	590	92	159	32	13	4	74	60	53	12	.269	.388
Charlie Gehringer	2B152	L	29	152	618	112	184	44	11	19	107	68	34	9	.298	.497
Billy Rogell	SS139, 3B4	B	27	144	554	88	150	29	6	9	61	50	38	14	.271	.394
Heinie Schuble	3B76, SS16	R	25	102	340	58	97	19	8	3	51	39	18	1	.287	.417
2 Earl Webb	OF85	L	34	88	338	49	97	19	3	6	36	35	29	0	.287	.426
Gee Walker	OF116	R	24	127	480	71	155	32	6	8	78	13	38	30	.323	.465
John Stone	OF142	L	26	145	582	106	173	35	12	17	108	58	64	2	.297	.486
Ray Hayworth	C106	R	28	109	338	41	99	24	2	2	44	31	22	1	.293	.382
Billy Rhiel	3B37, 1B12, OF8, 2B1	R	31	85	250	30	70	13	3	3	38	17	23	2	.280	.392
Jo-Jo White	OF48	L	23	80	208	25	54	6	3	2	21	22	19	6	.260	.346
Nolen Richardson	3B65, SS4	R	29	69	155	13	34	5	1	0	12	9	13	1	.219	.277
Muddy Ruel	C49	L	36	51	136	10	32	4	2	0	18	17	6	1	.235	.294
1 Roy Johnson	OF48	L	29	49	195	33	49	14	3	2	22	20	26	7	.251	.390
Gene Desautels	C24	R	25	28	72	8	17	2	0	0	3	13	11	0	.236	.264
Bill Lawrence	OF15	R	26	25	46	10	10	1	0	0	3	5	5	0	.217	.239
1 Dale Alexander	1B2	R	29	23	16	0	4	0	0	0	4	6	2	0	.250*	
Frank Doljack	OF6	R	24	8	26	5	10	1	2	0	5	1	3	0	.385	.538
George Susce	C2	R	24	3	1	0	0	0	0	0	0	0	1	0	—	—

*Alexander, also with Boston, league leader in BA with .367

NAME	T	AGE	W	L	PCT	SV	G	GS	CG	IP	H	BB	SO	SHO	ERA
		27	76	75	.503	17	153	153	66	1363	1421	592	521	9	4.30
Earl Whitehill	L	32	16	12	.571	0	33	32	17	244	255	93	81	3	4.54
Tommy Bridges	R	25	14	12	.538	1	34	26	10	201	174	119	108	4	3.36
Vic Sorrell	R	31	14	14	.500	0	32	31	13	234	234	77	84	1	4.04
Chief Hogsett	L	28	11	9	.550	7	47	15	7	178	201	66	56	0	3.54
Whit Wyatt	R	24	9	13	.409	1	43	22	10	206	228	102	82	0	5.02
George Uhle	R	33	6	6	.500	5	33	15	6	147	152	42	51	1	4.47
Izzy Goldstein	R	24	3	2	.600	0	16	6	2	56	63	41	14	0	4.50
Buck Marrow	R	22	2	5	.286	1	18	6	1	64	70	29	31	0	4.78
Art Herring	R	25	1	2	.333	2	12	0	0	25	25	12	5	0	5.32
2 Rip Sewell	R	25	0	0	—	0	5	0	0	11	19	8	2	0	12.28

ST. LOUIS — 6th 63-91 .409 44 — BILL KILLEFER

NAME	G by Pos	B	AGE	G	AB	R	H	2B	3B	HR	RBI	BB	SO	SB	BA	SA
TOTALS			27	154	5449	736	1502	274	69	67	684	507	528	69	.276	.388
Jack Burns	1B150	L	24	150	617	111	188	33	8	11	70	61	43	17	.305	.438
Oscar Melillo	2B153	R	32	154	612	71	148	19	11	3	66	36	42	6	.242	.324
Jim Levey	SS152	B	25	152	568	59	159	30	8	4	63	21	48	6	.280	.382
Art Scharein	3B77, SS3, 2B2	R	27	81	303	43	92	19	2	0	42	25	10	4	.304	.380
2 Bruce Campbell	OF137	L	22	137	585	83	169	35	11	14	85	40	100+	7	.289	.458
Fred Schulte	OF129, 1B5	R	31	146	565	106	166	35	9	5	73	71	44	5	.294	.425
Goose Goslin	OF149, 3B1	L	31	150	572	88	171	28	9	17	104	92	35	12	.299	.469
Rick Ferrell	C120	R	26	126	438	67	138	30	5	2	65	66	18	1	.315	.420
Benny Bengough	C47	R	33	54	139	13	35	7	1	0	15	12	4	0	.252	.317
Lin Storti (BF)	3B51	B	25	53	193	19	50	11	2	3	26	5	20	1	.259	.383
Debs Garms	OF33	L	25	34	134	20	38	7	1	3	8	17	7	4	.284	.373
Ed Grimes (JJ)	OF18, 2B2, SS1	R	26	31	68	7	16	0	1	0	13	6	12	0	.235	.265
Larry Bettencourt	OF4, 3B2	R	26	27	30	4	4	1	0	1	3	7	6	1	.133	.267
Tom Jenkins	OF12	L	34	25	62	5	20	1	0	0	5	4	6	0	.323	.339
Nap Kloza	OF3	R	28	19	13	4	2	0	0	0	2	4	4	0	.154	.154
Showboat Fisher	OF5	L	33	18	22	2	4	0	0	0	2	3	1	0	.182	.182
1 Johnny Schulte	C6	R	35	15	24	1	5	2	0	0	3	1	6	0	.208	.292
1 Red Kress	3B14	R	27	14	52	2	9	0	1	2	9	4	6	1	.173	.327
Jim McLaughlin	3B1	R	30	1	1	0	0	0	0	0	0	0	0	0	.000	.000

+Campbell, also with St. Louis and Chicago, league leader in SO with 104

NAME	T	AGE	W	L	PCT	SV	G	GS	CG	IP	H	BB	SO	SHO	ERA
		27	63	91	.409	11	154	154	63	1377	1592	574	496	7	5.00
George Blaeholder	R	28	14	14	.500	0	42	36	16	258	304	76	80	1	4.71
Lefty Stewart	L	31	14	19	.424	1	41	31	18	260	269	99	86	2	4.61
2 Bump Hadley	R	27	13	20#	.394	1	40	33	12	230	244	163#	132	1	5.52
Sam Gray	R	34	12	12	.400	4	52	19	7	207	250	53	79	3	4.52
1 Dick Coffman	R	25	5	3	.625	0	9	6	3	61	66	21	14	0	3.10
2 Chad Kimsey	R	25	4	2	.667	3	33	0	0	78	85	33	13	0	4.04
2 Carl Fischer	R	26	3	7	.300	0	24	11	4	97	122	45	35	0	5.57
Bob Cooney	R	24	1	2	.333	1	23	3	1	71	94	36	23	0	6.98
Wally Hebert	L	24	1	12	.077	1	35	15	2	108	145	45	29	0	6.50
Lou Polli	R	30	0	0	—	0	5	0	0	7	13	3	5	0	5.14

#Hadley, also with St. Louis and Chicago, league leader in L(21) BB(171)

CHICAGO — 7th 49-102 .325 56.5 — LEW FONSECA

NAME	G by Pos	B	AGE	G	AB	R	H	2B	3B	HR	RBI	BB	SO	SB	BA	SA
TOTALS			28	152	5336	667	1426	274	56	36	607	459	386	89	.267	.360
Lu Blue	1B105	B	35	112	373	51	93	21	2	0	43	64	21	17	.249	.316
Jackie Hayes	2B97, SS10, 3B10	R	25	117	475	53	122	26	4	2	54	30	28	7	.257	.333
Luke Appling	SS85, 3B14	R	25	139	489	66	134	20	10	3	63	40	36	9	.274	.374
Carey Selph	3B71, 2B26	R	30	116	396	50	112	19	8	0	51	31	9	7	.283	.371
2 Bob Seeds	OF112	R	25	116	434	53	126	18	6	2	45	31	37	5	.290	.373
Liz Funk	OF120	L	27	122	440	59	114	21	5	2	40	43	19	11	.259	.343
Bob Fothergill	OF86	R	34	116	346	36	102	24	1	7	50	27	10	4	.295	.431
Frank Grube	C92	R	27	93	277	36	78	16	2	0	31	33	13	6	.282	.354
2 Red Kress	OF64, SS53, 3B19	R	27	135	515	83	147	42	4	9	57	47	36	6	.285	.435
Billy Sullivan (RL)	1B52, 3B17, C5, OF3	L	21	93	307	31	97	11	1	4	45	20	9	1	.316	.384
2 Charlie Berry	C70	R	29	72	226	33	69	15	6	4	31	21	23	3	.305	.478
2 Johnny Hodapp	OF31, 2B5, 3B4	R	26	68	176	21	40	8	0	3	20	11	3	1	.227	.324
1 Jack Rothrock	OF19, 3B8, 1B1	B	27	39	64	8	12	2	1	0	6	5	9	1	.188	.250
Charlie English	3B13, SS1	R	22	24	63	7	20	3	1	1	3	1	7	0	.317	.444
Lew Fonseca	OF8, P1	R	33	18	37	0	5	2	0	0	6	1	7	0	.135	.462
1 Johnny Watwood	OF13	L	26	13	49	5	15	2	0	0	9	1	3	0	.306	.347
Evar Swanson	OF14	L	29	14	52	9	16	3	1	0	2	8	3	3	.308	.404
Bill Norman	OF13	R	21	13	48	6	11	3	1	0	2	2	5	0	.229	.333
1 Bill Cissell	SS11	R	28	12	43	7	11	1	1	1	5	1	6	0	.256	.395
1 Smead Jolley	OF11	L	30	12	42	3	15	4	0	0	7	3	0	1	.357	.429
Hal Anderson	OF9	R	29	9	32	4	8	0	0	0	2	0	1	0	.250	.250
1 Bruce Campbell	OF6	R	22	9	26	3	4	1	0	0	2	0	4	4	.154	.192
Mel Simons	OF6	L	32	7	0	0	0	0	0	0	0	0	0	0	.000	.000

Fabian Kowalik 24 L 5-13, 1 Bennie Tate 30 L 1-10, Greg Mulleavy 26 R 0-3
+ Campbell, also with St. Louis, league leader in SO with 104

NAME	T	AGE	W	L	PCT	SV	G	GS	CG	IP	H	BB	SO	SHO	ERA
		31	49	102	.325	12	152	152	50	1349	1550	579	377	2	4.82
Ted Lyons	R	31	10	15	.400	2	33	26	19	231	243	71	58	1	3.28
Sad Sam Jones	R	36	10	15	.400	3	28	20	10	200	217	75	64	0	4.23
Milt Gaston	R	36	7	17	.292	1	28	25	7	167	183	73	44	1	3.99
Paul Gregory	R	23	5	3	.625	0	33	9	3	118	125	51	39	0	4.50
1 Tommy Thomas	R	32	3	3	.500	0	12	3	1	44	55	11	15	0	6.14
Vic Frasier	R	26	3	13	.188	0	29	21	4	146	180	70	33	0	6.23
Pete Daglia	R	26	2	4	.333	0	12	5	2	50	60	20	16	0	5.76
Pat Caraway	R	26	2	6	.250	0	19	4	1	65	80	37	13	0	6.79
Red Faber	R	43	2	11	.154	6	42	5	3	106	123	38	26	0	3.74
Clarence Fieber	L	18	1	0	1.000	0	3	0	0	5	5	1	1	0	1.80
2 Chad Kimsey	R	25	1	1	.500	2	7	0	0	12	16	8	3	0	2.45
Charlie Biggs	R	25	1	1	.500	0	6	4	0	25	32	12	1	0	6.84
1 Bump Hadley	R	27	1	1#	.500	1	7	2	0	33	45	8#	12	0	3.79
Phil Gallivan	R	25	1	3	.250	0	13	3	1	33	49	24	12	0	7.63
Fabian Kowalik	R	24	0	0	—	0	6	0	0	12	17	4	4	0	7.20
Art Smith	R	26	0	0	—	0	2	0	0	7	17	4	1	0	11.57
Ed Walsh	R	27	0	2	.000	0	5	2	0	26	13	7	0	0	8.55
Bill Chamberlain	L	25	0	0	—	0	5	0	0	41	39	25	11	0	4.61
Hal McKain	R	25	0	0	—	0	11	0	0	11	17	5	1	0	11.46
Art Evans	L	20	0	0	—	0	1	0	0	3	3	1	0	0	3.00
Grant Bowler	R	24	0	0	—	0	6	0	0	6	15	2	2	0	16.50
Les Bartholomew	L	29	0	0	—	0	2	0	0	5	6	3	2	0	5.40
Archie Wise	R	19	0	0	—	0	1	0	0	5	5	4	4	0	5.14
Bob Poser	R	22	0	0	—	0	1	0	0	4	8	4	2	0	18.00

Lew Fonseca 33 R 0-0, Jim Moore 28 R 0-0
Hadley, also with St. Louis, league leader in L(21), BB(171)

BOSTON — 8th 43-111 .279 64 — SHANO COLLINS 11-44 .200   MARTY McMANUS 32-67 .323

NAME	G by Pos	B	AGE	G	AB	R	H	2B	3B	HR	RBI	BB	SO	SB	BA	SA
TOTALS			29	154	5295	566	1331	253	57	53	530	469	539	46	.251	.351
2 Dale Alexander	1B101	R	29	101	376	58	140	27	4	8	56	55	19	4	.372*	.524
Marv Olson	2B106, 3B1	R	25	115	403	58	100	14	6	0	25	61	26	1	.248	.313
Rabbit Warstler	SS107	R	28	115	388	26	82	15	6	0	34	22	43	9	.211	.276
Urban Pickering	3B126, C1	R	29	132	457	47	119	28	5	2	40	39	57	3	.260	.357
2 Roy Johnson	OF85	L	29	94	348	70	104	24	4	11	47	44	41	13	.299	.486
Tom Oliver	OF116	L	29	122	455	39	120	23	3	0	37	25	12	1	.264	.327
2 Smead Jolley	OF126, C5	L	30	137	531	57	164	27	5	18	99	27	29	0	.309	.480
2 Bennie Tate	C76	L	30	81	273	26	67	12	5	2	26	20	6	1	.245	.348
2 Johnny Watwood	OF46, 1B18	L	26	95	266	26	66	11	0	0	30	20	11	7	.248	.289
Marty McManus	2B49, 3B30, SS2, 1B1	R	32	99	302	39	71	19	4	5	24	30	30	1	.235	.374
George Stumpf	OF51	L	22	79	169	18	34	2	2	1	18	18	21	1	.201	.254
Ed Connolly	C75	R	23	77	222	19	50	8	4	0	21	20	22	0	.225	.297
Hal Rhyne	SS55, 3B4	R	33	71	207	26	47	12	5	0	14	23	14	3	.227	.333
2 Earl Webb	OF50, 1B2	L	34	52	192	23	54	9	1	5	27	25	15	0	.281	.417
Al Van Camp	1B25	R	28	34	103	10	23	4	2	0	17	4	4	2	.223	.301
Johnny Reder	1B10, 3B1	R	22	17	34	9	6	1	0	0	4	6	6	0	.176	.206
Andy Spognardi	2B9, SS3, 3B2	R	23	17	34	9	10	1	0	0	2	9	2	3	.294	.324
2 Jack Rothrock	OF12	B	27	13	48	5	10	3	0	0	4	2	6	0	.208	.229
1 Charlie Berry	C10	R	29	10	32	0	6	1	0	0	6	4	4	0	.188	.219
Howie Storie	C5	R	21	5	8	0	3	0	0	0	1	1	0	0	.375	.375
Otto Miller		R	31	4	6	0	0	0	0	0	0	0	0	0	.000	.000
Johnny Lucas		R	29	3											.000	.000
Hank Patterson	C1	R	24	2	1	0	0	0	0	0	0	0	1	0	.000	.000

*Alexander, also with Detroit, league leaguer in BA with .367

NAME	T	AGE	W	L	PCT	SV	G	GS	CG	IP	H	BB	SO	SHO	ERA
		27	43	111	.279	7	154	154	42	1362	1574	612	365	2	5.02
Bob Kline	R	22	11	13	.459	2	47	19	4	172	203	76	31	1	5.28
2 Ivy Andrews	R	25	8	6	.571	2	25	19	8	142	144	53	30	0	3.80
Ed Durham	R	24	6	13	.316	0	34	22	7	196	231	97	63	0	4.50
Bob Weiland	R	26	6	16	.273	1	43	27	7	196	204	97	93	0	4.51
Johnny Welch	R	26	4	6	.400	0	20	8	3	72	93	38	26	1	5.25
1 Wilcy Moore	R	35	4	10	.286	4	37	7	2	84	98	42	28	0	5.25
John Michaels	L	24	1	6	.143	0	28	8	1	81	101	27	16	0	5.11
1 Jack Russell	R	26	1	7	.125	0	15	6	1	43	61	20	11	0	6.75
2 Gordon Rhodes	R	24	1	8	.111	0	12	11	2	79	91	31	22	0	5.13
1 Danny MacFayden	R	27	1	10	.091	0	12	11	8	79	98	29	29	0	5.08
Gordon McNaughton	R	21	0	1	.000	0	6	1	0	12	20	11	3	0	6.43
Pete Donohue	R	31	0	1	.000	0	9	1	0	17	22	9	3	0	7.61
2 Pete Appleton	R	28	0	3	.000	0	11	3	0	46	49	26	15	0	4.11
Ed Gallagher	L	21	0	3	.000	0	9	4	0	25	37	27	14	0	12.38
Larry Boerner	R	27	0	4	.000	0	21	2	0	61	71	37	19	0	5.02
Hod Lisenbee	R	33	0	4	.000	0	13	3	0	73	87	25	13	0	5.67
Regis Leheny	L	24	0	0	—	0	3	0	0	5	4	0	1	0	15.00
Jud McLaughlin	L	20	0	0	—	0	2	0	0	3	5	4	0	0	15.00

Ed Morris (DD)32

CHICAGO 1ST 90-64 .584 — ROGERS HORNSBY 53-46 .535 — CHARLIE GRIMM 37-18 .673

NAME	G by Pos	B	AGE	G	AB	R	H	2B	3B	HR	RBI	BB	SO	SB	BA	SA
TOTALS			28	154	5462	720	1519	296	60	69	665	398	514	48	.278	.392
Charlie Grimm	1B149	L	33	149	570	66	175	42	2	7	80	35	22	2	.307	.425
Billy Herman	2B154	R	22	154	656	102	206	42	7	1	51	40	33	14	.314	.404
Billy Jurges (GW)	SS108, 3B5	R	24	115	396	40	100	24	4	2	52	19	26	1	.253	.328
Woody English	3B93, SS38	R	25	127	522	70	142	23	7	3	47	55	73	5	.272	.360
Kiki Cuyler (BF)	OF109	L	33	110	446	58	130	19	9	10	77	29	43	9	.291	.442
Johnny Moore	OF109	L	30	119	443	59	135	24	5	13	64	22	38	4	.305	.470
Riggs Stephenson	OF147	R	34	147	583	86	189	49	4	4	85	54	27	3	.324	.443
Gabby Hartnett	C117, 1B1	R	31	121	406	52	110	25	3	12	52	51	59	0	.271	.436
Stan Hack	3B51	L	22	72	178	32	42	5	6	2	19	17	16	2	.236	.365
Rollie Hemsley	C47, OF1	R	25	60	151	27	36	10	3	4	20	10	16	2	.238	.424
Marv Gudat	OF14, 1B8, P1	L	26	60	94	15	24	4	1	1	15	16	10	0	.255	.351
Lance Richbourg	OF33	L	34	44	148	22	38	2	2	1	21	8	4	0	.257	.318
Vince Barton	OF34	L	24	36	134	19	30	2	3	3	15	8	22	0	.224	.351
Mark Koenig	SS31	B	29	33	102	15	36	5	1	3	11	3	5	0	.353	.510
Frank Demaree	OF17	R	22	23	56	4	14	3	0	0	6	2	7	0	.250	.304
Zack Taylor	C14	R	33	21	30	2	6	1	0	0	3	1	4	0	.200	.233
Rogers Hornsby	OF10, 3B6	R	36	19	58	10	13	2	0	1	7	10	4	0	.224	.310
Harry Taylor	1B1	L	24	10	8	1	1	0	0	0	0	1	1	0	.125	.125
1 Danny Taylor	OF6	R	31	6	22	3	5	2	0	0	3	3	1	1	.227	.318

NAME	T	AGE	W	L	PCT	SV	G	GS	CG	IP	H	BB	SO	SHO	ERA
		31	90	64	.584	7	154	154	79	1401	1444	409	527	9	3.44
Lon Warneke	R	23	22	6	.786	0	35	32	25	277	247	64	106	4	2.37
Guy Bush	R	30	19	11	.633	0	40	30	15	239	262	70	73	1	3.20
Charlie Root	R	33	15	10	.600	3	39	24	11	216	211	55	96	0	3.58
Pat Malone	R	29	15	17	.469	2	37	32	17	237	222	78	120	2	3.38
Burleigh Grimes	R	38	6	11	.353	1	30	18	5	141	174	50	36	1	4.79
Bud Tinning	R	26	5	3	.625	0	21	9	3	93	93	24	30	0	2.81
Bob Smith	R	37	4	3	.571	2	34	11	4	119	136	35	35	1	4.61
Leroy Herrmann	R	26	2	1	.667	0	7	0	0	13	18	9	5	0	6.23
Jakie May	L	36	2	2	.500	1	35	0	0	54	61	19	20	0	4.33
Carroll Yerkes	L	29	0	0	—	0	2	0	0	9	5	3	4	0	3.00
Ed Baecht	R	25	0	0	—	0	1	0	0	1	1	1	0	0	0.00
Marv Gudat	L	26	0	0	—	0	1	0	0	1	0	1	2	0	0.00
Bobo Newsom	R	24	0	0	—	0	1	0	0	2	1	0	0	0	0.00

PITTSBURGH 2nd 86-68 .558 4 — GEORGE GIBSON

NAME	G by Pos	B	AGE	G	AB	R	H	2B	3B	HR	RBI	BB	SO	SB	BA	SA
TOTALS			27	154	5421	701	1543	274	90	48	653	358	385	71	.285	.395
Gus Suhr	1B154	L	26	154	581	78	153	31	16	5	81	63	39	7	.263	.398
Tony Piet	2B154	R	25	154	574	66	162	25	8	7	85	46	56	19	.282	.390
Arky Vaughan	SS128	L	20	129	497	71	158	15	10	4	61	39	26	10	.318	.412
Pie Traynor	3B127	R	33	135	513	74	169	27	10	2	68	32	20	6	.329	.433
Paul Waner	OF154	L	29	154	630	107	215	62	10	8	82	56	24	13	.341	.510
Lloyd Waner	OF131	L	26	134	565	90	188	27	11	2	38	31	11	6	.333	.428
Adam Comorosky	OF92	R	27	108	370	54	106	18	4	4	46	25	20	7	.286	.389
Earl Grace	C114	L	25	115	390	41	107	17	5	8	55	14	23	0	.274	.405
Dave Barbee	OF78	R	27	97	327	37	84	22	6	5	55	18	38	1	.257	.407
Tommy Thevenow (BG)	SS29, 3B22	R	28	59	194	12	46	3	3	0	26	7	12	0	.237	.284
Gus Dugas	OF20	L	25	55	97	13	23	3	3	1	12	7	11	0	.237	.423
Tom Padden	C43	R	23	47	118	13	31	6	1	0	10	9	7	0	.263	.331
Hal Finney (EJ)	C11	R	26	31	33	14	7	3	0	0	4	3	4	1	.212	.303
Howdy Groskloss	SS1	R	26	17	20	1	2	0	0	0	0	3	0	0	.100	.100
Bill Brenzel	C9	R	22	9	24	0	1	1	0	0	2	0	1	0	.042	.083
Bill Brubaker	3B7	R	21	7	24	3	10	3	0	1	4	4	1	1	.417	.542
Woody Jensen	OF1	L	24	7	5	2	0	0	0	0	0	0	2	0	.000	.000

NAME	T	AGE	W	L	PCT	SV	G	GS	CG	IP	H	BB	SO	SHO	ERA
		29	86	68	.558	12	154	154	79	1377	1472	338	377	12	3.75
Larry French	L	24	18	16	.529	4	47	33	19	274	301	62	72	3	3.02
Bill Swift	R	24	14	10	.583	4	39	23	11	214	205	26	64	0	3.62
Heinie Meine	R	36	12	9	.571	1	28	25	13	172	193	45	32	1	3.87
Steve Swetonic	R	28	11	6	.647	0	24	19	11	163	134	55	39	4	2.82
Bill Harris	R	32	11	9	.526	2	37	17	4	168	178	38	63	0	3.64
Leon Chagnon	R	29	9	6	.600	0	30	17	4	128	140	34	52	1	3.94
Ray Kremer	R	39	4	3	.571	0	11	10	3	57	61	16	6	1	4.26
Glenn Spencer	R	26	4	8	.333	1	39	13	5	138	167	44	35	1	4.96
Erv Brame	R	30	3	1	.750	0	23	3	0	51	84	16	10	0	7.41
Hal Smith	R	30	1	0	1.000	0	7	2	0	12	9	2	4	1	0.75

BROOKLYN 3rd 81-73 .526 9 — MAX CAREY

NAME	G by Pos	B	AGE	G	AB	R	H	2B	3B	HR	RBI	BB	SO	SB	BA	SA
TOTALS			30	154	5433	752	1538	296	59	110	703	388	574	61	.283	.420
George Kelly	1B62, OF1	R	36	64	202	23	49	9	1	4	22	22	27	0	.243	.356
Tony Cuccinello	2B154	R	24	154	597	76	168	32	6	12	77	46	47	5	.281	.415
Glenn Wright	SS122, 1B2	R	31	127	446	50	122	31	5	11	60	12	57	1	.274	.439
Joe Stripp	3B93, 1B43	R	29	138	534	94	162	36	9	6	64	36	30	14	.303	.438
Hack Wilson	OF125	R	32	135	481	77	143	37	5	23	123	51	85	2	.297	.538
2 Danny Taylor	OF96	R	31	105	395	84	128	22	7	11	48	33	41	13	.324	.499
Lefty O'Doul	OF148	L	35	148	595	120	219	32	8	21	90	50	20	11	.368	.555
Al Lopez	C125	R	23	126	404	44	111	18	6	1	43	34	35	3	.275	.356
Johnny Frederick	OF88	L	30	118	384	54	115	28	2	16	56	25	35	1	.299	.508
Gordon Slade	SS55, 3B23	R	27	79	254	23	60	15	1	1	23	11	26	3	.240	.320
Neal Finn	3B50, 2B2, SS1	R	30	65	189	22	45	5	2	0	14	11	15	2	.238	.286
Clyde Sukeforth	C36	L	30	59	111	14	26	4	4	0	12	6	10	1	.234	.342
Bud Clancy	1B53	L	31	53	196	14	60	4	2	0	16	6	13	0	.306	.347
Val Picinich	C24	R	35	41	70	8	18	6	0	1	11	4	8	0	.257	.386
Max Rosenfeld	OF30	L	29	34	39	8	14	3	0	2	7	0	10	2	.359	.590
Ike Boone	OF8	L	35	13	21	2	3	1	0	0	2	5	2	0	.143	.190
Alta Cohen	OF8	L	23	9	32	1	5	1	0	0	1	3	7	0	.156	.188
Bruce Caldwell	1B6	R	26	7	11	2	1	0	0	0	2	2	0	0	.091	.091
Dick Siebert	1B2	L	20	6	7	1	2	0	0	0	0	0	2	0	.286	.286
Paul Richards	C3	R	23	3	8	0	0	0	0	0	0	0	0	0	.000	.000
Fresco Thompson		R	30	3	1	0	0	0	0	0	0	0	0	0	.000	.000
Bobby Reis	3B1	R	23	1	4	0	1	0	0	0	0	0	0	0	.250	.250
Del Bissonnette (LJ) 32																

NAME	T	AGE	W	L	PCT	SV	G	GS	CG	IP	H	BB	SO	SHO	ERA
		32	81	73	.526	16	154	154	61	1380	1538	403	497	7	4.27
Watty Clark	L	30	20	12	.625	0	40	36	19	273	282	49	99	2	3.49
Van Lingle Mungo	R	21	13	11	.542	2	39	33	11	223	224	115	107	1	4.44
Sloppy Thurston	R	33	13	8	.600	0	28	19	10	153	174	38	35	2	4.06
Dazzy Vance	R	41	12	11	.522	1	27	24	9	176	171	57	103	1	4.19
Fred Heimach	L	31	9	4	.692	0	36	15	7	168	203	28	30	0	3.96
Joe Shaute	L	32	7	7	.500	4	34	9	1	117	147	21	32	0	4.54
Ray Phelps	R	28	4	5	.444	0	20	9	4	79	101	27	21	1	5.92
Jack Quinn	R	48	3	7	.300	8	42	0	0	87	102	24	28	0	3.31
1 Waite Hoyt	R	32	1	3	.250	1	8	4	2	27	38	12	7	0	7.67
Fay Thomas	R	28	1	0	1.000	0	7	2	0	17	22	8	9	0	7.41
Ed Pipgras	R	28	1	0	1.000	0	5	1	0	16	16	6	5	0	5.40
Cy Moore	R	27	0	3	.000	0	20	2	1	49	56	17	21	0	4.78
Art Jones	R	26	0	0	—	0	1	0	0	1	2	1	0	0	18.00

PHILADELPHIA 4th 78-76 .506 12 — BURT SHOTTON

NAME	G by Pos	B	AGE	G	AB	R	H	2B	3B	HR	RBI	BB	SO	SB	BA	SA
TOTALS			27	154	5510	844	1608	330	67	122	780	446	547	71	.292	.442
Don Hurst	1B150	L	26	150	579	109	196	41	4	24	143	65	27	10	.339	.547
Les Mallon	2B88, 3B5	R	26	103	347	44	90	16	0	5	31	28	28	1	.259	.349
Dick Bartell	SS154	R	24	154	614	118	189	48	7	1	53	64	47	8	.308	.414
Pinky Whitney	3B151, 2B5	R	27	154	624	93	186	33	11	13	124	35	66	6	.298	.449
Chuck Klein	OF154	L	27	154	650	152	226	50	15	38	137	60	49	20	.348	.646
Kiddo Davis	OF133	R	30	137	576	100	178	39	6	5	57	44	56	16	.309	.424
Hal Lee	OF148	R	27	149	595	80	180	42	10	18	85	36	45	6	.303	.497
Spud Davis	C120	R	27	125	402	44	135	24	5	14	70	40	39	1	.336	.522
Harry McCurdy	C42	L	32	62	136	13	32	6	1	1	14	17	13	0	.235	.316
Barney Friberg	2B56	R	32	61	154	17	37	8	2	0	14	19	23	0	.240	.318
Fred Brickell	OF12	L	25	45	66	9	22	6	1	0	2	4	5	2	.333	.455
Al Todd	C25	R	28	33	70	8	16	5	0	0	9	1	9	1	.229	.300
2 Eddie Delker	2B27	R	26	30	62	7	10	1	1	1	7	6	14	0	.161	.258
2 Cliff Heathcote	1B7	L	34	30	39	7	11	2	0	1	5	3	6	0	.282	.410
1 Rube Bressler	OF18	L	37	27	83	9	19	6	1	0	4	15	3	0	.229	.325
Russ Scarritt	OF1	R	29	11	11	0	2	0	0	0	1	0	2	0	.182	.182
George Knothe	2B5	R	34	6	12	2	1	1	0	0	1	0	4	0	.083	.167
Doug Taitt		L	29	4	2	0	0	0	0	0	1	0	0	0	.000	.000
Hugh Willingham		R	26	4	0	0	0	0	0	0	0	0	0	0	.000	.000

NAME	T	AGE	W	L	PCT	SV	G	GS	CG	IP	H	BB	SO	SHO	ERA
		30	78	76	.506	17	154	154	69	1384	1589	450	459	4	4.47
Phil Collins	R	30	14	12	.538	3	43	21	6	273	231	65	66	0	5.28
Ray Benge	R	30	13	12	.520	6	41	28	13	222	247	58	89	2	4.05
2 Flint Rhem	R	31	11	7	.611	1	26	20	10	169	177	49	35	0	3.73
Jumbo Jim Elliott	L	31	11	10	.524	0	39	22	8	166	210	47	62	0	5.42
Ed Holley	R	32	11	14	.440	0	34	30	16	228	247	55	87	2	3.95
Snipe Hansen	L	25	10	10	.500	2	35	18	5	191	215	51	56	0	3.72
Ad Liska	R	25	2	0	1.000	0	14	0	0	27	22	10	6	0	1.67
Reggie Grabowski	R	24	2	2	.500	0	14	2	0	34	38	22	15	0	3.71
Hal Elliott	R	33	2	4	.333	0	16	7	0	58	70	38	13	0	5.74
Clise Dudley	R	28	1	0	1.000	1	13	0	0	18	23	8	5	0	7.00
Jack Berly	R	29	1	2	.333	2	21	1	1	46	61	21	15	0	7.63
Chet Nichols	R	34	1	2	.333	0	11	0	0	19	23	14	5	0	7.11
Stew Bolen	L	29	0	0	—	0	6	0	0	16	18	10	3	0	2.81
Bob Adams	R	25	0	0	—	0	7	0	0	6	7	2	1	0	1.50

BOSTON 5th 77-77 .500 13 — BILL McKECHNIE

NAME	G by Pos	B	AGE	G	AB	R	H	2B	3B	HR	RBI	BB	SO	SB	BA	SA
TOTALS			29	155	5506	649	1460	262	53	63	594	347	496	36	.265	.366
Art Shires (BK)	1B80	L	24	82	298	32	71	9	3	5	30	25	21	1	.238	.339
Rabbit Maranville	2B149	R	40	149	571	67	134	20	4	0	37	46	28	4	.235	.284
Billy Urbanski	SS136	R	29	136	563	80	153	25	8	8	46	28	60	8	.272	.387
Fritz Knothe	3B87	R	29	89	344	45	82	16	3	1	36	39	37	5	.238	.308
Wes Schulmerich	OF101	R	30	119	404	47	105	22	5	11	57	27	61	5	.260	.421
Wally Berger	OF134, 1B11	R	26	145	602	90	185	34	6	17	73	36	66	5	.307	.468
Red Worthington (BN)	OF104	R	26	105	439	62	132	35	8	6	61	15	24	1	.303	.476
Al Spohrer	C100	R	29	104	335	31	90	12	2	0	33	15	26	2	.269	.316
Randy Moore	OF41, 3B31, 1B22, C1	L	27	107	351	41	103	21	5	4	43	15	11	1	.293	.390
Freddy Leach	OF50	L	34	84	223	21	55	9	1	2	29	18	10	1	.247	.318
Pinky Hargrave (BN)	C73	B	36	82	217	20	57	14	3	4	33	24	18	1	.263	.410
Earl Clark	OF16	R	24	50	44	11	11	2	0	0	4	2	7	1	.250	.295
Buck Jordan	1B49	L	25	49	212	27	68	12	3	2	29	4	5	1	.321	.434
2 Hod Ford	2B29, SS16, 3B2	R	34	40	95	9	26	5	2	0	6	4	9	0	.274	.368
Dutch Holland	OF39	R	29	39	156	15	46	11	1	1	12	10	20	0	.295	.397
Bill Akers	3B20, 2B5, SS5	R	27	36	93	8	24	3	1	2	17	10	15	0	.258	.344
Bucky Walters	3B22	R	23	22	75	8	14	3	1	0	8	1	8	0	.187	.253
2 Johnny Schulte	C10	R	35	10	9	1	2	0	0	1	0	2	4	0	.222	.556
Ox Eckhardt		L	30	4	4	1	1	0	0	0	0	0	0	0	.250	.250

NAME	T	AGE	W	L	PCT	SV	G	GS	CG	IP	H	BB	SO	SHO	ERA
		30	77	77	.500	8	155	155	72	1414	1483	420	440	8	3.53
Ed Brandt	L	27	16	16	.500	1	35	31	19	254	271	57	79	2	3.97
Bob Brown	R	21	14	7	.667	3	35	28	9	218	187	104	110	0	3.30
Ben Cantwell	R	30	13	11	.542	5	37	9	3	146	133	33	33	1	2.96
Huck Betts	R	35	13	11	.542	1	31	27	16	222	229	35	32	3	2.80
Tom Zachary	L	36	12	11	.522	0	32	24	12	212	231	55	67	1	3.10
Fred Frankhouse	R	28	4	6	.400	0	37	3	1	109	113	45	35	0	3.55
Socks Seibold	R	36	3	10	.231	0	28	20	6	137	173	41	33	1	4.66
Bruce Cunningham	R	26	1	0	1.000	0	18	3	0	47	50	19	21	0	3.45
Hub Pruett (LJ)	L	31	0	0	—	0	18	7	4	63	76	30	27	0	5.19
Leo Mangum	R	36	0	0	—	0	7	0	0	10	17	0	3	0	5.40
1 Bill Sherdel	L	35	0	0	—	0	3	0	0	3	3	0	0	0	—

NEW YORK — Batting

NAME	G by Pos	B	AGE	G	AB	R	H	2B	3B	HR	RBI	BB	SO	SB	BA	SA
NEW YORK 6th(Tie) 72-82 .468 18	JOHN McGRAW 17-23 .425 BILL TERRY 55-59 .482															
TOTALS			25	154	5530	755	1527	263	54	116	718	348	391	31	.276	.406
Bill Terry	1B154	L	33	154	643	124	225	42	11	28	117	32	23	4	.350	.580
Hughie Critz	2B151	R	31	151	659	90	182	32	7	2	50	34	27	2	.276	.355
Doc Marshall	SS63	R	26	68	226	18	56	8	1	0	28	6	11	1	.248	.292
Johnny Vergez	3B111, SS1	R	25	118	376	42	94	21	3	6	43	25	36	1	.261	.380
Mel Ott	OF154	L	23	154	566	119	180	30	8	38	123	100	39	6	.318	.601
Fred Lindstrom	OF128, 3B15	R	26	144	595	80	161	26	5	15	92	27	28	6	.271	.407
Jo-Jo Moore	OF86	L	23	86	361	53	110	15	2	2	27	20	18	4	.305	.374
Shanty Hogan	C136	R	26	136	502	36	144	18	2	7	77	26	22	0	.287	.387
Chick Fullis	OF55, 2B1	R	28	96	235	35	70	14	3	1	21	11	12	1	.298	.396
Sam Leslie	1B2	L	26	77	75	5	22	4	0	1	15	2	5	0	.293	.387
Gil English	3B39, SS23	R	22	59	204	22	46	7	5	2	19	5	20	0	.225	.338
Ethan Allen	OF24	R	28	54	103	13	18	6	2	1	7	1	12	0	.175	.301
Travis Jackson (BK)	SS52	R	28	52	195	23	50	17	1	4	38	13	16	1	.256	.415
Bob O'Farrell	C41	R	35	50	67	7	16	3	0	0	8	11	10	0	.239	.284
Len Koenecke	OF35	L	28	42	137	33	35	5	0	4	14	11	13	3	.255	.380
Eddie Moore	SS21, 3B6, 2B5	R	33	37	87	9	23	3	0	1	6	9	6	1	.264	.333
Francis Healy	C11	R	22	14	32	5	8	2	0	0	4	2	8	0	.250	.313
Art McLarney	SS9	B	23	9	23	2	3	1	0	0	3	1	3	0	.130	.174

Pat Veltman 26 R 0-1, Jack Tobin 25 R 0-1

NEW YORK — Pitching

NAME	T	AGE	W	L	PCT	SV	G	GS	CG	IP	H	BB	SO	SHO	ERA
		30	72	82	.468	16	154	154	57	1375	1533	387	506	3	3.83
Carl Hubbell	L	29	18	11	.621	2	40	32	22	284	260	40	137	0	2.50
Freddie Fitzsimmons	R	30	11	11	.500	0	35	31	11	238	287	83	65	0	4.42
Hi Bell	R	34	8	4	.667	2	35	10	5	120	132	16	25	0	3.68
Bill Walker	L	28	8	12	.400	2	31	22	9	163	177	55	74	0	4.14
Dolf Luque	R	41	6	7	.462	5	28	5	1	110	128	32	32	0	4.01
Jim Mooney	L	25	6	10	.375	0	29	18	4	125	154	42	37	1	5.04
Hal Schumacher	R	21	5	6	.455	0	27	13	2	101	119	39	38	1	3.56
2 Waite Hoyt	R	32	5	7	.417	0	18	12	3	97	103	25	29	0	3.43
Sam Gibson	R	32	4	8	.333	3	41	5	1	82	107	30	39	1	4.83
Clarence Mitchell	L	41	1	3	.250	2	8	1	1	30	41	11	7	0	4.20
Roy Parmelee	R	25	0	3	.000	0	8	3	0	25	25	14	23	0	3.96

ST. LOUIS — Batting

NAME	G by Pos	B	AGE	G	AB	R	H	2B	3B	HR	RBI	BB	SO	SB	BA	SA
ST. LOUIS 6th(Tie) 72-82 .468 18	GABBY STREET															
TOTALS			30	156	5458	684	1467	307	51	76	626	420	514	92	.269	.385
Ripper Collins	1B81, OF60	B	28	149	549	82	153	28	8	21	91	38	67	4	.279	.474
Jimmy Reese	2B77	R	30	90	309	38	82	15	0	2	26	20	19	4	.265	.333
Charlie Gelbert	SS122	R	26	122	455	60	122	28	9	1	45	39	30	8	.268	.376
Jake Flowers	3B54, SS7, 2B2	R	30	67	247	35	63	11	1	2	18	31	18	7	.255	.332
George Watkins	OF120	L	32	127	458	67	143	35	3	9	63	45	46	18	.312	.461
Pepper Martin (BG)	OF69, 3B15	R	28	85	323	47	77	19	6	4	34	30	31	9	.238	.372
Ernie Orsatti (SJ)	OF96, 1B1	R	29	101	375	44	126	27	6	2	44	18	29	5	.336	.456
Gus Mancuso	C82	R	26	103	310	25	88	23	1	5	43	30	15	0	.284	.413
Frankie Frisch	2B75, 3B37, SS4	B	33	115	486	59	142	26	2	3	60	25	13	18	.292	.372
Jimmie Wilson	C75, 1B3, 2B1	R	31	92	274	36	68	16	2	2	28	15	18	0	.248	.343
Jim Bottomley	1B74	L	32	91	311	45	92	16	3	11	48	25	32	2	.296	.473
Ray Blades	OF62, 3B1	R	35	80	201	35	46	10	1	3	29	34	31	2	.229	.333
Sparky Adams (KJ)	3B30	R	37	31	127	22	35	3	1	0	13	14	5	0	.276	.315
George Puccinelli	OF30	R	25	31	108	17	30	8	0	3	11	12	13	1	.278	.444
1 Harvey Hendrick	3B12, OF5	L	34	28	72	8	18	2	0	1	5	5	9	0	.250	.319
Joe Medwick	OF26	R	20	26	106	13	37	12	1	2	12	2	10	3	.349	.538
Charlie Wilson	SS24	B	27	24	96	7	19	3	1	1	2	3	8	0	.198	.323
Ray Pepper	OF17	R	21	57	3	14	2	1	0	7	5	13	1	.246	.316	
1 Eddie Delker	2B10, 3B5, SS4	R	26	20	42	1	5	4	0	0	2	8	7	0	.119	.214
Mike Gonzalez	C7	R	41	14	0	2	0	0	0	3	0	2	0	.143	.143	
Joel Hunt	OF5	R	26	12	21	0	4	1	0	0	3	4	3	0	.190	.238
Ray Cunningham	3B8, 2B2	R	27	11	22	4	4	1	0	0	0	3	4	0	.182	.227
Wattie Holm	OF4	R	30	11	17	3	3	1	0	0	1	3	1	0	.176	.235

2 Rube Bressler 37 R 3-19, Bill DeLancey 20 L 5-26, 1 Hod Ford 34 R 0-2, Skeeter Webb 22 R 0-0

ST. LOUIS — Pitching

NAME	T	AGE	W	L	PCT	SV	G	GS	CG	IP	H	BB	SO	SHO	ERA
		29	72	82	.468	9	156	156	70	1396	1533	455	681	13	3.97
Dizzy Dean	R	22	18	15	.545	2	46	33	16	286	280	102	191	4	3.30
Wild Bill Hallahan	L	29	12	7	.632	1	25	22	13	176	169	69	108	1	3.12
Paul Derringer	R	25	11	14	.440	0	39	30	14	233	296	67	78	1	4.06
Tex Carleton	R	25	10	13	.435	0	44	22	9	196	198	70	113	3	4.09
Syl Johnson	R	31	5	14	.263	2	32	22	7	165	199	35	70	1	4.91
1 Flint Rhem	R	31	4	2	.667	0	6	6	5	50	48	10	18	1	3.06
Allyn Stout	R	27	4	5	.444	1	36	3	1	74	87	28	32	0	4.38
Jesse Haines	R	38	3	5	.375	0	20	10	4	85	116	16	27	1	4.76
Jim Lindsey	R	34	3	3	.500	3	33	5	0	89	96	38	31	0	4.96
Jim Winford	R	22	1	1	.500	0	4	0	0	8	9	5	4	0	6.75
Ray Starr	R	26	1	1	.500	0	3	2	1	20	19	10	6	1	2.70
1 Benny Frey	R	26	0	2	.000	0	3	0	0	3	6	2	0	0	12.00
2 Bill Sherdel	L	35	0	—		0	3	0	0	6	7	1	1	0	4.50
Bud Teachout	L	28	0	0		0	1	0	0	1	2	0	0	0	0.00
Dick Terwilliger	R	26	0	0		0	1	0	0	2	2	1	0	0	4.50

CINCINNATI — Batting

NAME	G by Pos	B	AGE	G	AB	R	H	2B	3B	HR	RBI	BB	SO	SB	BA	SA
CINCINNATI 8th 60-94 .390 30	DAN HOWLEY															
TOTALS			30	155	5443	575	1429	265	68	47	546	436	436	35	.263	.362
2 Harvey Hendrick	1B94	L	34	94	398	56	120	30	3	4	40	23	29	3	.302	.422
George Grantham	2B115, 1B10	L	32	126	493	81	144	29	6	4	39	56	40	3	.292	.412
Leo Durocher	SS142	R	26	143	457	43	99	22	5	1	33	36	40	3	.217	.293
Wally Gilbert	3B111	R	31	114	420	35	90	18	2	1	40	20	23	2	.214	.274
Babe Herman	OF146	L	29	148	577	87	188	38	19	16	87	60	45	7	.326	.541
Estel Crabtree	OF95	R	28	108	402	38	110	14	9	2	35	23	26	2	.274	.368
Wally Roettger	OF94	R	29	106	347	26	96	18	3	3	43	23	24	0	.277	.372
Ernie Lombardi	C110	R	24	118	413	43	125	22	9	11	68	41	19	0	.303	.479
Taylor Douthit	OF88	R	31	96	333	28	81	12	1	0	25	31	29	3	.243	.285
Jo-Jo Morrissey	SS45, 2B42, 3B12, OF1	R	28	89	269	15	65	10	1	0	13	14	15	2	.242	.286
Andy High	3B46, 2B12	L	34	84	191	16	36	4	1	0	12	23	6	1	.188	.230
Chick Hafey (IL)	OF65	R	29	83	253	34	87	19	3	2	36	22	20	4	.344	.466
Red Lucas	P31	L	30	76	150	13	43	11	2	0	19	10	9	0	.287	.387
Clyde Manion	C47	R	35	49	135	7	28	4	0	0	12	14	16	0	.207	.237
Mickey Heath (IL)	1B39	L	28	39	134	14	27	1	3	0	15	20	23	0	.201	.254
Casper Asbjornson	C16	R	23	29	58	5	10	2	0	1	4	0	15	0	.172	.259
Harry Heilmann (IL)	1B6	R	37	15	31	3	8	2	0	0	6	4	4	0	.258	.323
Jimmy Shevlin	1B7	L	22	7	24	3	5	2	0	0	4	0	1	0	.208	.292

1 Cliff Heathcote 34 L 0-3, Otto Bluege 22 R 0-0

CINCINNATI — Pitching

NAME	T	AGE	W	L	PCT	SV	G	GS	CG	IP	H	BB	SO	SHO	ERA
		32	60	94	.390	6	155	155	83	1395	1505	276	359	6	3.79
Si Johnson	R	25	13	15	.464	2	42	27	14	245	246	57	94	2	3.27
Red Lucas	R	30	13	17	.433	0	31	31	28	269	261	35	63	0	2.94
Ownie Carroll	R	29	10	19	.345	1	32	26	15	210	245	44	55	0	4.50
Ray Kolp	R	37	10	10	.375	1	32	18	7	160	176	27	42	2	3.88
Larry Benton	R	34	6	13	.316	2	35	22	7	180	201	27	35	0	4.30
Eppa Rixey	L	41	5	2	.500	0	25	11	6	112	108	16	14	2	2.65
2 Benny Frey	R	26	4	10	.286	0	28	15	5	131	159	30	27	0	4.33
Jack Ogden	R	34	2	2	.500	0	24	3	1	57	72	22	20	0	5.21
Biff Wysong	R	27	1	0	1.000	0	7	0	0	12	13	8	5	0	3.75
Whitey Hilcher	R	29	0	3	.000	0	11	2	0	19	24	10	4	0	7.58

WORLD SERIES — NEW YORK (AL) 4   CHICAGO (NL) 0

LINE SCORES

TEAM	1	2	3	4	5	6	7	8	9	10	11	12	R	H	E

Game 1   September 28 at New York

| CHI (NL) | 2 | 0 | 0 | 0 | 0 | 0 | 2 | 2 | 0 | | | | 6 | 10 | 1 |
| NY (AL) | 0 | 0 | 0 | 3 | 0 | 5 | 3 | 1 | X | | | | 12 | 8 | 2 |

Bush, Grimes (6), Smith (8)   **Ruffing**

Game 2   September 29 at New York

| CHI | 1 | 0 | 1 | 0 | 0 | 0 | 0 | 0 | 0 | 2 | 9 | 0 |
| NY | 2 | 0 | 2 | 0 | 1 | 0 | 0 | 0 | X | 5 | 10 | 1 |

Warneke   Gomez

Game 3   October 1 at Chicago

| NY | 3 | 0 | 1 | 0 | 2 | 0 | 0 | 0 | 1 | 7 | 8 | 1 |
| CHI | 1 | 0 | 2 | 1 | 0 | 0 | 0 | 0 | 1 | 5 | 9 | 4 |

Pipgras, Pennock (9)   Root, Malone (5), May (8) Tinning (9)

Game 4   October 2 at Chicago

| NY | 1 | 0 | 2 | 0 | 0 | 2 | 4 | 0 | 4 | 13 | 19 | 4 |
| CHI | 4 | 0 | 0 | 0 | 0 | 1 | 0 | 0 | 1 | 6 | 9 | 1 |

Allen, **W. Moore** (1), Pennock (7)   Bush, Warneke (1), **May** (4) Tinning (7), Grimes (9)

COMPOSITE BATTING

NAME	POS	G	AB	R	H	2B	3B	HR	RBI	BA
New York (AL)										
Totals		4	144	37	45	6	0	8	36	.313
Gehrig	1B	4	17	9	9	1	0	3	8	.529
Chapman	OF	4	17	9	5	2	0	0	6	.294
Lazzeri	2B	4	17	4	5	0	0	2	5	.294
Dickey	C	4	16	2	7	0	0	0	4	.438
Combs	OF	4	16	8	6	1	0	1	4	.375
Ruth	OF	4	15	6	5	0	0	2	6	.333
Sewell	3B	4	15	4	5	1	0	0	3	.333
Crosetti	SS	4	15	2	2	1	0	0	1	.133
Pipgras	P	1	5	0	0	0	0	0	0	.000
Ruffing	P	2	4	0	0	0	0	0	0	.000
W. Moore	P	3	0	0	1	0	0	0	0	.333
Gomez	P	1	3	0	0	0	0	0	0	.000
Pennock	P	2	1	0	0	0	0	0	0	.000
Byrd	OF	1	0	0	0	0	0	0	0	—
Hoag	PR	1	0	1	0	0	0	0	0	—
Allen	P	1	1	0	0	0	0	0	0	.000
Chicago (NL)										
Totals		4	146	19	37	8	2	3	16	.253
Stephenson	OF	4	18	2	8	0	0	0	4	.444
Cuyler	OF	4	18	5	5	1	1	1	2	.278
Herman	2B	4	18	5	4	1	0	0	1	.222
English	3B	4	17	2	3	0	0	0	1	.176
Hartnett	C	4	16	2	5	2	0	1	1	.313
Grimm	1B	4	15	2	5	2	0	0	1	.333
Jurges	SS	3	11	1	4	1	0	0	3	.364
Demaree	OF	2	7	1	2	0	0	0	4	.286
J. Moore	OF	2	7	1	0	0	0	0	0	.000
Koenig	SS	2	4	1	1	0	0	0	1	.250
Warneke	P	3	4	0	0	0	0	0	0	.000
Hemsley	C	2	3	0	0	0	0	0	0	.000
Gudat	PH	2	2	0	0	0	0	0	0	.000
May	P	1	2	0	0	0	0	0	0	.000
Root	P	1	2	0	0	0	0	0	0	.000
Bush	P	2	2	0	0	0	0	0	0	.000
Grimes	P	2	1	0	0	0	0	0	0	.000
Tinning	P	2	2	1	0	0	0	0	0	.000
Hack	PR	1	1	0	0	0	0	0	0	—
Malone	P	1	0	0	0	0	0	0	0	—
Smith	P	1	1	0	0	0	0	0	0	—

COMPOSITE PITCHING

NAME	G	IP	H	BB	SO	W	L	SV	ERA
New York (AL)									
Totals	4	36	37	11	24	4	0	2	3.25
Gomez	1	9	9	1	8	1	0	0	1.00
Ruffing	1	9	10	6	10	1	0	0	4.00
Pipgras	1	8	9	3	1	1	0	0	4.50
W. Moore	1	5.1	2	0	1	1	0	0	2.25
Pennock	2	4	2	1	4	0	0	2	2.25
Allen	1	0.2	5	0	0	0	0	0	40.50
Chicago (NL)									
Totals	4	34	45	23	26	0	4	0	9.26
Warneke	2	10.2	15	5	8	0	1	0	5.91
Bush	2	5.2	5	6	2	0	1	0	14.29
May	2	4.2	9	3	4	0	1	0	11.57
Root	1	4.1	6	3	4	0	1	0	10.38
Malone	1	2.2	1	4	0	0	0	0	0.00
Grimes	2	2.2	7	2	0	0	0	0	23.63
Tinning	2	2.1	0	3	0	0	0	0	0.00
Smith	1	1	2	1	0	0	0	0	9.00

1933 A Starry Conglomerate

John McGraw was there and so was Connie Mack. There was also Ruth, Gehrig, Simmons, Dykes, Cronin, Gomez, Grove, Frisch, Klein, Terry, Traynor, Hubbell, Hartnett, and Paul Waner. They didn't all belong to the same team or league, but nevertheless they, with several other of their prominent colleagues, were assembled at Comiskey Park in Chicago on July 6, for the first All-Star Game.

McGraw came out of retirement to pilot the Nationals. Mack, at 61, had been around even before the junior circuit dawned and was an obvious choice to lead the Americans. The idea for *the game* came from Grantland Rice, dean of sportswriters. Baseball fans endorsed the idyllic scheme by sending 49,000 of their breed to pay homage to the event.

It was a game which millions of fans throughout the country had long conceived in fantasy, never daring to hope beyond their imaginative scribbling of dream lineups that it would suddenly turn into disbelieving reality. But there it was—plunk in the middle of a depression—a mastermind of a promotion that pitted the best against the best. Fostered as a benefit to raise funds for the National Association of Professional Baseball Players, the game was an instant success.

McGraw regarded the "dream game" for what it simply seemed to be— a dream game. Mack had different notions and a better team . Once he got the lead in the second inning on Lefty Grove's single, he coldly decided to play baseball and not shuttle his players, save for the pitchers and Earl Averill, who pinch-hit for General Crowder in the sixth. Mack's other players, Jimmie Foxx, Tony Lazzeri, Bill Dickey, Oral Hildebrand, and Wes Ferrell, spent the game in the best seats in the house—the dugout. Matters were decided in the third inning when Babe Ruth, playing on 38-year-old legs, delivered a home run with Charlie Gehringer on board for what turned out to be the go-ahead run in a 4-2 game.

In the regular business at hand, Washington captured the American League pennant in easy fashion behind rookie manager Joe Cronin, who also spent the season at shortstop with a .309 average. Washington's drive to the pennant was strongly aided by several off- season trades which brought to the team Goose Goslin, Fred Schulte, Lefty Stewart, Luke Sewell, Jack Russell,

and Earl Whitehill.

The Yankees gave up the chance to repeat due to poorer pitching and age beginning to catch up with Ruth. The A's traded away their pennant hopes when Al Simmons, Jimmy Dykes, and Mule Haas were sent to the White Sox. Only Lefty Grove, 24-8, and Jimmie Foxx, winner of the Triple Crown, saved Mack from a totally disgraceful season.

The Giants matched Washington's stunt of winning a pennant with a playing-manager in Bill Terry, who led the team with a .322 average and a five-game victory over Pittsburgh for the Jints' first National League flag since 1924. Terry was the main offensive threat on a squad which relied heavily on strong pitching by aces Carl Hubbell and Hal Schumacher. Reversing the New York story, the hot-hitting Pirates were hurt by a weak mound staff. The Cubs looked like they would easily repeat when they got Babe Herman from Cincinnati, but despite taking the Reds' best hitter they could do no better than tie their season series with the tail-enders and finish third, six games off the pace. The Phillies, although finishing seventh, helped make history behind Chuck Klein's Triple Crown performance, which made Philadelphia the only city ever to produce in one year two men to lead their leagues in average, home runs, and runs batted in.

When it came to the World Series, Washington and Cronin were the favorite, but the spirit which Terry instilled in bringing the Giants from sixth in 1932, was enough for a five-game Series victory. Both playing-managers played well, but the hero's laurels went to Carl Hubbell, who pitched two complete game victories, and 24-year-old Mel Ott, who led both teams in batting and clouted a tenth-inning homer to wrap up the final game for New York.

In another of the interesting highlights of the season, an energetic young man, Tom Yawkey, purchased the Red Sox in February. Yawkey's determination to bring a winning team to Boston often culminated—as history would prove in the many years to come—in spending exorbitant dollars for veteran players and hot prospects alike. But as fate would have it, Yawkey's dollars, more often than not, fell far short of the value he received. In fact, Yawkey's misfortunes did not wait long to visit him. When he purchased aging, but brilliant Lefty Grove from Connie Mack for the 1934 season, the hard luck was well underway.

1933 AMERICAN LEAGUE

NAME	G by Pos	B	AGE	G	AB	R	H	2B	3B	HR	RBI	BB	SO	SB	BA	SA
WASHINGTON 1st 99-53 .651				**JOE CRONIN**												
TOTALS			30	153	5524	850	1586	281	86	60	793	539	395	65	.287	.402
Joe Kuhel	1B153	L	27	153	602	89	194	34	10	11	107	59	48	17	.322	.467
Buddy Myer	2B129	L	29	131	530	95	160	29	15	4	61	60	29	9	.302	.436
Joe Cronin	SS152	R	26	152	602	89	186	45	11	5	118	87	49	5	.309	.445
Ossie Bluege	3B128	R	32	140	501	63	131	14	0	6	71	55	34	6	.261	.325
Goose Goslin	OF128	L	32	132	549	97	163	35	10	10	64	42	35	5	.297	.452
Fred Schulte	OF142	R	32	144	550	98	162	30	7	5	87	61	27	10	.295	.402
Heinie Manush	OF150	L	31	153	658	115	221	32	17	5	95	36	18	6	.336	.459
Luke Sewell	C141	R	32	141	474	64	125	30	4	2	61	48	24	7	.264	.357
Dave Harris	OF45, 1B6, 3B2	R	33	82	177	33	46	9	2	5	38	25	26	3	.260	.418
Sam Rice	OF39	L	43	73	85	19	25	4	3	1	12	3	7	0	.294	.447
Bob Boken	2B31, 3B19, SS10	R	25	55	133	19	37	5	2	3	26	9	16	0	.278	.414
Moe Berg	C35	R	31	40	65	8	12	3	0	2	9	4	5	0	.185	.323
Cliff Bolton	C9, OF1	L	26	33	39	4	16	1	1	0	6	6	3	0	.410	.487
John Kerr	2B16, 3B1	R	34	28	40	5	8	0	0	0	3	2	1	0	.200	.200
Cecel Travis	3B15	L	19	18	43	7	13	1	0	0	2	2	5	0	.302	.326
Nick Altrock		B	56	1	1	0	0	0	0	0	0	0	0	0	.000	.000

NAME	T	AGE	W	L	PCT	SV	G	GS	CG	IP	H	BB	SO	SHO	ERA
		30	99	53	.651	26	153	153	68	1390	1415	452	447	5	3.82
General Crowder	R	34	24	15	.615	4	52	35	17	299	311	81	110	0	3.97
Earl Whitehill	L	33	22	8	.733	1	39	37	19	270	271	100	96	2	3.33
Lefty Stewart	L	32	15	6	.714	0	34	31	11	231	227	60	69	1	3.82
Jack Russell	R	27	12	6	.667	13	50	7	3	124	119	32	28	0	2.69
Monty Weaver	R	27	10	5	.667	0	23	21	12	152	167	53	45	1	3.26
Tommy Thomas	R	33	7	7	.500	3	35	14	2	135	149	49	35	0	4.80
Bobby Burke	L	26	4	3	.571	0	23	6	4	64	64	31	28	1	3.23
Bill McAfee	R	25	3	2	.600	5	27	1	0	53	64	21	14	0	6.62
Alex McColl	R	39	1	0	1.000	0	4	1	1	17	13	7	5	0	2.65
Ed Linke	R	21	1	0	1.000	0	3	2	0	16	15	11	6	0	5.06
Ray Prim	L	26	0	1	.000	0	2	1	0	14	13	2	6	0	3.21
Ed Chapman	R	27	0	0	—	0	6	1	0	9	10	4	4	0	8.00
Bud Thomas	R	22	0	0		0	2	0	0	4	11	2	1	0	15.75
John Campbell	R	25	0	0		0	1	0	0	1	1	0	0	0	0.00

NAME	G by Pos	B	AGE	G	AB	R	H	2B	3B	HR	RBI	BB	SO	SB	BA	SA
NEW YORK 2nd 91-59 .607 7				**JOE McCARTHY**												
TOTALS			29	152	5274	927	1495	241	75	144	849	700	506	74	.283	.440
Lou Gehrig	1B152	L	30	152	593	138	198	41	12	32	139	92	42	9	.334	.605
Tony Lazzeri	2B138	R	29	139	523	94	154	22	12	18	104	73	62	15	.294	.486
Frankie Crosetti	SS133	R	22	136	451	71	154	22	9	4	55	40	4	3	.253	.379
Joe Sewell	3B131	L	34	135	524	87	143	18	1	2	54	71	4	2	.273	.323
Babe Ruth	OF132, 1B1, P1	L	38	137	459	97	138	21	3	34	103	114	90	4	.301	.582
Earle Combs	OF104	L	34	122	419	86	125	22	16	5	60	47	19	6	.298	.463
Ben Chapman	OF147	R	24	147	565	112	176	36	4	9	98	72	45	27	.312	.437
Bill Dickey	C127	L	26	130	478	58	152	24	8	14	97	47	14	3	.318	.490
Dixie Walker	OF77	R	22	98	328	68	90	15	7	15	51	26	28	2	.274	.500
Sammy Byrd	OF71	R	26	85	107	26	30	6	1	2	11	15	12	0	.280	.411
Red Ruffing	P35	R	29	55	115	10	29	3	1	2	13	7	15	0	.252	.348
Lyn Lary	3B28, SS16, 1B3, OF1	R	27	52	127	25	28	3	3	0	13	28	17	2	.220	.291
Doc Farrell	SS22, 3B20	R	31	44	93	16	25	0	0	0	6	16	6	0	.269	.269
Art Jorgens	C19	R	28	21	50	9	11	3	0	2	13	12	3	1	.220	.400
Tony Rensa	C8	R	31	8	29	4	9	2	1	0	1	3	1	3	.310	.448
Joe Glenn	C5	R	24	5	21	1	3	0	0	0	1	3	0	0	.143	.143
1 Bill Werber	3B1	R	25	3	2	0	0	0	0	0	0	0	0	0	.000	.000

NAME	T	AGE	W	L	PCT	SV	G	GS	CG	IP	H	BB	SO	SHO	ERA
		30	91	59	.607	22	152	152	70	1355	1426	612	711	8	4.36
Lefty Gomez	L	24	16	10	.615	2	35	30	14	235	218	106	163	4	3.18
Johnny Allen	R	28	15	7	.682	1	25	24	10	185	171	87	119	1	4.38
Russ Van Atta	L	27	12	4	.750	1	26	22	10	157	160	63	76	1	4.18
Red Ruffing	R	29	9	14	.391	3	35	28	18	235	230	93	122	0	3.91
Jumbo Brown	R	26	7	5	.583	0	21	8	1	74	78	52	55	0	5.23
Herb Pennock	L	39	7	4	.636	4	23	5	2	65	96	21	22	1	5.54
3 George Uhle	R	34	6	1	.857	0	12	6	4	61	63	20	26	0	5.16
Don Brennan	R	29	5	1	.833	3	18	10	3	85	92	47	46	0	4.98
Wilcy Moore	R	36	5	6	.455	3	35	0	0	62	92	20	17	0	5.52
Danny MacFayden	R	28	3	2	.600	0	25	6	2	90	120	37	28	0	5.90
Charlie Devens	R	23	3	3	.500	0	14	8	2	62	59	50	23	0	4.35
1 George Pipgras	R	33	2	2	.500	0	4	4	3	33	32	12	14	0	3.27
Babe Ruth	L	38	1	0	1.000	0	1	1	1	9	12	3	0	0	5.00
Pete Appleton	R	29	0	0	—	0	1	0	0	2	3	1	0	0	0.00

NAME	G by Pos	B	AGE	G	AB	R	H	2B	3B	HR	RBI	BB	SO	SB	BA	SA
PHILADELPHIA 3rd 79-72 .523 19.5				**CONNIE MACK**												
TOTALS			27	152	5330	875	1519	299	56	139	829	625	618	33	.285	.440
Jimmie Foxx	1B149, SS1	R	25	149	573	125	204	37	9	48	163	96	93	2	.356	.703
Max Bishop	2B113	L	33	117	391	80	115	27	4	1	42	106	46	1	.294	.399
Dib Williams	SS84, 2B29, 1B2	R	23	115	408	52	118	20	5	11	64	32	35	1	.289	.444
Pinky Higgins	3B152	R	24	152	567	85	178	35	11	13	99	61	53	2	.314	.483
Ed Coleman	OF89	L	31	102	388	48	109	26	3	6	68	19	51	0	.281	.410
Doc Cramer	OF152	R	27	152	661	109	195	27	8	8	75	36	24	5	.295	.396
Bob Johnson	OF142	R	27	142	535	103	155	44	4	21	93	85	74	8	.290	.505
Mickey Cochrane	C128	L	30	130	429	104	138	30	4	15	60	106	22	8	.322	.515
Eric McNair	SS46, 2B28	R	24	89	310	57	81	15	4	7	48	15	32	2	.261	.403
Lou Finney	OF63	L	22	74	240	26	59	12	3	3	22	13	17	1	.267	.371
Bing Miller	OF30, 1B6	R	38	67	120	22	33	7	1	2	17	12	7	4	.275	.400
Ed Madjeski	C41	R	24	51	142	17	40	4	0	1	17	4	21	0	.282	.310
Ed Cihocki	SS28, 2B1, 3B1	R	23	33	97	6	14	2	0	1	6	3	12	0	.144	.227
Frankie Hayes	C3	R	18	2	1	0	0	0	0	0	0	0	0	0	.000	.000
Joe Zapustas	OF2	R	25	2	5	0	1	0	0	0	0	0	0	0	.200	.200

NAME	T	AGE	W	L	PCT	SV	G	GS	CG	IP	H	BB	SO	SHO	ERA
		29	79	72	.523	14	152	152	69	1344	1523	644	423	6	4.81
Lefty Grove	L	33	24	8	.750	6	45	28	21	275	280	83	114	2	3.21
Roy Mahaffey	R	29	13	10	.565	0	33	23	9	179	198	74	66	0	5.18
Sugar Cain	R	26	13	12	.520	1	38	32	16	218	244	137	43	1	4.25
Rube Walberg	L	36	9	13	.409	4	40	20	10	201	224	95	68	1	4.88
George Earnshaw	R	33	5	10	.333	0	21	18	4	118	153	58	37	0	5.95
Dick Barrett	R	26	4	4	.500	0	15	7	3	70	74	49	26	0	5.79
Johnny Marcum	R	23	3	2	.600	0	5	3	2	37	28	10	14	0	4.50
Jim Peterson	R	24	2	5	.286	0	32	5	0	91	114	36	18	0	4.95
Tony Freitas	L	25	2	4	.333	1	19	9	2	64	90	24	15	0	7.31
Gowell Claset	L	25	1	0	1.000	0	11	0	0	11	23	11	1	0	9.82
1 Hank McDonald	R	22	1	0	1.000	0	12	0	0	14	14	4	1	0	5.25
Tim McKeithan	R	26	1	0	1.000	0	9	0	0	9	10	4	3	0	4.00
Bobby Coombs	R	26	0	0	—	0	2	0	0	31	47	20	8	0	7.55
Bill Dietrich	R	23	0	1	.000	0	13	1	0	13	19	4	5	0	5.02
Emile Roy	R	26	0	1	.000	0	2	0	0	3	5	3	1	0	31.50
Hank Winston	R	29	0	0		0	1	0	0	3	6	2	1	0	6.43

Batting

NAME	G by Pos	B	AGE	G	AB	R	H	2B	3B	HR	RBI	BB	SO	SB	BA	SA
CLEVELAND 4th 75-76 .497 23.5 ROGER PECKINPAUGH 26-25 .510 WALTER JOHNSON 49-51 .490																
TOTALS			27	151	5240	654	1366	218	77	50	611	448	426	36	.261	.360
Harley Boss	1B110	L	24	112	438	54	118	17	7	1	50	53	25	27	2	.269	.347
Odell Hale	2B73, 3B21	R	22	98	351	49	97	19	8	10	64	30	37	2	.276	.462
Bill Knickerbocker (JJ)	SS80	R	21	80	279	20	63	16	3	2	32	11	30	1	.226	.326
Willie Kamm	3B131	R	33	133	447	59	126	17	2	1	47	54	27	7	.282	.336
Dick Porter	OF124	L	31	129	499	73	133	19	6	0	41	51	42	4	.267	.329
Earl Averill	OF149	L	31	151	599	83	180	39	16	11	92	54	29	3	.301	.474
Joe Vosmik	OF113	R	23	119	438	53	115	20	10	4	56	42	13	0	.263	.381
Roy Spencer	C72	R	33	75	227	26	46	5	2	0	23	23	17	0	.203	.242
1 Bill Cissell	2B62, SS46, 3B1	R	29	112	409	53	94	21	3	6	33	31	29	6	.230	.340
John Burnett	SS41, 2B17, 3B12	L	28	83	261	39	71	11	2	1	29	23	14	3	.272	.341
Frankie Pytlak	C69	R	24	80	248	36	77	10	6	2	33	17	10	3	.310	.423
Wes Ferrell (SA)	P28, 1/13	R	25	61	140	26	38	7	0	7	26	20	22	0	.271	.471
Milt Galatzer	OF40, 1B5	L	26	57	160	19	38	2	1	1	17	23	21	2	.238	.281
Glenn Myatt	C27	L	35	40	77	10	18	4	0	0	7	15	8	0	.234	.286
Eddie Morgan	1B32, OF1	R	29	39	121	10	32	3	1	1	13	7	9	1	.264	.364
Mike Powers	OF11	R	22	47	47	6	13	2	1	0	3	2	6	2	.277	.362
Johnny Oulliber	OF18	R	22	22	75	9	20	1	0	0	3	4	2	0	.267	.280
Hal Trosky	1B11	L	20	11	44	6	13	1	2	1	8	2	12	0	.295	.477
DETROIT 5th 75-79 .487 25 BUCKY HARRIS 73-79 .480 DEL BAKER 2-0 1.000																
TOTALS			26	155	5502	722	1479	283	78	57	676	475	523	68	.269	.380
Hank Greenberg	1B117	R	22	117	449	59	135	33	3	12	87	46	78	6	.301	.468
Charlie Gehringer	2B155	L	30	155	628	103	204	42	6	12	105	68	27	5	.325	.468
Billy Rogell	SS155	B	28	155	587	67	173	42	11	0	57	79	33	6	.295	.404
Marv Owen	3B136	R	27	138	550	77	144	24	9	2	65	44	56	2	.262	.349
John Stone	OF141	L	27	148	574	86	161	33	11	11	80	54	37	1	.280	.434
Pete Fox	OF124	R	23	128	535	82	154	26	13	7	57	23	38	9	.288	.424
Gee Walker	OF113	R	25	127	483	68	135	29	7	9	64	15	49	26	.280	.424
Ray Hayworth	C133	R	29	134	425	37	104	14	3	1	45	35	28	0	.245	.299
Jo-Jo White	OF54	L	24	91	234	43	59	9	5	2	34	27	26	5	.252	.359
Harry Davis	1B44	L	25	66	173	24	37	8	2	0	14	22	8	2	.214	.283
Heinie Schuble	3B23, SS2, 2B1	R	26	49	96	12	21	4	4	0	6	5	17	2	.219	.281
Frank Doljack	OF37	R	25	42	147	18	42	5	2	0	22	14	13	2	.286	.347
Gene Desautels	C30	R	26	30	42	5	6	1	0	0	4	4	5	0	.143	.167
Johnny Pasek	C28	R	28	28	61	6	15	4	0	0	4	7	7	2	.246	.311
Billy Rhiel	OF1	R	28	21	17	1	3	0	1	0	1	1	3	0	.176	.294
Frank Reiber	C6	R	23	13	18	3	5	1	0	1	3	2	3	0	.278	.556
1 Earl Webb	OF2	L	35	6	11	1	3	0	0	0	0	3	2	0	.273	.273
CHICAGO 6th 67-83 .447 31 LEW FONSECA																
TOTALS			29	151	5318	683	1448	251	53	43	642	539	416	43	.272	.360
Red Kress	1B111, OF8	R	28	129	467	47	116	20	5	10	58	40	44	4	.248	.377
Jackie Hayes	2B138	R	26	138	535	69	138	23	4	2	47	55	36	2	.258	.331
Luke Appling	SS151	R	26	151	612	90	197	36	10	6	85	56	29	6	.322	.443
Jimmy Dykes	3B151	R	36	151	554	49	144	22	6	1	68	69	37	3	.260	.327
Evar Swanson	OF139	R	30	144	539	102	165	25	7	1	63	93	35	19	.306	.384
Mule Haas	OF146	L	29	146	585	97	168	33	4	1	51	65	41	0	.287	.362
Al Simmons	OF145	R	31	146	605	85	200	29	10	14	119	39	45	5	.331	.481
Frank Grube	C83	R	28	85	256	23	59	13	0	0	23	38	20	1	.230	.281
Charlie Berry	C83	R	30	86	271	25	69	8	3	2	28	17	16	0	.255	.328
2 Earl Webb	OF16, 1B10	L	35	58	107	16	31	5	1	1	8	16	13	0	.290	.364
Billy Sullivan (RL)	1B22, C8	L	22	54	125	9	24	5	0	1	13	10	5	0	.192	.208
Ted Lyons	P36	B	32	51	91	11	26	2	1	1	11	4	6	0	.286	.363
Hal Rhyne	2B19, 3B13, SS2	R	34	39	83	9	22	1	1	0	10	5	9	1	.265	.301
Lew Fonseca (NJ)	1B12	R	34	23	59	8	12	2	0	0	7	6	1	0	.203	.339
Milt Bocek	OF6	R	24	11	22	3	8	1	0	1	3	4	6	0	.364	.545
John Stoneham	OF9	L	24	10	25	4	3	0	0	0	3	2	2	0	.120	.240
Liz Funk	OF2	L	28	10	9	1	2	0	0	0	1	1	1	0	.222	.222
Charlie English	2B3	R	23	3	9	2	4	2	0	0	1	1	1	0	.444	.667
Mem Lovett		R	21	1	1	0	0	0	0	0	0	0	0	0	.000	.000
BOSTON 7th 63-86 .423 34.5 MARTY McMANUS																
TOTALS			28	149	5201	700	1407	294	56	50	647	519	464	62	.271	.377
Dale Alexander (LJ)	1B79	R	30	94	313	40	88	14	1	5	40	25	22	0	.281	.380
Johnny Hodapp	2B101, 1B10	R	27	115	413	55	129	27	5	3	54	33	14	1	.312	.424
Rabbitt Warstler	SS87	R	29	92	322	44	70	17	4	2	17	42	36	1	.217	.273
Marty McManus	3B76, 2B26, 1B4	R	33	106	366	51	104	30	4	3	36	49	21	3	.284	.413
Roy Johnson	OF125	L	30	133	483	88	151	30	7	10	95	55	36	13	.313	.466
Dusty Cooke	OF118	L	26	119	454	86	132	35	10	5	54	67	71	7	.291	.445
Smead Jolley	OF102	L	31	118	411	47	116	32	4	9	65	24	20	1	.282	.445
1 Rick Ferrell	C116	R	27	118	421	50	125	19	4	3	72	58	19	2	.297	.382
2 Bill Werber	SS71, 3B38, 2B2	R	25	108	425	64	110	30	6	3	39	33	39	15	.259	.379
Tom Oliver	OF86	R	30	90	244	25	63	9	1	0	23	13	7	1	.258	.303
Bob Seeds	1B41, OF32	R	26	88	230	26	56	13	4	0	23	21	20	1	.243	.335
Bucky Walters	3B43, 2B7	R	24	52	195	27	50	8	3	4	28	19	24	1	.256	.390
Johnny Gooch	C26	B	35	37	77	6	14	1	2	0	11	7	7	0	.182	.221
2 Joe Judge	1B28	L	39	34	104	20	32	8	1	0	22	13	4	2	.308	.404
Bob Fothergill	OF4	R	35	28	32	1	11	1	0	0	5	4	2	0	.344	.375
George Stumpf	OF15	L	22	22	41	8	14	3	0	0	5	4	2	4	.341	.415
Barney Friberg	2B6, 3B5, SS2	R	33	17	41	5	13	3	0	0	9	6	1	0	.317	.390
1 Merv Shea	C16	R	32	16	56	1	8	3	0	0	8	4	7	0	.143	.196
Freddie Muller	2B14	R	25	15	48	6	9	1	1	0	3	5	11	5	.188	.250
Mel Almada	OF13	L	20	14	44	11	15	0	0	1	3	11	3	4	.341	.409
Johnny Watwood	OF9	L	27	13	30	2	4	1	0	0	3	0	3	0	.133	.133
Lou Legett	C2	R	32	8	5	1	1	0	0	0	1	0	0	0	.200	.400
Tom Winsett	OF4	L	23	6	12	1	1	0	0	0	0	0	6	0	.083	.083
Marv Olson	2B1	R	26	3	1	1	0	0	0	0	0	1	0	0	.000	.000
Greg Mulleavy		R	27													
ST. LOUIS 8th 55-96 .364 43.5 BILL KILLEFER 34-57 .374 ALLAN SOTHORON 2-6 .250 ROGERS HORNSBY 19-33 .365																
TOTALS			28	153	5285	669	1337	244	64	64	605	520	556	70	.253	.360
Jack Burns	1B143	L	25	144	556	89	160	43	4	5	71	56	51	11	.288	.417
Oscar Melillo	2B130	R	33	132	496	50	145	23	6	3	79	29	18	12	.292	.381
Jim Levey	SS138	B	26	141	529	43	103	10	4	2	36	26	68	4	.195	.240
Art Scharein	3B95, SS24, 2B7	R	28	123	471	49	96	13	3	0	26	41	21	7	.204	.244
Bruce Campbell	OF144	L	23	148	567	87	157	38	6	16	106	69	77	10	.277	.457
Sammy West	OF127	L	28	133	517	93	155	25	12	11	48	54	25	9	.300	.458
Carl Reynolds	OF124	R	30	135	475	81	136	26	14	8	71	50	25	5	.286	.451
2 Merv Shea	C85	R	32	94	279	26	73	11	1	1	27	43	26	2	.262	.319
Ted Gullic	OF36, 3B33, 1B16	R	26	104	304	34	74	18	3	5	35	15	38	3	.243	.372
Debs Garms	OF47	L	26	78	189	35	60	10	2	4	24	30	21	2	.317	.455
Lin Storti	3B32, 2B24	B	26	70	210	26	41	7	4	3	21	25	31	2	.195	.310
Muddy Ruel	C28	R	37	63	63	13	12	2	0	0	8	24	4	0	.190	.222
2 Rollie Hemsley	C27	R	26	32	95	7	23	2	1	0	15	11	12	0	.242	.316
1 Rick Ferrell	C21	R	27	22	72	8	18	2	0	1	5	12	4	2	.250	.319
1 Jack Crouch	C9	R	29	19	30	1	9	1	0	0	5	0	1	0	.167	.267
2 Rogers Hornsby		R	37	11	9	1	3	0	0	0	0	1	1	0	.333	.778

Pitching

NAME	T	AGE	W	L	PCT	SV	G	GS	CG	IP	H	BB	SO	SHO	ERA
CLEVELAND TOTALS		27	75	76	.497	7	151	151	74	1350	1382	465	437	12	3.71
Oral Hilderbrand	R	26	16	11	.593	0	36	31	15	220	205	88	90	6	3.76
Mel Harder	R	23	15	17	.469	4	43	31	14	253	254	67	81	2	2.95
Wes Ferrell (SA)	R	25	11	12	.478	0	28	26	16	201	225	70	41	1	4.21
Clint Brown	R	29	11	12	.478	1	33	23	10	185	202	34	47	2	3.41
Monte Pearson	R	24	10	5	.667	0	19	16	10	135	111	55	54	0	2.33
Willis Hudlin	R	27	5	13	.278	1	34	17	6	147	161	61	44	0	3.98
Sarge Connally	R	34	5	3	.625	1	41	1	1	103	112	49	30	0	4.89
Belve Bean	R	28	1	2	.333	0	27	2	0	70	80	20	41	0	5.27
Thorton Lee	L	26	1	1	.500	0	3	2	2	17	13	11	7	0	4.24
Howard Craghead	R	25	0	0	—	0	11	0	0	17	19	10	2	0	6.35
DETROIT TOTALS		28	75	79	.487	17	155	155	69	1398	1415	561	575	6	3.96
Firpo Marberry	R	28	16	11	.593	2	37	32	15	238	232	61	84	1	3.29
Tommy Bridges	R	26	14	12	.538	2	33	28	17	233	192	110	120	2	3.09
Vic Sorrell	R	32	11	15	.423	1	36	28	13	233	233	78	75	1	3.79
Carl Fischer	L	27	11	15	.423	1	35	22	9	183	176	84	93	0	3.54
Schoolboy Rowe (SJ)	R	23	7	4	.636	0	19	15	8	123	129	31	75	1	3.59
Chief Hogsett	L	29	6	10	.375	9	45	2	0	116	137	56	39	0	4.50
2 Vic Frasier	R	28	5	5	.500	0	20	14	4	104	129	59	26	0	6.66
Elden Auker	R	22	3	3	.500	0	15	6	2	55	63	25	17	1	5.24
Luke Hamlin	R	28	1	0	1.000	0	3	1	0	17	20	10	10	0	4.76
Art Herring	R	27	1	2	.333	0	24	3	1	61	61	20	20	0	3.84
1 Whit Wyatt	R	25	1	1	.000	0	10	0	0	17	20	9	9	0	4.24
Roxie Lawson	R	27	0	1	.000	0	4	2	0	16	17	17	6	0	7.31
Bots Nekola	L	26	0	0	—	0	2	0	0	1	4	1	0	0	36.00
1 George Uhle	R	34	0	0	—	0	2	0	0	3	5	2	1	0	18.00
CHICAGO TOTALS		32	67	83	.447	13	151	151	53	1371	1505	519	423	8	4.45
Ed Durham	R	25	10	6	.625	0	24	21	6	139	137	46	65	0	4.47
Sad Sam Jones	R	40	10	12	.455	0	27	25	11	177	181	65	60	2	3.36
Ted Lyons	R	32	10	21	.321	1	36	27	14	228	260	74	74	2	4.48
Milt Gaston	R	37	8	12	.400	0	30	25	7	167	177	60	39	1	4.85
Joe Heving	R	32	7	5	.583	6	40	6	3	118	113	47	30	1	2.67
Jake Miller	L	35	6	8	.455	0	26	14	4	106	130	47	30	2	5.60
Chad Kimsey	R	26	4	1	.800	0	28	2	0	96	124	36	19	0	5.53
Paul Gregory	R	24	4	11	.267	0	23	17	5	104	124	47	18	0	4.93
Red Faber	R	44	3	4	.429	3	36	2	0	86	92	28	18	0	3.45
2 Whit Wyatt	R	25	3	4	.429	1	26	7	2	88	91	45	31	0	4.60
Les Tietje	R	22	2	0	1.000	0	3	3	1	22	16	15	9	0	2.45
1 Vic Frasier	R	28	1	1	.500	0	10	1	0	20	32	11	4	0	9.00
Hal Haid	R	35	0	0	—	0	6	0	0	15	18	13	7	0	7.80
Ira Hutchinson	R	22	0	0	—	0	1	0	0	4	7	3	2	0	13.50
George Murray	R	34	0	0	—	0	2	0	0	3	2	0	0	0	9.00
BOSTON TOTALS		27	63	86	.423	14	149	149	60	1328	1396	591	473	4	4.34
Gordon Rhodes	R	25	12	15	.444	0	34	29	14	232	242	93	85	0	4.03
2 George Pipgras	R	33	9	8	.529	1	29	28	9	128	140	45	56	2	4.08
Hank Johnson	R	27	8	6	.571	1	25	21	7	155	156	74	65	0	4.06
1 Lloyd Brown	L	28	8	8	.421	1	33	21	9	163	180	64	37	2	4.03
Bob Weiland	R	27	8	14	.364	3	39	27	12	216	197	100	97	0	3.87
Bob Kline	R	23	7	8	.467	4	46	8	1	127	197	67	16	0	4.54
Ivy Andrews	R	26	7	13	.350	1	34	17	5	140	157	61	44	0	4.95
Johnny Welch	R	27	6	9	.308	1	47	7	1	129	142	67	68	0	4.60
Curt Fullerton	R	34	0	2	.000	0	6	0	0	25	36	13	10	0	8.64
Jud McLaughlin	L	21	0	0	—	0	6	0	0	9	14	5	1	0	6.00
Mike Meola	R	27	0	0	—	0	6	2	2	5	2	1	0	0	27.00
ST. LOUIS TOTALS		28	55	96	.364	10	153	153	55	1361	1574	531	426	7	4.82
George Blaeholder	R	29	15	19	.441	0	38	36	14	256	283	93	85	3	4.71
Bump Hadley	R	28	15	20	.429	3	45	36	19	317	309	141	149	2	3.92
Sam Gray	R	35	7	4	.636	4	38	6	0	112	131	45	36	0	4.10
Ed Wells	L	33	6	14	.300	1	36	22	10	204	230	63	50	0	4.19
Wally Hebert	L	25	6	13	.300	0	33	10	3	88	114	35	19	0	5.32
Rollie Stiles	R	26	3	7	.300	1	34	5	1	115	154	47	29	1	5.01
Dick Coffman	R	26	3	7	.300	1	21	13	3	81	114	39	19	1	5.89
1 Lloyd Brown	L	28	1	6	.143	0	9			39	57	17	7	0	7.15
Jack Knott	R	26	1	8	.111	0	20	6	2	83	88	33	19	0	4.99
Garland Braxton	L	33	0	1	.000	0	8	1	0	11	8	5	10	0	10.13
2 Hank McDonald	R	22	0	0	—	0	25	0	0	58	83	34	22	0	8.69

NEW YORK — 1ST 91-61 .599 — BILL TERRY

NAME	G by Pos	B	AGE	G	AB	R	H	2B	3B	HR	RBI	BB	SO	SB	BA	SA
TOTALS			29	156	5481	636	1437	204	41	82	598	377	477	31	.263	.361
Bill Terry (BW)	1B117	L	34	123	475	68	153	20	5	6	58	40	23	3	.322	.423
Hughie Critz	2B133	R	32	133	558	68	137	18	5	2	33	23	24	4	.246	.306
Blondy Ryan	SS146	R	27	146	525	47	125	10	5	3	48	15	62	0	.238	.293
Johnny Vergas (IL)	3B123	R	26	123	458	57	124	21	6	16	72	39	66	1	.271	.448
Mel Ott	OF152	L	24	152	580	98	164	36	1	23	103	75	48	1	.283	.467
Kiddo Davis	OF120	R	31	126	434	61	112	20	4	7	37	25	30	10	.258	.371
Jo-Jo Moore	OF132	L	24	132	524	56	153	16	5	0	42	21	27	4	.292	.342
Gus Mancuso	C142	R	27	144	481	39	127	17	2	6	56	48	21	0	.264	.345
Homer Peel	Of45	R	30	84	148	16	38	1	1	1	12	14	10	0	.257	.297
2 Lefty O'Doul	OF63	L	36	78	229	31	70	9	1	9	35	29	17	1	.306	.472
Bernie James	2B26, SS6, 3B5	R	27	60	125	22	28	2	1	1	10	8	12	5	.224	.280
Travis Jackson	SS21, 3B21	R	29	53	122	11	30	5	0	0	12	8	11	2	.246	.287
Paul Richards	C36	R	24	51	87	4	17	3	0	0	10	3	12	0	.195	.230
1 Sam Leslie	1B35	R	27	40	137	21	44	12	3	3	27	12	9	0	.321	.518
Chuck Dressen	3B16	R	34	16	45	3	10	4	0	0	3	1	4	0	.222	.311
Joe Malay	1B8	L	27	8	24	0	3	0	0	0	0	0	0	0	.125	.125
Phil Weintraub	OF6	R	25	8	10	1	2	0	0	1	1	3	2	0	.200	.400
Hank Leiber	OF1	R	22	6	10	1	2	0	0	0	0	0	2	0	.200	.200
Harry Danning	C1	R	21	2	0	0	0	0	0	0	0	0	0	0	.000	.000

NAME	T	AGE	W	L	PCT	SV	G	GS	CG	IP	H	BB	SO	SHO	ERA
		31	91	61	.599	15	156	156	75	1409	1280	400	555	23	2.71
Carl Hubbell	L	30	23	12	.657	5	45	33	22	309	256	47	156	10	1.66
Hal Schumacher	R	22	19	12	.613	1	35	33	21	259	199	84	96	7	2.15
Freddie Fritzsimmons	R	31	16	11	.593	0	36	35	13	252	243	72	65	1	2.89
Roy Parmelee	R	26	13	8	.619	0	32	32	14	218	191	77	132	3	3.18
Dolf Luque	R	42	8	2	.800	4	35	0	0	80	75	19	23	0	2.70
Hi Bell	R	35	6	5	.545	5	38	7	1	105	100	20	24	1	2.06
2 Watty Clark	L	31	3	4	.429	0	16	5	0	44	58	11	11	0	4.70
Bill Shores	R	29	2	1	.667	0	8	3	1	37	41	14	20	0	3.89
2 George Uhle	R	34	1	1	.333	0	6	1	0	14	16	6	4	0	7.71
1 Ray Starr	R	27	0	1	.000	0	6	2	0	13	19	10	2	0	5.54
Glenn Spencer	R	27	0	2	.000	0	17	3	1	47	52	26	14	0	5.17
Jack Salveson	R	19	0	2	.000	0	5	3	1	31	30	14	8	0	3.77

PITTSBURGH — 2nd 87-67 .565 5 — GEORGE GIBSON

NAME	G by Pos	B	AGE	G	AB	R	H	2B	3B	HR	RBI	BB	SO	SB	BA	SA
TOTALS			27	154	5429	667	1548	249	84	39	618	366	334	34	.285	.383
Gus Suhr	1B154	L	27	154	566	72	151	31	11	10	75	72	52	2	.267	.413
Tony Piet	2B97	R	26	107	362	45	117	21	5	1	42	19	28	12	.323	.417
Arky Vaughan	SS152	L	21	152	573	85	180	29	19	9	97	64	23	3	.314	.478
Pie Traynor	3B154	R	34	154	624	85	190	27	6	1	82	35	24	5	.304	.372
Paul Waner	OF154	L	30	154	618	101	191	38	16	7	70	60	20	3	.309	.456
Fred Lindstrom	OF130	R	27	138	538	78	167	39	10	5	55	33	22	1	.310	.448
Lloyd Waner	OF114	L	27	121	500	59	138	14	5	0	26	22	8	3	.276	.324
Earl Grace	C88	L	26	93	291	22	84	13	1	3	44	26	23	0	.289	.371
Tommy Thevenow	2B61, SS3, 3B1	R	29	73	253	20	79	5	1	0	34	3	5	2	.312	.340
Woody Jensen	OF40	L	25	70	196	29	58	7	3	0	15	8	2	1	.296	.362
Adam Comorosky	OF30	R	28	64	162	18	46	8	1	1	15	4	9	2	.284	.364
Hal Finney	C47	R	27	56	133	17	31	4	1	1	18	3	19	0	.233	.301
Tom Padden	C27	R	24	30	90	5	19	2	0	0	8	2	6	0	.211	.233
Pep Young	2B1, SS1	R	25	25	20	3	6	1	1	0	0	0	5	0	.300	.450
2 Val Picinich	C16	R	36	16	52	6	13	4	0	1	7	5	10	0	.250	.385
Bill Brubaker	3B1	R	22	2	2	0	0	0	0	0	0	0	0	0	.000	.000
Red Nonnenkamp		R	21	1	1	0	0	0	0	0	0	0	1	0	.000	.000

NAME	T	AGE	W	L	PCT	SV	G	GS	CG	IP	H	BB	SO	SHO	ERA
		30	87	67	.565	12	154	154	70	1373	1417	313	401	16	3.27
Larry French	L	25	18	13	.581	1	47	35	21	291	290	55	88	5	2.72
Heinie Meine	R	37	15	8	.652	0	32	29	12	207	227	50	50	2	3.65
Bill Swift	R	25	14	10	.583	0	37	29	12	218	214	36	64	2	3.14
Steve Swetonic	R	29	12	12	.500	0	31	31	8	165	166	64	37	3	3.49
Hal Smith	R	31	8	7	.533	1	28	19	8	145	149	31	40	2	2.86
Leon Chagnon	R	30	6	4	.600	1	39	5	1	100	100	17	35	0	3.69
Waite Hoyt	R	33	5	7	.417	4	36	8	4	117	118	19	44	1	2.92
Ralph Birkofer	L	24	4	2	.667	0	9	8	3	51	43	17	20	1	2.92
Bill Harris	R	33	4	4	.500	5	31	0	0	59	68	14	19	0	3.20
Ray Kremer	R	40	1	1	1.000	0	7	0	0	20	36	9	4	0	10.35
Clise Dudley	R	29	0	0	—	0	1	0	0	.1	6	1	0	0	135.00

CHICAGO — 3rd 86-68 .558 6 — CHARLIE GRIMM

NAME	G by Pos	B	AGE	G	AB	R	H	2B	3B	HR	RBI	BB	SO	SB	BA	SA
TOTALS			29	154	5255	646	1422	256	51	72	608	392	475	52	.271	.380
Charlie Grimm	1B104	L	34	107	384	38	95	15	2	3	37	23	15	1	.247	.320
Billy Herman	2B153	R	23	153	619	82	173	35	2	0	44	45	34	5	.279	.342
Billy Jurges	SS143	R	25	143	448	49	131	17	6	5	50	26	39	3	.269	.359
Woody English	3B103, SS1	R	26	105	398	54	104	19	2	3	41	53	44	5	.261	.342
Babe Herman	OF131	L	30	137	540	77	147	36	12	16	93	50	57	6	.289	.502
Frank Demaree	OF133	R	23	134	515	68	140	24	6	6	51	22	42	4	.272	.377
Riggs Stephenson	OF91	R	35	97	346	45	113	14	4	4	51	34	16	5	.329	.436
Gabby Hartnett	C140	R	32	140	490	55	135	21	4	16	88	37	51	1	.276	.433
Mark Koenig	3B37, SS26, 2B2	B	30	80	218	32	62	12	1	3	25	15	9	5	.284	.390
Kiki Cuyler (BN)	OF69	R	34	70	262	37	83	13	3	5	31	21	29	4	.317	.447
Harvey Hendrick	1B38, OF8, 3B1	L	35	69	189	30	55	13	3	4	23	13	17	4	.291	.455
Gilly Campbell	C20	R	25	46	89	11	25	3	1	1	10	7	4	0	.281	.371
Lon Warneke	P36	R	24	39	100	9	30	6	1	2	13	3	13	0	.300	.440
Jim Mosolf	OF22	L	27	31	82	13	22	5	1	1	9	5	8	0	.268	.390
2 Taylor Douthit	OF18	R	32	27	71	8	13	5	0	0	5	11	7	2	.225	.296
Stan Hack	3B17	R	23	20	60	10	21	3	1	1	2	4	3	0	.350	.483
Dolph Camilli	1B16	L	26	16	58	8	13	2	1	2	7	4	11	3	.224	.397
Zack Taylor	C12	R	34	16	11	0	0	0	0	0	0	0	1	0	.000	.000
Babe Phelps	C2	L	25	3	7	0	2	0	0	0	0	0	0	0	.286	.286

NAME	T	AGE	W	L	PCT	SV	G	GS	CG	IP	H	BB	SO	SHO	ERA
		29	86	68	.558	9	154	154	95	1366	1316	411	488	16	2.92
Guy Bush	R	31	20	12	.625	2	41	32	20	259	261	68	84	4	2.75
Lon Warneke	R	24	18	13	.581	1	26	34	26	287	262	75	133	4	2.01
Charlie Root	R	34	15	10	.600	0	25	30	20	242	232	61	86	2	2.60
Rud Tinning	R	27	13	6	.684	1	32	21	10	175	169	60	59	3	3.19
Pat Malone	R	30	10	14	.417	0	31	26	13	186	186	59	72	2	3.92
Lynn Nelson	R	28	5	5	.500	1	24	3	1	76	65	30	20	0	3.20
1 Burleigh Grimes	R	39	3	6	.333	3	17	7	3	70	71	29	12	1	3.47
Roy Henshaw	L	21	2	1	.667	0	21	0	0	39	32	20	16	0	4.15
Leroy Herrmann	R	27	0	1	.000	1	9	1	0	21	26	8	4	0	5.57
Beryl Richmond	L	25	0	0	—	0	1	0	0	5	10	0	0	0	1.80
Carroll Yerkes	L	30	0	0	—	0	1	0	0	2	2	1	0	0	4.50

BOSTON — 4th 83-71 .539 9 — BILL McKECHNIE

NAME	G by Pos	B	AGE	G	AB	R	H	2B	3B	HR	RBI	BB	SO	SB	BA	SA
TOTALS			29	156	5243	552	1320	217	56	54	511	326	428	25	.252	.345
Buck Jordan	1B150	L	26	152	588	77	168	29	9	4	46	34	22	4	.286	.388
Rabbit Maranville	2B142	R	41	143	478	46	104	15	4	0	38	36	34	2	.218	.266
Billy Urbanski	SS143	R	30	144	566	65	142	21	4	0	35	33	48	4	.251	.302
2 Pinky Whitney	3B85, 2B18	R	28	100	382	42	94	17	2	8	49	25	23	2	.246	.364
Randy Moore	OF122, 1B10	L	28	135	497	64	150	23	7	8	70	40	16	3	.302	.425
Wally Berger	OF136	R	27	137	528	84	165	37	8	27	106	41	77	2	.313	.566
1 Hal Lee	OF87	R	28	88	312	32	69	15	9	1	28	18	26	1	.221	.337
Shanty Hogan	C95	R	27	96	328	15	83	7	0	3	30	13	9	0	.253	.302
Joe Mowry	OF64	R	25	86	249	25	55	8	5	0	20	15	22	1	.221	.293
Al Spohrer	C65	R	30	67	184	11	46	6	1	1	12	11	13	3	.250	.310
Dick Gyselman	3B42, 2B5, SS1	R	25	58	155	10	37	6	2	0	12	7	21	0	.239	.303
Ed Brandt	P41	R	28	47	97	9	30	4	0	0	6	4	7	0	.309	.351
Pinky Hargrave	C25	B	37	45	73	5	13	0	0	0	6	5	7	1	.178	.178
1 Fritz Knothe	3B33, SS9	R	30	44	158	15	36	5	2	1	6	13	25	1	.228	.304
1 Wes Schulmerich	OF21	R	31	29	85	10	21	6	1	1	13	5	10	0	.247	.376
Tommy Thompson	OF24	R	23	24	97	6	18	1	0	0	6	4	9	0	.186	.196
Red Worthington (BL)	OF10	R	27	17	45	3	7	4	0	0	1	0	3	0	.156	.244
Dutch Holland	OF7	R	29	13	31	3	8	3	0	0	3	0	2	1	.258	.355
Earl Clark	OF6	R	25	7	23	3	8	1	0	0	3	2	1	0	.348	.391
Hod Ford	SS5	R	35	5	15	0	1	0	0	0	0	0	1	0	.067	.067
Al Wright	2B3	R	22	4	1	0	1	0	0	0	0	0	0	0	1.000	1.000

NAME	T	AGE	W	L	PCT	SV	G	GS	CG	IP	H	BB	SO	SHO	ERA
		33	83	71	.539	16	156	156	85	1403	1391	355	383	15	2.96
Ben Cantwell	R	31	20	10	.667	2	40	29	18	255	242	54	57	2	2.61
Ed Brandt	L	28	18	14	.583	4	41	32	23	288	256	77	104	3	2.59
Fred Frankhouse	R	29	16	15	.516	2	43	30	14	245	249	77	83	2	2.79
Huck Betts	R	36	11	11	.500	4	35	26	17	242	225	55	40	2	2.79
Tom Zachary	L	37	4	9	.458	2	26	20	6	125	134	35	22	1	3.53
Leo Mangum	R	37	4	3	.571	0	25	5	2	84	93	11	28	1	3.32
2 Bob Smith	R	38	4	3	.571	1	14	4	3	59	68	7	16	1	3.20
Ed Fallenstein	R	24	2	1	.667	0	9	4	1	35	43	13	5	1	3.60
Socks Seibold	R	37	1	4	.200	1	11	5	1	37	43	14	10	0	3.65
2 Ray Starr	R	27	0	1	.000	0	9	1	0	28	32	9	15	0	3.86
Bob Brown (AJ)	R	22	0	0	—	0	5	0	0	6	3	3		0	2.57

ST. LOUIS — 5th 82-71 .536 9.5 — GABBY STREET 46-45 .505 FRANKIE FRISCH 36-26 .581

NAME	G by Pos	B	AGE	G	AB	R	H	2B	3B	HR	RBI	BB	SO	SB	BA	SA
TOTALS			30	154	5387	687	1486	256	61	57	629	391	528	99	.276	.378
Ripper Collins	1B123	B	29	132	493	66	153	26	7	10	68	38	49	7	.310	.452
Frankie Frisch	2B132, SS15	B	34	147	585	74	177	32	6	4	66	48	16	18	.303	.398
2 Leo Durocher	SS123	R	27	123	395	45	102	18	4	2	41	26	32	3	.258	.339
Pepper Martin	3B145	R	29	145	599	122	189	36	12	8	57	67	46	26	.316	.456
George Watkins	OF135	L	33	138	525	66	146	24	5	5	62	39	62	11	.278	.371
Ernie Orsatti	OF101, 1B3	L	29	120	436	53	130	30	3	0	38	33	33	14	.298	.374
Joe Medwick	OF147	R	21	148	595	92	182	40	10	18	98	26	56	5	.306	.497
Jimmie Wilson	C107	R	32	113	369	34	94	17	0	1	45	23	33	6	.255	.309
Ethan Allen	OF67	R	29	91	261	25	63	7	3	0	36	13	22	3	.241	.291
Pat Crawford	1B29, 2B15, 3B7	L	31	79	224	24	60	8	2	0	21	14	9	1	.268	.321
Bob O'Farrell	C50	R	36	55	163	16	39	4	2	2	20	15	25	0	.239	.325
1 Rogers Hornsby	2B17	R	37	46	83	9	27	6	0	2	21	12	6	1	.325	.470
Gordon Slade	SS31, 2B1	R	28	39	62	6	7	1	0	0	3	6	7	1	.113	.129
Estel Crabtree	OF7	R	29	23	34	6	9	3	0	0	3	2	5	1	.265	.353
Bill Lewis	C8	R	28	15	35	8	14	1	0	1	8	2	3	1	.400	.514
Burgess Whitehead	SS9, 2B3	R	23	12	12	1	2	1	0	0	0	1	1	0	.167	.250
Gene Moore	OF10	R	23	11	38	6	15	3	2	0	8	4	10	1	.395	.579
1 Sparky Adams	SS5, 3B3	R	38	8	12	0	2	0	0	0	0	0	1	0	.167	.200
Ray Pepper	OF2	R	27	3	9	2	2	0	0	0	1	0	0	0	.222	.222
Joe Sprinz	C3	R	30	3	5	1	1	0	0	0	0	0	2	0	.200	.200
Charlie Wilson	SS1	R	28	3	7	0	2	0	0	0	1	0	0	0	.286	.286
Charlie Gelbert (LJ) 27																

NAME	T	AGE	W	L	PCT	SV	G	GS	CG	IP	H	BB	SO	SHO	ERA
		31	82	71	.536	16	154	154	73	1383	1391	452	635	11	3.37
Dizzy Dean	R	23	20	18	.526	4	48	34	26	293	279	64	199	3	3.04
Tex Carleton	R	26	17	11	.607	3	44	33	15	277	263	97	147	4	3.38
Wild Bill Hallahan	L	30	16	13	.552	0	36	32	16	244	245	98	93	2	3.50
Bill Walker	L	29	9	10	.474	0	29	20	6	158	168	67	41	2	3.42
Jesse Haines	R	39	9	6	.600	1	32	10	5	115	113	37	37	0	2.50
Dazzy Vance	R	42	6	2	.750	3	28	11	2	99	105	28	67	0	3.55
Syl Johnson	R	32	3	3	.500	3	31	3	1	84	89	16	28	0	4.29
Jim Mooney	L	26	2	5	.286	1	21	8	2	77	87	26	14	0	3.74
2 Burleigh Grimes	R	39	3	1	.750	5	18	4	0	55	51	18	8	0	5.14
1 Paul Derringer	R	26	0	2*	.000	0	3	2	1	17	24	9	3	0	4.24
1 Allyn Stout	R	28	0	0	—	0	2	1	0	6	3	3	2	0	0.00
Jim Lindsey	R	35	0	0	—	0	3	1	0	8	16	2	5	0	4.50

*Derringer, also with Cincinnati, League leader in L with 27.

BROOKLYN   6th 65-88 .425 26.5   MAX CAREY

NAME	G by Pos	B	AGE	G	AB	R	H	2B	3B	HR	RBI	BB	SO	SB	BA	SA
TOTALS			29	157	5367	617	1413	224	51	62	566	397	453	82	.263	.359
2 Sam Leslie	1B95	L	27	96	364	41	104	11	4	5	46	23	14	1	.286	.379
Tony Cuccinello	2B120,3B14	R	25	134	485	58	122	31	4	9	65	44	40	4	.252	.388
Glenn Wright (AJ)	SS51,1B9,3B2	R	32	71	192	19	49	13	0	1	18	11	24	1	.255	.339
Joe Stripp	3B140	R	30	141	537	69	149	20	7	1	51	26	23	5	.277	.346
Johnny Frederick	OF138	L	31	147	556	65	171	22	7	7	64	36	14	9	.308	.410
Danny Taylor	OF91	L	32	103	358	75	102	23	9	9	40	47	45	11	.285	.469
Hack Wilson	OF90,2B5	R	33	117	360	41	96	13	2	9	54	52	50	7	.267	.389
Al Lopez	C124,2B1	R	24	126	372	39	112	11	4	3	41	21	39	10	.301	.379
Buzz Boyle	OF90	L	25	93	338	38	101	13	4	0	31	16	24	1	.299	.361
Chink Outen	C56	R	28	93	153	20	38	10	0	4	17	20	15	1	.248	.392
Jake Flowers	SS36,2B19,3B8,OF1	R	31	78	210	28	49	11	2	2	22	24	15	13	.233	.333
Jimmy Jordan (BH)	SS51,2B11	R	25	70	211	16	54	12	1	0	17	4	6	3	.256	.322
Joe Hutcheson	OF45	L	28	55	184	19	43	4	1	6	21	15	13	1	.234	.364
1 Lefty O'Doul	OF41	L	36	43	159	14	40	5	1	5	21	15	6	1	.252	.390
1 Joe Judge	1B28	L	28	42	112	7	24	2	1	0	9	7	10	0	.214	.250
Del Bissonette	1B32	L	33	35	114	9	28	7	0	1	10	2	17	1	.246	.307
Lonny Frey	SS34	B	22	34	135	25	43	5	3	0	12	13	13	4	.319	.400
Clyde Sukeforth	C18	L	31	20	36	1	2	0	0	0	0	2	1	0	.056	.056
Bert Delmas	2B10	L	22	12	28	4	7	0	0	0	0	0	1	0	.250	.250
1 Val Picinich	C6	R	36	6	6	1	1	1	0	0	0	0	1	0	.167	.333
Max Rosenfeld	OF2	R	30	5	9	0	1	0	0	0	0	0	1	1	.111	.111
Lu Blue	1B1	B	36	1	1	0	0	0	0	0	0	0	0	0	.000	.000

NAME	T	AGE	W	L	PCT	SV	G	GS	CG	IP	H	BB	SO	SHO	ERA
		29	65	88	.425	10	157	157	71	1386	1502	374	415	9	3.73
Van Lingle Mungo	R	22	16	15	.516	0	45	35	19	248	223	84	110	3	2.72
Ownie Carroll	R	30	13	15	.464	0	33	31	11	226	248	54	45	0	3.78
Boom-Boom Beck	R	28	12	20	.375	1	43	35	15	257	270	69	89	3	3.54
Ray Benge	R	31	10	17	.370	1	37	30	16	229	238	55	74	2	3.42
Sloppy Thurston	R	34	8	4	.429	3	32	15	5	131	171	34	22	0	4.53
Joe Shaute	L	33	4	4	.429	2	41	4	0	108	121	31	26	0	3.50
Dutch Leonard	R	24	3	4	.429	0	23	4	0	40	42	10	6	0	2.93
1 Watty Clark (AJ)	L	31	2	4	.333	1	11	8	4	51	61	6	14	1	4.76
Rosy Ryan	R	35	1	1	.500	2	30	0	0	61	69	16	22	0	4.57
Fred Heimach (BN)	L	32	0	1	.000	0	10	3	0	30	49	11	7	0	9.90
Ray Lucas	R	24	0	0	—	0	2	0	0	5	6	4	1	0	7.20

PHILADELPHIA   7th 60-92 .395 31   BURT SHOTTON

NAME	G by Pos	B	AGE	G	AB	R	H	2B	3B	HR	RBI	BB	SO	SB	BA	SA
TOTALS			28	152	5261	607	1439	240	41	60	570	381	479	55	.274	.369
Don Hurst	1B142	L	27	150	550	58	147	27	8	8	76	48	32	3	.267	.389
Jack Warner	2B71,3B30,SS1	R	29	107	340	31	76	15	1	0	22	48	33	1	.224	.274
Dick Bartell	SS152	R	25	152	587	78	159	25	5	1	37	56	46	6	.271	.336
Jim McLeod	3B67,SS1	R	24	67	232	20	45	6	1	0	15	12	25	1	.194	.228
Chuck Klein	OF152	L	28	152	606	101	223	44	7	28	120	56	36	15	.368	.602
Chick Fullis	OF151,3B1	R	29	151	647	91	200	31	9	1	45	36	34	18	.309	.380
2 Wes Schulmerich	OF97	R	31	97	365	53	122	19	4	8	59	32	45	1	.334	.474
Spud Davis	C132	R	28	141	495	51	173	28	3	9	65	32	24	1	.349	.503
Al Todd	C34,OF2	R	29	73	136	13	28	4	0	0	10	4	18	1	.206	.235
Harry McCurdy	C2	L	33	73	54	9	15	1	0	2	12	16	6	0	.278	.407
Neal Finn (DD)	2B51	R	31	51	169	15	40	12	0	2	13	10	14	2	.237	.272
1 Hal Lee	OF45	R	28	46	167	25	40	12	2	0	12	18	13	1	.287	.383
2 Fritz Knothe	3B32,2B4	R	30	41	113	10	17	2	0	0	11	6	19	2	.150	.168
Gus Dugas	1B11,OF1	L	26	37	71	4	12	3	0	0	9	1	8	1	.169	.211
1 Pinky Whitney	3B30	R	28	31	121	12	32	4	0	3	19	8	8	1	.264	.372
Mickey Haslin	2B26	R	23	26	89	3	21	2	0	0	9	3	5	1	.236	.258
Eddie Delker	2B17,3B4	R	27	25	41	6	7	3	1	0	1	0	12	0	.171	.293
Alta Cohen	OF7	L	24	19	32	6	6	1	0	0	1	6	4	0	.188	.219
Fred Brickell	OF4	L	26	8	13	2	4	1	1	0	1	0	0	0	.308	.538
Hugh Willingham		R	27	1	1	0	0	0	0	0	0	0	0	0	.000	.000

NAME	T	AGE	W	L	PCT	SV	G	GS	CG	IP	H	BB	SO	SHO	ERA
		29	60	92	.395	13	152	152	52	1338	**1563**	410	341	10	4.34
Ed Holley	R	29	13	15	.464	0	30	28	12	207	219	62	56	3	3.52
Cy Moore	R	28	8	9	.474	1	36	18	9	161	177	42	53	3	3.75
Phil Collins	R	31	8	13	.381	6	42	13	5	151	178	57	40	1	4.11
Jumbo Jim Elliott	L	32	6	10	.375	2	35	21	6	162	188	49	40	0	3.83
Snipe Hansen	L	26	6	14	.300	1	32	22	8	168	199	30	47	0	4.45
Frank Pearce	R	28	5	4	.556	0	20	7	3	82	78	29	18	1	3.62
Flint Rhem	R	32	5	14	.263	2	28	19	3	125	162	33	27	0	6.62
Ad Liska	R	26	3	2	.750	0	45	0	7	76	96	26	23	0	4.50
John Jackson	R	23	2	2	.500	0	10	7	1	54	74	35	11	0	6.00
Jack Berly	R	30	2	3	.400	0	13	6	1	50	62	22	4	1	5.04
Clarence Pickrel	R	22	1	0	1.000	0	14	2	0	20	23	6	3	0	3.86
Reggie Grabowski	R	25	1	3	.250	0	10	5	4	48	38	10	9	1	2.44
Frank Ragland	R	29	0	4	.000	0	11	5	0	38	51	16	4	0	6.87
Charlie Butler	L	28	0	0	—	0				1	1	2	0	0	9.00

CINCINNATI   8th 58-94 .382 33   DONIE BUSH

NAME	G by Pos	B	AGE	G	AB	R	H	2B	3B	HR	RBI	BB	SO	SB	BA	SA
TOTALS			30	153	5156	496	1267	208	37	34	455	349	354	30	.246	.320
Jim Bottomley	1B145	L	33	145	549	57	137	23	9	13	83	42	28	3	.250	.395
Jo-Jo Morrissey	2B88,SS63,3B15	R	29	148	534	43	123	20	0	0	26	20	22	3	.230	.268
Otto Bluege	SS95,2B10,3B1	R	23	108	291	17	62	6	2	0	18	26	29	0	.213	.247
4 Sparky Adams	3B132,SS8	R	38	137	538	59	141	21	1	0	22	44	20	3	.262	.310
Harry Rice	OF141,3B1	L	32	143	510	44	133	19	6	0	54	35	24	4	.261	.322
Chick Hafey	OF144	R	30	144	568	77	172	34	6	7	62	40	44	3	.303	.421
Johnny Moore	OF132	R	31	135	514	60	135	19	5	1	44	29	16	4	.263	.325
Ernie Lombardi	C95	R	25	107	350	30	99	21	4	4	47	16	17	2	.283	.382
George Grantham (BL)	2B72,1B17	L	33	87	260	32	53	14	3	0	28	38	21	4	.204	.327
Wally Roettger	OF55	R	30	84	209	13	50	7	1	1	17	8	10	0	.239	.297
Red Lucas	P29	L	31	75	122	14	35	6	1	1	15	12	6	0	.287	.377
1 Rollie Hemsley	C41	R	26	49	116	9	22	8	0	0	7	6	8	0	.190	.259
Clyde Manion	C34	R	36	36	84	3	14	1	0	0	6	3	8	1	.167	.179
Andy High	3B11,2B2	L	35	24	43	4	9	2	0	1	6	5	4	0	.209	.326
1 Leo Durocher	SS16	R	27	51	61	6	11	1	0	1	3	4	5	0	.216	.294
Tommy Robello	2B11,3B2	R	20	14	30	1	7	3	0	0	3	1	5	0	.233	.333
2 Jack Crouch	C6	R	29	10	16	5	2	0	0	0	0	0	1		.125	.125
Eddie Hunter	3B1	R	28	4	0	0	0	0	0	0	0	0	0	0	—	—
1 Taylor Douthit		R	32	1	1	0	0	0	0	0	0	0	0	0	.000	.000

NAME	T	AGE	W	L	PCT	SV	G	GS	CG	IP	H	BB	SO	SHO	ERA
		32	58	94	.382	8	153	153	74	1352	1470	257	310	13	3.42
Larry Benton	R	35	10	11	.476	2	34	19	7	153	160	36	33	2	3.71
Red Lucas	R	31	10	16	.385	0	29	29	21	220	248	18	40	3	3.40
Si Johnson	R	26	7	18	.280	1	34	28	14	211	212	54	51	4	3.50
2 Paul Derringer	R	26	7	25*	.219	1	33	31	16	231	240	51	86	2	3.23
Eppa Rixey	L	42	6	3	.667	0	16	12	5	94	118	12	10	1	3.16
Benny Frey	R	27	6	4	.600	0	37	9	1	132	144	21	12	1	3.82
Ray Kolp	R	38	6	4	.400	3	30	14	4	150	168	23	28	0	3.54
1 Bob Smith	R	38	4	4	.500	0	16	6	4	74	75	11	18	0	2.19
2 Allyn Stout	R	28	2	3	.400	0	23	5	2	71	85	26	29	0	3.80
Jack Quinn	R	49	0	1	.000	0	14	0	0	16	20	5	3	0	3.94

*Derringer, also with St. Louis, league leader in L with 27

WORLD SERIES — NEW YORK (NL) 4   WASHINGTON (AL) 1

LINE SCORES

TEAM	1	2	3	4	5	6	7	8	9	10	11	12	R	H	E

Game 1 October 3 at New York

	1	2	3	4	5	6	7	8	9	R	H	E
WAS	0	0	0	1	0	0	0	0	1	2	5	3
NY (NL)	2	0	2	0	0	0	0	0	X	4	10	2

Stewart, Russell (3), Thomas (8)   **Hubbell**

Game 2 October 4 at New York

	1	2	3	4	5	6	7	8	9	R	H	E
WAS	0	0	1	0	0	0	0	0	0	1	5	0
NY	0	0	0	0	0	6	0	0	X	6	10	0

Crowder, Thomas (6), McColl (7)   **Schumacher**

Game 3 October 5 at Washington

	1	2	3	4	5	6	7	8	9	R	H	E
NY	0	0	0	0	0	0	0	0	0	0	5	0
WAS	2	1	0	0	0	1	0	X		4	9	1

Fitzsimmons, Bell (8)   **Whitehill**

Game 4 October 6 at Washington

	1	2	3	4	5	6	7	8	9	10	11	R	H	E
NY	0	0	1	0	0	0	0	0	0	0	1	2	11	1
WAS	0	0	0	0	0	1	0	0	0	0	0	1	8	0

Hubbell   Weaver, Russell (11)

Game 5 October 7 at Washington

	1	2	3	4	5	6	7	8	9	10	R	H	E
NY	0	2	0	0	0	1	0	0	0	1	4	11	1
WAS	0	0	0	3	0	0	0	0	0		3	10	0

Schumacher, **Luque** (6)   Crowder, Russell (6)

COMPOSITE BATTING

NAME	POS	G	AB	R	H	2B	3B	HR	RBI	BA
New York (NL)										
Totals		5	176	16	47	5	0	3	16	.267
Terry	1B	5	22	3	6	1	0	1	1	.273
Moore	OF	5	22	1	5	1	0	0	1	.227
Critz	2B	5	22	2	3	0	0	0	0	.136
Davis	OF	5	19	1	7	1	0	0	0	.368
Ott	OF	5	18	3	7	0	0	2	4	.389
Jackson	3B	5	18	3	4	1	0	0	0	.222
Ryan	SS	5	18	0	5	0	0	0	0	.278
Mancuso	C	5	17	2	2	1	0	0	2	.118
Schumacher	P	2	7	0	2	0	0	0	3	.286
Hubbell	P	2	7	0	2	0	0	0	0	.286
Fitzsimmons	P	1	2	0	1	0	0	0	0	.500
Peel	OF	2	2	0	1	0	0	0	0	.500
O'Doul	PH	1	1	1	1	0	0	0	2	1.000
Luque	P	1	1	0	1	0	0	0	0	1.000
Bell	P	1	0	0	0	0	0	0	0	—
Washington (AL)										
Totals		5	173	11	37	4	0	2	11	.214
Cronin	SS	5	22	1	7	0	0	0	2	.318
Schulte	OF	5	21	1	7	1	0	0	4	.333
Myer	2B	5	20	2	6	1	0	0	2	.300
Goslin	OF	5	20	2	5	1	0	1	2	.250
Kuhel	1B	5	20	1	3	0	0	0	0	.150
Manush	OF	5	18	2	2	0	0	0	0	.111
Sewell	C	5	17	1	3	1	0	0	0	.176
Bluege	3B	5	16	1	2	1	0	0	1	.125
Crowder	P	2	4	0	1	0	0	0	0	.250
Weaver	P	1	4	0	0	0	0	0	0	.000
Whitehill	P	1	3	0	0	0	0	0	0	.000
Bolton	PH	2	2	0	0	0	0	0	0	.000
Harris	OF	1	2	0	0	0	0	0	0	.000
Russell	P	3	2	0	0	0	0	0	0	.000
Rice	PH	1	1	0	1	0	0	0	0	1.000
Stewart	P	1	1	0	0	0	0	0	0	.000
Kerr	PR	1	0	0	0	0	0	0	0	—
McColl	P	1	0	0	0	0	0	0	0	—
Thomas	P	2	0	0	0	0	0	0	0	—

COMPOSITE PITCHING

NAME	G	IP	H	BB	SO	W	L	SV	ERA
New York (NL)									
Totals	5	47	37	13	24	4	1	0	1.53
Hubbell	2	20	13	6	15	2	0	0	0.00
Schumacher	2	14.2	13	4	5	1	1	0	2.45
Fitzsimmons	1	7	9	0	1	0	1	0	5.14
Luque	1	4.1	2	2	5	1	0	0	0.00
Bell	1	1	0	1	0	0	0	0	0.00
Washington (AL)									
Totals	5	46	47	11	21	1	4	0	2.74
Crowder	2	11	16	5	7	0	1	0	7.36
Russell	3	10.1	8	0	7	0	1	0	0.87
Weaver	1	10.1	11	4	3	0	1	0	1.74
Whitehill	1	9	7	2	3	1	0	0	0.00
McColl	1	2	1	0	2	0	0	0	0.00
Stewart	1	2	6	0	1	0	1	0	9.00
Thomas	2	1.1	0	2	0	0	0	0	0.00

1934 Dizzy and Daffy and Dizzy

Giant fans had a taste of first place for 127 days during the season, while Cardinal fans had only 11 days alone in the hallowed. The first nine days occurred during the period from May 28 to June 5. The playing of the Giants was such that it seemed the Cardinals would never get around to having those other two days.

But, on September 28, Dizzy Dean shut out Cincinnati, 4-0, to leave the Cardinals and Giants with identical 93-58 records. The next day brother Paul, or more affectionately known as Daffy to complement his brother's nickname, defeated Cincinnati, 6-1, while in New York the Dodgers' Van Lingle Mungo beat the Giants, 5-1. Dizzy returned the next day to again shut out the hapless Reds, this time by a 9-0 score, to clinch the flag as the fading Giants bowed to Brooklyn, 8-5.

In capturing the pennant, playing-manager Frankie Frisch was the recipient of a 21-7 September compared to a 14-13 showing for the Giants. The Dean brothers had produced 49 victories, with the older Dizzy winning a league high of 30 and capturing the MVP honors.

The Cardinals had five of their regulars who batted .300 or better. Detroit, in winning their pennant, went one better by producing six regular men in the .300 bracket, and the other two, Billy Rogell and Pete Fox, had respective .296 and .285 averages. Mickey Cochrane, the manager-catcher, was purchased from Connie Mack during the winter and installed a winning spirit which enabled the Tigers, a Western team, to finally uproot their Eastern rivals after 14 years. Cochrane was greatly aided by pitchers Schoolboy Rowe and Tommy Bridges, the former winning 24 games, of which 16 were won consecutively from June 15 to August 25.

The runner-up Yankees, although victims of costly injuries in the stretch, overshadowed the Tigers when it came to gathering personal honors. Lefty Gomez led all American League pitchers with 26 wins and a 2.33 E.R.A., while first baseman Lou Gehrig swept the Triple Crown with 49 home runs, 165 runs batted in, and a .363 average —accomplishing a feat that had always eluded his fabled teammate, Babe Ruth. The one distinction Ruth did accomplish during the season was on July 13, when he briefly put the Yankees in first place with his 700th lifetime home run.

When it came to the World Series, the Dean brothers continued to provide the same one-two consistency which allowed the Cardinals entry into the fall classic. But the human interest story of the fracas did not come from the brotherly duo. Although both came away from the Series with two victories and impressive earned run averages, the historic spotlight found its way on Joe Medwick, the St. Louis leftfielder who managed to bring the wrath and the soiled fruit of the Detroit fans upon his head.

With the Tigers behind 7-0 in the top half of the sixth-inning of the final game, Medwick jumped on the ball and ended on third base after sliding hard into the bag. Medwick's aggressive running got him into a near-fight with third baseman Marv Owen. Although the umpires managed to quiet the two players, they could do nothing to hush the screaming of the Detroit crowd whose team entered the bottom of the sixth nine runs back. Medwick attempted to take his position three times but on each occasion oranges, apples, newspapers, and other assorted debris drove him back. Fortunately, for the good of Medwick, Commissioner Landis was at the game. After speaking to the umpires, Landis summoned Medwick and Owen to his box. A few moments later Medwick left the game for his own protection. It was a move which pacified the steaming crowd, and gave them the only victory they would have in what turned out to be a very long 11-0 afternoon.

1934 AMERICAN LEAGUE

NAME	G by Pos	B	AGE	G	AB	R	H	2B	3B	HR	RBI	BB	SO	SB	BA	SA
DETROIT 1st 101-53 .656	MICKEY COCHRANE		28	154	5475	958	1644	349	53	74	872	639	528	124	.300	.424
TOTALS			28	154	5475	958	1644	349	53	74	872	639	528	124	.300	.424
Hank Greenberg	1B153	R	23	153	593	118	201	63	7	26	139	63	93	9	.339	.600
Charlie Gehringer	2B154	L	31	154	601	134	214	50	7	11	127	99	25	11	.356	.517
Billy Rogell	SS154	B	29	154	592	114	175	32	8	3	100	74	36	13	.296	.392
Mary Owen	3B154	R	28	154	565	79	179	34	9	8	96	59	37	9	.317	.431
Pete Fox	OF121	R	24	128	516	101	147	31	2	2	45	49	53	25	.285	.364
Jo-Jo White	OF100	L	25	115	384	97	120	18	5	0	44	69	39	28	.313	.385
Goose Goslin	OF149	L	33	151	614	106	187	38	7	13	100	65	38	5	.305	.453
Mickey Cochrane	C124	L	31	129	437	74	140	32	1	2	76	78	26	8	.320	.412
Gee Walker	OF80	R	26	98	347	54	104	19	2	6	39	19	20	20	.300	.418
Frank Doljack	OF30, 1B3	R	26	56	120	15	28	7	1	1	19	13	15	2	.233	.333
Ray Hayworth	C54	R	30	54	167	20	49	5	2	0	27	16	22	0	.293	.347
Schoolboy Rowe	P45	R	24	51	109	15	33	8	1	2	22	6	20	0	.303	.450
Flea Clifton	3B4, 2B1	R	24	16	16	3	1	0	0	0	1	1	2	0	.063	.063
Heinie Schuble	SS3, 3B2, 2B1	R	27	11	15	2	4	2	0	0	1	4	0	0	.267	.400
Rudy York	C2	R	20	3	6	0	1	0	0	0	0	1	3	0	.167	.167
Frank Reiber		R	24	3	1	0	0	0	0	0	0	2	0	0	.000	.000
Cy Perkins		R	38	1	1	0	0	0	0	0	0	0	0	0	.000	.000
Icehouse Wilson		R	21	1	1	0	0	0	0	0	0	0	1	0	.000	.000
NEW YORK 2nd 94-60 .610 7	JOE McCARTHY		28	154	5368	842	1494	226	61	135	791	700	597	71	.278	.419
TOTALS			28	154	5368	842	1494	226	61	135	791	700	597	71	.278	.419
Lou Gehrig	1B153, SS1	L	31	154	579	128	210	40	6	49	165	109	31	9	.363	.708
Tony Lazzeri	2B92,3B30	R	30	154	438	59	117	24	6	14	67	71	64	11	.267	.445
Frankie Crosetti	SS119, 3B23, 2B1	R	23	138	554	85	147	22	10	11	67	61	58	5	.265	.401
Jack Saltzgaver	3B84, 1B4	L	29	94	350	64	95	8	1	6	36	48	29	8	.271	.351
Babe Ruth	OF111	L	39	125	365	78	105	17	4	22	84	104	63	1	.288	.537
Ben Chapman	OF149	R	25	149	588	82	181	21	13	5	86	67	68	26	.308	.413
Myril Hoag	OF86	R	26	97	251	45	67	8	2	3	34	21	21	1	.267	.351
Bill Dickey (BG)	C104	R	27	104	395	56	127	24	4	12	72	38	18	0	.322	.494
Sammy Byrd	OF104	R	27	106	191	32	47	8	0	3	23	18	22	1	.246	.335
Red Rolfe	SS46, 3B26	L	25	89	279	54	80	13	2	0	18	26	16	2	.287	.348
Don Heffner	2B68	R	23	72	241	29	63	8	3	0	25	25	18	1	.261	.320
Earle Combs (FS)	OF62	L	35	63	251	47	80	13	5	2	25	40	14	1	.319	.434
Art Jorgens	C56	R	29	58	183	14	38	6	1	0	20	23	24	1	.208	.251
George Selkirk	OF46	L	26	46	176	23	55	7	1	5	38	15	17	1	.313	.449
Dixie Walker	OF1	L	23	17	17	2	2	0	0	0	1	0	1	3	.118	.118
Zack Taylor	C3	R	35	4	7	0	1	0	0	0	0	0	1	0	.143	.143
1 Lyn Lary	1B1	R	28	1	0	0	0	0	0	0	0	1	0	0	—	—
CLEVELAND 3rd 85-69 .552 16	WALTER JOHNSON		27	154	5396	814	1550	340	46	100	763	526	433	52	.287	.423
TOTALS			27	154	5396	814	1550	340	46	100	763	526	433	52	.287	.423
Hal Trosky	1B154	L	21	154	625	117	206	45	9	35	142	58	49	2	.330	.598
Odell Hale	2B137, 3B5	R	25	143	563	82	170	44	6	13	101	48	50	8	.302	.471
Bill Knickerbocker	SS146	R	22	146	593	82	188	32	5	4	67	25	40	6	.317	.408
Willie Kamm	3B118	R	34	121	386	42	104	23	3	0	42	62	38	7	.269	.345
Sam Rice	OF78	L	44	97	335	48	98	19	1	1	33	28	9	5	.293	.364
Earl Averill	OF154	L	32	154	598	128	187	48	6	31	113	99	44	4	.313	.569
Joe Vosmik	OF104	R	24	104	405	71	138	33	2	6	78	35	10	1	.341	.477
Frankie Pytlak	C88	R	25	91	289	46	75	12	4	0	35	36	11	11	.260	.329
John Burnett	3B42, SS9, 2B3, OF2	L	29	72	208	28	61	11	2	3	30	19	11	1	.293	.409
2 Bob Seeds	OF48	R	27	61	186	28	46	8	1	0	18	21	13	2	.247	.301
Dutch Holland	OF31	R	30	50	128	19	32	12	1	2	13	13	11	0	.250	.406
Milt Galatzer	OF49	L	27	49	196	29	53	10	2	0	15	21	8	3	.270	.342
Glenn Myatt (BN)	C34	L	36	36	107	18	34	6	1	0	12	13	5	1	.318	.393
2 Moe Berg	C28	R	32	29	97	4	25	3	0	0	9	1	7	0	.258	.309
Eddie Moore	2B18, 3B3, SS2	R	35	27	65	4	10	2	0	0	8	10	4	0	.154	.185
Bill Brenzel	C15	R	24	15	51	4	11	3	0	0	6	4	5	0	.216	.275
1 Dick Porter	OF10	R	32	13	44	9	10	2	1	1	6	4	5	0	.227	.386
Kit Carson	OF4	L	21	5	16	1	4	1	1	0	1	0	3	1	.250	.500
Bob Garbark (JJ)	C5	R	24	5	11	1	0	0	0	0	2	0	1	0	.000	.000
Roy Spencer	C4	R	34	5	7	1	1	0	0	0	2	0	1	0	.143	.286

NAME	T	AGE	W	L	PCT	SV	G	GS	CG	IP	H	BB	SO	SHO	ERA
		28	101	53	.656	14	154	154	74	1370	1467	488	640	11	4.06
Schoolboy Rowe	R	24	24	8	.750	1	45	30	20	266	259	81	149	3	3.45
Tommy Bridges	R	27	22	11	.667	1	36	35	23	275	249	104	151	3	3.67
Firpo Marberry	R	35	15	5	.750	3	38	19	6	156	174	48	64	1	4.56
Elden Auker	R	23	15	7	.682	1	43	18	10	205	234	56	86	2	3.42
Vic Sorrell	R	33	6	9	.400	2	28	19	6	130	146	45	46	0	4.78
Carl Fischer	L	24	6	4	.600	1	20	15	4	95	107	38	39	1	4.36
2 General Crowder	R	35	5	1	.833	0	9	9	3	67	81	20	30	1	4.16
Chief Hogsett	L	30	3	2	.600	3	26	0	0	50	61	19	23	0	4.32
Luke Hamlin	R	29	2	3	.400	1	20	5	1	75	87	44	30	0	5.40
Red Phillips	R	25	2	0	1.000	1	7	1	1	23	31	16	3	0	6.28
Vic Frasier	R	29	1	3	.250	0	8	2	0	23	30	12	11	0	5.87
Steve Larkin	R	23	0	0	—	0	2	1	0	6	8	5	8	0	1.50
		26	94	60	.610	10	154	154	83	1383	1349	542	656	13	3.75
Lefty Gomez	L	25	26	5	.839	1	38	33	25	282	223	96	158	6	2.33
Red Ruffing	R	30	19	11	.633	0	36	31	19	256	232	104	149	5	3.94
Johnny Murphy	R	25	14	10	.583	4	40	20	10	208	193	76	70	0	3.12
Johnny Broaca	R	24	12	9	.571	0	26	24	13	177	203	65	74	1	4.17
Jimmie DeShong	R	24	6	7	.462	3	31	12	6	134	126	56	40	0	4.10
Johnny Allen (SA)	R	29	5	2	.714	0	13	10	4	72	62	32	54	0	2.88
Danny MacFayden	R	29	4	3	.571	0	22	11	4	96	110	31	41	0	4.50
Russ Van Atta	L	28	3	5	.375	0	28	9	0	88	107	46	39	0	6.34
George Uhle	R	35	2	4	.333	0	10	2	0	16	30	7	10	0	10.13
Charlie Devens	R	24	1	0	1.000	0	1	1	1	11	9	5	4	0	1.64
Vito Tamulis	L	22	1	0	1.000	0	1	1	1	9	7	1	5	1	0.00
3 Burleigh Grimes	R	40	1	2	.333	1	10	0	0	18	22	14	5	0	5.50
1 Harry Smythe	L	29	0	2	.000	1	8	0	0	15	24	8	7	0	7.80
Floyd Newkirk	R	25	0	0	—	0	1	0	0	1	1	1	0	0	0.00
		27	85	69	.552	19	154	154	72	1367	1476	582	554	8	4.28
Mel Harder	R	24	20	12	.625	4	44	29	17	255	246	81	91	6	2.61
Monte Pearson	R	25	18	13	.581	2	39	33	19	255	257	130	140	0	4.52
Willis Hudlin	R	28	15	10	.600	4	36	26	15	195	210	65	58	1	4.75
Oral Hildebrand	R	27	11	9	.550	1	33	28	10	198	225	99	72	1	4.50
Belve Bean	R	29	5	1	.833	0	21	1	0	51	53	21	20	0	3.88
Ralph Winegarner	R	24	5	4	.556	0	22	6	4	78	91	39	32	0	5.54
Lloyd Brown	L	29	5	10	.333	6	38	15	5	117	116	51	39	0	3.85
Clint Brown (BW)	R	30	4	3	.571	1	17	2	0	50	83	14	15	0	5.94
Thornton Lee	L	27	1	1	.500	0	24	6	0	88	105	44	41	0	5.02
2 Bob Weiland	L	28	1	5	.167	0	16	7	2	70	71	30	42	0	4.11
Bill Perrin	R	24	0	1	.000	0	1	1	0	5	13	2	3	0	14.40
Sarge Connally	R	35	0	0	—	0	5	0	0	5	4	5	1	0	5.40
Denny Galehouse	R	22	0	0	—	0	1	0	0	1	1	1	1	0	18.00

BOSTON — 4th 76-76 .500 24 — BUCKY HARRIS

NAME	G by Pos	B	AGE	G	AB	R	H	2B	3B	HR	RBI	BB	SO	SB	BA	SA
TOTALS			30	153	5339	820	1465	287	70	51	756	610	535	116	.274	.383
Eddie Morgan	1B137	R	30	138	528	95	141	28	4	3	79	81	46	7	.267	.352
Bill Cissell	2B96, SS7, 3B2	R	30	102	416	71	111	13	4	4	44	28	23	11	.267	.346
2 Lyn Lary	SS129	R	28	129	419	58	101	20	4	2	54	66	51	12	.241	.322
Bill Werber	3B130, SS22	R	26	152	623	129	200	41	10	11	67	77	37	40	.321	.472
Moose Solters	OF89	R	28	116	365	61	109	25	4	7	58	18	50	9	.299	.447
Carl Reynolds	OF100	R	31	113	413	61	125	26	9	4	86	27	28	5	.303	.438
Roy Johnson	OF137	L	31	143	569	85	182	43	10	7	119	54	36	11	.320	.467
Rick Ferrell	C128	R	28	132	437	50	130	29	4	1	48	66	20	0	.297	.389
Max Bishop	2B57, 1B15	L	34	97	253	65	66	13	1	1	22	82	22	3	.261	.332
2 Dick Porter	OF75	L	32	80	265	30	80	13	6	0	56	21	15	5	.302	.396
Dusty Cooke	OF44	L	27	74	168	34	41	8	5	1	26	36	25	7	.244	.369
Wes Ferrell	P26	R	26	34	78	12	22	4	0	4	17	7	15	1	.282	.487
Gordie Hinkle	C26	R	29	27	75	7	13	6	1	0	9	7	23	0	.173	.280
Mel Almada	OF23	L	21	23	90	7	21	2	1	0	10	6	8	3	.233	.278
1 Bucky Walters	3B23	R	25	23	88	10	19	4	4	4	18	3	12	0	.216	.489
Lou Legett	C17	R	33	19	38	4	11	0	0	0	1	2	4	0	.289	.289
Skinny Graham	OF13	L	24	13	47	7	11	2	1	0	3	6	13	2	.234	.319
Joe Judge	1B2	L	40	10	15	3	5	2	0	0	2	2	1	0	.333	.467
Al Niemiec	2B9	R	23	9	32	2	7	0	0	0	3	3	4	0	.219	.219
Don Kellett	SS4, 2B2, 3B1	R	24	9	9	0	0	0	0	0	0	1	5	0	.000	.000
1 Bob Seeds	OF1	R	27	8	6	0	1	0	0	0	1	0	1	0	.167	.167
Freddie Muller	3B1, 2B1	R	26	2	1	1	0	0	0	0	0	0	0	0	.000	.000

NAME	T	AGE	W	L	PCT	SV	G	GS	CG	IP	H	BB	SO	SHO	ERA
		30	76	76	.500	9	153	153	68	1361	1527	543	538	8	4.32
Wes Ferrell	R	26	14	5	.737	1	26	23	17	181	205	49	67	3	3.63
Johnny Welch	R	27	13	15	.464	0	41	22	8	206	223	76	91	1	4.50
Gordon Rhodes	R	26	12	12	.500	2	44	31	10	219	247	98	79	0	4.56
Fritz Ostermueller	L	26	10	13	.435	3	33	23	10	199	200	99	75	0	3.48
Lefty Grove (SA)	L	34	8	8	.500	0	22	12	5	109	149	32	43	0	6.52
Rube Walberg	L	37	6	7	.462	1	30	10	2	105	118	41	38	0	4.03
Hank Johnson	R	28	6	8	.429	1	31	14	7	124	162	53	66	1	5.37
Herb Pennock	L	40	2	0	1.000	1	30	2	1	62	68	16	16	0	3.05
George Hockette	R	26	2	1	.667	0	3	3	3	27	22	6	14	2	1.67
Joe Mulligan	R	20	1	0	1.000	0	14	2	1	45	46	27	13	0	3.60
Spike Merena	L	24	1	2	.333	0	4	3	2	25	20	16	7	1	2.88
1 Bob Weiland	R	28	1	5	.167	0	11	7	2	56	63	27	29	0	5.46
George Pipgras	R	34	0	0	—	0	2	0	0	3	4	1	0	0	9.00

PHILADELPHIA — 5th 68-82 .453 31 — CONNIE MACK

NAME	G by Pos	B	AGE	G	AB	R	H	2B	3B	HR	RBI	BB	SO	SB	BA	SA
TOTALS			27	153	5317	764	1491	236	50	144	708	491	584	57	.280	.425
Jimmie Foxx	1B140, 3B9	R	26	154	539	120	180	28	6	44	130	111	75	11	.334	.653
Rabbit Warstler	2B107, SS2	R	30	117	419	56	99	19	3	1	36	51	30	9	.236	.303
Eric McNair	SS131	R	25	151	599	80	168	20	4	17	82	35	42	5	.280	.412
Pinky Higgins	3B144	R	25	144	543	89	179	37	6	16	90	56	70	9	.330	.508
Ed Coleman	OF86	L	32	101	329	53	92	14	6	14	60	29	34	0	.280	.486
Doc Cramer	OF152	L	28	153	649	99	202	29	9	6	46	40	35	1	.311	.411
Bob Johnson	OF139	R	28	137	469	111	168	26	6	34	92	58	60	12	.307	.563
Charlie Berry	C99	R	31	99	269	14	72	10	2	0	34	22	23	1	.268	.320
Lou Finney	OF54, 1B15	L	23	92	272	32	76	11	4	1	28	14	17	4	.279	.360
Frankie Hayes	C89	R	19	92	248	24	56	10	0	6	30	20	44	2	.226	.339
Bing Miller	OF46	R	39	81	177	22	43	10	2	1	22	16	14	1	.243	.339
Dib Williams	2B53, SS2	R	24	66	205	25	56	10	1	2	17	21	18	0	.273	.361
Johnny Marcum	P37	R	24	58	112	10	30	4	0	1	13	3	5	0	.268	.330
Charlie Moss	C6	R	23	10	10	3	2	0	0	0	1	0	0	0	.200	.200
1 Ed Madjeski	C1	R	25	8	8	1	3	1	0	0	2	0	2	0	.375	.500
Jerry McQuaig	OF6	R	22	7	16	2	1	0	0	0	1	2	4	0	.063	.063

NAME	T	AGE	W	L	PCT	SV	G	GS	CG	IP	H	BB	SO	SHO	ERA
		26	68	82	.453	8	153	153	68	1337	1429	693	480	8	5.01
Johnny Marcum	R	24	14	11	.560	0	37	31	17	232	257	88	92	2	4.52
Joe Cascarella	R	27	12	15	.444	1	42	22	9	194	214	104	71	2	4.69
Bill Dietrich	R	24	11	12	.478	3	39	23	14	208	201	114	88	4	4.67
Sugar Cain	R	27	9	17	.346	0	36	32	15	231	235	128	66	0	4.40
Al Benton	R	23	7	9	.438	1	32	21	7	155	145	88	58	0	4.88
1 Bob Kline	R	24	6	2	.750	1	20	0	0	40	50	13	14	0	6.30
Roy Mahaffey	R	30	6	7	.462	2	37	14	3	129	142	55	37	0	5.37
George Caster	R	26	3	2	.600	0	5	3	2	32	14	15	10	0	3.41
Whitey Wilshere	R	21	0	1	.000	0	9	2	0	22	39	15	19	0	11.86
Jack Wilson	R	22	0	2	.000	0	14	3	0	31	34	33	6	0	5.81
Mort Flohr	R	24	0	0	—	0	3	0	0	9	15	9	2	0	12.00
Harry Matuzak	R	24	0	3	.000	0	11	0	0	24	28	10	9	0	4.88
Ed Lagger	R	21	0	0	—	0	8	0	0	18	27	14	2	0	11.00
Tim McKeithan	R	27	0	0	—	0	3	0	0	4	7	5	0	0	15.75
Roy Vaughn	R	22	0	0	—	0	3	0	0	8	5	6	1	0	2.25

ST. LOUIS — 6th 67-85 .441 33 — ROGERS HORNSBY

NAME	G by Pos	B	AGE	G	AB	R	H	2B	3B	HR	RBI	BB	SO	SB	BA	SA
TOTALS			27	154	5288	674	1417	252	59	62	631	514	631	43	.268	.373
Jack Burns	1B154	R	26	154	612	86	157	28	8	13	73	62	47	9	.257	.392
Oscar Melillo	2B141	R	34	144	552	54	133	19	3	2	55	28	27	4	.241	.297
Alan Strange	SS125	R	27	127	430	39	100	17	2	1	45	48	28	3	.233	.288
Harlond Clift	3B141	R	21	147	572	104	149	30	10	14	56	84	100	7	.260	.421
Bruce Campbell	OF123	L	24	138	481	62	134	25	6	9	74	51	64	5	.279	.412
Sammy West	OF120	L	29	122	482	90	157	22	10	9	55	62	55	3	.326	.469
Ray Pepper	OF136	R	28	143	564	71	168	24	6	7	101	29	67	1	.298	.399
Rollie Hemsley	C114, OF6	R	27	123	431	47	133	31	7	2	52	29	37	6	.309	.427
Ollie Bejma	SS32, 2B14, 3B13, OF9	R	26	95	262	39	71	16	3	2	29	40	36	3	.271	.378
Debs Garms	OF56	L	27	91	232	25	68	14	4	0	31	27	19	0	.293	.388
Frank Grube	C55	R	29	65	170	22	49	10	0	0	11	24	11	2	.288	.347
Rogers Hornsby	3B1, OF1	R	38	24	23	2	7	2	0	1	11	7	4	0	.304	.522
Earl Clark	OF9	R	26	13	41	4	7	2	0	0	1	1	3	0	.171	.207
George Puccinelli	OF6	R	27	10	26	4	6	1	0	2	5	1	8	0	.231	.500
Grover Hartley	C2	R	45	5	3	0	1	0	0	0	0	1	0	0	.333	.667
Art Scharein		R	29	4	1	0	0	0	0	0	0	2	0	0	.500	.500
Charley O'Leary		R	51	1	1	1	1	0	0	0	0	0	0	0	1.000	1.000

NAME	T	AGE	W	L	PCT	SV	G	GS	CG	IP	H	BB	SO	SHO	ERA
		28	67	85	.441	20	154	154	50	1350	1499	632	499	6	4.49
Bobo Newsom	R	26	16	20	.444	5	47	32	15	262	259	149	135	2	4.02
George Blaeholder	R	30	14	18	.438	3	39	33	14	234	276	68	66	1	4.23
Jack Knott	R	27	10	3	.769	4	45	10	2	138	149	67	56	0	4.96
Bump Hadley	R	29	10	16	.385	1	39	32	7	213	212	127	79	2	4.35
Dick Coffman	R	27	9	10	.474	3	40	21	6	173	212	59	55	1	4.53
Ivy Andrews	R	27	4	11	.267	3	43	13	2	139	166	65	51	0	4.96
1 Jim Weaver	R	30	2	0	1.000	0	5	2	0	17	20	11	0	0	6.30
Bill McAfee	R	26	1	0	1.000	0	28	0	0	62	84	26	11	0	5.81
Ed Wells	L	34	1	7	.125	1	33	8	2	92	108	35	27	0	4.79
Lefty Mills	L	24	0	0	—	0	4	0	0	9	10	11	2	0	4.00
Jim Walkup	R	24	0	0	—	0	8	0	0	8	6	5	6	0	2.25
Sam Gray (IL) 36															

WASHINGTON — 7th 66-86 .434 34 — JOE CRONIN

NAME	G by Pos	B	AGE	G	AB	R	H	2B	3B	HR	RBI	BB	SO	SB	BA	SA
TOTALS			30	155	5448	729	1512	278	70	51	682	567	447	49	.278	.382
Joe Kuhel (BN)	1B63	L	28	63	263	49	76	12	3	3	25	30	14	2	.289	.392
Buddy Myer	2B135	L	30	139	524	103	160	33	8	3	57	102	32	6	.305	.416
Joe Cronin (BA)	SS127	R	27	127	504	68	143	30	9	7	101	53	28	8	.284	.421
Cecil Travis	3B99	L	20	109	392	48	125	12	4	1	53	24	37	1	.319	.402
John Stone (NJ)	OF112	L	28	113	419	77	132	28	7	7	67	52	26	1	.315	.465
Fred Schulte	OF134	R	33	134	524	72	156	32	6	3	73	53	34	3	.298	.399
Heinie Manush	OF131	L	32	137	556	88	194	42	11	11	89	36	23	7	.349	.523
Eddie Phillips	C53	R	33	56	169	6	33	6	1	2	19	26	24	1	.195	.278
Ossie Bluege	3B41, SS30, 2B5, OF5	R	33	99	285	39	70	9	0	2	11	23	16	2	.246	.291
Dave Harris	OF64, 3B5	R	34	97	235	28	59	14	3	2	37	39	40	2	.251	.362
Luke Sewell (BG)	C50, OF7, 1B6, 2B1, 3B1	R	33	72	207	21	49	7	3	2	21	22	10	0	.237	.329
Pete Susko	1B58	R	29	58	224	25	64	5	2	3	25	18	10	3	.286	.362
2 Red Kress	1B30, OF10, 2B6, SS1, 3B1	R	29	56	171	18	39	4	3	4	24	17	19	3	.228	.357
Cliff Bolton	C39	L	27	42	148	12	40	9	1	1	17	11	9	2	.270	.365
1 Moe Berg	C31	R	32	33	86	5	21	4	0	0	6	6	4	2	.244	.291
John Kerr	3B17, 2B13	R	35	31	103	8	28	4	0	0	12	8	13	1	.272	.311
Gus Dugas	OF2	L	27	24	19	2	1	1	0	0	1	3	3	0	.053	.105
Johnny Gill	OF13	R	29	13	53	7	13	3	0	2	7	2	3	0	.245	.415
Elmer Klumpp	C11	R	27	12	15	2	2	0	0	0	1	0	3	0	.133	.133
1 Bob Boken	3B6, 2B1	R	26	11	27	5	6	1	1	0	6	3	1	2	.222	.333
Jake Powell	OF9	R	25	9	35	6	10	2	0	0	6	4	2	1	.286	.343
Fred Sington	OF9	R	24	9	35	2	10	2	0	0	6	1	4	2	.286	.343

NAME	T	AGE	W	L	PCT	SV	G	GS	CG	IP	H	BB	SO	SHO	ERA
		32	66	86	.434	12	155	155	61	1381	1622	503	412	3	4.68
Earl Whitehill	L	34	14	11	.560	0	32	31	15	235	269	94	96	0	4.52
Monty Weaver	R	28	11	15	.423	0	31	31	11	205	255	63	51	0	4.79
Bobby Burke	L	27	8	8	.500	0	37	15	7	168	155	72	52	1	3.21
Tommy Thomas	R	34	8	9	.471	1	33	18	7	133	154	58	42	1	5.48
Lefty Stewart	L	33	7	11	.389	0	24	22	7	152	184	36	36	1	4.03
Jack Russell	R	28	5	10	.333	7	54	4	3	158	179	56	38	0	4.16
1 General Crowder	R	35	4	10	.286	3	29	13	4	101	142	38	39	0	6.77
Alex McColl	R	40	3	4	.429	1	22	4	1	112	129	36	29	0	3.86
Ed Linke	R	22	2	2	.500	0	7	4	2	35	38	9	9	0	4.11
2 Bob Kline	R	24	1	0	1.000	0	6	0	0	4	10	4	1	0	15.75
Orville Armbrust	R	26	1	0	1.000	0	6	0	0	18	25	6	6	0	2.08
Sid Cohen	L	28	1	1	.500	0	3	2	1	18	26	5	6	0	7.50
Reese Diggs	R	18	1	3	.333	0	4	3	2	21	26	15	2	0	6.86
Allen Benson	R	26	0	1	.000	0	2	2	0	10	19	5	4	0	11.70
Ray Prim	L	27	0	2	.000	0	5	1	0	15	19	8	3	0	6.60
John Milligan	R	30	0	0	—	0	2	0	0	3	6	0	1	0	9.00
Marc Filley	R	22	0	0	—	0	1	0	0	1	1	1	0	0	27.00

CHICAGO — 8th 53-99 .349 47 — LEW FONSECA 4-11 .269 JIMMY DYKES 49-88 .358

NAME	G by Pos	B	AGE	G	AB	R	H	2B	3B	HR	RBI	BB	SO	SB	BA	SA
TOTALS			29	153	5301	704	1395	237	40	71	662	565	524	36	.263	.363
Zeke Bonura	1B127	R	25	127	510	86	154	35	4	27	110	64	31	0	.302	.545
Jackie Hayes (BG)	2B61	R	27	62	226	19	58	9	1	1	31	23	20	3	.257	.319
Luke Appling (FJ)	SS110, 2B8	R	27	118	452	75	137	28	6	2	61	59	27	3	.303	.405
Jimmy Dykes	3B74, 1B27, 2B27	R	37	127	456	52	122	17	4	7	82	64	28	1	.268	.368
Evar Swanson	OF105	R	31	117	426	71	127	9	5	0	34	59	31	10	.298	.344
Mule Haas	OF89	L	30	101	354	54	94	16	3	2	37	36	18	1	.268	.348
Al Simmons	OF138	R	32	138	558	102	192	36	7	18	104	53	58	3	.344	.530
2 Ed Madjeski	C79	R	25	85	281	36	62	14	2	5	32	14	31	2	.221	.338
2 Bob Boken	2B57, SS22	R	26	81	297	30	70	9	1	3	40	15	32	2	.236	.303
2 Marty Hopkins	3B63	R	27	67	210	22	45	7	2	0	28	22	26	0	.214	.276
Jocko Conlan	OF54	L	34	63	225	35	56	11	3	0	16	19	7	2	.249	.324
Merv Shea	C60	R	33	62	176	9	28	4	0	0	5	24	19	0	.159	.176
Frenchy Uhalt	OF40	L	24	57	165	28	40	5	1	0	16	29	12	6	.242	.285
Ted Lyons	P30	R	33	50	97	9	20	4	0	1	16	3	19	0	.206	.278
Joe Chamberlain	SS26, 3B14	R	24	43	141	13	34	5	1	2	17	6	38	1	.241	.333
Frenchy Bordagaray	OF17	R	24	29	87	12	28	3	1	0	2	3	4	1	.322	.379
Muddy Ruel	C21	R	38	22	57	4	12	3	0	0	7	8	5	0	.211	.263
Milt Bocek	OF10	R	21	19	38	3	8	1	0	0	3	0	5	0	.211	.237
Charlie Uhlir	OF6	L	24	18	27	3	4	0	0	0	3	0	2	0	.148	.148
Rip Radcliff	OF14	L	28	14	56	7	15	2	0	0	3	0	4	0	.268	.304
Mark Mauldin	3B10	R	19	10	38	3	10	1	0	0	3	0	8	0	.263	.395
1 Red Kress	2B3	R	29	8	14	3	4	0	0	0	1	2	2	0	.286	.286
Sidel Caithamer	C5	R	23	5	19	1	6	1	0	0	2	1	1	0	.316	.368
Johnny Pasek	C4	R	24	5	9	1	3	0	0	0	1	1	0	0	.333	.333
Bill Fehring	C1	B	22	1	1	0	0	0	0	0	0	0	0	1	.000	.000

NAME	T	AGE	W	L	PCT	SV	G	GS	CG	IP	H	BB	SO	SHO	ERA
		32	53	99	.349	8	153	153	72	1355	1599	628	506	4	5.41
George Earnshaw	R	34	14	11	.560	0	33	30	16	227	242	104	97	2	4.52
Ted Lyons	R	33	11	13	.458	1	30	24	21	205	249	66	53	0	4.87
Sadd Sam Jones	R	41	8	12	.400	0	27	26	11	183	217	60	60	1	5.11
Milt Gaston	R	38	6	19	.240	0	29	28	10	194	247	84	44	1	5.85
Les Tietje	R	23	5	14	.263	0	34	22	6	176	174	96	81	0	4.81
Phil Gallivan	R	26	3	7	.364	1	35	7	3	127	155	64	55	0	5.60
Whit Wyatt	R	26	4	11	.267	2	23	6	2	68	83	37	36	0	7.15
Joe Heving	R	34	2	1	.125	4	33	2	0	88	133	48	40	0	7.26
Harry Kinzy	R	23	0	1	.000	0	13	2	1	34	38	31	12	0	5.03
Vern Kennedy	R	27	0	0	.000	0	3	3	1	19	21	9	7	0	3.72
Hugo Klaerner	R	25	0	2	.000	0	3	3	1	17	24	16	9	0	11.12
Lee Stine	R	21	0	0	—	0	4	0	0	11	11	10	8	0	8.18
John Pomorski	R	28	0	0	—	0	4	0	0	11	13	6	4	0	4.50
Monty Stratton	R	22	0	0	—	0	1	0	0	3	4	1	0	0	6.00
Ed Durham (IL) 26															

ST. LOUIS 1ST 95-58 .621 — FRANKIE FRISCH

NAME	G by Pos	B	AGE	G	AB	R	H	2B	3B	HR	RBI	BB	SO	SB	BA	SA
TOTALS			28	154	5502	799	1582	294	75	104	748	392	535	69	.288	.425
Ripper Collins	1B154	B	30	154	600	116	200	40	12	35	128	57	50	2	.333	.615
Frankie Frisch	2B115, 3B25	B	35	140	550	74	168	30	6	3	75	45	10	11	.305	.390
Leo Durocher	SS146	R	28	146	500	62	130	26	5	3	70	33	40	2	.260	.350
Pepper Martin	3B107, P1	R	30	110	454	76	131	25	11	5	49	32	41	23	.289	.425
Jack Rothrock	OF154, 2B1	B	29	154	647	106	184	35	3	11	72	49	56	10	.284	.399
Ernie Orsatti	OF90	L	31	105	337	39	101	14	4	0	31	27	31	6	.300	.365
Joe Medwick	OF149	R	22	149	620	110	198	40	18	18	106	21	83	3	.319	.529
Spud Davis	C94	R	29	107	347	45	104	22	4	9	65	34	27	0	.300	.464
Burgess Whitehead	2B48, SS29, 3B28	R	24	100	332	55	92	13	5	1	24	12	19	5	.277	.355
Bill DeLancey	C77	L	22	93	253	41	80	18	3	13	40	41	37	1	.316	.565
2 Chick Fullis	OF56	R	30	69	199	21	52	9	1	0	26	14	11	4	.261	.317
Pat Crawford	3B9, 2B4	L	32	61	70	3	19	2	0	0	16	5	3	0	.271	.300
Buster Mills	OF18	R	25	29	72	7	17	4	1	1	8	4	11	0	.236	.361
1 Kiddo Davis	OF9	R	32	16	33	6	10	3	0	1	4	3	1	1	.303	.485
Francis Healy	C2, 3B1, OF1	R	24	15	13	1	4	1	0	0	1	0	2	0	.308	.385
Gene Moore	OF3	L	24	9	18	2	5	1	0	0	1	2	2	0	.278	.333
Lew Riggs		L	24	2	1	0	0	0	0	0	0	0	1	0	.000	.000
2 Red Worthington		R	28	1	1	0	0	0	0	0	0	0	1	0	.000	.000
Charley Gelbert (LJ) 28																

NAME	T	AGE	W	L	PCT	SV	G	GS	CG	IP	H	BB	SO	SHO	ERA
TOTALS		30	95	58	.621	16	154	154	78	1387	1463	411	689	15	3.69
Dizzy Dean	R	24	30	7	.811	7	50	33	24	312	288	75	195	7	2.65
Paul Dean	R	20	19	11	.633	2	39	26	16	233	225	52	150	5	3.44
Tex Carleton	R	27	16	11	.593	2	40	31	16	241	260	52	103	0	4.26
Bill Walker	L	30	12	4	.750	0	24	19	10	163	160	66	76	1	3.12
Wild Bill Hallahan	L	31	8	12	.400	0	32	26	10	163	195	66	70	2	4.25
Jesse Haines	R	40	4	4	.500	1	37	6	0	90	86	19	17	0	3.50
1 Burleigh Grimes	R	42	2	1	.667	0	4	0	0	8	5	2	1	0	3.38
Jim Mooney	L	27	2	4	.333	1	32	7	1	82	114	49	27	0	5.49
1 Flint Rhem	R	33	1	0	1.000	1	5	1	0	16	26	7	6	0	4.50
2 Dazzy Vance	R	43	1	1	.500	1	19	4	1	59	62	14	33	0	3.66
Jim Lindsey	R	36	0	1	.000	1	11	0	0	14	21	3	7	0	6.43
Jim Winford	R	24	0	2	.000	0	5	1	0	13	17	6	3	0	7.61
Clarence Heise	L	26	0	0	—	0	1	0	0	2	3	0	1	0	4.50
Pepper Martin	R	30	0	0	—	0	2	1	0	2	1	0	0	0	4.50

NEW YORK 2nd 93-60 .608 2 — BILL TERRY

NAME	G by Pos	B	AGE	G	AB	R	H	2B	3B	HR	RBI	BB	SO	SB	BA	SA
TOTALS			30	153	5396	760	1485	240	41	126	716	406	526	19	.275	.405
Bill Terry	1B153	L	35	153	602	109	213	30	6	8	83	60	47	0	.354	.463
Hughie Critz	2B137	R	33	137	571	77	138	17	1	6	40	19	24	3	.242	.306
Travis Jackson	SS130, 3B9	R	30	137	523	75	140	26	7	16	101	37	71	1	.268	.436
Johnny Vergez	3B104	R	27	108	320	31	64	18	1	7	27	28	55	1	.200	.328
Mel Ott	OF153	L	25	153	582	119	190	29	10	35	135	85	43	0	.326	.591
George Watkins	OF81	L	34	105	296	38	73	18	3	6	33	24	34	2	.247	.389
Jo-Jo Moore	OF131	L	25	139	580	106	192	37	4	15	61	31	23	5	.331	.486
Gus Mancuso	C122	R	28	122	383	32	94	14	0	7	46	27	19	0	.245	.337
Blondy Ryan	3B65, SS30, 2B25	R	28	110	385	35	93	19	0	2	41	19	68	3	.242	.306
Lefty O'Doul	OF38	L	37	83	177	30	56	4	3	9	46	18	7	2	.316	.525
Hank Leiber	OF51	R	23	63	187	17	45	5	3	2	25	4	13	1	.241	.332
Harry Danning	C37	R	22	53	97	8	32	7	0	1	7	1	9	1	.330	.433
Hal Schumacher	P41	R	23	44	117	19	28	5	1	6	15	2	26	0	.239	.453
Paul Richards	C37	R	25	42	75	10	12	1	0	0	3	13	8	0	.160	.173
Phil Weintraub	OF20	L	26	31	74	13	26	2	0	0	15	15	10	0	.351	.378
George Grantham	1B4, 3B2	L	34	32	29	5	7	2	0	1	4	8	6	0	.241	.414
Homer Peel	OF10	R	31	21	41	7	8	1	0	0	3	1	2	0	.195	.268
Fresco Thompson		R	32	1	1	0	0	0	0	0	0	0	0	0	.000	.000

NAME	T	AGE	W	L	PCT	SV	G	GS	CG	IP	H	BB	SO	SHO	ERA
TOTALS		30	93	60	.608	30	153	153	68	1370	1384	351	499	13	3.19
Hal Schumacher	R	23	23	10	.697	0	41	36	18	297	299	89	112	2	3.18
Carl Hubbell	L	31	21	12	.636	8	49	35	25	313	286	37	118	5	2.30
Freddie Fitzsimmons	R	32	18	14	.563	1	38	37	14	263	266	51	73	3	3.05
Roy Parmalee (IL)	R	27	10	6	.625	2	22	21	7	153	134	60	83	2	3.41
Joe Bowman	R	24	5	4	.556	3	30	10	3	107	119	36	36	0	3.62
Dolf Luque	R	43	4	3	.571	7	26	0	0	42	54	17	12	0	3.86
Hi Bell	R	36	4	3	.571	6	22	2	0	54	72	12	9	0	3.67
Jack Salveson	R	20	3	1	.750	0	12	4	0	38	43	13	18	0	3.55
Al Smith	L	26	3	5	.375	5	30	4	0	67	70	21	27	0	4.30
Slick Castleman	R	20	1	0	1.000	0	7	0	0	17	18	10	5	0	5.29
1 Watty Clark	L	32	1	2	.333	0	5	4	1	19	23	5	6	0	6.63

CHICAGO 3rd 86-65 .570 8 — CHARLIE GRIMM

NAME	G by Pos	B	AGE	G	AB	R	H	2B	3B	HR	RBI	BB	SO	SB	BA	SA
TOTALS			28	152	5347	705	1494	263	44	101	664	375	630	59	.279	.402
Charlie Grimm	1B74	L	35	75	267	24	79	8	1	5	47	16	12	1	.296	.390
Billy Herman	2B11	R	24	113	456	79	138	21	6	3	42	34	31	6	.303	.395
Billy Jurges	SS98	R	26	100	358	43	88	15	2	8	33	19	34	1	.246	.366
Stan Hack	3B109	L	24	111	402	54	116	16	6	1	21	45	42	11	.289	.366
Babe Herman	OF113, 1B7	L	31	125	467	65	142	34	5	14	84	35	71	1	.304	.488
Kiki Cuyler	OF142	R	35	142	559	80	189	42	8	6	69	31	62	15	.338	.474
Chuck Klein	OF110	L	29	115	435	78	131	27	2	20	80	47	38	3	.301	.510
Gabby Hartnett	C129	R	33	130	438	58	131	21	1	22	90	37	46	0	.299	.502
Woody English	SS56, 3B46, 2B7	R	27	109	421	65	117	26	5	3	31	48	65	6	.278	.385
Tuck Stainback	OF96, 3B1	R	22	104	359	47	110	14	3	2	46	8	42	7	.306	.379
Augie Galan	2B43, 3B3, SS1	B	22	66	192	31	50	6	2	5	22	16	15	4	.260	.391
2 Don Hurst	1B48	L	28	51	151	13	30	5	0	3	12	8	18	0	.199	.291
Babe Phelps	C18	R	26	44	70	7	20	5	2	2	12	1	4	0	.286	.500
Riggs Stephenson	OF15	R	36	38	74	5	16	0	0	0	7	7	5	0	.216	.216
1 Dolph Camilli	1B32	L	27	32	120	17	33	8	0	4	19	5	25*	1	.275	.442
2 Bob O'Farrell	C22	R	37	22	67	3	15	3	0	0	5	3	11	0	.224	.269
Bennie Tate	C8	L	32	11	24	1	3	0	0	0	1	1	3	0	.125	.125
Phil Cavarretta	1B5	L	17	7	21	5	8	0	1	1	6	2	3	1	.381	.619

*Camilli, also with Philadelphia, league leader in SO with 94

NAME	T	AGE	W	L	PCT	SV	G	GS	CG	IP	H	BB	SO	SHO	ERA
TOTALS		29	86	65	.570	9	152	152	73	1361	1432	417	633	11	3.76
Lon Warneke	R	25	22	10	.688	3	43	35	23	291	273	66	143	3	3.22
Guy Bush	R	32	18	10	.643	2	40	27	15	209	213	54	75	1	3.83
Pat Malone	R	31	14	7	.667	0	34	21	8	191	200	55	111	1	3.53
Bill Lee	R	24	13	14	.481	1	35	29	16	214	218	74	104	4	3.41
2 Jim Weaver	R	30	11	9	.555	0	27	20	10	159	163	54	98	1	3.91
Bud Tinning	R	28	4	6	.400	3	39	7	1	129	134	46	44	1	3.35
Charlie Root	R	35	4	7	.364	0	34	9	2	118	141	53	46	0	4.27
Roy Joiner	L	27	1	0	1.000	0	20	2	0	34	61	8	9	0	8.21
Lynn Nelson	R	29	0	1	.000	0	2	1	0	1	4	1	0	0	36.00
Chick Wiedemeyer	R	20	0	0	—	0	4	1	0	8	16	4	2	0	10.13
Dick Ward	R	25	0	0	—	0	4	0	0	6	9	2	1	0	3.00

BOSTON 4th 78-73 .517 16 — BILL McKECHNIE

NAME	G by Pos	B	AGE	G	AB	R	H	2B	3B	HR	RBI	BB	SO	SB	BA	SA
TOTALS			30	152	5370	683	1460	233	44	83	649	375	440	30	.272	.378
Buck Jordan	1B117	L	27	124	489	68	152	26	9	2	58	35	19	2	.311	.413
Marty McManus	2B73, 3B37	R	34	119	435	56	120	18	0	8	47	32	42	5	.276	.372
Billy Urbanski	SS145	R	31	146	605	104	177	30	6	7	53	56	37	4	.293	.397
Pinky Whitney	3B111, 2B36, SS2	R	29	146	563	58	146	26	2	12	79	25	54	7	.259	.377
Tommy Thompson	OF82	R	24	105	343	40	91	12	3	0	37	13	19	2	.265	.318
Wally Berger	OF150	R	28	150	615	92	183	35	8	34	121	49	65	2	.298	.546
Hal Lee	OF128, 2B4	R	29	139	521	70	152	23	6	8	79	41	43	3	.292	.405
Al Spohrer	C98	R	31	100	265	25	59	15	0	0	17	14	18	1	.223	.279
Randy Moore	OF72, 1B37	L	29	123	422	55	120	21	2	7	64	40	16	2	.284	.391
Shanty Hogan	C90	R	28	92	279	20	73	5	2	4	34	16	13	0	.262	.337
Les Mallon	2B42	R	28	42	166	23	49	6	1	0	18	15	12	0	.295	.343
1 Red Worthington	OF11	R	28	41	65	6	16	5	0	0	6	6	5	0	.246	.323
Joe Mowry	OF20, 2B1	R	26	25	79	9	17	3	0	1	6	3	13	0	.215	.291
Dick Gyselman	3B15, 2B2	R	26	24	36	7	6	1	1	0	4	2	11	0	.167	.250
Elbie Fletcher	1B1	R	18	8	4	4	2	0	0	0	0	0	2	1	.500	.500
Dan McGee	SS7	R	22	7	22	2	3	0	0	0	1	3	6	0	.136	.136
Johnnie Tyler	OF1	R	27	3	6	0	1	0	0	0	0	0	3	0	.167	.167
Rabbit Maranville (BL) 42																

NAME	T	AGE	W	L	PCT	SV	G	GS	CG	IP	H	BB	SO	SHO	ERA
TOTALS		33	78	73	.517	20	152	152	62	1360	1512	405	462	13	4.11
Fred Frankhouse	R	30	17	9	.654	1	37	30	13	234	239	77	78	2	3.19
Huck Betts	R	37	17	10	.630	3	40	27	10	213	258	42	69	2	4.06
Ed Brandt	L	29	16	14	.533	5	40	29	20	255	249	83	106	3	3.53
2 Flint Rhem	R	33	8	8	.500	0	25	20	5	153	164	38	56	2	3.59
Bob Smith	R	39	6	9	.400	3	39	5	3	122	133	36	26	0	4.65
Leo Mangum	R	38	5	3	.625	1	29	3	1	94	127	23	28	0	5.74
Ben Cantwell	R	32	5	11	.313	5	27	19	6	143	163	34	45	1	4.34
1 Tom Zachary	L	38	1	2	.333	0	5	4	2	24	27	8	4	1	3.38
Bob Brown	R	23	1	3	.250	0	16	8	2	58	59	36	21	1	5.74
Dick Oliver	R	27	1	3	.250	0	15	3	0	32	50	12	14	0	6.75
2 Jumbo Jim Elliott	R	33	1	1	.500	0	10	1	0	15	19	9	6	0	6.00
Clarence Pickrel	R	23	0	0	—	0	10	1	0	16	24	7	9	0	5.06

PITTSBURGH 5th 74-76 .493 19.5 — GEORGE GIBSON 27-24 .529 PIE TRAYNOR 47-52 .475

NAME	G by Pos	B	AGE	G	AB	R	H	2B	3B	HR	RBI	BB	SO	SB	BA	SA
TOTALS			27	151	5361	735	1541	281	57	52	679	440	398	44	.287	.398
Gus Suhr	1B151	L	28	151	573	67	162	36	13	13	103	66	52	4	.283	.459
Cookie Lavagetto	2B83	R	21	87	304	41	67	16	3	3	46	32	39	6	.220	.322
Arky Vaughan	SS149	L	22	149	558	115	186	41	11	12	94	94	38	10	.333	.511
Pie Traynor	3B110	R	35	119	444	62	137	22	10	1	61	21	27	3	.309	.410
Paul Waner	OF145	L	31	146	599	122	217	32	16	14	90	68	24	8	.362	.539
Lloyd Waner	OF139	L	28	140	611	95	173	27	6	1	48	38	12	6	.283	.352
Fred Lindstrom	OF92	R	28	97	383	59	111	24	4	4	49	23	21	1	.290	.405
Earl Grace	C83, 1B1	L	27	95	289	27	78	17	1	4	24	20	19	0	.270	.377
Tommy Thevenow	2B75, 3B44, SS1	R	30	122	446	37	121	16	2	0	54	20	20	0	.271	.316
Woody Jensen	OF66	L	26	88	283	34	82	13	4	0	27	4	13	2	.290	.364
Tom Padden	C76	R	25	82	237	27	76	12	2	0	22	30	23	1	.321	.388
Red Lucas	P29	L	32	68	105	11	23	5	1	0	8	6	16	1	.219	.286
Wally Roettger	OF23	R	31	47	106	7	26	5	1	0	11	3	8	0	.245	.311
Pep Young	2B2, SS2	R	26	19	17	3	4	0	0	0	2	1	6	0	.235	.235
Pat Veltman	C11	R	28	12	28	1	3	0	0	0	1	0	2	0	.107	.107
Hal Finney	C1	R	28	5	2	0	0	0	0	0	0	0	0	0	—	—
Bill Brubaker	3B3	R	23	3	6	0	1	0	0	1	0	0	2	0	.333	.500

NAME	T	AGE	W	L	PCT	SV	G	GS	CG	IP	H	BB	SO	SHO	ERA
TOTALS		31	74	76	.493	8	151	151	63	1330	1523	354	487	8	4.19
Waite Hoyt	R	34	15	6	.714	5	48	17	8	191	184	43	105	3	2.92
Larry French	L	26	12	18	.400	1	49	34	16	264	299	59	103	3	3.58
Ralph Birkofer	L	25	11	12	.478	1	41	23	11	204	227	66	71	0	4.10
Bill Swift	R	26	11	13	.458	0	37	25	13	213	244	46	81	1	3.97
Red Lucas	R	32	10	9	.526	0	29	22	12	173	198	40	44	1	4.37
Heinie Meine	R	38	7	6	.538	0	26	14	2	106	134	25	22	0	4.33
Leon Chagnon	R	31	4	1	.800	1	33	0	0	58	68	24	19	0	4.81
Hal Smith (IL)	R	32	3	4	.429	0	20	5	1	50	72	18	15	0	7.20
2 Burleigh Grimes	R	40	3	2	.667	0	8	1	0	27	36	10	9	0	7.33
Cy Blanton	R	25	1	0	1.000	0	1	1	0	3	4	5	1	0	3.38
Steamboat Struss	R	25	1	0	1.000	0	3	0	0	8	10	6	3	0	6.43
2 Ed Holley	R	34	0	0	—	0	2	0	0	9	20	6	2	0	16.00
Bill Harris	R	34	0	1	—	0	11	1	0	19	28	7	8	0	6.63
Lloyd Johnson	L	23	0	0	—	0	2	0	0	2	1	0	0	0	0.00

BROOKLYN 6th 71-81 .487 23.5 CASEY STENGEL

NAME	G by Pos	B	AGE	G	AB	R	H	2B	3B	HR	RBI	BB	SO	SB	BA	SA
TOTALS			29	153	5427	748	1526	284	52	79	699	548	555	55	.281	.396
Sam Leslie	1B138	L	28	146	546	75	181	29	6	9	102	69	34	5	.332	.456
Tony Cuccinello	2B101, 3B43	R	26	140	528	59	138	32	2	14	94	49	45	0	.261	.409
Lonny Frey	SS109, 3B13	B	23	125	490	77	139	24	5	8	57	52	54	11	.284	.402
Joe Stripp (NJ)	3B96, 1B7, SS1	R	31	104	384	50	121	19	6	1	40	22	20	2	.315	.404
Buzz Boyle	OF121	L	26	128	472	88	144	26	10	7	48	51	44	8	.305	.447
Len Koenecke	OF121	L	30	123	460	79	147	31	7	14	73	70	38	8	.320	.509
Danny Taylor	OF108	R	33	120	405	62	121	24	6	7	57	63	47	12	.299	.440
Al Lopez	C137, 2B2, 3B2	R	25	140	439	58	120	23	2	7	54	49	44	2	.273	.383
Johnny Frederick	OF77, 1B1	L	32	104	307	51	91	20	1	4	35	33	13	4	.296	.407
Jimmy Jordan	SS51, 2B41, 3B9	R	26	97	369	34	98	17	2	0	43	9	32	1	.266	.336
1 Hack Wilson	OF43	R	34	67	172	24	45	5	0	6	27	40	33	0	.262	.395
Glenn Chapman	OF40, 2B14	R	28	67	93	19	26	5	1	5	10	7	19	1	.280	.387
Jim Bucher (BN)	2B20, 3B6	L	23	47	84	12	19	5	2	0	8	4	7	1	.226	.333
Ray Berres	C37	R	26	39	79	7	17	4	0	0	3	1	16	0	.215	.266
Clyde Sukeforth	C18	L	32	27	43	5	7	1	0	0	1	1	6	0	.163	.186
Johnny McCarthy	1B13	L	24	17	39	7	7	2	0	1	5	2	2	0	.179	.308
Nick Tremark	OF9	L	21	17	28	3	7	1	0	0	6	2	2	0	.250	.286
Wally Millies	C2	R	27	2	1	0	0	0	0	0	0	0	0	0	.000	.000
Bert Hogg	3B1	R	21	2	1	0	0	0	0	0	0	0	0	0	.000	.000

NAME	T	AGE	W	L	PCT	SV	G	GS	CG	IP	H	BB	SO	SHO	ERA
		29	71	81	.467	12	153	153	66	1354	1540	475	520	6	4.48
Van Lingle Mungo	R	29	18	16	.529	3	45	38	22	315	300	104	184	3	3.37
Dutch Leonard	R	25	14	11	.560	5	44	21	11	184	210	33	58	2	3.28
Ray Benge	R	32	14	12	.538	0	36	32	14	227	252	61	64	1	4.32
Johnny Babich	R	21	7	11	.389	1	35	18	7	135	148	51	62	0	4.20
2 Tom Zachary	L	38	5	8	.455	2	22	12	4	102	122	21	28	0	4.41
Les Munns	R	25	3	7	.300	0	33	9	4	99	106	60	41	0	4.73
2 Watty Clark	L	32	8	2	.800	0	20	8	2	91	99	28	26	0	5.40
Art Herring	R	28	2	4	.333	0	14	4	2	49	63	29	15	0	6.24
Boom-Boom Beck	R	29	2	6	.250	0	22	9	2	57	72	32	24	0	7.42
Phil Page	L	28	1	0	1.000	0	6	0	0	10	13	6	4	0	5.40
Ray Lucas	R	25	1	1	.500	0	10	2	0	31	39	14	3	0	6.68
2 Harry Smythe	L	29	1	1	.500	0	8	2	1	21	30	8	1	0	6.00
Ownie Carroll	R	31	1	1	.250	1	26	5	0	74	108	33	17	0	6.45
Charlie Perkins	L	28	0	1	.000	0	11	2	0	24	37	14	5	0	8.63

PHILADELPHIA 7th 56-93 .376 37 JIMMIE WILSON

NAME	G by Pos	B	AGE	G	AB	R	H	2B	3B	HR	RBI	BB	SO	SB	BA	SA
TOTALS			28	149	5218	675	1480	286	35	56	634	398	534	52	.284	.384
2 Dolph Camilli	1B102	L	27	102	378	52	100	20	3	12	68	44	89*	3	.265	.429
Lou Chiozza	2B85, 3B26, OF17	L	24	134	484	64	147	28	5	0	44	34	35	9	.304	.382
Dick Bartell	SS146	R	26	146	604	102	187	30	4	0	37	64	59	13	.310	.373
2 Bucky Walters	3B80, 2B3, P2	R	25	83	300	36	78	20	3	4	38	19	54	1	.260	.387
3 Johnny Moore	OF115	L	32	116	458	68	157	34	6	11	93	40	18	7	.343	.515
2 Kiddo Davis	OF100	R	32	100	393	50	115	25	5	3	48	27	28	1	.293	.405
Ethan Allen	OF145	R	30	145	581	87	192	42	4	10	85	33	47	6	.330	.468
Al Todd	C82	R	30	91	302	33	96	22	2	4	41	10	39	1	.318	.444
Jimmie Wilson	C77, 1B1, 2B1	R	33	91	277	25	81	11	0	3	35	14	10	1	.292	.365
Mickey Haslin	3B26, 2B21, SS4	R	24	72	166	28	44	8	2	1	11	16	13	1	.265	.355
Harvey Hendrick	OF12, 1B7, 3B7	L	36	59	116	12	34	8	0	0	19	16	15	0	.293	.362
Irv Jeffries	3B52, 3B7	R	28	56	175	28	43	16	0	4	19	15	10	2	.246	.349
Andy High	3B14, 2B2	L	36	47	68	4	14	2	0	0	6	9	5	0	.206	.235
1 Don Hurst	1B34	L	28	40	130	16	34	9	0	2	21	12	7	1	.262	.377
1 Chick Fullis	OF27	R	30	28	102	8	23	6	0	0	12	10	4	2	.225	.284
Bud Clancy	1B10	L	33	20	49	8	12	0	1	0	7	6	4	0	.245	.306
Art Ruble	OF14	L	31	19	54	7	15	4	0	0	8	7	3	0	.278	.352
1 West Schulmerich	OF13	R	32	15	52	2	13	1	0	0	4	3	5	0	.250	.269
1 Marty Hopkins	3B9	R	27	14	25	2	3	2	0	0	3	1	5	0	.120	.200
Joe Holden	C6	L	21	10	14	1	1	0	0	0	0	0	2	0	.071	.071

Ed Boland 26 L 9-30, 2 Hack Wilson 34 R 2-20, Prince Oana 26 R 5-21, Fred Frink 22 R 0-0

NAME	T	AGE	W	L	PCT	SV	G	GS	CG	IP	H	BB	SO	SHO	ERA
		30	56	93	.376	15	149	149	52	1297	1501	437	416	8	4.76
Curt Davis	R	30	19	17	.528	5	51	31	18	274	283	60	99	3	2.96
Phil Collins	R	32	13	18	.419	1	45	32	15	254	277	87	72	0	4.18
Snipe Hansen	L	27	6	12	.333	3	50	16	5	151	194	61	40	2	5.42
Euel Moore	R	26	5	7	.417	1	20	16	3	122	145	41	38	0	4.06
2 Syl Johnson	R	33	5	9	.357	3	42	10	4	134	122	24	54	3	3.49
Cy Moore	R	29	4	9	.308	0	35	15	3	127	163	65	55	0	6.45
George Darrow	L	26	2	6	.250	1	17	8	2	49	57	28	14	0	5.51
Reggie Grabowski	R	26	1	3	.250	0	27	5	0	65	114	23	13	0	9.28
1 Ed Holley	R	34	1	8	.111	0	15	13	2	73	85	31	14	0	7.15
Bill Lohrman	R	21	0	1	.000	0	4	1	0	8	13	4	3	0	4.50
1 Jumbo Jim Elliott	L	33	0	1	.000	0	7	1	0	20	25	4	4	0	10.80
Frank Pearce	L	29	0	2	.000	0	7	1	0	20	25	5	4	0	7.20
1 Ted Kleinhans	R	35	0	0	—	0	5	0	0	6	11	3	2	0	9.00
Bucky Walters	R	25	0	0	—	0	2	0	0	7	10	2	4	0	1.29
Cy Malis	R	27	0	0	—	0	1	0	0	2	4	2	1	0	4.50

*Camilli, also with Chicago, league leader in SO with 94

CINCINNATI 8th 52-99 .344 42 BOB O'FARRELL 30-60 .333 BURT SHOTTON 1-0 1.000 CHUCK DRESSEN 21-39 .350

NAME	G by Pos	B	AGE	G	AB	R	H	2B	3B	HR	RBI	BB	SO	SB	BA	SA
TOTALS			30	152	5361	590	1428	227	65	55	560	313	532	34	.266	.364
Jim Bottomley	1B139	L	34	142	556	72	158	31	11	11	78	33	40	1	.284	.439
Tony Piet	2B49, 3B51	R	27	106	421	58	109	20	5	1	38	23	44	6	.259	.337
Gordon Slade	SS97, 2B39	R	29	138	555	61	158	19	8	4	52	25	34	6	.285	.369
Mark Koenig	3B64, SS58, 2B26, 1B4	B	31	151	633	60	172	26	6	1	67	15	24	5	.272	.336
Adam Comorosky	OF122	R	29	127	446	46	115	12	6	0	40	34	23	1	.258	.312
Chick Hafey	OF140	R	31	140	535	75	157	29	6	18	67	52	63	4	.293	.471
Harlin Pool	OF94	L	26	99	358	38	117	22	5	2	50	17	18	3	.327	.434
Ernie Lombardi	C111	R	26	132	417	42	127	19	4	9	62	16	22	0	.305	.434
Sparky Adams	3B38, 2B29	R	39	87	278	38	70	16	1	0	14	20	10	2	.252	.317
2 Wes Schulmerich	OF56	R	32	74	209	21	55	8	3	5	19	22	43	1	.263	.402
1 Bob O'Farrell	C42	R	37	44	123	10	30	8	3	1	9	11	19	0	.244	.382
Linc Blakely	OF28	R	22	34	102	11	23	7	1	0	10	5	14	1	.225	.255
Clyde Manion	C24	R	37	25	54	4	10	0	0	0	4	4	7	0	.185	.185
Alex Kampouris	2B16	R	21	19	66	6	13	1	0	3	3	3	18	0	.197	.212
Ivey Shiver	OF15	R	27	19	59	6	12	1	0	2	6	3	15	1	.203	.322
Jimmy Shevlin	1B10	L	31	18	39	6	12	2	0	0	6	6	5	0	.308	.359
1 Johnny Moore	OF10	L	32	16	42	5	8	2	0	0	5	1	1	0	.190	.262
Jake Flowers		R	32	13	9	1	3	0	0	0	0	1	1	1	.333	.333
Frankie McCormick	1B2	R	23	12	16	1	5	0	0	0	3	1	3	0	.313	.563
Ted Petoskey	OF2	R	23	13	9	1	0	0	0	0	0	2	5	0	.000	.000

Harry McCurdy 34 L 0-6, Tommy Robello 21 R 0-2, Bill Marshall 22 R 1-8

NAME	T	AGE	W	L	PCT	SV	G	GS	CG	IP	H	BB	SO	SHO	ERA
		31	52	99	.344	19	152	152	51	1347	1645	389	438	3	4.37
Paul Derringer	R	27	15	21	.417	4	47	31	18	261	297	59	122	1	3.59
Benny Frey	R	28	11	16	.407	2	39	30	12	245	288	42	33	2	3.53
Si Johnson	R	27	7	22	.241	3	46	31	9	216	264	84	89	0	5.21
Allyn Stout	R	29	6	8	.429	1	41	16	4	141	170	47	51	0	4.85
Tony Freitas	L	26	6	12	.333	1	30	18	5	153	194	25	37	0	4.00
Don Brennan	R	30	4	3	.571	2	28	7	2	78	89	35	31	0	3.81
2 Ted Kleinhans	L	35	2	6	.250	0	24	9	0	80	107	38	23	0	5.74
Beryl Richmond	L	26	2	3	.333	0	21	3	2	19	23	10	9	0	3.79
Larry Benton	R	36	1	0	1.000	0	16	1	0	29	53	7	5	0	6.52
Lee Grissom	L	26	0	1	.000	0	4	1	0	13	7	4	4	0	15.43
Whitey Wistert	R	22	0	1	.000	0	4	1	0	8	5	1	1	0	1.13
Ray Kolp	R	39	0	2	.000	3	28	2	0	62	78	12	19	0	4.50
Joe Shaute	L	34	0	2	.000	0	17	1	0	17	19	3	2	0	4.23
2 Dazzy Vance	R	43	0	2	.000	0	4	0	0	18	28	11	9	0	7.50
1 Jim Lindsey	R	36	0	0	—	0	4	0	0	7	9	0	0	0	4.50
1 Syl Johnson	R	33	0	0	—	0	1	0	0	2	3	0	2	0	2.57
Junie Barnes	L	22	0	0	—	0	1	0	0	1	4	0	0	0	0.00
Sherman Edwards	R	24	0	0	—	0	1	0	0	1	0	1	0	0	3.00

WORLD SERIES —ST. LOUIS (NL) 4   DETROIT (AL) 3

LINE SCORES

TEAM	1 2 3	4 5 6	7 8 9	10 11 12	R	H	E
Game 1 October 3 at Detroit							
STL (NL)	0 2 1	0 1 4	0 0 0		8	13	2
DET (AL)	0 0 1	0 0 1	0 1 0		3	8	5

D. Dean — Crowder, Marberry (6), Hogsett (6)

TEAM	1 2 3	4 5 6	7 8 9	10 11 12	R	H	E
Game 2 October 4 at Detroit							
STL	0 1 1	0 0 0	0 0 0	0 0 0	2	7	3
DET	0 0 0	1 0 0	0 0 1	0 0 1	3	7	0

Hallahan, B. Walker (9) — Rowe

TEAM	1 2 3	4 5 6	7 8 9	R	H	E
Game 3 October 5 at St. Louis						
DET	0 0 0	0 0 0	0 0 1	1	8	2
STL	1 1 0	0 2 0	0 0 X	4	9	1

Bridges, Hogsett (5) — P. Dean

TEAM	1 2 3	4 5 6	7 8 9	R	H	E
Game 4 October 6 at St. Louis						
DET	0 0 3	1 0 0	1 5 0	10	13	1
STL	0 1 1	2 0 0	1 0 0	4	10	5

Auker — Carleton, Vance (3), B. Walker (6), Haines (8), Mooney (9)

TEAM	1 2 3	4 5 6	7 8 9	R	H	E
Game 5 October 7 at St. Louis						
DET	0 1 0	0 0 2	0 0 0	3	7	0
STL	0 0 0	0 0 1	0 0 0	1	7	1

Bridges — D. Dean, Carleton (9)

TEAM	1 2 3	4 5 6	7 8 9	R	H	E
Game 6 October 8 at Detroit						
STL	1 0 0	0 2 0	1 0 0	4	10	2
DET	0 0 1	0 0 2	0 0 0	3	7	1

P. Dean — Rowe

TEAM	1 2 3	4 5 6	7 8 9	R	H	E
Game 7 October 9 at Detroit						
STL	0 0 7	0 0 2	2 0 0	11	17	1
DET	0 0 0	0 0 0	0 0 0	0	6	3

D. Dean — Auker, Rowe (3), Hogsett (3), Bridges (3), Marberry (8), Crowder (9)

COMPOSITE BATTING

NAME	POS	G	AB	R	H	2B	3B	HR	RBI	BA
St. Louis (NL)										
Totals		7	262	34	73	14	5	2	32	.279
Martin	3B	7	31	8	11	3	1	0	4	.355
Frisch	2B	7	31	2	6	1	0	0	4	.194
Collins	1B	7	30	4	11	1	0	0	6	.367
Rothrock	OF	7	30	3	7	3	1	0	6	.233
Medwick	OF	7	29	4	11	0	1	1	5	.379
DeLancey	C	7	29	3	5	3	0	1	4	.172
Durocher	SS	7	27	4	7	1	1	0	5	.259
Orsatti	OF	7	22	3	7	1	0	0	0	.318
D. Dean	P	4	12	3	3	0	0	0	2	.250
P. Dean	P	2	6	0	1	0	0	0	0	.167
Fullis	OF	3	5	0	2	0	0	0	0	.400
Hallahan	P	1	3	0	0	0	0	0	0	.000
S. Davis	PH	2	2	0	2	0	0	0	1	1.000
Crawford	PH	2	2	0	0	0	0	0	0	.000
B. Walker	P	3	2	0	0	0	0	0	0	.000
Carleton	P	2	1	0	0	0	0	0	0	.000
Haines	P	1	1	0	0	0	0	0	0	—
Mooney	P	1	1	0	0	0	0	0	0	.000
Vance	P	1	1	0	0	0	0	0	0	.000
Whitehead	SS	1	1	0	0	0	0	0	0	.000
Detroit (AL)										
Totals		7	250	23	56	12	1	2	20	.224
Gehringer	2B	7	29	5	11	1	0	1	2	.379
Rogell	SS	7	29	3	8	1	0	0	4	.276
Goslin	OF	7	29	2	7	1	0	0	4	.241
Owen	3B	7	29	0	2	0	0	0	1	.069
Greenberg	1B	7	28	4	9	2	1	1	7	.321
Fox	OF	7	28	1	8	6	0	0	2	.286
Cochrane	C	7	28	2	6	1	0	0	1	.214
White	OF	7	23	6	3	0	0	0	0	.130
Bridges	P	3	7	0	1	0	0	0	0	.143
Rowe	P	3	7	0	0	0	0	0	0	.000
Auker	P	2	4	0	0	0	0	0	0	.000
G. Walker	PH	3	3	0	1	0	0	0	0	.333
Hogsett	P	3	2	0	0	0	0	0	0	.000
Doljack	OF	2	2	0	0	0	0	0	0	.000
Crowder	P	2	1	0	0	0	0	0	0	.000
Hayworth	C	1	0	0	0	0	0	0	0	—
Marberry	P	2	0	0	0	0	0	0	0	—

COMPOSITE PITCHING

NAME	G	IP	H	BB	SO	W	L	SV	ERA
St. Louis (NL)									
Totals	7	65.1	56	25	43	4	3	0	2.34
D. Dean	3	26	20	5	17	2	1	0	1.73
P. Dean	2	18	15	7	11	2	0	0	1.00
Hallahan	1	8.1	6	4	6	0	0	0	2.16
B. Walker	2	6.1	6	6	2	0	0	0	7.11
Carleton	2	3.2	5	2	2	0	0	0	7.36
Vance	1	1.1	1	1	3	0	0	0	0.00
Mooney	1	1	1	0	0	0	0	0	0.00
Haines	1	0.2	1	0	2	0	0	0	0.00
Detroit (AL)									
Totals	7	65	73	11	31	3	4	0	3.74
Rowe	3	21.1	19	0	12	1	1	0	2.95
Bridges	3	17.1	21	1	12	1	1	0	3.63
Auker	2	11.1	16	5	2	1	1	0	5.56
Hogsett	3	7.1	6	3	0	0	0	0	1.23
Crowder	2	6	6	1	4	0	0	0	1.50
Marberry	2	1.2	5	1	0	0	0	0	21.60

1935 A Last Hurrah and a First Championship

Two of the biggest stories of the season took place in the cellars of both leagues. Connie Mack's Athletics had Jimmie Foxx, who batted .346 and hit 36 homers to tie for home run honors with Detroit's Hank Greenberg. There was also Doc Cramer, .332; Bob Johnson, .299; Pinky Higgins, .296; and rookie Wally Moses, who hit .325 before being shelved with a broken arm. The pitching wasn't much, although Johnny Marcum managed to win 17 games. All in all, Mack had the distinction of fielding one of the strongest tail-enders in league history.

By contrast, Boston of the National League was not as strong. In fact, their 115 losses was the greatest number of league defeats since the Cleveland Spiders' 134 setbacks in 1899. But Boston started the season with Babe Ruth, who was beginning his National League career with 708 home runs. Ruth, released from the Yankees because of age, had an auspicious start in his first at bat with a home run off Giant ace, Carl Hubbell. The four-bagger, however, did not prove an omen of things to come and in June, with an anemic .181 average, Ruth removed himself from the lineup. He had managed to collect six home runs for a career total of 714—a number that would defy challenge for decades to come.

If Ruth supplied the dramatics in the early going, the Cubs more than equaled the excitement in the last month of the season. After spending most of the year watching the Giants and Cardinals fighting it out, the Cubs put on a drive in September; their 21 straight wins proved enough to carry them to a National League pennant. Their final victims in the streak were the runner-up Cardinals. The Cubs entered St. Louis on September 25, with 18 consecutive victories and a five-game series. They needed two wins to clinch the flag and had to face the Dean brothers who, at about the same time the previous year, put the Cards over the top. In the first game, Lou Warneke beat Paul Dean, 1-0 and, in the first game of a doubleheader a day later, Bill Lee beat Dizzy Dean, 6-2. The Cubs iced the cake by winning the next game for their streak—the best since the Giants won 26 in a row in 1916.

MVP honors went to the Cubs' catcher Gabby Hartnett, who hit .344. Cincinnati, although finishing sixth, made baseball history by putting lights in the stadium and playing seven night games.

Before the American League season got underway, Tom Yawkey of the Red Sox shelled out $250,000 to Washington for Joe Cronin. When the season ended, the Red Sox had two pitchers who shared 45 wins and an outstanding manager-shortstop in Cronin, all of which was good for three more wins than 1934 and the same fourth-place finish. But with Yawkey's money, Lefty Grove's comeback of 20 wins, the E.R.A. crown of 2.70, and Wes Ferrell's league high of 25 wins, hopes remained high for the 1936 season

Mickey Cochrane, Detroit's manager-catcher, was more concerned with 1935 and proving that his 1934 pennant victory was no fluke. His Tigers began the season dismally and fell to the cellar before being able to put a drive together behind MVP Greenberg, second baseman Charlie Gehringer, outfielders Pete Fox and Goose Goslin, and a fine pitching staff including Schoolboy Rowe, Tommy Bridges, General Crowder, and Eldon Auker. Detroit's pennant gave Cochrane an enviable record. In seven years and with two different teams, he had been a member of five pennant winning teams.

The red-hot Cubs started the World Series with a 3-0 win behind Warneke and looked as if they would easily beat the Tigers—especially after Greenberg broke his wrist in the second game which Detroit won, 8-3. But the Tigers would not quit, going on to win four games to two for their first championship ever.

1935 AMERICAN LEAGUE

DETROIT 1st 93-58 .616 — MICKEY COCHRANE

NAME	G by Pos	B	AGE	G	AB	R	H	2B	3B	HR	RBI	BB	SO	SB	BA	SA
TOTALS			29	152	5423	919	1573	301	83	106	837	627	456	70	.290	.436
Hank Greenberg	1B152	R	24	152	619	121	203	46	16	36	170	87	91	4	.328	.628
Charlie Gehringer	2B149	R	32	150	610	123	201	32	8	19	108	79	16	11	.330	.502
Billy Rogell	SS150	B	30	150	560	88	154	23	11	6	71	80	29	3	.275	.388
Marv Owen	3B131	R	29	134	483	52	127	24	5	2	71	43	37	1	.263	.346
Pete Fox	OF125	R	25	131	517	116	166	38	8	15	73	45	52	14	.321	.513
Jo-Jo White	OF98	L	26	114	412	82	99	13	12	2	32	68	42	19	.240	.345
Goose Goslin	OF144	L	34	147	590	88	172	34	6	9	109	56	31	5	.292	.415
Mickey Cochrane	C110	L	32	115	411	93	131	33	3	5	47	96	15	5	.319	.450
Gee Walker	OF85	R	27	98	362	52	109	22	6	7	53	15	21	6	.301	.453
Ray Hayworth	C48	R	31	51	175	22	54	14	2	0	22	9	14	0	.309	.411
Schoolboy Rowe	P42	R	25	45	109	19	34	3	2	3	28	12	12	0	.312	.459
Flea Clifton	3B21, 2B5, SS4	R	25	43	110	15	28	5	0	0	9	5	13	2	.255	.300
Chet Morgan	OF4	R	25	14	23	2	4	1	0	0	1	0	0	0	.174	.217
Heinie Schuble	3B2, 2B1	R	28	11	8	3	2	0	0	0	0	1	0	0	.250	.250
Hub Walker	OF7	L	28	9	25	4	4	3	0	0	1	3	4	0	.160	.280
Frank Reiber	C5	R	25	8	11	3	3	0	0	0	1	3	3	0	.273	.273
Hugh Shelley	OF5	R	24	7	8	1	2	0	0	0	0	0	1	0	.250	.250

NAME	T	AGE	W	L	PCT	SV	G	GS	CG	IP	H	BB	SO	SHO	ERA
		28	93	53	.616	11	152	152	87	1364	1440	522	584	16	3.82
Tommy Bridges	R	28	21	10	.677	1	36	34	23	274	277	113	163	4	3.51
Schoolboy Rowe	R	25	19	13	.594	3	42	34	21	276	272	68	140	6	3.68
Elden Auker	R	24	18	7	.720	0	36	25	13	195	213	61	63	2	3.83
General Crowder	R	36	16	10	.615	0	33	32	16	241	269	67	59	2	4.26
Chief Hogsett	L	31	6	6	.500	5	40	0	0	97	109	49	39	0	3.53
Joe Sullivan	L	24	6	6	.500	0	25	12	5	126	119	71	53	0	3.50
Vic Sorrell	R	34	4	3	.571	0	12	6	4	51	65	25	22	0	4.06
Roxie Lawson	R	29	3	1	.750	2	7	4	4	40	34	24	16	2	1.58
Firpo Marberry	R	36	0	1	.000	0	5	2	1	19	22	9	7	0	4.26
1 Carl Fischer	L	29	0	1	.000	0	3	1	0	12	16	5	7	0	6.00
Clyde Hatter	L	26	0	0	—	0	8	2	0	33	44	30	15	0	7.64

NEW YORK 2nd 89-60 .597 3 — JOE McCARTHY

NAME	G by Pos	B	AGE	G	AB	R	H	2B	3B	HR	RBI	BB	SO	SB	BA	SA
TOTALS			29	149	5214	818	1462	255	70	104	755	604	469	68	.280	.416
Lou Gehrig	1B149	L	32	149	535	125	176	26	10	30	119	132	38	8	.329	.583
Tony Lazzeri	2B118, SS9	R	31	130	477	72	130	18	6	13	83	63	75	11	.275	.417
Frankie Crosetti	SS87	R	24	87	305	49	78	17	6	8	50	41	27	3	.256	.430
Red Rolfe	3B136, SS17	L	26	149	639	108	192	33	9	5	67	57	39	7	.300	.404
George Selkirk	OF127	L	27	128	491	64	153	29	12	11	94	44	36	2	.312	.487
Ben Chapman	OF138	R	26	140	553	118	160	38	8	4	74	61	39	17	.289	.430
Jesse Hill	OF94	R	28	107	392	69	115	20	3	4	33	42	32	14	.293	.390
Bill Dickey	C118	L	28	120	448	54	125	26	6	14	81	35	11	1	.279	.458
Earle Combs (BC)	OF70	L	36	89	298	47	84	7	4	3	35	36	10	1	.282	.362
Jack Saltzgaver	2B25, 3B18, 1B6	L	30	61	149	17	39	6	0	3	18	23	12	0	.262	.362
Red Ruffing	P30	R	31	50	109	13	37	10	0	2	18	3	9	0	.339	.486
Myril Hoag	OF37	R	27	48	110	13	28	4	1	1	13	12	19	4	.255	.336
Art Jorgens	C33	R	30	36	84	6	20	2	0	0	8	12	10	0	.238	.262
2 Blondy Ryan	SS30	R	29	30	105	12	25	1	3	0	11	3	10	0	.238	.305
Joe Glenn	C16	R	26	17	43	7	10	4	0	0	6	4	1	0	.233	.326
Nolen Richardson	SS12	R	32	12	46	3	10	1	1	0	5	3	1	0	.217	.283
Don Heffner	2B10	R	24	10	36	3	11	3	1	0	3	4	1	0	.306	.444
Dixie Walker (SJ)	OF2	L	24	8	13	1	2	1	0	0	1	0	1	0	.154	.231

NAME	T	AGE	W	L	PCT	SV	G	GS	CG	IP	H	BB	SO	SHO	ERA
		27	89	60	.597	13	149	149	76	1331	1276	516	594	12	3.60
Red Ruffing	R	31	16	11	.593	0	30	29	19	222	201	76	81	2	3.12
Johnny Broaca	R	25	15	7	.682	0	29	27	14	201	199	79	78	2	3.58
Johnny Allen	R	30	13	6	.684	0	23	23	12	167	149	58	113	2	3.61
Lefty Gomez	L	26	12	15	.444	1	34	30	15	246	223	86	138	2	3.18
Vito Tamulis	L	23	10	5	.667	1	30	19	9	161	178	55	57	3	4.08
Johnny Murphy	R	26	10	5	.667	5	40	8	4	117	110	55	28	0	4.08
Jumbo Brown	R	28	6	5	.545	0	20	8	3	87	94	37	41	0	3.62
Jimmie DeShong	R	25	4	1	.800	3	29	3	0	69	64	33	30	0	3.26
Pat Malone	R	32	3	3	.500	3	29	2	0	56	53	33	25	0	5.46
1 Russ Van Atta	L	29	0	0	—	0	5*	0	0	5	4	3	0		3.60

*Van Atta, also with St. Louis, League leader in G with 58

CLEVELAND 3rd 82-71 .536 12 — WALTER JOHNSON 46-48 .489 STEVE O'NEILL 36-23 .610

NAME	G by Pos	B	AGE	G	AB	R	H	2B	3B	HR	RBI	BB	SO	SB	BA	SA
TOTALS			27	156	5534	776	1573	324	77	93	737	460	567	63	.284	.421
Hal Trosky	1B153	L	22	154	632	84	171	33	7	26	113	46	60	1	.271	.468
Boze Berger	2B120, SS3, 1B2, 3B1	R	25	124	461	62	119	27	5	6	43	34	97	1	.258	.371
Bill Knickerbocker	SS128	R	23	132	540	77	161	34	5	2	57	27	31	2	.298	.380
Odell Hale	3B149, 2B1	R	26	150	589	80	179	37	11	6	101	52	55	15	.304	.486
Bruce Campbell (IL)	OF75	L	25	80	308	56	100	26	3	7	54	45	35	3	.325	.497
Earl Averill	OF139	L	33	140	563	109	162	34	13	19	79	70	58	8	.288	.496
Joe Vosmik	OF150	R	25	152	620	93	216	47	20	10	110	59	30	2	.348	.537
Eddie Phillips	C69	R	34	70	220	18	60	16	1	1	41	15	21	0	.273	.368
Milt Galatzer	OF81	L	28	93	259	45	78	9	3	0	19	35	8	4	.301	.359
Roy Hughes	2B40, SS29, 3B1	R	24	82	266	40	78	15	3	0	14	18	17	13	.293	.372
Ab Wright	OF47	R	28	67	160	17	38	11	1	2	18	10	17	2	.238	.356
R. Winegarner	P25, OF4, 3B3, 1B1	R	25	65	84	11	26	4	1	3	17	9	12	1	.310	.488
Frankie Pytlak	C48	R	26	55	149	14	44	6	1	1	12	11	4	3	.295	.369
Bill Brenzel	C51	R	25	52	142	12	31	5	1	0	14	6	10	0	.218	.268
Willis Hudlin	P36	R	29	37	86	10	24	7	0	1	8	6	19	0	.279	.395
Kit Carson	OF4	L	22	16	22	1	5	2	0	0	1	0	1	0	.227	.318
1 Glenn Myatt	C10	L	37	10	36	1	3	0	0	0	1	2	6	0	.083	.111
Bob Garbark	C6	R	25	8	18	4	6	1	0	0	4	5	1	0	.333	.389
Willie Kamm	3B4	R	35	6	18	2	6	0	0	0	1	0	2	0	.333	.333
Greek George	C1	R	22	2	1	0	0	0	0	0	0	0	0	0	—	—

NAME	T	AGE	W	L	PCT	SV	G	GS	CG	IP	H	BB	SO	SHO	ERA
		28	82	71	.536	21	156	156	67	1396	1527	457	498	11	4.15
Mel Harder	R	25	22	11	.667	2	42	35	17	287	313	53	95	3	3.29
Willia Hudlin	R	29	15	11	.577	5	36	29	14	232	252	61	45	3	3.69
Oral Hildebrand	R	28	9	8	.529	5	34	20	8	171	171	63	49	0	3.81
Lloyd Brown	L	30	8	7	.533	4	42	8	4	122	123	37	45	2	3.61
Monte Pearson	R	26	8	13	.381	0	30	24	10	182	199	103	90	1	4.90
Thornton Lee	L	28	7	10	.412	1	22	8	8	181	179	71	81	1	4.03
2 Lefty Stewart	L	34	6	6	.500	2	24	10	2	91	122	17	24	1	5.44
Clint Brown	R	31	4	3	.571	2	23	5	1	49	61	14	20	0	5.14
Ralph Winegarner (AJ)	R	25	2	2	.500	0	25	4	2	67	89	29	41	0	5.78
Denny Galehouse	R	23	1	1	.000	0	5	1	1	13	16	9	8	0	9.00
1 Belve Bean	R	30	0	0	—	0	1	0	1	2	0	1	0		9.00

BOSTON — 4th 78-75 .516 16 — JOE CRONIN

NAME	G by Pos	B	AGE	G	AB	R	H	2B	3B	HR	RBI	BB	SO	SB	BA	SA
TOTALS			28	154	5288	718	1458	281	63	69	660	609	470	91	.276	.392
Babe Dahlgren	1B149	R	23	149	525	77	138	27	7	9	63	56	67	6	.263	.392
2 Oscar Melillo	2B105	R	35	106	399	45	104	13	2	1	39	38	22	3	.261	.311
Joe Cronin	SS139	R	28	144	556	70	164	37	14	9	95	63	40	3	.295	.460
Bill Werber	3B123	R	27	124	462	84	118	30	3	14	61	69	41	29	.255	.424
Dusty Cooke	OF82	L	28	100	294	51	90	18	6	3	34	46	24	6	.306	.439
Mel Almada	OF149, 1B3	L	22	151	607	85	176	19	6	3	59	55	34	20	.290	.379
Roy Johnson	OF142	L	32	145	553	70	174	33	9	3	66	74	34	11	.315	.423
Rick Ferrell	C131	R	29	133	458	54	138	34	4	3	61	65	15	5	.301	.413
Carl Reynolds	OF64	R	32	78	244	33	66	13	4	6	35	24	20	4	.270	.430
Bing Miller	OF29	R	40	78	138	18	42	8	1	3	26	10	8	0	.304	.442
2 Dib Williams	3B30, 2B29, SS15, 1B1	R	25	75	251	26	63	12	0	3	25	24	23	2	.251	.335
Wes Ferrell	P41	R	27	75	150	25	52	5	1	7	32	21	16	0	.347	.533
Max Bishop	2B34, 1B11, 332	L	35	60	122	19	28	3	1	1	14	28	14	0	.230	.295
Moe Berg	C37	R	33	38	98	13	28	5	0	2	12	5	3	0	.286	.398
1 Moose Solters	OF21	R	29	24	79	15	19	6	1	0	8	2	7	1	.241	.342
Skinny Graham	OF2	L	23	8	10	1	3	0	0	0	1	1	3	1	.300	.300
George Dickey	C4	B	19	5	11	1	0	0	0	0	1	1	3	0	.000	.000
Doc Farrell	2B4	R	33	4	7	1	2	1	0	0	1	0	0	0	.286	.429
John Kroner	3B2	R	26	2	4	1	1	0	0	0	0	1	1	0	.250	.250
Lou Legett		R	34	2	0	1	0	0	0	0	0	0	0	0	—	—

NAME	T	AGE	W	L	PCT	SV	G	GS	CG	IP	H	BB	SO	SHO	ERA
		29	78	75	.516	11	154	154	82	1376	1520	520	470	6	4.05
Wes Ferrell	R	27	25	14	.641	0	41	38	31	322	336	108	110	3	3.52
Lefty Grove	L	35	20	12	.625	1	35	30	23	273	269	65	121	1	2.70
Johnny Welch	R	28	10	9	.526	2	31	19	10	143	155	53	48	1	4.47
Fritz Ostermueller	L	27	7	8	.467	1	22	19	10	138	135	78	41	0	3.91
Rube Walberg	R	38	5	9	.357	3	44	10	4	161	152	54	44	0	3.90
Jack Wilson	R	23	4	4	.429	1	23	6	2	64	72	36	19	0	4.22
Hank Johnson	R	29	2	1	.667	1	13	2	0	31	41	14	14	0	5.52
Stew Bowers	R	20	2	1	.667	0	10	2	1	24	26	17	5	0	3.38
George Hockette	L	27	2	3	.400	0	23	4	0	61	83	12	11	0	5.16
Gordon Rhodes	R	27	2	10	.167	2	34	19	1	146	195	60	44	0	5.42
George Pipgras	R	35	0	1	.000	0	1	0	0	1	3	2	0	0	14.40
2 Joe Cascarella	R	28	0	0	—	0	5	0	0	17	25	11	9	0	6.88
Hy Vandenberg	R	27	0	0	—	0	3	0	0	5	15	4	2	0	21.60
Walt Ripley	R	18	0	0	—	0	2	0	0	4	7	3	0	0	9.00

CHICAGO — 5th 74-78 .487 19.5 — JIMMY DYKES

NAME	G by Pos	B	AGE	G	AB	R	H	2B	3B	HR	RBI	BB	SO	SB	BA	SA
TOTALS			30	153	5314	738	1460	262	42	74	690	580	405	46	.275	.382
Zeke Bonura	1B138	R	26	138	550	107	162	34	4	21	92	57	28	4	.295	.485
Jackie Hayes	2B85	R	28	89	329	45	88	14	0	4	45	29	15	3	.267	.347
Luke Appling	SS153	R	28	153	525	94	161	28	6	1	71	122	40	12	.307	.389
Jimmy Dykes	3B98, 1B16, 2B3	R	38	117	403	45	116	24	2	4	61	59	28	4	.288	.387
Mule Haas (WJ)	OF84	L	31	92	327	44	95	22	1	2	40	37	14	4	.291	.382
Al Simmons	OF126	R	33	128	525	68	140	22	7	16	79	33	43	4	.267	.427
Rip Radcliff	OF142	L	29	146	623	95	178	28	8	10	68	53	21	3	.286	.404
Luke Sewell	C112	R	34	118	421	52	120	19	3	2	67	32	18	3	.285	.359
George Washington	OF79	L	28	108	339	40	96	22	3	8	47	10	18	1	.283	.437
2 Tony Piet	2B59, 3B17	R	28	77	292	47	87	17	5	3	27	33	27	2	.298	.421
Jocko Conlan	OF37	L	35	65	140	20	40	7	1	0	15	14	6	3	.286	.350
Marty Hopkins	3B49, 2B5	R	28	59	144	20	32	9	0	2	17	36	23	1	.222	.285
Merv Shea	C43	R	34	46	122	8	28	2	0	0	13	30	9	0	.230	.246
Fred Tauby	OF7	R	29	13	32	5	4	1	0	0	2	2	7	1	.125	.156
Glenn Wright	2B7	R	34	9	25	1	3	1	0	0	1	0	0	0	.120	.160
2 Frank Grube	C9	R	30	9	19	1	7	2	0	0	6	3	2	0	.368	.474
Mike Kreevich	3B6	R	27	6	23	3	10	2	0	0	2	1	0	1	.435	.522
1 Bud Hafey		R	22	2	0	0	0	0	0	0	0	0	0	0	—	—

NAME	T	AGE	W	L	PCT	SV	G	GS	CG	IP	H	BB	SO	SHO	ERA
		29	74	78	.487	8	153	153	80	1361	1443	574	436	8	4.38
Ted Lyons	R	34	15	8	.652	0	23	22	19	191	194	56	54	3	3.02
John Whitehead	R	26	13	13	.500	0	28	27	18	222	209	101	72	1	3.73
Vern Kennedy	R	28	11	11	.500	1	31	25	16	212	211	95	65	2	3.91
Les Tietje	R	24	9	15	.375	0	30	21	17	170	184	81	64	1	4.29
Sad Sam Jones	R	42	8	7	.533	0	21	19	7	140	162	51	38	0	4.05
2 Carl Fischer	L	29	5	5	.500	0	24	11	3	89	102	39	31	1	6.17
Whit Wyatt	R	27	4	3	.571	5	30	1	1	52	65	25	22	0	6.75
Ray Phelps	R	31	4	3	.333	1	27	17	4	125	126	55	38	0	4.82
Joe Vance	R	29	2	2	.500	0	10	0	0	31	36	21	12	0	6.68
2 Jack Salveson	R	21	2	2	.333	1	20	2	2	67	79	23	22	0	4.84
Monty Stratton	R	23	1	2	.333	0	5	5	2	38	44	11	8	0	4.03
1 George Earnshaw	R	35	1	2	.333	1	8	1	1	26	11	8	0		9.00
1 Talo Chelini	L	20	0	0	—	0	2	0	0	5	7	4	1	0	12.60
Lee Stine	R	21	0	0	—	0	1	0	0	3	2	3	1	0	9.00
Joe Heving (DP) 34															

WASHINGTON — 6th 67-86 .438 27 — BUCKY HARRIS

NAME	G by Pos	B	AGE	G	AB	R	H	2B	3B	HR	RBI	BB	SO	SB	BA	SA
TOTALS			29	154	5592	823	1591	255	95	32	763	595	406	54	.285	.381
Joe Kuhel	1B151	L	29	151	633	99	165	25	9	2	74	78	44	5	.261	.338
Buddy Myer	2B151	L	31	151	616	115	215	36	11	5	100	96	40	7	.349	.468
Ossie Bluege	SS58, 3B25, 2B4	R	34	100	320	44	84	14	3	0	34	37	21	2	.263	.325
Cecil Travis	3B114, OF16	L	21	138	534	85	170	27	6	0	61	41	28	4	.318	.397
John Stone	OF114	L	29	125	454	78	143	27	18	1	78	39	29	4	.315	.460
Jake Powell	OF136, 2B2	R	26	139	551	88	172	26	10	6	98	37	37	15	.312	.428
Heinie Manush	OF111	L	33	119	479	68	131	26	4	4	56	35	17	2	.273	.390
Cliff Bolton	C106	L	28	110	375	47	114	18	11	2	55	56	13	0	.304	.427
Red Kress	SS53, 1B5, P3, OF2, 2B1	R	30	84	252	32	75	13	4	2	42	25	16	3	.298	.405
Fred Schulte	OF55	R	34	75	224	33	60	6	4	2	23	26	22	0	.268	.357
Dee Miles	OF44	L	26	60	216	28	57	5	2	0	29	7	13	6	.264	.306
Sammy Holbrook	C47	R	24	52	135	20	35	2	2	2	25	30	16	0	.259	.348
Ed Linke	P40	R	23	40	68	14	20	4	0	1	9	7	6	0	.294	.397
1 Lyn Lary	SS30	R	29	39	103	8	20	4	1	0	7	12	10	3	.194	.233
Jack Redmond	C15	L	24	22	34	8	6	1	0	1	7	3	1	0	.176	.294
2 Alan Strange	SS16	R	28	20	54	3	10	2	1	0	5	4	1	0	.185	.259
Fred Sington	OF4	R	25	20	22	1	4	0	0	0	3	5	1	0	.182	.182
Bobby Estalella	3B15	R	24	15	51	7	16	2	0	2	10	17	7	1	.314	.471
Chick Starr	C12	R	24	12	24	1	5	0	0	0	1	0	1	0	.208	.208
Buddy Lewis	3B6	L	18	8	28	0	3	0	0	0	2	0	5	0	.107	.107
John Mihalic	SS6	R	23	6	22	4	5	3	0	0	6	2	3	1	.227	.364
Red Marion	OF3	R	21	4	11	2	2	1	0	1	1	0	2	0	.182	.545

NAME	T	AGE	W	L	PCT	SV	G	GS	CG	IP	H	BB	SO	SHO	ERA
		29	67	86	.438	12	154	154	67	1379	1672	613	456	5	5.25
Earl Whitehill	L	35	14	13	.519	0	34	34	19	279	318	104	102	1	4.29
Ed Linke	R	23	11	7	.611	3	40	22	10	178	211	80	51	0	5.01
2 Bobo Newsom (BK)	R	27	11	12+	.478	2	38	23	17	198	222	84	65	2	4.45
Bump Hadley	R	30	10	15	.400	0	35	32	13	230	268	102	77	0	4.93
Leon Pettit	R	33	8	5	.615	3	41	7	1	109	129	58	45	0	4.95
Jack Russell	R	29	4	9	.308	3	43	7	2	126	170	37	30	0	5.71
Henry Coppola	R	22	3	4	.429	0	19	5	2	59	72	29	19	1	5.95
2 Belve Bean	R	30	2	0	1.000	0	10	2	0	31	43	19	6	0	7.26
Jim Hayes	R	23	2	4	.333	0	7	4	1	28	38	23	9	0	8.36
Monty Weaver (IL-SA)	R	29	1	1	.500	0	5	2	1	30	32	17	8	0	5.25
Bobby Burke	L	28	1	8	.111	0	15	10	2	66	90	27	16	0	7.50
Buck Rogers	L	22	0	1	.000	0	6	1	0	16	16	6	7	0	7.20
1 Lefty Stewart	L	34	0	1	.000	0	1	0	0	3	8	1	0	0	12.00
Phil Hensiek	R	33	0	3	.000	0	6	1	0	13	21	9	6	0	9.69
Dick Lanahan	L	23	0	3	.000	0	3	0	0	21	27	17	10	0	5.57
Mac McLean	R	22	0	0	—	0	1	0	0	9	12	5	3	0	7.00
Red Kress	R	30	0	0	—	0	3	0	0	6	8	5	0	0	12.00
1 Tommy Thomas	R	35	0	0	—	0	1	0	0	1	3	0	0	0	54.00

+Newsom, also with St. Louis, league leader in L with 18

ST. LOUIS — 7th 65-87 .428 28.5 — ROGERS HORNSBY

NAME	G by Pos	B	AGE	G	AB	R	H	2B	3B	HR	RBI	BB	SO	SB	BA	SA
TOTALS			28	155	5365	718	1446	291	51	73	675	593	561	45	.270	.384
Jack Burns	1B141	L	27	143	549	77	157	28	1	5	67	68	49	3	.286	.368
Tom Carey	2B76	R	26	76	296	29	86	18	4	0	42	13	11	0	.291	.378
2 Lyn Lary	SS93	R	29	93	371	78	107	25	7	2	35	64	43	25	.288	.410
Harlond Clift	3B127, 2B6	R	22	137	475	101	140	26	4	11	69	83	64	8	.295	.436
2 Ed Coleman	OF102	L	33	108	397	66	114	15	9	7	71	53	41	0	.287	.499
Sammy West	OF135	L	30	138	527	93	158	37	4	10	70	75	46	1	.300	.442
2 Moose Solters	OF127	R	29	127	552	59	182	39	6	18	104	34	35	10	.330	.520
Rollie Hemsley	C141	R	28	144	504	57	146	32	7	0	48	44	41	3	.290	.381
Ray Pepper	OF57	R	27	92	261	20	66	15	3	4	37	20	32	0	.253	.379
Beau Bell	OF37, 1B15, 3B3	R	27	76	220	20	55	8	2	3	17	16	16	1	.250	.345
John Burnett	3B31, SS18, 2B12	R	27	103	206	17	46	10	1	0	26	19	16	1	.223	.282
Ollie Bejma	2B47, SS8, 3B2	R	27	64	198	18	38	8	2	2	26	27	21	1	.192	.283
1 Alan Strange	SS49	R	28	49	147	8	34	6	1	0	17	17	7	0	.231	.286
Tommy Heath	C37	R	21	47	93	10	22	3	0	2	9	20	13	0	.237	.269
1 Oscar Melillo	C38	R	35	19	63	8	13	3	0	0	5	8	4	0	.206	.254
Heinie Mueller	1B2, OF2	R	35	16	27	0	5	1	0	0	1	4	1	0	.185	.222
Mike Mazzera	OF10	R	21	12	30	4	7	2	0	1	2	4	9	0	.233	.400
Rogers Hornsby	1B3, 2B2, 3B1	R	39	10	24	1	5	3	0	0	3	3	6	0	.208	.333
Debs Garms	OF2	L	28	10	15	1	4	0	0	0	2	0	0	0	.267	.267
Hal Warnock	OF2	L	23	7	7	2	2	1	0	0	1	0	0	0	.286	.571
1 Frank Grube	C3	R	30	3	6	1	2	1	0	0	0	3	0	0	.333	.500

NAME	T	AGE	W	L	PCT	SV	G	GS	CG	IP	H	BB	SO	SHO	ERA
		28	65	87	.428	15	155	155	42	1380	1667	640	435	4	5.26
Ivy Andrews	R	28	13	7	.650	1	50	20	10	213	231	53	43	0	3.55
Jack Knott	R	28	11	8	.579	7	48	19	7	188	219	78	45	2	4.60
2 Sugar Cain	R	28	9	8	.529	0	31	24	8	168	197	104*	68	0	5.25
2 Russ Van Atta	L	29	9	16	.360	3	53=	17	1	170	201	86	87	0	5.35
Fay Thomas	R	31	9	15	.375	1	49	19	4	147	165	89	67	0	4.78
Jim Walkup	R	25	6	9	.400	0	55	20	4	181	226	104	44	1	6.27
Dick Coffman	R	28	5	11	.313	2	41	18	5	144	206	46	34	0	6.13
Earl Caldwell	R	30	3	2	.600	0	6	5	2	37	34	17	5	1	3.65
1 George Blaeholder	R	31	1	1	.500	0	6	2	0	18	20	5	5	0	7.00
Bob Poser	R	25	1	1	.000	0	10	4	0	27	26	4	1	0	9.00
2 Snipe Hansen	L	29	0	2	.000	0	10	4	0	27	44	9	8	0	8.67
Bob Weiland	L	29	0	2	.000	0	14	4	0	32	39	31	11	0	9.56
1 Bobo Newsom	R	27	0	6+	.000	0	7	6	1	35	54	13	22	0	4.81

*Cain, also with St. Louis, league leader in BB with 123

=Van Atta, also with New York, league leader in G with 58

+Newsom, also with Washington, league leader in L with 18

PHILADELPHIA — 8th 58-91 .389 34 — CONNIE MACK

NAME	G by Pos	B	AGE	G	AB	R	H	2B	3B	HR	RBI	BB	SO	SB	BA	SA
TOTALS			27	149	5269	710	1470	243	44	112	671	475	602	42	.279	.406
Jimmie Foxx	1B121, C26, 3B2	R	27	147	535	118	185	33	7	36	115	114	99	6	.346	.636
Rabbit Warstler	2B136, 3B2	R	31	138	496	62	124	20	7	3	59	56	53	8	.250	.337
Eric McNair	SS121, 3B11, 1B2	R	26	137	526	55	142	22	4	7	57	35	53	3	.270	.342
Pinky Higgins	3B131	R	26	133	524	69	155	32	4	23	94	42	62	6	.296	.504
Wally Moses (BA)	OF80	L	24	105	345	60	112	21	3	5	35	25	18	3	.325	.446
Doc Cramer	OF149	L	29	149	644	96	214	17	7	0	70	37	34	6	.332	.416
Bob Johnson	OF147	R	29	147	582	103	174	29	5	28	109	78	76	2	.299	.510
2 Paul Richards	C79	R	26	85	257	31	63	10	4	1	29	24	12	0	.245	.339
Lou Finney	OF76, 1B18	L	24	109	410	45	112	11	6	0	31	18	18	7	.273	.329
Johnny Marcum	P39	L	25	64	119	13	37	7	3	1	17	9	5	0	.311	.395
Charlie Berry	C56	R	32	62	190	14	48	7	3	3	29	10	20	0	.253	.368
Skeeter Newsome	SS24, 2B13, 3B4, OF1	R	24	59	145	18	30	7	1	0	11	12	13	0	.207	.290
Alex Hooks	1B10	L	28	15	44	4	10	3	0	0	4	3	10	0	.227	.295
Bernie Snyder	2B5, SS4	R	21	10	32	5	11	2	0	0	3	0	3	0	.344	.469
Jack Peerson	OF1	R	23	10	13	0	1	0	0	0	1	0	1	0	.077	.077
1 Ed Coleman	OF1	R	33	10	13	0	3	1	0	0	1	3	4	0	.231	.308
Bill Patton	C3	R	22	9	10	1	3	1	0	0	1	1	0	0	.300	.400
1 Dib Williams	2B2	R	25	5	10	0	1	0	0	0	1	0	0	0	.100	.100
Charlie Moss	C2	R	24	3	4	1	1	0	0	0	1	1	0	0	.250	.250
Jack Owens	C2	R	24	3	8	1	2	1	0	0	2	0	0	0	.250	.500
Bill Conroy	C1	R	20	1	4	1	1	0	0	0	1	0	0	0	.250	.500

NAME	T	AGE	W	L	PCT	SV	G	GS	CG	IP	H	BB	SO	SHO	ERA
		26	58	91	.389	10	149	149	58	1326	1486	704	469	7	5.12
Johnny Marcum	R	26	17	12	.586	3	39	27	19	243	256	83	99	2	4.07
Whitey Wilshere	L	22	9	9	.500	0	27	18	7	142	136	78	80	3	4.06
Roy Mahaffey	R	31	9	4	.667	0	27	17	5	136	153	42	39	0	3.90
Bill Dietrich	R	25	7	13	.350	3	43	15	8	185	203	101	59	1	5.40
2 George Blaeholder	R	31	6	10	.375	0	22	22	10	149	173	49	22	1	3.99
Al Benton	R	24	3	4	.429	0	27	7	0	78	110	47	42	0	7.73
Carl Doyle	R	22	2	7	.222	0	14	9	3	80	86	72	34	0	5.96
Earl Huckleberry	R	25	1	0	1.000	0	1	1	1	9	8	2	3	0	2.00
Dutch Lieber	R	26	1	1	.500	2	18	1	0	47	45	19	14	0	3.06
Vallie Eaves	R	23	0	2	.333	2	18	4	1	14	12	15	6	0	5.14
Bill Ferrazzi	R	28	1	2	.333	0	7	2	0	7	7	6	0	0	5.14
George Caster	R	27	1	4	.200	1	25	1	0	65	78	24	21	0	6.29
1 Joe Cascarella	R	28	0	1	.143	0	7	3	0	32	33	21	11	0	5.34
Woody Upchurch	L	24	0	2	.000	0	6	2	0	32	27	15	6	0	5.14
Wedo Martini	R	24	0	0	—	0	3	0	0	8	11	6	1	0	18.00
Al Veach	L	25	0	0	—	0	2	0	0	2	6	5	0	0	9.00
George Turbeville	L	22	0	0	—	0	6	2	0	24	24	24	9	0	7.59
Herman Fink	R	23	0	0	—	0	6	1	0	16	18	10	2	0	9.00
1 Sugar Cain	R	28	0	0	—	0	6	1	0	26	39	19*	8	0	6.75

*Cain, also with St. Louis, league leader in BB with 123

CHICAGO — 1ST 100-54 .649 — CHARLIE GRIMM

NAME	G by Pos	B	AGE	G	AB	R	H	2B	3B	HR	RBI	BB	SO	SB	BA	SA
TOTALS			27	154	5486	847	1581	303	62	88	782	464	471	66	.288	.414
Phil Cavarretta	1B145	L	18	146	589	85	162	28	12	8	82	39	61	4	.275	.404
Billy Herman	2B154	R	25	154	666	113	227	57	6	7	83	42	29	6	.341	.404
Billy Jurges	SS146	R	27	146	519	69	125	33	1	1	59	42	39	3	.241	.314
Stan Hack	3B111, 1B7	L	25	124	427	75	133	23	9	4	64	65	17	14	.311	.436
Chuck Klein	OF111	L	30	119	434	71	127	14	4	21	73	41	42	4	.293	.488
Frank Demaree	OF98	R	25	107	385	60	125	19	4	2	66	26	23	6	.325	.410
Augie Galan	OF154	B	23	154	646	133	203	41	11	12	79	87	53	22	.314	.467
Gabby Hartnett	C110	R	34	116	413	67	142	32	6	13	91	41	46	1	.344	.545
Fred Lindstrom	OF50, 3B33	R	29	90	342	49	94	22	4	3	62	10	13	1	.275	.389
Ken O'Dea	C63	L	22	76	202	30	52	13	2	6	38	26	18	0	.257	.431
Tuck Stainback	OF28	R	23	47	94	16	24	4	0	3	11	0	13	1	.255	.394
1 Kiki Cuyler	OF42	R	36	45	157	22	42	5	1	4	18	10	16	3	.268	.389
Woody English	3B16, SS12	R	28	34	84	11	17	2	0	2	8	20	4	1	.202	.298
Walter Stephenson	C6	R	24	16	26	2	10	1	1	0	2	1	5	0	.385	.500
Johnny Gill		L	30	3	3	2	1	1	0	0	1	0	1	0	.333	.667
Charlie Grimm	1B2	L	36	2	8	0	0	0	0	0	0	0	1	0	.000	.000

NAME	T	AGE	W	L	PCT	SV	G	GS	CG	IP	H	BB	SO	SHO	ERA
		27	100	54	.649	14	154	154	81	1394	1417	400	589	12	3.26
Bill Lee	R	25	20	6	.769	1	39	32	18	252	241	84	100	3	2.96
Lon Warneke	R	26	20	13	.606	4	42	30	20	262	257	50	120	1	3.06
Larry French	L	27	17	10	.630	2	42	30	16	246	279	44	90	4	2.96
Charlie Root	R	36	15	8	.652	2	38	18	11	201	193	47	94	1	3.09
Roy Henshaw	L	23	13	5	.722	1	31	18	7	143	135	68	53	3	3.27
Tex Carleton	R	28	11	8	.579	1	31	22	8	171	169	60	84	0	3.89
Fabian Kowalik	R	27	2	2	.500	7	21	1	0	55	60	19	20	0	4.42
Clyde Shoun	L	23	1	0	1.000	0	5	1	0	13	14	5	5	0	2.77
Clay Bryant	R	23	1	0	.667	2	9	1	0	23	34	7	13	0	5.09
Hugh Casey	R	21	0	0	—	0	13	0	0	26	29	14	10	0	3.81
Roy Joiner	L	28	0	0	—	0	3	0	0	3	6	2	0	0	6.00

ST. LOUIS — 2nd 96-58 .623 4 — FRANKIE FRISCH

NAME	G by Pos	B	AGE	G	AB	R	H	2B	3B	HR	RBI	BB	SO	SB	BA	SA
TOTALS			25	154	5457	829	1548	286	59	86	762	404	521	71	.284	.405
Ripper Collins	1B150	B	31	150	578	109	181	36	10	23	122	65	45	0	.313	.529
Frankie Frisch	2B88, 3B5	B	36	103	354	52	104	16	2	1	55	33	16	2	.294	.359
Leo Durocher	SS142	R	29	143	513	62	136	23	5	8	78	29	46	2	.265	.376
Pepper Martin	3B114, OF16	R	31	135	539	121	161	41	6	9	54	34	58	20	.299	.447
Jack Rothrock	OF127	B	30	129	502	76	137	18	5	3	56	57	29	7	.273	.347
Terry Moore	OF117	R	23	119	456	63	131	34	3	6	53	15	40	13	.287	.414
Joe Medwick	OF154	R	23	154	634	132	224	46	13	23	126	30	59	4	.353	.576
Bill DeLancey	C83	L	23	103	301	31	84	14	5	6	41	42	34	0	.279	.419
Burgess Whitehead	2B80, 3B8, SS6	R	25	107	338	45	89	10	2	0	33	11	14	5	.263	.305
Spud Davis	C81, 1B5	R	30	102	315	28	100	24	2	1	60	33	30	0	.317	.416
Ernie Orsatti	OF60	L	32	90	221	28	53	9	3	1	24	18	25	0	.240	.321
Charlie Gelbert	3B37, SS21, 2B3	R	29	62	168	24	49	7	2	2	21	17	18	0	.292	.393
Dizzy Dean	P50	R	24	53	128	18	30	4	0	2	21	1	16	2	.234	.313
Charlie Wilson	3B8	B	30	16	31	1	10	0	0	1	1	2	2	0	.323	.323
Bob O'Farrell	C8	R	38	14	10	0	0	0	0	0	0	2	0	0	.000	.000
Lynn King	OF6	L	27	8	22	6	4	0	0	0	0	4	1	2	.182	.182
Lyle Judy	2B5	R	21	8	11	2	0	0	0	0	0	2	2	0	.000	.000
Tom Winsett	OF2	L	25	7	12	2	6	1	0	0	2	2	3	0	.500	.500
Sam Narron	C1	R	21	4	7	0	3	0	0	0	0	0	0	0	.429	.429
Gene Moore		L	25	1	0	0	0	0	0	0	0	0	1	0	.000	.000

NAME	T	AGE	W	L	PCT	SV	G	GS	CG	IP	H	BB	SO	SHO	ERA
		30	96	58	.623	18	154	154	73	1384	1447	382	594	10	3.54
Dizzy Dean	R	25	28	12	.700	5	50	36	29	324	326	82	182	3	3.11
Paul Dean	R	21	19	12	.613	5	46	33	19	270	261	55	143	2	3.37
Wild Bill Hallahan	L	32	15	8	.652	1	40	23	8	181	196	57	73	2	3.43
Bill Walker	L	31	13	8	.619	1	37	25	8	193	222	78	79	2	3.82
2 Phil Collins	R	33	7	6	.538	2	26	9	2	83	96	26	18	0	4.55
Jesse Haines	R	41	6	5	.545	2	30	11	3	115	110	28	24	0	3.60
Ed Heusser	R	26	5	5	.500	2	33	11	2	123	125	27	39	0	2.93
Bill McGee	R	25	1	0	1.000	0	2	1	1	9	3	1	2	0	1.00
Ray Harrell	R	23	1	1	.500	0	11	1	0	30	39	11	13	0	6.60
Mike Ryba	R	32	1	1	.500	0	2	1	1	16	15	1	6	0	3.38
Nubs Kleinke	R	24	0	0	—	0	4	2	0	13	19	3	5	0	4.85
Jim Winford	R	25	0	0	—	0	11	1	0	11	13	5	7	0	4.09
Bud Tinning	R	29	0	0	—	0	4	0	0	11	13	5	2	0	5.63
Tony Kaufmann	R	34	0	0	—	0	4	1	0	4	1	0	0	0	2.25
Al Eckert	L	29	0	2	.000	0	3	1	0	7	1	1	0	0	12.00
Mays Copeland	R	21	0	0	—	0	2	0	0	2	1	0	0	0	13.50
Dick Ward	R	26	0	0	—	0	1	0	0	3	1	0	1	0	0.00

NEW YORK — 3rd 91-62 .595 8.5 — BILL TERRY

NAME	G by Pos	B	AGE	G	AB	R	H	2B	3B	HR	RBI	BB	SO	SB	BA	SA
TOTALS			29	156	5623	770	1608	248	56	123	703	392	479	32	.286	.416
Bill Terry	1B143	L	36	145	596	91	203	32	8	6	64	41	55	7	.341	.451
Mark Koenig	2B64, SS21, 3B15	B	32	107	396	40	112	12	0	3	37	13	18	0	.283	.336
Dick Bartell	SS137	R	27	137	539	60	141	28	4	14	53	37	52	5	.262	.406
Travis Jackson	3B128	R	31	128	511	74	154	20	12	9	80	29	64	3	.301	.440
Mel Ott	OF137, 3B15	L	26	152	593	113	191	33	6	31	114	82	58	7	.322	.555
Hank Leiber	OF154	R	24	153	613	110	203	37	4	22	107	48	29	0	.331	.512
Jo-Jo Moore	OF155	R	26	155	681	108	201	28	9	15	71	53	24	5	.295	.429
Gus Mancuso	C126	R	29	128	447	33	133	18	2	5	56	30	16	1	.298	.380
Hughie Critz	2B59	R	34	65	219	19	41	0	3	2	14	3	10	2	.187	.242
Harry Danning	C44	R	23	65	152	16	37	11	1	2	20	9	16	0	.243	.368
Phil Weintraub	1B19, OF7	L	27	64	112	18	27	3	3	1	6	17	13	0	.241	.348
Al Cuccinello	2B48, 3B2	R	20	54	165	27	41	7	1	4	20	1	20	0	.248	.376
Kiddo Davis	OF21	R	33	47	91	16	24	7	1	2	6	10	4	2	.264	.429
Hal Schumacher	P33	R	24	38	107	8	21	3	0	2	21	1	25	0	.196	.280
2 Glenn Myatt	C4	L	37	13	18	2	4	0	1	1	6	0	3	0	.222	.500
1 Paul Richards	C4	R	26	7	4	0	1	0	0	0	0	0	2	0	.250	.250
Joe Malay		L	29	1	1	0	1	0	0	0	0	0	0	0	1.000	1.000

NAME	T	AGE	W	L	PCT	SV	G	GS	CG	IP	H	BB	SO	SHO	ERA
		27	91	62	.595	11	156	156	76	1404	1433	411	524	10	3.78
Carl Hubbell	L	32	23	12	.657	0	42	35	24	303	314	49	150	1	3.27
Hal Schumacher	R	24	19	9	.679	0	33	33	19	262	235	70	79	3	2.89
Slick Castleman	R	21	15	6	.714	0	29	25	9	174	186	64	64	1	4.09
Roy Parmelee	R	28	14	10	.583	0	34	31	13	226	214	97	79	0	4.22
Al Smith	R	27	10	8	.556	5	40	10	4	124	125	32	44	1	3.41
F. Fitzsimmons (AJ)	R	33	4	8	.333	0	18	15	6	94	104	22	23	4	4.02
Frank Gabler	R	23	2	1	.667	0	26	1	0	60	79	20	24	0	5.70
2 Euel Moore	R	27	1	0	1.000	0	6	0	0	8	9	4	3	0	5.63
Dolf Luque	R	44	1	0	1.000	2	2	0	0	4	1	1	2	0	0.00
Harry Gumbert	R	25	1	2	.333	0	6	3	1	24	35	10	11	0	6.00
Allyn Stout	R	30	1	1	.200	5	40	2	0	88	99	37	29	0	4.91
Leon Chagnon	R	32	0	2	.000	1	4	1	0	38	32	5	16	0	3.55

PITTSBURGH — 4th 86-67 .562 13.5 — PIE TRAYNOR

NAME	G by Pos	B	AGE	G	AB	R	H	2B	3B	HR	RBI	BB	SO	SB	BA	SA
TOTALS			28	153	5415	743	1543	255	90	66	682	457	437	30	.285	.402
Gus Suhr	1B149, OF2	L	29	153	529	68	144	33	12	10	81	70	54	6	.272	.437
Pep Young	2B107, 3B6, OF6, SS4	R	27	128	494	60	131	25	10	7	82	21	59	2	.265	.399
Arky Vaughan	SS137	L	23	137	499	108	192	34	10	19	99	97	18	4	.385	.607
Tommy Thevenow	3B82, SS13, 2B8	R	31	110	408	38	97	9	0	0	47	12	23	1	.238	.304
Paul Waner	OF136	L	32	139	549	98	176	29	12	11	78	61	22	2	.321	.477
Lloyd Waner	OF121	L	29	122	537	83	166	22	14	0	46	22	10	1	.309	.402
Woody Jensen	OF140	R	27	143	627	97	203	28	7	8	62	15	14	9	.324	.429
Tom Padden	C94	R	26	97	302	35	82	9	1	1	30	48	26	1	.272	.318
Cookie Lavagetto	2B42, 3B15	R	22	78	231	27	67	9	4	0	19	18	15	1	.290	.364
Earl Grace	C69	L	28	77	224	19	59	8	1	3	29	32	17	1	.263	.348
2 Bud Hafey	OF47	R	22	58	184	29	42	11	2	6	16	16	48	0	.228	.408
Pie Traynor (JJ)	3B49, 1B1	R	36	57	204	24	57	10	3	1	36	10	17	2	.279	.373
Red Lucas	P20	L	33	47	66	6	21	6	0	0	10	7	11	0	.318	.409
1 Babe Herman	OF15, 1B3	L	32	26	81	8	19	8	1	0	7	5	3	0	.235	.358
Earl Browne	1B9	L	24	9	32	6	8	2	0	0	6	2	8	0	.250	.313
Bill Brubaker	3B5	R	24	6	11	1	0	0	0	0	0	2	5	0	.000	.000
Aubrey Epps	C1	R	23	1	4	1	3	0	1	0	3	0	0	0	.750	1.250
Steve Swetonic		R	31	1	0	1	0	0	0	0	0	0	0	0		

NAME	T	AGE	W	L	PCT	SV	G	GS	CG	IP	H	BB	SO	SHO	ERA
		30	86	67	.562	11	153	153	76	1366	1428	312	549	15	3.42
Cy Blanton	R	26	18	13	.581	1	35	30	23	254	220	55	149	4	2.59
Bill Swift	R	27	15	8	.652	1	39	22	11	204	193	37	74	3	2.69
Jim Weaver	R	31	14	8	.636	0	33	22	11	176	177	58	87	4	3.43
Guy Bush	R	33	11	11	.500	2	41	25	8	204	237	40	42	1	4.32
Ralph Birkofer	L	26	9	7	.563	1	37	18	8	150	173	42	80	1	4.08
Red Lucas	R	33	8	6	.571	0	20	19	8	126	136	23	29	2	3.43
Waite Hoyt	R	35	7	11	.389	6	39	11	5	164	187	27	63	0	3.40
Mace Brown	R	26	4	1	.800	0	18	5	2	73	84	22	28	0	3.58
1 Jack Salveson	R	21	0	1	.000	0	7	0	0	11	5	2	0	0	9.00
Claude Passeau	R	26	0	1	.000	0	1	1	0	3	7	2	1	0	12.00
Hal Smith	R	33	0	0	—	0	2	0	0	3	3	2	1	0	3.00
Wayne Osborne	R	22	0	0	—	0	1	0	0	1	2	0	0	0	9.00

BROOKLYN — 5th 70-83 .458 29.5 — CASEY STENGEL

NAME	G by Pos	B	AGE	G	AB	R	H	2B	3B	HR	RBI	BB	SO	SB	BA	SA
TOTALS			28	154	5410	711	1496	235	62	59	666	430	520	60	.277	.376
Sam Leslie	1B138	L	29	142	520	72	160	30	7	5	93	55	19	4	.308	.421
Tony Cuccinello	2B64, 3B36	R	27	102	360	49	105	20	4	8	53	40	35	3	.292	.431
Lonny Frey	SS127, 2B4	B	24	131	515	88	135	35	11	11	77	66	68	6	.262	.437
Joe Stripp	3B88, 1B15, OF1	R	32	109	373	44	114	13	5	3	43	22	15	2	.306	.391
Buzz Boyle	OF124	L	27	127	475	51	129	17	4	4	44	43	45	7	.272	.371
Frenchy Bordagaray	OF105	R	25	120	422	69	119	19	6	1	39	17	16	18	.282	.363
Danny Taylor	OF99	R	34	112	352	51	102	19	5	7	59	46	32	6	.290	.432
Al Lopez	C126	R	26	128	379	50	95	12	4	3	39	35	36	2	.251	.327
Jim Bucher	2B41, 3B39, OF37	L	24	123	473	72	143	22	1	7	58	30	33	4	.302	.397
Len Koenecke (DD)	OF91	L	31	100	325	43	92	13	2	4	27	43	45	0	.283	.372
Jimmy Jordan	2B46, SS28, 3B5	R	27	94	295	42	82	7	0	0	30	9	17	3	.278	.302
Bobby Reis	OF21, P14, 2B4, 1B1, 3B1	R	26	52	85	10	21	3	2	0	6	6	13	2	.247	.329
Babe Phelps	C34	L	27	47	121	17	44	7	2	5	22	9	5	0	.364	.579
Van Lingle Mungo	P37	R	24	44	90	9	26	3	0	0	19	1	10	0	.289	.322
Zack Taylor	C26	R	36	26	54	2	7	3	0	0	4	4	5	0	.130	.185
John McCarthy	1B19	L	25	22	48	9	12	1	0	0	2	2	9	1	.250	.313
Buster Mills	OF17	R	26	17	56	6	12	5	0	0	7	5	11	0	.214	.339
Johnny Cooney	OF10	R	34	10	29	3	9	2	1	0	1	4	4	0	.310	.379
Nick Tremark	OF4	L	22	10	13	1	3	1	0	0	6	1	1	1	.231	.308
Vince Sherlock	2B8	R	25	9	26	4	12	1	0	0	6	1	1	1	.462	.500
Frank Skaff	3B3	R	24	6	11	1	6	1	0	0	1	0	1	0	.545	.818
Rod Dedeaux	SS2	R	21	4	4	0	1	0	0	0	1	0	0	0	.250	.250
Whitey Ock	C1	R	23	3	3	0	0	0	0	0	0	0	2	0	.000	.000
Curly Onis	C1	R	26	1	1	0	1	0	0	0	0	0	0	0	1.000	1.000

NAME	T	AGE	W	L	PCT	SV	G	GS	CG	IP	H	BB	SO	SHO	ERA
		31	70	83	.458	20	154	154	62	1358	1519	436	480	11	4.22
Van Lingle Mungo	R	24	16	10	.615	2	37	26	18	214	205	90	143	4	3.66
Watty Clark	L	33	13	8	.619	0	33	25	11	207	215	28	35	1	3.30
Ray Benge	R	33	9	9	.500	1	23	17	5	125	142	47	39	1	4.46
2 George Earnshaw	R	35	8	12	.400	1	25	22	6	166	175	53	72	2	4.12
Tom Zachary	L	39	7	7	.368	4	25	21	9	158	193	35	33	1	3.59
Johnny Babich	R	24	7	14	.333	0	37	24	7	143	191	52	55	2	6.67
Dazzy Vance	R	44	3	2	.600	2	20	0	0	51	55	16	28	0	4.41
Bobby Reis	R	26	3	2	.600	2	14	2	1	41	46	24	7	0	2.85
Dutch Leonard	R	26	2	9	.182	8	43	11	4	138	152	29	41	0	3.91
Tom Baker	R	22	1	0	1.000	0	11	1	1	42	48	20	10	0	4.29
Les Munns	R	26	1	3	.250	1	21	5	0	58	74	33	13	0	5.59
Harry Eisenstat	L	19	0	1	—	0	2	0	0	4	4	3	1	0	12.60
Bob Logan	L	25	0	0	—	0	1	0	0	3	7	2	1	0	3.00
Frank Lamanske	L	28	0	0	—	0	4	0	0	6	9	4	1	0	6.75
Bob Barr	R	22	0	0	—	0	3	1	0	6	8	4	2	0	4.50
Harvey Green	R	20	0	0	—	0	1	0	0	3	3	0	1	0	9.00

NAME	G by Pos	B	AGE	G	AB	R	H	2B	3B	HR	RBI	BB	SO	SB	BA	SA
CINCINNATI 6th 68-85 .444 31.5				CHUCK DRESSEN												
TOTALS			28	154	5296	646	1403	244	68	73	605	392	547	72	.265	.378
Jim Bottomley	1B97	L	35	107	399	44	103	21	1	1	49	18	24	3	.258	.323
Alex Kampouris	2B141, SS6	R	22	148	499	46	123	26	5	7	62	32	84	8	.246	.361
Billy Myers	SS112	R	24	117	445	60	119	15	10	5	36	29	81	10	.267	.380
Lew Riggs	3B135	L	25	142	532	73	148	26	8	5	46	43	32	8	.278	.385
1 Val Goodman	OF146	L	24	148	592	86	159	23	18	12	72	35	50	14	.269	.429
Sammy Byrd	OF115	R	28	121	416	51	109	25	4	9	52	37	51	5	.262	.406
2 Babe Herman	OF76, 1B14	L	32	92	349	44	117	23	5	10	58	35	25	5	.335	.416
Ernie Lombardi	C82	R	27	120	332	36	114	23	3	12	64	16	6	0	.343	.539
Gilly Campbell	C66, 1B5, OF1	L	27	88	218	26	56	7	0	3	30	42	7	3	.257	.330
Billy Sullivan	1B40, 3B15, 2B6	L	24	85	241	29	64	9	4	2	36	19	16	4	.266	.361
Gordon Slade	SS30, 2B19, OF8, 3B7	R	30	71	196	22	55	10	0	1	14	16	16	0	.281	.347
2 Kiki Cuyler	OF57	R	36	62	236	36	56	8	3	2	22	27	18	5	.251	.341
Adam Comorosky	OF40	R	30	59	137	22	34	3	1	2	14	7	14	1	.248	.328
Hank Erickson	C25	R	27	37	88	9	23	3	2	1	4	6	4	0	.261	.375
Harlin Pool	OF18	L	27	28	68	8	12	6	2	0	11	2	2	0	.176	.324
Chick Hafey (SJ)	OF15	R	32	15	59	10	20	6	1	1	9	4	5	1	.339	.525
Calvin Chapman	SS12, 2B4	L	24	15	53	6	18	1	0	0	3	4	5	2	.340	.358
1 Tony Piet	OF1	R	28	6	5	2	1	1	0	0	2	0	0	0	.200	.400
Les Scarsella	1B2	L	21	6	10	4	2	1	0	0	0	0	3	1	.200	.300
Ted Petoskey	OF2	R	24	4	5	0	2	0	0	0	0	0	1	1	.400	.400
Lee Gamble	OF2	L	25	3	4	2	2	1	0	0	1	0	0	0	.500	.750
PHILADELPHIA 7th 64-89 .418 35.5				JIMMIE WILSON												
TOTALS			30	156	5442	6851	1466	249	32	92	624	392	661	52	.269	.378
Dolph Camilli	1B156	L	28	156	602	88	157	23	5	25	83	65	113	9	.261	.440
Lou Chiozza	2B120, 3B2	L	25	124	472	71	134	26	6	3	47	33	44	5	.284	.383
Mickey Haslin (IL)	SS87, 3B11, 2B9	R	25	110	407	53	108	17	3	3	52	19	25	5	.265	.344
Johnny Vergez	3B148, SS2	R	28	148	546	56	136	27	4	9	63	46	67	8	.249	.363
Johnny Moore	OF150	L	33	153	600	84	194	33	3	19	93	45	50	4	.323	.483
Ethan Allen	OF156	R	31	156	645	90	198	46	1	8	63	43	54	5	.307	.419
George Watkins	OF148	R	35	150	600	80	164	25	5	17	76	40	78	3	.270	.413
Al Todd	C87	R	31	107	328	40	95	18	3	4	42	19	35	2	.290	.390
Jimmie Wilson	C78, 2B1	R	34	93	290	38	81	20	0	1	37	19	19	4	.279	.359
Chile Gomez	SS36, 2B32	R	26	67	222	24	51	3	0	0	16	17	34	2	.230	.243
Bucky Walters	P24, OF5, 2B2, 3B1	R	26	49	96	14	24	2	1	0	6	9	12	0	.250	.292
1 Blondy Ryan	SS35, 2B1, 3B1	R	29	39	129	13	34	5	1	0	10	7	20	1	.264	.310
Ed Boland	OF10	L	27	30	47	5	10	0	0	0	4	4	3	0	.213	.213
Fred Lucas	OF10	R	32	20	34	1	9	0	0	0	2	3	6	0	.265	.265
Joe Holden	C4	L	22	6	9	0	1	0	0	0	0	0	3	1	.111	.111
Art Bramhall	SS1, 3B1	R	26	2	1	0	0	0	0	0	0	0	0	0	.000	.000
Dino Chiozza	SS2	L	23	2	1	0	1	0	0	0	0	0	0	0		
Bubber Jonnard	C1	R	35	1	1	0	0	0	0	0	0	0	0	0	.000	.000
BOSTON 8th 38-115 .248 61.5				BILL McKECHNIE												
TOTALS			29	153	5309	575	1396	233	33	75	544	353	436	20	.263	.362
Buck Jordan	1B95, 3B8, OF2	L	28	130	470	62	131	24	5	4	35	19	17	3	.279	.383
Les Mallon	2B73, 3B36, OF1	R	29	116	412	48	113	24	2	2	25	28	37	3	.274	.357
Billy Urbanski	SS129	R	32	132	514	53	118	17	0	4	30	40	32	3	.230	.286
Pinky Whitney	3B74, 2B49	R	30	128	458	41	125	23	4	4	60	24	36	2	.273	.367
Randy Moore	OF78, 1B21	L	30	125	407	42	112	24	4	4	42	26	16	1	.275	.373
Wally Berger	OF149	R	29	150	589	91	174	39	4	34	130	50	83	3	.295	.548
Hal Lee	OF110	R	30	112	422	49	128	18	6	0	39	18	25	0	.303	.374
Al Spohrer	C90	R	32	92	260	22	63	7	1	1	16	9	12	0	.242	.288
Tommy Thompson	OF85	L	25	112	297	34	81	7	1	4	30	36	17	2	.273	.343
Joe Coscarart	3B41, SS27, 2B15	R	25	86	284	30	67	11	2	1	29	18	28	2	.236	.299
Joe Mowry	OF45	B	27	81	136	17	36	8	1	0	13	11	13	0	.265	.360
Shanty Hogan	C56	R	29	59	163	9	49	9	2	0	25	21	8	0	.301	.387
Ray Mueller	C40	R	23	42	97	10	22	5	0	3	11	3	11	0	.227	.371
Elbie Fletcher	1B39	L	19	39	148	12	35	7	1	1	9	7	13	1	.236	.318
Babe Ruth	OF26	L	40	28	72	13	13	0	0	6	12	20	24	0	.181	.431
Rabbit Maranville	2B20	R	43	23	67	3	10	2	0	0	5	3	3	0	.149	.179
Johnnie Tyler	OF11	B	28	13	47	7	16	2	1	2	11	4	3	0	.340	.553
Ed Moriarty	2B8	R	22	8	34	4	11	2	1	1	6	0	6	0	.324	.529
Bill Lewis	C1	R	30	6	4	1	0	0	0	0	0	0	1	0	.000	.000
Art Doll	C3	R	23	3	10	0	1	0	0	0	0	0	5	0	.100	.100

NAME	T	AGE	W	L	PCT	SV	G	GS	CG	IP	H	BB	SO	SHO	ERA
		28	68	85	.444	12	154	154	59	1356	1490	438	500	9	4.30
Paul Derringer	R	28	22	13	.629	2	45	33	20	277	295	49	120	3	3.51
Gene Schott	R	21	8	11	.421	0	33	19	9	159	153	64	49	1	3.91
Benny Frey	R	29	6	10	.375	2	38	13	3	114	164	32	24	1	6.87
Al Hollingsworth	L	27	9	13	.316	0	38	22	8	173	165	76	89	0	3.90
Don Brennan	R	31	5	5	.500	5	38	5	2	114	101	44	48	1	3.16
Tony Freitas	L	27	5	10	.333	2	31	18	5	144	174	38	51	0	4.56
Si Johnson	R	28	5	11	.313	0	30	20	4	130	155	59	40	1	6.23
Emmett Nelson	R	30	4	4	.500	1	19	7	3	60	70	23	14	1	4.35
Leroy Herrmann	R	29	3	5	.375	0	29	8	2	108	124	31	30	0	3.58
Whitey Hilcher	R	26	2	0	1.000	0	4	1	1	19	19	5	9	1	2.84
1 Danny MacFayden	R	30	1	1	.500	0	3	1	1	21	31	4	13	0	3.86
Lee Grissom	L	27	1	1	.500	0	3	1	0	18	16	9	5	0	4.75
		27	64	89	.418	15	156	156	53	1375	1652	505	475	8	4.76
Curt Davis	R	31	16	14	.533	2	44	27	19	231	264	47	74	3	3.66
Syl Johnson	R	34	10	8	.556	6	37	18	8	175	182	31	89	1	3.55
Orville Jorgens	R	27	10	15	.400	2	53	24	6	188	216	96	57	0	4.84
Bucky Walters	R	26	9	9	.500	0	24	22	8	151	168	68	40	2	4.17
Joe Bowman	R	25	7	10	.412	1	33	17	6	148	157	56	58	1	4.26
Ray Prim	L	28	3	4	.429	0	29	6	1	73	110	15	27	0	5.79
Pretzels Pezzullo	L	24	5	8	.375	1	41	7	2	84	115	45	24	0	6.43
Hal Kelleher	R	22	0	0	1.000	0	3	3	2	25	26	12	12	1	1.80
Jim Bivin	R	25	2	9	.182	1	47	14	0	162	220	65	54	0	5.78
Hugh Mulcahy	R	21	1	5	.167	1	18	5	0	53	62	25	11	0	4.75
1 Euel Moore	R	26	1	6	.143	0	15	8	1	40	63	20	15	0	7.88
2 Tommy Thomas	R	35	0	1	.000	0	4	1	0	12	15	5	3	0	5.25
1 Snipe Hansen	L	28	0	0	.000	0	4	1	0	8	8	5	0	0	13.50
1 Phil Collins	R	33	0	0	.000	1	3	0	0	15	24	9	4	0	11.40
Frank Pearce	R	30	0	0	.000	0	3	0	0	13	22	6	7	0	8.31
		33	38	115	.248	5	153	153	54	1330	1645	404	355	6	4.93
Fred Frankhouse	R	31	11	15	.423	0	40	29	10	231	278	81	64	1	4.75
Bob Smith	R	40	8	18	.308	5	46	20	8	203	232	61	58	2	3.95
2 Danny MacFayden	R	30	5	13	.278	0	28	20	7	152	200	34	46	1	5.09
Ed Brandt	L	30	5	19	.208	0	29	25	12	175	224	66	61	0	4.99
Ben Cantwell	R	33	4	25	.138	0	39	24	13	211	235	44	34	0	4.61
Larry Benton	R	37	2	3	.400	0	29	1	1	72	103	24	21	0	6.88
Huck Betts	R	38	2	9	.182	0	44	19	2	160	213	40	40	1	5.46
Bob Brown	R	24	1	8	.111	0	15	10	2	65	79	36	17	1	6.37
Flint Rhem	R	34	0	5	.000	0	10	6	0	40	61	11	10	0	5.40
Al Blanche	R	25	0	0	—	0	6	0	0	17	14	5	4	0	1.59
Leo Mangum	R	39	0	0	—	0	3	0	0	5	6	2	0	0	3.60

WORLD SERIES — DETROIT (AL) 4   CHICAGO (NL) 2

LINE SCORES

TEAM	1	2	3		4	5	6		7	8	9		10	11	12		R	H	E
Game 1 October 2 at Detroit																			
CHI (NL)	2	0	0		0	0	0		0	0	0						3	7	0
DET (AL)	0	0	0		0	0	0		0	0	0						0	4	3
Warneke									Rowe										
Game 2 October 3 at Detroit																			
CHI	0	0	0		0	1	0		2	0	0						3	6	1
DET	4	0	0		3	0	0		1	0	X						8	9	2
Root, Henshaw (1), Kowelik (4)									Bridges										
Game 3 October 4 at Chicago																			
DET	0	0	0		0	1	0		0	4	0		0	1			6	12	2
CHI	0	2	0		0	0	2		0	0	0		5	10	3				
Auker, Hogsett (7), Rowe (8)									Lee, Warneke (8), French (10)										
Game 4 October 5 at Chicago																			
DET	0	0	1		0	0	1		0	0	0						2	7	0
CHI	0	1	0		0	0	0		0	0	0						1	5	2
Crowder									Carleton, Root (8)										
Game 5 October 6 at Chicago																			
DET	0	0	0		0	0	0		0	0	1						1	7	1
CHI	0	0	2		0	0	0		1	0	X						3	8	0
Rowe									Warneke, Lee (7)										
Game 6 October 7 at Detroit																			
CHI	0	0	1		0	2	0		0	0	0						3	12	0
DET	1	0	0		1	0	1		0	0	1						4	12	1
French									Bridges										

COMPOSITE BATTING

NAME	POS	G	AB	R	H	2B	3B	HR	RBI	BA
Detroit (AL)										
Totals		6	206	21	51	11	1	1	18	.248
Fox	OF	6	26	1	10	3	1	0	4	.385
Gehringer	2B	6	24	4	9	3	0	0	4	.375
Cochrane	C	6	24	3	7	1	0	0	1	.292
Rogell	SS	6	24	1	7	2	0	0	1	.292
Goslin	OF	6	22	2	6	1	0	0	3	.273
Owen	3B-1B	6	20	2	1	0	0	0	1	.050
White	OF	5	19	3	5	0	0	0	1	.263
Clifton	3B	4	16	1	0	0	0	0	0	.000
Rowe	P	3	8	0	2	1	0	0	0	.250
Bridges	P	2	8	1	1	0	0	0	0	.125
Greenberg	1B	2	6	1	1	0	0	0	2	.167
Walker	OF	3	4	1	1	0	0	0	0	.250
Crowder	P	1	3	1	1	0	0	0	0	.333
Auker	P	1	2	0	0	0	0	0	0	.000
Hogsett	P	1	0	0	0	0	0	0	0	—
Chicago (NL)										
Totals		6	202	18	48	6	2	5	17	.238
Galan	OF	6	25	2	4	1	0	0	2	.160
Herman	2B	6	24	3	8	2	1	0	6	.333
Hartnett	C	6	24	1	7	0	0	1	2	.292
Demaree	OF	6	24	2	6	1	0	2	2	.250
Cavarretta	1B	6	24	1	3	0	0	0	0	.125
Hack	3B-SS	6	22	2	5	1	1	0	0	.227
Jurges	SS	6	16	3	4	0	0	0	1	.250
Lindstrom	OF-3B	4	15	0	3	1	0	0	0	.200
Klein	OF	5	12	2	4	0	0	1	2	.333
Warneke	P	3	5	0	1	0	0	0	0	.200
French	P	2	4	1	1	0	0	0	0	.250
Kowalik	P	2	2	1	1	0	0	0	0	.500
O'Dea	PH	1	1	0	1	0	0	0	1	1.000
Henshaw	P	2	1	0	0	0	0	0	0	.000
Lee	P	2	2	0	0	0	0	0	0	.000
Stephenson	PH	1	1	0	0	0	0	0	0	.000
Carleton	P	1	1	0	0	0	0	0	0	.000
Root	P	2	0	0	0	0	0	0	0	—

COMPOSITE PITCHING

NAME	G	IP	H	BB	SO	W	L	SV	ERA
Detroit (AL)									
Totals	6	55	48	11	29	4	2	0	2.29
Rowe	3	21	19	1	14	1	2	0	2.57
Bridges	2	18	18	4	9	2	0	0	2.50
Crowder	1	9	5	3	5	1	0	0	1.00
Auker	1	6	6	2	1	0	0	0	3.00
Hogsett	1	1	0	1	0	0	0	0	0.00
Chicago (NL)									
Totals	6	54.2	51	25	27	2	4	1	2.96
Warneke	3	16.2	9	4	5	2	0	0	0.54
French	2	10.2	15	2	6	0	0	0	3.38
Lee	2	10.1	11	5	5	0	0	1	3.48
Carleton	1	7	6	7	4	0	1	0	1.29
Kowalik	2	4.1	3	1	1	0	0	0	2.10
Henshaw	1	3.2	5	5	2	0	1	0	7.36
Root	2	2	5	1	2	0	1	0	18.00

1936 Pains and Streaks and Tears

It was a memorable year, made up of a costly broken wrist, two 15-game winning streaks, one 16-game winning streak, two rookies of fantastic potential, S300,000 paid for the privilege of finishing sixth, and the Hall of Fame in Cooperstown, New York, which opened its doors to enshrine Ty Cobb, Babe Ruth, Honus Wagner, Christy Mathewson, and Walter Johnson.

Item No. 1 was Detroit. After winning two successive pennants, the Tigers finished a noble second, but a dismal 19 1/2 games behind the New York Yankees. The Tigers' problems began early as their powerhouse first baseman, Hank Greenberg, broke his wrist after playing 12 games. Then in mid-season, manager-catcher Mickey Cochrane broke down and had to go to Wyoming to regain his health.

In winning their first pennant since 1932, the Yankees unveiled Joe DiMaggio, a 21-year-old from Martinez, California. Well primed in the Pacific Coast League before making his debut he finished third on the club in batting to Bill Dickey and Gehrig and second in home runs to Lou Gehrig, who led the league with 49 and captured the MVP Award.

The other rookie news came out of Cleveland and was even more spectacular. Indian fans watched in disbelief as a 17-year-old kid from Van Meter, Iowa, struck out 15 Browns in his major league bow on August 23. Three weeks later, Bob Feller made believers of everyone as he tied an American League strikeout record by fanning 17 Athletics. In Chicago, Luke Appling helped the White Sox to third place behind his league-leading .388 average, thus becoming the first shortstop and the first White Sox player to win an American League batting title. In Boston, there were tears all over owner Tom Yawkey's bank book. After spending large sums in 1934 and 1935 to bolster the Red Sox, Yawkey shelled out S300,000 to Connie Mack and the A's to get Jimmie Foxx, Doc Cramer, Eric McNair, and John Marcum, only to finish a dismal sixth, 28 1/2 games out.

The National League couldn't boast of the same rookie finds as the American League, but they did have several notable streaks and a three-team pennant struggle from the Giants, Cubs, and Cardinals. St. Louis broke on top and looked something like the Gashouse Gang of 1934, but when Paul Dean developed arm trouble and brother Dizzy discovered he could not keep up his winning pace of the last two years, the Cards found themselves a disappointing tie for second with the Cubs, five games off the Giants. Aside from the Dean brothers putting together only 29 wins, compared to 47 in 1935, St. Louis could not contend with last-place Boston, which took their season series, 13-9.

The Cubs had replaced St. Louis at the top after a great June which had included a 15-game winning streak and seemed to be out of reach until the Giants awakened in late July and also fashioned a 15-game winning streak. In going for their second straight pennant, the Cubs traded back Chuck Klein, their big disappointment of 1935, to the Phillies for Ethan Allen and Curt Davis. But the Giants, with MVP Carl Hubbell, who won his last 16 games of the season, proved too much—especially after the Giants took three out of four at the end of August and destroyed whatever morale Chicago had left.

The Giants' and Yankees' victory marked the first time since 1923 that two New York Clubs met in the Series. Hubbell continued his season form by beating the Yankees in the Series opener, 6-1, and allowing seven scattered hits and no fielding chances for his outfielders. The Yankees then recovered by blasting the Giants, 18-4, and going on to win the Series—the same as in 1923—four games to two.

1936 AMERICAN LEAGUE

NEW YORK — 1st 102-51 .667 — JOE McCARTHY

NAME	G by Pos	B	AGE	G	AB	R	H	2B	3B	HR	RBI	BB	SO	SB	BA	SA
TOTALS			28	155	5591	1065	1676	315	83	182	995	700	594	76	.300	.483
Lou Gehrig	1B155	L	33	155	579	167	205	37	7	49	152	130	46	3	.354	.696
Tony Lazzeri	2B148, SS2	R	32	150	537	82	154	29	6	14	109	97	65	8	.287	.441
Frankie Crosetti	SS151	R	25	151	632	137	182	35	7	15	78	90	83	18	.288	.437
Red Rolfe	3B133	R	27	135	568	116	181	39	15	10	70	68	38	3	.319	.493
George Selkirk	OF135	L	28	137	493	93	152	28	9	18	107	94	60	13	.308	.511
2 Jake Powell	OF84	R	27	87	324	62	99	13	3	7	48	33	30	16	.306	.429
Joe DiMaggio	OF138	R	21	138	637	132	206	44	15	29	125	24	39	4	.323	.576
Bill Dickey	C107	R	29	112	423	99	153	26	8	22	107	46	16	0	.362	.617
Roy Johnson	OF33	L	33	63	147	21	39	8	2	1	19	21	14	3	.265	.367
Red Ruffing	P33	R	32	53	127	14	37	5	0	5	22	11	12	0	.291	.449
Myril Hoag (YJ)	OF39	R	28	45	156	23	47	9	4	3	34	7	16	3	.301	.468
Joe Glenn	C44	R	27	44	129	21	35	7	0	1	20	20	10	1	.271	.349
1 Ben Chapman	OF36	R	27	36	139	19	37	14	3	1	21	15	20	1	.266	.432
Jack Saltzgaver	3B16, 2B6, 1B4	L	31	34	90	14	19	5	0	1	13	13	18	2	.211	.300
Monte Pearson	P33	R	26	33	91	12	23	4	0	1	20	8	13	0	.253	.330
Art Jorgens	C30	R	31	31	66	5	18	3	1	0	5	2	3	0	.273	.348
Don Heffner	3B8, 2B5, SS3	R	25	19	48	7	11	2	1	0	6	6	5	0	.229	.313
Bob Seeds	OF9, 3B3	R	29	13	42	12	11	1	0	4	10	5	3	1	.262	.571
1 Dixie Walker	OF5	L	25	6	20	3	7	0	2	1	5	1	3	1	.350	.700

NAME	T	AGE	W	L	PCT	SV	G	GS	CG	IP	H	BB	SO	SHO	ERA
TOTALS		30	102	51	.667	21	155	155	77	1401	1474	663	624	6	4.17
Red Ruffing	R	32	20	12	.625	0	33	33	25	271	274	90	102	3	3.85
Monte Pearson	R	27	19	7	.731	1	33	31	15	223	191	135	118	1	3.71
Bump Hadley	R	31	14	4	.778	1	31	17	8	174	194	89	74	1	4.34
Lefty Gomez	L	27	13	7	.650	0	31	30	10	189	184	122	105	0	4.38
Pat Malone	R	33	12	4	.750	9	35	9	5	135	144	60	72	1	3.80
Johnny Broaca	R	26	12	7	.632	3	37	27	12	206	235	66	84	1	4.24
Johnny Murphy (JJ)	R	27	9	3	.750	5	27	5	2	88	90	36	34	0	3.38
Ted Kleinhans	L	37	1	1	.500	1	19	0	0	29	36	23	10	0	5.90
Kemp Wicker	L	29	1	2	.333	0	7	0	0	20	31	11	5	0	7.65
Jumbo Brown	R	29	1	4	.200	1	20	3	0	64	93	29	19	0	5.91
Steve Sundra	R	26	0	0	—	0	1			2	2	1	0	0	0.00

DETROIT — 2nd 83-71 .539 19.5 — MICKEY COCHRANE

NAME	G by Pos	B	AGE	G	AB	R	H	2B	3B	HR	RBI	BB	SO	SB	BA	SA
TOTALS			31	154	5464	921	1638	326	55	94	847	640	462	76	.300	.431
2 Jack Burns	1B138	L	28	138	558	96	158	36	3	4	63	79	45	4	.283	.380
Charlie Gehringer	2B154	L	33	154	641	144	227	60	12	15	116	83	13	4	.354	.555
Billy Rogell	SS146, 3B1	B	31	146	585	85	160	27	5	6	68	73	41	14	.274	.368
Mary Owen	3B153, 1B2	R	30	154	583	72	172	20	4	9	105	53	41	9	.295	.389
Gee Walker	OF125	R	28	134	550	105	194	55	5	12	93	23	30	17	.353	.536
Al Simmons	OF138, 1B1	R	34	143	568	96	186	38	6	13	112	49	35	6	.327	.484
Goose Goslin	OF144	L	35	147	572	122	180	33	8	24	125	85	50	14	.315	.526
Ray Hayworth	C81	R	32	81	250	31	60	10	0	1	30	39	18	0	.240	.292
Pete Fox	OF55	R	26	73	220	46	67	12	1	4	26	34	23	1	.305	.423
Jo-Jo White	OF18	L	27	58	51	11	14	3	0	0	6	9	12	2	.275	.333
Mickey Cochrane (IL)	C42	L	33	44	126	24	34	8	0	2	17	46	15	1	.270	.381
Eldon Auker	P35	R	25	35	78	7	24	1	2	0	15	7	24	0	.308	.372
Glenn Myatt	C27	R	38	27	78	5	17	1	0	0	5	11	4	0	.218	.231
Frank Reiber	C17, OF1	R	26	20	55	7	15	2	0	1	5	5	7	0	.273	.364
Flea Clifton	SS6, 3B2, 2B1	R	26	13	26	5	5	1	0	0	1	4	3	0	.192	.231
Hank Greenberg (BW)	1B12	R	25	12	46	10	16	6	2	1	16	9	6	1	.348	.630
Salty Parker	SS7, 1B2	R	23	11	25	6	7	2	0	0	4	2	3	0	.280	.360
Birdie Tebbetts	C10	R	26	10	33	7	10	1	2	1	4	5	3	0	.303	.545
Gil English	3B1	R	26	1	1	0	0	0	0	0	0	0	0	0	.000	.000

NAME	T	AGE	W	L	PCT	SV	G	GS	CG	IP	H	BB	SO	SHO	ERA
TOTALS		28	83	71	.539	13	154	154	76	1360	1568	562	526	13	5.00
Tommy Bridges	R	29	23	11	.676	1	39	38	26	295	289	115	175	5	3.60
Schoolboy Rowe	R	26	19	10	.655	3	41	35	19	245	266	64	115	4	4.52
Elden Auker	R	25	13	16	.448	0	35	31	14	215	263	83	66	2	4.89
Roxie Lawson	R	30	8	6	.571	3	41	8	3	128	139	71	34	0	5.48
Vic Sorrell	R	35	6	7	.462	3	30	14	5	131	153	64	37	1	5.29
General Crowder	R	37	4	3	.571	0	9	7	1	44	64	21	10	0	8.39
Jake Wade	L	24	4	5	.444	0	13	11	4	78	93	52	30	1	5.31
Chad Kimsey	R	29	2	3	.400	3	22	0	0	52	58	29	11	0	4.85
Red Phillips	R	27	2	4	.333	0	22	6	3	87	124	22	15	0	6.52
Joe Sullivan	L	25	2	5	.286	1	26	4	1	80	111	40	32	0	6.75
1 Chief Hogsett	L	32	0	1	.000	0	3	0	0	4	8	1	1	0	9.00

CHICAGO — 3rd 81-70 .536 20 — JIMMY DYKES

NAME	G by Pos	B	AGE	G	AB	R	H	2B	3B	HR	RBI	BB	SO	SB	BA	SA
TOTALS			30	153	5466	920	1597	282	56	60	862	684	417	66	.292	.397
Zeke Bonura	1B146	R	27	148	587	120	194	39	7	12	137	94	29	4	.330	.482
Jackie Hayes	2B89, SS13, 3B2	R	29	108	417	53	130	34	3	5	84	35	25	4	.312	.444
Luke Appling	SS137	R	29	138	526	111	204	31	7	6	128	85	25	10	.388	.508
Jimmy Dykes	3B125	R	39	127	435	62	116	16	3	1	60	61	36	1	.267	.366
Mule Haas	OF96, 1B7	L	32	119	408	75	116	26	2	0	46	64	29	1	.284	.358
Mike Kreevich	OF133	R	28	137	550	99	169	32	11	5	69	61	46	10	.307	.433
Rip Radcliff	OF132	L	30	138	618	120	207	31	7	8	82	44	12	6	.335	.447
Luke Sewell	C126	R	35	128	451	59	113	20	5	5	73	54	16	11	.251	.350
Tony Piet	2B68, 3B32	R	29	109	352	69	96	15	2	7	42	66	48	15	.273	.386
Larry Rosenthal	OF80	L	26	85	317	71	89	15	8	3	47	59	37	2	.281	.407
Vern Kennedy	P35	R	29	36	113	12	32	8	0	0	11	1	13	0	.283	.354
Frank Grube	C32	R	31	33	93	6	15	2	1	0	6	6	9	1	.161	.204
2 Dixie Walker (SJ)	OF17	L	25	26	70	12	19	2	0	0	11	14	6	1	.271	.300
George Washington	OF12	L	29	20	49	6	8	3	0	0	5	2	8	0	.163	.265
Jo-Jo Morrissey (BY)	3B9, SS4, 2B1	R	32	17	38	3	7	1	0	0	6	2	5	0	.184	.211
Merv Shea	C14	R	35	14	24	3	3	0	0	0	1	6	6	0	.125	.125
George Stumpf	OF4	L	25	10	22	3	6	1	0	0	1	0	1	0	.273	.318
Les Rock	1B2	L	23	2	1	0	0	0	0	0	0	1	0	0	.000	.000

NAME	T	AGE	W	L	PCT	SV	G	GS	CG	IP	H	BB	SO	SHO	ERA
TOTALS		29	81	70	.536	8	153	153	80	1365	1603	578	414	5	5.06
Vern Kennedy	R	29	21	9	.700	0	35	34	20	274	282	147	99	1	4.63
2 Sugar Cain	R	29	14	10	.583	0	30	26	14	195	228	75	42	1	4.75
John Whitehead	R	27	13	13	.500	1	34	32	15	231	254	98	70	1	4.64
Ted Lyons	R	35	10	13	.435	0	26	24	15	182	227	45	48	1	5.14
Clint Brown	R	32	6	2	.750	5	38	2	0	83	106	24	19	0	4.99
Monty Stratton	R	24	5	7	.417	0	16	14	3	95	117	46	37	0	5.21
Italo Chelini	L	21	4	3	.571	0	18	6	5	84	100	30	16	0	4.93
3 Bill Dietrich	R	26	4	4	.500	0	14	11	6	83	93	36	39	1	4.66
Ray Phelps	R	32	4	6	.400	0	15	4	2	69	91	42	17	0	6.00
Red Evans	R	29	0	3	.000	0	17	0	0	47	70	22	19	0	7.86
Bill Shores	R	32	0	0	—	0	3	0	0	17	26	8	5	0	9.53
Whit Wyatt	R	28	0	0	—	0	3	1	0	3	0	0	0	0	0.00
1 Les Tietje	R	25	0	2	.000	0	6	2	1	6	5	3	3	0	31.50

WASHINGTON 4th 82-71 .536 20 — BUCKY HARRIS

NAME	G by Pos	B	AGE	G	AB	R	H	2B	3B	HR	RBI	BB	SO	SB	BA	SA
	TOTALS		29	153	5433	889	1601	293	84	62	822	576	398	103	.295	.414
Joe Kuhel	1B149, 3B1	L	30	149	588	107	189	42	8	16	118	64	30	15	.321	.502
Ossie Bluege	2B52, SS23, 3B15	R	35	90	319	43	92	12	1	1	55	38	16	5	.288	.342
Cecil Travis	SS71, OF53, 1B4, 3B2	L	22	138	517	77	164	34	10	2	92	39	21	4	.317	.433
Buddy Lewis	3B139	L	19	143	601	100	175	21	13	6	67	47	46	4	.291	.399
Carl Reynolds	OF72	R	33	89	293	41	81	18	2	4	41	21	22	8	.276	.392
2 Ben Chapman	OF97	R	27	97	401	91	133	36	7	4	60	69	18	19	.332	.486
John Stone	OF114	L	30	123	437	95	149	22	11	15	90	60	26	8	.341	.545
Cliff Bolton	C83	L	29	86	289	41	84	18	4	2	51	25	12	1	.291	.401
Red Kress	SS64, 2B33, 1B5	R	31	109	391	51	111	20	6	8	51	39	25	6	.284	.427
Jesse Hill	OF60	R	29	85	233	50	71	19	5	0	34	29	23	11	.305	.429
Wally Millies	C72	R	29	74	215	26	67	10	2	0	25	11	8	1	.312	.377
1 Jake Powell	OF53	R	27	53	214	40	62	11	5	1	30	19	21	10	.290	.402
Buddy Myer (IL)	2B43	L	32	51	156	31	42	5	2	0	15	42	11	7	.269	.327
John Mihalic	2B25	R	24	25	88	15	21	2	1	0	8	14	14	2	.239	.284
Fred Sington	OF25	R	26	25	94	13	30	8	0	1	28	15	9	0	.319	.436
Dee Miles	OF10	L	27	25	59	8	14	1	2	0	7	1	5	0	.237	.322
Shanty Hogan	C19	R	30	19	65	8	21	4	0	1	7	11	2	0	.323	.431
Bobby Estalella		R	25	13	9	2	2	0	2	0	4	5	0	0	.222	.667
Alex Sabo	C4	R	26	4	8	1	3	0	0	0	1	0	2	1	.375	.375
Chick Starr	C1	R	25	1	0	0	0	0	0	0	0	0	0	0	—	—

NAME	T	AGE	W	L	PCT	SV	G	GS	CG	IP	H	BB	SO	SHO	ERA
		30	82	71	.536	14	153	153	78	1346	1484	588	462	8	4.58
Jimmie DeShong	R	26	18	10	.643	2	34	31	16	224	255	96	59	2	4.62
Bobo Newsom	R	28	17	15	.531	2	43	38	24	286	294	146	156	4	4.31
Pete Appleton	R	32	14	9	.609	3	38	20	12	202	199	77	77	1	3.52
Earl Whitehill	L	36	14	11	.560	0	28	28	14	212	252	89	63	0	4.88
2 Joe Cascarella	R	29	9	8	.529	1	22	16	7	139	147	54	34	1	4.08
Monty Weaver	R	30	6	4	.600	1	26	5	3	91	92	38	15	0	4.35
1 Jack Russell	R	30	3	2	.600	3	18	5	1	50	66	25	6	0	6.30
Ed Linke	R	24	1	5	.167	0	13	6	1	52	73	14	11	0	7.10
2 Bill Dietrich	R	26	0	1	.000	0	5	0	0	8	13	6	4	0	10.13
Sid Cohen	L	29	0	2	.000	1	19	1	0	36	44	14	21	0	5.25
2 Firpo Marberry	R	37	0	2	.000	0	5	1	0	14	11	3	4	0	3.86
Joe Bokina	R	26	0	2	.000	0	5	1	0	8	15	6	5	0	9.00
Henry Coppola	R	23	0	0	—	0	6	0	0	14	17	12	2	0	4.50
Bill Phebus	R	26	0	0	—	0	2	1	0	7	4	4	0	0	2.57
Ken Chase	L	22	0	0	—	0	2	0	0	2	4	4	1	0	13.50

CLEVELAND 5th 80-74 .519 22.5 — STEVE O'NEILL

NAME	G by Pos	B	AGE	G	AB	R	H	2B	3B	HR	RBI	BB	SO	SB	BA	SA
	TOTALS		26	157	5646	921	1715	357	82	123	852	514	470	66	.304	.461
Hal Trosky	1B151, 2B1	L	23	151	629	124	216	45	9	42	162	36	58	6	.343	.644
Roy Hughes	2B152	R	25	152	638	112	188	35	9	0	63	57	40	20	.295	.378
Bill Knickerbocker	SS155	R	24	155	618	81	182	35	3	8	73	56	30	5	.294	.400
Odell Hale	3B148, 2B3	R	27	153	620	126	196	50	13	14	87	64	43	8	.316	.506
Roy Weatherly	OF84	R	21	84	349	64	117	28	6	8	53	16	29	3	.335	.519
Earl Averill	OF150	L	34	152	614	136	232	39	15	28	126	65	35	3	.378	.627
Joe Vosmik	OF136	R	26	138	506	76	145	29	4	7	94	79	21	5	.287	.413
Billy Sullivan	C72, 3B5, 1B3, OF1	L	25	93	319	39	112	32	6	2	48	16	9	5	.351	.508
Bruck Campbell (IL)	OF47	L	26	76	172	35	64	15	2	6	30	19	17	2	.372	.587
Frankie Pytlak (BJ)	C58	R	27	75	224	35	72	15	4	0	31	24	11	5	.321	.424
Milt Galatzer	OF42, 1B1, P1	L	29	49	97	12	23	4	1	0	6	13	8	1	.237	.299
Jim Gleeson	OF33	B	24	41	139	26	36	9	2	4	12	18	17	2	.259	.439
Boze Berger	1B8, 2B8, 3B7, SS2	R	26	28	52	1	9	2	0	0	3	1	14	0	.173	.212
George Uhle	P7	R	37	24	21	1	8	1	0	1	4	2	0	0	.381	.571
Greek George	C22	R	23	23	77	3	15	3	0	0	5	9	16	0	.195	.234
Joe Becker (BG)	C15	R	27	22	50	5	9	3	1	1	11	5	4	0	.180	.340
Jeff Heath	OF12	L	21	12	41	6	14	3	1	3	8	3	4	1	.341	.634

NAME	T	AGE	W	L	PCT	SV	G	GS	CG	IP	H	BB	SO	SHO	ERA
		29	80	74	.519	12	157	157	74	1389	1604	607	619	5	4.83
Johnny Allen	R	31	20	10	.667	1	36	31	19	243	234	97	165	4	3.44
Mel Harder	R	26	15	15	.500	1	36	30	13	225	294	71	84	0	5.16
Orel Hildebrand	R	29	10	11	.476	4	36	21	9	175	197	83	65	0	4.89
George Blaeholder	R	32	8	4	.667	0	35	16	6	134	158	47	30	0	5.10
Denny Galehouse	R	24	8	7	.533	1	36	15	5	148	161	68	71	0	4.86
Lloyd Brown (IL)	R	31	8	10	.444	1	24	16	12	140	166	45	34	1	4.18
Bob Feller	R	17	5	3	.625	1	14	8	5	62	52	47	76	0	3.34
Thornton Lee	L	29	3	5	.375	3	43	8	2	127	138	67	49	0	4.89
Bill Zuber	R	23	1	1	.500	0	2	2	1	14	14	15	5	0	6.43
Al Milnar	R	22	1	2	.333	0	4	3	1	22	26	18	9	0	7.36
Willis Hudlin	R	30	1	5	.167	0	27	7	1	64	112	31	20	0	9.00
George Uhle	R	37	1	0	.000	7	0	0	13	26	5	5	0	8.53
Ralph Winegarner	R	26	0	0	—	0	9	0	0	15	18	6	3	0	4.80
Paul Kardow	R	20	0	0	—	0	2	0	0	2	1	2	0	0	4.50
Milt Galatzer	L	29	0	0	—	0	1	0	0	2	4	0	0	0	4.50

BOSTON 6th 74-80 .481 28.5 — JOE CRONIN

NAME	G by Pos	B	AGE	G	AB	R	H	2B	3B	HR	RBI	BB	SO	SB	BA	SA
	TOTALS		29	155	5383	775	1485	288	62	86	718	584	465	54	.276	.400
Jimmie Foxx	1B139, OF16, 3B1	R	28	155	585	130	198	32	8	41	143	105	119	13	.338	.631
Oscar Melillo	2B93	R	36	98	327	39	74	12	4	0	32	28	16	0	.226	.287
Eric McNair	SS84, 2B35, 3B11	R	27	128	484	68	141	36	2	4	74	27	34	3	.285	.391
Bill Werber	3B101, OF45, 2B1	R	28	145	535	89	147	29	6	10	67	89	37	23	.275	.407
Mel Almada	OF81	L	23	96	320	40	81	16	4	1	21	24	15	2	.253	.338
Doc Cramer	OF154	L	30	154	643	99	188	31	7	0	41	49	20	4	.292	.362
Dusty Cooke	OF91	L	29	111	341	58	93	20	3	6	47	72	48	4	.273	.402
Rick Ferrell	C121	R	30	121	410	59	128	27	5	8	55	65	17	0	.312	.461
John Kroner	2B38, 3B28, SS18, OF1	R	27	84	298	40	87	17	8	4	62	26	24	2	.292	.443
Heinie Manush (BG)	OF72	L	34	82	313	43	91	15	5	0	45	17	11	1	.291	.371
Joe Cronin	SS60, 3B21	R	29	81	295	36	83	22	4	2	43	32	21	1	.281	.403
Wes Ferrell	P39	R	28	61	135	20	36	6	1	5	24	14	10	0	.267	.437
Moe Berg	C39	R	34	39	125	9	30	4	1	0	19	2	6	0	.240	.288
Bing Miller	OF13	R	41	30	47	9	14	2	1	1	6	5	5	0	.298	.447
Babe Dahlgren	1B16	R	24	16	57	6	16	3	1	1	7	7	1	2	.281	.421
Fabian Gaffke	OF15	R	22	15	55	5	7	2	0	1	3	4	5	0	.127	.218
George Dickey	C10	B	20	10	23	0	1	0	0	0	2	2	3	0	.043	.087

NAME	T	AGE	W	L	PCT	SV	G	GS	CG	IP	H	BB	SO	SHO	ERA
		30	74	80	.481	9	155	155	78	1373	1501	552	584	11	4.39
Wes Ferrell	R	28	20	15	.571	0	39	38	28	301	330	119	106	3	4.19
Lefty Grove	L	36	17	12	.586	2	35	30	22	253	237	65	130	6	2.81
Fritz Ostermueller	L	28	10	16	.385	2	43	23	7	181	210	84	90	1	4.87
Johnny Marcum	R	26	8	13	.381	1	31	23	9	174	194	52	57	1	4.81
Jack Wilson	R	24	6	8	.429	3	43	9	2	136	152	86	74	0	4.43
Jim Henry	R	26	5	1	.833	0	21	8	2	76	75	40	36	0	4.62
Rube Walberg	R	39	5	4	.556	0	24	9	5	100	98	36	49	0	4.41
1 Johnny Welch	R	29	2	1	.667	0	9	3	1	33	43	8	9	0	5.45
Ted Olson	R	23	1	1	.500	0	5	3	1	18	24	8	5	0	7.50
Joe Cascarella	R	29	0	2	.000	0	10	1	0	21	27	9	7	0	6.86
2 Mike Meola	R	30	0	2	.000	1	6	3	1	21	29	10	8	0	5.57
Jennings Poindexter	L	25	0	2	.000	0	3	3	0	11	13	16	2	0	6.54
2 Jack Russell	R	30	0	3	.000	2	23	0	0	40	57	16	9	0	5.63
Stew Bowers	R	21	0	0	—	0	5	0	0	6	10	2	0	0	9.00
Emerson Dickman	R	21	0	0	—	0	1	0	0	2	1	2	2	0	9.00

ST. LOUIS 7th 57-95 .375 44.5 — ROGERS HORNSBY

NAME	G by Pos	B	AGE	G	AB	R	H	2B	3B	HR	RBI	BB	SO	SB	BA	SA
	TOTALS		29	155	5391	804	1502	299	66	79	761	625	627	62	.279	.403
Jim Bottomley	1B140	L	36	140	544	72	162	39	11	12	95	44	55	0	.298	.476
Tom Carey	2B128, SS1	R	27	134	488	58	133	27	6	1	57	27	25	2	.273	.359
Lyn Lary	SS155	R	30	155	620	112	179	30	6	2	52	117	54	37	.289	.366
Harlond Clift	3B152	R	23	153	572	145	174	40	11	20	73	115	68	12	.302	.514
Beau Bell	OF142, 1B17	R	28	155	616	100	212	40	12	11	123	60	55	4	.344	.502
Sammy West	OF148	L	31	152	533	78	148	26	4	7	70	94	70	2	.278	.381
Moose Solters	OF147	R	30	152	628	100	183	45	7	17	134	41	76	3	.291	.467
Rollie Hemsley	C114	R	29	116	377	43	99	27	2	2	39	46	30	2	.263	.353
Ed Coleman	OF18	L	34	92	137	13	40	5	4	2	34	15	17	0	.292	.431
Ray Pepper	OF18	R	30	75	124	13	35	5	0	2	23	5	23	0	.282	.371
Tony Giuliani	C66	R	23	71	198	17	43	3	0	0	13	11	13	0	.217	.232
Ollie Bejma	2B32, 3B7, SS1	R	28	67	139	19	36	2	3	2	18	27	21	0	.259	.360
1 Jack Burns	1B2	L	28	9	14	2	3	1	0	0	1	3	1	0	.214	.286
Rogers Homsby	1B1	R	40	2	5	1	2	0	0	0	2	1	0	0	.400	.400

NAME	T	AGE	W	L	PCT	SV	G	GS	CG	IP	H	BB	SO	SHO	ERA
		31	57	95	.375	13	154	154	54	1348	1776	609	399	3	6.24
2 Chief Hogsett	L	32	13	15	.464	1	39	29	10	215	278	90	67	0	5.53
Tommy Thomas	R	36	11	9	.550	0	36	21	8	180	219	72	40	1	5.25
Jack Knott	R	29	9	17	.346	6	47	23	9	193	272	93	60	0	7.27
Ivy Andrews	R	29	7	12	.368	1	36	25	11	191	221	50	33	0	4.85
Earl Caldwell	R	31	7	16	.304	2	41	25	10	189	252	83	59	2	6.00
Russ Van Atta	L	30	4	7	.364	2	52	9	2	123	164	68	59	0	6.59
2 Les Tietje	R	25	3	5	.375	0	14	7	2	50	65	30	16	0	6.66
Roy Mahaffey	R	32	2	6	.250	1	21	9	1	60	82	40	13	0	8.10
1 Sugar Cain	R	29	1	1	.500	0	4	3	1	16	20	9	8	0	6.75
1 Mike Meola	R	30	0	1	.000	0	9	0	0	19	23	13	6	0	9.47
Sig Jakucki	R	26	0	3	.000	0	7	2	0	21	32	12	9	0	8.57
Jim Walkup	R	27	0	3	.000	0	6	5	0	30	57	22	7	0	7.88
Glenn Liebhardt	R	25	0	0	—	0	24	0	0	55	98	27	20	0	8.84
Harry Kimberlin	R	27	0	0	—	0	13	0	0	20	24	16	4	0	5.40

PHILADELPHIA 8th 53-100 .346 49 — CONNIE MACK

NAME	G by Pos	B	AGE	G	AB	R	H	2B	3B	HR	RBI	BB	SO	SB	BA	SA
	TOTALS		26	154	5373	714	1443	240	60	72	663	524	590	59	.269	.376
Lou Finney	1B78, OF73	L	26	154	653	100	197	26	10	1	41	47	22	7	.302	.377
1 Rabbit Warstler	2B66	R	32	66	236	27	59	8	1	0	24	36	16	0	.250	.347
Skeeter Newsome	SS123, 2B2, 3B1, OF1	R	25	127	471	41	106	15	2	0	46	25	27	13	.225	.265
Pinky Higgins	3B145	R	27	146	550	89	159	32	2	12	80	67	61	7	.289	.420
George Puccinelli	OF117	R	29	135	457	83	127	30	3	11	78	65	70	2	.278	.459
Wally Moses	OF144	L	25	146	585	98	202	35	11	7	66	62	32	12	.345	.479
Bob Johnson	OF131, 2B22, 1B1	R	30	153	566	91	165	29	14	25	121	88	71	6	.292	.525
Frankie Hayes	C142	R	21	146	505	59	137	25	2	10	67	46	58	3	.271	.388
Chubby Dean	1B77	L	20	111	342	41	98	21	3	1	48	24	24	3	.287	.374
Al Niemiec	2B52, SS5	R	25	69	203	22	40	3	2	1	20	26	16	2	.197	.246
Rusty Peters	SS25, 3B10, OF2, 2B1	R	21	45	119	12	26	3	2	3	16	4	28	1	.218	.353
Charlie Moss	C19	R	25	33	44	2	11	1	0	0	10	6	5	1	.250	.318
Emil Mailho	OF1	L	26	21	18	5	1	0	0	0	1	6	2	0	.056	.056
Charlie Berry	C12	R	33	13	17	0	1	0	0	0	1	6	2	0	.059	.118
Bill Nicholson	OF1	L	21	11	12	2	0	0	0	0	0	1	5	0	.000	.000
Dick Culler	2B7, SS2	R	21	9	38	3	9	1	0	0	1	3	3	0	.237	.237
Hugh Luby	3B9	R	22	9	38	3	7	1	0	0	3	5	0	0	.184	.211
Jack Peerson	SS7, 2B1	R	25	9	34	7	11	3	0	1	5	0	0	0	.324	.412
Jim Oglesby	1B3	L	30	3	11	0	2	0	0	0	2	0	1	0	.182	.182
Bill Conroy	C1	R	21	4	2	0	1	0	0	0	0	2	1	0	.500	.500

NAME	T	AGE	W	L	PCT	SV	G	GS	CG	IP	H	BB	SO	SHO	ERA
		26	53	100	.346	12	154	154	68	1352	1645	696	405	3	6.08
Harry Kelley	R	30	15	12	.556	3	35	27	20	235	250	75	82	1	3.87
Buck Ross	R	21	9	14	.391	0	30	27	12	201	253	83	47	1	5.82
Gordon Rhodes	R	28	9	20	.310	1	35	28	13	216	266	102	61	1	5.75
1 Herman Fink	R	24	8	16	.333	1	34	24	9	189	222	78	53	0	6.50
Bill Dietrich	R	26	4	6	.400	3	21	4	0	72	91	40	34	0	6.50
Fred Archer	L	26	3	2	.400	0	6	5	2	37	41	15	9	0	6.32
George Turbeville	R	21	2	5	.286	0	12	6	2	44	42	32	10	0	6.34
Eddie Smith	L	22	1	1	.500	0	2	1	0	8	9	6	4	0	1.89
Randy Gumpert	R	18	1	2	.333	2	22	3	0	62	74	32	9	0	4.79
Whitey Wilshere (AJ)	R	23	1	3	.333	0	5	3	0	18	21	19	4	0	7.00
Hod Lisenbee	R	37	1	7	.125	0	19	7	4	86	115	24	17	0	6.17
Pete Naktenis	L	22	0	1	.000	0	7	1	0	13	23	8	4	0	12.32
Harry Matuzak	R	26	0	1	.000	0	10	0	0	15	21	14	8	0	7.20
Dutch Lieber	R	28	0	1	.000	0	12	0	0	19	37	7	6	0	7.50
Red Bullock	L	24	0	1	.000	0	12	2	0	19	39	7	7	0	13.76
Woody Upchurch	L	25	0	2	.000	0	4	1	0	14	21	9	6	0	9.82
Hank Johnson	R	30	0	0	—	0	4	0	0	8	11	5	3	0	4.50
Carl Doyle	R	24	0	1	.000	1	13	0	0	39	66	29	14	0	10.85
Stu Flythe	R	24	0	0	—	0	17	3	0	39	49	61	14	0	13.15

NEW YORK — 1ST 92-62 .597 — BILL TERRY

NAME	G by Pos	B	AGE	G	AB	R	H	2B	3B	HR	RBI	BB	SO	SB	BA	SA
TOTALS			29	154	5449	742	1529	237	48	97	687	431	452	31	.281	.395
Sam Leslie	1B99	L	30	117	417	49	123	19	5	6	54	23	16	0	.295	.408
Burgess Whitehead	2B153	R	26	154	632	99	176	31	3	4	47	29	32	14	.278	.356
Dick Bartell	SS144	R	28	145	510	71	152	31	3	8	42	40	36	6	.298	.418
Travis Jackson	3B116, SS9	R	32	145	465	41	107	8	1	7	53	18	56	0	.230	.297
Mel Ott	OF148	L	27	150	534	120	175	28	6	33	135	111	41	6	.328	.588
Hank Leiber	OF86, 1B1	R	25	101	337	44	94	19	7	9	67	37	41	1	.279	.457
Jo-Jo Moore	OF149	L	27	152	649	110	205	29	9	7	63	37	27	2	.316	.421
Gus Mancuso	C138	R	30	139	519	55	156	21	3	9	63	39	28	0	.301	.405
Jimmy Ripple	OF76	B	26	96	311	42	95	17	2	7	47	28	15	1	.305	.441
Bill Terry (KJ)	1B56	L	37	79	229	36	71	10	5	2	39	19	19	0	.310	.424
Kiddo Davis	OF22	R	34	47	67	6	16	1	0	0	5	6	5	2	.239	.254
Eddie Mayo	3B40	R	26	46	141	11	28	4	1	1	8	11	12	0	.199	.262
Mark Koenig	SS10, 2B8, 3B3	B	33	42	58	7	16	4	0	1	7	8	4	0	.276	.397
Harry Danning	C24	R	24	32	69	3	11	2	2	0	4	1	5	0	.159	.246
Roy Spencer	C14	R	36	19	18	3	5	1	0	0	3	2	3	0	.278	.333
Joe Martin	3B7	R	24	7	15	0	4	1	0	0	2	0	4	0	.267	.333
Charlie English	2B1	R	26	6	1	0	0	0	0	0	0	0	0	0	.000	.000
Johnny McCarthy	1B4	L	26	4	16	1	7	0	0	1	2	0	1	1	.438	.625
Jim Sheehan	C1	R	23	1	4	0	0	0	0	0	0	0	0	2	.000	.000
Babe Young		L	21	1	1	0	0	0	0	0	0	0	0	0	.000	.000

NAME	T	AGE	W	L	PCT	SV	G	GS	CG	IP	H	BB	SO	SHO	ERA
		28	92	62	.597	22	154	154	60	1385	1458	401	500	12	3.46
Carl Hubbell	L	33	26	6	.813	3	42	34	25	304	265	57	123	3	2.31
Al Smith	L	28	14	13	.519	2	43	30	9	209	217	69	89	4	3.79
Harry Gumbert	R	26	11	3	.786	0	39	15	3	141	157	54	52	0	3.89
Hal Schumacher	R	24	11	13	.458	1	35	30	9	215	234	69	75	3	3.47
Freddie Fitzsimmons	R	34	10	7	.588	2	28	17	7	141	147	39	35	0	3.32
Frank Gabler	R	24	9	8	.529	6	43	14	5	162	170	34	46	0	3.11
Dick Coffman	R	29	7	5	.583	7	40	2	0	102	119	23	26	0	3.88
Slick Castleman	R	22	4	7	.364	1	29	12	2	112	148	56	54	1	5.63
1 Firpo Marberry	R	37	0	0	—	0	1	0	0	1	1	0	0	0	0.00

CHICAGO — 2nd(Tie) 87-67 .5655 — CHARLIE GRIMM

NAME	G by Pos	B	AGE	G	AB	R	H	2B	3B	HR	RBI	BB	SO	SB	BA	SA
TOTALS			27	154	5409	755	1545	275	36	76	707	491	462	68	.286	.392
Phil Cavarretta	1B115	L	19	124	458	55	125	18	1	9	56	17	36	8	.273	.376
Billy Herman	2B153	R	26	153	632	101	211	57	7	5	93	59	30	5	.334	.470
Billy Jurges	SS116	R	28	118	429	51	120	25	1	1	42	23	25	4	.280	.350
Stan Hack	3B140, 1B11	L	26	149	561	102	167	27	4	6	78	89	39	17	.298	.392
Frank Demaree	OF154	R	26	154	605	93	212	34	3	16	96	49	30	4	.350	.496
Augie Galan	OF145	B	24	145	575	74	152	26	4	8	81	67	50	16	.264	.365
2 Ethan Allen	OF89	R	32	91	373	47	110	18	6	3	39	13	30	12	.295	.399
Gabby Hartnett	C114	R	35	121	424	49	130	25	6	7	64	30	36	0	.307	.443
Ken O'Dea	C55	L	23	80	189	36	58	10	3	2	38	38	18	0	.307	.423
Johnny Gill	OF41	L	31	71	174	20	44	8	0	7	28	13	19	0	.253	.420
Woody English	SS42, 3B17, 2B1	R	29	64	182	33	45	9	0	0	20	40	28	1	.247	.297
Tuck Stainback	OF26	R	24	44	75	13	13	3	0	1	5	6	14	1	.173	.253
Charlie Grimm	1B35	L	37	39	132	13	33	4	0	1	16	5	8	0	.250	.303
1 Chuck Klein	OF29	L	31	29	109	19	32	5	0	5	18	16	14	0	.294	.477
Gene Lillard	SS4, 3B15	R	22	19	34	6	7	1	0	0	2	3	8	0	.206	.235
Walter Stephenson	C4	R	25	6	12	0	1	0	0	0	1	0	5	0	.083	.083

NAME	T	AGE	W	L	PCT	SV	G	GS	CG	IP	H	BB	SO	SHO	ERA
		28	87	67	.656	10	154	154	77	1383	1413	434	597	18	3.53
Larry French	L	28	18	9	.667	3	43	28	16	252	262	54	104	4	3.39
Bill Lee	R	26	18	11	.621	1	43	33	20	259	238	93	102	4	3.30
Lon Warneke	R	27	16	13	.552	1	40	29	13	240	246	76	113	4	3.45
Tex Carleton	R	29	14	10	.583	1	35	26	12	197	204	67	88	4	3.65
2 Curt Davis	R	32	11	9	.550	1	24	19	10	153	146	31	52	0	3.00
Roy Henshaw	L	24	5	5	.545	1	39	16	6	129	152	56	69	0	3.98
Charlie Root	R	37	3	6	.333	1	33	3	0	74	81	20	32	0	4.14
Clay Bryant	R	24	1	2	.333	0	26	0	0	57	57	24	35	0	3.32
1 Fabian Kowalik	R	28	0	2	.000	1	6	0	0	16	24	7	1	0	6.75
Clyde Shoun	L	24	0	0	—	0	3	0	0	3	6	1	0	0	13.50

ST. LOUIS — 2nd(Tie) 87-67 .5655 — FRANKIE FRISCH

NAME	G by Pos	B	AGE	G	AB	R	H	2B	3B	HR	RBI	BB	SO	SB	BA	SA
TOTALS			30	155	5537	795	1554	332	60	88	733	422	577	69	.281	.410
Johnny Mize	1B97, OF8	L	23	126	414	76	136	30	8	19	93	50	32	1	.329	.577
Stu Martin	2B83, SS3	L	23	92	332	63	99	21	4	6	41	29	27	17	.298	.440
Leo Durocher	SS136	R	30	136	510	57	146	22	3	1	58	29	47	3	.286	.347
Charlie Gelbert	3B60, SS28, 2B8	R	30	93	280	33	64	15	2	3	27	25	26	2	.229	.339
Pepper Martin	OF127, 3B15, P1	R	32	145	572	121	177	36	11	11	76	58	66	23	.309	.469
Terry Moore	OF133	R	24	143	590	85	156	39	4	5	47	37	52	9	.264	.369
Joe Medwick	OF155	R	24	155	636	115	223	64	13	18	138	34	33	3	.351	.577
Spud Davis	C103, 3B2	R	31	112	363	24	99	26	2	4	59	35	34	0	.273	.388
Ripper Collins	1B61, OF9	B	32	103	277	48	81	15	3	13	48	48	30	1	.292	.509
Brusie Ogrodowski	C85	R	24	94	237	28	54	15	1	1	20	10	20	0	.228	.312
Frankie Frisch	2B61, 3B22, SS1	B	37	93	303	40	83	10	0	1	26	36	10	2	.274	.317
Lynn King	OF34	L	28	78	100	12	19	2	1	0	10	9	14	2	.190	.230
Art Garibaldi	3B46, 2B24	R	28	71	232	30	64	12	0	1	20	16	30	3	.276	.341
Chick Fullis	OF26	R	32	47	89	15	25	6	1	0	6	7	11	0	.281	.371
Don Gutteridge	3B23	R	24	23	91	13	29	3	4	3	16	1	14	3	.319	.538
Eddie Morgan	OF4	L	21	8	18	4	5	0	0	1	3	2	4	0	.278	.444
2 Johnny Vergez	3B8	R	29	8	18	1	3	1	0	0	1	1	3	0	.167	.222
Lou Scoffic	OF3	R	23	4	7	2	3	0	0	0	2	1	2	0	.429	.429
Heinie Schuble	3B1	R	29	2	0	0	0	0	0	0	0	0	0	0	—	—
Walt Alston	1B1	R	24	1	1	0	0	0	0	0	0	0	1	0	.000	.000
Pat Ankenman	SS1	R	23	1	3	0	0	0	0	0	0	0	3	0	.000	.000
Bill DeLancey (IL) 24																

NAME	T	AGE	W	L	PCT	SV	G	GS	CG	IP	H	BB	SO	SHO	ERA
		30	87	67	.565	24	155	155	65	1398	1610	434	559	5	4.47
Dizzy Dean	R	26	24	13	.649	11	51	34	28	315	310	53	195	2	3.17
Jim Winford	R	26	11	10	.524	3	39	23	10	192	203	68	72	1	3.80
Roy Parmelee	R	29	11	11	.500	2	33	26	9	221	226	107	79	0	4.56
Ed Heusser	R	27	7	3	.700	3	42	3	0	104	130	38	26	0	5.45
Jesse Haines	R	42	7	5	.583	1	25	9	4	99	110	21	19	0	3.91
Mike Ryba	R	33	5	1	.833	0	14	0	0	45	55	16	25	0	5.40
2 Si Johnson	R	29	5	3	.625	0	12	9	3	62	82	11	21	1	4.35
Paul Dean (SA)	R	22	5	5	.500	1	17	14	5	92	113	20	28	0	4.60
Bill Walker	L	32	5	6	.455	1	21	13	4	80	106	27	22	1	5.85
2 George Earnshaw	R	36	2	1	.667	0	20	6	1	58	80	20	28	0	6.36
Flint Rhem	R	35	2	1	.667	0	10	4	0	27	49	9	7	0	6.67
1 Wild Bill Hallahan	L	33	2	2	.500	0	9	6	1	37	58	17	16	0	6.32
Bill McGee	R	26	1	1	.500	0	7	2	0	16	23	4	8	0	7.88
Cotton Pippen	R	26	0	2	.000	0	4	2	0	21	37	8	8	0	7.71
Les Munns	R	27	0	3	.000	0	7	1	0	24	23	12	4	0	3.00
Bill Cox	R	23	0	0	—	0	2	0	0	3	4	1	1	0	6.00
Pepper Martin	R	32	0	0	—	0	1	0	0	2	1	2	0	0	0.00
Nels Potter	R	24	0	0	—	0	1	0	0	1	0	0	0	0	0.00

PITTSBURGH — 4th 84-70 .545 8 — PIE TRAYNOR

NAME	G by Pos	B	AGE	G	AB	R	H	2B	3B	HR	RBI	BB	SO	SB	BA	SA
TOTALS			29	156	5586	804	1596	283	80	60	732	517	502	37	.286	.397
Gus Suhr	1B156	L	30	156	583	111	182	33	12	11	118	95	34	8	.312	.467
Pep Young	2B123	R	28	125	475	47	118	23	10	6	77	29	52	3	.248	.377
Arky Vaughan	SS156	L	24	156	568	122	190	30	11	9	78	118	21	6	.335	.474
Bill Brubaker	3B145	R	25	148	554	77	160	27	4	6	102	50	96	5	.289	.384
Paul Waner	OF145	L	33	148	585	107	218	53	9	5	94	74	25	7	.373	.520
Lloyd Waner	OF92	L	30	106	414	67	133	13	8	1	31	31	5	1	.321	.399
Woody Jensen	OF153	R	28	153	696	98	197	34	10	10	58	16	19	2	.283	.404
Tom Padden	C87	R	27	88	281	22	70	9	2	1	31	22	41	0	.249	.306
Al Todd (BG)	C70	R	32	76	267	28	73	10	5	2	28	11	24	4	.273	.371
Fred Schulte	OF55	R	35	74	238	28	62	7	3	1	17	20	20	1	.261	.328
Red Lucas	P27	R	34	69	108	11	26	4	1	0	14	8	17	0	.241	.296
Cooke Lavagetto	2B37, 3B13, SS1	R	23	60	197	21	48	15	2	2	26	15	13	0	.244	.371
Bill Swift	P45	R	28	45	105	6	31	10	0	2	15	2	9	0	.295	.448
Bud Hafey	OF29	R	23	39	118	19	25	3	1	4	13	10	27	0	.212	.381
Hal Finney	C14	R	30	21	35	3	0	0	0	0	0	0	8	0	.000	.000
Johnny Dickshot	OF1	R	26	9	9	2	2	0	0	0	1	0	0	1	.222	.222
Earle Browne	OF4, 1B1	L	25	8	23	7	7	1	2	0	3	1	4	0	.304	.522

NAME	T	AGE	W	L	PCT	SV	G	GS	CG	IP	H	BB	SO	SHO	ERA
		31	84	70	.545	12	156	156	67	1395	1475	379	559	5	3.89
Bill Swift	R	28	16	16	.500	2	45	31	17	262	275	63	92	0	4.02
Red Lucas	R	34	15	4	.789	0	27	22	12	176	178	26	53	0	3.17
Jim Weaver	R	32	14	8	.636	0	38	31	11	226	239	74	108	1	4.30
Cy Blanton	R	27	13	15	.464	3	44	32	15	238	235	55	127	4	3.51
Mace Brown	R	27	10	11	.476	3	47	10	3	165	178	55	56	0	3.87
Ralph Birkofer	L	27	7	5	.583	0	34	13	2	109	130	41	44	0	4.71
Waite Hoyt (IL)	R	36	7	5	.583	1	22	9	6	117	115	20	37	0	2.69
Guy Bush	R	34	1	3	.250	2	16	0	0	35	49	11	10	0	5.91
Jack Tising	R	32	1	3	.250	0	10	6	1	47	52	24	27	0	4.21
Johnny Welch	R	29	0	0	—	1	9	1	0	22	22	6	5	0	4.50
Russ Bauers	R	22	0	0	—	0	1			2	4			0	45.00

CINCINNATI — 5th 74-80 .481 18 — CHUCK DRESSEN

NAME	G by Pos	B	AGE	G	AB	R	H	2B	3B	HR	RBI	BB	SO	SB	BA	SA
TOTALS			28	154	5393	722	1476	224	73	82	674	410	584	68	.274	.388
Les Scarsella	1B115	L	22	115	485	63	152	21	9	3	65	14	36	6	.313	.412
Alex Kampouris	2B119, OF1	R	23	122	355	43	85	19	3	5	46	24	46	3	.239	.332
Billy Myers	SS98	R	25	98	323	45	87	9	6	6	27	28	56	6	.269	.390
Lew Riggs	3B140	R	26	141	538	69	138	20	12	6	57	38	33	5	.257	.372
Ival Goodman	OF120	L	27	136	489	81	139	15	14	17	71	38	53	6	.284	.476
Kiki Cuyler	OF140	R	37	144	567	96	185	29	11	7	74	47	67	16	.326	.453
Babe Herman	OF92, 1B4	L	33	119	380	59	106	23	7	13	71	39	36	4	.279	.458
Ernie Lombardi	C105	R	28	121	387	42	129	23	2	12	68	19	16	1	.333	.496
Tommy Thevenow	SS68, 2B33, 3B12	R	32	106	321	25	75	7	2	0	36	15	23	2	.234	.268
Calvin Chapman	OF31, 2B23, 3B1	L	25	96	219	35	54	7	3	1	22	16	19	2	.247	.320
Hub Walker	OF73, 1B1, C1	L	29	92	258	49	71	18	1	4	23	33	32	8	.275	.399
Gilly Campbell	C71, 1B1	L	28	89	235	28	63	13	1	9	40	43	14	2	.268	.345
Sammy Byrd	OF37	R	29	59	141	17	35	8	0	2	13	11	11	0	.248	.348
George McQuinn	1B38	R	27	38	134	5	27	2	0	0	13	10	22	0	.201	.284
Al Hollingsworth	P29	L	28	34	73	7	23	2	0	1	11	5	8	0	.315	.384
Lee Handley	2B16, 3B7	R	22	24	78	10	24	1	0	0	6	7	16	3	.308	.397
Eddie Joost	SS7, 2B5	R	20	13	26	1	4	0	0	0	1	1	6	0	.154	.192
Eddie Miller	SS4, 2B1	R	19	5	10	1	1	0	0	0	0	0	4	0	.100	.100
Chick Hafey (IL) 33																

NAME	T	AGE	W	L	PCT	SV	G	GS	CG	IP	H	BB	SO	SHO	ERA
		28	74	80	.481	23	154	154	50	1367	1576	418	459	6	4.22
Paul Derringer	R	29	19	19	.500	5	51	37	13	282	331	42	121	2	4.02
Gene Schott	R	22	11	11	.500	7	31	23	8	180	184	73	65	0	3.80
Benny Frey	R	30	10	8	.556	0	31	12	5	131	164	30	20	0	4.26
Al Hollingsworth	L	28	9	10	.474	0	29	25	9	184	204	66	76	0	4.16
Peaches Davis	R	31	8	8	.500	5	26	15	5	126	139	36	32	0	3.57
Don Brennan	R	32	5	2	.714	9	41	3	0	94	117	35	40	0	4.40
2 Wild Bill Hallahan	R	33	5	9	.357	0	23	19	5	135	150	57	32	2	4.33
Lee Stine	R	22	3	3	.273	2	40	12	5	122	157	41	26	0	5.02
Emmett Nelson	R	31	1	0	1.000	0	17	1	0	24	31	17	3	0	3.18
Whitey Moore	R	24	1	0	1.000	0	1	1	0	5	5	4		0	5.40
Lee Grissom	L	18	1	1	.500	0	14	3	0	33	34	9	13	0	6.37
Whitey Hilcher	R	27	1	2	.333	0	14	1	0	35	44	14	10	0	6.17
Tony Freitas	L	28	0	0	.000	0	1	1	0	4	7	4	1	0	1.29
Jake Mooty	R	22	0	0	—	0	4	1	0	14	14	11		0	3.86
Dee Moore	R	23	0	0	—	0	1	0	0	1	0	0	0	0	0.00
1 Si Johnson	R	29	0	0	—	0	2	0	0	7	8	0	0	0	13.50

BOSTON — 6th 71-83 .461 21 — BILL McKECHNIE

NAME	G by Pos	B	AGE	G	AB	R	H	2B	3B	HR	RBI	BB	SO	SB	BA	SA
TOTALS			29	157	5478	631	1450	207	45	67	594	433	582	23	.265	.356
Buck Jordan	1B136	L	29	138	555	81	179	27	5	3	66	45	22	2	.323	.405
Tony Cuccinello	2B150	R	28	150	565	68	174	26	3	7	86	58	49	1	.308	.402
Billy Urbanski	SS80,3B38	R	33	122	494	55	129	17	5	0	26	31	42	2	.261	.316
Joe Coscarart	3B97,SS6,2B1	R	26	104	367	28	90	11	2	2	44	19	37	0	.245	.302
Gene Moore	OF151	L	26	151	637	91	185	38	12	13	67	40	80	6	.290	.449
Wally Berger	OF133	R	30	138	534	88	154	23	3	25	91	53	84	1	.288	.449
Hal Lee	OF150	R	31	152	565	46	143	24	7	3	64	52	50	1	.253	.336
Al Lopez	C127,1B1	R	27	128	426	46	103	12	5	7	50	41	41	1	.242	.343
Tommy Thompson	OF39,1B25	L	26	106	266	37	76	9	0	4	36	31	12	3	.286	.365
2 Rabbit Warstler	SS74	R	32	74	304	27	64	6	0	0	17	22	33	2	.211	.230
2 Mickey Haslin	3B17,2B7	R	26	36	104	14	29	1	2	1	11	5	9	2	.279	.385
Bill Lewis	C21	R	31	29	62	11	19	2	0	0	3	12	7	0	.306	.339
Ray Mueller	C23	R	24	71	5	14	4	0	0	5	5	17	0	.197	.254	
Pinky Whitney	3B10	R	31	10	40	1	7	0	0	0	5	2	4	1	.175	.175
Ed Moriarty		R	23	6	6	0	1	0	0	0	0	0	1	0	.167	.167
Swede Larsen	2B2	R	23	3	1	0	0	0	0	0	0	0	1	0	.000	.000
Andy Pilney		R	23	3	2	0	0	0	0	0	0	0	0	0	.000	.000

NAME	T	AGE	W	L	PCT	SV	G	GS	CG	IP	H	BB	SO	SHO	ERA
		32	71	83	.461	13	157	157	61	1413	1566	451	421	7	3.94
Danny MacFayden	R	31	17	13	.567	0	37	32	21	267	268	66	86	2	2.87
Tiny Chaplin	R	30	10	15	.400	2	40	31	14	232	273	62	86	0	4.11
Ben Cantwell	R	34	9	9	.500	2	34	11	4	133	127	35	42	0	3.05
1 Ray Benge	R	34	7	9	.438	0	21	19	2	115	161	38	32	0	5.79
Johnny Lanning	R	29	7	11	.389	0	20	20	3	153	154	55	33	1	3.65
Bobby Reis	R	27	6	5	.545	0	35	5	3	139	152	74	25	0	4.47
Bob Smith	R	41	6	7	.462	2	35	15	5	136	142	35	36	2	3.77
Roy Weir	L	25	4	3	.571	0	12	7	3	57	53	24	29	2	2.84
2 Guy Bush	R	34	4	5	.444	0	15	11	5	90	98	20	28	0	3.40
Wayne Osborne	R	23	1	1	.500	0	5	3	0	20	31	9	8	0	5.85
Al Blanche	R	26	0	1	.000	1	11	0	0	16	20	8	4	0	6.19
3 Fabian Kowalik	R	28	0	1	.000	0	1	0	0	8	11	2	2	0	8.00
Art Doll	R	24	0	1	.000	0	2	1	0	8	8	3	1	0	3.38
Bob Brown	R	25	0	2	.000	0	2	0	0	8	10	3	5	0	5.63
Amby Murray	L	23	0	0	—	0	4	1	0	11	14	3	4	0	11.25
Irish McCloskey	R	24	0	0	—	0	1	0	0	8	14	3	2	0	10.50
Johnny Babich	R	23	0	0	—	0	3	0	0	6	11	6	1	0	4.50
Bill Ford	R	20	0	0	—	0	1	0	0	2	1	0	0	0	4.50
Gene Ford	R	24	0	0	—	0	2	0	0	3	6	3	0	0	∞
Hal Weafer	R	23	0	0	—	0	1	0	0	2	1	0	0	0	12.00

BROOKLYN — 7th 67-87 .435 25 — CASEY STENGEL

NAME	G by Pos	B	AGE	G	AB	R	H	2B	3B	HR	RBI	BB	SO	SB	BA	SA
TOTALS			29	156	5574	662	1518	263	43	33	596	390	458	55	.273	.353
Buddy Hassett	1B156	L	24	156	635	79	197	29	11	3	82	35	17	5	.310	.405
Jimmy Jordan	2B98,3B6,SS9	R	28	115	398	26	93	15	1	2	28	15	21	1	.234	.291
Lonny Frey	SS117,2B30,OF1	B	25	148	524	63	146	29	4	4	60	71	56	7	.279	.372
Joe Stripp	3B106	R	33	110	439	51	139	31	1	1	60	22	12	1	.317	.399
Frenchy Bordagaray	OF92,2B11	R	26	125	372	63	117	21	3	4	31	17	42	12	.315	.419
Johnny Cooney	OF130	L	35	130	507	71	143	17	5	0	30	24	15	3	.282	.335
2 George Watkins	OF98	L	36	105	364	54	93	24	6	4	43	38	34	5	.255	.387
Ray Berres	C105	R	26	105	267	16	64	10	1	1	34	14	35	1	.240	.296
Babe Phelps	C98,OF1	R	28	115	319	36	117	23	2	5	57	27	16	1	.367	.498
Jim Bucher	3B39,2B32,OF30	R	25	110	370	49	93	12	8	2	41	29	27	5	.251	.343
Sid Gautreaux	C15	B	24	75	71	8	19	3	0	0	16	9	7	0	.268	.310
Eddie Wilson (FS)	OF47	L	26	52	173	28	60	8	1	3	25	14	25	3	.347	.457
Ben Geraghty	SS31,2B9,3B5	R	22	51	129	11	25	4	0	0	9	9	16	4	.194	.225
Danny Taylor	OF31	R	35	43	116	12	34	6	0	2	15	11	14	2	.293	.397
Randy Moore		R	31	42	46	5	13	3	0	0	14	8	1	0	.239	.273
Jack Radtke	2B14,3B5,SS4	R	23	33	31	3	3	0	0	0	5	4	9	3	.097	.097
Fred Lindstrom (LJ)	OF26	R	30	26	106	12	28	4	0	0	5	7	1	1	.264	.302
Tom Winsett	OF21	L	26	21	85	13	20	7	0	1	18	11	14	0	.235	.353
Ox Eckhardt	OF14	L	34	16	44	5	8	1	0	1	6	5	2	0	.182	.273
Nick Tremark	OF8	R	23	8	32	6	8	3	2	0	3	3	2	0	.250	.313
Johnny Hudson	SS4,2B1	R	24	6	12	1	2	0	0	0	1	0	4	0	.167	.167
Dick Siebert	OF1	L	24	2	2	0	0	0	0	0	0	0	0	0	.000	.000

NAME	T	AGE	W	L	PCT	SV	G	GS	CG	IP	H	BB	SO	SHO	ERA
		28	67	87	.435	18	156	156	59	1403	1466	528	651	7	3.98
Van Lingle Mungo	R	25	18	19	.486	3	45	38	22	312	275	118	238	2	3.35
Fred Frankhouse	R	32	13	10	.565	2	41	31	9	234	236	89	84	1	3.65
Ed Brandt	L	31	11	13	.458	2	38	29	12	234	246	65	104	1	3.50
Watty Clark	L	34	7	11	.389	2	33	16	1	120	162	28	28	1	4.43
Max Butcher	R	25	6	6	.500	2	38	14	5	148	154	59	55	0	3.95
George Jeffcoat	R	22	5	6	.455	3	40	5	3	96	84	63	46	0	4.50
1 George Earnshaw	R	36	4	9	.308	1	19	13	4	93	113	30	40	1	5.32
Harry Eisenstat	L	20	2	3	.333	0	5	2	1	14	22	6	5	0	5.79
Hank Winston	R	32	1	3	.250	0	14	0	0	32	40	16	8	0	6.19
Tom Baker	R	23	1	8	.111	2	35	8	2	88	98	48	35	0	4.70
Dutch Leonard (AJ)	R	27	0	0	—	1	16	0	0	32	34	5	8	0	3.66
1 Tom Zachary	L	40	0	0	—	0	1	0	0	2	1	0	0	0	54.00

PHILADELPHIA — 8th 54-100 .351 38 — JIMMIE WILSON

NAME	G by Pos	B	AGE	G	AB	R	H	2B	3B	HR	RBI	BB	SO	SB	BA	SA
TOTALS			29	154	5465	726	1538	250	46	103	682	451	586	50	.281	.401
Dolph Camilli	1B150	L	29	151	530	106	167	29	13	28	102	116	84	5	.315	.577
Chile Gomez	2B71,SS40	R	27	108	332	24	77	4	9	0	28	14	32	0	.232	.250
Leo Norris	SS121,2B38	R	28	154	581	64	154	27	4	11	76	39	79	4	.265	.382
2 Pinky Whitney	3B111,2B1	R	31	114	411	44	121	17	3	6	59	37	33	2	.294	.394
2 Chuck Klein	OF117	L	31	117	492	83	152	30	7	20	86	33	45	6	.309	.520
Lou Chiozza	OF90,2B33,3B26	L	26	144	572	83	170	32	6	1	48	37	39	17	.297	.379
Johnny Moore	OF112	L	34	124	472	85	151	24	3	16	66	26	22	1	.328	.494
Earl Grace	C65	R	29	86	221	24	55	11	0	4	32	34	20	0	.249	.353
Ernie Sulik	OF105	L	25	122	404	69	116	14	4	6	36	40	22	4	.287	.386
Jimmie Wilson	C63,1B1	R	35	85	230	25	64	12	0	1	27	12	21	5	.278	.343
Bill Atwood	C53	R	24	71	192	21	58	9	2	2	29	11	15	0	.302	.401
Bucky Walters	P40,2B1,3B1	R	27	64	121	12	29	10	1	1	16	7	15	0	.240	.364
Claude Passeau	P49	R	27	50	78	6	22	3	0	2	7	2	29	0	.282	.397
2 Fabian Kowalik	P22,OF3	R	28	42	57	2	13	1	0	0	7	2	8	0	.228	.246
Charlie Sheerin	2B17,3B13,SS5	R	27	39	72	4	19	4	0	0	4	7	18	0	.264	.319
Ethan Allen	OF30	L	22	30	125	21	37	3	1	1	9	4	5	0	.296	.360
Stan Sperry	2B15	L	22	20	37	2	5	3	0	0	4	3	5	0	.135	.216
1 George Watkins	OF17	L	36	19	70	7	17	4	2	0	5	5	13	2	.243	.386
1 Mickey Haslin	2B12,3B5	R	26	16	64	6	22	1	1	0	5	3	0	0	.344	.391
1 Johnny Vergez	3B12	R	29	15	40	4	11	2	0	1	5	3	11	0	.275	.400
Morrie Arnovich	OF13	R	25	13	48	4	15	3	0	1	7	2	6	0	.313	.438

Walt Bashore 26 R 2-10, Gene Corbett 22 L 3-21, Joe Holden 23 L 0-1

NAME	T	AGE	W	L	PCT	SV	G	GS	CG	IP	H	BB	SO	SHO	ERA
		28	54	100	.351	14	154	154	51	1365	1630	515	454	7	4.64
Claude Passeau	R	27	11	15	.423	3	49	21	8	217	247	55	85	2	3.48
Bucky Walters	R	27	11	21	.344	0	40	33	15	258	284	115	66	4	4.26
Joe Bowman	R	26	9	20	.310	1	40	28	12	204	243	53	80	0	5.03
Orville Jorgens	R	28	8	8	.500	0	39	21	4	167	196	69	59	0	4.80
Syl Johnson	R	35	5	7	.417	7	39	8	1	111	129	29	48	0	4.30
Pete Sivess	R	22	3	4	.429	0	17	6	2	65	84	36	22	0	4.57
Euel Moore	R	28	2	3	.400	1	20	5	1	54	76	12	19	0	7.00
1 Curt Davis	R	32	2	4	.333	0	10	8	3	60	71	19	18	0	4.65
Hugh Mulcahy	R	22	1	1	.500	0	3	2	0	23	20	12	2	0	3.13
2 Ray Benge	R	34	1	4	.200	1	15	6	0	46	70	19	13	0	4.70
2 Fabian Kowalik	R	28	1	5	.167	0	22	8	1	77	100	31	19	0	5.38
2 Tom Zachary	L	40	0	1	.000	0	3	2	0	20	28	11	8	0	8.10
Hal Kelleher	R	23	0	5	.000	0	14	4	1	44	60	29	13	0	5.32
Herb Harris	L	23	0	0	—	0	4	0	0	7	14	5	0	0	10.29
Elmer Burkart	R	19	0	0	—	0	2	0	0	4	12	2	0	0	3.38
Pretzels Pezzullo	L	25	0	0	—	0	2	1	0	2	6	4	0	0	4.50
Lefty Bertrand	L	27	0	0	—	0	2	1	0	3	2	1	0	0	9.00

WORLD SERIES — NEW YORK (AL) 4 NEW YORK (NL) 2

LINE SCORES

TEAM	1	2	3	4	5	6	7	8	9	10	11	12	R	H	E

Game 1   September 30 at New York (NL)
NY (AL) 0 0 0 0 0 0 0 0 0 — 1 7 2
NY (NL) 0 0 0 0 1 1 0 4 X — 6 9 1
Ruffing / Hubbell

Game 2   October 2 at New York (NL)
NY (AL) 2 0 7 0 0 1 2 0 6 — 18 17 0
NY (NL) 0 1 0 3 0 0 0 0 0 — 4 6 1
Gomez / Schumacher, Smith (3), Coffman (3), Gabler (5), Gumbert (9)

Game 3   October 3 at New York (AL)
NY (NL) 0 0 0 0 1 0 0 0 0 — 1 11 0
NY (AL) 0 0 0 0 0 1 0 1 X — 2 4 0
Fitzsimmons / **Hadley**, Malone (9)

Game 4   October 4 at New York (AL)
NY (NL) 0 0 0 1 0 0 0 1 0 — 2 7 1
NY (AL) 0 1 3 0 0 0 0 1 X — 5 10 1
Hubbell, Gabler (8) / **Pearson**

Game 5   October 5 at New York (AL)
NY (NL) 3 0 0 0 0 0 1 0 0 0 — 5 8 3
NY (AL) 0 1 1 0 0 2 0 0 0 0 — 4 10 1
Schumacher / Ruffing, **Malone** (7)

Game 6   October 6 at New York (NL)
NY (AL) 0 2 1 2 0 0 0 1 7 — 13 17 2
NY (NL) 2 0 0 0 0 1 1 1 0 — 5 9 1
Gomez, Murphy (7) / **Fitzsimmons**, Castleman (4), Coffman (9), Gumbert (9)

COMPOSITE BATTING

NAME	POS	G	AB	R	H	2B	3B	HR	RBI	BA
New York (AL) Totals		6	215	43	65	8	1	7	41	.302
DiMaggio	OF	6	26	3	9	3	0	0	3	.346
Crosetti	SS	6	26	5	7	2	0	0	1	.269
Rolfe	3B	6	25	5	10	0	0	0	4	.400
Dickey	C	6	25	5	3	0	0	1	5	.120
Selkirk	OF	6	24	6	8	0	1	2	3	.333
Gehrig	1B	6	24	5	7	1	0	2	7	.292
Powell	OF	6	22	8	10	1	0	1	5	.455
Lazzeri	2B	6	20	4	5	0	0	1	7	.250
Gomez	P	2	8	1	2	0	0	0	3	.250
Ruffing	P	3	5	0	0	0	0	0	0	.000
Pearson	P	1	4	0	2	1	0	0	0	.500
Murphy	P	1	2	1	1	0	0	0	0	.500
Hadley	P	1	2	0	0	0	0	0	0	.000
Malone	P	2	1	0	1	0	0	0	0	1.000
Johnson	PR-PH	2	1	0	0	0	0	0	0	.000
Seeds	PR	1	0	0	0	0	0	0	0	—
New York (NL) Totals		6	203	23	50	9	0	4	20	.246
Moore	OF	6	28	4	6	2	0	0	1	.214
Terry	1B	6	25	1	6	0	0	0	5	.240
Ott	OF	6	23	4	7	2	0	1	3	.304
Bartell	SS	6	21	5	8	3	0	0	1	.381
Jackson	3B	6	21	1	4	0	0	0	2	.190
Whitehead	2B	6	21	1	1	0	0	0	0	.048
Mancuso	C	6	19	3	5	2	0	0	2	.263
Ripple	OF	5	12	3	4	1	0	1	3	.333
Hubbell	P	2	6	0	2	0	0	0	1	.333
Leiber	OF	2	6	0	0	0	0	0	0	.000
Fitzsimmons	P	2	4	0	2	0	0	0	0	.500
Schumacher	P	2	4	1	1	0	0	0	2	.250
Leslie	PH	3	3	0	2	0	0	0	1	.667
Koenig	2B	2	3	0	1	0	0	0	0	.333
Castleman	P	2	2	0	1	0	0	0	0	.500
Davis	PR-PH	4	2	2	1	0	0	0	0	.500
Danning	C	1	1	0	0	0	0	0	0	.000
Mayo	3B	1	1	0	0	0	0	0	0	.000
Coffman	P	2	1	0	0	0	0	0	0	—
Gabler	P	2	1	0	0	0	0	0	0	—
Gumbert	P	2	0	0	0	0	0	0	0	—
Smith	P	1	0	0	0	0	0	0	0	—

COMPOSITE PITCHING

NAME	G	IP	H	BB	SO	W	L	SV	ERA
New York (AL) Totals	6	54	50	21	33	4	2	2	3.33
Gomez	2	15.1	14	11	9	2	0	0	4.70
Ruffing	2	14	16	5	12	1	1	0	4.50
Pearson	1	9	7	2	7	1	0	0	2.00
Hadley	1	8	10	1	2	1	0	0	1.12
Malone	2	5	2	1	2	0	1	1	1.80
Murphy	1	2.2	1	2	1	0	0	1	3.38
New York (NL) Totals	6	53	65	26	35	2	4	0	6.79
Hubbell	2	16	15	2	10	1	1	0	2.25
Schumacher	2	12	13	10	11	1	1	0	5.25
Fitzsimmons	2	11.2	13	2	5	0	2	0	5.40
Gabler	2	5	7	4	0	0	0	0	7.20
Castleman	2	4.1	3	2	5	0	0	0	2.08
Gumbert	2	1.2	4	3	2	0	0	0	36.00
Coffman	2	1.2	5	1	0	0	1	0	32.40
Smith	1	0.1	2	1	0	0	0	0	81.00

1937 The Battery Trouble in Detroit

The Detroit Tigers had hoped to improve on their second-place finish of 1936 and, once again, claim the junior circuit crown. But battery trouble shorted out their acceleration before they began. Star right-hander Schoolboy Rowe, who had won 19 games in the previous year, spent most of 1937 on the sidelines with an ailing wing. With Rowe's career up in the air, Mickey Cochrane's came to a sudden, but definite end on May 25, when a pitched ball fractured the catcher-manager's skull and placed his life in doubt. He recovered in time to resume control of the team late in the season, but never again would the great backstop catch. Rookie Rudy York was thrown into the catching breach and responded with 35 homers and 103 runs batted in, offsetting his defensive limitations behind the plate. Hank Greenberg socked 40 homers and a league-leading 183 RBI's, Gee Walker drove in 113 runs, and Charlie Gehringer led the loop with a .371 batting average. But the Tigers finished 13 games behind New York, consigned to second place by a mediocre pitching staff which missed Rowe badly.

No one was surprised at the repeat of the Yankees as champions, but the development of Joe DiMaggio into the premier American League outfielder raised some eyebrows. In his second season, Joltin' Joe polled 46 homers, tops in the league, and drove 167 Yankees home with his .346 batting. In addition, his center fielding was flawless and his base running heads-up. Lou Gehrig and Bill Dickey both had big years in average and power, and the Yankee lineup proved just as potent as Detroit's. But unlike the Tigers, New York also had pitching and boasted of the league's only two 20-game winners in Lefty Gomez and Red Ruffing. Gomez, in addition, won the E.R.A. title with a 2.33 mark. The rest of the staff was plagued by injuries, but Johnny Murphy made manager Joe McCarthy's job easier with effective relief work behind his ten saves. Ex-Yankee Johnny Allen continued to shine in a Cleveland uniform as he experienced a sensational season, winning 15 games before losing his only game.

Manager Bill Terry led his charges to a third National League pennant in his sixth year at the rudder of the Giant ship, edging the Cubs by defeating them head-on in late September in a series in New York. The repeat pennant was engineered without any super heroics. Terry got consistently good seasons from the entire squad, while Mel

Ott provided the offensive leadership with 31 home runs and 95 runs batted in. Additionally, Ott unselfishly consented to move to third base in mid-season to plug up a sore gap at the hot corner. While Dick Bartell held the infield together with his solid play at shortstop, the Jints flashed two left-handed aces in Carl Hubbell and rookie Cliff Melton. Hubbell used his screwball to rack up a league-high 22 wins, while Melton chalked up 20 victories in his maiden season.

The Cubs had enough hitting to finish only three games out, but they missed the pitching of Lon Warneke, whom they had traded to St. Louis during the winter. Pittsburgh finished third with the Waners, Big Poison and Little Poison, while the batting of Joe "Ducky" Medwick, who won the Triple Crown, and Johnny Mize, who brought close behind, brought the Cardinals home in the first division despite an injury to Dizzy Dean. The ace pitcher suffered a broken toe in the All-Star Game when hit by Earl Averill's line drive. When he tried to resume pitching before the toe fully healed, he strained his arm and his brilliant, but short, career was effectively finished. Boston had no attack but came up with two 30-year-old rookies who won 20 games in Lou Fette and Jim Turner, the last of whom captured the league E.R.A. title with a 2.38 performance.

Whereas the Yanks beat the Giants in six games in 1936, they needed only five games to turn the trick in 1937. Yankee thunder, as usual, drove home a plethora of runs, scoring 28 to the Giants' 12. While Lefty Gomez made two complete winning appearances, 34-year-old Tony Lazzeri starred offensively by hitting .400 in his final fling as a Yankee before joining the Cubs as a player-coach.

1937 AMERICAN LEAGUE

NAME	G by Pos	B	AGE	G	AB	R	H	2B	3B	HR	RBI	BB	SO	SB	BA	SA
NEW YORK	1st 102-52 .662			JOE McCARTHY												
	TOTALS		29	157	5487	979	1554	282	73	174	922	709	607	60	.283	.456
Lou Gehrig	1B157	L	34	157	569	138	200	37	9	37	159	127	49	4	.351	.643
Tony Lazzeri	2B125	R	33	126	446	56	109	21	3	14	70	71	76	7	.244	.399
Frankie Crosetti	SS147	R	26	149	611	127	143	29	5	11	49	86	105	13	.234	.352
Red Rolfe	3B154	L	28	154	648	143	179	34	10	4	62	90	53	4	.276	.378
Myril Hoag	OF99	R	29	106	362	48	109	19	8	3	46	33	33	4	.301	.423
Joe DiMaggio	OF150	R	22	151	621	151	215	35	15	46	167	64	37	3	.346	.673
Jake Powell (IL)	OF94	R	29	97	365	54	96	22	3	3	45	25	36	7	.263	.364
Bill Dickey	C137	L	30	140	530	87	176	35	2	29	133	73	22	3	.332	.570
George Selkirk (BC)	OF69	L	29	78	256	49	84	13	5	18	68	34	24	8	.328	.629
Tommy Henrich (JJ)	OF59	L	27	67	206	39	66	14	5	8	42	35	17	4	.320	.553
Don Heffner	2B38, SS13, 3B3, 1B1, OF1	R	26	60	201	23	50	6	5	0	21	19	19	1	.249	.328
Red Ruffing	P31	R	33	54	129	11	26	3	0	1	10	13	21	0	.202	.248
Joe Glenn	C24	R	28	25	53	6	15	2	2	0	4	4	10	1	.283	.396
Jack Saltzgaver	1B4	L	32	17	11	6	2	0	0	0	0	3	4	0	.182	.182
Art Jorgens	C11	R	32	13	23	3	3	1	0	0	3	2	5	0	.130	.174
1 Roy Johnson	OF12	L	34	12	51	5	15	3	0	0	6	3	2	1	.294	.353
Babe Dahlgren		R	25	1	1	0	0	0	0	0	0	0	0	0	.000	.000
DETROIT	2nd 89-65 .578 13			MICKEY COCHRANE												
	TOTALS		29	155	5516	935	1611	309	62	150	873	656	711	89	.292	.452
Hank Greenberg	1B154	R	26	154	594	137	200	49	14	40	183	102	101	8	.337	.668
Charlie Gehringer	2B142	L	34	144	564	133	209	40	1	14	96	90	25	11	.371	.520
Billy Rogell	SS146	B	32	146	536	85	148	30	7	8	64	83	48	5	.276	.403
Mary Owen	3B106	R	31	107	396	48	114	22	5	1	45	41	24	3	.288	.376
Pete Fox	OF143	R	27	148	628	116	208	39	8	12	82	41	43	12	.331	.476
Jo-Jo White	OF82	L	28	94	305	50	75	5	7	0	21	50	40	12	.246	.308
Gee Walker	OF151	R	29	151	635	105	213	42	4	18	113	41	74	23	.335	.499
Rudy York	C54, 3B41	R	23	104	375	72	115	18	3	35	103	41	52	3	.307	.651
Goose Goslin	OF40, 1B1	L	36	79	181	30	43	11	1	4	35	35	18	0	.238	.376
Chet Laabs	OF62	R	25	72	242	31	58	13	5	8	37	24	66	6	.240	.434
Birdie Tebbetts	C48	R	24	50	162	15	31	5	3	2	16	10	13	0	.191	.290
Ray Hayworth	C28	R	33	30	78	9	21	2	0	1	8	14	15	0	.269	.333
Mickey Cochrane (PB)	C27	L	34	27	98	27	30	10	1	2	12	25	4	0	.306	.490
Cliff Bolton	C13	L	30	27	57	6	15	2	0	1	7	8	6	0	.263	.351
2 Charlie Gelbert	SS16	R	31	20	47	4	4	2	0	0	1	5	4	0	.085	.128
1 Gil English	2B38, 3B6	R	27	18	65	6	17	1	0	1	6	6	4	1	.262	.323
Babe Herman	OF2	L	34	17	20	2	6	3	0	0	3	1	6	2	.300	.450
Flea Clifton	3B7, SS4, 2B3	R	27	15	43	4	5	1	0	0	1	4	10	1	.116	.140
CHICAGO	3rd 86-68 .558 16			JIMMY DYKES												
	TOTALS		30	154	5277	780	1478	280	76	67	726	549	447	70	.280	.400
Zeke Bonura	1B115	R	28	116	447	79	154	41	2	19	100	49	24	5	.345	.573
Jackie Hayes	2B143	R	30	143	573	63	131	27	4	2	79	41	37	1	.229	.300
Luke Appling	SS154	R	30	154	574	98	182	42	8	4	77	86	28	18	.317	.439
Tony Piet	3B86, 2B13	R	30	100	332	34	78	15	1	4	38	32	36	14	.235	.322
Dixie Walker	OF154	L	26	154	593	105	179	28	16	9	95	78	26	1	.302	.449
Mike Kreevich	OF138	R	29	144	583	94	176	29	16	12	73	43	45	10	.302	.468
Rip Radcliff	OF139	L	31	144	584	105	190	38	10	4	79	53	25	6	.325	.445
Luke Sewell	C118	R	36	122	412	51	111	21	6	1	61	46	18	4	.269	.357
Larry Rosenthal (LJ)	OF25	L	27	58	97	20	28	5	5	4	9	9	20	1	.289	.402
Mule Haas	1B32, OF2	L	33	54	111	18	23	3	3	0	15	16	10	1	.207	.288
Boze Berger	3B40, 2B1, SS1	R	27	52	130	19	31	5	0	5	13	15	24	1	.238	.392
Jimmy Dykes	1B15, 3B11	R	40	30	85	10	26	5	0	1	23	9	7	0	.306	.400
Merv Connors	3B28	R	23	28	103	12	24	4	1	2	14	19	19	2	.233	.350
Tony Rensa	C23	R	35	26	57	10	17	5	1	0	5	8	4	0	.298	.421
Hank Steinbacher	OF15	L	24	26	73	13	19	4	1	0	9	4	7	2	.260	.384
Merv Shea	C25	R	36	25	71	7	15	5	0	0	15	10	11	0	.211	.225

NAME	T	AGE	W	L	PCT	SV	G	GS	CG	IP	H	BB	SO	SHO	ERA
		30	102	52	.662	21	157	157	82	1396	1417	506	652	15	3.65
Lefty Gomez	L	28	21	11	.656	0	34	34	25	278	233	93	194	6	2.33
Red Ruffing (HO)	R	33	20	7	.741	0	31	31	22	256	242	68	131	4	2.99
Johnny Murphy	R	28	13	4	.765	10	39	4	0	110	121	50	36	0	4.17
Bump Hadley	R	32	11	8	.579	0	29	25	6	178	199	83	70	0	5.31
Monte Pearson	R	28	9	3	.750	1	22	20	7	145	145	64	71	1	3.17
Kemp Wicker	L	30	7	3	.700	0	16	10	6	88	107	26	14	1	4.40
Spud Chandler	R	29	7	4	.636	0	12	10	6	82	79	20	31	2	2.85
Frank Makosky	R	27	5	2	.714	3	26	1	1	58	64	24	27	0	4.97
Pat Malone	R	34	4	4	.500	6	28	9	3	92	109	35	49	0	5.48
2 Ivy Andrews	R	30	3	2	.600	1	11	5	3	49	49	17	17	1	3.12
Joe Vance	R	31	1	0	1.000	0	2	2	0	15	11	9	3	0	3.00
Johnny Broaca (JT)	R	27	1	4	.200	0	7	6	3	44	58	17	9	0	4.70
		27	89*	65	.578	11	155	155	70	1378	1521	635	485	6	4.87
Roxie Lawson	R	31	18	7	.720	1	37	29	15	217	236	115	68	0	5.27
Elden Auker	R	26	17	9	.654	1	39	32	19	253	250	97	73	1	3.88
Tommy Bridges	R	30	15	12	.556	0	34	31	18	245	267	91	138	3	4.08
George Gill	R	28	11	4	.733	1	31	10	4	128	146	42	40	1	4.50
Boots Poffenberger	R	22	10	5	.667	3	29	16	5	137	147	79	35	0	4.66
Slick Coffman	R	26	7	5	.583	0	28	5	1	101	121	39	22	0	4.37
Jack Wade	L	25	7	10	.412	0	33	25	7	165	160	107	69	1	5.40
Jack Russell	R	31	5	2	.286	4	25	0	0	40	63	20	10	0	7.65
Clyde Hatter	L	28	1	0	1.000	0	9	0	0	9	17	11	4	0	12.00
Schoolboy Rowe (AJ)	R	27	1	4	.200	0	10	2	1	31	49	9	6	0	8.71
Pat McLaughlin	R	26	0	2	.000	0	10	2	0	33	39	16	8	0	6.27
Vic Sorrell	R	36	0	2	.000	1	7	2	0	17	25	8	11	0	9.00
1 Bob Logan	L	27	0	0	—	0	1	0	0	1	1	1	1	0	0.00

*1 win by forfeit

		29	86	68	.558	21	154	154	70	1351	1435	532	533	15	4.17
Monte Stratton	R	25	15	5	.750	0	22	21	14	165	142	37	69	5	2.40
Vern Kennedy	R	30	14	13	.519	0	32	30	15	221	238	124	114	1	5.09
Ted Lyons	R	36	12	7	.632	0	22	22	11	169	182	45	45	0	4.15
Thornton Lee	L	30	12	10	.545	0	30	25	13	205	209	60	80	2	3.51
John Whitehead	R	28	11	8	.579	0	26	24	8	166	191	56	45	3	4.07
Bill Dietrich	R	27	8	10	.444	1	29	20	7	143	162	72	62	1	4.91
Clint Brown	R	33	7	7	.500	18	53	0	0	100	92	36	51	0	3.42
Sugar Cain	R	30	4	2	.667	0	18	6	1	69	88	15	17	0	6.13
Johnny Rigney	R	22	2	5	.286	1	22	4	0	31	107	46	38	0	4.95
Bill Cox	R	24	1	0	1.000	1	3	2	1	13	9	5	8	0	0.69
Italo Chelini	L	22	0	0	—	0	9	0	0	15	10	3	9	0	10.00
George Gick	R	21	0	0	—	1	2	0	0	7	6	5	3	0	0.00

CLEVELAND — 4th 83-71 .539 19 — STEVE O'NEILL

NAME	G by Pos	B	AGE	G	AB	R	H	2B	3B	HR	RBI	BB	SO	SB	BA	SA
TOTALS			28	156	5353	817	1499	304	76	103	754	570	551	76	.280	.423
Hal Trosky	1B152	L	28	153	601	104	179	36	9	32	128	65	60	3	.298	.547
John Kroner	2B64, 3B11	R	28	86	283	29	67	14	1	2	26	22	25	1	.237	.314
Lyn Lary	SS156	R	30	156	644	110	187	46	7	8	77	88	64	18	.290	.421
Odell Hale	3B90, 2B64	R	28	154	561	74	150	32	4	6	62	56	41	9	.267	.371
Bruce Campbell	OF123	L	27	134	448	82	135	42	11	4	61	67	49	4	.301	.471
Earl Averill	OF156	R	35	156	609	121	182	33	11	21	92	88	65	5	.299	.493
Moose Solters	OF149	R	31	152	589	90	190	42	11	20	109	42	56	6	.323	.533
Frankie Pytlak	C115	R	28	125	397	60	125	15	6	1	44	52	15	16	.315	.390
Roy Hughes	3B58, 2B32	R	26	104	346	57	96	12	6	1	40	40	22	11	.277	.355
Billy Sullivan	C38, 1B4, 3B1	L	26	72	168	26	48	12	3	3	22	17	7	1	.286	.446
Roy Weatherly	OF38, 3B1	L	22	53	134	19	27	4	0	5	13	6	14	1	.201	.343
Jeff Heath	OF14	L	22	20	61	8	14	1	4	0	8	0	9	0	.230	.377
Joe Becker	C12	R	29	18	33	3	11	2	1	0	2	3	4	0	.333	.485
Hugh Alexander	OF3	R	19	7	11	0	1	0	0	0	0	0	5	1	.091	.091
Blas Monaco	2B3	B	21	5	7	0	2	0	1	0	2	0	0	0	.286	.571
Ken Keltner	3B1	R	20	1	1	0	0	0	0	0	1	0	0	0	.000	.000
Bill Sodd		R	22	1	0	0	0	0	0	0	0	0	0	0	.000	.000

NAME	T	AGE	W	L	PCT	SV	G	GS	CG	IP	H	BB	SO	SHO	ERA
TOTALS		30	83	71	.539	15	156	156	64	1365	1529	566	630	4	4.39
Johnny Allen (IL)	R	32	15	1	.938	0	24	20	14	173	157	60	87	0	2.55
Mel Harder	R	27	15	12	.556	2	38	30	13	234	269	86	95	0	4.27
Willis Hudlin	R	31	12	11	.522	2	35	23	10	176	213	43	31	2	4.09
Bob Feller (AJ)	R	18	9	7	.563	1	26	19	9	149	116	106	150	0	3.38
Denny Galehouse	R	25	9	14	.391	3	36	29	7	201	238	83	78	0	4.57
Joe Herving	R	36	8	4	.667	5	40	0	0	73	92	30	35	0	4.81
Earl Whitehill	L	37	8	8	.500	2	33	22	6	147	189	80	53	1	6.49
Ivy Andrews	R	30	3	4	.429	0	12	4	1	60	76	9	16	1	4.35
Whit Wyatt	R	29	2	3	.400	0	29	4	2	73	67	40	52	0	4.44
Lloyd Brown	L	32	2	6	.250	0	31	5	2	77	107	27	32	0	6.55
1 Carl Fischer	L	31	0	1	.000	0	2	0	0	3	2	1	1	0	18.00
Ken Jungels	R	21	0	0	—	0	3	0	0	3	3	1	0	0	6.00

BOSTON — 5th 80-72 .526 21 — JOE CRONIN

NAME	G by Pos	B	AGE	G	AB	R	H	2B	3B	HR	RBI	BB	SO	SB	BA	SA
TOTALS			28	154	5354	821	1506	269	64	100	769	601	557	79	.281	.411
Jimmie Foxx	1B150, C1	R	29	150	569	111	162	24	6	36	127	99	96	10	.285	.583
Eric McNair	2B106, SS9, 3B4, 1B1	R	28	126	455	60	133	29	4	12	76	30	33	10	.292	.453
Joe Cronin	SS148	R	30	148	570	102	175	40	4	18	110	84	73	5	.307	.486
Pinky Higgins	3B152	R	28	153	570	88	172	33	5	9	106	76	51	2	.302	.425
2 Ben Chapman	OF112, SS1	R	28	113	423	76	130	23	11	7	57	57	35	27*	.307	.463
Doc Cramer	OF133	L	31	143	560	90	171	22	11	0	51	35	14	8	.305	.384
Buster Mills	OF120	R	28	123	505	85	149	26	8	7	58	48	42	11	.295	.418
Gene Desautels	C94	R	30	96	305	33	74	10	3	0	27	36	26	1	.243	.295
Dom Dallessandro	OF35	L	23	68	147	18	34	7	1	0	11	27	16	2	.231	.292
Bobby Doerr	2B47	R	19	55	147	22	33	5	1	2	14	18	25	2	.224	.313
Fabian Gaffke	OF50	R	23	54	184	32	53	10	4	6	34	15	25	1	.288	.484
Moe Berg	C47	R	35	47	141	13	36	3	1	0	20	5	4	0	.255	.291
1 Mel Almada	OF27, 1B4	L	24	32	110	17	26	6	2	1	9	15	6	0	.236	.355
Oscar Melillo	SS2, 3B2	R	37	26	56	8	14	2	0	0	6	5	4	0	.250	.286
1 Rick Ferrell	C18	R	31	18	65	8	20	2	0	1	4	15	4	0	.308	.385
Johnny Peacock	C9	R	27	9	32	3	10	2	1	0	3	1	0	0	.313	.438
Stew Bowers		R	22	10	1	0	0	0	0	0	0	0	0	0	—	—
Bob Daughters		R	22	11	0	0	0	0	0	0	0	0	0	0	—	—

NAME	T	AGE	W	L	PCT	SV	G	GS	CG	IP	H	BB	SO	SHO	ERA
TOTALS		30	80	72	.526	14	154	154	74	1366	1518	597	682	5	4.48
Lefty Grove	L	37	17	9	.654	0	32	32	21	262	269	83	153	2	3.02
Jack Wilson	R	25	16	10	.615	7	51	21	14	221	209	119	137	1	3.71
2 Bobo Newsom	R	29	13	10	.565	0	30	27#14	14	208	193	119#	127	1	4.37
Johnny Marcum	R	27	13	11	.542	3	37	23	9	184	230	47	59	1	4.84
Archie McKain	L	26	8	8	.500	2	36	18	3	137	152	64	66	0	4.66
Rube Walberg	L	40	5	7	.417	1	32	11	3	105	143	46	46	0	5.57
1 Wes Ferrell	R	29	3	6	.333	0	12	11	5▣	73▣	111▣	34	31	0	7.64
Fritz Ostermueller	L	29	3	7	.300	1	25	7	2	87	101	44	29	0	4.97
Jim Henry	R	27	1	0	1.000	0	3	1	1	15	15	11	8	0	5.40
2 Joe Gonzales	R	22	1	2	.333	0	8	2	2	31	37	11	11	0	4.35
Tommy Thomas	R	37	2	0	.000	0	3	2	1	11	16	4	4	0	4.09
Ted Olson	R	24	0	—		0	2	0	0	12	15	11	0	0	7.31

* Chapman, also with Washington, league leader in SB with 35

Newsom, also with Washington, league leader in GS (37) and BB (167)

▣ Ferrell, also with Washington, league leader in CG (26) IP (281), and H (325)

WASHINGTON — 6th 73-80 .477 28.5 — BUCKY HARRIS

NAME	G by Pos	B	AGE	G	AB	R	H	2B	3B	HR	RBI	BB	SO	SB	BA	SA
TOTALS			29	158	5578	757	1559	245	84	47	691	591	503	61	.279	.379
Joe Kuhel	1B136	L	31	136	547	73	155	24	11	6	61	63	39	6	.283	.400
Buddy Myer	2B119, OF1	L	33	125	430	54	126	16	10	1	65	78	41	2	.293	.384
Cecil Travis	SS129	L	23	135	526	72	181	27	7	3	66	39	34	3	.344	.439
Buddy Lewis	3B156	L	20	156	668	107	210	32	6	10	79	52	44	11	.314	.425
John Stone	OF137	L	31	139	542	84	179	33	15	6	88	66	36	6	.330	.480
2 Mel Almada	OF100	L	24	100	433	74	134	21	4	8	33	38	21	12	.309	.404
Al Simmons	OF102	R	35	103	419	60	117	21	10	8	84	27	35	3	.279	.434
2 Rick Ferrell	C84	R	31	86	279	31	64	6	1	1	32	50	18	1	.229	.262
Fred Sington	OF64	R	27	78	228	27	54	15	4	3	36	37	33	1	.237	.377
Wally Millies	C56	R	30	59	179	21	40	7	1	0	28	9	15	1	.223	.274
2 Wes Ferrell	P25	R	29	53	106	7	27	5	0	0	16	9	18	0	.255	.302
Ossie Bluege	SS28, 1B2, 3B2	R	36	42	127	12	36	4	2	1	13	13	19	1	.283	.370
John Mihalic	2B28, SS3	R	25	38	107	13	27	5	2	0	8	17	9	2	.252	.336
1 Ben Chapman	OF32	R	28	35	130	23	34	7	1	0	12	26	7	8*	.262	.331
1 Jesse Hill	OF21	R	30	33	92	24	20	2	1	1	4	13	16	2	.217	.293
Jimmy Wasdell	1B21, OF7	L	23	32	110	13	28	4	4	2	12	7	13	0	.255	.418
Geroge Case	OF22	R	21	22	90	14	26	6	2	0	11	3	5	2	.289	.400
Shanty Hogan	C21	R	31	21	66	4	10	4	0	0	5	6	8	0	.152	.212
Jimmy Bloodworth	2B14	R	19	15	50	3	11	2	1	0	3	8	5	0	.220	.300
1 Johnny Riddle	C8	R	31	8	26	2	7	0	0	0	3	0	2	0	.269	.269
Herb Crompton	C2	R	25	2	3	0	1	0	0	0	0	0	0	0	.333	.333
Milt Gray	C2	R	23	2	6	0	0	0	0	0	0	0	1	0	.000	.000
Mike Guerra	C1	R	24	1	3	0	0	0	0	0	0	0	0	0	.000	.000
Jerry Lynn	2B1	R	21	1	3	0	2	1	0	0	0	0	0	0	.667	1.000
Alex Sabo	C1	R	24	1	0	0	0	0	0	0	0	0	1	0	—	—
Frank Trechock	SS1	R	21	1	4	0	2	0	0	0	0	0	1	0	.500	.500

NAME	T	AGE	W	L	PCT	SV	G	GS	CG	IP	H	BB	SO	SHO	ERA
TOTALS		29	73	80	.477	14	158	158	75	1399	1498	676	535	5	4.57
Jimmy DeShong	R	27	14	15	.483	1	37	34	20	264	290	124	86	0	4.91
Monty Weaver	R	31	12	9	.571	0	30	26	9	189	197	70	44	0	4.19
2 Wes Ferrell	R	29	11	13	.458	0	25	24	21▣	208▣	214▣	88	92	0	3.93
Pete Appleton	R	33	8	15	.348	2	35	18	7	168	167	72	62	4	4.93
Ed Linke	R	25	6	1	.857	3	36	7	0	129	158	59	61	0	5.58
Joe Krakauskas	L	22	4	1	.800	0	5	4	3	40	33	22	18	0	2.70
Ken Chase	L	23	4	3	.571	0	14	9	4	76	74	60	43	0	4.14
2 Carl Fischer	L	31	4	5	.444	2	17	11	2	72	74	31	30	0	4.38
Bill Phebus	R	27	3	2	.600	1	6	5	1	41	33	24	12	1	2.20
1 Bobo Newsom	R	29	3	4	.429	0	11	10#	3	68	76	48#	39	0	5.82
Sid Cohen	L	30	2	4	.333	4	33	0	0	55	64	7	22	0	3.11
Joe Kohlman	R	24	1	0	1.000	0	2	1	0	13	15	3	0	0	4.15
Bucky Jacobs	R	24	1	1	.500	0	11	1	0	22	26	11	6	0	4.91
Dick Lanahan	L	25	0	1	.000	0	2	1	0	11	16	13	2	0	13.10
Red Anderson	R	24	0	1	.000	0	2	1	0	11	11	11	3	0	6.54
1 Joe Cascarella	R	30	0	5	.000	0	10	4	1	32	50	23	10	0	8.15

* Chapman, also with Boston, league leader in SB with 35

Newsom, also with Boston, league leader in GS (37) and BB (167)

▣ Ferrell, also with Boston, league leader in CG (26), IP (281), and H (325)

PHILADELPHIA — 7th 54-97 .358 46.5 — CONNIE MACK

NAME	G by Pos	B	AGE	G	AB	R	H	2B	3B	HR	RBI	BB	SO	SB	BA	SA
TOTALS			27	154	5228	699	1398	278	60	94	649	583	557	95	.267	.397
Chubby Dean	1B78, P2	L	21	104	309	36	81	14	4	2	31	42	10	2	.262	.353
Rusty Peters	2B70, 3B31, SS13	R	22	116	339	39	88	17	6	3	43	41	59	4	.260	.372
Skeeter Newsome	SS122	R	26	122	438	53	111	22	1	1	30	37	22	11	.253	.315
Bill Werber	3B125, OF3	R	29	128	493	85	144	31	4	7	70	74	39	35*	.292	.414
Wally Moses	OF154	L	26	154	649	113	208	48	13	25	86	54	38	9	.320	.550
2 Jesse Hill	OF68	R	30	70	242	32	71	12	3	1	37	31	20	16	.293	.380
Bob Johnson	OF133, 2B2	R	31	138	477	91	146	32	6	25	108	98	56	9	.306	.556
Earle Brucker (BH)	C92	R	36	102	317	40	82	16	5	8	37	48	30	1	.259	.397
Lou Finney	1B50, OF39, 2B1	L	26	92	379	53	95	14	9	1	20	20	16	2	.251	.343
Jack Rothrock	OF58, 2B1, 3B1	B	32	88	233	28	62	15	0	0	21	28	15	1	.267	.332
Lynn Nelson	P30, OF6	R	32	74	113	18	40	6	2	4	29	6	13	1	.354	.549
Frankie Hayes	C56	R	22	56	162	3	35	5	0	0	11	13	8	1	.216	.247
Wayne Ambler	2B16, SS15, 3B2	R	23	38	94	5	7	3	0	0	3	2	9	0	.130	.185
Warren Huston	SS19, 2B9, OF5	R	25	38	94	8	11	0	1	2	13	4	17	0	.117	.202
Ace Parker	2B33	R	33	34	117	15	31	7	0	1	14	17	10	0	.265	.350
Bill Cissell	2B33	R	33	34	117	15	31	6	3	3	14	13	14	1	.306	.520
Gene Hasson	1B28	L	21	28	98	12	30	6	3	3	14	11	14	1	.306	.520
Bill Conroy	C18, 1B1	R	22	26	60	4	12	1	1	0	5	7	9	1	.200	.250
Babe Barna	OF9, 1B1	L	22	14	36	10	14	2	0	2	9	2	5	0	.389	.611
Doyt Morris	OF3	R	20	6	13	0	2	0	0	0	0	3	1	0	.154	.154
Eddie Yount	OF2	R	21	4	7	1	2	0	0	0	1	0	1	0	.286	.286
Hal Wagner	C1	L	21	4	0	0	0	0	0	0	0	0	0	0	.000	.000

NAME	T	AGE	W	L	PCT	SV	G	GS	CG	IP	H	BB	SO	SHO	ERA
TOTALS		26	54	97	.358	9	154	154	65	1335	1490	613	469	6	4.85
Harry Kelley	R	31	13	21	.382	0	41	29	14	205	267	79	68	0	5.29
George Caster	R	29	12	19	.387	0	34	33	19	232	227	107	100	3	4.42
Bud Thomas	R	26	8	15	.348	0	35	26	6	170	208	52	54	0	4.98
Buck Ross	R	22	5	10	.333	0	28	22	7	147	183	63	37	1	4.90
Al Williams	R	23	4	1	.800	1	16	8	2	75	88	49	27	0	5.40
Lynn Nelson	R	32	4	9	.308	2	30	4	1	116	140	51	49	0	5.90
Eddie Smith	R	23	4	17	.190	5	38	23	14	197	178	90	79	3	3.93
Herman Fink	R	25	2	1	.667	1	28	3	1	80	82	35	18	0	4.05
Bill Kalfass	R	21	1	0	1.000	0	3	1	1	12	16	9	4	0	4.00
Chubby Dean	L	21	1	0	1.000	0	2	0	0	9	7	6	4	0	4.00
George Turbeville	R	22	0	4	.000	0	31	3	0	77	98	56	17	0	4.79
Randy Gumpert	R	19	0	0	—	0	10	1	0	12	16	15	5	0	12.00
Fred Archer	R	27	0	0	—	0	1	0	0	2	6	4	0	0	6.00
Woody Upchurch (AA) 26															

ST. LOUIS — 8th 46-108 .299 56 — ROGERS HORNSBY 25-52 .325 — JIM BOTTOMLEY 21-56 .273

NAME	G by Pos	B	AGE	G	AB	R	H	2B	3B	HR	RBI	BB	SO	SB	BA	SA
TOTALS			28	156	5510	715	1573	327	44	71	682	514	510	30	.285	.399
Harry Davis	1B112, OF1	L	29	137	489	89	124	25	3	1	35	71	26	7	.276	.364
Tom Carey	2B87, SS44, 3B1	R	28	130	487	54	134	24	1	1	40	21	26	1	.275	.335
Bill Knickerbocker	SS115, 2B6	R	25	121	441	53	128	29	5	4	61	30	32	3	.261	.365
Harlond Clift	3B155	R	24	155	571	103	175	36	7	29	118	98	80	8	.306	.546
Beau Bell	OF131, 1B26, 3B2	R	29	156	642	82	218	51	8	14	117	53	54	2	.340	.509
Sammy West	OF105	L	32	122	457	68	150	37	4	7	58	46	28	1	.328	.473
Joe Vosmik	OF143	R	27	144	594	81	193	47	9	4	93	49	38	2	.325	.455
Rollie Hemsley	C94, 1B2	R	30	104	334	30	74	12	3	3	28	25	29	0	.222	.302
Ethan Allen	OF78	R	33	103	320	39	101	18	4	0	31	21	17	3	.316	.378
Ben Huffman	C42	R	22	76	176	18	48	9	1	0	24	10	7	1	.273	.341
Jim Bottomley	1B24	L	37	65	109	10	26	9	1	1	12	18	15	1	.239	.330
Jerry Lipscomb	2B27, P3, 3B1	R	26	36	96	11	31	9	1	0	10	5	10	0	.323	.438
Red Barkley	2B24	R	24	31	101	9	27	6	0	0	14	4	17	1	.267	.327
Eddie Silber	OF21	R	23	22	83	10	26	5	2	0	7	5	13	0	.313	.337
Rogers Hornsby	2B17	R	41	20	56	7	18	3	0	1	11	7	5	0	.321	.429
Tony Giuliani	C19	R	24	19	53	4	16	2	1	0	4	6	2	0	.302	.321
Tommy Heath	C14	R	24	17	43	4	10	2	0	0	2	7	5	0	.233	.279
Mike Mazzera		L	23	7	7	1	2	0	0	0	1	0	1	0	.286	.571
Sam Harshany	C4	R	27	5	11	0	1	0	0	0	0	3	4	0	.091	.182
Tom Cafego	OF1	L	25	4	4	0	0	0	0	0	0	0	1	0	.000	.000

NAME	T	AGE	W	L	PCT	SV	G	GS	CG	IP	H	BB	SO	SHO	ERA
TOTALS		32	46	108	.299	8	156	156	55	1363	1770	653	468	2	6.00
Jim Walkup	R	27	9	12	.429	0	27	18	6	150	218	83	46	0	7.38
Oral Hildebrand	R	30	8	17	.320	1	28	27	12	201	228	87	75	1	5.15
Jack Knott	R	30	8	18	.308	2	38	22	8	191	220	91	74	0	4.90
Chief Hogsett	L	33	6	19	.240	2	37	26	8	177	245	75	68	1	6.31
Lou Koupal (BG)	R	38	6	9	.308	0	28	15	5	100	150	55	24	0	6.54
Julio Bonetti	R	25	4	11	.267	1	28	16	7	143	190	60	43	0	5.85
1 Sheriff Blake	R	37	2	2	.500	1	5	3	1	30	42	10	5	0	6.30
Bill Trotter	R	28	2	9	.182	1	14	12	3	122	150	50	37	0	5.83
Lefty Mills	L	27	1	1	.500	0	7	2	1	30	26	29	23	0	6.23
Russ Van Atta	L	31	1	3	.333	0	16	6	1	59	74	32	34	0	5.49
Les Tietje	R	26	1	3	.333	0	5	4	2	30	32	15	10	0	4.20
1 Tommy Thomas	R	37	1	1	.500	0	2	1	1	13	13	2	3	0	6.75
George Hennessey	R	26	0	1	.000	0	7	1	0	15	16	10	10	0	10.29
Emil Bildilli	R	24	0	1	.000	0	2	1	0	10	13	10	2	0	10.13
Bill Miller	R	27	0	1	.000	0	5	1	0	9	18	15	3	0	13.50
Harry Kimberlin	R	28	0	2	.000	0	15	2	0	49	73	19	11	0	6.43
Earl Caldwell	R	32	0	3	.000	0	9	2	1	39	39	13	8	0	6.83
Bill Strickland	R	30	0	0	—	0	4	0	0	8	12	3	1	0	4.50
Ed Baecht	R	30	0	0	—	0	3	1	0	11	16	7	4	0	13.50
Jerry Lipscomb	R	26	0	0	—	0	3	0	0	7	15	6	3	0	6.30
Bob Muncrief	R	21	0	0	—	0	2	1	0	8	7	7	2	0	4.50

NEW YORK — 1ST 95-57 .625 — BILL TERRY

NAME	G by Pos	B	AGE	G	AB	R	H	2B	3B	HR	RBI	BB	SO	SB	BA	SA
TOTALS			28	152	5329	732	1484	251	41	111	677	412	492	45	.278	.403
Johnny McCarthy	1B110	L	27	114	420	53	117	19	3	10	65	24	37	2	.279	.410
Burgess Whitehead	2B152	R	27	152	574	64	164	15	6	5	52	28	20	7	.286	.359
Dick Bartell	SS128	R	29	128	516	91	158	38	2	14	62	40	38	5	.306	.469
Lou Chiozza	3B93, OF12, 2B2	R	27	117	439	49	102	11	2	4	29	20	30	6	.232	.294
Mel Ott	OF91, 3B60	L	28	151	545	99	160	28	2	31	95	102	69	7	.294	.523
Jimmy Ripple	OF111	L	27	121	426	70	135	23	3	5	66	29	20	3	.317	.420
Jo-Jo Moore	OF140	L	28	151	580	89	180	37	10	6	57	46	27	7	.310	.440
Harry Danning	C86	R	25	93	292	30	84	12	4	8	51	18	20	1	.288	.438
Gus Mancuso (BG)	C81	R	31	86	287	30	80	17	1	4	39	17	20	1	.279	.387
Sam Leslie	1B44	L	31	72	191	25	59	7	2	3	30	20	12	1	.309	.414
2 Wally Berger	OF52	R	31	59	199	40	58	11	2	12	43	18	30	1	.291	.548
1 Kiddo Davis	OF37	R	35	56	76	20	20	0	0	0	9	10	7	1	.263	.395
Hank Leiber (PB)	OF46	R	26	51	184	24	54	7	3	4	32	15	27	1	.293	.429
Mickey Haslin	SS9, 2B4, 3B4	R	27	27	42	8	8	1	0	0	5	9	3	1	.190	.214
Blondy Ryan	SS19, 2B1, 3B1	R	31	21	75	10	18	3	1	1	13	6	8	0	.240	.347
2 Phil Weintraub	OF1	L	29	6	9	3	3	2	0	0	1	1	1	0	.333	.556
Ed Madjeski	C5	R	28	5	15	0	3	0	0	0	3	0	2	0	.200	.200

NAME	T	AGE	W	L	PCT	SV	G	GS	CG	IP	H	BB	SO	SHO	ERA
		28	95	57	.625	17	152	152	67	1361	1341	404	653	11	3.43
Carl Hubbell	L	34	22	8	.733	4	39	32	18	262	261	55	159	4	3.19
Cliff Melton	L	25	20	9	.690	7	46	27	14	248	216	55	142	2	2.61
Slick Castleman (AJ)	R	23	11	6	.647	0	23	23	10	160	148	33	78	2	3.32
Harry Gumbert	R	26	13	12	.520	1	38	29	10	218	222	89	100	1	3.59
Dick Coffman	R	30	8	3	.727	3	42	1	0	80	93	31	30	0	3.04
Al Smith	L	29	5	4	.556	0	33	9	2	86	91	30	41	0	4.19
1 Freddie Fitzsimmons	R	35	2	2	.500	0	7	7	1	27	28	8	13	1	4.67
2 Tom Baker	R	24	1	0	1.000	0	13	0	0	31	30	16	11	0	4.06
2 Don Brennan	R	33	1	0	1.000	0	6	0	0	9	12	9	1	0	7.00
2 Jumbo Brown	R	30	1	0	1.000	0	6	0	0	9	5	5	4	0	1.00
Bill Lohrman	R	24	1	1	.500	0	2	1	1	10	5	2	3	0	0.90
1 Ben Cantwell	R	35	0	1	.000	0	1	1	0	4	6	1	1	0	9.00
Hy Vandenberg	R	29	0	0	.000	0	8	1	1	8	10	6	2	0	7.88
1 Frank Gabler	R	25	0	0	—	0	6	0	0	9	20	2	3	0	10.00

CHICAGO — 2nd 93-68 .604 3 — CHARLIE GRIMM

NAME	G by Pos	B	AGE	G	AB	R	H	2B	3B	HR	RBI	BB	SO	SB	BA	SA
TOTALS			27	154	5349	811	1537	253	74	96	762	538	496	71	.287	.416
Ripper Collins (BN)	1B111	B	33	115	456	77	125	16	5	16	71	32	46	2	.274	.436
Billy Herman	2B137	R	27	138	564	106	189	35	5	8	65	56	22	2	.335	.479
Billy Jurges	SS128	R	29	129	450	53	134	18	10	1	65	42	41	2	.298	.389
Stan Hack	3B150, 1B4	L	27	154	582	106	173	27	6	2	63	83	42	16	.297	.375
Frank Demaree	OF154	R	27	154	615	104	199	36	6	17	115	57	31	6	.324	.485
Joe Marty	OF84	R	23	88	290	41	84	17	2	5	44	20	44	5	.290	.414
Augie Galan	OF140, 2B8, SS2	B	25	147	611	104	154	24	10	18	78	79	48	23	.252	.412
Gabby Hartnett	C103	R	36	110	356	47	126	21	6	12	82	43	19	0	.354	.548
Phil Cavarretta	OF55, 1B43	L	20	106	329	43	94	18	7	5	56	32	35	7	.286	.429
Ken O'Dea	C64	L	24	83	219	31	66	7	5	4	32	24	26	1	.301	.434
Lonny Frey	SS30, 2B13, 3B9, OF5	L	26	98	198	33	55	9	3	1	22	33	10	6	.278	.369
Tuck Stainback	OF49	R	25	72	160	18	37	7	1	0	14	7	16	3	.231	.425
John Bottarini	C18, OF1	R	28	26	40	3	11	3	0	1	7	5	0	0	.275	.425
Carl Reynolds	OF2	R	34	7	11	0	3	1	0	0	1	2	2	0	.273	.364
Bob Garbark (BW)		R	27	1	1	0	0	0	0	0	0	0	0	0	.000	.000
Dutch Meyer		R	21	1	0	0	0	0	0	0	0	0	0	0		

NAME	T	AGE	W	L	PCT	SV	G	GS	CG	IP	H	BB	SO	SHO	ERA
		30	93	61	.604	13	154	154	73	1381	1434	502	596	11	3.98
Tex Carleton	R	30	16	8	.667	0	32	27	18	208	183	94	105	4	3.16
Larry French	L	29	16	10	.615	0	42	28	11	208	229	65	100	4	3.98
Bill Lee	R	27	14	15	.483	3	42	34	17	272	289	73	108	2	3.54
Charlie Root	R	38	13	5	.722	5	43	15	5	179	173	32	74	0	3.37
Curt Davis (IL)	R	33	10	5	.667	1	28	14	8	124	138	30	32	0	4.06
Clay Bryant	R	25	9	3	.750	3	38	9	4	135	117	78	75	1	4.27
Clyde Shoun	L	25	7	7	.500	7	54	0	0	93	118	45	43	0	5.61
Roy Parmelee	R	30	7	8	.467	0	33	18	8	146	165	79	55	0	5.12
Kirby Higbe	R	22	1	0	1.000	0	5	1	0	9	5	4	2	0	5.40
2 Bob Logan	L	27	0	0	—	1	4	0	0	6	6	4	2	0	1.50
Newt Kimball	R	22	0	0	.000	0	2	0	0	5	12	1	0	0	10.80

PITTSBURGH — 3rd 86-68 .558 10 — PIE TRAYNOR

NAME	G by Pos	B	AGE	G	AB	R	H	2B	3B	HR	RBI	BB	SO	SB	BA	SA
TOTALS			29	154	5433	704	1550	223	86	47	649	463	480	32	.285	.384
Gus Suhr	1B151	L	29	151	575	69	160	28	14	5	97	83	42	2	.278	.402
Lee Handley	2B126, 3B1	R	23	127	480	59	120	21	12	3	37	37	40	5	.250	.363
Arky Vaughan	SS108, OF12	L	25	126	469	71	151	17	17	5	72	54	22	7	.322	.463
Bill Brubaker	3B115, SS3, 1B1	R	26	120	413	57	105	20	4	6	48	47	51	2	.254	.366
Paul Waner	OF150, 1B3	L	34	154	619	94	219	30	9	2	74	63	34	4	.354	.441
Lloyd Waner	OF123	L	31	129	537	80	177	23	4	1	45	34	12	3	.330	.393
Woody Jensen	OF120	L	29	124	509	77	142	23	9	5	45	15	29	2	.279	.389
Al Todd	C128	R	33	133	514	51	158	18	10	8	86	16	36	2	.307	.428
Pep Young	SS45, 3B39, 2B30	R	29	113	408	43	106	20	4	9	54	26	63	4	.260	.390
Johnny Dickshot	OF64	R	27	82	264	42	67	8	4	3	33	26	36	5	.254	.348
Red Lucas	P20	L	35	59	82	8	22	3	0	0	17	7	6	0	.268	.305
Tom Padden	C34	R	28	35	98	14	28	2	0	0	8	13	11	1	.286	.306
Fred Schulte	OF4	R	36	29	20	5	2	0	0	0	3	4	3	0	.100	.100
Pie Traynor	3B3	R	38	5	12	3	2	0	0	0	0	1	0	0	.167	.167
Bill Schuster	SS2	R	24	3	10	2	5	0	0	0	1	1	0	0	.500	.500
Ray Barres	C2	R	29	2	6	0	1	0	0	0	0	1	0	0	.167	.167

NAME	T	AGE	W	L	PCT	SV	G	GS	CG	IP	H	BB	SO	SHO	ERA
		29	86	68	.558	17	154	154	67	1367	1398	428	643	12	3.56
Cy Blanton	R	29	14	12	.538	0	36	34	14	243	250	76	143	4	3.30
Russ Bauers	R	23	13	6	.684	1	34	19	11	188	174	80	118	2	2.87
Ed Brandt	L	32	11	10	.524	2	33	25	7	176	177	67	74	3	3.12
Bill Swift	R	29	9	10	.474	3	36	17	9	164	160	34	84	0	3.95
Jim Weaver	R	33	8	5	.615	0	32	9	2	110	106	31	44	1	3.19
Joe Bowman	R	27	8	8	.500	1	30	19	7	128	161	35	38	0	4.57
Red Lucas	R	35	8	10	.444	0	20	20	9	126	150	23	20	1	4.29
Mace Brown	R	28	7	2	.778	7	50	2	0	108	109	45	60	0	4.17
Jim Tobin	R	24	6	3	.667	1	8	7	7	87	74	28	37	0	3.00
Ken Heintzelman	R	21	1	0	1.000	0	1	1	1	9	6	3	4	0	2.00
1 Waite Hoyt	R	37	1	2	.333	2	11	0	0	28	31	6	21	0	4.50

ST. LOUIS — 4th 81-73 .526 15 — FRANKIE FRISCH

NAME	G by Pos	B	AGE	G	AB	R	H	2B	3B	HR	RBI	BB	SO	SB	BA	SA
TOTALS			26	156	5476	789	1543	264	67	94	731	385	569	78	.282	.406
Johnny Mize	1B144	L	24	145	560	103	204	40	7	25	113	56	57	2	.364	.595
Jimmy Brown	2B112, SS25, 3B1	B	27	138	525	86	145	20	9	2	53	27	29	10	.276	.360
Leo Durocher	SS134	R	31	135	477	46	97	11	3	1	47	38	36	6	.203	.295
Don Gutteridge	3B105, SS8	R	25	119	447	66	121	19	7	6	61	25	66	12	.271	.421
Don Padgett	OF109	L	25	123	446	62	140	22	6	10	74	30	43	4	.314	.457
Terry Moore	OF106	R	25	115	461	76	123	19	4	5	43	32	41	13	.267	.349
Joe Medwick	OF156	R	25	156	633	111	237	56	10	31	154	41	50	4	.374	.641
Brusie Ogrodowski	C87	R	25	90	279	37	65	10	3	3	31	11	17	2	.233	.323
Pepper Martin	OF82, 3B5	R	33	98	339	60	103	27	8	5	38	33	50	9	.304	.475
Frenchy Bordagaray	3B50, OF28	R	27	96	300	43	88	11	4	1	37	15	25	11	.293	.367
Stu Martin	2B48, 1B9, SS1	L	24	90	223	34	56	6	1	1	17	32	18	3	.260	.309
Mickey Owen (JJ)	C78	R	21	80	234	17	54	4	2	0	20	15	13	1	.231	.265
Dick Siebert	1B7	L	25	22	38	3	7	2	0	0	2	4	8	1	.184	.237
Frankie Frisch	2B5	B	38	17	32	3	7	2	0	0	4	1	0	0	.219	.281
Herb Bremer	C10	R	23	11	33	2	7	1	0	0	3	2	4	0	.212	.242
2 Randy Moore	OF1	L	32	8	7	0	0	0	0	0	0	0	0	0	.000	.000
Bill Delancy (IL) 35																

NAME	T	AGE	W	L	PCT	SV	G	GS	CG	IP	H	BB	SO	SHO	ERA
		31	81*	73	.526	4	156	156	81	1392	1546	448	571	10	3.95
Lon Warneke	R	28	18	11	.621	0	36	33	18	239	280	69	87	2	4.52
Bob Weiland	L	31	15	14	.517	0	41	34	21	264	283	94	105	2	3.55
Dizzy Dean (BT)	R	27	13	10	.565	1	27	25	17	197	200	33	120	4	2.70
Si Johnson	R	30	12	12	.500	1	38	21	12	172	222	43	64	1	3.33
Mike Ryba	R	34	9	6	.600	0	38	8	5	135	152	40	57	0	4.13
Howie Kirst	R	21	1	0	.750	0	6	4	1	28	34	10	6	0	4.18
Jesse Haines	R	43	3	3	.500	0	16	6	2	66	81	23	18	0	4.50
Ray Harrell	R	25	3	7	.300	1	35	15	1	97	99	59	41	1	5.85
Jim Winford	R	27	2	4	.333	0	16	4	0	46	56	27	17	0	5.87
Bill McGee	R	27	1	0	1.000	1	14	3	1	14	13	4	9	0	2.57
Nubs Kleinke	R	26	1	1	.500	0	5	2	1	21	25	7	9	0	4.72
Abe White	L	33	1	0	1.000	0	3	0	0	3	2	1	1	0	7.00
2 Sheriff Blake	R	37	0	3	.000	0	14	2	2	44	45	18	20	0	3.68
Tom Sunkel	L	24	0	0	—	0	1	0	0	29	24	11	9	0	2.79
Nate Andrews	R	23	0	0		0	4	0	0	9	12	3	6	0	4.00
Johnnie Chambers	R	23	0	0		0	1	0	0	1	2	1	0	0	18.00
Paul Dean (SA)	R	23	0	0		0	1	0	0	1	2	1	0		T

* Win by forfiet

BOSTON — 5th 79-73 .520 16 — BILL McKECHNIE

NAME	G by Pos	B	AGE	G	AB	R	H	2B	3B	HR	RBI	BB	SO	SB	BA	SA
TOTALS			28	152	5124	579	1265	200	41	63	534	485	707	45	.247	.339
Elbie Fletcher	1B148	L	21	148	539	56	133	22	4	1	38	56	64	3	.247	.308
Tony Cuccinello	2B151	R	29	152	575	77	156	36	4	11	80	61	40	2	.271	.405
Rabbit Warstler	SS149	R	33	149	555	57	124	20	4	1	36	51	62	4	.223	.276
Gil English	3B71	R	27	79	269	25	78	5	2	2	37	23	27	3	.290	.346
Gene Moore	OF148	R	27	148	561	88	159	29	10	16	70	61	73	11	.283	.456
Vince DiMaggio	OF130	R	24	132	493	56	126	18	4	13	69	39	111	8	.256	.387
Debs Garms	OF81, 3B36	L	30	125	478	60	124	16	5	2	37	37	33	2	.259	.337
Al Lopez	C102	R	28	105	334	31	68	11	1	3	38	35	57	1	.204	.269
2 Roy Johnson	OF63, 3B1	L	34	85	260	24	72	8	3	3	22	38	29	5	.277	.365
Eddie Mayo	3B50	R	27	65	172	19	39	6	1	1	18	15	20	1	.227	.291
Ray Mueller	C57	R	25	64	187	21	47	9	2	2	26	18	36	1	.251	.353
Bobby Reis	OF18, 1B4, P4	R	28	45	86	10	21	5	0	0	8	13	12	2	.244	.302
1 Wally Berger	OF28	R	31	30	113	14	31	9	1	5	22	11	33	0	.274	.504
Tommy Thevenow	SS12, 3B6, 2B2	R	33	21	34	5	4	0	1	0	1	4	2	0	.118	.176
Beauty McGowan	OF2	L	35	9	12	0	1	0	0	0	1	2	2	0	.083	.083
1 Buck Jordan		R	30	8	4	0	1	0	0	0	0	1	0	0	.250	.250
2 Johnny Riddle	C2	R	31	3	3	0	0	0	0	0	0	0	0	0	.000	.000
Link Wasem	C2	R	26	1	1	0	0	0	0	0	0	0	0	0	.000	.000
Billy Urbanski (BN)		R	34	1	0	0	0	0	0	0	0	0	0	0		

NAME	T	AGE	W	L	PCT	SV	G	GS	CG	IP	H	BB	SO	SHO	ERA
		32	79	73	.520	16	152	152	85	1359	1344	372	387	16	3.22
Lou Fette	R	30	20	10	.667	0	35	33	23	259	243	81	70	5	2.88
Jim Turner	R	33	20	11	.645	1	33	30	24	257	228	52	69	5	2.38
Danny MacFayden	R	32	14	14	.500	0	32	32	16	246	250	60	33	1	2.93
Guy Bush	R	35	8	15	.348	1	32	20	11	181	201	48	56	1	3.53
Johnny Lanning	R	26	5	7	.417	2	32	11	4	117	107	40	37	1	3.92
Ira Hutchinson	R	26	4	6	.400	0	31	4	1	92	99	35	29	0	3.72
2 Frank Gabler	R	25	4	7	.364	2	19	9	2	76	84	16	19	1	5.09
Milt Shoffner	L	31	3	1	.750	1	6	5	3	43	38	9	13	1	2.51
Roy Weir (SA)	L	26	1	1	.500	0	10	4	1	37	19	8	9	3	3.82
Bob Smith	R	42	1	0	.000	3	18	0	0	44	52	6	14	0	4.09
Bobby Reis	R	28	0	0	—	0	4	0	0	9	8	1	0	0	1.80
Vic Frasier	R	32	0	0	—	0	3	0	0	8	12	1	2	0	5.63

BROOKLYN 6th 62-91 .405 33.5 — BURLEIGH GRIMES

NAME	G by Pos	B	AGE	G	AB	R	H	2B	3B	HR	RBI	BB	SO	SB	BA	SA
TOTALS			29	155	5295	616	1401	258	53	37	554	469	583	69	.265	.354
Buddy Hassett	1B131, OF7	L	25	137	556	71	169	31	6	1	70	20	19	13	.304	.387
Cookie Lavagetto	2B100, 3B45	R	24	149	503	64	142	26	6	8	70	74	41	13	.282	.406
Woody English	SS116, 2B11	R	30	129	378	45	90	16	2	1	42	65	55	4	.238	.299
Joe Stripp	3B66, 1B14, SS3	R	34	90	300	37	73	10	2	1	26	20	18	1	.243	.300
Heinie Manush	OF123	L	35	132	466	57	155	25	7	4	73	40	24	6	.333	.442
Johnny Cooney	OF111, 1B2	R	36	120	430	61	126	18	5	0	37	22	10	5	.293	.358
Gib Brack	OF101	R	29	112	372	60	102	27	9	5	38	44	93	9	.274	.435
Babe Phelps	C111	L	29	121	409	42	128	37	3	7	58	25	28	2	.313	.469
Jim Bucher	2B49, 3B43, OF6	R	26	125	380	44	96	11	2	4	37	20	18	5	.253	.324
Tom Winsett	OF101, P1	L	27	118	350	32	83	15	5	5	42	45	64	3	.237	.351
Roy Spencer	C45	R	37	51	117	5	24	2	2	0	4	8	17	0	.205	.256
Lindsay Brown	SS45	R	25	48	115	16	31	3	1	0	6	3	17	1	.270	.313
Eddie Wilson	OF21	L	27	36	54	11	12	4	1	1	8	17	14	1	.222	.389
Tony Malinosky	3B13, SS11	R	27	35	79	7	18	2	0	0	3	9	11	0	.228	.253
Eddie Morgan	1B7, OF7	L	22	31	48	4	9	3	0	0	5	9	7	0	.188	.250
Paul Chervinko	C26	R	26	30	48	1	7	0	1	0	2	3	16	0	.146	.188
Goody Rosen	OF21	L	24	22	77	10	24	5	1	0	6	6	6	2	.312	.403
George Cisar	OF13	R	24	20	29	8	6	0	0	0	4	2	6	3	.207	.207
Bert Haas	OF4, 1B3	R	23	16	25	2	10	3	0	0	2	1	1	0	.400	.520
Johnny Hudson	SS11, 2B1	R	25	13	27	5	5	4	0	0	2	3	9	0	.185	.333
1 Randy Moore	C10	L	32	13	22	3	3	1	0	0	2	3	2	0	.136	.182
Jake Daniel	1B7	L	25	12	27	3	5	1	0	0	3	3	4	0	.185	.222

Sid Gauteaux 25 B 1-10, Nick Polly 20 R 4-18, Art Parks 25 L 5-16, Elmer Klumpp 30 R 1-11, George Fallon 22 R 2-8

NAME	T	AGE	W	L	PCT	SV	G	GS	CG	IP	H	BB	SO	SHO	ERA
		30	62	91	.405	8	155	155	63	1363	1470	476	592	5	4.13
Luke Hamlin	R	32	11	13	.458	1	39	25	11	180	183	48	93	1	3.58
Max Butcher (JJ)	R	26	11	15	.423	0	39	24	8	192	203	75	57	1	4.27
Fred Frankhouse	R	33	10	13	.435	0	33	25	9	179	214	78	64	1	4.27
Van Lingle Mungo (AJ)	R	26	9	11	.450	3	25	21	14	161	136	56	122	0	2.91
2 Waite Hoyt	R	37	7	7	.500	0	27	19	10	167	180	30	44	1	3.23
Roy Henshaw	L	25	5	12	.294	2	42	16	5	156	176	69	98	0	5.08
2 F. Fitzsimmons (BG)	R	35	4	8	.333	0	13	13	4	91	91	32	29	0	4.25
Harry Eisenstat	L	21	3	3	.500	3	13	5	0	48	61	11	12	0	3.94
Buck Marrow	R	27	1	2	.333	0	6	3	1	16	19	9	2	0	6.75
George Jeffcoat (IL)	R	23	1	3	.250	0	21	3	1	54	58	27	29	1	5.17
Jim Lindsey	R	39	0	1	.000	2	20	0	0	38	43	12	15	0	3.55
1 Tom Baker	R	24	0	1	.000	0	7	0	0	8	14	5	2	0	9.00
Ralph Birkofer	L	28	0	2	.000	0	11	1	0	30	45	9	9	0	6.60
2 Ben Cantwell	R	35	0	0	—	0	13	0	0	27	32	8	12	0	4.67
Jim Peterson	R	28	0	0	—	0	3	0	0	6	8	2	4	0	7.50
Watty Clark	L	35	0	0	—	0	2	0	0	2	3	2	0	0	9.00
Tom Winsett	L	27	0	0	—	0	1	0	0	1	3	2	0	0	18.00

PHILADELPHIA 7th 61-92 .399 34.5 — JIMMIE WILSON

NAME	G by Pos	B	AGE	G	AB	R	H	2B	3B	HR	RBI	BB	SO	SB	BA	SA
TOTALS			28	154	5424	724	1482	258	37	103	668	478	640	66	.273	.391
Dolph Camilli	1B131	L	30	131	475	101	161	23	7	27	80	90	82	6	.339	.587
Del Young	2B108	R	25	109	360	30	70	9	2	0	24	18	55	0	.194	.237
George Scharein	SS146	R	22	146	511	44	123	20	1	0	57	36	47	13	.241	.284
Pinky Whitney	3B130	R	32	138	487	56	166	19	4	8	79	43	44	6	.341	.446
Chuck Klein	OF139	L	32	115	406	74	132	20	2	15	57	39	21	3	.325	.495
Hersh Martin	OF139	R	27	115	466	57	155	35	7	8	49	69	66	11	.283	.442
Morrie Amovich	OF107	R	26	117	410	60	119	27	4	10	60	34	52	6	.290	.449
Bill Atwood	C80	R	25	87	279	27	68	15	1	2	32	30	27	1	.244	.326
Leo Norris	2B74, 3B24, SS20	R	29	116	381	45	98	24	3	9	36	21	53	3	.257	.407
Earl Brown	OF54, 1B32	R	26	105	332	42	97	19	3	6	52	21	41	4	.292	.422
Johnny Moore	OF72	L	35	96	307	16	98	16	2	9	59	18	18	2	.319	.472
Earl Grace	C64	L	30	80	223	19	47	10	1	6	29	33	15	0	.211	.345
Bucky Walters	P37, 3B8	R	28	56	137	15	38	6	1	1	16	5	16	1	.277	.343
Jimmie Wilson	C22, 1B2	R	36	39	87	15	24	3	0	1	8	6	4	1	.345	.345
Howie Gorman	OF7	L	24	13	19	3	4	1	0	0	1	1	1	1	.211	.263
Fred Tauby	OF7	R	31	11	20	2	0	0	0	0	3	0	5	1	.000	.000

Walter Stephenson 26 R 6-23, Gene Corbett 23 L 4-12, Bill Andrus 29 R 0-2

NAME	T	AGE	W	L	PCT	SV	G	GS	CG	IP	H	BB	SO	SHO	ERA
		28	61	92*	.399	15	154	154	59	1371	1629	501	529	6	5.06
Wayne LaMaster	L	30	15	19	.441	4	50	30	10	220	255	82	135	1	5.32
Bucky Walters	R	28	14	15	.483	0	37	34	15	246	292	86	87	3	4.76
Claude Passeau	R	28	14	18	.438	2	50	34	18	292	348	79	135	1	4.35
Hugh Mulcahy	R	23	8	18	.308	3	56	26	9	216	256	97	54	1	5.13
Syl Johnson	R	36	8	10	.286	3	32	15	4	138	155	22	46	0	5.02
Orville Jorgens	R	29	3	4	.429	3	52	9	1	141	159	68	34	0	4.40
Hal Kelleher	R	24	2	4	.333	0	27	2	1	58	72	31	20	0	6.67
Pete Sivess	R	23	1	1	.500	0	6	2	1	20	30	11	4	0	8.10
Bub Allen	R	22	1	1	.500	0	3	1	0	12	18	8	8	0	6.75
Leon Pettit	R	35	0	1	.000	0	3	1	0	4	6	1	0	0	11.25
Elmer Burkart	R	20	0	1	—	0	7	0	0	16	20	9	4	0	6.19
Larry Crawford	R	23	0	0	—	0	6	0	0	6	12	1	2	0	15.00
Bobby Burke	L	30	0	0	—	0	3	0	0	0	1	2	0	0	
Walt Masters	R	30	0	0	—	0	1	0	0	5	1	5	1	0	36.00

*1 loss by forfeit

CINCINNATI 8th 56-98 .364 40 — CHUCK DRESSEN 51-78 .395 BOBBY WALLACE 5-20 .200

NAME	G by Pos	B	AGE	G	AB	R	H	2B	3B	HR	RBI	BB	SO	SB	BA	SA
TOTALS			29	155	5230	612	1329	215	59	73	567	437	586	53	.254	.360
2 Buck Jordan	1B76	L	30	98	316	45	89	14	3	1	28	25	14	6	.282	.345
Alex Kampouris	2B146	R	24	146	458	62	114	21	4	17	71	60	65	2	.249	.424
Bill Myers	SS121, 2B6	R	26	124	335	35	84	13	3	7	43	44	57	0	.251	.370
Lew Riggs	3B100, 2B4, SS1	L	27	122	384	43	93	17	5	6	45	24	24	10	.242	.359
Ival Goodman	OF141	R	28	147	579	102	164	25	12	12	55	55	58	10	.283	.428
Chick Hafey	OF64	R	34	89	257	39	67	11	5	9	41	23	42	2	.261	.447
Kiki Cuyler	OF106	R	38	117	406	48	107	12	4	0	32	36	50	10	.271	.320
Ernie Lombardi	C90	R	29	120	368	41	123	22	1	9	59	14	17	1	.334	.473
Les Scarsella	1B65, OF14	L	23	110	329	35	81	11	4	3	34	17	26	5	.246	.331
Hub Walker	OF58, 2B3	L	30	78	221	33	55	9	4	1	19	34	24	7	.249	.339
Spud Davis	C59	R	32	76	209	19	56	10	1	3	33	23	15	0	.268	.368
1 Phil Weintraub	OF47	L	29	49	177	27	48	10	4	3	20	19	25	1	.271	.424
Jimmy Outlaw	3B41	R	24	49	165	18	45	7	3	0	11	3	31	2	.273	.352
1 Charlie Gelbert	SS37, 2B9, 3B1	R	31	43	114	12	22	4	0	1	13	15	12	1	.193	.254
2 Kiddo Davis	OF35	R	35	40	136	19	35	6	0	1	5	16	6	1	.257	.324
Eddie Miller	SS30, 3B4	R	20	36	60	3	9	3	1	0	5	3	8	0	.150	.233
Frank McCormick	1B20, 2B4, OF1	R	26	24	83	5	27	5	0	0	9	3	5	0	.325	.386
Charlie English	3B15, 2B2	R	27	17	63	1	15	3	0	0	5	1	7	0	.238	.317

Gilly Campbell 29 L 11-40, Double Joe Dwyer 34 (BA) L 3-11, Harry Craft 22 R 13-42, Dee Moore 23 R 1-13, Eddie Joost 21 L 1-12, Pinky Jorgensen 22 R 4-14, Dutch Mele 22 L 2-14, Arnie Moser 21 R 0-5, Gus Brittain 27 R 1-6, Harry Chozen 21 R 1-4

NAME	T	AGE	W	L	PCT	SV	G	GS	CG	IP	H	BB	SO	SHO	ERA
		28	56	98	.364	18	155	155	64	1358	1428	533	581	10	3.94
Lee Grissom	L	29	12	17	.414	6	50	30	14	224	193	93	149	5	3.25
Peaches Davis	R	32	11	13	.458	3	42	24	11	218	252	51	59	1	3.59
Paul Derringer	R	30	10	14	.417	1	43	26	12	223	240	55	94	1	4.04
Al Hollingsworth	L	29	9	15	.375	5	43	24	11	202	224	73	74	1	3.92
Gene Schott	R	23	4	13	.235	1	37	16	7	154	150	48	56	2	2.98
Johnny Vander Meer	L	22	3	5	.375	0	19	10	4	84	63	69	52	0	3.86
Wild Bill Hallahan	R	34	3	9	.250	0	21	9	2	63	90	29	18	0	6.14
1 Jumbo Brown	R	30	1	0	1.000	0	4	1	0	16	16	3	4	0	8.10
1 Don Brennan	R	33	1	1	.500	0	10	0	0	16	25	10	6	0	6.75
2 Jos Cascarella	R	30	1	2	.333	1	11	3	2	44	44	22	16	0	3.89
Ted Kleinhans	L	38	1	2	.333	0	7	3	1	27	29	12	13	0	2.33
Paul Gehrman	R	25	0	1	.000	1	9	1	0	9	11	5	1	0	3.00
Jake Mooty	R	24	0	3	.000	1	14	2	0	39	54	22	11	0	8.31
Whitey Moore	R	25	0	3	.000	0	13	6	0	39	32	39	27	0	4.85
Red Barrett	R	22	0	0	—	0	6	0	0	6	5	2	1	0	1.50

WORLD SERIES — NEW YORK (AL) 4 NEW YORK (NL) 1

LINE SCORES

TEAM	1	2	3	4	5	6	7	8	9	10	11	12	R	H	E

Game 1 October 6 at Yankee Stadium

													R	H	E
NY (NL)	0	0	0	0	0	0	1	0	0				1	6	2
NY (AL)	0	0	0	0	0	7	0	1	X				8	7	0

Hubbell, Gumbert (6), Coffman (6), Smith (8)   Gomez

Game 2 October 7 at Yankee Stadium

NY (NL)	1	0	0	0	0	0	0	0	0				1	7	0
NY (AL)	0	0	0	0	2	4	2	0	X				8	12	0

Melton, Gumbert (5), Coffman (6)   Ruffing

Game 3 October 8 at Polo Grounds

NY (AL)	0	1	2	1	1	0	0	0	0				5	9	0
NY (NL)	0	0	0	0	0	0	1	0	0				1	5	4

Pearson, Murphy (9)   Schumacher, Melton (7), Brennan (9)

Game 4 October 9 at Polo Grounds

NY (AL)	1	0	1	0	0	0	0	0	1				3	6	0
NY (NL)	0	6	0	0	0	0	1	0	X				7	12	3

Hadley, Andrews (2), Wicker (8)   Hubbell

Game 5 October 10 at Polo Grounds

NY (AL)	0	1	1	0	2	0	0	0	0				4	8	0
NY (NL)	0	0	2	0	0	0	0	0	0				2	10	0

Gomez   Melton, Smith (6), Brennan (8)

COMPOSITE BATTING

NAME	POS	G	AB	R	H	2B	3B	HR	RBI	BA
New York (AL)										
Totals		5	169	28	42	6	4	4	25	.249
DiMaggio	OF	5	22	2	6	0	0	1	4	.273
Crosetti	SS	5	21	2	1	0	0	0	0	.048
Hoag	OF	5	20	4	6	1	0	1	2	.300
Rolfe	3B	5	20	3	6	2	1	0	1	.300
Selkirk	OF	5	19	5	5	1	0	0	6	.263
Dickey	C	5	19	3	4	0	0	0	1	.211
Gehrig	1B	5	17	4	5	1	1	1	3	.294
Lazzeri	2B	5	15	3	6	0	1	1	2	.400
Gomez	P	2	6	2	1	0	0	0	0	.167
Ruffing	P	1	4	0	2	1	0	0	3	.500
Pearson	P	1	3	0	0	0	0	0	0	.000
Andrews	P	1	2	0	0	0	0	0	0	.000
Powell	PH	1	1	0	0	0	0	0	0	.000
Hadley	P	1	0	0	0	0	0	0	0	—
Murphy	P	1	0	0	0	0	0	0	0	—
Wicker	P	1	0	0	0	0	0	0	0	—
New York (NL)										
Totals		5	169	12	40	6	0	1	12	.237
Moore	OF	5	23	1	9	1	0	0	1	.391
Bartell	SS	5	21	3	5	1	0	0	1	.238
Ott	3B	5	20	1	4	0	0	0	0	.200
Mccarthy	1B	5	19	1	4	1	0	0	1	.211
Ripple	OF	5	17	2	5	1	0	0	4	.294
Whitehead	2B	5	16	1	4	2	0	0	0	.250
Danning	C	3	12	0	3	1	0	0	2	.250
Leiber	OF	3	11	2	4	0	0	0	0	.364
Mancuso	C	3	8	0	0	0	0	0	0	.000
Chiozza	OF	2	7	0	2	0	0	0	0	.286
Hubbell	P	2	6	1	0	0	0	0	0	.000
Berger	PH	3	3	0	0	0	0	0	0	.000
Melton	P	3	3	0	0	0	0	0	0	.000
Leslie	PH	2	3	0	0	0	0	0	0	.000
Coffman	P	2	2	1	0	0	0	0	0	.000
Ryan	PH	1	1	0	0	0	0	0	0	.000
Schumacher	P	1	1	0	0	0	0	0	0	.000
Brennan	P	2	0	0	0	0	0	0	0	—
Gumbert	P	2	0	0	0	0	0	0	0	—
Smith	P	2	0	0	0	0	0	0	0	—

COMPOSITE PITCHING

NAME	G	IP	H	BB	SO	W	L	SV	ERA
New York (AL)									
Totals	5	44	40	11	21	4	1	1	2.45
Gomez	2	18	16	2	8	2	0	0	1.50
Ruffing	1	9	7	3	8	1	0	0	1.00
Pearson	1	8.2	5	2	4	1	0	0	1.04
Andrews	1	5.2	6	4	1	0	0	0	3.18
Hadley	1	1.1	6	0	0	0	1	0	33.75
Wicker	1	1	0	0	0	0	0	0	0.00
Murphy	1	0.1	0	0	0	0	0	1	0.00
New York (NL)									
Totals	5	43	42	21	21	1	4	0	4.81
Hubbell	2	14.1	12	4	7	1	1	0	3.77
Melton	3	11	12	6	7	0	2	0	4.91
Schumacher	1	6	9	4	3	0	1	0	6.00
Coffman	2	4.1	2	5	1	0	0	0	4.15
Brennan	2	3	1	1	0	0	0	0	0.00
Smith	2	3	2	0	1	0	0	0	3.00
Gumbret	2	1.1	4	1	1	0	0	0	27.00

1938 The Struggle for Second Fiddle

The season, as so many others before it, consisted of winning spurts and losing streaks, as well as injuries, sore arms, bad breaks, an abundance of cheers and boos, new faces making good, and similiar and tried faces doing well enough to hang around for another year. Yet, when all the finery was cleared away, the 1938 season got down to seven games.

The highlights of the year included such grandeur and tragedy as Cincinnati's Johnny Vander Meer earning immortality with back-to-back no-hit performances, and Monty Stratton, the 26-year-old star of the Whlte Sox pitching staff, blowing his leg off in a hunting accident after the season. The year also saw Brooklyn joining the night baseball scene, a $200,000 trade for a sore arm pitcher, and the fantastic return to form of the Red Sox's Jimmie Foxx—who went from a .285 batting average in 1937 to a league-leading .349 MVP performance. There was also Detroit's Hank Greenberg hitting 58 homers and the Reds' first baseman Frank McCormick who became the third modern player in his first full season to collect over 200 hits with his 209 tallies (Lloyd Waner turned the trick in 1927 with 223 and Johnny Frederick with 206 in 1929).

Injuries took their toll in both leagues and altered the outcome for several teams. The Giants' Carl Hubbell developed a sore arm and was shelved in August with a 13-10 record, losing his chance for a sixth straight 20-game season. Lefty Grove had 14 victories for the Red Sox when he was sidelined in mid-July, displaying a form which eventually earned him the American League's E.R.A. title with 3.07. The White Sox also suffered when Luke Appling broke his ankle in spring training and was lost for half the season and Clint Brown, their star reliever, chipped a bone in his pitching arm. Another victim of arm trouble was Cleveland's Johnny Allen, whose injury in the thick of the race finished whatever chance the Indians had for the pennant.

Of the seven games which capped the season, three took place between Pittsburgh and Chicago in late September to decide the National League pennant. Chicago, after replacing manager Charlie Grimm with catcher Gabby Hartnett, started a miraculous climb toward the Pirates and found themselves a game-and-a-half out when both clubs convened at Wrigley Field on September 27, for a three-game set. (The Giants and Reds had been eliminated two days before.)

Dizzy Dean, the sore arm pitcher for whom the Cubs paid the Cardinals $200,000,

was picked to start the game—his first since August 20. Dean surprised everyone by lasting until two out in the ninth giving the Cubs and their 42,223 fans a 2-1 triumph. The next day Hartnett provided all the heroics in the ninth inning when, with two outs and darkness threatening to end the game, he hit a home run to break a 5-5 tie and put the Cubs in first place. On the 29th, the Cubs made it ten straight with a 10-1 win, which all but broke the back of the Pirates and earned the Cubs a two-game pennant margin capped by a sizzling finishing record of 21-4.

In the World Series, which made up those other four games of 1938, the Cubs welcomed the Yankees into Wrigley Field. Unlike the tough, senior circuit dogfight, New York easily won their third straight American League title by 9 1/2 games over the Red Sox. In the first game the Cubs called on Bill Lee while the Yankees sent in their ace, 21-game winner Red Ruffing. With a brisk wind blowing in and preventing any home runs, the Yankees' infield sparkled and won, 3-1, on an attack paced by Bill Dickey's four singles. The next day, while the Yankees gave the nod to 18-game wumer Lefty Gomez, the Cubs responded with sore-armed Dean who, mostly relying on pitching savvy and guts, took a 3-2 lead into the eighth inning when he was greeted by a Frank Crosetti two-run homer. Joe DiMaggio applied the finishing touch in the ninth with another two-run shot which sent Dean out of the game and the Yankees to a final, 6-3 victory.

In the third game the action moved to New York where Joe Gordon provided most of the fireworks wlth a home run and bases-loaded single to give the Yankees a 5-2 victory. In the fourth and final game the Cubs used six pitchers to no avail as the Yankees scored eight times to sweep the Series and become the first team in baseball to win three straight world's championships.

1938 AMERICAN LEAGUE

NAME	G by Pos	B	AGE	G	AB	R	H	2B	3B	HR	RBI	BB	SO	SB	BA	SA
NEW YORK	1st 99-53 .651		JOE McCARTHY													
	TOTALS		28	157	5410	966	1480	283	63	174	917	749	616	91	.274	.446
Lou Gehrig	1B157	L	35	157	576	115	170	32	6	29	114	107	75	6	.295	.523
Joe Gordon	2B126	R	23	127	458	83	117	24	7	25	97	56	72	11	.255	.502
Frankie Crosetti	SS157	R	27	157	631	113	166	35	9	9	55	106	97	27	.263	.371
Red Rolfe	3B151	L	29	151	631	132	196	36	8	10	80	74	44	13	.311	.441
Tommy Henrich	OF130	L	28	131	471	109	127	24	7	22	91	92	32	6	.270	.490
Joe DiMaggio	OF145	R	23	145	599	129	194	32	13	32	140	59	21	6	.324	.581
George Selkirk	C95	L	30	99	335	58	85	12	5	10	62	68	52	9	.254	.409
Bill Dickey	C126	L	31	132	454	84	142	27	4	27	115	75	22	3	.313	.568
Myril Hoag	OF70	R	30	85	267	28	74	14	3	0	48	25	31	4	.277	.352
Bill Knickerbocker	2B34, SS3	R	26	46	128	15	32	4	1	1	21	11	10	0	.250	.383
Jake Powell	OF43	R	29	45	164	27	42	12	1	2	20	15	20	3	.256	.378
Joe Glenn	C40	R	29	41	123	10	32	7	2	0	25	10	14	1	.260	.350
Babe Dahlgren	3B8, 1B6	R	26	27	43	8	8	1	0	0	1	1	7	0	.186	.209
Art Jorgens	C8	R	33	9	17	3	4	2	0	0	3	3	3	0	.235	.353

NAME		T	AGE	W	L	PCT	SV	G	GS	CG	IP	H	BB	SO	SHO	ERA
			30	99	53	.651	13	157	157	91	1382	1436	566	567	11	3.91
Red Ruffing		R	34	21	7	.750	0	31	31	22	247	246	82	127	3	3.32
Lefty Gomez		L	29	18	12	.600	0	32	32	20	239	239	99	129	4	3.35
Monte Pearson		R	29	16	7	.696	0	28	27	17	202	198	113	98	1	3.97
Spud Chandler		R	30	14	5	.737	0	23	23	14	172	183	47	36	2	4.03
Bump Hadley		R	33	9	8	.529	1	29	17	8	167	165	66	61	1	3.61
Johnny Murphy		R	29	8	2	.800	11	32	2	1	91	90	41	43	0	4.25
Steve Sundra		R	28	6	4	.600	0	25	8	3	94	107	43	33	0	4.79
Joe Beggs		R	27	3	2	.600	0	14	9	4	58	69	20	8	0	5.43
2 Wes Ferrell		R	30	2	2	.500	0	5	4	1	30	52	18	7	0	8.10
Kemp Wicker		L	31	1	0	1.000	1	3	0	0	1	0	1	0	0	0.00
Ivy Andrews		R	31	1	3	.250	1	19	1	1	48	51	17	13	0	3.00
Atley Donald		R	27	0	1	.000	0	2	2	0	12	7	14	6	0	5.25
Lee Stine		R	24	0	0	—	0	4	0	0	9	9	1	4	0	4.50
Joe Vance		R	32	0	0	—	0	3	1	0	11	20	4	2	0	7.36

NAME	G by Pos	B	AGE	G	AB	R	H	2B	3B	HR	RBI	BB	SO	SB	BA	SA
BOSTON	2nd 88-61 .591 9.5		JOE CRONIN													
	TOTALS		28	150	5230	902	1566	298	56	98	860	650	463	55	.299	.434
Jimmie Foxx	1B149	R	30	149	565	139	197	33	9	50	175	119	76	5	.349	.704
Bobby Doerr	2B145	R	20	145	509	70	147	26	7	5	80	59	39	5	.289	.397
Joe Cronin	SS142	R	31	143	530	98	172	51	5	17	94	91	60	7	.325	.536
Pinky Higgins	3B129	R	29	139	524	77	159	29	5	5	106	71	55	10	.303	.406
Ben Chapman	OF126, 3B1	R	29	127	480	92	163	40	6	5	80	65	33	13	.340	.494
Doc Cramer	OF148, P1	L	32	148	658	116	198	36	8	0	71	51	19	4	.301	.380
Joe Vossmik	OF146	R	28	146	621	121	201	37	6	9	86	59	26	0	.324	.446
Gene Desautels	C81	R	31	108	333	47	97	16	2	2	48	57	31	1	.291	.369
Red Nonnenkamp	OF39, 1B5	L	26	87	180	37	51	4	1	0	18	21	13	6	.283	.317
Johnny Peacock	C57, 1B1, OF1	L	28	72	195	29	59	7	1	1	39	17	4	1	.303	.364
Eric McNair	SS15, 2B14, 3B3	R	29	46	96	9	15	1	1	0	7	3	6	0	.156	.188
Jim Tabor	3B11, SS2	R	24	19	57	8	18	3	2	1	8	1	6	2	.316	.491
Fabian Gaffke	OF2, C1	R	24	15	10	2	1	0	0	0	1	3	2	1	.100	.100
Moe Berg	C7, 1B1	R	36	10	12	0	4	0	0	0	1	0	1	0	.333	.333

NAME		T	AGE	W	L	PCT	SV	G	GS	CG	IP	H	BB	SO	SHO	ERA
			30	88	61	.591	15	150	150	67	1316	1472	528	484	10	4.46
Jim Bagby		R	21	15	11	.577	2	43	25	10	199	218	90	73	1	4.21
Jack Wilson		R	26	15	15	.500	1	37	27	11	195	200	91	96	3	4.29
Lefty Grove (SA)		L	38	14	4	.778	1	24	21	12	164	169	52	99	1	3.07
Fritz Ostermueller		L	30	13	5	.772	2	31	18	10	177	199	58	46	1	4.58
2 Joe Heving		R	37	8	1	.889	2	16	11	7	82	94	22	34	1	3.73
Archie McKain		L	27	5	4	.556	6	37	5	1	100	119	44	27	0	4.50
Emerson Dickman		R	23	5	5	.500	0	32	11	3	104	117	54	22	1	5.28
Bill Harris		R	38	5	5	.500	1	13	11	5	80	83	21	26	1	4.05
Johnny Marcum		R	28	5	6	.455	0	15	11	7	92	113	25	20	0	4.11
James Midkiff		R	23	1	1	.500	0	13	2	0	35	43	21	10	0	5.19
1 Lee Rogers		L	24	1	1	.500	0	14	2	0	28	32	18	7	0	6.43
Charlie Wagner		R	25	1	3	.250	0	13	6	1	37	47	24	14	0	8.27
Al Baker		R	32	0	0	—	0	1	0	0	8	13	2	2	0	9.00
Doc Cramer		L	32	0	0	—	0	1	0	0	4	3	3	1	0	4.50
Bill Humphrey		R	27	0	0	—	0	2	0	0	2	5	1	0	0	9.00
Bill LeFebvre		L	22	0	0	—	0	1	0	0	4	8	0	0	0	13.50
Ted Olson		R	25	0	0	—	0	2	0	0	7	9	2	1	0	6.43

NAME	G by Pos	B	AGE	G	AB	R	H	2B	3B	HR	RBI	BB	SO	SB	BA	SA
CLEVELAND	3rd 86-66 .566 13		OSSIE VITT													
	TOTALS		28	153	5356	847	1506	300	89	113	797	550	605	83	.281	.434
Hal Trosky	1B148	L	25	150	554	106	185	40	9	19	110	67	40	5	.334	.542
Odell Hale	2B127	R	29	130	496	69	138	32	2	8	69	44	39	8	.278	.399
Lyn Lary	SS141	R	32	141	568	94	152	36	4	3	51	88	65	23	.268	.361
Ken Keltner	3B149	R	21	149	576	86	159	31	9	26	113	33	75	4	.276	.497
Bruce Campbell	OF122	L	28	133	511	90	148	27	12	12	72	53	57	11	.290	.460
Earl Averill	OF131	L	36	134	482	101	159	27	15	14	93	81	48	5	.330	.535
Jeff Heath	OF122	L	23	126	502	104	172	31	18	21	112	33	55	3	.343	.602
Frankie Pytlak	C99	R	29	113	364	46	112	14	7	1	43	36	15	9	.308	.393
Roy Weatherly	OF55	L	23	83	210	32	55	14	3	2	18	14	14	8	.262	.386
Moose Solters	OF46	R	32	67	199	30	40	6	3	2	22	13	28	4	.201	.291
Rollie Hemsley (BG)	C58	R	31	66	203	27	60	11	3	2	28	23	14	1	.296	.409
John Kroner	2B31, 1B7, 3B3, SS1	R	29	51	117	13	29	16	0	1	17	19	6	0	.248	.410
Skeeter Webb	SS13, 3B3, 2B2	R	28	20	58	11	16	2	0	0	2	8	7	1	.276	.310
Hank Helf	C5	R	24	13	13	1	1	0	0	0	1	1	4	0	.077	.077
Oscar Grimes	2B2, 1B1	R	23	4	10	2	2	0	0	0	1	2	1	0	.200	.400
Tommy Irwin	SS3	R	25	3	9	1	1	0	0	0	0	3	1	0	.111	.111
Ray Mack	2B2	R	21	2	6	2	2	0	0	0	2	0	1	0	.333	.667
Lloyd Russell		R	25	2	1	0	0	0	0	0	0	0	0	0	.000	.000
Chuck Workman	OF1	L	23	1	5	1	2	0	0	0	0	0	2	0	.400	.400
Lou Boudreau	3B1	R	20	1	1	0	0	0	0	0	0	0	0	0	.000	.000

NAME		T	AGE	W	L	PCT	SV	G	GS	CG	IP	H	BB	SO	SHO	ERA
			28	86	66	.566	17	153	153	68	1353	1416	681	717	5	4.60
Mel Harder		R	28	17	10	.630	4	38	29	15	240	257	62	102	2	3.83
Bob Feller		R	19	17	11	.607	1	39	36	20	278	225	208	240	2	4.08
Johnny Allen (AJ)		R	33	14	8	.636	0	30	27	13	200	189	81	112	0	4.19
John Humphries		R	23	9	8	.529	6	45	6	1	103	105	63	56	0	5.24
Earl Whitehill		L	38	9	8	.529	0	26	23	4	160	187	83	60	0	5.57
Willis Hudlin		R	32	8	8	.500	1	29	15	8	127	158	45	27	0	4.89
Denny Glenhouse		R	26	7	8	.467	3	36	12	5	114	119	65	66	1	4.34
Al Milnar		L	24	3	1	.750	1	23	5	2	68	90	26	29	0	5.03
Ken Jungels		R	22	1	0	1.000	0	9	0	0	15	21	18	7	0	9.00
1 Joe Heving		R	37	1	0	1.000	0	6	0	0	6	10	5	0	0	9.00
Bill Zuber		R	25	0	3	.000	1	15	0	0	29	33	20	14	0	36.00
Clay Smith		R	23	0	0	—	0	4	0	0	11	18	2	3	0	4.97
Charley Suche		R	22	0	0	—	0	1	0	0	4	3	1	1	0	6.55

DETROIT — 4th 84-70 .545 16 — MICKEY COCHRANE 47-51 .480 — DEL BAKER 37-19 .661

NAME	G by Pos	B	AGE	G	AB	R	H	2B	3B	HR	RBI	BB	SO	SB	BA	SA
TOTALS			28	155	5270	862	1434	219	52	137	804	695	581	76	.272	.411
Hank Greenberg	1B155	R	27	155	556	144	175	23	4	58	146	119	92	7	.315	.683
Charlie Gehringer	2B152	L	35	152	568	133	174	32	5	20	107	112	21	14	.306	.486
Billy Rogell	SS134	B	33	136	501	76	130	22	8	3	55	86	37	3	.259	.353
Don Ross	3B75	R	28	77	265	22	69	7	1	1	30	28	11	1	.260	.306
Pete Fox	OF154	R	28	155	634	91	186	35	10	7	96	31	39	16	.293	.413
Chet Morgan	OF74	L	28	74	306	50	87	6	1	0	27	20	12	5	.284	.310
Dixie Walker	OF114	L	27	127	454	84	140	27	6	6	43	65	32	5	.308	.434
Rudy York	C116, OF14, 1B1	R	24	135	463	85	138	27	2	33	127	92	74	1	.298	.579
Mark Christman	3B69, SS21	R	24	95	318	35	79	6	4	1	44	27	21	5	.248	.302
Jo-Jo White	OF55	L	29	78	206	40	54	6	1	0	15	29	15	9	.262	.301
Chet Laabs	OF53	R	26	64	211	26	50	7	3	7	37	15	52	3	.237	.398
Birdie Tebbetts	C53	R	25	53	143	16	42	6	2	1	25	12	13	1	.294	.385
Tony Piet	3B18, 2B1	R	31	41	80	9	17	6	0	0	14	15	11	2	.213	.288
Vern Kennedy	P33	L	31	37	79	10	23	3	0	0	8	1	11	0	.291	.329
Roy Cullenbine	OF17	R	24	25	67	12	19	1	3	0	9	12	9	2	.284	.388
1 Ray Hayworth	C7	R	34	8	19	1	4	0	0	0	5	3	4	1	.211	.211
Benny McCoy	2B6, 3B1	L	22	7	15	2	3	1	0	0	0	1	2	0	.200	.267
George Archie		R	24	3	2	0	0	0	0	0	0	0	1	0	.000	.000
Clyde Hatter (DD) 29																

NAME	T	AGE	W	L	PCT	SV	G	GS	CG	IP	H	BB	SO	SHO	ERA
TOTALS		28	84	70	.545	11	155	155	75	1348	1532	608	435	2	4.79
Tommy Bridges	R	31	13	9	.591	1	25	20	13	151	171	58	101	0	4.59
George Gill	R	29	12	9	.571	0	24	23	13	164	195	50	30	1	4.12
Vern Kennedy (SA)	R	31	12	9	.571	2	33	26	11	190	215	113	53	0	5.07
Elden Auker	R	27	11	10	.524	0	27	24	12	161	184	56	46	1	5.25
Harry Eisenstat	L	22	9	6	.600	4	32	9	5	125	131	29	37	0	3.74
Rosie Lawson	R	27	7	5	.583	2	27	16	5	127	154	82	46	0	5.46
Boots Poffenberger	R	23	6	7	.462	1	25	15	8	125	147	66	28	0	4.82
Al Benton	R	27	5	3	.625	0	19	10	6	95	93	39	33	0	3.32
Slick Coffman	R	27	4	4	.500	2	39	6	1	96	120	48	31	0	6.00
Jake Wade	L	26	3	2	.600	0	27	2	0	70	73	48	23	0	6.56
Bob Harris	R	23	1	0	1.000	0	3	1	1	10	14	4	7	0	7.20
Schoolboy Rowe (AJ)	R	28	0	2	.000	0	4	3	0	21	20	11	4	0	3.00
Woody Davis	R	25	0	0	.000	0	2	0	0	6	3	4	1	0	1.50
Joe Rogalski	R	25	0	0	.000	0	2	0	0	7	12	2	4	0	2.57

WASHINGTON — 5th 75-76 .497 23.5 — BUCKY HARRIS

NAME	G by Pos	B	AGE	G	AB	R	H	2B	3B	HR	RBI	BB	SO	SB	BA	SA
TOTALS			28	152	5474	814	1602	278	72	85	767	573	379	65	.293	.416
Zeke Bonura	1B129	R	29	137	540	72	156	27	3	22	114	44	29	2	.289	.472
Buddy Myer	2B121	L	34	127	437	79	147	22	6	1	71	93	32	9	.336	.465
Cecil Travis	SS143	L	24	146	467	96	190	30	5	5	67	58	22	6	.335	.432
Buddy Lewis	3B151	L	21	151	656	122	194	35	9	12	91	58	35	17	.296	.431
George Case	OF101	R	22	107	433	69	132	27	3	2	40	39	28	11	.305	.395
2 Sammy West	OF85	R	33	92	344	51	104	19	5	5	47	33	21	1	.302	.430
Al Simmons	OF117	R	36	125	470	79	142	23	6	21	95	38	40	2	.302	.461
Rick Ferrell	C131	R	32	135	411	55	120	24	5	1	58	75	17	1	.292	.382
Taffy Wright	OF60	L	26	100	263	37	92	18	10	2	36	13	17	1	.350	.517
Ossie Bluege	2B38, SS10, 1B1, 3B1	R	37	58	184	25	48	12	1	0	21	21	11	0	.261	.337
John Stone (IL)	OF53	L	32	56	213	24	52	12	4	3	28	30	16	2	.244	.380
Jimmy Wasdell	1B26, OF6	L	24	53	140	19	33	2	1	2	16	12	12	5	.236	.307
Mel Almada	OF47	L	25	47	197	24	48	7	4	1	15	8	16	4	.244	.335
Tony Giuliani	C46	R	25	46	115	10	25	4	0	0	15	8	1	0	.217	.252
Goose Goslin	OF13	L	37	38	57	6	9	3	0	2	8	8	5	0	.158	.316
Mickey Livingston	C2	R	23	4	4	1	3	1	0	0	0	0	1	0	.750	1.250

NAME	T	AGE	W	L	PCT	SV	G	GS	CG	IP	H	BB	SO	SHO	ERA
TOTALS		30	75	76	.497	11	152	152	59	1360	1472	655	515	6	4.94
1 Wes Ferrell	R	30	13	8	.619	0	23	22	9	149	193	68	36	0	5.92
Dutch Leonard	R	29	12	15	.444	0	33	31	15	223	221	53	68	3	3.43
Ken Chase	L	24	9	10	.474	1	32	21	7	150	151	113	64	0	5.58
1 Harry Kelley	R	32	9	8	.529	1	38	14	7	148	162	46	44	2	4.50
Joe Krakauskas	L	23	7	5	.583	0	29	10	5	121	99	88	104	1	3.12
Monty Weaver	R	32	7	6	.538	0	31	18	7	139	157	74	43	0	5.24
Pete Appleton	R	34	7	9	.438	5	43	10	5	164	175	61	62	0	4.61
Chief Hogsett	L	34	5	6	.455	3	31	9	1	91	107	36	33	0	6.03
Jimmie DeShong	R	28	5	8	.385	0	31	14	1	131	160	83	41	0	6.60
Rene Monteagudo	L	22	1	1	.500	0	5	3	2	22	26	15	13	0	5.73
Joe Kohlman	R	25	0	0	.000	0	7	0	0	14	12	11	5	0	6.43
Bill Phebus	R	28	0	0	.000	1	5	0	0	9	7	7	2	0	12.00

CHICAGO — 6th 65-83 .439 32 — JIMMY DYKES

NAME	G by Pos	B	AGE	G	AB	R	H	2B	3B	HR	RBI	BB	SO	SB	BA	SA
TOTALS			31	149	5199	709	1439	239	55	67	657	514	489	56	.277	.383
Joe Kuhel	1B111	L	31	117	412	67	110	27	4	8	51	72	35	9	.267	.410
Jackie Hayes (KJ)	2B61	R	31	62	238	40	78	21	2	1	20	24	6	3	.328	.445
Luke Appling (BN)	SS78	R	31	81	294	41	89	14	0	0	44	42	17	1	.303	.350
Marv Owen	3B140	R	32	141	577	84	162	23	6	6	55	45	31	6	.281	.373
Hank Steinbacher	OF101	L	25	106	399	59	132	23	8	4	61	41	19	1	.331	.459
Mike Kreevich	OF127	R	30	129	489	73	145	26	12	6	73	56	23	13	.297	.436
Gee Walker	OF107	R	30	120	442	69	135	23	6	16	87	38	32	9	.305	.493
Luke Sewell	C65	R	37	65	211	23	45	4	1	0	27	20	20	0	.213	.242
Rip Radcliff	OF99, 1B23	R	32	129	503	64	166	23	6	5	81	36	17	5	.330	.429
Boze Berger	SS67, 2B42, 3B9	R	28	118	470	60	102	15	3	3	36	43	80	4	.217	.281
Larry Rosenthal	OF22	L	28	61	105	14	30	5	1	1	12	13	20	0	.286	.381
Tony Rensa	C57	R	36	59	165	15	41	5	0	3	19	25	16	1	.248	.333
Norm Schlueter	C34	R	21	35	118	11	27	5	1	0	16	0	23	0	.229	.288
Thornton Lee	P33	L	31	34	97	14	25	3	1	4	16	0	23	0	.258	.433
Jimmy Dykes	2B33, 3B1	R	41	26	89	9	27	4	2	2	13	10	8	0	.303	.461
Merv Connors	1B16	R	24	24	62	14	22	4	0	6	13	9	17	0	.355	.710
George Meyer	2B24	R	28	24	81	10	24	2	2	0	9	11	17	3	.296	.370
Tommy Thompson	1B1	R	28	19	18	2	2	0	0	0	2	1	0	0	.111	.111
Mike Tresh	C10	R	24	10	29	3	7	2	0	0	2	8	4	0	.241	.310
John Gerlach	SS8	R	21	9	25	2	7	0	0	0	1	4	2	0	.280	.280
Jesse Landrum	2B3	R	25	4	6	0	0	0	0	0	1	0	2	0	.000	.000
Joe Martin		R	26	1	0	0	0	0	0	0	0	0	0	0	.000	---

NAME	T	AGE	W	L	PCT	SV	G	GS	CG	IP	H	BB	SO	SHO	ERA
TOTALS		29	65	83	.439	9	149	149	83	1316	1449	550	432	5	4.36
Monty Stratton (LA)	R	26	15	9	.625	2	26	22	17	186	186	56	82	0	4.02
Thornton Lee	L	31	13	12	.520	2	33	30	18	245	252	94	77	1	3.49
John Whitehead	R	29	10	11	.476	2	32	24	10	183	218	80	38	1	4.77
Johnny Rigney	R	23	9	9	.500	1	38	12	7	167	164	72	84	0	3.56
Ted Lyons	R	37	9	11	.450	0	23	23	17	195	238	52	54	1	3.69
2 Jack Knott	R	31	5	10	.333	0	20	18	9	131	135	54	35	0	4.05
Bill Dietrich (AJ)	R	28	2	4	.333	0	8	7	1	48	49	31	11	0	5.44
Clint Brown (AJ)	R	34	1	3	.250	7	24	0	0	14	16	9	2	0	4.50
2 Frank Gabler	R	26	1	7	.125	0	18	7	3	69	101	34	17	0	9.13
Sugar Cain	R	31	0	1	.000	0	5	3	0	20	26	18	6	0	4.50
1 Bill Cox	R	25	0	2	.000	0	7	1	0	12	11	13	5	0	6.75
Harry Boyles	R	26	0	0	---	0	3	1	0	29	31	25	18	0	5.28
Gene Ford	R	26	0	0	---	0	1	0	0	14	21	12	2	0	10.29
Goerge Gick	R	22	0	0	---	0	1	0	0	1	0	1	0	0	0.00
Bob Uhl	L	24	0	0	---	0	1	0	0	2	1	0	0	0	0.00

ST. LOUIS — 7th 55-97 .362 44 — GABBY STREET 53-90 .371 — OSCAR MELILLO 2-7 .222

NAME	G by Pos	B	AGE	G	AB	R	H	2B	3B	HR	RBI	BB	SO	SB	BA	SA
TOTALS			28	156	5333	755	1498	273	36	92	713	590	528	51	.281	.397
George McQuinn	1B148	L	29	148	602	100	195	42	7	12	82	58	49	4	.324	.477
Don Heffner	2B141	R	27	141	473	47	116	23	3	7	69	65	53	1	.245	.319
Red Kress	SS150	R	33	150	566	74	171	33	3	7	79	69	47	5	.302	.408
Harlond Clift	3B149	R	25	149	534	119	155	25	7	34	118	118	67	10	.290	.554
Beau Bell	OF132, 1B4	R	30	147	526	91	138	35	3	13	84	71	46	1	.262	.414
2 Mel Almada	OF101	L	25	102	436	77	149	22	3	2	37	38	22	9	.342	.422
Buster Mills	OF113	R	29	123	466	66	133	24	4	3	46	43	46	7	.285	.373
Billy Sullivan	C99, 1B6	R	27	111	375	35	104	16	1	7	49	20	10	8	.277	.381
Mike Mazzera	OF47	L	24	86	204	33	57	8	2	6	29	12	25	1	.279	.426
Tommy Heath	C65	R	24	70	194	22	44	13	0	2	22	35	24	0	.227	.325
Roy Hughes	2B21, 3B5, SS2	R	27	58	96	16	27	3	0	2	13	12	11	3	.281	.375
1 Sammy West	OF41	L	33	44	165	17	51	8	2	1	27	14	9	1	.309	.400
Glenn McQuillan	OF30	R	23	43	116	14	33	6	0	0	13	4	12	0	.284	.319
Ethan Allen	OF7	L	34	19	33	4	10	3	1	0	4	2	4	0	.303	.455
Joe Grace	OF12	L	24	12	47	7	16	1	0	0	4	2	3	2	.340	.362
Sam Harshany	C10	R	28	11	24	2	7	0	0	0	3	0	2	0	.292	.292
Sig Gryska	SS7	R	23	7	21	3	10	2	1	0	4	3	3	0	.476	.667
Johnny Lucadello	3B6	B	19	7	20	1	3	1	0	0	1	1	5	0	.150	.200

NAME	T	AGE	W	L	PCT	SV	G	GS	CG	IP	H	BB	SO	SHO	ERA
TOTALS		30	56	97	.362	7	156	156	71	1345	1584	737	632	3	5.80
Bobo Newsom	R	30	20	16	.556	1	44	40	31	330	334	192	226	0	5.07
Lefty Mills	L	28	10	12	.455	0	30	27	15	210	216	116	134	1	5.31
Oral Hildebrand	R	31	8	10	.444	0	23	23	10	163	194	73	66	0	5.69
Russ VanAtta	L	32	7	7	.364	0	25	12	3	104	118	61	35	0	6.06
Fred Johnson	R	44	3	7	.300	3	17	6	3	69	91	27	24	0	5.61
Julio Bonetti	R	26	2	3	.400	0	28	4	1	74	113	38	28	0	6.43
Les Tietje	R	27	2	5	.286	0	17	8	2	62	83	38	15	1	7.55
1 Jack Knott	R	31	2	3	.333	0	7	4	0	30	55	15	4	0	4.80
Emil Bildilli	L	25	1	2	.333	0	5	3	2	33	11	11	10	0	6.95
2 Bill Cox	R	25	1	4	.200	0	22	7	1	63	81	35	16	0	7.00
Ed Cole	R	29	1	5	.167	3	36	6	1	89	116	48	26	0	5.16
Ed Linke	R	28	1	12	.077	0	21	2	0	40	60	33	18	0	7.88
Jim Walkup	R	29	0	1	.000	0	18	13	1	94	127	53	28	0	6.80
Bill Trotter	R	23	0	1	.000	0	1	1	0	8	9	4	0	0	5.63
1 Jim Weaver	R	34	0	1	.000	0	1	1	0	8	9	4	0	0	9.00
1 Vito Tamulis	L	26	0	3	.000	0	4	2	0	15	26	10	11	0	7.80
Glenn Liebhardt	R	27	0	0	.000	0	3	0	0	8	4	0	1	0	6.00
Harry Kimberlin	R	29	0	2	.000	0	8	2	0	28	31	13	10	0	3.38

PHILADELPHIA — 8th 53-99 .349 46 — CONNIE MACK

NAME	G by Pos	B	AGE	G	AB	R	H	2B	3B	HR	RBI	BB	SO	SB	BA	SA
TOTALS			27	154	5229	726	1410	243	62	98	686	605	590	65	.270	.396
Lou Finney	1B64, OF46	R	27	122	454	61	125	21	12	10	48	39	25	5	.275	.441
Dario Lodigiani	2B80	R	22	93	325	36	91	15	1	6	44	34	25	3	.280	.388
Wayne Ambler	SS116, 2B4	R	22	120	393	42	92	21	2	0	38	48	31	2	.234	.298
Bill Werber	3B134	R	30	134	499	79	129	22	7	11	69	93	37	19	.259	.397
Wally Moses	OF139	L	27	142	589	86	181	29	9	14	58	51	71	14	.307	.424
Bob Johnson	OF150, 2B3, 3B1	R	32	152	563	114	176	27	9	30	113	87	73	9	.313	.552
Sam Chapman	OF114	R	22	114	406	60	105	17	7	17	63	55	94	3	.259	.461
Frankie Hayes	C90	R	23	99	316	56	92	19	3	11	55	54	51	0	.291	.475
Lynn Nelson	P32	L	33	67	112	12	31	0	0	3	15	7	12	0	.277	.277
Stan Sperry	2B60	R	24	60	253	28	69	6	3	0	27	15	9	1	.273	.320
Ace Parker	SS26, 2B9, 3B9	R	26	56	113	12	26	5	0	0	10	16	16	1	.230	.274
Earle Brucker	C44, 1B1	R	37	53	171	26	64	21	1	3	35	19	16	1	.374	.561
2 Dick Siebert (KJ, AJ)	1B46	L	26	48	194	24	55	8	3	0	28	10	9	2	.284	.356
Mule Haas	OF12, 1B6	L	34	40	78	7	16	3	0	0	12	12	10	0	.205	.231
Hal Wagner	C30	L	22	33	88	10	20	2	1	0	8	8	9	0	.227	.273
Nick Etten	1B22	L	22	22	81	6	21	2	1	0	11	9	7	1	.259	.383
Gene Hasson	1B19	L	22	19	69	10	19	4	0	2	12	12	7	0	.275	.464
Skeeter Newsome (PB)	SS15	R	27	17	13	1	6	1	0	0	1	1	5	0	.271	.354
Chubby Dean	P6	L	22	16	20	3	6	1	0	0	2	1	3	0	.300	.400
Irv Bartling	SS13, 3B1	R	24	14	46	5	8	0	0	0	6	1	6	0	.174	.239
Babe Barna	OF7	L	23	9	30	4	4	0	1	0	1	2	6	0	.133	.133
Paul Esterling	OF1	R	32	4	7	1	2	0	0	0	1	1	1	0	.286	.286
Rusty Peters	SS2	R	23	3	3	0	0	0	0	0	0	0	2	0	.000	.000
Charlie Berry	C1	R	35	1	1	0	0	0	0	0	0	0	0	0	.000	.000

NAME	T	AGE	W	L	PCT	SV	G	GS	CG	IP	H	BB	SO	SHO	ERA
TOTALS		26	53	99	.349	12	154	154	56	1324	1573	599	473	4	5.48
George Caster	R	30	16	20	.444	1	42	40	20	281	310	117	112	2	4.36
Lynn Nelson	R	33	10	11	.476	2	32	23	13	191	215	79	75	0	5.65
Bud Thomas	R	27	9	14	.391	0	42	29	7	212	259	62	48	1	4.92
Buck Ross	R	23	9	16	.360	0	29	28	10	184	218	80	54	0	5.33
Eddie Smith	L	24	3	10	.231	4	43	1	0	131	151	76	78	0	5.91
Dave Smith	R	23	2	1	.667	0	21	0	0	44	50	28	13	0	5.11
Chubby Dean	L	22	2	6	.667	0	23	22	15	3	0	3.52			
Nels Potter	R	26	2	12	.143	1	35	9	4	111	139	49	43	0	6.49
Ralph Buxton	R						9		5				5		5.00
Randy Gumpert	R	20	0	2	.000	0	12			24	10	11	1		11.25
1 Harry Kelley	R	32	0	2	.000	0	8			17	10	3	0		16.88
Jim Reninger	R	23	0	2	.000		1			23	28	14	9	0	7.04
Al Williams	R	24	0	7	.000	0	30		1	93	128	54	25	0	6.97

CHICAGO — 1ST 89-63 .586 — CHARLIE GRIMM 45-36 .556 — GABBY HARTNETT 44-27 .620

NAME	G by Pos	B	AGE	G	AB	R	H	2B	3B	HR	RBI	BB	SO	SB	BA	SA
TOTALS			29	154	5333	713	1435	242	70	65	673	522	476	49	.269	.377
Ripper Collins	1B135	B	34	143	490	78	131	22	8	13	61	54	48	1	.267	.424
Billy Herman	2B151	R	28	152	624	86	173	34	7	1	56	59	31	3	.277	.359
Billy Jurges	SS136	R	30	137	465	53	114	18	3	1	47	58	53	3	.245	.303
Stan Hack	3B152	L	28	152	609	109	195	34	11	4	67	94	39	16	.320	.432
Frank Demaree	OF125	R	28	129	476	63	130	15	7	8	62	45	34	1	.273	.384
Carl Reynolds	OF125	R	35	125	497	59	150	28	10	3	67	22	32	9	.302	.416
Augie Galan	OF103	B	26	110	395	52	113	16	9	6	69	49	17	4	.286	.418
Gabby Hartnett	C83	R	37	88	299	40	82	19	1	10	59	48	17	1	.274	.445
Phil Cavarretta	OF52, 1B28	L	21	92	268	29	64	11	4	1	28	14	27	4	.239	.321
Ken O'Dea	C71	L	25	86	247	22	65	12	1	3	33	12	18	1	.263	.356
Joe Marty	OF68	R	24	76	235	32	57	8	3	7	35	18	26	0	.243	.391
Tony Lazzeri	SS25, 3B7, 2B4, OF1	R	34	54	120	21	32	5	0	5	23	22	30	0	.267	.433
Bob Garbark	C20, 1B1	R	28	23	54	2	14	0	0	0	5	1	0	0	.259	.259
Jim Asbell	OF10	R	24	17	33	6	6	2	0	0	3	3	9	0	.182	.242
Coaker Triplett	OF9	R	26	12	36	4	9	2	1	0	2	0	1	0	.250	.361
Steve Mesner	SS1	R	20	2	4	2	1	0	0	0	0	0	1	0	.250	.250
Bobby Mattick	SS1	R	22	1	1	0	1	0	0	0	0	0	1	0	01.000	1.000

NAME	T	AGE	W	L	PCT	SV	G	GS	CG	IP	H	BB	SO	SHO	ERA
		31	89	63	.586	18	154	154	67	1397	1414	454	583	16	3.37
Bill Lee	R	28	22	9	.710	2	44	37	19	291	281	74	121	9	2.66
Clay Bryant	R	26	19	11	.633	2	44	30	17	270	235	125	135	3	3.10
Tex Carleton	R	31	10	9	.526	0	33	24	9	168	213	74	80	0	5.41
Larry French	L	30	10	19	.345	0	43	27	10	201	210	62	83	3	3.81
Charlie Root	R	39	8	7	.533	8	44	11	5	161	163	30	70	0	2.85
Dizzy Dean (AJ)	R	28	7	1	.875	0	13	10	3	75	63	8	22	1	1.80
Jack Russell	R	32	6	1	.857	2	42	0	0	102	100	30	29	0	3.35
Vance Page	R	34	5	4	.566	1	13	9	3	68	90	13	18	0	3.84
Al Epperly	R	20	2	0	1.000	0	9	4	1	27	28	15	10	0	3.67
Bob Logan	L	28	0	2	.000	2	14	0	0	23	18	17	10	0	2.74
Kirby Higbe	R	23	0	0	—	0	2	0	0	10	10	6	4	0	5.40
Newt Kimball	R	23	0	0	—	0	1	0	0	1	3	1	1	0	9.00

PITTSBURGH — 2nd 86-64 .573 — 2 — PIE TRAYNOR

NAME	G by Pos	B	AGE	G	AB	R	H	2B	3B	HR	RBI	BB	SO	SB	BA	SA
TOTALS			30	152	5422	707	1511	265	66	65	659	485	409	47	.279	.388
Gus Suhr	1B145	L	32	145	530	82	156	35	14	3	64	87	37	4	.294	.434
Pep Young	2B149	R	30	149	562	58	156	36	5	4	79	40	64	1	.278	.381
Arky Vaughan	SS147	L	26	148	541	88	174	35	5	7	68	104	21	14	.322	.444
Lee Handley	3B136	R	24	139	570	91	153	29	6	4	51	53	31	17	.268	.372
Paul Waner	OF147	L	35	148	625	77	175	31	6	6	69	47	28	2	.280	.378
Lloyd Waner	OF144	L	32	147	619	79	194	25	7	5	57	28	11	5	.313	.401
Johnny Rizzo	OF140	R	25	143	555	97	167	31	9	23	111	54	61	1	.301	.514
Al Todd	C132	R	34	133	491	52	130	19	7	7	75	18	31	2	.265	.375
Woody Jensen	OF38	L	30	68	125	12	25	4	0	0	10	1	3	0	.200	.232
Bill Brubaker	3B18, 1B9, SS3, OF1	R	27	45	112	18	33	5	0	3	19	9	14	2	.295	.420
Ray Berres	C40	R	30	40	100	7	23	2	0	0	6	8	10	0	.230	.250
Red Lucas	P13	L	36	33	46	1	5	0	0	0	2	3	1	0	.109	.109
Johnny Dickshot	OF10	R	28	29	35	3	8	0	0	0	4	8	5	3	.229	.229
2 Heinie Manush		L	36	15	13	2	4	1	1	0	4	2	0	0	.308	.538
Tommy Thevenow	2B9, SS4, 3B1	R	34	15	25	2	5	0	0	0	0	1	5	0	.200	.200

NAME	T	AGE	W	L	PCT	SV	G	GS	CG	IP	H	BB	SO	SHO	ERA
		29	86	64	.573	15	152	152	57	1380	1406	432	557	8	3.46
Mace Brown	R	29	15	9	.625	5	51	2	0	133	155	44	55	0	3.79
Jim Tobin	R	25	14	12	.538	0	40	33	14	241	254	66	70	2	3.47
Russ Bauers	R	24	13	14	.481	3	40	34	12	243	207	99	117	3	3.07
Bob Klinger	R	30	12	5	.706	2	28	21	10	159	152	42	58	1	3.00
Cy Blanton	R	29	11	7	.611	0	29	26	10	173	190	46	80	1	3.69
Bill Swift	R	30	7	5	.583	4	36	9	2	150	155	40	77	0	3.24
Red Lucas	R	36	6	3	.667	0	13	13	4	84	90	16	19	0	3.54
Ed Brandt	L	33	5	4	.556	0	24	13	5	96	93	35	38	1	3.47
Joe Bowman (SA)	R	28	3	4	.429	1	17	1	0	60	68	20	25	0	4.65
Rip Sewell	R	31	0	1	.000	1	17	0	0	38	41	21	17	0	4.26
Ken Heintzelman	L	22	0	0	—	0	3	0	0	2	1	3	1	0	9.00

NEW YORK — 3rd 83-67 .553 — 5 — BILL TERRY

NAME	G by Pos	B	AGE	G	AB	R	H	2B	3B	HR	RBI	BB	SO	SB	BA	SA
TOTALS			28	152	5255	705	1424	210	36	125	672	465	528	31	.271	.396
Johnny McCarthy	1B125	L	28	134	470	55	128	13	4	8	59	39	28	3	.272	.368
2 Alex Kampouris	2B79	R	25	82	268	55	66	9	1	5	37	27	50	0	.246	.343
Dick Bartell	SS127	R	30	127	481	67	126	23	4	6	52	44	30	6	.262	.376
Mel Ott	3B113, OF37	R	29	150	527	116	164	23	6	36	116	118	47	2	.311	.583
Jimmy Ripple	OF131	L	28	134	501	68	131	21	3	10	60	49	21	2	.261	.375
Hank Leiber	OF89	R	27	98	360	50	97	18	4	12	65	31	45	0	.269	.442
Jo-Jo Moore	OF114	L	29	125	506	76	153	23	6	11	56	22	27	2	.302	.437
Harry Danning	C114	R	26	120	448	59	137	26	3	9	60	23	40	1	.306	.438
Bob Seeds	OF76	R	31	81	296	35	86	12	3	9	52	20	33	0	.291	.443
Sam Leslie	1B32	L	32	76	154	12	39	7	1	1	16	11	6	0	.253	.331
Lou Chiozza (BL)	2B43, OF16, 3B1	L	28	57	179	15	42	7	2	3	17	12	17	5	.235	.346
Gus Mancuso	C44	R	32	58	152	19	55	8	0	2	15	17	13	0	.348	.437
George Myatt	SS24, 3B19	R	24	43	170	27	52	2	1	3	10	14	13	10	.306	.382
Bill Cissell	2B33, 3B6	R	34	38	149	19	40	6	0	2	18	6	11	1	.268	.349
Mickey Haslin	3B15, 2B13	R	32	31	102	13	33	3	0	3	15	4	4	0	.324	.441
1 Wally Berger	OF9	R	32	16	32	5	6	0	0	0	4	2	4	0	.188	.188
Blondy Ryan	2B5, 3B3, SS2	R	32	12	24	1	5	0	0	0	0	1	3	0	.208	.208
Les Powers		L	28	2	3	0	0	0	0	0	0	0	1	0	.000	.000
Burgess Whitehead (IL) 28																

NAME	T	AGE	W	L	PCT	SV	G	GS	CG	IP	H	BB	SO	SHO	ERA
		28	83	67	.553	18	152	152	59	1349	1370	389	497	8	3.62
Harry Gumbert	R	28	15	13	.536	0	38	33	14	236	238	84	84	0	4.00
Cliff Melton	L	26	14	14	.500	2	38	31	10	243	266	61	101	1	3.89
Hal Schumacher	R	27	13	8	.619	0	28	28	12	185	178	50	54	4	3.50
Carl Hubbell (SA)	L	35	13	10	.565	1	24	22	13	179	171	33	104	1	3.07
Bill Lohrman	R	25	9	6	.600	0	31	14	3	152	152	33	52	0	3.32
Dick Coffman	R	31	8	4	.667	12	51	3	1	111	116	21	21	1	3.49
Jumbo Brown	R	31	8	3	.625	5	43	0	0	90	65	28	42	0	1.80
Slick Castleman	R	24	4	5	.444	0	21	14	4	91	108	37	18	0	4.15
Johnnie Wittig	R	24	3	3	.400	0	13	6	2	39	41	26	14	0	4.85
Tom Baker	R	25	0	0	—	0	2	0	0	4	1	3	1	0	9.00
Oscar Georgy	R	31	0	0	—	0	1	0	0	1	2	1	0	0	18.00
Hy Vandenberg	R	30	0	1	.000	0	6	1	0	18	28	12	7	0	7.50

CINCINNATI — 4th 82-68 .547 — 6 — BILL McKECHNIE

NAME	G by Pos	B	AGE	G	AB	R	H	2B	3B	HR	RBI	BB	SO	SB	BA	SA
TOTALS			28	151	5391	723	1495	251	57	110	679	366	518	19	.277	.406
Frank McCormick	1B151	R	27	151	640	99	209	40	4	5	106	18	17	1	.327	.425
Lonny Frey	1B121, SS3	R	27	124	501	76	133	26	4	6	36	49	50	4	.265	.365
Billy Myers	2B123, 2B11	R	27	134	442	57	112	18	6	12	47	41	80	2	.253	.403
Lew Riggs	3B142	R	28	142	531	53	134	21	13	2	55	40	32	3	.252	.352
Ival Goodman	OF142	L	29	145	568	103	166	27	10	30	92	53	51	3	.292	.533
Harry Craft	OF151	R	23	151	612	70	165	28	9	15	83	29	46	3	.307	.418
2 Wally Berger	OF98	R	32	99	407	74	125	23	4	16	56	24	44	2	.307	.501
Ernie Lombardi	C123	R	30	129	489	60	167	30	1	19	95	40	14	0	.342	.524
Dusty Cooke	OF51	L	31	82	233	41	64	15	1	2	33	28	36	0	.275	.373
Lee Gamble	OF35	L	25	53	75	13	24	3	1	0	5	0	6	0	.320	.387
Willard Hershberger	3B39, 2B1	R	28	49	105	12	29	3	1	0	12	5	6	1	.276	.324
Nolen Richardson	SS35	R	35	35	100	8	29	4	0	0	10	3	4	0	.290	.330
1 Alex Kampouris	2B21	R	25	21	74	13	19	1	0	2	7	10	13	0	.257	.351
Don Lang	3B15, 2B1, SS1	R	23	21	50	5	13	3	1	1	11	2	7	0	.260	.420
1 Spud Davis	C11	R	33	12	36	3	6	1	0	0	1	0	1	0	.167	.194
2 Justin Stein	SS7, 2B2	R	26	11	18	3	6	1	0	0	1	0	3	0	.333	.389
1 Buck Jordan		L	31	9	7	0	2	0	0	0	0	0	0	0	.286	.286
Kiddo Davis	OF5	R	36	5	18	3	5	1	0	0	0	0	4	0	.278	.333
Jimmy Outlaw		R	25	4	0	1	0	0	0	0	0	0	0	0	—	—
Nino Bongiovanni	OF2	L	26	2	7	0	2	1	0	0	0	0	1	0	.286	.429
Dick West		R	22	1	4	0	0	0	0	0	0	0	1	0	.000	.000

NAME	T	AGE	W	L	PCT	SV	G	GS	CG	IP	H	BB	SO	SHO	ERA
		29	82	68	.547	16	151	151	72	1362	1329	463	542	11	3.62
Paul Derringer	R	31	21	14	.600	3	41	37	26	307	315	49	132	4	2.93
Johnny Vander Meer	R	23	15	10	.600	0	32	29	16	225	177	103	125	3	3.12
2 Bucky Walters	R	29	11	6	.647	1	27	22	11	168	168	66	65	2	3.70
Peaches Davis	R	33	7	12	.368	1	29	19	11	168	193	40	28	1	3.96
Whitey Moore	R	26	6	4	.600	0	19	11	3	90	66	42	38	1	3.50
2 Jim Weaver	R	34	6	4	.600	3	30	15	2	129	109	54	64	0	3.14
Gene Scott	R	24	5	5	.500	2	31	4	1	83	89	32	21	0	4.45
Joe Cascarella	R	31	4	7	.364	4	33	1	0	61	66	22	30	0	4.57
Red Barrett	R	23	2	0	1.000	0	6	2	2	29	28	15	5	0	3.10
1 Al Hollingsworth	L	30	2	2	.500	0	9	4	1	34	43	12	13	0	7.15
Lee Grissom (KJ)	L	30	2	3	.400	0	14	7	0	51	60	22	16	0	5.29
Ray Benge	R	36	1	1	.500	2	18	0	0	15	13	6	5	0	4.20
Ted Kleinhans	L	39	0	0	—	0	1	0	0	1	2	0	0	0	9.00

BOSTON — 5th 77-75 .507 — 12 — CASEY STENGEL

NAME	G by Pos	B	AGE	G	AB	R	H	2B	3B	HR	RBI	BB	SO	SB	BA	SA
TOTALS			27	153	5250	561	1311	199	39	54	519	424	548	49	.250	.333
Elbie Fletcher	1B146	L	22	147	529	71	144	24	7	6	48	60	40	5	.272	.378
Tony Cuccinello	2B147	R	30	147	555	62	147	35	2	9	76	52	32	4	.265	.366
Rabbit Warstler	SS135, 2B7	R	34	142	467	37	108	10	4	0	40	48	38	3	.231	.270
2 Joe Stripp	3B58	R	35	99	229	19	63	10	0	1	19	10	7	2	.275	.332
Johnny Cooney	OF110, 1B16	L	37	120	432	45	117	25	5	0	17	22	12	2	.271	.352
Vince DiMaggio	OF149, 2B1	R	25	150	540	71	123	28	3	14	61	65	134	11	.228	.369
Max West	OF109, 1B7	L	21	123	418	49	98	16	5	10	63	38	38	5	.234	.368
Ray Mueller (BG)	C75	R	26	83	274	23	65	8	6	4	35	16	28	1	.237	.354
Debs Garms	OF63, 3B54, SS1	L	31	117	428	62	135	19	1	0	47	34	22	4	.315	.364
Al Lopez (BG)	C71	R	29	71	236	19	63	6	1	1	14	11	24	5	.267	.314
Harl Maggert	OF10, 3B8	R	28	66	89	12	25	3	0	0	6	3	16	0	.281	.416
Gene Moore (KJ)	OF47	L	28	54	180	27	49	8	3	3	19	16	20	1	.272	.400
Gil English	3B43, OF3, 2B2, SS2	R	29	53	165	17	41	6	0	2	21	15	19	1	.248	.321
Bobby Reis	P16, OF10, SS3, 2B1, C1	R	29	34	49	6	9	0	0	0	4	1	3	1	.184	.184
Jim Hitchcock	SS24, 3B2	R	24	28	76	2	13	0	0	0	7	2	11	1	.171	.171
Johnny Riddle	C19	R	32	19	57	6	16	1	0	0	2	0	6	0	.281	.298
Bob Kahle		R	32	8	6	0	2	0	0	0	0	0	3	0	.333	.333
Eddie Mayo	3B6, SS2	R	28	8	14	2	3	1	0	0	1	0	4	0	.214	.429
Roy Johnson	OF7	L	35	7	29	2	5	0	0	0	4	1	5	1	.172	.172
Ralph McLeod		L	21	6	7	1	2	1	0	0	2	0	1	0	.286	.429
Butch Sutcliffe	C3	R	22	4	4	1	1	0	0	0	2	0	1	0	.250	.250
Joe Walsh	SS4	R	21	4	9	0	0	0	0	0	0	0	1	0	.000	.000
Tom Kane	2B2	R	31	2	3	2	0	0	0	0	0	1	1	0	.000	.000

NAME	T	AGE	W	L	PCT	SV	G	GS	CG	IP	H	BB	SO	SHO	ERA
		30	77	75	.507	12	153	153	83	1380	1375	465	413	15	3.40
Danny MacFayden (BH)	R	33	14	9	.609	0	29	29	19	220	208	64	58	5	2.95
Jim Turner	R	34	14	18	.438	0	35	34	22	268	267	54	71	3	3.46
Lou Fette	R	31	11	13	.458	1	33	32	17	240	235	79	83	3	3.15
Dick Errickson	R	26	9	7	.563	6	34	10	6	123	113	56	40	1	3.15
Ira Hutchinson	R	27	8	8	.529	4	36	12	4	151	150	61	38	1	2.74
Johnny Lanning	R	31	8	7	.533	0	32	18	4	138	146	52	39	1	3.72
Milt Shoffner (IL)	L	32	8	7	.533	1	26	15	9	140	147	38	49	1	3.54
Roy Weir	R	27	1	0	1.000	0	9	0	0	13	14	6	3	0	6.92
Tom Earley	R	21	1	0	1.000	0	2	1	1	11	8	1	4	0	3.27
Johnny Niggeling	R	34	1	0	1.000	0	4	1	0	8	8	5	4	0	9.00
Bobby Reis	R	29	1	6	.143	0	16	2	1	58	61	41	20	0	4.97
2 Tommy Reis	R	23	0	0	—	0	9	0	0	14	21	9	1	0	7.50
Art Doll	R	23	0	0	—	0	2	0	0	3	5	1	1	0	2.25
Art Kenney	L	22	0	0	—	0	1	0	0	1	2	0	0	0	18.00
Hiker Moran	R	28	0	0	—	0	1	0	0	3	5	4	0	0	9.00
Mike Balas	R	28	0	0	—	0	1	0	0	1	2	0	1	0	9.00
1 Frank Gabler	R	26	0	0	—	0	1	0	0	1	4	0	0	0	81.00

ST. LOUIS — 6th 71-80 .470 17.5 — FRANKIE FRISCH 63-72 .467 — MIKE GONZALEZ 8-8 .500

NAME	G by Pos	B	AGE	G	AB	R	H	2B	3B	HR	RBI	BB	SO	SB	BA	SA
TOTALS			27	156	5528	725	1542	288	74	91	680	412	492	55	.279	.407
Johnny Mize	1B140	L	25	149	531	85	179	34	16	27	102	74	47	0	.337	.614
Stu Martin	2B99	R	25	114	417	54	116	26	2	1	27	30	28	4	.278	.357
Lynn Myers	SS69	R	24	70	227	18	55	10	2	1	9	9	25	9	.242	.317
Don Gutteridge	3B73, SS68	R	26	142	552	61	141	21	15	9	64	24	49	14	.255	.397
Enos Slaughter	OF92	L	22	112	395	59	109	20	10	8	58	32	38	1	.276	.438
Terry Moore	OF75, 3B6	R	26	94	312	49	85	21	3	4	21	46	19	4	.272	.397
Joe Medwick	OF144	R	26	146	590	100	190	47	8	21	122	42	41	0	.322	.536
Mickey Owen	C116	R	22	122	397	45	106	25	2	4	36	32	14	2	.267	.370
Don Padgett	OF71, 1B16, C6	L	26	110	388	59	105	26	5	8	65	18	28	0	.271	.425
Jimmy Brown	2B49, SS30, 3B24	B	28	108	382	50	115	12	6	0	38	27	9	7	.301	.364
Pepper Martin	OF62, 3B4	R	34	91	269	34	79	18	2	2	38	18	34	4	.294	.398
Frenchy Bordagaray	OF29, 3B4	R	28	81	156	19	44	5	1	0	21	8	9	2	.282	.327
1 Joe Stripp	3B51	R	25	54	199	24	57	7	0	0	18	18	10	0	.286	.322
Herb Bremer	C50	R	24	50	151	14	33	5	1	2	14	9	36	1	.219	.305
Lon Warneke	P31	R	29	31	71	5	23	3	0	0	6	2	7	0	.324	.366
Jim Bucher	2B14, 3B1	R	27	17	57	7	13	3	1	0	7	2	3	0	.228	.316
Hal Epps	OF10	L	24	17	50	8	15	0	0	1	3	2	4	2	.300	.360
Creepy Crespi	SS7	R	20	7	19	2	5	2	0	0	0	0	7	0	.263	.368
1 Tuck Stainback	OF2	R	26	6	10	2	0	0	0	0	0	0	3	0	.000	.000
1 Dick Siebert		L	26	1	1	0	1	0	0	0	0	0	0	0	1.000	1.000

Bill DeLancey (IL) 26

NAME	T	AGE	W	L	PCT	SV	G	GS	CG	IP	H	BB	SO	SHO	ERA
TOTALS		27	71	80	.470	16	156	156	58	1384	1482	474	534	10	3.84
Bob Weiland	L	32	16	11	.593	1	35	29	11	228	248	67	117	1	3.59
Lon Warneke	R	29	13	8	.619	1	31	26	12	197	199	64	89	4	3.97
Curt Davis	R	34	12	8	.600	3	40	21	8	173	187	27	36	2	3.64
Bill McGee	R	28	7	12	.368	5	47	25	10	216	216	78	104	1	3.21
Clyde Shoun	L	26	6	6	.500	1	40	12	3	117	130	43	37	0	4.15
Roy Henshaw	L	26	5	11	.313	0	27	15	4	130	132	48	34	0	4.02
Max Macon	L	22	4	11	.267	2	38	12	5	129	133	61	39	1	4.12
Paul Dean	R	24	3	1	.750	0	5	4	2	31	37	5	14	1	2.61
Mort Cooper	R	25	2	1	.667	1	4	3	1	24	17	12	11	0	3.00
Ray Harrell	R	26	2	3	.400	2	32	3	1	63	78	29	32	0	4.86
Mike Ryba	R	35	1	1	.500	0	3	0	0	5	8	1	0	0	5.40
Guy Bush	R	36	0	1	.000	1	6	0	0	6	6	3	1	0	4.50
Max Lanier	L	22	0	3	.000	0	18	3	1	45	57	28	14	0	4.20
Si Johnson	R	33	0	3	.000	0	6	3	0	16	27	6	4	0	7.31
Howie Krist	R	22	0	0	—	0	2	0	0	1	3	2	1	0	0.00
Preacher Roe	L	23	0	0	—	0	1	0	0	3	6	2	1	0	12.00

BROOKLYN — 7th 69-81 .463 17.5 — BURLEIGH GRIMES

NAME	G by Pos	B	AGE	G	AB	R	H	2B	3B	HR	RBI	BB	SO	SB	BA	SA
TOTALS			29	151	5142	704	1322	225	79	61	647	611	615	66	.257	.367
Dolph Camilli	1B145	L	31	146	509	106	128	25	11	24	100	119	101	6	.251	.485
Johnny Hudson	2B132, SS3	R	26	135	498	59	130	21	5	2	37	39	76	7	.261	.335
Leo Durocher	SS141	R	32	141	479	41	105	18	5	1	56	47	30	3	.219	.284
Cookie Lavagetto	3B132, 2B4	R	25	137	487	68	133	34	6	6	79	68	31	15	.273	.405
Goody Rosen	OF113	L	25	138	473	75	133	17	11	4	51	65	43	0	.281	.389
Ernie Koy	OF135, 3B1	R	28	142	521	78	156	29	13	11	76	38	76	15	.299	.468
Buddy Hassett	OF71, 1B8	L	26	115	335	49	98	11	6	0	40	32	19	3	.293	.361
Babe Phelps	C55	R	30	66	208	33	64	12	2	5	46	23	15	2	.308	.457
Kiki Cuyler	OF68	R	39	82	253	45	69	10	8	2	23	34	23	6	.273	.399
Gilly Campbell	C44	L	30	54	126	10	31	5	0	0	11	19	9	0	.246	.286
Merv Shea	C47	R	37	48	120	14	22	5	0	0	12	28	20	1	.183	.225
1 Gib Brack	OF13	R	30	40	56	10	12	2	1	1	6	4	14	1	.214	.339
3 Tuck Stainback	OF23	R	26	35	104	15	34	6	3	0	20	2	4	1	.327	.442
Woody English	3B21, 2B3, SS3	R	31	34	72	9	18	2	0	0	7	8	11	2	.250	.278
Pete Coscarart	2B27	R	25	32	79	10	12	3	0	0	6	9	18	0	.152	.190
Packy Rogers	SS9, 3B8, 2B3, OF1	R	25	23	37	3	7	1	1	0	5	6	6	0	.189	.270
Oris Hockett	OF17	L	28	21	70	8	23	5	1	1	6	4	9	0	.329	.471
Woody Williams	SS18, 3B1	R	25	20	51	6	17	1	1	0	6	1	1	1	.333	.392
Fred Sington	OF17	R	28	17	53	10	19	6	1	2	5	13	5	0	.358	.623
1 Heinie Manush	OF12	L	36	17	51	9	12	3	1	0	6	5	6	0	.235	.333
Roy Spencer	C16	R	38	16	45	2	12	1	0	0	6	5	6	0	.267	.333
Paul Chervinko	C12	R	27	12	27	0	4	0	0	0	3	2	0	0	.148	.148
Tom Winsett	OF9	L	28	12	30	6	9	1	0	1	7	6	4	0	.300	.300
Greek George	C7	R	25	7	20	0	4	0	1	0	2	1	0	0	.200	.300

2 Ray Hayworth 34 R 0-4, Ray Thomas 27 R 1-3, Bert Haas 24 R 0-0

NAME	T	AGE	W	L	PCT	SV	G	GS	CG	IP	H	BB	SO	SHO	ERA
TOTALS		30	69	80	.463	14	151	151	56	1332	1464	446	469	12	4.07
Luke Hamlin	R	33	12	15	.444	0	44	30	10	237	243	65	97	0	3.68
2 Vito Tamulis	L	26	12	6	.667	2	38	18	9	160	181	40	70	0	3.83
Freddie Fitzsimmons	R	36	11	8	.579	0	27	36	12	203	205	43	38	1	3.01
Tot Pressnell	R	31	11	14	.440	3	43	19	6	192	209	56	57	1	3.56
Bill Posedel	R	31	8	9	.471	1	33	17	6	140	178	46	49	1	5.66
1 Max Butcher	R	27	4		.556	2	24	8	3	73	104	39	21	1	6.53
Van Lingle Mungo	R	27	4	11	.267	0	24	18	6	133	133	72	72	2	3.92
Fred Frankhouse	R	34	3		.375	0	30	8	2	94	92	44	32	1	4.02
John Gaddy	R	24	2	0	1.000	0	2	2	1	13	13	4	3	0	0.69
Sam Nahem	R	22	1	0	1.000	0	1	1	0	9	6	4	2	0	3.00
Buck Marrow	R	29	1	0	.000	1	15	0	0	20	23	11	6	0	4.50
2 Wayne LaMaster	L	31	1	0	.000	0	3	0	0	11	17	3	3	0	4.91
Jim Winford	R	28	0	1	.000	2	7	1	0	16	9	4	10	0	10.50
2 Lee Rogers	L	24	0	2	.000	0	12	2	0	24	23	10	11	0	5.63
Waite Hoyt	R	38	0	3	.000	0	1	0	0	16	24	5	5	1	5.07
Dykes Potter	R	27	0	0		0	1	0	0	4	4	0	0	0	4.50

PHILADELPHIA — 8th 45-105 .300 43 — JIMMIE WILSON 45-103 .304 — HANS LOBERT 0-2 .000

NAME	G by Pos	B	AGE	G	AB	R	H	2B	3B	HR	RBI	BB	SO	SB	BA	SA
TOTALS			28	151	5192	550	1318	233	29	40	503	423	507	38	.254	.333
Phil Weintraub	1B98	L	30	100	351	51	109	23	2	4	45	64	43	1	.311	.422
Emmett Mueller	2B111, 3B1	B	25	136	444	53	111	12	4	4	34	64	43	2	.250	.322
Del Young	SS87, 2B17	R	26	108	340	27	78	13	2	0	21	20	35	0	.229	.279
Pinky Whitney	3B75, 1B4, 2B2	R	33	129	300	27	83	9	1	3	38	27	22	0	.277	.343
Chuck Klein	OF119	L	33	129	458	53	113	22	2	8	61	38	50	7	.247	.356
Hersh Martin	OF116	B	28	129	466	58	139	36	6	3	39	34	48	8	.298	.421
Morrie Arnovich	OF133	R	27	139	502	47	138	29	4	4	72	42	37	2	.275	.357
Bill Atwood	C94	R	26	102	281	27	55	8	1	3	28	25	26	0	.196	.263
George Scharein	SS77, 2B39, 3B1	R	23	147	390	47	93	16	4	1	29	16	33	11	.238	.308
2 Buck Jordan	3B58, 1B17	L	31	87	310	31	93	18	1	0	18	17	4	1	.300	.365
2 Gib Brack	C68	R	30	72	282	40	81	20	4	4	28	18	30	2	.287	.429
2 Spud Davis	C63	R	33	70	215	11	53	7	0	2	23	14	14	1	.247	.307
Cap Clark	C29	R	31	52	74	11	19	1	1	0	4	9	10	0	.257	.297
2 Tuck Stainback	OF25	R	26	30	81	9	21	3	0	1	11	3	3	1	.259	.333
Gene Corbett	1B22	L	24	24	75	7	6	1	0	2	7	4	5	0	.080	.173
Earl Browne	1B16, OF2	R	27	21	74	4	19	4	0	0	8	5	11	0	.257	.311
1 Justin Stein	3B7, 2B3	R	26	11	39	6	10	1	0	0	4	2	6	0	.256	.308
Eddie Feinberg	SS4, O42	L	20	10	20	0	3	0	0	0	0	1	7	0	.150	.150
Ray Stoviak	OF4	L	23	10	10	1	0	0	0	0	0	0	4	0	.000	.000

Alex Pitko 23 R 6-19, Art Rebel 24 L 2-9, Jimmie Wilson 37 R 0-2, Howie Gorman 25 L 0-1

NAME	T	AGE	W	L	PCT	SV	G	GS	CG	IP	H	BB	SO	SHO	ERA
TOTALS		28	45	105	.300	6	151	151	68	1329	1516	582	492	3	4.93
Claude Passeau	R	29	11	18	.379	1	44	33	15	239	281	93	100	0	4.52
Hugh Mulcahy	R	24	10	20	.333	1	46	34	15	267	294	120	90	0	4.62
2 Al Hollingsworth	L	30		0	.238	0	24	21	11	174	177	77	80	1	3.83
1 Wayne LaMaster	L	31	4	7	.364	0	18	12	1	64	80	31	35	1	2.94
2 Max Butcher	R	27	4		.333	0	12	12	11	98	94	31	29	0	7.73
1 Bucky Walters	R	29	4	8	.333	0	12	12	9	83	91	42	28	1	5.20
Pete Sivess	R	24	3	6	.333	1	39	8	2	116	143	69	32	0	5.51
Syl Johnson	R	37	2	7	.222	0	22	6	2	83	87	11	21	0	4.23
Al Smith	L	30	2		.200	1	37	1	0	86	115	40	46	0	6.28
Wild Bill Hallahan	R	35	1	8	.111	0	21	10	1	89	107	45	22	0	5.46
Tommy Reis	R	23	0		.000	0	4	0	0	5	8	4	2	0	18.00
Tom Lanning	R	29	0	1	.000	0	3	0	0	2	6	2	1	0	6.43
Elmer Burkart	R	21	0		.000	2	1	1	0	10	12	5	1	0	4.50
Hal Kelleher	R	25	0	0	—	0	7	0	0	16	16	4	4	0	19.29
Ed Heusser	R	29	0	0	—	0	2	0	0	2	1	0	0	0	27.00

WORLD SERIES — NEW YORK (AL) 4 CHICAGO (NL) 0

LINE SCORES

TEAM	1	2	3	4	5	6	7	8	9	10	11	12	R	H	E

Game 1 October 5 at Chicago

	1	2	3	4	5	6	7	8	9	R	H	E
NY (AL)	0	2	0	0	0	0	1	0	0	3	12	1
CHI (NL)	0	0	1	0	0	0	0	0	0	1	9	1

Ruffing   Lee, Russell (9)

Game 2 October 6 at Chicago

	1	2	3	4	5	6	7	8	9	R	H	E
NY	0	2	0	0	0	0	0	2	2	6	7	2
CHI	1	0	2	0	0	0	0	0	0	3	11	0

Gomez, Murphy (8)   Dean, French (9)

Game 3 October 8 at Chicago

	1	2	3	4	5	6	7	8	9	R	H	E
CHI	0	0	0	0	0	0	0	1	0	2	5	1
NY	0	0	0	0	2	2	0	1	X	5	7	2

Bryant, Russell (6), French (7)   **Pearson**

Game 4 October 9 at New York

	1	2	3	4	5	6	7	8	9	R	H	E
CHI	0	0	0	0	0	1	0	2	0	3	8	1
NY	0	3	0	0	0	1	0	4	X	8	11	1

Lee, Root (4), Page (7), French (8), Carleton (8), Dean (8)   **Ruffing**

COMPOSITE BATTING

NAME	POS	G	AB	R	H	2B	3B	HR	RBI	BA
New York (AL)										
Totals		4	135	22	37	6	1	5	21	.274
Rolfe	3B	4	18	0	3	0	0	0	0	.167
Crosetti	SS	4	16	1	4	2	1	0	6	.250
Henrich	OF	4	16	3	4	1	0	1	1	.250
Dickey	C	4	15	2	6	0	0	0	2	.400
Gordon	2B	4	15	3	6	2	0	1	6	.400
DiMaggio	OF	4	15	4	4	0	0	1	2	.267
Gehrig	1B	4	14	4	4	0	0	0	0	.286
Selkirk	OF	3	10	4	2	0	0	0	1	.200
Ruffing	P	2	6	1	1	0	0	0	1	.167
Hoag	OF	2	5	3	2	1	0	0	1	.400
Pearson	P	1	3	1	1	0	0	0	0	.333
Gomez	P	1	2	0	0	0	0	0	0	.000

Powell OF 0-0, Murphy P 0-0

NAME	POS	G	AB	R	H	2B	3B	HR	RBI	BA
Chicago (NL)										
Totals		4	136	9	33	4	1	2	8	.243
Hack	3B	4	17	3	8	1	0	0	1	.471
Herman	2B	4	16	1	3	0	0	0	1	.188
Collins	1B	4	15	1	2	0	0	0	0	.133
Cavarretta	OF	4	13	1	6	0	0	0	0	.462
Jurges	SS	4	13	0	3	1	0	0	1	.231
Marty	OF	3	12	1	6	1	0	0	5	.500
Reynolds	OF	4	12	0	0	0	0	0	0	.000
Hartnett	C	3	11	0	1	0	0	1	2	.091
Demaree	OF	3	10	1	1	0	0	0	0	.100
O'Dea	C	3	5	1	1	0	0	1	2	.200
Dean	P	2	3	0	2	0	0	0	0	.667
Lee	P	2	3	0	1	0	0	0	0	.333
Galan	PH	2	3	0	0	0	0	0	0	.000
Lazzeri	PH	1	2	0	1	0	0	0	0	.500
Bryant	P	1	2	0	0	0	0	0	0	.000

French P 0-0, Russell P 0-0, Carleton P 0-0, Page P 0-0, Root P 0-0

COMPOSITE PITCHING

NAME	G	IP	H	BB	SO	W	L	SV	ERA
New York (AL)									
Totals	4	36	33	6	26	4	0	1	1.75
Ruffing	2	18	17	2	11	2	0	0	1.50
Pearson	1	9	5	2	9	1	0	0	1.00
Gomez	1	7	9	1	5	1	0	0	3.86
Murphy	1	2	2	1	1	0	0	0	0.00

NAME	G	IP	H	BB	SO	W	L	SV	ERA
Chicago (NL)									
Totals	4	34	37	11	16	0	4	0	5.03
Lee	2	11	15	1	8	0	2	0	2.45
Dean	2	8.1	6	1	2	0	1	0	6.48
Bryant	1	5.1	6	5	3	0	1	0	6.75
French	3	3.1	1	2	0	0	0	0	2.70
Root	1	3	3	0	1	0	0	0	3.00
Russell	2	1.2	1	1	0	0	0	0	0.00
Page	1	1.1	2	1	1	0	0	0	13.50
Carleton	1								

1939 McCarthy's Final Walk

For the first three days of the season, the rain accomplished what both leagues had failed to do for three years—stop the Yankees. It was not until April 20, that Joe McCarthy and his men could get their first game in. When they did, it was enough to catapult them from a cellar-dwelling zero percentage to a first-place tie. Then, after floating between first and second place until May 11, they cut themselves loose from the rest of the league.

Although the final standings of a 17-game margin over Boston gave the impression of a trouble-free season, there were some problems for a time from the Red Sox. In early July, on the brink of the All-Star break, the Bostonians came to Yankee Stadium and shocked McCarthy, his Yankees, and their fans with five straight triumphs—four of the wins occurring in a pair of doubleheaders. After the All-Star break the Yankees went to Detroit and lost their sixth straight. But then McCarthy pulled his forces together and won eight in a row, which was enough to offset Boston's 23-10 July record.

In spite of finishing a poor second, the Red Sox got the chance to unveil a 20-year-old Californian who would keep Boston on the map for many years to come. Ted Williams made his major league debut and batted .327, hit 31 home runs, and drove in 145 runs, the last of which was enough to lead the league. On the other end of the yardstick for Boston was Lefty Grove who, despite his 39 years of age, turned in a fine 15-4 performance behind his league-leading 2.54 E.R.A. While Cleveland's season was heightened by the hitting of Hal Trosky, Odell Hale, and Ken Keltner—all .300 hitters, and the brilliant pitching of 20-year-old Bob Feller, who led the league in wins with 24 and strikeouts with 246, the club could do no more than limp home a distant third, 20 1/2 games back.

In the National League, the Cincinnati Reds finished first, a feat they had been unable to accomplish since 1919—the year they were unknowingly winning a "fixed" Series. The Rhinelanders' rise to the top was a dramatic one, considering their last-place finish in 1937. The only real challenge all year came from upstart St. Louis, who wound up sixth in 1938 and almost overtook the Reds at the wire, had it not been for the pitching of Paul Derringer—who clinched the pennant with a 5-3 win on September 29. It was Derringer, with 25 wins, and Bucky Walters, a former infielder with 27 wins, who spearheaded the Reds' success.

Dethroned Chicago suffered a collapse of their mound staff and finished fourth, the first time since 1927, mostly due to Dizzy Dean's being unable to regain his form. The Dodgers, after a six-year hiatus in the second division, began to show signs of life behind the presence of shortstop Leo Durocher, who took over the field leadership of the club and guided them to third place in his first managerial attempt. Durocher, while turning in a .277 average to help his own cause, got additional offensive help from Doug Camilli and Cookie Lavagetto, and good pitching out of 20-game winner Luke Hamlin. New York and Pittsburgh, both plagued with pitching problems and unable to get going, fell into the second division.

Bill McKechnie ushered his Reds into Yankee Stadium for the first Series game on October 4, and it was tied until the ninth inning when Bill Dickey's single drove in the winning run. McCarthy called on Monte Pearson to start the second game, and the Oakland native came within five outs of World Series history. Pearson had allowed one walk all day when Ernie Lombardi singled with one out in the eighth to spoil the no-hit bid. Then, in the ninth inning with two out, Werber, who had the only walk before Lombardi's clean hit, singled sharply to left to deny Pearson even a record performance one-hitter. The Yankees took the next two, running into a mild obstacle in the last game when they had to go to the tenth inning before wrapping up their second successive, four-game World Series sweep—thus giving Joe McCarthy the distinction of being the first man in baseball ever to win four straight championships. The Yankee victory also culminated in an impressive 16-3, four-year Series record.

The one Yankee tragedy for the year, a tragic footnote to all of baseball, was Lou Gehrig's voluntary retirement on May 2, after playing in only eight games. Gehrig quit the Yankees after playing in a miraculous 2,130 consecutive games and left behind a lifetime .340 batting average, 493 home runs, and a spirit of dedication hard to equal. On June 21, the Mayo Clinic announced that Gehrig was suffering from a rare neuromuscular disease, amyotrophic lateral sclerosis, that would claim his life two years later.

1939 AMERICAN LEAGUE

NAME	G by Pos	B	AGE	G	AB	R	H	2B	3B	HR	RBI	BB	SO	SB	BA	SA
NEW YORK	1st 106-45 .702		JOE McCARTHY													
	TOTALS		27	152	5300	967	1521	259	55	166	903	701	543	72	.287	.451
Babe Dahlgren	1B144	R	27	144	531	71	125	18	6	15	89	57	54	2	.235	.377
Joe Gordon	2B151	R	24	151	567	92	161	32	5	28	111	75	57	11	.284	.506
Frankie Crosetti	SS152	R	28	152	656	109	153	25	5	10	56	65	81	11	.233	.332
Red Rolfe	3B152	L	30	152	648	139	213	46	10	14	80	81	41	7	.329	.495
Charlie Keller	OF105	L	22	111	398	87	133	21	6	11	83	81	49	6	.334	.500
Joe DiMaggio (LJ)	OF117	R	24	120	462	108	176	32	6	30	126	52	20	3	.381	.671
George Selkirk	OF124	L	31	128	418	103	128	17	4	21	101	103	49	12	.306	.517
Bill Dickey	C126	L	32	128	480	98	145	23	3	24	105	77	37	5	.302	.513
Tommy Henrich	OF88, 161	L	29	99	347	64	96	18	4	9	57	51	23	7	.277	.429
Red Ruffing	P28	R	35	44	114	12	35	1	0	1	20	7	18	1	.307	.342
Buddy Rosar	C35	R	24	43	105	18	29	5	1	0	12	13	10	4	.276	.343
Jake Powell	OF23	R	30	31	86	12	21	4	1	1	9	3	8	1	.244	.349
1 Joe Gallagher	OF12	R	25	14	41	8	10	0	1	2	9	3	8	1	.244	.439
Lou Gehrig (IL)	1B8	L	36	8	28	2	4	0	0	0	1	5	1	0	.143	.143
Bill Knickerbocker	2B2, SS2	R	27	6	13	2	2	1	0	0	1	0	0	0	.154	.231
Art Jorgens	C2	R	34	3	1	0	0	0	0	0	0	0	0	0	—	—
BOSTON	2nd 89-62 .589 17		JOE CRONIN													
	TOTALS		28	152	5308	890	1543	287	57	124	833	591	505	42	.291	.436
Jimmie Foxx	1B123, P1	R	31	124	467	130	168	31	10	35	105	89	72	4	.360	.694
Bobby Doerr	2B126	R	21	127	525	75	167	28	2	12	73	38	32	1	.318	.448
Joe Cronin	SS142	R	32	143	520	97	160	33	3	19	107	87	48	6	.308	.492
Jim Tabor	3B148	R	25	149	577	76	167	33	8	14	95	40	54	16	.289	.447
Ted Williams	OF149	L	20	149	565	131	185	44	11	31	145	107	64	2	.327	.609
Doc Cramer	OF135	L	33	137	589	110	183	30	6	0	56	36	17	3	.311	.382
Joe Vosmik	OF144	R	29	145	554	89	153	29	6	7	84	66	33	4	.276	.388
Johnny Peacock	C84	R	29	92	274	33	76	11	4	0	36	29	11	1	.277	.347
2 Lou Finney	1B32, OF24	L	28	95	249	43	81	18	3	1	46	24	11	2	.325	.434
Gene Desautels	C73	R	32	76	226	26	55	14	0	0	21	33	13	1	.243	.305
Red Nonnenkamp	OF15	L	27	58	75	12	18	2	1	0	5	12	6	0	.240	.293
Tom Carey	2B35, SS10	R	30	54	161	17	39	6	2	0	20	3	9	0	.242	.304
Boze Berger	SS10, 3B5, 2B2	R	29	20	30	4	9	2	0	0	2	1	10	0	.300	.267
Moe Berg	C13	R	37	14	33	4	9	1	0	1	5	2	3	0	.273	.394
Fabian Gafke		R	25	1	0	1	0	0	0	0	0	0	0	0	.000	.000
CLEVELAND	3rd 87-67 .565 20.5		OSSIE VITT													
	TOTALS		27	154	5316	797	1490	291	79	85	730	557	574	72	.280	.413
Hal Trosky	1B118	L	26	122	448	89	150	31	4	25	104	52	28	2	.335	.589
Odell Hale	2B73, 2B2	R	30	108	253	36	79	16	2	4	48	25	18	4	.312	.439
Skeeter Webb	SS81	R	29	81	269	28	71	14	1	2	26	15	24	1	.264	.346
Ken Keltner	3B154	R	22	154	587	84	191	35	11	13	97	51	41	6	.325	.489
Bruce Campbell	OF115	L	29	130	450	84	129	23	13	8	72	67	48	7	.287	.449
Ben Chapman	OF146	R	30	149	545	101	158	31	6	6	82	97	30	18	.290	.494
Jeff Heath	OF108	L	24	121	431	64	126	31	7	14	69	41	64	8	.292	.494
Rollie Hemsley	C106	R	32	107	395	58	104	17	4	2	36	26	26	2	.263	.342
Oscar Grimes	2B48, 1B43, SS37	R	24	119	364	51	98	20	5	4	56	56	61	8	.269	.385
Roy Weatherly	OF76	L	24	95	323	43	100	16	6	1	32	19	23	7	.310	.406
Frankie Pytlak	C51	R	30	63	183	20	49	2	3	0	14	20	5	4	.286	.333
Lou Boudreau	SS53	R	21	53	225	42	58	15	4	0	19	28	24	2	.258	.360
1 Moose Solters	OF25	R	33	41	102	19	28	7	2	2	19	9	15	2	.275	.441
Ray Mack	2B34, 3B1	R	22	36	112	12	17	5	2	1	6	12	19	0	.152	.323
1 Jim Shilling	2B27, SS3	R	25	31	98	8	27	7	2	0	12	7	9	1	.276	.388
1 Earl Averill	OF11	L	37	24	55	8	15	8	0	1	7	6	12	1	.273	.473
Luke Sewell	C15, 1B1	R	38	16	20	1	3	1	0	0	1	3	0	0	.150	.200
1 Lyn Lary	SS2	R	33	3	2	0	0	0	0	0	0	1	0	0	.000	.000

NAME	T	AGE	W	L	PCT	SV	G	GS	CG	IP	H	BB	SO	SHO	ERA
		30	106	45	.702	26	152	152	87	1349	1208	567	565	15	3.31
Red Ruffing	R	35	21	7	.750	0	28	28	22	233	211	75	95	5	2.94
Atley Donald	R	28	13	3	.813	1	24	20	11	153	144	60	55	2	3.71
Monte Pearson	R	30	12	5	.706	0	22	20	8	146	151	70	76	0	4.50
Bump Hadley	R	34	12	6	.667	2	26	18	7	154	132	85	65	1	2.98
Lefty Gomez	L	30	12	8	.600	0	26	26	14	198	173	84	102	2	3.41
Steve Sundra	R	29	11	1	.917	0	24	11	8	121	110	56	27	1	2.75
Oral Hildebrand	R	32	10	4	.714	2	21	15	7	127	102	41	50	1	3.05
Marius Russo	L	24	8	3	.727	2	21	11	9	116	86	41	55	2	2.41
Spud Chandler (BL)	R	31	3	0	1.000	0	11	0	0	19	26	9	4	0	2.84
Johnny Murphy	R	30	3	6	.333	19	38	0	0	61	57	28	30	0	4.43
Wes Ferrell	R	31	1	2	.333	0	3	3	1	19	14	17	6	0	4.70
Marv Breuer	R	25	0	0	—	0	1	0	0	1	2	1	0	0	9.00
		29	89	62	.589	20	152	152	52	1351	1533	543	539	4	4.56
Lefty Grove	L	39	15	4	.789	0	23	23	17	191	180	58	81	2	2.54
Joe Heving	R	38	11	3	.786	7	46	5	1	107	124	34	43	0	3.70
Fritz Ostermueller	L	31	11	7	.611	4	34	20	8	159	173	58	61	0	4.25
Jack Wilson	R	27	11	11	.500	2	36	22	6	177	198	75	80	0	4.68
Elden Auker	R	28	9	10	.474	0	31	25	6	151	183	61	43	1	5.36
Denny Galehouse	R	27	9	10	.474	0	30	18	6	147	160	52	68	1	4.53
Emerson Dickman	R	24	8	3	.727	5	48	1	0	114	126	43	46	0	4.42
Jim Bagby	R	22	5	5	.500	0	21	11	3	80	119	36	35	0	7.09
Woody Rich (SA)	R	23	4	3	.571	1	21	12	3	77	78	35	24	0	4.91
Charlie Wagner	R	26	3	1	.750	0	9	5	0	38	49	14	13	0	4.26
Bill LeFebvre	L	23	1	1	.500	0	5	3	0	26	35	14	8	0	5.88
1 Jake Wade	R	27	1	4	.200	0	20	6	1	48	68	37	21	0	6.19
Monty Weaver	R	33	1	0	1.000	0	9	1	1	20	26	13	6	0	6.75
Jimmie Foxx	R	31	0	0	—	0	1	1	0	1	1	0	1	0	0.00
Bill Sayles	R	21	0	0	—	0	5	0	0	14	14	13	9	0	7.07
		26	87	67	.565	13	154	154	69	1365	1394	602	614	10	4.08
Bob Feller	R	20	24	9	.727	1	39	35	24	297	227	142	246	4	2.85
Mel Harder	R	29	15	9	.625	1	29	26	12	208	213	64	67	1	3.50
Al Milnar	L	25	14	12	.538	3	37	26	12	209	212	99	76	2	3.79
Johnny Allen	R	34	9	7	.563	0	28	26	9	175	199	56	79	2	4.58
Willis Hudlin	R	33	9	10	.474	3	27	20	7	143	175	42	28	0	4.91
2 Harry Eisenstat	L	23	7	7	.462	2	26	11	4	104	109	28	38	1	3.29
Johnny Broaca	R	29	4	2	.667	0	22	2	0	46	53	28	13	0	4.70
Bill Zuber	R	26	2	0	1.000	0	16	1	0	32	41	19	16	0	5.91
Joe Dobson	R	22	2	3	.400	1	35	3	0	78	87	51	27	0	5.88
John Humphries	R	24	2	4	.333	2	15	1	0	28	30	32	12	0	8.36
Tom Drake (AJ)	R	26	0	1	.000	0	6	1	0	15	23	19	1	0	9.00
Mike Naymick	R	21	0	1	.000	0	5	1	0	5	3	5	3	0	1.80
Floyd Stromme	R	22	0	1	.000	0	5	0	0	13	13	13	4	0	4.85
Lefty Sullivan	L	22	0	1	.000	0	7	1	0	9	13	9	4	0	4.15

CHICAGO 4th 85-69 .552 22.5 JIMMY DYKES

NAME	G by Pos	B	AGE	G	AB	R	H	2B	3B	HR	RBI	BB	SO	SB	BA	SA
TOTALS			31	155	5279	755	1451	220	56	64	681	579	502	113	.275	.374
Joe Kuhel	1B136	L	33	139	546	107	164	24	9	15	56	64	51	18	.300	.460
Ollie Bejma	2B81, SS1, 3B1	R	31	90	307	52	77	9	3	8	44	36	27	1	.251	.378
Luke Appling	SS148	R	32	148	516	82	162	16	6	0	56	105	37	16	.314	.368
Eric McNair	3B103, 2B19, SS9	R	30	129	479	62	155	18	5	3	82	38	41	17	.324	.426
Larry Rosenthal	OF93	L	27	107	324	50	86	21	5	10	51	53	46	6	.265	.454
Mike Kreevich	OF139, 3B4	R	31	145	541	85	175	30	4	5	77	59	40	23	.323	.436
Gee Walker	OF147	R	31	149	598	95	174	30	11	13	111	28	43	17	.291	.454
Mike Tresh	C119	R	25	119	352	49	91	5	2	0	38	64	30	3	.259	.284
Rip Radcliff	OF78, 1B20	L	33	113	397	49	105	25	2	2	53	26	21	6	.264	.353
Jackie Hayes	2B69	R	32	72	269	34	67	12	3	0	23	27	10	0	.249	.316
Hank Steinbacher	OF22	L	26	71	111	16	19	2	1	1	15	21	8	0	.171	.234
Marv Owen	3B55	R	33	58	194	22	46	9	0	0	15	16	15	4	.237	.284
Norm Schlueter	C32	R	22	34	56	5	13	2	1	0	8	1	11	2	.232	.304
Ken Silvestri	C20	B	23	22	75	6	13	3	0	2	5	6	13	0	.173	.293
Tony Rensa	C13	R	37	14	25	3	5	0	0	0	2	1	2	0	.200	.200
John Gerlach	3B1	R	22	3	2	1	2	0	0	0	0	0	0	0	1.000	1.000
Bob Kennedy	3B2	R	18	3	8	0	2	0	0	0	1	0	0	0	.250	.250
Jimmy Dykes	3B2	R	42	2	1	0	0	0	0	0	0	0	0	0	.000	.000
1 Tommy Thompson		L	29	1	0	0	0	0	0	0	0	0	0	0	—	—

NAME	T	AGE	W	L	PCT	SV	G	GS	CG	IP	H	BB	SO	SHO	ERA
		30	85	69	.552	21	155	155	62	1377	1470	454	535	5	4.31
Johnny Rigney	R	24	15	8	.652	0	35	29	11	219	208	84	119	2	3.70
Thornton Lee	R	32	15	11	.577	3	33	29	15	235	260	70	81	2	4.21
Ted Lyons	R	38	14	6	.700	0	21	21	16	173	162	26	65	0	2.76
Jack Knott	R	32	11	6	.647	0	25	23	8	150	157	41	56	0	4.14
Clint Brown	R	35	11	10	.524	18	61	0	0	118	127	27	41	0	3.89
2 Eddie Smith	L	25	9	11	.450	0	29	22	7	177	161	90	67	1	3.66
Bill Dietrich	R	24	7	8	.467	0	25	19	2	128	134	56	43	0	5.20
2 Johnny Marcum	R	29	3	3	.500	2	9	4	1	90	125	19	32	0	6.00
Vic Frasier (PB)	R	34	0	1	.000	0	10	1	0	24	45	11	7	0	10.13
Jess Dobernic	R	21	0	1	.000	0	4	0	0	3	3	6	1	0	15.00
Vallie Eaves	R	27	0	3	.000	0	2	1	1	12	11	8	5	0	4.50
1 John Whitehead	R	30	0	3	.000	0	4	1	0	32	60	5	9	0	8.16
Art Herring	R	33	0	0	—	0	14	0	0	14	13	5	8	0	5.79
Harry Boyles	R		0	0	—					3	4	6	1	0	12.00

DETROIT 5th 81-73 .526 26.5 DEL BAKER

NAME	G by Pos	B	AGE	G	AB	R	H	2B	3B	HR	RBI	BB	SO	SB	BA	SA
TOTALS			29	155	5326	849	1487	277	67	124	806	620	592	88	.279	.426
Hank Greenberg	2B136	R	28	138	500	112	156	42	7	33	112	91	95	8	.312	.622
Charlie Gehringer	2B107	R	36	118	406	86	132	29	6	16	86	68	16	4	.325	.544
Frank Croucher	SS93, 2B3	R	24	97	324	38	87	15	0	5	40	16	42	2	.269	.361
Pinky Higgins	3B130	R	30	132	489	57	135	23	2	8	76	56	41	7	.276	.380
Pete Fox	OF126	R	29	141	519	69	153	24	4	7	66	35	41	23	.295	.405
Barney McCosky	OF145	L	22	147	611	120	190	33	14	4	58	70	45	20	.311	.430
2 Earl Averill	OF80	R	37	87	309	58	81	20	6	10	58	43	30	4	.262	.463
Birdie Tebbetts	C100	R	28	106	341	37	89	22	4	4	53	25	20	1	.261	.372
Rudy York	C67, 1B19	R	25	102	329	66	101	16	1	20	68	41	50	5	.307	.544
Roy Cullenbine	OF46, 1B2	R	25	75	179	31	43	9	2	6	33	34	29	0	.240	.413
Billy Rogell	SS43, 3B21, 2B2	B	34	74	174	24	40	6	3	2	23	26	14	3	.230	.333
Johnny McCoy	2B34, SS16	L	23	55	192	38	58	13	6	1	33	29	26	3	.302	.448
2 Beau Bell	OF37	R	31	54	134	14	32	4	2	0	24	24	16	0	.239	.299
2 Red Kress (BL)	SS25, 2B16, 3B4	R	34	51	157	19	38	7	0	1	22	17	16	2	.242	.306
1 Dixie Walker	OF37	L	28	43	154	30	47	4	5	4	19	15	8	1	.305	.474
Les Fleming	OF3	L	23	8	16	0	0	0	0	0	0	0	4	0	.000	.000
1 Mark Christman	3B6	R	25	6	16	0	4	0	0	0	2	0	5	0	.250	.375
1 Chet Laabs	OF5	R	27	5	16	1	5	1	0	2	2	0	2	0	.313	.500
Dixie Parsons	C4	R	23	5	1	0	0	0	0	0	0	0	0	0	.000	.000
Merv Shea	C4	R	38	4	2	0	0	0	0	0	0	0	0	0	.000	.000

NAME	T	AGE	W	L	PCT	SV	G	GS	CG	IP	H	BB	SO	SHO	ERA
		29	81	73	.526	16	155	155	64	1367	1430	574	633	8	4.29
Tommy Bridges	R	32	17	7	.708	2	29	26	16	198	181	61	129	2	3.50
2 Bobo Newsom	R	31	17	10	.630	2	35	31◆	21◆	246	222	104	164	3	3.37
Schoolboy Rowe	R	29	10	12	.455	0	28	24	8	164	192	61	51	1	4.99
Dizzy Trout	R	24	9	10	.474	2	33	22	6	162	168	74	72	0	3.61
3 Bud Thomas	R	28	7	0	1.000	1	27	0	0	45	45	20	14	0	4.21
Al Benton	R	28	6	8	.429	5	37	16	3	150	182	58	67	0	4.56
Archie McKain	L	28	6	5	.455	4	32	11	4	130	120	54	49	1	3.67
Fred Hutchinson	R	19	3	6	.333	0	13	12	3	85	95	51	22	0	5.19
Slick Coffman	R	28	2	1	.667	0	23	1	0	42	51	22	10	0	6.43
1 Harry Eisenstat	L	23	2	2	.500	0	10	2	1	30	39	9	6	0	6.90
Floyd Giebell	R	29	1	1	.500	0	3	3	1	19	19	12	9	0	3.00
1 Bob Harris	R	24	1	1	.500	0	5	1	0	18	18	8	4	0	4.00
1 Roxie Lawson	R	33	1	1	.500	0	11	1	1	11	7	7	4	0	4.91
1 George Gill	R	30	0	1	.000	0	1	0	0	8	8	0	5	0	8.00
1 Red Lynn	R	25	0	0	—	0	8	0	0	8	11	3	3	0	9.00
Hal Newhouser	L	18	0	1	.000	0	1	1	0	5	3	4	4	0	5.40
2 Cotton Pippen	R	29	0	0	—	0	3	0	0	14	18	6	5	0	7.07
2 Jim Walkup	R	29	0	1	.000	0	1	0	0	8	8	6	1	0	7.50
1 Vern Kennedy	R	32	0	3*	.000	0	4	4	1	21	25	9	6	0	6.43

* Kennedy, also with St. Louis, league leader in L with 20
◆ Newsom, also with St. Louis, League leader in GS (37) and CG (24)

WASHINGTON 6th 65-87 .428 41.5 BUCKY HARRIS

NAME	G by Pos	B	AGE	G	AB	R	H	2B	3B	HR	RBI	BB	SO	SB	BA	SA
TOTALS			27	153	5334	702	1483	249	79	44	648	547	460	94	.278	.379
Mickey Vernon	1B75	L	21	76	276	23	71	15	4	1	30	24	28	1	.257	.351
Jimmy Bloodworth	2B73, OF5	R	21	83	318	34	92	24	1	4	40	10	26	3	.289	.409
Cecil Travis	SS118	L	25	130	476	55	139	20	9	5	64	34	25	0	.292	.403
Buddy Lewis	3B134	L	22	140	536	87	171	23	16	10	75	72	27	10	.319	.478
George Case	OF123	R	23	128	530	103	160	20	7	2	35	56	36	51	.302	.377
Sammy West	OF89, 1B17	L	34	115	390	52	110	20	4	3	52	67	29	1	.282	.397
Taffy Wright	OF123	L	27	129	499	77	154	29	11	4	90	38	19	1	.309	.435
Rick Ferrell	C83	R	33	87	274	32	77	13	1	0	31	41	12	1	.281	.336
Buddy Myer	2B65	L	35	83	258	33	78	10	4	1	32	40	18	4	.302	.376
Bobby Estalella	OF74	R	28	82	280	51	77	18	6	8	41	40	27	2	.275	.468
Charlie Gelbert	SS28, 3B20, 2B1	R	33	68	188	36	48	7	5	3	29	30	11	2	.255	.394
Johnny Welaj	OF55	R	25	63	201	23	55	11	2	1	33	13	20	13	.274	.363
Tony Giuliani	C50	R	26	54	172	20	43	6	2	0	18	4	7	1	.250	.308
Jake Early	C24	L	23	32	84	8	22	7	2	0	14	5	14	0	.262	.393
Jimmy Wasdell	1B28	L	25	29	109	12	33	5	1	0	13	9	16	3	.303	.367
Bob Prichard	1B26	L	21	26	85	8	20	5	0	0	8	19	16	0	.235	.294
Ossie Bluege	1B11, 2B2, SS2, 3B2	R	39	18	59	5	9	0	0	0	3	7	2	1	.153	.153
Hal Quick	SS10	R	19	12	41	3	10	1	0	0	2	4	1	1	.244	.268
Ed Leip	2B8	L	23	9	32	4	11	1	0	0	4	2	6	0	.344	.375
Morrie Aderholt	3B7	L	23	7	25	5	5	0	1	0	4	2	6	0	.200	.320
Al Evans	C6	R	22	7	21	2	7	0	0	0	1	5	2	0	.333	.333

Elmer Gedeon 22 R 3-15, Alex Pitko 24 R 1-8, Bobby Loane 24 R 0-9

NAME	T	AGE	W	L	PCT	SV	G	GS	CG	IP	H	BB	SO	SHO	ERA
		27	65	87	.428	10	153	153	72	1355	1420	602	521	4	4.60
Dutch Leonard	R	30	20	8	.714	0	34	34	21	269	273	59	88	2	3.55
Joe Krakauskas	L	24	11	17	.393	1	39	29	12	217	230	114	110	0	4.60
Ken Chase	L	25	10	19	.345	0	32	31	15	232	215	114	118	1	3.80
Joe Haynes	R	21	8	12	.400	0	27	20	10	173	186	78	64	1	5.36
Alex Carrasquel	R	26	5	9	.357	2	40	17	7	159	165	68	41	0	4.70
Pete Appleton	R	35	5	10	.333	6	40	4	2	103	104	48	50	0	4.54
Harry Kelley (KJ-GJ)	R	33	4	3	.571	1	15	3	2	54	69	14	20	0	4.67
Walt Masterson	R	19	2	5	.286	0	24	5	1	58	66	48	12	0	5.59
Bill Holland	L	32	1	0	1.000	0	4	0	0	6	6	5	2	0	11.25
Dick Bass	R	21	1	0	1.000	0	1	1	0	7	6	1	1	0	6.75
Early Wynn	R	19	2	2	.000	0	3	2	0	20	26	10	1	0	5.85
Jimmie DeShong	R	29	0	0	—	0	7	0	0	41	56	31	12	0	8.56
2 Bud Thomas	R	28	0	0	—	0	1	0	0	2	6	1	0	0	6.00
Lou Thuman	R	22	0	0	—	0	4	0	0	5	2	1	0	0	9.00
Bucky Jacobs	R	22	0	0	—	0	3	1	0	3	3	1	0	1	6.00
Mike Palagyi	R	21	0	0	—	0	1	0	0						□

Tom Baker (AJ) 26

PHILADELPHIA 7th 55-97 .362 51.5 CONNIE MACK

NAME	G by Pos	B	AGE	G	AB	R	H	2B	3B	HR	RBI	BB	SO	SB	BA	SA
TOTALS			27	153	5309	711	1438	282	55	98	666	503	532	60	.271	.400
Dick Siebert	1B99	L	27	101	402	58	118	28	3	6	47	21	22	4	.294	.423
Sep Gantenbein	2B76, 3B14, SS5	R	23	128	468	42	120	24	3	4	36	32	22	1	.290	.388
Skeeter Newsome	SS93, 2B2	R	28	99	248	22	55	9	1	0	17	19	12	5	.222	.266
Dario Lodigiani	3B89, 2B28	R	23	121	393	46	102	22	4	6	44	42	18	2	.260	.382
Wally Moses	OF103	L	28	115	437	68	134	28	7	3	33	44	23	7	.307	.423
Sam Chapman	OF117, 1B19	R	23	140	498	74	134	24	6	15	64	51	62	11	.269	.432
Bob Johnson	OF150, 2B1	R	33	150	544	115	184	30	9	23	114	99	59	15	.338	.553
Frankie Hayes	C114	R	24	124	431	66	122	28	5	20	83	64	40	4	.283	.510
Dee Miles	OF77	R	30	106	320	49	96	17	6	1	37	15	17	3	.300	.400
Bill Nagel	2B56, 3B43, P1	R	23	105	341	39	86	19	4	12	39	25	86	2	.252	.437
Wayne Ambler	SS77, 2B19	R	23	95	227	15	48	13	0	0	24	22	25	1	.211	.269
Chubby Dean	P54	L	23	80	72	12	27	4	0	0	19	8	4	0	.351	.403
Earle Brucker	C47	R	38	62	172	18	50	15	1	3	31	24	16	0	.291	.442
Eric Tipton	OF34	L	24	47	104	12	24	4	2	1	14	13	7	2	.231	.337
Nick Etten	1B41	L	25	43	155	20	39	11	2	3	29	16	11	0	.252	.406
Eddie Collins	OF6, 2B1	R	22	32	21	6	5	1	0	0	8	4	1	0	.238	.286
Al Brancato	3B20, SS24	R	20	21	68	12	14	5	0	1	8	4	11	0	.206	.324
Fred Chapman	SS15	R	22	15	49	5	14	1	1	0	1	1	3	1	.286	.347
1 Lou Finney	OF4	L	28	9	22	1	3	0	0	0	1	0	2	0	.136	.136

Bob McNamara 22 R 2-9, Bill Lillard 21 R 6-19, Hal Wagner 23 L 1-8, Harry O'Neill 22 R 0-0

NAME	T	AGE	W	L	PCT	SV	G	GS	CG	IP	H	BB	SO	SHO	ERA
		28	55	97	.362	12	153	153	50	1343	1687	579	397	6	5.79
Lynn Nelson	R	34	10	13	.435	1	35	24	12	198	233	64	75	2	4.77
George Caster (IL)	R	31	9	9	.500	0	28	17	7	136	144	45	59	1	4.90
Nels Potter	R	27	8	12	.400	2	41	25	9	196	258	88	60	0	6.61
Bill Beckman	R	31	7	11	.389	0	27	19	7	155	198	41	20	2	5.40
Bucky Ross	R	24	6	14	.300	0	29	28	6	174	216	95	43	1	6.00
Chubby Dean	L	23	5	8	.385	7	54	1	0	117	132	80	39	0	5.23
1 Cotton Pippen	R	29	4	11	.267	1	25	17	5	119	169	43	33	0	5.97
Bob Joyce	R	24	3	7	.300	0	30	6	1	108	156	37	25	0	6.67
1 Eddie Smith	L	25	1	0	1.000	0	3	1	0	8	3	3	9	0	9.00
Les McCrabb	R	24	1	1	.333	0	5	2	1	36	42	10	11	0	4.00
Roy Parmelee	R	32	1	6	.143	0	5	5	0	45	42	15	6	0	6.40
1 Bud Thomas	R	28	0	0	—	0	2	1	0	13	24	1	5	0	15.75
Jim Reninger	R	23	0	2	.000	0	2	2	0	11	12	9	7	0	7.88
Sam Page	R	23	0	3	.000	0	22	0	0	34	34	15	11	0	6.95
Walt Masters	R	32	0	0	—	0	3	1	0	8	14	8	4	0	6.55
Bill Nagel	R	23	0	0	—	0	1	0	0	1	0	0	0	0	12.00
Dave Smith	R	24	0	0	—	0	1	0	0						□
Jim Schelle	R	22	0	0	—	0	2								

ST. LOUIS 8th 43-111 .279 64.5 FRED HANEY

NAME	G by Pos	B	AGE	G	AB	R	H	2B	3B	HR	RBI	BB	SO	SB	BA	SA
TOTALS			27	156	5422	733	1453	287	50	91	696	559	606	48	.268	.381
George McQuinn	1B154	L	30	154	617	101	195	37	13	20	94	65	42	6	.316	.515
Johnny Berardino	2B114, 3B8, SS2	R	22	126	468	42	120	24	5	5	58	37	36	6	.256	.361
Don Heffner	SS73, 2B32	R	28	110	375	45	100	10	2	1	35	48	39	1	.267	.312
Harlond Clift	3B149	R	26	151	526	90	142	25	2	15	84	111	55	4	.270	.411
Myril Hoag	OF117, P1	R	31	129	482	58	142	23	4	10	75	24	35	9	.295	.421
2 Chet Laabs	OF79	R	27	95	317	52	95	20	5	10	62	33	62	4	.300	.489
2 Joe Gallagher	OF67	R	25	71	266	41	75	17	2	9	40	17	42	0	.282	.462
Joe Glenn	C82	R	30	88	286	29	78	13	1	4	29	31	40	4	.273	.367
Billy Sullivan	OF59, C19, 1B4	L	28	118	332	53	96	17	5	5	50	34	18	3	.289	.416
2 Mark Christman	SS64, 2B1	R	25	79	222	27	48	6	3	0	20	20	10	2	.216	.270
Joe Grace	OF53	L	25	74	207	35	63	11	2	3	22	19	24	3	.304	.420
Hal Spindel	C32	R	26	48	119	13	32	7	1	0	11	8	7	0	.269	.311
Sam Harshany	C36	R	29	42	145	15	35	2	0	0	15	9	8	0	.241	.255
1 Mel Almada	OF34	R	26	43	134	17	27	6	1	0	7	10	8	1	.239	.291
2 Moose Solters	OF30	R	33	40	131	14	27	5	1	0	9	5	9	0	.206	.267
Mike Mazzera	OF25	L	25	34	91	11	27	6	1	0	7	7	5	1	.297	.459
2 Tommy Thompson	OF23	L	29	30	86	23	26	7	2	0	23	12	9	5	.302	.395
Sig Gryska	SS14	R	25	23	73	5	19	3	0	0	5	7	8	0	.260	.315
1 Roy Hughes	2B6, SS1	R	28	17	23	1	2	0	0	0	0	1	3	0	.087	.087
1 Red Kress	SS13	R	34	13	41	4	9	3	0	0	2	2	4	0	.220	.293
1 Beau Bell	OF9	R	31	11	32	4	7	1	0	0	5	4	5	0	.219	.344
Johnny Lucadello	2B7	B	20	7	30	4	7	4	2	0	4	2	4	0	.233	.500

Bob Neighbors 21 R 2-11, Eddie Silber 25 R 0-1

NAME	T	AGE	W	L	PCT	SV	G	GS	CG	IP	H	BB	SO	SHO	ERA
		30	43	111	.279	3	156	156	56	1371	1724	739	516	3	6.01
Jack Kramer	R	31	9	16	.360	0	40	31	10	212	269	127	68	2	5.82
2 Vern Kennedy	R	32	9	17*	.346	0	33	27	12	192	229	115	54	1	5.72
Bill Trotter	R	30	8	13	.316	0	41	13	4	157	205	54	61	0	5.33
Lefty Mills	L	29	4	11	.267	2	34	14	4	144	147	113	103	0	6.56
2 Bobo Newsom	R	31	3	1	.750	0	4	6◆	3◆	46	52	20	28	0	4.70
2 Roxie Lawson	R	33	3	7	.300	0	28	16	6	151	181	83	43	0	5.30
2 Bob Harris	R	24	3	12	.200	0	28	16	6	126	162	71	48	0	5.71
1 Johnny Marcum	R	29	2	5	.286	0	12	6	2	48	66	10	14	0	7.69
Emil Bildilli	L	26	1	1	.500	2	19	2	1	33	32	23	13	0	5.49
Harry Kimberlin	R	30	1	3	.333	1	23	1	0	41	59	19	11	0	5.86
2 John Whitehead	R	30	1	3	.250	0	11	4	0	66	88	17	9	0	5.86
2 George Gill	R	30	1	12	.077	0	24	11	5	95	139	34	24	0	7.11
Fred Johnson	R	45	1	1	.500	0	12	5	1	41	63	9	10	0	6.43
Roy Hanning	R	21	0	1	.000	0	8	1	0	13	13	8	3	0	3.60
1 Jim Walkup	R	28	0	0	—	0	1	0	0	2	6	2	0	0	13.50
Ewald Pyle	L	28	0	0	—	0	3	0	0	7	6	1	0	0	7.50
Ed Cole	R	29	0	0	—	0	3	0	0	9	8	9	1	0	11.25
2 Jake Wade	L	27	0	0	—	0	1	0	0	16	26	19	9	0	11.25
Bill Cox	R	30	0	0	—	0	3	0	0	2	2	1	1	0	10.00
Russ Van Atta (SA)	L	33	0	0	—	0	9	0	0	9	21	9	6	0	11.57
Bob Muncrief	R	23	0	0	—	0	6	0	0	9	15	5	5	0	15.00
Myril Hoag	R	31	0	0	—	0	1	0	0	9	8	5	2	0	0.00

* Kennedy and Newsom (See Detroit)

CINCINNATI — 1ST 97-57 .630 — BILL McKECHNIE

NAME	G by Pos	B	AGE	G	AB	R	H	2B	3B	HR	RBI	BB	SO	SB	BA	SA
TOTALS			29	156	5378	767	1493	269	60	98	714	500	538	46	.278	.405
Frank McCormick	1B156	R	28	156	630	99	209	41	4	18	128	40	16	1	.332	.495
Lonny Frey	2B124	L	28	125	484	95	141	27	9	11	55	72	46	5	.291	.452
Billy Myers	SS151	R	28	151	509	79	143	18	6	9	56	71	90	4	.281	.393
Bill Werber	3B147	R	31	147	599	115	173	35	5	5	57	91	46	15	.289	.389
Ival Goodman	OF123	L	30	124	470	85	152	37	16	7	84	54	32	2	.323	.515
Harry Craft	OF134	R	24	134	502	58	129	20	7	13	67	27	54	5	.257	.402
Wally Berger	OF95	R	33	97	329	36	85	15	1	14	44	36	63	1	.258	.438
Ernie Lombardi	C120	R	31	130	450	43	129	26	2	20	85	35	19	0	.287	.487
Lee Gamble	OF56	L	29	72	221	24	59	7	2	0	14	9	14	5	.267	.317
Nino Bongiovanni	OF39	L	27	66	159	17	41	6	0	0	16	9	8	0	.258	.296
Willard Hershberger	C60	R	29	63	174	23	60	9	2	0	32	9	4	1	.345	.420
Frenchy Bordagaray	OF43, 2B2	R	29	63	122	19	24	5	1	0	12	9	10	3	.197	.254
Eddie Joost	2B32, SS6	R	23	42	143	23	36	6	3	0	14	12	15	1	.252	.336
Bucky Walters	P39	R	30	40	120	16	39	8	1	1	16	5	12	1	.325	.433
Lew Riggs	3B11	L	29	22	38	5	6	1	0	0	1	5	4	1	.158	.184
Les Scarsella (KJ)		L	25	16	14	0	2	0	0	0	2	0	2	0	.143	.143
2 Al Simmons	OF5	R	37	9	21	0	3	0	0	0	1	2	3	0	.143	.143
Vince DiMaggio	OF7	R	26	8	14	1	1	1	0	0	2	1	10	0	.071	.143
Dick West	OF5, C1	R	23	8	19	1	4	0	0	0	4	1	4	0	.211	.211
1 Bud Hafey	OF4	R	26	6	13	1	2	1	0	0	1	0	4	0	.154	.231
Jimmie Wilson	C1	R	38	4	3	0	1	0	0	0	0	0	0	0	.333	.333
Milt Galatzer	1B2	L	32	3	5	0	0	0	0	0	0	0	1	0	.000	.000
Nolen Richardson	SS1	R	36	1	3	0	0	0	0	0	0	0	0	0	.000	.000

NAME	T	AGE	W	L	PCT	SV	G	GS	CG	IP	H	BB	SO	SHO	ERA
		29	97	57	.630	9	156	156	86	1404	1340	499	637	13	3.27
Bucky Walters	R	30	27	11	.711	0	39	36	31	319	250	109	137	2	2.29
Paul Derringer	R	32	25	7	.781	0	38	35	28	301	321	35	128	5	2.93
Junior Thompson	R	22	13	5	.722	2	42	11	5	152	130	55	87	3	2.55
Whitey Moore	R	27	13	12	.520	3	42	24	9	186	177	95	81	2	3.45
Lee Grissom	R	31	9	7	.563	0	33	21	3	154	145	56	53	0	4.09
Johnny Vander Meer	R	24	5	9	.357	0	30	21	8	129	128	95	102	0	4.67
Johnny Niggeling	R	35	2	1	.667	0	10	5	2	40	51	13	20	1	5.85
2 Milt Shoffner	L	33	2	2	.500	0	10	3	0	38	43	11	6	0	3.32
Peaches Davis	R	34	1	0	1.000	0	20	0	0	31	43	11	4	0	6.39
Hank Johnson	R	33	0	3	.000	0	20	0	0	31	30	13	10	0	2.03
Wes Livengood	R	28	0	0	—	0	5	0	0	6	9	3	4	0	9.00
Pete Naktenis	L	25	0	0	—	0	3	0	0	4	2	1	2	0	2.25
Jim Weaver	R	35	0	0	—	0	3	0	0	3	3	1	3	0	3.00
Red Barrett	R	24	0	0	—	0	1	0	0	2	5	1	0	0	1.80
Elmer Riddle	R	24	0	0	—	0	1	0	0	2	1	0	0	0	0.00
Art Jacobs (SJ)	R	36	0	0	—	0	1	0	0	1	2	1	0	0	9.00

ST. LOUIS — 2nd 92-61 .601 4.5 — RAY BLADES

NAME	G by Pos	B	AGE	G	AB	R	H	2B	3B	HR	RBI	BB	SO	SB	BA	SA
TOTALS			27	155	5447	779	1601	332	62	98	732	475	566	44	.294	.432
Johnny Mize	1B152	L	26	153	564	104	197	44	14	28	108	92	49	0	.349	.626
Stu Martin	2B107, 1B1	L	26	120	425	60	114	26	7	3	80	33	40	4	.268	.384
Jimmy Brown	SS104, 2B50	B	29	147	645	88	192	31	8	3	51	32	18	4	.298	.384
Don Gutteridge	3B143, SS2	R	27	148	524	71	141	27	4	7	54	27	70	5	.269	.376
Enos Slaughter	OF149	R	23	149	604	95	193	52	5	12	86	44	53	2	.320	.482
Terry Moore	OF121, P1	R	27	130	417	65	123	25	2	17	77	43	38	6	.295	.487
Joe Medwick	OF149	R	27	150	606	98	201	48	8	14	117	45	44	6	.332	.507
Mickey Owen	C126	R	23	131	344	32	89	18	2	3	35	43	28	1	.259	.349
Don Padgett	C61, 1B6	L	27	92	233	38	93	15	3	5	53	18	11	1	.399	.554
Lynn King	OF44	L	31	89	85	10	20	2	0	0	11	15	3	2	.235	.259
Pepper Martin	OF51, 3B22	R	35	88	281	48	86	17	7	3	37	30	35	6	.306	.448
Lynn Myers	SS36, 3B13, 2B5	R	25	74	117	24	28	6	1	0	10	12	23	1	.239	.308
Curt Davis	P49	R	35	63	105	10	40	5	0	1	17	3	22	0	.381	.457
3 Lyn Lary	SS30, 3B3	R	33	34	75	11	14	3	0	0	9	16	15	1	.187	.227
Herman Franks	C13	L	25	17	17	1	1	0	0	0	3	3	3	0	.059	.059
Creepy Crespi	2B6, SS4	R	21	15	29	3	5	1	0	0	6	3	6	0	.172	.207
Herb Brenner	C	R	25	9	9	0	1	0	0	0	1	0	2	0	.111	.111
Joe Orengo	SS7	R	24	7	3	0	0	0	0	0	0	1	1	0	.000	.000
Johnny Hopp	1B2	L	22	6	4	1	2	1	0	0	1	1	1	0	.500	.750

Bob Repass 21 R 2-6, Buster Adams 24 R 0-1, Johnny Echols 22 R 0-0, Eddie Lake 23 R 1-4, Bill DeLancey (IL) 27

NAME	T	AGE	W	L	PCT	SV	G	GS	CG	IP	H	BB	SO	SHO	ERA
		29	92	61	.601	32	155	155	45	1385	1377	498	603	18	3.59
Curt Davis	R	35	22	16	.579	7	49	31	13	248	279	48	70	3	3.63
Bob Bowman	R	28	13	5	.722	9	51	15	4	169	241	60	78	2	2.61
Lon Warneke	R	30	13	7	.650	2	34	21	6	162	160	49	59	3	3.78
Bill McGee	R	29	12	5	.706	0	43	17	5	156	155	59	56	4	3.81
Mort Cooper	R	26	12	6	.667	4	45	26	7	211	208	97	130	2	3.24
Bob Weiland	L	33	10	12	.455	1	32	23	6	146	146	50	63	3	3.58
Tom Sunkel	L	26	4	4	.500	0	20	11	2	85	79	56	54	1	4.24
Clyde Shoun	L	27	3	1	.750	9	53	2	0	103	98	42	50	0	3.76
Max Lanier	L	23	2	1	.667	0	7	6	2	38	29	13	14	0	2.37
Nate Andrews	R	25	1	2	.333	0	11	1	0	16	24	12	6	0	6.75
Paul Dean	R	25	1	0	1.000	0	16	2	0	43	54	10	16	0	6.07
Frank Barrett	R	26	0	1	.000	0	2	1	1	3	2	1	3	0	4.50
Murray Dickson	R	22	0	0	—	0	1	0	0	4	1	1	2	0	0.00
Terry Moore	R	27	0	0	—	0	1	0	0	1	0	1	0	0	0.00
Ken Raffensberger	L	21	0	0	—	0	1	0	0	1	1	0	1	0	0.00

BROOKLYN — 3rd 84-69 .549 12.5 — LEO DUROCHER

NAME	G by Pos	B	AGE	G	AB	R	H	2B	3B	HR	RBI	BB	SO	SB	BA	SA
TOTALS			29	157	5350	708	1420	265	57	78	653	564	631	59	.265	.380
Dolph Camilli	1B157	L	32	157	565	105	164	30	12	26	104	110	107	1	.290	.524
Pete Coscarart	2B107, 3B4, SS2	R	26	115	419	59	116	22	4	4	43	40	56	10	.277	.386
Leo Durocher	SS113, 3B1	R	33	116	390	42	108	21	6	1	34	27	24	2	.277	.369
Cookie Lavagetto	3B149	R	26	153	587	93	176	28	5	10	87	78	30	14	.300	.416
Art Parks	OF65	L	27	71	239	27	65	13	2	1	19	28	14	2	.272	.356
Gene Moore	OF86, 1B1	L	29	107	306	45	69	13	6	3	39	40	50	4	.225	.337
Ernie Koy	OF114	R	29	125	425	57	118	37	5	8	67	39	64	11	.278	.445
Babe Phelps	C92	L	31	98	325	39	92	21	2	6	42	24	20	0	.285	.418
Johnny Hudson	SS50, 2B45, 3B1	R	27	109	343	46	87	17	3	2	32	30	36	1	.254	.338
Al Todd	C73	R	35	86	245	28	68	10	0	5	32	13	16	1	.278	.380
Tuck Stainback	OF55	R	27	68	201	22	54	7	0	3	19	4	23	5	.269	.348
Dixie Walker (KJ)	OF59	L	28	61	225	27	63	6	4	2	38	20	10	1	.280	.369
Goody Rosen	OF47	L	26	54	183	22	46	6	4	1	12	23	21	4	.251	.344
2 Mel Almada	OF32	L	26	39	112	11	24	4	0	0	3	9	17	2	.214	.250
Fred Sington	OF22	R	29	32	84	13	23	5	0	1	7	15	15	0	.274	.369
2 Lyn Lary	SS12, 3B7	R	33	29	31	7	5	1	1	0	1	12	6	1	.161	.258
1 Jimmy Ripple	OF28	L	23	28	106	18	35	8	4	0	28	11	8	0	.330	.481
1 Ray Hayworth	C18	R	35	21	26	0	4	2	0	0	1	4	7	0	.154	.231
1 Tony Lazzeri	2B11, 3B2	R	35	14	39	6	11	2	0	3	6	6	10	7	.282	.564
Chris Hartje	C8	R	24	9	16	2	5	1	0	0	5	1	0	0	.313	.375
Oris Hockett	OF1	L	29	6	13	3	3	0	0	0	1	1	2	0	.231	.231
Lindsey Deal	OF1	L	27	4	7	0	0	0	0	0	0	0	0	0	.000	.000
2 Gene Schott		R	25	1	0	0	0	0	0	0	0	0	0	0	—	—

NAME	T	AGE	W	L	PCT	SV	G	GS	CG	IP	H	BB	SO	SHO	ERA
		27	84	69	.549	13	157	157	69	1410	1431	399	528	9	3.64
Luke Hamlin	R	34	20	13	.606	0	40	36	19	270	255	54	88	2	3.64
Hugh Casey	R	25	15	10	.600	4	40	25	15	227	228	54	79	0	2.93
Tot Pressnell	R	32	9	7	.563	2	31	18	10	157	171	33	43	2	4.01
Vito Tamulis	L	27	9	8	.529	4	39	17	8	159	177	45	83	1	4.36
Whit Wyatt	R	31	8	3	.727	0	16	14	6	109	88	39	52	2	2.31
Freddie Fitzsimmons	R	37	7	9	.438	3	27	20	5	151	178	28	44	0	3.87
Ira Hutchinson	R	28	5	2	.714	4	41	1	0	106	103	51	46	0	4.33
Bill Crouch	R	29	1	0	1.000	0	6	3	3	38	37	14	10	0	2.60
Van Lingle Mungo (BL)	R	28	4	5	.444	0	14	10	1	77	70	33	34	0	3.27
2 Al Hollingsworth	L	31	1	2	.333	0	8	5	1	27	33	11	11	0	5.33
Carl Doyle	R	26	1	2	.333	1	5	1	1	18	8	7	1	0	1.00
Red Evans	R	32	1	8	.111	1	24	6	0	64	74	26	28	0	5.20
Boots Poffenberger (ST)	R	24	0	0	—	0	3	1	0	5	7	4	2	0	5.40
George Jeffcoat	R	25	0	0	—	0	1	0	0	2	2	0	1	0	0.00

CHICAGO — 4th 84-70 .545 13 — GABBY HARTNETT

NAME	G by Pos	B	AGE	G	AB	R	H	2B	3B	HR	RBI	BB	SO	SB	BA	SA
TOTALS			29	156	5293	724	1407	263	62	91	671	523	553	61	.266	.391
Rip Russell	1B43	R	24	143	542	55	148	24	5	9	79	36	56	2	.273	.386
Billy Herman	2B156	R	29	156	623	111	191	34	18	7	70	66	31	9	.307	.453
Dick Bartell	SS101, 3B1	R	31	105	336	37	80	24	2	3	34	42	25	6	.238	.348
Stan Hack	3B156	L	29	156	641	112	191	28	6	8	56	65	35	17	.298	.398
Jim Gleeson	OF91	R	27	111	332	43	74	19	6	4	45	39	46	7	.223	.352
Hank Leiber	OF98	R	28	112	365	65	113	16	1	24	88	59	42	1	.310	.556
Angie Galan	OF145	B	27	148	549	104	167	36	8	6	71	75	26	8	.304	.432
Gabby Hartnett	C86	R	38	97	306	36	85	18	2	12	59	37	32	0	.278	.467
Carl Reynolds	OF72	R	36	88	281	33	69	10	6	4	44	16	38	5	.246	.367
Gus Mancuso	C76	R	33	80	251	17	58	10	2	0	17	24	19	0	.231	.295
Bill Nicholson	OF58	L	24	58	220	37	65	15	5	5	38	20	29	0	.295	.464
Bobby Mattick	SS48	R	23	51	178	16	51	12	1	0	23	6	19	1	.287	.365
Bob Garbark	C21	R	24	24	21	1	3	0	0	0	0	3	0	0	.143	.143
1 Joe Marty	OF21	R	25	23	76	6	10	1	0	2	10	4	13	2	.132	.224
Phil Cavarretta (BN)	1B13, OF1	L	22	22	55	4	15	3	1	0	4	8	3	2	.273	.364
Steve Mesner	SS12, 2B1, 3B1	R	21	17	43	7	12	4	0	0	5	3	4	0	.279	.372

NAME	T	AGE	W	L	PCT	SV	G	GS	CG	IP	H	BB	SO	SHO	ERA
		32	84	70	.545	13	156	156	72	1392	1504	430	584	8	3.80
Bill Lee	R	29	19	15	.559	0	37	36	20	282	295	85	105	1	3.45
Larry French	L	31	15	8	.652	3	36	21	10	194	205	50	98	2	3.29
Claude Passeau	R	30	13	9	.591	3	34	27	13	221	215	48	108*	1	3.05
Charlie Root	R	40	8	7	.533	4	35	16	8	167	189	34	65	0	4.04
Vance Page	R	35	7	7	.500	1	27	17	8	139	169	37	43	1	3.88
Dizzy Dean	R	29	6	4	.600	0	19	13	7	96	98	17	27	2	3.38
Jack Russell	R	33	4	3	.571	9	33	0	0	69	78	24	32	0	3.65
Earl Whitehill (BG)	R	39	4	7	.364	1	24	11	2	89	102	50	42	1	5.16
Gene Lillard	R	25	3	5	.375	0	20	7	2	55	66	31	30	0	6.55
Clay Bryant (SA)	R	27	2	1	.667	0	4	2	1	31	42	14	9	0	5.81
1 Kirby Higbe	R	24	2	1	.667	0	9	2	0	23	12	22•	16	0	3.13
Vern Olsen	L	21	1	0	1.000	0	4	2	1	17	7	3	0	0	0.00
1 Ray Harrell	R	27	0	2	.000	0	4	2	0	17	29	6	5	0	8.47

* Passeau, also with Philadelphia, league leader in SO with 137
• Higbe, also with Philadelphia, league leader in BB with 123

NEW YORK — 5th 77-74 .510 18.5 — BILL TERRY

NAME	G by Pos	B	AGE	G	AB	R	H	2B	3B	HR	RBI	BB	SO	SB	BA	SA
TOTALS			29	151	5129	703	1395	211	38	116	651	498	499	26	.272	.396
Zeke Bonura	1B122	R	30	123	455	55	148	26	6	11	85	46	22	1	.321	.477
Burgess Whitehead	2B91, SS4, 3B1	R	29	95	335	31	80	6	3	0	24	24	19	1	.239	.293
Billy Jurges	SS137	R	31	138	543	84	155	21	11	6	63	47	34	3	.285	.398
Tom Hafey	3B70	R	25	70	256	37	62	10	1	6	26	10	44	1	.242	.359
Mel Ott	OF96, 3B20	L	30	125	396	85	122	23	2	27	80	100	50	2	.308	.581
Frank Demaree	OF150	R	29	150	560	68	170	27	2	11	79	66	40	2	.304	.446
Jo-Jo Moore	OF136	L	30	138	562	80	151	23	2	10	47	45	17	5	.269	.370
Harry Danning	C132	R	27	135	520	79	163	28	5	16	74	35	42	4	.313	.479
Alex Kampouris	2B62, 3B11	R	26	74	201	23	50	12	2	5	29	30	41	0	.249	.403
1 Jimmy Ripple	OF23	L	29	66	123	10	28	4	0	1	9	8	9	0	.228	.285
Bob Seeds	OF50	R	32	63	173	33	46	5	1	5	26	22	31	1	.266	.393
Ken O'Dea	C30	L	26	52	97	17	17	1	0	3	11	10	16	0	.175	.278
Johnny McCarthy	1B12, OF4, P1	L	29	50	80	12	21	5	1	0	12	9	10	0	.263	.400
Lou Chiozza (BL)	3B30, SS8	L	29	40	142	19	38	3	1	3	12	9	10	3	.268	.366
George Myatt (KJ)	3B14	L	25	22	53	7	10	2	0	0	3	4	6	2	.189	.226
Babe Young	1B22	L	24	22	75	8	23	4	0	3	14	5	6	0	.307	.480
2 Tony Lazzeri	3B13	R	35	13	41	5	14	1	0	0	3	8	4	0	.350	.364
Skeeter Scalzi	SS5, 3B1	R	26	11	18	4	4	3	0	0	2	2	4	0	.222	.389
Johnny Dickshot	OF10	R	29	10	34	2	8	1	0	0	4	2	6	0	.235	.294
Al Glossop	2B10	R	24	10	32	1	6	2	0	0	2	1	6	0	.188	.281
2 Ray Hayworth	C2	R	25	5	13	1	3	0	0	0	0	0	2	0	.231	.231

NAME	T	AGE	W	L	PCT	SV	G	GS	CG	IP	H	BB	SO	SHO	ERA
		29	77	74	.510	20	151	151	55	1319	1412	477	505	6	4.07
Harry Gumbert	R	29	18	11	.621	0	36	34	14	244	257	81	81	2	4.32
Hal Schumacher	R	28	13	10	.565	0	29	27	8	182	199	89	58	0	4.80
Bill Lohrman	R	26	13	13	.480	1	38	24	9	186	200	45	70	1	4.60
Cliff Melton	L	27	12	15	.444	3	41	23	9	207	214	65	95	2	3.57
Carl Hubbell	L	36	11	9	.550	2	29	18	10	154	150	24	62	0	2.75
Jumbo Brown	R	32	4	0	1.000	7	31	0	0	56	69	25	24	0	4.18
Manny Salvo	R	27	4	10	.286	0	32	18	4	136	150	75	69	0	4.63
2 Red Lynn	R	26	2	0	1.000	1	26	0	0	50	44	21	23	0	3.06
Dick Coffman	R	32	2	3	.333	2	27	0	0	38	50	6	9	0	3.08
Slick Castleman	R	25	1	2	.333	0	12	4	0	34	36	23	6	0	4.50
Johnnie Wittig	R	24	1	2	.000	0	5	2	1	17	18	14	4	0	7.41
Tom Gorman	L	20	0	0	—	0	5	1	1	19	18	10	6	0	7.20
Hy Vandenberg	R	31	0	0	—	0	6	0	0	10	6	3	8	0	6.00
Johnny McCarthy	L	29	0	0	—	0	1	0	0	1	1	2	0	0	7.20

NAME	G by Pos	B	AGE	G	AB	R	H	2B	3B	HR	RBI	BB	SO	SB	BA	SA
PITTSBURGH 6th 68-85 .444 28.5	**PIE TRAYNOR**		29	153	5269	666	1435	261	60	63	617	477	420	44	.276	.384
TOTALS																
2 Ebie Fletcher	1B101	L	23	102	370	49	112	23	4	12	71	48	28	3	.303	.484
Pep Young	2B84	R	31	84	293	34	81	14	3	3	29	23	29	1	.276	.375
Arky Vaughan	SS152	L	27	152	595	94	182	30	11	6	62	70	20	12	.306	.424
Lee Handley	3B100	R	25	101	376	43	107	14	5	1	42	32	20	17	.285	.356
Paul Waner	OF106	L	36	125	461	62	151	30	6	3	45	35	18	0	.328	.408
Lloyd Waner	OF92, 3B1	L	33	112	379	49	108	15	3	0	24	17	13	0	.285	.340
Johnny Rizzo	OF86	R	26	94	330	49	86	23	3	6	54	42	27	1	.261	.403
Ray Berres	C80	R	31	81	231	22	53	6	1	0	16	11	25	1	.229	.264
Bill Brubaker	2B65, 3B32, SS1	R	28	100	345	41	80	23	1	7	43	29	51	3	.232	.365
Ray Mueller	C81	R	27	86	180	14	42	8	1	2	18	14	22	4	.233	.322
Chuck Klein	OF66	L	34	85	270	37	81	16	4	11	47	26	17	1	.300	.511
Fern Bell	OF67, 3B1	R	26	83	262	44	75	5	8	2	34	42	18	2	.286	.389
Joe Bowman	P37	R	29	70	96	9	33	8	1	0	18	5	9	0	.344	.448
1 Gus Suhr	1B52	L	33	63	204	23	59	10	2	1	31	25	23	4	.289	.373
Bob Elliott	OF30	R	22	32	129	18	43	10	3	3	19	9	4	0	.333	.527
George Susce	1B31	R	31	31	75	8	17	3	1	1	4	12	5	0	.227	.333
Maurice Van Robays	OF25, 3B1	R	24	27	105	13	33	9	0	2	16	6	10	0	.314	.457
Frankie Gustine	3B22	R	19	22	70	5	13	3	0	0	6	3	4	1	.186	.229
Jack Juelich	2B10, 3B2	R	22	17	46	5	11	0	2	0	2	4	1	0	.239	.326

Woody Jensen 31 L 2-12, Heinie Manush 37 L 0-12, Joe Schultz 20 L 4-14, Eddie Yount 23 R 0-2

NAME	T	AGE	W	L	PCT	SV	G	GS	CG	IP	H	BB	SO	SHO	ERA
		28	68	85	.444	15	153	153	53	1354	**1537**	423	464	10	4.15
Bob Klinger	R	31	14	17	.452	0	37	33	10	225	251	81	64	2	4.36
Rip Sewell	R	32	10	9	.526	2	52	15	7	176	177	73	69	1	4.09
Joe Bowman	R	29	10	14	.417	1	37	27	10	185	217	43	58	1	4.48
Jim Tobin	R	26	9	9	.500	1	25	18	9	145	194	33	43	0	4.53
Mace Brown	R	30	9	13	.409	7	47	19	8	200	232	52	71	1	3.38
Bill Swift	R	31	5	7	.417	4	36	8	2	130	150	28	56	1	3.88
2 Max Butcher	R	28	4	4*	.500	0	14	12	5	87	104	23	21	2	3.41
Cy Blanton (SA)	R	30	2	3	.400	0	10	6	1	42	45	10	11	0	4.29
Russ Bauers (SA)	R	25	2	4	.333	1	15	8	1	54	46	25	12	0	3.33
Ken Heintzelman	L	23	1	1	.500	0	17	2	1	36	35	18	18	1	5.00
Oad Swigart	R	24	1	1	.500	0	3	3	1	24	27	6	8	1	4.50
Johnny Gee (SA)	L	23	1	2	.333	0	3	3	2	20	16	10	16	0	4.05
Bill Clemensen	R	20	0	1	.000	0	12	1	0	27	32	20	13	0	7.33
Pep Rambert	R	22	0	0	—	0	2	0	0	4	7	1	4	0	9.00

*Butcher, also with Philadelphia, league leader in L with 17

NAME	G by Pos	B	AGE	G	AB	R	H	2B	3B	HR	RBI	BB	SO	SB	BA	SA
BOSTON 7th 63-88 .417 32.5	**CASEY STENGEL**		29	152	5286	572	1395	199	39	56	534	366	494	41	.264	.348
TOTALS																
Buddy Hassett	1B23, OF23	L	27	148	590	72	182	15	3	2	60	29	14	13	.308	.344
Tony Cuccinello (NJ)	2B80	R	31	81	310	42	95	17	1	2	40	26	26	5	.306	.387
Eddie Miller (BL)	SS77	R	22	77	296	32	79	12	4	1	31	16	21	4	.267	.361
Hank Majeski	3B99	R	22	106	367	35	100	16	1	7	54	18	30	2	.272	.379
Debs Garms	OF96, 3B37	L	32	132	513	68	153	24	4	2	37	39	20	2	.298	.392
Johnny Cooney	OF116, 1B2	L	38	118	368	39	101	8	1	2	27	21	8	2	.274	.318
Max West	OF124	L	22	130	449	67	128	26	4	19	82	51	55	4	.285	.497
Al Lopez	C129	R	30	131	412	32	104	22	1	8	49	40	45	1	.252	.369
Rabbit Warstler	SS49, 2B43, 3B21	R	35	114	342	34	83	11	3	0	24	24	31	2	.243	.292
1 Al Simmons	OF82	R	37	93	330	39	93	17	5	7	43	22	40	0	.282	.427
Jimmy Outlaw	OF39, 3B22	R	26	65	133	15	35	2	0	0	5	10	14	1	.263	.278
Sibby Sisti	2B34, 3B17, SS10	R	18	63	215	19	49	7	1	1	11	12	38	1	.228	.284
Phil Masi	C42	R	22	46	114	14	29	7	2	1	14	9	15	0	.254	.377
1 Elbie Fletcher	1B31	L	23	106	144	14	26	2	0	0	8	19	5	1	.245	.264
Ralph Hodgin	OF9	L	24	32	48	4	10	1	0	0	4	3	4	0	.208	.229
Whitey Wietelmann	SS22, 2B1	R	20	33	69	2	14	1	0	0	5	2	9	1	.203	.217
Bama Rowell	OF16	L	23	21	59	5	11	2	2	0	6	1	4	0	.186	.288
Stan Andrews	C10	R	22	13	26	1	6	0	0	0	1	1	2	0	.231	.231
Red Barkely	SS7, 3B4	R	26	12	11	1	0	0	0	0	0	1	4	0	.000	.000

Otto Huber 25 R 6-22, Chet Ross 27 R 10-31, Chet Clemens 22 R 5-23, Oliver Hill 29 L 1-2, Bill Schuster 26 R 0-3

NAME	T	AGE	W	L	PCT	SV	G	GS	CG	IP	H	BB	SO	SHO	ERA
		31	63	88	.417	15	152	152	68	1358	1400	513	430	11	3.71
Bill Posedel	R	32	15	13	.536	0	33	29	18	221	221	78	73	5	3.91
Lou Fette	R	32	10	10	.500	2	27	26	11	146	123	61	35	6	2.96
Danny MacFayden	R	24	8	14	.364	2	33	28	8	192	221	59	46	0	3.98
Dick Errickson	R	27	6	9	.400	2	28	11	3	128	143	54	33	0	4.01
Joe Sullivan	L	28	6	9	.400	1	31	11	7	114	114	50	46	0	3.63
Johnny Lanning	R	32	5	6	.455	4	37	6	3	129	120	53	45	0	3.42
1 Milt Shoffner	L	33	4	6	.400	5	25	11	7	132	133	42	51	0	3.14
Jim Turner (BY)	R	35	4	11	.267	0	25	22	9	158	181	51	50	0	4.27
George Barnicle	R	21	2	2	.500	0	9	1	0	18	16	8	15	0	5.00
Joe Callahan	R	22	1	0	1.000	0	4	1	1	17	17	3	8	0	3.18
Hiker Moran	R	27	1	1	.500	0	7	1	0	20	21	11	4	0	4.50
Tom Earley	R	22	1	4	.200	0	14	2	0	40	49	19	9	0	4.73
Al Veigel	R	22	0	1	.000	0	2	0	0	3	3	5	1	0	6.00
Fred Frankhouse	R	35	0	2	.000	0	23	0	0	38	37	18	12	0	2.61
Roy Weir	L	28	0	0	—	0	3	1	1	2	0	0	0	0	0.00

NAME	G by Pos	B	AGE	G	AB	R	H	2B	3B	HR	RBI	BB	SO	SB	BA	SA
PHILADELPHIA 8th 45-106 .298 50.5	**DOC PROTHRO**		28	152	5133	553	1341	232	40	49	510	421	486	47	.261	.351
TOTALS																
2 Gus Suhr	1B60	L	33	60	198	21	63	12	2	3	24	34	14	1	.318	.444
2 Roy Hughes	2B65	R	28	65	237	22	54	5	1	1	16	21	18	4	.228	.270
George Scharein	SS117	R	24	118	399	35	95	17	1	1	33	13	40	4	.238	.293
Pinky May	3B132	R	28	135	464	49	133	27	3	2	62	41	20	1	.287	.371
2 Joe Marty	OF79, P1	R	25	91	299	32	76	12	6	9	44	24	27	1	.254	.425
Hersh Martin	OF95	B	29	111	393	59	111	28	5	1	22	42	27	4	.282	.387
Morrie Arnovich	OF132	R	28	134	491	68	159	25	2	5	67	58	28	7	.324	.413
Spud Davis	C85	R	34	87	202	10	62	8	1	0	23	9	10	0	.307	.356
Emmett Mueller	2B51, 3B17, OF17, SS1	R	26	115	341	46	95	19	4	9	43	33	34	4	.279	.437
Gib Brack	OF48, 1B19	R	31	91	270	40	78	21	4	6	41	26	49	1	.289	.468
Wally Millies	C84	R	34	84	205	12	48	3	0	0	12	9	5	0	.234	.249
Del Young	SS55, 2B17	R	27	77	217	22	57	9	2	3	20	8	24	1	.263	.364
LeGrant Scott	OF55	L	28	76	232	31	65	15	1	1	26	12	24	5	.280	.366
Jack Bolling	1B48	L	22	69	211	27	61	11	0	3	13	11	10	6	.289	.384
Pinky Whitney (IL)	1B12, 2B8, 3B2	R	34	34	75	9	14	0	1	1	6	7	4	0	.187	.253
1 Chuck Klein	OF11, 1B1	L	34	25	47	8	9	2	1	1	9	10	4	1	.191	.340
Les Powers	1B13	L	29	19	52	7	18	1	1	0	5	8	5	0	.346	.404
2 Bud Hafey	OF13, P2	R	26	18	51	3	9	1	0	0	3	3	12	0	.176	.196
Bonnie Warren	C17	R	27	18	56	4	13	0	1	0	7	7	7	0	.232	.286
Bud Bates	OF14	R	27	18	58	4	15	2	0	1	2	2	8	1	.259	.345

Dave Coble 26 R 7-25, Stan Benjamin 25 R 7-50, Charlie Letchas 23 R 10-44, S Jim Shilling (LJ) R 10-33.
Eddie Feinberg 21 B 4-18, Len Gabrielson (JJ) 23 L 4-18, Joe Kracher 25 R 1-5, Bill Atwood 27 R 0-6, Johnny Watwood 33 L 1-6

NAME	T	AGE	W	L	PCT	SV	G	GS	CG	IP	H	BB	SO	SHO	ERA
		28	45	106	.298	12	152	152	67	1327	1502	**579**	447	3	5.17
2 Kirby Higbe	R	24	10	14	.417	2	34	26	14	187	208	101	79	1	4.86
Hugh Mulcahy	R	25	9	16	.360	2	38	32	14	226	246	93	59	1	4.98
Syl Johnson	R	38	8	8	.500	3	32	13	6	111	112	15	37	0	3.81
Boom-Boom Beck	R	34	7	14	.333	3	34	16	12	183	203	64	77	0	4.72
2 Ray Harrell	R	27	3	7	.300	0	22	10	4	95	101	56	35	0	5.40
1 Claude Passeau	R	30	2	4	.333	0	8	4	3	53	54	25	29*	1	4.24
Ike Pearson	R	22	2	13	.133	0	26	13	4	125	144	56	29	0	5.76
1 Max Butcher	R	28	2	13*	.133	0	19	16	3	104	131	51	27	0	5.63
Elmer Burkart	R	22	1	0	1.000	0	5	0	0	11	2	2	4	0	4.50
1 Al Hollingsworth	L	31	1	9	.100	0	15	10	3	60	78	27	24	0	5.85
Jim Henry	R	29	0	1	.000	1	9	1	0	23	24	8	7	0	5.09
1 Gene Schott	R	25	0	1	.000	0	4	0	0	11	14	5	1	0	4.91
Bill Kerksieck	R	25	0	2	.000	0	23	2	1	63	81	32	13	0	7.14
Roy Bruner	R	22	0	4	.000	0	4	2	0	27	38	13	11	0	6.67
Jennings Poindexter	L	28	0	0	—	0	11	1	0	30	29	15	12	0	4.20
Al Smith	L	31	0	0	—	0	5	0	0	9	11	5	2	0	4.50
Bill Hoffman	R	21	0	0	—	0	6	0	0	6	8	7	1	0	13.50
2 Bud Hafey	R	26	0	0	—	0	2	0	0	1	7	1	1	0	45.00
2 Joe Marty	R	25	0	0	—	0	1	0	0	4	2	3	1	0	4.50

*Butcher (see Pittsburgh) • Passeau (see Chicago) Higbe (see Chicago)

WORLD SERIES — NEW YORK (AL) 4 CINCINNATI (NL) 0

LINE SCORES

TEAM	1	2	3	4	5	6	7	8	9	10	11	12	R	H	E
Game 1 October 4 at New York															
CIN (NL)	0	0	0		1	0	0		0	0	0		1	4	0
NY (AL)	0	0	0		0	1	0		0	0	1		2	6	0
Derringer							**Ruffing**								
Game 2 October 5 at New York															
CIN	0	0	0		0	0	0		0				0	2	0
NY	0	0	3		1	0	0		0 0 X				4	9	0
Walters							**Pearson**								
Game 3 October 7 at Cincinnati															
NY	2	0	2		0	3	0		0	0	0		7	5	1
CIN	1	2	0		0	0	0		0	0	0		3	10	0
Gomez, **Hadley** (2)							Thompson, Grissom (5)								
							Moore (7)								
Game 4 October 8 at Cincinnati															
NY	0	0	0		0	0	0		2	0	2	3	7	7	1
CIN	0	0	0		0	3	1		0	0	0		4	11	4
Hildebrank, Sundra (5),							Derringer, **Walters** (8)								
Murphy (7)															

COMPOSITE BATTING

NAME	POS	G	AB	R	H	2B	3B	HR	RBI	BA
New York (AL)										
Totals		4	131	20	27	4	1	7	18	.206
Keller	OF	4	16	8	7	1	1	3	6	.438
DiMaggio	OF	4	16	3	5	0	0	1	3	.313
Rolfe	3B	4	16	2	2	0	0	0	0	.125
Crosetti	SS	4	16	1	1	0	0	0	0	.063
Dickey	C	4	15	2	4	0	0	2	5	.267
Dahlgren	1B	4	14	2	3	2	0	1	4	.214
Gordon	2B	4	14	1	2	0	0	0	1	.143
Selkirk	OF	4	12	0	2	1	0	0	0	.167
Ruffing	P	1	3	0	1	0	0	0	0	.333
Hadley	P	1	3	0	0	0	0	0	0	.000
Murphy	P	1	2	0	0	0	0	0	0	.000
Pearson	P	1	2	0	0	0	0	0	0	.000
Gomez	P	1	1	0	0	0	0	0	0	.000
Hildebrand	P	1	1	0	0	0	0	0	0	.000
Sundra	P	1								—
Cincinnati (NL)										
Totals		4	133	8	27	3	1	0	8	.203
Frey	2B	4	17	0	0	0	0	0	0	.000
Weber	3B	4	16	1	4	0	0	0	0	.250
McCormick	1B	4	15	1	6	1	0	0	1	.400
Goodman	OF	4	15	3	5	0	0	0	0	.333
Berger	OF	4	15	0	0	0	0	0	0	.000
Lombardi	C	4	14	0	3	0	0	0	2	.214
Myers	SS	4	12	2	4	0	1	0	0	.333
Craft	OF	4	11	0	1	0	0	0	0	.091
Derringer	P	2	5	0	1	0	0	0	0	.200
Simmons	OF	1	4	1	1	0	0	0	0	.250
Walters	P	2	3	0	0	0	0	0	1	.000
Hershberger	C	4	2	0	1	0	0	0	1	.500
Bongiovanni	PH	1	1	0	0	0	0	0	0	.000
Gamble	PH	1	1	0	0	0	0	0	0	.000
Moore	P	1	1	0	0	0	0	0	0	.000
Thompson	P	1	1	0	1	0	0	0	0	1.000
Bordagaray	PR	2	0	0	0	0	0	0	0	.000
Grissom	P	1								.000

COMPOSITE PITCHING

NAME	G	IP	H	BB	SO	W	L	SV	ERA
New York (AL)									
Totals	4	37	27	6	22	4	0	0	1.22
Pearson	1	9	2	1	8	1	0	0	0.00
Ruffing	1	9	4	1	4	1	0	0	1.00
Hadley	1	8	7	3	2	1	0	0	2.25
Hildebrand	1	4	2	0	3	0	0	0	0.00
Murphy	1	3.1	5	0	2	1	0	0	2.70
Sundra	1	2.2	4	1	2	0	0	0	0.00
Gomez	1	1	3	1	0	0	0	0	9.00
Cincinnati (NL)									
Totals	4	35.2	27	9	20	0	4	0	4.29
Derringer	2	15.1	9	3	9	0	1	0	2.35
Walters	2	11	13	1	6	0	2	0	4.91
Thompson	1	4.2	5	4	3	0	1	0	13.50
Moore	1	3	0	0	0	0	0	0	0.00
Grissom	1	1.2	0	1	2	0	0	0	0.00

1940 Bakers Shift and McKechnie's Dozen

Del Baker took over as manager of Detroit toward the end of the 1938 season and posted a 37-20 record. In 1939 he remained at the helm all season and won 81 while losing 73, enough for a slip from fourth to fifth place. Then, in the spring of 1940, Baker simply shifted Hank Greenberg from first to left field and Rudy York from a part-time backstop to a full-time first baseman. Presto—a pennant! Yet, for all the honors of being tops in the best race the junior circuit staged up to 1940, Baker and his Tigers were again overshadowed by the omnipotent presence of the Yankees, who found themselves floundering in the league's basement in May only to make a fantastic dash down the stretch to wind up in third place, two games off the leaders.

If the Yankees threw a giant shadow, the Indians projected an even more stifling silhouette.

Bob Feller no-hit the White Sox on opening day and then went on to notch a league high 27 wins and league low 2.62 E.R.A. Lou Boudreau knocked in 101 runs and hit .295, good enough to take Rookie of the Year honors. But the Indians also suffered from incompatibility, which was enough of a problem to shatter their day in the sun. In a time when the status quo was more a way of life than something to throw stones at, Cleveland players found the courageous audacity to present a petition for the release of manager Ossie Vitt. The Cleveland establishment, ignoring the majority of 25 for the minority of one, refused the demand and watched a dispirited team make a faint-hearted stretch drive to finish a frustrating one-game off the Tigers.

Regardless of Cleveland's morale and the Yankees' Joe DiMaggio, who put his second straight batting title together, the Tigers had the MVP in Greenberg and the kind of power which unnerved the league—smashing 26 homers in 17 games. Aside from Greenberg's 41 home runs and York's 33, there was also Schoolboy Rowe's return to form (16-3) after three years of arm misery, and Bobo Newsom, 21-5, who finally managed to land on a pennant winner after six teams in ten years.

In contrast to the American League pennant struggle, the National League winner reversed roles and had a cakewalk. But the senior circuit, always seeming to have a lock on baseball's theatrics, presented a winner which was made to wear both masks of the traditional theater. After the Dodgers got off in perfect form with nine straight wins climaxed by Tex Carleton's no-hitter over the Reds on April 30, Cincinnati began their pennant drive and, in early July, went in front to stay.

St. Louis, which had provided most of the competition in 1939, got off to a poor

start and replaced manager Ray Blades with Billy Southworth. They also traded Joe Medwick and Curt Davis to the Dodgers for Ernie Koy, Carl Doyle, and Newt Kimball, plus picking up $100,000 in the swap. But the Dodgers' thrust to second was credited more to 38-year-old Freddie Fitzsimmons' 16-2 record than to the trades.

Whatever chance the Dodgers might have had was denied when rookie shortstop Pee Wee Reese broke his foot in mid-August and Cookie Lavagetto was sidelined at about the same time with appendicitis.

The Reds finished the season 12 games in front for manager Bill McKechnie. The statistics, though, tell little of the drama which unfolded at Cincinnati. While visiting Boston on August 2, catcher Willard Hershberger committed suicide. Then, in mid-September, starting catcher Ernie Lombardi sprained an ankle. It took 39-year-old coach Jimmie Wilson to rekindle the team's spirits. He took over the catching chores for the remainder to the season and turned in a fine job.

As the Reds entered the World Series, they still relied heavily on the catching of Wilson. In the first game Detroit routed Paul Derringer, one of Cincinnati's aces, in a five-run second-inning barrage and went on to win 7-2 behind Bobo Newsom. Bucky Walters, the other half of the Reds pitching power, evened matters the next day with a three-hit, 5-3 victory over Schoolboy Rowe. The Tigers got the upper hand in game three before Derringer returned in the fourth contest to knot up the Series with a 5-2 win. Newsom again gave the Tigers an edge in games, but after Walters bested Rowe—who didn't last through the first—the outcome came down to a second rematch between Derringer and Newsom. After Detroit got an unearned run in the third, Derringer held on and picked up two runs in the seventh to give the Reds a 2-1 win for their first championship in 21 years. In Wilson, who provided a steady hand behind the plate—especially in the important sixth-game shutout—there was no disappointment as he finished the Series with an impressive .353 batting average.

1940 AMERICAN LEAGUE

NAME	G by Pos	B	AGE	G	AB	R	H	2B	3B	HR	RBI	BB	SO	SB	BA	SA
DETROIT 1st 90-64 .584						DEL BAKER										
TOTALS			29	155	5418	888	1549	312	65	134	829	664	556	66	.286	.442
Rudy York	1B155	R	26	155	588	105	186	46	6	33	134	89	88	3	.316	.583
Charlie Gehringer	2B138	L	37	139	515	108	161	33	3	10	81	101	17	10	.313	.447
Dick Bartell	SS139	R	32	139	528	76	123	24	3	7	53	76	53	12	.233	.330
Pinky Higgins	3B129	R	31	131	480	70	130	24	3	13	76	61	31	4	.271	.415
Pete Fox	OF85	R	30	93	350	49	101	17	4	5	48	21	30	7	.289	.403
Barney McCosky	OF141	L	23	143	589	123	200	39	19	4	57	67	41	13	.340	.491
Hank Greenberg	OF148	R	29	148	573	129	195	50	8	41	150	93	75	6	.340	.670
Birdie Tebbetts	C107	R	27	111	379	46	112	24	4	4	46	35	14	4	.296	.412
Bruce Campbell	OF74	L	30	103	297	56	84	15	5	8	44	45	28	2	.283	.448
Billy Sullivan	C57, 3B6	L	29	78	220	36	68	14	4	3	41	31	11	2	.309	.450
Earl Averill	OF22	L	38	64	118	10	33	4	1	2	20	5	14	0	.280	.381
Frank Croucher	SS26, 2B7, 3B1	R	25	37	57	3	6	0	0	0	2	4	5	0	.105	.105
Red Kress	3B17, SS12	R	35	33	99	13	22	3	1	1	11	10	12	0	.222	.303
Scat Metha	2B10, 3B6	R	26	26	37	6	9	0	1	0	3	2	6	0	.243	.297
Dutch Meyer	2B21	R	24	23	58	12	15	3	0	0	6	4	10	2	.259	.310
Tuck Stainback	OF9	R	28	15	40	4	9	2	0	0	1	1	9	0	.225	.275
Pat Mullin	OF1	L	22	4	4	0	0	0	0	0	0	0	1	0	.000	.000
Frank Secory		R	27	1	1	0	0	0	0	0	0	0	1	0	.000	.000
CLEVELAND 2nd 89-65 .578 1						OSSIE VITT										
TOTALS			27	155	5361	710	1422	287	61	101	660	519	597	53	.265	.398
Hal Trosky	1B139	L	27	140	522	85	154	39	4	25	93	79	45	1	.295	.529
Ray Mack	2B146	R	23	146	530	60	150	21	5	12	69	51	77	4	.283	.409
Lou Boudreau	SS155	R	22	155	627	97	185	46	10	9	101	73	39	6	.295	.443
Ken Keltner	3B148	R	23	149	543	67	138	24	10	15	77	51	56	10	.254	.418
Beau Bell	OF97, 1B14	R	32	120	444	55	124	22	2	4	58	34	41	2	.279	.365
Roy Weatherly	OF135	L	25	135	578	90	175	35	11	12	59	27	26	9	.303	.464
Ben Chapman	OF140	R	31	143	548	82	157	40	6	4	50	78	45	13	.286	.403
Rollie Hemsley	C117	R	33	119	416	46	111	20	5	4	42	22	25	1	.267	.368
Jeff Heath	OF90	L	25	100	356	55	78	16	3	14	50	40	62	5	.219	.399
Frankie Pytlak (IL)	C58, OF1	R	31	62	149	16	21	2	1	0	16	17	5	0	.141	.168
Odell Hale	3B3	R	31	48	50	3	11	3	1	0	6	5	7	0	.220	.320
Soup Campbell	OF16	L	25	35	62	8	14	1	0	0	2	7	12	0	.226	.242
Rusty Peters	2B9, SS6, 3B6, 1B1	R	25	30	71	5	17	3	2	0	7	4	14	1	.239	.338
Oscar Grimes (BY)	1B4, 3B1	R	25	11	13	3	0	0	0	0	0	5	4	0	.000	.000
Hank Helf	C1	R	26	1	1	0	0	0	0	0	0	0	0	0	.000	.000
NEW YORK 3rd 88-66 .571 2						JOE McCARTHY										
TOTALS			28	155	5286	817	1371	243	66	155	757	648	606	59	.259	.418
Babe Dahlgren	1B155	R	28	155	568	51	150	24	4	12	73	46	54	1	.264	.384
Joe Gordon	2B155	R	25	155	616	112	173	32	10	30	103	52	57	18	.281	.511
Frankie Crosetti	SS145	R	29	145	546	84	106	23	4	4	31	72	77	14	.194	.273
Red Rolfe	3B138	L	31	139	588	102	147	26	6	10	53	50	48	4	.250	.366
Charlie Keller	OF136	L	23	138	500	102	143	18	15	21	93	106	65	8	.286	.508
Joe DiMaggio	OF130	R	25	132	508	93	179	28	9	31	133	61	30	1	.352	.626
George Selkirk	OF111	L	32	118	379	68	102	19	5	19	71	84	43	3	.269	.491
Bill Dickey	C102	L	33	106	372	45	92	11	1	9	54	48	32	0	.247	.355
Tommy Henrich	OF76, 1B2	L	30	90	293	57	90	28	5	10	53	48	30	1	.307	.539
Buddy Rosar	C63	R	25	73	228	34	68	11	3	4	37	19	11	7	.298	.425
Bill Knickerbocker	SS19, 3B17	R	28	45	124	17	30	4	1	1	10	14	8	1	.242	.347
Buster Mills	OF14	R	31	34	63	10	25	5	1	0	15	7	5	0	.397	.587
Jake Powell (CN)	OF57	R	31	12	27	3	5	1	0	0	3	6	4	0	.185	.185
Mike Chartak	OF3	L	24	11	15	2	2	1	0	0	3	5	5	0	.133	.200

NAME	T	AGE	W	L	PCT	SV	G	GS	CG	IP	H	BB	SO	SHO	ERA
		27	90	64	.584	23	155	155	59	1375	1425	570	752	10	4.01
Bobo Newsom	R	32	21	5	.808	0	36	34	20	264	235	100	164	3	2.83
Schoolboy Rowe	R	30	16	3	.842	0	27	23	11	169	170	43	61	1	3.46
Tommy Bridges	R	33	12	9	.571	0	29	28	12	198	171	88	133	2	3.36
Hal Newhouser	L	19	9	9	.500	0	28	20	7	133	149	76	89	0	4.87
Johnny Gorsica	R	25	7	7	.500	0	29	20	5	160	170	57	68	2	4.33
Al Benton	R	29	6	10	.375	17	42	0	0	79	93	36	50	0	4.44
Archie MaKain	L	29	5	0	1.000	3	27	0	0	51	48	25	24	0	2.82
Dizzy Trout	R	25	3	7	.300	2	33	10	1	101	125	54	64	0	4.46
Fred Hutchinson	R	20	3	7	.300	0	17	10	1	76	85	26	32	0	5.68
Floyd Giebell	R	30	2	0	1.000	0	2	2	2	18	14	4	11	1	1.00
Tom Seats	L	29	2	2	.500	1	26	2	0	56	67	21	25	0	4.66
Dick Conger	R	19	1	0	1.000	0	2	0	0	3	2	3	1	0	3.00
Clay Smith	R	25	1	0	1.000	1	14	1	0	28	32	13	14	0	5.14
Lynn Nelson	R	35	1	1	.500	0	6	2	0	14	23	9	7	0	10.93
Cotton Pippen	R	30	1	2	.333	0	4	3	0	21	29	10	9	0	6.86
Bud Thomas	R	29	0	1	.000	0	3	0	0	4	8	3	0	0	9.00
Bob Uhl	L	26	0	0	—	0	1	0	0	4	2	0	0	0	0
		27	89	65	.578	22	155	155	72	1375	1328	512	686	13	3.63
Bob Feller	R	21	27	11	.711	4	43	37	31	320	245	118	261	4	2.62
Al Milnar	L	26	18	10	.643	4	37	33	15	242	242	99	99	4	3.27
Al Smith	L	32	15	7	.682	2	31	24	11	183	187	55	46	1	3.44
Mel Harder	R	30	12	11	.522	0	31	25	5	186	200	59	76	0	4.06
Johnny Allen	R	35	9	8	.529	5	32	17	5	139	126	48	62	3	3.43
Joe Dobson	R	23	3	7	.300	3	40	7	2	100	101	48	57	1	4.95
1 Willis Hudlin	R	34	2	1	.667	0	4	4	2	24	31	2	8	0	4.88
Bill Zuber	R	27	1	1	.500	0	17	0	0	24	25	14	12	0	5.63
Mike Naymick	R	22	1	1	.500	0	13	4	0	30	34	17	15	0	5.10
Harry Eisenstat	L	24	1	4	.200	4	27	3	0	72	78	12	27	0	3.13
Nate Andrews	R	26	0	1	.000	0	6	0	0	12	16	6	3	0	6.00
John Humphries	R	25	0	2	.000	1	19	1	1	34	35	29	17	0	8.21
Dixie Howell	R	20	0	1	.000	0	3	0	0	5	2	4	2	0	1.80
Ken Jungels	R	24	0	0	—	0	3	0	0	3	3	1	1	0	3.00
Cal Dorsett	R	27	0	0	—	0	1	0	0	1	1	1	0	0	9.00
		31	88	66	.571	14	155	155	76	1373	1389	511	559	10	3.89
Red Ruffing	R	36	15	12	.556	0	30	30	20	226	218	76	97	3	3.38
Marius Russo	L	25	14	8	.636	0	30	24	15	189	181	55	87	0	3.29
Ernie Bonham	R	26	9	3	.750	0	12	12	10	99	83	13	37	1	1.91
Atley Donald	R	29	8	3	.727	0	24	11	6	119	113	59	60	1	3.03
Johnny Murphy	R	31	8	4	.667	9	35	1	0	63	58	15	23	0	3.71
Spud Chandler	R	32	8	7	.533	0	27	24	6	172	184	60	56	1	4.60
Marv Breuer	R	26	8	9	.471	0	27	22	10	164	175	61	71	0	4.55
Monte Pearson	R	31	7	5	.583	0	16	16	7	110	108	44	43	1	3.68
Steve Sundra	R	30	4	6	.400	2	27	8	2	99	121	42	26	0	5.55
Lefty Gomez (SA)	L	31	3	3	.500	0	9	5	0	27	37	18	14	0	6.67
Bump Hadley	R	35	3	5	.375	2	25	2	0	80	88	52	39	0	5.74
Oral Hildebrand	R	33	1	1	.500	0	10	1	0	19	19	14	5	0	1.89
1 Lee Grissom	L	32	1	0	—	0	1	0	0	5	4	1	0	0	0.00

Batting

NAME	G by Pos	B	AGE	G	AB	R	H	2B	3B	HR	RBI	BB	SO	SB	BA	SA
BOSTON 4th(tie) 82-72 .532 8																
TOTALS			28	154	5481	872	1566	301	80	145	810	590	597	55	.266	.449
Jimmie Foxx	1B95, C42, 3B1	R	32	144	515	106	153	30	4	36	119	101	87	4	.297	.581
Bobby Doerr	2B151	R	22	151	595	87	173	37	10	22	105	57	53	10	.291	.497
Joe Cronin	SS146, 3B2	R	33	149	548	104	156	35	6	24	111	83	65	7	.285	.502
Jim Tabor (IL)	3B120	R	26	120	459	73	131	28	6	21	81	42	58	14	.285	.210
Dom DiMaggio	OF94	R	23	108	418	81	126	32	6	8	46	41	46	7	.301	.464
Doc Cramer	OF149	L	34	150	661	94	200	27	12	1	51	36	29	3	.303	.384
Ted Williams	OF143, P1	L	21	144	561	134	193	43	14	23	113	96	54	4	.344	.594
Gene Desautels	C70	R	33	71	222	19	50	7	1	0	17	32	13	0	.225	.266
Lou Finney	OF69, 1B51	L	29	130	534	73	171	31	15	5	73	33	13	5	.320	.463
Johnny Peacock	C48	L	30	63	131	20	37	4	1	0	13	23	10	1	.282	.328
Stan Spence	OF15	L	25	51	68	5	19	2	1	2	13	4	9	0	.279	.426
Tom Carey	SS20, 2B4, 3B4	R	31	43	62	4	20	4	0	0	7	2	1	0	.323	.387
2 Charlie Gelbert	3B29, SS1	R	34	30	91	9	18	2	0	0	8	5	7	0	.198	.220
Joe Glenn	C19	R	31	22	47	3	6	1	0	0	4	5	7	0	.128	.149
Marv Owen	3B9, 1B8	R	34	20	57	4	12	0	0	0	6	8	4	0	.211	.211
Tony Lupien	1B8	L	23	10	19	5	9	3	2	0	4	1	1	0	.474	.842
Red Nonnenkamp		L	28	9	7	0	0	0	0	0	1	1	4	0	.000	.000
CHICAGO 4th(tie) 82-72 .532 8																
TOTALS			30	155	5386	735	1499	283	63	73	671	496	569	52	.278	.387
Joe Kuhel	1B155	L	34	155	603	111	169	28	8	27	94	87	59	12	.280	.488
Skeeter Webb	2B74, SS7, 3B1	R	30	84	334	33	79	11	2	1	29	30	33	3	.237	.290
Luke Appling	SS250	R	33	150	566	96	197	27	13	0	79	69	35	3	.348	.442
Bob Kennedy	3B154	R	19	154	606	74	153	23	3	3	52	42	58	3	.252	.315
Taffy Wright	OF144	L	28	147	581	79	196	31	9	5	88	43	25	4	.337	.448
Mike Kreevich	OF144	R	32	144	582	86	154	27	10	8	55	34	49	15	.265	.387
Moose Solters	OF107	R	34	116	428	65	132	28	3	12	80	27	54	3	.308	.472
Mike Tresh	C135	R	26	135	480	62	135	15	5	1	64	49	42	1	.281	.340
Larry Rosenthal	OF92	L	30	107	276	46	83	14	5	6	42	64	32	2	.301	.453
Eric McNair	2B65, 3B1	R	31	66	251	26	57	13	1	7	31	12	26	1	.227	.371
Tom Turner	C29	R	23	37	96	11	20	1	2	0	6	3	12	1	.208	.260
Ken Silvestri	C1	R	24	28	24	5	6	2	0	2	10	4	7	0	.250	.583
Jackie Hayes (IJ)	2B15	R	33	18	41	2	8	0	1	0	1	2	11	0	.195	.244
Don Kolloway	2B10	R	21	10	40	5	9	1	0	0	3	0	1	1	.225	.250
Dave Short		L	23	3	3	1	1	0	0	0	0	1	0	0	.333	.333
ST. LOUIS 6th 67-87 .435 23																
TOTALS			28	156	5416	757	1423	278	58	118	716	556	642	51	.263	.401
George McQuinn	1B150	L	31	151	594	78	166	39	10	16	84	57	58	3	.279	.460
Don Heffner	2B125	R	29	126	487	52	115	21	2	3	53	39	37	5	.236	.310
Johnny Berardino	SS112, 2B13, 3B9	R	23	142	523	71	135	31	4	16	85	32	46	6	.258	.424
Harlond Clift	3B147	R	27	150	523	92	143	29	5	20	87	104	62	9	.273	.463
Chet Laabs	OF63	R	28	105	218	32	59	11	5	10	40	34	59	3	.271	.505
Walt Judnich	OF133	L	24	137	519	97	157	27	7	24	89	54	71	8	.303	.520
Rip Radcliff	OF139, 1B4	L	34	150	584	83	200	33	9	7	81	47	20	6	.342	.466
Bob Swift	C128	R	25	130	398	37	97	20	1	0	39	28	39	1	.244	.299
2 Roy Cullenbine	OF57, 1B6	B	26	86	257	41	59	11	2	7	31	50	34	0	.230	.370
Joe Grace	OF51, C12	L	26	80	229	45	59	14	2	5	25	26	23	2	.258	.402
Myril Hoag	OF46	R	32	76	191	20	50	11	0	3	26	13	30	2	.262	.366
George Susce	C61	R	32	61	113	6	24	4	0	0	13	9	7	1	.212	.248
Alan Strange	SS35, 2B4	R	30	54	167	26	31	8	3	0	6	22	12	2	.186	.269
Vern Kennedy	P34	L	33	35	84	12	25	3	1	2	12	3	13	0	.298	.429
Lyn Lary	SS12, 2B1	R	34	27	54	5	3	1	1	0	3	4	7	0	.056	.111
1 Joe Gallagher	OF15	R	26	23	70	14	19	3	1	2	8	4	12	1	.271	.429
Johnny Lucadello	2B16	B	21	17	63	15	20	4	2	1	10	6	4	1	.317	.540
Sam Harshany	C2	R	30	3	1	0	0	0	0	0	0	1	0	0	.000	.000
Fuzz White		L	24	2	2	0	0	0	0	0	0	0	0	0	.000	.000
WASHINGTON 7th 64-90 .416 26																
TOTALS			27	154	5365	665	1453	226	67	52	600	468	504	94	.271	.374
1 Zeke Bonura	1B79	R	31	79	311	41	85	16	3	3	45	40	13	2	.273	.373
Jimmy Bloodworth	2B96, 1B17, 3B6	R	22	119	469	47	115	17	8	11	70	16	71	3	.245	.386
Jimmy Pofahl	SS112,2B4	R	23	119	406	34	95	23	5	2	36	37	55	2	.234	.330
Cecil Travis	3B113, SS23	L	26	136	528	60	170	37	11	2	76	48	23	0	.322	.445
Buddy Lewis	OF112, 3B36	L	23	148	600	101	190	38	10	6	63	74	36	15	.317	.443
George Case	OF154	R	24	154	656	109	192	29	5	5	56	52	39	35	.293	.375
Gee Walker	OF140	R	32	140	595	87	175	29	7	13	96	24	58	21	.294	.432
Rick Ferrell	C99	R	34	103	326	35	89	18	2	0	28	47	15	1	.273	.340
Johnny Welaj	OF53	R	26	88	215	31	55	9	3	0	21	19	20	8	.256	.340
Jake Early	C56	L	25	80	206	26	53	8	4	5	14	23	22	0	.257	.408
Buddy Myer	2B54	L	36	71	210	28	61	14	4	0	29	34	10	6	.290	.395
Sammy West	1B12, OF9	L	35	57	99	7	25	6	1	1	18	16	13	0	.253	.364
Jack Sanford	1B34	R	23	34	122	5	24	4	2	0	10	6	17	0	.197	.262
1 Charlie Gelbert	SS12, P2, 2B1	R	34	22	54	7	20	7	1	0	7	4	3	0	.370	.537
Al Evans	C9	R	23	14	25	1	8	2	0	0	6	7	1	1	.320	.400
1 Jimmy Wasdell	1B8	L	26	10	35	3	3	1	0	0	0	5	6	0	.086	.114
Sherry Robertson	SS10	L	21	10	33	4	7	0	1	0	5	1	8	1	.212	.273
Mickey Vernon	1B4	L	22	5	19	0	3	0	0	0	0	0	1	0	.158	.158
Jim Mallory	OF3	R	21	4	12	2	2	0	0	0	1	0	4	0	.167	.167
Dick Hahn	C1	R	23	1	3	0	0	0	0	0	0	0	0	0	.000	.000
Morrie Aderholt	2B1	L	24	1	1	0	0	0	0	0	0	0	0	0	.000	.000
PHILADELPHIA 8th 54-100 .351 36																
TOTALS			26	154	5304	703	1391	242	53	105	648	556	656	48	.262	.387
Dick Siebert	1B154	L	28	154	595	69	170	31	6	5	77	33	34	8	.286	.383
Benny McCoy	2B130, 3B1	L	24	134	490	56	126	26	5	7	62	65	44	2	.257	.373
Al Brancato	SS80, 2B10	R	21	107	298	42	57	11	2	1	23	28	36	3	.191	.252
Al Rubeling	3B98, 2B10	R	27	108	376	49	92	16	6	4	38	48	58	4	.245	.351
Wally Moses	OF133	L	29	142	537	91	166	41	9	9	50	75	44	6	.309	.469
Sam Chapman	OF129	R	24	134	508	88	140	26	3	23	75	46	96	2	.276	.474
Bob Johnson	OF136	R	34	138	512	93	137	23	4	31	103	83	64	8	.268	.514
Frankie Hayes	C134, 1B2	R	25	136	465	73	143	23	4	16	70	61	59	0	.308	.477
Dee Miles	OF50	L	31	88	236	36	71	9	6	1	23	8	18	1	.301	.403
Sep Gantenbein	3B45, 1B6, SS3, OF1	R	24	75	197	21	47	6	2	4	23	11	21	1	.239	.350
Bill Lillard	SS69, 2B1	R	22	73	206	26	49	8	2	1	21	28	28	0	.238	.311
Chubby Dean	P30, 1B1	L	24	67	90	6	26	2	0	0	6	16	9	0	.289	.311
Al Simmons	OF18	R	38	37	81	7	25	4	0	1	19	4	8	0	.309	.395
Hal Wagner (BG)	C28	L	24	34	75	9	19	5	1	0	10	11	6	0	.253	.347
Fred Chapman	SS25	R	23	26	69	6	11	1	0	0	4	6	10	1	.159	.174
Crash Davis	2B19, SS1	R	20	23	67	4	18	1	1	0	9	3	10	1	.269	.313
Earle Brucker	C13	R	39	23	46	3	9	1	1	0	2	8	5	0	.196	.261
Elmer Valo	OF6	L	19	6	23	2	8	1	0	0	2	4	3	0	.348	.348
Jack Wallaesa	SS6	R	20	6	20	0	3	0	0	0	1	0	6	0	.150	.150
Eric Tipton	OF2	R	24	1	8	0	1	0	0	0	0	0	3	0	.125	.375
Dario Lodigiani		R	24	1	1	0	0	0	0	0	0	0	0	0	.000	.000
Buddy Hancken	C1	R	25	1	0	0	0	0	0	0	0	0	0	0	.000	—

Pitching

NAME	T	AGE	W	L	PCT	SV	G	GS	CG	IP	H	BB	SO	SHO	ERA
BOSTON		29	82	72	.532	16	154	154	51	1380	1568	625	613	4	4.88
Jack Wilson	R	28	12	6	.667	5	41	16	9	158	170	87	102	0	5.07
Joe Hevring	R	39	12	7	.632	3	39	7	4	119	129	42	55	0	4.01
Jim Bagby	R	23	10	16	.385	2	36	21	6	183	217	83	57	1	4.72
Emerson Dickman	R	25	8	6	.571	3	35	9	2	100	121	38	40	0	6.03
Lefty Grove	L	40	7	6	.538	0	22	21	9	153	159	50	62	1	4.00
Herb Hash	R	29	7	7	.500	3	34	12	3	120	123	84	36	1	4.95
Earl Johnson	L	21	6	2	.750	0	17	10	2	70	69	39	26	0	4.11
Denny Galehouse	R	28	6	6	.500	0	21	20	5	120	155	41	53	0	5.18
Fritz Ostermueller	L	32	5	9	.357	0	31	16	5	144	166	70	80	0	4.94
Mickey Harris	R	23	4	2	.667	0	13	9	3	68	83	26	36	0	5.03
Bill Fleming	R	26	1	2	.333	0	10	6	1	46	53	20	24	0	4.89
Bill Butland	R	22	1	2	.333	0	3	3	1	21	27	10	5	0	5.57
Charlie Wagner	R	27	1	0	1.000	0	12	1	0	29	45	8	13	0	5.59
Yank Terry	R	29	1	0	1.000	0	4	1	0	19	24	11	9	0	9.00
Woody Rich	R	24	1	0	1.000	0	3	1	1	12	9	1	8	0	0.75
Alex Mustaikis	R	31	0	1	.000	0	6	1	0	15	15	16	6	0	9.00
Ted Williams	R	21	0	0	—	0	1	0	0	2	3	1	1	0	4.50
CHICAGO		32	82	72	.532	18	155	155	83	1387	1335	480	574	10	3.74
Eddie Smith	L	26	14	9	.609	0	32	28	12	207	179	95	119	0	3.22
Johnny Rigney	R	25	14	18	.438	3	39	33	19	281	240	90	141	2	3.11
Ted Lyons	R	39	12	8	.600	0	22	22	17	186	188	37	72	4	3.24
Thornton Lee	L	33	12	13	.480	2	28	27	24	228	223	56	87	1	3.47
Jack Knott	R	33	11	9	.550	0	25	23	4	158	166	52	44	2	4.56
Bill Dietrich	R	30	10	6	.625	0	23	17	6	150	154	65	43	1	4.02
Pete Appleton	R	36	4	0	1.000	5	25	0	0	58	54	28	21	0	5.59
Clint Brown	R	36	4	6	.400	10	37	0	0	66	75	16	23	0	3.68
Jack Hallett	R	25	1	1	.500	0	7	2	1	14	15	6	9	0	6.43
Vallie Eaves	R	28	0	2	.000	0	5	3	0	19	22	24	11	0	6.63
Ed Weiland	R	25	0	0	—	0	5	0	0	14	15	7	3	0	9.00
Orval Grove	R	20	0	0	—	0	1	0	0	6	4	1	1	0	3.00
ST. LOUIS		30	67	87	.435	9	156	156	64	1373	1592	646	439	4	5.13
Elden Auker	R	29	16	11	.593	0	38	35	20	264	299	96	78	2	3.95
Vern Kennedy	R	33	12	17	.414	0	34	32	18	222	263	122	70	0	5.59
Bob Harris	R	25	11	15	.423	1	35	28	8	194	225	85	49	1	4.92
Bill Trotter	R	31	7	6	.538	2	36	4	1	98	117	31	29	0	3.77
Johnny Niggeling	R	36	7	11	.389	0	28	20	10	154	148	69	82	0	4.44
Roxie Lawson	R	34	5	3	.625	4	30	2	0	72	77	54	18	0	5.13
Jack Kramer	R	22	3	7	.300	0	16	9	1	65	86	26	12	0	6.23
Slick Coffman	R	29	2	2	.500	1	31	4	1	75	108	23	26	0	6.24
Emil Bildilli	L	27	2	4	.333	1	28	11	3	97	113	52	32	0	5.57
Maury Newlin	R	26	1	0	1.000	0	1	1	0	6	4	2	3	0	6.00
John Whitehead (NJ)	R	31	1	3	.250	0	15	4	1	40	46	14	11	1	5.40
Bill Cox	R	27	0	1	.000	0	12	0	0	17	23	12	7	0	7.41
3 Willis Hudlin	R	34	0	1	.000	0	6	1	0	11	19	8	4	0	11.46
Lefty Mills	L	30	0	6	.000	0	26	5	1	59	64	52	18	0	7.78
WASHINGTON		25	64	90	.416	7	154	154	74	1350	1494	618	618	6	4.59
Sid Hudson	R	25	17	16	.515	1	38	31	19	252	272	81	96	3	4.57
Ken Chase	L	26	15	17	.469	0	35	34	20	262	260	143	129	1	3.23
Dutch Leonard	R	31	14	19	.424	0	35	35	23	289	328	78	124	2	3.49
Alex Carrasquel	R	27	6	2	.750	0	28	0	0	48	42	29	19	0	4.88
Joe Haynes	R	22	3	6	.333	0	22	7	1	63	85	34	23	0	6.57
Walt Masterson	R	20	3	13	.188	2	31	19	3	130	128	88	68	0	4.92
Rene Monteagudo	L	24	2	6	.250	2	27	8	3	101	128	52	64	0	6.06
Al Hollingsworth	L	32	1	0	1.000	0	3	0	0	18	18	11	7	0	5.50
Red Anderson	R	28	1	1	.500	0	2	1	1	14	12	5	3	0	3.86
2 Willis Hudlin	R	34	1	3	.333	0	8	1	1	37	50	5	9	0	6.57
Joe Krakauskas	R	24	1	6	.143	2	32	10	2	109	137	73	68	0	6.44
Bucky Jacobs	R	27	0	1	.000	0	6	1	0	15	16	9	6	0	6.00
Lou Thuman	R	23	0	1	.000	0	5	0	0	10	7	7	0	0	14.40
1 Charlie Gelbert	R	34	0	0	—	0	2	0	0	4	5	1	1	0	9.00
Gil Torres	R	24	0	0	—	0	1	0	0	0	0	0	0	0	0.00
PHILADELPHIA		27	54	100	.351	12	154	154	72	1345	1543	534	488	4	5.22
Johnny Babich	R	27	14	13	.519	0	31	30	16	229	222	80	94	1	3.73
Nels Potter	R	28	9	14	.391	0	31	25	13	201	213	71	73	0	4.43
Bill Beckmann	R	32	8	4	.667	1	34	9	6	127	132	35	47	2	4.18
Chubby Dean	L	24	6	13	.316	1	30	19	8	159	220	63	38	1	6.62
Ed Heusser	R	31	6	13	.316	5	41	6	2	110	144	42	39	0	4.99
Buck Ross	R	25	5	10	.333	1	24	19	10	156	160	60	43	0	4.38
George Caster	R	32	4	19	.174	2	36	24	11	178	234	69	75	0	6.57
Potter Vaughan	L	21	2	9	.182	2	18	15	5	99	104	61	46	0	5.36
Phil Marchildon	R	26	2	3	.400	0	2	2	1	10	12	4	9	0	7.20
Herman Besse	L	29	0	3	.000	0	1	1	0	53	70	34	19	0	8.83
Les McCrabb	R	25	0	0	—	0	6	0	0	12	19	2	4	0	6.75
Carl Miles	L	22	0	0	—	0	8	0	0	8	4	1	4	0	13.50
Pat McLaughlin	R	29	0	0	—	0	2	0	0	4	4	1	1	0	13.50

CINCINNATI — 1ST 100-53 .654 — BILL McKECHNIE

NAME	G by Pos	B	AGE	G	AB	R	H	2B	3B	HR	RBI	BB	SO	SB	BA	SA
TOTALS			28	155	5372	707	1427	264	3	89	649	453	503	72	.266	.379
Frank McCormick	1B155	R	29	155	618	93	191	44	3	19	127	52	26	2	.309	.482
Lonny Frey	2B150	L	29	150	563	102	150	23	6	8	54	80	48	22	.266	.371
Bill Myers	SS88	R	29	90	282	33	57	14	2	5	30	30	56	0	.202	.319
Bill Werber	3B143	R	32	143	584	105	162	35	5	12	48	68	40	16	.277	.416
Ival Goodman	OF135	L	31	136	519	78	134	20	6	12	63	60	54	9	.258	.389
Harry Craft	OF109, 1B2	R	25	115	422	47	103	18	5	6	48	17	46	2	.244	.353
Mike McCormick	OF107	R	23	110	417	48	125	20	0	1	30	13	36	8	.300	.355
Ernie Lombardi	C101	R	32	109	376	50	120	22	0	14	74	31	14	0	.319	.489
Eddie Joost	SS78, 2B7, 3B4	R	24	88	278	24	60	7	2	1	24	32	40	4	.216	.266
2 Morrie Arnovich	OF60	R	29	62	211	17	60	10	2	0	21	13	10	1	.284	.351
Willard Hershberger (DD)	C37	R	30	48	123	6	38	4	2	0	26	6	6	0	.309	.374
Lew Riggs	3B11	L	30	41	72	8	21	7	1	1	9	2	4	0	.292	.458
Lew Gamble	OF10	L	30	38	42	12	6	1	0	0	0	0	1	0	.143	.167
2 Jimmy Ripple	OF30	L	30	32	101	15	31	10	0	4	20	13	5	1	.307	.525
2 Johnny Rizzo	OF30	R	27	31	110	17	31	6	0	4	17	14	14	1	.282	.445
Bill Baker	C24	R	29	27	69	5	15	1	1	0	7	4	8	2	.217	.261
Jimmie Wilson	C16	R	39	16	37	2	9	2	0	0	3	2	1	1	.243	.297
Mike Dejan	OF2	R	25	12	16	1	3	0	1	0	2	3	3	0	.188	.313
Dick West	C7	R	24	7	28	4	11	2	0	1	6	0	2	1	.393	.571
1 Wally Berger		R	34	2	2	0	0	0	0	0	0	0	0	0	.000	.000
1 Vince DiMaggio	OF1	R	27	1	4	0	1	0	0	0	0	0	1	0	.250	.250

NAME	T	AGE	W	L	PCT	SV	G	GS	CG	IP	H	BB	SO	SHO	ERA
		29	100	53	.654	11	155	155	91	1408	1263	445	557	10	3.05
Bucky Walters	R	31	22	10	.688	0	36	36	29	305	241	92	115	3	2.48
Paul Derringer	R	33	20	12	.625	0	37	37	26	297	280	48	115	3	3.06
Junior Thompson	R	23	16	9	.640	0	31	31	17	225	197	96	103	3	3.32
Jim Turner	R	36	14	7	.667	0	24	23	11	187	187	32	53	0	2.89
Joe Beggs	R	29	12	3	.800	7	37	1	0	77	68	21	25	0	1.99
Whitey Moore	R	28	8	8	.500	1	25	15	5	117	100	56	60	1	3.62
Johnny Vander Meer	L	25	3	1	.750	1	10	7	2	48	38	41	41	0	3.75
Johnny Hutchings	R	24	2	1	.667	0	19	4	0	54	53	18	18	0	3.50
Milt Shoffner	L	34	1	0	1.000	0	20	0	0	54	56	18	17	0	5.67
Red Barrett	R	25	1	0	1.000	0	3	0	0	3	5	1	0	0	6.00
Elmer Riddle	R	25	1	2	.333	2	15	1	1	34	30	17	9	0	1.85
Witt Guise	L	31	0	0	.000	0	2	0	0	8	8	5	1	0	1.13

BROOKLYN — 2nd 88-65 .575 12 — LEO DUROCHER

NAME	G by Pos	B	AGE	G	AB	R	H	2B	3B	HR	RBI	BB	SO	SB	BA	SA
TOTALS			28	156	5470	697	1421	256	70	93	653	522	569	56	.260	.383
Dolph Camilli	1B140	L	33	142	512	92	147	29	13	23	96	89	83	9	.287	.529
Pete Coscarart	2B144	R	27	143	506	55	120	24	4	9	58	53	59	5	.237	.354
Pee Wee Reese (BF)	SS83	R	21	84	312	58	85	8	4	5	28	45	42	15	.272	.372
Cookie Lavagetto (IL)	3B116	R	27	118	448	56	115	21	3	4	43	70	32	4	.257	.344
Joe Vosmik	OF99	R	30	116	404	45	114	14	6	1	42	22	21	0	.282	.354
Dixie Walker	OF136	L	29	143	556	75	171	37	8	6	66	42	21	3	.308	.435
2 Joe Medwick	OF103	R	28	106	423	62	127	18	12	14	66	26	28	2	.300	.499
Babe Phelps	C99, 1B1	L	32	118	370	47	109	24	5	13	61	30	27	2	.295	.492
Johnny Hudson	SS38, 2B27, 3B1	R	28	85	179	13	39	4	3	0	19	9	26	2	.218	.274
2 Jimmy Wasdell	OF42, 1B17	L	26	77	230	35	64	14	4	3	37	18	24	4	.278	.413
Herman Franks	C43	L	26	65	131	11	24	4	0	1	14	20	6	2	.183	.237
Loe Durocher	SS53, 2B4	R	34	62	160	10	37	9	1	1	14	12	13	1	.231	.319
Gus Mancuso	C56	R	34	60	144	16	33	8	0	0	16	13	7	0	.229	.285
Pete Reiser	3B30, OF17, SS5	R	21	58	225	34	66	11	4	3	20	15	33	2	.293	.418
Charlie Gilbert	OF43	L	21	57	142	23	35	9	1	2	8	8	13	0	.246	.366
2 Joe Gallagher	OF31	R	26	57	110	10	29	6	1	3	16	2	14	1	.264	.418
1 Ernie Koy	OF19	R	30	24	48	9	11	2	1	1	8	3	3	1	.229	.375
1 Roy Cullenbine	OF19	B	26	22	61	8	11	1	0	1	9	23	11	2	.180	.246
Don Ross	3B10	R	25	10	38	4	11	2	0	1	3	3	3	1	.289	.421
1 Gene Moore	OF6	L	30	10	26	3	7	2	0	0	2	1	3	0	.269	.346
1 Jimmy Ripple	OF3	L	30	7	13	0	3	0	0	0	0	2	2	0	.231	.231
Tony Giuliani	C1	R	27	4	2	0	0	0	0	0	0	0	0	0	.000	.000

NAME	T	AGE	W	L	PCT	SV	G	GS	CG	IP	H	BB	SO	SHO	ERA
		32	88	65	.575	14	156		65	1433	1366	393	639	17	3.50
Freddie Fitzsimmons	R	38	16	2	.889	1	20	18	11	134	120	25	35	4	2.82
Whit Wyatt	R	32	15	14	.517	0	37	34	16	239	233	62	124	5	3.46
Hugh Casey	R	26	11	8	.579	2	44	10	5	154	136	51	53	2	3.62
Luke Hamlin	R	35	9	8	.529	0	33	25	9	182	183	34	91	2	3.63
Vito Tamulis	L	28	6	5	.615	2	41	12	4	154	147	34	55	1	3.10
2 Curt Davis	R	36	8	7	.533	2	22	18	9	137	135	19	46	0	3.81
Tot Pressnell	R	33	6	5	.545	2	24	4	1	68	58	17	21	1	3.71
Tex Carleton	R	33	6	6	.500	2	34	17	4	149	140	47	88	1	3.81
1 Newt Kimball	R	25	3	1	.750	1	21	0	0	34	29	15	21	0	3.18
2 Lee Grissom	L	32	2	5	.286	0	14	10	3	74	59	34	56	1	2.80
Ed Head	R	22	1	2	.333	0	13	5	2	39	40	18	13	0	4.15
Van Lingle Mungo (AJ)	R	29	1	0	1.000	1	7	0	0	22	24	10	9	0	2.45
Max Macon	L	24	1	0	1.000	0	2	0	0	2	5	0	1	0	22.50
Wes Flowers	R	26	1	1	.500	0	5	2	0	21	23	10	8	0	3.43
Steve Rachunok	R	23	0	1	.000	0	2	1	1	9	10	9	5	0	4.50
1 Carl Doyle	R	27	0	0	—	0	6	0	0	6	18	6	4	0	25.50
2 Lou Fette	R	33	0	0	—	0	1	0	0	3	3	3	2	0	0.00
Wes Ferrell	R	32	0	0	—	0	1	0	0	4	4	4	1	0	6.75

ST. LOUIS — 3rd 84-69 .549 16 — RAY BLADES 14-24 .368   MIKE GONZALES 1-5 .167   BILLY SOUTHWORTH 69-40 .633

NAME	G by Pos	B	AGE	G	AB	R	H	2B	3B	HR	RBI	BB	SO	SB	BA	SA
TOTALS			27	156	5499	747	1514	266	61	119	709	479	610	97	.275	.411
Johnny Mize	1B153	L	27	155	579	111	182	31	13	43	137	82	49	7	.314	.636
Joe Orengo	2B77, 3B34, SS19	R	25	129	415	59	119	20	4	7	56	65	90	9	.287	.412
Marty Marion	SS125	R	22	125	435	44	121	18	1	3	46	12	34	9	.278	.345
Stu Martin	3B73, 2B33	R	27	120	369	45	88	12	6	4	32	33	35	4	.238	.336
Enos Slaughter	OF132	L	24	140	516	96	158	25	13	17	73	50	35	8	.306	.504
Terry Moore	OF133	R	28	136	537	92	163	33	4	17	64	42	44	18	.304	.475
Mickey Owen	C113	R	24	117	307	27	81	16	2	0	27	34	13	4	.264	.329
Jimmy Brown (BZ)	2B48, 3B41, SS28	B	30	107	454	56	127	17	4	0	30	24	15	9	.280	.335
Don Padgett	C72, 1B2	L	28	93	240	24	58	15	1	6	41	26	14	1	.242	.388
Pepper Martin	OF63, 3B2	R	36	86	228	28	72	15	4	3	39	22	24	6	.316	.456
Johnny Hopp	OF39, 1B10	L	23	80	152	24	41	7	4	1	14	9	21	3	.270	.388
Don Gutteridge	3B39	R	28	69	168	19	29	5	0	3	14	5	15	3	.269	.369
1 Joe Medwick	OF37	R	28	37	158	21	48	12	0	3	20	6	8	0	.304	.437
Eddie Lake	2B17, SS6	R	24	32	66	12	14	3	0	2	7	12	17	1	.212	.348
Bill DeLancey	C12	L	28	15	18	0	4	1	0	0	2	0	2	0	.222	.222
Red Jones	OF1	L	28	12	11	0	1	0	0	0	0	0	4	0	.091	.091
Hal Epps	OF3	L	26	11	15	6	3	0	0	0	0	3	0	0	.200	.200
Harry Walker	OF7	L	23	7	27	2	5	2	0	0	6	0	4	0	.185	.259
Carden Gillenwater	OF7	R	23	7	25	1	4	1	0	0	5	0	5	0	.160	.200
Walker Cooper	C6	R	25	6	19	3	6	1	0	0	2	2	1	1	.316	.368
Creepy Crespi	3B2, SS1	R	22	3	11	2	3	1	0	0	0	0	1	0	.273	.364

NAME	T	AGE	W	L	PCT	SV	G	GS	CG	IP	H	BB	SO	SHO	ERA
		29	84	69	.549	14	156		71	1395	1457	488	550	10	3.83
Bill McGee	R	30	16	10	.615	0	38	31	15	218	222	96	78	3	3.80
Lon Warneke	R	31	16	10	.615	0	33	31	17	232	235	47	85	1	3.14
Clyde Shoun	L	28	13	11	.542	5	54	19	13	197	193	46	82	1	3.93
Mort Cooper	R	27	11	12	.478	3	38	29	16	231	225	86	95	3	3.62
Max Lanier	L	24	9	6	.600	3	35	11	4	105	113	38	49	2	3.34
Bob Bowman	R	29	7	5	.583	0	28	17	7	114	118	43	43	0	4.34
Ira Hutchinson	R	29	4	2	.667	0	21	2	1	63	68	19	19	0	3.14
2 Carl Doyle (BW)	R	27	3	3	.500	0	21	5	1	81	99	41	44	0	5.89
Jack Russell	R	34	3	4	.429	1	26	0	0	54	53	26	16	0	2.50
2 Newt Kimball	R	25	1	0	1.000	0	2	1	1	14	11	6	6	0	2.57
Ernie White	L	23	1	1	.500	0	8	1	0	22	29	14	15	0	4.09
Gene Lillard	R	26	0	1	.000	0	2	1	0	12	18	12	3	0	12.60
1 Curt Davis	R	36	0	0	.000	0	14	7	0	54	73	19	12	0	5.17
Harry Brecheen	L	25	0	0	—	0	3	0	0	3	2	4	0	0	0.00
Murry Dickson	R	23	0	0	—	0	3	0	0	6	5	1	0	0	13.50
Bob Weiland	L	34	0	0	—	0	1	0	0	2	5	1	0	0	27.00

PITTSBURGH — 4th 78-76 .506 22.5 — FRANKIE FRISCH

NAME	G by Pos	B	AGE	G	AB	R	H	2B	3B	HR	RBI	BB	SO	SB	BA	SA
TOTALS			29	156	5466	809	1511	276	68	76	740	553	494	69	.276	.394
Elbie Fletcher	1B147	L	24	147	510	94	139	22	7	16	104	119	54	5	.273	.437
Frankie Gustine	2B130	R	20	133	524	59	147	32	7	1	55	35	39	7	.281	.374
Arky Vaughan	SS155, 3B2	L	28	156	594	113	178	40	15	7	95	88	25	12	.300	.453
Lee Handley	3B80, 2B2	R	26	99	302	50	85	7	4	1	19	27	16	7	.281	.341
Bob Elliott	OF147	R	23	148	551	88	161	34	11	5	64	45	28	13	.292	.421
2 Vince DiMaggio	OF108	R	27	110	356	59	103	26	0	19	54	37	83	11	.289	.522
Maurice Van Robays	OF143, 1B1	R	25	145	572	82	156	24	7	11	116	33	58	2	.272	.402
Spud Davis	C87	R	35	99	285	23	93	14	1	3	39	35	20	0	.326	.435
Debs Garms	3B64, OF19	L	33	103	358	76	127	23	7	5	57	23	6	3	.355	.500
Paul Waner	OF45	L	37	89	238	32	69	16	1	1	32	23	14	0	.290	.378
Lloyd Waner	OF42	L	34	72	166	30	43	3	0	0	5	7	5	3	.259	.277
2 Al Lopez	C59	R	31	59	174	15	45	6	2	0	13	13	5	0	.259	.333
Joe Bowman	P32	R	29	57	90	11	22	5	1	1	14	14	14	1	.244	.356
Pep Young	2B33, SS7, 3B5	R	32	54	136	19	34	8	2	2	20	12	23	1	.250	.382
Bill Brubaker	3B19, SS8, 1B4	R	29	38	78	8	15	3	1	0	5	8	16	0	.192	.256
Ed Fernandes	C27	B	22	28	33	1	4	1	0	0	2	1	0	0	.121	.152
1 Ray Berres	C21	R	32	21	32	2	6	0	0	0	2	1	5	0	.188	.188
Joe Schultz	C13	L	21	16	36	2	7	1	0	0	1	6	0	0	.194	.250
1 Johnny Rizzo	OF7	R	27	9	28	1	5	1	0	0	3	0	5	0	.179	.214

Fern Bell 27 R 0-3, Ray Mueller 28 R 1-3, Ed Leip 29 R 1-5, Frank Kalin 22 R 0-3

NAME	T	AGE	W	L	PCT	SV	G	GS	CG	IP	H	BB	SO	SHO	ERA
		30	78	76	.506	24	156		49	1388	1569	492	491	8	4.36
Rip Sewell	R	33	16	5	.762	1	33	23	14	190	169	67	60	2	2.79
Mace Brown	R	31	10	9	.526	7	48	17	5	173	181	49	73	2	3.49
Joe Bowman	R	30	9	10	.474	2	32	24	10	188	209	66	57	0	4.45
Ken Heintzelman	L	24	8	8	.500	3	39	16	5	165	193	65	71	2	4.47
Max Butcher	R	29	8	9	.471	2	35	24	6	136	161	46	40	2	6.02
Bob Klinger	R	32	8	13	.381	3	39	22	3	142	196	53	48	0	5.39
Johnny Lanning	R	33	8	4	.667	2	38	7	2	116	119	39	42	0	4.03
Dick Lanahan	L	28	8	4	.429	2	40	8	4	108	121	42	45	0	4.25
Danny MacFayden	R	35	5	4	.556	2	35	8	0	91	112	27	24	0	3.56
Dutch Dietz	R	28	0	1	.000	0	15	2	0	15	22	9	8	0	6.00
Pep Rambert	R	23	0	1	.000	0	2	2	0	7	11	6	6	0	7.88
Russ Bauers	R	25	0	2	.000	0	15	2	0	31	42	18	11	0	7.55
Oad Swigart	L	25	0	0	—	0	3	1	0	22	27	10	9	0	4.50
Ray Harrell	R	28	0	0	—	0	3	0	0	5	2	3	0	0	9.00
Johnny Gee (SA) 24															

CHICAGO — 5th 75-79 .487 25.5 — GABBY HARTNETT

NAME	G by Pos	B	AGE	G	AB	R	H	2B	3B	HR	RBI	BB	SO	SB	BA	SA
TOTALS			30	154	5389	681	1441	272	48	86	627	482	566	63	.267	.384
Phil Cavarretta (JJ)	1B52	L	23	65	193	34	54	11	4	2	22	31	18	2	.280	.409
Billy Herman	2B135	R	30	135	558	77	163	24	4	5	57	47	30	1	.292	.376
Bobby Mattick	SS126, 3B1	R	24	128	441	30	96	15	0	0	33	19	33	5	.218	.252
Stan Hack	3B148, 1B1	L	30	149	603	101	191	38	6	8	40	75	24	21	.317	.439
Bill Nicholson	OF123	L	25	135	491	78	146	27	7	25	98	50	67	2	.297	.534
Hank Leiber	OF103, 2B12	R	29	117	440	68	133	24	2	17	86	45	68	1	.302	.482
Jim Gleeson	OF123	R	28	129	485	76	152	39	11	5	61	54	52	4	.313	.470
Al Todd	C104	R	36	104	381	31	97	13	2	6	42	11	29	1	.255	.346
Dom Dallessandro	OF74	L	26	107	287	33	77	19	6	1	36	34	13	4	.268	.387
Rip Russell (IL)	1B51, 3B3	R	25	68	215	15	53	7	2	5	33	8	23	1	.247	.367
Augie Galan (BK)	OF54, 2B2	B	28	68	209	33	48	14	2	3	22	37	23	9	.230	.359
2 Zeke Bonura	1B44	R	31	49	182	20	48	14	0	4	24	10	4	1	.264	.407
Bob Collins	C42	R	30	47	120	11	25	3	0	1	14	14	18	1	.208	.258
2 Rabbit Warstler	SS28, 2B17	R	36	46	139	11	26	4	1	0	12	18	9	1	.187	.230
Gabby Hartnett	C22, 1B1	R	39	37	64	8	17	3	0	1	12	6	5	1	.266	.359
Billy Rogell	SS14, 3B9, 2B3	B	35	33	59	7	8	0	0	1	5	8	5	1	.136	.186
Clyde McCullough	C7	R	23	9	26	4	4	1	0	0	1	0	5	0	.154	.192
Bobby Sturgeon	SS7	R	20	7	21	1	4	1	0	0	1	0	3	0	.190	.238

NAME	T	AGE	W	L	PCT	SV	G	GS	CG	IP	H	BB	SO	SHO	ERA
		30	75	79	.487	14	154		69	1393	1418	430	564	12	3.54
Claude Passeau	R	31	20	13	.606	5	46	31	20	281	259	59	124	4	2.50
Larry French	L	32	14	14	.500	2	40	33	18	246	240	64	107	3	3.29
Vern Olsen	L	22	13	9	.591	0	34	20	9	173	172	62	71	4	2.97
Bill Lee	R	30	9	17	.346	0	37	30	11	211	246	70	71	1	5.03
Ken Raffensberger	L	22	7	9	.438	3	43	10	3	115	120	29	55	0	3.37
Jake Mooty	R	27	6	6	.500	6	42	6	3	114	101	49	42	0	2.92
Dizzy Dean (SA)	R	30	3	3	.500	0	10	9	3	54	68	20	18	0	5.17
Charlie Root	R	41	2	4	.333	1	36	8	1	112	118	33	50	0	3.86
Vance Page	R	36	1	3	.250	2	19	1	0	59	65	26	22	0	4.42
Clay Bryant (SA)	R	28	1	0	.000	0	2	0	1	26	26	14	5	0	4.85
Julio Bonetti	R	28	0	0	—	0	1	0	0	3	4	1	0	0	27.00

NEW YORK 6th 72-80 .474 27.5   BILL TERRY

NAME	G by Pos	B	AGE	G	AB	R	H	2B	3B	HR	RBI	BB	SO	SB	BA	SA
	TOTALS		29	152	5324	663	1423	201	46	91	614	453	478	45	.267	.374
Babe Young	1B147	L	25	149	556	75	159	27	4	17	101	69	28	4	.286	.441
2 Tony Cuccinello	2B47, 3B37	R	32	88	307	26	64	9	2	5	36	16	42	1	.208	.300
Mickey Witek	SS89, 2B32	R	24	119	433	34	111	7	0	3	31	24	17	2	.256	.293
Burgess Whitehead	3B74, 2B57, SS4	R	30	133	586	68	160	9	6	4	36	26	17	9	.282	.340
Mel Ott	OF111, 3B42	L	31	151	536	89	155	27	3	19	79	100	50	6	.289	.457
Frank Demaree	OF119	R	30	121	460	68	139	18	6	7	61	45	39	5	.302	.413
Jo-Jo Moore	OF133	L	31	138	543	83	160	33	4	6	40	43	35	7	.276	.385
Harry Danning	C131	R	28	140	524	65	157	34	4	13	91	35	31	3	.300	.454
Johnny Rucker	OF57	L	23	86	277	38	82	7	5	4	23	7	32	4	.296	.401
Billy Jurges (PB)	SS63	R	32	63	214	23	54	3	3	2	36	15	14	2	.252	.322
Bob Seeds	OF40	R	33	56	155	18	45	5	2	4	16	17	19	0	.290	.426
Johnny McCarthy	1B6	L	30	51	67	6	16	4	0	0	12	16	15	0	.240	.302
Ken O'Dea	C31	L	27	48	96	9	23	4	1	0	12	16	15	0	.240	.302
1 Al Glossop	2B24	B	25	27	91	16	19	3	0	4	8	10	16	1	.209	.374
Glen Stewart	3B6, SS5	R	23	15	29	1	4	1	0	0	1	0	2	0	.138	.172
Buster Maynard	OF7	R	27	7	29	6	8	2	2	1	2	2	6	0	.276	.586
Red Tramback	OF1	L	24	2	4	1	1	0	0	0	0	1	1	1	.250	.250

NAME	T	AGE	W	L	PCT	SV	G	GS	CG	IP	H	BB	SO	SHO	ERA
		30	72	80	.474	18	152	152	57	1360	1383	473	606	11	3.79
Hal Schumacher	R	29	13	13	.500	1	34	30	12	227	218	96	123	1	3.25
Harry Gumbert	R	30	12	14	.462	2	35	30	14	237	230	81	77	2	3.76
Carl Hubbell	L	37	11	12	.478	0	31	28	11	214	220	59	86	2	3.66
Cliff Melton	R	28	10	11	.476	2	37	21	4	167	185	68	91	1	4.90
Bill Lohrman	R	27	10	15	.400	1	31	27	11	195	200	43	73	5	3.78
Red Lynn	R	26	4	3	.571	3	33	0	0	42	40	24	25	0	3.86
Paul Dean	R	26	4	4	.500	0	27	7	2	99	119	29	32	0	3.91
Roy Joiner	R	33	3	2	.600	0	53	66	17	25	0				3.40
Jumbo Brown	R	33	2	4	.333	7	41	0	0	55	49	25	31	0	3.44
Bob Carpenter	R	22	2	0	1.000	0	5	3	2	33	29	14	25	0	2.73
Hy Vandenberg	R	32	1	1	.500	0	13	3	1	32	27	16	17	0	3.94
4 Willis Hudlin	R	34	0	0	.000	0	5	5	1	9	1	1	0	10.80

BOSTON 7th 65-87 .428 34.5   CASEY STENGEL

NAME	G by Pos	B	AGE	G	AB	R	H	2B	3B	HR	RBI	BB	SO	SB	BA	SA
	TOTALS		27	152	5329	623	1366	219	50	59	588	402	581	48	.256	.349
Buddy Hassett	1B98, OF13	L	28	124	458	59	107	19	4	0	27	25	16	4	.234	.293
Bama Rowell	2B115, 0F7	L	24	130	486	46	148	19	8	3	58	18	22	12	.305	.395
Eddie Miller	SS151	R	23	151	569	78	157	33	14	79	41	43	8	.276	.418
Sibby Sisti	3B102, 2B16	R	19	123	459	73	115	19	5	6	34	36	64	4	.251	.353
Max West	OF102, 1B36	L	23	139	524	72	137	27	5	7	72	65	54	2	.261	.372
Johnny Cooney	OF99, 1B7	L	39	108	365	40	116	14	3	0	21	29	9	3	.318	.373
Chet Ross	OF149	R	23	149	569	84	160	23	14	17	89	59	127	4	.281	.460
2 Ray Berres	C85	R	32	85	229	12	44	4	1	0	14	18	19	0	.192	.218
2 Gene Moore	OF94	L	30	103	363	46	106	24	4	5	39	25	32	2	.292	.405
Phil Masi	C52	R	23	63	138	11	27	4	1	1	14	14	14	0	.196	.261
2 Al Glossop	2B18, 3B18, SS1	B	25	60	148	17	35	2	1	1	14	17	22	1	.236	.324
2 Al Lopez	C36	R	31	36	119	20	35	3	1	2	17	6	8	1	.294	.387
Whitey Wietelmann	2B15, 3B9, SS3	R	21	36	41	3	8	1	0	0	3	6	5	0	.195	.220
1 Tony Cuccinello	3B33	R	32	34	126	14	34	9	0	1	19	8	9	1	.270	.341
1 Rabbit Warstler	2B24, 3B2, SS1	R	36	33	57	6	12	0	0	0	4	10	5	0	.211	.211
Stan Andrews	C14	R	23	19	33	1	6	0	0	0	1	0	6	0	.182	.182
Les Scarsella	1B15	L	26	18	60	7	18	1	3	0	8	3	5	2	.300	.417
Bobby Loane	OF10	R	25	13	22	4	5	2	0	0	5	2	5	1	.227	.364
Mel Preibisch	OF11	R	27	11	40	3	9	2	0	0	5	2	4	0	.225	.275
Siggy Broskie	C11	R	29	11	22	1	6	1	0	0	4	3	2	0	.273	.318

Claude Welborn 27 L 0-7, Buddy Gremp 20 R 2-9, Don Manno 25 R 2-7, Hank Majeski 23 R 0-3

NAME	T	AGE	W	L	PCT	SV	G	GS	CG	IP	H	BB	SO	SHO	ERA
		28	65	87	.428	12	152	152	76	1359	1444	573	435	9	4.36
Dick Errickson	R	28	12	13	.480	4	34	29	17	236	241	90	34	3	3.17
Bill Posedel	R	33	12	17	.414	1	35	32	18	233	263	81	89	0	4.13
Manny Salvo	R	28	10	9	.526	0	21	20	14	161	151	43	60	5	3.07
Joe Sullivan	L	29	10	14	.417	1	36	22	7	177	157	89	64	0	3.56
Jim Tobin (KJ)	R	27	7	3	.700	0	15	11	9	96	102	24	29	0	3.84
Nick Strincevich	R	25	4	8	.333	1	32	14	5	129	142	63	54	0	5.51
Tom Earley	R	23	2	0	1.000	1	4	1	1	16	16	3	5	1	3.94
Al Javery	R	22	4	4	.333	0	29	4	1	83	99	36	42	0	5.53
Al Piechota	R	26	2	5	.286	0	21	8	2	61	68	41	18	0	5.75
George Barnicle	R	22	1	0	1.000	0	13	2	1	33	28	31	11	0	7.36
Frank LaManna	R	20	1	0	1.000	0	11	1	1	13	13	8	3	0	4.85
Dick Coffman	R	33	1	3	.167	3	31	0	0	48	63	11	9	0	5.44
Bill Swift	R	32	1	1	.500	1	4	0	0	9	12	7	7	0	3.00
Art Johnson	L	23	1	0	1.000	0	1	0	0	6	10	3	1	0	10.50
Joe Callahan	R	23	0	2	.000	0	6	2	0	15	20	13	3	0	10.20
1 Lou Fette	R	33	0	5	.000	0	7	5	0	32	38	18	2	0	5.63
Ace Williams	L	23	0	0	.000	0	9	0	0	21	12	5	6	0	16.00

PHILADELPHIA 8th 50-103 .327 50   DOC PROTHRO

NAME	G by Pos	B	AGE	G	AB	R	H	2B	3B	HR	RBI	BB	SO	SB	BA	SA
	TOTALS		27	153	5137	494	1225	180	35	75	459	435	527	25	.238	.331
Art Mahan	1B145, P1	L	27	146	544	55	133	24	4	2	39	40	37	4	.244	.318
Ham Schulte	2B119, SS1	R	29	138	436	44	103	18	2	1	27	32	30	3	.236	.294
Bobby Bragan	SS132, 3B2	R	22	132	474	36	105	14	1	4	44	28	34	2	.222	.300
Pinky May	3B135, SS1	L	29	136	501	59	147	24	1	1	48	58	33	2	.293	.355
Chuck Klein	OF96	L	35	116	354	39	77	16	2	7	37	44	30	2	.218	.333
Joe Marty	OF118	R	27	123	455	52	123	21	8	13	50	17	50	2	.270	.437
Johnny Rizzo	OF91, 3B7	R	27	103	367	53	107	12	2	20	53	37	31	2	.292	.499
Bennie Warren	C97, 1B1	R	28	106	289	30	71	6	1	12	34	40	46	1	.246	.398
Emmett Mueller	2B34, OF31, 3B13, 1B2	B	27	97	263	24	65	13	2	3	28	37	23	2	.247	.346
Bill Atwood	C89	L	28	78	203	7	39	9	0	0	22	25	18	0	.192	.236
Mike Mazzera	OF42, 1B11	L	26	69	156	16	37	5	4	0	13	19	15	1	.237	.321
1 Morrie Arnovich	OF37	R	29	39	141	13	28	2	1	0	12	14	15	0	.199	.227
Danny Litwhiler	OF34	R	23	36	142	10	49	2	2	5	17	3	13	1	.345	.493
Hersh Martin	OF23	B	30	33	83	10	21	6	1	0	4	9	9	1	.253	.349
Wally Millies	C24	R	33	26	43	1	3	0	0	0	0	4	4	0	.070	.070
2 Wally Berger	OF11, 1B1	R	34	20	41	3	13	2	0	1	5	4	8	1	.317	.439
Al Monchak	SS9, 2B1	R	23	19	14	1	2	0	0	0	0	0	6	1	.143	.143
Del Young	SS6, 2B5	R	23	15	33	2	8	0	1	0	1	2	6	0	.242	.303
George Jumonville	SS10, 3B1	R	23	11	34	4	3	0	0	0	0	1	6	0	.088	.088
Hal Marnie	2B11	R	21	11	34	4	6	0	0	0	4	5	5	0	.176	.176
Neb Stewart	OF9	R	22	10	31	3	4	0	0	0	0	2	5	0	.129	.129
Gus Suhr	1B7	L	34	10	25	4	4	0	0	0	1	6	3	0	.160	.400

Stan Benjamin 26 R 2-9, George Scharein 25 R 5-17, Sam File 18 R 1-13, Ed Levy 23 R 0-1, Roy Hughes 29 R 0-0

NAME	T	AGE	W	L	PCT	SV	G	GS	CG	IP	H	BB	SO	SHO	ERA
		30	50	103	.327	8	153	153	66	1357	1429	475	485	5	4.40
Kirby Higbe	R	25	14	19	.424	1	41	36	20	283	242	121	137	1	3.72
Hugh Mulcahy	R	26	13	22	.371	0	36	36	21	280	283	91	82	3	3.60
Si Johnson	R	33	5	14	.263	1	37	14	5	138	145	42	58	0	4.89
Cy Blanton	R	31	4	3	.571	0	13	10	5	77	82	21	24	0	4.32
Boom-Boom Beck	R	35	4	9	.308	0	29	15	4	129	147	41	38	0	4.33
Ike Pearson	R	23	3	14	.176	1	29	20	5	145	160	57	43	1	5.46
Syl Johnson	R	39	2	2	.500	2	17	2	2	41	37	5	13	0	4.17
Lefty Smoll	L	26	2	8	.200	0	33	9	0	109	145	36	31	0	5.37
Frank Hoerst	L	22	1	0	1.000	0	6	0	0	12	12	3	4	0	5.25
Lloyd Brown	L	35	1	3	.250	3	18	2	0	38	58	16	16	0	6.16
Johnny Podgajny	R	20	1	3	.250	0	4	4	3	35	33	1	12	0	2.83
Charlie Frye	R	25	0	0	.000	0	15	5	1	50	58	26	18	0	4.68
Maxie Wilson	L	24	0	0	—	0	7	16	2	3	0				12.86
Roy Bruner	R	23	0	0	—	0	2	0	0	6	5	6	4	0	6.00
Paul Masterson	L	24	0	0	—	0	2	0	0	5	5	2	3	0	7.20
Art Mahan		27	0	0	—	0	1	0	0	1	1	1	1	0	0.00

WORLD SERIES — CINCINNATI (NL) 4 DETROIT (AL) 3

LINE SCORES

TEAM	1	2	3	4	5	6	7	8	9	10 11 12	R	H	E

Game 1 October 2 at Cincinnati

DET (AL)	0	5	0	0	2	0	0	0	0		7	10	1
CIN (NL)	0	0	0	1	0	0	0	1	0		2	8	3

Newsom   Derringer, Moore (2), Riddle (9)

Game 2 October 3 at Cincinnati

DET	2	0	0	0	0	1	0	0	0		3	3	1
CIN	0	2	2	1	0	0	0	0	X		5	9	0

Rowe, Gorsica (4)   Walters

Game 3 October 4 at Detroit

CIN	1	0	0	0	0	0	0	1	2		4	10	1
DET	0	0	0	1	0	0	4	2	X		7	13	1

Turner, Moore (7), Beggs (8)   **Bridges**

Game 4 October 5 at Detroit

CIN	2	0	1	1	0	0	0	1	0		5	11	1
DET	0	0	1	0	0	1	0	0	0		2	5	1

Derringer   Trout, Smith (3), McKain (7)

Game 5 October 6 at Detroit

CIN	0	0	0	0	0	0	0	0	0		0	3	0
DET	0	0	3	4	0	0	0	1	X		8	13	0

Thompson, Moore (4), **Newsom**   Vander Meer (5), Hutchings (8)

Game 6 October 7 at Cincinnati

DET	0	0	0	0	0	0	0	0	0		0	5	0
CIN	2	0	0	0	0	1	0	1	X		4	10	2

Rowe, Gorsica (1), Hutchinson (8)   **Walters**

Game 7 October 8 at Cincinnati

DET	0	0	1	0	0	0	0	0	0		1	7	0
CIN	0	0	0	0	0	0	2	0	X		2	7	1

Newsom   Derrringer

COMPOSITE BATTING

NAME	POS	G	AB	R	H	2B	3B	HR	RBI	BA
Cincinnati (NL)										
Totals		7	232	22	58	14	0	2	21	.250
M. McCormick	OF	7	29	1	9	3	0	0	2	.310
Goodman	OF	7	29	5	8	2	0	0	5	.276
F. McCormick	1B	7	28	2	6	1	0	0	0	.214
Werber	3B	7	27	5	10	4	0	0	0	.370
Joost	2B	7	25	0	5	0	0	0	2	.200
Myers	SS	7	23	0	3	0	0	0	1	.130
Ripple	OF	7	21	3	7	2	0	1	6	.333
Wilson	C	6	17	2	6	0	0	0	1	.353
Walters	P	2	7	2	2	1	0	1	2	.286
Derringer	P	3	7	0	0	0	0	0	0	.000
Baker	C	3	4	1	1	0	0	0	0	.250
Lombardi	C	2	3	0	1	0	0	0	0	.333
Riggs	PH	3	3	1	0	0	0	0	0	.000
Frey	PH	3	2	0	0	0	0	0	0	.000
Moore	P	3	2	0	0	0	0	0	0	.000
Turner	P	1	1	0	0	0	0	0	0	.000
Arnovich	OF	1	1	0	0	0	0	0	0	.000
Craft	PH	3	1	0	0	0	0	0	0	.000
Thompson	P	1	1	0	0	0	0	0	0	.000

Beggs P 0-0, Hutchings P 0-0, Riddle P 0-0, Vander Meer P 0-0

NAME	POS	G	AB	R	H	2B	3B	HR	RBI	BA
Detroit (AL)										
Totals		7	228	28	56	9	3	4	24	.246
Greenberg	OF	7	28	5	10	2	1	1	6	.357
Gehringer	2B	7	28	3	6	0	0	0	1	.214
Bartell	SS	7	26	2	7	0	0	0	3	.269
York	1B	7	26	2	6	0	1	1	2	.231
Campbell	OF	7	25	4	9	1	0	1	5	.360
Higgins	3B	7	24	2	9	3	1	1	6	.375
McCosky	OF	7	23	5	7	1	0	0	0	.304
Sullivan	C	7	13	3	1	0	0	0	0	.077
Tebbetts	C	4	11	0	0	0	0	0	0	.000
Newsom	P	3	10	1	1	0	0	0	0	.100
Gorsica	P	2	4	0	0	0	0	0	0	.000
Averill	PH	3	3	0	0	0	0	0	0	.000
Bridges	P	2	3	0	0	0	0	0	0	.000
Fox	PH	2	2	0	0	0	0	0	0	.000
Rowe	P	2	2	0	0	0	0	0	0	.000
Smith	P	1	1	0	0	0	0	0	0	.000
Trout	P	1	1	0	0	0	0	0	0	.000
Croucher	SS	2	0	0	0	0	0	0	0	—
Hutchinson	P	1	0	0	0	0	0	0	0	—
McKain	P	1	0	0	0	0	0	0	0	—

COMPOSITE PITCHING

NAME	G	IP	H	BB	SO	W	L	SV	ERA
Cincinnati (NL)									
Totals	7	61	56	30	30	4	3	0	3.69
Derringer	3	19.1	17	10	6	2	1	0	2.79
Walters	2	18	8	6	2	2	0	0	1.50
Moore	3	8.1	8	6	7	0	0	0	3.24
Turner	1	6	8	0	4	0	1	0	7.50
Thompson	1	3.1	4	2	0	0	1	0	16.20
Vander Meer	1	3	2	3	2	0	0	0	0.00
Beggs	1	1	3	2	0	0	0	0	9.00
Hutchings	1	1	3	1	0	0	0	0	9.00
Riddle	1	1	0	0	2	0	0	0	0.00

NAME	G	IP	H	BB	SO	W	L	SV	ERA
Detroit (AL)									
Totals	7	60	58	15	30	3	4	0	3.00
Newsom	3	26	18	4	17	2	1	0	1.38
Gorsica	2	11.1	6	4	0	0	0	0	0.79
Bridges	2	9	10	1	5	1	0	0	3.00
Smith	1	4	3	3	1	0	0	0	2.25
Rowe	2	3.2	12	1	1	0	2	0	17.18
McKain	1	3	4	0	0	0	0	0	3.00
Trout	1	2	6	1	1	0	1	0	9.00
Hutchinson	1	1	1	1	1	0	0	0	9.00

1941 That Magnificent Streak

When the season of 1941 is recalled, it is mostly because of one man and the incredible record he achieved. Records that are made or broken over a lifetime are significant, but hardly ever as dramatic or immediate as those records attained in a single season. In 1941, the Yankees' Joe DiMaggio hit safely in 56 consecutive games—a feat considered by most to be monumental in view of the pressures and the lack of consistency characteristic of baseball. DiMaggio started his streak on May 15, and continued it through the most stringent of official scoring decisions until July 17.

The highlight of the streak came when DiMaggio tied Willie Keeler's major league mark of 44 consecutive games, achieved in 1897, by getting a hit in the second inning of what turned out to be a rain-shortened, five-inning affair. The day after the 56 game streak was stopped on great plays by Ken Keltner and Lou Boudreau, DiMaggio started a new streak of 16 games. Earlier in his career, while in the Pacific Coast League in 1933, DiMaggio had hit safely in 61 straight games.

Aside from personal glory, the streak contributed to a rousing Yankee comeback and a pennant victory by 17 games over the Red Sox. Boston's own Ted Williams also had a miraculous year by winning the batting title with a .406 average—the first major league batter to turn the trick since Bill Terry's .401 in 1930—and the home run crown with 37 round-trippers. Williams' 120 RBI's fell five short of DiMaggio's league-leading 125 and cost him the Triple Crown. In fact, DiMaggio's performance was such that it overshadowed the Boston slugger in the MVP voting. Williams' one moment alone in the limelight away from DiMaggio came in the All-Star Game when, with two outs and two on in the ninth inning, he hit a home run to give the American League a 7-5 win.

The raging war in Europe had slowly started to exact its toll on baseball and was most noticeable with the 1940 pennant-winning Detroit Tigers. They lost Hank Creenberg, their 1940 MVP, after he played 19 games and wound up in a dismal tie for fourth, 26 games out.

Cincinnati was looking for its third straight pennant in the National League but got off to a poor start and could never recover well enough to catch the Dodgers and Cardinals, who fought it out until the close of the season when the Dodgers finally nailed down the flag in late September. The Dodgers' big men offensively, were Dolph Camilli and Pete Reiser. Camilli led the league in home runs, 34, and RBI's, 120, and was named MVP while Reiser, playing his first full year, took league batting honors with a .343 average. Kirby Higbe, and Whit Wyatt provided the bulk of Brooklyn's pitching as they shared league honors with 22 wins each The pennant, which was the Dodgers' third but their first since 1920, brought great joy to the borough of Brooklyn. But the World Series proved another matter and brought nothing but tears.

In the first game of the Series, 68,540 fans showed up at Yankee Stadium—the largest Series-crowd to that time—and the Yankees won 3-2, mostly because of Pee Wee Reese trying to reach third on a foul out in front of the Yankee bench in the seventh inning. Game two uplifted Dodger hearts with a 3-2 win behind Wyatt, but the third game again sent Brooklyn's hopes scurrying as the old ace and favorite, Freddie Fitzsimmons, was struck by a savage line drive on the leg in the seventh inning and forced to leave a scoreless game, which the Yankees won in the eighth, 2-1.

All of the Dodger heartbreak that had occurred until the fourth game was infinitesimal when compared with the disastrous ninth inning. With Brooklyn leading 4-3 and two men out, Tommy Henrich swung and missed the low third strike, but Mickey Owen could not stop the ball and Henrich wound up on first, opening the door for four runs and a 7-4 Yankee victory.

The demoralized Dodgers collected four hits in the final 3-1 loss and gave the Yankees a happy winter send-off with a five-game Series victory.

1941 AMERICAN LEAGUE

NAME	G by Pos	B	AGE	G	AB	R	H	2B	3B	HR	RBI	BB	SO	SB	BA	SA
NEW YORK 1st 101-53 .658			JOE McCARTHY													
TOTALS			27	156	5444	830	1464	243	60	151	774	616	565	51	.269	.419
Johnny Sturm	1B124	L	25	124	524	58	125	17	3	3	36	37	50	3	.239	.300
Joe Gordon	2B131, 1B30	R	26	156	588	104	162	26	7	24	87	72	80	10	.276	.466
Phil Rizzuto	SS128	R	23	133	515	65	158	20	9	3	46	27	36	14	.307	.398
Red Rolfe	3B134	R	32	136	561	106	148	22	5	8	42	57	38	5	.264	.364
Tommy Henrich	OF139	L	31	144	538	106	149	27	5	31	85	81	40	3	.277	.519
Joe DiMaggio	OF139	R	26	139	541	122	193	43	11	30	125	76	13	4	.357	.643
Charlie Keller	OF137	L	24	140	507	102	151	24	10	33	122	102	65	6	.298	.580
Bill Dickey	C104	L	34	109	348	35	99	15	5	7	71	45	17	2	.284	.417
Goerge Selkirk	OF47	L	33	70	164	30	36	5	0	6	25	28	30	1	.220	.360
Buddy Rosar	C60	R	26	67	209	25	60	17	2	1	36	22	10	0	.287	.402
Jerry Priddy	2B31, 1B10	R	21	56	174	18	37	7	0	1	26	18	16	4	.213	.270
Frankie Crosetti	SS32, 3B13	R	30	50	148	13	33	2	1	2	22	18	14	0	.223	.284
Red Ruffing	P23	R	37	38	89	10	27	8	1	2	22	4	12	0	.303	.483
Frenchy Bordagaray	OF19	L	31	36	73	10	19	1	0	0	4	6	1	1	.260	.274
Ken Silvestri (IL)	C13	B	25	17	40	6	10	5	0	1	4	7	6	0	.250	.450
Johnny Lindell		R	24	1	1	0	0	0	0	0	0	0	0	0	.000	.000
BOSTON 2nd 84-70 .545 17			JOE CRONIN													
TOTALS			29	155	5359	865	1517	304	55	124	805	685	567	67	.283	.430
Jimmie Foxx	1B124, 3B5, OF1	R	33	135	487	87	146	27	8	19	105	93	103	2	.300	.505
Bobby Doerr	2B132	R	23	132	500	74	141	28	4	16	93	43	43	1	.282	.450
Joe Cronin	SS119, 3B22, OF1	R	34	143	518	98	161	38	8	16	95	82	55	1	.311	.508
Jim Tabor	3B125	R	27	126	498	65	139	29	3	16	101	36	48	17	.279	.446
Lou Finney	OF92, 1B24	L	30	127	497	83	143	24	10	4	53	38	17	2	.288	.400
Dom DiMaggio	OF144	R	24	144	584	117	165	37	6	8	58	90	57	13	.283	.408
Ted Williams	OF133	L	22	143	456	135	185	33	3	37	120	147	27	2	.406	.735
Frankie Pytlak	C91	R	32	106	336	36	91	23	1	2	39	28	19	5	.271	.383
Skeeter Newsome	SS69, 2B23	R	30	93	227	28	51	6	0	2	17	22	11	10	.225	.278
Stan Spence	OF52, 1B1	L	26	86	203	22	47	10	3	2	28	18	14	1	.323	.340
Johnny Peacock	C70	L	31	79	261	28	74	20	1	0	27	21	3	2	.284	.365
Pete Fox	OF62	R	31	73	268	38	81	12	7	0	31	21	32	9	.302	.399
Tom Carey	2B9, SS8, 3B1	R	32	25	21	7	4	0	0	0	2	0	2	0	.190	.190
1 Odell Hale	3B6, 2B1	R	32	12	24	5	5	2	0	1	3	4	0	0	.208	.417
Al Flair	1B8	R	24	10	31	3	6	2	1	0	2	1	1	0	.200	.333
Paul Campbell		L	23	1	0	0	0	0	0	0	0	0	0	0	.000	.000
CHICAGO 3rd 77-77 .500 24			JIMMY DYKES													
TOTALS			30	156	5404	638	1376	245	47	47	569	510	476	91	.255	.343
Joe Kuhel	1B151	L	35	153	600	99	150	39	5	12	63	70	55	20	.250	.392
Bill Knickerbocker	2B88	R	29	89	343	51	84	23	2	7	29	41	27	6	.245	.385
Luke Appling	SS154	R	34	154	592	93	186	26	8	1	57	82	32	12	.314	.390
Dario Lodigiani	3B86	R	25	87	322	39	77	19	2	4	40	31	19	0	.239	.348
Taffy Wright	OF134	L	29	136	513	71	165	35	5	10	97	60	27	3	.322	.468
Mike Kreevich	OF113	R	33	121	436	44	101	18	6	0	37	35	26	17	.232	.305
2 Myril Hoag	OF99	R	33	106	380	30	97	13	3	1	44	27	29	6	.255	.313
Mike Tresh	C115	R	27	115	390	38	98	10	1	0	33	38	27	1	.251	.282
Bob Kennedy	3B71	R	20	76	257	16	53	9	3	1	29	17	23	5	.206	.276
Mose Solters (IJ)	OF63	R	35	76	251	24	65	9	4	4	43	18	31	3	.259	.375
Don Kolloway	2B32, 1B4	R	22	71	280	33	76	8	3	3	24	6	12	11	.271	.354
2 Ben Chapman	OF49	R	32	57	190	26	43	14	7	1	19	19	14	2	.226	.316
Tom Turner	C35	R	24	38	126	7	30	5	0	0	8	9	15	2	.238	.278
George Dickey	C17	B	25	32	55	6	11	1	0	2	8	5	7	0	.200	.327
Skeeter Webb	2B18, SS5, 3B3	R	31	29	84	7	16	2	0	0	6	3	9	1	.190	.214
1 Larry Rosenthal	OF18	L	31	20	59	9	14	4	0	0	1	12	5	0	.237	.305
Dave Philley	OF2	L	21	7	9	4	2	1	0	0	0	0	0	0	.222	.333
Stan Goletz		L	23	5	5	0	3	0	0	0	0	1	1	0	.600	.600
Jake Jones	1B3	R	20	3	11	0	0	0	0	0	0	1	4	0	.000	.000
Dave Short (MS)	OF2	L	44	5	8	0	0	0	0	0	0	0	2	1	.000	.000
Chet Hajduk		R	22	1	3	0	0	0	0	0	0	0	1	0	.000	.000

NAME	T	AGE	W	L	PCT	SV	G	GS	CG	IP	H	BB	SO	SHO	ERA
(New York)		29	101	53	.656	26	156	156	75	1396	1309	598	589	13	3.53
Lefty Gomez	L	32	15	5	.750	0	23	23	8	156	151	103	76	2	3.75
Red Ruffing	R	37	15	6	.714	0	23	23	13	186	177	54	60	2	3.53
Marius Russo	L	26	14	10	.583	1	28	27	17	210	195	87	105	3	3.09
Spud Chandler	R	33	10	4	.714	4	28	20	11	164	146	60	60	4	3.18
Atley Donald	R	30	9	5	.643	0	22	19	9	159	141	69	71	0	3.57
Ernie Bonham	R	27	9	6	.600	2	23	14	7	127	118	31	43	1	2.88
Marv Breuer	R	27	9	7	.563	2	26	18	7	141	131	49	77	1	4.09
Johnny Murphy	R	32	8	3	.727	15	35	0	0	77	68	40	29	0	1.99
Norm Branch	R	26	5	1	.833	2	27	0	0	47	37	26	28	0	2.87
Steve Peek	R	26	4	2	.667	0	17	5	2	80	85	39	18	0	5.06
Charley Stanceu	R	25	3	3	.500	0	22	0	0	48	58	35	21	0	5.60
Goerge Washburn	R	26	0	1	.000	0	1	1	0	2	2	5	1	0	13.50
(Boston)		29	84*	70	.545	11	155	155	70	1372	1453	611	574	8	4.19
Dick Newsome	R	31	19	10	.655	0	36	29	17	214	235	79	58	2	4.12
Joe Dobson	R	24	12	5	.706	0	27	18	7	134	136	67	69	1	4.50
Charlie Wagner	R	28	12	8	.600	0	29	25	12	187	175	85	51	3	3.08
Mickey Harris	L	24	8	14	.364	1	35	22	11	194	189	86	111	1	3.25
Mike Ryba	R	38	7	3	.700	6	40	3	0	121	143	42	54	0	4.46
Lefty Grove (LJ)	L	41	7	7	.500	0	21	21	10	134	155	42	54	0	4.37
Tex Hughson	R	25	5	3	.625	0	12	4	1	61	70	13	22	0	4.13
Earl Johnson	L	22	4	5	.444	0	17	12	4	94	90	51	48	0	4.50
Jack Wilson	R	29	4	13	.235	2	27	12	4	116	140	70	55	1	5.03
2 Nels Potter	R	29	2	0	1.000	0	10	0	0	20	21	16	6	0	4.50
Herb Hash	R	30	1	0	1.000	0	4	0	0	8	7	3	0		5.63
Bill Fleming	R	27	1	1	.500	1	16	1	0	41	32	24	20	0	3.95
Emerson Dickman (MS)	R	26	1	1	.500	0	9	3	1	31	37	17	16	0	6.39
Oscar Judd	L	33	0	0	—	1	7	0	0	12	15	10	5	0	9.00
Woody Rich	R	25	0	0	—	0	3	1	0	18	8	2	4	0	15.75
*1 win by forfeit															
(Chicago)		30	77	77	.500	4	156	156	106	1416	1362	521	564	14	3.52
Thornton Lee	L	34	22	11	.667	0	35	34	30	300	258	92	130	3	2.37
Johnny Rigney	R	28	13	13	.500	1	35	34	19	237	224	92	119	3	3.84
Eddie Smith	R	27	13	17	.433	1	34	33	21	263	243	114	111	1	3.18
Ted Lyons	R	40	12	10	.545	0	22	22	19	187	199	37	63	2	3.71
Jack Hallett	R	26	5	5	.500	0	22	6	3	75	96	38	25	0	6.00
Bill Dietrich	R	31	8	8	.385	0	19	15	4	109	114	50	26	1	5.37
John Humphries (BT)	R	26	4	2	.667	1	14	6	4	73	63	22	25	4	1.85
2 Buck Ross	R	27	3	8	.373	0	20	11	7	108	99	43	30	3	3.17
Pete Appleton	R	37	0	3	.000	1	13	0	0	27	17	12	0		5.33
Joe Haynes	R	23	0	0	—	1	8	0	0	28	30	11	18	0	3.86
Orval Grove	R	21	0	0	—	0	2	0	0	0	9	5	5	0	0.00

CLEVELAND 4th(tie) 75-79 .487 26 ROGER PECKINPAUGH

NAME	G by Pos	B	AGE	G	AB	R	H	2B	3B	HR	RBI	BB	SO	SB	BA	SA
TOTALS			28	155	5283	677	1350	249	84	103	618	512	605	63	.256	.393
Hal Trosky (BG)	1B85	L	28	89	310	43	91	17	0	11	51	44	21	1	.294	.455
Ray Mack	2B145	R	24	145	500	54	114	22	4	9	44	54	69	1	.228	.342
Lou Boudreau	SS147	R	23	148	579	95	149	45	8	10	56	85	57	9	.257	.415
Ken Keltner	3B149	R	24	149	581	83	156	31	13	23	84	51	56	2	.269	.485
Jeff Heath	OF151	L	26	151	585	89	199	32	20	24	123	50	69	18	.340	.586
Roy Weatherly	OF88	L	26	102	363	59	105	21	5	3	37	32	20	2	.289	.399
Gee Walker	OF105	R	33	121	445	56	126	26	11	6	48	18	46	12	.283	.431
Rollie Hemsley	C96	R	34	98	288	29	69	10	5	2	24	18	19	2	.240	.330
Soup Campbell	0F78	L	26	104	328	36	82	10	4	3	35	31	21	1	.250	.332
Oscar Grimes	1B62, 2B13, 3B1	R	26	77	244	28	58	9	3	4	24	39	47	4	.238	.348
Gene Desautels (LJ)	C66	R	34	66	189	20	38	5	1	1	17	14	12	1	.201	.254
Beau Bell	OF14, 1B10	R	33	48	104	12	20	4	3	0	9	10	8	1	.192	.288
2 Larry Rosenthal	OF14, 1B1	L	31	45	75	10	14	3	1	1	8	9	10	1	.187	.293
Rusty Peters	SS11, 3B9, 2B3	R	26	29	63	6	12	2	0	0	2	7	10	0	.206	.238
Hank Edwards	OF16	L	22	16	68	10	15	1	1	1	6	2	4	0	.221	.309
Jim Hegan	C16	R	20	16	47	4	15	2	0	0	5	4	7	0	.319	.426
Red Howell		R	32	11	7	0	2	0	0	0	2	1	1	0	.286	.286
Chuck Workman		L	26	9	4	2	0	0	0	0	0	1	1	0	.000	.000
Buck Frierson	OF3	R	23	5	11	2	3	1	0	0	2	1	1	0	.273	.364
Bob Lemon	3B1	L	20	5	4	0	1	0	0	0	0	0	1	0	.250	.250
Fabian Gaffke	OF2	R	27	5	4	0	1	0	0	0	1	0	1	0	.250	.250

Jack Conway 22 R 1-2, Les Fleming 25 L 2-8, Vern Freiburger 17 R 1-8, Oris Hockett 31 L 2-6, George Susce 33 R 0-0

NAME	T	AGE	W	L	PCT	SV	G	GS	CG	IP	H	BB	SO	SHO	ERA
		30	75	79	.487	19	155	155	68	1377	1366	660	617	10	3.90
Bob Feller	R	22	25	13	.658	2	44	40	28	343	284	194	260	6	3.15
Al Smith	L	33	12	13	.480	0	29	27	13	207	204	75	76	2	3.83
Al Milnar	L	27	12	19	.387	0	35	30	9	229	236	116	82	1	4.36
Jim Bagby	R	24	9	15	.375	2	33	27	12	201	214	76	53	0	4.03
Joe Heving	R	40	5	2	.714	5	27	3	2	71	63	31	18	1	2.28
Mel Harder (SA)	R	31	5	4	.556	1	15	10	1	69	76	37	21	0	5.22
Clint Brown	R	37	3	3	.500	5	41	0	0	74	77	28	22	0	3.28
Harry Eisenstat	L	25	1	1	.500	0				34	43	16	11	0	4.24
Steve Gromek	R	21	1	1	.500	2	9	1	1	23	25	11	19	0	4.30
Joe Krakauskas	L	26	1	2	.333	0	12	5	0	42	39	25	25	0	4.07
2 Chubby Dean	L	25	1	4	.200	0	8	2	1	53	57	24	14	0	4.42
Cal Dorsett	R	28	0	1	.000	0	5	2	0	11	21	10	5	0	10.64
Fred Embree	R	23	0	0	—	0	1	0	0	4	7	3	4	0	6.75
Ken Jungels	R	25	0	0	—	0	2	0	0	14	17	8	6	0	7.07
Nate Andrews	R	27	0	0	—	0	2	0	0	3	2	1	0	0	13.50

DETROIT 4th(tie) 75-79 .487 26 DEL BAKER

NAME	G by Pos	B	AGE	G	AB	R	H	2B	3B	HR	RBI	BB	SO	SB	BA	SA
TOTALS			29	155	5370	686	1412	247	55	81	637	602	584	43	.263	.375
Rudy York	1B155	R	27	155	590	91	153	29	3	27	111	92	88	3	.259	.456
Charlie Gehringer	2B116	L	38	127	436	65	96	19	4	3	46	95	26	1	.220	.303
Frank Croucher	SS136	R	26	136	489	51	124	21	4	2	39	33	72	2	.254	.325
Pinky Higgins	3B145	R	32	147	540	79	161	28	3	11	73	67	45	5	.298	.422
Bruce Campbell	OF133	R	31	141	512	72	141	28	10	15	93	68	67	3	.275	.457
Barney McCosky	OF122	L	24	127	494	80	160	25	8	3	55	61	33	8	.324	.425
2 Rip Radcliff	OF87	R	35	96	379	47	120	14	5	3	40	19	13	4	.317	.404
Birdie Tebbetts	C98	R	28	110	359	28	102	19	4	2	47	38	29	1	.284	.376
Tuck Stainback	OF80	R	29	94	200	19	49	8	1	2	10	3	21	6	.245	.325
Billy Sullivan	C63	L	30	85	234	29	66	15	1	3	29	35	11	0	.282	.393
Pat Mullin	OF51	L	24	54	220	42	76	11	5	5	23	18	18	5	.345	.509
Dutch Meyer	2B40	R	25	46	153	12	29	9	1	1	14	8	13	1	.190	.281
Boyd Perry	SS25, 2B11	R	27	36	83	9	15	5	0	0	11	10	9	1	.181	.241
Ned Harris	OF12	L	24	26	61	11	13	3	1	1	4	6	13	1	.213	.344
Eric McNair	3B11, SS3	R	32	23	59	5	11	1	0	0	3	4	4	0	.186	.203
Hank Greenberg (MS)	OF19	R	30	19	67	12	18	5	1	2	12	16	12	1	.269	.463
Murray Franklin	SS4, 3B1	R	27	13	10	1	3	1	0	0	0	0	2	0	.300	.400
Dick Wakefield	OF1	L	20	7	7	0	1	0	0	0	0	0	1	0	.143	.143
1 Dick Bartell	SS5	R	33	5	12	0	2	1	0	0	1	2	2	0	.167	.250
Bob Patrick	OF3	R	23	5	7	2	2	0	0	0	0	1	0	0	.286	.286

Fred Hutchinson 21 L 0-2, Hoot Evers 20 R 0-4

NAME	T	AGE	W	L	PCT	SV	G	GS	CG	IP	H	BB	SO	SHO	ERA
		29	75	79	.487	16	155	155	52	1382	1399	645	697	8	4.18
Al Benton	R	30	15	6	.714	7	38	14	7	158	130	65	63	1	2.96
Bobo Newsom	R	33	12	20	.375	2	43	36	12	250	265	118	175	2	4.61
Dizzy Trout	R	26	9	9	.500	2	37	18	6	152	144	84	88	1	3.73
Johnny Gorsica	R	26	9	11	.450	2	33	21	8	171	193	55	59	1	4.47
Hal Newhouser	L	20	9	11	.450	0	33	27	5	173	166	137	106	1	4.79
Tommy Bridges	R	34	9	12	.429	0	25	22	10	148	128	70	90	1	3.41
Schoolboy Rowe	R	31	8	6	.571	1	27	14	7	139	155	33	54	0	4.14
1 Archie McKain	R	30	2	1	.667	0	15	0	0	43	58	11	14	0	5.02
Hal Manders	R	24	1	0	1.000	0	8	0	0	15	13	8	7	0	2.40
Bud Thomas	R	30	1	3	.250	2	18	1	0	73	74	22	17	0	4.19
Flyod Giebell	R	31	0	0	—	0	17	2	0	34	45	26	10	0	6.09
Les Mueller	R	22	0	0	—	0	4	0	0	13	9	10	8	0	4.85
Hal White	R	22	0	0	—	0	4	0	0	9	11	6	2	0	6.00
Earl Cook	R	32	0	0	—	0	2	0	0	4	5	1	0	0	4.50
Virgil Trucks	R	24	0	0	—	0	2	0	0	1	3	2	1	0	9.00

ST. LOUIS 6th(tie) 70-84 .455 31 FRED HANEY 15-29 .341 LUKE SEWELL 55-55 .500

NAME	G by Pos	B	AGE	G	AB	R	H	2B	3B	HR	RBI	BB	SO	SB	BA	SA
TOTALS			28	157	5408	765	1440	281	58	91	729	775	552	50	.266	.390
George McQuinn	1B125	L	32	130	495	93	147	28	4	18	80	74	30	5	.297	.479
Don Heffner	2B105	R	30	110	399	48	93	14	2	0	17	38	27	5	.233	.278
Johnny Berardino	SS123, 3B1	R	24	128	469	48	127	30	4	5	89	41	27	3	.271	.384
Harlond Clift	3B154	R	28	154	584	108	149	38	9	17	84	113	93	6	.255	.430
Chet Laabs	OF100	R	29	118	392	64	109	23	6	15	59	51	59	1	.278	.482
Walt Judnich	OF140	L	25	146	546	90	155	40	6	14	83	80	45	5	.284	.456
Roy Cullenbine	OF120, 1B22	B	27	149	501	82	159	29	9	9	98	121	43	6	.317	.465
2 Rick Ferrell	C98	R	35	100	321	30	81	14	3	2	23	52	22	2	.252	.333
Joe Grace	OF88, C9	L	27	115	362	53	112	17	4	6	60	57	31	1	.309	.428
Johnny Lucadello	2B70, SS12, 3B6, OF1	B	22	107	351	58	98	22	4	2	31	48	23	5	.279	.382
Bob Swift	C58	R	26	63	170	13	44	7	0	0	21	22	11	2	.259	.300
Bobby Estalella	OF17	R	30	46	83	7	20	6	1	0	14	18	13	0	.241	.337
Alan Strange	SS32, 1B2, 3B1	R	35	44	112	14	26	4	0	0	11	15	5	1	.232	.268
1 Rip Radcliff	OF14, 1B3	L	35	19	71	12	20	2	2	2	14	10	1	1	.282	.451
Frank Grube	C18	R	36	18	39	1	6	2	0	0	1	2	4	0	.154	.205
2 George Archie	1B8	R	27	9	29	3	11	3	0	0	5	7	3	2	.379	.483
Glenn McQuillen	OF6	R	26	7	21	4	7	2	0	1	3	1	0	1	.333	.524
Chuck Stevens	1B4	B	22	4	13	2	2	0	0	0	2	0	1	0	.154	.154
Vern Stephens	SS1	R	20	3	2	0	1	0	0	0	0	0	0	0	.500	.500
Myril Hoag		R	33	1	1	0	0	0	0	0	0	0	0	0	.000	.000

NAME	T	AGE	W	L	PCT	SV	G	GS	CG	IP	H	BB	SO	SHO	ERA
		30	70	84	.455	10	157	157	65	1389	1563	549	454	7	4.72
Elden Auker	R	30	14	15	.483	0	34	31	13	216	268	85	60	0	5.50
Bob Muncrief	R	25	13	9	.591	2	36	24	12	214	221	53	67	2	3.66
Bob Harris	R	26	12	14	.462	1	34	29	9	187	237	85	57	2	5.20
Denny Galehouse	R	29	9	10	.474	0	30	24	11	190	183	68	60	2	3.65
Johnny Niggeling	R	37	7	9	.438	0	24	20	13	168	168	63	68	1	3.80
Bill Trotter	R	32	4	2	.667	0	29	0	0	50	68	19	17	0	5.94
Jack Kramer	R	23	4	3	.571	2	29	3	0	59	69	40	20	0	5.19
George Caster	R	33	3	7	.300	3	32	1	0	104	105	37	36	0	5.02
1 Vern Kennedy	R	34	2	4	.333	1	6	6	2	45	44	27	6	0	4.40
1 Johnny Allen	R	36	2	5	.286	1	20	9	2	67	89	29	27	0	6.58
2 Archie McKain	R	30	1	0	1.000	0	10	0	0	10	16	4	2	0	8.10
Maury Newlin	R	27	0	2	.000	0	14	0	0	28	43	12	10	0	6.43
Fritz Ostermueller	L	33	0	3	.000	0	15	2	0	46	45	23	20	0	4.50
Emil Bildilli	L	28	0	0	—	0	2	0	0	5	3	1	1	0	13.50
Hooks Lott	L	21	0	0	—	0	2	0	0	2	2	1	0	0	9.00

WASHINGTON 6th(tie) 70-84 .455 31 BUCKY HARRIS

NAME	G by Pos	B	AGE	G	AB	R	H	2B	3B	HR	RBI	BB	SO	SB	BA	SA
TOTALS			26	156	5521	728	1502	257	80	52	672	470	488	79	.272	.376
Mickey Vernon	1B132	L	23	138	531	73	159	27	11	9	93	43	51	9	.299	.443
Jimmy Bloodworth	2B132, 3B6, SS1	R	23	142	506	59	124	24	3	7	66	41	58	1	.245	.346
Cecil Travis	SS136, 3B16	L	27	152	608	106	218	39	19	7	101	52	25	2	.359	.520
1 Geoge Archie	3B73, 1B23	R	25	105	379	45	102	20	4	3	48	30	42	8	.269	.367
Buddy Lewis	OF96, 3B49	L	24	149	569	97	169	29	11	9	72	82	30	10	.297	.434
Doc Cramer	OF152	L	35	154	660	93	180	20	7	2	66	37	15	4	.273	.338
George Case	OF151	R	25	153	649	95	176	32	8	7	51	42	54	33	.271	.354
Jake Early	C100	R	26	104	355	42	102	20	7	10	54	24	38	0	.287	.468
Al Evans	C51	R	24	53	159	16	44	8	4	1	19	9	18	0	.277	.396
Buddy Myer	2B24	L	37	53	107	14	27	3	1	0	9	18	10	2	.252	.299
Johnny Welaj	OF19	R	23	49	96	16	20	4	0	0	5	6	16	3	.208	.250
1 Ben Chapman	OF26	R	32	28	110	9	28	6	0	1	10	10	6	2	.255	.336
Sammy West	OF8	R	36	26	37	3	10	0	0	0	4	1	5	0	.270	.270
Roberto Ortiz	OF21	R	26	22	79	10	26	1	2	1	17	3	10	0	.329	.430
Jimmy Pofahl	SS21	R	24	22	75	9	14	3	2	0	6	6	11	1	.187	.280
1 Rick Ferrell	C21	R	35	26	61	8	18	5	0	1	13	15	4	1	.273	.348
Cliff Bolton	C3	L	34	14	11	0	0	0	0	0	0	0	0	0	.000	.000
Hilly Lane	3B13	L	25	45	46	3	14	2	0	0	6	1	5	0	.280	.320
Morrie Aderholt	2B2, 3B1	L	25	11	14	3	2	0	0	0	1	0	0	0	.143	.143

Jack Sanford 24 R 2-5, Charlie Letchas 25 R 1-8, Sherry Robertson 22 L 0-3

NAME	T	AGE	W	L	PCT	SV	G	GS	CG	IP	H	BB	SO	SHO	ERA
		28	70	84*	.455	7	156	156	69	1389	1524	603	544	8	4.36
Dutch Leonard	R	32	18	13	.581	2	34	33	19	256	271	54	91	4	3.45
Sid Hudson	R	26	13	14	.481	0	33	33	17	250	242	97	108	3	3.46
Steve Sundra	R	31	9	13	.409	0	28	23	11	168	203	61	50	0	5.30
Alex Carrasquel	R	28	6	6	.500	2	36	7	1	97	103	49	30	0	3.43
Bill Zuber	R	28	6	4	.600	2	36	7	1	96	110	61	51	0	5.44
Ken Chase	L	27	6	18	.250	0	33	30	8	206	228	115	98	1	5.07
Walt Masterson	R	21	4	3	.571	3	34	6	1	78	101	53	40	0	6.00
Red Anderson	R	29	4	6	.400	0	32	6	1	112	127	53	34	0	4.18
Early Wynn	R	21	3	1	.750	0	5	4	3	40	35	10	15	0	1.58
2 Vern Kennedy	R	34	1	7	.125	0	17	7	2	66	77	39	22	0	5.73
Danny MacFayden	R	36	0	1	.000	0	7	2	0	12	5	3	1	0	10.29
Dick Mulligan	R	23	0	0	—	0	1	0	0	9	11	2	2	0	5.00
Harry Dean	L	26	0	0	—	0	2	0	0	4	4	1	0	0	4.50
Ronnie Miller	R	22	0	0	—	0	1	0	0	3	4	5	2	0	4.50
Lou Thuman (MS) 24	R														

*1 loss by forfeit

PHILADELPHIA 8th 64-90 .416 37 CONNIE MACK

NAME	G by Pos	B	AGE	G	AB	R	H	2B	3B	HR	RBI	BB	SO	SB	BA	SA
TOTALS			27	154	5336	713	1431	240	69	85	660	574	588	27	.268	.387
Dick Siebert	1B123	L	29	123	467	63	156	28	8	5	79	37	22	1	.334	.460
Benny McCoy	2B135	L	22	141	517	86	140	12	7	8	61	95	50	3	.271	.368
Al Brancato	SS139, 3B7	R	22	144	530	60	124	20	9	4	49	59	49	1	.234	.317
Pete Suder	3B136, SS3	R	25	139	531	45	130	20	9	4	52	19	47	1	.245	.339
Wally Moses	OF109	L	30	116	438	78	132	31	4	4	35	62	27	3	.301	.418
Sam Chapman	OF141	R	25	148	552	97	178	29	9	25	106	47	49	6	.322	.543
Bob Johnson	OF122, 1B28	R	35	149	552	90	153	30	8	22	107	95	75	6	.275	.478
Frankie Hayes	C123	R	26	126	439	66	123	27	4	12	63	62	56	2	.280	.442
Eddie Collins	OF50	L	24	80	219	29	53	6	3	0	12	20	24	2	.242	.297
Dee Miles	OF35	L	32	80	170	14	53	7	1	0	16	4	10	1	.312	.365
Hal Wagner	C42	L	25	46	131	18	29	8	2	1	15	19	11	0	.221	.336
Crash Davis	2B20, 1B12	R	21	39	105	8	23	4	0	0	11	16	10	0	.219	.248
Fred Chapman	SS28, 3B2, 2B1	R	24	35	69	1	11	1	0	0	4	4	15	1	.159	.174
Elmer Valo	OF10	L	20	15	50	13	21	0	1	2	6	10	6	0	.420	.580
Don Richmond	3B9	L	21	9	35	3	7	1	0	0	3	2	6	0	.200	.286
Al Simmons	OF5	R	39	9	24	2	3	0	0	0	1	1	4	0	.125	.167
Al Rubeling	3B6	R	24	9	19	2	5	0	0	0	1	0	5	0	.263	.263
Felix Mackiewicz	OF1	L	24	7	14	3	4	1	0	0	3	1	5	0	.286	.429

Ray Poole 21 L 0-2, John Leovich 23 1-2, Eric Tipton 26 R 2-4

NAME	T	AGE	W	L	PCT	SV	G	GS	CG	IP	H	BB	SO	SHO	ERA
		29	64	90	.416	18	154	154	64	1365	1516	557	386	3	4.83
Jack Knott	R	34	13	11	.542	0	27	26	11	194	212	81	54	0	4.41
Phil Marchildon	R	27	10	15	.400	0	30	27	14	204	188	118	74	1	3.57
Les McCrabb	R	26	5	13	.409	2	26	23	11	157	188	49	40	1	5.50
Tom Ferrick	R	26	8	10	.444	7	36	4	2	119	130	33	30	1	3.78
Bill Beckmann	R	33	5	9	.357	1	22	15	4	130	141	33	28	0	4.57
Lum Harris	R	26	4	4	.500	2	33	10	5	132	134	51	49	0	4.77
2 Bump Hadley	R	36	4	4	.400	2	25	9	1	102	131	47	31	0	5.04
Herman Besse	L	29	2	0	1.000	0	5	4	0	43	45	14	7	0	2.93
Fred Caligiuri	R	22	2	1	.500	0	5	4	2	34	28	12	8	0	4.50
1 Chubby Dean	L	25	2	4	.333	0	18	7	2	76	90	35	22	0	6.16
Johnny Babich	R	28	2	7	.222	0	16	14	4	78	85	31	19	0	6.12
Rankin Johnson	R	24	1	1	1.000	0	4	0	0	10	11	5	3	0	3.60
1 Nels Potter	R	29	1	1	.500	0	7	2	1	24	26	8	7	0	9.39
Dick Fowler	R	20	1	1	.500	0	3	1	0	24	26	8	7	0	3.38
Tex Shirley	R	22	1	0	—	0	5	1	1	20	18	17	6	0	6.30
1 Buck Ross	R	26	0	1	.000	0	4	1	0	15	24	4	9	0	18.00
Porter Vaughan	L	21	0	0	—	0	5	2	0	30	36	12	6	0	7.83
Roger Wolff	R	30	0	0	—	0	1	0	0	17	15	4	2	0	3.18
Pat Tobin	R	25	0	0	—	0	1	0	0	4	6	3	1	0	36.00

BROOKLYN — 1ST 100-54 .649 — LEO DUROCHER

NAME	G by Pos	B	AGE	G	AB	R	H	2B	3B	HR	RBI	BB	SO	SB	BA	SA
TOTALS			28	157	5485	800	1494	286	69	101	747	600	535	36	.272	.405
Dolph Camilli	1B148	L	34	149	529	92	151	29	6	34	120	104	115	3	.285	.556
2 Billy Herman	2B133	R	31	133	536	77	156	19	4	3	41	58	38	1	.291	.379
Pee Wee Reese	SS151	R	22	152	595	76	136	23	5	2	46	68	56	10	.229	.294
Cookie Lavagetto	3B120	R	28	132	441	75	122	24	7	1	78	80	21	1	.277	.370
Dixie Walker	OF146	L	30	148	531	88	165	32	8	9	71	70	18	4	.311	.452
Pete Reiser	OF133	L	22	137	536	117	184	39	17	14	76	46	71	4	.343	.558
Joe Medwick	OF131	R	29	133	538	100	171	33	10	18	88	38	35	2	.318	.517
Mickey Owen	C128	R	25	128	386	32	89	15	2	1	44	34	14	1	.231	.288
Jimmy Wasdell	OF54, 1B15	L	27	94	265	39	79	14	3	4	48	16	15	2	.298	.419
Lew Riggs	3B43, 1B1, 2B1	L	31	77	197	27	60	13	4	5	36	16	12	1	.305	.487
Herman Franks	C54, OF1	L	27	57	139	10	28	7	0	4	11	14	13	0	.201	.273
Pete Coscarart	2B19, SS1	R	28	43	62	13	8	1	0	0	5	7	12	1	.129	.145
Whit Wyatt	P38	R	33	40	109	10	26	5	0	3	22	4	12	0	.239	.367
Joe Vosmik	OF18	R	31	25	56	0	11	0	0	0	4	4	0		.196	.196
Leo Durocher	SS12, 2B1	R	35	18	42	2	12	1	0	0	6	1	3	0	.286	.310
2 Augie Galan	OF6	B	29	17	27	3	7	3	0	0	4	3	1	0	.259	.370
Alex Kampouris (XJ)	2B15	R	28	16	51	8	16	4	2	2	9	11	8	0	.314	.588
Babe Phelps (JT)	C11	L	33	16	30	3	7	3	0	2	4	1	2	0	.233	.533
1 Paul Waner	OF9	L	38	11	35	5	6	0	0	0	4	8	0	0	.171	.171
Tommy Tatum	OF4	R	21	8	12	1	2	1	0	0	1	1	3	0	.167	.250

Tony Giulani 28 R 0-2, Geroge Pfister 22 R 0-2, Joe Gallagher (MS) 27

NAME	T	AGE	W	L	PCT	SV	G	GS	CG	IP	H	BB	SO	SHO	ERA
TOTALS		31	100	54	.649	22	157	157	66	1421	1236	495	603	17	3.14
Kirby Higbe	R	26	22	9	.710	3	48	39	19	298	244	132	121	2	3.14
Whit Wyatt	R	33	22	10	.688	1	38	35	23	288	223	82	176	7	2.34
Hugh Casey	R	27	14	11	.560	7	45	18	4	162	155	57	61	1	3.89
Curt Davis	R	37	13	7	.650	2	28	16	10	154	141	27	50	5	2.98
Luke Hamlin	R	36	8	8	.500	1	30	20	5	136	139	41	58	1	4.24
F. Fitzsimmons (AJ)	R	39	6	1	.857	0	13	7	3	83	78	26	19	1	2.06
2 Johnny Allen	R	36	3	0	1.000	0	11	4	1	57	50	12	21	0	2.53
Bill Swift	R	33	3	0	1.000	0	9	0	0	22	26	7	9	0	3.27
Newt Kimball	R	26	3	1	.750	1	15	5	1	52	43	29	17	0	3.63
2 Mace Brown (NJ)	R	32	3	2	.600	3	24	0	0	43	31	26	22	0	3.14
Bob Chipman	L	22	1	0	1.000	0	1	0	0	5	3	1	3	0	0.00
Tom Drake	R	28	1	1	.500	0	10	2	0	25	26	9	12	0	4.32
Kemp Wicker	L	34	1	2	.333	1	16	2	0	32	30	14	8	0	3.66
Ed Albosta	R	22	0	2	.000	0	2	2	0	13	11	8	5	0	6.23
2 Vito Tamulis	L	29	0	0	—	1	12	0	0	22	21	10	8	0	3.38
2 Larry French	L	33	0	0	—	0	6	1	0	16	16	4	8	0	3.38
1 Lee Grissom	L	33	0	0	—	1	4	1	0	11	10	8	5	0	2.46
Van Lingle Mungo	R	30	0	0	—	0	2	1	0	2	1	2	0	0	4.50

ST. LOUIS — 2nd 97-56 .634 2.5 — BILLY SOUTHWORTH

NAME	G by Pos	B	AGE	G	AB	R	H	2B	3B	HR	RBI	BB	SO	SB	BA	SA
TOTALS			28	155	5457	734	1482	254	56	70	664	540	543	47	.272	.371
Johnny Mize	1B122	L	28	126	473	67	150	39	8	16	100	70	45	4	.317	.535
Creepy Crespi	2B145	R	23	146	560	85	156	24	2	4	46	57	58	3	.279	.350
Marty Marion	SS155	R	23	155	547	50	138	22	3	3	58	42	48	8	.252	.320
Jimmy Brown	3B123, 2B11	B	31	132	549	93	168	28	9	3	56	45	22	2	.306	.406
Enos Slaughter (BC)	OF108	L	25	113	425	71	132	22	9	13	76	53	28	4	.311	.496
Terry Moore	OF129	R	29	122	493	86	145	26	4	6	68	52	31	3	.294	.400
Johnny Hopp	OF91, 1B39	L	24	134	445	83	135	25	11	4	50	50	63	15	.303	.436
Gus Mancuso	C105	R	35	106	328	25	75	13	1	2	37	37	19	0	.229	.293
Don Padgett	OF62, C18, 1B2	L	29	107	324	39	80	18	0	5	44	21	16	0	.247	.349
Estel Crabtree	OF50, 3B1	R	37	77	167	27	57	6	3	5	28	26	24	1	.341	.503
Coaker Triplett	OF46	R	29	76	185	29	53	6	3	3	21	18	27	0	.286	.400
Walker Cooper (BS)	C63	R	26	68	200	19	49	9	1	1	20	13	14	1	.245	.315
Eddie Lake	SS15, 3B15, 2B5	R	25	45	76	9	8	2	0	0	6	15	22	3	.105	.132
Steve Mesner	3B22	R	23	24	69	8	10	1	0	0	10	5	6	0	.145	.159
1 Ernie Koy	OF12	R	31	13	40	5	8	0	0	2	4	1	8	0	.200	.375
Stan Musial	OF11	L	20	12	47	8	20	4	0	1	7	2	1	1	.426	.574
Harry Walker	OF5	L	24	7	15	3	4	1	0	0	1	2	1	0	.267	.333
Erv Dusak	OF4	R	20	6	14	1	2	0	0	0	3	2	6	1	.143	.143
Whitey Kurowski	3B4	R	23	5	9	1	3	2	0	0	2	0	2	0	.333	.556

Walter Sessi 22 L 0-13, 2 Pep Young 33 R 0-2, Charlie Marshall 21 R 0-0

NAME	T	AGE	W	L	PCT	SV	G	GS	CG	IP	H	BB	SO	SHO	ERA
TOTALS		28	97	56	.634	20	155	155	64	1417	1289	502	659	15	3.19
Ernie White	L	24	17	7	.708	2	32	25	12	210	169	70	117	3	2.40
Lon Warneke	R	32	17	9	.654	0	37	30	12	246	227	82	83	4	3.15
Mort Cooper (EJ)	R	28	13	9	.591	0	29	25	12	187	175	69	118	0	3.90
2 Harry Gumbert	R	31	11	5	.688	1	33	17	8	144	139	30	53	3	2.75
Howie Krist	R	25	10	0	1.000	2	37	4	2	114	107	35	36	0	4.03
Max Lanier	R	25	10	8	.556	3	35	18	8	153	126	59	93	2	2.82
Sam Nahem	R	25	5	2	.714	1	26	8	2	82	76	38	31	0	2.96
Howie Pollet	L	20	5	2	.714	0	9	8	6	70	55	27	37	2	1.93
Clyde Shoun	R	29	3	5	.375	0	26	6	0	70	98	20	34	0	5.66
Johnny Grodizicki	R	24	2	1	.667	0	5	1	0	13	6	11	10	0	1.38
1 Hank Gornicki	R	30	1	0	1.000	0	5	1	1	8	6	2	1	0	3.28
Johnny Beazley	R	23	1	0	1.000	0	1	1	1	9	10	3	4	0	1.00
2 Bill Crouch	R	30	1	2	.333	6	18	4	0	45	45	14	15	0	3.00
Ira Hutchinson	R	30	1	5	.167	5	29	0	0	47	32	19	19	0	3.83
Bill McGee	R	31	0	0	.000	0	1	0	0	3	4	3	2	0	5.14
Hersh Lyons	R	25	0	0	—	0	1	0	0	1	3	1	1	0	

CINCINNATI — 3rd 88-66 .571 12 — BILL McKECHINIE

NAME	G by Pos	B	AGE	G	AB	R	H	2B	3B	HR	RBI	BB	SO	SB	BA	SA
TOTALS			29	154	5281	616	1288	213	33	64	567	477	428	68	.247	.337
Frank McCormick	1B154	R	30	156	603	77	162	31	5	17	97	40	13	2	.269	.421
Lonny Frey	2B145	R	30	146	544	78	138	29	5	6	59	72	37	16	.254	.359
Eddie Joost	SS147, 2B4, 1B2, 3B1	R	25	152	537	67	136	25	4	4	40	69	59	9	.253	.337
Bill Werber	3B107	R	33	109	418	56	100	9	2	4	46	53	24	14	.239	.299
Jim Gleeson	OF84	R	29	102	301	47	70	10	0	3	34	45	30	7	.233	.296
Harry Craft	OF115	R	26	119	413	48	103	15	2	10	59	33	43	4	.249	.368
Mike McCormick	OF101	R	24	110	369	52	106	17	3	4	31	30	24	4	.287	.382
Ernie Lombardi	C116	R	33	117	398	33	105	12	1	10	60	36	14	1	.264	.374
2 Ernie Koy	OF49	R	31	67	204	20	51	11	2	2	27	14	22	1	.250	.353
Dick West	C64	R	25	67	172	15	37	5	2	1	17	6	23	4	.215	.285
3 Lloyd Waner	OF35	L	35	55	164	17	42	4	1	0	6	3	4	0	.256	.293
Chuck Aleno	3B40, 1B2	R	24	54	169	23	41	7	3	1	18	11	16	3	.243	.337
Ival Goodman (IL)	OF40	L	32	42	149	14	40	5	2	1	12	16	15	1	.268	.349
Jimmy Ripple	OF25	L	31	38	102	10	22	6	1	1	9	4	4	1	.216	.324
Eddie Lukon	OF22	L	20	23	86	6	23	3	0	0	3	6	9	1	.267	.302
Bobby Mattick	SS12, 3B5, 2B1	R	25	20	60	8	11	3	0	0	7	8	7	1	.183	.233
Johnny Riddle	C10	R	35	10	10	2	3	0	0	0	0	1	0	0	.300	.300
Hank Sauer	OF8	R	24	9	33	4	10	4	0	0	5	1	4	0	.303	.424
Benny Zientara	2B6	R	23	9	21	3	6	0	0	0	1	1	4	1	.286	.286
1 Pep Young	3B3	R	33	8	24	4	4	1	2	0	0	0	1	0	.167	.167

1 Bill Baker 30 R 0-1, Ray Lamanno 21 R 0-0, Eddie Shokes 21 L 0-1

NAME	T	AGE	W	L	PCT	SV	G	GS	CG	IP	H	BB	SO	SHO	ERA
TOTALS		30	88	66	.571	12	154	154	89	1387	1300	510	627	19	3.17
Elmer Riddle	R	26	19	4	.826	1	33	22	15	217	180	59	80	4	2.24
Bucky Walters	R	32	19	15	.559	2	37	35	27	302	292	88	129	5	2.83
Johnny Vander Meer	R	26	16	13	.552	0	33	32	18	226	172	126	202	6	2.83
Paul Derringer	R	34	12	14	.462	1	29	28	17	228	233	54	76	2	3.83
Jim Turner (NJ)	R	37	6	4	.600	3	23	10	3	113	120	24	34	0	3.11
Junior Thompson	R	24	6	6	.500	1	27	15	4	109	117	57	46	0	4.87
Joe Beggs	R	30	4	3	.571	5	37	0	0	57	57	27	19	0	3.79
Ray Starr	R	35	3	2	.600	0	7	4	3	34	28	6	11	2	2.65
Whitey Moore	R	29	2	1	.667	0	23	4	1	62	62	45	17	0	4.35
Monte Pearson	R	32	1	3	.250	0	7	1	0	24	22	15	8	0	5.25
Bob Logan	L	31	1	0	1.000	0	3	0	0	5	5	0	0	0	9.00
1 Johnny Hutchings	R	25	0	0	—	0	8	0	0	11	12	4	5	0	4.09

PITTSBURGH — 4th 81-73 .526 19 — FRANKIE FRISCH

NAME	G by Pos	B	AGE	G	AB	R	H	2B	3B	HR	RBI	BB	SO	SB	BA	SA
TOTALS			27	156	5297	690	1417	233	65	56	634	547	516	59	.268	.368
Elbie Fletcher	1B151	L	25	151	524	95	150	29	13	11	74	118	54	5	.288	.450
Frankie Gustine	2B104, 3B15	R	21	121	463	46	125	24	7	1	46	28	38	5	.270	.359
Arky Vaughan	SS97, 3B3	R	29	106	374	69	118	20	7	6	38	50	13	8	.316	.455
Lee Handley	3B114	R	27	124	439	59	132	18	4	0	33	35	22	16	.288	.344
Bob Elliott	OF139	R	24	141	527	74	144	24	10	3	76	44	49	4	.273	.374
Vince DiMaggio	OF151	R	28	151	528	73	141	27	5	21	100	68	100	10	.267	.456
Maurice Van Robays	OF121	R	26	129	457	62	129	23	4	5	78	41	29	0	.282	.381
Al Lopez	C114	R	32	114	317	33	84	9	1	5	43	31	23	0	.265	.347
Stu Martin	2B53, 3B2, 1B1	R	28	88	233	37	71	13	2	0	19	10	17	2	.305	.378
Debs Garms	3B29, OF24	L	34	83	220	27	58	9	3	3	42	22	12	0	.264	.373
Bud Stewart	OF41	L	25	73	172	27	46	7	0	0	10	12	17	3	.267	.308
Alf Anderson	SS58	R	27	70	223	32	48	7	2	1	10	14	30	2	.215	.278
Spud Davis	C49	R	36	57	107	3	27	4	1	0	6	11	11	0	.252	.308
2 Bill Baker	C33	R	30	35	67	5	15	3	0	0	6	11	0	0	.224	.269
Ed Leip	2B7, 3B1	R	30	15	25	1	5	0	2	0	3	1	2	1	.200	.360
Billy Cox	SS10	R	21	10	37	4	10	3	1	0	4	2	3	1	.270	.405
Vinnie Smith	C9	R	26	9	33	3	10	1	0	0	5	1	5	0	.303	.333
Cully Rikard	OF5	L	27	6	20	1	4	1	0	0	0	1	1	0	.200	.250
1 Lloyd Waner	OF1	L	35	3	4	2	1	0	0	0	0	0	0	0	.250	.250
Joe Schultz		L	22	2	2	1	1	0	0	0	0	0	0	0	.500	.500

NAME	T	AGE	W	L	PCT	SV	G	GS	CG	IP	H	BB	SO	SHO	ERA
TOTALS		30	81	73	.526	12	156	156	71	1374	1392	492	410	8	3.48
Max Butcher	R	30	17	12	.586	0	33	32	19	236	249	66	61	0	3.05
Rip Sewell	R	24	14	17	.452	2	39	32	18	249	225	84	76	2	3.72
Ken Heintzelman	L	25	11	11	.500	0	35	24	13	196	206	83	81	2	3.44
Johnny Lanning	R	34	11	11	.500	1	34	23	9	176	175	47	41	0	3.12
Bob Klinger	R	33	9	4	.692	4	35	9	3	117	127	30	36	0	3.92
Dutch Dietz	R	29	7	2	.778	1	33	6	4	100	88	33	22	1	2.34
2 Joe Sullivan	L	30	4	1	.800	1	16	4	0	39	40	22	10	0	3.00
Joe Bowman	R	31	3	2	.600	1	18	7	1	94	77	28	22	1	3.00
Lefty Wilkie	L	26	2	4	.333	2	26	4	2	79	90	40	16	1	4.56
Bill Clemensen	R	22	1	0	1.000	0	3	1	1	7	7	4	2	0	2.77
2 Nick Strincevich	R	26	1	2	.333	0	12	3	0	31	35	13	12	0	5.23
Russ Bauers	R	27	1	3	.250	0	11	5	1	37	40	25	20	0	5.59
Dick Lanahan	L	29	0	1	.000	0	7	0	0	12	13	9	3	0	5.25
Bill Brandt	R	26	0	1	.000	0	6	1	0	7	11	5	3	0	3.86
Johnny Gee	L	25	0	0	—	0	3	1	0	11	9	2	6	0	6.43
Dick Conger	R	20	0	0	—	0	2	0	0	8	8	0	0	0	0.00
1 Mace Brown	R	32	0	0	—	0	7	0	0	13	7	4	4	0	

Oad Swigert (MS) 26

NEW YORK — 5th 74-79 .484 25.5 — BILL TERRY

NAME	G by Pos	B	AGE	G	AB	R	H	2B	3B	HR	RBI	BB	SO	SB	BA	SA
TOTALS			30	156	5395	667	1401	248	35	95	625	504	518	36	.260	.371
Babe Young	1B150	L	26	152	574	90	152	28	5	25	104	66	39	1	.265	.462
Burgess Whitehead	2B104, 3B15	R	31	116	403	41	92	15	4	1	23	14	10	7	.228	.293
Billy Jurges	SS134	R	34	134	471	50	138	25	2	5	61	47	36	0	.293	.386
2 Dick Bartell	3B84, SS21	R	33	104	373	44	113	20	0	5	36	52	29	6	.303	.397
Mel Ott	OF145	L	32	148	525	89	150	29	0	27	90	100	68	5	.286	.495
Johnny Rucker	OF142	L	24	142	622	95	179	38	9	1	42	39	61	8	.288	.383
Jo-Jo Moore	OF116	L	32	121	428	47	117	16	2	7	40	30	35	1	.273	.369
Harry Danning	C116, 1B1	R	29	130	459	58	112	22	4	7	56	30	25	1	.244	.355
Morrie Arnovich	OF61	R	30	85	207	25	58	8	3	2	22	23	14	2	.280	.377
Joe Orengo	3B59, SS9, 2B6	R	26	77	252	23	54	11	2	4	25	28	49	1	.214	.321
Gabby Hartnett	C34	R	40	64	150	20	45	5	0	5	26	12	14	0	.300	.433
Ken O'Dea	C14	L	28	59	89	13	19	5	1	3	17	8	20	0	.213	.393
2 Odell Hale	2B29	R	32	41	102	13	20	3	0	0	9	18	13	1	.196	.225
Mickey Witek	2B35	R	25	26	94	11	34	1	0	1	16	4	2	0	.362	.447
John Davis	3B21	R	25	21	70	8	15	1	1	0	6	1	5	0	.214	.257
1 Frank Demaree	OF10	R	31	14	35	4	6	1	0	0	2	5	1	0	.171	.171
Johnny McCarthy	1B8, OF1	L	31	14	40	1	13	1	0	2	6	1	1	0	.325	.400
Babe Barna	OF10	L	26	12	28	2	6	1	0	0	2	2	6	0	.214	.357
Sid Gordon	OF9	R	23	9	31	4	8	1	0	0	3	3	6	0	.258	.355

Rae Blaemire 30 R 2-5, Jack Aragon 25 R 0-0

NAME	T	AGE	W	L	PCT	SV	G	GS	CG	IP	H	BB	SO	SHO	ERA
TOTALS		30	74	79	.484	12	156	156	55	1392	1455	539	566	12	3.94
Hal Schumacher	R	30	12	10	.545	1	30	26	12	206	187	79	63	3	3.36
Bob Carpenter	R	23	11	6	.647	2	29	19	8	132	138	42	42	1	3.82
Carl Hubbell	L	38	11	9	.550	1	26	22	11	164	169	53	75	1	3.57
Bill Lohrman	R	28	11	8	.579	1	33	20	6	159	184	40	61	2	4.02
Cliff Melton	L	29	8	11	.421	1	42	12	7	194	181	61	100	3	3.02
Bob Bowman	R	30	6	7	.462	2	29	6	2	80	100	36	25	0	5.74
Ace Adams	R	31	4	1	.800	1	38	0	0	71	84	35	16	0	4.82
Johnnie Wittig	R	27	3	5	.375	0	9	8	5	85	111	45	47	0	5.61
2 Bill McGee	R	31	2	2	.182	0	22	14	1	106	117	54	41	0	4.92
1 Bump Hadley	R	36	1	0	1.000	0	13	1	0	19	19	9	6	0	6.23
Rube Fischer	R	24	1	0	1.000	0	9	1	0	13	16	13	9	0	2.45
1 Harry Gumbert	R	31	1	1	.500	0	5	1	1	32	34	14	9	0	4.50
Harry Feldman	R	21	1	1	.500	0	7	1	0	20	19	9	4	0	4.05
Hugh East	R	21	1	1	.500	0	2	1	0	16	19	9	3	0	3.38
Tom Sunkel	L	21	1	1	.500	0	3	1	0	24	17	10	12	0	1.88
Dave Koslo	L	21	0	0	—	0	3	0	0	2	3	0	2	0	3.00
Jumbo Brown	R	34	1	5	.167	8	31	0	0	57	49	21	30	0	3.32
Paul Dean	R	28	0	0	—	0	2	0	0	3	6	3	0	0	

CHICAGO — 6th 70-84 .455 30 — JIMMIE WILSON

NAME	G by Pos	B	AGE	G	AB	R	H	2B	3B	HR	RBI	BB	SO	SB	BA	SA
TOTALS			26	155	5230	666	1323	239	25	99	610	559	670	39	.253	.365
2 Babe Dahlgren	1B98	R	29	99	359	50	101	20	1	16	59	43	39	2	.281	.476
Lou Stringer	2B137, SS7	R	24	145	512	59	126	31	4	5	53	59	86	3	.246	.352
Bobby Sturgeon	SS126, 2B1, 3B1	R	21	129	433	45	106	15	3	0	25	9	30	5	.245	.293
Stan Hack	3B150, 1B	L	31	151	586	111	186	33	5	7	45	99	40	10	.317	.427
Bill Nicholson	OF143	L	26	147	532	74	125	26	1	26	98	82	91	1	.254	.453
Phil Cavarretta	OF66, 1B33	L	24	107	346	46	99	18	4	6	40	53	28	2	.286	.413
Dom Dallessandro	OF131	L	27	140	486	73	132	36	2	6	85	68	37	3	.272	.391
Clyde McCullough	C119	R	24	125	418	41	95	9	2	9	53	34	67	5	.227	.323
1 Augie Galan	OF31	B	29	65	120	18	25	3	0	1	13	22	10	0	.208	.258
Lou Novikoff	OF54	R	25	62	203	22	49	8	0	5	24	11	15	0	.241	.335
Hank Leiber (CN)	OF29, 1B15	R	30	53	162	20	35	5	0	7	25	16	25	0	.216	.377
Bob Scheffing	C34	R	27	51	132	9	32	8	0	1	20	5	19	2	.242	.326
Johnny Hudson	SS17, 2B13, 3B10	R	29	50	99	8	20	4	0	0	6	3	15	3	.202	.242
Charlie Gilbert	OF22	L	21	39	86	11	24	2	1	0	12	11	6	1	.279	.326
Greek George	C18	R	28	35	64	4	10	2	0	0	4	2	10	0	.156	.188
Barney Olsen	OF23	R	21	24	73	13	21	6	1	1	4	4	11	0	.288	.438
Billy Myers	SS19, 2B1	R	30	24	63	10	14	1	1	0	4	7	25	1	.222	.286
Eddie Waitkus	1B9	L	21	12	28	1	5	0	0	0	0	0	3	0	.179	.179
1 Billy Herman	2B11	R	31	11	36	4	7	0	1	0	9	5	1	0	.194	.250
Lennie Merullo	SS7	R	24	7	17	3	6	1	0	0	1	2	1	0	.353	.412
Rip Russell	1B5	R	26	6	17	1	5	0	0	0	1	1	5	0	.294	.353

Al Todd 37 R 1-6, Frank Jelincich 23 R 1-8, Zeke Bonura (MS) 32

NAME	T	AGE	W	L	PCT	SV	G	GS	CG	IP	H	BB	SO	SHO	ERA
		32	70	84	.455	9	155	155	74	1365	1431	449	548	8	3.72
Claude Passeau	R	32	14	14	.500	0	34	30	20	231	262	52	80	3	3.35
Vern Olsen	L	23	10	8	.556	1	37	23	10	186	202	59	73	2	3.15
Charlie Root	R	42	8	7	.533	0	19	15	6	107	133	37	46	0	5.38
Jake Mooty	R	28	8	9	.471	4	33	14	7	153	143	56	45	1	3.35
Bill Lee	R	31	8	14	.364	1	28	22	12	167	179	43	62	0	3.77
Tot Pressnell	R	34	5	3	.625	1	29	1	0	70	69	23	27	0	3.09
1 Larry French	L	33	5	14	.263	2	26	18	6	138	161	43	60	1	4.63
Vallie Eaves	R	29	3	3	.500	0	12	7	4	59	56	21	24	0	3.51
Johnny Schmitz	L	20	2	0	1.000	0	5	3	1	21	12	9	11	0	1.29
Vance Page	R	37	2	2	.500	1	25	3	1	48	48	30	17	0	4.31
Ken Raffensberger	R	23	0	1	.000	0	10	1	0	18	17	7	5	0	4.50
Walt Lanfranconi	R	24	0	1	.000	0	2	1	0	6	7	2	1	0	3.00
Russ Meers	L	22	0	1	.000	0	3	1	0	8	5	0	5	0	1.13
Wimpy Quinn	R	23	0	0	—	0	3	0	0	5	3	3	2	0	7.20
Emil Kush	R	24	0	0	—	0	2	0	0	4	2	0	2	0	2.25
Dizzy Dean (SA)	R	31	0	0	—	0	1	0	0	1	3	0	1	0	18.00
2 Hank Gornicki	R	30	0	0	—	0	1	0	0	2	3	0	2	0	4.50

BOSTON — 7th 62-92 .403 38 — CASEY STENGEL

NAME	G by Pos	B	AGE	G	AB	R	H	2B	3B	HR	RBI	BB	SO	SB	BA	SA
TOTALS			28	156	5414	592	1357	231	38	48	552	471	608	61	.251	.334
Buddy Hassett	1B99	L	29	118	405	59	120	9	4	1	33	36	15	10	.296	.346
Bama Rowell	2B112, OF14, 3B2	L	24	154	483	49	129	23	6	7	60	39	36	11	.267	.383
Eddie Miller	SS154	R	24	154	585	54	140	27	3	6	68	35	72	8	.239	.326
Sibby Sisti	3B137, 2B2, SS2	R	20	140	541	72	140	24	3	1	45	38	76	7	.259	.320
Gene Moore	OF110	L	31	129	397	42	108	17	8	5	43	45	37	5	.272	.393
Johnny Cooney	OF111, 1B4	R	40	123	442	52	141	25	2	0	29	27	15	3	.319	.385
Max West	OF132	L	24	138	484	63	134	28	4	12	68	72	68	5	.277	.426
Ray Berres	C120	R	33	120	279	21	56	10	0	1	19	17	20	2	.201	.247
2 Paul Waner	OF77, 1B1	L	38	95	294	40	82	10	2	2	46	47	14	1	.279	.347
Phil Masi	C83	R	24	87	180	17	40	8	2	3	18	16	13	4	.222	.339
Skippy Roberge	2B46, 3B5, SS2	R	24	55	167	12	36	6	0	0	15	9	18	0	.216	.251
2 Frank Demaree	OF28	R	31	48	113	20	26	5	2	2	15	12	5	2	.230	.363
1 Babe Dahlgren	1B39, 3B5	R	29	44	166	20	39	8	1	7	30	16	13	0	.235	.422
Al Montgomery	C30	R	20	44	52	4	10	1	0	0	4	3	9	0	.192	.212
Buddy Gremp	1B21, 2B6, C3	R	21	37	75	7	18	3	0	0	10	5	3	0	.240	.280
Chet Ross (NJ)	OF12	R	24	29	50	1	6	1	0	0	3	9	17	0	.120	.140
Don Manno	OF5, 3B3, 1B1	R	26	22	30	2	5	1	0	0	4	3	4	0	.167	.200
Hank Majeski	3B11	R	24	19	55	5	8	5	0	0	3	1	13	0	.145	.236
2 Lloyd Waner	OF15	L	35	19	51	7	21	1	0	0	4	2	1	1	.412	.431
Whitey Wietelmann	2B10, SS5, 3B2	R	22	16	33	1	3	0	0	0	0	1	9	0	.091	.091
John Dudra	2B5, 3B5, 1B1, SS1	R	25	14	25	3	3	1	0	0	3	1	4	0	.118	.560
Earl Averill	OF4	R	39	8	17	2	2	0	0	0	1	1	5	0	.118	.118

Mel Preibisch 26 R 0-4, Buster Bray 28 L 1-11

NAME	T	AGE	W	L	PCT	SV	G	GS	CG	IP	H	BB	SO	SHO	ERA
		27	62	92	.403	9	156	156	62	1386	1440	554	446	10	3.95
Jim Tobin	R	28	12	12	.500	0	33	26	20	238	229	60	61	3	3.10
Al Javery	R	23	10	11	.476	1	34	23	9	161	181	65	54	1	4.30
Art Johnson	L	24	7	15	.318	1	43	18	6	183	189	71	70	0	3.54
Manny Salvo	R	29	7	16	.304	0	35	27	11	195	192	93	67	2	4.06
Tom Earley	R	24	6	8	.429	3	33	13	6	139	120	46	54	1	2.53
Dick Errickson	R	29	6	12	.333	1	38	23	5	166	192	62	45	2	4.77
Frank Lamanna	R	21	4	4	.556	1	35	4	0	73	77	56	23	0	5.30
Bill Posedel	R	34	4	4	.500	0	18	9	3	57	61	30	10	0	4.89
Wes Ferrell	R	33	2	1	.667	0	3	3	1	14	13	9	10	0	5.14
1 Joe Sullivan	L	30	2	2	.500	0	16	2	0	52	60	26	11	0	4.16
2 Johnny Hutchings	R	25	1	6	.143	2	36	7	1	96	110	22	36	1	4.13
George Barnicle	R	23	0	1	.000	0	1	1	0	7	5	4	2	0	6.43
1 Nick Strincevich	R	26	0	0	—	0	2	0	0	3	7	6	1	0	12.00
Eddie Carnett	L	24	0	0	—	0	2	0	0	1	4	3	2	0	27.00
Al Piechota	R	27	0	0	—	0	1	0	0	1	1	0	0	0	0.00

PHILADELPHIA — 8th 43-111 .279 57 — DOC PROTHRO

NAME	G by Pos	B	AGE	G	AB	R	H	2B	3B	HR	RBI	BB	SO	SB	BA	SA
TOTALS			26	155	5233	501	1277	188	38	64	467	451	596	65	.244	.331
Nick Etten	1B150	L	27	151	540	78	168	27	4	14	79	82	33	9	.311	.454
Danny Murtaugh	2B85, SS1	R	23	85	347	34	76	8	1	0	11	26	31	18	.219	.248
Bobby Bragan	SS154, 2B2, 3B1	R	23	157	557	37	140	19	3	4	69	26	29	7	.251	.318
Pinky May	3B140	R	30	142	490	46	131	17	4	0	39	55	30	2	.267	.318
Stan Benjamin	OF110, 1B8, 2B2, 3B1	R	27	129	480	47	113	20	7	3	27	20	81	17	.235	.325
Joe Marty	OF132	R	27	137	477	60	128	19	3	8	39	51	41	6	.268	.371
Danny Litwhiler	OF150	R	24	151	590	72	180	29	6	18	66	39	43	1	.305	.466
Bennie Warren	C110	R	29	121	345	34	74	13	2	9	35	44	66	0	.214	.342
Johnny Rizzo	OF62, 3B2	R	28	99	235	20	51	9	0	4	24	24	34	1	.217	.323
Mickey Livingston	C71, 1B1	R	26	95	207	16	42	6	1	0	18	20	38	2	.203	.242
Emmett Mueller (BG)	2B29, OF21, 3B19	B	28	93	233	21	53	11	1	1	22	22	24	2	.227	.296
Hal Marnie	2B39, SS16, 3B3	R	22	61	158	12	38	3	0	0	11	13	25	0	.241	.297
Chuck Klein	OF14	L	36	50	73	6	9	0	0	1	3	10	6	0	.123	.164
Bill Nagel	2B12, OF2, 3B1	R	25	17	56	2	8	1	1	0	6	3	14	0	.143	.196
Jim Carlin	OF9, 3B2	L	25	16	21	2	3	1	0	1	2	3	4	0	.143	.333
Bill Harman	C5, P5	R	22	15	14	1	1	0	0	0	0	0	3	0	.071	.071
Paul Busby	OF3	L	22	10	16	3	5	0	1	0	0	3	5	0	.313	.313

George Jumonville 24 R 3-7, Wally Millies 34 R 0-2

NAME	T	AGE	W	L	PCT	SV	G	GS	CG	IP	H	BB	SO	SHO	ERA
		28	43	111	.279	9	155	155	35	1372	1499	606	552	4	4.50
Johnny Padgajny	R	21	9	12	.429	0	34	24	8	181	191	70	53	0	4.62
Tommy Hughes	R	21	9	14	.391	0	34	24	5	170	187	82	59	2	4.45
Cy Blanton	R	32	6	13	.316	0	28	25	7	164	186	57	64	1	4.50
Si Johnson	R	34	5	12	.294	2	39	21	6	163	207	54	80	1	4.53
Ike Pearson	R	24	4	14	.222	6	46	10	0	136	139	70	38	0	3.57
Frank Hoerst	L	23	3	10	.231	0	37	11	1	106	111	50	33	0	5.18
1 Bill Crouch	R	30	2	3	.400	1	20	5	1	59	65	17	26	0	4.42
2 Lee Grissom	L	33	2	13	.133	0	29	18	2	131	120	70	74	0	3.99
Paul Masterson	L	25	1	0	1.000	0	3	1	1	11	11	6	8	0	4.91
Rube Melton	R	24	1	5	.167	0	25	5	2	84	81	47	57	0	4.71
Boom-Boom Beck	R	36	1	9	.100	0	34	7	2	95	104	35	34	0	4.64
1 Vito Tamulis	L	29	0	1	.000	0	10	1	0	12	21	7	5	0	9.00
Dale Jones	R	22	0	1	.000	0	2	1	0	8	13	6	2	0	7.88
Gene Lambert	L	20	0	1	.000	0	2	1	0	9	11	2	2	0	3.00
Roy Bruner (MS)	R	24	0	3	.000	0	13	1	0	29	37	25	13	0	4.97
Bill Harman	R	22	0	0	—	0	5	0	0	13	15	8	3	0	4.85

Hugh Mulcahy (MS) 27

WORLD SERIES — NEW YORK (AL) 4 BROOKLYN (NL) 1

LINE SCORES

TEAM	1 2 3	4 5 6	7 8 9	10 11 12	R	H	E
Game 1 October 1 at New York							
BKN (NL)	0 0 0	0 1 0	1 0 0		2	6	0
NY (AL)	0 1 0	1 0 1	0 0 X		3	6	1

Davis, Casey (6), Allen (7) — Ruffing

TEAM	1 2 3	4 5 6	7 8 9	10 11 12	R	H	E
Game 2 October 2 at New York							
BKN	0 0 0	0 2 1	0 0 0		3	6	2
NY	0 1 1	0 0 0	0 0 0		2	9	1

Wyatt — Chandler, Murphy (6)

TEAM	1 2 3	4 5 6	7 8 9	10 11 12	R	H	E
Game 3 October 4 at Brooklyn							
NY	0 0 0	0 0 0	0 2 0		2	8	0
BKN	0 0 0	0 0 0	0 1 0		1	4	0

Russo — Fitzsimmons, Casey (8), French (8) — Allen

TEAM	1 2 3	4 5 6	7 8 9	10 11 12	R	H	E
Game 4 October 5 at Brooklyn							
NY	1 0 0	2 0 0	0 0 4		7	12	0
BKN	0 0 0	2 2 0	0 0 0		4	9	1

Donald, Breuer (5), Murphy (8) — Higbe, French (4), Allen (5), Casey (5)

TEAM	1 2 3	4 5 6	7 8 9	10 11 12	R	H	E
Game 5 October 6 at Brooklyn							
NY	0 2 0	0 1 0	0 0 0		3	6	0
BKN	0 0 1	0 0 0	0 0 0		1	4	1

Bonham — Wyatt

COMPOSITE BATTING

NAME	POS	G	AB	R	H	2B	3B	HR	RBI	BA
New York (AL) Totals		5	166	17	41	5	1	2	16	.247
Sturm	1B	5	21	0	6	0	0	0	2	.286
Rolfe	3B	5	20	2	6	0	0	0	0	.300
DiMaggio	OF	5	19	1	5	0	0	0	1	.263
Keller	OF	5	18	5	7	2	0	0	5	.389
Henrich	OF	5	18	4	3	1	0	1	1	.167
Dickey	C	5	18	3	3	1	0	0	1	.167
Rizzuto	SS	5	18	0	2	0	0	0	0	.111
Gordon	2B	5	14	2	7	1	1	1	5	.500
Bonham	P	1	4	0	0	0	0	0	0	.000
Russo	P	1	4	0	0	0	0	0	0	.000
Ruffing	P	1	3	0	1	0	0	0	1	.333
Chandler	P	1	2	0	1	0	0	0	1	.500
Selkirk	PH	2	2	0	1	0	0	0	0	.500
Murphy	P	2	2	0	0	0	0	0	0	.000
Donald	P	1	2	0	0	0	0	0	0	.000
Bruuer	P	1	1	0	0	0	0	0	0	.000
Rosar	C	1	0	0	0	0	0	0	0	—
Bordagary	PR	1	0	0	0	0	0	0	0	—
Brooklyn (NL) Totals		5	159	11	29	7	2	1	11	.182
Reiser	OF	5	20	1	4	1	1	1	3	.200
Reese	SS	5	20	1	4	0	0	0	0	.200
Walker	OF	5	18	3	4	2	0	0	0	.222
Camilli	1B	5	18	1	3	0	0	0	3	.167
Medwick	OF	5	17	1	4	1	0	0	0	.235
Owen	C	5	12	1	2	0	0	0	2	.167
Lavagetto	3B	3	10	1	1	0	0	0	0	.100
Riggs	3B	2	8	0	2	1	0	0	0	.250
Herman	2B	4	8	0	1	0	0	0	0	.125
Coscarart	2B	3	7	1	0	0	0	0	0	.000
Wyatt	P	2	6	1	1	0	0	0	1	.167
Wasdell	OF	3	5	0	1	1	0	0	2	.200
Casey	P	3	2	0	0	0	0	0	0	.000
Galan	PH	2	2	0	0	0	0	0	0	.000
Davis	P	1	2	0	0	0	0	0	0	.000
Fitzsimmons	P	1	2	0	0	0	0	0	0	.000
Higbe	P	2	1	0	1	0	0	0	0	1.000
Franks	C	1	1	0	0	0	0	0	0	.000
Allen	P	3	0	0	0	0	0	0	0	—
French	P	2	0	0	0	0	0	0	0	—

COMPOSITE PITCHING

NAME	G	IP	H	BB	SO	W	L	SV	ERA
New York (AL) Totals	5	45	29	14	21	4	1	0	1.80
Bonham	1	9	4	2	5	1	0	0	1.00
Ruffing	1	9	6	3	5	1	0	0	1.00
Russo	1	9	4	2	5	1	0	0	1.00
Murphy	2	6	2	1	3	1	0	0	0.00
Chandler	1	5	4	2	2	0	1	0	3.60
Donald	1	4	6	3	2	0	0	0	9.00
Breuer	1	3	3	1	2	0	0	0	0.00
Brooklyn (NL) Totals	5	44	41	23	18	1	4	0	2.66
Wyatt	2	18	15	10	14	1	1	0	2.50
Fitzsimmons	1	7	4	3	1	0	0	0	0.00
Casey	3	5.1	9	2	3	0	2	0	3.38
Davis	1	5.1	6	3	1	0	1	0	5.06
Allen	3	3.2	1	3	0	0	0	0	0.00
Higbe	2	3.2	6	2	1	0	0	0	7.36
French	2	1	0	0	0	0	0	0	0.00

1942 Branch Rickey and His Victory Garden

Branch Rickey made his reputation at St. Louis by providing homegrown ball players to fill the Cardinal lineup. While other teams usually purchased young, but seasoned, talent from independent minor league clubs, Rickey decided to develop a farm system where green talent could be inexpensively signed by Cardinal scouts and then nurtured on St. Louis-owned farm clubs. The success of the Mahatma's scheme manifested itself in the bumper crop of young talent which arrived in St. Louis in this first war year. A 21-year-old left-hand batter, whose stance at the plate resembled a corkscrew, hit .315 while holding down the left field spot, his name, Stan Musial. Enos Slaughter and Terry Moore were established stars in the other two garden posts, but the main outfield reserve was another young batting student, Harry "the Hat" Walker. Whitey Kurowski came up to furnish another big bat in the lineup, and Johnny Beazley won 21 games as the farm system's representative on the mound staff. Marty Marion and the Cooper brothers, Walker and Mort, lent stability to the squad with Mort on the throwing end of the battery and brother combination, especially shining by winning 22 games and picking up the league's MVP Award.

The Brooklyn Dodgers, nevertheless, seemed sure to repeat as pennant winners when they held a 10 1/2 game edge over the Birds in mid-August. But after sweeping a doubleheader from Brooklyn on August 4, the Cardinals caught fire, and the youthful squad went on to win 43 of its final 51 contests. Brooklyn held on as best it could in the face of the onslaught, yet soon found they were unable to keep pace. A St. Louis sweep of a two-game series at Ebbets Field in mid-September pulled the Cardinals into a first-place tie. The flying Redbirds then took the undisputed lead on September 13, and held it the rest of the way, despite a spirited fight from the Dodgers.

While Mort Cooper monopolized the league pitching honors, all the hitting awards went to players on also-ran teams. Boston's Ernie Lombardi, by hitting the ball harder than anyone else in captivity, won the batting title despite having a pair of cast iron legs. Giant skipper Mel Ott led the loop with 30 home runs, and new teammate Johnny Mize paced all sluggers with 110 runs batted in.

Joe McCarthy's Yankees served early notice on the American League that they planned to retain their crown, and proved it by seizing a quick lead that no one could whittle down all year. Finishing with a nine-game bulge over the runner-up Red Sox, the Yankees packed plenty of wallop as Joe DiMaggio, Charlie Keller, and Joe Gordon all knocked in over 100 tallies. The defense down the middle was impeccable, with DiMaggio in center field, Gordon and Phil Rizzuto around second, and veteran Bill Dickey behind the plate. As if that weren't enough, Tiny Bonham, Spud Chandler, and Hank Borowy gave the Bronx Bombers the best starting pitching in the loop, and Johnny Murphy the best relief pitching with a league-leading 11 saves.

The second-place Red Sox monopolized the individual honors, as Ted Williams followed up his .406 mark in 1941 by winning the Triple Crown with a .356 average, 36 homers, and 137 RBI's, and Tex Hughson led all pitchers with 22 wins. Despite Williams' marks, he was again denied the MVP Award, as it was given to the Yankees' Gordon for his "batting and fielding excellence".

The Yankees tabbed 37-year-old Red Ruffing to start the Series, and the veteran hurler did not allow a Cardinal hit until the eighth inning, as New York took the opener, 7-4. But the loss did nothing to dampen the Cardinals' spirit as they scored their four runs in the ninth inning and then swept the next four tilts behind the batting of Slaughter and Walker Cooper and Beazley's two complete games. This was to be the only Series loss McCarthy would suffer as manager of the Yankees.

After the season, more players started being drafted and began enlisting in the armed forces. Although the Cardinals, with a farm system chock-full of young talent, figured to weather the war-absences better than most clubs, the man most responsible for their success decided not to stick around to enjoy the fruits of his labor. During the winter, Branch Rickey jumped to a new challenge as general manager of the rival Brooklyn Dodgers—a move that would have vast repercussions on the game of baseball.

1942 AMERICAN LEAGUE

NAME	G by Pos	B	AGE	G	AB	R	H	2B	3B	HR	RBI	BB	SO	SB	BA	SA
NEW YORK	**1st 103-51 .669**				JOE McCARTHY											
TOTALS			28	154	5305	801	1429	223	57	108	744	591	556	69	.269	.394
Buddy Hassett	1B132	L	30	132	538	80	153	16	6	5	48	32	16	5	.284	.364
Joe Gordon	2B147	R	27	147	538	88	173	29	4	18	103	79	95	12	.322	.491
Phil Rizzuto	SS144	R	24	144	553	79	157	24	7	4	68	44	40	22	.284	.374
Frankie Crosetti	3B62, SS8, 2B2	R	31	74	285	50	69	5	5	4	23	31	31	1	.242	.337
Tommy Henrich (MS)	OF119, 1B1	L	32	127	483	77	129	30	5	13	67	58	42	4	.267	.431
Joe DiMaggio	OF154	R	27	154	610	123	186	29	13	21	114	68	36	4	.305	.498
Charlie Keller	OF152	L	25	152	544	106	159	24	9	26	108	114	61	14	.292	.513
Bill Dickey (SJ)	C80	L	35	82	268	28	79	13	1	2	37	26	11	2	.295	.373
Red Rolfe (IL)	3B60	L	33	69	265	42	58	8	2	8	25	23	18	1	.219	.355
Buddy Rosar	C58	R	27	69	209	18	48	10	0	2	34	17	20	1	.230	.308
Jerry Priddy	3B35, 1B11, 2B8, SS3	R	22	59	189	23	53	9	2	2	28	31	27	0	.280	.381
George Selkirk	OF19	L	34	42	78	15	15	3	0	0	10	16	8	1	.192	.231
2 Rollie Hemsley	C29	R	35	31	85	12	25	3	1	0	15	5	9	1	.294	.353
3 Roy Cullenbine	OF19, 1B1	B	28	21	77	16	28	7	0	2	17	18	2	0	.364	.532
Tuck Stainback	OF3	R	30	15	10	0	2	0	0	0	0	0	0	0	.200	.200
Ed Levy	1B13	R	25	13	41	5	5	0	0	0	3	4	5	1	.122	.122
Ed Kearse	C11	R	26	11	26	2	5	0	0	0	2	3	1	1	.192	.192
1 Mike Chartak		L	26	5	5	0	0	0	0	0	0	0	0	0	.000	.000
BOSTON	**2nd 93-59 .612 9**				JOE CRONIN											
TOTALS			27	152	5248	761	1451	244	55	103	699	591	508	68	.276	.403
Tony Lupien	1B121	L	25	128	463	63	130	25	7	3	70	50	20	10	.281	.384
Bobby Doerr	2B142	R	24	144	545	71	158	35	5	15	102	67	55	4	.290	.455
Johnny Pesky	SS147	L	22	147	620	105	205	29	9	2	51	42	36	12	.331	.416
Jim Tabor	3B138	R	28	139	508	56	128	18	2	12	75	37	47	6	.252	.366
Lou Finney	OF95, 1B21	L	31	113	397	58	113	16	7	3	61	29	11	3	.285	.383
Dom DiMaggio	OF151	R	25	151	622	110	178	36	8	14	48	70	52	16	.286	.437
Ted Williams	OF150	L	23	150	522	141	186	34	5	36	137	145	51	3	.356	.648
Bill Conroy	C83	R	27	83	250	22	50	4	2	4	20	40	47	2	.200	.280
Johnny Peacock	C82	L	32	82	286	17	76	7	3	0	25	21	11	1	.266	.311
Pete Fox	OF71	R	32	77	256	42	67	15	5	3	42	20	28	8	.262	.395
Joe Cronin	3B11, 1B5, SS1	R	35	45	79	7	24	3	0	4	24	15	11	0	.304	.494
1 Jimmie Foxx	1B27	R	34	30	100	18	27	4	0	5	14	18	15	0	.270	.460
Skeeter Newsome	3B12, 2B10, SS7	R	31	29	95	7	26	6	0	0	9	9	5	2	.274	.337
Paul Campbell	OF4	L	24	26	15	4	1	0	0	0	1	0	1	1	.067	.067
Andy Gilbert	OF5	R	27	6	11	0	1	0	0	0	1	1	3	0	.091	.091
Tom Carey	2B1	R	33	1	1	0	1	0	0	0	1	0	0	0	1.000	1.000
ST. LOUIS	**3rd 82-69 .543 19.5**				LUKE SEWELL											
TOTALS			28	151	5229	730	1354	239	62	98	688	609	607	37	.259	.385
George McQuinn	1B144	L	33	145	554	86	145	32	5	12	78	60	77	1	.262	.403
Don Gutteridge	2B145, 3B2	R	29	147	616	90	157	27	11	1	50	59	54	16	.255	.339
Vern Stephens	SS144	R	21	145	575	84	169	26	6	14	92	41	53	1	.294	.433
Harland Clift	3B141, SS1	R	29	143	541	108	148	39	4	7	55	106	48	6	.274	.399
Chet Laabs	OF139	R	30	144	520	90	143	21	7	27	99	88	88	0	.275	.498
Walt Judnich	OF122	L	26	132	457	78	143	22	6	17	82	74	41	3	.313	.499
Glenn McQuillen	OF77	R	27	100	339	40	96	15	12	3	47	10	17	1	.283	.425
Rick Ferrell	C95	R	36	99	273	20	61	6	1	0	26	33	13	0	.223	.253
Tony Criscola	OF52	L	26	91	158	17	47	9	2	1	13	8	13	2	.297	.399
3 Mike Chartak	OF64	L	26	73	237	37	59	11	2	9	43	40	27	3	.249	.426
2 Frankie Hayes	C51	R	27	56	159	14	40	6	0	2	17	28	39	0	.252	.327
1 Roy Cullenbine	OF27, 1B5	B	28	38	109	15	21	7	1	2	14	30	20	0	.193	.330
Johnny Berardino (MS)	SS6, 3B6, 1B5, 2B4	R	25	29	74	11	21	6	0	1	10	4	2	3	.284	.405
1 Bob Swift	C28	R	27	29	76	3	15	4	0	1	6	5	7	0	.197	.289
Don Heffner	2B6, 1B4	R	31	19	36	4	6	2	0	0	1	7	3	0	.167	.222
Alan Strange	3B10, SS3, 2B1	R	35	19	37	3	10	2	0	0	5	3	7	0	.270	.324
2 Luke Sewell	C6	R	41	6	12	1	1	1	0	0	1	1	5	0	.083	.083
2 Babe Dahlgren		R	30	2	1	0	0	0	0	0	0	0	1	0	.000	.000
Ray Hayworth		R	38	1	1	0	1	0	0	0	0	0	0	0	1.000	1.000

NAME	T	AGE	W	L	PCT	SV	G	GS	CG	IP	H	BB	SO	SHO	ERA
		30	103	51	.669	17	154	154	88	1375	1259	431	558	18	2.91
Ernie Bonham	R	28	21	5	.808	0	28	27	22	226	199	24	71	6	2.27
Spud Chandler	R	34	16	5	.762	0	24	24	17	201	176	74	74	3	2.37
Hank Borowy	R	26	15	4	.789	1	25	21	13	178	157	66	85	4	2.53
Red Ruffing	R	38	14	7	.667	0	24	24	16	194	183	41	80	4	3.20
Atley Donald	R	31	11	3	.786	0	20	19	10	148	133	45	53	1	3.10
Marv Breuer	R	28	8	9	.471	1	27	19	6	164	157	37	72	0	3.07
Lefty Gomez	L	33	6	4	.600	0	13	13	2	80	67	65	41	0	4.28
Marius Russo (SA)	L	27	4	1	.800	0	9	5	2	45	41	14	15	0	2.80
Johnny Murphy	R	33	4	10	.286	11	31	0	0	58	66	23	24	0	3.41
Johnny Lindell	R	25	2	1	.667	1	23	2	0	53	52	22	28	0	3.74
Mel Queen	R	24	1	0	1.000	0	4	0	0	6	6	3	0	0	0.00
2 Jim Turner	R	38	1	1	.500	1	5	0	0	7	4	1	2	0	1.29
Norm Branch (MS)	R	27	0	1	.000	2	10	0	0	16	18	16	13	0	6.19
		30	93	59	.612	17	152	152	84	1359	1260	553	500	11	3.44
Tex Hughson	R	26	22	6	.786	4	38	30	22	281	258	75	113	4	2.59
Charlie Wagner	R	29	14	11	.560	2	29	26	17	205	184	95	52	2	3.29
Joe Dobson	R	25	11	9	.550	0	30	23	10	183	155	68	72	3	3.30
Mace Brown	R	33	9	3	.750	6	34	0	0	60	56	28	20	0	3.45
Oscar Judd	L	34	8	10	.444	2	31	19	11	150	135	90	70	0	3.90
Dick Newsome	R	32	8	10	.444	0	24	23	11	158	174	67	40	0	5.01
Bill Butland	R	24	7	1	.875	1	23	10	6	111	85	33	46	2	2.51
Yank Terry	R	31	6	5	.545	1	20	11	3	85	82	43	37	0	3.92
Ken Chase	L	28	5	1	.833	1	13	10	4	80	82	41	37	0	3.83
Mike Ryba	R	39	3	2	.500	3	18	0	0	44	49	13	16	0	3.89
		32	82	69	.543	13	151	151	68	1363	1387	505	488	12	3.59
Johnny Niggeling	R	38	15	11	.577	0	28	27	16	206	173	93	107	3	2.67
Elden Auker	R	31	14	13	.519	0	35	34	17	249	273	86	62	2	4.08
Denny Galehouse	R	30	12	12	.500	1	32	28	12	192	193	79	75	3	3.61
Al Hollingsworth	L	34	10	6	.625	4	33	18	7	161	173	52	60	1	2.96
George Caster	R	34	8	2	.800	5	39	0	0	80	62	39	34	0	2.81
2 Steve Sundra	R	32	8	3	.727	0	20	13	6	111	122	29	36	0	3.81
Bob Muncrief	R	26	8	4	.429	0	24	18	7	134	149	31	39	1	3.90
Fritz Ostermueller	L	24	3	1	.750	0	14	4	4	46	41	21	13	0	3.68
Stan Ferens	L	27	3	4	.429	0	19	3	1	69	76	21	23	0	3.78
2 Pete Appleton	R	38	1	1	.500	2	14	0	0	21	15	11	12	0	3.00
Loy Hanning	R	24	1	1	.500	0	11	0	0	17	26	12	9	0	7.94
1 Bob Harris	R	27	1	5	.167	0	6	5	3	34	37	17	9	0	5.56
Frank Biscan (MS)	R	22	0	1	.000	1	11	0	0	27	13	11	10	0	2.33
1 Bill Trotter	R	33	0	1	.000	0	3	0	0	5	8	1	0	0	18.00
John Whitehead	R	33	0	1	—	0	3	0	0	4	5	4	1	0	6.75
Ewald Pyle	L	31	0	0	—	0	1	0	0	5	6	4	1	0	7.20
Jack Kramer (WW) 24															

CLEVELAND — 4th 75-79 .487 28 — LOU BOUDREAU

NAME	G by Pos	B	AGE	G	AB	R	H	2B	3B	HR	RBI	BB	SO	SB	BA	SA
TOTALS			28	156	5317	590	1344	223	58	50	541	500	544	69	.253	.345
Les Fleming	1B156	L	26	156	548	71	160	27	4	14	82	106	57	6	.292	.432
Ray Mack	2B143	R	25	143	481	43	108	14	6	2	45	41	51	5	.225	.291
Lou Boudreau	SS146	R	24	147	506	57	143	18	10	2	58	75	39	7	.283	.370
Ken Keltner	3B151	R	25	152	624	72	179	34	4	6	78	20	36	4	.287	.383
Oris Hockett	OF145	L	32	148	601	85	150	22	7	7	48	45	45	12	.250	.344
Roy Weatherly	OF117	L	27	143	473	61	122	23	7	5	39	35	25	8	.258	.368
Jeff Heath	OF146	L	27	147	568	82	158	37	13	10	76	62	66	9	.278	.442
Otto Denning	C78, OF2	R	29	92	214	51	45	14	0	1	19	18	14	0	.210	.290
Buster Mills	OF53	R	33	80	195	19	54	4	2	1	26	23	18	5	.277	.333
Chubby Dean	P27	L	26	70	101	4	27	1	0	0	7	11	7	0	.267	.277
Jim Hegan	C66	R	21	68	170	10	33	5	0	0	11	11	31	1	.194	.224
Gene Desautels (BN)	C61	R	35	62	162	14	40	5	0	0	9	12	13	1	.247	.278
Oscar Grimes	2B24, 3B8, 1B1, SS1	R	27	51	84	10	15	2	0	0	2	13	17	3	.179	.202
Fabian Gaffke	OF16	R	28	40	67	4	11	2	0	0	3	6	13	1	.164	.194
Rusty Peters	SS24, 2B1, 3B1	R	27	34	58	6	13	5	1	0	2	2	14	0	.224	.345
Hank Edwards	OF12	L	23	13	48	6	12	2	1	0	7	5	8	2	.250	.333
Eddie Robinson	1B1	L	21	8	8	1	1	0	0	0	2	1	0	0	.125	.125
Bob Lemon	3B1	L	21	5	5	0	0	0	0	0	1	0	3	0	.000	.000
Ted Sepkowski	2B2	L	18	5	10	0	1	0	0	0	0	0	1	0	.100	.100
George Susce	C2	R	34	2	1	1	1	0	0	0	0	0	1	0	1.000	1.000
Hal Trosky (IL) 29																

NAME	T	AGE	W	L	PCT	SV	G	GS	CG	IP	H	BB	SO	SHO	ERA
TOTALS		30	75	79	.487	11	156	156	61	1403	1353	560	448	12	3.59
Jim Bagby	R	30	17	9	.654	1	38	35	16	271	267	64	54	4	2.96
Mel Harder	R	32	13	14	.481	1	29	29	13	199	179	82	74	4	3.44
Al Smith	L	34	10	15	.400	0	30	24	7	168	163	71	66	1	3.96
Chubby Dean	L	26	8	11	.421	1	27	27	8	173	170	66	46	0	3.80
Al Milnar	R	28	6	8	.429	0	28	19	8	157	146	85	35	2	4.13
Joe Heving	R	41	5	3	.625	3	27	2	0	46	52	25	13	0	4.89
Vern Kennedy	R	35	4	8	.333	1	28	12	4	108	99	50	37	0	4.08
Tom Ferrick	R	27	3	2	.600	3	31	0	0	81	56	32	28	0	2.00
Red Embree	R	24	3	4	.429	0	19	6	2	63	58	31	44	0	3.86
Steve Gromek	R	22	2	0	1.000	0	14	0	0	44	46	23	14	0	3.68
Harry Eisenstat	L	26	2	1	.667	2	29	1	0	48	58	6	19	0	2.44
Clint Brown	R	38	1	1	.500	0	7	0	0	9	16	2	4	0	6.00
Ray Poat	R	24	1	3	.250	0	4	1	0	18	24	9	8	1	5.50
Joe Krakauskas	L	27	0	0	—	0	2	0	0	7	7	4	2	0	3.86
Allie Reynolds	R	27	0	0	—	0	2	0	0	5	5	4	2	0	0.00
Paul Calvert	R	24	0	0	—	0	1	0	0	3	7	4	0	0	18.00
Pete Center	R	20	0	0	—	0	1	0	0	3	7	4	0	0	18.00

DETROIT — 5th 73-81 .474 30 — DEL BAKER

NAME	G by Pos	B	AGE	G	AB	R	H	2B	3B	HR	RBI	BB	SO	SB	BA	SA
TOTALS			27	156	5327	589	1313	217	37	76	548	509	476	39	.246	.344
Rudy York	1B152	R	28	153	577	81	150	26	4	21	90	73	71	3	.260	.428
Jimmy Bloodworth	2B134, SS2	R	24	137	533	62	129	23	4	13	57	35	63	3	.242	.362
Billy Hitchcock	SS80, 3B1	R	25	87	280	27	59	8	1	0	29	26	21	2	.211	.246
Pinky Higgins	3B137	R	33	143	499	65	133	34	2	11	79	72	21	3	.267	.409
Ned Harris	OF104	L	25	121	398	53	108	16	10	9	45	49	35	5	.271	.430
Doc Cramer	OF150	L	36	151	630	71	166	26	4	0	43	43	18	4	.263	.317
Barney McCosky	OF154	L	25	154	600	75	176	28	11	7	50	68	37	11	.293	.412
Birdie Tebbetts	C97	R	29	99	308	24	76	11	0	1	27	39	17	4	.247	.292
Don Ross	OF38, 3B20	R	27	87	226	29	62	10	2	3	30	36	16	2	.274	.376
Dixie Parsons	C62	R	26	63	188	8	37	4	0	2	11	13	22	1	.197	.250
Rip Radcliff	OF24, 1B4	L	36	62	144	13	36	5	0	1	20	9	6	0	.250	.306
Murray Franklin	SS32, 2B7	R	28	48	154	24	40	7	0	2	16	7	5	0	.260	.344
Charlie Gehringer (MS)	2B3	L	39	45	45	6	12	0	0	1	7	7	4	0	.267	.333
Johnny Lipon	SS34	R	19	34	131	5	25	0	0	0	9	7	7	1	.191	.206
Eric McNair	SS21	R	33	26	68	5	11	2	0	1	4	3	6	0	.162	.235
Dutch Meyer	2B14	R	26	14	52	5	17	3	0	2	9	4	4	0	.327	.500
Hank Riebe	C11	R	20	11	35	1	11	2	0	0	2	0	6	0	.314	.371
Bob Patrick (BK)	OF3	R	24	4	8	1	2	1	0	1	3	1	0	0	.250	.750
Al Unser	C4	R	29	4	24	3	9	0	0	0	0	0	2	0	.375	.375

NAME	T	AGE	W	L	PCT	SV	G	GS	CG	IP	H	BB	SO	SHO	ERA
TOTALS		27	73	81	.474	14	156	156	65	1399	1321	598	671	12	3.13
Virgil Trucks	R	23	14	8	.636	0	28	20	8	168	147	74	91	2	2.73
Hal White	R	23	12	12	.500	1	34	25	12	217	212	82	93	4	2.90
Dizzy Trout	R	27	12	18	.400	0	35	29	13	223	214	89	91	1	3.43
Tommy Bridges	R	35	9	7	.563	1	23	22	11	174	164	61	97	2	2.74
Hal Newhouser	L	21	8	14	.364	5	38	23	11	184	137	114	103	1	2.45
Al Benton	R	31	7	13	.350	2	35	30	9	227	210	84	110	1	2.89
Johnny Gorsica	R	27	3	2	.600	4	28	0	0	53	63	26	19	0	4.75
Charley Fuchs	R	28	3	3	.500	0	9	4	1	37	43	19	15	1	6.57
Hal Manders	R	25	2	1	1.000	0	18	0	0	33	39	15	14	0	4.09
Roy Henshaw	L	30	2	4	.333	1	23	2	0	62	63	27	24	0	4.06
1 Schoolboy Rowe	R	32	1	0	1.000	0	2	1	0	10	9	2	7	0	0.00
2 Jack Wilson	R	30	0	0	—	0	3	0	0	13	20	5	7	0	4.85

CHICAGO — 6th 66-82 .446 34 — JIMMY DYKES

NAME	G by Pos	B	AGE	G	AB	R	H	2B	3B	HR	RBI	BB	SO	SB	BA	SA
TOTALS			30	148	4949	538	1215	214	36	25	487	497	427	114	.246	.318
Joe Kuhel	1B112	L	36	115	413	60	103	14	4	4	52	60	22	22	.249	.332
Don Kolloway	2B116, 1B33	R	23	147	601	72	164	40	4	3	60	30	39	16	.273	.368
Luke Appling	SS141	R	35	142	543	78	142	26	4	3	53	63	23	17	.262	.341
Bob Kennedy (MS)	3B96, OF16	R	21	113	412	37	95	18	5	0	38	22	41	11	.231	.299
Wally Moses	OF145	L	31	146	577	73	156	28	4	7	49	74	27	16	.270	.369
Myril Hoag	OF112	R	34	113	412	47	99	18	2	2	37	36	21	17	.240	.308
Taffy Wright	OF81	L	30	85	300	43	100	13	5	0	47	48	9	1	.333	.410
Mike Tresh	C72	R	28	72	233	21	54	8	1	0	15	28	24	2	.232	.275
Dario Lodigiani	3B43, 2B7	R	26	59	168	9	47	7	0	0	15	18	10	3	.280	.321
George Dickey (MS)	C29	B	26	59	116	6	27	3	0	1	17	9	11	0	.233	.284
Tom Turner	C54	R	25	56	182	18	44	9	1	3	21	19	15	0	.242	.352
Sammy West	OF45	L	37	49	151	14	35	5	0	0	25	31	18	2	.232	.265
Leo Wells	SS12, 3B6	R	24	35	62	8	12	2	0	1	4	4	5	1	.194	.274
Skeeter Webb	2B29	R	32	32	94	5	16	2	1	0	4	4	13	1	.170	.213
Bill Mueller	OF26	R	21	26	85	5	14	1	0	0	5	12	9	2	.165	.176
Val Heim (MS)	OF12	L	21	13	45	6	9	1	1	0	7	5	3	1	.200	.267
Bud Sketchley	OF12	L	23	13	36	1	7	1	0	0	3	7	4	0	.194	.222
Jimmy Grant	3B10	L	23	12	36	0	6	1	1	0	1	5	6	0	.167	.250
Jake Jones (MS)	1B5	R	21	7	20	2	3	1	0	0	0	2	4	0	.150	.200
Thruman Tucker	OF5	L	24	7	24	2	3	0	1	0	0	0	4	1	.125	.208
Moose Solters (VR) 36																

NAME	T	AGE	W	L	PCT	SV	G	GS	CG	IP	H	BB	SO	SHO	ERA
TOTALS		30	66	82	.446	8	148	148	86	1314	1304	473	432	8	3.58
Ted Lyons	R	41	14	6	.700	0	20	20	20	180	167	26	50	1	2.10
John Humphries	R	27	12	12	.500	2	28	28	17	228	227	59	71	2	2.68
Joe Haynes	R	24	8	5	.615	6	40	1	1	106	88	47	35	0	2.62
Eddie Smith	L	28	7	20	.259	1	29	28	18	215	223	86	78	2	3.98
Bill Dietrich	R	32	6	11	.353	0	26	23	6	160	173	70	39	0	4.89
Jake Wade	L	30	5	5	.500	0	15	10	3	86	84	56	32	0	4.08
Buck Ross	R	27	5	7	.417	1	22	14	4	113	118	39	37	2	5.02
Orval Grove (KJ)	R	22	4	6	.400	0	12	8	4	66	77	33	21	0	5.18
Johnny Rigney (MS)	R	27	3	3	.500	0	7	7	6	59	40	16	34	0	3.20
Thornton Lee	L	35	2	6	.250	0	11	8	6	76	82	31	25	1	3.32
Len Perme	L	24	1	0	1.000	0	4	1	1	13	5	4	4	0	1.38
Ed Weiland	R	27	0	0	—	0	5	0	0	10	18	3	4	0	7.20
1 Pete Appleton	R	38	0	0	—	0	4	0	0	5	2	3	2	0	3.60

WASHINGTON — 7th 62-89 .411 39.5 — BUCKY HARRIS

NAME	G by Pos	B	AGE	G	AB	R	H	2B	3B	HR	RBI	BB	SO	SB	BA	SA
TOTALS			26	151	5295	653	1364	224	49	40	593	581	536	98	.258	.341
Mickey Vernon	1B151	L	24	151	621	76	168	34	6	9	86	39	63	25	.271	.388
Ellis Clary	2B69, 3B2	R	25	76	240	34	66	9	0	0	16	45	25	2	.275	.313
John Sullivan	SS92	R	21	94	357	38	84	16	1	0	42	25	30	2	.235	.286
Bobby Estalella	3B78, OF36	R	31	133	429	68	119	24	5	8	65	85	42	5	.277	.413
Bruce Campbell (MS)	OF87	L	32	122	378	41	105	17	5	5	63	37	34	0	.278	.389
Stan Spence	OF149	L	27	149	629	94	203	27	15	4	79	62	16	5	.323	.432
George Case	OF120	R	26	125	513	101	164	26	2	5	43	44	30	44	.320	.407
Jake Early	C98	L	27	104	353	31	72	14	2	3	46	37	37	0	.204	.280
Jimmy Pofahl	SS49, 2B15, 3B14	R	25	84	283	22	59	7	2	0	28	29	30	4	.208	.247
Bob Repass	2B33, 3B29, SS11	R	24	81	259	30	62	11	1	2	23	33	30	6	.239	.313
Al Evans	C67	R	25	74	223	22	51	4	1	0	10	25	36	3	.229	.256
2 Roy Cullenbine	OF35, 3B28	B	28	64	241	30	69	19	0	2	35	44	18	1	.286	.390
Frank Croucher (SA)	2B18	R	27	26	65	2	18	1	1	0	5	3	9	0	.277	.323
Chile Gomez	2B23, 3B1	R	33	25	73	8	14	2	2	0	6	9	7	1	.192	.274
2 Mike Chartak	OF24	L	26	24	92	11	20	4	2	1	8	14	16	0	.217	.337
Roberto Ortiz	OF9	R	27	20	42	4	7	3	1	1	4	5	11	0	.167	.405
Stan Galle (MS)	3B3	R	23	13	18	3	2	0	0	0	0	3	6	0	.111	.111
Ray Hoffman	3B6	R	25	7	19	2	1	0	0	0	1	0	5	0	.053	.053
Al Kvashak (MS)	OF3	L	21	5	11	3	2	1	0	0	0	2	3	0	.182	.182
Gene Moore	OF1	L	32	2	0	0	0	0	0	0	0	0	0	0	.000	.000

NAME	T	AGE	W	L	PCT	SV	G	GS	CG	IP	H	BB	SO	SHO	ERA
TOTALS		28	62	89	.411	11	151	151	68	1347	1496	558	496	12	4.58
1 Bobo Newsom	R	34	11	17	.393	0	30	29	15	214	236	92	113	2	4.92
Early Wynn	R	22	10	16	.385	0	30	28	10	190	246	73	58	1	5.12
Sid Hudson	R	29	10	17	.370	2	35	31	19	239	266	70	72	1	4.37
Bill Zuber	R	29	9	9	.500	1	37	7	3	127	115	82	64	1	3.83
Alex Carrasquel	R	29	7	7	.500	3	35	15	7	152	161	53	40	1	3.43
Walt Masterson	R	22	5	5	.357	2	25	15	8	143	138	54	63	4	3.34
2 Bill Trotter	R	33	3	1	.750	0	7	4	0	41	52	14	13	0	5.71
Ray Scarborough	R	24	2	1	.667	0	7	1	0	63	68	32	16	1	4.14
Dutch Leonard (BN)	R	33	2	2	.500	0	6	5	1	35	28	5	15	1	4.11
Hardin Cathey	R	22	1	1	.500	0	12	2	0	30	44	16	8	0	7.50
1 Steve Sundra	R	32	1	3	.250	0	6	4	2	34	43	15	5	0	5.56
1 Jack Wilson	R	30	1	4	.200	0	12	6	1	42	57	23	18	0	6.64
Bill Kennedy	L	23	0	1	.000	0	7	1	1	18	21	10	8	0	8.00
Lou Bevil	R	20	0	1	.000	0	1	0	0	9	11	2	6	0	6.00
Dewey Adkins	R	24	0	1	.000	0	1	0	0	6	13	4	3	0	10.50
Phil McCullough	R	24	0	0	—	0	1	0	0	2	6	1	0	0	6.00

PHILADELPHIA — 8th 55-99 .357 48 — CONNIE MACK

NAME	G by Pos	B	AGE	G	AB	R	H	2B	3B	HR	RBI	BB	SO	SB	BA	SA
TOTALS			29	154	5285	549	1315	213	46	33	517	440	490	44	.249	.325
Dick Siebert	1B152	L	30	153	612	57	159	25	7	2	74	24	17	4	.260	.333
Bill Knickerbocker (BG)	2B81, SS1	R	30	87	289	25	73	12	0	1	19	29	30	1	.253	.304
Pete Suder	SS69, 3B34, 2B31	R	26	128	476	46	122	20	4	4	54	24	39	4	.256	.340
Buddy Blair	3B126	L	31	137	484	48	135	26	8	5	66	30	30	1	.279	.397
Elmer Valo	OF122	L	21	133	459	64	115	13	10	2	40	70	21	13	.251	.336
Mike Kreevich	OF107	R	34	116	444	57	113	19	1	1	30	47	31	7	.255	.309
Bob Johnson	OF149	L	36	149	550	78	160	35	7	13	80	82	61	3	.291	.451
Hal Wagner	C94	L	26	104	288	26	68	17	1	0	30	24	29	1	.236	.313
Dee Miles	OF81	L	33	99	346	41	94	12	5	0	22	12	10	5	.272	.335
Crash Davis	2B57, SS26, 1B3	R	22	80	272	31	61	8	1	2	26	21	30	1	.224	.283
2 Bob Swift	C60	R	27	60	192	9	44	3	0	0	15	13	17	1	.229	.245
Jack Wallaesa	SS36	R	22	36	117	13	30	4	1	2	13	8	26	0	.256	.359
2 Eric McNair	SS29, 2B1	R	33	34	103	6	25	2	0	0	4	11	5	1	.243	.262
1 Frankie Hayes	C20	R	27	21	63	8	15	4	0	1	5	7	13	0	.238	.302
Eddie Collins (MS)	OF9	R	25	20	34	6	8	2	0	0	1	2	6	0	.235	.294
Jim Castiglia (MS)	C3	L	23	9	18	2	7	0	0	0	1	3	3	0	.389	.389
Larry Eschen	SS7, 2B1	R	21	12	11	0	0	0	0	0	0	4	1	0	.000	.000
Felix Mackiewicz	OF3	R	24	6	14	2	5	2	0	0	1	1	3	0	.214	.357
Ken Richardson	OF3, 1B1, 3B1	R	27	6	15	1	1	0	0	0	0	0	3	0	.067	.067
George Yankowski	C6	R	19	6	13	0	2	0	0	0	1	0	4	0	.154	.231
Bruce Konopka	1B3	L	22	5	10	0	3	0	0	0	0	0	5	0	.300	.300
Dick Adkins	SS3	R	22	3	7	2	1	0	0	0	0	1	1	0	.143	.143

NAME	T	AGE	W	L	PCT	SV	G	GS	CG	IP	H	BB	SO	SHO	ERA
TOTALS		27	55	99	.357	9	154	154	67	1375	1404	639	546	5	4.44
Phil Marchildon	R	28	17	14	.548	1	38	31	18	244	215	140	110	4	4.20
Roger Wolff	R	31	12	15	.444	3	32	25	15	214	206	69	94	2	3.32
Lum Harris	R	27	11	15	.423	0	35	26	10	266	246	70	60	1	3.74
Dick Fowler	R	21	6	11	.353	1	31	17	4	140	159	45	38	0	4.95
Russ Christopher	R	24	4	13	.235	1	31	18	10	165	154	99	58	0	3.82
Herman Besse	L	30	2	9	.182	1	30	14	4	133	163	69	78	0	6.50
Jack Knott (MS	R	35	2	10	.167	0	23	14	6	95	127	36	31	0	5.59
2 Bob Harris	R	27	1	5	.167	0	16	8	2	78	77	24	26	1	2.88
Tex Shirley	R	24	1	0	1.000	0	4	1	0	36	37	22	10	0	5.25
Bob Savage	R	20	0	1	.000	0	3	0	0	12	24	31	10	0	3.20
1 Bill Beckmann	R	34	0	1	.000	0	10	0	0	20	24	9	10	0	7.20
Joe Coleman	R	19	0	1	.000	0	7	0	0	3	6	3	0	0	3.00
Fred Caligiuri	R	23	0	3	.000	1	3	0	0	37	45	18	20	0	6.33
Tal Abernathy	L	20	0	1	.000	0	1	0	0	3	3	0	1	0	9.00
Sam Lowry	R	22	0	0	—	0	2	0	0	3	4	1	2	0	6.00
Les McCrabb	R	27	0	0	—	0	4	1	1	14	24	2	7	0	31.50

ST. LOUIS — 1ST 106-48 .688 — BILLY SOUTHWORTH

NAME	G by Pos	B	AGE	G	AB	R	H	2B	3B	HR	RBI	BB	SO	SB	BA	SA
TOTALS			26	156	5421	755	1454	282	69	60	682	551	507	71	.268	.379
Johnny Hopp	1B88	L	25	95	314	41	81	16	7	3	37	36	40	14	.258	.382
Creepy Crespi	2B83, SS5	R	24	93	292	33	71	4	2	0	35	27	29	4	.243	.271
Marty Marion	SS147	R	24	147	485	66	134	38	5	0	54	48	50	8	.276	.375
Whitey Kurowski	3B104, SS1, OF1	R	24	115	366	51	93	17	3	9	42	33	60	7	.254	.391
Enos Slaughter	OF151	L	26	152	591	100	188	31	17	13	98	88	30	9	.318	.494
Terry Moore	OF126, 3B1	R	30	130	489	80	141	26	3	6	49	56	26	10	.288	.391
Stan Musial	OF135	L	21	140	467	87	147	32	10	10	72	62	25	6	.315	.490
Walker Cooper	C115	R	27	125	438	58	123	32	7	7	65	29	29	4	.281	.434
Jimmy Brown	2B82, 3B66, SS12	B	32	145	606	75	155	28	4	1	71	52	11	4	.256	.320
Ray Sanders	1B77	L	25	95	282	37	71	17	2	5	39	42	31	2	.252	.379
Harry Walker	OF56, 2B2	L	25	74	191	38	60	12	2	0	16	11	14	2	.314	.398
Coaker Triplett	OF46	L	30	64	154	18	42	7	4	1	23	17	15	1	.273	.390
Ken O'Dea	C49	L	29	58	192	22	45	7	1	5	32	17	23	0	.234	.359
Buddy Blattner	SS13, 2B3	R	22	19	23	3	1	0	0	0	1	3	6	0	.043	.043
Erv Dusak	OF8, 3B1	R	21	12	27	4	5	3	0	0	3	3	7	0	.185	.296
Sam Narron	C2	R	28	10	10	0	4	0	0	0	1	0	0	0	.400	.400
Estel Crabtree		B	38	10	9	1	3	2	0	0	2	1	3	0	.333	.556
1 Gus Mancuso	C3	R	36	5	13	0	1	0	0	0	1	0	0	0	.077	.077
Jeff Cross	SS1	R	23	1	4	0	1	0	0	0	1	0	0	0	.250	.250

NAME	T	AGE	W	L	PCT	SV	G	GS	CG	IP	H	BB	SO	SHO	ERA
TOTALS		26	106	48	.688	15	156	156	70	1409	1192	473	651	18	2.55
Mort Cooper	R	29	22	7	.759	0	37	35	22	279	207	68	152	10	1.77
Johnny Beazley	R	24	21	6	.778	3	43	23	13	215	181	73	91	3	2.14
Howie Krist	R	26	13	3	.813	1	34	8	3	118	103	43	47	0	2.52
Max Lanier	L	26	13	8	.619	2	34	20	8	161	137	60	93	2	2.96
Harry Gumbert	R	32	9	5	.643	5	38	19	5	163	156	59	52	0	3.26
Howie Pollet	L	21	7	5	.583	0	27	13	5	109	102	39	42	2	2.89
Ernie White (SA)	L	25	7	5	.583	2	26	19	7	128	113	41	67	1	2.53
Murry Dickson	R	25	6	3	.667	3	36	7	2	121	91	61	66	0	2.90
1 Lon Warneke	R	33	6	4	.600	0	12	12	5	82	76	15	31	0	3.29
2 Bill Beckmann	R	34	1	0	1.000	0	2	0	0	7	4	1	3	0	0.00
1 Bill Lohrman	R	29	1	1	.500	0	5	0	0	13	11	2	6	0	1.39
2 Whitey Moore	R	30	0	0	.000	0	9	0	0	12	10	11	1	0	4.50
1 Clyde Shoun	L	30	0	0	—	0	2	0	0	2	1	0	0	0	0.00

BROOKLYN — 2nd 104-50 .675 2 — LEO DUROCHER

NAME	G by Pos	B	AGE	G	AB	R	H	2B	3B	HR	RBI	BB	SO	SB	BA	SA
TOTALS			29	155	5285	742	1398	263	34	62	678	572	484	79	.265	.362
Dolph Camilli	1B150	L	35	150	524	89	132	23	7	26	109	97	85	10	.252	.471
Billy Herman	2B153, 1B3	R	32	155	571	76	146	34	2	2	65	72	52	6	.256	.333
Pee Wee Reese	SS151	R	23	151	564	87	144	24	5	3	53	82	55	15	.255	.332
Arky Vaughan	3B119, SS5, 2B1	L	30	128	495	82	137	18	4	2	49	51	17	8	.277	.341
Dixie Walker	OF110	L	31	118	393	57	114	28	1	6	54	47	15	1	.290	.412
Pete Reiser (YJ)	OF125	L	23	125	480	89	149	33	5	10	64	48	45	20	.310	.463
Joe Medwick	OF140	R	30	142	553	69	166	37	4	4	96	32	25	2	.300	.403
Mickey Owen	C133	R	26	133	421	53	109	16	3	0	44	44	17	10	.259	.311
Johnny Rizzo	OF70	R	29	78	217	31	50	8	0	4	27	24	25	2	.230	.323
Lew Riggs	3B46, 1B1	L	32	70	180	20	50	5	0	3	22	13	9	0	.278	.356
Augie Galan	OF55, 1B4, 2B3	B	30	69	209	24	55	16	0	0	22	24	12	2	.263	.340
Frenchy Bordagaray	OF17	R	32	48	58	11	14	2	0	0	5	3	3	2	.241	.276
Billy Sullivan	C41	L	31	43	101	11	27	2	1	1	14	12	6	1	.267	.337
3 Babe Dahlgren	1B10	R	30	17	19	2	1	0	0	0	3	2	4	0	.053	.053
Alex Kampouris	2B9	R	29	10	21	3	5	2	1	0	3	4	4	0	.238	.429
Cliff Dapper	C8	R	22	8	17	2	8	1	0	1	9	2	2	0	.471	.706
Stan Rojek		R	23	1	0	0	0	0	0	0	0	0	0	0	—	—

NAME	T	AGE	W	L	PCT	SV	G	GS	CG	IP	H	BB	SO	SHO	ERA
TOTALS		31	104	50	.675	24	155	155	67	1399	1205	493	612	16	2.84
Whit Wyatt	R	34	19	7	.731	0	31	30	16	217	185	63	104	0	2.74
Kirby Higbe	R	27	16	11	.593	0	38	32	13	222	180	106	115	2	3.24
Larry French	L	34	15	4	.789	0	38	14	8	148	127	36	62	4	1.82
Curt Davis	R	38	15	6	.714	2	32	26	13	206	179	51	60	5	3.26
Ed Head	R	24	10	6	.625	4	36	15	5	137	118	47	78	1	3.55
Johnny Allen	R	37	10	6	.625	3	27	15	5	118	106	39	50	1	3.20
Hugh Casey	R	28	6	3	.667	13	50	2	0	112	91	44	54	0	2.25
Max Macon	L	26	5	3	.625	1	14	8	4	84	67	33	27	1	1.93
Les Webber	R	27	3	2	.600	1	19	3	1	52	46	22	23	0	2.94
Newt Kimball	R	27	2	0	1.000	0	14	1	0	29	27	19	8	0	3.72
2 Bobo Newsom	R	34	2	2	.500	0	6	5	2	32	28	14	21	1	3.38
2 Schoolboy Rowe	R	32	1	0	1.000	0	9	2	0	30	36	12	6	0	5.40
Chet Kehn	R	20	0	0	—	0	3	1	0	8	8	3	4	0	6.75
Bob Chipman	L	23	0	0	—	0	2	0	0	1	1	2	1	0	0.00
Freddie Fitzsimmons	R	40	0	0	—	0	1	0	0	3	6	1	0	0	15.00

NEW YORK — 3rd 85-67 .559 20 — MEL OTT

NAME	G by Pos	B	AGE	G	AB	R	H	2B	3B	HR	RBI	BB	SO	SB	BA	SA
TOTALS			29	154	5210	675	1323	162	35	109	630	558	511	39	.254	.361
Johnny Mize	1B138	L	29	142	541	97	165	25	7	26	110	60	39	3	.305	.521
Mickey Witek	2B147	R	26	148	553	72	144	19	6	5	48	36	20	2	.260	.344
Billy Jurges	SS124	R	34	127	464	45	119	7	1	2	30	43	42	1	.256	.289
Bill Werber	3B93	R	34	98	370	51	76	9	2	1	13	51	22	9	.205	.249
Mel Ott	OF152	L	33	152	549	118	162	21	0	30	93	109	61	6	.295	.497
Willard Marshall	OF107	L	21	116	401	41	103	9	2	11	59	26	20	1	.257	.372
Babe Barna	OF89	L	27	104	331	39	85	8	7	6	58	48	48	3	.257	.378
Harry Danning	C116	R	30	119	408	45	114	20	3	1	34	34	29	3	.279	.350
Babe Young	OF54, 1B18	L	27	101	287	37	80	17	1	11	59	34	22	1	.279	.460
Dick Bartell	3B52, SS31	R	34	90	316	53	77	10	3	5	24	44	34	4	.244	.342
Buster Maynard	OF58, 3B10, 2B1	R	29	89	190	17	47	4	1	4	32	19	19	3	.247	.342
Hank Leiber	OF41, P1	R	31	58	147	11	32	6	0	4	23	19	27	0	.218	.340
2 Gus Mancuso	C38	R	36	39	109	4	21	1	0	0	8	14	7	1	.193	.220
Ray Berres	C12	R	34	12	32	0	6	0	0	0	1	2	3	0	.188	.188
Connie Ryan	2B11	R	22	11	27	4	5	0	0	0	2	4	3	1	.185	.185
Howie Moss	OF3	R	23	7	14	0	0	0	0	0	0	0	4	0	.000	.000
Sid Gordon	3B6	R	24	6	19	4	6	0	1	0	2	3	1	0	.316	.421
Charlie Fox	C3	R	20	3	7	3	3	0	0	0	3	1	0	0	.429	.429

NAME	T	AGE	W	L	PCT	SV	G	GS	CG	IP	H	BB	SO	SHO	ERA
TOTALS		28	85	67*	.559	13	154	154	70	1370	1299	493	497	12	3.31
2 Bill Lohrman	R	29	13	4	.765	0	26	19	12	158	143	33	41	2	2.56
Hal Schumacher	R	31	12	13	.480	0	29	29	12	216	208	82	49	3	3.04
Cliff Melton (EJ)	L	30	11	5	.688	1	23	17	12	144	122	33	61	2	2.63
Carl Hubbell	L	29	11	8	.579	0	24	20	11	157	158	34	61	0	3.96
Bob Carpenter	R	24	11	10	.524	0	28	25	12	186	192	51	53	2	3.15
Harry Feldman	R	22	7	1	.875	0	31	6	2	114	100	73	49	1	3.16
Ace Adams	R	32	7	4	.636	11	61	0	0	88	69	31	33	0	1.84
Bill McGee	R	32	6	3	.667	1	31	8	2	104	95	46	40	1	2.94
Dave Koslo	L	22	3	6	.333	0	19	11	3	78	79	32	42	1	5.08
Tom Sunkel	L	29	3	6	.333	0	19	11	3	64	65	41	29	0	4.78
Van Lingle Mungo	R	31	1	2	.333	0	9	5	0	36	38	21	27	0	6.00
Bill Voiselle	R	23	1	0	1.000	0	2	1	0	9	6	4	5	0	2.00
Hank Leiber	R	31	0	1	.000	0	1	0	0	1	9	5	5	0	6.00
Hugh East	R	22	0	2	.000	0	4	1	0	7	15	7	2	0	10.29

*1 loss by forfeit

CINCINNATI — 4th 76-76 .500 29 — BILL McKECHNIE

NAME	G by Pos	B	AGE	G	AB	R	H	2B	3B	HR	RBI	BB	SO	SB	BA	SA
TOTALS			29	154	5260	527	1216	198	39	66	488	483	549	42	.231	.321
Frank McCormick	1B144	R	29	145	564	58	146	24	0	13	89	45	18	1	.277	.388
Lonny Frey	2B140	L	31	141	523	66	139	23	6	2	39	87	38	9	.266	.344
Eddie Joost	SS130, 2B15	R	26	142	562	65	126	30	3	6	41	62	57	9	.224	.320
Bert Haas	3B146, 1B6, OF2	R	28	154	585	59	140	21	6	6	54	59	54	6	.239	.326
Max Marshall	OF129	L	28	131	530	49	135	17	6	7	43	34	38	4	.255	.349
Gee Walker	OF110	R	34	119	422	40	97	20	2	5	50	31	44	11	.230	.322
Eric Tipton	OF158	R	27	63	207	22	46	5	5	4	18	25	14	1	.222	.353
Ray Lamanno	C104	R	22	111	371	40	98	12	2	12	43	31	54	0	.264	.404
Ivel Goodman	OF57	L	33	87	226	21	55	18	1	0	15	24	32	0	.243	.332
Mike McCormick (BL)	OF38	R	25	40	135	18	32	2	3	1	11	13	7	0	.237	.319
Frankie Kelleher	OF30	R	25	38	110	13	20	3	1	3	12	16	20	0	.182	.309
Harry Craft	OF33	R	27	37	113	7	20	2	1	0	6	3	11	0	.177	.212
1 Rollie Hemsley	C34	R	35	36	115	7	13	1	2	0	7	4	11	0	.113	.157
Dick West	C17, OF6	R	26	33	79	9	14	3	0	1	9	8	13	1	.177	.253
Damon Phillips	SS27	R	23	28	84	4	17	2	0	0	6	7	5	0	.202	.226
Al Lakeman	C17	R	23	20	38	0	6	1	0	0	4	1	5	0	.158	.184
Clyde Vollmer	OF11	R	20	12	43	2	4	0	0	1	4	1	6	0	.093	.163
Joe Abreu	3B6, 2B2	R	29	9	28	4	6	1	0	1	3	4	4	0	.214	.357
Jim Gleeson	OF5	R	30	9	20	3	4	0	0	0	2	2	2	0	.200	.200
Hank Sauer	1B4	R	25	7	20	4	5	0	0	2	4	2	5	0	.250	.550
Chuck Aleno	3B2, 2B1	R	25	7	14	1	2	1	0	0	3	0	1	0	.142	.214
Bobby Mattick	SS3	R	26	6	10	0	2	1	0	0	3	3	1	0	.200	.300
1 Ernie Koy		R	32	3	2	0	0	0	0	0	0	0	0	0	.000	.000
Frank Secory	OF2	R	29	2	1	0	0	0	0	0	0	0	0	0	.000	.000

NAME	T	AGE	W	L	PCT	SV	G	GS	CG	IP	H	BB	SO	SHO	ERA
TOTALS		31	76	76	.500	8	154	154	80	1412	1213	526	616	12	2.82
Johnny Vander Meer	L	27	18	12	.600	0	33	33	21	244	188	102	186	5	2.43
Ray Starr	R	36	15	13	.536	2	37	33	17	277	228	106	83	4	2.66
Bucky Walters	R	33	15	14	.517	0	34	32	21	254	223	73	109	2	2.66
Paul Derringer	R	35	10	11	.476	0	29	27	13	209	203	49	68	1	3.06
Elmer Riddle	R	27	7	11	.389	0	29	19	7	158	157	79	78	1	3.70
Joe Beggs	R	31	6	5	.545	8	38	0	0	89	65	33	24	0	2.12
Junior Thompson	R	25	4	7	.364	0	29	10	1	102	86	53	35	0	3.35
2 Clyde Shoun	L	30	1	3	.250	0	34	0	0	73	55	24	32	0	2.22
1 Jim Turner	R	38	0	0	—	0	3	0	0	3	5	3	0	0	12.00
Ewell Blackwell	R	19	0	0	—	0	2	0	0	3	3	1	0	0	6.00
1 Whitey Moore	R	30	0	0	—	0	1	0	0	1	0	1	0	0	0.00

PITTSBURGH — 5th 68-81 .449 38.5 — FRANKIE FRISCH

NAME	G by Pos	B	AGE	G	AB	R	H	2B	3B	HR	RBI	BB	SO	SB	BA	SA
TOTALS			28	151	5104	585	1250	173	49	54	544	537	536	41	.245	.330
Elbie Fletcher	1B144	L	28	145	506	86	146	22	5	7	57	105	60	0	.289	.393
Frankie Gustine	2B108, SS2, 3B2, C1	R	22	119	388	34	89	11	4	2	29	20	27	5	.229	.294
Pete Coscarart	SS108, 2B25	R	29	133	487	57	111	12	4	3	29	38	56	2	.228	.287
Bob Elliott	3B142, OF1	R	25	143	560	75	166	26	7	9	89	52	35	2	.296	.416
Johnny Barrett	OF94	L	28	111	332	56	83	11	6	0	26	48	42	10	.247	.316
Vince DiMaggio	OF138	R	29	143	496	57	118	22	3	15	75	52	87	10	.238	.385
Jimmy Wasdell	OF97, 1B7	L	28	122	409	44	106	11	2	3	38	47	22	1	.259	.318
Al Lopez	C99	R	33	103	289	17	74	8	2	1	26	34	17	0	.256	.308
Maurice Van Robays	OF84	R	27	100	328	29	76	13	5	1	46	30	24	0	.232	.311
Babe Phelps	C72	L	34	95	257	21	73	11	1	9	41	20	24	2	.284	.440
Bud Stewart	OF34, 3B10, 2B6	L	26	82	183	21	40	8	4	0	20	22	16	2	.219	.306
Alf Anderson	SS48	R	28	54	166	24	45	4	1	0	7	18	19	4	.271	.307
Stu Martin (MM)	2B30, 1B1, SS1	R	29	42	120	16	27	4	2	1	12	8	10	1	.225	.317
Cully Rikard (BW)	OF16	L	28	38	52	6	10	2	1	0	5	7	8	0	.192	.269
Bill Baker (BH)	C11	R	30	18	17	1	2	0	0	1	2	3	4	0	.118	.118
Frank Colman	OF8	L	24	10	37	2	5	0	0	1	2	2	4	0	.135	.216
Johnny Wyrostek	OF8	L	23	9	35	2	4	0	1	0	3	2	3	0	.114	.171
Huck Geary (IL)	SS8	R	25	9	22	3	5	2	0	0	2	3	1	0	.227	.227
Jim Russell	OF3	B	23	5	14	2	1	0	0	0	0	0	3	0	.071	.071
Ed Leip (MS)		R	31	3	3	0	0	0	0	0	0	0	0	0	.000	.000
Lee Handley (SJ) 28																

NAME	T	AGE	W	L	PCT	SV	G	GS	CG	IP	H	BB	SO	SHO	ERA
TOTALS		32	66	81	.449	11	151	151	64	1351	1376	435	426	13	3.58
Rip Sewell	R	35	17	15	.531	2	40	33	18	248	259	72	69	5	3.41
Bob Klinger	R	34	8	11	.421	1	37	19	8	153	151	45	58	1	3.24
Ken Heintzelman (EJ)	L	26	8	11	.421	0	37	16	5	130	143	63	39	3	4.57
Lefty Wilkie	R	27	7	7	.462	1	35	6	3	107	112	37	18	0	4.21
Johnny Lanning	R	35	6	8	.429	1	34	2	1	119	125	26	31	1	3.33
Dutch Dietz	R	30	5	9	.400	2	40	13	7	134	139	57	35	0	3.96
Hank Gornicki	R	31	5	6	.455	2	25	14	7	112	89	40	48	2	2.57
Max Butcher (SA)	R	31	5	8	.385	1	24	18	9	151	144	44	49	2	2.92
Luke Hamlin	R	37	4	4	.500	0	23	14	6	112	128	19	38	1	3.94
Bill Brandt	R	27	1	1	.500	0	3	1	1	16	23	5	4	0	5.06
Jack Hallett	R	27	1	0	1.000	0	3	2	2	23	23	8	16	0	4.91
Ken Jungels	R	26	0	0	—	0	14	0	0	14	12	4	7	0	6.43
Nick Strincevich	R	27	0	0	—	0	7	1	0	22	19	9	10	0	2.86
Dick Conger	R	21	0	0	—	0	3	0	0	8	9	2	3	0	2.25
Harry Shuman	R	27	0	0	—	0	6	0	0	8	10	4	2	0	0.00
Johnny Gee (AJ) 26															

CHICAGO   6th 70-84 .455 30   JIMMIE WILSON

NAME	G by Pos	B	AGE	G	AB	R	H	2B	3B	HR	RBI	BB	SO	SB	BA	SA
TOTALS			27	155	5352	591	1360	224	41	75	532	509	607	63	.254	.353
Phil Cavarretta	1B61, OF70	L	25	136	482	59	130	24	4	3	54	71	42	7	.270	.363
Lou Stringer	2B113, 3B1	R	25	121	406	45	96	10	5	9	41	31	55	3	.236	.352
Lennie Merullo	SS143	R	25	143	515	53	132	23	3	2	37	35	45	14	.256	.324
Stan Hack	3B139	L	32	140	553	91	166	36	3	6	39	94	40	9	.300	.409
Bill Nicholson	OF151	L	27	152	558	83	173	22	11	21	78	76	80	8	.294	.476
Dom Dallessandro	OF66	L	28	96	264	30	69	12	4	4	43	36	18	4	.261	.383
Lou Novikoff	OF120	R	26	128	483	48	145	25	5	7	64	24	28	3	.300	.416
Clyde McCullough	C97	R	25	109	337	39	95	22	1	5	31	25	47	7	.282	.398
Rip Russell	1B35, 2B24, 3B10, OF3	R	27	102	302	32	73	9	0	8	41	17	21	0	.242	.351
Charlie Gilbert	OF47	L	22	74	179	18	33	6	3	0	7	25	24	1	.184	.251
2 Jimmie Foxx (BR)	1B52, C1	R	34	70	205	25	42	8	0	3	19	22	55	1	.205	.288
Bobby Sturgeon (LJ)	2B32, SS29, 3B2	R	22	63	162	8	40	7	1	0	7	4	13	2	.247	.302
Chico Hernandez	C43	R	26	47	118	6	27	5	0	0	7	11	13	0	.229	.271
Bob Scheffing	C32	R	28	44	102	7	20	3	0	2	12	7	11	2	.196	.284
Peanuts Lowrey	OF19	R	24	27	58	4	11	0	0	1	4	4	4	0	.190	.241
1 Babe Dahlgren	1B14	R	30	17	56	4	12	1	0	0	6	4	2	0	.214	.232
Cy Block	3B8, 2B1	R	23	9	33	6	12	1	1	0	4	3	2	3	.364	.455
Marv Rickert	OF6	L	21	8	26	5	7	0	0	1	0	1	5	0	.269	.269
Paul Gillespie	C4	L	21	5	16	3	4	0	0	2	4	1	2	0	.250	.625
Whitey Platt	OF4	R	21	4	16	1	1	0	0	0	2	0	3	0	.063	.063
Marv Felderman	C2	R	26	3	12	6	0	0	0	0	0	0	0	0	.167	.167

NAME	T	AGE	W	L	PCT	SV	G	GS	CG	IP	H	BB	SO	SHO	ERA
		29	68	86	.442	14	155	155	71	1401	1447	525	507	10	3.60
Claude Passeau	R	33	19	14	.576	0	35	34	24	278	284	74	89	3	2.69
Bill Lee (AJ)	R	32	13	13	.500	0	32	30	18	220	221	67	75	1	3.85
Hi Bithorn	R	26	9	14	.391	2	38	16	9	171	191	81	65	0	3.68
Vern Olsen	L	24	6	9	.400	1	32	17	4	140	161	55	46	1	4.50
Bill Fleming	R	28	5	6	.455	2	33	14	4	134	117	63	59	2	3.02
2 Lon Warneke	R	33	5	7	.417	2	15	12	8	99	97	21	28	1	2.27
Johnny Schmitz	L	21	3	7	.300	2	23	10	1	87	70	45	51	0	3.41
Hank Wyse	R	24	2	1	.667	0	4	4	1	28	33	6	8	1	1.93
Jake Mooty	R	29	2	5	.286	1	19	10	1	84	89	44	28	0	4.71
Tot Pressnell	R	35	1	1	.500	0	39	0	0	39	40	5	9	0	5.54
2 Dick Errickson	R	30	1	1	.500	0	13	0	0	24	39	8	9	0	4.13
Ed Hanyzewski	R	21	1	1	.500	0	6	1	0	19	17	8	6	0	3.79
Paul Erickson	R	26	1	6	.143	0	18	7	1	63	70	41	46	0	5.43
Jesse Flores	R	27	0	1	.000	0	4	0	0	5	5	2	6	0	3.60
Joe Berry	R	37	0	0	—	0	2	0	0	2	7	2	1	0	18.00
Vallie Eaves	R	30	0	0	—	0	2	0	0	3	4	0	0	0	9.00
Bob Bowman	R	31	0	0	—	0	1	0	0	1	1	0	0	0	0.00
Emil Kush	R	25	0	0	—	0	1	0	0	1	1	1	1	0	0.00

BOSTON   7th 59-89 .399 44   CASEY STENGEL

NAME	G by Pos	B	AGE	G	AB	R	H	2B	3B	HR	RBI	BB	SO	SB	BA	SA
TOTALS			28	150	5077	515	1216	210	19	68	479	474	507	49	.240	.329
Max West	1B85, OF50	L	25	134	452	54	115	22	0	16	56	68	59	4	.254	.409
Sibby Sisti	2B124, OF1	R	21	129	407	50	86	11	4	4	35	45	55	5	.211	.287
Eddie Miller	SS142	R	25	142	534	47	130	28	2	6	47	22	42	11	.243	.337
Nanny Fernandez	3B98, OF44	R	23	145	577	63	147	29	3	6	55	38	61	15	.255	.347
Paul Waner	OF94	L	39	114	333	43	86	17	1	1	39	62	20	2	.258	.324
Tommy Holmes	OF140	L	25	141	558	56	155	24	4	4	41	64	10	2	.278	.357
Chet Ross	OF57	R	26	76	220	20	43	7	2	5	19	16	37	0	.195	.314
Ernie Lombardi	C85	R	34	105	309	32	102	14	0	11	46	37	12	1	.330	.482
Johnny Cooney	OF54, 1B23	R	41	74	198	23	41	6	0	0	7	23	5	2	.207	.237
Skippy Roberge	2B29, 3B27, SS6	R	25	74	172	19	37	7	0	1	12	9	19	1	.215	.273
Clyde Kluttz	C57	R	24	72	210	21	56	10	1	1	31	7	13	0	.267	.338
Buddy Gremp (MS)	1B63, 3B1	R	22	72	207	12	45	11	0	3	19	13	21	1	.217	.314
Frank Demaree	OF49	R	32	64	187	18	42	5	0	3	24	17	10	2	.225	.299
Phil Masi	C39, OF4	R	25	57	87	14	19	3	1	0	9	12	4	2	.218	.276
Jim Tobin	P37	R	29	47	114	14	28	2	0	3	15	16	23	1	.246	.421
Tony Cuccinello	3B20, 2B14	R	34	40	104	8	21	3	0	1	8	9	11	1	.202	.260
Whitey Wietelmann	SS11, 2B1	B	23	13	34	4	7	2	0	0	4	5	0	0	.206	.265
Ducky Detweiler	3B12	R	23	12	34	5	12	4	0	0	6	1	3	0	.318	.409

Frank McElyea 23 R 0-4, Mike Sandlock 26 B 1-1, Al Mongomery (DD) 21

NAME	T	AGE	W	L	PCT	SV	G	GS	CG	IP	H	BB	SO	SHO	ERA
		26	59*	89	.339	8	150	150	84	1334	1326	518	414	9	3.76
Al Javery	R	24	12	16	.429	0	42	37	19	261	251	78	85	5	3.03
Jim Tobin	R	29	12	21	.364	0	37	33	28	288	283	96	71	1	3.97
Lou Tost	L	31	10	10	.500	0	35	22	5	148	146	52	43	1	3.53
Manny Salvo	R	30	7	8	.467	0	25	14	6	131	129	41	25	1	3.02
Tom Earley	R	25	6	11	.353	1	27	18	6	113	120	55	28	0	4.70
Johnny Sain	R	24	4	7	.364	6	40	3	0	97	79	63	68	0	3.90
Bill Donovan	L	25	3	6	.333	0	31	10	2	89	97	32	23	1	3.44
1 Dick Errickson	R	30	2	5	.286	1	21	4	0	59	76	20	15	0	5.03
Johnny Hutchings	R	26	1	0	1.000	0	3	0	0	66	66	34	27	0	4.38
Lefty Wallace	L	20	1	3	.250	0	19	3	1	49	39	24	20	0	3.86
Frank Lamanna	R	22	1	1	.500	0	5	0	0	7	5	3	2	0	5.14
Jim Hickey	R	21	1	0	1.000	0	5	1	0	1	3	3	2	0	27.00
Art Johnson (MS)	L	25	0	0	—	0	4	1	0	5	4	5	0	0	1.50
Warren Spahn	L	21	0	0	—	0	4	2	1	16	25	11	7	0	5.63
Geroge Diehl	R	24	0	0	—	0	4	2	0	8	7	2	0	0	2.25

*1 win by forfeit

PHILADELPHIA   8th 42-109 .278 62.5   HANS LOBERT

NAME	G by Pos	B	AGE	G	AB	R	H	2B	3B	HR	RBI	BB	SO	SB	BA	SA
TOTALS			27	151	5060	394	1174	168	37	44	354	392	488	37	.232	.306
Nick Etten	1B135	L	28	139	459	37	121	21	3	8	41	67	26	3	.264	.375
Al Glossop	2B118, 3B1	R	27	121	454	33	102	15	1	4	40	29	35	3	.225	.289
Bobby Bragan	SS78, C22, 2B4, 3B3	R	24	109	335	17	73	12	2	2	15	20	21	0	.218	.284
Pinky May	3B107	R	31	115	345	25	82	15	0	0	18	51	17	3	.238	.281
Ron Northey	OF109	L	22	127	402	31	101	13	2	5	31	28	33	2	.251	.331
Lloyd Waner	OF75	L	36	101	287	23	75	9	3	0	10	16	6	1	.261	.307
Danny Litwhiler	OF151	R	25	151	591	59	160	25	9	9	56	27	42	2	.271	.389
Bennie Warren	C78, 1B1	R	30	90	225	19	47	6	3	6	20	24	36	0	.209	.356
Danny Murtaugh	SS60, 3B53, 2B32	R	24	144	506	48	122	16	4	0	27	49	39	13	.241	.289
2 Ernie Koy	OF78	R	32	91	258	21	63	9	4	4	26	14	50	3	.244	.349
Mickey Livingston	C78, 1B6	R	27	89	239	20	49	6	1	2	22	25	20	0	.205	.264
Stan Benjamin	OF45, 1B15	R	28	78	210	24	47	8	3	8	10	27	34	5	.224	.319
Earl Naylor	OF34, P20, 1B1	R	23	76	168	9	33	4	1	0	14	11	18	1	.196	.232
Bill Burich	SS19, 3B3	R	24	25	80	3	23	1	0	0	7	6	13	2	.288	.300
Hal Marnie	SB11, SS7, 3B1	R	24	24	30	3	5	0	0	0	1	2	1	0	.167	.167
Chuck Klein		L	37	14	14	0	1	0	0	0	0	0	0	0	.071	.071
Ed Freed	OF11	R	22	13	33	3	10	3	1	0	1	4	3	1	.303	.455
Ed Murphy	1B8	R	23	13	28	2	7	2	0	0	3	2	5	0	.250	.321
Bert Hodge	3B2	L	25	8	11	0	2	0	0	0	0	1	0	0	.182	.182

Benny Culp 28 R 0-0, Bill Peterman 21 R 1-1

NAME	T	AGE	W	L	PCT	SV	G	GS	CG	IP	H	BB	SO	SHO	ERA
		27	42	109	.278	6	151	151	51	1341	1328	605	472	2	4.12
Tommy Hughes	R	22	12	18	.400	1	40	31	19	253	224	99	77	0	3.06
Rube Melton	R	25	9	20	.310	4	42	29	10	209	180	114	107	1	3.70
Si Johnson	R	35	8	19	.296	0	39	26	10	195	198	72	78	1	3.69
Johnny Podgajny	R	22	6	14	.300	0	43	23	6	187	191	63	40	0	3.90
Frank Hoerst	L	24	4	16	.200	1	33	22	5	151	162	78	52	0	5.19
George Hennessey	R	31	1	1	.500	0	5	1	0	17	11	10	2	0	2.65
Sam Nahem	R	26	1	3	.250	0	35	4	0	75	72	40	38	0	4.92
Ike Pearson	R	25	1	6	.143	0	35	7	0	85	87	50	21	0	4.55
Boom-Boom Beck	R	37	0	0	—	0	26	1	0	53	69	17	10	0	4.75
Andy Lapihuska	R	19	0	2	.000	0	7	1	0	17	13	8	0	0	5.14
Cy Blanton	R	33	0	4	.000	0	3	3	0	22	30	13	15	0	5.73
Earl Naylor	R	23	0	5	.000	0	20	4	1	60	68	29	19	0	6.15
Paul Masterson	L	26	0	0	—	0	3	0	0	6	3	6	2	1	9.00
Hilly Flitcraft	L	18	0	0	—	0	3	0	0	3	6	2	1	0	9.00
Gene Lambert	R	21	0	0	—	0	1	0	0	3	2	0	0	0	9.00

WORLD SERIES — ST. LOUIS (NL) 4 NEW YORK (AL) 1

LINE SCORES

TEAM	1	2	3	4	5	6	7	8	9	10	11	12	R	H	E
Game 1 September 30 at St. Louis															
NY (AL)	0	0	0	1	1	0	0	3	2				7	11	0
STL (NL)	0	0	0	0	0	0	0	0	4				4	7	4

Ruffing, Chandler (9)   M. Cooper, Gumbert (8)
Lanier (9)

TEAM	1	2	3	4	5	6	7	8	9	R	H	E
Game 2 October 1 at St. Louis												
NY	0	0	0	0	0	0	0	3	0	3	10	2
STL	2	0	0	0	0	0	0	1	X	4	6	0

Bonham   Beazley

TEAM	1	2	3	4	5	6	7	8	9	R	H	E
Game 3 October 3 at New York												
STL	0	0	1	0	0	0	0	0	1	2	5	1
NY	0	0	0	0	0	0	0	0	0	0	6	1

White   Chandler, Breuer (9), Turner (9)

TEAM	1	2	3	4	5	6	7	8	9	R	H	E
Game 4 October 4 at New York												
STL	0	0	0	6	0	0	2	0	1	9	12	1
NY	0	0	0	0	0	5	0	1	0	6	10	1

M. Cooper, Gumbert (6),   Borowy, Donald (4),
Pollett (6), Lanier (7)   Bonham (7)

TEAM	1	2	3	4	5	6	7	8	9	R	H	E
Game 5 October 5 at New York												
STL	0	0	0	1	0	1	0	0	2	4	9	4
NY	1	0	0	1	0	0	0	0	0	2	7	1

Beazley   Ruffing

COMPOSITE BATTING

St. Louis (NL)

NAME	POS	G	AB	R	H	2B	3B	HR	RBI	BA
Totals		5	163	23	39	4	2	2	23	.239
W. Cooper	C	5	21	3	6	1	0	0	4	.286
Brown	2B	5	20	2	6	0	0	0	0	.300
Slaughter	OF	5	19	3	5	1	0	1	2	.263
Musial	OF	5	18	2	4	1	0	0	2	.222
Marion	SS	5	18	2	2	0	1	0	3	.111
T. Moore	OF	5	17	2	5	1	0	0	2	.294
Hopp	1B	5	17	3	3	0	0	0	0	.176
Kurowski	3B	5	15	3	4	0	1	1	5	.267
Beazley	P	2	7	0	1	0	0	0	0	.143
M. Cooper	P	2	5	1	1	0	0	0	2	.200
White	P	1	2	0	0	0	0	0	0	.000
Lanier	P	2	1	0	1	0	0	0	1	1.000
O'Dea	PH	1	1	0	1	0	0	0	1	1.000
Sanders	PH	2	1	1	0	0	0	0	0	.000
Walker	PH	1	1	0	0	0	0	0	0	.000
Crespi	PR	1	0	1	0	0	0	0	0	—
Gumbert	P	2	0	0	0	0	0	0	0	—
Pollet	P	1	0	0	0	0	0	0	0	—

New York (AL)

NAME	POS	G	AB	R	H	2B	3B	HR	RBI	BA
Totals		5	178	18	44	6	0	3	14	.247
Rizzuto	SS	5	21	2	8	0	0	1	1	.381
DiMaggio	OF	5	21	3	7	0	0	0	3	.333
Gordon	2B	5	21	1	2	1	0	0	5	.095
Keller	OF	5	20	2	4	0	0	2	5	.200
Cullenbine	OF	5	19	3	5	1	0	0	2	.263
Dickey	C	5	19	1	5	0	0	0	0	.263
Rolfe	3B	5	17	5	6	2	0	0	1	.353
Priddy	3B-1B	5	10	0	1	1	0	0	0	.100
Hassett	1B	3	9	1	3	1	0	0	2	.333
Ruffing	P	2	9	0	2	0	0	0	0	.222
Crosetti	3B	3	3	0	0	0	0	0	0	.000
Bonham	P	2	2	0	0	0	0	0	0	.000
Chandler	P	2	2	0	0	0	0	0	0	.000
Donald	P	2	2	0	0	0	0	0	0	.000
Rosar	PH	1	1	0	1	0	0	0	0	1.000
Selkirk	PH	1	1	0	0	0	0	0	0	.000
Borowy	P	1	1	0	0	0	0	0	0	.000
Stainback	PR	2	0	0	0	0	0	0	0	—
Breuer	P	2	0	0	0	0	0	0	0	—
Turner	P	1	0	0	0	0	0	0	0	—

COMPOSITE PITCHING

St. Louis (NL)

NAME	G	IP	H	BB	SO	W	L	SV	ERA
Totals	5	45	44	8	22	4	1	0	2.60
Beazley	2	18	17	3	6	2	0	0	2.50
M. Cooper	2	13	17	4	9	0	1	0	5.54
White	1	9	6	6	6	1	0	0	0.00
Lanier	2	4	3	1	1	1	0	0	0.00
Gumbert	2	0.2	1	0	0	0	0	0	0.00
Pollet	1	0.1	0	0	0	0	0	0	0.00

New York (AL)

NAME	G	IP	H	BB	SO	W	L	SV	ERA
Totals	5	44	39	17	19	1	4	1	4.50
Ruffing	2	17.2	14	7	11	1	1	0	4.08
Bonham	2	11	9	3	3	0	1	0	4.09
Chandler	2	8.1	4	5	3	1	0	1	1.08
Donald	2	3	3	2	1	0	1	0	6.00
Borowy	1	3	6	3	1	0	0	0	18.00
Turner	1	1	1	0	0	0	0	0	0.00
Breuer	1	0	2	0	0	0	0	0	0.00

1943 The Lesser Struggle

As war raged throughout Europe and the Pacific, those remaining on the home front found their lives touched in a myriad of ways. As players, stars, and scrubs alike were drafted into the military in droves, baseball was forced to scramble to preserve the continuity it had enjoyed since 1876. Clubs had to operate with oldsters, youngsters, and draft deferred stars or not operate at all. When a government order forbade the teams to conduct spring training below the Mason-Dixon line, such picturesque towns as Asbury Park, New Jersey, became the hosting ground for the spring sweat sessions. During the season itself, each club promoted the sales of war bonds, and sizable contributions were handed over to various war charities. Although the National Pastime served as an escape from the violent overseas' headlines, the game itself became as altered as the other facets of American life.

The farm system which made the Cardinals into champions also served in the star-shortage year to make them pre-season favorites to cop the National League pennant, and the Redbirds waltzed through the circuit to an anticipated repeat championship. Enos Slaughter, Jimmy Brown, Terry Moore, and Johnny Beazley all had marched off into the armed forces, and Howie Pollet joined them after a sterling first half of the season. Harry Brecheen and Al Brazle appeared from the legendary Cardinal farm chain to shore up the pitching, while Lou Klein came to do an outstanding job at second base. Stan Musial grabbed his first batting title with a .357 mark, Walker Cooper swung a big stick, and Mort Cooper and Max Lanier starred on the pitching hill. Second-place Cincinnati finished 18 games back, and Branch Rickey suffered the frustration of having his new Brooklyn club limp home a distant 23 1/2 lengths behind the Cardinal club he had largely put together. Chicago's Bill "Swish" Nicholson copped the home run and RBI crowns but lost out in MVP honors to the 22-year-old Musial.

The American League also produced a repeat pennant winner as Joe McCarthy's New York Yankees pulled away from the Washington Senators after a close first half. Although the Yankees lost Joe DiMaggio, Phil Rizzuto, Tommy Henrich, Buddy Hassett, and Red Ruffing to Uncle Sam, their subs and veterans glowed bright enough with a steady competence that boosted the pinstripes to their seventh crown in eight years. After rookie Snuffy Stirnweiss failed to fill the shortstop gap, veteran Frankie Crosetti plugged the hole in time for the club's spurt. The Yankee attack remained the class of the league, as 36-year-old Bill Dickey batted .351, Charlie Keller slugged 31 home runs, and Hassett's replacement, Nick Etten, knocked in 107 runs.

The Yankees also had the cream of the league's pitching in the arm of Spud Chandler, the winner of 20 out of 24 decisions and the owner of a 1.64 E.R.A., the lowest mark in the American league in 24 years—a performance which earned him the MVP Award. The 1942 Triple Crown winner, Ted Williams, was not faced with the frustration of post-season honors, as he spent the year in the cockpit of a fighter plane. Chicago's Luke Appling picked up the Splendid Splinter's batting title, and Detroit's Rudy York the other two pieces of the Triple Crown, with 34 homers and 118 runs batted in.

Both clubs in the World Series reached on a return ticket, but the result of the confrontation was a reversal from 1942. The Yankees knocked out the Cardinals this time in five games by limiting them to nine runs for the entire Series.

1943 AMERICAN LEAGUE

NAME	G by Pos	B	AGE	G	AB	R	H	2B	3B	HR	RBI	BB	SO	SB	BA	SA
NEW YORK 1st 98-56 .636			**JOE McCARTHY**													
TOTALS			29	155	5282	669	1350	218	59	100	636	624	562	46	.256	.376
Nick Etten	1B154	L	29	154	583	78	158	35	5	14	107	76	31	3	.271	.470
Joe Gordon	2B152	R	28	152	543	82	135	28	5	17	69	98	75	4	.249	.413
Frankie Crosetti (SU)	SS90	R	32	95	348	36	81	8	1	2	20	36	47	4	.233	.279
Billy Johnson	3B155	R	24	155	592	70	166	24	6	5	94	53	30	3	.280	.367
Bud Metheny	OF91	L	28	103	360	51	94	18	2	9	36	39	34	2	.261	.397
Johnny Lindell	OF122	R	26	122	441	53	108	17	12	4	51	51	55	2	.245	.365
Charlie Keller	OF141	L	26	141	512	97	139	15	11	31	86	106	61	4	.271	.525
Bill Dickey	C71	L	36	85	242	29	85	18	2	4	33	41	12	2	.351	.492
Snuffy Stirnweiss	SS68, 2B4	R	24	83	274	34	60	8	4	1	25	47	37	11	.219	.288
Roy Weatherly	OF68	L	28	77	280	37	74	8	3	7	28	18	9	4	.264	.389
Tuck Stainback	OF61	R	31	71	231	31	60	11	2	0	10	7	16	3	.260	.325
Rollie Hemsley	C52	R	36	62	180	12	43	6	3	2	24	13	9	0	.239	.339
Ken Sears	C50	L	25	60	187	22	52	7	0	2	22	11	18	1	.278	.348
Oscar Grimes	SS3, 1B1	R	28	9	20	4	3	0	0	0	1	3	7	0	.150	.150
Aaron Robinson (MS)		L	28	1	1	0	0	0	0	0	0	0	1	0	.000	.000
WASHINGTON 2nd 84-69 .549 13.5			**OSSIE BLUEGE**													
TOTALS			28	153	5233	666	1328	245	50	47	617	605	579	142	.254	.347
Mickey Vernon	1B143	L	25	145	553	89	148	29	8	7	70	67	55	24	.268	.387
Jerry Priddy	2B134, SS15, 3B1	R	23	149	560	68	152	31	3	4	62	67	76	5	.271	.359
Johnny Sullivan	SS133	R	22	134	456	49	95	12	2	1	55	57	59	6	.208	.250
1 Ellis Clary	3B68, SS1	R	26	73	254	36	65	19	1	0	19	44	31	6	.256	.339
George Case	OF140	R	27	141	613	102	180	36	5	1	52	41	27	61	.294	.374
Stan Spence	OF148	L	28	149	570	72	152	23	10	12	88	84	39	8	.267	.405
Bob Johnson	OF88, 3B19, 1B10	R	37	117	438	65	116	22	8	7	63	64	50	11	.265	.400
Jake Early	C122	R	28	126	423	37	109	23	3	6	60	53	43	5	.258	.362
Gene Moore	OF57, 1B1	L	33	92	254	41	68	14	3	2	34	19	29	0	.268	.370
Sherry Robertson	3B27, SS1	L	24	59	120	22	26	4	1	3	14	17	19	0	.217	.342
2 Alex Kampouris	3B33, 2B10, OF1	R	30	51	145	24	30	4	0	2	13	30	25	7	.207	.276
Tony Giuliani	C49	R	30	49	133	5	30	4	1	0	20	12	14	0	.226	.271
George Myatt	2B11, SS2, 3B2	L	29	42	53	11	13	3	0	0	3	13	7	3	.245	.302
Early Wynn	P37	R	23	38	98	6	29	3	1	1	11	1	11	0	.296	.378
Jake Powell	OF33	R	34	37	132	14	35	10	2	0	20	5	13	3	.265	.371
Red Marion	OF4	R	29	14	17	2	3	0	0	0	1	3	1	0	.176	.176
Red Roberts	SS6, 3B1	R	24	9	23	1	6	1	0	1	3	4	2	0	.261	.435
2 Harlond Clift	3B8	R	30	8	30	4	9	0	0	0	4	5	3	0	.300	.300
Ed Butka	1B3	R	27	3	9	1	3	0	0	0	1	0	3	0	.333	.444
2 Tom Padden	C2	R	34	3	3	1	0	0	0	0	0	1	1	0	.000	.000
Red Barbary		R	23	1	1	0	0	0	0	0	0	0	1	0	.000	.000
Roberto Ortiz	OF1	R	28	1	4	0	1	0	0	0	0	0	0	0	.250	.250
CLEVELAND 3rd 82-71 .536 15.5			**LOU BOUDREAU**													
TOTALS			28	153	5269	600	1344	246	45	55	564	567	521	47	.255	.350
Mickey Rocco	1B108	R	27	108	405	43	97	14	4	5	46	51	40	1	.240	.331
Ray Mack	2B153	R	26	153	545	56	120	25	2	7	62	47	61	6	.220	.312
Lou Boudreau	SS152, C1	R	25	152	539	69	154	32	7	3	67	90	31	4	.286	.388
Ken Keltner	3B107	R	26	110	427	47	111	31	3	4	39	36	20	2	.260	.375
Roy Cullenbine	OF121, 1B13	B	29	134	488	66	141	24	4	8	56	96	58	3	.289	.404
Oris Hockett	OF139	L	33	141	601	70	166	33	4	2	51	45	45	13	.276	.354
Jeff Heath	OF111	L	28	118	424	58	116	22	6	18	79	63	58	5	.274	.481
Buddy Rosar	C114	R	28	115	382	53	108	17	1	1	41	33	12	0	.283	.340
Hank Edwards (BC)	OF74	L	24	92	297	38	82	18	6	3	28	30	34	4	.276	.407
Rusty Peters	3B46, SS14, 2B6, OF2	R	28	79	215	22	47	4	2	1	19	18	29	1	.219	.279
Gene Desautels	C66	R	36	68	185	14	38	6	1	0	19	11	16	2	.205	.249
Chubby Dean (MS)	P17	L	27	41	46	2	9	0	0	0	4	2	4	0	.196	.196
Otto Denning	1B34	R	30	37	109	8	31	6	0	0	13	5	1	0	.240	.287
Pat Seerey	OF16	R	20	26	72	8	16	3	0	1	5	4	19	0	.222	.306
2 Jimmy Grant	3B5	L	24	15	22	3	3	2	0	0	1	4	7	1	.136	.227
Eddie Turchin	3B4, SS2	R	26	11	13	4	3	0	0	0	1	9	5	0	.231	.231
Gene Wooding (MS)	OF6	L	20	8	5	2	1	1	0	0	0	1	2	0	.320	.600
Frank Doljack (IL)	OF3	R	35	3	7	0	0	0	0	0	0	0	0	0	.000	.000
George Susce (IL)	C3	R	35	3	1	0	0	0	0	0	0	0	0	0	.000	.000
Jim McDonnell	C1	L	20	2	1	1	0	0	0	0	0	1	0	0	.000	.000
Hal Trosky (IL) 30																

NAME	T	AGE	W	L	PCT	SV	G	GS	CG	IP	H	BB	SO	SHO	ERA
		31	98	56	.636	13	155	155	83	1415	1229	489	653	14	2.93
Spud Chandler	R	35	20	4	.833	0	30	30	20	253	197	54	134	5	1.64
Ernie Bonham	R	29	15	8	.652	1	28	26	17	226	197	52	71	4	2.27
Hank Borowy	R	27	14	9	.609	0	29	27	14	217	195	72	113	3	2.82
Butch Wensloff	R	27	13	11	.542	1	29	27	18	223	179	70	105	1	2.54
Johnny Murphy	R	34	12	4	.750	8	37	0	0	68	44	30	31	0	2.51
Bill Zuber	R	30	8	4	.667	1	20	13	7	118	100	74	57	0	3.89
Atley Donald	R	32	6	4	.600	0	22	15	2	119	134	38	57	0	4.61
Marius Russo	L	28	5	10	.333	1	24	14	5	102	89	45	42	1	3.71
Jim Turner	R	39	3	0	1.000	1	18	0	0	43	44	13	15	0	3.56
Tommy Byrne	R	23	2	1	.667	1	11	2	0	32	28	35	22	0	6.47
Marv Breuer	R	29	0	1	.000	0	5	1	0	14	22	6	6	0	8.36
		28	84	69	.549	21	153	153	61	1388	1293	540	495	16	3.18
Early Wynn	R	23	18	12	.600	1	37	33	12	257	232	83	89	3	2.91
Mickey Haefner	L	30	11	5	.688	6	36	13	8	155	126	60	65	1	2.29
Alex Carrasquel	R	30	11	7	.611	5	39	13	4	144	160	54	48	1	3.69
Milo Candini	R	25	11	7	.611	1	28	21	8	166	144	65	67	3	2.49
Dutch Leonard	R	34	11	13	.458	1	31	30	15	220	218	46	51	2	3.27
Jim Mertz	R	26	7	9	.437	3	33	10	2	117	109	58	53	0	4.62
2 Johnny Niggeling	R	39	4	2	.667	0	6	6	5	51	27	17	24	3	0.88
Ray Scarborough (MS)	R	25	4	4	.500	2	24	6	2	86	93	46	43	0	2.83
Ewald Pyle	L	32	4	8	.333	1	18	11	2	73	70	45	25	1	4.07
3 Bobo Newsom	R	35	3	5	.500	0	9	6	2	40	38	21	11	0	3.83
Bill LeFebvre	R	27	2	1	.667	0	6	3	1	32	33	16	10	0	4.50
Lefty Gomez (WW)	L	34	0	1	.000	0	1	1	0	5	4	5	0	0	5.40
Dewey Adkins	R	25	0	0	—	0	7	0	0	10	9	5	1	0	7.00
Owen Scheetz	R	29	0	0	—	0	4	0	0	9	16	4	5	0	9.00
Len Carpenter	R	29	0	0	—	0	4	0	0	3	4	1	0	0	
1 Ox Miller	R	28	0	0	—	0	6	1	0	10	15	1	1	0	10.50
Vern Curtis	R	23	0	0	—	0	2	0	0	4	3	6	1	0	6.75
		30	82	71	.536	20	153	153	64	1406	1234	606	585	14	3.15
Al Smith	L	35	17	7	.708	1	29	29	14	208	186	72	72	3	2.55
Jim Bagby	R	26	17	14	.548	1	36	33	16	273	248	80	70	3	3.10
Allie Reynolds	R	28	11	12	.478	3	34	21	11	199	140	109	151	3	2.98
Vern Kennedy	R	36	10	7	.588	0	28	17	8	147	130	59	63	1	2.45
Mel Harder (BW)	R	33	8	7	.533	0	19	18	6	135	126	61	40	1	3.07
Jack Salveson	R	29	5	3	.625	3	23	11	4	86	87	26	24	3	3.35
Chubby Dean (MS)	L	27	5	5	.500	0	17	9	3	76	83	34	29	0	4.50
Mike Naymick	R	25	4	4	.500	2	24	6	3	63	32	47	41	0	2.29
Ray Poat	R	25	2	5	.286	0	17	4	1	45	44	20	31	0	4.40
Joe Heving	R	42	1	1	.500	9	30	0	0	72	58	34	34	0	2.75
Pete Center (MS)	R	21	1	2	.333	1	24	1	0	42	29	18	10	0	2.79
1 Al Milnar	L	29	1	3	.250	0	16	6	0	39	51	35	12	0	8.08
Eddie Klieman	R	25	0	0	1.000	0	4	0	0	6	4	6	4	0	4.50
Paul Calvert	R	25	0	0	—	0	3	0	0	7	6	4	6	0	9.00
Steve Gromek	R	23	0	0	—	0	3	0	0						
Red Embree (VR) 25															

216

CHICAGO — 4th 82-72 .532 16 — JIMMY DYKES

NAME	G by Pos	B	AGE	G	AB	R	H	2B	3B	HR	RBI	BB	SO	SB	BA	SA
TOTALS			29	155	5254	573	1297	193	46	33	509	561	581	173	.247	.320
Joe Kuhel	1B153	L	37	153	531	55	113	21	1	5	46	76	45	14	.213	.284
Don Kolloway (MS)	2B85	R	24	85	348	29	75	14	4	1	33	9	30	11	.216	.287
Luke Appling	SS155	R	36	155	585	63	192	33	2	3	80	90	29	27	.328	.407
Ralph Hodgin	3B56, OF42	L	28	117	407	52	128	22	8	1	50	20	24	3	.314	.415
Wally Moses	OF148	L	32	150	599	82	147	22	12	3	48	55	47	56	.245	.337
Thurman Tucker	OF132	R	25	139	528	81	124	15	6	3	39	79	72	29	.235	.303
Guy Curtright	OF128	R	30	138	488	67	142	20	7	3	48	69	60	13	.291	.379
Mike Tresh	C85	R	29	86	279	20	60	3	0	0	20	37	20	2	.215	.226
Skeeter Webb	2B54	R	33	58	213	15	50	5	2	0	22	6	19	5	.235	.277
1 Jimmy Grant	3B51	L	24	58	197	23	51	9	2	4	22	18	34	4	.259	.386
Dick Culler	3B26, 2B19, SS3	R	28	53	148	9	32	5	1	0	11	16	11	4	.216	.264
Tom Turner	C49	R	26	51	154	16	37	7	1	2	11	13	21	1	.240	.338
Moose Solters	OF21	R	37	42	97	6	15	0	0	1	8	7	5	0	.155	.186
2 Tony Cuccinello	3B30	R	35	34	103	5	28	5	0	2	11	13	13	3	.272	.379
Vince Castino	C30	R	25	33	101	14	23	1	0	2	16	12	11	0	.228	.297
John Humphries	P28	R	28	28	69	6	20	6	0	0	5	3	25	1	.290	.377
Don Hanski	1B5, P1	L	27	9	21	1	5	1	0	0	2	0	5	0	.238	.286
Frank Kalin (MS)		R	25	4	4	0	0	0	0	0	0	0	0	0	.000	.000
Cass Michaels	3B2	R	17	2	1	0	0	0	0	0	0	0	0	0	.000	.000

NAME	T	AGE	W	L	PCT	SV	G	GS	CG	IP	H	BB	SO	SHO	ERA
		30	82	72	.532	19	155	155	70	1400	1352	501	476	12	3.20
Orval Grove	R	23	15	9	.625	2	32	25	18	216	192	72	76	3	2.75
Bill Dietrich	R	33	12	10	.545	0	26	26	12	187	180	53	52	2	2.79
Buck Ross	R	28	11	7	.611	0	21	21	7	149	140	56	41	1	3.20
John Humphries	R	28	11	11	.500	0	28	27	8	188	198	54	51	2	3.30
Eddie Smith	L	29	11	11	.500	0	25	25	14	188	197	76	66	2	3.69
Joe Haynes	R	25	7	11	.389	3	35	4	1	109	114	32	37	0	2.97
Gordon Maltzberger	R	30	7	4	.636	14	37	0	0	99	86	24	48	0	2.45
Thornton Lee	L	36	5	9	.357	0	19	19	7	127	129	50	35	1	4.18
Jake Wade	R	31	3	7	.300	0	21	9	3	84	66	54	41	1	3.00
Bill Swift	R	35	0	2	.000	0	18	1	0	51	48	27	28	0	4.24
Bon Hanski	L	27	0	0	—	0	1	0	0	1	1	1	0	0	0.00
Floyd Speer	R	30	0	0	—	0	1	0	0	1	2	1	0	0	9.00

DETROIT — 5th 78-76 .506 20 — STEVE O'NEILL

NAME	G by Pos	B	AGE	G	AB	R	H	2B	3B	HR	RBI	BB	SO	SB	BA	SA
TOTALS			29	155	5364	632	1401	200	47	77	571	483	553	40	.261	.116
Rudy York	1B155	R	29	155	571	90	155	22	11	34	118	34	88	5	.271	.527
Jimmy Bloodworth	2B129	R	25	129	474	41	114	23	4	6	52	29	59	4	.241	.344
Joe Hoover	SS144	R	28	144	575	78	140	15	8	4	38	36	101	6	.243	.318
Pinky Higgins	3B138	R	34	138	523	62	145	20	1	10	84	57	31	2	.277	.377
Ned Harris	OF96	L	26	114	354	43	90	14	3	6	32	47	29	6	.254	.362
Doc Cramer	OF138	L	37	140	606	79	182	18	4	1	43	31	13	4	.300	.348
Dick Wakefield	OF155	L	22	155	633	91	200	38	8	7	79	62	60	1	.316	.434
Paul Richards	C100	R	34	100	313	32	69	7	1	5	33	38	35	1	.220	.297
Don Ross	OF38, SS18, 2B7, 3B1	R	28	89	247	19	66	13	0	0	18	20	3	2	.267	.320
Rip Radcliff	OF19, 1B1	R	37	70	115	3	30	4	0	0	10	13	3	1	.261	.296
Joe Wood	2B22, 3B18	R	23	60	164	22	53	4	4	1	17	6	13	2	.323	.415
Charlie Metro	OF14	R	24	44	40	12	8	0	0	0	2	3	6	1	.200	.200
Dixie Parsons	C40	R	27	40	106	2	15	3	0	0	4	6	10	0	.142	.170
Al Unser	C37	R	30	38	101	14	25	5	0	0	4	15	15	0	.248	.297
Jimmy Outlaw	OF16	R	30	20	67	8	18	1	0	1	6	8	4	0	.269	.342
John McHale (MS)		L	21	4	3	0	0	0	0	0	0	0	1	0	.000	.000

NAME	T	AGE	W	L	PCT	SV	G	GS	CG	IP	H	BB	SO	SHO	ERA
		27	78	76	.506	20	155	155	67	1412	1226	549	706	18	3.00
Dizzy Trout	R	28	20	12	.625	6	44	30	18	247	204	101	111	5	2.48
Virgil Trucks	R	26	16	10	.615	2	33	25	10	203	170	52	118	2	2.84
Tommy Bridges	R	36	12	7	.632	0	25	22	11	192	159	61	124	3	2.39
Hal Newhouser	L	22	8	17	.320	1	37	25	10	196	163	111	144	1	3.03
Stubby Overmire	L	24	7	6	.583	1	29	18	8	147	135	38	48	3	3.18
Hal White	R	24	7	12	.368	2	32	24	7	178	150	71	58	2	3.39
Johnny Gorsica	R	28	4	5	.444	1	35	4	1	96	88	40	45	0	3.38
Prince Oana	R	35	3	2	.600	0	10	0	0	34	34	19	15	0	4.50
Rufe Gentry	R	25	1	3	.250	0	4	4	2	29	30	12	8	0	3.72
Roy Henshaw	L	31	0	0	.000	2	36	0	0	71	75	33	33	0	3.80
Joe Orrell	R	26	0	0	—	1	10	0	0	19	18	11	2	0	3.79

ST. LOUIS — 6th 72-80 .474 25 — LUKE SEWELL

NAME	G by Pos	B	AGE	G	AB	R	H	2B	3B	HR	RBI	BB	SO	SB	BA	SA
TOTALS			30	153	5175	596	1269	229	36	78	552	569	646	37	.245	.349
George McQuinn	1B122	L	34	125	449	53	109	19	2	12	74	56	65	4	.243	.374
Don Gutteridge	2B132	R	31	132	538	77	147	35	4	1	36	50	46	10	.273	.366
Vern Stephens	SS123, OF11	R	22	137	512	75	148	27	3	22	91	54	73	3	.289	.482
Harlond Clift (IL)	3B104	R	30	105	379	43	88	11	3	0	25	54	37	5	.232	.301
Mike Chartak	OF77, 1B18	L	27	108	344	38	88	16	2	10	37	39	51	1	.256	.401
Milt Byrnes	OF114	R	26	129	429	58	120	28	7	4	50	54	49	1	.280	.406
Chet Laabs	OF150	R	31	155	580	83	145	27	7	17	85	73	105	5	.250	.409
Frankie Hayes	C76, 1B1	R	28	88	250	16	47	7	0	5	30	37	36	1	.188	.276
Mark Christman	3B37, SS24, 1B20, 2B14	R	29	98	336	31	91	11	5	2	35	19	19	0	.271	.351
Rick Ferrell	C70	R	37	74	209	12	50	7	0	0	20	34	14	0	.239	.273
Al Zarilla	OF60	L	24	70	228	27	58	7	1	2	17	17	20	1	.254	.320
Mike Kreevich	OF51	R	35	60	161	24	41	6	0	0	10	26	13	4	.255	.292
Joe Schultz	C26	L	24	46	92	6	22	5	0	0	8	9	3	0	.239	.393
Tony Criscola	OF13	L	27	29	52	4	8	0	0	0	1	8	7	0	.154	.154
2 Ellis Clary	3B14, 2B3	R	26	23	69	15	19	2	0	0	5	11	6	1	.275	.304
Floyd Baker	SS10, 3B1	L	26	22	46	5	8	2	0	0	4	6	4	0	.174	.217
1 Don Heffner	2B13, 1B1	R	32	18	33	2	4	1	0	0	2	2	2	0	.121	.152
Hal Epps	OF8	L	29	8	35	2	10	4	0	0	1	3	4	1	.286	.400
Hank Schmulbach		L	18	1	0	1	0	0	0	0	0	0	0	0	—	—

NAME	T	AGE	W	L	PCT	SV	G	GS	CG	IP	H	BB	SO	SHO	ERA
		33	72	80	.474	14	153	153	64	1385	1397	488	572	10	3.41
Steve Sundra	R	33	15	11	.577	0	32	29	13	208	212	66	44	3	3.25
Bob Muncrief	R	27	13	12	.520	1	35	27	12	205	211	48	80	3	2.81
Denny Galehouse	R	31	11	11	.500	1	31	28	14	224	217	74	114	2	2.77
Nels Potter	R	31	10	5	.667	1	33	13	8	168	146	54	80	0	2.79
George Caster	R	35	6	8	.429	8	35	0	0	76	69	41	43	0	2.13
1 Johnny Niggeling	R	39	6	8	.429	0	20	17	7	150	122	57	73	0	3.18
Al Hollingsworth	L	35	6	13	.316	3	35	20	9	154	169	51	63	1	4.21
Sid Peterson	R	25	2	1	1.000	0	10	1	0	15	15	3	0	0	2.70
Archie McKain	L	32	1	1	.500	0	16	0	0	16	16	6	6	0	3.94
2 Al Milnar	R	29	1	2	.333	0	3	2	1	15	23	9	7	0	5.40
2 Bobo Newsom	R	35	1	6	.143	0	10	9	0	52	69	35	37	0	7.44
Al LaMacchia	R	21	0	0	.000	0	1	1	0	4	9	2	2	0	11.25
1 Fritz Ostermueller	L	35	0	2	.000	0	11	0	0	13	13	10	11	0	4.97
2 Charley Fuchs	R	29	0	0	—	0	13	0	0	36	42	11	9	0	4.00
Paul Dean	R	29	0	0	—	0	3	1	0	13	16	3	1	0	3.46
Jack Kramer (MS)	R	25	0	0	—	0	3	0	0	9	11	4	4	0	8.00
Fred Sanford	R	23	0	0	—	0	3	0	0	7	7	4	2	0	2.00
2 Ox Miller	R	28	0	0	—	0	2	0	0	6	7	3	3	0	12.00

BOSTON — 7th 68-84 .447 29 — JOE CRONIN

NAME	G by Pos	B	AGE	G	AB	R	H	2B	3B	HR	RBI	BB	SO	SB	BA	SA
TOTALS			27	155	5392	563	1314	233	42	57	510	486	591	86	.244	.332
Tony Lupien	1B153	L	26	154	608	65	155	21	9	4	47	54	23	16	.255	.339
Bobby Doerr	2B155	R	25	155	604	78	163	32	3	16	75	62	59	8	.270	.412
Skeeter Newsome	SS98, 3B15	R	32	114	449	48	119	21	2	1	22	21	41	5	.265	.327
Jim Tabor	3B133, OF2	R	29	137	537	57	130	26	3	13	85	43	54	7	.242	.374
Pete Fox	OF125	R	33	127	489	54	141	24	4	2	44	34	40	22	.288	.366
Catfish Metkovich	OF76, 1B2	L	21	78	321	34	79	14	4	5	27	19	38	1	.246	.361
Leon Culberson (NJ)	OF79	R	23	81	312	36	85	16	6	3	34	30	35	13	.272	.391
Roy Partee	C91	R	25	96	299	30	84	14	2	0	31	39	33	0	.281	.341
Johnny Lazor	OF63	L	30	83	208	21	47	10	2	0	13	22	25	6	.226	.293
Eddie Lake	SS63	R	27	75	216	26	43	10	0	3	16	47	35	3	.199	.287
Joe Cronin	3B10	R	26	59	77	8	24	4	0	5	29	11	4	0	.312	.558
Johnny Peacock	C32	R	33	48	114	7	23	3	1	0	7	10	9	1	.202	.246
Dee Miles	OF25	L	34	45	121	9	26	2	2	0	10	3	3	0	.215	.264
Al Simmons	OF33	R	41	40	133	9	27	5	0	1	12	8	21	0	.203	.263
Bill Conroy	C38	R	28	39	89	13	16	5	0	1	6	18	19	0	.180	.270
Ford Garrison	OF32	R	27	36	129	13	36	5	1	1	11	5	14	0	.279	.357
2 Babe Barna	OF29	L	28	30	112	19	19	4	1	0	7	14	15	2	.170	.277
Tom McBride	OF24	R	28	26	96	11	23	3	1	0	5	4	4	0	.240	.292
Danny Doyle	C13	B	26	13	43	2	9	1	0	0	7	6	7	0	.209	.233
Lou Finney (VR) 32																

NAME	T	AGE	W	L	PCT	SV	G	GS	CG	IP	H	BB	SO	SHO	ERA
		31	68	84	.447	16	155	155	62	1426	1369	615	513	13	3.45
Tex Hughson	R	27	12	15	.444	2	35	32	20	266	242	73	114	4	2.64
Oscar Judd	L	35	11	6	.647	0	23	20	8	155	131	69	53	1	2.90
Dick Newsome	R	33	8	13	.381	0	25	22	8	154	166	68	40	2	4.50
Mike Ryba	R	40	7	5	.583	2	40	8	4	144	142	57	50	1	3.25
Yank Terry	R	32	7	9	.438	1	30	22	7	164	147	63	63	0	3.51
Joe Dobson	R	26	7	11	.389	0	25	20	9	164	144	67	63	3	3.13
Mace Brown	R	34	6	6	.500	9	49	0	0	93	71	51	40	0	2.13
Pinky Woods	R	28	5	6	.455	1	23	12	2	101	109	55	32	0	4.90
Lou Lucier	R	25	3	4	.429	0	16	9	3	74	94	33	23	0	3.89
1 Andy Karl	R	29	1	1	.500	1	10	0	0	26	31	13	6	0	3.46
Emmett O'Neill	R	24	1	4	.200	0	11	5	1	58	56	46	20	0	4.50
1 Ken Chase	L	29	0	4	.000	0	7	5	0	27	36	30	9	0	7.00

PHILADELPHIA — 8th 49-105 .318 49 — CONNIE MACK

NAME	G by Pos	B	AGE	G	AB	R	H	2B	3B	HR	RBI	BB	SO	SB	BA	SA
TOTALS			29	155	5244	497	1219	174	44	26	462	430	465	55	.232	.297
Dick Siebert	1B145	L	31	146	558	50	140	26	7	1	72	33	21	6	.251	.328
Pete Suder	2B95, 3B32, SS5	R	27	131	475	30	105	14	5	3	41	14	40	1	.221	.291
Irv Hall	SS148, 2B1, 3B1	R	24	151	544	37	139	15	4	0	54	22	42	10	.256	.298
Eddie Mayo	3B123	L	33	128	471	49	103	10	1	0	28	34	32	2	.219	.244
Johnny Welaj (MS)	OF72	R	29	93	281	45	68	16	1	0	15	15	17	12	.242	.306
Jo-Jo White	OF133	L	34	139	500	69	124	17	7	1	30	61	51	12	.248	.316
Bobby Estalella	OF97	R	32	117	367	43	95	14	4	11	63	52	44	1	.259	.409
Hal Wagner	C99	L	27	111	289	22	69	17	1	1	26	36	17	3	.239	.315
Bob Swift	C77	R	28	77	224	16	43	5	1	1	11	35	16	0	.192	.237
Elmer Valo (MS)	OF63	L	22	77	249	31	55	6	2	3	18	35	13	2	.221	.297
Jim Tyack	OF38	L	32	54	155	11	40	8	1	0	23	14	9	1	.258	.323
2 Don Heffner	2B47, 1B1	R	32	52	178	17	37	6	0	0	8	18	12	3	.208	.242
Jimmy Ripple	3B32	L	33	32	126	8	30	3	1	0	15	7	7	0	.238	.278
Frank Skaff	1B18, 3B3, SS1	R	32	32	64	8	18	2	1	1	9	2	8	0	.281	.391
George Staller	OF20	L	27	21	85	14	23	1	3	3	12	5	6	1	.271	.459
Bill Burgo	OF17	L	23	17	70	12	26	4	2	0	6	4	9	0	.371	.529
Joe Rullo	2B16	R	27	16	55	2	16	3	0	0	6	8	7	1	.291	.345
Felix Mackiewicz	OF3	R	25	9	16	1	1	0	0	0	2	0	5	0	.063	.063
Woody Wheaton	OF57	L	28	7	30	2	8	2	0	0	2	3	10	0	.267	.267
Tony Parisse	C5	R	32	6	17	0	3	0	0	0	1	2	6	0	.176	.176
Ed Busch	SS4	R	25	4	17	4	5	0	0	0	0	0	2	0	.294	.294
Vern Benson (MS)		L	18	2	7	0	0	0	0	0	0	1	3	0	.000	.000
Bruce Konopka (MS)		L	23	3	1	0	0	0	0	0	0	0	1	0	.000	.000
Earle Brucker		R	42	1	1	0	0	0	0	0	0	0	0	0	.000	.000
Lew Flick	OF1	L	28	5	5	1	3	0	0	0	2	0	1	0	.600	.600
George Kell	3B1	R	20	1	5	1	1	0	0	0	0	0	0	0	.200	.200

NAME	T	AGE	W	L	PCT	SV	G	GS	CG	IP	H	BB	SO	SHO	ERA
		28	49	105	.318	13	155	155	73	1394	1421	536	503	5	4.05
Jesse Flores	R	28	12	14	.462	0	31	27	13	231	208	70	113	0	3.12
Roger Wolff	R	32	10	15	.400	4	41	26	13	221	232	72	91	2	3.54
Lum Harris	R	28	7	21	.250	1	32	27	15	216	241	63	55	1	4.21
Don Black	R	26	6	16	.273	1	33	26	12	208	193	110	65	1	4.20
Russ Christopher	R	25	5	8	.385	2	24	15	5	133	120	58	56	0	3.45
Orie Arntzen	R	33	4	13	.235	0	32	20	9	164	172	69	66	0	4.23
Everett Fagan (MS)	R	26	2	6	.250	3	18	2	0	37	41	14	9	0	6.32
Herman Besse	L	31	1	1	.500	0	5	1	0	16	17	4	4	0	3.38
Charlie Bowles (MS)	R	26	1	1	.500	0	3	2	1	18	17	4	4	0	3.00
Lou Ciola	R	20	1	3	.250	0	6	3	2	44	48	22	7	0	5.52
Bert Kucyznski (MS)	R	23	0	1	.000	0	6	2	0	25	36	9	8	0	3.96
Carl Scheib	R	16	0	1	.000	0	6	0	0	19	24	3	3	0	4.26
1 John Burrows	L	29	0	1	.000	0	4	1	1	11	14	9	5	0	7.88
Bud Mains	R	21	0	1	.000	0	2	0	0	5	8	5	1	0	12.60
Tal Abernathy	R	21	0	0	—	0	1	0	0	1	5	1	1	0	9.00
Sam Lowry	R	23	0	0	—	0	4	0	0	18	18	9	3	0	5.00
Tom Clyde	L	19	0	0	—	0	1	0	0	2	5	1	1	0	9.00
Norm Brown	R	20	0	0	—	0	1	0	0	1	1	0	0	0	0.00

St. Louis

NAME	G by Pos	B	AGE	G	AB	R	H	2B	3B	HR	RBI	BB	SO	SB	BA	SA
ST. LOUIS 1ST 105-49 .682	BILLY SOUTHWORTH															
TOTALS			27	157	5438	679	1515	259	72	70	638	428	438	40	.279	.391
Ray Sanders	1B141	L	26	144	478	69	134	21	5	11	73	77	33	1	.280	.414
Lou Klein	2B126, SS51	R	24	154	627	91	180	28	14	7	62	50	70	9	.287	.410
Marty Marion	SS128	R	25	129	418	38	117	15	3	1	52	32	37	1	.280	.337
Whitey Kurowski	3B137, SS2	R	25	139	522	69	150	24	8	13	70	31	54	3	.287	.439
Stan Musial	OF155	L	22	157	617	108	220	48	20	13	81	72	18	9	.357	.562
Harry Walker	OF144, 2B1	L	26	148	564	76	166	28	6	2	53	40	24	5	.295	.376
2 Danny Litwhiler	OF70	R	26	80	258	40	72	14	3	7	31	19	31	1	.279	.438
Walker Cooper	C112	R	28	122	449	52	143	30	4	9	81	19	19	1	.319	.463
Johnny Hopp	OF52, 1B27	L	26	91	241	33	54	10	2	2	25	24	22	8	.224	.307
Debs Garms	OF47, 3B23, SS1	L	36	90	249	26	64	10	2	0	22	13	8	2	.257	.313
Ken O'Dea	C56	L	30	71	203	15	57	11	2	3	25	19	25	0	.281	.399
Frank Demaree	OF23	R	33	39	86	5	25	2	0	0	9	8	4	1	.291	.314
George Fallon	2B36	R	28	36	78	6	18	1	0	0	5	2	9	0	.231	.244
Jimmy Brown	2B19, 3B9, SS6	B	33	34	110	6	20	4	2	0	8	6	1	0	.182	.255
Sam Narron	C3	R	29	10	11	0	1	0	0	0	0	1	2	0	.091	.091
1 Coaker Triplett	OF6	R	31	9	25	1	2	0	0	1	4	1	6	0	.080	.200
1 Buster Adams	OF6	R	28	8	11	1	1	0	0	0	1	0	2	0	.091	.182

NAME	T	AGE	W	L	PCT	SV	G	GS	CG	IP	H	BB	SO	SHO	ERA
		27	105	49	.682	15	157	157	94	1427	1246	477	639	21	2.57
Mort Cooper	R	30	21	8	.724	3	37	32	24	274	228	79	141	6	2.30
Max Lanier	L	27	15	7	.682	3	32	25	14	213	195	75	123	2	1.90
Howie Krist	R	27	11	5	.688	3	34	17	9	164	141	62	57	2	2.91
Harry Gembert	R	33	10	5	.667	0	21	19	7	133	115	32	40	2	2.84
George Munger	R	24	9	5	.643	2	32	9		93	101	42	45	0	3.97
Harry Brecheen	L	28	9	6	.600	4	29	13	8	135	98	39	68	1	2.27
Murry Dickson	R	26	8	2	.800	0	31	7	2	116	119	49	44	0	3.57
Al Brazle	L	29	8	2	.800	1	9	8	7	88	74	29	26	1	1.53
Howie Pollet	L	22	8	4	.667	0	16	14	12	118	83	32	61	5	1.75
Ernie White (SA)	L	26	5	5	.500	0	14	10	5	79	78	33	28	1	3.76
Bud Byerly	R	22	1	0	1.000	2	2	0	1	13	14	5	6	0	3.46

Cincinnati

NAME	G by Pos	B	AGE	G	AB	R	H	2B	3B	HR	RBI	BB	SO	SB	BA	SA
CINCINNATI 2nd 87-67 .565 18	BILL McKECHNIE															
TOTALS			31	155	5329	608	1362	229	47	43	558	445	476	49	.256	.340
Frank McCormick	1B120	R	32	126	472	56	143	28	0	8	59	29	15	2	.303	.413
Lonny Frey	2B144	R	32	144	586	78	154	20	8	2	43	76	56	7	.263	.334
Eddie Miller	SS154	R	26	154	576	49	129	26	4	2	71	33	43	8	.224	.293
Steve Mesner	3B130	R	25	137	504	53	137	26	1	0	52	26	20	1	.272	.327
Max Marshall	OF129	L	29	132	508	55	120	11	8	4	39	34	52	6	.236	.313
Gee Walker	OF106	R	35	114	429	48	105	23	2	3	54	12	38	6	.245	.329
Eric Tipton	OF139	R	28	140	493	82	142	26	7	9	49	85	36	1	.288	.424
Ray Mueller	C140	R	31	141	427	50	111	19	4	8	52	56	42	1	.260	.379
Bert Haas	1B44, 3B23, OF18	R	29	101	332	39	87	17	6	4	44	22	26	6	.262	.386
Estel Crabtree	OF64	L	39	95	254	25	70	12	0	2	26	25	17	1	.276	.346
Dain Clay	OF33	R	30	49	93	19	25	2	4	0	9	8	14	1	.269	.376
Tony DePhillips	C35	R	30	35	20	0	2	1	0	0	2	1	5	0	.100	.150
Woody Williams	2B12, 3B7, SS5	R	30	30	46	8	26	2	1	0	11	1	3	0	.377	.435
Al Lakeman	C21	R	24	22	55	14	14	2	1	0	6	3	11	0	.255	.327
Frankie Kelleher	OF1	R	26	9	10	1	0	0	0	0	0	2	0	0	.000	.000
Chuck Aleno	OF2	R	26	7	10	0	3	0	0	0	1	1	1	0	.300	.300
1 Charlie Brewster	2B2	R	26	7	8	1	1	0	0	0	0	0	2	0	.125	.125
Lonnie Goldstein	1B2	L	25	5	5	1	1	0	0	0	0	1	0	0	.200	.200

Mike McCormick (MS) 26 R 2-15, Dick West 27 R 0-0

NAME	T	AGE	W	L	PCT	SV	G	GS	CG	IP	H	BB	SO	SHO	ERA
		32	87	67	.565	17	155	155	78	1404	1299	581	498	18	3.13
Elmer Riddle	R	28	21	11	.656	3	36	33	19	260	235	107	69	5	2.63
Bucky Walters	R	34	15	15	.500	0	34	34	21	246	244	109	80	5	3.55
Johnny Vander Meer	L	28	15	16	.484	0	36	36	21	289	228	162	174	3	2.87
Clyde Shoun	L	31	14	5	.737	7	45	5	2	147	131	46	61	0	3.06
Ray Starr	R	37	11	10	.524	1	36	33	9	217	201	91	41	2	3.65
Joe Beggs	R	32	7	6	.538	6	39	4	4	115	121	25	28	2	2.35
Ed Heusser	R	34	7	6	.538	1	26	10	2	91	97	23	28	1	3.46
Rocky Stone	R	24	0	1	.000	0	13	0	0	25	23	8	11	0	4.32
Bob Malloy	R	25	0	0	—	0	6	0	0	10	14	8	4	0	6.30
Jack Niemes	R	23	0	0	—	3	3	0	0	3	5	1	1	0	6.00
Junior Thompson (VR) 26															

Brooklyn

NAME	G by Pos	B	AGE	G	AB	R	H	2B	3B	HR	RBI	BB	SO	SB	BA	SA
BROOKLYN 3rd 81-72 .529 23.5	LEO DUROCHER															
TOTALS			30	153	5309	716	1444	263	35	39	660	580	422	58	.272	.357
Dolph Camilli (VR)	1B95	L	36	95	353	56	87	15	6	6	43	65	48	2	.246	.374
Billy Herman	2B117, 3B37	R	33	153	585	76	193	41	2	2	100	66	26	4	.330	.415
Arky Vaughan	SS99, 3B55	R	31	149	610	112	186	39	6	5	66	60	13	20	.305	.413
Frenchy Bordagaray	3B25, OF53	R	33	89	268	47	81	18	2	0	19	30	15	6	.302	.384
Dixie Walker	OF136	L	32	138	540	83	163	32	6	5	71	49	24	3	.302	.411
Augie Galan	OF124, 1B13	L	31	139	483	83	142	26	3	9	67	103	39	6	.287	.406
Luis Olmo	OF57	R	23	57	238	39	72	6	4	4	37	10	20	3	.303	.412
Mickey Owen	C100, 3B3, SS1	R	27	106	365	31	95	11	2	0	54	25	15	4	.260	.301
Al Glossop	SS23, 2B24, 3B17, OF1	B	28	87	217	28	37	9	0	3	21	28	27	0	.171	.253
Paul Waner	OF57	L	40	82	225	29	70	16	0	1	26	35	9	0	.311	.396
Bobby Bragan	C57, 3B12, SS5	R	25	71	227	17	58	7	2	2	24	15	16	0	.264	.341
1 Joe Medwick	OF42	R	31	48	173	14	47	10	0	0	25	10	8	1	.272	.329
Howie Schultz	1B45	R	20	45	182	20	49	12	0	1	34	6	24	3	.269	.352
Max Macon	P25, 1B3	L	27	45	55	7	9	0	0	0	6	0	1	1	.164	.164
1 Dee Moore	C15, 3B9	R	29	37	79	8	20	3	0	0	12	11	8	1	.253	.291
Johnny Cooney	1B3, OF2	L	42	37	34	7	7	0	0	0	2	4	3	1	.206	.206
Red Barkley	SS18	R	30	32	51	6	16	3	0	0	7	4	7	1	.314	.373
1 Alex Kampouris	2B18	R	30	19	44	9	10	4	1	0	4	17	6	0	.227	.364
Gene Hermanski (MS)	OF17	L	23	18	60	6	18	2	1	0	12	11	7	1	.300	.367
Boyd Bartley (MS)	SS9	R	23	9	21	0	1	0	0	0	1	1	3	0	.048	.048
Bill Hart	3B6, SS1	R	30	8	19	0	3	0	0	0	1	0	2	0	.158	.158
Carden Gillenwater	OF5	R	26	8	17	1	3	0	0	0	2	4	5	0	.176	.176
Al Campanis	2B7	B	26	7	20	3	2	0	0	0	2	0	4	1	.100	.100
2 Joe Orengo	3B6	R	27	7	15	1	3	2	0	0	1	4	2	0	.200	.333
Leo Durocher	SS6	R	37	6	18	1	4	0	0	0	1	1	2	0	.222	.222

Pat Ankenman (MS) 30 R 1-2, Gil Hodges 19 R 0-2, Hal Peck 26 L 0-1, Lloyd Waner (WW) 37

NAME	T	AGE	W	L	PCT	SV	G	GS	CG	IP	H	BB	SO	SHO	ERA
		31	81	72	.529	22	153	153	50	1370	1326	637	585	13	3.88
Whit Wyatt (SA)	R	35	14	5	.737	0	26	26	13	181	139	43	80	3	2.49
Kirby Higbe	R	28	13	10	.565	0	35	27	8	185	189	95	108	1	3.70
Curt Davis (BG)	R	39	10	13	.435	3	31	21	8	164	182	39	47	2	3.79
1 Bobo Newsom	R	35	9	4	.692	1	22	12	6	125	113	57	75	1	3.02
Ed Head	R	25	9	10	.474	0	47	18	7	170	166	66	83	3	3.65
Max Macon	R	27	5	5	.583	0	25	9	0	77	91	32	21	0	5.96
1 Johnny Allen (SU)	R	38	5	1	.833	1	17	1	0	38	42	25	15	0	4.26
Rube Melton	R	26	5	8	.385	0	30	17	4	119	106	79	63	2	3.93
Freddie Fitzsimmons	R	41	3	4	.429	0	9	7	1	45	50	21	12	1	5.40
Les Webber	R	28	2	2	.500	10	54	0	1	109	112	69	24	0	3.80
Rex Barney	R	18	2	2	.500	0	9	8	1	45	36	41	23	0	6.40
2 Fritz Ostermueller	L	35	1	1	.500	0	7	1	0	27	21	12	15	0	3.33
1 Newt Kimball	R	28	1	1	.500	1	5	0	0	11	9	5	2	0	1.64
Chirs Haughey	R	17	0	1	.000	0	1	1	0	5	5	10	5	0	3.86
2 Bill Lohrman	R	30	0	2	.000	0	6	2	2	28	29	10	5	0	3.54
Hal Gregg	R	21	0	3	.000	0	5	4	0	19	21	7	9	0	9.47
2 Bill Sayles	R	25	0	0	—	0	5	1	0	12	13	10	5	0	7.50
Bob Chipman	L	24	0	0	—	0	1	0	0	2	2	1	1	0	0.00

Pittsburgh

NAME	G by Pos	B	AGE	G	AB	R	H	2B	3B	HR	RBI	BB	SO	SB	BA	SA
PITTSBURGH 4th 80-74 .519 25	FRANKIE FRISCH															
TOTALS			28	157	5353	669	1401	240	73	42	623	573	566	64	.262	.357
Elbie Fletcher	1B154	L	27	157	544	91	154	24	5	9	70	95	49	1	.283	.395
Pete Coscarart	2B85, SS47, 3B1	R	30	133	491	57	119	19	6	0	48	46	48	4	.242	.305
Frankie Gustine	SS68, 2B40, 1B1	R	23	112	414	40	120	21	3	0	43	32	36	12	.290	.355
Bob Elliott	3B151, 2B2, SS1	R	26	156	581	82	183	30	12	7	101	56	24	4	.315	.444
Johnny Barrett	OF99	L	27	130	290	41	67	12	3	1	32	32	23	5	.231	.303
Vince DiMaggio	OF156, SS1	R	30	157	580	64	144	41	2	15	88	70	126	11	.248	.403
Jim Russell	OF134, 1B6	B	24	146	533	79	138	19	11	4	44	77	67	12	.259	.358
Al Lopez	C116, 3B1	R	34	117	372	40	98	9	4	1	39	44	25	2	.263	.317
Tommy O'Brien	OF48, 3B9	R	24	89	232	35	72	12	7	2	28	15	24	1	.310	.448
Maurice Van Robays	OF60	R	28	69	236	32	68	17	7	1	35	18	19	0	.288	.432
Bill Baker	C56	R	32	72	172	12	47	6	3	1	26	22	6	3	.273	.360
Johnny Wyrostek (SJ)	OF20, 3B2, 1B1, 2B1	L	23	51	79	7	12	3	0	0	1	3	15	0	.152	.190
Al Rubeling	2B44, 3B1	R	30	47	168	23	44	8	4	0	9	8	17	0	.262	.357
Huck Geary	SS46	R	26	46	166	17	25	4	0	1	13	18	6	3	.151	.193
Rip Sewell	P35	R	36	41	140	9	30	4	1	0	17	2	21	7	.286	.343
Frank Colman	OF11	L	25	32	59	9	16	2	2	0	4	8	7	1	.271	.373

1 Jimmy Wasdell 29 L 1-2, Hank Camelli 28 R 0-3, Tony Ordenna 24 R 2-4, Bud Stewart (VR) 27

NAME	T	AGE	W	L	PCT	SV	G	GS	CG	IP	H	BB	SO	SHO	ERA
		31	80	74	.519	12	157	157	74	1404	1424	421	396	11	3.05
Rip Sewell	R	36	21	9	.700	3	35	31	25	265	267	75	65	3	2.55
Bob Klinger	R	35	11	8	.579	2	33	18	10	195	185	58	65	3	2.72
Max Butcher	R	32	10	8	.556	1	33	21	10	194	191	57	45	2	2.60
Wally Hebert	L	35	10	11	.476	3	34	23	12	184	197	45	41	1	2.98
Hank Gornicki	R	32	9	13	.409	4	42	18	4	147	165	47	63	1	3.98
Xavier Rescigno	R	30	9	6	.400	2	37	14	5	133	125	45	41	1	3.05
Bill Brandt	R	28	4	1	.800	0	29	3	0	57	57	19	17	0	3.16
Johnny Gee	L	27	4	4	.500	0	15	10	2	82	89	27	18	0	4.28
Jack Hallett (MS)	R	32	4	2	.333	1	9	4	2	48	36	11	11	1	6.43
Cookie Cuccurullo	L	25	0	0	—	0	7	0	0	7	10	3	3	0	6.43
1 Dutch Dietz	R	31	0	3	.000	0	4	0	0	8	14	6	4	0	6.00
2 Johnny Podgajny	R	23	0	0	—	0	15	5	0	34	37	13	7	0	4.76
Harry Shuman	R	28	0	0	—	0	18	0	0	35	35	5	10	0	5.32

Chicago

NAME	G by Pos	B	AGE	G	AB	R	H	2B	3B	HR	RBI	BB	SO	SB	BA	SA
CHICAGO 5th 74-79 .484 30.5	JIMMIE WILSON															
TOTALS			31	154	5279	632	1380	207	56	52	579	574	522	53	.261	.351
Phil Cavarretta	1B134, OF7	L	26	143	530	93	154	27	9	8	73	75	42	3	.291	.421
Eddie Stanky	2B131, SS12, 3B2	R	26	153	544	92	154	15	1	0	47	92	42	4	.245	.278
Lennie Merullo	SS125, 3B2, 2B1	R	26	129	453	37	115	18	3	1	25	26	42	1	.254	.313
Stan Hack	3B136	L	33	144	533	78	154	24	4	3	35	82	27	5	.289	.366
Bill Nicholson	OF154	L	28	154	608	95	188	30	9	29	128	71	86	4	.309	.531
Peanuts Lowrey	OF113, SS16, 3B2	R	25	144	580	59	140	25	12	1	63	35	24	3	.292	.400
Ival Goodman	OF61	L	34	80	225	30	72	10	5	3	45	24	20	3	.320	.449
Clyde McCullough (BN)	C81	R	26	87	266	20	63	5	2	2	23	24	33	6	.237	.293
Dom Dallessandro	OF45	L	29	87	176	13	39	8	3	1	31	40	14	1	.222	.318
Lou Novikoff (HO)	OF61	R	27	78	233	22	65	7	3	0	28	18	15	0	.279	.335
Stu Martin	2B22, 3B8, 1B2	R	30	64	118	13	26	4	0	0	5	10	15	1	.220	.254
Chico Hernandez	C41	R	27	43	126	10	34	4	0	0	9	5	19	0	.270	.302
2 Mickey Livingston	C31, 3B6	R	28	36	111	10	29	5	1	4	16	12	8	1	.261	.432
Heinz Becker	1B18	B	27	24	69	5	10	0	0	0	2	8	2	0	.145	.145
Al Todd	C17	R	39	21	45	1	6	0	0	0	4	1	6	0	.133	.133
Whitey Platt	OF14	R	22	20	41	2	7	3	0	0	5	1	7	1	.171	.244
Ed Sauer	OF13, 3B1	R	24	14	55	3	15	3	0	0	3	1	5	0	.273	.327
Andy Pafko	SS13	R	22	13	58	7	22	3	0	0	10	2	5	1	.379	.431
Bill Schuster	SS13	R	30	13	34	3	10	2	0	0	2	1	7	1	.294	.373
Don Johnson	2B10	R	31	10	42	3	8	1	0	0	3	1	4	0	.190	.238
John Ostrowski	OF5, 3B4	R	25	10	29	1	6	2	0	0	2	1	7	0	.207	.276
Pete Elko	3B9	R	25	9	30	2	4	1	0	0	4	1	5	0	.133	.133
Charlie Gilbert	OF6	L	23	8	20	1	3	0	0	0	2	4	2	0	.150	.150
Billy Holm	C7	R	31	7	15	0	1	0	0	0	0	1	5	0	.067	.067
Mickey Kreitner	C3	R	20	3	8	0	3	0	0	0	2	1	1	0	.375	.375

NAME	T	AGE	W	L	PCT	SV	G	GS	CG	IP	H	BB	SO	SHO	ERA
		31	74	79	.484	14	154	154	67	1386	1379	394	513	13	3.24
Hi Bithorn	R	27	18	12	.600	2	39	30	19	250	227	65	86	7	2.59
Claude Passeau	R	34	15	12	.556	1	35	31	18	257	247	66	93	1	2.91
Paul Derringer	R	36	10	14	.417	3	32	22	10	174	184	39	75	2	3.57
Hank Wyse	R	25	9	7	.563	3	38	15	8	156	159	34	45	2	2.94
Ed Hanyzewski	R	22	7	3	.533	0	33	16	3	130	120	45	55	0	2.56
Ray Prim	L	36	4	3	.571	0	20	6	0	67	14	27	0		3.58
Lon Warneke	R	34	4	4	.444	0	21	10	4	88	82	18	30	0	3.17
1 Bill Lee	R	33	3	7	.300	0	13	12	4	78	83	27	18	0	3.58
Walter Singer	R	32	2	1	.667	0	4	3	1	25	24	4	5	0	2.88
Paul Erickson	R	29	1	3	.250	0	15	4	0	43	47	22	24	0	6.07
Bill Fleming	R	29	1	0	1.000	0	11	0	0	32	41	12	12	0	6.47
Dale Alderson	R	29	0	1	.000	1	4	0	0	13	25	16	18	0	3.82
2 John Burrows	L	29	0	0	—	0	23	0	0	35	33	25	16	0	3.82
1 Dick Barrett	R	36	0	0	—	0	15	4	0	45	52	28	20	0	4.80
Jake Mooty	R	30	0	0	—	0	1	0	0	1	1	0	0	0	0.00

BOSTON 6th 68-85 .444 36.5 — BOB COLEMAN 21-25 .457 — CASEY STENGEL 47-60 .439

NAME	G by Pos	B	AGE	G	AB	R	H	2B	3B	HR	RBI	BB	SO	SB	BA	SA
TOTALS			27	153	5196	465	1213	202	36	39	431	469	604	56	.233	.309
Johnny McCarthy (BN-MS)	1B78	L	33	78	313	32	95	24	6	2	33	10	19	1	.304	.438
Connie Ryan	2B100, 3B30	R	23	132	457	52	97	10	2	1	24	58	56	7	.212	.249
Whitey Wietelmann	SS153	B	24	153	534	33	115	14	1	0	39	46	40	9	.215	.245
Eddie Joost	3B67, 2B60, SS1	R	27	124	421	34	78	16	3	2	20	68	80	5	.185	.252
Chuck Workman	OF149, 1B3, 3B1	L	28	153	615	71	153	17	1	10	67	53	72	12	.249	.328
Tommy Holmes	OF152	L	26	152	629	75	170	33	10	5	41	58	20	7	.270	.378
Butch Nieman	OF93	L	25	101	335	39	84	15	8	7	46	39	39	4	.251	.406
Phil Masi	C73	R	26	80	238	27	65	9	1	2	28	27	20	7	.273	.345
Chet Ross	OF73	R	26	94	285	27	62	12	2	7	32	26	67	1	.218	.347
Kerby Farrell	1B69, P5	L	29	85	280	11	75	14	1	0	21	16	15	1	.268	.325
Clyde Kluttz	C55	R	25	66	207	13	51	7	0	0	20	15	9	0	.246	.280
Joe Burns	3B34, OF4	R	28	52	135	12	28	3	0	1	5	8	25	2	.207	.252
Jim Tobin	P33, 1B1	R	30	46	107	8	30	4	0	2	12	6	16	0	.280	.374
2 Hugh Poland	C38	L	30	44	141	5	27	7	0	1	13	4	11	0	.191	.241
Heinie Heltzel	3B29	R	29	29	86	6	13	3	0	0	5	7	13	0	.151	.186
Bill Brubaker	3B5, 1B3	R	32	13	19	3	8	3	0	0	3	4	4	0	.421	.579
1 Tony Cuccinello	3B4, 2B2, SS1	R	35	13	19	0	0	0	0	0	2	3	1	0	.000	.000
Buck Etchison	1B6	L	28	10	19	2	6	3	0	0	2	2	7	0	.316	.474
Sam Gentile		R	26	8	4	1	1	1	0	0	0	0	0	0	.250	.500
Ben Geraghty	2B1, SS1, 3B1	R	30	8	1	2	0	0	0	0	0	0	0	0	.000	.000
Connie Creeden			27	1	4	1	1	0	0	0	1	0	1	0	.250	.250

NAME	T	AGE	W	L	PCT	SV	G	GS	CG	IP	H	BB	SO	SHO	ERA
		28	68	85	.444	4	153	153	87	1398	1361	440	409	13	3.24
Al Javery	R	25	17	16	.515	0	41	35	19	303	288	99	134	5	3.21
Jim Tobin	R	30	14	14	.500	0	33	30	24	250	241	69	52	1	2.66
Nate Andrews	R	29	14	20	.412	0	36	34	23	284	253	75	80	3	2.57
Red Barrett	R	28	12	18	.400	0	38	31	14	255	240	63	64	3	3.18
13Manny Salvo	R	31	5	7	.417	0	21	14	5	99	99	31	26	1	3.46
Danny MacFayden	R	38	2	1	.667	0	10	1	0	21	31	9	5	0	6.00
Allyn Stout	R	38	1	0	1.000	0	9	0	0	17	17	9	3	0	7.00
Bill Donovan (MS)	L	26	1	0	1.000	0	7	0	0	15	17	9	1	0	1.80
John Dagenhard	R	26	1	0	1.000	0	2	1	1	11	9	4	2	0	0.00
George Jeffcoat	R	29	1	2	.333	0	8	1	0	18	15	10	10	0	3.00
Kerby Farrell	L	29	1	0	1.000	0	5	0	0	23	24	9	4	0	4.30
Lou Tost	L	32	0	1	.000	0	1	0	0	7	10	4	3	0	5.14
Carl Lindquist	R	24	0	2	.000	0	2	0	0	13	17	4	1	0	6.23
Dave Odom	R	25	0	3	.000	0	22	3	1	55	54	30	17	0	5.24
Ben Cardoni	R	22	0	1	—	1	11	0	0	28	38	14	5	0	6.43
Ray Martin (MS)	R	18	0	0	—	0	2	0	0	3	3	1	1	0	9.00
George Diehl	R	25	0	0	—	0	1	0	0	4	4	3	1	0	4.50
Roy Talcott	R	23	0	0	—	0	1	0	0	1	2	0	0	0	18.00

PHILADELPHIA 7th 64-90 .416 41 — BUCKY HARRIS 38-52 .422 — FREDDIE FITZSIMMONS 26-38 .406

NAME	G by Pos	B	AGE	G	AB	R	H	2B	3B	HR	RBI	BB	SO	SB	BA	SA
TOTALS			28	157	5297	571	1321	186	36	66	529	499	556	29	.249	.335
2 Jimmy Wasdell	1B82, OF56	L	29	141	522	54	136	19	6	4	67	46	22	6	.261	.343
Danny Murtaugh (MS)	2B113	R	25	113	451	65	123	17	4	1	35	57	23	4	.273	.345
Glen Stewart	SS77, 2B18, 1B8, C1	R	30	110	336	23	71	10	1	2	24	32	41	1	.211	.265
Pinky May	3B132	R	32	137	415	31	117	19	2	8	48	56	21	2	.282	.345
Ron Northey	OF145	L	23	147	586	72	163	31	5	16	68	51	52	2	.278	.430
2 Buster Adams	OF107	R	28	111	418	48	107	14	7	4	38	39	67	2	.256	.352
2 Coaker Triplett	OF90	R	31	105	360	45	98	16	4	14	52	28	28	2	.272	.456
1 Mickey Livingston	C84, 1B2	R	28	84	265	25	66	9	2	3	18	19	18	1	.249	.332
Babe Dahlgren	1B73, 3B35, SS25, C1	R	31	136	508	55	146	19	2	5	56	50	39	2	.287	.362
Schoolboy Rowe	P27	R	33	82	120	14	36	7	0	4	19	8	15	0	.300	.458
2 Charlie Brewster	SS46	R	29	49	159	13	35	2	0	0	12	10	19	1	.220	.233
Ray Hamrick	2B31, SS12	R	21	44	160	12	32	3	1	0	9	8	28	0	.200	.231
2 Dee Moore	C21, OF6, 3B5, 1B1	R	29	37	113	13	27	4	1	1	8	15	8	0	.239	.319
1 Danny Litwhiler	OF34	R	26	36	139	23	36	6	0	5	17	11	14	1	.259	.410
Earl Naylor	OF33	R	24	33	120	12	21	2	0	2	14	12	16	1	.175	.267
Bob Finley	C24	R	27	28	81	9	21	2	0	1	5	2	12	0	.259	.321
Paul Busby	OF10	L	24	26	40	13	10	1	0	0	5	2	1	2	.250	.275
Andy Seminick	C22, OF1	R	22		72	9	13	2	0	2	5	7	12	0	.181	.292
1 Tom Padden	C16	R	34	17	41	5	12	0	0	0	1	2	6	0	.293	.293
Chuck Klein	OF2	L	38	12	20	0	2	0	0	0	3	0	3	0	.100	.100
Benny Culp	C10	R	29	10	24	4	5	1	0	0	1	5	2	0	.208	.250
Garton Del Savio	SS4	R	29	4	11	0	1	0	0	0	0	1	0	0	.091	.091

NAME	T	AGE	W	L	PCT	SV	G	GS	CG	IP	H	BB	SO	SHO	ERA
		31	64	90	.416	14	157	157	66	1393	1436	451	431	11	3.79
Schoolboy Rowe	R	33	14	8	.636	1	27	25	11	199	196	29	52	3	2.94
2 Dick Barrett	R	36	10	9	.526	1	23	20	10	169	137	51	65	2	2.40
Al Gerheauser	L	26	10	19	.345	0	38	31	15	215	222	70	92	2	3.60
Tex Kraus	L	25	9	15	.375	2	34	25	10	200	197	78	48	1	3.15
Si Johnson (MS)	R	36	8	3	.727	2	21	14	9	113	110	25	46	1	3.27
1 Johnny Podgajny	R	23	4	4	.500	0	13	5	3	64	77	16	13	0	4.22
1 Charley Fuchs	R	29	2	7	.222	1	17	9	4	78	76	34	12	1	4.27
Dick Conger	R	22	2	7	.222	0	13	10	2	55	72	24	18	0	6.05
Rogers McKee	L	16	1	0	1.000	0	4	1	1	13	12	5	1	0	6.23
2 Dutch Dietz	R	31	1	1	.500	2	21	0	0	36	42	15	10	0	6.50
2 Andy Karl	R	29	1	2	.333	0	9	2	0	27	44	11	4	0	7.00
2 Bill Lee	R	33	1	5	.167	3	13	7	2	61	70	21	17	0	4.57
1 Newt Kimball	R	28	1	6	.143	2	34	6	2	90	85	42	33	0	4.10
Ken Raffensberger	R	25	0	1	.000	0	7	1	0	18	7	2	3	0	1.13
Dale Matthewson	R	20	0	3	.000	0	11	1	0	26	28	8	8	0	4.85
George Eyrich (MS)	R	18	0	0	—	0	9	0	0	17	27	9	5	0	3.32
Boom-Boom Beck	R	38	0	0	—	0	4	0	0	14	24	5	3	0	9.64
Deacon Donahue	R	23	0	0	—	0	2	0	0	4	4	1	1	0	4.50
Andy Lapihuska	R	20	0	0	—	0	2	0	0	2	5	3	0	0	27.00
2 Manny Salvo	R	31	0	0	—	0	1	0	0	2	3	1	0	0	27.00
Bill Webb	R	29	0	0	—	0	1	0	0	1	6	4	0	0	9.00

NEW YORK 8th 55-98 .359 49.5 — MEL OTT

NAME	G by Pos	B	AGE	G	AB	R	H	2B	3B	HR	RBI	BB	SO	SB	BA	SA
TOTALS			31	156	5292	558	1309	153	33	81	517	480	470	35	.247	.335
1 Joe Orengo	1B82	R	28	83	266	28	58	8	2	6	29	36	46	1	.218	.331
Mickey Witek	2B153	R	27	153	622	68	195	17	6	5	55	41	23	1	.314	.370
Billy Jurges	SS99, 3B28	R	35	136	481	46	110	18	2	4	29	53	38	2	.229	.279
Dick Bartell	3B54, SS33	R	35	99	337	48	91	14	0	5	28	47	27	5	.270	.356
Mel Ott	OF111, 3B1	L	34	125	380	65	89	12	2	18	47	95	48	7	.234	.418
Johnny Rucker	OF117	L	26	132	505	56	138	19	4	2	46	22	44	4	.273	.339
2 Joe Medwick	OF74, 1B3	R	31	78	324	41	91	20	3	5	45	9	14	0	.281	.407
Gus Mancuso	C77	R	37	94	252	11	50	5	0	2	28	16	10	0	.198	.242
Sid Gordon	3B53, 1B41, OF28, 2B3	R	25	131	474	50	119	9	11	9	63	43	32	2	.251	.373
Buster Maynard	OF74, 3B22	R	30	121	393	43	81	8	2	9	32	24	27	3	.206	.305
Ernie Lombardi	C73	R	35	104	295	19	90	7	0	10	51	16	11	1	.305	.431
Nap Reyes	1B38, 3B1	R	23	40	125	13	32	4	2	0	13	4	12	2	.256	.320
1 Babe Barna	OF31	L	28	40	113	11	23	5	1	1	12	16	9	3	.204	.292
Charlie Mead	OF37	L	22	37	146	9	40	6	1	1	13	10	15	1	.274	.349
Buddy Kerr	SS27	R	20	27	98	14	28	3	0	2	12	8	5	1	.286	.378
Ray Berres	C17	R	35	20	28	1	4	1	0	0	1	6	3	0	.143	.179
Joe Stephenson	C6	R	22	9	24	4	6	1	0	0	1	4	5	0	.250	.292
Vic Bradford	OF1	R	28	6	5	1	1	0	0	0	1	0	0	0	.200	.200
1 Hugh Poland	C4	L	30	4	12	0	1	0	0	0	1	1	0	0	.083	.250

NAME	T	AGE	W	L	PCT	SV	G	GS	CG	IP	H	BB	SO	SHO	ERA
		30	55	98	.359	19	156	156	35	1395	1474	626	588	6	4.08
Ace Adams	R	33	11	7	.611	9	70	3	1	140	121	55	46	0	2.83
Cliff Melton (EJ)	R	31	9	13	.409	0	34	28	6	186	184	69	55	2	3.19
1 Bill Lohrman	R	30	5	6	.455	1	17	12	3	80	110	25	16	0	5.18
Rube Fischer	R	26	5	10	.333	2	22	17	4	131	140	59	47	0	4.60
Johnny Wittig	R	29	5	15	.250	4	40	22	4	164	172	76	56	1	4.23
Carl Hubbell (SA)	L	40	4	4	.500	0	12	11	3	66	87	24	31	0	4.91
Harry Feldman	R	23	4	5	.444	0	31	10	1	105	114	58	49	0	4.29
2 Ken Chase	R	29	4	12	.250	0	21	20	4	129	140	74	86	1	4.12
Van Lingle Mungo	R	32	3	7	.300	2	45	13	2	154	140	79	83	2	3.92
Bill Voiselle	R	24	2	3	.333	1	4	4	3	31	18	14	19	0	2.03
1 Bill Sayles	R	25	1	3	.250	0	18	3	1	53	60	23	38	0	4.75
Hugh East (MS)	R	23	1	3	.250	0	13	5	1	40	51	25	21	0	5.40
2 Johnny Allen	R	38	1	3	.250	2	15	0	0	41	37	14	24	0	3.07
Ken Trinkle	R	23	1	5	.167	0	11	6	1	46	51	15	10	0	3.72
Bobby Coombs	R	35	0	0	—	0	16	3	3	8	5	1	0	12.94
Frank Seward	R	22	0	1	.000	0	9	1	0	12	9	12	5	0	3.00
Tom Sunkel	L	30	0	1	.000	0	1	1	0	3	4	3	1	0	9.00

WORLD SERIES — NEW YORK (AL) 4 ST. LOUIS (NL) 1

LINE SCORES

TEAM	1	2	3	4	5	6	7	8	9	10	11	12	R	H	E

Game 1 October 5 at New York

| STL (NL) | 0 | 1 | 0 | 0 | 1 | 0 | 0 | 0 | 0 | | | | 2 | 7 | 2 |
| NY (AL) | 0 | 0 | 0 | 2 | 0 | 2 | 0 | 0 | X | | | | 4 | 8 | 2 |

Lanier, Brecheen (8)   Chandler

Game 2 October 6 at New York

| STL | 0 | 0 | 1 | 3 | 0 | 0 | 0 | 0 | 0 | | | | 4 | 7 | 2 |
| NY | 0 | 0 | 0 | 1 | 0 | 0 | 0 | 0 | 2 | | | | 3 | 6 | 0 |

M. Cooper   Bonham, Murphy (9)

Game 3 October 7 at New York

| STL | 0 | 0 | 0 | 2 | 0 | 0 | 0 | 0 | 0 | | | | 2 | 6 | 4 |
| NY | 0 | 0 | 0 | 0 | 0 | 1 | 0 | 5 | X | | | | 6 | 8 | 0 |

Brazle, Krist (8), Brecheen (8)   Borowy, Murphy (9)

Game 4 October 10 at St. Louis

| NY | 0 | 0 | 0 | 1 | 0 | 0 | 0 | 1 | 0 | | | | 2 | 6 | 2 |
| STL | 0 | 0 | 0 | 0 | 0 | 1 | 0 | 0 | 0 | | | | 1 | 7 | 1 |

Russo   Lanier, Brecheen (8)

Game 5 October 11 at St. Louis

| NY | 0 | 0 | 0 | 0 | 0 | 2 | 0 | 0 | 0 | | | | 2 | 7 | 1 |
| STL | 0 | 0 | 0 | 0 | 0 | 0 | 0 | 0 | 0 | | | | 0 | 10 | 1 |

Chandler   M. Cooper, Lanier (8), Dickson (9)

COMPOSITE BATTING

NAME	POS	G	AB	R	H	2B	3B	HR	RBI	BA
New York (AL) Totals		5	159	17	35	5	2	2	14	.220
Johnson	3B	5	20	3	6	1	1	0	3	.300
Etten	1B	5	19	2	2	0	0	0	0	.105
Dickey	C	5	18	1	5	0	0	1	4	.278
Crosetti	SS	5	18	4	5	0	0	0	2	.278
Keller	OF	5	18	3	4	0	1	0	1	.222
Gordon	2B	5	17	2	4	0	1	0	2	.235
Stainback	OF	5	17	0	3	0	0	0	0	.176
Lindell	OF	4	9	1	1	0	0	0	0	.111
Metheny	OF	5	8	0	1	0	0	0	0	.125
Chandler	P	2	6	0	1	0	0	0	0	.167
Russo	P	1	3	1	2	2	0	0	0	.667
Borowy	P	1	2	1	1	0	0	0	0	.500
Bonham	P	1	2	0	0	0	0	0	0	.000
Stirnweiss	PH	1	1	0	0	0	0	0	0	.000
Weatherly	PH	1	1	0	0	0	0	0	0	—
Murphy	P	2	0	0	0	0	0	0	0	—
St. Louis (NL) Totals		5	165	9	37	5	0	2	8	.224
Klein	2B	5	22	0	3	0	0	0	0	.136
Musial	OF	5	18	2	5	0	0	0	2	.278
Kurowski	3B	5	18	2	4	1	0	0	2	.222
Walker	OF	5	18	0	3	0	0	0	1	.167
Sanders	1B	5	17	3	5	0	0	1	3	.294
W. Cooper	C	5	17	1	5	0	0	0	0	.294
Litwhiler	OF	5	15	0	4	1	0	0	2	.267
Marion	SS	5	14	1	5	2	0	0	1	.357
Garms	OF	5	2	0	0	0	0	0	0	.000
M. Cooper	P	2	5	0	0	0	0	0	0	.000
Lanier	P	2	4	0	1	0	0	0	0	.250
Hopp	OF	1	4	0	0	0	0	0	0	.000
O'Dea	C	2	3	0	2	0	0	0	2	.667
Brazle	P	1	3	0	0	0	0	0	0	.000
Demaree	PH	2	2	0	0	0	0	0	0	.000
Narron	PH	1	1	0	0	0	0	0	0	.000
Brecheen	P	3	0	0	0	0	0	0	0	—
Dickson	P	1	0	0	0	0	0	0	0	—
Krist	P	1	0	0	0	0	0	0	0	—
White	PR	1	0	0	0	0	0	0	0	—

COMPOSITE PITCHING

NAME	G	IP	H	BB	SO	W	L	SV	ERA
New York (AL) Totals	5	45	37	11	26	4	1	1	1.40
Chandler	2	18	17	3	10	2	0	0	0.50
Russo	1	9	7	3	4	1	0	0	0.00
Borowy	1	8	6	3	4	1	0	0	2.25
Bonham	1	8	6	3	0	0	1	0	4.50
Murphy	2	2	1	1	1	0	0	1	0.00
St. Louis (NL) Totals	5	43	35	12	30	1	4	0	2.51
M. Cooper	2	16	11	3	10	1	1	0	2.81
Lanier	3	15.1	13	3	13	0	1	0	1.76
Brazle	1	7.1	5	2	4	0	1	0	3.68
Brecheen	3	3.2	5	3	3	0	1	0	2.45
Dickson	1	0.2	0	1	0	0	0	0	0.00
Krist	1	1	0	0	0	0	0	0	0.00

1944 Meet Me in St. Louis, Louie...

Part of the story of 1944 was the war and the absentee stars. But there were more intricate parts to the tale than the war itself. The main theme was whether or not a 44-year-old tenant of the junior circuit would finally win a pennant. The protagonists in the affair were the St. Louis Browns. The Detroit Tigers assumed the role of antagonists, and the New York Yankees chose the part of catalyst. It was a perfect script with an outcome so exciting that if it hadn't unfolded before the eyes of the country, no one would have believed it.

The main characters included Detroit's Hal Newhouser and Dizzy Trout, and the Browns' Vern Stephens, Nels Potter, and Sig Jakucki, the last of whom pitched in seven games in 1936, went to the minors until 1938, and then voluntarily retired until showing up again in 1944 with a lifetime 0-3 major league record. Jakucki's return, if anything, was simply for the benefit of giving the Browns a full squad.

An indication of what September would bring began early in April as the Browns jumped off to a sudden hot start. It was so sudden, in fact, that the experts considered it a fluke. What the Browns did was to win their first nine games, a feat no previous American League team had been able to accomplish.

Until late September, the American League race was a four-team fight among Boston, St. Louis, Detroit, and New York, but the Red Sox—after losing Tex Hughson and Bobby Doerr to the war—could not maintain the blistering pace. In the final week of the season, a blanket could literally be thrown over the other three contenders. Then, on the 27th, Detroit opened a little daylight by moving one game over the Browns and three over the Yankees. Rain washed out the games the next day and, on the 29th, the Yankees moved into St. Louis for a twin bill, while Detroit hooked up with Washington for two games. After the Browns came from behind to take the opener, Nels Potter pitched a brilliant six-hit, 1-0 shutout in the night-cap. Detroit could only manage a split and entered the final two days of the season with the same 87-65 record as St. Louis.

On the 30th, Denny Galehouse blanked the Yankees, 2-0, while Newhouser kept the Tigers even with his 29th victory. On closing day, October 1, Detroit sent Trout after his 28th victory, but Washington and Dutch Leonard proved too much as the Tigers lost 4-1. At Sportsman's Park, the Browns gave the call to Jakucki, who was looking for his 13th victory. The Browns were behind, 2-0, in the fourth inning without a hit off Yankee rookie Mel Queen when Mike Kreevich got things started with a single and Chet Laabs followed with a homer. Then, in the fifth inning, Kreevich came up with two outs and again singled, followed by Laabs, who hit a 3-1 pitch into the bleachers. The Browns added another run in the eighth on Vern Stephens' homer and suddenly found themselves going to a World Series. Detroit's one consolation came when Newhouser won MVP honors—beating out Trout by four points.

Accompanying the Browns in the fall classic were their city rivals—the St. Louis Cardinals—who won their third pennant in a row in the most one-sided race in the National League in 40 years. In chalking up their 105 victories, the Cardinals proved untouchable. They spent only four days out of first place all season, won 73 of their first 100 games, and had more victories on September 1, (91), than the American League winner had at the close. The team also established an all-time record for fewest errors, with 112, and became the first National League team to win over 100 games three years in a row. To top it off, shortstop Marty Marion beat out Chicago's Bill Nicholson 190-189 in the MVP voting to give the Cardinals the distinction of capturing the honors for the third straight time.

The magic which carried the Browns to a pennant was not enough when it came to contending with the Cardinals. The Browns lost the World Series in six games, but for the fans of St. Louis it was not a difficult thing to swallow. After all, how could they get worked up when the final result showed St. Louis as champions of the world?

1944 AMERICAN LEAGUE

NAME	G by Pos	B	AGE	G	AB	R	H	2B	3B	HR	RBI	BB	SO	SB	BA	SA
ST. LOUIS 1st 89-65 .579		LUKE SEWELL														
TOTALS			30	154	5269	684	1328	223	45	72	628	531	604	44	.252	.352
George McQuinn	1B146	L	35	146	516	83	129	26	3	11	72	85	74	4	.250	.376
Don Gutteridge	2B146	R	32	148	603	89	148	27	11	3	36	51	63	20	.245	.342
Vern Stephens	SS143	R	23	145	559	91	164	32	1	20	109	62	54	2	.293	.462
Mark Christman	3B145, 1B3	R	30	148	547	56	148	25	4	6	83	47	37	5	.271	.353
Gene Moore	OF98, 1B1	L	34	110	390	56	93	13	6	6	58	24	37	0	.238	.349
Milt Byrnes	OF122	R	27	128	407	63	120	20	4	4	45	68	50	1	.295	.393
Mike Kreevich	OF100	R	36	105	402	55	121	15	6	5	44	27	24	3	.301	.405
Red Hayworth	C86	R	28	90	270	20	60	11	1	1	25	10	13	0	.222	.281
Al Zarilla	OF79	L	25	100	288	43	86	13	6	6	45	29	33	1	.299	.448
Frank Mancuso	C87	R	26	88	244	19	50	11	0	1	24	20	32	1	.205	.262
Chet Laabs (WW)	OF55	R	32	66	201	28	47	10	2	5	23	29	33	3	.234	.378
Floyd Baker	2B17, SS16	L	27	44	97	10	17	3	0	0	5	11	5	2	.175	.206
Mike Chartak	1B12, OF7	L	28	35	72	8	17	2	1	1	7	6	9	0	.236	.333
Ellis Clary	3B11, 2B6	R	27	25	49	6	13	1	1	0	4	12	9	1	.265	.327
1 Hal Epps	OF18	L	30	22	62	15	11	1	1	0	3	14	14	0	.177	.226
Frank Demaree	OF16	R	34	16	51	4	13	2	0	0	6	6	3	0	.255	.294
2 Tom Turner	C11	R	27	15	25	2	8	1	0	0	4	2	5	0	.320	.360
Tom Hafey	OF4, 1B1	R	30	8	14	1	5	2	0	0	2	1	4	0	.357	.500
Joe Schultz	C3	R	25	3	8	1	2	0	0	0	0	0	0	1	.250	.250
Babe Martin	OF1	R	24	2	4	0	3	1	0	0	1	0	0	0	.7501	.000
Len Schulte		R	27	1	0	0	0	0	0	0	0	1	0	0		

NAME	T	AGE	W	L	PCT	SV	G	GS	CG	IP	H	BB	SO	SHO	ERA
		31	89	65	.578	17	154	154	71	1397	1392	469	581	16	3.17
Nels Potter	R	32	19	7	.731	0	32	29	16	232	211	70	91	3	2.83
Jack Kramer	R	26	17	13	.567	0	33	31	18	257	233	75	124	1	2.49
Bob Muncrief	R	28	13	8	.619	1	33	27	12	219	216	50	88	3	3.08
Sig Jakucki	R	34	13	9	.591	3	35	24	12	198	211	54	67	4	3.55
Denny Galehouse (WW)	R	32	9	10	.474	0	24	19	6	153	162	44	80	2	3.12
George Caster	R	36	6	6	.500	12	42	0	0	81	91	33	46	0	4.16
Tex Shirley	R	26	5	4	.556	0	23	11	2	80	59	64	35	1	4.16
Al Hollingsworth	L	36	5	7	.417	1	26	10	3	93	108	37	22	2	4.45
Steve Sundra (MS)	R	34	2	0	1.000	0	3	3	2	19	15	4	1	0	1.42
Willis Hudlin (MS)	R	38	0	1	.000	0	1	0	0	2	3	0	1	0	4.50
Sam Zoldak	L	25	0	0	—	0	18	0	0	39	49	19	15	0	3.69
Lefty West	L	28	0	0	—	0	11	0	0	24	34	19	11	0	6.37

NAME	G by Pos	B	AGE	G	AB	R	H	2B	3B	HR	RBI	BB	SO	SB	BA	SA
DETROIT 2nd 88-66 .571 1		STEVE O'NEILL														
TOTALS			32	156	5344	658	1405	220	44	60	591	532	500	61	.263	.354
Rudy York	1B151	R	30	151	583	77	161	27	7	18	98	68	73	5	.276	.439
Eddie Mayo	2B143, SS11	L	34	154	607	76	151	18	3	5	63	57	23	9	.249	.313
Joe Hoover	SS119, 2B1	R	29	120	441	67	104	20	2	0	29	35	66	7	.236	.290
Pinky Higgins	3B146	R	35	148	543	79	161	32	4	7	76	81	39	4	.297	.409
Jimmy Outlaw	OF137	R	31	139	535	69	146	20	6	3	57	41	40	7	.273	.350
Doc Cramer	OF141	L	38	143	578	69	169	20	9	2	42	37	21	6	.292	.369
Dick Wakefield (MS)	OF78	L	23	78	276	53	98	15	5	12	53	55	29	2	.355	.576
Paul Richards	C90	R	35	95	300	24	71	13	0	3	37	35	30	8	.237	.310
Chuck Hostetler	OF65	L	40	90	265	42	79	9	2	0	20	21	31	4	.298	.347
Bob Swift	C76	R	29	80	247	15	63	11	1	1	19	27	27	2	.255	.320
Don Ross	OF37, SS2, 1B1	R	29	66	167	14	35	5	0	2	15	14	9	2	.210	.275
Dizzy Trout	P49	R	29	51	133	18	36	4	1	5	24	9	28	2	.271	.429
Joe Orengo	SS29, 3B11, 1B5, 2B2	R	29	46	154	14	31	10	0	0	15	20	29	1	.201	.266
1 Charlie Metro	OF20	R	25	38	78	8	15	0	1	0	5	3	10	1	.192	.218
Al Unser	2B5, C1	R	31	11	25	2	3	0	1	1	5	3	2	0	.120	.320
Red Borom	2B4, SS1	L	28	7	14	1	1	0	0	0	1	2	2	0	.071	.071
Don Heffner	2B3	R	33	6	19	0	4	1	0	0	1	5	1	0	.211	.263
Hack Miller	C5	R	33	5	5	1	1	0	0	1	3	1	1	0	.200	.800
Bubba Floyd	SS3	R	27	3	9	1	4	1	0	0	1	0	1	0	.444	.556
John McHale	1B1	L	22	1	1	0	0	0	0	0	0	0	1	0	.000	.000
Jack Sullivan	2B1	R	26	1	1	0	0	0	0	0	0	0	0	0	.000	.000

NAME	T	AGE	W	L	PCT	SV	G	GS	CG	IP	H	BB	SO	SHO	ERA
		29	88	66	.571	8	156	156	87	1400	1373	452	586	20	3.09
Hal Newhouser	L	23	29	9	.763	2	47	34	25	312	264	102	187	6	2.22
Dizzy Trout	R	29	27	14	.659	0	49	40	33	352	314	83	144	7	2.12
Rufe Gentry	R	26	12	14	.462	0	37	30	10	204	211	108	68	3	4.24
Stubby Overmire	L	25	11	11	.500	1	32	28	11	200	214	41	57	3	3.06
Johnny Gorsica	R	29	6	14	.300	4	34	19	8	162	192	32	47	1	4.11
Joe Orrell	R	27	2	1	.667	0	10	2	0	22	26	11	10	0	4.50
Boom-Boom Beck	R	39	1	2	.333	1	28	2	0	74	67	27	25	0	3.89
Bob Gillespie	R	24	0	1	.000	0	7	0	0	11	7	12	4	0	6.55
Jake Mooty	R	31	0	0	—	0	15	0	0	28	35	18	7	0	4.50
Roy Henshaw	L	32	0	0	—	0	7	1	0	12	17	6	10	0	9.00
Zeb Eaton	R	24	0	0	—	0	6	0	0	16	19	8	4	0	5.63
Chief Hogsett	L	40	0	0	—	0	1	0	0	6	7	4	5	0	0.00

NAME	G by Pos	B	AGE	G	AB	R	H	2B	3B	HR	RBI	BB	SO	SB	BA	SA
NEW YORK 3rd 83-71 .539 6		JOE McCARTHY														
TOTALS			30	154	5331	674	1410	216	74	96	631	523	627	91	.264	.387
Nick Etten	1B154	L	30	154	573	88	168	25	4	22	91	97	29	4	.293	.466
Snuffy Stirnweiss	2B154	R	25	154	643	125	205	35	16	8	43	73	87	55	.319	.460
Mike Milosevich	SS91	R	29	94	312	27	77	11	4	0	32	30	37	1	.247	.308
Oscar Grimes	3B97, SS20	R	29	116	387	44	108	17	8	5	44	59	57	6	.279	.403
Bud Metheny	OF132	L	29	137	518	72	124	16	1	14	67	56	57	5	.239	.355
Johnny Lindell	OF149	R	27	149	594	91	178	33	16	18	103	44	56	5	.300	.500
Hersh Martin	OF80	B	34	85	328	49	99	12	4	9	47	34	26	5	.302	.445
Mike Garbark	C85	R	28	89	299	23	78	9	4	1	33	25	27	0	.261	.328
Rollie Hemsley (MS)	C76	R	37	81	284	23	76	12	5	2	26	9	13	0	.268	.366
Don Savage	3B60	R	25	71	239	31	63	7	5	4	24	20	41	1	.264	.385
Frankie Crosetti (VR)	SS55	R	33	55	197	20	47	4	2	5	30	11	21	3	.239	.355
Ed Levy	OF36	R	27	40	153	12	37	11	2	4	29	6	19	1	.242	.418
Russ Derry	OF28	L	27	38	114	14	29	3	0	4	14	20	19	1	.254	.386
1 Larry Rosenthal	OF26	L	34	36	101	9	20	5	0	3	9	19	15	1	.198	.328
Tuck Stainback	OF24	R	32	30	78	13	17	3	0	0	3	6	11	2	.218	.256
2 Johnny Cooney	OF2	L	43	10	8	1	1	0	0	0	1	2	1	0	.125	.125
2 Paul Waner		L	41	9	7	1	1	0	0	0	2	3	1	0	.143	.143
Bill Drescher	C1	R	23	4	7	1	1	0	0	0	0	0	1	0	.143	.143
Bob Collins	C3	R	34	4	3	0	1	0	0	0	0	0	0	0	.333	.333
Charlie Keller (MM) 27																

NAME	T	AGE	W	L	PCT	SV	G	GS	CG	IP	H	BB	SO	SHO	ERA
		30	83	71	.539	13	154	154	78	1390	1351	532	529	9	3.39
Hank Borowy	R	28	17	12	.586	2	35	30	19	253	224	88	107	3	2.63
Atley Donald	R	33	13	10	.565	0	30	19	9	159	173	59	48	0	3.34
Monk Dubiel	R	26	13	13	.500	0	30	28	19	232	217	86	79	3	3.38
Ernie Bonham	R	30	12	9	.571	0	26	25	17	214	228	41	54	1	2.99
Mel Queen	R	26	6	3	.667	0	10	10	4	82	68	34	30	1	3.29
Bill Zuber	R	31	5	7	.417	0	22	13	2	107	101	54	59	1	4.21
Joe Page	L	26	5	7	.417	0	19	16	4	103	100	52	63	0	4.54
Bill Bevens	R	27	4	1	.800	0	8	5	3	44	44	13	16	0	2.68
Steve Roser	R	26	4	3	.571	1	16	6	1	84	80	34	34	0	3.86
Jim Turner	R	40	4	4	.500	7	35	0	0	42	42	12	13	0	3.43
Johnny Johnson	L	29	0	2	.000	3	22	1	0	27	25	24	11	0	4.00
Al Lyons (MS)	R		0	0	—	0	11	0	0	40	43	24	14	0	4.50
Spud Chandler (MS)	R	36	0	0	—	0	1	0	0	6	6	1	1	0	4.50
Johnny Murphy (WW) 35																
Butch Wensloff (VR) 28																

BOSTON   4th 77-77 .500 12   JOE CRONIN

NAME	G by Pos	B	AGE	G	AB	R	H	2B	3B	HR	RBI	BB	SO	SB	BA	SA
TOTALS			30	156	5400	739	1456	277	56	69	691	522	505	60	.270	.380
Lou Finney (VR)	1B59, OF2	L	33	68	251	37	72	11	2	0	32	23	7	1	.287	.347
Bobby Doerr (MS)	2B125	R	26	125	468	95	152	30	10	15	81	58	31	5	.325	.528
Skeeter Newsome	SS126, 2B8, 3B1	R	33	136	472	41	114	26	3	0	41	33	21	4	.242	.309
Jim Tabor (MS)	3B114	R	30	116	438	58	125	25	4	3	72	31	38	4	.285	.445
Pete Fox	OF119	R	34	121	496	70	156	37	6	1	64	27	24	10	.315	.419
Catfish Metkovich	OF82, 1B50	L	22	134	549	94	152	28	8	9	59	31	57	13	.277	.406
Bob Johnson	OF142	R	38	144	525	106	170	40	8	17	106	95	67	2	.324	.528
Roy Partee	C85	R	26	89	280	18	68	12	0	2	41	37	29	0	.243	.307
Jim Bucher	3B44, 2B21	L	33	80	277	39	76	9	2	4	31	19	13	3	.274	.365
Joe Cronin	1B49	R	37	76	191	24	46	7	0	5	28	34	19	1	.241	.356
Leon Culberson	OF72	R	24	75	282	41	67	11	5	2	21	20	20	6	.238	.333
Tom McBride	OF57, 1B5	R	29	71	216	29	53	7	3	0	24	8	13	2	.245	.306
2 Hal Wagner (MS)	C64	L	28	66	223	21	74	13	4	1	38	29	14	1	.332	.439
Joe Bowman	P26	L	34	59	100	7	20	5	2	0	16	5	19	1	.200	.290
Eddie Lake	SS41, P6, 2B3, 3B1	R	28	57	126	21	26	5	0	0	8	23	22	5	.206	.246
Bill Conroy	C19	R	29	19	47	6	10	2	0	0	4	11	9	0	.213	.255
Johnny Lazor	OF6, C1	L	31	16	24	0	2	1	0	0	1	0	4	0	.083	.125
1 Ford Garrison	OF12	R	28	13	49	5	12	3	0	0	2	6	4	0	.245	.306
1 Johnny Peacock	C2	L	34	4	4	0	0	0	0	0	0	0	1	0	.000	.000

NAME	T	AGE	W	L	PCT	SV	G	GS	CG	IP	H	BB	SO	SHO	ERA
TOTALS		31	77	77	.500	17	156	156	58	1394	1404	592	524	5	3.82
Tex Hughson (MS)	R	28	18	5	.783	5	28	23	19	203	172	41	112	2	2.26
Mike Ryba	R	41	12	7	.632	2	42	7	2	138	119	39	50	0	3.33
Joe Bowman	R	34	12	8	.600	0	26	24	10	168	175	64	53	1	4.82
Frank Barrett	R	31	8	7	.533	8	38	2	0	90	93	42	40	0	3.70
Yank Terry	R	33	6	10	.375	0	27	17	3	133	142	65	50	0	4.20
Emmett O'Neill	R	26	6	11	.353	0	28	22	8	152	154	89	68	1	4.62
Rex Cecil	R	27	4	5	.444	0	11	9	4	61	72	33	33	0	5.16
Clem Hausmann	R	24	4	7	.364	2	32	12	3	137	139	69	43	0	3.42
Pinky Woods	R	29	4	8	.333	0	38	20	5	171	171	88	56	1	3.26
Clem Dreisewerd	L	28	2	4	.333	1	7	7	3	49	52	9	9	0	4.04
Oscar Judd	L	36	1	1	.500	0	9	6	1	30	30	15	9	0	3.60
Joe Wood	R	28	0	1	.000	0	1	0	0	10	13	3	5	0	6.30
Vic Johnson	L	23	0	3	.000	0	7	5	0	27	42	15	7	0	6.33
Eddie Lake	R	28	0	0	—	0	6	0	0	19	20	11	7	0	4.26
1 Lou Lucier	R	26	0	0	—	0	3	0	0	5	7	7	2	0	5.40
Stan Partenheimer	L	21	0	0	—	0	1	0	0	1	3	2	0	0	18.00

CLEVELAND   5th(tie) 72-82 .468 17   LOU BOUDREAU

NAME	G by Pos	B	AGE	G	AB	R	H	2B	3B	HR	RBI	BB	SO	SB	BA	SA
TOTALS			28	155	5481	643	1458	270	50	70	611	512	593	48	.266	.372
Mickey Rocco	1B155	L	28	155	653	87	174	29	7	13	70	56	51	4	.266	.392
Ray Mack	2B83	R	27	83	284	24	66	15	3	0	29	28	45	4	.232	.306
Lou Boudreau	SS149, C1	R	26	150	584	91	191	45	5	3	67	73	39	11	.327	.437
Ken Keltner	3B149	R	27	149	573	74	169	41	9	13	91	53	39	4	.295	.466
Roy Cullenbine	OF151	B	30	154	571	98	162	34	5	16	80	87	49	4	.284	.445
Oris Hockett	OF110	L	34	124	457	47	132	29	5	1	50	35	27	8	.289	.381
Pat Seerey	OF86	R	21	101	342	39	80	16	0	15	39	19	99	1	.234	.412
Buddy Rosar (WW)	C98	R	29	99	331	29	87	9	3	0	30	34	17	1	.263	.308
Rusty Peters	2B63, SS13, 3B8	R	29	88	282	23	63	13	3	1	24	15	35	2	.223	.301
Paul O'Dea	OF41, 1B3, P3	L	23	76	173	25	55	9	0	0	13	23	21	2	.318	.370
2 Myril Hoag	OF66	R	36	67	277	33	79	9	3	1	27	25	23	6	.285	.350
Jimmy Grant	2B20, 3B4	R	25	61	99	12	27	4	1	1	12	11	20	1	.273	.404
Jeff Heath	OF37	L	29	60	151	20	50	5	2	5	33	18	12	0	.331	.490
Norm Schlueter	C43	R	27	49	122	2	15	4	0	0	11	12	22	0	.123	.156
George Susce	C29	R	36	29	61	3	14	1	0	0	4	2	5	0	.230	.246
Jim McDonnell	C13	L	21	20	43	5	10	0	0	0	4	4	3	0	.233	.233
Russ Lyon	C3	R	31	7	11	1	2	0	0	0	0	1	1	0	.182	.182

Hank Ruszkowski 18 3-8, Steve Biras 22 R 2-2, Jim Devlin 21 L 0-1, Les Fleming (VR) 28

NAME	T	AGE	W	L	PCT	SV	G	GS	CG	IP	H	BB	SO	SHO	ERA
TOTALS		31	72	82	.468	18	155	155	48	1491	1428	621	524	7	3.65
Mel Harder	R	34	12	10	.545	0	30	27	12	196	211	69	64	2	3.72
Allie Reynolds	R	29	11	8	.579	1	28	21	5	158	141	91	84	1	3.30
Eddie Klieman	R	26	11	13	.458	5	47	19	5	178	185	70	44	1	3.39
Steve Gromek	R	24	10	9	.526	1	35	21	12	204	160	70	115	2	2.56
Joe Heving	R	43	8	3	.727	6	63	1	0	120	106	41	46	0	1.95
Al Smith	L	36	7	13	.350	0	28	26	7	182	197	69	44	1	3.41
Jim Bagby (MM)	R	27	4	5	.444	0	13	10	2	79	101	34	12	0	4.33
Ray Poat	R	26	4	8	.333	1	36	6	1	81	82	37	40	0	5.11
1 Vern Kennedy	R	37	2	5	.286	0	12	10	2	59	66	37	17	0	5.03
Earl Henry	R	27	1	1	.500	0	2	1	0	18	18	3	5	0	4.50
Hal Klein	L	21	1	1	.333	0	11	6	1	41	38	36	13	0	5.71
Paul Calvert	R	26	1	3	.250	0	35	4	0	77	89	38	31	0	4.56
Red Embree	R	26	0	1	.000	0	3	1	0	9	6	5	4	0	15.00
Bill Bonness	R	20	0	1	.000	0	1	1	1	5	11	5	1	0	7.71
1 Mike Naymick	R	26	0	0	—	0	7	0	0	13	16	10	4	0	9.69
Paul O'Dea	L	23	0	0	—	0	3	0	0	4	5	6	0	0	2.25

PHILADELPHIA   5th(tie) 72-82 .468 17   CONNIE MACK

NAME	G by Pos	B	AGE	G	AB	R	H	2B	3B	HR	RBI	BB	SO	SB	BA	SA
TOTALS			30	155	5312	525	1364	169	47	36	475	422	490	42	.257	.327
Bill McGhee	1B75	L	38	77	287	27	83	12	0	1	19	21	20	2	.289	.341
Irv Hall	2B97, SS40, 1B4	R	25	143	559	60	150	20	8	0	45	31	46	2	.268	.333
Ed Busch	SS111, 2B27, 3B4	R	26	140	484	41	131	11	3	0	40	29	17	5	.271	.306
George Kell	3B139	R	21	139	514	51	138	15	3	0	44	22	23	5	.268	.309
1 Jo-Jo White	OF74, SS1	L	35	85	267	30	59	4	2	1	21	40	27	5	.221	.262
Bobby Estalella	OF128, 1B6	R	33	140	506	54	151	17	9	7	60	59	60	3	.298	.409
2 Ford Garrison	OF119	R	28	121	449	58	121	13	2	4	37	22	40	10	.269	.334
Frankie Hayes	C155, 1B1	R	29	155	581	62	144	18	6	13	78	57	59	2	.248	.367
Dick Siebert	1B74, OF58	L	32	132	468	52	143	27	5	6	52	62	17	2	.306	.423
2 Hal Epps	OF60	L	30	67	229	27	60	8	8	0	13	18	18	2	.262	.367
Joe Rullo	2B33, 1B1	R	28	35	96	5	16	0	0	0	5	6	19	1	.167	.167
2 Larry Rosenthal	OF19	L	34	32	54	5	11	2	0	1	6	5	9	0	.204	.296
Woody Wheaton	P11, OF8	R	30	30	59	1	11	2	0	0	5	3	13	1	.186	.220
Joe Burns	3B17, 2B9	R	29	28	75	5	18	2	0	1	8	4	8	0	.240	.307
Bill Burgo	OF22	R	24	27	88	6	21	2	0	1	3	7	3	1	.239	.295
2 Charlie Metro	OF11, 3B5, 2B2	R	25	24	40	4	4	0	0	0	1	7	6	1	.100	.100
Bobby Wilkins	SS9	R	21	24	25	7	6	0	0	0	3	1	4	0	.240	.240
Lew Flick	OF6	L	29	19	35	1	4	0	0	0	2	1	2	1	.114	.114
Bob Garbark	C15	R	34	18	23	2	6	2	0	0	2	1	0	0	.261	.348
Bill Mills	C1	R	23	5	4	0	1	0	0	0	0	1	0	0	.250	.250
1 Hal Wagner	C1	L	28	5	4	0	1	0	0	0	0	0	2	0	.250	.250

Tony Parisse 33 R 0-4, Al Simmons 42 R 3-6, Jim Pruett 26 R 1-4, Hal Peck 27 L 2-8

NAME	T	AGE	W	L	PCT	SV	G	GS	CG	IP	H	BB	SO	SHO	ERA
TOTALS		30	72	82	.468	14	155	155	72	1398	1345	390	534	9	3.26
Russ Christopher	R	26	14	14	.500	1	35	24	13	215	200	63	84	1	2.97
Bobo Newsom	R	36	13	15	.464	1	37	33	18	265	243	82	142	2	2.82
Joe Berry	R	39	10	8	.556	12	53	0	0	111	78	23	44	0	1.95
Lum Harris	R	29	10	8	.526	0	23	22	12	174	193	26	33	2	3.31
Don Black	R	27	10	12	.455	0	29	27	8	177	177	75	78	0	4.07
Jesse Flores	R	29	9	11	.450	2	27	25	11	186	172	49	65	2	3.39
Luke Hamlin	R	39	6	12	.333	0	29	23	9	190	204	38	58	2	3.74
Woody Wheaton	R	29	0	1	.000	0	11	1	1	38	36	20	15	0	3.55
Carl Scheib	R	17	0	0	—	0	15	0	0	36	36	11	13	0	4.25
John McGillen	R	26	0	0	—	0	2	0	0	1	1	2	0	0	18.00
Tal Abernathy	L	22	0	0	—	0	1	0	0	3	5	1	2	0	3.00

CHICAGO   7th 71-83 .461 18   JIMMY DYKES

NAME	G by Pos	B	AGE	G	AB	R	H	2B	3B	HR	RBI	BB	SO	SB	BA	SA
TOTALS			31	154	5292	543	1307	210	55	35	495	439	448	66	.247	.320
Hal Trosky	1B130	L	31	135	497	55	120	32	2	10	70	62	30	3	.241	.374
Ray Schalk	2B142, SS5	R	35	146	587	47	129	14	4	1	44	45	52	5	.220	.282
Skeeter Webb	SS135, 2B5	R	34	139	513	44	108	19	6	0	30	20	39	7	.211	.271
Ralph Hodgin	3B82, OF33	L	29	121	465	56	137	25	7	1	51	21	14	3	.295	.385
Wally Moses	OF134	L	33	136	535	82	150	26	9	3	34	52	22	21	.280	.379
Thurman Tucker	OF120	L	26	124	446	59	128	15	6	2	46	57	40	13	.287	.361
Eddie Carnett	OF88, 1B25, P2	L	27	126	457	51	126	18	8	1	60	26	35	5	.276	.357
Mike Tresh	C93	R	30	93	312	22	81	8	1	0	25	37	15	0	.260	.292
Guy Curtright	OF51	R	31	72	198	22	50	8	2	2	23	23	21	4	.253	.343
Grey Clarke	3B45	R	31	63	169	14	44	10	1	0	27	22	6	2	.260	.331
Johnny Dickshot	OF40	L	34	62	162	18	41	8	5	0	15	13	10	2	.253	.364
Tony Cuccinello	3B30, 2B6	R	36	38	130	5	34	3	0	0	17	8	16	0	.262	.285
1 Tom Turner	C36	R	27	36	113	9	26	6	0	2	13	5	16	0	.230	.336
Ed Lopat	P27	L	26	29	81	8	25	1	1	0	6	3	3	0	.309	.346
Vince Castino	C26	R	26	29	78	4	18	5	0	0	3	10	13	0	.231	.295
Cass Michaels	SS21, 3B3	R	18	27	68	4	12	4	1	0	5	2	5	0	.176	.265
1 Myril Hoag	OF14	R	36	17	48	5	11	1	0	0	4	10	1	1	.229	.250
Tom Jordan	C14	R	24	14	45	2	12	1	1	0	3	1	4	0	.267	.333
Bill Metzig	2B5	R	25	5	16	1	2	0	0	0	1	1	1	0	.125	.125

NAME	T	AGE	W	L	PCT	SV	G	GS	CG	IP	H	BB	SO	SHO	ERA
TOTALS		31	71	83	.461	17	154	154	64	1391	1411	420	481	5	3.58
Bill Dietrich	R	34	16	17	.485	0	36	36	15	246	269	68	70	2	3.62
Orval Grove	R	24	14	15	.483	0	34	33	11	235	237	71	105	2	3.71
Ed Lopat	L	26	11	10	.524	0	27	25	13	210	217	59	75	1	3.26
G. Maltzberger (AJ)	R	31	10	5	.667	12	46	0	0	91	81	19	49	0	2.97
John Humphries	R	29	8	10	.444	1	30	20	8	169	170	57	42	0	3.67
Joe Haynes	R	26	6	9	.400	1	33	12	8	154	148	43	44	0	2.57
Thornton Lee (BA)	L	37	3	9	.250	0	15	14	6	113	105	25	39	0	3.03
Jake Wade	L	32	4	4	.333	2	19	5	1	75	75	41	35	0	4.80
Buck Ross	R	29	2	7	.222	0	20	9	2	90	97	35	20	0	5.20
Eddie Carnett	L	27	0	0	—	0	2	0	0	1	1	0	1	0	9.00
Don Hanski	R	22	0	0	—	0	1	0	0	2	3	1	0	0	12.00
Floyd Speer	R	31	0	0	—	0	2	0	0	2	4	0	1	0	9.00

WASHINGTON   8th 64-90 .416 25   OSSIE BLUEGE

NAME	G by Pos	B	AGE	G	AB	R	H	2B	3B	HR	RBI	BB	SO	SB	BA	SA
TOTALS			31	154	5319	592	1386	186	42	33	531	470	477	127	.261	.330
Joe Kuhel	1B138	L	38	139	518	90	144	26	7	4	51	68	40	11	.278	.378
George Myatt	2B121, SS15, OF3	R	30	140	538	86	153	19	6	0	40	54	44	26	.284	.342
John Sullivan	SS138	R	28	134	471	49	118	12	1	0	30	52	43	3	.251	.280
Gil Torres	3B123, 2B10, 1B4	R	28	134	524	42	140	20	6	0	58	21	24	10	.267	.328
Jake Powell	OF90, 3B1	R	35	94	367	29	88	9	1	1	37	16	26	7	.240	.278
Stan Spence	OF150, 1B3	L	29	153	592	83	187	31	8	18	100	69	28	3	.316	.486
Goerge Case	OF114	R	28	119	464	63	116	14	2	2	32	49	22	49	.250	.302
Rick Ferrell	C96	R	38	99	339	14	94	11	1	0	25	46	13	2	.277	.316
Roberto Ortiz	OF80	R	29	85	316	36	80	11	4	5	35	19	47	4	.253	.361
Mike Guerra	C58, OF1	R	31	75	210	29	59	7	2	1	29	13	14	8	.281	.348
Bill LeFebvre	P24, 1B2	L	28	60	62	4	16	2	2	0	8	12	9	0	.258	.355
Hilly Layne	3B18, 2B3	L	26	33	87	6	17	2	0	0	4	8	6	2	.195	.218
Fred Vaughn	2B26, 3B3	R	25	30	109	10	28	2	1	1	21	9	24	2	.257	.321
Ed Boland	OF14	L	36	19	59	4	16	4	0	0	14	0	6	0	.271	.339
Ed Butka	1B14	L	28	15	41	1	8	1	0	0	2	6	1	0	.195	.220
Al Evans (MS)	C8	R	27	14	22	5	2	0	0	0	0	4	2	0	.091	.091
Joe Vosmik	OF12	R	34	14	36	2	7	2	0	0	9	4	4	0	.194	.250
Harlond Clift	3B12	R	31	12	44	4	7	3	0	0	3	6	3	0	.159	.227
Rene Monteagudo	OF9	L	28	10	38	2	11	2	0	0	4	0	6	0	.289	.342
Preston Gomez	2B2, SS2	R	21	8	7	2	2	1	0	0	1	0	2	0	.286	.429
Eddie Yost	3B3, SS2	R	17	7	14	1	2	0	0	0	0	0	4	0	.143	.143
George Binks	OF3	L	29	5	12	0	3	0	0	0	0	1	0	0	.250	.250

Luis Suarez 27 R 0-2, Roy Valdes 24 R 0-1

NAME	T	AGE	W	L	PCT	SV	G	GS	CG	IP	H	BB	SO	SHO	ERA
TOTALS		31	64	90	.416	11	154	154	83	1381	1410	475	503	12	3.49
Dutch Leonard	R	35	14	14	.500	0	32	31	17	229	222	37	62	3	3.07
Mickey Haefner	L	31	12	15	.444	1	31	28	18	228	221	71	86	3	3.04
Johnny Niggeling	R	40	10	8	.556	0	24	24	14	206	164	88	121	2	2.32
Alex Carrasquel	R	31	7	7	.533	2	43	7	3	134	143	50	35	0	3.43
Early Wynn (MS)	R	24	8	17	.320	0	33	25	19	208	221	67	65	2	3.38
Milo Candini	R	26	6	7	.462	1	28	10	4	103	110	49	31	2	4.11
Roger Wolff	R	33	4	15	.211	2	33	21	15	155	186	60	73	0	4.99
Bill LeFebvre	L	28	2	4	.333	3	24	4	2	70	86	21	18	0	4.50
Vern Curtis (MS)	R	24	0	1	.000	0	3	1	0	5	4	3	2	0	2.70
Baby Ortiz	R	24	0	0	—	0	2	0	0	13	13	6	4	0	6.23
Jug Thesenga	R	29	0	0	—	0	2	0	0	11	18	12	2	0	5.25
Sandy Ullrich	R	22	0	0	—	0	10	0	0	17	14	12	6	0	9.00
Bill Zinser	R	26	0	0	—	0	1	0	0	1	5	1	0	0	18.00
Walt Holborow	R	30	0	0	—	0	1	1	0	4	4	0	0	0	0.00

Batting

NAME	G by Pos	B	AGE	G	AB	R	H	2B	3B	HR	RBI	BB	SO	SB	BA	SA
ST. LOUIS	**1ST 105-49 .682**					**BILLY SOUTHWORTH**										
TOTALS			27	157	5475	772	1507	274	59	100	720	544	473	37	.275	.402
Ray Sanders	1B152	L	27	154	601	87	177	34	9	12	102	71	50	2	.295	.441
Emil Verban	2B146	R	28	146	498	51	128	14	2	0	43	19	14	0	.257	.293
Marty Marion	SS144	R	26	144	506	50	135	26	2	6	63	43	50	1	.267	.362
Whitey Kurowski	3B146, 2B9, SS1	R	26	149	555	95	150	25	7	20	87	58	40	2	.270	.449
Stan Musial	OF146	L	23	146	568	112	197	51	14	12	94	90	28	7	.347	.548
Johnny Hopp	OF131, 1B6	L	27	139	527	106	177	35	9	11	72	58	47	15	.336	.499
Danny Litwhiler	OF136	R	27	140	492	53	130	25	5	15	82	37	56	2	.264	.427
Walker Cooper	C97	R	29	112	397	56	126	25	5	13	72	20	19	4	.317	.504
Ken O'Dea	C69	L	31	85	265	35	66	11	2	6	37	37	29	1	.249	.374
Augie Bergamo	OF50, 1B2	L	26	80	192	35	55	6	3	2	19	35	23	0	.286	.380
Debs Garms	OF23, 3B21	L	37	73	149	17	30	3	0	0	5	13	8	0	.201	.221
George Fallon	2B38, SS24, 3B6	R	29	69	141	16	28	6	0	1	9	16	11	1	.199	.262
Pepper Martin	OF29	R	40	40	86	15	24	4	0	2	4	15	11	2	.279	.395
John Antonelli	1B3, 3B3, 2B2	R	28	8	21	0	4	1	0	0	1	0	4	0	.190	.238
Bob Keely	C1	R	34	1	0	0	0	0	0	0	0	0	0	0	—	—
PITTSBURGH	**2nd 90-63 .588 14.5**					**FRANKIE FRISCH**										
TOTALS			28	158	5428	744	1441	248	80	70	706	573	616	87	.265	.379
Babe Dahlgren	1B158	R	28	158	599	67	173	28	7	12	101	47	56	2	.289	.419
Pete Coscarart	2B136, SS4, OF1	R	31	139	554	89	146	30	4	4	42	41	57	10	.264	.354
Frankie Gustine	SS116, 2B11, 3B1	R	24	127	405	42	93	18	3	2	42	33	41	8	.230	.304
Bob Elliott	3B140, SS1	R	27	143	538	85	160	28	16	10	108	75	42	9	.297	.465
Johnny Barrett	OF147	L	28	149	568	99	153	24	19	7	83	86	56	28	.269	.415
Vince DiMaggio	OF101, 3B1	R	31	109	342	41	82	20	4	9	50	33	83	6	.240	.401
Jim Russell	OF149	B	25	152	560	109	181	34	14	8	66	79	63	6	.312	.460
Al Lopez	C115	R	35	115	331	27	76	12	1	1	34	34	24	4	.230	.281
Frank Coleman	OF53, 1B6	L	26	99	226	30	61	9	5	6	33	25	27	0	.270	.434
Al Rubeling	OF18, 2B17, 3B16	R	31	92	184	22	45	7	2	4	30	19	19	4	.245	.370
Frankie Zak	SS67	R	22	87	160	33	48	3	1	0	11	22	18	6	.300	.331
Tommy O'Brien	OF48, 3B1	R	25	85	156	27	39	6	2	3	20	21	12	1	.250	.372
Hank Camelli	C61	R	29	63	125	14	37	5	1	1	10	18	12	0	.296	.376
Spud Davis	C35	R	39	54	93	6	28	7	0	2	14	10	8	0	.301	.441
Lee Handley	2B19, 3B11, SS3	R	30	40	86	7	19	2	0	0	5	3	5	1	.221	.244
2 Lloyd Waner	OF7	L	38	19	14	2	5	0	0	0	2	2	0	0	.357	.357
Al Gionfriddo	OF1	L	22	4	6	1	1	0	0	0	0	1	1	0	.167	.167
Bill Rogers	OF1	L	21	2	4	1	1	0	0	0	0	0	0	0	.250	.250

Vic Barnhart 21 R 1-2, Hank Sweeney 28 L 0-2, Bud Stewart (VR-MS) 28

NAME	G by Pos	B	AGE	G	AB	R	H	2B	3B	HR	RBI	BB	SO	SB	BA	SA
CINCINNATI	**3rd 89-65 .578 16**					**BILL McKECHNIE**										
TOTALS			30	155	5271	573	1340	229	31	51	528	423	391	51	.254	.338
Frank McCormick	1B153	R	33	155	581	85	177	37	3	20	102	57	7	3	.305	.482
Woody Williams	2B155	R	31	155	653	73	157	23	3	1	35	44	24	7	.240	.289
Eddie Miller	SS155	R	27	155	536	48	112	21	5	4	55	41	41	9	.209	.289
Steve Mesner	3B120	R	26	121	414	31	100	17	4	1	47	34	20	1	.242	.309
Gee Walker	OF117	R	36	121	478	56	133	21	3	5	62	23	48	7	.278	.366
Dain Clay	OF98	R	24	110	356	51	89	15	0	0	17	17	18	8	.250	.292
Eric Tipton	OF139	R	29	140	479	62	144	28	3	3	36	59	32	5	.301	.390
Ray Mueller	C155	R	32	155	555	54	159	24	4	10	73	53	47	4	.286	.398
Max Marshall (MS)	OF59	L	30	66	229	36	56	13	2	4	23	21	10	3	.245	.371
Tony Criscola	OF35	L	28	64	157	14	36	3	2	0	14	14	12	0	.229	.274
Estel Crabtree	OF19, 1B8	L	40	58	98	7	28	4	1	0	11	13	3	0	.286	.347
Chuck Aleno	3B42, 1B3, SS3	R	27	50	127	10	21	3	0	1	15	15	15	0	.165	.213
Bucky Walters	P34	R	35	37	107	9	30	4	0	3	13	8	18	0	.280	.318
2 Jo-Jo White	OF23	L	35	24	85	9	20	2	0	0	5	10	7	2	.235	.259
Buck Fausett	3B6, P2	L	36	13	23	3	3	0	1	0	1	1	2	0	.097	.161
Joe Just	C10	R	28	11	11	0	2	0	0	0	2	0	2	0	.182	.182
Len Rice	C5	R	25	10	4	1	0	0	0	0	0	1	0	0	.000	.000
Chucho Ramos	OF3	R	26	4	10	1	5	1	0	0	0	0	0	0	.500	.600
Kermit Wahl	3B1	R	21	4	1	0	0	0	0	0	0	0	0	0	.000	.000
Jodie Beeler	2B1, 3B1	R	22	3	3	0	0	0	0	0	0	0	2	0	.000	.000
Mike Kosman		R	26	1	0	0	0	0	0	0	0	0	0	0	—	—
Al Lakeman		R	25	1	0	0	0	0	0	0	0	0	0	0	.000	.000
Johnny Riddle	C1	R	38	1	0	0	0	0	0	0	0	0	0	0	—	—

NAME	G by Pos	B	AGE	G	AB	R	H	2B	3B	HR	RBI	BB	SO	SB	BA	SA
CHICAGO	**4th 75-79 .487 30**					**JIMMIE WILSON 1-9 .100 ROY JOHNSON 0-1 .000 CHARLIE GRIMM 74-69 .517**										
TOTALS			29	155	5462	702	1425	236	46	71	639	520	521	53	.261	.360
Phil Cavarretta	1B139, OF13	L	27	152	614	106	197	35	15	5	82	67	42	4	.321	.451
Don Johnson	2B154	R	32	154	569	169	37	1	2	71	28	48	8	.278	.332	
Lennie Merullo	SS56, 1B1	R	27	66	193	20	41	8	1	1	16	16	18	3	.212	.280
Stan Hack	3B75, 1B19	L	34	98	383	65	108	16	1	3	32	53	21	5	.282	.352
Bill Nicholson	OF156	L	29	156	582	116	167	35	8	33	122	93	71	3	.287	.545
Andy Pafko	OF123	R	23	128	469	47	126	16	2	6	62	28	23	2	.269	.350
Dom Dallessandro	OF106	L	30	117	381	53	116	19	4	8	74	61	29	1	.305	.438
Dewey Williams	C77	R	28	79	262	23	63	7	2	0	27	23	18	2	.240	.282
Roy Hughes	3B66, SS29	R	33	126	478	86	137	16	6	1	28	35	30	16	.287	.351
Lou Novikoff	OF29	R	28	71	139	15	39	4	2	3	19	10	11	1	.281	.403
Ival Goodman	OF35	L	35	62	144	24	37	8	1	1	16	23	15	0	.257	.354
Bill Schuster	SS38, 2B6	R	31	60	154	14	34	7	1	1	14	12	16	4	.221	.299
Bill Holm	C50	R	31	54	132	10	18	2	0	0	6	16	19	1	.136	.152
Mickey Kreitner	C39	R	21	39	85	3	13	2	0	0	1	8	6	1	.152	.176
Tony York	SS15, 3B12	R	31	28	85	4	20	1	0	0	7	4	11	0	.235	.247
Ed Sauer	OF12	R	25	23	50	3	11	0	0	0	5	2	6	0	.220	.300
Frank Secory	OF17	R	31	22	56	10	18	1	0	4	17	6	8	1	.321	.554
Roy Easterwood	C12	R	29	20	43	1	7	2	0	1	2	1	11	0	.212	.364
Jimmie Foxx	3B2, C1	R	36	15	20	0	1	1	0	0	2	2	5	0	.050	.100
1 Eddie Stanky	2B3, SS3, 3B3	R	27	13	25	4	6	0	1	0	2	5	2	0	.240	.320
Charlie Brewster	SS10	R	27	10	44	4	11	2	0	0	5	5	7	0	.250	.295
Paul Gillespie	C7	L	23	9	26	2	7	1	0	1	2	3	4	0	.269	.423
John Ostrowski	OF2	R	26	8	13	2	2	1	0	0	3	0	3	0	.154	.231
Pete Elko	3B6	R	26	7	22	3	5	1	0	0	3	1	6	0	.227	.273
Joe Stephenson (MS)	C3	R	23	4	8	1	1	0	0	0	0	0	1	0	.125	.125
Benn Mann		R	28	1	0	0	0	0	0	0	0	0	0	0	—	—

NAME	G by Pos	B	AGE	G	AB	R	H	2B	3B	HR	RBI	BB	SO	SB	BA	SA
NEW YORK	**5th 67-87 .435 38**					**MEL OTT**										
TOTALS			31	155	5306	682	1398	191	47	93	646	512	480	39	.263	.370
Phil Weintraub	1B99	L	36	104	361	59	114	18	9	13	77	59	59	0	.316	.524
George Hausmann	2B122	R	28	131	466	70	124	20	4	1	30	40	25	3	.266	.333
Buddy Kerr	SS149	R	21	150	548	68	146	31	4	9	63	37	32	14	.266	.387
Hugh Luby	3B65, 2B45, 1B1	R	31	111	323	30	82	10	2	3	35	52	15	2	.254	.316
Mel Ott	OF103, 3B4	L	35	120	399	91	115	16	4	26	82	90	47	2	.288	.544
Johnny Rucker	OF139	R	27	144	587	79	143	14	8	6	39	24	49	3	.244	.325
Joe Medwick	OF122	R	32	128	490	64	165	24	3	7	85	38	24	2	.337	.441
Ernie Lombardi	C100	R	36	117	373	37	95	13	0	10	58	33	25	0	.255	.370
Nap Reyes	1B63, 3B37, OF3	R	24	116	374	38	108	16	5	8	53	15	24	2	.289	.422
Billy Jurges	3B61, SS10, 2B1	R	36	85	284	28	52	2	1	1	23	23	20	2	.211	.240
Gus Mancuso	C72	R	38	78	195	15	49	4	1	1	25	30	20	0	.251	.297
Bruce Sloan	OF21	R	29	59	104	7	28	4	1	1	9	13	8	0	.269	.356
Red Treadway	OF38	L	24	50	170	23	51	5	2	3	16	13	11	2	.300	.353
Danny Gardella	OF25	L	24	47	112	20	28	2	6	14	11	13	5	0	.250	.464
Charlie Mead	OF23	L	23	39	78	5	14	2	1	0	4	7	9	0	.179	.231
Ray Berres	C12	R	36	17	17	4	8	1	0	0	2	2	1	0	.471	.647
Steve Filipowicz	OF10, C1	R	23	15	41	10	8	2	1	0	1	6	4	1	.195	.293
Roy Nichols	2B1, 3B1	R	23	11	9	3	2	1	0	0	1	0	2	0	.222	.333

Pitching

NAME	T	AGE	W	L	PCT	SV	G	GS	CG	IP	H	BB	SO	SHO	ERA
		28	105	49	.682	12	157	157	89	1427	1228	468	637	26	2.67
Mort Cooper	R	31	22	7	.759	1	34	33	22	286	227	60	97	7	2.46
Ted Wilks	R	28	17	4	.810	0	36	21	16	208	173	49	70	4	2.64
Max Lanier	L	28	17	12	.586	0	33	30	16	224	192	71	141	5	2.65
Harry Brecheen	L	29	16	5	.762	0	30	22	13	189	174	46	88	3	2.86
George Munger (MS)	R	25	11	3	.786	2	21	12	7	121	92	41	55	2	1.34
Freddy Schmidt	R	28	7	3	.700	5	37	9	3	114	94	58	58	2	3.16
Al Jurisich	R	22	7	9	.438	1	30	14	5	130	102	65	53	2	3.39
1 Harry Gumbert	R	34	4	2	.667	1	10	7	3	61	60	19	16	0	2.51
Blix Donnelly	R	30	2	1	.667	2	27	4	2	76	61	34	45	1	2.13
Bud Byerly	R	23	2	2	.500	0	9	4	2	42	37	20	13	0	3.43
Bill Trotter	R	35	0	1	.000	0	2	1	0	6	14	4	0	0	13.50
2 Mike Naymick	R	26	0	0	—	0	2	0	0	2	1	1	1	0	4.50

NAME	T	AGE	W	L	PCT	SV	G	GS	CG	IP	H	BB	SO	SHO	ERA
		32	90	63	.588	19	158	158	77	1414	1466	435	452	10	3.44
Rip Sewell	R	37	21	12	.630	2	38	33	24	286	263	99	87	3	3.18
Nick Strincevich	R	29	14	7	.667	2	40	26	11	190	190	37	47	0	3.08
Preacher Roe	R	29	13	11	.542	1	39	25	7	185	182	59	88	1	3.11
Max Butcher	R	33	13	11	.542	1	35	27	13	199	216	46	43	5	3.12
2 Fritz Ostermueller	L	36	11	7	.611	1	28	24	14	205	201	65	80	1	2.72
Xavier Rescigno	R	31	10	8	.556	5	48	6	2	124	146	34	45	0	4.35
Ray Starr	R	38	6	5	.545	3	27	12	5	90	116	36	25	0	5.00
Cookie Cuccurullo	L	26	2	1	.667	4	32	4	0	106	110	44	31	0	4.08
Len Gilmore	R	26	0	1	.000	0	1	1	1	8	13	0	0	0	7.88
1 Johnny Gee	L	28	0	0	—	0	4	0	0	11	20	5	3	0	7.36
Joe Vitelli	R	36	0	0	—	0	3	0	0	7	5	7	2	0	2.57
Roy Wise	R	18	0	0	—	0	2	0	0	3	4	3	1	0	9.00

NAME	T	AGE	W	L	PCT	SV	G	GS	CG	IP	H	BB	SO	SHO	ERA
		32	89	65	.578	12	155	155	93	1398	1292	384	359	17	2.97
Bucky Walters	R	35	23	8	.742	1	34	32	27	285	233	87	77	6	2.40
Clyde Shoun	L	32	13	10	.565	2	38	21	14	203	193	42	55	1	3.01
Ed Heusser	R	35	13	11	.542	2	30	23	17	193	165	42	42	4	2.38
Arnold Carter	L	26	11	7	.611	3	33	18	9	149	143	40	33	3	2.60
Harry Gumbert	R	34	10	8	.556	2	24	19	11	155	157	40	40	2	3.31
Tommy de la Cruz	R	32	9	9	.500	1	34	20	9	191	170	45	65	0	3.25
Jim Konstanty	R	27	6	4	.600	0	20	12	5	113	113	33	19	1	2.79
Elmer Riddle (SJ)	R	29	2	2	.500	0	4	4	2	27	25	12	6	0	4.00
Joe Beggs (MS)	R	33	1	0	1.000	1	9	1	1	9	8	0	2	0	2.00
Bob Malloy (MS)	R	26	1	1	.500	0	9	0	0	23	22	11	4	0	3.13
Bob Katz	R	33	0	1	.000	0	2	0	0	18	17	7	4	0	4.00
2 Bill Lohrman	R	31	0	1	.000	0	3	1	0	9	13	2	2	0	22.50
Bob Ferguson	R	25	0	3	.000	0	2	0	0	16	24	10	9	0	9.00
Buck Fausett	R	36	0	0	—	0	2	0	0	11	7	3	0	0	5.73
Howie Fox	R	23	0	0	—	0	2	0	0	2	0	0	0	0	0.00
Jake Eisenhardt	L	21	0	0	—	0	2	0	0	3	6	4	0	0	9.00
Joe Nuxhall	L	15	0	0	—	0	1	0	0	2	5	5	0	0	45.00
Kent Peterson	L	18	0	0	—	0	1	0	0	1	0	2	0	0	0.00

NAME	T	AGE	W	L	PCT	SV	G	GS	CG	IP	H	BB	SO	SHO	ERA
		31	75	79	.487	13	157	157	70	1401	1481	452	535	11	3.58
Hank Wyse	R	26	16	15	.516	1	41	34	14	257	277	57	86	3	3.15
Claude Passeau	R	35	15	9	.625	3	34	27	18	227	234	50	89	2	2.89
Bob Chipman	L	25	9	9	.500	2	26	21	8	129	147	40	41	1	3.49
Bill Fleming	R	30	9	10	.474	0	39	18	9	158	163	62	42	1	3.13
Hy Vandenberg	R	38	7	4	.636	2	35	9	2	126	123	51	54	0	3.64
Paul Derringer	R	37	7	13	.350	3	42	16	7	180	205	39	69	0	4.15
Red Lynn	R	30	5	4	.556	1	22	7	4	84	80	37	35	1	4.07
Paul Erickson	R	28	5	9	.357	1	33	15	5	124	113	67	82	3	3.56
Ed Hanyzewski (AJ)	R	23	2	5	.286	0	14	7	3	58	61	20	19	0	4.50
Charlie Gassaway	L	25	0	1	.000	0	2	2	0	20	10	7	7	0	7.50
Dale Alderson (MS)	R	26	0	0	—	0	12	1	0	22	31	9	7	0	6.55
Mack Stewart	R	29	0	0	—	0	3	0	0	12	11	4	3	0	1.50
John Burrows	L	30	0	0	—	0	3	0	0	1	7	3	1	0	18.00
Hank Miklos	L	33	0	0	—	0	1	0	0	7	9	3	0	0	7.71

NAME	T	AGE	W	L	PCT	SV	G	GS	CG	IP	H	BB	SO	SHO	ERA
		30	67	87	.435	21	155	155	47	1364	1413	587	499	4	4.29
Bill Voiselle	R	25	21	16	.568	2	43	41	25	313	276	118	161	1	3.02
Harry Feldman	R	24	11	13	.458	2	40	27	8	205	214	91	70	1	4.17
Ace Adams	R	34	8	11	.421	13	65	4	1	138	149	58	32	0	4.24
Ewald Pyle	L	33	7	10	.412	0	31	21	3	164	152	68	79	0	4.35
Rube Fischer	R	27	6	14	.300	2	38	18	2	129	128	87	39	1	5.16
Johnny Allen	R	39	7	0	—	0	18	13	2	84	88	24	33	1	4.07
Frank Seward	R	23	3	2	.600	0	25	7	0	78	98	32	16	0	5.42
Andy Hansen	R	19	3	3	.500	1	23	4	0	53	63	32	15	0	6.45
Cliff Melton	L	32	2	2	.500	0	13	10	1	64	78	19	15	0	4.08
Bob Barthelson	R	19	1	1	.500	0	7	1	0	13	15	4	4	0	4.50
Jack Brewer	R	26	1	4	.200	0	14	7	2	55	66	16	21	0	5.56
Ken Brondell	R	22	0	1	.000	0	3	1	0	19	27	8	1	0	8.53
Ken Miller	R	20	0	0	—	0	1	0	0	1	1	0	1	0	0.00
Lou Polli	R	42	0	2	.000	3	19	0	0	36	42	20	9	0	4.50
2 Johnny Gee	L	28	0	0	—	0	5	1	0	9	8	4	0	0	3.00
Frank Rosso	R	22	0	0	—	0	3	0	0	2	4	5	1	0	9.00
Walter Ockley	R	23	0	0	—	0	3	2	1	4	5	2	3	0	3.00

BOSTON   6th   65-89   .422   40   BOB COLEMAN

NAME	G by Pos	B	AGE	G	AB	R	H	2B	3B	HR	RBI	BB	SO	SB	BA	SA
TOTALS			28	155	5282	593	1299	250	39	79	558	456	509	37	.246	.353
Buck Etchison	1B85	L	29	109	308	30	66	16	0	8	33	33	50	1	.214	.344
Connie Ryan (MS)	2B80,3B14	R	24	88	332	56	98	18	5	4	25	36	40	13	.295	.416
Whitey Wietelmann	SS103,2B23,3B1	B	25	125	417	46	100	18	1	2	32	33	25	0	.240	.302
Damon Phillips	3B90,SS60	R	25	140	489	35	126	30	1	1	53	28	34	1	.258	.329
Chuck Workman	OF103,3B19	L	28	140	418	46	87	18	3	11	53	42	41	1	.208	.344
Tommy Holmes	OF155	L	27	155	631	93	195	42	6	13	73	61	11	4	.309	.456
Butch Nieman	OF126	L	26	134	468	65	124	16	6	16	65	47	47	5	.265	.427
Phil Masi	C63,1B12,3B2	R	27	89	251	33	69	13	5	3	23	31	20	4	.275	.402
Max Macon	1B72,OF22,P1	L	28	106	366	38	100	15	3	3	36	12	23	7	.273	.355
Clyde Kluttz	C58	R	26	81	229	20	64	12	2	2	19	13	14	0	.279	.376
Ab Wright	OF47	R	37	71	195	20	50	9	0	7	35	18	31	0	.256	.410
Stew Hofferth	C47	R	31	66	180	14	36	8	0	1	26	11	5	0	.200	.267
Chet Ross	OF38	R	27	54	154	20	35	9	2	5	26	12	23	1	.227	.409
Frank Drews	2B46	R	28	46	141	14	29	9	1	0	10	25	14	0	.206	.284
Warren Huston	3B20,2B5,SS4	R	30	33	55	7	11	1	0	1	8	5	0		.200	.218
Mike Sandlock	3B22,SS7	L	28	30	30	1	3	0	0	0	2	5	3	0	.100	.100
Roland Gladu	3B15,OF3	L	33	21	66	5	16	2	1	1	7	3	8	0	.242	.348
Chet Clemens (MS)	OF7	R	27	19	17	7	3	1	1	0	2	2	2	0	.176	.353
Steve Shemo	2B16,3B2	R	29	18	31	3	9	2	0	0	0	1	2	0	.290	.355
Ben Geraghty	2B4,3B3	R	31	11	16	3	4	0	0	0	0	1	2	0	.250	.250

Dick Culler 29 R 2-28, Hugh Poland 31 L 3-23, Pat Capri 25 R 0-1, Gene Patton 17 L 0-0, Eddie Joost (VR) 28

NAME	T	AGE	W	L	PCT	SV	G	GS	CG	IP	H	BB	SO	SHO	ERA
		29	65	89	.422	12	155	155	70	1388	1430	527	454	13	3.67
Jim Tobin	R	29	18	19	.486	3	43	36	28	299	271	97	83	5	3.01
Nate Andrews	R	30	16	15	.516	2	37	34	16	257	263	74	76	2	3.22
Al Javery	R	26	10	19	.345	3	40	33	11	254	248	137	137	3	3.54
Ira Hutchinson	R	33	7	7	.563	1	40	8	1	120	136	53	22	1	4.20
Red Barrett	R	29	9	16	.360	2	42	30	11	230	257	63	54	1	4.07
Woody Rich	R	28	1	1	.500	0	7	2	1	25	32	12	6	0	5.76
Stan Klopp	R	33	1	2	.333	0	24	0	0	46	47	33	17	0	4.30
Johnny Hutchings	R	28	1	4	.200	0	14	1	1	57	55	26	26	0	3.95
Ben Cardoni	R	23	0	6	.000	0	22	5	1	76	83	37	24	0	3.91
Jim Hickey (MS)	R	23	0	0	—	0	9	0	0	9	15	5	3	0	5.00
Carl Lindquist	R	25	0	0	—	0	3	0	0	9	2	4	4	0	3.00
George Woodend	R	26	0	0	—	0	3	0	0	2	5	5	0	0	13.50
Max Macon	L	28	0	0	—	0	1	0	0	3	10	1	1	0	21.00
Harry MacPherson	R	17	0	0	—	0	1	0	0	1	1	1	1	0	0.00

BROOKLYN   7th   63-91   .409   42   LEO DUROCHER

NAME	G by Pos	B	AGE	G	AB	R	H	2B	3B	HR	RBI	BB	SO	SB	BA	SA
TOTALS			29	155	5393	690	1450	255	51	56	631	486	451	43	.269	.366
Howie Schultz	1B136	R	21	138	526	59	134	32	3	11	83	24	67	6	.255	.390
2 Eddie Stanky	2B58,SS35,3B1	R	27	89	261	32	72	9	2	0	16	44	13	3	.276	.326
Bobby Bragan	SS51,C35,3B6,2B1	R	26	94	266	26	71	8	4	0	17	13	14	2	.267	.327
Frenchy Bordagaray	3B98,OF25	R	34	130	501	55	141	26	4	6	51	36	22	2	.281	.385
Dixie Walker	OF140	L	33	147	535	77	191	37	8	13	91	72	27	6	.357	.529
Goody Rosen	OF65	R	31	89	264	38	69	8	3	0	23	26	27	0	.261	.314
Augie Galan	OF147,2B2	L	32	151	547	96	174	43	9	12	93	101	23	4	.318	.494
Mickey Owen	C125,2B1	R	28	130	461	43	126	20	3	1	42	36	17	1	.273	.336
Luis Olmo	OF64,2B42,3B31	R	24	136	520	65	134	20	5	9	85	17	30	10	.258	.367
1 Paul Waner	OF32	L	41	83	136	16	39	4	1	0	16	27	7	0	.287	.331
Jack Bolling (MS)	1B27	L	27	56	131	21	46	14	1	1	25	14	4	0	.351	.496
Tommy Brown	SS46	R	16	46	146	17	24	4	0	0	8	8	17	0	.164	.192
Eddie Basinski	2B37,SS3	R	21	39	105	13	27	4	1	0	9	6	10	1	.257	.314
Barney Koch	2B29,SS1	R	21	33	96	11	21	2	0	0	1	3	9	1	.219	.240
Bill Hart	SS25,3B2	R	31	29	90	8	16	4	2	0	9	4	9	7	.178	.267
Gil English	SS13,3B11,2B2	R	34	27	79	4	12	3	0	1	7	6	7	0	.152	.228
Eddie Miksis	3B15,SS10	R	17	26	91	12	20	2	0	0	11	6	11	4	.220	.264
Morrie Aderholt	OF13	R	28	17	59	9	16	2	3	0	10	4	4	1	.271	.407
1 Lloyd Waner	OF4	L	38	15	14	3	4	0	0	0	0	3	0	0	.286	.286
Pat Ankenman	2B11,SS2	R	31	15	24	1	6	1	0	0	3	2	3	0	.250	.292
Red Durrett	OF9	L	23	11	32	3	5	1	0	0	2	1	9	1	.156	.281

1 Johnny Cooney 43 R 3-4, Ray Hayworth 40 R 0-10, Gene Mauch (MS) 18 R 2-15, Lou Rochelli (MS) 25 R 3-17
Clancy Smyres 22 B 0-2, Stan Andrews 27 R 1-8, Fats Dantonio 25 R 1-7, Roy Jarvis (MS) 18 0-1, Arky Vaughan (VR) 32

NAME	T	AGE	W	L	PCT	SV	G	GS	CG	IP	H	BB	SO	SHO	ERA
		25	63	91	.409	13	155	155	50	1368	1471	660	487	4	4.68
Curt Davis	R	40	10	11	.476	4	31	23	12	194	207	39	49	1	3.34
Rube Melton	R	27	9	13	.409	0	37	23	6	187	178	96	91	1	3.47
Hal Gregg	R	22	9	16	.360	2	39	31	6	198	201	137	92	0	5.45
Les Webber	R	29	7	8	.467	3	48	9	1	140	157	64	42	0	4.95
Ben Chapman	R	35	5	3	.625	0	11	9	6	79	75	33	37	0	3.42
Ed Head (MS)	R	26	4	3	.571	0	8	5	3	63	54	19	17	1	2.71
1 Bob Chipman	L	25	3	1	.750	0	11	3	1	36	38	24	20	0	4.25
Art Herring	R	38	3	4	.429	1	12	6	3	55	59	17	19	1	3.44
Cal McLish	R	18	3	10	.231	0	23	13	3	84	110	48	24	0	7.82
Clyde King	R	20	2	1	.667	0	14	3	1	44	42	12	14	0	3.07
1 Fritz Ostermueller	L	36	2	1	.667	1	10	4	3	42	46	12	17	0	3.21
Whit Wyatt (SA)	R	36	2	6	.250	0	9	9	1	38	51	16	4	0	7.11
Charley Fuchs	R	30	1	0	1.000	0	8	0	0	16	25	9	5	0	5.63
Wes Flowers	L	31	1	0	.500	0	7	0	0	17	26	13	4	0	7.94
Tom Sunkel	L	31	1	3	.250	1	12	3	0	24	39	10	6	0	7.50
Tommy Warren	R	26	1	4	.200	0	22	4	2	69	74	40	18	0	4.96
Ralph Branca	R	18	0	2	.000	1	21	0	0	45	46	32	16	0	7.00
John Wells	R	21	0	2	.000	0	10	0	0	10	7	3	0		5.40
Chink Zachary	R	26	0	2	.000	0	8	0	0	20	10	10	7	0	9.58
1 Bill Lohrman	R	31	0	3	.000	0	3	0	0	3	4	1	1	0	10.80
Claude Crocker	R	19	0	0	—	0	3	0	0	3	6	5	1	0	10.80
Charlie Osgood	R	17	0	0	—	0	1	0	0	2	2	3	0	0	4.50
Jack Franklin	R	24	0	0	—	0	1	0	0	1	3	2	4	0	13.50
Frank Worm	L	20	0	0	—	0	1	0	0	0.1	1	5	1	0	108.00

PHILADELPHIA   8th   61-92   .399   43.5   FREDDIE FITZSIMMONS

NAME	G by Pos	B	AGE	G	AB	R	H	2B	3B	HR	RBI	BB	SO	SB	BA	SA
TOTALS			29	154	5301	539	1331	199	42	55	495	470	500	32	.251	.336
Tony Lupien	1B151	L	27	153	597	82	169	23	9	5	52	56	29	18	.283	.377
Moon Mullen	2B114,3B1,C1	L	27	118	464	51	124	9	4	0	31	28	32	4	.267	.304
Ray Hamrick (MS)	SS74	R	22	74	292	22	60	10	1	1	23	23	34	1	.205	.257
Glen Stewart	2B83,SS32,2B1	R	31	118	377	32	83	11	5	0	29	28	40	0	.220	.276
Ron Northey	OF151	L	24	152	570	72	164	35	9	22	104	67	51	6	.288	.496
Buster Adams	OF151	R	28	155	584	86	165	35	3	17	64	74	74	2	.283	.440
Jimmy Wasdell	OF121,1B4	L	30	133	451	47	125	20	3	4	40	45	17	0	.277	.355
Bob Finley	C74	R	28	94	281	18	70	11	1	1	21	12	25	1	.249	.306
Charlie Letchas	2B47,3B32,SS29	R	28	116	396	29	94	8	0	0	33	32	27	0	.237	.298
Ted Cieslak	3B48,OF5	R	31	85	220	18	54	10	0	2	11	21	17	1	.245	.318
Coaker Triplett	C73,2B1	R	32	84	184	15	43	5	1	1	25	19	10	1	.234	.288
2 Johnny Peacock	OF44	R	34	83	253	21	57	9	3	0	21	31	5	1	.225	.285
Andy Seminick	C11,OF7	R	23	22	63	9	14	2	1	0	4	6	17	2	.222	.286
Granny Hamner	SS21	R	17	21	77	6	19	1	0	0	3	3	10	0	.247	.260
Heinie Heltzel	SS10	R	30	11	32	3	5	1	0	0	1	2	3	0	.182	.227

Merv Shea 43 R 4-15, Joe Antolik 28 R 2-6, Putsy Caballero 16 R 0-4, Benny Culp (MS) 30 R 0-2,
Chuck Klein 39 L 1-7, Lee Riley 37 L 1-12, Nick Goulish 27 L 0-1, Turkey Tyson 29 L 0-1

NAME	T	AGE	W	L	PCT	SV	G	GS	CG	IP	H	BB	SO	SHO	ERA
		29	61	92	.399	6	154	154	66	1395	1407	459	496	11	3.64
Charlie Schanz	R	25	13	16	.448	3	40	30	13	241	231	103	84	1	3.32
Ken Raffensberger	L	26	13	20	.394	0	37	31	18	259	257	45	136	3	3.06
Dick Barrett	R	37	12	18	.400	2	37	27	11	221	223	88	74	1	3.87
Bill Lee	R	34	10	11	.476	1	31	28	11	208	199	57	50	3	3.16
Al Gerheauser	L	27	8	16	.333	2	30	29	10	183	210	65	66	2	4.57
Andy Karl	R	30	3	2	.600	2	38	1	0	89	76	21	26	0	2.33
Chet Covington	L	33	1	1	.500	0	19	0	0	39	46	8	13	0	4.62
2 Vern Kennedy	R	37	1	5	.167	0	12	7	3	55	60	20	23	0	4.25
Barney Mussill	L	24	0	1	.000	1	16	0	0	19	20	13	5	0	6.16
Deacon Donahue	R	24	0	2	.000	0	18	0	0	27	26	11	4	0	8.00
Harry Shuman	R	29	0	0	—	0	18	0	0	27	26	11	4	0	4.00
Dale Mattewson	R	21	0	1	.000	0	3	0	0	32	27	16	8	0	3.94
John Fick	R	23	0	1	.000	0	4	0	0	3	5	2	2	0	3.60
2 Lou Lucier	R	26	0	0	—	0	7	0	0	10	13	5	6	0	13.50
Rogers McKee	L	17	0	0	—	0	2	0	0	4	5	2	1	0	4.50
Charlie Ripple	L	23	0	0	—	0	3	0	0	2	3	6	2	0	18.00
Al Verdel	R	23	0	0	—	0	1	0	0	1	2	1	0	0	0.00

WORLD SERIES — ST. LOUIS (NL) 4   ST. LOUIS (AL) 2

LINE SCORES

TEAM	1	2	3	4	5	6	7	8	9	10	11	12	R	H	E

Game 1   October 4 at Sportsman's Park
STL (AL)   0 0 0   2 0 0   0 0 0   2 2 0
STL (NL)   0 0 0   0 0 0   0 0 1   1 7 0
Galehouse   M. Cooper, Donnelly (8)

Game 2   October 5 at Sportsman's Park
STL (AL)   0 0 0   0 0 0   2 0 0   0 0   2 7 4
STL (NL)   1 0 0   1 0 0   0 0 0   0 1   3 7 0
Potter, Muncrief (7)   Lanier, Donnelly (8)

Game 3   October 6 at Sportsman's Park
STL (NL)   1 0 0   0 0 0   1 0 0   2 7 0
STL (AL)   0 0 4   0 0 0   2 0 X   6 8 2
Wilks, Schmidt (3), Jurisich (7),   Kramer
Byerly (7)

Game 4   October 7 at Sportsman's Park
STL (NL)   2 0 2   0 0 1   0 0 0   5 12 0
STL (AL)   0 0 0   0 0 0   0 1 0   1 9 1
Brecheen   Jakucki, Hollingworth (4)
Shirley (8)

Game 5   October 8 at Sportsman's Park
STL (AL)   0 0 0   0 0 0   0 0 0   0 7 1
STL (NL)   0 0 0   0 0 1   0 1 0   2 6 1
M. Cooper   Galehouse

Game 6   October 9 at Sportsman's Park
STL (AL)   0 1 0   0 0 0   0 0 0   1 3 2
STL (NL)   0 0 0   3 0 0   0 0 X   3 10 0
Potter, Muncrief (4), Kramer (7)   Wilks

COMPOSITE BATTING

NAME	POS	G	AB	R	H	2B	3B	HR	RBI	BA
St. Louis (NL) Totals		6	204	16	49	9	1	3	15	.240
Hopp	OF	6	27	2	5	0	0	0	1	.185
Musial	OF	6	23	2	7	2	0	1	2	.304
Kurowski	3B	6	23	2	5	1	0	0	1	.217
W. Cooper	C	6	22	1	7	2	1	0	2	.318
Marion	SS	6	22	1	5	3	0	0	2	.227
Sanders	1B	6	21	5	6	0	0	1	1	.286
Litwhiler	OF	5	20	2	4	1	0	1	1	.200
Verban	2B	6	17	1	7	0	0	0	2	.412
Bergamo	OF	3	6	0	0	0	0	0	0	.000
Lanier	P	3	4	0	2	0	0	0	0	.500
M. Cooper	P	2	4	0	0	0	0	0	0	.000
Brecheen	P	1	3	0	0	0	0	0	0	.000
O'Dea	PH	3	3	0	1	0	0	0	2	.333
Fallon	2B	2	3	0	1	0	0	0	0	.333
Garms	PH	2	2	0	0	0	0	0	0	.000
Wilks	P	2	2	0	0	0	0	0	0	.000
Donnelly	P	2	1	0	0	0	0	0	0	.000
Schmidt	P	1	1	0	0	0	0	0	0	.000
Byerly	P	1	0	0	0	0	0	0	0	—
Jurisich	P	1	0	0	0	0	0	0	0	—
St. Louis (AL) Totals		6	197	12	36	9	1	1	9	.183
Kreevich	OF	6	26	0	6	3	0	0	0	.231
Stephens	SS	6	22	2	5	0	0	0	2	.227
Moore	OF	6	22	4	4	0	0	0	1	.182
Christman	3B	6	22	0	2	0	0	0	1	.091
Gutteridge	2B	6	21	1	3	1	0	0	0	.143
Hayworth	C	6	17	1	2	1	0	0	0	.118
McQuinn	1B	6	16	2	7	2	0	1	5	.438
Laabs	OF	5	15	1	3	1	0	0	2	.200
Zarilla	OF	4	10	1	1	0	0	0	0	.100
Galehouse	P	2	4	0	0	0	0	0	0	.000
Kramer	P	2	4	0	1	0	0	0	0	.000
Potter	P	2	3	0	0	0	0	0	0	.000
Mancuso	C	2	3	0	2	0	0	0	0	.667
Baker	2B	2	2	0	0	0	0	0	0	.000
Byrnes	PH	3	2	0	0	0	0	0	0	.000
Chartak	PH	2	2	0	0	0	0	0	0	.000
Muncrief	P	2	1	0	0	0	0	0	0	.000
Clary	P	1	0	0	0	0	0	0	0	—
Turner	PH	1	1	0	0	0	0	0	0	.000

Hollingsworth P 0-1, Shirley P 0-0, Jakucki P 0-0

COMPOSITE PITCHING

NAME	G	IP	H	BB	SO	W	L	SV	ERA
St. Louis (NL) Totals	6	55	36	23	49	4	2	0	1.96
M. Cooper	2	16	9	5	16	1	1	0	1.12
Lanier	2	12.1	8	8	11	1	0	0	2.19
Brecheen	1	9	9	4	4	1	0	0	1.00
Wilks	2	6.1	5	3	7	0	1	0	5.68
Donnelly	2	4	2	3	7	1	0	0	0.00
Schmidt	1	3.1	1	0	1	0	0	0	0.00
Byerly	1	1.1	0	0	1	0	0	0	0.00
Jurisich	1	0.2	2	1	0	0	0	0	27.00
St. Louis (AL) Totals	6	54.1	49	19	43	2	4	0	1.49
Galehouse	2	18	13	5	15	1	1	0	1.50
Kramer	2	11	9	4	12	1	0	0	0.00
Potter	2	9.2	10	3	6	0	1	0	0.93
Muncrief	2	6.2	5	4	6	0	1	0	1.35
Hollingsworth	1	4	5	2	4	0	0	0	2.25
Jakucki	1	3	2	1	0	0	1	0	9.00
Shirley	1	2	2	1	0	0	0	0	0.00

1945 Greenberg's Grand Return

War-time travel restrictions canceled the All-Star Game, the St. Louis Browns signed Pete Gray, a one-armed outfielder, and baseball had a new commissioner. Judge Kennesaw Mountain Landis, the only commissioner the game had known since 1920, died November 25, 1944. Although controversial and sometimes questioningly stern, Landis had given baseball the discipline necessary to survive the holocaust of 1919—a year when it was learned that the World Series could be fixed and the sport could not be isolated from the other pressures which comprised American life.

The club owners named Albert B. (Happy) Chandler, a U.S. Senator from Kentucky, to replace the iron-handed Judge. Chandler's first year was tinged with even greater excitement than the Judge had enjoyed in 1944. Once again, the Detroit Tigers were involved in the nerve-splitting action. The outcome happily for Tiger fans, was a reversal of the disappointment of the previous September. On the final day of the season, Detroit found themselves in front by one game over Washington, which had already finished its schedule. The tigers had waited since September 26, to clinch the pennant, but could not compete with the rain, which brought their momentum to a grinding halt. They had two chances to put the flag away and, at the same time, revenge themselves against the Browns. But it started to rain again on the afternoon of the 30th, causing Detroit to wonder if the skies of St. Louis would ever permit another baseball game, let alone a doubleheader. Pitchers Nels Potter of St. Louis, and Detroit's Virgil Trucks, who was released from the Navy in time to pitch the first game, warmed up three times waiting for the skies to clear. They never did, but the rain stopped, and the game got underway .

In the sixth inning Trucks gave way to ace Hal Newhouser, who quelled a St. Louis rally with one out and the bases loaded to momentarily keep a 2-1 lead intact. Then in the seventh, the Browns got a run to tie the game and added another in the eighth to go ahead. Detroit found themselves against the wall in the ninth. With the skies getting darker, they loaded the bases with one out. Veteran Hank Greenberg, who had joined the team in mid-season after a four year military stint, found himself at the plate. The count was 1-1 when Greenberg met the next pitch head on and sent it into the left field bleachers to make the second game unnecessary and to give the Tigers the lowest percentage pennant winner (.575) in major league history. The victory was the 25th for Newhouser, who was again named MVP, thereby becoming the only man since Jimmie Foxx's 1932-33 performances to win the honors back-to-back.

The National League story was not as dramatic as the one the junior circuit offered. Brooklyn, led by Leo Durocher, surprised everyone and finished third, and the Chicago Cubs—led by field captain Phil Cavarretta's MVP pcrformance—won the pennant by three games over the Cardinals, who lost Stan Musial to the army and the chance to make it four flags in a row. En route to their tenth flag in the twentieth century, the Cubs set a record by sweeping 20 doubleheaders and further helped themselves by taking 21 out of the 22 games with Cincinnati.

Cavaretta led his teammates into the World Series and batted a sizzling .423. Claude Passeau picked up a victory on a one-hitter over the Tigers, and Hank Borowy, who led the league with a 2.14 E.R.A., collected two wins. But it was not enough as Newhouser returned in the finale to win his second game of the Series over a tired Borowy—pitching on one day's rest—and giving the Tigers the championship.

1945 AMERICAN LEAGUE

NAME	G by Pos	B	AGE	G	AB	R	H	2B	3B	HR	RBI	BB	SO	SB	BA	SA
DETROIT 1st 88-65 .575		STEVE O'NEILL														
TOTALS			33	155	5257	633	1345	227	47	77	588	517	533	60	.256	.361
Rudy York	1B155	R	31	155	595	71	157	25	5	18	87	60	85	6	.264	.143
Eddie Mayo	2B154	L	35	134	501	71	143	24	3	10	54	47	29	7	.285	.405
Skeeter Webb	SS104, 2B11	R	35	118	407	43	81	12	2	0	21	30	35	8	.199	.238
Bob Maier	3B124, OF5	R	29	132	486	58	128	25	7	1	34	38	32	7	.263	.350
2 Roy Cullenbine	OF146	B	31	146	523	80	145	27	5	18	93	101*	36	2	.277	.451
Doc Cramer	OF140	L	39	141	541	62	149	12	8	6	58	36	21	2	.275	.379
Jimmy Outlaw	OF105, 3B21	R	32	132	446	56	121	16	5	0	34	45	33	6	.271	.330
Bob Swift	C94	R	30	95	279	19	65	5	0	0	24	26	22	1	.233	.251
Paul Richards	C83	R	36	83	234	26	60	12	1	3	32	19	31	4	.256	.355
Hank Greenberg (MS)	OF72	R	34	78	270	47	84	20	2	13	60	42	40	3	.311	.544
Joe Hoover	SS68	R	30	74	222	33	57	10	5	1	17	21	35	6	.257	.360
Red Borum	2B28, 3B4, SS2	L	29	55	130	19	35	4	0	0	9	7	8	4	.269	.300
Chuck Hostetler	OF8	L	41	42	44	3	7	3	0	0	2	7	8	0	.159	.227
Hub Walker	OF7	L	38	28	23	4	3	0	0	0	1	9	4	1	.130	.130
John McHale	1B3	L	23	19	14	0	2	0	0	0	1	1	4	0	.143	.143
Ed Mierkkowicz	OF6	R	21	10	15	0	2	2	0	0	2	1	3	0	.133	.267
1 Don Ross	3B8	R	30	8	29	3	11	4	0	0	4	5	1	2	.379	.517
Hack Miller	C2	R	34	2	4	0	3	0	0	0	1	0	0	0	.750	.750
Russ Kerns		L	24	1	1	0	0	0	0	0	0	0	0	0	.000	.000
Carl McNabb		R	28	1	1	0	0	0	0	0	0	0	0	0	.000	.000
Milt Welch	C1	R	20	1	2	0	0	0	0	0	0	0	1	0	.000	.000

NAME	T	AGE	W	L	PCT	SV	G	GS	CG	IP	H	BB	SO	SHO	ERA
		29	88	65	.575	16	155	155	78	1394	1305	538	588	19	2.99
Hal Newhouser	L	24	25	9	.735	2	40	36	29	313	239	110	212	8	1.81
Dizzy Trout	R	30	18	15	.545	2	41	31	18	246	252	79	97	4	2.13
Al Benton (BN)	R	34	13	8	.619	3	31	27	12	192	175	63	76	5	2.02
Stubby Overmire	L	26	9	9	.500	1	31	22	9	162	189	42	36	0	3.89
Les Mueller	R	26	6	8	.429	1	26	18	6	135	117	58	42	2	3.67
2 George Caster	R	37	5	1	.833	2	22	0	0	51	47	27	23	0	3.88
Zeb Eaton	R	25	4	2	.667	0	17	3	0	53	48	40	15	0	4.08
2 Jim Tobin	R	32	4	5	.444	1	14	6	2	58	61	28	14	0	3.57
Joe Orrell	R	28	2	3	.400	0	12	5	1	48	46	24	14	0	3.00
Tommy Bridges (MS)	R	38	1	0	1.000	0	4	1	0	11	14	2	6	0	3.27
Walter Wilson	R	31	1	3	.250	0	25	4	1	70	76	35	28	0	4.63
Art Houtteman	R	17	0	2	.000	0	13	0	0	25	27	11	9	0	5.40
Billy Pierce	L	18	0	0	—	0	5	0	0	10	6	10	10	0	1.80
Prince Oana	R	37	0	0	—	1	3	1	0	11	3	7	3	0	1.64
Pat McLaughlin	R	34	0	0	—	0	1	0	0	1	2	0	0	0	9.00
Virgil Trucks (MS)	R	28	0	0	—	0	1	1	0	5	3	2	3	0	1.80
Rufe Gentry (HO) 27															

*Cullenbine, also with Cleveland, league leader in BB with 112

NAME	G by Pos	B	AGE	G	AB	R	H	2B	3B	HR	RBI	BB	SO	SB	BA	SA
WASHINGTON 2nd 87-67 .565 1.5		OSSIE BLUEGE														
TOTALS			32	156	5326	622	1375	197	63	27	570	545	489	110	.258	.334
Joe Kuhel	1B141	L	39	142	533	73	152	29	13	2	75	79	31	10	.285	.400
George Myatt	2B94, OF32, 3B6, SS1	L	31	133	490	81	145	17	7	1	39	63	43	30	.296	.365
Gil Torres	SS145, 3B2	R	29	147	562	39	133	12	5	0	48	21	29	7	.237	.276
Harlond Clift	3B111	R	32	119	375	49	79	12	0	8	53	76	58	2	.211	.307
Buddy Lewis (MS)	OF69	L	28	69	258	42	86	14	7	2	37	37	15	1	.333	.465
George Binks	OF128, 1B20	L	30	145	550	82	153	32	6	6	81	34	52	11	.278	.391
George Case	OF123	R	29	123	504	73	148	19	5	1	31	49	27	30	.294	.357
Rick Ferrell	C83	R	39	91	286	33	76	12	1	1	38	43	13	2	.266	.325
Fred Vaughn	2B76, SS1	R	26	80	268	28	63	7	4	1	25	23	48	0	.235	.302
Hilly Layne	3B33	L	27	61	147	23	44	5	4	1	14	10	7	0	.299	.408
Mike Guerra	C38	R	32	56	138	11	29	1	1	1	15	10	12	4	.210	.254
Jose Zardon	OF43	R	22	54	131	13	38	5	3	0	13	7	11	3	.290	.374
Al Evans	C41	R	28	51	150	19	39	11	2	1	19	17	22	2	.260	.400
2 Mike Kreevich	OF40	R	37	45	158	22	44	8	2	1	23	21	11	7	.278	.373
1 Jake Powell	OF27	R	36	31	98	4	19	2	0	0	3	6	9	1	.194	.214
Dick Kimble	SS15	L	29	20	49	5	12	1	1	0	1	5	2	0	.245	.306
Vince Ventura	OF15	R	28	18	58	4	12	0	0	0	2	4	4	0	.207	.207
Walt Chipple	OF13	R	28	18	44	4	6	0	0	0	5	5	6	0	.136	.136
Cecil Travis (MS)	3B14	L	31	15	54	4	13	2	1	0	10	4	5	0	.241	.315
Howie McFarland	OF3	R	35	6	11	0	1	0	0	0	0	0	3	0	.091	.091
Roberto Ortiz (VR) 30																

NAME	T	AGE	W	L	PCT	SV	G	GS	CG	IP	H	BB	SO	SHO	ERA
		32	87	67	.585	11	156	156	82	1413	1307	440	550	19	2.92
Roger Wolff	R	24	20	10	.667	2	33	29	21	250	200	53	108	4	2.12
Dutch Leonard	R	26	17	7	.708	1	31	29	12	216	208	35	96	4	2.13
Mickey Haefner	L	32	16	14	.533	3	37	28	19	238	226	69	83	1	3.48
Marino Pieretti	R	24	14	13	.519	2	44	27	14	233	235	91	66	3	3.32
Alex Carrasquel	R	32	7	5	.583	1	35	7	5	123	105	40	38	2	2.71
Johnny Niggeling	R	41	7	12	.368	0	26	25	8	177	161	73	90	2	3.15
Sandy Ullrich	R	23	3	3	.500	1	28	6	0	81	91	34	26	0	4.36
2 Pete Appleton	R	41	1	0	1.000	0	6	2	1	21	16	11	12	0	3.43
Walt Holborow	R	31	1	1	.500	0	15	1	1	31	20	16	14	1	2.32
Walt Masterson (MS)	R	25	1	2	.333	0	4	2	1	25	21	10	14	1	1.08
Dick Stone	R	33	0	0	—	0	5	0	0	6	2	0	0	0	0.00
Armando Roche	R	18	0	0	—	0	1	0	0	6	10	2	0	0	6.00
Joe Cleary	R	26	0	0	—	0	1	0	0	0.1	5	3	1	0	189.00
Bert Shepard	L	25	0	0	—	0	1	0	0	5	3	1	2	0	1.80

NAME	G by Pos	B	AGE	G	AB	R	H	2B	3B	HR	RBI	BB	SO	SB	BA	SA
ST. LOUIS 3rd 81-70 .536 6		LUKE SEWELL														
TOTALS			30	154	5227	597	1302	215	37	63	557	500	555	25	.249	.341
George McQuinn	1B136	L	35	139	483	69	134	31	3	7	61	65	51	1	.277	.398
Don Gutteridge	2B128, OF14	R	33	143	543	72	129	24	3	2	49	43	46	9	.238	.304
Vern Stephens	SS144, 3B4	R	24	149	571	90	165	27	3	24	89	55	70	2	.289	.473
Mark Christman	3B77	R	31	78	289	32	80	7	4	4	34	19	19	1	.277	.370
Gene Moore	OF100	L	35	110	354	48	92	16	2	5	50	40	26	1	.260	.359
1 Mike Kreevich	OF81	R	37	84	295	34	70	11	1	2	31	37	27	4	.237	.302
Milt Byrnes	OF125, 1B2	L	28	133	442	53	110	29	4	8	59	78	84	1	.249	.387
Frank Mancuso	C115	R	27	119	365	39	98	13	3	1	38	46	44	0	.268	.329
Len Schulte	3B71, 2B37, SS14	R	28	119	430	37	106	16	1	0	36	24	35	0	.247	.288
Pete Gray	OF61	L	30	77	234	26	51	6	2	0	13	13	11	5	.218	.261
2 Lou Finney	OF36, 1B22, 3B1	L	34	57	213	24	59	8	4	2	22	21	6	0	.277	.380
Red Hayworth	C55	R	29	56	160	7	31	4	0	0	17	7	6	0	.194	.219
Babe Martin	OF48, 1B6	R	25	54	185	13	37	5	2	2	16	11	24	0	.200	.281
Tex Shirley	P32	R	27	43	70	7	20	1	0	0	3	5	8	0	.286	.300
Joe Schultz	C4	L	26	41	44	4	13	2	0	0	8	1	1	0	.295	.341
Chet Laabs (MS)	OF35	R	33	35	109	15	26	4	3	5	18	16	17	0	.239	.358
Nels Potter	P32	L	33	32	92	3	28	2	0	0	8	1	7	0	.304	.326
Ellis Clary	3B16, 2B3	R	28	26	38	6	8	1	0	1	2	5	1	1	.211	.316

NAME	T	AGE	W	L	PCT	SV	G	GS	CG	IP	H	BB	SO	SHO	ERA
		30	81	70	.536	8	154	154	91	1383	1307	506	570	10	3.14
Nels Potter	R	33	15	11	.577	0	32	32	21	255	212	68	129	3	2.47
Bob Muncrief	R	29	13	4	.765	1	27	15	10	166	132	44	54	0	2.71
Al Hollingsworth	L	37	12	9	.571	1	26	22	15	173	164	68	64	1	2.71
Sig Jakucki	R	35	12	10	.545	2	30	24	15	192	188	65	51	3	3.52
Jack Kramer	R	27	10	15	.400	2	29	25	15	193	190	73	99	3	3.36
Tex Shirley	R	27	8	12	.400	0	32	24	10	184	191	93	77	2	3.62
Sam Zoldak	L	26	3	4	.429	0	24	8	1	74	71	31	38	0	3.65
Lefty West	L	29	3	4	.429	0	24	8	1	74	71	31	38	0	3.65
Al LaMacchia	R	23	2	0	1.000	0	5	0	0	9	6	3	2	0	2.00
Ox Miller	R	30	2	1	.667	0	4	3	0	28	23	5	4	0	1.61
1 George Caster	R	37	1	2	.333	1	19	0	0	16	20	7	9	0	6.75
Earl Jones	L	26	0	0	—	1	10	0	0	28	18	18	13	0	2.57
Cliff Fannin	R	21	0	0	—	0	5	0	0	10	8	5	5	0	2.70
Dee Sanders	R	24	0	0	—	0	2	0	0	1	1	1	0	0	54.00
1 Pete Appleton (MS)	R	41	0	0	—	0	1	0	0	1	7	1	0	0	18.00

224

NEW YORK — 4th 81-71 .533 6.5 — JOE McCARTHY

NAME	G by Pos	B	AGE	G	AB	R	H	2B	3B	HR	RBI	BB	SO	SB	BA	SA
TOTALS			30	152	5176	676	1343	189	61	93	639	618	567	64	.259	.373
Nick Etten	1B152	L	31	152	565	77	161	24	4	18	111	90	23	2	.285	.437
Snuffy Stirnweiss	2B152	R	26	152	632	107	195	32	22	10	64	78	62	33	.309	.476
Frankie Crosetti	SS126	R	34	130	441	57	105	12	0	4	48	59	65	7	.238	.293
Oscar Grimes	3B141, 1B1	R	30	142	480	64	127	19	7	4	45	97	73	7	.265	.358
Bud Metheny	OF128	L	30	133	509	64	126	18	2	8	53	54	31	5	.248	.338
Tuck Stainback	OF83	R	33	95	327	40	84	12	2	5	32	13	20	0	.257	.352
Hersh Martin	OF102	B	35	117	408	53	109	18	6	7	53	65	31	4	.267	.392
Mike Garbark	C59	R	29	60	176	23	38	5	3	1	26	23	12	0	.216	.295
Russ Derry	OF68	L	28	78	253	37	57	6	2	13	45	31	49	1	.225	.419
Aaron Robinson (MS)	C45	R	30	50	160	19	45	8	4	8	24	21	23	0	.281	.481
Bill Drescher	C33	L	24	48	126	10	34	3	1	0	15	8	5	0	.270	.310
Charlie Keller (MM)	OF44	R	28	44	163	26	49	7	4	10	34	31	21	0	.301	.577
Johnny Lindell (MS)	OF41	R	28	41	159	26	45	6	3	1	20	17	10	2	.283	.377
Herb Crompton	C33	R	33	36	99	6	19	3	0	0	12	2	7	0	.192	.222
Don Savage	3B14, OF2	R	26	34	58	5	13	1	0	0	3	3	14	1	.224	.241
Joe Buzas	SS12	R	25	30	65	8	17	2	1	0	6	2	5	2	.262	.323
Mike Milosevich	SS22, 2B1	R	30	30	69	5	15	2	0	0	7	6	6	0	.217	.246
Paul Waner (MS)			42	1	0	0	0	0	0	0	0	1	0	0	.000	.000

NAME	T	AGE	W	L	PCT	SV	G	GS	CG	IP	H	BB	SO	SHO	ERA
		30	81	71	.533	14	152	152	78	1355	1277	485	474	9	3.45
Bill Bevens	R	28	13	9	.591	0	29	25	14	184	174	68	76	2	3.67
1 Hank Borowy	R	29	10	5	.667	0	18	18	7	132	107	58	35	1	3.14
Monk Dubiel	R	27	10	9	.526	0	26	20	9	151	157	62	45	1	4.65
Al Gettel	R	27	9	8	.529	3	27	17	9	155	141	53	67	0	3.89
Ernie Bonham	R	31	8	11	.421	0	23	23	12	181	186	22	42	0	4.55
Red Ruffing	R	41	7	3	.700	0	11	11	8	87	85	20	24	1	2.90
Joe Page	L	27	6	3	.667	0	20	9	4	102	95	46	50	0	2.82
Atley Donald (IJ-EJ)	R	34	5	4	.556	0	9	9	6	64	62	25	19	2	2.95
Bill Zuber	R	32	5	11	.313	1	21	14	7	127	121	56	50	0	3.19
Ken Holcombe	R	26	3	3	.500	0	23	2	0	55	43	27	20	0	1.80
Jim Turner	R	41	3	4	.429	10	30	0	0	54	45	31	22	0	3.67
Spud Chandler (MS)	R	37	2	1	.667	0	4	4	2	31	30	7	12	1	4.65
Steve Roser	R	27	0	0	—	0	7	0	0	27	27	8	11	0	3.67
Paul Schreiber	R	42	0	0	—	0	2	0	0	4	4	2	1	0	4.50
Johnny Murphy (WW) 36															

CLEVELAND — 5th 77-72 .503 11 — LOU BOUDREAU

NAME	G by Pos	B	AGE	G	AB	R	H	2B	3B	HR	RBI	BB	SO	SB	BA	SA
TOTALS			27	147	4898	557	1249	216	48	65	519	505	578	19	.255	.359
Mickey Rocco	1B141	L	29	143	565	81	149	28	6	10	56	52	40	0	.264	.388
Dutch Meyer	2B130	R	29	130	524	71	153	29	8	7	48	40	32	2	.292	.418
Lou Boudreau (BN)	SS97	R	27	97	345	50	106	24	1	3	48	35	20	0	.307	.409
2 Don Ross	3B106	R	30	106	363	26	95	15	1	2	43	42	15	0	.262	.325
Pat Seerey	OF117	R	22	126	414	56	98	22	2	14	56	66	97	1	.237	.401
Felix Mackiewicz	OF112	R	27	120	359	42	98	14	7	3	37	44	41	5	.273	.368
Jeff Heath (KJ)	OF101	R	30	102	370	60	113	16	7	15	61	56	39	3	.305	.508
2 Frankie Hayes	C119	R	30	119	385	39	91	15	6	6	43	53	52	1	.236	.353
Al Cihocki	SS41, 3B29, 2B23	R	21	92	283	21	60	9	3	0	24	11	48	2	.212	.265
Paul O'Dea	OF53, P1	L	24	87	221	21	52	2	2	1	21	20	26	3	.235	.276
Ed Wheeler	3B14, SS11, 2B3	R	30	46	72	12	14	2	0	0	2	8	13	1	.194	.222
Les Fleming	OF33, 1B5	L	29	42	140	18	46	10	2	3	22	11	5	0	.329	.493
Myril Hoag	OF33, P2	R	37	40	128	10	27	5	3	0	3	11	18	1	.211	.297
Eddie Carnett (MS)	OF16, P2	L	28	30	73	5	16	7	0	0	7	2	9	2	.219	.315
Jim McDonnell	C23	R	22	28	51	3	10	2	0	0	8	2	4	1	.196	.235
Elmer Weingartner	SS20	R	26	20	39	5	9	1	0	0	1	4	11	0	.231	.256
Pop Williams	1B3	R	31	16	19	0	4	0	0	0	0	0	1	2	.211	.211
Hank Ruszkowski (MS)	C14	R	19	14	49	2	10	0	0	0	5	4	9	0	.204	.204
Stan Benjamin	OF4	R	31	14	21	1	7	2	0	0	3	0	0	0	.333	.429
1 Red Steiner	C4	L	30	12	20	0	3	0	0	0	2	1	4	0	.150	.150
Gene Desautels (MS)	C10	R	38	10	9	1	1	0	0	0	0	0	2	0	.111	.111
1 Roy Cullenbine	OF4, 3B3	B	31	8	13	3	1	1	0	0	11*	0	0	0	.077	.154
Bob Rothel	3B4	R	21	4	10	0	2	0	0	0	0	2	0	0	.200	.200

NAME	T	AGE	W	L	PCT	SV	G	GS	CG	IP	H	BB	SO	SHO	ERA
		29	73	72	.503	12	147	147	76	1302	1269	501	497	14	3.31
Steve Gromek	R	25	19	9	.679	1	33	30	21	251	229	66	101	3	2.55
Allie Reynolds	R	30	18	12	.600	4	44	30	16	247	227	130	112	2	3.21
Jim Bagby	R	28	8	11	.421	1	25	19	11	159	171	59	38	3	3.74
Pete Center	R	23	6	3	.667	1	31	8	2	86	89	28	34	0	3.98
Bob Feller (MS)	R	26	5	3	.625	0	9	9	7	72	50	35	59	1	2.50
Eddie Klieman	R	27	5	4	.385	4	38	12	4	126	123	49	33	1	3.86
Al Smith	L	37	5	12	.294	1	21	19	8	134	141	48	34	3	3.83
Red Embree (MS)	R	27	4	4	.500	0	7	7	5	70	56	26	42	1	1.93
Mel Harder	R	35	3	7	.300	0	11	11	2	76	93	23	16	0	3.67
Earl Henry	R	28	0	3	.000	0	15	1	0	22	20	20	10	0	5.32
Jack Salveson	R	31	0	0	—	0	19	0	0	44	52	6	11	0	3.86
Hal Klein	R	22	0	0	—	0	3	0	0	7	8	7	5	0	3.86
Eddie Carnett (MS)	R	28	0	0	—	0	2	0	0	8	3	6	1	0	0.00
Myril Hoag	R	37	0	0	—	0	3	0	0	3	1	0	0	0	0.00
Paul Calvert	R	27	0	0	—	0	1	0	0	2	4	1	1	0	18.00
Paul O'Dea	L	24	0	0	—	0	1	0	0	2	4	2	0	0	13.50
Ray Poat (VR) 27															

*Cullenbine, also with Detroit, league leader in BB with 112

CHICAGO — 6th 71-78 .477 15 — JIMMY DYKES

NAME	G by Pos	B	AGE	G	AB	R	H	2B	3B	HR	RBI	BB	SO	SB	BA	SA
TOTALS			32	150	5077	596	1330	204	55	22	545	470	467	78	.262	.337
Kerby Farrell	1B97	L	31	103	396	44	102	11	3	0	34	24	18	4	.258	.301
Roy Schalk	2B133	R	36	133	513	50	127	23	1	1	65	32	41	3	.248	.301
Cass Michaels	SS126, 2B1	R	19	129	445	47	109	8	5	2	54	37	28	8	.245	.299
Tony Cuccinello	3B112	R	37	118	402	50	124	25	3	2	49	45	19	6	.308	.400
Wally Moses	OF139	L	34	140	569	79	168	35	15	2	50	69	33	11	.295	.420
Oris Hockett	OF106	R	35	106	417	46	122	23	4	2	55	27	30	0	.293	.381
Johnny Dickshot	OF124	R	35	130	486	74	147	19	10	4	58	48	41	18	.302	.407
Mike Tresh	C150	R	31	150	458	50	114	12	0	0	47	65	37	6	.249	.275
Guy Curtright	OF84	R	32	98	324	51	91	15	7	4	32	39	29	3	.281	.407
Floyd Baker	3B58, 2B11	R	28	82	208	22	52	8	0	0	19	23	12	3	.250	.288
Bill Nagel	1B57, 3B1	R	29	67	220	21	46	10	3	3	27	15	41	3	.209	.323
Ed Lopat	P26	R	27	32	82	13	24	4	0	1	13	2	9	0	.293	.378
Danny Reynolds	SS14, 2B11	R	25	29	72	6	12	2	1	0	4	3	8	1	.167	.222
Vince Castino	C25	R	27	26	36	2	8	1	0	0	4	3	7	0	.222	.250
Luke Appling (MS)	SS17	R	38	18	57	12	21	2	2	1	10	12	7	1	.368	.526
Joe Orengo (MS)	3B7, 2B1	R	30	17	15	5	1	0	0	0	1	3	2	0	.067	.067
Bill Mueller (MS)	OF7	R	24	9	9	3	0	0	0	0	0	2	1	1	.000	.000
Hal Trosky (IL) 32																	

NAME	T	AGE	W	L	PCT	SV	G	GS	CG	IP	H	BB	SO	SHO	ERA
		32	71	78	.477	13	150	150	84	1331	1400	448	486	13	3.69
Thornton Lee	L	38	15	12	.556	0	29	28	19	228	208	76	108	1	2.45
Orval Grove	R	25	14	12	.538	1	33	30	16	217	233	68	54	4	3.44
Ed Lopat	R	27	10	13	.435	1	26	24	17	199	226	56	74	1	4.12
Bill Dietrich (EJ)	R	35	7	10	.412	0	18	16	6	122	136	36	43	3	4.20
Earl Caldwell	R	40	6	7	.462	4	27	11	5	105	108	37	45	1	3.60
John Humphries	R	30	6	14	.300	1	22	21	10	153	172	48	33	1	4.24
Joe Haynes (BL)	R	27	5	5	.500	1	14	13	8	104	92	29	34	1	3.55
Frank Papish	L	27	4	4	.500	1	19	5	3	84	75	40	45	0	3.75
Johnny Johnson	R	30	3	0	1.000	0	29	0	0	70	85	35	38	0	4.24
Buck Ross	R	30	1	1	.500	0	13	2	0	37	51	17	8	0	5.84
Clay Touchstone	R	42	0	0	—	0	6	0	0	10	14	6	4	0	5.40

BOSTON — 7th 71-83 .461 17.5 — JOE CRONIN

NAME	G by Pos	B	AGE	G	AB	R	H	2B	3B	HR	RBI	BB	SO	SB	BA	SA
TOTALS			30	157	5367	599	1393	225	44	50	561	541	534	72	.260	.346
Catfish Metkovich	1B97, OF42	L	23	138	539	65	140	26	3	5	62	51	70	19	.260	.347
Skeeter Newsome	2B82, SS33, 3B11	R	34	125	438	45	127	30	1	1	48	20	15	6	.290	.370
Eddie Lake	SS130, 2B1	R	29	133	473	81	132	27	1	11	51	106	37	9	.279	.410
Jack Tobin	3B72, 2B5, OF1	R	24	84	273	26	70	6	2	0	21	26	24	2	.252	.304
Johnny Lazor	OF81	L	32	101	335	35	104	19	2	5	45	18	17	3	.310	.424
Leon Culberson	OF91	R	25	97	331	26	91	21	6	6	45	20	37	4	.275	.429
Bob Johnson	OF140	R	39	143	529	71	148	27	7	12	74	63	56	5	.280	.425
Bob Garbark	C67	R	35	68	199	21	52	6	0	0	17	18	10	0	.261	.291
Tom McBride	OF81, 1B11	R	30	100	374	38	105	11	7	1	47	26	17	2	.305	.387
Ben Steiner	2B77	R	23	78	304	39	78	8	3	3	20	31	29	9	.257	.332
Pete Fox	OF57	R	35	66	208	21	51	4	1	0	20	11	18	2	.245	.275
Dolph Camilli (MS)	1B54	L	38	63	198	24	42	5	2	2	19	35	38	2	.212	.288
Boo Ferriss	P35	R	23	60	120	16	32	7	1	1	19	14	11	0	.267	.367
Billy Holm	C57	R	32	58	135	12	25	6	1	1	9	23	17	1	.185	.215
Ty LaForest	3B45, OF5	R	28	52	204	25	51	7	4	2	16	10	35	4	.250	.353
Jim Bucher	3B32, 2B2	L	34	52	151	19	34	4	3	0	11	7	13	1	.225	.291
Fred Walters	C38	R	32	40	93	2	16	2	0	0	5	10	9	1	.172	.194
2 Red Steiner	C24	L	30	26	59	6	12	1	0	0	4	14	2	0	.203	.220
Frankie Pytlak (MS)	C6	R	36	9	17	1	2	0	0	0	1	3	0	0	.118	.118
1 Lloyd Christopher	OF3	R	25	14	4	4	0	0	0	0	1	0	1	0	.286	.286
Nick Polly	3B2	R	28	4	7	0	1	0	0	0	0	1	1	0	.143	.143
Joe Cronin (BL)	3B3	R	38	3	8	1	3	0	0	0	1	3	2	0	.375	.375
1 Lou Finney (VR)		L	34	2	2	0	0	0	0	0	0	0	1	0	.000	.000

NAME	T	AGE	W	L	PCT	SV	G	GS	CG	IP	H	BB	SO	SHO	ERA
		28	71	83	.461	13	157	157	71	1391	1389	656	490	15	3.80
Boo Ferriss	R	23	21	10	.677	2	35	31	26	265	263	85	94	5	2.95
Emmett O'Neill	R	27	8	11	.421	0	24	22	10	142	134	117	55	1	5.13
Mike Ryba	R	42	6	5	.538	2	34	9	4	123	122	33	44	1	2.49
Vic Johnson	L	24	6	4	.600	2	26	9	4	85	90	46	21	1	4.02
Jim Wilson (FS)	R	23	6	8	.429	0	23	21	8	144	121	88	50	2	3.31
Clem Hausmann	R	25	5	7	.417	2	31	13	4	125	131	60	30	2	5.04
Frank Barrett	R	32	4	3	.571	3	37	0	0	86	77	29	35	0	2.62
Otie Clark	R	30	4	4	.500	0	12	9	4	82	86	19	20	1	3.07
Pinky Woods (JJ)	R	30	4	7	.364	2	24	12	3	107	102	63	36	0	4.21
Randy Heflin	R	26	4	10	.286	0	20	14	6	102	102	61	39	2	4.06
Rex Cecil	R	28	2	5	.286	0	7	1	0	45	46	27	30	0	5.20
Clem Dreisewerd (MS)	L	29	0	1	.000	2	2	0	0	10	13	2	3	0	4.50
1 Oscar Judd	R	37	0	0	—	0	2	0	0	12	18	9	9	0	9.00
1 Joe Bowman	R	35	0	2	.000	0	5	0	0	12	18	9	9	0	9.00
Yank Terry	R	34	0	0	—	0	4	0	0	57	64	14	28	0	4.11

PHILADELPHIA — 8th 52-98 .347 34.5 — CONNIE MACK

NAME	G by Pos	B	AGE	G	AB	R	H	2B	3B	HR	RBI	BB	SO	SB	BA	SA
TOTALS			29	153	5296	494	1297	201	37	33	440	449	463	25	.245	.316
Dick Siebert	1B147	L	33	147	573	62	153	29	1	7	51	50	33	2	.267	.358
Irv Hall	2B151	R	26	151	616	62	161	17	5	0	50	35	42	3	.261	.305
Ed Busch	SS116, 3B5, 2B2, 1B1	R	27	126	416	37	104	10	3	0	35	32	9	2	.250	.288
George Kell	3B147	R	22	147	567	50	154	30	3	4	56	27	15	2	.272	.356
Hal Peck	OF110	R	28	112	449	51	124	22	9	5	39	37	28	5	.276	.399
Bobby Estalella	OF124	R	34	126	451	45	135	25	6	8	52	74	46	1	.299	.435
Mayo Smith	OF65	R	30	73	203	18	43	5	0	0	11	36	13	0	.212	.236
Buddy Rosar (VR)	C85	R	30	92	300	23	63	12	1	1	25	20	16	2	.210	.267
Bill McGhee	OF48, 1B8	L	39	87	250	24	63	6	1	0	19	24	16	3	.252	.284
Charlie Metro	OF57	R	26	65	200	18	42	10	1	3	15	23	33	1	.210	.315
Bobby Wilkins	SS40, OF4	R	22	62	154	22	40	6	0	0	4	10	17	2	.260	.299
Greek George (SU)	C46	R	32	51	138	8	24	4	1	0	11	17	29	0	.174	.217
Ernie Kish	OF30	R	27	43	110	10	27	5	1	0	10	9	9	0	.245	.309
1 Frankie Hayes	C32	R	30	12	110	12	25	7	2	1	14	18	14	1	.227	.345
Joe Burns	OF19, 3B5, 1B1	R	30	31	90	7	23	1	0	0	8	4	17	0	.256	.289
Larry Rosenthal	OF21	L	35	28	75	9	15	3	0	1	6	18	13	2	.200	.293
Joe Cicero	OF7	R	34	12	19	3	3	1	0	0	1	0	3	0	.158	.158
Joe Astroth	C8	R	22	6	17	1	1	0	0	0	0	4	3	0	.059	.059
Al Brancato (MS)	SS10	R	26	10	34	4	4	0	0	0	2	3	5	0	.118	.147
Sam Chapman (MS)	OF8	R	29	8	25	2	6	1	0	0	3	4	3	1	.240	.280
Ford Garrison (MS)	OF5	R	29	6	23	3	7	1	0	0	6	4	1	3	.304	.478
Jim Pruett	C4	R	26	5	9	1	2	0	0	0	2	2	2	0	.222	.222
Larry York	OF1	L	24	1	2	0	0	0	0	0	0	0	0	0	.000	.000

NAME	T	AGE	W	L	PCT	SV	G	GS	CG	IP	H	BB	SO	SHO	ERA
		30	52	98	.347	8	153	153	65	1381	1380	571	531	11	3.62
Russ Christopher	R	27	13	13	.500	2	33	27	17	227	213	75	100	2	3.17
Joe Berry	R	40	8	7	.533	5	52	0	0	130	114	38	51	0	2.35
Bobo Newsom	R	37	8	20	.286	0	36	34	16	257	255	103	127	3	4.29
Jesse Flores	R	30	7	10	.412	1	29	24	9	191	180	63	52	4	3.44
Lou Knerr	R	23	5	11	.313	0	27	17	5	130	142	74	41	0	4.22
Don Black (ST)	R	26	5	4	.556	0	18	8	1	125	154	69	47	0	5.18
Charlie Gassaway	L	26	4	7	.364	0	24	11	4	118	114	55	50	0	3.74
Bill Connelly	R	20	1	1	.500	0	7	3	2	36	40	30	16	0	4.50
Dick Fowler (MS)	R	24	1	2	.333	0	7	3	1	37	41	18	21	1	4.86
Phil Marchildon (MS)	R	31	0	1	.000	0	1	1	0	9	7	7	2	0	5.00
Charlie Bowles (MS)	R	29	0	8	.000	0	8	4	1	33	35	23	11	0	5.18
Steve Gerkin	R	32	0	12	.000	0	21	12	3	102	112	27	25	0	3.62
Carl Scheib (MS)	R	18	0	0	—	0	4	0	0	3	3	1	3	0	3.00
Woody Crowson	R	26	0	0	—	0	1	0	0	6	6	1	1	0	6.00

CHICAGO 1ST 96-56 .636   CHARLIE GRIMM

NAME	G by Pos	B	AGE	G	AB	R	H	2B	3B	HR	RBI	BB	SO	SB	BA	SA
TOTALS			29	155	5298	735	1465	229	52	57	674	554	462	69	.277	.372
Phil Cavarretta	1B120, OF11	L	28	132	498	94	177	34	10	6	97	81	34	5	.355	.500
Don Johnson	2B138	R	33	138	557	94	168	23	4	2	58	32	34	9	.302	.361
Lennie Merullo	SS118	R	28	121	394	40	94	18	0	2	37	31	30	7	.239	.299
Stan Hack	3B146,1B5	L	35	150	597	110	193	29	7	2	43	99	30	12	.323	.405
Bill Nicholson	OF151	L	30	151	559	82	136	28	4	13	88	92	73	4	.243	.377
Andy Pafko	OF140	R	24	144	534	64	159	24	12	12	110	45	36	5	.298	.455
Peanuts Lowrey	OF138, SS2	R	27	143	523	72	148	22	4	7	89	48	27	11	.283	.392
Mickey Livingston	C68, 1B1	R	30	71	224	19	57	4	2	2	23	19	6	2	.254	.317
Paul Gillespie	C45, OF1	L	24	75	163	12	47	6	0	3	25	18	9	2	.288	.380
Roy Hughes (KJ)	SS36, 2B21, 3B9, 1B2	R	34	69	222	34	58	8	1	0	8	16	18	6	.261	.306
Heinz Becker	1B28	R	29	67	133	25	38	8	2	2	27	17	16	0	.286	.421
Dewey Williams	C54	R	29	59	100	16	28	2	2	2	5	13	13	0	.280	.400
Ed Sauer	OF26	R	26	49	93	8	24	4	1	2	11	8	23	2	.258	.387
Bill Schuster	SS22, 2B3, 3B1	R	32	45	47	.8	9	2	1	0	2	7	4	2	.191	.277
Frank Secory	OF12	R	32	35	57	4	9	1	0	0	6	2	7	0	.158	.175
Len Rice (CN)	C29	R	26	32	99	10	23	3	0	0	5	5	8	2	.232	.263
Reggie Otero	1B8	L	29	14	23	1	9	0	0	0	5	2	2	0	.391	.391
John Ostrowski	3B4	R	27	7	10	4	3	2	0	0	1	0	0	0	.300	.500
Johnny Moore		R	43	7	6	0	1	0	0	0	2	1	1	0	.167	.167

Cy Block (MS) 26 R 1-7, 2 Lloyd Christopher 25 R 0-0

NAME	T	AGE	W	L	PCT	SV	G	GS	CG	IP	H	BB	SO	SHO	ERA
		32	98	56	.636	14	155	155	86	1366	1301	385	541	15	2.98
Hank Wyse	R	27	22	10	.688	0	38	34	23	278	272	55	77	2	2.69
Claude Passeau	R	36	17	9	.654	0	34	27	19	227	205	59	98	5	2.46
Paul Derringer	R	38	16	11	.593	4	35	30	15	214	223	51	86	1	3.45
Ray Prim	R	38	13	8	.619	2	34	19	9	165	142	23	88	2	2.40
2 Hank Borowy	R	29	11	2	.846	1	15	14	11	122	105	47	47	1	2.14
Hy Vandenberg	R	39	7	3	.700	2	30	7	3	95	91	33	51	1	3.51
Paul Erickson	R	29	7	4	.636	2	28	9	3	108	94	48	53	0	3.33
Bob Chipman	L	26	4	5	.444	0	25	10	3	72	63	34	29	1	3.50
2 Ray Starr	R	39	1	0	1.000	0	9	1	0	13	17	7	5	0	7.62
Mack Stewart	R	30	0	1	.000	0	16	1	0	28	37	14	9	0	4.82
Lon Warneke	R	35	0	1	.000	0	9	1	0	14	16	1	6	0	3.86
Jorge Comellas	R	28	0	2	.000	0	7	1	0	12	11	6	6	0	4.50
Walter Signer	R	34	0	0	—	1	6	0	0	8	11	5	0	0	3.38
Ed Hanyzewski	R	24	0	0	—	0	2	1	0	5	7	1	2	0	5.40
George Hennessey	R	34	0	0	—	0	2	0	0	4	7	1	2	0	6.75

ST. LOUIS 2nd 95-59 .617 3   BILLY SOUTHWORTH

NAME	G by Pos	B	AGE	G	AB	R	H	2B	3B	HR	RBI	BB	SO	SB	BA	SA
TOTALS			27	155	5487	756	1498	256	44	64	698	515	488	55	.273	.371
Ray Sanders	1B142	L	28	143	537	85	148	29	3	8	78	83	55	3	.276	.385
Emil Verban	2B155	R	28	155	597	59	166	22	8	0	72	19	15	4	.278	.342
Marty Marion	SS122	R	27	123	430	63	119	27	5	1	59	39	39	2	.277	.370
Whitey Kurowski	3B131, SS6	R	27	133	511	84	165	27	4	21	102	45	45	1	.323	.511
Johnny Hopp	OF104, 1B15	L	28	124	446	67	129	22	8	3	44	49	24	14	.289	.395
2 Buster Adams	OF140	R	30	140	578	98	169	26	0	20	101	57	75	3	.292	.441
Red Schoendienst	OF118, SS10, 2B1	B	22	137	565	89	157	22	6	1	47	21	11	26	.278	.343
Ken O'Dea	C91	L	32	100	307	36	78	18	2	4	43	50	31	0	.254	.365
Augie Bergamo	OF77, 1B2	L	27	94	304	51	96	17	2	3	44	43	21	0	.316	.414
Del Rice	C77	R	22	83	253	27	66	17	3	1	24	12	15	1	.261	.364
Debs Garms	3B32, OF10	L	38	74	146	23	49	7	2	0	18	31	3	0	.336	.411
Pep Young	SS11, 3B9, 2B3	R	37	27	47	5	7	1	0	1	4	1	8	0	.149	.234
Art Rebel	OF18	L	31	26	72	12	25	4	0	0	5	6	4	1	.347	.403
Dave Bartosch	OF11	R	28	24	47	9	12	1	0	0	1	6	3	0	.255	.277
George Fallon (MS)	SS20, 2B4	R	30	24	55	4	13	2	1	0	7	6	6	1	.236	.309
Lou Klein (MS)	SS7, OF7, 3B4, 2B2	R	26	19	57	12	13	4	1	1	6	14	9	0	.228	.386
1 Jim Mallory	OF11	R	26	13	43	3	10	1	0	0	5	0	2	0	.233	.279
Gene Crumling	C6	R	23	6	12	0	1	0	0	0	1	0	4	0	.083	.083
Walker Cooper (MS)	C4	R	30	4	18	3	7	1	0	0	3	0	0	0	.389	.389

1 Glenn Crawford 31 L 0-3, 1 John Antonelli 29 R 0-3, Bob Keely 35 R 0-1

NAME	T	AGE	W	L	PCT	SV	G	GS	CG	IP	H	BB	SO	SHO	ERA
		28	95	59	.619	9	155	155	77	1409	1351	497	510	18	3.24
2 Red Barrett	R	30	21*	9	.700	0	36	29	22*	247*	244*	38	63	3	2.73
Ken Burkhart	R	28	18	8	.692	2	42	22	12	217	206	66	67	4	2.90
Harry Brecheen	L	30	15	4	.789	2	24	18	13	157	136	44	63	3	2.52
George Dockins	L	28	8	6	.571	0	31	12	9	126	132	38	33	2	3.21
Blix Donnelly	R	31	8	10	.444	2	31	23	5	166	157	87	76	4	3.52
Jack Creel	R	29	5	4	.556	2	26	8	2	87	78	45	34	0	4.14
Bud Byerly	R	24	5	4	.556	0	33	8	2	95	111	41	39	0	4.74
Ted Wilks (SA)	R	29	4	7	.364	0	18	16	4	98	103	29	28	1	2.94
Glenn Gardner	R	29	3	1	.750	1	17	4	2	55	50	27	20	1	3.27
Al Jurisich	R	23	3	3	.500	0	27	6	1	72	61	41	42	0	5.13
2 Mort Cooper (EJ)	R	32	2	0	1.000	0	4	3	1	24	20	7	14	0	1.50
Max Lanier (MS)	L	29	2	2	.500	0	4	3	1	26	22	8	16	0	1.73
Bill Crouch	R	34	1	0	1.000	0	6	0	0	13	12	7	4	0	3.46
Art Lopatka	R	26	1	0	1.000	0	4	2	0	13	12	11	6	0	1.50
Stan Partenheimer	R	22	0	0	—	0	4	2	0	13	12	16	6	0	6.23

*Barrett, also with Boston, league leader in W (23), CG (24), IP (285), H (287)

BROOKLYN 3rd 87-67 .565 11   LEO DUROCHER

NAME	G by Pos	B	AGE	G	AB	R	H	2B	3B	HR	RBI	BB	SO	SB	BA	SA
TOTALS			28	155	5418	795	1468	257	71	57	720	629	434	75	.271	.376
Augie Galan	1B66, OF49, 3B40	B	33	152	576	114	177	36	7	9	92	114	27	13	.307	.441
Eddie Stanky	2B153, SS1	R	28	153	555	128	143	29	5	1	39	148	42	6	.258	.333
Eddie Basinski	SS101, 2B6	R	22	108	336	30	88	9	4	0	33	11	33	0	.262	.313
Frenchy Bordagaray	3B57, OF22	R	35	113	273	32	70	9	6	2	49	29	15	7	.256	.355
Dixie Walker	OF153	L	34	154	607	102	182	42	9	8	124	75	16	6	.300	.438
Goody Rosen	OF141	L	32	145	606	126	197	24	11	12	75	50	36	4	.325	.460
Luis Olmo	OF106, 3B31, 2B1	R	25	141	556	62	174	27	13	10	110	36	33	15	.313	.462
Mike Sandlock	C47, SS22, 2B4, 3B2	B	29	80	195	21	55	14	2	2	17	18	19	2	.282	.405
Bill Hart	3B39, SS8	R	32	58	161	27	37	6	2	3	27	14	21	7	.230	.348
Tommy Brown	2B55, OF1	R	17	57	196	13	48	3	4	2	19	6	16	3	.245	.332
Ed Stevens	1B55	L	20	55	201	29	55	14	3	4	29	32	20	0	.274	.433
2 Johny Peacock	C38	R	35	48	110	11	28	5	1	0	14	24	10	2	.255	.318
Fats Dantonio	C45	R	26	47	128	12	32	6	1	0	12	11	6	3	.250	.313
Howie Schultz	1B38	R	22	39	142	18	34	8	2	1	19	10	14	2	.239	.345
1 Morrie Aderholt	OF8	L	29	39	60	4	13	1	0	0	6	3	10	0	.217	.233
Babe Herman	OF3	L	42	37	34	6	9	1	0	1	9	5	7	0	.265	.382
Mickey Owen (MS)	C24	R	29	24	84	5	24	9	0	0	11	10	2	0	.286	.393
1 Stan Andrews	C21	R	28	21	49	5	8	0	1	0	2	4	1	0	.163	.204
Clyde Sukeforth	C13	L	43	18	51	2	15	1	0	0	1	4	1	0	.294	.314
Red Durrett	OF4	L	24	8	16	2	2	0	0	0	0	0	3	0	.125	.125
John Douglas	1B4	L	27	9	10	0	0	0	0	0	0	2	4	0	.000	.000

Don Lund 22 R 0-3, Barney White 22 R 0-1, Claude Corbitt 29 R 2-4, Leo Durocher 39 R 1-5, Ray Hayworth 26 R 0-2, Erv Palica 17 R 0-0, Arky Vaughan (VR) 33

NAME	T	AGE	W	L	PCT	SV	G	GS	CG	IP	H	BB	SO	SHO	ERA
		28	87	67	.565	12	155	155	61	1392	1357	586	557	7	3.70
Hal Gregg	R	23	18	13	.581	2	42	34	13	254	221	120	139	2	3.47
Tom Seats	L	34	10	7	.588	0	31	18	6	122	127	37	44	2	4.35
Curt Davis	R	41	10	10	.500	0	24	18	10	150	171	21	39	0	3.24
Vic Lombardi	L	22	10	11	.476	4	38	24	9	204	195	86	64	0	3.31
Cy Buker	R	26	7	2	.778	5	42	4	0	87	90	45	48	0	3.31
Les Webber	R	30	7	3	.700	0	17	7	5	75	69	25	30	0	3.60
Art Herring	R	39	7	4	.636	2	22	15	7	124	103	43	34	2	3.48
Clyde King	R	21	5	5	.500	3	42	2	0	112	131	48	29	0	4.10
Ralph Branca	R	19	5	6	.455	1	16	15	7	110	73	79	69	0	3.03
Lee Pfund	R	25	3	2	.600	0	15	10	2	62	69	35	27	0	5.23
1 Ben Chapman	R	36	3	3	.500	0	10	7	2	54	64	32	23	0	5.50
Nick Nicholas	R	36	1	0	1.000	0	3	3	1	19	19	1	4	0	5.21
Ernie Rudolph	R	36	1	0	1.000	1	9	0	0	12	7	3	5	0	5.00
Ray Hathaway	R	28	0	1	.000	0	4	1	0	9	11	6	3	0	4.00
Claude Crocker	R	20	0	1	—	1	1	0	0	2	1	1	0	0	0.00

PITTSBURGH 4th 82-72 .532 16   FRANKIE FRISCH

NAME	G by Pos	B	AGE	G	AB	R	H	2B	3B	HR	RBI	BB	SO	SB	BA	SA
TOTALS			28	155	5343	734	1425	259	56	72	695	590	480	81	.267	.377
Babe Dahlgren	1B144	R	33	144	531	57	133	24	8	5	75	51	51	1	.250	.354
Pete Coscarart	2B122, SS1	R	32	123	392	59	95	17	2	8	38	55	55	2	.242	.357
Frankie Gustine	SS104, 2B29, C1	R	25	128	478	67	134	27	5	2	66	37	33	8	.280	.370
Bob Elliott	3B131, OF61	R	28	144	541	80	157	36	6	8	108	64	38	5	.290	.423
Johnny Barrett	OF132	L	29	142	507	97	130	29	4	15	67	79	68	25	.256	.418
Al Gionfriddo	OF106	L	23	122	409	74	116	18	9	2	42	60	22	12	.284	.386
Jim Russell	OF140	B	26	146	510	88	145	24	8	12	77	71	40	15	.284	.433
Al Lopez	C91	R	36	91	243	22	53	8	0	0	18	35	12	1	.218	.251
Lee Handley	3B79	R	31	98	312	39	93	16	2	1	32	20	16	7	.298	.372
Bill Salkeld	C86	R	28	95	267	43	83	16	1	15	52	50	16	2	.311	.547
Frank Colman	1B22, OF12	L	27	77	153	18	32	11	1	4	30	9	16	0	.209	.373
Vic Barnhart	SS60, 3B4	R	22	71	201	21	54	7	0	0	19	9	11	2	.269	.303
Tommy O'Brien (IL)	O45	R	26	58	161	23	54	6	5	0	19	19	13	3	.335	.435
Jack Saltzgaver	2B31, 3B1	L	40	52	117	20	38	5	3	0	10	8	8	0	.325	.419
Rip Sewell	P33	R	38	35	64	10	20	3	0	0	6	6	7	11	.313	.359
Spud Davis	C13	R	40	23	42	3	8	2	0	0	6	2	2	0	.242	.303
Lloyd Waner	OF3	L	39	23	19	5	5	0	0	0	3	4	1	0	.263	.263
Frankie Zak	SS10, 2B1	R	23	15	28	2	4	0	0	0	3	3	5	0	.143	.214

Hank Camelli 30 R 0-2, Bill Rodgers (MS) 22 L 1-1, Joe Vitelli 37 R 0-0

NAME	T	AGE	W	L	PCT	SV	G	GS	CG	IP	H	BB	SO	SHO	ERA
		31	82	72	.532	16	155	155	61	1387	1477	455	518	8	3.76
Nick Strincevich	R	30	16	10	.615	2	36	29	18	228	235	49	74	1	3.32
Preacher Roe	L	30	14	13	.519	1	33	31	15	235	228	46	148	3	2.87
Ken Gables	R	26	11	7	.611	1	29	16	6	139	139	46	49	0	4.14
Rip Sewell	R	38	11	9	.550	1	33	24	9	188	212	91	60	1	4.07
Max Butcher	R	34	10	8	.556	0	28	20	12	169	184	46	37	3	3.04
2 Boom-Boom Beck	R	40	6	1	.857	0	14	5	4	63	54	14	20	0	2.14
F. Ostermueller (MS)	L	37	5	4	.556	0	14	11	4	81	74	37	29	1	4.56
Al Gerheauser	R	28	5	10	.333	1	32	11	4	140	170	54	55	0	3.92
Xavier Rescigno	R	32	3	5	.375	9	44	1	0	79	95	34	29	0	5.70
Cookie Cuccurullo	L	27	3	1	.250	1	29	4	0	57	68	34	17	0	5.21
1 Ray Starr	R	39	0	0	—	0	7	0	0	10	4	0	0	0	9.00
Johnny Lanning (MS)	R	38	0	0	—	0	1	0	0	1	8	0	0	0	36.00

NEW YORK 5th 78-74 .513 19   MEL OTT

NAME	G by Pos	B	AGE	G	AB	R	H	2B	3B	HR	RBI	BB	SO	SB	BA	SA
TOTALS			30	154	5350	668	1439	175	35	114	626	501	457	38	.269	.379
Phil Weintraub	1B77	L	37	82	263	45	77	9	1	10	42	54	29	2	.272	.417
George Hausmann	2B154	R	29	154	623	98	174	15	8	2	45	73	46	7	.279	.339
Buddy Kerr	SS148	R	22	149	546	53	136	20	3	4	40	41	34	5	.249	.319
Nap Reyes	3B115, 1B5	R	25	122	431	39	124	15	3	4	44	25	26	1	.288	.376
Mel Ott	OF118	L	36	135	451	73	139	23	5	21	79	71	41	1	.308	.499
Johnny Rucker	OF98	R	28	105	429	58	117	19	11	7	51	20	36	7	.273	.417
Danny Gardella	OF94, 1B15	L	25	121	430	54	117	10	1	18	71	46	55	2	.272	.426
Ernie Lombardi	C96	R	37	115	386	46	113	7	1	19	70	43	11	0	.307	.446
Red Treadway	OF60	L	25	88	224	31	54	4	3	2	23	20	13	3	.241	.330
2 Clyde Kluttz	C57	R	27	73	222	25	62	14	0	4	21	15	10	1	.279	.396
Billy Jurges	3B44, SS8	R	37	61	176	22	57	3	1	3	24	24	11	2	.324	.403
2 Jim Mallory	OF21	R	26	37	94	10	28	1	0	0	9	5	8	1	.298	.309
Steve Filipowicz	OF31	R	24	35	112	14	23	5	0	4	15	8	25	0	.205	.304
Whitey Lockman (MS)	OF32	L	18	32	129	16	44	9	0	3	18	10	11	3	.341	.481
Mike Schemer	1B27	L	27	32	86	10	28	6	0	0	2	4	4	0	.333	.407
Johnny Hudson	3B5, 2B2	R	33	28	11	0	0	0	0	0	0	0	1	0	.000	.000
Roy Zimmerman	1B25, OF1	R	28	26	58	4	14	0	0	1	8	6	8	1	.276	.439
1 Joe Medwick	OF23	R	33	26	92	14	28	6	3	1	11	2	2	0	.304	.446
Ray Berres	C20	R	37	23	62	4	11	3	0	0	5	6	1	0	.167	.161
Al Gardella	1B9, OF1	L	27	16	26	2	4	0	0	0	3	4	3	0	.077	.077
Charlie Mead	OF1	L	24	10	37	4	10	1	0	0	4	4	6	0	.270	.378
Bill DeKoning	C2	R	26	4	0	0	0	0	0	0	0	0	0	0	.000	.000

NAME	T	AGE	W	L	PCT	SV	G	GS	CG	IP	H	BB	SO	SHO	ERA
		27	78	74	.513	21	154	154	53	1375	1401	529	530	13	4.06
Van Lingle Mungo	R	34	14	7	.667	0	26	24	7	183	161	71	101	2	3.20
Bill Voiselle	R	26	14	14	.500	0	41	35	14	232	249	97	115	4	4.50
Harry Feldman	R	25	12	13	.480	1	35	30	10	218	213	69	74	3	3.26
Ace Adams	R	35	11	9	.550	15	65	0	0	113	109	44	39	0	3.42
Jack Brewer	R	27	8	6	.571	0	28	21	8	160	162	58	49	0	3.83
Sal Maglie	R	28	5	4	.556	1	13	7	3	84	72	22	32	3	2.36
Andy Hansen (MS)	R	20	4	3	.571	3	23	13	4	93	98	28	37	0	4.65
Slim Emmerich	R	24	4	4	.500	0	7	1	1	39	47	18	20	0	4.86
Rube Fischer	L	28	3	8	.273	0	40	16	4	77	90	49	27	0	5.61
Adrian Zabala	L	28	2	4	.333	0	11	5	1	43	46	20	14	0	4.81
Don Fisher	R	29	1	0	1.000	0	2	1	1	18	12	7	8	1	2.00
Roy Lee	R	27	0	0	—	0	3	0	0	6	9	1	0	0	11.57
Ray Harrell	R	33	0	0	—	0	2	0	0	25	34	14	7	0	5.04
1 Ewald Pyle	L	34	0	0	—	0	1	0	0	6	9	2	1	0	18.00
Loren Bain	R	22	0	0	—	0	1	0	0	7	7	8	1	0	7.88
Johnny Gee (VR)	L	30	0	0	—	0	1	0	0	2	1	0	0	0	9.00
John Phillips	R	26	0	0	—	0	2	0	0	4	6	5	0	0	11.25

Cliff Melton (ST) 33

BOSTON 6th 67-85 .441 30 — BOB COLEMAN 42-51 .452 — DEL BISSONETTE 25-34 .424

NAME	G by Pos	B	AGE	G	AB	R	H	2B	3B	HR	RBI	BB	SO	SB	BA	SA
TOTALS			29	154	5441	721	1453	229	25	101	668	520	510	82	.267	.374
Vince Shupe	1B77	L	23	78	283	22	76	8	0	0	15	17	16	3	.269	.297
Whitey Wietelmann (BG)	2B87,SS39,3B2,P1	B	26	123	428	53	116	15	4	3	33	39	27	4	.271	.348
Dick Culler	SS126,3B6	R	30	136	527	87	138	12	1	2	30	50	35	7	.262	.300
Chuck Workman	3B107,OF24	L	30	139	514	77	141	16	2	25	87	51	58	4	.274	.457
Tommy Holmes	OF154	L	28	154	636	125	224	47	6	28	117	70	9	15	.352	.577
Carden Gillenwater	OF140	R	28	144	517	74	149	20	2	7	72	73	70	8	.288	.375
Butch Nieman	OF57	L	27	97	247	43	61	15	0	14	56	43	33	1	.247	.478
Phil Masi	C95, 1B7	R	28	114	371	55	101	25	4	7	46	42	32	9	.272	.472
Bill Ramsey	OF43	R	24	78	137	16	40	8	0	1	12	4	22	1	.292	.372
Joe Mack	1B65	R	33	66	260	30	60	13	1	3	44	34	39	1	.231	.323
2 Joe Medwick	OF38, 1B15	R	33	66	218	17	62	13	0	0	26	12	12	3	.284	.344
Stew Hofferth	C45	R	32	50	170	13	40	2	0	3	15	14	11	1	.235	.282
Frank Drews (KJ)	2B48	R	29	49	147	13	30	4	1	0	19	16	18	0	.204	.245
Tom Nelson	3B20, 2B12	R	28	40	121	6	20	2	0	0	6	4	13	1	.165	.182
Eddie Joost (BT-BW)	2B19,3B16	R	29	35	141	16	35	7	1	0	9	13	7	0	.248	.312
2 Morrie Aderholt	OF24, 2B1	L	29	31	102	15	34	4	0	2	11	9	6	0	.333	.431
1 Clyde Kluttz	C19	R	27	25	81	9	24	4	1	0	10	2	6	0	.296	.370
Steve Shemo	2B12, 3B3, SS1	R	30	17	46	4	11	1	0	0	7	1	3	1	.239	.261
Mike Ulisney	C4	R	27	11	18	4	7	1	0	1	4	1	0	0	.389	.611
Stan Wentzel	OF4	R	28	4	19	3	4	1	0	0	1	0	3	1	.211	.316
Norm Wallen	3B4	R	28	4	15	1	2	0	1	0	1	1	1	0	.133	.267

NAME	T	AGE	W	L	PCT	SV	G	GS	CG	IP	H	BB	SO	SHO	ERA
		31	67	85	.441	13	154	154	57	1392	1474	557	404	7	4.03
1 Jim Tobin	R	32	9	14	.391	0	27	25	16	197	220	56	38	0	3.84
Ed Wright	R	26	8	3	.727	0	15	12	7	111	104	33	24	1	2.51
2 Mort Cooper (EJ)	R	32	7	4	.636	1	20	11	4	78	77	27	45	1	3.35
Johnny Hutchings	R	29	7	6	.538	3	57	12	3	185	173	75	99	2	3.75
Bob Logan	L	35	7	11	.389	1	34	25	5	187	213	53	53	1	3.18
Nate Andrews	R	31	7	12	.368	0	21	19	8	138	160	52	26	0	4.57
2 Bill Lee	R	35	6	3	.667	0	13	6	4	73	74	39	14	0	4.93
Don Hendrickson	R	29	4	8	.333	5	37	2	1	73	74	33	14	0	4.93
Tom Earley	R	28	2	1	.667	0	11	2	1	41	36	19	4	0	4.61
1 Red Barrett	R	30	2*	3	.400	2	9	5	2*	38*	43*	16	13	0	4.74
Ira Hutchinson	R	34	2	3	.400	1	11	0	0	29	33	8	4	0	4.97
Al Javery (CJ)	R	27	2	7	.222	0	17	14	2	77	92	51	18	1	6.31
Lefty Wallace	L	23	1	0	1.000	0	5	3	1	20	18	9	4	0	4.50
Charlie Cozart	R	25	1	0	1.000	0	3	0	0	6	10	15	4	0	10.13
Joe Heving	R	44	1	0	1.000	0	9	0	0	15	18	3	1	0	3.60
Elmer Singleton	R	27	1	4	.200	0	7	5	1	37	35	14	14	0	4.86
Hal Schacker	R	20	1	4	.200	0	6	0	0	15	14	9	6	0	5.40
2 Ewald Pyle	L	34	0	1	.000	0	4	2	0	16	18	18	10	0	7.07
Bob Whitcher	L	28	0	2	.000	0	6	3	0	16	12	12	6	0	2.81
Lou Fette	R	38	0	2	.000	0	5	1	0	11	16	7	4	0	5.73
Ben Cardoni	R	24	0	0	—	0	3	0	0	5	4	3	1	0	9.00

Whitey Wietelmann 26 R 0-0 *Barrett (see STL)

CINCINNATI 7th 61-93 .396 37 — BILL McKECHNIE

NAME	G by Pos	B	AGE	G	AB	R	H	2B	3B	HR	RBI	BB	SO	SB	BA	SA
TOTALS			29	154	5283	536	1317	221	26	56	498	392	532	71	.249	.333
Frank McCormick	OF151	R	34	152	580	68	160	33	0	10	81	56	22	6	.276	.384
Woody Williams	2B133	R	32	133	481	46	114	14	0	2	27	39	24	6	.237	.266
Eddie Miller (BK)	SS115	R	28	115	421	46	100	27	2	13	49	18	38	4	.238	.404
Steve Mesner	3B148, 2B3	R	27	150	540	52	137	19	1	1	52	52	18	4	.254	.298
Al Libke	OF108, P4, 1B2	L	27	130	449	41	127	23	5	4	53	34	62	6	.283	.383
Dain Clay	OF152	R	25	153	656	81	184	29	2	1	50	37	58	19	.280	.335
Eric Tipton	OF83	R	30	108	331	32	80	17	1	5	34	40	37	11	.242	.344
Al Lakeman	C74	R	26	76	258	22	66	9	4	8	31	17	45	0	.256	.415
Gee walker	OF67, 3B3	R	37	106	316	28	80	11	2	2	21	16	38	8	.253	.320
Dick Sipek	OF31	L	22	82	156	14	38	6	2	0	13	9	15	0	.244	.308
Kermit Wahl	2B32, SS31, 3B7	R	22	71	194	18	39	6	3	0	23	22	22	2	.201	.263
Al Unser	C61	R	32	67	204	23	54	10	3	3	21	14	24	0	.265	.387
Hank Sauer (MS)	OF28, 1B3	R	28	31	116	18	34	1	0	5	20	6	16	2	.293	.431
Johnny Riddle	C23	R	39	23	45	0	8	0	0	0	2	4	6	0	.178	.178
1 Wally Flager	SS15	L	23	21	52	5	11	1	0	0	3	5	7	0	.212	.231
Joe Just	C14	R	29	14	34	2	5	0	0	0	2	4	7	0	.147	.147

Eddie Lukon (MS) 24 L 1-8, Ray Mederios 19 R 0-0

NAME	T	AGE	W	L	PCT	SV	G	GS	CG	IP	H	BB	SO	SHO	ERA
		33	61	93	.396	6	154	154	77	1366	1439	534	372	11	4.00
2 Joe Bowman	R	35	11	13	.458	0	25	24	15	186	198	68	71	1	3.58
Ed Heusser	R	36	11	16	.407	1	31	30	18	223	248	60	56	4	3.71
Bucky Walters	R	36	10	10	.500	0	22	22	12	168	166	51	45	3	2.68
Howie Fox	R	24	8	13	.381	0	45	15	7	164	169	77	54	0	4.94
2 Vern Kennedy	R	38	5	12	.294	1	24	20	11	158	170	69	38	1	3.99
Frank Dasso	R	27	4	5	.444	0	16	12	6	96	89	53	39	0	3.66
Mel Bosser	R	31	2	0	1.000	0	7	2	0	16	9	17	3	0	3.38
Arnold Carter	L	27	2	3	.400	0	13	6	2	47	54	13	4	1	3.06
Earl Harrist	R	25	2	4	.333	0	14	5	1	62	60	27	15	0	3.63
1 Boom-Boom Beck	R	40	2	4	.333	1	11	5	2	48	42	12	9	0	3.38
Mike Modak	R	23	1	2	.333	0	20	3	1	42	52	23	7	1	5.79
Johnny Hetki	R	23	1	2	.333	0	5	3	2	33	28	11	6	0	3.55
Hod Lisenbee	R	46	1	3	.250	0	31	3	0	80	97	16	14	0	5.51
Elmer Riddle (ST)	R	30	1	4	.200	0	12	3	0	30	39	27	5	0	8.10
Herm Wehmeier	R	18	0	1	.000	0	5	0	0	10	4	9	2	0	12.60
Guy Bush	R	43	0	0	—	0	4	0	0	5	3	1	0	0	9.00
Al Libke	R	27	0	0	—	0	4	0	0	10	11	9	6	0	5.40

PHILADELPHIA 8th 46-108 .299 52 — FREDDIE FITZSIMMONS 18-51 .261 — BEN CHAPMAN 28-57 .329

NAME	G by Pos	B	AGE	G	AB	R	H	2B	3B	HR	RBI	BB	SO	SB	BA	SA
TOTALS			30	154	5203	548	1278	197	27	56	503	449	501	54	.246	.326
Jimmy Wasdell	1B63, OF65	L	31	134	500	65	150	19	7	6	60	32	11	9	.300	.412
Fred Daniels	2B75, 3B1	R	26	76	230	15	46	3	2	0	10	12	22	1	.200	.230
Bitsy Mott	SS63, 2B27, 3B7	R	27	90	289	21	64	8	0	0	22	27	25	2	.221	.249
2 John Antonelli	3B108, 2B23, 1B1, SS1	R	29	125	504	50	129	27	2	1	28	24	24	1	.256	.323
Vance Dinges	OF65, 1B42	R	30	109	397	46	114	15	4	1	36	35	17	3	.287	.353
Vince DiMaggio	OF121	R	32	127	452	64	115	25	3	19	84	43	91	12	.257	.451
Coaker Triplett	OF92	R	33	120	363	36	87	11	1	7	46	40	27	1	.240	.333
Andy Seminick	C70, 3B4, OF1	R	24	80	188	18	45	7	2	6	26	18	38	1	.239	.394
Rene Monteagudo	OF35, P14	L	29	114	193	26	58	6	0	0	15	28	7	2	.301	.332
Jimmie Foxx	1B40, 3B14, P9	R	37	89	224	30	60	11	1	7	38	23	39	0	.268	.420
2 Glenn Crawford	OF38, SS34, 2B14	L	31	82	302	41	89	13	2	2	24	36	15	5	.295	.371
Gus Mancuso	C70	R	39	70	176	11	35	6	0	0	16	28	10	2	.199	.227
2 Wally Flager	SS48, 2B1	L	23	49	168	21	42	4	1	2	15	17	15	1	.250	.321
2 Jake Powell	OF44	R	36	48	173	14	40	5	1	1	14	8	13	1	.231	.277
Nick Picciuto	3B30, 2B4	R	23	36	89	7	12	6	0	0	6	6	17	0	.135	.202
Hal Spindel	C31	R	32	36	87	7	20	3	0	0	6	6	5	0	.230	.264
1 Johnny Peacock	C23	L	35	33	74	6	15	6	0	0	5	9	2	0	.203	.284
Garvin Hamner	2B21, SS9, 3B1	R	21	32	101	12	20	5	0	0	5	7	9	2	.198	.228
2 Ben Chamman	OF10, 3B4, P3	R	36	24	51	4	16	2	0	0	4	2	5	1	.314	.353
Ed Walczak	2B17, SS2	R	29	20	57	6	12	3	0	0	6	3	6	0	.211	.263
Tony Lupien (MS)	1B15	L	28	15	54	1	17	1	0	0	3	5	2	2	.315	.333
1 Buster Adams	OF14	R	30	14	56	6	13	5	3	0	7	5	6	0	.232	.429
Granny Hamner (MS)	SS13	R	18	14	41	3	7	2	0	0	3	0	1	0	.171	.220

2 Stan Andrews 28 R 11-33, Nick Goulish 28 L 3-11, Putsy Caballero 17 R 0-1, Don Hasenmayer (MS) 18 R 2-18

NAME	T	AGE	W	L	PCT	SV	G	GS	CG	IP	H	BB	SO	SHO	ERA
		30	46	108	.299	26	154	154	31	1353	1545	608	433	4	4.64
Andy Karl	R	31	8	8	.500	15	67	2	1	181	175	50	51	0	2.98
Dick Barrett	R	38	8	20	.286	1	36	30	8	191	216	92	72	0	5.42
Dick Mauney	R	25	6	10	.375	1	20	10	5	123	127	27	35	2	3.07
2 Oscar Judd	L	37	5	4	.556	2	23	9	3	83	80	40	36	1	3.80
Tex Kraus	R	27	4	9	.308	0	19	13	7	82	96	40	28	0	5.38
Charlie Sproull	R	26	4	10	.286	1	34	19	2	130	168	80	47	0	5.95
Charley Schanz (IL)	R	26	4	15	.211	5	35	21	5	145	165	87	56	1	4.34
1 Bill Lee	R	35	3	6	.333	1	13	13	2	77	107	30	13	0	4.68
Dick Coffman	R	38	2	1	.667	0	14	0	0	26	39	2	7	0	5.19
Jimmie Foxx	R	37	1	0	1.000	0	9	2	1	23	13	14	10	0	1.57
Hugh Mulcahy (MS)	R	31	1	3	.250	0	5	4	1	28	33	9	2	0	3.86
Lou Lucier	R	27	0	1	.000	0	9	1	0	23	24	6	5	0	2.25
Don Grate	R	21	0	1	.000	0	8	1	0	18	12	6	6	0	18.00
Charlie Ripple	L	24	0	1	.000	0	7	0	0	8	7	10	5	0	6.75
Lefty Scott	L	29	0	2	.000	0	5	2	0	12	29	12	5	0	4.50
2 Vern Kennedy	R	38	0	3	.000	0	12	3	0	16	26	9	5	0	5.50
Ken Raffensberger (MS)	R	27	0	0	—	0	3	0	0	24	28	14	6	0	4.50
Izzy Leon	R	34	0	1	.000	0	10	4	0	39	49	19	11	0	5.31
Whit Wyatt	R	37	0	1	.000	0	10	10	2	51	72	14	10	0	5.29
Rene Monteagudo	L	29	0	0	—	0	14	0	0	46	67	28	16	0	7.43
Mitch Chetkovich	R	27	0	0	—	0	3	0	0	7	7	6	4	0	0.00
2 Ben Chapman	R	36	0	0	—	0	3	0	0	7	7	6	4	0	7.71

WORLD SERIES — DETROIT (AL) 4 CHICAGO (NL) 3

LINE SCORES

TEAM	1	2	3	4	5	6	7	8	9	10	11	12	R	H	E

Game 1 October 3 at Detroit
CHI (NL) 4 0 3 | 0 0 0 | 2 0 0 | | 9 13 0
DET 0 0 0 | 0 0 0 | 0 0 0 | | 0 6 0
Borowy — Newhouser, Benton (3), Tobin (5), Mueller (8)

Game 2 October 4 at Detroit
CHI 0 0 0 | 1 0 0 | 0 0 0 | | 1 7 0
DET 0 0 0 | 0 4 0 | 0 0 X | | 4 7 0
Wyse, Erickson (7) — **Trucks**

Game 3 October 5 at Detroit
CHI 0 0 0 | 2 0 0 | 1 0 0 | | 3 8 0
DET 0 0 0 | 0 0 0 | 0 0 0 | | 0 1 2
Passeau — Overmire, Benton (7)

Game 4 October 6 at Chicago
DET 0 0 0 | 4 0 0 | 0 0 0 | | 4 7 1
CHI 0 0 0 | 0 0 1 | 0 0 0 | | 1 5 1
Trout — Prim, Derringer (4), Vandenberg (6), Erickson

Game 5 October 7 at Chicago
DET 0 0 1 | 0 0 4 | 1 0 2 | | 8 11 0
CHI 0 0 1 | 0 0 0 | 2 0 1 | | 4 7 2
Newhouser — Borowy, Vanderberg (6), Chipman (6), Derringer (7), Erickson (9)

Game 6 October 8 at Chicago
DET 0 1 0 | 0 0 0 | 2 4 0 | 0 0 0 | 7 13 3
CHI 0 0 0 | 0 4 1 | 2 0 0 | 0 0 1 | 8 15 3
Trucks, Caster (5), Bridges (6), Passeau, Wyse (9) — Benton (7), **Trout** (9) — Prim (8), **Borowy** (9)

Game 7 October 10 at Chicago
DET 5 1 0 | 0 1 0 | 1 2 0 | | 9 9 1
CHI 1 0 0 | 1 0 0 | 0 1 0 | | 3 10 1
Newhouser — Borowy, Derringer (1), Vandenberg (2), Erickson (6), Passeau (8), Wyse (9)

COMPOSITE BATTING

NAME	POS	G	AB	R	H	2B	3B	HR	RBI	BA
Detroit (AL)										
Totals		7	242	32	54	10	0	2	32	.223
Cramer	OF	7	29	7	11	0	0	0	4	.379
Mayo	2B	7	28	4	7	1	0	0	2	.250
Outlaw	3B	7	28	1	5	0	0	0	3	.179
York	1B	7	28	1	5	1	0	0	3	.179
Webb	SS	7	27	4	5	0	0	1	0	.185
Greenberg	OF	7	23	7	7	3	0	2	7	.304
Cullenbine	OF	7	22	5	5	2	0	0	4	.227
Richards	C	7	19	0	4	2	0	0	6	.211
Newhouser	P	3	8	0	0	0	0	0	1	.000
Trout	P	2	6	0	1	0	0	0	0	.167
Swift	C	3	4	1	1	0	0	0	0	.250
Trucks	P	2	4	0	0	0	0	0	0	.000
Hoover	SS	2	3	0	1	0	0	0	1	.333
Hostetler	PH	3	3	0	0	0	0	0	0	.000
McHale	PH	3	2	1	1	0	0	0	1	.500
Walker	PH	2	1	0	1	0	0	0	0	1.000
Maier	PH	1	1	0	0	0	0	0	0	.000
Borom	PH	2	0	2	0	0	0	0	0	.000
Eaton	PH	1	0	0	0	0	0	0	0	.000

Overmire P 0-1, Tobin P 0-0, Mierkowicz OF 0-0, Benton P 0-0, Bridges P 0-0, Caster P 0-0, Mueller P 0-0

NAME	POS	G	AB	R	H	2B	3B	HR	RBI	BA
Chicago (NL)										
Totals		7	247	29	65	16	3	1	27	.263
Hack	3B	7	30	1	11	3	0	0	4	.367
Lowrey	OF	7	29	4	9	1	0	0	0	.310
Johnson	2B	7	29	4	5	2	0	0	0	.172
Nicholson	OF	7	28	1	6	1	1	0	8	.214
Pafko	OF	7	28	5	6	2	0	0	2	.214
Cavarretta	1B	7	26	7	11	2	1	1	5	.423
Livingston	C	6	22	3	8	3	0	0	4	.364
Hughes	SS	6	17	1	5	1	0	0	3	.294
Passeau	P	2	6	0	0	0	0	0	0	.000
Borowy	P	4	6	0	1	0	0	0	0	.167
Gillespie	C	2	5	0	0	0	0	0	0	.000
Sacory	PH	3	5	0	2	0	0	0	0	.400
Wyse	P	3	4	0	0	0	0	0	0	.000
Becker	PH	3	2	0	1	0	0	0	0	.500
Merullo	SS	2	2	0	0	0	0	0	0	.000
Sauer	PH	2	2	1	0	0	0	0	0	.000
Williams		2	2	0	0	0	0	0	0	.000

Schuster SS 0-1, Vanderberg P 0-0, McCullough PH 0-1, Erickson P 0-0, Derringer P 0-0, Prim P 0-0, Block PR 0-0, Chipman P 0-0

COMPOSITE PITCHING

NAME	G	IP	H	BB	SO	W	L	SV	ERA
Detroit (AL)									
Totals	7	65.2	65	19	48	4	3	0	3.84
Newhouser	3	20.2	25	4	22	2	1	0	6.10
Trout	2	13.2	9	3	9	1	1	0	0.66
Trucks	2	13.1	14	5	7	1	0	0	3.38
Overmire	1	6	4	3	3	0	0	0	3.00
Benton	3	4.2	6	0	5	0	0	0	1.93
Tobin	1	3	4	1	0	0	0	0	6.00
Mueller	1	2	0	1	0	0	0	0	0.00
Bridges	1	1.2	3	3	1	0	0	0	16.20
Caster	1	0.2	0	0	1	0	0	0	0.00

NAME	G	IP	H	BB	SO	W	L	SV	ERA
Chicago (NL)									
Totals	7	65	54	33	22	3	4	0	4.15
Borowy	4	18	21	6	8	2	2	0	4.00
Passeau	3	16.2	7	8	3	1	0	0	2.70
Wyse	3	7.2	8	4	1	0	2	0	7.04
Erickson	3	7	7	4	3	0	0	0	3.86
Vandenberg	3	6	1	3	4	0	0	0	0.00
Derringer	3	5.1	5	7	1	0	0	0	6.75
Prim	2	4	4	1	0	0	0	0	9.00
Chipman	1	0.1	1	0	0	0	0	0	0.00

WORLD WAR II MILITARY SERVICE — AMERICAN LEAGUE

Full seasons missed by active players who played in at least one major league game before entering military service.

Boston

42	43	44	45	Player
				Pitchers
		44	45	Mace Brown
	43	44	45	Bill Butland
42				Emerson Dickman
		44	45	Joe Dobson
42	43	44	45	Mickey Harris
			45	Tex Hughson
42	43	44	45	Earl Johnson
	43	44	45	Charlie Wagner
				Catchers
			45	Bill Conroy
		44	45	Danny Doyle
			45	Roy Partee
42	43	44		Frankie Pytlak
			45	Hal Wagner
				Infielders
	43	44	45	Paul Campbell
	43	44	45	Tom Carey
			45	Bobby Doerr
42	43	44	45	Al Flair
	43	44	45	Johnny Pesky
			45	Jim Tabor
				Outfielders
	43	44	45	Dom DiMaggio
	43	44	45	Andy Gilbert
	43	44	45	Ted Williams

Chicago

42	43	44	45	Player
				Pitchers
42	43	44	45	Stan Goletz
			45	Don Hanski
42	43	44	45	Ted Lyons
			45	Gordon Maltzberger
42	43	44	45	Len Perme
	43	44	45	Johnny Ridgney
		44	45	Eddie Smith
	43	44	45	Ed Weiland
				Catchers
	43	44	45	George Dickey
			45	Ed Fernandes
				Infielders
		44		Luke Appling
	43	44	45	Jake Jones
	43	44	45	Bob Kennedy
		44	45	Don Kolloway
	43	44	45	Dario Lodigiani
			45	Bill Metzig
	43			Roy Schalk
	43	44	45	Leo Wells
				Outfielders
	43	44	45	Val Heim
	43			Myril Hoag
			45	Ralph Hodgin
		44	45	Frank Kalin
	43	44		Bill Mueller
	43	44	45	Dave Philley
42	43	44		Dave Short
			45	Thurman Tucker
	43	44	45	Sammy West
	43	44	45	Taffy Wright

Cleveland

42	43	44	45	Player
				Pitchers
		44		Pete Center
		44	45	Chubby Dean
42	43	44	45	Cal Dorsett
42	43	44	45	Harry Eisenstat
42	43	44		Bob Feller
	43	44	45	Tom Ferrick
	43	44	45	Joe Krakauskas
				Catchers
		44		Gene Desautels
	43	44	45	Jim Hegan
				Infielders
42	43	44	45	Jack Conway
			45	Ken Keltner
	43	44	45	Bob Lemon
			45	Ray Mack
			45	Rusty Peters
	43	44	45	Eddie Robinson
		44	45	Ted Sepkowski
				Outfielders
42	43	44	45	Soup Campbell
		44	45	Hank Edwards
	43	44	45	Buster Mills
		44	45	Gene Woodling

Detroit

42	43	44	45	Player
				Pitchers
	43	44		Al Benton
		44		Tommy Bridges
			45	Johnny Gorsica
42	43	44	45	Fred Hutchinson
				Les Mueller
		44		Virgil Trucks
		44	45	Hal White
				Catchers
	43	44	45	Hank Riebe
	43	44	45	Birdie Tebbetts
				Infielders
		44	45	Jimmy Bloodworth
	43	44	45	Murray Franklin
	43	44	45	Charlie Gahringer
			45	Pinky Higgins
	43	44	45	Billy Hitchcock
	43	44	45	Johnny Lipon
	43	44		Dutch Meyer
		44	45	Joe Wood
				Outfielders
	43	44	45	Hoot Evers
42	43	44		Hank Greenberg
		44	45	Ned Harris
	43	44	45	Barney McCosky
42	43	44	45	Pat Mullin
	43	44	45	Bob Patrick
		44	45	Rip Radcliff (also 46)
			45	Dick Wakefield
42	43	44		Hub Walker

New York

42	43	44	45	Player
				Pitchers
	43	44	45	Norm Branch
		44	45	Tommy Byrne
	43	44	45	Randy Gumpert
			45	Al Lyons
42	43	44	45	Steve Peek
			45	Mel Queen
	43	44		Red Ruffing
		44	45	Marius Russo
42	43	44		Charlie Stanceau
			45	Jake Wade
			45	Butch Wensloff (also 46)
				Catchers
		44	45	Bill Dickey
			45	Rollie Hemsley
		44		Aaron Robinson
		44	45	Ken Sears
42	43	44	45	Ken Silvestri
				Infielders
		44	45	Joe Gordon
	43	44	45	Buddy Hassett
		44	45	Billy Johnson
	43	44	45	Hank Majeski
	43	44	45	Phil Rizzuto
42	43	44	45	Johnny Sturm
				Outfielders
	43	44	45	Joe DiMaggio
	43	44	45	Tommy Henrich
	43	44	45	George Salkirk
		44	45	Roy Weatherly

Philadelphia

42	43	44	45	Player
				Pitchers
		44	45	Herman Besse
		44		Charlie Bowles
		44	45	Norm Brown
		44	45	Fred Caligiuri (also 46)
		44	45	Lou Ciola (also 46)
		44	45	Tom Clyde (also 46)
42	43	44	45	Joe Coleman
		44	45	Everett Fagan
	43	44		Dick Fowler
	43	44		Bob Harris
			45	Lum Harris
42	43	44	45	Rankin Johnson
	43	44	45	Jack Knott
		44	45	Bert Kuczynski (also 46)
		44	45	Sam Lowry (also 46)
	43	44	45	Phil Marchildon
42	43	44	45	Bob Savage
42	43	44	45	Porter Vaughan
				Catchers
	43	44	45	Jim Castiglia
	43	44	45	George Yankowski (also 46)
				Infielders
	43	44	45	Buddy Blair
42	43	44		Al Brancato
	43	44	45	Crash Davis
		44	45	Bruce Konopka
42	43	44	45	Benny McCoy
42	43	44	45	Don Richmond
		44	45	Pete Suder
	43	44	45	Jack Wallaesa
				Outfielders
		44	45	Vern Benson
42	43	44		Sam Chapman
	43	44	45	Eddie Collins
			45	Hal Epps
42	43	44	45	Ray Poole
		44	45	George Staller
		44	45	Elmer Valo
		44	45	Johnny Welaj

St. Louis

42	43	44	45	Player
				Pitchers
42				Pete Appleton
	43	44	45	Frank Biscan
			45	Denny Galehouse
			45	Hooks Iott
	43	44	45	Al Milnar
		44	45	Maury Newlin
			45	Fred Sanford
			45	Steve Sundra
				Catchers
		44	45	Hank Helf
			45	Tom Turner
				Infielders
42	43	44	45	George Archie
	43	44	45	Johnny Berardino
42	43	44	45	Johnny Lucadello
		44	45	Hank Schmulbach (also 46)
	43	44	45	Chuck Stevens
				Outfielders
42	43	44	45	Joe Grace
	43	44	45	Walt Judnich
	43	44	45	Glenn McQuillen
			45	Al Zarilla

Washington

42	43	44	45	Player
				Pitchers
				Red Anderson
	43	44	45	Lou Bevil
			45	Milo Candini
			45	Vern Curtis
	43	44	45	Sid Hudson
	43	44	45	Bill Kennedy
			45	Bill LeFebvre
	43	44		Walt Masterson
	43	44	45	Phil McCullough
		44	45	Jim Mertz (also 46)
		44	45	Ronnie Miller
		44	45	Ray Scarborough
42	43	44	45	Lou Thurman (also 41)
	43	44	45	Maxie Wilson
			45	Early Wynn
				Catchers
		44	45	Jake Early
	43			Al Evans
				Infielders
	43	44	45	Frank Croucher
		44	45	Stan Galle
		44	45	Alex Kampouris
			45	Hilly Layne
		44	45	Jerry Priddy
		44	45	Sherry Robertson
42	43	44	45	Jack Sanford
		44	45	John Sullivan (also 46)
42	43	44		Cacil Travis
		44	45	Mickey Vernon
			45	Eddie Yost
				Outfielders
	43	44	45	Bruce Campbell
	43	44	45	Al Kvasnak
42	43	44		Buddy Lewis
42	43	44		Jim Mallory
			45	Stan Spence

Total American League: 1942=40 1943=119 1944=168 1945=180

WORLD WAR II MILITARY SERVICE — NATIONAL LEAGUE

Full seasons missed by active players who played in at least one major league game before entering military service.

Boston

Pitchers

Player	42	43	44	45
Bill Donovan			44	45
Tom Earley		43	44	
Art Johnson		43	44	45
Frank LaManna		43	44	45
Ray Martin (also 46)			44	45
Bill Posedel	42	43	44	45
Woody Rich				45
Johnny Sain		43	44	45
Warren Spahn		43	44	45
Lou Tost			44	45
Letty Wallace		43	44	
Ace Williams		43	44	45

Catchers

Player	42	43	44	45
Hugh Poland				45

Infielders

Player	42	43	44	45
Ducky Detweiler		43	44	45
John Dudra	42	43	44	45
Nanny Fernandez		43	44	45
Buddy Gremp		43	44	45
Max Macon (also 46)				45
Johnny McCarthy			44	45
Gene Patton				45
Damon Phillips				45
Skippy Roberge		43	44	45
Bama Rowell	42	43	44	45
Connie Ryan				45
Sibby Sisti		43	44	45
Tom York				45

Outfielders

Player	42	43	44	45
Chet Clemens				45
Sam Gentile			44	45
Frank McElyea		43	44	45
Chet Ross				45
Max West		43	44	45

Brooklyn

Pitchers

Player	42	43	44	45
Rex Barney			44	45
Hugh Casey		43	44	45
Dutch Dietz			44	45
Larry French		43	44	45
Chris Haughey			44	45
Ed Head				45
Kirby Higbe			44	45
Chet Kehn		43	44	
Cal McLish				45
Rube Melton				45
Bill Sayles			44	45

Catchers

Player	42	43	44	45
Cliff Dapper		43	44	45
Herman Franks	42	43	44	45
Gil Hodges			44	45
Don Padgett	42	43	44	45

Infielders

Player	42	43	44	45
Boyd Bartley			44	45
Jack Bolling				45
Bobby Bragan (also 46)				45
Dolf Camilli			44	
Alex Campanis			44	45
Billy Herman			44	45
Cookie Lavagetto	42	43	44	45
Gene Mauch				45
Eddie Miksis				45
Pee Wee Reese		43	44	45
Lew Riggs		43	44	45
Lou Rochelli (also 46)				45
Stan Rojek		43	44	45

Outfielders

Player	42	43	44	45
Joe Gallagher (also 41)	42	43	44	45
Gene Hermanski			44	45
Pete Reiser		43	44	45
Johnny Rizzo		43	44	45
Tommy Tatum	42	43	44	45

Chicago

Pitchers

Player	42	43	44	45
Dale Alderson				45
Hi Bithorn			44	45
Bill Fleming				45
Emil Kush		43	44	45
Walt Lanfranconi	42	43	44	45
Red Lynn				45
Russ Meers	42	43	44	45
Vern Olsen		43	44	45
Johnny Schmitz		43	44	45
Lon Warneke			44	

Catchers

Player	42	43	44	45
Marv Felderman		43	44	
Mickey Livingston			44	
Clyde McCullough			44	45
Bob Scheffing		43	44	45
Joe Stephenson				45
Bennie Warren		43	44	45

Infielders

Player	42	43	44	45
Cy Block			44	45
Al Glossop		43	44	45
Lou Stringer		43	44	45
Bobby Sturgeon		43	44	45
Eddie Waitkus	42	43	44	45

Outfielders

Player	42	43	44	45
Dom Dallessandro				45
Charlie Gilbert			44	45
Peanuts Lowrey			44	
Lou Novikoff				45
Whitey Platt			44	45
Marv Rickert		43	44	45

Cincinnati

Pitchers

Player	42	43	44	45
Joe Beggs				45
Ewell Blackwell		43	44	45
Harry Gumbert				45
Jim Konstanty				45
Bob Malloy				45
Jack Niemes			44	45
Kent Peterson (also 46)				45
Clyde Shoun				45
Junior Thompson			44	45
Johnny Vander Meer			44	45

Catchers

Player	42	43	44	45
Ray Lamanno		43	44	45
Ray Mueller				45
Dick West			44	45

Infielders

Player	42	43	44	45
Lonny Frey			44	45
Lonnie Goldstein				45
Bert Haas			44	45
Hank Sauer			44	
Eddie Shokes		43	44	45
Benny Zientara	42	43	44	45

Outfielders

Player	42	43	44	45
Frankie Kelleher			44	45
Eddie Lukon		43	44	
Max Marshall				45
Mike McCormick			44	45
Clyde Vollmer		43	44	45

New York

Pitchers

Player	42	43	44	45
Bob Carpenter		43	44	45
Hugh East			44	45
Dave Koslo		43	44	45
Hal Schumacher	42	43	44	45
Ken Trinkle	42			
Johnnie Wittig			44	45

Catchers

Player	42	43	44	45
Jack Aragon	42	43	44	
Harry Danning		43	44	45
Charlie Fox		43	44	45

Infielders

Player	42	43	44	45
Dick Bartell			44	45
Buddy Blattner		43	44	45
John Davis	42	43	44	45
Sid Gordon			44	45
Hugh Luby				45
Johnny Mize		43	44	45
Mickey Witek			44	45
Babe Young		43	44	45

Outfielders

Player	42	43	44	45
Morrie Arnovich	42	43	44	45
Vic Bradford (also 46)			44	45
Willard Marshall		43	44	45
Buster Maynard			44	45

Philadelphia

Pitchers

Player	42	43	44	45
Roy Bruner	42	43	44	45
Dick Conger			44	45
George Eyrich (also 46)			44	45
Lee Grissom	42	43	44	45
Bill Harman			44	45
Frank Hoerst		43	44	45
Tommy Hughes		43	44	45
Si Johnson			44	45
Dale Jones	42	43	44	45
Tex Kraus			44	
Gene Lambert		43	44	45
Andy Lapihuska			44	45
Rogers McKee				45
Hugh Mulcahy (also 41)	42	43	44	45
Dick Mulligan		43	44	45
Sam Nahem		43	44	45
Ike Pearson		43	44	45
Schoolboy Rowe			44	45

Catchers

Player	42	43	44	45
Benny Culp				45
Dee Moore			44	45
Bill Peterman		43	44	45

Infielders

Player	42	43	44	45
Bill Burich				45
Ray Hamrick (also 46)				45
Charlie Letchas				45
Hal Marnie		43	44	45
Pinky May			44	45
Emmett Mueller	42	43	44	45
Moon Mullen (also 46)				45
Ed Murphy		43	44	45
Danny Murtaugh			44	45

Outfielders

Player	42	43	44	45
Jim Carlin	42	43	44	45
Ed Freed		43	44	45
Ernie Koy		43	44	45
Joe Marty	42	43	44	45
Ron Northey				45

Pittsburgh

Pitchers

Player	42	43	44	45
Ed Albosta		43	44	45
Russ Bauers			44	45
Bill Brandt			44	45
Bill Clemensen	42	43	44	45
Hank Gornicki			44	45
Jack Hallett			44	45
Ken Heintzelman		43	44	45
Bob Klinger			44	45
Johnny Lanning			44	
Oad Swigert (also 41)	42	43	44	45
Lefty Wilkie		43	44	45

Catchers

Player	42	43	44	45
Bill Baker			44	45
Roy Jarvis				45
Vinnie Smith			44	45
Billy Sullivan (also 46)			44	45

Infielders

Player	42	43	44	45
Alf Anderson			44	45
Billy Cox		43	44	45
Elbie Fletcher			44	45
Huck Geary			44	45
Ed Leip		43	44	45
Burgess Whitehead	42	43	44	45

Outfielders

Player	42	43	44	45
Culley Rikard		43	44	45
Bud Stewart			44	45
Maurice Van Robays			44	45

St. Louis

Pitchers

Player	42	43	44	45
Johnny Beazley		43	44	45
Al Brazle			44	45
Murry Dickson			44	45
Johnny Grodzicki	42	43	44	45
Howie Krist			44	45
Whitey Moore		43	44	45
George Munger				45
Howie Pollet			44	45
Freddy Schmidt				45
Ernie White			44	45

Catchers

Infielders

Player	42	43	44	45
Jimmy Brown			44	45
Creepy Crespi (also 46)		43	44	45
Jeff Cross		43	44	45
Lou Klein			44	

Outfielders

Player	42	43	44	45
Erv Dusak		43	44	45
Danny Litwhiler				45
Terry Moore		43	44	45
Stan Musial				45
Earl Naylor				45
Walter Sessi	42	43	44	45
Enos Slaughter		43	44	45
Harry Walker			44	45
Johnny Wyrostek			44	45

Total National League: 1942=31 1943=100 1944=174 1945=204

USE NAME - GIVEN NAMES (NICKNAMES)	TEAM BY YEAR	BIRTH DATE	BIRTH PLACE	DEATH DATE	B	T	HGT	WGT	G	AB	R	H	2B	3B	HR	RBI	BB	SO	SB	BA	SA
Abreu, Joe-Joseph Lawrence (The Magician)	42CinN	05-24-13	Oakland, Cal.	03-17-93	R	R	5'8	160	9	28	4	6	1	0	1	3	4	4	0	.214	.357
Adair, Jimmy-James Audrey (Choppy)	31ChiN	01-25-07	Waxahachie, Tex.	12-09-82	R	R	5'10	154	18	76	9	21	3	1	0	3	1	8	1	.276	.342
Adams, Buster-Elvin Clark	39,43StLN 43-45PhiN 45-46StLA 47PhiN	06-24-15	Trinidad, Colo.	09-01-90	R	R	6'	180	576	2003	282	532	96	12	50	249	234	281	12	.266	.400
Adams, Sparky-Earl John	22-27ChiN 28-29PitN 30-33StLN 33-34CinN	08-26-94	Zerbe, Pa.	02-24-89	R	R	5'6	151	1424	5557	844	1588	249	48	9	394	453	223	154	.286	.353
Adams, Spencer Dewey (Sparky)	23PitN 25WasA 26NYA 27StLN	06-21-98	Layton, Utah	11-24-70	L	R	5'9	165	180	395	61	101	16	5	0	38	38	50	5	.256	.322
Aderholt, Morrie-Morris Woodrow	39-41WasA 44-45BknN 45BosN	09-13-15	Mt. Olive, N.C.	03-18-55	L	R	6'1	188	106	262	36	70	7	3	3	32	19	29	3	.267	.351
Adkins, Dick-Richard Earl	03-03-20	Electra, Tex.	09-12-55	R	R	5'10	165	3	7	2	1	0	0	0	0	0	2	0	.143	.143
Akers, Bill-William G. (Bump)	29-31DetA 32BosN	12-25-04	Chattanooga, Tenn.	04-13-62	R	R	5'11	178	174	475	64	124	17	9	11	69	63	64	7	.261	.404
Aleno, Chuck-Charles	41-44CinN	02-19-17	St. Louis, Mo.	02-10-03	R	R	6'2	215	118	320	34	67	11	3	2	34	31	35	3	.209	.281
Alexander, Dale-David Dale (Moose)	29-32DetA 32-33BosA	04-26-03	Greenville, Tenn.	03-02-79	R	R	6'3	210	662	2450	369	811	164	30	61	459	248	197	20	.331	.497
Alexander, Hugh-Hugh	37CleA	07-10-17	Buffalo, Mo.	11-25-00	R	R	6'	190	7	11	0	1	0	0	0	0	0	5	1	.091	.091
Allen, Ethan-Ethan Nathan	26-30CinN 30-32NYN 33StLN 34-36PhiN 36ChiN 37-38StLA	01-01-04	Cincinnati, Ohio	09-15-93	R	R	6'1	180	1281	4418	623	1325	255	45	47	501	223	301	84	.300	.410
Almada, Mel-Baldomero Melo [Quiros]	33-37BosA 37-38WasA 38-39StLA 39BknN	02-07-13	Hwatabampo, Mexico	08-13-88	L	L	6'	170	646	2483	363	706	107	27	15	197	214	150	56	.284	.367
Alston, Walt-Walter Emmons (Smokey)	36StLN M54-57BknN M58-76LAN	12-01-11	Venice, Ohio	10-01-84	R	R	6'2	195	1	1	0	0	0	0	0	0	0	1	0	.000	.000
Ambler, Wayne-Wayne Harper	37-39PhiA	11-08-15	Abington, Pa.	01-03-98	R	R	5'9	165	271	782	60	175	39	2	0	73	83	64	4	.224	.269
Anderson, Hal-Harold	32ChiA	02-10-04	St. Louis, Mo.	05-01-74	R	R	5'11	160	9	32	4	8	0	0	0	2	0	1	0	.250	.250
Andrews, Stan-Stanley Joseph (Polo)	39-40BosN 44-45BknN 45PhiN	04-17-17	Lynn, Mass.	06-10-95	R	R	5'11	178	70	149	11	32	2	1	1	12	8	16	2	.215	.262
Andrus, Bill-William Morgan	31WasA 37PhiN	07-25-07	Beaumont, Tex.	03-12-82	R	R	6'	185	6	9	0	0	0	0	0	0	0	0	0	.000	.000
Angley, Tom-Thomas Samuel	29CinN	10-02-04	Baltimore, Md.	10-26-52	L	R	5'8	190	5	16	1	4	1	0	0	6	2	2	0	.250	.313
Ankenman, Pat-Fred Norman	36StLN 43-44BknN	12-23-12	Houston, Tex.	01-13-89	R	R	5'4	125	15	29	2	7	1	0	0	3	0	5	0	.241	.276
Antolick, Joe-Joseph	44PhiN	04-11-16	Hokendaugua, Pa.	06-25-02	R	R	6'	185	4	6	1	2	0	0	0	0	1	0	0	.333	.333
Antonelli, John-John Lawrence	44-45StLN 45PhiN	07-15-15	Memphis, Tenn.	04-18-90	R	R	5'10	165	135	528	50	133	28	2	1	29	24	29	1	.252	.318
Appling, Luke-Lucius Benjamin (Old Aches and Pains)	30-43ChiA 44MS 45-50ChiA M67KCA	04-02-07	High Point, N.C.	01-03-91	R	R	5'10	183	2422	8856	1319	2749	440	102	45	1118	1302	528	179	.310	.398
Aragon, Jack-Angel Valdes [Reyes]	41NYN 42-44MS	11-20-15	Havana, Cuba	04-04-88	R	R	5'10	176	1	0	0	0	0	0	0	0	0	0	0	—	—
Archdeacon, Maurice-Maurice John (Flash)	23-25CleA	12-14-97	St. Louis, Mo.	09-05-54	L	L	5'8	153	127	384	84	128	14	4	0	29	48	39	13	.333	.391
Archie, George-George Albert	38DetA 41WasA 41,46StLA 42-45MS	04-27-14	Nashville, Tenn.	09-20-01	R	R	6'1	170	121	421	49	115	24	4	3	53	37	47	10	.273	.371
Arlett, Buzz-Russell Loris	31PhiN	01-03-99	Elmhurst, Cal.	05-16-64	B	R	6'3	225	121	418	65	131	26	7	18	72	45	39	3	.313	.538
Arnovich, Morrie-Morris (Snooker)	36-40PhiN 40CinN 41NYN 42-45MS 46NYN	01-20-10	Superior, Wis.	07-20-59	R	R	5'10	168	590	2013	234	577	104	12	22	261	185	139	17	.287	.383
Asbell, Jim-James Marion (Big Jim)	38ChiN	06-22-14	Dallas, Tex.	07-06-67	R	R	6'	210	17	33	6	6	2	0	1	3	3	9	0	.182	.242
Asbjornson, Casper-Robert Anthony	28-29BosA 31-32CinN	06-19-09	Concord, Mass.	01-21-70	R	R	6'1	196	97	221	19	52	10	1	1	27	9	45	0	.235	.303
Atkinson, Lefty-Hubert Burley	27WasA	06-04-04	Chicago, Ill.	02-12-61	L	L	5'7	149	1	0	0	0	0	0	0	0	0	0	0	.000	.000
Attreau, Dick-Richard Gilbert	26-27PhiN	04-08-97	Chicago, Ill.	07-05-64	L	L	6'	160	61	144	26	31	2	2	1	16	20	23	1	.215	.278
Atwood, Bill-William Franklin	36-40PhiN	09-25-11	Rome, Ga.	09-14-93	R	R	6'	190	342	961	82	220	41	4	7	112	93	89	4	.229	.302
Autry, Martin-Martin Gordon (Chick)	24NYA 26-28CleA 29-30ChiA	03-05-03	Martindale, Tex.	01-26-50	R	R	6'	180	120	277	21	68	17	3	2	25	15	29	0	.245	.350
Averill, Earl-Howard Earl	29-39CleA 39-40DetA 41BosN	05-21-02	Snohomish, Wash.	08-16-83	L	R	5'10	172	1669	6358	1224	2020	401	128	238	1165	775	518	69	.318	.533
Badgro, Red-Morris Hiram 27-28, 30-36 played in N.F.L.	29-30StLA	12-01-02	Kent, Wash.	07-13-98	L	R	6'	190	143	382	57	98	30	3	2	45	24	42	4	.257	.368
Bagwell, Bill-William Mallory (Big Bill)	23BosN 25PhiA	02-24-95	Choudrant, La.	10-05-76	L	L	6'1	175	92	143	12	42	6	3	2	20	8	14	0	.294	.420
Bailey, Gene-Arthur Eugene	17PhiA 18MS 19-20BosN 20BosA 23-24BknN	11-25-93	Pearsall, Tex.	11-14-73	R	R	5'8	160	213	634	95	156	16	7	2	52	63	61	13	.246	.303
Baker, Bill-William Presley	40-41CinN 41-43,46PitN 44-45MS 48-49StLN	02-11-11	Paw Creek, N.C.	04-13-06	R	R	6'	200	263	588	45	145	25	5	2	68	68	30	6	.247	.316
Baldwin, Henry-Henry Clay (Ted)	27PhiN	06-13-94	Chadds Ford, Pa.	02-24-64	R	R	5'11	180	6	16	1	5	0	0	0	1	2	0	0	.313	.313
Ballenger, Pelham-Pelham Ashby	28WasA	02-06-94	Gilreath Mill, S.C.	12-08-48	R	R	5'11	180	3	9	1	1	0	0	0	0	0	1	0	.111	.111
Bancroft, Dave-David James (Beauty)	15-20PhiN 20-23NYN 24-27,M24BosN 28-29BknN 30NYN	04-20-91	Sioux City, Iowa	10-09-72	B	R	5'9	160	1913	7182	1048	2004	320	77	32	591	827	487	145	.279	.358
Barbare, Walter-Walter Lawrence (Dinty)	14-16CleA 18BosA 19-20PhiN 21-22BosN	08-11-91	Greenville, S.C.	10-28-65	R	R	6'	162	500	1777	173	462	52	21	1	156	88	121	37	.260	.315
Barbary, Red-Donald Odell	43WasA	06-20-20	Simpsonville, S.C.	09-27-03	R	R	6'3	190	1	0	0	0	0	0	0	0	0	0	0	.000	.000
Barbee, Dave-David Monroe	26PhiA 32PitN	05-07-05	Greensboro, N.C.	01-01-68	R	R	6'	178	116	374	44	92	23	7	6	60	20	42	1	.246	.393
Barber, Turner-Tyrus Turner	15-16WasA 17-22ChiN 23BknN	07-09-93	Lavinia, Tenn.	10-20-68	L	R	5'11	170	491	1531	189	442	47	21	2	185	115	112	28	.289	.351
Barkley, Red-John Duncan	37StLA 39BosN 43BknN	09-19-12	Childress, Tex.	12-12-00	R	R	5'11	160	63	163	16	43	9	0	0	21	19	26	2	.264	.319
Barna, Babe-Herbert Paul	37-38PhiA 41-43NYN 43BosA	03-02-15	Clarksburg, W.Va.	05-18-72	L	R	6'2	210	207	664	88	154	22	9	12	96	76	98	9	.232	.346
Barnes, Eppie-Everett Duane	23-24PhiN	12-01-00	Ossining, N.Y.	11-17-80	L	R	5'9	175	4	8	1	0	0	0	0	0	0	0	0	.000	.000
Barnes, Honey-John Francis	26NYA	01-31-00	Fulton, N.Y.	06-18-81	R	R	5'10	175	1	0	0	0	0	0	0	0	0	0	0	.143	.143
Barnes, Red-Emile Deering	27-30WasA 30ChiA	12-25-03	Suggsville, Ala.	07-03-59	L	R	5'10	158	286	836	152	224	41	24	8	97	95	76	12	.268	.403
Barnes, Sammy-Samuel Thomas	21DetA	12-18-99	Suggsville, Ala.	02-19-81	L	R	5'8	150	7	11	2	2	1	0	0	0	2	1	0	.182	.273
Barnhart, Clyde-Clyde Lee (Pooch)	20-28PitN	12-29-95	Buck Valley, Pa.	01-21-80	R	R	5'10	155	814	2673	405	788	123	62	27	436	265	149	35	.295	.418
Barnhart, Vic-Victor Dee	44-46PitN	09-01-22	Hagerstown, Md.	04-05-03	R	R	6'	188	74	204	21	55	7	0	0	19	10	12	2	.270	.304
Barett, Bill-William Joseph (Whispering Bill)	21PhiA 23-29ChiA 29-30BosA 30WasA	05-28-00	Cambridge, Mass.	01-26-51	R	R	6'	175	718	2395	318	690	151	30	23	328	211	239	80	.288	.405
Barrett, Bob-Robert Schley (Jumbo)	23-25ChiN 25,27BknN 29BosA	01-27-99	Atlanta, Ga.	01-18-82	R	R	5'11	175	239	650	57	169	23	5	10	86	32	61	6	.260	.357
Barrett, Johnny-John Joseph	42-46PitN 46BosN	12-18-15	Lowell, Mass.	08-17-74	L	L	5'10	170	588	1811	303	454	82	32	23	220	265	201	69	.251	.369
Barron, Red-David Irenus	29BosN	06-21-00	Clarksville, Ga.	10-04-82	R	R	6'	185	10	21	3	4	1	0	0	1	1	4	2	.190	.238
Bartell, Dick-Richard William (Rowdy Richard, Pepper)	27-30PitN 31-34PhiN 35-38NYN 39ChiN 40-41DetA 41-43,46NYN 44-45MS	11-22-07	Chicago, Ill.	08-04-95	R	R	5'9	160	2016	7629	1130	2165	442	71	79	710	748	627	109	.284	.391
Bartley, Boyd-Boyd Owen	43BknN 44-46MS	02-11-20	Chicago, Ill.		R	R	5'9	165	9	21	0	1	0	0	0	1	1	9	0	.048	.048
Bartling, Irv-Henry Irving	38PhiN	06-27-14	Bay City, Mich.	06-12-73	R	R	6'	175	14	46	5	8	1	1	0	5	3	7	0	.174	.239
Barton, Vince-Vincent David	31-32CinN	02-01-08	Edmonton, Canada	09-13-73	L	R	6'	180	102	373	64	87	12	4	16	65	29	62	1	.233	.416
Bartosch, Dave-David Robert	45StLN	03-24-17	St. Louis, Mo.	04-30-06	R	R	6'1	190	24	47	9	12	1	0	0	1	6	3	0	.255	.277
Bashore, Walt-Walter Franklin	36PhiN	10-06-09	Harrisburg, Pa.	09-26-84	R	R	6'	190	10	10	1	2	0	0	0	0	1	3	0	.200	.200
Basinski, Eddie-Edwin Frank (Fiddler)	44-45BknN 47PitN	11-04-22	Buffalo, N.Y.		R	R	6'1	172	203	602	58	147	19	7	4	59	35	70	1	.244	.319
Bassler, Johnny-John Landis	13-14CleA 21-27DetA	06-03-95	Mechanics Grove, Pa.	06-29-79	L	R	5'9	170	811	2319	250	704	99	16	1	318	437	81	13	.304	.361
Bates, Bud-Hubert Edgar	39PhiN	03-16-12	Los Angeles, Cal.	04-29-87	R	R	5'11	165	15	58	8	15	2	0	1	2	2	8	1	.259	.345
Bates, Charlie-Charles William	27PhiA	09-17-07	Philadelphia, Pa.	01-29-80	R	R	5'10	165	9	38	5	9	2	0	0	3	0	1	0	.237	.395
Battle, Jim-James Milton	27ChiA	03-26-01	Bailer, Tex.	09-30-65	R	R	6'1	170	6	8	1	3	0	0	0	0	0	0	0	.375	.625
Beck, Clyde-Clyde Eugene (Jersey)	26-30ChiN 31CinN	01-06-00	Bassett, Cal.	07-15-88	R	R	5'10	150	468	1525	203	354	56	11	12	162	184	180	9	.232	.307
Becker, Heinz-Heinz Reinhard (Dutch)	43,45-46ChiN 46-47CleA	08-26-15	Berlin, Germany	11-11-91	R	R	6'2	200	152	358	45	94	18	3	2	47	50	42	1	.236	.346
Becker, Joe-Joseph Edward	36-37CleA	06-25-08	Chicago, Ill. Bats Left 46	01-11-98	R	R	6'1	180	40	83	8	20	5	2	1	13	8	8	0	.241	.386
Bedford, Gene-William Eugene (Blink) 25-26 played in N.F.L.	25CleA	12-02-96	Commerce, Tex.	10-06-77	R	R	5'9	165	2	5	2	1	1	0	0	0	1	0	0	.200	.400
Beeler, Jodie-Joseph Sam	44CinN	11-26-21	Dallas, Tex.	10-08-02	R	R	6'	170	3	3	0	1	0	0	0	2	0	1	0	.333	.333
Begley, Jim-James Lawrence (Imp)	24CinN	09-13-02	San Francisco, Cal.	02-22-57	R	R	5'8	140	2	5	1	1	0	0	0	1	0	0	0	.200	.200
Bejma, Ollie(Alojzy)-Aloysius Frank	34-36StLA 37ChiA	09-12-07	South Bend, Ind.	01-03-95	R	R	5'10	165	316	906	128	222	35	11	14	117	130	105	5	.245	.354
Bell, Beau-Roy Chester	35-39StLA 39DetA 40-41CleA	08-20-07	Bellville, Tex.	09-14-77	R	R	6'2	185	767	2718	378	806	165	32	46	437	272	239	11	.297	.432
Bell, Fern-Fernando Jerome Lee (Danny)	39-40PitN	01-21-13	Ada, Okla.	08-29-00	R	R	6'	180	89	265	44	75	5	8	2	35	43	19	2	.283	.385
Bell, Les-Lester Rowland	23-27StLN 28-29BosN 30-31CinN	12-14-01	Harrisburg, Pa.	12-26-85	R	R	5'11	185	896	3239	404	938	184	49	66	509	276	322	25	.290	.438
Benes, Joe-Joseph Anthony (Bananas)	31StLN	01-08-01	Queens, N.Y.	03-07-75	R	R	5'8	158	10	12	1	2	0	0	0	1	0	2	0	.167	.167
Bengough, Benny-Bernard Oliver	23-30NYA 31-32StLA	07-27-98	Niagara Falls, N.Y.	12-22-68	R	R	5'7	168	411	1125	83	287	46	12	0	108	62	45	2	.255	.317
Benjamin, Stan-Alfred Stanley	39-42PhiN 43CleA	05-20-14	Framingham, Mass.		R	R	6'2	194	241	770	77	176	32	11	5	41	32	115	23	.229	.318
Bennett, Fred-James Fred (Red)	28StLA 31PitN	03-15-02	Atkins, Ark.	05-12-57	R	R	5'9	165	39	97	6	27	6	0	1	7	7	6	0	.278	.371
Bennett, Herschel-Herschel Emmett	23-27StLA	09-21-06	Elwood, Mo.	09-06-64	L	R	5'9	164	312	877	135	242	41	13	7	104	58	65	13	.276	.375
Bennett, Joe-Joseph Rosenblum	23PhiN	07-02-00	New York, N.Y.	07-11-87	R	R	5'9	168	1	0	0	0	0	0	0	0	0	0	0		
Bentley, Jack-John Needles (See P20-45)	13-18WasA 23-25NYN 26PhiN 26-27NYN	03-08-95	Sandy Spring, Md.	10-24-69	L	L	6'	200	287	584	58	170	30	8	7	71	21	39	0	.291	.406
Benton, Stan-Stanley (Rabbit)	22PhiN	09-29-01	Cannel City, Ky.	06-07-84	L	R	5'7	160	6	19	1	4	1	0	0	3	2	1	0	.211	.263
Berg, Moe-Morris	23BknN 26-30ChiA 31CleA 32-34WasA 34CleA 35-39BosA	03-02-02	New York, N.Y.	05-29-72	R	R	6'1	185	663	1812	150	441	71	6	6	206	78	117	11	.243	.299
Bergamo, Augie-August Samuel	44-45StLN	02-14-18	Detroit, Mich.	09-19-74	L	L	5'9	165	174	496	86	151	23	5	5	63	78	44	0	.304	.401
Berger, Boze-Louis William	32,35-36CleA 37-38ChiA 39BosA	05-13-10	Baltimore, Md.	11-03-92	R	R	6'2	180	343	1144	146	270	51	8	13	97	94	226	12	.236	.329

USE NAME - GIVEN NAMES (NICKNAMES)	TEAM BY YEAR	BIRTH DATE	BIRTH PLACE	DEATH DATE	B	T	HGT	WGT	G	AB	R	H	2B	3B	HR	RBI	BB	SO	SB	BA	SA
Berger, Johnny-John Henne	22PhiA 27WasA	08-27-01	Philadelphia, Pa.	05-09-79	R	R	5'9	165	11	16	1	5	0	0	0	1	2	3	1	.313	.313
Berger, Wally-Walter Antone	30-37BosN 37-38NYN 38-40CinN 40PhiN	10-10-05	Chicago, Ill.	11-30-88	R	R	6'2	198	1350	5163	809	1550	299	59	242	898	435	694	36	.300	.522
Berres, Ray-Raymond Frederick	34,36BknN 37-40PitN 40-41BosN 42-45NYN	08-31-07	Kenosha, Wis.		R	R	5'9	170	561	1330	96	287	37	3	3	78	70	134	4	.216	.255
Berry, Charlie-Charles Francis	25PhiA 28-32BosA 32-33ChiA 34-36,38PhiA 25-26 played in N.F.L.	10-18-02	Phillipsburg, N.J.	09-06-72	R	R	6'	185	709	2018	196	539	88	29	23	256	160	196	13	.267	.374
Berry, Howard-Joseph Howard Jr. (Nig)	21-22NYN 21 played in N.F.L.	12-31-94	Philadelphia, Pa.	04-29-76	B	R	5'11	165	15	6	0	2	0	1	0	2	1	1	0	.333	.667
Bettencourt, Larry-Lawrence Joseph 33 played in N.F.L.	28,31-32StLA	09-22-05	Newark, Cal.	09-15-78	R	R	5'11	195	168	395	61	102	19	6	8	53	60	60	7	.258	.397
Bigbee, Carson-Carson Lee (Skeeter)	16-26PitN	03-31-95	Waterloo, Ore.	10-17-64	L	R	5'9	157	1147	4192	629	1205	139	75	17	324	344	161	182	.287	.369
Bigelow, Elliot-Elliot Allardice (Babe, Gilly)	29BosA	10-13-98	Tarpon Springs, Fla.	08-13-33	L	L	5'11	185	100	211	23	60	16	0	1	26	23	18	1	.284	.374
Biras, Steve-Stephen Alexander	44CleA	02-26-22	East St. Louis, Ill.	04-21-65	R	R	5'11	185	2	2	0	2	0	0	0	2	0	0	0	1.000	1.000
Bischoff, George-John George (Smiley)	25ChiA 25-26BosA	10-28-94	Edwardsville, Ill.	12-28-81	R	R	5'8	160	107	271	20	71	20	3	1	35	22	32	2	.262	.369
Bishop, Max-Max Frederick (Tilly, Camera Eye)	24-33PhiA 34-35BosA	09-05-99	Waynesboro, Pa.	02-24-62	L	R	5'8	165	1338	4494	966	1216	236	35	41	379	1153	452	43	.271	.366
Bissonette, Del-Adelphia Louis	28-31BknN 32LJ 33BknN M45BosN	09-06-99	Winthrop, Me.	06-09-72	L	L	5'11	180	604	2291	359	699	117	50	65	391	233	269	17	.305	.485
Black, Bill-John William (Jiggy)	24CinN	08-12-99	Philadelphia, Pa.	01-14-68	L	R	5'11	168	6	5	0	1	0	0	0	0	2	0	0	.200	.200
Blackerby, George-George Franklin	28ChiA	11-10-03	Gluther, Okla.	05-30-87	R	R	6'1	176	30	83	8	21	0	0	0	12	4	10	2	.253	.253
Blades, Ray-Francis Raymond	22-28,30-32,M39-40StLN M8BknN	08-06-96	Mt. Vernon, Ill.	05-18-79	R	R	5'8	163	767	2415	467	726	133	51	50	340	331	310	33	.301	.460
Blaemire, Rae-Rae Bertram	41NYN	12-23-75	Gary, Ind.		R	R	6'	185	2	5	0	2	0	0	0	0	0	0	0	.400	.400
Blair, Buddy-Louis Nathan	42PhiA 43-45MS	09-10-10	Columbia, Miss.	06-07-96	L	R	6'	186	137	484	48	135	26	8	5	66	30	30	1	.279	.397
Blair, Footsie-Clarence Vick	29-31ChiN	07-13-00	Interprise, Okla.	07-01-82	R	R	6'1	180	246	890	138	243	48	17	10	96	37	88	11	.273	.399
Blakely, Linc-Lincoln Howard (Blink)	34CinN	02-12-12	Oakland, Cal.	09-28-76	R	R	6'	180	34	102	11	23	1	1	0	10	5	14	1	.225	.255
Block, Cy-Seymour	42ChiN 43-44MS 45-46ChiN	05-04-19	Brooklyn, N.Y.	09-22-04	R	R	5'11	180	17	53	9	16	1	1	0	5	7	3	2	.302	.358
Bloodworth, Jimmy-James Henry	37,39-41WasA 42-43DetA 44-45MS 46DetA 47PitN 49-50CinN 50-51PhiN	07-26-17	Tallahassee, Fla.	08-17-02	R	R	5'11	180	1002	3519	347	874	160	20	62	451	202	407	19	.248	.358
Blott, Jack-John Leonard	24CinN	08-24-02	Girard, Ohio	06-11-64	R	R	6'	210	2	1	0	0	0	0	0	0	0	0	0	.000	.000
Blue, Lu-Luzerne Atwell	21-27DetA 28-30StLA 31-32ChiA 33BknN	03-05-97	Washington, D.C.	07-28-58	B	L	5'10	165	1615	5904	1151	1696	319	109	44	692	1092	436	150	.287	.401
Bluege, Ossie-Oswald Louis	22-39,M43-47WasA	10-24-00	Chicago, Ill.	10-14-85	R	R	5'11	162	1867	6440	883	1751	276	67	43	848	724	525	140	.272	.356
Bluege, Otto-Otto Adam (Squeaky)	32-33CinN	07-20-09	Chicago, Ill.	06-28-77	R	R	5'10	154	109	291	18	62	6	2	1	18	26	29	0	.213	.247
Bocek, Milt-Milton Francis	33-34ChiA	07-16-12	Chicago, Ill.		R	R	6'1	185	30	60	6	16	2	0	1	6	9	11	0	.267	.350
Boeckel, Tony-Norman Doxie (Elmer)	17PitN 18MS 19PitN 19-23BosN	08-25-92	Los Angeles, Cal.	02-16-24	R	R	5'10	175	777	2880	372	813	130	36	27	337	237	218	90	.282	.381
Bohne (Cohen), Sammy-Samuel Arthur	16StLN 21-26CinN 26BknN	10-22-96	San Francisco, Cal.	05-23-77	R	R	5'8	170	663	2315	309	605	87	45	16	228	193	154	75	.261	.359
Boken, Bob-Robert Anthony	33-34WasA 34CinN	02-23-08	Maryville, Ill.	10-06-88	R	R	6'2	165	147	457	54	113	15	4	6	72	27	49	4	.247	.337
Boland, Ed-Edward John	34-35PhiN 44BosN	04-18-08	Queens, N.Y.	02-05-93	L	L	5'10	165	57	136	11	35	5	1	0	23	4	14	2	.257	.309
Boley (Bolinsky), Joe-John Peter	27-32PhiA 32CleA	07-19-96	Mahanoy City, Pa.	12-30-62	R	R	5'11	170	540	1780	203	478	88	22	7	227	130	84	15	.269	.354
Bolling, Jack-John Edward	39PhiN 44BknN 45-46MS	02-20-17	Mobile, Ala.	04-13-98	L	L	5'11	168	125	342	48	107	25	1	4	38	25	14	6	.313	.427
Bolton, Cliff-William Clifton	31,33-36WasA 37DetA 41WasA	04-10-07	High Point, N.C.	04-21-79	L	R	5'9	160	335	962	113	280	49	18	6	143	108	50	3	.291	.398
Bolton, Glenn-Cecil Glenford (Lefty)	28CleA	02-13-04	Booneville, Miss.	08-25-93	L	L	6'4	195	4	13	1	2	0	2	0	2	0	1	0	.154	.462
Bongiovanni, Nino-Anthony Thomas	38-39CinN	12-21-11	New Orleans, La.		L	L	5'10	175	68	166	17	43	7	0	0	16	9	8	0	.259	.301
Bonura, Zeke-Henry John	34-37ChiA 38WasA 39NYN 40WasA 40CinN 41-45MS	09-20-08	New Orleans, La.	03-09-87	R	R	6'	210	917	3582	600	1099	232	29	119	703	404	180	19	.307	.487
Bool, Al-Albert	28WasA 30PitN 31BosN	08-24-97	Lincoln, Neb.	09-27-81	R	R	6'	185	129	308	35	73	13	4	7	53	34	42	0	.237	.373
Boone, Ike-Isaac Morgan	22NYN 23-25BosA 27ChiA 30-32BknN	02-17-97	Samantha, Ala.	08-01-58	L	R	5'11	195	356	1159	176	370	78	11	26	192	140	68	3	.319	.473
Bordagaray, Frenchy-Stanley George	34ChiA 35-36BknN 37-38StLN 39CinN 41NYA 42-45BknN	01-03-10	Coalinga, Cal.	04-13-00	R	R	5'7	175	930	2632	410	745	120	28	14	270	173	186	65	.283	.366
Borom, Red-Edward Jones	44-45DetA	10-30-15	Spartanburg, S.C.		L	R	5'11	180	62	144	20	36	4	0	0	10	9	10	4	.250	.278
Boss, Harley-Elmer Harley (Lefty)	28-30WasA 33CleA	11-19-08	Hodge, La.	05-15-64	L	L	5'11	190	155	519	64	139	19	8	1	61	30	34	2	.268	.341
Bottarini, John-John Charles	37ChiN	09-14-08	Crockett, Cal.	10-08-76	R	R	6'	190	26	40	3	11	3	0	1	7	5	10	0	.275	.425
Bottomley, Jim-James LeRoy (Sunny Jim)	22-32StLN 33-35CinN 36-37,M37StLA	04-23-00	Oglesby, Ill.	12-11-59	L	L	6'	180	1991	7471	1177	2313	465	151	219	1422	664	591	58	.310	.500
Boudreau, Lou-Louis	38-50,M42-50CleA 51-52,M52-54BosA M55-57KCA M60CnN 38-39 played in N.B.L., 39-40 head coach in N.B.L.	07-17-17	Harvey, Ill.	08-10-01	R	R	5'11	185	1646	6029	861	1779	385	66	68	789	796	309	51	.295	.415
Bowman, Elmer-Elmari Wilhelm	20WasA	03-19-97	Proctor, Vt.	12-17-85	R	R	6'	193	2	1	0	0	0	0	0	0	0	0	0	.000	.000
Bowman, Joe-Joseph Emil (See P20-45)	32PhiA 34NYN 35-36PhiN 37-41PitN 44-45BosA 45CinN	03-17-10	Argentine, Kans.	11-22-90	L	R	6'2	190	430	639	62	141	24	8	2	75	46	90	3	.221	.293
Boyle, Buzz-Ralph Francis	29-30BosN 33-35BknN	02-09-08	Cincinnati, Ohio	11-12-78	L	L	5'11	170	366	1343	185	389	58	24	12	125	116	125	24	.290	.395
Boyle, Jim-James John	26NYN	01-19-04	Cincinnati, Ohio	12-24-58	R	R	6'	190	1	0	0	0	0	0	0	0	0	0	0	—	—
Brack, Gib-Gilbert Herman (Gibby)	37-38BknN 38-39PhiN	03-29-08	Chicago, Ill.	01-20-60	R	R	5'9	170	315	980	150	273	70	18	16	113	92	186	13	.279	.436
Bradford, Vic-Henry Victor	43NYN 44-46MS	03-05-15	Brownsville, Tenn.	06-10-94	R	R	6'2	190	6	5	1	1	0	0	0	1	1	1	0	.200	.200
Brady, Cliff-Clifford Francis	20BosA	03-06-97	St. Louis, Mo.	09-25-74	R	R	5'6	140	53	180	16	41	5	1	0	12	13	12	0	.228	.267
Bragan, Bobby-Robert Randall	40-42PhiN 43-44BknN 45-46MS 47-48BknN M56-57PitN M58CleA M63-65MilN M66AtLN	10-30-17	Birmingham, Ala.		R	R	5'10	175	597	1900	136	456	62	12	15	172	110	117	12	.240	.309
Bramhall, Art-Arthur Washington	35PhiN	02-22-09	Oak Park, Ill.	09-04-85	R	R	5'11	170	2	1	0	0	0	0	0	0	0	0	0	.000	.000
Brancato, Al-Albert	39-41PhiA 42-44MS 45PhiA	05-29-19	Philadelphia, Pa.		R	R	5'10	188	282	930	117	199	37	11	4	80	96	92	5	.214	.290
Brannan, Otis-Otis Owen	28-29StLA	03-13-99	Greenbrier, Ark.	06-06-67	R	R	5'9	160	158	534	72	133	19	3	11	74	64	23	3	.249	.358
Branom, Dud-Edgar Dudley	27PhiA	11-30-97	Sulphur Springs, Tex.	02-04-80	L	R	6'1	190	30	94	8	22	3	0	0	13	2	5	2	.234	.254
Bratcher, Joe-Joseph Warlick (Goobers)	24StLN	07-22-98	Grand Saline, Tex.	10-13-77	L	R	5'8	140	4	1	1	0	0	0	0	0	0	0	0	.000	.000
Bratschi, Fred-Frederick Oscar (Fritz)	21ChiA 26-27BosA	01-10-92	Alliance, Ohio	01-16-62	R	R	5'9	175	89	196	12	54	11	1	0	22	14	17	0	.276	.342
Bray, Buster-Clarence Wilbur	41BosN	04-01-13	Birmingham, Ala.	09-04-82	L	L	6'	170	4	11	2	1	0	0	0	1	1	2	0	.091	.182
Brazill, Frank-Frank Leo	21-22PhiA	08-11-99	Spangler, Pa.	11-03-76	L	L	5'11	175	72	190	17	49	3	1	0	20	23	22	2	.258	.284
Bremer, Herb-Herbert Frederick	37-39StLN	10-26-13	Chicago, Ill.	11-28-79	R	R	6'2	195	70	193	16	41	6	1	2	18	11	42	1	.212	.285
Brenzel, Bill-William Richard	32PitN 34-35CleA	03-03-10	Oakland, Cal.	06-12-79	R	R	5'10	173	76	217	16	43	9	1	0	19	8	15	2	.198	.249
Bessler, Rube-Raymond Bloom (See P01-19)	14-16PhiA 17-27CinN 28BknN 32PhiN 32StLN	10-23-94	Coder, Pa.	11-07-66	L	L	6'	187	1305	3881	544	1171	164	87	32	586	449	246	47	.302	.414
Brewster, Charlie-Chales Lawrence	43CinN 44PhiN 44CinN 46CleA	12-27-16	Marthaville, La.	10-01-00	R	R	5'9	175	69	213	17	47	4	0	0	14	16	28	1	.221	.239
Brickell, Fred-George Frederick	26-30PitN 30-33PhiN	11-09-06	Saffordville, Kans.	04-08-61	L	R	5'7	160	501	1448	221	407	54	23	6	131	106	121	19	.281	.363
Brittain, Gus-August Schuster	37CinN	11-29-09	Wilmington, N.C.	02-16-74	R	R	5'10	192	3	6	0	1	0	0	0	0	1	1	0	.167	.167
Brooks (Brozek), Mandy-Jonathan Joseph	25-26ChiN	08-19-97	Milwaukee, Wis.	06-17-62	R	R	5'9	165	116	397	62	107	26	7	15	78	24	33	10	.270	.484
Broskie, Siggy-Sigmund Theodore (Chaps)	40BosN	03-23-11	Iselin, Pa.	05-17-75	R	R	5'11	200	11	22	1	6	1	0	0	4	1	2	0	.273	.318
Brottem, Tony-Anton Christian	16,18StLN 21WasA 21PitN	04-30-91	Halstad, Minn.	08-05-29	R	R	6'	176	62	135	10	29	3	1	0	13	9	22	1	.215	.237
Brower, Frank-Frank Willard (Turkeyfoot)	20-22WasA 23-24CleA	03-26-93	Gainesville, Va.	11-20-60	R	R	6'2	180	450	1297	206	371	74	20	30	205	168	84	17	.286	.443
Brower, Lou-Louis Lester	31DetA	07-01-00	Cleveland, Ohio	03-04-94	R	R	5'10	155	21	62	3	10	1	0	0	6	8	5	1	.161	.177
Brown, Eddie-Edward William (Glass Arm Eddie)	20-21NYN 24-25BknN 26-28BosN	07-17-91	Milligan, Neb.	09-10-56	R	R	6'	190	790	2902	341	878	170	33	16	407	127	109	29	.303	.400
Brown, Jimmy-James Roberson	37-43StLN 44-45MS 46PhiN	04-25-10	Jamesville, N.C.	12-29-77	B	R	5'8	165	890	3512	465	980	146	42	9	319	231	110	39	.279	.352
Brown, Lindsay-John Lindsay (Red)	37BknN	07-22-11	Mason, Tex.	01-01-67	R	R	5'10	160	48	115	16	31	3	1	0	6	3	17	1	.270	.313
Browne, Earl-Earl James (Snitz)	35-36PhiN 37-38PhiN	03-05-11	Louisville, Ky.	01-12-93	L	L	6'	175	143	461	59	131	26	5	6	69	29	64	4	.284	.401
Brubaker, Bill-Wilbur Lee	32-40PitN 43BosN	11-07-10	Cleveland, Ohio	04-02-78	R	R	6'2	190	479	1564	208	413	85	10	22	225	151	239	13	.264	.373
Brucker, Earle-Earle Francis Sr.	37-40,43PhiA M52CinN	05-06-01	Albany, N.Y.	05-08-81	R	R	5'11	175	241	707	87	205	53	8	12	105	97	65	2	.290	.438
Bruggy, Frank-Frank Leo	21PhiN 22-24PhiA 25CinN	05-04-91	Elizabeth, N.J.	04-05-59	R	R	5'11	195	259	620	53	172	27	2	6	52	43	72	12	.277	.356
Bubser, Hal-Harold Frederick	22ChiA	09-28-95	Chicago, Ill.	06-22-59	R	R	5'11	170	3	0	0	0	0	0	0	0	0	0	0	.000	.000
Bucher, Jim-James Quinter	34-37BknN 38StLN 44-45BosN	03-24-11	Manassas, Va.	10-21-04	L	R	5'11	170	554	1792	242	474	66	19	17	193	91	113	19	.265	.351
Burgo, Bill-William Ross	43-44PhiA	11-15-19	Johnstown, Pa.	10-19-88	R	R	5'8	185	44	158	18	47	8	2	2	12	11	4	1	.297	.399
Burich, Bill-William Max	42PhiN 43-45MS 46PhiN	05-29-18	Calumet, Mich.		R	R	6'	180	27	81	4	23	1	0	0	7	6	13	2	.284	.296
Burke, Les-Leslie Kingston (Buck)	23-26DetA	12-18-02	Lynn, Mass.	05-06-75	R	R	5'9	168	194	506	73	131	17	7	0	47	46	32	7	.259	.320
Burke, Pat-Patrick Edward	24StLA	05-13-01	St. Louis, Mo.	07-07-65	R	R	5'11	170	1	3	0	0	0	0	0	0	0	0	0	.000	.000
Burnett, Johnny-John Henderson	27-34CleA 35StLA	11-01-04	Bartow, Fla.	08-12-59	L	R	5'11	175	558	1835	288	521	94	19	9	213	163	107	15	.284	.366
Burns, George-George Henry (Tioga George)	14-17PhiA 18-20BosA 22-23BosA 24-28CleA 28-29NYN 29PhiA	01-31-93	Niles, Ohio	01-07-78	R	R	5'11	175	1866	6573	901	2018	444	72	72	948	363	433	153	.307	.429
Burns, Jack-John Irving (Slug)	30-36StLA 36DetA	08-31-07	Cambridge, Mass.	04-18-75	L	L	6'1	175	890	3516	541	980	199	31	44	417	376	299	63	.279	.391
Burns, Joe-Joseph Francis	24ChiA	02-25-00	Trenton, N.J.	01-07-86	R	R	6'	175	8	19	1	2	0	0	0	0	1	2	0	.105	.105

USE NAME - GIVEN NAMES (NICKNAMES)	TEAM BY YEAR	BIRTH DATE	BIRTH PLACE	DEATH DATE	B	T	HGT	WGT	G	AB	R	H	2B	3B	HR	RBI	BB	SO	SB	BA	SA
Burns, Joe-Joseph James	43BosN 44-45PhiA	06-17-15	Bryn Mawr, Pa.	06-24-74	R	R	5'10	175	111	300	24	69	6	1	2	16	16	50	2	.230	.277
Burrus, Dick-Maurice Lennon	20-21PhiA 25-28BosN	01-29-98	Hatteras, N.C.	02-02-72	L	L	5'11	175	560	1760	206	513	87	12	11	211	138	95	18	.291	.373
Busby, Paul-Paul Miller (Red)	41,43PhiN	08-25-18	Waynesboro, Miss.		R	R	6'1	175	36	56	16	15	1	0	0	7	2	2	2	.268	.286
Busch, Ed-Edgar John	43-45PhiA	11-16-17	Lebanon, Ill.	01-11-87	R	R	5'10	175	270	917	80	240	21	6	0	75	62	28	7	.262	.298
Buskey, Joe-Joseph Henry (Jazzbow)	26PhiN	12-18-02	Cumberland, Md.	04-11-49	R	R	5'10	175	5	8	1	0	0	0	0	0	0	1	0	.000	.000
Butka, Ed-Edward Luke (Babe)	43-44WasA	01-07-16	Canonsburg, Pa.	04-21-05	R	R	6'3	193	18	50	1	11	2	0	0	2	2	14	0	.220	.260
Butler, Johnny-John Stephen (Trolley Line)	26-27BknN 28ChiN 29StLN	03-20-93	Fall River, Kans.	04-29-67	R	R	6'	175	375	1251	115	315	48	12	3	146	11	89	17	.252	.317
Buzas, Joe-Joseph John	45NYA	10-02-19	Alpha, N.J.	03-19-03	R	R	6'1	180	30	65	8	17	2	1	0	6	2	5	2	.262	.323
Byrd, Sammy-Samuel Dewey (Babe Ruth's Legs)	29-34NYA 35-36CinN	10-15-06	Bremen, Ga.	05-11-81	R	R	5'10	175	745	1700	304	465	101	10	38	220	198	178	17	.274	.412
Byrnes, Milt-Milton John (Skippy)	43-45StLA	11-15-16	St. Louis, Mo.	02-01-79	L	L	5'10	170	390	1278	174	350	77	15	16	154	200	183	3	.274	.395
Cafego, Tom-Thomas	37StLA	08-21-11	Whipple, W.Va.	10-29-61	L	R	5'10	160	4	4	1	0	0	0	0	0	0	1	0	.000	.000
Caithamer, Sidel-George Theodore	34ChiA	07-22-10	Chicago, Ill.	06-01-54	R	R	5'8	160	5	19	1	6	1	0	0	3	1	5	0	.316	.368
Caldwell, Bruce-Bruce 28 played in N.F.L.	28CleA 32BknN	02-08-06	Ashton, R.I.	02-15-59	R	R	6'	195	25	38	4	7	1	1	0	5	4	4	1	.184	.263
Callaghan, Marty-Martin Francis	22-23ChiN 28,30CinN	06-09-00	Norwood, Mass.	06-24-75	L	R	5'10	157	295	767	106	205	28	13	0	74	71	70	10	.267	.338
Callaway, Frank-Frank Burnett	21-22PhiA	02-26-98	Knoxville, Tenn.	08-21-87	R	R	6'	170	43	98	12	25	1	3	0	6	2	24	1	.255	.327
Camilli, Dolph-Adolph Louis	33-34ChiN 34-37PhiN 38-43BknN 44MS 45BosA	04-23-07	San Francisco, Cal.	10-21-97	L	L	5'10	185	1490	5353	936	1482	261	86	239	950	947	961	60	.277	.492
Campanis(Campani), Al(Alessandro)-Alexander Sebastian	43BknN 44-45MS	11-02-16	Kos, Greece	06-21-98	B	R	6'	185	7	20	3	2	0	0	0	0	4	5	0	.100	.100
Campbell, Bruce-Bruce Douglas	30-32ChiA 32-34StLA 35-39CleA 40-41DetA 42WasA 43-45MS	10-20-09	Chicago, Ill.	06-17-95	R	R	6'1	185	1360	4762	759	1382	295	87	106	766	548	584	53	.290	.455
Campbell, Gilly-William Gilthorpe	33ChiN 35-37CinN 38BknN	02-13-08	Kansas City, Kans.	02-21-73	L	R	5'11	176	295	708	78	186	30	2	5	93	116	35	5	.263	.332
Campbell, Soup-Clarence	40-41CleA 42-46MS	03-07-15	Sparta, Va.	02-16-00	L	R	6'1	188	139	390	44	96	11	4	3	37	38	33	1	.246	.318
Capri, Pat-Patrick Nicholas	44BknN	11-27-18	New York, N.Y.	06-14-89	R	R	6'	170	7	1	1	0	0	0	0	0	0	0	0	.000	.000
Carey (Carnarius), Max (Maximilian)-Max George (Scoops)	10-26PitN 26-29,M32-33BknN	01-11-90	Terre Haute, Ind.	05-30-76	B	R	5'11	170	2476	9363	1545	2665	419	159	69	800	1040	695	738	.285	.385
Carey, Tom-Thomas Francis Aloysious (Scoops)	35-37StLA 39-42,46BosA 43-45MS	10-11-08	Hoboken, N.J.	02-21-70	R	R	5'8	175	466	1521	169	418	79	13	2	169	66	75	3	.275	.348
Carlin, Jim-James Arthur	41PhiN 42-45MS	02-23-18	Wylam, Ala.		L	R	5'11	165	16	21	2	3	1	0	1	2	3	4	0	.143	.333
Carlyle, Cleo-Hiram Cleo	27BosA	09-07-02	Fairburn, Ga.	11-12-67	L	R	6'	195	95	278	31	65	12	8	1	28	36	40	4	.234	.345
Carlyle, Roy-Roy Edward (Dizzy)	25WasA 25-26BosA 26NYA	12-10-00	Buford, Ga.	11-22-56	L	R	6'2	195	174	494	61	157	31	6	9	76	24	57	1	.318	.460
Carnett, Eddie-Edwin Elliott (Lefty) (See P20-45)	41BosN 44ChiA 45CleA 46MS	10-21-16	Springfield, Mo.		L	L	6'	185	158	530	56	142	25	8	1	67	28	44	5	.268	.351
Carson, Kit-Walter Lloyd	34-35CleA	11-15-12	Colton, Cal.	06-21-83	L	L	6'	180	21	40	5	10	4	1	0	2	4	9	0	.250	.400
Carter, Blackie-Otis Leonard	25-26NYN	09-30-02	Langley, S.C.	09-10-76	R	R	5'10	175	6	21	4	4	1	0	1	1	1	1	0	.190	.381
Carter, Howard-John Howard (Nick)	26CinN	10-13-04	New York, N.Y.	07-24-91	R	R	5'10	154	5	1	0	0	0	0	0	0	0	0	0	.000	.000
Case, George-George Washington	37-45WasA 46CleA 47WasA	11-11-15	Trenton, N.J.	01-23-89	R	R	6'	183	1226	5016	785	1415	233	43	21	377	426	297	349	.282	.358
Castiglia, Jim-James Vincent 41,45-48 played in N.F.L. 47 played in A.A.F.C.	42PhiA 43-45MS	09-30-18	Passaic, N.J.		L	R	5'11	200	16	18	2	7	0	0	0	2	1	3	0	.389	.389
Castino, Vince-Vincent Charles	43-45ChiA	10-11-17	Willisville, Ill.	03-06-67	R	R	5'9	175	88	215	24	49	7	0	2	23	25	31	0	.228	.288
Cather, Ted-Theodore Physick	12-14StLN 14-15BosN	05-20-89	Chester, Pa.	04-09-45	R	R	5'10	178	201	548	60	138	30	8	2	72	34	90	21	.252	.347
Cavarretta, Phil-Philip Joseph	34-53,M51-53ChiN 54-55ChiA	07-19-16	Chicago, Ill.		L	L	5'11	175	2030	6754	990	1977	347	99	95	920	820	598	65	.293	.416
Caveney, Ike-James Christopher	22-25CinN	12-10-94	San Francisco, Cal.	07-06-49	R	R	5'9	168	466	1577	173	410	61	24	13	196	97	126	15	.260	.354
Chamberlain, Joe-Joseph Jeremiah	34ChiA	05-10-10	San Francisco, Cal.	01-28-83	R	R	6'1	170	43	141	13	34	5	1	2	17	6	38	1	.241	.333
Chaplin (Chapman), Bert-Bert Edgar (Chappy)	20-22BosA	09-25-93	Pelzer, S.C.	08-15-78	L	R	5'7	158	35	76	10	14	2	1	0	7	13	11	2	.184	.237
Chapman, Ben-William Benjamin (See P20-45)	30-36NYA 36-37WasA 37-38BosA 39-40CleA 41WasA 41CinN 44-45BknN 45-46,M45StLA	12-25-08	Nashville, Tenn.	07-07-93	R	R	6'	190	1717	6478	1144	1958	407	107	90	977	824	556	287	.302	.440
Chapman, Calvin-Calvin Louis	35-36CinN	12-20-10	Courtland, Miss.	04-01-83	R	R	5'9	160	111	272	41	72	8	3	1	25	20	24	7	.265	.327
Chapman, Fred-William Fred (Chappie)	34-41PhiA 42-45MS	07-17-16	Liberty, N.Y.	03-27-97	R	R	6'1	185	76	187	12	36	3	1	0	9	11	28	3	.193	.219
Chapman, Glenn-Glenn Justice (Pete)	34BknN	01-26-06	Cambridge City, Ind.	11-05-88	R	R	5'11	170	67	93	19	26	5	1	1	10	7	19	1	.280	.387
Chapman, John-John Joseph	24PhiN	10-15-99	Centralia, Pa.	11-03-53	R	R	5'10	175	19	71	7	20	4	1	0	6	3	3	0	.282	.366
Chartak, Mike-Michael George (Shotgun)	40,42NYA 42WasA 42-44StLA	04-28-16	Brooklyn, N.Y.	07-25-67	L	L	6'2	180	256	765	96	186	34	7	21	98	104	112	4	.243	.388
Chatham, Buster-Charles L.	30-31BosN	12-25-01	West, Tex.	12-15-75	R	R	5'5	150	129	448	52	118	21	11	6	59	43	47	8	.263	.400
Chervinko, Paul-Paul	37-38BknN	07-23-10	Trauger, Pa.	06-03-76	R	R	5'8	185	42	75	1	11	0	1	0	5	5	16	0	.147	.173
Chiozza, Dino-Dino Joseph (Dynamo)	35PhiN	06-30-12	Memphis, Tenn.	04-23-72	L	R	6'	170	2	0	1	0	0	0	0	0	0	0	0	--	--
Chiozza, Lou-Louis Peo	34-36PhiN 37-39NYN	05-11-10	Tallulah, La.	02-28-71	L	R	6'	172	616	2288	303	633	107	22	14	197	145	165	45	.277	.361
Chipple (Chlipala), Walt-Walter John	45WasA	09-26-18	Utica, N.Y.	06-08-88	R	R	6'	168	18	44	4	6	0	0	0	5	5	6	0	.136	.136
Chozen, Harry-Harry (Choz)	37CinN	09-27-15	Winnebago, Minn.	09-16-94	R	R	5'9	190	1	4	0	1	0	0	0	0	0	0	0	.250	.250
Christenbury, Lloyd-Lloyd Reid (Low)	19-22BosN	10-19-93	Mecklenburg Co., N.C.	12-13-44	L	R	5'7	165	205	414	78	113	14	6	4	47	54	32	5	.273	.365
Christensen, Cuckoo-Walter Neils (Seacap)	26-27CinN	10-24-99	San Francisco, Cal.	12-20-84	L	L	5'6	156	171	514	66	162	21	7	0	57	60	34	12	.315	.383
Christman, Mark-Marquette Joseph	38-39DetA 39,43-46StLA 47-49WasA	10-21-13	Maplewood, Mo.	10-09-76	R	R	5'11	175	911	3081	294	781	113	23	19	348	220	179	17	.253	.344
Churry, John-John	24-27ChiN	11-26-00	Johnstown, Pa.	02-08-70	R	R	5'9	172	12	18	1	5	1	0	0	3	0	3	0	.278	.333
Cicero, Joe-Joseph Francis (Dode)	29-30BosA 45PhiA	11-18-10	Atlantic City, N.J.	03-30-83	R	R	5'8	167	40	81	14	18	3	4	0	8	2	13	0	.222	.358
Cieslak, Ted-Theodore Walter	44PhiN	11-22-12	Milwaukee, Wis.	05-09-93	R	R	5'10	175	85	220	18	54	10	0	2	11	21	17	1	.245	.318
Cihocki, Al-Albert Joseph	45CleA	05-07-24	Nanticoke, Pa.		R	R	5'11	185	92	283	21	60	9	3	0	24	11	48	2	.212	.265
Cihocki, Ed-Edward Joseph (Cy)	32-33PhiA	05-09-07	Wilmington, Del.	11-09-87	R	R	5'8	163	34	98	6	14	2	1	0	9	7	16	0	.143	.224
Cisar, George-George Joseph	37BknN	08-25-12	Chicago, Ill.		R	R	6'	175	20	29	8	6	0	0	0	2	4	6	3	.207	.207
Cissell, Bill-Chalmer William	28-32ChiA 32-33CleA 34BosA 37PhiA 38NYN	01-03-04	Perryville, Mo.	03-15-49	R	R	5'11	170	956	3706	516	990	173	43	29	423	212	250	114	.267	.368
Clabaugh, Moose-John William	26BknN	11-13-01	Albany, Mo.	07-11-84	L	R	6'	185	11	14	2	1	0	0	0	0	0	5	0	.071	.143
Claire, Dave-David Matthew	20CleA	11-17-97	Ludington, Mich.	01-07-56	R	R	5'7	170	3	7	1	1	0	0	0	0	0	0	0	.143	.143
Clancy, Bud-John William	24-30ChiA 32BknN 34PhiN	09-15-00	Odell, Ill.	09-27-68	L	L	6'	170	522	1796	204	504	69	26	12	198	111	106	19	.281	.368
Clanton, Uke-Ucal (Cat)	22CleA	12-01-98	Powell, Mo.	02-24-60	L	L	5'8	160	1	2	0	0	0	0	0	1	0	1	0	.000	.000
Clark, Cap-John Carrol	38PhiN	09-19-06	Snow Camp, N.C.	02-16-57	L	R	5'11	180	52	74	11	19	1	0	0	4	9	10	0	.257	.297
Clark, Danny-Daniel Curran	22DetA 24BosA 27StLN	01-18-94	Meridian, Miss.	05-23-37	L	R	5'9	167	245	582	75	161	36	8	5	93	74	37	5	.277	.392
Clark, Earl-Bailey Earl	27-33BosN 34StLA	11-06-07	Washington, D.C.	01-16-38	R	R	5'10	170	293	826	122	240	41	7	4	81	37	79	11	.291	.372
Clarke, Grey-Richard Grey (Noisy)	44ChiA	09-26-12	Fulton, Ala.	11-25-93	R	R	5'9	183	63	169	14	44	10	1	0	27	22	6	0	.260	.331
Clarke, Stu-William Stuart	29-30PhiN	12-04-06	San Francisco, Cal.	08-26-85	R	R	5'8	160	61	187	22	51	5	8	2	23	20	21	3	.273	.417
Clarke, Sumpter-Sumpter Mills	20ChiN 23-24BosN	10-18-97	Savannah, Ga.	03-16-62	R	R	5'11	170	37	110	17	25	4	1	1	11	6	13	0	.227	.300
Clary, Ellis-Ellis (Cat)	42-43WasA 43-45StLA	09-11-16	Valdosta, Ga.	06-02-00	R	R	5'8	160	223	650	97	171	32	2	1	46	114	74	12	.263	.323
Clay, Dain-Dain Elmer (Ding-a-Ling)	43-46CinN	07-10-19	Hicksville, Ohio	08-28-94	R	R	5'10	160	433	1540	203	397	63	6	3	98	115	130	39	.258	.312
Clemens, Chet-Spurgeon Chester	39,44BosN 45-46MS	05-10-17	San Fernando, Cal.	02-10-02	R	R	6'	175	28	40	9	8	3	0	0	3	3	5	1	.200	.275
Clemons, Verne-Verne James (Fats, Tubby, Stinger)	16StLA 19-24StLN	09-08-91	Clemons, Iowa	05-05-59	R	R	5'10	190	474	1271	78	364	56	11	5	140	119	62	6	.286	.380
Clift, Harlond-Harlond Benton (Darkie)	34-43StLA 43-45WasA	08-12-12	El Reno, Okla.	04-27-92	R	R	5'11	180	1582	5730	1070	1558	309	62	178	829	1070	713	69	.272	.441
Clifton, Flea-Herman Earl	34-37DetA	12-12-09	Cincinnati, Ohio	12-22-97	R	R	5'10	160	87	195	27	39	7	0	0	13	17	28	5	.200	.236
Clough, Ed-Edgar George (Spec) (See P20-45)	24-26StLN	10-28-06	Wiconisco, Pa.	01-30-44	L	L	6'2	188	11	19	0	2	0	0	0	1	0	3	0	.105	.105
Coble, Dave-David Lamar	39PhiN	12-24-12	Monroe, N.C.	10-15-71	R	R	6'1	183	15	25	2	7	1	0	0	4	5	0	0	.280	.320
Cochrane, Mickey-Gordon Stanley (Black Mike)	25-33PhiA 34-37,M34-38DetA	04-06-03	Bridgewater, Mass.	06-28-62	L	R	5'10	180	1482	5169	1041	1652	333	64	119	832	857	217	64	.320	.478
Cohen, Alta-Alta Albert	31-32BknN 33PhiN	12-25-08	New York, N.Y.	03-11-03	L	L	5'10	170	29	67	8	13	2	0	0	2	9	11	0	.194	.224
Cohen, Andy-Andrew Howard	26,28-29NYN M60PhiN	10-25-04	Baltimore, Md.	10-29-88	R	R	5'8	155	262	886	106	249	36	10	14	114	43	34	6	.281	.392
Coleman, Ed-Parke Edward	32-35PhiA 36-37StLA	12-01-01	Canby, Ore.	08-05-64	L	R	6'2	200	439	1337	193	381	67	23	40	246	117	152	1	.285	.459
Collins, Bob-Robert Joseph (Rip)	40ChiN 44NYA	09-18-09	Pittsburgh, Pa.	04-19-89	R	R	5'11	176	50	123	11	26	3	0	1	14	15	18	4	.211	.260
Collins, Eddie-Edward Trowbridge Jr.	39,41-42PhiA 43-45MS	11-23-16	Lansdowne, Pa.	11-02-00	R	R	5'10	175	132	274	41	66	9	3	0	16	24	29	4	.241	.296
Collins, Pat-Tharon Leslie	19-24StLA 26-28NYA 29BosN	09-13-96	Sweet Springs, Mo.	05-20-60	R	R	5'10	175	542	1203	146	306	46	6	33	168	235	201	4	.240	.385
Collins, Ripper-James Anthony	31-36StLN 37-38ChiN 41PhiN	03-30-04	Altoona, Pa.	04-16-70	B	L	5'9	165	1084	3784	615	1121	205	65	135	659	356	373	18	.296	.492
Colman, Frank-Frank Lloyd	42-48PitN 46-47NYA	03-02-18	London, Canada	02-19-83	L	L	5'11	186	271	571	66	130	25	8	15	106	49	68	0	.228	.378
Combs, Earle-Earle Bryan (The Kentucky Colonel, The Mail Carrier)	24-35NYA	05-04-99	Pebworth, Ky.	07-21-76	L	R	6'	185	1455	5746	1186	1866	309	154	58	632	670	278	96	.325	.462
Comorosky, Adam-Adam Anthony	26-33PitN 34-35CinN	12-09-04	Swoyersville, Pa.	03-02-51	R	R	5'11	170	813	2787	404	795	134	51	28	417	214	158	57	.285	.400
Conlan, Jocko-John Bertrand	34-35ChiA	12-06-99	Chicago, Ill.	04-16-89	L	L	5'7	165	128	365	55	96	18	4	0	31	33	13	5	.263	.334
Conlon, Art-Arthur Joseph (Jocko)	23BosN	12-10-97	Woburn, Mass.	08-05-87	R	R	5'7	145	59	147	23	32	3	0	0	17	11	11	0	.218	.238

USE NAME - GIVEN NAMES (NICKNAMES)	TEAM BY YEAR	BIRTH DATE	BIRTH PLACE	DEATH DATE	B	T	HGT	WGT	G	AB	R	H	2B	3B	HR	RBI	BB	SO	SB	BA	SA
Connatser, Bruce-Broadus Milburn	31-32CleA	09-19-02	Sevierville, Tenn.	01-27-71	R	R	5'11	170	35	109	13	28	6	1	0	8	6	11	1	.257	.330
Connell, Gene-Eugene Joseph	31PhiN	05-10-06	Hazelton, Pa.	08-31-37	R	R	6'	180	6	12	1	3	0	0	0	0	0	5	0	.250	.250
Connell, Joe-Joseph Bernard	26NYN	01-16-02	Bethlehem, Pa.	09-21-77	L	L	5'8	165	2	1	1	0	0	0	0	0	0	0	0	.000	.000
Connelly, Tom-Thomas Martin	20-21NYA	10-20-97	Chicago, Ill.	02-18-41	R	R	5'11	165	5	6	0	1	0	0	0	0	1	0	0	.167	.167
Connolly, Bud-Mervin Thomas (Mike)	25BosA	05-25-01	San Francisco, Cal.	06-12-64	R	R	5'8	154	43	107	12	28	7	1	0	21	23	9	0	.262	.346
Connolly, Ed-Edward Joseph Sr.	29-32BosA	07-17-08	Brooklyn, N.Y.	11-12-63	R	R	5'9	180	149	371	13	66	11	4	0	31	29	50	0	.178	.229
Connolly, Joe-Joseph George (Coaster Joe)	21NYN 22-23CleA 24BosA	06-04-96	San Francisco, Cal.	03-30-60	R	R	6'	180	80	168	32	45	12	2	3	32	21	18	2	.268	.417
Connors, Merv-Mervin James	37-38ChiA	01-23-14	Berkeley, Cal.	01-10-06	R	R	6'2	192	52	165	26	46	8	1	8	25	23	36	2	.279	.485
Conroy, Bill-William Gordon	35-37PhiA 42-44BosA 45MS	02-26-15	Bloomington, Ill.	11-13-97	R	R	6'	185	169	452	45	90	13	3	5	33	77	85	3	.199	.274
Conroy, Pep-William Frederick	23WasA	01-09-99	Chicago, Ill.	01-23-70	R	R	5'8	160	18	60	6	8	2	2	0	2	4	9	0	.133	.233
Cooke, Dusty-Allen Lindsey	30-32NYA 33-36BosA 38CinN M48PhiN	06-23-07	Swepsonville, N.C.	11-21-87	L	R	6'1	205	608	1745	324	488	109	28	24	229	290	276	32	.280	.415
Cooney, Jimmy-James Edward (Scoops)	17BosA 18MS 19NYN 24-25StLN 26-27ChiN 27PhiN 28BosN	08-24-94	Cranston, R.I.	08-07-91	R	R	5'11	160	448	1575	181	413	64	16	2	150	76	58	30	.262	.327
Cooney, Johnny-John Walter (See P20-45)	21-30,38-42BosN 35-37,43-44BknN 44NYA M49BosN	03-18-01	Cranston, R.I.	07-08-86	R	L	5'10	165	1172	3372	408	965	130	26	2	219	208	107	30	.286	.342
Corbett, Gene-Eugene Louis	36-38PhiN	10-25-13	Winona, Minn.		L	R	6'2	190	37	108	12	13	3	0	2	10	8	14	0	.120	.204
Corgan, Chuck-Charles Howard 24-27 played in N.F.L.	25,27BknN	12-04-02	Wagoner, Okla.	06-13-28	B	R	6'	185	33	104	7	23	2	1	0	1	7	13	0	.221	.260
Cortazzo, Shine-John Francis	23ChiA	09-26-04	Wilmerding, Pa.	03-04-63	R	R	5'4	142	1	1	0	0	0	0	0	0	0	0	0	.000	.000
Coscarart, Joe-Joseph Marvin	35-36BosN	11-18-09	Escondido, Cal.	04-05-93	R	R	6'	185	190	651	58	157	22	4	3	73	35	65	2	.241	.301
Coscarart, Pete-Pete Joseph	38-41BknN 42-46PitN	06-16-13	Escondido, Cal.	07-24-02	R	R	5'11	175	864	2992	399	728	129	22	28	269	295	361	34	.243	.329
Cote, Pete-Warren Peter	26NYN	08-30-02	Cambridge, Mass.	10-17-87	R	R	5'6	148	2	1	0	0	0	0	0	0	0	0	0	.000	.000
Cotter, Ed-Edward Christopher	26PhiN	07-04-04	Hartford, Conn.	06-14-59	R	R	6'	185	17	26	3	8	0	1	0	1	1	4	1	.308	.385
Cotter, Harvey-Harvey Louis (Hooks)	22,24ChiN	05-22-00	Holden, Mo.	08-06-55	L	L	5'10	160	99	311	39	82	17	4	4	33	36	31	3	.264	.383
Cousineau, Dee-Edward Thomas (Ed)	23-25BosN	12-16-98	Watertown, Mass.	07-14-51	R	R	6'	170	5	4	1	2	0	0	0	2	0	0	0	.500	.500
Cox, Dick-Elmer Joseph	25-26BknN	09-30-95	Pasadena, Cal.	06-01-66	R	R	5'7	158	246	832	121	261	40	14	8	109	83	49	10	.314	.424
Crabtree, Estel-Estel Crayton (Crabby)	29,31-32CinN 33,41-42StLN 43-44CinN	08-19-03	Crabtree, Ohio	01-04-67	L	R	6'	168	489	1408	174	396	53	25	13	142	113	109	8	.281	.382
Craft, Harry-Harry Francis	37-42CinN M57-59KCA M61ChiN M62-64HouN	04-19-15	Ellisville, Miss.	08-03-95	R	R	6'1	185	566	2104	237	533	85	25	44	267	110	203	14	.253	.380
Cramer, Doc-Roger Maxwell (Flit)	29-35PhiA 36-40BosA 41WasA 42-48DetA	07-22-05	Beach Haven, N.J.	09-09-90	L	R	6'2	185	2239	9140	1357	2705	396	109	37	842	572	345	62	.296	.375
Crawford, Glenn-Glenn Martin (Shorty)	45StLN 45-46PhiN	12-02-13	North Beach, Mich.	01-02-72	L	R	5'9	165	87	306	41	89	13	2	2	24	37	15	5	.291	.366
Crawford, Pat-Clifford Rankin	29-30NYN 30CinN 33-34StLN	01-28-02	Society Hill, S.C.	01-25-94	L	R	5'11	170	318	651	75	182	23	5	9	104	60	29	4	.280	.372
Creeden, Connie-Cornelius Stephen	43BosN	07-21-15	Danvers, Mass.	11-30-69	L	R	6'	190	5	4	0	1	0	0	0	1	1	0	0	.250	.250
Creeden, Pat-Patrick Francis (Whoops)	31BosA	05-23-06	Newburyport, Mass.	04-20-92	L	R	5'8	175	5	8	0	0	0	0	0	0	1	3	0	.000	.000
Cespi, Creepy-Frank Angelo Joseph	38-42StLN 43-46NMS	02-16-18	St. Louis, Mo.	03-01-90	R	R	5'9	175	264	911	125	240	32	4	1	88	90	102	8	.263	.321
Criscola, Tony-Anthony Paul	42-43StLA 44CinN	09-09-15	Walla Walla, Wash.	07-10-01	L	R	5'11	180	184	367	35	91	12	4	1	28	30	32	2	.248	.311
Critz, Hughie-Hugh Melville	24-30CinN 30-35NYN	09-17-00	Starkville, Miss.	01-10-80	R	R	5'8	147	1478	5930	832	1591	195	95	38	531	289	257	109	.268	.352
Crompton, Herb-Herbert Bryan (Workhorse)	37WasA 45NYA	11-07-11	Taylor Ridge, Ill.	08-05-63	R	R	6'	185	38	102	6	20	3	0	0	12	2	7	0	.196	.225
Cronin, Bill-William Patrick (Crungy)	28-31BosN	12-26-02	West Newton, Mass.	10-06-66	R	R	5'9	167	126	296	28	68	15	2	0	27	12	13	0	.230	.294
Cronin, Jim-James John	29PhiN	08-07-05	Richmond, Cal.	06-10-83	B	R	5'10	150	25	56	7	13	2	1	0	4	5	7	0	.232	.304
Cronin, Joe-Joseph Edward	26-27PitN 28-34,M33-34WasA 35-45,M35-47BosA	10-12-06	San Francisco, Cal.	09-07-84	R	R	5'11	180	2124	7579	1233	2285	515	118	170	1424	1059	700	87	.302	.468
Crosetti, Frankie-Frank Peter Joseph (The Crow)	32-48NYN	02-11-10	San Francisco, Cal.		R	R	5'10	165	1683	6277	1006	1541	260	65	98	649	792	799	113	.245	.354
Crouch, Jack-Jack Albert (Roxy)	30-31,33StLA 33CinN	10-12-03	Cooleemee, N.C.	08-25-72	R	R	5'9	165	43	72	7	9	1	0	0	8	3	13	1	.125	.181
Croucher, Frank-Frank Donald (Dingle)	39-41DetA 42WasA 43-45MS	07-23-14	San Antonio, Tex.	05-21-80	R	R	5'11	165	296	935	94	235	37	5	7	86	56	128	4	.251	.324
Crouse, Buck-Clyde Ellsworth	23-30ChiN	01-06-97	Anderson, Ind.	10-23-83	L	R	5'8	185	470	1306	128	342	54	6	8	160	114	68	14	.262	.331
Crowley, Ed-Edgar Jewel	28WasA	08-06-06	Watkinsville, Ga.	04-14-70	R	R	6'1	180	2	1	0	0	0	0	0	0	0	0	0	.000	.000
Crumling, Gene-Eugene Leon	45StLN	04-05-22	Wrightsville, Pa.		R	R	6'	180	6	12	0	1	0	0	0	1	0	1	0	.083	.083
Crump, Buddy-Arthur Elliott	24NYN	11-29-01	Norfolk, Va.	09-26-76	L	L	5'10	156	1	4	0	0	0	0	0	0	0	0	0	.000	.000
Cuccinello, Al-Alfred Edward	35NYN	08-26-14	Queens, N.Y.	03-29-04	R	R	5'10	165	54	165	27	41	7	1	4	20	1	20	0	.248	.376
Cuccinello, Tony-Anthony Francis	30-31CinN 32-35BknN 36-40BosN 40NYN 42-43BosN 43-45ChiA	11-08-07	Queens, N.Y.	09-21-95	R	R	5'7	160	1704	6184	730	1729	334	46	94	884	579	497	42	.280	.394
Culberson, Leon-Delbert Leon	43-47BosA 48WasA	08-06-19	Hall's Station, Ga.	09-24-89	R	R	5'11	180	371	1217	148	324	59	18	14	131	107	126	28	.266	.379
Cullenbine, Roy-Roy Joseph	38-39DetA 40BknN 40-42StLA 42WasA 42NYA 43-45CleA 45-47DetA	10-18-13	Nashville, Tenn.	05-28-91	B	R	6'1	195	1181	3879	627	1072	209	32	110	599	853	399	26	.276	.432
Cullop(Kolop), Nick(Heinrich)-Henry Nicholas	26NYA 27WasA 27CleA 29BknN 30-31CinN	10-16-00	Weldon Spring, Mo.	12-08-78	R	R	6'	200	173	490	49	122	29	12	11	67	40	128	1	.249	.424
Culp, Benny-Benjamin Baldy	42-44PhiN 45MS	01-19-14	Philadelphia, Pa.	11-23-00	R	R	5'9	175	15	26	5	5	1	0	0	2	3	3	0	.192	.231
Cummings, Jack-John William	26-29NYN 29PhiN	04-01-04	Pittsburgh, Pa.	10-05-62	R	R	6'	195	89	132	15	45	11	1	4	28	12	18	0	.341	.530
Cunningham, Bill-William Aloysius	21-23NYN 24BosN	07-30-94	San Francisco, Cal.	09-26-53	R	R	5'8	155	318	945	113	270	39	12	9	112	52	48	17	.286	.381
Cunningham, Ray-Raymond Lee	31-32StLN	01-17-05	Mesquite, Tex.	07-30-05	R	R	5'7	150	14	26	4	4	1	0	0	1	3	4	0	.154	.192
Curtright, Guy-Guy Paxton	43-46ChiA	10-18-12	Holliday, Mo	08-23-97	R	R	5'11	200	331	1065	147	294	45	16	9	106	142	124	20	.276	.374
Cuyler, Kiki-Hazen Shirley	21-27PitN 28-35ChiN 35-37CinN 38BknN	08-30-98	Harrisville, Mich.	02-11-50	R	R	5'11	180	1879	7161	1305	2299	394	157	128	1065	676	752	328	.321	.474
Dahlgren, Babe-Ellsworth Tenney	35-36BosA 37-40NYA 41BosN 41-42ChiN 42StLA 42BknN 43PhiN 44-45NSL	06-15-12	San Francisco, Cal.	09-04-96	R	R	6'	190	1137	4045	470	1056	174	37	82	569	390	401	18	.261	.383
Dallessandro, Dom-Nicholas Dominic (Dim Dom)	37BosA 40-44ChiN 45MS 46-47ChiN	10-03-13	Reading, Pa.	04-29-88	L	L	5'6	168	746	1945	242	520	101	18	22	303	310	150	16	.267	.381
Daniel, Jake-Handley Jacob	37BknN	04-22-11	Roanoke, Ala.	04-23-96	L	L	5'11	175	12	27	3	5	1	0	0	3	3	4	0	.185	.222
Daniels, Fred-Fred Clinton (Tony)	12-28-24	Gastonia, N.C.		R	R	5'10	185	76	230	15	46	3	2	0	12	12	22	1	.200	.230
Danning, Harry-Harry (Harry the Horse)	33-42NYN 43-45MS	09-06-11	Los Angeles, Cal.	11-29-04	R	R	6'1	190	890	2971	363	847	162	26	57	397	187	217	13	.285	.415
Danning, Ike-Isaac	28StLA	01-20-05	Los Angeles, Cal.	03-30-83	R	R	5'10	160	2	6	0	3	0	0	0	1	1	2	0	.500	.500
Dantonio Fats-John James	44-45BknN	12-31-18	New Orleans, La.	05-28-93	R	R	5'8	165	50	135	12	33	6	1	0	12	11	7	3	.244	.304
Dapper, Cliff-Clifford Roland	42BknN 43-45MS	01-02-20	Jewett, Tex.		R	R	6'2	190	8	17	2	8	1	0	1	9	2	2	0	.471	.706
Dashiell, Wally-John Wallace	24ChiA	05-09-02	Jewett, Tex.	05-20-72	R	R	5'9	170	1	2	0	0	0	0	0	0	0	0	0	.000	.000
Daughters, Bob-Robert Francis (Red)	37BosA	04-03-02	Cincinnati, Ohio	08-22-88	R	R	6'2	185	1	0	1	0	0	0	0	0	0	0	0	—	—
Davis, Crash-Lawrence Columbus	40-42PhiA 43-45MS	07-14-19	Canon, Ga.	08-31-01	R	R	6'	173	148	444	43	102	12	2	2	43	35	56	2	.230	.279
Davis, Harry-Harry Albert (Stinky)	32-33DetA 37StLA	05-07-08	Shreveport, La.	03-03-97	L	L	5'10	175	327	1213	205	320	65	18	7	123	153	87	21	.264	.354
Davis, Ike-Isaac Marion	19WasA 24-25ChiA	06-14-95	Pueblo, Colo.	04-02-84	R	R	5'7	155	164	609	110	143	32	10	0	65	73	69	19	.235	.320
Davis, John-John Humphrey (Red)	41NYN 42-44ChiN	07-15-15	Wilkes-Barre, Pa.	04-26-02	R	R	5'11	212	21	70	8	15	3	0	0	5	8	12	0	.214	.257
Davis, Kiddo-George Willis	26NYA 32PhiN 33,35-37NYN 34PhiN 37-38CinN	02-12-02	Bridgeport, Conn.	03-04-83	R	R	5'11	178	575	1824	281	515	112	16	19	171	142	141	32	.282	.393
Davis, Spud-Virgil Lawrence	28StLN 28-33PhiN 34-36StLN 37-38CinN 38-39PhiN 40-41,44-45,M46PhiN	12-20-04	Birmingham, Ala.	08-14-84	R	R	6'1	197	1458	4255	388	1312	244	22	77	647	386	326	6	.308	.430
Deal, Lindsay-Lindsay Fred	39BknN	09-03-11	Lenoir, N.C.	04-18-79	L	R	6'	175	4	7	0	0	0	0	0	0	0	2	0	.000	.000
Dean, Chubby-Alfred Lovill (See P20-45)	36-41PhiA 41-43CleA 44-46MS	08-24-15	Mt. Airy, N.C.	12-21-70	L	L	5'11	188	533	1047	106	287	47	7	3	128	115	65	5	.274	.341
Dear, Buddy-Paul Stanford	27WasA	12-01-05	Norfolk, Va.	08-29-89	R	R	5'8	143	2	7	0	0	0	0	0	0	0	1	0	.000	.000
DeBerry, Hank-John Herman	16-17CleA 18MS 22-30BknN	12-29-94	Savannah, Tenn.	09-10-51	R	R	5'11	195	648	1850	170	494	81	16	11	234	148	119	13	.267	.346
Dedeaux, Rod-Raoul Martial	35BknN	02-17-14	New Orleans, La.	01-05-06	R	R	5'11	160	2	4	0	1	0	0	0	1	0	0	0	.250	.250
Deitrick, Bill-William Alexander	27-28PhiN	04-30-02	Hanover Co., Va.	05-06-46	R	R	5'10	160	57	106	14	21	6	0	0	7	17	10	1	.198	.255
Dejan, Mike-Mike Dan	40CinN	01-13-15	Cleveland, Ohio	02-02-53	L	L	6'1	180	12	16	1	3	0	0	0	2	3	3	0	.188	.313
DeKoning, Bill-William Callahan	45NYN	12-19-18	Brooklyn, N.Y.	07-26-79	R	R	5'11	185	3	1	0	0	0	0	0	0	0	0	0	.000	.000
DeLancey, Bill-William Pinkney	32,34-35,40StLN 36-39IL	11-28-11	Greensboro, N.C.	11-28-46	L	R	5'11	185	219	598	79	173	32	10	19	85	85	74	1	.289	.472
Delker, Eddie-Edward Alberts	29,31-32StLN 32-33PhiN	04-17-06	Palo Alto, Pa.	05-14-97	R	R	5'10	170	98	187	19	29	8	1	0	15	16	45	0	.156	.251
Delmas, Bert-Albert Charles	33BknN	05-20-11	San Francisco, Cal.	12-04-79	R	R	5'11	165	12	28	4	7	0	0	0	1	1	4	0	.250	.250
Del Savio, Garton-Garton Orville	43PhiN	11-26-13	New York, N.Y.		R	R	5'9	165	4	11	1	1	0	0	0	0	0	0	0	.091	.091
Demaree, Frank-Joseph Franklin	32-33,35-38CinN 39-41NYN 41-42BosN 43StLN 44StLA	06-10-10	Winters, Cal.	08-30-58	R	R	5'11	185	1155	4144	578	1241	190	36	72	591	359	269	33	.299	.415
Dennehey, Tod-Thomas Francis	23BosN	05-12-99	Philadelphia, Pa.	08-08-77	L	L	5'10	180	19	24	4	7	2	0	0	2	1	3	0	.292	.375
Denning, Otto-Otto George (Dutch)	42-43CleA	12-28-12	Hays, Kans.	05-25-92	R	R	6'	180	129	343	23	76	20	0	1	32	23	15	3	.222	.287
DePhillips, Tony-Anthony Andrew	43CinN	09-20-12	New York, N.Y.	05-05-94	R	R	6'2	185	35	20	0	2	0	0	0	3	1	3	0	.100	.150
Derry, Russ-Alva Russell	44-45NYA 48PhiA 49StLN	10-07-16	Princeton, Mo.	10-26-04	L	R	6'1	180	187	553	68	124	17	7	17	73	78	124	2	.224	.373

USE NAME - GIVEN NAMES (NICKNAMES)	TEAM BY YEAR	BIRTH DATE	BIRTH PLACE	DEATH DATE	B	T	HGT	WGT	G	AB	R	H	2B	3B	HR	RBI	BB	SO	SB	BA	SA
Desautels, Gene-Eugene Abraham (Red)	30-33DetA 37-40BosA 41-43CleA 44MS 45CleA 46PhiA	06-13-07	Worcester, Mass.	11-05-94	R	R	5'11	170	712	2012	211	469	71	11	3	186	233	167	12	.233	.285
Detore(de Tore), George-George Francis	30-31CleA	11-06-06	Utica, N.Y.	02-07-91	R	R	5'8	170	33	68	3	17	7	0	0	9	8	2	2	.250	.353
Detweiler, Ducky-Robert Sterling	42BosN 43-45MS 46BosN	02-15-19	Trumbauersville, Pa.		R	R	5'11	178	13	45	3	14	2	1	0	5	2	7	0	.311	.400
Devine, Mickey-William Patrick	18PhiN 20BosA 25NYN	05-09-92	Albany, N.Y.	10-01-37	R	R	5'10	165	33	53	7	12	4	0	0	4	3	6	1	.226	.302
deViveiros, Bernie-Bernard John	24ChiA 27DetA	04-19-01	Oakland, Cal.	07-05-94	R	R	5'7	160	25	23	4	5	1	0	0	2	2	8	1	.217	.261
Devlin, Jim-James Raymond	44CleA	08-25-22	Plains, Pa.	01-15-04	L	R	5'11	165	1	1	0	0	0	0	0	0	0	0	0	.000	.000
DeVormer, Al-Albert E.	18ChiA 21-22NYA 23BosA 27NYN	08-19-91	Grand Rapids, Mich.	08-29-66	R	R	6'	175	196	477	50	123	20	5	2	57	20	46	7	.258	.333
Dickey, Bill-William Malcolm	28-43NYA 44-45MS 46,M46NYA	06-06-07	Bastrop, La.	11-12-93	L	R	6'1	185	1789	6300	930	1969	343	72	202	1209	678	289	36	.313	.486
Dickshot (Dicksus), Johnny-John Oscar	36-38PittN 39NYN 44-45ChiA	01-24-10	Waukegan, Ill.	11-04-97	R	R	6'	195	322	990	142	273	35	19	7	116	101	97	23	.276	.371
Dillhoefer, Pickles-William Martin	17ChiN 18PhiN 19-21StlN	10-13-93	Cleveland, Ohio	02-23-22	R	R	5'7	154	247	600	59	134	16	10	0	48	35	30	12	.223	.283
DiMaggio, Joe-Joseph Paul (The Yankee Clipper, Joltin' Joe)	36-42NYA 43-45MS 46-51NYA	11-25-14	Martinez, Cal.	03-08-99	R	R	6'2	193	1736	6821	1390	2214	389	131	361	1537	790	369	30	.325	.579
DiMaggio, Vince-Vincent Paul	37-38BosN 39-40CinN 40-44PittN 45-46PhiN 46NYN	09-06-12	Martinez, Cal.	10-03-86	R	R	5'11	183	1110	3849	491	959	209	24	125	584	412	837	79	.249	.413
Dinges, Vance-Vance (George)	45-46PhiN	05-29-15	Elizabeth, N.J.	04-10-90	L	L	6'2	175	159	501	53	146	20	3	2	46	44	29	7	.291	.363
Dixon, Leo-Leo Moses	25-27StlA 29CinN	09-04-94	Chicago, Ill.	04-11-84	R	R	5'11	170	159	427	40	88	10	9	3	41	45	69	4	.206	.372
Doerr, Bobby-Robert Pershing	37-44BosA 45MS 46-51BosA	04-07-18	Los Angeles, Cal.		R	R	5'11	185	1865	7093	1094	2042	381	89	223	1247	809	608	54	.288	.461
Doljack, Frank-Frank Joseph (Dolie)	30-34DetA 43CleA	10-05-07	Cleveland, Ohio	01-23-48	R	R	5'11	185	192	561	68	151	31	7	9	85	47	60	8	.269	.398
Doll, Art-Arthur James (Moose) (See P20-45)	35-36,38BosN	05-07-12	Chicago, Ill.	04-28-78	R	R	6'1	200	7	13	0	2	0	0	0	0	0	3	0	.154	.154
Donahue, John-John Frederick (Jiggs)	23BosA	04-19-94	Roxbury, Mass.	10-03-49	B	R	5'8	170	10	36	5	10	4	0	0	1	4	5	0	.278	.389
Dondero, Len-Leonard Peter (Mike)	29StlA	09-12-03	Newark, Cal.	01-01-99	R	R	5'11	178	19	31	2	6	0	0	1	8	0	4	0	.194	.290
Doran, Bill-William James	22CleA	06-14-98	San Francisco, Cal.	03-09-78	L	R	5'11	175	3	2	0	1	0	0	0	0	1	0	0	.500	.500
Dorman, Charlie-Charles William (Slats)	23ChiA	04-23-98	San Francisco, Cal.	11-15-28	R	R	6'2	185	1	2	0	1	0	0	0	0	0	0	0	.500	.500
Dorman, Red-Charles Dwight	28CleA	10-03-00	Jacksonville, Ill.	12-07-74	R	R	5'11	180	25	77	12	28				11	9	6	1	.364	.442
Douglas, John-John Franklin	45BknN	09-14-17	Thayer, W. Va.	02-11-84	L	L	6'2	195	5	9	0	0	0	0	0	0	2	4	0	.000	.000
Douglass, Astyanax-Astyanax Saunders	21,25CinN	11-21-01	Covington, Tex.	01-26-75	R	R	6'1	190	11	24	2	4	0	0	0	1	2	4	0	.167	.167
Douthit, Taylor-Taylor Lee (The Ballhawk)	23-31StlN 31-33CinN 33ChiN	04-22-01	Little Rock, Ark.	05-30-86	R	R	5'11	175	1074	4127	665	1201	220	38	29	396	443	312	67	.291	.384
Doyle, Danny-Howard James	43BosA 44-45MS	01-24-17	McLoud, Okla.	12-14-04	B	R	6'1	195	13	43	2	9	1	0	0	6	7	9	0	.209	.233
Dreesen, Bill-William Richard	31BknN	07-26-04	New York, N.Y.	11-09-71	L	R	5'7	160	48	180	38	40	10	4	1	10	23	23	1	.222	.339
Drescher, Bill-William Clayton (Dutch, Moose)	44-46NYA	05-23-21	Congers, N.Y.	05-15-68	R	R	6'2	190	57	139	10	37	4	1	0	16	8	5	0	.266	.309
Dressen, Chuck-Charles Walter 20,22,23 played in N.F.L.	25-31CinN 33NYN M34-37CinN M52-53BknN M55-57WasA M60-61MilN M63-66DetA	09-20-98	Decatur, Ill.	08-10-66	R	R	5'6	146	646	2215	313	603	123	29	11	221	219	118	30	.272	.369
Drews, Frank-Frank John	44-45BosN	05-25-16	Buffalo, N.Y.	04-22-72	R	R	5'10	175	95	288	27	59	13	2	0	24	41	32	0	.205	.264
Dudley, Dud (See Dud Lee)	20StlA																				
Dudra, John-John Joseph	41BosN 42-45MS	05-27-16	Assumption, Ill.	10-24-65	R	R	5'11	175	14	25	3	9	3	1	0	3	3	4	0	.360	.560
Dugan, Joe-Joseph Anthony (Jumping Joe)	17-21PhiA 22BosA 22-28NYA 29BosA 31DetA	05-12-97	Mahanoy City, Pa.	07-07-82	R	R	5'11	160	1446	5405	664	1515	277	46	42	571	250	418	37	.280	.372
Dugas, Gus-Augustin Joseph	30PittN 31BJ 32PhiN 33PhiN 34WasA	03-24-07	St. Jean-de-Matha,Can.	04-14-97	L	L	5'9	165	125	218	27	45	9	3	3	23	18	27	0	.206	.317
Duncan, Pat-Louis Baird	15PittN 18MS 19-24CinN	10-06-93	Coalton, Ohio	07-17-60	R	R	5'9	170	727	2695	361	827	137	50	23	374	184	164	55	.307	.420
Dunham, Lee-Leland Huffield	26PhiA	06-09-02	Atlanta, Ill.	05-11-61	L	L	5'11	185	5	4	0	1	0	0	0	1	0	1	0	.250	.250
Dunlap, Bill-William James	29-30BosN	05-01-09	Palmer, Mass.	11-29-80	R	L	5'11	175	26	58	9	14	1	1	1	4	4	10	0	.241	.345
Durning, George-George Dewey	25PhiN	05-09-98	Philadelphia, Pa.	04-18-86	R	R	5'11	175	5	14	3	5	0	0	0	1	3	4	0	.357	.357
Durocher, Leo-Leo Ernest (The Lip, Speedy)	25,28-29NYA 30-33CinN 33-37BknN 38,41,43,45,M39-46BknN 47SL M48BknN M48-55NYN M66-72ChiN M72-73HouN	07-27-05	W. Springfield, Mass.	10-07-91	R	R	5'10	160	1637	5350	575	1320	210	56	24	567	377	480	31	.247	.320
Durrett, Red-Elmer Cable	44-45BknN	02-03-21	Sherman, Tex.	01-17-92	L	L	5'10	170	19	48	5	7	1	0	1	1	10	13	0	.146	.229
Durst, Cedric-Cedric Montgomery	22-23,26StlA 27-30NYA 30BosA	08-23-96	Austin, Tex.	02-16-71	L	L	5'11	160	481	1103	146	269	39	17	15	122	75	100	7	.244	.351
Dwyer, Double Joe-Joseph Michael	37CinN	03-27-03	Orange, N.J.	10-21-92	L	L	5'9	186	12	11	2	3	0	0	0	1	1	0	0	.273	.273
Dykes, Jimmy-James Joseph	18-32PhiA 33-39,M34-46ChiA M51-53PhiA M54BalA M58CinN M59-60DetA M60-61CleA	11-10-96	Philadelphia, Pa.	06-15-76	R	R	5'9	185	2282	8046	1108	2256	453	90	108	1071	955	849	70	.280	.399
Early, Jake-Jacob Willard	39-43WasA 44-45MS 46WasA 47StlA 48-49WasA	05-19-15	King's Mountain, N.C.	05-31-85	L	R	5'11	160	747	2208	216	532	98	23	32	264	281	259	7	.241	.350
East, Carl-Carlton William (See P01-19)	15StlA 24WasA	08-27-94	Marietta, Ga.	01-15-53	R	R	6'2	178	11	28	0	8	2	1	0	2	2	1	0	.286	.429
Easterling, Paul-Paul	28,30DetA 38PhiA	09-28-05	Reidsville, Ga.	03-15-93	R	R	5'11	180	76	200	25	55	13	1	4	26	15	44	2	.275	.410
Easterwood, Roy-Roy Charles (Shag)	44CleA	01-12-15	Waxahachie, Tex.	08-24-84	R	R	6'	196	17	33	1	7	2	0	1	2	1	11	0	.212	.364
Eayrs, Eddie-Edwin (See P20-45)	13PitN 20-21BosN 21BknN	11-10-90	Blackstone, Mass.	11-30-69	L	L	5'7	190	114	271	32	83	5	2	1	26	32	23	4	.306	.351
Echols, Johnny-John Gresham	39StlN	01-09-17	Atlanta, Ga.	11-13-72	R	R	5'10	175	2	0	0	0	0	0	0	0	0	0	0	—	—
Eckhardt, Ox-Oscar George 28 played in N.F.L.	32BosN 36BknN	12-23-01	Yorktown, Tex.	04-22-51	L	R	6'1	185	24	52	6	10	1	0	1	7	5	3	0	.192	.269
Eggert, Elmer-Elmer Albert (Mose)	27BosA	01-29-02	Rochester, N.Y.	04-09-71	R	R	5'9	160	5	3	0	0	0	0	0	0	0	0	0	.000	.000
Eibel, Hack-Henry Hack	12CleA 20BosA	12-06-93	Brooklyn, N.Y.	10-16-45	L	L	5'11	220	30	46	4	8	2	0	0	6	3	6	1	.174	.217
Eichrodt, Fred-Frederick George (Ike)	25-27CleA 31ChiA	01-06-03	Chicago, Ill.	07-14-65	R	R	5'11	167	171	516	51	121	34	5	0	51	21	51	3	.234	.320
Elko, Pete-Peter (Piccolo Pete)	43-44ChiN	06-17-18	Wilkes-Barre, Pa.	09-17-93	R	R	5'11	185	16	52	3	9	1	0	0	3	1	9	0	.173	.192
Ellerbe, Frank-Francis Rogers (Governor)	19-21WasA 21-24StlA 24CleA	12-25-95	Marion, S.C.	07-07-88	R	R	5'10	165	420	1453	179	389	58	22	4	152	72	136	12	.268	.346
Elliott, Allen-Allen Clifford (Ace)	23-24ChiN	12-25-97	St. Louis, Mo.	05-06-79	L	R	6'	170	63	182	21	44	8	2	2	29	2	13	3	.242	.341
Elliott, Carter-Carter Ward	21ChiN	11-29-93	Atchison, Kans.	05-21-59	R	R	5'11	165	12	28	5	7	2	0	0	0	3	0	0	.250	.321
Elmore, Ellie-Verdo Wilson	24StlA	12-10-99	Gordo, Ala.	08-05-69	L	R	6'	190	7	17	2	3	3	0	0	0	1	0	0	.176	.353
Elsh, Roy-Eugene Raybold (Dory)	23-25ChiA	03-01-91	Penns Grove, N.J.	11-12-78	R	R	5'9	165	173	404	55	106	17	3	0	39	31	44	23	.262	.319
Emery, Spoke-Herrick Smith	24PhiN	12-10-96	Bay City, Mich.	06-02-75	R	L	5'9	165	5	3	3	2	0	0	0	0	0	0	0	.667	.667
Emmer, Frank-Frank William	16,26CinN	12-17-96	Crestline, Ohio	10-18-63	R	R	5'8	150	122	313	30	57	10	7	0	20	20	57	2	.182	.259
Emmerich, Bob-Robert George	23BosN	03-01-97	New York, N.Y.	11-23-48	R	R	5'3	155	13	24	3	2	0	0	0	0	2	3	1	.083	.083
Engle, Charlie-Charles August (Cholly)	25-26PhiN 30PitN	08-27-03	Brooklyn, N.Y.	10-12-83	R	R	5'8	155	87	235	41	59	10	1	0	15	32	26	1	.251	.302
English, Charlie-Charles Dewie	32-33ChiA 36NYN 37CinN	04-08-10	Darlington, S.C.	06-25-99	R	R	5'9	160	50	136	10	39	8	2	1	13	4	10	0	.287	.397
English, Gil-Gilbert Raymond	31-32NYN 36-37DetA 37-38BosN 44BknN	07-02-09	Glenola, N.C.	08-31-96	R	R	5'11	180	240	791	74	194	22	7	8	90	56	78	5	.245	.321
English, Woody-Elwood George	27-36ChiN 37-38BknN	03-02-07	Fredonia, Ohio	09-19-97	R	R	5'10	155	1261	4746	801	1356	236	52	32	422	571	536	57	.286	.378
Ennis, Russ-Russell Elwood (Hack)	26WasA	03-10-97	Superior, Wis.	01-29-49	R	R	5'11	160	1	0	0	0	0	0	0	0	0	0	0	—	—
Ens, Jewel-Jewel Winklemeyer	22-25,M29-31PittN	08-24-89	St. Louis, Mo.	01-17-50	R	R	6'	172	67	186	25	54	8	4	1	24	7	16	5	.290	.392
Epps, Aubrey-Aubrey Lee (Yo-Yo)	35PitN	03-03-12	Memphis, Tenn.	11-13-84	R	R	5'10	170	1	4	1	3	0	1	0	3	0	0	0	.750	1.250
Epps, Hal-Harold Franklin	38,40StlN 43-44StlA 44PhiA 45-46MS	03-26-14	Athens, Ga.	08-25-04	L	L	6'	175	125	391	58	99	13	9	1	21	37	43	5	.253	.340
Erickson, Hank-Henry Nels (Popeye)	35CinN	11-11-07	Chicago, Ill.	12-19-64	R	R	6'1	185	37	88	9	23	3	2	1	6	4	6	0	.261	.375
Eschen, Larry-Lawrence Edward	42PhiA	09-22-20	Suffern, N.Y.		R	R	6'	160	12	11	0	0	0	0	0	0	0	2	0	.000	.000
Estalella, Bobby-Roberto (Ventoza) (Mendez)	35-36,39WasA 41StlA 42WasA 43-45PhiA 46-48SM 49PhiN	04-25-11	Cardenas, Cuba	01-06-91	R	R	5'8	185	680	2196	279	620	106	33	44	308	350	246	13	.282	.421
Etchison, Buck-Clarence Hampton	43-44BosN	01-27-15	Baltimore, Md.	01-24-80	L	L	6'1	190	119	327	32	72	19	0	8	35	35	52	1	.220	.352
Etten, Nick-Nicholas Raymond Thomas	38-39PhiA 41-42PhiN 43-46NYA 47PhiN	09-19-13	Spring Grove, Ill.	10-18-90	L	L	6'2	198	937	3320	426	921	167	25	89	526	480	199	22	.277	.423
Evans, Joe-Joseph Patton (Doc)	15-22CleA 23WasA 24-25StlA	05-15-95	Meridian, Miss.	08-08-53	R	R	5'9	160	733	2043	306	529	71	31	3	210	212	152	64	.259	.328
Ewing (Cohen), Reuben-Reuben	21StlN	11-30-99	Odessa, Russia	10-05-70	R	R	5'5	150	3	1	0	0	0	0	0	0	0	1	0	.000	.000
Ezzell, Homer-Homer Estell	23StlA 24-25BosA	02-28-96	Victoria, Tex.	08-03-76	R	R	5'10	158	236	734	104	196	20	8	0	61	47	58	25	.267	.316
Falk, Bibb-Bibb August (Jockey)	20-28ChiA 29-31CleA	01-27-99	Austin, Tex.	06-08-89	L	L	6'	175	1354	4656	656	1463	300	59	69	785	412	279	46	.314	.448
Fallon, George-George Decatur (Flash)	37BknN 43-45StlN	07-08-14	Jersey City, N.J.	10-25-94	R	R	5'9	155	133	282	26	61	10	1	0	21	25	26	2	.216	.270
Farrell, Doc-Edward Stephen	25-27NYN 27-29BosN 29NYN 30StlN 30ChiN 32-33NYA 35BosA	12-26-01	Johnson City, N.Y.	12-20-66	R	R	5'8	160	591	1799	181	467	63	8	10	213	109	120	14	.260	.320
Farrell, Kerby-Major Kerby	43BosA 45ChiA M57CleA	09-03-13	Leapwood, Tenn.	12-17-75	L	L	5'11	172	188	676	55	177	25	4	0	55	40	33	5	.262	.311
Fausett, Buck-Robert Shaw (Leaky)	44CinN	04-08-08	Sheridan, Ark.	05-02-94	R	R	5'10	170	13	31	2	3	1	1	0	1	1	4	0	.097	.161
Fehring, Bill-William Paul (Dutch)	34ChiA	05-31-12	Columbus, Ind.	04-13-06	B	R	6'	195	1	1	0	0	0	0	0	0	0	0	0	.000	.000
Feinberg, Eddie-Edward Isadore (Itzy)	38-39PhiN	09-29-17	Philadelphia, Pa.	08-06-86	B	R	5'9	160	16	38	2	7	0	1	0	1	0	9	0	.184	.211
Felderman, Marv-Marvin Wilfred (Coonie)	42CinN 43-45MS	12-20-15	Bellevue, Iowa	08-06-00	R	R	6'1	187	3	6	0	1	0	0	0	0	1	2	0	.167	.167
Felix, Gus-August Guenther	23-25BosN 26-27BknN	05-24-95	Cincinnati, Ohio	05-12-60	R	R	6'	180	583	2046	256	561	91	25	12	230	189	194	28	.274	.361
Fernandes, Ed-Edward Paul	40PitN 45MS 46ChiA	03-11-18	Oakland, Cal.	11-27-68	B	R	5'9	185	42	65	5	12	3	0	0	6	15	13	0	.185	.231
Ferrell, Rick-Richard Benjamin	29-33StlA 33-37BosA 37-41WasA 41-43StlA 44-45,47WasA	10-12-05	Durham, N.C.	07-27-95	R	R	5'10	160	1884	6028	687	1692	324	45	28	734	931	277	29	.281	.363

USE NAME - GIVEN NAMES (NICKNAMES)	TEAM BY YEAR	BIRTH DATE	BIRTH PLACE	DEATH DATE	B	T	HGT	WGT	G	AB	R	H	2B	3B	HR	RBI	BB	SO	SB	BA	SA
Ferrell, Wes-Wesley Cheek (See P20-45)	27-33CleA 34-37BosA 37-38WasA 38-39NYA 40BknN 41BosN	02-02-08	Greensboro, N.C.	12-09-76	R	R	6'2	195	548	1176	175	329	57	12	38	208	129	185	2	.280	.446
Fewster, Chick-Wilson Lloyd	17-22NYA 22-23BosA 24-25CleA 26-27BknN	11-10-95	Baltimore, Md.	04-16-45	R	R	5'11	160	644	1963	282	506	91	12	6	167	240	264	57	.258	.326
File, Sam-Samuel Lawrence	40PhiN	05-18-22	Chester, Pa.		R	R	5'11	160	7	13	0	1	0	0	0	1	0	2	0	.077	.077
Filipowicz, Steve-Stephen Charles (Flip) 45-46 played in N.F.L.	44-45NYN 48CinN	06-28-21	Donora, Pa.	02-21-75	R	R	5'8	195	57	179	24	40	7	2	2	26	9	21	0	.223	.318
Finley, Bob-Robert Edward	43-44PhiN	11-25-15	Ennis, Tex.	01-02-86	R	R	6'1	200	122	362	27	91	13	1	2	28	16	35	1	.251	.309
Finn, Neal-Cornelius Francis (Mickey)	30-32BknN 33PhiN	01-24-02	New York, N.Y.	07-07-33	R	R	5'11	168	321	1044	125	274	44	5	3	102	68	89	9	.262	.323
Finney, Hal-Harold Wilson	31-34,36PitN	07-30-05	Lafayette, Ala.	12-20-91	R	R	5'11	170	123	227	39	46	8	1	1	27	6	32	1	.203	.260
Finney, Lou-Louis Klopsche	31,33-39PhiA 39-42BosA 43VR 44-45BosA 45-46StLA 47PhiN	08-13-10	Buffalo, Ala.	04-22-66	L	R	6'	180	1270	4631	643	1329	203	85	31	494	329	186	39	.287	.388
Fisher, Showboat-George Aloys	23-24WasA 30StLN 32StLA	01-16-99	Wesley, Iowa	05-15-94	L	R	5'10	170	138	340	62	114	21	6	8	71	37	35	6	.335	.503
Fitzberger, Charlie-Charles Casper (Hon)	24-25BosN	02-13-04	Baltimore, Md.	01-25-65	L	L	6'1	190	7	7	0	2	0	0	0	0	0	3	0	.286	.286
Fitzgerald, Howie-Howard Chumney (Lefty)	22,24ChiN 26BosA	05-16-02	Mathews, Tex.	02-27-59	L	L	5'11	163	48	140	15	36	3	0	0	14	8	11	2	.257	.279
Fitzgerald, Ray-Raymond Francis	31CinN	12-05-04	Chicopee, Mass.	09-06-77	R	R	5'9	168	1	1	0	0	0	0	0	0	0	1	0	.000	.000
Flager, Wally-Walter Leonard	45CinN 45PhiN	11-03-21	Chicago Heights, Ill.	12-16-90	R	R	5'11	160	70	220	26	53	5	1	2	21	25	20	1	.241	.300
Flagstead, Ira-Ira James (Pete)	17DetA 18MS 19-23DetA 23-29BosA 29WasA 29-30PitN	09-22-93	Montague, Mich.	03-13-40	R	R	5'9	165	1218	4139	644	1201	261	49	40	450	467	288	71	.290	.460
Flair, Al-Albert Deli (Broadway)	41BosA 42-45BosA	07-24-16	New Orleans, La.	07-26-88	L	L	6'4	195	10	30	3	6	2	1	0	2	1	1	1	.200	.333
Flaskamper, Ray-Raymond Harold (Flash)	27ChiA	10-31-01	St. Louis, Mo.	02-03-78	B	R	5'7	140	26	95	12	21	5	0	0	6	3	8	0	.221	.274
Fletcher, Elbie-Elburt Preston	34-35,37-39BosN 39-43PitN 45MS 46-47PitN 49BosN	03-18-16	Milton, Mass.	03-09-94	L	L	6'	180	1415	4879	723	1323	228	58	79	616	851	495	32	.271	.390
Flick, Lew-Lewis Miller	43-44PhiA	02-18-15	Bristol, Tenn.	12-07-90	L	L	5'11	155	20	40	3	7	0	0	0	2	1	2	1	.175	.175
Florence, Paul-Paul Robert (Pep) 20 played in N.F.L.	26NYN	04-22-00	Chicago, Ill.	05-28-86	B	R	6'1	185	76	188	19	43	4	3	2	14	23	12	2	.229	.314
Flowers, Jake-D'Arcy Raymond	23,26StLN 27-31BknN 31-32StLN 33BknN 34CinN	03-16-02	Cambridge, Md.	12-27-62	R	R	5'11	170	583	1693	229	433	75	18	16	201	190	139	58	.256	.350
Floyd, Bubba-Leslie Roe	44DetA	06-23-17	Dallas, Tex.	12-15-00	R	R	5'11	160	3	9	1	4	1	0	0	1	0	1	0	.444	.556
Foley, Ray-Raymond Kirwin	28NYN	06-23-06	Naugatuck, Conn.	03-22-80	L	R	5'11	173	2	1	1	0	0	0	0	0	0	1	0	.000	.000
Fonseca, Lew-Lewis Albert	21-24CinN 25PhiN 27-31CleA 31-33,M32-34ChiA	01-21-99	Oakland, Cal.	11-26-89	R	R	5'11	180	937	3404	518	1075	203	50	31	485	186	199	64	.316	.432
Ford, Hod-Horace Hills	19-23BosN 24PhiN 25BknN 26-31CinN 32StLN 32-33BosN	07-23-97	New Haven, Conn.	01-29-77	R	R	5'10	165	1446	4833	484	1269	200	55	16	494	351	354	21	.263	.337
Foss, George-George Dueward (Deeby)	21WasA	06-13-97	Register, Ga.	11-10-69	R	R	5'10	170	4	7	0	0	0	0	0	0	0	3	0	.000	.000
Fothergill, Bob-Robert Roy (Fats)	22-30DetA 30-32ChiA 33BosA	08-16-97	Massillon, Ohio	03-20-38	R	R	5'10	230	1105	3265	453	1064	225	52	36	582	202	177	40	.326	.460
Fournier, Jack(John)-Jacques Frank	12-17CinA 18NYA 20-22StLN 23-26BknN 27BosN	09-28-89	Au Sable, Mich.	09-05-73	L	R	6'	195	1530	5207	821	1631	252	113	136	859	587	408	145	.313	.483
Fowler, Boob-Joseph Chester	23-25CinN 26BosA	11-11-00	Waco, Tex.	10-08-88	R	R	5'11	180	78	175	30	57	7	2	1	18	6	19	3	.326	.406
Fox, Charlie-Charles Francis (Irish)	42NYN 43-45MS M70-74SFN M76MonN M83ChiN	10-07-21	New York, N.Y.	02-16-04	R	R	5'11	180	3	7	1	3	0	0	1	1	1	2	0	.429	.429
Fox, Pete-Ervin	33-40DetA 41-45BosA	03-08-09	Evansville, Ind.	07-05-66	R	R	5'11	165	1461	5636	895	1678	314	75	65	694	392	471	158	.298	.415
Foxx, Jimmie-James Emory (Double X, The Beast) (See P20-45)	25-35PhiA 36-42ChiN 45PhiN	10-22-07	Sudlersville, Md.	07-21-67	R	R	6'	195	2317	8134	1751	2646	458	125	534	1921	1452	1311	87	.325	.609
Franklin, Murray-Murray Asher (Moe)	41-42DetA 43-45MS 46-49SM	04-01-14	Chicago, Ill.	03-16-78	R	R	6'	175	61	164	25	43	8	0	2	16	9	7	0	.262	.348
Franks, Herman-Herman Louis	39StLN 40-41BknN 42-45MS 47-48PhiA 49NYN M65-68SFN M77-79ChiN	01-04-14	Price, Utah		L	R	5'10	187	188	403	35	80	18	2	3	43	57	37	2	.199	.275
Frederick, Johnny-John Henry	29-34BknN	02-26-01	Denver, Colo.	06-18-77	L	L	5'11	165	805	3102	498	954	200	35	85	377	210	176	23	.308	.477
Freed, Ed-Edwin Charles	42PhiN 43-45MS	08-02-19	Centre Valley, Pa.	11-15-02	R	R	5'6	165	13	33	3	10	3	1	0	1	4	3	1	.303	.455
Freeman, John-John Edward (Buck)	27BosA	01-24-01	Boston, Mass.	04-14-58	R	R	5'8	160	4	2	0	0	0	0	0	0	1	0	0	.000	.000
Freiburger, Vern-Vern Donald	41CleA	12-19-23	Detroit, Mich.	02-27-90	R	L	6'1	175	2	8	0	1	0	0	0	1	0	2	0	.125	.125
Freigau, Howard-Howard Earl (Ty)	22-25StLN 25-27ChiN 28BknN	08-01-02	Dayton, Ohio	07-18-32	R	R	5'10	160	579	1974	224	537	99	25	15	226	138	161	32	.272	.370
French, Ray-Raymond Edward	20NYA 23BknN 24ChiA	01-09-95	Alameda, Cal.	04-03-78	R	R	5'9	158	82	187	29	36	8	1	0	19	14	21	3	.193	.235
French, Walt-Walter Edward (Fitz) 22,25 played in N.F.L.	23,25-29PhiA	07-12-99	Moorestown, N.J.	05-13-84	L	R	5'8	155	398	981	142	297	45	12	2	109	44	62	13	.303	.379
Frey, Lonny-Linus Reinhar (Junior)	33-36BknN 37CinN 38-43CinN 44-45MS 46CinN 47ChiN 47-48NYA 48NYN	08-23-10	St. Louis, Mo.						Bats Both 33-38	1535	5517	848	1482	263	69	61	549	752	525	105	.269	.374
Friberg, Barney-Augustaf Bernhard	19-20,22-25ChiN 25-32PhiN 33BosA	08-18-99	Manchester, N.H.	12-08-58	R	R	5'11	178	1299	4169	544	1170	181	44	38	471	471	498	51	.281	.373
Frierson, Buck-Robert Lawrence	41CleA	07-29-17	Chicota, Tex.	06-26-96	R	R	6'3	195	5	11	2	3	1	0	0	2	1	1	0	.273	.364
Frink, Fred-Frederick Ferdinand	34PhiN	06-19-11	Macon, Ga.	05-19-95	R	R	6'1	180	2	2	0	0	0	0	0	0	0	0	0	—	—
Frisch, Frankie-Frank Francis (The Fordham Flash)	19-26NYN 27-37,M33-38StLN M40-46PitN M49-51ChiN	09-09-98	Bronx, N.Y.	03-12-73	B	R	5'11	165	2310	9112	1532	2880	466	138	105	1244	728	272	419	.316	.432
Fuhrman, Ollie-Alfred George	22PhiN	07-20-96	Jordan, Minn.	01-11-69	B	R	5'11	185	6	6	1	2	0	0	0	1	0	0	0	.330	.500
Fulghum, Dot-James Lavoisier	21PhiN	07-04-00	Valdosta, Ga.	11-11-67	R	R	5'10	170	2	2	0	0	0	0	0	0	1	1	0	.000	.000
Fullis, Chick-Charles Philip	28-32NYN 33-34PhiN 34,36StLN	02-27-04	Giardville, Pa.	03-28-46	R	R	5'9	170	590	1855	305	548	92	14	12	167	132	113	46	.295	.380
Funk, Liz-Elias Calvin	29NYA 30DetA 32-33ChiA	10-28-04	La Cygne, Kans.	01-16-68	L	L	5'9	160	273	976	134	261	47	16	6	105	73	58	29	.267	.367
Gabrielson, Len-Leonard Hilborne	39PhiN	09-08-15	Oakland, Cal.	11-14-00	L	L	6'3	210	5	18	3	4	0	0	0	1	2	3	0	.222	.222
Gaffke, Fabian-Fabian Sebastian (Fabe)	36-39BosA 41-42CleA	08-05-13	Milwaukee, Wis.	02-08-92	R	R	5'10	170	129	321	43	73	14	4	7	42	30	47	2	.227	.361
Gagnon, Chick-Harold Dennis	22DetA 24WasA	09-27-97	Milbury, Mass.	04-30-70	R	R	5'8	158	13	9	3	2	0	0	0	1	2	1	0	.222	.222
Galan, Augie-August John (Frenchy)	34-40ChiN 41-46BknN 47-48CinN 49NYN 49PhiA	05-23-12	Berkeley, Cal.	12-28-93					Bats Left 44-49, part of 43	1742	5937	1004	1706	336	74	100	830	979	393	123	.287	.419
Galatzer, Milt-Milton	33-36CleA 39CinN	05-04-07	Chicago, Ill.	01-29-76	L	L	5'10	168	251	717	105	192	25	7	1	57	92	46	10	.268	.326
Gallagher, Gil-Lawrence Kirby	22BosN	09-05-96	Washington, D.C.	01-06-57	R	R	5'8	155	7	22	1	1	0	0	0	2	1	7	0	.045	.091
Gallagher, Jackie-John Laurence	23CleA	01-28-02	Providence, R.I.	09-10-84	L	L	5'10	175	1	1	0	1	0	0	0	0	0	0	0	1.000	1.000
Gallagher, Joe-Joseph Emmett (Muscles)	39NYA 39-40StLA 40BknN 41-45MS	03-07-14	Buffalo, N.Y.	02-25-98	R	R	6'2	210	165	487	73	133	26	5	16	73	26	76	4	.273	.446
Galle, Stan-Stanley Joseph (Galezewski)	42WasA 43-45MS	07-27-19	Milwaukee, Wis.	01-28-06	R	R	5'7	165	13	18	3	2	0	0	0	1	1	0	0	.111	.111
Galloway, Chick-Clarence Edward	19-27PhiA 28DetA	08-04-96	Manning, S.C.	11-07-69	R	R	5'8	160	1076	3583	381	946	136	46	17	407	274	224	79	.264	.342
Galvin, Jim-James Joseph	30BosA	08-11-07	Somerville, Mass.	09-30-69	R	R	6'1	180	2	2	0	0	0	0	0	0	0	1	0	.000	.000
Gamble, Lee-Lee Jesse	35,38-40CinN	11-03-10	Renovo, Pa.	10-05-94	L	R	6'1	170	165	342	51	91	12	3	0	21	10	21	6	.266	.319
Gantenbein, Sep-Joseph Steven	39-40PhiA	08-25-15	San Francisco, Cal.	08-02-93	L	R	5'9	168	186	545	68	148	20	6	8	59	43	43	2	.272	.374
Ganzel, Babe-Foster Pirie	27-28WasA	05-22-01	Malden, Mass.	02-06-78	R	R	5'11	172	23	74	7	23	5	2	1	17	8	7	0	.311	.473
Garbark, Bob-Robert Michael	34-35CleA 37-39ChiN 44PhiA 45BosA	11-13-09	Houston, Tex.	08-15-90	R	R	5'11	178	145	327	31	81	9	0	0	28	26	17	0	.248	.275
Garbark, Mike-Nathaniel Michael	44-45NYA	02-02-16	Houston, Tex.	08-31-94	R	R	6'	200	149	475	46	116	14	7	2	59	48	39	0	.244	.316
Gardella, Al-Alfred Stephen	45NYN	01-11-18	New York, N.Y.		L	L	5'10	172	16	26	2	2	0	0	0	1	4	3	0	.077	.077
Gardella, Danny-Daniel Lewis	44-45NYN 46-49SM 50StLN	02-26-20	New York, N.Y.	03-06-05	L	L	5'8	160	169	543	74	145	13	5	24	85	57	68	2	.267	.433
Gardner, Ray-Raymond Vincent	29-30CleA	10-25-01	Frederick, Md.	05-03-68	R	R	5'8	145	115	269	35	68	8	3	1	25	29	17	10	.253	.290
Garibaldi, Art-Arthur Edward	36StLN	08-21-07	San Francisco, Cal.	10-19-67	R	R	5'8	175	71	232	30	64	12	0	1	20	16	30	3	.276	.341
Garms, Debs-Debs C. (Tex)	32-35StLA 37-39BosN 40-41PitN 43-45StLN	06-26-07	Bangs, Tex.	12-16-84	R	R	5'9	165	1010	3111	489	910	141	39	17	328	288	161	18	.293	.379
Garrison, Ford-Robert Ford (Snapper, Rocky)	43-44BosA 44-46PhiA	08-29-15	Greenville, S.C.	06-01-01	R	R	5'10	180	185	687	80	180	22	3	6	56	37	67	11	.262	.329
Garrity, Hank-Francis Joseph	31ChiA	02-04-08	Boston, Mass.	09-01-62	R	R	6'1	185	8	14	0	3	1	0	0	2	1	2	0	.214	.286
Gaston, Alex-Alexander Nathaniel	20-23NYN 26,29BosA	03-13-93	New York, N.Y.	02-08-79	R	R	5'9	170	215	514	50	112	13	6	3	41	29	56	5	.218	.284
Gautreau, Doc-Walter Paul (Punk)	25PhiA 25-28BosN	07-26-01	Cambridge, Mass.	08-23-70	R	R	5'4	130	261	806	122	207	34	10	0	52	99	63	40	.257	.324
Gautreaux, Sid-Sidney Allen (Pudge)	36-37BknN	05-04-12	Schriever, La.	04-19-80	B	R	5'8	190	86	81	8	20	4	0	0	18	10	8	2	.247	.296
Gazella, Mike-Michael	23,26-28NYA	09-11-96	Olyphant, Pa.	08-11-78	R	R	5'7	165	160	352	51	85	14	4	0	32	56	50	8	.241	.304
Geary, Huck-Eugene Francis Joseph	42-43PitN 44-45MS	01-22-17	Buffalo, N.Y.	01-27-81	R	R	5'10	170	55	188	20	30	4	1	0	15	20	9	3	.160	.197
Gedeon, Elmer-Elmer John (Jack)	39WasA 41-44MS	04-15-17	Cleveland, Ohio	04-20-44	R	R	6'4	196	5	15	1	3	0	0	0	1	0	4	0	.200	.200
Gehrig, Lou (Heinrich Ludwig)-Henry Louis (The Iron Horse, Columbia Lou, Larruping Lou)	23-39NYA	06-19-03	New York, N.Y.	06-02-41	L	L	6'	200	2164	8001	1888	2721	535	162	493	1995	1508	790	102	.340	.632
Gehringer, Charlie-Charles Leonard (The Mechanical Man)	24-42DetA 43-45MS	05-11-03	Fowlerville, Mich.	01-21-93	L	R	5'11	180	2323	8860	1774	2839	574	146	184	1427	1185	372	181	.320	.480
Gelbert, Charley-Charles Magnus	29-32StLN 33-34LJ 35-36StLN 37CinN 37DetA 39-40WasA 40BosN	01-26-06	Scranton, Pa.	01-13-67	R	R	5'11	170	876	2869	398	766	169	43	17	350	290	245	34	.267	.374
Gentile, Sam-Samuel Christopher	43BosN 44-45MS	10-12-16	Charlestown, Mass.	05-04-98	L	R	5'11	180	8	4	1	1	0	0	0	0	1	0	0	.250	.500
George, Greek-Charles Peter	35-36ChiA 38BknN 41ChiN 45PhiN	12-25-12	Waycross, Ga.	08-15-99	R	R	6'2	190	118	299	15	53	9	2	0	24	28	59	0	.177	.221
Geraghty, Ben-Benjamin Raymond	36BknN	07-19-12	Jersey City, N.J.	06-18-63	R	R	5'11	175	70	146	16	29	4	0	0	9	18	14	1	.199	.226
Gerber, Wally-Walter (Spooks)	14-15PitN 17-28StLA 28-29BosA	08-18-91	Columbus, Ohio	06-19-51	R	R	5'10	152	1522	5099	558	1309	172	46	6	476	465	357	41	.257	.313
Gerken, George-George Herbert (Pickles)	27-28CleA	07-28-03	Chicago, Ill.	10-23-77	R	R	5'11	175	44	129	17	29	7	0	0	11	13	25	3	.225	.310
Gerlach, John-John Glenn	38-39ChiA	05-11-17	Shullsburg, Wis.	08-28-99	R	R	5'9	165	12	27	3	9	0	0	0	1	1	4	0	.333	.333

USE NAME - GIVEN NAMES (NICKNAMES)	TEAM BY YEAR	BIRTH DATE	BIRTH PLACE	DEATH DATE	B	T	HGT	WGT	G	AB	R	H	2B	3B	HR	RBI	BB	SO	SB	BA	SA
Geygan, Chappie-James Edward	24-26BosA	06-03-03	Ironton, Ohio	03-15-66	R	R	5'11	170	40	103	7	26	5	2	0	4	5	19	0	.252	.340
Gharrity, Patsy-Edward Patrick	16-23WasA 24-28DE 29-30WasA	03-13-92	Parnell, Iowa	10-10-66	R	R	5'10	170	676	1961	237	513	92	26	20	249	188	231	32	.262	.368
Gibson, Charlie-Charles Griffin		11-21-99	LaGrange, Ga.	12-18-90	R	R	5'8	160	12	15	1	2	0	0	0	1	0	0	0	.133	.133
Gibson, Frank-Frank Gilbert	13DetA 21-27BosN	09-27-90	Omaha, Neb.	04-27-61	B	R	6'1	172	468	1155	121	317	57	19	8	146	55	127	12	.274	.377
Gilbert, Andy-Andrew	42BosA 43-45MS 46BosA	07-18-14	Bradenville, Pa.	08-29-92	R	R	6'1	203	8	12	1	1	0	0	0	1	1	3	0	.083	.083
Gilbert, Charlie-Charles Mader	40BknN 41-43ChiN 44-45MS 46ChiN 46-47PhiN	07-08-19	New Orleans, La.	08-13-83	L	L	5'9	165	364	852	109	195	27	9	5	55	86	82	7	.229	.299
Gilbert, Wally-Walter John 23-26 played in N.F.L.		12-19-00	Oscada, Mich.	09-08-58	R	R	6'1	190	591	2317	301	624	112	17	7	214	162	131	21	.269	.341
Gilham, George-George Louis	20-21StLN	09-17-99	Shamokin, Pa.	04-25-37	R	R	5'11	164	2	4	0	0	0	0	0	0	0	1	0	.000	.000
Gill, Johnny-John Wesley (Patcheye)	27-28CleA 31,34WasA 35-36CinN	03-27-05	Nashville, Tenn.	12-26-84	L	R	6'2	190	118	322	39	79	17	1	10	45	23	43	1	.245	.398
Gillenwater, Carden-Carden Edison	40StLN 43BknN 45-46BosN 48WasA	05-13-17	Riceville, Tenn.	05-10-00	R	R	6'1	175	335	1004	129	261	41	7	11	114	153	138	20	.260	.348
Gillsepie, Paul-Paul Allen	42,44-45ChiN	09-18-20	Sugar Valley, Ga.	08-11-70	L	R	6'2	180	89	205	17	58	7	0	6	31	22	14	2	.283	.405
Gillis, Grant-Grant	27-28WasA 29BosA	01-24-01	Grove Hill, Ala.	02-04-81	R	R	5'10	165	62	196	26	48	12	2	0	23	12	13	0	.245	.327
Gionfriddo, Al-Albert Francis	44-47PittN 47BknN	03-08-22	Dysart, Pa.	03-14-03	L	L	5'6	165	228	680	95	154	22	12	2	58	91	39	15	.266	.355
Giuliani, Tony-Angelo John	36-37StLA 38-39WasA 40-41BknN 43WasA	11-24-12	St. Paul, Minn.	10-28-04	R	R	5'11	175	243	674	58	157	18	3	0	69	38	40	1	.233	.269
Gladu, Roland-Roland Edouard	44BosN	05-10-11	Montreal, Canada	07-26-94	L	R	5'9	185	21	66	5	16	2	1	1	7	3	8	0	.242	.348
Gleason, Billy-William Patrick	16-17PhiN 21StLA	09-06-94	Chicago, Ill.	01-09-57	R	R	5'6	157	40	118	9	26	1	1	0	8	11	11	1	.220	.246
Gleeson, Jim-James Joseph (Gee-Gee)	36CleA 39-40ChiN 41-42CinN	03-05-12	Kansas City, Mo.	05-01-96	B	R	6'1	191	392	1277	195	336	77	19	16	154	158	147	20	.263	.391
Gleich, Frank-Frank Elmer (Inch)	19-20NYA 21IL	03-07-94	Columbus, Ohio	03-27-49	R	R	5'11	175	29	45	6	6	0	0	0	4	7	10	0	.133	.133
Glenn (Gurzensky), Joe-Joseph Charles (Gabber)	32-33,35-38NYA 39StLA 40StLA	11-19-08	Dickson City, Pa.	05-06-85	R	R	5'11	181	248	718	77	181	34	5	5	89	81	91	6	.252	.334
Glossop, Al-Alban	39-40NYN 40BosN 42PhiN 43BknN 44-45MS 46CinN	07-12-14	Christopher, Ill.	07-02-91	B	R	6'	170	309	952	99	199	29	2	15	86	89	105	5	.209	.291
Goebel, Ed-Wilbur Edwin	22WasA	09-01-98	Brooklyn, N.Y.	08-12-59	R	R	5'11	170	37	59	13	16	1	0	1	3	6	8	1	.271	.339
Goldman, Jonah-Jonah John	28,30-31CleA	08-29-06	New York, N.Y.	08-17-80	R	R	5'7	170	148	389	33	87	20	0	1	49	35	31	4	.224	.283
Goldstein, Lonnie-Leslie Elmer	43CinN 45MS 46CinN	05-13-18	Austin, Tex.	05-10-00	L	L	6'2	190	11	10	2	1	0	0	0	0	3	2	0	.100	.100
Goletz, Stan-Stanley (Stash)	41ChiA 42-45MS	05-21-18	Crescent, Ohio	06-07-97	L	L	6'3	200	5	5	0	3	0	0	0	0	0	2	0	.600	.600
Golvin, Walt-Walter George	22ChiN	02-01-94	Hershey, Neb.	06-11-73	L	L	6'	165	2	2	0	0	0	0	0	0	1	0	0	.000	.000
Gomez, Chile-Jose Luis [Gonzales]	35-36PhiN 42WasA	05-23-09	Mazatlan, Mexico	12-01-92	R	R	5'10	165	200	627	56	142	9	3	0	50	40	73	3	.226	.250
Gomez, Preston-Pedro [Martinez]	44WasA M69-72DN M74-75HouN M80ChiN	04-20-23	Preston, Cuba		R	R	5'11	170	8	7	2	2	0	0	0	2	0	4	0	.286	.429
Gonzalez, Mike-Miguel Angel [Codero]	12BknN 14CinN 15-18StLN 19-21NYN 24-25StLN 25-29ChiN 31-32,M38,40StLN	09-24-90	Havana, Cuba	02-19-77	R	R	6'1	200	1042	2829	283	717	123	19	13	263	231	198	52	.253	.324
Gooch, Charlie-Charles Purman	29WasA	06-05-02	Smyrna, Tenn.	05-30-82	R	R	5'9	170	39	57	6	16	2	1	0	5	7	8	0	.281	.351
Gooch, Johnny-John Beverley	21-28PittN 28-29BknN 29-30CinN 33BosA	11-09-97	Smyrna, Tenn.	05-15-75	B	R	5'11	175	805	2363	227	662	98	29	7	293	206	141	11	.280	.355
Goodman, Ival-Ival Richard (Goodie)	35-42CinN 43-44CubN	07-23-08	Northview, Mo.	11-25-84	L	L	5'11	175	1107	3928	609	1104	188	85	95	525	382	380	49	.281	.445
Gordon, Joe-Joseph Lowell (Flash)	38-43NYA 44-45MS 46NYA 47-50,M58-60CleA M60DetA M61KCA M69KCA	02-18-15	Los Angeles, Cal.	04-14-78	R	R	5'10	180	1566	5707	914	1530	264	52	253	975	759	702	89	.268	.466
Gorman, Howie-Howard Paul (Lefty)	37-38PhiN	05-14-13	Pittsburgh, Pa.	04-29-84	L	L	6'2	160	14	20	3	4	1	0	0	1	1	1	1	.200	.250
Goslin, Goose-Leon Allen	21-30WasA 30-32StLA 33WasA 34-37DetA 38WasA	10-16-00	Salem, N.J.	05-15-71	L	L	5'11	185	2287	8654	1483	2735	500	173	248	1609	949	585	175	.316	.500
Goulish, Nick-Nicholas Edward	44-45PhiN	11-13-16	Punxsutawney, Pa.	05-15-84	L	L	6'1	179	14	12	4	3	0	0	0	2	1	3	0	.250	.250
Grabowski, Johnny-John Patrick (Nig)	24-26ChiA 27-29NYA 31DetA	01-07-00	Ware, Mass.	05-23-46	R	R	5'11	180	296	816	84	206	25	8	3	86	47	84	1	.252	.314
Grace, Earl-Robert Earl	29,31ChiN 31-35PittN 36-37PhiN	02-24-07	Barlow, Ky.	12-22-80	L	R	6'	175	627	1877	169	493	83	10	31	251	185	130	1	.263	.367
Grace, Joe-Joseph LaVerne	38-41StLA 42-45MS 46StLA 46-47WasA	01-05-14	Gorham, Ill.	09-18-69	L	R	6'2	180	484	1561	225	442	76	18	20	172	179	135	9	.283	.393
Graham, Roy-Roy Vincent	22-23ChiA	02-22-97	San Francisco, Cal.	04-26-33	R	R	5'10	175	41	85	3	16	2	0	0	6	9	6	0	.188	.212
Graham, Skinny-Arthur William	34-35BosA	08-12-09	Somerville, Mass.	07-10-67	L	R	5'7	162	21	57	8	14	2	1	0	4	7	16	3	.246	.316
Grant, Jimmy-James Charles	42-43ChiA 43-44CleA	10-06-18	Racine, Wis.	07-08-70	L	R	5'8	166	146	354	38	87	16	6	5	6	38	67	5	.246	.367
Grantham, George-George Farley (Boots)	22-24ChiN 25-31PittN 32-33CinN 34NYN	05-20-00	Galena, Kans.	03-16-54	L	R	5'10	170	1444	4989	912	1508	292	93	105	712	717	526	132	.302	.461
Graves, Joe-Joseph Ebenezer	26CinN	02-26-06	Marblehead, Mass.	12-22-80	L	R	6'	160	2	5	0	0	0	0	0	0	0	1	0	.000	.000
Graves, Sid-Sidney (Whitey)	27BosN	11-30-01	Marblehead, Mass.	12-28-83	R	R	6'	175	7	20	5	5	1	0	0	0	1	1	1	.250	.400
Gray, Milt-Milton Marshall	37WasA	02-21-14	Louisville, Ky.	06-30-69	R	R	6'1	180	2	6	0	0	0	0	0	0	0	0	0	.000	.000
Gray (Wyshner), Pete-Peter J.	45StLA	03-06-15	Nanticoke, Pa.	06-30-02	L	L	6'1	169	77	234	26	51	6	2	0	13	13	11	5	.218	.261
Greene (Green), Joe-Joseph Henry (Tilly)	24PhiA	09-17-97	Philadelphia, Pa.	02-04-72	R	R	6'2	170	1	1	0	0	0	0	0	0	0	0	0	.000	.000
Greenberg, Hank-Henry Benjamin (Hammerin' Hank)	30,33-41DetA 42-44MS 45-46DetA 47PittN	01-01-11	New York, N.Y.	09-04-86	R	R	6'4	210	1394	5193	1051	1628	379	71	331	1276	852	844	58	.313	.605
Gremp, Buddy-Louis Edward	40-42BosN 43-45MS	08-05-19	Denver, Colo.	01-30-95	R	R	6'1	175	113	291	19	65	14	0	3	31	18	24	1	.223	.302
Griesenbeck, Tim-Carlos Phillippe Timothy	20StLN	12-10-97	San Antonio, Tex.	03-25-53	R	R	5'11	185	5	3	1	1	0	0	0	0	0	0	0	.333	.333
Griffin, Ivy-Ivy Moore	19-21PhiA	11-16-96	Thomasville, Ala.	08-25-57	L	L	5'11	180	185	638	65	164	21	5	0	39	23	65	4	.257	.306
Griffith, Bert-Bartholomew Joseph (Buck)	22-23BknN 24WasA	03-09-96	St. Louis, Mo.	05-05-73	L	R	6'	188	191	581	69	174	30	12	4	72	18	28	6	.299	.413
Grigsby, Denver-Denver Clarence	23-25ChiN	03-24-01	Jackson, Ky.	11-10-73	L	R	5'9	155	199	620	86	179	28	4	3	73	57	64	12	.289	.361
Grimes, Ed-Edward Adelbert	31-32StLA	09-08-05	Chicago, Ill.	10-04-74	R	R	5'10	165	74	125	16	31	1	3	0	18	15	15	1	.248	.304
Grimes, Oscar-Oscar Ray Jr.	38-42CleA 43-46NYA 46PhiA	05-08-15	Minerva, Ohio	05-19-93	R	R	5'11	178	602	1832	235	469	73	24	18	200	297	303	30	.256	.352
Grimes, Ray-Oscar Ray Sr.	20BosA 21-24ChiN 26PhiN	09-11-93	Bergholz, Ohio	05-25-53	R	R	6'	175	433	1537	269	505	101	25	27	263	204	133	21	.329	.480
Grimes, Roy-Roy Austin (Bummer)	20NYN	09-11-93	Bergholz, Ohio	09-13-54	R	R	6'1	165	26	57	5	9	1	0	0	3	3	8	1	.158	.175
Grimm, Charlie-Charles John (Jolly Cholly)	16PhiA 18StLN 19-24PittN 25-36,M32-38,44-49ChiN M52BosN M53-56MilN M60ChiN	08-28-98	St. Louis, Mo.	11-15-83	L	L	5'11	173	2164	7917	908	2299	394	108	79	1078	578	410	57	.290	.397
Groskloss, Howdy-Howard Hoffman	30-32PittN	04-10-06	Pittsburgh, Pa.	07-15-06	R	R	5'9	176	72	184	14	48	7	2	0	21	11	19	1	.261	.321
Gross, Turkey-Ewell	25BosA	02-21-96	Mesquite, Tex.	01-11-36	R	R	6'	165	9	32	3	3	0	0	0	2	2	2	0	.094	.156
Grube, Frank-Franklin Thomas (Hans) 28 played in N.F.L.	31-33ChiA 34-35StLA 35-36ChiA 41StLA	01-07-05	Easton, Pa.	07-02-45	R	R	5'9	190	394	1125	121	274	59	5	1	107	131	88	12	.244	.308
Gryska, Sig-Sigmund Stanley	38-39StLA	11-04-14	Chicago, Ill.	08-27-94	R	R	5'11	173	25	70	7	23	4	1	0	12	9	13	3	.329	.414
Gudat, Marv-Marvin John (See P20-45)	29CinN 32ChiN	08-27-05	Goliad, Tex.	03-01-54	L	L	5'11	176	69	104	15	26	4	1	1	15	16	10	0	.250	.337
Guisto, Lou-Louis Joseph	16-17CleA 18MS 21-23CleA	11-16-95	Napa, Cal.	10-15-89	R	R	5'11	193	156	449	35	88	19	3	0	59	46	44	5	.196	.252
Gulley, Tom-Thomas Jefferson	23-24CleA 26ChiA	12-25-99	Garner, N.C.	11-24-66	R	R	5'11	178	26	58	10	12	4	2	0	9	8	4	0	.207	.345
Gullic, Ted-Tedd Jasper	30,33StLA	01-02-07	Koshkonong, Mo.	01-28-00	R	R	6'2	175	196	612	73	151	25	8	9	79	42	81	7	.247	.358
Gustine, Frankie-Frank William	39-48PittN 49ChiN 50StLA	02-20-20	Hoopeston, Ill.	04-01-91	R	R	6'	175	1261	4582	553	1214	222	47	38	480	369	427	60	.265	.359
Gutteridge, Don-Donald Joseph (Firpo)	36-40StLN 42-45StLA 46-47BosA 48PittN M69-70ChiA	06-19-12	Pittsburg, Kans.		R	R	5'10	165	1151	4202	586	1075	200	64	39	391	309	444	95	.256	.362
Gyselman, Dick-Richard Renald	33-34BosN	04-06-08	San Francisco, Cal.	09-20-90	R	R	6'2	170	82	191	17	43	7	3	0	16	9	32	0	.225	.293
Haas, Mule-George William	25PittN 28-32PhiA 33-37ChiA 38PhiA	10-15-03	Montclair, N.J.	06-30-74	L	R	6'1	175	1168	4303	706	1257	254	45	43	496	433	299	12	.292	.402
Hack, Stan-Stanley Camfield (Smiling Stan)	32-47,M54-56ChiN M58StLN	12-06-09	Sacramento, Cal.	12-15-79	L	R	6'	170	1938	7278	1239	2193	363	81	57	642	1092	466	165	.301	.397
Haeffner, Bill-William Bernhard	15PhiA 20PittN 28NYN	07-18-94	Philadelphia, Pa.	01-27-82	R	R	5'9	165	59	180	8	35	4	1	0	14	8	15	1	.194	.228
Hafey, Bud-Daniel Albert	35ChiA 35-36PittN 39CinN 39PhiN	08-06-12	Berkeley, Cal.	07-27-86	R	R	6'	185	123	366	53	78	19	3	10	33	30	91	2	.213	.363
Hafey, Chick-Charles James	24-31StLN 32-35CinN 36IL 37CinN	02-12-03	Berkeley, Cal.	07-02-73	R	R	6'	185	1283	4625	777	1466	341	67	164	833	372	477	70	.317	.526
Hafey, Tom-Thomas Francis (The Arm)	39NYN 44StLA	07-12-13	Berkeley, Cal.	10-02-96	R	R	6'1	180	78	270	38	67	12	1	6	28	11	48	1	.248	.367
Hahn, Dick-Richard Frederick	40WasA	07-24-16	Canton, Ohio	11-05-92	R	R	5'11	176	1	1	0	0	0	0	0	0	0	0	0	.000	.000
Haines, Hinkey-Henry Luther 25-29,31 played in N.F.L.	23NYA	12-23-98	Red Lion, Pa.	01-09-79	R	R	5'10	170	28	25	4	4	2	0	0	3	4	5	3	.160	.240
Hajduk, Chet-Chester	41ChiA	07-21-18	Chicago, Ill.	07-04-06	R	R	6'	195	1	1	0	0	0	0	0	0	0	0	0	.000	.000
Hale, Odell-Arvel Odell (Bad News, Chief)	31,33-40CleA 41BosA 41NYN	08-10-08	Hosston, La.	06-09-80	R	R	5'10	175	1062	3701	551	1071	240	51	73	573	353	315	57	.289	.441
Hale, Sammy-Samuel Douglas	20-21DetA 23-29PhiA 30StLA	09-10-96	Glen Rose, Tex.	09-06-74	R	R	5'9	160	883	2915	422	880	157	54	30	392	130	218	41	.302	.424
Hall, Irv-Irvin Gladstone	43-46PhiA	10-07-18	Alberton, Md.		R	R	5'10	160	508	1904	178	496	58	19	0	168	97	148	16	.261	.311
Hamby, Sam-James Sanford (Cracker)	26-27NYN	09-29-97	Wilkesboro, N.C.	10-21-91	R	R	6'	170	22	55	6	10	0	0	0	2	3	6	0	.182	.218
Hamner, Garvin-Wesley Garvin (Wes)	45PhiN	03-18-24	Richmond, Va.	12-15-03	R	R	5'11	172	32	101	12	20	3	0	0	5	7	9	2	.198	.228
Hamrick, Ray-Raymond Bernard	43-44PhiN 45-46MS	08-01-21	Nashville, Tenn.		R	R	5'11	160	118	452	34	92	13	2	1	32	31	62	1	.204	.248
Hancken, Buddy-Morris Medlock	40PhiN	08-30-14	Birmingham, Ala.		R	R	6'1	175	1	0	0	0	0	0	0	0	0	0	0	—	—
Handley, Lee-Lee Elmer (Jeep)	36CinN 37-41,44-46PittN 47PhiN	07-31-13	Clarion, Iowa	04-08-70	R	R	5'7	160	968	3356	418	902	122	45	15	297	267	204	68	.269	.345
Haney, Fred-Fred Girard (Pudge)	22-25DetA 26-27BosA 27CinN 29StLN M39-41StLA M53-55PittN M56-59MilN	04-25-98	Albuquerque, N.M.	11-09-77	R	R	5'6	170	622	1977	338	544	66	21	8	228	282	123	50	.275	.342
Hanski (Hanyzewski), Don-Donald Thomas	43-44ChiA 45MS	02-27-16	La Porte, Ind.	09-02-57	L	L	5'11	180	11	22	1	5	1	0	0	2	0	5	0	.227	.273
Happenny, John-John Clifford (Cliff)	23ChiA	05-18-01	Waltham, Mass.	12-29-88	R	R	5'11	165	32	86	7	19	1	0	0	10	3	13	0	.221	.279

USE NAME - GIVEN NAMES (NICKNAMES)	TEAM BY YEAR	BIRTH DATE	BIRTH PLACE	DEATH DATE	B	T	HGT	WGT	G	AB	R	H	2B	3B	HR	RBI	BB	SO	SB	BA	SA
Hargrave, Bubbles-Eugene Franklin	13-15ChiN 21-28CinN 30NYA	07-15-92	New Haven, Ind.	02-23-69	R	R	5'10	174	852	2533	314	786	155	58	29	376	217	165	29	.310	.452
Hargrave, Pinky-William McKinley	23-25WasA 25-26PhiA 28-30DetA 30-31WasA 32-33BosN	01-31-96	New Haven, Ind.	10-03-42	B	R	5'9	180	650	1602	177	445	91	16	39	265	140	165	17	.278	.428
							Bats Right 23-26														
Hargreaves, Charlie-Charles Russell	23-28BknN 28-30PitN	12-14-96	Trenton, N.J.	05-09-79	R	R	6'	170	423	1188	96	321	44	11	4	139	77	49	6	.270	.336
Harper, George-George Washington	16-18DetA 22-24CinN 24-26PhiN 27-28NYN 28StLN 29BosN	06-24-92	Arlington, Ky.	08-18-78	L	R	5'8	167	1073	3398	505	1030	158	43	91	528	389	208	58	.303	.455
Harrington, Andy-Andrew Matthew	25DetA	02-12-03	Mountain View, Cal.	01-26-79	R	R	5'11	170	1	1	0	0	0	0	0	0	0	0	0	.000	.000
Harris, Bucky-Stanley Raymond	19-28,M24-28WasA 29,31M29-33DetA M34BosN M35-42WasA M43PhiN M47-48NYA M50-54WasA M55-56DetA	11-08-96	Port Jervis,N.Y.	11-08-77	R	R	5'9	156	1264	4736	722	1297	224	64	9	506	472	310	166	.274	.354
Harris, Dave-David Stanley (Sheriff)	25,28BosN 30ChiA 30-34WasA	06-14-00	Summerfield, N.C.	09-18-73	R	R	5'11	190	542	1477	243	406	74	33	32	247	196	245	28	.281	.444
Harris, Joe-Joseph (Moon)	14NYA 17CleA 18MS 19CleA 20-21DO 22-25BosA 25-26WasA 27-28PitN 28BknN	05-20-91	Coulters, Pa.	12-10-59	R	R	5'9	170	970	3035	461	963	201	64	47	517	418	188	35	.317	.472
Harris, Ned-Robert Ned	41-43DetA 44-45MS 46DetA	07-09-16	Ames, Iowa	12-18-76	L	L	5'11	175	262	814	107	211	33	14	16	81	102	77	12	.259	.393
Harris, Spence-Spencer Anthony	25-26ChiA 29WasA 30PhiA	08-12-00	Duluth, Minn.	07-03-82	L	L	5'9	160	164	377	53	94	15	3	3	46	39	33	10	.249	.329
Harshany(Harshaney), Sam-Samuel	37-40StLA	04-24-10	Madison, Ill.	02-01-01	R	R	6'	180	61	181	17	43	3	0	0	15	16	10	0	.238	.254
Hart, Bill-William Woodrow	43-45BknN	03-04-13	Wisconsin, Pa.	07-29-68	R	R	6'	175	95	270	35	56	10	4	3	32	24	30	8	.207	.307
Hartje, Chris-Christian Henry	39BknN	03-25-15	San Francisco, Cal.	06-26-46	R	R	5'11	180	9	16	2	5	1	0	0	5	1	0	0	.313	.375
Hartnett, Gabby-Charles Leo (Old Tomato Face)	22-40,M38-40ChiN 41NYN	12-20-00	Woonsocket, R.I.	12-20-72	R	R	6'1	195	1990	6432	867	1912	396	64	236	1179	703	697	28	.297	.489
Harvel, Luther-Luther Raymond (Red)	28CleA	09-30-05	Cambria, Ill.	04-10-86	R	R	5'11	180	40	136	12	30	6	1	0	12	4	17	1	.221	.279
Hassenmayer, Don-Donald Irvin	45-46PhiN	04-04-27	Roslyn, Pa.		R	R	5'10	180	11	30	1	3	1	0	0	1	2	3	0	.100	.133
Haslin (Haslinsky), Mickey-Michael Joseph	33-36PhiN 36BosN 37-38NYN	10-25-09	Wilkes-Barre, Pa.	03-07-02	R	R	5'8	165	318	974	125	265	33	8	9	109	59	64	8	.272	.350
Hassett, Buddy-John Aloysius	36-38BknN 39-41BosN 42NYA 43-46MS	09-05-11	New York, N.Y.	08-23-97	L	L	5'11	180	929	3517	469	1026	130	40	12	343	209	116	53	.292	.362
Hassler, Joe-Joseph Frederick	28-29PhiA 30StLA	04-07-05	Fort Smith, Ark.	09-04-71	R	R	6'	165	37	46	9	11	2	0	0	4	2	7	0	.239	.283
Hasson, Gene-Charles Eugene	37-38PhiA	07-20-15	Connellsville, Pa.	07-30-03	L	L	6'	197	47	167	22	49	12	5	4	26	25	21	0	.293	.497
Hauser, Joe-Joseph John (Unser Choe)	22-24,26,28PhiA 25BK 29CleA	01-12-99	Milwaukee, Wis.	07-11-97	L	L	5'10	175	629	2044	351	580	103	29	79	356	250	228	19	.284	.478
Hausmann, George-George John	44-45NYN 46-48SM 49NYN	02-11-16	St. Louis, Mo.	06-16-04	R	R	5'5	145	301	1136	173	304	35	13	3	78	120	77	10	.268	.329
Hawks, Chicken-Nelson Louis	21NYA 25PhiN	02-03-96	San Francisco, Cal.	05-26-73	L	L	5'11	167	146	393	68	124	17	8	7	60	37	45	3	.316	.453
Hayes, Frankie-Franklin Whitman (Blimp)	33-34,36-42PhiA 42-43StLA 42-43StLA 45-48CleA 46ChiA 47BosN	10-13-14	Jamesburg, N.J.	06-22-55	R	R	6'	200	1364	4493	545	1164	213	32	119	628	564	627	30	.259	.400
Hayes, Jackie-Minter Carney	27-31WasA 32-40ChiA	07-19-06	Clanton, Ala.	02-09-83	R	R	5'10	165	1091	4040	494	1069	196	33	20	493	309	241	34	.265	.344
Hayworth, Ray-Raymond Hall	26,29-38DetA 38-39BknN 39NYN 42StLN 44-45BknN	01-29-04	High Point, N.C.	09-25-02	R	R	6'	180	699	2062	221	546	92	16	5	238	198	188	2	.265	.332
Hayworth, Red-Myron Claude	44-45StLA 46-48MS	05-14-16	High Point, N.C.		R	R	6'1	200	146	430	27	91	15	1	1	42	17	19	0	.212	.259
Healy, Francis-Francis Xavier Paul	30-32NYN 34StLN	06-29-10	Holyoke, Mass.	02-12-97	L	R	5'10	175	42	54	9	13	3	0	0	5	2	10	0	.241	.296
Heath, Jeff-John Geoffrey	36-45CleA 46WasA 46-47StLA 48-49BosN	04-01-15	Fort William, Canada	12-09-75	L	R	5'11	200	1383	4937	777	1447	279	102	194	887	593	670	56	.293	.509
Heath, Mickey-Minor Wilson	31-32CinN	10-30-03	Toledo, Ohio	07-30-86	L	L	5'11	175	46	160	16	34	1	3	0	18	22	28	0	.213	.256
Heath, Tommy-Thomas George	35,37-38StLN	08-18-13	Akron, Ohio	02-26-37	R	R	5'11	185	134	330	36	76	16	2	3	34	65	40	0	.230	.318
Heathcote, Cliff-Clifton Earl	18-22StLN 22-30ChiN 31-32CinN 32PhiN	01-24-98	Glen Rock, Pa.	01-18-39	L	L	5'10	160	1415	4443	643	1222	206	55	42	448	367	325	190	.275	.375
Heffner, Don-Donald Henry (Jeep)	34-37NYA 38-43StLA 43PhiA 44DetA M66CinN	02-08-11	Rouzerville, Pa.	08-01-89	R	R	5'10	155	743	2526	275	610	99	19	6	248	270	218	15	.241	.303
Heilmann, Harry-Harry Edwin (Slug)	14,16-29DetA 30CinN 30NL 31IL 32CinN	08-03-94	San Francisco, Cal.	07-09-51	R	R	6'1	200	2146	7787	1291	2660	542	151	183	1537	856	550	112	.342	.520
Heim, Val-Val Raymond	42ChiA 43-45MS	11-04-20	Plymouth, Wis.		L	R	5'11	170	13	45	6	9	1	1	0	7	5	3	1	.200	.267
Heine, Bud-William Henry	21NYN	09-22-00	Elmira, N.Y.	09-02-76	L	R	5'8	145	1	2	0	0	0	0	0	0	0	0	0	.000	.000
Heltzel, Heinie-William Wade	43BosN 44PhiN	12-21-13	York, Pa.	05-01-98	R	R	5'11	150	40	108	7	17	4	0	0	5	9	16	0	.157	.194
Hemsley, Rollie-Ralston Burdett	28-31PitN 31-32PhiN 33CinN 33-37StLA 38-41CleA 42CinN 42-44NYA 45MS 46-47PhiN	06-24-07	Syracuse, Ohio	07-31-72	R	R	5'10	180	1593	5047	562	1321	257	72	31	555	357	395	29	.262	.360
Hendrick, Harvey-Harvey (Gink)	23-24NYA 25CleA 27-31BknN 31CinN 32StLN 33CinN 34PhiN	11-09-97	Mason, Tenn.	10-29-41	L	R	6'2	190	922	2910	434	896	157	46	48	413	239	243	75	.308	.443
Henline, Butch-Walter John	21NYN 21-26PhiN 27-29BknN 30-31ChiA	12-20-94	Fort Wayne, Ind.	10-09-57	R	R	5'10	175	740	2101	58	611	96	21	40	268	192	156	19	.291	.414
Henrich, Fritz-Frank Wilde	24PhiN	05-08-99	Cincinnati, Ohio	05-01-59	R	R	5'10	160	36	90	4	19	4	0	0	4	2	12	0	.211	.256
Henrich, Tommy-Thomas David (Old Reliable)	37-42NYA 43-45MS 46-50NYA	02-20-10	Massillon, Ohio		L	L	6'	180	1284	4603	901	1297	269	73	183	795	712	383	37	.282	.491
Henry, Snake-Frederick Marshall	22-23BosN	07-19-95	Waynesville, N.C.	10-12-87	L	L	6'	170	29	75	6	14	4	1	0	7	3	9	2	.187	.267
Herman, Babe-Floyd Caves	26-31BknN 32CinN 33-34ChiN 35PitN 35-36CinN 37DetA 45BknN	06-26-03	Buffalo, N.Y.	11-27-87	L	L	6'4	190	1552	5603	882	1818	399	110	181	997	520	553	94	.324	.532
Herman, Billy-William Jennings Bryan	31-41ChiN 41-43BknN 44-45MS 46BknN 46BosN 47,M47PitN M64-66BosA	07-07-09	New Albany, Ind.	09-05-92	R	R	5'11	180	1922	7707	1163	2345	486	82	47	839	737	428	67	.304	.407
Hermann, Al-Albert Bartel (Duke)	23-24BknN	03-28-99	Milltown, N.J.	08-02-80	R	R	6'	180	32	94	2	22	4	0	0	11	0	8	3	.234	.277
Hernandez, Chico-Salvadore Jose [Ramos]	42-43ChiN	01-03-16	Havana, Cuba	01-03-86	R	R	6'	195	90	244	16	61	9	0	0	16	20	22	0	.250	.287
Herrara, Mike-Ramon	25-26Bos	12-19-97	Havana, Cuba	02-03-78	R	R	5'6	147	84	276	22	76	14	1	0	27	17	15	1	.275	.333
Hershberger, Willard-Willard McKee	38-40CinN	05-28-10	Lemon Cove, Cal.	08-03-40	R	R	5'10	167	160	402	41	127	16	5	0	70	20	16	2	.316	.381
Heving, Johnnie-John Aloys	20StLA 24-25,28-30BosA 31-32PhiA	04-29-96	Covington, Ky.	12-24-68	R	R	6'	175	399	985	103	261	37	12	1	90	65	59	4	.265	.330
Higbe, Mahlon-Mahlon Jesse	22NYN	08-16-01	Louisville, Ky.	04-07-68	R	R	5'11	165	3	10	2	4	0	0	1	5	0	2	0	.400	.700
Higgins, Pinky-Michael Franklin	30,33-36PhiA 37-38BosA 39-44DetA 45MS 46DetA 46,M55-59,M60-62BosA	05-27-09	Red Oak, Tex.	03-21-69	R	R	6'1	185	1802	6636	930	1941	375	50	140	1075	800	590	61	.292	.427
High, Andy-Andrew Aird (Handy Andy)	22-25BknN 25-27BosN 28-31StLN 32-33CinN 34PhiN	11-21-97	Ava, Ill.	02-22-81	L	R	5'6	155	1314	4400	618	1250	195	65	44	482	425	130	33	.284	.388
High, Charlie-Charles Edwin	19-20PhiA	12-01-98	Ava, Ill.	09-11-60	L	R	5'9	170	28	94	9	22	2	1	1	7	6	10	2	.234	.309
Hill, Jesse-Jesse Terrill	35NYA 36-37WasA 37PhiA	01-20-07	Yates, Mo.	08-31-93	R	R	5'9	165	295	959	175	277	53	12	6	108	115	91	43	.289	.388
Hill, Oliver-Oliver Clinton	39BosN	10-16-09	Powder Springs, Ga.	09-20-70	R	R	5'11	178	2	2	1	1	0	0	0	0	0	0	0	.500	1.000
Hiller, Hob-Harvey Max	20-21BosA	05-12-93	E. Mauch Chunk, Pa.	12-27-56	R	R	5'8	162	18	30	4	5	1	1	0	2	2	5	0	.167	.267
Hillis, Mack-Malcolm David	24NYA 28PitN	07-23-01	Cambridge, Mass.	06-16-61	R	R	5'10	165	12	37	7	9	2	3	1	7	0	6	1	.243	.541
Hinkle, Gordie-Daniel Gordon	34BosA	04-03-05	Toronto, Ohio	03-19-72	R	R	6'	185	27	75	7	13	6	1	0	9	7	23	0	.173	.280
Hinson, Paul-James Paul	28BosA	05-09-04	Vanleer, Tenn.	09-23-60	R	R	5'10	150	3	5	0	0	0	0	0	0	0	0	0	—	—
Hitchcock, Jim-James Franklin	38BosN	05-09-11	Inverness, Ala.	06-23-59	R	R	5'11	178	28	76	2	13	0	0	0	7	2	11	1	.171	.171
Hoag, Myril-Myril Oliver	31-32,34,38NYA 39-41StLN 41-42ChiA 43MS 44ChiA 44-45CleA	03-09-08	Davis, Cal.	07-28-71	R	R	5'11	180	1020	3147	384	854	141	33	28	401	252	298	59	.271	.371
Hock, Ed-Edward Francis	20StLN 23-24CinN	03-27-99	Franklin Furnace, Ohio	11-21-63	L	R	5'10	165	19	10	1	1	0	0	0	0	0	2	0	.100	.100
Hockett, Oris-Oris Leon (Brown)	38-39BknN 41-44CleA 45ChiA	09-29-09	Amboy, Ind.	03-23-69	L	R	5'9	182	551	2165	259	598	112	21	13	214	159	157	43	.276	.365
Hodapp, Johnny-Urban John	25-32CleA 32ChiA 33BosA	09-26-05	Cincinnati, Ohio	06-14-80	R	R	6'	185	791	2826	378	880	169	34	28	429	163	136	18	.311	.425
Hodge(Hodges), Bert-Edward Burton	42PhiN	05-25-17	Knoxville, Tenn.	01-08-01	L	R	5'11	170	8	11	0	2	0	0	0	0	1	0	0	.182	.182
Hodgin, Ralph-Elmer Ralph	39BosN 43-44ChiA 45MS 46-48ChiA	02-15-17	Greensboro, N.C.		L	R	5'10	167	530	1689	198	481	79	24	4	188	97	63	7	.285	.367
Hofferth, Stew-Stewart Edward	44-46BosN	01-27-13	Logansport, Ind.	03-07-94	R	R	6'2	195	136	408	30	88	11	1	4	51	28	22	1	.216	.277
Hoffman, Dutch-Clarence Casper	29ChiA	01-28-04	Freeburg, Ill.	12-06-62	R	R	6'	175	107	337	27	87	16	5	3	37	24	28	6	.258	.362
Hoffman, Ray-Raymond Lamont	42WasA	06-04-17	Detroit, Mich.		R	R	6'	180	7	19	2	1	0	0	0	2	1	1	0	.053	.053
Hofmann, Fred-Fred (Bootnose)	19-25NYA 27-28BosA	06-10-94	St. Louis, Mo.	11-19-64	R	R	5'11	175	378	1000	98	247	49	11	7	93	77	120	6	.247	.339
Hogan, Kenny-Kenneth Slyvester	21CinN 23-24CleA	10-09-02	Cleveland, Ohio	01-02-80	L	R	5'9	145	4	3	0	0	0	0	0	0	0	0	0	.000	.000
Hogan, Shanty-James Francis	25-27BosN 28-32NYN 33-35BosN 36-37WasA	03-21-06	Somerville, Mass.	04-07-67	R	R	6'1	240	989	3180	288	939	146	12	61	474	220	188	6	.295	.406
Hogg, Bert-William George (Sonny)	34BknN	04-21-13	Detroit, Mich.	11-05-73	R	R	5'11	162	2	1	0	0	0	0	0	0	0	1	0	.000	.000
Hohman, Bill-William Henry	27PhiN	11-27-03	Brooklyn, Md.	10-29-68	R	R	6'	178	7	18	1	5	0	0	0	0	0	1	0	.278	.278
Holbrook, Sammy-James Marbury	35WasA	07-17-10	Meridan, Miss.	04-10-91	R	R	5'11	189	52	135	20	35	4	2	0	16	25	30	16	.259	.348
Holden, Joe-Joseph Francis (Socks)	34-36PhiN	06-04-13	St. Clair, Pa.	05-10-96	R	R	5'11	175	17	24	1	2	0	0	0	0	5	1	0	.083	.083
Holke, Walter-Walter Henry (Union Man)	14,16-18NYN 19-22BosN 23-25PhiN 25CinN	12-25-92	St. Louis, Mo.	10-12-54	B	L	6'2	185	1212	4456	464	1278	153	58	24	487	191	304	81	.287	.363
Hollahan, Bill-Willis James (Happy)	20WasA	11-22-96	New York, N.Y.	11-27-65	R	R	5'9	165	3	4	0	1	0	0	0	1	1	2	1	.250	.250
Holland, Dutch-Robert Clyde	32-33BosN 34CleA	10-12-03	Middlesex, N.C.	06-16-67	R	R	6'1	190	102	315	37	86	26	2	3	34	28	39	1	.273	.397
Hollocher, Charlie-Charles Jacob	18-24ChiN	06-11-96	St. Louis, Mo.	08-14-40	L	R	5'7	154	760	2936	411	894	145	35	14	241	277	94	99	.304	.392
Holm, Billy-William Frederick Henry	43-44ChiN 45BosA	07-21-12	Chicago, Ill.	07-27-77	R	R	5'10	168	119	282	22	44	4	1	0	15	41	40	2	.156	.177
Holm, Wattie-Roscoe Albert	24-29,32StLN	12-28-01	Peterson, Iowa	05-19-50	R	R	5'9	160	436	1493	207	410	73	26	6	174	100	86	11	.275	.370
Holt, Red-James Emmett Madison	25PhiA	07-25-94	Dayton, Tenn.	02-02-61	L	L	5'11	175	27	88	13	24	7	0	1	8	12	9	0	.273	.386
Hood, Abie-Abie Larrison	25BosN	01-31-03	Sanford, N.C.	10-14-88	L	R	5'8	152	5	21	2	6	2	0	1	2	1	0	0	.286	.524

USE NAME - GIVEN NAMES (NICKNAMES)	TEAM BY YEAR	BIRTH DATE	BIRTH PLACE	DEATH DATE	B	T	HGT	WGT	G	AB	R	H	2B	3B	HR	RBI	BB	SO	SB	BA	SA
Hood, Wally-Wallace James Sr.	20PitN 20-22BknN	02-09-95	Whittier, Cal.	05-02-65	R	R	5'11	160	67	80	23	19	2	2	1	5	14	18	5	.238	.350
Hooks, Alex-Alexander Marcus	35PhiA	08-29-06	Edgewood, Tex.	06-19-93	L	L	6'1	183	15	44	4	10	3	0	0	4	3	10	0	.227	.295
Hoover, Joe-Robert Joseph	43-45DetA	04-15-15	Brawley, Cal.	09-02-65	R	R	5'11	175	338	1238	178	301	45	15	5	84	92	202	19	.243	.316
Hopkins, Marty-Meredith Hilliard	34PhiN 34-35ChiA	02-22-07	Wolfe City, Tex.	11-20-63	R	R	5'11	175	136	379	48	80	12	0	4	48	85	54	1	.211	.274
Horan, Shags-Joseph Patrick	24NYA	09-06-95	St. Louis, Mo.	02-13-69	R	R	5'10	170	22	31	4	9	1	0	0	7	1	5	0	.290	.323
Hornsby, Rogers-Rogers (Rajah)	15-26,M25-26StLN 27NYN,M27NYN 28,M28BosN 29-32,M30-32ChiN 33StLN 33-37,M33-37,52StLA M52-53CinN	04-27-96	Winters, Tex.	01-05-63	R	R	5'11	175	2259	8173	1579	2930	541	169	301	1584	1038	679	135	.358	.577
Hostetler, Chuck-Charles Cloyd	44-45DetA	09-22-03	McClellandtown, Pa.	02-18-71	L	R	6'	175	132	309	45	86	12	2	0	22	28	39	4	.278	.330
Howell, Red-Murray Donald (Porky)	41CleA	01-29-09	Atlanta, Ga.	10-01-50	R	R	6'	215	11	7	0	2	0	0	0	2	4	2	0	.286	.286
Huber, Clarence-Clarence Bill (Gilly)	20-21DetA 25-26PhiN	10-28-95	Tyler, Tex.	02-22-65	R	R	5'10	165	254	854	95	225	47	13	6	93	59	67	12	.263	.370
Huber, Otto-Otto	39BosN	03-12-14	Garfield, N.J.	04-09-89	R	R	5'10	165	11	22	2	6	1	0	0	1	0	1	0	.273	.318
Hudgens, Jimmy-James Price	23StLN 25-26CinN	08-24-02	Newburg, Mo.	08-26-55	L	L	6'	180	26	39	4	11	3	1	0	1	5	4	0	.282	.410
Hudson, Johnny-John Wilson (Mr. Chips)	36-40BknN 41ChiN 45NYN	06-30-12	Bryan, Tex.	11-07-70	R	R	5'10	165	426	1169	138	283	50	11	4	96	87	164	17	.242	.314
Huffman, Ben-Benjamin Franklin	37StLA	07-08-14	Rileyville, Va.	02-22-05	L	R	5'11	175	76	176	18	48	9	0	1	24	10	7	1	.273	.324
Hughes, Roy-Roy John (Jeep, Sage)	35-37CleA 38-39StLA 39-40PhiN 44-45ChiN 46PhiN	01-11-11	Cincinnati, Ohio	03-05-95	R	R	5'10	167	763	2582	396	705	105	27	5	205	222	175	80	.273	.340
Hughes, Tom-Thomas Franklin	30DetA	08-06-07	Emmet, Ark.	08-10-89	L	R	6'1	190	17	59	8	22	2	3	0	5	4	8	0	.373	.508
Hungling, Bernie-Bernard Herman (Bud)	22-23BknN 30StLA	03-05-96	Dayton, Ohio	03-30-68	R	R	6'2	180	51	137	13	33	3	2	1	15	11	25	2	.241	.314
Hunnefield, Bill-William Fenton (Wild Bill)	26-30ChiA 31CleA 31BosN 31NYN	01-05-99	Dedham, Mass.	08-28-76	B	R	5'10	165	511	1664	230	452	75	9	9	144	117	111	67	.272	.344
Hunt, Joel-Oliver Joel (Jodie)	31-32StLN	10-11-05	Texico, N.M.	07-24-78	R	R	5'10	165	16	22	4	4	1	0	0	3	4	4	0	.182	.227
Hunter, Eddie-Edison Franklin	33CinN	02-06-05	Bellevue, Ky.	03-14-67	R	R	5'8	150	1	0	0	0	0	0	0	0	0	0	0	—	—
Hurst, Don-Frank O'Donnell	28-34PhiN 34ChiN	08-12-05	Maysville, Ky.	12-06-52	L	L	6'	215	905	3275	510	976	190	28	115	610	391	210	41	.298	.478
Husta, Carl-Carl Lawrence (Sox) 25-31 played in A.B.L.	25PhiA	04-08-02	Egg Harbor City, N.J.	11-06-51	R	R	5'11	176	6	22	3	3	0	0	0	2	2	3	0	.136	.136
Huston, Warren-Warren Llewellyn	37PhiA 44BosN	10-31-13	Newtonville, Mass.	08-30-99	R	R	6'	170	71	109	12	18	4	0	0	4	10	14	0	.165	.202
Hutcheson, Joe-Joseph Johnson (Poodles)	33BknN	02-05-05	Springtown, Tex.	02-23-93	R	R	6'2	200	55	184	19	43	4	1	6	21	15	13	1	.234	.364
Hutson, Roy-Roy Lee	25BknN	02-27-02	Luray, Mo.	05-20-57	L	R	5'9	165	7	8	1	4	0	0	0	1	1	1	0	.500	.500
Ingram, Mel-Melvin David	29PitN	07-04-04	Asheville, N.C.	10-28-79	R	R	5'11	175	3	0	1	0	0	0	0	0	0	0	0	—	—
Irwin, Tommy-Thomas Andrew	38CleA	12-20-12	Altoona, Pa.	04-25-96	R	R	5'11	165	3	9	1	1	0	0	0	0	3	1	0	.111	.111
Irwin,Walt-Walter Kingsley (Lightning)	21StLN	07-18-14	Henrietta, Pa.	08-18-76	R	R	5'10	170	4	1	1	0	0	0	0	0	0	1	0	.000	.000
Jackson, Travis-Travis Calvin (Stonewall, The Arkansas Traveler)	22-36NYN	11-02-03	Waldo, Ark.	07-27-87	R	R	5'10	160	1656	6086	833	1768	291	86	135	929	412	565	71	.291	.433
Jacobs, Ray-Raymond Frederick	28ChiN	04-02-02	Salt Lake City, Utah	04-04-52	R	R	6'	160	2	2	0	1	0	0	0	0	0	0	0	.500	.500
Jacobson, Baby Doll-William Chester	15DetA 15,17StLA 18MS 19-23StLA 26-27BosA 27CleA 27PhiA	08-16-90	Cable, Ill.	01-16-77	R	R	6'3	215	1472	5507	787	1714	328	94	83	819	355	410	86	.311	.450
Jacobson, Merwin-Merwin John William (Jake)	15NYN 16ChiN 26-27BknN	03-07-94	New Britain, Conn.	01-13-78	L	L	5'11	165	133	331	47	76	9	2	0	24	38	34	7	.230	.269
Jahn, Art-Arthur Charles	25ChiN 28NYN 28PhiN	12-02-95	Struble, Iowa	01-09-48	R	R	6'	180	104	349	45	97	15	8	1	55	17	36	2	.278	.375
James, Bernie-Robert Byrne	29-30BosN 33NYN	03-30-05	Angleton, Tex.	08-01-94	R	R	5'9	150	137	237	35	61	6	3	1	20	17	26	8	.257	.321
Jamieson, Charlie-Charles Devine (The Jersey Comet) (See P01-19)	15-17WasA 17-18PhiA 19-32CleA	02-07-93	Paterson, N.J.	10-27-69	L	L	5'9	165	1779	6560	1062	1990	322	80	18	550	748	345	132	.303	.385
Jeanes, Tex-Ernest Lee	21-22CleA25-26WasA27NYN	12-19-00	Maypearl, Tex.	04-05-73	R	R	6'	176	52	72	15	19	3	0	1	9	7	7	1	.264	.347
Jeffries, Irv-Irvine Franklin	30-31ChiA 34PhiN	09-10-05	Louisville, Ky.	06-08-82	R	R	5'10	175	175	495	71	116	19	4	8	46	32	21	6	.234	.321
Jelincich, Frank-Frank Anthony (Jelly)	41ChiN 42-45MS	03-17-19	San Jose, Cal.	06-27-92	R	R	6'2	198	4	8	0	1	0	0	0	1	0	2	0	.125	.125
Jenkins, John-John Robert	22ChiA	03-21-92	Bosworth, Mo.	08-03-68	R	R	5'8	160	5	3	0	0	0	0	0	0	1	0	0	.000	.000
Jenkins, Tom-Thomas Griffin (Tut)	25-26BosA 26PhiA 29-32StLA	04-10-98	Camden, Ala.	05-03-79	L	R	6'1	174	171	459	42	119	14	6	3	44	28	53	1	.259	.336
Jensen, Woody-Forrest Docenus	31-39PitN	08-11-07	Bremerton, Wash	10-05-01	L	L	5'10	160	738	2720	392	774	114	37	26	235	69	100	20	.285	.382
Jessee, Dan-Daniel Edward	29CleA	02-22-01	Olive Hill, Ky.	04-30-70	L	R	5'10	165	1	0	0	0	0	0	0	0	0	0	0	—	—
Johnson, Bob-Robert Lee (Indian Bob)	33-42PhiA 43WasA 44-45BosN	11-26-05	Pryor, Okla.	07-06-82	R	R	6'	180	1863	6920	1239	2051	396	95	288	1283	1075	851	96	.296	.506
Johnson, Don-Donald Spore (Pep)	43-48CinN	12-07-11	Chicago, Ill.	04-06-00	R	R	6'	170	511	1935	219	528	89	6	8	175	112	171	26	.273	.374
Johnson, Ed-Edwin Cyril	20WasA	03-31-99	Morganfield, Ky.	07-03-75	R	R	5'9	160	2	8	0	2	0	0	0	1	0	0	0	.250	.250
Johnson, Ernie-Ernest Rudolph	12ChiA 15StLF 16-18StLA 21-23ChiA 23-25NYA	04-29-88	Chicago, Ill.	05-01-52	R	R	5'9	151	811	2619	372	697	91	36	19	256	181	118	114	.266	.350
Johnson, Paul-Paul Oscar	20-21PhiA	09-02-96	N. Grosvenordale, Conn.	02-14-73	R	R	5'8	160	67	199	23	55	6	2	1	15	13	25	2	.276	.342
Johnson, Roy-Roy Cleveland	29-32PhiA 32-35BosA 36-37NYA 37-38BosN	02-23-03	Pryor, Okla.	09-11-73	R	R	5'9	175	1153	4358	717	1292	275	83	58	556	489	380	135	.296	.438
Johnston, Fred-Wilfred Ivy (Red Top)	24ChiN	07-09-99	Charlotte, N.C.	07-14-59	R	R	5'11	170	4	1	1	0	0	0	0	0	0	1	0	.000	.000
Johnston, Jimmy-James Harle	11ChiA 14ChiN 16-25BknN 26BosN 26NYN	12-10-89	Cleveland, Tenn.	02-14-67	R	R	5'10	160	1377	5070	754	1493	185	75	22	410	391	246	169	.294	.374
Jolley, Smead-Smead Powell (Smudge)	30-32ChiA 32-33BosA	01-14-02	Wesson, Ark.	11-17-91	L	R	6'3	210	473	1710	188	521	111	21	46	313	89	105	5	.305	.475
Jones, Binky-John Joseph	24BknN	07-11-99	St. Louis, Mo.	05-13-61	R	R	5'9	154	10	37	0	4	1	0	0	2	0	3	0	.108	.135
Jones, Bob-Robert Walter (Ducky)	17-25DetA	12-02-89	Clayton, Cal.	08-30-64	L	R	6'	170	853	2990	399	791	120	38	7	316	208	156	49	.265	.337
Jones, Cobe-Dyas Coburn	28-29PitN	08-21-05	Denver, Colo.	06-03-69	B	R	5'7	155	27	65	6	17	5	1	0	4	1	5	1	.262	.369
Jones(Painter), Howie-Howard	21StLN	03-01-97	Irwin, Pa.	07-15-72	L	L	5'11	185	3	5	0	0	0	0	0	0	0	0	0	.000	.000
Jones, John-John William (Skins)	23,32PhiA	05-13-01	Coatesville, Pa.	11-03-56	L	L	6'	170	5	10	0	2	0	0	0	0	1	1	0	.200	.200
Jones, Red-Morris E.	40StLN	11-02-11	Timpson,Tex.	06-30-74	R	R	6'3	190	12	11	0	1	0	0	0	0	1	1	0	.091	.091
Jonnard, Bubber-Clarence James	20ChiA 22PitN 26-27PhiN 29StLN 35BosN	11-23-97	Nashville, Tenn.	08-23-77	R	R	6'1	185	103	235	26	54	7	1	0	20	12	23	0	.230	.268
Jordan, Buck-Baxter Byerly	27,29NYN 31WasA 32-37BosN 37-38CinN 38PhiN	01-16-07	Cooleemee, N.C.	03-18-93	L	R	6'	170	811	2980	396	890	153	35	17	281	182	109	20	.299	.391
Jordan, Jimmy-James William (Lord)	33-36BknN	01-13-08	Tucapau, S.C.	12-04-57	R	R	5'9	157	376	1273	102	327	51	4	2	118	37	76	8	.257	.308
Jorgens, Art-Arndt Ludwig	29-39NYA	05-18-05	Modum, Norway	03-01-80	R	R	5'9	160	307	738	79	176	31	5	4	89	85	73	3	.238	.310
Jorgensen, Pinky-Carl	37CinN	11-21-14	Laton, Cal.	05-02-96	R	R	6'1	195	6	14	1	4	0	0	0	1	1	2	0	.286	.286
Jourdan, Ted-Theodore Charles	16-18,20ChiA	09-05-95	New Orleans, La.	09-23-61	L	L	6'	175	75	196	19	42	6	2	0	11	19	21	5	.214	.265
Judge, Joe-Joseph Ignatius	15-32WasA 33BknN 33-34BosA	05-25-94	Brooklyn, N.Y.	03-11-63	L	L	5'8	155	2170	7894	1184	2352	433	159	71	1034	965	478	213	.298	.420
Judnich, Walt-Walter Franklin	40-42StLA 43-45MS 46-47StLA 48CleA 49PitN	06-24-16	San Francisco, Cal.	07-12-71	L	L	6'1	205	790	2786	424	782	150	29	90	420	385	298	20	.281	.452
Judy, Lyle-Lyle LeRoy (Punch)	35StLN	11-15-13	Lawrenceville, Ill.	01-15-91	R	R	5'11	180	8	11	2	0	0	0	0	0	2	2	2	.000	.000
Juelich, Jack-John Samuel (Red)	39PitN	09-20-16	St. Louis, Mo.	12-25-70	R	R	5'11	180	17	46	5	11	0	2	0	4	2	4	0	.239	.326
Jumonville, George-George Benedict	40-41PhiN	05-16-17	Mobile, Ala.	12-12-96	R	R	6'	170	41	41	1	6	0	0	1	2	1	6	0	.146	.220
Jurges, Billy-William Frederick	31-38ChiN 39-45NYN 46-47ChiN M59-60BosA	05-09-08	Bronx, N.Y.	03-03-97	R	R	5'11	175	1816	6253	721	1613	245	55	43	656	568	530	36	.258	.335
Just (Juszczak), Joe-Joseph Erwin	44-45CinN	01-08-16	Milwaukee, Wis.	11-22-03	R	R	5'11	185	25	45	2	7	1	0	0	2	2	4	0	.156	.156
Kahdot, Ike-Isaac Leonard (Chief)	22CleA	10-22-99	Georgetown, Okla.	03-31-99	R	R	5'6	160	4	2	2	0	0	0	0	0	0	0	1	.000	.000
Kahle, Bob-Robert Wayne	38BosN	11-23-15	New Castle, Ind.	12-16-88	R	R	6'	170	8	3	2	1	0	0	0	0	1	0	0	.333	.333
Kahn, Owen-Owen Earle (Jack)	30BosN	06-05-05	Richmond,Va.	01-17-81	R	R	5'11	160	1	0	0	0	0	0	0	0	0	0	0	—	—
Kalin (Kalinkiewicz), Frnak-Frank Bruno (Fats)	40PitN 43ChiA 44-45MS	06-05-05	Steubenville, Ohio	01-12-75	R	R	6'	200	7	2	0	0	0	0	0	0	0	1	0	.000	.000
Kamm, Willie-William Edward	23-31ChiA 31-35CleA	02-02-00	San Francisco, Cal.	12-21-88	R	R	5'10	170	1692	5851	802	1643	348	85	29	826	824	405	126	.281	.384
Kampouris, Alex-Alexis William	34-38CinN 38-39NYN 41-43BknN 43BosN 44-45MS	11-13-12	Sacramento, Cal.	05-29-93	R	R	5'8	155	708	2182	272	531	94	20	45	284	244	360	22	.243	.367
Kane, John-John Francis	25ChiA	02-19-00	Chicago, Ill.	07-25-56	R	R	5'10	162	14	56	6	10	1	0	0	3	0	3	0	.179	.196
Kane, Tom-Thomas Joseph (Sugar)	38BosN	12-15-06	Chicago, Ill.	11-26-73	R	R	5'10	160	2	2	0	0	0	0	0	0	0	0	0	.000	.000
Karlon, Bill-William John (Hank)	30NYA	01-21-09	Palmer, Mass.	12-07-64	R	R	6'1	190	4	2	0	0	0	0	0	0	0	0	0	.000	.000
Karow(Karowsky), Marty-Martin Gregory	27BosA	07-18-04	Braddock, Pa.	04-28-86	R	R	5'10	170	6	10	0	2	1	0	0	1	0	2	0	.200	.300
Kaufmann, Tony-Anthony Charles (See P20-45)	21-27ChiN 27PhiN 27-28StLN 29NYN 30-31,35StLN	12-16-00	Chicago, Ill.	06-04-82	R	R	5'11	165	260	414	62	91	19	1	9	57	28	82	4	.220	.374
Kearns, Ted-Edward Joseph 25-30 played in A.B.L.	20PhiA 24-25CinN	01-01-00	Trenton, N.J.	12-21-49	R	R	5'11	180	8	19	0	5	0	0	0	1	1	0	0	.263	.368
Kearse, Ed-Paul Edward (Trick)	42NYA	02-23-16	San Francisco, Cal.	07-15-68	R	R	6'1	195	11	26	2	5	0	0	0	3	1	1	0	.192	.192
Keely, Bob-Robert William	44-45StLN	08-22-09	St. Louis, Mo.	05-20-01	R	R	6'	175	1	0	0	0	0	0	0	0	0	0	0	.000	.000
Keesey, Jim-James Ward	25,30PhiA	10-27-02	Perryville, Md.	09-05-51	R	R	6'	170	16	17	3	5	1	0	0	1	3	4	0	.294	.353
Kelleher, Frankie-Francis Eugene	42-43CinN 44-45MS	08-22-16	San Francisco, Cal.	04-13-79	R	R	6'1	195	47	120	14	20	3	1	2	12	18	20	0	.167	.283
Kelleher, John-John Patrick	12StLN 16BknN 21-23ChiN 24BosN	09-13-93	Brookline, Mass.	08-21-60	R	R	5'11	150	235	703	81	206	29	8	10	89	45	42	9	.293	.400
Keller, Charlie-Charles Ernest (King Kong)	39-43NYA 44MM 45-49NYA 50-51DetA 52NYA	09-12-16	Middletown, Md.	05-23-90	L	R	5'10	185	1170	3790	725	1085	166	72	189	760	784	499	45	.286	.518
Kellett, Don-Donald Stafford (Red)	34BosA	07-15-09	Brooklyn, N.Y.	11-03-70	R	R	6'	170	8	8	1	0	0	0	0	0	0	0	0	.000	.000
Kelly, Bill-William Henry (Big Bill)	20PhiN 28PhiN	12-28-98	Syracuse, N.Y.	04-08-90	R	R	6'	190	32	84	6	15	2	1	0	5	7	22	0	.179	.226
Kelly, George-George Lange (Highpockets)	15-17NYN 17PhiN 18MS 19-26NYN 27-30CinN 30ChiN 32BknN	09-10-95	San Francisco, Cal.	10-13-84	R	R	6'4	190	1622	5993	819	1778	337	76	148	1020	386	694	65	.297	.452
Kelly, Joe-Joseph James	26,28ChiN	04-23-00	New York, N.Y.	11-24-67	L	L	6'	180	97	228	19	70	16	3	1	39	8	14	0	.307	.417

USE NAME - GIVEN NAMES (NICKNAMES)	TEAM BY YEAR	BIRTH DATE	BIRTH PLACE	DEATH DATE	B	T	HGT	WGT	G	AB	R	H	2B	3B	HR	RBI	BB	SO	SB	BA	SA
Keltner, Ken-Kenneth Frederick	37-44CleA 45MS 46-49CleA 50BosA	10-31-16	Milwaukee, Wis.	12-12-91	R	R	6'	190	1526	5683	737	1570	308	69	163	852	514	480	39	.276	.441
Kenna, Ed-Edward Aloysius (Scrap Iron)	28WasA	09-30-97	San Francisco, Cal.	08-21-72	R	R	5'8	145	41	118	14	35	4	2	1	20	14	8	1	.297	.390
Kerns, Russ-Russell Eldon	45DetA	11-10-20	Fremont, Ohio	08-21-00	L	R	6'	188	1	1	0	0	0	0	0	0	0	0	0	.000	.000
Kerr, John-John Francis	23-24DetA 29-31ChiA 32-34WasA	11-26-98	San Francisco, Cal.	10-19-93	R	R	5'8	158	471	1457	172	388	59	13	6	145	115	92	26	.266	.337
			Bats Both 23-24																		
Kerr, Mel-John Melville	25ChiN	05-22-03	Souris, Canada	08-09-80	L	L	5'11	155	1	0	0	0	0	0	0	0	0	0	0		
Kibbie, Hod-Horace Kent	25BosN	07-18-03	Fort Worth, Tex.	10-19-75	R	R	5'10	150	11	41	5	11	0	0	0	2	5	6	0	.268	.317
Kilduff, Pete-Peter John	17NYN 17-19ChiN 19-21BknN	04-04-93	Wier City, Kans.	02-14-30	R	R	5'10	150	428	1384	163	374	62	28	4	159	134	132	28	.270	.364
Kimble, Dick-Richard Louis	45WasA	07-27-15	Buchtel, Ohio	05-07-01	L	R	5'9	160	20	49	5	12	1	1	0	1	5	2	0	.245	.306
Kimmick, Wally-Wally Lyons	19StLN 21-23CinN 25-26PhiN	05-30-97	Turtle Creek, Pa.	07-24-89	R	R	5'11	174	163	345	39	90	9	5	1	31	34	61	4	.261	.325
King, Lee-Edward Lee	16-18PitN 19-21NYN 21-22PhiN 22NYN	12-26-92	Hundred, W.Va.	09-16-67	R	R	5'8	160	411	1189	134	294	60	18	15	144	82	175	16	.247	.366
King, Lynn-Lynn Paul (Dig)	35-36,39StLN	11-28-07	Villisca, Iowa	05-11-72	L	R	5'8	160	175	207	28	43	4	1	0	21	28	18	6	.208	.237
Kingdon, Wes-Wescott William	32WasA	07-04-00	Los Angeles, Cal.	04-19-75	R	R	5'8	148	18	34	10	11	3	1	0	3	5	2	0	.324	.471
Kish, Ernie-Ernest Alexander	45PhiA	02-06-18	Washington, D.C.	12-21-93	L	R	5'10	170	43	110	10	27	5	1	0	10	9	9	0	.245	.309
Klee, Ollie-Ollie Chester (Babe)	25CinN	05-20-00	Piqua, Ohio	02-09-77	L	R	5'9	160	3	1	0	0	0	0	0	0	0	1	0	.000	.000
Klein, Chuck-Charles Herbert	28-33PhiN 34-36ChiN 36-39PhiN 39PitN 40-44PhiN	10-07-04	Indianapolis, Ind.	03-28-58	L	R	6'	185	1753	6486	1168	2076	398	74	300	1201	601	521	79	.320	.543
Klein, Lou-Louis Frank	43StLN 44MS 45-46StLN 47-48SM 49StLN 51CleA 51PhiA M61-62,65ChiN	10-22-18	New Orleans, La.	06-20-76	R	R	5'11	167	305	1037	162	269	48	15	16	101	105	119	10	.259	.381
Klinger, Joe-Joseph John	27NYN 30ChiA	08-02-02	Canonsburg, Pa.	07-31-60	R	R	6'	190	7	13	0	5	0	0	0	1	0	2	0	.385	.385
Kloza, Nap-John Clarence	31-32StLA	09-07-03	Poland	06-11-62	R	R	5'11	180	22	20	5	3	0	1	0	2	5	8	0	.150	.250
Klugman, Joe-Josie	21-22ChiN 24BknN 25CleA	03-26-95	St. Louis, Mo.	07-18-51	R	R	5'11	175	77	187	22	47	11	3	0	17	11	15	3	.251	.342
Klumpp, Elmer-Elmer Edward	34WasA 37BknN	08-26-06	St. Louis, Mo.	10-18-96	R	R	6'	184	17	26	2	3	0	0	0	2	1	5	0	.115	.115
Knickerbocker, Bill-William Hart	33-36CleA 37StLA 38-40NYA 41ChiA 42PhiA	12-29-11	Los Angeles, Cal.	09-08-63	R	R	5'11	170	907	3418	423	943	198	27	28	368	244	328	25	.276	.374
Knode, Mike-Kenneth Thomson	20StLN	11-08-95	Westminster, Md.	12-20-80	L	R	5'10	160	42	65	11	15	1	1	0	12	5	6	0	.231	.277
Knode, Ray-Robert Traxell (Bob)	23-26CleA	01-28-01	Westminster, Md.	04-13-82	L	L	5'10	160	109	207	32	55	7	1	2	21	17	11	6	.266	.338
Knothe, Fritz-Wilfred Edgar	32-33BosN 33PhiN	05-01-03	Passaic, N.J.	03-27-63	R	R	5'10	180	174	615	70	135	26	3	2	53	58	81	8	.220	.281
Knothe, George-George Bertram (Whitey)	32PhiN	01-12-98	Bayonne, N.J.	07-03-81	R	R	5'10	170	6	12	2	1	1	0	0	0	0	2	0	.083	.167
Knox, Cliff-Clifford Hiram (Bud)	24PitN	01-07-02	Coalville, Iowa	09-24-65	B	R	5'11	178	6	18	1	4	0	0	0	2	2	0	0	.222	.222
Koch, Barney-Barnett	44BknN	03-23-23	Cambell, Neb.	01-06-87	R	R	5'8	140	33	96	11	21	2	0	0	3	9	5	0	.219	.240
Koehler, Pip-Horace Levering	26-31 played in A.B.L.	01-16-02	Gilbert, Pa.	12-08-86	R	R	5'10	165	1	2	1	0	0	0	0	0	0	0	0	.000	.000
Koenecke, Len-Leonard George	32NYN 34-35BknN	01-18-04	Baraboo, Wis.	09-17-35	L	R	5'11	190	265	922	155	274	49	9	22	114	124	96	11	.297	.441
Koenig, Mark-Mark Anthony	25-30NYA 30-31DetA 32-33ChiN 34CinN 35-36NYN	07-19-02	San Francisco, Cal.	04-22-93	B	R	6'	180	1162	4271	572	1190	195	49	28	443	222	190	31	.279	.367
Kopf, Wally-Walter Henry	21NYN	07-10-99	Stonington, Conn.	04-30-79	B	R	5'11	168	2	3	0	1	0	0	0	0	1	1	0	.333	.333
Kopshaw, George-George Karl	23StLN	07-05-95	Passaic, N.J.	12-26-34	R	R	5'11	176	2	5	1	1	0	0	0	0	0	0	0	.200	.400
Kosman, Mike-Michael Thomas	44CinN	11-26-17	Hamtramck, Mich.	12-20-02	R	R	5'9	160	1	0	0	0	0	0	0	0	0	0	0		
Koster, Fred-Frederick Charles (Fritz)	31PhiN	12-21-05	Louisville, Ky.	04-24-79	L	L	5'11	165	76	151	21	34	2	2	0	8	14	21	4	.225	.266
Koy, Ernie-Ernest Anyz (Chief)	38-40BknN 40-41StLN 41-42CinN 42PhiN 43-45MS	09-17-09	Sealy, Tex.		R	R	6'	200	558	1846	238	515	108	29	36	260	137	284	40	.279	.427
Kracher, Joe-Joseph Peter (Jug)	39PhiN	11-04-13	Philadelphia, Pa.	12-24-81	R	R	5'11	185	5	5	0	1	0	0	0	0	2	1	0	.200	.200
Kreevich, Mike-Michael Andreas	31ChiN 35-41ChiA 42PhiA 43-45StLA 45BraA 43-44ChiN	06-10-08	Mount Olive, Ill.	04-25-94	R	R	5'8	168	1241	4676	676	1321	221	75	45	514	446	341	115	.283	.391
Kreitner, Mickey-Albert Joseph	43-44ChiN	10-09-22	Nashville, Tenn.	03-06-03	R	R	6'3	190	42	93	3	16	2	0	0	3	9	18	0	.172	.194
Kress, Red-Ralph (See P20-45)	27-32StLA 32-34ChiA 34-36WasA 38-39StLA 39-40DetA 46NYN	01-02-05	Columbia, Cal.	11-29-62	R	R	5'11	165	1391	5087	690	1454	298	58	89	799	474	453	47	.286	.420
Kroner, John-John Harold	35-36BosA 37-38CleA	11-13-08	St. Louis, Mo.	08-26-68	R	R	6'	165	223	702	83	184	47	9	7	105	68	56	3	.262	.385
Krug, Marty-Martin John	12BosA 22ChiN	09-10-88	Coblenz, Germany	06-27-66	R	R	5'9	180	143	489	73	136	25	5	4	67	48	43	9	.278	.374
Kuhel, Joe-Joseph Anthony	30-37WasA 38-43ChiA 44-46WasA 46-47ChiA M48-49WasA	06-25-06	Cleveland, Ohio	02-26-84	L	L	6'	180	2104	7984	1236	2212	412	11	131	1049	980	611	178	.277	.406
Kurowski, Whitey-George John	41-49StLN	04-19-18	Reading, Pa.	12-09-99	R	R	5'11	193	916	3229	518	925	162	32	106	529	369	332	19	.286	.455
Kvasnak, Al-Alexander	42WasA 43-45MS	01-11-21	Sagamore, Pa.	09-26-02	R	R	6'1	170	5	11	3	2	0	0	0	0	2	1	0	.182	.182
Laabs, Chet-Chester Peter	37-39DetA 39-46StLA 47PhiA	04-30-12	Milwaukee, Wis.	01-26-83	R	R	5'8	175	950	3102	467	813	151	44	117	509	389	595	32	.262	.452
Lacy, Guy-Osceola Guy	26CleA	06-12-97	Cleveland, Tenn.	11-19-53	L	R	5'11	170	13	24	2	4	0	0	1	2	2	2	0	.167	.292
LaForest, Ty-Biron Joseph	45BosA	04-18-17	Edmondston, Canada	05-05-47	R	R	5'9	165	52	204	25	51	7	4	2	16	10	35	4	.250	.353
Lakeman, Al-Albert Wesley (Moose)	42-47CinN 47-48PhiN 49BosN 54DetA	12-31-18	Cincinnati, Ohio	05-25-76	R	R	6'2	195	239	646	40	131	17	5	15	66	36	137	0	.203	.314
Lamar, Bill-William Harmong (Good Time Bill)	17-19NYA 19BosA 20-21BknN 24-27PhiA	03-21-97	Rockville, Md.	05-24-70	L	R	5'11	185	550	2040	303	633	114	23	19	245	86	78	25	.310	.417
Lamb, Lyman-Lyman Raymond	20-21StLN	03-17-95	Lincoln, Neb.	10-05-55	R	R	5'7	150	54	158	22	43	11	2	1	21	4	19	2	.272	.386
LaMotte, Bobby-Robert Eugene	20-22WasA 25-26StLA	02-15-98	Savannah, Ga.	11-02-70	R	R	5'11	160	221	693	99	175	34	9	3	85	66	50	11	.253	.341
Land, Doc-Mickey Gilbert	29WasA	05-14-03	Bennsville, Miss.	04-14-86	L	L	5'11	165	1	3	0	0	0	0	0	1	0	0	0	.000	.000
Landrum, Jesse-Jesse Glenn	38ChiA	07-31-12	Crockett, Tex.	06-27-83	R	R	5'11	175	4	6	0	0	0	0	0	0	1	2	0	.000	.000
Lane, Hunter-James Hunter (Dodo)	24BosN	07-20-00	Pulaski, Tenn.	09-12-94	R	R	5'11	165	7	15	0	1	0	0	0	0	1	1	0	.067	.067
Langford, Sam-Elton	26BosA 27-28CleA	05-21-00	Briggs, Tex.	07-31-93	L	R	6'	180	131	495	61	136	22	8	5	57	26	42	3	.275	.342
Lapan, Pete-Peter Nelson	22-23WasA	06-25-91	Easthampton, Mass.	01-05-53	R	R	5'7	165	13	36	7	11	1	0	1	6	3	4	1	.306	.417
Larsen, Swede-Erling Adeli	36BosN	11-15-13	Jersey City, N.J.	10-08-05	R	R	5'11	170	3	3	1	0	0	0	0	0	0	0	0	.000	.000
Lary, Lyn-Lynford Hobart (Broadway)	29-34NYA 34BosA 35WasA 35-36StLA 37-39CleA 39BknN 38StLN 40StLA	01-28-06	Armona, Cal.	01-09-73	R	R	6'	165	1302	4604	805	1239	247	56	38	526	705	470	162	.269	.372
Lavagetto, Cookie-Harry Arthur	34-36PitN 37-41BknN 42-45MS 46-47BknN M57-60WasA M61MinA	12-01-12	Oakland, Cal.	08-10-90	R	R	6'	170	1043	3509	487	945	183	37	40	486	485	244	63	.269	.377
Lawrence, Bill-William Henry	32DetA	03-11-06	San Mateo, Cal.	06-15-97	R	R	6'4	194	25	46	10	10	1	0	0	3	5	5	0	.217	.239
Layne, Herman-Herman	27PitN	02-13-01	New Haven, W.Va.	08-27-73	L	R	6'	170	11	6	3	0	0	0	0	1	0	0	0	.000	.000
Layne, Hilly-Ivoria Hillis	41WasA 42-43MS 44-45WasA	02-23-18	Whitewell, Tenn.		L	R	6'	170	107	284	37	75	9	4	1	28	20	22	3	.264	.335
Lazor, Johnny-John Paul	43-46BosA	09-09-12	Taylor, Wash.	12-09-02	L	R	5'10	180	223	596	57	157	30	4	6	62	41	53	8	.263	.357
Lazzeri, Tony-Anthony Michael (Poosh 'Em Up)	26-37NYA 38ChiN 39BknN 39NYN	12-06-03	San Francisco, Cal.	08-06-46	R	R	5'11	170	1740	6297	986	1840	334	115	178	1191	870	864	148	.292	.467
Leach, Freddy-Frederick M.	23-28PhiN 29-31NYN 32BosN	11-23-97	Springfield, Mo.	12-10-81	L	R	5'11	183	991	3733	543	1147	196	53	72	509	163	189	32	.307	.446
Leathers, Hal-Harold Langford (Chuck)	20ChiN	12-02-98	Selma, Cal.	04-12-77	L	R	5'7	152	9	23	3	7	0	1	0	1	1	1	1	.304	.478
LeBourveau, Bevo-DeWitt Wiley	19-22PhiN 29PhiA	08-24-96	Dana, Cal.	12-09-47	L	R	5'11	175	280	788	100	217	27	11	11	70	79	125	15	.275	.379
Lee, Cliff-Clifford Walker	19-20PitN 21-24PhiN 24CinN 25-26CleA	08-04-96	Lexington, Neb.	08-25-80	R	R	6'1	190	521	1583	216	475	87	28	38	216	104	186	14	.300	.462
Lee, Dud-Ernest Holford (played as Dud Dudley 1920)	20-21StLA 24-26BosA	08-22-99	Denver, Colo.	01-07-71	L	R	5'9	150	253	732	80	163	20	9	0	60	88	70	12	.223	.275
Lee, Hal-Harold Burnham (Sheriff)	31-33PhiN 33-36BosN	02-15-05	Ludlow, Miss.	09-04-89	R	R	5'11	180	752	2750	316	755	144	40	33	323	203	225	15	.275	.392
Lees, George-George Edward	21ChiA	02-02-95	Bethlehem, Pa.	01-02-80	R	R	5'9	150	20	42	3	9	2	0	0	4	0	3	0	.214	.262
Lefevre, Al-Alfred Modesto	20NYN	09-16-98	New York, N.Y.	01-21-82	L	R	5'10	160	17	27	5	4	0	1	0	0	6	13	0	.148	.222
Lefler, Wade-Wade Hampton	24BosN 24WasA	06-05-96	Cooleemee, N.C.	03-06-81	L	R	5'11	162	6	9	0	5	3	0	0	6	0	0	0	.556	.889
Legett, Lou-Louis Alfred (Doc)	29BosN 33-35BosA	06-01-01	New Orleans, La.	03-06-88	R	R	5'10	166	68	124	13	25	3	0	0	8	5	22	2	.202	.226
Leiber, Hank-Henry Edward	33-38NYN 39-41ChiN 42NYN	01-17-11	Phoenix, Ariz.	11-08-93	R	R	6'1	205	813	2805	410	808	137	24	101	518	274	319	5	.288	.462
Leifer, Elmer-Elmer Edwin	21ChiA	05-23-93	Clarington, Ohio	09-26-48	R	R	5'9	170	9	10	0	3	0	0	0	1	0	4	0	.300	.300
Leip, Ed-Edgar Ellsworth	39WasA 40-42PitN 43-45MS	11-29-10	Trenton, N.J.	11-24-83	R	R	5'9	160	30	62	7	17	2	1	0	7	6	6	1	.274	.355
Leovich, John-John Joseph	41PhiN	05-05-18	Portland, Ore.	02-03-00	R	R	6'	200	1	2	0	1	0	0	0	0	0	0	0	.500	1.000
Lerian, Walt-Walter Irvin (Peck)	28-29PhiN	02-10-03	Baltimore, Md.	10-22-29	R	R	6'	190	201	512	56	126	29	4	8	50	94	66	1	.246	.365
Leslie, Roy-Roy Reid	17ChiN 19StLN 22PhiN	08-23-94	Bailey, Tex.	04-09-72	R	R	6'1	190	160	556	47	148	24	2	6	55	42	57	4	.266	.349
Leslie, Sam-Samuel Andrew (Sambo)	29-33NYN 33-35BknN 36-38NYN	07-26-05	Moss Point, Miss.	01-21-79	L	L	6'	192	822	2460	311	749	123	28	36	389	216	118	14	.304	.421
Letchas, Charlie-Charlie	39PhiN 41WasA 44PhiN 45MS 46PhiN	10-03-15	Thomasville, Ga.	03-14-95	R	R	5'10	150	136	461	32	108	10	1	0	37	35	31	0	.234	.262
Levey, Jim-James Julius	30-33StLA	09-13-06	Pittsburgh, Pa.	03-14-70	B	R	5'10	154	440	1632	162	375	61	14	11	140	85	201	23	.230	.306
	34-36 played in N.F.L.		Bats Right 30-31																		
Levy (Whitner), Ed-Edward Clarence	40PhiN 42,44NYA	10-28-16	Birmingham, Ala.		R	R	6'	190	54	195	17	42	11	2	4	32	10	24	2	.215	.354
Lewis, Bill-William Henry (Buddy)	33StLN 35-36BosN	10-15-04	Ripley, Tenn.	10-24-77	R	R	5'9	165	50	101	20	33	4	1	0	11	15	11	0	.327	.386
Lewis, Buddy-John Kelly	35-41WasA 42-44MS 45-47,49WasA	08-10-16	Gastonia, N.C.		L	R	6'1	175	1349	5261	830	1563	249	93	71	607	573	303	83	.297	.420
Libke, Al-Albert Walter (Big Al)	45-46CinN	06-02-18	Tacoma, Wash.	03-07-03	R	R	6'4	215	254	880	73	236	45	6	9	95	77	112	6	.268	.364
Lillard, Bill-William Beverly	39-40PhiA	01-10-18	Goleta, Cal.		R	R	5'10	170	80	225	30	55	9	2	1	22	31	29	0	.244	.316
Lillard, Gene-Robert Eugene (See P20-45)	36,39ChiN 40StLN	11-12-13	Santa Barbara, Cal.	04-12-91	R	R	6'	190	44	44	9	8	1	0	2	5	4	6	0	.182	.205
Lind, Carl-Henry Carl (Hooks)	27-30CleA	09-19-03	New Orleans, La.	08-02-46	R	R	6'	170	256	981	131	267	53	5	1	73	57	79	9	.272	.340
Lindstrom, Fred (Frederick Anthony)-Frederick Charles (Lindy)	24-32NYN 33-34PitN 35ChiN 36BknN	11-21-05	Chicago, Ill.	10-04-81	R	R	5'11	170	1438	5611	895	1747	301	81	103	779	334	276	84	.311	.449

USE NAME - GIVEN NAMES (NICKNAMES)	TEAM BY YEAR	BIRTH DATE	BIRTH PLACE	DEATH DATE	B	T	HGT	WGT	G	AB	R	H	2B	3B	HR	RBI	BB	SO	SB	BA	SA
Linton, Bob-Claud Clarence	29PitN	04-18-02	Emerson, Ark.	04-03-80	L	R	6'	185	17	18	0	2	0	0	0	1	1	2	0	.111	.111
Lipscomb, Jerry-Gerald (Nig)	37StLA	02-24-11	Rutherfordton, N.C.	02-27-78	R	R	6'	175	36	96	11	31	9	1	0	8	11	10	0	.323	.438
Litwhiler, Danny-Daniel Webster	40-43PhiN 43-44StLN 45MS 46StLN 47-48BosN 48-51CinN	08-31-16	Ringtown, Pa.		R	R	5'10	198	1057	3494	428	982	162	32	107	451	299	377	11	.281	.438
Livingston, Mickey-Thompson Orville	38WasA 41-43PhiN 43ChiN 44MS 45-47ChiN 47-49NYN 49BosN 51BknN	11-15-14	Newberry, S.C.	04-03-83	R	R	6'1	185	561	1490	128	354	56	9	19	153	144	141	7	.238	.326
Loane, Bobby-Robert Kenneth	39WasA 40BosN	08-05-14	Berkeley, Cal.	12-11-02	R	R	6'	190	16	31	6	5	3	0	0	2	6	9	2	.161	.258
Lodigiani, Dario-Dario Joseph (Lodi)	38-40PhiA 41-42ChiA 45-46ChiA	06-06-16	San Francisco, Cal.		R	R	5'8	150	405	1364	142	355	71	7	16	156	141	86	12	.260	.358
Loepp, George-George Herbert	28BosA 30WasA	09-11-01	Detroit, Mich.	09-04-67	R	R	6'	170	65	185	29	46	10	2	0	17	25	21	0	.249	.324
Loftus, Dick-Richard Joseph	24-25BknN	03-07-01	Concord, Mass.	01-21-72	L	R	6'	155	97	212	34	53	12	0	0	21	12	7	3	.250	.307
Lombardi, Ernie-Ernesto Natali (Schnozz)	31BknN 32-41CinN 42BosN 43-47NYN	04-06-08	Oakland, Cal.	09-26-77	R	R	6'3	230	1853	5855	601	1792	277	27	190	990	430	262	8	.306	.460
Long, Jimmie-James Albert	22ChiA	06-29-98	Fort Dodge, Iowa	09-14-70	R	R	5'11	160	3	0	0	0	0	0	0	0	1	0	0	.000	.000
Lopez, Al-Alfonso Ramon	28,30-35BknN 36-40BosN 40-46PitN 47,M51-56CleA M57-65,68-69CinN	08-20-08	Tampa, Fla.	10-30-05	R	R	5'11	165	1950	5916	613	1547	206	43	51	652	556	538	46	.261	.337
Lord, Carl-William Carlton	23PhiN	01-07-00	Philadelphia, Pa.	08-15-47	R	R	5'11	170	17	47	3	11	2	0	0	2	3	2	0	.234	.277
Lovelace, Tom-Thomas Rivers	22PitN	10-19-97	Wolfe City, Tex.	07-12-79	R	R	5'11	167	1	1	0	0	0	0	0	0	0	0	0	.000	.000
Lovett, Mem-Merritt Marwood	33ChiA	06-15-12	Chicago, Ill.	09-19-95	R	R	5'9	165	1	1	0	0	0	0	0	0	0	1	0	.000	.000
Luby, Hugh-Hugh Max (Hal)	36PhiA 44NYN 45MS	06-13-13	Blackfoot, Ida.	05-04-86	R	R	5'10	185	120	361	33	89	11	2	2	38	52	22	4	.247	.305
Lucadello, Johnny-John	38-41StLA 42-45MS 46StLA 47NYA	02-22-19	Thurber, Tex.	10-30-01	R	R	5'11	160	239	686	95	181	36	7	5	60	93	56	6	.264	.359
Lucas, Fred-Frederick Warrington (Fritz)	35PhiN	03-11-87	Vineland, N.J.		R	R	5'10	165	20	34	1	9	0	0	0	3	3	6	0	.265	.265
Lucas, Johnny-John Charles (Buster)	31-32BosA	02-10-03	Glen Carbon, Ill.	10-31-70	L	R	5'10	186	4	3	0	0	0	0	0	0	0	1	0	.000	.000
Lucas, Red-Charles Fred (The Nashville Narcissus) (See P20-45)	23NYN 24-25BosN 26-33CinN 34-38PitN	04-28-02	Columbia, Tenn.	07-09-86	L	R	5'10	170	907	1439	155	404	61	13	3	190	124	133	2	.281	.347
Luce, Frank-Frank Edward	23PitN	12-06-96	Spencer, Ohio	02-03-42	R	R	5'11	180	9	12	2	6	0	0	0	3	2	2	0	.500	.500
Lucey, Joe-Joseph Earl (Scootch) (See P20-45)	20NYA 25BosA	03-27-97	Holyoke, Mass.	07-30-80	R	R	6'	168	13	18	0	2	0	0	0	0	4	0	0	.111	.111
Luebbe, Roy-Roy John	25NYA	09-17-00	Parkersburg, Iowa	08-21-85	B	R	6'1	183	8	15	1	0	0	0	0	3	2	6	0	.000	.000
Lupien, Tony-Ulysses John	40,42-43BosA 44-45PhiN 48ChiA	04-23-17	Chelmsford, Mass.	07-09-04	L	L	5'11	185	614	2358	285	632	92	30	18	230	241	111	57	.268	.355
Lutz, Red-Louis William	22CinN	12-17-98	Cincinnati, Ohio	02-22-84	R	R	5'10	170	1	1	0	1	0	0	0	0	0	0	0	1.000	2.000
Lutzke, Rube-Walter John	23-27CleA	11-17-97	Milwaukee, Wis.	03-06-38	R	R	5'11	175	572	1876	216	468	87	18	4	223	179	196	24	.249	.321
Lynch, Jabber-Walter Edward	22BosA	04-15-97	Buffalo, N.Y.	12-21-76	R	R	6'	176	3	2	1	1	0	0	0	0	0	0	0	.500	.500
Lynn, Jerry-Jerome Edward	37WasA	04-14-16	Scranton, Pa.	09-25-72	R	R	5'10	164	1	3	0	2	1	0	0	0	0	0	0	.667	1.000
Lyon, Russ-Russell Mayo	44CleA	06-26-13	Ball Ground, Ga.	12-24-75	R	R	6'1	230	7	11	1	2	0	0	0	1	1	0	0	.182	.182
Lyons, Terry -Terence Hilbert	29PhiN	12-14-08	New Holland, Ohio	09-09-59	R	R	6'	165	1	0	0	0	0	0	0	0	0	0	0	—	—
MacDonald, Harvey-Harvey Forsyth	28PhiN	05-18-98	New York, N.Y.	10-04-65	L	L	5'11	170	13	16	0	4	0	0	0	2	3	0	0	.250	.250
Mack (Maciarz), Joe-Joseph John	45BosN	01-04-12	Chicago, Ill.	12-19-98	B	L	5'11	185	66	260	30	60	13	1	3	44	34	39	1	.231	.323
Mack (Mickovsky), Ray-Raymond James	38-44CleA 45MS 46CleA 47NYA 47ChiN	08-31-16	Cleveland, Ohio	05-07-69	R	R	6'	190	791	2707	273	629	113	24	34	278	261	365	35	.232	.330
Mackiewicz, Felix-Felix Thaddeus	41-43PhiA 45-47CleA 47WasA	11-20-17	Chicago, Ill.	12-20-93	R	R	6'2	197	223	672	85	174	32	12	2	55	63	88	10	.259	.351
Macon, Max-Max Cullen (See P20-45)	38StLN 40,42-43BknN 44BosN 45-46MS 47BosN	10-14-15	Pensacola, Fla.	08-05-89	L	R	6'3	175	226	502	54	133	17	4	3	46	16	32	9	.265	.333
MacPhee, Waddy-Walter Scott 26 played in N.F.L.		12-23-99	Brooklyn, N.Y.	01-20-80	R	R	5'8	155	2	7	2	2	1	0	0	0	0	0	0	.286	.571
Madjeski (Majewski), Ed-Edward William	32-34PhiA 34ChiA 37NYN	07-20-08	Queens, N.Y.	11-11-94	R	R	6'	170	166	481	58	116	19	2	5	56	21	61	2	.241	.320
Maggert, Harl-Harl Warren	38BosN	05-04-14	Los Angeles, Cal.	07-10-86	R	R	6'	190	66	89	12	25	3	0	3	19	10	20	0	.281	.416
Maguire, Freddie-Fred Edward	22-23NYN 28ChiN 29-31BosN	05-10-99	Roxbury, Mass.	11-03-61	R	R	5'11	165	618	2120	226	545	90	22	1	163	82	131	23	.257	.322
Mahady, Jim-James Bernard	21NYN	04-22-01	Cortland, N.Y.	08-09-36	R	R	5'11	170	1	0	0	0	0	0	0	0	0	0	0	—	—
Mahan, Art-Arthur Leo	40PhiN	06-08-13	Somerville, Mass.		L	L	5'11	178	146	544	55	133	24	5	2	39	40	37	4	.244	.318
Maier, Bob-Robert Phillip	45DetA	09-05-15	Dunellen, N.J.	08-04-93	R	R	5'8	180	132	486	58	128	25	7	1	34	38	32	7	.263	.350
Mailho, Emil-Emil Pierre (Lefty)	35PhiA	12-16-09	Berkeley, Cal.		L	L	5'11	170	21	18	5	1	0	0	0	0	5	3	0	.056	.056
Maisel, George-George John	13StLA 16DetA 21-22ChiN	03-12-92	Catonsville, Md.	11-20-68	R	R	5'10	180	167	500	67	141	10	3	0	50	20	24	18	.282	.314
Malay, Joe-Joseph Charles	33,35NYN	10-25-05	Brooklyn, N.Y.	03-19-89	L	L	6'	175	9	25	0	4	0	0	0	2	0	0	0	.160	.160
Malinosky, Tony-Anthony Francis	37BknN	10-05-09	Collinsville, Ill.		R	R	5'10	165	35	79	7	18	2	0	0	3	9	11	0	.228	.253
Mallon, Les-Leslie Clyde	31-32PhiN 34-35BosN	11-21-05	Sweetwater, Tex.	04-17-91	R	R	5'8	160	383	1300	156	368	65	5	8	119	100	117	4	.283	.359
Mallonee, Ben-Howard Bennett (Lefty)	21PhiA	03-31-94	Baltimore, Md.	02-19-78	L	L	5'6	150	7	24	2	6	1	0	0	0	1	1	1	.250	.292
Mallonee, Jule-Julius Norris	25ChiA	04-04-00	Charlotte, N.C.	12-26-34	L	R	6'2	180	2	3	1	0	0	0	0	0	0	0	0	.333	.333
Mallory, Jim-James Baugh (Sunny Jim)	40WasA 42-44MS 45StLN 45NYN	09-01-18	Lawrenceville, Va.	08-06-01	R	R	6'1	170	54	149	15	40	3	0	0	14	7	10	1	.268	.289
Mancuso, Frank-Frank Octavius	44-46StLA 47WasA	05-23-18	Houston, Tex.		R	R	6'	195	337	1002	85	241	37	7	5	98	101	118	2	.241	.306
Mancuso, Gus-August Rodney (Blackie)	28,30-32StLN 33-38NYN 39ChiN 40BknN 41-42StLN 42-44NYN 45PhiN	12-05-05	Galveston, Tex.	10-26-84	R	R	5'10	185	1460	4505	386	1194	197	16	53	543	418	264	8	.265	.351
Manion, Clyde-Clyde Jennings (Pete)	20-24,26-27DetA 28-30StLA 32-34CinN	10-30-96	Big River, Mo.	09-04-67	R	R	5'11	175	477	1145	96	250	25	3	3	112	118	102	5	.218	.253
Mann, Ben-Ben Garth (Red)	44CinN	11-16-15	Brandon, Tex.	09-11-80	R	R	6'	155	1	0	0	0	0	0	0	0	0	0	0	—	—
Mann, Johnny-John Leo	28ChiA	02-04-98	Fontanet, Ind.	03-31-77	R	R	5'11	160	6	6	0	2	0	0	0	0	1	0	0	.333	.333
Manno, Don-Donald D.	40-41BosN	05-04-15	Williamsport, Pa.	03-11-95	R	R	6'1	180	19	37	5	7	3	1	0	1	8	9	0	.189	.297
Manush, Heinie-Henry Emmett	23-27DetA 28-30StLA 30-35WasA 36BosA 37-38BknN 38-39PitN	07-20-01	Tuscumbia, Ala.	05-12-71	L	L	6'1	200	2009	7653	1287	2524	491	160	110	1173	506	345	114	.330	.479
Maple, Howie-Howard Albert 30 played in N.F.L.	32WasA	07-20-03	Adrian, Mo.	11-09-70	L	R	5'7	175	44	41	6	10	0	1	0	7	7	7	0	.244	.293
Maranville, Rabbit-Walter James Vincent	12-20BosN 21-24PitN 25,M25ChiN 26BknN 27-28StLN 29-33BosN 34BL 35BosN	11-11-91	Springfield, Mass.	01-05-54	R	R	5'5	155	2670	10078	1255	2605	380	177	28	884	839	756	291	.258	.340
Marion, Marty-Martin Whiteford (Slats, The Octopus)	40-50StLN M51StLN 51XJ 52-53,M52-53StLA M54-56CinA	12-01-17	Richburg, S.C.		R	R	6'2	170	1572	5506	602	1448	272	37	36	624	470	537	35	.263	.345
Marion, Red-John Wyeth	35,43WasA	03-14-14	Richburg, S.C.	03-13-75	R	R	6'2	175	18	28	3	5	1	0	1	2	3	3	0	.179	.321
Marnie, Hal-Harry Sylvester	40-42PhiN 43-45MS	07-06-18	Philadelphia, Pa.	01-07-02	R	R	5'11	178	96	222	19	49	3	3	0	15	18	29	1	.221	.261
Marquardt, Ollie-Albert Ludwig	31BosA	09-22-02	Toledo, Ohio	02-07-68	R	R	5'9	160	17	39	4	7	1	0	0	3	3	3	0	.179	.205
Marriott, Bill-William Earl	17ChiN 18MS 20-21ChiN 25BosN 26-27BknN	04-18-93	Pratt, Kans.	08-11-69	R	R	6'	170	264	826	86	220	27	14	4	95	57	55	16	.266	.347
Marshall, Bill-William Henry	31BosA 34CinN	02-14-12	Dorchester, Mass.	05-05-77	R	R	5'8	156	7	8	1	1	0	0	0	0	0	0	0	.125	.125
Marshall (Marchlewicz), Charlie-Charles Anthony	41StLN	08-28-19	Wilmington, Del.		R	R	5'10	178	1	0	0	0	0	0	0	0	0	0	0	—	—
Marshall, Doc-Edward Harbert	29-32NYN	06-04-06	New Albany, Miss.	09-01-99	R	R	5'11	150	219	658	72	170	21	6	0	61	28	28	2	.258	.309
Marshall, Max-Milo May	42-44CinN 45NYN	09-18-13	Randolph, Iowa	09-16-93	L	R	6'1	180	329	1267	140	311	41	16	15	105	89	100	15	.245	.339
Martin (Martinovich), Babe-Boris Michael	44-46StLA 48-49BosA 53StLA	03-28-20	Seattle, Wash.		R	R	5'11	194	69	206	13	44	6	2	2	18	13	27	0	.214	.291
Martin, Hersh-Hershel Ray	37-40PhiN 44-45NYA	09-19-09	Birmingham, Ala.	11-17-80	B	R	6'2	190	607	2257	331	643	135	29	28	215	253	207	33	.285	.408
Martin, Joe-William Joseph (Smokey Joe)	36NYN 38ChiA	08-28-11	Seymour, Mo.	09-28-60	R	R	5'11	181	8	15	0	4	1	0	0	2	0	4	0	.267	.333
Martin, Pepper-Johnny Leonard Roosevelt (The Wild Hoss of the Osage)	28,30-40,44StLN	02-29-04	Temple, Okla.	03-05-65	R	R	5'8	170	1189	4117	756	1227	270	75	59	501	369	438	146	.298	.443
Martin, Stu-Stuart McGuire	36-40StLN 41-42PhiN 43CinN	11-19-12	Rich Square, N.C.	01-11-97	L	R	6'	175	722	2237	322	599	112	24	16	183	190	185	36	.268	.361
Marty, Joe-Joseph Anton	37-39ChiN 39-41PhiN 42-45MS	09-01-13	Sacramento, Cal.	10-04-84	R	R	6'	182	538	1832	223	478	78	22	44	222	142	187	14	.261	.400
Matthews, Wid-Wid Curry	23PhiA 24-25WasA	10-20-96	Raleigh, Ill.	10-05-65	L	L	5'8	160	192	663	79	188	21	10	1	39	61	32	19	.284	.350
Mattick, Bobby-Robert James	38-40ChiN 41-42CinN M80-81TorA	12-05-15	Sioux City, Iowa	12-16-04	R	R	5'11	178	206	690	54	161	31	1	0	64	33	60	7	.233	.281
Mattox, Cloy-Cloy Mitchell (Monk)	29PhiA	11-21-02	Leesville, Va.	08-31-85	L	R	5'8	168	3	6	0	1	0	0	0	0	1	0	0	.167	.167
Mattox, Jim-James Powell	22-23PitN	12-17-96	Leesville, Va.	10-12-73	L	R	5'9	168	51	83	15	21	2	0	0	4	1	8	0	.253	.325
Mauldin, Mark-Marshall Reese	34ChiA	11-05-14	Atlanta, Ga.	09-02-90	R	R	5'11	170	10	38	3	10	2	0	0	2	0	5	0	.263	.395
May, Pinky-Merrill Glend	39-43PhiN 44-45MS	01-18-11	Laconia, Ind.	09-04-00	R	R	5'11	165	665	2215	210	610	102	11	4	215	261	121	13	.275	.337
Maynard, Buster-James Walter	40,42-43NYN 44-45MS 46NYN	03-25-13	Henderson, N.C.	09-07-77	R	R	6'1	170	224	616	68	136	14	5	14	66	46	53	6	.221	.328
Maynard, Chick-Leroy Evans	22BosA	11-02-96	Turners Falls, Mass.	01-31-57	L	R	5'9	150	12	24	1	3	0	0	0	0	3	2	0	.125	.125
Mayo (Mayoski), Eddie-Edward Joseph	36NYN 37-38BosN 43PhiA 44-48DetA	04-15-10	Holyoke, Mass.		L	R	5'11	178	834	3013	350	759	119	16	26	287	257	175	29	.252	.328
Mazzera, Mike-Melvin Leonard	35,37-39StLA 40PhiN	01-31-14	Stockton, Cal.	12-17-97	L	L	5'11	180	208	508	75	136	22	8	10	66	45	71	2	.268	.402
McBride, Tom-Thomas Raymond	43-47BosA 47-48WasA	11-02-14	Bonham, Tex.	12-26-01	R	R	6'	180	408	1186	140	326	39	16	2	141	93	63	13	.275	.340
McCann, Emmett-Robert Emmett	20-21PhiA 26BosA	03-04-02	Philadelphia, Pa.	04-15-37	R	R	6'	175	71	194	19	44	4	1	0	18	8	8	2	.227	.268
McCarren, Bill-William Joseph	23BknN	11-04-95	Fortenia, Pa.	09-11-83	R	R	5'11	170	69	216	28	53	10	1	3	27	22	39	0	.245	.343
McCarthy, Johnny-John Joseph	34-35BknN 36-41NYN 43BosN 44-45MS 46BosN 48NYN	01-07-10	Chicago, Ill.	09-13-73	L	L	6'2	185	542	1557	182	432	72	16	25	209	90	114	8	.277	.392

USE NAME - GIVEN NAMES (NICKNAMES)	TEAM BY YEAR	BIRTH DATE	BIRTH PLACE	DEATH DATE	B	T	HGT	WGT	G	AB	R	H	2B	3B	HR	RBI	BB	SO	SB	BA	SA
McClanahan, Pete-Robert Hugh	31PitN	10-24-06	Coldspring, Tex.	10-28-87	R	R	5'9	170	7	4	2	2	0	0	0	2	0	0	0	.500	.500
McClellan, Harvey-Harvey McDowell	19-24ChiA 25IL	12-22-94	Cynthia, Ky.	11-06-25	R	R	5'10	150	344	1162	130	257	54	8	4	98	68	103	23	.210	.292
McCormick, Frank-Frank Andrew (Buck)	34,37-45CinN 46-47PhiN 47-48BosN	06-09-11	New York, N.Y.	11-21-82	R	R	6'4	205	1534	5723	722	1711	334	26	128	954	399	189	27	.299	.434
McCoy, Benny-Benjamin Jenison	38-39DetA 40-41PhiA 42-45MS	11-09-15	Jenison, Mich.		L	R	5'9	170	337	1214	182	327	52	18	16	156	190	122	8	.269	.381
McCrea, Frank-Francis William	25CleA	09-06-96	Jersey City, N.J.	02-25-81	R	R	5'9	155	1	5	1	1	0	0	0	0	0	0	0	.200	.200
McCue, Frank-Frank Aloysius	22PhiA	10-04-98	Chicago, Ill.	07-05-53	B	R	5'9	150	2	5	0	0	0	0	0	0	0	0	0	.000	.000
McCurdy, Harry-Harry Henry (Hank)	22-23StLN 26-28ChiA 30-33PhiN 34CinN	09-15-99	Stevens Point, Wis.	07-21-72	L	R	5'11	187	543	1157	148	326	71	12	9	148	129	108	12	.282	.387
McDonnell, Jim-James William (Mack)	43-45CleA	08-15-22	Gagetown, Mich.	04-24-93	L	R	5'11	165	50	95	9	20	2	0	0	12	8	8	0	.211	.232
McElyea, Frank-Frank	42BosN 43-45MS	08-04-18	Hawthorne Twp., Ill.	04-19-87	R	R	6'6	220	7	4	0	0	0	0	0	0	0	0	0	.000	.000
McFarland, Howie-Howard Alexander	45WasA	03-07-10	El Reno, Okla.	04-07-93	R	R	6'	175	6	11	0	1	0	0	0	2	0	3	0	.091	.091
McGee, Dan-Daniel Aloysius	34BosN	09-29-11	New York, N.Y.	12-04-91	R	R	5'8	152	7	22	2	3	0	0	0	1	3	6	0	.136	.136
McGee, Tubby-Francis De Sales	25WasA	04-28-99	Columbus, Ohio	01-30-34	R	R	5'11	175	2	3	0	0	0	0	0	0	0	1	0	.000	.000
McGhee, Bill-William Mac (Fibber)	44-45PhiA	09-05-05	Shawmut, Ala.	03-10-84	L	L	5'11	183	170	537	51	146	18	1	1	38	45	36	5	.272	.315
McGowan, Beauty-Frank Bernard	22-23PhiA 28-29StLA 37BosN	11-08-01	Branford, Conn.	05-06-82	L	R	5'11	190	375	1208	174	316	58	16	6	108	154	122	17	.262	.351
McHenry, Austin-Austin Bush (Mac)	18-22StLN	09-22-95	Wrightsville, Ohio	11-27-22	R	R	6'	175	543	1959	262	592	105	39	34	286	117	229	35	.302	.448
McLarney, Art-Arthur James	32NYN	12-20-08	Fort Worden, Wash.	12-20-84	B	R	5'11	168	9	23	2	3	1	0	0	3	1	3	0	.130	.174
McLaughlin, Jim-James Robert	32StLA	01-03-02	St. Louis, Mo.	12-18-68	R	R	5'10	168	1	1	0	0	0	0	0	1	0	0	0	.000	.000
McLeod, Jim-Soule James	30,32WasA 33PhiN	09-12-08	Jones, La.	08-03-81	R	R	6'	187	92	266	24	54	7	1	0	16	14	30	2	.203	.237
McLeod, Ralph-Ralph Alton	38BosN	10-19-16	North Quincy, Mass.		L	L	6'	170	6	7	1	2	1	0	0	0	2	0	0	.286	.429
McManus, Marty-Martin Joseph	20-26StLA 27-31DetA 31-33,M32-33BosA 34BosN		Chicago, Ill.	02-18-66	R	R	5'10	160	1831	6660	1008	1926	401	88	120	996	675	558	126	.289	.430
McMillan, Norm-Norman Alexis (Bub)	22NYA 23BosA 24StLA 28-29CinN	10-05-95	Latta, S.C.	09-28-69	R	R	6'	175	413	1356	157	353	74	16	6	147	95	133	36	.260	.352
McMullen, Hugh-Hugh Raphael	25-26NYN 28WasA 29CinN	12-16-01	La Cygne, Kans.	05-23-86	B	R	5'11	180	64	108	6	19	3	0	0	6	2	22	1	.176	.204
McNabb, Carl-Carl Mac (Skinny)	45DetA	01-25-17	Stevenson, Ala.		R	R	5'9	155	1	1	0	0	0	0	0	0	0	1	0	.000	.000
McNair, Eric-Donald Eric (Boob, Rabbit)	29-35,42PhiA 36-38BosA 39-40ChiA 41-42DetA	04-12-09	Meridian, Miss.	03-11-49	R	R	5'8	160	1251	4519	592	1240	229	29	82	633	261	328	59	.274	.392
McNally, Mike-Michael Joseph	15-17BosA 18MS 19-20BosA 21-24NYA 25WasA	09-13-93	Minooka, Pa.	05-29-65	R	R	5'11	150	492	1078	169	257	16	6	1	85	92	97	39	.238	.267
McNamara, Bob-Robert Maxey	39PhiA	09-19-16	Denver, Colo.		R	R	5'10	170	9	9	0	2	1	0	0	3	1	1	0	.222	.333
McNamara, Dinny-John Raymond	27-28BosN	09-16-05	Lexington, Mass.	12-20-63	L	R	5'9	165	20	13	5	1	0	0	0	0	0	4	0	.077	.077
McNamara, George-George Francis	22WasA	01-11-01	Chicago, Ill.	06-12-90	L	R	6'	175	3	11	3	3	0	0	0	1	1	2	1	.273	.273
McNamara, Tom-Thomas Henry	22PitN	11-05-95	Roxbury, Mass.	05-05-74	R	R	6'2	200	1	1	0	0	0	0	0	0	0	0	0	.000	.000
McNeely, Earl-George Earl	24-27WasA 28-31StLA	05-12-98	Sacramento, Cal.	07-16-71	L	R	5'9	140	683	2254	369	614	107	33	4	213	183	187	68	.272	.354
McNulty, Pat-Patrick Howard	22,24-27CleA	02-27-99	Cleveland, Ohio	05-04-63	L	R	5'11	160	308	820	132	238	36	9	6	84	98	62	22	.290	.378
McQuaig, Jerry-Gerald Joseph	34PhiN	01-31-12	Douglas, Ga.	02-05-01	R	R	5'11	183	7	16	2	1	0	0	0	1	2	4	0	.063	.063
McQuillen, Glenn-Glenn Richard (Red)	38,41-42StLA 43-45MS 46-47StLA	04-19-15	Strasburg, Va.	06-08-89	R	R	6'	198	210	643	82	176	24	16	4	75	34	49	1	.274	.379
McQuinn, George-George Hartley	36CinN 38-45StLA 46PhiA 47-48NYA	05-29-09	Arlington, Va.	12-24-78	L	L	5'11	165	1550	5747	832	1588	315	64	135	794	712	634	32	.276	.424
McWilliams, Bill-William Henry	31BosA	11-28-10	Dubuque, Iowa	01-21-97	R	R	6'1	180	2	2	0	0	0	0	0	0	0	1	0	.000	.000
Mead, Charlie-Charles Richard	43-45NYN	04-09-21	Vermilion, Canada		L	R	6'2	185	87	261	18	64	8	3	1	27	20	24	3	.245	.318
Medeiros, Ray-Ray Antone (Pep)	45CinN	05-09-26	Oakland, Cal.	06-06-03	R	R	5'10	163	1	0	0	0	0	0	0	0	0	0	0	--	--
Medwick, Joe-Joseph Michael (Ducky, Muscles)	32-40StLN 40-43BknN 43-45NYN 45BosN 46BknN 47-48StLN	11-24-11	Carteret, N.J.	03-21-75	R	R	5'10	187	1984	7635	1198	2471	540	113	205	1383	437	551	42	.324	.505
Mele, Dutch-Albert Ernest	37CinN	01-11-15	New York, N.Y.	02-12-75	L	L	5'11	195	6	14	1	2	1	0	0	1	1	1	0	.143	.143
Melillo, Oscar-Oscar Donald (Ski, Spinach)	26-35StLA 35-37BosA M38StLA	04-04-99	Chicago, Ill.	11-14-63	R	R	5'8	150	1377	5063	590	1316	210	64	22	548	327	306	69	.260	.340
Meliana, Joe-Joseph Peter	27PhiA	03-11-05	Oakland, Cal.	11-01-69	R	R	5'10	180	4	7	1	2	0	0	0	2	0	1	0	.286	.286
Menosky, Mike-Michael William (Leaping Mike)	14-15PitF 16-17WasA 18MS 19WasA 20-23BosA	10-16-94	Glen Campbell, Pa.	04-11-83	L	R	5'10	163	809	2465	382	685	98	38	18	250	295	260	90	.278	.370
Merewether, Art-Arthur Francis (Merry)	22PitN	07-07-02	E. Providence, R.I.	02-02-97	R	R	5'9	155	1	1	0	0	0	0	0	0	0	0	0	.000	.000
Merritt, Herm-Herman G.	21DetA	11-12-00	Independence, Kans.	05-26-27	R	R			20	46	3	17	1	2	0	6	1	5	1	.370	.478
Merullo, Lennie-Leonard Richard	41-47ChiN	05-05-17	Boston, Mass.		R	R	5'11	165	639	2071	191	497	92	8	6	152	136	174	38	.240	.301
Mesner, Steve-Stephen Mathias	38-39ChiN 41StLN 43-45CinN	01-13-18	Los Angeles, Cal.	04-06-61	R	R	5'9	178	451	1574	153	397	67	6	2	167	121	69	11	.252	.306
Metha, Scat-Frank Joseph	40DetA	12-13-13	Los Angeles, Cal.	03-02-75	R	R	5'11	165	26	37	6	9	0	0	0	3	2	9	0	.243	.297
Metheny, Bud-Arthur Beauregard	43-46NYA	06-01-15	St. Louis, Mo.	01-02-03	L	L	5'11	190	376	1390	187	344	52	5	31	156	149	122	12	.247	.359
Metro (Moreskonich), Charlie-Charles	43-44DetA 44-45PhiA M62ChiN M70KCA	04-28-19	Nanty-Glo, Pa.		R	R	5'11	175	171	358	42	69	10	2	3	23	36	55	3	.193	.257
Metz, Lenny-Leonard Ray	23-25PhiN	07-06-99	Superior, Colo.	02-24-53	R	R	5'11	175	30	58	6	10	0	0	0	4	5	0	0	.172	.172
Metzig, Bill-William Andrew	44ChiA	12-04-18	Fort Dodge, Iowa	03-12-06	R	R	6'1	180	5	16	1	2	0	0	0	1	1	4	0	.125	.125
Metzler, Alex-Alexander	25ChiN 26PhiA 27-30ChiA 30StLA	01-04-03	Fresno, Cal.	11-30-73	L	R	5'9	167	560	1965	290	561	85	41	9	207	260	144	48	.285	.384
Meusel, Bob-Robert William (Long Bob)	20-29NYA 30CinN	07-19-96	San Jose, Cal.	11-28-77	R	R	6'3	190	1407	5475	826	1693	368	95	156	1067	375	619	139	.309	.497
Meusel, Irish-Emil Frederick	14WasA 18-21PhiN 21-26NYN 27BknN	06-09-93	Oakland, Cal.	03-01-63	R	R	5'11	178	1289	4900	700	1521	250	93	106	819	269	199	113	.310	.464
Meyer, Dutch-Lambert Daniel	37ChiN 40-42DetA 43-44MS 45-46DetA	10-06-15	Waco, Tex.	11-19-03	R	R	5'11	178	286	994	113	262	49	12	10	93	82	75	5	.264	.367
Meyer, George-George Francis	38ChiA	08-03-09	Chicago, Ill.	01-03-92	R	R	5'9	160	24	81	10	24	2	2	0	9	11	17	3	.296	.370
Michaels, Ralph-Ralph Joseph	24-26ChiN	05-03-02	Etna, Pa.	08-05-88	R	R	5'10	178	32	61	11	18	1	0	0	8	6	10	1	.295	.311
Mihalic, John-John Michael	35-37WasA	11-13-11	Cleveland, Ohio	04-24-87	R	R	5'11	172	69	217	32	53	10	3	0	22	33	26	5	.244	.318
Miles, Dee-Wilson Daniel	35-36WasA 39-42PhiA 43-45PhiA	02-15-09	Kellerman, Ala.	11-02-76	L	L	6'	175	503	1468	175	411	53	24	2	143	50	74	15	.280	.353
Miller, Bing-Edmund John	21WasA 22-26PhiA 26-27StLA 28-34PhiA 35-36BosA	08-30-94	Vinton, Iowa	05-07-66	R	R	6'	185	1820	6212	946	1937	389	96	116	990	383	340	128	.312	.461
Miller, Eddie-Edward Robert (Eppie)	36-37CinN 39-42BosN 43-47CinN 48-49PhiN 50StLN	11-26-16	Pittsburgh, Pa.	07-31-97	R	R	5'9	180	1510	5337	539	1270	263	28	97	640	351	465	64	.238	.352
Miller, Hack-James Eldridge	44-45DetA	02-13-16	Celeste, Tex.	11-21-66	R	R	5'11	215	7	9	1	4	0	0	1	4	1	1	0	.444	.778
Miller, Hack-Laurence H.	16BknN 18BosA 22-25ChiN	01-01-94	New York, N.Y.	09-16-71	R	R	5'9	195	349	1200	164	387	65	11	38	205	64	103	10	.323	.490
Miller (Munzing), Jake-Jacob George	22PitN	12-01-95	Baltimore, Md.	08-24-74	R	R	5'10	170	3	11	0	1	0	0	0	0	0	1	0	.091	.091
Miller, Otto-Otis Louis	27StLA 30-32BosA	02-02-01	Belleville, Ill.	07-26-59	R	R	5'10	168	272	837	95	229	39	6	0	91	49	46	3	.274	.335
Miller, Ralph-Ralph Joseph 25-31 played in A.B.L.	20-21PhiN 24WasA	02-29-96	Fort Wayne, Ind.	03-18-39	R	R	6'	190	163	557	48	138	24	1	3	54	18	43	6	.248	.311
Miller, Rudy-Rudel Charles	29PhiA	07-12-00	Kalamazoo, Mich.	01-22-94	R	R	6'1	180	2	4	1	1	0	0	0	1	3	0	0	.250	.250
Millies, Wally-Wally Louis	34BknN 36-37WasA 39-41PhiN	10-18-06	Chicago, Ill.	02-28-95	R	R	5'10	170	246	651	60	158	20	3	0	65	33	32	2	.243	.283
Mills, Bill-William Henry	44PhiA	11-20-20	Boston, Mass.		R	R	5'10	170	3	1	0	0	0	0	0	0	0	0	0	.000	.000
Mills, Buster-Colonel Buster	34StLN 35BknN 37BosA 38StLA 40NYA 42CleA 43-45MS 46CleA	09-16-08	Ranger, Tex.	12-01-91	R	R	5'11	195	415	1379	200	396	62	19	14	163	131	137	23	.287	.390
Milosevich, Mike-Michael (Mollie)	44-45NYA	01-13-15	Ziegler, Ill.	02-03-66	R	R	5'10	172	124	381	32	92	13	4	0	39	36	43	5	.241	.297
Mitchell, Clarence-Clarence Elmer (See P20-45)	11DetA 16-17CinN 18-22BknN 23-28PhiN 28-30StLN 30-32NYN	02-22-91	Franklin, Neb.	11-06-63	L	L	5'11	190	650	1287	138	324	41	10	7	133	72	92	9	.252	.316
Mitchell, Johnny-John Franklin	21-22NYA 22-23BosA 24StLA	08-09-94	Detroit, Mich.	11-04-65	R	R	5'8	155	329	1175	152	288	38	8	2	63	119	81	14	.245	.296
Mize, Johnny-John Robert (Big Jawn, The Big Cat)	36-41StLN 42NYN 43-45MS 46-49NYN 49-53NYA	01-07-13	Demorest, Ga.	06-02-93	L	R	6'2	215	1884	6443	1118	2011	367	83	359	1337	856	524	28	.312	.562
Mizeur, Bill-William Francis (Bad Bill)	23-24StLA	06-22-97	Nokomis, Ill.	08-27-76	L	R	6'2	190	2	2	0	0	0	0	0	0	0	0	0	.000	.000
Mohardt, Johnny-John Henry 22-25 played in N.F.L.	22DetA	01-21-98	Pittsburgh, Pa.	11-24-61	L	R	5'10	165	5	2	1	2	1	0	0	0	1	0	0	1.000	1.000
Moken, Johnny-John Leo	21-22PitN 22-27PhiN	09-23-95	Buffalo, N.Y.	02-10-85	R	R	5'7	190	582	1936	282	563	98	17	32	273	206	150	26	.291	.409
Monaco, Blas-Blas	37,46CleA	11-16-15	San Antonio, Tex.	02-10-00	B	R	5'11	170	17	13	5	2	0	0	0	3	9	3	0	.154	.308
Moncewicz, Freddie-Frederick Alfred	28BosA	09-01-03	Brockton, Mass.	04-23-69	R	R	5'9	175	3	1	0	0	0	0	0	0	0	0	0	.000	.000
Monchak, Al-Alex	40PhiN	03-05-17	Bayonne, N.J.		R	R	6'	180	19	14	1	2	0	0	0	0	0	4	0	.143	.143
Monroe, John-John Allen	21NYN 21PhiN	08-24-98	Farmersville, Tex.	06-19-56	L	R	5'9	160	60	154	17	41	4	2	0	14	14	15	2	.266	.357
Montague, Ed-Edward Francis	28,30-32CleA	07-24-05	San Francisco, Cal.	06-17-88	R	R	5'10	165	220	615	105	161	18	7	2	69	85	91	7	.262	.324
Monteagudo, Rene-Rene [Miranda] (See P20-45)	38,40,44WasA 45PhiN	03-12-16	Havana, Cuba	09-14-73	L	L	5'7	165	156	270	32	78	9	1	0	21	29	12	2	.289	.330
Montgomery, Al-Alvin Atlas	41BosN	07-03-20	Loving, N.M.	04-26-42	R	R	5'10	185	42	52	4	10	5	0	0	9	6	9	0	.192	.212
Moore, Al-Albert James	25-26NYN	08-04-02	Brooklyn, N.Y.	11-29-74	R	R	5'10	174	30	89	12	19	4	0	0	6	6	9	5	.213	.258
Moore, Bill-William Henry (Willie)	25CleA	12-12-01	Kansas City, Mo.	05-24-72	L	R	6'	180	49	87	9	18	2	0	0	8	7	13	2	.207	.230
Moore, Dee-DC	36-37CinN 43BknN 43PhiN 44-45MS 46PhiN	04-06-14	Hadley, Tex.	07-02-97	R	R	6'	200	98	228	29	53	9	2	1	22	34	24	1	.232	.303
Moore, Eddie-Graham Edward	23-26PitN 26-28BosN 29-30BknN 32NYN 34CleA	01-18-99	Barlow, Ky.	02-10-76	R	R	5'7	165	748	2474	360	706	106	26	13	257	272	121	52	.285	.366
Moore, Gene-Eugene Jr. (Rowdy)	31CinN 33-35StLN 36-38BosN 39-40BknN 40-41BosN 42-43WasA 44-45StLA	08-26-09	Lancaster, Tex.	03-12-78	L	L	5'11	175	1042	3543	497	958	179	53	58	436	317	401	31	.270	.400

USE NAME - GIVEN NAMES (NICKNAMES)	TEAM BY YEAR	BIRTH DATE	BIRTH PLACE	DEATH DATE	B	T	HGT	WGT	G	AB	R	H	2B	3B	HR	RBI	BB	SO	SB	BA	SA
Moore, Jimmy-James William	30ChiA 30-31PhiA	04-24-03	Paris, Tex.	03-07-86	R	R	6'	187	80	232	32	59	10	1	4	35	19	20	1	.254	.358
Moore, Johnny-John Francis	28-29,31-32ChiN 33-34CinN 34-37PhiN 45ChiN	03-23-02	Waterville, Conn.	04-04-91	L	R	5'11	175	846	3013	439	926	155	26	73	452	195	176	23	.307	.449
Moore, Jo-Jo-Joseph Gregg (The Gause Ghost)	30-41NYN	12-25-08	Gause, Tex.	04-01-01	L	R	5'11	155	1335	5427	809	1615	258	53	79	513	348	247	46	.298	.408
Moore, Randy-Randolph Edward	27-28ChiA 30-35BosN 36-37BknN 37StlN	06-21-05	Naples, Tex.	06-12-92	L	R	6'	185	749	2253	258	627	110	17	27	308	158	85	11	.278	.378
Moore, Terry-Terry Bluford	35-42StlN 43-45MS 46-48StlN M54PhiN	05-27-12	Vernon, Ala.	03-29-95	R	R	511	195	1298	4700	719	1318	263	28	80	513	406	368	82	.280	.399
Morehart, Ray-Raymond Anderson	24,26ChiA 27NYA	12-02-99	Abner, Tex.	01-13-89	L	R	5'9	157	177	487	82	131	21	7	1	49	57	40	10	.269	.347
Morgan, Chet-Chester Collins (Chick)	35,38DetA	07-09-10	Cleveland, Miss.	09-20-91	L	R	5'9	160	88	329	52	91	7	1	0	28	25	12	5	.277	.304
Morgan, Eddie-Edward Carre	28-33CleA 34BosA	05-22-04	Cairo, Ill.	04-09-30	R	R	6'	180	771	2810	512	879	186	45	52	474	385	252	36	.313	.467
Morgan, Eddie-Edwin Willis (Pepper)	36StlN 37BknN	11-19-14	Brady Lake, Ohio	06-27-82	L	L	5'10	160	39	66	8	14	3	0	1	8	11	11	0	.212	.303
Moriarty, Ed-Edward Jerome	35-36BosN	10-12-12	Holyoke, Mass.	09-29-91	R	R	5'10	160	14	40	4	12	2	1	1	1	0	7	0	.300	.475
Morris, Doyt-Doyt Theodore	37PhiA	07-15-16	Stanley, N.C.	07-04-84	R	R	6'4	195	6	13	0	2	0	0	0	0	0	3	0	.154	.154
Morrissey, Jo-Jo-Joseph Anselm	32-33CinN 36ChiA	01-16-04	Warren, R.I.	05-02-50	R	R	6'3	178	254	841	61	195	31	1	0	45	36	40	7	.232	.271
Morse, Bud-Newell Obediah	29PhiA	09-04-04	Berekley, Cal.		R	R	5'9	180	8	27	1	2	0	0	0	0	0	4	0	.074	.074
Moser, Arnie-Arnold Robert	37CinN	08-09-15	Houston, Tex.	08-15-02	R	R	5'11	165	5	5	0	0	0	0	0	0	0	2	0	.000	.000
Moses, Wally-Wallace	35-41PhiA 42-46ChiA 46-48BosA 49-51PhiA	10-08-10	Uvalda, Ga.	10-10-90	L	L	5'10	160	2012	7356	1114	2138	435	110	89	679	821	457	174	.291	.416
Mosolf, Jim-James Frederick	29-31PitN 33ChiN	08-21-05	Puyallup, Wash.	12-28-79	L	R	5'10	186	118	190	39	56	9	3	2	28	22	21	0	.295	.405
Moss, Charlie-Charles Crosby	34-36PhiA	03-20-11	Meridian, Miss.	10-09-91	R	R	5'10	160	47	57	6	14	1	1	0	12	7	5	1	.246	.298
Mostil, Johnny-John Anthony	18,21-29ChiA	06-01-96	Chicago, Ill.	12-10-70	B	R	5'9	168	972	3507	618	1054	209	82	23	376	415	336	176	.301	.427
Mott, Bitsy-Elisha Matthew	45PhiN	02-25-01	Arcadia, Fla.		R	R	5'11	165	90	289	21	64	8	0	0	22	27	25	2	.221	.249
Mowry, Joe-Joseph Aloysius	33-35BosN	04-06-08	St. Louis, Mo.	02-09-94	B	R	6'	198	192	464	51	108	19	6	2	37	29	48	1	.233	.313
Mueller, Bill-William Lawrence (Hawk)	42ChiA 43-44MS 45ChiA	11-09-20	Bay City, Mich.	10-24-01	R	R	6'2	180	39	94	8	14	1	0	0	5	14	10	3	.149	.160
Mueller, Emmett-Emmett Jerome (Heinie)	38-41PhiN 42-45MS	07-20-12	St. Louis, Mo.	10-03-86	B	R	5'6	167	441	1281	144	324	55	11	17	127	156	124	10	.253	.353
Mueller, Heinie-Clarence Francis	20-26StlN 26-27NYN 28-29BosN 36StlA	09-16-99	St. Louis, Mo.	01-23-75	L	L	5'8	158	693	2118	296	597	87	37	22	272	168	147	37	.282	.389
Mueller, Ray-Ray Coleman (Iron Man)	35-38BosN 39-40PitN 43-44CinN 44MS 46-49CinN 49-50NYN 50PitN 51BosN	03-08-12	Pittsburg, Kans.	06-29-94	R	R	5'9	175	985	2911	281	733	123	23	56	373	250	322	14	.252	.368
Mueller, Walter-Walter John	22-24,26PitN	12-06-94	Central, Mo.	08-16-71	R	R	5'8	160	121	345	46	95	10	7	2	49	13	19	4	.275	.362
Mulleavy, Greg-Gregory Thomas (Moe)	30,32ChiA 33BosA	09-25-05	Detroit, Mich.	02-01-80	R	R	5'9	160	79	292	28	76	14	5	0	28	20	23	5	.260	.342
Mullen, Billy-William John	20-21StlA 23BknN 26DetA 28StlA	03-13-96	St. Louis, Mo.	05-04-71	R	R	5'8	160	35	47	5	11	1	0	0	2	10	6	1	.234	.255
Mullen, Moon-Ford Parker	44PhiN 45-46MS	02-09-17	Olympia, Wash.	05-04-71	R	R	5'9	165	118	464	51	124	9	4	0	31	28	32	4	.267	.304
Muller, Freddie-Frederick William	33-34BosA		Newark, Cal.	10-20-76	R	R	5'10	170	17	49	7	9	1	1	0	3	6	5	1	.184	.245
Mulligan, Eddie-Edward Joseph	15-16ChiN 21-22ChiA 28PitN	08-27-94	St. Louis, Mo.	03-15-82	R	R	5'9	152	351	1235	143	287	41	24	1	88	70	120	23	.232	.307
Munson (Carlson), Joe-Joseph Martin Napoleon	25-26ChiN	11-06-99	Renovo, Pa.	02-24-91	L	R	5'9	184	42	136	22	39	5	3	3	18	11	5	1	.287	.434
Murphy, Ed-Edward Joseph	42PhiN 43-45MS	03-23-18	Joliet, Ill.	12-10-91	R	R	5'11	180	13	28	2	7	2	0	0	4	2	4	0	.250	.321
Murray, Bobby-Robert Hayes	23WasA	07-04-94	St. Albans, Vt.	01-04-79	R	R	5'8	160	10	39	2	7	1	0	0	2	1	3	0	.179	.205
Murray, Tony-Anthony John	23ChiN	04-30-04	Chicago, Ill.	03-19-74	R	R	5'10	154	2	4	0	1	0	0	0	0	0	0	0	.250	.250
Muser, Danny-William Daniel	32WasA	09-05-05	Zion, Pa.	03-02-00	L	R	5'9	160	1	2	0	1	0	0	0	0	0	0	0	.500	.500
Myatt, George-George Edward (Mercury, Foghorn)	43-47WasA M68-69PhiN	06-14-14	Denver, Colo.	09-14-00	L	R	5'11	167	407	1345	220	381	44	14	4	99	156	120	72	.283	.346
Myatt, Glenn-Glenn Calvin	20-21PhiA 23-35CleA 35NYN 36DetA	07-09-97	Argenta, Ark.	08-09-69	L	R	5'11	165	1004	2678	346	722	137	37	38	387	249	195	18	.270	.391
Myer, Buddy-Charles Solomon	25-27WasA 27-28BosA 29-41WasA	03-16-04	Ellisville, Miss.	10-31-74	L	R	5'10	163	1923	7038	1174	2131	353	130	38	850	965	428	156	.303	.406
Myers, Billy-William Harrison	35-40CinN 41ChiN	08-14-10	Enola, Pa.	04-10-95	R	R	5'8	168	738	2399	319	616	88	33	45	243	250	445	23	.257	.379
Myers, Lynn-Lynnwood Lincoln	38-39StlN	02-23-14	Enola, Pa.	01-19-00	R	R	5'6	145	144	344	42	83	16	3	1	29	21	48	10	.241	.314
Nagel, Bill-William Taylor	39PhiA 41PhiN 43ChiA	08-19-15	Memphis, Tenn.	10-08-81	R	R	6'1	190	189	617	62	140	30	8	15	72	43	141	5	.227	.374
Naleway, Frank-Frank (Chick)	24ChiA	07-04-01	Chicago, Ill.	01-28-49	R	R	5'9	165	1	2	0	0	0	0	0	0	0	0	0	.000	.000
Narleski, Bill-William Edward (Cap)	29-30BosA	03-09-00	Perth Amboy, N.J.	07-20-64	R	R	5'9	160	135	358	41	95	25	1	0	32	28	27	4	.265	.341
Narron, Sam-Samuel Woody	35,42-43StlN	08-25-13	Middlesex, N.C.	12-31-96	R	R	5'10	180	24	28	0	8	0	0	0	1	1	2	0	.286	.286
Naylor, Earl-Earl Eugene (See P20-45)	42-43PhiN 44-45MS 46BknN	05-19-19	Kansas City, Mo.	01-16-90	R	R	6'	190	112	290	22	54	6	1	3	28	23	35	2	.186	.245
Neighbors, Bob-Robert Otis	39StlA	11-09-17	Talahina, Okla.	08-08-52	R	R	5'11	165	7	11	3	2	0	0	0	1	0	1	0	.182	.455
Neis, Bernie-Bernard Edmund	20-24BknN 25-26BosA 27CleA 27ChiA	09-26-95	Bloomington, Ill. (Bats Right 20-21)	11-29-72	B	R	5'7	160	677	1825	297	496	84	18	25	210	201	186	46	.272	.379
Neitzke, Ernie-Ernest Fredrich	21BosA		Toledo, Ohio	04-27-77	R	R	5'10	180	11	25	3	6	0	0	0	1	4	4	0	.240	.240
Nelson, Tom-Thomas Cousineau (Hollywood)	45BosN	05-01-17	Chicago, Ill.	09-24-73	R	R	5'11	180	40	121	6	20	2	0	0	6	4	13	1	.165	.182
Neun, Johnny-John Henry (Flip)	25-28DetA 30-31BosN M46NYA M47-48CinN	10-28-00	Baltimore, Md.	03-28-90	B	L	5'10	175	432	945	171	273	42	17	2	85	110	93	41	.289	.376
Newsome, Skeeter-Lamar Ashby	35-39PhiA 41-45BosA 46-47PhiN	10-18-10	Phenix City, Ala.	08-31-89	R	R	5'9	155	1128	3716	381	910	164	15	9	292	246	194	67	.245	.304
Nichols, Roy-Roy	44ChiA	02-15-19	Little Rock, Ark.	04-03-02	R	R	5'11	155	11	9	3	2	0	0	0	0	2	2	0	.222	.333
Nicholson, Bill-William Beck (Swish)	36PhiA 39-48ChiN 49-53PhiN	12-11-14	Chestertown, Md.	03-08-96	L	R	6'	205	1677	5546	837	1484	272	60	235	948	800	828	27	.268	.465
Nicholson, Fred-Fred	17DetA 18MS 19-20PitN 21-22BosN	09-01-94	Honey Grove, Tex.	01-23-72	R	R	5'10	173	303	794	112	247	34	21	12	105	65	97	21	.311	.452
Niebergall, Charlie-Charles Arthur (Nig)	21-24StlN	09-06-02	New York, N.Y.	08-29-62	R	R	5'10	160	54	92	9	21	7	0	0	8	5	11	0	.228	.304
Niehaus, Al-Albert Bernard	25PitN 25CinN	06-01-99	Cincinnati, Ohio	10-14-31	R	R	5'11	175	68	211	23	58	18	2	0	21	14	15	1	.275	.379
Nieman, Butch-Elmer LeRoy	43-45BosN	02-08-18	Herkimer, Kans.	11-02-93	L	L	6'2	195	332	1050	147	269	46	14	37	167	129	119	20	.256	.432
Niemiec, Al-Alfred Joseph	34BosA 36PhiA	05-18-11	Meriden, Conn.	10-29-95	R	R	5'11	178	78	235	24	47	3	2	1	23	29	20	2	.200	.243
Nixon, Al-Albert Richard	15-16,18BknN 21-23BosN 26-28PhiN	04-11-86	Atlantic City, N.J.	11-09-60	R	R	5'8	164	422	1345	180	372	60	13	7	118	66	77	19	.277	.356
Nonnenkamp, Red-Leo William	33PitN 38-40BosA	07-07-11	St. Louis, Mo.	12-03-00	L	L	5'11	165	155	263	49	69	6	2	0	24	34	24	6	.262	.308
Norman, Bill-Henry Willis Patrick	31-32ChiA M58-59DetA	07-16-10	St. Louis, Mo.	04-21-62	R	R	6'2	190	37	103	13	21	5	1	0	8	6	13	0	.204	.272
Norris, Leo-Leo John	36-37PhiN	05-17-08	Bay St. Louis, Miss.	02-13-87	R	R	5'11	165	270	962	109	252	51	7	20	112	60	132	7	.262	.392
Novikoff, Lou-Louis Alexander (The Mad Russian)	41-44ChiN 44MS 46PhiN	10-12-15	Glendale, Ariz.	09-30-70	R	R	5'10	185	356	1081	107	305	45	10	15	138	64	71	4	.282	.393
Oana, Prince-Henry Kawaihoa (See P20-45)	34PhiN 43,45DetA	01-22-08	Waipahu, Hawaii	06-19-76	R	R	6'2	193	30	52	8	16	3	1	1	10	1	3	0	.308	.462
O'Brien, Mickey-Frank Andrew	23PhiN	09-13-94	San Francisco, Cal.	11-04-71	R	R	5'8	160	15	21	3	7	2	0	0	3	3	0	0	.333	.429
O'Brien, Tommy-Thomas Edward (Obie)	43-45PhiN 49-50BosA 50WasA	12-19-18	Anniston, Ala.	11-05-71	R	R	5'11	195	293	714	110	198	30	14	8	78	70	66	2	.277	.392
Ock, Whitey-Harold David	35BosA	03-17-12	Brooklyn, N.Y.	03-18-75	R	R	5'11	180	1	3	0	0	0	0	0	0	0	0	0	.000	.000
O'Connell, Jimmy-James Joseph	23-24NYN 24SL	02-11-01	Sacramento, Cal.	11-11-76	L	R	5'10	175	139	356	66	96	13	4	8	57	45	48	9	.270	.396
O'Connell, John-John Charles	28-29PitN	06-13-04	Verona, Pa.	10-17-92	R	R	6'	175	3	8	1	1	0	0	0	0	0	1	0	.125	.250
O'Dea, Ken-James Kenneth	35-38ChiN 39-41NYN 42-46StlN 46BosN	03-16-13	Lima, N.Y.	12-12-85	L	R	6'	180	832	2195	262	560	101	20	40	323	273	251	4	.255	.374
O'Dea, Paul-Paul (Lefty)	44-45CleA	03-23-20	Cleveland, Ohio	12-11-78	L	L	6'	200	163	394	46	107	11	2	1	34	43	47	5	.272	.317
Odom, Heinie-Herman Boyd	25NYA	10-13-00	Rusk, Tex.	08-31-70	B	R	6'	170	1	1	0	1	0	0	0	0	0	0	0	1.000	1.000
O'Donnell, Harry-Harry Herman (Butch)		04-02-94	Philadelphia, Pa.	01-31-58	R	R	5'10	165	16	16	1	1	0	0	0	0	2	0	0	.063	.063
O'Doul, Lefty-Francis Joseph (See P20-45)	19-20,22NYA 23BosA 28NYN 29-30PhiN 31-33BknN 34NYN	03-04-97	San Francisco, Cal.	12-07-69	L	L	6'	180	970	3264	624	1140	175	41	113	542	333	122	36	.349	.532
O'Farrell, Bob-Robert Arthur	15-25ChiN 25-28,M27StlN 28-32NYN 33StlN 34,M34CinN 34ChiN 35StlN	10-19-96	Waukegan, Ill.	02-20-88	R	R	5'9	180	1492	4101	517	1120	201	58	51	549	547	408	35	.273	.390
Oglesby, Jim-James Dorn	36StlN	08-10-05	Schofield, Mo.	09-01-55	L	L	6'	190	3	11	0	2	0	0	0	2	0	0	0	.182	.182
Ogrodowski, Brusie-Ambrose Francis	36-37StlN	02-17-12	Hoytville, Pa.	03-05-56	R	R	5'11	175	184	516	65	119	25	4	4	51	21	37	2	.231	.318
Oliver, Tom-Thomas Noble (Rebel)	30-33BosA	01-15-03	Montgomery, Ala.	02-26-88	R	R	6'	184	514	1931	202	534	101	11	0	176	105	61	12	.277	.340
Olmo(Rodriguez), Luis-Luis Francisco Rodriguez [Olmo] (Jibaro)	43-45,49BknN 46-48SM 50-51BknN	08-11-19	Arecibo, P.R.		R	R	5'11	185	462	1629	208	458	65	25	29	272	88	128	33	.281	.405
Olsen, Barney-Bernard Charles	41ChiN	09-11-19	Everett, Mass.	03-30-77	L	R	5'11	180	24	73	13	21	6	1	1	4	4	11	0	.288	.438
Olson, Marv-Marvin Clement (Sparky)	31-33BosA	05-28-07	Gayville, S.D.	02-05-98	L	R	5'7	160	133	457	67	110	15	6	0	30	70	30	1	.241	.298
O'Neil, Mickey-George Michael	19-25BosN 26BknN 27WasA 27NYN	04-12-98	St. Louis, Mo.	04-08-64	R	R	5'9	180	672	1995	177	475	41	23	4	179	139	127	18	.238	.288
O'Neill, Harry-Harry Mink	39PhiA	05-08-17	Philadelphia, Pa.	03-06-45	R	R	6'3	205	1												
O'Neill, Jim-James Leo	20,23WasA	02-23-93	Minooka, Pa.	09-05-76	R	R	5'10	165	109	327	33	94	18	7	1	43	14	33	7	.287	.394
Onis, Curly-Manuel Dominguez (Ralph)	35BknN	02-23-00	Tampa, Fla.	01-04-95	R	R	5'9	160	1	1	0	1	0	0	0	0	0	0	0	1.000	1.000
Ordenana, Tony-Antonio [Rodriguez] (Mosquito)	43PitN	10-30-18	Guanabacoa, Cuba	09-29-88	R	R	5'9	158	2	4	1	2	0	0	0	0	1	0	0	.500	.500
Orengo, Joe-Joseph Charles	39-40StlN 41,43NYN 43BknN 44DetA 45ChiA	11-29-14	San Francisco, Cal.	07-24-88	R	R	6'	185	366	1120	129	266	54	8	17	122	156	219	4	.238	.346
Orme, George-George William	20BosN	09-16-91	Lebanon, Ind.	03-16-62	R	R	5'10	160	4	3	1	1	0	0	0	1	0	0	0	.333	.333
O'Rourke, Frank-Francis James (Blackie)	12BosN 17-18BknN 20-21WasA 22BosA 24-26DetA 27-31StlA	11-28-91	Hamilton, Canada	05-14-86	R	R	5'10	165	1131	4069	547	1032	196	42	15	430	314	377	101	.254	.333

USE NAME - GIVEN NAMES (NICKNAMES)	TEAM BY YEAR	BIRTH DATE	BIRTH PLACE	DEATH DATE	B	T	HGT	WGT	G	AB	R	H	2B	3B	HR	RBI	BB	SO	SB	BA	SA
O'Rourke, Joe-Joseph Leo, Jr.	29PhiN	10-28-04	Philadelphia, Pa.	06-27-90	L	R	5'7	145	3	3	0	0	0	0	0	0	0	1	0	.000	.000
Orsatti, Ernie-Ernest Ralph	27-35StLN	09-08-02	Los Angeles, Cal.	09-04-68	L	L	5'8	154	701	2165	306	663	129	39	10	237	176	218	46	.306	.416
Ortiz, Roberto-Roberto Gonzalo (Nunez) (Bob)	41-44WasA 45VR 46-48SM 49-50WasA 50PhiA	06-30-15	Camaguey, Cuba	09-15-71	R	R	6'4	210	213	659	67	168	18	10	8	78	43	95	4	.255	.349
Orwoll, Ossie-Oswald Christian (See P20-45) 26 played in N.F.L.	28-29PhiA	11-17-00	Portland, Ore.	05-08-67	L	L	5'11	165	94	221	34	65	15	3	0	28	18	35	3	.294	.289
Ostergard, Red-Roy Lund	21ChiA	05-16-96	Denmark, Wis.	01-13-77	R	R	5'10	175	12	11	2	4	0	0	0	0	0	2	0	.364	.364
Otero, Reggie-Regino Jose [Gomez]	45ChiN	09-07-15	Havana, Cuba	10-21-88	L	R	5'11	160	14	23	1	9	0	0	0	5	2	2	0	.391	.391
Ott, Mel-Melvin Thomas (Master Melvin)	26-47,M42-48NYN	03-02-09	Gretna, La.	11-21-58	L	R	5'9	170	2730	9456	1859	2876	488	72	511	1860	1708	896	89	.304	.533
Oulliber, Johnny-John Andrew	33CleA	02-24-11	New Orleans, La.	12-26-80	R	R	5'11	165	22	75	9	20	1	0	0	3	4	5	0	.267	.280
Outen, Chink-William Austin	33BknN	06-17-05	Mount Holly, N.C.	09-11-61	L	R	6'	200	93	153	20	38	10	0	4	17	20	15	1	.248	.392
Outlaw, Jimmy-James Paulus	37-38CinN 39BosN 43-49DetA	01-20-13	Orme, Tenn.	04-09-06	R	R	5'8	165	650	1974	257	529	79	17	6	184	188	176	24	.268	.334
Owen, Marv-Marvin James (Freck)	31,33-37DetA 38-39ChiA 40BosA	03-22-06	Agnew, Cal.	06-22-91	R	R	6'1	175	1011	3782	473	1040	167	44	31	497	338	283	30	.275	.367
Owen, Mickey-Arnold Malcolm	37-40StLN 41-45BknN 46-48SM 49-51ChiN 54BosA	04-14-16	Nixa, Mo.	07-13-05	R	R	5'10	170	1209	3649	338	929	163	21	14	378	326	181	36	.255	.322
Owens, Jack-Furman Lee	35PhiA	05-06-08	Converse, S.C.	11-14-58	R	R	5'10	210	2	8	0	2	0	0	0	1	0	1	0	.250	.250
Padden, Tom-Thomas Francis	32-37PitN 43PhiN 43WasA	10-06-08	Manchester, N.H.	06-11-73	R	R	6'	185	399	1170	122	318	40	6	2	110	127	121	5	.272	.321
Padgett, Don-Don Wilson	37-41StLN 42-46MS 46BknN 46BosN 47-48PhiN	12-05-11	Caroleen, N.C.	12-09-80	L	R	6'	190	699	1991	247	573	111	16	37	338	141	130	6	.288	.415
Padgett, Ernie-Ernest Kitchen (Red)	23-25BosN 26-27CleA	03-01-99	Philadelphia, Pa.	04-15-57	R	R	5'8	155	271	838	84	223	34	17	1	81	61	75	8	.266	.351
Palmisano, Joe-Joseph A.	31PhiA	11-19-02	West Point, Ga.	11-05-71	R	R	5'8	160	19	44	5	10	2	0	0	4	6	3	0	.227	.273
Parisee, Tony-Louis Peter	43-44PhiA	06-25-11	Philadelphia, Pa.	06-02-56	R	R	5'10	165	10	21	0	3	0	0	0	1	2	3	0	.143	.143
Parker, Ace-Clarence McKoy	37-41,45 played in N.F.L. 46 played in A.A.F.C.	05-17-12	Portsmouth, Va.		R	R	6'	180	94	207	20	37	5	1	2	25	14	33	1	.179	.242
Parker, Dixie-Douglas Woolley	23PhiN	04-24-95	Forest Home, Ala.	05-15-72	L	R	5'11	160	4	5	0	1	0	0	0	0	1	0	0	.200	.200
Parker, Salty-Francis James	36DetA M67NYN M72HouN	07-08-12	East St. Louis, Ill.	07-27-92	R	R	6'	173	11	25	6	7	2	0	0	4	2	3	0	.280	.360
Parkinson, Frank-Frank Joseph (Parky)	21-24PhiN	03-23-95	Dickson City, Pa.	07-04-60	R	R	6'	180	378	1311	157	335	57	8	24	149	95	233	9	.256	.336
Parks, Art-Artie William	37,39BknN	01-01-11	Paris, Ark.	12-06-89	R	R	5'9	170	78	255	29	70	15	2	1	19	30	16	2	.275	.361
Parsons, Dixie-Edward Dixon	39,42-43DetA	05-12-16	Talladega, Ala.	10-31-91	R	R	6'2	180	108	295	10	52	7	0	2	15	20	39	1	.176	.220
Partee, Roy-Roy Robert	43-44BosA 45MS 46-47BosA 48StLA	09-17-17	Los Angeles, Cal.	12-27-00	R	R	5'11	160	367	1090	89	273	41	5	2	114	132	120	2	.250	.303
Partridge, Jay-James Bugg	27-28BknN	11-15-02	Mountville, Ga.	01-14-74	R	R	5'11	160	183	645	90	167	17	7	7	52	33	42	11	.259	.340
Paschal, Ben-Benjamin Edwin	15CleA 20BosA 24-29NYA	10-13-95	Enterprise, Ala.	11-10-74	R	R	5'11	185	364	787	143	243	47	11	24	138	72	93	24	.309	.488
Pasek, Johnny-John Paul	33DetA 34ChiA	06-25-05	Niagara Falls, N.Y.	03-13-76	R	R	5'10	175	32	70	7	18	4	0	0	4	8	8	2	.257	.314
Patrick, Bob-Robert Lee	41-42DetA 43-45MS	10-27-17	Fort Smith, Ark.	10-06-99	R	R	6'2	190	9	15	3	4	1	0	1	3	1	1	0	.267	.533
Patterson, Bill-William Jennings Bryan (Pat)	21NYN	01-29-97	Belleville, Ill.	10-01-77	R	R	6'1	175	23	35	5	14	1	0	0	5	2	5	0	.400	.486
Patterson, Hank-Henry Joseph Colquit	32BosA	07-17-07	San Francisco, Cal.	09-30-70	R	R	5'11	170	1	1	0	0	0	0	0	0	0	0	0	.000	.000
Patton, Bill-George William	35PhiA	10-07-12	Cornwall, Pa.	03-15-86	R	R	6'2	180	9	10	1	3	1	0	0	2	2	3	0	.300	.400
Patton, Gene-Gene Tunney	44BosN 45BknN	07-08-26	Coatesville, Pa.		R	R	5'10	165	1	0	0	0	0	0	0	0	0	0	0	—	—
Peacock, Johnny-John Thomas	37-44BosA 44-45PhiN 45BknN	01-10-10	Wilson, N.C.	10-17-81	L	R	5'11	165	619	1734	175	455	74	16	1	194	183	63	14	.262	.325
Peel, Homer-Homer Hefner	27StLN 29PhiN 30StLN 33-34NYN	10-10-02	Port Sullivan, Tex.	04-08-97	R	R	5'9	170	186	420	48	100	15	2	2	44	30	24	1	.238	.298
Peerson, Jack-Jack Chiles	35-36PhiA	08-28-10	Brunswick, Ga.	10-23-66	R	R	5'10	165	18	53	10	17	2	1	0	6	1	4	0	.321	.396
Pence, Elmer-Elmer Clair	22ChiA	09-17-68	Valley Springs, Cal.		R	R	6'	185	1	0	0	0	0	0	0	0	0	0	0	—	—
Peploski, Henry-Henry Stephen	29BosN	09-15-05	Garlin, Poland	01-28-82	L	R	5'9	155	6	10	1	2	0	0	0	1	1	3	0	.200	.200
Pepper, Ray-Raymond Watson	32-33StLN 34-36StLA	08-05-05	Decatur, Ala.	03-24-96	R	R	6'2	195	339	1015	109	285	46	10	14	170	59	136	2	.281	.387
Perkins, Cy-Ralph Foster	15,17-30PhiA 31NYA 34DetA	02-27-96	Gloucester, Mass.	10-02-63	R	R	5'10	158	1171	3604	329	933	175	35	30	409	301	221	18	.259	.352
Perrin, Jack-John Stephenson 26 played in N.F.L.	21BosA	02-04-98	Escanaba, Mich.	06-24-69	L	R	5'9	160	4	13	3	3	0	0	0	1	0	2	0	.231	.231
Perry, Boyd-Boyd Glenn	41DetA	03-21-14	Snow Camp, N.C.	06-29-90	R	R	5'10	158	36	83	9	15	5	0	0	11	10	9	1	.181	.241
Peterman, Bill-William David	42PhiN 43-45MS	04-20-21	Philadelphia, Pa.	03-13-99	R	R	6'2	185	1	1	0	1	0	0	0	0	0	0	0	1.000	1.000
Peters, John-John William (Shotgun, Big Pete)	15DetA 18CleA 21-22PhiN	07-14-93	Kansas City, Kans.	02-21-32	R	R	6'4	220	112	302	22	80	13	1	7	47	16	33	1	.265	.384
Peters, Rusty-Russell Dixon	36-38PhiA 40-44CleA 45MS 46CleA 47StLA	12-14-14	Roanoke, Va.	02-21-03	R	R	5'11	170	417	1222	123	289	53	16	8	117	98	199	9	.236	.326
Petoskey, Ted-Frederick Lee	34-35CinN	01-05-11	St. Charles, Mich.	11-30-96	R	R	5'11	183	10	12	0	2	0	0	0	1	0	6	1	.167	.167
Pfister, George-George Edward	41BknN	09-04-18	Bound Brook, N.J.	08-14-97	R	R	6'	200	1	2	0	0	0	0	0	0	0	1	0	.000	.000
Phelps, Babe-Ernest Gordon (Blimp)	31WasA 33-34ChiN 35-41BknN 42PitN	04-19-08	Odenton, Md.	12-10-92	L	R	6'2	225	726	2117	239	657	143	19	54	345	160	157	9	.310	.472
Phillips, Damon-Damon Roswell (Dee)	42CinN 44BosN 45MS 46BosN	06-08-19	Corsicana, Tex.	11-04-04	R	R	6'	176	170	575	39	144	32	1	1	59	35	39	1	.250	.315
Phillips, Eddie-Edward David	24BosN 29DetA 31PitN 32NYA 34WasA 35CleA 45PhiN	02-17-01	Worcester, Mass.	01-26-68	R	R	6'	178	312	997	82	236	54	6	14	126	104	115	3	.237	.345
Picciuto, Nick-NicholasThomas	45PhiN	08-27-21	Newark, N.J.	01-10-97	R	R	5'8	160	36	89	7	12	6	0	0	6	6	17	0	.135	.202
Picinich, Val-Valentine John	16-17PhiA 18-22WasA 23-25BosA 26-28CinN 29-33BknN 33PitN	09-08-96	New York, N.Y.	12-05-42	R	R	5'9	165	1037	2877	298	743	166	25	27	298	314	382	31	.258	.361
Pick, Eddie-Edgar Everett	23-24CinN 27ChiN	05-07-99	Attleboro, Mass.	05-13-67	B	R	6'	185	66	191	25	34	5	2	2	17	23	30	0	.178	.257
Pickering, Urban-Urbane Henry (Pick)	31-32BosA	06-03-99	Hoxie, Kans.	05-13-70	R	R	5'11	175	235	798	95	205	41	9	11	92	72	124	6	.257	.372
Piet (Pietruszka), Tony-Anthony Francis	31-33PitN 34-35CinN 35-37ChiA 38DetA	12-07-06	Berwick, Pa.	12-01-81	R	R	6'	175	744	2585	352	717	132	30	23	312	247	274	80	.277	.378
Pilney, Andy-Antone James	36CinN	01-19-13	Frontenac, Kans.	09-15-96	R	R	5'11	174	3	2	1	0	0	0	0	0	0	0	0	.000	.000
Pinelli, Babe-Ralph Arthur (Rinaldo Angelo)	18ChiA 20DetA 22-27CinN	10-18-95	San Francisco, Cal.	10-22-84	R	R	5'9	165	774	2617	327	723	101	33	5	298	182	162	71	.276	.346
Pipp, Wally-Walter Clement	13DetA 15-25NYA 26-28CinN	02-17-93	Chicago, Ill.	01-11-65	L	L	6'1	180	1872	6914	974	1941	311	148	90	996	596	551	125	.281	.408
Pitko, Alex-Alexander (Spunk)	38PhiN 39WasA	01-22-14	Burlington, N.J.		R	R	5'10	170	11	27	2	7	1	0	0	3	4	6	1	.259	.296
Pittinger, Pinky-Clarke Alonzo	21-23BosA 25ChiN 27-29CinN	02-24-99	Hudson, Mich.	11-04-77	R	R	5'10	160	373	959	118	252	32	3	1	83	37	50	27	.263	.306
Pofahl, Jimmy-James Willard	40-42WasA	06-18-17	Faribault, Minn.	09-14-84	R	R	5'11	173	225	764	65	168	33	9	2	70	76	96	7	.220	.295
Poland, Hugh-Hugh Reid	43NYN 43-44BosN 45MS 46BosN 47-48CinN	01-19-13	Tompkinsville, Ky.	03-29-84	R	R	5'11	185	83	211	8	39	10	1	0	19	6	16	0	.185	.242
Polly (Polachanin), Nick-Nicholas Joseph	37BknN 45BosA	04-18-17	Chicago, Ill.	01-17-93	R	R	5'11	190	14	25	2	5	0	0	0	3	0	2	0	.200	.200
Pool, Harlin-Harlin Welty (Samson)	34-35CinN	03-13-08	Lakeport, Cal.	02-15-63	L	R	5'10	195	127	426	46	129	28	7	2	61	19	20	3	.303	.415
Poole, Jim-James Robert (Easy)	25-27PhiA	05-12-95	Taylorsville, N.C.	01-02-75	L	R	5'10	170	283	940	118	271	54	13	13	140	59	68	9	.288	.415
Porter, Dick-Richard Twilley (Twitchy)	29-34CleA 34BosA	12-30-01	Princess Anne, Md.	09-24-74	L	R	5'10	170	675	2515	426	774	159	37	11	282	268	186	23	.308	.414
Post, Sam-Samuel Gilbert	22BknN	11-17-96	Richmond, Va.	03-31-71	L	L	6'1	170	9	25	3	7	0	0	0	4	1	4	1	.280	.280
Powell, Jake-Alvin Jacob	30,34-36WasA 36-40NYA 43-45WasA 45PhiN	07-15-08	Silver Spring, Md.	11-04-48	R	R	5'11	180	688	2540	353	689	116	26	22	327	174	219	65	.271	.363
Powell, Ray-Raymond Reath (Rabbit)	13DetA 17-24BosN	11-20-88	Siloam Springs, Ark.	10-16-62	L	R	5'9	160	875	3324	467	890	117	67	35	276	321	461	51	.268	.375
Powers, Les-Leslie Edwin	38NYN 39PhiN	11-05-09	Seattle, Wash.	11-13-83	L	L	6'1	185	21	55	7	18	5	0	0	7	3	8	0	.327	.382
Powers, Mike-Ellis Foree	32-33CleA	03-02-06	Toddspoint, Ky.	12-02-83	L	L	6'1	185	38	80	10	19	4	0	1	8	8	2	2	.238	.338
Pratt, Frank-Francis Bruce (Truckhorse)	21ChiA	08-24-97	Blocton, Ala.	03-08-74	R	R	5'9	155	1	0	0	0	0	0	0	0	0	0	0	.000	.000
Preibisch, Mel-Melvin Adolphus (Primo)	40-41BosN	11-23-14	Sealy, Tex.	04-12-80	R	R	5'11	185	16	44	3	9	2	0	0	5	3	6	0	.205	.250
Price, Joe-Joseph Preston (Lumber)	28NYN	04-10-97	Milligan Coll., Tenn.	01-15-61	R	R	6'2	187	1	1	0	0	0	0	0	0	0	1	0	.000	.000
Prichard, Bob-Robert Alexander	39WasA	10-21-17	Paris, Tex.	09-25-91	L	L	6'1	195	26	85	8	20	5	0	0	8	19	16	0	.235	.294
Propst, Jake-William Jacob	23WasA	03-10-95	Kennedy, Ala.	02-24-67	L	R	5'10	165	1	1	0	0	0	0	0	0	0	1	0	.000	.000
Prothro, Doc-James Thompson	20,23-24WasA 25BosA 26CinN M39-41PhiN	07-16-93	Memphis, Tenn.	10-14-71	R	R	5'10	175	180	600	66	191	34	10	0	81	69	40	13	.318	.408
Pruess, Earl-Earl Henry (Gibby)	20StLA	04-02-95	Chicago, Ill.	08-26-79	R	R	5'10	170	1	0	1	0	0	0	0	0	1	0	0	—	—
Pruett, Urban-Jim James Calvin	44-45PhiA	12-16-17	Nashville, Tenn.	07-29-03	R	R	5'10	198	3	13	0	3	0	0	0	0	0	3	0	.231	.231
Puccinelli, George-George Lawrence (Count, Pooch)	30,32StLN 34StLA 36PhiA	06-22-07	San Francisco, Cal.	04-16-56	R	R	6'	190	187	607	109	172	40	3	19	102	78	92	3	.283	.453
Purdy, Pid-Everett Virgil 26-27 played in N.F.L.	26ChiA 27-29CinN	06-15-02	Beatrice, Neb.	01-16-51	L	R	5'8	160	181	499	74	146	22	11	2	59	48	25	3	.293	.393
Pytlak, Frankie-Frank Anthony (Pity)	32-40CleA 41BosA 42-44MS 45-46BosA	07-30-08	Buffalo, N.Y.	05-08-77	R	R	5'7	160	795	2399	316	677	100	36	7	272	247	97	56	.282	.363
Quellich, George-George William	31DetA	02-10-06	Johnsville, Cal.	08-31-58	R	R	6'1	180	13	54	6	12	5	0	1	11	3	4	1	.222	.370
Quick, Hal-James Harold (Blondie)	39WasA	10-04-17	Rome, Ga.	03-09-74	R	R	5'10	163	12	41	3	10	1	0	0	2	1	1	0	.244	.268
Rabbitt, Joe-Joseph Patrick	22CleA	07-24-00	Frontenac, Kans.	12-05-69	L	R	5'9	156	2	5	1	1	0	0	0	0	1	0	0	.333	.333
Radcliff, Rip-Raymond Allen	34-39ChiA 40-41StLA 41-43DetA 44-46MS	01-19-06	Kiowa, Okla.	05-23-62	L	L	5'10	170	1081	4074	598	1267	205	50	42	533	310	141	40	.311	.417
Rader, Don-Donald Russell	13ChiA 21PhiN	09-05-93	Wolcott, Ind.	06-26-83	R	R	5'10	164	11	35	5	10	3	0	0	3	0	5	0	.286	.371
Radtke, Jack-Jack William	36BknN	04-14-13	Denver, Colo.		B	R	5'8	155	33	31	8	3	0	0	0	0	2	4	3	.097	.097
Ramos, Chucho-Jesus Manuel [Garcia]	44CinN	04-12-18	Maturin, Venezuela	09-02-77	R	R	5'10	167	4	10	1	5	0	0	0	2	1	0	0	.500	.600
Ramsey, Bill-William Thrace (Square Jaw)	45BosN	10-20-20	Osceola, Ark.		R	R	6'	175	78	137	16	40	8	0	1	12	4	22	1	.292	.372

USE NAME - GIVEN NAMES (NICKNAMES)	TEAM BY YEAR	BIRTH DATE	BIRTH PLACE	DEATH DATE	B	T	HGT	WGT	G	AB	R	H	2B	3B	HR	RBI	BB	SO	SB	BA	SA
Rapp, Goldie-Joseph Aloysius	21NYN 21-23PhiN	02-06-94	Cincinnati, Ohio	07-01-66	B	R	5'10	165	276	1064	134	269	47	5	2	73	75	64	16	.253	.312
Rawlings,Johnny-John William (Red)	14 CinN 14-15KCF 17-20BosN 20-21PhiN 21-22NYN 23-26PhiN	08-17-92	Bloomfield, Iowa	10-16-72	R	R	5'8	158	1080	3721	408	927	122	28	14	302	257	210	92	.249	.308
Rebel, Art-Arthur Anthony	38PhiN 45StLN	03-04-14	Cincinnati, Ohio	07-10-04	L	L	5'8	180	33	81	14	27	4	0	0	6	7	5	1	.333	.383
Reder, Johnny-John Anthony	32BosA	09-24-09	Lublin, Poland	04-12-90	R	R	6'	184	17	37	4	5	1	0	0	3	6	6	0	.135	.162
Redfern, Buck-George Howard	28-29ChiA	04-07-02	Asheville, N.C.	09-08-64	R	R	5'11	165	107	307	22	67	6	3	0	38	15	22	9	.218	.257
Redmond, Jack-John McKittrick (Red)	35WasA	09-03-10	Florence, Ariz.	07-27-68	L	R	5'11	185	22	34	8	6	1	0	1	7	3	1	0	.176	.294
Reese, Andy-Andrew Jackson	27-30NYN	02-07-04	Tupelo, Miss.	01-10-66	R	R	5'11	180	331	1142	166	321	47	11	14	111	51	107	21	.281	.378
Reese (Soloman), Jimmie-James Herman	30-31NYA 32StLN	10-01-01	New York, N.Y.	07-13-94	L	R	5'11	165	232	742	123	209	39	4	8	70	48	37	7	.278	.373
Reeves, Bobby-Robert Edwin (Gunner)	26-28WasA 29-31BosA	06-24-04	Hill City, Tenn.	06-04-93	R	R	5'11	170	502	1598	260	402	55	22	8	135	175	218	21	.252	.329
Regan, Bill-William Wright	26-30BosA 31PitN	01-23-99	Pittsburgh, Pa.	06-11-68	R	R	5'10	155	641	2364	236	632	158	36	18	292	122	245	38	.267	.387
Rego (DeRego), Tony-Antone (Mighty Midget)	24-25StLA	10-31-97	Wailuku, Hawaii	09-29-01	R	R	5'5	140	44	91	10	26	3	1	0	8	4	5	0	.286	.341
Reiber, Frank-Frank Bernard (Tubby)	33-36DetA	09-19-09	Huntington, W.Va.	12-26-02	R	R	5'8	170	44	85	13	23	2	1	2	9	12	13	0	.271	.388
Reichle, Dick-Richard Wendell 23 played in N.F.L.	22-23BosA	11-23-96	Lincoln, Ill.	06-13-67	L	R	6'	185	128	385	43	99	18	3	1	39	22	36	3	.257	.327
Reinholz, Art-Arthur August	28CleA	01-27-03	Detroit, Mich.	12-29-80	R	R	5'10	175	2	3	0	1	0	0	0	0	1	0	0	.333	.333
Reis, Bobby-Robert Joseph Thomas (See P20-45)	31-32,35BknN 36-38BosN	01-02-09	Queens, N.Y.	05-01-73	R	R	6'1	190	175	301	32	70	10	2	0	21	25	35	5	.233	.279
Reiss, Al-Albert Allen	32PhiA	01-08-09	Elizabeth, N.J.	05-13-89	B	R	5'10	165	9	5	0	1	0	0	0	1	1	1	0	.200	.200
Rensa, Tony-Tony George Anthony (Pug)	30DetA 30-31PhiN 33NYA 37-39ChiA	09-21-06	Parsons, Pa.	01-04-87	R	R	5'10	180	200	514	71	134	26	5	7	65	57	54	5	.261	.372
Repass, Bob-Robert Willis	39StLN 42WasA	11-06-17	West Pittston, Pa.	11-16-06	R	R	6'1	185	84	265	30	64	12	1	2	24	33	32	6	.242	.317
Reyes, Nap-Napoleon [Aguilera]	43-45NYN 46-49SM 50NYN	11-24-19	Santiago, Cuba	09-15-95	R	R	6'1	205	279	931	90	264	35	11	13	110	44	62	5	.284	.387
Reynolds, Carl-Carl Nettles	27-31ChiA 32,36WasA 33StLA 34-35BosA 37-39CinN	02-01-03	La Rue, Tex.	05-29-78	R	R	6'	194	1222	4495	672	1357	247	107	80	699	262	308	112	.302	.458
Reynolds, Danny-Daniel Vance (Squirrel)	45CinN	11-27-19	Stony Point, N.C.		R	R	5'11	158	29	72	6	12	2	1	0	4	3	8	1	.167	.222
Rhiel, Billy-William Joseph	29BknN 30BosN 32-33DetA	08-16-00	Youngstown, Ohio	08-16-46	R	R	5'11	175	200	519	61	138	26	8	7	68	43	57	2	.266	.387
Rhyne, Hal-Harold J.	26-27PitN 29-32BosA 33ChiA	03-30-99	Paso Robles, Cal.	01-07-71	R	R	5'8	163	655	2031	252	508	98	22	2	192	184	127	13	.250	.323
Rice, Bob-Robert Turnbull		03-30-99	Philadelphia, Pa.	02-20-86	R	R	5'10	170	19	54	3	8	0	1	0	10	3	4	0	.148	.185
Rice, Harry-Harry Francis	23-27StLA 28-30DetA 30NYA 31WasA 33CinN	11-22-00	Ware Station, Ill.	01-01-71	L	R	5'9	185	1024	3740	620	1118	186	63	48	506	376	194	60	.299	.421
Rice, Len-Leonard Oliver	44CinN 45CubN	09-02-18	Lead, S.D.	06-13-92	R	R	6'	175	42	103	11	23	3	0	0	7	5	8	2	.223	.252
Rice, Sam-Edgar Charles (See P01-19)	15-33WasA 34CleA	02-20-90	Morocco, Ind.	10-13-74	L	R	5'9	150	2404	9269	1514	2987	497	184	34	1078	709	275	351	.322	.427
Richards, Paul-Paul Rapier	32BknN 33-35NYN 35PhiA 43-45ChiA M51-54ChiA M55-61BalA M76ChiA	11-21-08	Waxahachie, Tex.	05-04-86	R	R	6'2	180	523	1417	140	321	51	5	15	155	157	149	15	.227	.301
Richardson, Nolen-Clifford Nolen	29,31-32DetA 35NYA 38-39CinN	01-18-03	Chattanooga, Tenn.	09-25-51	R	R	6'1	170	168	473	39	117	19	5	0	45	23	22	8	.247	.309
Richbourg, Lance-Lance Clayton	21PhiN 24WasA 27-31BosN 32CinN	12-18-97	DeFuniak Spr., Fla.	09-10-75	L	R	5'10	160	698	2619	378	806	101	51	13	247	174	153	65	.308	.400
Riconda, Harry-Henry Paul	23-24PhiA 26BosN 28BknN 29PitN 30CinN 26-27,28-30 played in A.B.L.	03-17-97	New York, N.Y.	11-15-58	R	R	5'10	175	243	765	83	189	44	11	4	70	61	91	13	.247	.349
Riddle, Johnny-John Ludy (Mutt)	30ChiA 37WasA 37-38BosN 41,44-45CinN 48PitN	10-03-05	Clinton, S.C.	12-15-98	R	R	5'11	190	98	214	18	51	4	1	0	11	13	19	0	.238	.266
Riggs, Lew-Lewis Sidney	34StLN 35-40CinN 41-43BknN 43-45MS 46BknN	04-22-10	Mebane, N.C.	08-12-75	L	R	6'	175	760	2477	298	650	110	43	28	271	181	140	22	.262	.375
Rigney, Topper-Emory Elmo	22-25DetA 26-27BosA 27WasA	05-25-95	Groveton, Tex.	01-06-72	R	R	5'9	150	694	2326	324	669	113	39	13	314	377	176	44	.288	.387
Riley, Jim-James Norman	21StLA 23WasA	05-25-95	Bayfield, Canada	05-25-69	L	R	5'10	185	6	14	1	0	0	0	0	0	3	3	0	.000	.000
Riley, Lee-Leon Francis	44PhiN	08-20-06	Princeton, Neb.	09-13-70	L	R	6'1	185	4	12	1	1	1	0	0	1	0	0	0	.083	.167
Ripple, Jimmy-James Albert	36-39NYN 39-40BknN 40-41CinN 43BosA	10-14-09	Export, Pa.	07-16-59	L	R	5'10	170	554	1809	241	510	92	14	28	251	156	89	7	.282	.396
Rizzo, Johnny-John Costa	38-40PitN 40CinN 40-41PhiN 42BknN 43-46MS	07-30-12	Houston, Tex.	12-04-77	R	R	6'	190	557	1842	268	497	90	16	61	288	200	197	7	.270	.435
Robello, Tommy-Thomas Vardasco (Tony)	33-34CinN	02-09-13	San Leandro, Cal.	12-25-94	R	R	5'10	175	16	32	1	7	3	0	0	3	1	6	0	.219	.313
Roberge, Skippy-Joseph Albert Armand	41-42BosN 43-45MS 46BosN	05-19-17	Lowell, Mass.	06-07-93	R	R	5'11	185	177	508	35	112	19	2	3	47	25	49	2	.220	.283
Roberts, Red-Charles Emory	36ChiA	08-08-18	Carrollton, Ga.	12-02-98	R	R	6'	170	9	23	1	6	1	0	1	3	4	2	0	.261	.435
Robertson, Gene-Eugene Edward	19,22-26StLA 28-29NYA 29-30BosN	12-25-98	St. Louis, Mo.	10-21-81	L	R	5'7	152	656	2200	311	615	101	23	20	249	205	79	29	.280	.384
Rocco, Mickey-Michael Dominick	43-46CleA	03-02-16	St. Paul, Minn.	06-01-97	L	L	5'11	188	440	1721	219	444	73	17	30	186	174	146	6	.258	.372
Rochelli, Lou-Louis Joseph	44BknN 45-46MS	10-23-92	Staunton, Ill.	10-23-92	R	R	6'1	175	5	17	0	3	0	0	0	2	2	6	0	.176	.294
Rock (Schwarzrock), Les-Lester Henry	36ChiA	08-19-12	Springfield, Minn.	09-09-91	R	R	6'2	184	2	1	0	0	0	0	0	1	0	0	0	.000	.000
Rodgers, Bill-William Sherman	44-45PitN	12-05-22	Harrisburg, Pa.	05-13-02	L	L	6'	162	3	5	1	2	0	0	0	0	0	1	0	.400	.400
Roettger, Oscar-Oscar Frederick Louis (See P20-45)	23-24NYA 27BknN 32CinN	02-19-00	St. Louis, Mo.	07-04-86	R	R	6'	170	37	66	7	14	1	0	0	6	6	5	0	.212	.227
Roettger, Wally-Walter Henry	27-29StLN 30NYN 31CinN 31StLN 32-33CinN 34PitN	08-28-02	St. Louis, Mo.	09-14-51	R	R	6'2	190	599	1949	192	556	96	23	19	245	99	143	4	.285	.387
Roetz,Ed-Edward Bernard	29StLA	08-06-05	Philadelphia, Pa.	03-16-65	R	R	5'10	160	16	45	7	11	4	1	0	4	4	6	0	.244	.378
Rogell, Billy-William George	25,27-28BosA 30-39DetA 40ChiN	11-24-04	Springfield, Ill.	08-09-03	B	R	5'10	163	1482	5149	755	1375	258	75	42	609	649	416	82	.267	.370
Rogers (Hazinski), Packy-Stanley Frank	38BknN	04-26-13	Swoyersville, Pa.	05-15-98	R	R	5'8	175	23	37	3	7	1	1	0	5	6	6	0	.189	.270
Rohwer, Ray-Ray	21-22PitN	06-05-95	Dixon, Cal.	01-24-88	L	L	5'10	155	83	169	25	48	9	5	3	28	14	25	1	.284	.450
Rolfe, Red-Robert Abial 46-47 head coach in B.A.A.	31,34-42NYA M49-52DetA	10-17-08	Penacook, N.H.	07-08-69	L	R	5'11	170	1175	4827	942	1394	257	67	69	497	526	335	44	.289	.413
Rollings, Red-William Russell	27-28BosA 30BosN	03-31-04	Mobile, Ala.	12-31-64	L	R	5'11	167	184	355	36	89	13	2	0	28	27	23	5	.251	.299
Rosar, Buddy-Warren Vincent	39-42NYA 43-44CleA 45-49PhiA 50-51BosA	07-03-14	Buffalo, N.Y.	03-13-94	R	R	5'9	190	988	3198	335	836	147	15	18	367	315	161	17	.261	.334
Rosen, Goody-Goodwin George	37-39,44-46BknN 46NYN	08-28-12	Toronto, Canada	04-06-94	L	L	5'10	155	551	1916	310	557	71	34	22	197	218	166	12	.291	.398
Rosenberg, Harry-Harry	30NYN	06-22-08	San Francisco, Cal.	04-13-97	R	R	5'10	180	9	5	1	0	0	0	0	0	1	1	0	.000	.000
Rosenberg, Lou-Louis	23ChiA	03-05-04	San Francisco, Cal.	09-08-91	R	R	5'7	155	3	4	1	1	0	0	0	0	0	1	0	.250	.250
Rosenfeld, Max-Max	31-33BknN	12-23-02	New York, N.Y.	03-10-69	R	R	5'8	175	42	57	8	17	4	0	2	7	2	12	2	.298	.474
Rosenthal, Larry-Lawrence John	36-41ChiA 41CleA 44NYA 44-45PhiA	05-21-10	St. Paul, Minn.	03-04-92	L	L	6'	190	579	1483	240	390	75	25	22	190	251	195	13	.263	.392
Rosenthal, Si-Simon	25-26BosA	11-13-03	Boston, Mass.	04-07-69	L	R	5'9	165	126	357	40	95	17	5	4	42	26	21	5	.266	.378
Roser, Bunny-John William Joseph (Jack)	22BosN	11-15-01	St. Louis, Mo.	05-06-79	L	L	5'11	175	32	113	13	27	3	3	0	16	10	19	2	.239	.336
Ross, Chet-Chester James	39-44BosN 45MS	04-01-17	Buffalo, N.Y.	02-21-89	R	R	6'1	195	413	1309	156	316	53	21	34	170	124	281	6	.241	.392
Ross, Don-Donald Raymond	38DetA 40BknN 42-45DetA 45-46CleA	07-16-14	Pasadena, Cal.	03-28-96	R	R	6'1	185	498	1488	129	390	63	4	12	162	165	70	10	.262	.334
Rothel, Bob-Robert Burton	45CleA	09-17-23	Columbia Sta., Ohio	05-21-84	R	R	5'10	170	10	10	0	2	0	0	0	0	3	1	0	.200	.200
Rothrock, Jack-John Houston	25-32BosA 32ChiA 34-35StLN 37PhiA	03-14-05	Long Beach, Cal.	02-02-80	B	R	5'11	165	1014	3350	498	924	162	35	28	327	299	312	75	.276	.370
Roush, Edd-Edd J.	13ChiA 14IndF 15NwkF 16NYN 16-26CinN 27-29NYN 30VR 31CinN	05-08-93	Oakland City, Ind.	03-21-88	L	L	5'11	170	1967	7363	1099	2376	339	182	68	981	484	260	268	.323	.446
Rowe, Schoolboy-Lynwood Thomas (See P20-45)	33-42DetA 42BknN 43PhiN 44-45MS 46-49PhiN	01-11-10	Waco, Tex.	01-08-61	R	R	6'4	210	491	909	116	239	36	9	18	153	86	157	3	.263	.382
Rowell, Bama-Carvel William	39-41BosN 42-45MS 46-47BosN 48PhiN	01-13-16	Citronelle, Ala.	08-16-93	R	R	5'11	185	574	1901	200	523	95	26	19	217	113	105	37	.275	.384
Rowland, Chuck-Charlie Leland	23PhiA	07-23-99	Warrenton, N.C.	01-21-92	R	R	6'1	185	5	6	0	0	0	0	0	0	0	2	0	.000	.000
Rubeling, Al-Albert William	40-41PhiA 43-44PitN	05-10-13	Baltimore, Md.	01-29-88	R	R	6'	185	253	747	94	186	31	12	8	79	77	95	8	.249	.355
Ruble, Art-William Arthur (Speedy)	27DetA 34PhiN	03-11-03	Knoxville, Tenn.	11-01-83	L	R	5'10	168	75	145	23	30	4	2	0	19	21	18	2	.207	.290
Rucker, Johnny-John Joel (The Crabapple Comet)	40-46NYN	01-15-17	Crabapple, Ga.	08-07-85	L	R	6'2	175	705	2617	354	711	105	39	21	214	109	248	35	.272	.366
Ruel, Muddy-Herold Dominic	15StLA 17-20NYA 21-22BosA 23-30WasA 31BosA 31-32DetA 33StLA 34ChiA M47StLA	02-20-96	St. Louis, Mo.	11-13-63	R	R	5'9	150	1470	4514	494	1242	187	29	4	532	606	238	61	.275	.332
Ruether, Dutch-Walter Henry (See P20-45)	17CinN 17-20CinN 21-24BknN 25-26WasA 26-27NYA	09-13-93	Alameda, Cal.	05-16-70	L	L	6'1	180	487	969	83	250	30	12	7	111	77	129	3	.258	.335
Ruffing, Red-Charles Herbert (See P20-45)	24-30BosA 30-42NYA 43-44MS 45-46NYA 47ChiA	05-03-04	Granville, Ill.	02-17-86	R	R	6'2	205	882	1937	207	521	98	13	36	273	97	266	1	.269	.389
Rullo, Joe-Joseph Vincent	43-44PhiA	06-16-16	New York, N.Y.	10-28-69	R	R	5'11	168	51	151	7	32	3	0	0	11	14	26	1	.212	.232
Russell, Lloyd-Lloyd Opal (Tex)	38CleA	04-10-13	Atoka, Okla.	05-24-88	R	R	5'11	166	2	0	0	0	0	0	0	0	0	0	0		
Russell, Reb-Ewell Albert (See P01-19)	13-19ChiA 22-23PitN	09-30-73	Jackson, Miss.	09-30-73	L	L	5'11	185	417	976	142	262	48	25	21	172	42	130	8	.268	.433
Russell, Rip-Glen David	39-42ChiN 46-47BosN	01-26-15	Los Angeles, Cal.	09-26-76	R	R	6'	195	425	1402	133	344	52	8	29	192	83	142	4	.245	.356
Ruszkowski, Hank-Henry Alexander	44-45CleA 46MS 47CleA	11-10-25	Cleveland, Ohio	05-31-00	R	R	6'	190	40	84	8	20	0	0	3	10	6	16	0	.238	.369
Ruth, Babe-George Herman (See P01-19) (The Sultan of Swat, The Bambino)	14-19BosA 20-34NYA 35BosN	02-06-95	Baltimore, Md.	08-16-48	L	L	6'2	215	2503	8399	2174	2873	506	136	714	2213	2062	1330	123	.342	.690
Ryan, Blondy-John Collins	30ChiA 33-34NYN 35PhiN 35NYA 37-38NYN	01-04-06	Lynn, Mass.	11-28-59	R	R	6'1	178	386	1330	127	318	36	13	6	133	57	184	6	.239	.304
Ryan, Jack-John Francis	29BosA		West Mineral, Kans.	09-02-67	R	R	6'	185	3	0	0	0	0	0	0	0	0	0	0	.000	.000
Rye (Mercantelli), Gene-Eugene Rudolph (Half Pint)	31BosA	11-15-06	Chicago, Ill.	01-21-80	L	R	5'6	165	17	39	3	7	0	0	0	4	2	5	0	.179	.179
Sabo (Szabo), Alex-Alexander (Giz)	36-37WasA	02-14-10	New Brunswick, N.J.	01-03-01	R	R	6'	192	39	8	1	3	0	0	0	0	2	3	0	.375	.375
Saltzgaver, Jack-Otto Hamlin	32,34-37NYA 45PitN	01-23-05	Croton, Iowa	02-01-78	L	R	5'11	165	278	764	131	199	26	5	10	82	105	90	9	.260	.347
Sandberg, Gus-Gustave Emanuel	23-24CinN	02-23-95	New York, N.Y.	02-03-30	R	R	6'1	189	31	69	2	12	1	0	0	4	3	8	0	.174	.188

USE NAME - GIVEN NAMES (NICKNAMES)	TEAM BY YEAR	BIRTH DATE	BIRTH PLACE	DEATH DATE	B	T	HGT	WGT	G	AB	R	H	2B	3B	HR	RBI	BB	SO	SB	BA	SA
Sand, Heinie-John Henry	23-28PhiN	07-03-97	San Francisco, Cal.	11-03-58	R	R	5'8	160	848	3033	457	781	145	32	18	251	382	340	21	.258	.344
Sanders, Ray-Raymond Floyd	42-45StLN 46BosN 47BA 48-49BosN	12-04-16	Bonne Terre, Mo.	10-28-83	L	R	6'2	185	630	2182	321	597	114	19	42	329	328	216	8	.274	.401
Sandlock, Mike-Michael Joseph	42,44BosN 45-46BknN 53PitN	10-17-15	Old Greenwich, Conn.		B	R	6'1	180 (Bats Left 44)	195	446	34	107	19	2	2	31	38	45	2	.240	.305
Sanford, Jack-John Doward	40-41WasA 42-45MS 46WasA	06-23-17	Chatham, Va.	01-04-05	R	R	6'3	195	47	153	13	32	4	4	0	11	9	24	0	.209	.288
Sankey, Ben-Benjamin Turner	29-31PitN	09-02-07	Nauvoo, Ala.	10-14-01	R	R	5'10	155	72	169	21	36	2	5	0	14	16	14	0	.213	.284
Sargent, Joe-Joseph Alexander (Horse Belly)	21DetA	09-24-93	Rochester, N.Y.	07-05-50	R	R	5'10	165	66	178	21	45	8	5	2	22	24	26	2	.253	.388
Saunders, Rusty-Russell Collier 25-31 played in A.B.L. 40-41,45-46 played in N.B.L.	27PhiA	03-12-06	Trenton,N.J.	11-24-67	R	R	6'2	205	5	15	2	2	1	0	0	2	3	2	0	.133	.200
Savage, Don-Donald Anthony	44-45NYA	03-05-19	Bloomfield, N.J.	12-25-61	R	R	6'	180	105	297	36	76	8	5	4	27	23	55	2	.256	.357
Sax, Ollie-Erik Oliver	23StLA	11-05-04	Branford, Conn.	03-21-82	R	R	5'8	164	16	17	4	3	0	0	0	0	5	3	0	.176	.176
Scalzi, Johnny-John Anthony 31 played in N.F.L.	31BosN	03-22-07	Stamford, Conn.	09-27-62	R	R	5'7	170	2	1	1	0	0	0	0	0	0	1	0	.000	.000
Scalzi, Skeeter-Frank Joseph	39NYN	06-16-13	Lafferty, Ohio	08-15-84	R	R	5'6	160	11	18	3	6	1	0	0	3	2	1	1	.333	.333
Scarritt, Russ-Stephen Russell Mallory	29-31BosA 32PhiN	01-14-03	Pensacola, Fla.	12-04-94	L	R	5'10	165	285	1037	139	296	44	25	3	121	49	91	17	.285	.385
Scarsella, Les-Leslie George	35-37,39CinN 40BosN	11-23-13	Santa Cruz, Cal.	12-16-58	L	L	5'11	185	265	898	109	255	34	16	6	109	37	70	13	.284	.378
Schalk, Roy-LeRoy John	32NYA 43MS 44-45ChiA	11-09-08	Chicago, Ill.	03-11-90	R	R	5'10	168	282	1112	100	259	38	5	2	109	79	95	8	.233	.281
Schang, Wally-Walter Henry	13-17PhiA 18-20BosA 21-25NYA 26-29StLA 30PhiA 31DetA	08-22-89	South Wales, N.Y.	03-06-65	B	R	5'10	180	1839	5306	769	1506	264	90	59	710	849	573	120	.284	.401
Scharein, Art-Arthur Otto (Scoop)	32-34StLA	06-30-05	Decatur, Ill.	07-02-69	R	R	6'	180	205	776	92	189	32	5	0	70	66	31	11	.244	.298
Scharein, George-George Albert (Tom)	37-40PhiN	11-21-14	Decatur, Ill.	12-23-81	R	R	6'1	174	388	1317	126	316	53	6	2	119	65	123	28	.240	.294
Scheer, Heinie-Henry	22-23PhiA	07-31-00	New York, N.Y.	03-21-76	R	R	5'8	146	120	345	36	73	11	1	6	33	20	66	4	.212	.301
Schemer, Mike-Michael (Lefty)	45-46NYN	11-20-17	Baltimore, Md.	04-22-83	L	L	6'	180	32	109	10	36	3	1	1	10	6	1	2	.330	.404
Schindler, Bill-William Gibbons	20StLN	07-10-96	Perryville, Mo.	02-06-79	R	R	5'11	160	1	0	0	0	0	0	0	0	0	1	0	.000	.000
Schliebner, Dutch-Frederick Paul	23BknN 23StLA	05-19-91	Berlin, Germany	04-15-75	R	R	5'8	180	146	520	61	141	23	6	4	56	44	67	4	.271	.362
Schlueter, Norm-Norman John	38-39ChiA 44CleA	09-25-16	Belleville, Ill.	10-06-04	R	R	5'10	175	118	296	18	55	11	2	0	26	17	48	3	.186	.236
Schmandt, Ray-Raymond Henry	15StLA 18-22BknN	01-25-96	St. Louis, Mo.	02-02-69	R	R	6'1	175	317	1054	122	284	36	13	3	122	46	75	11	.269	.337
Schmidt, Walter-Walter Joseph	16-24PitN 25StLA	03-20-87	Coal Hill, Ark.	07-04-73	R	R	5'9	160	766	2411	213	619	63	20	3	234	137	105	57	.257	.303
Schmulbach, Hank-Henry Alrives	43StLA 44-46MS	01-17-25	East St. Louis, Ill.	05-03-01	L	R	5'11	165	1	0	0	0	0	0	0	0	0	0	0	---	---
Schuble, Heinie-Henry George	27StLN 29,32-35DetA 36StLN	11-01-06	Houston, Tex.	10-02-90	R	R	5'8	160	332	935	139	235	43	16	11	116	57	108	19	.251	.367
Schulmerich, Wes-Edward Wesley	31-33BosN 33-34PhiN 34CinN	08-21-01	Hillsboro, Ore.	06-26-85	R	R	5'11	210	429	1442	169	417	73	20	27	192	118	197	7	.289	.424
Schulte (Schult), Fred-Fred William (Fritz)	27-32StLA 33-35WasA 36-37PhiN	01-13-01	Belvidere, Ill.	05-20-83	R	R	6'1	183	1178	4257	686	1241	249	54	47	593	462	361	56	.292	.409
Schulte (Schultenhenrich), Ham-Herman Joseph	40PhiN	09-01-12	St. Louis, Mo.	12-21-93	R	R	5'8	158	120	436	44	103	18	2	1	21	32	30	3	.236	.294
Schulte, Johnny-John Clement	23StLA 27StLN 28PhiN 29ChiN 32StLA 32BosN	07-31-96	Fredericktown, Mo.	06-28-78	R	R	5'11	190	192	374	59	98	15	4	14	64	76	49	1	.262	.436
Schulte (Schultenhenrich), Len-Leonard Bernard	44-46StLA	12-05-16	St. Charles, Mo.	05-06-86	R	R	5'10	160	124	435	38	108	16	1	0	38	25	35	0	.248	.290
Schultz, Howie-Howard Henry (Stretch, Steeple) 46-49 played in N.B.L. 49-50,51-53 played in N.B.A.	43-47BknN 47-48PhiN 48CinN	07-03-22	St. Paul, Minn.		R	R	6'6	200	470	1588	163	383	85	7	24	208	82	218	15	.241	.349
Schultz, Joe-Joseph Charles Sr. (Germany)	12-13BosN 15BknN 15CinN 16PitN 19-24StLN 24-25PhiN 25CinN	07-24-93	Pittsburgh, Pa.	04-13-41	R	R	5'11	172	703	1959	235	558	83	19	15	249	116	102	35	.285	.370
Schultz, Joe-Joseph Charles Jr. (Dode)	39-41PitN 43-48StLA M69SeaA M73DetA	08-29-18	Chicago, Ill.	01-10-96	L	R	5'11	180	240	328	18	85	13	1	1	46	37	21	0	.259	.314
Schuster, Bill-William Charles (Broadway)	37PitN 39BosN 43-45ChiN	08-04-12	Buffalo, N.Y.	06-28-87	R	R	5'9	164	123	261	27	61	11	3	1	17	23	23	6	.234	.310
Scoffic, Lou-Louis (Weaser)	36StLA	05-20-13	Herrin, Ill.	08-28-97	R	R	5'10	182	4	7	1	3	0	0	0	2	1	1	0	.429	.429
Scott, Everett-Lewis Everett (Deacon)	14-21BosA 22-25NYA 25WasA 26ChiA 26CinN	11-19-92	Bluffton, Ind.	11-02-60	R	R	5'8	142	1654	5837	552	1455	208	58	20	549	243	282	69	.249	.315
Scott, LeGrant-LeGrant Edward	39PhiN	07-25-10	Cleveland, Ohio	11-12-93	L	L	5'9	170	76	232	31	65	15	1	1	26	22	14	5	.280	.366
Scott, Pete-Floyd John	26-27ChiN 28PitN	12-21-97	Woodland, Cal.	05-03-53	R	R	5'11	175	208	522	95	158	41	6	8	88	59	63	5	.303	.450
Sears, Ken-Kenneth Eugene (Ziggy)	43NYA 44-45MS 46StLA	07-06-17	Streator, Ill.	07-17-68	L	R	6'1	200	67	202	23	57	7	0	2	23	14	18	1	.282	.347
Secory, Frank-Frank Edward	40DetA 42CinN 44-46ChiN	08-24-12	Mason City, Iowa	04-07-95	R	R	6'1	200	93	162	21	37	5	0	7	36	17	24	1	.228	.289
See, Charlie-Charles Henry (Chad)	19-21CinN	10-13-96	Pleasantville, N.Y.	07-19-48	R	R	5'10	175	92	202	21	55	9	1	1	23	9	12	5	.272	.342
Seeds, Bob-Ira Robert (Suitcase Bob)	30-32CleA 32ChiA 33-34BosA 34CleA 36NYA 38-40NYN	02-24-07	Ringgold, Tex.	10-28-93	R	R	6'	180	615	1937	268	537	77	21	28	233	160	190	14	.277	.382
Seibold, Socks-Harry (See P20-45)	15-17PhiA 18MS 19PhiA 29-33BosN	05-31-96	Philadelphia, Pa.	09-21-65	R	R	5'8	162	207	395	27	76	7	1	1	27	25	43	1	.192	.223
Selkirk, George-George Alexander (Twinkletoes)	34-42NYA 43-45MS	01-04-08	Huntsville, Canada	01-19-87	L	R	6'1	182	846	2790	503	810	131	41	108	576	486	319	49	.290	.483
Selph, Carey-Carey Isom	29StLN 32ChiA	12-05-01	Donaldson, Ark.	02-24-76	R	R	5'9	175	141	447	58	124	20	9	0	58	37	13	8	.277	.362
Severeid, Hank-Henry Levai	11-13CinN 15-25StLA 25-26WasA 26NYA	06-01-91	Story City, Iowa	12-17-68	R	R	6'	175	1390	4312	408	1245	204	42	17	539	331	169	35	.289	.367
Sewell, Joe-Joseph Wheeler	20-30CleA 31-33NYA	10-09-98	Titus, Ala.	03-06-90	L	R	5'7	155	1903	7132	1141	2226	436	68	49	1051	844	114	74	.312	.413
Sewell, Luke-James Luther	21-32CleA 33-34WasA 35-38ChiA 39CleA 42,M41-46StLA M49-52CleA	01-05-01	Titus, Ala.	05-14-87	R	R	5'10	160	1630	5383	653	1393	272	56	20	696	486	307	65	.259	.341
Sewell.Tommy-Thomas Wesley	27ChiN	04-16-06	Titus, Ala.	07-30-56	L	R	5'7	155	1	1	0	0	0	0	0	0	0	0	0	.000	.000
Shaner, Wally-Walter Dedaker (Skinny)	23CleA 26-27BosA 29CinN	05-24-00	Lynchburg, Va.	11-13-92	R	R	6'2	195	207	629	80	175	45	8	4	74	43	54	13	.278	.394
Shay, Marty-Arthur Joseph	24-25BosN	04-25-96	Boston, Mass.		R	R	5'7	148	21	75	4	18	3	1	0	2	5	6	2	.240	.307
Shea, Merv-Mervin John	27-29DetA 33BosA 33StLA 34-37ChiA 38BknN 39DetA 44WasA	09-05-00	San Francisco, Cal.	01-27-53	R	R	5'11	175	439	1197	105	263	39	7	5	115	189	145	8	.220	.277
Sheehan, Jack-John Thomas	20-21BknN	04-15-93	Chicago, Ill.	05-29-87	B	R	5'8	165	8	17	2	2	1	0	0	0	1	1	0	.118	.176
Sheehan, Jim-James Thomas (Big Jim)	36NYN	06-03-13	New Haven, Conn.	12-02-03	R	R	6'2	196	1	4	0	0	0	0	0	0	0	0	0	.000	.000
Sheely, Earl-Earl Homer (Whitey)	21-27ChiA 29PitN 31BosN	02-12-93	Bushnell, Ill.	09-16-52	R	R	6'3	195	1234	4471	572	1340	244	27	48	747	563	205	33	.300	.399
Sheerin, Charlie-Charles Joseph	36PhiN	04-17-09	Brooklyn, N.Y.	09-27-86	R	R	6'	188	39	72	4	19	4	0	0	4	7	18	0	.264	.319
Shelley, Hugh-Hubert Leneirre	35DetA	10-26-10	Rogers, Tex.	06-16-78	R	R	6'	170	7	4	2	1	0	0	0	1	0	1	0	.250	.250
Shemo, Steve-Stephen Michael	44-45BosN	04-09-15	Swoyersville, Pa.	04-13-92	R	R	5'11	175	35	77	7	20	3	2	0	8	2	6	0	.260	.364
Shepardson, Ray-Raymond Francis	24StLN	05-03-97	Little Falls, N.Y.	11-08-75	R	R	5'11	170	3	6	1	0	0	0	0	0	0	3	0	.000	.000
Sherling, Ed-Edward Creech (Shine)	24PhiA	07-18-97	Coalburg, Ala.	11-16-65	R	R	6'1	180	4	2	2	1	1	1	0	1	0	0	0	.500	1.500
Sherlock, Monk-John Clinton	30PhiN	10-26-04	Buffalo, N.Y.	11-26-85	R	R	5'10	175	92	299	51	97	18	2	0	38	27	28	0	.324	.398
Sherlock, Vince-Vincent Thomas	35BknN	03-27-10	Buffalo, N.Y.	05-11-97	R	R	6'	180	9	26	4	12	1	0	0	6	1	0	1	.462	.500
Shevlin, Jimmy-James Cornelius	30DetA 32,35CinN	07-09-09	Cincinnati, Ohio	10-30-74	L	L	5'10	155	53	77	13	19	4	0	0	12	12	8	4	.247	.299
Shilling, Jim-James Robert	39CleA 39PhiN	05-14-14	Tulsa, Okla.	09-12-86	R	R	5'11	175	42	131	11	37	8	5	0	16	8	13	1	.282	.420
Shinault, Ginger-Enoch Erskine	21-22CleA	09-07-92	Benton, Ark.	12-29-30	R	R	6'1	168	35	44	6	13	2	0	0	3	6	7	1	.295	.341
Shinners, Ralph-Ralph Peter	22-23NYN 25StLN	10-04-95	Monches, Wis.	07-23-62	R	R	6'	180	163	399	60	110	14	4	7	51	19	42	11	.276	.383
Shires, Art-Charles Arthur (Art the Great)	28-30ChiA 30WasA 32BosN	08-13-07	Italy, Tex.	07-13-67	L	R	6'2	190	290	986	118	287	45	12	11	119	81	62	8	.291	.395
Shirley, Mule-Ernest Raeford	24-25WasA	05-24-01	Snow Hill, N.C.	08-03-55	L	L	5'11	180	44	100	14	21	3	2	0	8	4	14	0	.210	.280
Shiver, Ivey-Ivey Merwin (Chick)	31DetA 34CinN	01-22-07	Sylvester, Ga.	08-31-72	R	R	6'2	200	21	68	8	13	1	0	2	6	3	18	1	.191	.294
Short, Dave-David Orvis	40-41ChiA 42-45MS	05-11-17	Magnolia, Ark.	11-19-99	L	L	5'10	162	7	11	1	1	0	0	0	0	3	0	0	.091	.091
Shorten, Chick-Charles Henry	15-17BosA 18MS 19-21DetA 22StLA 23VR 24CinN	04-19-92	Scranton, Pa.	10-23-65	L	L	6'	175	527	1345	161	370	51	20	3	134	110	68	12	.275	.349
Shupe, Vince-Vincent William	45BosN	09-05-21	East Canton, Ohio	04-05-62	L	L	5'11	180	78	283	22	76	8	0	0	15	17	16	3	.269	.297
Siebert, Dick-Richard Walther	32,36BknN 37-38StLN 38-45PhiA 46HO	02-19-12	Fall River, Mass.	12-09-78	L	L	6'	170	1035	3917	439	1104	204	40	32	482	276	185	30	.282	.379
Siemer, Oscar-Oscar Sylvester (Cotton)	25-26BosN	08-14-01	St. Louis, Mo.	12-05-59	R	R	5'9	162	47	119	8	29	5	1	0	11	3	7	0	.244	.294
Sigafoos, Frank-Francis Leonard	26PhiA 29DetA 29ChiA 31CinN	03-21-04	Easton, Pa.	04-12-68	R	R	5'9	170	55	134	14	27	3	0	0	6	5	9	0	.201	.224
Sigman, Tripp-Wesley Triplett	29-30PhiN	01-17-99	Mooresville, N.C.	03-08-71	L	R	6'	180	62	129	23	42	5	1	5	19	9	10	1	.326	.519
Silber, Eddie-Edward James	37,39StLA	06-06-14	Philadelphia, Pa.	10-26-76	R	R	5'11	170	23	84	10	26	2	0	1	12	5	14	0	.310	.333
Silvestri, Ken-Kenneth Joseph (Hawk)	39-40ChiA 41,46-47NYA 42-45MS 49-51PhiN	05-03-16	Chicago, Ill.	03-31-92	B	R	6'1	200	102	203	26	44	11	1	5	25	31	41	0	.217	.355
Simmons (Szymanski), Al (Alois)-Aloysius Harry (Bocketfoot Al)	24-32PhiA 33-35ChiA 36DetA 37-38WasA 39BosN 39CinN 40-41PhiA 43BosA 44PhiA	05-22-02	Milwaukee, Wis.	05-26-56	R	R	5'11	190	2215	8761	1507	2927	539	149	307	1827	615	737	87	.334	.535
Simon, Syl-Sylvester Adam	23-24StLA	12-14-97	Chandler, Ind.	02-28-73	B	R	5'10	170	24	33	5	8	1	1	0	0	12	12	0	.242	.333
Simons, Mel-Melbern Ellis (Butch)	31-32ChiA	10-10-74	Carlyle, Ill.		L	R	5'9	170	55	194	24	52	9	0	0	12	12	18	1	.268	.314
Sington, Fred-Frederic William	34-37WasA 38-39BknN	02-24-10	Birmingham, Ala.	08-20-98	R	R	6'2	215	181	516	66	140	36	5	7	85	89	86	2	.271	.401
Sipek, Dick-Richard Francis	45CinN	01-16-23	Chicago, Ill.	07-17-05	R	R	5'9	170	82	156	14	38	6	0	0	12	8	14	0	.244	.308
Sisler, George-George Harold (Gorgeous George) (See P01-19)	15-22StLA 23IJ 24-27,M24-26StLA 28WasA 28-30BosN	03-24-93	Manchester, Ohio	03-26-73	L	L	5'11	170	2055	8267	1284	2812	425	164	102	1175	472	327	375	.340	.468
Skaff, Frank-Francis Michael	35BknN 43PhiA M66DetA	09-30-10	LaCrosse, Wis.	04-12-88	R	R	5'10	185	38	75	12	24	3	2	1	11	6	13	0	.320	.453
Sketchley, Bud-Harry Clement	42ChiA	03-30-19	Virden, Canada	12-19-79	L	L	5'10	180	13	36	1	7	1	0	0	3	7	4	0	.194	.222

USE NAME - GIVEN NAMES (NICKNAMES)	TEAM BY YEAR	BIRTH DATE	BIRTH PLACE	DEATH DATE	B	T	HGT	WGT	G	AB	R	H	2B	3B	HR	RBI	BB	SO	SB	BA	SA
Skiff, Bill-William Franklin	21PitN 26NYA	10-16-95	New Rochelle, N.Y.	12-25-76	R	R	5'10	170	22	56	7	14	2	0	0	11	0	5	1	.250	.286
Skinner, Camp-Elisha Harrison	22NYA 23BosA	06-25-97	Douglasville, Ga.	08-04-44	L	R	5'11	165	34	46	2	9	2	0	0	3	0	4	1	.196	.239
Slade, Gordon-Gordon Leigh (Oskie)	30-32BknN 33StLN 34-35CinN	10-09-04	Salt Lake City, Utah	01-02-74	R	R	5'10	160	437	1372	147	353	60	11	8	123	84	116	12	.257	.335
Slayback, Scottie-Elbert	26NYN	10-05-01	Paducah, Ky.	11-30-79	R	R	5'8	165	2	8	0	0	0	0	0	0	0	0	0	.000	.000
Sloan, Bruce-Bruce Adams (Fatso)	44NYN	10-14-18	McAlester, Okla.	09-24-73	L	L	5'9	195	59	104	7	28	4	1	1	9	13	8	0	.269	.356
Small, Charlie-Charles Albert	30BosA	10-24-05	Auburn, Me.	01-14-53	L	R	5'11	180	25	18	1	3	0	0	0	0	5	5	1	.167	.222
Smith, Bob-Robert Eldridge (See P20-45)	23-30BosN 31-32ChiN 33CinN 33-37BosN	04-22-95	Rogersville, Tenn.	07-19-87	R	R	5'10	175	742	1689	154	409	64	17	5	166	52	110	16	.242	.309
Smith, Carr-Emanuel Carr	23-24WasA	04-08-01	Kernersville, N.C.	06-11-77	R	R	6'	175	10	9	1	3	1	0	0	1	0	3	0	.158	.211
Smith, Earl-Earl Leonard (Sheriff)	16ChiN 17-20StLA 21-22WasA	01-20-91	Oak Hill, Ohio	03-14-43	B	R	6'	175	495	1580	176	429	72	32	9	186	82	127	36	.272	.375
Smith, Earl-Earl Sutton (Oil)	19-23NYN 23-24BosN 24-27PitN 28-30StLN	02-14-97	Sheridan, Ark.	06-09-63	L	R	5'10	180	860	2264	225	686	115	19	46	355	247	106	18	.303	.432
Smith, Elmer-Elmer John	14-16CleA 16-17WasA 17CleA 18MS 19-21CleA 22BosA 22-23NYA 25CinN	09-21-92	Sandusky, Ohio	08-03-84	L	R	5'10	165	1012	3195	469	881	181	62	70	540	319	359	54	.276	.437
Smith (Schmidt), Ernie-Ernest Henry (The Kansas City Kid)	30ChiA	10-11-01	Totowa, N.J.	04-06-73	R	R	5'9	165	24	79	5	19	3	0	0	3	5	6	2	.241	.278
Smith (Smadt), Jack-John (Jan)	15-26StLN 26-29BosN	06-23-95	Chicago, Ill.	05-02-72	L	L	5'8	165	1406	4532	783	1301	182	71	40	382	334	348	228	.287	.385
Smith, Jack-John Marshall	31BosA	12-08-00	Washington, D.C.	05-09-82	B	R	6'1	180	4	15	2	2	0	0	0	1	2	1	1	.133	.133
Smith, Mayo-Edward Mayo	45PhiA M55-58PhiN M59CinN M67-70DetA	01-17-15	New London, Mo.	11-24-77	L	R	6'	183	73	203	18	43	5	0	0	11	36	13	0	.212	.236
Smith, Mike-Elwood Hope	11-16-04	Norfolk, Va.	05-31-81																			
Smith, Mike-Elwood Hope	26NYN	11-16-04	Norfolk, Va.	05-31-81	L	R	5'11	170	4	7	0	1	0	0	0	0	0	0	0	.143	.143
Smith, Paddy-Lawrence Patrick	20BosA	05-16-94	Pelham, N.Y.	12-02-90	L	R	6'	195	2	2	0	0	0	0	0	0	0	0	0	.000	.000
Smith, Red-Marvin Harold	25PhiA	07-17-99	Ashley, Ill.	02-19-61	R	R	5'7	165	20	14	0	4	0	0	0	1	2	5	0	.286	.286
Smith, Red-Richard Paul 27-31 played in N.F.L.	27NYN	05-18-04	Brokaw, Wis.	03-08-78	R	R	5'10	185	1	0	0	0	0	0	0	0	0	0	0	—	—
Smith, Vinnie-Vincent Ambrose	41PitN 42-45MS 46PitN	12-07-15	Richmond, Va.	12-14-79	R	R	6'1	176	16	54	5	14	1	0	0	5	2	10	0	.259	.278
Smyres, Clancy-Clarence Melvin	44BknN	05-24-22	Culver City, Cal.		B	L	5'11	175	5	2	1	0	0	0	0	0	0	0	0	.000	.000
Snipes, Roxy-Wyatt Eure (Rock)	23ChiA	10-28-96	Marion, S.C.	05-01-41	L	R	6'	185	3	3	0	0	0	0	0	0	0	0	0	.000	.000
Snyder, Bernie-Bernard Austin	35PhiA	08-25-13	Philadelphia, Pa.	04-15-99	R	R	6'	175	10	32	5	11	1	0	0	3	1	9	0	.344	.375
Snyder, Frank-Frank Elton (Pancho)	12-19StLN 19-26NYN 27StLN	05-27-94	San Antonio, Tex.	01-05-62	R	R	6'2	185	1392	4229	331	1122	170	44	47	525	281	416	37	.265	.360
Sodd, Bill-William	37CleA	09-18-14	Fort Worth, Tex.	05-14-98	R	R	6'2	210	1	1	0	0	0	0	0	0	0	0	0	.000	.000
Solomon, Mose-Mose Hirsch (The Rabbi of Swat, Hickory)	23NYN	12-08-00	New York, N.Y.	06-25-66	L	L	5'10	180	2	8	0	3	1	0	0	1	0	1	0	.375	.500
Solters (Soltesz), Moose-Julius Joseph (Lemons)	34-35BosA 35-36StLA 37-39CleA 39StLA 40-41ChiA 42VR 43ChiA	03-22-06	Pittsburgh, Pa.	09-28-75	R	R	6'	190	938	3421	503	990	213	42	83	599	221	377	42	.289	.449
Sorrells, Chick-Raymond Edwin (Red)	22CleA	07-31-96	Stringtown, Okla.	07-20-83	R	R	5'9	155	2	1	0	0	0	0	0	0	0	0	0	.000	.000
Sothern (Southern), Denny-Dennis Elwood	26,28-30PhiN 30PitN 31BknN	01-20-04	Washington, D.C.	12-07-77	R	R	5'11	175	357	1355	219	379	80	9	19	115	83	136	38	.280	.394
Southworth, Billy-William Harrison	13,15CleA 18-20PitN 21-23BosN 24-26NYN 26-27,29,40-45StLN M41-51BosN	03-09-93	Harvard, Neb.	11-15-69	L	R	5'9	170	1192	4359	661	1296	173	91	52	561	402	148	138	.297	.415
Spalding, Dick-Charles Harry	27PhiN 28WasA	10-13-93	Philadelphia, Pa.	02-03-50	L	L	5'11	185	131	465	69	139	16	3	0	25	38	44	5	.299	.346
Spence, Stan-Stanley Orvil	40-41BosA 42-44WasA 45MS 46-47WasA 48-49BosA 49StLA	03-20-15	S. Portsmouth, Ky.	01-09-83	L	L	5'10	180	1112	3871	541	1090	196	60	95	575	520	248	21	.282	.437
Spencer, Roy-Roy Hampton	25-27PitN 29-32WasA 33-34CleA 36NYN 37-38BknN	02-22-00	Scranton, Pa.	02-08-73	R	R	5'10	168	636	1814	177	448	57	13	3	203	128	130	4	.247	.298
Spencer, Vern-Vernon Murray	20NYN	02-04-93	Wixom, Mich.	06-03-71	R	R	5'7	165	45	140	15	28	2	3	0	19	11	17	4	.200	.257
Speraw, Paul-Paul Bachman (Polly, Birdie)	20StLA	05-15-93	Annville, Pa.	02-22-62	R	R	5'8	145	1	2	0	0	0	0	0	0	0	0	0	.000	.000
Sperber, Ed-Edwin George	24-25BosN	01-21-95	Cincinnati, Ohio	01-05-76	L	L	5'11	175	26	61	8	17	2	0	1	12	10	9	3	.279	.361
Sperry, Stan-Stanley Kenneth	36PhiN 38PhiA	02-19-14	Evansville, Wis.	09-27-62	L	R	5'10	164	80	290	30	74	9	3	0	31	18	14	1	.255	.307
Spindel, Hal-Harold Stewart	39StLA 45-46PhiN	05-27-13	Chandler, Okla.	07-28-02	R	R	6'	185	85	209	20	53	6	1	0	20	14	14	0	.254	.292
Spognardi, Andy-Andrea Ettore	32BosA	10-18-08	Boston, Mass.	01-01-00	R	R	5'9	160	17	34	9	10	1	0	0	1	6	6	0	.294	.324
Spohrer, Al-Alfred Ray	28NYN 28-35BosN	12-03-02	Philadelphia, Pa.	07-17-72	R	R	5'10	175	756	2218	213	575	103	25	6	199	124	166	13	.259	.334
Spotts, Jim-James Russell	30PhiN	04-10-09	Honeybrook, Pa.	06-15-64	R	R	5'10	175	3	2	1	0	0	0	0	0	0	0	0	.000	.000
Sprinz, Joe-Joseph Conrad (Mule)	30-31CleA 33StLN	08-03-02	St. Louis, Mo.	01-11-94	R	R	5'11	185	21	53	6	9	1	0	0	2	5	5	0	.170	.189
Spurgeon, Freddie-Fred	24-27CleA	10-09-01	Wabash, Ind.	11-05-70	R	R	5'11	160	316	1177	181	335	47	7	1	100	60	71	23	.285	.339
Stainback, Tuck-George Tucker	34-37ChiN 38StLN 38PhiN 38-39BknN 40-41DetA 42-45NYA 46PhiA	08-04-11	Los Angeles, Cal.	11-29-92	R	R	5'11	175	817	2261	284	585	90	14	17	204	64	213	27	.259	.333
Staley, Gale-George Gaylord	25CinN	05-02-99	DePere, Wis.	04-19-89	R	R	5'8	167	7	26	2	11	2	0	0	3	2	1	0	.423	.500
Staller, George-George Walborn (Stopper)	43PhiA 44-45MS	04-01-16	Rutherford Hgts., Pa.	07-03-92	L	L	5'11	190	21	85	14	23	1	3	3	12	5	6	1	.271	.459
Standaert, Jerry-Jerome John	25-26BknN 29BosA	04-01-16	Chicago, Ill.	08-04-64	R	R	5'10	168	86	132	14	42	10	2	0	18	8	10	0	.318	.424
Stanton, Buck-George Washington	31StLA	06-19-06	Stantonsburg, N.C.	01-01-92	L	L	5'10	150	13	15	3	3	2	0	0	0	0	1	0	.200	.333
Starr, Chick-William	35-36WasA	02-26-11	Brooklyn, N.Y.	08-12-91	R	R	6'1	175	13	24	1	5	0	0	0	1	0	1	0	.208	.208
Statz, Jigger-Arnold John	19-20NYN 20BosA 22-25ChiN 27-28BknN	10-20-97	Waukegan, Ill.	03-16-88	R	R	5'7	150	683	2585	376	737	114	31	17	215	194	211	77	.285	.373
Stein, Justin-Justin Marion (Ott)	38PhiN 38CinN	08-09-11	St. Louis, Mo.	05-01-92	R	R	5'11	185	29	57	9	16	1	1	0	3	2	5	0	.281	.333
Steinbacher, Hank-Henry John	37-39ChiA	03-22-13	Sacramento, Cal.	04-03-77	L	R	5'11	180	203	583	88	170	29	10	6	85	66	34	3	.292	.407
Steinecke, Bill-William Robert	31PitN	02-07-07	Cincinnati, Ohio	07-17-88	R	R	5'8	175	4	4	0	0	0	0	0	0	0	0	0	.000	.000
Steiner, Ben-Benjamin Saunders	45-46BosA 47DetA	07-28-21	Alexandria, Va.	10-27-88	L	R	5'11	165	82	308	41	79	8	3	3	20	31	29	10	.256	.331
Steiner, Red-James Harry	45CleA 45BosA 46-49SM	01-07-15	Los Angeles, Cal.	11-16-01	R	R	5'11	175	38	79	6	15	1	0	0	6	15	6	0	.190	.203
Stephenson, Riggs-Jackson Riggs (Old Hoss)	21-25CleA 26-34ChiN	01-05-98	Akron, Ala.	11-15-85	R	R	5'10	185	1310	4508	714	1515	321	54	63	773	494	247	54	.336	.473
Stephenson, Walter-Walter McQueen (Tarzan, Stevie)	35-36ChiN 37PhiN	03-27-11	Saluda, N.C.	07-04-93	R	R	6'	180	32	61	3	17	1	0	0	5	6	8	0	.279	.328
Stevens, Bobby-Robert Jordan	31PhiN	04-17-07	Chevy Chase, Md.	12-30-05	L	R	5'8	149	12	35	3	12	0	0	0	4	2	0	0	.343	.343
Stewart, Glen-Geln Weldon (Gabby)	40NYN 43-44PhiN	09-29-12	Tullahoma, Tenn.	02-11-97	R	R	6'	175	243	742	56	158	22	6	2	53	61	83	1	.213	.267
Stewart, Neb-Walter Nesbitt	40PhiN	05-21-18	S. Charleston, Ohio	06-08-90	R	R	6'1	195	10	31	3	4	0	0	0	1	0	5	0	.129	.129
Stewart, Stuffy-John Franklin	16-17StLN 22PitN 23BknN 25-27,29WasA	01-31-94	Jasper, Fla.	12-30-84	R	R	5'9	160	176	265	74	63	14	3	1	18	17	32	21	.238	.325
Stock, Milt-Milton Joseph	13-14NYN 15-18PhiN 19-23StLN 24-26BknN	07-11-93	Chicago, Ill.	07-16-77	R	R	5'8	154	1628	6249	839	1806	270	58	22	696	455	321	155	.289	.361
Stokes (Stocek), Al-Albert John	25-26BosA	01-01-00	Chicago, Ill.	12-19-86	R	R	5'10	170	47	138	14	25	3	4	0	7	12	36	0	.181	.261
Stone, John-John Thomas (Rocky)	28-33DetA 34-38WasA	10-10-05	Lynchburg, Tenn.	11-11-55	L	R	6'1	178	1199	4490	739	1391	268	105	77	707	463	352	45	.310	.468
Stone, Tige-William Arthur	23StLN	09-18-01	Macon, Ga.	01-01-60	R	R	5'8	145	5	1	0	1	0	0	0	0	0	0	0	1.000	1.000
Stoneham, John-John Andrew	33ChiA	11-08-08	Wood River, Ill.	01-01-04	L	R	5'9	168	10	25	4	3	0	0	0	0	2	0	0	.120	.240
Storie, Howie-Howard Edward	31-32BosA	05-15-11	Pittsfield, Mass.	07-27-68	R	R	5'10	175	12	25	2	5	0	0	0	3	2	1	0	.200	.200
Storti, Lin-Lindo Ivan	30-33StLA	12-05-06	Santa Monica, Cal.	07-24-82	B	R	5'10	162	216	704	83	160	34	11	9	75	47	107	3	.227	.345
Stoviak, Ray-Raymond Thomas	38PhiN	06-06-15	Scottdale, Pa.	02-23-98	L	L	6'1	195	10	10	1	0	0	0	0	0	0	2	0	.000	.000
Strand, Paul-Paul Edward (See P01-19)	13-15BosN 24PhiA	12-19-93	Carbonado, Wash.	07-02-74	R	L	6'	190	96	219	20	49	11	4	0	18	5	18	3	.224	.311
Strange, Alan-Alan Cochrane (Inky)	34-35WasA 35WasA 40-42StLA	12-04-06	Philadelphia, Pa.	06-27-94	R	R	5'9	162	314	947	93	211	39	7	5	89	109	54	6	.223	.282
Stringer, Lou-Louis Bernard	41-42ChiN 43-45MS 46CinN 48-50BosA	05-13-17	Grand Rapids, Mich.		R	R	5'11	180	409	1196	148	290	49	10	19	122	121	192	7	.242	.348
Stripp, Joe-Joseph Valentine (Jersey Joe)	28-31CinN 32-37BknN 38StLN 38BosN	02-03-03	Harrison, N.J.	06-10-89	R	R	5'11	175	1146	4211	575	1238	219	43	24	464	280	226	50	.294	.384
Stroner, Jim-James Melvin	29PhiN	05-29-01	Chicago, Ill.	12-06-75	R	R	6'	185	6	8	0	3	1	0	0	1	0	0	0	.375	.500
Stuart, Luke-Luther Lane	21StLA	05-23-92	Alamance County, N.C.	06-15-47	R	R	5'8	165	3	3	2	1	0	0	0	2	0	0	0	.333	1.333
Stumpf, George-George Frederick	31-33BosA 36ChiA	12-15-10	New Orleans, La.	03-06-93	L	L	5'8	155	118	260	31	61	7	3	1	32	25	26	5	.235	.296
Sturdy, Guy-Guy	27-28StLA	08-07-99	Sherman, Tex.	05-04-65	L	L	6'	180	59	66	8	19	2	0	1	13	9	4	2	.288	.364
Sturgeon, Bobby-Robert Harwood	40-42ChiN 43-45MS 46-47ChiN 48BosN	08-01-19	Clinton, Ind.		R	R	6'	175	420	1220	106	313	48	12	1	80	34	79	7	.257	.318
Sturm, Johnny-John Peter Joseph	41NYA 42-45MS	01-23-16	St. Louis, Mo.	10-08-04	L	L	6'1	185	124	524	58	125	17	3	3	36	37	50	3	.239	.300
Stutz, George-George (Kid)	26PhiN	02-12-93	Philadelphia, Pa.	12-29-30	R	R	5'5	150	6	6	0	0	0	0	0	0	0	0	0	.000	.000
Styles, Lena-William Graves	19-21PhiA 30-31CinN	11-27-99	Gurley, Ala.	03-14-56	R	R	6'1	185	77	176	14	44	7	2	0	16	16	24	1	.250	.313
Suarez, Luis-Luis Abelardo	44WasA	08-23-16	Alto Songo, Cuba	06-05-91	R	R	5'11	170	1	2	0	0	0	0	0	0	0	0	0	.000	.000
Suhr, Gus-August Richard	30-39PitN 39-40PhiN	01-03-06	San Francisco, Cal.	01-15-04	L	R	6'	180	1435	5176	714	1446	288	114	84	818	718	433	53	.279	.428
Sukeforth, Clyde-Clyde LeRoy (Sukey)	26-31CinN 32-34,45,M47BknN	11-30-01	Washington, Me.	09-03-00	R	R	5'10	170	486	1237	122	326	50	14	2	96	95	57	12	.264	.331
Sulik, Ernie-Ernest Richard	36PhiN	07-10-10	San Francisco, Cal.	05-31-63	L	L	5'10	178	122	404	69	116	14	4	0	36	40	22	4	.287	.386
Sullivan, Billy-William Joseph Jr.	31-33ChiA 35CinN 36-37CleA 38-39StLA 40-41DetA 42BknN 44-46MS 47PitN	10-23-10	Chicago, Ill.	01-04-94	L	R	6'	170	962	2840	347	820	152	32	29	388	240	119	30	.289	.417
Sullivan, Jack-Carl Mancel	44DetA	02-22-18	Princeton, Tex.	10-15-92	R	R	5'11	172	1	1	0	0	0	0	0	0	0	0	0	.000	.000
Sullivan, John-John Lawrence	20-21BosN 21CinN	03-03-90	Williamsport, Pa.	04-01-66	R	R	6'	185	162	495	64	153	28	8	5	67	48	55	6	.309	.428
Sullivan, John-John Paul	42-44WasA 45-46MS 47-48WasA 49StLA	11-02-20	Chicago, Ill.		R	R	5'10	170	605	1833	203	422	59	7	7	167	162	206	10	.230	.270
Sullivan, Tom-Thomas Brandon	25CinN	12-19-06	Nome, Alaska	08-16-44	R	R	6'	190	1	1	0	0	0	0	0	0	0	1	0	.000	.000
Summa, Homer-Homer Wayne	20PitN 22-28CleA 29-30PhiA	11-03-98	Gentry, Mo.		L	R	5'11	175	840	3001	413	905	166	34	18	361	166	88	44	.302	.398
Sumner, Carl-Carl Ringdahl (Lefty)	28BosA	09-28-08	Cambridge, Mass.	02-08-99	L	L	5'8	170	16	29	6	8	1	0	0	3	5	6	0	.276	.379
Susce, George-George Cyril Methodius (Good Kid)	29PhiN 32DetA 39PitN 40StLA 41-44CleA	08-13-07	Pittsburgh, Pa.	02-05-86	R	R	5'11	200	146	268	23	61	11	1	2	22	25	21	1	.228	.299

USE NAME - GIVEN NAMES (NICKNAMES)	TEAM BY YEAR	BIRTH DATE	BIRTH PLACE	DEATH DATE	B	T	HGT	WGT	G	AB	R	H	2B	3B	HR	RBI	BB	SO	SB	BA	SA
Susko, Pete-Peter Jonathan	34WasA	07-02-04	Laura, Ohio	05-22-78	L	R	5'11	172	58	224	25	64	5	3	2	25	18	10	3	.286	.362
Sutcliffe, Butch-Charles Inigo	38BosN	07-22-15	Fall River, Mass.	03-02-94	R	R	5'9	165	4	4	1	1	0	0	0	2	2	1	0	.250	.250
Swanson, Evar-Ernest Evar 24-27 played in N.F.L.	29-30CinN 32-34ChiA	10-15-02	DeKalb, Ill.	07-17-73	R	R	5'9	170	518	1892	325	573	87	28	7	170	212	133	69	.303	.390
Swanson, Karl-Karl Edward	28-29ChiA	12-17-00	N. Henderson, Ill.	04-03-02	L	R	5'10	155	24	65	2	9	1	0	0	6	4	7	3	.138	.154
Sweeney, Bill-William Joseph	28DetA 30-31BosA	12-29-03	Cleveland, Ohio	04-18-57	R	R	5'11	185	308	1050	127	300	58	8	5	107	44	73	22	.286	.370
Sweeney, Hank-Henry Leon	44PitN	12-28-15	Franklin, Tenn.	05-06-80	L	L	6'	185	1	2	0	0	0	0	0	0	0	1	0	.000	.000
Swentor, Augie-August William	22ChiA	11-21-99	Seymour, Conn.	11-10-69	R	R	6'	185	1	1	0	0	0	0	0	0	0	0	0	.000	.000
Swift, Bob-Robert Virgil	42-43PhiA 44-53,M66DetA	03-06-15	Salina, Kans.	10-07-66	R	R	5'11	180	1001	2750	212	635	86	3	14	238	324	233	10	.231	.280
Tabor, Jim-James Reubin (Rawhide)	38-44BosA 45MS 46-47PhiN	11-05-13	Owens Crossroads, Ala.	08-22-53	R	R	6'2	175	1005	3788	473	1021	191	29	104	598	286	377	69	.270	.418
Taitt, Doug-Douglas John (Poco)	28-29BosA 29ChiA 31-32PhiN	08-03-02	Bay City, Mich.	12-12-70	L	R	6'	176	258	824	81	217	43	16	4	95	58	64	13	.263	.369
Tankersley, Leo-Lawrence William (Tank)	25ChiA	06-08-01	Terrell, Tex.	09-18-80	R	R	6'	180	1	1	0	0	0	0	0	0	0	0	0	.000	.000
Tarbert, Arlie-Wilber Arlington	27-28BosA	09-10-04	Cleveland, Ohio	11-27-46	R	R	6'	160	39	86	6	16	2	0	0	7	4	13	1	.186	.209
Tate, Bennie-Henry Bennett	24-30WasA 30-32ChiA 34CinN	12-03-01	Whitwell, Tenn.	10-27-73	L	R	5'8	165	566	1560	144	435	68	16	4	173	118	51	5	.279	.351
Tauby, (Taubensee), Fred-Fred Joseph	35ChiA 37PhiN	03-27-06	Canton, Ohio	11-23-55	L	R	5'9	168	24	52	7	4	1	0	0	5	2	8	1	.077	.096
Tavener, Jackie-John Adam	21,25-28DetA 29CleA	12-27-97	Celina, Ohio	09-14-69	L	R	5'5	138	632	2131	254	543	88	53	13	242	186	231	47	.255	.364
Taylor, Chink-C. L.	25ChiA	02-09-98	Burnet, Tex.	07-07-80	R	R	5'9	160	8	6	2	0	0	0	0	0	0	0	0	.000	.000
Taylor, Danny-Daniel Turney	26WasA 29-32ChiN 32-36BknN	12-23-00	Lash, Pa.	10-11-72	R	R	5'10	190	674	2190	388	650	121	37	44	305	267	268	56	.297	.446
Taylor, Eddie-Edward James	26BosN	11-17-01	Chicago, Ill.	01-30-92	R	R	5'6	160	92	272	37	73	8	2	0	33	38	26	4	.268	.313
Taylor, Harry-Harry Warren (Handsome Harry)	32ChiN	12-26-07	McKeesport, Pa.	04-27-69	L	L	6'1	185	10	8	1	1	0	0	0	0	1	0	0	.125	.125
Taylor, Leo-Leo Thomas	23ChiA	05-13-01	Walla Walla, Wash.	05-20-82	R	R	5'10	150	1	0	0	0	0	0	0	0	0	0	0	---	---
Taylor, Tommy-Thomas Livingston Carlton	24WasA	09-17-92	Mexia, Tex.	04-05-56	R	R	5'10	176	26	73	11	19	3	1	0	10	2	8	2	.260	.329
Taylor, Zack-James Wren	20-25BknN 26-27BosN 27NYN 28-29BosN 29-33ChiN 34NYA 35BknN M46,48-51StLA	07-27-98	Yulee, Fla.	09-19-74	R	R	5'11	180	918	2865	258	748	113	28	9	311	161	192	9	.261	.329
Terry, Bill-William Harold (Memphis Bill)	23-36,M32-41NYN	10-30-98	Atlanta, Ga.	01-09-89	L	L	6'1	200	1721	6428	1120	2193	373	112	154	1078	537	449	56	.341	.506
Terry, Zeb-Zebulon Alexander	16-17ChiA 18BosN 19PitN 20-22ChiN	06-17-91	Denison,Tex.	03-14-88	R	R	5'8	130	640	2327	254	605	90	24	2	216	179	133	32	.260	.322
Thevenow, Tommy-Thomas Joseph	24-28StLN 29-30PhiN 31-35PitN 36CinN 37BosN 38PitN	09-06-03	Madison, Ind.	07-29-57	R	R	5'10	170	1229	4164	380	1030	124	32	2	456	210	222	23	.247	.294
Thomas, Herb-Herbert Mark	24-25,27BosN 27NYN	05-26-02	Sampson City, Fla.	12-04-91	R	R	5'5	157	74	235	27	52	11	4	1	15	15	18	7	.221	.315
Thomas, Ray-Raymond Joseph	38BosN	07-09-10	Dover, N.H.	12-06-93	R	R	5'10	175	1	3	1	1	0	0	0	0	0	0	0	.333	.333
Thomas, Red-Robert William	21ChiN	04-25-98	Harvgrove, Ala.	03-22-62	R	R	5'11	165	8	30	5	8	3	0	1	5	4	5	0	.267	.467
Thompson, Frank-Frank E.	20StLA	07-02-95	Springfield, Mo.	06-27-40	R	R	5'8	155	22	53	7	9	0	0	0	5	13	10	1	.170	.170
Thompson, Fresco-Lafayette Fresco (Tommy)	25PitN 26NYN 27-30PhiN 31-32BknN 34NYN	06-06-02	Centreville, Ill.	11-20-68	R	R	5'8	150	669	2560	400	762	149	34	13	249	215	143	69	.298	.398
Thompson, Tommy-Rupert Luckhart	33-36BosN 38-39ChiA 39StLA	05-19-10	Elkhart, Ill.	05-24-71	L	R	5'11	175	397	1107	142	294	34	4	9	119	108	63	7	.266	.328
Tierney, Cotton-James Arthur	20-23PitN 23PhiN 24BosN 25BknN	02-10-94	Kansas City, Kans.	04-18-53	R	R	5'8	175	630	2299	266	681	119	30	31	331	109	187	28	.296	.415
Tipton, Eric-Eric Gordon (Dukie, Blue Devil)	39-41PhiA 42-45CinN	02-05-15	Petersburg, Va.	08-29-01	R	R	5'11	190	501	1626	212	439	80	19	22	151	223	127	20	.270	.383
Tobin, Jack-John Martin (Tip)	32NYN	09-15-06	Jamaica Plain, Mass.	08-06-83	R	R	6'3	187	1	1	0	0	0	0	0	1	0	0	0	.000	.000
Tobin, Jack-John Thomas	14-15StLF 16,18-25StLA 26WasA 26-27BosA	05-04-92	St. Louis, Mo.	12-10-69	L	L	5'9	150	1617	6173	934	1908	297	101	64	581	498	172	147	.309	.421
Tobin, Jack-John Patrick (Jackie)	45BosA	01-08-21	Oakland, Cal.	01-18-82	R	R	6'	165	84	278	25	70	6	2	0	21	26	24	2	.252	.288
Todd, Al-Alfred Chester	32-35PhiN 36-38PitN 39BknN 40-41,43StLA	01-07-04	Troy, N.Y.	03-08-85	R	R	6'1	198	863	2785	286	768	119	29	35	366	104	243	18	.276	.377
Todt, Phil-Philip Julius	24-30BosA 31PhiA	08-09-01	St. Louis, Mo.	11-15-73	L	L	6'	175	957	3415	372	880	183	58	57	452	207	229	29	.258	.395
Tolson, Chick-Charles Julius (Slug)	25CleA 26-27,29-30ChiN	11-06-98	Washington, D.C.	04-16-65	R	R	6'	185	144	275	23	78	16	1	4	45	26	39	1	.284	.393
Toporcer, (Toporczer), Specs-George	21-28StLN	02-09-99	New York, N.Y.	05-17-89	L	R	5'10	165	546	1566	223	437	76	22	9	151	150	93	22	.279	.373
Torphy, Red-Walter Anthony	20BosN	11-06-91	Fall River, Mass.	02-11-80	R	R	5'11	169	3	15	1	3	0	0	0	2	0	1	0	.200	.333
Torres, Gil-Don Gilberto (Nunez) (See P20-45)	40,44-46WasA	08-23-15	Regla, Cuba	01-10-83	R	R	6'	155	346	1271	99	320	40	11	0	119	53	65	20	.252	.301
Torres, Ricardo-Ricardo J. [Martinez]	20-22WasA	04-16-93	Havana, Cuba	04-17-60	R	R	5'11	160	22	37	9	11	1	0	0	3	2	6	0	.297	.324
Tamback, Red-Stephen Joseph	40NYN	11-01-15	Iselin, Pa.	12-28-79	R	R	6'	175	2	4	0	1	0	0	0	0	0	1	1	.250	.250
Travis, Cecil-Cecil Howell	33-41WasA 42-44MS 45-47WasA	08-08-13	Riverdale, Ga.		L	R	6'1	185	1328	4914	665	1544	265	78	27	657	402	291	23	.314	.416
Traynor, Pie-Harold Joseph	20-35,37,M34-39PitN	11-11-98	Framingham, Mass.	03-16-72	R	R	6'	170	1941	7559	1183	2416	371	164	58	1273	472	278	158	.320	.435
Treadway, Ray-Edgar Raymond	30Was	10-31-07	Ragland, Ala.	10-12-35	R	R	5'7	170	6	19	1	4	2	0	0	2	0	3	0	.211	.316
Treadway, Red-Thadford Leon	44-45NYN	04-28-20	Athalone, N.C.	05-26-94	L	L	5'10	175	138	394	54	105	9	4	0	28	33	24	5	.266	.340
Trechock, Frank-Frank Adam	37WasA	12-24-15	Windber, Pa.	01-16-89	R	R	5'10	175	1	4	0	2	0	0	0	0	0	1	0	.500	.500
Tremark, Nick-Nicholas Joseph	34-36BknN	10-15-12	Yonkers, N.Y.	09-07-00	L	L	5'5	150	35	73	10	18	4	0	0	10	6	5	2	.247	.301
Tremper, Overton-Carlton Overton	27-28BknN	03-22-06	Brooklyn, N.Y.	01-09-96	R	R	5'10	163	36	91	5	20	7	0	0	8	4	9	0	.220	.264
Trash, Mike-Michael	38-48ChiA 49CleA	02-23-14	Hazelton, Pa.	10-04-66	R	R	5'11	170	1027	3169	326	788	75	14	2	297	402	263	19	.249	.283
Triplett, Coaker-Herman Coaker	38ChiN 41-43StLN 43-45PhiN	12-18-11	Boone, N.C.	01-30-92	R	R	5'11	185	470	1307	148	334	47	14	27	173	123	114	10	.256	.375
Trosky (Trojovsky), Hal-Harold Arthur Sr.	33-41CleA 42-43IL 44ChiA 45IL 46ChiA	11-11-12	Norway, Iowa	06-18-79	L	R	6'2	207	1347	5161	835	1561	331	58	228	1012	545	440	28	.302	.552
Tucker, Ollie-Oliver Dinwiddie	27WasA 28CleA	01-27-02	Radiant, Va.	07-13-40	L	R	5'11	180	34	71	6	11	2	0	1	10	11	5	0	.155	.225
Turchin, Eddie-Edward Lawrence (Smiley)	43CleA	02-10-17	New York, N.Y.	02-08-82	R	R	5'10	165	11	13	4	3	0	0	0	1	3	1	0	.231	.231
Turgeon, Pete-Eugene Joseph	23ChiN	01-03-97	Minneapolis, Minn.	01-24-77	R	R	5'6	145	3	6	1	1	0	0	0	0	1	0	0	.167	.167
Turner, Tom-Thomas Richard	40-44ChiA 44StLA 45MS	09-18-16	Custer, Okla.	05-14-86	R	R	6'2	195	233	696	63	165	29	4	7	63	51	84	4	.237	.320
Twombly, Babe-Clarence Edward	20-21ChiN	01-18-96	Jamaica Plain, Mass.	11-23-74	L	R	5'10	165	165	358	47	109	9	2	3	32	28	30	9	.304	.366
Tyack, Jim-James Fred	43PhiA	01-09-11	Florence, Mont.	01-03-95	L	R	6'2	195	54	155	11	40	8	1	0	23	14	9	1	.258	.323
Tyler (Tylka), Johnnie-John Anthony (Ty Ty)	34-35BosN	07-30-06	Mt. Pleasant, Pa.	07-11-72	R	R	6'	175	16	53	7	17	2	1	2	12	4	6	0	.321	.509
Tyson, Turkey-Cecil Washington	44PhiN	12-06-14	Elm City, N.C.	02-17-00	R	R	6'5	225	1	1	0	0	0	0	0	0	0	0	0	.000	.000
Tyson, Ty-Albert Thomas	26-27NYN 28BknN	06-01-92	Wilkes-Barre, Pa.	08-16-53	R	R	5'9	169	199	704	89	197	34	4	5	73	35	61	14	.280	.361
Uhalt, Frenchy-Bernard Bartholomew	34ChiA	04-27-10	Bakersville, Cal.	09-03-04	L	R	5'10	180	57	165	28	40	4	1	0	16	29	12	6	.242	.285
Uhle, George-George Ernest (Bull) (See P20-45)	19-28CleA 29-33DetA 33NYN 33-34NYA 36CleA	09-18-98	Cleveland, Ohio	02-26-85	R	R	6'	190	722	1360	172	393	60	21	9	187	98	112	6	.289	.384
Uhlir, Charlie-Charles Karel	34ChiA	07-30-12	Chicago, Ill.	07-09-84	L	L	5'7	150	14	27	3	4	0	0	0	3	2	6	0	.148	.148
Ulisney (Ulicny), Mike-Michael Edward (Slugs)	45BosN	09-28-17	Greenwald, Pa.	09-22-05	R	R	5'9	165	11	18	4	7	1	0	0	4	1	0	0	.389	.611
Unser, Al-Albert Bernard	42-44DetA 45CinN	10-12-12	Morrisonville, Ill.	07-07-95	R	R	6'1	175	120	338	41	85	15	4	4	39	32	43	0	.251	.355
Urban, Luke-Louis John 21-24 played in N.F.L.	27-28BosN	03-22-97	Fall River, Mass.	12-07-80	R	R	5'8	168	50	128	11	35	4	0	0	12	3	7	1	.273	.313
Urbanski, Billy-William Michael	31-37BosN	06-05-03	Staten Island, N.Y.	07-12-73	R	R	5'8	165	763	3046	379	791	123	27	19	207	198	252	24	.260	.337
Ussat, Dutch-William August	25,27CleA	04-11-04	Dayton, Ohio	05-29-59	R	R	6'1	170	17	4	3	0	1	0	0	2	2	1	0	.176	.294
Vache, Tex-Ernest Lewis	25BosA	11-17-88	Santa Monica, Cal.	06-11-53	R	R	5'11	185	110	252	41	79	15	7	3	48	21	33	2	.313	.464
Valdes, Roy-Rogelio Lazaro [Rojas]	44WasA	02-20-20	Havana, Cuba		R	R	5'11	175	1	1	0	0	0	0	0	0	0	0	0	.000	.000
Van Camp, Al-Albert Joseph	28CleA 31-32BosA	11-29-03	Moline, Ill.	02-02-81	R	R	5'11	175	140	444	44	116	20	6	0	41	24	42	4	.261	.333
Van Robays, Maurice-Maurice Rene (Bomber)	39-43PitN 44-45MS 46PitN	11-15-14	Detroit, Mich.	03-01-65	R	R	6'	190	529	1844	232	493	94	27	20	303	139	155	2	.267	.380
Vaughan, Arky-Joseph Floyd	32-41PitN 42-43BknN 44-46VR 47-48BknN	03-09-12	Clifty, Ark.	08-30-52	L	R	5'10	175	1817	6622	1173	2103	356	128	96	926	937	276	118	.318	.453
Vaughn, Fred-Frederick Thomas (Muscles)	44-45WasA	10-18-18	Coalinga, Cal.	03-02-64	R	R	5'10	185	110	377	38	91	9	5	2	46	32	72	2	.241	.308
Veltman, Pat-Arthur Patrick	26ChiA 28-29NYN 31BosN 32NYN 34PhiN	03-24-06	Mobile, Ala.	10-01-80	R	R	6'	190	23	38	4	5	0	1	0	2	4	9	0	.132	.184
Ventura, Vince-Vincent	45WasA	04-18-17	New York, N.Y.	09-11-01	R	R	6'1	190	18	58	4	12	2	0	0	2	3	6	0	.207	.207
Vergez, Johnny-Jean Louis	31-34NYN 35-36PhiN 36StLN	07-09-06	Oakland, Cal.	07-15-91	R	R	5'8	165	672	2323	258	593	114	16	52	292	171	303	22	.255	.385
Vick, Ernie-Henry Arthur 25,27-28 played in N.F.L.	22,24-26StLN	07-16-80	Toledo, Ohio	07-02-00	R	R	5'10	180	57	112	12	26	7	1	0	7	6	8	0	.232	.313
Vogel, Otto-Otto Henry	23-24ChiN	10-26-99	Mendota, Ill.	07-19-69	R	R	6'	185	111	253	38	63	11	3	2	30	17	37	6	.249	.340
Vosmik, Joe-Joseph Franklin	30-36CleA 37StLA 38-39BosA 40-41BknN 44WasA	04-04-10	Cleveland, Ohio	01-27-62	R	R	6'	185	1414	5472	818	1682	335	92	65	874	514	272	23	.307	.438
Voyles, Phil-Philip Vance	29BosN	05-12-00	Murphy, N.C.	11-03-72	L	R	5'11	175	20	68	9	16	4	0	0	7	2	3	0	.235	.294
Waddey, Frank-Frank Orum	31StLA	08-21-05	Memphis, Tenn.	10-21-90	L	L	5'10	185	14	22	3	6	1	0	0	2	0	0	0	.273	.318
Wade, Rip-Richard Frank	23WasA	01-12-98	Duluth, Minn.	06-15-57	L	R	5'11	174	33	69	8	16	2	2	1	14	5	10	0	.232	.406
Wagner, Hal-Harold Edward	37-44PhiA 44,46-47BosA 45MS 47-48DetA 48-49PhiN	07-02-15	East Riverton, N.J.	08-07-79	L	R	6'	165	672	1849	179	458	90	12	15	227	253	152	10	.248	.353
Walczak, Ed-Edwin Joseph (Husky)	45PhiN	09-21-15	Arctic, R.I.	03-10-98	R	R	5'11	180	20	57	6	12	3	0	0	7	3	3	0	.211	.263
Walker, Curt-William Curtis	19NYA 20-21PhiN 21-24PhiN 24-30CinN	07-03-96	Beeville, Tex.	12-09-55	L	R	5'9	170	1359	4858	714	1475	235	117	64	688	535	254	96	.304	.440
Walker, Dixie-Fred (The People's Cherce)	31,33-36NYA 36-37ChiA 38-39DetA 39-47BknN 48-49PitN	09-24-10	Villa Rica, Ga.	05-17-82	L	R	6'1	175	1905	6740	1037	2064	376	96	105	1023	817	325	59	.306	.437
Walker, Frank-Frank Charles Franklin	17-18DetA 20-21PhiA 25NYN	09-22-94	Enoree, S.C.	09-16-74	R	R	5'11	165	139	407	38	87	16	5	3	41	29	66	5	.214	.300
Walker, Gee-Gerald Holmes	31-37DetA 38-39ChiA 40WasA 41CleA 42-45CinN	03-19-08	Gulfport, Miss.	03-20-81	R	R	5'11	188	1784	6771	954	1991	399	76	124	997	330	600	223	.294	.453
Walker, Hub-Harvey Willos	31,35DetA 36-37CinN 42-44MS 45DetA	11-26-06	Gulfport, Miss.	11-27-82	L	R	5'10	175	297	779	117	205	43	6	5	60	104	89	26	.263	.353
Walker, Johnny-John Miles	19-21PhiA	12-11-96	Toulon, Ill.	08-19-76	R	R	6'	175	125	454	41	114	15	5	2	50	9	32	5	.251	.319
Walker, Speed-Joseph Richard	23StLN	01-23-98	Munhall, Pa.	06-20-59	R	R	6'	175	1	1	0	0	0	0	0	0	0	0	0	.286	.286

USE NAME - GIVEN NAMES (NICKNAMES)	TEAM BY YEAR	BIRTH DATE	BIRTH PLACE	DEATH DATE	B	T	HGT	WGT	G	AB	R	H	2B	3B	HR	RBI	BB	SO	SB	BA	SA
Wallen (Walentoski), Norm-Norman Edward	45BosN	02-13-17	Milwaukee, Wis.	06-20-94	R	R	5'11	175	4	15	1	2	0	1	0	1	1	1	0	.133	.267
Walsh, Joe-Joseph Patrick (Tweet)	38BosN	03-13-17	Boston, Mass.	10-05-96	R	R	5'10	165	4	8	0	0	0	0	0	0	0	2	0	.000	.000
Walsh, Walt-Walter William	20PhiN	04-30-97	Newark, N.J.	01-15-66	R	R	5'11	170	2	0	0	0	0	0	0	0	0	0	0	——	——
Walters, Bucky-William Henry (See P20-45)	31-32BosN 33-34BosA 34-38PhiN 38-48,M48-49CinN 50BosN	04-19-09	Philadelphia, Pa.	04-20-91	R	R	6'1	180	715	1966	227	477	99	16	23	234	114	303	12	.243	.344
Walters, Fred-Fred James (Whale)	45BosN	09-04-12	Laurel, Miss.	02-01-80	R	R	6'1	210	40	93	2	16	2	0	0	5	10	9	1	.172	.194
Walters, Roxy-Alfred John	15-18NYA 19-23CleA 24-25CleA	11-05-92	San Francisco, Cal.	06-03-56	R	R	5'8	160	498	1426	119	317	41	6	0	115	97	151	13	.222	.259
Wambsganss, Bill-William Adolph	14-23CleA 24-25BosA 26PhiA	03-19-94	Garfield Hts., Ohio	12-08-85	R	R	5'11	175	1492	5241	710	1359	215	59	7	519	490	357	142	.259	.327
Waner, Lloyd-Lloyd James (Little Poison)	27-41PitN 41BosN 41CinN 42PhiN 43WW 44BknN 44-45PitN	03-16-06	Harrah, Okla.	07-22-82	L	R	5'9	150	1993	7772	1201	2459	281	118	27	598	420	173	67	.316	.393
Waner, Paul-Paul Glee (Big Poison)	26-40PitN 41BknN 41-42BosN 43-44BknN 44-45NYA	04-16-03	Harrah, Okla.	08-29-65	L	R	5'9	153	2549	9459	1626	3152	603	190	113	1309	1091	376	104	.333	.473
Wanninger, Pee Wee-Paul Louis	25NYA 27BosA 27CinN	12-12-02	Birmingham, Ala.	03-07-81	R	R	5'7	150	163	556	53	130	15	8	1	31	23	43	5	.234	.295
Ward, Aaron-Aaron Lee	17-26NYA 27ChiA 28CleA	08-28-96	Booneville, Ark.	01-30-61	R	R	5'10	160	1059	3611	457	966	158	54	50	446	339	457	37	.268	.383
Warner, Jack-John Ralph	25-28DetA 29-31BknN 33PhiN	08-29-03	Evansville, Ind.	03-13-86	R	R	5'9	165	478	1546	199	387	52	20	1	120	142	137	32	.250	.312
Warnock, Hal-Harold Charles	35StlA	01-06-12	New York, N.Y.	02-08-97	L	R	6'2	180	6	7	1	2	0	0	0	0	0	3	0	.286	.571
Warren, Bennie-Bennie Louis	39-42PhiN 43-45MS 46-47NYN	03-02-12	Elk City, Okla.	05-11-94	R	R	6'1	184	377	989	97	217	26	7	33	104	129	177	1	.219	.360
Warstler, Rabbit-Harold Burton	30-33BosA 34-36PhiA 36-40BosN 40CleN	09-13-03	North Canton, Ohio	05-31-64	R	R	5'7	150	1205	4088	431	935	133	36	11	332	405	414	42	.229	.287
Warwick, Bill-Firman Newton	21PitN 25-26StlN	11-26-97	Philadelphia, Pa.	12-19-84	R	R	6'	180	23	56	8	17	1	2	1	8	5	7	0	.304	.446
Wasdell, Jimmy-James Charles	37-40WasA 40-41BknN 42-43PitN 43-46PhiN 46-47CleA	05-15-14	Cleveland, Ohio	08-06-83	L	L	5'11	185	888	2866	339	782	109	34	29	341	243	165	29	.273	.365
Wassem, Link-Lincoln William	37BosN	01-30-11	Birmingham, Ohio	03-06-79	R	R	5'9	180	2	1	0	0	0	0	0	0	0	0	0	.000	.000
Washington, George-George Sloan Vernon	35-36ChiA	08-07-07	Linden, Tex.	02-17-85	L	R	5'11	190	128	388	46	104	24	3	9	52	11	22	1	.268	.415
Watkins, George-George Archibald (Watty)	30-33StlN 34NYN 35-36PhiN 36BknN	06-04-00	Palestine, Tex.	06-01-70	L	R	5'11	170	894	3207	490	925	192	42	73	420	246	382	61	.288	.443
Watson, Johnny-John Thomas	30DetA	01-16-08	Tazewell, Va.	04-29-65	L	R	6'	175	4	12	1	3	2	0	0	3	1	2	0	.250	.417
Watt, Allie-Albert Bailey	20WasA	12-12-99	Philadelphia, Pa.	03-15-68	R	R	5'8	154	1	1	0	1	0	0	0	1	0	0	0	1.000	2.000
Watwood, Johnny-John Clifford (Lefty)	29-32ChiA 32-33BosA 39PhiN	08-17-05	Alexander City, Ala.	03-01-80	L	L	6'1	186	469	1423	192	403	66	16	5	158	154	103	27	.283	.363
Way, Bobby-Robert Clinton	27ChiA	04-02-06	Emlenton, Pa.	06-20-74	R	R	5'10	168	5	3	3	1	0	0	0	1	0	1	0	.333	.333
Weatherly, Roy-Cyril Roy (Stormy)	36-42CleA 43NYA 44-45MS 46NYA 50NYN	02-25-15	Warren, Tex.	09-19-91	L	R	5'7	170	811	2781	415	794	152	44	43	290	180	170	42	.286	.418
Webb, Earl-William Earl	25NYN 27-28ChiN 30-32BosA 32-33DetA 33ChiA	09-17-97	Bon Air, Tenn.	05-23-65	L	R	6'1	185	650	2161	326	661	155	25	56	333	260	202	8	.306	.478
Webb, Skeeter-James Laverne	32StlN 38-39CleA 40-44ChiA 45-47DetA 48PhiA	11-04-09	Meridian, Miss.	07-08-86	R	R	5'9	150	699	2274	216	498	73	15	3	166	132	215	33	.219	.268
Weingartner, Elmer-Elmer William (Dutch)	45CleA	08-03-18	Cleveland, Ohio		R	R	5'11	178	20	39	5	9	1	0	1	1	4	11	0	.231	.256
Weintraub, Phil-Philip (Mickey)	33-35NYN 37CinN 37NYN 38PhiN 44-45NYN	10-12-07	Chicago, Ill.	06-21-87	L	L	6'1	195	444	1382	215	407	67	19	32	207	232	182	4	.295	.440
Weis, Butch-Arthur John	22-25ChiN	02-01-01	St. Louis, Mo.	05-04-97	L	L	5'11	180	128	341	39	92	14	4	2	50	43	44	6	.270	.352
Welaj, Johnny-John Ludwig	39-41WasA 43PhiA 44-45MS	05-27-14	Moss Creek, Pa.	09-13-03	R	R	6'	164	293	793	115	198	40	3	4	74	53	73	36	.250	.323
Welch, Frank-Frank Tiguer (Bugger)	19-26PhiA 27BosA	08-10-97	Birmingham, Ala.	07-25-57	R	R	5'9	175	738	2310	310	634	100	31	41	295	250	225	18	.274	.398
Welch, Herb-Herbert M. (Dutch)	25BosA	10-19-00	Roellen, Tenn.	04-13-67	L	R	5'6	154	13	38	2	11	0	1	0	2	6	0	0	.289	.342
Welch, Milt-Milton Edward	45DetA	07-26-24	Farmersville, Ill.		R	R	5'10	175	1	2	0	0	0	0	0	0	0	1	0	.000	.000
Welsh, Jim-James Daniel	25-27BosN 28-29NYN 29-30BosN	10-09-02	Denver, Colo.	10-30-70	L	R	6'1	170	715	2684	387	778	127	47	35	288	156	144	37	.290	.411
Wendell, Lew-Lewis Charles	15-16NYN 24-26PhiN	02-22-92	New York, N.Y.	07-11-53	R	R	5'11	178	62	100	3	18	2	1	0	10	6	17	0	.180	.220
Wentzel, Stan-Stanley Aaron	45BosN	01-03-17	Lorain, Pa.	11-28-91	R	R	6'1	200	4	19	3	4	1	0	1	0	0	3	1	.211	.316
Wera, Julie-Julian Valentine	27,29NYA	02-09-02	Winona, Minn.	12-12-75	R	R	5'8	164	43	54	8	15	3	0	1	10	2	6	0	.278	.389
Werber, Bill-William Murray	30,33NYA 33-36BosA 37-38PhiA 39-41CinN 42NYN	06-20-08	Berwyn, Md.	03-13-96	R	R	5'10	170	1295	5024	875	1363	271	50	78	239	701	363	215	.271	.392
West, Dick-Richard Thomas	38-43CinN 44-45MS	11-24-15	Louisville, Ky.		R	R	6'2	180	119	299	30	66	10	2	3	35	12	42	6	.221	.288
West, Max-Max Edward	38-42BosN 43-45MS 46BosN 48PhiN	11-28-16	Dexter, Mo.	12-31-03	L	R	6'1	182	824	2676	338	681	136	20	77	380	353	340	19	.254	.407
West, Max-Maxwell Walter	28-29BknN	07-14-04	Sunset, Tex.	04-25-71	R	R	5'11	175	12	29	5	8	0	0	0	2	5	1	0	.276	.414
West, Sammy-Samuel Filmore	27-32WasA 33-38StlA 38-41WasA 42ChiA 43-45MS	10-05-04	Longview, Tex.	11-23-85	L	L	5'11	165	1753	6148	934	1838	347	101	75	838	696	540	53	.299	.425
Weston, Al-Alfred John	29BosN	12-11-05	Lynn, Mass.	11-13-97	R	R	6'	195	3	3	0	0	0	0	0	0	0	0	0	.000	.000
Wetzel, Dutch-Franklin Burton	20-21StlA	07-07-93	Columbus, Ind.	03-05-42	R	R	5'9	177	67	138	21	34	3	1	2	15	13	21	0	.246	.326
Whaley, Bill-William Carl	23StlA	02-10-99	Indianapolis, Ind.	03-03-43	R	R	5'11	178	23	50	5	12	2	1	0	1	4	2	0	.240	.320
Wheaton, Woody-Elwood Pierce (See P20-45)	43-44PhiA	10-03-14	Philadelphia, Pa.	12-11-95	L	L	5'8	160	37	89	3	17	4	0	0	7	8	5	1	.191	.236
Wheeler, Ed-Edward Raymond	45CleA	05-24-15	Los Angeles, Cal.	08-04-83	R	R	5'9	160	46	72	12	14	2	0	0	2	8	13	1	.194	.222
Whelan, Tom-Thomas Joseph 20-21 played in N.F.L.	20BosN	01-03-94	Lynn, Mass.	06-26-57	R	R	5'10	180	1	1	0	0	0	0	0	0	0	1	0	.000	.000
White, Barney-William Barney (Bear)	45BknN	06-25-23	Paris, Tex.	07-24-02	R	R	5'11	190	1	1	0	0	0	0	0	0	0	0	0	.000	.000
White, Jack-John Peter	27-28CinN	08-31-05	New York, N.Y.	06-19-71	B	R	5'7	135	6	7	1	0	0	0	0	0	0	1	0	.000	.000
White, Jo-Jo-Joyner Clifford	32-38DetA 43-44PhiA 44CinN M60CleA	06-01-09	Red Oak, Ga.	10-08-86	L	R	5'11	165	878	2652	456	678	83	42	8	229	384	276	92	.256	.328
Whitehead, Burgess-Burgess Urquhart (Whitey)	33-35StlN 36-37NYN 38IL 39-41NYN 42-45MS 46PitN	06-29-10	Tarboro, N.C.	11-25-93	R	R	5'10	160	924	3316	415	883	100	31	17	245	150	138	51	.266	.331
Whitney, Pinky-Arthur Carter	28-33PhiN 33-36BosN 36-39PhiN	01-02-05	San Antonio, Tex.	09-01-87	R	R	5'10	165	1539	5765	696	1701	303	56	93	927	400	438	45	.295	.465
Wietelmann, Whitey-William Frederick Bats Right 39-41	39-46BosN 47PitN	03-15-19	Zanesville, Ohio	03-26-02	B	R	6'	190	580	1762	170	409	55	6	7	122	156	131	14	.232	.282
Wilborn, Claude-Claude Edward	40BosN	09-01-12	Woodsdale, N.C.	11-13-92	L	R	6'1	180	5	7	0	0	0	0	0	0	0	1	0	.000	.000
Wilke, Harry-Henry Joseph	27ChiN	12-14-00	Cincinnati, Ohio	06-21-91	R	R	5'10	171	3	9	0	0	0	0	0	0	0	1	0	.000	.000
Wilkins, Bobby-Robert Linwood	44-45PhiA	08-11-22	Denton, N.C.		R	R	5'9	165	86	179	29	46	6	0	0	7	11	21	2	.257	.291
Williams, Cy-Fred	12-17ChiN 18-30PhiN	12-21-87	Wadena, Ind.	04-23-74	L	R	6'2	180	2002	6780	1024	1981	306	74	251	1005	690	721	115	.292	.470
Williams, Denny-Evon Daniel	21CinN 24-25,28BosA	12-13-96	Portland, Ore.	03-23-29	L	R	5'8	150	119	328	46	85	4	3	0	18	28	19	5	.259	.290
Williams, Dewey-Dewey Edgar (Dee)	44-47ChiN 48CinN	02-05-16	Durham, N.C.	03-19-00	R	R	6'	160	193	464	48	106	11	4	3	37	46	52	2	.233	.293
Williams, Dib-Edwin Dibrell	30-35PhiA 35BosA 36StlN	01-19-10	Greenbrier, Ark.	04-02-92	R	R	5'11	175	475	1574	198	421	74	12	29	201	133	140	7	.267	.389
Williams, Earl-Earl Baxter	28BosN	01-27-03	Cumberland Gap, Tenn.	03-10-58	R	R	6'	185	2	3	0	0	0	0	0	0	0	0	0	.000	.000
Williams, Ken-Kenneth Roy	15-16CinN 18-27StlA 28-29BosA	06-28-90	Grants Pass, Ore.	01-22-59	R	R	6'	170	1397	4860	860	1552	285	77	196	914	566	287	154	.319	.531
Williams, Pap-Fred	45CleA	07-17-13	Meridian, Miss.	11-02-93	R	R	6'1	200	16	19	0	4	0	0	0	1	2	0	0	.211	.211
Williams, Woody-Woodrow Wilson	38BknN 43-45CinN	08-21-12	Pamplin, Va.	02-24-95	R	R	5'11	175	338	1255	133	314	40	5	1	79	88	52	14	.250	.292
Williamson, Howie-Nathaniel Howard	28StlN	12-23-04	Little Rock, Ark.	08-15-69	L	L	6'	170	10	9	0	2	0	0	0	0	1	3	0	.222	.222
Willingham, Hugh-Thomas Hugh	30ChiA 31-33PhiN	05-30-06	Dalhart, Tex.	06-15-88	R	R	6'	180	31	42	7	10	2	1	1	3	4	10	0	.238	.405
Willson, Kid-Frank Hoxie	18,27ChiA	11-03-95	Bloomington, Neb.	04-17-64	L	R	6'1	190	11	11	3	1	0	0	0	0	0	0	0	.091	.091
Wilson, Charlie-Charles Woodrow (Swamp Baby)	31BosN 32-33,35StlN	03-13-05	Clinton, S.C.	12-19-70	B	R	5'10	178	57	186	15	40	7	3	2	14	8	16	0	.215	.317
Wilson, Eddie-Edward Francis	36-37BknN	09-07-09	Hamden, Conn.	04-11-79	L	R	5'11	165	88	227	39	72	12	2	4	33	31	39	4	.317	.441
Wilson, Frank-Francis Edward (Squash)	24-26BosN 28CleA 28StlA	04-19-01	Malden, Mass.	11-25-74	L	R	5'11	170	168	489	46	120	19	4	7	48	37	44	8	.245	.307
Wilson, Hack-Lewis Robert	23-25NYN 26-31ChiN 32-34BknN 34PhiN	04-26-00	Ellwood City, Pa.	11-23-48	R	R	5'6	190	1348	4760	884	1461	266	67	244	1063	674	713	52	.307	.545
Wilson, Icehouse-George Peacock	34DetA	09-14-12	Maricopa, Cal.	10-13-73	R	R	6'	186	1	1	0	0	0	0	0	0	0	0	0	.000	.000
Wilson, Jimmie-James (Ace)	23-28PhiN 28-33StlN 34-38,M34-38PhiN 39-40CinN M41-44CinN	07-23-00	Philadelphia, Pa.	05-31-47	R	R	6'1	200	1525	4778	580	1358	252	32	32	621	356	280	86	.284	.370
Wilson, Mike-Samuel Marshall 23-25 played in N.F.L.	21PitN	12-02-96	Edge Hill, Pa.	05-16-78	R	R	5'10	160	5	4	0	0	0	0	0	0	0	0	0	.000	.000
Windle, Bill-Willis Brewer	28-29PhiN	12-13-04	Galena, Kans.	12-08-81	L	L	5'10	170	3	2	1	1	1	0	0	0	0	0	0	.500	1.000
Winegarner, Ralph-Ralph Lee (See P20-45)	30,32,34-36CleA 49StlA	10-29-09	Benton, Kans.	04-14-88	R	R	6'	182	136	185	28	51	7	1	5	28	15	43	1	.276	.405
Wingo, Al-Absalom Holbrook (Red)	19PhiA 24-28DetA	05-06-98	Norcross, Ga.	10-09-64	L	R	5'11	180	493	1326	224	409	87	19	9	191	211	119	23	.308	.423
Wingo, (LaRiviere), Ed-Edmond Armand	20PhiA	08-21-95	Ste. Anne, Canada	12-05-64	R	R	5'5	160	1	4	0	1	0	0	0	0	0	0	0	.250	.250
Winsett, Tom-John Thomas (Long Tom)	30-31,33BosA 35StlN 36-38BknN	11-24-09	McKenzie, Tenn.	07-20-87	L	R	6'2	190	230	566	60	134	25	5	8	76	69	113	2	.237	.341
Wirts, Kettle-Elwood Vernon	21-23ChiN 24ChiA	10-30-97	Consume, Cal.	07-12-68	R	R	5'11	170	49	86	9	14	2	0	0	8	16	20	1	.163	.221
Wise, Hughie-Hugh Edward	30DetA	02-06-06	Campbellsville, Ky.	07-21-87	B	R	6'	178	2	6	0	2	0	0	0	0	0	1	0	.333	.333
Witek, Mickey-Nicholas Joseph	40-43NYN 44-45MS 46-47NYN 49NYA	12-19-15	Luzerne, Pa.	08-24-90	R	R	5'10	170	581	2147	239	595	65	9	22	196	148	84	7	.277	.347
Withrow, Frank-Frank Blaine (Kid)	20,22PhiN	06-14-91	Greenwood, Mo.	09-05-66	R	R	5'11	187	58	153	11	31	6	1	0	15	11	31	0	.203	.255
Witt (Wittkowski), Whitey (Ladislaw Waldemar)-Lawton Walter	16-17PhiA 18MS 19-21PhiA 22-25NYA 26PhiA	09-28-95	Orange, Mass.	07-14-88	L	R	5'7	150	1139	4171	632	1195	144	62	18	302	489	309	78	.287	.364
Woehr, Andy-Andrew Emil	23-24PhiN	02-04-96	Fort Wayne, Ind.	07-24-90	R	R	5'11	165	63	193	14	47	6	5	0	20	6	9	2	.244	.326
Wolf, Ray-Raymond Bernard	27CinN	05-15-05	Chicago, Ill.	10-06-79	R	R	5'11	180	1	1	0	0	0	0	0	0	0	0	0	.000	.000
Womack, Sid-Sidney Kirk (Tex)	26BosN	10-02-96	Greensburg, La.	08-28-58	R	R	5'10	200	1	3	0	0	0	0	0	0	0	0	0	.000	.000
Wood, Doc-Charles Spencer	20DetA	02-28-00	Batesville, Miss.	11-03-74	R	R	5'9	160	1	3	0	1	0	0	0	0	0	0	0	.333	.333
Wood, Joe-Joseph Perry (The Little General)	43DetA 44-45MS	10-03-19	Houston, Tex.	03-25-85	R	R	5'9	160	60	164	22	53	4	1	7	17	6	21	1	.323	.415
Woodall, Larry-Charles Lawrence	20-29DetA	07-26-94	Staunton, Va.	05-16-63	R	R	5'9	165	548	1317	161	353	50	15	1	160	159	67	16	.268	.331

USE NAME - GIVEN NAMES (NICKNAMES)	TEAM BY YEAR	BIRTH DATE	BIRTH PLACE	DEATH DATE	B	T	HGT	WGT	G	AB	R	H	2B	3B	HR	RBI	BB	SO	SB	BA	SA
Workman, Chuck-Charles Thomas	38,41CleA 43-46BosN 46PitN	01-06-15	Leeton, Mo.	01-03-53	L	R	6'	175	526	1749	213	423	57	7	50	230	161	202	24	.242	.368
Worthington, Red-Robert Lee (Bob)	31-34BosN 34StLN	04-24-06	Alhambra, Cal.	12-08-63	R	R	5'11	170	292	1037	118	298	69	18	12	111	48	71	2	.287	.423
Wright, Ab-Albert Owen 30 played in N.F.L.	35Cle 44BosN	11-16-06	Terlton, Okla.	05-23-95	R	R	6'1	190	138	355	37	88	20	1	9	53	28	48	2	.248	.386
Wright, Al-Albert Edgar (A-1)	33BosN	11-11-12	San Francisco, Cal.	11-13-98	R	R	6'1	170	4	1	0	1	0	0	0	0	0	0	0	1.000	1.000
Wright, Glenn-Forrest Glenn (Buckshot)	24-28PitN 29-33BknN 35ChiA	02-06-01	Archie, Mo.	04-06-84	R	R	5'11	170	1119	4153	584	1219	203	76	94	723	209	407	38	.294	.447
Wright, Taffy-Taft Shedron	38-39WasA 40-42ChiA 43-45MS 46-48ChiA 49PhiA	08-10-11	Tabor City, N.C.	10-22-81	L	R	5'10	180	1029	3583	465	1115	175	55	38	553	347	155	32	.311	.423
Wrightstone, Russ-Russell Guy	20-28PhiN 28NYN	03-18-93	Bowmansdale, Pa.	02-25-69	L	R	5'10	176	929	2992	427	889	152	34	60	425	215	152	35	.297	.431
Wuestling, Yats-George	29-30DetA 30NYA	10-18-03	St. Louis, Mo.	04-26-70	R	R	5'11	167	83	217	18	41	4	2	0	19	15	41	0	.189	.226
Wyatt, Joe-Loral John	24CleA	04-06-01	Petersburg, Ind.	12-05-70	R	R	6'1	175	4	11	1	2	0	0	0	1	2	1	0	.182	.182
Yaran, Yam-Clarence Everett	21-22ChiA	11-05-92	Knowlton, Iowa	11-16-64	R	R	5'10	180	81	173	20	45	10	2	2	24	15	26	1	.260	.376
York, Rudy-Rudolph Preston	34,37-45DetA 46-47BosA 47ChiA 48PhiA M59BosA	08-17-13	Ragland, Ala.	02-05-70	R	R	6'1	220	1603	5891	876	1621	291	52	277	1152	792	867	38	.275	.483
York, Tony-Tony Batton	44ChiN 45MS	11-27-12	Irene, Tex.	04-18-70	R	R	5'10	165	28	85	4	20	1	0	0	7	4	11	0	.235	.247
Yoter, Elmer-Elmer Ellsworth	21PhiA 24CleA 27-28ChiN	06-26-00	Plainfield, Pa.	07-26-66	R	R	5'7	155	36	96	5	24	2	2	0	12	9	13	0	.250	.313
Young, Babe-Norman Robert	36,39-42NYN 43-45MS 46-47NYN 47-48CinN 48StLN	07-01-15	Queens, N.Y.	12-25-83	L	L	6'2	185	728	2403	320	656	121	17	79	415	274	161	9	.273	.436
Young, Del-Delmer Edward	37-40PhiN	05-11-12	Cleveland, Ohio	12-08-79	B	R	5'11	168	309	950	87	213	31	7	3	76	48	115	7	.224	.281
Young, Pep-Lemuel Floyd	33-40PitN 41CinN 41,45StLN	08-29-07	Jamestown, N.C.	01-14-62	R	R	5'9	162	730	2466	274	645	128	34	32	347	152	312	18	.262	.380
Young, Russ-Russell Charles 25-26 played in N.F.L.	31StLA	09-15-02	Bryan, Ohio	05-13-84	B	R	6'	190	16	34	2	4	0	0	1	2	2	4	0	.118	.206
Youngs, Ross (Royce)-Ross Middlebrook (Pep)	17-26NYN	04-10-97	Shiner, Tex.	10-22-27	L	R	5'8	162	1211	4627	812	1491	236	93	42	592	550	390	153	.322	.441
			Bats Both 17																		
Yount, Eddie-Floyd Edwin	37PhiA 39PitN	12-19-15	Newton, N.C.	10-26-73	R	R	6'1	185	6	9	1	2	0	0	0	1	0	3	0	.222	.222
Zak, Frankie-Frank Thomas	44-46PitN	02-22-22	Passaic, N.J.	02-06-72	R	R	5'10	150	123	208	43	56	5	1	0	14	26	23	6	.269	.303
Zapustas, Joe-Joseph John 33 played in N.F.L.	33PhiA	07-25-07	Boston, Mass.	01-14-01	R	R	6'1	185	2	5	0	1	0	0	0	0	0	0	0	.200	.200
Zardon, Jose-Jose Antonio [Valdes] (Guineo)	45WasA	05-20-23	Havana, Cuba		R	R	6'	150	54	131	13	38	5	3	0	13	7	11	3	.290	.374
Zimmerman, Roy-Roy Franklin (Dutch)	45NYN 46-49SM	09-13-16	Pine Grove, Pa.	11-22-91	L	L	6'2	187	27	98	14	27	1	0	5	15	5	16	1	.276	.439
Zitzman, Billy-William Arthur	19PitN 19,25-29CinN	11-19-97	Queens, N.Y.	05-29-85	R	R	5'10	175	406	1004	197	268	38	11	3	89	83	85	42	.267	.336

USE NAMES - GIVEN NAMES (NICKNAMES)	TEAM BY YEAR	BIRTH DATE	BIRTHPLACE	DEATH DATE	B	T	HGT	WGT	W	L	Pct.	SV	G	GS	CG	IP	H	BB	SO	ShO	ERA
Abernathy, Tal-Talmadge Lafayette	42-44PhiA	10-30-21	Bynum, N.C.	11-16-01	R	L	6'2	210	0	3	.000	0	7	2	1	20	31	17	13	0	11.07
Abrams, George-George Allen	23CinN	11-09-97	Seattle, Wash.	12-05-86	R	R	5'9	170	0	0	—	0	3	0	0	5	10	3	1	0	9.00
Acosta, Jose-Jose (Acostica)	20-21WasA 22ChiA	03-04-91	Havana, Cuba	11-16-77	R	R	5'6	134	10	10	.500	4	55	13	6	213	265	68	45	1	4.51
Adams, Ace-Ace Townsend	41-46NYN	03-02-10	Willows, Cal.	02-26-06	R	R	5'11	182	41	33	.554	49	302	7	2	553	541	224	171	0	3.47
Adams, Bob-Robert Andrew	31-32PhiN	01-20-07	Birmingham, Ala.	03-06-70	R	R	6'2	165	0	1	.000	0	5	1	0	12	21	3	5	0	5.25
Adams, Bob-Robert Burdette	25BosA	07-24-01	Holyoke, Mass.	10-17-96	R	R	5'11	168	0	0	—	0	2	0	0	6	10	3	1	0	7.50
Adkins, Grady-Grady Emmett (Butcher Boy)	28-29ChiA	06-29-97	Jacksonville, Ark.	03-31-66	R	R	5'11	175	12	27	.308	1	67	42	19	363	401	156	78	0	4.34
Alderson, Dale-Dale Leonard	43-44ChiN 45MS	03-09-18	Belden, Neb.	02-12-82	R	R	5'10	190	0	1	.000	0	16	3	0	36	52	12	11	0	6.56
Aldridge, Vic-Victor Eddington	17-18,22-24ChiN 25-27PitN 28NYN	10-25-93	Indian Springs, Ind.	04-17-73	R	R	5'10	175	97	80	.548	6	248	205	102	1601	1671	512	526	8	3.76
Allen, Bob-Robert Earl (Thin Man)	37PhiN	07-02-14	Smithville, Tenn.	10-30-05	R	R	6'1	165	0	1	.000	0	3	1	0	12	18	8	4	0	6.75
Allen, Johnny-John Thomas (Big Chin)	32-35NYA 36-40CleA 41StLA 41-43BknN 44-44NYN	09-30-04	Lenoir, N.C.	03-29-59	R	R	6'	180	142	75	.654	18	352	241	109	1950	1849	738	1070	17	3.75
Alten, Ernie-Ernest Matthias (Lefty)	20DetA	12-01-94	Avon, Ohio	09-09-81	R	L	6'	175	0	1	.000	0	14	1	0	23	40	9	4	0	9.00
Anderson, Bill-William Edward (Lefty)	25BosN	12-03-95	Boston, Mass.	03-13-83	R	L	6'1	165	0	0	—	0	2	0	0	3	5	2	1	0	9.00
Anderson, Red-Arnold Revola	37,40-41WasA 42MS	06-19-12	Lawton, Iowa	08-07-72	R	R	6'3	210	5	8	.385	2	36	9	3	137	150	69	40	0	4.35
Andrews, Elbert-Elbert DeVore	25PhiA	12-11-01	Greenwood, S.C.	11-25-79	L	R	6'	175	0	0	—	0	6	0	0	8	12	11	0	0	10.13
Andrews, Ivy-Ivy Paul (Poison)	31-32NYA 32-33BosA 34-36StLA 37CleA 37-38NYA	05-06-07	Dora, Ala.	11-24-70	R	R	6'3	210	50	59	.459	8	249	108	43	1041	1151	342	257	2	4.14
Andrews, Nate-Nathan Hardy	37,39StLA 40-41CleA 43-45BosN 46CinN 46NYN	09-30-13	Pembroke, N.C.	04-26-91	R	R	6'	195	41	54	.432	5	127	98	51	773	798	236	216	5	3.46
Appleton, Pete-Peter William	27-28CinN 30-32CleA 32BosA 33NYA 36-39WasA 40-42ChiA 42,45StLA 43-44MS 45WasA	05-20-04 (Played as Pete Jablonowski 27-33)	Terryville, Conn.	01-18-74	R	R	5'11	180	57	66	.463	26	341	73	34	1141	1187	486	420	6	4.30
Archer, Fred-Frederick Marvin (Lefty)	36-37PhiA	03-07-10	Johnson City, Tenn.	10-31-81	L	L	6'	193	2	3	.400	0	7	5	2	40	45	15	11	0	6.35
Armbrust, Orville-Orville Martin	34WasA	03-02-08	Beverly, Ark.	10-02-67	R	R	5'10	195	1	0	1.000	0	3	0	0	13	10	3	3	0	2.08
Arntzen, Orie-Orie Edgar (Old Folks)	43PhiA	10-18-09	Beverly, Ill.	01-28-70	R	R	6'1	200	4	13	.235	2	32	20	9	164	172	69	66	0	4.23
Ash, Ken-Kenneth Lowther	28-30CinN	09-16-01	Anmoore, W.Va.	11-15-79	R	R	5'11	165	6	8	.429	2	55	13	5	161	178	59	47	0	4.96
Auker, Elden-Elden LeRoy (Big Six)	33-38DetA 39BosA 40-42StLA	09-21-10	Norcatur, Kans.	08-04-06	R	R	6'2	194	130	101	.563	2	333	261	126	1963	2230	706	594	14	4.42
Babich, Johnny-John Charles	34-35BknN 36BosN 40-41PhiA	05-14-13	Albion, Cal.	01-19-01	R	R	6'1	180	30	45	.400	1	112	86	34	592	657	220	231	3	4.93
Baecht, Ed-Edward Joseph	26-28PhiN 31-32ChiN 37StLA	05-15-07	Paden, Okla.	08-15-57	R	R	6'2	195	5	6	.455	2	64	9	3	160	200	78	61	0	5.56
Bagby, Jim-James Charles Jacob Jr.	38-40BosA 41-45CleA 46BosA 47PitN	09-18-16	Cleveland, Ohio	09-02-88	R	R	6'2	170	97	96	.503	2	303	198	84	1666	1815	608	431	13	3.96
Bailey, Sweetbreads-Abraham Lincoln	19-21ChiN 21BknN	02-12-95	Joliet, Ill.	09-27-39	R	R	6'	184	4	7	.364	2	52	6	1	137	154	40	35	0	4.59
Bain, Loren-Herbert Loren	45NYN	07-04-22	Staples, Minn.	11-24-96	R	R	6'	190	0	0	—	0	8	0	0	8	10	4	1	0	7.88
Baker, Al-Albert Jones	38BosA	02-28-06	Batesville, Miss.	11-06-82	R	R	5'11	170	0	0	—	0	1	0	0	8	13	2	4	0	9.00
Baker, Neal-Neal Vernon	27PhiA	06-11-01	La Porte, Tex.	01-05-82	R	R	6'1	175	0	0	—	0	11	1	0	27	27	7	3	0	5.82
Baker, Tom-Thomas Calvin (Rattlesnake)	35-37BknN 37-38NYN 39AJ	06-11-13	Nursery, Tex.	01-03-91	R	R	6'	180	3	9	.250	2	68	3	1	173	195	92	58	0	4.73
Balas (Balaski), Mike-Mitchell Francis	38BosN	05-09-10	Lowell, Mass.	10-15-96	R	R	6'	195	0	0	—	0	1	0	0	1	3	0	0	0	9.00
Baldwin, Harry-Howard Edward	25BosN	06-03-00	Baltimore, Md.	01-23-58	R	R	5'11	160	3	1	.750	0	7	4	3	35	45	12	5	0	4.37
Ballou, Win-Noble Winfred (Old Pard)	25WasA 26-27StLA 29BknN	11-30-97	Mount Morgan, Ky.	01-29-63	R	R	5'10	170	19	20	.487	2	99	27	10	330	398	168	109	0	5.10
Barfoot, Clyde-Clyde Raymond	22-23StLN 26DetA	07-08-91	Richmond, Va.	03-11-71	R	R	6'	170	8	10	.444	5	86	5	2	250	293	66	49	1	4.10
Barnabe, Charlie-Charles Edward	27-28ChiA	06-12-00	Russell Gulch, Colo.	08-16-77	L	L	5'11	164	0	7	.000	0	24	7	1	71	103	20	8	0	5.48
Barnes, Bob-Robert Avery (Lefty)	24CinN	01-06-02	Washburn, Ill.	12-08-93	L	L	5'11	150	0	0	—	0	5	0	0	14	14	0	1	0	19.80
Barnes, Frank-Frank Samuel (Lefty)	29DetA 30NYA	01-09-00	Dallas, Tex.	09-27-67	L	L	6'3	195	0	2	.000	0	6	3	0	17	23	16	2	0	7.79
Barnes, Jesse-Jesse Lawrence (Nubby)	15-17BosN 18-23NYN 23-25BosN 26-27BknN	08-26-92	Perkins, Okla.	09-09-61	L	R	6'	170	153	149	.507	13	422	312	180	2570	2686	515	653	26	3.22
Barnes, Junie-Junie Shoaf (Lefty)	34CinN	12-01-11	Linwood, N.C.	12-31-63	L	L	6'	170	0	0	—	0	2	0	0	0.1	0	1	0	0	0.00
Barnes, Virgil-Virgil Jennings (Zeke)	19-20,22-28NYN 28BosN	03-05-97	Ontario, Kans.	07-24-58	R	R	6'6	165	61	59	.508	11	205	134	58	1094	1192	293	275	7	3.66
Barnhart, Ed-Edgar Vernon	24StLA	09-16-04	Providence, Mo.	09-14-84	R	R	5'10	160	0	0	—	0	1	0	0	1	2	0	0	0	6.75
Barnhart, Les-Leslie Earl (Barney)	28,30CleA	02-23-05	Hoxie, Kans.	10-11-71	R	R	6'	180	1	1	.500	0	17	2	1	25	18	2	6	0	6.75
Barnicle, George-George Bernard	39-41BosN	08-26-17	Fitchburg, Mass.	10-10-90	R	R	6'2	175	3	3	.500	2	20	4	1	58	49	43	28	0	6.55
Barr, Bob-Robert Alexander	35BknN	03-12-08	Newton, Mass.	08-01-02	R	R	6'	175	0	0	—	0	2	0	0	2	5	2	0	0	4.50
Barrett, Dick-Tracey Souter (Kewpie) (Played as Dick Oliver 33-34)	33PhiA 34BosN 43ChiN 43-45PhiN	09-28-06	Montoursville, Pa.	10-30-66	R	R	5'9	175	35	58	.376	2	141	91	32	729	752	320	271	3	4.30
Barrett, Frank-Francis Joseph	39StLN 44-45BosA 46BosN 50PitN	07-01-13	Ft. Lauderdale, Fla.	03-06-98	R	R	6'2	173	15	17	.469	12	104	2	1	218	211	90	69	0	3.51
Barrett, Red-Charles Henry	37-40CinN 43-45BosN 45-46StLN 47-49BosN	02-14-15	Santa Barbara, Cal.	07-28-90	R	R	5'11	183	69	69	.500	7	253	149	67	1263	1292	312	333	11	3.53
Barthelson, Bob-Robert Edward	44NYN	07-15-24	New Haven, Conn.	04-14-00	R	R	6'	185	1	1	.500	0	7	1	0	13	13	5	4	0	4.50
Bartholomew, Les-Lester Justin	28PitN 32ChiA	04-04-03	Madison, Wis.	09-19-72	R	L	6'	195	0	0	—	0	9	0	0	28	36	15	7	0	6.75
Bass, Dick-Richard William	39WasA	07-07-06	Rogersville, Tenn.	03-03-89	R	R	6'2	175	0	1	.000	0	1	1	0	8	7	6	4	0	6.75
Batchelder, Joe-Joseph Edmund (Win)	23-25BosN	07-11-98	Wentham, Mass.	05-05-89	R	L	5'7	165	1	0	1.000	0	11	1	0	21	26	4	6	0	5.66
Bauers, Russ-Russell Lee	36-41PitN 44-45MS 46CinN 50StLA	05-10-14	Townsend, Wis.	01-21-95	L	R	6'3	195	31	30	.508	6	129	71	27	599	562	271	300	5	3.53
Baumgartner, Harry-Harry Edward	20DetA	10-08-92	S. Pittsburg, Tenn.	12-03-30	R	R	5'11	175	0	1	.000	0	18	0	0	18	18	6	7	0	4.00
Baumgartner, Stan-Stanwood Fulton	14-16,21-22PhiN 17-20VR 24-26PhiA	12-14-92	Houston, Tex.	10-04-55	L	L	6'1	185	27	21	.563	7	143	42	18	506	553	185	129	3	3.70
Bayne, Bill-William Lear (Beverly)	19-24StLA 28CleA 29-30BosA	04-18-99	Pittsburgh, Pa.	05-22-81	L	L	5'9	160	31	32	.492	8	198	55	22	661	710	296	259	2	4.82
Beall, Walter-Walter Esau	24-27NYA 29WasA	07-29-99	Washington, D.C.	01-28-59	R	R	5'10	178	5	5	.500	1	36	12	1	124	110	111	85	0	4.43
Bean, Belve-Beveric Benton (Bill)	30-31,33-35CleA 35WasA	04-23-05	Mullin, Tex.	06-01-88	R	R	6'2	197	11	7	.611	2	86	8	2	235	288	96	89	0	5.32
Beazley, Johnny-John Andrew	41-42,46StLN 43-45MS 47-49BosN	05-25-18	Nashville, Tenn.	04-21-90	R	R	6'2	190	31	12	.721	3	76	46	21	374	349	157	147	3	3.01
Beck, Boom-Boom-Walter William	24,27-28StLA 33-34BknN 39-43PhiN 44DetA 45CinN 45PitN	10-16-04	Decatur, Ill.	05-07-87	R	R	6'2	200	38	69	.355	6	265	101	44	1034	1121	342	352	3	4.30
Beckman (Boeckman), Jim-(Reinhardt)-James Joseph	27-28CinN	03-01-05	Cincinnati, Ohio	12-05-74	R	R	5'10	172	0	2	.000	0	10	1	0	28	37	15	4	0	5.86
Beckmann, Bill-William Aloys	39-42PhiA 42StLN	12-08-07	Clayton, Mo.	01-02-90	R	R	6'	175	21	25	.457	2	90	44	17	440	499	119	108	4	4.79
Bedgood, Phil-Philip Burlette	22-23CleA	03-08-99	Harrison, Ga.	05-08-27	R	R	6'3	218	1	2	.333	0	10	3	1	28	23	18	12	0	4.88
Bedner, Andy-Andrew Jackson	30-31PitN	08-16-08	Streator, Ill.	11-25-37	R	R	5'11	180	0	0	—	0	5	0	0	5	14	1	3	0	15.19
Beggs, Joe-Joseph Stanley	38NYA 40-44,46-47CinN 45MS 47-48BosN	11-04-10	Rankin, Pa.	07-19-83	R	R	6'2	182	48	35	.578	29	238	41	23	694	687	189	178	4	2.96
Behan, Petie-Charles Frederick	21-23PhiN	12-11-87	Dallas City, Pa.	01-22-57	R	R	5'10	160	7	15	.318	2	40	24	9	189	248	72	43	1	4.76
Bell, Hi-Herman S.	24,26-27,29-30StLN 32-34BknN	07-16-97	Mt. Sherman, Ky.	06-07-49	R	R	6'	185	32	34	.485	24	221	47	14	663	743	143	191	1	3.69
Benge, Ray-Raymond Adelphia (Silent Cal)	25-26CleA 28-32PhiN 33-35BknN 36BosN 36PhiN 38CinN	04-22-02	Jacksonville, Tex.	06-27-97	R	R	5'9	160	101	130	.437	19	346	247	102	1875	2177	598	655	12	4.52
Bennett, Bugs-Joseph Harley (Played as Bugs Morris 21)	18,21StLA 21ChiA	04-19-92	Kansas City, Mo.	11-21-57	R	R	6'	163	0	5	.000	0	10	5	1	34	42	29	5	0	6.68
Bennett, Frank-Francis Allen (Chip)	27-28BosA	10-27-04	Mardela Springs, Md.	03-18-66	R	R	5'10	163	0	1	.000	0	13	1	0	36	16	6	1	0	2.70
Benson, Allen-Allen Wilbert (Bullet Ben)	34WasA	03-28-08	Hurley, S.D.	11-16-99	R	R	6'1	185	0	1	.000	0	2	2	0	10	19	5	4	0	11.70
Bentley, Jack-John Needles (See B20-45)	13-16WasA 23-25NYN 26PhiN 26-27NYN	03-08-95	Sandy Spring, Md.	10-24-69	L	L	6'	200	46	34	.575	9	138	89	39	714	761	263	259	4	4.01
Benton, Al-John Alton	34-35PhiA 38-42,45-48DetA 43-44MS 49-50CleA 52BosA	03-18-11	Noble, Okla.	04-14-68	R	R	6'5	220	98	88	.527	66	455	167	58	1689	1672	733	697	10	3.66
Benton, Larry-Lawrence James	23-27,35BosN 27-30NYN 30-34CinN	11-20-97	St. Louis, Mo.	04-03-53	R	R	5'11	165	127	128	.498	22	455	261	123	2297	2559	691	670	13	4.03
Benton, Sid-Sidney Wright	22WasA	08-04-94	Buckner, Ark.	03-08-77	R	R	6'2	170	0	0	—	0	3	0	0	2	4	6	1	0	9.00
Berly, Jack-John Chambers	24StLN 31NYN 32-33PhiN	05-24-03	Natchitoches, La.	06-26-77	R	R	6'	190	10	13	.435	2	65	18	6	215	245	98	66	2	5.02
Berry, Joe-Jonas Arthur (Jittery Joe)	42ChiN 44-46PhiA 46CleA	12-16-04	Huntsville, Ark.	09-27-58	R	R	5'10	145	21	22	.488	18	133	0	0	294	246	87	117	0	2.45
Bertrand, Lefty-Roman Mathias	36PhiN	02-28-09	Cobden, Minn.	03-17-02	R	L	6'	180	0	0	—	0	3	0	0	4	2	1	1	0	9.00
Besse, Herman-Herman (Long Herm)	40-43,46PhiA 44-45MS	08-16-11	St. Louis, Mo.	08-13-72	L	L	6'2	190	5	15	.250	2	65	25	5	243	298	128	118	0	6.96
Betts, Huck-Walter McKinley	20-25PhiN 32-35BosN	02-18-97	Millsboro, Del.	06-13-87	L	R	5'11	170	61	68	.473	16	307	125	53	1581	321	323	323	8	3.93
Bevil (Bevilacqua), Lou-Louis Eugene	42WasA 43-45MS	11-27-22	Nelson, Ill.	02-01-73	B	R	6'	190	0	1	.000	0	4	1	0	10	11	2	4	0	6.30
Biemiller, Harry-Harry Lee	20WasA 25ChiN	10-09-97	Baltimore, Md.	05-25-65	R	R	6'1	171	1	0	1.000	0	7	2	1	16	34	19	0	0	4.22
Bigbee, Lyle-Lyle Randolph (Al) 22 played in N.F.L.	20PhiA 21PitN	08-22-94	Waterloo, Ore.	08-05-42	L	R	6'	180	1	3	.250	0	17	0	0	53	70	29	13	0	6.96
Biggs, Charlie-Charls Orval	32ChiA	09-15-06	Franch Lick, Ind.	05-24-54	R	R	6'1	185	1	1	.500	0	6	4	0	25	32	12	1	0	6.84
Bildilli, Emil-Emil (Hill Billy)	37-41StLA	09-16-12	Diamond, Ind.	09-16-46	L	R	5'10	170	4	8	.333	1	41	17	7	148	184	75	55	0	5.84
Billings, Haskell-Haskell Clark	27-29DetA	04-26-07	New York, N.Y.	12-26-83	R	R	5'11	170	10	15	.400	1	39	25	8	197	209	107	67	1	5.03
Bird, Red-James Edward	21WasA	04-25-90	Stephenville, Tex.	03-23-72	L	L	5'11	170	0	0	—	0	1	0	0	5	5	5	0	0	5.40
Birkofer, Ralph-Ralph Joseph (Lefty)	33-36PitN 37BknN	11-05-08	Cincinnati, Ohio	03-16-71	L	L	5'11	213	31	28	.525	2	132	63	24	544	618	175	224	2	4.19

USE NAMES - GIVEN NAMES (NICKNAMES)	TEAM BY YEAR	BIRTH DATE	BIRTHPLACE	DEATH DATE	B	T	HGT	WGT	W	L	Pct.	SV	G	GS	CG	IP	H	BB	SO	ShO	ERA
Bishop, Bill-William Henry (Lefty)	21PhiA	10-22-00	Houtzdale, Pa.	02-14-56	L	L	5'9	185	0	0	—	0	2	0	0	7	8	10	4	0	9.00
Bishop, Jim-James Morton	23-24PhiN	01-28-98	Montgomery City, Mo.	09-17-73	R	R	6'	185	0	4	.000	0	22	1	0	50	72	18	8	0	6.30
Bithorn, Hi-Hiram Gabriel [Sosa]	42-43ChiN 44-45MS 46ChiN 47ChiA	03-18-16	Santurce, P.R.	12-30-51	R	R	6'1	200	34	31	.523	5	105	53	30	510	517	171	185	8	3.16
Bivin, Jim-James Nathaniel	35PhiN	12-11-09	Jackson, Miss.	11-07-82	R	R	6'	155	2	9	.182	1	47	14	0	162	220	65	54	0	5.78
Black, Don-Donald Paul	43-45PhiA 46-48CleA	07-20-16	Salix, Iowa	04-21-59	R	R	6'	185	34	55	.382	1	154	113	37	797	803	400	293	4	4.35
Blackburne, Lena-Russell Aubrey (Slats) (See B01-19)	29,M28-29ChiA	10-23-86	Clifton Hts., Pa.	02-29-68	R	R	5'11	160	0	0	—	0	1	0	0	0.1	1	0	0	0	0.00
Blaeholder, George-George Franklin	25,27-35StLA 35PhiA 36CleA	01-26-04	Orange, Cal.	12-29-47	R	R	5'11	175	104	125	.454	12	338	251	106	1913	2220	535	572	13	4.54
Blake, Sheriff-John Frederick	20PitN 24-31ChiN 31PhiN 37StLA 37StLN	09-17-99	Ansted, W.Va.	10-31-82	B	R	6'	180	87	102	.460	8	304	195	81	1619	1766	767	621	11	4.14
Blanche (Bilangio), Al-Prosper Albert	35-36BosN	09-21-09	Somerville, Mass.	04-02-97	R	R	6'	178	0	1	.000	1	17	0	0	33	34	13	8	0	3.82
Blankenship, Homer-Homer (Si)	22-23ChiA 28PitN	08-04-02	Bonham, Tex.	06-22-74	R	R	6'	185	1	3	.250	1	13	2	1	40	57	15	10	0	5.18
Blankenship, Ted-Theodore	22-30ChiA	05-10-01	Bonham, Tex.	01-14-45	R	R	6'1	170	77	79	.494	4	241	156	73	1321	1462	489	378	8	4.32
Blanton, Cy-Darrel Elijah	34-39PitN 40-42PhiN	07-06-08	Waurika, Okla.	09-13-45	L	R	5'11	180	68	71	.489	2	202	167	70	1219	1243	337	611	14	3.55
Blethen, Clarence-Clarence Waldo (Climax)	23BosA 29BknN	07-11-93	Dover-Foxcroft, Me.	04-11-73	L	R	5'11	165	0	0	—	0	3	0	0	20	33	10	2	0	7.20
Blume, Clint-Clinton Willis	22-23NYN	10-17-98	Brooklyn, N.Y.	06-12-73	R	R	5'11	175	3	0	1.000	0	13	2	1	33	29	21	4	0	3.00
Boerner, Larry-Lawrence Hyer	32BosA	01-21-05	Staunton, Va.	10-16-69	R	R	6'4	175	0	4	.000	0	21	5	0	61	71	37	19	0	5.02
Bogart, John-John Renzie (Big John)	20DetA	09-21-00	Bloomsburg, Pa.	12-07-86	R	R	6'2	195	2	1	.667	0	4	2	0	24	16	18	5	0	3.00
Boggs, Ray-Raymond Joseph (Lefty)	28BosN	12-12-04	Reamsville, Kans.	11-27-89	L	L	6'	170	0	0	—	0	5	2		10	12	7	0	0	5.40
Bokina, Joe-Joseph	36WasA	04-04-10	Northampton, Mass.	10-25-91	R	R	6'	184	0	2	.000	0	5	1	0	8	15	6	5	0	9.00
Bolen, Stew-Stewart O'Neal	26-27StLA 31-32PhiN	10-12-02	Jackson, Ala.	08-30-69	L	L	5'11	180	3	13	.188	0	41	17	3	140	170	84	72	1	6.04
Bonetti, Julio-Julio Giacomo	37-38StLA 40ChiN	07-14-11	Genoa, Italy	06-18-52	R	R	6'	180	6	14	.300	1	46	16	7	172	234	77	50	0	6.07
Boney, Hank-Henry Tate	27NYN	10-28-03	Wallace, N.C.	06-12-02	R	R	5'11	176	0	0	—	0	3	0	0	4	4	2	0	0	2.25
Bonham, Ernie-Ernest (Tiny)	40-46NYA 47-49PitN	08-16-13	Ione, Cal.	09-15-49	R	R	6'2	215	103	72	.589	9	231	193	110	1553	1501	287	478	21	3.06
Bonness, Bill-William John (Lefty)	44CleA	12-15-23	Cleveland, Ohio	12-03-77	R	L	6'4	200	0	1	.000	0	1	0	0	7	11	5	1	0	7.71
Bono, Gus-Adlai Wendell	20WasA	08-29-94	Doe Run, Mo.	12-03-48	R	R	5'11	175	0	2	.000	0	4	1	0	12	17	6	4	0	9.00
Boone, Danny-James Albert	19PhiA 21DetA 22-23CleA	01-19-95	Samantha, Ala.	05-11-68	R	R	6'2	190	8	13	.381	1	42	16	4	162	205	62	25	0	5.11
Borowy, Hank-Henry Ludwig	42-45NYA 45-48ChiN 45-50PhiN 50PitN 50-51DetA	05-12-16	Bloomfield, N.J.	08-23-04	R	R	6'	175	108	82	.568	7	314	214	94	1715	1660	623	690	17	3.50
Bosser, Mel-Melvin Edward	45CinN	02-08-14	Johnstown, Pa.	03-26-86	R	R	6'	173	2	0	1.000	0	7	2	0	16	9	17	3	0	3.38
Bowers, Stew-Stewart Cole (Doc)	35-37BosA	02-26-15	New Freedom, Pa.	12-14-05	B	R	6'	170	2	1	.667	0	15	2	1	30	36	19	5	0	4.50
Bowler, Grant-Grant Tierney (Moose)	31-32ChiA	10-24-07	Denver, Colo.	06-25-68	R	R	6'	190	0	1	.000	0	17	3	1	41	55	27	17	0	7.02
Bowles, Charlie-Charles James	43PhiA 44MS 45PhiA	03-15-17	Norwood, Mass.	12-23-03	R	R	6'3	180	1	4	.200	0	10	6	3	51	52	27	17	0	4.41
Bowles, Emmett-Emmett Jerome (Chief)	22ChiA	08-02-98	Wanette, Okla.	09-03-59	R	R	6'	180	0	0	—	0	1	0	0	1	2	1	0	0	27.00
Bowman, Bob-Robert James	39-40StLN 41NYN 42ChiN	10-03-10	Keystone, W.Va.	09-04-72	R	R	5'10	160	26	17	.605	10	109	38	13	364	360	139	146	2	3.83
Bowman, Joe-Joseph Emil (See B20-45)	32PhiA 34NYN 35-36PhiN 37-41PhiN 44-45BosA 45CinN	06-17-10	Argentine, Kans.	11-22-90	L	R	6'2	190	77	96	.445	11	298	184	74	1465	1656	484	502	5	4.40
Boyles, Harry-Harry (Stretch)	38-39ChiA	11-29-11	Granite City, Ill.	01-07-05	R	R	6'5	185	0	4	.000	0	11	2	1	32	35	31	19	0	5.91
Bradley, Herb-Herbert Theodore	27-29BosA	01-03-03	Agenda, Kans.	10-16-58	R	R	6'	170	1	4	.200	0	24	7	3	74	87	25	20	1	5.96
Bradshaw, Joe-Joe Siah	29BknN	08-17-97	Ro Ellen, Tenn.	01-30-85	R	R	6'4	200	0	0	—	0	2	0	0	4	3	4	1	0	4.50
Brady, Neal-Cornelius Joseph	15,17NYA 18MS 25CinN	03-04-97	Covington, Ky.	06-19-47	R	R	6'	197	2	3	.400	1	24	5	2	82	88	32	22	0	4.17
Brame, Erv-Ervin Beckham	28-32PitN	10-12-01	Big Rock, Tenn.	11-22-49	L	R	6'2	190	52	37	.584	1	142	91	62	793	946	232	188	3	4.76
Branch, Norm-Norman Downs (Red)	41-42NYA 43-45MS	03-22-15	Spokane, Wash.	11-21-75	R	R	6'3	200	5	2	.714	4	37	0	0	63	55	42	41	0	3.71
Brandt, Bill-William George	41-43PitN 44-45MS	03-21-15	Augora, Ind.	05-16-68	R	R	5'8	170	5	3	.625	4	34	7	1	80	85	27	21	0	3.60
Brandt, Ed-Edward Arthur (Dutch)	28-35BosN 36BknN 37-38PitN	02-17-05	Spokane, Wash.	11-01-44	L	L	6'	175	121	146	.453	17	378	279	150	2268	2342	778	877	18	3.86
Braxton, Garland-Edgar Garland — Bats Left 27-30	21-22BosN 25-26NYA 27-30WasA 30-31ChiA 31,33StLA	06-10-00	Snow Camp, N.C.	02-25-66	B	L	5'11	152	50	53	.485	32	283	71	28	938	1014	276	412	2	4.13
Breckinridge, Bill-William Robertson	29PhiA	10-16-07	Tulsa, Okla.	08-23-58	R	R	5'11	175	0	0	—	0	3	1	0	10	10	16	2	0	8.10
Brennan, Don-James Donald	33NYA 34-37CinN 37NYN	12-02-03	Augusta, Me.	04-26-53	R	R	6'	220	21	12	.636	19	141	26	7	396	436	180	172	1	4.20
Brenton, Lynn-Lynn Davis (Buck, Herb)	13,15CleA 20-21CinN	10-07-89	Peoria, Ill.	10-14-68	R	R	5'10	165	5	12	.294	2	34	15	4	131	161	41	52	1	3.98
Brett, Herb-Herbert James (Duke)	24-25ChiN	05-23-00	Lawrenceville, Va.	11-25-74	R	R	6'	175	1	1	.500	0	17	2	0	22	18	10	7	0	4.09
Breuer, Marv-Marvin Howard (Baby Face)	39-43NYA	04-29-14	Rolla, Mo.	01-17-91	R	R	6'2	185	25	26	.490	3	86	60	23	484	487	154	226	1	4.04
Brewer, Jack-Jack Herndon (Buddy)	44-46NYN	04-21-18	Spokane, Wash.	11-30-03	R	R	6'2	170	9	10	.474	4	43	28	10	217	231	76	73	0	4.35
Bridges, Tommy-Thomas Jefferson Davis	30-46DetA 44MS 45-46DetA	12-28-06	Gordonsville, Tenn.	04-19-68	R	R	5'10	155	194	138	.584	14	424	362	200	2827	2675	1192	1674	32	3.57
Brillheart, Jim-James Benson (Buck)	22-23WasA 27ChiN 31BosN	09-28-03	Dublin, Va.	09-02-72	R	L	5'11	170	8	9	.471	1	86	23	7	287	314	137	98	0	4.17
Broaca, Johnny-John Joseph	34-37NYA 39CleA	10-03-09	Lawrence, Mass.	05-16-85	R	R	5'11	190	44	29	.603	3	121	86	42	674	748	255	258	4	4.09
Brondell, Ken-Kenneth LeRoy	44NYN	10-17-21	Bradshaw, Neb.	10-03-04	R	R	6'1	195	0	1	.000	0	7	1	0	19	27	8	1	0	8.53
Brown, Bob-Robert Murray	30-36BosN	04-01-11	Dorchester, Mass.	08-17-90	R	R	6'	190	16	21	.432	1	79	49	13	363	360	193	159	2	4.49
Brown, Clint-Clinton Harold	28-35CleA 36-40ChiA 41-42CleA	07-08-03	Blackash, Pa.	12-31-55	R	R	6'	190	89	93	.489	64	434	130	67	1485	1740	368	410	7	4.27
Brown, Joe-Joseph Henry (Smokey, Bullet)	27ChiA	07-03-00	Little Rock, Ark.	03-07-50	R	R	6'	176	0	0	—	0	1	0	0	0	2	1	0	0	∞
Brown, Jumbo-Walter George (Curley)	25ChiN 27-28CleA 32-33,35-36NYA 37CinN 37-41NYN	04-30-07	Greene, R.I.	10-02-66	R	R	6'4	260	33	31	.516	29	249	23	7	598	619	300	301	1	4.06
Brown, Lloyd-Lloyd Andrew (Gimpy)	25BknN 28-32WasA 33StLA 33BosA 34-37CleA 40PhiN	12-25-04	Beeville, Tex.	01-14-74	L	L	5'9	170	91	105	.464	21	404	181	77	1693	1899	590	510	10	4.20
Brown, Mace-Mace Stanley	35-41PitN 41BknN 42-43,46BosA 44-45MS	05-21-09	N. English, Iowa	03-24-02	R	R	6'1	190	76	57	.571	48	387	55	18	1075	1125	388	435	3	3.47
Brown, Myrl-Myrl Lincoln	22PhiN	10-10-94	Waynesboro, Pa.	02-23-81	R	R	5'11	172	3	1	.750	0	7	5	2	35	42	13	9	0	5.91
Bruner, Roy-Walter Roy	39-41PhiN 42-45MS	02-10-17	Cecilia, Ky.	11-30-86	R	R	6'	165	0	7	.000	0	19	5	2	62	80	44	28	0	5.81
Bryant, Clay-Claiborne Henry	35-40ChiN	11-16-11	Madison Hts., Va.	04-09-99	R	R	6'2	195	32	20	.615	7	129	44	23	542	511	262	272	4	3.74
Buckeye, Garland-Garland Maiers (Gob) — 20-24 played in N.F.L., 26 played in A.F.L.	18WasA 25-28CleA 28NYN	10-16-97	Heron Lake, Minn.	11-14-75	B	L	6'	260	30	39	.435	1	108	67	29	565	622	214	134	4	3.90
Buker, Cy-Cyril Owen	45BknN	02-05-19	Greenwood, Wis.		R	R	5'11	190	7	2	.778	3	42	4	1	87	90	45	48	0	3.31
Bullock, Red-Malton Joseph	36PhiA	10-12-11	Biloxi, Miss.	06-27-88	L	L	6'1	192	0	2	.000	0	12	2	0	17	19	37	7	0	13.76
Burkart, Elmer-Elmer Robert (Swede)	36-39PhiN	02-01-17	Philadelphia, Pa.	02-06-95	R	R	6'2	190	1	1	.500	0	16	3	1	42	47	26	9	0	4.93
Burke, Bobby-Robert James (Lefty)	27-35WasA 37PhiN	01-23-07	Joliet, Ill.	02-08-71	L	L	6'2	150	38	46	.452	5	253	88	27	917	926	360	299	4	4.30
Burns, Denny-Dennis Jr.	23-24PhiA	05-24-98	Tiff City, Mo.	05-21-69	R	R	5'10	180	8	9	.471	1	41	20	9	181	212	75	34	0	4.62
Burrows, John-John	43PhiA 43-44ChiN	10-30-13	Winnfield, La.	04-27-87	R	L	5'10	200	0	3	.000	2	30	2	0	43	40	28	22	0	5.65
Burwell, Bill-William Edwin	20-21StLA 28,M47PitN	03-27-95	Jarbalo, Kans.	06-11-73	L	R	5'11	175	9	8	.529	6	70	6	1	218	253	79	49	0	4.38
Bush, Guy-Guy Terrell (The Mississippi Mudcat)	23-34ChiN 35-36PitN 36-37BosN 38StLN 38StLA 45CinN	08-23-01	Aberdeen, Miss.	07-02-85	R	R	6'	175	176	136	.564	34	542	308	151	2722	2950	859	850	16	3.86
Bush, Bullet Joe-Leslie Ambrose	12-17PhiA 18-21BosA 22-24NYA 25StLA 26WasA 26-27PitN 27NYN 28PhiA	11-27-92	Brainerd, Minn.	11-01-74	R	R	5'9	173	195	183	.516	18	489	370	225	3093	3001	1263	1319	35	3.51
Bushey, Frank-Francis Clyde	27,30BosA	08-01-06	Wheaton, Kans.	03-18-72	R	R	6'	180	0	1	.000	0	12	0	0	31	36	17	4	0	6.39
Butcher, Max-Albert Maxwell	36-38BknN 38-39PhiN 39-45PitN	09-21-10	Holden, W.Va.	09-15-57	R	R	6'2	220	95	106	.473	9	334	228	104	1787	1935	583	485	15	3.73
Butland, Bill-Wilburn Rue	40,42BosA 43-45MS 46-47PhiN	03-22-18	Terre Haute, Ind.	09-19-97	R	R	6'5	180	9	3	.750	1	32	15	7	150	138	56	62	2	3.90
Butler, Charlie-Charles Thomas (Lefty)	33PhiN	05-12-05	Green Cove Spr., Fla.	05-10-64	R	L	6'	210	0	0	—	0	1	0	0	1	1	2	0	0	9.00
Byrne, Jerry-Gerald Wilford	29ChiA	02-02-07	Parnell, Mich.	08-11-55	R	R	6'	170	0	1	.000	0	2	1	1	11	6	1	1	0	7.71
Cadore, Leon-Leon Joseph	15-23BknN 23ChiN 24NYN	11-20-90	Chicago, Ill.	03-16-58	R	R	6'1	190	68	72	.486	3	192	147	83	1257	1273	289	445	10	3.14
Cain, Sugar-Merritt Patrick — Bats Both 32-33	32-35PhiA 35-36StLA 36-38ChiA	04-05-07	Macon, Ga.	04-03-75	B	R	5'11	190	53	60	.469	1	178	137	58	989	1119	569	279	2	4.82
Caldwell, Charlie-Charles William	25NYA	08-02-01	Bristol, Va.	11-01-57	R	R	5'11	190	0	0	—	0	3	0	0	3	7	1	1	0	15.00
Caldwell, Earl-Earl Walton (Teach)	28PhiN 35-37StLA 45-48ChiA 48BosA	04-09-05	Sparks, Tex.	09-15-81	R	R	6'1	178	33	43	.434	25	200	49	18	582	656	259	202	5	4.68
Caligiuri, Fred-Frederick John	41-42PhiA 43-46MS	10-22-18	West Hickory, Pa.		R	R	6'	190	2	5	.286	1	18	7	4	80	90	32	24	0	4.50
Callahan, Joe-Joseph Thomas	39-40BosN	10-18-16	East Boston, Mass.	05-24-49	R	R	6'2	170	1	2	.333	0	13	3	1	32	37	16	11	0	6.47
Campbell, Archie-Archibald Stewart (Iron Man)	28NYA 29WasA 30CinN	10-20-03	Maplewood, N.J.	11-22-89	R	R	6'	180	2	6	.250	1	40	4	1	86	111	47	29	0	5.86
Campbell, John-John Millard	33WasA	09-13-07	Washington, D.C.	04-24-95	R	R	6'1	184	0	0	—	0	1	1	0	1	1	0	0	0	0.00
Cantrell, Guy-Guy Dewey (Gunner)	25BknN	04-09-04	Clarita, Okla.	01-31-61	R	R	6'	190	2	7	.222	3	38	9	1	99	115	47	45	0	4.27
Cantwell, Ben-Benjamin Caldwell	27-28NYN 28-36BosN 37NYN 37BknN	04-13-02	Milan, Tenn.	12-04-62	R	R	6'1	168	76	108	.413	21	316	163	75	1533	1640	382	348	6	3.91
Caraway, Pat-Cecil Bradford Patrick	30-32ChiN	09-26-05	Gordon, Tex.	06-09-74	L	L	6'4	180	22	40	.355	3	108	62	21	478	542	195	151	2	5.35
Cardoni, Ben-Armond Joseph (Big Ben)	43-45BosN	08-21-20	Jessup, Pa.	04-02-69	R	R	6'	195	0	6	.000	1	17	1	0	108	127	54	34	0	4.75
Carleton, Tex-James Otto	32-34StLN 35-38ChiN 40BknN	08-19-06	Comanche, Tex.	01-11-77	R	R	6'1	180	100	76	.568	2	293	202	91	1607	1630	561	808	16	3.91
Carlson, Hal-Harold Gust	17-23PitN 24-27PhiN 27-30ChiN	05-17-92	Rockford, Ill.	05-28-30	R	R	6'	180	114	120	.487	19	377	235	121	2002	2256	498	590	17	3.97
Carlson, Leon-Leon Alton (Swede)	20WasA	02-17-95	Jamestown, N.Y.	09-15-61	R	R	6'3	195	0	0	—	0	3	0	0	12	14	2	3	0	3.75

USE NAMES - GIVEN NAMES (NICKNAMES)	TEAM BY YEAR	BIRTH DATE	BIRTHPLACE	DEATH DATE	B	T	HGT	WGT	W	L	Pct.	SV	G	GS	CG	IP	H	BB	SO	ShO	ERA
Carnett, Eddie-Edwin Elliott (Lefty)	41BosN 44ChiA 45CleA 46MS	10-21-16	Springfield, Mo.		L	L	6'	185	0	0	—	0	6	0	0	5	7	3	4	0	9.00
Carpenter, Bob-Robert Louis	40-42NYN 43-45MS 46-47NYN 47ChiN	12-12-17	Chicago, Ill.	10-19-05	R	R	6'3	195	25	20	.556	2	80	54	23	400	411	132	134	4	3.60
Carpenter, Lew-Lewis Emmett	43WasA	08-16-13	Woodstock, Ga.	04-25-79	R	R	6'2	195	0	0	—	0	4	0	0	3	1	4	1	0	4.00
Carrasquel, Alex-Alejandro Eloy [Aparicio]	39-45WasA 46-48SM 49ChiA	07-24-12	Caracas, Venezuela	08-19-69	R	R	6'1	182	50	39	.562	16	258	64	30	861	887	347	252	4	3.73
Carroll, Ed-Edgar Fleischer	29BosA	07-27-07	Baltimore, Md.	10-13-84	R	R	6'3	185	1	0	1.000	0	24	2	0	67	77	20	13	0	5.64
Carroll, Ownie-Owen Thomas	25,27-30DetA 30NYA 30-32CinN 33-34BknN	11-02-06	Kearny, N.J.	06-08-75	R	R	5'10	185	65	89	.422	5	248	153	71	1330	1532	486	311	2	4.43
Carter, Arnold-Arnold Lee (Lefty, Hook)	44-45CinN	03-14-18	Rainelle, W.Va.	04-12-89	L	L	5'10	170	13	11	.542	3	46	24	11	195	197	53	37	4	2.72
Carter, Sol-Solomon Mobley (Buck)	31PhiA	12-23-08	Picayune, Miss.	05-22-02	R	R	6'4	178	0	0	—	0	2	0	0	2	1	4	1	0	22.50
Cascarella, Joe-Joseph Thomas (Crooning Joe)	34-35PhiA 35-36BosA 36-37WasA 37-38CinN	06-28-07	Philadelphia, Pa.		R	R	5'10	175	27	48	.360	8	143	54	20	540	602	267	192	3	4.85
Casey, Hugh-Hugh Thomas	35CinN 39-42BknN 43-45MS 46-48BknN 49PitN 49NYA	10-14-13	Atlanta, Ga.	07-03-51	R	R	6'1	207	75	42	.641	55	343	56	24	940	935	321	349	3	3.45
Caster, George- George Jasper	34-35,37-40PhiA 41-45StLA 45-46DetA	08-04-07	Colton, Cal.	12-18-55	R	R	6'1	180	76	100	.432	39	376	127	62	1376	1469	597	595	6	4.55
Castleman, Slick-Clydell	34-39NYN	09-08-13	Donelson, Tenn.	03-02-98	R	R	6'2	180	36	26	.581	4	121	78	25	588	644	223	225	4	4.24
Castner, Paul-Paul Henry (Lefty)	23ChiA	02-16-97	St. Paul, Minn.	03-03-86	L	L	5'11	187	0	0	—	0	6	0	0	10	14	5	0	0	6.30
Cathey, Hardin-Hardin Abner (L'il Abner)	23ChiA	07-16-19	Burns, Tenn.	07-27-97	R	R	6'	190	1	1	.500	0	2	2	0	30	44	16	8	0	7.50
Causey, Red-Cecil Algernon	18-19NYN 19BosN 20-21PhiN 21-22NYN	08-11-93	Georgetown, Fla.	11-11-60	R	R	6'2	190	39	35	.527	6	131	80	35	649	666	230	139	3	3.59
Cecil, Rex-Rex Holston	44-45BosA	10-08-16	Lindsay, Okla.	10-30-66	L	R	6'3	195	6	10	.375	0	18	16	5	106	118	60	63	0	5.18
Center, Pete-Marvin Earl	42-43CleA 44MS 45-46CleA	04-22-12	Hazel Green, Ky.	08-08-04	R	R	6'4	205	7	7	.500	3	77	9	2	160	154	70	50	0	4.11
Chagnon, Leon-Leon Wilbur (Shag)	29-30,32-34PitN 35NYN	09-28-02	Pittsfield, N.H.	07-30-53	R	R	6'	182	19	16	.543	3	135	21	8	393	443	104	153	1	4.51
Chamberlain, Bill-William Vincent	32ChiA	04-21-09	Stoughton, Mass.	02-06-94	R	L	5'10	173	0	5	.000	0	12	5	0	41	39	25	11	0	4.61
Chambers, Johnnie-Johnnie Monroe	37StLN	09-09-10	Copperhill, Tenn.	05-11-77	L	L	6'	185	0	0	—	0	2	0	0	2	5	2	1	0	18.00
Chandler, Spud-Spurgeon Ferdinand	37-47NYN	09-12-07	Commerce, Ga.	01-09-90	R	R	6'	181	109	43	.717	6	211	184	109	1485	1327	463	614	26	2.84
Chaplin, Tiny-James Bailey	28,30-31NYN 36BosN	07-13-05	Los Angeles, Cal.	03-25-39	R	R	6'1	195	15	23	.395	4	87	43	18	371	428	102	118	0	4.25
Chapman, Ben-William Benjamin (See B20-45)	44-45BknN 45-46, M45-48PhiN	12-25-08	Nashville, Tenn.	07-07-93	R	R	6'	190	8	6	.571	0	25	16	8	141	147	71	65	0	4.40
Chapman, Ed-Edwin Volney	33WasA	11-28-05	Courtland, Miss.	05-03-00	B	R	6'1	185	0	0	—	0	6	1	0	9	10	2	4	0	8.00
Chase, Ken-Kendall Fay (Lefty)	36-41WasA 42-43BosA 43NYN	10-06-13	Oneonta, N.Y.	01-16-85	R	L	6'2	210	53	84	.387	1	188	160	62	1165	1188	694	582	4	4.27
Cheeves, Virgil-Virgil Earl (Chief)	20-23ChiN 24CleA 27NYN	02-12-01	Oklahoma City, Okla.	05-05-79	R	R	6'	175	26	27	.491	2	111	55	18	458	526	188	98	2	4.74
Chelini, Italo-Italo Vincent (Lefty)	35-37ChiA	10-10-14	San Francisco, Cal.	08-25-72	L	L	5'10	175	4	4	.500	0	24	6	5	98	122	34	20	0	5.79
Chetkovich, Mitch-Mitchell	45PhiN	07-21-17	Fairpoint, Ohio	08-24-71	R	R	6'4	225	0	0	—	0	4	0	0	3	3	3	0	0	0.00
Child, Harry-Harry Patrick	30WasA	05-23-05	Baltimore, Md.	11-08-72	R	R	5'11	175	0	0	—	0	5	0	0	10	10	5	5	0	6.30
Christopher, Russ-Russell Ormand	42-47PhiA 48CleA 49IL		Richmond, Cal.	12-05-54	R	R	6'3	170	54	64	.458	35	241	97	46	999	931	399	424	3	3.37
Ciola, Lou-Louis Alexander	43PhiA 44-45MS	09-06-22	Norfolk, Va.	10-18-81	R	R	5'9	175	1	3	.250	0	12	3	2	44	48	22	7	0	5.52
Clark, Bob-Robert William	20-21CleA	08-22-97	Newport, R.I.	05-18-44	R	R	6'3	188	1	2	.333	1	16	2	2	51	82	19	10	1	5.47
Clark, Otie-William Otis	45BosA	04-25-15	Boscobel, Wis.		R	R	6'1	190	4	4	.500	0	12	9	4	82	86	19	20	1	3.07
Clark, Watty-William Watson (Lefty)	24CleA 27-33BknN 33-34NYN 34-37BknN	05-16-02	St. Joseph, La.	03-04-72	L	L	6'	175	111	97	.534	16	355	209	91	1748	1897	383	643	14	3.66
Clarke, Alan-Alan Thomas (Lefty)	21CinN	03-08-96	Clarksville, Md.	03-11-75	B	L	5'11	180	0	1	.000	0	1	1	1	5	7	2	1	0	5.40
Clarke, Rufe-Rufus Rivers	23-24DetA	04-13-00	Estill, S.C.	02-08-83	R	R	6'1	203	1	1	.500	0	7	0	0	11	9	11	3	0	5.40
Clarkson, Bill-William Henry (Blackie)	27-28NYN 28-29BosN	09-27-98	Portsmouth, Va.	08-27-71	R	R	5'11	160	3	12	.200	2	51	10	2	134	171	79	39	0	5.44
Claset, Gowell-Gowell Sylvester (Lefty)	33PhiA	11-16-07	Battle Creek, Mich.	03-08-81	B	L	6'3	210	0	1	0.000	0	8	1	0	11	23	11	1	0	9.82
Cleary, Joe-Joseph Christopher (Fire)	45WasA	12-03-18	Cork, Ireland	06-03-04	R	R	5'9	150	0	0	—	0	1	0	0	0.1	5	3	1	0	189.00
Clemensen, Bill-Wiliam Melville	39,41PitN 42-45MS 46PitN	06-20-19	New Brunswick, N.J.	02-18-94	R	R	6'1	193	1	1	.500	0	15	2	1	42	39	27	19	0	5.57
Clough, Ed-Edgar Goerge (Spec) (See B20-45)	25-26StLN	10-28-06	Wiconisco, Pa.	01-30-44	L	L	6'2	188	0	1	.000	0	4	0	0	12	16	8	3	0	10.50
Clowers, Bill-William Perry	26BosA	08-14-98	San Marcos, Tex.	01-13-78	L	L	5'11	175	0	0	—	0	2	0	0	2	2	0	0	0	0.00
Clyde, Tom-Thomas Knox	43PhiA 44-45MS	08-17-23	Wachapreague, Va.	10-01-05	R	R	6'3	190	4	0	—	0	4	0	0	6	7	4	0	0	9.00
Cobb, Herb-Herbert Edward	29StLA	08-06-04	Pinetops, N.C.	01-08-80	R	R	5'11	150	0	0	—	0	1	0	0	1	3	1	0	0	36.00
Coffman, Dick-Samuel Richard	27WasA 28-32StLA 32WasA 33-35StLA 36-39NYN 40BosN	12-18-06	Veto, Ala.	03-24-72	R	R	6'2	195	72	95	.431	38	472	132	47	1460	1782	463	372	9	4.65
Coffman, Slick-George David	37-39DetA 40StLA	12-11-10	Veto, Ala.	05-08-03	R	R	5'11	160	15	12	.556	3	121	16	3	314	400	132	89	0	5.59
Cohen, Sid-Sydney Harry	34,36-37WasA	05-07-06	Baltimore, Md.	04-09-88	B	L	5'11	180	3	7	.300	5	55	3	2	109	133	37	49	0	4.54
Cole, Bert-Albert George	21-25DetA 25CleA 27ChiA	07-01-96	San Francisco, Cal.	05-30-75	L	L	6'1	180	28	32	.467	10	176	47	17	605	734	230	119	4	4.67
Cole, (Kisleauskas), Ed-Edward William	38-39StLA	03-22-09	Wilkes-Barre, Pa.	07-28-99	R	R	5'11	170	1	7	.125	0	42	6	1	95	124	54	31	0	5.31
Collard, Hap-Earl Clinton	27-28CleA 30PhiN	08-29-98	Williams, Ariz.	07-07-68	R	R	6'	170	6	12	.333	2	35	15	4	136	200	46	28	0	6.62
Collier, Orlin-Orlin Edward	31DetA	02-17-07	East Prairie, Mo.	09-09-44	R	R	5'11	180	2	0	1.000	0	2	2	0	10	17	7	3	0	8.10
Collins, Phil-Philip Eugene (Fidgety Phil)	23ChiN 29-35PhiN 36StLN	08-27-01	Chicago, Ill.	08-14-48	R	R	5'11	175	80	85	.485	24	292	142	64	1323	1541	497	423	4	4.67
Collins, Rip-Harry Warren (Two Gun)	20-21NYA 22BosA 23-27DetA 29-31StLA	02-26-96	Weatherford, Tex.	05-27-68	R	R	6'1	205	108	82	.568	5	311	220	86	1712	1795	674	569	15	3.99
Comellas, Jorge-Jorge [Pous] (Pancho)	45ChiN	12-07-16	Havana, Cuba	09-13-01			Bats Both 20-23	185	0	2	.000	0	7	1	0	12	11	6	6	0	4.50
Conger, Dick-Richard	40DetA 41-42PitN 43PhiN 44-46MS	04-03-21	Los Angeles, Cal.	02-16-70	R	R	6'	185	3	7	.300	0	19	12	2	70	86	35	24	0	5.14
Conkwright, Allen-Allen Howard (Red)	20DetA	12-04-96	Sedalia, Mo.	07-30-91	R	R	5'10	170	2	1	.667	1	5	3	0	19	29	16	4	0	7.11
Connally, Sarge-George Walter	21,23-29ChiA 31-34CleA	08-31-98	McGregor, Tex.	01-27-78	R	R	5'11	170	49	60	.450	31	303	67	33	996	1108	453	346	2	4.30
Conway, Jerry-Jerome Patrick	20WasA	06-07-01	Holyoke, Mass.	04-16-80	L	L	6'2	190	0	0	—	0	1	0	0	2	1	1	0	0	0.00
Cook, Earl-Earl Davis	41DetA	12-10-08	Stouffville, Canada	11-21-96	R	R	6'	195	0	0	—	0	2	4	0	1	4	0	1	0	4.50
Coombs, Bobby-Raymond Franklin	33PhiA 43NYN	02-02-08	Goodwins Mills, Me.	10-21-91	R	R	5'9	160	0	2	.000	2	30	0	0	47	80	28	13	0	9.38
Cooney, Bob-Robert Daniel	31-32StLA	07-12-07	Glens Falls, N.Y.	05-04-76	R	R	5'11	160	1	5	.167	1	28	7	2	110	140	56	36	0	5.97
Cooney, Johnny-John Walter (See B20-45)	21-26,28,30BosN M49BosN 49ChiN	03-18-01	Cranston, R.I.	07-08-86	R	L	5'10	165	34	44	.436	4	159	75	44	796	858	223	224	7	3.72
Cooper, Mort-Morton Cecil	38-45StLN 45-47BosN 47NYN 49CinN	03-02-13	Atherton, Mo.	11-17-58	R	R	6'2	210	128	75	.631	14	295	239	128	1842	1666	571	913	32	2.97
Copeland, Mays-Mays	35StLN	08-31-13	Mt. View, Ark.	11-29-82	R	R	6'	180	0	0	—	0	1	0	0	1	2	0	0	0	9.00
Coppola, Henry-Henry Peter	35-36WasA	08-04-12	East Douglas, Mass.	07-10-90	R	R	5'11	175	3	4	.429	1	25	5	2	73	89	41	21	1	5.67
Couch, Johnny-John Daniel	17DetA 18MS 22-23CinN 23-25PhiN	03-31-91	Vaughn, Mont.	12-08-75	L	R	6'	180	29	34	.460	0	147	62	26	642	785	171	112	3	4.64
Courtney, Harry-Harry Seymour	19-22WasA 22ChiA	11-19-98	Asheville, N.C.	12-11-54	B	L	6'4	185	22	27	.449	1	94	53	21	444	518	213	112	2	4.91
Coveleski (Kowalewski), Stan (Stanislaus)-Stanley Anthony	12PhiA 16-24CleA 25-27WasA 28NYA	07-13-89	Shamokin, Pa.	03-20-84	R	R	5'11	166	216	143	.602	20	450	384	226	3092	3055	802	981	38	2.88
Covington, Chet-Chester Rogers (Chesty, The Great)	44PhiN	11-06-10	Cairo, Ill.	06-11-76	B	L	6'2	225	1	1	.500	0	19	0	0	39	46	8	13	0	4.62
Cox, Bill-William Donald	36StLN 37-38ChiA 38-40StLA	06-23-13	Ashmore, Ill.	02-16-88	R	R	6'1	185	2	9	.182	0	50	12	3	117	138	74	45	0	6.54
Cox, Ernie-Ernest Thompson (Elmer)	22ChiA	02-19-94	Birmingham, Ala.	04-29-74	L	R	6'1	180	0	0	—	0	1	0	0	1	1	2	0	0	18.00
Cox, George-George Melvin	28DetA	11-15-04	Sherman, Tex	12-17-95	R	R	6'	170	1	2	.330	0	26	2	0	89	110	39	22	0	5.26
Cox, Les-Lesie Warren	26ChiA	08-14-05	Junction, Tex.	10-12-34	R	R	6'	164	0	1	.000	0	2	0	0	5	6	5	3	0	5.40
Cox, Red-Plateau Preston Rex	20DetA	02-16-95	Laurel Springs, N.C.	10-15-84	L	R	6'2	190	0	0	—	0	3	0	0	5	9	3	1	0	5.40
Cozart, Charlie-Charles Rhubin	45BosN	10-17-19	Lenoir, N.C.	12-31-04	R	R	6'2	190	1	0	1.000	0	8	0	0	10	14	4	5	0	10.13
Craghead, Howard-Howard Oliver (Judge)	31,33CleA	05-25-08	Selma, Cal.	07-14-62	R	R	6'2	200	0	0	—	0	15	0	0	23	27	12	4	0	6.26
Crawford, Larry-Charles Lowrie	37PhiN	04-27-14	Swissvale, Pa.	12-20-94	L	L	6'	165	0	0	—	0	6	0	0	6	12	1	2	0	15.00
Creel, Jack-Jack Dalton (Tex)	45StLN	04-23-16	Kyle, Tex.	08-13-02	R	R	6'	165	5	4	.556	2	26	8	2	87	78	45	34	0	4.14
Cremins, Bob-Robert Anthony (Lefty, Crooked Arm)	27BosA	02-15-06	Pelham Manor, N.Y.	03-27-04	L	L	5'11	178	0	0	—	0	4	0	0	5	5	3	0	0	5.40
Crocker, Claude-Claude Arthur	44-45BknN	07-20-24	Caroleen, N.C.	12-19-02	R	R	6'2	185	0	0	—	0	3	0	0	5	5	4	1	0	7.20
Crouch, Bill-William Elmer	39BknN 41PhiN 41,45StLN	08-20-10	Wilmington, Del.	12-26-80	B	R	6'	180	8	5	.615	7	50	12	4	155	159	52	55	0	3.48
Crowder, General-Alvin Floyd	26-27,30-34WasA 34-35StLA 34-36DetA	01-11-99	Winston-Salem, N.C.	04-03-72	L	R	5'10	170	167	115	.592	22	402	292	150	2344	2453	800	799	16	4.12
Crowson, Woody-Thomas Woodrow	45PhiA	09-19-18	Fuquay Springs, N.C.	08-14-47	R	R	6'2	185	0	0	—	0	3	0	0	3	2	3	2	0	6.00
Crumpler, Roy-Roy Maxton	20DetA 25PhiN	07-08-96	Clinton, N.C.	10-06-69	L	L	6'1	195	1	0	1.000	0	5	3	1	18	25	13	3	0	6.00
Cuccurullo, Cookie-Arthur Joseph	43-45PitN	02-08-18	Asbury Park, N.J.	01-23-83	L	L	5'10	168	3	5	.375	5	62	6	0	170	188	81	51	0	4.55
Culloton, Bud-Bernard Aloysius	25-26PitN	05-19-97	Kingston, N.Y.	11-09-76	R	R	5'11	180	1	0	1.000	0	13	1	0	25	22	7	4	0	3.24
Cunningham, Bruce-Bruce Lee	29-32BosN	09-29-05	San Francisco, Cal.	03-08-84	R	R	5'10	165	13	24	.351	0	104	33	12	383	428	146	103	1	4.63
Curtis, Vern-Vernon Eugene (Turk)	43-44WasA 45MS 46WasA	05-24-20	Cairo, Ill.	06-24-92	R	R	6'	170	0	1	.000	0	16	1	0	30	30	19	10	0	5.70
Cvengros, Mike-Michael John	22NYN 23-25ChiA 27PitN 29ChiN	12-01-00	Pana, Ill.	08-02-70	L	L	5'8	160	25	40	.385	6	144	61	21	553	587	285	201	0	4.57
Dagenhard, John-John Douglas	43BosN	04-25-17	Magnolia, Ohio	07-16-01	R	R	6'2	195	1	0	1.000	0	2	1	0	7	3	4	2	0	0.00
Daglia, Pete-Peter George	32ChiA	02-28-06	Napa, Cal.	03-11-52	R	R	6'1	200	2	4	.333	0	12	5	2	50	67	24	16	0	5.76
Dailey, Sam-Samuel Laurence	29PhiN	03-31-04	Oakford, Ill.	12-02-79	R	R	5'11	168	2	2	.500	2	20	4	0	51	74	23	18	0	7.59

USE NAMES - GIVEN NAMES (NICKNAMES)	TEAM BY YEAR	BIRTH DATE	BIRTHPLACE	DEATH DATE	B	T	HGT	WGT	W	L	Pct.	SV	G	GS	CG	IP	H	BB	SO	ShO	ERA
Daney, Art-Arthur Lee (Chief Whitehorn)	28PhiA	07-09-04	Talihina, Okla.	03-11-88	R	R	5'11	165	0	0	—	0	1	1	0	1	0	0	0	0	0.00
Danforth, Dave-David Charles (Dauntless Dave)	11-12PhiA 16-19ChiA 22-25StLA	03-07-90	Granger, Tex.	09-19-70	L	L	6'	167	72	67	.518	24	286	114	44	1187	1235	455	484	3	3.88
Darrow, George-George Oliver (Lefty)	34PhiW	07-12-03	Beloit, Kans.	03-24-83	L	L	6'	180	2	6	.250	1	17	8	2	49	57	28	14	0	5.51
Dasso, Frank-Francis Joseph Nicholas	45-46CinN	08-31-17	Chicago, Ill.		R	R	5'11	185	4	5	.444	0	18	12	6	97	91	55	40	0	3.90
Davenport, Claude-Claude Edwin	20NYN	05-28-98	Runge, Tex.	06-13-76	R	R	6'6	193	0	0	—	0	1	0	0	2	2	1	0	0	4.50
Davenport, Lum-Joubert Lum	21-24ChiA	06-26-00	Tucson, Ariz.	04-21-61	L	L	6'1	165	1	4	.200	0	25	3	0	58	63	51	20	0	7.76
Davies, Chick-Lloyd Garrison (See B01-19)	14-15PhiA 25-26NYN	03-06-92	Peabody, Mass.	09-05-73	L	L	5'8	145	4	6	.400	6	45	5	1	120	137	54	38	0	4.50
Davis, Curt-Curtis Benton (Coonskin)	34-36PhiN 36-37ChiN 38-40StLN 40-46BknN	09-07-03	Greenfield, Mo.	10-12-65	R	R	6'2	185	158	131	.547	33	429	280	141	2324	2459	479	684	24	3.42
Davis, Dixie-Frank Talmadge	12CinN 15ChiA 18PhiN 20-26StLA	10-12-90	Wilsons Mills, N.C.	02-04-44	R	R	5'11	155	75	71	.514	2	239	164	77	1317	1311	688	460	10	3.97
Davis, Peaches-Roy Thomas	36-39CinN	05-31-05	Glen Rose, Tex.	04-28-95	L	R	6'3	190	27	33	.450	11	117	58	27	543	627	138	123	2	3.86
Davis, Woody-Woddrow Wilson (Babe)	38DetA	04-25-13	Nicholas, Ga.	07-18-99	L	R	6'1	200	0	0	—	0	2	0	0	6	3	4	1	0	1.50
Dawson, Joe-Ralph Fenton (Aviator)	24CleA 27-29PhiN	03-09-97	Bow, Wash.	01-04-78	R	R	5'11	182	11	17	.393	3	59	18	5	239	233	112	62	0	4.14
Day, Pea Ridge-Henry Clyde	24-25StLN 26CinN 31BknN	08-25-99	Pea Ridge, Ark.	03-22-34	R	R	6'	190	5	7	.417	2	46	9	3	122	163	28	48	0	5.31
Dean, Chubby-Alfred Lovill (See B20-45)	37-41PhiA 41-43CleA 44-46MS	08-24-15	Mt. Airy, N.C.	12-21-70	L	L	5'11	188	30	46	.395	9	162	68	23	686	781	232	195	1	5.08
Dean, Dizzy-Jay Hanna	30,32-37StLN 38-41ChiN 47StLA	01-16-10	Lucas, Ark.	07-17-74	R	R	6'2	182	150	83	.644	30	317	230	154	1966	1921	458	1155	26	3.04
Dean, Harry-James Harry	41WasA	05-12-15	Rockmart, Ga.	06-01-60	R	R	6'4	185	0	0	—	0	2	0	0	2	3	0	0	0	4.50
Dean, Paul-Paul Dee (Daffy)	34-39StLN 40-41NYN 43StLA	08-14-13	Lucas, Ark.	03-17-81	R	R	6'	175	50	34	.595	8	159	87	44	787	825	179	387	8	3.75
Dean, Wayland-Wayland Ogden	24-25NYN 26-27PhiN 27ChiN	06-20-02	Richwood, W.Va.	04-11-30	B	R	6'2	180	24	36	.400	7	96	60	27	486	559	188	147	2	4.87
DeBerry, Joe-Joseph Gaddy	20-21StLA	11-29-96	Mt. Gilead, N.C.	10-09-44	L	R	6'1	175	2	5	.286	0	20	8	3	67	80	30	13	1	5.24
Decatur, Art-Arthur Rue	22-25BknN 25-27PhiN	01-14-94	Cleveland, Ohio	04-25-66	R	R	6'	190	23	34	.404	7	153	37	11	539	653	145	152	0	4.51
de la Cruz, Tommy-Tomas [Rivero]	44CinN	09-18-11	Marianao, Cuba	09-06-58	R	R	6'1	168	9	9	.500	2	34	20	9	191	170	45	65	0	3.25
Delaney (Helenius), Art-Arthur Dewey	28-29BosN	01-05-95	Chicago, Ill.		R	R	5'10	178	13	22	.371	2	67	31	12	287	319	97	64	1	4.26
Derringer, Paul-Samuel Paul (Duke, 'Oom Paul)	31-33StLN 33-42CinN 43-45ChiN	10-17-06	Springfield, Ky.	11-17-87	R	R	6'3	205	223	212	.513	29	579	445	251	3646	3912	761	1507	32	3.46
DeShong, Jimmie-James Brooklyn	32PhiA 34-35NYA 36-39WasA	11-30-09	Harrisburg, Pa.	10-16-93	R	R	5'11	165	47	44	.516	9	175	100	44	873	968	432	273	2	5.08
Devens, Charlie-Charles	32-34NYA	01-01-10	Milton, Mass.	08-13-03	R	R	6'1	180	5	3	.625	0	16	10	4	82	74	62	31	0	3.73
Deviney, Hal-Harold John	20BosA	04-11-91	Newton, Mass.	01-04-33	R	R			0	0	—	0	1	0	0	3	7	2	0	0	15.00
Dibut, Pedro-Pedro [Villafana]	24-25CinN	11-18-92	Cienfuegos, Cuba	12-04-79	R	R	5'8	190	3	0	1.000	1	8	2	2	37	27	12	15	0	2.68
Dickerman, Leo-Leo Louis	23-24BknN 24-25StLN	10-31-96	DeSoto, Mo.	04-30-82	R	R	6'4	192	19	27	.413	1	89	53	22	430	443	218	135	4	4.00
Dickman, Emerson-George Emerson	36,38-41BosA 42MS	11-12-14	Buffalo, N.Y.	04-27-81	R	R	6'2	175	22	16	.595	8	125	24	6	350	403	153	126	1	5.32
Diehl, George-George Krause	42-43BosN	02-25-18	Emmaus, Pa.	03-24-86	R	R	6'2	196	0	0	—	0	2	0	0	8	6	5	1	0	3.38
Dietrich, Bill-William John (Bullfrog)	33-36PhiA 36WasA 36-46ChiA 47-48PhiN	03-29-10	Philadelphia, Pa.	06-20-78	R	R	6'	200	108	128	.458	11	366	253	92	2004	2117	890	660	17	4.48
Dietz, Dutch-Lloyd Arthur	40-43PitN 43PhiN	02-19-12	Cincinnati, Ohio	10-29-72	R	R	6'	180	14	16	.467	6	106	21	7	294	303	113	79	1	3.89
Diggs, Reese-Reese Wilson (Diggsy)	34WasA	09-22-15	Matthews, Va.	10-30-78	R	R	6'2	185	1	2	.333	1	3	2	1	21	26	15	2	0	6.86
Dobb, John-John Kenneth (Lefty)	24ChiA	11-15-01	Muskegon, Mich.	07-31-91	R	L	6'2	180	0	0	—	0	2	0	0	2	4	1	2	0	9.00
Dobens, Ray-Raymond Joseph (Lefty)	29BosA	07-28-06	Nashua, N.H.	04-21-80	L	L	5'8	175	0	0	—	0	11	1	0	28	32	0	4	0	3.86
Dockins, George-George Woodrow (Lefty)	45StLN 47BknN	05-05-17	Clyde, Kans.	01-22-97	R	L	6'	175	8	6	.571	0	35	12	5	131	142	40	34	2	3.57
Dodge, Sam-Samuel Edward	21-22BosA	12-19-89	Neath, Pa.	04-05-66	R	R	6'1	170	0	0	—	0	4	0	0	7	12	4	3	0	5.14
Doll, Art-Arthur James (Moose) (See B20-45)	36,38BosN	05-07-12	Chicago, Ill.	04-28-78	R	R	6'	200	1	0	1.000	0	4	2	1	12	15	5	3	0	3.00
Donahue, Deacon-John Stephen Michael	43-44PhiN		Chicago, Ill.		R	R	6'	180	0	2	.000	0	8	0	0	13	22	3	4	0	6.92
Donald, Atley-Richard Atley (Swampy)	38-45NYA	08-19-10	Morton, Miss.	10-19-92	L	R	6'1	186	65	33	.663	1	153	115	54	953	907	369	369	6	3.52
Donohue, Pete-Peter Joseph	21-30CinN 30-31NYN 31CleA 32BosA	11-05-00	Athens, Tex.	02-23-88	R	R	6'2	185	134	118	.532	7	344	267	137	2112	2439	422	571	16	3.87
Donovan, Bill-Willard Earl	42-43BosN 44-45MS	07-06-16	Maywood, Ill.	09-25-97	R	L	6'2	190	4	6	.400	2	38	10	2	104	114	41	24	1	3.20
Dorsett, Cal-Calvin Leavelle (Preacher)	40-41CleA 42-45MS 45CleA	06-10-13	Lone Oak, Tex.	10-22-70	R	R	6'1	185	0	1	.000	0	8	2	0	13	25	13	6	0	12.46
Doyle, Carl-William Carl	35-36PhiA 39-40BknN 40StLN	07-30-12	Knoxville, Tenn.	09-04-51	R	R	6'1	185	6	15	.286	2	51	21	6	224	277	155	101	1	6.91
Doyle, Jess-Jesse Herbert	25-27DetA 31StLA	04-14-98	Knoxville, Tenn.	04-15-61	R	R	5'11	175	4	7	.364	9	55	3	0	135	183	57	38	0	6.27
Drake, Logan-Logan Gaffney (L.G.)	22-24CleA	12-26-99	Spartanburg, S.C.	06-01-40	R	R	5'10	165	1	0	1.000	0	10	1	0	18	24	17	11	0	8.00
Drake, Tom-Thomas Kendall	39CleA 41BknN 42-45MS	08-07-12	Birmingham, Ala.	07-02-88	R	R	6'1	185	1	2	.333	0	18	3	0	40	49	28	13	0	6.08
Dudley, Clise-Elzie Clise	29-30BknN 31-32PhiN 33PitN	08-08-03	Graham, N.C.	01-12-89	R	R	6'1	195	17	33	.340	2	100	51	18	421	540	156	106	1	5.02
Duff, Larry-Cecil Elba	22ChiA	11-20-96	Radersburg, Mont.	11-10-69	L	R	6'1	175	1	1	.500	0	3	1	0	13	16	3	7	0	4.85
Dugan, Dan-Daniel Phillip	28-29ChiA	02-22-07	Plainfield, N.J.	06-25-68	L	L	6'1	187	1	4	.200	1	8	7	1	55	77	19	15	0	6.65
Dumovich, Nick-Nicholas	23ChiN	01-02-02	Sacramento, Cal.	12-12-78	L	L	6'	170	3	5	.375	1	28	8	1	94	118	45	23	0	4.60
Durham, Ed-Edward Fant (Bull)	29-32BosA 33ChiA 34IL	08-17-07	Chester, S.C.	04-27-76	R	R	5'11	170	29	44	.397	1	143	71	23	641	677	202	204	3	4.45
Dyer, Eddie-Edwin Hawley	22-27,M46-50StLN	10-11-99	Morgan City, La.	04-20-64	L	L	5'11	168	15	15	.500	3	69	23	10	256	316	96	63	2	4.75
Early, Tom-Thomas Francis Aloysius (Chick)	38-42BosN 43-44MS 45BosN	02-19-17	Boston, Mass.	04-05-88	R	R	6'	180	11	17	.393	9	81	37	15	360	349	143	104	2	3.78
Earnshaw, George-George Livingston (Moose)	28-33PhiA 34-35ChiA 35-36BknN 36StLN	02-15-00	New York, N.Y.	12-01-76	R	R	6'4	210	127	93	.577	12	319	249	114	1916	1981	809	1002	17	4.38
East, Hugh-Gordon Hugh	41-43NYN 44-45MS	07-07-19	Birmingham, Ala.	11-02-81	R	R	6'2	185	2	6	.250	0	19	8	1	63	85	41	27	0	5.43
Eaton, Zeb-Zebulon Vance (Red)	44-45DetA	02-02-20	Cooleemee, N.C.	12-17-89	R	R	5'10	185	4	2	.667	0	23	3	0	69	67	48	19	0	4.43
Eaves, Vallie-Vallie Herbert (Chief)	35DetA 38-40ChiA 41-42ChiN	09-06-11	Allen, Okla.	04-19-60	R	R	6'2	180	4	8	.333	0	24	14	6	107	105	70	46	0	4.54
Eayrs, Eddie-Edwin (See B20-45)	13PitN 20-21BosN	11-10-90	Blackstone, Mass.	11-30-69	L	L	5'7	160	1	2	.333	1	11	3	0	39	53	27	13	0	6.23
Eckert, Al-Albert George (Obbie)	30-31CinN 35StLN	05-17-06	Milwaukee, Wis.	04-20-74	L	L	5'10	174	0	2	.000	0	18	2	0	27	40	14	7	0	9.00
Eckert, Charlie-Charles William (Buzz)	19-20,22PhiA	08-08-97	Philadelphia, Pa.	08-22-86	R	R	5'11	180	0	0	—	0	25	1	1	72	86	27	22	0	4.50
Edelen, Ed-Edward Joseph (Doc)	32WasA	03-16-12	Bryanstown, Md.	02-01-82	R	R	6'	191	0	0	—	0	1	0	0	1	1	6	0	0	27.00
Edmonson, George-George Henderson (Big Ed)	22-24CleA	05-18-96	Waxahachie, Tex.	07-11-73	R	R	6'1	179	0	0	—	0	2	0	0	4	6	2	1	0	9.64
Edwards, Foster-Foster Hamilton (Eddie)	25-28BosN 30NYA	09-01-03	Holstein, Iowa	01-04-80	R	R	6'3	175	4	6	.400	0	56	17	4	170	193	84	60	0	4.76
Edwards, Jim Joe-James Corbette	22-25CleA 25-26ChiA 28CinN	12-14-94	Banner, Miss.	01-19-65	R	L	6'2	185	26	37	.413	4	145	59	23	579	666	278	211	6	4.41
Edwards, Sherman-Sherman Stanley	34CinN	07-25-09	Mt. Ida, Ark.	03-08-92	R	R	6'	165	0	0	—	0	1	0	0	3	4	1	1	0	3.00
Ehmke, Howard-Howard Jonathan (Bob)	15BufF 16-17DetA 18MS 19-22DetA 23-26BosA 26-30PhiA	04-24-94	Silver Creek, N.Y.	03-17-59	R	R	6'3	190	166	166	.500	14	427	338	199	2822	2873	1042	1030	19	3.75
Ehrhardt, Rube-Welton Claude	24-28BknN 29CinN	11-20-94	Beecher, Ill.	04-27-80	R	R	6'2	190	22	34	.393	10	193	41	22	588	633	200	128	3	4.15
Eisenhart, Jake-Jacob Henry (Hank)	44CinN	10-03-22	Perkasie, Pa.	12-20-87	L	L	6'3	195	0	0	—	0	1	0	0	0.1	0	1	0	0	0.00
Eisenstat, Harry-Harry	35-37BknN 38-39DetA 39-42CleA 43-46MS	10-10-15	Brooklyn, N.Y.	03-21-03	L	L	5'11	180	25	27	.481	14	165	33	11	479	550	114	157	1	3.83
Elliott, Hal-Harold William (Ace)	29-32PhiN	05-29-99	Mt. Clemens, Mich.	04-25-63	R	R	6'1	200	11	24	.314	4	120	30	4	322	453	174	90	0	6.96
Elliott, Jumbo Jim-James Thompson	23StLA 25,27-30BknN 31-34PhiN 34BosN	10-22-00	St. Louis, Mo.	01-07-70	R	L	6'3	235	63	74	.460	12	252	144	51	1207	1338	414	453	8	4.24
Ellison, George-George Russell	20CleA	01-24-97	San Francisco, Cal.	01-20-78	R	R	6'3	195	0	0	—	0	1	0	0	1	2	0	0	0	0.00
Embry, Slim-Charles Akin	23ChiA	08-17-01	Columbia, Tenn.	10-10-47	R	R	6'4	190	0	0	—	0	1	0	0	3	7	2	1	0	9.00
Emmerich, Slim-William Peter	45-46NYN	09-29-19	Allentown, Pa.	09-17-98	R	R	6'1	170	0	4	.500	0	33	7	1	104	117	33	28	0	4.85
Epperly, Al-Albert Paul (Pard)	38ChiN 50BknN	05-07-18	Glidden, Iowa	04-14-03	R	R	6'2	194	2	0	1.000	1	14	4	1	36	42	19	13	0	4.00
Erickson, Eric-Eric George Adolph	14NYN 16,18-19DetA 19-22WasA	03-13-92	Goteborg, Sweden	05-19-65	R	R	6'2	190	34	56	.378	4	145	94	42	822	805	379	367	3	3.85
Erickson, Paul-Paul Walford (Li'l Abner)	41-48ChiN 48PhiN 48NYN	12-14-15	Zion, Ill.	04-05-02	R	R	6'2	200	37	48	.435	6	207	86	21	814	774	425	432	5	3.86
Erickson, Ralph-Ralph Lief	29-30PitN	06-25-02	Dubois, Idaho	06-27-02	L	L	6'1	175	0	0	—	0	15	0	0	23	12	4	2	0	8.40
Errickson, Dick-Richard Merriwell (Lief)	38-42BosN 42ChiN	03-05-12	Vineland, N.J.	11-28-99	L	R	6'1	175	36	47	.434	13	168	77	31	736	804	290	176	6	3.85
Estrada, Oscar-Oscar	29StLA	02-15-04	Havana, Cuba	01-02-78	L	L	6'	160	0	0	—	0	1	0	0	2	1	0	0	0	0.00
Eubanks, Uel-Uel Melvin (Poss)	22CinN	02-14-03	Quinlan, Tex.	11-22-54	R	R	6'3	175	0	0	—	0	2	0	0	5	4	1	1	0	22.50
Evans, Art-William Arthur	32ChiA	08-03-11	Elvins, Mo.	01-08-52	B	L	6'1	181	0	0	—	0	7	0	0	18	19	10	6	0	3.00
Evans, Red-Russell Edison	36ChiA 39BknN	11-12-06	Chicago, Ill.	06-14-82	R	R	5'11	180	1	11	.083	1	41	6	0	111	144	48	47	0	6.24
Eyrich, George-George Lincoln	43PhiN 44-46MS	03-03-25	Reading, Pa.		R	R	5'11	175	0	0	—	0	19	0	0	27	19	14	5	0	3.32
Faber, Red-Urban Clarence	14-33ChiA	09-06-88	Cascade, Iowa	09-25-76	B	R	6'2	180	254	212	.545	28	669	483	275	4087	4106	1213	1471	29	3.15
Faeth, Tony-Anthony Joseph	19-20CleA	07-09-93	Aberdeen, S.D.	12-22-87	R	R	6'	180	0	0	—	0	19	0	0	43	44	30	21	0	2.72
Falk, Chet-Chester Emmanuel (Spot)	25-27StLA	05-15-05	Austin, Tex.	01-07-82	L	L	6'2	170	5	6	.556	0	32	13	5	115	158	54	16	0	6.03
Fallenstein (Valestin), Ed-Edward Joseph (Jack)	31PhiN 33BosN	12-22-08	Newark, N.J.	11-24-71	R	R	6'3	180	2	1	.667	0	33	4	1	77	99	39	20	1	5.49
Faulkner, Jim-James LeRoy (Lefty)	27-28NYN 30BknN	07-27-99	Beatrice, Neb.	06-01-61	Bats Left 27				8	5	.556	3	30	9	1	127	146	47	34	0	3.76
Feldman, Harry-Harry	41-46NYN 47-49SM	11-10-19	New York, N.Y.	03-16-62	R	R	5'11	175	35	35	.500	3	143	78	22	666	671	300	254	6	3.80
Fenner, Hod-Horace Alfred	21ChiN	07-12-97	Martin, Mich.	11-20-54	R	R	5'10	165	0	0	—	0	2	0	0	7	14	3	1	0	7.71
Ferguson, Alex-James Alexander	18,21NYA 22-25BosA 25NYA 25-26WasA 27-29PhiN 29BknN	02-16-97	Montclair, N.J.	04-26-78	R	R	6'	180	61	85	.418	10	257	166	62	1242	1455	482	397	2	4.93

USE NAMES - GIVEN NAMES (NICKNAMES) TEAM BY YEAR	BIRTH DATE	BIRTHPLACE	DEATH DATE	B	T	HGT	WGT	W	L	Pct.	SV	G	GS	CG	IP	H	BB	SO	ShO	ERA
Ferguson, Bob-Robert Lester 44CinN	04-18-19	Birmingham, Ala.		R	R	6'1	180	0	3	.000	1	9	2	0	16	24	10	9	0	9.00
Ferrazzi, Bill-William Joseph 35PhiA	04-19-07	West Quincy, Mass.	08-10-93	R	R	6'2	200	1	2	.333	0	3	2	0	7	7	5	0	0	5.14
Ferrell, Wes-Wesley Cheek 27-33CleA 34-37BosA 37-38WasA	02-02-08	Greensboro, N.C.	12-09-76	R	R	6'2	195	193	128	.601	13	374	323	227	2623	2845	1040	985	17	4.04
(See B20-45) 38-39NYA 40BknN 41BosN																				
Fette, Lou-Louis Henry William 37-40BosN 40BknN 45BosN	03-15-07	Alma, Mo.	01-03-81	R	R	6'1	200	41	40	.506	1	109	97	51	691	658	248	194	14	3.15
Fick, John-John Ralph 44PhiN	05-18-21	Baltimore, Md.	06-09-58	L	L	5'10	150	0	0	—	0	4	0	0	5	3	2	0	0	3.60
Fieber, Clarence-Clarence Thomas (Lefty) 32ChiA	09-04-13	San Francisco, Cal.	08-20-85	L	L	6'4	187	0	0	—	0	4	0	0	5	6	3	2	0	1.80
Filley, Marc-Marcus Lucius 34WasA	02-28-12	Lansingburgh, N.Y.	01-20-95	R	R	5'11	172	1	0	1.000	0	3	0	0	5	6	3	1	0	1.80
Fillingim, Dana-Dana 15PhiA 18-23BosN 25PhiN	11-06-93	Columbus, Ga.	02-03-61	L	R	5'10	175	47	72	.395	2	200	114	59	1076	1170	313	270	10	3.56
Fink, Herman-Herman Adam 35-37PhiA	08-22-11	Concord, N.C.	08-24-80	R	R	6'2	198	10	20	.333	4	67	30	10	285	322	123	73	0	5.21
Fischer, Carl-Charles William 30-32WasA 32StLN 33-35DetA	11-05-05	Medina, N.Y.	12-10-63	R	L	6'	180	46	50	.479	11	191	105	31	824	900	372	376	3	4.62
35ChiA 37CleA 37WasA																				
Fischer, Rube-Reuben Walter 41,43-46NYN	09-19-16	Carlock, S.D.	07-16-97	R	R	6'4	190	16	34	.320	4	108	41	7	384	416	222	136	1	5.09
Fisher, Clarence-Clarence Henry 19-20WasA	08-27-98	Letart, W.Va.	11-02-65	R	R	6'	174	0	1	.000	0	4	0	0	8	13	8	1	0	11.25
Fisher, Don-Donald Raymond 45NYN	02-06-16	Cleveland, Ohio	07-29-73	R	R	6'	210	1	0	1.000	0	2	1	1	18	12	7	4	1	2.00
Fitzke, Bob (Frederick Herman)-Paul Robert 24CleA	07-30-00	La Crosse, Wis.	06-30-50	R	R	5'11	195	0	0	—	0	1	0	0	4	5	3	1	0	4.50
25 played in N.F.L.																				
Fitzsimmons, Freddie-Frederick Landis (Fat Freddie) 25-37NYN	07-28-01	Mishawaka, Ind.	11-18-79	R	R	5'11	195	217	146	.598	13	513	425	186	3225	3335	846	870	30	3.51
37-43BknN M43-45PhiN																				
Fleming, Bill-Lesie Fletchard 40-41BosA 42-44ChiN 45MS 46ChiN	07-31-13	Rowland, Cal.	06-04-06	R	R	6'	190	16	21	.432	3	123	40	14	440	443	163	167	3	3.80
Flitcraft, Hilly-Hildreth Milton 42PhiN	08-21-23	Woodstown, N.J.	04-02-03	L	L	6'2	180	0	0	—	0	3	0	0	3	6	2	1	0	9.00
Flohr, Mort-Moritz Herman (Dutch) 34PhiN	08-15-11	Canisteo, N.Y.	06-02-94	L	L	6'	173	0	2	.000	0	14	3	0	31	34	33	6	0	5.81
Flores, Jesse-Jesse [Sandoval] 42ChiN 43-47PhiA 50CleA	11-02-14	Guadalajara, Mex.	12-17-91	R	R	5'10	175	44	59	.427	4	176	113	46	972	904	306	352	11	3.19
Flowers, Wes-Charles Wesley 40,44BknN	08-13-13	Vanndale, Ark.	12-31-88	L	L	6'1	190	2	2	.500	0	14	3	0	38	49	23	11	0	5.45
Flythe, Stu-Stuart McGuire 36PhiA	12-05-11	Conway, N.C.	10-18-63	R	R	6'2	175	0	6	.000	0	17	3	0	39	49	61	14	0	13.15
Ford, Bill-William Brown 36BosN	10-14-15	Buena Vista, Pa.	04-06-94	R	R	6'2	200	0	0	—	0	3	0	0	6	11	5	3	0	9.00
Ford, Gene-Eugene Matthew 36BosN 38DetA	06-23-12	Fort Dodge, Iowa	09-07-70	R	R	6'2	195	0	0	—	0	5	1	0	14	21	15	2	0	4.50
Foreman, Happy-August G. 24ChiA 26BosA	07-20-97	Memphis, Tenn.	02-13-53	L	L	5'7	160	0	0	—	0	6	0	0	11	10	9	4	0	11.57
Fortune, Gary-Garrett Reese 16,18PhiN 20BosA	10-11-94	High Point, N.C.	09-23-55	R	R	5'11	176	0	5	.000	0	20	6	2	78	89	46	23	0	6.58
Fowler, Jesse-Jesse Peter (Pete) 30BosN	10-30-98	Spartanburg, S.C.	09-23-73	R	L	5'10	158	1	1	.500	1	13	3	0	33	28	18	5	0	4.36
Foxx,Jimmie-James Emory (Double X, The Beast) (See B20-45) 39BosA 45PhiN	10-22-07	Sudlersville, Md.	07-21-67	R	R	6'	195	1	0	1.000	0	10	2	0	23	14	14	11	0	1.50
Francis, Ray-Ray James 22WasA 23DetA 25NYA 25BosA	03-08-93	Sherman, Tex.	07-06-34	L	L	6'1	182	12	28	.300	3	82	36	15	337	409	110	96	2	4.65
Frankhouse, Fred-Frederick Meloy 27-30StLN 30-35BosN 36-38BknN 39BosN	04-09-04	Port Royal, Pa.	08-17-89	R	R	5'11	175	106	97	.522	12	402	212	81	1888	2033	701	622	10	3.92
Franklin, Jack-Jack Wilford 44BknN	10-20-19	Paris, Ill.	11-15-91	R	R	5'11	170	0	0	—	0	1	0	0	2	2	4	0	0	13.50
Frasier (Frazier), Vic-Victor Patrick 31-33ChiA 33-34DetA 37BosN 39ChiA	08-05-04	Ruston, La.	01-10-77	R	R	6'	182	23	38	.377	4	126	68	21	580	686	291	170	2	5.76
Freeman, Buck-Alexander Vernon 21-22ChiN	07-05-97	Mart, Tex.	02-21-53	B	R	5'10	167	9	11	.450	4	49	21	6	203	236	80	52	0	4.70
Freeman, Harvey-Harvey Bayard (Buck) 21PhiA	12-22-97	Mottville, Mich.	01-10-70	R	R	5'10	145	1	4	.200	1	18	4	2	51	65	35	5	0	7.24
Freeze, Jake-Carl Alexander 25ChiA	04-25-00	Huntington, Ark.	04-09-83	R	R	5'8	165	0	0	—	0	2	0	0	4	5	3	1	0	2.25
Freitas, Tony-Antonio 32-33PhiA 34-36CinN	05-05-08	Mill Valley, Cal.	03-14-94	R	L	5'8	161	25	33	.431	4	107	63	22	518	614	137	135	1	4.48
French, Larry-Lawrence Herbert 29-34PitN 35-41ChiN 41-42BknN	11-01-07	Visalia, Cal.	02-09-87	R	L	6'1	195	197	171	.535	17	570	383	198	3152	3375	819	1187	40	3.44
43-45MS				Bats Both 34,40-42																
Frey, Benny-Benjamin Rudolph 26-31CinN 32StLN 32-36CinN	04-06-06	Dexter, Mich.	11-01-37	L	R	5'10	165	57	82	.410	7	256	127	49	1159	1415	263	179	7	4.50
Friday, Skipper-Grier William 23WasA	10-26-97	Gastonia, N.C.	08-25-62	R	R	5'11	170	0	1	.000	0	7	2	1	30	35	22	9	0	6.00
Fried, Cy-Arthur Edwin 20DetA	07-23-97	San Antonio, Tex.	10-10-70	L	L	5'11	150	0	0	—	0	2	0	0	4	4	0	0	0	13.50
Friedrich(Friedrichs), Bob-Robert George 32WasA	08-30-06	Cincinnati, Ohio	04-15-97	R	R	5'11	165	0	0	—	0	2	0	0	4	4	7	2	0	11.25
Fry, Johnson-Johnson (Jay) 23CleA	11-21-01	Huntington, W.Va.	04-07-59	R	R	6'1	150	0	0	—	0	1	0	0	4	4	3	1	0	11.25
Frye, Charlie-Charles Andrew 40PhiN	07-17-14	Hickory, N.C.	05-25-45	R	R	6'1	175	0	6	.000	0	15	5	1	50	58	26	18	0	4.68
Fuchs, Charley-Charles Thomas 42DetA 43PhiN 43StLA 44BknN	11-18-13	Union Hill, N.J.	06-10-69	B	R	5'10	175	6	10	.375	1	47	13	5	166	186	73	41	2	4.88
Fuhr, Oscar-Oscar Lawrence 21ChiN 24-25BosA	08-22-93	Defiance, Mo.	03-27-75	L	L	6'	176	3	12	.200	0	63	15	4	175	249	69	59	1	6.38
Fullerton, Curt-Curtis Hooper 21-25,33BosA	09-13-98	Ellsworth, Me.	01-09-75	R	R	6'	162	10	37	.213	3	115	44	19	421	483	211	104	0	5.13
Fussell, Fred-Frederick Morris (Moonlight Ace) 22-23ChiN 28-29PitN	12-29-94	Sheridan, Mo.	10-07-95	L	L	5'10	155	14	17	.452	5	80	27	11	295	365	88	103	2	4.85
Gabler, Frank-Frank Harold (The Great Gabbo) 35-37NYN 37-38BosN	11-06-11	E. Highlands, Cal.	11-01-67	R	R	6'1	175	16	23	.410	8	113	31	10	377	457	107	109	1	5.25
38ChiA																				
Gables, Ken-Kenneth Harlin (Coral) 40-47PitN	01-21-19	Walnut Grove, Mo.	01-02-60	R	R	5'11	210	13	11	.542	5	62	23	6	240	255	88	88	0	4.69
Gaddy, John-John Wilson (Sheriff) 42BknN	02-15-14	Wadesboro, N.C.	05-03-66	R	R	6'	182	2	0	1.000	0	2	1	0	13	13	4	3	0	0.69
Gaines, Nemo-Willard Roland 21WasA	12-23-97	Alexandria, Va.	01-26-79	L	L	6'	180	0	0	—	0	4	0	0	5	5	2	1	0	0.00
Galehouse, Denny-Dennis Ward 34-38CleA 39-40BosA 41-44StLA 45MS 46-47StLA 47-49BosA	12-07-11	Marshallville, Ohio	10-12-98	R	R	6'1	195	109	118	.480	13	375	258	100	2003	2148	735	851	17	3.98
Gallagher, Ed-Edward Michael (Lefty) 28BosA	11-28-10	Dorchester, Mass.	12-22-81	B	L	6'2	197	0	3	.000	0	9	3	0	24	30	28	6	0	12.38
Gallivan, Phil-Philip Joseph 31BknN 32,34ChiA	05-29-07	Seattle, Wash.	11-24-69	R	R	6'	180	5	11	.313	1	54	11	4	175	227	95	68	0	5.97
Gardiner, Art-Arthur Cecil 23PhiN	12-26-99	Brooklyn, N.Y.	10-21-54	R	R			0	0	—	0	1	0	0	1	1	0	0	0	0.00
Gardner, Glenn-Glenn Glenn 45StLN	01-25-16	Burnsville, N.C.	07-07-64	R	R	5'11	180	3	1	.750	1	7	4	1	55	50	27	20	1	3.27
Garland, Lou-Louis Lyman 31ChiA	07-16-05	Archie, Mo.	08-30-90	R	R	6'2	200	0	2	.000	0	7	2	0	17	30	14	0	0	10.06
Garrison, Cliff-Clifford William 28BosA	08-13-06	Belmont, Okla.	08-25-94	R	R	6'	195	0	0	—	0	6	0	0	16	22	6	4	0	7.88
Gassaway, Charlie-Charles Cason (Sheriff) 44ChiN 45PhiA 46CleA	08-12-18	Gassaway, Tenn.	01-15-92	L	L	6'2	210	5	9	.357	2	39	19	4	181	188	91	80	0	4.03
Gaston, Milt-Nathaniel Milton 24NYA 25-27StLA 28WasA 29-31BosA	01-27-96	Ridgefield Park, N.J.	04-26-96	R	R	6'1	185	97	164	.372	4	355	269	127	2106	2338	836	615	10	4.55
32-34ChiN				Bats Both 33																
Gaw, Chippy-George Joseph 20ChiN	03-13-92	West Newton, Mass.	05-26-68	R	R	5'11	180	1	1	.500	1	2	1	0	13	16	3	4	0	4.85
Gearin, Dinty-Dennis John 23-24NYN 24BosN	10-15-97	Providence, R.I.	03-11-59	L	L	5'4	148	2	4	.333	1	13	6	3	53	56	28	13	0	3.74
Gee, Johnny-John Alexander (Whiz) 39PitN 40SA 41PitN 42AJ 46-47 played in N.B.L. 43-45PitN 44-46NYN	10-07-15	Syracuse, N.Y.	01-23-88	L	L	6'9	225	7	12	.368	1	44	21	4	175	209	64	65	0	4.42
Gehrman, Paul-Paul Arthur (Dutch) 37CinN	05-03-12	Marquam, Ore.	10-23-86	R	R	6'	195	0	1	.000	0	2	1	0	9	11	5	1	0	3.00
Genewich, Joe-Joseph Edward 22-28BosN 28-30NYN	01-15-97	Elmira, N.Y.	12-21-85	R	R	6'	174	73	92	.442	12	272	166	71	1401	1610	402	316	8	4.29
Gentry, Rufe-James Ruffus 43-44DetA 45HO 46-48DetA	05-18-18	Daisy Station, N.C.	07-03-97	R	R	6'1	180	13	17	.433	0	48	34	12	243	251	134	78	3	4.37
Georgy, Oscar-Oscar John 38NYN	11-25-16	New Orleans, La.	01-15-99	R	R	6'3	180	0	0	—	0	1	0	0	2	1	0	0	0	18.00
Gerheauser, Al-Albert (Lefty) 43-44PhiN 45-46PitN 48StLA	06-24-17	St. Louis, Mo.	05-28-72	L	L	6'3	190	25	50	.333	1	149	79	27	643	726	224	255	4	4.13
Gerkin, Steve-Stephen Paul (Splinter) 45PhiA	11-19-12	Grafton, W.Va.	11-09-78	R	R	6'11	162	0	12	.000	0	21	12	3	102	112	27	25	0	3.62
Giard, Joe-Joseph Oscar (Peco) 25-26StLA 27NYA	10-07-98	Ware, Mass.	07-10-56	L	L	5'10	170	13	15	.464	3	68	37	11	278	330	173	71	4	5.96
Gibson, Sam-Samuel Braxton 26-28DetA 30NYA 32NYN	08-05-99	King, N.C.	01-31-83	R	R	6'2	198	32	38	.457	5	131	75	33	594	676	249	208	4	4.24
Gick, George-George Edward 37-38ChiA	10-18-15	Dunnington, Ind.		B	R	6'	190	0	0	—	0	3	0	0	2	2	0	0	0	0.00
Giebell, Floyd-Floyd George 39-41DetA	12-10-09	Pennsboro, W.Va.	04-28-04	L	R	6'2	172	3	1	.750	0	28	4	2	67	78	42	30	1	4.03
Gill, George-George Lloyd 37-39DetA 39StLA	02-13-09	Catchings, Miss.	02-21-99	R	R	6'1	185	24	26	.480	1	85	45	22	396	494	129	95	2	5.05
Gill, Haddie-Harold Edmund 23CinN	01-23-99	Brockton, Mass.	08-01-32	L	L	5'10	145	0	0	—	0	3	0	0	4	7	4	1	0	4.50
Gillenwater, Claral-Claral Lewis 22ChiA	05-20-00	Sims, Ind.	02-26-78	R	R	6'	187	1	3	.250	0	5	3	1	21	28	6	4	0	5.57
Gillespie, John-John Patrick (Silent John) 22CinN	02-25-00	Oakland, Cal.	02-15-54	R	R	5'11	172	3	3	.500	0	31	4	1	78	84	29	21	0	4.50
Gilmore, Len-Leonard Preston (Meow) 44PitN	11-03-17	Fairview Park, Ind.		R	R	6'3	175	0	1	.000	0	1	1	0	8	13	10	0	0	7.88
Glaiser, John-John Burke (Bert) 20DetA	07-28-94	Yoakum, Tex.	03-07-59	R	R	5'8	165	0	0	—	0	9	1	0	17	23	8	3	0	6.35
Glass, Tom-Thomas Joseph 25PhiA	04-29-98	Greensboro, N.C.	12-15-81	R	R	6'3	170	1	0	1.000	0	4	0	0	5	9	2	1	0	7.20
Glazner, Whitey-Charles Franklin 20-23PitN 23-24PhiN	09-17-93	Sycamore, Ala.	06-06-89	R	R	5'9	165	41	48	.461	4	142	102	46	784	895	249	266	6	4.21
Gleason, Joe-Joseph Paul 20,22WasA	07-09-95	Phelps, N.Y.	09-08-90	R	R	5'10	175	2	2	.500	0	11	5	3	49	67	24	14	0	6.06
Glenn, Bob-Burdette 20StLN	06-16-94	West Sunbury, Pa.	06-03-77	R	R			0	0	—	0	2	0	0	4	6	0	1	0	0.00
Gliatto, Sal-Salvador Michael 30CleA	05-07-02	Chicago, Ill.	11-02-95	R	R	5'8	150	1	1	.500	0	5	1	0	15	21	9	7	0	6.60
Goldsmith, Hal-Harold Eugene 26-28BosN 29StLN	08-18-98	Peconic, N.Y.	10-20-85	R	R	6'	174	6	10	.375	2	47	20	6	185	235	56	30	0	4.04
Goldstein, Izzy-Isidore 32DetA	06-06-08	Odessa, Ukraine	09-24-93	R	R	6'	160	3	2	.600	0	16	6	2	56	63	41	14	0	4.50
Gomez, Lefty-Vernon Louis (Goofy, The Gay Castillian) 30-42NYA 43WasA	11-26-08	Rodeo, Cal.	02-17-89	L	L	6'2	173	189	102	.649	9	368	320	173	2503	2290	1095	1468	27	3.34
Gonzales, Joe-Joseph Madrid 37BosA	03-19-15	San Francisco, Cal.	11-16-96	R	R	5'9	175	1	2	.333	0	8	2	1	31	37	11	11	0	4.35
Goodell, John-John Henry William (Lefty) 28ChiA	04-05-07	Muskogee, Okla.	09-21-93	R	L	5'10	165	0	1	.000	0	4	1	0	8	14	9	1	0	18.00
Gordinier, Ray-Raymond Cornelius 21-22BknN	11-15-60	Rochester, N.Y.		B	R	5'8	172	1	0	1.000	0	6	1	0	9	7	4	0	0	7.04
Gorman, Tom-Thomas David (Big Tom) 39NYN	03-16-19	New York, N.Y.	08-11-86	R	R	6'2	200	0	0	—	0	1	0	0	1	4	0	0	0	27.00
Gornicki, Hank-Henry Frank 41StLN 41ChiN 42-43PitN 44-45MS 46PitN	01-14-11	Niagara Falls, N.Y.	02-16-96	R	R	6'1	180	15	19	.441	9	79	33	12	285	275	107	123	4	3.38
Gorsica (Gorczyca), Johnny-John Joseph Perry 40-44,46-47DetA 45MS	03-29-15	Bayonne, N.J.	12-16-98	R	R	6'2	180	31	39	.443	17	204	64	22	724	778	247	272	4	4.18
Grabowski, Al-Alfons Francis (Hook) 29-30StLN	09-04-01	Syracuse, N.Y.	10-29-68	L	L	5'11	175	9	6	.600	1	39	14	5	156	165	58	67	2	4.10

USE NAMES - GIVEN NAMES (NICKNAMES)	TEAM BY YEAR	BIRTH DATE	BIRTHPLACE	DEATH DATE	B	T	HGT	WGT	W	L	Pct.	SV	G	GS	CG	IP	H	BB	SO	ShO	ERA
Grabowski, Reggie-Reginald John	32-34PhiN	07-16-07	Syracuse, N.Y.	04-02-55	R	R	6'	185	4	8	.333	0	51	12	4	147	190	55	37	1	5.76
Graham, Kyle-Kyle (Skinny)	24-26BosN 29DetA	08-14-99	Oak Grove, Ala.	12-01-73	R	R	6'2	172	11	22	.333	2	67	37	9	278	334	125	61	0	5.02
Grampp, Hank-Henry Erchardt	27,29ChiN	09-28-03	New York, N.Y.	03-24-86	R	R	6'1	175	0	1	.000	0	3	1	0	5	8	4	3	0	16.20
Grant, George-George Addison	23-25StLA 27-29CleA 31PitN	09-08-03	E. Tallassee, Ala.	03-25-86	R	R	5'11	175	15	20	.429	1	114	23	8	347	460	182	89	1	5.65
Grant, Jim-James Ronald	23PhiN	08-04-94	Coalville, Iowa	11-30-85	R	L	5'11	180	0	0	—	0	2	0	0	4	10	4	0	0	13.50
Grate, Don-Donald (Buckeye) 47-48 played in N.B.L. 49-50 played in N.B.A.	45-46PhiN	08-27-23	Greenfield, Ohio		R	R	6'2	180	1	1	.500	0	7	2	0	16	22	14	8	0	9.56
Gray, Sam-Samuel David (Sad Sam)	24-27PhiA 28-33StLA	10-15-97	Van Alstyne, Tex.	04-16-53	R	R	5'10	175	110	115	.489	22	379	232	101	1945	2196	639	730	16	4.19
Green, Harvey-Harvey George (Buck)	35BknN	02-09-15	Kenosha, Wis.	07-24-70	B	R	6'2	185	0	0	—	0	2	0	0	1	2	3	0	0	9.00
Greene, June-Julius Foust	28-29PhiN	06-26-00	Greensboro, N.C.	03-19-74	L	R	6'	185	0	0	—	0	6	0	0	16	38	9	4	0	18.00
Greene, Nelson-Nelson George (Lefty)	24-25BknN	09-20-99	Philadelphia, Pa.	05-06-83	L	L	6'	185	2	1	.667	1	15	1	0	31	59	9	7	0	8.71
Greenfield, Kent-Kent	24-27NYN 27-29BosN 29BknN	07-01-02	Guthrie, Ky.	03-14-78	R	R	6'1	180	41	48	.461	1	152	98	36	776	871	297	242	2	4.53
Gregg, Hal-Harold Dane	43-47BknN 48-50PitN 52NYN	07-11-21	Anaheim, Cal.	05-13-91	R	R	6'3	195	40	48	.455	9	200	115	27	826	805	443	401	5	4.54
Gregory, Paul-Paul Edwin (Pop)	32-33ChiA	09-02-08	Tomnolen, Miss.	09-16-99	R	R	6'2	180	9	14	.391	0	56	26	8	222	249	98	57	0	4.70
Griffin, Marty-Martin John	28BosN	09-02-01	San Francisco, Cal.	11-19-51	R	R	6'2	200	0	3	.000	0	11	3	0	38	42	17	9	0	4.97
Grimes, Burleigh-Burleigh Arland (Ol' Stubbleard)	16-17PitN 18-26BknN 27NYN 28-29PitN 30BosN 30-31StLN 32-33ChiN 33-34StLN 34PitN 34NYA M37-38BknN	08-18-93	Clear Lake, Wis.	12-06-85	R	R	5'10	175	270	212	.560	18	615	497	314	4178	4406	1295	1512	35	3.52
Grissom, Lee-Lee Theo	34-39CinN 40NYA 40-41BknN 41PhiN 42-45MS	10-23-07	Sherman, Tex.	10-04-98	B	L	6'3	200	29	48	.377	7	162	95	23	702	668	305	384	6	3.88
			Bats Right 34,37																		
Grove, Lefty-Robert Moses (Mose)	25-33PhiA 34-41BosA	03-06-00	Lonaconing, Md.	05-22-75	L	L	6'3	190	300	141	.680	55	616	457	300	3940	3849	1187	2266	33	3.06
Grove, Orval-Orval LeRoy	40-49ChiA	08-29-19	Mineral, Kans.	04-20-92	R	R	6'3	196	63	73	.463	4	207	152	66	1177	1237	444	374	11	3.78
Grubbs, Tom-Thomas Dillard (Judge)	20NYN	02-22-94	Mt. Sterling, Ky.	01-28-86	R	R	6'2	165	0	1	.000	0	1	1	0	5	9	0	0	0	7.20
Gudat, Marv-Marvin John (See B20-45)	29CinN 32CinN	08-27-05	Goliad, Tex.	03-01-54	L	L	5'11	176	1	1	.500	0	2	0	0	28	30	4	2	0	3.21
Guise, Witt-Witt Orison (Lefty)	40CinN	09-18-08	Driggs, Ark.	08-13-68	L	L	6'2	172	0	0	—	0	3	0	0	8	8	5	1	0	1.13
Gumbert, Harry-Harry Edwards (Gunboat)	35-41NYN 41-44StLN 44CinN 45-46CinN 49-50PitN	11-05-09	Elizabeth, Pa.	01-04-95	R	R	6'2	185	143	113	.559	48	508	235	96	2158	2186	721	709	12	3.68
Hadley, Bump-Irving Darius	26-31WasA 32ChiA 32-34StLA 35WasA 36-40NYA 41NYN 41PhiA	07-05-04	Lynn, Mass.	02-15-63	R	R	5'11	190	161	165	.494	25	528	355	135	2945	2980	1442	1318	12	4.25
Haid, Hal-Harold Augustine	19StLA 28-30StLN 31BosN 33ChiA	12-21-97	Barberton, Ohio	08-13-52	R	R	5'10	150	14	15	.483	12	119	14	8	308	330	123	103	0	4.15
Haines, Jesse-Jesse Joseph (Pop)	18CinN 20-37StLN	07-22-93	Clayton, Ohio	08-05-78	R	R	6'	190	210	158	.571	10	555	386	208	3208	3460	871	981	23	3.64
Hallahan, Wild Bill-William Anthony	25-26,29-36StLN 36-37CinN 38PhiN	08-04-02	Binghamton, N.Y.	07-08-81	R	L	5'10	170	102	94	.520	8	324	224	90	1740	1838	777	856	13	4.03
Hallett, Jack-Jack Price	40-41ChiA 42-43,46PitN 44-45MS 48NYN	11-13-14	Toledo, Ohio	06-11-82	R	R	6'4	215	12	16	.429	0	73	24	11	278	280	106	128	2	4.05
Hamann, Doc-Elmer Joseph	22CleA	12-21-00	New Ulm, Minn.	01-11-73	R	R	6'1	180	0	0	—	0	1	0	0	0	3	3	0	0	∞
Hamlin, Luke-Lewis Dennison (Hot Potato)	33-34DetA 37-41BknN 42PitN 44PhiA	07-03-04	Ferris Cen., Mich.	02-18-78	R	R	6'2	168	73	76	.490	2	261	181	70	1405	1442	353	563	9	3.77
Hankins, Don-Donald Wayne	27DetA	02-09-02	Pendleton, Ind.	05-16-63	R	R	6'3	183	2	1	.667	2	20	1	0	42	67	13	10	0	6.43
Hanning, Loy-Loy Vernon	39,42StLA	10-18-17	Bunker, Mo.	06-24-86	R	R	6'2	175	1	2	.333	0	15	1	0	27	32	16	17	0	6.33
Hansen, Snipe-Roy Emil Frederick	30,32-35PhiN 35StLA	02-21-07	Chicago, Ill.	09-11-78	B	L	6'3	195	22	45	.328	3	155	71	19	625	783	194	176	2	5.01
			Bats Left 30																		
Hanski (Hanyzewski), Don-Donald Thomas (See B20-45)	43-44ChiA 44MS	02-27-16	LaPorte, Ind.	09-02-57	L	L	5'11	180	0	0	—	0	3	0	0	6	6	3	0	0	9.00
Hanson, Ollie-Earl Sylvester	21ChiN	01-19-96	Holbrook, Mass.	08-19-51	R	R	5'9	178	0	2	.000	0	2	1	1	9	9	6	2	0	7.00
Hanyzewski, Ed-Edward Michael	42-46ChiN	09-18-20	Union Mills, Ind.	10-08-91	R	R	6'1	200	12	13	.480	0	58	25	6	218	213	79	81	0	3.30
Harder, Mel-Melvin LeRoy (Wimpy, Chief)	28-47,M61CleA	10-15-09	Beemer, Neb.	10-20-02	R	R	6'1	195	223	186	.545	23	582	433	181	3426	3706	1118	1160	24	3.80
Harman, Bill-William Bell	41PhiN 42MS	01-02-19	Bridgewater, Va.		R	R	6'4	200	0	0	—	0	13	15	8	3	0	4.85			
Harrell, Ray-Raymond James (Cowboy)	35,37-38StLN 39ChiN 39PhiN 40PitN 45NYN	02-16-12	Petrolia, Tex.	01-28-84	R	R	6'1	185	9	20	.310	3	119	31	6	330	385	177	136	1	5.70
Harris, Bill-William Milton	23-24CinN 31-34PitN 38BosA	06-23-00	Wylie, Tex.	08-21-65	R	R	6'1	180	24	22	.522	8	121	36	13	434	467	109	149	2	3.92
Harris, Bob-Robert Arthur	38-39DetA 39-42StLA 42PhiA 43-45MS	05-01-15	Gillette, Wyo.	08-08-89	R	R	6'	185	30	52	.366	2	127	89	26	647	770	294	205	4	4.95
Harris, Herb-Herbert Benjamin (Hub, Lefty)	36PhiN	04-24-13	Chicago, Ill.	01-18-91	L	L	6'1	175	0	0	—	0	4	0	0	7	14	5	0	0	10.29
Harris, Lum-Chalmer Luman	41-44PhiA 44MS 46PhiA 47WasA M61BalA M64-65HouN M68-72AtlN	01-17-15	New Castle, Ala.	11-11-96	R	R	6'1	180	35	63	.357	3	151	91	46	819	874	265	232	4	4.16
Harriss, Slim-William Jennings Bryan	20-26PhiA 26-28BosA	12-11-96	Brownwood, Tex.	09-19-63	R	R	6'6	180	95	135	.413	16	349	228	89	1750	1963	630	644	6	4.25
Hash, Herb-Herbert Howard	40-41BosA	02-13-11	Woolwine, Va.		R	R	6'3	210	8	7	.533	4	38	12	3	128	130	91	39	1	4.99
Hasty, Bob-Robert Keller	19-24PhiA	05-03-96	Canton, Ga.	05-28-72	R	R	6'3	210	29	53	.354	1	146	94	35	751	900	215	167	2	4.64
Hathaway, Ray-Ray Wilson	45BknN	10-13-16	Greenville, Ohio		R	R	6'	165	1	0	1.000	0	4	1	0	9	11	6	3	0	4.00
Hatter, Clyde-Clyde Melnow (Mad)	35-37DetA	08-07-08	Poplar Hill, Ky.	10-16-37	R	L	5'11	170	1	0	1.000	1	11	2	0	42	61	41	19	0	8.57
Haughey, Chris-Christopher Francis (Bud)	43BknN 44-45MS	10-03-25	Queens, N.Y.		R	R	6'1	180	0	1	.000	0	7	5	10	0	0	3.86			
Hausmann, Clem-Clemens Raymond	44-45BosA 49PhiA	08-17-19	Houston, Tex.	08-29-72	R	R	5'9	165	9	14	.391	4	64	25	7	263	270	131	73	2	4.21
Hayes, Jim-James Millard (Whitey)	35WasA	02-25-12	Montevallo, Ala.	11-27-93	L	R	5'11	168	4	7	.364	0	28	14	3	28	23	9	0	8.36	
Head, Ed-Edward Marvin	40,42-44BknN 45MS 46BknN	01-25-18	Selma, Ala.	01-31-80	R	R	6'1	175	27	23	.540	11	118	53	22	465	434	174	208	5	3.48
Head, Ralph-Ralph	23PhiN	08-30-93	Tallapoosa, Ga.	10-08-62	R	R	5'10	175	2	9	.182	0	35	13	5	132	185	57	24	0	6.68
Hearn, Bunny-Elmer Lafayette	26-29BosN	01-13-04	Brooklyn, N.Y.	03-31-74	L	L	5'8	160	7	11	.389	2	59	13	3	158	161	82	65	0	4.39
Heath, Spencer-Spencer Paul	20ChiA	11-05-93	Chicago, Ill.	01-25-30	B	R	6'	170	0	0	—	0	7	19	2	0	15.43				
Hebert, Wally-Wallace Andrew (Preacher)	31-33StLA 43PitN	08-21-07	Lake Charles, La.	12-08-99	L	L	6'1	195	21	36	.368	1	125	61	22	483	584	168	115	1	4.64
Heflin, Randy-Randolph Rutherford	45-46BosA	09-11-18	Fredericksburg, Va.	08-17-99	L	R	6'1	175	4	11	.267	0	25	15	6	117	118	73	45	2	3.85
Heimach, Fred-Fred Amos (Lefty)	20-26PhiA 26BosA 28-29NYA 30-33BknN	01-27-01	Camden, N.J.	06-01-73	L	L	6'	175	62	69	.473	4	296	127	56	1289	1510	360	334	5	4.46
Heise, Clarence-Clarence Edward (Lefty)	34StLN	08-07-07	Topeka, Kans.	05-30-99	L	L	5'10	172	0	0	—	0	2	0	0	3	3	0	1	0	4.50
Henderson, Bernie-Bernard (Barnyard)	21CleA	04-12-99	Douglasville, Tex.	06-06-66	R	R	5'9	175	0	0	—	0	2	1	0	3	5	0	1	0	9.00
Henderson, Bill-William Maxwell	30NYA	11-04-01	Altha, Fla.	10-06-66	R	R	6'6	185	0	0	—	0	3	0	0	8	7	4	2	0	4.50
Hendrickson, Don-Donald William	45BknN	07-14-13	Kewanna, Ind.	01-19-77	R	R	6'2	195	4	9	.308	5	39	2	1	75	78	41	16	0	4.92
Hennessey, George-George (Three Star)	37StLA 42PhiN 45ChiN	10-28-07	Slatington, Pa.	01-15-88	R	R	5'10	168	1	2	.333	0	12	1	0	28	33	17	8	0	5.14
Henry, Dutch-Frank John	21-22StLA 23-24BknN 27-29NYN 29-30ChiN	05-12-02	Cleveland, Ohio	08-23-68	L	L	6'1	173	27	43	.386	6	164	62	25	646	809	190	170	3	4.39
Henry, Earl-Earl Clifford (Hook)	44-45CleA	06-10-17	Roseville, Ohio	12-10-02	L	L	5'11	172	1	4	.200	0	17	3	1	40	38	23	15	0	4.95
Henry, Jim-James Francis	36-37BosA 39PhiN	06-26-10	Danville, Va.	08-15-76	R	R	6'2	175	6	2	.750	4	33	11	3	114	114	59	51	0	4.82
Henshaw, Roy-Roy Knikelbine (Kid)	33,35-36ChiN 37BknN 38StLN 42-44DetA	07-29-11	Chicago, Ill.	06-08-93	R	L	5'8	155	33	40	.452	7	216	71	20	742	782	327	337	3	4.16
Hensiek, Phil-Philip Frank (Sid)	35WasA	10-13-01	St. Louis, Mo.	02-21-72	R	R	6'	160	0	3	.000	0	13	2	1	9	6	0	5.69		
Herring, Art-Arthur L. (Sandy)	29-33DetA 34BknN 39ChiA 44-46BknN 47PitN	03-10-06	Altus, Okla.	12-02-95	R	R	5'7	168	34	38	.472	13	199	56	25	697	754	284	243	3	4.33
Herrmann, Leroy-Leroy George	32-33ChiN 35CinN	02-27-06	Steward, Ill.	07-03-72	R	R	5'10	185	5	7	.417	1	45	9	2	142	168	48	39	0	4.12
Heusser, Ed-Edward Burlton (The Wild Elk of the Wasatch)	35-36StLN 38PhiN 40PhiA 43-46CinN 48PhiN	05-07-09	Salt Lake Co., Utah	03-01-56	B	R	6'	187	56	67	.455	18	266	104	50	1087	1167	300	299	10	3.69
			Bats Right 35-38																		
Heving, Joe-Joseph William	30-31WasA 33-34ChiA 35DP 37-38CleA 38-40BosA 41-44CleA 45BosN	09-02-00	Covington, Ky.	04-11-70	R	R	6'1	185	76	48	.613	63	430	40	17	1039	1136	380	429	1	3.90
Hickey, Jim-James Robert (Sid)	44BosN 45MS	08-22-20	N. Abington, Mass.	09-20-97	R	R	6'1	204	0	1	.000	0	9	0	0	10	9	7	3	0	7.20
Higbe, Kirby-Walter Kirby	37-39ChiN 39-40PhiN 41-43BknN 44-45MS 46-47BknN 47-49PitN 49-50NYN	04-08-15	Columbia, S.C.	05-06-85	R	R	5'11	190	118	101	.539	24	418	238	98	1954	1763	979	971	11	3.68
Hilcher, Whitey-Walter Frank	31-32,35-36ChiN	02-28-09	Chicago, Ill.	11-21-62	R	R	6'	174	3	6	.333	1	31	6	1	85	103	33	28	1	5.29
Hildebrand, Oral-Oral Clyde	31-36CleA 37-38StLA 39-40NYA	04-07-07	Bridgeport, Ind.	09-08-77	R	R	6'3	175	83	78	.516	13	258	182	80	1430	1490	623	527	9	4.36
Hill, Carmen-Carmen Proctor (Specs)	15-16,18-19PitN 22NYN 26-29PitN 29-30StLN	10-01-95	Royalton, Minn.	01-01-90	R	R	6'1	180	49	33	.598	4	147	85	47	788	769	267	264	5	3.44
Hockette, George-George Edward (Lefty)	34-35BosA	04-07-08	Perth, Miss.	01-20-74	L	L	6'	174	4	4	.500	0	26	7	3	88	105	18	25	0	4.09
Hodge, Shavel-Clarence Clement	20-22ChiA	07-06-93	Clayton, Ala.	12-31-67	R	R	6'4	190	14	15	.483	9	75	21	9	302	360	131	67	0	5.16
Hoerst, Frank-Francis Joseph (Lefty)	40-42PhiN 43-45MS 46-47PhiN	08-11-17	Philadelphia, Pa.		L	L	6'3	192	10	33	.233	1	98	41	9	348	381	175	105	0	5.17
Hoffman, Bill-William Joseph	39PhiN	03-03-18	Philadelphia, Pa.	05-14-04	L	L	5'9	170	0	0	—	0	3	0	0	6	8	7	1	0	13.50
Hogsett, Chief-Elon Chester	29-36DetA 36-37StLA 38WasA 44DetA	11-02-03	Brownell, Kans.	07-17-01	L	L	6'	190	63	87	.420	33	330	114	37	1221	1511	501	441	0	5.03
Holborow, Walt-Walter Albert (Wally)	44-45WasA 48PhiA	11-30-13	New York, N.Y.	07-14-86	R	R	5'11	187	2	3	.400	0	21	2	1	51	52	25	18	1	3.35
Holland, Bill-William David	29PhiA	06-04-15	Varina, N.C.	04-05-97	L	L	6'1	185	0	0	—	0	13	0	0	23	33	16	5	0	11.25
Holland, Mul-Howard Arthur	26CinN 27NYN 29StLN	01-06-03	Franklin, Va.	02-16-69	R	R	6'4	185	1	1	.500	0	13	0	0	26	15	15	5	0	6.26
Hollaway, Ken-Kenneth Eugene	22-28DetA 29-30CleA 30NYN	08-08-97	Barwick, Ga.	10-26-68	L	R	6'1	185	64	52	.552	18	285	100	43	1159	1370	397	293	4	4.40
Holley, Ed-Edward Edgar	28ChiN 32-34PhiN 34PitN	07-23-99	Benton, Ky.		R	R	6'1	195	33	42	.440	0	97	76	30	548	602	170	169	5	4.40
Holling, Carl-Carl Theodore	21-22DetA	07-09-96	Dixon, Cal.	07-18-62	R	R	6'1	172	4	8	.333	4	40	12	4	145	183	63	40	0	5.03
Hollingsworth, Al-Albert Wayne (Boots)	35-38CinN 38-39PhiN 39BknN 40WasA 42-46StLA 46ChiA	02-25-08	St. Louis, Mo.	04-28-96	L	L	6'2	185	70	104	.402	15	315	185	78	1519	1642	587	608	7	3.99

USE NAMES - GIVEN NAMES (NICKNAMES)	TEAM BY YEAR	BIRTH DATE	BIRTHPLACE	DEATH DATE	B	T	HGT	WGT	W	L	Pct.	SV	G	GS	CG	IP	H	BB	SO	ShO	ERA
Hollingsworth, Bonnie-John Burnette	22PitN 23WasA 24BknN 28BosN	12-26-95	Jacksboro, Tenn.	01-04-90	R	R	5'10	170	4	9	.308	0	36	11	2	118	127	81	50	0	4.88
Holloway, Jim-James Madison	29PhiN	09-22-08	Plaquemine, La.	04-15-97	R	R	6'1	165	0	0	—	0	3	0	0	5	10	5	1	0	12.60
Holshouser, Herm-Herman Alexander	30StLA	01-20-07	Rockwell, N.C.	07-26-94	R	R	6'	170	0	1	.000	1	25	1	0	62	103	28	37	0	7.84
Hopkins, Paul-Paul Henry	27,29WasA 29StLA	09-25-04	Cheter, Conn.	01-02-04	R	R	6'	170	1	1	.500	0	11	1	0	27	28	15	11	0	3.00
Horne, Trader-Berlyn Dale (Sonny)	29ChiN	04-12-99	Bachman, Ohio	02-03-83	B	R	5'9	155	1	1	.500	0	11	1	0	23	24	21	6	0	5.09
Howe, Les-Lester Curtis (Lucky)	23-24BosA	08-24-95	Brooklyn, N.Y.	07-16-76	R	R	5'11	170	2	0	1.000	0	16	2	1	37	34	9	10	0	3.41
Hoyt, Waite-Waite Charles (Schoolboy)	18NYN 19-20BosA 21-30NYA 30-31DetA 31PhiA 32BknN 32NYN 33-37PitN 37-38BknN	09-09-99	Brooklyn, N.Y.	08-25-84	R	R	6'	180	237	182	.566	52	674	424	226	3762	4037	1003	1206	25	3.59
25-26 played in A.B.L.																					
Hubbell, Bill-Wilbert William	19-20NYN 20-25PhiN 25BknN	06-17-97	San Francisco, Cal.	08-03-80	R	R	6'2	205	40	63	.388	10	204	108	50	930	1207	225	167	5	4.68
Hubbell, Carl-Carl Owen (The Meal Ticket, King Carl)	28-43NYN	06-22-03	Carthage, Mo.	11-21-88	R	L	6'	170	253	154	.622	33	535	433	260	3591	3461	725	1677	36	2.98
Huckleby, Earl-Earl Eugene	35PhiA		Konawa, Okla.	02-25-99	R	R	5'11	165	1	0	1.000	0	1	0	0	7	8	4	2	0	9.00
Hudlin, Willis-George Willis (Ace)	26-40CleA 40WasA 40StLA 40NYN 44StLA	05-23-06	Wagoner, Okla.	08-05-02	R	R	6'	190	158	156	.503	31	491	328	154	2613	3011	843	677	11	4.41
Hughes, Bill-William Nesbert	21PitN	11-18-96	Philadelphia, Pa.	02-25-63	R	R	5'10	155	0	0	—	0	1	0	0	2	3	1	2	0	4.50
Hughson, Tex-Cecil Carlton	41-44BosA 45MS 46-49BosA	02-09-16	Buda, Tex.	08-06-93	R	R	6'3	198	96	54	.640	17	225	156	99	1376	1270	372	693	15	2.94
Hulihan, Harry-Harry Joseph	22BosN	04-18-99	Rutland, Vt.	09-11-80	R	L	5'11	170	2	3	.400	1	7	6	2	40	40	26	16	0	3.15
Hulvey, Hank-James Hensel	23PhiA	07-18-97	Mt. Sidney, Va.	04-09-82	B	R	6'	180	0	1	.000	0	1	1	0	7	10	2	2	0	7.71
Humphrey, Bill-Bryon William	38BosA	06-17-11	Vienna, Mo.	02-13-92	R	R	6'	180	0	0	—	0	2	0	0	2	5	1	0	0	9.00
Humphries, John-John William	38-40CleA 41-45ChiA 46PhiN	06-23-15	Clifton Forge, Va.	06-24-65	R	R	6'1	185	52	63	.452	12	211	111	49	1001	1024	373	317	9	3.79
Huntzinger, Walter-Walter Henry (Shakes)	23-25NYN 26StLN 26ChiN	02-06-99	Pottsville, Pa.	08-11-81	R	R	6'	150	7	8	.467	3	60	8	2	167	179	49	40	0	3.61
Hutchings, Johnny-John Richard Joseph	40-41CinN 41-42,44-46BosN	04-14-16	Chicago, Ill.	04-27-63	R	R	6'2	250	12	18	.400	6	155	34	5	472	474	180	212	3	3.95
Hutchinson, Ira-Ira Kendall	33ChiA 37-38BosN 39ChiN 39BknN 40-41StLN 44-45BosN	08-31-10	Chicago, Ill.	08-21-73	R	R	5'10	180	34	33	.507	13	209	32	7	612	628	249	179	2	3.75
Jablonowski, Pete (See Pete Appleton)																					
Jackson, John-John Lewis	33PhiN	07-15-09	Philadelphia, Pa.	10-22-56	R	R	6'2	180	2	2	.500	0	10	7	1	54	74	35	11	0	6.00
Jacobs, Art-Arthur Edward (Lefty)	39CinN	08-28-02	Luckey, Ohio	06-08-67	L	L	5'10	170	0	0	—	1	1	0	0	1	2	1	0	0	9.00
Jacobs, Bucky-Newton Smith	37,39-40WasA	03-21-13	Altavista, Va.	06-15-90	R	R	5'11	150	1	2	.333	0	22	1	0	40	43	20	15	0	4.95
Jaeger, Joe-Joseph Peter (Zip)	20ChiN	03-03-95	St.Cloud, Minn.	12-13-63	R	R	6'1	190	0	0	—	0	2	0	0	3	6	4	0	0	12.00
Jakucki, Sig-Sigmund (Jack)	36,44-45StLA	08-20-09	Camden, N.J.	05-28-79	R	R	6'2	198	25	22	.532	5	72	50	27	411	431	131	131	5	3.79
Jamerson, Charley-Charles Dewey (Lefty)	26 played in N.F.L.	24BosA	01-26-00	Enfield, Ill.	08-04-80	L	L	6'1	195	0	0	—	0	1	0	0	1	3	0	0	0	18.00
Javery, Al-Alva William (Bear Tracks)	40-46BosN	06-05-18	Worcester, Mass.	03-16-77	R	R	6'3	183	53	74	.417	5	205	147	61	1142	1164	452	470	15	3.81
Jeffcoat, George-George Edward	36-37,39BknN 43BosN	12-24-13	New Brookland, S.C.	10-13-78	R	R	5'11	175	7	11	.389	3	70	9	4	170	159	100	86	1	4.50
Johns, Augie-Augustus Francis (Lefty)	26-27DetA	09-10-99	St. Louis, Mo.	12-12-75	L	L	5'9	170	6	4	.600	1	36	14	3	114	118	70	41	1	5.37
Johnson, Art-Arthur Gilbert	27NYN	02-15-97	Warren, Pa.	06-07-82	B	L	6'	167	0	0	—	0	3	1	1	0	0	0	0	0	0.00
Johnson, Art-Arthur Henry (Lefty)	40-42BosN 43-45MS	07-16-16	Winchester, Mass.		L	L	6'2	185	7	16	.304	1	49	19	6	195	203	79	71	0	3.69
Johnson, Fred-Frederick Edward (Cactus, Deacon)	22-23NYN 38-39StLA	03-10-94	Hanley, Tex.	06-14-73	R	R	5'11	180	5	10	.333	3	27	12	6	118	145	44	39	0	5.26
Johnson, Hank-Henry Ward	25-26,28-32NYA 33-35BosA 36PhiA 39CinN	05-21-06	Bradenton, Fla.	08-20-82	R	R	5'11	175	63	56	.529	11	249	116	45	1065	1107	567	568	4	4.76
	Bats Both 33																				
Johnson, Johnny-John Clifford (Swede)	44NYA 45ChiA 46AJ	09-29-14	Belmore, Ohio	06-26-91	R	R	6'	182	3	2	.600	7	51	1	0	97	110	59	49	0	4.18
Johnson, Lloyd-Lloyd William (Eppa)	34PhiN	12-24-10	Santa Rosa, Cal.	10-08-80	L	L	6'4	220	0	0	—	0	1	0	0	1	1	0	0	0	0.00
Johnson, Rankin-Adam Rankin Jr.	41PhiA 42-45MS	03-01-17	Hayden, Ariz.	02-11-06	R	R	6'3	177	1	0	1.000	0	7	0	0	10	14	3	2	0	3.60
Johnson, Si-Silas Kenneth	28-36CinN 36-38StLN 40-43PhiN 44-45MS 46PhiN 46-47BosN	10-05-06	Danway, Ill.	05-12-94	R	R	5'11	180	101	165	.380	15	492	272	108	2280	2510	687	840	13	4.09
Johnson, Syl-Sylvester	22-25DetA 26-33StLN 34CinN 34-40PhiN	12-31-00	Portland, Ore.	02-20-85	R	R	5'11	180	112	117	.489	43	542	209	82	2166	2290	488	920	13	4.06
Johnson, Vic-Victor Oscar	44-45BosA 46CleA	08-30-20	Eau Claire, Wis.	05-10-05	R	L	6'	160	6	8	.429	2	42	15	4	126	152	69	31	1	5.07
Joiner, Roy-Roy Merrill (Pop, Lefty)	34-35ChiN 40NYN	10-30-06	Red Bluff, Cal.	12-26-89	L	L	6'	170	3	3	.500	1	52	4	0	90	133	27	34	0	5.30
Jones, Art-Arthur Lennox	32BknN	02-07-06	Kershaw, S.C.	11-25-80	R	R	6'	165	0	0	—	0	3	0	0	5	5	7	1	0	9.00
Jones, Broadway-Jesse Frank	23PhiN	11-15-98	Millsboro, Del.	09-07-77	R	R	5'9	154	0	0	—	0	3	0	0	1	2	1	0	0	18.00
Jones, Dale-Dale Eldon (Nubs)	41PhiN 42-45MS	12-17-18	Marquette, Neb.	11-08-80	R	R	6'1	172	0	1	.000	0	2	1	0	8	13	6	2	0	7.88
Jones, Dick-Decatur Poindexter	26-27WasA	05-22-02	Meadville, Miss.	08-02-94	L	R	6'	184	2	1	.667	0	6	3	1	24	28	16	4	0	6.75
Jones, Earl-Earl Leslie (Lefty)	45StLA	06-11-19	Fresno, Cal.	01-24-89	L	L	5'10	190	0	0	—	1	10	0	0	28	18	18	13	0	2.57
Jones, Johnny-John Paul (Admiral)	19NYN 20BknN	08-25-92	Arcadia, La.	06-05-80	R	R	6'	150	1	0	1.000	0	17	5	8	9	5	8	0	5.82
Jones, Ken-Kenneth Frederick (Broadway)	24DetA 30BknN	04-13-03	Dover, N.J.	05-15-91	R	R	6'3	193	0	1	.000	0	9	1	0	22	29	5	4	0	5.82
Jones, Percy-Percy Lee	20-22,25-28ChiN 29BosN 30PitN	10-28-99	Harwood, Tex.	03-18-79	R	L	5'11	175	53	57	.482	6	251	114	49	1026	1137	494	381	8	4.34
Jones, Sad Sam-Samuel Pond	14-15CleA 16-21BosA 22-26NYA 27StLA 28-31WasA 32-35ChiA	07-26-92	Woodsfield, Ohio	07-06-66	R	R	6'	170	228	216	.514	31	647	487	250	3884	4084	1396	1223	35	3.84
Jonnard, Claude-Claude Alfred	21-24NYN 26StLN 29CinN	11-23-97	Nashville, Tenn.	08-27-59	R	R	6'2	185	14	12	.538	17	137	9	2	350	372	122	160	0	3.78
Jorgens, Orville-Orville Edward	35-37PhiN	06-04-08	Rockford, Ill.	01-11-92	R	R	6'1	180	21	27	.438	1	144	54	11	496	571	233	149	0	4.70
Joyce, Bob-Robert Emmett	39PhiN 46NYN	01-14-15	Stockton, Cal.	12-10-81	R	R	6'1	180	6	9	.400	0	44	13	3	169	235	57	49	0	6.18
Judd, Oscar-Thomas William Oscar (Ossie)	41-45BosA 45-48PhiN	02-14-08	Rebecca, Canada	12-27-95	L	L	6'	180	40	51	.440	7	161	99	43	708	744	397	304	4	3.90
Judd, Ralph-Ralph Wesley	27WasA 29-30NYN	12-07-01	Perrysburg, Ohio	05-06-57	L	R	5'10	170	3	0	1.000	1	21	0	0	63	70	16	23	0	3.29
Jungels, Ken-Kenneth Peter (Curly)	37-38,40-41CleA 42PitN	06-23-16	Aurora, Ill.	09-09-75	R	R	6'1	180	1	0	1.000	0	25	0	0	49	56	32	21	0	6.80
Jurisich, Al-Alvin Joseph	44-45StLN 46-47PhiN	08-25-21	New Orleans, La.	11-03-81	R	R	6'2	193	15	22	.405	4	104	42	13	388	344	189	177	3	4.24
Kalfass, Bill-William Phillip (Lefty)	37PhiA	03-03-16	New York, N.Y.	09-08-68	R	L	6'3	190	1	0	1.000	0	3	1	1	12	10	10	9	0	3.00
Kamp, Ike-Alphonse Francis	24-25BknN	09-05-00	Roxbury, Mass.	02-26-55	B	L	6'	170	2	5	.286	1	65	7	1	77	77	40	24	0	5.12
Kardow, Paul-Paul Otto (Tex)	36CleA	09-19-15	Humble, Tex.	04-27-68	R	R	6'6	210	0	0	—	0	2	0	0	1	2	0	0	0	4.50
Karl, Andy-Anton Andrew	43BosA 43-46PhiN 47BosN	04-08-14	Mt.Vernon, N.Y.	04-08-89	R	R	6'1	175	18	23	.439	26	191	4	1	423	451	130	107	0	3.51
Karr, Benn-Benjamin Joyce (Baldy)	20-22BosA 25-27CleA	11-28-93	Mt. Pleasant, Miss.	12-08-68	L	R	6'	175	35	48	.422	5	177	58	29	781	921	260	180	1	4.60
Katz,Bob-Robert Clyde	44CinN	01-30-11	Lancaster, Pa.	12-14-62	R	R	5'11	190	0	0	—	0	6	0	0	18	17	7	4	0	4.50
Kaufmann, Tony-Anthony Charles	21-27ChiN 27PhiN 27-28,30-31,35StLN (See B20-45)	12-16-00	Chicago,Ill.	06-04-82	R	R	5'11	165	64	62	.508	12	202	124	71	1086	1198	368	345	9	4.18
Keck, Cactus-Frank Joseph	22CinN	01-13-99	St. Louis, Mo.	02-06-81	R	R	5'11	170	10	12	.455	3	62	21	6	218	222	61	43	1	3.51
Keefe, Dave-David Edwin	17PhiA 18MS 19-21PhiA 22CleA	01-09-97	Williston, Vt.	02-04-78	R	R	5'9	165	9	17	.346	1	97	27	12	353	403	113	126	1	4.16
Keen, Vic-Howard Victor	18PhiA 21-25ChiN 26-27StLN	03-16-99	Bel Air, Md.	12-10-76	R	R	5'9	165	42	44	.488	6	165	81	41	749	888	248	202	1	4.11
Keenan, Jimmie-James William (Sparkplug)	20-21PhiN	05-25-98	Avon, N.Y.	06-05-80	L	L	5'7	155	1	2	.333	0	16	2	0	35	51	16	9	0	6.43
Kehn, Chet-Chester Lawrence	42BknN 43-45MS	10-30-21	San Diego, Cal.	04-05-84	R	R	5'11	168	0	0	—	0	5	0	0	8	8	4	3	0	6.75
Kelleher, Hal-Harold Joseph	35-38PhiN	06-24-13	Philadelphia, Pa.	08-27-89	R	R	6'	165	4	9	.308	1	50	6	3	134	174	81	49	1	5.98
Kellett, Al-Alfred Henry	26-31 played in A.B.L.	23PhiA 24BosA	10-30-01	Red Bank, N.J.	07-14-60	R	R	6'3	200	0	1	.000	0	6	0	0	10	11	10	1	0	8.10
Kelley, Harry-Harry Leroy	25-26WasA 36-38PhiA 38-39WasA	02-13-06	Parkin, Ark.	03-23-58	R	R	5'9	190	42	47	.472	3	146	78	43	676	812	244	230	3	4.86
Kelly, Mike-Michael J.	26PhiN	11-09-08	St. Louis, Mo.	04-26-82	R	R	6'1	178	0	0	—	0	4	0	0	7	7	4	2	0	9.00
Kelly, Ren-Reynolds Joseph	23PhiN	11-18-99	San Francisco, Cal.	08-24-63	R	R	6'	183	0	0	—	0	7	1	0	7	7	4	1	0	2.57
Kemner, Dutch-Herman John	29CinN	03-04-99	Quincy, Ill.	01-16-88	R	R	5'10	175	0	0	—	0	15	1	0	15	19	8	10	0	7.80
Kennedy, Vern-Lloyd Vernon	34-37ChiA 38-39DetA 39-41StLA 41WasA 42-44CleA 44-45PhiN 45CinN	03-20-07	Kansas City, Mo.	01-28-93	L	R	6'	175	104	132	.441	5	344	263	126	2025	2173	1049	691	7	4.68
Kenney, Art-Arthur Joseph	38BosN	04-29-16	Milford, Mass.		L	L	6'	175	0	0	—	0	2	0	0	3	8	2	0	0	18.00
Kirksieck, Bill-Wayman William	39PhiN	12-06-13	Ulm, Ark.	03-11-70	R	R	6'1	183	0	2	.000	0	23	2	1	63	81	32	13	0	7.14
Kerr, Dickie-Richard Henry	19-21ChiA 22HO 23-24SL 25StLN	07-03-93	St. Louis, Mo.	05-04-63	L	L	5'7	155	53	35	.602	4	140	83	55	812	876	250	235	7	3.83
Ketchum, Gus-Augustus Franklin	22PhiA	03-21-97	Royce City, Tex.	09-06-80	R	R	5'9	170	0	0	—	0	6	0	0	16	19	8	4	0	5.63
Kiefer, Joe-Joseph William (Smoke, Harlem Joe)	20ChiA 25-26BosA	07-19-99	West Layden, N.Y.	07-05-75	R	R	5'11	190	0	5	.000	0	15	4	0	50	56	30	9	0	6.12
Kimball, Newt-Newell W.	37-38ChiN 40StLN 40-43BknN 43PhiN	03-27-15	Logan, Utah	03-22-01	R	R	6'2	190	11	9	.550	4	94	13	4	236	219	117	88	0	3.78
Kimberlin, Harry-Harry Lydle (Murphy)	36-39StLA	07-08-06	Sullivan, Mo.	12-31-99	R	R	6'	190	1	4	.200	1	34	6	2	84	107	47	21	0	4.71
Kime, Hal-Harold Lee (Lefty)	20StLN	03-15-98	West Salem, Ohio	05-16-39	L	L	5'9	160	0	0	—	0	2	0	0	7	3	7	1	0	2.57
Kimsey, Chad-Clyde Elias (Slim)	29-32StLA 32-33ChiA 36DetA	08-06-06	Copperhill, Tenn.	12-03-42	L	R	6'3	200	24	29	.453	17	198	10	2	508	623	194	121	0	5.08
Kinzy, Harry-Harry Hersel (Slim)	34ChiA	07-19-10	Hallsville, Tex.	06-22-03	R	R	6'4	185	0	1	.000	0	13	2	1	34	38	31	12	0	5.03
Kircher, (Kerscher), Mike (Wolfgang)-Michael Andrew	19PhiA 20-21StLN	09-30-97	Rochester, N.Y.	06-26-72	B	R	6'	185	2	2	.500	0	14	4	1	48	69	9	9	0	6.00
Klaerner, Hugo-Hugo Emil (Dutch)	34ChiA	10-15-08	Fredericksburg, Tex.	02-03-82	R	R	5'11	190	0	0	—	0	1	0	0	5	5	0	2	0	3.60
Kleine, Hal-Harold John	44-45CleA	06-08-23	St. Louis, Mo.	12-10-57	L	L	6'2	193	1	2	.333	0	7	4	0	48	46	43	18	0	5.44
Kleinhans, Ted-Theodore (Traugott)Otto	34PhiN 34CinN 36NYA 37-38CinN	04-08-99	Deer Park, Wis.	07-24-85	R	L	6'1	185	4	7	.364	1	56	12	1	143	185	76	48	0	5.29
Kleinke, Nubs-Norbert George	35,37StLN	05-19-11	Fond du Lac, Wis.	03-16-50	R	R	6'1	170	1	1	.500	0	34	4	1	34	44	10	14	0	4.76

USE NAMES - GIVEN NAMES (NICKNAMES)	TEAM BY YEAR	BIRTH DATE	BIRTHPLACE	DEATH DATE	B	T	HGT	WGT	W	L	Pct.	SV	G	GS	CG	IP	H	BB	SO	ShO	ERA
Kline, Bob-Robert George (Junior)	30-33BosA 34PhiA 34WasA	12-09-09	Enterprise, Ohio	03-16-87	R	R	6'3	200	30	28	.517	7	148	37	8	442	501	195	87	1	5.05
Klinger, Bob-Robert Harold	38-43PitN 44-45MS 46-47BosA	06-04-08	Allenton, Mo.	08-19-77	R	R	6'	180	66	61	.520	23	265	130	48	1090	1153	358	357	7	3.68
Klopp, Stan-Stanley Harold (Betz)	44BosN	12-22-10	Womelsdorf, Pa.	03-11-80	R	R	6'1	180	1	2	.333	0	24	0	0	46	47	33	17	0	4.30
Kneisch, Rudy-Rudolph Frank	26DetA	04-10-99	Baltimore, Md.	04-06-65	R	L	5'10	175	0	1	.000	0	2	2	1	17	18	6	4	0	2.65
Knight, Jack-Elmer Russell	22StLN 25-26PhiN 27BosN	01-12-95	Pittsboro, Miss.	07-30-76	L	R	6'	175	10	18	.357	5	72	27	9	255	382	89	49	0	6.85
Knott, Jack-John Henry	33-38StLA 38-40ChiA 41-42,46PhiA 43-45MS	03-02-07	Dallas, Tex.	10-13-81	R	R	6'2	200	82	103	.443	19	325	192	62	1557	1787	642	484	4	4.97
Knowlton, Bill-William Young	20PhiA	08-18-92	Philadelphia, Pa.	02-25-44	R	R			0	1	.000	0	1	1	0	6	9	3	5	0	4.50
Kohlman, Joe-Joseph James (Blackie)	37-38WasA	01-28-13	Philadelphia, Pa.	03-16-74	R	R	5'11	172	1	0	1.000	0	9	2	1	27	27	14	8	0	5.33
Kolp, Ray-Raymond Carl (Jockey)	21-24StLA 27-34CinN	10-01-94	New Berlin, Ohio	07-29-67	R	R	5'10	187	79	95	.454	18	383	172	66	1688	1918	424	439	11	4.08
Koupal, Lou-Louis Laddie	25-26PitN 28-29BknN 29-30PhiN 37StLA	12-19-98	Tabor, S.D.	12-08-61	R	R	5'11	175	10	21	.323	1	101	34	12	336	436	156	87	0	5.57
Kowalik, Fabian-Fabian Lorenz	32ChiA 35-36ChiN 36PhiN 36BosN	04-22-08	Falls City, Tex.	08-14-54	B	R	5'11	185	3	11	.214	2	51	12	4	167	218	63	42	0	5.44
	Bats Right 36																				
Krakauskas, Joe-Joseph Victor Lawrence	37-40WasA 41-42CleA 43-45MS 46CleA	03-28-15	Montreal, Canada	07-08-60	L	L	6'1	203	26	36	.419	4	149	63	22	583	605	355	347	1	4.54
Kraus, Tex-John William (Texas Jack)	43PhiN 44MS 45PhiN 46NYN	04-26-18	San Antonio, Tex.	01-02-76	R	L	6'4	190	15	25	.375	2	70	39	10	307	318	133	83	1	3.99
Krausse, Lew-Lewis Bernard Sr.	31-32PhiA	06-08-12	Media, Pa.	09-06-88	R	R	6'	167	5	1	.833	0	23	4	3	68	70	30	17	1	4.50
Kremer, Ray-Remy Peter (Wiz)	24-33PitN	03-23-93	Oakland, Cal.	02-08-65	R	R	6'	190	143	85	.627	10	308	247	134	1955	2108	483	516	14	3.77
Kress, Red-Ralph (See B20-45)	35WasA 46NYN	01-02-05	Columbia, Cal.	11-29-62	R	R	5'11	165	0	1	.000	0	10	13	6	6	0	11.70
Krist, Howie-Howard Wilbur (Spud)	37-38,41-43StLN 44-45MS 46StLN	02-28-16	W. Henrietta, N.Y.	04-23-89	R	R	6'1	175	37	11	.771	6	128	37	15	444	408	158	150	2	3.32
Kuczynski, Bert-Bernard Carl	43PhiN 44-46MS	01-08-20	Philadelphia, Pa.	01-19-97	R	R	6'	195	0	1	.000	0	6	1	0	25	36	9	8	0	3.96
	43,46 played in N.F.L.																				
Kuhn, Bob-Robert Daniel	24CleA	10-12-99	Vicksburg, Mich.	11-20-56	L	R	6'1	182	0	1	.000	0	1	0	0	1	4	0	0	0	27.00
Kunz, Earl-Earl Dewey (Pinch)	23PitN	12-25-98	Sacramento, Cal.	04-14-63	R	R	5'10	170	1	2	.333	1	21	2	1	46	48	24	12	0	5.48
Lagger, Ed-Edwin Joseph	34PhiA	07-14-12	Joliet, Ill.	11-10-81	R	R	6'3	200	0	0	—	0	2	0	0	18	27	14	2	0	11.00
Lamanna, Frank-Frank (Hank)	40-42BosN 43-45MS	08-22-19	Waterton, Pa.	09-01-80	R	R	6'2	195	6	5	.545	4	45	5	1	93	95	67	28	0	5.23
Lamanske, Frank-Frank James (Lefty)	35BknN	09-30-06	Oglesby, Ill.	08-04-71	L	L	5'11	170	0	0	—	0	2	0	0	4	5	1	1	0	6.75
LaMaster, Wayne-Wayne Lee	37-38PhiN 38BknN	02-13-07	Speed, Ind.	08-04-84	L	L	5'8	170	19	27	.413	4	71	42	11	295	352	116	173	2	5.83
Lambert, Gene-Eugene Marion	41-42PhiN 43-45MS	04-26-21	Crenshaw, Miss.	02-10-00	R	R	5'11	175	0	1	.000	0	3	1	0	10	14	2	4	0	2.70
Lanahan, Dick-Richard Anthony	35-37WasA 40-41PitN	09-27-11	Washington, D.C.	03-12-75	L	L	6'1	170	6	13	.316	2	56	14	3	152	177	75	62	0	5.15
Lang, Marty-Martin John (Lefty)	30PitN	09-27-05	Hooper, Neb.	01-13-68	R	L	5'11	160	0	0	—	0	2	0	0	2	9	3	2	0	45.00
Lanier, Max-Hubert Max	38-46,49-51StLN 47-48SM 52-53NYN 53StLA	08-18-15	Denton, N.C.		R	L	5'11	190	108	82	.568	17	327	204	91	1619	1490	611	821	21	3.01
Lanning, Johnny-John Young (Tobacco Chewin' Johnny)	36-39BosN 40-43PitN 44MS 45-46PitN 47BosN	04-22-07	Asheville, N.C.	11-08-89	R	R	6'1	185	58	60	.492	13	278	104	30	1072	1078	358	295	4	3.58
Lanning, Tom-Thomas Newton	38PhiN	04-22-09	Biltmore, N.C.	11-04-67	L	L	165		0	1	.000	0	7	3	2	2	6	4	3	0	6.43
Lansing, Gene-Eugene Hewitt (Jigger)	22BosN	01-11-98	Albany, N.Y.	01-18-45	R	R	6'1	185	0	1	.000	0	15	1	0	41	46	22	14	0	5.93
Lapihuska, Andy-Andrew (Apples)	42-43PhiN 44-45MS	11-01-22	Delmont, N.J.	02-17-96	L	R	5'10	175	0	2	.000	0	4	2	0	23	22	16	8	0	7.04
Larkin, Steve-Stephen Patrick	34DetA	12-09-10	Cincinnati, Ohio	05-02-69	R	R	6'1	195	0	0	—	0	2	0	0	5	8	5	8	0	1.50
Lasley, Bill-Willard Almond	24StLA	07-13-02	Gallipolis, Ohio	08-24-90	B	R	6'	175	0	0	—	0	2	0	0	4	7	2	0	0	6.75
Lawrence, Bob-Robert Andrew (Larry)	24ChiA	12-14-99	Brooklyn, N.Y.	11-06-83	R	R	5'11	180	0	0	—	0	1	1	1	1	1	1	0	0	9.00
Lawson, Roxie-Alfred Voyle	30-31CleA 33,35-39DetA 39-40StLA	12-14-06	Donnellson, Iowa	04-09-77	R	R	6'	180	47	39	.547	11	208	83	34	852	963	512	258	2	5.37
Lee, Bill-William Crutcher (Big Bill)	34-43ChiN 43-45PhiN 45-46BosN 47ChiN	10-21-09	Plaquemine, La.	06-15-77	R	R	6'3	195	169	157	.518	13	462	379	182	2863	2953	893	998	29	3.54
Lee, Roy-Roy Edwin	45NYN	09-28-17	Elmira, N.Y.	11-11-85	L	L	5'11	175	0	2	.000	0	4	1	0	9	11	4	1	0	11.57
Lee, Thornton-Thornton Starr (Lefty)	33-36CleA 37-47ChiA 48NYN	09-13-06	Sonoma, Cal.	06-09-97	L	L	6'3	205	117	124	.485	10	374	272	155	2331	2327	838	937	14	3.56
LeFebvre(Lefebvre), Bill-Wilfrid Henry (Lefty)	38-39BosA 43-44WasA 44MS	11-11-15	Natick, R.I.		L	L	5'11	180	5	5	.500	3	36	10	3	132	162	51	36	0	5.05
Leheny, Regis-Regis Francis	32BosA	01-05-08	Pittsburgh, Pa.	11-02-76	L	L	6'	180	0	0	—	0	3	0	0	3	5	3	1	0	15.00
Lehr, Norm-Norman Carl Michael (King)	26CleA	05-28-01	Rochester, N.Y.	07-17-68	R	R	6'	168	0	0	—	0	4	0	0	15	11	4	4	0	3.00
Lennon, Ed-Edward Francis	28PhiN	08-17-97	Philadelphia, Pa.	09-13-47	R	R	5'11	170	0	0	—	0	5	0	0	12	19	10	6	0	9.00
Leon, Izzy-Isidoro (Becerra)	45PhiN	01-04-11	Cruces, Cuba	07-25-02	R	R	5'10	175	0	4	.000	0	14	4	0	39	49	19	11	0	5.31
Leonard, Dutch-Emil John	33-36BknN 38-46WasA 47-48PhiN 49-53CinN	03-25-09	Auburn, Ill.	04-17-83	R	R	6'	185	191	181	.513	44	640	374	192	3220	3304	737	1170	30	3.25
Leopold, Rudy-Rudolph Matas	28PhiA	07-27-05	Grand Cane, La.	09-03-65	L	L	6'	160	0	0	—	0	2	0	0	2	4	2	2	0	4.50
Leverett, Dixie-Gorham Vance	22-24,26ChiA 29BosN	03-29-94	Georgetown, Tex.	02-20-57	R	R	5'11	190	29	34	.460	6	122	77	33	639	725	221	193	4	4.49
Leverette, Hod-Horace Wilbur (Levy)	20StLA	02-04-89	Shreveport, La.	04-10-58	R	R	6'	200	0	0	—	0	3	2	0	10	9	12	0	0	5.40
Levsen, Emil-Emil Henry (Dutch)	23-28CleA	04-29-98	Wyoming, Iowa	03-12-72	R	R	6'	180	21	26	.447	0	80	51	23	402	426	173	88	3	4.19
Lewis, Bert-William Burton	24PhiN	10-03-95	Tonawanda, N.Y.	03-24-50	R	R	6'2	176	0	0	—	0	12	0	0	18	23	7	3	0	6.00
Lieber, Dutch-Charles Edwin	35-36PhiA	02-01-10	Alameda, Cal.	12-31-61	R	R	6'	180	1	2	.333	2	21	1	0	59	62	25	15	0	3.97
Liebhardt, Glenn-Glenn Ignatius (Sandy)	30PhiA 36,38StLA	07-31-10	Cleveland, Ohio	03-14-92	R	R	5'10	170	0	1	.000	0	31	0	0	67	116	35	23	0	9.00
Lillard, Gene-Robert Eugene (See B20-45)	39ChiN 40StLN	11-12-13	Santa Barbara, Cal.	04-12-91	R	R	5'10	170	3	6	.333	0	22	8	2	60	76	40	33	0	7.05
Lindquist, Carl-Carl Emil (Lindy)	43-44BosN	05-09-19	Morris Run, Pa.	09-13-01	R	R	6'2	185	0	2	.000	0	7	2	0	25	25	6	5	0	4.91
Lindsay, Jim-James Kendrick	22,24CleA 29-33StLN 34CinN 34StlN 37BknN	01-24-98	Greensburg, La.	10-25-63	R	R	6'1	175	21	20	.512	19	177	20	5	431	507	176	175	1	4.70
Linke, Ed-Edward Karl (Babe)	33-37WasA 38StLA	11-09-11	Chicago, Ill.	06-21-88	R	R	5'11	180	22	20	.524	9	120	43	13	450	555	206	156	0	5.00
Lisenbee, Hod-Horace Milton	27-28WasA 29-22BosA 36PhiA 45CinN	09-23-98	Clarksville, Tenn.	11-14-87	R	R	5'11	170	37	58	.389	1	207	107	48	969	1076	314	253	4	4.81
Liska, Ad-Adolph James	29-31WasA 32-33PhiN	07-10-06	Dwight, Neb.	11-30-98	R	R	5'11	160	17	18	.486	3	111	28	11	352	354	150	104	1	3.86
Littlejohn, Carlisle-Charles Carlisle	27-28StLN	10-06-01	Martens, Tex.	10-27-77	R	R	5'11	175	5	2	.714	0	26	4	2	74	83	28	22	0	4.14
Livengood, Wes-Wesley Amos	39CinN	09-18-10	Salisbury, N.C.	09-02-96	R	R	6'2	172	0	0	—	0	5	0	0	6	9	4	0	0	9.00
Llewellyn, Clem-Clement Manly (Lew)	22NYA	08-01-95	Dobson, N.C.	11-27-69	L	R	6'3	195	0	0	—	0	2	0	0	2	4	1	0	0	9.00
Loftus, Pat-Francis Patrick	26WasA	03-10-98	Scranton, Pa.	10-27-80	R	R	5'9	190	0	0	—	0	1	0	0	1	1	1	0	0	9.00
Logan, Bob-Robert Dean (Lefty)	35BknN 37DetA 37-38ChiN 41CinN 45BosN	05-20-10	Thompson, Neb.	05-20-78	R	L	5'11	175	7	15	.318	4	57	25	5	223	245	81	67	1	3.15
Lohrman, Bill-William LeRoy	34PhiN 37-43NYN 43-44BknN 44CinN	05-22-13	Brooklyn, N.Y.	09-13-99	R	R	6'1	185	60	59	.504	8	198	120	47	991	1048	240	330	10	3.69
Long, Tommy-Thomas Francis (Little Hawk)	24BknN	04-22-98	Memphis, Tenn.	09-16-73	L	L	5'7	140	0	0	—	0	1	0	0	2	2	2	0	0	9.00
Lopatka, Art-Arthur Joseph	45StLN 46PhiN	05-28-19	Chicago, Ill.		B	L	5'10	170	1	1	.500	0	17	2	0	20	7	9	0	6.35
Lowe, George-George Wesley (Doc)	20CinN	04-25-95	Ridgefield Park, N.J.	09-02-81	R	R	6'2	180	0	0	—	0	2	1	1	2	1	1	0	0	9.00
Lowry, Sam-Samuel Joseph (Mose)	42-43PhiA 44-45PhiN	03-25-20	Philadelphia, Pa.	12-01-92	R	R	5'11	175	0	0	—	0	21	21	10	45	5	0	5.14
Lucas, Ray-Ray Wesley (Luke)	29-31NYN 33-34BknN	10-02-08	Springfield, Ohio	10-09-69	R	R	6'2	175	1	1	.500	0	22	2	0	56	58	32	5	0	5.79
Lucas, Red-Charles Fred (The Nashville Narcissus)	23NYN 24BosN 26-33CinN 34-38PitN	04-28-02	Columbia, Tenn.	07-09-86	L	R	5'10	170	157	135	.538	7	396	302	204	2543	2736	455	602	22	3.72
Lucey, Joe-Joseph Earl (Scootch) (See B20-45)	25BosA	03-27-97	Holyoke, Mass.	07-30-80	R	R	6'	168	0	1	.000	0	7	2	0	11	18	14	2	0	9.00
Lucier, Lou-Louis Joseph	43-44BosA 44-45PhiN	23-18-13	Northbridge, Mass.		R	R	5'8	160	3	5	.375	1	33	9	3	101	118	47	31	0	3.83
Ludolph, Willie-William Francis (Wee Willie)	24DetA	01-21-00	San Francisco, Cal.	04-07-52	R	R	6'1	170	0	0	—	0	6	5	2	1	5	1	0	4.50
Lundgren, Del-Ebin Delmar	24PitN 26-27BosA	09-21-99	Lindsborg, Kans.	10-19-84	R	R	5'8	160	5	15	.250	2	55	20	5	182	220	114	53	2	6.52
Luque, Dolf-Adolfo Domingo de Guzman (The Pride of Havana)	14-15BosN 18-29CinN 30-31BknN 32-35NYN	08-04-90	Havana, Cuba	07-03-57	R	R	5'7	160	193	179	.519	28	550	367	206	3221	3231	918	1130	26	3.24
Lyle, Jim-James Charles	25WasA		Lake, Miss.	10-10-77	R	R	6'1	180	0	0	—	0	1	0	0	3	5	1	3	0	6.00
Lynch, Adrian-Adrian Ryan	20StLA	02-09-97	Laurens, Iowa	03-16-34	B	R			2	0	1.000	0	5	3	1	22	23	17	8	0	5.32
Lynn, Red-Japhet Monroe	39DetA 39-40NYN 44ChiN 45MS	12-27-13	Kenney, Tex.	10-27-77	R	R	6'	162	10	8	.556	5	85	7	4	184	175	85	85	1	3.96
Lyons, George-George Tony (Smooth)	20StLN 24BosN	01-25-91	Bible Grove, Mo.	12-81-81	R	R	5'11	180	5	3	.625	3	33	8	3	101	118	54	30	0	4.72
Lyons, Hersh-Herschel Englebert	41StLN	07-23-15	Fresno, Cal.		R	R	5'11	195	0	0	—	0	3	1	0	9	15	5	1	0	4.00
Lyons, Ted-Theodore Amar	23-42ChiA 43-45MS 46,M46-48ChiA	12-28-00	Lake Charles, La.	07-25-86	B	R	5'11	200	260	230	.531	23	594	484	356	4161	4489	1121	1073	27	3.67
MacFayden, Danny-Daniel Knowles (Deacon Danny)	26-32BosA 32-34NYA 35CinN 35-39BosN 40PitN 41WasA 43BosN	06-10-05	North Truro, Mass.	08-26-72	R	R	5'11	170	132	159	.454	9	465	334	157	2706	2981	872	797	17	3.96
Mack, Frank-Frank George (Stubby)	22-23,25ChiA	02-02-00	Oklahoma City, Okla.	07-02-71	R	R	6'1	180	2	3	.400	0	27	4	1	70	83	40	23	1	5.01
Macon, Max-Max Cullen (See B20-45)	38StLA 40,42-43BknN 44BosN 45-46MS 47BosN	10-14-15	Pensacola, Fla.	08-05-89	L	L	6'3	175	17	19	.472	3	81	29	9	297	307	128	90	2	4.24
MacPherson, Harry-Harry William	44BosN	07-10-26	N. Andover, Mass.		R	R	5'10	150	0	0	—	0	1	0	0	1	1	0	0	0	0.00
Mahaffey, Roy-Le Roy (Popeye)	26-27PitN 30-35PhiA 36StLA	02-09-03	Belton, S.C.	07-23-69	R	R	6'	195	67	49	.578	7	180	129	45	1056	1161	452	365	1	5.01
Mahon, Al-Alfred Gwinn (Lefty)	30PhiA	09-23-09	Albion, Mich.	12-26-77	L	L	5'11	160	0	0	—	0	4	0	0	4	11	7	0	0	24.75
Mails, Duster-John Walter (The Great)	15-16BknN 17-18MS 20-22CleA 25-26StLN	10-01-94	San Quentin, Cal.	07-05-74	L	L	6'	195	32	25	.561	2	104	61	29	515	554	220	242	5	4.11

USE NAMES - GIVEN NAMES (NICKNAMES)	TEAM BY YEAR	BIRTH DATE	BIRTHPLACE	DEATH DATE	B	T	HGT	WGT	W	L	Pct.	SV	G	GS	CG	IP	H	BB	SO	ShO	ERA
Mains, Bud-James Royal	43PhiA	06-12-22	Bridgeton, Me.	03-17-69	R	R	6'2	190	0	1	.000	0	1	1	1	8	9	3	4	0	5.6
Makosky, Frank-Frank (Dins)	37NYA	01-10-87	Boonton, N.J.	01-12-71	R	R	6'1	185	5	2	.714	3	26	1	1	58	64	24	27	0	4.9
Malis, Cy-Cyrus Sol	34PhiN	02-26-07	Philadelphia, Pa.	01-12-71	R	R	5'11	175	0	0	—	0	1	0	0	4	4	2	1	0	4.5
Malone, Pat-Perce Leigh	28-34ChiN 35-37NYA	09-25-02	Altoona, Pa.	05-13-43	R	R	6'2	200	134	92	.593	26	357	219	115	1915.	1934	705	1024	16	3.7
					Bats Both 35-37																R
Maltzberger, Gordon-Gordon Ralph (Maltzy)	43-44,46-47ChiA 45MS	09-04-12	Utopia, Tex.	12-11-74	R	6'	170	20	13		.606	33	135	0	0	294	258	75	136	0	2.6
Manders, Hal-Harold Carl	41-42,46DetA 46ChiN	06-14-17	Waukee, Iowa		R	R	6'	187	3	1	.750	0	30	1	0	60	71	28	28	0	4.8
Mangum, Leo-Leo Allan (Blackie)	24-25ChiA 28NYN 32-35BosN	05-24-96	Durham, N.C.	07-09-74	R	R	6'1	187	11	10	.524	1	85	16	4	258	343	72	78	1	5.3
Marberry, Firpo-Fred	23-32WasA 33-35DetA 36NYN 36WasA	11-30-98	Streetman, Tex.	06-30-76	R	R	6'1	190	147	89	.623	101	551	186	86	2066	2049	686	822	7	3.6
Marcum, Johnny-John Alfred (Footsie)	33-35PhiA 36-38BosA 39StLA 39ChiN	09-09-09	Campbellsburg, Ky.	09-10-84	R	L	5'11	197	65	63	.508	7	195	132	69	1100	1269	344	392	8	4.6
Markle, Cliff-Clifford Monroe	15-16NYA 21-22CinN 24NYA	05-03-94	Dravosburg, Pa.	05-24-74	R	R	5'9	163	12	17	.414	0	56	21	12	235	235	110	90	2	4.1
Marquis, Jim-James Milburn	11-18-00	Yoakum, Tex.	08-05-92	25NYA		R	R	5'11	174	0	0	—	0	2	0	0	7	12	6	0	0	10.2
Marrow, Buck-Charles Kennon	32DetA 37-38BknN	08-29-09	Tarboro, N.C.	11-21-82	R	R	6'4	200	3	8	.273	1	39	9	2	100	112	49	39	0	5.0
Martin, Pat-Patrick Francis	19-20PhiA	04-13-92	Brooklyn, N.Y.	02-01-49	L	L	5'11	170	1	6	.143	0	10	7	3	43	59	33	20	0	5.1
Martin, Speed-Elwood Good	17StLA 18-22CinN	05-15-93	Wawawai, Wash.	06-14-83	R	R	6'	183	29	43	.403	6	126	63	30	593	645	191	207	4	3.7
Martina, Joe-Joseph John (Oyster Joe)	24WasA	07-08-89	New Orleans, La.	03-22-62	R	R	6'	183	6	8	.429	0	24	14	8	125	129	56	57	0	4.6
Martini, Wedo-Guido Joe (Southern)	35PhiA	07-01-13	Birmingham, Ala.	10-28-70	R	R	5'10	165	0	2	.000	0	3	2	0	6	8	11	1	0	18.00
Masters, Walt-Walter Thomas	31WasA 37PhiN 39PhiA	03-28-07	Pen Argyle, Pa.	07-10-92	R	R	5'10	180	0	0	—	1	8	0	0	21	27	13	3	0	6.0
36,43-44 played in N.F.L.																					
Masterson(Nastasowski), Paul-Paul Nicholas	40-42PitN	11-27-97	Chicago, Ill.		L	L	5'11	165	1	0	1.000	0	8	1	1	24	26	13	14	0	6.0
Matthews, Joe-John Joseph (Lefty)	22BosN	09-29-98	Baltimore, Md.	02-08-68	B	L	6'	170	0	1	.000	0	3	1	0	10	5	6	0	0	3.6
Matthewson, Dale-Dale Wesley	43-44PhiN	05-15-23	Catasauqua, Pa.	02-20-84	R	R	5'11	145	0	3	.000	0	28	2	0	58	53	24	16	0	4.3
Mattingly, Earl-Laurence Earl	31BknN	11-04-04	New Port, Md.	09-08-93	R	R	5'10	164	0	1	.000	0	8	0	0	14	15	10	6	0	2.5
Matuzak, Harry-Harry George (Matty)	34,36PhiA	01-27-10	Omer, Mich.	11-16-78	R	R	5'11	185	0	4	.000	0	17	1	0	39	49	14	17	0	5.7
Maun, Ernie-Ernest Gerald	24NYN 26PhiN	02-03-01	Clearwater, Kans.	01-01-87	R	R	6'	165	2	5	.286	1	36	5	0	73	103	28	14	0	6.1
Mauney, Dick-Richard	45-47PhiN	01-26-20	Concord, N.C.	02-06-70	R	R	5'11	164	12	14	.462	4	53	24	9	229	240	52	72	3	2.9
May, Buckshot-William Herbert	24PitN	12-13-99	Bakersfield, Cal.	03-15-84	L	R	6'2	170	0	0	—	0	1	0	0	1	2	1	0	0	0.0
May, Jakie-Frank Spruiell	17-21StLN 24-30CinN 31-32ChiN	11-25-95	Youngsville, N.C.	06-03-70	R	L	5'8	178	72	95	.431	19	410	160	70	1563	1645	617	765	7	3.8
Mays, Carl-Carl William (Sub)	15-19BosA 19-23NYA 24-28CinN 29NYN	11-12-91	Liberty, Mo.	04-04-71	R	R	5'11	195	207	127	.620	29	490	325	228	3021	2912	734	862	29	2.9
McAfee, Bill-William Fort	30ChiN 31BosN 32-33WasA 34StLA	09-07-07	Smithville, Ga.	07-08-58	R	R	6'2	186	10	4	.714	5	83	7	2	187	237	81	44	0	5.6
McBee, Pryor-Pryor Edward (Lefty)	26ChiA	06-20-01	Blanco, Okla.	04-19-65	R	L	6'1	190	0	0	—	0	1	0	0	1	1	3	1	0	9.0
McCloskey, Irish-James Ellwood	36BosN	05-26-10	Danville, Pa.	08-18-71	L	L	5'10	180	0	0	—	0	4	1	0	8	14	3	2	0	11.2
McColl, Alex-Alexander Boyd (Red)	33-34WasA	03-29-94	Eagleville, Ohio	02-06-91	R	R	6'1	178	4	4	.500	1	46	3	2	129	142	43	34	0	3.7
McCrabb, Les-Lester William (Buster)	39-42,50PhiA	11-04-14	Wakefield, Pa.		R	R	5'11	175	10	15	.400	2	38	27	13	210	270	63	57	1	5.9
McCullough, Paul-Paul Willard	29WasA	07-28-98	New Castle, Pa.	11-07-70	R	R	5'10	190	0	0	—	0	3	0	0	7	2	3	2	0	9.0
McCullough, Phil-Pinson Lamar	42WasA 43-45MS	07-22-17	Stockbridge, Ga.	01-16-03	R	R	6'4	204	0	0	—	0	1	0	0	3	5	2	2	0	9.0
McDonald, Hank-Henry Monroe	31,33PhiA 33StLA	01-16-11	Santa Monica, Cal.	10-17-82	R	R	6'3	200	3	9	.250	0	48	16	1	141	159	79	46	1	5.8
McEvoy, Lou-Louis Anthony	30-31NYA	05-30-02	Williamsburg, Kans.	12-17-53	R	R	6'2	203	1	3	.250	4	34	1	0	64	83	41	17	0	7.8
McGee, Bill-William Henry (Fiddler Bill)	35-41StLN 41-42NYN	11-16-09	Batchtown, Ill.	02-11-87	R	R	6'2	215	46	41	.529	6	197	102	31	853	861	355	340	9	3.7
McGillen, John-John Joseph	44PhiA	08-06-17	Eddystone, Pa.	08-11-87	L	L	6'	175	0	0	—	0	2	0	0	1	1	2	0	0	18.00
McGraw, Bob-Robert Emmett	17-19NYA 19BosA 20NYA 25-27BknN 27StLN 28-29PhiN	04-10-95	La Veto, Colo.	06-02-78	R	R	6'2	160	26	38	.406	6	168	47	17	591	677	265	164	1	4.8
McGrew, Slim-Walter Howard	22-24WasA	08-05-99	Yoakum, Tex.	08-21-67	R	R	6'7	235	0	1	.000	0	10	2	0	30	40	17	10	0	6.6
McIlree, Vance-Vance Elmer	21WasA	10-14-97	Riverside, Iowa	05-06-59	R	R	6'	160	0	0	—	0	1	0	0	1	6	2	1	0	9.0
McKain, Archie-Archie Richard (Happy)	37-38BosA 39-41DetA 41,43StLA	05-12-11	Delphos, Kans.	05-21-85	L	L	5'10	170	26	21	.553	16	165	34	8	487	529	208	188	1	4.2
					Bats Left 41,43																
McKain, Hal-Harold Leroy	27CleA 29-32ChiA	07-10-06	Logan, Iowa	01-24-70	L	R	5'11	185	18	23	.439	6	103	24	7	381	435	193	136	1	4.9
McKee, Rogers-Rogers Hornsby	43-44PhiN 45-46MS	09-16-26	Shelby, N.C.		L	L	6'1	160	1	0	1.000	0	5	1	1	15	14	6	1	0	6.0
McKeithan, Tim-Emmett James	32-34PhiA	11-02-06	Shelby, N.C.	08-30-69	R	R	6'2	182	1	1	.500	0	10	3	0	26	35	14	3	0	7.2
McLaughlin, Jud-Justin Theodore	31-33BosA	03-24-12	Brighton, Mass.	09-27-64	L	L	5'11	155	0	0	—	0	7	0	0	24	42	17	4	0	10.13
McLaughlin, Pat-Patrick Elmer	37DetA 40PhiA 45DetA	08-17-10	Taylor, Tex.	11-01-99	R	R	6'2	175	0	2	.000	0	12	3	0	36	45	17	8	0	6.7
McLean, Mac-Albert Elrod	35WasA	09-20-12	Chicago, Ill.	09-29-90	R	R	6'	175	0	0	—	0	4	0	0	9	12	5	3	0	7.00
McNamara, Tim-Timothy Augustine	22-25BosN 26NYN	11-20-98	Millville, Mass.	11-05-94	R	R	5'11	170	14	29	.326	4	98	42	13	396	495	92	88	4	4.7
McNaughton, Gordon-Gordon Joseph	32BosA	07-10-10	Chicago, Ill.	08-06-42	R	R	6'1	190	0	1	.000	0	6	2	0	21	21	22	6	0	6.4
McQuaid, Herb-Herbert George	23CinN 26NYA	03-29-99	San Francisco, Cal.	04-04-66	R	R	6'2	185	2	0	1.000	0	29	2	0	72	79	23	15	0	4.3
McQuillan, Hugh-Alvin Hugh (Handsome Hugh)	18-22BosN 22-27NYN 27BosN	09-15-95	New York, N.Y.	08-26-47	R	R	6'	170	88	94	.484	16	279	204	95	1562	1703	489	446	10	3.8
McWeeny, Doug-Douglas Lawrence (Buzz)	21-22ChiA 23ST 24ChiN 26-29BknN 30CinN	08-17-96	Chicago, Ill.	01-01-53	R	R	6'2	180	37	57	.394	6	206	117	38	948	980	450	386	5	4.1
Meador, Johnny-John Davis	20PitN	12-04-92	Madison, N.C.	04-11-70	R	R	5'10	165	2	2	.500	0	12	2	0	36	48	7	5	0	4.2
Meadows, Lee-Henry Lee (Specs)	15-19StLN 19-23PhiN 23-29PitN	07-12-94	Oxford, N.C.	01-29-63	L	R	6'	190	188	180	.511	7	490	405	219	3150	3280	956	1063	25	3.3
Meadows, Rufe-Rufus Rivers	26CinN	08-25-07	Chase City, Va.	05-10-70	Bats Both 20-21,26,29	L	L	5'11	175	0	0	—	0	1	0	0	0.1	0	0	0	0	0.0
Meeker, Roy-Charles Roy (Lefty)	23-24PhiA 26CinN	09-15-00	Lead Mine, Mo.	03-25-29	L	L	5'9	175	8	14	.364	0	42	17	8	192	214	103	54	1	4.7
Meine, Heinie-Henry William (The Count of Luxemburg)	22StLA 29-34PitN	05-01-96	St. Louis, Mo.	03-18-68	R	R	5'11	180	66	50	.569	3	165	132	60	998	1125	287	199	7	3.9
Melton, Cliff-Clifford George (Mountain Music)	37-44NYN 45ST	01-03-12	Brevard, N.C.	07-28-86	L	L	6'5	203	86	80	.518	16	272	179	65	1453	1446	431	660	13	3.4
Melton, Rube-Reuben Franklin	41-42PhiN 43-44BknN 45MS 46-47BknN	02-27-17	Cramerton, N.C.	09-11-71	R	R	6'5	205	30	50	.375	1	162	87	25	704	624	395	363	6	3.6
Meola, Mike-Emile Michael	33BosA 36StLA 36BosA	10-19-05	New York, N.Y.	09-01-76	R	R	5'11	175	0	3	.000	0	18	3	1	43	63	25	15	0	4.8
Merena, Spike-John Joseph	34BosA	11-18-09	Paterson, N.J.	03-08-77	L	L	6'	185	1	2	.333	0	4	3	2	25	20	16	7	1	2.8
Mertz, Jim-James Verlin	43WasA 44-46MS	08-10-16	Lima, Ohio	02-04-03	R	R	5'10	170	5	7	.417	3	33	10	2	117	109	58	53	0	4.6
Messenger, Bud-Andrew Warren	24CleA	02-01-98	Grand Blanc, Mich.	11-04-71	R	R	6'	175	2	0	1.000	0	5	2	0	25	28	14	4	0	4.3
Metivier, Dewey-George Dewey	22-24CleA	05-06-98	Cambridge, Mass.	03-02-47	R	R	5'11	175	7	7	.500	4	54	13	4	167	239	75	24	0	5.7
Michaels, John-John Joseph	32BosA	07-10-07	Bridgeport, Conn.	11-18-96	L	L	5'10	154	1	6	.143	0	28	8	2	81	101	27	16	0	5.1
Michaelson, John-John August (Mike)	21ChiA	08-12-93	Tivalkoski, Finland	04-16-68	R	R	5'9	165	0	0	—	0	3	4	1	9	14	7	3	0	4.5
Middleton, Jim-James Blaine (Rifle Jim)	17NYN 21DetA	05-28-89	Argos, Ind.	01-12-74	R	R	6'1	165	7	12	.368	8	51	10	2	158	184	52	40	0	4.5
Middleton, John-John Wayne (Lefty)	22CleA	04-11-00	Mt. Calm, Tex.	11-03-86	L	L	6'1	195	0	0	—	0	7	8	6	2	0	7.7				
Midkiff, James-Richard James	38DetA	09-28-14	Gonzales,Tex.	10-30-56	R	R	6'2	195	1	1	.500	0	13	2	0	35	43	21	10	0	5.1
Miklos, Hank-John Joseph	44ChiN	11-27-10	Chicago, Ill.	03-29-00	L	L	5'11	165	0	0	—	0	7	0	0	9	3	6	0	0	7.7
Miles, Carl-Carl Thomas	40PhiA	03-22-18	Trenton, Mo.		B	L	5'11	178	0	0	—	0	2	0	0	8	8	6	0	0	13.5
Miljus, Johnny-John Kenneth (Big Serb, Jovo)	15PitF 17BknN 18MS 20-21BknN 27-29PitN 28-29CleA	06-30-95	Pittsburgh, Pa.	02-11-76	R	R	6'	178	29	26	.527	5	127	45	15	457	526	173	166	2	3.9
Miller, Bill-William Francis (Wild Bill)	37StLA	04-12-10	Hannibal, Mo.	02-26-82	R	R	6'	180	1	0	1.000	0	4	1	0	4	7	4	1	0	13.50
Miller, Elmer-Elmer Joseph (Lefty)	29PhiN	04-17-03	Detroit, Mich.	01-08-87	L	L	5'11	165	0	1	.000	0	11	12	21	15	0	11.45				
Miller, Jake-Walter	24-31CleA 33ChiA	02-28-98	Wagram, Ohio	08-20-75	L	L	6'	185	60	58	.508	4	200	138	57	1069	1260	340	305	8	4.0
Miller, Ken-Kenneth Albert (Whitey)	44NYN	04-03-91	St. Louis, Mo.		R	R	6'	195	0	0	—	0	5	1	4	2	0	0.00				
Miller, Ralph-Ralph Henry (Lefty)	21WasA	01-14-99	Vinton, Iowa	02-18-67	R	L	6'1	195	1	0	1.000	0	2	1	0	5	3	2	0	0	0.00
Miller, Red-Leo Alphonso	23PhiN	02-11-97	Philadelphia, Pa.	10-20-73	R	R	5'11	195	0	0	—	0	1	0	0	1	2	5	1	0	27.00
Miller, Ronnie-Roland Arthur	41WasA 42-45MS	08-28-18	Mason City, Iowa	01-06-98	R	R	5'11	167	0	0	—	0	1	1	0	1	0	4	1	0	4.50
Miller, Russ-Russell Lewis	27-28PhiN	03-25-00	Etna, Ohio	04-30-62	R	R	5'11	165	1	13	.071	1	35	14	2	123	158	37	23	0	5.4
Milligan, John-John Alexander	28-31PhiN 34WasA	01-22-04	Schuylerville, N.Y.	05-15-72	L	L	5'10	172	3	8	.273	0	35	12	4	117	141	67	38	0	5.2
Mills, Art-Arthur Grant	27-28BosN	03-02-03	Utica, N.Y.	07-23-75	R	R	5'10	155	0	1	.000	0	19	1	0	46	58	26	7	0	5.28
Mills, Lefty-Howard Robinson	34,37-40StLA	05-12-10	Dedham, Mass.	09-23-82	L	L	6'1	187	15	30	.333	2	96	48	21	435	453	302	267	1	6.06
Milnar, Al-Albert Joseph (Happy)	36,38-43CleA 43StLA 44-45MS 46StLA 46PhiN	12-26-13	Cleveland, Ohio	06-30-05	L	L	6'2	195	57	58	.496	7	188	127	49	996	1043	495	350	10	4.22
Milstead, George-George Earl (Cowboy, Lefty)	24-26ChiN	06-26-03	Cleburne, Tex.	08-09-77	L	L	5'9	142	3	7	.300	2	36	9	2	106	130	45	27	0	4.1
Miner, Ray-Raymond Theodore (Lefty)	21PhiA	04-04-97	Glens Falls, N.Y.	09-15-63	R	L	5'11	160	0	0	—	0	1	0	0	2	3	0	1	0	36.00
Mitchell, Clarence-Clarence Elmer	11DetA 16-17CinN 18-22BknN 23-28PhiN 28-30StLN 30-32NYN	02-22-91	Franklin, Neb.	11-06-63	L	L	5'11	190	125	139	.473	9	390	278	145	2217	2613	624	543	12	4.12
Mitchell, Monroe-Monroe Barr (See B20-45)	23WasA	09-11-01	Starkville, Miss.	09-04-76	R	R	6'1	170	2	4	.333	0	10	6	3	42	57	22	8	1	6.4
Modak, Mike-Michael	45CinN 46MS	05-18-22	Campbell, Ohio	12-12-95	R	R	5'10	170	2	2	.333	1	7	4	0	42	44	22	8	0	5.7
Mogridge, George-George Anthony	11-12ChiA 15-20NYA 21-25WasA 25StLA 26-27BosN	02-18-89	Rochester, N.Y.	03-04-62	L	L	6'2	165	133	130	.506	18	399	260	138	2275	2350	565	679	19	3.20
Mohart, George-George Benjamin	20-21BknN	03-06-92	Buffalo, N.Y.	10-02-70	R	R	5'9	165	0	1	.000	0	15	1	0	43	41	8	14	0	3.20

USE NAMES - GIVEN NAMES (NICKNAMES)	TEAM BY YEAR	BIRTH DATE	BIRTHPLACE	DEATH DATE	B	T	HGT	WGT	W	L	Pct.	SV	G	GS	CG	IP	H	BB	SO	ShO	ERA
Monteagudo, Rene-Rene [Miranda] (See B20-45)	38,40WasA 45PhiN	03-12-16	Havana, Cuba	09-14-73	L	L	5'7	165	3	7	.300	2	46	11	5	169	221	95	93	0	6.39
Moon, Leo-Leo (Lefty)	32CleA	06-22-99	Bellemont, N.C.	08-25-70	R	L	6'	175	0	0	—	0	1	0	0	6	11	7	1	0	10.50
Mooney, Jim-Jim Irving	31-32NYN 33-34StLN	09-04-06	Mooresburg, Tenn.	04-27-79	R	L	5'11	168	17	20	.459	2	92	41	13	356	426	133	116	3	4.25
Moore, Bill-William Christopher	25DetA	09-03-02	Corning, N.Y.	01-24-84	R	R	6'3	195	0	0	—	0	1	0	0	0	0	3	0	0	∞
Moore, Carlos-Carlos Whitman	30WasA	08-03-06	Clinton, Tenn.	07-02-58	R	R	6'1	180	0	0	—	0	4	0	0	12	9	4	2	0	2.25
Moore, Cy-William Austin	29-32BknN 33-34PhiN	02-07-05	Elberton, Ga.	03-28-72	R	R	6'1	190	16	26	.381	3	147	39	13	467	547	168	181	3	4.86
Moore, Euel-Euel Walton (Chief)	34-35PhiN 35NYN 36PhiN		Reagan, Okla.	02-12-89	R	R	6'2	185	9	16	.360	3	61	29	5	224	293	77	75	0	5.50
Moore, Jim-James Stanford	28-29CleA 30-32ChiA	12-14-03	Prescott, Ark.	05-08-73	R	R	6'	165	2	4	.333	1	46	10	3	140	147	49	29	0	4.50
Moore, Roy-Roy Daniel	20-22PhiA 22-23DetA	10-21-98	Austin, Tex.	04-05-51	B	L	6'	185	11	26	.297	3	80	48	19	407	476	239	154	0	4.98
Moore, Whitey-Lloyd Albert	36-42CinN 42StLN 43-45MS	06-10-12	Tuscarawas,Ohio	12-10-87	R	R	6'1	195	30	29	.508	4	133	60	18	514	450	292	228	4	3.75
Moore, Wilcy-William Wilcy (Cy)	27-29NYA 31-32BosA 32-33NYA	05-20-97	Bonita,Tex.	03-29-63	R	R	6'	195	51	44	.537	49	261	32	14	691	732	232	204	2	3.69
Mooty, Jake-Jake T	36-37CinN 40-43ChiN 44DetA	04-13-13	Bennett, Tex.	04-20-70	R	R	5'10	170	16	23	.410	8	111	38	14	433	434	194	145	1	4.03
Moran, Hiker-Albert Thomas	38-39BosN	01-01-12	Rochester, N.Y.	01-07-98	R	R	6'4	185	1	1	.500	0	7	2	1	23	22	12	4	0	3.91
Morgan, Cy-Cyril Arlon	21-22BosN	11-11-95	Lakeville, Mass.	09-11-46	R	R	6'	170	1	1	.500	1	19	0	0	31	45	19	8	0	7.55
Morrell, Bill-Willard Blackmer (Bats Right 26)	26WasA 30-31NYN	04-09-93	Hyde Park, Mass.	08-05-75	L	R	6'	172	8	6	.571	2	48	9	3	144	172	57	35	0	4.63
Morris, Bugs (See Bugs Bennett)																					
Morris, Ed-Walter Edward	22ChiN 28-31BosA	12-07-99	Foshee, Ala.	03-03-32	R	R	6'2	185	42	45	.483	6	140	78	43	674	702	293	256	2	4.19
Morrisette, Bill-William Lee	15-16PhiA 20DetA	11-21-94	Baltimore, Md.	03-25-66	R	R	6'	176	3	1	.750	0	13	4	2	51	46	29	28	0	3.35
Morrison, Guy-Walter Guy	27-28BosN		Hinton, W.Va.	08-14-34	R	R	5'11	185	1	2	.333	0	12	3	1	37	44	18	6	0	5.11
Morrison, Johnny-John Dewey (Jughandle Johnny)	20-27PitN 29-30BknN	10-22-95	Pelleville, Ky.	03-20-66	R	R	5'11	188	103	80	.563	23	297	164	90	1536	1574	506	546	13	3.64
Morrison, Phil-Philip Melvin	21PitN	10-18-94	Rockport, Ind.	01-18-55	B	R	6'2	190	0	0	—	0	1	0	0	1	1	0	1	0	0.00
Moss, Mal-Charles Malcolm	30ChiN	04-18-05	Sullivan, Ind.	02-05-83	R	L	6'	175	0	0	—	1	12	1	0	19	18	14	4	0	6.16
Moss, Ray-Raymond Earl	26-31BknN 31BosN	12-05-01	Chattanooga, Tenn.	08-09-98	R	R	6'1	185	22	18	.550	2	112	42	13	415	474	189	109	3	4.97
Mueller, Les-Leslie Clyde	41DetA 42-44MS 45DetA	03-04-19	Belleville, Ill.		R	R	6'3	190	6	8	.429	1	30	18	6	148	126	68	50	2	3.77
Muich, Joe-Ignatius Andrew	24BosN	11-23-03	St. Louis, Mo.	07-02-93	R	R	6'2	175	0	0	—	0	9	0	0	9	19	5	1	0	11.00
Mulcahy, Hugh-Hugh Noyes (Losing Pitcher)	35-40PhiN 41-44MS 45-46PhiN 47PitN	09-09-13	Brighton, Mass.	10-19-01	R	R	6'2	190	45	89	.336	9	220	145	63	1163	1271	487	314	5	4.48
Mulligan, Joe-Joseph Ignatius (Big Joe)	34BosA	07-31-13	E. Weymouth, Mass.	06-05-86	R	R	6'4	210	1	0	1.000	0	14	2	1	45	46	27	13	0	3.60
Mulrenan, Dominic-Dominic Joseph	21ChiA	12-18-93	Woburn, Mass.	07-27-64	R	R	5'11	170	2	8	.200	0	12	10	3	56	84	36	10	0	7.23
Mulroney, Frank-Frank Joseph	30BosN	04-08-03	Mallard, Iowa	11-11-85	R	R	6'	170	0	1	.000	0	3	0	0	3	2	0	2	0	3.00
Muncrief, Bob-Robert Cleveland	37,39,41-47StLA 48CleA 49PhiN 49ChiN 51NYA	01-28-16	Madill, Okla.	02-06-96	R	R	6'2	190	80	82	.494	9	288	165	67	1400	1503	392	525	11	3.81
Mungo, Van Lingle-Van Lingle (Vandy)	31-41BknN 42-43,45NYN	06-08-11	Pageland, S.C.	02-12-85	R	R	6'2	185	120	115	.511	16	364	260	123	2111	1957	862	1242	20	3.47
Munns, Les-Leslie Ernest (Nemo)	34-35BknN 36StLN	11-01-08	Fort Bragg, Cal.	02-28-97	R	R	6'5	212	4	13	.235	2	64	15	4	181	203	105	58	0	4.77
Murchison, Tim-Thomas Malcolm	17StLN 20CleA	10-08-96	Liberty, N.C.	10-20-62	R	L	6'	185	0	0	—	0	6	3	0	6	3	6	2	0	0.00
Murphy, Johnny-John Joseph (Fireman, Grandma, Fordham Johnny)	32,34-43NYA 44-45WW 46NYA 47BosA	07-14-08	New York, N.Y.	01-14-70	R	R	6'2	190	93	53	.637	107	415	40	17	1044	985	444	378	0	3.50
Murphy, Walter-Walter Joseph	31BosN	09-27-07	New York, N.Y.	03-23-76	R	R	6'1	180	0	0	—	0	2	0	0	2	4	1	0	0	9.00
Murray, Amby-Ambrose Joseph	36BosN	06-04-13	Fall River, Mass.	02-06-97	L	L	5'7	150	0	0	—	0	4	1	0	11	15	3	2	0	4.09
Murray, George-George King (Smiler)	22NYA 23-24BosA 26-27WasA 33ChiA	09-23-98	Charlotte, N.C.	10-18-55	R	R	6'	200	20	26	.435	0	110	43	10	416	450	199	114	0	5.39
Murray, Jim-James Francis (Big Jim)	22BknN	12-31-00	Scranton, Pa.	07-15-73	B	L	6'2		0	0	—	1	4	0	0	6	8	3	1	0	4.50
Mussill, Barney-Bernard James	44PhiN	10-01-19	Bowerhill, Pa.		R	L	6'1	200	0	1	.000	0	16	0	0	19	20	13	5	0	6.16
Mustaikis, Alex-Alexander Dominick	40BosA	03-26-09	Chelsea, Mass.	01-17-70	R	R	6'4	196	0	1	.000	0	15	1	0	15	15	15	6	0	9.00
Nahem, Sam-Samuel Ralph (Subway)	38BknN 41StLN 42PhiN 43-45MS 48PhiN	10-19-15	New York, N.Y.	04-19-04	R	R	6'1	185	10	8	.556	1	90	12	3	225	222	127	101	0	4.48
Naktenis, Pete-Peter Ernest	36PhiA 39CinN	02-12-14	Aberdeen, Wash.		L	L	6'1	185	0	1	.000	0	10	1	0	23	26	27	19	0	10.57
Napier, Buddy-Skelton LeRoy	12StLA 18CinN 20-21CinN	12-18-89	Byromville, Ga.	03-29-68	R	R	6'	180	4	6	.400	2	39	13	6	138	162	29	43	1	3.91
Naylor, Earl-Earl Eugene (See B20-45)	42PhiN	05-19-19	Kansas City, Mo.	01-16-90	R	R	6'	180	0	5	.000	0	20	4	1	60	68	29	19	0	6.15
Naylor, Rollie-Roleine Cecil	17,19-24PhiA	02-04-92	Krum, Tex.	06-18-66	R	R	6'1	180	42	83	.336	0	181	136	67	1010	1174	346	282	2	3.94
Naymick, Mike-Michael John	39-40,43-44CleA 44StLN	08-26-17	Berlin, Pa.	10-12-05	R	R	6'8	225	5	7	.417	2	52	9	1	113	89	80	64	0	3.90
Nehf, Art-Arthur Neukom	15-19BosN 19-26NYN 26-27CinN 27-29ChiN	07-31-92	Terre Haute, Ind.	12-18-60	L	L	5'9	176	184	120	.605	13	451	320	182	2708	2715	640	844	30	3.20
Nekola, Bots-Francis Joseph	29NYA 33DetA	03-11-07	New York, N.Y.	03-11-87	L	L	5'11	175	0	0	—	0	11	1	0	20	25	16	2	0	5.85
Nelson, Emmett-George Emmett (Ramrod)	35-36CinN	02-26-05	Viborg, S.D.	08-25-67	R	R	6'3	180	5	4	.556	1	25	8	3	77	94	27	17	1	4.09
Nelson, Lynn-Lynn Bernard (Line Drive)	30,33-34ChiN 37-39PhiA 40DetA	02-24-05	Sheldon, N.D.	02-15-55	R	R	5'10	175	33	42	.440	6	166	60	29	677	777	262	255	2	5.25
Neubauer, Hal-Harold Charles	25BosA	05-13-02	Hoboken, N.J.	09-09-49	R	R	6'1	190	1	0	1.000	0	7	0	0	10	17	11	4	0	12.60
Nevers, Ernie-Ernest Alonzo (26-27,29-31 played in N.F.L.)	26-28StLA	06-11-03	Willow River, Minn.	05-03-76	R	R	6'	205	6	12	.333	2	44	12	6	179	196	61	39	0	4.63
Newkirk, Floyd-Floyd Elmo (Three Fingers)	34NYA	07-16-08	Norris City, Ill.	04-15-76	R	R	5'11	178	0	0	—	0	1	0	0	1	1	0	0	0	0.00
Newkirk, Joel-Joel Ivan (Sailor)	19-20CinN	05-01-96	Kyana, Ind.	11-22-66	R	R	6'	180	0	1	.000	0	3	1	0	9	10	9	3	0	7.00
Newlin, Maury-Maurice Milton (Newt)	40-41StLA 42-45MS	06-22-14	Bloomingdale, Ind.	08-14-78	R	R	6'	176	1	2	.333	1	15	1	0	34	47	14	13	0	6.35
Newsom, Bobo-Norman Louis (Buck)	29-30BknN 32ChiN 34-35StLA 35-37WasA 37BosA 38-39StLA 39-41DetA 42WasA 42-43BknN 43StLA 43WasA 44-46PhiA 46-47WasA 47NYA 48NYN 52WasA 52-53PhiA	08-11-07	Hartsville, S.C.	12-07-62	R	R	6'3	210	211	222	.487	21	600	483	246	3759	3769	1732	2082	31	3.98
Newsome, Dick-Heber Hampton	41-43BosA	12-13-09	Ahoskie, N.C.	12-15-65	R	R	6'	185	35	33	.515	0	85	74	36	526	575	214	138	4	4.50
Nichols, Chet-Chester Raymond Sr.	26-27PitN 28NYN 30-32PhiN	07-02-97	Woonsocket, R.I.	07-11-82	R	R	5'11	160	1	8	.111	0	44	5	1	124	167	56	33	0	7.11
Niemes, Jack-Jack Leland	43CinN 44-46MS	10-19-19	Cincinnati, Ohio	03-04-66	R	L	6'1	180	0	0	—	0	3	0	0	5	2	1	0	0	6.00
Niggeling, Johnny-John Arnold	38BosN 39CinN 40-43StLA 43-46WasA 46BosA	07-10-03	Remsen, Iowa	09-16-63	R	R	6'	170	64	69	.481	0	184	161	81	1250	1111	516	620	12	3.22
Nitcholas, Nick-Otho James	45BknN	09-13-08	McKinney, Tex.	09-11-86	R	R	6'	195	1	0	1.000	0	7	0	0	19	19	1	4	0	5.21
North, Lou-Louis Alexander	13DetA 17StLN 18MS 20-24StLN 24BosN	06-15-91	Elgin, Ill.	05-15-74	R	R	5'11	175	21	16	.568	13	172	25	8	463	509	200	199	0	4.43
Oana, Prince-Henry Kawaihoa (See B20-45)	43-45DetA		Waipahu, Hawaii	06-19-76	R	R	6'2	193	3	2	.600	1	13	1	0	45	37	26	18	0	3.80
Ockey, Walter-Walter Andrew (Footie)	44NYN	07-04-20	New York, N.Y.	12-04-71	R	R	6'	175	0	0	—	0	2	0	0	2	2	1	0	0	3.00
Odenwald, Ted-Theodore Joseph (Lefty)	21-22CleA	01-04-02	Hudson, Wis.	10-23-65	R	L	5'10	147	1	0	1.000	0	11	0	0	18	22	8	6	0	4.50
Odom, Dave-David Everett (Porky)	43BosN	06-05-18	Dinuba, Cal.	11-19-87	R	R	5'10	185	0	3	.000	2	22	3	1	55	54	30	17	0	5.24
O'Doul, Lefty-Francis Joseph (See B20-45)	19-20,22NYA 23BosA	03-04-97	San Francisco, Cal.	12-07-69	L	L	6'	180	1	1	.500	0	34	0	0	78	104	49	19	0	4.85
Oeschger, Joe-Joseph Carl	14-19PhiN 19NYN 19-23BosN 24NYN 24PhiN 25BknN	05-24-92	Chicago, Ill.	07-28-86	R	R	6'	190	82	116	.414	3	365	197	99	1818	1936	651	535	18	3.81
Ogden, Curly-Warren Harvey	22-24PhiA 24-26WasA	01-24-01	Ogden, Pa.	08-06-64	R	R	6'1	180	18	19	.486	0	93	38	19	377	378	186	88	4	3.80
Ogden, Jack-Jack Mahlon	18NYN 28-29StLA 31-32CinN	11-05-97	Ogden, Pa.	11-09-77	R	R	6'1	180	25	34	.424	3	123	57	29	529	570	181	144	2	4.24
Ogrodowski, Joe-Joseph Anthony	25BosN	02-17-12	Hoytville, Pa.	06-24-59	R	R	5'11	165	0	0	—	0	1	0	0	1	6	3	0	0	54.00
Okie, Frank-Frank Anthony (Lefty)	20DetA	10-27-96	Detroit, Mich.	10-16-59	L	L	5'11	175	1	2	.333	0	21	1	1	41	44	18	9	0	5.27
Oldham, Red-John Cyrus (Bats Left 22, 25-26)	14-15,20-22DetA 25-26PitN	07-15-93	Zion, Md.	01-28-61	B	L	6'	176	39	48	.448	12	176	94	39	854	978	292	267	2	4.15
Oliver, Dick (See Dick Barrett)																					
Olsen, Ole-Arthur Ole	22-23DetA	09-12-94	S. Norwalk, Conn.	09-12-80	R	R	5'10	163	8	7	.533	3	54	17	6	178	189	57	64	0	4.96
Olsen, Vern-Vern Jarl	39-42ChiN 43-45MS 47ChiN	03-16-18	Hillsboro, Ore.	07-13-89	R	L	6'	175	30	26	.536	2	112	60	23	517	547	192	201	7	3.39
Olson, Ted-Theodore Otto	36-38BosA	08-27-12	Quincy, Mass.	12-09-80	R	R	6'2	185	1	1	.500	0	18	1	0	57	75	25	18	0	7.26
O'Neal, Skinny-Oran Herbert	25,27PhiN	05-02-99	Gatewood, Mo.	06-02-81	R	R	5'8	140	0	0	—	0	13	1	0	25	44	14	8	0	9.36
O'Neill, Emmett-Robert Emmett (Pinky)	43-45BosA 46ChiN 46ChiA	01-13-18	San Mateo, Cal.	10-11-93	R	R	6'3	185	15	26	.366	0	66	49	19	357	348	260	144	2	4.74
O'Neill, Harry-Joseph Henry	22-23PhiA	11-20-92	Lindsay, Canada	09-05-69	R	R	6'	180	0	0	—	0	5	3	2	8	10	1	1	0	1.80
Orrell, Joe-Forrest Gordon	43-45DetA	03-06-17	National City, Cal.	01-12-93	R	R	6'4	210	4	4	.500	1	28	7	1	89	90	46	26	0	3.03
Ortiz, Baby-Oliverio Ortiz	44WasA		Camaguey, Cuba	03-27-84	R	R	6'	190	0	2	.000	1	13	1	0	13	13	6	4	0	6.23
Orwoll, Ossie-Oswald Christian (26 played in N.F.L.) (See B20-45)	28-29PhiA	11-17-00	Portland, Ore.	05-08-67	L	L	5'11	165	6	7	.462	3	39	8	3	136	142	56	65	0	4.63
Osborn, Bob-John Bode	25-27,29-30ChiN 31PitN	04-17-03	San Diego, Tex.	04-19-60	R	R	6'1	175	27	17	.614	2	121	43	11	447	528	181	140	4	4.31
Osborne, Tiny-Earnest Preston	22-24ChiN 24-25BknN	04-06-93	Porterdale, Ga.	01-05-69	R	R	6'4	215	31	40	.437	6	142	74	31	646	693	315	263	2	4.72
Osborne, Wayne-Wayne Harold (Ossie, Fish)	35PitN 36BosN	10-11-12	Watsonville, Cal.	03-13-87	L	R	6'2	190	1	1	.500	0	8	1	0	21	32	9	9	0	6.00
Osgood, Charlie-Charles Benjamin	44BknN	11-23-26	Somerville, Mass.		R	R	5'10	180	0	0	—	0	1	0	0	3	2	3	0	0	3.00
Ostermueller, Fritz-Frederick Raymond	34-40BosA 41-43StLA 43-44BknN 44-48PitN	09-15-07	Quincy, Ill.	12-17-57	L	L	5'11	185	114	115	.498	15	390	246	113	2068	2170	835	774	11	3.99
Ozmer, Doc-Horace Robert	23PhiA	05-25-01	Atlanta, Ga.	12-28-70	R	R	6'2	185	0	0	—	0	4	0	0	3	1	3	0	0	4.50
Page, Phil-Philippe Rausac	28-30DetA 34BknN	08-23-05	Springfield, Mass.	06-26-58	R	L	6'2	190	2	3	.400	3	69	6	3	69	86	44	15	0	6.26
Page, Sam-Samuel Walter	39PhiA	02-11-16	Woodruff, S.C.	05-29-02	R	R	6'	172	0	3	.000	0	4	3	0	22	34	15	11	0	6.95
Page, Vance-Vance Linwood	38-41ChiN	09-15-03	Elm City, N.C.	07-14-51	R	R	6'1	185	15	16	.484	5	95	30	12	314	372	106	100	1	4.04

USE NAMES - GIVEN NAMES (NICKNAMES)	TEAM BY YEAR	BIRTH DATE	BIRTHPLACE	DEATH DATE	B	T	HGT	WGT	W	L	Pct.	SV	G	GS	CG	IP	H	BB	SO	ShO	ERA
Palagyi, Mike-Michael Raymond	39WasA	07-04-17	Conneaut, Ohio		R	R	6'2	185	0	0	—	0	1	0	0	0	0	3	0	0	∞
Palmero, Emilio-Emilio Antonio (Pal)	15-16NYN 21StLA 26WasA 28BosN	06-13-95	Guanabacoa, Cuba	07-15-70	L	L	5'11	157	6	15	.286	0	41	17	5	142	172	83	48	0	5.13
Bats Both 15-16																					
Parks, Slicker-Vernon Henry	21DetA	11-10-95	Dallas, Mich.	02-21-78	R	R	5'9	168	3	2	.600	0	10	1	0	25	33	16	10	0	5.76
Parmalee, Roy-LeRoy Earl (Tarzan)	29-35NYN 36StLN 37ChiN 39PhiA	04-25-07	Lambertville, Mich.	08-03-81	R	R	6'1	190	59	55	.518	3	206	145	55	1121	1075	531	514	5	4.27
Partenheimer, Stan-Stanwood Wendell (Party)	44BosA 45StLN	10-21-22	Chicopee Falls, Mass.	01-28-89	R	L	5'11	175	0	0	—	0	9	3	0	15	18	16	6	0	7.07
Passeau, Claude-Claude William	35PitN 36-39PhiN 39-47ChiN	04-09-09	Waynesboro, Miss.	08-30-03	R	R	6'3	198	162	150	.519	21	444	331	188	2718	2856	728	1104	26	3.32
Pate, Joe-Joseph William	26-27PhiA	06-06-92	Alice, Tex.	12-26-48	L	L	5'10	184	9	3	.750	12	79	2	0	167	176	72	38	0	3.50
Pattison, Jimmy-James Wells	29BknN	12-18-08	Bronx, N.Y.	02-22-91	L	L	6'	185	0	1	.000	0	6	0	0	12	9	4	5	0	4.50
Paulsen, Gil-Guilford Paul Hans	25StLN	11-14-02	Graettinger, Iowa	04-02-94	R	R	6'2	190	0	0	—	0	1	0	0	2	1	0	1	0	0.00
Payne, George-George Washington	20ChiA	05-23-89	Mt. Vernon, Ky.	01-24-59	R	R	5'11	172	1	1	.500	0	12	0	0	30	39	9	7	0	5.40
Pearce, Frank-Frank Thomas	33-35PhiN	08-31-05	Middletown, Ky.	09-03-50	R	R	6'	170	5	6	.455	0	32	8	3	115	125	40	29	1	4.77
Pearson, Ike-Isaac Overton	39-42PhiN 43-45MS 46PhiN 48ChiA	03-01-17	Grenada, Miss.	03-17-85	R	R	6'1	180	13	50	.206	8	165	54	10	558	611	268	149	2	4.84
Pearson, Monte-Montgomery Marcellus	32-35CleA 36-40NYA 41CinN	09-02-08	Oakland, Cal.	01-27-78	R	R	6'	175	100	62	.617	4	224	191	94	1430	1392	740	703	5	4.00
Peek, Steve-Stephen George	41NYA 42-45MS	07-30-14	Springfield, Mass.	09-20-91	B	R	6'2	195	4	2	.667	0	17	8	2	80	85	39	18	0	5.06
Peery, Red-George Allan	27PitN 29BosN	08-15-06	Payson, Utah	05-06-85	L	L	5'11	160	0	1	.000	0	10	1	0	45	53	10	3	0	5.00
Pence, Rusty-Russell William	21ChiA	03-11-00	Marine, Ill.	08-11-71	R	R	6'	185	0	0	—	0	4	0	0	5	6	7	2	0	9.00
Penner, Ken-Kenneth William	16CleA 29ChiN	04-24-96	Booneville, Ind.	05-28-59	R	R	5'11	170	0	1	.000	0	9	2	0	26	28	10	8	0	3.46
Pennock, Herb-Herbert Jefferis (The Knight of Kennett Square)	12-15PhiA 15-17BosA 18MS 19-22BosA 23-33NYA 34BosA	02-10-94	Kennett Sq., Pa.	01-30-48	B	L	6'	160	241	161	.600	33	617	419	247	3572	3900	916	1227	35	3.60
Perkins, Charlie-Charles Sullivan (Lefty)	30PhiA 34BknN	09-09-05	Ensley, Ala.	05-25-88	R	L	6'	175	0	3	.000	0	19	3	0	48	62	29	20	0	7.50
Perme, Len-Leonard John	42ChiA 43-45MS 46ChiA	11-25-17	Cleveland, Ohio		L	L	6'	170	0	1	.000	0	8	1	1	17	11	11	6	0	3.18
Perrin, Bill-William Joseph (Lefty)	34CleA	06-23-10	New Orleans, La.	06-30-74	R	L	5'11	172	0	1	.000	0	1	0	0	5	13	2	3	0	14.40
Pertica, Bill-William Andrew	18BosA 21-23StLN	08-17-98	Santa Barbara, Cal.	12-28-67	R	R	5'9	165	22	18	.550	2	74	47	17	330	370	138	98	2	4.28
Peterson, Jim-James Niels	31,33PhiA 37BknN	08-18-09	Philadelphia, Pa.	04-08-75	R	R	6'	200	2	6	.250	0	41	6	1	110	140	42	29	0	5.24
Peterson, Sid-Sidney Herbert	43StLA	01-31-18	Havelock, N.D.	08-29-01	R	R	6'3	200	2	0	1.000	0	3	0	0	10	15	3	0	0	2.70
Pettit, Leon-Leon Arthur (Lefty)	35WasA 37PhiN	06-23-02	Waynesburg, Pa.	11-21-74	L	L	5'10	180	8	6	.571	3	44	8	1	113	135	62	45	0	5.18
Petty, Jesse-Jesse Lee	21CleA 25-28BknN 29-30PitN 30CinN	11-23-94	Orr, Okla.	10-23-71	R	L	6'1	195	67	78	.462	4	207	153	76	1209	1286	296	407	6	3.68
Pezzullo, Pretzels-John	35-36PhiN	12-10-10	Bridgeport, Conn.	05-16-90	L	L	5'11	180	3	5	.375	1	42	7	2	86	116	51	24	0	6.38
Pfund, Lee-LeRoy Herbert	42BknN	10-10-19	Oak Park, Ill.		R	R	6'	185	3	2	.600	0	15	10	2	62	69	35	27	0	5.23
Phebus, Bill-Raymond William	36-38WasA	08-02-09	Cherryvale, Kans.	10-11-89	R	R	5'9	170	3	2	.600	2	13	6	4	54	46	35	18	1	3.33
Phelps, Ray-Raymond Clifford	30-32BknN 35-36ChiA	12-11-03	Dunlap, Tenn.	07-07-71	R	R	6'2	200	33	35	.485	1	126	80	24	602	700	220	190	5	4.93
Phillips, Buz-Albert Abenathy	30PhiN	05-25-04	Newton, N.C.	11-06-64	R	R	5'11	185	0	2	.000	0	14	1	0	44	68	18	9	0	7.98
Phillips, John-John Stephen (Jack)	45NYN	05-24-19	St. Louis, Mo.	06-16-58	R	R	6'1	185	0	0	—	0	1	0	0	1	3	5	1	0	11.25
Phillips, Red-Clarence Lemuel	34,36DetA	11-03-08	Pauls Valley, Okla.	02-01-88	R	R	6'3	195	4	4	.500	1	29	7	4	110	155	38	18	0	6.46
Phillips, Tom-Thomas Gerald	15StLA 19CleA 21-22WasA	04-01-89	Philipsburg, Pa.	04-12-29	R	R	6'2	190	8	12	.400	0	45	15	6	161	164	71	44	1	3.75
Pickrel, Clarence-Clarence Douglas	33PhiN 34BosN	03-28-11	Gretna, Va.	11-04-83	R	R	6'	180	1	0	1.000	0	19	1	0	30	44	10	15	0	4.50
Piechota, Al-Aloysius Edward	40-41BosN	01-19-14	Chicago, Ill.	06-13-96	R	R	6'1	195	2	5	.286	0	22	8	2	62	68	42	18	0	5.66
Pierce, Ray-Raymond Lester (Lefty)	24ChiN 25-26PhiN	06-06-97	Emporia, Kans.	05-04-63	L	L	5'7	156	7	11	.389	0	66	15	5	182	269	63	38	0	5.64
Piercy, Bill-William Benton (Wild Bill)	17,21NYA 22-24BosA 26BknN	05-02-96	El Monte, Cal.	08-28-51	R	R	6'	170	27	43	.386	0	116	70	28	611	677	268	165	2	4.26
Pierotti, Al-Albert Felix	20-21BosN	10-24-95	Boston, Mass.	12-12-64	R	R	5'10	195	1	2	.333	0	8	2	2	27	26	12	13	0	4.00
20,22-24,27-29 played in N.F.L.																					
Pillette, Herman-Herman Polycarp (Old Folks)	17CinN 22-24DetA	12-26-96	St. Paul, Ore.	04-30-60	R	R	6'2	190	34	32	.515	3	107	77	33	564	600	192	148	4	3.45
Pinto, Lerton-William Lerton	22,24PhiN	04-08-99	Chillicothe, Ohio	05-13-83	L	L	6'	190	0	1	.000	0	12	0	0	29	38	14	5	0	5.40
Pipgras, Ed-Edward John (Pip)	32BknN	06-15-04	Schleswig, Iowa	04-13-64	R	R	6'2	185	0	0	—	0	5	1	0	10	16	6	4	0	5.40
Pipgras, George-George William (Pip)	23-24,27-33NYA 33-35BosA	12-20-99	Ida Grove, Iowa	10-19-86	R	R	6'1	185	102	73	.583	12	276	189	93	1487	1529	598	714	15	4.09
Pippen, Cotton-Henry Harold	36StLN 39PhiA 39-40DetA	04-02-10	Cisco, Tex.	02-15-81	R	R	6'2	180	5	16	.238	1	38	25	5	175	253	64	55	0	6.38
Planeta, Emil-Emil Joseph	31NYN	01-13-09	Higganum, Conn.	02-02-63	R	R	6'	190	0	0	—	0	2	0	0	5	7	4	0	0	10.80
Plitt, Norman-Norman William (Duke)	18,27BknN 27NYN	02-21-93	York, Pa.	02-01-54	R	R	5'11	180	3	6	.333	0	23	8	1	72	85	38	9	0	4.75
Podgajny, Johnny-John Sigmund (Specs)	40-43PhiN 43PitN 46CleA	06-10-20	Chester, Pa.	03-02-71	R	R	6'	173	20	37	.351	0	115	61	20	510	542	165	129	0	4.20
Poetz, Joe-Joseph Frank (Bull Montana)	26NYN	06-22-00	St. Louis, Mo.	02-07-42	R	R	5'10	175	0	1	.000	0	2	1	0	8	8	0	0	0	3.38
Poffenberger, Boots-Cletus Elwood (The Baron)	37-38DetA 39BknN	07-01-15	Williamsport, Md.	09-01-99	R	R	5'10	178	16	12	.571	4	57	32	13	267	301	149	65	0	4.75
Poindexter, Jennings-Chester Jennings (Jinx)	36BosA 39PhiN	09-30-10	Pauls Valley, Okla.	03-03-83	L	L	5'10	165	0	2	.000	0	14	4	0	41	42	34	14	0	4.83
Polli, Lou-Louis Americo (Crip)	32StLA 44NYN	07-09-01	Baveno, Italy	12-19-00	R	R	5'10	165	0	2	.000	0	24	0	0	43	55	23	11	0	4.60
Pomorski, John-John Leon	34ChiA	12-30-05	Brooklyn, N.Y.	12-06-77	R	R	6'	178	0	0	—	0	3	0	0	2	1	2	0	0	4.50
Ponder, Elmer-Charles Elmer	17PitN 18MS 19-21PitN 21ChiN	06-26-93	Reed, Okla.	04-20-74	R	R	6'	178	17	27	.386	0	69	42	20	378	395	72	113	3	3.21
Porter, Ned-Ned Swindell	26-27NYN	05-06-05	Apalachicola, Fla.	06-30-68	R	R	6'	173	0	0	—	0	3	0	0	4	5	1	1	0	2.25
Posedel, Bill-William John (Barnacle Bill)	38BknN 39-41BosN 42-45MS 46BosN	08-02-06	San Francisco, Cal.	11-28-89	R	R	5'11	175	41	43	.488	0	138	87	45	679	757	248	227	6	4.56
Poser, Bob-John Falk	32ChiA 35StLA	03-16-10	Columbus, Wis.	05-21-02	L	R	6'	173	1	1	.500	0	5	0	15	29	6	2	0	0	9.60
Pott, Nellie-Nelson Adloph (Lefty)	22CleA	07-16-99	Cincinnati, Ohio	12-03-63	L	L	6'	185	0	0	—	0	2	0	0	2	7	2	0	0	31.50
Potter, Dykes-Marland Dykes	38BknN	11-18-10	Ashland, Ky.	02-27-02	R	R	6'	185	0	0	—	0	2	0	0	2	4	0	1	0	4.50
Potter, Nels-Nelson Thomas	36StLN 38-41PhiA 41BosA 43-48StLA 48PhiA 48-49BosN	08-23-11	Mt. Morris, Ill.	09-30-90	R	L	5'11	180	92	97	.487	22	349	177	89	1685	1721	582	747	6	4.00
Potter, Squire-Robert	23WasA	03-18-02	Flatwoods, Ky.	01-27-83	R	R	6'2	185	0	0	—	0	1	0	0	3	11	4	1	0	21.00
Powers, Ike-John Lloyd	27-28PhiA	03-13-06	Hancock, Md.	12-22-68	R	R	6'	188	2	1	.667	0	20	1	0	38	34	17	7	0	4.50
Pressnell, Tot-Forest Charles	38-40BknN 41-42ChiN	08-08-06	Findlay, Ohio	11-06-01	R	R	5'10	175	32	30	.516	12	154	42	17	526	547	134	157	4	3.80
Prim, Ray-Raymond Lee (Pop)	33-34WasA 35PhiN 43,45-46ChiN	12-30-06	Salitpa, Ala.	04-29-95	R	L	6'	178	22	21	.512	4	116	34	10	350	379	72	161	2	3.57
Proctor, Red-Noah Richard	23CinN	10-27-00	Williamsburg, Va.	12-17-54	R	R	6'1	165	0	0	—	0	4	0	0	4	11	2	0	0	13.50
Prudhomme, Augie-John Olgus (Johnny)	29DetA	11-20-02	Frierson, La.	10-04-92	R	R	6'	186	1	6	.143	0	34	6	2	94	119	53	26	0	6.22
Pruett, Hub-Hubert Shelby (Shucks)	22-24StLA 27-28PhiN 30NYN 32BknN	09-01-00	Malden, Mo.	01-28-82	R	L	5'8	165	29	48	.377	13	211	69	28	745	816	396	357	1	4.63
Pumpelly, Spence-Spencer Armstrong	25WasA	04-11-93	Owego, N.Y.	12-05-73	R		5'11	175	0	0	—	0	1	1	0	1	1	1	0	0	9.00
Pyle, Ewald-Ewald (Lefty)	39,42StLA 43WasA 44-45NYN 45BosN	08-27-10	St. Louis, Mo.	01-10-04	L	L	6'	175	11	21	.344	1	67	36	5	270	277	150	122	1	5.03
Pyle, Harlan-Harlan Albert (Firpo)	28CinN	11-29-05	Burchard, Neb.	01-13-93	R	R	6'2	180	0	0	—	0	2	0	0	1	4	1	1	0	27.00
Quinn (Picus), Jack (John Quinn)-John Picus	09-12NYA 13BosN	07-05-83	Janesville, Pa.	04-17-46	R	R	6'	196	247	219	.530	59	756	443	243	3935	4243	863	1331	28	3.29
14-15BalF 18ChiA 19-21NYA 22-25BosA 25-30PhiA 31-32BknN 33ChiA																					
Quinn, Wimpy-Wellington Hunt	41ChiN	05-14-18	Birmingham, Ala.	09-01-54	R	R	6'2	187	0	0	—	0	3	0	0	5	3	3	2	0	7.20
Rachunok, Steve-Stephen Stepanovich (The Mad Russian)	40BknN	12-05-16	Rittman, Ohio	05-11-02	R	R	6'4	200	1	1	.000	0	2	1	1	10	9	5	10	0	4.50
Rader, Drew-Drew Leon (Lefty)	21PhiN	05-14-01	Elmira, N.Y.	06-05-75	L	R	6'	187	0	0	—	0	2	0	0	2	2	1	0	0	0.00
Ragland, Frank-Frank Roland	32WasA 33PhiN	05-14-06	Water Valley, Miss.	07-28-59	R	R	6'1	186	1	4	.200	0	23	6	0	76	105	31	15	0	7.11
Rambert, Pep-Elmer Donald	39-40PitN	08-01-16	Cleveland, Ohio	11-16-74	R	R	6'	190	0	0	—	0	5	1	0	12	19	5	4	0	8.25
Rambo, Pete-Warren Dawson	26PhiN	11-01-06	Thorofare, N.J.	06-19-91	R	R	5'9	150	0	0	—	0	4	1	0	4	11	4	4	0	13.50
Reinhart, Art-Arthur Conrad	19,25-28StLN	05-29-99	Ackley, Iowa	11-11-46	L	L	6'1	170	30	18	.625	3	92	45	31	445	470	157	79	4	3.60
Reis, Bobby-Robert Joseph Thomas (See B20-45)	35BknN 36-38BosN	01-02-09	Queens, N.Y.	05-01-73	R	R	6'	190	10	13	.435	2	69	9	5	243	262	144	52	0	4.36
Reis, Tommy-Thomas Edward	38PhiN 38BosN	08-06-14	Newport, Ky.		R	R	6'	180	0	1	.000	0	11	0	0	16	16	9	6	0	12.27
Reninger, Jim-James David	38-39PhiA	03-07-15	Aurora, Ill.	08-23-93	R	R	6'3	210	0	4	.000	0	7	3	0	39	52	26	12	0	7.38
Rescigno, Xavier-Xavier Frederick (Mr. X)	43-45PitN	10-13-12	New York, N.Y.	12-24-05	R	R	5'10	175	19	22	.463	16	129	21	7	336	366	113	115	1	4.15
Rettig, Otto-Adolph John	22PhiA	01-29-94	New York, N.Y.	06-17-77	R	R	5'11	165	1	2	.333	0	4	2	1	18	18	12	3	0	5.00
Rhem, Flint-Charles Flint (Shad)	24-28,30-32StLN 32-33PhiN 34StLN 34-35BosN 36StLN	01-24-01	Georgetown, S.C.	07-30-69	R	R	6'	190	105	97	.520	10	294	230	91	1726	1958	529	534	9	4.20
Rhodes, Gordon-John Gordon (Dusty)	29-32NYA 32-35BosA 36PhiA	08-11-07	Winnemucca, Nev.	03-22-60	R	R	6'	187	43	74	.368	5	200	135	47	1048	1196	477	346	1	4.85
Rich, Woody-Woodrow Earl	39-41BosA 44BosN 45MS	03-09-16	Morganton, N.C.	04-18-83	R	R	6'2	185	6	4	.600	1	33	16	5	118	127	50	42	0	5.03
Richmond, Beryl-Beryl Justice	33ChiN 34CleA	04-24-07	Glen Easton, W.Va.	04-24-80	B	L	6'1	185	1	2	.333	0	11	2	1	24	33	12	11	0	3.33
Bats Right 33																					
Richmond, Ray-Raymond Sinclair (Bud)	20-21StLA	06-05-96	Fillmore, Il.	10-21-69	R	R	6'	170	2	1	.667	0	3	1	1	32	41	23	11	0	8.72
Riddle, Elmer-Elmer Ray	39-45CinN 46VR 47CinN 48-49PitN	07-31-14	Columbus, Ga.	05-14-84	R	R	5'11	170	65	52	.556	8	190	124	57	1023	974	458	342	13	3.40
Rigney, Johnny-John Dungan (Dunc)	37-42ChiA 43-45MS 46-47ChiA	10-28-14	Oak Park, Ill.	10-21-84	R	R	6'2	190	64	64	.500	5	197	132	66	1188	1101	450	605	9	3.58
Ring, Jimmy-James Joseph	17-20CinN 21-25PhiN 26NYN 27StLN 28PhiN	02-15-95	Brooklyn, N.Y.	07-06-65	R	R	6'1	180	118	149	.442	9	389	294	154	2354	2545	953	835	9	4.12
Ripley, Walt-Walter Franklin	35BosA	11-26-16	Worcester, Mass.	10-07-90	R	R	6'	168	0	0	—	0	1	0	0	7	3	0	0	0	9.00
Ripple, Charlie-Charles Dawson	44-46PhiN	12-01-20	Bolton, N.C.	05-06-79	L	L	6'2	210	1	0	.500	0	11	1	0	18	20	10	6	0	9.69
Riviere, Tink-Arthur Bernard	21StLN 25ChiA	08-02-99	Liberty, Tex.	09-27-65	R	R	5'10	167	1	0	1.000	0	20	1	0	40	51	27	16	0	7.65

USE NAMES - GIVEN NAMES (NICKNAMES)	TEAM BY YEAR	BIRTH DATE	BIRTHPLACE	DEATH DATE	B	T	HGT	WGT	W	L	Pct.	SV	G	GS	CG	IP	H	BB	SO	ShO	ERA
Rixey, Eppa-Eppa Jr. (Eppa Jeptha)	12-17,19-20PhiN 18MS 21-33CinN	05-03-91	Culpeper, Va.	02-28-63	R	L	6'5	210	266	251	.515	14	692	553	290	4495	4633	1082	1350	38	3.15
Roberts, Jim-James Newson (Big Jim)	24-25BknN	10-13-95	Artesia, Miss.	06-24-84	R	R	6'3	205	0	3	.000	0	12	5	0	26	42	8	10	0	7.27
Robertson, Charlie-Charles Culbertson	19,22-25ChiA 26StLA 27-28BosN	01-31-96	Dexter, Tex.	08-23-84	L	R	6'	175	49	80	.380	1	166	141	60	1004	1149	377	310	6	4.45
Roche, Armando-Armando [Baez]	45WasA	12-07-26	Havana, Cuba	06-26-97	R	R	6'	190	0	0	—	0	2	0	0	6	10	2	0	0	6.00
Roe, Clay-James Clay (Shad)	23WasA	01-07-04	Green Brier, Tenn.	04-04-56	L	L	6'2	180	0	1	.000	0	1	1	0	2	6	2	0	0	0.00
Roettger, Oscar-Oscar Frederick Louis (See B20-45)	23-24NYA	02-09-00	St. Louis, Mo.	07-04-86	R	R	6'	170	0	0	—	1	6	0	0	12	17	14	7	0	8.25
Rogalski, Joe-Joseph Anthony	38DetA	07-16-12	Ashland, Wis.	11-20-51	R	R	6'1	187	0	0	—	0	2	1	0	7	12	0	2	0	2.57
Rogers, Buck-Orlin Woodrow (Lefty)	35WasA	11-05-12	Spring Garden, Va.	02-20-99	R	L	5'8	164	0	1	.000	0	2	1	0	10	16	6	7	0	7.20
Rogers, Lee-Lee Otis (Buck, Lefty)	38BosA 38BknN	10-08-13	Tuscaloosa, Ala.	11-23-95	R	L	5'11	170	1	3	.250	0	26	4	0	51	55	28	18	0	6.18
Rommel, Eddie-Edwin Americus	20-32PhiA	09-13-97	Baltimore, Md.	08-26-70	R	R	6'2	197	171	119	.590	29	500	249	147	2557	2729	724	599	18	3.54
Root, Charlie-Charle Henry (Chinski)	23StLA 26-41CinN	03-17-99	Middletown, Ohio	11-05-70	R	R	5'10	190	201	160	.557	40	632	341	177	3197	3252	889	1459	21	3.59
Roser, Steve-Emerson Corey	44-46NYA 46BosN	01-25-18	Rome, N.Y.	02-08-02	R	R	6'4	220	6	5	.545	2	45	8	1	149	147	64	64	0	4.05
Ross, Buck-Lee Ravon	36-41PhiA 41-45ChiA	02-03-15	Norwood, N.C.	11-23-78	R	R	6'2	170	56	95	.371	2	237	182	65	1363	1545	573	360	6	4.95
Ross, Buster-Chester Franklin	24-26BosA	03-11-03	Kuttawa, Ky.	04-24-82	L	L	5'8	150	7	12	.368	1	64	10	1	190	233	74	31	1	5.02
Rosso, Frank-Francis James	44NYA	01-26-80	Agawam, Mass.	01-26-80	R	R	5'11	180	0	0	—	0	2	0	0	4	11	3	1	0	9.00
Rowe, Schoolboy-Lynwood Thomas (See B20-45)	32-42DetA 42BknN 43PhiN 44-45MS 46-49PhiN	01-11-10	Waco, Tex.	01-08-61	R	R	6'4	210	158	101	.610	12	382	278	137	2219	2332	558	913	22	3.87
Roy, Emile-Emil Arthur	33PhiA	03-26-07	Brighton, Mass.	01-05-97	R	R	5'11	180	0	1	.000	0	1	1	0	2	4	4	3	0	31.50
Roy, Luther-Luther Franklin	24-25CleA 27ChiN 29PhiN 29BknN	07-29-02	Ootewah, Tenn.	07-24-63	R	R	5'10	161	6	12	.333	0	56	17	3	171	231	92	36	0	7.16
Rudolph, Ernie-Ernest William	45BknN	02-13-09	Black R. Falls, Wis.	01-13-03	R	R	5'8	165	1	0	1.000	0	7	0	0	9	12	7	3	0	5.00
Ruether, Dutch-Walter Henry (See B20-45)	17ChiN 17-20CinN 21-24BknN 25-26WasA 26-27NYA	09-13-93	Alameda, Cal.	05-16-70	L	L	6'1	180	137	95	.591	8	309	272	154	2124	2244	739	708	17	3.50
Ruffing, Red-Charles Herbert (See B20-45)	24-30BosA 30-42NYA 43-44MS 45-46PhiN 47ChiA	05-03-04	Granville, Ill.	02-17-86	R	R	6'2	205	273	225	.548	16	624	538	335	4344	4284	1541	1987	45	3.80
Rush, Andy-Jesse Howard	25BknN	12-26-89	Hartland, Kans.	03-16-69	R	R	6'3	180	0	1	.000	0	4	2	0	10	16	5	4	0	9.00
Russell, Allen-Allen E.	15-19NYA 19BosA 23-25WasA	07-31-93	Baltimore, Md.	10-20-72	B	R	5'9	165	69	76	.476	41	345	113	55	1393	1382	610	603	5	3.52
Russell, Jack-Jack Erwin	26-32BosA 32CleA 33-36WasA 36BosA 37DetA 38-39ChiN 40StLN	10-24-05	Paris, Tex.	11-03-90	R	R	6'1	178	85	141	.376	38	557	182	71	2051	2454	571	418	3	4.47
Russell, Jack-John Albert	17-18BknN 21-22ChiN	10-20-94	San Mateo, Cal.	11-19-30	L	L	6'2	195	2	7	.222	1	21	10	5	90	103	46	19	0	5.40
Russo, Marius-Marius Ugo (Lefty)	39-43NYA 44-45MS 46NYA	07-19-14	Brooklyn, N.Y.	03-26-05	L	L	6'1	190	45	34	.570	5	120	84	48	681	618	253	311	6	3.13
Ryan, Rosy-Wilfred Patrick Dolan	19-24NYN 25-26BosN 28NYA 33BknN	03-15-98	Worcester, Mass.	12-10-80	R	R	6'	185	52	47	.525	19	248	75	29	881	941	278	315	1	4.14
Ryba, Mike-Dominic Joseph	35-38StLN 41-46BosA	06-09-03	DeLancey, Pa.	12-13-71	R	R	5'11	180	52	34	.605	16	240	36	16	784	817	247	307	2	3.66
Sale, Freddy-Frederick Link	24PitN	05-02-02	Chester, S.C.	05-27-56	R	R	5'9	160	0	0	—	0	1	0	0	1	0	1	0	0	0.00
Salveson, Jack-John Theodore	33-34NYN 35PitN 35CleA 43,45CleA	01-05-14	Fullerton, Cal.	12-28-74	R	R	6'	180	9	9	.500	4	87	19	8	273	302	87	85	3	3.99
Salvo, Manuel-Manuel (Gyp)	39NYN 40-43BosN 43PhiN 43BknN	06-30-12	Sacramento, Cal.	02-07-97	R	R	6'4	210	33	50	.398	1	135	93	40	722	723	284	247	9	3.69
Samuels, Joe-Joseph Jonas (Skabotch)	30DetA	23-01-05	Scranton, Pa.	10-28-96	R	R	6'1	196	0	0	—	0	6	0	0	6	10	6	1	0	16.50
Sanders, Dee-Dee Wilma	45StLA	04-08-21	Quitman, Tex.		R	R	6'1	180	0	0	—	0	1	0	0	1	1	1	0	0	54.00
Savidge, Don-Donald Snyder	29WasA	08-28-08	Berwick, Pa.	03-22-83	R	R	6'1	180	0	0	—	0	3	0	0	6	12	2	2	0	9.00
Sayles, Bill-William Nisbeth	39BosA 43NYN 43BknN 44-45MS	07-27-17	Portland, Ore.	11-20-96	R	R	6'2	175	1	3	.250	1	28	3	1	79	87	46	52	0	5.58
Schacht, Al-Alexander (The Clown Prince of Baseball)	19-21WasA	11-12-92	New York, N.Y.	07-14-84	R	R	5'11	142	14	10	.583	3	53	18	8	197	254	61	38	1	4.48
Schacker, Hal-Harold	45BosA	04-06-25	Brooklyn, N.Y.		R	R	6'	180	0	0	—	0	15	14	9	6	6	5	0	5.40
Schanz, Charley-Charles Murrell	44-47PhiN 50BosN	06-08-19	Anacortes, Wash.	05-28-92	R	R	6'3	215	28	43	.394	14	155	72	23	627	658	332	243	2	4.33
Scheetz, Owen-Owen Franklin	43WasA	12-24-13	New Bedford, Ohio	09-28-94	R	R	6'	190	0	0	—	0	6	0	0	9	16	4	5	0	7.00
Schelle, Jim-Gerard Anthony	39PhiA	04-13-17	Baltimore, Md.	05-04-90	R	R	6'3	204	0	0	—	0	1	0	0	1	3	0	0	0	∞
Schemanske, Fred-Frederick George (Buck)	23WasA	04-28-03	Detroit, Mich.	02-18-60	R	R	6'2	190	0	0	—	0	1	0	0	3	0	0	0	0	27.00
Schesler, Dutch-Charles	31PhiN	06-01-00	Frankfurt, Germany	11-19-53	R	R	6'2	180	0	0	—	0	17	0	0	38	65	18	14	0	7.34
Schillings, Red-Elbert Isaiah	22PhiA	03-29-00	Deport, Tex.	01-07-54	R	R	5'10	180	0	0	—	0	4	0	0	8	10	11	4	0	6.75
Schmidt, Freddy-Frederick Albert	44,46-47StLN 45MS 45ChiN 47PhiN	02-09-16	Hartford, Conn.		R	R	6'1	185	13	11	.542	5	85	15	3	225	206	122	98	2	3.76
Schnell, Karl-Karl Otto	22-23CinN	09-20-99	Los Angeles, Cal.	05-31-92	R	R	6'1	176	0	0	—	0	11	0	0	21	23	20	5	0	4.29
Schott, Gene-Arthur Eugene	35-38CinN 39PhiN 39BknN 36CinN	07-14-13	Batavia, Ohio	11-16-92	R	R	6'2	185	28	41	.406	4	136	62	24	587	590	222	192	3	3.73
Schreiber, Paul-Paul Frederick (Von)	22-23BknN 45NYA	10-08-02	Jacksonville, Fla.	01-28-82	R	R	6'2	180	0	0	—	1	20	0	0	22	25	10	5	0	4.05
Schultz, Webb-Wilbert Carl	24ChiA	01-31-98	Wautoma, Wis.	07-26-86	R	R	5'11	172	0	0	—	0	1	0	0	1	1	0	0	0	9.00
Schulz, Walt-Walter Frederick	20StLN	04-16-00	St. Louis, Mo.	02-27-28	R	R	6'	170	0	0	—	0	2	0	0	6	10	2	0	0	6.00
Schumacher, Hal-Harold Henry (Prince Hal)	31-42NYN 43-45MS 46NYN	11-23-10	Hinckley, N.Y.	04-21-93	R	R	6'	190	158	121	.566	7	391	329	138	2482	2424	902	906	28	3.36
Scott, George-George Wilson	20StLN	11-17-95	Appanoose Co., IA	12-03-62	R	R	6'1	175	0	0	—	0	2	0	0	2	3	1	1	0	4.50
Scott, Jack-John William	16PitN 17,19-21BosN 22CinN 22-23,25-26NYN 27PhiN 28-29NYN	04-18-92	Ridgeway, N.C.	11-30-59	L	R	6'2	215	103	109	.486	19	356	195	115	1816	1969	493	657	11	3.85
Scott, Lefty-Marshall	07-15-15	Roswell, N.M.		R	L	6'	165	0	2	.000	0	3	2	0	22	29	12	5	0	4.50
Seats, Tom-Thomas Edward	40DetA 45BknN	09-24-10	Farmington, N.C.	05-10-92	R	L	5'11	190	12	9	.571	1	57	20	6	178	194	58	69	2	4.45
					Bats Both 40																
Sedgwick, Duke-Henry Kenneth	21PhiN 23WasA	06-01-98	Martins Ferry, Ohio	12-04-82	R	R	6'	175	1	4	.200	0	21	7	2	87	108	38	25	0	5.48
Seibold, Socks-Harry (See B20-45)	16-17PhiA 18MS 19PhiA 29-33BosN	05-31-96	Philadelphia, Pa.	09-21-65	R	R	5'8	162	48	86	.358	5	191	135	64	1065	1179	405	296	8	4.42
Sell, Epp-Elwood Lester	22-23StLN	04-26-97	Llewellyn, Pa.	02-19-61	R	R	6'	175	4	3	.571	0	12	4	0	48	63	14	7	0	6.56
Settlemire, Merle-Edgar Merle (Lefty)	28BosA	01-19-03	Santa Fe, Ohio	06-12-88	L	L	5'9	156	0	6	.000	0	30	6	0	82	116	34	12	0	5.49
Seward, Frank-Frank Martin	43-44NYN	04-07-21	Pennsauken, N.J.	04-12-04	R	R	6'3	200	3	3	.500	0	8	9	3	87	110	37	18	0	5.17
Sewell, Rip-Truett Banks	32DetA 38-49PitN	05-11-07	Decatur, Ala.	09-03-89	R	R	6'1	180	143	97	.596	15	390	243	137	2119	2101	748	636	18	3.48
Shanner, Bill-Wilfred William (W.W.)	11-04-94	Oakland City, Ind.	12-18-86	R	R	6'		0	0	—	0	1	0	0	4	6	1	1	0	6.75
Shaute, Joe-Joseph Benjamin (Lefty)	22-30CleA 31-33BknN 34CinN	08-01-99	Peckville, Pa.	02-21-70	L	L	6'	190	99	109	.476	18	360	209	103	1819	2097	534	512	5	4.15
Shawkey, Bob-James Robert	13-15PhiA 15-27,M30NYA	12-04-90	Sigel, Pa.	12-31-80	R	R	5'11	168	198	150	.569	28	488	331	194	2938	2722	1018	1360	32	3.09
Shea, John-John Michael Joseph (Lefty)	28DetA	12-27-04	Everett, Mass.	12-01-56	R	L	5'10	170	0	0	—	0	1	1	1	1	0	1	0	0	18.00
Shea, Red-Patrick Henry	18PhiA 21-22NYN	11-29-98	Ware, Mass.	11-17-81	R	R	6'	165	5	5	.500	0	23	4	1	64	64	15	17	0	3.80
Shealy, Al-Albert Berley	28NYA 30ChiN	05-24-00	Chapin, S.C.	03-07-67	R	R	5'11	175	8	6	.571	2	47	5	3	123	161	56	53	0	5.71
Sheehan, Tom-Thomas Clancy (Long Tom)	15-16PhiA 21NYA 24-25CinN 25-26PitN M60SFN	06-27-94	Grand Ridge, Ill.	10-29-82	R	R	6'2	190	17	37	.315	5	146	50	26	607	677	242	169	3	4.00
Shepard, Bert-Bert Robert	45WasA	06-28-20	Dana, Ind.		L	L	5'11	195	0	0	—	0	1	0	0	5	3	3	2	0	1.80
Sherdel, Bill-William Henry (Wee Willie)	18-30,32StLN 30-32BosN	08-15-96	McSherrystown, Pa.	11-14-68	L	L	5'10	160	165	146	.531	26	514	273	159	2709	3018	661	839	11	3.72
Sherid, Roy-Royden Richard	29-31NYA	02-28-82	Norristown, Pa.		R	R	6'2	185	23	24	.489	7	87	44	20	418	473	166	149	0	4.65
Shields, Ben-Benjamin Cowen (Lefty)	24-25NYA 30BosA 31PhiN	06-17-03	Huntersville, N.C.	01-24-82	B	L	6'1	195	4	0	1.000	0	13	2	2	41	55	27	9	0	8.34
Shields, Vince-Vincent William	24StLN	11-18-00	Fredericton, Can.	10-17-52	L	R	5'11	175	1	1	.500	1	2	1	1	12	10	3	4	0	3.00
Shirey, Duke-Clair Lee	20WasA	06-29-98	Jersey Shore, Pa.	09-01-62	R	R	5'11	175	0	1	.000	0	2	1	0	4	5	2	0	0	6.75
Shirley, Tex-Alvis Newman	44-46StLA	04-25-18	Birthright, Tex.	11-07-93	B	R	6'1	175	19	30	.388	2	102	54	19	447	443	290	168	3	4.25
					Bats Right 41-42																
Shocker (Shockcor), Urban, (Urbain Jacques)-Urban James	16-17NYA 18-24StLA 25-28NYA	09-22-90	Cleveland, Ohio	09-09-28	R	R	5'10	180	188	117	.616	25	412	319	202	2681	2709	657	983	28	3.17
Shoffner, Milt-Milburn James	29-31CleA 37-39BosN 39-40CinN	11-13-05	Sherman, Tex.	01-19-78	L	L	6'1	184	25	26	.490	3	134	51	22	578	647	214	180	4	4.58
Shores, Bill-William David	28-31PhiA 33NYN 36CinN	05-26-04	Abilene, Tex.	02-19-84	R	R	6'	210	26	15	.634	9	96	39	14	396	425	168	129	2	4.16
Shoun, Clyde-Clyde Mitchell (Hardrock)	35-37ChiN 38-42StLN 42-44CinN 45MS 46-47CinN 47-49BosN 49ChiA	03-20-12	Mountain City, Tenn.	03-20-68	L	L	6'1	188	73	59	.553	29	454	85	34	1286	1325	404	483	3	3.91
Shriver, Harry-Harry Graydon (Pop)	22-23BknN	09-02-96	Wadestown, W.Va.	11-21-70	R	R	6'2	190	4	6	.400	2	26	14	4	112	122	48	39	2	3.13
Shuman, Harry-Harry (Handsome Harry)	42-43PitN 44PhiN	03-05-15	Philadelphia, Pa.	10-25-96	R	R	6'2	195	0	0	—	0	30	0	0	51	56	20	10	0	4.41
Signer, Walter-Walter Donald Aloyisius	43,45CinN	10-12-10	New York, N.Y.	07-23-74	R	R	6'	165	2	1	.667	1	10	2	1	33	35	9	5	0	3.86
Simmons (Simoni), Pat-Patrick Clement	28-29BosA	11-29-08	Watervliet, N.Y.	07-03-68	R	R	5'11	172	0	2	.000	0	33	3	0	76	75	41	18	0	3.67
Singleton, John-John Edward (Sheriff)	22PhiN	11-27-96	Gallipolis, Ohio	10-24-37	R	R	5'11	171	1	10	.091	0	28	8	5	93	127	38	27	1	5.90
29 played in N.F.L.																					
Sivess, Pete-Peter	36-38PhiN	09-23-13	South River, N.J.	06-01-03	R	R	6'3	195	7	11	.389	2	62	16	5	201	257	116	58	0	5.46
Slappey, John-John Henry	20PhiA	08-08-98	Albany, Ga.	06-10-57	R	R	6'4	195	0	0	—	0	4	0	0	8	15	4	1	0	7.50
Slayton, Steve-Foster Herbert	28BosA	04-26-02	Barre, Vt.	12-20-84	R	R	6'	163	0	0	—	0	3	0	0	6	4	3	2	0	3.86
Smith, Al-Alfred John	34-37NYN 38-39PhiN 40-45CleA	10-12-07	Belleville, Ill.	04-28-77	L	L	5'11	180	99	101	.495	17	356	201	75	1663	1707	587	587	16	3.72
Smith, Al-Alfred Kendricks	26NYN	12-13-03	Norristown, Pa.	08-11-95	R	R	6'	170	0	0	—	0	4	0	0	9	9	7	1	0	9.00
Smith, Art-Arthur Laird	32ChiA	06-21-06	Boston, Mass.	11-22-95	R	R	6'	175	0	1	.000	0	3	0	0	4	11	3	0	0	11.57
Smith, Bob-Robert Eldridge (See B20-45)	25-30BosN 31-32ChiN 33CinN 33-37BosN	04-22-95	Rogersville, Tenn.	07-19-87	R	R	5'10	175	106	139	.433	40	577	229	128	2246	2472	670	618	10	3.94
Smith, Clay-Clay Jamieson	38CleA 40DetA	09-11-14	Cambridge, Kans.	03-05-02	R	R	6'2	190	1	0	.500	0	18	1	0	39	50	15	11	0	5.54
Smith, Dave-David Merwin	38-39PhiA	12-17-14	Sellers, S.C.	04-01-98	R	R	5'10	170	2	1	.667	0	22	6	0	44	51	30	13	0	5.11
Smith, Eddie-Edgar	36-39PhiA 39-43ChiA 44-45MS 46-47ChiA 47BosA	12-14-13	Mansfield, N.J.	01-02-94	B	L	5'10	174	73	113	.392	12	282	197	91	1595	1554	739	694	7	3.82

USE NAMES - GIVEN NAMES (NICKNAMES)	TEAM BY YEAR	BIRTH DATE	BIRTHPLACE	DEATH DATE	B	T	HGT	WGT	W	L	Pct.	SV	G	GS	CG	IP	H	BB	SO	ShO	ERA
Smith, George-George Allen (Columbia George)	16-17NYN 18CinN 18NYN 18BknN 19NYN 19-22PhiN 23BknN	05-31-92	Byram, Conn.	01-07-65	R	R	6'2	163	41	81	.336	4	229	115	52	1144	1321	255	263	6	3.89
Smith, George-George Shelby	26-29DetA 30BosA	10-17-01	Louisville, Ky.	05-26-81	R	R	6'2	175	10	8	.556	3	132	7	1	331	354	218	135	0	5.33
Smith, Hal-Harold Lavern	32-35PitN	06-30-02	Creston, Iowa	09-27-92	R	R	6'3	195	12	11	.522	1	51	25	10	210	232	52	59	3	3.77
Smith, Rufus-Rufus Frazier (Shirt)	27DetA	01-24-05	Guilford Coll., N.C.	08-21-84	R	L	5'8	180	0	0	—	0	1	1	0	8	8	3	2	0	3.38
Smith, Sherry-Sherrod Malone	11-12PitN 15-17BknN 18MS 19-22BknN 22-27CleA	02-18-91	Monticello, Ga.	09-12-49	L	L	6'1	170	114	118	.491	21	373	226	142	2052	2234	440	428	16	3.32
Smoll, Lefty-Clyde Hetrick	40PhiN	04-17-14	Quakertown, Pa.	08-31-85	B	L	5'10	175	2	8	.200	0	33	9	0	109	145	36	31	0	5.37
Smythe, Harry-William Henry	29-30PhiN 34NYA 34BknN	10-24-04	Augusta, Ga.	08-28-80	L	L	5'10	179	5	12	.294	4	60	12	2	155	232	62	33	0	6.39
Snyder, Bill-William Nicholas	19-20WasA	01-28-98	Mansfield, Ohio	10-08-34	R	R			2	2	.500	1	18	5	1	62	65	31	22	0	3.77
Songer, Don-Donald C.	24-27PitN 27NYN	01-31-99	Walnut, Kans.	10-03-62	L	L	6'	165	10	14	.417	4	71	17	5	202	204	98	44	1	3.39
Sorrell, Vic-Victor Garland	28-37DetA	04-09-01	Morrisville, N.C.	05-04-72	R	R	5'10	180	92	101	.477	10	280	216	95	1673	1820	706	619	7	4.43
Sothoron, Allan-Allan Sutton (Dixie)	14-15,17-21StLA 21BosA 21-22CleA 24-26StLN M33StLA	04-27-93	Bradford, Ohio	06-17-39		R	5'11	182	92	100	.479	9	264	194	102	1583	1583	596	576	17	3.31
	Bats Right 24-26																				
Speece, By-Byron Franklin	24WasA 25-26CleA 30PhiN	09-29-74	West Baden, Ind.	09-29-74	R	R	5'11	170	5	6	.455	1	62	4	3	167	208	61	51	0	4.74
Speer, Floyd-Floyd Vernie	43-44ChiA	01-27-13	Booneville, Ark.	03-22-69	R	R	6'	180	0	0	—	0	3	0	0	3	5	3	2	0	9.00
Spencer, Glenn-Glenn Edward	28,30-32PitN 33NYN	09-11-05	Corning, N.Y.	12-30-58	R	R	5'11	155	23	31	.426	8	139	45	22	535	588	201	162	2	4.53
Springer, Brad-Bradford Louis	25StLA 26CinN	05-09-04	Detroit, Mich.	01-04-70	L	L	6'	155	0	0	—	0	3	0	0	4	3	9	1	0	4.50
Sproull, Charlie-Charles William	45PhiN	01-09-19	Taylorsville, Ga.	01-13-80	R	R	6'3	185	4	10	.286	1	34	19	2	130	158	80	47	0	5.95
Starr, Ray-Raymond Francis (Iron Man)	32StLN 33NYN 33BosN 41-43CinN 44-45PitN 45ChiN	04-23-06	Nowata, Okla.	02-09-63	R	R	6'1	178	37	35	.514	4	138	88	35	699	670	279	189	9	3.53
Stauffer, Ed-Charles Edward	23ChiN 25StLA	01-10-98	Emsworth, Pa.	07-02-79	R	R	5'11	185	0	1	.000	0	21	1	0	32	39	22	13	0	5.91
Steengrafe, Milt-Milton Henry	24,26ChiA	05-26-98	San Francisco, Cal.	06-02-77	R	R	6'	170	1	1	.500	0	16	1	0	44	58	23	13	0	5.11
Stein, Irv-Irvin Michael	32PhiN	05-21-11	Madisonville, La.	01-07-81	R	R	6'2	170	0	0	—	0	1	0	0	3	7	1	0	0	12.00
Steineder, Ray-Raymond	23-24PitN 24PhiN	11-13-94	Salem, N.J.	08-25-82	R	R	6'	160	3	2	.600	0	29	2	1	86	95	39	34	0	4.92
Stewart, Frank-Frank	27ChiA	09-08-06	Minneapolis, Minn.	04-30-01	R	R	6'	178	0	1	.000	0	1	1	0	4	5	4	0	0	9.00
Stewart, Lefty-Walter Cleveland	21DetA 27-32StLA 33-35WasA 35CleA	09-23-00	Sparta, Tenn.	09-26-74	R	L	5'10	160	100	98	.505	8	279	215	107	1724	1895	498	503	9	4.19
Stewart, Mack-William Macklin	44-45ChiN	09-23-14	Stevenson, Ala.	03-21-60	R	R	6'	167	0	1	.000	0	24	1	0	40	48	18	12	0	3.83
Stiely, Fred-Fred Warren (Lefty)	29-31StLA	06-01-01	Pillow, Pa.	01-06-81	L	L	5'8	170	1	1	.500	1	9	3	2	35	45	14	9	0	5.91
Stiles, Rollie-Rolland Mays (Lena)	30-31,33StLA	11-17-06	Ratcliff, Ark.		R	R	6'1	180	9	14	.391	1	85	18	9	298	402	148	86	1	5.92
Stimson, Carl-Carl Remus	23BosA	07-18-94	Hamburg, Iowa	11-09-36	B	R	6'5	190	0	0	—	0	2	0	0	4	12	5	1	0	22.50
Stine, Lee-Lee Elbert	34-35ChiA 36CinN 38NYA	11-17-13	Stillwater, Okla.	05-06-05	R	R	6'	180	3	8	.273	2	49	12	5	144	179	55	39	0	5.06
Stokes, Art-Arthur Milton	25PhiA	09-13-96	Emmitsburg, Md.	06-03-62	R	R	5'10	155	1	1	.500	0	12	0	0	24	24	10	7	0	4.13
Stone, Arnie-Edwin Arnold	23-24PhiN	12-19-92	North Creek, N.Y.	07-24-48	R	L	6'	180	4	3	.571	0	35	2	1	76	76	19	9	0	3.79
Stone, Dick-Charles Richard	45WasA	12-05-11	Oklahoma City, Okla.	02-18-80	L	L	5'9	153	0	0	—	0	3	0	0	5	6	2	0	0	0.00
Stone, Rocky-John Vernon	43CinN	08-23-18	Redding, Cal.	11-12-86	R	R	6'	200	0	1	.000	0	13	0	0	25	23	8	11	0	4.32
Stoner, Lil-Ulysses Simpson Grant	24,24-29DetA 30PitN 31PhiN	02-28-99	Bowie, Tex.	06-26-66	R	R	5'10	180	50	58	.463	14	229	111	45	1005	1180	374	298	1	4.76
Stout, Allyn-Allyn McClelland (Fish Hook)	31-33StLN 33-34CinN 35NYN 43BosN	10-31-04	Peoria, Ill.	12-22-74	R	R	5'10	167	20	20	.500	11	180	29	8	458	546	177	185	0	4.54
Stratton, Monty-Monty Franklin Pierce (Gander)	34-38ChiA 38LA	05-21-12	Wagner, Tex.	09-29-82	R	R	6'5	180	36	23	.610	2	70	62	36	487	489	149	196	5	3.71
Strelecki, Ed-Edward Harold	28-29StLA 31CinN	04-10-08	Newark, N.J.	01-09-68	R	R	5'11	180	1	3	.250	1	42	2	1	85	98	32	13	0	5.82
Strickland, Bill-William Goss	37StLA	03-29-08	Ray City, Ga.	11-26-00	R	R	6'2	170	0	0	—	0	9	0	0	21	28	15	6	0	6.00
Strincevich, Nick-Nicholas (Jumbo)	40-41BosN 41-42,44-48PitN 48PhiN	03-01-15	Gary, Ind.		R	R	6'1	180	46	49	.484	6	203	103	46	889	958	270	274	4	4.05
Stromme, Floyd-Floyd Marvin (Rock)	39CleA	08-01-16	Cooperstown, N.D.	02-07-93	R	R	5'11	170	0	1	.000	0	5	0	0	13	13	13	4	0	4.85
Struss, Steamboat-Clarence Herbert	34PhiN	02-24-09	Riverdale, Ill.	09-12-85	R	R	5'11	163	0	1	.000	0	1	1	0	7	7	6	3	0	6.43
Stryker, Dutch-Sterling Alpa	24BosN 26BknN	07-29-95	Atl. Highlands, N.J.	11-05-64	R	R	5'11	182	0	3	.000	0	22	10	2	75	98	23	22	0	6.60
Stuart, Johnny-John Davis (Stud)	22-25StLN	04-27-01	Clinton, Tenn.	05-13-70	R	R	5'11	170	20	18	.526	3	82	34	21	358	360	156	124	1	4.75
Stueland, George-George Anton	21-23,25CinN	03-02-99	Alonga, Iowa	09-09-64	B	R	6'1	174	9	6	.600	4	44	12	4	135	153	64	52	0	5.73
Suche, Charley-Charles Morris	38CleA	08-05-15	Cranes Mill, Tex.	02-11-84	R	L	6'2	190	0	0	—	0	1	0	0	1	4	3	1	0	36.00
Sullivan, Charlie-Charles Edward	28,30-31DetA	05-23-03	Yadkin Valley, N.C.	05-28-35	L	R	6'1	185	4	9	.308	5	74	9	4	205	239	105	68	0	5.66
Sullivan, Jim-James Richard	21-22PhiA 23CleA	04-05-94	Mine Run, Va.	02-12-72	R	R	5'11	170	0	5	.000	0	25	4	3	73	106	37	27	0	5.55
Sullivan, Joe-Joe	35-36DetA 39-41BosN 41PitN	09-26-10	Mason City, Ill.	04-28-85	L	L	5'11	175	30	37	.448	13	150	55	20	589	601	298	216	0	4.00
Sullivan, Lefty-Paul Thomas	39CleA	09-07-16	Nashville, Tenn.	11-01-88	L	L	6'3	204	0	1	.000	0	7	1	0	13	9	9	4	0	4.15
Sullivan, Tom-Thomas Augustin	22PhiN	10-18-95	Boston, Mass.	09-23-62	L	L	5'11	178	0	0	—	0	3	0	0	8	16	5	0	0	11.25
Sundra, Steve-Stephen Richard (Smokey)	36,38-40NYA 41-42WasA 42-44StLA 45MS 46StLA	03-27-10	Luxor, Pa.	03-23-52	B	R	6'1	185	56	41	.577	2	168	99	47	858	944	321	214	4	4.17
	Bats Right 41-43																				
Sunkel, Tom-Thomas Jacob (Lefty)	37,39StLN 41-43NYN 44BknN	08-09-12	Paris, Ill.	04-06-02	L	L	6'1	190	9	15	.375	2	63	29	6	230	218	133	112	2	4.34
Sutherland, Suds-Harvey Scott	21DetA	02-20-94	Eugene, Ore.	04-11-72	R	R	6'	180	6	2	.750	0	13	8	3	58	80	18	18	0	4.97
Swartz, Dazzy-Vernon Monroe (Monty)	20CinN	01-01-97	Farmersville, Ohio	01-13-80	R	R	5'11	182	0	1	.000	0	1	1	1	12	17	2	2	0	4.50
Sweetland, Les-Leo	27-30PhiN 31CinN	08-14-01	St. Ignace, Mich.	03-04-74	R	L	5'11	155	33	58	.363	4	161	96	38	740	992	358	159	2	6.11
	Bats Both 30-31																				
Swetonic, Steve-Stephen Albert	29-33,35PitN	08-13-03	Mt. Pleasant, Pa.	04-22-74	R	R	5'11	185	37	36	.507	11	133	58	25	597	607	212	154	8	3.80
Swift, Bill-William Vincent	32-39PitN 40BosN 41BknN 43ChiA	06-19-08	Elmira, N.Y.	02-23-69	R	R	6'1	192	95	82	.537	20	336	165	78	1637	1682	351	636	7	3.58
Swigart, Oad-Oadis Vaughn	39-40PitN 41-45MS	02-13-15	Archie, Mo.	08-08-97	L	R	6'	175	1	3	.250	0	9	5	1	46	54	16	17	1	4.50
Taber, Lefty-Edward Timothy	26-27PhiN	01-11-00	Rock Island, Ill.	11-05-83	L	L	6'	180	0	1	.000	0	11	1	0	16	16	10	0	0	11.36
Talcott, Roy-LeRoy Everett	43BosN	01-16-20	Brookline, Mass.	12-06-99	R	R	6'1	175	0	0	—	0	1	0	0	1	1	6	0	0	18.00
Tamulis, Vito-Vitautis Casimirus	34-35NYA 38StLA 38-40BknN 41PhiN 41BknN	07-11-11	Cambridge, Mass.	05-05-74	L	L	5'9	170	40	28	.588	10	170	70	31	692	758	202	294	6	3.97
Tauscher, Walt-Walter Edward	28PitN 31WasA	11-22-01	LaSalle, Ind.	11-27-92	R	R	6'1	186	1	0	1.000	0	23	0	0	41	52	16	12	0	5.71
Taylor, Arlas-Arlas Walter (Lefty, Foxy)	21PhiA	03-16-96	Warrick Co., Ind.	09-10-58	R	L	5'11		0	1	.000	0	2	0	0	2	7	2	0	0	22.50
Teachout, Bud-Arthur John	30-31ChiN 32StLN	08-27-04	Los Angeles, Cal.	05-11-85	R	L	6'2	183	12	6	.667	0	68	19	7	215	259	76	73	0	4.52
Tennent, Jim-James McDonnell	29NYN	03-03-08	Shepherdstown, W.Va.	04-16-67	R	R	6'1	190	0	0	—	0	1	0	0	3	1	0	1	0	4.50
Terry, Yank-Lancelot Yank	40,42-45BosA	02-11-11	Bedford, Ind.	11-04-79	R	R	6'1	170	20	28	.417	1	93	55	14	458	463	196	167	0	4.09
Terwilliger, Dick-Richard Martin	32StLN	06-27-06	Sand Lake, Mich.	01-21-69	R	R	5'11	178	0	0	—	0	1	0	0	3	1	2	2	0	0.00
Theis, Jack-John Louis	20CinN	07-23-91	Georgetown, Ohio	07-06-41	R	R	6'	190	0	1	.000	0	1	0	0	3	3	0	0	0	0.00
Thesenga, Jug-Arnold Joseph	44WasA	03-16-14	Jefferson, S.D.	12-03-02	R	R	6'1	180	0	0	—	0	5	1	0	12	18	12	2	0	5.25
Thomas, Bud-Luther Baxter	32-33WasA 37-39PhiA 39WasA 39-41DetA	09-09-10	Faber, Va.	05-20-01	R	R	6'	180	25	34	.424	3	143	58	13	526	625	166	135	1	4.96
Thomas, Fay-Fay Wesley (Scow)	27NYN 31CleA 32BknN 35StLA	10-10-03	Holyrood, Kans.	08-12-90	R	R	6'2	195	9	20	.310	1	81	23	5	229	269	133	112	0	4.95
Thomas, Lefty-Clarence Fletcher	25-26WasA	10-04-03	Glade Springs, Va.	03-21-52	L	L	6'2	190	0	2	.000	0	8	2	1	22	22	17	13	0	3.27
Thomas, Myles-Myles Lewis	26-29NYA 29-30WasA	10-22-97	State College, Pa.	12-12-63	R	R	5'9	170	23	22	.511	2	105	40	11	435	499	189	121	0	4.64
Thomas, Tommy-Alphonse	26-32ChiA 32-35WasA 35PhiN 36-37StLA 37BosA	12-23-99	Baltimore, Md.	04-27-88	R	R	5'10	175	117	128	.478	12	397	267	128	2174	2339	712	735	15	4.12
Thompson, Junior-Eugene Earl	39-42CinN 43VR 44-45MS 46-47NYN	06-07-17	Latham, Ill.	08-24-06	R	R	6'1	185	47	35	.573	7	185	68	27	687	602	328	315	6	3.26
Thompson, Lee-John Dudley (Lefty)	21ChiA	02-26-98	Smithfield, Utah	02-17-63	L	L	6'	185	0	3	.000	0	4	4	0	21	32	6	4	0	8.14
Thuman, Lou-Louis Charles Frank	39-40WasA 41-45MS	12-13-16	Baltimore, Md.	12-19-00	R	R	6'2	185	0	1	.000	0	9	0	0	9	15	9	1	0	12.00
Thurston, Sloppy-Hollis John	23StLA 23-26ChiA 27WasA 30-33BknN	06-02-99	Fremont, Neb.	09-14-73	R	R	5'11	165	89	86	.509	13	288	177	95	1534	1859	369	306	8	4.26
Tietje, Les-Leslie William (Toots)	33-36ChiA 36-38StLA	09-11-10	Sumner, Iowa	10-02-96	R	R	6'1	185	22	44	.349	0	105	65	22	513	560	282	193	2	5.11
Tinning, Bud-Lyle Forrest	32-34ChiN 35StLN	03-12-06	Pilger, Neb.	01-17-61	B	R	5'11	198	22	15	.595	4	99	35	13	405	405	135	135	4	3.20
	Bats Right 34-35																				
Tising, Jack-Johnnie Joseph	36PitN	10-09-03	High Point, Mo.	09-05-67	R	R	6'2	180	1	3	.250	0	10	6	1	47	52	24	27	0	4.21
Tobin, Jim-James Anthony (Abba Dabba)	37-39PitN 40-45BosN 45DetA	12-27-12	Oakland, Cal.	05-19-69	R	R	6'	185	105	112	.484	5	287	227	156	1899	1929	557	498	12	3.44
Tobin, Pat-Marion Brooks	41PhiN	01-28-16	Hermitage, Ark.	01-21-75	R	R	6'	180	0	0	—	0	5	0	0	10	13	3	3	0	36.00
Torres, Gil-Don Gilberto [Nunez] (See B20-45)	40,46WasA	08-23-15	Regla, Cuba	01-10-83	R	R	6'	155	0	0	—	0	5	0	0	12	12	3	3	0	5.40
Tost, Lou-Louis Eugene	42-43BosN 44-45MS 47PitN	06-01-11	Cumberland, Wash.	02-21-67	L	L	6'	175	10	11	.476	0	39	23	5	156	159	56	46	1	3.63
Touchstone, Clay-Clayton Maffitt	28-29BosN 45ChiA	01-24-03	Moores, Pa.	04-28-49	R	R	6'	175	0	0	—	0	12	0	0	21	35	8	6	0	6.43
Townsend, Ira-Ira Dance (Pat)	20-21BosN	01-09-94	Weimar, Tex.	07-21-65	R	R	6'1	180	0	0	—	0	14	21	1	14	21	6	1	0	6.43
Townsend, Leo-Leo Alphonse (Lefty)	20-21BosN	01-15-91	Mobile, Ala.	12-03-76	L	L	5'10	160	1	2	.400	0	11	1	0	25	20	5	0	0	2.88
Trotter, Bill-William Felix	37-42StLA 42WasA 44StLN	08-10-08	Cisne, Ill.	08-26-84	R	R	6'2	180	16	23	.410	12	163	31	9	484	619	174	158	0	5.39
Trout, Dizzy-Paul Howard	39-52DetA 52BosA 57BalA	06-29-15	Sandcut, Ind.	02-28-72	R	R	6'2	205	170	161	.514	35	521	322	158	2726	2641	1046	1256	28	3.23
Turbeville, George-George Elkins	35-37PhiA	08-24-14	Turbeville, S.C.	10-05-83	R	R	6'1	175	2	12	.143	0	62	15	4	185	196	157	47	0	6.13
Turk, Lucas-Lucas Newton (Chief)	22WasA	05-02-98	Homer, Ga.	01-11-94	R	R	6'	165	0	0	—	0	5	0	0	12	16	5	1	0	6.75

USE NAMES - GIVEN NAMES (NICKNAMES)	TEAM BY YEAR	BIRTH DATE	BIRTHPLACE	DEATH DATE	B	T	HGT	WGT	W	L	Pct.	SV	G	GS	CG	IP	H	BB	SO	ShO	ERA
Turner, Jim-James Riley (Milkman)	37-39BosN 40-42CinN 42-45NYA	08-06-03	Antioch, Tenn.	11-29-98	L	R	6'	185	69	60	.535	20	231	119	69	1132	1123	283	329	8	3.22
Turner, Ted-Theodore Holhot	20ChiN	05-04-92	Lawrenceburg, Ky.	02-04-58	R	R	6'	180	0	0	—	0	1	0	0	1	2	1	0	0	18.00
Tutwiler, Elmer-Elmer Strange	28PitN	11-09-05	Carbon Hill, Ala.	05-03-76	R	R	5'11	158	0	0	—	0	2	0	0	4	4	0	1	0	4.50
Twombly, Cy-Edwin Parker	21ChiA	06-15-97	Groveland, Mass.	12-03-74	R	R	5'10	170	1	2	.333	0	7	4	0	28	26	25	7	0	5.79
Uchrinscko, Jimmie-James Emerson	26WasA	10-20-00	West Newton, Pa.	03-17-95	L	R	6'	185	0	0	—	0	3	0	0	8	13	8	0	0	10.13
Uhle, Bob-Robert Ellwood (Lefty)	38ChiA 40DetA	09-17-13	San Francisco, Cal.	08-21-90	B	L	5'11	175	0	0	—	0	2	5	2	0	0	1	0	0	18.00
Uhle, George-George Ernest (Bull) (See B20-45)	19-28CleA 29-33DetA 33NYA 33-34NYA 36CleA	09-18-98	Cleveland, Ohio	02-26-85	R	R	6'	190	200	166	.546	25	513	368	232	3120	3417	966	1135	20	3.99
Ullrich, Sandy-Carlos Santiago [Castello]	44-45WasA	07-25-21	Havana, Cuba	04-21-01	R	R	6'	175	3	3	.500	1	31	6	0	91	108	38	28	0	5.04
Ulrich, Dutch-Frank W.	25-27PhiN 28IL	11-18-99	Baltimore, Md.	02-12-29	R	R	6'2	195	19	27	.413	2	98	38	24	406	452	89	123	3	3.48
Underhill, Willie-Willie Vern	27-28CleA	09-06-04	Yowell, Tex.	10-26-70	R	R	6'2	185	1	4	.200	0	15	4	1	36	45	31	20	0	5.75
Upchurch, Woody-Jefferson Woodrow	35-36PhiA 37AA	04-13-11	Buies Creek, N.C.	10-23-71	R	L	6'	180	0	4	.000	0	10	5	2	43	59	26	8	0	7.53
Van Alstyne, Clay-Clayton Emery (Spike)	27-28WasA	05-24-00	Stuyvesant, N.Y.	01-05-60	R	R	5'11	180	0	0	—	0	6	0	0	24	29	13	5	0	5.25
Van Atta, Russ-Russell (Sheriff)	33-35NYA 35-39StLA	06-21-06	Augusta, N.J.	10-10-86	L	L	6'	184	33	41	.446	6	207	76	17	713	838	367	339	1	5.59
Vance, Dazzy-Clarence Arthur	15PitN 15,18NYA 22-32BknN 33StlN 34CinN 34StLN 35BknN	03-04-91	Orient, Iowa	02-16-61	R	R	6'2	200	197	140	.585	11	442	349	216	2967	2809	840	2045	30	3.24
Vance, Joe-Joseph Albert (Sandy) 31 played in N.F.L.	35ChiA 37-38NYN	09-16-05	Devine, Tex.	07-04-78	R	R	6'1	190	3	2	.600	0	15	3	0	57	67	34	17	0	5.84
Vandenberg, Hy-Harold Harris	35BosA 37-40NYN 44-45ChiN	03-17-06	Abilene, Kans.	07-31-94	R	R	6'2	195	15	10	.600	5	90	22	7	290	304	128	120	1	4.34
Vander Meer, Johnny-John Samuel (Double No-Hit, The Dutch Master)	37-43CinN 44-45MS 46-49CinN 50ChiN 51CleA	11-02-14	Prospect Park, N.J.	10-06-97	B	L	6'1	190	119	121	.496	2	346	286	131	2104	1799	1132	1294	30	3.44
Vangilder, Elam-Elam Russell	19-27StLA 28-30DetA	04-23-96	Cape Girardeau, Mo.	04-30-77	R	R	6'1	192	100	102	.495	19	367	187	90	1714	1894	700	474	13	4.29
Vargus, Bill-William Fay	25-26BosN	11-11-99	N. Scituate, Mass.	02-12-79	L	L	6'	165	1	3	.250	0	15	2	1	39	49	14	5	0	3.92
Vaughan, Porter-Cecil Porter (Lefty)	40-41PhiA 42-45MS 46PhiA	05-11-19	Stevensville, Va.		R	L	6'1	178	2	11	.154	2	24	18	6	122	137	74	52	0	5.83
Vaughn, Roy-Clarence LeRoy	34PhiA	09-04-11	Sedalia, Mo.	03-01-37	B	R	6'2	178	0	0	—	0	2	0	0	4	3	3	1	0	2.25
Veach, Al-Alvis Lindel	35PhiA	08-06-09	Maylene, Ala.	09-06-90	R	R	5'11	178	0	2	.000	0	2	2	1	10	20	9	3	0	11.70
Vedder, Lou-Louis Edward	20DetA	04-20-97	Oakville, Mich.	03-09-90	R	R	5'10	175	0	0	—	0	1	0	0	2	0	1	0	0	0.00
Veigel, Al-Allen Francis	39BosN	01-30-17	Dover, Ohio		R	R	6'1	180	0	1	.000	0	3	0	0	3	5	1	0	0	6.00
Verdel, Al-Albert Alfred (Stumpy)	44PhiN	06-10-21	Punxsutawney, Pa.	04-16-91	R	R	5'9	186	0	0	—	0	1	0	0	1	0	0	0	0	0.00
Vines, Bob-Robert Earl	24StLN 25PitN	02-25-97	Waxahachie, Tex.	10-18-82	R	R	6'4	184	0	0	—	0	9	0	0	15	32	3	0	0	9.60
Vitelli, Joe-Antonio Joseph	44-45PitN	04-12-08	McKees Rocks, Pa.	02-07-67	R	R	6'1	195	0	0	—	0	5	0	0	7	5	7	2	0	2.57
Voigt, Ollie-Olen Edward	24StLA	01-29-99	Wheaton, Ill.	04-07-70	R	R	6'1	170	1	0	1.000	0	8	1	0	16	21	13	4	0	5.63
Wade, Jake-Jacob Fields (Whistlin' Jake)	36-38DetA 39BosA 39StLA 42-44ChiA 45ChiA 46WasA	04-01-12	Morehead City, N.C.	02-01-06	L	L	6'2	175	27	40	.403	3	171	71	20	669	690	440	291	3	4.99
Wagner, Charlie-Charles Thomas (Broadway)	38-42,46BosA 43-45MS	12-03-12	Reading, Pa.	08-31-06	R	R	5'11	170	32	23	.582	2	100	67	30	527	532	245	157	5	3.91
Walberg, Rube-George Elvin	23NYN 23-33PhiA 34-37BosA	07-27-96	Pine City, Minn.	10-27-78	L	L	6'1	190	156	141	.525	32	544	306	140	2645	2795	1031	1085	14	4.17
Walker, Bill-William Henry	27-32NYN 33-36StLN	10-07-03	E. St. Louis, Ill.	06-14-68	L	L	6'	175	97	77	.557	8	272	192	83	1489	1578	538	626	15	3.59
Walker, Marty-Martin Van Buren (Buddy)	28PhiN	03-27-99	Philadelphia, Pa.	04-24-78	L	L	6'	170	0	1	.000	0	1	0	0	2	3	0	0	0	∞
Walker, Roy-James Roy (Dixie)	12,15CleA 17-18ChiN 21-22StLN	04-13-93	Lawrenceburg, Tenn.	02-10-62	R	R	6'1	180	18	27	.400	5	91	48	17	386	408	157	148	0	3.99
			Bats Both 17-18, 22																		
Walkup, Jim-James Elton	34-39StLA39DetA	12-14-09	Havana, Ark.	02-07-97	R	R	6'1	170	16	38	.296	0	116	53	11	462	614	260	134	1	6.74
Walkup, Jim-James Huey	27DetA	11-03-95	Havana, Ark.	06-12-90	R	L	5'8	150	0	0	—	0	2	0	0	3	0	0	0	0	4.50
Wallace, Lefty-James Harold	42BosN 43-44MS 45-46BosN	08-12-21	Evansville, Ind.	07-28-72	L	L	5'11	160	5	6	.455	0	51	14	4	144	133	64	51	0	4.13
Walsh, Augie-August Sothley	27-28PhiN	08-17-04	Wilmington, Del.	11-12-85	R	R	6'	175	4	10	.286	2	39	12	3	132	172	45	38	0	6.07
Walsh, Ed-Edward Arthur	28-30,32ChiA	02-11-05	Meriden, Conn.	10-31-37	R	R	6'1	180	11	24	.314	0	79	38	15	331	399	149	107	0	5.57
Walsh, Jim-James Thomas	21DetA	07-10-94	Roxbury, Mass.	05-13-67	L	L	5'11	175	0	0	—	0	4	0	0	4	2	1	0	0	2.25
Walter, Bernie-James Bernard	30PitN	08-15-08	Dover, Tenn.	10-30-88	R	R	6'1	175	0	0	—	0	1	0	0	1	0	0	0	0	0.00
Walters, Bucky-William Henry (See B20-45)	34-38PhiN 38-48,M48-49CinN 50BosN	04-19-09	Philadelphia, Pa.	04-20-91	R	R	6'1	180	198	160	.553	4	428	398	242	3104	2990	1121	1107	42	3.30
Walton, Zack (See Tom Zachary)																					
Ward, Dick-Richard Ole	34ChiN 35StLN	05-21-09	Herrick, S.D.	05-30-66	R	R	6'1	198	0	0	—	0	4	0	0	6	9	3	1	0	3.00
Warmoth, Cy-Wallace Walter	16StLN 22-23WasA	02-02-93	Bone Gap, Ill.	06-23-57	L	L	5'11	158	8	5	.615	0	29	14	4	129	130	89	54	0	4.26
Warneke, Lon-Lonnie (The Arkansas Humming Bird)	30-36ChiN 37-42StLN 42-43ChiN 44MS 45ChiN	03-28-09	Mount Ida, Ark.	06-23-76	R	R	6'2	185	192	121	.613	13	445	343	192	2781	2726	739	1140	31	3.18
Warren, Tommy-Thomas Gentry	44BknN	07-15-17	Tulsa, Okla.	01-02-68	B	L	6'1	180	1	4	.200	0	22	4	0	69	74	40	18	0	4.96
Washburn, George-George Edward	41NYA	10-06-14	Solon, Me.	01-05-79	R	R	6'1	175	0	1	.000	0	1	1	0	2	2	5	1	0	13.50
Watson, Mule-John Reaves	18-19PhiA 20BosN 20PitN 20-23BosN 23-24NYN	10-15-96	Arizona, La.	08-25-49	R	R	6'1	185	49	53	.480	4	178	124	53	940	1062	256	208	8	4.04
Watt, Frank-Frank Marion (Kilo)	31PhiN	12-15-02	Washington, D.C.	08-31-56	R	R	6'1	205	5	5	.500	2	38	12	5	123	147	49	25	0	4.83
Wayenberg, Frank-Frank	24CleA	08-27-98	Franklin, Kans.	04-16-75	R	R	6'	170	0	0	—	0	2	0	0	7	7	5	3	0	5.14
Weafer, Hal-Kenneth Albert (Al)	36BosA	02-06-13	Woburn, Mass.	06-04-05	R	R	6'	180	0	0	—	0	1	0	0	1	4	1	0	0	12.00
Weaver, Jim-James Dement (Big Jim)	28WasA 31NYA 34StLA 34ChiN 35-37PitN 38StLA 38-39CinN	11-25-03	Obion Co., Tenn.	12-12-83	R	R	6'6	230	57	36	.613	4	189	108	38	894	891	336	449	7	3.88
Weaver, Monte-Montie Morton (Prof)	31-38WasA 39BosA	06-15-06	Helton, N.C.	06-14-94	L	R	6'	170	71	50	.587	4	201	135	57	1052	1137	435	297	4	4.36
Webb, Bill-Willie Fred	43PhiN	12-12-13	Atlanta, Ga.	06-01-94	R	R	6'2	180	0	0	—	0	1	0	0	1	1	0	0	0	9.00
Webber, Les-Lester Elmer	42-46BknN 46,48CleA	05-06-15	Kelseyville, Cal.	11-13-86	R	R	6'	180	23	19	.548	14	154	25	7	432	434	201	141	0	4.19
Wehde, Biggs-Wilbur	30-31ChiA	11-23-06	Holstein, Iowa	09-21-70	R	R	5'10	180	1	0	1.000	0	12	0	0	22	26	17	6	0	7.78
Weiland, Bob-Robert George (Lefty)	28-31ChiA 32-34BosA 34CleA 35StLA 37-40StLN	12-14-05	Chicago, Ill.	11-09-88	L	L	6'4	215	62	94	.397	7	277	179	66	1388	1463	611	614	7	4.24
Weiland, Ed-Edwin Nicholas	40,42ChiA 43-45MS	11-26-14	Evanston, Ill.	07-12-71	L	R	5'11	180	0	4	.000	0	24	0	0	33	10	7	0	0	8.25
Weinert, Lefty-Philip Walter	19-24PhiN 27-28ChiN 31NYA	04-21-02	Philadelphia, Pa.	04-07-73	L	L	6'1	195	18	33	.353	2	131	49	19	438	528	222	160	0	4.58
Weir, Roy-William Franklin (Bill)	36-39BosN	02-25-11	Portland, Me.	09-30-89	L	L	5'8	170	6	4	.600	0	29	11	4	106	95	50	42	0	3.57
Welch, Johnny-John Vernon	26-28,31ChiN 32-36BosA 36PitN	12-02-06	Washington, D.C.	09-02-40	R	R	6'3	184	35	41	.461	6	172	63	24	648	735	262	257	3	4.66
Wells, Ed-Edwin Lee	23-27DetA 29-32NYA 33-34StLA	06-07-00	Ashland, Ohio	05-01-86	L	L	6'1	183	68	69	.496	13	291	140	54	1233	1417	468	403	7	4.65
Wells, John-John Frederick	44BknN	11-25-22	Junction City, Kans.	10-23-93	R	R	5'11	180	0	2	.000	0	4	2	0	15	18	11	7	0	5.40
Welzer, Tony-Anton Frank	26-27BosA	04-05-99	Germany	03-18-71	R	R	5'11	180	14	14	.417	1	77	24	9	323	381	128	86	1	4.60
Wensloff, Butch-Charles William	43NYA 44VR 45-46MS 47NYA 48CleA	12-03-15	Sausalito, Cal.	01-18-01	R	R	6'2	185	16	13	.552	4	41	32	19	277	222	95	125	1	2.60
Werts, Johnny-Henry Levi	26-29BosN	04-20-98	Pomaria, S.C.	09-24-90	R	R	5'10	180	15	21	.417	2	88	40	11	377	460	111	111	1	4.30
West, Lefty-Weldon Edison	44-45StLA	09-03-15	Gibsonville, N.C.	07-23-79	R	L	6'	165	3	4	.429	1	35	6	2	98	105	50	49	0	4.32
Wetzel, Buzz-Charles Edward	27PhiA	08-25-94	Jay, Okla.	03-07-41	R	R	6'1	162	0	0	—	0	1	0	0	3	2	1	0	0	7.20
Wheaton, Woody-Elwood Pierce (See B20-45)	44PhiA	10-03-14	Philadelphia, Pa.	12-11-95	L	L	5'8	160	0	1	.000	0	11	1	0	38	36	20	15	0	3.55
Wheeler, Rip-Floyd Clark	21-22PitN 23-24ChiN	03-02-98	Marion, Ky.	09-18-68	R	R	6'	180	4	8	.333	1	34	7	1	129	138	29	21	0	4.19
Whitcher, Bob-Robert Arthur	45BosN	04-29-17	Berlin, N.H.	05-08-97	L	L	5'8	165	0	2	.000	0	6	3	0	16	12	12	6	0	2.81
White, Abe-Adel	37StLN	05-16-04	Winder, Ga.	10-01-78	R	L	6'	185	0	0	—	0	9	0	0	14	14	3	2	0	6.00
White, Ernie-Ernest Daniel	40-43StLN 44-45MS 46-48BosN	09-05-16	Pacolet Mills, S.C.	05-22-74	R	L	5'11	175	30	21	.588	6	108	57	24	490	425	188	244	5	2.77
Whitehead, John-John Henderson (Silent John)	35-39ChiA 39-40,42StLA	04-27-09	Coleman, Tex.	10-20-64	R	R	6'2	195	49	54	.476	4	172	119	52	944	1074	372	254	7	4.60
Whitehill, Earl-Earl Oliver	23-32DetA 33-36WasA 37-38CleA 39ChiN	02-07-00	Cedar Rapids, Iowa	10-22-54	L	L	5'9	174	218	185	.541	11	541	474	227	3563	3917	1431	1350	17	4.36
Wicker (Whicker), Kemp-Kemp Caswell	36-38NYA 41BknN	08-13-06	Kernersville, N.C.	06-11-73	R	L	5'11	182	10	7	.588	4	40	12	6	141	168	52	27	1	4.66
Wiedemeyer, Chick-Charles John	34ChiN	01-31-14	Chicago, Ill.	10-27-79	L	L	6'3	180	0	0	—	0	4	1	0	8	16	4	2	0	10.13
Wieneke, Jack-John	21ChiN	03-10-94	Saltsburg, Pa.	03-16-33	R	L	6'	182	0	1	.000	0	10	0	0	25	39	17	10	0	8.28
Wigington, Fred-Fred Thomas (Wig)	23StLN	12-16-97	Rogers, Neb.	05-08-80	R	R	5'10	168	0	0	—	0	3	0	0	8	11	5	2	0	3.38
Wilkie, Lefty-Aldon Jay	41-42PitN 43-45MS 46PitN	10-31-14	Zealandia, Canada	08-05-92	L	L	5'11	175	8	11	.421	1	68	12	5	194	215	80	37	1	4.59
Wilkinson, Roy-Roy Hamilton	18CleA 19-22ChiA	05-08-93	Canandaigua, N.Y.	07-02-56	R	R	6'1	170	12	31	.279	2	79	36	21	380	466	142	88	1	4.67
Williams, Ace-Robert Fulton	40BosN 43-45MS 46BosN	03-08-17	Montclair, N.J.	09-16-99	R	R	6'2	174	0	0	—	0	9	0	0	22	13	13	5	0	16.00
Williams, Al-Almon Edward	37-38PhiA	05-11-14	Valhermosa Spr., Ala.	07-19-69	R	R	6'3	200	0	8	.333	1	46	16	3	169	216	103	52	0	6.23
Williams, Leon-Leon Theo	26BknN	12-05-05	Macon, Ga.	11-20-84	L	L	5'10	154	0	0	—	0	1	0	0	2	0	1	0	0	5.63
Williamson, Al-Silas Albert	28ChiA	02-20-00	Buckville, Ark.	11-29-78	R	R	5'11	160	0	0	—	0	1	0	0	1	3	0	0	0	9.00
Willis, Lefty-Charles William	25-27PhiA	11-04-05	Leetown, W.Va.	05-10-62	L	R	6'	175	3	1	.750	1	64	5	2	72	25	23	17	0	3.94
			Bats Right 25																		
Willoughby, Claude-Claude William (Weeping Willie)	25-30PhiN 31PitN	11-14-98	Buffalo, Kans.	08-14-73	R	R	5'9	180	38	58	.396	9	219	102	33	842	1111	406	175	4	5.84
Wilshere, Whitey-Vernon Sprague	34-36PhiA	08-03-12	Poplar Ridge, N.J.	05-23-85	L	L	6'	180	10	12	.455	1	41	23	7	182	196	112	103	3	5.29
Wilson, Jack-John Francis (Black Jack)	34PhiA 35-41BosA 42WasA 42DetA	04-12-12	Portland, Ore.	04-19-95	R	R	5'11	210	68	72	.486	20	281	121	50	1131	1233	601	590	5	4.59

USE NAMES - GIVEN NAMES (NICKNAMES)	TEAM BY YEAR	BIRTH DATE	BIRTHPLACE	DEATH DATE	B	T	HGT	WGT	W	L	Pct.	SV	G	GS	CG	IP	H	BB	SO	ShO	ERA
Wilson, John-John Samuel	27-28BosA	04-25-03	Coal City, Ala.	08-27-80	R	R	6'2	164	0	2	.000	0	3	0	0	4	4	3	1	0	4.50
Wilson, Mutt-William Clarence	20DetA	07-20-96	Keyser, N.C.	08-31-62	R	R	6'3	167	1	1	.500	0	3	2	1	13	12	5	4	0	3.46
Wilson, Roy-Roy Edward (Lefty)	28ChiA	09-13-96	Foster, Iowa	12-03-69	L	L	6'	175	0	0	—	0	1	0	0	3	2	3	2	0	0.00
Wilson, Tex-Gomer Russell	24DetN	07-08-01	Trenton, Tex.	09-15-46	R	L	5'10	170	0	0	—	0	2	0	0	4	7	1	1	0	13.50
Wilson, Walter-Walter Wood	45DetA	11-24-13	Glenn, Ga.	04-17-94	L	R	6'4	190	1	3	.250	0	25	4	1	70	76	35	28	0	4.63
Wiltse, Hal-Harold James (Whitey)	26-28BosA 28StLA 31PhiN	08-06-03	Clay City, Ill.	11-02-83	L	L	5'9	168	20	40	.333	1	102	65	23	500	589	211	134	2	4.88
Wineapple, Ed-Edward (Lefty) 29-30 played in A.B.L.	29WasA	08-10-05	Boston, Mass.	07-23-96	L	L	6'	195	0	0	—	0	1	0	0	4	7	3	1	0	4.50
Winegarner, Ralph-Ralph Lee (See B20-45)	32,34-36CleA 49StLA	10-29-09	Benton, Kans.	04-14-88	R	R	6'	182	8	6	.571	0	70	11	7	194	229	89	89	0	5.34
Winford, Jim-James Head (Cowboy)	32,34-37StLN 38BknN	10-09-09	Shelbyville, Tenn.	12-16-70	R	R	6'1	180	14	18	.438	3	68	31	10	276	307	115	107	1	4.57
Wingard, Ernie-Ernest James (Jim)	24-27StLA	10-17-00	Prattville, Ala.	01-17-77	L	L	6'2	176	29	43	.403	4	145	77	36	696	800	317	101	0	4.55
Wingfield, Ted-Frederick Davis	23-24WasA 24-27BosA	08-07-99	Bedford, Va.	07-18-75	R	R	5'11	168	24	44	.353	5	113	58	31	554	624	181	68	3	4.18
Winn, George-George Benjamin (Breezy, Lefty)	19BosA 22-23CleA	10-26-97	Perry, Ga.	11-01-69	L	L	5'11	170	1	2	.333	0	12	3	1	41	50	7	7	0	4.61
Winston, Hank-Henry Rudolph	33PhiA 36BknN	06-15-04	Youngsville, N.C.	02-07-74	R	R	6'3	226	1	3	.250	0	15	0	0	39	47	22	10	0	6.23
Winters, Clarence-Clarence John	24BosN	09-07-98	Detroit, Mich.	06-29-45	R				0	1	.000	0	4	2	0	7	22	4	3	0	20.57
Winters, Jesse-Jesse Franklin (T-Bone)	19-20NYN 21-23PhiN	12-22-93	Stephenville, Tex.	06-05-86	L	R	6'1	165	13	24	.351	6	110	31	15	404	510	164	94	0	5.06
Wise, Archie-Archibald Edwin	32ChiA	07-31-12	Waxahachie, Tex.	02-02-78	R	R	6'	165	0	0	—	0	2	0	0	7	8	5	2	0	5.14
Wise, Roy-Roy Ogden	44PitN	11-18-25	Springfield, Ill.		B	R	6'2	170	0	0	—	0	2	0	0	3	4	3	1	0	9.00
Wisner, John-John Henry (Jack)	19-20PhiA 25-26NYN	11-05-99	Grand Rapids, Mich.	12-15-81	R	R	6'3	195	4	5	.444	0	51	6	4	132	112	41	35	0	3.20
Wistert, Whitey-Francis Michael	34CinN	02-20-12	Chicago, Ill.	04-23-85	R	R	6'4	210	0	1	.000	0	2	1	0	8	5	5	1	0	1.13
Wittig, Johnnie-John Carl (Hans)	38-39,41,43NYN 44-45MS 49BosA	06-16-14	Baltimore, Md.	02-24-99	R	R	6'	180	10	25	.286	4	84	39	7	307	342	163	121	1	4.90
Wolf, Lefty-Walter Francis	21PhiA	06-10-00	Hartford, Conn.	09-25-71	R	L	5'10	163	0	0	—	0	8	0	0	15	15	16	12	0	7.20
Wolfe, Chuck-Charles Hunt	23PhiA	02-15-97	Wolfsburg, Pa.	11-27-57	L	R	5'7	175	0	0	—	0	3	0	0	10	6	8	1	0	3.60
Wolff, Roger-Roger Francis	41-43PhiA 44-46WasA 47CleA	04-10-11	Evansville, Ind.	03-23-94	R	R	6'1	208	52	69	.430	13	182	128	63	1025	1018	316	430	8	3.41
Wood, Joe-Joe Frank	44BosN	05-20-16	Shohola, Pa.	10-10-02	R	R	6'	190	0	1	.000	0	3	1	0	10	13	3	5	0	6.30
Wood, Spades-Charles Asher	30-31PitN	01-13-09	Spartanburg, S.C.	05-18-86	L	L	5'10	150	6	9	.400	2	24	17	6	122	130	78	56	0	5.61
Woodend, George-George Anthony	44BosN	12-09-17	Hartford, Conn.	02-06-80	R	R	6'	200	0	0	—	0	3	0	0	2	5	5	0	0	13.50
Woods, John-John Fulton (Abe)	24BosN	01-18-98	Princeton, W.Va.	10-04-46	R	R	5'11	150	0	0	—	0	1	0	0	1	0	3	0	0	0.00
Woods, Pinky-George Rowland	43-45BosA	05-22-15	Waterbury, Conn.	10-29-82	R	R	6'5	225	13	21	.382	3	85	44	10	379	388	206	124	1	3.97
Workman, Hoge-Harry Hallworth (Sonny) 24,31-32 played in N.F.L.	24BosA	09-25-99	Huntington, W.Va.	05-20-72	R	R	5'11	170	0	0	—	0	11	0	0	18	25	11	7	0	8.50
Wright, Jiggs-James	27-28StLA	09-19-00	Hyde, England	04-11-63	R	R	6'3	195	1	0	1.000	0	4	1	1	14	11	6	6	0	5.79
Wright, Rasty-Wayne Bromley	17-19,22-23StLA	11-05-95	Ceredo, W.Va.	06-12-48	R	R	5'11	160	24	18	.571	5	109	43	17	451	481	132	114	1	4.05
Wurm, Frank-Frank James	44BknN	04-27-24	Cambridge, N.Y.	09-19-93	B	L	6'1	175	0	0	—	0	1	0	0	0.1	1	5	1	0	108.00
Wyatt, Whit-John Whitlow	29-33DetA 33-36ChiA 37CleA 39-44BknN 45PhiN	09-27-07	Kensington, Ga.	07-16-99	R	R	6'1	185	106	95	.527	13	360	210	97	1762	1684	642	872	17	3.79
Wyse, Hank-Henry Washington (Hooks)	42-47ChiN 50-51PhiA 51WasA	03-01-18	Lunsford, Ark.	10-22-00	R	R	5'11	185	79	70	.530	8	251	159	67	1257	1338	373	362	11	3.52
Wysong, Biff-Harlin	30-32CinN	04-13-05	Clarksville, Ohio	08-08-51	L	L	6'3	195	1	3	.250	0	20	3	0	36	44	34	11	0	7.25
Yarnall, Rusty-Waldo Ward	26PhiN	10-22-02	Chicago, Ill.	10-09-85	R	R	6'	175	0	1	.000	0	1	0	0	1	3	1	0	0	18.00
Yarrison, Rube-Byron Wordsworth	22PhiA 24BknN	03-09-96	Montgomery, Pa.	04-22-77	R	R	5'11	165	1	4	.200	0	21	3	0	45	62	15	12	0	7.80
Yde, Emil-Emil Ogden	24-27PitN 29DetA	01-28-00	Great Lakes, Ill.	12-05-68	B	L	5'11	165	49	25	.662	0	141	80	43	705	751	296	160	6	4.02
					Bats Left 25																
Yeargin, Al-James Almond (Grapefruit)	22,24BosN	10-16-01	Maudlin, S.C.	05-08-37	R	R	6'2	175	1	12	.077	0	33	13	7	148	167	44	35	0	4.93
Yellowhorse, Chief-Moses J.	21-22PitN	03-28-98	Pawnee, Okla.	04-10-64	R	R	5'10	180	8	4	.667	1	38	8	3	126	137	33	43	0	3.93
Yerkes, Carroll-Charles Carroll (Lefty)	27-29PhiA 32-33ChiN	06-13-03	McSherrystown, Pa.	12-20-50	R	L	5'11	180	1	1	.500	1	25	3	1	58	61	20	16	0	3.88
York, Lefty-James Edward	19PhiA 21CinN	11-01-92	West Fork, Ark.	04-09-61	L	L	5'10	185	5	11	.313	1	42	13	4	143	183	68	59	1	5.35
Youngblood, Chief-Albert Clyde	22WasA	06-13-00	Hillsboro, Tex.	07-06-68	R	R	6'3	202	0	0	—	0	2	0	0	4	9	7	0	0	15.75
Yowell, Carl-Carl Columbus (Sundown)	24-25CleA	12-20-02	Madison, Va.	07-27-85	L	L	6'4	180	3	4	.429	0	16	6	3	63	77	30	20	0	5.43
Zabala, Adrian-Adrian [Rodriguez]	45NYN 46-48SM 49NYN	08-26-16	San Antonio, Cuba	01-04-02	L	L	5'11	165	4	7	.364	1	26	9	3	84	90	30	27	1	5.04
Zachary, (Zarski), Chink-Albert Myron	44BknN	10-19-17	Brooklyn, N.Y.		R	R	5'11	182	0	2	.000	0	4	2	0	10	10	7	3	0	9.90
Zachary, Tom-Jonathan Thompson Walton	18PhiA19-25WasA 26-27StLA 27-28WasA 28-30NYA 30-34BosN 34-36BknN 36PhiN	05-07-96	Graham, N.C.	01-24-69	L	L	6'1	187	185	191	.492	22	533	407	185	3136	3580	914	720	23	3.72
	(Played as Zach Walton 18)																				
Zahniser, Paul-Paul Vernon	23-24WasA 25-26BosA 29CinN	09-06-98	Sac City, Iowa	09-26-64	R	R	5'10	170	25	47	.347	1	125	80	29	619	746	284	145	4	4.66
Zink, Walt-Walter Noble	21NYN	11-21-98	Pittsfield, Mass.	06-12-64	R	R	6'	165	0	0	—	0	2	0	0	4	4	3	1	0	2.25
Zinn, Jimmy-James Edward	19PhiA 20-22PitN 29CleA	01-31-95	Benton, Ark.	02-26-91	L	R	6'	195	13	16	.448	7	66	26	15	299	390	80	108	2	4.30
					Bats Right 29																
Zinser, Bill-William Francis	44WasA	01-06-18	Queens, N.Y.	02-16-93	R	R	6'1	185	0	0	—	0	2	0	0	1	1	5	1	0	18.00
Zuber, Bill-William Henry (Goober)	36,38-40CleA 41-42WasA 43-46NYA 46-47BosA	03-26-13	Middle Amana, Iowa	11-02-82	R	R	6'2	195	43	42	.506	6	224	65	23	785	767	468	383	3	4.29

1946-1960
Goin' for the Pump

In the age where the home run ball became the shortest distance between anonymity and newspaper headlines, baseball's ethnic imbalance was finally corrected. The racial mix began in 1947 when 28-year-old Jackie Robinson stepped on the playing field for the Brooklyn Dodgers. This was the doing of Branch Rickey, the team's imaginative general manager. Before coming to the parent club, Robinson spent the 1946 season with Montreal - the Dodgers' farm club, in a move more for "transitional" purposes of bringing a black man to baseball than to sharpen Robinson's skills. The fleet-footed Georgia native spent the first year of his life in the majors at first base, not his ordinary position, and led the National League in stolen bases. He also led the Dodgers to a pennant while taking home Rookie of the Year honors.

The entry of black athletes into baseball, while proving the most historic highlight of the period, also signaled the start of many changes. The pitcher's plight, as it had begun in 1920, did not improve, Instead, it only got worse as light bats became the mainstay of the batter's arsenal. Armed with a light weapon that responded to a good pair of wrists and could help negate the blazing fastball, the batter was able to continue his dominance over the pitcher. The result was that choking up on the bat became a rarity and nearly everyone went for the pump, or home run. Even a scuffed ball, which gave the pitcher some advantage, was no longer allowed. All this new-found power was sharply reflected in stolen base and home run totals, which seemed to be going in opposite directions. While stolen bases per game for both teams continued their downward spiral of less than one theft per game for both teams, home runs climbed to nearly two per game. Home run status also culminated in a healthier paycheck, and such were the state of affairs that they led to hardy power men driving Cadillacs while their counterparts on the mound had to find less expensive means of transportation.

Yet, what the home run ball did for the batter's prestige, it did not do for his batting average. Going for the long ball, while increasing strikeouts to almost five per nine innings, also lowered batting averages to below the .260 mark. Another factor that contributed to a reduction in base hits, was night baseball, which began in Cincinnati in 1935 and became a major part of most team schedules during the fifties. Only the Chicago Cubs, with the help of owner Phil Wrigley, managed to starve off the intrusion of the twentieth century.

Beyond the effects of a changing strategy, there was even a more profound upheaval taking place at the core of the game itself. Until the late forties, the only way to see a ball game was by going out to the ball park. If that was not possible, there was also the option of keeping an ear to the radio., It was these limited accesses that helped preserve the structure of the two eight-team circuits, as well as keeping baseball locked in the same geographical pattern it had chosen at the turn of the century. In fact, not since the Baltimore franchise itself as the American League's entry into New York for the start of the 1903 season had there been any franchise activity.

But a new technological giant - television - was on the rise and the tranquillity of five decades slowly began to disintegrate. Also, as television evolved as a major force in the affairs of American life, so did the airplane. As radio had served to protect a franchise structure that extended no further than the Mississippi River, so did train travel, which was often long, tedious, and tiring. But as the country entered the fifties it was evident how quickly life was changing and baseball, always parallel to the events outside its domain, was no exception. Suddenly, those franchises that had been previously locked in and forced to accept low attendance found there was a means of escape.

The first of the franchise shifts took place in the National League in 1953 when the Boston Braves, unable to compete with Ted Williams and the neighboring Red Sox, moved to Milwaukee, which oddly enough had first hosted a National League club for the 1878 season. The Braves also held the distinction, along with the Chicago Cubs, of being original tenants of the National League and remaining in their respective cities without any interruption or changes in franchise since 1876. A year after the Braves changed homes, the hapless St. Louis Browns moved to Baltimore - a city that had lost its major league representation in 1902. The year after the Browns departed, the Philadelphia Athletics, once American League powerhouses, picked up and moved to Kansas City for the start of the 1955 season.

The next and last changes that occurred in the period took place three years later in the National League stronghold of New York, and were perhaps the most dramatic of any of the franchise shifts. The Brooklyn Dodgers and New York Giants, teams which had more emotional and historic ties with their patrons than any other clubs, shocked the baseball world and their followers alike by moving to California. While the Dodgers took residency in Los Angeles, the Giants moved to the northern reaches of San Francisco. Although the Giants' sliding attendance gave some justification for their departure, there seemed to be none for the Dodgers, who had enjoyed a near-fanatical following. Walter O'Malley, the Dodgers' president, claimed that insufficient parking and an aging stadium - Ebbets Field - as his reasons for the move. But even if New York politicians would have granted a new stadium - which they did not - it would be doubtful that O'Malley would have turned down the potential awaiting him three thousand miles away.

Suddenly, in the course of five years, from 1953-1958, baseball found itself drastically altered. In three cities that had been represented by two teams each - St. Louis, Boston, and Philadelphia - there was now only one tenant per city. And New York, which had been able to support three teams, found itself with only the Yankees, which did neither the economics of the city nor the heart of National League fans any good. Although the tremors of such abrupt change would seems to have repercussions that would take another lifetime to heal, they proved only a tiny glimpse of what was to take place when the 1960's first dawned.

1946 South of the Border

Although World War II was officially over and baseball's finest were back in their familiar ranks, tranquillity no longer had a place in the major leagues. What had happened was that the new Mexican League, headed by millionaire Jorge Pasquel, had lured a cluster of players from the majors. The Cardinals lost pitchers Max Lanier and Freddie Martin, and second baseman Lou Klein. Mickey Owen jumped from the Dodgers, along with Luis Olmo. Vern Stephens of the Browns also joined the exodus but immediately returned before the season started to escape Commissioner Chandler's decree that all jumpers would be barred from organized ball for five years. The first player to learn of Chandler's seriousness was Mickey Owen, who returned in August, asked for clemency, and was refused.

There were other players of marginal significance that fled to Mexico, making it almost impossible to predict how the balance of the pennant race would be upset. The one clear case of imbalance was the New York Giants, who lost eight players—four of them pitchers—and wound up in last place, although leading the league with 121 home runs, 40 ahead of their nearest rival. Those leaving the Giants included pitchers Sal Maglie, Harry Feldman, and Ace Adams, and outfielder Danny Gardella.

Yet, regardless of the defection, the show went on. The victorious Cubs of 1945 were plagued by slumps, as well as injuries to Andy Pafko, Stan Hack, and Don Johnson, and finished a poor third to both the Cardinals and Dodgers who, for the first time in major league history, forced a play-off to decide the National League winner.

Both clubs entered the final day of the season with 96-57 records but could not avert the deadlock as the Cubs thrashed the Cardinals 8-3, while Boston's Mort Cooper was shutting out the Dodgers, 4-0. The Dodgers journeyed to St. Louis for the first of three play-off games without the services of their most exciting player, Pete Reiser, who broke an ankle three weeks before. Brooklyn

lost, 4-2, to the pitching arm of Howie Pollet. The Cardinals then came Eas for the second game and won the pennant, 8-4.

In Boston, the Red Sox finally made it to the altar after finishing secon to the Yankees in 1938, 1939, 1941, and 1942 due mainly to the return of Te Williams. A bit rusty from his three-year wartime layoff, he finished secon in the Triple Crown categories, but won the praise of the sportswriters an was named MVP.

The World Series began with Ted Williams and Stan Musial as the me most likely to succeed. When it was over, after seven hectic games William had a .200 average and Musial a .222 mark. Even Howie Pollet, the league biggest winner, failed to win a game. The honors, instead, went to Harr Brecheen, a regular season .500 pitcher who picked up three victories, an Enos Slaughter, who proved victory could outweigh pain.

Early in the fifth game Slaughter was clipped on the elbow by a pitch an later forced to leave the game for what turned out to be a broken elbow. On th return train trip to St. Louis, where the Series resumed the next day Slaughter got his elbow patched and played in the Cardinals' 4-1 serie evener. The next day Slaughter played again but did not manage a hit unt the bottom of the eighth with the score at 3-3.

In Boston's part of the inning, they had managed to score the tying ru although losing Dom DiMaggio because of a sprained ankle. Leon Culberso took DiMaggio's place in center. Slaughter was still on first base with two ou when Harry Walker hit a line drive over Johnny Pesky's head. Slaughte continued to circle the bases as Culberson's throw came into Pesky. Th Boston shortstop was either not believing his eyes or thinking of things othe than baseball. But whatever his thoughts were, they were enough to caus him to hesitate for a moment in relaying the throw to the plate as Slaughte slid home with what turned out to be the world's championship.

1946 AMERICAN LEAGUE

NAME	G by Pos	B	AGE	G	AB	R	H	2B	3B	HR	RBI	BB	SO	SB	BA	SA
BOSTON	**1st 104-50 .675**		**JOE CRONIN**													
	TOTALS		30	156	5318	792	1441	268	50	109	736	687	661	45	.271	.402
Rudy York	1B154	R	32	154	579	78	160	30	6	17	119	86	93	3	.276	.437
Bobby Doerr	2B151	R	28	151	583	95	158	34	9	18	116	66	67	5	.271	.453
Johnny Pesky	SS153	L	26	153	621	115	208	43	4	2	55	65	29	9	.335	.427
Rip Russell	3B70, 2B3	R	31	80	274	22	57	10	1	6	35	13	30	1	.208	.318
Catfish Metkovich	OF81	L	24	86	281	42	69	15	2	4	25	36	39	8	.246	.356
Dom DiMaggio	OF142	R	29	142	534	85	169	24	7	7	73	66	58	10	.316	.427
Ted Williams	OF150	L	27	150	514	142	176	37	8	38	123	156	44	0	.342	.667
Hal Wagner	C116	L	30	117	370	39	85	12	2	6	52	69	32	3	.230	.322
2 Pinky Higgins	3B59	R	37	64	200	18	55	11	1	2	28	24	24	0	.275	.370
Tom McBride	OF43	R	31	61	153	21.	46	5	2	0	19	9	6	0	.301	.359
Leon Culberson	OF49, 3B4	R	26	59	179	34	56	10	1	3	18	16	19	0	.313	.430
2 Wally Moses	OF44	L	35	48	175	13	36	11	3	2	17	14	15	2	.206	.337
Roy Partee	C38	R	28	40	111	13	35	5	2	0	9	13	14	0	.315	.396
Paul Campbell	1B5	L	28	26	26	3	3	1	0	0	2	0	7	0	.115	.154
Johnny Lazor	OF7	L	33	23	29	1	4	0	0	1	4	2	11	0	.138	.241
Eddie Pellagrini	3B14, SS9	R	28	22	71	7	15	3	1	2	4	3	18	1	.211	.366
Don Gutteridge	2B9, 3B8	R	34	22	47	8	11	3	0	1	6	2	7	0	.234	.362
Ernie Andres	3B15	R	28	15	41	0	4	2	0	0	1	3	5	0	.098	.146
Ed McGah	C14	R	24	15	37	2	8	1	0	0	1	7	7	0	.216	.297
Frankie Pytlak 37 R 2-14, Tom Carey 37 R 1-5, Ben Steiner 24 L 1-4, Andy Gilbert 31 R 0-1																
DETROIT	**2nd 92-62 .597 12**		**STEVE O'NEILL**													
	TOTALS		31	155	5318	704	1373	212	41	108	644	622	616	65	.258	.374
Hank Greenberg	1B140	R	35	142	523	91	145	29	5	44	127	80	88	5	.277	.604
Jimmy Bloodworth (MS)	2B71	R	28	76	249	26	61	8	1	5	36	12	26	3	.245	.345
Eddie Lake	SS155	R	29	155	587	105	149	24	1	8	31	103	69	15	.254	.339
2 George Kell	3B105, 1B1	R	23	105	434	67	142	19	9	4	41	30	14	3	.327	.440
Roy Cullenbine	OF81, 1B21	B	32	113	328	63	110	21	0	15	56	88	39	3	.335	.537
Hoot Evers (BN)	OF76	R	25	81	304	42	81	8	4	4	33	34	43	7	.266	.359
Dick Wakefield	OF104	L	25	111	396	64	106	11	5	12	59	59	55	3	.268	.412
Birdie Tebbetts	C87	R	33	87	280	20	68	11	2	1	34	28	23	1	.243	.307
Pat Mullin	OF75	L	28	93	276	34	68	13	4	3	35	25	36	3	.246	.355
Jimmy Outlaw	OF43, 3B38	R	32	92	299	36	78	14	2	2	31	29	24	5	.261	.341
Doc Cramer	OF50	L	40	68	204	26	60	8	2	1	26	15	8	1	.294	.368
Skeeter Webb	2B50, SS8	R	36	64	169	12	37	1	1	0	17	9	18	1	.219	.237
Paul Richards	C54	R	37	57	139	13	28	5	2	0	11	23	18	2	.201	.266
Eddie Mayo (TJ)	2B49	L	36	51	202	21	51	9	2	0	22	14	12	6	.252	.317
Anse Moore	OF32	L	28	51	134	16	28	4	0	1	8	12	9	1	.209	.261
Bob Swift	C42	R	31	42	107	13	25	2	0	2	10	14	7	0	.234	.308
Fred Hutchinson	P28	R	26	40	89	11	28	4	0	0	13	6	1	0	.315	.360
1 Barney McCosky	OF24	L	29	25	91	11	18	5	0	1	11	17	9	0	.198	.286
1 Pinky Higgins	3B17	R	37	18	60	2	13	3	1	0	8	5	6	0	.217	.300
Johnny Lipon	SS8, 3B1	R	23	14	20	4	6	0	0	0	1	5	3	0	.300	.300
Johnny Groth 19 R 0-9, 1 Billy Hitchcock 29 R 0-3, Ned Harris 29 L 0-1, Rip Radcliff (MS) 40																
NEW YORK	**3rd 87-67 .565 17**		**JOE McCARTHY 22-13 .629**		**BILL DICKEY 57-48 .543**		**JOHNNY NEUN 8-6 .571**									
	TOTALS		30	154	5139	684	1275	208	50	136	649	627	706	48	.248	.387
Nick Etten	1B84	L	32	108	323	37	75	14	1	9	49	49	38	0	.232	.365
Joe Gordon	2B108	R	31	112	376	35	79	15	0	11	47	49	72	2	.210	.338
Phil Rizzuto	SS125	R	28	126	471	53	121	17	1	2	38	34	39	14	.257	.310
Snuffy Stirnweiss	3B79, 2B46, SS4	R	27	129	487	75	122	19	7	0	37	66	58	18	.251	.318
Tommy Henrich	OF111, 1B41	L	33	150	565	92	142	25	4	19	83	67	63	5	.251	.411
Joe DiMaggio	OF131	R	31	132	503	81	146	20	8	25	95	59	24	1	.290	.511
Charlie Keller	OF149	L	29	150	538	98	148	29	10	30	101	113	101	1	.275	.533
Aaron Robinson	C95	L	31	100	330	32	98	17	2	16	64	48	40	0	.297	.506
Johnny Lindell	OF74, 1B14	R	29	102	332	41	86	10	5	10	40	32	47	4	.259	.410
Billy Johnson (MS)	3B74	R	27	85	296	51	77	14	5	4	35	31	42	1	.260	.382
Bill Dickey	C39	L	39	54	134	10	35	8	0	2	10	19	12	0	.261	.366
Steve Souchock	1B20	R	27	47	86	15	26	3	3	2	10	7	13	0	.302	.477
Gus Niarhos	C29	R	25	37	40	11	9	1	1	0	3	6	2	1	.225	.300
Frankie Crosetti	SS24	R	35	28	59	4	17	3	0	0	3	8	5	0	.288	.339
Tommy Byrne	P4	L	26	17	9	2	2	0	0	0	1	0	3	0	.222	.222
1 Oscar Grimes	SS7, 2B5	R	31	14	39	1	8	1	0	0	4	1	7	0	.205	.231
Ken Silvestri	C12	B	30	13	21	1	6	1	0	0	1	2	8	0	.286	.333
1 Hank Majeski	3B2	R	29	9	11	1	1	0	0	0	1	1	1	0	.083	.250
Yogi Berra	C6	L	21	7	22	3	8	1	0	2	4	1	1	0	.364	.682
Bobby Brown 21 L 8-24, 2 Frank Colman 28 L 4-15, Bill Drescher 25 L 2-6, Eddie Bockman 25 R 1-12,																
Bud Metheny 31 L 0-3, Roy Weatherly 31 L 1-2, Butch Wensloff (MS) 30																

NAME	T	AGE	W	L	PCT	SV	G	GS	CG	IP	H	BB	SO	SHO	ERA
		31	104	50	.675	20	156	156	79	1397	1359	501	667	15	3.38
Boo Ferriss	R	24	25	6	.806	3	40	35	26	274	274	71	106	6	3.25
Tex Hughson	R	30	20	11	.645	3	39	35	21	278	252	51	172	6	2.75
Mickey Harris	L	29	17	9	.654	0	34	30	15	223	236	76	131	0	3.63
Joe Dobson	R	29	13	7	.650	0	32	24	9	167	148	68	91	1	3.23
Jim Bagby	R	29	7	6	.538	0	21	11	6	107	117	49	16	1	3.70
2 Bill Zuber	R	33	5	1	.833	0	15	7	2	57	37	39	29	1	2.53
Earl Johnson	L	27	5	4	.556	3	29	5	0	80	78	39	40	0	3.71
Clem Dreisewerd	L	30	4	1	.800	0	20	1	0	47	50	15	19	0	4.21
Mace Brown	R	37	3	1	.750	1	18	0	0	26	26	16	10	0	2.08
Bob Klinger	R	38	3	2	.600	9	28	1	0	57	49	25	16	0	2.37
Charlie Wagner	R	33	1	0	1.000	0	8	4	0	31	32	19	14	0	5.81
Bill Butland	R	28	1	0	1.000	0	5	2	0	16	23	13	10	0	11.25
Mel Deutsch	R	30	0	0	—	0	3	0	0	6	7	3	2	0	6.00
Jim Wilson	R	24	0	0	—	0	1	0	0	1	2	0	0	0	18.00
Mike Ryba	R	43	0	1	.000	0	9	1	0	13	12	5	5	0	3.46
Randy Heflin	R	27	0	1	.000	0	5	1	0	15	16	12	6	0	2.40
		30	92	62	.597	15	155	155	94	1402	1277	497	896	18	3.22
Hal Newhouser	L	25	26	9	.743	1	37	34	29	293	215	98	275	6	1.94
Dizzy Trout	R	31	17	13	.567	3	38	32	23	276	244	97	151	5	2.35
Virgil Trucks	R	29	14	9	.609	0	32	29	15	237	217	75	161	2	3.23
Fred Hutchinson	R	26	14	11	.560	2	28	26	18	207	184	66	138	3	3.09
Al Benton	R	35	11	7	.611	1	38	15	6	141	132	58	60	1	3.64
Stubby Overmire	L	27	6	4	.600	1	24	13	3	97	106	29	34	0	4.79
George Caster	R	38	2	1	.667	4	26	0	0	41	42	24	19	0	5.71
Lou Kretlow	R	25	1	0	1.000	0	1	1	1	7	2	4	0	0	3.00
Hal White	R	27	1	1	.500	0	11	1	0	27	34	15	12	0	5.67
Tommy Bridges	R	39	1	1	.500	1	9	1	0	21	24	8	17	0	6.60
Johnny Gorsica (MS)	R	31	0	0	—	1	14	0	0	24	28	11	14	0	4.50
Rufe Gentry	R	28	0	0	—	0	2	0	0	3	4	1	0	0	15.00
1 Hal Manders	R	29	0	0	—	0	2	0	0	6	8	2	3	0	10.50
Art Houtteman	R	18	0	1	.000	1	1	0	0	8	15	6	2	0	9.00
Ted Gray	L	21	0	1	.000	1	3	2	0	12	17	5	5	0	8.25
		30	87	67	.565	17	154	154	68	1361	1232	552	653	17	3.13
Spud Chandler	R	38	20	8	.714	2	34	32	20	257	200	90	138	6	2.10
Bill Bevens	R	29	16	13	.552	0	31	31	18	250	213	78	120	3	2.23
Randy Gumpert	R	28	11	3	.786	1	33	13	4	133	113	32	63	0	2.30
Joe Page	L	28	9	8	.529	3	31	17	6	136	126	72	77	1	3.57
Al Gettel	R	28	6	7	.462	0	26	11	5	103	89	40	54	2	2.97
Red Ruffing	R	42	5	1	.833	0	8	4	3	61	37	23	19	2	1.77
Ernie Bonham	R	32	5	8	.385	3	18	14	6	105	97	23	30	2	3.69
Johnny Murphy	R	37	4	2	.667	7	27	0	0	45	40	19	19	0	3.40
Cuddles Marshall	R	21	3	4	.429	0	23	11	1	81	96	56	32	0	5.33
Vic Raschi	R	27	2	0	1.000	0	2	2	1	15	14	5	11	0	3.94
1 Jake Wade	L	34	2	1	.667	1	13	1	0	35	33	14	22	0	2.31
Bill Wight	L	24	2	1	.500	0	14	4	0	44	30	11	0	0	4.50
Mel Queen (MS)	R	28	1	0	1.000	0	14	3	1	30	40	21	26	0	6.60
1 Steve Roser	R	28	1	0	1.000	0	9	0	0	7	8	5	0	0	6.00
Tommy Byrne	L	26	0	1	.000	0	4	1	0	9	7	4	5	0	6.00
Karl Drews	R	26	0	0	—	0	1	0	0	6	10	3	3	0	9.00
1 Bill Zuber	R	33	0	0	—	0	5	0	0	10	10	13	8	0	12.00
Al Lyons	R	28	0	0	—	0	2	0	0	6	4	6	0	0	5.40
1 Charley Stanceau	R	30	0	0	—	0	2	0	0	5	6	3	2	0	10.80
Herb Karpel	L	28	0	0	—	0	2	0	0	2	3	2	0	0	4.50
Marius Russo	L	31	0	0	—	0	19	1	0	26	11	7	0	0	4.34
Frank Hiller (EJ)	R	25	0	0	—	0	1	0	0	11	13	6	4	0	4.76

WASHINGTON — 4th 76-78 .494 28 | OSSIE BLUEGE

NAME	G by Pos	B	AGE	G	AB	R	H	2B	3B	HR	RBI	BB	SO	SB	BA	SA
TOTALS			30	155	5337	608	1388	260	63	60	553	511	641	51	.260	.366
Mickey Vernon	1B147	L	28	148	587	88	207	51	8	8	85	49	64	14	.353	.508
Jerry Priddy	2B138	R	26	138	511	54	130	23	4	8	58	57	73	9	.254	.364
Cecil Travis	SS75,3B56	L	32	137	465	45	117	22	3	1	56	45	47	2	.252	.318
2 Billy Hitchcock	SS53,3B46	R	29	98	354	27	75	8	3	0	25	26	52	2	.212	.251
Buddy Lewis	OF145	L	29	150	582	82	170	28	13	7	45	59	26	5	.292	.421
Stan Spence	OF150	L	31	152	578	83	169	50	10	16	87	62	31	1	.292	.497
2 Joe Grace	OF74	L	32	77	321	39	97	17	4	2	31	24	19	1	.302	.399
Al Evans	C81	R	29	88	272	30	69	10	4	2	30	30	28	1	.254	.342
S. Robertson	3B38,2B14,SS12,OF1	R	27	74	230	30	46	6	3	6	19	30	42	6	.200	.330
George Binks	OF28	R	31	65	134	13	26	3	0	0	12	6	16	1	.194	.216
Jake Early	C64	L	31	64	189	13	38	6	0	4	18	23	27	0	.201	.296
Gil Torres	SS31,3B18,2B7,P3	R	30	63	185	18	47	8	0	0	13	11	12	3	.254	.297
Gil Coan	OF29	L	24	59	134	17	28	3	2	3	9	7	37	2	.209	.328
1 Jeff Heath	OF47	L	31	48	166	23	47	12	3	4	27	36	36	1	.283	.464
Mike Guerra	C27	R	33	41	83	3	21	2	1	0	4	5	6	1	.253	.301
George Myatt	3B7,2B2	L	32	15	34	7	8	1	0	0	4	2	3	0	.235	.265
1 Joe Kuhel	1B6	L	40	14	20	2	3	1	0	0	1	2	2	0	.150	.150

Jack Sanford 29 R 6-26, Eddie Yost (MS) 19 R 2-25, Ray Goolsby 26 R 0-4, Roberto Ortiz (SM) 31, John Sullivan (MS) 25

NAME	T	AGE	W	L	PCT	SV	G	GS	CG	IP	H	BB	SO	SHO	ERA
		31	76	78	.494	10	155	155	71	1396	1459	547	537	8	3.74
Mickey Haefner	L	33	14	11	.560	1	33	27	17	228	220	80	85	2	2.84
2 Bobo Newsom	R	38	11	8	.579	1	24	22	14	178	163	60	82	2	2.78
Dutch Leonard	R	37	10	10	.500	0	26	23	7	162	182	36	62	3	2.63
Early Wynn (MS)	R	26	8	5	.615	0	17	12	9	107	112	33	36	0	3.11
Sid Hudson	R	31	8	11	.421	1	31	15	6	142	160	37	35	1	3.61
Ray Scarborough	R	28	7	11	.389	1	32	20	6	156	176	74	46	1	4.04
Walt Masterson	R	26	5	6	.455	1	29	9	2	91	105	67	61	0	6.03
Roger Wolff	R	35	5	8	.385	0	21	17	6	122	115	30	50	0	2.58
1 Johnny Niggeling	R	42	3	2	.600	0	8	6	3	38	39	21	10	0	4.03
Milo Candini	R	28	2	0	1.000	1	9	0	0	22	15	4	8	0	2.04
Marino Pieretti	R	25	2	2	.500	0	30	2	1	62	70	40	20	0	5.95
Bill Kennedy	L	27	1	2	.333	1	21	2	0	39	40	29	18	0	6.00
Vern Curtis	R	26	0	0	—	0	16	1	0	16	19	10	7	0	7.31
2 Jake Wade	L	34	0	0	—	0	6	0	0	11	12	12	9	0	4.91
Gil Torres	R	30	0	1	.000	0	3	0	0	7	9	3	2	0	7.71
Maxie Wilson	L	30	0	1	.000	0	13	0	0	13	16	9	8	0	6.92
2 Al LaMacchia	R	24	0	1	.000	0	2	0	0	3	6	2	0	0	15.00

Alex Carrasquel (SM) 33, Jim Mertz (MS) 30

CHICAGO — 5th 74-80 .481 30 | JIMMY DYKES 10-20 .333 | TED LYONS 64-60 .516

NAME	G by Pos	B	AGE	G	AB	R	H	2B	3B	HR	RBI	BB	SO	SB	BA	SA
TOTALS			31	155	5312	562	1364	206	44	37	515	501	600	78	.257	.333
Hal Trosky	1B80	L	33	88	299	22	76	12	3	2	31	34	37	4	.254	.334
Don Kolloway	2B90,3B31	R	27	123	482	45	135	23	4	3	53	9	29	14	.280	.363
Luke Appling	SS149	R	39	149	582	59	180	27	5	1	55	71	41	6	.309	.378
Dario Lodigiani (EJ)	3B44	R	30	44	155	12	38	8	0	0	13	16	14	4	.245	.297
Taffy Wright (IL)	OF107	L	34	115	422	46	116	19	4	7	52	42	17	10	.275	.389
Thurman Tucker	OF110	L	28	121	438	62	126	20	3	1	36	54	45	9	.288	.354
Bob Kennedy	OF75,3B29	R	25	113	411	43	106	13	5	5	34	24	62	6	.258	.350
Mike Tresh	C79	R	30	80	217	28	47	5	2	0	21	36	24	0	.217	.258
Cass Michaels	2B66,3B13,SS6	R	20	91	291	37	75	8	0	1	22	29	36	9	.258	.296
Ralph Hodgin	OF57	L	31	87	258	32	65	10	1	0	25	19	6	0	.252	.298
Whitey Platt	OF61	R	25	84	247	28	62	8	5	3	32	17	34	1	.251	.360
2 Joe Kuhel	1B62	L	40	64	238	24	65	9	3	4	20	21	24	4	.273	.387
1 Wally Moses	OF36	L	35	56	168	20	46	9	1	4	16	17	20	2	.274	.411
2 Frankie Hayes	C50	R	31	53	179	15	38	6	0	2	16	29	33	1	.212	.279
Leo Wells	3B38,SS2	R	28	45	127	11	24	4	1	1	11	12	34	3	.189	.260
George Dickey	C	B	30	37	78	8	15	1	0	0	1	12	13	0	.192	.205
Jake Jones (BW)	1B20	R	25	24	79	10	21	5	1	3	13	2	13	0	.266	.468
Guy Curtright	OF15	R	33	23	55	7	11	2	0	0	5	11	14	0	.200	.236
Dave Philley	OF17	B	26	17	68	10	24	2	1	0	7	4	4	5	.353	.471
Frank Whitman	SS6,2B1,1B1	R	21	17	16	7	1	0	0	0	1	2	6	0	.063	.063
Ed Fernandes	C12	R	28	14	32	4	8	2	0	0	2	6	3	0	.250	.313

1 Tom Jordan (AJ) 26 R 4-15, Floyd Baker 29 R 6-24, Joe Smaza 22 L 1-5

NAME	T	AGE	W	L	PCT	SV	G	GS	CG	IP	H	BB	SO	SHO	ERA
		31	74	80	.481	16	155	155	62	1392	1348	508	550	9	3.10
Earl Caldwell	R	41	13	4	.765	8	39	0	0	91	60	29	42	0	2.08
Ed Lopat	L	28	13	13	.500	0	29	29	20	231	216	48	89	2	2.73
Eddie Smith	L	32	8	11	.421	1	24	21	3	145	135	60	59	1	2.86
Orval Grove	R	26	8	13	.381	0	33	26	10	205	213	78	60	1	3.03
Frank Papish	L	28	7	5	.583	0	31	15	6	138	122	63	66	2	2.74
Joe Haynes	R	28	7	9	.438	2	32	23	9	177	203	60	60	0	3.76
Johnny Rigney (SJ)	R	31	5	5	.500	0	15	11	3	83	76	35	51	2	4.01
2 Al Hollingsworth	L	38	3	2	.600	1	21	2	0	55	63	22	22	0	4.58
Bill Dietrich (BG)	R	36	3	3	.500	1	11	9	3	62	63	24	20	0	2.61
G. Maltzberger (MS)	R	33	2	0	1.000	2	19	0	0	40	30	6	17	0	1.58
Thornton Lee (EJ)	R	39	2	4	.333	0	7	7	2	43	39	23	23	0	3.56
Ralph Hammer	R	29	2	7	.222	1	25	7	1	71	80	39	29	0	4.43
Ted Lyons	R	45	1	4	.200	0	5	5	5	43	38	9	10	0	2.30
Len Perme	L	28	0	0	—	0	4	0	0	4	6	7	2	0	9.00
2 Emmett O'Neill	R	28	0	0	—	0	4	0	0	4	4	5	1	0	9.00

Johnny Johnson (AJ) 31

CLEVELAND — 6th 68-86 .442 36 | LOU BOUDREAU

NAME	G by Pos	B	AGE	G	AB	R	H	2B	3B	HR	RBI	BB	SO	SB	BA	SA
TOTALS			28	156	5374	537	1285	233	56	79	496	506	697	57	.245	.356
Les Fleming	1B80,OF1	L	30	99	306	40	85	17	5	8	42	50	42	1	.278	.444
Dutch Meyer	2B64	R	30	72	207	13	48	5	3	0	16	26	16	0	.232	.285
Lou Boudreau	SS139	R	28	140	515	51	151	30	6	6	62	40	14	6	.293	.410
Ken Keltner	3B113	R	29	116	398	47	96	17	1	13	45	30	38	0	.241	.387
Hank Edwards	OF123	L	27	124	458	62	138	33	16	10	54	43	48	1	.301	.509
Pat Seerey	OF115	R	23	117	404	57	91	17	2	26	62	65	101	2	.225	.496
George Case	OF118	R	30	118	484	46	109	23	4	1	22	34	38	28	.225	.295
Jim Hegan	C87	R	25	88	271	29	64	11	5	0	17	17	44	1	.236	.314
Felix Mackiewicz	OF72	R	28	78	258	35	67	15	4	0	16	16	32	5	.260	.349
Jack Conway	2B50,SS14,3B3	R	27	68	258	24	58	6	2	0	18	20	36	2	.225	.264
Ray Mack	2B61	R	29	61	171	13	35	6	2	1	9	23	27	2	.205	.281
Gene Woodling	OF37	L	23	61	133	8	25	1	4	0	9	16	13	1	.188	.256
Don Ross	3B41,OF2	R	31	55	153	12	41	7	0	3	14	17	12	0	.268	.373
Bob Lemon	P32,OF12	L	25	55	89	9	16	3	0	1	4	7	18	0	.180	.247
1 Frankie Hayes	C50	R	31	51	156	11	40	12	0	3	18	21	26	1	.256	.391
2 Heinz Becker	1B44	L	30	50	147	15	44	10	1	0	17	23	18	1	.299	.381
Mickey Rocco	1B27	L	30	34	98	8	24	2	0	2	14	15	15	1	.245	.327
2 Jimmy Wasdell	1B44,OF3	L	32	41	112	11	30	4	0	0	4	4	4	1	.268	.268
Sherm Lollar	C24	R	21	28	62	7	15	6	0	1	9	6	3	0	.242	.387

2 Tom Jordan 26 R 7-35, Blas Monaco 30 B 0-6, Dale Mitchell 24 L 19-44, Buster Mills 37 R 6-22, Rusty Peters (MS) 31 R 6-21, 2 Howie Moss 27 R 2-32, Jackie Price 33 L 3-13, Eddie Robinson 25 L 12-30 Ralph Weigel 24 R 2-12, Charlie Brewster 29 R 0-2, Ted Sepkoski 22 L 4-8, Eddie Carnett (MS) 29, Hank Ruszkowski (MS) 20

NAME	T	AGE	W	L	PCT	SV	G	GS	CG	IP	H	BB	SO	SHO	ERA
		29	68	86	.442	13	156	156	63	1389	1282	649	789	16	3.62
Bob Feller	R	27	26	15	.634	4	48	42	36	371	277	153	348	10	2.18
Allie Reynolds	R	31	11	15	.423	0	31	28	9	183	180	108	107	3	3.89
Red Embree (MS)	R	28	8	12	.400	0	28	26	8	200	170	79	87	0	3.47
Mel Harder (HJ)	R	36	5	4	.556	0	13	12	4	92	85	31	21	1	3.42
Steve Gromek	R	26	5	15	.250	4	29	21	5	154	159	47	75	0	4.32
Bob Lemon	R	25	4	5	.444	1	32	5	1	94	77	68	39	0	2.49
2 Joe Berry	R	41	3	6	.333	1	21	0	0	37	32	16	14	0	3.41
Joe Krakauskas	L	31	2	5	.286	1	29	5	0	47	60	25	20	0	5.55
Bob Kuzava	L	23	1	0	1.000	0	2	2	0	12	9	11	4	0	3.00
Charlie Gassaway	L	27	1	1	.500	0	13	6	0	51	54	26	23	0	3.88
2 Les Webber	R	31	1	1	.500	0	18	0	0	44	45	21	15	0	5.20
Don Black	R	29	1	2	.333	0	18	4	0	44	45	21	15	0	4.50
1 Tom Ferrick	R	31	0	0	—	0	9	0	0	15	18	6	2	0	6.60
Eddie Klieman	R	28	0	0	—	0	15	0	0	18	18	10	2	0	6.00
Johnny Podgajny	R	25	0	0	—	0	1	0	0	14	20	8	3	0	9.00
Vic Johnson	L	25	0	0	—	0	1	0	0	14	20	8	3	0	9.00
Ray Flanigan	R	22	0	0	—	0	1	0	0	2	1	1	0	0	0.00
Ralph McCabe	R	27	0	1	.000	0	1	1	0	5	6	3	1	0	11.25
Pete Center	R	24	0	1	.000	0	3	0	0	29	20	6	16	0	4.97

ST. LOUIS — 7th 66-88 .429 38 | LUKE SEWELL 53-71 .427 | ZACK TAYLOR 13-17 .433

NAME	G by Pos	B	AGE	G	AB	R	H	2B	3B	HR	RBI	BB	SO	SB	BA	SA
TOTALS			29	156	5373	621	1350	220	46	84	576	465	713	23	.251	.356
Chuck Stevens	1B120	B	27	122	432	53	107	17	4	2	27	47	62	4	.248	.326
Johnny Berardino	2B143	R	29	144	582	70	154	29	5	5	68	34	58	2	.265	.357
Vern Stephens	SS112	R	25	115	450	67	138	19	4	14	64	35	49	0	.307	.460
Mark Christman	3B77,SS47	R	32	128	458	40	118	22	2	1	41	22	29	0	.258	.321
Al Zarilla	OF107	R	27	125	371	46	96	14	9	4	43	27	37	3	.259	.377
Walt Judnich	OF137	L	30	142	527	60	134	23	4	15	72	60	54	0	.262	.411
2 Jeff Heath	OF83	L	31	86	316	46	87	20	4	12	57	37	37	0	.275	.478
Frank Mancuso	C85	R	28	87	262	22	63	8	3	3	23	30	31	1	.240	.328
Johnny Lucadello	3B37,2B19	B	27	87	210	21	52	7	1	1	15	36	20	0	.248	.305
Bill Dillinger	3B54,SS1	R	27	83	225	33	63	6	3	0	11	19	32	4	.280	.333
Chet Laabs	OF72	R	34	80	264	40	69	13	0	16	52	20	50	3	.261	.492
Hank Helf	C69	R	32	71	182	17	35	11	0	6	21	9	40	0	.192	.352
Glenn McQuillen	OF48	R	31	59	166	24	40	3	3	1	12	19	18	0	.241	.313
1 Joe Grace	OF43	L	32	48	161	21	37	7	2	1	13	16	20	1	.230	.317
Joe Schultz	C17	R	27	42	57	1	22	4	0	0	14	11	2	0	.386	.456
Babe Dahlgren	1B24	R	34	28	80	2	14	1	0	0	9	6	13	0	.175	.188
Jerry Witte	1B18	R	30	18	73	7	14	2	0	2	9	4	18	0	.192	.301
Lou Finney	OF7	L	35	16	30	0	9	0	0	0	3	2	1	0	.300	.300
Paul Lehner	OF12	L	26	12	20	3	4	1	0	0	2	2	5	0	.222	.333
Les Moss	C12	R	21	12	35	4	13	3	0	1	6	5	3	0	.371	.457

Ken Sears 28 L 5-15, George Archie 32 R 2-11, George Bradley 32 R 2-12, Len Schulte 29 R 2-5, Babe Martin 25 R 2-9, Hank Schmulbach (MS) 21, Dick Siebert (HO) 34

NAME	T	AGE	W	L	PCT	SV	G	GS	CG	IP	H	BB	SO	SHO	ERA
		29	66	88	.429	12	156	156	63	1382	1465	573	574	13	3.95
Jack Kramer	R	28	13	11	.542	0	31	28	13	195	190	68	69	3	3.18
Sam Zoldak	L	27	9	11	.450	2	35	21	9	170	166	57	51	2	3.44
Nels Potter	R	34	8	9	.471	0	23	19	10	145	152	59	72	0	3.72
Denny Galehouse	R	34	8	12	.400	0	30	24	11	180	194	52	90	2	3.65
Tex Shirley	R	28	6	12	.333	0	27	18	7	140	148	105	43	1	4.95
Cliff Fannin	R	22	5	2	.714	2	7	7	4	87	76	42	52	1	5.00
2 Tom Ferrick	R	31	4	1	.800	5	25	4	1	82	26	5	13	0	2.81
Ellis Kinder	R	31	3	3	.500	1	33	7	1	87	78	36	59	0	3.31
Bob Muncrief	R	30	3	12	.200	0	29	14	4	115	149	31	49	1	4.50
Fred Sanford	R	26	2	1	.667	0	3	2	0	19	19	9	8	0	2.05
Stan Ferens	L	31	2	9	.182	0	34	6	1	88	100	38	28	0	4.50
Frank Biscan	L	26	1	1	.500	1	16	0	0	21	19	15	9	0	5.09
1 Al Milnar	L	32	1	1	.500	0	2	1	0	15	15	6	1	1	2.40
Ox Miller	R	28	1	3	.250	1	15	5	2	52	55	19	12	0	6.94
1 Al LaMacchia	R	24	0	0	—	0	4	0	0	15	17	7	3	0	6.00
1 Al Hollingsworth	L	38	0	0	—	0	4	0	0	18	20	13	8	0	5.00
Chet Johnson	L	28	0	0	—	0	2	0	0	5	6	8	1	0	11.25
Steve Sundra	R	36	0	0	—	0	1	0	0	3	1	2	1	0	0.00
Ray Shore	R	25	0	0	—	0	2	0	0	3	5	7	0	0	18.00

PHILADELPHIA — 8th 49-105 .318 55 | CONNIE MACK

NAME	G by Pos	B	AGE	G	AB	R	H	2B	3B	HR	RBI	BB	SO	SB	BA	SA
TOTALS			30	155	5200	529	1317	220	51	40	481	482	594	39	.253	.338
George McQuinn	1B134	L	37	136	484	47	109	23	6	3	35	64	62	4	.225	.316
Gene Handley	2B68,3B4,SS1	R	31	89	251	31	63	8	5	0	21	22	29	5	.251	.323
Pete Suder	SS67,3B33,2B12,1B3	R	30	128	455	38	128	20	3	2	50	18	37	1	.281	.352
2 Hank Majeski	3B72	R	29	78	264	25	66	14	3	1	25	26	13	3	.250	.337
Elmer Valo	OF90	L	25	108	348	59	107	21	6	1	31	60	18	9	.307	.411
2 Barney McCosky	OF85	L	29	92	308	33	109	17	4	1	34	43	13	2	.354	.445
Sam Chapman	OF145	R	30	146	545	79	142	22	5	20	67	54	66	1	.261	.429
Buddy Rosar	C117	R	31	121	424	34	120	22	2	0	47	36	17	1	.283	.330
Tuck Stainback	OF66	R	34	91	291	35	71	10	2	0	20	7	20	3	.244	.292
Russ Derry	OF50	L	29	69	184	19	38	5	0	8	14	27	54	0	.207	.304
Irv Hall	2B40,SS7	R	27	63	184	16	45	9	5	0	11	17	19	2	.249	.303
Jack Wallaesa	SS59	R	26	63	194	16	38	4	2	0	11	14	47	1	.196	.314
2 Oscar Grimes	2B43,3B6,SS4	R	31	59	190	18	50	12	0	2	21	40	16	2	.263	.358
Gene Desautels	C52	R	39	52	130	10	29	4	0	0	16	10	20	0	.215	.254
Hal Peck (DF)	OF35	L	29	45	126	17	28	5	0	3	10	11	14	2	.247	.349
John Caulfield	SS31,3B1	R	28	44	94	13	26	6	0	0	10	4	11	0	.277	.362
Bruce Konopka	1B20,OF1	R	27	23	87	3	18	3	0	0	10	10	15	0	.207	.310
1 George Kell	3B26	R	23	26	87	13	28	5	2	0	9	10	10	0	.299	.391
Don Richmond	3B16	L	24	16	31	3	4	0	0	0	2	2	7	0	.129	.129
Ford Garrison	OF8	R	30	9	37	1	4	0	0	0	0	2	2	0	.108	.108

George Armstrong 22 R 1-6, Vern Benson 21 L 0-5, Joe Astroth 23 R 1-7, Bobby Estalella (SM) 35, George Yankowski (MS) 23

NAME	T	AGE	W	L	PCT	SV	G	GS	CG	IP	H	BB	SO	SHO	ERA
		28	49	105	.318	5	155	155	61	1343	1371	577	562	10	3.90
Phil Marchildon	R	32	13	16	.448	1	36	29	16	227	197	114	95	1	3.49
Jesse Flores	R	31	9	7	.563	1	29	15	8	155	147	38	48	4	2.32
Dick Fowler	R	25	9	16	.360	0	32	28	14	206	213	75	89	1	3.28
Russ Christopher	R	28	5	7	.417	0	31	11	9	119	114	44	79	0	4.31
1 Bobo Newsom	R	38	5	5	.375	0	10	9	3	59	61	30	32	1	3.36
Lum Harris	R	31	3	14	.176	0	34	12	4	125	153	48	33	0	5.26
Bob Savage	R	24	3	15	.167	2	40	19	7	164	164	93	78	1	4.06
Lou Knerr	R	24	3	16	.158	0	30	22	6	148	171	67	58	0	5.41
Bill McCahan	R	25	1	1	.500	0	7	2	0	18	16	16	9	0	1.00
Everett Fagan (MS)	R	28	0	1	.000	0	15	4	0	47	42	42	24	1	6.40
1 Joe Berry	R	41	0	0	—	0	5	0	0	13	13	5	3	0	2.77
Norm Brown	R	27	0	0	—	0	3	0	0	9	11	3	4	0	6.00
Jack Knott	R	39	0	1	.000	0	8	0	0	14	18	8	3	0	6.00
Lee Griffeth	R	28	0	0	—	0	4	0	0	6	9	2	2	0	3.00
Pat Cooper	R	28	0	0	—	0	1	0	0	5	7	5	0	0	5.14
Porter Vaughan	L	27	0	0	—	0	2	0	0	3	3	5	1	0	9.00
Herman Besse	L	34	0	0	—	0	3	0	0	21	19	9	10	0	5.14
Joe Coleman	R	23	0	1	.000	0	2	1	0	6	9	5	4	0	5.54

Fred Caligiuri (MS) 27, Lou Ciola (MS) 23, Tom Clyde (MS) 22, Burt Kuczynski (MS) 26, Sam Lowry (MS) 26, Carl Scheib (MS) 19

1946 NATIONAL LEAGUE

ST. LOUIS — 1ST 98-58 .628 — EDDIE DYER (Defeated Brooklyn in playoff 2 games to 0)

NAME	G by Pos	B	AGE	G	AB	R	H	2B	3B	HR	RBI	BB	SO	SB	BA	SA
TOTALS			27	156	5372	712	1426	265	56	81	665	530	537	58	.265	.381
Stan Musial	1B114, OF42	L	25	156	624	124	228	50	20	16	103	73	31	7	.365	.587
Red Schoendienst	2B128, 3B12, SS4	B	23	142	606	94	170	28	5	0	34	37	27	12	.281	.343
Marty Marion	SS145	R	28	146	498	51	116	29	4	3	46	59	53	1	.233	.325
Whitey Kurowski	3B138	R	28	142	519	76	156	32	5	14	89	72	47	2	.301	.462
Enos Slaughter	OF156	L	30	156	609	100	183	30	8	18	130	69	41	9	.300	.465
Terry Moore (KJ)	OF66	R	34	91	278	32	73	14	1	3	28	18	26	0	.263	.353
Harry Walker	OF92, 1B8	L	29	112	346	53	82	14	6	3	27	30	29	12	.237	.338
Joe Garagiola	C70	L	20	74	211	21	50	4	1	3	22	23	25	0	.237	.308
Erv Dusak	OF77, 3B11, 2B2	R	25	100	275	38	66	9	1	9	42	33	63	7	.240	.378
Dick Sisler	1B37, OF29	L	25	83	235	17	61	11	2	3	42	14	28	0	.260	.362
Buster Adams	OF58	R	31	81	173	21	32	6	0	5	22	29	27	3	.185	.306
Del Rice	C53	R	23	55	139	10	38	8	1	1	12	8	16	0	.273	.367
2 Clyde Kluttz	C49	R	28	52	136	8	36	7	0	0	14	10	10	0	.265	.316
Jeff Cross	SS17, 2B8, 3B1	R	27	49	69	17	15	3	0	0	6	10	8	4	.217	.261
Lou Klein (SM)	2B23	R	27	23	93	12	18	3	0	1	4	9	7	1	.194	.258
1 Ken O'Dea (XJ)	C22	L	33	22	57	2	7	2	0	1	3	8	8	0	.123	.211
Bill Endicott	OF2	L	27	20	20	2	4	3	0	0	3	4	4	0	.200	.350
Nippy Jones	2B3	R	21	16	12	3	4	0	0	0	1	2	1	0	.333	.333
Walter Sessi		L	28	14	21	2	3	0	0	0	4	2	4	0	.143	.357

1 Danny Litwhiler (MS) 29 R 0-5, Del Wilber 27 R 0-4, 1 Emil Verban 30 R 0-1, Creepy Crespi (MS) 28

NAME	T	AGE	W	L	PCT	SV	G	GS	CG	IP	H	BB	SO	SHO	ERA
		30	98	58	.628	15	156	156	75	1397	1326	493	607	18	3.01
Howie Pollet	L	25	21	10	.677	5	40	32	22	266	228	86	107	4	2.10
Murray Dickson	R	29	15	6	.714	1	47	19	12	184	160	56	82	2	2.88
Harry Brecheen	L	31	15	15	.500	3	36	30	14	231	212	67	117	5	2.49
Al Brazle	R	32	11	10	.524	0	37	15	6	153	152	55	58	2	3.29
Ted Wilks	R	30	8	0	1.000	1	40	4	0	95	88	38	40	0	3.41
Johnny Beazley (SA)	R	28	7	5	.583	0	19	18	5	103	109	55	36	0	4.46
Max Lanier (SM)	L	30	6	0	1.000	0	6	6	5	56	45	19	36	2	1.93
Ken Burkhart	R	29	6	3	.667	2	25	13	6	100	111	36	32	2	2.88
Red Barrett	R	31	3	2	.600	2	23	9	1	67	75	24	22	1	4.03
Freddie Martin (SM)	R	31	2	1	.667	0	6	3	2	28	19	8	19	0	4.03
George Munger (MS)	R	27	2	2	.500	1	10	7	2	49	47	12	28	0	3.31
Freddy Schmidt	R	30	1	0	1.000	0	16	0	0	27	27	15	14	0	3.33
1 Blix Donnelly	R	32	1	1	.333	1	13	0	0	14	17	10	11	0	3.86
Johnny Grodzicki	R	29	0	0	—	0	3	0	0	4	4	4	2	0	9.00
Howie Krist	R	30	0	2	.000	0	15	0	0	19	22	8	3	0	6.63

(LJ-from MS)

BROOKLYN — 2nd 96-60 .615 2 — LEO DUROCHER (Defeated by St. Louis in playoff 2 games to 0)

NAME	G by Pos	B	AGE	G	AB	R	H	2B	3B	HR	RBI	BB	SO	SB	BA	SA
TOTALS			28	157	5285	701	1376	233	66	55	642	691	575	100	.260	.361
Ed Stevens	1B99	L	21	103	310	34	75	7	1	10	60	27	45	2	.242	.426
Eddie Stanky	2B141	L	29	144	483	98	132	24	7	0	36	137	56	6	.273	.352
Pee Wee Reese	SS152	R	27	152	542	79	154	16	10	5	60	87	71	10	.284	.378
Cookie Lavagetto	3B67	R	33	88	242	36	57	10	1	3	27	38	17	3	.236	.318
Dixie Walker	OF149	L	35	150	576	80	184	29	9	9	116	67	28	14	.319	.448
Carl Furillo	OF112	R	24	117	335	29	95	18	6	3	35	31	20	6	.284	.400
Pete Reiser (BN)	OF97, 3B15	L	27	122	423	75	117	21	5	11	73	55	58	34	.277	.428
Bruce Edwards	C91	R	22	92	292	24	78	13	5	1	25	34	20	1	.267	.356
Dick Whitman	OF85	L	25	104	265	39	69	15	3	2	31	22	19	5	.260	.362
Augie Galan	OF60, 3B19, 1B2	L	34	99	274	53	85	22	5	3	38	68	21	8	.310	.460
Howie Schultz	1B87	R	23	90	249	27	63	14	1	3	27	16	34	2	.253	.353
Ferrell Anderson	C70	R	28	79	199	19	51	10	0	2	14	18	21	1	.256	.337
Gene Hermanski	OF34	L	26	64	110	15	22	2	0	2	8	17	10	2	.200	.255
Bob Ramazotti	3B30, 2B16	R	29	62	120	10	25	4	0	0	7	9	13	0	.208	.242
1 Billy Herman	3B29, 2B16	R	36	46	184	24	53	8	4	0	28	16	10	2	.288	.375
Stan Rojek	SS15, 2B6, 3B4	R	27	45	47	11	13	2	1	0	3	6	4	1	.277	.362
Joe Medwick	OF18, 1B1	R	34	41	77	7	24	4	0	2	18	6	5	0	.312	.442
Eddie Miksis (MS)	3B13, 2B1	R	19	23	48	3	7	0	0	0	5	3	6	1	.146	.146
1 Don Padgett	C10	L	34	19	30	2	5	1	0	0	3	4	0	0	.167	.300
Mike Sandlock	C17, 3B1	B	30	19	34	1	5	0	0	0	4	4	3	0	.147	.147

Joe Tepsic 22 R 0-5, Earl Naylor 27 R 0-2, 1 Goody Rosen 33 L 1-3, 1 Jack Graham 29 L 1-5, John Corriden 28 B 0-0, Tommy Brown (MS) 18,
Otis Davis 25 L 0-0, Lew Riggs 36 L 0-4, Luis Olmo (SM) 26, Mickey Owen (SM) 30, Arky Vaughan (VR) 30, Bobby Bragan (MS) 28, Lou Rochelli (MS) 27

NAME	T	AGE	W	L	PCT	SV	G	GS	CG	IP	H	BB	SO	SHO	ERA
		27	96	60	.615	28	157	157	52	1416	1280	671	647	14	3.05
Kirby Higbe	R	31	17	8	.680	1	42	29	11	211	178	107	134	3	3.03
Joe Hatten	L	29	14	11	.560	2	42	30	13	222	207	110	85	0	2.84
Vic Lombardi	L	23	13	10	.565	3	41	25	13	193	170	84	60	2	2.89
Hank Behrman	R	25	11	5	.688	4	47	11	2	151	138	69	78	0	2.92
Hugh Casey	R	32	11	5	.688	5	46	1	0	100	101	33	31	0	1.98
Art Herring	R	39	7	2	.778	5	35	2	0	86	91	29	34	0	3.35
Rube Melton (MS)	R	29	6	3	.667	1	24	12	3	100	72	52	44	2	1.98
Hal Gregg	R	24	6	4	.600	2	26	16	4	117	103	44	54	2	3.00
Ralph Branca	R	20	3	1	.750	3	24	10	2	67	62	41	42	2	3.90
Ed Head (SA)	R	28	3	2	.600	1	13	7	3	56	56	24	17	1	3.21
1 Les Webber	R	31	3	3	.500	0	11	4	0	43	34	15	16	0	2.30
Rex Barney	R	21	2	5	.286	0	16	9	1	54	46	51	36	0	5.83
Harry Taylor	R	27	0	0	—	0	1	0	0	5	5	1	6	0	3.60
Jean Pierre Roy	R	26	0	0	—	0	3	1	0	6	5	5	6	0	10.50
Curt Davis	R	42	0	0	—	0	3	0	0	2	2	1	1	0	13.50
Glen Moulder	R	28	0	0	—	0	1	0	0	2	2	1	1	0	4.50
Cal McLish (MS)	L	20	0	1	.000	0	1	1	0	1	0	0	0	0	∞
Paul Minner (SJ)	L	22	0	1	.000	0	2	1	0	4	8	2	1	0	6.75

CHICAGO — 3rd 82-71 .536 14.5 — CHARLIE GRIMM

NAME	G by Pos	B	AGE	G	AB	R	H	2B	3B	HR	RBI	BB	SO	SB	BA	SA
TOTALS			30	155	5298	626	1344	223	50	56	566	586	599	43	.254	.346
Eddie Waitkus	1B106	L	26	113	441	50	134	24	5	4	55	29	14	4	.304	.408
Don Johnson (BH)	R	34	83	314	37	76	10	1	1	19	26	39	6	.242	.290
Billy Jurges	SS73, 3B7, 2B2	R	38	82	221	26	49	9	2	0	17	43	28	1	.222	.281
Stan Hack (BG)	R	36	92	323	55	92	13	4	0	26	83	32	5	.285	.350
Phil Cavarretta	OF86, 1B51	L	29	130	510	89	150	28	10	8	78	88	54	2	.294	.435
Peanuts Lowrey	OF126, 3B20	R	28	144	540	75	139	24	5	4	54	56	22	10	.257	.343
Marv Rickert	OF104	L	25	111	392	44	103	18	3	7	47	28	54	3	.263	.378
Clyde McCullough	C89	R	29	90	307	38	88	18	5	4	34	22	39	2	.287	.417
Bill Nicholson	OF80	L	31	105	296	36	65	13	2	8	41	44	44	1	.220	.358
Bobby Sturgeon	SS72, 2B21	R	26	100	294	26	87	12	2	1	21	10	18	0	.296	.361
Lou Stringer	2B62, SS1, 3B1	R	29	80	209	26	51	3	1	3	19	26	34	0	.244	.311
Mickey Livingston (NJ)	C56	R	31	66	176	14	45	14	0	2	20	20	19	0	.256	.369
Andy Pafko (BN-BA)	OF64	R	25	65	234	18	66	6	4	3	30	27	15	4	.282	.380
Lennie Merullo	SS44	R	29	65	126	14	19	4	0	0	6	14	25	2	.151	.214
Dom Dallessandro	OF20	L	32	65	89	4	20	2	2	1	9	23	12	1	.225	.326
John Ostrowski	3B50, OF3	R	30	64	160	20	34	4	2	3	16	13	19	1	.213	.319
Bob Scheffing	C43	R	32	63	115	8	32	4	1	0	18	12	18	0	.278	.330
Frank Secory		R	33	33	43	6	10	3	0	1	8	6	8	0	.233	.512

1 Charlie Gilbert 26 L 1-13, 1 Heinz Becker 30 B 2-7, Cy Block 27 R 3-13, Rabbit Garriott 29 L 0-5, Hank Schenz 27 R 2-11,
Al Glossop 31 B 0-10, Ted Pawelek 26 L 1-4, Dewey Williams 30 R 1-5, Clarence Maddern 24 R 0-3

NAME	T	AGE	W	L	PCT	SV	G	GS	CG	IP	H	BB	SO	SHO	ERA
		30	82	71	.536	11	155	155	59	1393	1370	527	609	15	3.24
Hank Wyse	R	28	14	12	.538	1	40	27	12	201	206	52	52	2	2.69
Hank Borowy	R	30	12	10	.545	0	32	28	8	201	220	61	95	1	3.76
Johnny Schmitz	L	25	11	11	.500	2	41	21	14	224	184	94	135	2	2.61
Emil Kush	R	29	9	2	.818	2	40	6	1	130	120	43	50	1	3.05
Paul Erickson	R	30	9	7	.563	0	32	14	9	137	119	65	70	1	2.43
Claude Passeau	R	37	9	8	.529	0	21	21	10	129	118	42	47	2	3.14
Bob Chipman	L	27	6	5	.545	2	34	10	5	109	103	54	42	3	3.14
Hi Bithorn	R	30	6	5	.545	1	26	7	2	87	97	25	34	1	3.83
Russ Bauers	R	32	2	1	.667	1	15	2	2	43	45	19	22	0	3.56
Ray Prim (AJ)	L	39	2	3	.400	1	14	2	0	23	28	10	10	0	5.87
Ed Hanyzewski	R	25	1	0	1.000	0	4	0	0	9	11	6	1	0	4.50
Russ Meers	L	27	1	2	.333	1	7	1	0	11	10	9	3	0	3.27
Vern Olsen	L	28	0	0	—	0	6	0	0	9	11	5	4	0	2.70
Russ Meyer	R	22	0	0	—	0	1	0	0	17	21	10	10	0	3.18
1 Emmett O'Neill	R	28	0	0	—	0	1	0	0	3	1	9	1	0	6.21
Bill Fleming	R	32	0	1	.000	0	14	1	0	29	37	12	10	0	6.21
Red Adams	R	24	0	1	.000	0	8	1	0	12	18	7	3	0	8.25
2 Hal Manders	R	29	0	1	.000	1	9	0	0	14	16	9	9	0	9.00
Doyle Lade	R	25	0	0	—	0	2	1	0	15	15	3	8	0	4.20

BOSTON — 4th 81-72 .529 15.5 — BILLY SOUTHWORTH

NAME	G by Pos	B	AGE	G	AB	R	H	2B	3B	HR	RBI	BB	SO	SB	BA	SA
TOTALS			29	154	5225	630	1377	238	48	44	596	558	468	60	.264	.353
Ray Sanders (BA)	1B77	L	29	80	235	29	56	12	0	6	35	50	38	0	.243	.359
Connie Ryan	2B120, 3B24	R	26	143	502	59	121	28	8	1	48	55	63	7	.241	.335
Dick Culler	SS132	R	31	134	482	70	123	15	3	0	33	62	18	7	.255	.299
Nanny Fernandez	3B81, SS18, OF14	R	27	115	372	37	95	15	2	2	42	30	44	1	.255	.323
Tommy Holmes	OF146	L	29	149	568	80	176	35	6	6	79	58	14	7	.310	.424
Carden Gillenwater	OF78	R	29	99	264	31	51	10	1	1	14	39	27	3	.228	.295
Bama Rowell	OF85	L	30	95	293	37	82	12	6	3	31	29	15	5	.280	.392
Phil Masi	C124	R	29	133	397	52	106	17	5	3	62	55	41	5	.267	.358
Johnny Hopp	1B68, OF58	L	29	129	445	71	148	20	8	3	44	34	34	21	.333	.440
2 Danny Litwhiler	OF65, 3B2	R	29	79	247	29	72	12	4	8	38	19	23	1	.291	.453
2 Billy Herman	2B44, 1B22, 3B5	R	36	75	252	32	77	23	1	2	42	43	13	1	.306	.440
2 Mike McCormick (KJ)	OF48	R	29	59	164	23	43	6	2	1	16	11	7	0	.262	.341
Skippy Roberge	3B48	R	29	48	169	13	39	6	2	2	20	7	12	1	.231	.325
2 Don Padgett	C26	L	34	44	98	6	25	3	0	2	21	5	7	0	.255	.347
Whitey Wietelmann	SS16, 3B8, 2B4, P3	R	27	44	78	7	16	0	0	0	4	9	6	0	.205	.205
Johnny Sain	P37	R	28	40	94	6	28	2	1	0	17	0	0	0	.298	.340
1 Chuck Workman	OF12	L	31	25	49	4	7	1	0	0	8	6	12	0	.167	.333
2 Johnny Barrett (KJ)	OF17	L	27	24	43	3	10	3	0	0	6	12	1	4	.233	.302
Stew Hofferth	C15	R	31	24	58	3	12	1	0	0	5	4	9	0	.207	.259

Al Dark 24 R 3-13, Tommy Neill 26 L 12-45, 2 Ken O'Dea 33 L 7-32, Hugh Poland 33 L 1-6, Bob Brady 23 L 1-5,
Johnny McCarthy 36 L 1-7, Damon Phillips 27 R 1-2, Ducky Detweiler 26 R 0-1, Sibby Sisti 25 R 0-0, 1 Max West 29 L 0-1, Max Macon (MS) 30

NAME	T	AGE	W	L	PCT	SV	G	GS	CG	IP	H	BB	SO	SHO	ERA
		31	81	72	.529	12	154	154	74	1371	1291	478	531	10	3.37
Johnny Sain	R	28	20	14	.588	2	37	34	24	265	225	87	129	3	2.21
Mort Cooper	R	33	13	11	.542	1	25	23	13	199	181	39	83	3	3.12
Ed Wright	R	27	12	9	.571	0	36	21	9	176	164	71	44	2	3.53
Bill Lee	R	36	10	9	.526	0	25	21	8	140	148	45	32	0	4.18
Warren Spahn (MS)	L	25	8	5	.615	1	24	16	8	126	107	36	67	0	2.93
2 Si Johnson	R	39	6	5	.545	1	28	12	5	127	134	35	41	1	2.76
Lefty Wallace	L	24	3	3	.500	0	17	8	2	75	76	31	27	0	4.20
Bill Posedel	R	39	2	0	1.000	0	19	0	0	34	43	19	9	0	7.07
Frank Barrett	R	33	4	4	.333	1	23	0	0	35	35	17	12	0	5.14
2 Johnny Niggeling	R	42	2	5	.286	0	8	8	5	58	54	21	24	0	3.26
Dick Mulligan	R	28	1	0	1.000	0	15	0	0	19	14	7	12	0	2.40
Earl Reid	R	33	1	0	1.000	2	13	0	0	30	33	7	4	0	3.00
Steve Roser	R	28	1	1	.500	1	14	1	0	33	34	21	17	0	3.71
Elmer Singleton	R	27	1	2	.333	0	8	4	1	27	21	17	17	0	3.71
Ernie White	L	29	0	0	—	0	12	0	0	24	22	12	8	0	4.13
Jim Konstanty	R	29	0	1	.000	0	9	0	0	17	19	5	5	0	5.40
Dan Hendrickson	R	30	0	1	.000	0	4	0	0	4	9	4	2	0	4.50
Al Javery	R	30	0	1	.000	0	9	0	0	6	9	8	0	0	15.00
Johnny Hutchings	R	30	0	1	.000	0	3	0	0	11	16	7	1	0	9.00

Whitey Wietelmann 27 R 0-0, Ace Williams 29 L 0-0, Ray Martin (MS) 21

PHILADELPHIA — 5th 69-85 .448 28 — BEN CHAPMAN

NAME	G by Pos	B	AGE	G	AB	R	H	2B	3B	HR	RBI	BB	SO	SB	BA	SA
TOTALS			29	155	5233	560	1351	209	40	80	517	417	590	41	.258	.359
Frank McCormick	1B134	R	35	135	504	46	143	20	2	11	66	36	21	2	.284	.397
2 Emil Verban	2B138	R	30	138	473	44	130	17	2	0	34	21	18	5	.275	.322
Skeeter Newsome	SS107, 2B3, 3B2	R	35	112	375	35	87	10	1	3	34	35	23	4	.232	.277
Jim Tabor	3B124	R	32	124	463	53	124	15	2	10	50	36	51	3	.268	.374
Ron Northey	OF111	L	26	128	438	55	109	24	6	16	62	59	47	1	.249	.441
Johnny Wyrostek	OF142	L	26	145	545	59	153	30	6	4	45	70	42	7	.281	.383
Del Ennis	OF138	R	21	141	540	70	169	30	6	17	73	39	65	5	.313	.485
Andy Seminick	C118	R	25	124	406	55	107	15	5	12	54	39	86	2	.264	.414
Roy Hughes	SS34, 3B31, 2B7, 1B1	R	35	89	276	29	65	11	0	0	22	19	16	3	.236	.283
2 Charlie Gilbert	OF69	L	26	88	260	34	63	5	7	1	17	25	18	2	.242	.288
Vance Dinges	1B26, OF1	L	31	50	104	7	32	5	3	1	11	9	10	2	.308	.404
Rollie Hemsley (BW)	C45	R	39	49	139	7	31	6	1	0	11	9	10	0	.223	.266
Oscar Judd	P30	L	38	46	19	7	5	1	0	0	1	1	3	0	.316	.405
John O'Neil	SS32	R	25	46	94	12	25	1	0	0	5	10	6	0	.266	.298
1 Jimmy Wasdell	OF11, 1B2	L	32	44	73	9	17	2	0	1	9	6	4	1	.233	.301
Lou Novikoff	OF3	R	30	23	14	2	4	0	0	0	1	3	0	0	.234	.348

Dee Moore 32 R 1-13, 1 Vince DiMaggio 33 L 4-19, Don Hasenmayer 19 R 1-12, Charlie Letchas (MS) 30 R 3-13,
Danny Murtaugh 28 R 4-19, Ken Richardson 31 R 3-20, Bill Burich 28 R 0-1, Granny Hamner 19 R 1-7,
Glenn Crawford 32 L 0-1, Hal Spindel 33 L 1-3, Ray Hamrick (MS) 24, Moon Mullen (MS) 29

NAME	T	AGE	W	L	PCT	SV	G	GS	CG	IP	H	BB	SO	SHO	ERA
		30	69	85	.448	23	155	155	55	1369	1442	542	490	11	3.99
Schoolboy Rowe	R	36	11	4	.733	0	17	16	9	136	112	21	51	2	2.12
Oscar Judd	L	38	11	12	.478	2	30	24	12	173	169	90	65	1	3.54
Ken Raffensberger	L	28	8	15	.348	6	39	23	14	196	203	39	73	2	3.63
Dick Mauney	R	26	6	4	.600	2	37	3	1	90	98	18	31	1	2.70
Charley Schanz	R	27	6	6	.500	2	32	15	4	116	130	71	47	0	5.82
Tommy Hughes	R	26	6	9	.400	1	29	13	3	111	123	44	34	2	4.38
Al Jurisich	R	24	4	3	.571	1	13	7	1	71	61	31	34	1	3.71
2 Blix Donnelly	R	32	3	4	.429	1	12	2	2	76	64	24	38	0	2.96
Andy Karl	R	32	3	7	.300	5	39	0	0	65	84	22	15	0	4.98
1 Dick Mulligan	R	28	1	0	1.000	0	5	0	0	16	11	9	3	0	4.75
Hugh Mulcahy	R	32	2	4	.333	0	16	5	1	63	69	33	12	0	4.43
2 Charley Stanceu	R	30	2	4	.333	0	14	7	1	70	71	39	23	0	4.63
Charlie Ripple	L	26	1	0	1.000	0	5	1	0	14	9	9	3	0	12.00
Ike Pearson	R	29	1	0	1.000	0	11	1	0	24	25	14	10	0	3.86
Don Grate	R	23	0	0	—	0	2	1	0	11	6	7	1	0	1.13
Lou Possehl	R	25	0	0	—	0	1	0	0	1	2	0	1	0	5.93
Frank Hoerst	L	29	1	6	.143	0	12	7	1	68	77	36	17	0	4.61

Art Lopatka 27 L 0-1, Eli Hodkey 28 L 0-1, Dick Koecher 20 L 0-1, John Humphries 31 R 0-0,
Ben Chapman 37 R 0-0, 1 Si Johnson 39 R 0-0, 2 Al Milnar 32 L 0-0,
George Eyrich (MS) 21, Rogers McKee (MS) 19

CINCINNATI 6th 67-87 .435 30   BILL McKECHNIE

NAME	G by Pos	B	AGE	G	AB	R	H	2B	3B	HR	RBI	BB	SO	SB	BA	SA
TOTALS			28	156	5291	523	1262	206	33	65	481	493	604	82	.239	.327
Bert Haas	1B131, 3B6	R	32	140	535	57	141	24	7	3	50	33	42	12	.264	.351
Bobby Adams	2B74, OF2, 3B1	R	24	94	311	35	76	13	3	4	24	18	32	16	.244	.344
Eddie Miller	SS88	R	29	91	299	30	58	10	0	6	35	25	34	5	.194	.288
Grady Hatton	3B116, OF2	L	23	116	436	56	118	18	3	14	69	66	53	4	.271	.422
Al Libke	OF115, P1	R	28	124	431	32	109	22	1	5	42	43	50	0	.253	.340
Dain Clay	OF120	R	26	121	435	52	99	17	0	2	22	53	40	11	.228	.280
Eddie Lukon	OF83	L	25	102	312	37	78	8	8	12	34	26	29	3	.250	.442
Ray Mueller	C100	R	34	114	378	35	96	18	4	8	48	27	37	0	.254	.386
Lonny Frey	2B65, OF28	L	35	111	333	46	82	10	3	3	24	63	31	5	.246	.321
Bob Usher	OF80, 3B1	R	21	92	152	16	31	5	1	1	14	13	27	2	.204	.270
Ray Lamanno	C61	R	26	85	239	18	58	12	0	1	30	11	26	3	.243	.305
Claude Corbitt	SS77	R	30	82	274	25	68	10	1	1	16	23	13	3	.248	.303
Benny Zientara	2B39, 3B36	R	28	78	280	26	81	10	2	0	16	14	11	3	.289	.339
2 Max West	OF58	L	29	72	202	16	43	13	0	5	18	32	36	1	.213	.351
Eddie Shokes	1B29	L	26	31	83	3	10	1	0	0	5	18	21	1	.120	.133
Al Lakeman	C6	R	27	23	30	4	4	0	0	0	4	2	7	0	.133	.133
1 Mike McCormick	OF21	R	29	23	74	10	16	4	2	0	6	4	16	2	.216	.243

Clyde Vollmer 24 R 4-22, 1 Howie Moss 27 R 5-26, Lonnie Goldstein (MS) 28 L 0-5, 1 Garland Lawing 27 R 0-3

NAME	T	AGE	W	L	PCT	SV	G	GS	CG	IP	H	BB	SO	SHO	ERA
		31	67	87	.435	11	156	156	69	1414	1334	467	506	17	3.07
Joe Beggs	R	35	12	10	.545	11	28	14	2	190	175	39	38	3	2.32
Bucky Walters	R	37	10	7	.588	0	22	22	10	151	146	64	60	2	2.56
Johnny Vander Meer	R	31	10	12	.455	0	29	25	11	204	175	78	94	5	3.18
Ewell Blackwell	R	23	9	13	.409	0	33	25	10	194	160	79	100	6	2.46
Ed Heusser	R	37	7	14	.333	2	29	21	9	168	167	39	47	1	3.21
Johnny Hetki	R	24	6	6	.500	3	32	11	4	126	121	31	41	0	3.00
Harry Gumbert	R	36	6	8	.429	4	36	10	5	119	112	42	44	0	3.25
Clay Lambert	R	29	2	2	.500	1	23	4	2	53	48	20	20	0	4.25
1 Nate Andrews	R	32	2	4	.333	0	7	7	3	43	50	8	13	0	3.98
Bob Malloy (MS)	R	28	2	5	.286	2	27	3	1	72	71	26	24	0	2.75
Clyde Shoun	L	34	1	6	.143	0	27	5	0	79	87	26	20	0	4.10
Howie Fox	R	25	0	0	—	0	4	0	0	5	12	5	1	0	18.00
George Burpo	L	24	0	0	—	0	2	0	0	2	4	5	1	0	18.00
Frank Dasso	R	28	0	0	—	0	2	0	0	2	1	2	1	0	27.00
Al Libke	R	28	0	0	—	0	1	0	0	5	4	3	2	0	3.60

Elmer Riddle (VR) 31, Mike Modak (MS) 24, Kent Peterson (MS) 20

PITTSBURGH 7th 63-91 .409 34   FRANKIE FRISCH 62-89 .411   SPUD DAVIS 1-2 .333

NAME	G by Pos	B	AGE	G	AB	R	H	2B	3B	HR	RBI	BB	SO	SB	BA	SA
TOTALS			29	155	5199	552	1300	202	52	60	508	592	555	48	.250	.344
Elbie Fletcher	1B147	L	30	148	532	72	136	25	8	4	66	111	37	4	.256	.355
Frankie Gustine	2B113, SS13, 3B7	R	26	131	495	60	128	23	6	3	54	40	52	2	.259	.378
Billy Cox	SS114	R	26	121	411	32	119	22	6	2	36	26	15	4	.290	.387
Lee Handley	3B102, 2B3	R	32	116	416	43	99	8	7	1	28	29	20	4	.238	.298
Bob Elliott	OF92, 3B43	R	29	140	502	68	143	25	3	5	68	64	44	6	.285	.403
Jim Russell	OF134, 1B5	B	27	146	516	68	143	29	6	8	50	67	54	11	.277	.403
Ralph Kiner	OF140	R	23	144	502	63	124	17	3	23	81	74	109	3	.247	.430
Al Lopez (BH)	C56	R	37	56	150	13	46	2	0	1	12	23	14	1	.307	.340
Jimmy Brown	SS30, 2B21, 3B9	B	36	79	241	23	58	6	0	0	12	18	5	3	.241	.266
Bill Salkeld	C51	R	29	69	160	18	47	8	0	3	19	39	16	2	.294	.400
Al Gionfriddo (IL)	OF33	L	24	64	102	11	26	2	0	0	14	15	1		.255	.314
Maurice Van Robays	OF37, 1B2	R	31	59	146	14	31	5	3	1	12	11	15	0	.212	.308
2 Chuck Workman	OF40, 3B1	R	31	58	145	11	32	4	1	2	16	11	19	2	.221	.303
Burgess Whitehead	2B30, 3B4, SS1	R	36	55	127	10	28	1	2	0	5	6	12	6	.220	.260
Bill Baker	C41, 1B1	R	35	53	113	7	27	4	0	1	13	8	19	0	.239	.301
Hank Camelli	C39	R	31	42	96	8	20	2	2	0	5	8	13	0	.208	.271
1 Johnny Barrett	OF21	R	30	32	71	7	12	3	0	0	6	8	11	1	.169	.211
Fritz Ostermueller	P27	R	38	28	64	7	21	3	0	2	5	8		0	.328	.375
1 Frank Colman	OF8, 1B2	L	28	26	53	3	9	3	0	1	6	2	5	0	.170	.283
Frankie Zak	SS10	R	24	21	20	8	4	0	0	0	1	0			.200	.200

Vinnie Smith (KJ) 30 R 4-21, Pete Coscarart 33 R 1-2, Alf Anderson 32 R 0-1, Vic Barnhart 23 R 0-1, Ben Guintini 27 R 0-3, Roy Jarvis (MS) 20 R 1-4, Billy Sullivan (MS) 35

NAME	T	AGE	W	L	PCT	SV	G	GS	CG	IP	H	BB	SO	SHO	ERA
		32	63	91	.409	6	155	155	61	1370	1406	541	458	10	3.72
Fritz Ostermueller	L	38	13	10	.565	0	27	25	16	193	193	56	57	2	2.84
Nick Strincevich	R	31	10	15	.400	1	32	22	11	176	185	44	49	3	3.58
Ed Bahr	R	26	8	6	.571	0	27	14	7	137	128	52	44	0	2.63
Ken Heintzelman	L	30	8	12	.400	1	32	24	6	158	165	86	57	2	3.76
Rip Sewell	R	39	8	12	.400	0	25	20	11	149	140	53	33	0	3.68
Jack Hallett	R	31	5	7	.417	0	35	6	3	115	107	39	64	1	3.29
Johnny Lanning	R	39	4	5	.444	1	27	9	3	97	97	31	16	0	3.07
Preacher Roe	L	31	3	8	.273	2	21	10	1	70	83	25	28	0	5.14
Al Gerheauser	R	29	2	2	.500	0	35	3	1	82	92	25	32	0	3.95
Ken Gables	R	27	2	4	.333	1	32	7	0	101	113	52	39	0	5.14
Hank Gornicki	R	35	0	0	—	0	7	0	0	13	13	11	4	0	3.46
Lefty Wilkie	L	31	0	0	—	0	6	0	0	13	8	13	3	0	10.13
Bill Clemensen	R	27	0	1	.000	0	2	1	0	10	7	10	2	0	5.40
Junior Walsh	R	22	0	1	.000	0	3	2	1	14	9	6	6	0	2.08
Lee Howard	L	27	0	1	.000	0	1	1	0	5	4	5	1	0	11.25
Jim Hopper	R	27	0	1	.000	0	2	1	0	6	4	3	3	0	5.00
Al Tata	R	28	0	1	.000	0	2	1	0	7	9	5	6	0	6.08
Ed Albosta	R	27	0	6	.000	0	8			40	41	35	19		6.08

NEW YORK 8th 61-93 .396 36   MEL OTT

NAME	G by Pos	B	AGE	G	AB	R	H	2B	3B	HR	RBI	BB	SO	SB	BA	SA
TOTALS			30	154	5191	612	1326	176	37	121	576	532	546	46	.255	.374
Johnny Mize (BH)	1B101	L	33	101	377	70	122	18	3	22	70	62	26	2	.337	.576
Buddy Blattner	2B114, 1B1	R	26	126	420	43	107	18	6	11	49	56	52	3	.255	.405
Buddy Kerr	SS126, 3B18	R	23	145	497	50	124	20	3	6	40	53	31	7	.249	.338
Bill Rigney	3B73, SS33	R	28	110	360	38	85	9	1	3	31	36	29	9	.236	.292
2 Goody Rosen	OF84	L	33	100	310	39	87	11	4	5	30	48	32	2	.281	.390
Willard Marshall	OF125	L	25	131	510	64	143	18	3	13	48	33	29	3	.282	.406
Sid Gordon	OF101, 3B30	R	28	135	450	64	132	15	4	5	60	57	27	1	.293	.378
Walker Cooper (EJ)	C73	R	31	74	280	29	75	10	1	8	46	17	12	6	.268	.396
Babe Young	1B49, OF24	L	31	104	291	30	81	11	0	7	33	30	21	1	.278	.388
2 Jack Graham	OF62, 1B7	L	29	100	270	34	59	6	4	14	47	23	37	1	.219	.426
Johnny Rucker	OF54	L	29	95	197	28	52	8	2	1	13	7	27	2	.264	.340
Ernie Lombardi	C63	R	38	88	238	19	69	4	1	12	39	18	24	0	.290	.466
Mickey Witek (BA)	2B42, 3B35	R	30	82	284	32	75	13	2	4	29	28	10	1	.264	.366
Bennie Warren	C30	R	34	39	69	7	11	1	1	4	8	14	21	0	.159	.377
Mel Ott	OF16	L	37	31	68	2	5	1	0	1	4	8	15	0	.074	.132
Bobby Thomson	3B16	R	22	18	54	8	17	4	1	2	4	5	5	0	.315	.537
Jess Pike	OF10	L	30	16	41	4	7	1	1	1	6	6	13	0	.171	.317
2 Vince DiMaggio	OF13	R	33	15	25	2	0	0	0	0	0	5	2	0	.000	.000
2 Garland Lawing	OF5	R	27	8	12	2	2	0	0	0	0	1	6	0	.167	.167

Mickey Grasso 26 R 3-22, Buster Maynard 33 R 0-4, Dick Lajeskie 20 R 2-10, Dick Bartell 38 R 0-2, 1 Clyde Kluttz 28 R 3-8, Jim Gladd 23 R 1-11, Morrie Arnovich 35 R 0-3, Mike Schemer 28 L 0-1, Danny Gardella (SM) 26, George Hausmann (SM) 30, Nap Reyes (SM) 26, Vic Bradford (MS) 31, Whitey Lockman (MS) 19

NAME	T	AGE	W	L	PCT	SV	G	GS	CG	IP	H	BB	SO	SHO	ERA
		28	61	93	.396	13	154	154	48	1353	1299	660	581	8	3.92
Dave Koslo	L	26	14	19	.424	1	40	35	17	265	251	101	121	3	3.63
Monte Kennedy	L	24	9	10	.474	1	38	27	10	187	153	116	71	1	3.42
Bill Voiselle	R	27	9	15	.375	0	36	25	10	178	171	85	89	2	3.74
Ken Trinkle	R	26	7	14	.333	2	48	13	2	151	146	74	49	0	3.87
Hal Schumacher	R	35	4	4	.500	1	24	13	2	97	95	52	48	0	3.90
Junior Thompson	R	29	4	6	.400	4	39	1	0	63	36	40	31	0	5.31
Bob Joyce	R	31	3	4	.429	0	14	7	2	61	79	20	24	0	5.31
Tex Kraus	L	28	2	1	.667	0	17	1	0	25	15	15	7	0	6.12
Mike Budnick	R	26	2	3	.400	3	35	1	1	88	75	48	36	1	3.17
Johnny Gee	L	30	2	4	.333	0	6	3	0	47	60	15	22	0	4.02
2 Nate Andrews	R	32	1	0	1.000	0	3	2	0	12	17	4	5	0	6.00
Woody Abernathy	L	31	1	1	.500	1	5	1	0	18	22	9	6	0	3.38
Rube Fischer	R	29	1	2	.333	0	15	1	0	36	48	21	14	0	6.25
Sheldon Jones	R	24	1	2	.333	0	6	4	1	29	21	17	24	0	3.21
Bob Carpenter (JJ)	R	28	1	3	.250	0	12	6	1	39	37	18	13	1	4.85
Ace Adams (SM)	R	36	0	1	.000	0	3	0	0	9	5	3	9	0	15.00
Marv Grissom	R	28	0	2	.000	0	3	0	0	19	17	9	9	0	4.26
Harry Feldman (SM)	L	26	0	2	.000	0	3	1	0	18	18	11	6	0	18.00

Slim Emmerich 26 R 0-0, Jack Brewer 28 R 0-0, John Carden 25 R 0-0, Red Kress 41 R 0-0, Sal Maglie (SM) 29, Adrian Zabala (SM) 29, Andy Hansen (MS) 21

WORLD SERIES — ST. LOUIS (NL) 4   BOSTON (AL) 3

LINE SCORES

TEAM	1	2	3	4	5	6	7	8	9	10	11	12	R	H	E

Game 1   October 6 at St. Louis
BOS (AL) 0 1 0   0 0 0   0 0 1   1   3 9 2
STL (NL) 0 0 0   0 0 1   0 1 0   0   2 7 0
Hughson, Johnson (9)   **Pollet**

Game 2   October 7 at St. Louis
BOS 0 0 0   0 0 0   0 0 0   0 4 1
STL 0 0 1   0 2 0   0 0 X   3 6 0
Harris, Dobson (8)   **Brecheen**

Game 3   October 9 at Boston
STL 0 0 0   0 0 0   0 0 0   0 6 1
BOS 3 0 0   0 0 1   0 0 X   4 8 0
Dickson, Wilks (8)   **Ferriss**

Game 4   October 10 at Boston
STL 0 3 3   0 1 0   1 0 4   12 20 1
BOS 0 0 0   1 0 0   0 2 0   3 9 0
Munger   **Hughson**, Bagby (3), Zuber (6), Brown (8), Ryba (9), Dreisewerd (9)

Game 5   October 11 at Boston
STL 0 1 0   0 0 0   0 0 2   3 4 1
BOS 1 1 0   0 0 1   3 0 X   6 11 3
Pollet, **Brazle** (1), Beazle   **Dobson**

Game 6   October 13 at St. Louis
BOS 0 0 0   0 0 0   1 0 0   1 7 0
STL 0 0 3   0 0 0   0 1 X   4 8 0
Harris, Hughson (3)   **Brecheen**
Johnson (8)

Game 7   October 15 at St. Louis
BOS 1 0 0   0 0 0   0 2 0   3 8 0
STL 0 0 1   0 0 1   0 2 X   4 9 1
Ferriss, Dobson (5), **Klinger** (8), Johnson (8)   Dickson, **Brecheen** (8)

COMPOSITE BATTING

NAME	POS	G	AB	R	H	2B	3B	HR	RBI	BA
St. Louis (NL)										
Totals		7	232	28	60	19	2	1	27	.259
Schoendienst	2B	7	30	3	7	1	0	0	1	.233
Kurowski	3B	7	27	5	8	3	0	0	2	.296
Musial	1B	7	27	3	6	4	1	0	4	.222
Moore	OF	7	27	4	4	0	0	0	0	.148
Slaughter	OF	7	25	5	8	1	1	1	2	.320
Marion	SS	7	24	4	6	0	0	0	4	.250
Garagiola	C	5	19	2	6	2	0	0	4	.316
Walker	OF	7	17	3	7	2	0	0	6	.412
Brecheen	P	3	8	2	1	0	0	0	0	.125
Rice	C	3	6	2	3	1	0	0	1	.500
Dickson	P	2	5	1	2	2	0	0	0	.400
Dusak	OF	4	4	0	1	0	0	0	0	.250
Munger	P	2	4	0	1	0	0	0	0	.250
Pollet	P	2	4	0	0	0	0	0	0	.000
Sisler	PH	2	2	0	0	0	0	0	0	.000
Brazle	P	2	2	0	0	0	0	0	0	.000
Jones	PH	1	1	0	0	0	0	0	0	.000
Beazley	P	1	1	0	0	0	0	0	0	.000
Wilks	P	1	0	0	0	0	0	0	0	—
Boston (AL)										
Totals		7	233	20	56	7	1	4	18	.240
Pesky	SS	7	30	2	7	0	1	0	0	.233
DiMaggio	OF	7	27	2	7	3	0	0	3	.259
Williams	OF	7	25	2	5	0	0	0	1	.200
Higgins	3B	7	24	1	5	1	0	0	2	.208
York	1B	7	23	6	6	1	0	2	5	.261
Doerr	2B	6	22	1	9	1	0	1	3	.409
H. Wagner	C	5	13	0	0	0	0	0	0	.000
Moses	OF	4	12	1	5	1	0	0	1	.417
McBride	OF	5	12	1	2	0	0	0	0	.167
Partee	C	5	10	1	1	0	0	0	1	.100
Culberson	OF	5	9	1	2	0	0	0	0	.222
Ferriss	P	2	5	0	0	0	0	0	0	.000
Gutteridge	2B	3	5	1	2	0	0	0	0	.400
Harris	P	2	3	0	1	0	0	0	0	.333
Hughson	P	3	3	0	1	0	0	0	0	.333
Dobson	P	3	3	0	0	0	0	0	0	.000
Russell	3B	2	2	0	2	0	0	0	0	1.000
Metkovich	PH	2	2	0	1	0	0	0	0	.500
Johnson	P	3	1	0	0	0	0	0	0	.000
Bagby	P	2	1	0	0	0	0	0	0	.000

Brown P 0-0, Campbell PR 0-0, Dreisewerd P 0-0, Klinger P 0-0, Ryba P 0-0, Zuber P 0-0

COMPOSITE PITCHING

NAME	G	IP	H	BB	SO	W	L	SV	ERA
St. Louis (NL)									
Totals	7	62	56	22	28	4	3	0	2.32
Brecheen	3	20	14	5	11	3	0	0	0.45
Dickson	2	14	11	4	7	1	0	0	3.86
Pollet	2	10.1	12	4	3	0	1	0	3.48
Munger	1	9	9	3	2	1	0	0	1.00
Brazle	1	6.2	6	4	5	0	0	0	5.40
Beazley	1	1	1	0	0	0	0	0	0.00
Wilks	1	2	1	0	0	0	0	0	0.00
Boston (AL)									
Totals	7	61	60	19	30	3	4	0	2.95
Hughson	3	14.1	14	3	8	0	1	0	3.14
Ferriss	2	13.1	13	2	4	1	0	0	2.02
Dobson	3	12.2	4	1	10	1	0	0	0.00
Harris	2	9.2	11	4	5	0	2	0	3.72
Johnson	3	3.1	4	2	5	0	0	0	2.70
Bagby	2	1	1	0	0	0	0	0	3.00
Zuber	1	1	4	2	0	0	0	0	4.50
Brown	1	1	1	1	0	0	0	0	27.00
Ryba	1	.2	2	1	0	0	0	0	13.50
Klinger	1	.2	2	1	0	0	1	0	13.50
Dreisewerd	1	.1	0	0	0	0	0	0	0.00

1947 Never a Dull Moment

Before the season got underway, it seemed to at least promise some good races and the usual array of dramatics. Certainly no one expected anything unusual before the season started.

One of the Yankee owners, Larry MacPhail, made the mistake of luring Charlie Dressen away from a Brooklyn coaching spot. Brooklyn manager Leo Durocher and general manager Branch Rickey then made the greater mistake of criticizing MacPhail publicly and compounded the mistake by accusing the Yankee executive of having alleged gamblers in his box at an exhibition game between the Yankees and Dodgers at Havana, Cuba, in March. As part of Durocher's communication program, he used his column in *The Brooklyn Eagle*, ghost-written by road secretary Harold Parrott.

MacPhail denied any gambler connections and filed libel charges with Commissioner Happy Chandler. The results: Durocher suspended for entire season for "conduct detrimental to baseball"; Dressen suspended for 30 days for "violating a verbal agreement to coach with Brooklyn"; Parrott fined $5,000 for the "statement in the *Eagle* column"; and the Yankees and Dodgers each fined $2,000 for "engaging in public feuding".

The Yankee-Dodger feud, while having its lighter side, was by no means an historic footnote to baseball. But there was another event underway in Brooklyn which was to have as much historical impact as the beginning of baseball itself. And for many, 1947 marked the *real* beginning of baseball—at least on a national level—as the doors were finally opened to the black athlete. The man responsible for the initiative was Branch Rickey, and the first black player was a 28-year-old infielder by the name of Jackie Robinson. Later in the year, the Dodgers repeated the experiment with Dan Bankhead, while Cleveland added Larry Doby, and the St. Louis Browns took on Hank Thompson and Willard Brown.

At the end of 1947, baseball found that it no longer had to *experiment* with the black man. Jackie Robinson firmly convinced one and all that talent was too great an asset to hide behind the excuse of dark skin pigmentation, as he hit .297, was named Rookie of the Year, and led the Dodgers to a five-game pennant victory over St. Louis.

The Boston Red Sox installed lights in Fenway Park, produced the second man in baseball history to win a second Triple Crown in Ted Williams, and finished third because of arm trouble to pitchers Tex Hughson, Mickey Harris and Dave Ferris. The Yankees obtained pitcher Bobo Newsom from Washington, recalled Vic Raschi from the minors, and returned to the pennant after a four-year layoff. Joe DiMaggio supplied the offensive muscle as he again beat out Williams for MVP honors, despite being well bathed in the shadow of the Boston slugger's statistics.

The Yankees and Dodgers provided a treat in the fall classic, which was filled with enough dramatics to guarantee them a place in World Series history. After winning the first two games without too much trouble, the Yankees lost the third, 9-8, despite the first pinch-hit homer in Series history—hit by rookie catcher-outfielder Yogi Berra.

The fourth game caused adrenaline to overflow, as Yankee pitcher Bill Bevens went into the bottom of the ninth with two outs and two on needing only to retire pinch hitter Cookie Lavagetto to become the first man ever in post-season play to hurl a no-hitter. Such was not destined to be, as Lavagetto doubled off the right field wall to not only break the no-hitter, but also drive in two runs to give the Dodgers a 3-2 Series equalizer.

New York took the fifth game, and might have won the sixth, save for Al Gionfriddo's great catch of a DiMaggio clout ear-marked home run with two on in the sixth and the score 8-5. Joe Page, who saved a league high 17 games for the Yankees during the season, came out of the bullpen in the fifth inning of the seventh game to preserve a 5-2 Series victory.

1947 AMERICAN LEAGUE

NEW YORK 1st 97-57 .630 BUCKY HARRIS

NAME	G by Pos	B	AGE	G	AB	R	H	2B	3B	HR	RBI	BB	SO	SB	BA	SA
TOTALS			31	155	5308	794	1439	230	72	115	746	610	581	27	.271	.407
George McQuinn	1B142	L	38	144	517	84	157	24	3	13	80	78	66	0	.304	.437
Snuffy Stirnweiss	2B148	R	28	148	571	102	146	18	8	5	41	89	47	5	.256	.342
Phil Rizzuto	SS151	R	29	153	549	78	150	26	9	2	60	57	31	11	.273	.364
Billy Johnson	3B132	R	28	132	494	67	141	19	8	10	95	44	43	1	.285	.417
Tommy Henrich	OF132, 1B6	L	37	142	550	109	158	35	13	16	98	71	54	3	.287	.485
Joe DiMaggio	OF139	R	32	141	534	97	168	31	10	20	97	64	32	3	.315	.522
Johnny Lindell	OF118	R	30	127	476	66	131	18	7	11	67	32	70	1	.275	.412
Aaron Robinson	C74	L	32	82	252	23	68	11	5	5	36	40	26	0	.270	.413
Yogi Berra	C51, OF25	L	22	83	293	41	82	15	3	11	54	13	12	0	.280	.464
Bobby Brown	3B27, SS11, OF3	L	22	69	150	21	45	6	1	1	18	21	9	0	.300	.373
Charlie Keller (XJ)	OF43	L	30	45	151	36	36	6	1	13	36	41	18	0	.238	.550
Ralph Houk	C41	R	27	41	92	7	25	3	1	0	12	11	5	0	.272	.326
Allie Clark	OF16	R	24	24	67	9	25	5	0	1	14	5	2	0	.373	.493
2 Lonny Frey	2B8	L	36	24	28	10	5	2	0	0	2	10	1	3	.179	.250
Frank Colman	OF6	L	29	22	28	2	3	0	0	2	6	2	6	0	.107	.321
Jack Phillips	1B10	R	25	16	36	5	10	0	1	1	2	3	5	0	.278	.417
Johnny Lucadello	2B5	R	28	12	12	0	1	0	0	0	0	0	2	0	.083	.083
Sherm Lollar	C9	R	22	11	32	4	7	0	1	0	6	1	5	0	.219	.375

Frankie Crosetti 36 R 0-1, Ken Silvestri 31 B 2-10, 2 Ted Sepkowski 23 L 0-0, 1 Ray Mack 30 R 0-0

NAME	T	AGE	W	L	PCT	SV	G	GS	CG	IP	H	BB	SO	SHO	ERA
		30	97	57	.630	21	155	155	73	1374	1221	628	691	14	3.39
Allie Reynolds	R	32	19	8	.704	2	34	30	17	242	207	123	129	4	3.20
Spec Shea	R	26	14	5	.737	1	27	23	13	179	127	89	89	3	3.07
Joe Page	L	29	14	8	.636	17	56	2	0	141	105	72	116	0	2.49
Spud Chandler (AJ)	R	39	9	5	.643	0	17	16	13	128	100	41	68	2	2.46
Vic Raschi	R	28	7	2	.778	0	15	14	6	105	89	38	51	1	3.86
2 Bobo Newsom	R	39	7	5	.583	0	17	15	6	116	109	30	42	2	2.79
Bill Bevens	R	30	7	13	.350	0	28	23	11	165	167	77	77	1	3.82
Karl Drews	R	27	6	6	.500	1	30	10	0	92	92	55	45	0	4.89
Randy Gumpert	R	29	4	1	.800	0	24	6	2	56	71	28	25	0	5.46
Don Johnson	R	20	4	3	.571	0	15	8	2	54	57	23	16	0	3.67
Butch Wensloff	R	31	3	1	.750	0	11	5	1	52	41	22	18	0	2.60
1 Al Lyons	R	28	1	0	1.000	0	6	0	0	11	18	9	7	0	9.00
Dick Starr	R	26	1	0	1.000	0	4	1	1	12	12	8	1	0	1.50
Bill Wight	L	25	1	0	1.000	0	1	1	1	9	8	2	3	0	1.00
1 Mel Queen	R	29	0	0	—	0	5	0	0	7	9	4	2	0	9.00
Tommy Byrne	L	27	0	0	—	0	4	1	0	4	5	6	2	0	4.50
Rugger Ardizoia	R	27	0	0	—	0	1	0	0	2	4	1	0	0	9.00

DETROIT 2nd 85-69 .552 12 STEVE O'NEILL

NAME	G by Pos	B	AGE	G	AB	R	H	2B	3B	HR	RBI	BB	SO	SB	BA	SA
TOTALS			30	158	5276	714	1363	234	42	103	657	762	565	52	.258	.377
Roy Cullenbine	1B138	B	33	142	464	82	104	18	1	24	78	137	51	3	.224	.422
Eddie Mayo	2B142	L	37	142	535	66	149	28	4	4	48	48	28	3	.279	.379
Eddie Lake	SS158	R	31	158	602	96	127	19	6	12	46	120	54	11	.211	.322
George Kell	3B152	R	24	152	588	75	188	29	5	5	93	61	16	9	.320	.412
Pat Mullin	OF106	L	29	116	398	62	102	28	6	15	62	63	66	3	.256	.470
Hoot Evers	OF123	R	26	126	460	67	136	24	5	10	67	45	49	4	.296	.435
Dick Wakefield	OF101	L	26	112	368	59	104	15	5	8	51	80	44	1	.283	.416
Bob Swift	C97	R	32	97	279	23	70	11	0	1	21	33	16	2	.251	.301
Vic Wertz	OF82	L	22	102	333	60	96	22	4	6	44	47	66	2	.288	.432
Doc Cramer	OF35	L	41	73	157	21	42	2	2	2	30	20	5	2	.268	.344
2 Hal Wagner	C71	L	31	71	191	19	55	10	0	5	32	28	16	0	.288	.419
Jimmy Outlaw	OF37, 3B9	R	34	70	127	20	29	7	1	0	15	21	14	3	.228	.299
Fred Hutchinson	P33	R	27	56	106	8	32	5	2	2	15	6	6	2	.302	.443
Skeeter Webb	2B30, SS6	R	37	50	79	13	16	3	0	0	6	7	9	3	.203	.241
John McHale	1B25	L	25	39	95	10	20	1	0	3	11	7	24	1	.211	.316
Ed Mierkowicz	OF10	R	23	21	42	6	8	1	0	1	1	1	12	1	.190	.286
1 Birdie Tebbetts	C20	R	34	20	53	1	5	1	0	0	2	3	1	0	.094	.113
Hank Riebe	C3	R	25	8	15	0	0	0	0	0	0	0	2	0	.000	.000

Johnny Groth 20 R 1-4, Ben Steiner 25 L 0-0

NAME	T	AGE	W	L	PCT	SV	G	GS	CG	IP	H	BB	SO	SHO	ERA
		29	85	69	.552	18	158	158	77	1399	1382	531	648	15	3.57
Fred Hutchinson	R	27	18	10	.643	2	33	25	18	220	211	61	113	3	3.03
Hal Newhouser	L	26	17	17	.500	2	40	36	24	285	268	110	176	3	2.87
Stubby Overmire	L	28	11	5	.688	0	28	17	7	141	142	44	33	3	3.77
Dizzy Trout	R	32	10	11	.476	2	32	26	9	186	186	65	74	2	3.48
Virgil Trucks	R	30	10	12	.455	2	36	26	8	181	186	79	108	2	4.52
Art Houtteman	R	19	7	2	.778	0	23	9	7	111	106	36	58	2	3.41
Al Benton	R	36	6	7	.462	7	36	14	4	133	147	61	33	0	4.40
Hal White	R	28	4	5	.444	2	35	5	0	85	91	47	33	0	3.60
Johnny Gorsica	R	32	2	0	1.000	1	31	0	0	58	44	26	20	0	3.72
Rufe Gentry	R	29	0	0	—	0	1	0	0	.1	1	2	0	0	81.00

BOSTON 3rd 83-71 .539 14 JOE CRONIN

NAME	G by Pos	B	AGE	G	AB	R	H	2B	3B	HR	RBI	BB	SO	SB	BA	SA
TOTALS			29	157	5322	720	1412	206	54	103	674	666	590	41	.265	.382
2 Jake Jones	1B109	R	26	109	404	50	95	14	3	16	76	40	66	5	.235	.403
Bobby Doerr	2B146	R	29	146	561	79	145	23	10	17	95	59	47	3	.258	.426
Johnny Pesky	SS133, 3B22	L	27	155	638	106	207	27	8	0	39	72	22	12	.324	.392
Sam Dente	3B46	R	25	46	168	14	39	4	2	0	14	19	15	0	.232	.280
Sam Mele	OF115, 1B6	R	25	123	453	71	137	14	8	12	73	47	63	3	.302	.448
Dom DiMaggio	OF134	R	30	136	513	75	145	21	5	8	71	74	62	10	.283	.390
Ted Williams	OF156	L	28	156	528	125	181	40	9	32	114	162	47	0	.343	.634
2 Birdie Tebbetts	C89	R	34	90	291	22	87	10	0	1	28	21	30	2	.299	.344
Wally Moses	OF58	L	36	90	255	32	70	18	2	2	27	27	16	3	.275	.384
Eddie Pellegrini (FJ)	3B42, SS26	R	29	74	231	29	47	8	1	4	19	23	35	2	.203	.299
Roy Partee	C54	R	29	60	169	14	39	2	0	0	16	18	23	0	.231	.243
Don Gutteridge	2B20, 3B19	R	35	54	131	20	22	2	0	2	5	17	13	3	.168	.229
1 Rudy York	1B48	R	33	48	184	16	39	7	0	6	27	22	32	0	.212	.348
Leon Culberson	OF25, 3B4	R	27	47	84	10	20	1	0	0	11	12	10	1	.238	.250
Rip Russell	3B13	R	32	26	52	8	8	1	0	1	3	4	5	0	.154	.231
1 Hal Wagner	C21	L	31	21	65	5	15	3	0	0	6	9	5	0	.231	.277
Merrill Combs	3B17	L	27	17	68	8	15	1	0	1	6	9	9	1	.221	.279
Billy Goodman	OF1	L	21	12	11	1	2	0	0	0	1	2	1	0	.182	.182
Ed McGah	C7	R	25	7	5	0	1	0	0	0	0	0	1	0	.000	.000
Matt Batts	C6	R	25	7	16	3	8	1	0	0	5	1	1	0	.500	.750
Frankie Hayes	C4	R	32	5	13	1	2	1	0	0	1	2	0	0	.154	.154
Strick Shafner	3B4	R	27	5	13	1	2	1	0	0	1	2	0	0	.154	.308

Doyle Auld 26 R 1-4, 1 Tom McBride 32 R 1-5

NAME	T	AGE	W	L	PCT	SV	G	GS	CG	IP	H	BB	SO	SHO	ERA
		31	83	71	.539	19	157	157	64	1392	1383	575	586	13	3.81
Joe Dobson	R	30	18	8	.692	1	33	31	15	229	203	73	110	1	3.25
Earl Johnson	L	28	12	11	.522	4	45	17	6	142	129	62	65	3	2.98
Boo Ferriss	R	25	12	11	.522	0	33	28	14	218	241	92	64	1	4.05
Tex Hughson (RJ)	R	31	12	11	.522	0	29	26	13	189	173	71	119	3	3.33
2 Denny Galehouse	R	35	11	7	.611	0	21	21	11	149	150	34	38	3	3.32
Harry Dorish	R	25	7	8	.467	2	41	8	2	136	149	54	50	0	4.70
Mickey Harris (SJ)	L	30	5	4	.556	0	15	6	1	52	42	23	35	0	2.42
Mel Parnell	L	25	2	3	.400	1	15	5	1	51	60	27	23	0	6.35
Bill Zuber	R	34	1	0	1.000	0	10	1	0	51	60	31	23	0	5.29
Bob Klinger	R	39	1	1	.500	5	29	0	0	42	42	24	12	0	3.86
Tommy Fine	R	33	1	3	.333	0	9	7	1	36	41	19	10	0	5.50
2 Eddie Smith	L	33	1	3	.250	0	17	8	1	51	55	41	28	0	7.41
Johnny Murphy	R	38	0	0	—	3	32	0	0	55	41	28	9	0	2.78
Al Widmar	R	22	0	0	—	0	1	0	0	1	3	4	0	0	18.00
Bill Butland	R	29	0	0	—	0	4	0	0	6	10	5	2	0	4.50
Cot Deal	R	24	0	1	.000	0	2	1	0	13	20	7	6	0	9.00
Chuck Stobbs	L	17	0	1	.000	0	1	0	0	9	10	5	1	0	6.00

CLEVELAND   4th 80-74 .519 17   LOU BOUDREAU

NAME	G by Pos	B	AGE	G	AB	R	H	2B	3B	HR	RBI	BB	SO	SB	BA	SA
TOTALS			28	157	5367	687	1392	234	51	112	646	502	609	29	.259	.385
Eddie Robinson	1B87	L	26	95	318	52	78	10	1	14	52	30	18	1	.245	.415
Joe Gordon	2B155	R	32	155	562	89	153	27	6	29	93	62	49	7	.272	.496
Lou Boudreau	SS148	R	29	150	538	79	165	45	4	4	67	67	10	1	.307	.424
Ken Keltner	3B160	R	30	151	541	49	139	29	3	11	76	59	45	5	.257	.383
Hank Edwards (SJ)	OF100	L	28	108	393	54	102	12	3	15	59	31	55	1	.260	.420
Catfish Metkovich	OF119, 1B1	L	25	108	473	68	120	22	7	5	40	32	51	5	.254	.362
Dale Mitchell	OF115	L	25	123	493	69	156	16	10	1	34	23	14	2	.316	.396
Jim Hegan	C133	R	26	135	378	38	94	14	5	4	42	41	49	3	.249	.344
Hal Peck	OF97	L	28	114	392	58	115	18	2	8	44	27	31	3	.293	.411
Les Fleming	1B77	L	31	103	281	39	68	14	2	4	43	53	42	0	.242	.349
Pat Seerey	OF68	R	24	82	216	24	37	4	1	11	29	34	66	0	.171	.352
Al Lopez	C57	R	38	61	126	9	33	9	0	0	14	9	13	1	.262	.270
Eddie Bockman	3B12, 2B4, SS1, OF1	R	26	46	66	8	17	2	2	1	14	5	17	0	.258	.394
Jack Conway	SS24, 2B5, 3B1	R	28	34	50	3	9	2	0	0	5	3	8	0	.180	.220
Larry Doby	2B4, 1B1, SS1	L	23	29	32	3	5	1	0	0	2	1	11	0	.156	.188
Hank Ruszkowski	C16	R	23	27	5	7	2	0	3	4	2	6	0	.259	.667	
1 Ted Sepkowski	OF1	L	23	10	8	0	1	1	0	0	0	1	0	0	.125	.250
Joe Frazier	OF5	L	24	9	14	1	1	1	0	0	0	1	1	0	.071	.143
Al Rosen	3B2, OF1	R	23	7	9	1	1	0	0	0	0	1	0	3	.111	.111
Heinz Becker		B	31	2	2	0	0	0	0	0	0	0	0	0	.000	.000
1 Felix Mackiewicz	OF2	L	29	2	5	0	0	0	0	0	0	0	2	0	.000	.000
Jimmy Wasdell		L	33	1	1	0	0	0	0	0	0	0	0	0	.000	.000

NAME	T	AGE	W	L	PCT	SV	G	GS	CG	IP	H	BB	SO	SHO	ERA
TOTALS		30	80	74	.519	29	157	157	55	1402	1244	628	590	13	3.44
Bob Feller	R	28	20	11	.645	3	42	37	20	299	230	127	196	5	2.68
Al Gettel	R	29	11	10	.524	0	31	21	9	149	122	62	64	2	3.20
Bob Lemon	R	26	11	5	.688	3	37	15	6	167	150	97	65	1	3.45
Don Black	R	30	10	12	.455	0	30	28	8	191	177	85	72	3	3.91
Red Embree	R	29	8	10	.444	0	27	21	6	163	137	67	56	0	3.15
Mel Harder	R	37	6	4	.600	0	15	9	4	80	91	27	11	0	4.50
Eddie Klieman	R	29	5	4	.556	17	58	0	0	92	78	39	21	0	3.03
Bryan Stephens	R	26	5	10	.333	1	31	5	1	92	79	39	34	0	4.01
Steve Gromek	R	27	3	5	.375	4	29	7	0	84	77	36	39	0	3.75
Hal Peck	L	24	1	1	.500	0	4	4	1	22	22	9	9	1	4.09
1 Roger Wolff	R	36	0	0	—	0	7	2	0	16	15	10	5	0	3.94
Cal Dorsett	R	34	0	0	—	0	2	0	0	1	3	3	1	0	36.00
Ernie Groth	R	25	0	0	—	0	2	0	0	1	1	1	0	0	0.00
Gene Bearden	L	26	0	0	—	0	1	0	0	2	1	2	1	0	81.00
Lyman Linde	R	26	0	0	—	0	1	0	0	3	1	0	0	0	18.00
Les Willis	L	38	0	2	.000	1	22	2	0	44	58	24	10	0	3.48

PHILADELPHIA   5th 78-76 .506 19   CONNIE MACK

NAME	G by Pos	B	AGE	G	AB	R	H	2B	3B	HR	RBI	BB	SO	SB	BA	SA
TOTALS			30	156	5198	633	1311	218	52	61	581	605	563	37	.252	.349
Ferris Fain	1B132	L	26	136	461	70	134	28	6	7	71	95	34	4	.291	.423
Pete Suder	2B140, SS3, 3B2	R	31	145	528	45	127	28	4	5	60	35	44	0	.241	.337
Eddie Joost	SS151	R	31	151	540	76	111	23	3	13	64	114	110	6	.206	.330
Hank Majeski	3B134, SS4, 2B1	R	30	141	497	54	134	26	5	8	72	53	31	1	.280	.405
Elmer Valo	OF104	L	26	112	370	60	111	12	6	5	36	64	21	11	.300	.405
Sam Chapman	OF146	R	31	149	551	84	139	18	5	14	83	65	70	3	.252	.379
Barney McCosky	OF136	R	30	137	546	77	179	22	7	1	52	57	29	1	.328	.399
Buddy Rosar	C102	R	32	102	359	40	93	20	2	1	33	40	13	1	.259	.334
George Binks	OF75, 1B13	L	32	104	333	33	86	19	4	2	34	23	36	8	.258	.357
Mike Guerra	C62	R	34	72	209	20	45	2	2	0	18	10	15	1	.215	.244
Dick Adams	1B24, OF3	R	27	37	89	9	18	2	3	2	11	2	18	0	.202	.360
Gene Handley (KJ)	2B17, 3B10, SS1	R	32	36	90	10	23	2	1	0	8	10	2	1	.256	.300
Austin Knickerbocker	OF14	R	28	21	48	8	12	3	2	0	4	3	4	0	.250	.396
Don Richmond	3B4, 2B1	R	27	19	21	2	4	1	1	0	4	3	4	0	.190	.333
Chet Laabs	OF7	R	35	15	32	5	7	1	0	1	5	4	4	0	.219	.344
Pat Cooper	1B1	R	29	13	16	0	4	2	0	0	3	0	5	0	.250	.375
Ray Poole		L	27	13	13	1	3	0	0	0	1	1	4	0	.231	.231
Mickey Rutner	3B11	R	27	12	48	4	12	1	0	1	4	3	10	0	.250	.333
Herman Franks	C4	R	33	8	15	2	3	0	1	0	1	4	0	0	.200	.333
Nellie Fox	2B1	L	19	7	3	2	0	0	0	0	0	1	0	0	.000	.000
Tom Kirk		L	19	1	1	0	0	0	0	0	0	0	0	0	.000	.000
Bobby Estalella (SM) 36																

NAME	T	AGE	W	L	PCT	SV	G	GS	CG	IP	H	BB	SO	SHO	ERA
TOTALS		27	78	76	.506	15	156	156	70	1391	1291	597	493	12	3.51
Phil Marchildon	R	33	19	9	.679	0	35	35	21	277	228	141	128	2	3.22
Dick Fowler	R	26	12	11	.522	0	36	31	16	227	210	85	75	3	2.81
Bill McCahan	R	26	10	5	.667	0	29	19	10	165	160	62	47	1	3.33
Russ Christopher	R	29	10	7	.588	12	44	0	0	81	70	33	33	0	2.89
Bob Savage	R	25	8	10	.444	2	44	8	2	146	135	55	56	1	3.76
Joe Coleman	R	24	6	12	.333	1	32	21	9	160	171	62	65	2	4.33
Bill Dietrich	R	37	5	2	.714	0	11	9	2	61	48	40	18	1	3.10
Carl Scheib	R	20	4	6	.400	0	21	12	6	116	121	55	26	2	5.04
Jesse Flores	R	32	4	13	.235	0	28	20	4	151	139	59	41	0	3.40
Lou Brissie	L	23	0	0	—	1	1	1	0	7	9	5	4	0	6.43

CHICAGO   6th 70-84 .455 27   TED LYONS

NAME	G by Pos	B	AGE	G	AB	R	H	2B	3B	HR	RBI	BB	SO	SB	BA	SA
TOTALS			30	155	5274	553	1350	211	41	53	519	492	527	91	.256	.342
2 Rudy York	1B102	R	33	102	400	40	97	18	4	15	64	36	55	1	.243	.420
Don Kolloway	2B99, 1B11, 3B8	R	28	124	485	49	135	25	4	2	35	17	34	11	.278	.359
Luke Appling	SS129, 3B2	R	40	139	503	67	154	29	0	8	49	64	28	8	.306	.412
Floyd Baker	3B101, 2B1, SS1	L	30	105	371	61	98	12	3	0	22	66	28	9	.264	.313
Bob Kennedy	OF106, 3B1	R	26	115	428	47	112	19	3	6	48	18	38	3	.262	.362
Dave Philley	OF133, 3B4	B	27	143	551	55	142	25	11	2	45	35	39	21	.258	.354
Taffy Wright	OF100	L	35	124	401	48	130	13	0	4	54	48	17	8	.324	.387
Mike Tresh	C89	R	33	90	274	19	66	6	2	0	20	26	26	2	.241	.277
Cass Michaels	2B60, 3B44, SS2	R	21	110	355	31	97	15	4	3	34	39	28	10	.273	.363
Thurman Tucker	OF65	R	29	89	254	28	60	9	4	1	17	38	25	10	.236	.315
George Dickey	C80	B	31	83	211	15	47	6	0	1	27	34	25	4	.223	.265
Jack Wallaesa	SS27, OF22, 3B1	B	27	81	205	25	40	9	1	7	32	23	51	2	.195	.351
Ralph Hodgin (PB)	OF41	L	32	59	180	26	53	10	3	1	24	13	4	1	.294	.400
1 Jake Jones	1B43	R	26	45	171	15	41	7	1	3	20	13	25	1	.240	.345
Joe Stephenson	C13	R	26	16	35	3	5	0	0	0	3	1	7	0	.143	.143
Loyd Christopher	OF7	R	27	7	23	1	5	0	1	0	2	0	5	0	.217	.304
Joe Kuhel		L	41	3	3	0	0	0	0	0	0	0	2	0	.000	.000

NAME	T	AGE	W	L	PCT	SV	G	GS	CG	IP	H	BB	SO	SHO	ERA
TOTALS		31	70	84	.455	27	155	155	47	1391	1384	603	522	11	3.64
Ed Lopat	L	29	16	13	.552	0	31	31	22	253	241	73	109	3	2.81
Joe Haynes	R	29	14	6	.700	0	29	22	7	182	174	61	50	2	2.42
Frank Papish	L	29	12	12	.500	3	38	26	6	199	185	98	79	1	3.26
Orval Grove	R	27	6	8	.429	0	25	19	6	136	158	70	33	1	4.43
Bob Gillespie	R	27	5	8	.385	0	25	17	1	118	133	53	36	0	4.73
Red Ruffing (KJ)	R	43	3	5	.375	0	9	9	1	53	63	16	11	0	6.11
Thornton Lee	L	40	3	7	.300	1	21	11	2	87	86	56	57	1	4.45
Earl Harrist	R	27	3	8	.273	5	33	4	0	94	85	49	55	0	3.54
Pete Gebrian	R	23	2	4	.400	0	27	4	0	66	61	33	17	0	4.50
Johnny Rigney	R	32	2	3	.400	0	11	7	2	51	42	15	19	0	1.94
Hi Bithorn	R	31	1	0	1.000	0	2	0	0	2	2	0	0	0	0.00
1 Earl Smith	L	33	1	3	.250	0	15	5	0	33	40	24	12	0	7.36
Earl Caldwell	R	42	1	4	.200	8	40	0	0	54	53	30	22	0	3.67
Gordon Maltzberger	R	34	1	4	.200	5	33	0	0	64	61	25	22	0	3.38

WASHINGTON   7th 64-90 .416 33   OSSIE BLUEGE

NAME	G by Pos	B	AGE	G	AB	R	H	2B	3B	HR	RBI	BB	SO	SB	BA	SA
TOTALS			30	154	5112	496	1234	186	48	42	458	525	534	53	.241	.321
Mickey Vernon	1B154	L	29	154	600	77	159	29	12	7	85	49	42	12	.265	.388
Jerry Priddy	2B146	R	27	147	505	42	108	20	3	3	49	62	79	7	.214	.283
Mark Christman	SS106, 2B1	R	33	110	374	27	83	15	2	1	33	33	16	4	.222	.281
Eddie Yost	3B114	R	20	115	428	52	102	17	3	0	14	45	57	3	.238	.292
Buddy Lewis	OF130	L	30	140	506	67	132	15	4	6	48	51	27	6	.261	.342
Stan Spence	OF142	L	32	147	506	62	141	22	6	16	73	81	41	2	.279	.441
Joe Grace	OF67	L	33	78	234	25	58	9	4	3	17	35	15	1	.248	.359
Al Evans	C94	R	30	99	319	17	77	8	3	2	23	28	25	2	.241	.304
Sherry Robertson	OF55, 3B10, 2B4	R	28	95	266	25	62	9	3	1	23	32	52	4	.233	.301
Cecil Travis	3B39, SS15	L	33	74	204	10	44	4	1	0	18	16	19	1	.216	.240
2 Tom McBride	OF51, 3B1	R	32	56	166	19	45	4	2	0	15	15	9	3	.271	.319
Early Wynn	P33	R	27	54	120	6	33	6	2	0	13	1	19	0	.275	.375
John Sullivan	SS40, 2B1	R	29	49	133	13	34	0	1	0	5	22	14	0	.256	.271
Frank Mancuso	C35	R	29	43	131	13	30	1	0	0	13	5	11	0	.229	.282
Rick Ferrell	C37	R	41	37	99	10	30	11	0	0	12	14	7	0	.303	.414
George Case	OF21	R	31	36	80	11	12	1	0	0	2	8	8	5	.150	.163
George Myatt	2B1	L	33	12	7	1	0	0	0	0	0	0	0	0	.000	.000
Gil Coan	OF11	L	25	11	42	5	21	3	2	0	9	2	6	2	.500	.667
Ed Lyons	2B7	R	24	7	26	2	4	0	0	0	0	2	2	0	.154	.154
Earl Wooten	OF6	L	23	6	24	0	2	0	0	0	1	0	4	1	.083	.083
2 Felix Mackiewicz	OF3	R	29	3	6	1	1	0	0	0	1	0	3	0	.167	.333
Cal Ermer	2B1	R	23	1	0	0	0	0	0	0	0	0	0	0	.000	.000
Roberto Ortiz (SM) 32																

NAME	T	AGE	W	L	PCT	SV	G	GS	CG	IP	H	BB	SO	SHO	ERA
TOTALS		29	64	90	.416	12	154	154	67	1362	1408	579	551	15	3.97
Early Wynn	R	27	17	15	.531	0	33	31	22	247	251	90	73	2	3.64
Walt Masterson	R	27	12	16	.429	1	35	31	14	253	215	97	135	4	3.13
Mickey Haefner	L	34	10	14	.417	1	31	28	14	193	195	85	77	4	3.64
Sid Hudson (HJ)	R	32	6	9	.400	0	20	17	5	106	113	58	37	1	5.60
Ray Scarborough	R	29	6	13	.316	3	33	18	8	161	165	67	63	2	3.41
1 Bobo Newsom	R	39	4	6	.400	0	14	13	1	84	99	37	40	0	4.07
Scott Cary	L	24	3	1	.750	0	23	3	1	55	73	20	25	0	5.89
Milo Candini	R	29	3	4	.429	1	38	2	0	87	96	35	31	0	5.17
Marino Pieretti	R	26	2	4	.333	0	23	10	2	83	97	47	32	1	4.23
Tom Ferrick	R	32	1	7	.125	9	31	0	0	60	57	20	23	0	3.15
Lou Knerr	R	25	0	0	—	0	6	0	0	9	17	6	1	0	11.00
Lum Harris	R	32	0	1	.000	0	6	0	0	9	18	3	3	0	9.00
Buzz Dozier	R	18	0	0	—	0	1	0	0	2	1	4	0	0	3.00
Bill Kennedy	L	28	0	0	—	0	7	1	0	7	10	5	1	0	7.71
Hal Toenes	R	29	0	0	—	0	5	0	0	7	11	4	5	0	6.43
Alex Carrasquel (SM) 34																

ST. LOUIS   8th 59-95 .383 38   MUDDY RUEL

NAME	G by Pos	B	AGE	G	AB	R	H	2B	3B	HR	RBI	BB	SO	SB	BA	SA
TOTALS			28	154	5145	564	1238	189	52	90	626	583	664	69	.241	.350
Walt Judnich	1B129, OF15	L	31	144	500	58	129	24	3	18	64	60	62	2	.258	.426
Johnny Berardino (JJ)	2B86	R	30	90	306	29	80	22	1	1	20	44	26	6	.261	.350
Vern Stephens	SS149	R	26	155	562	74	157	18	4	15	83	70	61	8	.279	.406
Bob Dillinger	3B137	R	28	137	571	70	168	23	6	3	37	56	38	34	.294	.371
Al Zarilla	OF110	L	28	127	380	34	85	15	6	3	38	40	45	3	.224	.318
Paul Lehner	OF127	L	27	135	483	59	120	25	9	7	48	28	29	5	.248	.381
Jeff Heath	OF140	L	32	141	491	81	123	20	9	27	85	88	87	2	.251	.485
Les Moss	C96	R	22	96	274	17	43	5	2	6	27	35	48	0	.157	.255
Ray Coleman	OF93	R	25	110	343	39	86	9	7	2	30	26	32	2	.259	.344
Jake Early	C85	R	32	87	214	25	48	9	3	3	19	54	34	1	.224	.336
Billy Hitchcock	2B46, 3B17, SS7, 1B5	R	30	80	275	25	61	2	2	1	28	21	34	3	.222	.255
Joe Schultz		B	28	43	38	3	7	0	0	0	4	5	4	0	.184	.263
Rusty Peters	2B13, SS2	R	32	34	103	11	35	7	4	1	12	11	22	0	.340	.485
Jerry Witte	1B27	R	31	34	99	4	14	2	1	2	12	11	22	1	.141	.242
Hank Thompson	2B19	L	21	27	78	10	20	1	1	0	5	7	24	0	.256	.295
Willard Brown	OF18	R	32	21	67	4	12	3	0	1	6	1	5	0	.179	.269
Perry Currin	SS1	R	18	5	4	0	0	0	0	0	0	0	0	0	.000	.000
Glenn McQuillen		R	32	1	0	0	0	0	0	0	0	0	0	0	.000	.000

NAME	T	AGE	W	L	PCT	SV	G	GS	CG	IP	H	BB	SO	SHO	ERA
TOTALS		30	59	95	.383	13	154	154	50	1365	1426	604	552	7	4.33
Jack Kramer	R	29	11	16	.407	1	33	28	9	199	206	89	77	1	4.97
Sam Zoldak	L	28	9	10	.474	1	35	19	6	171	162	76	36	1	3.47
Bob Muncrief	R	31	8	14	.364	0	31	23	7	176	210	51	74	0	4.91
Ellis Kinder	R	32	8	15	.348	1	34	26	10	194	201	82	110	2	4.50
Fred Sanford	R	27	7	16	.304	4	34	23	9	187	186	76	62	0	3.71
Cliff Fannin	R	23	6	8	.429	1	26	18	6	146	134	77	77	2	3.58
Glen Moulder	R	29	4	2	.667	2	32	3	0	73	78	43	23	0	3.82
Nels Potter	R	35	4	10	.286	2	32	10	3	123	130	44	65	0	4.02
Walter Brown	R	32	1	1	1.000	0	19	0	0	46	50	28	10	0	4.89
1 Denny Galehouse	R	35	0	3	.250	0	9	4	2	42	46	11	10	0	6.19
Bud Swartz	L	18	0	1	—	0	6	1	0	5	7	12	1	0	7.20
Dizzy Dean	R	37	0	0	—	0	1	0	0	4	3	1	0	0	0.00
1 Hooks Iott	R	27	0	0	—	0	1	0	0	5	15	14	6	0	16.88

BROOKLYN 1ST 94-60 .610 CLYDE SUKEFORTH 2-0 1.000 BURT SHOTTON 92-60 .605

NAME	G by Pos	B	AGE	G	AB	R	H	2B	3B	HR	RBI	BB	SO	SB	BA	SA
TOTALS			28	155	5249	774	1428	241	50	83	719	732	561	88	.272	.384
Jackie Robinson	1B151	R	28	151	590	125	175	31	5	12	48	74	36	29	.297	.427
Eddie Stanky	2B146	R	30	146	559	97	141	24	5	3	53	103	39	3	.252	.329
Pee Wee Reese	SS142	R	28	142	476	81	135	24	4	12	73	104	67	7	.284	.426
Spider Jorgensen	3B128	L	27	129	441	57	121	29	8	5	67	58	45	4	.274	.410
Dixie Walker	OF147	L	36	148	529	77	162	31	3	9	94	97	26	6	.306	.427
Carl Furillo	OF121	R	25	124	437	61	129	24	7	8	88	34	24	7	.295	.437
Pete Reiser (CN)	OF108	L	28	110	388	68	120	23	2	5	46	68	41	14	.309	.418
Bruce Edwards	C128	R	23	130	471	53	139	15	8	9	80	49	55	2	.295	.418
Gene Hermanski	OF66	R	27	79	189	36	52	7	1	7	39	28	7	5	.275	.434
Arky Vaughan	OF22,3B10	L	35	64	126	24	41	5	2	2	25	27	11	4	.325	.444
Eddie Miksis	2B13,OF11,3B5,SS2	R	20	45	86	18	23	1	0	4	10	9	8	0	.267	.419
Cookie Lavagetto	3B18,1B3	R	34	41	69	6	18	1	0	3	11	12	5	0	.261	.406
Duke Snider	OF25	L	20	40	83	6	20	3	1	0	5	3	24	2	.241	.301
2 Al Gionfriddo	OF17	L	25	37	62	10	11	2	1	0	6	16	11	2	.177	.242
Stan Rojak	SS17,3B9,2B7	R	28	32	80	7	21	0	1	0	7	7	3	1	.263	.288
Gil Hodges	C24	R	23	28	77	9	12	3	1	1	7	14	19	0	.156	.260
Bobby Bragan	C24	R	29	25	36	3	7	2	0	0	3	7	3	1	.194	.250
Marv Rackley	OF2	L	25	18	9	2	2	0	0	0	2	1	0	0	.222	.222
Tommy Brown (MS)	3B6,OF3,SS1	R	19	15	34	3	8	1	0	0	2	1	6	0	.235	.265
Don Lund	OF5	R	24	11	20	5	6	2	0	2	5	3	7	0	.300	.700
Ed Stevens	1B4	L	22	5	13	0	2	1	0	0	1	1	5	0	.154	.231
1 Tommy Tatum	OF3	R	27	4	6	0	0	0	0	0	0	0	1	0	.000	.000

Dick Whitman 26 L 4-10, 1 Howie Schultz 24 R 0-1, Leo Durocher (SL) 41, Luis Olmo (SM) 27, Mickey Owen (SM) 31

NAME	T	AGE	W	L	PCT	SV	G	GS	CG	IP	H	BB	SO	SHO	ERA
TOTALS		26	94	60	.610	34	155	155	47	1375	1299	626	592	14	3.82
Ralph Branca	R	21	21	12	.636	1	43	36	15	280	251	98	148	4	2.67
Joe Hatten	L	30	17	8	.680	1	42	32	11	225	211	105	76	3	3.64
Vic Lombardi	L	24	12	11	.522	3	33	20	7	175	156	65	72	3	2.98
Hugh Casey	R	33	10	4	.714	18	46	0	0	77	75	29	40	0	3.97
Harry Taylor	R	28	10	5	.667	1	33	20	10	162	130	83	58	2	3.11
Clyde King	R	23	6	5	.545	0	29	9	2	88	85	29	31	0	2.76
Rex Barney	R	22	5	2	.714	0	28	9	0	78	66	59	36	0	4.96
13 Hank Behrman	R	26	5	3	.625	8	40	6	0	92	97	48	33	0	5.48
Hal Gregg	R	25	4	5	.444	1	37	16	2	104	115	55	59	1	5.88
1 Kirby Higbe	R	32	2	0	1.000	0	3	0	0	16	18	12*	10	0	5.06
Phil Haugstad	R	23	1	0	1.000	0	6	1	0	13	14	4	4	0	2.77
Willie Ramsdell	R	31	1	1	.500	0	2	0	0	3	4	3	3	0	6.00
Dan Bankhead	R	27	0	0	—	1	4	0	0	10	15	8	6	0	7.20
George Dockins	R	30	0	0	—	0	4	0	0	5	10	2	1	0	12.60
Johnny Van Cuyk	L	25	0	0	—	0	2	0	0	3	5	1	2	0	6.00
Ed Chandler	R	25	0	1	.000	0	15	1	0	30	31	12	8	0	6.30
Rube Melton	R	30	0	1	.000	0	4	1	0	5	7	7	1	0	12.60
Jack Banta	R	22	0	1	.000	0	3	0	0	8	7	4	3	0	6.75
Erv Palica	R	19	0	1	.000	0	3	0	0	3	2	1	0	0	3.00

*Higbe, also with Pittsburgh, league leader in BB with 122

ST. LOUIS 2nd 89-65 .578 5 EDDIE DYER

NAME	G by Pos	B	AGE	G	AB	R	H	2B	3B	HR	RBI	BB	SO	SB	BA	SA
TOTALS			27	156	5422	780	1462	235	65	115	718	612	511	28	.270	.401
Stan Musial	1B149	L	26	149	587	113	183	30	13	19	95	80	24	4	.312	.504
Red Schoendienst	2B142,3B5,OF1	B	24	151	659	91	167	25	9	3	48	48	21	5	.253	.332
Marty Marion	SS149	R	29	149	540	57	147	19	6	4	74	49	58	3	.272	.352
Whitey Kurowski	3B141	R	29	146	513	108	159	27	6	27	104	87	56	4	.310	.544
Erv Dusak	OF89,3B7	R	26	111	328	56	93	7	3	6	28	50	34	1	.284	.378
Terry Moore	OF120	R	35	127	460	61	130	17	1	7	45	38	39	1	.283	.370
Enos Slaughter	OF142	L	31	147	551	100	162	31	13	10	86	59	27	4	.294	.452
Del Rice	C94	R	24	97	261	28	57	7	3	12	44	36	40	1	.218	.406
2 Ron Northey	OF94,3B2	L	27	110	311	52	91	19	3	15	63	48	29	0	.293	.518
Chuck Diering	OF75	R	24	105	74	22	16	3	1	2	11	19	22	3	.216	.365
Joe Garagiola	C74	L	21	77	183	20	47	10	2	5	25	40	14	0	.257	.415
Joe Medwick	OF43	R	35	75	150	19	46	12	0	4	28	16	12	0	.307	.467
Del Wilber	C34	R	28	51	99	7	23	8	1	0	12	5	13	0	.232	.333
Jeff Cross	3B15,SS14,2B2	R	28	51	49	4	5	1	0	0	3	10	6	0	.102	.122
Dick Sisler	1B10,OF5	L	26	46	74	4	15	2	1	0	9	3	8	0	.203	.257
Nippy Jones	2B13,OF2	R	22		73	6	18	4	0	1	5	2	10	0	.247	.342
Bernie Creger	SS13	R	20	15	16	3	3	1	0	0	0	5	1	0	.188	.250
1 Harry Walker	OF9	L	30	10	25	2	5	1	0*	0	0	4	2	0	.200*	.240

Lou Klein (SM) 28

NAME	T	AGE	W	L	PCT	SV	G	GS	CG	IP	H	BB	SO	SHO	ERA
TOTALS		29	89	65	.578	20	156	156	65	1398	1407	495	642	12	3.53
George Munger	R	28	16	5	.762	3	40	31	13	224	218	76	123	6	3.38
Harry Brecheen	L	32	16	11	.593	1	29	28	18	223	220	66	89	1	3.31
Al Brazle	L	33	14	8	.636	4	44	19	7	168	186	48	85	0	2.84
Murry Dickson	R	30	13	16	.448	3	47	25	11	232	211	88	111	4	3.06
Jim Hearn	R	26	12	7	.632	1	37	21	4	162	151	63	57	1	3.22
Howie Pollet	L	26	9	11	.450	2	31	24	9	176	195	87	73	0	4.35
Ted Wilks	R	31	4	1	.800	5	37	0	0	50	57	11	28	0	5.04
Ken Burkhart	R	30	3	6	.333	1	34	6	1	95	108	23	44	0	5.21
Ken Johnson	L	24	1	0	1.000	0	9	2	1	10	2	5	8	0	0.00
Gerry Staley	R	26	1	0	1.000	0	18	1	1	29	33	8	14	0	2.79
1 Freddy Schmidt	R	31	0	0	—	2	0	0	0	4	5	1	2	0	2.25
Johnny Grodzicki	R	30	0	1	.000	0	3	0	0	23	21	19	8	0	5.48

Max Lanier (SM) 31
Freddie Martin (SM) 32

*Walker, also with Philadelphia, league leader in 3B (16), BA (.363)

BOSTON 3rd 86-68 .558 8 BILLY SOUTHWORTH

NAME	G by Pos	B	AGE	G	AB	R	H	2B	3B	HR	RBI	BB	SO	SB	BA	SA
TOTALS			30	154	5253	701	1444	265	42	85	645	558	500	58	.275	.390
Earl Torgeson	1B117	L	23	128	399	73	112	20	6	16	78	82	59	11	.281	.481
Connie Ryan	2B150,SS1	R	27	150	544	60	144	33	5	5	69	71	60	5	.265	.371
Dick Culler	SS75	R	32	77	214	20	53	5	1	0	19	19	15	1	.248	.280
Bob Elliott	3B148	R	30	150	555	93	176	35	5	22	113	87	60	3	.317	.517
Tommy Holmes	OF147	L	30	150	618	90	191	33	9	9	53	44	16	3	.309	.416
Johnny Hopp	OF125	L	30	134	430	74	124	20	2	2	32	58	30	13	.288	.358
Bama Rowell	OF100,2B7,3B4	L	31	113	384	48	106	23	2	5	40	18	14	7	.276	.385
Phil Masi	C123	R	30	126	411	54	125	22	4	9	50	47	27	1	.304	.443
Mike McCormick	OF79	R	30	92	284	42	81	13	7	3	36	20	21	1	.285	.412
Danny Litwhiler	OF66	R	30	91	226	38	59	5	2	7	31	25	43	1	.261	.394
Nanny Fernandez	SS62,OF8,3B6	R	28	83	209	16	43	4	0	2	21	22	20	2	.206	.254
2 Frank McCormick	1B48	R	36	81	212	24	75	18	2	2	43	11	8	2	.354	.486
Sibby Sisti	SS51,2B1	R	26	56	153	22	43	8	2	0	15	20	17	2	.281	.373
Hank Camelli	C51	R	32	52	150	10	29	8	1	1	11	18	18	0	.193	.280
Johnny Sain	P38	R	29	40	107	13	37	7	0	0	18	3	1	0	.346	.411
Tommy Neill	OF2	R	27	7	10	1	2	0	1	0	0	1	2	0	.200	.400
Danny Murtaugh	2B2,3B2	R	29	8	8	0	1	0	0	0	0	1	2	0	.125	.125

Bob Brady 24 L 0-1, Ray Sanders (BA) 30

NAME	T	AGE	W	L	PCT	SV	G	GS	CG	IP	H	BB	SO	SHO	ERA
TOTALS		31	86	68	.558	13	154	154	74	1363	1352	453	494	14	3.62
Warren Spahn	L	26	21	10	.677	3	40	35	22	290	245	84	123	7	2.33
Johnny Sain	R	29	21	12	.636	1	38	35	22	266	265	79	132	3	3.52
Red Barrett	R	32	11	12	.478	1	36	30	12	211	200	53	53	3	3.54
2 Bill Voiselle	R	28	8	7	.533	0	22	20	7	131	146	51	59	0	4.33
Si Johnson	R	40	6	8	.429	2	36	10	3	113	124	34	27	0	4.22
2 Clyde Shoun	L	35	6	3	.625	1	26	3	1	74	73	21	23	1	4.38
Walt Lanfranconi	R	30	4	4	.500	1	36	4	1	64	65	27	18	0	2.95
Ed Wright	R	28	3	3	.500	0	23	6	1	65	80	35	14	0	6.37
Johnny Beazley (SA)	R	29	2	0	1.000	0	9	2	2	29	30	19	12	0	4.34
Andy Karl	R	33	2	3	.400	3	27	0	0	35	41	13	5	0	3.86
1 Mort Cooper	R	34	2	5	.286	0	10	7	2	47	48	13	15	0	4.02
Ray Martin	R	22	1	0	1.000	0	1	1	1	9	7	4	2	0	1.00
Johnny Lanning	R	40	1	0	—	0	3	0	0	4	2	1	1	0	9.00
Max Macon	R	31	0	0	—	0	4	0	0	4	1	1	1	0	0.00
Dick Mulligan	R	29	0	0	—	0	1	0	0	1	1	1	0	0	9.00
Ernie White (SA)	R	30	0	0	—	0	1	0	0	4	1	1	0	0	0.00
Glenn Elliott	L	27	0	1	.000	0	11	0	0	19	18	11	8	0	4.74

NEW YORK 4th 81-73 .526 13 MEL OTT

NAME	G by Pos	B	AGE	G	AB	R	H	2B	3B	HR	RBI	BB	SO	SB	BA	SA
TOTALS			27	155	5343	830	1446	220	48	221	790	494	568	29	.271	.454
Johnny Mize	1B154	L	32	154	586	137	177	26	2	51	138	74	42	2	.302	.614
Bill Rigney	2B72,3B41,SS24	R	29	130	531	84	142	24	3	17	59	51	54	7	.267	.420
Buddy Kerr	SS138	R	24	138	547	73	157	23	5	7	49	36	49	2	.287	.386
Lucky Lohrke	3B111	R	23	112	329	44	79	12	4	11	35	46	29	3	.240	.401
Willard Marshall	OF155	L	26	155	587	102	171	19	6	36	107	67	30	3	.291	.528
Bobby Thomson	OF127,2B9	R	23	138	545	105	154	26	5	29	85	40	78	1	.283	.508
Sid Gordon	OF124,3B2	R	29	130	437	57	119	19	8	13	57	50	21	2	.272	.442
Walker Cooper	C132	R	32	140	515	79	157	24	8	35	122	24	43	2	.305	.586
Lloyd Gearhart	OF44	R	23	73	179	26	44	9	0	6	17	17	30	1	.246	.397
Joe Lafata	OF19,1B2	L	25	62	95	13	21	4	2	0	18	15	18	1	.221	.295
Buddy Blattner	2B34,3B11	R	27	55	153	28	40	9	2	0	13	21	19	4	.261	.346
Mickey Witek (BA)	2B40,3B3	R	31	51	160	22	35	4	1	3	17	15	12	1	.219	.313
Ernie Lombardi	C24	R	39	48	110	8	31	5	0	4	21	7	9	0	.282	.436
Clint Hartung	P23,OF7	R	24		94	13	29	4	3	4	13	3	21	0	.309	.543
1 Babe Young		L	32	14	14	0	1	1	0	0	1	0	0	0	.071	.143
Bobby Rhawn	2B8,3B5	R	28	13	45	7	14	3	0	0	3	1	4	0	.311	.444
Fuzz White	OF5	L	31	7	13	3	3	0	0	0	0	1	0	0	.231	.231
Wes Westrum	C2	R	24	6	12	1	5	1	0	0	1	5	1	0	.417	.500
2 Mickey Livingston	C2	R	32	5	6	0	1	0	0	0	1	0	2	0	.167	.167
Mel Ott		L	38	4	4	0	0	0	0	0	0	1	0	0	.000	.000

Bennie Warren 35 R 1-5, Whitey Lockman (BN) 20 L 1-2, Sal Yvars 23 R 1-5, Danny Gardella (SM) 27, George Hausmann (SM) 31, Nap Reyes (SM) 27

NAME	T	AGE	W	L	PCT	SV	G	GS	CG	IP	H	BB	SO	SHO	ERA
TOTALS		27	81	73	.526	14	155	155	58	1364	1418	590	553	6	4.44
Larry Jansen	R	26	21	5	.808	1	42	30	20	248	241	57	104	1	3.16
Dave Koslo	L	27	15	10	.600	0	39	31	10	217	223	82	86	3	4.40
Clint Hartung	R	24	9	7	.563	0	23	20	8	138	140	69	54	1	4.57
Monte Kennedy	L	25	9	12	.429	0	34	24	9	148	158	88	60	0	4.86
Ken Trinkle	R	27	8	4	.667	10	62	0	0	94	100	48	37	0	3.73
Junior Thompson	R	30	4	2	.667	0	15	0	0	36	36	27	13	0	4.25
Ray Poat	R	29	4	3	.571	0	7	5	0	60	53	13	25	0	2.55
2 Joe Beggs	R	36	3	3	.500	2	32	0	0	66	81	18	23	0	4.23
2 Hooks Iott	L	27	2	2	.273	0	9	9	2	71	67	52	46	1	5.96
Sheldon Jones	R	25	2	2	.500	0	15	6	1	56	51	29	24	0	3.86
1 Bill Voiselle	R	28	1	4	.200	0	11	5	1	43	44	22	20	0	4.60
Andy Hansen	R	22	1	5	.167	0	27	9	1	82	87	38	18	0	4.39
2 Mort Cooper	R	34	1	5	.167	0	9	7	1	37	51	13	12	0	7.05
Hub Andrews	R	24	0	0	—	0	7	0	0	12	16	10	6	0	6.00
Mike Budnick	R	23	0	0	—	0	12	1	0	12	16	10	6	0	10.50
1 Bob Carpenter	R	29	0	0	—	0	2	0	0	7	10	2	1	0	12.00
Mario Picone	R	32	0	0	—	0	1	0	0	7	10	2	1	0	7.71
Woody Abernathy	R	32	0	0	—	0	9	0	0	9	12	9	0	0	9.00
Bill Ayers	R	27	0	0	.000	0	13	4	1	35	46	14	22	0	8.23

Sal Maglie (SM) 30, Adrian Zabala (SM) 30, Harry Feldman (SM) 27, Ace Adams (SM) 35

CINCINNATI 5th 73-81 .474 21 JOHNNY NEUN

NAME	G by Pos	B	AGE	G	AB	R	H	2B	3B	HR	RBI	BB	SO	SB	BA	SA
TOTALS			29	154	5299	681	1372	242	43	95	637	539	530	46	.259	.375
2 Babe Young	1B93	L	32	95	364	55	103	21	3	14	79	35	26	0	.283	.473
Benny Zientara	2B100,3B13	R	29	117	418	60	108	18	1	2	24	23	23	2	.258	.321
Eddie Miller	SS151	R	30	151	545	69	146	38	4	19	87	49	46	5	.268	.457
Grady Hatton	3B136	L	24	146	524	91	147	26	4	16	77	81	50	7	.281	.448
Frankie Baumholtz	OF150	L	28	151	643	96	182	32	9	5	45	56	53	6	.283	.384
Bert Haas	OF69,1B53	R	33	135	482	58	138	17	7	3	67	42	27	9	.286	.369
Augie Galan	OF118	L	35	124	392	60	123	18	2	6	61	94	19	3	.314	.416
Ray Lamanno	C109	R	27	118	413	33	106	21	3	5	50	28	39	0	.257	.358
Eddie Lukon	OF55	R	26	86	200	26	41	6	1	11	33	36	36	2	.205	.410
Bobby Adams	2B69	R	25	81	217	39	59	11	2	4	20	25	23	9	.272	.396
Clyde Vollmer	OF66	R	25	78	155	19	34	10	0	1	9	18	29	0	.219	.303
Ray Mueller	C55	R	35	71	192	17	48	11	0	6	33	16	25	1	.250	.401
2 Tommy Tatum	OF49,2B1	R	27	69	176	19	48	5	2	1	16	16	16	7	.273	.341
2 Kermit Wahl	3B20,SS9,2B2	R	24	39	81	8	14	0	1	0	4	12	12	1	.173	.210
2 Hugh Poland	C3	L	25	11	27	4	9	0	0	0	4	0	4	0	.333	.389
Charlie Kress	1B8	L	24	11	27	4	4	0	0	0	4	4	5	0	.148	.148
Ted Kluszewski	1B2	L	22	9	10	1	1	0	0	0	0	2	1	0	.100	.100
Bob Usher	OF8	R	22	9	22	4	4	1	0	0	2	1	5	0	.182	.318
Virgil Stallcup	SS1	R	25	3	1	0	0	0	0	0	0	0	0	0	.000	.000
1 Al Lakeman																

NAME	T	AGE	W	L	PCT	SV	G	GS	CG	IP	H	BB	SO	SHO	ERA
TOTALS		28	73	81	.474	13	154	154	54	1365	1442	589	633	13	4.41
Ewell Blackwell	R	24	22	8	.733	0	33	33	23	273	227	95	193	6	2.47
Harry Gumbert	R	37	10	10	.500	10	46	0	0	90	88	47	43	0	3.90
Johnny Vander Meer	L	32	9	14	.391	0	30	29	9	186	186	87	79	3	4.40
Bucky Walters	R	38	8	8	.500	0	26	20	5	122	137	49	43	2	5.75
2 Ken Raffensberger	L	29	8	5	.615	1	19	15	7	107	132	29	38	0	4.12
Kent Peterson	L	21	6	13	.316	0	37	17	3	152	156	62	78	1	4.26
Bud Lively	R	22	7	4	.364	0	38	17	3	123	126	63	52	1	4.68
Eddie Erautt	R	22	4	4	.308	0	30	10	2	119	146	53	43	0	5.07
Johnny Hetki	R	25	3	4	.429	0	37	5	2	96	110	48	33	0	5.81
1 Elmer Riddle	R	32	1	0	1.000	0	5	0	0	10	14	16	5	0	8.40
1 Clyde Shoun	L	30	1	0		0	5			14	16			0	5.14
Clay Lambert	R	30													15.00
Harry Perkowski	L	25								12					3.86
Ken Polivka	R	24													4.50
Bob Malloy	R	22													18.00
Mike Schultz	L	25													0.00
Herm Wehmeier	R	20					3			32	42	6	11	0	4.50
1 Joe Beggs	R	36													5.34

NAME	G by Pos	B	AGE	G	AB	R	H	2B	3B	HR	RBI	BB	SO	SB	BA	SA
CHICAGO 6th 69-85 .448 25																
TOTALS			31	155	5305	567	1373	231	48	71	540	471	578	22	.259	.361
Eddie Waitkus	1B126	L	27	130	514	60	150	28	6	2	35	32	17	3	.292	.381
Don Johnson	2B108, 3B6	R	35	120	402	33	104	17	2	3	26	24	45	2	.259	.333
Lennie Merullo	SS108	R	30	108	373	24	90	16	1	0	29	15	26	4	.241	.290
Peanuts Lowrey	3B91, OF25, 2B6	R	29	115	448	56	126	17	5	5	37	38	26	2	.281	.375
Bill Nicholson	OF140	L	32	148	487	69	119	28	1	26	75	87	83	1	.244	.466
Andy Pafko	OF127	R	26	129	513	68	155	25	7	13	66	31	39	4	.302	.454
Phil Cavarretta	OF100, 1B24	L	30	127	459	56	144	22	5	2	63	58	35	2	.314	.397
Bob Scheffing	C97	R	33	110	363	33	96	11	5	5	50	25	25	2	.264	.364
Bobby Sturgeon	SS45, 2B30, 3B5	R	27	87	232	16	59	10	5	0	21	7	12	0	.254	.341
Clyde McCullough	C64	R	30	86	234	25	59	12	4	3	30	20	20	1	.252	.376
Stan Hack	3B66	L	37	76	240	28	65	11	2	0	12	41	19	0	.271	.333
Marv Rickert	OF30, 3B1	L	26	71	137	7	20	2	0	2	15	15	17	0	.146	.190
Dom Dallessandro	OF28	L	33	66	115	18	33	7	1	1	14	21	11	0	.287	.391
Cliff Aberson	OF40	R	25	47	140	24	39	6	3	4	20	20	32	5	.279	.450
1 Lonny Frey	2B9	R	36	24	43	4	9	0	0	0	3	4	6	0	.209	.209
2 Ray Mack	2B21	R	30	21	78	9	17	6	0	2	12	5	15	0	.218	.372
1 Mickey Livingston	C7	R	32	19	33	2	7	2	0	0	3	1	5	0	.212	.273
Billy Jurges	SS14	R	39	14	40	5	8	2	0	1	2	9	9	0	.200	.325
Sal Madrid	SS8	R	27	8	24	0	3	1	0	0	1	1	6	0	.125	.167
Hank Schenz 28 R 1-14, Dewey Williams 31 R 0-2																

NAME	T	AGE	W	L	PCT	SV	G	GS	CG	IP	H	BB	SO	SHO	ERA
		29	69	85	.448	15	155	155	46	1367	1449	618	571	8	4.10
Johnny Schmitz	L	26	13	18	.419	1	38	28	10	207	209	80	97	3	3.22
Doyle Lade	R	26	11	10	.524	3	34	25	7	187	202	79	62	1	3.95
Emil Kush	R	30	8	3	.727	5	47	1	1	91	80	53	44	0	3.36
Hank Borowy	R	31	8	12	.400	2	40	25	7	183	190	63	75	1	4.38
Bob Chipman	L	28	7	6	.538	0	32	17	5	135	135	66	51	1	3.67
Paul Erickson	R	31	7	12	.368	1	40	20	6	174	179	93	82	0	4.34
Hank Wyse	R	29	6	9	.400	1	37	19	5	142	158	64	53	1	4.31
Russ Meyer (NJ)	R	23	2	1	.600	0	23	2	1	45	43	14	22	0	3.40
Russ Meers	L	28	2	0	1.000	0	35	1	0	64	61	38	28	0	4.50
Claude Passeau	R	38	2	6	.250	2	19	6	1	63	97	24	26	1	6.29
Ox Miller	R	32	1	2	.333	0	4	4	1	16	31	5	7	0	10.13
Ralph Hamner	R	30	1	2	.333	0	3	3	2	25	24	16	14	0	2.52
3 Freddy Schmidt	R	31	0	1	.000	0	1	1	0	7	10	4	1	0	9.00
2 Bob Carpenter	R	29	0	1	.000	0	2	1	0	7	7	4	3	0	5.14
Bill Lee	R	37	0	2	.000	0	14	2	0	24	26	14	9	0	4.50

NAME	G by Pos	B	AGE	G	AB	R	H	2B	3B	HR	RBI	BB	SO	SB	BA	SA
PHILADELPHIA 7th(Tie) 62-92 .403 32																
TOTALS			29	155	5256	589	1354	210	52	60	544	464	594	60	.258	.352
2 Howie Schultz	1B114	R	24	114	403	30	90	19	1	6	35	21	70	0	.223	.320
Emil Verban	2B155	R	31	155	540	50	154	14	8	0	42	23	8	5	.285	.341
Skeeter Newsome	SS85, 2B6, 3B1	R	36	95	310	36	71	8	2	2	22	24	24	4	.229	.287
Lee Handley	3B83, 2B3, SS1	R	33	101	277	17	70	10	3	0	24	24	18	1	.253	.310
Johnny Wyrostek	OF126	R	28	128	454	68	124	24	7	5	51	61	45	7	.273	.390
2 Harry Walker	OF127, 1B4	L	30	130	488	79	181	28	16*	1	41	59	37	13	.371*	.500
Del Ennis	OF135	R	22	139	541	71	149	25	6	12	81	37	51	9	.275	.411
Andy Seminick	C109	R	26	111	337	48	85	16	2	13	50	58	69	4	.252	.427
Charlie Gilbert	OF37	L	27	83	152	20	36	5	2	2	10	13	14	1	.237	.336
Jim Tabor	3B67	R	33	75	251	27	59	14	0	4	31	20	21	2	.235	.339
Don Padgett	C39	L	35	75	158	14	50	8	1	0	24	16	5	0	.316	.380
Buster Adams	OF51	R	32	69	182	21	45	11	1	2	15	26	29	2	.247	.352
Ralph LaPointe	SS54	R	25	56	211	33	65	7	0	1	15	5	17	15	.308	.355
2 Al Lakeman	1B29, C23	R	28	55	182	11	29	3	0	6	19	5	39	0	.159	.275
Schoolboy Rowe	P31	R	37	43	79	9	22	2	0	2	11	13	18	0	.278	.380
Jack Albright (BL)	SS33	R	26	41	99	9	23	4	0	1	5	10	11	1	.232	.333
Willie Jones	3B17	R	21	18	62	5	14	0	1	0	7	0	2	0	.226	.258
1 Frank McCormick	1B12	R	36	15	40	7	9	0	0	1	8	3	2	0	.225	.300
Nick Etten	1B11	L	33	14	41	5	10	4	0	1	8	5	4	0	.244	.415
1 Ron Northey	OF13	L	27	13	47	7	12	3	0	1	6	3	1	0	.255	.319
Lou Finney 36 L 0-4, 1 Hugh Poland 34 L 0-8, Putsy Caballero 19 R 1-7, Granny Hamner 20 R 2-7, Rollie Hemsley 40 R 1-3, Jesse Levan 20 L 4-9																

NAME	T	AGE	W	L	PCT	SV	G	GS	CG	IP	H	BB	SO	SHO	ERA
		32	62	92	.403	14	155	155	70	1362	1399	501	514	8	3.96
Dutch Leonard	R	38	17	12	.586	0	32	29	19	235	224	57	103	3	2.68
Schoolboy Rowe	R	37	14	10	.583	1	31	28	15	196	232	45	74	1	4.32
2 Ken Heintzelman	R	31	7	10	.412	1	24	19	8	136	144	46	55	0	4.04
2 Freddy Schmidt	R	31	8	3	.385	0	29	11	3	77	76	43	24	0	4.68
Blix Donnelly	R	33	4	6	.400	5	38	10	5	121	113	46	31	1	2.98
Tommy Hughes	R	27	4	11	.267	1	29	15	4	127	121	59	44	1	3.47
Oscar Judd	L	39	4	15	.211	0	32	19	8	147	155	69	54	1	4.59
Charley Schanz	R	28	2	4	.333	2	34	6	1	102	107	47	42	0	4.15
1 Ken Raffensberger	R	29	2	6	.250	0	10	7	3	41	50	8	16	1	5.49
Curt Simmons	L	18	1	0	1.000	0	1	1	1	9	5	6	9	0	1.00
Frank Hoerst	L	29	1	1	.500	0	4	1	0	13	19	3	0	0	8.18
Al Jurisich	R	25	1	7	.125	1	34	12	5	118	110	52	48	0	4.96
Dick Mauney	R	27	0	0	—	0	1	0	0	16	15	7	6	0	3.94
Homer Spragins	R	26	0	0	—	0	2	0	0	5	3	3	1	0	7.20
Lou Possehl	R	21	0	0	—	0	2	1	0	6	8	5	2	0	4.50
Dick Koecher	R	21	0	2	.000	0	3	2	0	17	20	10	4	0	4.76

*Walker, also with St. Louis, league leader in 3B (16), BA (.363)

NAME	G by Pos	B	AGE	G	AB	R	H	2B	3B	HR	RBI	BB	SO	SB	BA	SA
PITTSBURGH 7th (Tie) 62-92 .403 32																
TOTALS			28	156	5307	744	1385	216	44	156	699	607	687	30	.261	.406
Hank Greenberg	1B119	R	36	125	402	71	100	13	2	25	74	104	73	0	.249	.478
Jimmy Bloodworth	2B87	R	30	88	316	27	79	9	0	7	48	16	39	1	.250	.345
Billy Cox	SS129	R	27	132	529	75	145	30	7	15	54	29	28	5	.274	.442
Frankie Gustine	3B156	R	27	156	616	102	183	30	6	9	67	63	65	5	.297	.409
Wally Westlake	OF109	R	26	112	407	59	111	17	4	17	69	27	63	4	.273	.459
Jim Russell	OF119	B	28	128	478	68	121	21	8	8	51	63	58	7	.253	.381
Ralph Kiner	OF152	R	24	152	565	118	177	23	4	51	127	98	81	1	.313	.639
Dixie Howell	C74	R	27	76	214	23	59	11	0	4	25	27	34	1	.276	.383
Culley Rikard	OF79	L	33	109	324	57	93	16	4	4	32	50	39	1	.287	.398
Clyde Kluttz	C69	R	29	73	232	26	70	9	2	6	42	17	18	1	.302	.435
Elbie Fletcher	1B50	L	31	69	157	22	38	9	1	1	22	29	24	2	.242	.331
Eddie Basinski	2B56	R	24	56	161	15	32	6	2	4	17	18	27	0	.199	.335
W. Wietelmann	SS22, 2B14, 3B6, 1B1	B	28	48	128	21	30	4	1	1	7	12	10	0	.234	.305
Bill Salkeld	C15	L	30	47	61	5	13	0	0	6	13	14	8	0	.213	.246
Billy Sullivan	C12	L	36	38	55	1	14	3	0	0	6	4	1	0	.255	.309
Gene Woodling	OF21	L	24	22	79	7	21	2	2	0	10	7	5	0	.266	.342
Roy Jarvis	C15	R	21	18	45	4	7	1	0	1	4	6	5	0	.156	.244
Gene Mauch	2B6, SS5	R	21	16	30	8	9	0	0	1	2	6	5	0	.300	.300
Billy Herman	2B10, 1B2	R	37	15	47	3	10	4	0	0	6	2	1	0	.213	.298
Pete Castiglione 26 R 14-50, 1 Al Gionfriddo 25 L 0-1																

NAME	T	AGE	W	L	PCT	SV	G	GS	CG	IP	H	BB	SO	SHO	ERA
		33	62	92	.403	13	156	156	44	1374	1488	592	530	9	4.68
Fritz Ostermueller	L	39	12	10	.545	0	26	24	12	183	181	68	66	3	3.84
Ernie Bonham	R	33	11	8	.579	3	33	18	7	150	167	35	63	3	3.84
2 Kirby Higbe	R	32	11	17	.393	5	46	30	10	225	204	110*	99	1	3.72
Rip Sewell	R	40	6	4	.600	0	24	12	4	121	121	36	36	1	3.57
Jim Bagby	R	30	5	4	.556	0	37	6	2	116	143	37	23	0	4.66
2 Preacher Roe	L	32	4	15	.211	2	38	22	4	144	156	63	59	1	5.25
Ed Bahr	R	27	3	5	.375	0	19	11	1	82	70	43	25	0	4.61
2 Mel Queen	R	29	3	7	.300	0	14	12	2	74	70	51	34	0	4.01
Elmer Singleton	R	29	2	2	.500	1	36	3	0	67	70	39	24	0	6.31
2 Al Lyons	R	28	1	2	.333	0	13	0	0	28	36	12	16	0	7.39
Art Herring	R	40	1	3	.250	2	11	0	0	11	18	4	8	0	8.18
Steve Nagy	L	28	1	3	.250	0	1	0	0	14	18	9	4	0	5.79
Roger Wolff	R	36	1	4	.200	0	13	6	1	30	49	18	7	0	8.70
Nick Strincevich	R	32	1	6	.143	0	32	7	1	89	111	37	22	0	5.26
1 Ken Heintzelman	L	31	0	0	—	0	2	0	0	2	2	1	0	0	20.25
Lee Howard	L	23	0	1	.000	0	3	1	0	3	3	2	0	0	3.00
Hugh Mulcahy	R	33	0	0	—	0	3	0	0	3	4	4	0	0	3.86
Ken Gables	R	28	0	0	—	0	1	0	0	1	1	0	0	0	54.00
2 Hank Behrman	R	—	0	0	—	0	1	0	0	2	2	2	2	0	9.00
Cal McLish 21 R 0-0, Lou Tost 36 L 0-0																

*Higbe, also with Brooklyn, league leader in BB with 122

WORLD SERIES — NEW YORK (AL) 4 BROOKLYN (NL) 3

LINE SCORES

TEAM	1	2	3	4	5	6	7	8	9	10	11	12	R	H	E
Game 1 September 30 at New York															
BKN (NL)	1	0	0		0	0	1		1	0	0		3	6	0
NY (AL)	0	0	0		0	5	0		0	0	X		5	4	0
Branca, Behrman (5), Shea, Page (6)															
Game 2 October 1 at New York															
BKN	0	0	1		1	0	0		0	0	1		3	9	2
NY	1	0	1		1	2	1		4	0	X		10	15	1
Lombardi, Gregg (5), Behrman (7), Reynolds, Barney (7)															
Game 3 October 2 at Brooklyn															
NY	0	0	2		2	2	1		0	0	0		8	13	0
BKN	0	6	1		2	0	0		0	0	X		9	13	1
Newsom, Raschi (2), Drews (3), Chandler (4), Page (6), Hatten, Branca (5), Casey (7)															
Game 4 October 3 at Brooklyn															
NY	1	0	0		1	0	0		0	0	0		2	8	1
BKN	0	0	0		0	0	1		0	0	2		3	1	3
Bevens, Taylor, Gregg (1), Behrman (8), Casey (9)															
Game 5 October 4 at Brooklyn															
NY	0	0	0		1	1	0		0	0	0		2	5	0
BKN	0	0	0		0	0	1		0	0	0		1	4	1
Shea, Barney, Hatten (5), Behrman (7), Casey (8)															
Game 6 October 5 at New York															
BKN	0	2	0		0	0	4		0	0	0		8	12	1
NY	0	0	4		1	0	0		0	0	1		6	15	2
Lombardi, Branca (3), Hatten (6), Casey (9), Reynolds, Drews (3), Page (5), Newsom (6), Raschi (7), Wensloff (8)															
Game 7 October 6 at New York															
BKN	0	2	0		0	0	0		0	0	0		2	7	0
NY	0	1	0		2	0	1		0	0	X		5	7	0
Gregg, Behrman (4), Hatten (6), Barney (6), Casey (7), Shea, Bevens (2), Page (5)															

COMPOSITE BATTING

NAME	POS	G	AB	R	H	2B	3B	HR	RBI	BA
New York (AL)										
Totals		7	238	38	67	11	5	4	36	.282
Henrich	OF	7	31	2	10	2	0	1	5	.323
Stimweiss	2B	7	27	1	7	0	1	0	3	.259
Rizzuto	SS	7	26	3	8	1	0	0	3	.308
Johnson	3B	7	26	8	7	0	3	0	2	.269
DiMaggio	OF	7	26	4	6	0	0	2	5	.231
McQuinn	1B	7	23	3	3	0	0	1	1	.130
Berra	C-OF	6	19	2	3	1	0	1	2	.158
Lindell	OF	6	18	3	9	3	1	0	7	.500
A. Robinson	C	3	10	2	2	1	0	0	1	.200
Shea	P	3	5	0	2	1	0	0	1	.400
Lollar	C	2	4	1	3	1	0	0	1	.750
Reynolds	P	2	4	0	2	0	0	0	1	.500
Page	P	4	4	0	0	0	0	0	0	.000
Bevens	P	2	3	0	1	0	0	0	0	.333
Brown	PH	4	3	2	3	0	0	0	3	1.000
Clark	OF	3	2	1	1	0	0	0	0	.500
Phillips	1B	2	2	0	0	0	0	0	0	.000
Drews	P	2	1	0	0	0	0	0	0	.000
Houk	PH	1	1	0	1	0	0	0	0	1.000
Frey	PH	1	1	0	0	0	0	0	0	.000
Newsom P 0-0, Raschi P 0-0, Chandler P 0-0, Wensloff P 0-0										
Brooklyn (NL)										
Totals		7	226	29	52	13	1	1	26	.230
J. Robinson	1B	7	27	3	7	2	0	0	3	.259
Walker	OF	7	27	1	6	0	1	0	4	.222
Edwards	C	7	27	3	6	1	0	0	2	.222
Stanky	2B	7	25	4	6	1	0	0	0	.240
Reese	SS	7	23	5	7	1	0	0	4	.304
Jorgensen	3B	7	20	1	4	2	0	0	1	.200
Hermanski	OF	7	19	4	3	1	0	0	2	.158
Furillo	OF	6	17	2	6	1	0	0	2	.353
Reiser	OF	5	12	3	3	1	0	0	4	.250
Lavagetto	3B	5	7	1	1	0	0	0	2	.143
Miksis	2B-OF	5	4	1	1	0	0	0	0	.250
Branca	P	3	4	0	0	0	0	0	0	.000
Hatten	P	4	3	0	1	0	0	0	0	.333
Gionfriddo	OF	4	3	1	0	0	0	0	0	.000
Gregg	P	3	3	0	0	0	0	0	0	.000
Lombardi	P	3	2	0	0	0	0	0	0	.000
Vaughan	PH	2	2	0	1	0	0	0	0	.500
Bragan	PH	1	1	0	1	0	0	0	1	1.000
Hodges PH 0-1, Casey P 0-1, Barney P 0-1, Taylor P 0-0, Bankhead PR 0-0										

COMPOSITE PITCHING

NAME	G	IP	H	BB	SO	W	L	SV	ERA
New York (AL)									
Totals	7	61.2	52	30	32	4	3	1	4.09
Shea	3	15.1	10	8	10	2	0	0	2.35
Page	4	13	12	2	7	1	1	1	4.15
Bevens	2	11.1	11	7	0	0	1	0	2.38
Reynolds	2	11.1	15	3	6	1	0	0	4.76
Drews	2	3	3	1	0	0	0	0	3.00
Newsom	2	2.1	6	2	0	0	1	0	19.29
Wensloff	1	2	0	2	1	0	0	0	0.00
Chandler	1	2	2	3	1	0	0	0	9.00
Raschi	1	1.1	0	1	2	0	0	0	6.75
Brooklyn (NL)									
Totals	7	60	67	38	37	3	4	1	5.55
Gregg	3	14.2	9	8	10	0	1	0	3.55
Casey	6	10.1	5	3	2	0	1	2	0.87
Hatten	4	9	12	7	5	0	0	0	7.00
Branca	3	8.1	12	5	8	1	1	0	8.64
Barney	3	6.2	4	10	3	0	1	0	2.70
Lombardi	2	6.2	14	1	5	0	0	0	12.15
Behrman	5	6.1	9	1	3	0	0	0	7.11
Taylor	1	0	2	1	0	0	0	0	0.00

1948 Nylons and Orchids

The Boston Red Sox and Cleveland Indians struggled through their 154-game schedule, only to find themselves having to play another game before the American League had a team to present to the World Series. What had happened for the first time in junior circuit history was a flat-footed tie for first place. Contributing to the excitement was the fact that the Yankees, led by Joe DiMaggio, stayed in the race until they were eliminated by the Red Sox on the next-to-last day of the season.

The winner-take-all playoff game was set in motion when Cleveland dropped their finale to Detroit, and Boston again got by New York. The climax was staged in Boston and was short-lived as Lou Boudreau poled two home runs, and rookie Gene Bearden allowed five hits in an 8-3 rout.

Despite producing the league batting champion in Ted Williams (.369), getting Joe McCarthy out of retirement, and making a great rush after a dismal 14-28 Memorial Day record, the Red Sox—in a sense—never stood a chance against the Cleveland spirit, promoted by Indian owner Bill Veeck. Included in Veeck's bag of surprises, which was vital and fresh enough to snap the turnstiles 2,260,627 times (a then all-time high) were: giving away nylons to women fans, flying in thousands of orchids from Hawaii, opening a nursery under the stands of Memorial Stadium so mothers could attend games, honoring Mr. Average Fan—Joe Earley—with gifts at home plate, having a special night and raising $40,000 for pitcher Don Black, who days before had suffered a cerebral hemorrhage while at bat, and signing the 41-year-old legendary black pitcher from the Kansas City Monarchs, Leroy Satchel Paige.

Stunts and promotions alone did not bring Veeck a pennant. In addition to Boudreau, who finished second in batting with .355 and won the MVP, there was Bearden, tops with a 2.43 E.R.A., Bob Lemon, and Bob Feller, as well as ace reliever Russ Christopher and southpaw Sam Zoldak, whom Veeck picked up in trades.

Stan Musial dominated the National League statistics and narrowly missed the Triple Crown by one home run, while the Braves climaxed an upsurge under manager Billy Southworth to clinch their first flag since their miraculous predecessors turned the trick in 1914. The story for the Braves began with a phrase glorifying two of their pitchers that is certain to be echoed whenever the National League winner of 1948 is mentioned—"Spahn and Sain and two days of rain", attributed to Warren Spahn and Johnny Sain, who combined for 39 victories with Sain contributing a league high of 24.

Also responsible for the Braves' success was shortstop Al Dark, who hit .322 in his first full season, and second baseman Eddie Stanky, who was acquired in a trade from Brooklyn during spring training and hit .320 before being sidelined in early July with a broken ankle.

In the Series opener, Feller allowed two hits and lost 1-0 to Sain on a run scored by Phil Masi after the Indians were sure that he had been picked off second base. The umpire disagreed and Tommy Holmes promptly singled Masi home. Lemon evened matters the next day with a 4-1 win over Spahn, and Bearden put the Indians in front to stay with a 2-0 win over the Braves in the third game. In the fourth game, Boston again got Sain only one run, but fell short as the Indians put two across for Steve Gromek. The Braves' last surge came in the next game as Bob Elliott hit two homers in leading an assault, before Lemon and Bearden combined with a 4-3 win to bring Cleveland their first Series win since 1920.

1948 AMERICAN LEAGUE

CLEVELAND — 1st 97-58 .626 — LOU BOUDREAU (Defeated Boston in a 1 game playoff)

NAME	G by Pos	B	AGE	G	AB	R	H	2B	3B	HR	RBI	BB	SO	SB	BA	SA
TOTALS			29	156	5446	840	1534	242	54	155	802	646	575	54	.282	.431
Eddie Robinson	1B131	L	27	134	493	53	125	18	5	16	83	36	42	1	.254	.408
Joe Gordon	2B144, SS2	R	33	144	550	96	154	21	4	32	124	77	68	5	.280	.507
Lou Boudreau	SS151, C1	R	30	152	560	116	199	34	6	18	106	98	9	3	.355	.534
Ken Keltner	3B153	R	31	153	558	91	166	24	4	31	119	89	52	2	.297	.522
Larry Doby	OF114	L	24	121	439	83	132	23	9	14	66	54	77	9	.301	.490
Thurman Tucker	OF66	L	30	83	242	52	63	13	2	1	19	31	17	11	.260	.343
Dale Mitchell	OF140	L	26	141	608	82	204	30	8	4	56	45	17	13	.336	.431
Jim Hegan	C142	R	27	144	472	60	117	21	6	14	61	48	74	6	.248	.407
Allie Clark	OF65, 3B5, 1B1	R	25	81	271	43	84	5	2	9	38	23	13	0	.310	.443
Walt Judnich	OF49, 1B20	L	32	79	218	36	56	13	3	2	29	56	23	2	.257	.372
J. Berardino	2B20, 1B18, SS12, 3B3	R	31	66	147	19	28	5	1	2	10	27	16	0	.190	.279
2 Bob Kennedy	OF50, 2B2, 1B1	R	27	66	73	10	22	3	2	0	5	4	6	0	.301	.397
Hank Edwards (SJ)	OF41	L	29	55	160	27	43	9	2	3	18	18	18	1	.269	.406
Bob Lemon	P43	R	27	52	119	20	34	9	0	5	21	8	23	0	.286	.487
Joe Tipton	C40	R	26	47	90	11	26	3	0	1	13	4	10	0	.289	.356
Hal Peck	OF9	L	31	45	63	12	18	3	0	0	8	4	8	1	.286	.333
1 Pat Seerey	OF7	R	25	10	23	7	6	0	0	1	6	7	8*	0	.261	.391
Ray Boone	SS4	R	24	6	5	0	2	1	0	0	1	0	2	0	.400	.600
Al Rosen	3B2	R	24	5	5	0	1	0	0	0	0	0	2	0	.200	.200
Ray Murray		R	30	4	4	0	0	0	0	0	0	0	3	0	.000	.000

NAME	T	AGE	W	L	PCT	SV	G	GS	CG	IP	H	BB	SO	SHO	ERA
		30	97	58	.626	30	156	156	66	1409	1246	625	593	26	3.23
Gene Bearden	L	27	20	7	.741	1	37	29	15	230	187	106	80	6	2.43
Bob Lemon	R	27	20	14	.588	2	43	37	20	294	231	129	147	10	2.82
Bob Feller	R	29	19	15	.559	3	44	38	18	280	255	116	164	2	3.57
Steve Gromek	R	28	9	3	.750	2	38	9	4	130	109	51	50	1	2.84
2 Sam Zoldak	L	29	9	6	.600	0	23	12	4	106	104	24	17	1	2.80
Satchel Paige	R	41	6	1	.857	1	21	7	3	73	61	22	43	2	2.47
Bob Muncrief	R	32	5	4	.556	0	21	9	1	72	76	31	24	1	4.00
Russ Christopher	R	30	3	2	.600	17	45	0	0	59	55	27	14	0	2.90
Eddie Klieman	R	30	3	2	.600	4	44	0	0	80	62	46	18	0	2.59
Don Black (QJ)	R	31	2	2	.500	0	18	10	1	52	57	40	16	0	5.37
1 Bill Kennedy	L	27	1	0	1.000	0	6	3	0	11	16	13	12	0	11.45
Lyman Linde	R	27	0	0	—	0	3	0	0	10	9	4	0	0	5.40
Ernie Groth	R	26	0	0	—	0	1	0	0	1	2	3	0	0	9.00
Mike Garcia	R	24	0	0	—	0	1	0	0	2	3	0	1	0	9.00
Les Webber	R	33	0	0	—	0	1	0	0	1	3	1	1	0	27.00
1 Al Gettel	R	30	0	1	.000	0	5	2	0	8	15	10	4	0	16.88
Butch Wensloff	R	32	0	1	.000	0	2	1	0	2	3	2	1	0	9.00

*Seerey, also with Chicago, league leader in SO with 102

BOSTON — 2nd 96-59 .619 1 — JOE McCARTHY (Defeated by Cleveland in a 1 game playoff)

NAME	G by Pos	B	AGE	G	AB	R	H	2B	3B	HR	RBI	BB	SO	SB	BA	SA
TOTALS			30	155	5363	907	1471	277	40	121	854	823	552	38	.274	.409
Billy Goodman	1B117, 2B2, 3B2	L	22	127	445	65	138	27	4	1	66	74	44	5	.310	.387
Bobby Doerr	2B138	R	30	140	527	94	150	23	6	27	111	83	49	3	.285	.505
Vern Stephens	SS155	R	27	155	635	114	171	25	8	29	137	77	56	1	.269	.471
Johnny Pesky	3B141	L	28	143	565	124	159	26	6	3	55	99	32	3	.281	.365
Stan Spence	OF92, 1B14	L	33	114	391	71	92	17	4	12	61	82	33	0	.235	.391
Dom DiMaggio	OF155	R	31	155	648	127	185	40	4	9	87	101	58	10	.285	.401
Ted Williams	OF134	L	29	137	509	124	188	44	3	25	127	126	41	4	.369	.615
Birdie Tebbetts	C126	R	35	128	446	54	125	26	2	5	68	62	32	5	.280	.381
Wally Moses	OF45	L	37	78	189	26	49	12	1	2	29	21	19	5	.259	.365
Sam Mele	OF55	R	26	80	180	25	42	12	1	2	25	13	21	1	.233	.344
Billy Hitchcock	2B15, 3B15	R	31	49	124	15	37	3	2	1	20	7	9	1	.298	.379
Matt Batts	C41	R	26	46	118	13	37	12	0	1	24	15	9	1	.314	.441
Jake Jones	1B31	R	27	36	105	3	21	4	0	1	8	11	26	1	.200	.267
Babe Martin	C1	R	28	4	4	0	2	0	0	0	0	1	0	0	.500	.500
Lou Stringer	2B2	R	31	4	11	1	1	0	0	0	1	0	3	0	.091	.364
Tom Wright		L	25	1	2	1	1	0	0	0	1	0	0	0	.500	1.500
Neill Sheridan		R	26	2	1	0	0	0	0	0	0	0	1	0	.000	.000
John Ostrowski		R	30	1	1	0	0	0	0	0	0	0	0	0	.000	.000

NAME	T	AGE	W	L	PCT	SV	G	GS	CG	IP	H	BB	SO	SHO	ERA
		30	96	59	.619	13	155	155	70	1379	1445	592	513	11	4.20
Jack Kramer	R	30	18	5	.783	0	29	29	14	205	233	64	72	2	4.35
Joe Dobson	R	31	16	10	.615	2	38	32	16	245	237	92	116	5	3.56
Mel Parnell	L	26	15	8	.652	0	35	27	16	212	205	90	77	1	3.14
Earl Johnson	L	29	10	4	.714	5	35	3	1	91	98	42	45	0	4.55
Ellis Kinder	R	33	10	7	.588	0	28	22	10	178	183	63	53	1	3.74
Denny Galehouse	R	36	8	8	.500	3	31	15	6	137	152	46	38	1	4.01
Boo Ferriss	R	26	7	3	.700	3	31	9	1	115	127	61	30	0	5.24
Mickey Harris	L	31	7	10	.412	0	20	17	6	114	120	59	42	1	5.29
Tex Hughson (SA)	R	32	3	1	.750	0	15	0	0	19	21	7	6	0	5.21
Cot Deal	R	25	1	0	1.000	0	4	3	2	0	3	3	2	0	0.00
2 Earl Caldwell	R	43	1	1	.500	0	8	0	0	11	11	5	0	0	13.00
Mickey McDermott	L	19	0	0	—	0	7	0	0	23	16	35	17	0	6.26
Chuck Stobbs	L	18	0	0	—	0	2	0	0	7	7	4	6	0	6.43
Mike Palm	R	23	0	0	—	0	3	0	0	3	6	5	1	0	6.00
Harry Dorish	R	26	0	1	.000	0	14	1	0	14	18	6	5	0	5.79
Windy McCall	L	22	0	0	—	0	1	0	0	1	1	1	0	0	27.00

NEW YORK — 3rd 94-60 .610 2.5 — BUCKY HARRIS

NAME	G by Pos	B	AGE	G	AB	R	H	2B	3B	HR	RBI	BB	SO	SB	BA	SA
TOTALS			30	154	5324	857	1480	251	75	139	806	623	478	24	.278	.432
George McQuinn	1B90	L	30	94	302	33	75	11	4	11	41	40	38	0	.248	.421
Snuffy Stirnweiss	2B141	R	29	141	515	90	130	20	7	3	32	86	62	5	.252	.336
Phil Rizzuto	SS128	R	30	128	464	65	117	13	2	6	50	60	24	6	.252	.328
Billy Johnson	3B118	R	29	127	446	59	131	26	6	12	64	41	30	0	.294	.446
Tommy Henrich	OF102, 1B46	L	35	146	588	138	181	42	14	25	100	76	42	2	.308	.554
Joe DiMaggio	OF152	R	33	153	594	110	190	26	11	39	155	67	30	1	.320	.598
Johnny Lindell	OF79	R	31	88	309	58	98	17	2	13	55	51	30	0	.317	.511
Gus Niarhos	C82	R	27	83	228	41	61	12	2	0	19	52	15	1	.268	.338
Yogi Berra	C71, OF50	L	23	125	469	70	143	24	10	14	98	25	24	3	.305	.488
Bobby Brown	3B41, SS26, 2B17, OF4	L	23	113	363	62	109	19	5	3	48	48	16	0	.300	.405
Charlie Keller (BH)	OF66	L	31	83	247	41	66	15	2	6	44	41	25	1	.267	.417
Cliff Mapes	OF21	L	26	53	88	19	22	11	1	1	12	6	13	1	.250	.432
Steve Souchock	1B32	R	29	44	118	11	24	3	1	3	11	7	13	3	.203	.322
Sherm Lollar	C10	R	23	22	38	0	8	0	0	0	1	1	6	0	.211	.211
Hank Bauer	OF14	R	25	19	50	6	9	1	1	0	9	6	13	1	.180	.300
Frank Crosetti	2B6, SS5	R	37	17	14	4	4	0	0	0	3	0	2	0	.286	.429
Ralph Houk	C14	R	28	14	29	3	8	2	0	0	3	0	0	0	.276	.345
1 Bud Stewart		L	32	6	5	1	1	0	0	0	1	0	2	0	.200	.400
Joe Collins		R	23	5	5	1	1	0	0	0	0	0	1	0	.200	.200
Charlie Silvera	C4	R	23	4	14	1	8	1	0	0	1	0	0	0	.571	.714
1 Lonny Frey		R	38	4	5	0	1	0	0	0	0	0	0	0	.200	.200
Jack Phillips	1B1	R	26	2	2	0	0	0	0	0	0	0	0	0	.000	.000

NAME	T	AGE	W	L	PCT	SV	G	GS	CG	IP	H	BB	SO	SHO	ERA
		29	94	60	.610	24	154	154	62	1366	1289	641	654	16	3.75
Vic Raschi	R	29	19	8	.704	1	36	31	18	223	208	74	124	6	3.83
Ed Lopat	L	30	17	11	.607	0	33	31	13	227	246	66	83	3	3.65
Allie Reynolds	R	33	16	7	.696	3	39	31	11	236	240	111	101	1	3.78
Spec Shea	R	27	9	10	.474	1	28	22	8	156	117	87	71	3	3.40
Tommy Byrne	L	28	8	5	.615	2	31	11	5	134	79	101	93	1	3.29
Joe Page	R	30	7	8	.467	16	55	1	0	108	116	66	77	0	4.25
Frank Hiller	R	27	5	2	.714	0	22	5	1	62	59	30	25	0	4.06
Red Embree	R	30	5	3	.625	0	20	8	4	77	77	30	25	0	3.74
Bob Porterfield	R	24	5	3	.625	0	16	12	2	78	85	34	30	1	4.50
1 Karl Drews	R	28	2	3	.400	1	19	2	0	38	35	31	11	0	3.79
1 Randy Gumpert	R	30	1	0	1.000	0	15	0	0	25	27	6	12	0	2.88
Cuddles Marshall	R	23	0	0	—	0	3	0	0	0	0	2	0	0	0.00
Dick Starr	R	27	0	0	—	0	2	0	0	2	0	2	0	0	4.50

PHILADELPHIA · 4th 84-70 .545 12.5 · CONNIE MACK

NAME	G by Pos	B	AGE	G	AB	R	H	2B	3B	HR	RBI	BB	SO	SB	BA	SA
TOTALS			30	154	5181	729	1345	231	47	68	685	726	523	40	.260	.362
Ferris Fain	1B145	L	27	145	520	81	146	27	6	7	88	113	37	10	.281	.396
Pete Suder	2B148	R	32	148	519	64	125	23	5	7	60	60	60	1	.241	.345
Eddie Joost	SS135	R	32	135	509	99	127	22	2	16	55	119	87	1	.250	.395
Hank Majeski	3B142, SS8	R	31	148	590	88	183	41	4	12	120	48	43	2	.310	.454
Elmer Valo	OF109	L	27	113	383	72	117	17	4	3	46	81	13	10	.305	.394
Sam Chapman	OF118	R	32	123	445	58	115	18	6	13	70	55	50	6	.258	.413
Barney McCosky	OF134	L	31	135	515	95	168	21	5	0	46	68	22	1	.326	.386
Buddy Rosar	C90	R	33	90	302	30	77	13	0	4	41	39	12	0	.255	.338
Don White	OF54, 3B17	R	29	86	253	29	62	14	2	1	28	19	16	0	.245	.328
2 Ray Coleman	OF53	L	26	68	210	32	51	6	6	0	21	31	17	4	.243	.329
Mike Guerra	C47	R	35	53	142	18	30	4	2	1	23	18	13	2	.211	.289
Carl Scheib	P32, OF2	R	21	52	104	14	31	8	3	2	21	8	17	0	.298	.490
Herman Franks	C27	L	34	40	98	10	22	7	1	1	14	16	11	0	.224	.347
Rudy York	1B14	R	34	31	51	4	8	0	0	0	6	7	15	0	.157	.157
Skeeter Webb	2B9, SS8	R	38	23	54	5	8	2	0	0	5	3	3	0	.148	.185
Billy DeMars	SS9, 2B1, 3B1	R	22	18	29	3	5	0	0	0	1	5	3	1	.172	.172
1 George Binks	OF14	L	33	17	41	2	4	1	0	0	2	2	2	1	.098	.122
Bob Wellman	1B2, OF1	R	22	4	10	1	2	0	1	0	0	3	2	0	.200	.400
Nellie Fox	2B3	L	20	3	13	0	2	0	0	0	0	1	0	1	.154	.154

Earle Brucker 22 L 1-6, Bobby Estalella (SM) 37

NAME	T	AGE	W	L	PCT	SV	G	GS	CG	IP	H	BB	SO	SHO	ERA
		26	84	70	.545	18	154	154	74	1369	1456	638	486	7	4.42
Dick Fowler (AJ)	R	27	15	8	.652	2	29	26	16	205	221	76	50	1	3.78
Carl Scheib	R	21	14	8	.636	0	32	24	15	199	219	76	44	1	3.93
Lou Brissie	L	24	14	10	.583	5	39	25	11	194	202	95	127	4	4.13
Joe Coleman	R	25	14	13	.519	0	33	29	13	216	224	90	86	3	4.08
Phil Marchildon	R	34	9	15	.375	0	33	30	12	226	214	131	66	1	4.54
Bob Savage	R	26	5	1	.833	5	33	1	0	75	98	33	26	0	6.24
Charlie Harris	R	22	5	2	.714	5	45	0	0	94	89	35	42	0	4.12
Bill McCahan (SA)	R	27	4	7	.364	0	17	15	5	87	98	65	20	0	5.69
2 Nels Potter	R	36	2	2	.500	1	8	0	0	18	17	5	13	0	4.00
Walt Holborow	R	34	1	2	.333	0	5	1	1	17	32	7	3	0	5.82
Bill Dietrich	R	38	1	2	.333	0	4	0	0	15	21	9	5	0	6.00
Alex Kellner	L	23	0	0	—	0	13	1	0	23	21	16	14	0	7.83

DETROIT · 5th 78-76 .506 18.5 · STEVE O'NEILL

NAME	G by Pos	B	AGE	G	AB	R	H	2B	3B	HR	RBI	BB	SO	SB	BA	SA
TOTALS			29	154	5235	700	1396	219	58	78	661	671	504	22	.267	.375
George Vico	1B142	L	24	144	521	50	139	23	9	8	58	39	39	2	.267	.392
Eddie Mayo	2B86, 3B10	R	38	106	370	35	92	20	1	2	42	30	19	1	.249	.324
Johnny Lipon	SS117, 2B1, 3B1	R	25	121	458	65	133	18	8	5	52	68	22	4	.290	.397
George Kell (BW-BJ)	3B92	R	25	92	368	47	112	24	3	2	44	33	15	2	.304	.402
Pat Mullin	OF131	L	30	138	496	91	143	16	11	23	80	77	57	1	.288	.504
Hoot Evers	OF138	R	27	139	538	81	169	33	6	10	103	51	31	3	.314	.454
Vic Wertz	OF98	L	23	119	391	49	97	19	9	7	67	48	70	0	.248	.396
Bob Swift	C112	R	33	113	292	23	65	6	0	4	33	51	29	1	.223	.284
Dick Wakefield	OF86	L	27	110	322	50	89	20	5	11	53	70	55	0	.276	.472
Neil Berry	SS41, 2B26	R	26	87	256	46	68	8	1	0	16	37	23	1	.266	.305
Fred Hutchinson	P33	R	28	76	112	11	23	1	0	1	12	23	9	3	.205	.241
Jimmy Outlaw	3B47, OF13	R	35	74	198	33	56	12	0	0	25	31	15	0	.283	.343
Eddie Lake (BG)	2B45, 3B17	R	32	64	198	51	52	6	0	2	18	57	20	3	.263	.323
Paul Campbell	1B27	L	30	59	83	15	22	1	1	1	11	10	1	0	.265	.337
Hal Wagner	C52	L	32	54	109	10	22	3	0	0	10	20	11	1	.202	.229
Hank Riebe	C24	R	26	25	62	0	12	0	0	0	5	3	5	0	.194	.194
Joe Ginsberg	C11	L	21	11	36	7	13	0	0	0	1	5	3	1	.361	.361
Johnny Groth	OF4	R	21	6	17	3	8	3	0	1	5	1	1	0	.471	.824
Johnny Bero	2B2	R	25	4	9	2	0	0	0	0	1	1	1	0	.000	.000
Doc Cramer	OF1	R	42	4	4	1	0	0	0	0	0	0	0	0	.000	.000
Ed Mierkowicz	OF1	R	24	3	5	0	1	0	0	0	1	2	1	0	.200	.200
John McHale	1B	L	27	1	1	0	0	0	0	0	0	0	0	0	.000	.000

NAME	T	AGE	W	L	PCT	SV	G	GS	CG	IP	H	BB	SO	SHO	ERA
		28	78	76	.506	22	154	154	60	1377	1367	589	678	5	4.15
Hal Newhouser	L	27	21	12	.636	1	39	35	19	272	249	99	143	2	3.01
Virgil Trucks	R	31	14	13	.519	2	43	26	7	212	190	85	123	0	3.78
Fred Hutchinson	R	28	13	11	.542	0	33	28	15	221	223	48	92	0	4.32
Dizzy Trout	R	33	10	14	.417	2	32	23	11	184	193	73	91	2	3.42
Ted Gray	L	23	6	2	.750	0	26	11	3	85	73	72	60	1	4.24
Billy Pierce	L	21	3	0	1.000	0	22	5	0	55	47	51	36	0	6.38
Stubby Overmire	L	29	3	4	.429	3	37	4	0	66	89	31	14	0	6.00
Hal White	R	29	2	1	.667	1	27	0	0	43	46	26	17	0	6.07
Lou Kretlow	R	27	1	1	.500	0	5	2	1	23	21	11	9	0	4.70
Al Benton	R	37	2	2	.500	3	30	0	0	44	45	36	18	0	5.73
Art Houtteman	R	20	2	16	.111	0	43	20	4	164	186	52	74	0	4.66
Rufe Gentry	R	30	0	0	—	0	4	0	0	7	5	5	1	0	2.57

ST. LOUIS · 6th 59-94 .386 37 · ZACK TAYLOR

NAME	G by Pos	B	AGE	G	AB	R	H	2B	3B	HR	RBI	BB	SO	SB	BA	SA
TOTALS			27	155	5303	671	1438	251	62	63	623	578	572	63	.271	.378
Chuck Stevens	1B85	B	29	85	287	34	75	12	4	1	26	41	26	2	.261	.341
Jerry Priddy	2B146	R	29	151	560	96	166	40	9	8	79	86	71	6	.296	.443
Eddie Pellagrini	SS98	R	30	105	290	31	69	8	3	2	27	34	40	1	.238	.307
Bob Dillinger	3B153	R	29	153	644	110	207	34	10	2	44	65	34	28	.321	.415
Al Zarilla	OF136	L	29	144	529	77	174	39	4	12	74	48	48	11	.329	.482
Paul Lehner	OF89, 1B2	L	28	103	333	23	92	15	4	1	46	30	19	0	.276	.363
Whitey Platt	OF114	R	27	123	454	57	123	22	10	7	82	39	51	1	.271	.410
Les Moss	C103	R	23	107	335	35	86	12	1	14	46	39	50	0	.257	.424
Sam Dente	SS76, 3B6	R	26	98	267	26	72	11	2	0	22	22	8	1	.270	.326
Roy Partee	C76	R	30	82	231	14	47	8	1	0	17	25	21	2	.203	.247
Dick Kokos	OF71	L	20	71	258	40	77	15	3	4	40	28	32	4	.298	.426
Hank Arft	1B69	R	26	69	248	25	59	10	3	5	38	45	43	1	.238	.363
2 Don Lund	OF45	R	25	63	161	21	40	7	4	3	25	10	17	0	.248	.398
Andy Anderson	2B21, SS10, 1B2	R	25	51	87	13	24	5	1	1	12	8	15	0	.276	.391
Joe Schultz		L	29	43	37	0	7	0	0	0	4	6	3	0	.189	.189
Pete Layden	OF30	R	28	41	104	11	26	2	1	0	4	6	10	4	.250	.288
1 Ray Coleman	OF5	L	26	17	29	2	5	0	0	0	1	2	1	0	.172	.241
2 George Binks	OF5, 1B4	L	33	15	23	2	5	0	0	0	1	2	1	0	.217	.217
Ken Wood	OF24	R	24	10	24	2	2	0	0	0	2	0	4	0	.083	.167
Jerry McCarthy	1B2	R	25	2	3	0	1	0	0	0	0	0	1	0	.333	.333
Tom Jordan		R	28	1	1	0	0	0	0	0	0	0	0	0	.000	.000

NAME	T	AGE	W	L	PCT	SV	G	GS	CG	IP	H	BB	SO	SHO	ERA
		27	59	94	.386	20	155	155	35	1373	1513	737	531	4	5.01
Fred Sanford	R	28	12	21	.364	2	42	33	9	227	250	91	79	1	4.64
Cliff Fannin	R	24	10	14	.417	1	34	29	10	214	198	104	102	3	4.16
2 Bill Kennedy	L	27	7	8	.467	0	26	20	3	132	132	104	77	0	4.70
Ned Garver	R	22	7	11	.389	5	38	24	7	198	200	95	75	0	3.41
Frank Biscan	L	28	6	7	.462	2	47	4	1	99	129	71	45	0	6.09
Joe Ostrowski	L	31	4	6	.400	3	26	9	3	78	108	17	20	0	6.08
2 Karl Drews	R	28	3	2	.600	0	20	2	0	38	43	38	11	0	8.05
Bryan Stephens	R	27	3	6	.333	3	43	12	2	123	141	67	35	0	6.00
1 Sam Zoldak	L	29	2	4	.333	0	11	9	0	54	64	19	13	0	4.67
Al Widmar	R	23	2	6	.250	1	49	0	0	83	88	48	34	0	4.45
Blackie Schwamb	R	21	1	1	.500	0	12	5	0	32	44	21	7	0	8.44
1 Nels Potter	R	36	1	1	.500	0	2	2	0	17	4	4	0		5.40
Ray Shore	R	27	1	2	.333	0	17	4	0	38	40	35	12	0	6.39
Jim Wilson	R	26	0	0	—	0	4	0	3	5	5	1		0	12.00
1 Clem Dreisewerd	L	32	0	2	.000	0	13	0	0	22	28	8	6	0	5.73
Al Gerheauser	L	31	0	0	.000	0	14	2	0	23	32	10	10	0	7.43

WASHINGTON · 7th 56-97 .366 40 · JOE KUHEL

NAME	G by Pos	B	AGE	G	AB	R	H	2B	3B	HR	RBI	BB	SO	SB	BA	SA
TOTALS			29	154	5111	578	1245	203	75	31	538	568	572	76	.244	.331
Mickey Vernon	1B150	L	30	150	558	78	135	27	7	3	48	54	43	15	.242	.332
Al Kozar	2B149	R	26	150	577	61	144	25	8	1	58	66	52	4	.250	.326
Mark Christman	SS102, 3B9, 2B3	R	34	120	409	38	106	17	2	1	40	25	19	0	.259	.318
Eddie Yost	3B145	R	21	145	555	74	138	32	11	2	50	82	51	4	.249	.357
2 Bud Stewart	OF114	L	32	118	401	56	112	17	13	7	69	49	27	8	.279	.439
Carden Gillenwater	OF67	R	31	77	221	23	54	10	4	3	21	39	36	4	.244	.367
Gil Coan	OF131	L	26	138	513	56	119	13	9	7	60	41	78	23	.232	.333
Jake Early	C92	L	33	97	246	22	54	7	2	1	28	36	33	2	.220	.276
Al Evans	C85	R	31	93	228	19	59	6	3	2	28	38	20	1	.259	.338
Tom McBride	OF55	R	33	92	206	22	53	9	1	1	29	28	15	2	.257	.325
Earl Wooten	OF73, 1B6, P1	R	24	88	258	34	66	8	3	2	23	24	21	2	.256	.322
John Sullivan	SS57, 2B4	R	27	85	173	25	36	4	1	0	12	22	25	2	.208	.243
Early Wynn	P33	R	28	73	106	9	23	3	1	0	16	14	22	0	.217	.264
Sherry Robertson	OF51	L	29	71	187	19	46	11	3	2	22	24	26	8	.246	.369
Sammy Meeks	SS10, 2B1	R	25	24	33	4	4	1	0	0	2	1	12	0	.121	.152
Len Okrie	C17	R	24	19	42	1	10	0	1	0	1	1	7	0	.238	.286
Angel Fleitas	SS7	R	33	15	13	1	1	0	0	0	0	3	2	0	.077	.077
Leon Culberson	OF11	R	28	12	29	1	5	1	0	0	4	0	5	0	.172	.172
Jim Clark	OF2	L	20	9	12	1	3	0	0	0	0	0	3	0	.250	.250
Larry Drake	OF2	L	27	4	7	0	2	0	0	0	0	1	3	1	.286	.286

Jay Difani R 25 0-2, 2 Clyde Vollmer R 26 2-5, Roberto Ortiz (SM) 33

NAME	T	AGE	W	L	PCT	SV	G	GS	CG	IP	H	BB	SO	SHO	ERA
		30	56	97	.366	22	154	154	42	1357	1439	734	446	4	4.66
Ray Scarborough	R	30	15	8	.652	1	31	26	9	185	166	72	76	0	2.82
Walt Masterson	R	28	8	15	.348	2	33	27	9	188	171	122	72	2	3.83
Early Wynn	R	28	8	19	.296	0	33	31	15	198	236	94	49	1	5.82
Forrest Thompson	L	30	6	10	.375	4	46	7	0	131	134	54	40	0	3.85
Mickey Haefner	L	35	5	13	.278	0	28	20	4	148	151	61	45	0	4.01
Sid Hudson	R	33	4	16	.200	1	39	29	4	182	217	107	53	0	5.88
2 Earl Harrist	R	28	3	3	.500	2	23	4	0	61	70	37	21	0	4.57
Dick Welteroth	R	21	2	1	.667	1	33	2	0	65	73	50	16	0	5.54
Milo Candini	R	30	2	3	.400	3	35	4	1	94	96	63	23	0	5.17
Tom Ferrick	R	33	2	5	.286	10	37	0	0	74	75	38	34	0	4.14
Dick Weik	R	21	1	1	.500	0	3	0	0	13	14	22	8	0	5.54
Ramon Garcia	R	24	0	1	—	0	3	0	0	4	11	4	2	0	15.75
Earl Wooten	L	24	0	0	—	0	2	0	0	2	2	1	1	0	9.00
Cal Cooper	R	25	0	0	—	0	1	0	0	2	4	2	0	0	45.00
1 Marino Pieretti	R	27	0	2	.000	0	9	1	0	12	18	7	6	0	10.50

Alex Carrasquel (SM) 35

CHICAGO · 8th 51-101 .336 44.5 · TED LYONS

NAME	G by Pos	B	AGE	G	AB	R	H	2B	3B	HR	RBI	BB	SO	SB	BA	SA
TOTALS			30	154	5192	559	1303	172	39	55	532	595	528	46	.251	.331
Tony Lupien	1B154	L	31	154	617	69	152	19	3	6	54	74	38	11	.246	.316
Don Kolloway	2B83, 3B18	R	29	119	417	60	114	14	4	6	38	18	18	2	.273	.369
Cass Michaels	SS85, 2B55, OF1	R	22	145	484	47	120	12	6	5	56	69	42	8	.248	.329
Luke Appling	3B72, SS64	R	41	139	497	63	156	16	2	0	47	94	35	10	.314	.354
Taffy Wright	OF114	L	36	134	455	50	127	15	4	1	61	39	18	2	.279	.365
Dave Philley	OF128	B	28	137	488	51	139	26	3	5	42	36	35	8	.287	.387
2 Pat Seerey	OF93	R	25	95	340	44	78	11	0	18	64	61	94*	1	.229	.421
Aaron Robinson	C92	L	33	98	326	47	82	14	2	8	39	46	30	0	.252	.380
Ralph Hodgin	OF79	L	32	104	331	28	88	11	5	1	34	21	11	0	.266	.338
Floyd Baker	3B71, 2B18, SS1	R	31	104	335	47	72	8	3	0	18	73	26	4	.215	.257
Ralph Weigel	C39, OF2	R	26	66	163	8	36	4	1	0	13	16	18	1	.233	.313
Mike Tresh	C34	R	34	39	108	10	27	1	0	0	11	9	5	0	.250	.287
Jack Wallaesa	SS5, OF1	R	28	33	48	2	9	2	0	1	6	5	15	0	.188	.250
1 Bob Kennedy	OF30	R	27	30	113	4	28	0	0	1	14	4	17	1	.248	.336
Jim Delsing	OF15	L	22	21	53	3	10	2	0	0	3	4	5	0	.190	.190
Herb Adams	OF4	L	20	5	11	3	3	0	0	0	0	0	0	0	.273	.364
Jerry Scala	OF2	L	21	3	6	1	0	0	0	0	0	0	3	0	.000	.000
Frank Whitman	SS1	R	24	3	4	0	0	0	0	0	0	0	0	0	.000	.000

NAME	T	AGE	W	L	PCT	SV	G	GS	CG	IP	H	BB	SO	SHO	ERA
		30	51	101	.336	23	154	154	35	1346	1454	673	403	2	4.89
Joe Haynes	R	30	9	10	.474	0	27	22	6	150	167	52	40	0	3.96
Bill Wight	L	26	9	20	.310	1	34	32	7	223	238	135	68	1	4.80
2 Al Gettel	R	30	8	10	.444	1	28	18	7	148	154	60	49	0	4.01
2 Marino Pieretti	R	27	6	10	.375	1	21	18	4	120	117	52	28	0	4.95
Howie Judson	R	22	4	5	.444	8	40	5	1	107	102	56	38	0	4.79
Glen Moulder	R	30	3	6	.333	2	33	9	2	83	108	54	26	0	6.38
Ike Pearson	R	31	2	3	.400	1	23	2	0	53	62	27	12	0	4.92
2 Randy Gumpert	R	30	2	2	.500	0	16	11	6	97	103	13	31	1	3.80
Frank Papish	L	28	3	2	.600	0	18	5	1	95	97	75	41	0	5.02
Orval Grove	R	28	2	10	.167	1	32	11	1	88	110	42	18	0	6.14
1 Earl Harrist	R	28	1	1	.250	0	11	1	0	23	23	13	14	0	5.87
1 Earl Caldwell	R	43	1	5	.167	3	23	0	0	30	41	12	10	0	5.31
Fred Bradley	R	27	0	0	—	0	6	1	0	16	11	4	2	0	4.50
Jim Goodwin	L	24	0	0	—	0	3	0	0	3	4	1	1	0	9.00
Marv Rotblatt	L	20	0	1	—	0	5	1	0	18	19	23	4	0	8.00
Bob Gillespie	R	29	0	0	—	0	4	0	0	7	8	1	3	0	5.13

*Seerey, also with Cleveland, league leader in SO with 102

BOSTON — 1st 91-62 .595 — BILLY SOUTHWORTH

NAME	G by Pos	B	AGE	G	AB	R	H	2B	3B	HR	RBI	BB	SO	SB	BA	SA
TOTALS			30	154	5297	739	1458	272	49	95	695	671	536	43	.275	.399
Earl Torgeson	1B129	L	24	134	438	70	111	23	5	10	67	81	54	19	.253	.397
Eddie Stanky (BN)	2B66	R	31	67	247	49	79	14	2	2	29	61	13	3	.320	.417
Al Dark	SS133	R	26	137	543	85	175	39	6	3	48	24	36	4	.322	.433
Bob Elliott	3B150	R	31	151	540	99	153	24	5	23	100	131	57	6	.283	.474
Tommy Holmes	OF137	L	31	139	585	85	190	35	7	6	61	46	20	1	.325	.439
Mike McCormick	OF100	R	31	115	343	45	104	22	7	1	39	32	34	1	.303	.417
Jeff Heath (BN)	OF106	R	33	115	364	64	116	26	5	20	76	51	46	2	.319	.582
Phil Masi	C109	R	31	113	376	43	95	19	0	5	44	35	26	2	.253	.343
Clint Conatser	OF76	R	26	90	224	30	62	9	3	3	23	32	27	0	.277	.384
Jim Russell (IL)	OF84	B	29	89	322	44	85	18	4	9	54	46	31	4	.264	.410
Sibby Sisti	2B44, SS26	R	27	83	221	30	54	6	2	0	21	31	34	4	.244	.290
Bill Salkeld	C59	R	31	78	198	26	48	8	1	8	28	42	37	1	.242	.414
Frank McCormick	1B50	R	37	75	180	14	45	9	2	4	34	10	9	0	.250	.389
Connie Ryan	2B40, 3B4	R	28	51	122	14	26	3	0	0	10	21	16	0	.213	.238
Bobby Sturgeon	2B18, SS4, 3B4	R	28	34	78	10	17	3	1	0	4	4	5	0	.218	.282
Al Lyons	P7, OF4	R	29	16	12	2	2	0	0	0	0	2	4	0	.167	.167
1 Danny Litwhiler	OF8	L	31	13	30	0	9	2	0	0	6	4	2	0	.273	.333
Ray Sanders		L	31	5	4	0	1	0	0	0	0	0	0	0	.250	.250
2 Marv Rickert	OF3	R	27	3	13	1	3	0	1	0	2	0	0	0	.231	.385
Paul Burris	C2	R	24	2	4	0	2	0	0	0	0	0	0	0	.500	.500

NAME	T	AGE	W	L	PCT	SV	G	GS	CG	IP	H	BB	SO	SHO	ERA
TOTALS		31	91	62	.595	17	154	154	70	1389	1354	430	579	10	3.38
Johnny Sain	R	30	24	15	.615	1	42	39	28	315	297	83	137	4	2.60
Warren Spahn	L	27	15	12	.556	1	36	35	16	257	237	77	114	3	3.71
Bill Voiselle	R	29	13	13	.500	2	37	30	9	216	226	90	89	2	3.63
Vern Bickford	R	27	11	5	.688	1	33	22	10	146	125	63	60	1	3.27
Bobby Hogue	R	27	8	2	.800	2	40	1	0	86	88	19	43	0	3.24
Red Barrett	R	33	7	8	.467	0	34	13	3	128	132	26	40	0	3.66
Clyde Shoun	L	36	5	1	.833	2	31	2	1	74	77	20	25	0	4.01
3 Nels Potter	R	36	5	2	.714	2	18	7	3	85	77	8	47	0	2.33
Al Lyons	R	29	1	0	1.000	0	7	0	0	13	17	8	5	0	7.62
Glenn Elliott	L	28	1	0	1.000	0	3	1	1	5	1	2	3	0	9.00
Jim Prendergast	L	30	1	1	.500	1	10	2	0	17	30	5	3	0	10.06
Johnny Antonelli	L	18	0	0	—	0	4	0	0	4	2	3	2	0	2.25
Ed Wright	R	29	0	0	—	0	5	0	0	5	9	2	2	0	1.80
Ray Martin	R	23	0	0	—	0	2	0	0	2	1	0	0	0	0.00
Johnny Beazley (SA)	R	30	0	1	.000	0	2	0	0	16	19	7	4	0	4.50
Ernie White	L	31	0	0	—	2	15	0	0	23	13	17	8	0	1.96

ST. LOUIS — 2nd 85-69 .552 6.5 — EDDIE DYER

NAME	G by Pos	B	AGE	G	AB	R	H	2B	3B	HR	RBI	BB	SO	SB	BA	SA
TOTALS			29	155	5302	742	1396	238	58	105	680	594	521	24	.263	.389
Nippy Jones	1B128	R	23	132	481	58	122	21	9	10	81	36	45	2	.254	.397
Red Schoendienst	2B96	B	25	119	408	64	111	21	4	4	36	28	16	1	.272	.373
Marty Marion	SS142	R	30	144	567	70	143	26	4	4	43	37	54	1	.252	.333
Don Lang	3B95, 2B2	R	33	117	323	30	87	14	1	4	31	47	38	2	.269	.356
Enos Slaughter	OF146	L	32	146	549	91	176	27	11	11	90	81	29	4	.321	.470
Terry Moore	OF71	R	36	91	207	30	48	11	0	4	18	27	12	0	.232	.343
Stan Musial	OF155, 1B2	L	27	155	611	135	230	46	18	39	131	79	34	7	.376	.702
Del Rice	C99	R	25	100	290	24	57	10	1	4	34	37	46	1	.197	.279
Erv Dusak	OF68, 2B29, 3B9, SS1, P1	R	27	114	311	60	65	9	2	6	19	49	55	3	.209	.309
Ron Northey	OF67	L	28	96	246	40	79	10	1	13	64	38	25	1	.321	.528
Ralph LaPointe	2B44, SS25, 3B1	R	26	87	222	27	50	3	0	0	15	18	19	1	.225	.239
Whitey Kurowski (AJ)	3B65	R	30	77	220	34	47	8	0	2	33	42	28	0	.214	.277
Bill Baker	C36	R	37	45	119	13	35	10	1	0	15	17	7	1	.294	.395
Murry Dickson	P42	R	31	43	96	7	27	2	0	0	11	1	1	0	.281	.302
2 Babe Young	1B35	L	33	41	111	14	27	5	2	1	13	16	6	0	.243	.351
Del Wilber	C26	R	29	27	58	5	11	2	0	0	10	4	9	0	.190	.224
Joe Garagiola	C23	L	22	24	56	9	6	1	0	2	7	12	9	0	.107	.232
Joe Medwick	OF1	R	36	20	19	0	4	0	0	0	2	1	0	0	.211	.211
Hal Rice	OF8	L	24	8	31	3	10	1	2	0	3	2	4	0	.323	.484
Chuck Diering	OF5	R	25	7	7	2	0	0	0	0	0	2	1	0	1.000	.000
Eddie Kazak	3B6	R	27	6	22	1	6	3	0	0	2	0	1	0	.273	.409

Bobby Young 23 L 0-1, Johnny Bucha 23 R 0-1, 1 Jeff Cross 29 R 0-0, Larry Miggins 22 R 0-1, Lou Klein (SM) 29

NAME	T	AGE	W	L	PCT	SV	G	GS	CG	IP	H	BB	SO	SHO	ERA
TOTALS		30	85	69	.552	18	155	155	60	1369	1392	476	635	13	3.91
Harry Brecheen	L	33	20	7	.741	1	33	30	21	233	193	49	149	7	2.24
Howie Pollet	L	27	13	8	.619	0	33	26	11	186	216	67	80	0	4.55
Murry Dickson	R	31	12	16	.429	1	42	29	11	252	257	85	113	1	4.14
Al Brazle	L	34	8	6	.625	1	42	23	6	156	171	50	55	2	3.81
George Munger	R	29	10	11	.476	0	39	25	7	166	199	74	72	2	4.50
Jim Hearn	R	27	8	6	.571	1	34	13	3	90	92	35	27	0	4.20
Ted Wilks	R	32	6	6	.500	13	57	2	1	131	143	39	71	0	2.61
Gerry Staley	R	27	4	4	.500	0	31	3	0	52	61	21	23	0	6.92
Ken Johnson	L	25	2	4	.333	0	13	4	0	45	43	30	20	0	4.80
1 Ken Burkhart	R	31	0	0	—	1	20	0	0	37	50	14	16	0	5.59
Clarence Beers	R	29	0	0	—	0	1	0	0	6	4	1	1	0	9.00
Erv Dusak	R	27	0	0	—	0	1	0	0	0	1	3	0	0	0.00
Ray Yochim	R	25	0	0	—	0	4	0	0	3	4	3	1	0	0.00
Al Papai	R	31	0	1	.000	0	10	0	0	16	14	7	8	0	5.06

Max Lanier (SM) 32, Freddie Martin (SM) 33

BROOKLYN — 3rd 84-70 .545 7.5 — LEO DUROCHER 35-37 .486 — RAY BLADES 1-0 1.000 — BURT SHOTTON 48-33 .593

NAME	G by Pos	B	AGE	G	AB	R	H	2B	3B	HR	RBI	BB	SO	SB	BA	SA
TOTALS			26	155	5328	744	1393	256	54	91	671	601	684	114	.261	.381
Gil Hodges	1B96, C38	R	24	134	481	48	120	18	5	11	70	43	61	7	.249	.376
Jackie Robinson	2B116, 1B30, 3B6	R	29	147	574	108	170	38	8	12	85	57	37	22	.296	.453
Pee Wee Reese	SS149	R	29	151	566	96	155	31	4	9	75	79	63	25	.274	.390
Billy Cox	3B70, SS6, 2B1	R	28	88	237	36	59	13	2	3	15	38	19	3	.249	.359
Gene Hermanski	OF119	L	28	133	400	63	116	22	7	15	60	64	46	15	.290	.493
Carl Furillo	OF104	R	26	108	364	55	108	20	4	4	44	43	32	6	.297	.407
Marv Rackley	OF74	L	26	88	281	55	92	13	5	0	15	19	25	8	.327	.409
Roy Campanella	C78	R	26	83	279	32	72	11	3	9	45	36	45	3	.258	.416
B. Edwards (SA)	C48, OF21, 3B14, 1B1	R	24	96	286	36	79	17	2	8	54	26	28	4	.276	.434
Eddie Miksis	2B54, 3B22, SS5	R	21	86	221	28	47	7	1	2	16	19	27	5	.213	.281
Arky Vaughan	OF26, 3B8	L	36	65	123	19	30	3	0	3	22	21	8	0	.244	.341
Pete Reiser (JJ)	OF30, 3B6	L	29	64	127	17	30	8	2	1	19	29	21	4	.236	.354
George Shuba	OF56	L	23	63	161	21	43	6	0	4	32	34	31	1	.267	.379
Dick Whitman	OF48	L	27	60	165	24	48	13	0	0	20	14	12	4	.291	.370
Tommy Brown	3B43, 1B1	R	20	54	145	18	35	4	0	2	20	7	17	1	.241	.310
Duke Snider	OF47	L	21	53	160	22	39	6	6	5	21	12	27	4	.244	.450
Preston Ward	1B38	L	21	42	146	9	38	9	2	1	21	15	23	0	.260	.370
Spider Jorgensen (AJ)	3B24	L	28	31	90	15	27	6	2	1	13	16	13	1	.300	.444
1 Don Lund	OF25	R	25	27	69	9	13	4	0	1	5	5	16	1	.188	.290
1 Gene Mauch	2B7, SS1	R	22	12	13	1	2	0	0	0	0	0	4	0	.154	.154
Bobby Bragan	C5	R	30	9	12	0	2	0	0	0	0	0	0	0	.167	.167
Bob Ramazzotti	3B2, 2B1	R	31	4	3	0	0	0	0	0	0	0	1	0	.000	.000

Luis Olmo (SM) 28, Mickey Owen (SM) 32

NAME	T	AGE	W	L	PCT	SV	G	GS	CG	IP	H	BB	SO	SHO	ERA
TOTALS		27	84	70	.545	22	155	155	52	1392	1316	633	670	9	3.76
Rex Barney	R	23	15	13	.536	0	44	34	12	247	193	122	138	4	3.10
Ralph Branca	R	22	14	9	.609	1	36	28	11	216	189	80	122	1	3.50
Joe Hatten	L	31	13	10	.565	0	42	30	11	209	228	94	73	1	3.57
Preacher Roe	L	33	12	8	.600	2	34	22	8	178	156	33	86	2	2.63
Carl Erskine	R	21	6	3	.667	0	17	9	3	64	51	35	29	0	3.23
Erv Palica	R	20	6	6	.500	3	41	10	3	125	111	58	74	0	4.46
Hank Behrman	R	27	5	4	.556	7	34	4	2	91	95	42	42	1	4.05
Paul Minner	L	24	4	3	.571	1	28	2	0	63	61	26	23	0	2.43
Willie Ramsdell	R	32	4	4	.500	4	27	1	0	50	48	41	34	0	5.22
Hugh Casey (XJ)	R	34	3	0	1.000	4	22	0	0	36	59	17	7	0	8.00
Harry Taylor (IL)	R	29	2	7	.222	0	17	13	2	81	90	61	32	0	5.33
Johnny Hall	R	24	0	0	—	0	4	0	0	4	2	6	2	0	6.75
Johnny Van Cuyk	L	26	0	0	—	0	3	0	0	5	4	1	1	0	3.60
Elmer Sexauer	R	22	0	0	—	0	2	0	0	1	2	1	0	0	9.00
Phil Haugstad	R	24	0	0	—	0	1	0	0	1	0	0	0	0	0.00
Clyde King	R	24	0	0	—	0	9	0	0	12	14	6	5	0	8.25
Dwain Sloat	L	29	0	1	.000	0	4	1	0	7	7	8	1	0	6.43
Jack Banta	R	23	0	1	.000	2	9	1	0	13	8	5	5	1	9.00

PITTSBURGH — 4th 83-71 .539 8.5 — BILLY MEYER

NAME	G by Pos	B	AGE	G	AB	R	H	2B	3B	HR	RBI	BB	SO	SB	BA	SA
TOTALS			28	156	5286	706	1388	191	54	108	650	580	578	68	.263	.380
Ed Stevens	1B117	L	23	128	429	47	109	19	6	10	69	43	61	7	.254	.396
Danny Murtaugh	2B146	R	30	146	514	56	149	21	5	1	71	60	40	10	.290	.356
Stan Rojek	SS156	R	29	156	641	85	186	27	5	4	51	61	41	24	.290	.367
Frankie Gustine	3B118	R	28	131	449	60	120	19	2	9	42	42	62	5	.267	.379
Dixie Walker	OF112	L	37	129	408	39	129	19	3	2	54	53	10	2	.316	.392
Wally Westlake	OF125	R	27	132	428	78	122	19	10	17	65	46	40	2	.285	.456
Ralph Kiner	OF154	R	25	156	555	104	147	19	5	40	123	112	61	1	.265	.533
Ed Fitz Gerald	C96	R	24	102	262	31	70	7	3	1	35	32	37	3	.267	.344
Johnny Hopp	OF80, 1B25	R	31	120	392	64	109	15	12	1	31	40	25	5	.278	.385
Clyde Kluttz	C91	R	30	94	271	26	60	12	2	4	20	20	19	3	.221	.325
Max West	1B32, OF16	L	31	87	146	19	26	4	0	8	21	27	28	1	.178	.370
Eddie Bockman	3B51, 2B1	R	27	70	176	23	42	7	1	4	23	17	35	2	.239	.358
Monte Basgall	2B22	R	26	38	51	12	11	1	0	2	6	3	16	0	.216	.353
Ted Beard	OF22	L	27	25	81	15	16	1	3	0	7	12	18	5	.198	.284
Grady Wilson	SS7	R	25	12	10	1	1	1	0	0	1	0	3	0	.100	.200
Johnny Riddle	C10	R	42	10	15	1	3	0	0	0	1	3	0	0	.200	.200
Pete Castiglione	SS1	R	27	4	2	0	0	0	0	0	0	1	0	0	.000	.000
Don Gutteridge		R	36	4	2	0	0	0	0	0	0	0	0	0	.000	.000
Earl Turner	C1	R	25	2	1	0	0	0	0	0	0	0	0	0	.000	.000

NAME	T	AGE	W	L	PCT	SV	G	GS	CG	IP	H	BB	SO	SHO	ERA
TOTALS		31	83	71	.539	19	156	156	65	1371	1373	564	519	5	4.15
Bob Chesnes	R	27	14	6	.700	0	25	23	15	194	180	90	69	0	3.57
Rip Sewell	R	41	13	3	.813	0	21	17	7	122	126	37	36	0	3.47
Elmer Riddle	R	33	12	10	.545	1	28	27	12	191	184	81	63	3	3.49
Vic Lombardi	L	25	10	9	.526	4	38	17	9	163	156	67	54	0	3.70
Kirby Higbe	R	33	8	7	.533	10	56	8	3	158	140	83	86	0	3.36
Fritz Ostermueller	L	40	8	11	.421	2	23	22	10	134	143	41	43	2	4.43
Ernie Bonham	R	34	6	10	.375	0	22	20	7	136	145	23	42	0	4.30
Mel Queen	R	30	4	4	.500	2	38	5	1	66	82	40	34	0	6.68
Elmer Singleton	R	30	4	6	.400	2	38	5	1	92	90	40	53	0	4.99
Hal Gregg	R	26	4	4	.333	1	21	8	1	74	72	34	25	0	4.62
Junior Walsh	R	29	1	0	1.000	0	4	0	0	4	5	9	1	0	11.25
Woody Main	R	26	1	1	.500	0	17	0	0	35	19	12	0	0	8.33
1 Nick Strincevich	R	33	0	0	—	0	4	0	0	4	8	2	1	0	9.00
Cal McLish	R	22	0	0	—	0	2	1	0	5	8	2	1	0	9.00

NEW YORK — 5th 78-76 .506 13.5 — MET OTT 37-38 .493 — LEO DUROCHER 41-38 .519

NAME	G by Pos	B	AGE	G	AB	R	H	2B	3B	HR	RBI	BB	SO	SB	BA	SA
TOTALS			28	155	5277	780	1352	210	49	164	733	599	648	51	.256	.408
Johnny Mize	1B152	L	35	152	560	110	162	26	4	40	125	94	37	4	.289	.564
Bill Rigney	2B105, SS7	R	30	113	424	72	112	17	3	10	43	47	54	4	.264	.389
Buddy Kerr	SS143	R	25	144	496	41	119	16	4	0	46	56	36	9	.240	.288
Sid Gordon	3B115, OF23	R	30	142	521	100	156	20	4	30	107	74	39	8	.299	.537
Willard Marshall	OF142	L	27	143	537	72	146	21	8	14	86	64	34	2	.272	.419
Whitey Lockman	OF144	L	21	146	584	117	167	24	10	18	59	68	37	8	.286	.454
Bobby Thomson	OF125	R	24	138	471	75	117	22	6	16	63	30	77	2	.248	.401
Walker Cooper (KJ)	C79	R	33	91	290	40	77	12	0	16	54	28	29	1	.266	.472
Lucky Lohrke	3B50, 2B36	R	24	97	280	35	70	15	1	5	31	30	30	3	.250	.364
Wes Westrum	C63	R	25	66	125	14	20	3	1	4	16	20	36	1	.160	.296
Les Layton	OF20	R	26	63	91	14	21	4	2	3	12	6	21	0	.231	.429
Johnny McCarthy	1B6	L	38	56	57	6	15	0	1	2	12	2	3	0	.263	.404
Mickey Livingston	C42	R	33	45	99	9	21	5	1	2	13	11	12	0	.212	.333
Don Mueller	OF22	L	21	36	81	12	29	2	0	2	9	4	7	0	.358	.469
Bobby Rhawn	SS14, 3B7	R	29	29	52	5	14	3	1	2	9	5	7	0	.273	.432
2 Lonny Frey	2B13	L	37	29	51	6	13	1	0	1	2	9	4	2	.255	.333
Jack Conway	2B13, SS6, 3B3	R	24	15	38	4	4	1	0	0	3	5	10	0	.245	.388
Sal Yvars	C15	R	24	15	38	4	8	0	0	0	2	0	8	0	.211	.316
Pete Milne	OF9	L	23	9	18	6	4	2	0	0	2	2	5	0	.222	.296
Buddy Blattner	2B7	R	28	8	20	3	4	1	0	0	2	0	3	0	.200	.250

Hal Bamberger 23 L 1-12, Jack Harshman 20 L 2-8, Joe Lafata 26 L 0-1, Danny Gardella (SM) 28, George Hausmann (SM) 32, Nap Reyes (SM) 28

NAME	T	AGE	W	L	PCT	SV	G	GS	CG	IP	H	BB	SO	SHO	ERA
TOTALS		26	78	76	.506	21	155	155	54	1373	1425	551	527	15	3.93
Larry Jansen	R	27	18	12	.600	2	42	36	15	277	283	54	126	4	3.61
Sheldon Jones	R	26	16	8	.667	5	55	21	8	201	204	90	82	3	3.36
Ray Poat	R	30	11	10	.524	0	39	24	7	158	162	67	57	3	4.33
Clint Hartung	R	25	8	8	.500	1	36	19	6	153	146	72	42	2	4.76
Dave Koslo	L	28	8	10	.444	3	35	18	5	149	168	62	58	3	3.87
Andy Hansen	R	23	5	3	.625	1	30	9	3	100	96	36	27	0	2.97
Ken Trinkle	R	28	4	5	.444	7	53	0	0	71	66	41	20	0	3.17
Monte Kennedy	L	26	3	9	.250	0	25	16	7	114	118	57	63	1	4.03
Red Webb	R	23	2	1	.667	0	9	3	0	28	27	10	9	0	3.21
Alex Konikowski	R	20	2	0	1.000	0	8	1	0	33	41	17	9	0	7.64
Thornton Lee	L	41	1	0	1.000	0	11	1	0	33	41	12	17	0	4.36
2 Clem Dreisewerd	L	32	0	0	—	0	4	0	0					0	5.54
Mickey McGowan	R	26	0	0	—	0	2	0	0					0	6.75
3 Paul Erickson	R	32	0	0	—	0	9	0	0					0	4.50
Jack Hallett	R	33	0	0	—	0	2	0	0					0	4.50
Lou Lombard	L	19	0	0	—	0	1	0	0					0	7.20
Hub Andrews	L	23	0	0	—	0	5							0	0.00
Joe Beggs	R	37	0	0	—	0	2							0	6.00
Bobo Newsom	R	40	0	0	.000	0	11			26	35	13	21	0	4.15

Sal Maglie (SM) 31, Adrian Zabala (SM) 31, Harry Feldman (SM) 28, Ace Adams (SM) 36

PHILADELPHIA 6th 66-88 .429 25.5 — BEN CHAPMAN 37-42 .468 — DUSTY COOKE 6-6 .500 — EDDIE SAWYER 23-40 .365

NAME	G by Pos	B	AGE	G	AB	R	H	2B	3B	HR	RBI	BB	SO	SB	BA	SA
TOTALS			27	155	5287	591	1367	227	39	91	548	440	598	68	.259	.368
Dick Sisler	1B120	L	27	121	446	60	122	21	3	11	56	47	46	1	.274	.408
Granny Hamner	2B87, SS37, 3B3	R	21	129	446	42	116	21	5	3	48	22	39	2	.260	.350
Eddie Miller	SS122	R	31	130	468	45	115	20	1	14	61	19	40	1	.246	.382
Putsy Caballero	3B79, 2B23	R	20	113	351	33	86	12	1	0	19	24	58	7	.245	.285
Del Ennis	OF151	R	23	152	589	86	171	40	4	30	95	47	58	2	.290	.525
Richie Ashburn (BG)	OF116	R	21	117	463	78	154	17	4	2	40	60	22	32	.333	.400
Johnny Blatnik	OF105	R	27	121	415	56	108	27	8	6	45	31	77	3	.260	.407
Andy Seminick	C124	R	27	125	391	49	88	11	3	13	44	58	68	4	.225	.368
Harry Walker	OF81, 1B4, 3B1	L	31	112	332	34	97	11	2	2	23	33	30	4	.292	.355
Bert Haas (CN)	3B54, 1B35	R	34	95	333	35	94	9	2	4	34	36	25	8	.282	.357
Bama Rowell	3B18, OF17, 2B12	L	32	97	196	15	47	16	2	1	22	8	14	2	.240	.357
1 Emil Verban	2B54	R	32	55	169	14	39	5	1	0	11	11	5	0	.231	.272
Don Padgett	C19	L	36	36	74	3	17	3	0	0	7	3	2	0	.230	.270
Al Lakeman	C22, P1	R	29	32	68	2	11	2	0	1	4	5	22	0	.162	.235
Willie Jones	3B17	R	22	17	60	9	20	2	0	2	9	3	5	0	.333	.467
Jackie Mayo	OF11	L	22	12	35	7	8	2	1	0	3	7	7	1	.229	.343
Stan Lopata	C4	L	22	6	15	2	2	1	0	0	2	4	4	0	.133	.200
1 Howie Schultz	1B3	R	25	6	13	0	1	0	0	0	1	1	2	0	.077	.077
2 Hal Wagner	C1	L	32	3	1	0	0	0	0	0	0	0	1	0	.000	.000

NAME	T	AGE	W	L	PCT	SV	G	GS	CG	IP	H	BB	SO	SHO	ERA
	R	30	66	88	.429	15	155	155	61	1362	1385	561	552	6	4.08
Dutch Leonard	R	39	17	17	.414	0	34	30	16	226	226	54	92	1	2.51
Schoolboy Rowe	R	38	10	10	.500	2	30	20	8	148	167	31	46	0	4.07
Monk Dubiel	R	30	8	10	.444	4	37	17	6	150	139	58	42	2	3.90
Robin Roberts	R	21	7	9	.438	0	20	20	9	147	148	61	84	0	3.18
Curt Simmons	L	19	7	13	.350	0	31	23	7	170	169	108	86	0	4.87
Ken Heintzelman	L	32	6	11	.353	2	27	16	5	130	117	45	57	2	4.29
Blix Donnelly	R	34	5	7	.417	2	26	19	8	132	125	49	46	1	3.68
Ed Heusser	R	39	3	2	.600	3	33	0	0	74	89	28	22	0	4.99
Sam Nahem	R	32	3	3	.500	0	28	1	0	59	68	45	30	0	7.02
2 Paul Erickson	R	32	2	0	1.000	0	4	2	0	17	19	17	5	0	5.29
Jim Konstanty	R	31	1	0	1.000	0	6	0	0	10	7	2	7	0	0.90
Jocko Thompson	L	31	1	0	1.000	0	2	2	1	13	10	9	7	0	2.77
Lou Possehl	R	22	1	0	.500	0	3	2	1	15	17	4	7	0	4.80
Al Porto	L	22	0	0	—	0	3	0	0	4	2	1	1	0	7.20
Lou Grasmick	R	23	0	0	—	0	2	0	0	5	3	8	2	0	7.20
Al Lakeman	R	29	0	0	—	0	1	0	0	1	1	0	0	0	9.00
Charlie Bicknell	R	19	0	1	.000	0	17	1	0	26	29	17	5	0	5.88
2 Nick Strincevich	R	33	0	1	.000	0	6	1	0	17	28	10	4	0	9.00
Dick Koecher	R	22	0	1	.000	0	3	0	0	6	4	3	2	0	3.00
Oscar Judd	L	40	0	1	.000	0	4	1	0	14	19	11	7	0	7.07

CINCINNATI 7th 64-89 .418 27 — JOHNNY NEUN 44-56 .440 — BUCKY WALTERS 20-33 .377

NAME	G by Pos	B	AGE	G	AB	R	H	2B	3B	HR	RBI	BB	SO	SB	BA	SA
TOTALS			28	153	5127	588	1266	221	37	104	548	478	586	42	.247	.365
Ted Kluszewski	1B98	L	28	113	379	49	104	23	4	12	57	18	32	1	.274	.451
Bobby Adams	2B64, 3B7	R	26	87	262	33	78	20	3	1	21	25	23	6	.298	.408
Virgil Stallcup	SS148	R	26	149	539	40	123	30	4	3	65	18	52	2	.228	.315
Grady Hatton	3B123, 2B3, SS2, OF1	L	25	133	458	58	110	17	2	9	44	72	50	7	.240	.345
Frankie Baumholtz	OF110	L	28	128	415	57	123	19	5	4	30	27	32	8	.296	.395
Johnny Wyrostek	OF130	L	28	136	512	74	140	24	9	17	76	52	63	7	.273	.455
Hank Sauer	OF132, 1B12	R	31	145	530	78	138	24	1	35	90	60	85	2	.260	.504
Ray Lamanno	C125	R	28	127	385	31	93	12	0	9	27	48	32	2	.242	.273
2 Danny Litwhiler	OF83, 3B15	R	31	106	338	51	93	19	2	14	44	48	41	1	.275	.467
Claude Corbitt	2B52, 3B16, SS11	R	32	87	258	24	66	11	0	0	18	14	16	4	.256	.298
Benny Zientara	2B60, 3B3, SS2	R	30	74	187	17	35	7	1	2	7	12	11	0	.187	.214
Augie Galan	OF18	L	36	54	77	18	22	3	2	2	16	26	4	0	.286	.455
1 Babe Young	1B31, OF1	L	33	49	130	11	30	7	2	1	12	19	12	0	.231	.338
Dewey Williams	C47	R	32	40	95	9	16	2	0	1	5	10	18	0	.168	.221
2 Howie Fox	1B26	R	25	36	72	9	12	0	0	2	9	4	7	2	.167	.250
Ray Mueller (BN)	C10	R	36	14	34	2	7	1	0	0	2	4	3	0	.206	.235
1 Marv Rickert	OF7	R	27	8	6	0	1	0	0	0	0	0	3	0	.167	.167
Steve Filipowicz	OF7	R	27	7	26	0	9	1	0	0	3	2	1	0	.346	.423
1 Clyde Vollmer	OF2	R	26	7	9	0	1	0	0	0	0	0	1	0	.111	.111
Hugh Poland		L	35	3	3	0	1	0	0	0	0	0	0	0	.333	.333

NAME	T	AGE	W	L	PCT	SV	G	GS	CG	IP	H	BB	SO	SHO	ERA
		28	64	89	.418	20	153	153	40	1343	1410	572	599	8	4.48
Johnny Vander Meer	L	33	17	14	.548	0	33	33	16	232	204	124	120	3	3.41
Herm Wehmeier	R	21	11	8	.579	0	33	24	6	147	179	75	56	0	5.88
Ken Raffensberger	L	30	11	12	.478	0	40	24	7	180	187	37	57	4	3.85
Harry Gumbert	R	38	10	8	.556	17	61	0	0	106	123	34	25	0	3.48
Ewell Blackwell (AJ)	R	25	7	9	.438	1	22	20	4	139	134	52	114	1	4.53
Howie Fox	R	27	6	9	.400	1	34	24	5	171	185	62	63	0	4.53
Kent Peterson	L	22	2	15	.118	1	43	17	2	137	146	59	64	0	4.60
Bud Lively	R	23	0	0	—	0	10	0	0	23	13	11	12	0	2.35
Eddie Erautt	R	29	0	0	—	0	2	0	0	2	3	0	2	0	6.00
Ken Holcombe	R	31	0	1	.000	0	30	2	1	60	60	42	33	0	4.50
Walker Cress	R	31	0	0	.000	0	2	0	0	3	5	4	0	0	9.00
Johnny Hetki	R	26	0	1	.000	0	7	3	3	32	38	14	10	0	4.22
Jim Blackburn	R	24	0	2	.000	0	16	0	0	32	38	14	10	0	6.86
2 Ken Burkhart	R	31	0	0	.000	0	16	0	0	42	46	16	14	0	6.86
Bucky Walters	R	39	0	0	.000	0	7	5	1	35	42	18	19	0	4.63
Tommy Hughes	R	28	0	0	.000	0	12	4	0	27	43	24	7	0	9.00

CHICAGO 8th 64-90 .416 27.5 — CHARLIE GRIMM

NAME	G by Pos	B	AGE	G	AB	R	H	2B	3B	HR	RBI	BB	SO	SB	BA	SA
TOTALS			28	155	5352	597	1402	225	44	87	564	443	578	39	.262	.369
Eddie Waitkus	1B116, OF20	L	28	139	562	87	166	27	10	7	44	43	19	11	.295	.416
Hank Schenz	2B78, 3B5	R	22	96	337	43	88	17	1	1	14	18	15	3	.261	.326
Roy Smalley	SS124	R	22	124	361	25	78	11	4	9	36	23	76	0	.216	.302
Andy Pafko	3B139	R	27	142	548	82	171	26	5	19	101	50	50	3	.312	.516
Bill Nicholson	OF136	L	33	143	494	68	129	24	5	19	67	81	60	2	.261	.445
Hal Jeffcoat	OF119	R	23	134	473	53	132	16	4	4	24	68	88	8	.279	.355
Peanuts Lowrey	OF103, 3B9, 2B2, SS1	R	30	129	435	47	128	12	3	2	54	34	31	2	.294	.349
Bob Scheffing	C78	R	34	102	293	23	88	18	2	5	45	22	27	0	.300	.427
Phil Cavarretta	1B41, OF40	L	31	111	334	41	93	16	5	3	40	35	29	4	.278	.383
Clarence Maddern	OF55	R	26	80	214	16	54	12	1	4	27	10	25	0	.252	.374
Rube Walker	C44	L	27	79	171	17	47	8	0	5	26	24	17	0	.275	.409
Clyde McCullough	C51	R	31	69	172	10	36	4	2	1	7	15	25	0	.209	.273
2 Emil Verban	2B56	R	32	56	248	37	73	15	1	1	16	4	7	2	.294	.375
2 Gene Mauch	2B26, SS19	R	22	53	138	18	28	3	2	1	7	26	10	1	.203	.275
Dick Culler	SS43, 2B21	R	33	48	89	4	15	2	0	0	5	13	3	0	.169	.191
2 Jeff Cross	SS9, 2B1	R	29	16	20	1	2	0	0	0	0	0	4	0	.100	.100
Cliff Aberson	OF8	R	26	12	32	1	6	1	0	1	1	1	5	0	.188	.313
Dummy Lynch	2B1	R	22	7	7	3	2	0	0	1	0	1	1	0	.286	.714
Don Johnson	2B2, 3B2	R	36	6	12	0	3	0	0	0	0	0	1	1	.250	.250
Carmen Mauro	OF2	L	21	3	5	2	1	0	0	1	0	1	1	0	.200	.800
Carl Sawatski		L	20	2	2	0	0	0	0	0	0	0	2	0	.000	.000

NAME	T	AGE	W	L	PCT	SV	G	GS	CG	IP	H	BB	SO	SHO	ERA
		28	64	90	.416	10	155	155	51	1356	1355	609	636	7	4.00
Johnny Schmitz	L	27	18	13	.581	1	34	30	19	242	186	97	100	2	2.64
Russ Meyer	R	24	10	10	.500	0	29	26	8	165	157	77	89	3	3.65
Jess Dobernic	R	30	7	2	.778	1	54	0	0	86	67	40	48	0	3.14
Doyle Lade	R	27	5	6	.455	0	19	12	8	87	99	31	29	0	4.03
Ralph Hamner	R	31	5	9	.357	0	27	17	5	111	110	69	53	0	4.70
Hank Borowy	R	32	5	10	.333	1	39	17	2	127	146	49	60	1	4.89
Bob Rush	R	22	5	11	.313	0	36	16	4	133	153	37	72	0	3.92
Dutch McCall	L	27	4	13	.235	0	30	20	5	151	158	85	89	0	4.83
Bob Chipman	L	29	2	1	.667	0	34	3	0	60	73	24	16	0	3.60
Cliff Chambers	L	26	2	9	.182	0	29	12	3	104	100	48	51	1	4.41
Emil Kush	R	31	1	4	.200	1	34	1	0	72	70	37	31	0	4.38
1 Paul Erickson	R	32	0	0	—	0	3	0	0	6	7	6	4	0	6.00
Don Carlsen	R	21	0	0	—	0	3	0	0	3	2	0	2	0	4.50
Tony Jacobs	R	22	0	0	—	0	1	0	0	1	3	3	0	0	21.00
Warren Hacker	R	23	0	1	.000	0	3	1	0	7	3	0	1	0	7.20
Ben Wade	R	25	0	0	.000	0	2	0	0	5	4	4	1	0	7.20
Hank Wyse (AJ) 30															

WORLD SERIES — CLEVELAND (AL) 4 BOSTON (NL) 2

LINE SCORES

TEAM	1	2	3	4	5	6	7	8	9	10	11	12	R	H	E
Game 1 October 6 at Boston															
CLE (AL)	0	0	0	0	0	0	0	0	0				0	4	0
BOS (NL)	0	0	0	0	0	0	0	1	X				1	2	2
Feller					Sain										
Game 2 October 7 at Boston															
CLE	0	0	0	2	1	0	0	0	1				4	8	1
BOS	1	0	0	0	0	0	0	0	0				1	8	3
Lemon					Spahn, Barrett (5), Potter (7)										
Game 3 October 8 at Cleveland															
BOS	0	0	0	0	0	0	0	0	0				0	5	1
CLE	0	0	1	1	0	0	0	0	X				2	5	0
Bickford, Voiselle (4), Barrett(8)					Bearden										
Game 4 October 9 at Cleveland															
BOS	0	0	0	0	0	0	1	0	0				1	7	0
CLE	1	0	1	0	0	0	0	0	X				2	5	0
Sain					Gromek										
Game 5 October 10 at Cleveland															
BOS	3	0	1	0	0	1	6	0	0				11	12	0
CLE	0	0	0	1	0	0	5	0	0				5	6	2
Potter, Spahn (4)					Feller, Klieman (7), Christopher (7), Paige (7), Muncrief (8)										
Game 6 October 11 at Boston															
CLE	0	0	1	0	0	2	0	1	0				4	10	0
BOS	0	0	0	1	0	0	0	2	0				3	9	0
Lemon, Bearden (8)					Voiselle, Spahn (8)										

COMPOSITE BATTING

NAME	POS	G	AB	R	H	2B	3B	HR	RBI	BA
Cleveland (AL)										
Totals		6	191	17	38	7	0	4	16	.199
Mitchell	OF	6	23	4	4	1	0	0	0	.174
Doby	OF	6	22	1	7	1	0	1	2	.318
Boudreau	SS	6	22	1	6	4	0	0	3	.273
Gordon	2B	6	22	3	4	0	0	1	2	.182
Keltner	3B	6	21	3	2	0	0	0	0	.095
Robinson	1B	6	20	0	6	0	0	0	1	.300
Hegan	C	6	19	2	4	0	0	1	5	.211
Judnich	OF	4	13	1	1	0	0	0	0	.077
Lemon	P	2	5	1	1	0	0	0	0	.200
Bearden	P	2	4	1	2	0	0	0	0	.500
Feller	P	2	4	0	0	0	0	0	0	.000
Tucker	OF	3	3	1	1	0	0	0	0	.333
Clark	OF	1	3	0	0	0	0	0	0	.000
Gromek	P	1	3	0	0	0	0	0	0	.000
Bob Kennedy	OF	3	2	0	1	0	0	0	0	.500
Boone	PH	1	1	0	0	0	0	0	0	.000
Rosen	PH	1	1	0	0	0	0	0	0	.000
Tipton	PH	1	1	0	0	0	0	0	0	.000
Peck	OF	1	0	0	0	0	0	0	0	—

Christopher P 0-0, Klieman P 0-0, Muncrief P 0-0, Paige P 0-0

NAME	POS	G	AB	R	H	2B	3B	HR	RBI	BA
Boston (NL)										
Totals		6	187	17	43	6	0	4	16	.230
Holmes	OF	6	26	3	5	0	0	0	1	.192
Dark	SS	6	24	2	4	1	0	0	0	.167
M. McCormick	OF	6	23	1	6	0	0	0	0	.261
Elliott	3B	6	21	4	7	0	0	2	5	.333
Rickert	OF	5	19	2	4	0	0	1	2	.211
Torgeson	1B	5	18	2	7	3	0	0	4	.389
Stanky	2B	6	14	0	4	1	0	0	1	.286
Salkeld	C	5	9	2	2	0	0	1	4	.222
Masi	C	5	8	1	1	0	0	0	0	.125
F. McCormick	1B	3	5	0	1	0	0	0	0	.200
Sain	P	2	5	0	1	0	0	0	0	.200
Conatser	OF	2	4	0	0	0	0	0	0	.000
Spahn	P	3	2	1	1	0	0	0	0	.500
Potter	P	2	2	0	1	0	0	0	0	.500
Voiselle	P	2	2	0	0	0	0	0	0	.000
Sisti	2B	2	1	0	0	0	0	0	0	.000
Ryan	PH	1	1	0	0	0	0	0	0	.000
Sanders	PH	1	1	0	0	0	0	0	0	.000
Barrett	P	2	0	0	0	0	0	0	0	—
Bickford	P	1	0	0	0	0	0	0	0	—

COMPOSITE PITCHING

NAME	G	IP	H	BB	SO	W	L	SV	ERA
Cleveland (AL)									
Totals	6	53	43	16	19	4	2	1	2.72
Lemon	2	16.1	16	7	6	2	0	0	1.65
Feller	2	14.1	10	5	7	0	2	0	5.02
Bearden	2	10.2	6	1	4	1	0	1	0.00
Gromek	1	9	7	1	2	1	0	0	1.00
Muncrief	1	2	1	0	0	0	0	0	0.00
Paige	1	.2	0	0	0	0	0	0	0.00
Klieman	1	0	1	2	0	0	0	0	∞
Christopher	1	0	2	0	0	0	0	0	∞
Boston (NL)									
Totals	6	52	38	12	26	2	4	0	2.60
Sain	2	17	9	0	9	1	1	0	1.08
Spahn	3	12	10	3	12	1	1	0	3.00
Voiselle	2	10.2	8	2	1	0	0	0	2.53
Potter	2	5.1	6	2	1	0	0	0	8.44
Barrett	2	3.2	1	1	0	1	0	0	0.00
Bickford	1	3.1	4	5	1	0	1	0	2.70

1949 The Arrival of Casey and His Magic Bag

The Yankees' dynasty showed every sign of having crumbled before the start of the season. The Bombers had fallen to third place the past season, age was slowing up several key pinstripers, and both Cleveland and Boston seemed stronger on paper than their 1948 contending squads. Add the fact that Joe DiMaggio would miss the first half of the campaign with a heel injury, and almost no one could realistically forecast a Yankee pennant. But the prognosticators did not take into account that the Yankees had a magician who could change the picture in any crystal ball. Double-talking paragraphs and fashioning a language that reporters struggled to comprehend, Casey Stengel, the 1890-Kansas City, Missouri, product, had little to recommend him for the task. Although he had been a successful manager in the minors, he was better known as a clown in his two previous managerial trials in the majors. But Stengel showed no regard for his past and quickly proved the alchemist as he made moves which turned everything to gold for New York from the opening game.

No one laughed, but Yankee fans smiled as the pinstripers tore out to a quick lead under Stengel's deft direction. Injuries began to knock regulars out of the lineup for sizeable periods, but Casey kept coming up with the right sub at the right time. DiMaggio returned to the lineup in June and belted the ball at a .346 clip the rest of the way. Yogi Berra missed a month with a broken finger but still found time to drive 91 runs across the plate. Only star shortstop Phil Rizzuto escaped the injury hex the entire year. Although Vic Raschi chalked up 21 wins to lead the starters, Stengel relied most heavily on fast-balling reliever Joe Page of all his hurlers.

A strong rush by the Red Sox brought the heavy-hitting Beantowners within shouting distance of the top late in the season, and Stengel had apparently hit the bottom of his magic bag when Boston swept three games from New York on the next-to-last weekend to dump the Yankees into second place. The Sox still held a one-game lead as they came into Yankee Stadium for the final two games of the season. The Bombers knotted the race with an inspirational 5-4 triumph on Saturday, and the next day Stengel proved his magic by taking the pennant on a 5-3 victory. The one prize Stengel did not have in his bag was most valuable player honors. Despite DiMaggio's second-half performance, Boston's Ted Williams was awarded the MVP for leading the Red Sox late season surge.

A veteran St. Louis Cardinal squad, featuring the batting of Stan Musial and Enos Slaughter, the fielding of Marty Marion, and the pitching of Howie Pollet, battled all season long for the top spot in the National League with the youthful Brooklyn Dodgers. Brooklyn, boasting of a fine attack which carried a mediocre pitching staff, was expected to fold at any juncture, but the Cardinals instead reacted to the pressure by dropping four straight tilts in the final week to give Brooklyn a chance to climb in front. The Dodgers applied the coup de grace with a tenth-inning 9-7 win over the Phillies in the curtain-dropper to clinch the title with a narrow one-game edge over the crestfallen Cardinals. The Dodgers' return to the top was spearheaded by Jackie Robinson, who led the league in batting and won the MVP Award, and Gil Hodges and Carl Furillo, who were blossoming into power threats.

The young Brooklyn squad squared off with the veteran Bronx Bombers in Yankee Stadium in game one of the Series and for eight innings both Newcombe and Yankee starter Allie Reynolds kept all runners away from home. Leading off the bottom of the ninth, Old Reliable Tommy Henrich clouted a home run to beat Newcombe and presage the final outcome. Despite a shutout victory behind Preacher Roe the next day, the Dodgers went on to drop the fall classic in five games to prove that Stengel's magic was no laughing matter.

1949 AMERICAN LEAGUE

NAME	G by Pos	B	AGE	G	AB	R	H	2B	3B	HR	RBI	BB	SO	SB	BA	SA
NEW YORK	1st 97-57 .630		**CASEY STENGEL**													
TOTALS			29	155	5196	829	1396	215	60	115	759	731	539	58	.269	.400
Tommy Henrich	OF61, 1B52	L	39	115	411	90	118	20	3	24	85	86	34	2	.287	.526
Jerry Coleman	2B122, SS4	R	24	128	447	54	123	21	5	2	42	63	44	5	.275	.358
Phil Rizzuto	SS152	R	31	153	614	110	169	22	7	5	65	72	34	18	.275	.358
Bobby Brown	3B86, OF3	L	24	104	343	61	97	14	4	6	61	38	18	4	.283	.399
Hank Bauer	OF95	R	26	103	301	56	82	6	6	10	45	37	42	5	.272	.432
Joe DiMaggio (FJ)	OF76	R	34	76	272	58	94	14	6	14	67	55	18	0	.346	.596
Gene Woodling	OF98	L	26	112	296	60	80	13	7	5	44	52	21	2	.270	.412
Yogi Berra (BG)	C109	L	24	116	415	59	115	20	2	20	91	22	25	2	.277	.480
Billy Johnson	3B81, 1B21, 2B1	R	30	113	329	48	82	11	3	8	56	48	44	1	.249	.374
Johnny Lindell	OF65	R	32	78	211	33	51	10	6	6	27	35	27	3	.242	.374
Cliff Mapes	OF108	L	27	111	304	56	75	13	3	7	38	58	50	6	.247	.378
Snuffy Stirnweiss	2B51, 3B4	R	30	70	157	29	41	8	2	0	11	29	20	3	.261	.338
Charlie Keller	OF31	L	32	60	116	17	29	4	1	3	16	25	15	2	.250	.379
Charlie Silvera	C51	R	24	58	130	8	41	2	0	0	13	18	5	2	.315	.331
Dick Kryhoski	1B51	L	24	54	177	18	52	10	3	1	27	9	17	2	.294	.401
1 Jack Phillips	1B38	R	27	45	91	16	28	4	1	1	10	12	9	1	.308	.407
Gus Niarhos	C30	R	28	32	43	7	12	2	1	0	6	13	8	0	.279	.372
2 Johnny Mize	1B6	L	36	13	23	4	6	1	0	1	2	4	2	0	.261	.435
Fenton Mole	1B8	L	24	10	27	2	5	2	1	0	2	3	5	0	.185	.333
Jim Delsing	OF5	L	23	9	20	5	7	1	0	1	3	1	2	0	.350	.550
Joe Collins	1B5	L	26	7	10	2	1	0	0	0	4	6	2	0	.100	.100
Ralph Houk 29 R 4-7, Mickey Witek 33 R 1-1																

NAME		T	AGE	W	L	PCT	SV	G	GS	CG	IP	H	BB	SO	SHO	ERA
			30	97	57	.630	36	155	155	59	1371	1231	812	671	12	3.70
Vic Raschi		R	30	21	10	.677	0	38	37	21	275	247	138	124	3	3.34
Allie Reynolds		R	34	17	6	.739	1	35	31	4	214	200	123	105	2	4.00
Tommy Byrne		L	29	15	7	.682	0	32	30	12	196	125	179	129	3	3.72
Ed Lopat		L	31	15	10	.600	1	31	30	14	215	222	69	70	4	3.27
Joe Page		L	31	13	8	.619	27	60	0	0	135	103	75	99	0	2.60
Fred Sanford		R	29	7	3	.700	0	29	11	3	95	100	57	51	0	3.88
Cuddles Marshall		R	24	3	0	1.000	3	21	2	0	49	48	48	13	0	5.14
Duane Pillette		R	26	2	4	.333	0	12	3	2	37	43	19	9	0	4.38
Bob Porterfield (AJ)		R	25	2	5	.286	0	12	8	3	58	53	29	25	0	4.03
2 Hugh Casey		R	35	1	0	1.000	0	4	0	0	8	11	8	5	0	7.88
Spec Shea		R	28	1	1	.500	1	20	3	0	52	48	43	22	0	5.37
Wally Hood		R	23	0	0	—	0	2	0	0	2	0	1	2	0	4.00
Ralph Buxton		R	38	0	1	.000	2	14	0	0	27	22	16	14	0	4.00
Frank Hiller		R	28	0	2	.000	1	4	1	0	8	9	7	3	0	5.63

NAME	G by Pos	B	AGE	G	AB	R	H	2B	3B	HR	RBI	BB	SO	SB	BA	SA
BOSTON	2nd 96-58 .623 1		**JOE McCARTHY**													
TOTALS			30	155	5320	896	1500	272	36	131	831	835	510	43	.282	.420
Billy Goodman	1B117	L	23	122	443	54	132	23	3	0	56	58	21	2	.298	.363
Bobby Doerr	2B139	R	31	139	541	91	167	30	9	18	109	75	33	2	.309	.497
Vern Stephens	SS155	R	28	155	610	113	177	31	2	39	159	101	73	2	.290	.539
Johnny Pesky	3B148	L	29	148	604	111	185	27	7	2	69	100	19	8	.306	.384
2 Al Zarilla	OF122	L	30	124	474	68	133	32	4	9	71	48	51	4	.281	.422
Dom DiMaggio	OF144	R	32	145	605	126	186	34	5	8	60	96	55	9	.307	.420
Ted Williams	OF155	R	30	155	566	150	194	39	3	43	159	162	48	1	.343	.650
Birdie Tebbetts	C118	R	36	122	403	42	109	14	0	5	48	62	22	8	.270	.342
Matt Batts	C50	R	27	60	157	23	38	9	1	3	31	25	22	1	.242	.369
Billy Hitchcock	1B29, 2B8	R	32	55	147	22	30	6	1	0	9	17	11	2	.204	.259
Tommy O'Brien	OF32	R	30	49	125	24	28	5	0	3	10	21	12	1	.224	.336
Lou Stringer	2B9	R	32	35	41	10	11	4	0	1	6	5	10	0	.268	.439
1 Sam Mele	OF5	R	27	18	46	1	9	1	1	0	7	1	7	14	2	.196	.261
Merrill Combs	3B9, SS1	R	29	14	24	5	5	1	0	0	1	9	0	0	.208	.250
Walt Dropo	1B11	R	26	11	41	3	6	2	0	0	1	3	7	0	.146	.195
1 Stan Spence	OF5	L	34	7	20	3	3	1	0	0	1	6	1	0	.150	.200
Tom Wright		L	25	5	4	1	1	1	0	0	1	1	1	0	.250	.500
Babe Martin	C1	R	29	2	1	0	0	0	0	0	0	0	0	0	.000	.000

NAME		T	AGE	W	L	PCT	SV	G	GS	CG	IP	H	BB	SO	SHO	ERA
			29	96	58	.623	16	155	155	84	1377	1375	661	598	16	3.97
Mel Parnell		L	27	25	7	.781	2	39	33	27	295	258	134	122	4	2.78
Ellis Kinder		R	34	23	6	.793	4	43	30	19	252	251	99	138	6	3.36
Joe Dobson		R	32	14	12	.538	2	33	27	12	213	219	97	87	2	3.85
Chuck Stobbs		L	19	11	6	.647	0	26	19	10	152	145	75	70	0	4.03
Jack Kramer		R	31	6	8	.429	1	21	18	7	112	126	49	24	2	5.14
Mickey McDermott		L	20	5	4	.556	0	12	12	6	80	63	52	50	2	4.05
Tex Hughson		R	33	4	2	.667	3	29	2	0	78	82	41	35	0	5.31
2 Walt Masterson		R	29	3	4	.429	4	18	5	1	55	58	35	19	0	4.25
Earl Johnson		L	30	3	6	.333	0	49	65	29	20	0	7.53				
1 Mickey Harris		L	32	2	3	.400	7	38	53	20	14	0	4.97				
Frank Quinn		R	21	0	0	—	0	22	18	9	4	0	2.86				
Harry Dorish		R	27	0	0	—	5	0	8	7	1	5	0	2.25			
Windy McCall		L	23	0	0	—	1	1	3	10	8	0	12.00				
Boo Ferriss (SA)		R	27	0	0	—	0	4	4	1	1	0	3.86				
Jack Robinson		R	28	0	0	—	0	4	1	1	1	0	2.25				
Denny Galehouse		R	37	0	0	—	0	2	6	1	0	0	13.50				
Johnnie Wittig		R	35	0	0	—	0	1	2	3	0	0	9.00				

NAME	G by Pos	B	AGE	G	AB	R	H	2B	3B	HR	RBI	BB	SO	SB	BA	SA
CLEVELAND	3rd 89-65 .578 8		**LOU BOUDREAU**													
TOTALS			29	154	5221	675	1358	194	58	112	640	601	534	44	.260	.384
Mickey Vernon	1B153	L	31	153	584	72	170	27	4	18	83	58	51	9	.291	.443
Joe Gordon	2B145	R	34	148	541	74	136	18	3	20	84	83	33	5	.251	.407
Lou Boudreau	SS88, 3B38, 1B6, 2B1	R	31	134	475	53	135	20	3	4	60	70	10	0	.284	.364
Ken Keltner	3B69	R	32	80	246	35	57	9	2	8	30	38	26	0	.232	.382
Bob Kennedy	OF98, 3B21	R	28	121	424	49	117	23	5	9	57	37	40	5	.276	.417
Larry Doby	OF147	L	25	147	547	106	153	25	3	24	85	91	90	10	.280	.468
Dale Mitchell	OF149	L	27	149	640	81	203	16	23	3	56	43	11	10	.317	.428
Jim Hegan	C152	R	28	152	468	54	105	19	5	8	55	49	89	1	.224	.338
Ray Boone	SS76	R	25	86	258	39	65	4	4	4	26	38	17	0	.252	.345
Thurman Tucker	OF42	L	31	80	197	28	48	5	2	0	14	18	19	4	.244	.289
Johnny Berardino	3B25, 2B8, SS3	R	32	50	116	11	23	6	0	1	13	14	14	0	.198	.267
Bob Lemon	P37	L	28	46	108	17	29	6	2	7	19	10	20	0	.269	.556
Mike Tresh	C38	R	35	38	37	4	8	0	0	0	1	5	7	0	.216	.216
Allie Clark	OF17, 1B1	R	26	35	74	8	13	4	0	1	9	4	7	0	.176	.270
Hal Peck (KJ)	OF2	L	32	33	29	1	9	1	0	0	9	3	3	0	.310	.345
Bobby Avila	2B5	R	25	31	14	3	3	0	0	0	3	1	3	0	.214	.214
Al Rosen	3B10	R	25	23	44	3	7	1	0	1	5	4	4	0	.159	.205
Luke Easter	OF12	L	33	21	45	6	10	3	0	0	2	6	8	0	.222	.289
Minnie Minoso	OF7	R	26	9	16	3	3	0	0	1	1	2	1	0	.188	.375
1 Hank Edwards	OF5	L	30	5	15	3	4	1	0	1	1	1	2	1	.267	.467
Milt Nielsen 24 L 1-9, Freddie Marsh 25 R 0-0, 2 Herm Reich 31 R 1-2																

NAME		T	AGE	W	L	PCT	SV	G	GS	CG	IP	H	BB	SO	SHO	ERA
			31	89	65	.578	19	154	154	65	1384	1275	611	594	10	3.36
Bob Lemon		R	28	22	10	.688	1	37	33	22	280	211	137	138	2	2.99
Bob Feller		R	30	15	14	.517	0	36	28	15	211	198	84	108	0	3.75
Mike Garcia		R	25	14	5	.737	2	41	20	8	176	154	60	94	5	2.35
Early Wynn		R	29	11	7	.611	0	26	23	6	165	186	57	62	0	4.15
Al Benton		R	38	9	6	.600	10	40	11	4	136	116	51	41	2	2.12
Gene Bearden		L	28	8	8	.500	0	32	19	5	127	140	92	41	0	5.10
Steve Gromek		R	29	4	6	.400	0	27	12	3	92	86	40	22	0	3.33
Satchel Paige		R	42	4	7	.364	5	31	5	1	83	70	33	54	0	3.04
Frank Papish		L	31	1	0	1.000	0	23	3	1	62	54	39	23	0	3.19
Sam Zoldak		L	30	1	2	.333	0	7	3	0	53	60	18	11	0	4.25
Russ Christopher (IL) 31																

DETROIT — 4th 87-67 .565 10 — RED ROLFE

NAME	G by Pos	B	AGE	G	AB	R	H	2B	3B	HR	RBI	BB	SO	SB	BA	SA
TOTALS			29	155	5259	751	1405	215	51	88	709	751	502	39	.267	.378
Paul Campbell	1B74	L	31	87	255	38	71	15	4	3	30	24	32	3	.278	.404
Neil Berry	2B95, SS4	R	27	109	329	38	78	9	1	0	18	27	24	4	.237	.271
Johnny Lipon	SS120	R	26	127	439	57	110	14	6	3	59	75	24	2	.251	.330
George Kell	3B134	R	26	134	522	97	179	38	9	3	59	71	13	7	.343	.467
Vic Wertz	OF155	L	24	155	608	96	185	26	6	20	133	80	61	2	.304	.465
Johnny Groth	OF99	R	22	103	348	60	102	19	5	11	73	65	27	3	.293	.471
Hoot Evers	OF123	R	28	132	432	68	131	21	6	7	72	70	38	6	.303	.428
Aaron Robinson	C108	R	34	110	331	38	89	12	0	13	56	73	21	0	.269	.423
2 Don Kolloway	2B62, 1B57, 3B7	R	30	126	483	71	142	19	3	2	47	49	25	7	.294	.358
Pat Mullin	OF79	L	31	104	310	55	83	8	6	12	59	42	29	1	.268	.448
Eddie Lake	SS38, 2B19, 3B18	R	33	94	240	38	47	9	1	1	15	61	33	1	.196	.254
Bob Swift	C69	R	34	74	189	16	45	6	0	2	18	26	20	0	.238	.302
George Vico	1B53	L	25	67	142	15	27	5	2	4	18	21	17	0	.190	.338
Dick Wakefield	OF32	L	28	59	126	17	26	3	1	6	19	32	24	0	.206	.389
Hank Riebe	C11	R	27	17	33	1	6	2	0	0	2	0	5	1	.182	.242
Jimmy Outlaw		R	36	5	4	1	1	0	0	0	0	0	1	0	.250	.250
Don Lund		R	26	2	2	0	0	0	0	0	0	0	0	0	.000	.000
Bob Mavis		L	31	4	0	0	0	0	0	0	0	0	0	1	—	—
1 Earl Rapp		L	28	1	0	0	0	0	0	0	0	0	1	0	—	—

NAME	T	AGE	W	L	PCT	SV	G	GS	CG	IP	H	BB	SO	SHO	ERA
		28	87	67	.565	12	155	155	70	1394	1338	628	631	19	3.77
Virgil Trucks	R	32	19	11	.633	4	41	32	17	275	209	124	153	6	2.81
Hal Newhouser	L	28	18	11	.621	1	38	35	22	292	277	111	144	3	3.36
Fred Hutchinson	R	29	15	7	.682	1	33	21	9	189	167	52	54	4	2.95
Art Houtteman (FS)	R	21	15	10	.600	2	34	25	13	204	227	59	85	2	3.71
Ted Gray	L	24	10	10	.500	1	34	27	8	195	163	103	96	3	3.51
Lou Kretlow	R	28	3	2	.600	0	25	10	1	76	85	69	40	0	6.16
Dizzy Trout	R	34	3	6	.333	3	33	0	0	59	68	21	19	0	4.42
Marv Grissom	R	31	2	4	.333	0	27	2	0	39	56	34	17	0	6.46
Hal White	R	30	1	0	1.000	2	9	0	0	12	5	4	4	0	0.00
Stubby Overmire	L	30	1	3	.250	0	14	1	0	17	29	9	3	0	10.06
Saul Rogovin	R	27	0	1	.000	0	6			13		7	2	0	13.50
Marlin Stuart	R	30	0	2	.000	1	2	0	0	30	39	35	14	0	9.00

PHILADELPHIA — 5th 81-73 .526 16 — CONNIE MACK

NAME	G by Pos	B	AGE	G	AB	R	H	2B	3B	HR	RBI	BB	SO	SB	BA	SA
TOTALS			31	154	5123	726	1331	214	49	82	680	783	493	36	.260	.369
Ferris Fain	1B150	L	28	150	525	81	138	21	5	3	78	136	51	8	.263	.339
Pete Suder	2B89, 3B36, SS2	R	33	118	445	44	119	24	6	10	75	23	35	0	.267	.416
Eddie Joost	SS144	R	33	144	525	128	138	25	3	23	81	149	80	2	.263	.453
Hank Majeski	3B113	R	32	114	448	62	124	26	5	9	67	29	23	0	.277	.417
Wally Moses	OF92	L	38	110	308	49	85	19	3	1	25	51	19	1	.276	.367
Sam Chapman	OF154	R	33	154	589	89	164	24	4	24	108	80	68	3	.278	.455
Elmer Valo	OF150	L	28	150	547	85	155	27	12	5	85	119	32	14	.283	.404
Mike Guerra	C95	R	36	98	298	41	79	14	1	3	31	37	26	3	.265	.349
Nellie Fox	2B77	L	21	88	247	42	63	6	2	0	21	32	9	2	.255	.296
Taffy Wright	OF35	L	37	59	149	14	35	2	5	2	25	16	6	0	.235	.356
Don White	OF48, 3B4	R	30	57	169	12	36	6	0	0	10	14	12	2	.213	.249
Joe Astroth	C44	R	26	55	148	18	36	4	1	0	12	21	13	1	.243	.284
Buddy Rosar	C31	R	34	32	95	7	19	2	0	0	6	16	5	0	.200	.221
Tod Davis	SS14, 3B12, 2B1	R	24	31	75	7	20	0	1	1	6	9	16	0	.267	.333
Hank Biasatti	1B8	R	27	21	24	6	2	2	0	0	2	3	6	0	.083	.167
2 Augie Galan	OF9	L	37	12	26	4	8	2	0	0	0	9	2	0	.308	.385
Bobby Estalella (SM)	OF6	R	38	8	20	2	5	1	0	0	3	1	2	0	.250	.250
Barney McCosky (XJ)	32															

NAME	T	AGE	W	L	PCT	SV	G	GS	CG	IP	H	BB	SO	SHO	ERA
		24	81	73	.526	11	154	154	85	1365	1359	758	490	9	4.23
Alex Kellner	L	24	20	12	.625	1	38	27	19	245	243	129	94	0	3.75
Lou Brissie	L	25	16	11	.593	2	34	29	18	229	220	118	118	0	4.28
Dick Fowler	R	28	15	11	.577	1	31	28	15	214	210	115	43	4	3.74
Joe Coleman	R	26	13	14	.481	1	33	30	18	240	249	127	109	1	3.86
Carl Scheib	R	22	9	12	.429	0	38	23	11	183	191	118	43	2	5.11
Bobby Shantz	L	23	6	8	.429	2	33	7	4	127	100	74	58	1	3.40
Charlie Harris	R	23	1	1	.500	3	37	0	0	84	92	42	18	0	5.46
Bill McCahan	R	28	1	1	.500	0	7	4	1	21	23	9	3	0	2.57
Jim Wilson	R	27	0	0	—	0	5			7		5	2	0	14.40
Clem Housmann	R	29	0	0	—	0	1	0		1	0		2	0	9.00
Phil Marchildon (SA)	R	35	0	3	.000	0	7	6	0	16	24	19	2	0	11.81

CHICAGO — 6th 63-91 .409 34 — JACK ONSLOW

NAME	G by Pos	B	AGE	G	AB	R	H	2B	3B	HR	RBI	BB	SO	SB	BA	SA
TOTALS			28	154	5204	648	1340	207	66	43	591	702	596	62	.257	.347
2 Charlie Kress	1B95	L	27	97	353	45	98	17	6	1	44	39	44	6	.278	.368
Cass Michaels	2B154	R	23	154	561	73	173	27	9	6	83	101	50	5	.308	.421
Luke Appling	SS141	R	42	142	492	82	148	21	5	5	58	121	24	7	.301	.394
Floyd Baker	3B122, SS3, 2B1	L	32	125	388	38	101	15	4	1	40	84	32	1	.260	.327
Dave Philley	OF145	B	29	146	598	84	176	20	8	0	44	54	51	13	.294	.346
Catfish Metkovich	OF87	L	27	93	338	50	80	9	4	5	45	41	24	5	.237	.331
Herb Adams (BG)	OF48	L	21	56	268	26	61	5	3	0	16	9	16	1	.293	.346
Don Wheeler	C58	R	26	67	192	17	46	9	2	1	22	27	19	2	.240	.323
Steve Souchock	OF39, 1B30	R	30	84	252	29	59	13	5	7	37	25	38	5	.234	.409
Gus Zernial	OF46	R	26	73	198	24	63	17	2	5	38	15	26	0	.318	.500
Joe Tipton	C53	R	27	67	191	20	39	5	3	3	19	27	17	1	.204	.309
Eddie Malone	C51	R	29	55	170	17	46	7	2	1	16	29	19	2	.271	.353
John Ostrowski	OF41, 3B8	R	31	49	158	19	42	9	4	3	31	15	41	4	.266	.468
Gordon Goldsberry	1B21	L	21	39	145	25	36	3	2	1	13	18	9	2	.248	.317
Fred Hancock	SS27, 3B3, OF1	R	29	39	52	7	7	2	1	0	9	8	9	0	.135	.212
Jerry Scala	OF37	L	22	37	120	17	30	7	1	1	13	17	19	3	.250	.350
Billy Bowers	OF20	L	27	26	78	5	15	2	1	0	6	4	5	1	.192	.244
3 Bobby Rhawn	3B19, SS3	R	30	24	73	12	15	4	1	0	5	12	8	0	.205	.288
2 Earl Rapp	OF13	L	28	19	54	3	14	1	1	0	11	5	6	1	.259	.315
Rocky Krsnich	3B16	R	21	16	55	7	12	3	1	1	9	6	4	0	.218	.364
Dick Lane	OF11	R	22	12	42	4	5	0	0	0	4	5	3	0	.119	.119
George Yankowski	C6	R	26	12	18	0	3	1	0	0	2	0	2	0	.167	.222
Bill Higdon	OF6	L	25	11	23	3	7	3	0	0	1	6	3	1	.304	.435
Jim Baumer	SS7	R	18	8	10	2	4	1	1	0	2	1	1	0	.400	.700
1 Don Kolloway	3B2	R	30	4	4	0	0	0	0	0	0	0	0	0	.000	.000
Pat Seerey	OF2	R	26	4	4	1	0	0	0	0	0	3	1	0	.000	.000

NAME	T	AGE	W	L	PCT	SV	G	GS	CG	IP	H	BB	SO	SHO	ERA
		28	63	91	.409	17	154	154	57	1363	1362	693	502	10	4.30
Bill Wight	L	27	15	13	.536	1	35	33	14	245	254	96	78	3	3.31
Randy Gumpert	R	31	13	16	.448	1	34	32	18	234	223	83	78	3	3.81
Bob Kuzava	R	26	10	6	.625	0	29	18	9	157	139	91	83	1	4.01
Billy Pierce	L	22	7	15	.318	0	32	26	8	172	145	112	95	0	3.87
Marino Pieretti	R	28	4	6	.400	4	39	9	0	116	131	54	25	0	5.51
2 Mickey Haefner	L	36	4	6	.400	1	14	12	4	80	84	41	17	1	4.39
Max Surkont	R	27	3	5	.375	4	44	2	0	96	92	60	38	0	4.78
2 Eddie Klieman	R	31	2	0	1.000	3	18	0	0	33	33	15	9	0	3.00
1 Al Gettel	R	31	2	5	.286	1	19	7	1	63	69	26	22	1	6.43
2 Clyde Shoun	L	37	1	1	.500	0	16	0	0	23	37	13	8	0	5.87
Jack Bruner	L	25	1	2	.333	4	2	8		10	8	4		0	7.88
Howie Judson	R	23	1	14	.067	1	26	12	3	108	114	70	36	0	4.58
Bob Cain	L	24	0	0	—	0	4			1	5	5		0	2.45
Alex Carrasquel (SM)	R	36	0	0	—	0	3			1		2		0	13.50
Fred Bradley	R	28	0	0	—	0	4			7		5		0	13.50
Orval Grove	R	29	0	0	—	0	1					1		0	36.00
Bill Evans	R	30	0	1	.000	0	6			6		3	1	0	7.50
Ernie Groth	R	27	0	0	—	0	2			1				0	5.40

ST. LOUIS — 7th 53-101 .344 44 — ZACK TAYLOR

NAME	G by Pos	B	AGE	G	AB	R	H	2B	3B	HR	RBI	BB	SO	SB	BA	SA
TOTALS			28	154	5112	667	1301	213	30	117	624	631	700	38	.254	.377
Jack Graham	1B136	L	32	137	500	71	119	22	1	24	79	61	62	0	.238	.430
Jerry Priddy	2B144	R	29	145	544	83	158	26	4	11	63	80	81	5	.290	.414
Eddie Pellagrini	SS76	R	31	79	235	26	56	8	1	2	15	14	24	2	.238	.306
Bob Dillinger	3B133	R	30	137	644	106	176	22	13	1	51	51	40	20	.324	.417
Dick Kokos	OF138	L	21	143	501	80	131	28	4	23	77	66	91	3	.261	.459
2 Stan Spence	OF87, 1B1	L	34	104	314	46	77	13	3	13	45	52	36	1	.245	.430
Roy Sievers	OF125, 3B7	R	22	140	471	84	144	28	4	16	91	70	75	4	.306	.471
Sherm Lollar	C93	R	24	109	284	28	74	9	1	8	49	32	22	0	.261	.384
John Sullivan	SS71, 3B23, 2B6	R	28	105	243	29	55	8	3	0	18	38	35	5	.226	.284
Paul Lehner	OF56, 1B18	L	29	104	297	25	68	13	0	3	37	16	20	0	.229	.303
Whitey Platt	OF59, 1B2	R	28	102	244	29	63	8	2	3	29	24	27	0	.258	.344
Les Moss	C83	R	24	97	278	28	81	11	0	10	39	49	32	0	.291	.439
Andy Anderson	SS44, 2B8, 3B8	R	26	71	136	10	17	3	0	1	5	14	21	0	.125	.169
George Elder	OF10	L	28	44	44	9	11	3	0	0	2	4	11	0	.250	.318
1 Al Zarilla	OF15	L	30	15	56	10	14	1	0	1	6	8	2	1	.250	.321
Ken Wood	OF3	R	25	7	6	0	0	0	0	0	0	1	2	0	.000	.000
Hank Arft		R	27	6	5	1	1	1	0	0	2	1	0	0	.200	.400
Owen Friend	2B2	R	21	3	8	0	0	0	0	0	1	0	0	0	.000	.000
Al Naples	SS2	R	21	2	7	0	1	1	0	0	1	0	1	0	.143	.286
Frankie Pack		L	21	2	1	0	0	0	0	0	0	0	0	0	.000	.000

NAME	T	AGE	W	L	PCT	SV	G	GS	CG	IP	H	BB	SO	SHO	ERA
		29	53	101	.344	16	155	155	43	1341	1583	685	432	3	5.21
Ned Garver	R	23	12	17	.414	3	41	32	16	224	245	102	70	1	3.98
Joe Ostrowski	L	32	8	8	.500	2	40	13	4	141	185	27	34	0	4.78
Cliff Fannin	R	25	8	14	.364	1	30	25	5	143	177	93	57	0	6.17
Tom Ferrick	R	34	6	4	.600	6	50	0	0	104	102	41	34	0	3.89
Bill Kennedy	L	28	4	11	.267	1	48	16	2	154	172	73	69	0	4.68
Al Papai	R	32	4	11	.267	2	42	15	6	142	175	81	31	0	5.07
Karl Drews	R	29	4	12	.250	0	31	23	3	140	180	66	35	1	6.62
Red Embree	R	31	3	13	.188	1	35	19	4	127	146	89	24	0	5.39
Ed Albrecht	R	20	1	0	1.000	0	1	1		5	1	1		0	5.40
Bob Malloy	R	31	1	1	.500	0	5	0	0	16	23	12	5	0	2.70
Ribs Raney	R	26	1	2	.333	0	3	1	0	16	23	12	5	0	7.88
Dick Starr (IL)	R	28	1	7	.125	0	21	8	0	83	96	48	44	1	4.34
Ralph Winegarner	R	39	0	0	—	0	4			17	22	14	2	0	6.43
Bob Savage	R	27	0	0	—	0	7			12		3	1	0	6.43
Irv Medlinger	L	22	0	0	—	0	4			11		3	4	0	27.00
Jim Bilbrey	R	25	0	1	.000	0	3				18			0	18.00
Ray Shore	R	28	0	1	.000	0	23			27	31	13		0	10.96

WASHINGTON — 8th 50-104 .325 47 — JOE KUHEL

NAME	G by Pos	B	AGE	G	AB	R	H	2B	3B	HR	RBI	BB	SO	SB	BA	SA
TOTALS			28	154	5234	584	1330	207	41	81	546	593	495	46	.254	.356
Eddie Robinson	1B143	L	28	143	527	66	155	27	3	18	78	67	30	3	.294	.459
Al Kozar	2B102	R	27	105	350	46	94	15	2	4	31	25	23	2	.269	.357
Sam Dente	SS153	R	27	153	590	48	161	24	4	1	53	31	24	3	.273	.332
Eddie Yost	3B122	R	22	124	435	57	110	19	7	9	45	91	41	3	.253	.391
Bud Stewart	OF105	L	33	118	388	58	110	23	4	8	43	49	33	6	.284	.425
Clyde Vollmer	OF114	R	27	129	443	58	112	17	1	14	59	53	62	1	.253	.391
Gil Coan	OF97	L	27	111	358	36	78	7	8	3	25	29	58	9	.218	.307
Al Evans	C107	R	32	109	321	32	87	12	3	2	42	50	19	4	.271	.346
Sherry Robertson	2B71, 3B19, OF13	L	30	114	359	59	94	17	3	11	42	42	35	10	.251	.401
Buddy Lewis	OF67	L	32	95	257	25	63	14	4	3	28	41	12	2	.245	.366
2 Sam Mele	OF63, 1B11	R	27	78	264	21	64	12	2	3	25	17	34	2	.242	.337
John Simmons	OF26	R	24	62	93	12	20	0	0	0	5	11	6	1	.215	.215
Jake Early	C53	R	34	53	130	12	34	4	0	1	11	26	11	0	.246	.297
Mark Christman	3B23, 1B6, SS4, 2B1	R	35	49	112	8	24	3	0	0	18	8	7	0	.214	.313
Roberto Ortiz (SM)	OF32	R	34	40	129	12	36	0	1	4	11	9	12	2	.279	.326
Ralph Weigel	C21	R	27	34	60	4	14	2	0	0	4	4	6	0	.233	.267
Hal Keller	C	R	21	3	3	1	1	0	0	0	0	3	1	0	.333	.333
Jay Difani	2B1	R	26	3	4	1	1	0	0	0	0	0	0	0	1.000	2.000
1 Herm Reich		R	31	2	1	0	0	0	0	0	0	0	0	0	.000	.000

NAME	T	AGE	W	L	PCT	SV	G	GS	CG	IP	H	BB	SO	SHO	ERA
		29	50	104	.325	9	154	154	44	1346	1438	779	451	9	5.10
Ray Scarborough	R	31	13	11	.542	0	34	27	11	200	204	88	81	1	4.59
Sid Hudson	R	34	8	17	.320	1	40	27	11	209	234	91	54	2	4.22
Paul Calvert	R	31	6	17	.261	1	34	23	5	161	175	86	52	0	5.42
1 Mickey Haefner	L	36	5	5	.500	0	19	12	4	92	85	53	23	1	4.40
Lloyd Hittle	L	25	5	7	.417	0	36	9	3	109	123	57	32	2	4.21
1 Walt Masterson	R	29	3	2	.600	0	7	3		42	21	17		0	3.23
Dick Weik	R	21	3	12	.200	1	27	14	2	95	78	103	58	2	5.40
Dick Welteroth	R	21	2	5	.286	2	52	2	0	95	107	89	37	0	7.39
Joe Haynes	R	31	2	9	.182	2	37	10	0	96	106	55	19	0	6.28
2 Mickey Harris	R	32	2	12	.143	0	23	19	4	129	151	55	54	0	5.16
Forrest Thompson	L	31	1	3	.250	0	1			16	22	9		0	4.50
Julio Gonzalez	R	28	0	0	—	0	34			47		5		0	4.76
Milo Candini	R	31	0	0	—	0	6			4		1		0	4.50
Buzz Dozier	R	20	0	1	.000	0	1			12				0	12.00
1 Eddie Klieman	R	31	0	0	—	0	8			18				0	18.00
Jim Pearce	R	24	0	1	.000	0	9							0	9.00
Dizzy Sutherland	R	31	0	0	—	0	2							0	45.00
2 Al Gettel	R	31	0	2	.000	1	16	3	0	35	43	24	7	0	5.40

BROOKLYN — 1st 97-57 .630 — BURT SHOTTON

NAME	G by Pos	B	AGE	G	AB	R	H	2B	3B	HR	RBI	BB	SO	SB	BA	SA
TOTALS			27	156	5400	879	1477	236	47	152	816	638	570	117	.274	.419
Gil Hodges	1B156	R	25	156	596	94	170	23	4	23	115	66	64	10	.285	.453
Jackie Robinson	2B156	R	30	156	593	122	203	38	12	16	124	86	27	37	.342	.528
Pee Wee Reese	SS155	R	30	155	617	132	172	27	3	16	73	116	59	26	.279	.410
Billy Cox	3B100	R	29	100	390	48	91	18	2	8	40	30	18	5	.233	.351
Carl Furillo	OF142	R	27	142	549	95	177	27	10	18	106	37	29	4	.322	.506
Duke Snider	OF145	L	22	146	552	100	161	28	7	23	92	56	92	12	.292	.493
Gene Hermanski	OF77	L	29	87	224	48	67	12	3	8	42	47	21	12	.299	.487
Roy Campanella	C127	R	27	130	436	65	125	22	2	22	82	67	36	3	.287	.498
Bruce Edwards	C41 OF4 3B1	R	25	64	148	24	31	3	0	8	25	25	15	0	.209	.392
13 Marv Rackley	OF47	L	27	63	150	25	45	5	1	1	15	14	8	1	.300	.367
Mike McCormick	OF49	R	32	55	139	17	29	5	1	2	14	14	12	1	.209	.302
Spider Jorgensen	3B36	L	29	53	134	15	36	5	1	1	14	23	13	0	.269	.343
Eddie Miksis	3B29 SS4 2B3 1B1	R	22	50	113	17	25	5	0	1	6	7	8	3	.221	.292
Tommy Brown	OF27	R	21	41	89	14	27	2	0	3	18	6	8	0	.303	.427
Luis Olmo (SM)	OF34	R	29	38	105	15	32	4	1	1	14	5	11	2	.305	.390
Dick Whitman	OF11	L	28	23	49	8	9	0	0	0	2	4	4	0	.184	.224
Cal Abrams	OF7	L	25	8	24	6	2	1	0	0	0	7	6	1	.083	.125
2 Johnny Hopp	OF4 1B2	L	32	8	14	0	0	0	0	0	0	0	3	0	.000	.000

1 Bob Ramazzotti 32 R 2-13, Chuck Connors 28 L 0-1, George Shuba 24 L 0-1

NAME	T	AGE	W	L	PCT	SV	G	GS	CG	IP	H	BB	SO	SHO	ERA
		25	97	57	.630	17	156	156	62	1409	1306	582	743	15	3.80
Don Newcombe	R	23	17	8	.680	1	38	31	19	244	223	73	149	5	3.17
Preacher Roe	L	34	15	6	.714	1	30	27	13	213	201	44	109	3	2.79
Ralph Branca	R	23	13	5	.722	0	34	27	9	187	181	91	109	4	4.38
Joe Hatten	L	32	12	8	.600	2	37	29	11	187	194	69	58	2	4.19
Jack Banta	R	24	10	6	.625	3	48	12	2	152	125	68	97	1	3.38
Rex Barney	R	24	9	8	.529	1	38	20	6	141	108	89	80	2	4.40
Carl Erskine	R	22	8	1	.889	0	23	2	2	80	68	51	49	0	4.61
Erv Palica	R	21	8	9	.471	6	49	1	0	97	93	49	44	0	3.62
Paul Minner	L	25	3	1	.750	2	27	1	0	47	49	18	17	0	3.83
Pat McGlothin	R	28	1	1	.500	0	7	0	0	16	13	5	11	0	4.50
Morrie Martin	L	26	1	3	.250	0	10	4	0	31	39	15	15	0	6.97
Johnny Van Cuyk	L	27	0	0	—	0	2	0	0	3	1	0	9	0	9.00
Bud Podbielan	R	25	0	1	.000	0	7	1	0	12	9	9	5	0	3.75

ST. LOUIS — 2nd 96-58 .623 1 — EDDIE DYER

NAME	G by Pos	B	AGE	G	AB	R	H	2B	3B	HR	RBI	BB	SO	SB	BA	SA
TOTALS			27	157	5463	766	1513	281	54	102	720	569	482	17	.277	.404
Nippy Jones	1B98	R	24	110	380	51	114	20	2	8	62	16	20	1	.300	.426
Red Schoendienst	2B138 SS14 3B6 OF2	R	26	151	640	102	190	25	8	3	54	51	18	8	.297	.356
Marty Marion	SS134	R	31	134	515	61	140	31	2	5	70	37	42	0	.272	.369
Eddie Kazak (JJ)	3B80 2B5	R	28	92	326	43	99	15	3	6	42	29	17	0	.304	.423
Stan Musial	OF156 1B1	L	28	157	612	128	207	41	13	36	123	107	38	3	.338	.624
Chuck Diering	OF124	R	26	131	369	60	97	21	3	3	38	35	49	1	.263	.388
Enos Slaughter	OF150	L	33	151	568	92	191	34	13	13	96	79	37	3	.336	.511
Del Rice	C92	R	26	92	284	25	67	16	1	4	29	30	40	0	.236	.342
Ron Northey	OF73	L	29	90	265	28	69	18	2	7	50	31	15	0	.260	.423
Tommy Glaviano	3B73 2B7	R	25	87	258	32	69	16	1	6	36	41	35	0	.267	.407
Rocky Nelson	1B70	L	24	82	244	28	54	8	4	4	32	11	12	1	.221	.336
Joe Garagiola	C80	R	23	81	241	25	63	14	0	3	26	31	19	0	.261	.357
Lou Klein (SM)	SS21 2B9 3B7	R	30	58	114	25	25	5	6	0	12	22	20	0	.219	.325
Hal Rice	OF10	L	25	40	46	3	9	2	1	1	9	3	7	0	.196	.348
1 Ed Sauer	OF10	R	30	24	45	5	10	2	1	0	5	3	8	0	.222	.311
Bill Baker	C10	R	38	20	30	2	4	1	0	0	4	2	2	0	.133	.167
Solly Hemus	2B16	R	26	20	33	8	11	1	0	0	7	7	3	0	.333	.364
Whitey Kurowski (EJ)	3B2	R	31	10	14	0	2	1	0	0	0	1	0	0	.143	.143
Bill Howerton	OF6	L	27	9	13	1	4	1	0	0	1	2	4	0	.308	.385

Steve Bilko 20 R 5-17, Russ Derry 32 L 0-2, Del Wilber 30 R 1-4, Erv Dusak 28 R 0-0

NAME	T	AGE	W	L	PCT	SV	G	GS	CG	IP	H	BB	SO	SHO	ERA
		31	96	58	.623	19	157	157	64	1408	1356	506	606	13	3.44
Howie Pollet	L	28	20	9	.690	1	39	28	17	231	228	59	108	5	2.77
George Munger	R	30	15	8	.652	2	35	28	12	188	179	87	82	2	3.88
Al Brazle	L	35	14	8	.636	0	39	25	9	206	208	61	75	1	3.19
Harry Brecheen	L	34	14	11	.560	1	32	31	14	215	207	65	88	2	3.35
Ted Wilks	R	33	10	3	.769	9	59	0	0	118	105	38	71	0	3.74
Gerry Staley	R	28	10	10	.500	6	45	17	5	171	154	41	55	2	2.74
Freddie Martin (SM)	R	34	6	0	1.000	0	21	5	3	70	65	20	30	0	2.44
Max Lanier (SM)	L	33	5	4	.556	0	15	15	4	92	92	35	37	1	3.82
Bill Reeder	R	27	1	1	.500	0	21	1	0	34	33	30	21	0	5.03
Jim Hearn	R	28	1	3	.250	0	17	4	0	42	48	23	18	0	5.14
Cloyd Boyer	R	21	0	0	—	0	4	1	0	3	5	7	0	0	12.00
Ray Yochim	R	26	0	0	—	0	3	0	0	2	3	4	3	0	18.00
Kurt Krieger	R	22	0	0	—	0	1	0	0	1	0	1	0	0	0.00
Ken Johnson	L	26	0	1	.000	0	14	2	0	34	29	35	18	0	6.35

PHILADELPHIA — 3rd 81-73 .526 16 — EDDIE SAWYER

NAME	G by Pos	B	AGE	G	AB	R	H	2B	3B	HR	RBI	BB	SO	SB	BA	SA
TOTALS			26	154	5307	662	1349	232	55	122	622	528	670	27	.254	.388
Dick Sisler	1B96	L	28	121	412	42	119	19	6	7	50	25	38	0	.289	.415
Eddie Miller	2B82 SS1	R	32	85	266	21	55	10	1	6	29	29	21	1	.207	.327
Granny Hamner	SS154	R	22	154	662	83	174	32	5	6	53	25	47	6	.263	.353
Willie Jones	3B145	R	23	149	532	71	130	35	1	19	77	65	66	3	.244	.421
Bill Nicholson	OF91	L	34	98	299	42	70	8	1	10	40	45	53	1	.234	.391
Richie Ashburn	OF154	L	22	154	662	84	188	18	11	1	37	58	38	9	.284	.349
Del Ennis	OF154	R	24	154	610	92	184	39	11	25	110	59	61	2	.302	.525
Andy Seminick	C98	R	28	109	384	52	81	11	2	24	68	69	74	0	.243	.503
Stan Lopata	C58	R	23	83	240	31	65	9	2	8	27	21	44	1	.271	.425
Stan Hollmig	OF66	R	23	81	251	28	64	11	6	2	26	20	43	1	.255	.371
Buddy Blattner	2B15 3B12 SS7	R	29	64	97	15	24	6	1	0	5	21	19	1	.247	.464
Mike Goliat	2B50 1B5	R	27	55	189	24	40	6	3	3	19	20	32	0	.212	.323
Eddie Waitkus (GW)	1B54	L	29	54	209	41	64	16	3	1	28	33	12	3	.306	.426
Jackie Mayo	OF25	L	23	45	39	3	5	0	0	0	2	4	5	0	.128	.128
Putsy Caballero	2B21 SS1	R	21	29	68	8	19	3	0	0	5	3	10	1	.279	.324
Bill Glynn	1B1	L	24	8	10	0	2	0	0	0	1	0	3	0	.200	.200
Ed Sanicki	OF6	R	25	7	13	4	3	0	0	3	7	1	4	0	.231	.923
Johnny Blatnik	OF2	R	28	6	8	3	1	0	0	0	0	4	1	0	.125	.125

Ken Silvestri 33 B 0-4, 1 Bert Haas R 0-1, Hal Wagner 33 L 0-4

NAME	T	AGE	W	L	PCT	SV	G	GS	CG	IP	H	BB	SO	SHO	ERA
		30	81	73*	.526	15	154	154	58	1392	1389	502	495	12	3.89
Russ Meyer	R	25	17	8	.680	1	37	28	14	213	199	70	78	2	3.08
Ken Heintzelman	L	33	17	10	.630	0	33	32	15	250	239	93	65	5	3.02
Robin Roberts	R	22	15	15	.500	4	43	31	11	227	229	75	95	3	3.69
Hank Borowy	R	33	12	12	.500	0	28	28	12	193	188	63	43	1	4.20
Jim Konstanty	R	32	9	5	.643	7	53	0	0	97	98	29	43	0	3.25
Curt Simmons	L	20	4	10	.286	1	38	14	2	131	133	55	83	0	4.60
Schoolboy Rowe	R	39	3	7	.300	0	23	6	2	65	68	17	22	0	4.85
Blix Donnelly	R	35	2	1	.667	0	23	10	1	78	84	40	36	0	5.08
Ken Trinkle	R	29	1	1	.500	2	42	0	0	74	79	30	14	0	4.04
Jocko Thompson	L	32	1	1	.250	0	8	5	1	31	38	11	12	0	6.97
Charlie Bicknell	R	20	0	0	—	0	13	0	0	28	32	17	4	0	7.71
Bob Miller	R	23	0	0	—	0	3	2	0	2	2	0	0	0	0.00

*1 loss by forfeit

BOSTON — 4th 75-79 .487 22 — BILLY SOUTHWORTH 55-54 .505 JOHNNY COONEY 20-25 .444

NAME	G by Pos	B	AGE	G	AB	R	H	2B	3B	HR	RBI	BB	SO	SB	BA	SA
TOTALS			29	157	5336	706	1376	246	33	103	654	684	656	28	.258	.374
Elbie Fletcher	1B121	L	33	122	413	57	108	19	1	5	51	84	65	1	.262	.402
Eddie Stanky	2B135	R	32	138	506	90	144	24	5	1	42	113	41	3	.285	.358
Al Dark	SS125 3B4	R	27	130	529	74	146	24	5	3	53	31	43	5	.276	.355
Bob Elliott	3B130	R	32	139	482	77	135	29	5	17	76	90	38	0	.280	.467
Tommy Holmes	OF103	R	32	117	380	47	101	24	2	8	59	39	6	1	.266	.403
Jim Russell	OF120	B	30	130	415	57	96	22	1	8	54	64	68	3	.231	.347
Marv Rickert	OF75 1B12	R	28	100	277	44	81	18	3	6	49	23	38	1	.292	.444
Del Crandall	C63	R	19	67	228	21	60	10	1	4	34	9	18	2	.263	.368
Sibby Sisti	OF48 2B21 SS18 3B1	R	28	101	268	39	69	12	0	5	22	34	42	1	.257	.358
Connie Ryan	3B25 SS18 2B16 1B3	R	29	85	208	28	52	13	1	6	30	31	30	1	.250	.409
Pete Reiser	OF63 3B4	B	30	84	221	32	60	8	3	8	40	33	42	3	.271	.443
2 Ed Sauer	OF71 3B2	R	32	79	214	26	57	12	0	3	31	17	34	0	.266	.364
Bill Salkeld	C63	L	32	66	161	17	41	5	0	5	25	44	24	1	.255	.379
Clint Conatser	OF44	R	27	53	152	10	40	9	0	3	16	14	19	0	.263	.362
1 Phil Masi	C37	R	32	37	105	13	22	2	0	0	6	14	10	1	.210	.229
Jeff Heath (BN)	OF31	L	34	36	111	17	34	7	0	9	23	15	26	0	.306	.613
2 Mickey Livingston (BG)	C22	R	34	28	64	6	15	2	1	2	8	8	7	0	.234	.297
Earl Torgeson (SJ)	1B25	L	25	25	100	17	26	5	1	4	19	13	4	4	.260	.450
Ray Sanders (BW)	1B7	L	32	9	21	0	3	1	0	0	4	4	9	0	.143	.190
Don Thompson	OF2	L	25	5	11	0	2	0	0	0	0	0	6	0	.182	.182

Al Lakeman 30 R 1-6, Steve Kuczek 24 R 1-1

NAME	T	AGE	W	L	PCT	SV	G	GS	CG	IP	H	BB	SO	SHO	ERA
		29	75	79	.487	11	157	157	68	1400	1466	520	591	12	3.99
Warren Spahn	L	28	21	14	.600	0	38	38	25	302	283	86	151	4	3.07
Vern Bickford	R	28	16	11	.593	0	37	36	15	231	246	106	101	2	4.25
Johnny Sain	R	31	10	17	.370	0	37	36	16	243	285	75	73	1	4.81
Bill Voiselle	R	30	7	8	.467	1	30	22	5	169	170	78	63	4	4.05
Bob Hall	R	25	4	6	.400	0	31	6	2	74	77	41	43	0	4.38
Nels Potter	R	37	6	11	.353	7	41	3	1	97	99	30	57	0	4.18
Glenn Elliott	L	29	3	4	.429	0	22	6	1	68	70	27	15	0	3.97
Johnny Antonelli	R	19	3	7	.300	0	22	10	3	96	99	42	48	1	3.56
Bobby Hogue	R	28	2	2	.500	3	33	0	0	72	78	25	23	0	3.13
Red Barrett	R	34	1	1	.500	0	23	0	0	44	58	10	17	0	5.73
Johnny Beazley	R	31	0	0	—	0	4	1	0	4	1	0	1	0	0.00
1 Clyde Shoun	L	37	0	0	—	0	1	0	0	1	0	0	0	0	0.00

NEW YORK — 5th 73-81 .474 24 — LEO DUROCHER

NAME	G by Pos	B	AGE	G	AB	R	H	2B	3B	HR	RBI	BB	SO	SB	BA	SA
TOTALS			28	156	5308	736	1383	203	52	147	690	613	523	43	.261	.401
1 Johnny Mize	1B101	L	36	106	388	59	102	15	0	18	62	50	19	1	.263	.441
Hank Thompson	2B69 3B21	L	23	75	275	51	77	10	4	9	34	42	30	5	.280	.444
Buddy Kerr	SS89	R	26	90	220	16	46	4	0	0	19	21	23	0	.209	.227
Sid Gordon	3B123 OF15 1B1	R	31	141	489	87	139	26	2	26	90	95	37	1	.284	.505
Willard Marshall	OF138	R	28	141	499	81	153	19	3	12	70	78	20	4	.307	.429
Bobby Thomson	OF156	R	25	156	641	99	198	35	9	27	109	44	45	10	.309	.518
Whitey Lockman	OF151	L	22	151	617	97	186	32	7	11	65	62	31	12	.301	.429
Wes Westrum	C62	R	26	64	169	23	41	4	1	7	28	37	39	1	.243	.402
Bill Rigney	SS81 2B26 3B14	R	31	122	389	53	108	19	6	6	47	47	38	3	.278	.404
Joe Lafata (IL)	1B47	L	27	64	140	18	33	2	2	3	16	9	23	1	.236	.343
2 Ray Mueller	C56	R	37	56	170	17	38	2	1	2	23	13	14	1	.224	.347
Lucky Lohrke	2B23 3B19 SS15	R	25	55	180	32	48	11	4	5	22	16	12	3	.267	.456
2 Bert Haas	1B23 3B11	R	35	54	104	12	27	2	3	1	10	5	8	1	.260	.365
Don Mueller	OF6	L	22	51	56	5	13	4	0	0	1	5	6	0	.232	.304
1 Walker Cooper	C40	R	34	42	147	14	31	4	2	4	21	7	8	0	.211	.347
Monte Irvin	OF10 3B5 1B5	R	30	36	76	7	17	2	1	0	7	11	9	0	.224	.316
Pete Milne	OF1	L	24	31	29	5	7	1	0	0	5	6	6	0	.241	.379
1 Augie Galan	1B3 OF1	L	37	32	17	0	1	1	0	0	3	5	0	0	.059	.118
Bobby Hofman	2B16	R	23	19	48	4	10	0	0	3	5	6	5	0	.208	.208
1 Mickey Livingston	C19	R	34	19	57	4	10	0	1	2	8	18	5	0	.175	.298
George Hausmann (SM)	2B13	R	33	16	47	9	6	0	0	0	3	4	6	1	.128	.170
Davey Williams	2B13	R	21	13	50	9	12	3	0	0	6	3	8	0	.240	.360

1 Bobby Rhawn 30 R 5-29, Dick Culler 34 R 0-1, Rudy Rufer 22 R 1-15, Sal Yvars 25 R 0-8, Herman Franks 35 L 2-3, Danny Gardella (SM) 29, Nap Reyes (SM) 29

NAME	T	AGE	W	L	PCT	SV	G	GS	CG	IP	H	BB	SO	SHO	ERA
		28	73*	81	.474	9	156	156	68	1374	1328	544	516	10	3.82
Sheldon Jones	R	27	15	12	.556	0	42	27	11	207	198	88	79	1	3.35
Larry Jansen	R	28	15	16	.484	0	37	35	17	260	271	62	113	3	3.84
Monte Kennedy	L	27	12	14	.462	1	38	32	14	223	208	100	95	4	3.43
Dave Koslo	L	29	11	14	.440	4	38	23	15	212	193	43	64	0	2.50
Clint Hartung	R	26	9	11	.450	0	33	25	8	155	156	86	48	0	4.99
Hank Behrman	R	28	3	3	.500	0	43	4	1	71	64	52	25	1	4.94
2 Kirby Higbe	R	34	2	0	1.000	2	37	2	0	80	72	41	38	0	3.49
Adrian Zabala (SM)	L	32	2	3	.400	1	15	4	2	40	40	13	13	1	5.27
Andy Hansen	R	24	2	6	.250	1	33	2	0	66	58	28	26	0	4.64
Red Webb	R	24	1	1	.500	0	20	0	0	45	41	21	9	0	4.00
Roger Bowman	L	21	0	0	—	0	4	0	0	4	6	4	0	0	4.50
1 Ray Poat	R	31	0	0	—	0	8	1	0	11	8	1	0	0	22.50
Andy Tomasic	R	29	0	0	.000	0	2	0	0	2	4	5	1	0	18.00

Sal Maglie (SM) 32, Ace Adams (SM) 37, Harry Feldman (SM) 29

* 1 win by forfeit

PITTSBURGH 6th 71-83 .461 26   BILLY MEYER

NAME	G by Pos	B	AGE	G	AB	R	H	2B	3B	HR	RBI	BB	SO	SB	BA	SA
TOTALS			29	154	5214	681	1350	191	41	126	626	548	554	48	.259	.384
13 Johnny Hopp	1B77 OF16	L	32	105	371	55	118	14	4	5	39	37	29	9	.318	.423
Monty Basgall	2B98 3B3	R	27	107	308	25	67	9	1	2	26	31	32	1	.218	.273
Stan Rojek	SS144	R	30	144	557	72	136	19	2	0	31	50	31	4	.244	.285
Pete Castiglione	3B98 SS17 OF2	R	28	118	448	57	120	20	8	6	43	20	43	2	.268	.362
Wally Westlake	OF143	R	28	147	525	77	148	24	8	23	104	45	69	6	.282	.490
Dino Restelli	OF61 1B1	R	24	72	232	41	58	11	0	12	40	35	26	3	.250	.453
Ralph Kiner	OF152	R	26	152	549	116	170	19	5	54	127	117	61	6	.310	.658
Clyde McCullough	C90	R	32	91	241	30	57	9	3	4	21	24	30	1	.237	.349
Dixie Walker	OF39 1B3	L	38	88	181	26	51	4	1	1	18	26	11	0	.282	.331
Eddie Bockman	3B8 2B5	R	28	79	220	21	49	6	1	6	19	23	31	1	.223	.341
Danny Murtaugh	2B74	R	31	75	236	16	48	7	2	2	24	29	17	2	.203	.275
Ed Fitz Gerald	C56	R	25	75	160	16	42	7	0	2	18	8	27	1	.263	.344
Tom Saffell	OF53	L	27	73	205	36	66	7	1	2	25	21	27	5	.322	.395
Ed Stevens	1B58	L	24	67	221	22	58	10	1	4	32	22	24	1	.262	.371
2 Phil Masi	C44 1B2	R	32	48	135	16	37	6	1	2	13	17	16	1	.274	.378
Les Fleming	1B5	L	33	24	31	0	8	0	2	0	7	6	2	0	.258	.387
2 Jack Phillips	1B16 3B1	R	27	18	56	6	13	3	1	0	3	4	6	1	.232	.321
Ted Beard	OF10	L	28	14	24	1	2	1	0	0	1	2	1	1	.083	.083

2 Marv Rackley 27 L 11-35, Walt Judnich 33 L 8-35, Jack Cassini 29 R 0-0, 2 Bobby Rhawn 30 R 1-7

NAME	T	AGE	W	L	PCT	SV	G	GS	CG	IP	H	BB	SO	SHO	ERA
		33	71	83	.461	15	154	154	53	1356	1452	535	556	9	4.57
Cliff Chambers	L	27	13	7	.650	0	34	21	10	177	186	58	93	1	3.97
Bill Werle	L	28	12	13	.480	0	35	29	10	221	243	51	106	2	4.24
Murry Dickson	R	32	12	14	.462	0	44	20	11	224	216	80	89	2	3.29
Ernie Bonham (DD)	R	35	7	4	.636	0	18	14	5	89	81	23	25	1	4.25
Bob Chesnes	R	28	7	13	.350	1	27	25	8	145	153	82	49	1	5.90
Rip Sewell	R	42	6	1	.857	1	28	6	2	76	82	32	26	1	3.91
Vic Lombardi	L	26	5	5	.500	3	34	12	4	134	149	68	64	0	4.57
1 Hugh Casey	R	35	4	1	.800	5	33	0	0	39	50	14	9	0	4.62
Hal Gregg	R	27	4	1	.500	0	8	1	0	19	20	8	9	0	3.32
2 Harry Gumbert	R	39	1	4	.200	3	16	0	0	28	30	18	5	0	5.79
Junior Walsh	R	30	1	4	.200	0	9	7	1	43	40	16	24	1	5.02
1 Bob Muncrief	R	33	1	5	.167	3	13	4	1	36	44	13	11	0	6.25
Elmer Riddle	R	34	1	8	.111	1	16	12	1	74	81	45	24	0	5.35
2 Ray Poat	R	31	0	0		0	11	2	0	36	52	15	17	0	6.25
1 Kirby Higbe	R	34	0	2	.000	1	7	1	0	15	25	12	5	0	13.80

CINCINNATI 7th 62-92 .403 35   BUCKY WALTERS 61-90 .404   LUKE SEWELL 1-2 .333

NAME	G by Pos	B	AGE	G	AB	R	H	2B	3B	HR	RBI	BB	SO	SB	BA	SA
TOTALS			29	156	5469	627	1423	264	35	86	588	429	559	31	.260	.368
Ted Kluszewski	1B134	L	24	136	531	63	164	26	2	8	68	19	24	3	.309	.411
Jimmy Bloodworth	2B92 1B23 3B8	R	31	134	452	40	118	27	1	9	59	27	36	1	.261	.385
Virgil Stallcup	SS141	R	27	141	575	49	146	28	5	3	45	9	44	5	.254	.336
Grady Hatton	3B136	R	26	137	537	71	141	38	5	11	69	62	48	4	.263	.413
Johnny Wyrostek	OF129	R	29	134	474	54	118	20	4	9	46	58	63	7	.249	.365
Lloyd Merriman	OF86	L	24	103	287	35	66	12	5	4	26	21	36	2	.230	.348
2 Peanuts Lowrey	OF78	R	31	89	309	48	85	16	2	2	25	37	11	1	.275	.359
2 Walker Cooper	C77	R	34	82	307	34	86	9	2	16	62	21	24	0	.280	.479
Bobby Adams	2B63 3B14	R	27	107	277	32	70	16	2	0	25	26	36	4	.253	.325
Danny Litwhiler	OF82 3B3	R	32	102	292	35	85	18	1	11	48	44	42	0	.291	.473
2 Harry Walker	OF77 1B1	R	32	86	314	53	100	15	2	1	23	34	17	4	.318	.389
Dixie Howell	C56	R	29	64	172	17	42	6	1	2	18	6	21	0	.244	.326
Claude Corbitt	SS18 2B17 3B11	R	33	44	94	10	17	1	0	0	3	9	1	1	.181	.191
1 Hank Sauer	OF39 1B1	R	32	42	152	22	36	6	0	4	16	18	19	0	.237	.355
1 Ray Mueller	C31	R	37	32	106	7	29	4	0	1	13	5	13	1	.274	.340
1 Frankie Baumholtz	OF20	L	30	27	81	12	19	5	3	1	6	8	6	0	.235	.407
1 Charlie Kress	1B16	L	27	27	29	3	6	3	0	0	3	3	5	0	.207	.310
Johnny Pramesa	C13	R	23	17	25	2	6	1	0	1	2	3	5	0	.240	.400
Sammy Meeks	2B8 SS3	R	26	16	36	10	11	2	0	2	6	2	6	1	.306	.528
Wally Post	OF3	R	19	6	4	1	1	0	0	0	1	0	3	0	.250	.250

NAME	T	AGE	W	L	PCT	SV	G	GS	CG	IP	H	BB	SO	SHO	ERA
		28	62	92	.403	6	156	156	55	1401	1423	640	538	10	4.34
Ken Raffensberger	L	31	18	17	.514	0	41	38	20	284	289	80	103	5	3.39
Herm Wehmeier	R	22	11	12	.478	0	33	29	11	213	202	117	80	1	4.69
Howie Fox	R	28	6	19	.240	0	38	30	9	215	221	77	60	0	3.98
Ewell Blackwell (IL)	R	26	5	5	.500	1	30	4	2	77	80	34	55	0	4.21
Johnny Vander Meer	L	34	5	10	.333	0	28	24	7	160	172	85	76	3	4.89
1 Harry Gumbert	R	39	4	3	.571	2	40	1	0	41	58	8	12	0	5.49
Kent Peterson	L	23	4	5	.444	0	30	7	2	66	66	46	28	0	6.27
Bud Lively	R	24	4	6	.400	1	31	10	3	103	91	53	30	1	3.93
Eddie Erautt	R	24	4	11	.267	1	39	9	1	113	99	61	43	0	3.35
Harry Perkowski	R	26	1	1	.500	0	5	3	2	24	21	14	3	0	4.50
2 Jess Dobernic	R	31	0	0	—	0	14	0	0	19	28	16	6	0	9.95
Ken Burkhart	R	32	0	0	—	1	11	0	0	28	29	10	8	0	3.21
Walker Cress	R	32	0	0		0	3	0	0	2	2	3	0	0	
Dixie Howell	R	29	0	1	.000	0	5	1	0	13	21	8	7	0	8.31
Frank Fanovich	L	27	0	2		0	29	1	0	48	51	22	8	0	5.44

CHICAGO 8th 61-93 .396 36   CHARLIE GRIMM 19-31 .380   FRANKIE FRISCH 42-62 .404

NAME	G by Pos	B	AGE	G	AB	R	H	2B	3B	HR	RBI	BB	SO	SB	BA	SA
TOTALS			29	154	5214	593	1336	212	53	97	539	396	573	53	.256	.373
3 Herm Reich	1B85 OF16	R	31	108	386	43	108	22	4	9	34	13	32	4	.280	.360
Emil Verban	2B88	R	33	98	343	38	99	11	1	0	22	8	2	3	.289	.327
Roy Smalley	SS132	R	23	135	477	57	117	21	10	8	35	36	77	2	.245	.382
Frankie Gustine	3B55 2B16	R	29	76	261	39	59	13	4	4	27	18	22	3	.226	.352
Hal Jeffcoat	OF101	R	24	108	363	43	89	18	6	2	26	20	48	12	.245	.344
Andy Pafko	OF98 3B16	R	28	144	519	79	146	29	2	18	69	63	63	4	.281	.449
2 Hank Sauer	OF96	R	32	96	357	59	104	17	1	27	83	37	47	0	.291	.571
Mickey Owen (SM)	C59	R	33	62	198	15	54	9	2	2	18	12	13	1	.273	.379
Phil Cavarretta	1B70 OF25	L	32	105	360	46	106	22	4	8	49	45	31	2	.294	.444
Gene Mauch	2B25 SS19 3B7	R	23	72	150	15	37	6	2	1	7	21	15	3	.247	.333
2 Bob Ramazzotti	3B36 SS12 2B4	R	32	65	190	14	34	3	1	0	6	5	33	9	.179	.205
2 Hank Edwards (SJ)	OF51	L	30	58	176	25	51	8	4	7	21	19	22	0	.290	.500
2 Frankie Baumholtz	OF43	L	30	58	164	15	37	4	2	1	15	9	21	0	.226	.293
Rube Walker	C43	L	23	56	172	11	42	4	1	3	22	9	18	0	.244	.331
Bob Scheffing (IL)	C40	R	35	55	149	12	40	6	1	3	19	9	9	0	.268	.383
Smoky Burgess	C8	L	22	46	56	4	15	0	0	1	12	4	4	0	.268	.321
1 Harry Walker	OF39	L	32	42	159	20	42	6	3	1	14	11	6	2	.264	.358
1 Peanuts Lowrey	OF31 3B1	R	31	38	111	18	30	5	0	2	10	9	8	3	.270	.369
Wayne Terwilliger	2B34	R	24	36	112	11	25	2	1	0	10	16	22	2	.223	.313
Rube Novotney	C20	R	24	22	67	4	18	2	1	0	6	3	6	0	.269	.328

Bill Serena 24 R 8-37, Clarence Maddern 27 R 3-9, Hank Schenz 30 R 6-14, Cliff Aberson 27 R 0-7, Jim Kirby 26 R 1-2

NAME	T	AGE	W	L	PCT	SV	G	GS	CG	IP	H	BB	SO	SHO	ERA
		30	61	93	.396	17	154	154	44	1358	1463	564	532	8	4.50
Johnny Schmitz	L	28	11	13	.458	3	36	31	9	207	227	92	75	3	4.35
Bob Rush	R	23	10	18	.357	4	35	27	9	201	197	79	80	1	4.07
Bob Chipman	L	30	4	8	.467	1	38	11	3	113	110	63	46	1	3.98
Dutch Leonard	R	40	7	16	.304	0	33	28	10	180	198	43	83	1	4.15
Monk Dubiel	R	31	6	9	.400	4	32	20	3	148	142	54	52	1	4.14
2 Bob Muncrief	R	33	5	6	.455	2	34	3	1	75	80	31	36	0	4.56
Warren Hacker	R	24	5	6	.385	0	30	12	3	126	141	53	40	0	4.49
Doyle Lade	R	28	4	5	.444	1	36	13	5	130	141	58	43	1	4.98
Emil Kush	R	32	3	3	.500	2	26	0	0	48	51	24	22	0	3.75
Dewey Adkins	R	31	2	4	.333	0	30	5	1	82	98	39	43	0	5.71
Cal McLish	R	23	1	1	.500	0	23	2	0	23	31	12	6	0	5.87
Dwain Sloat	L	30	0	0		0	5	1	0	9	14	3	3	0	7.00
1 Jess Dobernic	R	31	0	0	—	0	4	0	0	4	4	2	0	0	20.25
Mort Cooper	R	36	0	0		0	1	0	0	1	2	1	0	0	∞
Ralph Hamner	R	32	0	2	.000	0	12	1	1	22	22	8	3	0	9.00

WORLD SERIES — NEW YORK (AL) 4 BROOKLYN (NL) 1

LINE SCORES

TEAM	1 2 3	4 5 6	7 8 9	10 11 12	R	H	E
Game 1 — October 5 at New York							
BKN(NL)	0 0 0	0 0 0	0 0 0		0	2	0
NY(AL)	0 0 0	0 0 0	0 0 1		1	5	1

Newcombe / Reynolds

TEAM	1 2 3	4 5 6	7 8 9	R	H	E
Game 2 — October 6 at New York						
BKN	0 1 0	0 0 0	0 0 0	1	7	2
NY	0 0 0	0 0 0	0 0 0	0	6	1

Roe / Raschi, Page (9)

TEAM	1 2 3	4 5 6	7 8 9	R	H	E
Game 3 — October 7 at Brooklyn						
NY	0 0 1	0 0 0	0 0 3	4	5	0
BKN	0 0 0	0 1 0	0 0 2	3	5	0

Byrne, Page (4) / Branca, Banta (9)

TEAM	1 2 3	4 5 6	7 8 9	R	H	E
Game 4 — October 8 at Brooklyn						
NY	0 0 0	3 3 0	0 0 0	6	10	0
BKN	0 0 0	0 0 4	0 0 0	4	9	1

Lopat, Reynolds (6) / Newcombe, Hatten (4), Erskine (6), Banta (7)

TEAM	1 2 3	4 5 6	7 8 9	R	H	E
Game 5 — October 9 at Brooklyn						
NY	2 0 3	1 1 3	0 0 0	10	11	1
BKN	0 0 1	0 0 1	4 0 0	6	11	2

Raschi, Page (7) / Barney, Banta (3), Erskine (6), Hatten (6), Palica (7), Minner (9)

COMPOSITE BATTING

NAME	POS	G	AB	R	H	2B	3B	HR	RBI	BA
New York (AL) Totals		5	164	21	37	10	2	2	20	.226
Coleman	2B	5	20	0	5	3	0	0	4	.250
Henrich	1B	5	19	4	5	0	0	1	1	.263
Rizzuto	SS	5	18	2	3	0	0	0	1	.167
DiMaggio	OF	5	18	2	2	0	0	1	2	.111
Berra	C	4	16	2	1	0	0	0	1	.063
B.Brown	3B	4	12	4	6	1	2	0	5	.500
Woodling	OF	4	10	4	4	3	0	0	0	.400
Mapes	OF	4	10	3	1	1	0	0	2	.100
Johnson	3B	2	7	0	1	0	0	0	0	.143
Lindell	OF	2	7	0	1	0	0	0	0	.143
Bauer	OF	3	6	0	1	0	0	0	0	.167
Raschi	P	2	5	0	1	0	0	0	0	.200
Reynolds	P	2	4	0	2	0	0	0	0	.500
Page	P	2	4	0	0	0	0	0	0	.000
Lopat	P	1	3	0	1	0	0	0	0	.333
Mize	PH	2	2	0	2	0	0	0	2	1.000
Silvera	C	1	2	0	0	0	0	0	0	.000
Byrne	P	1	1	0	1	0	0	0	1	1.000

Stirnweiss PR 0-0, Nairhos C 0-0

NAME	POS	G	AB	R	H	2B	3B	HR	RBI	BA
Brooklyn (NL) Totals		5	162	14	34	7	1	4	14	.210
Snider	OF	5	21	2	3	1	0	0	0	.143
Reese	SS	5	19	2	6	0	1	0	2	.316
Hodges	1B	5	17	2	4	0	0	1	2	.235
Robinson	2B	5	16	2	3	1	0	0	2	.188
Campanella	C	5	15	2	4	1	0	0	2	.267
Hermanski	OF	4	13	1	4	1	0	0	0	.308
Olmo	OF	4	11	2	3	0	0	1	2	.273
Jorgensen	3B	4	11	1	2	2	0	0	1	.182
Furillo	OF	3	8	0	1	0	0	0	0	.125
Miksis	3B	3	7	0	2	1	0	0	0	.286
Rackley	OF	2	5	0	0	0	0	0	0	.000
Newcombe	P	2	4	0	0	0	0	0	0	.000
Cox	3B	2	3	0	1	0	0	0	0	.333
Branca	P	2	3	0	0	0	0	0	0	.000
Roe	P	2	3	0	0	0	0	0	0	.000
Edwards	PH	2	2	0	1	0	0	0	0	.500
T.Brown	PH	2	2	0	0	0	0	0	0	.000
Banta	P	3	1	0	0	0	0	0	0	.000
Whitman	PH	1	1	0	0	0	0	0	0	.000
Hatten	P	2	1	0	0	0	0	0	0	—

Barney P 0-0, Erskine P 0-0, Minner P 0-0, Palica P 0-0, McCormick OF 0-0

COMPOSITE PITCHING

NAME	G	IP	H	BB	SO	W	L	SV	ERA
New York (AL) Totals	5	45	34	15	38	4	1	2	2.80
Raschi	2	14.2	15	5	11	1	1	0	4.30
Reynolds	2	12.1	2	4	14	1	0	1	0.00
Page	3	9	6	3	8	1	0	1	2.00
Lopat	1	5.2	9	1	4	1	0	0	6.35
Byrne	1	3.1	2	1	1	0	0	0	2.70

NAME	G	IP	H	BB	SO	W	L	SV	ERA
Brooklyn (NL) Totals	5	44	37	18	27	1	4	0	4.30
Newcombe	2	11	10	3	11	0	2	0	3.09
Roe	1	9	6	3	1	1	0	0	0.00
Branca	2	8.2	4	4	6	0	1	0	4.15
Banta	3	5.2	5	1	4	0	0	0	3.18
Barney	1	2.2	3	6	2	0	1	0	16.88
Palica	1	2.1	3	1	2	0	0	0	3.86
Erskine	2	1.2	4	3	2	0	0	0	16.20
Hatten	2	1.2	4	1	2	0	0	0	16.20
Minner	1	1.1	2	1	0	0	0	0	0.00

1950 Whiz, Sweep, and a Couple of Farewells

The bandbox that was Ebbets Field pulsated as the 35,073 fans took their seats to watch their beloved Bums pull another pennant from the National League fires. It was Sunday, October 1. The schedule showed one remaining game for the Dodgers and Phillies. The standings told the tale: Philadelphia, 90-63; Brooklyn, 89-64. The prospects for Brooklyn looked excellent. The Phillies were skidding badly, having dissipated a seven-game lead in nine days. On Saturday, Erv Palica beat the Philadelphia Whiz Kids, 7-3. The Phils' manager Eddie Sawyer was forced to go with Robin Roberts, making his third start in the last five days, while Burt Shotton had his own iron man in Don Newcombe, who weeks before almost single-handedly beat the Phils in a doubleheader (a 2-0 shutout in the first game, and seven innings of the nightcap before departing for a pinch hitter!).

To further boost Brooklyn's hopes, the Phillies' catcher Andy Seminick was playing with a painful ankle injury suffered four days before when the Giants' Monte Irvin crashed into Seminick at the plate in the last play of a twin bill. Sawyer's troops were also without the services of their lefty pitching ace Curt Simmons, who was called to active military duty on September 10. Aside from MVP Jim Konstanty, who had already appeared in a league-high 74 games and had 22 saves to go along with his 16 wins, there was little else Sawyer could count on. His two promising rookie hurlers, Bubba Church and Bob Miller, were nursing their wounds. Miller had a bad arm, and Church was hit in the face by a line drive on September 15.

All of Brooklyn's dreams seemed assured when Pee Wee Reese wedged a freak homer between the scoreboard and the right field fence to tie the game at 1-1 in the sixth inning. The fact that the Dodgers threw away the game in the ninth when Richie Ashburn nailed Cal Abrams at the plate, and Roberts retired Carl Furillo and Gil Hodges with the bases loaded, did not completely destroy the rousing throng in the stands. Although the fans were feeling as empty as a Brooklyn heart could be, there was still the recent memory of 1949 when the Dodgers beat the Phils in ten innings, to win the pennant by one game over St. Louis. But 1950 was not 1949, and Dick Sisler climaxed a seven-year rebuilding program with a tenth-inning, three-run homer that brought the Whiz Kids their first pennant since 1915.

By comparison, the American League finish was ho-hum. Casey Stengel, traipsing on the magic that was to guide him to the Hall of Fame, brought up a southpaw sensation in late June by the name of Whitey Ford. That move, coupled with Joe DiMaggio's late season comeback, the clutch hitting of Big Jawn Mize, and Phil Rizzuto's MVP year at shortstop, was enough to edge Detroit, Boston, and Cleveland.

Stengel was also aided by a big trade with the St. Louis Browns, which brought him pitchers Tom Ferrick and Joe Ostrowski, plus a cleverly manuevered waiver deal which landed him Johnny Hopp from Pittsburgh, the then No. 2 batter in the National League with a .340 average. Detroit missed the flag by three games and blamed their woes on losing their ace, Virgil Trucks, to arm trouble early in the season. Boston's pennant hopes faded when Ted Williams fractured his elbow in the annual All-Star Game and Cleveland, never really able to get going, was destroyed when the lowly Browns beat them four straight in September.

The World Series had its excitement, although the Yankees swept the Whiz Kids four straight. Perhaps more significant than New York's victory was Luke Appling's retirement, after toiling at shortstop for the White Sox since 1931, and Connie Mack's finally stepping down as manager of the Athletics after 50 years of service.

1950 AMERICAN LEAGUE

NAME	G by Pos	B	AGE	G	AB	R	H	2B	3B	HR	RBI	BB	SO	SB	BA	SA
NEW YORK	**1st 98-56 .636**				CASEY STENGEL											
TOTALS			29	155	5361	914	1511	234	70	159	863	687	463	41	.282	.441
Johnny Mize	1B72	L	37	90	274	43	76	12	0	25	72	29	24	0	.277	.595
Jerry Coleman	2B152 SS6	R	25	153	522	69	150	19	6	6	69	67	38	3	.287	.381
Phil Rizzuto	SS155	R	32	155	617	125	200	36	7	7	66	92	39	12	.324	.439
Billy Johnson	3B100 1B5	R	31	108	327	44	85	16	2	6	40	42	30	1	.260	.376
Hank Bauer	OF110	R	27	113	415	72	133	16	2	13	70	35	41	2	.320	.463
Joe DiMaggio	OF137 1B1	R	35	139	525	114	158	33	10	32	122	80	33	0	.301	.585
Gene Woodling	OF118	L	27	122	449	81	127	20	10	6	60	70	31	0	.283	.412
Yogi Berra	C148	L	25	151	597	116	192	30	6	28	124	55	12	4	.322	.537
Cliff Mapes	OF102	L	28	108	356	60	88	14	6	12	61	47	61	1	.247	.421
Joe Collins	1B99 OF2	L	27	108	205	47	48	8	3	8	28	31	34	5	.234	.420
Bobby Brown	3B82	L	25	95	277	33	74	4	2	4	37	39	18	3	.267	.339
Tommy Henrich (KJ)	1B34	L	40	73	151	20	41	6	8	6	34	27	6	0	.272	.536
Jackie Jensen	OF23	R	23	45	70	13	12	2	2	1	5	7	8	4	.171	.300
Billy Martin	2B22 3B1	R	22	34	36	10	9	1	0	1	8	3	3	0	.250	.361
2 Johnny Hopp	1B12 OF6	L	33	19	27	9	9	2	1	1	8	8	1	0	.333	.593
Charlie Silvera	C15	R	25	18	25	2	4	0	0	0	1	1	2	0	.160	.160
1 Jim Delsing		L	24	12	10	2	4	0	0	0	2	2	0	0	.400	.400
Ralph Houk	C9	R	30	10	9	0	1	1	0	0	1	0	2	0	.111	.222
1 Johnny Lindell	OF6	R	33	7	21	2	4	0	0	0	2	4	2	0	.190	.190
1 Snuffy Stirnweiss	2B4	R	31	7	2	0	0	0	0	0	0	0	0	0	.000	.000
1 Dick Wakefield		L	29	3	2	0	1	0	0	0	1	1	1	0	.500	.500
Hank Workman	1B1	L	24	2	5	1	1	0	0	0	1	0	1	0	.200	.200
1 Gus Niarhos		R	29	1	0	0	0	0	0	0	0	0	0	0		
DETROIT	**2nd 95-59 .617 3**				RED ROLFE											
TOTALS			28	157	5381	837	1518	285	50	114	787	722	480	23	.282	.417
Don Kolloway	1B118 2B1	R	31	125	467	55	135	20	4	6	62	29	28	1	.289	.388
Jerry Priddy	2B157	R	30	157	618	104	177	26	6	13	75	95	95	2	.277	.401
Johnny Lipon	SS147	R	27	147	601	104	176	27	6	2	63	81	26	9	.293	.368
George Kell	3B157	R	27	157	641	114	218	56	6	8	101	66	18	3	.340	.484
Vic Wertz	OF145	L	25	149	559	99	172	37	4	27	123	91	55	0	.308	.533
Johnny Groth	OF157	R	23	157	566	95	173	30	8	12	85	95	27	1	.306	.451
Hoot Evers	OF139	R	29	143	526	100	170	35	11	21	103	71	40	5	.323	.551
Aaron Robinson	C103	L	35	107	283	37	64	7	0	9	37	75	35	0	.226	.346
Pat Mullin	OF32	L	32	69	142	16	31	5	0	6	23	20	23	1	.218	.380
Bob Swift	C66	R	35	67	132	14	30	4	0	2	9	25	6	0	.227	.303
Dick Kryhoski	1B47	L	25	53	169	20	37	10	0	4	19	8	11	0	.219	.349
Charlie Keller	OF6	L	33	50	51	7	16	1	3	2	16	13	6	0	.314	.569
Fred Hutchinson	P39	R	30	44	95	15	31	7	0	0	20	12	3	0	.326	.400
Neil Berry	SS12 2B2 3B1	R	28	39	40	9	10	1	0	0	7	6	11	0	.250	.275
Joe Ginsberg	C31	L	23	36	95	12	22	6	0	0	12	11	6	1	.232	.295
Eddie Lake	3B1 SS1	R	34	20	7	3	0	0	0	0	1	1	3	0	.000	.000
Frank House	C5	L	20	5	5	1	2	1	0	0	0	0	1	0	.400	.600
Paul Campbell		L	32	4	0	0	0	0	0	0	0	0	0	0		
BOSTON	**3rd 94-60 .610 4**			JOE McCARTHY 31-28 .525	STEVE O'NEILL 63-32 .663											
TOTALS			30	154	5516	1027	1665	287	61	161	974	719	582	32	.302	.464
Walt Dropo	1B134	R	27	136	559	101	180	28	8	34	144	45	75	0	.322	.583
Bobby Doerr	2B149	R	32	149	586	103	172	29	11	27	120	67	42	3	.294	.519
Vern Stephens	SS146	R	29	149	628	125	185	34	6	30	144	65	43	0	.295	.511
Johnny Pesky	3B116 SS8	L	30	127	490	112	153	22	6	1	49	104	31	2	.312	.388
Al Zarilla	OF128	L	31	130	471	92	153	32	10	9	74	76	47	2	.325	.493
Dom DiMaggio	OF140	R	33	141	588	131	193	30	11	7	70	82	68	15	.328	.452
Ted Williams (BE)	OF86	L	31	89	334	82	106	24	1	28	97	82	21	3	.317	.647
Birdie Tebbetts	C74	R	37	79	268	33	83	10	1	8	45	29	26	1	.310	.444
B. Goodman	OF45 3B27 1B21 2B5 SS1	L	24	110	424	91	150	25	3	4	68	52	25	2	.354	.455
Matt Batts	C73	R	28	75	238	27	65	15	3	4	34	18	19	0	.273	.412
2 Clyde Vollmer	OF39	R	28	57	169	35	48	10	0	7	37	21	35	1	.284	.467
Tom Wright	OF24	L	26	54	107	17	34	7	0	0	20	6	18	0	.318	.383
Buddy Rosar	C25	R	35	27	84	13	25	2	0	0	12	7	4	0	.298	.357
Lou Stringer	3B3 2B1 SS1	R	33	24	17	7	5	2	0	0	4	3	4	0	.294	.353
Ken Keltner	3B8 1B1	R	33	13	28	4	9	2	0	0	3	1	1	0	.321	.393
Fred Hatfield	3B3	R	25	10	12	3	3	0	0	0	2	3	1	0	.250	.250
1 Tommy O'Brien	OF9	R	31	9	31	0	4	1	0	0	3	5	1	0	.129	.161
Jimmy Piersall	OF2	R	20	6	2	1	0	0	0	0	0	0	1	0	.000	.000
Charlie Maxwell	OF2	L	23	3	4	1	0	0	0	0	0	1	1	0	.000	.000
1 Merrill Combs 30 L 0-0, Bob Scherbarth 24 R 0-0																

NAME		T	AGE	W	L	PCT	SV	G	GS	CG	IP	H	BB	SO	SHO	ERA
			31	98	56	.636	31	155	155	66	1373	1322	708	712	12	4.15
Vic Raschi		R	31	21	8	.724	1	33	32	17	257	232	116	155	2	3.99
Ed Lopat		R	32	18	8	.692	1	35	32	15	236	244	65	72	3	3.47
Allie Reynolds		R	35	16	12	.571	2	35	29	14	241	215	138	160	2	3.73
Tommy Byrne		L	30	15	9	.625	0	31	31	10	203	188	160	118	2	4.74
Whitey Ford		L	21	9	1	.900	1	20	12	7	112	87	52	59	2	2.81
2 Tom Ferrick		R	35	8	4	.667	9	30	0	0	57	49	22	20	0	3.63
Fred Sanford		R	30	5	4	.556	0	26	12	2	113	103	79	54	0	4.54
Joe Page		L	32	3	7	.300	13	37	0	0	55	66	31	33	0	5.07
2 Joe Ostrowski		L	33	1	1	.500	3	21	4	1	44	50	15	15	0	5.11
Bob Porterfield (AJ-BJ)		R	26	1	1	.500	1	10	2	0	20	28	8	9	0	8.55
1 Don Johnson		R	23	1	0	1.000	0	8	0	0	18	35	12	9	0	10.00
1 Duane Pillette		R	27	0	0	—	0	4	0	0	7	9	3	4	0	1.29
Lew Burdette		R	23	0	0	—	0	2	0	0	1	3	0	0	0	9.00
Dave Madison		R	29	0	0	—	0	1	0	0	3	3	1	1	0	6.00
Ernie Nevel		R	30	0	1	.000	0	3	1	0	6	10	6	3	0	10.50
			29	95	59	.617	20	157	157	72	1407	1444	553	576	9	4.13
Art Houtteman		R	22	19	12	.613	4	41	34	21	275	257	99	88	4	3.53
Fred Hutchinson		R	30	17	8	.680	0	39	26	10	232	269	48	71	1	3.96
Hal Newhouser		L	29	15	13	.536	3	35	30	15	214	232	81	87	1	4.33
Dizzy Trout		R	35	13	5	.722	4	34	20	11	185	190	64	88	1	3.75
Ted Gray (IL)		L	25	10	7	.588	1	27	21	7	149	139	72	102	0	4.41
Hal White		R	31	9	6	.600	1	42	8	3	111	96	65	53	1	4.54
Marlin Stuart		R	31	3	1	.750	2	19	1	0	44	59	22	19	0	5.52
Virgil Trucks (SA)		R	33	3	1	.750	0	7	7	2	48	45	21	25	1	3.56
Paul Calvert		R	32	2	2	.500	4	32	0	0	51	71	25	14	0	6.35
Saul Rogovin		R	28	2	1	.667	0	11	5	1	40	39	26	11	0	4.50
3 Hank Borowy		R	34	1	1	.500	0	13	2	1	33	23	16	12	0	3.27
Ray Herbert		R	20	1	2	.333	1	8	3	1	22	20	12	5	0	3.68
2 Bill Connelly		R	25	0	0	—	0	4	0	0	4	4	2	1	0	6.75
			27	94	60	.610	28	154	154	66	1362	1413	748	630	6	4.88
Mel Parnell		L	28	18	10	.643	3	40	31	21	249	244	106	93	2	3.61
Joe Dobson		R	33	15	10	.600	4	39	27	12	207	217	81	81	1	4.17
Ellis Kinder		R	35	14	12	.538	9	48	23	11	207	212	78	95	1	4.26
Chuck Stobbs		L	20	12	7	.632	1	32	21	6	169	158	88	78	0	5.11
Walt Masterson		R	30	8	6	.571	3	33	15	6	129	145	82	60	0	5.65
Willard Nixon		R	22	8	6	.571	2	22	15	2	101	126	58	57	0	6.06
Mickey McDermott		L	21	7	3	.700	5	38	15	4	130	119	124	96	0	5.19
1 Al Papai		R	33	4	2	.667	2	16	3	2	51	61	28	19	0	6.71
Charley Schanz		R	31	3	2	.600	0	14	0	0	23	25	24	13	0	8.22
Dick Littlefield		L	24	2	2	.500	1	15	5	1	27	24	13	0	9.39
Harry Taylor		R	31	2	0	1.000	0	7	2	1	19	13	8	1	1	1.42
Jim McDonald		R	23	1	0	1.000	0	3	3	1	21	23	10	5	0	3.79
Earl Johnson		L	31	0	0	—	0	11	0	0	14	18	8	6	0	7.07
Gordy Mueller		L	27	0	0	—	0	11	0	0	13	11	13	5	0	10.29
Jim Suchecki		R	27	0	0	—	0	2	0	0	4	4	4	0	0	4.50
Jim Atkins		L	29	0	0	—	0	2	0	0	3	3	3	0	0	9.00
Boo Ferriss		R	28	0	1	.000	0	1	0	0	1	6	2	1	0	18.00
Bob Gillespie		R	30	0	1	.000	0	1	0	0	1	3	3	0	0	27.00
Phil Marchildon		R	36	0	1	.000	0	1	0	0	1	3	4	0	0	9.00
Frank Quinn		R	22	0	0	—	0	1	0	0	1	1	0	0	0	9.00

CLEVELAND — 4th 92-62 .597 6 — LOU BOUDREAU

NAME	G by Pos	B	AGE	G	AB	R	H	2B	3B	HR	RBI	BB	SO	SB	BA	SA
TOTALS			29	155	5263	806	1417	222	46	164	758	693	624	40	.269	.422
Luke Easter	1B128 OF13	L	34	141	540	96	151	20	4	28	107	70	95	0	.280	.487
Joe Gordon	2B105	R	35	119	368	59	87	12	1	19	57	56	44	4	.236	.429
Ray Boone	SS102	R	26	109	365	53	110	14	6	7	58	56	27	1	.301	.430
Al Rosen	3B154	R	26	155	554	100	159	23	4	37	116	100	72	5	.287	.543
Bob Kennedy	OF144	R	29	146	540	79	157	27	5	9	54	53	31	3	.291	.409
Larry Doby	OF140	L	25	142	503	110	164	25	5	25	102	98	71	8	.326	.545
Dale Mitchell	OF127	L	28	130	506	81	156	11	5	3	49	67	21	3	.308	.399
Jim Hegan	C129	R	29	131	415	53	91	16	5	14	58	42	52	1	.219	.383
Lou Boudreau	SS61 1B8 2B2 3B2	R	32	81	260	23	70	13	2	1	29	31	5	1	.269	.346
Bobby Avila	2B62 SS2	R	26	80	201	39	60	10	2	1	21	29	17	5	.299	.383
Bob Lemon	P44	R	29	72	136	21	37	9	1	6	26	13	25	0	.272	.485
Allie Clark	OF41	R	27	59	163	19	35	6	1	6	21	11	10	0	.215	.374
Thurman Tucker	OF34	R	32	57	101	13	18	2	0	1	7	14	14	1	.178	.228
Ray Murray	C45	R	32	55	139	16	38	8	2	1	13	12	13	1	.273	.381
1 Mickey Vernon	1B25	L	32	28	90	8	17	0	0	0	10	12	10	2	.189	.189
Jim Lemon	OF10	R	22	12	34	4	6	1	0	1	3	1	2	0	.176	.294
Herb Conyers	1B1	R	29	7	9	2	3	0	0	1	1	1	2	1	.333	.667
1 Johnny Berardino	2B1 3B1	R	33	4	5	1	2	0	0	0	3	1	0	0	.400	.400

NAME	T	AGE	W	L	PCT	SV	G	GS	CG	IP	H	BB	SO	SHO	ERA
		31	92	62	.597	16	155	155	69	1379	1289	647	674	11	3.75
Bob Lemon	R	29	23	11	.676	3	44	37	22	288	281	146	170	3	3.84
Early Wynn	R	30	18	8	.692	0	32	28	14	214	166	101	143	2	3.20
Bob Feller	R	31	16	11	.593	0	35	34	16	247	230	103	119	3	3.43
Mike Garcia	R	26	11	11	.500	0	33	29	11	184	191	74	96	0	3.86
Steve Gromek	R	30	10	7	.588	0	31	13	4	113	94	36	43	1	3.66
Al Benton	R	39	4	2	.667	4	36	0	0	63	57	30	26	0	3.57
Sam Zoldak	L	31	4	2	.667	0	33	3	0	64	64	21	15	0	3.94
Jessie Flores	R	35	3	3	.500	4	28	2	1	53	53	25	27	1	3.74
1 Gene Bearden	L	29	1	3	.250	0	14	3	0	45	57	32	10	0	6.20
2 Dick Weik	R	22	1	3	.250	0	11	2	0	26	18	26	16	0	3.81
Al Aber	L	22	1	0	1.000	0	1	1	1	9	5	4	4	0	2.00
Dick Rozek	L	23	0	0	—	0	12	0	0	25	28	19	14	0	5.04
Marino Pieretti	R	29	0	0	.000	1	29	0	0	47	45	30	11	0	4.21

WASHINGTON — 5th 67-87 .435 31 — BUCKY HARRIS

NAME	G by Pos	B	AGE	G	AB	R	H	2B	3B	HR	RBI	BB	SO	SB	BA	SA
TOTALS			28	155	5251	690	1365	190	53	76	659	671	606	42	.260	.360
2 Mickey Vernon	1B85	L	32	90	327	47	100	17	3	9	65	50	29	6	.306	.459
2 Cass Michaels	2B104	R	24	106	388	48	97	8	4	4	47	55	39	2	.250	.322
Sam Dente	SS128 2B29	R	28	155	603	56	144	20	5	2	59	39	19	1	.239	.299
Eddie Yost	3B155	R	23	155	573	114	169	26	2	11	58	141	63	6	.295	.405
Bud Stewart	OF100	L	34	118	378	46	101	15	6	4	35	46	33	5	.267	.370
Irv Noren	OF121 1B17	L	25	138	542	80	160	27	10	14	98	67	77	5	.295	.450
Gil Coan (FS)	OF98	L	28	104	366	58	111	9	4	7	50	28	46	10	.303	.429
Al Evans	C88	R	33	90	289	24	68	8	3	2	30	29	21	0	.235	.304
Sam Mele	OF99 1B16	R	28	126	435	57	119	21	6	12	86	51	40	2	.274	.432
Mickey Grasso	C69	R	30	75	195	25	56	4	1	1	22	25	31	1	.287	.333
Sherry Robertson	OF14 2B12 3B1	L	31	71	123	19	32	3	3	2	16	22	18	1	.260	.382
2 John Ostrowski	OF45	R	32	55	141	16	32	2	1	4	23	20	31	2	.227	.340
1 Roberto Ortiz	OF19	R	35	39	75	4	17	2	1	0	8	7	12	0	.227	.280
2 Merrill Combs	SS30	R	30	37	102	19	25	1	0	0	6	22	16	0	.245	.255
1 Eddie Robinson	1B36	L	29	36	129	21	30	4	2	1	13	25	4	0	.233	.318
1 Al Kozar	2B15	R	28	20	55	7	11	1	0	0	3	5	8	0	.200	.218
Len Okrie	C17	R	26	17	27	1	6	0	0	0	2	6	7	0	.222	.222
Hal Keller	C8	L	22	11	28	1	6	3	0	1	5	2	2	0	.214	.429
Fred Taylor	1B3	R	25	6	16	1	2	0	0	0	2	0	1	0	.125	.125
1 Clyde Vollmer	OF3	R	28	6	14	4	4	0	0	0	1	2	3	1	.286	.286
2 Tommy O'Brien	OF3	R	31	3	9	1	1	0	0	0	0	0	1	0	.111	.111
George Genovese		R	28	3	1	1	0	0	0	0	0	1	0	0	.000	.000

NAME	T	AGE	W	L	PCT	SV	G	GS	CG	IP	H	BB	SO	SHO	ERA
		31	67	87	.435	18	155	155	59	1365	1479	648	486	7	4.65
Sid Hudson	R	35	14	14	.500	0	30	30	17	238	261	98	75	0	4.08
2 Bob Kuzava	L	27	8	7	.533	0	22	22	8	155	156	75	84	1	3.95
Joe Haynes	R	32	5	7	.417	0	27	10	1	102	124	46	15	1	5.82
Sandy Consuegra	R	29	7	8	.467	2	21	18	8	125	132	57	38	2	4.39
Connie Marrero	R	38	6	10	.375	1	27	19	8	152	159	55	63	1	4.50
Mickey Harris	L	33	5	9	.357	15	53	0	0	98	93	46	41	0	4.78
Al Sima	R	28	5	4	.444	0	17	9	1	77	89	26	23	0	4.79
2 Gene Bearden	L	29	3	5	.375	0	12	9	4	69	81	33	20	0	4.17
1 Ray Scarborough	R	32	3	5	.375	0	8	8	4	58	62	22	24	2	4.03
Jim Pearce	R	25	2	1	.667	0	3	1	0	57	58	37	18	0	6.00
Lloyd Hittle	L	26	2	4	.333	0	11	4	1	43	60	17	19	0	5.02
Steve Nagy	L	31	2	5	.286	0	9	5	2	53	69	29	17	0	6.62
Julio Moreno	R	29	1	1	.500	0	2	2	2	21	22	12	7	0	4.71
Carlos Pascual	R	19	1	1	.500	0	2	2	1	17	12	8	3	0	2.12
Elmer Singleton	R	32	1	2	.333	0	21	1	0	36	39	17	19	0	5.25
1 Dick Weik	R	22	1	3	.250	0	14	5	1	44	38	47	26	0	4.30
Dick Welteroth	R	22	0	0	—	0	5	0	0	6	5	6	1	0	3.00
Bob Ross	L	21	0	1	.000	0	6	2	0	15	15	2	2	0	8.31
Rogelio Martinez	R	31	0	1	.000	0	2	1	1	1	1	4	2	0	36.00

CHICAGO — 6th 60-94 .390 38 — JACK ONSLOW 8-22 .267   RED CORRIDEN 52-72 .419

NAME	G by Pos	B	AGE	G	AB	R	H	2B	3B	HR	RBI	BB	SO	SB	BA	SA
TOTALS			29	156	5260	625	1368	172	47	93	592	551	566	19	.260	.364
2 Eddie Robinson	1B119	L	29	119	424	62	133	11	2	20	73	60	28	0	.314	.491
Nellie Fox	2B121	L	22	130	457	45	113	12	7	0	30	35	17	4	.247	.304
Chico Carrasquel	SS115	R	22	141	524	72	148	21	5	4	46	66	46	0	.282	.365
Hank Majeski	3B112	R	33	122	414	47	128	18	2	6	46	42	34	1	.309	.406
2 Marv Rickert	OF78 1B1	R	29	84	278	38	66	9	2	4	27	21	42	0	.237	.327
Dave Philley	OF154	R	30	156	619	69	150	21	5	14	80	52	57	6	.242	.360
Gus Zernial	OF137	R	27	143	543	75	152	16	4	29	93	38	110	6	.280	.484
Phil Masi	C114	R	33	122	377	38	105	17	2	7	55	49	36	2	.279	.390
Floyd Baker	3B53 2B3 OF2	L	33	83	186	26	59	7	0	0	11	32	10	1	.317	.355
Gordon Goldsberry	1B40 OF3	L	22	82	127	19	34	8	2	0	25	26	18	0	.268	.409
2 Mike McCormick	OF44	R	33	55	138	16	32	4	3	0	10	16	6	0	.232	.304
Luke Appling	SS20 1B13 2B1	R	43	50	128	11	30	3	4	0	13	12	8	2	.234	.320
2 Gus Niarhos	C36	R	29	41	105	17	34	4	0	0	16	14	6	0	.324	.362
Jerry Scala	OF23	R	23	40	67	8	13	2	1	0	6	10	10	0	.194	.254
1 Cass Michaels	2B35	R	24	36	138	21	43	6	3	4	19	13	8	0	.312	.486
Herb Adams	OF33	R	22	34	118	12	24	2	3	0	2	12	7	3	.203	.271
Eddie Malone	C21	R	30	31	71	2	16	2	0	0	10	10	8	0	.225	.254
13 John Ostrowski	OF15	R	32	22	49	10	12	2	1	2	2	9	9	0	.245	.449
Jim Busby	OF12	R	23	18	48	5	10	0	0	0	4	1	5	0	.208	.208
Joe Erautt	C5	R	28	16	18	0	4	0	0	0	1	3	0	0	.222	.222
2 Al Kozar	2B4 3B1	L	28	10	10	4	3	0	1	0	2	0	3	0	.300	.600
Charlie Kress	1B2	L	28	3	8	0	0	0	0	0	0	1	0	0	.000	.000
Ed McGhee	OF1	R	25	3	6	1	1	0	0	0	0	2	1	0	.167	.500
Bill Wilson	OF2	R	21	3	6	0	0	0	0	0	0	2	2	0	.000	.000
Joe Kirrene	3B1	R	18	3	4	0	1	0	0	0	0	0	2	0	.250	.250
Bill Salkeld	C1	L	33	1	0	0	0	0	0	0	0	0	0	0	.000	.000
2 Dick Wakefield (HO) 29																

NAME	T	AGE	W	L	PCT	SV	G	GS	CG	IP	H	BB	SO	SHO	ERA
		29	60	94	.390	9	156	156	62	1366	1370	734	566	7	4.41
Billy Pierce	L	23	12	16	.429	1	33	29	15	219	189	137	118	1	3.99
2 Ray Scarborough	R	32	10	13	.435	1	27	23	8	149	160	62	70	1	5.28
Bill Wight	L	28	10	16	.385	0	30	28	13	206	213	79	62	3	3.58
Bob Cain	R	25	9	12	.429	2	34	23	11	172	153	109	77	1	3.92
Luis Aloma	R	27	7	2	.778	4	42	0	0	88	77	53	49	0	3.78
Randy Gumpert	R	32	5	12	.294	0	40	17	6	155	165	58	48	1	4.76
Ken Holcombe	R	31	3	10	.231	1	24	15	5	96	122	45	37	0	4.59
Howie Judson	R	24	2	3	.400	0	46	3	1	112	105	63	34	0	4.64
1 Bob Kuzava	L	27	1	3	.250	0	10	7	1	44	43	27	21	0	5.73
1 Mickey Haefner	L	37	1	6	.143	0	24	9	2	71	83	45	17	0	5.70
2 Lou Kretlow	R	29	1	0	—	0	11	0	0	21	17	27	14	0	3.86
1 Jack Bruner	L	26	0	0	—	0	2	0	0	12	7	14	8	0	3.75
1 Bill Connelly	R	25	0	0	—	0	2	0	0	2	5	1	0	0	13.50
Charlie Cuellar	R	32	0	0	—	0	1	0	0	2	4	0	0	0	45.00
Marv Rotblatt	L	22	0	0	—	0	9	0	0	11	5	6	6	0	6.00
John Perkovich	R	26	0	0	—	0	1	0	0	5	7	1	3	0	7.20
Gus Keriazakos	R	18	0	1	.000	0	2	1	1	7	5	1	0	0	22.50

ST. LOUIS — 7th 58-96 .377 40 — ZACK TAYLOR

NAME	G by Pos	B	AGE	G	AB	R	H	2B	3B	HR	RBI	BB	SO	SB	BA	SA
TOTALS			25	154	5163	684	1269	235	43	106	642	690	744	39	.246	.370
Don Lenhardt	1B86 OF39 3B10	R	27	139	480	75	131	22	6	22	81	90	94	3	.273	.481
Owen Friend	2B93 3B24 SS3	R	23	119	372	48	88	15	2	8	50	40	68	2	.237	.352
Tom Upton	SS115 2B32 3B1	R	23	124	389	50	92	5	6	2	30	52	45	7	.237	.296
Bill Sommers	3B37 2B21	R	27	65	137	24	35	5	1	0	14	25	14	0	.255	.307
Ken Wood	OF94	R	26	122	380	42	83	24	0	13	62	38	58	0	.225	.396
Ray Coleman	OF98	L	28	117	384	54	104	25	6	8	55	32	37	5	.271	.430
Dick Kokos	OF127	L	22	143	490	77	128	27	5	18	67	88	73	8	.261	.447
Sherm Lollar	C109	R	25	126	396	55	111	22	3	13	65	64	25	2	.280	.449
Roy Sievers	OF78 3B21	R	23	113	370	46	88	20	4	10	57	34	42	1	.238	.395
Hank Arft	1B84	R	28	95	261	45	75	16	4	1	32	46	48	3	.268	.364
2 Snuffy Stirnweiss	2B62 3B31 SS5	R	31	93	326	32	71	16	2	1	24	51	49	3	.218	.288
Les Moss	C60	R	25	84	222	24	59	6	0	8	34	26	32	0	.266	.401
Jim Delsing	OF53	R	24	69	209	25	55	5	2	0	15	20	23	1	.263	.306
Billy DeMars (NJ)	SS54 3B5	R	24	61	178	25	44	5	1	0	13	22	13	0	.247	.287
Ned Garver	P37 OF1	R	24	51	91	13	26	4	0	1	10	8	9	0	.286	.363
Leo Thomas	3B35	R	26	35	121	19	24	6	1	0	9	24	14	0	.198	.273
Frankie Gustine	3B6	R	30	9	19	1	3	0	0	0	0	1	5	0	.158	.211

NAME	T	AGE	W	L	PCT	SV	G	GS	CG	IP	H	BB	SO	SHO	ERA
		27	58	96	.377	14	154	154	56	1365	1629	651	448	7	5.20
Ned Garver	R	24	13	18	.419	0	37	31	22	260	264	108	85	2	3.39
Stubby Overmire	L	31	9	12	.429	0	31	19	8	161	200	45	39	2	4.19
Dick Starr	R	29	7	5	.583	2	32	16	4	124	140	74	30	1	5.01
Al Widmar	R	25	7	15	.318	4	36	26	8	195	211	74	78	1	4.75
2 Don Johnson	R	23	5	6	.455	1	25	12	4	96	126	55	31	1	6.09
Cliff Fannin	R	26	5	9	.357	1	25	16	3	102	116	58	42	0	6.53
Harry Dorish	R	28	4	9	.308	0	29	13	4	109	162	36	36	0	6.44
2 Duane Pillette	R	27	3	5	.375	2	24	7	1	74	104	44	18	0	7.05
1 Joe Ostrowski	L	33	2	4	.333	0	9	7	2	57	57	11	15	0	4.63
1 Jack Bruner	R	26	1	2	.333	1	13	1	0	35	36	23	16	0	4.63
Cuddles Marshall	R	24	1	3	.250	1	28	2	0	54	72	51	24	0	7.83
1 Tom Ferrick	R	35	1	3	.250	2	16	0	0	24	24	7	6	0	4.13
Sid Schacht	R	32	0	0	—	1	8	1	0	11	14	14	6	0	10.54
Tommy Fine	R	35	0	0	—	0	14	0	0	37	53	25	6	0	8.03
Ed Albrecht	R	21	0	1	.000	0	7	0	0	7	6	7	1	0	5.14
Ribs Raney	R	27	0	1	.000	0	2	0	0	9	14	10	10	0	4.50
1 Lou Kretlow	R	24	0	0	—	0	5	0	0	14	25	18	10	0	12.21

Russ Bauers 36 R 0-0, Bill Kennedy 29 L 0-0, Lou Sleater 23 L 0-0

PHILADELPHIA — 8th 52-102 .338 46 — CONNIE MACK

NAME	G by Pos	B	AGE	G	AB	R	H	2B	3B	HR	RBI	BB	SO	SB	BA	SA
TOTALS			32	154	5212	670	1361	204	53	100	627	685	493	42	.261	.378
Ferris Fain	1B151	L	29	151	522	83	147	25	4	10	83	133	26	8	.282	.402
Billy Hitchcock	2B107 SS1	R	33	115	399	35	109	22	5	1	54	45	32	3	.273	.361
Eddie Joost	SS131	R	34	131	476	79	111	12	3	18	58	103	68	5	.233	.384
1 Bob Dillinger	3B84	R	31	84	356	55	110	21	9	3	41	31	20	5	.309	.444
Elmer Valo	OF117	L	29	129	446	62	125	16	5	10	46	82	22	12	.280	.406
Sam Chapman	OF140	R	34	144	553	93	139	20	6	23	95	68	79	3	.251	.434
Paul Lehner	OF101	R	30	114	427	48	132	17	5	9	52	32	33	1	.309	.436
Mike Guerra	C78	R	37	87	252	25	71	10	4	2	26	16	12	1	.282	.377
Kermit Wahl	3B61 SS18 2B2	R	27	89	280	26	72	12	3	2	27	30	30	1	.257	.343
Wally Moses	OF62	L	39	88	265	47	70	16	5	2	21	40	17	0	.264	.385
Pete Suder	2B47 3B11 SS10 1B4	R	34	77	248	34	61	10	0	8	35	23	31	2	.246	.383
Barney McCosky	OF42	L	33	66	179	19	43	10	1	0	11	22	12	0	.240	.307
Joe Tipton	C59	R	28	64	164	16	37	8	1	5	20	19	16	0	.226	.402
Joe Astroth	C38	R	27	39	110	11	36	7	0	0	18	18	3	0	.327	.400
Bob Wellman	OF2	R	24	11	15	1	5	2	0	0	4	1	4	0	.333	.533
2 Roberto Ortiz	OF3	R	35	6	14	1	1	0	0	0	0	2	1	0	.071	.071
Gene Markland	2B5	R	30	5	8	2	1	0	0	0	0	3	1	0	.125	.125
Ben Guintini	OF1	R	31	4	0	0	0	0	0	0	0	1	0	0	.000	.000
Bob Rinker	C1	R	29	3	3	1	1	0	0	0	0	0	1	0	.333	.333

NAME	T	AGE	W	L	PCT	SV	G	GS	CG	IP	H	BB	SO	SHO	ERA
		26	52	102	.338	18	154	154	50	1346	1528	729	466	3	5.49
Bob Hooper	R	28	15	10	.600	5	45	20	3	170	181	91	58	0	5.03
Hank Wyse	R	32	9	14	.391	0	41	23	4	171	192	87	33	0	5.84
Bobby Shantz	L	24	8	14	.364	0	36	23	6	215	251	85	93	1	4.60
Alex Kellner	L	25	8	20	.286	2	36	29	15	225	253	112	85	0	5.48
Lou Brissie	L	26	7	19	.269	8	46	31	15	246	237	117	101	2	4.02
Carl Scheib	R	23	3	10	.231	3	43	8	1	106	138	70	37	0	7.22
Johnny Kucab	R	30	1	1	.500	0	7	0	0	26	29	8	8	0	3.46
Dick Fowler (AJ)	R	29	1	5	.167	0	11	6	2	67	75	56	15	0	6.45
Harry Byrd	R	25	0	0	—	0	9	0	0	11	25	9	2	0	16.36
Eddie Klieman	R	32	0	0	—	0	1	0	0	2	5	1	1	0	9.00
Les McCrabb	R	35	0	0	—	0	1	0	0	1	5	0	0	0	36.00
Moe Burtschy (EJ)	R	27	0	0	—	0	5	0	0	30	34	21	9	0	7.11
Joe Murray	L	29	0	1	.000	0	2	0	0	11	15	9	0	0	5.70
Joe Coleman	R	27	0	0	—	0	12	5	0	54	74	50	12	0	8.50

PHILADELPHIA 1st 91-63 .591 — EDDIE SAWYER

NAME	G by Pos	B	AGE	G	AB	R	H	2B	3B	HR	RBI	BB	SO	SB	BA	SA
TOTALS			26	157	5426	722	1440	225	55	125	673	535	569	33	.265	.396
Eddie Waitkus	1B154	L	30	154	641	102	182	32	5	2	44	55	29	3	.284	.359
Mike Goliat	2B145	R	28	145	483	49	113	13	6	13	64	53	75	3	.234	.366
Granny Hamner	SS157	R	23	157	637	78	172	27	5	11	82	39	35	2	.270	.380
Willie Jones	3B157	R	24	157	610	100	163	28	6	25	88	61	40	1	.267	.456
Del Ennis	OF149	R	25	153	595	92	185	34	8	31	126	56	59	2	.311	.551
Richie Ashburn	OF147	L	23	151	594	84	180	25	14	2	41	63	32	14	.303	.402
Dick Sisler	OF137	L	29	141	523	79	155	29	4	13	83	64	50	1	.296	.442
Andy Seminick	C124	R	29	130	393	55	113	15	3	24	68	68	50	0	.288	.524
Dick Whitman	OF32	L	29	75	132	21	33	7	0	0	12	10	10	1	.250	.303
Stan Lopata	C51	R	24	58	129	10	27	2	0	1	11	22	25	1	.209	.279
2 Jimmy Bloodworth	2B27, 1B7, 3B2	R	32	54	96	6	22	2	0	0	13	6	12	0	.229	.250
Putsy Caballero	2B5, 3B4, SS2	R	22	46	24	12	4	0	0	0	1	6	2	1	.167	.167
Bill Nicholson	OF15	L	35	41	58	3	13	2	1	3	10	8	16	0	.224	.448
Jackie Mayo	OF15	R	24	18	36	1	8	3	0	0	3	2	5	0	.222	.306
Ken Silvestri	C9	B	34	11	20	2	5	0	1	0	4	4	3	0	.250	.350
Stan Hollmig	OF3	R	24	11	12	1	3	2	0	0	1	0	3	0	.250	.417
1 Johnny Blatnik	OF1	R	29	4	4	0	1	0	0	0	0	2	3	0	.250	.250

NAME	T	AGE	W	L	PCT	SV	G	GS	CG	IP	H	BB	SO	SHO	ERA
		27	91	63	.591	27	157	157	57	1406	1324	530	620	13	3.50
Robin Roberts	R	23	20	11	.645	1	40	39	21	304	282	77	146	5	3.02
Curt Simmons	L	21	17	8	.680	1	31	27	11	215	178	88	146	2	3.39
Jim Konstanty	R	33	16	7	.696	22	74	0	0	152	108	50	56	0	2.66
Bob Miller	R	24	11	6	.647	1	35	22	7	174	190	57	44	2	3.57
Russ Meyer	R	26	9	11	.450	1	32	25	3	160	193	67	74	0	5.29
Bubba Church	R	25	8	6	.571	1	31	18	8	142	113	56	50	2	2.73
2 Ken Johnson	L	27	4	1	.800	0	14	8	3	61	61	43	32	1	3.98
Ken Heintzelman	L	34	3	9	.250	0	23	17	4	125	122	54	39	1	4.10
Blix Donnelly	R	36	2	4	.333	0	14	1	0	21	30	10	10	0	4.29
Milo Candini	R	32	1	0	1.000	0	18	0	0	30	32	15	10	0	2.70
1 Hank Borowy	R	34	0	0	—	0	6	5	4	30	32	16	10	0	6.00
Jack Brittin	R	26	0	0	—	0	3	0	0	4	2	1	0	0	4.50
Paul Stuffel	R	23	0	0	—	0	3	0	0	5	4	1	3	0	1.80
Jocko Thompson	L	33	0	0	—	0	2	0	0	4	1	4	2	0	0.00
Steve Ridzik	R	21	0	0	—	0	1	0	0	3	1	2	0	0	6.00

BROOKLYN 2nd 89-65 .578 2 — BURT SHOTTON

NAME	G by Pos	B	AGE	G	AB	R	H	2B	3B	HR	RBI	BB	SO	SB	BA	SA
TOTALS			28	155	5364	847	1461	247	46	194	774	607	632	77	.272	.444
Gil Hodges	1B153	R	26	153	561	98	159	26	2	32	113	73	73	6	.283	.508
Jackie Robinson	2B144	R	31	144	518	99	170	39	4	14	81	80	24	12	.328	.500
Pee Wee Reese	SS134, 3B7	R	31	141	531	97	138	21	5	11	52	91	62	17	.260	.380
Billy Cox	3B107, 2B13, SS9	R	30	119	451	62	116	17	2	8	44	35	24	6	.257	.357
Carl Furillo	OF153	R	28	153	620	99	189	30	6	18	106	41	40	8	.305	.460
Duke Snider	OF151	L	23	152	620	109	199	31	10	31	107	58	79	16	.321	.553
Gene Hermanski	OF78	L	30	94	289	36	86	17	3	7	34	36	26	2	.298	.450
Roy Campanella	C123	R	28	126	437	70	123	19	3	31	89	55	51	1	.281	.551
Jim Russell	OF55	B	31	77	214	37	49	8	2	10	32	31	36	1	.229	.425
Bobby Morgan	3B52, SS10	R	24	67	199	38	45	10	3	7	21	32	43	0	.226	.412
Eddie Miksis	2B15, SS15, 3B7	R	23	51	76	13	19	2	1	2	10	5	10	3	.250	.382
Bruce Edwards	C38, 3B1	R	26	50	142	16	26	4	1	8	16	13	22	1	.183	.394
Tommy Brown	OF16	R	22	48	86	15	25	2	1	8	20	11	9	0	.291	.616
Cal Abrams	OF15	L	26	38	44	5	9	1	0	0	4	9	13	0	.205	.227
George Shuba	OF27	L	25	34	111	15	23	8	2	3	12	13	22	2	.207	.396
Wayne Belardi	1B1	L	19	10	10	0	0	0	0	0	0	0	4	0	.000	.000
Steve Lembo	C5	R	24	7	6	0	1	0	0	0	1	1	0	0	.167	.167
1 Spider Jorgensen	3B1	L	30	3	2	0	0	0	0	0	1	1	0	0	.000	.000

NAME	T	AGE	W	L	PCT	SV	G	GS	CG	IP	H	BB	SO	SHO	ERA
		27	89	65	.578	21	155	155	62	1390	1397	591	772	10	4.28
Don Newcombe	R	24	19	11	.633	3	40	35	20	267	258	75	130	4	3.71
Preacher Roe	L	35	19	11	.633	1	36	32	16	251	245	66	125	2	3.30
Erv Palica	R	22	13	8	.619	1	43	19	10	201	176	98	131	2	3.58
Dan Bankhead	R	30	9	4	.692	3	41	12	2	129	119	88	96	1	5.51
Carl Erskine	R	23	7	6	.538	1	22	13	3	103	109	35	50	0	4.72
Ralph Branca	R	24	7	9	.438	1	43	15	5	142	152	55	100	0	4.69
Bud Podbielan	R	26	5	4	.556	1	20	10	2	73	93	29	28	0	5.30
Jack Banta (SA)	R	25	4	4	.500	2	16	5	1	41	39	36	15	0	4.39
Rex Barney	R	25	2	1	.667	0	20	1	0	34	25	48	23	0	6.35
Joe Hatten	L	33	2	2	.500	0	23	8	2	69	82	31	29	1	4.57
1 Willie Ramsdell	R	34	1	2	.333	1	5	0	0	6	7	2	2	0	3.00
Chris Van Cuyk	L	23	1	3	.250	0	12	4	1	33	33	12	21	0	4.91
Billy Loes	R	20	0	0	—	0	10	0	0	13	16	5	2	0	7.62
Joe Landrum	R	21	0	0	—	0	7	0	0	7	12	1	5	0	7.71
Al Epperly	R	32	0	0	—	0	5	0	0	9	14	5	3	0	5.00
Jim Romano	R	23	0	0	—	0	4	0	0	8	8	8	3	0	6.00
Mal Mallette	R	23	0	0	—	0	2	0	0	1	2	1	2	0	6.00
Clem Labine	R	23	0	0	—	0	1	0	0	2	1	2	0	0	4.50
Pat McGlothin	R	29	0	0	—	0	1	0	0	2	5	1	2	0	13.50

NEW YORK 3rd 86-68 .558 5 — LEO DUROCHER

NAME	G by Pos	B	AGE	G	AB	R	H	2B	3B	HR	RBI	BB	SO	SB	BA	SA
TOTALS			26	154	5238	735	1352	204	50	133	684	627	629	42	.258	.392
Tookie Gilbert	1B111	L	21	113	322	40	71	12	2	4	32	43	36	3	.220	.307
Eddie Stanky	2B151	R	33	152	527	115	158	25	5	8	51	144	50	9	.300	.412
Al Dark	SS154	R	28	154	587	79	164	36	5	16	67	39	60	9	.279	.440
Hank Thompson	3B138, OF10	L	24	148	512	82	148	17	6	20	91	83	60	8	.289	.463
Don Mueller	OF125	L	23	132	525	60	153	15	6	7	84	10	26	1	.291	.383
Bobby Thomson	OF149	R	26	149	563	79	142	22	7	25	85	55	45	3	.252	.449
Whitey Lockman	OF128	L	23	129	532	72	157	28	5	6	52	42	29	1	.295	.400
Wes Westrum	C139	R	27	140	437	68	103	13	3	23	71	92	73	2	.236	.437
Monte Irvin	1B59, OF49, 3B1	R	31	110	374	61	112	19	5	15	66	52	41	3	.299	.497
Bill Rigney	2B23, 3B11	R	32	56	83	8	15	2	0	0	8	8	13	0	.181	.205
Roy Weatherly	OF15	L	35	52	69	10	18	3	3	0	11	13	10	0	.261	.391
Sammy Calderone	C33	R	24	34	67	9	20	1	0	1	12	2	5	0	.299	.358
Lucky Lohrke	3B16, 2B1	R	26	30	43	4	8	0	0	0	4	4	8	0	.186	.186
Jack Maguire	OF9, 1B2	R	25	29	40	3	7	2	0	0	3	3	13	1	.175	.225
2 Spider Jorgensen	3B5	L	30	24	37	5	5	0	0	0	4	5	2	0	.135	.135
Rudy Rufer	SS8	R	23	15	11	1	1	0	0	0	0	1	3	0	.091	.091
Jack Harshman	1B9	L	22	9	32	3	4	0	0	2	4	3	6	0	.125	.313
Sal Yvars	C9	R	26	9	14	0	2	0	0	0	1	2	0	0	.143	.143
Pete Milne		L	25	4	4	1	1	0	1	0	1	0	1	0	.250	.750
1 Ray Mueller	C4	R	38	4	11	0	1	1	0	0	0	0	2	0	.091	.182
1 Mike McCormick		R	33	4	4	0	0	0	0	0	0	0	1	0	.000	.000
Marv Blaylock		L	20	1	1	0	0	0	0	0	0	0	0	0	.000	.000
Nap Reyes	1B1	R	30	1	1	0	0	0	0	0	0	0	0	0	.000	.000

NAME	T	AGE	W	L	PCT	SV	G	GS	CG	IP	H	BB	SO	SHO	ERA
		30	86	68	.558	15	154	154	70	1375	1268	536	596	19	3.71
Larry Jansen	R	29	19	13	.594	3	40	35	21	275	238	55	161	5	3.01
Sal Maglie	R	33	18	4	.818	1	47	16	12	206	169	86	96	5	2.71
Dave Koslo	L	30	13	15	.464	3	40	22	7	187	190	68	56	1	3.90
Sheldon Jones	R	28	13	16	.448	2	40	28	11	199	188	90	97	2	4.61
2 Jim Hearn	R	29	11	3	.786	0	16	16	11	125	72	38	54	5	1.94*
Monte Kennedy	L	28	5	4	.556	2	36	17	5	114	120	53	41	0	4.74
Clint Hartung	R	27	3	3	.500	0	20	8	1	65	87	44	23	0	6.65
Jack Kramer	R	32	3	6	.333	1	35	9	1	87	91	39	27	0	3.52
George Spencer	R	23	1	0	1.000	0	10	1	1	25	12	7	5	0	2.52
Andy Hansen	R	25	0	1	.000	3	31	1	0	57	64	26	19	0	5.53
Kirby Higbe	R	35	0	3	.000	1	18	1	0	35	37	30	17	0	4.86

*Hearn, also with St. Louis, league leader in ERA with 2.49

BOSTON 4th 83-71 .539 8 — BILLY SOUTHWORTH

NAME	G by Pos	B	AGE	G	AB	R	H	2B	3B	HR	RBI	BB	SO	SB	BA	SA
TOTALS			29	156	5363	785	1411	246	36	148	726	615	616	71	.263	.405
Earl Torgeson	1B156	L	26	156	576	120	167	30	3	23	87	119	69	15	.290	.472
Roy Hartsfield	2B96	R	24	107	419	62	116	15	2	7	24	27	61	7	.277	.372
Buddy Kerr	SS155	R	27	155	507	45	115	24	2	4	46	50	50	0	.227	.310
Bob Elliott	3B137	R	33	142	531	94	162	28	5	24	107	68	67	2	.305	.512
Tommy Holmes	OF88	L	33	105	322	44	96	20	1	9	51	33	8	0	.298	.450
Sam Jethroe	OF141	R	32	141	582	100	159	28	8	18	58	52	93	35	.273	.442
Sid Gordon	OF123, 3B10	R	32	134	481	78	146	33	4	27	103	78	31	2	.304	.557
2 Walker Cooper	C88	R	35	102	337	52	111	19	3	14	60	30	26	1	.329	.528
Willard Marshall	OF85	L	29	105	298	38	70	10	2	5	40	36	5	1	.235	.332
Del Crandall	C75, 1B1	R	20	79	255	21	56	11	0	4	37	13	24	0	.220	.310
Luis Olmo	OF55, 3B1	R	30	69	154	23	35	7	1	5	22	18	23	3	.227	.383
Sibby Sisti	SS23, 2B19, 3B13, 1B1, OF1	R	29	69	105	21	18	3	1	2	11	16	19	1	.171	.276
Pete Reiser	OF24, 3B1	R	31	53	78	12	16	2	0	1	10	18	22	1	.205	.269
Gene Mauch	2B28, 3B7, SS5	R	24	48	121	17	28	5	0	1	15	14	9	1	.231	.298
1 Connie Ryan	2B20	R	30	20	72	12	14	2	0	3	6	12	9	0	.194	.347
Bob Addis	OF7	L	24	16	28	7	7	1	0	0	2	3	5	1	.250	.286
Paul Burris	C8	R	26	10	23	1	4	1	0	0	3	1	2	0	.174	.217
2 Emil Verban	2B2	R	34	4	5	1	0	0	0	0	0	0	0	0	.000	.000
Walt Linden	C3	R	26	3	5	0	2	1	0	0	1	0	0	0	.400	.600

NAME	T	AGE	W	L	PCT	SV	G	GS	CG	IP	H	BB	SO	SHO	ERA
		27	83	71	.539	10	156	156	88	1385	1411	554	615	7	4.13
Warren Spahn	L	29	21	17	.553	1	41	39	25	293	248	111	191	1	3.16
Johnny Sain	R	32	20	13	.606	0	37	37	25	278	294	70	96	3	3.95
Vern Bickford	R	29	19	14	.576	0	40	39	27	312	293	122	126	2	3.46
Bob Chipman	R	31	7	7	.500	1	27	12	4	124	127	37	40	0	4.43
Max Surkont	R	28	5	2	.714	0	9	6	2	56	63	20	21	0	3.21
Norm Roy	R	21	4	3	.571	1	19	6	2	60	72	39	25	0	5.10
Bobby Hogue	R	29	3	5	.375	7	36	1	0	63	69	31	15	0	5.00
Ernie Johnson	R	26	2	0	1.000	0	16	1	0	21	37	13	15	0	6.86
Johnny Antonelli	L	20	2	3	.400	0	20	6	2	58	81	22	33	1	5.93
Dick Manville	R	23	0	0	—	0	1	0	0	3	0	2	1	0	0.00
Murray Wall	R	23	0	0	—	0	2	0	0	4	6	1	1	0	9.00
Bucky Walters	R	41	0	0	—	0	1	0	0	4	4	4	0	0	4.50
Dave Cole	R	19	0	1	.000	0	4	0	0	8	7	10	3	0	1.13
Bob Hall	R	26	0	2	.000	0	4	2	0	18	23	13	7	0	7.02
Dick Donovan	R	22	0	0	—	0	10	3	0	25	28	34	9	0	8.10
2 Mickey Haefner	L	37	0	0	—	0	8	0	0	24	23	12	10	0	5.63

ST. LOUIS 5th 78-75 .510 12.5 — EDDIE DYER

NAME	G by Pos	B	AGE	G	AB	R	H	2B	3B	HR	RBI	BB	SO	SB	BA	SA
TOTALS			29	153	5215	693	1353	255	50	102	646	606	604	23	.259	.386
Stan Musial	OF77, 1B69	L	29	146	555	105	192	41	7	28	109	87	36	5	.346	.596
Red Schoendienst	2B143, SS10, 3B1	B	27	153	642	81	177	43	9	7	63	33	32	3	.276	.403
Marty Marion	SS101	R	32	106	372	36	92	10	2	4	40	44	55	1	.247	.317
Tommy Glaviano	3B106, 2B5, SS1	R	26	115	410	92	117	29	2	11	44	90	74	6	.285	.446
Enos Slaughter	OF145	L	34	148	556	82	161	26	7	10	101	66	33	3	.290	.415
Chuck Diering (BE)	OF81	R	27	89	204	34	51	12	0	3	18	38	38	1	.250	.353
Bill Howerton	OF94	L	28	110	313	50	88	20	8	10	59	47	60	0	.281	.492
Del Rice	C130	R	27	130	414	39	101	20	3	9	54	43	65	0	.244	.372
Eddie Kazak	3B48	R	29	93	207	21	53	2	2	5	23	18	19	0	.256	.357
Rocky Nelson	1B70	L	25	76	235	27	58	10	4	1	20	26	9	4	.247	.336
Eddie Miller	SS51, 3B1	R	33	64	172	17	39	8	0	3	22	19	21	0	.227	.326
Harry Walker	OF46, 1B2	L	33	60	150	17	31	5	0	0	7	18	12	0	.207	.240
Hal Rice	OF37	R	26	44	128	12	27	3	1	2	11	10	10	0	.211	.297
Johnny Lindell	OF33	R	33	36	113	16	21	5	2	5	16	15	24	0	.186	.398
Joe Garagiola (SJ)	C30	R	24	34	88	8	28	6	1	2	20	10	7	0	.318	.477
Erv Dusak	P14, OF2	R	29	23	12	0	1	0	0	0	1	1	4	0	.083	.167
Johnny Bucha	C17	R	25	22	36	1	5	1	0	0	1	4	7	0	.139	.167
2 Peanuts Lowrey	2B6, 3B5, OF4	R	33	20	56	10	15	0	0	1	4	6	1	0	.268	.321
Nippy Jones (SJ)	1B8	R	25	13	26	0	6	1	0	0	6	6	5	0	.231	.269
Solly Hemus	3B5	L	27	11	15	1	2	1	0	0	0	6	2	0	.133	.200
Steve Bilko	1B9	R	21	10	33	1	6	1	0	2	4	4	10	0	.182	.212
2 Johnny Blatnik	OF7	R	29	9	20	4	3	0	0	0	3	2	5	0	.150	.150
Ed Mickelson	1B4	R	23	5	10	1	1	0	0	0	1	0	3	0	.100	.100
Don Bollweg	1B4	L	29	5	11	1	2	1	0	0	0	1	3	0	.182	.182
Danny Gardella		L	30	1	1	0	0	0	0	0	0	0	0	0		
Ed Mierkowicz		R	26	1	1	0	0	0	0	0	0	0	0	0	.000	.000

NAME	T	AGE	W	L	PCT	SV	G	GS	CG	IP	H	BB	SO	SHO	ERA
		32	78	75	.510	14	153	153	57	1356	1398	535	603	10	3.97
Howie Pollet	L	29	14	13	.519	2	37	30	14	232	228	68	117	2	3.30
Gerry Staley	R	29	13	13	.500	2	42	22	7	170	201	61	62	1	4.98
Al Brazle	L	36	11	9	.550	6	46	12	3	165	188	80	47	0	4.09
Max Lanier	L	34	11	9	.550	0	27	27	10	181	173	68	89	2	3.13
Harry Brecheen	L	35	8	11	.421	1	27	23	12	163	151	45	80	2	3.81
Cloyd Boyer	R	22	7	7	.500	1	36	14	6	120	105	49	82	1	3.53
George Munger	R	31	7	8	.467	0	32	20	5	155	158	70	61	1	3.89
Freddie Martin	R	35	4	2	.667	0	30	2	0	63	87	30	19	0	5.14
Ted Wilks (EJ)	R	34	2	0	1.000	0	18	0	0	24	27	9	15	0	6.75
2 Al Papai	R	33	1	0	1.000	0	13	0	0	19	21	14	7	0	5.21
Tom Poholsky	R	20	0	0	—	0	1	0	0	15	16	3	2	0	3.60
Cot Deal	R	27	0	0	—	0	3	1	0	3	2	1	0	0	18.00
1 Ken Johnson	R	27	0	1	.000	0	6	1	0	19	21	6	5	0	6.75
1 Jim Hearn	R	29	0	1	.000	0	9	6	2	36	27	27	16	0	10.00*
Erv Dusak	R	29	0	0	—	0	14	0	0	36	27	27	16	0	3.75

*Hearn, also with New York, league leader in ERA with 2.49

NAME	G by Pos	B	AGE	G	AB	R	H	2B	3B	HR	RBI	BB	SO	SB	BA	SA
CINCINNATI 6th 66-87 .431 24.5 **LUKE SEWELL**			27	153	5253	654	1366	257	27	99	617	504	497	37	.260	.376
TOTALS																
Ted Kluszewski	1B131	L	25	134	538	76	165	37	0	25	111	33	28	3	.307	.515
2 Connie Ryan	2B103	R	30	106	367	45	95	18	5	3	43	52	46	4	.259	.360
Virgil Stallcup	SS136	R	28	136	483	44	121	23	2	8	54	17	39	4	.251	.356
Grady Hatton	3B126 2B1 SS1	R	27	130	438	67	114	17	1	11	54	70	39	6	.260	.379
Johnny Wyrostek	OF129 1B4	L	30	131	509	70	145	34	5	8	76	52	38	1	.285	.418
Lloyd Merriman	OF84	L	25	92	298	44	77	15	3	2	31	30	23	6	.258	.349
Bob Usher	OF93	R	25	106	321	51	83	17	0	6	35	27	38	3	.259	.368
Dixie Howell	C81	R	30	82	224	30	50	9	1	2	22	32	31		.223	.299
Bobby Adams	2B53 3B42	R	28	115	348	57	98	21	8	3	25	43	29	7	.282	.414
Joe Adcock	OF75 1B24	R	22	102	372	46	109	16	1	8	55	24	24	2	.293	.406
1 Peanuts Lowrey	OF72 2B1	R	32	91	264	34	60	14	0	1	15	36	7	1	.227	.292
Johnny Pramesa	C73	R	24	74	228	14	70	10	1	5	30	10	15	0	.307	.425
Danny Litwhiler	OF29	R	33	54	112	15	29	4	0	6	12	20	21	1	.259	.455
Sammy Meeks	SS29 3B2	R	27	39	95	7	27	5	0	1	8	6	14	1	.284	.368
1 Ron Northey	OF24	L	30	27	77	11	20	5	0	5	9	15	6	0	.260	.519
2 Bob Scheffing	C11	R	36	21	47	4	13	0	0	2	6	4	2	0	.277	.404
1 Walker Cooper	C13	R	35	15	47	3	9	3	0	0	4	0	5	0	.191	.255
1 Jimmy Bloodworth	2B4	R	32	4	14	1	3	1	0	0	1	2	0	0	.214	.286
Jim Bolger 18 R 0-1, Hobie Landrith 20 L 3-14, Marv Rackley 28 L 1-2, Ted Tappe 19 L 1-5																
CHICAGO 7th 64-89 .418 26.5 **FRANKIE FRISCH**			27	154	5230	643	1298	224	47	161	615	479	767	46	.248	.401
TOTALS																
Preston Ward (NJ)	1B76	L	22	80	285	31	72	11	2	6	33	27	42	3	.253	.368
WayneTerwilliger	2B126 3B1 1B1 OF1	R	25	133	480	63	116	22	3	10	32	43	63	13	.242	.363
Roy Smalley	SS154	R	24	154	557	58	128	21	9	21	85	49	114	2	.230	.413
Bill Serena	3B125	R	25	127	435	56	104	20	4	17	61	65	75	1	.239	.421
Bob Borkowski	OF65 1B1	R	24	85	256	27	70	7	4	4	29	16	30	1	.273	.379
Andy Pafko	OF144	R	29	146	514	95	156	24	8	36	92	69	32	4	.304	.591
Hank Sauer	OF125 1B18	R	33	145	540	85	148	32	2	32	103	60	67	1	.274	.519
Mickey Owen	C86	R	34	86	259	22	63	11	0	2	21	13	16	2	.243	.309
Phil Cavarretta (BA)	1B67 OF3	L	33	82	256	49	70	11	1	10	31	40	31	1	.273	.441
Rube Walker	C62	L	24	74	213	19	49	7	1	6	16	18	34	2	.230	.357
Hal Jeffcoat (BC)	OF53	R	25	66	179	21	42	13	1	2	18	6	23	7	.235	.352
Carmen Mauro	OF49	L	23	62	185	19	42	4	3	1	10	13	31	3	.227	.297
Bob Ramazzotti	2B31 3B10 SS3	R	33	61	145	19	38	3	3	1	6	4	16	3	.262	.345
2 Ron Northey	OF27	L	30	53	114	11	32	9	0	4	20	10	9	0	.281	.465
1 Emil Verban	2B8 SS3 3B1 OF1	R	34	45	37	7	4	1	0	0	1	3	5	0	.108	.135
Hank Edwards	OF29	L	31	41	110	13	40	11	1	2	21	10	13	5	.364	.536
Carl Sawatski	C32	L	22	38	103	4	18	1	0	1	7	11	19	0	.175	.214
Randy Jackson	3B27	R	24	34	111	13	25	3	3	6	7	25		4	.225	.396
Harry Chiti 17 R 2-6, 1 Bob Scheffing 36 R 3-16																
PITTSBURGH 8th 57-96 .373 33.5 **BILLY MEYER**			30	154	5327	681	1404	227	59	138	634	564	693	43	.264	.406
TOTALS																
1 Johnny Hopp	1B70 OF7	L	33	106	318	51	108	24	5	8	47	37	7	3	.340	.522
Danny Murtaugh	2B108	R	32	118	367	34	108	20	5	2	37	47	42	2	.294	.392
Danny O'Connell	SS65 3B12	R	23	79	315	39	92	16	1	3	32	24	33	7	.292	.425
2 Bob Dillinger	3B51	R	31	58	222	23	64	8	2	1	9	13	22	4	.288	.356
Gus Bell	OF104	L	21	111	422	62	119	22	11	8	53	28	46	4	.282	.443
Wally Westlake	OF123	R	29	139	477	69	136	15	6	24	95	48	78	1	.285	.493
Ralph Kiner	OF150	R	27	150	547	112	149	21	6	47	118	122	79	2	.272	.590
Clyde McCullough (BW)	C100	R	33	103	279	28	71	16	4	6	34	31	35	3	.254	.405
Pete Castiglione	3B35 SS29 2B9 1B3	R	29	94	263	29	67	10	3	3	22	23	23	1	.255	.350
Stan Rojek	SS68 2B3	R	31	76	230	24	59	12	1	0	17	18	13	2	.257	.317
Jack Phillips	1B54 3B4 P1	R	28	69	208	25	61	7	6	5	34	20	17	1	.293	.457
Tom Saffell	OF43	L	28	67	182	18	37	7	0	2	6	14	34	1	.203	.275
2 Ray Mueller	C63	R	38	67	156	17	42	7	0	6	24	11	14	2	.269	.429
Nanny Fernandez	3B52	R	31	65	198	23	51	11	0	6	27	19	17	2	.258	.404
Ted Beard (BH)	OF49	L	29	61	177	32	41	6	2	4	12	27	45	3	.232	.356
Hank Schenz	2B21 3B12 SS4	R	31	58	101	17	23	4	1	1	5	6	7	2	.228	.337
Dale Coogan	1B32	L	19	53	129	19	31	6	1	1	13	17	24	0	.240	.326
2 Johnny Berardino	2B36 3B3	R	27	40	131	12	27	3	1	1	12	19	11	0	.206	.267
Earl Turner	C34	R	27	40	74	10	18	0	0	3	9	4	13	1	.243	.365
Cliff Chambers	P37	L	28	37	90	10	26	1	1	2	9	4	18	0	.289	.389
George Strickland	SS19 3B1	R	24	23	27	0	3	0	0	0	2	3	8	1	.111	.111
Ed Stevens	1B12	L	25	17	46	2	9	0	0	3	4	5	1	0	.196	.239
1 Marv Rickert 29 L 3-20, Ed Fitz Gerald 26 R 1-15																

NAME	T	AGE	W	L	PCT	SV	G	GS	CG	IP	H	BB	SO	SHO	ERA
		27	66	87	.431	0	153	153	67	1358	1363	582	686	7	4.31
Ewell Blackwell	R	27	17	15	.531	4	40	32	18	261	203	112	188	1	2.97
Ken Raffensberger	L	32	14	19	.424	0	38	35	18	239	271	40	87	4	4.26
Howie Fox	R	29	11	8	.579	1	34	22	10	187	196	85	64	1	4.33
Herm Wehmeier	R	23	10	18	.357	4	41	32	12	230	255	135	121	0	5.67
Willie Ramsdell	R	34	7	12	.368	0	27	24	8	157	151	75	83	1	3.73
Eddie Erautt	R	25	4	2	.667	1	33	2	1	65	82	22	35	0	5.68
Frank Smith	R	22	2	7	.222	3	32	1	0	91	73	39	55	0	5.09
Johnny Hetki	R	28	1	2	.333	0	22	1	0	53	53	27	21	0	5.09
Harry Perkowski	L	27	0	0	—	0	22	0	0	34	36	23	19	0	5.29
Jim Avrea	R	29	0	0	—	0	2	0	0	5	6	3	2	0	3.60
Bud Byerly	R	29	0	0	.000	0	4	1	0	15	12	4	5	0	2.40
Kent Peterson	L	24	0	3	.000	0	9	2	0	25	17	6	7	0	7.20
		30	64	89	.418	19	154	154	55	1371	1452	593	559	9	4.28
Bob Rush	R	24	13	20	.394	1	39	34	19	255	261	93	93	1	3.71
Frank Hiller	R	29	12	5	.706	1	38	17	9	153	153	32	55	2	3.53
Johnny Schmitz	L	29	10	16	.385	0	39	27	8	193	217	91	75	3	4.99
Paul Minner	R	26	8	13	.381	4	39	24	9	190	217	72	99	1	4.12
Monk Dubiel	R	32	6	10	.375	2	39	12	4	143	152	67	51	2	4.15
Dutch Leonard	R	41	5	1	.833	6	35	1	0	74	70	27	28	0	3.77
Doyle Lade	R	29	5	6	.455	2	34	12	2	118	126	50	36	0	4.73
Johnny Vander Meer	L	35	3	4	.429	1	32	6	0	74	80	59	41	0	3.77
Johnny Klippstein	R	22	2	9	.182	1	33	11	3	105	112	64	51	0	5.23
Andy Varga	L	19	0	0	—	0	2	1	0	1	0	1	0	0	0.00
Warren Hacker	R	25	0	1	.000	1	5	3	1	15	20	8	5	0	5.40
Bill Voiselle	R	31	0	4	.000	0	19	7	0	51	64	29	25	0	5.82
		28	57	96	.373	16	154	154	42	1369	1472	616	556	6	4.96
Cliff Chambers	L	28	12	15	.444	0	37	33	11	249	262	92	93	2	4.30
Murry Dickson	R	33	10	15	.400	3	51	22	8	225	227	83	76	0	3.80
Bill Macdonald	R	21	8	10	.444	1	32	20	6	153	138	88	60	2	4.29
Bill Werle	L	29	8	16	.333	8	48	22	6	215	249	65	78	0	4.60
Vern Law	R	20	7	9	.438	0	27	17	5	128	137	49	57	1	4.92
Mel Queen	R	32	5	14	.263	0	33	21	4	120	135	73	76	1	6.00
Bob Chesnes	R	29	3	3	.500	0	7	3	2	39	44	17	12	0	5.54
Woody Main	R	28	1	0	1.000	1	12	0	0	21	11	12	0	0	4.95
Junior Walsh	R	31	1	4	.500	2	38	2	0	62	56	34	33	0	5.08
Frank Barrett	R	37	1	2	.333	1	5	0	0	4	5	3	3	0	4.50
2 Hank Borowy	R	34	1	3	.250	0	11	3	0	25	32	9	9	0	6.48
Frank Papish	L	32	0	0	—	0	4	1	0	2	8	4	1	0	31.50
Windy McCall	L	24	0	0	—	0	7	0	0	12	4	5	5	0	9.00
Harry Gumbert	R	40	0	0	—	1	4	0	0	2	5	4	2	0	4.50
Jack Phillips	R	28	0	0	—	0	1	0	0	5	7	1	2	0	7.20
Hal Gregg	R	28	0	1	.000	0	5	1	0	10	7	3	3	0	14.40
Bill Pierro	R	24	0	1	.000	0	12	3	0	29	33	28	13	0	10.55
Vic Lombardi	L	27	0	5	.000	0	38	2	0	76	93	48	26	0	6.63

WORLD SERIES — NEW YORK (AL) 4   PHILADELPHIA (NL) 0

LINE SCORES

TEAM	1	2	3	4	5	6	7	8	9	10	11	12	R	H	E
Game 1 October 4 at Philadelphia															
NY (AL)	0	0	0		1	0	0		0	0	0		1	5	0
PHI (NL)	0	0	0		0	0	0		0	0	0		0	2	1
Raschi									Konstanty, Meyer (9)						
Game 2 October 5 at Philadelphia															
NY	0	1	0		0	0	0		0	0	1		2	10	0
PHI	0	0	0		0	1	0		0	0	0	0	1	7	0
Reynolds									Roberts						
Game 3 October 6 at New York															
PHI	0	0	0		0	0	1		1	0	0		2	10	2
NY	0	0	1		0	0	0		0	1	1		3	7	0
Heintzelman, Konstanty (8), Lopat, Ferrick (9)															
Meyer (9)															
Game 4 October 7 at New York															
PHI	0	0	0		0	0	0		0	0	2		2	7	1
NY	2	0	0		0	0	3		0	0	X		5	8	2
Miller, Konstanty (1) Ford, Reynolds (9)															
Roberts (8)															

COMPOSITE BATTING

NAME	POS	G	AB	R	H	2B	3B	HR	RBI	BA
New York (AL)										
Totals		4	135	11	30	3	1	2	10	.222
Berra	C	4	15	2	3	0	0	1	2	.200
Mize	1B	4	15	0	2	0	0	0	1	.133
Bauer	OF	4	15	2	2	0	0	0	1	.133
Woodling	OF	4	14	2	6	0	0	0	1	.429
Coleman	2B	4	14	2	4	0	0	0	3	.286
Rizzuto	SS	4	14	1	2	1	0	0	0	.143
DiMaggio	OF	4	13	2	4	1	0	1	2	.308
Brown	3B	4	12	1	4	1	1	0	1	.333
B. Johnson	3B	4	6	0	0	0	0	0	0	.000
Mapes	OF	1	4	0	0	0	0	0	0	.000
Raschi	P	1	3	0	1	0	0	0	0	.333
Reynolds	P	2	3	0	1	0	0	0	0	.333
Ford	P	1	2	0	0	0	0	0	0	.000
Lopat	P	2	2	0	1	0	0	0	0	.500
Hopp	1B	3	2	0	0	0	0	0	0	.000
Collins	1B	1	0	0	0	0	0	0	0	—
Ferrick	P	1	0	0	0	0	0	0	0	—
Jensen	PR	1	0	0	0	0	0	0	0	—
Philadelphia (NL)										
Totals		4	128	5	26	6	1	0	3	.203
Ashburn	OF	4	17	0	3	1	0	0	0	.176
Sisler	OF	4	17	0	1	0	0	0	0	.059
Waitkus	1B	4	15	0	4	1	0	0	0	.267
Hamner	SS	4	14	1	6	2	1	0	0	.429
Jones	3B	4	14	1	4	0	0	0	0	.286
Goliat	2B	4	14	1	3	0	0	0	1	.214
Ennis	OF	4	14	1	2	1	0	0	2	.143
Seminick	C	4	11	0	2	0	0	0	0	.182
Konstanty	P	3	4	0	1	0	0	0	0	.250
Roberts	P	2	3	0	0	0	0	0	0	.000
Heintzelman	P	1	2	0	0	0	0	0	0	.000
Whitman	PH	3	2	0	0	0	0	0	0	.000
Lopata	C	2	1	0	0	0	0	0	0	.000
Caballero	PH	3	1	0	0	0	0	0	0	.000
K.Johnson	PR	1	0	0	0	0	0	0	0	—
Silvestri	C	1	0	0	0	0	0	0	0	—
Bloodworth	2B	1	0	0	0	0	0	0	0	—
Mayo	OF	1	0	0	0	0	0	0	0	—
Meyer	P	2	0	0	0	0	0	0	0	—
Miller	P	1	0	0	0	0	0	0	0	—

COMPOSITE PITCHING

NAME	G	IP	H	BB	SO	W	L	SV	ERA
New York (AL)									
Totals	4	37	26	7	24	4	0	1	0.73
Reynolds	2	10.1	7	4	7	1	0	1	0.87
Raschi	1	9	2	1	5	1	0	0	0.00
Ford	1	8.2	7	1	7	1	0	0	0.00
Lopat	1	8.0	9	0	5	1	0	0	2.25
Ferrick	1	1.0	1	1	0	1	0	0	0.00
Philadelphia (NL)									
Totals	4	35.2	30	13	12	0	4	0	2.27
Kostanty	3	15	9	4	3	0	1	0	2.40
Roberts	2	11	11	3	5	0	1	0	1.64
Heintzelman	1	7.2	4	6	3	0	0	0	1.17
Meyer	2	1.2	6	0	1	0	0	0	5.40
Miller	1	0.1	0	0	0	0	1	0	27.00

1951: Ouch

The season began with Ford Frick succeeding Happy Chandler as Commissioner of Baseball. Midway through the campaign, Browns' owner Bill Veeck pulled the most famous stunt of his promotional career by unfurling, for one turn at bat, the smallest man ever to wear a major league uniform- 3'7" Eddie Gaedel.

At the season's end, there was a broken heart for every foot of trolley track in the borough of Brooklyn. The story of the Dodgers and their misery, and the Giants and their joy, began in April with no indications as to the outcome which would astonish the baseball world in October.

The Giants and their hated rival, the Brooklyn Dodgers, were both strong enough to take the pennant. But while the Dodgers, led by MVP Roy Campanella, sprinted out to a comfortable lead, the Giants lost 11 straight games after an opening day win. By August 12, the Dodgers lead over the second place Giants was 13 1/2 games .

Part two of the story began on that August date, as the Giants won again and again, running off 16 straight victories to climb up Brooklyn's back. Manager Leo Durocher masterfully guided the assault by whipping his charges into victory in 39 of the final 47 matches. Oddly enough, it was a 20-year-old rookie by the name of Willie Mays who proved the main spark of the team with his centerfield play and infectious enthusiasm. The second part of the story concluded as the Giants climbed into the top spot by winning their last seven contests, while the hapless Dodgers could only hang onto a tie by downing the Phils in 14 innings in the season's finale.

The feuding neighbors squared off in a three-game play-off for the flag to end the saddest story ever to be told in Brooklyn. A split of the first two tilts placed the issue directly on the line at the Polo Grounds on October 3. Those who now claim to have been present at the game number in the hundreds of thousands, but 34,320 ticket stubs were collected at the turnstiles on that overcast day in New York. Going into the bottom of the ninth, Giant fans were prepared to slink out into the street as quietly as possible, for Brooklyn was up 4-1 with big Don Newcombe needing only three more outs to wrap up the title. Alvin Dark opened

up the fateful frame with an apparently harmless single, but Don Mueller raised some hopes by lashing another single to right. The tiring Newcombe managed to coax Monte Irvin into popping out, but Whitey Lockman bashed a double to left, plating Dark and sending Mueller sliding into third. An ankle injury forced Durocher to send in a pinch-runner for Mueller, and Dodger Skipper Dressen took advantage of the delay to wave big Ralph Branca to the mound to bail Newcombe out.

Branca, the proud bearer of uniform number 13, entered the fray to face slugger Bobby Thomson at the plate. Although first base stood empty, Dressen decided against an intentional pass to Thomson, which would have put the potential winning run on base with Mays at bat. Branca dauntlessly fired the first pitch down the middle for strike one, but his second serve needed no umpire's decision. On the next pitch, Thomson swung and drilled a rising line drive into the left field stands to score the incredible winning runs. For a full second the crowd sat quietly stunned before spontaneously erupting into delirium at the realization that the Giants had pulled off the impossible. As Thomson circled the bases, Eddie Stanky hopped on manager Durocher's back in the third-base coaching box, typewriters clacked out headline stories, Mueller rejoiced from his stretcher in the dressing room, and the Dodgers could only wish quiet graves in their funeral march to the distant centerfield clubhouse.

With all the drama of the National League chase monopolizing the press coverage, the Yankees quietly retained the junior loop flag by outlasting threats from Cleveland and Boston—both of which died in the final two weeks. Phil Rizzuto and MVP Yogi Berra starred at bat and in the field, and Allie Reynolds hurled a pair of no-hitters in joining Vic Raschi and Eddie Lopat as Casey Stengel's mound aces. Only Joe DiMaggio's final year in pinstripes after a 13-season career, which netted him a .325 lifetime batting average, and the appearance of a green 19-year-old rookie outfielder named Mickey Mantle, gave Yankee fans any historical memory. The World Series, won by Stengel for the third time in as many tries, proved insignificant when compared to the miracle of Coogan's Bluff.

1951 AMERICAN LEAGUE

NEW YORK 1st 98-56 .636 — CASEY STENGEL

NAME	G by Pos	B	AGE	G	AB	R	H	2B	3B	HR	RBI	BB	SO	SB	BA	SA
	TOTALS		28	154	5194	798	1395	208	48	140	741	605	547	78	.269	.408
Johnny Mize	1B93	L	38	113	332	37	86	14	1	10	49	36	24	1	.259	.398
Jerry Coleman	2B102, SS18	R	26	121	362	48	90	11	2	3	43	31	36	6	.249	.315
Phil Rizzuto	SS144	R	33	144	540	87	148	21	6	2	43	58	27	18	.274	.346
Bobby Brown	3B90	R	26	103	313	44	84	15	2	6	51	47	18	1	.268	.387
Hank Bauer	OF107	R	28	118	348	53	103	9	3	10	54	42	39	5	.296	.454
Joe DiMaggio	OF113	R	36	116	415	72	109	22	4	12	71	61	36	0	.263	.422
Gene Woodling	OF116	L	28	120	420	65	118	15	8	15	71	62	37	0	.281	.462
Yogi Berra	C141	L	26	141	547	92	161	19	4	27	88	44	20	5	.294	.492
Gil McDougald	3B82, 2B55	R	23	131	402	72	123	23	4	14	68	56	54	14	.306	.488
Joe Collins	1B114, OF15	L	28	125	262	52	75	8	5	9	48	34	23	9	.286	.458
Mickey Mantle	OF86	B	19	96	341	61	91	11	5	13	65	43	74	4	.267	.443
Jackie Jensen	OF48	R	24	56	168	30	50	8	1	8	25	18	18	8	.298	.500
Billy Martin	2B23, SS6, 3B2, OF1	R	23	51	58	10	15	1	2	0	2	4	9	1	.259	.345
Johnny Hopp	1B25	L	34	46	63	10	13	1	0	2	9	11	2	2	.206	.317
1 Cliff Mapes	OF34	L	29	45	51	6	11	3	1	2	8	4	14	0	.216	.431
Charlie Silvera	C18	R	26	18	51	5	14	3	0	1	7	5	3	0	.275	.392
1 Billy Johnson	3B13	R	32	15	40	5	12	3	0	0	4	7	0	0	.300	.375
Bob Cerv	OF9	R	25	12	28	4	6	1	0	0	2	4	6	0	.214	.250
Archie Wilson	OF2	R	27	4	4	0	0	0	0	0	0	0	0	0	.000	.000

Ralph Houk 31 R 1-5, Jim Brideweser 24 R 3-8, Clint Courtney 24 L 0-2

NAME	T	AGE	W	L	PCT	SV	G	GS	CG	IP	H	BB	SO	SHO	ERA
		31	98	56	.636	22	154	154	66	1367	1290	562	664	24	3.56
Ed Lopat	L	33	21	9	.700	0	31	31	20	235	209	71	93	4	2.91
Vic Raschi	R	32	21	10	.677	0	35	34	15	258	233	103	164	4	3.28
Allie Reynolds	R	36	17	8	.680	7	40	26	16	221	171	100	126	7	3.05
Tom Morgan	R	21	9	3	.750	2	27	16	4	125	119	36	57	2	3.67
2 Bob Kuzava	L	28	8	4	.667	5	23	8	4	82	76	27	50	1	2.41
Joe Ostrowski	L	34	6	4	.600	5	34	3	2	95	103	18	30	0	3.51
Spec Shea	R	30	5	5	.500	0	25	11	2	96	112	50	38	2	4.33
Art Schallock	L	27	3	1	.750	0	11	6	1	46	50	20	19	0	3.91
1 Tommy Byrne	R	31	2	1	.667	0	9	3	0	21	16	36*	14	0	6.86
2 Johnny Sain	R	33	2	1	.667	1	7	4	1	37	41	8	21	0	4.14
3 Bobby Hogue	R	30	1	0	1.000	0	7	0	0	7	4	3	2	0	0.00
1 Tom Ferrick	R	36	1	1	.500	1	9	0	0	12	21	7	3	0	7.50
2 Stubby Overmire	L	32	1	1	.500	0	15	4	1	45	50	18	14	0	4.60
2 Jack Kramer	R	33	1	3	.250	0	19	3	0	41	46	21	15	0	4.61
Bob Wiesler (MS)	L	20	0	2	.000	0	4	3	0	9	13	11	3	0	14.00
1 Fred Sanford	R	31	0	0	—	0	11	2	0	27	15	25	10	0	5.17
Bob Muncrief	R	35	0	0	—	0	2	0	0	3	5	1	1	0	9.00
Ernie Nevel	R	31	0	0	—	0	1	0	0	4	4	1	1	0	4.50
1 Bob Porterfield	R	27	0	0	—	0	3	0	0	3	5	3	2	0	15.00
Whitey Ford (MS) 22															

*Byrne, also with St. Louis, league leader in BB with 150

CLEVELAND 2nd 93-61 .604 5 — AL LOPEZ

NAME	G by Pos	B	AGE	G	AB	R	H	2B	3B	HR	RBI	BB	SO	SB	BA	SA
	TOTALS		29	155	5250	696	1346	208	35	140	658	606	632	52	.256	.389
Luke Easter	1B125	L	35	128	486	65	131	12	5	27	103	37	71	0	.270	.481
Bobby Avila	2B136	R	27	141	542	76	165	21	3	10	58	60	31	14	.304	.410
Ray Boone	SS151	R	27	151	544	65	127	14	4	12	51	48	36	5	.233	.329
Al Rosen	3B154	R	27	154	573	82	152	30	1	24	102	85	71	7	.265	.447
Bob Kennedy	OF106	R	30	108	321	30	79	15	4	7	29	34	33	4	.246	.383
Larry Doby	OF132	L	27	134	447	84	132	27	5	20	69	101	81	4	.295	.512
Dale Mitchell	OF124	L	29	134	510	83	148	19	7	11	62	53	16	7	.290	.424
Jim Hegan	C129	R	30	133	416	60	99	17	5	6	43	38	72	0	.238	.346
Harry Simpson	OF68, 1B50	L	25	122	332	51	76	7	0	7	24	45	48	6	.229	.313
2 Sam Chapman	OF84, 1B1	R	35	94	246	24	56	9	1	6	36	27	32	3	.228	.346
Birdie Tebbetts	C44	R	38	55	137	8	36	6	0	2	18	8	7	0	.263	.350
Snuffy Stirnweiss	2B25, 3B2	R	32	50	88	10	19	1	1	0	4	22	5	1	.216	.261
3 Barney McCosky	OF16	L	34	31	61	8	13	3	0	0	4	5	3	1	.213	.262
Merrill Combs	SS16	R	31	19	28	2	5	2	0	0	2	2	3	0	.179	.250
Milt Nielsen		R	26	16	6	1	0	0	0	0	0	1	1	0	.000	.000
4 Paul Lehner	OF1	L	31	12	13	2	3	0	0	0	1	1	2	0	.231	.231
Clarence Maddern	OF1	R	29	11	12	0	2	0	0	0	2	1	0	0	.167	.167
Minnie Minoso	1B7	R	28	8	14	3	6	1	2	0*	1	2	1	1	.429	.571

1 Allie Clark 28 R 3-10, Hal Naragon 22 L 2-8, Doug Hansen 22 R 0-0, 1 Lou Klein 32 R 0-2, 1 Ray Murray 33 R 1-1, Thurman Tucker 33 L 0-1

NAME	T	AGE	W	L	PCT	SV	G	GS	CG	IP	H	BB	SO	SHO	ERA
		28	93	61	.604	19	155	155	76	1391	1287	577	642	10	3.38
Bob Feller	R	32	22	8	.733	0	33	32	16	250	239	95	111	4	3.49
Mike Garcia	R	27	20	13	.606	6	47	30	15	254	239	82	118	1	3.15
Early Wynn	R	31	20	13	.606	1	37	34	21	274	227	107	133	3	3.02
Bob Lemon	R	30	17	14	.548	2	42	34	17	263	244	124	132	1	3.52
Steve Gromek	R	31	7	4	.636	1	27	8	4	107	98	24	40	0	2.78
2 Lou Brissie	L	27	4	3	.571	9	54	4	1	112	90	61	50	0	3.21
Bob Chakales	R	23	3	4	.429	0	17	10	2	68	80	43	32	1	4.76
Sam Jones	R	25	0	1	.000	0	2	1	0	9	4	5	4	0	2.00
Johnny Vander Meer	L	36	0	1	.000	0	1	1	0	3	4	3	1	0	18.00
George Zuverink	R	26	0	0	—	0	16	0	0	25	24	13	14	0	5.40
Dick Rozek	L	24	0	0	—	0	7	1	0	15	18	11	5	0	3.00
Red Fahr	R	26	0	0	—	0	5	0	0	6	11	2	0	0	4.50
2 Charlie Harris	R	25	0	0	—	0	4	0	0	4	5	4	1	0	4.50
Al Aber (MS) 23															
Dick Weik (MS) 23															

*Minoso, also with Chicago, league leader in 3B(14) and SB(31)

BOSTON 3rd 87-67 .565 11 — STEVE O'NEILL

NAME	G by Pos	B	AGE	G	AB	R	H	2B	3B	HR	RBI	BB	SO	SB	BA	SA
	TOTALS		28	154	5378	804	1428	233	32	127	757	756	594	20	.266	.392
Walt Dropo	1B93	R	28	99	360	37	86	14	0	11	57	34	52	0	.239	.369
Bobby Doerr (XJ)	2B106	R	33	106	402	60	116	21	2	13	73	57	33	2	.289	.448
Johnny Pesky	SS106, 3B11, 2B5	L	31	131	480	93	150	20	6	3	41	84	15	2	.313	.398
Vern Stephens (LJ)	3B89, SS2	R	30	109	377	62	113	21	2	17	78	38	33	1	.300	.501
Clyde Vollmer	OF106	R	29	115	386	66	97	9	2	22	85	55	66	0	.251	.456
Dom DiMaggio	OF146	R	34	146	639	113	189	34	4	12	72	73	53	4	.296	.418
Ted Williams	OF143	L	32	148	531	109	169	28	4	30	126	144	45	1	.318	.556
2 Les Moss	C69	R	26	71	202	18	40	6	0	3	26	25	34	0	.198	.272
Billy Goodman	1B62, 2B44, OF38, 3B1	L	25	141	546	92	162	34	4	0	50	79	37	7	.297	.374
Lou Boudreau	SS52, 3B15, 1B2	R	33	82	273	37	73	18	1	5	47	30	12	1	.267	.396
Fred Hatfield	3B49	L	26	80	163	23	28	4	2	2	14	22	27	1	.172	.258
Buddy Rosar	C56	R	36	58	150	11	39	7	0	1	13	19	14	0	.229	.288
Charlie Maxwell	OF13	L	24	49	80	8	15	1	0	3	12	9	18	0	.188	.313
Mel Parnell	P36	L	29	37	81	12	25	5	0	0	7	5	10	0	.309	.346
Tom Wright	OF18	L	27	28	63	8	14	1	1	1	9	11	8	0	.222	.317
2 Aaron Robinson	C25	L	36	26	74	9	15	2	0	1	5	12	8	0	.203	.324
Al Evans	C10	R	34	12	24	1	3	1	0	0	3	4	1	0	.125	.167
1 Matt Batts	C11	R	29	11	26	2	3	1	0	0	1	4	2	0	.138	.172
1 Mike Guerra	C10	R	38	10	32	1	5	0	0	0	4	5	1	0	.156	.156

Mel Hoderlein 28 B 5-14, Norm Zauchin 21 R 2-12, Karl Olson 20 R 1-10, Al Richter 24 R 1-11, Sammy White R 23 2-11, Bob DiPietro 23 R 1-11

NAME	T	AGE	W	L	PCT	SV	G	GS	CG	IP	H	BB	SO	SHO	ERA
		28	87	67	.565	24	154	154	46	1399	1413	599	658	7	4.14
Mel Parnell	L	29	18	11	.621	2	36	29	11	221	229	77	77	3	3.26
Ray Scarborough	R	33	12	9	.571	0	37	22	8	184	201	61	71	0	5.09
Ellis Kinder	R	36	11	2	.846	14	63	2	1	127	108	46	84	0	2.55
Chuck Stobbs	L	21	10	9	.526	0	34	25	6	170	180	74	75	0	4.76
Mickey McDermott	L	22	8	8	.500	3	34	19	9	172	141	92	127	1	3.35
Willard Nixon	R	23	7	4	.636	0	34	17	4	118	128	63	38	2	5.11
Bill Wight	L	29	7	7	.500	0	34	17	4	118	128	56	70	1	4.90
Leo Kiely	L	21	7	7	.500	1	17	16	4	113	106	39	46	0	3.35
Harry Taylor	R	32	4	9	.308	2	31	8	1	81	100	42	22	0	5.78
Walt Masterson	R	31	3	0	1.000	2	30	1	0	59	53	32	39	0	3.36
Harley Hisner	R	24	0	1	.000	1	1	1	0	4	4	4	1	0	4.50
Bill Evans	R	24	0	0	—	0	6	0	0	15	15	9	4	0	4.20
Paul Hinrichs	R	25	0	0	—	0	3	0	0	3	1	1	1	0	24.00
Ben Flowers	R	23	0	0	—	0	1	0	0	2	2	0	1	0	0.00

Batting

NAME	G by Pos	B	AGE	G	AB	R	H	2B	3B	HR	RBI	BB	SO	SB	BA	SA
CHICAGO 4th 81-73 .526 17															PAUL RICHARDS	
TOTALS			29	155	5378	714	1453	229	64	86	668	596	524	99	.270	.385
Eddie Robinson	1B147	L	30	151	564	85	159	23	5	29	117	77	54	2	.282	.495
Nellie Fox	2B147	L	23	147	604	93	189	32	12	4	55	43	11	9	.313	.425
Chico Carrasquel	SS147	R	23	147	538	41	142	22	4	5	58	46	39	14	.264	.331
2 Bob Dillinger	3B70	R	32	89	299	39	90	6	4	0	20	15	17	5	.301	.348
Al Zarilla	OF117	L	32	120	382	56	98	21	2	10	60	60	57	2	.257	.401
Jim Busby	OF139	R	24	143	477	59	135	15	2	5	68	40	46	26	.283	.354
2 Minnie Minoso	OF82, 3B68, SS1	R	28	138	516	109	167	32	14♀	10	74	72	41	31♀	.324	.498
Phil Masi	C78	R	34	84	225	24	61	11	2	4	28	32	27	1	.271	.391
Bud Stewart	OF63	L	35	95	217	40	60	13	5	6	40	29	9	1	.276	.465
Floyd Baker	3B44, 2B5, SS3	L	34	82	133	24	35	6	0	1	14	25	12	0	.263	.323
Gus Niarhos (BW)	C59	R	30	66	168	27	43	6	0	1	10	47	9	4	.256	.310
2 Don Lenhardt	OF53, 1B2	R	28	64	199	23	53	9	1	10	45	24	25	1	.266	.472
Joe DeMaestri	SS27, 2B11, 3B8	R	22	56	74	8	15	0	2	1	3	5	11	0	.203	.297
2 Ray Coleman	OF51	L	29	51	181	21	50	8	7	3	21	15	14	2	.276	.448
Bud Sheely	C33	L	30	34	89	2	16	2	0	0	7	6	7	0	.180	.202
2 Paul Lehner	OF20	L	31	23	72	9	15	3	1	0	3	10	4	0	.208	.278
Bert Haas	1B7, OF4, 3B1	R	37	23	43	1	7	0	1	1	2	5	4	0	.163	.279
Joe Erautt	C12	R	29	16	25	3	4	1	0	0	3	2	0	.160	.200
1 Hank Majeski	3B9	R	34	12	35	4	9	4	0	0	6	1	0	3	.257	.371
Bob Boyd	1B6	L	31	12	18	3	3	0	1	0	0	3	3	0	.167	.278
1 Dave Philley	OF6	B	31	7	25	0	6	2	0	0	0	0	2	0	.240	.320
1 Gus Zernial	OF4	R	28	4	19	2	2	0	0	0#	4#	2	2#	0	.105	.105

Gordon Goldsberry 23 L 1-11, 3 Rocky Nelson 26 L 0-5, Sam Hairston 31 R 2-5, Red Wilson 22 R 3-11, Herb Adams (MS) 23, Bill Wilson (MS) 22

NAME	G by Pos	B	AGE	G	AB	R	H	2B	3B	HR	RBI	BB	SO	SB	BA	SA
DETROIT 5th 73-81 .474 25															RED ROLFE	
TOTALS			29	154	5336	685	1413	231	35	104	636	568	525	37	.265	.380
Dick Kryhoski	1B112	L	26	119	421	58	121	19	4	12	57	28	29	1	.287	.437
Jerry Priddy	2B154, SS1	R	31	154	619	66	161	22	6	8	57	69	73	4	.260	.360
Johnny Lipon	SS125	R	28	129	487	56	129	15	1	0	38	49	27	7	.265	.300
George Kell	3B147	R	28	147	598	92	191	36	3	2	59	61	18	10	.319	.400
Vic Wertz	OF131	L	26	138	501	86	143	24	4	27	94	78	61	0	.285	.511
Johnny Groth	OF112	R	24	118	428	41	128	29	1	3	49	31	32	1	.299	.393
Hoot Evers	OF108	R	30	116	393	47	88	15	2	11	46	40	47	5	.224	.356
Joe Ginsberg	C95	L	24	102	304	44	79	10	2	8	37	43	37	2	.260	.385
Pat Mullin	OF83	L	33	110	295	40	83	11	6	12	51	40	38	2	.281	.481
Steve Souchock	OF59, 3B3, 1B1, 2B1	R	32	91	188	33	46	10	3	11	48	20	27	0	.245	.505
Don Kolloway	1B59	R	32	78	212	28	54	7	0	1	17	15	12	2	.255	.302
Neil Berry	SS38, 2B10, 3B7	R	29	67	157	17	36	5	2	0	9	10	15	4	.229	.287
Charlie Keller	OF8	L	34	54	62	6	16	2	0	3	21	11	12	0	.258	.403
Bob Swift (IL)	C43	R	36	44	104	8	20	0	0	0	5	12	10	0	.192	.192
1 Aaron Robinson	C35	L	36	36	82	3	17	6	0	0	9	17	9	0	.207	.280
Frank House	C18	L	21	18	41	3	9	0	0	1	5	4	3	0	.220	.341

Russ Sullivan 28 L 5-26, Al Federoff 26 R 0-4, Doc Daugherty 23 R 0-1

NAME	G by Pos	B	AGE	G	AB	R	H	2B	3B	HR	RBI	BB	SO	SB	BA	SA
PHILADELPHIA 6th 70-84 .455 28															JIMMY DYKES	
TOTALS			31	154	5277	736	1381	262	43	102	685	677	565	47	.262	.386
Ferris Fain (BF)	1B108, OF11	L	30	117	425	63	146	30	7	6	57	80	20	0	.344	.471
Pete Suder	2B103, SS18, 3B3	R	35	140	553	49	160	18	1	4	42	30	42	5	.289	.415
Eddie Joost	SS140	R	35	140	553	107	160	28	5	19	78	106	70	10	.289	.461
Hank Majeski	3B88	R	34	89	274	22	75	19	4	2	42	35	24	1	.285	.415
Elmer Valo	OF116	L	30	123	444	75	134	27	8	7	55	75	24	1	.302	.446
2 Dave Philley	OF120, 3B2	B	31	125	468	71	123	18	7	7	53	63	38	9	.263	.385
2 Gus Zernial	OF138	R	28	139	552	90	151	30	5	33*	125*	61	99*	2	.274	.525
Joe Tipton	C72	R	29	72	213	23	51	9	0	3	20	51	25	1	.239	.324
Lou Limmer	1B58	R	26	84	214	26	34	9	1	5	30	28	40	1	.159	.280
Billy Hitchcock	3B45, 2B23, 1B1	R	34	77	222	27	68	10	4	1	36	21	23	2	.306	.401
Wally Moses	OF27	L	40	70	136	17	26	6	0	0	9	21	9	2	.191	.235
Joe Astroth	C57	R	28	64	187	30	46	10	1	4	22	15	7	2	.246	.353
2 Allie Clark	OF32, 3B10	R	28	56	161	20	40	10	1	4	22	5	17	0	.248	.398
2 Lou Klein	2B42	R	32	49	144	22	33	7	0	5	17	10	14	1	.229	.382
Carl Scheib	P46	R	24	48	53	9	21	2	2	2	8	1	5	0	.396	.623
2 Ray Murray	C39	R	33	40	122	10	26	6	0	0	13	14	8	0	.213	.262
1 Kermit Wahl	3B18	R	28	20	59	4	11	2	0	0	6	9	5	0	.186	.220
1 Sam Chapman	OF17	R	35	18	65	7	11	1	0	1	5	12	6	0	.169	.185
1 Barney McCosky	OF7	L	34	12	27	4	8	2	0	1	5	2	4	0	.296	.481

Tod Davis 26 R 1-15, 1 Paul Lehner 31 L 4-28, Eddie Samcoff 26 R 0-11

NAME	G by Pos	B	AGE	G	AB	R	H	2B	3B	HR	RBI	BB	SO	SB	BA	SA
WASHINGTON 7th 62-92 .403 36															BUCKY HARRIS	
TOTALS			29	154	5329	672	1399	242	45	54	627	560	515	45	.263	.355
Mickey Vernon	1B137	L	33	146	546	69	160	30	7	9	87	53	45	7	.293	.423
Cass Michaels	2B128	R	25	138	485	59	125	20	4	4	45	61	41	1	.258	.340
Pete Runnels	SS73	L	23	78	273	31	76	12	2	0	25	31	24	0	.278	.337
Eddie Yost	3B152, OF3	R	24	154	568	109	161	36	4	12	65	126	55	6	.283	.424
Sam Mele	OF124, 1B15	R	29	143	558	58	153	36	7	5	94	32	31	2	.274	.391
Irv Noren	OF126	L	26	129	509	82	142	33	5	8	86	51	35	10	.279	.411
Gil Coan	OF132	L	29	135	538	85	163	25	7	9	62	39	62	9	.303	.426
2 Mike Guerra	C	R	38	72	214	20	43	2	1	0	20	16	18	2	.201	.234
Sam Dente	SS65, 2B10, 3B5	R	29	88	273	21	65	8	1	0	29	25	10	3	.238	.275
Mike McCormick	OF62	R	34	81	243	31	70	9	1	3	23	29	21	1	.288	.362
Gene Verble	SS28, 2B19, 3B1	R	23	68	177	16	36	3	2	0	15	18	10	1	.203	.252
Sherry Robertson	OF22	L	32	62	111	14	21	2	1	1	10	9	22	2	.189	.252
2 Clyde Kluttz	C46	R	33	53	159	15	49	9	0	1	22	20	9	0	.308	.384
Mickey Grasso	C49	R	31	52	175	16	37	5	0	0	14	14	17	0	.211	.240
Dan Porter	OF7	L	19	13	19	2	4	0	0	0	2	0	1	0	.211	.211
Frank Campos	OF7	L	27	7	26	2	11	2	0	0	2	0	2	0	.423	.615
Willie Miranda	SS2, 1B1	B	25	6	9	2	4	0	0	0	0	1	0	1	.444	.444

Frank Sacka 26 R 4-16, Fred Taylor 26 L 2-12, Len Okrie 27 R 1-8, Roy Hawes 24 L 1-6

NAME	G by Pos	B	AGE	G	AB	R	H	2B	3B	HR	RBI	BB	SO	SB	BA	SA
ST. LOUIS 8th 52-102 .338 46															ZACK TAYLOR	
TOTALS			27	154	5219	611	1288	223	47	86	555	521	693	35	.247	.357
Hank Arft	1B97	R	29	112	345	44	90	16	5	7	42	41	34	4	.261	.397
Bobby Young	2B147	L	26	147	611	75	159	13	9	1	31	44	51	8	.260	.316
Bill Jennings	SS64	R	25	64	195	20	35	10	2	0	13	26	42	1	.179	.251
Freddie Marsh	3B117, SS3, 2B2	R	27	130	445	44	108	21	4	4	43	36	56	4	.243	.335
Ken Wood	OF100	R	26	109	333	40	79	19	0	15	44	27	64	1	.237	.429
Jim Delsing	OF87	L	25	93	341	49	96	16	5	5	55	34	32	5	.282	.408
1 Ray Coleman	OF	L	26	98	310	45	78	14	0	4	44	43	26	1	.252	.397
Sherm Lollar	C85, 3B1	R	26	98	310	44	78	14	0	4	44	43	26	1	.252	.397
2 Matt Batts	C64	R	29	79	248	26	75	17	1	5	31	21	21	2	.302	.440
Johnny Bero	SS55, 2B1	R	29	61	160	24	34	8	0	2	17	26	30	1	.213	.338
2 Cliff Mapes	OF53	L	29	56	201	32	55	7	2	9	32	33	52	0	.274	.433
Tom Upton	SS47	R	24	52	131	9	26	6	1	1	14	12	21	3	.198	.275
Ned Garver	P33	R	25	49	95	8	29	6	1	1	9	4	21	0	.305	.421
3 Jack Maguire	OF26, 3B5, 2B2	R	26	41	127	15	31	5	1	0	16	9	21	1	.244	.299
Johnny Berardino	3B31, 2B2, 1B1, OF1	R	34	39	119	13	27	3	0	3	13	17	13	1	.227	.303
2 Dale Long	1B28, OF1	L	23	34	105	11	25	5	1	1	11	10	22	0	.238	.362
Bennie Taylor	1B25	L	23	33	93	14	24	5	0	0	13	6	13	0	.258	.398
Roy Sievers (SJ)	OF25	R	24	31	89	10	20	7	0	0	5	8	22	0	.225	.303
1 Don Lenhardt	OF27, 1B1	R	28	31	103	19	27	3	1	5	18	16	6	13	.262	.437
2 Earl Rapp	OF23	L	34	28	98	14	32	5	1	0	14	11	11	1	.327	.500
3 Paul Lehner	OF18	L	31	21	67	2	9	1	0	0	5	4	4	0	.134	.254
Frank Saucier	OF3	L	25	18	14	1	2	1	0	0	0	0	1	0	.071	.143
1 Les Moss	C12	R	26	16	47	5	8	1	0	1	5	6	6	0	.170	.277
Joe Lutz	1B11	L	25	14	24	1	4	0	0	0	0	2	4	0	.167	.167
Bud Thomas	SS14	R	22	14	20	1	7	1	0	0	2	1	4	0	.350	.500
Bob Nieman	OF11	R	24	12	43	6	14	1	0	5	12	3	8	0	.326	.698
2 Kermit Wahl	3B6	R	28	12	18	4	6	0	0	0	3	1	3	0	.333	.444

2 Mike Goliat 29 R 2-11, Jim Dyck 29 R 1-15, 1 Clyde Kluttz 33 R 2-4, Billy DeMars 25 R 1-4, Eddie Gaedel 26 R 0-0, Owen Friend (MS) 24, Dick Kokos (MS) 23

Pitching

NAME	T	AGE	W	L	PCT	SV	G	GS	CG	IP	H	BB	SO	SHO	ERA
CHICAGO		29	81	73	.526	14	155	155	74	1418	1353	549	572	11	3.50
Billy Pierce	L	24	15	14	.517	2	37	28	18	240	237	73	113	1	3.04
2 Saul Rogovin	R	29	11	7	.611	0	22	17	11	193	166	67	77	3	2.47*
Ken Holcombe	R	32	11	12	.478	0	28	23	12	159	142	68	39	2	3.79
Randy Gumpert	R	34	9	8	.529	3	28	16	7	142	156	34	45	1	4.31
Joe Dobson	R	34	7	6	.538	3	28	21	6	147	136	51	67	0	3.61
Luis Aloma (AJ)	R	28	6	0	1.000	3	26	1	1	69	52	24	25	1	1.83
Lou Kretlow	R	30	6	9	.400	0	26	18	7	137	129	74	89	1	4.20
Harry Dorish	R	29	5	6	.455	0	32	4	2	97	101	31	29	1	3.53
Howie Judson	R	25	5	5	.455	2	27	14	3	122	124	55	43	0	3.76
Marv Rotblatt	L	23	4	2	.667	2	26	2	0	48	44	23	20	0	3.38
Dick Littlefield	L	25	1	1	.500	0	4	2	0	10	9	17	7	0	8.10
1 Bob Cain	L	26	1	2	.333	0	4	4	1	26	25	13	3	0	3.81
Ross Grimsley	R	29	0	0	—	0	7	0	0	14	12	10	8	0	3.86
Hal Brown	R	26	0	0	—	0	3	0	0	9	15	4	4	0	9.00
2 Bob Mahoney	R	23	0	0	—	0	3	0	0	7	5	3	0	0	5.14

*Rogovin, also with Detroit, league leader in ERA with 2.78

♀Minoso, also with Cleveland, league leader in 3B (14), SB (31)
#Zernial, also with Philadelphia, league leader in HR (33), RBI (129), SO (101)

NAME	T	AGE	W	L	PCT	SV	G	GS	CG	IP	H	BB	SO	SHO	ERA
DETROIT		31	73	81	.474	17	154	154	51	1384	1385	602	597	8	4.29
Virgil Trucks	R	34	13	8	.619	1	37	18	6	154	153	75	89	1	4.23
2 Bob Cain	L	26	11	10	.524	2	35	22	6	149	155	82	58	1	4.71
Fred Hutchinson	R	31	10	10	.500	2	31	20	9	188	204	27	53	2	3.69
Dizzy Trout	R	36	9	14	.391	5	42	22	7	192	172	75	89	0	4.03
Ted Gray	L	26	7	14	.333	1	34	28	9	157	194	95	131	1	4.07
Hal Newhouser (SA)	L	30	6	6	.500	0	15	14	7	96	98	19	37	1	3.94
Ray Herbert (MS)	R	21	0	0	1.000	0	5	0	0	13	8	9	9	0	1.38
Marlin Stuart	R	32	4	4	.400	1	29	15	5	124	119	71	46	0	3.77
Hal White	R	32	3	4	.429	4	38	4	0	76	74	49	23	0	4.74
2 Gene Bearden	L	30	3	4	.429	0	22			106	112	58	38	1	4.33
Hank Borowy	R	35	2	2	.500	0	18	5	0	45	58	27	16	0	7.00
1 Saul Rogovin	R	29	1	1	.500	0	2			11	20	4	5	0	5.25*
Wayne McLeland	R	26	0	1	.000	0	11			11	20	4	0	0	8.18
Dick Marlowe	R	22	0	1	.000	0	2	1	0	6	4	2	2	0	27.00
Earl Johnson	L	32	0	0	—	0	6	0	0	6	11	4	2	0	6.00
Paul Calvert	R	33	0	0	—	0	3	0	0	4	8	1	1	0	9.00

Art Houtteman (MS) 23

*Rogovin, also with Chicago, league leader in ERA with 2.78

NAME	T	AGE	W	L	PCT	SV	G	GS	CG	IP	H	BB	SO	SHO	ERA
PHILADELPHIA		28	70	84	.455	22	154	154	52	1358	1421	569	437	7	4.47
Bobby Shantz	L	25	18	10	.643	0	32	25	13	205	213	70	77	3	3.95
Bob Hooper	R	29	12	10	.545	5	38	23	9	189	192	61	64	0	4.38
Morrie Martin	L	28	11	4	.733	0	35	13	3	138	139	63	35	1	3.78
Alex Kellner	L	26	11	14	.440	2	33	29	11	210	233	93	94	1	4.46
Sam Zoldak	L	32	6	10	.375	0	26	18	8	128	127	24	18	1	3.16
Dick Fowler	R	30	5	11	.313	0	22	22	4	105	141	72	29	0	5.62
Johnny Kucab	R	31	4	3	.571	4	30	1	0	75	76	23	23	0	4.92
1 Hank Wyse	R	33	1	2	.333	0	9	1	0	25	31	7	9	0	7.80
Joe Coleman	R	28	1	6	.143	1	28	9	1	96	117	59	34	0	6.00
Carl Scheib	R	24	1	12	.077	0	46	11	3	143	132	71	49	0	4.47
1 Lou Brissie	L	27	0	0	.000	0	3	2	0	13	20	4	3	0	6.92
Moe Burtsyhy (EJ)	R	22	0	0	—	0	1	0	0	1	6	4	2	0	5.29
1 Charlie Harris	R	25	0	0	—	0	3	0	0	3	4	5	4	0	9.00

*Zernial, also with Chicago, league leader in HR (33), RBI (129), SO (101)

NAME	T	AGE	W	L	PCT	SV	G	GS	CG	IP	H	BB	SO	SHO	ERA
WASHINGTON		32	62	92	.403	13	154	154	58	1366	1429	630	475	6	4.49
Connie Marrero	R	39	11	9	.550	2	25	16	10	197	198	71	66	2	3.90
2 Bob Porterfield	R	27	9	8	.529	0	19	19	10	133	109	54	53	3	3.25
Sandy Consuegra	R	30	7	8	.467	3	40	12	5	146	140	63	31	0	3.60
2 Don Johnson	R	24	7	11	.389	0	21	20	8	144	138	58	52	1	3.94
Mickey Harris	R	34	5	4	.429	4	41	0	0	87	87	43	47	0	3.83
Julio Moreno	R	30	5	11	.313	2	31	18	5	133	132	80	37	0	4.87
Sid Hudson	R	36	5	12	.294	0	23	19	8	139	168	52	43	0	5.12
1 Bob Kuzava	L	28	8	7	.533	0	8	8	5	77	79	41	26	0	4.79
Al Sima	R	22	3	3	.500	0	8	3	2	42	36	17	10	2	2.36
2 Tom Ferrick	R	36	2	5	.286	2	22	0	0	42	43	17	7	0	6.57
2 Fred Sanford	R	32	1	2	.333	1	11	0	0	36	30	15	10	0	4.44
Joe Haynes	R	33	1	4	.200	2	26	3	1	61	76	37	18	0	5.61
2 Dick Starr	R	30	1	7	.125	0	11	9	1	61	76	37	18	0	6.47
Bob Ross	L	22	0	1	.000	0	11	1	1	12	14	10	6	0	6.47
Alton Brown	R	29	0	1	.000	0	2	0	0	9	10	5	0	0	10.00
2 Hank Wyse	R	32	0	1	.000	0	5	1	0	7	10	1	9	0	15.00
1 Gene Bearden	L	30	0	0	—	0	1	0	0	1	1	1	0	0	15.00

NAME	T	AGE	W	L	PCT	SV	G	GS	CG	IP	H	BB	SO	SHO	ERA
ST. LOUIS		28	52	102	.338	9	154	154	56	1370	1525	801	550	5	5.17
Ned Garver	R	25	20	12	.625	0	33	30	24	246	237	96	84	1	3.73
Duane Pillette	R	29	6	14	.300	0	35	24	6	191	205	115	65	1	4.99
Jim McDonald	R	24	7	11	.364	1	16	11	5	84	84	46	28	0	4.07
Al Widmar	R	24	7	15	.318	0	28	15	5	108	157	52	28	0	6.50
2 Tommy Byrne	L	31	4	10	.286	0	19	17	7	123	104	114*	57	2	3.80
Satchel Paige	R	45	3	4	.429	5	23	3	0	62	67	29	48	0	4.79
3 Fred Sanford	R	32	3	3	.333	0	17	7	0	66	67	37	30	0	4.44
2 Bob Mahoney	R	25	0	2	.000	0	15	0	0	52	66	46	22	0	5.10
2 Bobby Hogue	R	30	2	6	.250	0	15	9	0	82	96	42	26	0	5.10
Duke Markell	R	27	1	1	.500	1	30	1	0	33	35	20	10	0	6.43
Bill Kennedy	L	30	1	1	.500	0	5	1	0	23	25	20	11	0	5.79
1 Stubby Overmire	L	32	1	2	.333	0	16	0	0	53	61	21	13	0	3.57
Lou Sleater	L	25	1	3	.143	0	17	3	0	35	51	17	20	0	12.60
1 Don Johnson	R	24	1	0	—	0	4	0	0	27	18	18	8	0	12.60
Bob Turley	R	20	0	1	.000	0	5	0	0	10	12	5	11	0	7.71
Cliff Fannin	R	27	0	1	.000	0	1	1	0	7	9	10	6	0	6.60
Jim Suchecki	R	23	0	2	.000	0	6	1	0	20	27	18	8	0	6.60
Irv Medlinger	L	24	0	4	.000	0	25	6	0	90	113	42	47	0	5.40
1 Sid Schacht	R	33	0	0	—	0	6	0	0	6	14	6	4	0	21.00
	R		0	0	—	0	5	0	0	4	8	7	1	0	31.50

Dave Madison (MS) 30

*Byrne, also with New York, league leader in BB with 150

NEW YORK — 1st 98-59 .624 — LEO DUROCHER (Defeated Brooklyn in playoff 2 games to 1)

NAME	G by Pos	B	AGE	G	AB	R	H	2B	3B	HR	RBI	BB	SO	SB	BA	SA
TOTALS			27	157	5360	781	1396	201	53	179	734	671	624	55	.260	.418
Whitey Lockman	1B119, OF34	L	24	153	614	85	173	27	7	12	73	50	32	4	.282	.407
Eddie Stanky	2B140	R	34	145	515	88	127	17	2	14	43	127	63	6	.247	.369
Al Dark	SS156	R	29	156	646	114	196	41	7	14	69	42	39	12	.303	.454
Hank Thompson	3B71	R	25	87	264	37	62	8	4	8	33	43	23	1	.235	.386
Don Mueller	OF115	L	24	122	469	58	130	10	7	16	69	11	7	1	.277	.431
Willie Mays	OF121	R	20	121	464	59	127	22	5	20	68	56	60	7	.274	.472
Monte Irvin	OF112, 1B39	R	32	151	558	94	174	19	11	24	121	89	44	12	.312	.514
Wes Westrum	C122	R	28	124	361	59	79	12	0	20	70	104	93	1	.219	.418
Bobby Thomson	OF77, 3B69	R	27	148	518	89	152	27	8	32	101	73	57	5	.293	.562
Ray Noble	C41	R	32	55	141	16	33	6	0	5	26	6	26	0	.234	.383
Bill Rigney	3B12, 2B9	R	33	44	69	9	16	2	0	4	9	8	7	0	.232	.435
Davey Williams	2B22	R	23	30	64	17	17	1	0	2	8	5	8	1	.266	.375
Spider Jorgensen	OF11, 3B1	L	31	28	51	5	12	0	0	2	8	3	7	0	.235	.353
Sal Yvars	C23	R	27	25	41	9	13	2	0	2	3	5	7	0	.317	.512
Lucky Lohrke	3B17, SS1	R	27	23	40	3	8	0	0	1	3	10	2	0	.200	.275
Clint Hartung	OF12	R	28	21	44	4	9	1	0	0	2	1	9	0	.205	.227
Artie Wilson	2B3, SS3, 1B2	L	30	19	22	2	4	0	0	0	1	2	1	2	.182	.182
1 Jack Maguire	OF8	R	26	16	20	6	8	1	1	1	4	2	1	0	.400	.700
1 Earl Rapp	OF3	L	30	3	11	0	1	0	0	0	1	2	3	0	.091	.091

2 Hank Schenz 32 R 0-0, Sammy Calderone (MS) 25

NAME	T	AGE	W	L	PCT	SV	G	GS	CG	IP	H	BB	SO	SHO	ERA
		29	98	59	.624	18	157	157	64	1413	1334	482	625	9	3.48
Sal Maglie	R	34	23	6	.793	4	42	37	22	298	254	86	146	3	2.93
Larry Jansen	R	30	23	11	.676	0	39	34	18	279	254	56	145	3	3.03
Jim Hearn	R	30	17	9	.654	0	34	34	11	211	204	82	66	0	3.63
George Spencer	R	24	10	4	.714	6	57	4	2	132	125	56	36	0	3.75
Dave Koslo	L	31	10	9	.526	3	39	16	5	150	153	45	54	2	3.30
Sheldon Jones	R	29	6	11	.353	4	41	12	2	120	119	52	58	0	4.28
Al Corwin	R	24	5	1	.833	1	8	5	3	59	49	21	30	1	3.66
Roger Bowman	L	23	2	4	.333	0	9	5	0	26	35	22	24	0	6.23
Al Gettel	R	33	1	2	.333	1	30	1	0	57	52	25	36	0	4.89
Monte Kennedy	L	29	1	2	.333	0	29	5	1	68	68	31	22	0	2.25
1 Jack Kramer	R	33	0	0	—	0	4	1	0	5	11	3	2	0	14.40
Alex Konikowski	R	23	0	0	—	0	4	0	0	5	4	2	0	0	0.00
George Bamberger	R	25	0	0	—	0	2	0	0	2	4	1	0	0	18.00
Red Hardy	R	28	0	0	—	0	2	0	0	1	4	1	0	0	9.00

BROOKLYN — 2nd 97-60 .618 1 — CHUCK DRESSEN (Defeated by New York in playoff 2 games to 1)

NAME	G by Pos	B	AGE	G	AB	R	H	2B	3B	HR	RBI	BB	SO	SB	BA	SA
TOTALS			29	158	5492	855	1511	249	37	184	794	603	649	89	.275	.434
Gil Hodges	1B158	R	27	158	582	118	156	25	3	40	103	93	99	9	.268	.527
Jackie Robinson	2B150	R	32	153	548	106	185	33	7	19	88	79	27	25	.338	.527
Pee Wee Reese	SS154	R	32	154	616	94	176	20	8	10	84	81	57	20	.286	.393
Billy Cox	3B139, SS1	R	31	142	455	62	127	25	4	9	51	37	30	5	.279	.411
Carl Furillo	OF157	R	29	158	667	93	197	32	4	16	91	43	33	8	.295	.427
Duke Snider	OF150	L	24	150	606	96	168	26	6	29	101	62	97	14	.277	.483
2 Andy Pafko	OF76	R	30	84	277	42	69	11	0	18	58	35	27	1	.249	.484
Roy Campanella	C140	R	29	143	505	90	164	33	1	33	108	53	51	1	.325	.590
Don Thompson	OF61	L	27	80	118	25	27	3	0	0	6	12	12	2	.229	.254
Cal Abrams	OF34	L	27	67	150	27	42	8	0	3	19	36	26	3	.280	.393
Rocky Bridges	3B40, SS9	R	23	63	134	13	34	7	0	1	15	10	10	0	.254	.328
2 Wayne Terwilliger	2B24, 3B1	R	26	37	50	11	14	1	0	0	4	8	7	1	.280	.300
Rube Walker	C23	R	25	36	74	6	18	4	0	2	9	6	14	0	.243	.378
1 Hank Edwards	OF19	L	32	35	31	1	7	3	0	0	3	4	9	0	.226	.387
Gene Hermanski	OF19	L	31	31	80	8	20	4	0	1	5	10	12	0	.250	.338
Dick Williams	OF15	R	22	23	60	5	12	3	1	1	5	4	10	0	.200	.333
Eddie Miksis	3B6, 2B1	R	24	19	10	6	2	1	0	0	1	2	0		.200	.333
1 Bruce Edwards	C9	R	27	17	36	6	9	2	0	0	1	2	6	0	.250	.389
Jim Russell	OF4	B	32	16	13	2	4	0	0	0	0	4	6	0	.308	.308
1 Tommy Brown	OF5	R	23	11										0	.000	.000

Wayne Belardi 20 L 1-3, Mickey Livingston 36 R 2-5

NAME	T	AGE	W	L	PCT	SV	G	GS	CG	IP	H	BB	SO	SHO	ERA
		27	97	60	.618	13	158	158	64	1423	1360	549	693	10	3.88
Preacher Roe	L	36	22	3	.880	0	34	33	19	258	247	64	113	2	3.03
Don Newcombe	R	25	20	9	.690	0	40	36	18	272	235	91	164	3	3.28
Carl Erskine	R	24	16	12	.571	4	46	19	7	190	206	78	95	0	4.45
Clyde King	R	27	14	7	.667	6	48	3	1	121	118	50	33	0	4.17
Ralph Branca	R	25	13	12	.520	3	42	27	13	204	180	85	118	3	3.26
Clem Labine	R	24	5	1	.833	0	14	6	5	65	52	20	39	2	2.22
Bud Podbielan	R	27	2	2	.500	0	19	5	1	53	55	20	15	0	4.75
Erv Palica	R	23	2	6	.250	0	17	8	0	53	55	35	26	0	4.75
1 Joe Hatten	L	34	1	0	1.000	0	19	0	0	49	55	21	22	0	4.59
Chris Van Cuyk	L	24	1	2	.333	0	9	6	0	29	33	11	16	0	5.59
2 Johnny Schmitz	L	30	1	4	.200	0	16	7	0	56	55	28	20	0	5.30
Phil Haugstad	R	27	0	0	—	0	21	0	1	31	28	24	22	0	6.39
Dan Bankhead	R	31	0	1	.000	0	14	1	0	14	27	14	9	0	15.43
Earl Mossor	L	25	0	1	.000	0	3	0	0	2	7	7	1	0	27.00
Joe Landrum (VR) 22															
Billy Loes (MS) 21															

ST. LOUIS — 3rd 81-73 .526 15.5 — MARTY MARION (XJ)

NAME	G by Pos	B	AGE	G	AB	R	H	2B	3B	HR	RBI	BB	SO	SB	BA	SA
TOTALS			30	154	5317	683	1404	230	57	95	629	569	492	30	.264	.382
Nippy Jones	1B71	R	26	80	300	20	79	12	0	9	41	19	41	1	.263	.333
Red Schoendienst	2B124, SS8	B	28	135	553	88	160	32	7	6	54	35	23	1	.289	.405
Solly Hemus	SS105, 2B12	L	28	120	420	68	118	18	9	2	32	75	71	7	.281	.381
2 Billy Johnson	3B124	R	32	124	442	52	116	23	1	14	64	46	49	5	.262	.414
Enos Slaughter	OF106	L	35	123	409	48	115	17	8	4	64	67	25	7	.281	.391
Peanuts Lowrey	OF85, 3B11, 2B3	R	33	114	370	52	112	19	5	5	40	35	12	0	.303	.422
Stan Musial	OF91, 1B60	L	30	152	578	124	205	30	12	32	108	98	40	4	.355	.614
Del Rice	C120	R	28	122	374	34	94	23	1	7	47	34	26	0	.251	.364
2 Wally Westlake	OF68	R	30	73	267	36	68	8	5	6	39	24	42	1	.255	.390
Hal Rice	OF63	R	27	69	236	20	60	12	1	4	38	24	22	0	.254	.364
Chuck Diering	OF44	R	28	64	85	9	22	5	1	0	6	8	15	0	.259	.341
Tommy Glaviano	OF35, 2B9	R	27	54	104	20	19	4	0	1	4	18	16	3	.183	.250
2 Stan Rojek	SS51	R	32	51	186	21	51	7	3	0	14	10	10	0	.274	.344
Bill Sarni	C35	R	23	36	86	7	15	1	0	2	9	6	13	1	.174	.186
1 Joe Garagiola	C23	R	25	27	72	9	14	3	2	0	9	9	7	0	.194	.375
1 Bill Howerton	OF17	L	29	24	65	10	17	4	1	1	4	10	12	0	.262	.400
Steve Bilko	1B19	R	22	21	72	5	16	4	0	2	12	9	10	0	.222	.361
1 Dick Cole	SS24	R	25	15	36	4	7	1	0	0	3	6	5	0	.194	.222
Vern Benson	3B9, OF4	L	26	13	46	8	12	3	1	1	7	6	5	0	.261	.435
Don Richmond	3B11	L	31	12	34	3	3	1	0	1	1	7	3	0	.088	.265
2 Bob Scheffing	C11	R	37	12	18	0	2	0	0	0	1	4	3	0	.111	.111
Eddie Kazak	3B10	R	30	11	33	2	6	2	0	0	2	1	4	0	.182	.242
Harry Walker	OF6, 1B1	L	34	8	26	6	8	1	0	0	2	1	5	0	.308	.346

1 Rocky Nelson 26 L 4-18, Jay Van Noy 22 L 0-7, Don Bollweg 30 L 1-9, Larry Ciaffone 26 R 0-5

NAME	T	AGE	W	L	PCT	SV	G	GS	CG	IP	H	BB	SO	SHO	ERA
		29	81	73	.526	23	155	155	58	1388	1391	558	546	9	3.95
Gerry Staley	R	29	19	13	.594	3	42	30	10	227	244	74	67	4	3.81
2 Cliff Chambers	L	29	11	9	.647	0	21	16	7	129	120	56	45	1	3.84
Max Lanier	L	35	11	9	.550	1	31	23	9	160	149	50	59	2	3.26
Harry Brecheen	L	36	8	4	.667	2	24	16	5	139	134	54	57	0	3.24
Joe Presko	R	22	7	4	.636	2	15	12	5	89	86	20	38	0	3.44
Tom Poholsky	R	21	7	13	.350	1	38	26	10	195	204	68	70	1	4.43
Al Brazle	L	37	6	5	.545	7	56	6	5	154	139	60	66	0	3.10
George Munger	R	32	6	4	.600	0	23	11	3	95	106	46	44	0	5.31
Dick Bokelmann	R	24	3	3	.500	3	20	1	0	52	49	31	22	0	3.81
Jackie Collum	L	24	2	1	.667	0	3	1	0	17	11	10	5	1	1.59
Cloyd Boyer	R	23	2	5	.286	1	19	8	1	63	68	46	40	0	5.29
Jack Crimian	R	25	1	0	1.000	1	11	0	0	17	24	8	5	0	9.00
Dan Lewandowski	R	23	1	0	1.000	0	5	1	0	14	17	8	6	0	7.20
1 Howie Pollet	L	30	0	0	—	0	3	0	0	9	10	4	5	0	4.50
1 Ted Wilks	R	35	0	0	—	1*	17*			15	19	5	5	0	3.00
1 Erv Dusak	R	25	0	0	—	0	10	0	0	14	7	8	7	0	7.20
Bob Habenicht	R	25	0	0	—	0	3	0	0	5	6	3	2	0	7.20
Kurt Krieger	R	24	0	0	—	0	2			4	5	3	1	0	15.75

*Wilks, also with Pittsburgh, league leader in G with 65, SV with 13.

BOSTON — 4th 76-78 .494 20.5 — BILLY SOUTHWORTH 28-31 .475 TOMMY HOLMES 48-47 .505

NAME	G by Pos	B	AGE	G	AB	R	H	2B	3B	HR	RBI	BB	SO	SB	BA	SA
TOTALS			29	155	5293	723	1385	234	37	130	683	565	617	80	.262	.394
Earl Torgeson	1B155	L	27	155	610	99	153	27	4	24	92	102	70	20	.263	.437
Roy Hartsfield	2B114	R	25	120	450	63	122	11	4	6	31	41	73	4	.271	.344
Buddy Kerr	SS63, 2B5	R	28	69	172	18	32	4	0	1	18	22	20	0	.186	.227
Bob Elliott	3B127	R	34	136	480	73	137	29	4	15	70	65	56	2	.285	.448
Willard Marshall	OF136	L	30	136	469	65	132	24	7	11	62	48	18	0	.281	.420
Sam Jethroe	OF140	B	33	148	572	101	160	29	10	18	65	57	88	35	.280	.460
Sid Gordon	OF122, 3B34	R	33	150	556	96	158	24	1	29	109	80	42	2	.287	.500
Walker Cooper	C90	R	36	109	342	42	107	14	1	18	59	28	18	1	.313	.518
Sibby Sisti	SS55, 2B52, 3B6, OF1, 1B1	R	30	114	362	46	101	20	2	3	38	32	50	4	.279	.362
Bob Addis	OF46	L	25	85	199	23	55	7	0	1	24	9	10	3	.276	.327
Ebba St. Claire (BG)	C62	R	29	72	220	22	62	17	2	1	25	12	24	0	.282	.391
Luis Marquez	OF43	R	25	68	122	19	24	5	1	0	11	10	20	4	.197	.254
Johnny Logan	SS58	R	24	62	169	14	37	7	1	0	16	18	13	0	.219	.272
Ray Mueller	C23	R	39	28	70	8	11	2	0	1	7	9	7	0	.157	.229
Tommy Holmes	OF3	L	34	27	29	1	9	2	0	0	1	2	2	0	.172	.241
Luis Olmo	OF16	R	31	21	56	4	11	1	0	1	4	4	4	0	.196	.250
Gene Mauch	SS10, 3B3, 2B2	R	25	19	20	1	2	0	0	0	1	0	4	0	.100	.100
Bob Thorpe		R	24	2	2	1	1	0	0	0	1	0	1	0	.500	1.500

Del Crandall (MS) 21

NAME	T	AGE	W	L	PCT	SV	G	GS	CG	IP	H	BB	SO	SHO	ERA
		27	76	78	.494	12	155	155	73	1389	1378	595	604	16	3.75
Warren Spahn	L	30	22	14	.611	0	39	36	26	311	278	109	164	7	2.98
Max Surkont	R	29	12	16	.429	1	37	33	11	237	230	89	110	2	3.99
Chet Nichols	L	20	11	8	.579	2	33	19	12	156	142	69	71	3	2.88
Vern Bickford (BG)	R	31	11	9	.550	0	25	20	12	165	146	76	76	3	3.11
Jim Wilson	R	29	7	7	.500	1	20	15	5	110	131	40	63	1	5.40
1 Johnny Sain	R	33	5	13	.278	1	26	22	6	160	195	45	63	1	4.22
Bob Chipman	L	33	4	3	.571	4	33	4	2	52	59	19	17	0	4.85
Phil Paine	R	21	2	1	.667	0	21	0	0	23	20	13	9	0	3.09
Dave Cole	R	21	2	4	.333	0	23	4	1	68	64	64	33	0	4.24
Blix Donnelly	R	37	1	1	.500	1	37	0	0	60	56	37	11	0	4.35
George Estock	R	26	0	1	.000	0	37	0	0	60	56	37	11	0	7.71
2 Sid Schacht	R	33	0	2	.000	0	8	2	0	14	17	11	4	0	5.14
Dick Donovan	R	23	0	0	—	0	8							0	1.80
1 Bobby Hogue	R	30	0	0	—	0	9						5	0	5.40
Lew Burdette	R	24	0	0	—	0	3				4	5	1	0	6.75
Johnny Antonelli (MS) 21															

PHILADELPHIA — 5th 73-81 .474 23.5 — EDDIE SAWYER

NAME	G by Pos	B	AGE	G	AB	R	H	2B	3B	HR	RBI	BB	SO	SB	BA	SA
TOTALS			28	154	5332	648	1384	199	47	108	609	505	525	63	.260	.375
Eddie Waitkus	1B144	L	31	145	610	65	157	27	4	1	46	53	22	0	.257	.320
Putsy Caballero	2B54, SS3, 3B3	R	23	84	161	15	30	4	1	0	11	12	7	1	.186	.248
Granny Hamner	SS150	R	24	150	589	61	150	23	7	9	72	29	32	10	.255	.363
Willie Jones	3B147	R	25	148	564	79	161	28	5	22	81	60	47	6	.285	.470
Del Ennis	OF135	R	26	144	532	76	142	20	5	15	73	68	42	4	.267	.408
Richie Ashburn	OF154	L	24	154	643	92	221	31	5	4	63	50	37	29	.344	.426
Dick Sisler	OF111	L	30	123	428	46	123	20	5	8	52	40	39	1	.287	.414
Andy Seminick	C91	R	30	101	291	42	66	8	1	11	37	63	67	1	.227	.375
Eddie Pellagrini	2B53, SS8, 3B6	R	33	86	197	31	46	4	5	3	30	23	35	5	.234	.381
Bill Nicholson	OF47	L	36	85	170	23	41	9	2	5	25	30	24	0	.241	.459
Del Wilber	C73	R	32	84	245	30	68	7	3	8	34	17	26	0	.278	.429
2 Tommy Brown	OF32, 2B14, 1B12, 3B1	R	23	78	196	24	43	2	1	10	32	15	21	1	.219	.393
1 Mike Goliat	2B37, 3B2	R	25	68	138	14	31	4	1	3	11	17	20	0	.225	.312
Jimmy Bloodworth	2B8, 1B6	R	33	21	42	4	6	0	0	1	7	2	3	0	.143	.143
Dick Whitman	OF4	L	30	15	17	0	2	0	0	0	0	2	0		.118	.118
Dick Young	2B15	L	24	13	68	7	16	4	0	0	5	2	3	0	.235	.309
Ed Sanicki	OF10	R	27	10	4	1	2	0	0	1					.500	.750
Mel Clark	OF7	R	24	10	31	4	10	1	0	0	1	3	0		.323	.452

Jackie Mayo 25 L 1-7, Ken Silvestri 35 B 2-9, Stan Lopata 25 R 0-5, Stan Hollmig 25 R 0-2

NAME	T	AGE	W	L	PCT	SV	G	GS	CG	IP	H	BB	SO	SHO	ERA
		29	73	81	.474	15	154	154	57	1385	1373	496	570	19	3.81
Robin Roberts	R	24	21	15	.583	2	44	39	22	315	284	64	127	6	3.03
Bubba Church	R	26	15	11	.577	1	38	33	15	247	246	90	104	4	3.53
Russ Meyer	R	27	9	11	.471	0	28	24	7	168	172	55	65	2	3.48
Ken Heintzelman	L	35	6	12	.333	2	25	18	4	118	119	53	55	0	4.19
Ken Johnson	L	28	5	8	.385	0	20	18	4	106	103	68	58	3	4.58
Jocko Thompson	L	34	4	8	.333	1	29	14	3	119	102	59	60	2	3.86
Jim Konstanty	R	34	4	11	.267	9	58	1	0	116	127	31	27	0	4.03
Andy Hansen	R	26	3	1	.750	2	34	0	0	49	47	18	10	0	2.54
Bob Miller (SA)	R	25	1	1	.500	0	17	0	0	34	47	18	10	0	6.88
Niles Jordan	R	26	2	2	.400	1	5	3	0	34	47	18	10	1	3.16
Milo Candini	R	33	1	0	1.000	0	15	0	0	33	18	14	0	0	6.00
Karl Drews	R	31	1	0	1.000	0	10	2	0	29	7	13	6	0	6.26
Leo Cristante	R	24	1	0	1.000	0	10					4	9	0	4.91
Lou Possehl	R	30	0	0	—	0	3					9		0	6.00
Jack Brittin	R	27	0	0	—	0	2					3		0	9.00
Curt Simmons (MS) 22															

CINCINNATI 6th 68-86 .442 28.5   LUKE SEWELL

NAME	G by Pos	B	AGE	G	AB	R	H	2B	3B	HR	RBI	BB	SO	SB	BA	SA
TOTALS			27	155	5285	559	1309	215	33	88	528	415	577	44	.248	.351
Ted Kluszewski	1B154	L	26	154	607	74	157	35	2	13	79	33	33	6	.259	.387
Connie Ryan	2B121, 3B3, 1B2, OF1	R	31	136	473	75	112	17	4	16	53	79	72	11	.237	.391
Virgil Stallcup	SS117	R	29	121	428	33	103	17	2	8	49	6	40	2	.241	.346
Grady Hatton (BG)	3B87, OF2	L	28	96	331	41	84	9	3	4	37	33	32	4	.254	.335
Johnny Wyrostek	OF139	L	31	142	537	52	167	31	3	2	36	31	34	8	.242	.359
Lloyd Merriman	OF102	L	29	114	359	34	87	23	2	5	38	24	29	1	.243	.380
Joe Adcock	OF107	R	23	113	395	40	96	16	4	10	47	24	29	5	.251	.319
Dixie Howell	C73	R	31	77	207	22	52	6	1	2	18	15	34	0	.251	.319
Bobby Adams	3B60, 2B42, OF1	R	29	125	403	57	107	12	5	5	24	43	40	4	.266	.357
Bob Usher	OF98	R	26	114	303	27	63	12	5	2	25	19	36	4	.208	.310
Roy McMillan	SS54, 3B12, 2B1	R	21	85	199	21	42	4	0	1	8	17	26	0	.211	.246
Johnny Pramesa	C63	R	25	72	227	12	52	5	2	6	22	5	17	0	.229	.348
1 Bob Scheffing	C41	R	37	47	122	9	31	2	0	2	14	16	9	0	.254	.320
2 Hank Edwards (HJ)	OF34	L	32	41	127	14	40	9	1	3	20	13	17	0	.315	.472
Ewell Blackwell	P38	R	28	39	82	10	24	3	1	1	6	5	12	0	.293	.390
3 Barney McCosky	OF11	L	34	25	50	2	16	2	1	1	11	4	2	0	.320	.460
Sammy Meeks	3B4, SS1	R	28	23	35	4	8	0	0	0	2	3	4	1	.229	.229
Wally Post	OF9	R	21	15	41	6	9	3	0	1	9	1	9	0	.220	.366

Danny Litwhiler 34 R 8-29, Hobie Landrith 21 L 5-13, Ted Tappe 20 L 1-3, Jim Bolger 19 R 0-0

NAME	T	AGE	W	L	PCT	SV	G	GS	CG	IP	H	BB	SO	SHO	ERA
		29	68	86	.442	23	155	155	55	1391	1357	490	584	14	3.70
Ewell Blackwell	R	28	16	15	.516	2	38	32	11	233	204	97	120	2	3.44
Ken Raffensberger	L	33	16	17	.485	5	42	33	14	249	232	38	81	5	3.43
Howie Fox	R	30	9	14	.391	2	40	30	9	228	239	69	57	4	3.83
Willie Ramsdell	R	35	9	17	.346	0	31	31	10	196	204	70	88	1	4.04
Herm Wehmeier	R	24	7	10	.412	2	39	22	10	185	167	89	93	2	3.70
Frank Smith	R	23	5	5	.500	11	50	0	0	76	65	22	34	0	3.20
Harry Perkowski	L	28	3	6	.333	1	35	7	1	102	96	46	56	0	2.82
Bud Byerly	R	30	2	1	.667	0	46	0	0	66	69	25	28	0	3.27
Kent Peterson	L	25	1	1	.500	0	30	0	0	10	13	8	5	0	6.30
Eddie Erautt	R	26	0	0	—	0	30	0	0	39	50	23	20	0	5.77
Ed Blake	R	25	0	0	—	0	3	0	0	4	10	1	1	0	11.25
Jim Blackburn	R	27	0	0	—	0	3	0	0	4	8	2	1	0	15.75

PITTSBURGH 7th 64-90 .416 32.5   BILLY MEYER

NAME	G by Pos	B	AGE	G	AB	R	H	2B	3B	HR	RBI	BB	SO	SB	BA	SA
TOTALS			28	155	5318	689	1372	218	56	137	648	557	615	29	.258	.397
Jack Phillips	1B53, 3B4	R	29	70	156	12	37	7	3	0	12	5	17	1	.237	.321
Danny Murtaugh	2B65, 3B3	R	33	77	151	9	30	7	0	1	11	16	19	0	.199	.265
George Strickland	SS125, 2B13	R	25	138	454	59	98	12	7	9	47	59	63	1	.216	.333
Pete Castiglione	3B99, SS28	R	30	132	482	62	126	19	4	7	42	34	28	2	.261	.361
Gus Bell	OF145	L	22	149	600	80	167	27	12	16	89	42	41	1	.278	.443
Catfish Metkovich	OF69, 1B37	L	29	120	423	51	124	21	3	3	61	54	54	2	.293	.398
Ralph Kiner	OF94, 1B58	R	28	151	531	124	164	31	6	42	109	137	57	2	.309	.627
Clyde McCullough	C87	R	34	92	259	26	77	9	2	8	39	27	31	2	.297	.440
2 Bill Howerton	OF53, 3B4	L	29	80	219	29	60	12	2	11	37	26	44	1	.274	.498
Pete Reiser	OF27, 3B5	B	32	74	140	22	38	4	2	3	13	27	20	4	.271	.421
2 Joe Garagiola	C61	L	25	72	212	24	54	8	2	9	35	32	20	2	.255	.439
2 Rocky Nelson	1B32, OF1	L	26	71	195	29	52	7	4	1	19	23	19	0	.267	.359
Monty Basgall	2B55	R	29	55	153	15	32	5	2	0	12	3	10	1	.209	.288
Ed Fitz Gerald	C38	R	27	55	197	8	32	6	0	0	4	7	10	1	.227	.289
1 Wally Westlake	3B34, OF11	R	30	50	181	28	51	9	0	16	45	9	26	0	.282	.569
Tom Saffell	OF17	L	29	49	65	11	13	0	0	1	5	5	11	1	.200	.246
2 Dick Cole	2B34, SS8	R	25	42	106	19	25	4	0	0	11	15	9	0	.236	.302
Frank Thomas	OF37	R	22	39	148	21	39	9	2	2	16	9	15	0	.264	.392
1 Hank Schenz	2B19, 3B9	R	32	25	61	5	13	1	0	0	3	2	9	1	.213	.230
Ted Beard	OF15	L	30	22	48	7	9	1	0	1	3	6	14	0	.188	.271
Dino Restelli	OF11	R	26	21	38	4	7	1	0	0	3	2	4	0	.184	.289
2 Erv Dusak	OF12, P3, 2B2, 3B2	R	30	31	39	6	12	2	0	1	7	3	11	0	.308	.462
Jack Merson	2B13	R	29	13	50	6	18	2	1	1	14	1	7	0	.360	.540

Dick Smith 23 R 8-46, 1 Bob Dillinger 32 R 10-43, 1 Dale Long 25 L 2-12, 1 Stan Rojek 32 R 3-16, 2 Jack Maguire 26 R 0-5, Harry Fisher 25 L 0-3, Danny O'Connell (MS) 24

NAME	T	AGE	W	L	PCT	SV	G	GS	CG	IP	H	BB	SO	SHO	ERA
		29	64	90	.416	22	155	155	40	1380	1479	627	580	9	4.78
Murry Dickson	R	34	20	16	.556	2	45	35	19	289	294	101	112	3	4.02
Bill Werle	L	30	8	6	.571	6	59	9	2	150	181	51	57	0	5.64
Mel Queen	R	33	7	9	.438	0	39	21	4	168	149	99	123	1	4.45
Vern Law	R	21	6	9	.400	2	28	14	2	114	109	51	41	1	4.50
Bob Friend	R	20	6	10	.375	0	34	22	3	150	173	68	41	1	4.26
1 Howie Pollet	R	30	6	10	.375	0	21	21	4	129	149	51	47	1	5.02
2 Ted Wilks	R	35	3	5	.375	12*	48*	1	1	83	69	24	43	0	2.82
1 Cliff Chambers	R	29	3	6	.333	0	10	10	2	60	64	31	19	1	5.55
Don Carlsen	R	24	2	3	.400	0	7	6	2	43	50	14	20	0	4.19
Len Yochim	L	22	1	1	.500	0	3	2	0	9	10	11	5	0	8.00
Junior Walsh	R	32	1	1	.500	0	36	0	0	73	92	46	32	0	6.90
Paul LaPalme	L	27	1	1	.167	0	22	8	1	54	79	31	24	1	6.33
Bill Koski	R	19	0	1	.000	0	13	1	0	27	26	28	6	0	6.67
1 Erv Dusak	R	30	0	1	.000	0	9	1	0	16	11	7	5	0	11.57
Joe Muir	L	28	0	2	.000	0	3	0	0	6	11	4	1	0	2.81
Con Dempsey	R	27	0	2	.000	0	3	2	0	7	11	9	1	0	9.00
Paul Pettit	L	19	0	0	—	0	2	0	0	3	3	4	2	0	3.00

Bill Macdonald (MS) 22

*Wilks, also with St. Louis, league leader in G with 65, SV with 13.

CHICAGO 8th 62-92 .403 34.5   FRANKIE FRISCH 35-45 .438   PHIL CAVARRETTA 27-47 .365

NAME	G by Pos	B	AGE	G	AB	R	H	2B	3B	HR	RBI	BB	SO	SB	BA	SA
TOTALS			28	155	5318	614	1327	200	47	103	572	477	647	63	.250	.364
Chuck Connors	1B57	L	30	66	201	16	48	7	2	2	18	12	25	1	.239	.303
2 Eddie Miksis	2B102	R	24	102	421	48	112	13	3	4	35	33	36	11	.266	.340
Roy Smalley (BL)	SS74	R	25	79	238	24	55	7	4	3	31	25	53	0	.231	.395
Randy Jackson	3B143	R	25	145	557	78	153	24	6	16	76	47	44	14	.275	.425
Hal Jeffcoat	OF87	R	26	141	278	44	76	20	2	4	27	16	23	6	.273	.403
Frankie Baumholtz	OF140	L	32	146	560	62	159	28	10	2	50	49	36	5	.284	.380
Hank Sauer	OF132	R	34	141	525	77	138	19	4	30	89	45	77	2	.263	.486
Smoky Burgess	C64	L	24	94	219	21	55	4	2	2	20	21	12	2	.251	.315
Phil Cavarretta	1B53	L	34	89	206	24	64	7	1	6	28	27	28	0	.311	.442
2 Gene Hermanski	OF81	L	31	75	213	28	65	12	1	3	20	35	30	3	.281	.381
Bob Ramazzotti	SS51, 2B6, 3B1	R	34	73	158	13	39	5	2	1	15	10	23	0	.247	.323
Jack Cusick	SS56	R	23	65	164	16	29	3	2	2	16	17	29	2	.177	.256
Mickey Owen	C57	R	35	58	125	10	23	6	0	0	15	13	13	1	.184	.232
Bob Borkowski	OF25	R	25	58	89	9	14	1	0	1	10	3	16	0	.157	.169
2 Bruce Edwards	C28, 1B9	R	27	51	141	19	33	9	2	3	17	16	14	1	.234	.390
1 Wayne Terwilliger	2B49	R	26	50	192	26	41	6	0	0	10	29	21	3	.214	.245
1 Andy Pafko	OF48	R	30	49	178	26	47	5	3	12	35	16	20	1	.264	.528
Dee Fondy	1B44	R	27	40	170	23	46	7	2	3	20	11	20	5	.271	.388
1 Rube Walker	C31	L	25	37	107	9	25	3	0	2	15	12	13	0	.234	.327
Bill Serena (BW)	3B12	R	26	26	13	39	6	13	1	0	0	3	3	5	0	.333	.333

Carmen Mauro 24 L 5-29, Fred Richards 23 L 8-27, Harry Chiti 18 R 11-31, Carl Sawatski (MS) 23, Preston Ward (MS) 23

NAME	T	AGE	W	L	PCT	SV	G	GS	CG	IP	H	BB	SO	SHO	ERA
		29	62	92	.403	10	155	155	48	1386	1416	572	544	10	4.34
Bob Rush	R	25	11	12	.478	2	37	29	12	211	212	68	129	2	3.84
Dutch Leonard	R	42	10	6	.625	3	41	1	0	82	69	28	30	0	2.63
Bob Kelly	R	23	7	6	.538	0	35	11	4	124	130	55	48	0	4.65
Johnny Klippstein	R	23	6	6	.500	2	35	11	1	124	125	53	56	1	4.28
Frank Hiller	R	30	6	12	.333	1	24	21	6	141	147	31	50	2	4.85
Paul Minner	R	27	6	17	.261	1	33	28	14	202	219	64	68	3	3.79
Turk Lown	R	27	4	9	.308	0	31	18	3	127	125	90	39	1	5.46
Cal McLish	R	25	4	10	.286	0	30	17	5	146	159	52	46	1	4.44
Bob Schultz	L	27	3	6	.333	0	17	10	2	77	75	51	27	0	5.26
Monk Dubiel	R	33	2	2	.500	1	23	6	0	55	46	22	19	0	2.29
2 Joe Hatten	L	34	2	6	.250	0	23	6	1	75	82	37	23	0	5.16
1 Johnny Schmitz	L	30	1	3	.333	0	8	3	0	18	22	15	6	0	8.00
Warren Hacker	R	26	0	0	—	0	2	0	0	4	3	1	0	0	18.00
Andy Varga	L	20	0	0	—	0	2	0	0	3	2	6	1	0	3.00

WORLD SERIES — NEW YORK (AL) 4 NEW YORK (NL) 2

LINE SCORES

TEAM	1 2 3	4 5 6	7 8 9	10 11 12	R	H	E

Game 1   October 4 at Yankee Stadium

| NY (NL) | 2 0 0 | 0 0 3 | 0 0 0 | | 5 | 10 | 1 |
| NY (AL) | 0 1 0 | 0 0 0 | 0 0 0 | | 1 | 7 | 1 |

Koslo   Reynolds, Hogue (7), Morgan (8)

Game 2   October 5 at Yankee Stadium

| NY (NL) | 0 0 0 | 0 0 0 | 1 0 0 | | 1 | 5 | 1 |
| NY (AL) | 1 1 0 | 0 0 0 | 0 1 X | | 3 | 6 | 0 |

Jansen, Spencer (7)   Lopat

Game 3   October 6 at Polo Grounds

| NY (AL) | 0 0 0 | 0 0 0 | 0 1 1 | | 2 | 5 | 2 |
| NY (NL) | 0 1 0 | 0 5 0 | 0 0 X | | 6 | 7 | 2 |

Raschi, Hogue (5)   Hearn, Jones (8)
Ostrowski (7)

Game 4   October 8 at Polo Grounds

| NY (AL) | 0 1 0 | 1 2 0 | 2 0 0 | | 6 | 12 | 0 |
| NY (NL) | 1 0 0 | 0 0 0 | 0 0 1 | | 2 | 8 | 2 |

Reynolds   Maglie, Jones (6)
            Kennedy (9)

Game 5   October 9 at Polo Grounds

| NY (AL) | 0 0 5 | 2 0 2 | 4 0 0 | | 13 | 12 | 1 |
| NY (NL) | 1 0 0 | 0 0 0 | 0 0 0 | | 1 | 5 | 3 |

Lopat   Jansen, Kennedy (4)
         Spencer (6), Corwin (7),
         Konikowski (9)

Game 6   October 10 at Yankee Stadium

| NY (NL) | 0 0 0 | 0 1 0 | 0 0 2 | | 3 | 11 | 1 |
| NY (AL) | 1 0 0 | 0 0 3 | 0 0 X | | 4 | 7 | 0 |

Koslo, Heam (7),   Raschi, Sain (7), Kuzava (9)
Jansen (8)

COMPOSITE BATTING

NAME	POS	G	AB	R	H	2B	3B	HR	RBI	BA
New York (AL)										
Totals		6	199	29	49	7	2	5	25	.246
Rizzuto	SS	6	25	5	8	1	0	0	3	.320
DiMaggio	OF	6	23	3	6	2	0	1	5	.261
Berra	C	6	23	4	6	1	0	0	0	.261
McDougald	3B-2B	6	23	2	6	1	0	1	7	.261
Collins	1B-OF	6	18	2	4	0	0	1	3	.222
Bauer	OF	6	18	2	3	0	1	0	3	.167
Woodling	OF	6	18	6	3	1	1	1	1	.167
Brown	3B	5	14	1	5	1	0	0	1	.357
Coleman	2B	5	8	2	2	0	0	0	0	.250
Lopat	P	2	8	0	1	0	0	0	1	.125
Mize	1B	2	4	1	2	0	0	0	0	.286
Reynolds	P	2	3	0	1	0	0	0	0	.333
Mantle	OF	2	5	1	1	0	0	0	0	.200
Raschi	P	2	2	0	0	0	0	0	0	.000
Sain	P	1	1	0	0	0	0	0	0	.000
Martin	PR	1	0	1	0	0	0	0	0	—
Hopp	PH	1	0	0	0	0	0	0	0	—

Morgan P 0-0, Ostrowski P 0-0, Kuzava P 0-0, Hogue P 0-0

NAME	POS	G	AB	R	H	2B	3B	HR	RBI	BA
New York (NL)										
Totals		6	194	18	46	7	1	2	15	.237
Lockman	1B	6	25	6	6	1	0	0	4	.240
Irvin	OF	6	24	3	11	0	1	0	2	.458
Dark	SS	6	24	5	10	3	0	1	4	.417
Mays	OF	6	22	1	4	0	0	0	1	.182
Stanky	2B	6	22	3	3	0	0	0	1	.136
Thompson	3B	6	21	1	5	1	1	0	2	.238
Westrum	C	6	17	1	4	1	0	0	3	.235
Thomson	OF	5	14	3	2	1	0	0	3	.143
Koslo	P	2	5	0	0	0	0	0	0	.000
Rigney	PH	4	4	0	1	0	0	0	0	.250
Hartung	PH	2	4	0	2	0	0	0	0	
Hearn	P	2	3	0	0	0	0	0	0	.000
Noble	C	2	3	0	0	0	0	0	0	
Lohrke	PH	2	2	0	0	0	0	0	0	
Jansen	P	2	2	0	0	0	0	0	0	
Yvars	PH	2	1	0	0	0	0	0	0	
Williams	PH	1	1	0	0	0	0	0	0	
Maglie	P	1	1	1	1	0	0	0	0	
Schenz	PR	1	0	0	0	0	0	0	0	

Jones P 0-0, Kennedy P 0-0, Corwin P 0-0, Konikowski P 0-0, Spencer P 0-0

COMPOSITE PITCHING

NAME	G	IP	H	BB	SO	W	L	SV	ERA
New York (AL)									
Totals	6	53	46	25	22	4	2	1	1.87
Lopat	2	18	10	3	4	2	0	0	0.50
Reynolds	2	15	16	11	8	1	1	0	4.20
Raschi	2	10.1	12	8	4	1	1	0	0.87
Hogue	2	2.2	4	0	1	0	0	0	0.00
Morgan	1	2	1	1	1	0	0	0	0.00
Ostrowski	1	2	1	0	1	0	0	0	0.00
Sain	1	1	3	2	0	0	0	1	9.00
Kuzava	1	1	0	0	1	0	0	0	0.00

NAME	G	IP	H	BB	SO	W	L	SV	ERA
New York (NL)									
Totals	6	52	49	26	23	2	4	0	4.67
Koslo	2	15	12	7	6	1	1	0	3.00
Jansen	3	10	8	4	6	0	2	0	6.30
Hearn	2	8.2	5	8	1	1	0	0	1.04
Maglie	1	5	8	3	1	0	1	0	7.20
Jones	2	4.1	5	1	2	0	0	0	2.08
Spencer	2	3.1	6	3	0	0	0	0	18.90
Kennedy	2	3	6	3	0	0	1	0	6.00
Corwin	1	1.2	4	0	3	0	0	0	0.00
Konikowski	1	1	1	1	1	0	0	0	0.00

1952 A Lesson from the Old Professor

After winning three straight world championships, Casey Stengel was up against it as the season opened. Joe DiMaggio, after posting a lifetime .325 batting average, retired. Starting infielders Bobby Brown and Jerry Coleman were off to the service along with pitcher Tom Morgan. It was doubtful the Old Professor would achieve a fourth pennant. The experts didn't think so and neither did Cleveland, which was starting the campaign with the best pitching staff in the league.

Except for one demoralizing setback late in April, when St. Louis' Bob Cain bested the Indians' Bob Feller, 1-0, in a double one-hit game and unbelievably put the Browns in first place for a day, Cleveland got off to a fine start. By contrast, the Yankees were well off the pennant road, showing an 18-17 record at the end of May. To further complicate Stengel's life, Ed Lopat, his 1951 ace, hurt the shoulder of his pitching arm and could only post a mediocre 5-5 record when he was shelved at the All-Star break until mid-August.

But Stengel, who seemed to have a direct pipeline to the Gods, took Billy Martin off the bench and plugged up the vacancy Coleman left at second. Gil McDougald, who alternated between second and third in 1951, was made the regular at third and turned in a fine job. And a switch-hitting powerhouse by the name of Mickey Charles Mantle, out of Spavinaw, Oklahoma, took over DiMaggio's chores in center field and quickly blossomed in his second year in the majors, with 23 homers and a .311 batting average.

When Labor Day arrived, the Yankees found themselves 2 1/2 games ahead of the pack but were faced with 18 of their last 21 games on the road compared to runner-up Cleveland, which had 20 of 22 to play at home. Both clubs met in a showdown in mid-September before 73,609 fans—the largest crowd of the season—and the Yankees stopped Mike Garcia, 7-1.

A few days later Bobby Shantz, the A's 5'6", 139-pound wonder southpaw, shook the Yankees, 2-0, to whittle their lead to 1½ games. But Allie Reynolds, who led the league with a 2.07 E.R.A., assured New York of at least a tie when he beat Boston, 3-2, before Lopat and Johnny Sain combined to send them over the top with a 5-2 victory at Philadelphia.

The failure for the Indians came when they could not get together with their long-time ace Bob Feller who, after pitching winning ball for 13 years, ran into a disappointing 9-13 season.

Over in the National League, the Dodgers made good after their humiliating loss in 1951. It was mostly because of Joe Black, a 28-year-old rookie who wasn't even on the roster at spring, and their feasting on the National League's tail—the Pirates, Braves, and Reds—for a combined 54-11 record.

Giant fans thought their team would have no trouble repeating as National League winners after they watched Leo Durocher manage his way to a 16-2 start. Such was not the case, especially when it was remembered that Monte Irvin, the 1951 RBI leader, broke an ankle in spring training and would not be with the team until late in the year. And Willie Mays, the Giants' super soph, would only remain until May when he had to depart for military service. The arrival of rookie knuckle-baller Hoyt Wilhelm, who posted the best E.R.A. in the league with 2.43, was enough for at least a second-place finish.

As far as the Series was concerned, it took Stengel and his Yankees the full seven games to prove the pre-season experts wrong.

1952 AMERICAN LEAGUE

NAME	G by Pos	B	AGE	G	AB	R	H	2B	3B	HR	RBI	BB	SO	SB	BA	SA
NEW YORK	**1st 95-59 .619**				**CASEY STENGEL**											
	TOTALS		27	154	5294	727	1411	221	56	129	672	566	652	52	.267	.403
Joe Collins	1B119	L	29	122	428	69	120	16	8	18	59	55	47	4	.280	.481
Billy Martin (BN)	2B107	R	24	109	363	32	97	13	3	3	33	22	31	3	.267	.344
Phil Rizzuto	SS152	R	34	152	578	89	147	24	10	2	43	67	42	17	.254	.341
Gil McDougald	3B117, 2B38	R	24	152	555	65	146	16	5	11	78	57	73	6	.263	.369
Hank Bauer	OF139	R	29	141	553	86	162	31	6	17	74	50	61	6	.293	.463
Mickey Mantle	OF141, 3B1	B	20	142	549	94	171	37	7	23	87	75	111	4	.311	.530
Gene Woodling	OF118	L	29	122	408	58	126	19	6	12	63	59	31	1	.309	.463
Yogi Berra	C140	L	27	142	534	97	146	17	1	30	98	66	24	2	.273	.478
2 Irv Noren	OF60, 1B19	L	27	93	272	36	64	13	2	5	21	26	34	4	.235	.353
Johnny Mize	1B27	L	39	78	137	9	36	9	0	4	29	11	15	0	.263	.416
Jim Brideweser	SS22, 2B4, 3B1	R	25	42	38	12	10	0	0	0	2	3	5	0	.263	.263
Bob Cerv	OF27	R	26	36	87	11	21	3	2	1	8	9	22	0	.241	.356
Bobby Brown (MS)	3B24	L	27	29	89	6	22	2	0	1	14	9	6	1	.247	.303
Charlie Silvera	C20	R	27	20	55	4	18	3	0	0	11	5	2	0	.327	.382
Andy Carey	3B14, SS1	R	20	16	40	6	6	0	0	0	1	3	10	0	.150	.150
1 Johnny Hopp	1B12	L	35	15	25	4	4	0	0	0	2	4	3	2	.160	.160
Jerry Coleman (MS)	2B11	R	27	11	42	6	17	2	1	0	4	5	4	0	.405	.500

Kal Segrist 21 R 1-23, Loren Babe 24 L 2-6, 1 Jackie Jensen 25 R 2-19, 1 Archie Wilson 28 R 1-2, Charlie Keller 35 L 0-1

NAME		T	AGE	W	L	PCT	SV	G	GS	CG	IP	H	BB	SO	SHO	ERA
			30	95	59	.617	27	154	154	72	1381	1240	581	666	21	3.14
Allie Reynolds		R	37	20	8	.714	6	35	29	24	244	194	97	160	6	2.07
Vic Raschi		R	33	16	6	.727	0	31	31	13	223	174	91	127	4	2.78
Johnny Sain		R	34	11	6	.647	7	35	16	8	148	149	38	57	0	3.47
Ed Lopat (SJ)		L	34	10	5	.667	0	20	19	10	149	127	53	56	2	2.54
Bob Kuzava		L	29	8	8	.500	3	28	12	6	133	115	63	67	1	3.45
Tom Gorman		R	27	6	2	.750	1	12	6	1	61	63	22	31	1	4.57
2 Ray Scarborough		R	34	5	1	.833	0	9	4	1	34	27	15	13	0	2.91
Tom Morgan (MS)		R	22	5	4	.556	2	16	12	2	94	86	33	.35	1	3.06
Bill Miller		L	24	4	6	.400	0	21	13	5	88	78	49	45	2	3.48
Jim McDonald		R	25	3	4	.429	0	26	5	1	69	71	40	20	0	3.52
1 Bobby Hogue		R	31	3	5	.375	4	27	0	0	47	52	25	12	0	5.36
Joe Ostrowski		L	35	2	2	.500	2	20	1	0	40	56	14	17	0	5.63
2 Ewell Blackwell		R	29	1	0	1.000	1	5	2	0	16	12	12	7	0	0.56
2 Johnny Schmitz		L	31	1	1	.500	1	5	2	1	15	15	9	3	0	3.60
Harry Schaeffer		L	28	0	1	.000	0	5	2	0	17	18	18	15	0	5.29
Art Schallock		L	28	0	0	—	0	2	0	0	2	3	2	1	0	9.00
Whitey Ford (MS) 23																
Bob Wiesler (MS)21																

NAME	G by Pos	B	AGE	G	AB	R	H	2B	3B	HR	RBI	BB	SO	SB	BA	SA
CLEVELAND	**2nd 93-61 .604 2**				**AL LOPEZ**											
	TOTALS		29	155	5330	763	1399	211	49	148	721	626	749	46	.262	.404
Luke Easter	1B118	L	36	127	437	63	115	10	3	31	97	44	84	1	.263	.513
Bobby Avila	2B149	R	28	150	597	102	179	26	11	7	45	67	36	12	.300	.415
Ray Boone	SS96, 3B2, 2B1	R	28	103	316	57	83	8	2	7	45	53	33	0	.263	.367
Al Rosen	3B147, 1B4, SS3	R	28	148	567	101	171	32	5	28	105	75	54	8	.302	.524
Harry Simpson	OF127, 1B26	L	26	146	545	66	145	21	10	10	65	56	82	5	.266	.396
Larry Doby	OF136	L	28	140	519	104	143	26	8	32	104	90	111	5	.276	.541
Dale Mitchell	OF128	L	30	134	511	61	165	26	3	5	58	52	9	6	.323	.415
Jim Hegan	C107	R	31	112	333	39	75	17	2	4	41	29	47	0	.225	.324
Jim Fridley	OF54	R	27	62	175	23	44	2	0	4	16	14	40	3	.251	.331
Barney McCosky	OF19	L	35	54	80	14	17	4	1	1	6	8	5	1	.213	.325
Merrill Combs	SS49, 2B3	R	32	52	139	11	23	1	1	1	10	14	15	0	.165	.209
Bill Glynn	1B32	L	27	44	92	15	25	5	0	2	7	5	16	1	.272	.391
2 Joe Tipton	C35	R	30	43	105	15	26	2	0	6	22	21	21	1	.248	.438
Birdie Tebbetts	C37	R	39	42	101	4	25	4	0	1	18	8	9	0	.248	.317
2 Hank Majeski	3B11, 2B3	R	35	36	54	7	16	2	0	0	9	7	7	0	.296	.333
1 Johnny Berardino	2B8, SS8, 3B4, 1B2	R	35	35	32	5	3	0	0	0	2	10	8	0	.094	.094
Pete Reiser	OF10	B	33	34	44	7	6	1	0	3	7	4	16	1	.136	.364
2 George Strickland	SS30, 2B1	R	26	31	88	8	19	4	0	1	8	14	15	0	.216	.295
3 Wally Westlake	OF28	R	31	29	69	11	16	4	1	1	9	8	16	1	.232	.362
Bob Kennedy (MS)	OF13, 3B3	R	31	22	40	6	12	3	1	0	12	9	5	1	.300	.425
Dave Pope	OF10	L	31	12	34	9	10	1	1	1	4	1	7	0	.294	.471

Quincy Trouppe 39 B 1-10, Snuffy Stirnweiss 33 R 0-0, Hal Naragon (MS) 23

NAME		T	AGE	W	L	PCT	SV	G	GS	CG	IP	H	BB	SO	SHO	ERA
			31	93	61	.604	18	155	155	80	1407	1278	556	671	19	3.32
Early Wynn		R	32	23	12	.657	3	42	33	19	286	239	132	153	4	2.90
Mike Garcia		R	28	22	11	.667	4	46	36	19	292	284	87	143	6	2.37
Bob Lemon		R	31	22	11	.667	4	42	36	28	310	236	105	131	5	2.50
Bob Feller		R	33	9	13	.409	0	30	30	11	192	219	83	81	0	4.73
Steve Gromek		R	32	7	7	.500	1	29	13	3	123	109	28	65	1	3.66
1 Mickey Harris		L	35	3	0	1.000	1	29	0	0	47	42	21	23	0	4.60
Lou Brissie		L	28	3	2	.600	2	42	1	0	83	68	34	28	0	3.47
Sam Jones		R	26	2	3	.400	1	14	4	0	36	38	37	28	0	7.25
Dick Rozek		L	25	1	0	1.000	0	10	1	0	13	11	13	5	0	4.85
Bob Chakales		R	24	1	2	.333	—	1	7	0	12	19	8	7	0	9.75
2 Ted Wilks		R	36	0	0	—	1	7	0	0	12	8	7	6	0	3.75
Bill Abernathie		R	23	0	0	—	0	1	1	0	4	5	4	1	0	13.50
George Zuverink		R	27	0	0	—	0	1	0	0	1	0	1	0	0	0.00
Al Aber (MS) 24																
Dick Weik (MS) 24																

NAME	G by Pos	B	AGE	G	AB	R	H	2B	3B	HR	RBI	BB	SO	SB	BA	SA
CHICAGO	**3rd 81-73 .526 14**				**PAUL RICHARDS**											
	TOTALS		29	154	5316	610	1337	199	38	80	560	541	521	61	.252	.348
Eddie Robinson	1B155	L	31	155	594	79	176	33	1	22	104	70	49	2	.296	.466
Nellie Fox	2B151	L	24	152	648	76	192	25	10	0	39	34	14	5	.296	.366
Chico Carrasquel (BG)	SS99	R	24	100	359	36	89	7	1	4	42	33	27	2	.248	.298
Hector Rodriguez	3B113	R	32	124	407	55	108	14	1	0	40	47	22	7	.265	.307
2 Sam Mele	OF112, 1B3	R	30	123	423	46	105	18	2	14	59	48	40	1	.248	.400
2 Jim Rivera	OF53	L	29	53	201	27	50	7	3	3	18	21	27	13	.249	.358
Minnie Minoso	OF143, 3B9, SS1	R	29	147	569	96	160	24	9	13	61	71	46	22	.281	.424
Sherm Lollar	C120	R	27	132	375	35	90	15	0	13	50	54	34	1	.240	.384
Bud Stewart	OF60	L	36	92	225	23	60	10	0	5	30	28	17	3	.267	.378
1 Ray Coleman	OF73	L	30	85	195	19	42	7	1	2	14	13	17	0	.215	.292
13 Willie Miranda	SS54, 3B5, 2B2	B	26	70	150	14	33	4	1	0	7	13	14	1	.220	.260
Sam Dente	SS27, 3B18, 2B6, OF6, 1B2	R	30	62	145	12	32	2	1	0	21	16	16	1	.221	.234
2 Tom Wright	OF34	L	28	60	132	15	34	10	2	1	21	16	16	1	.258	.386
Rocky Krsnich	3B37	R	24	44	91	11	21	7	2	0	15	6	15	1	.231	.352
1 Al Zarilla	OF32	L	33	39	99	14	23	4	1	2	15	14	6	1	.232	.354
Bud Sheely	C31	L	31	36	75	1	18	2	0	0	14	10	3	0	.240	.267
Phil Masi	C25	R	35	30	49	1	12	2	0	0	7	10	10	0	.254	.302
2 Darrell Johnson	C21	R	23	22	37	3	4	0	0	0	1	5	9	1	.108	.108
2 Leo Thomas	3B9	R	28	19	24	1	4	1	0	0	5	6	5	1	.167	.167

1 Jim Busby 25 R 5-39, 2 Hank Edwards 33 L 6-18, 1 George Wilson 26 L 1-9, Don Nicholas 21 L 0-2, Ken Landenberger 23 L 1-5, Red Wilson 23 R 0-3, Sammy Esposito (MS) 20 R 1-4, Herb Adams (MS) 24, Joe Kirrene (MS) 20, Bill Wilson (MS) 23

NAME		T	AGE	W	L	PCT	SV	G	GS	CG	IP	H	BB	SO	SHO	ERA
			29	81	73	.526	28	156	156	53	1417	1251	578	774	15	3.25
Billy Pierce		L	25	15	12	.556	1	33	32	14	255	214	79	144	4	2.58
Saul Rogovin		R	30	14	9	.609	1	33	30	12	232	224	79	121	3	3.84
Joe Dobson		R	35	14	10	.583	1	29	25	11	201	164	60	101	3	2.51
Marv Grissom		R	34	12	10	.545	0	28	24	7	166	156	79	97	1	3.74
Harry Dorish		R	30	8	4	.667	11	39	1	1	91	66	42	47	0	2.47
Chuck Stobbs		L	22	7	12	.368	1	38	17	2	135	118	72	73	0	3.13
Lou Kretlow		R	31	4	4	.500	1	19	11	4	79	52	56	63	2	2.96
Luis Aloma (SA)		R	29	3	1	.750	6	25	0	0	40	42	11	18	0	4.28
Bill Kennedy		L	31	2	2	.500	5	47	1	0	71	54	38	46	0	2.79
Hal Brown		R	27	2	3	.400	0	24	8	1	72	82	21	31	0	4.25
Howie Judson		R	26	1	0	.000	1	21	0	0	34	30	22	15	0	4.24
1 Ken Holcombe		R	33	0	0	.000	0	7	1	0	35	38	18	12	0	6.17
2 Hal Hudson		L	25	0	0	—	0	2	0	0	4	7	1	4	0	2.25
Al Widmar		R	27	0	0	—	0	1	0	0	4	4	3	1	0	4.50

PHILADELPHIA   4th 79-75 .513 16   JIMMY DYKES

NAME	G by Pos	B	AGE	G	AB	R	H	2B	3B	HR	RBI	BB	SO	SB	BA	SA
TOTALS			31	155	5163	664	1305	212	35	89	634	683	561	52	.253	.359
Ferris Fain	1B144	L	31	145	538	82	176	43	3	2	59	105	26	3	.327	.429
Skeeter Kell	2B68	R	22	75	213	24	47	9	2	1	14	18	18	5	.221	.286
Eddie Joost	SS146	R	36	146	540	49	132	26	3	20	75	122	94	5	.244	.415
Billy Hitchcock	3B104, 1B13	R	35	119	407	45	100	26	4	5	47	39	45	1	.246	.292
Elmer Valo	OF121	R	31	129	388	69	109	26	4	5	47	101	16	12	.281	.407
Dave Philley	OF149, 3B2	L	32	151	586	80	154	25	4	7	71	59	35	11	.263	.355
Gus Zernial	OF141	R	29	145	549	76	144	15	5	29	100	70	87	5	.262	.452
Joe Astroth	C102	R	29	104	337	24	84	7	2	1	36	25	27	2	.249	.291
Kite Thomas	OF29	R	29	75	116	24	29	6	1	6	18	20	27	0	.250	.474
Pete Suder	2B43, SS17, 3B16	R	36	74	228	22	55	7	2	1	20	16	17	1	.241	.303
Allie Clark (BW)	OF48, 1B2	R	29	71	186	23	51	12	0	7	29	10	19	0	.274	.452
3 Cass Michaels	2B55	R	26	55	200	22	50	4	5	1	18	23	11	3	.250	.335
Ray Murray	C42	R	34	44	136	14	28	5	0	1	10	9	13	0	.206	.265
2 Sherry Robertson	2B8, OF7, 3B2	L	33	43	60	8	12	3	0	0	5	21	15	1	.200	.250
1 Hank Majeski	3B34	R	35	34	117	14	30	2	2	2	20	19	10	0	.256	.359
1 Joe Tipton	C23	R	30	23	68	6	13	4	0	3	15	11	5	0	.191	.382

Tom Hamilton 26 L 2-10, 2 Hal Bevan (BL) 21 R 6-17, Jack Littrell 23 R 0-2

NAME	T	AGE	W	L	PCT	SV	G	GS	CG	IP	H	BB	SO	SHO	ERA
		29	79	75	.513	15	155	155	73	1384	1402	526	562	11	4.16
Bobby Shantz	L	26	24	7	.774	0	33	33	27	280	230	63	152	5	2.48
Harry Byrd	R	27	15	15	.500	2	37	28	15	228	244	98	116	3	3.32
Alex Kellner	R	27	12	14	.462	0	34	33	14	231	223	86	105	2	4.36
Bob Hooper	R	30	8	15	.348	6	43	14	4	144	158	68	40	0	5.19
Carl Scheib	R	25	11	7	.611	2	30	19	8	158	153	50	42	1	4.39
2 Bobo Newsom	R	44	3	3	.500	1	24			48	38	23	22	0	3.59
Ed Wright	R	33	2	1	.667	1	24	0	0	41	55	20	9	0	6.59
Charlie Bishop	R	28	2	2	.500	0	5	1	0	31	36	17	16	0	6.39
Marion Fricano	R	28	1	0	1.000	0	5	1	0	5	1	0	1	0	1.80
Dick Fowler	R	31	1	1	.333	0	18	3	1	59	71	28	14	0	6.41
Johnny Kucab	R	32	0	1	.000	2	25	0	0	51	64	20	17	0	5.29
Morrie Martin (BG)	L	29	0	0	.000	0	5	5	0	25	32	15	13	0	6.48
Sam Zoldak	L	33	0	0	.000	1	16	10	2	75	86	25	12	0	4.08
Tex Hoyle	R	30	0	0	—	0	2	0	0	4	3	1	2	0	31.50
Walt Kellner	R	23	0	0	—	0	2	0	0	6	7	5	1	0	6.75
Len Matarazzo	R	23	0	0	—	0	1	0	0	1	1	0	0	0	0.00

WASHINGTON   5th 78-76 .506 17   BUCKY HARRIS

NAME	G by Pos	B	AGE	G	AB	R	H	2B	3B	HR	RBI	BB	SO	SB	BA	SA
TOTALS			29	157	5357	598	1282	225	44	50	555	580	607	48	.239	.326
Mickey Vernon	1B153	L	34	154	569	71	143	33	9	10	80	89	66	7	.251	.394
Floyd Baker	2B68, SS7, 3B1	L	35	79	263	27	69	8	0	0	33	30	17	1	.262	.293
Pete Runnels	SS147, 2B1	R	24	152	555	70	158	18	3	1	64	72	55	0	.285	.333
Eddie Yost	3B157	R	25	157	587	92	137	32	3	12	49	129	73	4	.233	.359
2 Jackie Jensen	OF143	R	25	144	570	94	163	19	5	10	80	63	40	17	.286	.407
2 Jim Busby	OF128	R	25	129	512	58	125	24	4	2	47	22	48	5	.244	.318
Gil Coan	OF86	L	30	107	332	50	68	11	4	6	20	32	35	9	.205	.319
Mickey Grasso	C114	R	32	115	361	22	78	14	0	0	27	29	36	1	.216	.241
Mel Hoderlein	2B58	R	29	72	208	16	56	8	2	0	17	18	22	2	.269	.327
2 Ken Wood	OF56	R	28	61	210	26	50	8	6	6	32	30	21	0	.238	.419
Clyde Kluttz	C52	R	34	58	144	7	33	5	0	1	11	12	11	0	.229	.285
Frank Campos	OF23	L	28	53	112	9	29	6	1	0	9	6	13	0	.259	.330
2 Earl Rapp	OF10	L	31	46	67	7	19	6	0	0	9	4	13	0	.284	.373
Jerry Snyder	OF24	R	28	36	57	5	9	2	0	0	2	5	11	1	.158	.193
2 Archie Wilson	OF24	R	28	26	96	8	20	2	3	0	14	5	11	0	.208	.292
1 Cass Michaels	2B22	R	26	22	86	10	20	4	1	1	7	1	15	0	.233	.337

1 Irv Noren 27 L 12-49, Hal Keller 24 L 4-23, George Bradshaw 27 R 5-23, Fred Taylor 27 L 5-19, 1 Sam Mele 30 R 12-28,
2 Freddie Marsh 28 R 1-24, Tom Upton 25 R 0-5, Buck Varner 21 L 0-4, 1 Sherry Robertson 33 L 0-0, Dan Porter (MS) 20

NAME	T	AGE	W	L	PCT	SV	G	GS	CG	IP	H	BB	SO	SHO	ERA
		32	78	76	.506	15	157	157	75	1430	1405	577	574	10	3.37
Bob Porterfield	R	28	13	14	.481	0	31	29	15	231	222	85	80	3	2.73
Spec Shea	R	31	11	7	.611	0	22	21	12	169	144	92	65	2	2.93
Connie Marrero	R	40	11	8	.579	0	22	22	16	184	175	53	77	2	2.89
2 Walt Masterson	R	32	9	9	.529	2	24	21	11	161	153	72	89	0	3.69
Julio Moreno	R	31	9	9	.500	0	26	22	7	147	154	52	62	0	3.98
Sandy Consuegra	R	31	6	0	1.000	5	30	2	0	74	80	27	19	0	3.04
2 Lou Sleater	L	25	3	3	.667	0	14	9	3	57	56	30	22	1	3.63
Tom Ferrick	R	37	4	3	.571	1	27	0	0	51	53	11	28	0	4.24
2 Randy Gumpert	R	34	3	3	.308	0	20	12	2	104	112	30	29	0	4.24
1 Sid Hudson	R	37	3	7	.429	0	7	7	6	63	59	29	24	0	2.71
2 Mike Fornieles	R	20	2	2	.500	0	4	2		26	13	11	12	1	1.38
1 Bobo Newsom	R	44	1	1	.500	2	10	0	0	13	16	9	5	0	4.85
Raul Sanchez	R	21	1	1	.500	0	5	1	0	13	13	7	5	0	3.46
Joe Haynes	R	34	0	3	.000	3	22	2	0	66	70	35	18	0	4.50
Don Johnson	R	25	0	5	.000	1	15	6	0	69	80	33	37	0	4.43
1 Mickey Harris	R	35	0	0	—	0	1	0	0	1	0	0	0	0	9.00
Harley Grossman	R	22	0	0	—	0	1	0	0	0.1	0	0	0	0	54.00
Bunky Stewart	L	21	0	0	—	0	1	0	0	2	3	3	2	0	18.00
Bob Ross (MS) 23															

BOSTON   6th 76-78 .494 19   LOU BOUDREAU

NAME	G by Pos	B	AGE	G	AB	R	H	2B	3B	HR	RBI	BB	SO	SB	BA	SA
TOTALS			27	154	5246	668	1338	233	34	113	628	542	739	59	.255	.377
Dick Gernert	1B99	R	23	102	367	58	89	20	2	19	67	35	83	4	.243	.463
Billy Goodman	2B103, 1B23, 3B5, OF4	L	26	138	513	79	157	27	3	4	56	48	23	6	.306	.394
2 Johnny Lipon	SS69, 3B7	R	29	79	234	25	48	8	1	0	18	32	20	1	.205	.248
George Kell	3B73	R	29	75	276	41	88	15	2	6	40	31	10	0	.319	.453
Faye Throneberry	OF86	L	21	98	310	38	80	11	3	5	23	33	67	16	.258	.377
Dom DiMaggio	OF123	R	35	128	486	81	143	20	1	6	33	57	61	6	.294	.377
2 Hoot Evers (BG)	OF105	R	31	106	401	53	105	17	4	14	59	39	55	5	.262	.429
Sammy White	C110	R	24	115	381	35	107	20	2	10	49	16	43	2	.281	.423
Vern Stephens (KJ)	SS53, 3B29	R	31	92	295	35	75	13	2	7	44	39	31	2	.254	.383
Clyde Vollmer	OF70	R	30	90	250	35	66	12	4	11	50	39	47	2	.264	.476
Ted Lepcio	2B57, 3B25, SS1	R	21	84	237	34	72	17	2	5	26	24	41	3	.263	.394
Jimmy Piersall (IL)	SS30, OF22, 3B1	R	22	56	161	28	43	8	0	1	16	28	26	3	.267	.335
Del Wilber	C39	R	33	72	135	7	36	10	1	3	23	7	20	1	.267	.422
2 George Schmees	OF29, 1B2, P2	L	27	42	64	8	13	3	0	0	3	10	11	0	.203	.250
1 Walt Dropo	1B35	R	29	37	132	13	35	7	1	6	27	11	22	0	.265	.470
1 Don Lenhardt	OF27	R	29	30	105	18	31	4	0	7	24	15	18	0	.295	.533
Gus Niarhos	C25	R	31	29	58	4	6	0	0	0	2	12	9	0	.103	.103
1 Johnny Pesky	3B19, SS2	L	32	25	67	10	10	2	0	1	2	15	5	0	.149	.179
Gene Stephens	OF13	L	19	21	53	10	12	5	0	0	7	6	8	4	.226	.321
3 Al Zarilla	OF19	L	33	21	60	9	11	0	1	0	4	9	5	0	.183	.317
1 Fred Hatfield	3B17	L	27	19	25	6	8	1	1	1	3	2	4	2	.320	.560
Ted Williams (MS)	OF2	R	33	6	10	2	4	1	0	1	3	2	2	1	.400	.900

3 Archie Wilson 28 R 10-38, 1 Ken Wood 28 R 2-20, Milt Bolling 21 8-36, Charlie Maxwell 25 L 1-15, Lou Boudreau 34 R 0-2,
Paul Lehner 32 L 2-3, 1 Hal Bevan 21 R 0-1, Len Okrie (MS) 21, Karl Olson (MS) 21, Norm Zauchin (MS) 22

NAME	T	AGE	W	L	PCT	SV	G	GS	CG	IP	H	BB	SO	SHO	ERA
		30	76	78	.494	24	154	154	53	1372	1332	623	624	7	3.80
Mel Parnell	L	30	12	12	.500	2	33	29	15	214	207	69	107	3	3.62
Mickey McDermott	L	23	10	9	.526	0	30	21	7	162	139	92	117	2	3.72
2 Dizzy Trout	R	37	9	8	.529	1	26	17	2	134	133	68	57	0	3.63
2 Sid Hudson	R	37	9	9	.438	0	21	18	7	134	145	36	50	0	3.63
Willard Nixon	R	24	4	4	.556	0	23	13	5	104	115	61	50	0	4.85
Bill Henry	L	24	4	4	.556	0	15	10	5	77	75	36	23	0	3.86
Dick Brodowski	R	19	5	5	.500	0	20	13	5	111	111	50	42	0	4.38
Ellis Kinder	R	37	5	6	.455	4	23	10	4	98	85	28	50	0	2.57
Al Benton	R	41	4	3	.571	6	24	0	0	42	38	17	20	0	2.37
Ike Delock	R	22	4	9	.308	5	39	7	1	95	88	50	46	1	4.72
Ralph Brickner	R	27	3	1	.750	1	14	1	0	33	24	14	5	0	2.18
1 Bill Wight	L	34	1	0	1.000	0	20	0	0	20	15	5	6	0	4.05
Hersh Freeman	R	24	1	0	1.000	0	2	1	0	10	6	1	0	0	1.80
Harry Taylor	R	33	1	0	1.000	0	2	1	0	6	6	1	0	0	3.00
1 Walt Masterson	R	32	1	1	.500	0	5	1	0	10	6	2	1	0	12.00
1 Ray Scarborough	R	34	1	5	.167	0	28	4	1	77	79	35	29	1	4.79
Jim Atkins	L	24	0	1	.000	0	2	1	0	6	9	3	2	0	3.60
2 George Schmees	L	27	0	0	—	0	2	1	0	9	6	2	2	0	3.00
Leo Kiely (MS) 22															

ST. LOUIS   7th 64-90 .416 31   1 ROGERS HORNSBY 22-29 .431   MARTY MARION 42-61 .408

NAME	G by Pos	B	AGE	G	AB	R	H	2B	3B	HR	RBI	BB	SO	SB	BA	SA
TOTALS			27	155	5353	604	1340	225	46	82	574	540	720	30	.250	.356
Dick Kryhoski	1B86	L	27	111	342	38	83	13	1	11	42	23	42	2	.243	.383
Bobby Young	2B149	L	27	149	575	59	142	15	9	4	39	56	48	3	.247	.325
Joe DeMaestri	SS77, 3B1, 2B1	R	23	81	186	13	42	9	1	1	18	8	25	0	.226	.301
Jim Dyck	3B74, OF48	R	30	122	402	60	108	22	3	15	64	50	68	0	.269	.450
Bob Nieman	OF125	R	25	131	478	64	137	18	2	18	74	46	73	0	.289	.456
1 Jim Rivera	OF88	L	29	97	336	45	86	13	6	4	30	29	59	8	.256	.366
1 Jim Delsing	OF85	L	26	93	298	34	76	13	4	5	34	25	29	3	.255	.349
Clint Courtney	C113	R	25	119	413	38	118	16	2	5	50	39	26	0	.286	.395
13 Freddie Marsh	SS60, 3B21, 2B9	R	24	86	247	28	69	9	1	2	27	27	33	3	.279	.348
Gordon Goldsberry	1B72, OF2	L	24	84	227	30	52	9	2	3	17	34	37	0	.229	.335
Marty Marion	SS63	R	34	67	186	16	46	11	0	2	19	19	17	0	.247	.339
2 Cass Michaels	3B42, 2B8	R	26	55	166	21	44	8	2	3	25	23	16	1	.265	.392
Les Moss	C39	R	27	52	118	11	29	3	0	3	12	15	13	0	.246	.347
2 Al Zarilla	OF35	L	33	48	130	10	31	6	0	0	9	27	15	2	.238	.308
1 Leo Thomas	3B37, SS3, 2B1	R	28	41	124	12	29	5	1	0	12	17	7	2	.234	.290
2 Vic Wertz	OF36	L	27	37	130	22	45	6	0	3	16	23	20	0	.346	.523
1 George Schmees	OF19, 1B2	L	27	34	61	9	8	1	1	0	5	7	10	0	.131	.180
Jay Porter	OF7	L	19	33	104	9	29	7	0	0	10	10	14	0	.250	.308
1 Earl Rapp	OF7	L	31	30	49	3	7	2	0	0	2	6	9	0	.143	.224
Darrell Johnson	C22	R	23	29	78	9	22	3	0	0	9	11	4	0	.282	.333

1 Tom Wright 28 L 16-66, Gene Bearden 31 L 23-65, 2 Ray Coleman 30 L 9-46, 3 Don Lenhardt 29 R 13-48, Hank Arft (PB) 30 L 4-28,
Roy Sievers (BC) 25 R 6-30, Stan Rojek 33 R 1-7, Rufus Crawford 24 R 2-11, 2 Willie Miranda 26 B 1-11, Mike Goliat 30 R 0-4,
Owen Friend (MS) 25, Dick Kokos (MS) 24, Frank Saucier (MS) 21

NAME	T	AGE	W	L	PCT	SV	G	GS	CG	IP	H	BB	SO	SHO	ERA
		32	64	90	.416	18	155	155	48	1399	1388	598	581	6	4.12
Satchel Paige	R	45	12	10	.545	10	46	6	3	138	116	57	91	2	3.07
Bob Cain	L	27	12	10	.545	2	29	27	8	170	169	62	70	1	4.13
Duane Pillette	R	29	10	13	.435	0	30	30	9	205	222	55	62	1	3.60
Gene Bearden	L	31	7	8	.467	0	34	16	3	151	158	78	45	0	4.29
1 Ned Garver	R	26	7	10	.412	0	21	21	7	149	130	55	60	2	3.68
Tommy Byrne	L	32	7	14	.333	0	29	24	14	196	182	112	91	0	4.68
1 Dave Madison	R	31	4	2	.667	0	31	4	0	78	78	48	35	0	4.38
2 Dick Littlefield	R	26	2	3	.400	0	7	5	3	46	35	17	34	0	2.74
Earl Harrist	R	32	2	8	.200	5	36	9	1	117	119	47	49	0	4.00
2 Marlin Stuart	R	33	1	1	.333	1	12	2	0	26	26	9	13	0	4.15
2 Bobby Hogue	R	31	1	0	1.000	0	8	1	0	16	13	2	9	0	2.76
1 Lou Sleater	L	25	1	3	.250	0	9	9	2	41	40	34	25	0	4.00
Johnny Hetki	R	30	0	1	.000	0	9	0	0	15	22	4	6	0	4.00
2 Ken Holcombe	R	28	0	2	.000	0	10	0	0	16	34	9	6	0	12.94
Cliff Fannin	R	28	0	2	.000	0	7	1	0	16	34	9	6	0	3.73
Stubby Overmire	L	33	0	0	—	0	17	0	0	4	4	7	10	0	12.00
1 Hal Hudson	L	25	0	1	.000	0	3	0	0	8	6	3	4	0	12.00
Bob Mahoney	R	24	0	0	—	0	3	0	0	4	4	4	1	0	18.00
Pete Taylor	R	22	0	0	—	0	1	0	0	1	3	1	0	0	13.50
Bob Turley (MS) 21															

DETROIT   8th 50-104 .325 45   RED ROLFE 23-49 .319   FRED HUTCHINSON 27-55 .329

NAME	G by Pos	B	AGE	G	AB	R	H	2B	3B	HR	RBI	BB	SO	SB	BA	SA
TOTALS			30	156	5258	557	1278	190	37	103	529	553	605	27	.243	.352
2 Walt Dropo	1B115	R	29	115	459	56	128	17	3	23	70	26	63	2	.279	.479
Jerry Priddy (BL)	2B75	R	32	75	279	37	79	23	3	4	29	40	29	1	.283	.430
Neil Berry	SS66, 3B2	R	30	73	189	22	43	6	0	0	13	22	19	1	.228	.280
2 Fred Hatfield	3B107, SS9	L	27	112	441	43	104	12	2	2	25	35	52	2	.236	.286
1 Vic Wertz	OF79	L	27	85	285	46	70	15	3	17	51	46	44	1	.246	.498
Johnny Groth	OF139	R	25	141	524	56	149	20	4	4	51	51	39	2	.284	.357
Pat Mullin	OF65	L	34	97	265	29	66	13	5	7	35	31	30	4	.251	.424
Joe Ginsberg	C101	R	25	113	307	29	68	13	2	6	36	51	21	1	.221	.336
Steve Souchock	OF56, 3B13, 1B9	R	33	92	265	40	66	16	4	13	45	21	28	1	.249	.487
Cliff Mapes	OF63	R	30	88	193	26	37	7	0	9	23	40	37	0	.197	.373
Al Federoff	2B70, SS7	R	27	74	231	14	56	7	0	0	14	16	13	1	.242	.277
2 Johnny Pesky	SS41, 2B22, 3B5	L	32	69	177	26	45	9	0	1	14	41	11	1	.254	.294
Don Kolloway	1B32, 2B8	R	33	65	173	19	42	9	2	1	21	12	19	0	.243	.329
Matt Batts (IL)	C55	R	30	56	173	11	41	12	3	0	13	28	10	0	.188	.278
2 Don Lenhardt	OF43	R	29	45	144	18	27	5	0	4	17	15	20	0	.188	.278
2 Johnny Hopp	OF4, 1B1	L	35	42	46	5	10	0	0	0	5	11	3	0	.217	.239
1 George Kell	3B39	R	30	39	154	18	42	7	1	0	15	15	10	2	.296	.368
1 Johnny Lipon	SS39	R	29	39	136	17	30	4	2	1	7	15	11	2	.221	.279
2 Jim Delsing	OF32	L	26	33	100	11	27	5	0	3	11	11	11	0	.274	.389

Bob Swift 37 R 8-58, Harvey Kuenn 21 R 26-80, Russ Sullivan 29 L 17-52, Don Lund 29 R 7-23, Bill Tuttle 22 R 6-25, Bennie Taylor 24 L 3-18,
George Lerchen 29 B 5-32, Carl Linhart 22 L 0-2, Alex Garbowski 27 R 0-0, 1 Hoot Evers 31 R 1-1, Frank House (MS) 22

NAME	T	AGE	W	L	PCT	SV	G	GS	CG	IP	H	BB	SO	SHO	ERA
		29	50	104	.325	14	156	156	51	1388	1394	591	702	10	4.25
Ted Gray	L	27	12	17	.414	0	35	32	13	224	212	101	138	2	4.14
Hal Newhouser	L	31	9	9	.500	0	25	19	8	154	148	47	57	0	3.74
Art Houtteman	R	24	8	20	.286	1	35	28	10	221	218	65	109	2	3.88
2 Bill Wight	L	30	5	9	.357	0	23	19	8	144	167	55	65	3	3.97
Virgil Trucks	R	35	5	19	.208	1	35	29	8	197	190	82	129	3	4.95
1 Marlin Stuart	R	33	2	3	.600	1	30	4	2	91	91	48	32	0	4.95
Fred Hutchinson	R	33	2	1	.667	0	12	5	1	45	40	10	13	0	3.41
Billy Hoeft	L	20	2	7	.222	0	34	10	1	125	123	63	67	0	4.32
2 Ned Garver	R	31	2	2	.500	0	10	5	3	51	61	27	33	0	3.69
2 Dave Madison	R	31	2	1	.667	0	10	0	0	15	16	10	7	0	7.80
2 Dizzy Trout	R	37	1	5	.167	1	10	2	0	30	30	19	20	0	5.33
Hal White	R	33	1	4	.111	5	41	0	0	63	53	39	18	0	3.71
Bill Black	R	23	0	1	.000	0	4	1	0	14	14	11	9	0	10.13
Dick Marlowe	R	23	0	0	—	0	7	1	0	18	18	14	5	0	7.36
1 Dick Littlefield	L	26	0	1	.000	0	4	1	0	8	12	11	10	0	6.55
Ken Johnson	L	29	0	0	—	0	2	1	0	5	11	10	6	0	9.00
Wayne McLeland	R	27	0	0	—	0	6	0	0	11	13	5	3	0	9.00
Ray Herbert (MS) 22															

BROOKLYN — 1st 96-57 .627 — CHUCK DRESSEN

NAME	G by Pos	B	AGE	G	AB	R	H	2B	3B	HR	RBI	BB	SO	SB	BA	SA
TOTALS			30	155	5266	775	1380	199	32	153	725	663	699	90	.262	.399
Gil Hodges	1B153	R	28	153	508	87	129	27	1	32	102	107	90	2	.254	.500
Jackie Robinson	2B146	R	33	149	510	104	157	17	3	19	75	106	40	24	.308	.465
Pee Wee Reese	SS145	R	33	149	559	94	152	18	8	6	58	86	59	30	.272	.365
Billy Cox (EJ)	3B100, SS10, 2B9	R	32	116	455	56	118	12	3	6	34	25	32	10	.259	.338
Carl Furillo	OF131	R	30	134	425	52	105	18	1	8	59	31	33	1	.247	.351
Duke Snider	OF141	L	25	144	534	80	162	25	7	21	92	55	77	7	.303	.494
Andy Pafko	OF139, 3B13	R	31	150	551	76	158	17	5	19	85	64	48	4	.287	.439
Roy Campanella	C122	R	30	128	468	73	126	18	1	22	97	57	59	8	.269	.453
George Shuba	OF67	L	27	94	256	40	78	12	1	9	40	38	29	1	.305	.465
Bobby Morgan	3B60, 2B5, SS4	R	26	67	191	36	45	8	0	7	16	46	35	2	.236	.387
Rocky Bridges	2B24, SS13, 3B6	R	24	51	56	9	11	3	0	0	2	7	9	0	.196	.250
Rube Walker	C40	L	26	46	139	9	36	8	0	1	19	8	17	0	.259	.338
Rocky Nelson	1B5	L	27	37	39	6	10	1	0	0	3	7	4	0	.256	.282
Dick Williams (JJ)	OF25, 1B1, 3B1	R	23	36	68	13	21	4	1	0	11	2	10	0	.309	.397
2 Tommy Holmes	OF6	L	35	31	36	2	4	1	0	0	1	4	1	0	.111	.139
Sandy Amoros	OF10	L	22	20	44	10	11	3	1	0	3	5	14	1	.250	.364
1 Cal Abrams	OF1	L	28	10	10	1	2	0	0	0	0	2	4	0	.200	.200
Steve Lembo	C2	R	25	2	5	0	1	0	0	0	0	1	1	0	.200	.200

NAME	T	AGE	W	L	PCT	SV	G	GS	CG	IP	H	BB	SO	SHO	ERA
		27	96	57	.627	24	155	155	45	1399	1295	544	773	11	3.53
Joe Black	R	28	15	4	.789	15	56	2	1	142	102	41	85	0	2.15
Carl Erskine	R	25	14	6	.700	2	33	26	10	207	167	71	131	4	2.70
Billy Loes	R	22	13	8	.619	1	39	21	8	187	154	71	115	4	2.70
Preacher Roe	L	37	11	2	.846	0	27	25	8	159	163	39	83	2	3.11
Ben Wade	R	29	11	9	.550	3	37	24	5	180	166	94	118	1	3.60
Clem Labine	R	27	8	4	.667	0	25	9	6	77	76	47	43	0	5.14
Johnny Rutherford	R	27	7	7	.500	2	22	11	4	97	97	29	29	0	4.27
Chris Van Cuyk	L	25	5	6	.455	1	23	16	4	98	104	40	66	0	5.14
Ralph Branca (SA)	R	26	4	2	.667	0	16	7	2	61	52	21	26	0	3.84
Clyde King	R	28	2	0	1.000	2	23	0	0	43	56	12	17	0	5.02
Jim Hughes	R	29	2	1	.667	0	6	0	0	19	16	11	8	0	1.42
1 Johnny Schmitz	L	31	1	1	.500	0	10	3	1	33	29	18	11	0	4.36
Ray Moore	R	26	1	1	.333	0	14	2	0	28	29	26	11	0	4.82
Ken Lehman	L	24	1	2	.333	0	4	0	0	15	19	6	7	0	5.40
Joe Landrum	R	23	1	3	.250	0	9	5	2	38	46	10	17	0	5.21
Ron Negray	R	22	0	0	—	0	3	1	0	13	15	5	5	0	3.46
1 Bud Podbielan	R	28	0	0	—	0	4	0	0	8	9	6	3	1	18.00
Don Newcombe (MS) 26															
Erv Palica (MS) 24															

NEW YORK — 2nd 92-62 .597 4.5 — LEO DUROCHER

NAME	G by Pos	B	AGE	G	AB	R	H	2B	3B	HR	RBI	BB	SO	SB	BA	SA
TOTALS			27	154	5229	722	1337	186	56	151	663	536	672	30	.256	.399
Whitey Lockman	1B154	L	25	154	606	99	176	21	4	13	58	67	52	2	.290	.396
Davey Williams	2B138	R	24	138	540	70	137	26	3	13	55	48	63	2	.254	.385
Al Dark	SS150	R	30	151	589	92	177	29	3	14	73	47	39	6	.301	.431
Bobby Thomson	3B91, OF63	R	28	153	608	89	164	29	14	24	108	52	74	5	.270	.482
Don Mueller	OF120	R	25	126	456	61	128	14	7	12	49	34	24	2	.281	.421
Hank Thompson	OF72, 3B46, 2B4	L	26	128	423	67	110	13	9	17	67	50	38	4	.260	.454
Bob Elliott	OF65, 3B13	R	35	98	272	33	62	6	2	10	35	36	20	1	.228	.375
Wes Westrum	C112	R	29	114	322	47	71	11	0	14	43	76	68	1	.220	.385
Dusty Rhodes	OF56	L	25	67	176	34	44	8	1	10	36	23	33	1	.250	.477
Sal Yvars	C59	R	28	66	151	15	37	3	0	4	18	10	16	0	.245	.344
2 George Wilson	OF21, 1B2	L	26	62	112	9	27	7	0	2	16	3	14	0	.241	.357
Bill Rigney	3B10, 2B9, SS4, 1B1	R	34	60	90	15	27	5	1	1	14	11	6	2	.300	.411
Monte Irvin (BN)	OF32	R	33	46	126	10	39	2	1	4	21	10	11	0	.310	.437
Chuck Diering	OF36	R	29	41	23	2	4	1	0	0	2	4	3	0	.174	.304
Willie Mays (MS)	OF34	R	21	34	127	17	30	2	4	4	23	16	17	1	.236	.409
Bobby Hofman	2B21, 3B2, 1B1	R	26	32	63	11	18	2	2	2	4	8	10	0	.286	.476
Clint Hartung	OF24	R	29	28	78	6	17	2	1	3	8	9	24	0	.218	.385
2 Bill Howerton	OF3	L	30	11	15	2	1	1	0	0	1	3	2	0	.067	.133
Ray Katt	C8	R	25	9	27	4	6	0	0	0	1	1	5	0	.222	.222
Daryl Spencer	SS3, 3B3	R	22	7	17	0	5	0	1	0	3	1	4	0	.294	.412
Ray Noble	C5	L	25	6	5	0	0	0	0	0	0	1	2	0	.000	.000
Dick Wakefield		L	31	3	2	0	0	0	0	0	0	0	1	0	.000	.000
Sammy Calderone (MS) 26																

NAME	T	AGE	W	L	PCT	SV	G	GS	CG	IP	H	BB	SO	SHO	ERA
		30	92	62	.597	31	154	154	49	1371	1282	538	655	12	3.59
Sal Maglie	R	35	18	8	.692	1	35	31	12	216	199	75	112	5	2.92
Hoyt Wilhelm	R	29	15	3	.833	11	71	0	0	159	127	57	108	0	2.43
Jim Hearn	R	31	14	7	.667	1	37	34	11	224	208	97	89	1	3.78
Larry Jansen (XJ)	R	31	11	11	.500	2	34	27	8	167	183	47	74	1	4.10
Dave Koslo	L	32	10	7	.588	5	41	17	8	166	154	47	67	2	3.20
Max Lanier	L	36	7	12	.368	5	37	16	6	137	124	65	47	1	3.94
Al Corwin	R	25	6	1	.857	2	21	7	1	68	58	36	36	0	2.65
Bill Connelly	R	27	5	0	1.000	0	11	4	0	32	22	25	22	0	4.50
Monte Kennedy	L	30	3	4	.429	0	31	6	2	83	73	31	48	1	3.04
George Spencer	R	25	3	5	.375	3	35	4	0	60	57	21	27	0	5.55
Hal Gregg	R	30	1	0	1.000	1	16	4	1	36	42	17	13	0	4.75
Mario Picone	R	25	0	1	.000	0	9	1	0	9	11	5	3	0	7.00
Jack Harshman	R	24	0	2	.000	0	7	2	0	6	12	6	6	0	15.00
George Bamberger	R	26	0	0	—	0	4	0	0	4	6	0	3	0	9.00
Roger Bowman	L	24	0	0	—	0	1	0	0	3	4	3	3	0	12.00
Alex Konikowski (MS) 24																

ST. LOUIS — 3rd 88-66 .571 8.5 — EDDIE STANKY

NAME	G by Pos	B	AGE	G	AB	R	H	2B	3B	HR	RBI	BB	SO	SB	BA	SA
TOTALS			31	154	5200	677	1386	247	54	97	643	537	479	33	.267	.391
2 Dick Sisler	1B114	L	31	119	418	48	109	14	5	13	60	29	35	3	.261	.411
Red Schoendienst	2B142, 3B11, SS3	B	29	152	620	91	188	40	7	7	67	42	30	9	.303	.424
Solly Hemus	SS148, 3B2	L	29	151	570	105	153	28	8	15	52	96	55	1	.268	.425
Billy Johnson	3B89	R	33	94	282	23	71	15	2	6	42	30	25	1	.252	.323
Enos Slaughter	OF137	L	36	140	510	73	153	17	12	11	101	70	25	6	.300	.445
Stan Musial	OF129, 1B25, P1	L	31	154	578	105	194	42	6	21	91	96	29	7	.336	.538
Peanuts Lowrey	OF106, 3B6	R	34	132	374	48	107	18	2	1	48	34	13	3	.286	.353
Del Rice	C147	R	29	147	495	43	128	27	2	11	65	33	38	0	.259	.388
Hal Rice	OF81	L	28	98	295	37	85	14	5	7	45	16	26	1	.288	.441
Tommy Glaviano	3B52, 2B1	R	28	80	162	30	39	5	1	3	19	27	26	0	.241	.340
Eddie Stanky	2B20	R	35	53	83	13	19	4	0	2	7	19	9	0	.229	.277
Larry Miggins	OF25, 1B1	R	26	42	96	7	22	5	1	2	10	6	19	0	.229	.365
Les Fusselman	C32	R	31	32	63	5	10	3	0	1	3	0	9	0	.159	.254
Virgil Stallcup	SS12	R	30	29	31	4	4	1	0	0	1	1	5	0	.129	.161
1 Wally Westlake	OF20	R	31	21	74	7	16	3	0	0	10	8	11	1	.216	.257
Steve Bilko (BA)	1B20	R	23	20	72	7	19	6	1	1	6	4	15	0	.264	.417
Vern Benson (BL)	3B15	L	27	24	47	6	9	2	0	2	5	5	9	0	.191	.362
Gene Mauch	SS2	R	26	7	3	0	0	0	0	0	0	2	0	0	.000	.000
1 Eddie Kazak	3B1	R	31	3	2	1	0	0	0	0	0	0	1	0	.000	.000
Bill Sarni	C3	R	24	5	5	1	1	0	0	0	0	1	0	0	.200	.200
Neal Hertweck	1B2	L	20	2	6	0	0	0	0	0	0	0	1	0	.000	.000
Herb Gorman		L	27	1	1	0	0	0	0	0	0	0	0	0	.000	.000

NAME	T	AGE	W	L	PCT	SV	G	GS	CG	IP	H	BB	SO	SHO	ERA
		29	88	66	.571	27	154	154	49	1361	1274	501	712	12	3.66
Gerry Staley	R	31	17	14	.548	2	35	33	15	240	238	52	93	0	3.26
Eddie Yuhas	R	27	12	2	.857	6	54	2	0	99	90	35	39	0	2.73
Al Brazle	L	38	12	5	.706	16	46	6	3	109	75	42	30	0	2.72
Vinegar Bend Mizell	R	21	10	8	.556	0	30	30	7	190	171	103	146	2	3.65
Harry Brecheen	L	37	7	5	.583	2	25	13	4	100	82	28	54	1	3.33
Joe Presko	R	23	7	10	.412	0	25	18	5	147	140	57	63	1	4.04
Stu Miller	R	24	6	3	.667	0	12	11	6	88	63	26	64	2	2.05
Cloyd Boyer	R	24	6	5	.500	0	23	14	4	110	108	47	44	2	4.25
Cliff Chambers	L	30	4	4	.500	1	26	13	2	98	110	33	47	1	4.13
Mike Clark	R	30	2	0	1.000	1	26	4	0	25	32	14	10	0	6.12
Harvey Haddix	L	26	2	2	.500	0	7	6	3	42	31	10	31	0	2.79
Willard Schmidt	R	24	2	3	.400	1	18	3	0	35	36	18	30	0	5.14
2 Bill Werle	L	31	1	2	.333	1	19	0	0	39	40	15	23	0	4.85
Dick Bokelmann	R	25	1	0	1.000	0	11	0	0	13	20	7	5	0	9.00
1 George Munger	R	33	1	0	—	0	1	0	0	1	1	1	1	0	13.50
Bobby Tiefenauer	R	22	0	0	—	0	6	0	0	8	12	7	3	0	7.88
Jack Crimian	R	26	0	0	—	0	3	0	0	8	15	4	4	0	10.13
Jackie Collum	L	25	0	0	—	0	4	1	0	4	5	3	5	0	0.00
Fred Hahn	R	25	0	0	—	0	1	0	0	1	0	1	1	0	0.00
Stan Musial	L	31	0	0	—	0	1	1	0	2	1	0	1	0	0.00
Tom Poholsky (MS) 22																

PHILADELPHIA — 4th 87-67 .565 9.5 — EDDIE SAWYER 28-35 .444   STEVE O'NEILL 59-32 .648

NAME	G by Pos	B	AGE	G	AB	R	H	2B	3B	HR	RBI	BB	SO	SB	BA	SA
TOTALS			28	154	5205	657	1353	237	45	93	606	540	534	60	.260	.376
Eddie Waitkus	1B146	L	32	146	499	51	144	29	4	7	49	64	23	2	.289	.375
Connie Ryan	2B154	R	32	154	577	81	139	24	6	12	49	69	72	13	.241	.366
Granny Hamner	SS151	R	25	151	596	74	164	30	5	17	87	27	51	7	.275	.428
Willie Jones	3B147	R	26	147	541	60	135	13	3	18	72	53	36	5	.250	.383
2 Johnny Wyrostek	OF88	L	32	98	321	45	88	16	3	1	37	44	26	1	.274	.352
Richie Ashburn	OF154	L	25	154	613	93	173	31	6	1	42	75	30	16	.282	.357
Del Ennis	OF149	R	27	151	592	90	171	30	10	20	107	47	65	6	.289	.475
Smoky Burgess	C104	L	25	110	451	49	110	21	6	7	56	49	21	3	.296	.429
Stan Lopata	C55	R	26	57	179	25	49	9	1	4	27	36	33	1	.274	.402
Bill Nicholson	OF19	L	37	55	88	17	24	3	0	8	19	14	26	0	.273	.511
Jackie Mayo	OF27, 1B6	R	26	50	119	13	29	5	0	1	4	12	17	1	.244	.311
Mel Clark	OF38, 3B1	R	25	47	155	20	52	6	4	1	15	6	13	2	.335	.445
Putsy Caballero	SS8, 2B7, 3B7	R	24	35	42	10	10	3	0	0	6	2	9	1	.238	.310
Lucky Lohrke	SS5, 3B3, 2B1	R	28	25	29	4	6	0	1	0	2	4	3	0	.207	.207
1 Tommy Brown	OF3, 1B3	R	24	18	25	2	4	1	1	0	2	4	3	0	.160	.320
Nippy Jones	1B8	R	27	9	30	3	5	0	0	0	5	0	4	0	.167	.267
Dick Young	2B2	B	24	9	9	3	2	0	0	0	0	1	3	0	.222	.333
1 Del Wilber		R	33	4	3	0	0	0	0	0	0	0	1	0	.000	.000

NAME	T	AGE	W	L	PCT	SV	G	GS	CG	IP	H	BB	SO	SHO	ERA
		29	87	67	.565	16	154	154	80	1387	1301	373	609	17	3.07
Robin Roberts	R	25	28	7	.800	2	39	37	30	330	292	45	148	3	2.59
Curt Simmons	L	23	14	8	.636	0	28	28	15	201	170	70	141	6	2.82
Karl Drews	R	32	14	15	.483	0	33	30	15	229	213	52	96	5	2.71
Russ Meyer	R	28	13	14	.481	1	37	32	14	232	235	65	92	1	3.14
Jim Konstanty	R	35	5	3	.625	6	42	2	2	80	87	21	16	1	3.94
Andy Hansen	R	23	4	2	.667	0	44	0	0	77	76	27	18	0	3.27
Steve Ridzik	R	23	4	2	.667	0	24	3	0	93	74	37	43	0	3.00
Howie Fox	R	31	2	7	.222	0	13	11	2	62	70	26	16	0	5.08
Paul Stuffel	R	26	1	0	1.000	0	3	1	0	8	7	8	3	0	3.00
Ken Heintzelman	L	36	1	3	.250	1	23	1	0	43	41	12	20	0	3.14
Lou Possehl	R	26	1	0	.000	0	1	0	0	2	3	1	0	0	4.85
Bob Miller	R	26	1	0	1.000	0	9	0	0	13	13	1	2	0	6.00
Kent Peterson	L	26	0	1	.000	0	2	0	0	7	11	1	5	0	0.00
1 Bubba Church	R	27	0	0	—	0	2	1	0	7	11	6	2	0	10.80

CHICAGO — 5th 77-77 .500 19.5 — PHIL CAVARRETTA

NAME	G by Pos	B	AGE	G	AB	R	H	2B	3B	HR	RBI	BB	SO	SB	BA	SA
TOTALS			28	155	5330	628	1408	223	45	107	595	422	712	50	.264	.383
Dee Fondy	1B143	L	27	145	554	69	156	27	9	10	67	28	60	13	.300	.424
Eddie Miksis	2B54, SS40	R	25	93	383	44	89	20	1	9	32	19	30	4	.232	.305
Roy Smalley	SS82	R	26	87	261	36	58	14	1	5	30	29	58	0	.222	.341
Randy Jackson	3B104, OF1	R	26	116	379	44	88	9	4	9	34	27	42	6	.232	.351
Frankie Baumholtz	OF101	L	33	103	409	59	133	17	4	4	35	27	25	4	.325	.416
Hal Jeffcoat	OF95	R	27	102	297	29	65	17	2	4	30	15	40	7	.219	.330
Hank Sauer	OF151	R	35	151	567	89	153	31	3	37	121	77	92	1	.270	.531
Toby Atwell	C101	L	28	107	362	36	105	16	3	2	31	40	22	2	.290	.367
Bill Serena	3B58, 2B49	R	27	122	390	49	107	21	5	15	61	39	83	1	.274	.469
Gene Hermanski	OF76	L	32	99	275	28	70	8	0	4	34	29	32	2	.255	.320
Bob Addis	OF79	L	26	93	292	38	86	13	2	1	28	23	30	4	.295	.363
2 Tommy Brown	SS39, 2B10, 1B5	R	24	61	200	24	64	11	0	3	12	14	14	3	.320	.420
Bob Ramazzotti (JJ)	2B50	R	35	50	183	26	52	5	3	1	12	14	14	3	.284	.361
Bruce Edwards (SA)	C22, 2B1	R	28	50	94	7	23	4	1	2	12	8	12	1	.245	.340
Phil Cavarretta	1B13	L	35	41	80	7	23	6	0	0	12	8	6	0	.238	.340
Bob Rush	P34	R	26	34	96	5	28	5	0	0	15	1	35	0	.292	.365
Harry Chiti	C32	R	19	32	113	14	31	6	0	5	13	6	15	0	.274	.451
Johnny Pramesa	C17	R	26	22	46	1	13	1	0	0	4	4	4	0	.283	.370
Leon Brinkopf	SS6	R	26	9	22	1	4	2	0	0	1	0	5	0	.182	.182
Bud Hardin (JJ)	SS2, 2B1	R	30	3	7	1	1	0	0	0	0	2	1	0	.143	.143
Ron Northey		L	32	5	1	0	0	0	0	0	0	0	0	0	.000	.000
Bob Usher		R	27	3	1	0	0	0	0	0	0	0	1	0	.000	.000
Carl Sawatski (MS) 24, Preston Ward (MS) 24																

NAME	T	AGE	W	L	PCT	SV	G	GS	CG	IP	H	BB	SO	SHO	ERA
		29	77	77	.500	15	155	155	59	1386	1265	534	661	15	3.58
Bob Rush	R	26	17	13	.567	0	34	32	17	250	205	81	157	4	2.70
Warren Hacker	R	27	15	9	.625	0	33	20	12	185	144	31	84	5	2.58
Paul Minner	L	28	14	9	.609	0	28	27	12	181	180	54	61	2	3.73
Johnny Klippstein	R	24	9	14	.391	3	41	25	7	203	208	89	110	2	4.43
Bob Schultz	L	28	3	3	.667	0	29	5	1	74	63	51	31	0	4.01
Joe Hatten	L	35	4	0	.500	0	13	8	2	50	65	25	15	0	6.12
Bob Kelly	R	24	4	9	.308	0	31	15	3	125	114	46	50	2	3.60
Turk Lown	R	28	4	11	.267	0	33	15	3	157	154	93	73	0	4.36
Dutch Leonard	R	43	2	1	.500	11	45	0	0	67	56	24	37	0	2.15
Willie Ramsdell	R	36	2	0	.400	0	11	0	0	17	41	24	30	0	2.42
Dick Manville	R	25	0	1	.000	0	11	0	0	13	15	12	6	0	7.94
Vern Fear	R	26	0	0	—	0	11	0	0	9	9	6	2	0	7.88
Monk Dubiel	R	34	0	0	—	0	3	0	0	2	2	1	1	0	0.00
Cal Howe	L	27	0	0	—	0	1	0	0	1	3	1	1	0	0.00

NAME	G by Pos	B	AGE	G	AB	R	H	2B	3B	HR	RBI	BB	SO	SB	BA	SA
CINCINNATI 6th 69-85 .448 27.5			LUKE SEWELL 39-59 .398		EARLE BRUCKER 3-2 .600		2 ROGERS HORNSBY 27-24 .529									
TOTALS			28	154	5234	615	1303	212	45	104	562	480	709	32	.249	.366
Ted Kluszewski	1B133	L	27	135	497	62	159	24	11	16	86	47	28	3	.320	.509
Grady Hatton	2B120	L	29	128	433	48	92	14	1	9	57	66	60	5	.212	.312
Roy McMillan	SS154	R	22	154	540	60	132	32	2	7	57	54	45	6	.244	.350
Bobby Adams	3B154	R	30	154	637	85	180	28	4	6	48	49	67	11	.283	.363
2 Willard Marshall	OF105	L	31	107	397	52	106	23	4	8	46	37	21	0	.267	.390
Bob Borkowski	OF103, 1B5	R	26	126	377	42	95	11	4	4	24	26	53	1	.252	.334
Joe Adcock	OF85, 1B17	R	24	117	378	43	105	22	4	13	52	23	38	1	.278	.460
Andy Seminick	C99	R	31	108	336	38	86	16	1	14	50	35	65	1	.256	.435
1 Hank Edwards	OF51	L	33	74	184	24	52	7	6	6	28	19	22	0	.283	.484
2 Cal Abrams	OF46	L	28	71	158	23	44	9	2	2	13	19	25	1	.278	.399
2 Wally Westlake	OF56	R	31	59	183	29	37	4	3	6	14	31	29	0	.202	.273
Joe Rossi	C46	R	34	55	145	14	32	0	1	1	6	20	20	1	.221	.255
Eddie Pellagrini	2B22, 1B8, 3B1, SS1	R	34	46	100	15	17	2	0	1	3	8	18	1	.170	.220
1 Johnny Wyrostek	OF29, 1B1	L	32	30	106	12	25	1	3	1	10	18	7	1	.236	.330
Johnny Temple	2B16	R	23	30	97	8	19	3	0	1	5	5	4	2	.196	.258
Wally Post (IL)	OF16	R	22	19	58	5	9	1	0	1	5	1	20	0	.155	.276
Jim Greengrass	OF17	R	24	18	68	10	21	2	1	5	24	7	12	0	.309	.588
Dixie Howell	C16	R	32	17	37	4	7	1	1	2	4	3	9	0	.189	.432
Hobie Landrith	C14	L	22	15	50	1	13	1	0	0	4	4	0	0	.260	.340
2 Eddie Kazak 31 R 1-15, 1 Dick Sisler 31 L 5-27, 1 Virgil Stallcup 30 R 0-1, Lloyd Merriman (MS) 27																

BOSTON 7th 64-89 .418 32			1 TOMMY HOLMES 13-22 .371		CHARLIE GRIMM 51-67 .432											
TOTALS			28	155	5221	569	1214	187	31	110	530	483	711	58	.233	.343
Earl Torgeson	1B105, OF5	L	28	122	382	49	88	17	0	5	34	86	31	11	.230	.314
Jack Dittmer	2B90	L	24	93	326	26	63	7	4	5	24	26	26	1	.193	.291
Johnny Logan	SS117	R	25	117	456	56	129	21	3	4	42	31	33	1	.283	.368
Eddie Mathews	3B142	L	20	145	528	80	128	23	5	25	58	59	115	6	.242	.447
Bob Thorpe	OF72	R	25	81	292	20	76	8	2	3	26	20	32	0	.260	.332
Sam Jethroe	OF151	B	34	151	608	79	141	19	7	13	58	68	112	28	.232	.357
Sid Gordon	OF142, 3B2	R	34	144	522	69	151	22	2	25	75	77	49	0	.289	.483
Walker Cooper	C89	R	37	102	349	33	82	12	1	10	55	22	32	1	.235	.361
Jack Daniels	OF87	L	24	106	219	31	41	5	1	2	14	28	30	3	.187	.247
Sibby Sisti	2B33, OF23, SS18, 3B9	R	31	90	245	19	52	7	1	4	24	14	43	2	.212	.310
George Crowe	1B55	L	31	73	217	25	56	13	1	4	20	18	25	5	.258	.382
Paul Burris	C50	R	28	55	168	14	37	4	0	2	21	7	19	0	.220	.280
Jack Cusick	SS28, 3B3	R	24	49	78	5	13	1	0	0	6	6	9	0	.167	.179
Ebba St. Claire	C34	B	30	39	108	5	23	2	0	2	4	5	12	0	.213	.287
Roy Hartsfield	2B29	R	26	38	107	13	28	2	0	1	7	4	13	1	.262	.355
Pete Whisenant	OF14	R	22	24	52	3	10	2	0	0	7	4	13	1	.192	.288
1 Willard Marshall	OF16	L	31	21	66	5	15	4	1	2	11	4	4	0	.227	.409
Billy Reed	2B14	L	29	15	52	4	13	1	0	0	0	5	3	1	.250	.250
Bus Clarkson	SS6, 3B2	R	34	14	25	3	5	1	0	0	2	3	3	0	.200	.200
Billy Klaus 23 L 0-4, Del Crandall (MS) 22																

PITTSBURGH 8th 42-112 .273 54.5			BILLY MEYER													
TOTALS			26	155	5193	515	1201	181	30	92	478	486	724	43	.231	.331
Tony Bartirome	1B118	L	24	124	355	32	78	10	3	0	16	26	37	3	.220	.265
Jack Merson	2B81, 3B27	R	30	111	398	41	98	20	3	6	38	22	38	1	.246	.344
Dick Groat	SS94	R	21	95	384	38	109	6	1	1	29	19	27	2	.284	.313
Pete Castiglione (BE)	3B57, 1B1, OF1	R	31	67	214	27	57	9	1	4	18	17	13	1	.266	.374
Gus Bell	OF123	L	23	131	468	53	117	21	5	16	59	36	72	1	.250	.419
Bobby Del Greco	OF93	R	19	99	341	34	74	14	2	1	20	38	70	6	.217	.279
Ralph Kiner	OF149	R	29	149	516	90	126	17	2	37	87	110	77	3	.244	.500
Joe Garagiola	C105	R	26	118	344	35	94	15	4	8	54	50	24	0	.273	.410
Catfish Metkovich	1B72, OF33	L	30	125	373	41	101	18	5	7	41	32	29	5	.271	.391
Clem Koshorek	SS33, 2B27, 3B26	R	27	98	322	27	84	17	0	0	15	26	39	4	.261	.314
1 G. Strickland	2B45, SS28, 3B1, 1B1	R	26	76	232	17	41	6	2	5	22	21	45	4	.177	.284
Clyde McCullough	C61, 1B1	R	35	66	172	10	40	5	1	1	15	10	18	0	.233	.291
Brandy Davis	OF29	R	24	55	95	14	17	1	0	1	7	8	22	9	.179	.211
Ed Fitz Gerald	C18, 3B2	R	28	51	73	4	17	1	0	1	7	5	8	0	.233	.288
Lee Walls	OF19	R	19	32	80	6	15	0	1	2	9	4	21	0	.188	.288
Sonny Senerchia	3B28	R	21	29	100	5	22	5	0	3	11	4	21	0	.220	.360
Dick Smith	3B16, SS4, 2B4	R	24	29	66	8	7	0	0	2	2	12	9	1	.106	.121
Dick Hall	OF14, 3B5	R	21	26	80	6	11	0	0	0	2	3	17	0	.138	.150
Erv Dusak	OF11	R	31	20	27	1	6	0	0	0	4	3	6	0	.222	.333
2 Johnny Berardino	2B18	R	35	19	56	2	8	4	0	0	3	4	4	0	.143	.214
Ted Beard	OF13	L	24	17	22	1	4	0	0	1	3	4	5	2	.182	.273
1 Bill Howerton 30 L 8-25, Jim Mangan 22 R 2-13, Frank Thomas 23 R 2-21, Jack Phillips 30 R 0-1, Danny O'Connell (MS) 25																

Pitching — Cincinnati:

NAME	T	AGE	W	L	PCT	SV	G	GS	CG	IP	H	BB	SO	SHO	ERA
		28	69	85	.448	12	154	154	56	1363	1377	517	579	11	4.00
Ken Raffensberger	L	34	17	13	.567	1	38	33	18	247	247	45	93	6	2.81
Harry Perkowski	L	29	12	10	.545	0	33	24	11	194	197	89	86	1	3.80
Frank Smith	R	24	12	11	.522	7	53	2	1	122	109	41	75	0	3.76
Herm Wehmeier	R	25	11	11	.450	0	33	26	6	190	197	103	83	1	5.16
Frank Hiller	R	31	5	8	.385	1	28	15	6	124	129	37	50	1	4.65
2 Bubba Church	R	27	5	9	.357	0	29	22	5	153	173	48	47	1	4.35
2 Bud Podbielan	R	28	5	7	.444	1	24	7	4	87	78	26	22	1	2.79
1 Ewell Blackwell	R	29	3	12	.200	0	17	13	0	102	107	60	48	0	5.38
3 Johnny Schmitz	L	31	1	0	1.000	0	3	0	0	5	3	3	3	0	0.00
Joe Nuxhall	L	23	1	4	.200	1	11	6	1	58	83	42	52	0	3.23
Bud Byerly	R	31	1	0	1.000	1	12	0	0	25	29	7	14	0	5.04
Niles Jordan	R	26	0	1	.000	1	5	1	0	6	14	3	2	0	10.50
Phil Haugstad	R	28	0	0	—	0	2	0	0	1	3	8	1	0	6.75
Ed Blake	R	26	0	0	—	0	2	0	0	3	3	3	1	0	0.00

Pitching — Boston:

NAME	T	AGE	W	L	PCT	SV	G	GS	CG	IP	H	BB	SO	SHO	ERA
		28	64	89	.418	13	155	155	63	1396	1388	525	687	11	3.78
Warren Spahn	L	31	14	19	.424	3	40	35	19	290	263	73	183	5	2.98
Max Surkont	R	30	12	13	.480	0	31	29	12	215	201	76	125	3	3.77
Jim Wilson	R	30	12	14	.462	0	33	33	14	234	234	90	104	0	4.23
Vern Bickford	R	31	7	12	.368	0	26	22	7	161	165	64	62	1	3.75
Ernie Johnson	R	25	6	3	.667	1	29	10	2	92	100	31	45	1	4.11
Lew Burdette	R	25	6	11	.353	7	45	9	5	137	138	47	47	0	3.61
Virgil Jester	R	24	3	5	.375	0	19	8	4	73	80	23	25	1	3.33
Bob Chipman	L	33	1	1	.500	2	29	0	0	45	38	20	16	0	2.79
Dave Cole	R	21	1	1	.500	0	22	9	1	45	42	42	22	0	4.00
Bert Thiel	R	26	1	1	.500	0	4	0	0	7	11	4	6	0	7.71
Sheldon Jones	R	30	1	4	.200	1	39	1	0	70	81	31	40	0	4.76
Dick Donovan	R	24	0	2	.000	0	18	0	0	18	18	12	6	0	5.54
Gene Conley	R	21	0	3	.000	0	4	3	0	13	23	9	6	0	7.62
Dick Hoover	R	26	0	0	—	0	2	0	0	5	5	1	0	0	7.20
Johnny Antonelli (MS) 22, Chet Nichols (MS) 21, Phil Paine (MS) 22															

Pitching — Pittsburgh:

NAME	T	AGE	W	L	PCT	SV	G	GS	CG	IP	H	BB	SO	SHO	ERA
		27	42	112	.273	8	155	155	43	1364	1395	625	564	5	4.65
Murry Dickson	R	35	14	21	.400	2	43	34	21	278	278	76	112	2	3.56
Howie Pollet	L	31	7	16	.304	0	31	30	9	214	217	71	90	1	4.12
Bob Friend	R	21	7	17	.292	0	35	23	6	185	186	84	75	1	4.18
1 Ted Wilks	R	36	5	5	.500	4	44	0	0	72	65	31	24	0	3.63
Joe Muir	L	29	2	3	.400	0	12	5	1	36	42	18	17	0	6.25
Woody Main	R	30	2	12	.143	0	48	11	2	153	149	52	79	0	4.47
Paul LaPalme	L	28	1	2	.333	0	31	2	0	60	56	37	25	0	3.90
Harry Fisher	R	26	1	2	.333	0	8	3	0	18	17	13	5	0	7.00
Jim Waugh	R	18	1	6	.143	0	17	7	1	52	61	32	31	0	6.40
Ron Necciai	R	20	1	6	.143	0	12	9	0	55	63	32	31	0	7.04
Cal Hogue	R	24	1	8	.111	0	19	12	3	84	79	68	34	0	4.93
Don Carlsen	R	25	0	1	.000	0	10	1	0	16	16	13	4	0	10.80
Bill Bell	R	18	0	1	.000	0	2	0	0	16	16	13	4	0	4.50
Mel Queen	R	34	0	0	—	0	10	0	0	6	9	8	4	0	33.00
2 George Munger	R	33	0	3	.000	0	8	3	0	50	57	27	23	0	7.27
Ron Kline	R	20	0	7	.000	0	27	11	0	79	74	66	27	0	5.47
1 Bill Werle	L	31	0	0	—	0	9	0	0	10	14	4	6	0	9.00
Jim Suchecki	R	29	0	0	—	0	3	0	0	10	14	4	6	0	5.40
Jim Dunn	R	23	0	0	—	0	3	1	0	14	16	4	4	0	3.60
Ed Wolfe	R	24	0	0	—	0	2	0	0	4	7	1	1	0	6.75
Bill Koski (MS) 20, Vern Law (MS) 22, Bill Macdonald (MS) 23															

WORLD SERIES —NEW YORK (AL) 4 BROOKLYN (NL) 3

LINE SCORES

TEAM	1	2	3	4	5	6	7	8	9	10	11	12	R	H	E
Game 1 October 1 at Brooklyn															
NY (AL)	0	0	1	0	0	0	0	1	0				2	6	2
BKN (NL)	0	1	0	0	0	2	0	1	X				4	6	0
Reynolds, Scarborough (8) Black															
Game 2 October 2 at Brooklyn															
NY	0	0	0	1	1	5	0	0	0				7	10	0
BKN	0	0	1	0	0	0	0	0	0				1	3	1
Raschi Erskine, Loes (6) Lehman (8)															
Game 3 October 3 at New York															
BKN	0	0	1	0	1	0	0	1	2				5	11	0
NY	0	1	0	0	0	0	1	1					3	6	2
Roe Lopat, Gorman (9)															
Game 4 October 4 at New York															
BKN	0	0	0	0	0	0	0	0	0				0	4	1
NY	0	0	0	1	0	0	0	0	X				2	4	1
Black, Rutherford (8) Reynolds															
Game 5 October 5 at New York															
BKN	0	1	0	0	3	0	0	1	0	0	1		6	10	0
NY	0	0	0	0	5	0	0	0	0	0	0		5	5	1
Erskine Blackwell, Sain (6)															
Game 6 October 6 at Brooklyn															
NY	0	0	0	0	0	0	2	1	0				3	9	0
BKN	0	0	0	0	0	1	0	1	0				2	8	1
Raschi, Reynolds (8) Loes, Roe (9)															
Game 7 October 7 at Brooklyn															
NY	0	0	0	1	1	1	1	0	0				4	10	4
BKN	0	0	0	1	1	0	0	0	0				2	8	1
Lopat, **Reynolds** (4), Black, Roe (6), Raschi (7), Kuzava (7) Erskine (8)															

COMPOSITE BATTING

NAME	POS	G	AB	R	H	2B	3B	HR	RBI	BA
New York (AL) Totals		7	232	26	50	5	2	10	24	.216
Mantle	OF	7	29	5	10	1	1	2	3	.345
Berra	C	7	28	2	6	1	0	2	3	.214
Rizzuto	SS	7	27	2	4	1	0	0	0	.148
McDougald	3B	7	25	5	5	0	0	1	3	.200
Woodling	OF	7	23	4	8	1	1	1	1	.348
Martin	2B	7	23	2	5	0	0	1	4	.217
Bauer	OF	7	18	2	1	1	0	0	1	.056
Mize	1B	5	15	3	6	1	0	3	6	.400
Collins	1B	6	12	1	0	0	0	0	0	.000
Noren	OF	4	10	0	3	0	0	0	0	.300
Reynolds	P	4	7	0	0	0	0	0	0	.000
Raschi	P	3	6	0	1	0	0	0	0	.167
Lopat	P	2	3	1	1	0	0	0	0	.333
Sain	P	2	3	0	0	0	0	0	0	.000
Houk	PH	1	1	0	0	0	0	0	0	.000
Blackwell	P	1	1	0	0	0	0	0	0	.000
Kuzava	P	1	1	0	0	0	0	0	0	.000
Scarborough	P	1	0	0	0	0	0	0	0	—
Gorman	P	1	0	0	0	0	0	0	0	—
Brooklyn (NL) Totals		7	233	20	50	7	0	6	18	.215
Snider	OF	7	29	5	10	2	0	4	8	.345
Reese	SS	7	29	4	10	1	0	1	4	.345
Campanella	C	7	28	0	6	1	0	0	1	.214
Cox	3B	7	27	4	8	2	0	0	2	.296
Robinson	2B	7	23	4	4	0	0	1	2	.174
Furillo	OF	7	23	0	4	1	0	0	1	.174
Pafko	OF	7	21	0	4	0	0	2	4	.190
Hodges	1B	7	21	1	0	0	0	0	0	.000
Shuba	OF	4	10	0	3	0	0	0	0	.300
Black	P	3	6	1	0	0	0	0	0	.000
Erskine	P	3	6	1	0	0	0	0	0	.000
Loes	P	3	6	0	2	1	0	0	0	.333
Nelson	PH	4	4	0	0	0	0	0	0	.000
Roe	P	2	3	0	0	0	0	0	0	.000
Holmes	OF	3	3	0	0	0	0	0	0	.000
Morgan	3B	3	1	0	0	0	0	0	0	.000
Lehman	P	2	0	0	0	0	0	0	0	—
Rutherford	P	1	0	0	0	0	0	0	0	—
Amoros	PR	1	0	0	0	0	0	0	0	—

COMPOSITE PITCHING

NAME	G	IP	H	BB	SO	W	L	SV	ERA
New York (AL) Totals	7	64	50	24	49	4	3	2	2.81
Reynolds	4	20.1	12	6	18	2	1	1	1.77
Raschi	3	17	12	8	18	2	0	0	1.59
Lopat	2	11.1	14	4	3	0	1	0	4.76
Sain	2	6	6	3	3	0	1	0	3.00
Blackwell	1	5	4	3	4	0	0	0	7.20
Kuzava	1	2.2	1	0	2	0	0	1	0.00
Scarborough	1	1	1	0	1	0	0	0	9.00
Gorman	1	0.2	1	0	0	0	0	0	0.00
Brooklyn (NL) Totals	7	64	50	31	32	3	4	0	3.52
Black	3	21.1	15	8	9	1	2	0	2.53
Erskine	3	18	12	10	10	1	1	0	4.50
Roe	3	11.1	9	6	7	1	0	0	3.18
Loes	2	10.1	11	5	5	0	1	0	4.35
Lehman	2	2	2	1	0	0	0	0	0.00
Rutherford	1	1	1	1	1	0	0	0	9.00

1953 One More Time

Casey Stengel wasn't waiting for anyone. Part of the reason may have been the scare of 1952 when the Yankees almost lost the pennant. But, more than proximity itself, Stengel realized he had one foot on the doorstep of history. He did not want to lose his footing nor the chance to become the first man to manage five straight pennant winners. After bowing in the opener, the Yankees went on to win nine out of ten, giving them a lead they never relinquished. Any thought that the runner-up Indians had a chance was dispelled in late May when the Yankees went on an 18-game winning streak, falling one short of the American League record established by the 1906 White Sox, but enough of a surge to assure Stengel his well-deserved place in the record books.

The Yankees' victory was attributed to a veteran pitching staff and the left arm of a 24-year-old youngster by the name of Whitey Ford, who rejoined the team after a two-year military absence. Ford led the staff with 18 victories, while 35-year old Ed Lopat led the league with a 2.43 E.R.A. Allie Reynolds, at 38, Vic Raschi, at 34, and Johnny Sain, at 35, were the other pitching mainstays. These five men combined for an impressive 74-30 record. Catcher Yogi Berra led the offense with 27 home runs and 108 runs batted in, while Mickey Mantle, in his third year, hit 21 home runs, one of which astounded the baseball world in mid-April, a prodigious 565-foot shot off Chuck Stobbs in Washington.

Yet, while the Yankees collected team honors, individual laurels were taken by Al Rosen of Cleveland who was named the MVP with a near Triple Crown performance, losing out only to Mickey Vernon of Washington, who won the batting title by one point. But the Browns' Bobo Holloman suffered a greater disappointment than Rosen. Holloman started his first major league game on May 6, and threw a no-hitter against Philadelphia. Then, in July, with a 3-7 record, he found himself optioned to Toronto, never again to return to the majors.

The National League headlines also belonged to New York. Not the Giants, but the Dodgers, who became the first team to repeat as pennant winners since the 1944 Cardinals. Led by MVP catcher Roy Campanella, the Brooklynites cracked the race open after the All-Star break and finished a strong 13 games in front of the surprising Braves. In their victory route, the Dodgers paced the league in runs, home runs, and batting average. Their 105 victories set an all-time high for the team, and Duke Snider's 42 home runs, coupled with Campanella's 41, marked the first time in the National League that two men on the same club went over the 40 home run mark. Carl Furillo won a lame duck batting title by hitting .344 and spending the last three weeks of the season on the sidelines after breaking his hand in a free-for-all with the Giants—a rhubarb which started after Furillo was hit by a pitch which he claimed Giants manager Leo Durocher had ordered.

The underlying story of the year came from Milwaukee, where owner Lou Perini had shifted his Braves from Boston, marking the first major league franchise transplant since 1903. The Braves, infused by new blood as the result of trades which brought Andy Pafko from the Dodgers and Joe Adcock from Cincinnati, and the blossoming of sophomore third baseman Eddie Mathews, who broke Ralph Kiner's seven-year hold on the home run title, produced a National League attendance mark of 1,826,397. It was a figure which was also greatly credited to the franchise shift and one which would start the machinery in many owners' heads whizzing for some time to come.

The Dodgers entered the fall classic with a regular lineup boasting of five .300-plus batters and seemed destined to win their first World Series. Such was not the case. Stengel had a lock on destiny and took the Series in six games to make it five world championships in five years. There seemed little remaining that the Old Professor had to prove.

1953 AMERICAN LEAGUE

NEW YORK — 1st 99-52 .656 — CASEY STENGEL

NAME	G by Pos	B	AGE	G	AB	R	H	2B	3B	HR	RBI	BB	SO	SB	BA	SA
Joe Collins	TOTALS		28	151	5194	801	1420	226	52	139	762	656	644	34	.273	.417
Joe Collins	1B113, OF4	L	30	127	387	72	104	11	2	17	44	59	36	2	.269	.439
Billy Martin	2B146, SS18	R	25	149	587	72	151	24	6	15	75	43	56	6	.257	.395
Phil Rizzuto	SS133	R	35	134	413	54	112	21	3	2	54	71	39	4	.271	.351
Gil McDougald	3B136, 2B26	R	25	141	541	82	154	27	7	10	83	60	65	3	.285	.416
Hank Bauer	OF126	R	30	133	437	77	133	20	6	10	57	59	45	2	.304	.446
Mickey Mantle	OF121, SS1	B	21	127	461	105	136	24	3	21	92	79	90	8	.295	.497
Gene Woodling	OF119	L	30	125	395	64	121	26	4	10	58	82	29	2	.306	.468
Yogi Berra	C133	L	28	137	503	80	149	23	5	27	108	50	32	0	.296	.523
Irv Noren	OF96	L	28	109	345	55	92	12	6	6	46	42	39	3	.267	.388
Johnny Mize	1B15	L	40	81	104	6	26	3	0	4	27	12	17	0	.250	.394
Don Bollweg	1B43	L	32	70	155	24	46	6	4	6	24	21	31	1	.297	.503
Bill Renna	OF40	R	28	61	121	19	38	6	3	2	13	13	31	1	.314	.463
Andy Carey	3B40, SS2, 2B1	R	21	51	81	14	26	5	0	4	8	9	12	2	.321	.531
2 Willie Miranda	SS45	B	27	48	58	12	13	0	0	1	5	5	10	1	.224	.276
Charlie Silvera	C39, 3B1	R	28	42	82	11	23	3	1	0	12	9	5	0	.280	.341
Gus Triandos	1B12, C5	R	22	18	51	5	8	2	0	1	6	3	9	0	.157	.255
Ralph Houk	C8	R	33	8	9	2	2	0	0	0	1	0	1	0	.222	.222
Jerry Coleman (MS)	2B7, SS1	R	28	8	10	1	2	0	0	0	0	0	2	0	.200	.200

Bob Cerv 27 R 0-6, Jim Brideweser 26 R 3-3, Art Schult 25 R 0-0, 1 Loren Babe 25 L 6-18, Frank Verdi 27 R 0-0, Bobby Brown (MS) 28

NAME	T	AGE	W	L	PCT	SV	G	GS	CG	IP	H	BB	SO	SHO	ERA
		32	99	52	.656	39	151	151	50	1358	1286	500	604	18	3.20
Whitey Ford	L	24	18	6	.750	0	32	30	11	207	187	110	110	3	3.00
Ed Lopat	L	35	16	4	.800	0	25	24	9	178	169	32	50	3	2.43
Johnny Sain	R	35	14	7	.667	9	40	19	10	189	189	45	84	1	3.00
Vic Raschi	R	34	13	6	.684	1	28	26	7	181	150	55	76	4	3.33
Allie Reynolds	R	38	13	7	.650	13	41	15	5	145	140	61	86	1	3.41
Jim McDonald	R	26	9	7	.563	0	27	18	6	130	128	39	43	2	3.81
Bob Kuzava	L	30	6	5	.545	4	33	6	2	92	92	34	48	2	3.33
Tom Gorman	R	28	4	5	.444	6	40	1	0	77	65	32	38	0	3.39
Ewell Blackwell (SA)	R	30	2	0	1.000	1	8	4	0	20	17	13	11	0	3.60
Bill Miller	L	25	2	1	.667	1	13	3	0	34	46	19	17	0	4.76
1 Ray Scarborough	R	35	2	2	.500	2	25	1	0	55	52	26	20	0	3.27
Steve Kraly	L	24	0	2	.000	1	5	3	0	25	19	16	8	0	3.24
Art Schallock	L	29	0	0	—	1	7	1	0	21	30	15	13	0	3.00
1 Johnny Schmitz	L	32	0	0	—	2	3	0	0	4	2	3	0	0	2.25
Tom Morgan (MS) 23															

CLEVELAND — 2nd 92-62 .597 8.5 — AL LOPEZ

NAME	G by Pos	B	AGE	G	AB	R	H	2B	3B	HR	RBI	BB	SO	SB	BA	SA
	TOTALS		30	155	5285	770	1426	201	29	160	729	609	683	33	.270	.410
Bill Glynn	1B135, OF2	L	28	147	411	60	100	14	2	3	30	44	65	1	.243	.309
Bobby Avila	2B140	R	29	141	559	85	160	22	3	8	55	58	27	10	.286	.379
George Strickland	SS122, 1B1	R	27	123	419	43	119	17	4	5	47	51	52	0	.284	.379
Al Rosen	3B154, 1B1	R	29	155	599	115	201	27	5	43	145	85	48	8	.336	.613
Wally Westlake	OF72	R	32	82	218	42	72	7	1	9	46	35	29	2	.330	.495
Larry Doby	OF146	L	29	149	513	92	135	18	5	29	102	96	121	3	.263	.487
Dale Mitchell	OF125	L	31	134	500	76	150	26	4	13	60	42	20	3	.300	.446
Jim Hegan	C106	R	32	112	299	37	65	10	1	9	37	25	41	1	.217	.348
Bob Kennedy	OF89	R	32	100	161	22	38	5	0	3	22	19	11	0	.236	.323
Harry Simpson	OF69, 1B2	L	27	82	242	25	55	3	4	1	22	18	27	0	.227	.335
Luke Easter (BF)	1B56	L	37	68	211	26	64	9	0	7	31	15	35	0	.303	.445
Hank Majeski	2B10, 3B7, OF1	R	36	50	50	6	15	1	0	2	12	3	8	0	.300	.440
Al Smith	OF39, 3B2	R	25	47	150	28	36	9	3	14	20	25	2	.240	.360
Joe Tipton	C46	R	31	47	109	17	25	2	0	6	13	19	13	0	.229	.413
2 Joe Ginsberg	C39	L	26	46	109	10	31	4	0	0	10	14	4	0	.284	.321
Early Wynn	P36	B	33	37	91	11	25	3	0	3	10	7	17	0	.275	.396
1 Ray Boone	SS31	R	29	34	112	21	27	1	2	4	21	24	21	1	.241	.393
2 Owen Friend	2B19, SS8, 3B1	R	26	34	68	7	16	2	0	2	13	5	16	0	.235	.353
Barney McCosky		L	36	22	21	3	4	3	0	0	3	1	4	0	.190	.333
Jim Lemon	OF11, 1B2	R	25	16	46	5	8	1	0	1	5	3	15	0	.174	.261
2 Hank Foiles	C7	R	24	7	7	2	1	0	0	1	5	3	0	0	.143	.143

Dick Aylward 28 R 0-3, 1 Dick Weik 25 R 0-0, Hal Naragon (MS) 24

NAME	T	AGE	W	L	PCT	SV	G	GS	CG	IP	H	BB	SO	SHO	ERA
		30	92	62	.597	15	155	155	81	1373	1311	519	586	11	3.64
Bob Lemon	R	32	21	15	.583	1	41	36	23	287	283	110	98	5	3.36
Mike Garcia	R	29	18	9	.667	0	38	35	21	272	260	81	134	3	3.24
Early Wynn	R	33	17	12	.586	0	36	34	16	252	234	107	138	1	3.93
Bob Feller	R	34	10	7	.588	0	25	25	10	176	163	60	60	1	3.58
Dave Hoskins	R	27	9	3	.750	1	26	7	3	113	102	38	55	0	3.98
2 Art Houtteman	R	25	7	7	.500	3	22	13	6	109	113	25	40	1	3.80
Bob Hooper	R	31	5	4	.556	7	43	0	0	69	50	38	16	0	4.04
2 Bill Wight	L	31	2	1	.667	1	20	0	0	27	29	16	14	0	3.67
Dick Tomanek	L	22	1	0	1.000	0	1	1	1	9	6	6	6	0	2.00
1 Al Aber	L	25	1	1	.500	0	6	0	0	6	6	6	2	0	7.50
1 Steve Gromek	R	33	1	1	.500	0	5	1	0	11	11	3	8	0	3.27
Bob Chakales	R	25	0	2	.000	0	7	3	1	27	28	10	6	0	2.67
Lou Brissie	L	29	0	0	—	2	16	0	0	13	21	13	5	0	7.62
Ted Wilks	R	37	0	0	—	4	4	0	0	4	3	2	0	0	6.75

CHICAGO — 3rd 89-65 .578 11.5 — PAUL RICHARDS

NAME	G by Pos	B	AGE	G	AB	R	H	2B	3B	HR	RBI	BB	SO	SB	BA	SA
	TOTALS		29	156	5212	716	1345	226	53	74	676	601	530	73	.258	.364
Ferris Fain	1B127	L	32	128	446	73	114	18	2	6	52	108	28	3	.256	.345
Nellie Fox	2B154	L	25	154	624	92	178	31	8	3	72	49	18	4	.285	.375
Chico Carrasquel	SS149	R	25	149	552	72	154	30	4	2	47	38	47	5	.279	.359
2 Bob Elliott	3B58, OF2	R	36	67	208	24	54	11	4	2	32	31	21	1	.260	.380
Sam Mele	OF138, 1B2	R	31	140	481	64	132	28	8	12	82	48	47	3	.274	.437
Jim Rivera	OF156	L	30	156	567	79	147	26	16	11	78	53	70	22	.259	.420
Minnie Minoso	OF147, 3B10	R	30	151	556	104	174	24	8	15	104	74	43	25	.313	.466
Sherm Lollar	C107, 1B1	R	28	113	334	46	96	19	0	8	54	47	29	1	.287	.416
Tom Wright	OF33	L	29	77	132	14	33	5	3	2	25	12	21	0	.250	.379
Red Wilson	C63	R	24	71	164	21	41	6	1	0	10	26	12	2	.250	.299
Freddie Marsh	3B32, SS17, 1B5, 2B2	R	29	67	95	22	19	1	0	0	8	13	26	0	.200	.274
Rocky Krsnich	3B25	R	25	64	129	9	26	8	0	1	14	12	11	0	.202	.287
Bob Boyd	1B29, OF16	L	33	55	165	20	49	6	2	3	23	13	11	0	.297	.412
Bud Stewart (IL)	OF16	L	37	53	59	16	16	2	2	2	14	13	4	1	.271	.407
1 Vern Stephens	3B38, SS3	R	32	44	129	14	24	6	0	1	14	13	18	0	.186	.256
Bud Sheely	C17	L	33	31	46	4	10	1	0	0	5	2	6	0	.217	.239
1 Tommy Bryne	P6	L	33	18	18	2	3	1	0	1	5	2	9	0	.167	.333
2 Connie Ryan	3B16	R	33	17	54	6	12	1	0	1	6	6	9	2	.222	.241
2 Allie Clark	OF1, 1B1	R	30	9	15	0	1	0	0	0	1	0	4	0	.067	.067

Bill Wilson 24 R 1-17, 2 Neil Berry 31 R 1-8, Sam Dente 31 R 0-0, Sammy Esposito (MS) 21, Joe Kirrene (MS) 21

NAME	T	AGE	W	L	PCT	SV	G	GS	CG	IP	H	BB	SO	SHO	ERA
		31	89	65	.578	33	156	156	57	1404	1299	583	714	17	3.41
Billy Pierce	L	26	18	12	.600	3	40	33	19	271	216	102	186	7	2.72
2 Virgil Trucks	R	36	15	6	.714	4	24	21	13	176	151	67	102	3	2.86
Harry Dorish	R	31	10	6	.625	18	55	6	1	146	140	52	69	0	3.39
Mike Fornieles	R	21	8	7	.533	3	39	16	5	153	160	61	72	0	3.59
2 Sandy Consuegra	R	32	7	5	.583	3	29	13	5	124	122	28	30	1	2.54
Bob Keegan (SA)	R	32	7	5	.583	1	22	11	4	99	80	33	32	2	2.73
Saul Rogovin (EJ)	R	31	7	12	.368	1	22	19	4	131	151	48	62	1	5.22
Joe Dobson	R	36	5	5	.500	1	23	15	3	101	96	37	50	1	3.65
Connie Johnson	R	30	4	4	.500	0	14	10	2	61	55	38	44	1	3.54
Gene Bearden	L	33	3	3	.500	0	25	3	0	58	48	33	24	0	2.95
Luis Aloma	R	30	2	0	1.000	2	24	0	0	38	41	23	23	0	4.74
1 Tommy Byrne	L	33	1	1	.500	1	7	3	1	26	18	26	4	0	10.13
1 Earl Harrist	R	33	1	0	1.000	0	9	1	0	16	18	6	4	0	7.88
1 Lou Kretlow	R	32	1	1	.500	2	12	2	1	29	21	12	30	15	3.43
Hal Hudson	L	26	0	1	.000	0	1	0	0	1	0	1	0	0	—

BOSTON — 4th 84-69 .549 16 — LOU BOUDREAU

NAME	G by Pos	B	AGE	G	AB	R	H	2B	3B	HR	RBI	BB	SO	SB	BA	SA
TOTALS			26	153	5246	656	1385	255	37	101	613	496	601	33	.264	.384
Dick Gernert	1B136	R	24	139	494	73	125	15	1	21	71	88	82	0	.253	.415
Billy Goodman	2B112, 1B20	L	27	128	514	73	161	33	5	2	41	57	11	1	.313	.409
Milt Bolling	SS109	R	22	109	323	30	85	12	1	5	28	24	41	1	.263	.353
George Kell	3B124, OF7	R	30	134	460	68	141	41	2	12	73	52	22	5	.307	.483
Jimmy Piersall	OF151	R	23	151	633	76	159	21	9	3	52	41	52	11	.272	.354
Tommy Umphlett	OF136	R	23	137	495	53	140	27	5	3	59	34	30	6	.283	.376
Hoot Evers	OF93	R	32	99	300	39	72	10	1	11	31	23	41	2	.240	.380
Sammy White	C131	R	25	130	414	59	113	34	2	13	64	29	48	3	.273	.435
2 Floyd Baker	3B37, 2B16	L	36	81	172	22	47	4	2	0	24	24	10	0	.273	.320
Gene Stephens	OF72	L	20	78	221	30	45	6	2	3	18	29	56	3	.204	.290
Ted Lepcio	2B34, SS20, 3B11	R	22	66	161	17	38	4	2	4	11	17	24	0	.236	.360
1 Johnny Lipon	SS58	R	30	60	145	18	31	7	0	0	13	14	16	1	.214	.262
Del Wilber	C28, 1B2	R	34	58	112	16	27	6	1	7	29	6	21	0	.241	.500
Al Zarilla	OF18	R	34	57	67	11	13	2	0	0	4	14	13	0	.194	.224
Billy Consolo	3B16, 2B11	R	18	47	65	9	14	2	1	1	6	2	23	1	.215	.323
Mickey McDermott	P32	L	24	45	93	9	28	8	0	1	13	2	13	0	.301	.419
Ted Williams (MS)	OF26	L	34	37	91	17	37	6	0	13	34	19	10	0	.407	.901
Karl Olson (MS)	OF24	R	22	25	57	5	7	2	0	1	6	1	9	0	.123	.211
Gus Niarhos	C16	R	25	16	35	6	7	1	0	0	4	0	2	0	.200	.286

Dom DiMaggio 36 R 1-3, Jack Merson 31 R 0-4, Al Richter 26 R 0-0, 1 Clyde Vollmer 31 R 0-0, Faye Throneberry (MS) 22, Norm Zauchin (MS) 23

NAME	T	AGE	W	L	PCT	SV	G	GS	CG	IP	H	BB	SO	SHO	ERA
		29	84	69	.549	37	153	153	41	1373	1333	584	642	15	3.59
Mel Parnell	L	31	21	8	.724	0	38	34	12	241	217	116	136	5	3.06
Mickey McDermott	L	24	18	10	.643	0	32	30	8	206	169	109	92	4	3.01
Hal Brown	R	28	11	6	.647	0	30	25	6	166	177	57	62	1	4.66
Ellis Kinder	R	38	10	6	.625	27	69	0	0	107	84	38	39	0	1.85
Sid Hudson	R	38	6	9	.400	2	30	17	4	156	164	49	60	0	3.52
Bill Henry	L	25	5	5	.500	1	21	12	4	86	86	33	56	1	3.24
Willard Nixon	R	25	4	8	.333	0	23	15	5	117	114	59	57	1	3.92
Ike Delock	R	23	3	1	.750	3	21	1	0	49	60	20	40	0	4.41
1 Marv Grissom	R	35	2	6	.250	0	13	11	1	59	61	30	31	1	4.73
Ken Holcombe	R	34	1	0	1.000	1	3	0	0	6	9	3	1	0	6.00
Frank Sullivan	R	23	1	1	.500	0	14	0	0	26	24	11	17	0	5.54
Ben Flowers	R	26	1	4	.200	3	32	6	1	79	87	24	36	1	3.87
Hersh Freeman	R	25	1	4	.200	0	18	2	0	39	50	17	15	0	5.54
Bill Werle	L	32	0	1	.000	2	6	0	0	12	7	1	4	0	1.50
Bill Kennedy	L	32	0	0	—	0	5	0	0	24	24	17	14	0	3.75

Dick Brodowski (MS) 20, Leo Kiely (MS) 23

WASHINGTON — 5th 76-76 .500 23.5 — BUCKY HARRIS

NAME	G by Pos	B	AGE	G	AB	R	H	2B	3B	HR	RBI	BB	SO	SB	BA	SA
TOTALS			29	152	5149	687	1354	230	53	69	647	596	604	65	.263	.368
Mickey Vernon	1B152	L	35	152	608	101	205	43	11	15	115	63	57	4	.337	.518
Wayne Terwilliger	2B133	R	28	134	464	62	117	24	4	4	46	64	65	7	.252	.347
Pete Runnels	SS121, 2B11	L	25	137	486	64	125	15	5	2	50	64	36	7	.257	.321
Eddie Yost	3B152	R	26	152	577	107	157	30	7	9	45	123	59	1	.272	.395
Jackie Jensen	OF146	R	26	147	552	87	147	32	8	10	84	73	51	18	.266	.408
Jim Busby	OF150	R	26	150	586	68	183	28	7	6	82	38	45	13	.312	.415
2 Clyde Vollmer	OF106	R	31	116	408	54	106	15	3	11	74	48	59	0	.260	.392
1 Ed Fitz Gerald	C85	R	29	88	288	23	72	13	0	3	39	19	34	2	.250	.326
Gil Coan	OF46	L	31	68	168	28	33	1	4	2	17	22	23	7	.196	.286
Mickey Grasso	C59	R	33	61	113	9	24	3	1	0	11	13	18	0	.209	.276
2 Kite Thomas	OF8, C1	R	30	38	58	10	17	3	2	1	12	11	7	0	.293	.466
Jerry Snyder	SS17, 2B4	R	29	29	62	10	21	4	0	0	4	5	6	0	.339	.403
Mel Hoderlein	2B11, SS2	B	30	23	47	5	9	0	0	0	5	6	9	1	.191	.191
Yo-Yo Davalillo	SS17	R	22	19	58	10	17	1	0	0	2	1	7	1	.293	.310
2 Carmen Mauro	OF6	R	26	17	23	1	4	0	1	0	3	2	6	0	.174	.261
2 Tommy Byrne	P6	L	33	14	17	0	1	0	0	0	1	3	4	0	.059	.059
Gene Verble	SS8	R	25	13	21	4	4	1	0	0	3	2	3	0	.190	.190
Ken Wood	OF7	R	29	12	33	0	7	1	0	0	2	1	5	0	.212	.242
Frank Campos	OF6	L	29	10	9	1	1	0	0	0	0	1	0	0	.111	.111
Les Peden	C8	R	29	9	8	4	2	1	0	0	1	3	4	0	.250	.393
1 Floyd Baker	3B1	L	36	4	7	0	0	0	0	0	0	4	1	0	.000	.000
Bob Oldis	C7	R	28	7	16	0	4	0	0	0	3	1	4	0	.250	.250
Frank Sacka	C6	R	28	7	18	2	5	0	0	0	1	1	3	0	.278	.278

Bruce Barmes 23 L 1-5, Tony Roig 24 R 1-8, Dan Porter (MS) 21

NAME	T	AGE	W	L	PCT	SV	G	GS	CG	IP	H	BB	SO	SHO	ERA
		31	76	76	.500	10	152	152	76	1345	1313	478	515	16	3.66
Bob Porterfield	R	29	22	10	.688	0	34	32	24	255	243	73	77	9	3.35
Spec Shea	R	32	12	7	.632	0	23	23	11	165	151	75	38	1	3.93
Chuck Stobbs	L	23	11	8	.579	0	27	20	8	153	146	44	67	0	3.93
Walt Masterson	R	33	10	12	.455	0	29	20	10	166	145	62	95	4	3.63
Connie Marrero	R	41	8	7	.533	2	22	20	10	146	130	48	65	2	3.02
Sonny Dixon	R	28	5	8	.385	3	43	6	3	120	123	31	40	0	3.75
Julio Moreno	R	32	3	1	.750	0	12	2	1	35	41	13	13	0	2.83
Al Sima	R	31	2	3	.400	1	31	5	1	68	63	31	25	0	3.44
2 Johnny Schmitz	L	32	2	7	.222	4	24	13	5	108	118	37	39	0	3.67
Jerry Lane	R	27	1	4	.200	0	20	2	0	57	64	16	26	0	4.89
Jim Pearce	R	28	1	0	1.000	0	9	1	0	13	15	6	5	0	8.00
Dean Stone	L	22	1	0	1.000	0	13	1	0	15	17	11	5	0	4.80
Bunky Stewart	L	22	0	0	—	0	6	0	0	9	13	5	5	0	8.00
2 Tommy Byrne	L	33	0	5	.000	0	6	5	2	34	35	22	24	0	4.24
1 Sandy Consuegra	R	32	0	0	—	0	9	0	0	7	9	4	0	0	10.80

Bob Ross (MS) 24

DETROIT — 6th 60-94 .390 40.5 — FRED HUTCHINSON

NAME	G by Pos	B	AGE	G	AB	R	H	2B	3B	HR	RBI	BB	SO	SB	BA	SA
TOTALS			29	158	5553	695	1479	259	44	108	660	506	603	30	.266	.387
Walt Dropo	1B150	R	30	152	606	61	150	30	3	13	96	29	69	2	.248	.371
Johnny Pesky	2B73	L	33	103	308	43	90	22	1	2	24	29	10	3	.292	.390
Harvey Kuenn	SS155	R	22	155	679	94	209	33	7	2	48	50	31	6	.308	.386
2 Ray Boone	3B97, SS3	R	29	101	385	73	120	16	6	22	93	48	47	2	.312	.556
Don Lund	OF123	R	30	131	421	51	108	21	4	9	47	39	65	3	.257	.390
Jim Delsing	OF133	L	27	138	479	77	138	26	6	11	62	66	39	1	.288	.436
Bob Nieman	OF135	R	26	142	508	72	143	32	5	15	69	57	57	0	.281	.453
Matt Batts	C103	R	31	116	374	38	104	24	3	6	42	34	36	2	.278	.406
Fred Hatfield	3B54, 2B28, SS1	L	28	109	311	41	79	11	1	3	19	40	34	3	.254	.325
Steve Souchock	OF80, 1B1	R	34	89	278	29	84	13	3	11	46	8	35	5	.302	.489
Pat Mullin	OF14	L	35	79	97	11	26	4	0	4	17	14	15	0	.268	.402
Jerry Priddy	2B45, 1B11, 3B2	R	33	65	196	14	46	6	2	1	24	17	19	1	.235	.301
Johnny Bucha	C56	R	28	60	158	17	35	9	0	1	14	20	14	1	.222	.297
1 Owen Friend	2B26	R	26	31	96	10	17	4	0	3	10	6	9	0	.177	.313
Al Kaline	OF20	R	18	30	28	9	7	0	0	1	2	1	5	1	.250	.357
Russ Sullivan	OF20	L	30	23	72	7	18	6	1	0	5	2	10	0	.250	.389
Billy Hitchcock	3B12, 2B1, SS1	R	36	22	38	8	8	0	0	0	3	3	3	0	.211	.211
1 Joe Ginsberg	C15	L	26	18	53	6	16	3	1	0	7	11	1	0	.302	.340
Frank Carswell	OF3	R	33	16	21	2	5	0	0	0	3	1	4	0	.238	.238
John Baumgartner	3B7	R	22	7	27	4	5	0	0	0	2	3	5	0	.185	.185

Bob Swift 38 R 1-3, Reno Bertoia 18 R 0-1, George Freese 26 R 0-1, Frank House (MS) 23

NAME	T	AGE	W	L	PCT	SV	G	GS	CG	IP	H	BB	SO	SHO	ERA
		27	60	94	.390	16	158	158	50	1415	1633	585	645	2	5.25
Ned Garver	R	27	11	11	.500	1	30	26	13	198	228	66	69	0	4.45
Ted Gray	L	28	10	15	.400	0	30	28	8	176	166	76	115	0	4.60
Billy Hoeft	L	21	9	14	.391	2	29	27	9	198	223	58	90	0	4.82
Dick Marlowe	R	24	6	7	.462	0	42	11	2	120	152	42	52	0	5.25
2 Steve Gromek	R	33	6	8	.429	1	19	17	6	126	138	36	59	1	4.50
2 Al Aber	L	25	4	3	.571	0	17	10	2	67	63	41	34	0	4.43
Ray Herbert	R	23	4	4	.400	6	43	3	0	88	109	46	37	0	5.22
2 Ralph Branca	R	27	4	7	.364	1	17	14	7	102	98	31	50	0	4.15
Dave Madison	R	32	3	4	.429	0	32	1	0	62	76	44	27	0	6.82
1 Art Houtteman	R	25	2	6	.250	1	16	9	3	69	87	29	28	1	5.87
Bob Miller	R	17	1	3	.333	0	13	0	0	36	43	21	9	0	6.00
Hal Erickson	R	33	1	0	1.000	2	18	0	0	33	43	10	19	0	4.78
2 Dick Weik	R	24	1	0	1.000	0	8	1	0	19	32	23	6	0	14.21
Milt Jordan	R	26	0	1	.000	0	8	1	0	17	26	5	4	0	5.82
Hal Newhouser (SA)	L	32	0	1	.000	0	7	1	0	22	34	6	6	0	6.95
2 Ray Scarborough	R	35	0	2	.000	2	13	0	0	21	34	11	12	0	8.14
2 Earl Harrist	R	33	0	2	.000	0	12	0	0	15	25	14	10	0	8.53
1 Bill Wight	L	31	0	3	.000	0	13	4	0	35	35	14	10	0	6.02
Paul Foytack	R	22	0	0	—	0	6	0	0	9	9	11	9	0	10.80
Fred Hutchinson	R	33	0	0	—	0	3	0	0	6	6	0	3	0	2.70

Bill Black (MS) 20

PHILADELPHIA — 7th 59-95 .383 41.5 — JIMMY DYKES

NAME	G by Pos	B	AGE	G	AB	R	H	2B	3B	HR	RBI	BB	SO	SB	BA	SA
TOTALS			30	157	5455	632	1398	205	38	116	588	498	602	41	.256	.372
Eddie Robinson	1B155	L	32	156	615	64	152	28	4	22	102	63	56	1	.247	.413
Cass Michaels	2B116	R	27	111	411	53	103	10	0	12	42	51	56	7	.251	.363
Joe DeMaestri	SS108	R	24	111	420	53	107	17	3	6	35	24	39	0	.255	.352
1 Loren Babe	3B93, SS1	L	25	103	343	34	77	16	2	0	20	35	20	0	.224	.283
2 Dave Philley	OF157, 3B1	B	33	157	620	80	188	30	9	9	59	51	35	13	.303	.434
Ed McGhee	OF99	R	28	104	358	36	94	11	4	1	29	17	46	4	.263	.304
Gus Zernial	OF141	R	30	147	556	65	158	21	3	42	108	57	79	0	.284	.559
Joe Astroth	C79	R	30	82	260	28	77	24	0	1	24	27	12	1	.296	.404
Pete Suder	3B72, 2B38	R	37	115	454	44	130	11	3	4	35	17	35	3	.286	.350
Ray Murray	C78	R	35	84	268	25	76	14	3	6	41	18	25	0	.284	.425
2 Carmen Mauro	OF49, 3B1	L	26	64	165	14	44	4	2	0	17	19	21	3	.267	.339
Tom Hamilton	1B7, OF2	R	27	58	56	8	11	2	0	0	5	5	11	0	.196	.232
Eddie Joost	SS51	R	37	51	177	39	44	6	0	6	15	45	24	3	.249	.384
Elmer Valo (BG)	OF25	L	32	50	85	15	19	3	0	2	3	6	10	0	.224	.259
1 Kite Thomas	OF15	R	30	24	49	1	6	0	0	0	2	3	6	0	.122	.122
Neal Watlington	C9	R	30	21	44	4	7	1	2	0	3	1	5	0	.159	.182
1 Allie Clark	OF19	R	30	20	74	6	15	4	0	0	3	13	5	0	.203	.378
Tommy Giordano	2B11	R	27	11	40	4	7	2	0	1	6	3	9	0	.175	.375

Spider Wilhelm 24 R 2-7, Don Kolloway 34 R 0-1

NAME	T	AGE	W	L	PCT	SV	G	GS	CG	IP	H	BB	SO	SHO	ERA
		30	59	95	.383	11	157	157	51	1409	1475	594	566	7	4.67
Alex Kellner	L	28	11	12	.478	0	25	25	14	202	210	51	81	2	3.92
Harry Byrd	R	28	11	20	.355	0	40	37	11	237	279	115	122	2	5.51
Morrie Martin	L	30	10	12	.455	7	58	11	2	156	158	59	64	0	4.44
Marion Fricano	R	29	9	12	.429	3	39	23	10	211	206	90	67	0	3.88
Bobby Shantz (SA)	R	27	5	9	.357	0	16	16	6	106	107	26	58	0	4.08
Joe Coleman (IL)	R	30	3	4	.429	0	21	9	2	90	85	49	18	1	4.00
Carl Scheib	R	26	3	7	.300	2	28	4	3	96	99	29	25	0	4.88
Charlie Bishop	R	29	3	14	.176	2	39	20	1	161	174	86	66	1	5.65
Bobo Newsom	R	45	2	6	.250	0	17	2	1	39	44	24	16	0	4.85
Bob Trice	R	27	2	1	.667	0	6	3	3	34	39	12	15	0	5.48
Frank Fanovich	L	31	0	0	—	0	26	0	0	62	62	37	37	0	5.52
Rinty Monahan	R	24	0	1	.000	0	5	1	0	11	14	8	3	0	4.09
Walt Kellner	R	24	0	0	—	0	7	1	0	11	8	4	6	0	4.91
Dick Rozek	L	25	0	1	.000	0	5	1	0	11	18	9	5	0	13.50
Bill Harrington (MS)	R	25	0	0	—	0	1	0	0	2	2	1	0	0	0.00
Johnny Mackinson	R	29													

ST. LOUIS — 8th 54-100 .351 46.5 — MARTY MARION

NAME	G by Pos	B	AGE	G	AB	R	H	2B	3B	HR	RBI	BB	SO	SB	BA	SA
TOTALS			28	157	5264	555	1310	214	25	112	522	507	644	17	.249	.363
Dick Kryhoski	1B88	L	28	104	338	35	94	18	4	16	50	26	33	0	.278	.497
Bobby Young	2B148	L	28	148	537	48	137	22	2	4	37	44	40	2	.255	.326
Billy Hunter	SS152	R	25	154	567	50	124	18	1	1	37	24	45	3	.219	.259
Jim Dyck	OF55, 3B51	R	31	112	334	38	71	15	1	9	38	38	56	2	.213	.344
Vic Wertz	OF121	L	28	128	440	61	118	18	6	19	70	72	44	1	.268	.466
Johnny Groth	OF141	R	26	141	557	65	141	29	4	10	57	42	53	5	.253	.370
Dick Kokos	OF83	L	25	107	299	41	72	12	0	13	38	56	53	0	.241	.411
Clint Courtney	C103	L	26	106	355	28	89	12	2	4	25	35	20	0	.251	.330
Don Lenhardt	OF77, 3B6	R	30	97	303	37	96	15	0	10	35	41	41	1	.317	.465
Roy Sievers	1B76	R	26	92	285	37	77	15	3	4	35	32	47	0	.270	.407
Les Moss	C71	R	28	78	239	21	66	14	1	2	28	18	31	0	.276	.388
Hank Edwards	OF21	L	34	65	106	16	21	3	2	0	9	13	9	1	.198	.226
2 Neil Berry	3B18, 2B15, SS6	R	31	57	99	14	28	1	2	0	11	9	10	1	.283	.333
1 Don Larsen	P38, OF1	R	23	50	81	11	23	2	0	0	4	6	28	0	.284	.457
1 Bob Elliott	3B45	R	36	48	160	19	40	7	0	2	29	30	18	0	.250	.400
1 Vern Stephens	3B46	R	32	46	165	16	53	13	0	7	24	17	18	0	.321	.442
1 Willie Miranda	SS8, 3B6	R	27	17	6	1	1	0	0	0	1	0	3	0	.167	.167
Dixie Upright		L	25	6	8	1	5	1	0	1	2	0	0	0	.625	.625
2 Johnny Lipon	3B6, 2B1	R	30	7	9	2	2	0	0	0	0	0	0	0	.222	.222

Ed Mickelson 26 R 2-15, Babe Martin 33 R 0-2, Jim Pisoni 23 R 1-12, Marty Marion 35 R 0-7, Frank Kellert 28 R 0-4, Jay Porter (MS) 20, Frank Saucier (MS) 27

NAME	T	AGE	W	L	PCT	SV	G	GS	CG	IP	H	BB	SO	SHO	ERA
		32	54	100	.351	24	154	154	28	1384	1467	626	639	10	4.47
Marlin Stuart	R	34	8	2	.800	7	60	2	0	114	136	44	46	0	3.95
Don Larsen	R	23	7	12	.368	2	38	22	7	193	201	64	96	2	4.15
Dick Littlefield	L	27	7	12	.368	0	36	22	2	152	153	84	104	0	5.09
Duane Pillette	R	30	7	13	.350	0	31	25	6	167	181	62	58	1	4.47
2 Virgil Trucks	R	36	5	4	.556	2	16	12	4	88	83	32	47	2	3.07
Harry Brecheen	L	38	5	13	.278	1	26	15	7	117	122	31	44	0	3.08
Bob Cain	L	28	4	10	.286	1	32	13	1	100	129	45	36	0	6.21
Bobo Holloman	R	30	3	7	.300	0	22	10	1	65	69	50	25	1	5.26
Satchel Paige	R	46	3	9	.250	11	57	4	0	117	114	39	51	0	3.54
Mike Blyzka	R	24	2	6	.250	0	27	10	3	94	110	39	44	0	6.41
Bob Turley (MS)	R	22	2	6	.250	0	10	10	4	60	39	54	61	1	3.77
2 Lou Kretlow	R	32	5	11	.313	2	22	11	0	81	93	52	37	0	5.11
2 Max Lanier	L	37	0	2	.000	0	10	2	0	22	28	19	8	0	7.50
1 Hal White	R	34	0	0	—	0	11	0	0	22	25	6	8	0	2.70
Bob Habenicht	R	27	0	0	—	0	6	0	0	6	14	5	4	0	4.50

BROOKLYN — 1st 105-49 .682 — CHUCK DRESSEN

NAME	G by Pos	B	AGE	G	AB	R	H	2B	3B	HR	RBI	BB	SO	SB	BA	SA
TOTALS			29	155	5373	955	1529	274	59	208	887	655	686	90	.285	.474
Gil Hodges	1B127, OF24	R	29	141	520	101	157	22	7	31	122	75	84	1	.302	.550
Jim Gilliam	2B149	B	24	151	605	125	168	31	17	6	63	100	38	21	.278	.415
Pee Wee Reese	SS135	R	34	140	524	108	142	25	7	13	61	82	61	22	.271	.420
Billy Cox	3B89, SS6, 2B1	R	33	100	327	44	95	18	1	10	44	37	21	2	.291	.443
Carl Furillo	OF131	R	31	132	479	82	165	38	6	21	92	34	32	1	.344	.580
Duke Snider	OF151	L	26	153	590	132	198	38	4	42	126	82	90	16	.336	.627
J. Robinson	OF76, 3B44, 2B9, 1B6, SS1	R	34	136	484	109	159	34	7	12	95	74	30	17	.329	.502
Roy Campanella	C140	R	31	144	519	103	162	26	3	41	142	67	58	4	.312	.611
Don Thompson	OF81	L	29	96	153	25	37	5	0	1	12	14	13	2	.242	.294
George Shuba	OF44	R	28	74	169	19	43	12	1	5	23	17	20	1	.254	.426
Bobby Morgan	3B36, SS21	R	27	69	196	35	51	6	2	7	33	33	47	2	.260	.418
Wayne Belardi (AJ)	1B38	L	22	69	163	19	39	3	2	11	34	16	40	1	.239	.485
Rube Walker	C28	L	27	43	95	5	23	6	0	3	9	7	11	0	.242	.400
Bill Antonello	OF25	R	26	40	43	9	7	1	1	1	4	2	11	0	.163	.302
Dick Williams	OF24	R	24	30	55	4	12	2	0	2	5	3	10	0	.218	.364
1 Carmen Mauro	OF1	L	26	8	9	1	0	0	0	0	0	0	0	0	.000	.000
Dixie Howell		R	33	1	1	0	0	0	0	0	0	0	1	0	.000	.000
Dick Teed		B	27	1	1	0	0	0	0	0	0	0	1	0	.000	.000

NAME	T	AGE	W	L	PCT	SV	G	GS	CG	IP	H	BB	SO	SHO	ERA
TOTALS		28	105	49	.682	29	155	155	51	1381	1337	509	817	11	4.10
Carl Erskine	R	26	20	6	.769	3	39	33	16	247	213	95	187	4	3.53
Russ Meyer	R	29	15	5	.750	0	34	32	10	191	201	63	106	2	4.57
Billy Loes	R	23	14	8	.636	0	32	25	9	163	165	53	75	1	4.53
Preacher Roe	L	38	11	3	.786	0	25	24	9	157	171	40	85	1	4.36
Clem Labine	R	26	11	6	.647	7	37	7	0	110	92	30	44	0	2.78
Johnny Podres	L	20	9	4	.692	0	33	18	3	115	126	64	82	1	4.23
Bob Milliken	R	26	8	4	.667	2	37	10	3	118	94	42	65	0	3.36
Ben Wade	R	30	7	5	.583	3	32	10	0	90	79	33	65	0	3.80
Joe Black	R	29	6	3	.667	5	34	3	0	73	74	27	42	0	5.30
Jim Hughes	R	30	4	3	.571	9	48	0	0	86	80	41	49	0	3.45
Glenn Mickens	R	22	0	1	.000	0	4	2	0	6	11	4	5	0	12.00
Ray Moore	R	27	0	1	.000	0	1	1	1	8	6	4	4	0	3.38
1 Ralph Branca	R	27	0	0	—	0	7	0	0	11	15	5	5	0	9.82
Erv Palica (MS)	R	25	0	0	—	0	4	0	0	6	10	8	3	0	12.00
Don Newcombe (MS) 27															

MILWAUKEE — 2nd 92-62 .597 13 — CHARLIE GRIMM

NAME	G by Pos	B	AGE	G	AB	R	H	2B	3B	HR	RBI	BB	SO	SB	BA	SA
TOTALS			27	157	5349	738	1422	227	52	156	691	439	637	46	.266	.415
Joe Adcock	1B157	R	25	157	590	71	168	33	6	18	80	42	82	3	.285	.453
Jack Dittmer	2B138	L	25	138	504	54	134	22	1	9	63	18	35	1	.266	.367
Johnny Logan	SS150	R	26	157	611	100	167	27	8	11	73	41	33	2	.273	.398
Eddie Mathews	3B157	L	21	157	579	110	175	31	8	47	135	99	83	1	.302	.627
Andy Pafko	OF139	R	32	140	516	70	153	23	4	17	72	37	33	2	.297	.455
Bill Bruton	OF150	L	27	151	613	82	153	18	14	1	41	44	100	26	.250	.330
Sid Gordon	OF137	R	35	140	464	67	127	22	4	19	75	71	40	1	.274	.461
Del Crandall	C108	R	23	116	382	55	104	13	1	15	51	33	47	2	.272	.429
Jim Pendleton	OF105, SS7	R	29	120	251	48	75	12	4	7	27	7	36	6	.299	.462
Walker Cooper	C35	R	38	53	137	12	30	6	0	3	16	12	15	1	.219	.328
Harry Hanebrink	2B21, 3B1	L	25	51	80	8	19	1	1	1	8	6	8	1	.238	.313
George Crowe	1B9	L	32	47	42	6	12	2	0	2	6	2	7	0	.286	.476
Sibby Sisti	2B13, SS6, 3B4	R	32	38	23	8	5	1	0	0	4	5	2	0	.217	.261
Ebba St. Claire	C27	B	31	33	80	7	16	3	0	2	5	3	9	0	.200	.313
Bob Thorpe	OF18	R	26	27	37	1	6	1	0	0	5	1	6	0	.162	.189
Mel Roach	2B1	R	20	5	2	1	0	0	0	0	0	0	1	0	.000	.000
Paul Burris	C2	R	29	2	1	0	0	0	0	0	0	0	0	0	.000	.000
Billy Klaus		L	24	2	2	1	0	0	0	0	0	1	0	0	.000	.000

NAME	T	AGE	W	L	PCT	SV	G	GS	CG	IP	H	BB	SO	SHO	ERA
TOTALS		28	92	62	.597	15	157	157	72	1387	1282	539	738	14	3.30
Warren Spahn	L	32	23	7	.767	3	35	32	24	266	211	70	148	5	2.10
Lew Burdette	R	26	15	5	.750	8	46	13	6	175	177	56	58	1	3.24
Bob Buhl	R	24	13	8	.619	0	30	18	8	154	133	73	83	3	2.98
Johnny Antonelli	R	23	12	12	.500	1	31	26	11	175	167	71	131	2	3.19
Max Surkont	R	31	11	5	.688	0	28	24	11	170	168	64	83	2	4.18
Don Liddle	L	28	7	6	.538	2	31	15	4	129	119	55	63	0	3.07
Ernie Johnson	R	29	4	3	.571	0	36	1	0	81	79	22	36	0	2.67
Jim Wilson	R	31	4	3	.308	0	20	18	5	114	107	43	71	0	4.34
Vern Bickford	R	32	2	5	.286	1	20	9	2	58	60	35	25	0	5.28
Joey Jay	R	17	1	0	1.000	0	3	1	1	10	6	5	4	1	0.00
Dave Jolly	R	28	0	1	.000	3	24	0	0	38	34	27	23	0	3.55
Dave Cole	R	22	0	1	.000	0	10	0	0	15	17	14	13	0	8.40
Virgil Jester	R	25	0	0	—	0	2	0	0	2	4	4	0	0	22.50
Chet Nichols (MS) 22															
Phil Paine (MS) 23															

PHILADELPHIA — 3rd(tie) 83-71 .539 22 — STEVE O'NEILL

NAME	G by Pos	B	AGE	G	AB	R	H	2B	3B	HR	RBI	BB	SO	SB	BA	SA
TOTALS			28	156	5290	716	1400	228	62	115	657	530	597	42	.265	.396
Earl Torgeson	1B105	L	29	111	379	58	104	25	8	11	64	53	57	7	.274	.470
Granny Hamner	2B93, SS71	R	26	154	609	90	168	30	8	21	92	32	28	2	.276	.455
Ted Kazanski	SS95	R	19	95	360	39	78	17	5	2	27	26	53	1	.217	.308
Willie Jones	3B147	R	27	149	481	61	108	16	2	19	70	85	45	1	.225	.385
Johnny Wyrostek	OF110	L	33	125	409	42	111	14	2	6	47	38	43	0	.271	.359
Richie Ashburn	OF156	L	26	156	622	110	205	25	9	2	57	61	35	14	.330	.408
Del Ennis	OF150	R	28	152	578	79	165	23	3	29	125	57	53	1	.285	.484
Smoky Burgess	C95	L	26	102	312	31	91	17	5	4	36	37	17	3	.292	.417
1 Connie Ryan	2B65, 1B2	R	33	90	247	47	73	14	6	5	26	30	35	5	.296	.462
Eddie Waitkus	1B59	L	33	81	247	24	72	9	2	1	16	13	23	1	.291	.356
Stan Lopata	C80	R	27	81	234	34	56	12	3	8	31	28	39	3	.239	.419
Mel Clark (KJ)	OF51	R	26	60	198	31	59	10	4	0	19	11	17	1	.298	.389
Tommy Glaviano	3B14, 2B12, SS1	R	29	53	74	17	15	1	2	3	5	24	20	2	.203	.392
Bill Nicholson	OF12	L	38		62	12	13	5	1	2	16	12	20	0	.210	.419
Lucky Lohrke	SS2, 2B2, 3B1	R	29	12	13	3	2	0	0	0	0	1	2	0	.154	.154
2 Johnny Lindell	P5, OF2	R	36	11	18	3	7	1	0	0	2	6	2	0	.389	.444
Jackie Mayo	OF1	R	27	5	4	0	0	0	0	0	0	0	1	0	.000	.000
Stan Palys	OF1	R	23	4	0	0	0	0	0	0	0	0	0	0	.000	.000

NAME	T	AGE	W	L	PCT	SV	G	GS	CG	IP	H	BB	SO	SHO	ERA
TOTALS		28	83	71	.539	15	156	156	76	1370	1410	410	637	13	3.80
Robin Roberts	R	26	23	16	.590	2	44	41	33	347	324	61	198	5	2.75
Curt Simmons (FJ)	L	24	16	13	.552	0	32	30	19	238	211	82	138	4	3.21
Jim Konstanty	R	36	14	10	.583	5	48	19	7	171	198	42	45	0	4.42
Steve Ridzik	R	24	9	6	.600	2	42	12	1	124	119	48	53	0	3.77
Karl Drews	R	33	9	10	.474	3	47	27	6	185	218	50	72	0	4.52
Bob Miller	R	27	4	9	.471	2	35	20	8	157	169	42	63	3	4.01
Thornton Kipper	R	24	3	3	.500	0	20	3	0	46	59	12	15	0	4.70
2 Johnny Lindell	R	36	1	1	.500	0	3	3	2	23	22	23*	16	0	4.30
Kent Peterson	L	27	0	1	.000	0	15	0	0	27	26	21	20	0	6.67
Andy Hansen	R	28	0	2	.000	3	30	1	0	51	60	24	17	0	4.06
Paul Stuffel	R	26	0	0	—	0	2	0	0	4	4	0	0	0	∞
Tom Qualters	R	18	0	0	—	0	1	0	0	0.1	4	1	0	0	162.00

*Lindell, also with Pittsburgh, league leader in BB with 139.

ST. LOUIS — 3rd(tie) 83-71 .539 22 — EDDIE STANKY

NAME	G by Pos	B	AGE	G	AB	R	H	2B	3B	HR	RBI	BB	SO	SB	BA	SA
TOTALS			30	157	5397	786	1474	281	56	140	722	574	617	18	.273	.424
Steve Bilko	1B154	R	24	154	570	72	143	23	3	21	84	70	125	0	.251	.412
Red Schoendienst	2B140	B	30	146	564	107	193	35	5	15	79	60	23	3	.342	.502
Solly Hemus	SS150, 2B3	L	30	154	585	110	163	32	11	14	61	86	40	2	.279	.443
Ray Jablonski	3B157	R	26	157	604	64	162	23	2	21	112	34	61	2	.268	.427
Enos Slaughter	OF137	L	37	143	492	64	143	34	9	6	89	80	28	4	.291	.433
Rip Repulski	OF153	R	24	153	567	75	156	25	4	15	66	33	71	3	.275	.413
Stan Musial	OF157	L	32	157	593	127	200	53	9	30	113	105	32	3	.337	.609
Del Rice	C135	R	30	135	419	32	99	22	1	6	37	48	49	0	.236	.337
Peanuts Lowrey	OF38, 2B10, 3B1	R	35	104	182	26	49	9	2	5	27	15	21	1	.269	.423
2 Pete Castiglione	3B51, 2B9, SS3	R	32	67	52	9	9	2	0	0	3	2	5	0	.173	.212
Harvey Haddix	P36	R	27	48	97	21	28	3	3	1	11	5	19	0	.289	.412
Dick Schofield	SS15	B	18	33	39	9	7	0	0	2	4	2	11	0	.179	.333
Dick Sisler	1B10	L	32	32	43	3	11	1	1	0	4	1	4	0	.256	.326
2 Sal Yvars	C26	R	29	30	57	4	14	2	0	1	6	4	6	0	.246	.333
Harry Elliott	OF17	R	28	24	59	6	15	6	1	1	6	3	8	0	.254	.441
Ferrell Anderson	C12	R	35	18	35	1	10	2	0	0	1	0	4	0	.286	.343
Eddie Stanky	2B8	R	36	17	30	5	8	0	0	0	1	6	4	0	.267	.267
Grant Dunlap	OF1	R	29	16	17	2	6	0	1	1	3	0	2	0	.353	.647
Vern Benson		L	28	13	4	2	0	0	0	0	0	0	1	0	.000	.000
Billy Johnson	3B11	R	34	11	5	0	1	0	0	0	1	2	1	1	.200	.400
Les Fusselman	C11	R	32	11	8	1	2	1	0	0	0	0	3	0	.250	.375
Dick Rand	C9	R	22	9	31	3	9	1	0	0	1	1	4	0	.290	.323
Ed Phillips		B	21	9	0	4	0	0	0	0	0	0	0	0	—	—
1 Hal Rice		L	29	8	8	0	2	0	0	0	0	1	0	0	.250	.250
Virgil Stallcup		R	31	4	0	0	0	0	0	0	0	0	0	0	.000	.000
Fred Marolewski	1B1	R	24	1	4	0	0	0	0	0	0	0	0	0	.000	.000
Herb Gorman (DD) 28																	

NAME	T	AGE	W	L	PCT	SV	G	GS	CG	IP	H	BB	SO	SHO	ERA
TOTALS		29	83	71	.539	36	157	157	51	1387	1406	533	732	11	4.22
Harvey Haddix	L	27	20	9	.690	1	36	33	19	253	220	69	163	6	3.06
Gerry Staley	R	32	18	9	.667	4	40	33	10	230	243	54	88	1	3.99
Vinegar Bend Mizell	L	22	13	11	.542	0	33	33	10	224	193	114	173	1	3.50
Stu Miller	R	25	7	8	.467	4	40	18	8	138	161	47	79	2	5.54
2 Hal White	R	34	6	5	.545	7	49	0	0	85	84	39	32	0	2.96
Al Brazle	L	39	6	7	.462	18	60	0	0	92	101	43	57	0	4.21
Joe Presko	R	24	6	13	.316	1	34	25	4	162	165	65	56	0	5.00
2 Eddie Erautt	R	28	1	7	.750	0	36	4	0	36	43	16	15	0	6.25
Cliff Chambers	L	31	3	6	.333	0	32	8	0	80	82	43	26	0	4.84
Mike Clark	R	31	1	0	1.000	3	23	2	0	36	46	21	17	0	4.75
Willard Schmidt	R	25	0	2	.000	0	7	0	0	18	21	13	11	0	9.00
1 Jackie Collum	L	26	0	0	—	0	7	0	0	11	15	4	5	0	6.55
Jack Faszholz	R	26	0	0	—	0	4	1	0	12	16	1	7	0	6.75
Dick Bokelmann	R	26	0	0	—	0	8	0	0	9	12	9	3	0	6.00
John Romonosky	R	23	0	0	—	0	4	1	0	7	3	5	3	0	4.50
Eddie Yuhas (SA)	R	28	0	0	—	0	3	0	0	3	0	1	0	0	18.00
Tom Poholsky (MS) 23															

NEW YORK — 5th 70-84 .455 35 — LEO DUROCHER

NAME	G by Pos	B	AGE	G	AB	R	H	2B	3B	HR	RBI	BB	SO	SB	BA	SA
TOTALS			27	155	5362	768	1452	195	45	176	739	499	608	31	.271	.422
Whitey Lockman	1B120, OF30	L	26	150	607	85	179	24	4	9	61	52	36	3	.295	.389
Davey Williams	2B95	R	25	112	340	51	101	11	2	3	34	44	19	2	.297	.368
Al Dark	SS110, 2B26, OF17, 3B8, P1	R	31	155	647	126	194	41	6	23	88	28	34	7	.300	.488
Hank Thompson	3B101, OF9, 2B1	L	27	114	388	80	117	15	8	24	74	60	39	6	.302	.567
Don Mueller	OF122	L	26	131	480	56	160	12	2	6	60	19	13	2	.333	.404
Bobby Thomson	OF154	R	29	154	608	80	175	22	6	26	106	43	57	4	.288	.472
Monte Irvin	OF113	R	34	124	444	72	146	21	5	21	97	55	34	2	.329	.541
Wes Westrum	C106, 3B1	R	30	113	300	40	65	5	0	12	30	56	73	2	.224	.366
Daryl Spencer	SS53, 3B36, 2B32	R	23	118	408	55	85	18	5	20	56	42	74	0	.208	.424
Dusty Rhodes	OF47	L	26	76	163	18	38	7	0	11	30	14	28	0	.233	.479
Bobby Hofman	3B23, 2B17	R	27	74	169	21	45	7	2	12	34	13	22	1	.266	.544
Tookie Gilbert	1B44	L	24	70	160	12	27	3	0	3	16	22	21	1	.169	.244
Ray Noble	C41	R	34	46	97	15	20	1	0	4	14	10	26	0	.206	.351
Sammy Calderone	C31	R	27	35	45	4	10	2	0	0	8	4	11	0	.222	.267
1 Sal Yvars	C20	R	29	24	27	5	6	1	0	1	7	1	7	0	.277	.277
Bill Rigney	3B2, 2B1	R	35	19	20	2	5	0	0	0	1	5	2	0	.250	.250
George Wilson		R	27	11	8	0	1	0	0	0	0	0	3	0	.125	.125
Ray Katt	C8	R	26	8	29	2	5	1	0	0	1	1	3	0	.172	.207
Willie Mays (MS) 22																	

NAME	T	AGE	W	L	PCT	SV	G	GS	CG	IP	H	BB	SO	SHO	ERA
TOTALS		31	70	84	.455	20	155	155	46	1366	1403	610	647	10	4.25
Ruben Gomez	R	25	13	11	.542	0	29	26	13	204	166	101	113	3	3.40
Larry Jansen	R	32	11	16	.407	1	36	26	6	185	185	55	88	0	4.14
Jim Hearn	R	32	9	12	.429	0	36	32	6	197	206	84	77	0	4.52
Sal Maglie	R	36	8	9	.471	0	27	24	9	145	158	47	80	3	4.16
Hoyt Wilhelm	R	30	7	8	.467	15	68	0	0	145	127	77	71	0	3.04
Al Corwin	R	26	6	4	.600	2	48	7	2	107	122	68	49	1	4.96
Dave Koslo	L	33	6	12	.333	2	37	12	2	112	135	36	36	0	4.74
2 Marv Grissom	R	35	4	2	.667	0	21	7	3	84	83	31	46	0	3.96
Al Worthington	R	24	4	8	.333	0	20	17	5	102	103	54	52	2	3.44
Frank Hiller	R	32	1	1	.667	0	19	1	0	34	43	15	10	0	6.69
Bill Connelly	R	28	0	1	.000	0	2	1	0	20	33	17	11	0	11.25
Monte Kennedy	L	31	0	0	—	0	18	0	0	29	30	19	11	0	7.04
1 Max Lanier	L	37	0	0	—	0	3	0	0	5	8	3	2	0	7.20
George Spencer	R	27	0	0	—	0	5	0	0	8	9	5	4	0	9.00
Al Dark	R	31	0	0	—	0	1	0	0	1	0	1	0	0	18.00
Alex Konikowski (MS) 25															

CINCINNATI 6th 68-86 .442 37 ROGERS HORNSBY 64-82 .438 BUSTER MILLS 4-4 .500

NAME	G by Pos	B	AGE	G	AB	R	H	2B	3B	HR	RBI	BB	SO	SB	BA	SA
TOTALS			27	155	5343	714	1396	190	34	166	669	485	701	25	.261	.403
Ted Kluszewski	1B147	L	28	149	570	97	180	25	0	40	108	55	34	2	.316	.570
Rocky Bridges	2B115, SS6, 3B3	R	25	122	432	52	98	13	2	1	21	37	42	1	.227	.273
Roy McMillan	SS155	R	23	155	557	51	130	15	4	5	43	43	52	2	.233	.302
Bobby Adams	3B150	R	31	150	607	99	167	14	6	8	49	58	67	3	.275	.357
Willard Marshall	OF95	L	32	122	357	51	95	14	6	17	62	41	28	0	.266	.482
Gus Bell	OF151	L	24	151	610	102	183	37	5	30	105	48	72	6	.300	.525
Jim Greengrass	OF153	R	25	154	606	86	173	22	7	20	100	47	83	6	.285	.444
Andy Seminick	C112	R	32	109	387	46	91	12	0	19	64	49	82	2	.235	.413
Bob Borkowski	OF67, 1B2	R	27	94	249	32	67	11	1	7	29	21	41	0	.269	.406
Grady Hatton	2B35, 1B10, 3B5	L	30	83	159	22	37	3	1	7	22	29	24	0	.233	.396
Johnny Temple	2B44	R	24	63	110	14	29	4	0	1	9	7	12	1	.264	.327
Hobie Landrith	C47	L	23	52	154	15	37	3	1	3	16	12	8	2	.240	.331
Bob Marquis	OF10	L	28	40	44	9	12	1	1	2	3	4	11	0	.273	.477
George Lerchen	OF1	L	30	22	17	2	5	1	0	0	2	5	6	0	.294	.353
Frank Baldwin	C6	R	24	16	20	0	2	0	0	0	0	1	9	0	.100	.100
Wally Post	OF11	R	23	11	33	3	8	1	0	1	4	4	6	1	.242	.364

1 Hank Foiles 24 R 2-13, Joe Szekely 28 R 1-13, Ed Bailey 22 L 3-8, Lloyd Merriman (MS) 28

NAME	T	AGE	W	L	PCT	SV	G	GS	CG	IP	H	BB	SO	SHO	ERA
		28	68	86	.442	15	155	155	47	1365	1484	488	506	7	4.64
Harry Perkowski	L	30	12	11	.522	2	33	25	7	193	204	62	70	2	4.52
2 Fred Baczewski		27	11	4	.733	1	24	18	10	138	125	52	58	1	3.46
Joe Nuxhall	L	24	9	11	.450	2	30	17	5	142	136	69	52	1	4.31
Frank Smith	R	25	8	9	.889	7	50	1	0	84	89	25	42	0	5.46
2 Jackie Collum	L	26	7	11	.389	3	30	12	4	125	123	39	51	1	3.74
Ken Raffensberger	L	35	7	14	.333	0	26	26	9	174	200	33	47	1	4.93
Bud Podbielan	R	29	6	16	.273	1	36	24	8	186	214	67	74	1	4.74
1 Bubba Church	R	28	3	3	.500	0	11	7	2	44	55	19	12	0	5.93
Clyde King	R	29	3	6	.333	0	10	1	0	76	78	32	21	0	5.21
2 Bob Kelly	R	25	1	2	.333	2	28	5	0	66	71	26	29	0	4.36
Herm Wehmeier	R	26	1	6	.143	0	28	10	2	82	100	47	32	0	7.13
Howie Judson	R	27	0	1	.000	0	10	6	0	39	58	11	11	0	5.54
Ernie Nevel	R	33	0	0	.000	0	10	0	0	10	16	1	5	0	6.30
1 Eddie Erautt	L	28	0	0	.000	0	4	0	0	5	11	3	1	0	5.40
Ed Blake	R	27	0	0	.000	0	1	0	0	0	1	1	0	0	T
Barney Martin	R	30	0	0	.000	0	2	0	0	2	3	1	1	0	9.00

CHICAGO 7th 65-89 .422 40 PHIL CAVARRETTA

NAME	G by Pos	B	AGE	G	AB	R	H	2B	3B	HR	RBI	BB	SO	SB	BA	SA
TOTALS			30	155	5272	633	1372	204	57	137	588	514	746	49	.260	.399
Dee Fondy	1B149	L	28	150	595	79	184	24	11	18	78	44	106	10	.309	.477
Eddie Miksis	2B92, SS53	R	26	142	577	61	145	17	6	9	39	33	59	1	.251	.343
Roy Smalley	SS77	R	27	82	253	20	63	9	0	6	25	28	57	0	.249	.356
Randy Jackson	3B133	R	27	139	498	61	142	22	8	19	66	42	61	0	.285	.476
Hank Sauer (BG)	OF105	R	36	108	346	51	104	16	5	19	60	50	56	0	.263	.473
Frankie Baumholtz	OF130	L	34	133	520	75	159	36	7	3	25	42	59	3	.306	.419
2 Ralph Kiner	OF116	R	30	117	414	73	117	14	2	28	87	75	67	1	.283	.529
Clyde McCullough	C73	R	36	77	229	21	59	3	2	6	23	15	23	0	.258	.367
Hal Jeffcoat	OF100	R	28	106	183	22	43	3	1	4	22	21	26	5	.235	.328
Bill Serena	2B49, 3B28	R	28	93	275	30	69	10	5	10	52	41	46	0	.251	.433
2 Joe Garagiola	C68	L	27	74	222	21	62	9	4	1	21	21	23	0	.272	.360
Tommy Brown	SS25, OF6	R	25	65	138	19	27	7	1	2	13	13	17	1	.196	.304
2 Catfish Metkovich	OF38, 1B7	L	31	61	124	19	29	9	2	2	16	16	10	2	.234	.355
Carl Sawatski	C15	R	25	43	59	5	13	3	0	1	5	7	13	0	.220	.322
1 Preston Ward	OF27, 1B7	L	25	33	100	10	23	5	0	4	12	18	21	3	.230	.400
Phil Cavarretta		L	36	27	21	3	6	3	0	0	3	6	3	0	.286	.429
Bob Ramazzotti (HJ)	2B18	R	36	26	39	3	6	2	0	0	4	3	4	1	.154	.205
1 Toby Atwell	C24	L	29	24	74	10	17	2	0	1	8	13	7	0	.230	.297
1 Gene Hermanski	OF13	L	33	18	40	1	6	1	1	0	1	4	7	1	.150	.175
Ernie Banks	SS10	R	22	10	35	3	11	1	1	2	6	4	5	0	.314	.571

1 Bob Addis 27 L 2-12, Dale Talbot 26 R 10-30, Gene Baker 28 R 5-22, Paul Schramka 25 L 0-0, Harry Chiti (MS) 20

NAME	T	AGE	W	L	PCT	SV	G	GS	CG	IP	H	BB	SO	SHO	ERA
		30	65	89	.422	22	155	155	38	1359	1491	554	623	3	4.79
Paul Minner	L	29	12	15	.444	1	31	27	9	201	227	40	64	2	4.21
Warren Hacker	R	28	12	19	.387	2	39	32	9	222	225	54	106	0	4.38
Johnny Klippstein	R	25	10	11	.476	6	48	19	5	168	169	107	113	0	4.82
Bob Rush	R	27	9	14	.391	0	29	28	8	167	177	66	84	1	4.53
Turk Lown	R	29	8	7	.533	3	49	12	2	148	166	84	76	0	5.17
2 Howie Pollet	L	32	5	6	.455	1	25	17	2	111	120	44	45	0	4.13
2 Bubba Church	R	28	4	5	.444	1	27	11	1	104	115	49	47	0	5.02
Jim Willis	R	26	2	1	.667	0	13	3	2	43	37	15	15	0	3.14
Dutch Leonard	R	44	2	3	.400	8	45	0	0	63	72	24	27	0	4.57
Duke Simpson	R	25	1	2	.333	0	30	1	0	45	60	25	21	0	8.00
1 Bob Kelly	R	25	0	0	.000	0	14	0	0	17	27	6	9	0	9.53
Don Elston	R	24	0	1	.000	0	2	0	0	1	2	1	0	0	14.40
Sheldon Jones	R	31	0	0	.000	0	22	2	0	38	47	16	9	0	5.45
1 Bob Schultz	L	29	0	2	.000	0	7	2	0	12	13	11	4	0	5.25
1 Fred Baczewski	L	27	0	0	—	0	9	0	0	10	20	6	3	0	6.30
Bill Moisan	R	27	0	0	.000	0	5	2	1	5	2	1	1	0	5.40

PITTSBURGH 8th 50-104 .325 55 FRED HANEY

NAME	G by Pos	B	AGE	G	AB	R	H	2B	3B	HR	RBI	BB	SO	SB	BA	SA
TOTALS			27	154	5253	622	1297	178	49	99	571	524	715	41	.247	.356
2 Preston Ward	1B78	L	25	88	281	35	59	7	1	8	27	44	39	1	.210	.327
Johnny O'Brien	2B77, SS1	R	22	89	279	28	69	13	2	2	21	24	36	1	.247	.330
Eddie O'Brien	SS81	R	22	89	221	21	62	5	3	0	14	17	30	6	.238	.280
Danny O'Connell	3B104, 2B47	R	26	149	588	88	173	26	8	7	55	57	42	3	.294	.401
Cal Abrams	OF112	L	29	119	448	66	128	10	6	15	43	58	70	4	.286	.482
Carlos Bernier	OF87	R	26	105	310	48	66	7	8	3	31	51	53	15	.213	.316
Frank Thomas	OF118	R	24	128	455	68	116	22	1	30	102	50	93	1	.255	.505
Mike Sandlock	C64	B	37	64	186	10	43	5	0	0	12	12	19	0	.231	.258
Paul Smith	1B74, OF19	L	22	118	389	41	110	12	7	4	44	24	23	2	.283	.380
Dick Cole	SS77, 2B7, 1B1	R	27	97	235	29	64	13	1	0	23	38	26	2	.272	.336
2 Hal Rice	OF70	L	29	78	286	39	89	16	1	4	42	17	22	0	.311	.416
Eddie Pellagrini	2B31, 3B12, SS3	R	35	78	174	16	44	3	2	4	19	14	20	1	.253	.362
1 Johnny Lindell	P27, 1B2	R	36	58	91	11	26	6	1	4	15	16	15	0	.286	.505
2 Toby Atwell	C45	L	29	53	139	11	34	6	0	0	17	20	12	0	.245	.288
1 Pete Castiglione	3B43	R	32	45	159	14	33	2	1	4	21	5	14	1	.208	.308
Vic Janowicz	C35	R	23	42	123	10	31	3	1	2	8	5	31	0	.252	.341
1 Ralph Kiner	OF41	R	30	41	148	27	40	6	1	7	29	25	21	1	.270	.446
2 Gene Hermanski	OF13	L	33	41	62	7	11	0	0	1	8	8	14	0	.177	.226
Felipe Montemayor	OF12	L	25	28	55	5	6	1	0	1	5	6	13	0	.109	.182
1 Joe Garagiola	C22	L	27	27	73	9	17	5	0	2	14	10	11	1	.233	.384
1 Catfish Metkovich	1B5, OF4	L	31	26	41	5	6	1	0	1	6	6	3	0	.146	.268
Dick Smith	SS13	R	25	13	43	4	7	1	0	0	3	2	6	0	.163	.209
Brandy Davis	OF9	L	25	12	39	5	8	2	0	0	1	3	11	4	.205	.256

Dick Hall 22 R 4-24, Nick Koback 17 R 2-16, Pete Naton (MS) 21 R 2-12, 1 Ed Fitz Gerald 29 R 2-17, 2 Bob Addis 27 L 0-3, Jack Shepard 22 R 1-4, Clem Koshorek 28 R 0-1, Tony Bartirome (MS) 21, Dick Groat (MS) 22, Jim Mangan (MS) 23

NAME	T	AGE	W	L	PCT	SV	G	GS	CG	IP	H	BB	SO	SHO	ERA
		28	50	104	.325	10	154	154	49	1358	1529	577	607	4	5.22
Murry Dickson	R	36	10	19	.345	4	45	26	10	201	240	58	88	1	4.52
Bob Friend	R	22	8	11	.421	0	32	24	8	171	193	57	66	0	4.89
Paul LaPalme	L	29	8	16	.333	2	35	24	7	176	191	64	86	1	4.60
Roy Face	R	25	6	8	.429	0	41	13	2	119	145	30	56	0	6.58
1 Johnny Lindell	R	36	5	16	.238	0	27	23	13	176	173	116*	102	1	4.70
Jim Waugh	R	19	4	5	.444	0	29	11	1	90	108	60	42	0	6.50
Johnny Hetki	R	31	3	6	.333	3	54	2	0	118	120	33	37	0	3.97
Bob Hall	R	29	3	12	.200	1	37	17	6	152	172	72	68	1	5.39
1 Howie Pollet	L	32	1	1	.500	0	5	2	0	13	27	6	8	0	10.38
Cal Hogue	R	25	1	1	.500	0	12	3	2	22	19	16	10	0	5.21
Paul Pettit	L	21	1	2	.333	0	10	5	0	28	33	20	14	0	7.71
Bill Macdonald	R	24	0	1	.000	0	4	1	0	12	8	4	2	0	12.86
2 Bob Schultz	L	29	0	0	.000	0	11	2	0	19	26	10	5	0	8.05
Roger Bowman	L	25	0	4	.000	0	30	2	0	65	65	29	36	0	4.85
Woody Main	R	31	0	0	—	0	2	0	0	4	5	2	4	0	11.25
Bill Bell (MS) 19															
Ron Kline (MS) 21															
Bill Koski (MS) 21															
Vern Law (MS) 23															
Ron Necciai (MS) 21															

*Lindell, also with Philadelphia, league leader in BB with 139.

WORLD SERIES —NEW YORK (AL) 4 BROOKLYN (NL) 2

LINE SCORES

Game 1 September 30 at New York

TEAM	1	2	3	4	5	6	7	8	9	10	11	12	R	H	E
BKN (NL)	0	0	0	1	3	1	0	0	—				5	12	2
NY	4	0	0	0	1	0	1	3	X				9	12	0

Erskine, Hughes (2), Reynolds, **Sain** (6)
Labine (6), Wade (7)

Game 2 October 1 at New York

BKN	0	0	0	2	0	0	0	0	0				2	9	1
NY	1	0	0	0	0	0	1	2	X				4	5	0

Roe   Lopat

Game 3 October 2 at Brooklyn

NY	0	0	0	0	1	0	0	1	0				2	6	0
BKN	0	0	0	0	1	1	0	1	X				3	9	0

Raschi   **Erskine**

Game 4 October 3 at Brooklyn

NY	0	0	0	0	2	0	0	0	1				3	9	0
BKN	3	0	0	1	0	2	1	0	X				7	12	0

Ford, Gorman (2), **Loes**, Labine (9)
Sain (5), Schallock (7)

Game 5 October 4 at Brooklyn

NY	1	0	5	0	0	0	3	1	1				11	11	1
BKN	0	1	0	0	1	0	0	4	1				7	14	1

McDonald, Kuzava (8), **Podres**, Meyer (3),
Reynolds (9) Wade (8), Black (9)

Game 6 October 5 at New York

BKN	0	0	0	0	0	1	0	0	2				3	8	3
NY	2	1	0	0	0	0	0	1					4	13	0

Erskine, Milliken (5), Ford, **Reynolds** (8)
Labine (7)

COMPOSITE BATTING

New York (AL)

NAME	POS	G	AB	R	H	2B	3B	HR	RBI	BA
Totals		6	201	33	56	6	4	9	32	.279
Martin	2B	6	24	5	12	1	2	2	8	.500
Mantle	OF	6	24	3	5	0	0	2	7	.208
McDougald	3B	6	24	2	4	0	1	1	2	.167
Collins	1B	6	24	4	4	1	0	1	2	.167
Bauer	OF	6	23	6	6	1	0	0	1	.261
Berra	C	6	21	3	9	1	0	1	4	.429
Woodling	OF	6	20	5	6	0	0	1	3	.300
Rizzuto	SS	6	19	4	6	1	0	0	3	.316
Ford	P	2	3	0	1	0	0	0	0	.333
Lopat	P	1	3	0	0	0	0	0	0	.000
Mize	PH	3	3	0	0	0	0	0	0	.000
McDonald	P	1	2	0	1	0	0	0	1	.500
Reynolds	P	3	2	0	1	0	0	0	0	.500
Sain	P	2	2	1	1	0	0	0	2	.500
Bollweg	1B	2	2	0	0	0	0	0	0	.000
Raschi	P	1	2	0	0	0	0	0	0	.000
Noren	PH	2	1	0	0	0	0	0	0	.000

Gorman P 0-1, Kuzava P 0-1, Schallock P 0-0

Brooklyn (NL)

NAME	POS	G	AB	R	H	2B	3B	HR	RBI	BA
Totals		6	213	27	64	13	1	8	26	.300
Gilliam	2B	6	27	4	8	3	0	2	4	.296
Snider	OF	6	25	3	8	3	0	1	5	.320
Robinson	OF	6	25	3	8	2	0	0	2	.320
Furillo	OF	6	24	4	8	2	0	1	4	.333
Reese	SS	6	24	0	5	0	1	0	1	.208
Cox	3B	6	23	3	7	3	0	0	6	.304
Hodges	1B	6	22	3	8	1	0	1	9	.364
Campanella	C	6	22	6	6	0	0	1	2	.273
Erskine	P	3	4	0	1	0	0	0	0	.250
Loes	P	1	3	0	2	0	0	0	0	.667
Roe	P	1	3	0	0	0	0	0	0	.000
Williams	PH	3	2	0	1	0	0	0	0	.500
Labine	P	2	2	0	0	0	0	0	0	.000
Belardi	PH	2	1	0	0	0	0	0	0	.000
Shuba	PH	3	1	0	1	0	0	0	1	1.000
Podres	P	1	1	0	0	0	0	0	0	.000
Hughes	P	2	1	0	0	0	0	0	0	.000
Meyer	P	1	1	0	0	0	0	0	0	.000
Morgan	PH	1	1	0	0	0	0	0	0	.000
Thompson	OF	2	0	0	0	0	0	0	0	.000

Black P 0-0, Milliken P 0-0, Wade P 0-0

COMPOSITE PITCHING

New York (AL)

NAME	G	IP	H	BB	SO	W	L	SV	ERA
Totals	6	52	64	15	30	4	2	1	4.50
Lopat	1	9	9	4	3	1	0	0	2.00
Raschi	2	8	9	3	4	1	1	0	3.38
Ford	2	8	9	2	7	0	1	0	4.50
Reynolds	3	8	9	4	9	1	1	0	6.75
McDonald	1	7.2	12	0	3	1	0	0	5.87
Sain	2	5.2	6	1	3	0	0	0	4.76
Gorman	1	3	4	0	1	0	0	0	3.00
Schallock	1	2	1	1	0	0	0	0	4.50
Kuzava	1	0.2	1	0	1	0	0	0	13.50

Brooklyn (NL)

NAME	G	IP	H	BB	SO	W	L	SV	ERA
Totals	6	51.1	56	25	43	2	4	1	4.91
Erskine	3	14	14	9	16	1	1	0	5.79
Loes	1	8	5	2	8	1	0	0	3.38
Roe	1	8	5	4	4	1	0	0	4.50
Labine	3	5	10	1	3	0	2	1	3.60
Meyer	1	4.1	4	1	5	0	0	0	6.23
Hughes	2	4	3	1	0	0	0	0	2.25
Podres	1	2.2	1	2	3	0	1	0	3.38
Wade	2	2.1	4	1	2	0	0	0	15.43
Milliken	1	2	2	1	0	1	0	0	0.00
Black	1	1	2	0	1	0	1	0	9.00

1954 The Year the Indians Almost Took It All Apart

There were two notable absences as the season opened. Chuck Dressen, after leading the Dodgers to two straight pennants, demanded a three-year contract from owner Walter O'Malley and was promptly fired. In his place came Walter Alston, an unassuming man with one major league at-bat to his credit. The other vacancy was in St. Louis. After the 1953 season, financially plagued Bill Veeck sold the team to a syndicate which moved the club to Baltimore—a town that hadn't been in the majors since 1902, when the franchise had been moved to New York.

Beyond the franchise shifts, which were beginning to unsettle baseball's grinning complacency, there was a more immediate problem to handle. Could anyone loosen the Yankees' grip on the pennant? After five years of dominance, people were beginning to wonder if Casey Stengel had a contract with some higher authority than the Yankee owners. As it turned out, Casey proved mortal, even though the Yankees registered 103 victories—more than any of his previous five pennant winners could claim. But the Cleveland Indians, with Bobby Avila, Larry Doby, and Al Rosen, plus pitchers Early Wynn, Bob Lemon, Mike Garcia, and Bob Feller, set a torrid pace and won 111 games to set a new American League record.

Part of the story of Cleveland's victory was pitching. While some of the Yankees hurlers were beginning to show signs of age, Cleveland came up with rookies Don Mossi and Ray Narleski, who accounted for nine wins and 20 saves, and Hal Newhouser, who decided not to retire and chalked up a 7-2 record with seven saves. Also, getting Vic Wertz from Baltimore and putting him on first base did no harm. The Yankees had to be content with an MVP performance from catcher Yogi Berra and 20 wins from rookie Bob Grim.

In the National League, the Dodgers were expected to repeat. Instead, the 1953 fifth-place Giants surprised everyone by winning the flag by five games over Brooklyn. The return of Willie Mays, after two years in the army, and the trade to the Braves of outfielder Bobby Thomson for pitcher Johnny Antonelli made the difference. While Mays got red hot after the All-Star-break and hit 41 home runs to win MVP honors, Antonelli came through with 21 wins and a league-low 2.29 E.R.A. Ruben Gomez and Sal Maglie also proved reliable starters, but the main thrust came from the bullpen, where Marv Grissom and Hoyt Wilhelm combined to win 22 games and save 26 more. Brooklyn's near miss could be traced to their pitching, especially Don Newcombe, who returned from the service and won only nine, and a hand injury to catcher Roy Campanella, which dropped his average by 105 points.

One departure and several new arrivals also added to the story of 1954. Arnold Johnson bought out the interests of Connie Mack and his family and transplanted the Philadelphia Athletics to Kansas City for the start of the 1955 season. In Milwaukee, Bobby Thomson broke an ankle and forced the Braves to try a young infielder by the name of Hank Aaron in left field. Wally Moon hit well enough for the Cardinals to cause them to trade Enos Slaughter to the Yankees, while Ernie Banks took over as shortstop for the Cubs and Al Kaline right field for the Tigers.

The World Series only lasted for four games, mostly because of the Giants' Mays and their ace pinch hitter Dusty Rhodes. In the first game, with the score knotted at 2-2 and two men on, Wertz of the Indians hit a booming fly ball to the deepest caverns of the Polo Grounds. Mays tore full speed with his back to the plate and caught the drive over his shoulder some 460 feet from home plate. Rhodes capped the game in the tenth inning with a three run pinch-hit homer. In the second game, Rhodes again provided the heroics with a pinch-hit single that tied the game before delivering an insurance homer in the seventh. The third game was again Rhodes', as he came in with the bases loaded and singled to score two runs to give the Giants a 3-0 lead in a 6-2 finale. The last game was all the Giants'. They jumped on the Indians for seven runs to capture the first championship for the National League since 1946.

1954 AMERICAN LEAGUE

NAME	G by Pos	B	AGE	G	AB	R	H	2B	3B	HR	RBI	BB	SO	SB	BA	SA
CLEVELAND	1st 111-43 .721	AL LOPEZ														
	TOTALS		30	156	5222	746	1368	188	39	156	714	637	668	30	.262	.403
2 Vic Wertz	1B83, OF5	L	29	94	295	33	81	14	2	14	48	34	40	0	.275	.484
Bobby Avila	2B141, SS7	R	30	143	555	112	189	27	2	15	67	59	31	9	.341	.477
George Strickland (BJ)	SS112	R	28	112	361	42	77	12	3	6	37	55	62	2	.213	.313
Al Rosen	3B87, 1B46, 2B1, SS1	R	30	137	466	76	140	20	2	24	102	85	43	6	.300	.506
Dave Philley	OF129	B	34	133	452	48	102	13	3	12	60	57	48	2	.226	.347
Larry Doby	OF153	L	30	153	577	94	157	18	4	32	126	85	94	3	.272	.484
Al Smith	OF109, 3B21, SS4	R	26	131	481	101	135	29	6	11	50	88	65	2	.281	.435
Jim Hegan	C137	R	33	139	423	56	99	12	7	11	40	34	48	0	.234	.374
Bill Glynn	1B96, OF1	L	29	111	171	19	43	3	2	5	18	12	21	3	.251	.380
Wally Westlake	OF70	R	33	85	240	36	63	9	2	11	42	26	37	0	.263	.454
Sam Dente	SS60, 2B7	R	32	68	169	18	45	7	1	1	19	14	4	0	.266	.337
Rudy Regalado	3B50, 2B2	R	24	65	180	21	45	5	0	2	24	19	16	0	.250	.311
Dave Pope	OF29	L	33	60	102	21	30	2	1	4	13	10	22	2	.294	.451
Hank Majeski	2B25, 3B10	R	37	57	121	10	34	4	0	3	17	7	14	0	.281	.388
Dale Mitchell	OF6, 1B1	L	32	53	60	6	17	1	0	1	6	9	1	0	.283	.350
Hal Naragon	C45	L	25	46	101	10	24	2	2	0	12	9	12	0	.238	.297

Mickey Grasso 34 R 2-6, Luke Easter 38 L 1-6, Rocky Nelson 29 L 0-4, Joe Ginsberg 27 L 1-2, Jim Dyck 32 R 1-1, 1 Bob Kennedy 33 R 0-0

NAME		T	AGE	W	L	PCT	SV	G	GS	CG	IP	H	BB	SO	SHO	ERA
			30	111	43	.721	36	156	156	77	1419	1220	486	678	12	2.78
Bob Lemon		R	33	23	7	.767	0	36	33	21	258	228	92	110	2	2.72
Early Wynn		R	34	23	11	.676	2	40	36	20	271	225	83	155	3	2.72
Mike Garcia		R	30	19	8	.704	5	45	34	13	259	220	71	129	5	2.64
Art Houtteman		R	26	15	7	.682	0	32	25	11	188	198	59	68	1	3.35
Bob Feller		R	35	13	3	.813	0	19	19	9	140	127	39	59	1	3.09
Hal Newhouser		L	33	7	2	.778	7	26	1	0	47	34	18	25	0	2.49
Don Mossi		L	25	6	1	.857	7	40	5	2	93	56	39	55	0	1.94
Ray Narleski		R	25	3	3	.500	13	42	2	1	89	59	44	52	0	2.22
1 Bob Chakales		R	26	2	0	1.000	0	3	0	0	10	4	12	3	0	0.90
Dave Hoskins		R	28	0	1	.000	0	14	1	0	27	29	10	9	0	3.00
Bob Hooper		R	32	0	0	—	2	17	0	0	35	39	16	12	0	4.89
Jose Santiago		R	25	0	0	—	0	1	0	0	2	1	1	0	0	0.00
Dick Tomanek		L	23	0	0	—	0	1	0	0	2	1	1	0	0	4.50

NAME	G by Pos	B	AGE	G	AB	R	H	2B	3B	HR	RBI	BB	SO	SB	BA	SA
NEW YORK	2nd 103-51 .669 8	CASEY STENGEL														
	TOTALS		28	155	5226	805	1400	215	59	133	747	650	632	34	.268	.408
Joe Collins	1B117	L	31	130	343	67	93	20	2	12	46	51	37	2	.271	.446
Gil McDougald	2B92, 3B35	R	26	126	394	66	102	22	2	12	48	47	51	12	.259	.416
Phil Rizzuto	SS126, 2B1	R	36	127	307	47	60	11	0	2	15	41	23	3	.195	.251
Andy Carey	3B120	R	22	122	411	60	124	14	6	8	65	43	68	5	.302	.423
Hank Bauer	OF108	R	31	114	377	73	111	16	5	12	54	40	42	4	.294	.459
Mickey Mantle	OF144, SS4, 2B1	B	22	146	543	129	163	17	12	27	102	102	107	5	.300	.525
Irv Noren	OF116, 1B1	L	29	125	426	70	136	21	6	12	66	43	38	4	.319	.481
Yogi Berra	C149, 3B1	L	29	151	584	88	179	28	6	22	125	56	29	0	.307	.488
Jerry Coleman	2B79, SS30, 3B1	R	29	107	300	39	65	7	1	3	21	29	29	3	.217	.277
Gene Woodling (HJ)	OF89	L	31	97	304	33	76	12	5	3	40	53	35	3	.250	.352
Willie Miranda	SS88, 2B4, 3B1	B	28	92	116	12	29	4	2	1	12	10	10	0	.250	.345
Bill Skowron	1B61, 3B5, 2B2	R	23	87	215	37	73	12	9	7	41	19	18	2	.340	.577
Eddie Robinson	1B29	L	33	85	142	11	37	9	0	3	27	19	21	0	.261	.387
Enos Slaughter (BW)	OF30	L	38	69	125	19	31	4	2	1	19	28	8	0	.248	.336
Bob Cerv	OF24	R	28	56	100	14	26	6	1	3	13	11	17	0	.260	.470
Bobby Brown (MS)	3B17	L	29	28	60	5	13	1	0	1	7	8	3	0	.217	.283
Charlie Silvera	C18	R	29	20	37	1	10	1	0	0	4	3	2	0	.270	.297
Frank Leja	1B6	L	18	12	5	2	1	0	0	0	0	0	1	0	.200	.200

Lou Berberet 24 L 2-5, Woodie Held 22 R 0-3, Gus Triandos 23 R 0-1, Ralph Houk 34 R 0-1, Billy Martin (MS) 26

NAME		T	AGE	W	L	PCT	SV	G	GS	CG	IP	H	BB	SO	SHO	ERA
			30	103	51	.669	37	155	155	51	1379	1284	552	655	16	3.26
Bob Grim		R	24	20	6	.769	0	37	20	8	199	175	85	108	1	3.26
Whitey Ford		L	25	16	8	.667	1	34	28	11	211	170	101	125	3	2.82
Allie Reynolds		R	39	13	4	.765	7	36	18	5	157	133	66	100	4	3.32
Ed Lopat		L	36	12	4	.750	0	26	23	7	170	189	33	54	0	3.55
Tom Morgan		R	24	11	5	.688	1	32	17	7	143	149	40	34	4	3.34
Harry Byrd		R	29	9	7	.563	0	25	21	5	132	131	43	52	1	3.00
Johnny Sain		R	36	6	6	.500	22	45	0	0	77	66	15	33	0	3.16
Jim McDonald (GJ)		R	27	4	1	.800	0	16	10	3	71	54	45	20	1	3.17
2 Marlin Stuart		R	35	3	0	1.000	1	10	0	0	18	28	12	2	0	5.50
Bob Wiesler		L	23	3	2	.600	0	5	5	0	30	28	30	25	0	4.20
Tommy Byrne		L	34	3	2	.600	0	5	5	4	40	36	19	24	1	2.70
2 Ralph Branca		R	28	1	0	1.000	0	5	3	0	13	9	13	7	0	2.77
2 Jim Konstanty		R	37	1	1	.500	2	7	0	0	18	11	6	3	0	1.00
1 Bob Kuzava		L	31	1	3	.250	1	20	3	0	40	46	18	22	0	5.40
Art Schallock		L	30	0	1	.000	0	6	1	1	17	20	11	9	0	4.24
Bill Miller		L	26	0	1	.000	0	2	1	0	6	9	1	6	0	6.00
Tom Gorman		R	29	0	0	—	2	23	0	0	37	30	14	31	0	2.19

NAME	G by Pos	B	AGE	G	AB	R	H	2B	3B	HR	RBI	BB	SO	SB	BA	SA
CHICAGO	3rd 94-60 .610 17	PAUL RICHARDS 91-54 .628		MARTY MARION 3-6 .333												
	TOTALS		30	155	5168	711	1382	203	47	94	655	604	536	98	.267	.379
Ferris Fain (KJ)	1B64	L	33	65	235	30	71	10	1	5	51	40	14	5	.302	.417
Nellie Fox	2B155	L	26	155	631	111	201	24	8	2	47	51	12	16	.319	.391
Chico Carrasquel	SS155	R	26	155	620	106	158	28	3	12	62	85	67	7	.255	.368
Cass Michaels (FS)	3B91, 2B2	B	28	101	282	35	74	13	2	7	44	56	31	10	.262	.397
Jim Rivera	OF143	L	31	145	490	62	140	16	8	13	61	49	68	18	.286	.431
Johnny Groth	OF125	R	27	125	422	41	116	20	0	7	60	42	37	3	.275	.372
Minnie Minoso	OF146, 3B9	R	31	153	568	119	182	29	18	19	116	77	46	18	.320	.535
Sherm Lollar	C93	R	29	107	316	31	77	13	0	7	34	37	28	0	.244	.351
2 George Kell (KJ)	1B32, 3B31, OF2	R	31	71	233	25	66	10	0	5	48	18	12	1	.283	.391
Phil Cavarretta	1B44, OF9	L	37	71	158	21	50	6	0	3	24	26	12	4	.316	.411
Freddie Marsh	3B36, SS3, 1B2, OF1	R	30	62	98	21	30	5	2	0	4	9	16	4	.306	.398
2 Matt Batts	C42	R	32	55	158	16	36	7	1	3	19	17	15	0	.228	.342
Willard Marshall	OF29	L	33	47	71	7	18	2	0	1	7	11	9	0	.254	.324
Carl Sawatski	C33	L	26	43	109	6	20	3	3	1	12	15	20	0	.183	.294
2 Ed McGhee	OF34	R	29	42	75	12	17	1	0	0	5	12	8	5	.227	.240
Ron Jackson	1B35	R	20	40	93	10	26	4	0	4	10	6	20	2	.280	.452
Bob Boyd	OF13, 1B12	L	34	29	56	10	10	3	0	0	5	4	3	2	.179	.232
1 Bill Wilson	OF19	R	25	20	35	4	6	1	0	2	5	5	9	1	.171	.371
Bud Stewart	OF2	L	38	18	13	0	1	0	0	0	0	3	2	0	.077	.077
2 Grady Hatton	3B10, 1B3	L	31	13	30	5	5	2	0	0	4	6	3	1	.167	.200
Joe Kirrene	3B9	R	22	9	23	4	7	1	0	0	4	5	0	0	.304	.348

1 Red Wilson 25 R 4-20, Don Nicholas 23 L 0-0, 2 Stan Jok 28 R 2-12, Bob Cain 29 L 0-0, Sammy Esposito (MS) 22

NAME		T	AGE	W	L	PCT	SV	G	GS	CG	IP	H	BB	SO	SHO	ERA
			30	94	60	.610	3	155	155	60	1383	1255	517	701	23	3.05
Virgil Trucks		R	37	19	12	.613	3	40	33	16	265	224	95	152	5	2.78
Sandy Consuegra		R	33	16	3	.842	3	39	17	3	154	142	35	31	2	2.69
Bob Keegan		R	33	16	9	.640	2	31	27	14	210	211	82	61	2	3.09
Jack Harshman		R	26	14	8	.636	1	35	21	9	177	157	96	134	4	2.95
Billy Pierce		L	27	9	10	.474	3	36	26	12	189	179	86	148	4	3.48
Don Johnson		R	27	8	7	.533	7	46	16	3	144	129	43	68	3	3.13
Harry Dorish		R	32	6	4	.600	6	37	6	2	109	88	29	48	1	2.72
2 Morrie Martin		L	31	5	4	.556	5	35	2	1	70	52	24	31	0	2.06
Mike Fornieles		R	22	4	4	.333	1	15	6	0	42	41	14	18	0	4.29
1 Al Sima		L	32	1	0	1.000	1	15	0	0	7	11	2	1	0	5.14
Dick Strahs		R	30	0	0	—	1	9	0	0	14	16	8	8	0	5.79
Tom Flanigan		L	19	0	0	—	0	2	0	0	2	1	1	0	0	0.00
Vito Valentinetti		R	25	0	0	—	0	1	0	0	1	4	2	1	0	54.00

BOSTON — 4th 69-85 .448 42 — LOU BOUDREAU

NAME	G by Pos	B	AGE	G	AB	R	H	2B	3B	HR	RBI	BB	SO	SB	BA	SA
TOTALS			26	156	5399	700	1436	244	41	123	657	654	660	51	.266	.395
Harry Agganis	1B119	L	25	132	434	54	109	13	8	11	57	47	57	6	.251	.394
Ted Lepcio	2B80,3B24,SS14	R	23	116	398	42	102	19	4	8	45	42	62	3	.256	.384
Milt Bolling	SS107,3B5	R	23	113	370	42	92	20	3	6	36	47	55	2	.249	.368
3 Grady Hatton	3B93,SS1,1B1	L	31	99	302	40	85	12	3	5	33	58	25	1	.281	.391
Jimmy Piersall	OF126	R	24	133	474	77	135	24	2	8	38	36	42	5	.285	.395
Jackie Jensen	OF151	R	27	152	580	92	160	25	7	25	117	79	52	22	.276	.472
Ted Williams (BC)	OF115	L	35	117	386	93	133	23	1	29	89	136	32	0	.345	.635
Sammy White	C133	R	26	137	493	46	139	25	2	14	75	21	50	1	.282	.426
Billy Goodman	2B72,1B27,OF13,3B12	L	28	127	489	71	148	25	4	1	36	51	15	3	.303	.376
Karl Olson (MS)	OF23	R	23	101	227	25	59	12	2	1	20	12	23	2	.260	.344
Billy Consolo	SS50,3B18,2B12	R	19	91	242	23	55	7	1	1	11	33	69	2	.227	.277
Charlie Maxwell	OF27	L	27	74	104	9	26	4	1	0	5	12	21	3	.250	.308
2 Don Lenhardt	OF13,3B1	R	31	44	66	5	18	4	0	3	17	3	9	0	.273	.470
2 Sam Mele	1B22,OF4	R	32	42	132	22	42	6	0	7	23	12	12	0	.318	.523
Mickey Owen	C30	R	38	32	68	6	16	3	0	1	11	9	6	0	.235	.324
1 George Kell	3B25	R	31	26	93	15	24	3	0	0	10	15	3	0	.258	.290
Del Wilber	C18	R	35	24	61	2	8	2	1	1	7	4	6	0	.131	.246
1 Floyd Baker	3B7,2B1	L	37	21	20	1	4	2	0	0	3	0	1	0	.200	.300
Dick Gernert	1B6	R	25	14	23	2	6	2	0	0	1	6	4	0	.261	.348

1 Hoot Evers 33 R 0-8, Guy Morton 23 R 0-1, Faye Throneberry (MS) 23

NAME	T	AGE	W	L	PCT	SV	G	GS	CG	IP	H	BB	SO	SHO	ERA
		28	69	85	.448	22	156	156	41	1412	1434	612	707	10	4.02
Frank Sullivan	R	24	15	12	.556	1	36	26	11	206	185	66	124	3	3.15
Willard Nixon	R	26	11	12	.478	0	31	30	8	200	182	87	102	2	4.05
Tom Brewer	R	22	10	9	.526	0	33	23	7	163	152	95	69	0	4.64
Ellis Kinder	R	39	8	8	.500	15	48	2	0	107	106	36	47	0	3.62
Russ Kemmerer	R	22	5	3	.625	0	19	9	2	75	71	41	37	1	3.50
Leo Kiely	L	24	5	8	.385	0	28	19	4	131	153	58	59	1	3.50
Sid Hudson	R	39	3	4	.429	0	21	3	0	71	83	30	27	0	4.44
Bill Henry	L	27	3	3	.500	0	24	13	3	96	104	49	38	1	4.50
Mel Parnell (BA)	L	32	3	7	.300	0	19	15	4	92	104	35	38	1	3.72
Tom Hurd	R	30	2	0	1.000	1	16	0	0	30	21	12	14	0	3.00
Tex Clevenger	R	21	2	4	.333	0	23	8	1	68	67	29	43	0	4.76
Tom Herrin	R	24	1	2	.333	0	14	1	0	28	34	12	8	0	7.39
Hal Brown	R	29	1	8	.111	0	40	5	1	118	126	41	66	0	4.12
Bill Werle	L	33	0	1	.000	0	14	0	0	25	41	10	14	0	4.32
Joe Dobson	R	37	0	1	—	0	2	0	0	3	5	1	1	0	6.00

Dick Brodowski (MS) 21

DETROIT — 5th 68-86 .442 43 — FRED HUTCHINSON

NAME	G by Pos	B	AGE	G	AB	R	H	2B	3B	HR	RBI	BB	SO	SB	BA	SA
TOTALS			25	155	5233	584	1351	215	41	90	552	492	603	48	.258	.367
Walt Dropo	1B95	R	31	107	320	27	90	14	2	4	44	24	41	0	.281	.375
Frank Bolling	2B113	R	22	117	368	46	87	15	2	6	38	36	51	3	.236	.337
Harvey Kuenn	SS155	R	23	155	656	81	201	28	6	5	48	29	13	9	.306	.390
Ray Boone	3B148,SS1	R	30	148	543	76	160	19	7	20	85	71	53	4	.295	.466
Al Kaline	OF135	R	19	138	504	42	139	18	3	4	43	22	45	9	.276	.347
Bill Tuttle	OF145	R	24	147	530	64	141	20	11	7	58	62	60	5	.266	.385
Jim Delsing	OF108	L	28	122	371	39	92	24	2	6	38	49	38	4	.248	.372
Frank House	C107	L	24	114	352	35	88	12	1	9	38	31	34	2	.250	.366
Bob Nieman	OF62	R	27	91	251	24	66	14	1	8	35	22	32	0	.263	.422
2 Wayne Belardi	1B79	L	23	88	250	27	58	7	1	11	35	24	34	1	.232	.400
Fred Hatfield	2B54,3B15	L	29	81	218	31	64	12	0	2	25	28	24	4	.294	.376
Red Wilson	C53	R	25	54	170	22	48	11	1	2	22	27	12	3	.282	.394
Reno Bertoia	2B15,3B8,SS3	R	19	54	37	13	6	2	0	1	2	5	9	1	.162	.297
Don Lund	OF31	R	31	35	54	4	7	2	0	0	3	4	3	0	.130	.167
3 Hoot Evers	OF24	R	33	34	60	5	11	4	0	0	5	8	1		.183	.250
Steve Souchock (BW)	OF9,3B2	R	35	25	39	6	7	0	1	3	8	2	10	1	.179	.462
1 Charlie Kress	1B7,OF1	L	32	24	37	4	7	0	1	0	3	1	4	0	.189	.243
1 Johnny Pesky	3B2	L	34	20	17	5	3	0	0	1	1	3	1	0	.176	.353
1 Matt Batts	C8	R	32	12	21	1	6	1	0	0	5	2	4	0	.286	.333
Charlie King	OF7	R	23	11	28	4	6	0	1	0	3	3	8	0	.214	.286

Al Lakeman 35 R 0-6, George Bullard 25 R 0-1, Walt Streuli 18 R 0-0.

NAME	T	AGE	W	L	PCT	SV	G	GS	CG	IP	H	BB	SO	SHO	ERA
		26	68	86	.442	13	155	155	58	1383	1375	506	603	13	3.81
Steve Gromek	R	34	18	16	.529	1	36	32	17	253	236	57	102	4	2.74
Ned Garver	R	28	14	11	.560	1	35	32	16	246	216	62	93	3	2.82
2 George Zuverink	R	29	9	13	.409	4	35	25	9	203	201	62	70	2	3.59
Billy Hoeft	L	22	7	15	.318	1	34	25	10	175	180	59	114	4	4.58
Dick Marlowe	R	25	5	4	.556	2	38	2	0	84	76	40	39	0	4.18
Al Aber	L	26	5	11	.313	3	32	18	4	125	121	40	54	0	3.96
1 Ralph Branca	R	28	3	3	.500	0	17	5	0	45	63	30	15	0	5.80
Ted Gray (AJ)	L	29	3	5	.375	0	19	10	2	72	70	56	29	0	5.38
Ray Herbert	R	24	3	3	.333	0	42	4	0	84	114	50	44	0	5.86
Bob Miller	L	18	1	1	.500	1	32	1	0	70	62	26	27	0	2.44
Dick Weik	R	26	0	0	.000	0	16			23	16		9	0	7.31
Frank Lary	R	24	0	0	—	0	3	0	0	6	9	5	2	0	2.25
Dick Donovan	R	26	0	0	—	0	2	0	0	6	6	5	2	0	10.50

Bill Black (MS) 21

WASHINGTON — 6th 66-88 .429 45 — BUCKY HARRIS

NAME	G by Pos	B	AGE	G	AB	R	H	2B	3B	HR	RBI	BB	SO	SB	BA	SA
TOTALS			29	155	5249	632	1292	188	69	81	592	610	719	37	.246	.355
Mickey Vernon	1B148	L	36	151	597	90	173	33	14	20	97	61	61	1	.290	.492
Wayne Terwilliger	2B90,3B10,SS3	R	29	106	337	42	70	10	1	3	24	32	40	3	.208	.270
Pete Runnels	SS107,2B27,OF1	L	26	139	481	75	131	17	15	3	56	78	60	2	.268	.383
Eddie Yost	3B155	R	27	155	539	101	138	26	4	11	47	131	71	7	.256	.380
Tommy Umphlett	OF101	R	24	114	342	21	75	8	3	1	33	17	42	1	.219	.269
Jim Busby	OF155	R	27	155	628	83	187	22	7	7	80	43	56	17	.298	.389
Roy Sievers	OF133,1B8	R	27	145	514	75	119	26	6	24	102	80	77	2	.232	.446
Ed Fitz Gerald	C107	R	30	115	360	33	104	13	5	4	40	33	22	0	.289	.386
Tom Wright	OF43	L	30	76	171	13	42	4	4	1	17	18	38	1	.246	.333
Jerry Snyder	SS48,2B3	R	24	64	154	17	36	3	1	0	17	15	18	3	.234	.266
Clyde Vollmer	OF26	R	32	62	117	8	30	4	0	2	15	12	28	0	.256	.342
Joe Tipton	C52	R	32	54	157	9	35	6	1	1	10	30	30	1	.223	.293
Mickey McDermott	P30	L	25	54	99	7	19	3	0	0	4	7	12	0	.200	.232
2 Johnny Pesky	2B37,SS1	L	34	49	158	17	40	4	3	0	9	10	7	1	.253	.316
Jim Lemon	OF33	R	26	38	120	12	30	2	3	2	13	9	34	0	.234	.344
Mel Hoderlein	SS6,2B5	R	31	14	25	0	4	1	0	0	1	1	4	0	.160	.200
Bob Oldis	C8,3B2	R	26	11	24	0	8	1	0	0	0	1	3	0	.333	.375
Harmon Killebrew	2B3	R	18	9	13	1	4	1	0	0	3	2	3	0	.308	.385
Roy Dietzel	2B7,3B2	R	23	9	21	1	5	0	0	1	1	1	6	0	.238	.238

Carlos Paula 26 R 4-24, Jesse Levan 27 L 3-10, Steve Korcheck 21 R 1-7

NAME	T	AGE	W	L	PCT	SV	G	GS	CG	IP	H	BB	SO	SHO	ERA
		28	66	88	.429	7	155	155	69	1383	1396	573	562	10	3.84
Bob Porterfield	R	30	13	15	.464	0	32	31	21	244	249	77	82	2	3.32
Dean Stone	L	23	12	10	.545	0	31	23	10	179	161	69	87	2	3.22
Johnny Schmitz	L	33	11	8	.579	1	29	23	12	185	176	64	56	2	2.91
Chuck Stobbs	L	24	11	11	.500	0	31	24	10	182	189	67	67	3	4.10
Mickey McDermott	L	25	7	15	.318	1	30	26	11	196	172	110	95	1	3.44
Camilo Pascual	R	20	4	7	.364	3	48	4	1	119	126	61	60	0	4.24
Connie Marrero	R	42	3	6	.333	0	22	8	1	66	74	22	26	0	4.77
Gus Keriazakos	R	22	2	3	.400	0	22	3	2	60	59	30	33	0	3.75
Spec Shea	R	33	2	9	.182	0	23	11	1	71	97	34	22	0	6.21
1 Sonny Dixon	R	29	1	2	.333	1	16*	0	0	30	26	12	7	0	3.00
Bunky Stewart	L	23	0	2	.000	1	29	0	0	51	67	27	27	0	7.59

*Dixon, also with Philadelphia, league leader in G with 54

BALTIMORE — 7th 54-100 .351 57 — JIMMY DYKES

NAME	G by Pos	B	AGE	G	AB	R	H	2B	3B	HR	RBI	BB	SO	SB	BA	SA
TOTALS			30	154	5206	483	1309	195	49	52	451	468	634	30	.251	.338
Eddie Waitkus	1B78	L	34	95	311	35	88	17	4	2	33	28	25	0	.283	.383
Bobby Young	2B127	L	29	130	432	43	106	13	6	4	24	54	42	4	.245	.331
Billy Hunter	SS124	R	26	125	411	28	100	9	5	2	27	21	58	5	.243	.304
Vern Stephens	3B96	R	33	101	365	31	104	17	1	8	46	17	36	0	.285	.403
2 Cal Abrams	OF115	L	30	115	423	67	124	22	7	6	25	72	67	1	.293	.421
Chuck Diering	OF119	R	31	128	418	35	108	14	1	2	29	56	57	3	.258	.311
Gil Coan	OF67	L	32	94	265	29	74	11	2	2	20	16	17	7	.279	.351
Clint Courtney	C111	R	27	122	397	25	107	18	3	4	37	30	7	2	.270	.360
2 Bob Kennedy	3B71,OF21	R	33	106	323	37	81	13	2	6	45	28	43	2	.251	.359
Dick Kryhoski	1B69	L	29	100	302	32	78	13	2	1	34	19	24	0	.260	.327
Jim Fridley	OF67	R	29	85	240	25	59	8	5	4	36	21	41	0	.246	.371
Jim Brideweser	SS48,2B19	R	27	73	204	18	54	7	2	0	12	15	27	1	.265	.319
1 Sam Mele	OF62	R	32	72	230	17	55	9	4	5	32	18	26	1	.239	.378
Les Moss	C38	R	29	50	126	7	31	3	0	0	5	14	16	0	.246	.270
Chico Garcia	2B24	R	29	39	62	6	7	0	2	0	5	6	7	0	.113	.177
1 Vic Wertz	OF27	L	29	29	94	5	19	1	0	1	13	11	17	0	.202	.245
Ray Murray	C21	R	36	22	61	4	15	4	0	0	7	1	5	0	.246	.344
1 Don Lenhardt	OF7,1B2	R	31	13	33	2	5	0	0	0	3	1	4	0	.152	.182
Dick Kokos	OF1	L	26	11	10	1	2	0	0	0	0	0	3	0	.200	.500
Joe Durham	OF10	R	22	10	40	4	9	0	0	2	6	4	9	0	.225	.300
Frank Kellert	1B9	R	27	10	34	3	7	2	0	0	4	4	7	0	.206	.265
Neil Berry	SS5	R	32	5	9	1	1	0	0	0	1	1	1	0	.111	.111

Jay Porter (MS) 21, Frank Saucier (MS) 28

NAME	T	AGE	W	L	PCT	SV	G	GS	CG	IP	H	BB	SO	SHO	ERA
		29	54	100	.351	8	154	154	58	1373	1279	688	668	6	3.88
Bob Turley	R	23	14	15	.483	0	35	35	14	247	178	181	185	0	3.46
Joe Coleman	R	31	13	17	.433	0	33	32	15	221	184	96	103	4	3.50
Duane Pillette	R	31	10	14	.417	0	25	25	11	179	158	67	66	1	3.12
Lou Kretlow	R	33	10	14	.353	0	32	20	5	167	169	82	82	0	4.37
2 Bob Chakales	R	26	3	7	.300	3	38	6	0	89	81	43	44	0	3.74
Don Larsen	R	24	3	21	.125	0	29	28	12	202	213	89	80	1	4.37
Billy O'Dell	L	21	1	1	.500	0	7	2	1	16	15	5	6	0	2.81
Howie Fox	R	33	1	2	.333	2	38	0	0	74	80	34	27	0	3.65
1 Marlin Stuart	R	35	1	3	.333	2	22	0	0	38	46	15	13	0	4.50
2 Bob Kuzava	L	31	1	3	.250	0	4	4	0	24	30	11	15	0	4.71
Mike Blyzka	R	26	1	5	.167	1	27	5	0	86	83	51	35	0	4.71
1 Dave Koslo	L	34	0	1	.000	0	7	0	0	14	20	3	3	0	9.00
Vern Bickford	R	34	0	0	—	0	3	1	0	4	8	5	1	0	9.00
1 Dick Littlefield	L	28	0	0	—	0	2	0	0	5	5	2	0	0	10.50
Jay Heard	L	29	0	0	—	0	2	0	0	3	6	3	2	0	15.00
Ryne Duren	R	25	0	0	—	0	1	0	0	2	3	1	2	0	9.00

PHILADELPHIA — 8th 51-103 .331 60 — EDDIE JOOST

NAME	G by Pos	B	AGE	G	AB	R	H	2B	3B	HR	RBI	BB	SO	SB	BA	SA
TOTALS			29	156	5206	542	1228	191	41	94	503	504	677	30	.236	.342
Lou Limmer	1B79	L	29	115	316	41	73	10	3	14	32	35	57	2	.231	.415
Spook Jacobs	2B131	R	28	132	508	63	131	11	1	0	26	60	22	17	.258	.283
Joe DeMaestri	SS142,3B1,2B1	R	25	146	539	49	124	16	3	8	40	20	63	1	.230	.315
Jim Finigan	3B136	R	29	136	487	57	147	25	6	7	51	64	66	2	.302	.421
Bill Renna	OF115	R	29	123	422	52	98	15	4	13	53	41	60	1	.232	.379
2 Bill Wilson	OF91	R	25	114	323	43	77	10	1	15	53	39	59	1	.238	.415
Vic Power	OF101,1B21,3B1,SS1	R	26	127	462	36	118	19	4	8	38	19	19	2	.255	.366
Joe Astroth	C71	R	31	77	226	22	50	8	1	1	23	21	19	0	.221	.310
Don Bollweg	1B71	L	30	103	268	35	60	15	3	5	24	35	33	1	.224	.358
Gus Zernial (BC)	OF90,1B2	R	31	97	336	42	84	8	2	14	62	30	60	0	.250	.411
Elmer Valo	OF62	L	33	92	228	28	48	11	6	1	33	51	18	2	.214	.330
Pete Suder	2B35,3B20,SS2	R	38	69	205	8	41	11	0	0	16	7	16	0	.200	.263
Jim Robertson	C50	R	26	63	187	9	27	6	0	0	8	23	25	0	.184	.238
Billy Shantz	C51	R	26	51	164	13	42	9	1	1	17	13	23	0	.256	.366
1 Ed McGhee	OF13	R	29	21	55	2	9	1	0	0	4	2	8	0	.208	.258
Eddie Joost	SS9,3B5,2B1	R	38	19	47	9	17	2	1	1	5	10	10	0	.362	.489
Joe Taylor	OF16	R	28	18	58	5	13	1	1	3	6	3	13	0	.224	.328
Jack Littrell	SS9	R	25	14	30	1	9	1	0	0	3	6	4	0	.300	.467

NAME	T	AGE	W	L	PCT	SV	G	GS	CG	IP	H	BB	SO	SHO	ERA
		29	51	103	.331	13	156	156	49	1371	1523	685	555	3	5.18
Arnie Portocarrero	R	27	9	18	.333	0	34	33	16	248	233	114	132	1	4.06
Bob Trice	R	27	7	8	.467	0	19	18	8	119	146	48	22	1	5.60
Alex Kellner	R	29	6	17	.261	0	27	27	8	174	204	88	69	1	5.38
Moe Burtschy	R	32	4	4	.556	4	46	0	0	95	80	53	54	0	3.79
2 Sonny Dixon	R	29	5	11	.417	4	38*	0	1	107	136	27	42	0	4.88
Marion Fricano	R	30	5	11	.313	1	37	4	1	152	163	64	43	0	5.15
Charlie Bishop	R	30	4	1	.400	1	22	7	2	50	53	19	24	0	4.41
John Gray	R	26	3	12	.200	0	18	16	5	105	111	91	51	0	6.51
Morrie Martin	L	32	3	4	.333	0	13	6	2	53	57	19	24	0	5.43
2 Al Sima	R	32	2	5	.286	2	29	7	1	79	101	32	36	0	5.24
Bobby Shantz (SA)	L	28	1	0	1.000	0	2	1	0	18	12	6	7	0	7.88
Dutch Romberger	R	27	1	1	.500	0	11	1	0	39	50	14	20	0	6.46
Art Ditmar	R	25	1	4	.200	0	14	5	0	59	50	36	14	0	6.46
Bill Oster	L	21	0	1	.000	0	8	0	0	17	15	11	6	0	7.00
1 Carl Scheib	R	27	0	1	.000	0	2	1	0	4	11	2	1	0	22.50
Ozzie Van Brabant	R	24	0	1	.000	0	4	1	0	11	19	7	6	0	7.00
Lee Wheat	L	24	0	1	.000	0	2	1	0	8	14	5	7	0	5.79
Bill Upton	R	25	0	0	—	0	2	0	0	2	3	1	2	0	1.80

Dick Rozek 27 L 0-0, Hal Raether 21 R 0-0, Bill Harrington (MS) 26 *Dixon (See Washington)

NEW YORK — 1st 97-57 .630 — LEO DUROCHER

NAME	G by Pos	B	AGE	G	AB	R	H	2B	3B	HR	RBI	BB	SO	SB	BA	SA
TOTALS			28	154	5245	732	1386	194	42	186	701	522	561	30	.264	.424
Whitey Lockman	1B145, OF2	L	27	148	570	73	143	17	3	16	60	59	31	2	.251	.375
Davey Williams	2B142	R	26	142	544	65	121	18	3	9	46	43	33	1	.222	.316
Al Dark	SS154	R	32	154	644	98	189	26	6	20	70	27	40	5	.293	.446
Hank Thompson	3B130, 2B2, OF1	L	28	136	448	76	118	18	1	26	86	90	58	3	.263	.482
Don Mueller	OF153	L	27	153	619	90	212	35	8	4	71	22	17	2	.342	.444
Willie Mays	OF151	R	23	151	565	119	195	33	13	41	110	66	57	8	.345	.667
Monte Irvin	OF128, 3B1, 1B1	R	35	135	432	62	113	13	3	19	64	70	23	7	.262	.438
Wes Westrum	C98	R	31	98	246	25	46	3	1	8	27	45	60	0	.187	.305
Ray Katt	C82	R	27	86	200	26	51	7	1	9	33	19	29	1	.255	.435
Dusty Rhodes	OF37	L	27	82	164	31	56	7	3	15	50	18	25	1	.341	.695
Bobby Hofman	1B21, 2B10, 3B8	R	28	71	125	12	28	5	0	8	30	17	15	0	.224	.456
Billy Gardner	3B30, 2B13, SS5	R	26	62	108	10	23	5	0	1	7	6	19	0	.213	.287
Bill Taylor	OF9	L	24	55	65	4	12	1	0	2	10	3	15	0	.185	.292
Ebba St. Claire	C16	R	32	20	42	5	11	1	0	2	6	12	7	0	.262	.429
Foster Castleman	2B2	R	23	13	12	0	3	0	0	0	1	0	3	0	.250	.250
Joey Amalfitano	3B4, 2B1	R	20	9	5	2	0	0	0	0	0	0	4	0	.000	.000
2 Joe Garagiola	C3	L	28	5	11	1	3	2	0	0	1	1	2	0	.273	.455
Eric Rodin	OF3	R	24	5	6	0	0	0	0	0	0	1	0	0	.000	.000
Harvey Gentry		R	28	5	4	0	1	0	0	0	1	1	0	0	.250	.250
Bob Lennon		L	25	3	3	0	0	0	0	0	0	1	0	0	.000	.000
Daryl Spencer (MS) 24																

NAME	T	AGE	W	L	PCT	SV	G	GS	CG	IP	H	BB	SO	SHO	ERA
		30	97	57	.630	33	154	154	45	1390	1258	613	692	19	3.09
Johnny Antonelli	L	24	21	7	.750	2	39	37	18	259	209	94	152	6	2.29
Ruben Gomez	R	26	17	9	.654	0	37	32	10	222	202	109	106	4	2.88
Sal Maglie	R	37	14	6	.700	2	34	31	9	218	222	70	117	1	3.26
Hoyt Wilhelm	R	31	12	4	.750	7	57	0	0	111	77	52	64	0	2.11
Marv Grissom	R	36	10	7	.588	19	56	3	1	122	100	50	64	1	2.36
Don Liddle	L	29	9	4	.692	0	28	19	4	127	100	55	44	3	4.15
Jim Hearn	R	33	8	8	.500	1	29	18	3	130	137	66	45	2	4.15
Larry Jansen	R	33	2	2	.500	0	13	7	0	41	57	15	15	0	5.93
Windy McCall	L	28	2	5	.286	2	33	4	0	61	50	29	38	0	3.25
George Spencer	R	27	1	0	1.000	0	12	0	0	12	9	8	4	0	3.75
Al Corwin	R	27	1	3	.250	0	20	0	0	31	35	14	14	0	4.06
Al Worthington	R	25	0	2	.000	0	10	1	0	18	21	15	8	0	3.50
Alex Konikowski	R	26	0	0	—	0	10	0	0	12	10	12	6	0	7.50
Paul Giel	R	21	0	0	—	0	4	0	0	8	4	2	4	0	9.00
Ray Monzant	R	21	0	0	—	0	6	1	0	8	8	11	6	0	4.50
1 Mario Picone	R	27	0	0	—	0	5	1	0	14	13	11	6	0	5.14

BROOKLYN — 2nd 92-62 .597 5 — WALT ALSTON

NAME	G by Pos	B	AGE	G	AB	R	H	2B	3B	HR	RBI	BB	SO	SB	BA	SA
TOTALS			30	154	5251	778	1418	246	56	186	741	634	625	46	.270	.444
Gil Hodges	1B154	R	30	154	579	106	176	23	5	42	130	74	84	3	.304	.579
Jim Gilliam	2B143, OF4	B	25	146	607	107	171	28	8	13	52	76	30	8	.282	.418
Pee Wee Reese	SS153	R	35	141	554	98	171	35	8	10	69	90	62	8	.309	.455
Don Hoak	3B75	R	26	88	261	41	64	9	5	7	26	25	39	8	.245	.398
Carl Furillo	OF149	R	32	150	547	56	161	23	1	19	96	49	35	2	.294	.444
Duke Snider	OF148	L	27	149	584	120	199	39	10	40	130	84	96	6	.341	.647
Jackie Robinson	OF74, 3B50, 2B4	R	35	124	386	62	120	22	4	15	59	63	20	7	.311	.505
Roy Campanella (HJ)	C111	R	32	111	397	43	82	14	3	19	51	42	49	1	.207	.401
Sandy Amoros	OF70	L	24	79	263	44	72	18	6	9	34	31	24	1	.274	.490
Billy Cox	3B58, 2B11, SS8	R	34	77	226	26	53	9	2	2	17	21	13	0	.235	.319
Rube Walker	C47	L	28	50	155	12	28	7	0	5	23	24	17	0	.181	.323
Walt Moryn	OF20	L	28	48	91	16	25	4	2	2	14	7	11	0	.275	.429
George Shuba	OF13	L	29	45	65	3	10	5	0	2	10	7	10	0	.154	.323
Don Thompson	OF29	L	30	34	25	2	1	0	0	0	1	5	5	0	.040	.040
Don Zimmer	SS13	R	23	24	33	3	6	0	1	0	3	3	8	2	.182	.242
Dick Williams	OF14	R	25	16	34	5	5	0	0	1	3	2	7	0	.147	.235
2 Charlie Kress	1B1	L	32	13	12	1	1	0	0	0	1	1	3	0	.083	.083
1 Wayne Belardi		L	23	11	9	0	2	0	0	0	1	2	3	0	.222	.222
Tim Thompson	C2, OF1	L	30	10	13	2	2	1	0	0	1	0	1	0	.154	.231

NAME	T	AGE	W	L	PCT	SV	G	GS	CG	IP	H	BB	SO	SHO	ERA
		28	92	62	.597	36	154	154	39	1394	1399	533	762	8	4.31
Carl Erskine	R	27	18	15	.545	1	38	37	12	260	239	92	166	2	4.15
Billy Loes	R	24	13	5	.722	0	28	21	6	148	154	60	97	0	4.14
Russ Meyer	R	30	11	6	.647	0	36	28	6	180	193	49	70	2	4.00
Johnny Podres (IL)	L	21	11	7	.611	0	29	21	6	152	147	53	79	2	4.26
Don Newcombe	R	28	9	8	.529	0	29	25	6	144	158	49	82	0	4.56
Jim Hughes	R	31	8	4	.667	24	60	0	0	87	76	44	58	0	3.21
Clem Labine	R	27	7	6	.538	7	47	2	0	108	101	53	43	0	4.17
Bob Milliken	R	27	5	2	.714	2	24	3	0	63	58	18	25	0	4.00
Erv Palica	R	26	3	3	.500	0	25	5	0	68	77	31	25	0	5.29
Preacher Roe	L	39	3	4	.429	0	15	10	1	63	69	23	31	0	5.00
Karl Spooner	L	23	2	0	1.000	0	2	2	2	18	7	6	27	2	0.00
1 Ben Wade	R	31	1	1	.500	3	23	0	0	45	62	21	25	0	8.20
Pete Wojey	R	34	1	1	.500	1	14	0	0	28	24	14	21	0	3.21
Bob Darnell	R	23	0	0	—	0	6	1	0	14	15	7	5	0	3.21
Joe Black (SA)	R	30	0	0	—	0	7	0	0	11	15	3	9	0	11.57
Tommy Lasorda	L	26	0	0	—	0	4	0	0	9	5	5	5	0	5.00

MILWAUKEE — 3rd 89-65 .578 8 — CHARLIE GRIMM

NAME	G by Pos	B	AGE	G	AB	R	H	2B	3B	HR	RBI	BB	SO	SB	BA	SA
TOTALS			26	154	5261	670	1395	217	41	139	636	471	619	54	.265	.401
Joe Adcock	1B133	R	26	133	500	73	154	27	5	23	87	44	58	1	.308	.520
Danny O'Connell	2B103, 3B35, 1B8, SS1	R	27	146	541	61	151	28	4	7	37	38	46	2	.279	.357
Johnny Logan	SS154	R	27	154	560	66	154	17	7	8	66	51	51	2	.275	.373
Eddie Mathews	3B127, OF10	L	22	138	476	96	138	21	4	40	103	113	61	10	.290	.603
Andy Pafko	OF138	R	33	138	510	61	146	22	4	14	69	37	36	1	.286	.427
Bill Bruton	OF141	L	28	142	567	89	161	20	7	4	30	40	78	34	.284	.365
Hank Aaron (BN)	OF116	R	20	122	468	58	131	27	6	13	69	28	39	2	.280	.447
Del Crandall	C136	R	24	138	463	60	112	18	2	21	64	40	56	0	.242	.425
Jim Pendleton	OF50	R	30	71	173	20	38	3	1	1	16	4	21	2	.220	.266
Catfish Metkovich	1B18, OF13	L	32	68	123	7	34	5	1	1	15	15	15	0	.276	.358
Jack Dittmer	2B55	R	26	66	192	22	47	8	0	6	20	19	17	0	.245	.380
Charlie White	C28	L	26	50	93	14	22	4	0	1	8	9	8	0	.237	.312
Bobby Thomson (BN)	OF26	R	30	43	99	7	23	3	0	2	15	12	29	1	.232	.323
Roy Smalley	SS9, 2B7, 1B2	R	28	28	36	5	8	0	0	1	7	4	9	0	.222	.306
Sammy Calderone	C16	R	28	22	29	3	11	2	0	0	5	4	4	0	.379	.448
Sibby Sisti		R	33	9	6	0	0	0	0	0	0	0	1	0	.000	.000
Mel Roach	1B1	R	21	3	4	0	0	0	0	0	0	0	1	0	.000	.000
Billy Queen	OF1	R	25	3	2	0	0	0	0	0	0	0	0	0	.000	.000

NAME	T	AGE	W	L	PCT	SV	G	GS	CG	IP	H	BB	SO	SHO	ERA
		26	89	65	.578	21	154	154	63	1395	1296	553	698	13	3.19
Warren Spahn	R	33	21	12	.636	3	39	34	23	283	262	86	136	1	3.14
Lew Burdette	R	27	15	14	.517	0	38	32	13	238	224	62	79	4	2.76
Gene Conley	R	23	14	9	.609	0	28	27	12	194	171	79	113	2	2.97
Dave Jolly	L	29	11	6	.647	10	47	1	0	111	87	64	62	0	2.43
Chet Nichols	L	23	9	11	.450	1	35	20	5	122	132	65	55	1	4.43
Jim Wilson	R	32	8	2	.800	0	27	19	6	128	129	36	52	4	3.52
Ernie Johnson	R	30	5	2	.714	2	40	4	1	99	77	34	68	0	3.13
Bob Buhl	R	25	2	7	.222	3	31	14	2	110	117	65	57	1	4.01
Ray Crone	R	22	1	0	1.000	1	19	2	1	49	44	19	33	0	2.02
Joey Jay	R	18	1	0	1.000	0	15	2	1	28	21	16	13	0	6.50
Phil Paine	R	24	1	0	1.000	0	11	0	0	14	12	11	0	0	3.86
2 Dave Koslo	L	34	1	1	.500	1	12	3	1	17	13	9	7	0	3.18
Charlie Gorin	L	26	0	1	.000	0	5	0	0	10	6	12	6	0	1.80

PHILADELPHIA — 4th 75-79 .487 22 — STEVE O'NEILL 40-37 .519 TERRY MOORE 35-42 .455

NAME	G by Pos	B	AGE	G	AB	R	H	2B	3B	HR	RBI	BB	SO	SB	BA	SA
TOTALS			28	153	5184	659	1384	243	58	102	620	604	620	30	.267	.395
Earl Torgeson	1B133	L	30	135	490	63	133	28	3	16	60	75	52	7	.271	.371
Granny Hamner	2B152, SS1	R	27	152	596	83	178	39	11	13	89	53	44	1	.299	.466
Bobby Morgan	SS129, 3B8, 2B5	R	28	135	455	58	119	25	2	14	50	70	68	3	.262	.418
Willie Jones	3B141	R	28	142	535	64	145	28	3	12	56	61	54	4	.271	.402
Danny Schell	OF69	L	26	92	272	25	77	14	3	7	33	17	31	0	.283	.434
Richie Ashburn	OF153	L	27	153	559	111	175	16	8	1	41	125	46	11	.313	.376
Del Ennis	OF142, 1B1	R	29	145	556	73	145	23	2	25	119	50	60	2	.261	.444
Smoky Burgess	C91	L	27	108	345	41	127	27	5	4	46	42	11	1	.368	.510
Johnny Wyrostek	OF55, 1B22	L	34	92	259	28	62	12	4	3	28	29	39	0	.239	.351
Stan Lopata	C75, 1B1	R	28	86	259	42	75	14	5	14	42	33	37	1	.290	.544
Mel Clark	OF63	R	27	83	233	26	56	9	7	1	24	17	21	0	.240	.352
Ted Kazanski	SS38	R	20	39	104	7	14	2	0	1	8	4	14	0	.135	.183
2 Floyd Baker	3B7, 2B1	R	37	23	22	0	5	0	0	0	0	5	4	0	.227	.227
Bob Micelotta	SS1	R	25	13	3	2	0	0	0	0	0	0	0	0	.000	.000
Jim Command	3B6	R	25	9	18	1	4	1	0	1	6	2	4	0	.222	.444
Johnny Lindell		R	37	7	5	0	1	0	0	0	0	0	1	0	.200	.200
Gus Niarhos	C3	R	33	5	5	0	1	0	0	0	0	2	0	0	.200	.200
1 Stan Jok		R	28	3	0	0	0	0	0	0	0	0	0	0	.000	.000
Stan Palys	OF1	R	24	2	4	0	1	0	0	0	2	0	1	0	.250	.250

NAME	T	AGE	W	L	PCT	SV	G	GS	CG	IP	H	BB	SO	SHO	ERA
		29	75*	79	.487	12	153	153	78	1365	1329	450	570	14	3.59
Robin Roberts	R	27	23	15	.605	4	45	38	29	337	289	56	185	4	2.96
Curt Simmons	R	25	14	15	.483	1	34	33	21	253	226	98	125	3	2.81
2 Herm Wehmeier	R	27	10	8	.556	2	25	17	10	138	117	51	49	2	3.85
Murry Dickson	R	37	10	20	.333	2	40	31	12	226	256	73	64	4	3.78
Bob Miller	R	28	9	4	.438	0	30	16	5	150	176	39	42	0	4.56
Steve Ridzik	R	25	4	4	.444	0	35	6	0	81	72	44	45	0	4.11
1 Jim Konstanty	R	37	2	3	.400	3	33	1	0	50	62	12	11	0	3.78
1 Karl Drews	R	34	1	0	1.000	0	13	1	0	16	18	8	6	0	5.63
Ron Mrozinski	L	23	1	1	.500	0	15	4	1	48	49	25	26	0	4.50
Paul Penson	R	22	1	1	.500	0	8	2	0	14	14	14	9	0	4.50
Bob Greenwood (JJ)	R	26	1	2	.333	0	14	4	0	37	28	18	9	0	3.16
Thornton Kipper	R	25	0	1	.000	1	11	0	0	14	12	12	5	0	7.71
Tom Qualters (DP) 19															

*1 win by forfeit

CINCINNATI — 5th 74-80 .481 23 — BIRDIE TEBBETTS

NAME	G by Pos	B	AGE	G	AB	R	H	2B	3B	HR	RBI	BB	SO	SB	BA	SA
TOTALS			27	154	5234	729	1369	221	46	147	685	557	645	47	.262	.406
Ted Kluszewski	1B149	L	29	149	573	104	187	28	3	49	141	78	35	0	.326	.642
Johnny Temple	2B144	R	26	146	505	60	155	16	4	0	44	62	24	21	.307	.366
Roy McMillan	SS154	R	24	154	588	86	147	21	4	9	42	47	54	4	.250	.313
Bobby Adams	3B93, 2B2	R	32	110	390	69	105	25	6	3	23	53	46	6	.269	.387
Wally Post	OF116	R	24	130	451	46	115	21	3	18	83	26	70	2	.255	.435
Gus Bell	OF153	L	25	153	619	104	185	38	7	17	101	44	58	5	.299	.465
Jim Greengrass	OF137	R	26	139	542	79	152	27	4	27	95	41	81	0	.280	.494
Andy Seminick	C82	R	33	86	247	25	58	9	4	7	30	48	39	0	.235	.389
Chuck Harmon	3B67, 1B3	R	30	94	286	39	68	7	3	2	25	17	27	7	.238	.304
Ed Bailey	C61	L	23	73	183	21	36	3	2	9	20	35	34	1	.197	.388
Bob Borkowski	OF36, 1B3	R	28	73	162	13	43	12	1	1	19	8	18	0	.265	.370
Lloyd Merriman	OF25	L	29	73	112	12	30	8	1	0	16	23	10	3	.268	.357
Nino Escalera	OF14, 1B8, SS1	L	24	73	69	15	11	4	1	0	3	7	11	3	.159	.203
Rocky Bridges	SS20, 2B19, 3B13	R	27	53	52	4	12	1	0	0	5	7	7	2	.231	.250
Hobie Landrith	C42	L	24	48	81	10	16	0	0	2	14	18	9	1	.198	.259
Dick Murphy		L	22	5	0	0	0	0	0	0	0	0	0	0	.000	.000
Jim Bolger	OF2	R	22	5	3	1	1	0	0	0	0	0	1	0	.333	.333
1 Grady Hatton		L	31	5	0	0	0	0	0	0	0	0	0	0	.000	.000
Johnny Lipon		R	31	3	0	0	0	0	0	0	0	0	0	0	.000	.000
Connie Ryan		R	34	3	0	0	0	0	0	0	0	0	0	0	.000	.000

NAME	T	AGE	W	L	PCT	SV	G	GS	CG	IP	H	BB	SO	SHO	ERA
		27	74	80	.481	27	154	154	34	1367	1491	547	537	8	4.50
Joe Nuxhall	L	25	12	5	.706	0	35	14	5	167	188	59	85	1	3.88
Art Fowler	R	31	12	10	.545	0	40	29	8	228	256	85	93	1	3.83
Corky Valentine	R	25	12	11	.522	1	36	28	7	194	211	60	73	3	4.45
Jackie Collum	L	27	7	3	.700	0	36	2	1	79	86	32	28	0	3.76
Bud Podbielan	R	30	7	10	.412	0	27	24	4	131	157	58	42	0	5.36
Fred Baczewski	L	28	6	6	.500	0	29	22	4	130	159	53	43	1	5.26
Howie Judson	R	28	5	5	.500	4	41	9	1	93	86	42	27	0	3.97
Frank Smith	R	26	4	4	.500	20	50	0	0	81	60	29	51	0	2.67
2 Karl Drews	R	34	4	4	.500	2	16	7	1	60	79	19	29	1	6.00
Harry Perkowski	L	31	3	8	.200	0	28	12	3	96	100	62	32	1	6.09
Jerry Lane	R	28	1	0	1.000	1	19	0	0	37	41	19	15	0	1.64
Jim Pearce	R	29	1	0	1.000	0	7	1	0	19	22	8	9	0	4.26
2 Mario Picone	R	27	0	0	—	0	8	0	0	24	23	8	7	0	4.88
Moe Savransky	L	25	0	2	.000	0	16	1	0	34	38	21	13	0	8.10
Ken Raffensberger	L	36	0	0	—	0	4	0	0	8	10	2	5	0	6.62
Cliff Ross	R	25	0	0	—	0	2	0	0	4	6	3	0	0	9.00
1 George Zuverink	R	29	0	0	—	0	10	1	0	14	17	9	7	0	9.00

Batting

NAME	G by Pos	B	AGE	G	AB	R	H	2B	3B	HR	RBI	BB	SO	SB	BA	SA
ST. LOUIS 6th 72-82 .468 25																
TOTALS	**EDDIE STANKY**		28	153	5405	799	1518	285	58	119	748	582	586	63	.281	.421
Joe Cunningham	1B85	L	22	85	310	40	88	11	3	11	50	43	40	1	.284	.445
Red Schoendienst	2B144	B	31	148	610	98	192	38	8	5	79	54	22	4	.315	.428
Alex Grammas	SS142, 3B1	R	28	142	401	57	106	17	4	2	29	40	29	6	.264	.342
Ray Jablonski	3B149, 1B1	R	27	152	611	80	181	33	3	12	104	49	42	9	.296	.419
Stan Musial	OF152, 1B10	L	33	153	591	120	195	41	9	35	126	103	39	1	.330	.607
Wally Moon	OF148	L	24	151	635	106	193	29	9	12	76	71	73	18	.304	.435
Rip Repulski	OF152	R	25	152	619	99	175	39	5	19	79	43	75	8	.283	.454
Bill Sarni	C118	R	26	123	380	40	114	18	4	9	70	25	42	3	.300	.439
Solly Hemus	SS66, 3B27, 2B12	L	31	124	214	43	65	15	3	2	27	55	27	5	.304	.430
Joe Frazier	OF11, 1B1	L	31	81	88	8	26	5	2	3	18	13	17	0	.295	.500
Peanuts Lowrey	OF12	R	36	74	61	6	7	1	2	0	5	9	9	0	.115	.197
Tom Alston	1B65	L	28	66	244	28	60	14	2	4	34	24	41	3	.246	.369
Del Rice	C52	R	31	56	147	13	37	10	1	2	16	16	21	0	.252	.374
Dick Schofield	SS11	B	19	43	7	17	1	0	1	0	1	0	3	1	.143	.429
Sal Yvars	C21	R	30	38	57	8	14	4	0	2	8	6	5	1	.246	.421
Tom Burgess	OF4	L	26	17	21	2	1	1	0	0	1	3	9	0	.048	.095
1 Steve Bilko	1B6	R	25	8	14	1	2	0	0	0	1	3	1	0	.143	.143
Pete Castiglione	3B5	R	33	14												

CHICAGO 7th 64-90 .416 33																
TOTALS	**STAN HACK**		31	154	5359	700	1412	229	45	159	640	478	693	46	.263	.412
Dee Fondy	1B138	L	29	141	568	77	162	30	4	9	49	35	84	20	.285	.400
Gene Baker	2B134	R	29	135	541	68	149	32	5	13	61	47	55	4	.275	.425
Ernie Banks	SS154	R	23	154	593	70	163	19	7	19	79	40	50	6	.275	.427
Randy Jackson	3B124	R	28	126	484	77	132	17	6	19	67	44	55	2	.273	.450
Hank Sauer	OF141	R	37	142	520	98	150	18	1	41	103	70	68	2	.288	.563
Dale Talbot	OF111	R	27	114	403	45	97	15	4	1	19	16	25	1	.241	.305
Ralph Kiner	OF147	R	31	147	557	88	159	36	5	22	73	76	90	2	.285	.487
1 Joe Garagiola	C55	L	28	63	153	16	43	5	0	5	21	28	12	0	.281	.412
Frankie Baumholtz	OF71	L	35	90	303	38	90	12	6	4	28	20	15	1	.297	.416
2 Walker Cooper	C48	R	39	57	158	21	49	10	2	7	32	21	23	0	.310	.532
2 Hal Rice	OF24	L	30	51	72	5	11	0	0	0	5	8	15	0	.153	.153
2 Steve Bilko	1B22	R	25	47	92	11	22	8	1	4	12	11	24	2	.239	.478
El Tappe	C46	R	27	46	119	5	22	3	0	0	4	10	9	0	.185	.210
Bill Serena	3B12, 2B2	R	29	41	63	8	10	0	1	4	13	14	18	0	.159	.381
Eddie Miksis	2B21, 3B2, OF1	R	27	38	99	9	20	3	0	2	3	4	9	1	.202	.293
Bob Rush	P33	R	28	33	83	6	23	4	1	2	9	3	23	0	.277	.422
Clyde McCullough (SA)	C26, 3B3	R	37	31	81	9	21	7	0	3	17	5	5	0	.259	.457
Vern Morgan	3B15	L	25	24	64	3	15	2	0	0	2	1	10	0	.234	.266
1 Luis Marquez	OF14	R	28	17	12	2	1	0	0	0	0	2	1	3	.083	.083
Don Robertson	OF6	L	23	14	6	2	0	0	0	0	0	0	2	0	.000	.000
Jim Fanning	C11	R	26	11	38	2	7	0	0	0	0	5	6	0	.184	.184

Bruce Edwards 30 R 0-3, Chris Kitsos 26 B 0-0, Harry Chiti (MS) 21

PITTSBURGH 8th 53-101 .344 44																
TOTALS	**FRED HANEY**		26	154	5088	557	1260	181	57	76	526	566	737	21	.248	.350
Bob Skinner	1B118, OF2	L	22	132	470	67	117	15	9	8	46	47	59	4	.249	.370
Curt Roberts	2B131	R	24	134	496	47	115	18	7	1	36	55	49	6	.232	.302
Gair Allie	SS95, 3B19	R	22	121	418	38	83	8	6	3	30	56	84	1	.199	.268
Dick Cole	SS66, 3B55, 2B17	R	28	138	486	40	131	22	5	1	40	41	48	0	.270	.342
Sid Gordon	OF73, 3B40	R	36	131	363	38	111	12	0	12	49	67	24	0	.306	.438
Dick Hall	OF102	R	23	112	310	38	74	8	4	2	27	33	46	3	.239	.310
Frank Thomas	OF153	R	25	153	557	81	172	32	7	23	94	51	74	3	.298	.497
Toby Atwell	C88	L	30	96	287	36	83	8	4	3	26	43	21	2	.289	.376
Preston Ward	1B48, OF42, 3B11	L	26	117	360	37	97	16	2	7	48	39	61	0	.269	.383
Jerry Lynch	OF83	L	23	98	284	27	68	4	5	8	36	20	43	2	.239	.373
Jack Shepard	C67	R	23	82	227	24	69	8	2	3	22	26	33	0	.304	.396
Eddie Pellagrini	3B31, 2B7, SS1	R	36	73	125	12	27	6	0	0	16	9	21	0	.216	.264
Vic Janowicz	OF1	R	24	41	73	10	11	3	0	2	7	23	0		.151	.192
1 Hal Rice	OF24	L	30	28	81	10	14	4	1	1	9	14	24	0	.173	.284
1 Cal Abrams	OF13	L	30	17	42	6	6	1	1	0	2	10	9	1	.143	.214
Gail Henley	OF9	L	25	14	30	7	9	1	0	1	2	4	4	0	.300	.433
Jim Mangan (MS)	C7	R	24	14	26	2	5	0	0	0	2	4	6	0	.192	.192
2 Luis Marquez	OF4	R	28	14	9	3	1	0	0	0	0	4	1	0	.111	.111
1 Walker Cooper	C2	R	39	14	15	0	3	2	0	0	1	2	1	0	.200	.333
Dick Smith	3B9	R	26	12	33	4	3	0	1	0	3	0	7	0	.097	.194

Bill Hall 25 L 0-7, Nick Koback 18 R 0-10, Sam Jethroe 36 B 0-1, Tony Bartirome (MS) 22, Dick Groat (MS) 23, Pete Naton (MS) 22, Eddie O'Brien (MS) 23, Johnny O'Brien (MS) 23

Pitching

NAME	T	AGE	W	L	PCT	SV	G	GS	CG	IP	H	BB	SO	SHO	ERA
		30	72	82*	.468	18	153	153	40	1390	1484	535	680	11	4.50
Harvey Haddix	L	28	18	13	.581	0	43	35	13	260	247	77	184	3	3.57
Brooks Lawrence	R	29	15	6	.714	1	35	18	8	159	141	72	72	0	3.74
Vic Raschi	R	35	8	9	.471	0	30	29	6	179	182	71	73	2	4.73
Gerry Staley	R	33	7	13	.350	2	48	20	3	156	198	47	50	1	5.25
Al Brazle	L	40	5	4	.556	8	58	0	0	84	93	24	30	0	4.18
Tom Poholsky	R	24	5	7	.417	0	25	13	4	106	101	20	55	0	3.06
Gordon Jones	R	24	4	4	.500	0	11	10	4	81	78	19	48	2	2.00
Joe Presko	R	25	4	9	.308	0	37	6	1	72	97	41	36	1	6.88
Cot Deal	R	31	3	4	.400	1	33	0	0	72	85	36	25	0	6.25
Royce Lint	L	33	2	3	.400	0	30	4	1	70	75	30	36	1	4.89
Stu Miller	R	26	2	3	.400	2	19	4	0	47	55	29	22	0	5.74
2 Carl Scheib	R	27	0	1	.000	0	3	1	0	5	6	5	5	0	10.80
Willie Greason	R	29	0	1	.000	0	3	2	0	4	8	4	2	0	13.50
Memo Luna	L	24	0	1	.000	0	1	1	0	1	2	2	0	0	18.00
Ralph Beard	R	25	0	4	.000	0	13	10	0	58	62	28	17	0	3.72
2 Ben Wade	R	31	0	0	—	0	13	0	0	23	27	15	19	0	5.48
Mel Wright	R	26	0	0		0	9	0	0	10	16	11	4	0	10.80
Hal White	R	35	0	0		0	4	0	0	5	11	4	2	0	19.80
Vinegar Bend Mizell (MS) 23															

* 1 loss by forfeit

NAME	T	AGE	W	L	PCT	SV	G	GS	CG	IP	H	BB	SO	SHO	ERA
		28	64	90	.416	19	154	154	41	1374	1375	619	622	6	4.51
Bob Rush	R	28	13	15	.464	0	33	32	11	236	213	103	124	0	3.78
Jim Davis	L	29	11	7	.611	4	46	12	2	128	114	51	58	0	3.52
Paul Minner	L	30	11	11	.500	1	32	29	12	218	236	50	79	0	3.96
Howie Pollet	L	33	8	10	.444	0	20	20	4	128	131	54	58	2	3.59
Warren Hacker	R	29	6	13	.316	2	39	18	4	159	157	37	80	1	4.25
Hal Jeffcoat	R	26	4	11	.267	1	36	21	4	148	155	96	69	0	5.19
Johnny Klippstein	R	26	4	11	.267	0	36	21	4					0	5.29
Dave Cole (SA)	R	23	3	8	.273	0	18	14	2	84	74	62	37	1	5.36
Jim Brosnan	R	24	1	0	1.000	0	18	0	0	33	44	18	17	0	9.55
Bill Tremel	R	24	1	2	.333	1	33	0	0	51	45	28	21	0	4.24
Bubba Church	R	29	1	3	.250	0	7	3	1	15	21	13	8	0	9.60
Jim Willis	R	27	1	4	.200	0	14	1	0	23	22	18	5	0	3.91
John Pyecha	R	22	0	1	.000	0	1	0	0	0	2	1	0	0	9.00
Turk Lown	R	30	0	2	.000	0	15	0	0	22	23	15	16	0	6.14
Bob Zick	R	27	0	0	—	0	8	0	0	16	23	7	9	0	8.44
Al Lary	R	25	0	0		0	1	1	0	6	3	7	4	0	3.00

NAME	T	AGE	W	L	PCT	SV	G	GS	CG	IP	H	BB	SO	SHO	ERA
		27	53	101	.344	15	154	154	37	1346	1510	564	525	4	4.92
2 Dick Littlefield	L	28	10	11	.476	0	23	21	7	155	140	85	92	1	3.60
Vern Law	R	24	9	13	.409	3	39	18	7	162	201	56	57	0	5.50
Max Surkont	R	32	9	18	.333	2	33	29	11	208	216	78	78	0	4.41
Bob Friend	R	23	7	12	.368	2	35	20	4	170	204	58	73	2	5.08
Johnny Hetki	R	32	4	4	.500	9	58	1	0	83	102	30	27	0	4.99
Paul LaPalme	L	30	4	10	.286	2	33	15	2	121	147	54	57	0	5.50
Bob Purkey	R	24	3	8	.273	0	36	11	0	131	145	62	38	0	5.08
Jake Thies	R	28	3	9	.250	1	33	18	3	130	120	49	57	1	3.88
George O'Donnell	R	25	3	9	.250	1	21	10	3	87	105	21	8	0	4.55
Laurin Pepper	R	23	1	0	.000	0	14	8	0	51	63	43	17	0	7.94
Len Yochim	L	25	1	1	.000	0	10	1	0	20	30	8	7	0	7.20
Cal Hogue	R	26	0	1	.000	0	3	2	0	11	11	12	7	0	4.91
Joe Page	R	36	0	0		0	7	0	0	10	16	7	4	0	10.80
Nellie King	R	26	0	0	—	0	7	0	0	10	7	10	1	3	5.14
Bill Bell (MS) 20															
Ron Kline (MS) 22															
Bill Koski (MS) 22															

WORLD SERIES — NEW YORK (NL) 4 CLEVELAND (AL) 0

LINE SCORES

TEAM	1	2	3	4	5	6	7	8	9	10	11	12	R	H	E

Game 1 September 29 at New York
CLE (AL) 2 0 0   0 0 0   0 0 0   0   2 8 0
NY 0 0 2   0 0 0   0 0 1   X   5 9 3
Lemon   Maglie, Liddle (8), **Grissom** (8)

Game 2 September 30 at New York
CLE 1 0 0   0 0 0   0 0 0   1 8 0
NY 0 0 0   0 2 0   1 0 X   3 4 0
Wynn, Mossi (8)   **Antonelli**

Game 3 October 1 at Cleveland
NY 1 0 3   0 1 1   0 0 0   6 10 1
CLE 0 0 0   0 0 0   1 1 0   2 4 2
Gomez, Wilhelm (8)   **Garcia**, Houtteman (4), Narleski (6), Mossi (9)

Game 4 October 2 at Cleveland
NY 0 2 1   0 4 0   0 0 0   7 10 3
CLE 0 0 0   0 3 0   1 0 0   4 6 2
Liddle, Wilhelm (7), Antonelli (8)   **Lemon**, Newhouser (5), Narleski (5), Mossi (6), Garcia (8)

COMPOSITE BATTING

NAME	POS	G	AB	R	H	2B	3B	HR	RBI	BA
New York (NL) Totals		4	130	21	33	3	0	2	20	.254
Mueller	OF	4	18	4	7	0	0	1		.389
Lockman	1B	4	18	2	2	0	0	0	0	.111
Dark	SS	4	17	2	7	0	0	0	0	.412
Mays	OF	4	14	4	4	1	0	0	3	.286
Thompson	3B	4	11	6	4	1	0	0	2	.364
Westrum	C	4	11	0	3	0	0	0	3	.273
Williams	2B	4	11	0	0	0	0	1	0	.000
Irvin	OF	4	9	1	2	0	0	0	2	.222
Rhodes	OF	3	6	2	4	0	0	2	7	.667
Gomez	P	1	3	0	0	0	0	0	0	.000
Maglie	P	1	3	0	0	0	0	0	0	.000
Liddle	P	2	3	0	0	0	0	0	0	.000
Antonelli	P	2	3	0	0	0	0	0	1	.000
Wilhelm	P	2	2	0	0	0	0	0	0	.000
Grissom	P	1	1	0	0	0	0	0	0	.000
Cleveland (AL) Totals		4	137	9	26	5	1	3	9	.190
Wertz	1B	4	16	2	8	2	1	1	3	.500
Doby	OF	4	16	0	2	0	0	0	1	.125
Avila	2B	4	15	1	2	0	0	0	0	.133
Smith	OF	4	14	2	3	1	0	1	2	.214
Hegan	C	4	13	1	2	1	0	0	0	.154
Rosen	3B	3	12	0	3	0	0	0	2	.250
Strickland	SS	4	9	0	0	0	0	0	0	.000
Philley	OF	4	8	0	1	0	0	0	0	.125
Westlake	OF	2	7	0	1	0	0	0	0	.143
Majeski	3B	4	6	1	1	0	0	0	1	.167
Lemon	P	2	6	0	0	0	0	0	0	.000
Regalado	3B	3	3	0	1	0	0	0	0	.333
Dente	SS	3	3	1	0	0	0	0	0	.000
Pope	OF	3	3	0	0	0	0	0	0	.000
Wynn	P	1	2	0	1	0	0	0	0	.500
Glynn	1B	2	2	1	1	0	0	0	0	.500
Mitchell	PH	3	2	0	0	0	0	0	0	.000
Grasso	C	1	1	0	0	0	0	0	0	—
Naragon	C	1	1	0	0	0	0	0	0	—
Mossi	P	3	1	0	0	0	0	0	0	.000
Garcia	P	2	1	0	0	0	0	0	0	.000
Narleski	P	2	1	0	0	0	0	0	0	.000
Houtteman	P	1	0	0	0	0	0	0	0	—
Newhouser	P	1	0	0	0	0	0	0	0	—

COMPOSITE PITCHING

NAME	G	IP	H	BB	SO	W	L	SV	ERA
New York (NL) Totals	4	37	26	16	23	4	0	2	1.46
Antonelli	2	10.2	8	7	12	1	0	1	0.84
Gomez	1	7.1	4	3	2	1	0	0	2.45
Liddle	2	7	5	1	2	1	0	0	1.29
Maglie	1	7	7	2	2	0	0	0	2.57
Grissom	1	2.2	1	3	2	1	0	0	0.00
Wilhelm	2	2.1	1	0	3	0	0	1	0.00
Cleveland (AL) Totals	4	35.1	33	17	24	0	4	0	4.84
Lemon	2	13.1	16	8	11	0	2	0	6.75
Wynn	1	7	4	2	5	0	1	0	3.86
Garcia	2	5	6	4	4	0	1	0	5.40
Mossi	3	4	3	0	1	0	0	0	0.00
Narleski	2	4	1	1	2	0	0	0	2.25
Houtteman	1	2	2	1	1	0	0	0	4.50
Newhouser	1	0	1	1	0	0	0	0	T

1955 Forget about Next Year

After winning five championships in a row with teams that never topped 100 victories, Casey Stengel broke the barrier in 1954 only to finish a good second. In 1955, Stengel and the Yankees returned to their old ways and won less than 100 games—a feat which was good enough for a sixth pennant in seven years under the helm of the Old Professor. But Stengel, to his regret, was not the *big story* of the year. Baseball's dynamite, for once, belonged to Brooklyn. While the Yankees topped the American League with 175 home runs, the Dodgers outdid them by proving the powerhouse of the majors with 201 clouts.

The Dodgers, in fact, were devastating. They opened their campaign by reeling off ten wins in a row and taking 22 of their first 24 games to find themselves 12½ over the pack by July 4. Even an August slump couldn't harm them as they finished a strong 13½ games in front of Milwaukee, the pre-season favorites.

Roy Campanella recovered sufficiently from a 1954 hand injury and proved the anchor in his performance behind the plate, as well as behind the bat, as he hit .318, collected 32 home runs, and was voted league MVP. Duke Snider led the league with 136 RBI's while batting .309 and hitting 42 home runs, while Don Newcombe returned to form and posted a 20-5 season. Clem Labine led the relief corps with 13 victories and 11 saves to round out the most balanced Dodgers' attack in years. Milwaukee finished second mostly due to sophomore Hank Aaron's maturing year and Eddie Mathews' 41 home runs. Willie Mays again gave the Giants a good year with a league-leading 51 homers and a .319 average, but could not make up for the reversal of form by Johnny Antonelli and Ruben Gomez, who could only combine for 23 wins instead of the 38 they bunched in 1954.

While Campanella was leading the Dodgers to victory, Yogi Berra was doing the same for the Yankees. Although his batting stats did not compare with those of his Dodger rival, his performance was also good enough to earn him MVP

honors. The Yankees edged out Cleveland by three games, mostly due to a shakeup in the pitching department and Stengel's being able to compensate for off years and injuries. With Allie Reynolds retired, Bob Grim suffering from arm trouble, and Vic Raschi, Johnny Sain, and Eddie Lopat sold, Stengel brought Tommy Byrne back from the minors and got good mileage out of Bob Turley and Don Larsen, obtained during the winter from Baltimore as part of an 18-man trade. Stengel's big problem at shortstop, where Phil Rizzuto became a part-timer, was solved by using Billy Hunter until Jerry Coleman was able to recover from a broken collarbone.

Cleveland's one compensation for their regulars' off-year, and the polio which sidelined Vic Wertz in late August, was the debut of Herb Score, who created much excitement with his 16 victories and 245 strikeouts. Detroit produced a batting champion in 20-year-old sophomore Al Kaline—a feat which tied him with Ty Cobb as the youngest batting champion ever.

As the Series got underway, and the Yankees won the first two games, it seemed as if, indeed, the Dodgers would have to "wait till next year". But the Dodgers came home to Ebbets Field and won the next three games. Back at Yankee Stadium, Whitey Ford cooled off Brooklyn, 5-1, and the old rivals entered the final game. With Johnny Podres throwing shutout ball and the Dodgers up two runs on Gil Hodges' hitting, Billy Martin started off the sixth inning with a walk, followed by Gil McDougald's infield single. Berra then came up and hit a high fly ball into the left field corner. Sandy Amoros, playing in left center, started running toward the ball in desperation. At the last second, he made a lunge and speared the ball just inside the foul line. Amoros recovered in time to throw to Reese who, in turn, relayed the ball to Hodges to double McDougald off first base. Podres hung on to shut out the Yankees and to evoke the cry, "this is next year."

1955 AMERICAN LEAGUE

NAME	G by Pos	B	AGE	G	AB	R	H	2B	3B	HR	RBI	BB	SO	SB	BA	SA
NEW YORK	1st 96-58 .623													**CASEY STENGEL**	
TOTALS			28	154	5161	762	1342	179	55	175	722	609	658	55	.260	.418
Bill Skowron	1B74, 3B3	R	24	108	288	46	92	17	3	12	61	21	32	1	.319	.524
Gil McDougald	2B126, 3B17	R	27	141	533	79	152	10	8	13	53	65	77	6	.285	.407
Billy Hunter	SS98	R	27	98	255	14	58	7	1	3	20	15	18	9	.227	.298
Andy Carey	3B135	R	23	135	510	73	131	19	11	7	47	44	51	3	.257	.378
Hank Bauer	OF133, C1	R	32	139	492	97	137	20	5	20	53	56	65	8	.278	.461
Mickey Mantle	OF145, SS2	B	23	147	517	121	158	25	11	37	99	113	97	8	.306	.611
Irv Noren	OF126	L	30	132	371	49	94	19	1	8	59	43	33	5	.253	.375
Yogi Berra	C145	L	30	147	541	84	147	20	3	27	108	60	20	1	.272	.470
Joe Collins	1B73, OF27	L	32	105	278	40	65	9	1	13	45	44	32	0	.234	.414
Elston Howard	OF75, C9	R	26	97	279	33	81	8	7	10	43	20	36	0	.290	.477
Eddie Robinson	1B46	L	34	88	173	25	36	1	0	16	42	36	26	0	.208	.491
Phil Rizzuto	SS79, 2B1	R	37	81	143	19	37	4	1	1	9	22	18	7	.259	.322
Bob Cerv	OF20	R	29	55	85	17	29	4	2	3	22	7	16	4	.341	.541
Jerry Coleman (BC)	SS29, 2B13, 3B1	R	30	43	96	12	22	5	0	0	8	11	11	0	.229	.281
Billy Martin (MS)	2B17, SS3	R	27	20	70	8	21	2	0	1	9	7	9	1	.300	.371
Tommy Carroll	SS4	R	18	14	6	3	2	0	0	0	0	0	0	0	.333	.333

Charlie Silvera 30 R 5-26, Bobby Richardson 19 R 4-26, 1 Enos Slaughter 39 L 1-9, Frank Leja 19 L 0-2, Lou Berberet 25 L 2-5, Dick Tettelbach 26 R 0-5, Marv Throneberry 21 L 2-2, Johnny Blanchard 22 L 0-3

NAME	T	AGE	W	L	PCT	SV	G	GS	CG	IP	H	BB	SO	SHO	ERA
		28	96	58	.623	33	154	154	52	1372	1163	688	732	19	3.23
Whitey Ford	L	26	18	7	.720	2	39	33	18	254	188	113	137	5	2.62
Bob Turley	R	24	17	13	.567	1	36	34	13	247	168	177	210	6	3.06
Tommy Byrne	L	35	16	5	.762	2	27	22	9	160	137	87	76	3	3.15
Don Larsen	R	25	9	2	.818	2	19	13	5	97	81	51	44	1	3.06
Johnny Kucks	R	21	8	7	.533	0	29	13	3	127	122	44	49	1	3.40
Jim Konstanty	R	38	7	2	.778	11	45	0	0	74	68	24	19	0	2.31
Tom Morgan	R	25	7	3	.700	10	40	1	0	72	72	24	17	0	3.25
Bob Grim (SA)	R	25	7	5	.583	4	26	11	1	92	81	42	63	1	4.21
1 Ed Lopat	L	37	4	8	.333	0	16	12	3	87	101	16	24	1	3.72
Rip Coleman	L	23	2	1	.667	1	10	6	0	29	40	16	15	0	5.28
Tom Sturdivant	R	25	1	3	.250	0	33	1	0	68	48	42	48	0	3.18
Bob Wiesler	L	24	0	2	.000	0	16	7	0	53	39	49	22	0	3.91
1 Johnny Sain	R	37	0	0	—	0	3	0	0	5	6	1	5	0	7.20
1 Art Schallock	L	31	0	0	—	0	2	0	0	3	4	1	2	0	6.00
2 Gerry Staley	R	34	0	0	—	0	2	0	0	2	5	1	0	0	13.50
3 Ted Gray	L	30	0	0	—	0	1	1	0	3	3	0	1	0	3.00

CLEVELAND	2nd 93-61 .604 3													**AL LOPEZ**	
TOTALS			31	154	5146	698	1325	195	31	148	657	723	715	28	.257	.394
Vic Wertz (IL)	1B63, OF9	L	30	74	257	30	65	11	2	14	55	32	33	1	.253	.475
Bobby Avila	2B141	R	31	141	537	83	146	22	4	13	61	82	47	1	.272	.400
George Strickland	SS128	R	29	130	388	34	81	9	5	2	34	49	60	1	.209	.273
Al Rosen	3B106, 1B41	R	31	139	492	61	120	13	1	21	81	92	44	4	.244	.402
Al Smith	OF120, 3B45, SS5, 2B1	R	27	154	607	123	186	27	4	22	77	93	77	11	.306	.473
Larry Doby	OF129	L	31	131	491	91	143	17	5	26	75	61	100	2	.291	.505
Ralph Kiner	OF87	R	32	113	321	56	78	13	0	18	54	65	46	0	.243	.452
Jim Hegan	C111	R	34	116	304	30	67	5	2	9	40	34	33	0	.220	.339
2 Gene Woodling	OF70	L	32	79	259	33	72	15	1	5	35	36	15	2	.278	.402
Sam Dente	SS53, 3B13, 2B4	R	33	73	105	10	27	4	0	0	10	12	8	0	.257	.295
Hank Foiles	C41	R	26	62	111	13	29	9	0	1	7	17	18	0	.261	.369
Dale Mitchell	1B8, OF3	L	33	61	58	4	15	2	1	0	10	4	3	0	.259	.328
Hal Naragon	C52	L	26	57	127	12	41	9	2	1	14	15	8	1	.323	.449
2 Ferris Fain	1B51	L	34	56	118	9	30	3	0	0	8	42	13	3	.254	.280
1 Dave Philley	OF34	B	35	43	104	15	31	4	2	2	9	12	10	0	.298	.433
Joe Altobelli	1B40	L	23	42	75	8	15	3	0	2	5	5	14	0	.200	.320
2 Hoot Evers	OF25	R	34	39	66	10	19	7	1	2	9	3	12	0	.288	.515
1 Hank Majeski	3B9, 2B4	R	38	36	48	3	9	2	0	2	6	3	6	0	.188	.354
1 Dave Pope	OF31	L	34	35	104	17	31	5	0	6	22	12	31	0	.298	.519
2 Bobby Young	2B11, 3B1	L	30	18	45	7	14	1	1	0	6	1	2	0	.311	.378

1 Wally Westlake 34 R 5-20, Stu Locklin 26 L 3-18, Billy Harrell 26 R 8-19, Rudy Regalado 25 R 7-26, Rocky Colavito 21 R 4-9, Kenny Kuhn 18 L 2-6, 1 Harry Simpson 29 L 0-1, Stan Pawloski 23 R 1-8

NAME	T	AGE	W	L	PCT	SV	G	GS	CG	IP	H	BB	SO	SHO	ERA
		30	93	61	.604	36	154	154	45	1386	1285	558	877	15	3.39
Bob Lemon	R	34	18	10	.643	2	35	31	5	211	218	74	100	0	3.88
Early Wynn	R	35	17	11	.607	0	32	31	16	230	207	80	122	6	2.82
Herb Score	R	22	16	10	.615	0	33	32	11	227	158	154	245	2	2.85
Mike Garcia	R	31	11	13	.458	2	38	25	9	211	230	56	120	4	4.01
Art Houtteman	R	27	10	6	.625	0	35	12	3	124	126	44	53	1	3.99
Ray Narleski	R	26	9	1	.900	19	60	1	1	112	91	52	94	0	3.70
Don Mossi	L	26	4	3	.571	9	57	1	0	82	81	18	69	0	2.41
Bob Feller	R	36	4	4	.500	0	25	11	2	83	71	31	25	1	3.47
Jose Santiago	R	26	2	0	1.000	0	17	0	0	33	31	14	19	0	2.45
Hank Aguirre	L	24	2	0	1.000	1	13	6	1	12	6	1	1	1.38
Bud Daley	R	22	1	0	1.000	0	1	0	0	7	10	1	2	0	6.43
2 Sal Maglie	R	38	0	2	.000	2	10	2	0	26	26	7	11	0	3.81
1 Bill Wight	L	33	0	1	.000	1	17	0	0	24	24	9	9	0	2.63
2 Ted Gray	L	30	0	0	—	0	2	0	0	2	5	2	1	0	18.00
Hal Newhouser	L	34	0	0	—	0	2	0	0	2	1	4	1	0	0.00

CHICAGO	3rd 91-63 .591 5													**MARTY MARION**	
TOTALS			30	155	5220	725	1401	204	36	116	678	567	595	69	.268	.388
Walt Dropo	1B140	R	32	141	453	55	127	15	2	19	79	42	71	0	.280	.448
Nellie Fox	2B154	L	27	154	636	100	198	28	7	6	59	38	15	7	.311	.406
Chico Carrasquel	SS144	R	27	145	523	83	134	11	2	11	52	61	59	1	.256	.348
George Kell	3B105, 1B24, OF1	R	32	128	429	44	134	24	1	8	81	51	36	2	.312	.429
Jim Rivera	OF143	L	32	147	454	71	120	24	4	10	52	62	59	25	.264	.401
2 Jim Busby	OF99	R	28	99	334	38	82	13	4	1	27	25	37	7	.243	.315
Minnie Minoso	OF138, 3B2	R	32	139	517	79	149	26	7	10	70	76	43	19	.288	.424
Sherm Lollar	C136	R	30	138	426	67	111	13	1	16	61	68	34	2	.261	.408
Bob Nieman	OF78	R	28	99	272	36	77	11	2	11	53	36	37	1	.283	.460
2 Bob Kennedy	3B55, OF20, 1B3	R	34	83	214	28	65	10	2	3	43	16	16	0	.304	.495
Ron Jackson	1B29	R	21	40	74	10	15	1	1	2	7	8	22	1	.203	.324
Jim Brideweser	SS26, 3B3, 2B2	R	28	34	58	6	12	3	0	2	4	3	7	0	.207	.328
1 Johnny Groth	OF26	R	28	32	77	13	26	7	0	2	11	6	13	1	.338	.506
2 Les Moss	C32	R	30	32	55	7	14	3	0	1	9	4	4	0	.254	.390
2 Bobby Adams	3B9, 2B1	R	33	25	21	8	2	0	0	0	3	4	4	0	.095	.190
Ed McGhee	OF17	R	30	24	39	0	0	0	0	0	0	6	1	2	.077	.077
2 Vern Stephens	3B18	R	34	22	56	10	14	3	0	3	11	6	6	0	.250	.464
Willard Marshall	OF25	L	34	22	41	6	7	2	0	0	6	13	1	0	.171	.171
1 Clint Courtney	C17	L	28	19	37	7	14	3	0	1	10	7	0	0	.378	.541
2 Gil Coan	OF3	L	33	17	17	0	3	1	0	0	0	0	3	0	.176	.176

Ron Northey 35 L 5-14, Buddy Peterson 30 R 6-21, Stan Jok 29 R 1-4, Phil Cavarretta 38 L 0-4, Earl Battey 20 R 2-7, Sammy Esposito (MS) 23 R 0-4, Ed White 29 R 2-4, 1 Lloyd Merriman 30 L 0-1, Bob Powell 21 R 0-0

NAME	T	AGE	W	L	PCT	SV	G	GS	CG	IP	H	BB	SO	SHO	ERA
		31	91	63	.591	23	155	155	55	1378	1301	497	720	20	3.37
Dick Donovan	R	27	15	9	.625	0	29	24	11	187	186	48	88	5	3.32
Billy Pierce	L	28	15	10	.600	1	33	26	16	206	162	64	157	6	1.97
Virgil Trucks	R	38	13	8	.619	0	32	26	7	175	176	61	91	3	3.96
Jack Harshman	R	27	11	7	.611	0	32	23	9	179	144	97	116	0	3.37
Dixie Howell	R	35	8	3	.727	9	35	0	0	74	70	25	26	2	2.92
Connie Johnson	R	32	7	4	.636	0	17	16	5	99	95	52	72	2	3.45
Mike Fornieles	R	23	6	3	.667	2	26	9	2	86	84	29	23	0	3.87
Sandy Consuegra	R	34	6	5	.545	7	44	7	3	126	120	18	35	0	2.64
2 Harry Byrd	R	30	4	6	.400	1	25	12	1	91	85	30	44	1	4.65
1 Harry Dorish	R	33	2	0	1.000	1	17	0	0	16	9	6	6	0	3.75
Morrie Martin	L	32	2	3	.400	2	37	0	0	52	50	20	22	0	3.63
Bob Keegan (KJ)	R	34	2	5	.286	0	18	11	1	59	83	28	29	0	5.80
1 Bob Chakales	R	27	0	0	—	0	7	0	0	12	14	9	4	0	1.50
Al Papai	R	38	0	0	—	0	3	0	0	12	14	4	0	0	3.75
1 Ted Gray	L	30	0	0	—	0	3	0	0	5	3	6	1	0	18.00

302

BOSTON — 4th 84-70 .545 12 — PINKY HIGGINS

NAME	G by Pos	B	AGE	G	AB	R	H	2B	3B	HR	RBI	BB	SO	SB	BA	SA
TOTALS			28	154	5273	755	1392	241	39	137	710	707	733	43	.264	.402
Norm Zauchin	1B126	R	25	130	477	65	114	10	0	27	93	69	105	3	.239	.430
Billy Goodman	2B143, 1B5, OF1	L	29	149	599	100	176	31	2	0	52	99	44	5	.294	.352
Billy Klaus	SS126, 3B8	R	26	135	541	83	153	26	2	7	60	60	44	6	.283	.377
Grady Hatton	3B111, 2B1	L	32	126	380	48	93	11	4	4	49	76	28	0	.245	.326
Jackie Jensen	OF150	R	28	152	574	95	158	27	6	26	116	89	63	16	.275	.479
Jimmy Piersall	OF147	R	25	149	515	68	146	25	5	13	62	67	52	6	.283	.427
Ted Williams (RP)	OF93	L	36	98	320	77	114	21	3	28	83	91	24	2	.356	.703
Sammy White	C143	R	27	143	544	65	142	30	4	11	64	44	58	1	.261	.392
Gene Stephens	OF75	L	22	109	157	25	46	9	4	3	18	20	34	0	.293	.459
Faye Throneberry	OF34	R	24	60	144	20	37	7	3	6	27	14	31	0	.257	.472
Eddie Joost	SS20, 2B17, 3B2	R	39	55	119	15	23	2	0	5	17	17	21	0	.193	.336
Ted Lepcio	3B45	R	24	51	134	19	31	9	0	6	15	12	36	1	.231	.433
Karl Olson	OF21	R	24	26	48	7	12	1	2	0	1	1	10	0	.250	.354
Harry Agganis (DD)	1B20	L	26	25	83	11	26	10	1	0	10	10	10	1	.313	.458
Pete Daley	C14	R	25	17	50	4	11	2	1	0	5	3	6	0	.220	.300
1 Owen Friend	SS14, 2B1	R	28	14	42	3	11	3	0	1	4	2	11	0	.262	.333
1 Sam Mele	OF7	R	33	14	31	1	4	2	0	1	0	1	7	1	.129	.194

Billy Consolo 20 R 4-18, Dick Gernert 26 R 4-20, Frank Malzone 25 R 7-20, Milt Bolling (BE) 24 R 1-5, Haywood Sullivan 24 R 0-6, Jim Pagliaroni 17 R 0-0

NAME	T	AGE	W	L	PCT	SV	G	GS	CG	IP	H	BB	SO	SHO	ERA
		27	84	70	.545	34	154	154	44	1384	1333	582	674	9	3.72
Frank Sullivan	R	25	18	13	.581	0	35	35	16	260	235	100	129	3	2.91
Willard Nixon	R	27	12	10	.545	0	31	31	7	208	207	85	95	3	4.07
Tom Brewer	R	23	11	10	.524	0	31	28	9	193	198	87	91	2	4.20
Ike Delock	R	25	9	7	.563	3	29	18	6	144	136	61	88	0	3.75
George Susce	R	23	9	7	.563	0	29	15	6	144	123	49	60	1	3.06
Tom Hurd	R	31	8	6	.571	5	43	0	0	81	72	38	48	0	3.00
Ellis Kinder	R	40	5	5	.500	18	43	0	0	67	57	15	31	0	2.82
Leo Kiely	L	25	3	3	.500	6	33	4	0	90	91	37	36	0	2.80
Frank Baumann	L	22	2	1	.667	0	7	5	0	34	38	17	27	0	5.82
Mel Parnell	L	33	2	3	.400	1	13	9	0	46	62	25	18	0	7.83
Bill Henry	L	27	2	3	.333	0	17	7	0	60	56	21	23	0	3.30
Dick Brodowski	R	22	1	0	1.000	0	16	0	0	32	36	25	10	0	5.63
1 Hal Brown	R	30	1	0	1.000	0	4	2	2	2	2	2	0		2.25
Russ Kemmerer	R	23	1	1	.500	0	7	2	0	17	18	15	13	0	7.41
1 Hersh Freeman	R	27	0	0	—	0	2	0	0	2	1	1	1	0	0.00
Joe Trimble	R	24	0	0	—	0	2	0	0	3	3	1	0	0	0.00
Bob Smith	L	24	0	0	—	0	2	0	0	2	3	3	1	0	0.00

DETROIT — 5th 79-75 .513 17 — BUCKY HARRIS

NAME	G by Pos	B	AGE	G	AB	R	H	2B	3B	HR	RBI	BB	SO	SB	BA	SA
TOTALS			27	154	5283	755	1407	211	38	130	724	641	583	41	.266	.394
2 Earl Torgeson	1B83	L	31	89	300	58	85	10	4	9	50	61	29	9	.283	.413
Fred Hatfield	2B92, 3B16, SS14	L	30	122	413	51	96	15	3	8	33	61	49	3	.232	.341
Harvey Kuenn	SS141	R	24	145	620	101	190	38	8	8	62	40	27	8	.306	.423
Ray Boone	3B126	R	31	135	500	61	142	22	7	20	116	50	49	1	.284	.476
Al Kaline	OF152	R	20	152	588	121	200	24	8	27	102	82	57	6	.340	.546
Bill Tuttle	OF154	R	25	154	603	102	168	23	4	14	78	76	54	6	.279	.400
Jim Delsing	OF101	L	29	116	356	49	85	15	2	10	60	48	40	2	.239	.376
Frank House	C93	L	25	102	328	37	85	11	1	15	53	22	25	0	.259	.436
Bubba Phillips	OF65, 3B4	R	25	95	184	18	43	4	0	3	23	14	20	2	.234	.304
Red Wilson	C72	R	26	78	241	26	53	9	0	2	17	26	23	1	.220	.282
Harry Malmberg	2B65	R	29	67	208	25	45	5	2	0	19	29	19	0	.216	.260
1 Ferris Fain	1B44	L	34	58	140	23	37	8	2	0	23	52	12	2	.264	.364
Jack Phillips	1B35, 3B3	R	33	55	117	15	37	8	2	1	20	10	12	0	.316	.444
2 Charlie Maxwell	OF26, 1B2	L	28	55	109	19	29	7	1	7	18	20	20	0	.266	.541
Reno Bertoia	3B14, 2B6, SS5	R	20	38	68	13	14	2	1	1	10	5	11	0	.206	.309
Jay Porter	1B6, C4, OF1	R	22	22	69	7	15	2	0	5	1	6		0	.236	.273

Jim Small 18 L 0-4, Charlie King 24 R 5-21, Wayne Belardi 24 L 0-3, Walt Streuli 19 R 1-4, Ron Samford 25 R 0-1, Steve Souchock 36 R 1-1, Frank Bolling (MS) 23

NAME	T	AGE	W	L	PCT	SV	G	GS	CG	IP	H	BB	SO	SHO	ERA
		27	79	75	.513	12	154	154	66	1380	1381	517	629	16	3.79
Billy Hoeft	L	23	16	7	.696	0	32	29	17	220	187	75	133	7	2.99
Frank Lary	R	25	14	15	.483	1	36	31	16	235	232	89	98	2	3.10
Steve Gromek	R	35	13	10	.565	0	28	25	8	181	183	37	73	2	3.98
Ned Garver	R	29	12	16	.429	0	33	32	16	231	251	67	83	1	3.97
Al Aber	L	27	3	3	.667	0	39	1	0	80	86	28	37	0	3.38
Duke Maas	R	26	5	6	.455	0	18	16	5	87	91	50	42	2	4.86
Babe Birrer	R	25	4	3	.571	3	36	3	1	80	77	29	28	0	4.16
Jim Bunning	R	23	3	5	.375	1	15	8	0	51	59	32	37	0	6.35
2 Joe Coleman (SA)	R	32	2	1	.667	3	17	0	0	25	22	14	5	0	3.24
Bob Miller	R	19	2	1	.667	0	7	1	1	25	26	12	11	0	2.52
Dick Marlowe	R	26	1	0	1.000	1	4	1	1	15	12	4	9	0	1.80
Bill Black	R	22	1	1	.500	3	2	1	0	14	9	3	1	0	1.29
Paul Foytack	R	24	0	1	.000	0	22	1	0	50	48	36	38	0	5.22
Leo Cristante	R	28	0	1	.000	0	20	1	0	37	37	14	9	0	3.16
1 George Zuverink	R	30	0	0	—	0	14	1	0	28	34	14	13	0	7.07
Van Fletcher	R	30	0	0	—	0	9	0	0	12	13	4	3	0	6.00
1 Ben Flowers	R	28	0	0	—	0	2	0	0	2	1	2	1	0	0.00
Bill Froats	L	24	0	0	—	0	1	0	0	2	2	2	0	0	0.00
Bob Schultz	L	31	0	0	—	0	1	0	0	1	3	1	0	0	27.00

KANSAS CITY — 6th 63-91 .409 33 — LOU BOUDREAU

NAME	G by Pos	B	AGE	G	AB	R	H	2B	3B	HR	RBI	BB	SO	SB	BA	SA
TOTALS			29	155	5335	638	1395	189	46	121	593	463	725	22	.261	.382
Vic Power	1B144	R	27	147	596	91	190	34	10	19	76	35	27	0	.319	.505
Jim Finigan	2B90, 3B59	R	26	146	545	72	139	30	7	9	68	61	49	1	.255	.385
Joe DeMaestri	SS122	R	26	123	457	42	114	14	1	6	37	20	47	3	.249	.324
Hector Lopez	3B93, 2B36	R	25	128	483	50	140	15	2	15	68	33	58	1	.290	.422
Bill Wilson	OF82, P1	R	26	98	273	39	61	12	0	15	38	24	63	1	.223	.432
1 Harry Simpson	OF100, 1B3	L	29	112	396	42	119	16	7	5	52	34	61	3	.301	.414
Gus Zernial	OF103	R	32	120	413	62	105	9	3	30	84	30	91	0	.254	.508
Joe Astroth	C100	R	32	101	274	29	69	4	1	1	23	47	33	2	.252	.328
Elmer Valo	OF72	L	34	112	283	50	103	17	4	3	37	52	18	5	.364	.484
2 Enos Slaughter	OF77	L	39	108	267	49	86	12	4	5	34	40	17	2	.322	.453
Bill Renna	OF79	R	30	100	249	33	53	7	3	7	28	31	42	0	.213	.349
Billy Shantz	C78	R	27	79	217	18	56	4	1	1	12	11	14	0	.258	.300
Clete Boyer	SS12, 3B11, 2B10	R	18	47	79	3	19	1	0	0	6	3	17	0	.241	.253
Jack Littrell (NJ)	SS22, 1B6, 2B4	R	26	37	70	7	14	0	1	0	4	2	10	0	.200	.229
Dick Kryhoski	1B14	L	30	28	47	2	10	2	0	0	2	6	7	0	.213	.255
Pete Suder	2B35	R	39	26	81	3	17	4	0	1	5	2	13	0	.210	.284
Jerry Schypinski	SS21, 2B2	R	23	22	69	7	15	2	0	0	5	1	6	0	.217	.246
Spook Jacobs	2B7	L	30	13	16	3	4	0	0	0	1	3	0	1	.250	.250

Don Bollweg 34 L 1-9, Bill Stewart 27 R 2-18, 2 Tom Saffell 33 L 8-37, Don Plarski 25 R 1-11, Jim Robertson 27 R 2-8, Alex George 16 L 1-10, Hal Bevan 24 R 0-3, Eric MacKenzie 22 L 0-1

NAME	T	AGE	W	L	PCT	SV	G	GS	CG	IP	H	BB	SO	SHO	ERA
		29	63	91	.409	22	155	155	29	1382	1486	707	572	9	5.35
Art Ditmar	R	26	12	12	.500	1	35	22	7	175	180	86	79	1	5.04
Alex Kellner	L	30	11	8	.579	1	30	24	6	163	164	60	75	3	4.20
Tom Gorman	R	30	7	6	.538	18	57	0	0	109	98	36	46	0	3.55
Cloyd Boyer	R	27	5	9	.357	0	30	11	2	98	107	69	32	0	6.24
A. Portocarrero (SJ)	R	27	5	5	.500	0	31	11	2	111	109	67	54	1	4.78
Bobby Shantz	R	29	5	10	.333	0	23	17	4	125	124	66	58	1	4.54
2 Vic Raschi	R	36	4	6	.400	0	20	18	1	101	132	35	38	0	5.44
Art Ceccarelli	L	25	4	7	.364	0	31	16	3	124	123	71	68	1	5.30
Bill Harrington (MS)	R	27	3	3	.500	2	34	1	0	77	69	41	26	0	4.09
Moe Burtschy	R	33	2	0	1.000	0	11	1	0	11	17	10	9	0	10.64
1 Johnny Sain	R	37	2	5	.286	1	25	0	0	54	60	10	12	0	5.40
Charlie Bishop	R	31	1	0	1.000	0	7	0	0	7	6	8	4	0	5.14
Lou Sleater	L	28	1	1	.500	0	16	1	0	26	33	11	11	0	7.62
Ray Herbert	R	25	1	8	.111	0	23	1	0	88	99	40	30	0	6.24
Gus Keriazakos	R	23	0	1	.000	0	12	1	0	15	15	7	8	0	12.00
John Kume	R	23	0	0	—	0	4	0	0	24	35	15	7	0	7.88
Walt Craddock	R	23	0	0	—	0	2	0	0	4	10	5	2	0	7.80
Glenn Cox	R	24	0	0	—	0	2	0	0	2	11	1	2	0	36.00
John Gray	R	24	0	0	—	0	2	0	0	3	2	11	3	0	6.33

Ewell Blackwell 32 R 0-1, Marion Fricano 31 R 0-0, Bob Trice 28 R 0-0, Lee Wheat 25 R 0-0, Sonny Dixon 30 R 0-0, Bob Spicer 30 R 0-0, Ozzie Van Brabant 28 R 0-0, Bill Wilson 26 R 0-0

BALTIMORE — 7th 57-97 .370 39 — PAUL RICHARDS

NAME	G by Pos	B	AGE	G	AB	R	H	2B	3B	HR	RBI	BB	SO	SB	BA	SA
TOTALS			29	156	5283	540	1263	177	39	54	503	560	742	34	.240	.320
Gus Triandos	1B103, C36, 3B1	R	24	140	481	47	133	17	3	12	65	40	55	0	.277	.399
Freddie Marsh (BE-LJ)	2B76, 3B16, SS16	R	31	89	303	30	66	7	1	2	19	35	33	1	.218	.267
Willie Miranda	SS153, 2B1	R	29	153	487	42	124	12	6	1	38	42	58	4	.255	.310
Wayne Causey	3B55, 2B1, SS1	L	18	68	175	14	34	2	1	1	9	17	25	0	.194	.234
Cal Abrams	OF96, 1B4	L	31	118	309	56	75	12	3	6	32	89	69	2	.243	.359
Chuck Diering	OF107, 3B34, SS12	R	32	137	311	38	95	16	2	3	31	57	45	5	.256	.334
2 Dave Philley	OF82, 3B2	R	35	83	311	50	93	13	3	6	41	34	38	1	.299	.418
Hal Smith	C125	R	24	135	424	41	115	23	4	4	52	30	21	1	.271	.373
2 Dave Pope	OF73	L	34	86	222	21	55	8	4	1	30	16	34	5	.248	.333
Bob Hale	1B44	L	21	67	182	13	66	7	1	0	29	5	19	0	.357	.407
Jim Dyck	OF45, 3B17	R	33	61	197	32	55	13	1	2	22	28	21	1	.279	.386
1 Gil Coan	OF43	L	33	61	130	18	31	7	1	1	11	13	15	4	.238	.331
1 Hoot Evers	OF55	R	34	60	185	21	44	10	1	6	30	19	28	2	.238	.400
1 Billy Young	2B58	L	30	59	186	5	37	2	1	0	11	23	19	1	.199	.231
Billy Cox	3B37, 2B18, SS6	R	35	53	194	25	41	7	2	3	14	16	22	1	.211	.314
1 Gene Woodling	OF44	L	32	47	145	22	32	6	2	2	18	24	18	1	.221	.352
1 Eddie Waitkus	1B26	L	35	38	85	2	22	1	1	0	9	11	10	2	.259	.294
1 Les Moss	C17	R	30	29	56	5	19	1	0	2	5	10	10	0	.339	.464
1 Bob Kennedy	OF14, 1B6, 3B1	R	34	30	70	10	10	1	0	1	5	10	10	0	.143	.157
Bob Nelson	OF6, 1B6, 3B1	L	18	25	31	4	6	0	0	0	3	5	14	0	.194	.194
Tommy Gastall	C15	R	23	20	27	4	4	1	0	0	3	5	5	0	.148	.185
2 Hank Majeski	3B8, 2B5	R	38	16	41	2	7	1	0	0	4	4	8	0	.171	.195

2 Wally Westlake 34 R 3-24, Angie Dagres 20 L 4-15, Kal Segrist 24 R 3-9, Brooks Robinson 18 R 2-22, 1 Charlie Maxwell 28 L 0-4, 1 Vern Stephens 34 R 1-6, Roger Marquis 18 L 0-1, Joe Durham (MS) 23

NAME	T	AGE	W	L	PCT	SV	G	GS	CG	IP	H	BB	SO	SHO	ERA
		31	57	97	.370	20	156	156	35	1389	1403	625	594	10	4.21
Jim Wilson	R	33	12	18	.400	0	34	31	14	235	200	87	96	4	3.45
Ray Moore	R	29	10	10	.500	6	46	14	3	152	128	80	80	1	3.91
2 Bill Wight	L	33	8	9	.429	2	19	14	8	117	111	39	54	2	4.13
Erv Palica	R	27	5	11	.313	0	33	25	5	170	165	83	68	1	4.13
2 George Zuverink	R	30	4	4	.571	4	28	0	0	86	80	17	31	0	2.20
1 Harry Byrd	R	30	3	2	.600	1	14	8	1	65	64	28	25	1	4.57
2 Harry Dorish	R	33	3	4	.500	6	35	1	0	66	58	28	22	0	3.14
2 Ed Lopat	L	37	4	3	.429	0	10	7	1	49	57	9	10	0	4.22
2 Art Schallock	L	31	4	5	.375	0	21	8	1	80	92	42	33	0	4.16
Jim McDonald	R	28	4	5	.375	0	21	8	1	68	89	35	27	0	5.82
Don Johnson	R	28	2	4	.333	1	15	1	0	30	33	13	13	0	7.10
Bob Alexander	R	32	1	0	1.000	0	8	0	0	15	21	11	8	0	13.50
4 Ted Gray	L	30	1	2	.333	0	6	0	0	15	21	11	8	0	8.40
1 Saul Rogovin	R	33	1	8	.111	0	12	1	0	71	79	27	35	0	4.56
1 Joe Coleman	R	32	1	0	1.000	0	6	2	0	12	19	10	6	0	10.50
1 Bob Kuzava	L	32	0	2	.000	0	12	1	0	31	28	13	6	0	3.75
Bill Miller	L	27	0	1	.000	0	9	1	0	14	18	13	8	0	6.43
Duane Pillette	R	32	0	1	.000	0	4	0	0	12	9	10	4	0	13.50
2 Hal Brown	R	34	1	0	1.000	0	5	1	0	38	50	27	26	0	4.11
Lou Kretlow	R	34	0	0	—	0	8	0	0	15	13	15	3	0	3.00
Don Ferrarese	L	23	0	0	—	0	5	1	0	15	7	11	3	0	3.00
Charlie Locke	R	23	0	0	—	0	2	0	0	4	6	4	1	0	13.50
Bob Harrison	R	24	0	0	—	0	2	0	0	9	9	9	0		9.00

Billy O'Dell (MS) 22

WASHINGTON — 8th 53-101 .344 43 — CHUCK DRESSEN

NAME	G by Pos	B	AGE	G	AB	R	H	2B	3B	HR	RBI	BB	SO	SB	BA	SA
TOTALS			28	154	5142	598	1277	178	54	80	556	538	654	25	.248	.351
Mickey Vernon	1B144	L	37	150	538	74	162	23	8	14	85	74	50	0	.301	.452
Pete Runnels	2B132, SS2	L	27	134	503	66	143	16	4	2	49	55	51	3	.284	.344
Jose Valdivielso	SS94	R	21	94	294	32	65	12	5	2	28	21	38	1	.221	.316
Eddie Yost	3B107	R	28	122	375	64	91	17	5	7	48	95	54	4	.243	.371
Carlos Paula	OF85	R	27	115	351	34	105	20	7	6	45	17	42	3	.299	.447
Tommy Umphlett	OF103	L	28	144	509	54	138	20	10	0	41	24	35	2	.271	.366
Roy Sievers	OF129, 1B17, 3B2	R	28	144	509	74	138	18	0	25	106	73	66	1	.271	.489
Ed Fitz Gerald	C72	R	31	74	236	28	56	13	4	1	19	25	20	1	.237	.309
Ernie Oravetz	OF57	B	23	100	263	24	71	5	5	0	25	26	19	1	.270	.297
Bobby Kline	SS69, 2B4, 3B3, P1	R	26	77	140	12	31	5	0	0	9	11	27	0	.221	.257
2 Clint Courtney	C67	L	28	70	238	26	71	8	2	4	30	19	9	0	.298	.391
2 Mickey McDermott	P31	L	26	70	95	10	24	4	0	1	6	14	20	0	.253	.337
2 Johnny Groth	OF48	R	28	63	182	22	40	6	2	1	18	18	21	1	.219	.328
Juan Delis	3B24, OF8, 2B1	R	27	54	132	12	23	3	0	1	14	12	33	1	.189	.227
1 Jim Busby	OF28	R	28	47	133	21	30	6	2	1	14	6	14	3	.230	.271
Jerry Snyder	2B22, SS20	R	25	44	107	7	24	5	3	0	6	15	11	0	.224	.271
Harmon Killebrew	3B23, 2B3	R	19	38	80	12	30	3	0	4	7	9	31	0	.200	.363
Bruce Edwards	C22, 3B5	R	31	30	57	4	10	3	1	0	3	16	6	0	.175	.211
Tony Roig	SS21, 3B8, 2B1	R	26	24	57	4	13	2	0	0	5	1	5	0	.228	.263
Jerry Schoonmaker	OF15	R	21	20	46	5	7	1	0	1	5	1	11	0	.152	.261

Jesse Levan 28 L 3-16, Steve Korcheck 22 R 10-36, Jim Lemon 27 R 5-25, Julio Becquer 23 L 3-14, Tom Wright 31 L 0-7, Bob Oldis 27 R 0-6

NAME	T	AGE	W	L	PCT	SV	G	GS	CG	IP	H	BB	SO	SHO	ERA
		26	53	101	.344	16	154	154	37	1355	1450	634	607	10	4.62
Mickey McDermott	L	26	10	10	.500	1	31	20	8	156	140	100	78	1	3.75
Bob Porterfield	R	31	10	17	.370	0	30	27	8	178	197	54	74	2	4.45
Johnny Schmitz	L	34	7	10	.412	1	32	21	6	165	187	54	49	1	3.71
Dean Stone	L	24	6	13	.316	1	43	24	5	180	180	114	84	1	4.15
Ted Abernathy	R	22	5	9	.357	0	40	13	6	117	136	67	79	2	5.97
Pedro Ramos	R	20	5	11	.313	1	45	9	2	125	127	39	74	1	3.88
Chuck Stobbs	L	25	4	14	.222	3	41	16	2	140	169	57	60	0	5.00
Spec Shea	R	34	2	4	.333	1	11	5	1	56	53	27	16	1	4.02
2 Bob Chakales	R	27	2	4	.400	0	29	0	0	55	55	25	28	0	5.24
Camilo Pascual	R	21	2	12	.143	1	43	16	1	129	158	70	82	0	6.14
Bunky Stewart	L	24	1	1	.500	0	13	1	0	23	18	17	14	0	4.71
Webbo Clarke	L	27	1	1	.500	0	7	0	0	21	17	14	9	0	4.71
Bill Currie	R	23	0	0	—	0	2	0	0	4	6	2	1	0	13.50
Dick Hyde	R	27	0	0	—	0	4	0	0	4	5	4	2	0	4.50
Vince Gonzales	L	29	0	0	—	0	3	0	0	2	3	0	0	0	27.00
Bobby Kline	R	26	0	0	—	0	1	0	0	1	3	1	1	0	27.00

BROOKLYN 1st 98-55 .641 — WALT ALSTON

NAME	G by Pos	B	AGE	G	AB	R	H	2B	3B	HR	RBI	BB	SO	SB	BA	SA
TOTALS			30	154	5193	857	1406	230	44	201	800	674	718	79	.271	.448
Gil Hodges	1B139, OF16	R	31	150	546	75	158	24	5	27	102	80	91	4	.289	.500
Jim Gilliam	2B99, OF46	B	26	147	538	110	134	20	4	7	40	70	37	15	.249	.355
Pee Wee Reese	SS142	R	36	145	553	99	156	29	4	10	61	78	60	8	.282	.403
Jackie Robinson	3B84, OF10, 2B1, 1B1	R	36	105	317	51	81	6	2	8	36	61	18	12	.256	.363
Carl Furillo	OF140	R	33	140	523	83	164	24	3	26	95	43	43	4	.314	.520
Duke Snider	OF146	L	28	148	538	126	166	34	6	42	136	104	87	9	.309	.628
Sandy Amoros	OF109	L	25	119	388	59	96	16	7	10	51	55	45	10	.247	.402
Roy Campanella	C121	R	33	123	446	81	142	20	1	32	107	56	41	2	.318	.583
Don Hoak	3B78	R	27	94	279	50	67	13	3	5	19	46	50	9	.240	.362
Don Zimmer	2B62, SS21, 3B8	R	24	88	280	38	67	10	1	15	50	19	66	5	.239	.443
Don Newcombe	P34	L	29	57	117	18	42	9	1	7	23	6	18	1	.359	.632
Rube Walker	C35	L	30	44	103	6	26	5	0	2	13	15	11	0	.252	.359
George Shuba	OF9	L	30	44	51	8	14	2	0	1	8	11	10	0	.275	.373
Frank Kellert	1B22	R	30	39	80	12	26	4	2	4	19	9	10	0	.325	.575
Dixie Howell	C13	R	35	16	42	2	11	4	0	0	5	1	7	0	.262	.357
Walt Moryn	OF7	L	29	11	19	3	5	1	0	1	3	5	4	0	.263	.474
2 Bob Borkowski	OF9	L	29	9	19	2	2	0	0	0	0	1	6	0	.105	.105
Bert Hamric		L	27	2	1	0	0	0	0	0	0	0	1	.000	.000	

NAME	T	AGE	W	L	PCT	SV	G	GS	CG	IP	H	BB	SO	SHO	ERA
	R	26	98	55	.641	37	154	154	46	1378	1296	483	773	11	3.68
Don Newcombe	R	29	20	5	.800	0	34	31	17	234	222	38	143	1	3.19
Clem Labine	R	28	13	5	.722	11	60	8	1	144	121	55	67	0	3.25
Carl Erskine	R	28	11	8	.579	1	31	29	7	195	185	64	84	2	3.78
Billy Loes	R	25	10	4	.714	0	21	19	6	128	116	46	85	0	3.59
Johnny Podres	L	22	9	10	.474	0	27	24	5	159	160	57	114	2	3.96
Don Bessent	R	24	8	1	.889	3	24	2	1	63	51	21	29	0	2.71
Karl Spooner (SA)	L	24	8	6	.571	2	29	14	2	99	79	41	78	1	3.64
Russ Meyer (XJ)	R	31	6	2	.750	0	18	11	2	73	86	31	26	1	5.42
Roger Craig	R	25	5	3	.625	2	21	10	3	91	81	43	48	0	2.77
Ed Roebuck	R	23	5	6	.455	12	47	0	0	84	96	24	33	0	4.71
Sandy Koufax (NJ)	L	19	2	2	.500	0	12	5	2	42	33	28	30	2	3.00
1 Joe Black	R	31	1	0	1.000	0	6	0	0	15	15	5	9	0	3.00
Chuck Templeton	L	23	0	1	.000	0	4	0	0	5	5	3	1	0	10.80
Jim Hughes	R	32	0	0	.000	4	24	0	0	43	41	19	20	0	4.19
Tommy Lasorda	R	27	0	0	—	0	4	1	0	4	5	6	4	0	13.50

MILWAUKEE 2nd 85-69 .552 13.5 — CHARLIE GRIMM

NAME	G by Pos	B	AGE	G	AB	R	H	2B	3B	HR	RBI	BB	SO	SB	BA	SA
TOTALS			28	154	5277	743	1377	219	55	182	699	504	735	42	.261	.427
George Crowe	1B79	R	34	104	303	41	85	12	4	15	55	45	44	1	.281	.495
Danny O'Connell	2B114, 3B7, SS1	R	28	124	453	47	102	15	4	6	40	28	43	1	.225	.316
Johnny Logan	SS154	R	28	154	595	95	177	37	5	13	83	58	58	3	.297	.442
Eddie Mathews	3B137	L	23	141	499	108	144	23	5	41	101	109	98	3	.289	.601
Hank Aaron	OF126, 2B27	R	21	153	602	105	189	37	9	27	106	49	61	3	.314	.540
Bill Bruton	OF149	L	29	149	636	106	175	30	12	9	47	43	72	25	.275	.403
Bobby Thomson	OF91	R	31	101	343	40	88	12	3	12	56	34	52	2	.257	.414
Del Crandall	C131	R	25	133	440	61	104	15	2	26	62	40	56	2	.236	.457
Chuck Tanner	OF62	R	25	97	243	27	60	9	3	6	27	27	32	1	.247	.383
Andy Pafko	OF58, 3B12	R	34	86	252	29	67	3	5	5	34	7	23	1	.266	.377
Joe Adcock (BA)	1B78	R	27	84	288	40	76	14	0	15	45	31	44	0	.264	.469
Warren Spahn	P39	L	34	40	81	7	17	1	1	4	14	4	20	0	.210	.395
Jack Dittmer	2B28	R	27	38	72	4	9	1	1	1	4	4	15	0	.125	.208
2 Del Rice	C22	R	32	71	5	14	0	1	2	7	6	12	0	.197	.310	
Charlie White	C10	L	27	12	30	3	7	1	0	0	4	5	7	0	.233	.267
Bennie Taylor	1B1	R	27	12	10	2	1	0	0	0	0	2	1	0	.100	.100

Jim Pendleton 31 R 0-10, Bob Roselli 23 R 2-9, Mel Roach (MS) 22

NAME	T	AGE	W	L	PCT	SV	G	GS	CG	IP	H	BB	SO	SHO	ERA
	R	27	85	69	.552	12	154	154	61	1383	1339	591	654	5	3.85
Warren Spahn	L	34	17	14	.548	1	39	32	16	246	249	65	110	1	3.26
Lew Burdette	R	28	13	8	.619	2	42	33	11	230	253	73	70	2	4.03
Bob Buhl	R	26	13	11	.542	1	38	27	11	202	168	109	117	1	3.21
Gene Conley	R	24	11	7	.611	0	22	21	10	158	152	52	107	0	4.16
Ray Crone	R	23	10	9	.526	0	33	15	6	140	117	42	76	1	3.47
Chet Nichols	L	24	9	8	.529	1	34	21	6	144	139	67	44	0	4.00
Ernie Johnson	R	31	5	7	.417	4	40	2	0	92	81	55	43	0	3.42
Humberto Robinson	R	25	3	1	.750	2	13	2	1	38	31	25	19	0	3.08
Phil Paine	R	25	2	0	1.000	0	15	0	0	25	20	14	26	0	2.52
Dave Jolly	R	30	2	3	.400	1	36	0	0	58	58	51	23	0	5.74
Dave Koslo	L	35	0	1	.000	0	0	0	0	0	1	0	0	0	T
Roberto Vargas	L	26	0	0	—	0	25	0	0	25	39	14	13	0	8.64
Joey Jay	R	19	0	0		0	12	1	0	19	23	13	3	0	4.74
John Edelman	R	19	0	0		0	5	0	0	6	7	8	3	0	10.50
Charlie Gorin	L	27	0	0		0	2	0	0	0.1	1	3	1	0	54.00

NEW YORK 3rd 80-74 .519 18.5 — LEO DUROCHER

NAME	G by Pos	B	AGE	G	AB	R	H	2B	3B	HR	RBI	BB	SO	SB	BA	SA
TOTALS			28	154	5288	702	1377	173	34	169	643	497	581	38	.260	.402
Gail Harris	1B75	L	23	79	263	27	61	9	0	12	36	20	46	0	.232	.403
Wayne Terwilliger	2B78, SS1, 3B1	R	30	80	257	29	66	16	1	9	18	36	42	2	.257	.339
Al Dark (SJ)	SS115	R	33	115	475	77	134	20	3	9	45	22	32	3	.282	.394
Hank Thompson	3B124, 2B7, SS1	R	29	135	432	65	105	13	1	17	63	84	56	2	.245	.398
Don Mueller	OF146	R	28	147	605	67	185	21	4	8	83	19	12	1	.306	.393
Willie Mays	OF152	R	24	152	580	123	185	18	13	51	127	79	60	24	.319	.659
Whitey Lockman	OF81, 1B68	L	28	147	576	76	157	19	0	15	49	39	34	3	.273	.384
Ray Katt	C122	R	28	124	326	27	70	7	2	7	28	22	38	0	.215	.313
Bobby Hofman	1B24, 2B19, C19, 3B5	R	29	96	207	32	55	7	2	10	28	22	31	0	.266	.464
Dusty Rhodes	OF45	L	28	94	187	22	57	5	2	6	32	27	26	1	.305	.449
Davey Williams (XJ)	2B71	R	27	82	247	25	62	4	1	4	15	17	17	0	.251	.324
Wes Westrum	C68	R	32	69	137	11	29	1	0	4	18	24	18	0	.212	.307
2 Sid Gordon	3B31, OF17	R	37	66	144	19	35	6	1	7	25	25	15	0	.243	.444
Bill Taylor	OF2	L	25	65	64	9	17	4	0	4	12	1	16	0	.266	.516
Billy Gardner	SS38, 3B10, 2B4	R	27	59	187	26	38	10	1	3	17	9	27	0	.203	.316
Monte Irvin	OF45	R	36	51	150	16	38	7	1	1	17	17	15	3	.253	.333
Jim Hearn	P39	R	34	41	77	11	12	0	0	4	6	4	26	0	.156	.312
Johnny Antonelli	P38	L	25	38	82	8	17	1	0	4	15	3	18	0	.207	.366
Joey Amalfitano	SS5, 3B2	R	21	36	22	6	5	1	1	0	1	2	2	0	.227	.364
Foster Castleman	2B6, 3B1	R	24	15	28	3	6	1	0	2	4	2	4	0	.214	.464

3 Gil Coan 33 L 2-13, Mickey Grasso 35 R 0-2, Daryl Spencer (MS) 25

NAME	T	AGE	W	L	PCT	SV	G	GS	CG	IP	H	BB	SO	SHO	ERA
	R	30	80	74	.519	14	154	154	52	1387	1347	560	721	6	3.77
Jim Hearn	R	34	14	16	.467	0	39	33	11	227	225	66	86	1	3.73
Johnny Antonelli	L	25	14	16	.467	1	38	34	14	235	206	82	143	2	3.33
Don Liddle	L	30	10	4	.714	1	33	13	4	106	97	61	56	0	4.25
1 Sal Maglie	R	38	9	5	.643	0	23	21	6	130	142	48	71	0	3.74
Ruben Gomez	R	27	9	10	.474	1	33	31	9	185	207	63	79	3	4.57
Windy McCall	L	29	6	5	.545	3	42	4	0	95	86	37	50	0	3.69
Marv Grissom	R	37	5	4	.556	8	55	0	0	89	76	41	49	0	2.93
Hoyt Wilhelm	R	32	4	1	.800	0	59	0	0	103	104	40	71	0	3.93
Paul Giel	R	22	4	4	.500	0	34	2	0	82	70	50	47	0	3.40
Ray Monzant	R	22	4	8	.333	0	28	12	3	95	98	43	54	0	3.98
Pete Burnside	L	24	1	0	1.000	0	13	0	0	13	10	9	2	0	2.77
Al Corwin	R	28	0	1	.000	0	13	0	0	25	25	17	13	0	3.96
George Spencer	R	28	0	0		0	1	0	0	2	1	3	0	0	4.50

PHILADELPHIA 4th 77-77 .500 21.5 — MAYO SMITH

NAME	G by Pos	B	AGE	G	AB	R	H	2B	3B	HR	RBI	BB	SO	SB	BA	SA
TOTALS			27	154	5092	675	1300	214	50	132	631	652	673	44	.255	.395
Marv Blaylock	1B77, OF6	L	25	113	259	30	54	7	7	3	24	31	43	6	.208	.324
Bobby Morgan	2B88, SS41, 3B6, 1B1	R	29	136	483	61	112	20	2	10	49	73	72	6	.232	.344
Roy Smalley	SS87, 3B1, 2B1	R	29	92	260	33	51	11	1	7	39	59	46	5	.196	.327
Willie Jones	3B146	R	29	146	516	65	133	20	3	16	81	77	51	6	.258	.401
2 Jim Greengrass	OF83, 3B2	R	27	94	323	43	88	20	2	12	37	33	43	0	.272	.458
Richie Ashburn	OF140	L	28	140	533	91	180	32	9	3	42	105	36	12	.338	.448
Del Ennis	OF145	R	30	146	564	82	167	24	7	29	120	46	64	4	.296	.518
2 Andy Seminick	C88	R	34	93	289	32	71	12	1	11	34	32	59	1	.246	.408
Granny Hamner	2B82, SS32	R	28	104	405	57	104	12	4	5	43	41	30	0	.257	.343
Stan Lopata	C66, 1B24	R	29	99	303	49	82	9	3	22	58	58	62	4	.271	.538
2 Glen Gorbous	OF57	L	24	91	224	25	53	9	1	4	25	21	17	0	.237	.339
Peanuts Lowrey	OF28, 2B1, 3B1	R	37	54	106	9	20	4	0	0	8	7	10	2	.189	.226
1 Earl Torgeson	1B43	L	31	47	150	29	40	5	3	1	17	32	20	2	.267	.360
Herm Wehmeier	P31	R	28	34	72	10	20	1	0	7	2	2	26	0	.278	.319
2 Eddie Waitkus	1B31	L	35	33	107	10	30	5	0	2	14	17	7	0	.280	.383
1 Stan Palys	OF15	R	25	15	52	8	15	3	0	1	8	6	5	1	.288	.404
Mel Clark	OF8	R	28	10	32	3	5	3	0	0	1	3	4	1	.156	.250
Ted Kazanski	SS4, 3B4	R	21	9	12	1	1	0	0	1	0	1	1	0	.083	.333
Gus Niarhos	C7	R	34	7	9	1	1	0	0	0	0	1	1	0	.111	.111
1 Smoky Burgess	C6	L	28	7	7	1	1	1	0	0	1	3	4	0	.190	.429

Floyd Baker 38 L 0-8, Jim Command 26 L 0-5, Bob Micelotta 26 R 0-4, Bob Bowman 24 R 0-3, Danny Schell 27 R 0-2, John Easton 22 R 0-0, Fred Van Dusen 17 L 0-0, Jim Westlake 24 L 0-1

NAME	T	AGE	W	L	PCT	SV	G	GS	CG	IP	H	BB	SO	SHO	ERA
	R	28	77	77	.500	21	154	154	58	1357	1291	477	657	11	3.93
Robin Roberts	R	28	23	14	.622	0	41	38	26	305	292	53	160	1	3.28
Murry Dickson	R	38	12	11	.522	0	36	28	12	216	190	82	92	4	3.50
Herm Wehmeier	R	28	10	12	.455	0	31	29	10	194	176	67	85	1	4.41
Bob Miller	R	29	8	4	.667	1	40	0	0	90	80	28	28	0	2.40
Curt Simmons	L	26	8	8	.500	0	25	22	3	130	148	50	58	0	4.92
Jack Meyer	R	23	6	11	.353	16	50	5	0	110	75	66	97	0	3.44
2 Saul Rogovin	R	33	5	3	.625	0	12	11	5	73	60	17	27	2	3.08
Ron Negray	R	25	4	3	.571	0	19	10	2	72	71	21	30	0	3.50
2 Bob Kuzava	L	32	1	0	1.000	0	17	4	0	42	47	12	13	0	7.31
Thornton Kipper	R	26	0	1	.000	0	24	0	0	40	47	22	15	0	4.95
Lynn Lovenguth	R	32	0	1	.000	0	14	0	0	18	17	10	14	0	4.50
1 Steve Ridzik	R	26	0	1	.000	0	3	0	0	11	7	8	6	0	2.45
Jack Spring	L	22	0	1	.000	0	11	0	0	11	13	7	8	0	6.00
Ron Mrozinski	L	24	0	2	.000	0	22	1	0	34	38	19	18	0	6.62
Jim Owens	R	21	0	1	.000	0	9	0	0	13	7	6	8	0	8.00
Dave Cole	R	24	0	3	.000	0	18	2	0	18	21	14	6	0	6.50
Bob Greenwood	R	27	0	0	—	0	1	0	0	1	1	0	0	0	18.00

CINCINNATI 5th 75-79 .487 23.5 — BIRDIE TEBBETTS

NAME	G by Pos	B	AGE	G	AB	R	H	2B	3B	HR	RBI	BB	SO	SB	BA	SA
TOTALS			27	154	5270	761	1424	216	28	181	726	556	657	51	.270	.425
Ted Kluszewski	1B153	L	30	153	612	116	192	25	0	47	113	66	40	1	.314	.585
Johnny Temple	2B149, SS1	R	26	150	588	94	165	20	3	0	50	80	32	19	.281	.325
Roy McMillan	SS150	R	25	151	470	50	126	21	2	1	37	66	33	4	.268	.328
Rocky Bridges	2B59, SS26, 2B9	R	27	95	168	20	48	4	0	1	18	15	19	1	.286	.327
Wally Post	OF154	R	25	154	601	116	186	33	4	40	109	60	102	7	.309	.574
Gus Bell	OF154	L	26	154	610	88	188	30	6	27	104	54	57	4	.308	.510
2 Stan Palys	OF55, 1B1	R	25	79	222	29	51	14	0	7	30	12	35	1	.230	.387
2 Smoky Burgess	C107	L	28	116	421	67	129	15	3	20	77	47	35	1	.306	.499
Chuck Harmon	3B39, OF32, 1B6	R	31	96	198	31	50	6	3	5	28	26	24	9	.253	.389
Bob Thurman	OF36	L	38	82	152	19	33	2	3	7	22	17	26	0	.217	.408
Ray Jablonski	3B28, 2B28	R	28	74	221	28	53	9	0	9	28	13	35	0	.240	.403
1 Bobby Adams	3B42, 2B5	R	33	64	150	23	41	11	2	2	20	20	21	2	.273	.413
Hobie Landrith (BC)	C27	L	25	43	87	9	22	3	0	4	10	14	24	0	.253	.425
Milt Smith	3B28, 2B5	R	26	36	102	15	20	3	1	3	13	13	24	1	.196	.333
2 Sam Mele	OF13, 1B1	R	33	35	62	4	13	1	0	2	7	5	13	0	.210	.323
Matt Batts	C21	R	33	26	71	4	18	4	1	0	13	4	11	0	.254	.338
2 Bob Borkowski	OF11, 1B1	R	29	25	18	1	3	1	0	0	0	1	3	0	.167	.222
Ed Bailey	C11	L	24	22	19	3	4	1	0	1	4	6	4	0	.205	.359
Joe Brovia		L	33	21	18	1	3	1	0	0	1	1	4	0	.111	.111
1 Jim Greengrass	OF11	R	27	13	39	1	4	2	0	0	3	9	5	0	.103	.154
Al Silvera	OF1	R	19	13	7	1	1	0	0	0	2	0	1	0	.143	.143
1 Glen Gorbous	OF5	L	24	7	6	1	2	0	0	0	1	1	1	0	.333	.500
1 Andy Seminick	C5	R	34	6	15	1	2	0	0	0	1	1	3	0	.133	.133
Bob Hazle	OF3	L	24	6	13	0	3	1	0	0	0	0	3	0	.231	.231

NAME	T	AGE	W	L	PCT	SV	G	GS	CG	IP	H	BB	SO	SHO	ERA
	R	29	75	79	.487	22	154	154	38	1363	1373	443	576	12	3.95
Joe Nuxhall	L	26	17	12	.586	3	50	33	14	257	240	78	98	5	3.47
Art Fowler	R	32	11	10	.524	2	46	28	8	208	198	63	94	3	3.89
Jackie Collum	L	28	9	8	.529	1	32	17	5	134	128	37	49	0	3.63
Johnny Klippstein	R	27	9	10	.474	0	39	14	3	138	120	60	68	2	3.39
2 Hersh Freeman	R	27	7	4	.636	11	52	0	0	92	94	30	37	0	2.15
1 Joe Black	R	31	5	2	.714	3	32	11	1	102	106	25	54	0	4.24
1 Gerry Staley	R	34	5	8	.385	0	30	18	2	120	146	28	40	0	4.65
Rudy Minarcin	R	25	5	9	.357	1	41	12	3	116	116	51	45	1	4.89
Don Gross	L	24	4	5	.444	0	17	11	2	67	79	16	33	1	4.16
Corky Valentine	R	26	2	1	.667	0	10	5	0	29	36	14	10	0	7.33
Bud Podbielan (JJ)	R	31	2	3	.333	0	17	2	0	42	36	11	26	0	3.21
Jim Pearce	R	30	0	1	.000	0	4	0	0	11	11	6	9	0	12.00
Jerry Lane	R	29	0	0		0	11	1	0	15	20	6	6	0	4.91
Bob Hooper	R	33	0	0		0	13	0	0	13	20	6	9	0	7.62
2 Steve Ridzik	R	26	0	0		0	4	0	0	30	35	14	6	0	4.50
Fred Baczewski	L	27	0	0		0	3	0	0	6	13	3	1	0	18.00
Maury Fisher	R	24	0	0		0	2	0	0	1	2	1	1	0	6.00

CHICAGO 6th 72-81 .471 26 STAN HACK

NAME	G by Pos	B	AGE	G	AB	R	H	2B	3B	HR	RBI	BB	SO	SB	BA	SA
TOTALS			28	154	5214	626	1287	187	55	164	597	428	806	37	.247	.398
Dee Fondy	1B147	L	30	150	574	69	152	23	8	17	65	35	87	8	.265	.422
Gene Baker	2B154	R	30	154	609	82	163	29	7	11	52	49	57	9	.268	.392
Ernie Banks	SS154	R	24	154	596	98	176	29	9	44	117	45	72	9	.295	.596
Randy Jackson	3B134	R	29	138	499	73	132	13	7	21	70	58	58	6	.265	.445
Jim King	OF93	L	22	113	301	43	77	13	3	11	45	24	39	2	.256	.425
Eddie Miksis	OF111, 3B18	R	28	131	481	52	113	14	2	9	41	32	55	3	.235	.338
Hank Sauer	OF68	R	38	79	261	29	55	8	1	12	28	26	47	0	.211	.387
Harry Chiti	C113	R	22	113	338	24	78	6	1	11	41	14	68	0	.231	.352
Frankie Baumholtz	OF63	L	36	105	288	23	81	12	5	1	27	16	24	0	.289	.379
Bob Speake	OF55, 1B8	L	24	95	261	36	57	9	5	12	43	28	71	3	.218	.429
2 Lloyd Merriman	OF47	L	30	72	145	15	31	6	1	1	8	21	21	1	.214	.290
Jim Bolger	OF51	R	23	64	160	19	33	5	4	0	7	9	17	2	.206	.288
Walker Cooper	C31	R	40	54	111	11	31	8	1	7	15	6	19	0	.279	.559
Clyde McCullough	C37	R	38	44	81	7	16	0	0	0	10	8	15	0	.198	.198
Ted Tappe (FJ)	OF15	L	24	23	50	12	13	2	0	4	10	11	11	0	.260	.540
Gale Wade	OF9	L	26	9	33	5	6	1	0	1	1	4	3	0	.182	.303
Vern Morgan	3B2	R	26	7	7	1	1	0	0	0	1	3	4	1	.143	.143

2 Owen Friend 28 R 1-10, Jim Fanning 27 R 0-10, Al Lary 26 R 0-0, El Tappe 28 R 0-0

NAME	T	AGE	W	L	PCT	SV	G	GS	CG	IP	H	BB	SO	SHO	ERA
		30	72	81	.471	23	154	154	47	1378	1306	601	686	10	4.17
Sam Jones	R	29	14	20	.412	0	36	34	12	242	175	185	198	4	4.09
Bob Rush	R	29	13	11	.542	0	33	33	14	234	204	73	130	3	3.50
Warren Hacker	R	30	11	15	.423	3	35	30	13	213	202	43	80	0	4.27
Paul Minner	L	31	9	9	.500	0	22	22	7	158	173	47	53	1	3.47
Hal Jeffcoat	R	30	8	6	.571	6	50	1	0	101	107	53	32	0	2.94
Jim Davis	L	30	7	11	.389	3	40	16	0	134	122	58	62	0	4.43
Howie Pollet	L	34	4	3	.571	2	24	7	1	61	62	27	21	1	5.61
Bill Tremel	R	23	0	0	1.000	2	23	0	0	39	33	18	13	0	3.69
Harry Perkowski	L	32	3	4	.429	2	25	4	0	48	53	25	28	0	5.25
John Andre	R	32	0	1	.000	1	22	3	0	45	45	28	19	0	5.80
Vicente Amor	R	22	0	1	.000	0	6	1	0	9	11	3	4	0	4.50
Dave Hillman	R	27	0	0	—	0	25	3	0	58	63	25	28	0	5.28
Don Kaiser	R	20	0	1	.000	0	11	0	0	18	20	5	11	0	5.50
Hy Cohen	R	24	0	0	—	0	7	1	0	17	28	10	4	0	7.94
Bubba Church	R	30	0	0	—	0	2	0	0	4	3	1	0	0	6.00
Bob Thorpe	R	20	0	0	—	0	2	0	0	2	0	1	0	0	3.00

ST. LOUIS 7th 68-86 .442 30.5 EDDIE STANKY 17-19 .472 HARRY WALKER 51-67 .432

NAME	G by Pos	B	AGE	G	AB	R	H	2B	3B	HR	RBI	BB	SO	SB	BA	SA
TOTALS			29	154	5266	654	1375	228	36	143	608	458	597	64	.261	.400
Stan Musial	1B110, OF51	L	34	154	562	97	179	30	5	33	108	80	39	5	.319	.566
Red Schoendienst	2B142	B	32	145	553	68	148	21	3	11	51	54	28	1	.268	.376
Alex Grammas	SS126	R	29	128	366	32	88	19	2	3	25	33	36	4	.240	.328
Ken Boyer	3B139, SS18	R	24	147	530	78	140	27	2	18	62	37	67	6	.264	.425
Wally Moon	OF100, 1B51	L	25	152	593	86	175	24	8	19	76	47	65	11	.295	.434
Bill Virdon	OF142	L	24	144	534	58	150	18	6	17	68	36	64	2	.281	.433
Rip Repulski	OF141	R	26	147	512	64	138	28	2	23	73	49	66	5	.270	.467
Bill Sarni	C99	R	27	107	325	32	83	15	2	3	34	27	33	1	.255	.342
Solly Hemus	3B43, 2B10, SS2	L	32	96	206	36	50	10	2	5	21	27	22	1	.243	.383
Harry Elliott	OF28	R	31	68	117	9	30	4	0	1	12	11	9	0	.256	.316
Bobby Stephenson	SS48, 2B7, 3B1	R	26	67	111	9	27	3	0	0	6	5	18	2	.243	.270
Nels Burbrink	C55	R	33	58	170	11	47	8	1	0	15	14	13	1	.276	.335
Pete Whisenant	OF40	R	25	58	131	12	26	5	1	2	9	5	29	1	.198	.344
Joe Frazier	OF14	L	32	58	70	12	14	1	0	4	9	6	12	0	.200	.386
1 Del Rice	C18	R	32	20	59	6	12	3	0	1	7	0	6	0	.203	.305
Tom Alston	1B7	L	29	13	8	1	1	0	0	0	0	0	6	0	.125	.125
Dick Schofield	SS3	R	20	12	4	3	0	0	0	0	0	0	0	0	.000	.000
Harry Walker	OF1	L	38	11	14	2	5	2	0	0	1	1	0	0	.357	.500
Don Blasingame	2B3, SS2	L	23	5	16	4	6	1	0	0	0	6	1	1	.375	.438
Dick Rand	C3	R	24	3	10	1	3	0	1	0	1	0	3	0	.300	.600

NAME	T	AGE	W	L	PCT	SV	G	GS	CG	IP	H	BB	SO	SHO	ERA
		27	68	86	.442	15	154	154	42	1377	1376	549	730	10	4.56
Harvey Haddix	L	29	12	16	.429	1	37	30	9	208	216	62	150	2	4.46
Luis Arroyo	L	28	11	8	.579	0	35	24	9	159	162	63	68	1	4.19
Tom Poholsky	R	25	9	11	.450	0	30	24	8	151	143	35	66	2	3.81
Larry Jackson	R	24	9	14	.391	2	37	25	4	177	189	72	88	1	4.32
Willard Schmidt	R	27	7	6	.538	0	20	15	8	130	89	57	86	1	2.77
Paul LaPalme	L	31	4	3	.571	3	56	0	0	92	76	34	39	0	2.74
Frank Smith (AJ)	R	27	3	1	.750	1	28	0	0	39	27	23	17	0	3.23
Brooks Lawrence	R	30	3	8	.273	1	46	10	2	96	102	58	52	1	6.56
Mel Wright	R	27	2	2	.500	1	29	0	0	36	44	9	18	0	6.25
Floyd Wooldridge	R	26	2	4	.333	0	18	8	2	58	64	27	14	0	4.81
Al Gettel	R	37	1	0	1.000	0	17	0	0	17	26	10	7	0	9.00
2 Ben Flowers	R	28	1	1	.500	0	14	1	0	24	29	15	8	0	7.88
Herb Moford	R	26	1	1	.500	2	14	1	0	30	30	15	19	0	7.80
Barney Schultz	R	28	1	2	.333	4	19	0	0	30	31	10	16	0	4.36
Bobby Tiefenauer	R	25	1	4	.200	1	15	9	0	57	66	28	46	0	5.84
Gordon Jones	R	25	1	4	.200	0	15	6	0	57	66	28	46	0	5.84
Johnny Mackinson	R	31	0	1	.000	0	8	1	0	21	24	10	8	0	7.71
1 Vic Raschi	R	36	0	1	.000	—	0	5	1	0	5	1	5	1	18.00
Lindy McDaniel	R	19	0	0	—	0	4	2	0	19	22	7	7	0	4.74
Tony Jacobs	R	19	0	0	—	0	2	1	0	2	6	1	1	0	18.00

Vinegar Bend Mizell (MS) 24

PITTSBURGH 8th 60-94 .390 38.5 FRED HANEY

NAME	G by Pos	B	AGE	G	AB	R	H	2B	3B	HR	RBI	BB	SO	SB	BA	SA
TOTALS			25	154	5173	560	1262	210	60	91	532	471	652	22	.244	.361
Dale Long	1B119	L	29	131	419	59	122	19	13	16	79	48	72	0	.291	.513
Johnny O'Brien (MS-JJ)	2B78	R	24	84	278	22	83	15	2	1	25	20	19	1	.299	.378
Dick Groat	SS149	R	24	151	521	43	139	28	4	4	51	38	26	0	.267	.351
Gene Freese	3B65, 2B78	R	21	134	455	69	115	21	8	14	44	34	57	5	.253	.426
Roberto Clemente	OF118	R	20	124	474	48	121	23	11	5	47	18	60	2	.255	.382
Eddie O'Brien (MS)	OF56, 3B7, SS4	R	24	75	256	31	60	8	1	1	18	13	33	4	.233	.254
Frank Thomas	OF139	R	26	142	510	72	125	16	2	25	72	60	76	2	.245	.431
Jack Shepard	C77	R	24	94	264	24	63	10	2	2	23	33	25	1	.239	.314
Jerry Lynch	OF71, C2	L	24	88	282	43	80	18	6	5	28	22	33	2	.284	.443
Preston Ward	1B48, OF1	L	27	84	179	16	38	7	4	5	25	22	26	0	.212	.380
Dick Cole	3B33, 2B24, SS12	R	29	77	239	16	54	8	3	0	21	18	22	0	.226	.285
1 Tom Saffell	OF47	L	33	73	113	21	19	1	0	1	3	15	22	1	.168	.204
Toby Atwell	C67	L	31	71	207	21	44	8	0	1	18	40	16	0	.213	.266
Roman Mejias	OF44	R	24	71	167	14	36	8	1	3	21	9	13	1	.216	.329
George Freese	3B50	R	28	59	179	17	46	8	2	3	22	17	18	1	.257	.374
Felipe Montemayor	OF28	R	27	36	95	10	20	1	3	2	8	18	24	1	.211	.347
Hardy Peterson	C31	R	25	32	81	7	20	6	0	1	10	7	7	0	.247	.358
Dick Hall	P15, OF3	R	24	21	40	3	7	1	0	1	3	6	5	0	.175	.275
1 Sid Gordon	3B8, OF4	R	37	16	47	2	8	1	0	0	2	6	6	0	.170	.191
Curt Roberts	2B6	R	25	6	17	1	2	1	0	0	1	0	5	0	.118	.176
Earl Smith	OF5	R	27	5	16	1	1	0	0	0	0	4	2	0	.063	.063
Nick Koback	C2	R	19	5	7	1	2	0	0	0	1	0	2	0	.286	.286

Dick Smith 27 R 0-0, Johnny Powers 25 L 1-4, Paul Smith (MS) 24

NAME	T	AGE	W	L	PCT	SV	G	GS	CG	IP	H	BB	SO	SHO	ERA
		27	60	94	.390	16	154	154	41	1362	1480	536	622	5	4.39
Bob Friend	R	24	14	9	.609	2	44	20	9	200	178	52	98	2	2.84
Vern Law	R	25	10	10	.500	1	43	24	8	201	221	61	82	1	3.81
Max Surkont	R	33	7	14	.333	2	35	22	5	166	194	78	84	0	5.58
Dick Hall	R	24	6	6	.500	1	15	13	4	94	92	28	46	0	3.93
Ron Kline	R	23	6	13	.316	2	36	19	2	137	161	53	48	1	4.14
Roy Face	R	27	5	7	.417	5	42	10	4	126	128	40	84	0	3.57
Dick Littlefield	L	29	5	12	.294	0	35	17	4	130	148	68	70	1	5.12
Lino Donoso	L	32	4	6	.400	1	25	9	3	95	106	35	38	0	5.31
Bob Purkey	R	25	7	2	.222	1	14	10	2	68	77	25	24	0	5.29
Nellie King	R	27	1	3	.250	0	17	4	0	54	60	14	21	0	3.00
Laurin Pepper	R	24	1	0	1.000	0	14	1	0	20	30	25	7	0	10.35
Ben Wade	R	32	0	1	.000	1	14	0	0	28	26	14	7	0	3.21
Paul Martin	R	23	0	1	.000	0	7	1	0	13	17	13	3	0	14.14
Jake Thies	R	29	0	1	.000	1	10	0	0	17	17	17	5	0	4.50
Roger Bowman	L	27	0	3	.000	0	3	0	0	7	7	2	4	0	8.47
Al Grunwald	L	25	0	0	—	0	3	0	0	9	7	2	6	0	4.50
Fred Waters	L	28	0	0	—	0	2	1	0	7	1	0	1	0	3.60
Bill Bell	R	21	0	0	—	0	1	1	0	3	3	2	1	0	0.00
Red Swanson	R	18	0	0	—	0	1	0	0	2	4	0	2	0	18.00

WORLD SERIES — BROOKLYN (NL) 4 NEW YORK (AL) 3

LINE SCORES

TEAM	1	2	3	4	5	6	7	8	9	10	11	12	R	H	E
Game 1 September 28 at New York															
BKN (NL)	0	2	1	0	0	0	0	2	0				5	10	0
NY (AL)	0	2	1	1	0	2	0	0	X				6	9	1

Newcombe, Bessent (6), Labine (8)   Ford, Grim (9)

Game 2 September 29 at New York															
BKN	0	0	0	1	1	0	0	0	0				2	5	2
NY	0	0	0	4	0	0	0	0	X				4	8	0

Loes, Bessent (4), Spooner (5), Labine (8)   Byrne

Game 3 September 30 at Brooklyn															
NY	0	2	0	0	0	0	1	0	0				3	7	0
BKN	2	2	0	2	0	0	2	0	X				8	11	1

Turley, Morgan (2), Kucks (5), Sturdivant (7)   Podres

Game 4 October 1 at Brooklyn															
NY	1	1	0	1	0	2	0	0	0				5	9	0
BKN	0	0	1	3	3	0	1	0	X				8	14	0

Larsen, Kucks (5), R. Coleman (6), Sturdivant (8)   Erskine, Bessent (4), Labine (5)

Game 5 October 2 at Brooklyn															
NY	0	0	0	1	0	0	0	1	0				3	6	0
BKN	0	2	1	0	1	0	1	X					5	9	2

Grim, Turley (7), Morgan (7)   Craig, Labine (7)

Game 6 October 3 at New York															
BKN	0	0	0	1	0	0	0	0	0				1	4	1
NY	5	0	0	0	0	0	0	0	X				5	8	0

Spooner, Meyer (1), Roebuck (7)   Ford

Game 7 October 4 at New York															
BKN	0	0	0	1	0	1	0	0	0				2	5	0
NY	0	0	0	0	0	0	0	0	0				0	8	1

Podres   Byrne, Grim (6), Turley (8)

COMPOSITE BATTING

NAME	POS	G	AB	R	H	2B	3B	HR	RBI	BA
Brooklyn (NL)										
Totals		7	223	31	58	8	1	9	30	.260
Reese	SS	7	27	5	8	1	0	0	2	.296
Furillo	OF	7	27	4	8	1	0	1	3	.296
Campanella	C	7	27	4	7	3	0	2	4	.259
Snider	OF	7	25	5	8	1	0	4	7	.320
Gilliam	OF-2B	7	24	4	7	1	0	1	3	.292
Hodges	1B	7	24	2	7	0	0	1	5	.292
J. Robinson	3B	6	22	5	4	1	1	0	1	.182
Amoros	OF	5	12	3	4	0	0	1	3	.333
Zimmer	2B	4	9	0	2	0	0	0	2	.222
Podres	P	2	7	1	1	0	0	0	1	.143
Labine	P	4	4	0	0	0	0	0	0	.000
Kellert	PH	3	3	0	1	0	0	0	0	.333
Hoak	3B	2	3	0	1	0	0	0	0	.333
Newcombe	P	1	3	0	0	0	0	0	0	.000
Meyer	P	1	2	0	0	0	0	0	0	.000
Shuba	PH	1	1	0	0	0	0	0	0	.000
Bessent	P	3	1	0	0	0	0	0	0	.000
Loes	P	2	1	0	0	0	0	0	0	.000
Erskine	P	1	1	0	0	0	0	0	0	.000

Spooner P 0-0, Craig P 0-0, Roebuck P 0-0

NAME	POS	G	AB	R	H	2B	3B	HR	RBI	BA
New York (AL)										
Totals		7	222	26	55	4	2	8	25	.248
McDougald	3B	7	27	2	7	0	0	1	3	.259
Howard	OF	7	26	3	5	0	0	1	3	.192
Martin	2B	7	25	2	8	1	0	1	4	.320
Berra	C	7	24	5	10	1	0	1	2	.417
Cerv	OF	5	16	1	2	0	0	1	2	.125
Noren	OF	5	16	0	1	0	0	0	0	.063
Rizzuto	SS	7	15	2	4	0	0	0	0	.267
Bauer	OF	6	14	1	6	0	0	0	1	.429
Skowron	1B	5	12	3	4	0	0	1	3	.333
Collins	1B-OF	5	12	6	2	0	0	0	0	.167
Mantle	OF	3	10	1	2	0	0	1	1	.200
Byrne	P	2	6	0	1	0	0	0	2	.167
Ford	P	2	5	0	1	0	0	0	0	.200
E. Robinson	1B	2	3	0	2	0	0	0	0	.667
Carey	PH	2	2	0	1	0	0	0	0	.500
J. Coleman	SS	3	3	0	0	0	0	0	0	.000
Grim	P	3	3	0	0	0	0	0	0	.000
Larsen	P	2	2	0	0	0	0	0	0	.000
Turley	P	3	1	0	0	0	0	0	0	.000

Morgan P 0-0, Kucks P 0-0, Sturdivant P 0-0
R. Coleman P 0-0, Carroll PR 0-0

COMPOSITE PITCHING

NAME	G	IP	H	BB	SO	W	L	SV	ERA
Brooklyn (NL)									
Totals	7	60	55	22	39	4	3	1	3.75
Podres	2	18	15	4	10	2	0	0	1.00
Labine	4	9.1	6	2	2	1	0	1	2.89
Craig	1	6	4	5	4	1	0	0	3.00
Meyer	1	5.2	4	2	4	0	0	0	0.00
Newcombe	1	5.2	8	4	0	0	1	0	9.53
Loes	2	3.2	7	1	5	0	0	0	9.82
Bessent	3	3.1	3	1	1	0	0	0	0.00
Spooner	2	3.1	4	6	3	0	1	0	13.50
Erskine	1	3	3	2	3	0	0	0	9.00
Roebuck	1	1	1	0	0	0	0	0	0.00

NAME	G	IP	H	BB	SO	W	L	SV	ERA
New York (AL)									
Totals	7	60	58	33	38	3	4	1	4.20
Ford	2	17	13	8	10	2	0	0	2.12
Byrne	2	14.1	8	8	1	1	1	0	1.88
Grim	3	8.2	8	5	8	0	1	1	4.15
Turley	3	5.1	4	7	0	1	0	0	8.44
Larsen	1	4	5	2	2	0	1	0	11.25
Morgan	2	3.2	3	1	1	0	0	0	4.91
Kucks	2	3	4	1	0	0	0	0	6.00
Sturdivant	2	3	3	5	6	0	0	0	6.00
R. Coleman	1	1	1	0	3	0	0	0	9.00

1956 October's Revenge

Casey Stengel was not a man to hold a grudge. But as the season started, his Yankees were only the second best in the world to the Brooklyn Dodgers. Stengel had spent too many years getting used to being first, and began the season with that goal in mind. The Yankees roared to seven victories in their first eight matches, hovering near the top until permanently staking their claim to the lead on May 16, and waltzing home to their seventh pennant in the Old Professor's eight-year reign.

A successor to Ruth, Gehrig, and DiMaggio finally came to fruition in the person of Mickey Mantle. The 24-year-old Oklahoman hit 52 home runs en route to his Triple Crown and was voted the MVP. While Mantle provided the heavy artillery, Stengel had other key performers at his beck and call. Yogi Berra hit .298 with 30 homers and 105 RBI's, Hank Bauer belted 26 homers, and both Bill Skowron and Gil McDougald were .300 batters. The pitching did not come as easy, causing Stengel to again provide some magic. He patched up his pitching by coming up with two trump cards in the form of Tom Sturdivant and Johnny Kucks. With Don Larsen, Bob Turley, Tommy Byrne, and Bob Grim all disappointing, Sturdivant, a 26-year-old ex-minor league infielder, and Kucks, a 22-year-old-baby-faced sophomore, both came out of the bullpen to win 16 and 18 games respectively. Whitey Ford provided continuity to the staff by winning 19 games, missing the 20th only by losing on the final day of the season. Runner-up Cleveland boasted superior pitching by flashing three 20-game winners in Bob Lemon, Early Wynn, and strikeout phenom Herb Score, but could not keep pace with New York's offense.

In the National League, the Dodgers almost failed to accommodate Stengel for another showdown, winning the pennant only on the final day of the season by one game over the Milwaukee Braves and two over the Cincinnati Reds. All three teams battled for the top spot all season—Brooklyn's aging championship squad, Milwaukee's maturing young team, and Cincinnati's surprising Reds, who made a strong run on overwhelming home run power and not much else. Don

Newcombe chalked up 27 wins for Brooklyn in carrying them most of the way; his crackling fastball won him the MVP and the first Cy Young Award. Down the stretch, though, Sal Maglie booted the Dodgers home. Obtained on waivers from Cleveland in May, Sal the Barber won 13 games, threw a no-hitter against the Phils on September 25, in the peak of the flag fight, and won key games whenever they were there to win.

The Braves' attack centered around young Hank Aaron, whose .328 batting average led the league and whose 26 homers and 92 RBI's provided much firewater for the Braves' attack. Warren Spahn won 20 games for the Tribe but late season slumps by Bob Buhl, Lew Burdette, Eddie Mathews, and Joe Adcock took the edge off their fine season. The Reds' 221 homers, tying the 1947 Giants for the most ever by a team in one season, kept them in the race until the end. The final weekend of the season saw Milwaukee in front of Brooklyn by one game with three left to play. But, while the Dodgers, behind Clem Labine, Maglie, and Newcombe, were taking three straight from the Pirates, the Braves dropped two of three to St. Louis.

Finally, Stengel had his chance. But after the second World Series game was over, Stengel found himself on the bottom of a 13-8 score and a two-game deficit. As the experts pondered whether the Yankees would suddenly start chanting Brooklyn's cry of "wait till next year", Whitey Ford returned with the help of a three-run homer from Enos Slaughter to give the Yankees a 5-3 win. The muscle of Mantle and Bauer combined with Sturdivant's pitching to give the Yankees a 6-2 win. Game No. 5 made history. Don Larsen made his second Series start after being shelled in the second inning of the second game and threw an unprecedented perfect game. Although Labine restored Brooklyn's hopes in the sixth game with a brilliant 1-0 pitching triumph in ten innings over Bob Turley, who was the victim of a misjudged fly ball by Slaughter, the final game proved anticlimactic. Newcombe made his second start and again failed to go beyond the third inning, as the Yankees won in a 9-0 rout; which, of many things, gave proof through the night that Stengel and the Yankees were again supreme.

1956 AMERICAN LEAGUE

NAME	G by Pos	B	AGE	G	AB	R	H	2B	3B	HR	RBI	BB	SO	SB	BA	SA
NEW YORK	**1st 97-57 .630**								CASEY STENGEL							
TOTALS			28	154	5312	857	1433	193	55	190	788	615	755	51	.270	.434
Bill Skowron	1B120, 3B2	R	25	134	464	78	143	21	6	23	90	50	60	4	.308	.528
Billy Martin	2B105, 3B16	R	28	121	458	76	121	24	5	9	49	30	56	7	.264	.397
Gil McDougald	SS92, 2B31, 3B5	R	28	120	438	79	136	13	3	13	56	68	59	3	.311	.443
Andy Carey	3B131	R	24	132	422	54	100	18	2	7	50	45	53	9	.237	.339
Hank Bauer	OF146	R	33	147	539	96	130	18	7	26	84	59	72	4	.241	.445
Mickey Mantle	OF144	B	24	150	533	132	188	22	5	52	130	112	99	10	.353	.705
Elston Howard	OF65, C26	R	27	98	290	35	76	8	3	5	34	21	30	0	.262	.362
Yogi Berra	C135, OF1	R	31	140	521	93	155	29	2	30	105	65	29	3	.298	.534
Joe Collins	OF51, 1B43	L	33	100	262	38	59	5	3	7	43	34	33	3	.225	.347
Jerry Coleman	2B41, SS24, 3B18	R	31	80	183	15	47	5	1	0	18	12	33	1	.257	.295
Norm Siebern (KJ)	OF51	L	22	54	162	27	33	1	4	4	21	19	38	1	.204	.333
Bob Cerv (JJ)	OF44	R	30	54	115	16	35	5	6	3	25	18	13	0	.304	.530
Mickey McDermott	P23	L	27	46	52	4	11	0	0	1	4	8	13	0	.212	.269
Billy Hunter (NJ)	SS32, 3B4	R	28	39	75	8	21	3	4	0	11	2	4	0	.280	.427
Tommy Carroll	3B11, SS1	R	19	36	17	11	6	0	0	0	1	0	3	1	.353	.353
Tom Sturdivant	P32	R	26	32	64	5	20	1	1	0	5	0	7	0	.313	.359
Phil Rizzuto	SS30	R	38	31	52	6	12	0	0	0	6	6	5	0	.231	.231
Irv Noren (KJ)	OF10, 1B1	L	31	29	37	4	8	1	0	0	6	12	7	0	.216	.243
1 Eddie Robinson	1B14	L	35	26	54	7	12	1	0	5	11	5	3	0	.222	.519
2 Enos Slaughter	OF20	L	40	24	83	15	24	4	2	0	4	5	4	1	.289	.386
Jerry Lumpe	SS17, 3B1	L	23	20	62	12	16	3	0	0	4	5	11	1	.258	.306

2 George Wilson 30 L 2-12, Charlie Silvera 31 R 2-9, 1 Lou Skizas 24 R 1-6, Bobby Richardson 20 R 1-7

NAME	T	AGE	W	L	PCT	SV	G	GS	CG	IP	H	BB	SO	SHO	ERA
TOTALS		27	97	57	.630	35	154	154	50	1382	1285	652	732	10	3.63
Whitey Ford	L	27	19	6	.760	1	31	30	18	226	187	84	141	2	2.47
Johnny Kucks	R	22	18	9	.667	1	34	31	12	224	223	72	67	3	3.86
Tom Sturdivant	R	26	16	8	.667	5	32	17	6	158	134	52	110	2	3.30
Don Larsen	R	26	11	5	.688	1	38	20	6	180	133	96	107	1	3.25
Bob Turley	R	25	8	4	.667	1	27	21	5	132	138	103	91	1	5.05
Tommy Byrne	L	36	7	3	.700	6	37	8	1	110	108	72	52	0	3.35
Bob Grim	R	26	6	1	.857	5	26	6	1	75	64	31	48	0	2.76
Tom Morgan	R	26	6	7	.462	11	41	0	0	71	74	27	20	0	4.18
Rip Coleman	L	24	3	5	.375	2	29	9	0	88	97	42	42	0	3.68
Mickey McDermott	L	27	2	6	.250	0	23	9	1	87	85	47	38	0	4.24
Ralph Terry	R	20	1	2	.333	0	3	3	0	13	17	11	8	0	9.69
Sonny Dixon	R	31	0	1	.000	1	3	0	0	4	5	5	1	0	2.08
1 Jim Konstanty	R	39	0	0	—	2	8	0	0	11	15	6	6	0	4.91
1 Gerry Staley	R	35	0	0	—	0	1	0	0	0.1	4	1	0	0	108.00
Jim Coates	R	23	0	0	—	0	2	0	0	2	1	4	0		13.50

NAME	G by Pos	B	AGE	G	AB	R	H	2B	3B	HR	RBI	BB	SO	SB	BA	SA
CLEVELAND	**2nd 88-66 .571 9**								AL LOPEZ							
TOTALS			30	155	5148	712	1256	199	23	153	675	681	764	40	.244	.381
Vic Wertz	1B133	L	31	136	481	65	127	22	0	32	106	75	87	0	.264	.509
Bobby Avila	2B135	R	32	138	513	74	115	14	2	10	54	70	68	17	.224	.318
Chico Carrasquel	SS141, 3B1	R	28	141	474	60	115	15	1	7	48	52	61	0	.243	.323
Al Rosen	3B116	R	32	121	416	64	111	18	2	15	61	58	44	1	.267	.428
Rocky Colavito	OF98	R	22	101	322	55	89	11	4	21	65	49	46	0	.276	.531
Jim Busby	OF133	R	29	135	494	72	116	17	3	12	50	43	87	8	.235	.354
Al Smith	OF122, 3B28, 2B1	R	28	141	526	87	144	26	5	16	71	84	72	6	.274	.433
Jim Hegan	C118	R	35	122	315	42	70	15	2	6	34	49	54	1	.222	.340
Gene Woodling (IL)	OF85	L	33	100	316	56	83	17	0	8	38	69	29	2	.262	.391
2 Preston Ward	1B60, OF17	L	28	87	150	18	38	10	0	6	21	16	20	2	.253	.440
George Strickland	SS28, 2B28, 3B26	R	30	85	171	22	36	1	2	3	17	22	27	0	.211	.292
Sam Mele	OF20, 1B8	R	34	57	114	17	29	7	0	4	20	12	20	0	.254	.421
Hal Naragon	C48	L	27	53	122	11	35	3	1	3	18	13	9	0	.287	.402
Bob Lemon	P39	R	35	43	93	8	18	0	0	5	12	9	21	0	.194	.355
Earl Averill	C34	R	24	42	93	12	22	6	0	3	14	14	25	0	.237	.398
1 Dale Mitchell	OF1	L	34	38	30	2	4	0	0	0	6	7	2	0	.133	.133
2 Dave Pope	OF18	L	27	35	70	6	17	3	1	0	6	10	12	0	.243	.314

Kenny Kuhn 19 L 6-22, Rudy Regalado 26 R 11-47, Joe Caffie 25 L 13-38, Stu Locklin 27 L 1-6, 1 Hoot Evers 35 R 0-0, 1 Hank Foiles 27 R 0-0, Bobby Young 31 L 0-0

NAME	T	AGE	W	L	PCT	SV	G	GS	CG	IP	H	BB	SO	SHO	ERA
TOTALS		30	88	66	.571	24	155	155	67	1384	1233	564	845	17	3.32
Early Wynn	R	36	20	9	.690	2	38	35	18	278	233	91	158	4	2.72
Herb Score	L	23	20	9	.690	0	35	33	16	249	162	129	263	5	2.53
Bob Lemon	R	35	20	14	.588	2	39	35	21	255	230	89	94	2	3.04
Mike Garcia	R	32	11	12	.478	0	35	30	8	198	213	74	119	4	3.77
Don Mossi	L	27	6	5	.545	11	48	3	0	88	79	33	59	0	3.58
Ray Narleski (EJ)	R	27	3	2	.600	4	32	0	0	59	36	19	42	0	1.53
Hank Aguirre	L	25	3	5	.375	1	16	9	2	65	63	27	31	1	3.74
Art Houtteman	R	28	2	2	.500	1	22	4	0	47	60	31	19	0	6.51
Cal McLish	R	30	2	4	.333	1	37	2	0	62	67	32	27	0	4.94
Bud Daley	L	23	1	0	1.000	0	14	0	0	20	21	14	13	0	6.30
Bob Feller	R	37	0	4	.000	1	19	4	2	58	63	23	18	0	4.97
1 Sal Maglie	R	39	0	0	—	0	2	0	0	5	6	2	2	0	3.60

NAME	G by Pos	B	AGE	G	AB	R	H	2B	3B	HR	RBI	BB	SO	SB	BA	SA
CHICAGO	**3rd 85-69 .552 12**								MARTY MARION							
TOTALS			30	154	5286	776	1412	218	43	128	729	619	660	70	.267	.397
Walt Dropo	1B117	R	33	125	361	42	96	13	1	8	52	37	51	0	.266	.374
Nellie Fox	2B154	L	28	154	649	109	192	20	10	4	52	44	14	8	.296	.376
Luis Aparicio	SS152	R	22	152	533	69	142	19	7	3	56	34	63	21	.266	.341
2 Fred Hatfield	3B100, SS3	L	31	106	321	46	84	9	1	7	33	37	36	1	.262	.361
Jim Rivera	OF134	L	33	139	491	76	125	23	5	12	66	40	75	20	.255	.395
Larry Doby	OF137	L	32	140	504	89	135	22	3	24	102	102	105	0	.268	.466
Minnie Minoso	OF148, 3B8, 1B1	R	33	151	545	106	172	29	11	21	88	86	40	12	.316	.525
Sherm Lollar	C132	R	31	140	450	55	132	28	2	11	75	53	34	2	.293	.438
2 Dave Philley	1B51, OF30	B	36	86	279	44	74	14	2	4	47	28	27	1	.265	.373
Sammy Esposito	3B61, SS19, 2B3	R	24	81	184	30	42	8	2	3	25	41	19	1	.228	.342
Bubba Phillips	OF35, 3B2	R	26	67	99	16	27	6	2	3	11	6	12	1	.273	.394
Les Moss	C49	R	31	56	127	10	31	6	0	10	23	16	15	0	.244	.512
2 Jim Delsing	OF29	L	30	55	41	11	9	3	0	0	6	9	8	1	.122	.195
Ron Northey	OF4	L	36	53	48	4	13	2	0	4	15	6	7	0	.354	.583
Jack Harshman	P34	L	28	36	71	6	12	1	0	6	19	11	21	0	.169	.437
Ron Jackson	1B19	R	22	31	80	7	18	4	1	2	14	10	13	1	.214	.321
1 George Kell	3B18, 1B4	R	33	21	80	7	25	5	0	1	11	8	10	0	.313	.413
Bob Nieman	OF10	R	29	21	80	9	24	4	0	3	18	8	16	0	.300	.475

1 Jim Bridgeweser 29 R 2-11, 1 Bob Kennedy 35 R 1-13, Earl Battey 21 R 1-4, Cal Abrams 32 L 1-3, Bob Powell (MS) 22

NAME	T	AGE	W	L	PCT	SV	G	GS	CG	IP	H	BB	SO	SHO	ERA
TOTALS		33	85	69	.552	13	154	154	65	1389	1351	524	722	11	3.73
Billy Pierce	L	29	20	9	.690	1	35	33	21	276	261	100	192	1	3.33
Jack Harshman	L	28	15	11	.577	0	34	30	15	227	183	102	143	4	3.09
Dick Donovan	R	28	12	10	.545	0	34	31	14	235	212	59	120	3	3.64
2 Jim Wilson	R	34	9	12	.429	0	28	26	6	160	149	70	82	3	4.05
2 Gerry Staley	R	35	8	3	.727	0	26	10	5	102	98	20	25	0	2.91
Dixie Howell	R	36	5	6	.455	4	34	1	0	64	79	36	28	0	4.64
Bob Keegan	R	35	5	7	.417	0	20	16	4	105	119	35	32	0	3.94
2 Ellis Kinder	R	41	5	1	.750	3	29	0	0	30	33	8	19	0	2.70
3 Paul LaPalme	L	32	3	1	.750	0	26	1	0	49	31	27	23	0	2.35
1 Howie Pollet	L	35	2	1	.750	0	11	0	0	26	27	11	14	0	4.15
1 Morrie Martin	L	33	1	0	1.000	0	10	0	0	14	7	9	5	0	5.00
1 Sandy Consuegra	R	35	1	0	.333	2	28	0	0	38	45	11	7	0	5.21
1 Mike Fornieles	R	24	0	1	.000	1	12	0	0	14	22	6	4	0	4.50
1 Connie Johnson	R	33	0	0	—	0	9	0	0	24	21	14	17	0	3.75
Harry Byrd	R	31	0	0	—	0	1	0	0	4	7	2	1	0	11.25
Jim Derrington	L	16	0	1	.000	0	1	1	0	6	9	2	2	0	7.50
Jim McDonald	R	29	0	0	—	0	1	0	0	3	4	1	0	0	9.00
Jerry Dahlke	R	26	0	0	—	0	1	0	0	2	7	1	0	0	19.29
Bill Fischer	R	25	0	0	—	0	1	0	0	2	5	1	1	0	22.50
2 Dick Marlowe	R	27	0	0	—	0	1	0	0	3	5	2	1	0	9.00

BOSTON — 4th 84-70 .545 13 — PINKY HIGGINS

NAME	G by Pos	B	AGE	G	AB	R	H	2B	3B	HR	RBI	BB	SO	SB	BA	SA
TOTALS		L	29	155	5349	780	1473	261	45	139	752	727	687	28	.275	.419
Mickey Vernon	1B108	L	38	119	403	67	125	28	4	15	84	57	40	1	.310	.511
Billy Goodman	2B95	L	30	105	399	61	117	20	4	2	38	40	22	0	.293	.404
Don Buddin	SS113	R	22	114	377	49	90	24	0	5	37	65	62	2	.239	.342
Billy Klaus	3B106	R	27	135	520	91	141	29	5	7	59	90	43	1	.271	.387
Jackie Jensen	OF151	R	29	151	578	80	182	23	11	20	97	89	43	11	.315	.497
Jimmy Piersall	OF155	R	26	155	601	91	176	40	6	14	87	58	48	7	.293	.449
Ted Williams	OF110	L	37	136	400	71	138	28	2	24	82	102	39	0	.345	.605
Sammy White	C114	R	28	114	392	28	96	15	2	5	44	35	40	2	.245	.332
Dick Gernert	OF50, 1B37	R	27	106	306	53	89	11	0	16	68	56	57	1	.291	.484
Gene Stephens	OF71	R	23	104	63	22	17	2	0	1	7	12	12	0	.270	.349
Ted Lepcio	2B57, 3B22	R	25	83	284	34	74	10	0	15	51	30	77	1	.261	.454
Pete Daley	C57	R	26	59	187	22	50	11	3	5	29	18	30	1	.267	.439
Billy Consolo	2B25	R	21	48	11	13	2	0	0	0	1	3	5	0	.182	.182
Milt Bolling	SS26, 3B11, 2B1	R	25	45	118	19	25	3	2	1	8	18	20	0	.212	.347
Norm Zauchin	1B31	R	26	44	84	12	18	2	0	2	11	14	22	0	.214	.310
Tom Brewer	P32	R	24	38	94	14	28	0	1	1	13	5	19	0	.298	.351
Frank Malzone	3B26	R	26	27	103	15	17	3	1	2	11	9	8	1	.165	.272
Faye Throneberry (IL)	OF13	L	25	24	50	6	11	2	0	1	3	3	16	0	.220	.320
Gene Mauch	2B6	R	30	7	25	4	8	0	0	0	1	3	3	1	.320	.320

1 Grady Hatton 33 L 2-5, Marty Keough 22 L 0-2, Jim Pagliaroni (MS) 18

NAME	T	AGE	W	L	PCT	SV	G	GS	CG	IP	H	BB	SO	SHO	ERA
TOTALS		28	84	70	.545	20	155	155	50	1398	1354	668	712	8	4.17
Tom Brewer	R	24	19	9	.679	0	32	32	15	244	200	112	127	4	3.50
Frank Sullivan	R	26	14	7	.667	0	34	33	12	242	253	66	116	1	3.42
Ike Delock	R	26	13	7	.650	9	48	8	1	128	122	80	105	0	4.22
Dave Sisler	R	24	9	8	.529	3	39	14	3	142	120	72	93	0	4.63
Willard Nixon	R	28	9	8	.529	0	23	22	9	145	142	57	74	1	4.22
Mel Parnell (NJ)	L	34	7	6	.538	0	21	20	6	131	129	59	41	1	3.78
Tom Hurd	R	32	3	4	.429	5	40	0	0	76	84	47	34	0	5.33
Bob Porterfield	R	32	3	12	.200	0	25	18	4	126	127	64	53	1	5.14
Frank Baumann	L	23	2	1	.667	0	7	1	0	25	22	14	18	0	3.24
Leo Kiely	L	26	2	2	.500	3	23	0	0	31	47	14	9	0	5.23
George Susce (IL)	R	24	2	4	.333	0	21	6	0	70	71	44	26	0	6.17
Rudy Minarcin	R	26	1	0	1.000	0	9	1	0	10	9	8	5	0	2.70
1 Harry Dorish	R	34	0	2	.000	0	15	0	0	23	23	10	11	0	3.52
1 Johnny Schmitz	L	35	0	0	—	0	2	0	0	5	4	0	0	0	0.00

DETROIT — 5th 82-72 .532 15 — BUCKY HARRIS

NAME	G by Pos	B	AGE	G	AB	R	H	2B	3B	HR	RBI	BB	SO	SB	BA	SA
TOTALS			28	155	5364	789	1494	209	50	150	745	644	618	43	.279	.420
Earl Torgeson	1B83	L	32	117	318	61	84	9	3	12	42	78	47	6	.264	.425
Frank Bolling	2B102	R	24	102	366	53	103	21	7	7	45	42	51	6	.281	.434
Harvey Kuenn	SS141, OF1	R	25	146	591	96	196	32	7	12	88	55	34	9	.332	.470
Ray Boone	3B130	R	32	131	481	77	148	14	6	25	81	77	46	0	.308	.518
Al Kaline	OF153	R	21	153	617	96	194	32	10	27	128	70	55	7	.314	.530
Bill Tuttle	OF137	R	26	140	546	61	138	22	4	9	65	38	48	5	.253	.357
Charlie Maxwell	OF136	L	29	141	460	96	163	14	3	28	87	79	74	1	.326	.534
Frank House	C88	R	26	94	321	44	77	6	2	10	44	21	19	1	.240	.364
Wayne Belardi	1B31, OF2	L	25	79	154	24	43	3	1	6	15	15	13	0	.279	.429
Red Wilson	C78	R	27	78	228	32	66	12	2	7	38	42	18	2	.289	.452
2 Jim Brideweser	SS32, 2B31, 3B4	R	29	70	156	23	34	4	0	0	10	20	19	3	.218	.244
2 Bob Kennedy	OF29, 3B27	R	35	69	177	17	41	5	0	4	22	24	19	2	.232	.328
Jack Phillips	1B56, OF1, 2B1	R	34	67	224	31	66	13	2	1	20	21	19	1	.295	.384
Jim Small	OF26	L	19	58	91	13	29	4	2	0	10	6	10	0	.319	.407
Buddy Hicks	SS16, 2B6, 3B1	R	29	26	47	5	10	2	0	0	5	3	2	0	.213	.255
Reno Bertoia	2B18, 3B2	R	21	22	66	7	12	2	0	1	5	6	12	0	.182	.258
Jay Porter	C2, OF2	R	23	14	21	0	2	0	0	0	3	0	8	0	.095	.095
1 Jim Delsing	OF3	L	30	10	12	0	0	0	0	0	0	3	3	0	.000	.000

1 Fred Hatfield 31 L 3-12, Charlie King 25 R 2-9, Charlie Lau 23 L 2-9, Walt Streuli 20 R 2-8

NAME	T	AGE	W	L	PCT	SV	G	GS	CG	IP	H	BB	SO	SHO	ERA
TOTALS		29	82	72	.532	15	155	155	62	1379	1389	655	788	10	4.06
Frank Lary	R	26	21	13	.618	1	41	38	20	294	289	116	165	3	3.15
Billy Hoeft	L	24	20	14	.588	0	38	34	18	248	276	104	172	4	4.06
Paul Foytack	R	25	15	13	.536	1	43	33	16	256	211	142	184	1	3.59
Steve Gromek	R	36	8	6	.571	4	40	13	4	141	142	47	64	0	4.28
Virgil Trucks	R	39	6	5	.545	1	22	16	3	120	104	63	43	1	3.83
Jim Bunning	R	24	5	1	.833	1	15	3	0	53	55	28	34	0	3.74
Al Aber	L	28	4	4	.500	7	42	0	0	63	65	25	21	0	3.43
Walt Masterson	R	36	1	1	.500	0	35	0	0	50	54	32	28	0	4.14
1 Dick Marlowe	R	27	1	1	.500	0	7	1	0	11	12	9	4	0	5.73
Bill Black	R	23	1	1	.500	0	10	0	0	10	10	5	7	0	3.60
Bob Miller	R	20	0	2	.000	0	11	3	0	32	37	22	16	0	5.63
Ned Garver (SA)	R	30	0	2	.000	0	4	2	0	18	15	13	6	0	4.00
Hal Woodeshick	L	23	0	2	.000	0	2	2	0	5	12	3	1	0	14.40
Duke Maas	R	27	0	7	.000	0	26	7	0	63	81	32	34	0	6.57
Jim Brady	L	20	0	0	—	0	6	0	0	15	11	3	3	0	30.00
Pete Wojey	R	36	0	0	—	0	2	0	0	4	2	1	1	0	2.25
Gene Host	L	23	0	0	—	0	2	0	0	5	9	2	5	0	7.20

BALTIMORE — 6th 69-85 .448 28 — PAUL RICHARDS

NAME	G by Pos	B	AGE	G	AB	R	H	2B	3B	HR	RBI	BB	SO	SB	BA	SA
TOTALS			27	154	5090	571	1242	198	34	91	515	563	725	39	.244	.350
Bob Boyd (BE)	1B60, OF8	L	36	70	225	28	70	8	3	2	11	30	14	0	.311	.400
Billy Gardner	2B132, SS25, 3B6	R	28	144	515	53	119	16	2	11	50	29	53	5	.231	.334
Willie Miranda	SS147	B	30	148	461	38	100	16	4	4	34	46	73	3	.217	.282
2 George Kell	3B97, 1B21	R	33	102	345	45	90	17	2	8	37	25	31	0	.261	.391
2 Tito Francona	OF122, 1B21	L	22	139	445	62	115	16	4	9	57	51	60	1	.258	.373
2 Dick Williams	OF81, 1B10, 2B10, 3B4	R	27	87	353	45	101	18	4	11	37	30	40	5	.286	.453
2 Bob Nieman	OF114	R	29	114	388	60	125	20	6	12	64	86	59	1	.322	.497
Gus Triandos	C89, 1B52	R	25	131	452	47	126	18	1	21	88	48	73	0	.279	.462
Bob Hale	1B51	L	22	85	207	18	49	10	1	1	24	11	10	0	.237	.309
Jim Pyburn	OF77	R	25	84	156	23	27	3	0	2	11	17	26	4	.173	.269
1 Hal Smith	C71	R	25	77	229	16	60	14	0	3	18	17	22	1	.262	.362
Wayne Causey	3B30, 2B7	L	19	53	88	7	15	1	1	1	4	8	23	0	.170	.227
Chuck Diering	OF40, 3B2	R	33	50	97	15	18	4	0	1	4	23	19	2	.186	.258
2 Hoot Evers	OF36	R	35	48	112	20	27	3	1	0	11	11	20	1	.241	.295
1 Joe Frazier	OF19	L	33	45	74	7	19	6	0	1	12	11	6	0	.257	.378
Bobby Adams	3B24, 2B18	R	34	41	111	19	25	6	1	0	7	25	15	1	.225	.297
Bob Nelson	OF24	R	19	39	68	5	14	2	0	0	5	7	22	0	.206	.235
1 Dave Philley	OF31, 3B6	B	36	32	117	13	24	4	2	0	17	18	13	3	.205	.299
Tommy Gastall (DD)	C20	R	24	32	56	3	11	2	0	0	4	4	8	0	.196	.232
3 Grady Hatton	2B15, 3B12	L	33	27	61	4	9	1	0	0	3	13	6	0	.148	.213
Freddie Marsh	3B8, SS8, 2B5	R	32	20	24	2	3	0	0	0	0	4	3	1	.125	.125
Brooks Robinson	3B14, 2B1	R	19	15	44	5	10	4	0	1	1	1	5	0	.227	.386
2 Joe Ginsberg	C8	L	29	15	28	0	2	0	0	0	2	2	4	0	.071	.071

1 Jim Dyck 34 R 5-23, 1 Dave Pope 35 L 3-19, Joe Durham (MS) 24

NAME	T	AGE	W	L	PCT	SV	G	GS	CG	IP	H	BB	SO	SHO	ERA
TOTALS		30	69	85	.448	24	154	154	38	1361	1362	547	715	10	4.20
Ray Moore	R	30	12	7	.632	0	32	27	9	185	161	99	105	1	4.18
Hal Brown	R	31	9	7	.563	2	35	14	4	152	142	37	57	1	4.03
2 Connie Johnson	R	33	9	10	.474	0	26	25	9	184	165	82	130	2	3.42
Bill Wight	L	34	9	12	.429	0	35	26	7	175	198	72	84	1	4.01
George Zuverink	R	31	7	6	.538	16	62	0	0	97	112	34	33	0	4.18
1 Jim Wilson	R	34	4	2	.667	0	7	7	1	48	49	16	31	0	5.06
2 Mike Fornieles	R	24	4	7	.364	1	30	11	1	111	109	25	53	1	3.97
Don Ferrarese	L	27	4	10	.286	2	36	14	3	102	86	64	81	1	5.03
Erv Palica	R	28	4	11	.267	0	29	14	2	116	117	50	62	0	4.50
Charlie Beamon	R	21	2	0	1.000	0	2	1	1	13	9	8	14	1	1.38
2 Billy Loes	R	26	2	7	.222	3	21	6	1	57	65	23	22	0	4.74
Fred Besana	L	25	1	0	1.000	0	7	2	0	18	22	14	7	0	5.50
Morrie Martin	L	33	1	1	.500	0	5	0	0	9	10	2	3	0	10.80
1 Sandy Consuegra	R	35	1	1	.500	0	9	0	0	9	14	2	1	0	4.00
Ron Moeller	L	17	0	1	.000	0	4	0	0	2	5	5	1	0	9.00
2 Johnny Schmitz	L	35	0	3	.000	0	38	0	0	49	49	14	15	0	4.03
1 Harry Dorish	R	34	0	0	—	0	13	0	0	20	22	3	4	0	4.05
Babe Birrer	R	27	0	0	—	0	4	0	0	5	9	1	1	0	7.20
Mel Held	R	23	0	0	—	0	2	0	0	7	7	3	4	0	5.14
Billy O'Dell (MS)	R	23	0	1	.000	0	7	0	0	8	6	6	6	0	1.13
Bob Harrison	R	25	0	0	—	0	2	0	0	4	0	3	1	0	13.50
Gordie Sundin	R	18	0	0	—	0	1	0	0	0	1	2	0	0	
George Werley	R	17	0	0	—	0	1	0	0	1	3	2	1	0	9.00

WASHINGTON — 7th 59-95 .383 38 — CHUCK DRESSEN

NAME	G by Pos	B	AGE	G	AB	R	H	2B	3B	HR	RBI	BB	SO	SB	BA	SA
TOTALS			27	155	5202	652	1302	198	62	112	613	690	877	37	.250	.377
Pete Runnels	1B81, 2B69, SS3	L	28	147	578	72	179	29	9	8	76	58	64	5	.310	.433
Herb Plews	2B66, SS5, 3B2	L	28	91	256	29	69	10	7	1	25	26	40	1	.270	.375
Jose Valdivielso	SS90	R	22	90	246	18	58	8	2	4	29	29	36	3	.236	.333
Eddie Yost	3B135, OF6	R	29	152	515	94	119	17	2	11	53	151	82	8	.231	.336
Jim Lemon	OF141	R	28	146	538	77	146	21	11	27	96	65	138	2	.271	.502
Karl Olson	OF101	R	25	106	313	34	77	10	2	4	22	28	41	1	.246	.329
Whitey Herzog	OF103, 1B5	L	24	117	421	49	103	13	7	4	35	50	74	5	.245	.337
Clint Courtney	C76	L	29	101	283	31	85	20	3	5	44	20	10	0	.300	.445
Roy Sievers	OF78, 1B76	R	29	152	550	92	139	27	2	29	95	100	88	0	.253	.467
Lou Berberet	C59	L	26	95	207	25	54	6	3	4	27	46	33	0	.261	.377
Ernie Oravetz	OF31	B	24	88	137	20	34	3	2	0	11	27	20	1	.248	.299
Ed Fitz Gerald	C50	R	32	64	144	15	45	8	0	2	12	20	16	0	.304	.399
Tony Roig	2B27, SS19	R	27	44	119	11	25	5	2	0	7	20	29	2	.210	.286
Harmon Killebrew	3B20, 2B4	R	20	44	99	10	22	2	0	5	13	10	39	0	.222	.394
Jerry Snyder (BW)	SS35, 2B7	R	26	43	148	14	40	3	1	5	14	10	9	1	.270	.345
Lyle Luttrell	SS37	R	26	38	122	17	23	5	3	2	9	8	19	5	.189	.328
Carlos Paula	OF20	R	28	33	82	8	15	2	1	3	13	8	15	0	.183	.341
Dick Tettelbach	OF18	R	27	18	64	10	10	1	2	1	9	14	15	1	.156	.281

Tom Wright 32 L 0-1, Steve Korcheck (MS) 23, Jerry Schoonmaker (MS) 22

NAME	T	AGE	W	L	PCT	SV	G	GS	CG	IP	H	BB	SO	SHO	ERA
TOTALS		25	59	95	.383	18	155	155	36	1369	1539	730	663	1	5.33
Chuck Stobbs	L	26	15	15	.500	1	37	33	15	240	264	54	97	1	3.60
Pedro Ramos	R	21	12	10	.545	0	37	18	4	152	178	76	54	0	5.27
Camilo Pascual	R	22	6	18	.250	2	39	27	6	189	194	89	162	0	5.86
Dean Stone	L	25	5	7	.417	3	41	21	2	132	148	93	86	0	6.27
Bunky Stewart	L	25	5	7	.417	2	33	9	1	105	111	82	36	0	5.57
Bob Chakales	R	28	4	4	.500	4	43	1	0	96	94	57	33	0	4.03
Connie Grob	R	23	4	5	.444	1	37	1	0	79	126	27	27	0	7.86
Bob Wiesler	L	25	3	12	.200	0	37	21	3	123	141	112	69	0	6.44
Bud Byerly	R	35	2	4	.333	4	25	0	0	52	45	14	19	0	2.94
Evelio Hernandez	R	24	1	1	.500	0	4	4	0	24	24	9	4	0	4.70
Ted Abernathy (SA)	R	23	1	3	.250	0	9	4	2	30	35	10	18	0	6.00
Hal Griggs	R	27	1	6	.143	1	34	12	1	99	120	76	48	0	6.00
Dick Brodowski	R	23	0	3	.000	0	7	1	0	31	31	16	9	0	7.09
Tex Clevenger	R	23	0	0	—	0	17	0	0	32	33	31	15	0	5.34

KANSAS CITY — 8th 52-102 .338 45 — LOU BOUDREAU

NAME	G by Pos	B	AGE	G	AB	R	H	2B	3B	HR	RBI	BB	SO	SB	BA	SA
TOTALS			30	154	5256	619	1325	204	41	112	581	480	727	40	.252	.370
Vic Power	1B76, 2B47, OF7	R	28	127	546	77	164	21	5	14	63	24	16	2	.309	.447
Jim Finigan	2B52, 3B32	R	27	91	250	29	54	7	2	2	21	30	28	1	.216	.284
Joe DeMaestri	SS132, 2B2	R	27	133	434	41	101	16	1	6	39	25	73	3	.233	.316
Hector Lopez	3B121, OF20, 2B8, SS4	R	26	151	561	91	153	27	3	18	69	63	73	4	.273	.428
Harry Simpson	OF111, 1B32	L	30	141	543	76	159	22	11	21	105	47	82	2	.293	.490
Johnny Groth	OF84	R	29	95	244	22	63	13	3	5	37	30	31	1	.258	.398
2 Lou Skizas	OF74	R	24	99	344	39	94	11	3	11	39	15	17	3	.316	.485
Tim Thompson	C68	L	32	92	268	21	73	13	2	1	27	17	23	2	.272	.347
Gus Zernial	OF69	R	33	109	272	36	61	12	0	16	44	33	66	2	.224	.445
1 Enos Slaughter	OF56	L	40	91	237	37	62	14	3	2	23	29	20	1	.278	.395
2 Eddie Robinson	1B47	L	35	75	172	13	34	5	1	2	12	26	20	0	.198	.273
Mike Baxes	SS62, 2B1	R	25	73	106	9	24	5	1	0	6	9	27	0	.226	.302
1 Joe Ginsberg	C57	L	25	71	195	15	48	9	1	1	12	23	17	1	.246	.313
Al Pilarcik	OF67	L	25	69	129	15	28	6	0	0	4	11	14	0	.217	.279
Clete Boyer	2B51, 3B7	R	19	67	129	15	28	5	1	1	10	12	18	0	.217	.333
Rance Pless	1B15, 3B5	R	30	48	85	4	23	4	0	3	12	3	12	1	.275	.408
2 Hal Smith	OF?	R	31	48	135	19	39	6	1	3	10	5	10	1	.271	.407
Bill Renna	OF25	R	31	33	48	13	9	3	5	3	10	1			.216	.247
1 Spook Jacobs	2B31	R	31	30	83	12	17	3	0	0	5	3	10	3	.205	.241
Jim Pisoni	OF9	R	26	10	30	4	8	2	1	1	3	5	6	0	.267	.467
1 Elmer Valo	OF1	L	35	9	9	1	2	0	0	0	1	2	2	0	.222	.222

Joe Astroth 33 R 1-13, Dave Melton 27 R 1-3

NAME	T	AGE	W	L	PCT	SV	G	GS	CG	IP	H	BB	SO	SHO	ERA
TOTALS		29	52	102	.338	18	154	154	30	1370	1424	679	636	3	4.86
Art Ditmar	R	27	12	22	.353	1	44	34	14	254	254	108	126	2	4.43
Tom Gorman	R	31	9	10	.474	3	52	13	1	151	168	68	56	0	3.84
Alex Kellner	R	31	7	8	.636	0	20	17	5	92	103	33	44	0	4.30
Wally Burnette	R	27	6	8	.429	0	18	14	4	121	115	39	54	1	2.90
Jack Crimian	R	30	4	8	.333	3	54	7	0	122	129	49	70	0	5.29
Lou Kretlow	R	35	4	9	.308	0	25	20	3	119	121	74	61	0	5.29
Moe Burtschy	R	34	3	1	.750	0	29	1	0	42	38	26	21	0	3.98
Bill Harrington	R	28	2	1	.500	1	23	0	0	38	40	26	14	0	6.39
Bobby Shantz (XJ)	R	30	2	7	.222	2	23	9	1	101	95	37	67	0	4.37
Carl Duser	R	23	1	1	.500	2	6	0	0	6	14	2	5	0	9.00
Jose Santiago	R	28	1	1	.500	0	23	0	0	36	17	9	8	0	8.18
Troy Herriage	R	25	1	13	.071	0	31	16	1	103	135	64	59	0	6.64
Art Ceccarelli	L	26	1	0	1.000	0	4	1	0	10	11	7	2	0	7.20
Arnie Portocarrero	R	24	0	1	.000	0	4	1	0	10	14	6	3	0	10.13
Glenn Cox	R	21	0	2	.000	0	5	3	0	10	10	6	9	0	4.30
Walt Craddock	L	24	0	1	.000	0	4	0	0	7	7	2	1	0	7.00
Tommy Lasorda	R	28	0	0	—	0	18	0	0	45	39	22	13	0	6.15
2 Jack McMahan	L	24	0	5	.000	0	23	6	0	62	69	31	13	0	4.79
George Brunet	L	21	0	0	—	0	9	0	0	14	13	13	8	0	8.18
Bob Spicer	R	31	0	0	—	0	4	0	0	4	8	5	2	0	22.50
Bill Bradford	R	34	0	0	—	0	2	0	0	3	5	2	1	0	9.00

Batting

NAME	G by Pos	B	AGE	G	AB	R	H	2B	3B	HR	RBI	BB	SO	SB	BA	SA
BROOKLYN 1st 93-61 .604															**WALT ALSTON**	
TOTALS			32	154	5098	720	1315	212	36	179	680	649	738	65	.258	.419
Gil Hodges	1B138, OF30, C1	R	32	153	550	86	146	29	4	32	87	76	91	3	.265	.507
Jim Gilliam	2B102, OF56	B	27	153	594	102	178	23	8	6	43	95	39	21	.300	.396
Pee Wee Reese	SS136, 3B12	R	37	147	572	85	147	19	2	9	46	56	69	13	.257	.344
Randy Jackson	3B80	R	30	101	307	37	84	15	7	8	53	28	38	2	.274	.446
Carl Furillo	OF146	R	34	149	523	66	151	30	0	21	83	57	41	1	.289	.467
Duke Snider	OF150	L	29	151	542	112	158	33	2	43	101	99	101	3	.292	.598
Sandy Amoros	OF86	L	26	114	292	53	76	11	8	16	58	59	51	3	.260	.517
Roy Campanella	C121	R	34	124	388	39	85	6	1	20	73	66	61	1	.219	.394
Jackie Robinson	3B72, 2B22, 1B9, OF2	R	37	117	357	61	98	15	2	10	43	60	32	12	.275	.412
Gino Cimoli	OF62	R	26	73	36	3	4	1	0	0	4	1	8	1	.111	.139
Charlie Neal	2B51, SS1	R	25	62	136	22	39	5	1	2	14	14	19	2	.287	.382
Rube Walker	C43	L	30	54	146	15	31	6	1	3	20	7	18	0	.212	.329
Chico Fernandez	SS25	R	24	34	66	11	15	2	0	1	9	3	10	2	.227	.303
1 Rocky Nelson	1B25	L	31	31	96	7	20	2	0	4	15	4	10	0	.208	.354
2 Dale Mitchell	OF2	L	34	19	24	3	7	1	0	0	1	0	3	0	.292	.333
Don Zimmer (BY)	SS8, 3B3, 2B1	R	25	17	20	4	6	1	0	0	2	0	7	0	.300	.350
Dixie Howell	C6	R	36	7	13	0	3	2	0	0	1	1	3	0	.231	.385

1 Dick Williams 27 R 2-7, Don Demeter 21 R 1-3, Bob Aspromonte 18 R 0-1

NAME	G by Pos	B	AGE	G	AB	R	H	2B	3B	HR	RBI	BB	SO	SB	BA	SA
MILWAUKEE 2nd 92-62 .597 1															**CHARLIE GRIMM 24-22 .522 FRED HANEY 68-40 .630**	
TOTALS			28	155	5207	709	1350	212	54	177	667	486	714	29	.259	.423
Joe Adcock	1B129	R	28	137	454	76	132	23	1	38	103	32	86	1	.291	.597
Danny O'Connell	2B138, 3B4, SS1	R	29	139	498	71	119	17	9	2	42	76	42	3	.239	.321
Johnny Logan	SS148	R	29	148	545	69	153	27	5	15	46	46	49	3	.281	.431
Eddie Mathews	3B150	L	24	151	552	103	150	21	2	37	95	91	86	6	.272	.518
Hank Aaron	OF152	R	22	153	609	106	200	34	14	26	92	37	54	2	.328	.558
Bill Bruton	OF145	L	30	147	525	73	143	23	15	8	56	26	63	8	.272	.419
Bobby Thomson	OF136, 3B3	R	32	142	451	59	106	10	4	20	74	43	75	2	.235	.408
Del Crandall	C109	R	26	112	311	37	74	14	2	16	48	35	30	1	.238	.450
Frank Torre	1B89	L	24	111	159	17	41	6	0	0	16	11	4	1	.258	.296
Wes Covington	OF35	L	24	75	138	17	39	4	0	2	16	16	20	1	.283	.355
Del Rice	C65	R	33	71	188	15	40	9	1	3	17	18	34	0	.213	.319
Chuck Tanner	OF8	L	26	60	63	6	15	2	0	1	4	10	10	0	.238	.317
Andy Pafko	OF37	R	35	45	93	15	24	5	0	2	9	10	13	0	.258	.376
Jack Dittmer	2B42	L	28	44	102	8	25	4	0	1	6	8	8	0	.245	.314
Felix Mantilla	SS15, 3B3	R	21	35	53	9	15	1	1	0	3	1	8	1	.283	.340
2 Toby Atwell	C10	L	32	15	30	2	5	1	0	2	7	4	1	0	.167	.400
Jim Pendleton	SS3, 3B2, 2B1, 1B1	R	32	14	11	0	0	0	0	0	0	1	3	0	.000	.000

Earl Hersh 24 L 3-13, Bob Roselli 24 R 1-2, Mel Roach (MS) 23

NAME	G by Pos	B	AGE	G	AB	R	H	2B	3B	HR	RBI	BB	SO	SB	BA	SA
CINCINNATI 3rd 91-63 .591 2															**BIRDIE TEBBETTS**	
TOTALS			27	155	5291	775	1406	201	32	221	734	528	760	45	.266	.441
Ted Kluszewski	1B131	L	31	138	517	91	156	14	1	35	102	49	31	0	.302	.536
Johnny Temple	2B154, OF1	R	27	154	632	88	180	18	3	2	41	58	40	14	.285	.332
Roy McMillan	SS150	R	26	150	479	51	126	16	7	3	62	76	54	4	.263	.344
Ray Jablonski	3B127, 2B1	R	29	130	407	42	104	25	1	15	66	37	57	2	.256	.432
Wally Post	OF136	R	26	143	539	94	134	25	3	36	83	37	124	6	.249	.506
Gus Bell	OF149	L	27	150	603	82	176	31	4	29	84	50	46	6	.292	.501
Frank Robinson	OF152	R	20	152	572	122	166	27	6	38	83	64	95	8	.290	.558
Ed Bailey	C106	L	25	118	383	59	115	8	2	28	75	52	50	2	.300	.551
Smoky Burgess	C55	L	29	90	229	28	63	10	0	12	39	26	18	0	.275	.476
Bob Thurman	OF29	L	39	80	139	25	41	5	2	8	22	10	14	0	.295	.532
2 Alex Grammas	3B58, SS12, 2B5	R	30	77	140	17	34	11	0	0	16	16	18	0	.243	.321
George Crowe	1B32	L	35	77	144	22	36	2	1	10	23	11	28	0	.250	.486
Rocky Bridges	3B51, 2B8, SS7, OF1	R	28	71	19	9	4	0	0	0	1	5	4	1	.211	.211
Stan Palys	OF10	R	26	40	53	5	12	0	0	2	5	6	13	0	.226	.340
2 Jim Dyck	3B1, 1B1	R	34	18	11	5	1	0	0	0	0	3	5	0	.091	.091
1 Chuck Harmon	OF6, 1B2	R	32	13	4	2	0	0	0	0	1	0	0	0	.000	.000
2 Joe Frazier	OF4	L	33	10	17	2	4	0	0	1	2	1	7	0	.235	.412
Bruce Edwards	C2, 3B1, 2B1	R	32	7	5	1	0	0	0	0	0	2	0	0	.200	.200
Bobby Balcena	OF2	R	30	7	2	2	0	0	0	0	0	0	1	0	.000	.000

Art Schult 28 R 3-7, Curt Flood 18 R 0-1, Matt Batts 34 R 0-2, John Oldham 23 R 0-0, Al Silvera 20 R 0-0, Dick Murphy (MS) 24

NAME	G by Pos	B	AGE	G	AB	R	H	2B	3B	HR	RBI	BB	SO	SB	BA	SA
ST. LOUIS 4th 76-78 .494 17															**FRED HUTCHINSON**	
TOTALS			28	156	5378	678	1443	234	49	124	628	503	622	41	.268	.399
Stan Musial	1B103, OF53	L	35	156	594	87	184	33	6	27	109	75	39	2	.310	.522
Don Blasingame	2B98, SS49, 3B2	L	24	150	587	94	153	22	7	0	27	72	52	8	.261	.322
2 Al Dark	SS99	R	34	100	413	54	118	14	7	4	37	21	33	2	.286	.383
Ken Boyer	3B149	R	25	150	595	91	182	30	4	26	98	38	65	8	.306	.494
Wally Moon	OF97, 1B52	L	26	149	540	86	161	22	11	16	68	80	50	12	.298	.469
2 Bobby Del Greco	OF99	R	23	102	270	29	58	16	2	5	18	32	50	1	.215	.344
Rip Repulski	OF100	R	27	112	376	44	104	18	3	11	55	24	46	2	.277	.428
Hal Smith	C66	R	25	75	227	17	64	12	0	5	23	15	22	1	.282	.401
Hank Sauer	OF37	R	39	75	151	11	45	4	0	5	24	25	31	0	.298	.424
2 Whitey Lockman	OF57, 1B2	L	29	70	193	14	48	0	2	0	10	18	8	2	.249	.269
2 Bobby Morgan	2B13, 3B1, SS6	R	30	61	113	14	22	7	0	3	20	15	24	0	.195	.336
2 Ray Katt	OF29	R	29	47	158	11	41	4	0	6	20	6	24	0	.259	.399
2 Grady Hatton	2B13, 3B1	L	33	44	73	10	18	1	2	0	7	13	7	1	.247	.315
1 Bill Sarni	C41	R	28	43	148	12	43	7	2	5	22	8	15	1	.291	.466
1 Red Schoendienst	2B36	B	33	40	153	22	48	9	0	0	15	13	5	0	.314	.373
Walker Cooper	C16	R	41	40	68	5	18	5	1	2	14	3	8	0	.265	.456
2 Rocky Nelson	1B14, OF8	L	31	38	56	6	13	5	0	2	9	8	6	0	.232	.482
1 Jackie Brandt	OF26	R	22	27	42	9	12	3	0	1	3	2	8	0	.286	.429
1 Bill Virdon	OF24	L	25	24	71	10	15	2	0	2	6	5	8	0	.211	.324
Charlie Peete (DD)	OF21	L	27	23	52	3	10	2	2	0	6	6	10	0	.192	.308
2 Chuck Harmon	OF11, 1B2, 3B1	R	32	20	15	2	0	0	0	0	0	6	6	0	.000	.000
Dick Schofield	SS6	B	21	16	30	3	3	2	0	0	1	4	8	0	.100	.167
1 Joe Frazier	OF3	L	33	14	19	1	4	0	1	0	2	1	3	0	.211	.474
1 Alex Grammas	SS5	R	30	6	12	1	3	0	0	0	0	3	1	0	.250	.250

1 Solly Hemus 33 L 1-5, Joe Cunningham 24 L 0-3, Tom Alston 30 L 0-2

NAME	G by Pos	B	AGE	G	AB	R	H	2B	3B	HR	RBI	BB	SO	SB	BA	SA
PHILADELPHIA 5th 71-83 .461 22															**MAYO SMITH**	
TOTALS			30	154	5204	668	1313	207	49	121	616	585	673	45	.252	.381
Marv Blaylock	1B124, OF1	L	26	136	460	61	117	14	8	10	50	50	86	5	.254	.385
Ted Kazanski	2B116, SS1	R	22	117	379	35	80	11	4	3	34	20	41	0	.211	.277
Granny Hamner	SS110, 2B11, P3	R	29	122	401	42	90	24	3	4	42	30	42	2	.224	.329
Willie Jones	3B149	R	30	149	520	68	144	20	4	17	78	92	49	5	.277	.429
2 Elmer Valo	OF87	L	35	98	291	40	84	13	3	5	37	48	21	1	.289	.405
Richie Ashburn	OF154	L	29	154	628	94	190	26	8	3	50	79	45	10	.303	.384
Del Ennis	OF153	R	31	153	630	80	164	23	3	26	95	33	62	1	.260	.430
Stan Lopata	C102, 1B39	R	30	146	535	96	143	33	7	32	95	75	93	5	.267	.535
Jim Greengrass	OF62	R	28	86	215	24	44	8	0	5	20	31	36	0	.205	.335
2 Solly Hemus	2B49, 3B1	L	33	78	187	24	54	10	4	5	24	28	21	1	.289	.465
Frankie Baumholtz	OF15	L	37	76	100	13	27	6	0	0	5	8	9	0	.270	.270
Roy Smalley	SS60	R	30	65	168	14	38	9	0	3	16	23	29	0	.226	.315
Andy Seminick	C54	R	35	60	161	16	32	3	1	4	21	30	38	3	.199	.360
Joe Lonnett	C7	R	29	16	11	2	2	0	0	0	2	0	3	0	.182	.182
Glen Gorbous	OF8	L	25	15	33	1	6	0	0	0	1	2	6	0	.182	.182
Mack Burk	C1	R	21	5	1	0	1	0	0	0	0	0	0	0	1.000	1.000
Ed Bouchee	1B6	L	23	5	47	6	13	3	0	2	6	6	9	0	.277	.383
1 Bobby Morgan	3B5, 2B3	R	30	4	10	0	2	0	0	0	2	0	3	0	.200	.200
Bob Bowman	OF5	R	25	9	16	2	3	0	1	0	2	1	3	0	.188	.500
2 Wally Westlake		R	35	6	4	0	0	0	0	0	0	0	0	0		

Pitching

NAME	T	AGE	W	L	PCT	SV	G	GS	CG	IP	H	BB	SO	SHO	ERA
		27	93	61	.604	30	154	154	46	1369	1251	441	772	12	3.57
Don Newcombe	R	30	27	7	.794	0	38	36	18	268	219	46	139	5	3.06
2 Sal Maglie	R	39	13	5	.722	0	28	26	9	191	154	52	108	3	2.87
Carl Erskine	R	29	13	11	.542	0	31	28	8	186	189	57	95	1	4.26
Roger Craig	R	26	12	11	.522	1	35	32	8	199	169	87	109	2	3.71
Clem Labine	R	29	10	6	.625	19	62	3	1	116	111	39	75	0	3.34
Ed Roebuck	R	24	5	4	.556	1	43	0	0	89	83	29	60	0	3.94
Don Drysdale	R	19	5	5	.500	0	25	12	2	99	95	31	55	0	2.64
Don Bessent	R	25	4	3	.571	9	38	0	0	79	63	31	52	0	2.51
Ken Lehman	L	28	2	3	.400	0	25	4	0	49	65	23	29	0	5.69
Sandy Koufax	L	20	2	4	.333	0	16	10	0	59	66	29	30	0	4.88
Chuck Templeton	L	24	0	1	.000	0	6	2	0	16	20	10	8	0	6.75
1 Billy Loes	R	26	0	1	.000	1	1	1	0	1	5	1	2	0	54.00
1 Jim Hughes	R	33	0	0	—	0	5	0	0	12	10	4	8	0	5.25
Ralph Branca	R	30	0	0	—	0	1	0	0	2	1	2	2	0	0.00
Bob Darnell	R	25	0	0	—	0	1	0	0	1	1	0	0	0	0.00

Johnny Podres (MS) 23

NAME	T	AGE	W	L	PCT	SV	G	GS	CG	IP	H	BB	SO	SHO	ERA
		28	92	62	.597	27	155	155	64	1393	1295	467	639	12	3.11
Warren Spahn	L	35	20	11	.645	3	39	35	20	281	249	52	128	3	2.79
Lew Burdette	R	29	19	10	.655	1	39	35	16	256	234	52	110	6	2.71
Bob Buhl	R	27	18	8	.692	0	38	33	13	217	190	105	86	2	3.32
Ray Crone	R	24	11	10	.524	2	35	21	6	170	173	44	73	0	3.86
Gene Conley	R	25	8	9	.471	3	31	19	5	158	169	52	68	1	3.13
Taylor Phillips	L	23	5	3	.625	2	23	6	3	88	69	33	36	0	2.25
Ernie Johnson	R	32	4	3	.571	6	36	0	0	51	54	21	26	0	3.71
Bob Trowbridge	R	26	3	2	.600	0	19	4	1	51	38	34	40	0	2.65
Lou Sleater	L	29	2	2	.500	2	25	1	0	46	42	27	32	0	3.13
Dave Jolly	R	31	3	4	.400	7	29	0	0	46	39	35	20	0	3.72
Chet Nichols	L	25	0	1	.000	0	2	0	0	4	9	3	2	0	6.75
Red Murff (XJ)	R	35	0	0	—	1	14	1	0	24	25	7	18	0	4.50
Phil Paine	R	26	0	0	—	0	3	0	0	3	0	0	0	0	∞
Humberto Robinson	R	26	0	0	—	0	2	0	0	2	1	2	0	0	0.00

NAME	T	AGE	W	L	PCT	SV	G	GS	CG	IP	H	BB	SO	SHO	ERA
		29	91	63	.591	29	155	155	47	1389	1406	458	653	4	3.85
Brooks Lawrence	R	31	19	10	.655	9	49	30	11	219	210	71	96	1	3.99
Hersh Freeman	R	28	14	5	.737	18	64	0	0	109	112	34	50	0	3.39
Joe Nuxhall	L	27	13	11	.542	3	44	32	10	201	196	87	120	2	3.72
Johnny Klippstein	R	28	12	11	.522	1	37	29	11	211	219	82	86	0	4.09
Art Fowler	R	33	11	11	.500	1	45	23	8	178	191	35	86	0	4.04
Hal Jeffcoat	R	31	8	2	.800	2	38	16	2	171	189	55	55	0	3.84
Tom Acker	R	26	4	3	.571	1	29	7	1	84	60	29	54	1	2.36
Don Gross	L	25	3	0	1.000	0	19	7	2	69	69	20	47	0	1.96
Joe Black	R	32	3	2	.600	2	32	0	0	62	61	25	27	0	4.50
Larry Jansen	R	35	2	3	.400	1	8	7	2	35	39	9	16	0	5.14
2 Paul LaPalme	L	32	2	4	.333	0	11	2	0	27	26	4	4	0	4.67
Pat Scantlebury	L	38	0	1	.000	0	6	2	0	19	24	5	10	0	6.63
Frank Smith	R	28	0	0	—	0	3	0	0	3	2	1	0	0	12.00
2 Russ Meyer	R	32	0	0	—	0	1	0	0	1	0	1	1	0	0.00
Bill Kennedy	L	35	0	0	—	0	1	0	0	1	2	2	1	0	18.00

NAME	T	AGE	W	L	PCT	SV	G	GS	CG	IP	H	BB	SO	SHO	ERA
		30	76	78	.494	30	156	156	41	1389	1339	546	709	12	3.97
Vinegar Bend Mizell	L	25	14	14	.500	0	33	33	11	209	172	92	153	3	3.62
2 Murry Dickson	R	39	13	8	.619	0	28	27	12	196	175	57	109	3	3.08
2 Herm Wehmeier	R	29	12	9	.571	1	34	19	7	171	150	71	68	2	3.68
Tom Poholsky	R	26	9	14	.391	0	33	29	7	203	210	44	95	2	3.59
Willard Schmidt	R	28	6	8	.429	1	33	21	2	148	131	78	52	0	3.83
Lindy McDaniel	R	20	7	6	.538	0	39	7	1	116	121	42	59	0	3.41
1 Ellis Kinder	R	29	6	2	.750	7	38	1	0	66	63	27	17	0	4.20
Larry Jackson	R	25	2	2	.500	9	51	1	0	85	75	45	50	0	4.13
1 Harvey Haddix	L	30	1	0	1.000	0	4	4	1	24	28	10	16	1	5.25
1 Jim Konstanty	R	39	1	1	.500	5	27	0	0	39	46	6	7	0	4.62
1 Ben Flowers	R	29	1	1	.500	0	3	3	0	12	15	5	5	0	6.75
2 Don Liddle	L	31	1	2	.333	0	14	5	0	25	36	18	14	0	8.28
Bob Blaylock	R	21	1	6	.143	0	14	6	0	41	45	24	39	0	6.37
Stu Miller	R	28	0	1	.000	0	7	3	0	12	5	5	5	0	5.14
2 Dick Littlefield	L	30	0	0	—	0	2	0	0	10	4	4	6	0	7.20
Gordon Jones	R	26	0	0	—	0	2	0	0	6	6	5	5	0	5.73
2 Max Surkont	R	34	0	0	—	0	1	0	0	6	10	2	5	0	9.00
1 Paul LaPalme	L	32	0	0	—	0	1	0	0	1	6	3	0	0	54.00

NAME	T	AGE	W	L	PCT	SV	G	GS	CG	IP	H	BB	SO	SHO	ERA
		29	71	83	.461	15	154	154	57	1377	1407	437	750	4	4.20
Robin Roberts	R	29	19	18	.514	3	43	37	22	297	328	40	157	1	4.45
Curt Simmons	L	27	15	10	.600	0	33	27	14	198	186	65	68	0	3.36
2 Harvey Haddix	L	30	12	8	.600	2	31	26	11	207	196	55	154	2	3.48
Saul Rogovin	R	34	7	6	.538	0	22	18	3	107	122	27	48	0	4.96
Jack Meyer	R	24	7	11	.389	2	41	7	2	96	86	51	66	0	4.41
2 Stu Miller	R	28	6	3	.385	0	24	15	2	107	109	51	55	0	4.46
Bob Miller	R	30	3	6	.333	5	49	6	3	122	115	34	53	1	3.25
Ron Negray	R	26	2	3	.400	3	39	4	0	67	72	24	44	0	4.16
Jack Sanford	R	27	1	0	1.000	0	3	0	0	13	7	13	6	0	1.38
Granny Hamner	R	29	0	1	.000	0	3	3	0	8	10	2	4	0	4.50
Dick Farrell	R	22	0	1	.000	0	8	0	0	4	8	9	6	0	13.50
2 Ben Flowers	R	29	0	0	—	0	32	0	0	41	54	10	22	0	5.71
1 Herm Wehmeier	R	29	0	0	—	0	3	0	0	20	18	11	8	0	4.05
1 Murry Dickson	R	39	0	0	—	0	3	0	0	20	12	1	5	0	5.09
Jim Owens	R	22	0	0	—	0	10	0	0	30	35	22	17	0	7.20
Duane Pillette	R	33	0	0	—	0	20	0	0	18	12	10	6	0	6.65
Angelo LiPetri	R	26	0	0	—	0	3	0	0	11	7	3	8	0	3.27
Bob Ross	L	27	0	0	—	0	2	0	0	2	4	4	2	0	9.00

309

NEW YORK — 6th 67-87 .435 26 — BILL RIGNEY

Batting

NAME	G by Pos	B	AGE	G	AB	R	H	2B	3B	HR	RBI	BB	SO	SB	BA	SA
TOTALS			27	154	5190	540	1268	192	45	145	497	402	659	67	.244	.382
Bill White	1B138, OF2	L	22	138	508	63	130	23	7	22	59	47	72	15	.256	.459
2 Red Schoendienst	2B85	B	33	92	334	39	99	12	3	2	14	28	10	1	.296	.368
Daryl Spencer	2B70, SS66, 3B12	R	26	146	489	46	108	13	2	14	42	35	65	1	.221	.342
Foster Castleman	3B107, SS2, 2B1	R	25	124	385	33	87	16	3	14	45	15	50	2	.226	.392
Don Mueller	OF117	L	29	138	453	38	122	12	1	5	41	15	7	0	.269	.333
Willie Mays	OF152	R	25	152	578	101	171	27	8	36	84	68	65	40	.296	.557
2 Jackie Brandt	OF96	R	22	98	351	45	105	16	8	11	47	17	31	3	.299	.484
2 Bill Sarni (IL)	C75	R	28	78	238	16	55	9	3	5	23	20	31	0	.231	.357
Dusty Rhodes	OF68	L	29	111	244	20	53	10	3	8	33	30	41	0	.217	.381
Hank Thompson	3B44, OF10, SS1	L	30	83	183	24	43	9	0	8	29	31	26	2	.235	.415
Wes Westrum	C67	R	34	68	132	10	29	5	2	3	8	25	28	0	.220	.356
1 George Wilson	OF8	L	30	53	68	5	9	1	1	1	5	5	14	0	.132	.191
Ed Bressoud	SS48	R	24	49	163	15	37	4	2	0	9	12	20	1	.227	.276
Al Dark	SS48	R	34	48	206	19	52	12	0	2	17	8	13	0	.252	.340
1 Whitey Lockman	OF39, 1B7	L	29	48	169	13	46	7	1	1	10	16	17	1	.272	.343
Bobby Hofman	3B7, C7, 1B3, 2B2	R	30	47	56	1	10	1	0	0	2	6	9	0	.179	.196
1 Ray Katt	C37	R	29	37	101	10	23	4	0	7	14	6	16	0	.228	.475
Bob Lennon	OF21	L	27	26	55	3	10	1	0	1	4	4	17	0	.182	.200
Jim Mangan	C15	R	26	20	20	2	2	0	0	0	1	4	6	0	.100	.100
Wayne Terwilliger	2B6	R	31	14	18	0	4	1	0	0	0	0	5	0	.222	.278
Gail Harris	1B11	L	24	12	38	1	5	1	0	1	3	10	1	0	.132	.263

Gil Coan 34 L 0-1, Ozzie Virgil 23 R 5-12, Bill Taylor 26 L 1-4

Pitching

NAME	T	AGE	W	L	PCT	SV	G	GS	CG	IP	H	BB	SO	SHO	ERA
		30	67	87	.435	28	154	154	31	1378	1287	551	765	9	3.78
Johnny Antonelli	L	26	20	13	.606	1	41	36	15	258	225	75	145	5	2.86
Al Worthington (XJ)	R	27	7	14	.333	0	28	24	4	166	158	74	95	0	3.96
Ruben Gomez	R	28	7	17	.292	0	40	31	4	196	191	77	76	2	4.59
Steve Ridzik	R	27	6	2	.750	0	41	5	1	92	80	65	53	1	3.82
Joe Margoneri	L	26	6	6	.500	0	23	13	2	92	88	49	49	0	3.91
Jim Hearn	R	35	5	11	.313	1	30	19	2	129	124	44	66	0	3.98
3 Dick Littlefield	L	30	4	4	.500	2	31	7	0	97	78	39	65	0	4.08
Hoyt Wilhelm	R	33	4	9	.308	8	64	0	0	89	97	43	71	0	3.84
Windy McCall	L	30	3	4	.429	7	46	4	0	77	74	20	41	0	3.62
3 Max Surkont	R	34	2	2	.500	1	8	4	1	32	24	9	18	0	4.78
Ray Monzant	R	23	1	0	1.000	0	4	1	1	13	8	7	11	0	4.15
Marv Grissom	R	38	1	1	.500	7	43	2	0	81	71	16	49	0	1.56
1 Don Liddle	L	31	1	2	.333	1	11	5	1	41	45	14	21	0	3.95
Mike McCormick	L	17	0	1	.000	0	3	2	0	7	7	10	4	0	9.00
Roy Wright	R	22	0	1	.000	0	3	1	0	3	8	2	0	0	15.00
Jim Constable	L	23	0	0	—	0	3	0	0	4	9	7	1	0	15.75

Paul Giel (MS) 23

PITTSBURGH — 7th 66-88 .429 27 — BOBBY BRAGAN

Batting

NAME	G by Pos	B	AGE	G	AB	R	H	2B	3B	HR	RBI	BB	SO	SB	BA	SA
TOTALS			24	157	5221	588	1340	199	57	110	546	383	752	24	.257	.380
Dale Long	1B138	L	30	148	517	64	136	20	4	27	91	54	85	1	.263	.485
Bill Mazeroski	2B81	R	19	81	255	30	62	8	1	3	14	18	24	0	.243	.318
Dick Groat	SS141, 3B2	R	25	142	520	40	142	19	3	0	37	35	25	0	.273	.321
Frank Thomas	3B111, OF56, 2B4	R	27	157	588	69	166	24	3	25	80	36	65	0	.282	.461
Roberto Clemente	OF139, 2B2, 3B1	R	21	147	543	66	169	30	7	7	60	13	58	6	.311	.431
2 Bill Virdon	OF130	L	25	133	509	67	170	21	10	8	37	33	63	6	.334	.462
Lee Walls	OF133, 3B1	R	23	143	474	72	130	20	11	11	54	50	83	3	.274	.432
Jack Shepard	C86, 1B2	R	25	100	256	24	62	11	2	7	30	25	37	1	.242	.383
Bob Skinner	OF36, 1B23, 3B1	L	24	113	233	29	47	8	3	5	29	26	50	1	.202	.326
2 Hank Foiles	C73	R	27	79	222	24	47	10	2	7	25	17	56	0	.212	.369
Johnny O'Brien	2B53, P8, SS1	R	25	73	104	13	18	1	0	0	3	5	7	0	.173	.183
Dick Cole	3B18, 2B12, SS6	R	30	72	99	7	21	2	1	0	9	5	10	0	.212	.253
Gene Freese	3B47, 2B26	R	22	65	207	17	43	9	0	3	14	16	45	0	.208	.295
Eddie O'Brien	SS23, OF6, 3B4, 2B2, P1	R	25	63	53	17	14	2	0	0	3	2	1	0	.264	.302
Dick Hall	P19, 1B1	R	25	33	29	5	10	0	0	1	5	7	5	0	.345	.345
Danny Kravitz	C26, 3B2	L	25	32	68	6	18	2	2	1	10	5	5	0	.265	.441
Curt Roberts	2B27	R	26	31	62	6	11	5	2	0	4	5	12	1	.177	.323
Jerry Lynch (IL)	OF1	L	25	19	19	1	3	0	1	0	1	4	6	0	.158	.263
1 Preston Ward	OF5, 3B5	L	28	16	30	3	10	1	1	1	11	6	4	0	.333	.500
1 Bobby Del Greco	OF7, 3B3	R	23	14	20	4	4	0	2	0	1	4	3	0	.200	.500
Toby Atwell	C9	L	32	12	18	0	2	0	0	0	3	1	5	0	.111	.111
2 Spook Jacobs	2B11	R	30	11	37	4	6	2	0	0	1	2	5	0	.162	.216

Johnny Powers 26 L 1-21, Bill Hall 27 L 0-3, Paul Smith (MS) 25

Pitching

NAME	T	AGE	W	L	PCT	SV	G	GS	CG	IP	H	BB	SO	SHO	ERA
		28	66	88	.429	24	157	157	37	1376	1406	469	662	8	3.74
Bob Friend	R	25	17	17	.500	3	49	42	19	314	310	85	166	4	3.47
Ron Kline	R	24	14	18	.438	2	44	39	9	264	263	81	125	2	3.38
Roy Face	R	28	12	13	.480	6	68	3	0	135	131	42	96	0	3.53
Vern Law	R	26	8	16	.333	2	39	32	6	196	218	49	60	0	4.32
Nellie King	R	28	4	1	.800	5	38	0	0	60	54	19	25	0	3.15
Luis Arroyo	L	29	3	3	.500	0	18	2	1	29	36	12	17	0	4.66
George Munger	R	37	4	9	.429	2	35	13	0	107	126	41	45	0	4.04
Fred Waters	L	29	2	2	.500	0	23	5	1	51	48	30	14	0	2.82
Johnny O'Brien	R	25	1	0	1.000	0	8	0	0	19	8	9	9	0	2.84
Laurin Pepper	R	25	1	1	.500	0	11	7	0	30	35	25	12	0	3.00
Cholly Naranjo	R	21	1	2	.333	0	17	3	0	34	37	17	26	0	4.50
2 Howie Pollet	L	35	0	4	.000	1	19	0	0	23	18	8	10	0	3.13
Dick Hall (FJ)	R	25	0	7	.000	1	19	9	1	62	64	21	27	0	4.79
1 Jack McMahan	L	23	0	0	—	0	11	0	0	13	18	9	9	0	6.23
Red Swanson	R	19	0	0	—	0	2	0	0	12	21	8	5	0	9.75
1 Dick Littlefield	L	30	0	0	—	0	3	0	0	14	14	6	10	0	4.15
Lino Donoso	L	33	0	0	—	0	3	0	0	4	3	3	1	0	0.00
Bob Garber	R	27	0	0	—	0	2	0	0	4	3	2	3	0	2.25
Bob Purkey	R	26	0	0	—	0	1	0	0	4	4	1	1	0	2.25
1 Max Surkont	R	34	0	0	—	0	1	0	0	4	2	2	2	0	4.50
Eddie O'Brien	R	25	0	0	—	0	1	0	0	1	0	1	0	0	0.00

CHICAGO — 8th 60-94 .390 33 — STAN HACK

Batting

NAME	G by Pos	B	AGE	G	AB	R	H	2B	3B	HR	RBI	BB	SO	SB	BA	SA
TOTALS			28	157	5260	597	1281	202	50	142	563	446	776	55	.244	.382
Dee Fondy	1B133	L	31	137	543	52	146	22	9	9	46	20	74	9	.269	.392
Gene Baker	2B140	R	31	140	546	65	141	23	3	12	57	39	54	4	.258	.377
Ernie Banks	SS139	R	25	139	538	82	160	25	8	28	85	52	62	6	.297	.530
Don Hoak	3B110	R	28	121	424	51	91	18	4	5	37	41	46	2	.215	.311
Walt Moryn	OF141	L	30	147	529	69	151	27	3	23	67	50	67	4	.285	.478
Pete Whisenant	OF93	R	26	103	314	37	75	16	3	11	46	24	53	8	.239	.414
Monte Irvin	OF96	R	37	111	339	44	92	13	3	15	50	41	41	1	.271	.460
Hobie Landrith	C99	L	26	111	312	22	69	10	3	4	32	39	38	0	.221	.311
Jim King	OF82	L	23	118	317	32	79	13	2	15	54	30	44	4	.249	.445
Eddie Miksis	3B48, OF33, 2B19, SS2	R	29	114	356	54	85	10	3	9	27	32	40	4	.239	.360
Harry Chiti	C67	R	23	72	203	17	43	6	4	18	19	15	35	0	.212	.340
Frank Kellert	1B27	R	31	71	129	10	24	3	1	4	17	12	22	0	.186	.318
Solly Drake	OF53	B	25	65	215	29	55	9	1	2	15	23	35	9	.256	.335
Jerry Kindall	SS18	R	21	32	55	7	9	1	1	0	6	6	17	1	.164	.218
Ed Winceniak	3B4, 2B1	R	25	15	17	1	2	0	0	0	1	0	3	0	.118	.118
Clyde McCullough	C7	R	39	14	19	0	4	1	0	1	0	5	5	0	.211	.263

Gale Wade 27 L 0-12, Richie Myers 26 R 0-1, El Tappe 29 R 0-1, Owen Friend 29 R 0-2, Jim Fanning 28 R 1-4, Ted Tappe (IL) 25

Pitching

NAME	T	AGE	W	L	PCT	SV	G	GS	CG	IP	H	BB	SO	SHO	ERA
		29	60	94	.390	17	157	157	37	1392	1325	613	744	6	3.96
Bob Rush	R	30	13	10	.565	0	32	32	13	240	210	59	104	1	3.19
Turk Lown	R	32	9	8	.529	13	61	0	0	111	95	78	74	0	3.57
Sam Jones	R	30	9	14	.391	0	33	28	8	189	155	115	176	2	3.90
Vito Valentinetti	R	27	6	4	.600	1	42	2	0	95	84	36	26	0	3.79
Jim Davis	L	31	5	7	.417	2	46	11	2	120	116	59	66	1	3.68
Jim Brosnan	R	26	5	9	.357	1	30	10	1	95	95	45	51	1	3.79
Don Kaiser	R	21	3	4	.429	0	27	22	5	150	144	52	74	1	3.60
Warren Hacker	R	31	3	13	.188	0	34	24	4	168	190	44	65	0	4.66
Moe Drabowski	R	20	2	4	.333	0	9	7	3	51	37	39	36	0	2.47
Paul Minner (YJ)	L	32	2	5	.286	0	19	9	1	67	69	19	14	0	6.89
2 Jim Hughes	R	33	1	3	.250	0	25	1	0	45	43	30	20	0	5.20
1 Russ Meyer (SJ)	R	32	1	6	.143	0	20	9	0	57	71	26	28	0	6.32
Dave Hillman	R	28	0	2	.000	0	3	2	1	12	11	5	6	0	1.80
Johnny Briggs	R	22	0	0	—	0	3	0	0	5	5	4	1	0	1.80
George Piktuzis	L	24	0	0	—	0	3	0	0	5	6	2	3	0	7.20
Bill Tremel	R	26	0	0	—	0	3	0	0	3	3	4	0	0	9.00

WORLD SERIES — NEW YORK (AL) 4 BROOKLYN (NL) 3

LINE SCORES

TEAM	1	2	3	4	5	6	7	8	9	10	11	12	R	H	E
Game 1 October 3 at Brooklyn															
NY (AL)	2	0	0	1	0	0	0	0	0				3	9	1
BKN (NL)	0	2	3	1	0	0	0	0	X				6	9	0

Ford, Kucks (4), Morgan (6), Turley (8)   **Maglie**

Game 2 October 5 at Brooklyn															
NY	1	5	0	1	0	0	0	0	1				8	12	2
BKN	0	6	1	2	2	0	2	0	X				13	12	0

Larsen, Kucks (2), Byrne (2), Sturdivant (3), Morgan (3), Turley (5), McDermott (6)   Newcombe, Roebuck (2), **Bessent (3)**

Game 3 October 6 at New York															
BKN	0	1	0	0	0	1	0	0	1				3	8	1
NY	0	1	0	0	0	3	0	1	X				5	8	1

Craig, Labine (7)   **Ford**

Game 4 October 7 at New York															
BKN	0	0	0	1	0	0	0	0	1				2	6	0
NY	1	0	0	2	0	1	0	2	X				6	7	2

Erskine, Roebuck (5), Drysdale (7)   **Sturdivant**

Game 5 October 8 at New York															
BKN	0	0	0	0	0	0	0	0	0				0	0	0
NY	0	0	0	1	0	1	0	0	X				2	5	0

Maglie   **Larsen**

Game 6 October 9 at Brooklyn															
NY	0	0	0	0	0	0	0	0	0	0			0	7	0
BKN	0	0	0	0	0	0	0	0	0	1			1	4	0

Turley   **Labine**

Game 7 October 10 at Brooklyn															
NY	2	0	2	1	0	0	4	0	0				9	10	0
BKN	0	0	0	0	0	0	0	0	0				0	3	1

Kucks   Newcombe, Bessent (4), Craig (7), Roebuck (7), Erskine (9)

COMPOSITE BATTING

NAME	POS	G	AB	R	H	2B	3B	HR	RBI	BA
New York (AL) Totals		7	229	33	58	6	0	12	33	.253
Bauer	OF	7	32	3	9	0	0	1	3	.281
Martin	2B-3B	7	27	5	8	0	0	2	3	.296
Berra	C	7	25	5	9	2	0	3	10	.360
Mantle	OF	7	24	6	6	1	0	3	4	.250
Collins	1B	6	21	2	5	2	0	0	2	.238
McDougald	SS	7	21	0	3	0	0	0	1	.143
Slaughter	OF	6	20	6	7	0	0	1	4	.350
Carey	3B	7	19	2	3	0	0	0	0	.158
Skowron	1B	3	10	1	1	0	0	1	4	.100
Howard	OF	5	11	5	4	2	1	1	1	.400
Turley	P	3	4	0	0	0	0	0	0	.000
Ford	P	2	4	0	0	0	0	0	0	.000
Kucks	P	3	3	0	0	0	0	0	0	.000
Larsen	P	2	3	1	1	0	0	0	0	.333
Sturdivant	P	2	3	0	1	0	0	0	0	.333
J. Coleman	2B	2	3	0	0	0	0	0	0	.000
Cerv	PH	1	1	0	1	0	0	0	0	1.000
McDermott	P	1	1	0	1	0	0	0	0	1.000
Morgan	P	2	1	1	1	0	0	0	0	1.000
Siebern	PH	1	1	0	0	0	0	0	0	.000
Wilson	PH	1	1	0	0	0	0	0	0	.000
Byrne	P	2	0	0	0	0	0	0	0	.000
Brooklyn (NL) Totals		7	215	25	42	8	1	3	24	.195
Reese	SS	7	27	3	6	0	1	0	2	.222
Furillo	OF	7	25	2	6	2	0	1	2	.240
Robinson	3B	7	24	5	6	1	0	1	2	.250
Gilliam	2B-OF	7	24	2	2	0	0	0	2	.083
Snider	OF	7	23	5	7	1	0	1	4	.304
Hodges	1B	7	23	5	7	1	0	1	8	.304
Campanella	C	7	22	2	4	1	0	0	3	.182
Amoros	OF	6	19	1	1	0	0	0	0	.053
Maglie	P	2	5	0	0	0	0	0	0	.000
Labine	P	2	4	0	1	0	0	0	0	.250
Neal	2B	4	4	0	0	0	0	0	0	.000
Mitchell	PH	4	3	0	0	0	0	0	0	.000
Jackson	PH	2	2	0	1	0	0	0	0	.500
Bessent	P	2	2	0	0	0	0	0	0	.000
Craig	P	2	2	0	1	0	0	0	0	.500
Walker	PH	2	2	0	0	0	0	0	0	.000
Newcombe	P	2	1	0	0	0	0	0	0	.000
Erskine	P	2	1	0	0	0	0	0	0	.000
Cimoli	OF	1	1	0	0	0	0	0	0	—

Roebuck P 0-0, Drysdale P 0-0

COMPOSITE PITCHING

NAME	G	IP	H	BB	SO	W	L	SV	ERA
New York (AL) Totals	7	61.2	42	32	47	4	3	0	2.48
Ford	2	12	14	2	8	1	1	0	5.25
Turley	3	11	4	8	14	0	1	0	0.82
Kucks	3	11	6	3	2	1	0	0	0.82
Larsen	2	10.2	4	4	7	1	0	0	0.00
Sturdivant	2	9.2	8	9	9	1	0	0	2.79
Morgan	2	6	4	3	0	0	0	0	0.00
McDermott	1	3	2	3	0	0	0	0	3.00
Byrne	1	0.1	1	0	1	0	0	0	0.00
Brooklyn (NL) Totals	7	61	58	21	43	3	4	0	4.72
Maglie	2	17	14	6	15	1	1	0	2.65
Labine	2	12	8	3	4	1	0	0	0.00
Bessent	2	10	8	3	5	1	0	0	1.80
Craig	2	6	10	3	4	1	0	0	12.00
Erskine	2	5	4	2	2	0	1	0	5.40
Newcombe	2	4.2	11	3	4	0	1	0	21.21
Roebuck	3	4.1	1	0	5	0	0	0	2.08
Drysdale	1	2	1	1	0	0	0	0	9.00

1957 Glory for the Older Gentry and a Championship to the Young

Part of the scenery was gone. The Dodgers had wanted to trade Jackie Robinson to the Giants, but he retired instead. Along with baseball's first black performer went Bob Feller, Phil Rizzuto, and Al Rosen. All had left a heavy enough impression upon the game to give the feeling that the times were changing. For Fred Haney, things had changed for the better.

In 1955, Haney had little thought that he would manage a World Series winner two years later. From 1953 through 1955, Haney managed the Pirates to three straight last place finishes. Yet, when the Milwaukee Braves got off to a slow start in 1956, they gave him the nod to succeed Charlie Grimm as manager—and suddenly Haney found himself with a contending club to work with for the first time in his managerial career. After coming alive in mid-1956 but fading at the end to finish only one game behind Brooklyn, the 1957 Braves outlasted mid-summer challenges from St. Louis and Cincinnati to win the National League flag by a margin of eight games.

Brooklyn was plagued by age's toll on Pee Wee Reese, Don Newcombe, Carl Erskine, and Roy Campanella, and never made a serious run at the top. While the Braves were paced by sluggers Hank Aaron and Eddie Mathews, and a Big Three pitching staff of Warren Spahn, Lew Burdette, and Bob Buhl, Haney kept pulling rabbits out of his hat to stock the supporting cast. He sent three players to the Giants in June in exchange for Red Schoendienst, who proceeded to hit .310 and make all the plays at second base. Bill Bruton and Joe Adcock were put out of action in mid-season by injuries, only to see Wes Covington and Bob "Hurricane" Hazle recalled from Wichita. Covington knocked 21 homers and Hazle batted a torrid .403. When a relief pitcher was needed, Haney was able to come up with Don McMahon from Wichita. Aaron took the MVP Award, leading the senior circuit in homers and RBI's losing only the batting crown to 36-year-old Stan Musial.

In the American League, there was almost a final surprise, as the White Sox came out of the gate fast. But the Chicago attack, devoid of power and long on singles and stolen bases, could only support their strong pitching well enoug to remain on top through June. They proved no match for the Yankees, wh took 14 of 22 contests from Al Lopez's squad to win their eighth pennant in nin years. The Chicago guerrilla attack of Luis Aparicio, Nellie Fox, and Minni Minoso turned out to be no match for the big guns of Mickey Mantle, Yog Berra, and Bill Skowron. Mantle won a second consecutive MVP Award wit a .365 batting average and logs of 34 homers and 94 RBI's. Berra's 24 homers Skowron's .304 batting, and a .297 rookie season by Tony Kubek fleshed ou the Yankee offense, while Stengel again had to patch together a pitching staff. Whitey Ford was troubled by a bad shoulder and won only 11 games, but Tor Sturdivant continued his good work of 1956, Bob Turley made a comebac from an off-season, and Bobby Shantz, the diminutive left-hander obtaine from Kansas City during the winter, recovered from arm ills to lead th American League in E.R.A. with 2.45.

The rest of the league saw several key events. Boston's 38-year-old Te Williams took the batting crown with a .388 mark, becoming the oldest battin champ ever. Washington's Roy Sievers won the home run and RBI titles, bu the Senators still finished eighth. Cleveland lost baseball's most promisin young pitcher when lefty Herb Score was struck on the eye by a line drive hi by the Yankees' Gil McDougald on May 7.

The series saw the world championship flag fly west of the Hudson River fo the first time since 1948, as the Braves knocked off the Yanks in seven games Aaron hit a rousing .393, but the big story was Lew Burdette. In throwing thre complete game victories, Burdette became the first to perform that feat sinc Stan Coveleski in 1920.

Beyond Stengel's having to again settle for second-best, the most fa reaching story of the year was the decision of the Brooklyn Dodgers and th New York Giants to abandon their traditional turf for new California sod Unlike previous franchise shifts, both teams were still fairly good gate draws but each cited outmoded ball parks and inadequate parking facilities an wanted the unlimited potential which Los Angeles and San Francisco offered

1957 AMERICAN LEAGUE

NAME	G by Pos	B	AGE	G	AB	R	H	2B	3B	HR	RBI	BB	SO	SB	BA	SA
NEW YORK 1st 98-56 .636																**CASEY STENGEL**
TOTALS			29	154	5271	723	1412	200	54	145	682	562	709	49	.268	.409
Bill Skowron	1B115	R	26	122	457	54	139	15	5	17	88	31	60	3	.304	.470
Bobby Richardson	2B93	R	21	97	305	36	78	11	1	0	19	9	26	1	.256	.298
Gil McDougald	SS121, 2B21, 3B7	R	29	141	539	87	156	25	9	13	62	59	71	2	.289	.442
Andy Carey	3B81	R	25	85	247	30	63	6	5	6	33	15	42	2	.255	.393
Hank Bauer	OF135	R	34	137	479	70	124	22	9	18	65	42	64	7	.259	.455
Mickey Mantle	OF139	B	25	144	474	121	173	28	6	34	94	146	75	16	.365	.665
Enos Slaughter	OF64	L	41	96	209	24	53	7	1	5	34	40	19	0	.254	.368
Yogi Berra	C121, OF6	L	32	134	482	74	121	14	2	24	82	57	24	1	.251	.438
Tony Kubek	OF50, SS41, 3B38, 2B1	L	20	127	431	56	128	21	3	3	39	24	48	6	.297	.381
Elston Howard	OF71, C32, 1B2	R	28	110	356	33	90	13	4	8	44	16	43	2	.253	.379
Joe Collins	1B32, OF15	L	34	79	149	17	30	1	0	2	10	24	18	2	.201	.248
2 Harry Simpson	OF42, 1B21	L	31	75	224	27	56	7	3*	7	39	19	36	1	.250	.402
Jerry Coleman	2B45, 3B21, SS4	R	32	72	157	23	42	7	2	2	12	20	21	1	.268	.376
1 Billy Martin	2B26, 3B13	R	29	43	145	12	35	5	2	1	14	3	14	2	.241	.324
Jerry Lumpe	3B30, SS6	L	24	40	103	15	35	6	2	0	11	9	13	2	.340	.437
Darrell Johnson	C20	R	28	21	46	4	10	1	0	1	8	3	10	0	.217	.304
2 Bobby Del Greco	OF6	R	24	8	7	3	3	0	0	0	0	2	2	1	.429	.429
Zeke Bella	OF4	R	26	5	10	0	1	0	0	0	0	1	2	0	.100	.100
1 Woodie Held		R	25	1	1	0	0	0	0	0	0	0	0	0	.000	.000
CHICAGO 2nd 90-64 .584 8																**AL LOPEZ**
TOTALS			30	155	5265	707	1369	208	41	106	671	633	745	109	.260	.375
2 Earl Torgeson	1B70, OF1	L	33	86	251	53	74	11	2	7	46	49	44	7	.295	.438
Nellie Fox	2B155	L	29	155	619	110	196	27	8	6	61	75	13	5	.317	.415
Luis Aparicio	SS142	R	23	143	575	82	148	22	6	3	41	52	55	28	.257	.332
Bubba Phillips	3B97, OF20	R	27	121	393	38	106	13	3	7	42	28	32	5	.270	.372
Jim Rivera	OF86, 1B31	L	34	125	402	51	103	21	6	14	52	40	80	18	.256	.443
Larry Doby	OF110	L	33	119	416	57	120	27	4	14	79	56	79	2	.288	.464
Minnie Minoso	OF152, 3B1	R	34	153	568	96	176	36	5	12	103	79	54	18	.310	.454
Sherm Lollar (BW)	C96	R	32	101	351	33	90	11	2	11	70	35	24	2	.256	.393
Jim Landis	OF90	R	23	96	274	38	58	11	3	2	16	45	61	14	.212	.296
Sammy Esposito	3B53, SS22, 2B4, OF1	R	25	94	176	26	36	3	0	2	15	38	27	5	.205	.256
Walt Dropo	1B69	R	34	93	223	24	57	2	0	13	49	16	40	0	.256	.439
Fred Hatfield	3B44	L	32	69	114	14	23	3	0	0	8	15	20	1	.202	.228
Earl Battey	C43	R	22	48	115	12	20	2	3	2	12	20	18	0	.174	.322
Les Moss	C39	R	32	42	115	10	31	3	0	2	12	20	18	0	.270	.348
1 Ron Northey	OF28	L	37	40	27	0	5	1	0	0	7	18	14	3	.185	.222
Ted Beard	OF28	L	36	38	78	15	16	1	0	0	7	14	14	3	.205	.218
1 Dave Philley	OF17, 1B2	B	37	22	71	9	23	4	0	0	4	4	10	1	.324	.380
Ron Jackson	1B13	R	23	13	60	4	19	3	0	2	8	1	12	0	.317	.467
1 Bob Kennedy		R	36	4	2	0	0	0	0	0	0	0	1	0	.000	.000
Bob Powell		R	23	1	0	1	0	0	0	0	0	0	0	0	—	—
BOSTON 3rd 82-72 .532 16																**PINKY HIGGINS**
TOTALS			27	154	5267	721	1380	231	32	153	695	624	739	29	.262	.405
Dick Gernert	1B71, OF16	R	28	99	316	45	75	13	3	14	58	39	62	1	.237	.430
Ted Lepcio	2B68	R	26	79	232	24	56	10	2	9	37	29	61	0	.241	.418
Billy Klaus	SS118	L	28	127	477	76	120	18	4	10	42	55	53	2	.252	.369
Frank Malzone	3B153	R	27	153	634	82	185	31	5	15	103	31	41	2	.292	.427
Jackie Jensen	OF144	R	30	145	544	82	153	29	4	23	103	75	66	8	.281	.469
Jimmy Piersall	OF151	R	27	151	609	103	159	27	5	19	63	62	54	14	.261	.415
Ted Williams	OF125	L	38	132	420	96	163	28	1	38	87	119	43	0	.388	.731
Sammy White	C111	R	29	111	340	24	73	10	1	3	31	25	38	1	.215	.276
Gene Stephens	OF90	L	24	120	173	25	46	6	4	3	26	26	20	0	.266	.399
Mickey Vernon	1B70	L	39	102	270	36	65	18	1	7	38	41	35	0	.241	.393
Pete Daley	C77	R	27	78	191	17	43	10	0	3	25	16	31	0	.225	.325
Billy Consolo	SS42, 2B16, 3B2	R	22	68	196	26	53	6	1	4	19	23	48	1	.270	.372
Gene Mauch (VJ)	2B58	R	31	65	222	23	60	10	3	2	28	22	26	1	.270	.369
Norm Zauchin (BW)	1B36	R	27	52	91	11	24	3	0	4	14	9	13	0	.264	.396
Willard Nixon	P29	L	29	32	75	7	22	3	1	0	6	8	16	0	.293	.307
Ken Aspromonte	2B24	R	25	24	78	9	21	5	0	0	4	6	9	0	.269	.333
1 Billy Goodman		L	31	18	16	1	1	0	0	0	0	2	1	0	.063	.125
Marty Keough	OF7	L	22	9	17	1	1	0	0	0	0	4	5	0	.059	.059
Haywood Sullivan	C1	R	26	2	1	0	0	0	0	0	0	0	0	0	.000	.000
1 Milt Bolling		R	26	1	0	0	0	0	0	0	0	0	0	0	.000	.000

1 Faye Throneberry 26 L 0-1, Jim Pagliaroni (MS) 19

NAME	T	AGE	W	L	PCT	SV	GS	GS	CG	IP	H	BB	SO	SHO	ERA
		28	98	56	.636	42	154	154	41	1395	1198	580	810	13	3.00
Tom Sturdivant	R	27	16	6	.727	0	28	28	7	202	170	80	118	2	2.54
Bob Turley	R	26	13	6	.684	3	32	23	9	176	120	85	152	4	2.71
Bob Grim	R	27	12	8	.600	19	46	0	0	72	60	36	52	0	2.63
Bobby Shantz	L	31	11	5	.688	5	30	21	9	173	157	40	72	1	2.45
Whitey Ford (SJ)	L	28	11	5	.688	0	24	17	5	129	114	53	84	0	2.58
Don Larsen	R	27	10	4	.714	0	27	20	4	140	113	87	81	1	3.73
Art Ditmar	R	28	8	3	.727	6	46	11	0	127	128	35	64	0	3.26
Johnny Kucks	R	23	8	10	.444	2	37	23	4	179	169	56	78	1	3.57
Tommy Byrne	L	37	4	6	.400	2	30	4	1	85	70	60	57	0	4.34
2 Sal Maglie	R	40	2	0	1.000	3	6	3	1	26	22	7	9	1	1.73
Al Cicotte	R	27	2	2	.500	2	20	2	0	65	57	30	36	0	3.05
1 Ralph Terry	R	21	1	1	.500	0	7	2	1	21	18	8	7	1	3.00

*Simpson, also with Kansas City, tied for league lead in 3B with 9

NAME	T	AGE	W	L	PCT	SV	GS	GS	CG	IP	H	BB	SO	SHO	ERA
		31	90	64	.584	27	155	155	59	1402	1305	470	665	16	3.35
Billy Pierce	L	30	20	12	.625	2	37	34	16	257	228	71	171	4	3.26
Dick Donovan	R	29	16	6	.727	0	28	28	16	221	203	45	88	2	2.77
Jim Wilson	R	35	15	8	.652	0	30	29	12	202	189	65	100	5	3.44
Bob Keegan	R	36	10	8	.556	2	30	19	7	143	131	37	36	2	3.52
Jack Harshman	L	29	8	8	.500	1	30	26	6	151	142	82	83	0	3.41
Bill Fischer	R	26	7	8	.467	1	33	11	3	124	139	35	48	1	3.44
Dixie Howell	R	37	6	5	.545	6	37	0	0	68	64	30	37	0	3.31
Gerry Staley	R	36	5	1	.833	7	47	0	0	105	95	27	44	0	2.06
Don Rudolph	L	25	1	0	1.000	0	5	0	0	12	6	2	2	0	2.25
Barry Latman	R	21	1	0	1.000	1	7	2	0	12	12	13	9	0	8.25
Paul LaPalme	L	33	1	4	.200	7	35	0	0	40	35	19	19	0	3.38
Jim Hughes	R	34	0	0	—	0	4	0	0	5	12	3	2	0	10.80
Ellis Kinder	R	42	0	0	—	1	9	0	0	6	6	2	6	0	0.00
Stover McIlwain	R	17	0	0	—	0	1	0	0	3	3	2	0	0	0.00
Jim Derrington	L	17	0	1	.000	0	20	5	0	37	29	29	14	0	4.86
Jim McDonald	R	30	0	1	.000	0	10	0	0	22	18	10	12	0	2.04

NAME	T	AGE	W	L	PCT	SV	GS	GS	CG	IP	H	BB	SO	SHO	ERA
		27	82	72	.532	23	154	154	55	1377	1391	498	692	9	3.88
Tom Brewer	R	25	16	13	.552	0	32	32	15	238	225	93	128	2	3.86
Frank Sullivan	R	27	14	11	.560	0	31	30	14	241	206	48	127	3	2.73
Willard Nixon	R	29	12	13	.480	0	29	29	11	191	207	56	96	1	3.68
Ike Delock	R	27	9	8	.529	11	49	2	0	94	80	45	62	0	3.83
2 Mike Fornieles	R	25	8	7	.533	2	25	18	7	125	136	38	64	1	3.53
George Susce	R	25	7	3	.700	1	29	5	0	88	93	41	40	0	4.30
Dave Sisler	R	25	7	8	.467	1	22	19	5	122	135	61	55	0	4.72
Bob Porterfield	R	33	4	4	.500	1	28	9	3	102	107	30	28	1	4.06
Murray Wall	R	30	3	0	1.000	1	11	0	0	24	21	2	13	0	3.38
Frank Baumann	L	26	1	3	.250	0	12	4	0	24	12	13	3	7	3.75
2 Dean Stone	L	26	1	3	.250	0	17	8	0	51	56	35	32	0	5.12
Rudy Minarcin	R	27	0	0	—	2	26	0	0	45	44	30	20	0	4.40
Russ Meyer	R	33	0	0	—	0	5	0	0	5	10	3	1	0	5.40
1 Russ Kemmerer	R	25	0	0	—	0	5	0	0	13	13	3	7	0	4.50
Jack Spring	L	24	0	0	—	0	4	0	0	5	6	2	5	0	7.20
2 Bob Chakales	R	29	0	2	.000	3	18	0	0	32	53	11	16	0	8.16

310

DETROIT — 4th 78-76 .506 20 — JACK TIGHE

NAME	G by Pos	B	AGE	G	AB	R	H	2B	3B	HR	RBI	BB	SO	SB	BA	SA
TOTALS			28	154	5348	614	1376	224	37	116	574	504	643	36	.257	.378
Ray Boone	1B117,3B4	R	33	129	462	48	126	25	3	12	65	57	47	1	.273	.418
Frank Bolling	2B146	R	25	146	576	72	149	27	6	15	40	57	64	1	.259	.405
Harvey Kuenn	SS136,3B17,1B1	R	26	151	624	74	173	30	6	9	44	47	28	5	.277	.388
Reno Bertoia	3B83,SS7,2B2	R	22	97	295	28	81	16	2	4	28	19	43	2	.275	.383
Al Kaline	OF145	R	22	149	577	83	170	29	4	23	90	43	38	11	.295	.478
Bill Tuttle	OF128	R	27	133	451	49	113	12	4	5	47	44	41	2	.251	.328
Charlie Maxwell	OF137	L	30	138	492	75	136	23	3	24	82	76	84	3	.276	.482
Frank House	C97	L	27	106	348	31	90	9	0	7	36	35	26	1	.259	.345
2 Dave Philley	1B27,OF12,3B1	B	37	65	173	15	49	8	1	2	16	7	16	3	.283	.376
Jim Finigan	3B59,2B3	R	28	64	174	20	47	4	2	0	17	23	18	1	.270	.316
Red Wilson	C60	R	28	60	180	21	43	8	1	3	13	25	19	2	.239	.344
Jay Porter	OF27,C12,1B3	R	24	58	140	14	35	8	0	2	18	14	20	0	.250	.350
Ron Samford	SS35,2B11,3B4	R	27	54	91	6	20	1	2	0	5	6	15	1	.220	.275
2 Johnny Groth	OF36	R	30	38	103	11	30	10	0	0	16	6	7	0	.291	.388
Jim Small	OF14	L	20	36	42	7	9	2	0	0	0	2	11	0	.214	.262
1 Earl Torgeson	1B17	L	33	30	50	5	12	2	1	1	5	12	10	1	.240	.380
Steve Boros	3B9,SS5	R	20	24	41	4	6	1	0	0	2	1	9	0	.146	.171
Jack Dittmer	3B3,2B1	L	29	16	22	3	5	1	0	0	2	2	1	0	.227	.273
1 Eddie Robinson	1B1	L	36	13	9	0	0	0	0	0	0	3	0	0	.000	.000
Bobo Osborne	OF5,1B4	L	21	11	27	4	4	1	0	0	1	3	7	0	.148	.185
2 Bill Taylor	OF5	L	27	9	23	4	8	2	0	0	5	1	9	0	.348	.565

2 Karl Olson 26 R 2-14, Mel Clark 30 R 0-7, Jack Phillips 35 R 0-1, George Thomas 19 R 0-1, Tom Yewcic 25 R 0-1

NAME	T	AGE	W	L	PCT	SV	G	GS	CG	IP	H	BB	SO	SHO	ERA
		29	78	76	.506	21	154	154	52	1418	1330	505	756	9	3.56
Jim Bunning	R	25	20	8	.714	1	45	30	14	267	214	72	182	1	2.70
Paul Foytack	R	26	14	11	.560	1	38	27	8	212	175	104	118	1	3.14
Frank Lary	R	27	11	16	.407	3	40	35	12	238	250	72	107	2	3.97
Duke Maas	R	28	10	14	.417	6	45	26	8	219	210	65	116	2	3.29
Billy Hoeft	L	25	9	11	.450	1	34	28	10	207	188	69	111	1	3.48
Harry Byrd	R	32	4	3	.571	5	37	1	0	59	53	28	20	0	3.36
Lou Sleater	L	30	3	3	.500	2	41	0	0	69	61	28	43	0	3.78
1 Al Aber	L	29	3	3	.500	1	28	0	0	37	46	11	15	0	6.81
John Tsitouris	R	21	1	0	1.000	0	2	0	0	3	3	2	0	0	9.00
Jim Stump	R	25	1	0	1.000	0	6	0	0	13	11	8	2	0	2.08
Joe Presko	R	28	1	1	.500	0	11	0	0	30	30	4	10	0	1.64
Don Lee	R	23	1	3	.250	0	11	6	0	39	48	18	19	0	4.62
Pete Wojey	R	37	0	0	—	0	3	0	0	1	0	0	0	0	0.00
Chuck Daniel	R	23	0	0	—	0	2	0	0	2	3	0	2	0	9.00
Steve Gromek	R	37	0	1	.000	0	15	1	0	24	32	13	11	0	6.00
Bob Shaw	R	24	0	1	.000	0	7	0	0	10	11	7	4	0	7.20
Jack Crimian	R	31	0	1	.000	0	4	0	0	6	9	4	1	0	12.00

BALTIMORE — 5th 76-76 .500 21 — PAUL RICHARDS

NAME	G by Pos	B	AGE	G	AB	R	H	2B	3B	HR	RBI	BB	SO	SB	BA	SA
TOTALS			29	154	5264	597	1326	191	39	87	554	504	699	57	.252	.353
Bob Boyd	1B132,OF1	L	37	141	485	73	154	16	8	4	34	55	31	2	.318	.408
Billy Gardner	2B148,SS9	R	29	154	644	79	169	36	3	6	55	53	67	10	.262	.356
Willie Miranda	SS115	B	31	115	314	29	61	3	0	0	20	24	42	2	.194	.204
George Kell	3B80,1B22	R	34	99	310	28	92	9	0	9	44	25	16	2	.297	.413
Al Pilarcik	OF126	L	26	142	407	52	113	16	3	9	49	53	49	14	.278	.398
2 Jim Busby	OF85	R	30	86	288	31	72	10	1	3	19	23	36	6	.250	.323
Bob Nieman	OF120	R	30	129	445	61	123	17	6	13	70	63	86	4	.276	.429
Gus Triandos	C120	R	26	129	418	46	106	21	1	19	72	38	73	0	.254	.445
Tito Francona	OF73,1B4	L	23	97	279	35	65	8	3	7	38	29	48	7	.233	.358
Jim Brideweser	SS74,3B3,2B1	R	30	91	142	16	38	7	1	1	13	14	23	1	.268	.352
Joe Ginsberg	C66	L	30	85	175	15	48	8	2	1	18	18	19	2	.274	.360
Joe Durham	OF59	R	25	77	157	19	29	2	0	4	17	16	42	1	.185	.274
2 Billy Goodman	3B54,OF9,1B8,2B5,SS5	L	31	73	263	36	61	10	3	3	33	21	18	0	.308	.403
Brooks Robinson (KJ)	3B47	R	20	50	117	13	28	6	1	2	14	7	10	1	.239	.359
1 Dick Williams	OF26,3B15,1B12	R	28	47	167	16	39	10	2	1	17	14	21	0	.234	.335
Bob Hale	1B5	L	23	42	44	2	11	0	0	0	7	2	2	0	.250	.250
Jim Pyburn	OF28,C1	R	24	35	40	8	9	0	1	1	5	6	12	0	.225	.300
Lenny Green	OF15	L	23	19	33	2	6	1	1	1	3	5	1	4	.182	.364
Carl Powis	OF13	R	29	15	41	4	8	2	0	0	2	9	13	1	.195	.317
Bob Nelson	OF8	L	20	15	23	5	5	2	0	0	3	0	5	1	.217	.391

Wayne Causey 20 L 2-10, Frank Zupo 17 L 1-12, Buddy Peterson 32 R 3-17, 3 Eddie Robinson 36 L 0-3, 2 Eddie Miksis 30 R 0-1, Tom Patton 21 R 0-2

NAME	T	AGE	W	L	PCT	SV	G	GS	CG	IP	H	BB	SO	SHO	ERA
		30	76	76	.500	25	154	154	44	1408	1272	493	767	13	3.46
Connie Johnson	R	34	14	11	.560	0	35	30	14	242	212	66	177	3	3.20
Billy Loes	R	27	12	7	.632	4	31	18	8	155	142	37	86	3	3.25
Ray Moore	R	31	11	13	.458	0	34	32	7	227	196	112	117	1	3.73
George Zuverink	R	32	10	6	.625	9	56	0	0	113	105	39	36	0	2.47
2 Ken Lehman	L	29	8	3	.727	6	30	3	1	68	57	22	32	0	2.78
Hal Brown	R	32	7	8	.467	1	25	20	7	150	132	37	62	2	3.90
Bill Wight	L	35	6	6	.500	0	27	17	2	121	122	54	50	0	3.64
Billy O'Dell	L	24	4	10	.286	4	35	15	2	140	107	39	97	1	2.70
1 Mike Fornieles	R	25	2	6	.250	0	15	4	1	57	57	17	43	1	4.26
Jerry Walker	R	18	1	0	1.000	1	13	3	1	24	14	13	1		2.89
Don Ferrarese	L	28	1	1	.500	2	8	3	0	19	14	12	13	0	4.74
2 Art Houtteman	R	29	0	0	—	0	5	1	0	7	20	3	3	0	16.71
1 Sandy Consuegra	R	36	0	0	—	0	5	0	0	7	8	1	1	0	1.80
Charlie Beamon	R	22	0	0	—	0	1	0	0	2	5	0	0	0	5.00
Milt Pappas	R	18	0	0	—	0	4	0	0	4	5	3	2	1	1.00
Dizzy Trout	R	42	0	0	—	0	1	0	0	0.1	4	0	0	0	81.00
Art Ceccarelli	L	27	0	5	.000	0	18	5	1	58	62	31	30	0	4.50

CLEVELAND — 6th 76-77 .497 21.5 — KERBY FARRELL

NAME	G by Pos	B	AGE	G	AB	R	H	2B	3B	HR	RBI	BB	SO	SB	BA	SA
TOTALS			28	153	5171	682	1304	199	26	140	649	591	786	40	.252	.382
Vic Wertz	1B139	L	32	144	515	84	145	21	0	28	105	78	88	2	.282	.485
Bobby Avila	2B107,3B16	R	33	129	463	60	124	19	3	5	48	46	47	2	.268	.354
Chico Carrasquel	SS122	R	29	135	392	37	108	14	1	8	57	41	53	0	.276	.378
Al Smith	3B84,OF58	R	29	135	507	78	125	23	5	11	49	79	70	12	.247	.377
Rocky Colavito	OF130	R	23	134	461	66	116	26	0	25	84	71	80	1	.252	.471
Roger Maris	OF112	L	22	116	358	61	84	9	5	14	51	60	79	8	.235	.405
Gene Woodling	OF113	L	34	133	430	74	138	25	2	19	78	64	35	0	.321	.521
Jim Hegan	C58	R	36	58	148	14	32	7	0	4	15	16	23	0	.216	.345
Larry Raines	3B27,SS25,2B10,OF8	R	27	96	244	39	64	14	0	2	16	19	40	5	.262	.344
George Strickland	2B48,SS23,3B19	R	31	89	201	21	47	8	2	1	19	26	29	0	.234	.308
Joe Altobelli	1B56,OF7	L	25	83	87	9	18	3	2	0	9	5	14	3	.207	.287
2 Dick Williams	OF37,3B19	R	28	67	205	33	58	7	0	6	17	12	19	3	.283	.405
Russ Nixon	C57	B	22	62	185	15	52	7	1	2	18	12	12	0	.281	.362
Hal Naragon	C39	L	28	57	121	12	31	1	1	0	8	12	9	0	.256	.281
Kenny Kuhn	2B14,3B2,SS1	L	20	40	53	5	9	0	2	0	4	9	6	0	.170	.170
Dick Brown	C33	R	22	34	114	10	30	4	0	4	14	4	23	1	.263	.404
Joe Caffie	OF19	L	26	32	89	14	24	2	1	3	10	4	11	0	.270	.416
1 Jim Busby	OF26	R	30	30	74	9	14	2	1	2	6	4	6	3	.189	.324
Billy Harrell	SS14,3B6,2B1	R	28	22	57	6	15	1	1	1	5	4	7	3	.263	.368
2 Eddie Robinson	1B7	L	36	19	27	1	6	1	0	1	2	5	4	0	.222	.370
Preston Ward	1B1	L	29	10	11	2	2	1	0	0	2	0	3	0	.182	.273
1 Bob Usher	OF4,3B1	R	32	9	8	0	1	0	0	0	0	1	1	0	.125	.125

NAME	T	AGE	W	L	PCT	SV	G	GS	CG	IP	H	BB	SO	SHO	ERA
		30	76	77	.497	23	153	153	46	1381	1381	618	807	7	4.06
Early Wynn	R	37	14	17	.452	1	40	37	13	263	270	104	184	1	4.31
Mike Garcia	R	33	12	8	.600	0	38	27	9	211	221	73	110	1	3.75
Ray Narleski	R	28	11	5	.688	16	46	15	7	154	136	70	93	1	3.10
Don Mossi	L	28	11	10	.524	3	36	22	6	159	165	57	97	1	4.13
Cal McLish	R	31	9	7	.563	1	42	7	2	144	118	67	68	0	2.75
Bob Lemon	R	36	6	11	.353	0	21	17	2	117	129	64	45	0	4.62
Dick Tomanek	L	26	2	1	.667	0	34	2	0	70	67	37	55	0	5.66
Herb Score (IJ)	L	24	2	1	.667	0	5	5	3	36	18	26	39	1	2.00
Stan Pitula (AJ)	R	26	2	2	.500	0	23	5	1	60	67	32	17	0	4.95
2 Vito Valentinetti	R	28	2	2	.500	0	11	2	1	24	26	13	9	0	4.87
Bud Daley	L	24	2	8	.200	2	34	10	1	87	99	40	54	0	4.45
2 Hoyt Wilhelm	R	34	1	0	1.000	0	10	1	0	20	26	13	9	0	2.25
Hank Aguirre	L	26	1	1	.500	0	10	1	0	20	21	13	13	0	5.85
John Gray	R	29	1	3	.250	0	7	3	1	20	21	13	13	0	5.85
1 Art Houtteman	R	29	0	0	—	0	4	0	0	7	10	5	1	0	6.75
Bob Alexander	R	29	0	1	.000	0	6	0	0	7	15	1	0	0	9.00

KANSAS CITY — 7th 59-94 .386 38.5 — LOU BOUDREAU 36-67 .350 / HARRY CRAFT 23-27 .460

NAME	G by Pos	B	AGE	G	AB	R	H	2B	3B	HR	RBI	BB	SO	SB	BA	SA
TOTALS			29	154	5170	563	1262	195	40	166	535	364	760	35	.244	.394
Vic Power	1B113,OF6,2B4	R	29	129	467	48	121	15	1	14	42	19	21	3	.259	.385
Billy Hunter	2B64,SS35,3B17	R	29	116	319	39	61	10	4	8	29	27	43	1	.191	.323
Joe DeMaestri	SS134	R	28	135	461	44	113	19	4	9	33	22	82	6	.245	.360
Hector Lopez	3B111,2B4,OF3	R	27	121	391	51	115	19	4	11	35	41	66	1	.294	.448
Bob Cerv	OF89	R	31	124	345	55	94	14	2	11	44	20	57	1	.272	.420
2 Woodie Held	OF92	R	25	92	326	48	78	15	0	20	50	37	81	4	.239	.485
Gus Zernial	OF113,1B1	R	34	131	437	56	103	20	1	27	69	34	84	1	.236	.471
Hal Smith	C103	R	26	107	360	41	109	26	0	13	41	14	44	2	.303	.483
Lou Skizas	OF76,3B32	R	25	119	376	34	92	14	1	18	44	27	15	5	.245	.431
Tim Thompson	C62	L	33	81	230	24	47	10	2	3	19	18	26	0	.204	.339
1 Irv Noren	OF25,1B6	L	32	81	160	8	34	9	0	3	16	11	19	0	.213	.300
2 Billy Martin	2B52,3B20,SS2	R	29	73	265	33	68	9	3	9	27	12	29	1	.257	.415
Bob Martyn	OF49	L	26	58	131	10	35	2	4	1	12	11	20	1	.267	.366
Mickey McDermott	P29,1B2	L	28	58	49	6	12	1	0	1	9	7	16	0	.245	.510
Milt Graff	2B53	R	26	56	155	16	28	4	0	0	10	15	10	2	.181	.245
1 Johnny Groth	OF50	R	30	51	59	10	15	0	0	0	7	6	9	0	.254	.254
1 Harry Simpson	1B27,OF21	L	31	50	179	24	53	9	6*	4	24	12	28	0	.296	.514
Jim Pisoni	OF44	R	27	44	97	14	23	2	3	2	12	10	17	0	.237	.392
Clete Boyer	3B1,2B1	R	20	9	7	1	0	0	0	0	0	1	5	0	—	—

*Simpson, also with New York, tied for league lead in 3B with 9

NAME	T	AGE	W	L	PCT	SV	G	GS	CG	IP	H	BB	SO	SHO	ERA
		29	59	94	.386	19	154	154	26	1370	1344	565	626	6	4.19
Virgil Trucks	R	40	9	7	.563	7	48	7	0	116	106	62	55	0	3.03
Tom Morgan	R	27	9	7	.563	7	46	13	5	144	160	61	32	0	4.63
Jack Urban	R	28	7	4	.636	0	31	13	3	129	111	45	55	0	3.35
Wally Burnette	R	28	7	12	.368	1	38	9	1	113	115	44	57	0	4.30
Alex Kellner	L	32	6	5	.545	0	28	21	3	133	141	41	72	0	4.26
Ned Garver	R	31	6	13	.316	0	24	23	6	145	120	55	61	1	3.85
Tom Gorman	R	32	5	7	.357	3	38	12	3	125	123	36	66	1	3.82
Arnie Portocarrero	R	25	5	8	.385	0	24	18	3	115	103	34	42	0	3.91
2 Ralph Terry	R	21	4	11	.267	0	21	19	3	131	119	47	80	1	3.37
Glenn Cox	R	26	1	0	1.000	0	10	1	0	13	15	5	5	0	5.14
Mickey McDermott	L	28	1	4	.200	0	29	6	0	69	68	50	29	0	5.48
2 Al Aber	L	29	0	0	—	0	9	0	0	11	11	7	4	0	12.00
Ed Blake	R	31	0	0	—	0	4	0	0	6	4	2	0	0	4.50
Harry Taylor	R	37	0	0	—	0	2	0	0	2	4	1	0	0	4.50
Dave Hill	R	19	0	0	—	0	2	0	0	2	6	4	2	0	31.50
Hal Raether	R	21	0	0	—	0	1	0	0					0	0.00
George Brunet	L	22	0	0	—	0	4	0	0	11	13	9	3	0	5.73
Gene Host	L	22	0	0	—	0	3	0	0	5	8	7	3	0	7.12
Ryne Duren	R	28	0	0	—	0	14	0	0	43	37	30	37	0	5.23
Rip Coleman	L	25	0	0	—	0	9	1	0	41	53	25	15	0	5.93

WASHINGTON — 8th 55-99 .357 43 — CHUCK DRESSEN 4-16 .200 / COOKIE LAVAGETTO 51-83 .381

NAME	G by Pos	B	AGE	G	AB	R	H	2B	3B	HR	RBI	BB	SO	SB	BA	SA
TOTALS			26	154	5231	603	1262	215	38	111	576	527	733	13	.244	.363
Pete Runnels	1B72,3B32,2B23	L	29	134	473	53	109	18	4	5	55	51	51	2	.230	.298
Herb Plews	2B79,3B11,SS4	L	29	104	329	51	89	19	4	1	26	28	39	0	.271	.362
2 Rocky Bridges	SS108,2B14,3B1	R	29	120	391	40	89	17	2	3	47	40	32	0	.228	.304
Eddie Yost	3B107	R	30	110	414	47	104	13	9	8	38	73	49	1	.251	.372
Jim Lemon	OF131,1B3	R	29	137	518	58	147	23	6	17	64	49	94	1	.284	.450
2 Bob Usher	OF95	R	32	96	295	36	77	7	1	5	27	27	30	0	.261	.342
Roy Sievers	OF130,1B21	R	30	152	572	99	172	23	5	42	114	76	55	1	.301	.579
Lou Berberet	C77	L	27	99	264	24	69	11	2	7	36	41	38	0	.261	.398
Julio Becquer	1B43	L	25	105	186	14	42	6	2	2	22	10	29	3	.226	.312
2 Milt Bolling	SS37,2B9,3B1	R	26	91	277	29	63	12	1	4	19	18	59	2	.227	.321
Clint Courtney	C59	L	30	91	232	23	62	14	0	3	27	16	11	0	.267	.414
2 Art Schult	1B35,OF7	R	29	77	247	30	66	15	0	4	35	14	30	0	.263	.368
Faye Throneberry	OF58	L	26	68	195	21	36	8	2	4	19	17	37	0	.185	.277
Ed Fitz Gerald	C37	R	33	45	125	14	36	6	0	0	12	1	11	0	.272	.336
Jerry Snyder	SS15,2B13,3B1	R	27	42	93	6	14	1	0	0	4	9	14	0	.151	.194
Whitey Herzog	OF28	L	25	36	99	13	17	4	1	0	7	11	12	1	.167	.263
Jerry Schoonmaker	OF13	R	24	30	23	6	3	1	1	0	2	1	11	0	.087	.130
Neil Chrisley	OF11	L	25	19	49	5	9	0	2	1	5	6	13	0	.157	.235
Lyle Luttrell	SS17	R	27	19	45	4	9	3	0	0	8	8	5	0	.200	.289
Harmon Killebrew	3B7,2B1	R	21	9	31	4	9	2	0	2	5	2	8	0	.290	.548

Dick Tettelbach 28 R 2-11, 1 Karl Olson 26 R 2-12, Steve Korcheck (MS) 24

NAME	T	AGE	W	L	PCT	SV	G	GS	CG	IP	H	BB	SO	SHO	ERA
		26	55	99	.357	16	154	154	31	1377	1482	580	691	5	4.85
Pedro Ramos	R	22	12	16	.429	0	43	30	7	231	251	69	91	1	4.79
Camilo Pascual	R	23	8	17	.320	0	29	26	8	176	168	76	113	2	4.09
Chuck Stobbs	L	27	8	20	.286	1	42	31	5	212	235	80	114	2	5.35
Tex Clevenger	R	24	7	6	.538	8	52	3	2	140	139	47	75	0	4.18
2 Russ Kemmerer	R	25	7	11	.389	0	39	26	6	172	214	71	81	0	4.97
Bud Byerly	R	36	6	6	.500	4	47	0	0	95	94	22	39	0	3.13
Dick Hyde	R	28	4	3	.571	1	52	0	0	109	104	56	46	0	4.13
Ted Abernathy	R	24	2	10	.167	0	26	16	2	85	100	65	50	0	6.78
Bob Wiesler	L	26	1	1	.500	1	16	3	0	36	38	10	15	0	4.50
Evelio Hernandez	R	25	0	0	—	0	14	2	0	36	38	10	15	0	4.50
Garland Shifflett	R	21	0	0	—	0	17	0	0	32	40	22	12	0	9.00
1 Dean Stone	L	27	0	0	—	0									
Joe Black	R	33	0	1	.000	0	7	0	0	11	11	6	4	0	9.00
Dick Brodowski	R	24	0	1	.000	0	11	1	0	31	36	12	12	0	11.46
1 Bob Chakales	R	30	0	2	.000	0									5.50
Ralph Lumenti	L	20	0	1	.000	0	3	1	0	8	16	11	4	0	7.00
Hal Griggs	R	29	0	2	.000	0									3.21
Don Minnick	R	26	0	1	.000	0									5.00
Jim Heise	R	24	0	1	.000	0	19	1	0	25	16	8	9	0	8.05

MILWAUKEE — 1st 95-59 .617 — FRED HANEY

NAME	G by Pos	B	AGE	G	AB	R	H	2B	3B	HR	RBI	BB	SO	SB	BA	SA
TOTALS			28	155	5458	772	1469	221	62	199	722	461	729	35	.269	.442
Frank Torre	1B117	L	28	129	364	46	99	19	5	5	40	29	19	0	.272	.393
2 Red Schoendienst	2B92, OF2	B	34	93	394	56	122*	23	4	6	32	23	7	2	.310	.434
Johnny Logan	SS129	R	30	129	494	59	135	19	7	10	49	31	49	5	.273	.401
Eddie Mathews	3B147	L	25	148	572	109	167	28	9	32	94	90	79	3	.292	.540
Hank Aaron	OF150	R	23	151	615	118	198	27	6	44	132	57	58	1	.322	.600
Bill Bruton (KJ)	OF79	L	31	79	306	41	85	16	9	5	30	19	35	11	.278	.438
Wes Covington	OF89	L	25	96	328	51	93	4	8	21	65	29	44	4	.284	.537
Del Crandall	C102, OF9, 1B1	R	27	118	383	45	97	11	2	15	46	30	38	1	.253	.410
Andy Pafko	OF69	R	36	83	220	31	61	6	1	8	27	10	22	1	.277	.423
Felix Mantilla	SS35, 2B13, 3B7, OF1	R	22	71	182	28	43	9	1	4	21	14	34	2	.236	.363
Joe Adcock (BL)	1B56	R	29	65	209	31	60	13	2	12	38	20	51	0	.287	.541
Carl Sawatski	C28	L	29	58	105	13	25	4	0	6	17	10	15	0	.238	.448
Del Rice (BG)	C48	R	34	54	144	15	33	1	1	9	20	17	37	0	.229	.438
1 Danny O'Connell	2B48	R	30	48	183	29	43	9	1	1	8	19	20	1	.235	.311
Bob Hazle	OF40	L	26	41	134	26	54	12	0	7	27	18	15	1	.403	.649
1 Bobby Thomson	OF38	R	33	41	148	15	35	5	3	4	23	8	27	2	.236	.392
John DeMerit	OF13	R	21	33	34	8	5	0	0	0	1	0	8	1	.147	.147
Nippy Jones	1B20, OF1	R	32	30	79	5	21	2	1	2	8	3	7	0	.266	.392
1 Chuck Tanner	OF18	L	27	22	69	5	17	3	0	2	6	5	4	0	.246	.377
Dick Cole	2B10, 3B1, 1B1	R	31	15	14	1	1	0	0	0	0	3	5	0	.071	.071
Bobby Malkmus	2B7	R	25	13	22	6	2	0	1	0	0	3	3	0	.091	.182
Mel Roach	2B5	R	24	7	6	1	1	0	0	0	0	0	3	0	.167	.167
Hawk Taylor	C1	R	18	7	1	2	0	0	0	0	0	0	0	0	.000	.000
Harry Hanebrink	3B2	L	29	6	7	0	2	0	0	0	0	0	1	2	.286	.286
Ray Shearer	OF1	R	27	2	2	1	1	0	0	0	0	0	1	1	.500	.500

NAME	T	AGE	W	L	PCT	SV	G	GS	CG	IP	H	BB	SO	SHO	ERA
		28	95	59	.617	24	155	155	60	1411	1347	570	693	9	3.47
Warren Spahn	L	36	21	11	.656	3	39	35	18	271	241	78	111	4	2.69
Bob Buhl	R	28	18	7	.720	0	34	31	14	217	191	121	117	2	2.74
Lew Burdette	R	30	17	9	.654	0	37	33	14	257	260	59	78	1	3.71
Gene Conley	R	26	9	9	.500	1	35	18	6	148	133	64	61	1	3.16
Ernie Johnson	R	33	7	3	.700	4	30	0	0	65	67	26	44	0	3.88
Bob Trowbridge	R	27	7	5	.583	1	32	16	3	126	118	52	75	1	3.64
Juan Pizarro	L	20	5	6	.455	0	24	10	3	99	99	51	68	0	4.64
1 Ray Crone	R	25	3	1	.750	0	13	5	2	42	54	15	15	0	4.50
Taylor Phillips	L	24	3	2	.600	2	27	6	0	73	82	40	36	0	5.55
Red Murff	R	36	2	2	.500	2	12	1	0	26	31	11	13	0	4.85
Don McMahon	R	27	3	3	.400	9	32	0	0	47	33	29	46	0	1.53
Dave Jolly	R	32	1	1	.500	1	23	0	0	38	37	21	27	0	4.97
Joey Jay	R	21	0	0	—	1	1	0	0	1	0	0	0	0	0.00
Phil Paine	R	27	0	0	—	1	3	0	0	2	1	3	2	0	0.00

*Schoendienst, also with New York, league leader in H with 200

ST. LOUIS — 2nd 87-67 .565 8 — FRED HUTCHINSON

NAME	G by Pos	B	AGE	G	AB	R	H	2B	3B	HR	RBI	BB	SO	SB	BA	SA
TOTALS			28	154	5472	737	1497	235	43	132	685	493	672	58	.274	.405
Stan Musial	1B130	L	36	134	502	82	176	38	3	29	102	66	34	1	.351	.612
Don Blasingame	2B154	L	25	154	650	108	176	25	7	8	58	71	49	21	.271	.368
Al Dark	SS139, 3B1	R	35	140	583	80	169	25	4	8	64	29	56	3	.290	.381
Eddie Kasko	3B120, SS13, 2B1	R	25	134	479	59	131	16	5	1	35	33	53	6	.273	.334
Del Ennis	OF127	R	32	136	490	61	140	24	3	24	105	37	50	1	.286	.494
Ken Boyer	OF105, 3B41	R	26	142	544	79	144	18	3	19	62	44	77	12	.265	.414
Wally Moon	OF133	L	27	142	516	86	152	28	5	24	73	62	57	5	.295	.508
Hal Smith	C97	R	26	100	333	25	93	12	3	2	37	18	18	2	.279	.351
Joe Cunningham	1B57, OF46	L	25	122	261	50	83	15	0	9	52	56	29	3	.318	.479
Bobby Gene Smith	OF79	R	23	93	185	24	39	7	1	3	18	13	35	1	.211	.308
Hobie Landrith	C67	L	27	75	214	18	52	6	0	3	26	25	27	1	.243	.313
Dick Schofield	SS23	B	22	65	56	10	9	0	0	0	2	7	13	0	.161	.161
1 Eddie Miksis	OF31	R	30	49	38	3	8	0	0	1	2	7	7	0	.211	.289
Walker Cooper	C13	R	42	48	78	7	21	5	1	3	10	5	10	0	.269	.474
Jim King	OF8	L	24	22	35	1	11	0	0	0	2	4	2	0	.314	.314
1 Irv Noren	OF8	L	32	17	30	3	11	4	1	1	10	4	6	0	.367	.667
1 Chuck Harmon	OF8	R	33	9	3	2	1	0	0	0	1	0	0	1	.333	1.000
Tom Alston (IL)	1B6	L	31	9	17	2	5	1	0	0	2	3	3	0	.294	.353
Gene Green	OF3	R	24	6	15	0	3	1	0	0	2	0	3	0	.200	.267
Don Lassetter	OF3	R	24	4	13	2	2	0	1	0	1	0	4	0	.154	.308

NAME	T	AGE	W	L	PCT	SV	G	GS	CG	IP	H	BB	SO	SHO	ERA
		27	87	67	.565	29	154	154	46	1413	1385	506	778	11	3.78
Larry Jackson	R	26	15	9	.625	1	41	22	6	210	196	57	96	2	3.47
Lindy McDaniel	R	21	15	9	.625	0	30	26	10	191	196	53	75	1	3.49
Sam Jones	R	31	12	9	.571	0	37	28	10	183	164	71	154	2	3.59
Willard Schmidt	R	29	10	3	.769	0	40	8	1	117	146	49	63	0	4.77
Herm Wehmeier	R	30	10	7	.588	0	36	18	5	165	165	54	91	0	4.31
Vinegar Bend Mizell	L	26	8	10	.444	0	33	21	7	149	136	51	87	2	3.74
Von McDaniel	R	18	7	5	.583	0	17	13	4	87	71	31	45	2	3.21
Murry Dickson	R	40	5	3	.625	0	14	13	3	74	87	25	29	1	4.14
Billy Muffett	R	26	3	2	.600	8	23	0	0	44	35	13	21	0	2.25
Lloyd Merritt	R	24	1	2	.333	7	44	0	0	65	60	28	35	0	3.32
1 Hoyt Wilhelm	R	34	1	4	.200	11	40	0	0	55	52	21	29	0	4.25
1 Bob Smith	L	26	0	0	—	1	6	0	0	10	12	6	11	0	4.50
Bob Miller	R	18	0	0	—	0	5	0	0	9	13	5	7	0	7.00
Morrie Martin	L	34	0	0	—	0	4	0	0	5	4	2	2	0	2.45
2 Bob Kuzava	L	34	0	0	—	0	5	0	0	4	4	2	4	0	4.50
1 Jim Davis	L	32	0	1	.000	1	10	0	0	14	18	6	5	0	5.15
Tom Cheney	R	22	0	1	.000	0	3	0	0	9	6	15	10	0	4.50
Frank Barnes	R	30	0	1	.000	0	1	0	0	6	8	6	2	0	4.50
Lynn Lovenguth	R	34	0	0	—	0	2	1	0	9	6	6	6	0	2.00

BROOKLYN — 3rd 84-70 .545 11 — WALT ALSTON

NAME	G by Pos	B	AGE	G	AB	R	H	2B	3B	HR	RBI	BB	SO	SB	BA	SA
TOTALS			31	154	5242	690	1325	188	38	147	648	550	848	60	.253	.387
Gil Hodges	1B150, 3B2, 2B1	R	33	150	579	94	173	28	7	27	98	63	91	5	.299	.511
Jim Gilliam	2B148, OF2	B	28	149	617	89	154	26	4	2	37	84	37	26	.250	.314
Charlie Neal	SS100, 3B23, 2B3	R	26	128	448	62	121	13	7	12	62	53	83	11	.270	.411
Pee Wee Reese	3B75, SS23	R	38	103	330	33	74	3	1	1	29	39	32	5	.224	.248
Carl Furillo	OF107	R	35	119	395	61	121	17	4	12	66	29	33	0	.306	.461
Duke Snider	OF136	L	30	139	508	91	139	25	7	40	92	77	104	3	.274	.587
Gino Cimoli	OF138	R	27	142	532	88	156	22	5	10	57	39	86	3	.293	.410
Roy Campanella	C100	R	35	103	330	31	80	9	0	13	62	34	50	1	.242	.388
Sandy Amoros	OF66	L	27	106	238	40	66	7	1	7	26	46	42	3	.277	.403
Don Zimmer	3B39, SS37, 2B5	R	26	84	269	23	59	9	1	6	19	16	63	1	.219	.327
Elmer Valo	OF36	L	36	81	161	14	44	10	1	4	26	25	16	0	.273	.422
Rube Walker	C50	L	31	60	166	12	30	8	0	2	23	15	33	2	.181	.265
Randy Jackson (KJ)	3B34	R	31	48	131	7	26	1	0	2	16	9	20	0	.198	.252
Johnny Roseboro	C19, 1B5	L	24	35	69	6	10	2	0	2	6	10	20	1	.145	.261
2 Bob Kennedy	OF9, 3B3	R	36	19	31	5	4	1	0	1	4	1	5	0	.129	.258
Joe Pignatano	C6	R	27	8	14	0	3	1	0	0	1	1	3	0	.214	.286
Jim Gentile	1B2	L	23	4	6	1	1	0	0	1	1	1	1	0	.167	.667
Rod Miller		L	17	1	1	0	0	0	0	0	0	0	1	0	.000	.000

NAME	T	AGE	W	L	PCT	SV	G	GS	CG	IP	H	BB	SO	SHO	ERA
		27	84	70	.545	29	154	154	44	1399	1285	456	891	18	3.35
Don Drysdale	R	20	17	9	.654	0	34	29	9	221	197	61	148	4	2.69
Johnny Podres	L	24	12	9	.571	3	31	27	10	196	168	44	109	6	2.66
Don Newcombe	R	31	11	12	.478	0	28	28	12	199	199	33	90	4	3.48
Ed Roebuck	R	25	8	2	.800	8	44	1	0	96	70	46	73	0	2.72
Danny McDevitt	L	24	7	4	.636	0	22	17	5	119	105	72	90	2	3.25
1 Sal Maglie	R	40	6	6	.500	1	19	17	4	101	94	26	50	1	2.94
Roger Craig	R	27	6	9	.400	0	32	13	1	111	102	47	69	0	4.62
Carl Erskine (SA)	R	30	5	3	.625	0	15	7	1	66	62	20	26	0	3.55
Sandy Koufax	L	21	5	4	.556	0	34	13	2	104	83	51	122	0	3.89
Clem Labine	R	30	5	7	.417	17	58	0	0	105	104	27	67	0	3.43
Rene Valdez	R	28	1	1	.500	0	5	1	0	13	13	7	10	0	5.54
Don Bessent	R	26	1	3	.250	0	27	0	0	44	58	19	24	0	5.73
2 Jackie Collum	L	30	0	0	—	0	4	0	0	7	1	3	9	0	9.00
1 Ken Lehman	L	29	0	0	—	0	7	0	0	7	7	1	3	0	0.00
1 Don Elston	R	28	0	0	—	0	1	0	0	4	1	4	0	0	9.00
Fred Kipp	L	25	0	0	—	0	1	0	0	1	3	0	0	0	9.00
Bill Harris	R	25	0	0	.000	0	1	0	0	5	6	2	3	0	3.86

CINCINNATI — 4th 80-74 .519 15 — BIRDIE TEBBETTS

NAME	G by Pos	B	AGE	G	AB	R	H	2B	3B	HR	RBI	BB	SO	SB	BA	SA
TOTALS			29	154	5389	747	1452	251	33	187	713	546	752	51	.269	.432
George Crowe	1B120	L	36	133	494	71	134	20	1	31	92	32	62	1	.271	.504
Johnny Temple	2B145	R	28	145	557	95	158	24	4	0	37	94	34	19	.284	.341
Roy McMillan	SS151	R	27	151	448	50	122	25	5	1	55	66	44	5	.272	.357
Don Hoak	3B149, 2B1	R	29	149	529	78	155	39	2	19	89	74	54	8	.293	.482
Wally Post	OF124	R	27	134	467	68	114	26	2	20	74	33	84	2	.244	.437
Gus Bell	OF121	L	28	121	510	65	149	20	3	13	61	30	54	0	.292	.420
Frank Robinson	OF136, 1B24	R	21	150	611	97	197	29	5	29	75	44	92	10	.322	.529
Ed Bailey	C115	L	26	122	391	64	102	15	2	20	48	73	69	5	.261	.463
Smoky Burgess	C45	L	30	90	205	29	58	14	1	14	39	24	16	0	.283	.566
Bob Thurman	OF44	L	40	74	190	38	47	4	2	16	40	15	33	0	.247	.542
Alex Grammas	SS42, 2B20, 3B9	R	31	73	99	14	30	4	0	0	8	10	6	1	.303	.343
Ted Kluszewski (XJ)	1B23	L	32	69	127	12	34	7	0	6	21	5	5	0	.268	.465
Jerry Lynch	OF24, C2	L	26	67	124	11	32	4	1	4	13	6	18	0	.258	.403
Pete Whisenant	OF43	R	27	67	90	18	19	3	2	5	11	5	24	0	.211	.456
Joe Taylor	OF27	R	31	33	107	14	28	7	0	4	9	6	24	0	.262	.439
Bobby Henrich	SS7, OF6, 3B2, 2B1	R	18	29	10	4	2	0	0	0	1	1	4	0	.200	.200
1 Art Schult	OF5	R	29	21	34	4	9	2	0	0	4	0	2	0	.265	.324
1 Rocky Bridges	2B2, SS1, 3B1	R	29	5	1	1	0	0	0	0	0	0	0	0	.000	.000
Dutch Dotterer	C4	R	25	4	12	1	1	0	0	0	0	1	2	0	.083	.083
Curt Flood	3B2, 2B1	R	19	3	3	2	1	0	0	0	1	0	0	0	.333	.333

Bobby Durnbaugh 24 R 0-1, Don Pavletich (MS) 18 R 0-1, Dick Murphy (MS) 25

NAME	T	AGE	W	L	PCT	SV	G	GS	CG	IP	H	BB	SO	SHO	ERA
		30	80	74	.519	29	154	154	40	1396	1486	429	707	5	4.62
Brooks Lawrence	R	32	16	13	.552	4	49	32	12	250	234	76	121	1	3.53
Hal Jeffcoat	R	32	12	13	.480	7	37	31	10	207	236	46	63	1	4.52
Tom Acker	R	27	10	5	.667	4	49	6	1	109	122	41	67	0	4.95
Joe Nuxhall	L	28	10	10	.500	1	39	28	6	174	192	53	99	2	4.76
Johnny Klippstein	R	29	8	11	.421	3	46	18	3	146	146	68	99	1	5.05
Hersh Freeman	R	29	7	2	.778	8	52	0	0	84	90	14	36	0	4.50
Don Gross	L	26	7	9	.438	1	43	16	5	148	152	53	73	0	4.32
Art Fowler	R	34	3	0	1.000	0	33	7	1	88	111	24	45	0	6.44
Raul Sanchez	R	26	3	2	.600	5	38	0	0	62	61	25	37	0	4.79
1 Warren Hacker	R	32	3	2	.600	0	15	6	0	43	50	13	18	0	5.23
Vicente Amor	R	24	1	2	.333	0	9	1	0	27	39	10	9	0	6.00
Claude Osteen	L	17	0	0	—	0	4	0	0	4	1	4	1	0	2.25
Dave Skaugstad	L	17	0	0	—	0	1	0	0	2	1	0	1	0	1.50
Bud Podbielan	R	33	0	1	.000	0	7	1	0	10	12	6	4	0	4.50
Jay Hook	R	20	0	0	—	0	3	0	0	10	9	7	10	0	4.50
Charlie Rabe	L	25	0	1	.000	0	2	2	0	13	16	5	9	0	6.23
Bill Kennedy	L	36	0	0	—	0	3	0	0	13	16	5	9	0	6.23

PHILADELPHIA — 5th 77-77 .500 18 — MAYO SMITH

NAME	G by Pos	B	AGE	G	AB	R	H	2B	3B	HR	RBI	BB	SO	SB	BA	SA
TOTALS			28	156	5241	623	1311	213	44	117	569	534	758	57	.250	.375
Ed Bouchee	1B154	L	24	154	574	78	168	35	8	17	76	84	91	1	.293	.470
Granny Hamner	2B125, SS5, P1	R	30	133	502	59	114	19	5	10	62	34	42	3	.227	.345
Chico Fernandez	SS149	R	25	149	500	42	131	14	4	5	51	31	64	18	.262	.336
Willie Jones	3B126	R	31	133	440	58	98	19	2	9	47	61	41	1	.218	.332
Rip Repulski	OF130	R	28	134	516	65	134	23	4	20	68	19	74	7	.260	.436
Richie Ashburn	OF156	L	30	156	626	93	186	26	8	0	33	94	44	13	.297	.364
Harry Anderson	OF109	L	25	118	400	53	107	15	4	17	61	36	61	0	.268	.453
Stan Lopata	C108	R	31	116	388	50	92	18	2	18	67	56	81	0	.237	.433
Bob Bowman	OF81	R	26	99	237	31	63	8	2	6	23	27	50	0	.266	.392
Solly Hemus	2B24	L	34	70	108	8	20	1	0	1	5	20	13	1	.185	.259
Joe Lonnett	C65	R	30	67	160	11	27	5	0	5	22	12	39	0	.169	.294
Ted Kazanski	3B36, 2B22, SS3	R	23	62	185	19	49	7	1	3	11	17	20	1	.265	.362
2 Chuck Harmon	OF25, 3B5, 1B2	R	33	57	86	14	22	1	2	0	9	5	8	1	.256	.302
Harvey Haddix	P27	R	31	41	68	6	21	3	1	1	8	3	12	1	.309	.382
Marv Blaylock	1B12, OF1	L	27	33	26	4	4	1	0	2	6	4	14	0	.154	.385
2 Ron Northey		L	37	33	28	4	1	1	0	0	3	6	4	0	.161	.323
Roy Smalley	SS20	R	31	28	16	0	0	0	0	0	0	2	2	0	.161	.161
Andy Seminick	C8	R	36	8	11	0	1	0	0	0	0	0	1	0	.091	.091
John Kennedy	3B2	R	30	5	2	1	0	0	0	0	0	0	0	1	0	.000	.000
Glen Gorbous	OF2	L	26	4	2	1	0	0	0	0	0	1	0	2	0	.000	.000
Don Landrum	OF2	L	21	2	7	1	1	0	0	0	2	1	1	0	.143	.286

1 Bobby Morgan 31 R 0-0, Frankie Baumholtz 38 L 0-2

NAME	T	AGE	W	L	PCT	SV	G	GS	CG	IP	H	BB	SO	SHO	ERA
		28	77	77	.500	23	156	156	54	1402	1363	412	858	9	3.80
Jack Sanford	R	28	19	8	.704	0	33	33	15	237	194	94	188	3	3.08
Curt Simmons	L	28	12	11	.522	0	32	29	9	212	214	50	92	2	3.44
Dick Farrell	R	23	10	2	.833	10	52	0	0	83	74	36	54	0	2.39
Harvey Haddix	L	31	10	13	.435	0	27	25	8	171	176	39	136	1	4.05
Robin Roberts	R	30	10	22	.313	2	39	32	14	250	246	43	128	2	4.07
Jim Hearn	R	36	5	1	.833	3	36	4	1	74	79	18	46	0	3.65
2 Warren Hacker	R	32	4	4	.500	0	30	19	5	128	122	42	92	1	4.92
Don Cardwell	R	21	4	8	.333	1	30	19	5	128	122	42	92	1	4.92
Bob Miller	R	31	4	3	.571	0	32	6	1	60	61	17	12	0	2.70
Seth Morehead	L	22	1	1	.500	0	19	1	0	45	57	20	36	0	3.66
Tom Qualters	R	22	0	0	—	0	17	0	0	27	36	12	10	0	7.71
Saul Rogovin	L	35	0	0	—	0	4	0	0	4	11	5	2	0	9.00
Granny Hamner	R	30	0	0	—	0	1	0	0	2	2	2	0	0	0.00
Jack Meyer	R	25	0	3	.000	0	19	2	0	38	44	28	34	0	5.68

Jim Owens (MS) 23

NEW YORK — 6th 69-85 .448 26 — BILL RIGNEY

NAME	G by Pos	B	AGE	G	AB	R	H	2B	3B	HR	RBI	BB	SO	SB	BA	SA
TOTALS			30	154	5346	643	1349	171	54	157	612	447	669	64	.252	.393
Whitey Lockman	1B102, OF27	L	30	133	456	51	113	9	4	7	30	39	19	5	.248	.331
2 Danny O'Connell	2B68, 3B30	R	30	95	364	57	97	18	3	7	30	28	33	8	.266	.390
Daryl Spencer	SS110, 2B36, 3B6	R	27	148	534	65	133	31	2	11	50	50	50	3	.249	.376
Ray Jablonski	3B70, 1B6, OF1	R	30	107	305	37	88	15	1	9	50	31	47	0	.289	.433
Don Mueller	OF115	L	30	135	450	45	116	7	1	6	37	13	16	2	.258	.318
Willie Mays	OF150	R	26	152	585	112	195	26	20	35	97	76	62	38	.333	.626
Hank Sauer	OF98	R	40	127	378	46	98	14	1	26	76	49	59	1	.259	.508
Valmy Thomas	C88	R	28	88	241	30	60	10	3	6	31	16	29	0	.249	.390
Ozzie Virgil	3B62, OF24, SS1	R	24	96	226	26	53	0	2	4	24	14	27	2	.235	.305
Dusty Rhodes	OF44	L	30	92	190	20	39	5	1	4	19	18	34	0	.205	.305
Gail Harris	1B61	L	25	90	225	28	54	7	3	9	31	16	28	1	.240	.418
2 Bobby Thomson	OF71, 3B6	R	33	81	215	24	52	7	4	8	38	19	39	1	.242	.423
Ray Katt	C68	R	30	72	165	11	38	3	1	2	17	15	35	1	.230	.297
Wes Westrum	C63	R	34	63	91	4	15	1	0	1	2	10	24	0	.165	.209
1 Red Schoendienst	2B57	B	34	57	254	35	78*	8	4	3	33	10	8	2	.307	.476
Ed Bressoud	SS33, 3B12	R	25	49	127	11	34	2	2	5	10	4	19	0	.268	.433
Andre Rodgers	SS20, 3B8	R	22	32	86	8	21	2	1	3	9	9	21	0	.244	.395
Foster Castleman	3B7, SS1, 2B1	R	26	18	37	7	6	2	0	1	2	8		0	.162	.297

1 Bill Taylor 27 L 0-9, Bobby Hofman 31 R 0-2, Bill White (MS) 23

NAME	T	AGE	W	L	PCT	SV	G	GS	CG	IP	H	BB	SO	SHO	ERA
TOTALS		27	69	85	.448	20	154	154	35	1399	1436	471	701	9	4.01
Ruben Gomez	R	27	15	13	.536	0	38	36	16	238	233	71	92	3	3.78
Johnny Antonelli	L	27	12	18	.400	0	40	30	8	212	228	67	114	3	3.78
Curt Barclay	R	25	9	9	.500	0	37	28	5	183	196	48	67	2	3.44
Al Worthington	R	28	8	11	.421	0	55	12	1	158	140	56	90	1	4.22
Stu Miller	R	29	7	9	.438	1	38	13	0	124	110	45	60	0	3.63
Marv Grissom	R	39	4	4	.500	14	55	0	0	83	74	23	51	0	2.60
2 Ray Crone	R	25	4	2	.333	1	25	17	2	121	131	40	56	0	4.31
Mike McCormick	L	18	3	1	.750	0	24	5	1	75	79	32	50	0	4.08
Ray Monzant	R	24	3	2	.600	0	24	2	0	50	55	16	37	0	3.96
2 Jim Davis	L	32	1	0	1.000	0	10	0	0	11	13	5	6	0	6.55
Jim Constable	L	24	1	1	.500	0	16	0	0	28	27	7	13	0	2.89
Joe Margoneri	L	27	1	1	.500	0	13	2	1	34	44	21	18	0	5.29
Pete Burnside	L	26	1	4	.200	0	10	9	1	31	47	13	18	1	8.71
Windy McCall	L	31	0	0	—	0	5	0	0	3	8	2	2	0	15.00
2 Sandy Consuegra	R	36	0	0	—	0	4	0	0	5	7	1	1	0	2.25
Gordon Jones	R	27	0	0	.000	0	12	1	0	16	3	5	6	0	
Max Surkont	R	35	0	1	.000	0	5	0	0	6	9	2	7	0	10.50
Steve Ridzik	R	28	0	1	.000	0				27	19	19	13	0	4.67

Paul Giel (MS) 24

* Schoendienst, also with Milwaukee, league leader in H with 200

CHICAGO — 7th (tie) 62-92 .403 33 — BOB SCHEFFING

NAME	G by Pos	B	AGE	G	AB	R	H	2B	3B	HR	RBI	BB	SO	SB	BA	SA
TOTALS			28	156	5369	628	1312	223	31	147	590	461	989	28	.244	.380
2 Dale Long	1B104	L	31	123	397	55	121	19	0	21	62	52	63	1	.305	.511
2 Bobby Morgan	2B116, 3B12	R	31	125	425	43	88	20	2	5	27	52	87	5	.207	.299
Ernie Banks	SS100, 3B58	R	26	156	594	113	169	34	6	43	102	70	85	8	.285	.579
Bobby Adams	3B47, 2B1	R	35	60	187	21	47	10	2	1	10	17	28	0	.251	.342
Walt Moryn	OF147	L	31	149	568	76	164	33	0	19	88	50	90	0	.289	.447
2 Chuck Tanner	OF82	L	27	95	318	42	91	16	2	7	42	23	20	0	.286	.415
2 Lee Walls	OF94, 3B1	R	24	117	366	42	88	10	5	6	33	27	67	5	.240	.344
Cal Neeman	C118	R	28	122	415	37	107	11	1	10	39	22	87	0	.258	.376
Bob Speake	OF60, 1B39	L	26	129	418	65	97	14	5	16	50	38	68	5	.232	.404
Jim Bolger	OF63, 3B3	R	25	112	273	28	75	4	1	5	29	10	36	0	.275	.352
Jerry Kindall	2B28, 3B19, SS9	R	22	72	181	18	29	3	0	6	12	8	48	1	.160	.276
Bob Will	OF30	L	25	70	112	13	25	3	0	1	10	5	21	1	.223	.277
Jack Littrell	SS47, 2B6, 3B5	R	28	61	153	8	29	4	2	1	9	4	43	0	.190	.261
Jim Fanning	C35	R	29	47	106	12	19	3	1	0	4	4	17	0	.180	.264
Casey Wise	2B31, SS5	R	24	43	106	12	19	3	1	0	7	11	14	0	.179	.226
Charlie Silvera	C26	R	32	26	53	1	11	3	0	0	2	4	5	0	.208	.264
1 Bobby Del Greco	OF16	R	24	20	40	2	8	3	0	0	3	10	17	1	.200	.350
Frank Ernaga	OF10	R	26	20	35	9	11	3	2	2	7	9	14	0	.314	.686
Ed Winceniak	SS5, 3B4, 2B3	R	28	17	50	5	12	3	0	1	8	2	9	0	.240	.360
1 Gene Baker	3B12	R	32	12	44	4	11	3	1	1	10	6	3	0	.250	.432
1 Dee Fondy	1B11	L	32	11	51	3	16	3	1	0	2	0	5	1	.314	.412
Eddie Haas	OF4	L	22	14	24	1	5	1	0	0	4	1	5	0	.208	.250
Johnny Goryl	3B9	R	23	9	38	7	8	2	0	1	5	5	9	0	.211	.263
Bob Lennon	OF4	L	28	9	21	2	3	1	0	1	3	1	4	0	.143	.333

Gordon Massa 21 L 7-15, Ed Mickelson 30 R 0-12, Jim Woods 17 R 0-0

NAME	T	AGE	W	L	PCT	SV	G	GS	CG	IP	H	BB	SO	SHO	ERA
TOTALS		27	62	92	.403	26	156	156	30	1403	1397	601	859	5	4.13
Dick Drott	R	21	15	11	.577	0	38	32	7	229	200	129	170	3	3.58
Moe Drabowsky	R	21	13	15	.464	0	36	33	12	240	214	94	170	2	3.53
2 Don Elston	R	28	6	7	.462	8	39	14	2	144	139	55	102	0	3.56
Dave Hillman	R	29	6	11	.353	1	32	14	1	103	115	37	53	0	4.37
Bob Rush	R	31	6	16	.273	0	31	29	5	205	211	66	103	0	4.39
Jim Brosnan	R	27	5	5	.500	0	41	5	1	99	79	46	73	0	3.36
Turk Lown	R	33	5	7	.417	12	67	0	0	93	74	51	51	0	3.77
Dick Littlefield	L	31	2	3	.400	4	48	2	0	66	76	37	51	0	5.32
Don Kaiser	R	22	2	6	.250	0	20	13	1	72	91	28	23	0	5.00
1 Jackie Collum	L	30	1	1	.500	0	11	8	0					0	6.55
Tom Poholsky	R	27	1	7	.125	0	28	11	1	84	117	22	28	0	4.93
1 Vito Valentinetti	R	28	0	0	—	0	9	0	0	12	12	7	8	0	2.25
Ed Mayer	L	25	0	0	—	0	3	1	0	8	8	5	3	0	5.63
Glen Hobbie	R	21	0	0	—	0	2	0	0	4	6	5	3	0	11.25
Bob Anderson	R	21	0	0	.000	0	16	0	0	8	8	7	0	0	7.88
Elmer Singleton (EJ)	R	39	0	1	.000	0	5	2	0	13	20	2	6	0	6.92
Johnny Briggs	R	23	0	1	.000	0								0	13.50

PITTSBURGH — 7th (tie) 62-92 .403 33 — BOBBY BRAGAN 36-67 .350 — DANNY MURTAUGH 26-25 .510

NAME	G by Pos	B	AGE	G	AB	R	H	2B	3B	HR	RBI	BB	SO	SB	BA	SA
TOTALS			27	155	5402	586	1447	231	60	92	551	374	733	46	.268	.384
2 Dee Fondy	1B73	L	32	95	323	42	101	23	5	3	25	29	33	11	.313	.384
Bill Mazeroski	2B144	R	20	148	526	59	149	27	7	8	54	27	49	3	.283	.407
Dick Groat	SS123, 3B2	R	26	125	501	58	158	30	5	7	54	27	26	0	.315	.437
Gene Freese	3B74, 2B10, OF10	R	23	114	346	44	98	18	2	6	31	17	42	9	.283	.399
Roberto Clemente	OF109	R	22	111	451	42	114	17	7	4	30	23	45	0	.253	.348
Bill Virdon	OF141	L	26	144	564	59	141	28	11	8	50	33	69	3	.251	.383
Bob Skinner	OF93, 1B9, 3B1	L	25	126	387	58	118	12	6	13	45	38	50	10	.305	.468
Hank Foiles	C109	R	28	109	281	32	76	10	4	9	36	37	53	1	.270	.431
Frank Thomas	1B71, OF59, 3B31	R	28	151	594	72	172	30	1	23	89	44	66	3	.290	.460
2 Gene Baker	3B60, SS28, 2B13	R	32	111	365	36	97	19	4	2	36	29	29	3	.266	.356
Paul Smith	OF33, 1B1	L	26	81	150	22	38	4	0	3	11	12	17	0	.253	.340
Dick Rand	C57	R	26	60	105	7	23	2	1	1	9	11	24	0	.219	.286
Roman Mejias (VJ)	OF42	R	26	58	142	12	39	7	4	2	15	6	13	2	.275	.423
Jim Pendleton	OF9, 3B2, SS1	R	33	46	59	9	18	1	1	0	9	9	14	0	.305	.356
Johnny O'Brien	P16, SS8, 2B2	R	26	34	35	7	11	2	1	0	5	4	5	0	.314	.429
Hardy Peterson	C30	R	27	30	73	10	22	2	1	0	6	6	8	0	.301	.438
Johnny Powers	OF8, 2B1, 1B1	L	27	20	35	7	10	2	0	0	5	5	9	0	.286	.543
Danny Kravitz	C20	L	26	19	41	2	6	1	0	0	5	1	10	0	.146	.171

Buddy Pritchard 21 R 1-11, 1 Lee Walls 24 R 4-22, 1 Dale Long 31 L 4-22, Ken Hamlin 22 R 0-1

NAME	T	AGE	W	L	PCT	SV	G	GS	CG	IP	H	BB	SO	SHO	ERA
TOTALS		27	62	92	.403	15	155	155	47	1395	1463	421	663	9	3.88
Bob Friend	R	26	14	18	.438	0	40	38	17	277	273	68	143	3	3.38
Bob Purkey	R	27	11	14	.440	2	48	21	6	180	194	38	51	1	3.85
Vern Law	R	27	10	8	.556	1	31	25	9	173	172	32	55	3	2.86
Ron Kline	R	25	9	16	.360	0	40	31	11	205	214	61	88	2	4.04
Roy Face	R	29	4	6	.400	10	59	1	0	94	97	24	53	0	3.06
Red Swanson	R	20	3	3	.500	0	32	8	1	73	68	31	29	0	3.70
Whammy Douglas	R	22	3	3	.500	0	11	8	0	47	48	30	28	0	3.26
Luis Arroyo	L	30	3	11	.214	1	54	10	0	131	151	31	101	0	4.67
Nellie King	R	29	2	1	.667	1	36	0	0	52	69	16	23	0	4.50
2 Bob Smith (EJ)	R	26	2	4	.333	0	20	4	2	55	48	25	35	0	3.11
Eddie O'Brien	R	26	1	0	1.000	0	3	1	1	12	11	3	10	0	2.25
Dick Hall (AJ)	R	26	0	0	—	0	10	0	0	17	15	7	7	0	10.80
Chuck Churn	R	26	0	0	—	0	5	0	0	4	4	4	3	0	4.50
1 Bob Kuzava	L	34	0	0	—	0	7	0	0	9	9	6	4	0	9.00
Laurin Pepper	R	26	0	1	.000	0	8	1	0	12	16	8	5	0	8.00
Bennie Daniels	R	25	0	1	.000	0	5	1	0	7	9	8	6	0	1.29
George Witt	R	23	0	1	.000	0	1	1	0	5	7	1	5	0	54.00
Joe Trimble	R	26	0	2	.000	0	3	1	0	5	10	13	9	0	8.10
Johnny O'Brien	R	26	0	2	.000	0	16	1	0	40	46	24	13	0	6.08

WORLD SERIES — MILWAUKEE (NL) 4 NEW YORK(AL) 3

LINE SCORES

TEAM	1	2	3	4	5	6	7	8	9	10	11	12	R	H	E

Game 1 — October 2 at New York
MIL (NL) 0 0 0   0 0 0   1 0 0 — 1 5 0
NY (AL) 0 0 0   0 1 2   0 0 X — 3 9 1
Spahn, Johnson (6) / **Ford**
McMahon (7)

Game 2 — October 3 at New York
MIL 0 1 1   2 0 0   0 0 0 — 4 8 0
NY 0 1 1   0 0 0   0 0 0 — 2 7 2
Burdette / Shantz, Ditmar (4), Grim (8)

Game 3 — October 5 at Milwaukee
NY 3 0 2   2 0 0   5 0 0 — 12 9 0
MIL 0 1 0   0 2 0   0 0 0 — 3 8 1
Turley, **Larsen** (2) / Buhl, Pizarro (1), Conley (3), Johnson (5), Trowbridge (7), McMahon (8)

Game 4 — October 6 at Milwaukee
NY 1 0 0   0 0 0   0 0 3 1 — 5 11 0
MIL 0 0 0   4 0 0   0 0 0 3 — 7 7 0
Sturdivant, Shantz (5), Kucks (8), Byrne (8), Grim (10) / **Spahn**

Game 5 — October 7 at Milwaukee
NY 0 0 0   0 0 0   0 0 0 — 0 7 0
MIL 0 0 0   0 0 1   0 0 X — 1 6 1
Ford, Turley (8) / **Burdette**

Game 6 — October 9 at New York
MIL 0 0 0   1 0 0   1 0 0 — 2 4 0
NY 0 0 2   0 0 0   1 0 X — 3 7 0
Buhl, Johnson (3), McMahon (8) / **Turley**

Game 7 — October 10 at New York
MIL 0 0 4   0 0 0   0 1 0 — 5 9 1
NY 0 0 0   0 0 0   0 0 0 — 0 7 3
Burdette / Larsen, Shantz (3), Ditmar (4), Sturdivant (6), Byrne (8)

COMPOSITE BATTING

NAME	POS	G	AB	R	H	2B	3B	HR	RBI	BA
Milwaukee (NL) Totals		7	225	23	47	6	1	8	22	.209
Aaron	OF	7	28	5	11	0		3	7	.393
Logan	SS	7	27	5	5	1	0	1	2	.185
Covington	OF	7	24	1	5	1		0	1	.208
Mathews	3B	7	22	4	5	3	0	1	4	.227
Crandall	C	6	19	1	4	0	0		1	.211
Schoendienst	2B	5	18	0	5	1	0		2	.278
Adcock	1B	5	15	1	3	0	0		2	.200
Pafko	OF	6	14	1	3	0	0	0		.214
Hazle	OF	4	13	2	2	0	0			.154
Torre	1B	7	10	2	3	0	0	2	3	.300
Mantilla	2B	4	10	1	0	0	0			.000
Burdette	P	3	8	0	0	0	0			.000
Rice	C	2	6	1	1	0	0			.167
Spahn	P	2	5	0	1	0	0			.000
Jones	PH	3	2	0	0	0	0			.000
Sawatski	PH	2	2	0	0	0	0			.000
Johnson	P	3	1	0	0	0	0			.000
Buhl	P	2	1	0	0	0	0			.000
Pizarro	P	2	1	0	0	0	0			.000

Trowbridge P 0-0, McMahon P 0-0, Conley P 0-0, DeMerit PR 0-0

NAME	POS	G	AB	R	H	2B	3B	HR	RBI	BA
New York (AL) Totals		7	230	25	57	7	1	7	25	.248
Bauer	OF	7	31	3	8	2	1	2	6	.258
Kubek	OF-3B	7	28	4	8	0	0	2	4	.286
Berra	C	7	25	5	8	1	0			.320
McDougald	SS	7	24	3	6	0	0			.250
Coleman	2B	7	22	2	8	0	0		2	.364
Mantle	OF	6	19	3	5	0	0	1		.263
Lumpe	3B	6	14	0	4	0	0			.286
Slaughter	OF	5	12	2	3	1	0			.250
Simpson	1B	5	12	0	1	0	0			.083
Howard	1B	6	11	2	3	0	0			.273
Carey	3B	2	7	0	2	0	0			.286
Collins	1B	3	5	0	0	0	0			.000
Ford	P	2	5	0	0	0	0			.000
Skowron	1B	2	4	0	0	0	0			.000
Turley	P	3	4	0	0	0	0			.000
Byrne	P	2	2	0	0	0	0			.500
Larsen	P	2	2	0	0	0	0			.000
Shantz	P	2	2	0	0	0	0			.000
Sturdivant	P	2	1	0	0	0	0			.000
Richardson	2B	2	1	0	0	0	0			—

Shantz P 0-1, Ditmar P 0-1, Grim P 0-0, Kucks P 0-0

COMPOSITE PITCHING

NAME	G	IP	H	BB	SO	W	L	SV	ERA
Milwaukee (NL) Totals	7	62	57	22	34	4	3	0	3.48
Burdette	3	27	21	4	13	3	0	0	0.67
Spahn	2	15.1	18	2	2	1	1	0	4.70
Johnson	3	7	2	1	8	0	0	0	1.29
McMahon	3	5	3	3	5	0	0	0	0.00
Buhl	2	3.1	6	6	4	0	1	0	10.80
Pizarro	1	1.2	3	2	1	0	0	0	10.80
Conley	1	1.2	2	1	0	0	0	0	10.80
Trowbridge	1	1	1	3	1	0	0	0	45.00

NAME	G	IP	H	BB	SO	W	L	SV	ERA
New York (AL) Totals	7	62.1	47	22	40	3	4	0	2.89
Ford	2	16	11	5	7	1	1	0	1.13
Turley	3	11.2	7	6	12	1	0	0	2.31
Larsen	2	9.2	8	5	6	1	1	0	3.72
Shantz	3	6.2	8	2	7	0	1	0	4.05
Ditmar	2	6	7	2	0	0	0	0	0.00
Sturdivant	2	6	6	1	4	0	0	0	6.00
Byrne	2	3.1	2	1	2	0	1	0	5.40
Grim	2	2.1	3	0	2	0	1	0	7.71
Kucks	1	0.2	1	0	2	0	0	0	0.00

1958 O'Malley's Rambling Meadows

Ebbets Field felt the wrecker's steel ball, the Polo Grounds played only to yesterday's ghosts and the West coast had its first taste of major league baseball. Walter O'Malley's Dodgers set up shop in the Los Angeles Memorial Coliseum, which proved to be as colorful a home as Ebbets Field had been. The huge football stadium had a monstrously vast right field, ranging to 440 feet in the power lane, and a short 251-foot left field target, which was crowned by a 40-foot high screen extending 140 feet into left center, a concoction designed to present a feared flood of cheap home runs.

Opening day on Friday, April 18, saw the largest curtain-raising crowd in history; 78,672 turned out to see the Giants knock off the Dodgers in the first renewal of the newly transplanted geographical rivalry. The opening three-game series between the two teams additionally set an attendance record for a three-game series, 167,204. The 94,000 capacity coliseum counted 1,845,556 clicks of the turnstile during the season, surpassing the 1947 record attendance, and almost double the 1957 Polo Grounds' count.

The Giants new home was San Francisco's Seals Stadium, which seated only 22,900. Nevertheless 1,272,625 fans viewed the team, only 300,000 short of the Giant's 1947 record attendance, and almost double the 1957 Polo Grounds' count.

Both teams planned new stadiums. A municipally-built and owned Candlestick Park received quick approval in San Francisco and mid-1959 was a hoped-for time of occupancy. The Dodgers, of course, showed much more flair. An agreement was reached with the Los Angeles city fathers, in which the valuable Chavez Ravine land tract would be turned over to the Dodgers where they were to build themselves a $12 million stadium. Opponents to the project put the agreement onto a highly-contested referendum, which was approved and then brought into court, where it remained until the California Supreme Court passed the final decision approving the agreement in January, 1959.

On the field, the Dodgers and Giants passed each other in opposite directions. The Dodgers were expected to continue as strong contenders but got off to a slow start, spent most of the year in the basement, and limped home in seventh place. The Dodgers had lost their field leader during the winter, when catcher Roy Campanella was tragically paralyzed in an early-morning car accident in New York. Pee Wee Reese and Carl Erskine became part-time players and were obviously playing out the string. Don Newcombe started slowly and was traded to Cincinnati in June with an 0-6 record. Duke Snider had his bat taken out of his hands by the vast right field playing area in Los Angeles. Without the cozy Ebbets Field right field screen, and plagued by a bad knee, Snider fell from 40 homers in 1957 to a mere 15. Charging up from a sixth-place finish in New York, the Giants flashed a hand of six rookie aces, the most promising being Orlando Cepeda to finish a strong third.

Yet, while the Dodgers and Giants were moving, the National League pennant wasn't; it stayed put in Milwaukee. Overcoming injuries to Bob Buhl and Bill Bruton, and Red Schoendienst being disabled by tuberculosis, the Braves again won by eight games, spearheaded by Hank Aaron and Ed Mathews at bat, and Warren Spahn and Lew Burdette on the hill. A trio of young pitchers, Carl Willey, Joey Jay, and Juan Pizarro, took up the slack left by the injury to Buhl and the off-season of Gene Conley. The Pirates finished in the first division for the first time since 1948, by closing fast and winding up in second place. Bob Friend won 22 games for the Bucs, and several young hitters, such as Roberto Clemente, Dick Groat, and Bill Mazeroski matured into stardom. The second division boasted stars in the Cubs' Ernie Banks, the homer and RBI champ and MVP, and Richie Ashburn of the Phils, the batting champ.

The Yankees, as usual, took the American League pennant, this time by ten games over Chicago. Mickey Mantle and Bob Turley were the stars of this season's production, though Boston again boasted of the batting champ in Ted Williams, and the MVP-Jackie Jensen.

In the series, the Yanks dropped three of four to the Braves, then became the first team since 1925 to win the championship after being down 3 games to 1, to give Stengel his seventh world's title in ten years-making it, perhaps, the sweetest victory the Old Professor ever enjoyed.

1958 AMERICAN LEAGUE

NEW YORK — 1st 92-62 .597 — CASEY STENGEL

NAME	G by Pos	B	AGE	G	AB	R	H	2B	3B	HR	RBI	BB	SO	SB	BA	SA
TOTALS			27	155	5294	759	1418	212	39	164	715	537	822	48	.268	.416
Bill Skowron	1B118, 3B2	R	27	126	465	61	127	22	3	14	73	28	69	1	.273	.424
Gil McDougald	2B115, SS19	R	30	138	503	69	126	19	1	14	65	59	75	6	.250	.376
Tony Kubek	SS134, OF3, 2B1, 1B1	L	21	138	559	66	148	21	1	2	48	25	57	5	.265	.317
Andy Carey	3B99	R	26	102	315	39	90	19	4	12	45	34	43	1	.286	.486
Hank Bauer	OF123	R	35	128	452	62	121	22	6	12	50	32	56	3	.268	.423
Mickey Mantle	OF150	B	26	150	519	127	158	21	1	42	97	129	120	18	.304	.592
Norm Siebern	OF133	L	24	134	460	79	138	19	5	14	55	66	87	5	.300	.454
Yogi Berra	C88, OF21, 1B2	L	33	122	433	60	115	17	3	22	90	35	35	3	.266	.471
Elston Howard	C67, OF24, 1B5	R	29	103	376	45	118	19	5	11	66	22	60	1	.314	.479
Jerry Lumpe	3B65, SS5	L	25	81	232	34	59	8	4	3	32	23	21	1	.254	.362
Enos Slaughter	OF35	L	42	77	138	21	42	4	1	4	19	21	16	2	.304	.435
Bobby Richardson	2B51, 3B13, SS2	R	22	73	182	18	45	6	2	0	14	8	5	1	.247	.302
Marv Throneberry	1B40, OF5	L	24	60	150	30	34	5	2	7	19	19	40	1	.227	.427
Don Larsen (EJ)	P19	R	28	28	49	9	15	1	0	4	13	5	9	0	.306	.571
1 Harry Simpson	OF15	L	32	24	51	1	11	2	1	0	6	6	12	0	.216	.294
Bobby Del Greco	OF12	R	25	12	5	1	1	0	0	0	0	1	1	0	.200	.200
Darrell Johnson	C4	R	29	5	16	1	4	0	0	0	0	0	2	0	.250	.250

Fritzie Brickell 23 R 0-0, Tommy Carroll (MS) 21

NAME	T	AGE	W	L	PCT	SV	G	GS	CG	IP	H	BB	SO	SHO	ERA
		29	92	62	.597	33	155	155	53	1379	1201	557	796	21	3.22
Bob Turley	R	27	21	7	.750	1	33	31	19	245	178	128	168	6	2.98
Whitey Ford	L	29	14	7	.667	1	30	29	15	219	174	62	145	7	2.01
Don Larsen (EJ)	R	28	9	6	.600	0	19	19	5	114	100	52	55	3	3.08
Art Ditmar	R	29	9	8	.529	4	38	13	4	140	124	38	52	0	3.41
Johnny Kucks	R	24	8	8	.500	4	34	15	4	126	132	39	46	1	3.93
2 Duke Maas	R	29	7	3	.700	0	22	13	2	101	93	36	50	1	3.83
Bobby Shantz	L	32	7	6	.538	0	33	13	3	126	127	35	80	0	3.36
Ryne Duren	R	29	6	4	.600	20	44	1	0	76	40	43	87	0	2.01
Zack Monroe	R	26	4	2	.667	1	21	6	1	58	57	27	18	0	3.26
Tom Sturdivant (SA)	R	28	3	6	.333	0	15	10	0	71	77	38	41	0	4.18
2 Virgil Trucks	R	41	2	1	.667	1	25	0	0	40	40	24	26	0	4.50
1 Sal Maglie	R	41	1	1	.500	0	7	3	0	23	27	9	7	0	4.70
2 Murry Dickson	R	41	1	1	.333	1	6	2	0	20	18	12	9	0	5.85
Johnny James	R	24	0	0	—	0	2	0	0	3	2	4	1	0	0.00
1 Bob Grim	R	28	0	1	.000	0	11	0	0	16	12	10	11	0	5.63

CHICAGO — 2nd 82-72 .532 10 — AL LOPEZ

NAME	G by Pos	B	AGE	G	AB	R	H	2B	3B	HR	RBI	BB	SO	SB	BA	SA
TOTALS			30	155	5249	634	1348	191	42	101	600	518	669	101	.257	.367
2 Ray Boone	1B63	R	34	77	246	25	60	12	1	7	41	18	33	1	.244	.386
Nellie Fox	2B155	R	30	155	623	82	187	21	6	0	49	47	11	5	.300	.353
Luis Aparicio	SS145	R	24	145	557	76	148	20	9	2	40	35	38	29	.266	.345
Billy Goodman	3B111, 1B3, 2B1, SS1	L	32	116	425	41	127	15	5	0	40	37	21	1	.299	.358
Jim Rivera	OF99	L	36	116	276	37	62	8	4	9	35	24	49	21	.225	.380
Jim Landis	OF142	R	24	142	523	72	145	23	7	15	64	52	80	19	.277	.434
Al Smith	OF138, 3B1	R	30	139	480	61	121	23	5	12	58	48	77	3	.252	.396
Sherm Lollar	C116	R	33	127	421	53	115	16	0	20	84	57	37	2	.273	.454
Sammy Esposito	3B63, SS22, 2B2, OF1	R	26	98	81	16	20	3	0	0	3	12	6	1	.247	.284
Earl Torgeson	1B73	L	34	96	188	37	50	8	0	10	30	48	29	7	.266	.468
Bubba Phillips (BF)	3B47, OF37	R	28	84	260	26	71	10	4	5	30	15	14	3	.273	.369
Don Mueller	OF43	L	31	70	166	7	42	5	0	0	16	11	9	0	.253	.283
Earl Battey	C49	R	23	68	168	24	38	8	0	8	26	24	34	1	.226	.417
Ron Jackson	1B38	R	24	61	146	19	34	4	0	7	21	18	46	2	.233	.404
1 Tito Francona	OF35	L	24	41	128	10	33	3	2	1	10	14	24	2	.258	.336
1 Walt Dropo	1B16	R	35	28	52	3	10	1	0	2	8	5	11	0	.192	.327
Ted Beard	OF15	L	37	19	22	5	2	0	0	1	2	6	5	3	.091	.227
Johnny Callison	OF18	L	19	18	64	10	19	4	2	1	12	6	14	1	.297	.469
Norm Cash	OF4	L	23	13	8	2	2	0	0	0	0	1	0	0	.250	.250
Jim McAnany	OF3	R	21	5	13	0	0	0	0	0	0	0	5	0	.000	.000
Johnny Romano	C2	R	23	4	7	1	2	0	0	0	0	0	2	0	.286	.286

Les Moss 33 R 0-1, Chuck Lindstrom 21 R 1-1

NAME	T	AGE	W	L	PCT	SV	G	GS	CG	IP	H	BB	SO	SHO	ERA
		31	82	72	.532	25	155	155	55	1390	1296	515	751	15	3.61
Billy Pierce	L	31	17	11	.607	2	35	32	19	245	204	66	144	3	2.68
Dick Donovan	R	30	15	14	.517	0	34	34	16	248	240	53	127	4	3.01
Early Wynn	R	38	14	16	.467	2	40	34	11	240	214	104	179	4	4.13
Ray Moore	R	32	9	7	.563	2	32	20	4	137	107	70	73	2	3.81
Jim Wilson	R	36	9	9	.500	1	28	23	4	156	156	63	70	1	4.10
2 Bob Shaw	R	25	4	2	.667	1	29	3	0	64	67	28	18	0	4.64
Gerry Staley	R	37	4	5	.444	8	50	0	0	85	81	24	27	0	3.18
Barry Latman	R	22	3	0	1.000	0	13	3	1	48	27	17	28	1	0.75
3 Turk Lown	R	34	3	3	.500	8	27	0	0	41	49	28	40	0	3.90
1 Bill Fischer	R	27	2	3	.400	0	17	3	0	36	43	13	16	0	6.75
Don Rudolph	L	26	1	0	1.000	0	7	0	0	7	4	5	2	0	2.57
Hal Trosky	R	21	1	0	1.000	0	4	0	0	3	5	2	1	0	6.00
2 Tom Qualters	R	23	0	0	—	0	26	0	0	43	45	20	14	0	4.19
Jim McDonald	R	31	0	0	—	0	3	0	0	2	6	1	0	0	22.50
Dixie Howell	R	38	0	0	—	0	4	0	0	4	4	0	4	0	4.50
Stover McIlwain	R	18	0	0	—	1	8	0	0	5	8	6	1	0	2.25
Bob Keegan	R	37	0	0	.000	0	14	0	0	30	44	18	8	0	6.00

BOSTON — 3rd 79-75 .513 13 — PINKY HIGGINS

NAME	G by Pos	B	AGE	G	AB	R	H	2B	3B	HR	RBI	BB	SO	SB	BA	SA
TOTALS			29	155	5218	697	1335	229	30	155	665	638	820	29	.256	.400
Dick Gernert	1B114	R	34	124	431	59	102	19	1	20	69	59	78	2	.237	.425
Pete Runnels	2B106, 1B42	L	30	147	568	103	183	32	5	8	59	87	49	1	.322	.438
Don Buddin	SS136	R	24	136	497	74	118	25	2	12	43	82	106	0	.237	.368
Frank Malzone	3B155	R	28	155	627	76	185	30	2	15	87	33	53	1	.295	.421
Jackie Jensen	OF153	R	31	154	548	83	157	31	0	35	122	99	65	9	.286	.535
Jimmy Piersall	OF125	R	28	130	417	55	99	13	5	8	48	42	43	12	.237	.350
Ted Williams	OF114	L	39	129	411	81	135	23	2	26	85	98	49	1	.328	.584
Sammy White	C102	R	30	102	328	25	85	15	3	6	35	21	37	1	.259	.378
Gene Stephens	OF110	L	25	134	270	38	59	10	1	9	25	22	46	1	.219	.363
Marty Keough	OF25, 1B2	L	24	68	113	21	26	3	1	9	13	8	22	1	.230	.522
Billy Klaus	SS27	R	29	61	88	5	14	4	0	1	7	5	16	0	.159	.239
2 Lou Berberet	C49	L	28	57	167	11	35	5	1	6	23	20	23	0	.210	.311
Ted Lepcio	2B40	R	27	50	136	10	27	3	0	6	14	12	47	1	.199	.353
Billy Consolo	2B13, SS11, 3B1	R	23	46	72	13	9	2	1	0	4	18	14	0	.125	.181
Bill Renna	OF11	R	33	39	56	5	15	5	0	4	18	6	14	0	.268	.571
Pete Daley	C27	R	28	27	56	10	18	2	1	2	7	9	11	0	.321	.500
1 Ken Aspromonte	2B6	R	26	6	16	0	2	0	0	0	0	3	2	0	.125	.125

Haywood Sullivan (JJ) 27

NAME	T	AGE	W	L	PCT	SV	G	GS	CG	IP	H	BB	SO	SHO	ERA
		28	79	75	.513	28	155	155	44	1380	1396	521	695	5	3.92
Ike Delock	R	28	14	8	.636	2	31	19	6	160	155	56	82	1	3.38
Frank Sullivan	R	28	13	9	.591	3	32	29	10	199	216	49	103	2	3.57
Tom Brewer	R	26	12	12	.500	0	33	32	10	227	227	93	124	1	3.73
Murray Wall	R	31	8	9	.471	10	52	1	0	114	109	33	53	0	3.63
Dave Sisler	R	26	8	9	.471	0	30	25	4	149	157	79	71	1	4.95
Leo Kiely	L	28	8	7	.714	12	47	0	0	81	77	18	26	0	3.00
2 Ted Bowsfield	L	22	4	2	.667	0	16	10	2	66	58	36	38	0	3.82
Riverboat Smith	L	30	4	3	.571	0	17	7	1	67	61	45	43	0	3.76
Mike Fornieles	R	26	4	6	.400	1	37	7	1	111	123	33	49	0	4.95
Bill Monbouquette	R	21	3	4	.429	0	7	7	3	54	52	20	30	0	3.33
Frank Baumann	L	25	2	2	.500	0	11	7	0	52	56	27	31	0	4.50
2 Bud Byerly	R	37	1	3	.333	0	18	0	0	30	31	7	16	0	1.80
Willard Nixon (JJ)	R	30	1	1	.125	0	14	7	0	38	41	15	15	0	6.07
Al Schroll	R	26	0	0	—	0	4	0	0	10	6	7	2	0	4.50
Jerry Casale	R	24	0	0	—	0	4	0	0	4	4	4	1	0	4.50
1 Bob Porterfield	R	34	0	0	—	0	4	0	0	4	5	1	4	0	4.50
1 George Susce	R	27	0	0	—	0	1	0	0	1	0	3	0	0	18.00
Duane Wilson	L	24	0	0	—	0	2	0	0	6	10	7	2	0	6.00

CLEVELAND — 4th 77-76 .503 14.5 — BOBBY BRAGAN 31-36 .463 — JOE GORDON 46-40 .535

NAME	G by Pos	B	AGE	G	AB	R	H	2B	3B	HR	RBI	BB	SO	SB	BA	SA
TOTALS			28	153	5201	694	1340	210	31	161	653	494	819	50	.258	.403
Mickey Vernon	1B96	L	28	119	355	49	104	22	3	8	55	44	56	0	.293	.439
Bobby Avila	2B82,3B33	R	34	113	375	54	95	21	3	5	30	55	45	5	.253	.365
2 Billy Hunter	SS75,3B2	R	30	76	190	21	37	10	2	0	9	17	37	4	.195	.268
Billy Harrell	3B46,SS45,2B7,OF1	R	29	101	229	36	50	4	0	7	19	15	36	12	.218	.328
Rocky Colavito	OF129,1B11,P1	R	24	143	489	80	148	26	3	41	113	84	89	0	.303	.620
Larry Doby	OF68	L	34	89	247	41	70	10	1	13	45	26	49	0	.283	.490
Minnie Minoso	OF147,3B1	R	35	149	556	94	168	25	2	24	80	59	53	14	.302	.484
Russ Nixon	C101	L	23	113	376	42	113	17	4	9	46	13	38	0	.301	.439
Billy Moran	2B74,SS38	R	24	115	257	26	58	11	0	1	18	13	23	3	.226	.280
2 Vic Power	3B42,1B41,2B27,SS2,OF1	R	30	93	385	63	122	24	6*	12	53	13	11	2	.317	.504
Gary Geiger	OF53,3B2,P1	L	21	91	195	28	45	3	1	6	27	43	2	.231	.272	
Dick Brown	C62	R	23	68	173	20	41	5	0	7	20	14	27	1	.237	.387
2 Woodie Held	OF43,SS14,3B4	R	26	67	144	12	28	4	1	3	17	15	36	1	.194	.299
1 Roger Maris	OF47	L	23	51	182	26	41	5	1	9	27	17	33	4	.225	.412
1 Chico Carrasquel	SS32,3B14	R	30	49	156	14	40	6	0	2	21	14	12	0	.256	.333
1 Preston Ward	3B24,1B21	L	30	48	148	22	50	3	1	4	21	10	27	0	.338	.453
Jay Porter	C20,1B4,3B1	R	25	40	85	13	17	1	0	4	19	9	23	0	.200	.353
2 Randy Jackson	3B24	R	32	29	91	7	22	3	1	4	13	3	18	0	.242	.429
Carroll Hardy	OF17	R	25	27	49	10	10	3	0	1	6	6	14	1	.204	.327
Vic Wertz (BN)	1B8	L	33	25	43	5	12	1	0	3	12	5	7	0	.279	.512
Earl Averill	3B17	R	26	17	55	2	10	1	0	2	7	4	7	1	.182	.309
Hal Naragon		L	29	14	9	2	3	0	1	0	0	0	0	0	.333	.556

Larry Raines 28 R 0-9, Rod Graber 28 L 1-8, 1 Fred Hatfield 33 L 1-8, George Strickland (VR) 32

NAME	T	AGE	W	L	PCT	SV	G	GS	CG	IP	H	BB	SO	SHO	ERA
TOTALS		28	77	76	.503	20	153	153	51	1373	1283	604	766	2	3.73
Cal McLish	R	32	16	8	.667	1	39	30	13	226	214	70	97	2	2.99
Ray Narleski	R	29	13	10	.565	1	44	24	7	183	179	91	102	4	4.08
Gary Bell	R	21	12	10	.545	1	33	23	10	182	141	73	110	0	3.31
Mudcat Grant	R	22	10	11	.476	2	44	28	11	204	173	104	111	1	3.84
Don Mossi	L	29	7	8	.467	3	43	5	0	102	106	30	55	0	3.63
Hal Woodeshick	R	25	6	6	.500	1	14	9	3	72	71	25	27	0	3.63
Don Ferrarese	L	29	3	4	.429	1	28	10	2	95	91	46	62	0	3.69
2 Morrie Martin	L	35	2	1	.1000	1	19	0	0	19	20	8	8	0	2.37
1 Dick Tomanek	R	27	2	3	.400	0	18	6	2	58	61	28	42	0	5.59
Herb Score (IJ)	R	25	2	3	.400	3	12	5	2	41	29	34	48	1	3.95
1 Hoyt Wilhelm	R	35	2	7	.222	5	30	6	1	90	70	35	57	0	2.50
Mike Garcia (SA)	R	34	1	0	1.000	6	1	0	8	15	7	2	0	9.00	
Dick Brodowski	R	25	1	0	1.000	0	5	0	0	10	3	6	12	0	9.00
Chuck Churn	R	28	0	0	—	0	6	0	0	9	12	5	4	0	6.00
Rocky Colavito	R	24	0	0	—	0	3	0	0	3	0	3	1	0	0.00
Gary Geiger	R	21	0	0	—	0	1	0	0	0	0	0	0	0	0.00
Bob Lemon	R	37	0	1	.000	0	11	1	0	25	41	16	8	0	5.40
2 Jim Constable	L	25	0	1	.000	0	9	0	0	17	4	3	12	0	12.00
2 Bob Kelly	R	30	0	2	.000	0	13	3	0	28	29	13	12	0	5.14
Steve Ridzik	R	29	0	2	.000	0	9	0	0	9	5	6	5	0	2.00

*Power, also with Kansas City, league leader in 3B with 10

DETROIT — 5th 77-77 .500 15 — JACK TIGHE 21-28 .429 — BILL NORMAN 56-49 .533

NAME	G by Pos	B	AGE	G	AB	R	H	2B	3B	HR	RBI	BB	SO	SB	BA	SA
TOTALS			27	154	5194	659	1384	229	41	109	612	463	678	48	.266	.389
Gail Harris	1B122	L	26	134	451	63	124	18	4	20	83	36	60	1	.273	.481
Frank Bolling	2B154	R	26	154	610	91	164	25	4	14	75	54	54	6	.269	.392
Billy Martin	3B131	R	30	131	498	56	127	19	1	7	42	16	62	5	.255	.339
Reno Bertoia	3B68,SS5,OF1	R	23	86	240	28	56	6	0	6	27	20	35	5	.233	.333
Al Kaline	OF145	R	23	146	543	84	170	34	7	16	85	54	47	7	.313	.490
Harvey Kuenn	OF138	R	27	139	561	73	179	39	3	8	54	51	34	5	.319	.442
Charlie Maxwell	OF114,1B14	L	31	131	397	56	108	14	4	13	65	64	54	6	.272	.426
Red Wilson	C101	R	29	103	298	31	89	13	1	3	29	35	30	10	.299	.379
Johnny Groth	OF80	R	31	88	146	24	41	5	2	2	11	13	19	0	.281	.384
Gus Zernial	OF24	R	35	66	124	8	40	7	1	5	23	6	25	0	.323	.516
Coot Veal	SS58	R	25	58	207	29	53	10	2	0	16	14	21	1	.256	.324
Ozzie Virgil	3B49	R	25	49	193	19	47	10	2	3	19	8	20	1	.244	.363
2 Jim Hegan	C45	R	37	45	140	8	27	6	0	1	7	10	32	0	.192	.262
2 Tito Francona	OF18,1B1	L	24	45	69	11	17	5	0	0	10	15	16	0	.246	.319
2 Bob Hazle	OF12	L	27	43	69	7	17	3	0	0	5	5	13	0	.241	.379
1 Ray Boone	1B32	R	34	39	114	16	27	4	1	6	20	14	13	0	.237	.447
Charlie Lau	C25	R	30	68	8	10	1	2	0	6	12	15	0	.147	.221	
Milt Bolling	SS13,2B1,3B1	R	27	24	31	3	6	2	0	0	5	7	0	.194	.258	
Lou Skizas	OF5,3B4	R	26	23	33	4	8	2	0	1	2	5	1	0	.242	.394
Bill Taylor	OF1	L	28	8	8	1	3	0	0	1	0	2	0	0	.375	.375

Steve Boros 21 R 0-2, Tim Thompson 34 L 1-6, George Alusik 23 R 0-2, Bobo Osborne 22 L 0-2, Jack Feller 21 R 0-0, George Thomas 20 R 0-0

NAME	T	AGE	W	L	PCT	SV	G	GS	CG	IP	H	BB	SO	SHO	ERA
TOTALS		27	77	77	.500	19	154	154	59	1357	1294	437	797	8	3.59
Frank Lary	R	28	16	15	.516	1	39	34	19	260	249	68	131	3	2.91
Paul Foytack	R	27	15	13	.536	1	39	33	16	230	198	77	135	2	3.44
Jim Bunning	R	26	14	12	.538	0	35	34	10	220	188	79	177	3	3.52
Billy Hoeft	L	26	4	3	.526	3	36	21	6	143	148	49	94	0	4.15
2 George Susce	R	26	4	3	.571	1	27	10	2	91	90	26	42	0	3.60
Herb Moford	R	29	4	9	.308	1	25	11	6	110	83	42	58	0	3.60
2 Al Cicotte	R	28	3	1	.750	0	14	2	0	43	50	15	21	0	3.54
Hank Aguirre	R	27	3	4	.429	1	44	3	0	70	67	27	38	0	3.73
2 Bill Fischer	R	27	2	4	.333	2	22	0	0	31	46	13	16	0	7.55
Tom Morgan	R	28	2	5	.286	1	39	1	0	63	70	4	32	0	3.14
1 Vito Valentinetti	R	29	1	0	1.000	2	15	0	0	19	18	5	10	0	3.38
George Spencer	R	31	1	0	1.000	0	7	0	0	10	11	4	5	0	2.70
2 Herm Wehmeier	R	31	1	0	1.000	0	7	3	0	29	31	11	13	0	2.35
1 Bob Shaw	R	25	1	2	.333	0	11	3	0	27	32	13	17	0	5.00
Joe Presko	R	29	0	2	.000	0	11	0	0	11	13	6	4	0	3.27
1 Lou Sleater	L	31	0	0	—	0	3	0	0	6	6	0	4	0	7.20
Mickey McDermott	L	29	0	0	—	0	2	0	0	2	6	2	0	0	9.00
Don Lee	R	24	0	0	—	0	1	0	0	2	3	0	2	0	9.00

BALTIMORE — 6th 74-79 .484 17.5 — PAUL RICHARDS

NAME	G by Pos	B	AGE	G	AB	R	H	2B	3B	HR	RBI	BB	SO	SB	BA	SA
TOTALS			29	154	5111	521	1233	195	19	108	493	483	731	33	.241	.350
Bob Boyd	1B99	L	38	125	401	58	124	21	5	7	36	25	34	1	.309	.439
Billy Gardner	2B151,SS13	R	30	151	560	58	126	28	3	33	34	53	2	.225	.298	
Willie Miranda	SS102	B	32	102	214	15	43	6	0	1	8	14	25	1	.201	.243
Brooks Robinson	3B140,2B16	R	21	145	463	31	110	16	3	3	32	31	51	1	.238	.305
Al Pilarcik	OF119	L	27	141	379	40	92	21	0	4	24	42	37	7	.243	.306
Jim Busby	OF103,3B1	R	31	113	215	32	51	7	2	3	19	24	37	6	.237	.330
Gene Woodling	OF116	L	35	133	413	57	114	16	1	15	65	66	49	4	.276	.429
Gus Triandos	C132	R	27	137	474	59	116	10	0	30	79	60	65	1	.245	.456
Dick Williams	OF70,3B45,1B26,2B7	R	29	128	409	36	113	17	0	4	32	37	47	0	.276	.347
Bob Nieman (HJ)	OF100	R	31	105	366	56	119	20	2	16	60	44	57	2	.325	.522
Foster Castleman	SS91,2B4,3B4,OF1	R	27	98	200	15	34	5	0	3	14	16	34	2	.170	.240
1 Jim Marshall	1B52,OF8	L	26	85	191	17	41	4	3	5	19	18	30	1	.215	.346
Lenny Green	OF53	L	24	69	91	10	21	4	0	0	8	7	15	3	.231	.275
Joe Ginsberg	C39	L	31	61	109	4	23	1	0	3	16	13	14	0	.211	.303
Jack Harshman	P34,OF1	L	30	47	82	13	16	1	0	6	14	17	22	0	.195	.427
2 Joe Taylor	OF21	R	32	36	77	11	21	4	0	2	9	7	19	0	.273	.403
Bob Hale	1B2	L	25	24	20	1	7	2	0	0	3	2	1	0	.350	.450
Willie Tasby	OF16	R	25	18	50	6	10	3	0	1	5	1	7	15	.200	.320
Chuck Oertel	OF2	L	24	8	12	2	2	0	0	1	1	1	6	0	.167	.417
Jerry Adair	SS10,2B1	R	21	11	19	1	2	0	0	0	1	1	7	0	.105	.105

Ron Hansen 20 R 0-19, Bert Hamric 30 L 1-8, Leo Burke 24 R 5-11, 1 Eddie Miksis 31 R 0-2, Frank Zupo 18 L 0-2

NAME	T	AGE	W	L	PCT	SV	G	GS	CG	IP	H	BB	SO	SHO	ERA
TOTALS		28	74	79	.484	28	154	154	55	1370	1277	403	749	15	3.40
Arnie Portocarrero	R	26	15	11	.577	2	32	27	10	205	173	57	90	3	3.25
Billy O'Dell	L	25	14	11	.560	8	41	25	12	221	201	51	137	3	2.97
Jack Harshman	L	30	12	15	.444	4	34	29	17	236	204	75	161	3	2.90
Milt Pappas	R	19	10	10	.500	0	31	21	3	135	135	48	72	0	4.07
Hal Brown (JJ)	R	33	7	5	.583	1	19	17	4	97	96	20	44	2	3.06
Connie Johnson	R	35	6	9	.400	1	26	17	4	118	116	32	68	0	3.88
Billy Loes	R	28	3	9	.250	5	32	10	1	114	106	44	44	0	3.63
Ken Lehman	L	30	2	1	.667	3	31	1	1	62	64	18	36	0	3.48
George Zuverink	R	33	2	2	.500	7	45	0	0	69	74	17	22	0	3.39
2 Lou Sleater	L	31	1	0	1.000	0	6	0	0	14	2	5	0	12.86	
Charlie Beamon	R	23	1	3	.250	0	21	3	0	50	47	21	26	0	4.32
2 Hoyt Wilhelm	R	35	1	3	.250	0	9	4	3	41	35	15	35	1	1.98
Jerry Walker	R	19	0	1	.000	0	6	0	0	10	16	5	6	0	7.20
Ron Moeller	L	19	0	0	—	0	4	0	0	4	6	3	3	0	4.50

KANSAS CITY — 7th 73-81 .474 19 — HARRY CRAFT

NAME	G by Pos	B	AGE	G	AB	R	H	2B	3B	HR	RBI	BB	SO	SB	BA	SA
TOTALS			28	156	5261	642	1297	196	50	138	605	452	747	22	.247	.381
1 Vic Power	1B50,2B1	R	30	52	205	35	62	13	4*	4	27	7	3	1	.302	.463
Hector Lopez	2B96,3B55,SS1,OF1	R	29	151	564	84	147	28	4	17	73	49	61	2	.261	.415
Joe DeMaestri	SS137	R	29	139	442	32	97	11	5	9	38	16	84	1	.219	.290
Hal Smith	3B43,C31,1B1	R	27	99	315	32	86	19	2	5	46	25	47	0	.273	.394
2 Roger Maris	OF99	L	23	99	401	61	99	14	3	19	53	26	20	0	.247	.439
Bill Tuttle	OF145	R	28	148	511	77	118	14	9	11	51	74	58	7	.231	.358
Bob Cerv	OF136	R	32	141	515	93	157	20	7	38	104	50	82	3	.305	.592
Harry Chiti	C83	R	25	103	295	32	79	11	3	9	44	18	48	3	.268	.417
Bob Martyn	OF63	L	27	95	226	25	59	10	7	2	23	26	36	1	.261	.394
2 Whitey Herzog	OF37,1B22	L	26	88	96	11	23	1	2	9	16	21	0	.240	.292	
2 Preston Ward	1B39,3B34,OF2	L	30	81	268	28	68	10	1	6	24	27	36	0	.254	.366
2 Harry Simpson	1B43,OF11	L	32	78	212	21	56	7	1	7	27	26	33	0	.264	.406
Frank House	C55	L	28	76	202	16	51	6	3	4	24	12	13	1	.252	.371
Mike Baxes	2B61,SS4	R	27	73	231	31	49	10	1	0	8	21	24	1	.212	.264
2 Chico Carrasquel	3B32,SS22	R	30	59	160	19	34	5	1	2	13	21	15	0	.213	.294
1 Woodie Held	OF41,3B4,SS1	R	26	47	131	13	28	2	0	6	16	10	28	0	.214	.321
1 Billy Hunter	SS12,2B8,3B1	R	30	22	58	6	9	1	0	1	5	4	5	1	.155	.310
Dave Melton	OF2	R	29												.000	.000
Milt Graff	2B3	L	28	5	1	0	0	0	0	0	0	0	1	0	.000	.000
Kent Hadley	1B2	L	23	5	3	1	0	0	0	0	0	1	3	0	.182	.182

Lou Klimchock 18 L 2-10, Jim Small 21 L 0-4

NAME	T	AGE	W	L	PCT	SV	G	GS	CG	IP	H	BB	SO	SHO	ERA
TOTALS		30	73	81	.474	25	156	156	42	1398	1405	467	721	9	4.15
Ned Garver	R	32	12	11	.522	1	31	28	10	201	192	66	72	3	4.03
Ralph Terry	R	22	11	13	.458	2	40	33	8	217	217	61	134	3	4.23
1 Murry Dickson	R	41	9	5	.643	1	27	9	3	99	99	31	46	0	3.27
Ray Herbert	R	28	8	8	.500	3	42	16	5	175	161	55	108	0	3.50
Jack Urban	R	29	8	11	.421	0	30	24	5	132	150	51	54	1	5.93
2 Bob Grim	R	28	7	6	.538	0	26	14	5	114	118	41	54	1	4.50
2 Dick Tomanek	L	27	5	5	.500	5	36	2	1	72	69	28	50	0	3.63
Tom Gorman	R	33	4	4	.500	8	50	1	0	90	86	20	44	0	3.50
1 Duke Maas	R	29	4	4	.444	1	10	7	3	55	49	13	19	1	3.93
Bud Daley	R	25	3	2	.600	0	26	5	1	79	71	19	39	0	3.30
Howie Reed	R	21	1	0	1.000	0	3	1	1	10	5	4	5	0	0.90
Wally Burnette	R	28	1	1	.500	0	12	1	1	24	14	11	10	0	3.54
Glenn Cox	R	27	0	0	—	0	2	0	0	9	10	3	1	0	9.00
Ken Johnson	R	24	0	0	—	0	3	2	0	12	14	12	4	0	31.50
John Tsitouris	R	22	0	0	—	0	3	0	0	3	3	0	1	0	3.00
Carl Duser	L	24	0	0	—	0	3	0	0	7	9	4	0	0	4.50
1 Virgil Trucks	R	41	0	0	—	3	16	0	0	22	18	15	15	0	2.05
1 Alex Kellner	L	33	0	2	.000	3	16	0	0	40	41	20	22	0	5.82
Walt Craddock	L	26	0	3	.000	0	23	1	0	37	41	20	22	0	5.84
Bob Davis	R	24	0	3	.000	0	7	0	0	31	45	22	22	0	7.84

*Power-also with Cleveland, league leader in 3B with 10

WASHINGTON — 8th 61-93 .396 31 — COOKIE LAVAGETTO

NAME	G by Pos	B	AGE	G	AB	R	H	2B	3B	HR	RBI	BB	SO	SB	BA	SA
TOTALS			28	156	5153		1240	161	38	121	526	477	751	22	.240	.357
Norm Zauchin	1B91	R	28	96	303	35	69	8	2	15	37	38	68	0	.228	.416
2 Ken Aspromonte	2B72,3B11,SS1	R	26	94	253	15	57	9	1	5	27	25	28	1	.225	.328
Rocky Bridges	SS112,2B3,3B3	R	30	116	377	38	99	14	3	5	37	21	32	0	.263	.355
Eddie Yost	3B114,OF4,1B2	R	31	134	406	55	91	16	0	8	37	81	43	3	.224	.355
Jim Lemon	OF137	R	30	146	501	65	123	16	9	26	75	50	120	2	.246	.467
Albie Pearson	OF141	L	23	146	530	63	146	25	5	3	33	64	41	7	.275	.358
Roy Sievers	OF114,1B33	R	31	146	550	85	162	18	1	39	108	53	93	0	.295	.544
Clint Courtney	C128	L	31	134	450	45	113	18	0	6	62	48	23	1	.251	.344
Herb Plews	2B64,3B36	L	30	111	380	46	98	12	6	2	29	17	45	1	.258	.337
Neil Chrisley	OF69,3B1	L	26	103	233	19	50	7	4	5	26	16	18	1	.215	.343
Ossie Alvarez	SS64,2B14,3B3	R	24	87	196	20	39	5	0	0	16	26	26	1	.209	.224
Julio Becquer	1B42,OF1	L	26	88	164	10	39	3	0	0	13	6	15	1	.238	.256
Ed Fitz Gerald	C21,1B5	R	34	58	114	7	30	4	0	1	8	15	7	0	.263	.289
Faye Throneberry	OF27	L	27	56	164	19	30	5	2	4	20	18	47	0	.184	.396
Bobby Malkmus	2B26,3B2,SS1	R	26	41	70	6	13	4	0	0	3	5	13	0	.186	.243
Steve Korcheck	C29	R	25	16	35	1	6	1	0	0	5	6	4	0	.171	.200
Harmon Killebrew	3B9	R	22	13	31	2	6	0	0	0	2	10	12	0	.194	.194
Bob Allison	OF11	R	23	11	35	1	7	1	0	0	3	5	10	0	.200	.229
1 Whitey Herzog	OF7	L	26	8	10										.000	.000
Johnny Schaive	2B6	R	24	7	24	1	6	1	0	0	2	5	4	0	.250	.250

Jerry Snyder 28 R 1-9, 1 Lou Berberet 28 L 1-6

NAME	T	AGE	W	L	PCT	SV	G	GS	CG	IP	H	BB	SO	SHO	ERA
TOTALS		28	61	93	.396	28	156	156	28	1377	1443	558	762	6	4.53
Pedro Ramos	R	23	14	18	.438	3	43	37	10	259	277	77	132	4	4.24
Dick Hyde	R	29	10	3	.769	18	53	0	0	103	82	35	49	0	1.75
Tex Clevenger	R	25	9	9	.500	6	55	4	0	124	119	50	70	0	4.35
Camilo Pascual	R	24	8	12	.400	0	31	27	6	177	166	60	146	2	3.15
Russ Kemmerer	R	26	6	15	.286	0	40	30	6	224	234	74	111	0	4.62
2 Vito Valentinetti	R	29	4	6	.400	0	23	10	2	96	109	46	33	0	5.06
Hal Griggs	R	29	3	11	.214	0	32	21	3	137	138	74	69	0	5.52
1 Bud Byerly	R	37	3	1	.750	1	17	0	0	34	34	11	13	0	6.75
John Romonosky	R	28	2	2	.500	0	8	5	1	55	52	16	23	0	6.00
1 Chuck Stobbs	L	28	2	2	.500	0	19	5	0	57	87	16	23	0	6.00
Ralph Lumenti	L	21	1	3	.333	0	8	3	0	38	36	20	8	0	8.57
Joe Albanese	L	25	0	1	.000	0	4	1	0	6	6	4	1	0	4.50
Bob Wiesler	L	27	0	1	.000	0	4	1	0	7	16	11	9	0	7.00
Jack Spring	L	25	0	1	.000	0	7	0	0	6	13	6	3	0	14.14
2 Jim Constable	L	25	0	0	—	0	4	0	0	9	9	2	4	0	4.82
1 Al Cicotte	R	28	0	0	—	0	2	0	0	9	9	2	4	0	4.82
3 Bill Fischer	R	27	0	3	.000	0	9	2	0	36	36	14	14	0	3.86

MILWAUKEE 1st 92-62 .597 — FRED HANEY

NAME	G by Pos	B	AGE	G	AB	R	H	2B	3B	HR	RBI	BB	SO	SB	BA	SA
TOTALS			29	154	5225	675	1388	221	21	167	641	478	646	26	.266	.412
Frank Torre	1B122	L	26	138	372	41	115	22	5	6	54	42	14	2	.309	.444
Red Schoendienst (IL)	2B105	B	35	106	427	47	112	23	1	1	24	31	21	3	.262	.328
Johnny Logan	SS144	R	31	145	530	54	120	20	0	11	53	40	57	1	.226	.326
Eddie Mathews	3B149	L	26	149	546	97	137	18	1	31	77	85	85	5	.251	.458
Hank Aaron	OF153	R	24	153	601	109	196	34	4	30	95	59	49	4	.326	.546
Bill Bruton (KJ)	OF96	L	32	100	325	49	91	11	3	3	28	27	37	4	.280	.360
Wes Covington	OF82	L	26	90	294	43	97	12	1	24	74	20	35	0	.330	.622
Del Crandall	C124	R	28	131	427	50	116	23	1	18	63	48	38	2	.272	.457
Joe Adcock	1B71, OF22	R	30	105	320	40	88	15	1	19	54	21	63	0	.275	.506
Andy Pafko	OF93	R	37	95	164	17	39	7	1	3	23	15	17	0	.238	.348
Felix Mantilla	OF43, 2B21, SS5, 3B2	R	23	85	226	37	50	5	1	7	19	20	20	2	.221	.345
Harry Hanebrink	OF33, 3B7	L	30	63	133	14	25	3	0	4	10	13	9	0	.188	.301
Mel Roach (KJ)	2B27, OF7, 1B1	R	25	44	136	14	42	7	0	3	10	6	15	0	.309	.426
Del Rice	C38	R	35	43	121	10	27	7	0	1	8	6	30	0	.223	.306
Warren Spahn	P38	L	37	41	108	10	36	6	1	2	15	7	24	0	.333	.463
Casey Wise	2B10, SS7, 3B1	B	25	31	71	8	14	1	0	0	4	8	1		.197	.211
1 Bob Hazle	OF20	L	27	20	56	6	10	0	0	0	5	9	4	0	.179	.179
Joe Koppe	SS3	R	27	16	9	1	4	0	0	0	1	0	1	0	.444	.444
1 Carl Sawatski	C3	L	30	10	10	1	1	0	0	0	1	2	5	0	.100	.100
Eddie Haas	OF3	R	23	9	14	2	5	0	0	0	1	2	1	0	.357	.357
Hawk Taylor	OF4	R	19	8	8	1	1	1	0	0	0	0	3	0	.125	.250

John DeMerit 22 R 2-3, Bob Roselli 26 R 0-1

NAME	T	AGE	W	L	PCT	SV	G	GS	CG	IP	H	BB	SO	SHO	ERA
		29	92	62	.597	17	154	154	72	1376	1261	426	773	16	3.21
Warren Spahn	L	37	22	11	.667	1	38	36	23	290	257	76	150	2	3.07
Lew Burdette	R	31	20	10	.667	0	40	36	19	275	279	50	113	3	2.91
Bob Rush	R	32	10	6	.625	0	28	20	5	147	142	31	84	2	3.43
Carl Willey	R	27	9	7	.563	0	23	19	9	140	110	53	74	4	2.70
Don McMahon	R	28	7	2	.778	8	38	0	0	59	50	29	37	0	3.66
Joey Jay	R	22	7	5	.583	0	18	12	6	97	60	43	74	3	2.13
Juan Pizarro	L	21	6	4	.600	1	19	7		95	75	47	84	1	2.69
Bob Buhl (SA)	R	29	5	2	.714	0	11	10	3	73	74	27	41	0	3.45
Ernie Johnson	R	34	3	1	.750	5	15	0	0	23	35	10	13	0	8.22
Humberto Robinson	R	28	2	4	.333	1	19	0	0	42	30	13	26	0	3.00
Bob Trowbridge	R	28	1	3	.250	1	27	4	0	55	53	26	31	0	3.93
Dick Littlefield	L	32	1	0	1.000	1	4	0	0	6	7	1	7	0	4.50
Gene Conley (AJ)	R	27	0	6	.000	2	26	7	0	72	89	17	53	0	4.88

PITTSBURGH 2nd 84-70 .545 8 — DANNY MURTAUGH

NAME	G by Pos	B	AGE	G	AB	R	H	2B	3B	HR	RBI	BB	SO	SB	BA	SA
TOTALS			27	154	5247	662	1386	229	68	134	625	396	753	30	.264	.410
Ted Kluszewski	1B72	L	33	100	301	29	88	13	4	4	37	26	16	0	.292	.402
Bill Mazeroski	2B152	R	21	152	567	69	156	24	6	19	68	25	71	1	.275	.439
Dick Groat	SS149	R	27	151	584	67	175	36	9	3	66	23	32	2	.300	.408
Frank Thomas	3B139, OF8, 1B2	R	29	149	562	69	158	26	4	35	109	42	79	0	.281	.528
Roberto Clemente	OF135	R	23	140	519	69	150	24	10	6	50	31	41	8	.289	.408
Bill Virdon	OF143	L	27	144	604	75	161	24	11	9	46	52	70	5	.267	.387
Bob Skinner	OF141	L	26	144	529	93	170	33	9	13	70	58	55	12	.321	.491
Hank Foiles	C103	R	29	104	264	31	54	10	2	8	30	45	53	0	.205	.348
Roman Mejias	OF57	R	27	76	157	17	42	3	2	5	19	2	27	2	.268	.408
Dick Stuart	1B64	R	25	67	254	38	68	12	5	16	48	11	75	0	.268	.543
R C Stevens	1B52	R	23	59	90	16	24	3	1	7	18	5	25	0	.267	.556
Johnny Powers	OF14	L	28	57	82	6	15	1	0	2	8	9	19	0	.183	.268
Bill Hall	C51	R	29	51	116	15	33	6	0	1	15	15	13	0	.284	.362
Danny Kravitz	C37	L	27	45	100	9	24	3	2	1	5	11	10	0	.240	.340
Gene Baker (KJ)	3B11, 2B3	R	33	29	56	3	14	2	1	0	7	6	6	2	.250	.321
2 Dick Schofield	SS5, 3B2	B	23	26	27	4	4	0	1	0	2	3	6	0	.148	.222
1 Gene Freese	3B1	R	24	17	18	1	3	0	0	1	2	1	2	0	.167	.333
Harry Bright	3B7	R	28	15	24	4	6	1	0	1	3	4	6	0	.250	.417

1 Paul Smith 27 L 1-3, 1 Johnny O'Brien 27 R 0-1, Jim Pendleton 34 R 1-3, Hardy Peterson 28 R 2-6

NAME	T	AGE	W	L	PCT	SV	G	GS	CG	IP	H	BB	SO	SHO	ERA
		27	84	70	.545	41	154	154	43	1367	1344	470	679	10	3.56
Bob Friend	R	27	22	14	.611	0	38	38	16	274	299	61	135	1	3.68
Vern Law	R	28	14	12	.538	3	35	29	6	202	235	39	56	1	3.97
Ron Kline	R	26	13	16	.448	0	32	32	11	237	226	92	109	2	3.53
George Witt	R	24	9	2	.818	0	18	15	5	106	78	59	81	3	1.61
Curt Raydon	R	24	8	4	.667	1	31	20	2	134	118	61	85	1	3.63
Roy Face	R	30	5	2	.714	20	57	0	0	84	77	22	47	0	2.89
Don Gross	L	27	5	7	.417	7	40	3	0	75	67	38	59	0	3.96
2 Bob Porterfield	R	34	4	6	.400	5	37	6	2	88	78	19	39	1	3.27
Ron Blackburn	R	23	2	1	.667	3	38	2	0	64	61	27	31	0	3.38
Bob Smith	L	27	2	2	.500	1	35	4	0	61	61	31	24	0	4.43
Don Williams	R	26	0	0	—	0	2	0	0	4	3	2	1	0	6.75
Eddie O'Brien	R	27	0	0	—	0	2	0	0	2	4	1	1	0	13.50
George Perez	R	20	0	1	.000	0	4	2	0	11	9	7	4	0	5.63
Bennie Daniels	R	26	0	3	.000	0	8	5	1	28	31	15	7	0	5.46

Dick Hall (VR) 27

SAN FRANCISCO 3rd 80-74 .519 12 — BILL RIGNEY

NAME	G by Pos	B	AGE	G	AB	R	H	2B	3B	HR	RBI	BB	SO	SB	BA	SA
TOTALS			27	154	5318	727	1399	250	42	170	682	531	817	64	.263	.422
Orlando Cepeda	1B147	R	20	148	603	88	188	38	4	25	96	29	84	15	.312	.512
Danny O'Connell	2B104, 3B3	R	31	148	307	44	71	12	2	3	23	51	35	2	.232	.314
Daryl Spencer	SS134, 2B17	R	28	148	539	71	138	20	5	17	74	73	60	1	.256	.406
Jim Davenport	3B130, SS5	R	24	134	434	70	111	22	3	12	41	33	64	1	.256	.403
Willie Kirkland	OF115	L	24	122	418	48	108	25	6	14	56	43	69	3	.258	.447
Willie Mays	OF151	R	27	152	600	121	208	33	11	29	96	78	56	31	.347	.583
Felipe Alou	OF70	R	23	75	182	21	46	9	2	4	16	19	34	4	.253	.390
Bob Schmidt	C123	R	25	127	393	46	96	20	2	14	54	33	59	0	.244	.412
Whitey Lockman	OF25, 2B15, 1B7	L	31	92	122	15	29	5	0	2	7	13	8	0	.238	.328
Hank Sauer	OF67	R	41	88	236	27	59	8	0	12	46	15	37	0	.250	.436
Ray Jablonski	3B57	R	31	82	230	28	53	15	1	4	46	17	50	2	.230	.461
Leon Wagner	OF57	L	24	74	221	31	70	9	0	13	35	18	34	1	.317	.534
Ed Bressoud	2B57, 3B6, SS4	R	26	66	137	19	36	5	3	0	8	14	22	0	.263	.343
Bob Speake	OF10	L	27	66	71	9	15	3	0	3	10	13	15	0	.211	.380
Valmy Thomas	C61	R	29	63	143	14	37	5	0	3	16	13	24	1	.259	.357
Don Taussig	OF36	R	26	39	50	10	10	0	0	1	4	3	8	0	.200	.260
Jim King	OF15	L	25	34	56	8	12	1	2	1	8	8	10	0	.214	.393
Bill White (MS)	1B3, OF2	L	24	26	29	5	7	1	0	1	4	7	5	1	.241	.379
Jim Finigan	2B8, 3B4	R	29	23	25	3	5	2	0	0	1	3	5	0	.200	.280
Andre Rodgers	SS18	R	23	22	63	7	13	3	1	1	11	4	14	0	.206	.381
Jackie Brandt (MS)	OF14	R	24	18	52	7	13	1	0	0	3	6	5	1	.250	.269
Nick Testa	C1	R	30													

NAME	T	AGE	W	L	PCT	SV	G	GS	CG	IP	H	BB	SO	SHO	ERA
		29	80	74	.519	25	154	154	38	1389	1400	512	775	7	3.98
Johnny Antonelli	L	28	16	13	.552	3	41	34	13	242	216	87	143	0	3.21
Al Worthington	R	29	11	7	.611	6	54	12	1	151	152	57	76	0	3.64
Mike McCormick	L	19	11	8	.579	1	42	28	8	178	192	60	82	2	4.60
Ruben Gomez	R	30	10	12	.455	1	42	30	8	208	204	77	112	1	4.37
Ray Monzant	R	25	8	6	.421	1	43	16	4	151	160	57	93	1	4.71
Marv Grissom	R	40	7	5	.583	10	51	0	0	65	71	26	46	0	4.02
Stu Miller	R	30	6	9	.400	0	41	20	4	182	160	49	119	1	2.47
Paul Giel	R	25	4	4	.444	0	29	9	0	92	89	55	55	0	4.70
Gordon Jones	R	28	3	1	.750	1	11	1	0	30	33	5	8	0	2.40
1 Jim Constable	L	25	1	0	1.000	1	9	0	0	8	10	3	4	0	5.63
Curt Barclay	R	26	1	0	1.000	0	16			16	5	6		0	2.81
Dom Zanni	R	26	1	0	1.000	0	4			7	1	3		0	2.25
Ray Crone	R	26	1	2	.333	0	14	1	0	24	35	13	7	0	6.75
Pete Burnside	L	27	0	1	.000	1	11			20	5	4		0	6.55
John Fitzgerald	L	24	0	0	—	0	1			1	1	3		0	3.00
Joe Shipley	R	23	0	0	—	0	1			1	3			0	45.00
Don Johnson	R	31	0	1	.000	1	17	0	0	28	31	8	14	0	6.26

CINCINNATI 4th 76-78 .494 16 — BIRDIE TEBBETTS 52-61 .460 JIMMY DYKES 24-17 .585

NAME	G by Pos	B	AGE	G	AB	R	H	2B	3B	HR	RBI	BB	SO	SB	BA	SA
TOTALS			30	154	5273	695	1359	242	40	123	649	572	765	61	.258	.389
George Crowe	1B93, 2B1	L	37	111	345	31	95	12	5	7	61	41	51	1	.275	.400
Johnny Temple	2B141, 1B1	R	29	141	542	82	166	31	6	3	47	91	41	15	.306	.402
Roy McMillan	SS145	R	27	145	393	48	90	18	3	1	25	47	33	5	.229	.298
Don Hoak	3B112, SS11	R	30	114	417	51	109	30	0	6	50	43	36	6	.261	.376
Jerry Lynch	OF101	L	27	122	420	58	131	20	5	16	68	14	43	1	.312	.498
Gus Bell	OF107	L	29	112	385	42	97	16	2	10	46	36	40	2	.252	.382
Frank Robinson	OF138, 3B11	R	22	148	554	90	149	25	6	31	83	62	80	10	.269	.504
Ed Bailey	C99	R	27	112	360	39	90	23	1	11	59	47	61	2	.250	.411
Alex Grammas	SS61, 3B38, 2B14	R	32	105	216	25	47	8	0	0	12	34	24	2	.218	.255
Smoky Burgess	C58	L	31	99	251	28	71	12	1	6	31	22	20	0	.283	.410
Bob Thurman	OF41	L	41	94	178	23	41	7	4	4	20	20	38	1	.230	.382
Dee Fondy	1B36, OF22	L	33	89	124	23	27	1	1	1	11	5	27	7	.218	.266
Pete Whisenant	OF66, 3B5	R	28	85	203	33	48	9	2	11	40	18	37	3	.236	.463
2 Eddie Miksis	OF32, 3B14, 2B7, SS5, 1B1	R	31	69	50	15	7	1	0	0	6	7		1	.140	.140
2 Walt Dropo	1B43	R	35	63	162	18	47	7	2	7	31	12	31	0	.290	.488
2 Don Newcombe	P20	R	32	39	60	9	21	1	0	1	9	8	10	0	.350	.417
1 Steve Bilko	1B21	R	29	31	87	12	23	4	2	4	17	10	26	0	.264	.494
Vada Pinson	OF27	L	19	27	96	20	26	7	0	1	8	11	18	2	.271	.375
Dan Morejon	OF11	R	22	12	26	4	5	0	0	0	1	9	2	0	.192	.192
Dutch Dotterer	C8	R	26	11	28	1	7	1	0	1	2	2	4	0	.250	.393
Chuck Coles	OF4	R	27	5	11	0	2	1	0	0	0	0	5	0	.182	.273

Bobby Henrich 19 R 0-3, Jim Fridley 33 R 2-9, 2 Fred Hatfield 33 L 0-1, Don Pavletich (MS) 19

NAME	T	AGE	W	L	PCT	SV	G	GS	CG	IP	H	BB	SO	SHO	ERA
		31	76	78	.494	20	154	154	50	1385	1422	419	705	7	3.73
Bob Purkey	R	28	17	11	.607	0	37	34	17	250	259	49	70	3	3.60
Joe Nuxhall	R	29	12	11	.522	0	36	26	5	176	169	63	111	0	3.78
Harvey Haddix	L	32	8	7	.533	0	29	26	8	184	191	43	110	1	3.52
Brooks Lawrence	R	33	8	13	.381	4	46	23	6	181	194	55	74	2	4.13
2 Alex Kellner	L	33	7	3	.700	0	18	7	4	82	74	20	42	0	2.30
2 Don Newcombe	R	32	7	7	.500	0	20	18	7	133	159	28	53	0	3.86
Hal Jeffcoat	R	33	6	4	.429	9	49	0	0	75	76	26	35	0	3.72
Tom Acker	R	28	4	4	.571	3	38	10	3	125	126	43	90	0	4.54
1 Johnny Klippstein	R	30	3	2	.600	1	12	4	0	33	37	14	22	0	4.91
Willard Schmidt	R	30	3	5	.375	0	41	2	0	69	60	33	41	0	2.87
Orlando Pena	R	24	1	0	1.000	0	15			10	4	11		0	0.60
1 Hersh Freeman	R	30	0	0	—	0	3	0	0	4	5	1	4	0	4.50
Gene Hayden	L	23	0	0	—	0	3			4	1			0	4.50
1 Bob Kelly	R	30	0	0	—	0	3	0	0	4	3	1	3	0	3.38
Ted Wieand	R	25	0	0	—	0	2	0	0	2	5	4	1	0	9.00
1 Bill Wight	L	36	0	0	—	0	3	0	0	2	4	3	3	0	3.86
Jay Hook	R	21	0	1	.000	0	3							0	12.00
Jim O'Toole	R	21	0	0	—	0	3	0	0	9	10	6	9	0	1.29
2 Turk Lown	R	34	0	2	.000	0	11	0	0	12	12	12	9	0	5.25
Charlie Rabe	L	26	0	2	.000	0	9			19	25	10	10	0	4.26

CHICAGO 5th (tie) 72-82 .468 20 — BOB SCHEFFING

NAME	G by Pos	B	AGE	G	AB	R	H	2B	3B	HR	RBI	BB	SO	SB	BA	SA
TOTALS			29	154	5289	709	1402	207	49	182	666	487	853	39	.265	.426
Dale Long	1B137, C2	L	32	142	480	68	130	26	4	20	75	66	64	2	.271	.467
Tony Taylor	2B137, 3B1	R	22	140	497	63	117	15	7	27	40	93	21	23	.235	.314
Ernie Banks	SS154	R	27	154	617	119	193	23	11	47	129	52	87	4	.313	.614
2 Al Dark	3B111	R	36	114	464	54	137	16	4	3	43	29	23	1	.295	.366
Lee Walls	OF132	R	25	136	513	60	156	19	3	24	72	47	63	4	.304	.493
Bobby Thomson	OF148, 3B4	R	34	153	547	67	155	25	7	21	82	56	76	0	.283	.466
Walt Moryn	OF141	L	32	143	512	77	135	26	7	26	77	62	83	1	.264	.494
Sammy Taylor	C87	L	25	96	301	30	78	12	2	6	36	27	46	2	.259	.372
Jim Bolger	OF37	R	26	84	120	15	27	4	1	1	9	20		0	.225	.300
Johnny Goryl	3B44, 2B35	R	24	83	219	27	53	9	3	4	14	27	34	0	.242	.365
Cal Neeman	C71	R	29	76	201	30	52	7	0	12	29	21	41	0	.259	.473
Chuck Tanner	OF15	R	28	73	103	10	27	5	0	3	17	9	10	1	.262	.437
Bobby Adams	1B11, 3B9, 2B7	R	36	62	96	14	27	4	1	2	14	13	14	3	.281	.438
2 Jim Marshall	1B15, OF11	L	26	61	162	18	45	9	1	11	27	20	31	2	.278	.543
Lou Jackson	OF12	L	22	24	35	6	6	1	1	1	6	1	10	0	.171	.371
2 Paul Smith	1B4	L	27	18	20	1	3	0	0	0	1	1	5	0	.150	.150
El Tappe	C16	R	31	17	28	2	6	0	0	0	2	2	9	0	.214	.214
Moe Thacker	C9	R	24	11	17	0	2	0	0	0	1	1	3	0	.118	.118
Frank Ernaga	OF7	R	27	3	8	1	1	0	0	0	0	1	2	0	.125	.125
Charlie King	OF7	R	27	2	4	0	1	0	0	0	2	0	0		.250	.250

Dick Johnson 26 L 0-5, Bob Will 26 L 1-4, Jerry Kindall 23 R 1-6, Bill Gabler 27 L 0-3, Gordon Massa 22 L 0-2, Bobby Morgan 32 R 0-1

NAME	T	AGE	W	L	PCT	SV	G	GS	CG	IP	H	BB	SO	SHO	ERA
		26	72	82	.468	24	154	154	27	1361	1322	619	805	5	4.22
Glen Hobbie	R	22	10	6	.625	2	55	16	2	168	163	93	91	1	3.75
Don Elston	R	29	9	8	.529	10	69	0	0	97	75	39	84	0	2.88
Moe Drabowsky	R	23	9	11	.450	0	22	20	4	126	118	73	77	1	4.50
Taylor Phillips	L	25	7	10	.412	1	39	27	5	170	178	79	102	1	4.76
Dick Drott	R	21	7	11	.389	0	31	31	4	167	156	99	127	0	5.44
Bill Henry	L	30	5	4	.556	6	44	0	0	81	63	17	58	0	2.89
Johnny Briggs	R	24	5	5	.500	0	20	17	3	96	99	45	46	1	4.50
Dave Hillman	R	30	4	8	.333	1	31	16	3	126	132	31	65	0	3.14
John Buzhardt	R	21	3	2	.600	1	6	2	2	24	16	12	7	0	1.88
Bob Anderson	R	23	3	4	.429	0	18	2	0	52	54	29	51	0	3.95
Marcelino Solis	L	27	3	3	.500	0	15	3	1	52	74	20	15	0	6.06
1 Jim Brosnan	R	28	3	4	.429	0	18			30				0	3.12
Ed Mayer	L	26	2	2	.500	1	19	0	0	24	15	16	14	0	4.50
Elmer Singleton	R	40	1	0	1.000	0	7	0	0	8	11	1	4	0	3.75
Gene Fodge	R	27	1	1	.500	0	13	2	0	41	49	17	15	0	4.73
1 Turk Lown	R	34	0	0	—	0									4.50
Freddy Rodriguez	R	27	0	0	—	0	8	0	0	12	14	9	9	0	7.71
2 Hersh Freeman	R	30	0	0	—	0	3	0	0	13	23	3	7	0	8.31
Dick Ellsworth	L	18	0	1	.000	0	1	1	0	2				0	18.00
Dolan Nichols	R	28	0	4	.000	0	24	0	0	41	46	16	22	0	5.05

ST. LOUIS 5th (tie) 72-82 .468 20   FRED HUTCHINSON 69-75 .479   STAN HACK 3-7 .300

NAME	G by Pos	B	AGE	G	AB	R	H	2B	3B	HR	RBI	BB	SO	SB	BA	SA
TOTALS			28	154	5255	619	1371	216	39	151	570	533	637	44	.261	.380
Stan Musial	1B124	L	37	135	472	64	159	35	2	17	62	72	26	0	.337	.528
Don Blasingame	2B137	L	26	143	547	71	150	19	10	2	36	57	47	20	.274	.356
Eddie Kasko	SS77, 2B12, 3B1	R	26	104	259	20	57	8	1	2	21	21	25	1	.220	.282
Ken Boyer	3B144, OF6, SS1	R	27	150	570	101	175	21	9	23	90	49	53	11	.307	.496
Wally Moon	OF82	L	28	108	290	36	69	10	3	7	38	47	30	2	.238	.366
Curt Flood	OF120, 3B1	R	20	121	422	50	110	17	2	10	41	31	56	2	.261	.382
Del Ennis	OF84	R	33	106	329	22	86	18	1	3	47	16	35	0	.261	.350
Hal Smith	C71	R	27	77	220	13	50	4	1	1	24	14	14	0	.227	.268
Gene Green	OF75, C48	R	25	137	442	47	124	18	3	13	55	37	48	2	.281	.423
Joe Cunningham	1B67, OF66	L	26	131	337	61	105	20	3	12	57	82	23	4	.312	.496
Irv Noren	OF77	L	33	117	178	24	47	9	1	4	22	13	21	0	.264	.393
Hobie Landrith	C45	L	28	70	144	9	31	4	0	3	13	26	21	0	.215	.306
2 Gene Freese	SS28, 2B14, 3B3	R	24	62	191	28	49	11	1	6	16	10	32	1	.257	.419
Ruben Amaro	SS36, 2B1	R	22	40	76	8	17	2	1	0	5	8	4	0	.224	.276
1 Dick Schofield	SS27	B	23	39	108	16	23	4	0	1	8	23	15	0	.213	.278
Bobby Gene Smith	OF27	R	24	28	88	8	25	3	0	2	5	2	18	1	.284	.386
Ray Katt	C14	R	31	19	41	1	7	1	0	1	4	4	6	0	.171	.268
1 Al Dark	SS8, 3B8	R	36	18	64	7	19	0	0	1	5	2	6	0	.297	.344
1 Joe Taylor	OF5	R	32	18	23	2	7	3	0	1	3	2	4	0	.304	.565
Lee Tate	SS9	R	26	10	35	4	7	2	0	0	1	4	3	0	.200	.257

2 Johnny O'Brien 27 R 0-2, Benny Valenzuela 25 R 3-14, Ellis Burton 21 B 7-30

NAME	T	AGE	W	L	PCT	SV	G	GS	CG	IP	H	BB	SO	SHO	ERA
		29	72	82	.468	25	154	154	45	1382	1398	567	822	6	4.12
Sam Jones	R	32	14	13	.519	0	35	35	14	250	204	107	225	2	2.88
Larry Jackson	R	27	13	13	.500	8	49	23	11	198	211	51	124	1	3.68
Vinegar Bend Mizell	R	27	10	14	.417	0	30	29	8	190	178	91	80	2	3.41
Jim Brosnan	R	28	8	4	.667	2	33	12	2	115	107	50	65	0	3.44
Phil Paine	R	28	5	1	.833	1	46	0	0	73	70	31	45	0	3.58
Lindy McDaniel	R	22	5	7	.417	0	26	17	2	109	139	31	47	1	5.78
Billy Muffett	R	27	4	6	.400	5	35	6	1	84	107	42	41	0	4.93
2 Bill Wight	L	36	3	0	1.000	2	28	1	1	57	64	32	18	0	5.05
1 Morrie Martin	R	35	3	1	.750	0	17	0	0	25	19	12	16	0	4.68
Bob Mabe	R	28	3	9	.250	0	31	13	4	112	113	41	74	0	4.50
6 Sal Maglie	R	41	2	6	.250	0	10	10	2	53	46	25	21	0	4.75
Frank Barnes	R	31	1	1	.500	0	9	1	0	19	16	17	7	0	7.58
2 Chuck Stobbs	L	28	1	3	.250	1	17	0	0	40	40	14	25	0	3.60
Von McDaniel (SA)	R	19	0	0	—	0	2	1	0	2	5	5	0	0	13.50
2 Johnny O'Brien	R	27	0	0	—	0	2	0	0	2	7	2	2	0	22.50
Tom Flanigan	L	23	0	0	—	0	1	0	0	2	1	0	0	0	9.00
Nels Chittum	R	25	0	0	.000	0	13	2	0	29	31	7	13	0	6.52
Phil Clark	R	25	0	1	.000	0	7	0	0	8	11	3	1	0	3.38
1 Herm Wehmeier	R	31	0	1	.000	0	3	0	0	6	13	2	4	0	13.50
Bill Smith	L	24	0	1	.000	0	2	1	0	12	12	4	6	0	6.30

Tom Cheney (MS) 23

LOS ANGELES 7th 71-83 .461 21   WALT ALSTON

NAME	G by Pos	B	AGE	G	AB	R	H	2B	3B	HR	RBI	BB	SO	SB	BA	SA
TOTALS			29	154	5173	668	1297	166	50	172	627	495	850	73	.251	.402
Gil Hodges	1B122, 3B15, OF9, C1	R	34	141	475	68	123	15	1	22	64	52	87	8	.259	.434
Charlie Neal	2B132, 3B9	R	27	140	473	87	120	19	6	22	65	61	91	7	.254	.438
Don Zimmer	SS114, 3B12, 2B1, OF1	R	27	127	455	52	119	15	2	17	60	28	92	14	.262	.415
Dick Gray	3B55	R	26	58	197	25	49	5	6	9	30	19	30	1	.249	.472
Carl Furillo	OF119	R	36	122	411	54	119	19	3	18	83	35	28	0	.290	.482
Duke Snider	OF92	L	31	106	327	45	102	12	3	15	58	32	49	2	.312	.505
Gino Cimoli	OF104	R	28	109	325	35	80	6	3	9	27	18	49	3	.246	.366
Johnny Roseboro	C104, OF5	L	25	114	384	52	104	11	9	14	43	36	56	11	.271	.456
Jim Gilliam	OF75, 3B44, 2B32	B	29	147	555	81	145	25	5	2	43	78	22	18	.261	.335
Norm Larker	OF43, 1B35	L	27	99	253	32	70	16	5	4	29	29	21	1	.277	.427
Elmer Valo	OF26	L	37	65	101	9	25	2	1	1	14	12	11	0	.248	.317
Joe Pignatano	C57	R	28	63	142	16	31	4	0	4	17	16	26	1	.218	.437
Pee Wee Reese	SS22, 3B21	R	39	59	147	21	33	7	2	4	17	26	15	1	.224	.381
2 Steve Bilko	1B25	R	29	47	101	13	21	1	1	7	18	8	37	0	.208	.465
Don Drysdale	P24	R	21	47	66	9	15	1	1	3	12	3	25	0	.227	.591
Don Demeter	OF39	R	23	43	106	11	20	2	0	5	8	5	32	2	.189	.349
1 Randy Jackson	3B17	R	32	35	65	8	12	3	0	1	7	5	10	0	.185	.277
Rube Walker	C20	R	32	25	44	3	5	2	0	1	5	10	7	0	.114	.227
Bob Lillis	SS19	R	28	20	69	10	27	3	1	1	5	4	6	1	.391	.507
Ron Fairly	OF15	L	19	15	53	6	15	1	0	2	8	6	7	0	.283	.415
Jim Gentile	1B8	L	24	12	30	4	4	1	0	2	4	4	6	0	.133	.167

1 Don Newcombe 32 L 5-12, Frank Howard 21 R 7-29, Don Miles 22 L 4-22, Earl Robinson 21 R 3-15, Bob Wilson 33 R 1-5, Roy Campanella (BX) 36

NAME	T	AGE	W	L	PCT	SV	G	GS	CG	IP	H	BB	SO	SHO	ERA
		26	71	83	.461	31	154	154	30	1368	1399	606	855	7	4.47
Johnny Podres	L	25	13	15	.464	1	39	31	10	210	208	78	143	2	3.73
Don Drysdale	R	21	12	13	.480	0	44	29	6	212	214	72	131	1	4.16
Sandy Koufax	L	22	11	11	.500	1	40	26	5	159	132	105	131	0	4.47
Stan Williams	R	21	9	7	.563	0	27	21	3	119	119	65	80	2	4.01
Clem Labine	R	31	6	6	.500	14	52	2	0	104	112	33	43	0	4.15
Fred Kipp	L	26	6	6	.500	0	40	9	0	102	107	45	58	0	5.03
Carl Erskine	R	31	4	4	.500	0	22	9	2	98	115	35	54	1	5.14
2 Johnny Klippstein	R	31	4	5	.444	3	45	0	0	90	81	44	73	0	4.50
Roger Craig	R	28	2	1	.667	0	11	2	1	32	30	12	16	0	4.50
Danny McDevitt	L	25	2	6	.250	0	13	10	2	48	71	31	26	0	7.50
Don Bessent (SA)	R	27	1	0	1.000	0	19	0	0	24	24	17	13	0	3.38
Bob Giallombardo	L	21	1	1	.500	0	5	1	0	12	12	11	11	0	3.81
Ralph Mauriello	R	23	1	1	.500	0	3	1	0	12	10	8	11	0	4.50
Babe Birrer	R	28	0	0	—	1	16	0	0	34	43	7	16	0	4.50
Larry Sherry	R	22	0	0	—	0	5	0	0	5	4	7	2	0	13.50
Ron Negray	R	28	0	0	—	0	2	0	0	2	4	1	2	0	7.36
Jackie Collum	L	31	0	0	—	0	3	0	0	3	4	2	0	0	9.00
Ed Roebuck	R	26	0	0	.000	0	32	0	0	44	45	15	26	0	3.48
1 Don Newcombe	R	32	0	6	.000	0	11	8	1	34	53	16	15	0	7.94

PHILADELPHIA 8th 69-85 .448 23   MAYO SMITH 39-45 .464   EDDIE SAWYER 30-40 .429

NAME	G by Pos	B	AGE	G	AB	R	H	2B	3B	HR	RBI	BB	SO	SB	BA	SA
TOTALS			29	154	5363	664	1424	238	56	124	630	573	871	51	.266	.400
Ed Bouchee (IL)	1B89	L	25	89	334	55	86	19	5	9	39	51	74	1	.257	.425
Solly Hemus	2B84, 3B1	L	35	105	334	53	95	14	3	8	36	51	34	3	.284	.416
Chico Fernandez	SS148	R	26	148	522	38	120	18	5	6	51	37	48	12	.230	.318
Willie Jones	3B110, 1B1	R	28	118	398	52	108	15	1	14	60	49	45	1	.271	.420
Wally Post	OF91	R	28	110	379	51	107	21	3	12	62	32	74	0	.282	.449
Richie Ashburn	OF152	L	31	152	615	98	215	24	13	2	33	97	48	30	.350	.441
Harry Anderson	OF87, 1B49	L	26	140	515	80	155	34	6	23	97	59	95	1	.301	.524
Stan Lopata	C80	R	32	86	258	36	64	9	0	9	33	60	63	0	.248	.388
Ted Kazanski	2B59, SS22, 3B16	R	24	95	289	21	66	12	2	3	35	22	34	0	.228	.315
Dave Philley	OF24, 1B18	B	38	91	207	30	64	11	4	3	31	15	20	1	.309	.444
Bob Bowman	OF57	R	27	91	184	31	53	11	2	8	24	16	30	0	.288	.500
Rip Repulski	OF56	R	29	85	238	33	58	9	4	13	40	15	47	0	.244	.479
2 Carl Sawatski	C53	L	30	60	183	12	42	4	1	5	12	16	42	0	.230	.344
Chuck Essegian	OF30	R	26	39	114	15	28	5	2	5	16	12	34	0	.246	.456
Granny Hamner (KJ)	3B22, 2B11, SS3	R	31	33	133	18	40	7	3	2	18	8	16	0	.301	.444
Bobby Young	2B21	L	33	32	60	7	14	1	1	1	3	5	5	0	.233	.333
Pancho Herrera	3B16, 1B11	R	24	29	63	5	17	2	5	0	7	6	15	1	.270	.365
2 Jim Hegan	C25	R	37	25	59	5	13	6	0	1	6	16	16	0	.220	.322
Joe Lonnett	C15	R	31	17	50	0	7	2	0	0	2	3	9	0	.140	.180

Jimmie Coker 22 R 1-6, Roy Smalley 32 R 0-2, Mack Burk (MS) 23 R 0-1

NAME	T	AGE	W	L	PCT	SV	G	GS	CG	IP	H	BB	SO	SHO	ERA
		28	69	85	.448	15	154	154	51	1397	1480	446	778	6	4.32
Robin Roberts	R	31	17	14	.548	0	35	34	21	270	270	51	130	1	3.23
Ray Semproch	R	27	13	11	.542	0	36	30	12	204	211	58	92	2	3.93
Jack Sanford	R	29	10	13	.435	0	38	27	7	186	197	81	106	2	4.45
Dick Farrell	R	24	8	9	.471	11	54	0	0	94	84	40	73	0	3.35
Curt Simmons	L	29	7	14	.333	1	29	27	7	168	196	40	78	1	4.39
Jim Hearn	R	37	3	6	.333	2	37	5	1	90	77	33	87	0	3.60
Jack Meyer	R	26	3	6	.333	2	37	5	1	90	77	33	77	0	3.60
Don Cardwell	R	22	3	3	.500	0	16	14	3	108	99	37	77	0	4.50
Jim Owens (MS)	R	24	1	0	1.000	0	1	1	0	7	4	5	3	0	2.57
Bob Miller	R	32	1	1	.500	0	17	0	0	22	36	9	9	0	11.86
Seth Morehead	L	23	1	6	.143	0	27	11	0	92	121	26	54	0	5.87
John Gray	R	30	0	0	—	0	15	0	0	17	12	14	10	0	4.24
John Anderson	R	28	0	0	—	0	9	0	0	16	26	4	9	0	7.88
Angelo LiPetri	R	28	0	0	—	0	4	0	0	6	1	0	3	0	11.25
Bob Conley	R	24	0	0	—	0	2	0	0	2	6	1	0	0	7.88
1 Tom Qualters	R	23	0	0	—	0	1	0	0	2	2	4	1	0	3.00
Hank Mason	R	27	0	0	—	0	2	0	0	2	1	3	0	0	10.80
Warren Hacker	R	33	0	1	.000	0	12	0	0	11	24	8	4	0	7.41
Don Erickson	R	26	0	1	.000	0	12	0	0	11	11	9	9	0	4.50

WORLD SERIES — NEW YORK (AL) 4 MILWAUKEE (NL) 3

LINE SCORES

TEAM	1	2	3	4	5	6	7	8	9	10	11	12	R	H	E
Game 1				October 1 at Milwaukee											
NY (AL)	0	0	0	1	2	0	0	0	0	0			3	8	1
MIL (NL)	0	0	0	2	0	0	1	0	1				4	10	0

Ford, Duren (8)   Spahn

TEAM	1	2	3	4	5	6	7	8	9				R	H	E
Game 2				October 2 at Milwaukee											
NY	1	0	0	0	0	0	0	0	3				5	7	0
MIL	7	1	0	0	0	0	2	3	X				13	15	1

Turley, Maas (1), Kucks (1), Dickson (5), Monroe (8)   Burdette

TEAM	1	2	3	4	5	6	7	8	9				R	H	E
Game 3				October 4 at New York											
MIL	0	0	0	0	0	0	0	0	0				0	6	0
NY	0	0	0	0	2	0	2	0	X				4	4	0

Rush, McMahon (7)   Larsen, Duren (8)

TEAM	1	2	3	4	5	6	7	8	9				R	H	E
Game 4				October 5 at New York											
MIL	0	0	0	0	0	1	1	1	0				3	9	0
NY	0	0	0	0	0	0	0	0	0				0	2	1

Spahn   Ford, Kucks (8), Dickson (9)

TEAM	1	2	3	4	5	6	7	8	9				R	H	E
Game 5				October 6 at New York											
MIL	0	0	0	0	0	0	0	0	0				0	5	0
NY	0	0	1	0	0	6	0	0	X				7	10	0

Burdette, Pizarro (6), Willey (8)   Turley

TEAM	1	2	3	4	5	6	7	8	9	10			R	H	E
Game 6				October 8 at Milwaukee											
NY	1	0	0	0	0	0	1	0	0	2			4	10	1
MIL	1	1	0	0	0	0	0	0	0	1			3	10	4

Ford, Ditmar (2), Duren (6), Turley (10)   Spahn, McMahon (10)

TEAM	1	2	3	4	5	6	7	8	9				R	H	E
Game 7				October 9 at Milwaukee											
NY	0	2	0	0	0	0	0	4	0				6	8	0
MIL	0	0	0	1	0	0	0	0	1				2	5	2

Larsen, Turley (3)   Burdette, McMahon (9)

COMPOSITE BATTING

NAME	POS	G	AB	R	H	2B	3B	HR	RBI	BA
New York (AL) Totals		7	233	29	49	5	1	10	29	.210
Bauer	OF	7	31	6	10	0	0	4	8	.323
McDougald	2B	7	28	5	9	2	0	2	4	.321
Skowron	1B	7	27	3	7	0	0	2	7	.259
Berra	C	7	27	3	6	3	0	0	2	.222
Mantle	OF	7	24	4	6	0	1	2	3	.250
Kubek	SS	7	21	0	1	0	0	0	0	.048
Howard	OF	6	18	4	4	0	0	2	2	.222
Lumpe	3B-SS	6	12	0	2	0	0	0	0	.167
Carey	3B	5	12	1	1	0	0	0	0	.083
Siebern	OF	3	8	1	1	0	0	0	0	.125
Turley	P	3	5	0	1	0	0	0	2	.200
Richardson	3B	3	5	0	0	0	0	0	0	.000
Ford	P	3	4	1	0	0	0	0	0	.000
Duren	P	3	4	0	0	0	0	0	0	.000
Slaughter	PH	4	4	0	0	0	0	0	0	.000
Larsen	P	2	2	0	0	0	0	0	0	.000
Kucks	P	2	1	0	1	0	0	0	0	1.000
Throneberry	PH	1	1	0	0	0	0	0	0	.000
Ditmar	P	2	1	0	0	0	0	0	0	.000
Dickson	P	2	0	0	0	0	0	0	0	—
Maas	P	1	0	0	0	0	0	0	0	—
Monroe	P	1	0	0	0	0	0	0	0	—
Milwaukee (NL) Totals		7	240	25	60	10	1	3	24	.250
Schoendienst	2B	7	30	5	9	3	0	0	0	.300
Aaron	OF	7	27	3	9	2	0	0	2	.333
Covington	OF	7	26	2	7	0	0	0	4	.269
Mathews	3B	7	25	3	4	0	0	3	1	.160
Logan	SS	7	25	3	3	0	0	0	2	.120
Crandall	C	7	25	4	6	0	0	1	2	.240
Bruton	OF	7	17	2	7	1	0	0	2	.412
Torre	1B	7	17	0	3	0	0	0	0	.176
Adcock	1B	4	13	1	4	0	0	0	3	.308
Spahn	P	3	12	0	4	0	0	1	2	.333
Pafko	OF	4	9	0	3	0	0	0	1	.333
Burdette	P	3	9	1	1	0	0	1	2	.111
Hanebrink	PH	2	3	0	0	0	0	0	0	.000
Rush	P	1	3	0	0	0	0	0	0	.000
Wise	PH	2	2	0	0	0	0	0	0	.000
Mantilla	SS	3	3	0	0	0	0	0	0	.000
McMahon	P	3	0	0	0	0	0	0	0	—
Pizarro	P	1	0	0	0	0	0	0	0	—
Willey	P	1	0	0	0	0	0	0	0	—

COMPOSITE PITCHING

NAME	G	IP	H	BB	SO	W	L	SV	ERA
New York (AL) Totals	7	63.2	60	27	56	4	3	2	3.39
Turley	4	16.1	10	7	13	2	1	1	2.76
Ford	3	15.1	19	5	16	0	1	0	4.11
Larsen	2	9.1	9	6	9	1	0	0	0.96
Duren	3	9.1	7	6	14	1	1	1	1.93
Kucks	2	4.1	4	0	1	0	0	0	2.08
Dickson	2	4	2	4	0	1	0	0	4.50
Ditmar	1	3.2	9	2	2	0	0	0	27.00
Monroe	1	1	1	0	0	0	0	0	27.00
Maas	1	0.1	2	1	0	0	0	0	81.00
Milwaukee (NL) Totals	7	63	49	21	42	3	4	0	3.71
Spahn	3	28.2	19	8	18	2	1	0	2.20
Burdette	3	22.1	22	4	12	1	2	0	5.64
Rush	1	6	3	5	2	0	0	0	3.00
McMahon	3	3.1	3	3	5	0	0	0	5.40
Pizarro	1	1.2	3	1	0	0	0	0	5.40
Willey	1	1	0	2	0	0	0	0	0.00

1959 Don't Count Your Pennants Until They Hatch

Late in the season, San Francisco Giant officials were considering whether to play the World Series in Seals Stadium or to open the still-unfinished Candlestick Park. With eight games remaining on the schedule, the Giants led the Braves and Dodgers by two games. A decision would have to be made soon. It was, but not in the Giants' front office. The Dodgers came into Seals Stadium on the weekend of September 19-20, and bumped off the Jints three straight times, sending them reeling into third place. Milwaukee kept pace with the Dodgers the final week, each team winning and losing on alternate days, while the Giants were dropping four out of five to the Cubs and Cards, making it seven losses in their final eight games. On Sunday, Roger Craig and Bob Buhl hurled victories to end the National League race in a tie for the third time. The three-game play-off only went two games, as the Dodgers beat the Braves two straight to take the pennant and break their post-season jinx, after having been the victims in 1946 and 1951.

Shooting from seventh to the top in one year, the heart of the team consisted of two old Brooklyn veterans, one young veteran, one newly acquired veteran, and three mid-season recalls from Spokane. Duke Snider and Gil Hodges provided power, Don Drysdale won 17 games, and ex-Cardinal Wally Moon hit .302 with 74 RBI's. Roger Craig fit into the starting rotation, Larry Sherry was a strong reliever, and Maury Wills plugged a gaping hole in the infield at shortstop. A blend of old and new, the Dodgers had no standout stars, unlike their rivals. Hank Aaron and Eddie Mathews were the Brave offense; Spahn, Burdette, and Buhl were the hill staff. Willie Mays and Orlando Cepeda carried the Giant attack, joined in August by a young powerhouse named Willie McCovey. The Giants' five-man pitching staff of Johnny Antonelli, Sam Jones, Jack Sanford, Mike McCormick, and Stu Miller collapsed in the stretch due to overuse by manager Bill Rigney. The trailing teams boasted of a second straight MVP in Ernie Banks of Chicago—and the Pirates had an 18-1 relief pitcher in Elroy Face and a superb performance from Harvey Haddix, who threw 12 perfect innings only to be defeated in the 13th.

For once, all was not ho-hum in the American League. The fact that it was not became clear on May 20, when the New York Yankees shocked the world by falling into last place. While Cleveland and Chicago were fighting over first, the heavily-favored Yankees trailed the lowly Senators. New York was able to climb back into contention but never could forge ahead of the White Sox or Indians. The Go-Go Sox, with a high-octane running team, took over first for keeps on July 28, but could shake the Indians only by sweeping a four-game series from them August 28-30. MVP Nellie Fox and Luis Aparicio ran the guerrilla attack and provided an air-tight defense. Jim Landis and Sherm Lollar also starred, while 39-year-old Early Wynn won 22 games, Bob Shaw won 18 games and a starter's job, and oldsters Gerry Staley and Turk Lown provided solid relief work. Ted Kluszewski came over from the National League on waivers August 25, and provided punch in the stretch. Although Cleveland paced the loop in homers and batting, their pitching was no match for Chicago; Rocky Colavito belted 42 home runs for the Tribe, while Tito Francona hit .363 after coming off the bench.

The White Sox expected to run on the Dodgers in the World Series, but catcher Johnny Roseboro's arm put an end to Al Lopez's ideas. After Ted Kluszewski led Chicago to an 11-0 first-game victory, the Dodgers took four of the next five games behind Larry Sherry's two wins and two saves, to give California a championship in its second year in the majors.

The year also saw old-timers Stan Musial and Ted Williams experience the first off-seasons in their long careers, as both became part-time players. Another old-timer, former Brooklyn general manager Branch Rickey, attempted a comeback as president of the proposed Continental League. The threat of a new major league painfully forced big league owners to consider expansion—a move which baseball had avoided for 58 years.

1959 AMERICAN LEAGUE

NAME	G by Pos	B	AGE	G	AB	R	H	2B	3B	HR	RBI	BB	SO	SB	BA	SA
CHICAGO	1st 94-60 .610															AL LOPEZ
TOTALS			30	156	5297	669	1325	220	46	97	620	580	634	113	.250	.364
Earl Torgeson	1B103	L	35	127	277	40	61	5	3	9	45	62	55	7	.220	.357
Nellie Fox	2B156	L	31	156	624	84	191	34	6	2	70	71	13	5	.306	.389
Luis Aparicio	SS152	R	25	152	612	98	157	18	5	6	51	53	40	56	.257	.332
Bubba Phillips	3B100, OF23	R	29	117	379	43	100	27	1	5	40	27	28	1	.264	.380
Jim McAnany	OF67	R	22	67	210	22	58	9	3	0	27	19	26	2	.276	.348
Jim Landis	OF148	R	25	149	515	78	140	26	7	5	60	78	68	20	.272	.379
Al Smith	OF128, 3B1	R	31	129	472	65	112	16	4	17	55	46	74	7	.237	.396
Sherm Lollar	C122, 1B24	R	34	140	505	63	134	22	3	22	84	55	49	4	.265	.451
Billy Goodman	3B74, 2B3	L	33	104	268	21	67	14	1	1	28	19	20	3	.250	.321
Jim Rivera	OF69	L	36	80	177	18	39	4	4	4	19	11	19	5	.220	.384
Sammy Esposito	3B45, SS14, 2B2	R	27	69	66	12	11	1	0	1	5	11	16	0	.167	.227
Norm Cash	1B31	L	24	58	104	16	25	0	1	4	16	18	9	1	.240	.375
Johnny Romano	C38	R	24	53	126	20	37	5	1	5	25	23	18	0	.294	.468
Johnny Callison	OF41	L	20	49	104	12	18	3	0	3	12	13	20	0	.173	.288
2 Harry Simpson	OF12, 1B1	L	33	38	75	5	14	5	1	2	13	4	14	0	.187	.360
2 Ted Kluszewski	1B29	L	34	31	101	11	30	2	1	2	10	9	10	0	.297	.396
2 Del Ennis	OF25	R	34	26	96	10	21	6	0	2	7	4	10	0	.219	.344
Earl Battey	C20	R	24	26	64	9	14	1	2	2	7	8	13	0	.219	.391
2 Larry Doby (BN)	OF12, 1B2	L	35	21	58	1	14	1	1	0	9	2	13	1	.241	.293
Ron Jackson	1B5	R	25	10	14	3	3	1	0	1	2	1	0	0	.214	.500
1 Ray Boone	1B6	R	35	9	21	3	5	0	0	1	3	6	3	0	.238	.381

Lou Skizas 27 R 1-13, Joe Hicks 26 L 3-7, Don Mueller 32 L 2-4, J. C. Martin 22 L 1-4, Cam Carreon 21 R 0-1

NAME	T	AGE	W	L	PCT	SV	G	GS	CG	IP	H	BB	SO	SHO	ERA
		32	94	60	.610	36	156	156	44	1425	1297	525	761	13	3.29
Early Wynn	R	39	22	10	.688	0	37	37	14	256	202	119	179	5	3.16
Bob Shaw	R	26	18	6	.750	3	47	26	8	231	217	54	89	3	2.69
Billy Pierce	L	32	14	15	.483	0	34	33	12	224	217	62	114	2	3.62
Turk Lown	R	35	9	2	.818	15	60	0	0	93	73	42	63	0	2.90
Dick Donovan	R	31	9	10	.474	0	31	29	5	180	171	58	71	1	3.65
Gerry Staley	R	38	8	5	.615	14	67	0	0	116	111	25	54	0	2.25
Barry Latman	R	23	8	5	.615	0	37	21	5	156	138	72	97	2	3.75
Ray Moore	R	33	3	6	.333	0	29	8	0	90	86	46	49	0	4.10
Rudy Arias	L	28	2	0	1.000	2	34	0	0	44	49	20	28	0	4.09
Joe Stanka	R	27	1	0	1.000	0	2	0	0	5	2	4	3	0	3.60
1 Don Rudolph	L	27	0	1	—	0	4	0	0	3	4	2	0	0	0.00
Claude Raymond	R	22	0	0	—	0	3	0	0	4	5	2	1	0	9.00
Gary Peters	L	22	0	0	—	0	2	0	0	1	2	2	1	0	0.00
Ken McBride	R	23	0	1	.000	0	11	2	0	23	20	17	12	0	3.13

NAME	G by Pos	B	AGE	G	AB	R	H	2B	3B	HR	RBI	BB	SO	SB	BA	SA
CLEVELAND	2nd 89-65 .578 5															JOE GORDON
TOTALS			29	154	5288	745	1390	216	25	167	682	433	721	33	.263	.408
Vic Power	1B121, 2B21, 3B7	R	31	147	595	102	172	31	6	10	60	40	22	9	.289	.412
Billy Martin (SJ-BY)	2B67, 3B4	R	31	73	242	37	63	7	0	9	24	8	18	0	.260	.401
Woodie Held	SS103, 3B40, OF6, 2B3	R	27	143	525	82	132	19	3	29	71	46	118	1	.251	.465
George Strickland	3B80, SS50, 2B4	R	33	132	441	55	105	15	2	4	48	51	64	1	.238	.302
Rocky Colavito	OF154	R	25	154	588	90	151	24	0	42	111	71	86	3	.257	.512
Jimmy Piersall	OF91, 3B1	R	29	100	317	42	78	13	2	4	30	25	31	6	.246	.338
Minnie Minoso	OF148	R	36	148	570	92	172	32	0	21	92	54	46	8	.302	.468
Russ Nixon	C74	L	24	82	258	23	62	10	3	1	29	15	28	0	.240	.314
Tito Francona	OF64, 1B35	L	25	122	399	68	145	17	2	20	79	35	42	2	.363	.566
2 Jim Baxes	2B48, 3B22	R	30	77	247	35	59	11	0	15	34	21	47	0	.239	.466
2 Ed Fitz Gerald (BG)	C45	R	35	49	129	12	35	6	1	1	4	12	14	0	.271	.357
Dick Brown	C48	R	24	48	141	15	31	7	0	5	16	11	39	0	.220	.376
Ray Webster	2B24, 3B4	R	21	40	74	10	15	2	1	2	10	5	7	1	.203	.338
Elmer Valo	OF2	L	38	34	24	3	7	0	0	0	5	7	0	0	.292	.292
Carroll Hardy	OF15	R	26	32	53	12	11	1	0	0	2	3	7	1	.208	.226
2 Granny Hamner	SS10, 2B7, 3B5	R	32	27	67	4	11	1	1	1	3	1	8	0	.164	.254
1 Hal Naragon	C10	L	30	14	36	6	10	4	1	0	5	3	0	0	.278	.444
Chuck Tanner	OF10	L	29	14	48	6	12	2	0	1	5	2	9	0	.250	.354
Gene Leek	3B13, SS1	R	22	13	36	7	8	3	0	1	5	2	9	0	.222	.389

2 Willie Jones 33 R 4-18, Don Dillard 22 L 4-10, Billy Moran 25 R 5-17, 1 Jim Bolger 27 R 0-7, Gordy Coleman 24 L 8-15, 1 Randy Jackson 33 R 1-7

NAME	T	AGE	W	L	PCT	SV	G	GS	CG	IP	H	BB	SO	SHO	ERA
		27	89	65	.578	23	154	154	58	1384	1230	635	799	7	3.75
Cal McLish	R	33	19	8	.704	1	35	32	13	235	253	72	113	0	3.64
Gary Bell	R	22	16	11	.593	5	44	28	12	234	208	105	136	1	4.04
Jim Perry	R	23	12	10	.545	4	44	13	8	153	122	55	79	2	2.65
Mudcat Grant	R	23	10	7	.588	3	38	19	6	165	140	81	85	1	4.15
Herb Score	L	26	9	11	.450	0	30	25	9	161	123	115	147	1	4.70
3 Jack Harshman	R	31	5	1	.833	1	13	6	5	66	46	13	35	1	2.59
Don Ferrarese	L	30	5	3	.625	0	15	10	4	76	58	51	45	0	3.20
Al Cicotte	R	29	3	1	.750	1	26	1	0	44	46	25	23	0	5.32
Bobby Locke	R	25	3	2	.600	2	24	7	0	78	66	41	40	0	3.12
Mike Garcia	R	35	3	6	.333	1	29	8	1	72	72	31	49	0	4.00
Dick Brodowski	R	26	2	2	.500	5	18	0	0	30	19	21	9	0	1.80
1 Humberto Robinson	R	29	1	0	1.000	0	5	0	0	9	4	4	6	0	4.00
Jake Striker	L	25	1	0	1.000	0	1	1	0	7	8	4	5	0	2.57
2 Riverboat Smith	L	31	0	1	.000	0	12	3	0	29	31	12	17	0	5.28
Bud Podbielan	R	35	0	0	—	0	6	0	0	12	17	2	5	0	6.00
Johnny Briggs	R	25	0	0	.000	0	4	0	0	13	12	3	5	0	2.08

NAME	G by Pos	B	AGE	G	AB	R	H	2B	3B	HR	RBI	BB	SO	SB	BA	SA
NEW YORK	3rd 79-75 .513 15															CASEY STENGEL
TOTALS			28	155	5379	687	1397	224	40	153	651	457	828	45	.260	.402
Bill Skowron (XJ)	1B72	R	28	74	282	39	84	13	5	15	59	20	47	1	.298	.539
Bobby Richardson	2B109, SS14, 3B12	R	23	134	469	53	141	18	6	2	33	26	20	5	.301	.377
Tony Kubek	SS67, OF53, 3B17, 2B1	R	22	132	512	67	143	25	7	6	51	24	46	3	.279	.391
2 Hector Lopez	3B76, OF35	R	29	112	406	60	115	16	2	16	69	28	54	3	.283	.451
Hank Bauer	OF111	R	36	114	341	44	81	20	0	9	39	33	54	4	.238	.375
Mickey Mantle	OF143	R	27	144	541	104	154	23	4	31	75	93	126	21	.285	.514
Norm Siebern	OF93, 1B2	L	25	120	380	52	103	17	0	11	53	41	71	3	.271	.403
Yogi Berra	C116, OF7	L	34	131	472	64	134	25	1	19	69	43	38	1	.284	.462
Gil McDougald	2B53, SS52, 3B25	R	31	127	434	44	109	16	8	4	34	35	40	0	.251	.353
Elston Howard	1B50, C43, OF28	R	30	125	443	59	121	24	6	18	73	20	67	0	.273	.476
Marv Throneberry	1B54, OF13	L	25	80	192	27	46	5	0	8	22	18	51	0	.240	.391
1 Enos Slaughter	OF7	L	44	74	99	10	17	2	6	2	21	13	19	1	.172	.374
Johnny Blanchard	C12, OF8, 1B1	L	26	49	59	6	10	3	0	1	7	7	12	0	.169	.288
Clete Boyer	SS26, 3B16	R	22	47	114	4	20	7	0	0	4	8	22	0	.175	.193
Andy Carey (IL)	3B34	R	27	41	101	10	26	1	0	3	9	5	17	1	.257	.356
Fritzie Brickell	SS15, 2B3	R	24	18	39	4	10	1	0	1	4	1	10	0	.256	.359
1 Jerry Lumpe	3B12, SS4, 2B1	L	26	18	45	2	10	2	0	0	2	6	5	0	.222	.222
2 Jim Pisoni	OF15	R	29	17	17	2	3	0	1	1	5	3	9	1	.176	.294

Gordie Windhorn 25 R 0-11, Ken Hunt 24 R 4-12

NAME	T	AGE	W	L	PCT	SV	G	GS	CG	IP	H	BB	SO	SHO	ERA
		28	79	75	.513	28	155	155	38	1399	1281	594	836	15	3.60
Whitey Ford	L	30	16	10	.615	1	35	29	9	204	194	89	114	2	3.04
Duke Maas	R	30	14	8	.636	4	38	21	3	138	149	53	67	1	4.43
Art Ditmar	R	30	13	9	.591	1	38	25	7	202	156	52	96	1	2.90
Bob Turley	R	28	8	11	.421	0	33	22	7	154	141	83	111	3	4.32
Bobby Shantz	L	33	7	3	.700	3	33	4	2	95	64	33	66	2	2.37
Jim Coates	R	26	6	1	.857	3	37	4	2	100	89	36	64	0	2.88
Don Larsen	R	29	6	7	.462	0	25	18	3	125	122	76	69	1	4.32
Ryne Duren	R	30	3	6	.333	14	41	0	0	77	49	43	96	0	1.87
2 Ralph Terry	R	23	3	7	.300	0	24	16	5	127	130	50	55	1	3.40
Eli Grba	R	24	2	5	.286	0	19	6	0	50	52	39	23	0	6.48
John Gabler	R	28	1	1	.500	0	3	0	0	10	11	11	0	0	2.84
Zack Monroe	R	27	0	0	—	0	3	0	0	3	6	1	0	0	6.00
2 Mark Freeman	R	28	0	0	—	0	4	0	0	2	2	3	1	0	2.57
2 Gary Blaylock	R	27	0	0	.000	0	15	1	0	26	30	15	20	0	3.46
1 Johnny Kucks	R	25	0	0	—	0	6	0	0	11	7	6	3	0	8.47
1 Tom Sturdivant	R	29	0	2	—	0	15	2	0	35	20	16	21	0	5.04
Jim Bronstad	R	23	0	0	.000	0	9	1	0	34	33	13	14	0	5.28

DETROIT — 4th 76-78 .494 18 — BILL NORMAN 2-15 .118 — JIMMY DYKES 74-63 .540

NAME	G by Pos	B	AGE	G	AB	R	H	2B	3B	HR	RBI	BB	SO	SB	BA	SA
TOTALS			28	154	5211	713	1346	196	30	160	667	580	737	34	.258	.400
Gail Harris	1B93	L	27	114	349	39	77	4	3	9	39	29	49	0	.221	.327
Frank Bolling	2B126	R	27	127	459	56	122	18	3	13	55	45	37	2	.266	.403
Rocky Bridges	SS110, 2B5	R	31	116	381	38	102	16	3	3	35	30	35	1	.268	.349
Eddie Yost	3B146, 2B1	R	32	148	521	115	145	19	0	21	61	135	77	0	.278	.436
Harvey Kuenn	OF137	R	28	139	561	99	198	42	7	9	71	48	37	7	.353	.501
Al Kaline	OF136	R	24	136	511	86	167	19	2	27	94	72	42	10	.327	.530
Charlie Maxwell	OF136	L	32	145	518	81	130	12	2	31	95	81	91	2	.251	.461
Lou Berberet	C95	R	29	100	338	38	73	8	2	13	44	35	59	0	.216	.367
Bobo Osborne	1B56, OF1	L	23	86	209	27	40	7	1	3	21	16	41	1	.191	.278
Coot Veal	SS72	R	26	77	89	12	18	1	0	1	15	8	7	0	.202	.247
2 Ted Lepcio	SS35, 2B24, 3B11	R	28	76	215	25	60	8	0	7	24	17	49	2	.279	.414
Red Wilson	C64	R	30	67	228	28	60	17	2	4	35	10	23	2	.263	.408
Neil Chrisley	OF21	L	27	65	106	7	14	3	0	6	11	12	10	0	.132	.330
Gus Zernial	1B32, OF1	R	26	60	132	11	30	4	0	7	26	7	27	0	.227	.417
Johnny Groth	OF41	R	32	55	102	12	24	7	1	1	10	7	14	0	.235	.353
1 Larry Doby	OF16	L	35	18	55	5	12	3	1	0	4	8	9	0	.218	.309
Steve Demeter	3B4	R	24	11	18	1	2	1	0	0	1	0	1	0	.111	.167

Ossie Alvarez 25 R 1-2, Ron Shoop 27 R 1-7, Charlie Lau 26 L 1-6

NAME	T	AGE	W	L	PCT	SV	G	GS	CG	IP	H	BB	SO	SHO	ERA
		28	76	78	.494	24	154	154	53	1360	1327	432	829	9	4.20
Don Mossi	L	30	17	9	.654	0	34	30	15	228	210	49	125	3	3.36
Frank Lary	R	29	17	10	.630	0	32	32	11	223	225	46	137	3	3.55
Jim Bunning	R	27	17	13	.567	1	40	35	14	250	220	75	201	1	3.89
Paul Foytack	R	28	14	14	.500	1	39	37	11	240	239	64	110	2	4.65
Ray Narleski	R	30	4	12	.250	5	42	10	1	104	105	59	71	0	5.80
Jerry Davie	R	26	2	2	.500	0	11	5	1	37	40	17	20	0	4.14
1 Billy Hoeft	L	27	1	1	.500	0	2	2	0	9	6	4	2	0	5.00
Barney Schultz	R	32	1	3	.333	1	20	0	0	18	17	14	17	0	4.50
2 Dave Sisler	R	27	1	3	.250	7	32	0	0	52	46	36	29	0	3.98
Pete Burnside	L	28	1	3	.250	1	30	0	0	62	55	25	49	0	3.77
Tom Morgan	R	29	1	4	.200	9	46	1	0	93	94	18	39	0	3.97
George Susce	R	27	0	0	—	0	3			15	24	9	9	0	12.60
Jim Stump	R	27	0	0	—	0	9	0	0	11	12	4	6	0	2.45
Hank Aguirre	L	28	0	0	—	0	3	0	0	3	4	3	3	0	3.00
Bob Bruce	R	26	0	1	.000	0	2	1	0	2	2	3	1	0	9.00
Jim Proctor	R	23	0	1	.000	0	2	1	0	3	8	3	0	0	15.00
2 Bob Smith	R	28	0	3	.000	0	9	0	0	11	20	3	10	0	8.18

BOSTON — 5th 75-79 .487 19 — PINKY HIGGINS 31-42 .425 — RUDY YORK 0-1 .000 — BILLY JURGES 44-36 .550

NAME	G by Pos	B	AGE	G	AB	R	H	2B	3B	HR	RBI	BB	SO	SB	BA	SA
TOTALS			27	154	5225	726	1335	248	28	155	671	626	810	68	.256	.385
Dick Gernert	1B75, OF25	R	30	117	298	41	78	14	1	11	42	52	49	1	.262	.426
Pete Runnels	2B101, 1B44, SS9	L	31	147	560	95	176	33	6	6	57	95	48	6	.314	.427
Don Buddin	SS150	R	25	151	485	75	117	24	1	10	53	92	99	6	.241	.357
Frank Malzone	3B154	R	29	154	604	90	169	34	2	19	92	42	58	6	.280	.437
Jackie Jensen	OF146	R	32	148	535	101	148	31	0	28	112	88	67	20	.277	.492
Gary Geiger	OF95	L	22	120	335	45	82	10	4	11	48	21	55	9	.245	.397
Ted Williams	OF76	L	40	103	272	32	69	15	0	10	43	52	27	0	.254	.419
Sammy White	C119	R	31	119	377	34	107	13	4	1	42	23	39	4	.284	.347
Marty Keough	OF69, 1B3	L	25	96	251	40	61	13	5	7	27	26	40	3	.243	.418
Vic Wertz	1B64	L	34	94	247	38	68	13	0	7	49	22	32	0	.275	.413
Gene Stephens (BA)	OF85	L	26	92	270	34	75	13	1	3	39	29	33	5	.278	.367
Pete Daley	C58	R	29	65	169	9	38	7	0	1	11	13	31	1	.225	.284
Jim Busby	OF34	R	32	61	102	16	23	8	0	1	5	5	18	0	.225	.333
Pumpsie Green	2B45, SS1	R	25	50	172	30	40	6	3	1	10	29	22	4	.233	.320
Jim Mahoney	SS30	R	25	31	23	10	3	0	0	0	4	3	7	0	.130	.261
2 Bobby Avila	2B11	R	35	22	45	7	11	0	0	3	6	6	11	0	.244	.444
Bill Renna	OF7	R	34	14	22	2	2	0	0	0	2	5	6	0	.091	.091

1 Billy Consolo 24 R 3-14, Jerry Mallett 23 R 4-15, Haywood Sullivan 28 R 0-2, 1 Ted Lepcio 28 R 1-3, Don Gile 24 R 2-10, 2 Herb Plews 31 L 1-12

NAME	T	AGE	W	L	PCT	SV	G	GS	CG	IP	H	BB	SO	SHO	ERA
		27	75	79	.487	25	154	154	38	1364	1386	589	724	9	4.17
Jerry Casale	R	25	13	8	.619	0	31	26	9	180	162	89	93	3	4.30
Ike Delock	R	29	11	6	.647	0	28	17	4	134	120	62	55	0	2.96
Tom Brewer	R	27	10	12	.455	2	26	32	11	215	219	88	121	3	3.77
Frank Sullivan	R	29	9	11	.450	1	30	26	5	178	172	67	107	2	3.94
Bill Monbouquette	R	22	7	7	.500	0	34	17	4	152	165	33	87	0	4.14
Frank Baumann	L	26	6	4	.600	1	26	10	2	96	96	55	48	0	4.03
Mike Fornieles	R	27	5	3	.625	11	46	0	0	82	77	29	54	0	3.07
Nels Chittum	R	26	3	0	1.000	0	21	0	0	30	29	11	12	0	1.20
Leo Kiely	L	29	3	3	.500	7	41	0	0	56	67	18	30	0	4.18
2 Jack Harshman	L	31	2	3	.400	0	8	2	0	25	29	10	14	0	6.48
13 Murray Wall	R	32	2	5	.286	3	26	0	0	49	57	26	14	0	5.51
Ted Wills	L	25	2	6	.250	0	9	8	2	56	68	24	24	0	5.30
Earl Wilson	R	24	1	1	.500	0	9	4	2	21	21	31	17	0	6.00
2 Al Schroll	R	27	1	4	.200	0	14	5	1	46	47	22	26	0	4.70
1 Dave Sisler	R	27	0	0	—	0	3	0	0	7	9	1	3	0	6.43
Ted Bowsfield	L	23	0	1	.000	0	5	2	0	9	16	9	4	0	15.00
Herb Moford	R	30	0	2	.000	0	9			10	6	7		0	11.00
2 Billy Hoeft	L	27	0	3	.000	0	5	3	0	18	22	8	8	0	5.50

BALTIMORE — 6th 74-80 .481 20 — PAUL RICHARDS

NAME	G by Pos	B	AGE	G	AB	R	H	2B	3B	HR	RBI	BB	SO	SB	BA	SA
TOTALS			30	155	5208	551	1240	182	23	109	514	536	690	36	.238	.345
Bob Boyd	1B109	L	39	128	415	42	110	20	2	3	41	29	14	3	.265	.345
Billy Gardner	2B139, 3B1, SS1	R	31	140	401	34	87	13	2	6	27	38	61	2	.217	.304
Chico Carrasquel	SS89, 2B22, 3B2, 1B1	R	31	114	346	28	77	13	0	4	28	34	41	2	.223	.295
Brooks Robinson	3B87, 2B1	R	22	88	313	29	89	15	2	4	24	17	37	2	.284	.383
Gene Woodling	OF124	L	36	140	440	63	132	22	2	14	77	78	35	1	.300	.455
Willie Tasby	OF137	R	26	142	505	69	126	16	5	13	48	34	80	3	.250	.378
Bob Nieman	OF97	R	32	118	360	49	105	18	2	21	60	42	55	1	.292	.528
Gus Triandos	C125	R	28	126	393	43	85	7	1	25	73	65	56	0	.216	.430
Al Pilarcik	OF106	R	28	130	273	37	77	12	1	3	16	30	25	9	.282	.366
Billy Klaus	SS59, 3B49, 2B1	R	30	104	321	33	80	11	0	3	25	51	38	2	.249	.312
2 Albie Pearson	OF50	R	24	80	138	22	32	4	2	0	6	13	5	4	.232	.290
Joe Ginsberg	C62	R	32	65	166	14	30	2	0	1	14	21	13	1	.181	.211
Willie Miranda	SS47, 3B11, 2B5	B	33	65	88	8	14	5	0	0	7	7	16	0	.159	.216
2 Walt Dropo	1B54, 3B2	R	36	62	151	14	42	9	0	6	21	12	20	0	.278	.457
Jim Finigan	3B42, 2B6, SS2	R	30	48	119	14	30	6	0	1	10	9	10	1	.252	.328
Bob Hale	1B8	L	25	40	54	2	10	3	0	0	7	2	6	0	.185	.241
1 Whitey Lockman	1B22, 2B5, OF1	L	32	38	69	7	15	1	1	0	2	8	4	0	.217	.261
Barry Shetrone	OF23	L	20	33	79	8	16	1	1	0	5	5	9	3	.203	.241
1 Lenny Green	OF23	L	25	27	24	3	7	0	1	0	2	1	3	0	.292	.417
1 Bobby Avila	1B10, 2B8, 3B1	R	35	20	47	1	8	0	0	0	0	4	5	0	.170	.170
Joe Taylor	OF12	R	33	14	32	2	5	1	0	1	2	11	5	0	.156	.281
Jerry Adair	2B11, SS1	R	22	12	35	3	11	0	1	0	4	1	5	0	.314	.371

Fred Valentine 24 B 6-10, Leo Burke 25 R 2-10, Ron Hansen 21 R 0-4, Bob Saverine 18 B 0-0

NAME	T	AGE	W	L	PCT	SV	G	GS	CG	IP	H	BB	SO	SHO	ERA
		27	74	80	.481	30	155	155	45	1400	1290	476	735	15	3.56
Milt Pappas	R	20	15	9	.625	3	33	27	15	209	175	75	120	4	3.27
Hoyt Wilhelm	R	36	15	11	.577	0	32	27	13	226	178	77	139	3	2.19
Hal Brown	R	34	11	9	.550	3	31	21	2	164	158	32	81	0	3.79
Jerry Walker	R	20	11	10	.524	4	30	22	7	182	160	52	100	2	2.92
Billy O'Dell	L	26	10	12	.455	1	38	24	6	199	163	67	88	2	2.94
Ernie Johnson	R	35	4	1	.800	1	31	1	0	50	57	19	29	0	4.14
Billy Loes	R	29	4	7	.364	14	37	0	0	64	58	25	34	0	4.08
Arnie Portocarrero	R	27	2	7	.222	0	27	14	1	90	107	32	23	0	6.80
3 Billy Hoeft	R	27	1	1	.500	0	16	3	0	41	50	19	30	0	5.71
Jack Fisher	R	20	1	6	.143	2	27	7	1	89	76	38	52	1	3.03
Wes Stock	R	25	0	0	—	0	3			13	16	2	8	0	4.00
2 Rip Coleman	L	28	0	0	—	0	3	0	0	4	8	2	2	0	7.88
George Bamberger	R	33	0	0	—	0	3	1	0	8	15	2	2	0	7.00
George Zuverink (SJ)	R	34	0	1	.000	0	6	0	0	13	15	6	1	0	4.15
1 Jack Harshman	L	31	0	6	.000	0	18	6	0	47	58	28	24	0	6.89

KANSAS CITY — 7th 66-88 .429 28 — HARRY CRAFT

NAME	G by Pos	B	AGE	G	AB	R	H	2B	3B	HR	RBI	BB	SO	SB	BA	SA
TOTALS			30	154	5264	681	1383	231	43	117	638	481	780	34	.263	.390
Kent Hadley	1B95	L	24	113	288	40	73	11	1	10	39	24	74	1	.253	.403
Wayne Terwilliger	2B63, SS2, 3B1	R	34	114	307	48	77	11	0	2	18	19	31	2	.267	.361
Joe DeMaestri	SS115	R	30	118	352	31	86	16	5	6	34	20	65	1	.244	.369
Dick Williams	3B80, 1B32, OF23, 2B3	R	30	130	488	72	130	33	1	16	75	28	60	4	.266	.436
Roger Maris (IL)	OF117	L	24	122	433	69	118	21	7	16	72	58	53	2	.273	.464
Bill Tuttle	OF121	R	29	126	461	67	133	19	6	7	43	48	38	10	.300	.413
Bob Cerv	OF119	R	33	125	463	61	132	22	4	20	87	35	87	3	.285	.479
Frank House	C95	R	29	98	347	32	82	14	3	1	30	20	23	0	.236	.303
2 Jerry Lumpe	2B61, SS16	L	26	108	403	47	98	11	5	3	28	41	32	2	.243	.318
Hal Smith	3B77, C22	R	28	108	292	36	84	12	0	5	31	34	39	0	.288	.380
Russ Snyder	OF44	L	25	73	243	41	76	13	2	3	21	19	29	6	.313	.420
2 Ray Boone	1B38, 3B3	R	35	61	132	19	36	6	0	2	12	27	17	1	.273	.364
Preston Ward	1B22, OF1	L	31	58	109	8	27	4	1	2	19	7	12	0	.248	.358
Harry Chiti	C47	R	26	55	162	20	44	11	1	5	25	17	26	0	.272	.444
Zeke Bella	OF25, 1B1	R	28	47	82	10	17	2	1	1	9	9	14	0	.207	.293
Bud Daley	P39	L	26	39	78	5	23	1	0	0	13	2	11	0	.295	.308
Whitey Herzog (IL)	OF34, 1B1	L	27	38	123	25	36	7	1	1	9	34	23	1	.293	.390
1 Hector Lopez	2B33	R	29	35	115	22	38	10	3	6	24	8	23	1	.281	.533
Ned Garver	P32	R	33	32	71	9	20	2	1	2	9	1	7	0	.282	.423
2 Ray Jablonski	3B17	R	32	32	65	4	17	1	0	2	8	3	11	0	.262	.369
2 Joe Morgan	3B2	R	28	21	21	2	4	0	1	0	3	0	5	0	.190	.286
Lou Klimchock	2B16	R	19	17	26	7	7	3	0	1	4	0	13	1	.269	.470

Tommy Carroll 22 R 1-7, 1 Harry Simpson 33 L 4-14, Bob Martyn 28 L 0-1

NAME	T	AGE	W	L	PCT	SV	G	GS	CG	IP	H	BB	SO	SHO	ERA
		30	66	88	.429	21	154	154	44	1361	1452	492	703	8	4.35
Bud Daley	L	26	16	13	.552	1	39	29	12	216	212	62	125	2	3.17
Ray Herbert	R	29	11	11	.500	1	37	26	10	184	196	62	99	2	4.84
Ned Garver	R	33	10	13	.435	1	32	30	9	201	214	42	61	3	3.72
2 Johnny Kucks	R	25	8	11	.421	1	33	23	6	151	163	42	51	1	4.24
Bob Grim	R	29	6	10	.375	4	40	9	3	125	124	57	65	1	4.10
John Tsitouris	R	23	4	3	.571	0	24	10	0	83	90	35	50	0	4.99
Murry Dickson	R	42	2	6	.250	0	38	0	0	71	85	27	36	0	4.94
1 Ralph Terry	R	23	2	4	.333	0	9	7	2	46	56	19	35	0	5.28
2 Tom Sturdivant	R	29	2	6	.250	5	36	3	0	72	70	34	57	0	4.63
1 Rip Coleman	L	28	2	10	.167	2	29	11	2	81	85	34	54	0	4.56
Russ Meyer	R	35	1	0	1.000	1	18	0	0	24	24	14	9	0	7.20
Tom Gorman	R	34	1	0	1.000	1	17	0	0	24	14	9	7	0	4.09
Ken Johnson	R	26	1	1	.500	0	2	2	0	11	11	5	8	0	4.20
Evans Killeen	R	26	0	0	—	0	7			7	7	7	1	0	4.50
Marty Kutyna	R	26	0	0	—	0	6			7	7	1		0	7.00
1 Mark Freeman	R	28	0	0	—	0	5			10	7	3		0	10.80
George Brunet	L	24	0	0	—	0	5			10	7	7		0	6.43
Dick Tomanek	L	28	0	0	.000	2	16	0	0	21	27	12	13	0	6.43
Al Grunwald	L	29	0	1	.000	0	3	1	0	16	18	11	7	0	8.18
Howie Reed	R	22	0	0	—	0	2	0	0	21	26	10	11	0	7.29

WASHINGTON — 8th 63-91 .409 31 — COOKIE LAVAGETTO

NAME	G by Pos	B	AGE	G	AB	R	H	2B	3B	HR	RBI	BB	SO	SB	BA	SA
TOTALS			27	154	5092	619	1205	173	32	163	579	517	881	51	.237	.379
Roy Sievers	1B93, OF13	R	32	115	385	55	93	19	0	21	49	53	62	1	.242	.455
Reno Bertoia	2B71, 3B5, SS1	R	24	90	308	33	73	10	0	8	29	29	48	2	.237	.347
2 Billy Consolo	SS75, 2B4	R	24	79	202	25	43	5	3	0	10	36	54	1	.213	.267
Harmon Killebrew	3B150, OF4	R	23	153	546	98	132	20	2	42	105	90	116	3	.242	.516
Faye Throneberry	OF86	R	28	117	327	36	82	11	2	10	42	33	61	6	.251	.388
Bob Allison	OF149	R	24	150	570	83	149	18	9	30	85	60	92	13	.261	.482
Jim Lemon	OF142	R	31	147	531	73	148	18	3	33	100	46	99	5	.279	.510
2 Hal Naragon	C54	L	30	71	195	12	47	3	2	0	11	8	11	0	.241	.277
Julio Becquer	1B53	L	27	108	220	20	59	12	5	1	26	8	17	3	.268	.382
Ron Samford	SS64, 2B23	R	29	91	237	23	53	13	0	5	22	11	29	1	.224	.342
2 Lenny Green	OF58	L	25	88	190	29	46	6	1	2	15	20	15	9	.242	.316
Clint Courtney (IL)	C53	R	32	76	189	19	44	4	1	2	18	20	19	0	.233	.296
Ken Aspromonte	2B52, SS12, 1B1, OF1	R	27	70	225	31	55	12	0	1	14	26	39	2	.244	.324
1 Jay Porter	C34, 1B2	R	26	37	106	8	24	4	0	1	10	11	16	0	.226	.292
Camilo Pascual	P32	R	25	32	86	10	26	2	0	3	5	5	11	0	.302	.326
Zoilo Versalles	SS29	R	19	29	59	4	9	1	0	1	4	1	15	1	.153	.203
1 Herb Plews	2B6	L	31	27	40	4	9	2	0	0	3	6	7	0	.225	.225
1 Albie Pearson	OF21	L	25	25	40	4	9	2	0	0	3	6	7	0	.225	.225
Jose Valdivielso	SS21	R	25	24	14	1	4	0	0	0	1	1	3	0	.286	.286
Steve Korcheck	C22	R	26	19	35	5	5	1	0	0	3	3	8	0	.157	.196
1 Ed Fitz Gerald	C16	R	35	19	62	6	15	2	0	0	7	1	4	0	.194	.242
Norm Zauchin	1B19	R	29	19	41	6	9	2	1	1	8	6	11	0	.220	.394
Dan Dobbek	OF16	L	24	16	60	8	15	4	1	0	5	3	13	0	.250	.383
Johnny Schaive	2B16	R	25	16	59	7	9	1	0	1	4	3	17	0	.153	.186

Bobby Malkmus 27 R 0-0

NAME	T	AGE	W	L	PCT	SV	G	GS	CG	IP	H	BB	SO	SHO	ERA
		27	63	91	.409	21	154	154	46	1360	1358	467	694	10	4.01
Camilo Pascual	R	25	17	10	.630	0	32	30	17	239	202	69	185	6	2.64
Pedro Ramos	R	24	13	19	.406	0	37	35	11	234	232	52	95	0	4.15
Bill Fischer	R	28	9	11	.450	0	34	29	6	187	211	43	62	1	4.28
Tex Clevenger	R	26	8	5	.615	8	50	7	2	117	114	51	71	2	4.00
Russ Kemmerer	R	27	8	17	.320	1	37	28	8	206	221	71	89	0	4.50
Hal Woodeshick	R	26	2	4	.333	0	31	3	0	61	58	36	30	0	3.69
Dick Hyde (SA)	R	30	2	3	.286	4	27	0	0	54	56	27	29	0	5.00
Hal Griggs	R	30	2	8	.200	2	37	10	2	98	103	52	43	1	5.23
John Romonosky	R	29	2	1	.667	0	12	2	0	38	36	19	22	0	3.32
Chuck Stobbs	L	30	1	8	.111	7	41	7	0	91	82	24	50	0	2.97
Jack Kralick	L	24	0	1	.000	0	7	1	0	13	16	4	9	0	6.75
Ralph Lumenti	L	22	0	0	—	0	3			4	2	2		0	9.00
2 Murray Wall	R	32	0	0	—	0	1			2	1			0	9.00
Tom McAvoy	L	23	0	0	—	0	3			5	7	5	1	0	10.92
Vito Valentinetti	R	30	0	2	.000	0	9			7	5	1		0	7.45
Jim Kaat	L	20	0	2	.000	0	3	2	0	5	7	5	1	0	12.60

LOS ANGELES   1st 88-68   .564   WALT ALSTON (Defeated Milwaukee in playoff 2 games to 0)

NAME	G by Pos	B	AGE	G	AB	R	H	2B	3B	HR	RBI	BB	SO	SB	BA	SA
TOTALS			28	156	5282	705	1360	196	46	148	667	591	891	84	.257	.396
Gil Hodges	1B113, 3B4	R	35	124	413	57	114	19	2	25	80	58	92	3	.276	.513
Charlie Neal	2B151, SS1	R	28	151	616	103	177	30	11	19	83	43	86	17	.287	.464
Don Zimmer	SS88, 3B5, 2B1	R	28	97	249	21	41	7	1	4	28	37	56	3	.165	.249
Jim Gilliam	3B132, 2B8, OF4	B	30	145	553	91	156	18	4	3	34	96	25	23	.282	.345
Duke Snider	OF107	L	32	126	370	59	114	11	2	23	88	58	71	1	.308	.535
Don Demeter	OF124	R	24	139	371	55	95	11	1	18	70	16	87	5	.256	.437
Wally Moon	OF143, 1B1	L	29	145	543	93	164	26	11	19	74	81	64	15	.302	.495
Johnny Roseboro	C117	L	26	118	397	39	92	14	7	10	38	52	69	7	.232	.378
Ron Fairly	OF88	L	20	118	244	27	58	12	1	4	23	31	24	0	.238	.344
Norm Larker	1B55, OF30	L	28	108	311	37	90	14	1	8	49	26	25	0	.289	.418
Maury Wills	SS82	B	26	83	242	27	63	5	2	0	7	13	27	7	.260	.298
Rip Repulski	OF31	R	30	53	94	11	24	4	0	2	14	13	23	0	.255	.362
Joe Pignatano	C49	R	29	52	139	17	33	4	1	1	11	21	15	1	.237	.302
Carl Furillo	OF25	R	37	50	93	8	27	4	0	0	13	7	11	0	.290	.333
Don Drysdale	P44	R	22	46	91	9	15	1	1	4	12	4	31	0	.165	.330
Bob Lillis	SS20	R	29	30	48	7	11	2	0	0	2	3	4	0	.229	.271
2 Chuck Essegian	OF10	R	27	24	46	6	14	6	0	1	5	4	11	0	.304	.500
1 Dick Gray	3B11	R	27	21	52	8	8	1	0	2	4	6	12	0	.154	.288
1 Jim Baxes	3B10	R	30	11	33	4	10	1	0	2	5	4	7	1	.303	.515
Frank Howard	OF6	R	22	9	21	2	3	0	1	1	6	2	9	0	.143	.381
1 Solly Drake	OF4	B	28	9	8	2	2	0	0	0	0	1	3	1	.250	.250
Sandy Amoros	OF5	L	29	5	5	1	1	0	0	0	1	0	1	0	.200	.200

Norm Sherry 27 R 1-3, Tommy Davis 20 R 0-1

NAME	T	AGE	W	L	PCT	SV	G	GS	CG	IP	H	BB	SO	SHO	ERA
TOTALS		27	88	68	.564	26	156	156	43	1412	1317	614	1077	14	3.79
Don Drysdale	R	22	17	13	.567	2	44	36	15	271	237	93	242	4	3.45
Johnny Podres	L	26	14	9	.609	0	34	29	6	195	192	74	145	2	4.11
Roger Craig	R	29	11	5	.688	0	29	17	7	153	122	45	76	4	2.06
Danny McDevitt	L	26	10	8	.556	4	39	22	6	145	149	51	106	2	3.97
Sandy Koufax	L	23	8	6	.571	2	35	23	6	153	136	92	173	1	4.06
Larry Sherry	R	23	7	2	.778	3	23	9	1	94	75	43	72	1	2.20
Stan Williams	R	22	5	5	.500	0	35	15	2	125	102	86	89	0	3.96
Clem Labine	R	32	5	10	.333	9	56	0	0	85	91	25	37	0	3.92
Johnny Klippstein	R	31	4	0	1.000	2	28	0	0	46	48	33	30	0	5.87
Chuck Churn	R	29	3	2	.600	1	14	0	0	31	28	10	24	0	4.94
Art Fowler	R	36	3	4	.429	2	36	0	0	61	70	23	47	0	5.31
Gene Snyder	L	28	1	1	.500	0	11	2	0	26	32	20	20	0	5.54
Fred Kipp	L	27	0	0	—	0	2	0	0	3	2	3	1	0	0.00
Bill Harris	R	27	0	0	—	0	1	0	0	5	3	1	0	0	0.00
Carl Erskine	R	32	0	3	.000	1	10	3	0	23	33	13	15	0	7.83

MILWAUKEE   2nd 86-70   .551   2   FRED HANEY (Defeated by Los Angeles in playoff 2 games to 0)

NAME	G by Pos	B	AGE	G	AB	R	H	2B	3B	HR	RBI	BB	SO	SB	BA	SA
TOTALS			29	157	5388	724	1426	216	36	177	683	488	765	41	.265	.417
Joe Adcock	1B89, OF21	R	31	115	404	53	118	19	2	25	76	32	77	0	.292	.535
Felix Mantilla	2B60, SS23, 3B9, OF7	R	24	103	251	26	54	5	0	3	19	16	31	6	.215	.271
Johnny Logan	SS138	R	32	138	470	59	137	17	0	13	50	57	45	1	.291	.411
Eddie Mathews	3B148	L	27	148	594	118	182	16	8	46	114	80	71	2	.306	.593
Hank Aaron	OF152, 3B5	R	25	154	629	116	223	46	7	39	123	51	54	8	.355	.636
Bill Bruton	OF133	L	33	133	478	72	138	22	6	6	41	35	54	13	.289	.397
Wes Covington (KJ)	OF94	L	27	103	373	38	104	17	3	7	45	26	54	1	.279	.397
Del Crandall	C146	R	29	150	518	65	133	19	2	21	72	46	48	5	.257	.423
Frank Torre	1B87	L	27	115	263	23	60	15	1	1	33	35	12	0	.228	.304
Mickey Vernon	1B10, OF4	L	41	74	91	8	20	4	1	1	14	7	20	0	.220	.363
Andy Pafko	OF64	R	38	71	142	17	31	8	2	1	15	14	15	0	.218	.324
3 Bobby Avila	2B51	R	35	51	172	29	41	3	2	3	19	24	31	3	.238	.331
Lee Maye	OF44	L	24	51	140	17	42	5	1	4	16	7	26	2	.300	.436
Johnny O'Brien	2B37	R	28	44	116	16	23	4	0	1	8	11	15	0	.198	.259
Stan Lopata	C11, 1B2	R	33	25	48	0	5	0	0	1	5	3	13	0	.104	.104
Casey Wise	2B20, SS5	B	26	22	76	11	13	2	0	0	5	10	5	0	.171	.237
Mel Roach (KJ)	2B8, OF4, 3B1	R	26	19	31	1	3	0	0	0	2	4	9	0	.097	.097
Del Rice (BL)	C9	R	36	13	29	3	6	0	0	0	2	3	7	0	.207	.207
1 Joe Morgan	2B7	L	28	13	23	2	5	1	0	0	2	1	6	0	.217	.261
3 Ray Boone	1B3	R	35	13	15	3	3	0	0	0	2	4	2	0	.200	.400
2 Enos Slaughter	OF5	L	43	11	18	0	3	0	0	0	1	3	3	0	.167	.167
Chuck Cottier	2B10	R	23	10	24	1	3	1	0	0	0	3	7	0	.125	.167
1 Jim Pisoni	OF9	R	29	9	24	4	4	1	0	0	2	0	6	0	.167	.208
Al Spangler	OF4	L	25	6	12	3	5	0	1	0	1	1	4	0	.417	.583

John DeMerit 23 R 1-5, Red Schoendienst (IL) 36 B 0-3

NAME	T	AGE	W	L	PCT	SV	G	GS	CG	IP	H	BB	SO	SHO	ERA
TOTALS		29	86	70	.551	18	157	157	69	1401	1406	429	775	18	3.51
Lew Burdette	R	32	21	15	.583	1	41	39	20	290	312	38	105	4	4.07
Warren Spahn	L	38	21	15	.583	0	40	36	21	292	282	70	143	4	2.96
Bob Buhl (SA)	R	30	15	9	.625	0	31	25	13	198	181	74	105	4	2.86
Juan Pizarro	L	22	6	2	.750	0	29	14	6	134	117	70	126	2	3.76
Joey Jay	R	23	6	11	.353	0	34	19	4	136	130	64	88	1	4.10
Don McMahon	R	29	5	3	.625	15	60	0	0	81	81	37	55	0	2.56
Bob Rush	R	33	5	6	.455	0	31	9	1	101	102	23	64	1	2.41
Carl Willey	R	28	5	9	.357	0	26	15	5	117	126	31	51	2	4.15
Bob Trowbridge	R	29	1	1	1.000	0	16	0	0	30	45	10	22	0	6.00
Bob Giggie	R	25	1	0	1.000	0	13	0	0	20	24	10	15	0	4.05
Bob Hartman	L	21	0	0	—	0	3	0	0	2	6	2	1	0	22.50

SAN FRANCISCO   3rd 83-71   .539   4   BILL RIGNEY

NAME	G by Pos	B	AGE	G	AB	R	H	2B	3B	HR	RBI	BB	SO	SB	BA	SA
TOTALS			25	154	5281	705	1377	239	35	167	660	473	875	81	.261	.414
Orlando Cepeda	1B122, OF44, 3B4	R	21	151	605	92	192	35	4	27	105	33	100	23	.317	.522
Daryl Spencer	2B151, SS4	R	29	152	555	59	147	20	1	12	62	58	67	5	.265	.369
Ed Bressoud	SS92, 1B1, 2B1, 3B1	R	27	104	315	36	79	17	2	9	26	28	55	0	.251	.403
Jim Davenport	3B121, SS1	R	25	123	469	65	121	16	3	6	38	28	65	0	.258	.343
Willie Kirkland	OF117	L	25	126	463	64	126	23	3	22	68	42	84	5	.272	.475
Willie Mays	OF147	R	28	151	575	125	180	43	5	34	104	65	58	27	.313	.583
Jackie Brandt	OF116, 3B18, 1B3, 2B1	R	25	137	429	63	116	16	5	12	57	35	69	11	.270	.415
Hobie Landrith	C109	L	29	109	283	30	71	14	0	3	29	43	23	0	.251	.332
Felipe Alou	OF69	R	24	95	247	38	68	13	2	10	33	17	38	5	.275	.466
Leon Wagner	OF28	L	25	87	129	20	29	4	3	5	13	5	24	0	.225	.419
Andre Rodgers	SS66	R	24	71	228	32	57	12	1	6	24	32	50	2	.250	.390
Bob Schmidt	C70	R	26	71	181	17	44	7	1	5	20	13	24	0	.243	.376
Dusty Rhodes		L	32	54	48	1	9	2	0	0	7	5	13	0	.188	.229
Willie McCovey	1B51	L	21	52	192	32	68	9	5	13	38	22	35	2	.354	.656
Danny O'Connell	3B26, 2B8	R	32	34	58	6	11	3	0	0	6	5	15	0	.190	.241
Jose Pagan	3B18, SS5, 2B3	R	24	31	46	7	8	1	0	0	1	3	6	1	.174	.196
2 Jim Hegan	C21	R	38	21	30	0	4	1	0	0	1	4	10	0	.133	.167
Bob Speake		L	28	15	11	0	1	0	0	0	1	1	4	0	.091	.091
Hank Sauer	OF1	R	42	13	15	1	1	0	0	1	1	0	3	0	.067	.267
Roger McCardell	C3	R	26	4	4	0	0	0	0	0	0	1	0	0	.000	.000

NAME	T	AGE	W	L	PCT	SV	G	GS	CG	IP	H	BB	SO	SHO	ERA
TOTALS		28	83	71	.539	23	154	154	52	1376	1279	500	873	12	3.47
Sam Jones	R	33	21	15	.583	4	50	35	16	271	232	109	209	4	2.82
Johnny Antonelli	L	29	19	10	.655	4	40	38	17	282	247	76	165	4	3.10
Jack Sanford	R	30	15	12	.556	1	36	31	10	222	198	70	132	0	3.16
Mike McCormick	L	20	12	16	.429	4	47	31	7	226	213	86	151	3	3.98
Stu Miller	R	31	8	7	.533	8	59	9	2	168	164	57	95	0	2.84
Gordon Jones	R	29	3	2	.600	2	31	0	0	44	45	19	29	0	4.30
Al Worthington	R	30	2	3	.400	2	42	3	0	73	68	37	45	0	3.70
Eddie Fisher	R	22	2	6	.250	1	17	5	0	40	57	8	15	0	7.88
Bud Byerly	R	38	1	0	1.000	0	11	0	0	13	11	5	4	0	1.38
Joe Shipley	R	24	0	0	—	0	10	1	0	18	16	17	11	0	4.50
Dom Zanni	R	27	0	0	—	0	9	0	0	11	12	8	11	0	6.55
Billy Muffett	R	28	0	0	—	0	5	0	0	9	12	3	3	0	5.14
Curt Barclay	R	27	0	0	—	0	1	0	0	0.1	2	1	2	0	54.00
Marshall Renfroe	L	23	0	0	—	0	1	1	0	3	3	3	1	0	27.00

Ray Monzant (VR) 26

PITTSBURGH   4th 78-76   .506   9   DANNY MURTAUGH

NAME	G by Pos	B	AGE	G	AB	R	H	2B	3B	HR	RBI	BB	SO	SB	BA	SA
TOTALS			28	155	5369	651	1414	230	42	112	617	442	715	32	.263	.384
Dick Stuart	1B105, OF7	R	26	118	397	64	118	15	2	27	78	42	86	1	.297	.549
Bill Mazeroski	2B133	R	22	135	493	50	119	15	6	7	59	29	54	1	.241	.339
Dick Groat	SS145	R	28	147	593	74	163	22	7	5	51	32	35	0	.275	.361
Don Hoak	3B155	R	31	155	564	60	166	29	3	6	65	71	75	9	.294	.399
Roberto Clemente (EJ)	OF104	R	24	105	432	60	128	17	7	4	50	15	51	2	.296	.396
Bill Virdon	OF144	L	28	144	519	67	132	24	2	8	41	55	65	7	.254	.355
Bob Skinner	OF142, 1B1	L	27	143	547	78	153	18	4	13	61	67	65	10	.280	.399
Smoky Burgess	C101	L	32	114	377	41	112	28	5	11	59	31	16	0	.297	.485
Rocky Nelson	1B56, OF2	L	34	98	175	31	51	11	0	6	32	19	19	0	.291	.457
Roman Mejias	OF85	R	28	96	276	28	65	6	1	7	28	21	48	1	.236	.341
Dick Schofield	2B28, SS8, OF3	B	24	81	145	21	34	10	1	1	9	16	22	1	.234	.338
1 Ted Kluszewski	1B20	L	34	60	122	16	32	10	1	2	17	5	14	0	.262	.410
Hank Foiles (KJ)	C51	R	30	53	80	10	18	3	0	3	14	7	16	0	.225	.375
Danny Kravitz	C45	L	28	52	162	18	41	9	1	3	21	5	14	0	.253	.377
Harry Bright	OF4, 3B3, 2B1	R	29	40	48	4	12	1	0	3	8	5	10	0	.250	.458
Joe Christopher	OF9	R	23	15	12	6	0	0	0	0	1	3	3	1	.000	.000
3 Harry Simpson	OF9	L	33	15	12	4	0	0	0	1	0	0	0	0	.267	.400

Ken Hamlin 24 R 1-8, R C Stevens 24 R 2-7, Hardy Peterson 29 R 0-1, Gene Baker (KJ) 34

NAME	T	AGE	W	L	PCT	SV	G	GS	CG	IP	H	BB	SO	SHO	ERA
TOTALS		28	78	76	.506	17	155	155	48	1393	1432	418	730	7	3.90
Roy Face	R	31	18	1	.947	10	57	0	0	93	91	25	69	0	2.71
Vern Law	R	29	18	9	.667	0	34	33	20	266	245	53	110	2	2.98
Harvey Haddix	L	33	12	12	.500	0	31	29	14	224	189	49	149	2	3.13
Ron Kline	R	27	11	13	.458	0	33	29	7	186	186	70	91	0	4.26
Bob Friend	R	28	8	19	.296	0	35	35	7	235	267	52	104	2	4.02
Bennie Daniels	R	27	7	9	.438	1	34	12	0	101	115	39	67	0	5.44
Ron Blackburn (MS)	R	24	1	1	1.000	1	26	0	0	44	50	15	19	0	3.68
Don Gross	L	28	1	0	.500	2	21	0	0	33	28	10	15	0	3.55
13 Bob Porterfield	R	35	1	2	.333	1	36	0	0	41	51	19	19	0	4.39
Freddie Green	L	25	1	0	.333	1	17	0	0	37	37	15	20	0	3.16
1 Bob Smith	L	28	0	0	—	0	20	0	0	28	32	17	12	0	3.54
Al Jackson	L	24	0	0	—	0	8	4	0	18	24	8	13	0	6.50
Don Williams	R	27	0	0	—	0	6	0	0	12	17	6	3	0	6.75
Paul Giel	R	27	0	0	—	0	8	1	0	9	17	6	3	0	13.50
Dick Hall	R	28	0	0	—	0	9	0	0	12	13	1	3	0	3.00
Jim Umbricht	R	28	0	0	—	0	1	0	0	9	12	3	6	0	6.43
George Witt (SA)	R	25	0	7	.000	1	15	11	0	51	58	32	30	0	6.88

CHICAGO   5th (tie) 74-80   .481   13   BOB SCHEFFING

NAME	G by Pos	B	AGE	G	AB	R	H	2B	3B	HR	RBI	BB	SO	SB	BA	SA
TOTALS			30	155	5296	673	1321	209	44	163	635	498	911	32	.249	.398
Dale Long	1B85	L	33	110	296	34	70	13	3	14	37	31	53	0	.236	.432
Tony Taylor	2B149, SS2	R	23	150	624	96	175	30	8	8	38	45	86	23	.280	.393
Ernie Banks	SS154	R	28	155	589	97	179	25	6	45	143	64	72	2	.304	.596
Al Dark	3B131, 1B4, SS1	R	37	136	477	60	126	22	6	6	45	35	50	1	.264	.386
Lee Walls	OF119	R	26	120	354	43	91	18	3	8	42	42	73	0	.257	.393
George Altman	OF121	L	26	135	420	54	103	14	4	12	47	34	80	1	.245	.383
Bobby Thomson	OF116	R	35	122	374	55	98	15	2	11	52	35	50	1	.259	.398
Sammy Taylor	C109	L	26	110	353	41	95	13	2	13	43	35	47	1	.269	.428
Walt Moryn	OF104	L	33	117	381	41	89	14	1	14	48	44	66	0	.234	.386
Jim Marshall	1B72, OF8	L	27	108	294	39	75	10	1	11	40	33	39	0	.252	.406
Earl Averill	C32, 3B13, OF5, 2B2	R	27	74	186	22	44	10	0	10	34	15	39	0	.237	.452
2 Irv Noren	OF40, 1B1	L	34	65	156	27	50	6	4	9	19	24	23	2	.321	.462
Cal Neeman	C38	R	30	44	96	7	17	6	0	2	14	5	15	0	.162	.267
Art Schult	1B23, OF15	R	31	42	118	17	32	7	0	2	14	5	15	0	.271	.381
2 Johnny Goryl	2B11, 3B4	R	25	26	48	1	9	1	0	1	5	2	7	0	.188	.354
Billy Williams	OF10	L	21	18	33	0	5	1	0	0	2	2	11	0	.152	.212
Lou Jackson		L	23	6	16	2	4	0	0	1	1	1	5	0	.250	.250

Don Eddy 25 R 0-1, 1 Charlie King 28 R 0-3, Bobby Adams 37 R 0-2, Gordon Massa (MS) 23

NAME	T	AGE	W	L	PCT	SV	G	GS	CG	IP	H	BB	SO	SHO	ERA
TOTALS		28	74	80	.481	25	155	155	30	1391	1337	519	765	11	4.01
Glen Hobbie	R	23	16	13	.552	0	46	33	10	234	204	106	138	3	3.69
Bob Anderson	R	23	12	13	.480	0	37	36	7	235	245	77	113	1	4.14
Don Elston	R	30	10	8	.556	13	65	0	0	98	77	46	82	0	3.31
Bill Henry	L	31	9	8	.529	12	65	0	0	134	111	26	115	0	2.69
Dave Hillman	R	31	8	11	.421	0	39	24	4	191	178	43	88	1	3.53
Art Ceccarelli	L	29	5	5	.500	0	18	14	2	102	95	37	56	2	4.76
Moe Drabowsky	R	23	5	10	.333	0	31	23	3	142	138	75	70	1	4.12
John Buzhardt	R	22	4	5	.444	1	31	10	1	101	107	29	33	1	4.99
Elmer Singleton	R	41	2	1	.667	0	21	1	0	43	40	12	25	0	2.72
Joe Schaffernoth (EJ)	R	21	1	0	1.000	0	11	0	0	15	11	4	3	0	7.88
Ed Donnelly	R	26	1	1	.500	0	9	0	0	15	21	4	12	0	3.21
Dick Drott (BA)	R	23	1	1	.333	0	17	3	0	25	26	15	15	1	6.00
Ben Johnson	R	35	0	0	—	0	6	0	0	12	11	8	9	0	2.12
2 Bob Porterfield	R	35	0	0	—	0	2	0	0	5	9	3	1	0	12.00
Morrie Martin	L	36	0	0	—	0	9	0	0	7	9	8	3	0	22.50
1 Riverboat Smith	L	31	0	0	—	0	6	0	0	9	17	6	3	0	81.00
2 Seth Morehead	L	25	0	0	—	0	16	1	0	43	44	12	25	0	4.74
1 Taylor Phillips	L	26	0	0	—	0	4	0	0	9	12	11	5	0	7.41

CINCINNATI 5th (tie) 74-80 .481 13   MAYO SMITH 35-45 .438   FRED HUTCHINSON 39-35 .527

NAME	G by Pos	B	AGE	G	AB	R	H	2B	3B	HR	RBI	BB	SO	SB	BA	SA
TOTALS		28	154	5288	764	1448	258	34	161	721	499	763	65	.274	.427	
Frank Robinson	1B125, OF40	R	23	146	540	106	168	31	4	36	125	69	93	18	.311	.583
Johnny Temple	2B149	R	30	149	598	102	186	35	6	8	67	72	40	14	.311	.430
Roy McMillan (BC)	SS73	R	29	79	246	38	65	14	2	9	24	27	27	0	.264	.447
3 Willie Jones	3B68	R	33	72	233	33	58	12	1	7	31	28	26	0	.249	.399
Gus Bell	OF145	L	30	148	580	59	170	27	2	19	115	29	44	2	.293	.445
Vada Pinson	OF154	L	20	154	648	131	205	47	9	20	84	55	98	21	.316	.509
Jerry Lynch	OF98	L	28	117	379	49	102	16	3	17	58	29	50	2	.269	.462
Ed Bailey	C117	L	28	121	379	43	100	13	0	12	40	62	53	2	.264	.393
Frank Thomas	3B64, OF33, 1B14	R	30	108	374	41	84	18	2	12	47	27	56	0	.225	.380
Eddie Kasko	SS84, 3B31, 2B2	R	27	118	329	39	93	14	1	2	31	14	38	2	.283	.350
Jim Pendleton	OF24, 3B16, SS3	R	35	65	113	13	29	2	0	3	9	8	18	3	.257	.354
Don Newcombe	P30	R	33	61	105	10	32	2	0	3	21	17	23	0	.305	.410
Dutch Dotterer	C51	R	27	52	161	21	43	7	0	2	17	16	23	0	.267	.348
2 Whitey Lockman	1B20, 2B6, OF1, 3B1	L	32	52	84	10	22	5	1	0	7	4	6	0	.262	.345
Johnny Powers	OF5	L	29	43	43	8	11	2	1	2	4	3	13	0	.256	.488
Pete Whisenant	OF21	R	29	36	71	13	17	2	0	5	11	8	18	0	.239	.479
1 Walt Dropo	1B23	R	36	26	39	4	4	1	0	1	2	4	7	0	.103	.205
Cliff Cook	3B9	R	22	9	21	3	8	2	1	0	5	2	8	1	.381	.571

Bobby Henrich 20 R 0-3, Buddy Gilbert 23 L 3-20, 1 Del Ennis 34 R 4-12, Bob Thurman 42 L 1-4, Don Pavletich 20 R 0-

0

NAME	T	AGE	W	L	PCT	SV	G	GS	CG	IP	H	BB	SO	SHO	ERA
		29	74	80	.481	26	154	154	44	1357	1460	456	690	7	4.31
Don Newcombe	R	29	13	8	.619	1	30	29	17	222	216	27	100	2	3.16
Bob Purkey	R	29	13	18	.419	1	38	33	9	218	241	43	78	1	4.25
Joe Nuxhall	L	30	9	9	.500	1	28	21	6	132	155	35	75	1	4.23
2 Jim Brosnan	R	29	8	3	.727	2	26	9	1	83	79	26	56	1	3.36
Brooks Lawrence	R	34	7	12	.368	10	43	14	3	128	144	45	64	0	4.78
Jay Hook	R	22	5	5	.500	0	17	15	4	79	79	39	37	0	5.13
Jim O'Toole	L	22	5	5	.385	0	28	19	3	129	129	47	70	0	5.16
Orlando Pena	R	25	5	9	.357	5	46	8	1	136	150	39	76	0	4.76
Bob Mabe	R	29	4	2	.667	3	18	1	0	30	29	19	8	0	5.40
Willard Schmidt	R	31	3	2	.600	0	36	4	0	71	80	30	40	0	3.93
Luis Arroyo	L	32	1	0	1.000	0	10	0	0	14	17	11	8	0	3.86
Tom Acker	R	29	1	2	.333	2	37	0	0	63	57	37	45	0	4.14
2 Don Rudolph	L	27	0	0	—	0	7	1	0	7	13	3	8	0	5.14
Mike Cuellar	L	22	0	0	—	0	4	7	1	4	5	4	2	0	15.75
Claude Osteen	L	19	0	0	—	0	8	0	0	11	11	9	3	0	6.75
1 Hal Jeffcoat	R	34	0	1	.000	1	17	0	0	21	10	12	3	0	3.27
Jim Bailey	L	24	0	1	.000	0	3	1	0	12	17	6	7	0	6.00

ST. LOUIS 7th 71-83 .461 16   SOLLY HEMUS

NAME	G by Pos	B	AGE	G	AB	R	H	2B	3B	HR	RBI	BB	SO	SB	BA	SA
TOTALS		28	154	5317	641	1432	244	49	118	605	485	747	65	.269	.400	
Stan Musial	1B90, OF3	L	38	115	341	37	87	13	2	14	44	60	25	0	.255	.428
Don Blasingame	2B150	L	27	150	615	90	178	26	7	1	24	67	42	15	.289	.359
Alex Grammas	SS130	R	33	131	368	43	99	14	2	3	30	38	26	3	.269	.342
Ken Boyer	3B143, SS2	R	28	149	563	86	174	18	5	28	94	67	77	12	.309	.508
Joe Cunningham	OF121, 1B35	L	27	144	458	65	158	28	6	7	60	88	47	2	.345	.478
Gino Cimoli	OF141	R	29	143	519	61	145	40	7	8	72	37	83	7	.279	.430
Bill White	OF92, 1B71	L	25	138	517	77	156	33	9	12	72	34	61	15	.302	.470
Hal Smith	C141	R	28	142	452	35	122	15	3	13	50	15	28	1	.270	.403
Curt Flood	OF106, 2B1	R	21	121	208	24	53	7	3	7	26	16	35	2	.255	.418
George Crowe	1B14	R	38	77	103	14	31	6	0	8	29	5	12	0	.301	.592
Gene Oliver	OF42, C9, 1B5	R	23	68	172	14	42	9	0	6	28	7	41	3	.244	.401
1 Ray Jablonski	3B19, SS1	R	32	60	87	11	22	4	0	3	14	8	19	1	.253	.402
Wally Shannon	SS21, 2B10	L	26	47	95	5	27	5	0	0	5	0	12	0	.284	.337
Bobby Gene Smith	OF32	R	25	43	60	11	13	1	1	1	7	1	9	0	.217	.317
Lee Tate	SS39, 3B2, 2B2	R	27	41	50	5	7	1	1	1	4	5	7	0	.140	.260
2 Dick Gray	SS13, 3B6, 2B2, OF1	R	27	36	51	9	16	1	0	1	6	6	8	3	.314	.392
Gene Green	OF19, C11	R	26	30	74	8	14	6	0	1	5	3	18	0	.189	.311
Solly Hemus	2B1, 3B1	L	36	24	17	2	4	2	0	0	1	8	2	0	.235	.353
2 Jay Porter	C19, 1B1	R	26	23	33	5	7	3	0	1	2	1	4	0	.212	.394
1 Chuck Essegian	OF9	R	27	17	39	2	7	2	0	1	5	1	13	0	.179	.282
Ray Katt	C14	R	32	15	24	0	7	2	0	0	2	0	8	0	.292	.375
Duke Carmel	OF10	L	22	10	23	2	3	1	0	0	0	2	8	0	.130	.174
Tim McCarver	C6	L	17	8	24	3	4	1	0	0	0	2	1	0	.167	.208

1 Irv Noren 34 L 1-8, Joe Durham 27 R 0-5, 2 Charlie King 28 R 3-7, Charlie O'Rourke 22 R 0-2

NAME	T	AGE	W	L	PCT	SV	G	GS	CG	IP	H	BB	SO	SHO	ERA
		26	71	83	.461	21	154	154	36	1363	1427	564	846	8	4.34
Lindy McDaniel	R	23	14	12	.538	15	62	7	1	132	144	41	86	0	3.82
Larry Jackson	R	28	14	13	.519	0	40	37	12	256	271	64	145	3	3.30
Vinegar Bend Mizell	R	28	13	10	.565	0	31	30	8	201	196	89	108	1	4.21
Ernie Broglio	R	23	7	12	.368	0	35	25	6	181	174	89	133	4	4.72
Marshall Bridges	L	28	6	3	.667	1	27	4	1	76	67	37	76	0	4.26
Bob Miller	R	20	4	3	.571	0	11	10	3	71	66	21	43	0	3.30
1 Gary Blaylock	R	27	4	5	.444	0	26	12	3	100	117	43	61	0	5.13
Bob Gibson	R	23	3	5	.375	0	13	9	2	76	77	39	48	1	3.32
Alex Kellner (EJ)	L	34	2	1	.667	0	12	4	0	37	31	10	19	0	3.16
Howie Nunn	R	23	2	2	.500	1	16	0	0	21	23	15	20	0	7.71
1 Jim Brosnan	R	29	1	3	.250	2	20	1	0	33	34	15	18	0	4.91
Dick Ricketts	R	25	1	6	.143	0	12	9	0	56	68	30	25	0	5.79
Jack Urban	R	30	0	1	—	0	8	0	0	11	18	7	4	0	9.00
Bill Smith	L	25	0	1	—	0	6	0	0	8	11	3	4	0	1.13
Marv Grissom	R	41	0	0	—	0	3	0	0	2	6	3	0	0	22.50
Dean Stone	L	28	0	1	.000	0	18	0	0	30	36	16	17	0	4.20
2 Hal Jeffcoat	R	34	0	1	.000	0	11	0	0	18	17	9	7	0	6.75
Tom Cheney	R	24	0	1	.000	0	12	0	0	12	17	11	8	0	6.75
Bob Duliba	R	24	0	1	.000	0	11	0	0	23	19	12	14	0	2.74
Phil Clark	R	26	0	1	.000	0	10	0	0	6	11	7	3	0	12.86
Bob Blaylock	R	24	0	2	.000	0	3	1	0	9	6	3	4	0	4.00
Tom Hughes	R	24	0	2	.000	0	4	1	0	8	9	2	1	0	15.75

PHILADELPHIA 8th 64-90 .416 23   EDDIE SAWYER

NAME	G by Pos	B	AGE	G	AB	R	H	2B	3B	HR	RBI	BB	SO	SB	BA	SA
TOTALS		30	155	5109	599	1237	196	38	113	560	498	858	39	.242	.362	
Ed Bouchee	1B134	L	26	136	499	75	142	29	4	15	74	70	74	0	.285	.449
Sparky Anderson	2B152	R	25	152	477	42	104	9	3	0	34	42	53	6	.218	.249
Joe Koppe	SS113, 2B11	R	28	126	422	68	110	18	7	7	28	41	80	7	.261	.386
Gene Freese	3B109, 2B6	R	25	132	400	60	107	14	5	23	70	43	61	8	.268	.500
Wally Post	OF120	R	29	132	468	62	119	17	6	22	94	36	101	0	.254	.457
Richie Ashburn	OF149	L	32	153	564	86	150	16	2	1	20	79	42	9	.266	.307
Harry Anderson	OF137	L	27	142	508	50	122	28	6	14	63	43	95	1	.240	.402
Carl Sawatski	C69	L	31	74	198	15	58	10	0	9	43	32	36	0	.293	.480
Dave Philley	OF34, 1B24	B	39	99	254	32	74	18	2	7	37	18	27	0	.291	.461
2 Solly Drake	OF37	B	28	67	62	10	9	1	0	0	3	8	15	5	.145	.161
Valmy Thomas	C65, 3B1	R	30	66	140	5	28	2	0	1	7	9	19	1	.200	.236
Harry Hanebrink	2B15, 3B9, OF1	L	31	57	97	10	25	3	1	1	7	2	12	0	.258	.340
Bob Bowman	OF20, P5	R	28	57	79	7	10	0	2	5	5	23	0	.127	.203	
1 Willie Jones	3B46	R	33	47	160	23	43	7	1	7	24	19	14	0	.269	.469
Chico Fernandez	SS40, 2B2	R	27	45	123	15	26	5	1	0	3	10	11	2	.211	.268
Joe Lonnett	C43	R	32	43	93	8	16	1	0	1	10	14	17	0	.172	.215
2 Jim Bolger	OF9	R	27	35	48	1	4	1	0	1	3	8	0	.083	.104	
1 Jim Hegan	C25	R	38	25	51	1	10	1	0	0	3	3	10	0	.196	.216
1 Granny Hamner	SS15, 3B1	R	32	21	64	10	19	4	2	0	11	1	7	0	.297	.453
John Easton		R	26	3	3	0	0	0	0	0	0	0	0	0	.000	.000

NAME	T	AGE	W	L	PCT	SV	G	GS	CG	IP	H	BB	SO	SHO	ERA
		29	64	90	.416	15	155	155	54	1354	1357	474	769	8	4.27
Robin Roberts	R	32	15	17	.469	0	35	35	19	257	267	35	137	2	4.27
Gene Conley (BH)	R	28	12	7	.632	1	25	22	12	180	159	42	102	3	3.00
Jim Owens	R	25	12	12	.500	1	31	30	11	221	203	73	135	1	3.22
Don Cardwell	R	23	9	10	.474	0	25	25	5	153	135	65	106	1	4.06
Jack Meyer	R	27	5	3	.625	1	47	1	1	94	76	53	71	0	3.35
Ruben Gomez	R	31	3	8	.273	1	20	12	2	72	90	24	37	1	6.13
Ray Semproch	R	28	3	10	.231	0	30	18	2	112	119	59	54	0	5.38
2 Humberto Robinson	R	29	2	4	.333	1	31	4	1	73	70	24	32	0	3.33
1 Al Schroll	R	27	1	1	.500	0	9	0	0	12	6	4	9	0	9.00
2 Taylor Phillips	R	26	1	4	.200	1	32	3	1	63	72	31	35	0	4.74
Dick Farrell	R	25	1	6	.143	6	38	0	0	57	61	25	31	0	4.74
Curt Simmons (SA)	L	30	0	0	—	0	3	2	0	14	19	10	8	0	8.36
Chris Short	L	21	0	0		0	3	2	0	14	19	10	8	0	8.36
Freddy Rodriguez	R	31	0	0	—	0	4	0	0	4	0	1	0		13.50
Bob Bowman	R	28	0	1	.000	0	5	0	0	9	6	6	0	0	6.00
Jim Hearn	R	38	0	2	.000	0	5	0	0	10	15	3	6	0	5.73
1 Seth Morehead	L	24	0	2	.000	0	10	3	0	30	15	13	8	0	9.90
Ed Keegan	R	19	0	0	.000	0	3	1		9	19	13	13	0	18.00

WORLD SERIES — LOS ANGELES (NL) 4 CHICAGO (AL) 2

LINE SCORES

TEAM	1 2 3	4 5 6	7 8 9	10 11 12	R	H	E

Game 1   October 1 at Chicago

LA (NL)	0 0 0	0 0 0	0 0 0		0	8	3
CHI	2 0 7	2 0 0	0 0 X		11	11	0

Craig, Churn (3), Labine (4), Wynn, Stanley (8)
Koufax (5), Klippstein (7)

Game 2   October 2 at Chicago

LA	0 0 0	0 1 0	3 0 0	4	9	1
CHI	0 0 0	0 0 1	0 2 0	3	8	0

Podres, Sherry (7)   Shaw, Lown (7)

Game 3   October 4 at Los Angeles

CHI	0 0 0	0 0 0	0 1 0	1	12	0
LA	0 0 0	0 0 2	1 X	3	5	0

Donovan, Staley (7)   Drysdale, Sherry (8)

Game 4   October 5 at Los Angeles

CHI	0 0 0	0 0 0	4 0 0	4	10	3
LA	0 0 0	0 0 0	0 1 X	5	9	0

Wynn, Lown (3),   Craig, Sherry (8)
Pierce (4), Staley (7)

Game 5   October 6 at Los Angeles

CHI	0 0 0	1 0 0	0 0 0	1	5	0
LA	0 0 0	0 0 0	0 0 0	0	9	0

Shaw, Pierce (8),   Koufax, Williams (8)
Donovan (8)

Game 6   October 8 at Chicago

LA	0 0 2	6 0 0	0 0 1	9	13	0
CHI	0 0 0	3 0 0	0 0 0	3	6	1

Podres, Sherry (4)   Wynn, Donovan (4),
Lown (4), Staley (5),
Pierce (8), Moore (9)

COMPOSITE BATTING

Los Angeles (NL)

NAME	POS	G	AB	R	H	2B	3B	HR	RBI	BA
Totals		6	203	21	53	3	1	7	19	.261
Neal	2B	6	27	4	10	2	0	2	6	.370
Gilliam	3B	6	25	2	6	0	0	0	2	.240
Hodges	1B	6	23	2	9	0	1	1	2	.391
Moon	OF	6	23	3	6	0	0	1	2	.261
Roseboro	C	6	21	0	2	0	0	0	1	.095
Wills	SS	6	20	2	5	0	0	0	1	.250
Larker	OF	6	16	2	3	0	0	0	1	.188
Demeter	OF	6	12	3	3	0	0	1	2	.250
Snider	OF	4	10	1	2	0	0	1	2	.200
Sherry	P	5	4	1	2	0	0	0	1	.500
Podres	P	3	4	1	2	0	0	0	0	.500
Furillo	OF	4	4	0	1	0	0	0	2	.250
Essegian	PH	4	3	2	2	0	0	2	2	.667
Fairly	OF	6	3	1	1	0	0	0	1	.333
Craig	P	2	3	0	0	0	0	0	0	.000
Koufax	P	2	2	0	0	0	0	0	0	.000
Drysdale	P	1	2	0	0	0	0	0	0	.000
Zimmer	SS	1	1	0	0	0	0	0	0	.000
Pignatano	C	1	1	0	0	0	0	0	0	—
Repulski	PH	1	0	0	0	0	0	0	0	—

Churn P 0-0, Labine P 0-0, Klippstein P 0-0, Williams P 0-0

Chicago (AL)

NAME	POS	G	AB	R	H	2B	3B	HR	RBI	BA
Totals		6	199	23	52	10	0	4	19	.261
Aparicio	SS	6	26	1	8	1	0	0	0	.308
Fox	2B	6	24	4	9	3	0	0	0	.375
Landis	OF	6	24	6	7	0	0	0	1	.292
Kluszewski	1B	6	23	5	9	1	0	3	10	.391
Lollar	C	6	22	3	5	0	0	1	5	.227
Smith	OF	6	20	1	5	0	0	0	1	.250
Goodman	3B	5	13	1	3	0	0	0	1	.231
Rivera	OF	5	11	1	0	0	0	0	0	.000
Phillips	3B-OF	3	10	0	3	1	0	0	1	.300
Wynn	P	3	5	0	1	0	0	0	1	.200
McAnany	OF	3	5	0	0	0	0	0	0	.000
Shaw	P	2	4	0	1	0	0	0	0	.250
Cash	PH	3	4	0	0	0	0	0	0	.000
Donovan	P	3	3	0	1	0	0	0	0	.333
Esposito	3B	2	3	0	0	0	0	0	0	.000
Torgeson	1B	3	1	1	0	0	0	0	0	.000
Romano	PH	2	1	0	0	0	0	0	0	.000
Staley	P	4	1	0	0	0	0	0	0	.000

Lown P 0-0, Pierce P 0-0, Moore P 0-0

COMPOSITE PITCHING

Los Angeles (NL)

NAME	G	IP	H	BB	SO	W	L	SV	ERA
Totals	6	53	52	20	33	4	2	2	3.23
Sherry	4	12.2	8	2	5	2	0	2	0.71
Podres	2	9.1	7	6	4	1	0	0	4.82
Craig	2	9.1	15	5	8	0	1	0	8.68
Koufax	2	9	5	1	7	0	1	0	1.00
Drysdale	1	7	11	4	5	1	0	0	1.29
Williams	1	2	0	2	1	0	0	0	0.00
Klippstein	1	2	1	2	0	0	0	0	0.00
Labine	1	1	0	0	1	0	0	0	0.00
Churn	1	0.2	5	1	0	0	0	0	27.00

Chicago (AL)

NAME	G	IP	H	BB	SO	W	L	SV	ERA
Totals	6	52	53	12	27	2	4	2	3.46
Shaw	2	14	17	2	2	1	1	0	2.57
Wynn	3	13	19	4	10	1	1	0	5.54
Staley	4	8.1	8	0	3	0	1	1	2.16
Donovan	2	8.1	4	3	5	0	1	1	5.40
Pierce	3	4	2	2	3	0	0	0	0.00
Lown	3	3.1	1	1	3	0	0	0	0.00
Moore	1	1	1	1	0	0	0	0	9.00

1960 Stengel's Last Hurrah

On the eve of the Series opener, the Pirates had to be thirsting for revenge. Pittsburgh had last taken the National League flag in 1927, only to run up against the Yankees of Babe Ruth and Lou Gehrig and be blown out of the park in four games. And if the Pirates weren't giving much thought to the holocaust which had erupted 33 years before, the press was—if for no other reason than the fact that the 1960 rendition of the Yankees featured Mickey Mantle and Roger Maris.

The Pirates' seven-game margin over runner-up Milwaukee gave little evidence that they were a team of destiny. They had earned the chance to vindicate their image by leading the National League race practically the entire way and beating back challenges by Milwaukee and St. Louis. Pittsburgh had Roberto Clemente and Bill Mazeroski, league All-Stars, at right field and second base, a fiery inspirational leader in ex-Marine Don Hoak at third base, and the league batting champ in Dick Groat. The final balance of Danny Murtaugh's club was provided by pitching aces Vern Law, Bob Friend, and Roy Face, plus the healthy addition of left-hander Vinegar Bend Mizell, who came from the Cardinals in a May trade.

The Yankees began the season unlike a pennant contender, and it seemed as if Casey Stengel's magic was finally gone. After stumbling through May as the White Sox and Orioles led the pack, a repeat of 1959 looked imminent. But the weather warmed, and Stengel got his juggernaut going to make it a three-team race by the time August rolled around. Then, in typical Yankee fashion, they broke the race wide open by winning their last 15 in a row, a pace too rich for the rookie-laden Orioles and the newly-powerful White Sox.

Stengel's magic, which could be traced to his genius for knowing when to say "goodbye" and when to say "hello" to his players, cemented the Yankee cause by trading a few young players over the winter to Kansas City in return for Roger Maris. There was no doubt that the young lefty slugger was a perfect fit for a Yankee uniform and the short right field Yankee Stadium fence 301 feet away. While Maris endorsed Stengel's wizardry by hitting 39 homers and driving in a league-leading 112 runs to be named MVP, Mantle once again provided the

supercharge with his league-leading 40 home runs. It was a good thing for Yankee power, because Yankee pitching was not the name of the game. Art Ditmar led the starters with 15 wins and Bobby Shantz the relievers with 11 saves, but the offense led the American League record books with 193 round trippers.

The World Series opened at Pittsburgh, and the Pirates wasted no time in refurbishing their image with a 6-4 win. But reality and shades of 1927 occurred in games two and three, as the Yankees blasted the Bucs by embarrassing scores of 16-3 and 10-0. In the next game, the Pirates shook off the Yankees' savage attack and recovered for a 3-2 win to knot the Series. In the fifth game, Haddix and Face combined to give the Pirates a 5-2 victory, only to watch the Yankees rise up in arms in the next game for a 12-0 rout and the third Series tie. That left it all up to the seventh game.

Pittsburgh scored two runs in the first and second and were coasting on a 4-0 lead, when Bill Skowron and Yogi Berra homered in successive innings, to give New York a 5-4 lead. The Yankees added two more in their half of the eighth to bring a curtain of gloom over the Forbes Field crowd. But destiny was not to be denied. An apparent double play ground ball took a bad hop and hit shortstop Tony Kubek in the neck, opening the gates for five runs and a Pittsburgh 9-7 lead. Three more outs and the Pirates would be renewed, but the script was more involved as Friend, the old reliable, failed and allowed the Yankees to tie the score. Throats in Forbes Field were sore and expectations confused, as Bill Mazeroski stepped in to start the Pirates' last turn at bat in regulation play. Ralph Terry, who had finally put out the Pirates' fire in the eighth, was on the mound. He sadly watched his pitch sail over the left field wall, to end the grueling slugfest at 10-9.

Terry apologized to Stengel for failing the old master, but it mattered little at the Yankee front office as—after 12 years, ten pennants, and seven World Series victories—the services of Charles Dillon Stengel were no longer needed. The Yankees gave the reason as age, but most fans felt they knew better.

1960 AMERICAN LEAGUE

NAME	G by Pos	B	AGE	G	AB	R	H	2B	3B	HR	RBI	BB	SO	SB	BA	SA
NEW YORK	**1st 97-57 .630**										**CASEY STENGEL**					
	TOTALS		29	155	5290	746	1377	215	40	193	699	537	818	37	.260	.426
Bill Skowron	1B142	R	29	146	538	63	166	34	3	26	91	38	95	2	.309	.528
Bobby Richardson	2B141,3B11	R	24	150	460	45	116	12	3	1	26	35	19	6	.252	.298
Tony Kubek	SS136, OF29	L	23	147	568	77	155	25	3	14	62	31	42	3	.273	.401
Clete Boyer	3B99, SS33	R	23	124	393	54	95	20	1	14	46	23	85	2	.242	.405
Roger Maris	OF136	L	25	136	499	98	141	18	7	39	112	70	65	2	.283	.581
Mickey Mantle	OF150	B	28	153	527	119	145	17	6	40	94	111	125	14	.275	.558
Hector Lopez	OF106, 2B5, 3B1	R	30	131	408	66	116	14	6	9	42	46	64	1	.284	.414
Elston Howard	C91, OF1	R	31	107	323	29	79	11	3	6	39	28	43	3	.245	.353
Yogi Berra	C63, OF36	L	35	120	359	46	99	14	1	15	62	38	23	2	.276	.446
Gil McDougald	3B84, 2B42	R	32	119	337	54	87	16	4	8	34	38	45	2	.258	.401
2 Bob Cerv	OF51, 1B3	R	34	87	216	32	54	11	1	8	28	30	36	0	.250	.421
Kent Hadley	1B24	L	25	55	64	8	13	2	0	4	11	6	19	0	.203	.422
Johnny Blanchard (IL)	C28	L	27	53	99	8	24	3	1	4	14	6	17	0	.242	.414
Joe DeMaestri	2B19, SS17	R	31	49	35	8	8	1	0	0	2	0	9	0	.229	.257
2 Dale Long	1B11	L	34	26	41	6	15	3	1	3	10	5	6	0	.366	.707
Ken Hunt	OF24	R	25	25	22	4	6	2	0	0	1	4	6	0	.273	.364
Jim Pisoni	OF18	R	30	20	9	1	1	0	0	0	1	2	1	0	.111	.111

Deron Johnson 21 R 2-4, 1 Elmer Valo 39 L 0-5, Jesse Gonder 24 L 2-7, 1 Andy Carey 28 R 1-3, Billy Shantz 32 R 0-0

NAME	T	AGE	W	L	PCT	SV	G	GS	CG	IP	H	BB	SO	SHO	ERA
		29	97	57	.630	42	155	155	38	1398	1225	609	712	16	3.52
Art Ditmar	R	31	15	9	.625	0	34	28	8	200	195	56	65	1	3.57
Jim Coates	R	27	13	3	.813	1	35	18	6	149	139	66	73	2	4.29
Whitey Ford	L	31	12	9	.571	0	33	29	8	193	168	65	85	4	3.08
Ralph Terry	R	24	10	8	.556	1	35	23	7	167	149	52	92	3	3.40
Bob Turley	R	29	9	3	.750	5	34	24	4	173	138	87	87	1	3.28
Eli Grba	R	25	6	4	.600	1	24	9	1	81	65	46	32	0	3.67
Duke Maas	R	31	5	1	.833	4	35	1	0	70	70	35	28	0	4.11
Luis Arroyo	L	33	5	1	.833	7	29	0	0	41	30	22	29	0	2.85
Johnny James	R	26	5	1	.833	2	28	0	0	43	38	26	29	0	4.40
Bobby Shantz	L	34	5	4	.556	11	42	0	0	68	57	24	54	0	2.78
Bill Stafford	R	20	3	1	.750	0	11	8	2	60	50	18	36	1	2.25
John Gabler	R	29	3	3	.500	1	21	4	0	52	46	32	19	0	4.15
Ryne Duren	R	31	3	4	.429	9	42	1	0	49	27	49	67	0	4.96
Bill Short	L	22	3	5	.375	0	10	10	2	47	49	30	14	0	4.79
Hal Stowe	L	22	0	0	—	0	1	0	0	1	0	1	0	0	9.00
Fred Kipp	L	28	0	1	.000	0	4	0	0	4	4	0	2	0	6.75

NAME	G by Pos	B	AGE	G	AB	R	H	2B	3B	HR	RBI	BB	SO	SB	BA	SA
BALTIMORE	**2nd 89-65 .578 8**										**PAUL RICHARDS**					
	TOTALS		29	154	5170	682	1307	206	33	123	640	596	801	37	.253	.377
Jim Gentile	1B124	L	26	138	384	67	112	17	0	21	98	68	72	0	.292	.500
Marv Breeding	2B152	R	26	152	551	69	147	25	2	3	43	35	80	10	.267	.336
Ron Hansen	SS154	R	22	153	530	72	135	22	5	22	86	69	94	3	.255	.440
Brooks Robinson	3B152, 2B3	R	23	152	595	74	175	27	9	14	88	35	49	2	.294	.440
2 Gene Stephens	OF127	R	27	84	193	38	46	11	0	5	11	25	25	4	.238	.373
Jackie Brandt	OF142, 3B2, 1B1	R	26	145	511	73	130	24	6	15	65	47	69	5	.254	.413
Gene Woodling	OF124	L	37	140	435	68	123	18	3	11	62	84	40	3	.283	.414
Gus Triandos (HJ)	C105	R	29	109	364	36	98	18	0	12	54	41	62	0	.269	.418
Al Pilarcik	OF75	L	29	104	194	30	48	5	1	4	17	15	16	0	.247	.345
Clint Courtney	C58	L	33	83	154	14	35	3	0	1	12	30	14	0	.227	.266
Walt Dropo	1B67, 3B1	R	37	79	179	16	48	8	0	4	21	20	19	0	.268	.380
2 Jim Busby	OF71	R	33	79	159	25	41	7	1	0	12	20	14	2	.258	.314
Bob Boyd	1B17	L	34	71	82	9	26	5	2	0	9	6	5	0	.317	.427
Dave Nicholson	OF44	R	20	54	113	17	21	1	1	5	11	20	55	0	.186	.345
Albie Pearson	OF32	L	25	48	82	17	20	2	1	1	4	24	17	3	.244	.305
Billy Klaus	2B30, SS12, 3B2	L	31	46	43	8	9	2	0	1	6	9	9	0	.209	.326
1 Willie Tasby	OF36	R	27	39	85	9	18	2	1	1	5	4	9	12	1	.212	.259
3 Dave Philley	OF8, 3B1	B	40	14	34	6	9	2	1	1	5	4	5	1	.265	.471
1 Joe Ginsberg	C14	L	33	14	30	3	8	1	0	0	6	6	1	0	.267	.300
1 Johnny Powers	OF4	L	30	10	18	3	2	1	0	0	0	3	1	0	.111	.111
Valmy Thomas	C8	R	31	8	16	0	1	0	0	0	0	0	5	0	.063	.063

Ray Barker 24 L 0-6, Jerry Adair 23 R 1-5, 2 Bobby Thomson 36 R 0-6, Gene Green 27 R 1-4, 3 Del Rice 37 R 0-1, Barry Shetrone 21 L 0-0

NAME	T	AGE	W	L	PCT	SV	G	GS	CG	IP	H	BB	SO	SHO	ERA
		26	89	65	.578	22	154	154	48	1376	1222	552	785	11	3.52
Chuck Estrada	R	22	18	11	.621	2	36	25	12	209	162	101	144	1	3.57
Milt Pappas	R	21	15	11	.577	0	30	27	11	206	184	83	126	3	3.36
Hal Brown	R	35	12	5	.706	0	30	20	6	159	155	22	66	1	3.06
Jack Fisher	R	21	12	11	.522	2	40	20	8	198	174	78	99	3	3.41
Hoyt Wilhelm	R	37	11	8	.579	7	41	11	3	147	125	39	107	1	3.31
Steve Barber	L	22	10	7	.588	2	36	27	6	182	148	113	112	1	3.21
Arnie Portocarrero	R	28	3	2	.600	0	13	5	1	41	44	9	15	0	4.39
Jerry Walker	R	21	3	4	.429	5	29	18	1	118	107	56	48	0	3.74
Billy Hoeft	L	28	2	1	.667	0	19	0	0	19	18	14	14	0	4.26
Wes Stock	R	26	2	2	.500	2	17	0	0	34	26	14	23	0	2.91
Gordon Jones	R	30	1	1	.500	2	29	0	0	55	59	13	30	0	4.42
John Anderson	R	30	0	0	—	0	4	0	0	5	8	4	1	0	12.60
Bob Mabe	R	30	0	0	—	0	2	0	0	1	0	1	0	0	18.00
Rip Coleman	L	28	0	0	.000	0	4	0	0	8	15	6	0	0	11.25

NAME	G by Pos	B	AGE	G	AB	R	H	2B	3B	HR	RBI	BB	SO	SB	BA	SA
CHICAGO	**3rd 87-67 .565 10**										**AL LOPEZ**					
	TOTALS		31	154	5191	741	1402	242	38	112	684	567	648	122	.270	.396
Roy Sievers	1B114, OF6	R	33	127	444	87	131	22	0	28	93	74	69	1	.295	.534
Nellie Fox	2B149	L	32	150	605	85	175	24	10	2	59	50	13	2	.289	.372
Luis Aparicio	SS153	R	26	153	600	86	166	20	7	2	61	43	39	51	.277	.343
Gene Freese	3B122	R	26	127	455	60	124	32	6	17	79	29	65	10	.273	.481
Al Smith	OF141	R	32	142	536	80	169	31	3	12	72	50	65	8	.315	.451
Jim Landis	OF147	R	26	148	494	89	125	25	6	10	49	80	84	23	.253	.389
Minnie Minoso	OF154	R	37	154	591	89	184	32	4	20	105	52	63	17	.311	.481
Sherm Lollar	C123	R	35	129	421	43	106	23	0	7	46	42	39	2	.252	.356
Ted Kluszewski	1B39	L	35	81	181	20	53	9	0	5	39	22	10	0	.293	.425
Earl Torgeson	1B10	L	36	68	57	12	15	2	0	2	9	21	8	1	.263	.404
Sammy Esposito	3B37, SS11, 2B5	R	28	57	77	14	14	5	0	1	11	10	20	0	.182	.286
Jim Rivera	OF24	L	37	48	17	11	9	1	0	1	3	3	4	4	.294	.471
Joe Hicks	OF14	L	27	36	47	3	9	1	0	2	6	6	8	0	.191	.213
Billy Goodman	3B20, 2B7	L	34	30	77	5	18	4	0	0	2	5	8	0	.234	.286
2 Joe Ginsberg	C25	L	33	28	75	8	19	4	0	0	10	8	1	0	.253	.307
Floyd Robinson	OF17	L	24	22	46	7	13	0	0	0	5	9	3	0	.283	.283
Dick Brown	C14	R	25	16	43	4	7	3	0	0	3	1	6	0	.163	.372
2 Earl Averill	C5	R	28	10	14	2	3	0	0	0	1	0	4	0	.214	.214
Cam Carreon	C7	R	22	8	17	2	4	0	0	0	0	1	2	0	.235	.235

J.C. Martin 23 L 2-20, Stan Johnson 23 L 1-6, Jim McAnany 23 R 0-2

NAME	T	AGE	W	L	PCT	SV	G	GS	CG	IP	H	BB	SO	SHO	ERA
		33	87	67	.565	26	154	154	42	1381	1338	533	695	11	3.60
Billy Pierce	L	33	14	7	.667	0	32	30	8	196	201	46	108	1	3.63
Frank Baumann	L	27	13	6	.684	3	47	20	7	185	169	53	71	2	2.68
Gerry Staley	R	39	13	8	.619	10	64	0	0	115	94	25	52	0	2.43
Early Wynn	R	40	13	12	.520	1	36	35	13	237	220	112	158	4	3.49
Bob Shaw	R	27	13	13	.500	0	36	32	7	193	221	62	46	1	4.06
Dick Donovan	R	32	6	1	.857	3	33	8	0	79	87	25	30	0	5.35
2 Russ Kemmerer	R	28	6	3	.667	2	36	7	2	121	111	45	76	1	2.98
Herb Score	L	27	5	10	.333	0	23	22	5	114	91	87	78	1	3.71
Turk Lown	R	36	2	3	.400	5	45	0	0	67	60	34	39	0	3.90
1 Ray Moore	R	34	1	1	.500	1	14	0	0	21	19	11	3	0	5.57
2 Al Worthington	R	31	1	1	.500	1	11	0	0	18	16	13	6	0	3.60
Mike Garcia	R	36	0	0	—	2	15	0	0	18	23	10	8	0	4.50
2 Bob Rush	R	34	0	0	—	1	6	1	0	16	15	12	10	0	5.79
Gary Peters	L	23	0	0	—	0	2	0	0	4	4	4	1	0	9.00
Jake Striker	R	26	0	0	—	0	1	0	0	2	1	1	2	0	4.50
Don Ferrarese	L	31	0	0	.000	0	4	0	0	4	4	5	2	0	18.00
Ken McBride	R	24	0	0	—	0	2	0	0	6	3	4	5	0	3.60

CLEVELAND 4th 76-78 .494 21   1 JOE GORDON 49-46 .516   JO-JO WHITE 1-0 1.000   2 JIMMY DYKES 26-32 .448

NAME	G by Pos	B	AGE	G	AB	R	H	2B	3B	HR	RBI	BB	SO	SB	BA	SA
TOTALS			28	154	5296	667	1415	218	20	127	632	444	573	58	.267	.388
Vic Power	1B147, SS5, 3B4	R	32	147	580	69	167	26	3	10	84	24	20	9	.288	.395
2 Ken Aspromonte	2B80, 3B36	R	28	117	459	65	133	20	1	10	48	53	32	4	.290	.403
Woodie Held (BC)	SS109	R	28	109	376	45	97	15	1	21	67	44	73	0	.258	.471
Bubba Phillips	3B85, OF25, SS1	R	30	113	304	34	63	14	1	4	33	14	37	1	.207	.299
Harvey Kuenn	OF119, 3B5	R	29	126	474	65	146	24	0	9	54	55	25	5	.308	.416
Jimmy Piersall	OF134	R	30	138	486	70	137	12	4	18	66	64	38	18	.282	.414
Tito Francona	OF138, 1B13	L	26	147	544	84	159	36	2	17	79	67	67	4	.292	.460
Johnny Romano	C99	R	25	108	316	40	86	12	2	16	52	37	50	0	.272	.475
Johnny Temple	2B77, 3B17	R	31	98	381	50	102	13	1	2	19	32	20	11	.268	.323
Bob Hale	1B5	L	26	70	70	2	21	7	0	0	12	3	6	0	.300	.400
2 Marty Keough	OF42	L	26	65	149	19	37	5	0	3	11	9	23	2	.248	.342
Mike de la Hoz	SS38, 3B8	R	21	49	160	20	41	6	2	6	23	9	12	0	.256	.431
Walt Bond	OF36	L	22	40	131	19	29	2	1	5	18	13	14	4	.221	.366
2 Red Wilson	C30	R	31	32	88	5	19	3	0	1	10	6	7	0	.216	.284
George Strickland	SS14, 3B12, 2B2	R	34	32	42	4	7	0	0	1	3	4	8	0	.167	.238
1 Carroll Hardy	OF17	R	27	29	18	7	2	1	0	0	1	0	1	0	.111	.167
1 Russ Nixon	C25	L	25	25	82	6	20	5	0	1	6	6	6	0	.244	.341
2 Hank Foiles	C22	R	31	24	68	9	19	1	0	1	6	7	5	0	.279	.338
2 Joe Morgan	3B12, OF2	L	29	22	47	6	14	2	0	2	4	6	4	0	.298	.468
Chuck Tanner	OF4	L	30	21	25	2	7	1	0	0	4	4	6	1	.280	.320
2 Rocky Bridges	SS7, 3B3	R	32	10	27	1	9	0	0	0	3	1	2	0	.333	.333
1 Johnny Powers	OF5	L	30	8	12	2	2	1	0	0	2	2	1	0	.167	.417
Ty Cline	OF6	L	21	7	26	2	8	1	0	0	2	0	4	0	.308	.423

2 Pete Whisenant 30 R 1-6, Don Dillard 23 L 1-7, Steve Demeter 25 R 0-5

NAME	T	AGE	W	L	PCT	SV	G	GS	CG	IP	H	BB	SO	SHO	ERA
		27	76	78	.494	30	154	154	32	1382	1308	636	771	10	3.95
Jim Perry	R	24	18	10	.643	1	41	36	16	261	257	91	120	4	3.62
Mudcat Grant	R	24	9	8	.529	0	33	19	5	160	147	78	75	0	4.39
Gary Bell	R	23	9	10	.474	1	28	23	6	155	139	82	109	2	4.12
Barry Latman	R	24	7	7	.500	0	31	20	4	147	146	72	94	0	4.04
Johnny Klippstein	R	32	5	5	.500	14	49	7	0	74	53	35	46	0	2.92
Dick Stigman	L	24	5	11	.313	9	41	18	3	134	118	87	104	0	4.50
1 Johnny Briggs	R	26	4	2	.667	1	36	2	0	36	32	15	19	0	4.50
Frank Funk	R	24	4	2	.667	0	9	0	0	32	27	9	18	0	1.97
Wynn Hawkins	R	24	4	4	.500	0	15	9	1	66	68	39	39	0	4.23
2 Ted Bowsfield	L	24	3	4	.429	0	11	6	1	41	47	20	14	1	5.05
Bobby Locke	R	26	3	5	.375	2	32	11	2	123	121	37	53	2	3.37
2 Don Newcombe	R	34	2	3	.400	1	20	2	0	54	61	8	27	0	4.33
Jack Harshman	L	32	2	4	.333	0	15	8	0	54	50	30	25	0	4.00
Carl Thomas	R	28	1	0	1.000	0	7	0	0	8	10	5	7	0	7.20
Mike Lee	L	19	0	0	—	0	7	0	0	9	6	11	6	0	2.00
Carl Mathias	L	24	0	1	.000	0	5	1	0	15	14	8	13	0	3.60
Bobby Tiefenauer	R	30	0	0	—	0	9	0	0	9	8	3	2	0	0.00
1 Bob Grim	R	30	0	0	.000	0	2	0	0	2	6	1	2	0	13.50

WASHINGTON 5th 73-81 .474 24   COOKIE LAVAGETTO

NAME	G by Pos	B	AGE	G	AB	R	H	2B	3B	HR	RBI	BB	SO	SB	BA	SA
TOTALS			27	154	5248	672	1283	205	43	147	626	584	883	52	.244	.384
Julio Becquer	1B77, P1	L	28	110	298	41	75	15	7	4	35	12	35	1	.252	.389
Billy Gardner	2B145, SS13	R	32	145	592	71	152	26	5	9	56	43	76	0	.257	.363
Jose Valdivielso	SS115, 3B1	R	26	121	268	23	57	11	1	2	19	20	36	1	.213	.246
Reno Bertoia	3B112, 2B21	R	25	121	460	44	122	17	7	4	45	26	58	3	.265	.359
Bob Allison	OF140, 1B4	R	25	144	501	79	126	30	3	15	69	92	94	11	.251	.413
Lenny Green	OF100	L	26	127	304	62	97	16	7	5	33	43	45	21	.294	.430
Jim Lemon	OF145	R	32	148	528	81	142	10	1	38	100	67	114	2	.269	.508
Earl Battey	C136	R	25	137	466	49	126	24	2	15	60	48	68	4	.270	.427
Harmon Killebrew	1B71, 3B65	R	24	124	442	84	122	19	1	31	80	71	106	1	.276	.534
Dan Dobbek	OF78	L	25	110	248	32	54	8	2	10	30	35	41	4	.218	.387
Billy Consolo	SS82, 2B12, 3B2	R	25	100	174	23	36	4	2	3	15	25	29	1	.207	.305
Faye Throneberry	OF34	L	29	85	157	18	39	7	1	3	23	18	33	1	.248	.325
2 Elmer Valo	OF6	L	39	76	64	6	18	3	0	0	16	17	4	0	.281	.328
4 Pete Whisenant	OF47	R	30	58	115	19	26	9	0	3	19	9	14	2	.226	.383
Hal Naragon	C29	L	31	33	92	7	19	2	0	0	5	8	4	0	.207	.228
Don Mincher	1B20	L	22	27	79	10	19	4	1	2	5	11	11	0	.241	.392
Zoilo Versalles	SS15	R	20	15	45	2	6	1	0	1	4	2	10	1	.133	.267

Johnny Schaive 26 R 3-12, Lamar Jacobs 23 R 0-2, 1 Ken Aspromonte 28 R 0-3

NAME	T	AGE	W	L	PCT	SV	G	GS	CG	IP	H	BB	SO	SHO	ERA
		28	73	81	.474	35	154	154	34	1405	1392	538	775	10	3.77
Chuck Stobbs	L	30	12	7	.632	2	40	13	1	119	115	38	72	1	3.33
Camilo Pascual	R	26	12	8	.600	2	26	22	8	152	139	53	143	3	3.02
Pedro Ramos	R	25	11	18	.379	2	43	36	14	274	254	99	160	1	3.45
Jack Kralick	L	25	8	6	.571	1	35	18	7	151	139	45	71	2	3.04
Don Lee	R	26	8	7	.533	3	44	20	1	165	160	64	88	0	3.44
Tex Clevenger	R	27	5	11	.313	7	53	11	1	129	150	49	49	0	4.19
Rudy Hernandez	R	28	4	1	.800	0	21	0	0	35	34	21	22	0	4.37
Hal Woodeshick	L	27	4	5	.444	4	41	14	1	115	131	60	46	0	4.70
2 Ray Moore	R	34	3	2	.600	13	37	0	0	66	49	27	29	0	2.86
1 Bill Fischer	R	29	3	5	.375	0	20	7	1	77	85	17	31	0	4.91
Ted Sadowski	R	24	1	0	1.000	1	9	1	0	17	17	9	12	0	5.29
2 Tom Morgan	R	30	1	3	.250	0	14	0	0	24	36	7	8	0	3.75
Jim Kaat	L	21	1	5	.167	0	13	5	0	50	48	31	25	0	5.58
Ted Abernathy	R	27	0	0	—	0	3	0	0	4	4	1	0	0	12.00
Hector Maestri	R	25	0	0	—	0	1	0	0	2	1	1	1	0	0.00
Julio Becquer	L	28	0	0	—	0	1	0	0	1	1	0	0	0	9.00
Dick Hyde	R	31	0	0	.000	0	7	0	0	9	17	8	3	0	4.00
1 Russ Kemmerer	R	28	0	0	.000	3	17	18	10	17	18	10	7	0	7.94

DETROIT 6th 71-83 .461 26   1 JIMMY DYKES 44-52 .458   BILLY HITCHCOCK 1-0 1.000   2 JOE GORDON 26-31 .456

NAME	G by Pos	B	AGE	G	AB	R	H	2B	3B	HR	RBI	BB	SO	SB	BA	SA
TOTALS			29	154	5202	633	1243	188	34	150	601	636	728	66	.239	.375
Norm Cash	1B99, OF4	L	25	121	353	64	101	16	3	18	63	65	58	4	.286	.501
Frank Bolling	2B138	R	28	139	536	64	136	20	4	9	59	40	48	7	.254	.356
Chico Fernandez	SS130	R	28	133	435	44	105	13	3	4	35	39	50	13	.241	.343
Eddie Yost	3B142	R	33	143	497	78	129	23	2	14	47	125	69	5	.260	.398
Rocky Colavito	OF144	R	26	145	555	67	138	18	1	35	87	53	80	3	.249	.474
Al Kaline	OF142	R	25	147	551	77	153	29	4	15	68	65	47	19	.278	.426
Charlie Maxwell	OF120	L	33	134	482	70	114	16	5	24	81	58	75	5	.237	.440
Lou Berberet	C81	L	30	85	232	18	45	4	0	5	23	41	31	2	.194	.276
Neil Chrisley	OF47, 1B2	L	28	96	220	27	56	10	3	5	24	19	26	2	.255	.395
Steve Bilko	1B62	R	31	78	222	20	46	11	2	9	25	27	31	0	.207	.396
2 Sandy Amoros	OF10	L	30	65	67	7	10	0	0	1	7	12	10	0	.149	.194
Ozzie Virgil	3B42, 2B8, SS5, C1	R	27	62	132	16	30	4	2	3	13	4	14	1	.227	.356
1 Red Wilson	C45	R	31	45	134	17	29	4	0	1	14	16	14	3	.216	.269
2 Harry Chiti	C36	R	27	30	104	9	17	0	0	2	5	10	12	0	.163	.221
Casey Wise	2B17, SS10, 3B1	R	27	30	68	6	10	2	0	2	5	4	9	1	.147	.294
Coot Veal	SS22, 3B3, 2B1	R	27	26	64	8	19	5	1	0	8	11	7	0	.297	.406
3 Hank Foiles	C22	R	31	26	56	5	14	3	0	0	3	1	8	1	.250	.304
Johnny Groth	OF8	R	33	25	19	3	7	1	0	0	2	3	1	0	.368	.421
2 Dick Gernert	1B13, OF6	R	31	21	50	6	15	4	0	1	5	4	5	0	.300	.440
2 Rocky Bridges	3B7, SS3	R	32	10	5	0	1	0	0	0	0	0	0	0	.200	.200
Dick McAuliffe	SS7	L	20	8	27	2	7	1	0	0	3	1	6	0	.259	.333

Gail Harris 28 R 0-5, Em Lindbeck 24 L 0-1

NAME	T	AGE	W	L	PCT	SV	G	GS	CG	IP	H	BB	SO	SHO	ERA
		28	71	83	.461	25	154	154	40	1406	1336	474	824	7	3.64
Frank Lary	R	30	15	15	.500	1	38	36	15	274	262	62	149	2	3.51
Jim Bunning	R	28	11	14	.440	0	36	34	10	252	217	64	201	3	2.79
Don Mossi	L	31	9	8	.529	0	23	22	9	158	158	32	69	2	3.47
Dave Sisler	R	28	7	5	.583	6	41	0	0	80	56	45	47	0	4.26
Pete Burnside	L	29	7	7	.500	2	31	15	2	114	122	50	71	0	4.28
Hank Aguirre	L	29	5	3	.625	0	37	6	1	95	75	30	80	0	2.84
2 Bill Fischer	R	29	5	3	.625	0	20	6	1	55	50	18	24	0	3.44
Bob Bruce	R	27	4	7	.364	0	34	15	1	130	127	56	76	0	3.74
Ray Semproch	R	29	3	0	1.000	0	17	0	0	29	26	16	9	0	4.66
1 Tom Morgan	R	30	2	0	1.000	1	22	0	0	29	33	10	12	0	4.66
Paul Foytack	R	29	2	11	.154	2	28	13	1	97	108	49	38	0	6.12
George Spencer	R	33	0	0	—	0	5	0	0	8	10	5	4	0	3.38
2 Clem Labine	R	33	0	1	.000	0	14	0	0	19	19	12	6	0	5.21
Phil Regan	R	23	0	4	.000	0	17	7	0	68	70	25	38	0	4.50

BOSTON 7th 65-89 .422 32   BILLY JURGES 15-27 .357   DEL BAKER 2-5 .286   PINKY HIGGINS 48-57 .457

NAME	G by Pos	B	AGE	G	AB	R	H	2B	3B	HR	RBI	BB	SO	SB	BA	SA
TOTALS			28	155	5226	615	1359	234	32	124	570	570	798	34	.260	.389
Vic Wertz	1B117	L	35	131	443	45	125	22	0	19	103	37	54	0	.282	.460
Pete Runnels	2B129, 1B57, 3B3	L	32	143	528	80	169	29	2	2	35	71	51	5	.320	.394
Don Buddin	SS124	R	26	124	428	62	105	21	5	6	36	62	59	4	.245	.360
Frank Malzone	3B151	R	30	152	595	60	161	30	2	14	79	36	42	2	.271	.398
Lu Clinton	OF89	R	22	96	298	37	68	17	5	6	37	20	66	4	.228	.379
2 Willie Tasby	OF102	R	27	105	386	68	108	17	1	7	37	51	54	3	.281	.384
Ted Williams	OF87	L	41	113	310	56	98	15	0	29	72	75	41	1	.316	.645
2 Russ Nixon	C74	L	25	80	272	24	81	17	5	5	33	13	23	0	.298	.438
Pumpsie Green	2B69, SS41	B	26	133	260	36	63	10	3	3	21	44	47	5	.242	.338
Gary Geiger (IL)	OF66	L	23	77	245	32	74	13	3	9	33	23	38	2	.302	.490
2 Carroll Hardy	OF59	R	27	73	145	26	34	5	2	2	15	17	40	3	.234	.338
2 Rip Repulski	OF33	R	31	73	136	14	33	6	1	3	20	10	25	0	.243	.368
Haywood Sullivan	C50	R	29	52	124	9	20	1	0	3	10	16	24	0	.161	.242
1 Bobby Thomson	OF27, 1B1	R	36	40	114	9	30	3	1	5	20	11	15	0	.263	.439
1 Marty Keough	OF29	L	26	38	105	15	24	6	1	1	9	8	17	1	.228	.352
Eddie Sadowski (BG)	C36	R	29	38	93	10	20	2	0	3	10	3	22	0	.215	.333
1 Gene Stephens	OF31	L	27	35	109	9	25	4	0	1	8	14	14	5	.229	.321
2 Ray Boone	1B22	R	36	34	66	6	16	1	1	1	11	11	15	0	.205	.256
Don Gile	C15, 1B11	R	25	29	51	6	9	1	1	1	4	3	14	0	.176	.294
Jim Pagliaroni	C18	R	22	28	62	7	19	5	2	0	7	8	6	0	.306	.548
Ron Jackson	1B9	R	26	10	31	1	7	2	0	0	1	6	9	0	.226	.290

Marlan Coughtry 25 L 3-19, Ray Webster 22 R 0-3, 1 Jim Busby 33 R 0-0, Jackie Jensen (VR) 33, Sammy White (VR) 31

NAME	T	AGE	W	L	PCT	SV	G	GS	CG	IP	H	BB	SO	SHO	ERA
		28	65	89	.422	23	154	154	34	1361	1440	580	767	6	4.62
Bill Monbouquette	R	23	14	11	.560	0	35	30	12	215	217	68	134	3	3.64
Mike Fornieles	R	28	10	5	.667	14	70	0	0	109	86	49	64	0	2.64
Tom Brewer	R	28	10	15	.400	1	34	29	8	187	220	72	60	1	4.81
Ike Delock	R	30	9	10	.474	0	24	23	3	129	145	52	49	1	4.74
Billy Muffett	R	29	6	4	.600	0	23	14	4	125	116	36	75	1	3.24
Frank Sullivan	R	30	6	16	.273	1	40	22	4	154	164	52	98	0	5.08
Earl Wilson	R	25	3	2	.600	2	13	6	1	65	61	48	40	0	4.71
Tom Sturdivant	R	30	3	3	.500	1	40	3	0	101	106	45	67	0	4.99
Jerry Casale	R	26	2	9	.182	0	29	14	1	96	113	67	54	0	6.19
Ted Wills	L	26	1	1	.500	1	15	0	0	38	38	16	28	0	7.50
1 Ted Bowsfield	L	24	1	2	.333	2	17	2	0	21	20	13	18	0	5.14
Nels Chittum	R	27	0	0	—	0	4	0	0	4	6	5	4	0	4.50
Tracy Stallard	R	22	0	1	.000	0	4	0	0	4	6	5	5	0	6.53
1 Al Worthington	R	31	0	1	.000	0	12	1	0	17	11	7	7	0	7.00
Arnie Earley	L	27	0	0	—	0	13	1	0	13	12	4	11	0	4.15
Chat Nichols	L	29	0	0	.000	0	5	0	0	9	13	12	4	0	15.75
Dave Hillman (RJ)	R	30	0	0	.000	0	6	1	0	13	15	11	11	0	5.59
Tom Borland	L	27	0	4	.000	1	26	4	0	51	67	23	32	0	6.53

KANSAS CITY 8th 58-96 .377 39   BOB ELLIOTT

NAME	G by Pos	B	AGE	G	AB	R	H	2B	3B	HR	RBI	BB	SO	SB	BA	SA
TOTALS			29	155	5226	615	1303	212	34	110	566	513	744	16	.249	.366
Marv Throneberry	1B71	L	26	104	236	29	59	9	2	11	41	23	60	0	.250	.445
Jerry Lumpe	2B134, SS15	L	27	146	574	69	156	19	3	8	53	48	49	1	.272	.357
Ken Hamlin	SS139	R	25	140	428	51	96	10	2	2	24	44	48	1	.224	.271
2 Andy Carey	3B91	R	28	102	343	30	80	14	4	12	53	26	52	0	.233	.402
Russ Snyder	OF91	L	26	125	304	45	79	10	5	4	26	20	28	7	.260	.365
Bill Tuttle	OF148	R	30	151	565	74	153	21	3	8	40	66	52	1	.256	.347
Norm Siebern	OF75, 1B69	L	26	144	520	69	145	31	6	19	69	72	68	0	.279	.471
Pete Daley	C61, OF1	R	30	73	228	19	60	11	2	2	22	19	26	0	.263	.390
Dick Williams	3B57, 1B34, OF5	R	31	127	420	47	121	31	0	12	65	39	68	0	.288	.448
Hank Bauer	OF67	R	37	95	255	30	71	15	0	3	31	21	36	1	.275	.369
Whitey Herzog (IL)	OF69, 1B2	L	28	83	257	43	67	10	2	8	38	40	32	3	.261	.366
Bob Johnson	SS30, 2B27, 3B11	R	24	76	146	12	30	4	0	1	9	13	25	2	.205	.253
2 Danny Kravitz	C47	L	29	59	175	17	41	7	1	5	17	11	33	1	.234	.366
1 Harry Chiti	C52	R	27	58	190	16	42	7	0	7	19	17	33	1	.221	.337
1 Bob Cerv	OF21	R	34	23	78	14	20	1	1	2	10	5	17	0	.256	.526
Ray Jablonski	3B6	R	34	21	50	4	11	3	0	1	6	5	6	0	.220	.340
Jim Delsing	OF10	L	34	18	40	4	10	3	1	0	3	5	7	1	.250	.375
Leo Posada	OF9	R	24	17	40	4	9	2	0	1	5	6	6	0	.225	.350

Lou Klimchock 20 L 3-10, 1 Hank Foiles 31 R 4-7, Chet Boak 25 R 2-13, Jim McManus 23 L 4-13, Wayne Terwilliger 35 R 0-1

NAME	T	AGE	W	L	PCT	SV	G	GS	CG	IP	H	BB	SO	SHO	ERA
		29	58	96	.377	14	155	155	44	1374	1428	525	664	4	4.38
Bud Daley	L	27	16	16	.500	0	37	35	13	231	234	96	126	1	4.56
Ray Herbert	R	30	14	15	.483	1	37	33	14	253	256	72	122	0	3.27
Dick Hall	R	29	8	13	.381	2	29	28	9	182	183	38	79	1	4.05
Ken Johnson	R	27	5	10	.333	2	42	6	2	120	120	45	83	0	3.84
Ned Garver	R	34	4	9	.308	2	28	15	5	122	170	35	50	2	3.84
Johnny Kucks	R	27	4	10	.286	0	31	17	1	114	140	43	38	0	6.00
Marty Kutyna	R	27	3	2	.600	4	51	0	0	62	64	32	20	0	3.92
2 Bob Giggie	R	26	1	0	1.000	0	6	0	0	9	7	5	6	0	5.68
Leo Kiely	L	30	1	1	.500	0	21	2	1	35	30	15	13	1	1.75
Bob Trowbridge	R	30	1	1	.250	2	15	6	1	84	73	34	33	0	4.63
Don Larsen	R	30	1	10	.091	2	22	15	0	84	97	42	43	0	5.36
Bob Davis	R	26	0	0	—	0	1	0	0	3	3	3	2	0	3.66
Dave Wickersham	R	24	0	1	.000	0	4	0	0	8	9	7	4	0	1.13
Howie Reed	R	23	0	0	—	0	4	0	0	1	1	5	6	0	0.00
John Tsitouris (BJ)	R	24	0	1	.000	0	18	4	0	44	55	19	34	0	6.55
2 Johnny Briggs	R	26	0	2	.000	0	10	3	0	12	12	6	6	0	13.05
1 George Brunet	L	25	0	2	.000	0	7	2	0	10	12	14	4	0	4.50

PITTSBURGH — 1st 95-59 .617 — DANNY MURTAUGH

NAME	G by Pos	B	AGE	G	AB	R	H	2B	3B	HR	RBI	BB	SO	SB	BA	SA
TOTALS			29	155	5406	734	1493	236	56	120	689	486	747	34	.276	.407
Dick Stuart	1B108	R	27	122	438	48	114	17	5	23	83	39	107	0	.260	.479
Bill Mazeroski	2B151	R	23	151	538	58	147	21	5	11	64	40	50	4	.273	.392
Dick Groat	SS136	R	29	138	573	85	186	26	4	2	50	39	35	0	.325	.394
Don Hoak	3B155	R	32	155	553	97	156	24	9	16	79	74	74	4	.282	.445
Roberto Clemente	OF142	R	25	144	570	89	179	22	6	16	94	39	72	4	.314	.458
Bill Virdon	OF109	L	29	120	409	60	108	16	9	8	40	40	44	4	.264	.406
Bob Skinner	OF141	L	28	145	571	83	156	33	6	15	86	59	86	11	.273	.431
Smoky Burgess	C89	L	33	110	337	33	99	15	2	7	39	35	13	0	.294	.412
Gino Cimoli	OF91	R	30	101	307	36	82	14	4	0	28	12	43	1	.267	.339
Rocky Nelson	1B73	L	35	93	200	34	60	11	4	7	35	24	15	1	.300	.470
Hal Smith	C71	R	29	77	258	37	76	18	2	11	45	22	48	1	.295	.508
Dick Schofield	SS23, 2B10, 3B1	B	25	65	102	9	34	4	1	0	10	16	20	0	.333	.392
Joe Christopher	OF17	R	24	50	56	21	13	2	0	1	3	5	8	1	.232	.321
Gene Baker	3B7, 2B1	R	35	33	37	5	9	0	0	1	4	2	9	0	.243	.243
Bob Oldis	C22	R	32	22	20	1	4	1	0	0	3	4	1	0	.200	.250

R C Stephens 25 R 0-3, Mickey Vernon 42 L 1-8, 1 Danny Kravitz 29 L 0-6, Harry Bright 30 R 0-4, Dick Barone 27 R 0-6, Roman Mejias 29 R 0-1

NAME	T	AGE	W	L	PCT	SV	G	GS	CG	IP	H	BB	SO	SHO	ERA
		29	95	59	.617	33	155	155	47	1400	1363	386	811	11	3.49
Vern Law	R	30	20	9	.690	0	35	35	18	272	266	40	120	3	3.08
Bob Friend	R	29	18	12	.600	1	38	37	16	276	266	45	183	4	3.00
2 Vinegar Bend Mizell	L	29	13	5	.722	0	23	23	8	156	141	46	71	3	3.12
Harvey Haddix	L	34	11	10	.524	1	29	28	4	172	189	38	101	0	3.98
Roy Face	R	32	10	8	.556	24	68	0	0	115	93	29	72	0	2.90
Freddie Green	L	26	8	4	.667	3	45	0	0	70	61	33	49	0	3.21
Joe Gibbon	L	25	4	2	.667	0	27	9	0	80	87	31	60	0	4.05
3 Clem Labine	R	33	3	0	1.000	3	15	0	0	30	29	11	21	0	1.50
Paul Giel	R	27	2	0	1.000	0	16	0	0	33	33	15	21	0	5.73
Tom Cheney	R	25	2	2	.500	0	11	8	1	52	44	33	35	1	3.98
Earl Francis	R	23	1	0	1.000	0	7	0	0	18	14	4	8	0	2.00
Jim Umbricht	R	29	1	2	.333	1	17	3	0	41	40	27	26	0	5.05
George Witt	R	26	1	2	.333	0	10	6	0	30	33	12	15	0	4.20
Bennie Daniels	R	28	1	3	.250	0	10	6	0	40	52	17	16	0	7.88
Don Gross	L	29	0	0	—	0	5	0	0	5	5	0	3	0	3.60
Diomedes Olivo	L	41	0	0	—	0	10	0	0	10	8	5	10	0	2.70

MILWAUKEE — 2nd 88-66 .571 7 — CHUCK DRESSEN

NAME	G by Pos	B	AGE	G	AB	R	H	2B	3B	HR	RBI	BB	SO	SB	BA	SA
TOTALS			30	154	5263	724	1393	198	48	170	681	463	793	69	.265	.417
Joe Adcock	1B136	R	32	138	514	55	153	21	4	25	91	46	86	2	.298	.500
Chuck Cottier	2B92	R	24	95	229	29	52	8	0	3	19	14	21	1	.227	.301
Johnny Logan	SS136	R	33	136	482	52	118	14	4	7	42	40	40	1	.245	.334
Eddie Mathews	3B153	L	28	153	548	108	152	19	7	39	124	111	113	7	.277	.551
Hank Aaron	OF153, 2B1	R	26	153	590	102	172	20	11	40	126	60	63	16	.292	.566
Bill Bruton	OF149	L	34	151	629	112	180	27	13	12	54	41	97	22	.286	.428
Wes Covington	OF72	L	28	95	281	25	70	16	1	10	35	15	37	1	.249	.420
Del Crandall	C141	R	30	142	537	81	158	14	1	19	77	34	36	4	.294	.430
Al Spangler	OF92	L	26	101	105	26	28	5	2	0	6	14	17	6	.267	.352
Red Schoendienst	2B62	B	37	68	226	21	58	9	1	1	19	17	13	1	.257	.319
Felix Mantilla	2B26, SS25, OF8	R	26	63	148	21	38	7	0	3	11	7	16	3	.257	.365
2 Al Dark	OF25, 1B10, 3B4, 2B3	R	38	50	141	16	42	6	2	1	18	7	13	0	.298	.390
Mel Roach	OF21, 2B20, 3B1, 1B1	R	27	48	140	12	42	12	0	3	18	6	19	0	.300	.450
Lee Maye	OF19	L	25	41	83	14	25	6	0	2	7	2	21	5	.301	.373
Eddie Haas	OF2	R	25	32	32	4	7	2	0	1	5	5	14	0	.219	.375
Frank Torre	1B17	L	28	21	44	2	9	1	0	0	5	3	6	0	.205	.227
Charlie Lau	C16	L	27	21	53	4	10	2	0	0	2	6	10	0	.189	.226
1 Ray Boone	1B4	R	36	7	12	3	3	1	0	0	4	5	1	0	.250	.333
Stan Lopata	C4	R	34	7	8	0	1	0	0	0	0	1	3	0	.125	.125
Mike Krsnich	OF3	R	24	8	9	0	3	1	0	0	2	0	1	0	.333	.444

Len Gabrielson 20 L 0-3, Joe Torre 19 R 1-2

NAME	T	AGE	W	L	PCT	SV	G	GS	CG	IP	H	BB	SO	SHO	ERA
		29	88	66	.571	28	154	154	55	1387	1327	518	807	13	3.76
Warren Spahn	L	39	21	10	.677	2	40	33	18	268	254	74	154	4	3.49
Lew Burdette	R	33	19	13	.594	4	45	32	18	276	277	35	83	4	3.36
Bob Buhl	R	31	16	9	.640	0	36	33	11	239	202	103	121	2	3.09
Joey Jay	R	24	9	8	.529	1	32	11	3	133	128	59	90	0	3.25
Carl Willey	R	29	6	7	.462	0	28	21	2	145	136	65	109	1	4.34
Juan Pizarro	L	23	6	7	.462	0	21	17	3	115	105	72	88	0	4.54
Ron Piche	R	25	3	5	.375	9	37	0	0	48	48	23	38	0	3.56
Don McMahon	R	30	3	6	.333	10	48	0	0	64	66	32	50	0	5.91
2 George Brunet	L	25	2	0	1.000	0	17	6	0	50	53	22	39	0	5.04
3 Bob Rush	R	34	1	1	.500	0	15	2	0	24	25	8	15	0	4.20
Don Nottebart	R	24	1	0	1.000	1	5	0	0	15	14	5	8	0	4.20
Terry Fox	R	24	0	0	—	0	5	0	0	8	6	6	6	0	4.50
1 Bob Giggie	R	26	0	0	—	0	4	0	0	5	4	5	0	0	4.50
Ken MacKenzie	L	26	0	1	.000	0	9	0	0	8	9	3	6	0	6.75

ST. LOUIS — 3rd 86-68 .558 9 — SOLLY HEMUS

NAME	G by Pos	B	AGE	G	AB	R	H	2B	3B	HR	RBI	BB	SO	SB	BA	SA
TOTALS			30	155	5187	639	1317	213	48	138	592	501	792	48	.254	.393
Bill White	1B123, OF29	L	26	144	554	81	157	27	10	16	79	42	83	12	.283	.455
Julian Javier	2B119	R	23	119	451	55	107	19	8	4	21	21	72	19	.237	.341
Daryl Spencer	SS138, 2B16	R	30	148	507	70	131	20	8	11	58	81	74	1	.258	.404
Ken Boyer	3B146	R	29	151	552	95	168	26	10	32	97	56	77	8	.304	.562
Joe Cunningham	OF116, 1B15	L	29	139	492	68	138	28	3	6	59	59	59	1	.280	.386
Curt Flood	OF134, 3B1	R	22	140	396	37	94	20	1	8	38	35	54	0	.237	.354
Stan Musial	OF59, 1B29	L	39	116	331	49	91	17	1	17	63	41	34	1	.275	.486
Hal Smith	C124	R	29	127	337	20	77	16	0	2	28	29	33	1	.228	.294
Alex Grammas	SS40, 2B38, 3B13	R	34	102	196	20	48	4	1	4	17	12	15	0	.245	.337
Bob Nieman	OF55	R	33	81	188	19	54	13	5	4	31	24	31	0	.287	.473
Carl Sawatski	C67	L	32	78	179	16	41	4	0	6	27	22	24	0	.229	.352
2 Walt Moryn	OF62	L	34	75	200	24	49	4	3	11	35	17	38	0	.245	.460
George Crowe	1B5	L	39	73	72	5	17	3	0	4	13	5	16	0	.236	.444
Charlie James	OF37	R	22	43	50	5	9	1	0	2	5	1	12	0	.180	.320
Leon Wagner	OF32	L	26	39	98	12	21	2	0	4	11	17	17	0	.214	.357
John Glenn	OF28	R	31	32	31	4	8	0	1	0	5	0	8	0	.258	.323
Ellis Burton	OF23	B	23	29	28	5	6	1	0	0	2	4	14	0	.214	.250
Wally Shannon	2B15, SS1	L	27	18	23	2	4	0	0	0	1	3	6	0	.174	.174
Don Landrum	OF13	L	24	13	49	7	12	0	1	2	3	4	6	3	.245	.408
Tim McCarver	C5	L	18	10	10	3	2	0	0	0	1	0	2	0	.200	.200
Dick Gray	2B4, 3B1	R	28	9	5	1	0	0	0	0	0	2	2	0	.000	.000
Gary Kolb	OF2	L	20	9	3	1	0	0	0	0	0	0	0	0	.000	.000
Chris Cannizzaro	C6	R	22	7	9	0	2	0	0	0	1	0	3	0	.222	.222
Julio Gotay	SS2, 3B1	R	21	8	8	1	3	0	0	0	1	1	1	1	.375	.375
Ed Olivares	3B1	R	21	5	0	0	0	0	0	0	0	0	0	0	.000	.000

Darrell Johnson 31 R 0-2, Duke Carmel 23 L 0-3, 3 Rocky Bridges 32 R 0-0, 2 Del Rice 37 R 0-2, Bob Sadowski 23 L 0-1, Doug Clemens 21 L 0-0

NAME	T	AGE	W	L	PCT	SV	G	GS	CG	IP	H	BB	SO	SHO	ERA
		26	86	68	.558	30	155	155	37	1371	1316	511	906	11	3.64
Ernie Broglio	R	24	21	9	.700	0	52	24	9	226	172	100	188	3	2.75
Larry Jackson	R	29	18	13	.581	0	43	38	14	282	277	70	171	3	3.48
Lindy McDaniel	R	24	12	4	.750	26	65	2	1	116	85	24	105	0	2.09
Ray Sadecki	L	19	9	9	.500	0	26	26	7	157	148	86	95	1	3.78
2 Curt Simmons	L	31	7	4	.636	0	23	17	3	152	149	31	63	1	2.66
Bob Miller	R	21	4	3	.571	0	15	7	0	53	53	17	33	0	3.40
Bob Duliba (AA)	R	25	4	4	.500	0	27	0	0	41	49	16	23	0	4.17
Ron Kline	R	28	4	9	.308	1	34	17	1	118	133	43	54	0	6.03
Bob Gibson	R	24	3	6	.333	0	27	12	2	87	97	48	69	0	5.59
1 Marshall Bridges	L	29	2	2	.500	1	20	1	0	31	33	16	27	0	3.48
3 Bob Grim	R	30	1	0	1.000	0	15	0	0	17	26	8	15	0	5.82
1 Vinegar Bend Mizell	L	29	1	3	.250	0	9	0	0	55	64	28	42	0	4.58
Ed Bauta	R	25	0	0	—	0	16	0	0	16	14	11	6	0	6.19
Cal Browning	L	22	0	0	—	0	1	0	0	1	5	1	0	0	27.00
Frank Barnes	R	33	0	1	.000	0	4	1	0	8	8	9	8	0	3.38
Mel Nelson	L	24	0	1	.000	0	2	1	0	8	7	2	7	0	3.38

LOS ANGELES — 4th 82-72 .532 13 — WALT ALSTON

NAME	G by Pos	B	AGE	G	AB	R	H	2B	3B	HR	RBI	BB	SO	SB	BA	SA
TOTALS			28	154	5227	662	1333	216	38	126	606	529	837	95	.255	.383
Norm Larker	1B119, OF2	L	29	133	440	56	142	26	3	5	78	34	42	1	.323	.430
Charlie Neal	2B136, SS3	R	29	139	477	60	122	23	4	8	40	48	75	5	.256	.363
Maury Wills	SS145	B	27	148	516	75	152	15	2	0	27	35	47	50	.295	.331
Jim Gilliam	3B130, 2B30	B	31	151	557	96	138	20	4	8	40	96	28	12	.248	.348
Frank Howard	OF115, 1B4	R	23	117	448	54	120	15	2	23	77	32	108	0	.268	.464
Tommy Davis	OF87, 3B5	R	21	110	352	43	97	18	1	11	44	13	35	6	.276	.426
Wally Moon	OF127	L	30	138	469	74	140	21	6	13	69	67	53	6	.299	.452
Johnny Roseboro	C87, 1B1, 3B1	L	27	103	287	22	61	15	3	8	42	44	53	7	.213	.369
Duke Snider	OF75	L	33	101	235	38	57	13	5	14	36	46	54	1	.243	.519
Gil Hodges	1B92, 3B10	R	36	101	197	22	39	8	1	8	30	26	37	0	.198	.371
Don Demeter	OF62	R	25	64	168	23	46	7	1	9	29	8	34	0	.274	.488
Joe Pignatano	C40	R	30	58	90	11	21	4	0	2	9	15	17	1	.233	.344
Chuck Essegian	OF18	R	28	52	79	8	17	3	0	3	11	8	24	0	.215	.367
Bob Lillis	SS23, 3B14, 2B1	R	30	48	60	6	16	4	0	0	2	6	2	0	.267	.333
Norm Sherry	C44	R	28	47	138	22	39	4	1	8	19	12	29	0	.283	.500
2 Irv Noren		L	35	26	25	1	5	0	0	1	7	1	8	0	.200	.320
Willie Davis	OF22	L	20	22	88	12	28	6	1	2	10	4	12	3	.318	.477
Bob Aspromonte	SS15, 3B4	R	22	21	55	1	10	1	0	1	6	0	15	0	.182	.255
Charley Smith	3B18	R	22	18	60	2	10	1	1	0	5	1	15	0	.167	.217
Ron Fairly	OF13	L	21	14	37	6	4	0	3	1	3	7	12	0	.108	.351
Doug Camilli	C6	R	23	6	24	4	8	2	0	1	4	2	4	0	.333	.542
1 Sandy Amoros	OF3	L	30	9	14	1	2	0	0	0	2	4	1	0	.143	.143
Carl Furillo	OF2	R	38	8	10	1	2	0	0	0	1	0	2	0	.200	.200
1 Rip Repulski	OF2	R	31	4	5	0	1	0	0	0	0	0	1	0	.200	.200

NAME	T	AGE	W	L	PCT	SV	G	GS	CG	IP	H	BB	SO	SHO	ERA
		26	82	72	.532	20	154	154	46	1398	1218	564	1122	13	3.40
Don Drysdale	R	23	15	14	.517	2	41	36	15	269	214	72	246	5	2.84
Larry Sherry	R	24	14	10	.583	7	57	3	1	142	125	84	114	0	3.80
Stan Williams	R	23	14	10	.583	1	38	30	9	207	162	72	175	2	3.00
Johnny Podres	L	27	14	12	.538	0	34	33	8	228	217	71	159	1	3.08
Ed Roebuck	R	28	8	3	.727	8	58	0	0	117	109	38	77	0	2.77
Roger Craig (BS)	R	30	8	3	.727	0	21	15	6	116	99	43	69	1	3.26
Sandy Koufax	L	24	8	13	.381	1	37	26	7	175	133	100	197	2	3.91
Jim Golden	R	24	1	0	1.000	0	7	1	0	7	6	4	6	0	6.43
Phil Ortega	R	20	0	0	—	0	3	1	0	6	12	5	4	0	18.00
Ed Palmquist	R	27	0	1	.000	0	22	0	0	39	34	16	23	0	2.54
1 Clem Labine	R	33	0	1	.000	1	13	0	0	17	26	8	15	0	5.82
Ed Rakow	R	25	0	0	—	0	22	0	0	22	30	11	9	0	7.36
Danny McDevitt	L	27	0	4	.000	0	24	7	0	53	51	42	30	0	4.25

SAN FRANCISCO — 5th 79-75 .513 16 — BILL RIGNEY 33-25 .569 / TOM SHEEHAN 46-50 .479

NAME	G by Pos	B	AGE	G	AB	R	H	2B	3B	HR	RBI	BB	SO	SB	BA	SA
TOTALS			29	156	5324	671	1357	220	62	130	622	467	846	86	.255	.393
Willie McCovey	1B71	L	22	101	260	37	62	15	3	13	51	45	53	1	.238	.469
Don Blasingame	2B133	L	28	136	523	72	123	12	8	2	31	49	53	14	.235	.300
Ed Bressoud	SS115	R	28	116	386	37	87	19	6	9	43	35	71	1	.225	.376
Jim Davenport	3B103, SS7	R	26	112	363	43	91	15	3	6	38	26	58	0	.251	.358
Willie Kirkland	OF143	L	26	146	515	59	130	21	10	21	65	44	86	12	.252	.454
Willie Mays	OF152	R	29	153	595	107	190	29	12	29	103	61	70	25	.319	.555
Orlando Cepeda	OF91, 1B63	R	22	151	569	81	169	36	3	24	96	34	91	15	.297	.497
Bob Schmidt	C108	R	27	110	344	31	92	12	1	8	37	26	51	0	.267	.378
Joey Amalfitano	3B63, 2B33, SS3, OF1	R	26	106	328	47	91	15	3	1	27	26	31	2	.277	.351
Felipe Alou	OF95	R	25	106	322	48	85	17	3	8	44	16	42	10	.264	.410
Andre Rodgers	SS41, 3B21, 1B6, OF2	R	25	81	217	22	53	8	5	2	22	24	44	1	.244	.355
Jim Marshall	1B28, OF6	L	28	75	118	19	28	7	0	1	17	14	24	0	.237	.339
Hobie Landrith	C70	L	30	71	190	18	46	10	0	3	20	23	11	1	.242	.311
2 Dave Philley	OF10, 3B3	L	40	39	61	5	9	6	0	0	6	5	14	0	.164	.213
1 Dale Long	1B10	L	34	37	54	4	9	0	0	3	6	5	9	0	.167	.333
Jose Pagan	SS11, 3B1	R	25	32	49	8	14	2	2	0	5	3	2	2	.286	.408
Neil Wilson	C6	R	25	6	10	0	0	0	0	0	0	0	0	0	.000	.000
Matty Alou	OF1	L	21	4	3	1	1	0	0	0	0	1	0	0	.333	.333

NAME	T	AGE	W	L	PCT	SV	G	GS	CG	IP	H	BB	SO	SHO	ERA
		29	79	75	.513	26	156	155	55	1396	1288	512	897	16	3.44
Sam Jones	R	34	18	14	.563	0	39	35	13	234	200	91	190	3	3.19
Mike McCormick	L	21	15	12	.556	0	40	34	15	253	228	65	154	4	2.70
Jack Sanford	R	31	12	14	.462	0	37	34	11	219	199	99	125	6	3.82
Billy O'Dell	L	27	8	13	.381	2	43	24	6	203	198	72	145	1	3.19
Stu Miller	R	32	7	6	.538	2	47	3	2	102	100	31	65	0	3.88
Juan Marichal	R	22	6	2	.750	0	11	11	6	81	59	28	58	1	2.67
Johnny Antonelli	L	30	6	7	.462	1	41	10	1	112	106	47	57	1	3.78
Billy Loes	R	30	2	3	.600	5	37	0	0	46	40	17	28	0	4.89
Bud Byerly	R	39	1	0	1.000	2	19	0	0	32	36	6	13	0	5.32
Eddie Fisher	R	23	1	1	.500	0	13	2	1	26	25	11	12	0	3.46
Sherman Jones	R	25	1	1	.500	0	17	3	1	31	31	11	10	0	3.09
Georges Maranda	R	28	1	2	.200	0	17	1	0	51	50	20	28	0	4.59
Joe Shipley	R	25	0	0	—	0	15	0	0	20	20	9	5	0	5.40
Don Choate	R	21	0	0	—	0	4	0	0	8	4	4	4	0	2.25
Ray Monzant	L	27	0	0	—	0	2	0	0	4	7	2	6	0	9.00

CINCINNATI 6th 67-87 .435 28 FRED HUTCHINSON

NAME	G by Pos	B	AGE	G	AB	R	H	2B	3B	HR	RBI	BB	SO	SB	BA	SA
TOTALS			28	154	5289	640	1324	230	40	140	604	512	858	73	.250	.388
Frank Robinson	1B78, OF51, 3B1	R	24	139	464	86	138	33	6	31	83	82	67	13	.297	.595
Billy Martin	2B97	R	32	103	317	34	78	13	1	3	16	27	34	0	.246	.334
Roy McMillan	SS116, 2B10	R	30	124	399	42	94	12	2	10	42	35	40	2	.236	.351
Eddie Kasko	3B86, 2B33, SS15	R	28	126	479	56	140	21	1	6	51	46	37	9	.292	.378
Gus Bell	OF131	R	31	143	515	65	135	19	5	12	62	29	40	4	.262	.388
Vada Pinson	OF154	L	21	154	652	107	187	37	12	20	61	47	96	32	.287	.472
2 Wally Post	OF67	R	30	77	249	36	70	14	0	17	38	28	51	0	.281	.542
Ed Bailey	C129	L	29	133	441	52	115	19	3	13	67	59	70	1	.261	.406
Jerry Lynch	OF32	L	29	102	159	23	46	8	2	6	27	16	25	0	.289	.478
Willie Jones	3B46, 2B1	R	34	79	149	16	40	7	0	3	27	31	16	1	.268	.376
Gordy Coleman	1B66	L	25	66	251	26	68	10	1	6	32	12	32	1	.271	.390
Cliff Cook	3B47, OF4	R	23	54	149	9	31	7	0	3	13	8	51	0	.208	.315
Elio Chacon	2B43, OF2	R	23	49	116	14	21	1	0	0	7	14	23	7	.181	.190
Leo Cardenas	SS47	R	21	48	142	13	33	2	4	1	12	6	32	1	.232	.324
2 Harry Anderson	1B15, OF4	L	28	42	66	6	11	3	0	1	9	11	20	0	.167	.258
1 Tony Gonzalez	OF31	R	23	39	99	10	21	5	1	3	14	4	27	1	.212	.374
Dutch Dotterer	C31	R	28	33	79	4	18	5	0	2	11	13	10	0	.228	.367
1 Lee Walls	OF24, 1B2	R	27	29	84	12	23	3	2	1	7	17	20	2	.274	.393

Frank House 30 L 5-28, Whitey Lockman 33 L 2-10, Joe Azcue 20 R 3-31, Joe Gaines 23 R 3-15, Rogelio Alvarez 22 R 1-9, 1 Pete Whisenant 30 R 0-1

NAME	T	AGE	W	L	PCT	SV	G	GS	CG	IP	H	BB	SO	SHO	ERA
TOTALS		29	67	87	.435	35	154	154	33	1390	1417	442	740	8	4.00
Bob Purkey	R	30	17	11	.607	0	41	33	11	253	259	59	97	1	3.59
Jim O'Toole	L	23	12	12	.500	1	34	31	7	196	198	66	124	2	3.81
Jay Hook	R	23	11	18	.379	0	36	33	10	222	222	73	103	2	4.50
Jim Brosnan	R	30	7	2	.778	12	57	2	0	99	79	22	62	0	2.36
2 Marshall Bridges	L	29	4	2	.667	2	14	0	0	25	14	7	26	0	1.08
1 Don Newcombe	R	34	4	6	.400	0	16	15	1	83	99	14	36	0	4.50
Cal McLish	R	34	4	14	.222	0	37	21	2	151	170	48	56	1	4.17
2 Bob Grim	R	30	2	2	.500	2	26	0	0	32	10	22	0		4.50
Jim Maloney	R	20	2	6	.250	0	11	10	2	64	61	37	48	1	4.64
Raul Sanchez	R	29	1	0	1.000	0	15	12	11	5	0			0	4.80
Brooks Lawrence	R	35	1	0	1.000	1	7	0	0	9	8	4	2	0	10.13
Bill Henry	L	32	1	5	.167	17	51	0	0	68	62	20	58	0	3.18
Joe Nuxhall	L	31	1	8	.111	0	38	6	0	112	130	27	72	0	4.42
Duane Richards	R	23	0	0	—	2	0	0	3	5	2	2		0	9.00
Claude Osteen	L	20	0	1	.000	0	20	3	0	48	53	30	15	0	5.06
Ted Wieand	R	27	0	1	.000	0	5	0	0	9	8	3	5	0	11.25
Orlando Pena	R	26	0	1	.000	0	9	0	0	9	8	3	9	0	3.00

CHICAGO 7th 60-94 .390 35 CHARLIE GRIMM 6-11 .353 LOU BOUDREAU 54-83 .394

NAME	G by Pos	B	AGE	G	AB	R	H	2B	3B	HR	RBI	BB	SO	SB	BA	SA
TOTALS			28	156	5311	634	1293	213	48	119	600	531	897	51	.243	.369
2 Ed Bouchee	1B80	L	27	98	299	33	71	11	1	5	44	45	51	2	.237	.331
Jerry Kindall	2B82, SS2	R	25	89	246	17	59	16	2	2	23	5	52	4	.240	.346
Ernie Banks	SS156	R	29	156	597	94	162	32	7	41	117	71	69	1	.271	.554
Ron Santo	3B94	R	20	95	347	44	87	24	2	9	44	31	44	0	.251	.409
Bob Will	OF121	L	28	138	475	58	121	20	9	6	53	47	54	1	.255	.373
Richie Ashburn	OF146	L	33	151	547	99	159	16	5	0	40	116	50	16	.291	.338
George Altman	OF79, 1B21	L	27	119	334	50	89	16	4	13	51	32	67	4	.266	.455
El Tappe	C49	R	33	51	103	11	24	7	0	0	3	11	12	0	.233	.301
Frank Thomas	1B50, OF49, 3B33	R	31	135	479	54	114	12	1	21	64	28	74	1	.238	.399
Don Zimmer	2B75, 3B45, SS5, OF2	R	29	132	368	37	95	16	1	6	35	27	56	4	.258	.389
Sammy Taylor (AJ)	C43	L	27	74	150	14	31	9	0	3	17	6	18	0	.207	.327
Moe Thacker	C50	R	26	54	90	5	14	1	0	0	6	14	20	1	.156	.167
1 Earl Averill	C34, 3B1, OF1	R	28	52	102	14	24	4	0	1	13	11	16	1	.235	.304
1 Dick Gernert	1B18, OF5	R	31	52	96	8	24	3	0	0	10	10	11	0	.250	.281
Al Heist	OF33	R	32	41	102	11	28	5	3	1	6	10	12	3	.275	.412
1 Walt Moryn	OF30	L	34	38	109	12	32	4	0	3	13	9	13	1	.294	.385
Lou Johnson	OF25	R	25	34	68	6	14	2	1	0	1	5	19	3	.206	.265
2 Don Cardwell	P31	R	24	33	69	9	14	1	0	3	6	0	30	1	.203	.348
Danny Murphy	OF21	L	17	31	75	7	9	2	0	1	6	4	13	0	.120	.187
1 Tony Taylor	2B19	R	24	19	76	14	20	3	3	1	9	3	14	2	.263	.421

Grady Hatton 37 L 13-38, Jim Hegan 39 R 9-43, 1 Del Rice 37 R 12-52, Sammy Drake 25 B 1-15, Billy Williams 22 L 13-47, Art Schult 32 R 2-15, 1 Irv Noren 35 L 1-11, 1 Cal Neeman 31 R 2-13, Dick Bertell 24 R 2-15, Nelson Mathews 18 R 2-8, Jim McKnight 24 R 2-6

NAME	T	AGE	W	L	PCT	SV	G	GS	CG	IP	H	BB	SO	SHO	ERA
TOTALS		25	60	94	.390	25	156	156	36	1403	1393	565	805	6	4.35
Glen Hobbie	R	24	16	20	.444	1	46	36	16	259	253	101	134	4	3.96
Bob Anderson	R	24	9	11	.450	1	38	30	5	204	201	68	115	0	4.10
Don Elston	R	31	8	9	.471	11	60	0	0	127	109	55	85	0	3.40
2 Don Cardwell	R	24	8	14	.364	0	31	26	6	177	166	68	129	1	4.37
Dick Ellsworth	L	20	7	13	.350	0	31	27	6	177	170	72	94	0	3.71
Moe Drabowsky	R	24	3	1	.750	1	32	7	0	50	71	23	26	0	6.48
Mark Freeman	R	29	3	3	.500	1	30	8	1	77	70	33	50	0	5.61
Ben Johnson	R	29	2	1	.667	1	17	0	0	29	39	11	9	0	4.97
Joe Schaffernoth	R	22	2	4	.333	0	33	0	0	55	46	17	33	0	2.78
Seth Morehead	L	26	2	9	.182	4	45	7	2	123	123	46	64	0	3.95
Art Ceccarelli	L	30	2	3	.400	0	11	0	0	13	16	4	10	0	5.54
John Goetz	R	22	0	0	—	0	3	0	0	5	6	1	3	0	13.50
Dick Burwell	R	20	0	0	—	0	2	0	0	10	11	7	1	0	5.40
Al Schroll	R	28	0	0	—	0	2	0	0	2	1	0	1	0	9.00
Mel Wright	R	32	0	0	.000	2	16	0	0	16	17	3	8	0	5.06
Jim Brewer (BY)	R	22	0	3	.000	0	2	0	0	22	25	6	7	0	5.73
Jack Drott	R	24	0	6	.000	0	11	5	0	55	63	42	32	0	7.20

PHILADELPHIA 8th 59-95 .383 36 EDDIE SAWYER 0-1 1.000 ANDY COHEN 1-0 1.000 GENE MAUCH 58-94 .382

NAME	G by Pos	B	AGE	G	AB	R	H	2B	3B	HR	RBI	BB	SO	SB	BA	SA
TOTALS			26	154	5169	546	1235	196	44	99	503	448	1054	45	.239	.351
Pancho Herrera	1B134, 3B1	R	26	145	512	61	144	26	4	17	71	51	136	2	.281	.455
2 Tony Taylor	2B123, 3B4	R	24	127	505	66	145	22	4	4	35	33	66	24	.287	.370
Ruben Amaro	SS92	R	24	92	264	25	61	9	1	0	16	21	32	0	.231	.273
4 Al Dark	3B53, 1B1	R	38	55	198	29	48	5	1	3	14	19	14	1	.242	.323
Ken Walters	OF119	R	26	124	426	42	102	10	8	3	37	16	50	4	.239	.319
Bobby Del Greco	OF89	R	27	100	300	48	71	16	4	10	26	54	64	1	.237	.417
Johnny Callison (KL)	OF86	L	21	99	288	36	75	11	5	9	30	45	70	0	.260	.427
Jimmie Coker	C76	R	24	81	252	18	54	5	3	6	34	23	45	0	.214	.329
Bobby Gene Smith	OF70, 3B1	R	26	98	217	24	62	5	2	4	27	10	28	3	.286	.382
Tony Curry	OF64	L	21	95	245	26	64	14	2	6	34	16	53	0	.261	.408
Clay Dalrymple	C48	L	23	82	158	11	43	6	2	4	21	15	21	0	.272	.411
Bobby Malkmus	SS29, 2B23, 3B12	R	28	79	133	16	28	4	1	1	12	11	22	1	.211	.278
2 Tony Gonzalez	OF67	L	23	78	241	27	72	17	5	6	33	11	47	2	.299	.485
Ted Lepcio	3B50, SS14, 2B5	R	29	69	141	16	32	7	0	2	8	17	41	0	.227	.319
2 Lee Walls	3B34, OF13, 1B7	R	27	65	181	19	36	6	3	1	19	14	32	3	.199	.293
2 Cal Neeman	C52	R	31	59	160	13	29	6	2	4	13	16	42	0	.181	.319
Joe Koppe (WJ)	SS55, 3B2	R	29	58	170	13	29	6	1	1	13	23	47	1	.171	.235
1 Harry Anderson	OF16, 1B12	L	28	38	93	10	23	2	0	5	22	10	19	0	.247	.430
1 Wally Post	OF22	R	30	34	84	11	24	6	1	2	12	9	24	0	.286	.452
1 Joe Morgan	3B24	R	29	26	83	5	11	2	2	0	2	6	11	0	.133	.205
1 Ed Bouchee	1B22	L	27	22	65	1	17	4	0	2	9	8	9	1	.262	.323

1 Dave Philley 40 B 5-15, Jim Woods 20 R 6-34, 1 Don Cardwell 24 R 2-8, Bobby Wine 21 R 2-14

NAME	T	AGE	W	L	PCT	SV	G	GS	CG	IP	H	BB	SO	SHO	ERA
TOTALS		27	59	95	.383	16	154	154	45	1375	1423	439	736	6	4.01
Robin Roberts	R	33	12	16	.429	1	35	33	13	237	256	34	122	2	4.03
Dick Farrell	R	26	10	6	.625	11	59	0	0	103	88	29	70	0	2.71
Gene Conley	R	29	8	14	.364	0	29	25	9	183	192	42	117	2	3.69
Art Mahaffey	R	22	7	3	.700	0	14	12	5	93	78	34	56	1	2.32
Chris Short	L	22	6	9	.400	3	42	10	2	107	101	52	54	0	3.95
John Buzhardt	R	23	5	16	.238	0	30	29	5	200	198	68	73	3	3.87
Jim Owens	R	26	4	14	.222	0	31	22	6	150	182	64	83	0	5.04
Jack Meyer (XJ)	R	28	3	1	.750	0	7	4	0	25	11	18	4	0	4.32
Dallas Green	R	25	3	6	.333	0	23	10	5	109	100	44	51	1	4.05
1 Don Cardwell	R	24	1	2	.333	0	5	4	0	28	28	11	21	0	4.50
Al Neiger	L	21	0	0	—	0	4	2	0	13	16	4	3	0	5.54
1 Curt Simmons	L	31	0	0	—	0	3	2	0	13	16	4	6	0	18.00
Hank Mason	R	29	0	0	—	0	3	0	0	4	3	1	2	0	9.00
Taylor Phillips	L	27	0	1	.000	0	10	1	0	14	11	9	6	0	8.36
Ruben Gomez	R	32	0	0	.000	0	22	1	0	52	68	9	24	0	5.37
Humberto Robinson	R	30	0	4	.000	0	33	1	0	50	48	22	31	0	3.42

WORLD SERIES — PITTSBURGH (NL) 4 NEW YORK (AL) 3

LINE SCORES

TEAM	1	2	3	4	5	6	7	8	9	10	11	12	R	H	E

Game 1 October 5 at Pittsburgh
NY (AL) 1 0 0   1 0 0   0 0 2   4 13 2
PIT (NL) 3 0 0   2 0 1   0 0 X   6 8 0
Ditmar, Coates (1),   Law, Face (8)
Maas (5), Duren (7)

Game 2 October 6 at Pittsburgh
NY 0 0 0   1 2 7   3 0 1   16 19 1
PIT 0 0 0   1 0 0   0 0 2   3 13 1
Turley, Shantz (9)   Friend, Green (5), Labine (6), Witt (6), Gibbon (7), Cheney (9)

Game 3 October 8 at New York
PIT 0 0 0   0 0 0   0 0 0   0 4 0
NY 6 0 0   4 0 0   0 0 X   10 16 1
Mizell, Labine (1), Green (1), Ford   Witt (4), Cheney (6), Gibbon (8)

Game 4 October 9 at New York
PIT 0 0 0   0 3 0   0 0 0   3 7 0
NY 0 0 0   1 0 0   0 0 0   2 8 0
Law, Face (7)   Terry, Shantz (7), Coates (8)

Game 5 October 10 at New York
PIT 0 3 1   0 0 0   0 0 1   5 10 2
NY 0 1 1   0 0 0   0 0 0   2 5 2
Haddix, Face (7)   Ditmar, Arroyo (2), Stafford (3), Duren (8)

Game 6 October 12 at Pittsburgh
NY 0 1 5   0 0 2   2 2 0   12 17 1
PIT 0 0 0   0 0 0   0 0 0   0 7 1
Ford   Friend, Cheney (3), Mizell (4), Green (6), Labine (6), Witt (7)

Game 7 October 13 at Pittsburgh
NY 0 0 0   0 1 4   0 2 2   9 13 1
PIT 2 2 0   0 0 0   5 1   10 11 0
Turley, Stafford (2), Shantz (3), Coates (8), Terry (8)   Law, Face (6), Friend (9), Haddix (9)

COMPOSITE BATTING

Pittsburgh (NL)

NAME	POS	G	AB	R	H	2B	3B	HR	RBI	BA
Totals		7	234	27	60	11	0	4	26	.256
Clemente	OF	7	29	1	9	0	0	0	3	.310
Virdon	OF	7	29	2	7	3	0	0	5	.241
Groat	SS	7	28	3	6	2	0	0	2	.214
Mazeroski	2B	7	25	4	8	2	0	2	5	.320
Hoak	3B	7	23	3	5	2	0	0	3	.217
Cimoli	OF	7	20	1	5	0	0	0	0	.250
Stuart	1B	5	20	0	3	0	0	0	0	.150
Burgess	C	5	18	2	6	1	0	0	3	.333
Nelson	1B	4	9	2	3	0	0	1	2	.333
Smith	C	3	8	1	3	0	0	0	3	.375
Law	P	3	6	1	2	0	0	0	1	.333
Skinner	OF	2	5	2	1	0	0	0	1	.200
Schofield	SS	3	3	0	1	0	0	0	0	.333
Haddix	P	2	3	0	1	0	0	0	0	.333
Face	P	4	3	0	0	0	0	0	0	.000
Baker	PH	3	3	0	0	0	0	0	0	.000
Christopher	PR-PH	2	0	0	0	0	0	0	0	—
Oldis	C	2	0	0	0	0	0	0	0	—

Friend P 0-1, Green P 0-1, Cheney P 0-0, Labine P 0-0, Witt P 0-0, Gibbon P 0-0, Mizell P 0-0

New York (AL)

NAME	POS	G	AB	R	H	2B	3B	HR	RBI	BA
Totals		7	269	55	91	13	4	10	54	.338
Skowron	1B	7	32	7	12	2	0	2	6	.375
Richardson	2B	7	30	8	11	2	2	1	12	.367
Kubek	SS-OF	7	30	6	10	1	0	0	3	.333
Maris	OF	7	30	6	8	1	0	2	2	.267
Mantle	OF	7	25	8	10	1	0	3	11	.400
Berra	OF-C	7	22	6	7	0	0	1	8	.318
McDougald	3B	6	18	4	5	1	0	0	2	.278
Cerv	OF	4	14	1	5	1	0	0	1	.357
Howard	C	5	12	6	6	1	1	1	4	.462
Boyer	3B-SS	5	12	1	3	0	0	1	2	.250
Blanchard	C	5	11	2	5	2	0	0	4	.455
Ford	P	2	8	1	2	0	0	0	0	.250
Lopez	PH	2	5	1	2	0	0	0	1	.429
Turley	P	2	4	1	1	0	0	0	0	.250
Long	PH	2	4	0	1	0	0	0	0	.250
Shantz	P	3	3	0	1	0	0	0	0	.333
DeMaestri	SS	4	2	1	1	0	0	0	0	.500
Terry	P	2	2	0	0	0	0	0	0	.000

Coates P 0-1, Stafford P 0-1, Arroyo P 0-1, Ditmar P 0-0, Duren P 0-0, Maas P 0-0, Grba PR 0-0

COMPOSITE PITCHING

Pittsburgh (NL)

NAME	G	IP	H	BB	SO	W	L	SV	ERA
Totals	7	62	91	18	40	4	3	3	7.11
Law	3	18.1	22	3	8	2	0	0	3.44
Face	4	10.1	9	2	4	0	0	3	5.23
Haddix	2	7.1	6	2	6	2	0	0	2.45
Friend	2	6	13	3	7	0	2	0	13.50
Cheney	3	4	4	1	6	0	0	0	4.50
Labine	3	4	13	1	2	0	0	0	13.50
Green	3	4	11	1	3	0	0	0	22.50
Gibbon	2	3	4	1	2	0	0	0	9.00
Witt	3	2.2	1	0	0	0	0	0	0.00
Mizell	2	2.1	4	2	1	0	1	0	15.43

New York (AL)

NAME	G	IP	H	BB	SO	W	L	SV	ERA
Totals	7	61	60	12	26	3	4	1	3.54
Ford	2	18	11	2	8	2	0	0	0.00
Turley	2	9.1	15	4	0	1	0	0	4.82
Terry	2	6.2	7	1	5	0	2	0	5.40
Shantz	3	6.1	6	1	3	0	0	0	4.26
Coates	3	6.1	6	1	2	0	1	0	5.68
Stafford	2	6	5	1	2	0	0	0	1.50
Duren	2	4	2	1	5	0	0	0	2.25
Maas	1	2	2	4	2	0	0	0	4.50
Ditmar	1	1.2	6	1	0	0	2	0	21.60
Arroyo	1	0.2	1	1	0	0	0	0	13.50

USE NAME - GIVEN NAMES (NICKNAMES)	TEAM BY YEAR	BIRTH DATE	BIRTH PLACE	DEATH DATE	B	T	HGT	WGT	G	AB	R	H	2B	3B	HR	RBI	BB	SO	SB	BA	SA
Aberson, Cliff-Clifford Alexander	46 played in N.F.L. 47-49ChiN	08-28-21	Chicago,Ill.	06-23-73	R	R	6'	200	63	179	25	45	7	3	5	26	25	44	0	.251	.408
Abrams, Cal-Calvin Ross	49-52BknN 52CinN 53-54PitN 54-55BalA 56ChiA	03-02-24	Philadelphia, Pa.	02-25-97	L	L	6'	180	567	1611	257	433	64	19	32	138	304	290	12	.269	.392
Adams, Bobby-Robert Henry	46-55CinN 55ChiA 56BalA 57-59ChiN	12-14-21	Tuolumne, Cal.	02-13-97	R	R	5'10	170	1281	4019	591	1082	188	49	37	303	414	447	67	.269	.368
Adams, Dick-Richard Leroy	47PhiA	04-08-20	Tuolumne, Cal.		R	L	6'	185	37	89	9	18	2	3	2	11	2	18	0	.202	.360
Adams, Herb-Herbert Loren	48-50ChiA 51-52MS	04-14-28	Hollywood, Cal.		L	L	5'9	160	95	337	39	88	8	6	0	18	22	24	4	.261	.320
Adcock, Joe-Joseph Wilbur	50-52Cinn 53-62MilN 63CleA 64LAA 65-66CalA M67CleA	10-30-27	Coushatta, La.	05-03-99	R	R	6'4	220	1959	6606	823	1832	295	35	336	1122	594	1059	20	.277	.485
Addis, Bob-Robert Gordon	50-51BosN 52-53ChiN 53PitN	11-06-25	Mineral, Ohio		L	R	6'	180	208	534	70	150	22	2	2	47	37	47	8	.281	.341
Agganis, Harry-Harry (The Golden Greek)	54-55BosA	04-20-29	Lynn, Mass.	06-27-55	L	L	6'2	200	157	517	65	135	23	9	11	67	57	67	8	.261	.404
Albright, Jack-Harold John	47PhiN	07-22-21	St. Petersburg, Fla.	07-22-91	R	R	5'9	175	41	99	9	23	4	0	2	5	10	11	1	.232	.333
Allie, Gair-Gair Roosevelt	54PitN	10-29-31	Statesville, N.C.		R	R	6'1	190	121	418	38	83	8	6	3	30	56	84	1	.199	.268
Alston, Tom-Thomas Edison	54-57StLN	01-31-26	Greensboro, N.C.	12-30-93	L	R	6'5	210	91	271	30	66	15	2	4	36	25	46	3	.244	.358
Altobelli, Joe-Joseph Salvatore	55,57CleA 61MinA M77-79SFN M83-85BalA M91ChiN	05-26-32	Detroit, Mich.		L	L	6'	185	166	257	27	54	8	3	5	28	23	42	3	.210	.323
Alvarez, Ossie-Oswaldo [Gonzalez]	58WasA 59DetA	10-19-33	Bolondron, Cuba		R	R	5'10	165	95	198	20	42	3	0	0	5	16	27	1	.212	.227
Amoros, Sandy-Edmundo [Isasi]	52,54-57BknN 59-60LAN 60DetA	01-30-30	Havana, Cuba	06-27-92	L	L	5'7	170	517	1311	215	334	55	23	43	180	211	189	18	.255	.430
Anderson, Andy-Andy Holm	48-49StLA	11-13-22	Bremerton, Wash.	07-18-82	R	R	5'11	172	122	223	23	41	8	1	2	17	22	36	0	.184	.256
Anderson, Ferrell-Ferrell Jack	46BknN 53StLN	01-09-18	Maple City, Kans.	03-12-78	R	R	6'1	200	97	234	20	61	12	0	2	15	18	25	1	.261	.338
Anderson, Harry-Harry Walter	57-60PhiN 60-61CinN	09-10-31	North East, Md.	06-11-98	L	R	6'3	205	484	1586	199	419	82	16	60	242	159	291	3	.264	.450
Anderson, Sparky-George Lee	59PhiN M70-78CinN M79-95DetA	02-22-34	Bridgewater, S.D.		R	R	5'9	170	152	477	42	104	9	3	0	34	42	53	6	.218	.249
Andres, Ernie-Ernest Henry (Junie)	39-40,45-48 played in N.B.L.	46BosA	02-01-20	Jeffersonville, Ind.		R	R	6'1	200	15	41	0	4	2	0	0	1	3	5	0	.098	.146
Antonello, Bill-William James	53BknN	05-19-27	Brooklyn, N.Y.	03-04-93	R	R	5'11	185	40	43	9	7	1	1	1	4	2	11	0	.163	.302
Arft, Hank-Henry Irven (Bow Bow)	48-52StLA	01-28-22	Manchester, Mo.	12-14-02	L	L	5'11	190	300	906	116	229	46	13	13	118	137	133	8	.253	.375
Armstrong, George-Noble George (Dodo)	46PhiA	06-03-24	Orange, N.J.	07-24-93	R	R	5'10	190	8	6	0	1	1	0	0	0	0	3	0	.167	.333
Ashburn, Richie-Don Richard (Whitey)	48-59PhiN 60-61ChiN 62NYN	03-19-27	Tilden, Neb.	09-09-97	L	R	5'10	170	2189	8365	1322	2574	317	109	29	586	1198	571	234	.308	.382
Aspromonte, Ken-Kenneth Joseph	57-58BosA 58-60CleA 60CinN 61LAA 61-62CleA 62MilN 63ChiN M72-74CleA	09-22-31	Brooklyn, N.Y.		R	R	6'	180	475	1483	171	369	69	3	19	124	179	149	7	.249	.338
Astroth, Joe-Joseph Henry	45-46,49-54PhiA 55-56KCA	09-01-22	East Alton, Ill.		R	R	5'9	187	544	1579	163	401	51	10	13	156	177	124	6	.254	.324
Atwell, Toby-Maurice Dailey	52-53ChiN 53-56PitN 56MilN	09-08-24	Leesburg, Va.	01-25-03	R	R	5'9	185	378	1117	116	290	41	7	9	110	161	84	4	.260	.333
Aulds, Doyle-Leycester Doyle (Tex)	47BosA	12-28-20	Farmersville, La.	10-13-99	R	R	6'2	185	3	4	0	1	0	0	0	0	0	1	0	.250	.250
Avila, Bobby-Roberto Francisco [Gonzalez] (Beto)	49-58CleA 59BalA 59BosA 59MilN	04-02-24	Varacruz, Mexico	10-26-04	R	R	5'10	175	1300	4620	725	1296	185	35	80	467	561	399	78	.281	.388
Aylward, Dick-Richard John	53CleA	06-04-25	Baltimore, Md.	06-11-83	R	R	6'	190	4	3	0	0	0	0	0	0	0	0	0	.000	.000
Babe, Loren-Loren Rolland (Bee Bee)	52-53NYA 53PhiA	01-11-28	Pisgah, Iowa	02-14-84	L	R	5'10	180	120	382	37	85	18	2	2	26	39	26	1	.223	.296
Bailey, Ed-Lonas Edgar	53-61CinN 61-63SFN 64MilN 65SFN 65ChiN 66CalA	04-15-31	Strawberry Pl., Tenn.		L	R	6'2	205	1212	3581	432	915	128	15	155	540	545	577	17	.256	.429
Baker, Floyd-Floyd Wilson	43-44StLA 44-51ChiA 52-53WasA 53-54BosA 54-55PhiN	10-10-16	Luray, Va.	11-27-04	R	R	5'9	160	874	2280	285	573	76	13	1	196	382	165	23	.251	.297
Baker, Gene-Eugene Walter	53-57ChiN 57-58,60-61PitN	12-01-99	Davenport, Iowa		R	R	6'1	175	630	2230	265	590	109	21	39	227	184	219	21	.265	.385
Balcena, Bobby-Robert Rudolph	56CinN	08-01-25	San Pedro, Cal.	01-05-90	R	L	5'7	160	7	2	2	0	0	0	0	0	0	1	0	.000	.000
Baldwin, Frank-Frank DeWitt	53CinN	12-25-28	High Bridge, N.J.	11-18-04	R	R	5'11	195	16	20	0	2	0	0	0	0	1	5	0	.100	.100
Bamberger, Hal-Harold Earl (Dutch)	48NYN	10-29-24	Lebanon,Pa.		L	R	6'	173	7	12	0	1	0	0	0	0	0	1	0	.083	.083
Barnes, Bruce-Bruce Raymond (Squeaky)	53WasA	10-23-29	Vincennes, Ind.		R	R	5'8	165	5	5	1	1	0	0	0	0	0	2	0	.200	.200
Barone, Dick-Richard Anthony	60PitN	10-13-32	San Jose, Cal.		R	R	5'9	165	3	6	0	0	0	0	0	0	0	1	0	.000	.000
Bartirome, Tony-Anthony Joseph	52PitN 53-54MS	05-09-32	Pittsburgh, Pa.		R	R	5'10	155	124	355	32	78	10	3	0	16	26	37	3	.220	.265
Basgall, Monty-Romanus	48-49,51PitN	02-08-22	Pfeifer, Kans.	09-22-05	R	R	5'10	175	200	512	52	110	15	3	4	41	46	51	1	.215	.279
Batts, Matt-Matthew Daniel	47-51BosA 51StLA 52-54DetA 54ChiA 55-56DetA	10-16-21	San Antonio, Tex.		R	R	5'11	200	546	1605	163	432	95	11	26	219	143	163	6	.269	.391
Bauer, Hank-Henry Albert	48-59NYA 60-61,M61-62KCA M64-68BalA M69OakA	07-31-22	East St. Louis, Ill.		R	R	6'	192	1544	5145	833	1424	229	57	164	703	521	638	50	.277	.439
Baumgartner, John-John Edward	53DetA	05-29-31	Birmingham, Ala.		R	R	6'1	190	7	27	3	5	0	0	0	2	0	5	0	.185	.185
Baumholtz, Frankie-Frank Conrad	47-49CinN 49,51-55ChiN 56-57PhiN 45-46 played in N.B.L., 46-47 played in B.A.A.	10-07-18	Midvale, Ohio	12-14-97	L	L	5'10	175	1019	3477	450	1010	165	51	25	272	258	258	30	.290	.389
Baxes, Jim-Dimitrios Speros	59LAN 59CleA	07-05-28	San Francisco, Cal.	11-14-96	R	R	6'1	190	88	280	39	69	12	0	17	39	25	54	1	.246	.471
Baxes, Mike-Michael	56,58KCA	11-04-30	San Francisco, Cal.		R	R	5'10	175	146	337	40	73	13	2	1	13	39	39	1	.217	.276
Beard, Ted-Cramer Theodore	48-52PitN 57-58ChiA	01-07-21	Woodsboro, Md.		L	L	5'8	165	194	474	80	94	11	6	6	35	78	107	16	.198	.285
Becquer, Julio-Julio [Villegas]	55,57-60WasA 61LAA 61,63MinA	12-20-31	Havana, Cuba		L	L	5'11	178	488	974	100	238	37	16	12	114	41	120	8	.244	.352
Belardi, Wayne-Carroll Wayne (Footsie)	50-51,53-54BknN 54-56DetA	09-05-30	St. Helena, Cal.	10-21-93	L	L	6'1	185	263	522	71	143	13	5	28	74	66	97	1	.242	.422
Bell, Gus-David Russell	50-52PitN 53-61CinN 62NYN 62-64MilN	11-15-28	Louisville, Ky.	05-07-95	L	R	6'1	196	1741	6478	865	1823	311	66	206	942	470	636	30	.281	.445
Bella, Zeke-John	57NYA 59KCA	08-23-30	Greenwich, Conn.		R	L	5'11	185	52	98	10	18	2	1	1	9	10	16	0	.196	.272
Berson, Vern-Vernon Edward	43PhiA 44-45MS 46PhiA 51-53StLN M77AtlN	11-15-30	Granite Quarry, N.C.		R	R	5'11	185	55	104	17	21	5	1	3	12	13	22	0	.202	.356
Berardino, Johnny-John	39-42StLA 43-45StLA 46-47StLA 48-50CleA 50PitN 51StLA 52CleA 52PitN	05-01-17	Los Angeles, Cal.	05-19-96	R	R	5'11	175	912	3028	334	755	167	23	36	387	284	268	27	.249	.355
Berberet, Lou-Louis Joseph	54-55NYA 56-58WasA 58BosA 59-60DetA	11-20-29	Long Beach, Cal.	04-06-04	L	R	5'11	200	448	1224	118	281	34	10	31	153	200	195	2	.230	.350
Bernier, Carlos-Carlos [Rodriguez]	53PitN	01-28-27	Juana Diaz, P.R.	04-06-89	R	R	5'9	180	105	310	48	66	7	8	3	31	51	53	15	.213	.319
Bero, Johnny-John George	48DetA 51StLA	12-22-22	Gary, W.Va.		R	R	6'	170	65	169	26	34	5	0	5	17	27	31	1	.201	.320
Berra, Yogi-Lawrence Peter	46-63,M64NYA 65,M72-75NYN M84-85NYA	05-12-25	St. Louis, Mo.		L	R	5'8	195	2120	7555	1175	2150	321	49	358	1430	704	414	30	.285	.482
Berry, Neil-Cornelius John	48-52DetA 53StLA 53ChiA 54BalA	01-11-22	Kalamazoo, Mich.		R	R	5'10	168	442	1087	148	265	28	9	0	74	113	105	11	.244	.286
Bertoia, Reno-Reno Peter	53-58DetA 59-60WasA 61MinA 61KCA 61-62DetA	01-08-35	St. Vito Udine, Italy		R	R	5'11	185	612	1745	204	425	60	10	27	171	142	252	16	.244	.336
Bevan, Hal-Harold Joseph	52BosA 52PhiA 55KCA 61CinN	11-15-30	New Orleans, La.	10-05-68	R	R	6'2	198	15	24	2	7	0	0	1	0	3	2	0	.292	.417
Biasatti, Hank-Henry Arcado	46-47 played in B.A.A.	49PhiA	01-14-22	Beano, Italy	04-20-96	L	L	5'11	175	21	24	6	2	0	0	0	2	8	5	0	.083	.083
Bilko, Steve-Stephen Thomas	49-54StLN 54ChiN 54CinN 58LAN 60DetA 61-62LAA	11-13-28	Nanticoke, Pa.	03-07-78	R	R	6'1	230	600	1738	220	432	85	13	76	276	234	395	2	.249	.444
Binks (Binkowski), George-George Alvin (Bingo)	44-46WasA 47CleA 48StLA	07-11-14	Chicago, Ill.		L	L	6'	175	351	1093	112	277	55	10	8	130	67	108	21	.253	.344
Blasingame, Don-Don Lee (Blazer)	55-59StLN 60-61SFN 61-63CinN 63-66WasA 64KCA	03-16-32	Corinth, Miss.	04-13-05	L	R	5'10	160	1444	5296	731	1366	178	62	21	308	552	462	105	.258	.327
Blatnik, Johnny-John Louis (Chief)	48-50PhiN 50StLN	03-10-21	Bridgeport, Ohio	01-21-04	R	R	6'	195	138	447	59	113	27	8	6	46	40	83	3	.253	.389
Blattner, Buddy-Robert Garnett	42StLN 43-45MS 46-48NYN 49PhiN	02-08-20	St. Louis, Mo.		R	R	6'	180	272	713	112	176	34	8	16	84	102	96	18	.247	.389
Blaylock, Marv-Marvin Edward	50NYN 55-57PhiN	02-20-29	Fort Smith, Ark.	10-23-93	L	L	6'1	175	287	746	96	175	21	15	15	78	84	137	11	.235	.363
Boak, Chet-Chester Robert	60KCA 61WasA	06-19-35	New Castle, Pa.	11-28-83	R	R	6'	180	10	20	1	2	0	0	0	1	1	3	1	.100	.100
Bockman, Eddie-Joseph Edward	46NYA 47CleA 48-49PitN	07-26-20	Santa Ana, Cal.		R	R	5'9	175	249	474	54	109	16	4	11	56	46	87	5	.230	.304
Bolger, Jim-James Cyril (Dutch)	50-51,54CinN 55,57-58ChiN 59CleA 59PhiN	03-23-32	Cincinnati, Ohio		R	R	6'2	180	312	612	65	140	30	4	8	50	32	83	3	.229	.301
Bolling, Frank-Frank Elmore	54DetA 55MS 56-60DetA 61-65MilN 66AtlN	11-16-31	Mobile, Ala.		R	R	6'1	175	1540	5562	692	1415	221	40	106	556	462	558	40	.254	.366
Bolling, Milt-Milton Joseph	52-57BosA 57WasA 58DetA	08-09-30	Mississippi City, Miss.		R	R	6'1	177	400	1161	127	280	50	7	19	94	115	188	5	.241	.369
Bollweg, Don-Donald Raymond	50-51StLN 53NYA 54PhiN 55KCA	02-12-21	Wheaton, Ill.	05-26-96	L	L	6'1	190	195	452	62	110	22	7	11	53	60	68	2	.243	.396
Boone, Ray-Raymond Otis (Ike)	48-53CleA 53-58DetA 58-59ChiA 59KCA 59-60MilN 60BosA	07-27-23	San Diego, Cal.	10-17-04	R	R	6'	185	1373	4589	645	1260	162	46	151	737	608	463	21	.275	.429
Borkowski, Bob-Robert Vilarian (Bush)	50-51ChiN 52-55CinN 55BknN	01-27-26	Dayton, Ohio		R	R	6'	182	470	1170	126	294	43	10	16	112	76	166	2	.251	.389
Bouchee, Ed-Edward Francis	56-60PhiN 60-61ChiN 62NYN	03-07-33	Livingston, Mont.		L	L	6'	210	670	2199	298	583	114	21	61	290	340	401	5	.265	.419
Bowers, Billy-Grover Bill	49CinN	03-25-22	Parkin, Ark.	09-17-96	R	L	5'9	176	26	78	5	15	3	0	0	6	4	5	1	.192	.244
Bowman, Bob-Robert Leroy	55-59PhiN	05-10-31	Laytonville, Cal.		R	R	6'1	195	256	519	71	129	19	5	17	54	48	109	0	.249	.403
Boyd, Bob-Robert Richard (The Rope)	51,53-54ChiA 56-60BalA 61KCA 61MilN	10-01-19	Potts Camp, Miss.	09-07-04	L	L	5'10	170	693	1936	253	567	81	23	19	175	167	114	9	.293	.388
Bradley, George-George Washington	46StLA	04-01-14	Greenwood, Ark.	10-19-82	R	R	6'1	185	4	12	2	2	1	0	0	3	1	4	0	.167	.250
Bradshaw, George-George Thomas	52WasA	09-12-24	Salisbury, N.C.	11-04-94	R	R	6'2	185	10	23	3	5	2	1	0	6	1	2	0	.217	.304
Brady, Bob-Robert Jay	46-47BosN	11-08-22	Lewistown, Pa.	04-22-96	R	R	6'1	175	4	6	0	1	0	0	0	0	0	3	0	.167	.167
Brideweser, Jim-James Ehrenfeld	51-53NYA 54BalA 55-56ChiA 56DetA 57BalA	02-13-27	Lancaster, Ohio	08-25-89	R	R	6'	165	329	620	79	156	22	6	1	50	63	77	6	.252	.311
Bridges, Rocky-Everett Lamar	51-52BknN 52-57CinN 57-58WasA 59-60DetA 60CleA 60StLN 61LAA	08-07-27	Refugio, Tex.		R	R	5'8	176	919	2272	245	562	80	11	16	187	205	229	10	.247	.313
Brinkopf, Leon-Leon Clarence	52ChiN	10-20-26	Cape Girardeau, Mo.	07-02-98	R	R	5'11	185	9	22	1	4	1	0	0	2	4	0	0	.182	.182
Brovia, Joe-Joseph John (Ox)	55PhiN	02-18-22	Davenport, Cal.	08-15-94	R	R	6'3	195	21	18	0	2	1	0	0	0	4	5	0	.111	.111
Brown, Bobby-Robert William (Doc)	46-52NYA 53MS 54NYA	10-25-24	Seattle, Wash.		L	R	6'	180	548	1619	233	452	62	14	22	237	214	88	9	.279	.376
Brown, Tommy-Thomas Michael (Buckshot)	44-46BknN 46MS 47-51BknN 51-52PhiN 52-53ChiN	12-06-27	Brooklyn, N.Y.		R	R	6'1	170	494	1280	151	309	39	7	31	159	85	142	7	.241	.355
Brown, Willard-Willard Jessie	47StLA	06-26-15	Shreveport, La.	08-04-96	R	R	5'11	200	21	67	4	12	3	0	1	6	0	7	2	.179	.269
Brucker, Earle-Earle Francis	48PhiA	06-25-25	Los Angeles, Cal.		R	R	6'2	210	2	6	0	1	0	0	0	0	0	1	0	.167	.167
Bruton, Bill-William Haron	53-60MilN 61-64DetA	11-09-25	Panola, Ala.	12-05-95	L	R	6'	169	1610	6056	937	1651	241	102	94	545	482	793	207	.273	.393
Bucha, Johnny-John George	48,50StLN 53DetA	01-22-25	Allentown, Pa.	04-28-96	R	R	5'11	190	84	195	18	40	10	0	3	15	25	21	1	.205	.272
Buddin, Don-Donald Thomas	56,58-61BosA 62HouN 62DetA	05-05-34	Turbeville, S.C.		R	R	5'11	178	711	2289	342	551	123	12	41	225	410	404	15	.241	.359

USE NAME - GIVEN NAMES (NICKNAMES)	TEAM BY YEAR	BIRTH DATE	BIRTH PLACE	DEATH DATE	B	T	HGT	WGT	G	AB	R	H	2B	3B	HR	RBI	BB	SO	SB	BA	SA
Bullard, George-George Donald (Curly)	54DetA	10-24-28	Lynn, Mass.	12-23-02	R	R	5'9	165	4	1	0	0	0	0	0	0	0	0	0	.000	.000
Burbrink, Nels-Nelson Edward	55StLN	12-28-21	Cincinnati, Ohio	04-12-01	R	R	5'10	195	58	170	11	47	8	1	0	15	14	13	1	.276	.335
Burgess, Smoky-Forrest Harrill	49,51ChiN 52-55PhiN 55-58CinN 59-64PitN 64-67ChiA	02-06-27	Caroleen, N.C.	09-15-91	L	R	5'8	190	1691	4471	485	1318	230	33	126	673	477	270	13	.295	.446
Burk, Mack-Mack Edwin	56PhiN 57MS 58PhiN	04-21-35	Nacogdoches, Tex.		R	R	6'4	190	16	2	3	1	0	0	0	0	0	1	0	.500	.500
Burris, Paul-Paul Robert	48,50,52BosN 53MilN	07-21-23	Hickory, N.C.	10-03-99	R	R	6'	190	69	196	15	43	5	0	2	24	8	21	0	.219	.276
Busby, Jim-James Franklin	50-52ChiA 52-55WasA 55ChiA 56-57CleA 57-58BalA 59-60BosA 60-61BalA 62HouN	01-08-27	Kenedy, Tex.	07-08-96	R	R	6'1	175	1352	4250	541	1113	162	35	48	438	310	439	97	.262	.350
Caballero, Putsy-Ralph Joseph	44-45,47-52PhiN	11-05-27	New Orleans, La.		R	R	5'10	170	322	658	81	150	21	3	1	40	41	34	10	.228	.274
Caffie, Joe-Joseph Clifford (Rabbit)	56-57CleA	02-14-31	Ramer, Ala.		L	R	5'10	180	44	127	21	37	2	1	3	11	8	19	3	.291	.394
Calderone, Sammy-Samuel Francis	50NYN 51-52MS 53NYN 54MilN	02-06-26	Beverly, N.J.		R	R	5'10	185	91	141	16	41	5	0	1	25	7	13	0	.291	.348
Camelli, Hank-Henry Richard	43-46PitN 47BosN	12-09-14	Gloucester, Mass.	07-14-96	R	R	5'11	190	159	376	33	86	15	4	2	26	46	39	0	.229	.306
Campanella, Roy-Roy	48-57BknN 58BX	11-19-21	Philadelphia, Pa.	06-26-93	R	R	5'9	205	1215	4205	627	1161	178	18	242	856	533	501	25	.276	.500
Campbell, Paul-Paul McLaughlin	41-42BosA 43-45MS 46BosA 48DetA	09-01-17	Paw Creek, N.C.	06-22-06	L	L	5'10	185	204	380	61	97	17	5	4	41	28	54	4	.255	.358
Campos, Frank-Francisco Jose [Lopez]	51-53WasA	05-11-24	Havana, Cuba	01-28-06	L	L	5'10	170	71	147	13	41	9	2	0	13	2	14	0	.279	.367
Carey, Andy-Andrew Arthur	52-60NYA 60—61KCA 61ChiA 62LAN	10-18-31	Oakland, Cal.		R	R	6'1	190	938	2850	371	741	119	38	64	350	268	389	23	.260	.396
Carrasquel, Chico-Alfonso [Colon]	50-55ChiA 56-58CleA 58KCA 59BalA	01-23-28	Caracas, Venezuela	05-26-05	R	R	6'	170	1325	4644	568	1199	172	25	55	474	491	467	31	.258	.342
Carroll, Tommy-Thomas Edward	55-56NYA 58MS 59KCA	09-17-36	Queens, N.Y.		R	R	6'3	186	64	30	15	9	1	0	1	1	6	1	0	.300	.300
Carswell, Frank-Frank Willis (Wheels, Tex)	53DetA	11-06-19	Palestine, Tex.	10-16-98	R	R	6'	195	16	15	2	4	0	0	0	2	3	1	0	.267	.267
Cassini, Jack-Jack Dempsey (Scat)	49PitN	10-26-19	Dearborn, Mich.		R	R	5'10	175	8	3	0	0	0	0	0	0	0	0	0	—	—
Castiglione, Pete-Peter Paul	47-53PitN 53-54StLN	02-13-21	Greenwich, Conn.		R	R	5'11	175	545	1670	205	426	62	11	24	150	103	126	10	.255	.349
Castleman, Foster-Foster Ephraim	54-57NYN 58BalA	01-01-31	Nashville, Tenn.		R	R	6'	175	268	662	58	136	24	3	20	65	35	99	4	.205	.341
Caulfield, John-John Joseph (Jake)	46PhiA	11-23-17	Los Angeles, Cal.	12-16-86	R	R	6'	190	44	94	13	26	8	0	0	10	4	11	0	.277	.362
Cerv, Bob-Robert Henry	51-56NYA 57-60KCA 60NYA 61LAA 61-62NYA 62HouN	05-05-26	Weston, Neb.		R	R	6'	210	829	2261	320	624	96	26	105	374	212	392	12	.276	.481
Chapman, Sam-Samuel Blake	38-41PhiA 42-44MS 45-51PhiA 51CleA	04-11-16	Tiburon, Cal.		R	R	6'	190	1368	4988	754	1329	210	52	180	773	562	682	41	.266	.438
Chiti, Harry-Harry	50-52ChiN 53-54MS 55-56ChiN 58-60KCA 60-61DetA 62NYN	11-16-32	Kincaid, Ill.	01-31-02	R	R	6'2	221	502	1495	135	356	49	9	41	179	115	242	4	.238	.365
Chrisley, Neil-Barbra O'Neil	57-58WasA 59-60DetA 60MilN	12-16-31	Calhoun Falls, S.C.		L	R	6'3	187	302	619	60	130	22	8	16	64	55	62	3	.210	.349
Christopher, Loyd-Loyd Eugene	45BosA 45ChiN 47ChiA	12-31-19	Richmond, Cal.	09-05-91	R	R	6'2	190	16	37	5	9	0	1	0	4	5	6	0	.243	.297
Ciaffone, Larry-Lawrence Thomas (Symphony)	51StLN	08-17-24	Brooklyn, N.Y.	12-14-91	R	R	5'10	185	5	5	0	0	0	0	0	0	1	2	0	.000	.000
Cimoli, Gino-Gino Nicholas	56-57BknN 58LAN 59StLN 60-61PitN 61MilN 62-64KCA 64BalA 65CalA	12-18-29	San Francisco, Cal.		R	R	6'1	195	969	3054	370	808	133	48	44	321	221	474	21	.265	.383
Clark, Allie-Alfred Aloysius	47NYA 48-51CleA 51-53PhiA 53ChiA	06-16-23	South Amboy, N.J.		R	R	6'	195	358	1021	131	267	48	4	32	149	72	70	2	.262	.410
Clark, (Petrosky), Jim-James	48WasA	09-01-27	Baggaley, Pa.	10-24-90	R	R	5'9	160	9	12	1	3	0	0	0	0	0	2	0	.250	.250
Clark, Mel-Melvin Earl	51-55PhiN 57DetA	07-26-26	Letart, W.Va.		R	R	6'	187	215	656	82	182	29	15	3	63	37	61	3	.277	.381
Clarkson, Bus-James Buster	52BosN	03-13-15	Hopkins, S.C.	01-18-89	R	R	5'11	195	14	25	3	5	0	0	0	1	3	3	0	.200	.200
Coan, Gil-Gilbert Fitzgerald (Citation)	46-53WasA 54-55BalA 55ChiA 55-56NYN	05-18-22	Monroe, N.C.		L	R	6'	180	918	2877	384	731	98	44	39	278	232	384	83	.254	.359
Cole, Dick-Richard Roy	51StLN 51,53-56PitN 57MilN	05-06-26	Long Beach, Cal.		R	R	6'2	180	456	1215	106	303	50	10	2	107	132	124	2	.249	.312
Coleman, Jerry-Gerald Francis	49-57NYA M80SDN	09-14-24	San Jose, Cal.		R	R	6'	165	723	2119	267	558	77	18	16	217	235	218	22	.263	.339
Coleman, Ray-Raymond Leroy	47-48StLA 48PhiA 50-51StLA 51-52ChiA 52StLA	06-04-22	Dunsmuir, Cal.		L	R	6'	185	559	1729	208	446	74	33	20	199	148	158	19	.258	.374
Coles, Chuck-Charles Edward	58CinN	06-27-31	Fredericktown, Pa.	01-25-96	L	L	5'9	195	5	11	0	2	1	0	0	0	0	3	0	.182	.273
Collins (Kollinige), Joe-Joseph Edward	48-57NYA	12-03-22	Scranton, Pa.	08-30-89	L	L	6'	195	908	2329	404	596	79	24	86	329	338	263	27	.256	.421
Combs, Merrill-Merrill Russell	47,49-50BosA 50WasA 51-52CleA	12-11-19	Los Angeles, Cal.	07-07-81	R	R	6'	172	140	361	45	73	6	1	2	25	57	43	0	.202	.241
Command, Jim-James Dalton (Igor)	54-55PhiN	10-15-28	Grand Rapids, Mich.		L	R	6'2	200	14	23	1	4	1	0	1	6	2	4	0	.174	.348
Conatser, Clint-Astor Clinton (Connie)	48-49BosN	07-24-21	Los Angeles, Cal.		R	R	6'	182	143	376	40	102	15	3	6	39	46	46	0	.271	.375
Connors, Chuck-Kevin Joseph	45-46 played in N.B.L. 46-48 played in B.A.A. 49BknN 51ChiN	04-10-21	Brooklyn, N.Y.	11-10-92	L	L	6'5	190	67	202	16	48	5	1	2	18	12	25	4	.238	.302
Consolo, Billy-William Angelo	53-59BosA 59-60WasA 61MinA 62PhiN 62LAA 62KCA	08-18-34	Cleveland, Ohio		R	R	5'11	180	603	1178	158	260	31	11	9	83	161	297	9	.221	.289
Conway, Jack-Jack Clements	41CleA 42-45MS 46-47CleA 48NYN	07-30-18	Bryan, Tex.	06-11-93	R	R	5'11	175	128	359	35	80	10	3	1	27	28	54	2	.223	.276
Conyers, Herb-Herbert Leroy	50PitN	01-08-21	Cogwill, Mo.	09-16-64	L	R	6'5	210	7	9	2	3	0	0	1	1	0	1	0	.333	.667
Coogan, Dale-Dale Roger	50PitN	08-14-30	Los Angeles, Cal.	03-08-89	R	R	6'1	190	53	129	19	31	6	1	1	13	17	24	0	.240	.326
Cooper, Pat-Orge Patterson (See P46-60)	46-47PhiA	11-26-17	Albermarle, N.C.	03-15-93	R	R	6'3	180	14	16	0	4	2	0	0	3	1	6	0	.250	.375
Cooper, Walker-William Walker	40-45StLN 46-49NYN 49-50CinN 50-52BosN 53MilN 54PitN 54-55ChiN 56-57StLN	01-08-15	Atherton, Mo.	04-11-91	R	R	6'3	210	1473	4702	573	1341	240	40	173	812	309	357	19	.285	.464
Corbitt, Claude-Claude Elliott	45BknN 46,48-49CinN	07-21-15	Sunbury, N.C.	05-01-78	R	R	5'10	170	215	630	60	153	22	1	0	37	47	30	8	.243	.286
Corriden, John-John Michael Jr.	46BknN	01-06-18	Logansport, Ind.	06-04-01	B	R	5'6	160	1	0	0	0	0	0	0	0	0	0	0	—	—
Courtney, Clint-Clinton Dawson (Scrap Iron)	51NYA 52-53StLA 54BalA 55ChiA 55-59WasA 60BalA 61KCA 61BalA	03-16-27	Hall Summit, La.	06-16-75	L	R	5'8	180	946	2796	260	750	126	17	38	313	265	143	3	.268	.367
Cox, Billy-William Richard	41PitN 42-45MS 46-47PitN 48-54BknN 55BalA	08-29-19	Newport, Pa.	03-30-78	R	R	5'10	150	1058	3712	470	974	174	32	66	351	298	218	42	.262	.380
Crandall, Del-Delmar Wesley	49-50BosN 51-52MS 53-63MilN 64SFN 65PitN 66CleA M72-75MilA M83-84SeaA	03-05-30	Ontario, Cal.		R	R	6'1	200	1573	5026	585	1276	179	18	179	657	424	477	26	.254	.404
Crawford, Rufus-Rufus (Jake)	52StLN	03-20-28	Campbell, Mo.		R	R	6'1	185	7	11	1	2	0	0	0	0	1	0	0	.182	.273
Creger, Bernie-Bernard Odell	47StLN	03-21-27	Wytheville, Va.	11-30-97	R	R	6'	175	15	16	3	3	0	0	0	1	3	4	1	.188	.250
Cross, Jeff-Joffre James	42StLN 43-45MS 46-48StLN 48StLA	08-28-18	Tulsa, Okla.	07-23-97	R	R	5'11	160	119	142	22	23	4	0	0	10	20	18	4	.162	.190
Crowe, George-George Daniel	52BosN 53,55MilN 56-58CinN 59-61StLN 48-49 played in N.B.L.	03-22-21	Whiteland, Ind.		L	L	6'2	210	702	1727	215	467	70	12	81	299	159	246	3	.270	.466
Culler, Dick-Richard Broadus	36PhiA 43ChiA 44-47BosN 48ChiN 49NYN	01-25-15	High Point, N.C.	06-16-64	R	R	5'9	155	472	1527	195	372	39	6	2	99	166	87	19	.244	.281
Cunningham, Joe-Joseph Robert	54,56-61StLN 62-64ChiA 64-66WasA	08-27-31	Paterson, N.J.		L	L	6'	188	1141	3362	525	980	177	26	64	436	599	369	16	.291	.417
Currin, Perry-Perry Gilmore	47StLA	09-27-28	Washington, D.C.		L	L	6'	175	3	3	1	0	0	0	0	0	0	0	0	.000	.000
Curry, Tony-George Anthony	60-61PhiN 66CleA	12-22-38	Nassau, Bahamas		L	L	5'11	185	129	297	33	73	16	2	6	40	20	69	0	.246	.374
Cusick, Jack-John Peter	51ChiN 52BosN	06-12-28	Weehawken, N.J.	11-17-89	R	R	6'	170	114	242	21	42	4	2	2	22	23	38	2	.174	.231
Dagres, Angie-Angie George (Junior)	55BalA	08-22-34	Newburyport, Mass.		L	L	5'11	175	8	15	5	4	0	0	0	0	1	2	0	.267	.267
Daley, Pete-Peter Harvey	55-59BosA 60KCA 61WasA	01-14-30	Grass Valley, Cal.		R	R	6'	195	391	1084	93	259	49	8	18	120	87	187	2	.239	.349
Daniels, Jack-Harold Jack (Sour Mash)	52BosN	12-21-27	Chester, Pa.		L	L	5'10	165	106	219	31	41	5	1	2	14	28	30	3	.187	.247
Dark, Al-Alvin Ralph (Blackie)	46,48-49BosN 50-56NYN 56-58StLN 58-59CinN 60PhiN 60MilN M61-64SFN M66-67KCA M68-71CleA M74-75OakA M77SDN	01-07-22	Comanche, Okla.		R	R	5'11	185	1828	7219	1064	2089	358	72	126	757	430	534	59	.289	.411
Daugherty, Doc-Harold Ray	51DetA	10-12-27	Paris, Pa.		R	R	6'	180	1	1	0	0	0	0	0	0	0	0	0	.000	.000
Davalillo, Yo-Yo-Pompeyo Antonio [Romero]	53WasA	06-30-31	Caracas, Venezuela		R	R	5'3	140	19	58	10	17	1	0	0	2	1	7	1	.293	.310
Davis, Brandy-Robert Brandon	52-53PitN	09-10-27	Newark, Del.	06-12-05	R	R	6'	170	67	134	19	25	3	1	0	3	11	31	9	.187	.224
Davis, Otis-Otis Allen (Scat)	46BknN	09-24-20	Charleston, Ark.		L	R	6'	160	1	0	0	0	0	0	0	0	0	0	0	—	—
Davis, Tod-Thomas Oscar	49,51PhiA	07-24-24	Los Angeles, Cal.	12-31-78	R	R	6'2	190	42	90	7	21	0	1	0	10	16	19	0	.233	.289
Delis, Juan-Juan Francisco	55WasA	02-27-28	Santiago de Cuba, Cuba	07-23-03	R	R	5'10	185	54	132	12	25	3	1	0	11	3	15	1	.189	.227
Delsing, Jim-James Henry	48ChiA 49-50NYA 50-52StLA 52-56DetA	11-13-25	Rudolph, Wis.	05-04-06	L	R	5'10	175	822	2461	322	627	112	21	40	286	299	251	15	.255	.366
DeMaestri, Joe-Joseph Paul (Oats)	56ChiA 60KCA 51ChiA 52StLA 53-54PhiA 55-59KCA 60-61NYA	12-09-28	San Francisco, Cal.		R	R	6'	180	1121	3441	322	813	114	23	49	281	168	511	15	.236	.325
DeMars, Billy-William Lester (Kid)	48PhiA 50-51StLA	08-26-25	Brooklyn, N.Y.		R	R	5'10	160	80	211	29	50	5	1	0	14	28	16	0	.237	.270
Demeter, Steve-Stephen	59DetA 60CleA	01-27-35	Homer City, Pa.		R	R	5'11	185	15	23	1	2	1	0	0	1	0	2	0	.087	.130
Dente, Sam-Samuel Joseph (Blackie)	47BosN 48StlA 49-51WasA 52-53ChiA 54-55CleA	04-26-22	Harrison, N.J.	04-21-02	R	R	5'11	175	745	2320	205	585	78	16	4	214	167	96	9	.252	.305
Dickey, George-George Willard (Skeets)	35-36BosA 41-42ChiA 43-45MS 46-47ChiA	07-10-15	Kensett, Ark.	06-16-76	B	R	6'2	180	226	494	36	101	12	0	4	54	63	62	4	.204	.253
Diering, Chuck-Charles Edward Allen	47-51StLN 52NYN 54-56BalA	02-05-23	St. Louis, Mo.		R	R	5'10	165	752	1648	217	411	76	14	14	141	237	250	16	.249	.338
Dietzel, Roy-Leroy Louis	54WasA	01-09-31	Baltimore, Md.		R	R	6'	190	9	21	1	5	0	0	0	2	5	4	0	.238	.238
Difani, Jay-Clarence Joseph	48-49WasA	12-21-22	Crystal City, Mo.	12-03-03	R	R	6'	170	4	3	0	1	0	0	1	1	1	0	0	.333	.667
Dillinger, Bob-Robert Bernard	46-49StLA 50PhiA 50-51PitN 51ChiA	09-17-18	Glendale, Cal.		R	R	5'11	170	753	2904	401	888	123	47	10	213	251	203	106	.306	.391
DiMaggio, Dom-Dominic Paul (The Little Professor)	40-42BosA 43-45MS 46-53BosA	02-12-17	San Francisco, Cal.		R	R	5'9	168	1399	5640	1046	1680	308	57	87	618	750	571	100	.298	.419
DiPietro, Bob-Robert Louis Paul	51BosA	09-01-27	San Francisco, Cal.		R	R	5'11	185	4	11	0	1	0	0	0	1	0	2	0	.091	.091
Dittmer, Jack-John Douglas	52BosN 53-56MilN 57DetA	01-10-28	Elkader, Iowa		L	R	6'	190	395	1218	117	283	43	4	24	136	77	102	2	.232	.333
Dobbek, Dan-Daniel John	59-60WasA 61MinA	12-06-34	Ontonagon, Mich.		L	L	6'	195	198	433	52	90	12	5	14	49	53	72	5	.208	.363
Doby, Larry-Lawrence Eugene	47-55CleA 56-57ChiA 58CleA 59DetA 59ChiA	12-13-23	Camden, S.C.	06-18-03	L	R	6'1	180	1533	5348	960	1515	243	52	253	970	871	1011	47	.283	.490
Dotterer, Dutch-Henry John	57-60CinN 61WasA	11-11-32	Syracuse, N.Y.	12-09-90	R	R	6'2	209	107	299	27	74	15	0	5	33	35	44	0	.247	.348
Drake, Larry-Larry Francis	48WasA 48WasA	05-04-21	McKinney, Tex.	07-14-85	L	R	6'1	190	9	9	1	2	0	0	0	0	1	0	0	.222	.222
Drake, Solly-Solomon Louis	56ChiN 59LAN 59PhiN	10-23-30	Little Rock, Ark.		B	R	6'	170	141	285	44	66	10	2	1	18	32	53	15	.232	.295
Dropo, Walt-Walter (Moose)	49-52BosA 52-54DetA 55-58ChiA 58-59CinN 59-61BalA	01-30-23	Moosup, Conn.		R	R	6'5	220	1288	4124	478	1113	168	22	152	704	328	582	5	.270	.432
Dunlap, Grant-Grant Lester (Snap)	53StLN	12-20-23	Stockton, Cal.		R	R	6'2	180	16	17	2	6	0	0	0	0	2	0	0	.353	.647

USE NAME - GIVEN NAMES (NICKNAMES)	TEAM BY YEAR	BIRTH DATE	BIRTH PLACE	DEATH DATE	B	T	HGT	WGT	G	AB	R	H	2B	3B	HR	RBI	BB	SO	SB	BA	SA
Durham, Joe-Joseph Vann (Pop)	54BalA 55-56MS 57BalA 59StLN	07-31-31	Newport News, Va.		R	R	6'1	186	93	202	25	38	2	0	5	20	20	50	1	.188	.272
Dumbaugh, Bobby-Robert Eugene (Scroggy)	57CinN	01-15-33	Dayton, Ohio		R	R	5'8	170	2	1	0	0	0	0	0	0	0	0	0	.000	.000
Dusak, Erv-Ervin Frank (Four Sack) (See P46-60)	41-42StLN 43-45MS 46-51StLN 51-52PitN	07-29-20	Chicago, Ill.	11-06-94	R	R	6'2	185	413	1035	168	251	32	6	24	106	142	188	12	.243	.355
Dyck, Jim-James Robert	51-53StLA 54CleA 55-56BalA 56CinN	02-03-22	Omaha, Neb.	01-11-99	R	R	6'2	200	330	983	139	242	52	5	26	114	131	140	4	.246	.389
Eaddy, Don-Donald Johnson	59CinN	02-16-34	Grand Rapids, Mich.		R	R	5'11	165	15	1	3	0	0	0	0	0	0	1	0	.000	.000
Easter, Luke-Luscious Luke	49-54CleA	08-04-15	St. Louis, Mo.	03-29-79	L	R	6'4	240	491	1725	256	472	54	12	93	340	174	293	1	.274	.481
Easton, John-John David (Goose)	55,59PhiN	03-04-33	Trenton, N.J.	07-28-01	R	R	6'2	185	4	3	0	0	0	0	0	0	0	0	0	.000	.000
Edwards, Bruce-Charles Bruce (Bull)	46-51BknN 51-52,54ChiN 55WasA 56CinN	07-15-23	Quincy, Ill.	04-25-75	R	R	5'8	180	591	1675	191	429	67	20	39	241	190	179	9	.256	.309
Edwards, Hank-Henry Albert	41-43CleA 44-45MS 46-49CleA 49-50ChiN 51BknN 51-52CinN 52ChiA 53StLA	01-29-19	Elmwood Place, Ohio	06-22-88	L	L	6'	190	735	2191	285	613	116	41	51	276	208	264	9	.280	.440
Elder, George-George Rezin	49StLA	03-10-21	Lebanon, Ky.		L	R	5'11	180	41	44	9	11	3	0	0	2	4	11	0	.250	.318
Elliott, Bob-Robert Irving	39-46PitN 47-51BosN 52NYN 53StLA 53ChiA M60KCA	11-26-16	San Francisco, Cal.	05-04-66	R	R	6'	185	1978	7141	1064	2061	382	94	170	1195	967	604	60	.289	.440
Elliott, Harry-Harry Lewis	53,55StLN	12-30-23	San Francisco, Cal.		R	R	5'10	175	92	176	15	45	10	1	2	18	14	17	0	.256	.358
Endicott, Bill-William Franklin	46StLN	09-04-18	Acorn, Mo.		R	R	5'11	175	20	20	2	4	3	0	0	3	4	4	0	.200	.350
Ennis, Del-Delmer	46-56PhiN 57-58StLN 59CinN 59ChiA	06-08-25	Philadelphia, Pa.	02-08-96	R	R	6'	195	1903	7254	985	2063	358	69	288	1284	597	719	45	.284	.472
Erautt, Joe-Joseph Michael (Stubby)	50-51ChiA	09-01-21	Vibank, Canada	10-06-76	R	R	5'9	175	32	43	3	8	1	0	0	1	4	5	0	.186	.209
Ermer, Cal-Calvin Coolidge	47WasA M67-68MinA	11-10-23	Baltimore, Md.		R	R	5'7	175	1	3	0	0	0	0	0	0	0	0	0	.000	.000
Ernaga, Frank-Frank John	57-58ChiN	08-22-30	Susanville, Cal.		R	R	6'1	195	29	43	9	12	3	2	2	7	9	16	0	.279	.581
Escalera, Nino-Saturnino [Cuadrado]	54CinN	12-01-29	Santurce, P.R.		L	R	5'10	165	73	69	15	11	1	1	0	3	7	11	1	.159	.203
Esposito, Sammy-Samuel	52ChiA 53-54MS 55-63ChiA 63KCA	12-15-31	Chicago, Ill.		R	R	5'9	170	560	792	130	164	27	2	8	73	145	127	7	.207	.227
Evans, Al-Alfred Hubert	39-42WasA 43MS 44-50WasA 51BosA	09-28-16	Kenly, N.C.	04-06-79	R	R	5'11	190	704	2053	188	514	70	23	13	211	243	206	14	.250	.326
Evers, Hoot-Walter Arthur	41DetA 43-45MS 46-52DetA 52-54BosA 54NYN 54DetA 55BalA 55-56CleA 56BalA	02-08-21	St. Louis, Mo.	01-25-91	R	R	6'2	180	1142	3801	556	1055	187	41	98	565	415	420	45	.278	.426
Fain, Ferris-Ferris Roy (Burrhead)	47-52PhiA 53-54ChiA 55DetA 55CleA	03-29-21	San Antonio, Tex.	10-18-01	L	L	5'11	180	1151	3930	595	1139	213	30	48	570	904	261	46	.290	.396
Fanning, Jim-James James	54-57ChiN M81-82,84MonN	09-14-27	Chicago, Ill.		R	R	5'11	180	64	141	5	24	2	0	0	5	6	26	0	.170	.184
Federoff, Al-Alfred (Whitey)	51-52DetA	07-11-24	Bairford, Pa.		R	R	5'10	165	76	235	14	56	4	2	0	14	16	13	1	.238	.272
Feller, Jack-Jack Leland	58DetA	12-10-36	Adrian, Mich.		R	R	6'	185	1	0	0	0	0	0	0	0	0	0	0	—	—
Fernandez, Chico-Humberto [Perez]	56BknN 57-59PhiN 60-63DetA 63NYN	03-02-32	Havana, Cuba		R	R	6'	170	856	2778	270	666	91	19	40	259	213	338	68	.240	.329
Fernandez, Nanny-Froilan	42BosN 43-45MS 46-47BosN 50PitN	10-25-18	Wilmington, Cal.	09-19-96	R	R	5'9	170	408	1356	139	336	59	5	16	145	109	142	20	.248	.334
Finigan, Jim-James Leroy	54PhiA 55-56KCA 57DetA 58SFN 59BalA	08-19-28	Quincy, Ill.	05-16-81	R	R	5'11	175	512	1600	195	422	74	17	19	168	190	176	8	.264	.367
Fisher, Harry-Harry Deveraux (See P46-60)	51-52PitN	01-03-26	Newbury, Canada	09-20-81	L	R	6'	180	18	18	0	5	1	0	0	1	0	3	0	.278	.333
Fitz Gerald, Ed-Edward Raymond	48-53PitN 53-59WasA 59CinN	05-21-24	Santa Ynez, Cal.		R	R	6'	170	807	2086	199	542	82	10	19	217	185	235	9	.260	.336
Fleitas, Angel-Angel Felix [Husta]	48WasA	11-10-14	Los Abreus, Cuba	07-10-06	R	R	5'9	160	15	13	1	1	0	0	0	1	3	5	0	.077	.077
Fleming, Les-Leslie Harvey (Moe)	39DetA 41-42CleA 43-44VR 45-47CleA 49PitN	08-07-15	Singleton, Tex.	03-05-80	L	L	5'10	185	434	1330	168	369	69	15	29	199	226	152	7	.277	.417
Foiles, Hank-Henry Lee	53CinN 53,55-56CleA 56-59PitN 60KCA 60CleA 60DetA 61BalA 62-63CinN 63-64LAA	06-10-29	Richmond, Va.		R	R	6'	200	608	1455	171	353	59	10	46	166	170	295	3	.243	.392
Fondy, Dee-Dee Virgil	51-57ChiN 57PitN 58CinN	10-31-24	Slaton, Tex.	08-19-99	L	L	6'3	195	967	3502	437	1000	144	47	69	373	203	526	84	.286	.413
Fox, Nellie-Jacob Nelson	47-49PhiA 50-63ChiA 64-65HouN	12-25-27	St. Thomas, Pa.	12-01-75	L	R	5'10	160	2367	9232	1279	2663	355	112	35	790	719	216	76	.288	.363
Frazier, Joe-Joseph Filmore (Cobra Joe)	47CleA 54-56StLN 56CinN 56BalA M76-77NYN	10-06-22	Liberty, N.C.		L	R	6'	180	217	282	31	68	15	2	10	45	35	46	0	.241	.415
Freese, Gene-Eugene Lewis	55-58PitN 58StLN 59PhiN 60ChiA 61-63CinN 64-65PitN 65-66ChiA 66HouN	01-08-34	Wheeling, W.Va.		R	R	5'11	185	1115	3446	429	877	161	28	115	432	243	535	51	.254	.418
Freese, George-George Walter (Bud)	53DetA 55PitN 61ChiN	09-12-26	Wheeling, W.Va.		R	R	6'	197	61	187	17	48	8	2	3	23	18	22	1	.257	.369
Fridley, Jim-James Riley (Big Jim)	52CleA 54BalA 58CinN	09-06-24	Phillippi, W.Va.	02-28-03	R	R	6'2	205	154	424	50	105	12	5	8	53	35	83	3	.248	.356
Friend, Owen-Owen Lacey (Red)	49-50StLA 51-52MS 53DetA 53CleA 55BosA 55-56ChiN	03-21-27	Granite City, Ill.		R	R	6'1	180	208	598	69	136	24	2	13	76	55	109	2	.227	.339
Furillo, Carl-Carl Anthony (Skoonj, The Reading Rifle)	46-57BknN 58-60LAN	03-08-22	Stony Creek Mills, Pa.	01-21-89	R	R	6'	190	1806	6378	895	1910	324	56	192	1058	514	436	48	.299	.458
Fusselman, Les-Lester LeRoy	52-53StLN	03-07-21	Pryor, Okla.	05-21-70	R	R	6'1	195	43	71	6	12	4	0	1	3	0	9	0	.169	.268
Gabler, Bill-William Louis (Gabe)	58CinN	04-30-30	St. Louis, Mo.		L	L	6'1	190	3	3	0	0	0	0	0	0	0	3	0	.000	.000
Gaedel(Gaedele), Eddie-Edward Carl	51StLA	06-08-25	Chicago, Ill.	06-18-61	R	L	3'7	65	1	0	0	0	0	0	0	0	1	0	0	—	—
Garagiola, Joe-Joseph Henry	46-51StLN 51-53PitN 53-54ChiN 54NYN	02-12-26	St. Louis, Mo.		L	R	6'	190	676	1872	198	481	82	16	42	255	267	173	5	.257	.385
Garbowski, Alex-Alexander	52DetA	06-25-25	Yonkers, N.Y.		R	R	6'1	185	2	0	0	0	0	0	0	0	0	0	0	—	—
Garcia, Chico-Vincio [Uzcanga]	54BalA	12-24-24	Veracruz, Mexico		R	R	5'8	170	39	62	6	7	0	2	0	5	8	3	0	.113	.177
Gardner, Billy-William Frederick (Shotgun)	54-55NYN 56-59BalA 60WasA 61-62NYA 62-63BosA M81-85MinA M87KCA	07-19-27	Waterford, Conn.		R	R	6'	180	1034	3544	356	841	159	18	41	271	246	439	19	.237	.327
Garriott, Rabbit-Virgil Cecil	46CinN	08-15-16	Harristown, Ill.	02-20-90	L	R	5'8	165	6	5	1	0	0	0	0	0	0	2	0	.000	.000
Gastall, Tommy-Thomas Everett	55-56BalA	06-13-32	Fall River, Mass.	09-20-56	R	R	6'2	187	52	83	7	15	3	0	0	6	4	13	0	.181	.217
Gearhart, Lloyd-Lloyd William (Gary)	47NYN	08-10-23	New Lebanon, Ohio	04-02-01	R	L	5'11	180	73	179	26	44	9	0	1	17	17	30	1	.246	.397
Genovese, George-George Michael	50WasA	02-22-22	Staten Island, N.Y.		R	R	5'6	160	3	1	1	0	0	0	0	0	0	0	0	.000	.000
Gentry, Harvey-Harvey William	54NYN	05-27-26	Winston Salem, N.C.		L	R	6'	170	5	4	0	1	0	0	0	0	1	0	0	.250	.250
George, Alex-Alex Thomas M.	55KCA	09-27-38	Kansas City, Mo.		L	R	5'11	170	5	10	0	1	0	0	0	0	1	7	0	.100	.100
Gernert, Dick-Richard Edward	52-59BosA 60ChiN 60-61DetA 61CinN 62HouN	09-28-28	Reading, Pa.		R	R	6'3	209	835	2493	357	632	104	8	103	402	363	462	10	.254	.426
Gilbert, Buddy-Drew Edward	59CinN	07-26-35	Knoxville, Tenn.		R	R	6'3	195	7	20	4	3	0	0	2	2	3	4	0	.150	.450
Gilbert, Tookie-Harold Joseph	50,53NYN	04-24-29	New Orleans, La.	06-23-67	L	R	6'2	185	183	482	52	98	15	2	7	48	65	57	4	.203	.286
Gile, Don-Donald Loren (Bear)	59-62BosA	04-19-35	Modesto, Cal.		R	R	6'6	220	58	120	12	18	2	1	3	9	5	35	0	.150	.258
Gilliam, Jim-James William (Junior)	53-57BknN 58-66LAN	10-17-28	Nashville, Tenn.	10-08-78	B	R	5'11	180	1956	7119	1163	1889	304	71	65	558	1036	416	203	.265	.355
Ginsburg, Joe-Myron Nathan	48,50-53DetA 53-54CleA 56KCA 56-60BalA 60-61ChiA 61BosA 62NYN	10-11-26	New York, N.Y.		L	R	5'11	180	695	1716	168	414	59	8	20	182	226	125	7	.241	.320
Giordano, Tommy-Carmine Arthur (T-Bone)	53PhiA	10-09-25	Newark, N.J.		R	R	6'	175	11	40	6	7	2	0	2	5	0	6	0	.175	.375
Gladd, Jim-James Walter	46NYN	10-02-22	Fort Gibson, Okla.	11-08-77	R	R	6'2	190	4	11	0	1	0	0	0	0	1	4	0	.091	.091
Glaviano, Tommy-Thomas Giatano (Rabbit)	49-52StLN 53PhiN	10-26-23	Sacramento, Cal.	01-19-04	R	R	5'9	175	389	1008	191	259	55	6	24	108	208	173	11	.257	.395
Glenn, John-John	60StLN	07-10-28	Moultrie, Ga.		R	R	6'	180	32	31	4	8	0	1	0	5	0	9	0	.258	.323
Glynn, Bill-William Vincent	49PhiN 52-54CleA	01-30-25	Sussex, N.J.		L	L	6'	190	310	684	94	170	22	4	10	56	61	105	4	.249	.336
Goldsberry, Gordon-Gordon Frederick	49-51ChiA 52StLA	08-30-27	Sacramento, Cal.	02-23-96	L	L	6'	170	217	510	78	123	20	7	6	56	80	66	2	.241	.343
Goliat, Mike-Mike Mitchel	49-51PhiN 51-52StLA	11-03-25	Yatesboro, Pa.	01-13-04	R	R	6'	180	249	825	87	186	21	10	20	99	83	127	3	.225	.348
Goodman, Billy-William Dale	47-57BosA 57BalA 58-61ChiA 62HouN	03-22-26	Concord, N.C.	10-01-84	L	R	5'11	165	1623	5644	807	1691	299	44	19	591	669	329	37	.300	.378
Goolsby, Ray-Raymond Daniel (Ox)	46WasA	09-21-19	Florala, Ala.	11-13-99	R	R	6'1	185	3	4	0	0	0	0	0	0	0	2	0	.000	.000
Gorbous, Glen-Glen Edward	55CinN 55-57PhiN	07-08-30	Drumheller, Canada	06-12-90	R	R	6'2	175	117	277	29	66	13	1	4	29	25	19	0	.238	.336
Gordon, Sid-Sidney	41-43,46-49NYN 44-45MS 50-52BosN 53MilN 54-55PitN 55NYN	08-13-17	Brooklyn, N.Y.	06-17-75	R	R	5'10	185	1475	4992	735	1415	220	43	202	805	731	356	19	.283	.466
Gorman, Herb-Herbert Allan	52StLN	12-19-24	San Francisco, Cal.	04-05-53	L	L	5'11	180	1	1	0	0	0	0	0	0	0	0	0	.000	.000
Graber, Rod-Rodney Blaine	58CleA	06-20-30	Massillon, Ohio		L	L	5'11	175	4	8	0	1	0	0	0	0	0	3	0	.125	.125
Graff, Milt-Milton Edward	57-58KCA	12-30-30	Jefferson Center, Pa.	08-02-05	R	R	5'7	158	61	156	16	28	4	3	0	10	15	10	2	.179	.244
Graham, Jack-Jack Bernard	46BknN 46NYN 49StLA	12-24-16	Minneapolis, Minn.	12-30-98	L	L	6'2	200	239	775	105	179	28	5	38	126	84	99	1	.231	.427
Grammas, Alex-Alexander Peter	54-56StLN 56-58CinN 56-62StLN 62-63ChiN M69PitN M76-77MilA	04-03-26	Birmingham, Ala.		R	R	5'11	175	913	2073	236	512	90	10	12	163	208	192	17	.247	.317
Grasso, Mickey-Newton Michael	46NYN 50-53WasA 54CleA 55NYN	05-10-20	Newark, N.J.	10-15-75	R	R	6'	195	322	957	78	216	23	1	5	87	81	108	2	.226	.284
Gray, Dick-Richard Benjamin	58-59LAN 59-60StLN	07-11-31	Jefferson, Pa.		R	R	5'11	165	124	305	43	73	7	6	12	41	33	52	4	.239	.420
Green, Pumpsie-Elijah Jerry	59-62BosA 63NYN	10-27-33	Oakland, Cal.		B	R	6'	175	344	796	119	196	31	12	13	74	138	132	12	.246	.364
Greengras, Jim-James Raymond	52-55CinN 55-56PhiN	10-24-27	Addison, N.Y.		R	R	6'1	200	504	1793	243	482	82	16	69	282	165	271	6	.269	.434
Groth, Johnny-John Thomas	46-52DetA 53StLA 54-55ChiA 54WasA 56-57KCA 57-60DetA	07-23-26	Chicago, Ill.		R	R	6'	182	1248	3808	480	1064	197	31	60	486	419	329	19	.279	.395
Guerra, Mike-Fermin [Romero]	37,44-46WasA 47-50PhiA 51BosA 51WasA	10-11-12	Havana, Cuba	10-09-92	R	R	5'10	155	565	1581	168	382	42	14	9	168	131	123	24	.242	.303
Guintini, Ben-Benjamin John	46PitN 50PhiA	01-13-19	Los Banos, Cal.	12-02-98	R	R	6'1	190	5	7	0	0	0	0	0	0	0	0	0	.000	.000
Haas, Bert-Berthold John	37-38BknN 42-43CinN 44-45MS 46-47CinN 48-49PhiN 49NYN 51ChiA	02-08-14	Naperville, Ill.	06-23-99	R	R	5'11	178	721	2440	263	644	93	32	22	263	204	188	51	.264	.355
Haas, Eddie-Eddie Edwin	57ChiN 58,60MilN M85MinA	05-26-35	Paducah, Ky.		R	R	5'5	170	55	70	7	17	3	0	1	5	9	7	0	.243	.329
Hadley, Kent-Kent William	58-59KCA 60NYA	12-17-34	Pocatello, Idaho	03-10-05	L	L	6'3	190	171	363	49	88	13	1	14	50	30	97	1	.242	.399
Hairston, Sam-Samuel Harding	51ChiA	01-20-20	Crawford, Miss.	10-31-97	R	R	5'10	187	4	5	1	2	1	0	0	1	1	0	0	.400	.600
Hale, Bob-Robert Houston	55-59BalA 60-61CleA 61NYA	07-10-33	Sarasota, Fla.		L	L	6'	195	374	626	41	171	29	2	2	75	33	55	0	.273	.335
Hall, Bill-William Lemuel	54,56,58PitN	07-30-28	Moultrie, Ga.	01-01-86	L	R	5'11	165	57	126	15	33	6	0	1	15	15	14	0	.262	.335
Hall, Dick-Richard Wallace (Turkey Neck) (See P61-73)	52-57PitN 58VR 59PhiN 60KCA 61-66BalA 67-68PhiN 69-71BalA	09-27-30	St. Louis, Mo.		R	R	6'6	205	669	714	79	150	15	4	4	56	61	147	6	.210	.259

USE NAME - GIVEN NAMES (NICKNAMES)	TEAM BY YEAR	BIRTH DATE	BIRTH PLACE	DEATH DATE	B	T	HGT	WGT	G	AB	R	H	2B	3B	HR	RBI	BB	SO	SB	BA	SA
Hamilton, Tom-Thomas Ball (Ham)	52-53PhiA	09-29-25	Altoona, Kans.	11-28-73	L	R	6'4	213	67	66	9	13	3	0	0	6	8	12	0	.197	.242
Hamner, Granny-Granville Wilbur (See P46-60)	44-59PhiN 59CleA 62KCA	04-26-27	Richmond, Va.	09-12-93	R	R	5'10	163	1531	5839	711	1529	272	62	104	708	351	432	35	.262	.383
Hamric, Bert-Odbert Herman	55BknN 58BalA	03-01-28	Clarksburg, W.Va.	08-08-84	L	R	6'	165	10	9	0	1	0	0	0	0	0	7	0	.111	.111
Hancock, Fred-Fred James	49ChiA	03-28-20	Allenport, Pa.	03-12-86	R	R	5'8	170	39	52	7	7	2	2	1	9	8	9	0	.135	.212
Handley, Gene-Eugene Louis	46-47PhiA	11-25-14	Kennett, Mo.		R	R	5'10	165	125	341	41	86	10	6	0	29	32	27	9	.252	.317
Hanebrink, Harry-Harry Aloysius	53,57-58MilN 59PhiN	11-12-27	St. Louis, Mo.	09-09-96	L	R	6'	185	177	317	32	71	7	2	6	25	22	31	1	.224	.315
Hansen, Doug-Douglas William	51CleA	12-06-28	Los Angeles, Cal.	09-16-99	R	R	6'	180	3	0	0	2	0	0	0	0	0	0	0		
Hardin, Bud-William Edgar	52ChiN	06-14-22	Shelby, N.C.	07-28-97	R	R	5'10	165	3	7	1	1	0	0	0	0	0	0	0	.143	.143
Harmon, Chuck-Charles Byron	54-56CinN 56-57StLN 57PhiN	04-23-24	Washington, Ind.		R	R	6'2	175	289	592	90	141	15	8	7	59	46	57	25	.238	.326
Harrell, Billy-William	55,57-58CleA 61BosA	07-18-28	Norristown, Pa.		R	R	6'1	180	173	342	54	79	7	1	8	26	23	54	17	.231	.327
Harris, Gail-Boyd Gail	55-57NYN 58-60DetA	10-15-31	Abingdon, Va.		L	L	6'	200	437	1331	159	320	38	15	51	190	106	194	2	.240	.406
Harshman, Jack-John Elvin (See P46-60)	48,50,52NYN 54-57ChiA 58-59BalA 59BosA 59-60CleA	07-12-27	San Diego, Cal.		L	L	6'2	189	258	424	46	76	7	0	21	65	72	119	0	.179	.344
Hartsfield, Roy-Roy Thomas	50-52BosN M77-79TorA	10-25-25	Chattahoochee, Ga.		R	R	5'9	165	265	976	138	266	30	7	13	59	73	146	14	.273	.358
Hartung, Clint-Clinton Clarence (The Hondo Hurricane, Floppy) (See P46-60)	47-52NYN	08-10-22	Hondo, Tex.		R	R	6'5	210	196	378	42	90	10	6	14	43	25	112	0	.238	.407
Hatfield, Fred-Frederick James	50-52BosA 52-56DetA 56-57ChiA 58CleA 58CinN	03-18-25	Lanett, Ala.	05-22-98	L	R	6'1	171	722	2039	260	493	67	10	25	165	248	247	15	.242	.321
Hatton, Grady-Grady Edgebert	46-54CinN 54ChiA 54-56BosA 56StLN 56BalA 60ChiN M66-68HouN	10-07-22	Beaumont, Tex.		L	R	5'8	170	1312	4206	562	1068	166	33	91	533	646	430	42	.254	.374
Hawes, Roy-Roy Lee	51WasA	07-05-26	Shiloh, Ill.		L	L	6'2	190	3	6	0	1	0	0	0	0	0	2	0	.167	.167
Hazle, Bob-Robert Sidney (Hurricane)	55CinN 57-58MilN 58DetA	12-09-30	Laurens, S.C.	04-25-92	L	L	6'	190	110	261	37	81	14	0	9	37	32	35	1	.310	.467
Hegan, Jim-James Edward	41-42CleA 43-45MS 46-57CleA 58DetA 58-59PhiN 59SFN 60ChiN	08-03-20	Lynn, Mass.	06-17-84	R	R	6'2	195	1666	4772	550	1087	187	46	92	525	456	742	15	.228	.344
Helf, Hank-Henry Hartz	38,40CleA 44-45MS 46StLA	08-26-13	Austin, Tex.	10-27-84	R	R	6'1	196	78	196	18	36	11	0	6	22	10	41	0	.184	.332
Hemus, Solly-Solomon Joseph	49-56StLN 56-58PhiN 59,M59-61StLN	04-17-23	Phoenix, Ariz.		L	R	5'9	175	961	2694	459	736	137	41	51	263	456	247	21	.273	.411
Henley, Gail-Gail Curtice	54PitN	10-15-28	Wichita, Kans.		L	R	5'9	180	14	30	7	9	1	0	1	2	4	4	0	.300	.433
Henrich, Bobby-Robert Edward	57-59CinN	12-24-38	Lawrence, Kans.		R	R	6'1	185	48	16	13	2	0	0	0	1	1	9	0	.125	.125
Hermanski, Gene-Eugene Victor	43BknN 44-45MS 46-51BknN 51-53ChiN 53PitN	05-11-20	Pittsfield, Mass.		L	R	5'11	185	739	1960	276	533	85	18	46	259	289	212	43	.272	.404
Herrera, Pancho-Juan Francisco [Willavicencio]	58,60-61PhiN	06-16-34	Santiago, Cuba	04-28-05	R	R	6'3	220	300	975	122	264	46	8	31	128	113	271	8	.271	.430
Hersh, Earl-Earl Walter	56MilN	05-21-32	Ebbvale, Md.		L	L	6'	205	7	13	0	3	0	0	0	3	0	5	0	.231	.462
Hertweck, Neal-Neal Charles	52StLN	11-22-31	St. Louis, Mo.		L	L	6'1	175	2	6	0	0	0	0	0	0	0	0	0	.000	.000
Herzog, Whitey-Dorrel Norman Elvert (White Rat)	56-58WasA 58-60KCA 61-62BalA 63DetA M73TexA M74CalA M75-79KCA M80-90StLN	11-09-31	New Athens, Ill.		L	L	5'11	187	634	1614	213	414	60	20	25	172	241	261	13	.257	.365
Hicks, Buddy-Clarence Walter	56DetA	02-15-27	Belvedere, Cal.		B	R	5'10	170	26	47	5	10	2	0	0	5	3	2	0	.213	.255
Higdon, Bill-William Travis (Wild Bill)	49ChiA	04-27-24	Camp Hill, Ala.	08-30-86	L	R	6'2	193	11	23	3	7	0	0	1	6	3	1	1	.304	.435
Hitchcock, Billy-William Clyde	42DetA 43-45MS 46DetA 46WasA 47StLA 48-49BosA 50-52PhiA 53,M60DetA M62-63BalA M66-67AtlN	07-31-16	Inverness, Ala.	04-09-06	R	R	6'1	185	703	2249	231	547	67	22	5	257	206	230	15	.243	.299
Hoak, Don-Donald Albert (Tiger)	54-55BknN 56ChiN 57-58CinN 59PhiN 63-64PhiN	02-05-28	Roulette, Pa.	10-09-69	R	R	6'	180	1263	4322	598	1144	214	44	89	498	523	530	64	.265	.396
Hoderlein, Mel-Melvin Anthony	51BosA 52-54WasA	06-26-23	Mt. Carmel, Ohio	05-21-01	B	R	5'10	170	118	294	22	74	10	3	0	24	31	30	1	.252	.340
Hodges (Hodge), Gil-Gilbert Ray	43BknN 44-45MS 46-57BknN 58-61LAN 62-63NYN M63-67WasA M68-71NYN	04-04-24	Princeton, Ind.	04-02-72	R	R	6'2	200	2071	7030	1105	1921	295	48	370	1274	943	1137	63	.273	.487
Hofman, Bobby-Robert George	49,52-57NYN	10-05-25	St. Louis, Mo.	04-05-94	R	R	5'10	178	341	670	81	166	22	6	32	101	70	94	1	.248	.442
Hollmig, Stan-Stanley Ernest (Hondo)	49PhiN	01-02-26	Fredericksburg, Tex.	12-04-81	R	R	6'2	190	94	265	29	67	13	6	2	27	20	46	1	.253	.370
Holmes, Tommy-Thomas Francis (Kelly)	42-51,M51-52BosN 52BknN	03-29-17	Brooklyn, N.Y.		L	L	5'10	180	1320	4992	698	1507	292	47	88	581	480	122	40	.302	.432
Hopp, Johnny-John Leonard (Hippity)	39-45StLN 46-47BosN 48-49PitN 49BknN 49-50PitN 50-52NYA 52DetA	07-18-16	Hastings, Neb.	06-01-03	L	R	5'10	170	1393	4260	698	1262	216	74	46	458	464	378	128	.296	.414
Houk, Ralph-Ralph George (Major)	47-54,M61-63, 66-73NYA M74-78DetA M81-84BosA	08-09-19	Lawrence, Kans.		R	R	5'11	193	91	158	12	43	6	1	0	20	12	10	0	.272	.323
House, Frank-Henry Franklin (Pig)	50-51DetA 52-53MS 54-57DetA 58-59KCA 60CinN 61DetA	02-18-30	Bessemer, Ala.	03-13-05	L	R	6'1	190	653	1994	202	494	64	11	47	235	151	147	6	.248	.362
Howell, Dixie-Homer Elliott (Bats Both 47)	47PitN 49-52CinN 53,55-56BknN	04-24-20	Louisville, Ky.	10-05-90	R	R	5'11	190	340	910	98	224	39	4	12	93	87	140	1	.246	.337
Howerton, Bill-William Ray (Hopalong)	49-51StLN 51-52PitN 52NYN	12-12-21	Lompoc, Cal.	12-18-01	L	R	5'11	185	247	650	95	178	39	12	22	106	92	125	1	.274	.472
Hunter, Billy-Gordon William	53StLA 54BalA 55-56NYA 57-58KCA 58CleA M77-78TexA	06-04-28	Punxsutawney, Pa.		R	R	6'	180	630	1875	166	410	58	18	16	144	111	192	23	.219	.294
Hutchinson, Fred-Frederick Charles (Big Bear)(See P46-60)	39-41DetA 42-45MS 46-53,M52-54DetA M56-58StLN M59-64CinN	08-12-19	Seattle, Wash.	11-12-64	L	R	6'2	190	354	650	71	171	23	3	4	83	67	30	6	.263	.326
Irvin, Monte-Monford	49-55NYN 56ChiN	02-25-19	Haleburg, Ala.		R	R	6'1	195	764	2499	366	731	97	31	99	443	351	220	28	.293	.475
Jablonski, Ray-Raymond Leo (Jabbo)	53-54StLN 55-56CinN 57NYN 58SFN 59StLN 59-60KCA	12-17-26	Chicago, Ill.	11-25-85	R	R	5'10	180	806	2562	297	987	126	11	83	438	196	330	16	.268	.423
Jackson, Lou-Louis Clarence	58-59ChiN 64BalA	07-26-35	Riverton, La.	05-27-69	L	R	5'10	168	34	47	7	10	2	1	1	7	1	13	0	.213	.362
Jackson, Randy-Ransom Joseph (Handsome Ransom)	50-55ChiN 56-57BknN 58LAN 58-59CinN 59ChiN	02-10-26	Little Rock, Ark.		R	R	6'1	185	955	3203	412	835	115	44	103	415	281	382	36	.261	.421
Jackson, Ron-Ronald Harris	54-59ChiA 60BosA	10-22-33	Kalamazoo, Mich.		R	R	6'7	235	196	474	54	116	18	1	17	52	45	119	6	.245	.395
Jacobs, Spook-Robert Forrest Vandergrift	54PhiA 55-56KCA 56PitN	11-04-25	Cheswold, Del.		L	R	5'8	155	188	665	87	164	16	1	0	33	80	32	22	.247	.274
Janowicz, Vic-Victor Felix 54-55 played in N.F.L.	53-54PitN	02-26-30	Elyria, Ohio	02-27-96	R	R	5'9	185	83	196	20	42	6	1	2	10	12	54	0	.214	.286
Jarvis, Roy-Leroy Gilbert	44BknN 45MS 46-47PitN	06-07-26	Shawnee, Okla.	01-13-90	R	R	5'9	160	21	50	4	8	1	0	1	4	7	7	0	.160	.240
Jeffcoat, Hal-Harold Bentley (See P46-60)	48-55ChiN 56-59CinN 59StLN	09-06-24	West Columbia, S.C.		R	R	5'10	185	918	1963	249	487	95	18	26	188	114	289	49	.248	.355
Jennings, Bill-William Lee	51StLA	09-28-25	St. Louis, Mo.		R	R	6'2	175	64	195	20	35	10	2	0	13	26	42	1	.179	.251
Jensen, Jackie-Jack Eugene	50-52NYA 52-53WasA 54-59BosA 60VR 61BosA	03-09-27	San Francisco, Cal.	07-14-82	R	R	5'11	190	1438	5236	810	1463	259	45	199	929	750	546	143	.279	.460
Jethroe, Sam-Samuel (Jet)	50-52BosN 54PitN	01-20-18	East St. Louis, Ill.	06-16-01	B	R	6'1	178	442	1763	280	460	80	25	49	181	177	293	98	.261	.418
Johnson, Billy-William Russell (Bull)	43NYA 44-45MS 46-51NYA 51-53StLN	08-30-18	Montclair, N.J.	06-20-06	R	R	5'9	180	964	3253	419	882	141	33	61	487	347	290	13	.271	.391
Johnson, Darrell-Darrell Dean	52StLA 52ChiA 57-58NYA 60StLN 61PhiN 61-62CinN 62BalA M74-76BosA M77-80SeaA M82TexA	08-30-28	Horace, Neb.	05-03-04	R	R	6'1	180	134	320	24	75	11	2	2	28	26	39	1	.234	.278
Johnson, Dick-Richard Allan (Footer, Treads)	58CinN	02-15-32	Dayton, Ohio		L	L	5'11	175	8	5	1	0	0	0	0	0	0	2	0	.000	.000
Johnson, Stan-Stanley Lucius	60ChiA 61KCA	12-02-37	Dallas, Tex.		L	R	5'10	180	8	9	2	1	0	0	1	1	2	2	0	.111	.444
Jok, Stan-Stanley Edward (Tucker)	54PhiN 54-55ChiA	05-03-26	Buffalo, N.Y.	03-06-72	R	R	6'	190	12	19	4	3	0	0	1	5	0	5	0	.158	.316
Jones, Jake-James Murrell	41-42ChiA 43-46MS 46-47ChiA 47-48BosA	11-23-20	Epps, La.	12-13-00	R	R	6'3	197	224	790	80	181	31	5	23	117	69	130	8	.229	.368
Jones, Nippy-Vernal Leroy	46-51StLN 52PhiN 57MilN	06-29-25	Los Angeles, Cal.	10-03-95	R	R	6'1	185	412	1381	146	369	60	12	25	209	71	102	4	.267	.382
Jones, Willie-Willie Edward (Puddin' Head)	47-59PhiN 59CleA 59-61CinN	08-16-25	Dillon, S.C.	10-18-83	R	R	6'2	205	1691	5826	786	1502	252	33	190	812	755	541	40	.258	.410
Joost, Eddie-Edwin David	36-37,39-42CinN 43BosN 44VR 45BosN 47-54,M54PhiA 55BosA	06-05-16	San Francisco, Cal.		R	R	6'	175	1574	5606	874	1339	238	35	134	601	1043	827	61	.239	.366
Jordan, Tom-Thomas Jefferson	44,46CleA 46CleA 48StLA	09-05-19	Lawton, Okla.		R	R	6'2	195	39	96	5	23	4	2	1	6	4	2	1	.240	.344
Jorgensen, Spider-John Donald	47-50BknN 50-51NYN	11-03-19	Folsom, Cal.	11-16-03	L	R	5'9	155	267	755	97	201	40	11	9	107	106	75	5	.266	.384
Katt, Ray-Raymond Frederick	52-56NYN 56StLN 57NYN 58-59StLN	05-09-27	New Braunfels, Tex.	10-19-99	R	R	6'2	200	417	1071	92	248	29	4	32	120	74	164	2	.232	.356
Kazak (Tkazcuk), Eddie-Edward Terrance	48-52StLN 52CinN	07-18-20	Steubenville, Ohio	12-15-99	R	R	5'11	175	218	605	69	165	22	6	11	75	52	45	0	.273	.383
Kazanski, Ted-Theodore Stanley	53-58PhiN	01-25-34	Hamtramck, Mich.		R	R	6'1	180	417	1329	118	288	49	9	14	116	90	163	4	.217	.299
Kell, George-George Clyde	43-46PhiA 46-52DetA 52-54BosA 54-56ChiA 56-57BalA	08-23-22	Swifton, Ark.		R	R	5'9	175	1795	6702	881	2054	385	50	78	870	621	287	51	.306	.414
Kell, Skeeter-Everett Lee	52PhiA	10-11-29	Swifton, Ark.		R	R	5'9	160	75	213	24	47	9	0	0	17	14	18	1	.221	.286
Keller, Hal-Harold Kefauver	49-50,52WasA	07-07-27	Middletown, Md.		L	R	6'1	200	25	54	4	11	5	0	1	5	3	3	0	.204	.352
Kellert, Frank-Frank William	53StLA 54BalA 55BknN 56DetA	07-06-24	Oklahoma City, Okla.	11-19-76	R	R	6'2	193	122	247	25	57	9	3	8	47	26	36	0	.231	.364
Kennedy, Bob-Robert Daniel	39-42ChiA 43-45MS 46-48ChiA 48-54CleA 54-55BalA 55-56ChiA 56DetA 57ChiN 57BknN M63-65ChiN M68OakA	08-18-20	Chicago, Ill.	04-07-05	R	R	6'2	193	1483	4624	514	1176	196	41	63	514	364	443	45	.254	.355
Kennedy, John-John Irvin	57PhiN	10-12-26	Jacksonville, Fla.	04-27-98	R	R	5'10	175	5	2	1	0	0	0	0	0	0	2	0	.000	.000
Kerr, Buddy-John Joseph	43-49NYN 50-51BknN	11-06-22	Queens, N.Y.		R	R	6'2	175	1067	3631	378	903	145	25	31	333	324	280	38	.249	.328
Kiner, Ralph-Ralph McPherran	46-53PitN 53-54ChiN 55CleA	10-27-22	Santa Rita, N.M.		R	R	6'2	195	1472	5205	971	1451	216	39	369	1015	1011	749	22	.279	.548
King, Charlie-Charles Gilbert (Chick)	54-56DetA 58-59ChiN 59StLN	11-10-30	Paris, Tenn.		R	R	6'2	190	45	76	11	18	0	1	1	9	4	13	0	.237	.263
Kirby, Jim-James Herschel	49ChiN	05-05-23	Nashville, Tenn.		R	R	5'11	175	2	4	0	1	0	0	0	0	2	1	0	.500	.500
Kirk, Tom-Thomas Daniel	47PhiA	09-27-27	Philadelphia, Pa.	08-01-74	L	L	5'10	182	1	0	0	0	0	0	0	0	0	1	0	.000	.000
Kirrene, Joe-Joseph John	50ChiA 52-53MS 54ChiA	10-04-31	San Francisco, Cal.		R	R	6'2	195	10	27	4	8	0	0	0	3	1	6	0	.296	.333
Kitsos, Chris-Christopher Anestos	54ChiN	02-11-28	New York, N.Y.	06-07-04	R	R	5'11	165	13	5	0	0	0	0	0	0	1	0	0		
Klaus, Billy-William Joseph	52BosN 53MilN 55-58BosA 59-60BalA 61WasA 62-63PhiN	12-09-28	Spring Grove, Ill.		R	R	5'9	165	821	2513	357	626	106	15	40	250	331	285	14	.249	.351
Kline, Bobby-John Robert	55WasA	01-27-29	St. Petersburg, Fla.		R	R	6'	179	77	140	16	31	5	0	0	9	11	22	0	.221	.257
Kluszewski, Ted-Theodore Bernard (Klu)	47-57CinN 58-59PhiN 59-60ChiA 61LAA	09-10-24	Argo, Ill.	03-29-88	L	L	6'2	235	1718	5929	848	1766	290	29	279	1028	492	365	20	.298	.498
Kluttz, Clyde-Clyde Franklin	42-45BosN 45-46NYN 46StLN 47-48PhiN 51StLA 51-52WasA	12-12-17	Rockwell, N.C.	05-12-79	R	R	6'	193	656	1903	172	510	90	8	19	212	132	119	5	.268	.354
Knickerbocker, Austin-Austin Jay	47PhiA	10-15-18	Bangall, N.Y.	02-18-97	R	R	5'11	185	21	48	8	12	3	2	0	2	3	4	0	.250	.396

USE NAME - GIVEN NAMES (NICKNAMES) — TEAM BY YEAR	BIRTH DATE	BIRTH PLACE	DEATH DATE	B	T	HGT	WGT	G	AB	R	H	2B	3B	HR	RBI	BB	SO	SB	BA	S
Koback, Nick-Nicholas Nicholie 53-55PitN	07-19-35	Hartford, Conn.		R	R	6'	187	16	33	1	4	0	1	0	1	1	13	0	.121	.18
Kokos (Kokoszka), Dick-Richard Jerome 48-50StLA 51-52MS 53StLA 54BalA	02-28-28	Chicago, Ill.	04-09-86	L	L	5'8	170	475	1558	239	410	82	9	59	223	242	252	15	.263	.40
Kolloway, Don-Donald Martin (Butch, Cab) 40-43ChiA 44-45MS 46-49ChiA 49-52DetA 53PhiA	08-04-18	Posan, Ill.	06-30-94	R	R	6'3	200	1079	3993	466	1081	180	30	29	393	189	251	76	.271	.38
Konopka, Bruce-Bruno Bruce 42-43PhiA 44-45MS 46PhiA	09-16-19	Hammond, Ind.	09-27-96	L	L	6'2	190	45	105	9	25	4	1	0	10	5	9	0	.238	.29
Korcheck, Steve-Stephen Joseph (Hoss) 54-55WasA 56-57MS 58-59WasA	08-11-32	McClellandtown, Pa.		R	R	6'1	205	58	145	12	23	6	1	0	7	6	36	0	.159	.21
Koshorek, Clem-Clement John (Scooter) 52-53PitN	06-20-25	Royal Oak, Mich.	09-08-91	R	R	5'4	165	99	323	27	84	17	0	0	15	26	40	4	.260	.31
Kozar, Al-Albert Kenneth 48-50WasA 50ChiA	08-29-21	McKees Rocks, Pa.		R	R	5'9	173	285	992	118	252	41	10	6	94	96	86	6	.254	.34
Kravitz, Danny-Daniel (Beek, Dusty) 56-60PitN 60KCA	12-21-30	Lopez, Pa.		L	R	5'11	200	215	552	52	130	22	7	10	54	35	64	1	.236	.35
Kress, Charlie-Charles Steven (Chuck) 47,49CinN 49-50ChiA 54DetA 54BknN	12-09-21	Philadelphia, Pa.		L	L	6'	190	175	466	57	116	20	7	1	52	49	59	6	.249	.32
Krsnich, Rocky-Rocco Peter 49,52-53ChiA	08-05-27	West Allis, Wis.		R	R	6'	180	120	275	27	59	18	3	3	38	30	24	0	.215	.33
Kryhoski, Dick-Richard David 49NYA 50-51DetA 52-53StLA 54BalA 55KCA	03-24-25	Leonia, N.J.		L	L	6'2	205	569	1794	203	475	85	14	45	231	119	163	5	.265	.40
Kuczek, Steve-Stanislaw Leo 49BosN	12-28-24	Amsterdam, N.Y.		R	R	6'	160	1	1	0	1	0	0	0	0	0	0	0	1.000	2.00
Kuenn, Harvey-Harvey Edward 52-59DetA 60CleA 61-65SFN 65-66ChiN 66PhiN M75,82-83MilA	12-04-30	West Allis, Wis.	02-28-88	R	R	6'2	192	1833	6913	951	2092	356	56	87	671	594	404	68	.303	.40
Kuhn, Kenny-Kenneth Harold 55-57CleA	03-20-37	Louisville, Ky.		L	R	5'10	175	71	81	12	17	1	0	0	7	5	13	1	.210	.22
Kwietniewski, Cass (See Cass Michaels)																				
Lafata, Joe-Joseph Joseph 47-49NYN	08-03-21	Detroit, Mich.	05-06-04	L	L	6'	163	127	236	31	54	3	2	5	34	24	42	2	.229	.32
Lajeskie, Dick-Richard Edward 46NYN	01-08-26	Passaic, N.J.	08-15-76	R	R	5'11	175	6	10	3	2	0	0	0	0	3	2	0	.200	.20
Lake, Eddie-Edward Erving 39-41StLN 43-45BosA 46-50DetA	03-18-16	Antioch, Cal.	06-07-95	R	R	5'7	159	835	2595	442	599	105	9	39	193	546	312	52	.231	.43
Lamanno, Ray-Raymond Simond 41-42CinN 43-45MS 46-48CinN	11-17-19	Oakland, Cal.	02-09-94	R	R	6'	185	442	1408	122	355	57	5	18	150	118	151	2	.252	.33
Landenberger, Ken-Kenneth Henry (Red) 52ChiA	07-29-28	Lyndhurst, Ohio	07-28-60	L	L	6'3	200	2	5	0	1	0	0	0	0	0	2	0	.200	.20
Landrith, Hobie-Hobert Neal 50-55CinN 57-58StLN 59-61SFN 62NYN 62-63BalA 63WasA	03-16-30	Decatur, Ill.		L	R	5'10	170	772	1929	179	450	69	5	34	203	253	188	5	.233	.32
Lane, Dick-Richard Harrison 49ChiA	06-28-27	Highland Park, Mich.		R	R	5'11	178	12	42	4	5	0	0	0	4	5	3	0	.119	.11
Lang, Don-Donald Charles 38CinN 48StLN	03-15-15	Selma, Cal.		R	R	6'	175	138	373	35	100	17	2	5	42	49	45	2	.268	.34
LaPointe, Ralph-Ralph Robert 47PhiN 48StLN	01-08-22	Winooski, Vt.	09-13-67	L	R	5'11	185	143	433	60	115	10	0	1	30	35	34	9	.266	.29
Larker, Norm-Norman Howard John 58-61LAN 62HouN 63MilN 63SFN	12-27-30	Beaver Meadows, Pa.		L	L	6'	185	667	1953	227	538	97	15	32	271	211	165	3	.275	.39
Lassetter, Don-Donald O'Neal 57StLN	03-27-33	Newnan, Ga.		R	R	6'3	200	4	13	2	2	0	0	0	0	1	3	0	.154	.30
Lawing, Garland-Garland Fred (Knobby) 46CinN 46NYN	08-26-18	Gastonia, N.C.	09-27-96	R	R	6'1	180	10	15	2	2	0	0	0	0	0	5	0	.133	.13
Layden, Pete-Peter John 48-49 played in A.A.F.C. 50 played in N.F.L. 48StLA	11-18-21	Dallas, Tex.	07-18-82	R	R	5'11	185	41	104	11	26	2	1	0	4	6	10	4	.250	.28
Layton, Les-Lester Lee 48NYN	11-18-21	Nardin, Okla.		R	R	6'	165	63	91	14	21	4	2	4	12	6	21	1	.231	.42
Lehner, Paul-Paul Eugene 46-49StLA 50-51PhiA 51ChiA 51StLA 51CleA 52BosA	07-01-20	Dolomite, Ala.	12-27-67	L	L	5'9	160	540	1768	175	455	80	21	22	197	127	118	6	.257	.37
Leja, Frank-Frank John 54-55NYA 62LAA	02-07-36	Holyoke, Mass.		L	L	6'4	215	26	23	3	1	0	0	0	0	1	5	0	.043	.04
Lembo, Steve-Stephen Neal 50,52BknN	11-13-26	Brooklyn, N.Y.	12-04-89	R	R	6'	185	7	11	0	2	0	0	0	0	1	5	0	.182	.18
Lemon, Bob-Robert Granville (See P46-60) 41-42,46-58CleA 43-45MS M70-72KCA M77-78ChiA M78-79,81-82NYA	09-22-20	San Bernardino, Cal.	01-11-00	L	R	6'	180	615	1183	148	274	54	9	37	147	93	241	2	.232	.38
Lemon, Jim-James Robert 50,53CleA 54-60WasA 61-63MinA 63PhiN 63ChiA M68WasA	03-23-28	Covington, Va.	05-14-06	R	R	6'4	205	1010	3445	446	901	121	35	164	529	363	787	13	.262	.44
Lenhardt, Don-Donald Eugene (Footsie) 50-51StLA 51ChiA 52BosA 52DetA 52-53StLA 54BalA 54BosA	10-04-22	Alton, Ill.		R	R	6'3	190	481	1481	192	401	64	9	61	239	214	235	4	.271	.45
Lennon, Bob-Robert Albert (Arch) 54,56NYN 57CinN	09-15-28	Brooklyn, N.Y.	06-14-05	L	L	6'	200	38	79	5	13	2	0	1	4	5	26	0	.165	.22
Lepcio, Ted-Thaddeus Stanley 52-59BosA 59DetA 60PhiN 61ChiA 61MinA	07-28-30	Utica, N.Y.		R	R	5'10	177	729	2092	233	512	91	11	69	251	209	471	11	.245	.39
Leppert, Don-Don Eugene (Tiger) 55BalA	07-28-30	Memphis, Tenn.		L	R	5'8	175	40	70	6	8	1	0	0	2	9	10	1	.114	.14
Lerchen, George-George Edward 52DetA 53CinN	12-01-22	Detroit, Mich. Bats Left 53		B	R	5'11	175	36	49	3	10	2	0	1	5	12	16	1	.204	.30
Levan, Jesse-Jesse Roy 47PhiN 54-55WasA	07-15-26	Reading, Pa.	11-30-98	L	L	6'	205	25	35	5	10	0	0	1	5	0	2	0	.286	.34
Limmer, Lou-Louis 51,54PhiA	03-10-25	New York, N.Y.		L	L	6'2	190	209	530	66	107	19	4	19	62	63	77	3	.202	.36
Lindbeck, Em-Emerit Desmond 60DetA	08-27-35	Kewanee, Ill.		L	R	6'	185	2	1	0	0	0	0	0	0	1	0	0	.000	.00
Lindell, Johnny-John Harlan (See P46-60) 41-50NYA 50StLN 53PitN 53-54PhiN	08-30-16	Greeley, Colo.	08-27-85	R	R	6'4	217	854	2795	401	762	124	48	72	404	289	366	17	.273	.42
Linden, Walt-Walter Charles 50BosN	03-27-24	Chicago, Ill.		R	R	6'1	190	3	5	0	2	1	0	0	0	1	0	0	.400	.60
Lindstrom, Chuck-Charles William 58ChiA	09-07-36	Chicago, Ill.		R	R	5'11	175	1	1	1	1	0	1	0	1	0	0	0	1.000	3.00
Linhart, Carl-Carl James 52DetA	12-14-29	Zborow, Czechoslovakia		L	R	5'11	184	3	2	0	0	0	0	0	0	0	1	0	.000	.00
Lipon, Johnny-John Joseph (Skids) 42DetA 43-45MS 46,48-52DetA 52-53BosA 53StLA 54CinN M71CleA	11-10-22	Martins Ferry, Ohio	08-17-98	R	R	6'	175	758	2661	351	690	95	24	10	266	347	152	28	.259	.32
Littrell, Jack-Jack Napier 52,54PhiA 55KCA 57ChiN	01-22-29	Louisville, Ky.		R	R	6'	185	111	255	22	52	6	3	2	17	20	60	1	.204	.27
Locklin, Stu-Stuart Carlton 55-56CleA	07-22-28	Appleton, Wis.		L	L	6'1	190	25	24	4	4	1	0	0	0	3	5	0	.167	.21
Lockman, Whitey-Carroll Walter 45NYN 46MS 47-56NYN 56StLN 57NYN 58SFN 59BalA 59-60CinN M72-74ChiN	07-25-26	Lowell, N.C.		L	R	6'1	180	1666	5940	836	1658	222	49	114	563	552	383	43	.279	.39
Logan, Johnny-John (Yatcha) 51-52BosN 53-61MilN 61-63PitN	03-23-27	Endicott, N.Y.		R	R	5'11	175	1503	5244	651	1407	216	41	93	547	451	472	19	.268	.37
Lohrke, Lucky-Jack Wayne 47-51NYN 52-53PhiN	02-25-24	Los Angeles, Cal.		R	R	6'	180	354	914	125	221	38	9	22	96	111	86	9	.242	.37
Lollar, Sherm-John Sherman 46CleA 47-48NYA 49-51StLA 52-63ChiA	08-23-24	Durham, Ark.	09-24-77	R	R	6'	195	1752	5351	623	1415	244	14	155	808	671	453	20	.264	.40
Long, Dale-Richard Dale 51PitN 51StLA 55-57PitN 57-59ChiN 60SFN 60NYA 61-62WasA 62-63NYA	02-06-26	Springfield, Mo.	01-27-91	L	L	6'4	212	1013	3020	384	805	135	33	132	467	353	460	10	.267	.46
Lonnett, Joe-Joseph Paul 56-59PhiN	02-07-27	Beaver Falls, Pa.		R	R	5'10	185	143	325	22	54	8	0	6	27	40	74	0	.166	.24
Lopata, Stan-Stanley Edward 48-58PhiN 59-60MilN	09-12-25	Delray, Mich.		R	R	6'2	210	853	2601	375	661	116	25	116	397	393	497	18	.254	.45
Lopez, Hector-Hector Headley [Swainson] 55-59KCA 59-66NYA	07-09-29	Colon, Panama		R	R	5'11	180	1450	4644	623	1251	193	37	136	591	418	696	16	.269	.41
Lowrey, Peanuts-Harry Lee 42-43,45-49ChiN 44MS 49-50CinN 50-54StLN 55PhiN	08-27-17	Culver City, Cal.	07-02-86	R	R	5'8	170	1401	4317	564	1177	186	45	37	479	403	226	48	.273	.34
Lukon, Eddie-Edward Paul (Mongoose) 41CinN 43-44MS 45-47CinN	08-05-20	Burgettstown, Pa.	11-07-96	L	L	5'10	168	213	606	64	143	17	9	23	70	60	72	4	.236	.40
Lund, Don-Donald Andrew 45,47-48BknN 48StLA 49,52-54DetA	05-18-23	Detroit, Mich.		R	R	6'	200	281	753	91	181	36	8	15	86	65	113	5	.240	.36
Luttrell, Lyle-Lyle Kenneth 56-57WasA	02-22-30	Bloomington, Ill.	07-11-84	R	R	6'	180	57	167	21	32	9	3	2	14	11	27	5	.192	.31
Lutz, Joe-Rollin Joseph 51StLA	02-18-25	Keokuk, Iowa		L	L	6'	195	14	36	7	6	0	0	0	2	6	9	0	.167	.22
Lynch, Dummy-Matthew Daniel 48ChiN	02-07-26	Dallas, Tex.	06-30-78	R	R	5'11	174	7	7	3	2	0	0	1	1	1	1	0	.286	.71
Lynch, Jerry-Gerald Thomas 54-56PitN 57-63CinN 63-66PitN	07-17-30	Bay City, Mich.		L	R	6'1	190	1184	2879	364	798	123	34	115	470	224	416	12	.277	.44
Lyons, Ed-Edward Hoyte (Mouse) 47WasA	05-12-23	Winston-Salem, N.C.		R	R	5'9	165	7	26	2	4	0	0	0	0	2	4	0	.154	.15
MacKenzie, Eric-Eric Hugh 55KCA	08-29-32	Glendon, Canada		R	R	6'	185	1	1	0	0	0	0	0	0	0	0	0	.000	.00
Maddern, Clarence-Clarence James 46,48-49ChiN 51CleA	09-26-21	Lowell, Ariz.	05-09-86	R	R	6'1	185	104	238	17	59	12	1	5	29	12	26	0	.248	.37
Madrid, Sal-Salvador 47ChiN	06-19-20	El Paso, Tex.	02-24-77	R	R	5'9	165	8	24	0	3	1	0	0	1	1	6	0	.125	.16
Maguire, Jack-Jack 50-51NYN 51PitN 51StLA	02-05-25	St. Louis, Mo.	09-28-01	R	R	5'11	165	94	192	25	46	5	2	2	21	18	36	1	.240	.31
Majeski, Hank-Henry (Heinie) 39-41BosN 43-45MS 46NYA 46-49PhiA 50-51ChiA 51-52PhiA 52-55CleA 55BalA	12-13-16	Staten Island, N.Y.	08-09-91	R	R	5'9	185	1069	3421	404	956	181	27	57	501	299	260	10	.279	.39
Mallett, Jerry-Gerald Gordon 59BosA	09-18-35	Bonne Terre, Mo.		R	R	6'5	208	4	15	1	4	0	0	0	1	1	3	0	.267	.26
Malmberg, Harry-Harry William (Swede) 55DetA	07-31-25	Fairfield, Ala.	10-29-76	R	R	6'1	190	67	208	25	45	5	2	0	19	29	19	0	.216	.28
Malone, Eddie-Edward Russell 49-50ChiA	06-16-20	Chicago, Ill.	06-01-06	R	R	5'10	175	86	241	19	62	9	4	0	26	39	27	2	.257	.33
Mangan, Jim-James Daniel 52PitN 53MS 56PitN 56-57ChiN	05-10-30	San Francisco, Cal.		R	R	5'10	190	45	59	5	9	0	0	0	2	9	6	0	.153	.15
Mantle, Mickey-Mickey Charles (The Commerce Comet) 51-68NYA	10-20-31	Spavinaw, Okla.	08-13-95	B	R	5'11	195	2401	8102	1677	2415	344	72	536	1509	1733	1710	153	.298	.55
Mapes, Cliff-Cliff Franklin (Tiger) 48-51NYA 51StLA 52DetA	03-13-22	Sutherland, Neb.	12-05-96	L	R	6'3	205	459	1193	199	289	55	13	38	172	168	213	8	.242	.40
Markland, Gene-Cleneth Eugene (Mousy) 50PhiA	12-26-19	Detroit, Mich.	06-15-99	R	R	5'10	160	8	8	2	1	0	0	0	0	4	5	0	.125	.12
Marolewski, Fred-Fred Daniel (Fritz) 55MS	10-06-28	Chicago, Ill.		R	R	6'2	205	1	1	0	0	0	0	0	0	0	0	0	—	—
Marquez, Luis-Luis Angel [Sanchez] (Canena) 51BosN 54ChiN 54PitN	10-28-25	Aguadilla, P.R.	03-01-88	R	R	5'10	174	99	143	24	26	5	1	0	11	16	24	7	.182	.23
Marquis, Bob-Robert Rudolph 53CinN	12-23-24	Oklahoma City, Okla.		L	L	6'1	170	40	44	9	12	1	1	2	3	4	11	0	.273	.47
Marquis, Roger-Roger Julian (Noonie) 55BosA	04-05-37	Holyoke, Mass.	07-19-04	L	L	6'	190	1	1	0	0	0	0	0	0	0	0	0	.000	.00
Marsh, Freddie-Fred Francis 49CleA 51-52StLA 52WasA 52StLA 53-54ChiA 55-56BalA	01-05-24	Valley Falls, Kans.		R	R	6'	180	465	1236	148	296	43	8	10	96	125	171	13	.239	.31
Marshall, Jim-Rufus James 58BalA 58-59ChiN 60-61SFN 62PitN M74-76ChiN M79OakA	05-25-32	Danville, Ill.		L	L	6'1	195	410	852	111	206	24	2	29	106	101	139	5	.242	.38
Marshall, Willard-Willard Warren 42NYN 43-45MS 46-49NYN 50-52BosN 52-53CinN 54-55ChiA	02-08-21	Richmond, Va.	11-05-00	L	R	6'1	205	1246	4233	583	1160	163	39	130	604	458	219	14	.274	.44
Martin (Pesano), Billy-Alfred Manuel 50-53NYA 54MS 55-57NYA 57KCA 58DetA 59CleA 60CinN 61MilN 61,M69MinA M71-73DetA M73-75TexA M75-79NYA M80-82OakA M83,85,88NYA	05-16-28	Berkeley, Cal.	12-25-89	R	R	5'11	165	1021	3419	425	877	137	28	64	333	188	355	34	.257	.36
Martyn, Bob-Robert Gordon 57-59KCA	08-15-30	Weiser, Idaho		L	R	6'	176	154	358	39	94	12	11	3	35	37	56	2	.263	.34
Masi, Phil-Philip Samuel 39-49BosN 49PitN 50-52ChiA	01-06-17	Chicago, Ill.	03-29-90	R	R	5'10	185	1229	3468	420	917	164	31	47	417	410	311	45	.264	.37
Massa, Gordon-Gordon Richard (Moose, Duke) 57-59ChiN 59MS	09-02-35	Cincinnati, Ohio		R	R	6'3	200	8	17	2	7	1	0	0	4	0	5	0	.412	.52
Mathews, Eddie-Edwin Lee 52BosN 53-65MilN 66AtlN 67HouN 67-68DetA M72-74AtlN	10-13-31	Texarkana, Tex.	02-18-01	L	R	6'1	200	2391	8537	1509	2315	354	72	512	1453	1444	1487	68	.271	.50

USE NAME - GIVEN NAMES (NICKNAMES)	TEAM BY YEAR	BIRTH DATE	BIRTH PLACE	DEATH DATE	B	T	HGT	WGT	G	AB	R	H	2B	3B	HR	RBI	BB	SO	SB	BA	SA
Mauch, Gene-Gene William (Skip)	44BknN 45MS 47PitN 48BknN 48-49ChiN 50-51BosN 52StLN 56-57BosA M60-68PhiN M69-75MonN M76-80MinA M81-82,85-87CalA	11-18-25	Salina, Kans.	08-08-05	R	R	5'10	165	304	737	93	176	25	7	5	62	104	82	6	.239	.312
Mauro, Carmen-Carmen Louis	48,50-51ChiN 53BknN 53WasA 53PhiA	11-10-26	St. Paul, Minn.	12-19-03	L	R	6'	167	167	416	40	96	9	8	2	33	37	65	6	.231	.305
Mavis, Bob-Robert Henry	49DetA	04-08-18	Milwaukee, Wis.	03-01-05	L	R	5'7	160	1	0	0	0	0	0	0	0	0	0	0	—	.000
Maxwell, Charlie-Charles Richard	50-52,54BosA 55BalA 55-62DetA 62-64ChiA	04-08-27	Lawton, Mich.		L	L	5'11	190	1133	3245	478	856	110	26	148	532	484	545	18	.264	.451
Mayo, Jackie-John Lewis	48-53PhiN	07-26-25	Litchfield, Ill.		R	R	6'1	190	139	240	25	51	10	1	1	12	25	35	2	.213	.275
McAnany, Jim-James	58-60ChiA 61-62ChiN	09-04-36	Los Angeles, Cal.		R	R	5'10	196	93	241	23	61	10	3	0	27	21	38	2	.253	.320
McCardell, Roger-Roger Morton	59SFN	08-29-32	Gorsuch Mills, Md.	11-13-96	R	R	6'	200	4	4	0	0	0	0	0	0	0	0	0	.000	.000
McCarthy, Jerry-Jerome Francis	48StLA	10-03-65	Brooklyn, N.Y.		L	L	6'1	195	2	3	0	1	0	0	0	0	0	0	0	.333	.333
McCormick, Mike-Myron Winthrop	40-43CinN 44-45MS 46CinN 46-48BosN 49BknN 50NYN 50ChiA 51WasA	05-06-17	Angels Camp, Cal.	04-13-76	R	R	6'	195	748	2325	302	640	100	29	14	215	188	174	16	.275	.361
McCosky, Barney-William Barney	39-42DetA 43-45MS 46DetA 46-48,50-51PhiA 49XJ 51CinN 51-53CleA	04-11-17	Coal Run, Pa.	09-06-96	L	R	6'1	184	1170	4172	664	1301	214	71	24	397	497	261	58	.312	.414
McCullough, Clyde-Clyde Edward (1945-played in World Series game ChiN)	40-43ChiN 44-45MS 46-48ChiN 49-52PitN 53-56ChiN	03-04-17	Nashville, Tenn.	09-18-82	R	R	5'11	190	1098	3121	308	785	121	28	52	339	265	398	27	.252	.358
McDermott, Mickey-Maurice Joseph (See P46-60)	48-53BosA 54-55WasA 56NYA 57KCA 58DetA 61StLN 61KCA	08-29-28	Poughkeepsie, N.Y.	08-07-03	L	L	6'2	185	443	619	71	156	29	2	9	74	52	112	1	.252	.349
McDougald, Gil-Gilbert James	51-60NYA	05-19-28	San Francisco, Cal.		R	R	6'	180	1336	4676	697	1291	187	51	112	576	559	623	45	.276	.410
McGah, Ed-Edward Joseph	46-47BosA	09-30-21	Oakland, Cal.		R	R	6'	183	24	51	3	8	1	1	0	3	10	7	0	.157	.216
McGhee, Ed-Warren Edward	50ChiA 53-54PhiA 54-55ChiA	09-29-24	Perry, Ark.	02-13-86	R	R	5'11	182	196	505	59	124	14	5	3	43	54	61	11	.246	.311
McHale, John-John Joseph	43-45,47-48DetA	09-21-21	Detroit, Mich.		L	R	6'	200	64	114	10	22	1	0	3	12	9	29	1	.193	.281
McManus, Jim-James Michael	60KCA	07-20-36	Brookline, Mass.		L	L	6'4	215	5	13	3	4	0	0	1	2	1	2	0	.308	.538
McMillan, Roy-Roy David	51-60CinN 61-64MilN 64-66NYN M72MilA M75NYN	07-17-29	Bonham, Tex.	11-02-97	R	R	5'11	170	2093	6752	739	1639	253	35	68	594	665	711	41	.243	.321
Meeks, Sammy-Samuel Mack	48WasA 49-51CinN	04-23-23	Anderson, S.C.		R	R	5'9	160	102	199	25	50	8	3	3	18	9	36	3	.251	.312
Mele, Sam-Sabath Anthony	47-49BosA 49-52WasA 52-53ChiA 54BalA 54-55BosA 55CinN 56CleA M61-67MinA	01-21-22	Queens, N.Y.		R	R	6'1	183	1046	3437	406	916	168	39	80	544	311	342	15	.267	.408
Melton, Dave-David Olin	56,58KCA	10-03-28	Pampa, Tex.		R	R	6'	185	12	9	0	1	0	0	0	0	0	5	0	.111	.111
Merriman, Lloyd-Lloyd Archer (Citation)	49-51,54CinN 54-55MS 54ChiN	08-02-24	Clovis, Cal.	01-20-04	L	L	6'	190	455	1202	140	291	64	12	12	117	126	124	20	.242	.345
Merson, Jack-John Warren	51-52PitN 53BosA	01-17-22	Elkridge, Md.	04-28-00	R	R	5'11	175	125	452	47	116	22	4	6	52	23	45	1	.257	.363
Metkovich, Catfish-George Michael	43-46BosA 47CleA 49ChiA 51-53PitN 53ChiN 54MilN	10-08-21	Angel's Camp, Cal.	05-17-95	L	L	6'1	185	1055	3585	476	934	167	36	47	373	307	342	61	.261	.367
Micelotta, Bob-Robert Peter (Mickey)	54-55PhiN	10-20-28	Queens, N.Y.		R	R	5'11	185	7	7	2	0	0	0	0	0	1	1	0	.000	.000
Michaels, Cass-Casimir Eugene (Kwietniewski) (Played as Cass Kwietniewski 43)	43-50ChiA 50-52WasA 52StLA 52-53PhiA 54ChiA	03-04-26	Detroit, Mich.	11-12-82	R	R	5'11	175	1288	4367	508	1142	147	46	53	501	566	406	64	.262	.353
Mickelson, Ed-Edward Allen	50StLN 53StLA 57ChiN	09-09-26	Ottawa, Ill.		R	R	6'3	205	18	37	2	3	1	0	0	3	4	13	0	.081	.108
Mierkowicz, Ed-Edward Frank (Butch)	45,47-48DetA 50StLN	03-06-24	Wyandotte, Mich.		R	R	6'4	205	35	63	6	11	3	0	1	4	4	18	1	.175	.270
Miggins, Larry-Lawrence Edward (Irish)	48,52StLN	08-20-25	Bronx, N.Y.		R	R	6'4	198	43	97	8	22	2	1	2	10	3	19	0	.227	.361
Miksis, Eddie-Edward Thomas	44BknN 45MS 46-51BknN 51-56ChiN 57StLN 57-58BalA 58CinN	09-11-26	Burlington, N.J.	04-08-05	R	R	6'	185	1042	3053	383	722	95	17	44	228	215	313	52	.236	.322
Miles, Don-Donald Ray	58LAN	03-13-36	Indianapolis, Ind.		L	L	6'1	210	8	22	2	4	0	0	0	0	0	6	0	.182	.182
Miller, Rod-Rodney Carter	57BknN	01-16-40	Portland, Ore.		L	R	5'10	160	1	1	0	0	0	0	0	0	0	1	0	.000	.000
Milne, Pete-William James	48-50NYN	01-16-26	Mobile, Ala.	04-11-99	L	R	6'1	180	47	60	6	14	1	2	1	9	4	13	0	.233	.367
Minoso, Minnie-Saturnino Orestes Arrieta [Armas]	49,51CleA 51-57ChiA 58-59CleA 60-61ChiA 62StLN 63WasA 64,76,80ChiA	11-29-22	Havana, Cuba		R	R	5'10	175	1835	6579	1136	1963	336	83	186	1023	814	584	205	.298	.459
Miranda, Willie-Guillermo [Perez]	51WasA 52ChiA 52StLA 52ChiA 53StLA 53-54NYA 55-59BalA	05-24-26	Velasco, Cuba	09-07-96	B	R	5'9	150	824	1914	176	423	50	14	6	132	165	250	13	.221	.271
Mitchell, Dale-Loren Dale	46-56CleA 56BknN	08-23-21	Colony, Okla.	01-05-87	L	R	6'1	195	1127	3984	555	1244	169	61	41	403	346	119	45	.312	.416
Mole, Fenton-Fenton LeRoy (Muscles)	49NYA	06-14-25	San Leandro, Cal.		L	L	6'1	200	10	27	2	5	2	1	0	2	3	5	0	.185	.333
Montemayor, Felipe-Felipe Angel (Monty)	53,55PhiN	02-07-28	Monterrey, Mexico		L	L	6'2	185	64	150	15	26	5	3	2	10	22	37	1	.173	.287
Moon, Wally-Wallace Wade	54-58StLN 59-65LAN	04-03-30	Bay, Ark.		L	R	6'	175	1457	4843	737	1399	212	60	142	661	644	591	89	.289	.445
Moore, Anse-Anselm Winn	46DetA	09-22-17	Delhi, La.	10-29-93	L	R	6'1	190	51	134	16	28	4	0	1	8	12	9	1	.209	.261
Morejon, Dan-Daniel [Torres]	58CinN	07-21-30	Havana, Cuba		R	R	6'1	175	12	26	4	5	0	0	0	1	9	2	1	.192	.192
Morgan, Bobby-Robert Morris	50,52-53BknN 54-56PhiN 56StLN 57PhiN 57-58CinN	06-29-26	Oklahoma City, Okla.		R	R	5'10	180	671	2088	286	487	96	11	53	217	327	381	18	.233	.366
Morgan, Joe-Joseph Michael	59MilN 59KCA 60PhiN 60-61CleA 64StLN M88-91BosA	11-19-30	Walpole, Mass.		R	R	5'10	170	88	187	15	36	5	3	2	10	18	31	0	.193	.283
Morgan, Vern-Vernon Thomas	54-55CinN	08-08-28	Emporia, Va.	11-08-75	R	R	6'1	190	31	71	4	16	2	0	0	3	4	14	0	.225	.254
Morton, Guy-Guy Jr. (Moose)	54BosA	11-04-30	Tuscaloosa, Ala.		R	R	6'2	200	1	0	0	0	0	0	0	0	0	1	0	.000	.000
Moryn, Walt-Walter Joseph (Moose)	54-55BknN 56-60ChiN 60-61StLN 61PitN	04-12-26	St. Paul, Minn.	07-21-96	L	R	6'2	210	785	2506	324	667	116	16	101	354	251	393	7	.266	.446
Moss, Howie-Howard Glenn	42NYN 45MS 46CinN 46CleA	10-17-18	Gastonia, N.C.	05-07-89	R	R	5'11	195	22	72	3	7	0	0	4	1	3	17	0	.097	.097
Moss, Les-John Lester	46-51StLA 52-53StLA 54-55BalA 55-58,M68ChiA M79DetA	05-14-25	Tulsa, Okla.		R	R	5'11	205	824	2234	210	552	75	4	63	276	282	316	2	.247	.369
Mueller, Don-Donald Frederick (Mandrake the Magician)	48-57NYN 58-59CinN	04-14-27	St. Louis, Mo.		L	R	6'	185	1245	4364	499	1292	139	37	65	520	167	146	11	.296	.400
Mullin, Pat-Patrick Joseph	40-41DetA 42-45MS 46-53DetA	11-01-17	Trotter, Pa.	08-14-99	L	R	6'2	190	864	2493	381	676	106	43	87	385	330	312	20	.271	.453
Murphy, Dick-Richard Lee	54CinN 55-57MS	10-25-31	Cincinnati, Ohio		L	L	5'11	170	6	1	1	0	0	0	0	0	0	0	0	.000	.000
Murray, Ray-Raymond Lee (Deacon)	48,50-51CleA 51-53PhiA 54BalA	10-12-17	Spring Hope, N.C.	04-09-03	R	R	6'3	204	250	731	69	184	37	6	8	80	55	67	1	.252	.352
Murtaugh, Danny-Daniel Edward	41-43PhiN 44-45MS 46PhiN 47BosN 48-51,M57-64,67,70-71,73-76PitN	10-08-17	Chester, Pa.	12-02-76	R	R	5'9	165	767	2599	263	661	97	21	8	219	287	215	49	.254	.317
Musial, Stan-Stanley Frank (Stan the Man)	41-44StLN 45MS 46-63StLN	11-21-20	Donora, Pa.		L	L	6'	175	3026	10972	1949	3630	725	177	475	1951	1599	696	78	.331	.559
Myers, Richie-Richard	56ChiN	04-07-30	Sacramento, Cal.		R	R	5'6	150	4	2	1	0	0	0	0	0	0	0	0	.000	.000
Naples, Al-Aloysius Francis	49StLA	08-29-27	Staten Island, N.Y.		R	R	5'9	168	2	7	0	1	1	0	0	0	1	0	0	.143	.286
Naragon, Hal-Harold Richard	51CleA 52-53MS 54-59CleA 59-60WasA 61-62MinA	10-01-28	Zanesville, Ohio		L	R	6'	180	424	985	83	262	27	11	6	87	76	62	1	.266	.334
Naton, Pete-Peter Alphonsus	53PitN 54MS	09-03-31	Queens, N.Y.		R	R	6'1	200	6	12	2	2	1	0	0	1	2	1	0	.167	.167
Neal, Charlie-Charles Lenard	56-57BknN 58-61LAN 62-63NYN 63CinN	01-30-31	Longview, Tex.	11-18-96	R	R	5'10	165	970	3316	461	858	113	38	87	391	337	557	48	.259	.394
Neeman, Cal-Calvin Amandus	57-60CinN 60-61PhiN 62PitN 63CleA 63WasA	02-18-29	Valmayer, Ill.		R	R	6'1	192	376	1002	93	224	35	4	30	97	79	221	1	.224	.306
Neill, Tommy-Thomas White	46-47BosN	11-07-19	Hartsdale, Ala.	09-22-80	L	R	6'2	190	20	55	9	14	2	1	0	7	3	3	0	.255	.327
Nelson, Bob-Robert Sidney (Tex, Babe)	55-57BalA	08-07-36	Dallas, Tex.		L	L	6'3	205	79	122	11	25	2	2	5	11	15	40	0	.205	.254
Nelson, Rocky-Glenn Richard	49-51StLN 51PitN 51ChiA 52BknN 54CleA 56BknN 56StLN 59-61PitN	11-18-24	Portsmouth, Ohio		L	L	5'10	175	620	1394	186	347	61	14	31	173	130	94	7	.249	.379
Niarhos, Gus-Constantine Gregory	46,48-50NYA 50-51ChiA 52-53BosA 54-55PhiN	12-06-20	Birmingham, Ala.	12-29-04	R	R	6'	160	315	691	114	174	26	5	1	59	153	56	6	.252	.308
Nicholas, Don-Donald Leigh	52,54ChiA	10-30-30	Phoenix, Ariz.		L	R	5'7	150	10	2	3	0	0	0	0	0	0	0	0	.000	.000
Nielsen, Milt-Milton Robert	49,51CleA	02-08-25	Tyler, Minn.		L	L	5'11	175	19	15	2	1	0	0	0	0	3	5	0	.067	.067
Nieman, Bob-Robert Charles	51-52StLA 53-54DetA 55-56ChiA 56-59BalA 60-61StLN 61-62CleA 62SFN	01-26-27	Cincinnati, Ohio	03-10-85	R	R	5'11	195	1113	3452	455	1018	180	32	125	544	435	512	10	.295	.474
Noble, Ray-Rafael Miguel [Magee]	51-53NYN	03-15-19	Central Hatillo, Cuba	05-09-98	R	R	5'11	210	107	243	31	53	6	1	9	40	25	41	1	.218	.362
Noren, Irv-Irving Arnold (46-47 played in N.B.L.)	50-52WasA 52-56NYA 57KCA 57-59StLN 59-60CinN 60-61LAN	11-29-24	Jamestown, N.Y.		L	L	6'	190	1093	3119	443	857	157	35	65	453	335	350	34	.275	.410
Northey, Ron-Ronald James (The Round Man)	42-44PhiN 44MS 46-47PhiN 47-49StLN 50CinN 50,52ChiA 55-57PhiN 57ChiA	04-26-20	Mahanoy City, Pa.	04-16-71	L	R	5'10	195	1084	3172	385	874	172	28	108	513	361	297	7	.276	.450
Novotney, Rube-Ralph Joseph	49ChiN	08-05-24	Streator, Ill.	07-16-87	R	R	6'	187	22	67	4	18	2	1	0	6	8	11	0	.269	.328
O'Brien, Eddie-Edward Joseph (See P46-60)	53,55-58PitN 54MS 58StLN 59MilN	12-11-30	South Amboy, N.J.		R	R	5'9	168	231	554	64	131	10	4	0	25	37	45	11	.236	.269
O'Brien, Johnny-John Thomas (See P46-60)	53,55-58PitN 54MS 58StLN 59MilN	12-11-30	South Amboy, N.J.		R	R	5'9	170	339	815	90	204	35	5	4	59	59	82	2	.250	.320
O'Connell, Danny-Daniel Francis	50PitN 51-52MS 53PitN 54-57MilN 57NYN 58-59SFN 61-62WasA	01-21-27	Paterson, N.J.	10-02-69	R	R	5'11	180	1143	4035	527	1049	181	35	39	320	431	396	48	.260	.351
Oertel, Chuck-Charles Frank (Snuffy, Ducky)	58BalA	03-12-31	Coffeyville, Kans.		L	L	5'8	165	14	12	4	2	0	0	0	1	1	1	0	.167	.417
Okie, Len-Leonard Joseph	48,50-51DetA 52PhiA	07-16-23	Detroit, Mich.		R	R	6'1	185	42	78	3	17	3	1	0	3	9	16	0	.218	.256
Oldham, John-John Hardin	56CinN	11-06-32	Salinas, Cal.		R	L	6'3	198	1	0	0	0	0	0	0	0	0	0	0	—	—
Olson, Karl-Karl Arthur (Ole)	51BosA 52MS 53-55BosA 56-57WasA 57DetA	07-06-30	Kentfield, Cal.		R	R	6'3	210	279	681	74	160	25	6	8	50	43	94	3	.235	.316
O'Neil, John-John Francis	46PhiA	04-19-20	Shelbiana, Ky.		R	R	5'9	155	46	94	12	27	4	1	0	8	9	8	0	.287	.298
Oravetz, Ernie-Ernest Eugene	55-56WasA	01-24-32	Johnstown, Pa.		B	L	5'4	145	188	400	44	105	4	3	0	36	53	39	2	.263	.298
O'Rourke, Charlie-James Patrick	59StLN	06-22-37	Walla Walla, Wash.		R	R	6'2	195	2	0	0	0	0	0	0	0	0	0	0	.000	.000
Ostrowski, John-John Thaddeus	43-46ChiN 48BosA 49-50ChiA 50WasA 50CleA	10-17-17	Chicago, Ill.	11-13-92	R	R	5'11	180	216	561	73	131	20	9	14	74	68	125	7	.234	.376
Pack, Frankie-Frank	49StLA	04-10-28	Morristown, Tenn.	01-26-00	R	R	6'	190	1	1	0	0	0	0	0	0	0	0	0	.000	.000
Pafko, Andy-Andrew (Handy Andy, Pruschka)	43-51ChiN 51-52BknN 53-59MilN	02-25-21	Boyceville, Wis.		R	R	6'	190	1852	6292	844	1796	264	62	213	976	561	477	38	.285	.449
Palys, Stan-Stanley Francis	53-55PhiN 55-56CinN	05-01-30	Blakely, Pa.		R	R	6'2	190	138	333	42	79	17	5	9	46	26	54	2	.237	.378
Patton, Tom-Tommy Allen		09-05-35	Honey Brook, Pa.		R	R	5'9	185	1	2	0	0	0	0	0	0	0	0	0	.000	.000
Paula, Carlos-Carlos [Conill]	54-56WasA	11-28-27	Havana, Cuba	04-25-83	R	R	6'3	195	157	457	64	124	23	8	9	60	27	62	2	.271	.416
Pawelek, Ted-Theodore John (Porky)	46ChiN	08-15-19	Chicago Heights, Ill.	02-12-64	R	R	5'11	202	4	4	1	1	0	0	0	0	0	1	0	.250	.500
Pawloski, Stan-Stanley Walter	55CleA	09-06-31	Wanamie, Pa.		R	R	6'1	175	2	8	0	1	0	0	0	0	0	1	0	.125	.125

USE NAME - GIVEN NAMES (NICKNAMES)	TEAM BY YEAR	BIRTH DATE	BIRTH PLACE	DEATH DATE	B	T	HGT	WGT	G	AB	R	H	2B	3B	HR	RBI	BB	SO	SB	BA	SA
Peck, Hal-Harold Arthur	43BknN 44-46PhiA 47-49CleA	04-20-17	Big Bend, Wis.	04-13-95	L	L	5'11	175	355	1092	136	305	52	13	15	112	87	86	10	.279	.392
Peden, Les-Leslie Earl	53WasA	09-17-23	Azle, Tex.	02-11-02	R	R	6'1	212	9	28	4	7	1	0	1	1	4	3	0	.250	.393
Peete, Charlie-Charles (Mule)	56StlN	02-22-29	Franklin, Va.	11-27-56	L	R	5'10	190	23	52	3	10	2	2	0	6	6	10	0	.192	.308
Pellagrini, Eddie-Edward Charles	46-47BosA 48-49StlA 51PhiN 52ChiN 53-54PitN	03-13-18	Boston, Mass.		R	R	5'9	160	563	1423	167	321	42	13	20	133	128	201	13	.226	.316
Pendleton, Jim-James Edward	53-56MilN 57-58PitN 59CinN 62HouN	01-07-24	St. Charles, Mo.	03-20-96	R	R	6'	185	444	941	120	240	30	8	19	97	43	151	11	.255	.365
Pesky (Paveskovich), Johnny-John Michael	42BosA 43-45MS 46-52BosA 52-54DetA 54WasA M63-64,80BosA	09-27-19	Portland, Ore.		L	R	5'9	168	1270	4745	867	1455	226	50	17	404	662	218	53	.307	.386
Peterson, Buddy-Carl Francis	55ChiA 57BalA	04-23-25	Portland, Ore.		R	R	5'9	170	13	38	8	9	3	0	0	2	5	4	0	.237	.316
Peterson, Hardy-Harding William (Pete)	55,57-59PitN	10-17-29	Perth Amboy, N.J.		R	R	6'	205	66	161	17	44	8	1	3	21	17	17	0	.273	.391
Philley, Dave-David Earl	41ChiA 43-45MS 46-51ChiA 51-53PhiA 54-55CleA 55-56BalA 56-57ChiA 57DetA 58-60PhiN 60SFN 60-61BalA 62BosA	05-16-20	Paris, Tex.		B	R	6'	188	1904	6296	789	1700	276	72	84	729	594	551	102	.270	.377
Phillips, Bubba-John Melvin	55DetA 56-59ChiA 60-62CleA 63-64DetA	02-24-30	West Point, Miss.	06-22-93	R	R	5'9	180	1062	3278	348	835	135	8	62	356	182	314	25	.255	.358
Phillips, Ed-Howard Edward	53StlN	07-08-31	St. Louis, Mo.		B	R	6'1	180	6	0	0	0	0	0	0	0	0	0	0	—	—
Phillips, Jack-Jack Dorn (Stretch)	49-52PhiN 55-57DetA	09-06-21	Clarence, N.Y.		R	R	6'4	193	343	892	111	252	42	16	9	101	85	86	5	.283	.396
Piersall, Jimmy-James Anthony	50,52-58BosA 59-61CleA 62-63WasA 63NYN 63-64LAA 65-67CalA	11-14-29	Waterbury, Conn.		R	R	6'	190	1734	5890	811	1604	256	52	104	591	524	583	115	.272	.386
Pignatano, Joe-Joseph Benjamin	57BknN 58-60LAN 61KCA 62SFN 62NYN	08-04-29	Brooklyn, N.Y.		R	R	5'10	180	307	689	81	161	25	4	16	62	94	116	8	.234	.351
Pike, Jess-Jess Willard	46NYN	07-31-15	Dustin, Okla.	03-28-84	L	L	6'3	180	16	41	4	7	1	1	1	6	6	9	0	.171	.317
Pilarcik, Al-Alfred James	56KCA 57-60BalA 61KCA 61ChiA	07-03-30	Whiting, Ind.		L	L	5'10	180	668	1614	205	413	66	7	22	143	185	150	41	.256	.346
Pisoni, Jim-James Pete	53StlA 56-57KCA 59MilN 59-60NYA	08-14-29	St. Louis, Mo.		R	R	5'10	169	103	189	26	40	3	3	6	20	16	47	0	.212	.354
Plarski, Don-Donald Joseph	55KCA	11-09-29	Chicago, Ill.	12-29-81	R	R	5'6	160	8	11	0	1	0	0	0	0	0	2	1	.091	.091
Platt, Whitey-Mizell George	42-43ChiN 44-45MS 46ChiN 48-49StlA	08-21-20	W. Palm Beach, Fla.	07-27-70	R	R	6'2	215	333	1002	117	256	41	17	13	147	81	122	2	.255	.369
Pless, Rance-Rance	56KCA	12-06-25	Greeneville, Tenn.		R	R	6'	195	48	85	4	23	3	1	0	9	10	13	0	.271	.329
Plews, Herb-Herbert Eugene	56-59WasA 59BosA	06-14-28	Helena, Mont.		L	R	5'11	165	346	1017	125	266	42	17	4	82	74	133	3	.262	.348
Poole, Ray-Raymond Herman	41PhiA 42-45MS 47PhiA	01-16-20	Salisbury, N.C.	03-01-06	R	R	6'	180	15	15	1	3	0	0	0	1	1	5	0	.200	.200
Pope, Dave-David	52,54-55CleA 55-56BalA 56CleA	06-17-21	Talladega, Ala.	08-28-99	L	R	5'10	170	230	551	75	146	19	7	12	73	40	113	7	.265	.390
Porter, Dan-Daniel Edward	51WasA 52-53MS	10-17-31	Decatur, Ill.		L	L	6'	164	13	19	2	4	0	0	0	0	2	4	0	.211	.211
Porter, Jay-J W	52StlA 53-54MS 55-57DetA 58CleA 59WasA 59StlN	01-17-33	Shawnee, Okla.		R	R	6'2	180	229	544	58	124	22	1	8	62	53	96	4	.228	.316
Post, Wally-Walter Charles	49,51-57CinN 58-60PhiN 60-63CinN 63MinA 64CleA	07-09-29	St. Wendelin, Ohio	01-06-82	R	R	6'1	203	1204	4007	594	1064	194	28	210	699	331	813	19	.266	.485
Powell, Bob-Robert Leroy	55ChiA 56MS 57ChiA	10-17-33	Flint, Mich.		R	R	6'1	190	2	0	0	0	0	0	0	0	0	0	0	—	—
Power, Vic-Victor Felipe Pellot [Pove]	54PhiA 55-58KCA 58-61CleA 62-64MinA 64PhiN 65CalA	11-01-27	Arecibo, P.R.	11-29-05	R	R	6'	195	1627	6046	765	1716	290	49	126	658	279	247	45	.284	.411
Powers, Johnny-John Calvin	55-58PitN 59CinN 60CalA 60CleA	07-08-29	Birmingham, Ala.	09-25-01	L	R	6'1	197	151	215	26	42	7	2	6	14	22	48	0	.195	.330
Powis, Carl-Carl Edgar (Jug)	57BalA	01-11-28	Philadelphia, Pa.	05-10-99	R	R	6'	185	15	41	4	8	3	1	0	2	7	9	2	.195	.341
Pramesa, Johnny-John Steven	49-51CinN 52ChiN	08-28-25	Barton, Ohio	09-09-96	R	R	6'2	210	185	526	29	141	17	3	13	59	31	41	0	.268	.386
Price, Jackie-John Thomas Reid	46CleA	11-13-12	Winborn, Miss.	10-02-67	L	R	5'10	150	7	13	1	3	0	0	0	0	1	0	0	.231	.231
Priddy, Jerry-Gerald Edward	41-42NYA 43WasA 44-45MS 46-47WasA 48-49StlA 50-53DetA	11-09-19	Los Angeles, Cal.	03-03-80	R	R	5'11	180	1296	4720	612	1252	232	46	61	541	624	639	44	.265	.373
Pritchard, Buddy-Harold William	57PitN	01-25-36	South Gate, Cal.		R	R	6'	165	23	11	1	1	0	0	0	0	4	0	0	.091	.091
Pyburn, Jim-James Edward	55-57BalA	11-01-32	Fairfield, Ala.		R	R	6'	190	158	294	36	56	5	5	3	20	34	56	6	.190	.272
Queen, Billy-Billy Eddleman (Doc)	54MilN	11-28-28	Gastonia, N.C.	04-23-06	R	R	6'1	185	3	2	0	0	0	0	0	0	0	1	0	.000	.000
Rackley, Marv-Marvin Eugene	47-49BknN 49PitN 49BknN 50CinN	07-25-21	Seneca, S.C.		L	L	5'10	170	185	477	87	151	20	6	1	35	36	36	10	.317	.390
Raines, Larry-Lawrence Glenn Hope	57-58CleA	03-09-30	St. Albans, W.Va.	01-28-78	R	R	5'10	165	103	253	39	64	14	0	2	16	19	45	5	.253	.332
Ramazzotti, Bob-Robert Louis	46,48-49BknN 49-53ChiN	01-16-17	Elanora, Pa.	02-15-00	R	R	5'9	175	346	851	86	196	22	9	4	53	45	107	15	.230	.291
Rand, Dick-Richard Hilton	53,55StlN 57PitN	03-07-31	South Gate, Cal.	01-22-96	R	R	6'2	185	72	146	11	35	3	1	2	13	14	31	0	.240	.315
Rapp, Earl-Earl Wellington	49DetA 49ChiA 51NYN 51-52StlA 52BosN	05-09-21	Corunna, Mich.	02-13-92	L	R	6'2	185	135	279	27	73	16	4	2	39	25	41	2	.262	.369
Reed, Billy-William Joseph	46-47 played in N.B.L. 52BosN	11-12-22	Shawano, Wis.	12-05-05	R	R	5'		14	52	4	13	0	0	0	0	0	5	0	.250	.250
Reese, Pee Wee-Harold Henry (The Little Colonel)	40-42BknN 43-45MS 46-57BknN 58LAN	07-23-18	Ekron, Ky.	08-14-99	R	R	5'10	175	2166	8058	1338	2170	330	80	126	885	1210	890	232	.269	.377
Regalado, Rudy-Rudolph Valentino	54-56CleA	05-21-30	Los Angeles, Cal.		R	R	6'1	185	91	253	27	63	8	0	2	31	25	21	0	.249	.304
Reich, Herm-Herman Charles	49WasA 49CleA 49CinN	11-23-17	Bell, Cal.		R	L	6'2	200	111	390	43	109	18	2	3	34	14	33	4	.279	.359
Reiser, Pete-Harold Patrick (Pistol Pete)	40-42BknN 43-45MS 46-48BknN 49-51PitN 52CleA (Bats Both parts of 40, 48-52)	03-17-19	St. Louis, Mo.	10-25-81	L	R	5'11	185	861	2662	473	786	155	41	58	368	343	369	87	.295	.450
Renna, Bill-William Benedito (Big Bill)	53NYA 54PhiA 55-56KCA 58-59BosA	10-14-24	Hanford, Cal.		R	R	6'3	218	370	918	123	219	36	10	28	119	99	166	2	.239	.391
Repulski, Rip-Eldon John	53-56StlN 57-58PhiN 59-60LAN 60-61BosA	10-04-28	Sauk Rapids, Minn.	02-10-93	R	R	6'	195	928	3088	407	830	153	23	106	416	207	433	25	.269	.436
Restelli, Dino-Dino Paolo (Dingo)	49,51PitN	09-23-24	St. Louis, Mo.	08-08-06	R	R	5'10	191	93	270	42	65	12	0	13	43	37	30	3	.241	.430
Rhawn, Bobby-Robert John (Rocky)	47-49NYN 49PitN 49ChiA	02-13-19	Catawissa, Pa.	06-09-84	R	R	5'8	180	90	198	38	47	9	2	1	18	35	17	4	.237	.333
Rhodes, Dusty-James Lamar	52-57NYN 59SFN	05-13-27	Matthews, Ala.		L	R	6'	178	576	1172	146	296	44	10	54	207	131	196	3	.253	.445
Rice, Del-Delbert	45-55StlN 55-59MilN 60ChiN 60StlN 60BalA 61LAA M72CalA (45-46 played in N.B.L.)	10-27-22	Portsmouth, Ohio	01-26-83	R	R	6'2	190	1309	2826	342	908	177	20	79	441	382	522	2	.237	.356
Rice, Hal-Harold Housten (Hoot)	48-53StlN 53-54PitN 54ChiN	02-11-24	Morganette, W.Va.	12-22-97	R	R	6'1	195	424	1183	129	307	52	12	19	162	94	133	1	.260	.372
Richards, Fred-Fred Charles (Fuzzy)	51ChiN	11-03-27	Warren, Ohio		L	L	6'1	185	10	27	1	8	2	0	0	4	2	3	0	.296	.370
Richardson, Ken-Kennth Franklin	42PhiA 46PhiN	05-02-15	Orleans, Ind.	12-07-87	R	R	5'11	187	12	35	2	4	1	0	0	2	2	2	0	.114	.143
Richmond, Don-Donald Lester	41PhiA 42-45MS 46-47PhiA 51StlN	10-27-19	Gillett, Pa.	05-24-81	L	R	6'1	175	56	152	11	32	6	2	2	22	10	7	0	.211	.316
Richter, Al-Allen Gordon	51,53BosA	02-07-27	Norfolk, Va.		R	R	5'11	165	6	11	1	1	0	0	0	0	3	0	0	.091	.091
Rickert, Marv-Marvin August (Twitch)	42ChiN 43-45MS 46-47ChiN 48CinN 48-49BosN 50PitN 50ChiA	01-08-21	Longbranch, Wash.	06-03-78	L	R	6'2	195	402	1149	139	284	45	9	19	145	88	161	4	.247	.352
Riebe, Hank-Harvey Donald	42DetA 43-45MS 47-49DetA	10-10-21	Cleveland, Ohio	04-16-01	R	R	5'9	175	61	137	2	29	4	0	0	11	3	18	1	.212	.241
Rigney, Bill-William Joseph (Specs, Cricket)	46-53,M56-57NYN M58-60SFN M61-64LAA M65-69CalA M70-72MinA M76SFN	01-29-18	Alameda, Cal.	02-20-01	R	R	6'1	178	654	1966	281	510	78	14	41	212	208	206	25	.259	.380
Rikard, Culley-Culley	41-42PitN 43-45MS 47PitN	05-09-14	Oxford, Miss.	02-25-00	L	R	6'	183	153	396	64	107	19	5	4	37	58	48	1	.270	.374
Rinker, Bob-Robert John	49PhiA	04-21-21	Audenried, Pa.	12-19-02	R	R	6'	190	3	3	0	1	0	0	0	0	1	1	0	.333	.333
Rivera, Jim-Manuel Joseph (Jungle Jim)	52StlA 52-61ChiA 61KCA	07-22-22	Bronx, N.Y.		L	L	6'	196	1171	3552	503	911	155	56	83	422	365	523	160	.256	.426
Rizzuto, Phil-Philip Francis (Scooter)	41-42NYA 43-45MS 46-56NYA	09-25-17	Brooklyn, N.Y.		R	R	5'6	160	1661	5816	877	1588	239	62	38	563	651	398	149	.273	.355
Roach, Mel-Melvin Earl	53-54MilN 55-56MS 57-61MilN 61ChiN 62PhiN	11-25-33	Richmond, Va.		R	R	6'1	190	227	499	42	119	25	0	7	43	24	75	1	.238	.331
Roberts, Curt-Curtis Benjamin	54-56PitN	08-16-29	Pineland, Tex.	11-14-69	R	R	5'8	165	171	575	54	128	24	9	1	40	62	62	7	.223	.301
Robertson, Don-Donald Alexander	54ChiN	10-15-30	Harvey, Ill.		L	L	5'10	180	14	9	1	0	0	0	0	0	1	3	0	.000	.000
Robertson, Jim-James Edward	54PhiA 55KCA	11-22-28	Chicago, Ill.		R	R	5'9	183	69	155	19	29	8	0	2	8	24	27	0	.187	.239
Robertson, Sherry-Sherrard Alexander	40-41,43WasA 44-45MS 46-52WasA 52PhiA	01-01-19	Montreal, Canada	10-23-70	L	R	6'	180	597	1507	200	346	55	18	26	151	202	238	32	.230	.342
Robinson, Aaron-Aaron Andrew	43NYA 44MS 45-47NYA 48-49DetA 51BosA	06-23-15	Lancaster, S.C.	03-09-66	L	R	6'2	205	610	1839	208	478	74	11	61	272	337	194	0	.260	.412
Robinson, Eddie-William Edward	42CleA 43-45MS 46-48CleA 49-50WasA 50-52ChiA 53PhiA 54-56NYA 56KCA 57DetA 57CleA 57BalA	12-15-20	Paris, Tex.		L	R	6'2	210	1315	4282	546	1146	172	24	172	723	521	359	10	.268	.440
Robinson, Jackie-Jack Roosevelt	47-56BknN	01-31-19	Cairo, Ga.	10-24-72	R	R	5'11	195	1382	4877	947	1518	273	54	137	734	740	291	197	.311	.474
Rodin, Eric-Eric Chapman	54NYN	02-05-30	Orange, N.J.	01-04-01	R	R	6'2	215	5	6	0	0	0	0	0	0	0	3	0	.000	.000
Rodriguez, Hector-Hector Antonio [Ordenana]	52ChiA	06-13-20	Alquizar, Cuba	09-01-03	B	R	5'8	165	124	407	55	108	14	0	1	40	47	22	7	.265	.307
Roig, Tony-Anton Ambrose	53,55-56WasA	03-24-28	New Orleans, La.		R	R	6'2	180	76	184	14	39	7	3	0	11	22	45	2	.212	.283
Rojek, Stan-Stanley Andrew	42,46-47BknN 43-45MS 48-51PitN 51StlN 52StlA	04-21-19	N.Tonawanda, N.Y.	07-09-97	R	R	5'10	170	522	1764	225	470	67	13	4	122	152	100	32	.266	.326
Rosen, Al-Albert Leonard (Flip)	47-56CleA	02-29-24	Spartanburg, S.C.		R	R	5'10	180	1044	3725	603	1063	165	20	192	717	587	385	39	.285	.495
Rossi, Joe-Joseph Anthony	52CinN	03-13-21	Oakland, Cal.	02-20-99	R	R	6'1	205	55	145	14	32	8	1	1	16	20	20	1	.221	.255
Rufer, Rudy-Rudolph Joseph	49-50NYN	10-28-28	Queens, N.Y.		R	R	6'	165	12	26	3	2	0	0	0	1	6	5	0	.077	.077
Runnels, Pete-James Edward (Runnels)	51-57WasA 58-62BosA 63-64HouN M66BosA	01-28-28	Lufkin, Tex.	05-20-91	L	R	6'	170	1799	6373	876	1854	282	64	49	630	844	627	37	.291	.378
Russell, Jim-James William	42-47PitN 48-49BosN 50-51BknN	10-01-18	Fayette City, Pa.	11-24-87	B	R	6'1	181	1033	3595	554	959	171	51	67	428	503	427	59	.267	.400
Rutner, Mickey-Milton	47ChiA	03-18-20	Hampstead, N.Y.		R	R	5'11	180	12	48	4	12	1	1	0	4	3	2	0	.250	.333
Ryan, Connie-Cornelius Joseph	42NYN 43-44BosN 45MS 46-50BosN 50-51CinN 52-53PhiN 53ChiA 54CinN M75AtlN M77TexA	02-27-20	New Orleans, La.	01-03-96	R	R	5'11	175	1184	3982	535	988	181	42	56	381	518	514	69	.248	.357
Sacka, Frank-Frank	51,53WasA	08-30-24	Romulus, Mich.	12-07-94	R	R	6'	195	14	34	3	9	0	0	0	3	6	6	0	.265	.265
Saffell, Tom-Tomas Judson	49-51,55PitN 55KCA	07-26-21	Etowah, Tenn.		L	R	5'11	170	271	602	91	143	15	9	6	40	59	108	9	.238	.296
St. Clair, Ebba-Edward Joseph	51-52BosN 54NYN	08-05-21	Whitehall, N.Y.	08-22-82	R	R	6'1	219	164	450	39	112	23	2	7	46	25	49	0	.249	.356
Salkeld, Bill-William Franklin	45-47PitN 48-49BosN 50CinN	03-08-17	Pocatello, Idaho	04-22-67	L	R	5'10	190	356	850	111	232	39	2	31	132	182	101	6	.273	.448
Samcoff, Eddie-Edward William	51PhiA	09-01-24	Sacramento, Cal.		R	R	5'10	165	4	11	0	0	0	0	0	0	0	2	0	.000	.000
Samford, Ron-Ronald Edward	54NYN 55,57DetA 59WasA	02-28-30	Dallas, Tex.		R	R	5'11	156	158	334	31	73	14	2	5	27	17	46	2	.219	.317
Sanicki, Ed-Edward Robert (Butch)	49,51PhiN	07-07-23	Wallington, N.J.	07-06-98	R	R	5'9	195	16	17	9	5	1	0	3	7	8	8	0	.294	.882
Sarni, Bill-William Fiorine	51-52,54-56StlN 56NYN	09-19-27	Los Angeles, Cal.	04-15-83	R	R	5'11	185	390	1182	107	311	50	11	22	151	89	135	6	.263	.380
Saucier, Frank-Frank Field	51StlA 52-54MS	05-28-26	Leslie, Mo.		L	R	6'1	180	18	14	4	1	0	0	0	0	5	4	0	.071	.143

USE NAME - GIVEN NAMES (NICKNAMES)	TEAM BY YEAR	BIRTH DATE	BIRTH PLACE	DEATH DATE	B	T	HGT	WGT	G	AB	R	H	2B	3B	HR	RBI	BB	SO	SB	BA	SA
Sauer, Ed-Edward (Hon)	43-45ChiN 49StLN 49BosN	01-03-19	Pittsburgh, Pa.	07-01-88	R	R	6'1	188	189	457	45	117	25	2	5	57	33	77	3	.256	.352
Sauer, Hank-Henry John	41-42CinN 44MS 45,48-49CinN 49-55CinN 56StLN 57NYN 58-59SFN	03-17-17	Pittsburgh, Pa.	08-24-01	R	R	6'3	198	1399	4796	709	1278	200	19	288	876	561	714	11	.266	.496
Sawatski, Carl-Carl Ernest (Swats)	48,50ChiN 51-52MS 53CinN 54ChiA 57-58MilN 58-59PhiN 60-63StLN	11-04-27	Shickshinny, Pa.	11-24-91	L	R	5'10	220	633	1449	133	351	46	5	58	213	191	251	2	.242	.401
Scala, Jerry-Gerard Michael	48-50ChiA	09-27-26	Bayonne, N.J.	12-14-93	L	R	5'11	178	80	193	26	43	9	2	1	19	27	32	3	.223	.306
Scheffing, Bob-Robert Boden	41-42ChiN 43-45MS 46-50ChiN 50-51CinN 51StLN M57-59ChiN M61-63DetA	08-11-13	Overland, Mo.	10-26-85	R	R	6'2	180	517	1357	105	357	53	9	20	187	103	127	6	.263	.360
Schell, Danny-Clyde Daniel	54-55PhiN	12-26-27	Fostoria, Mich.	05-11-72	R	R	6'1	195	94	274	25	77	14	3	7	33	17	32	0	.281	.431
Schenz, Hank-Henry Leonard	46-49ChiN 50-51PitN 51NYN	04-11-19	New Richmond, Ohio	05-12-88	R	R	5'9	175	207	538	70	133	22	3	2	24	27	25	6	.247	.310
Scherbarth, Bob-Robert Elmer	50BosA	01-18-26	Milwaukee, Wis.		R	R	6'	180	1	0	0	0	0	0	0	0	0	0	0	—	—
Schmees, George-George Edward (Rocky)	52StLA 52BosA	09-06-24	Cincinnati, Ohio	10-30-98	L	L	6'	190	76	125	17	21	4	1	0	6	12	29	0	.168	.216
Schmidt, Bob-Robert Benjamin	58-61SFN 61CinN 62-63WasA 65NYA	04-22-33	St. Louis, Mo.		R	R	6'2	205	454	1305	133	317	55	4	39	150	100	199	2	.243	.381
Schoendienst, Red-Albert Frederick	45-56StLN 56-57NYN 57-60MilN 61-63,M65-76,80,90StLN	02-02-23	Germantown, Ill.		B	R	6'	170	2216	8479	1223	2449	427	78	84	773	606	346	89	.289	.387
Schoonmaker, Jerry-Jerald Lee	55WasA 56MS 57WasA	12-14-33	Seymour, Mo.		R	R	5'11	190	50	69	10	9	1	1	1	4	7	22	1	.130	.217
Schramka, Paul-Paul Edward	53ChiN	03-22-28	Milwaukee, Wis.		R	L	6'	185	2	0	0	0	0	0	0	0	0	0	0	—	—
Schult, Art-Arthur William (Dutch)	53NYA 56-57CinN 57WasA 59-60ChiN	06-20-28	Brooklyn, N.Y.		R	R	6'3	210	164	421	58	111	24	0	6	56	23	50	0	.264	.363
Schypinski, Jerry-Gerald Albert	55KCA	09-16-31	Detroit, Mich.		R	R	5'10	170	22	69	7	15	2	0	0	5	1	8	0	.217	.246
Seerey, Pat-James Patrick	43-48CleA 48-49ChiA	03-17-23	Wilburton, Okla.	04-28-86	R	R	5'10	200	561	1815	236	406	73	5	86	261	259	485	3	.224	.412
Segrist, Kal-Kal Hill	52NYA 55BalA	04-14-31	Greenville, Tex.		R	R	6'	180	20	32	4	4	0	0	0	1	5	1	0	.125	.125
Seminick, Andy-Andrew Wasal	43-51PhiN 52-55CinN 55-57PhiN	09-12-20	Pierce, W.Va.	02-22-04	R	R	5'11	187	1304	3921	495	953	139	26	164	556	582	780	23	.243	.417
Senerchia, Sonny-Emanuel Robert	52PitN	04-06-31	Newark, N.J.	11-01-03	R	R	6'1	195	29	100	5	22	5	0	3	11	4	21	0	.220	.360
Sepkowski, Ted-Theodore Walter	42CleA 44-45MS 46-47CleA 47NYA	11-09-23	Baltimore, Md.	03-08-02	L	R	5'11	190	19	26	3	6	2	0	0	1	1	4	0	.231	.308
Serena, Bill-William Robert	49-54ChiN	10-02-24	Alameda, Cal.	04-17-96	R	R	5'9	180	408	1239	154	311	57	16	48	198	177	235	2	.251	.439
Sessi, Walter-Walter Anthony (Watsie)	41StLN 42-45MS 46StLN	07-23-18	Finleyville, Pa.	04-18-98	L	L	6'3	225	20	27	4	2	0	0	1	2	2	6	0	.074	.185
Shannon, Wally-Walter Charles	59-60StLN	01-23-33	Cleveland, Ohio	02-08-92	L	R	6'	178	65	118	7	31	5	0	0	6	3	18	0	.263	.305
Shantz, Billy-Wilmer Ebert	54PhiA 55KCA 60NYA	07-31-27	Pottstown, Pa.	12-13-93	R	R	6'1	160	131	381	31	98	13	4	2	29	28	37	0	.257	.328
Shearer, Ray-Ray Solomon	57MilN	09-19-29	Jacobus, Pa.	02-21-82	R	R	6'	200	2	2	1	1	0	0	0	0	0	1	0	.500	.500
Sheely, Bud-Hollis Kimball	51-53ChiA	11-26-20	Spokane, Wash.	10-17-85	L	R	6'1	200	101	210	7	44	5	0	0	12	27	22	0	.210	.233
Shepard, Jack-Jack Leroy	53-56PitN	05-13-31	Clovis, Cal.	12-31-94	R	R	6'2	195	278	751	72	195	29	6	12	75	84	97	2	.260	.362
Sheridan, Neill-Neill Rawlins (Wild Horse)	48BosA	11-20-21	Sacramento, Cal.		R	R	6'1	195	2	1	0	0	0	0	0	0	0	0	0	.000	.000
Shetrone, Barry-Barry Steven	59-62BalA 63WasA	07-06-38	Baltimore, Md.	07-18-01	L	R	6'2	190	60	112	12	23	7	1	1	7	5	16	3	.205	.268
Shofner, Strick-Frank Strickland	47BosA	07-23-20	Crawford, Tex.	10-10-98	R	R	5'11	172	5	13	1	2	0	1	0	0	0	3	0	.154	.308
Shokes, Eddie-Edward Christopher	41CinN 43-45MS 46CinN	01-27-20	Charlestown, S.C.	09-14-02	L	L	6'	170	32	84	3	10	1	0	0	5	18	22	1	.119	.131
Shoop, Ron-Ronald Lee	59DetA	09-19-31	Rural Valley, Pa.	03-14-03	R	R	5'11	180	3	7	1	1	0	0	0	1	0	1	0	.143	.143
Shuba, George-George Thomas (Shotgun)	48-50,52-55BknN	12-13-24	Youngstown, Ohio		L	R	5'11	180	355	814	106	211	45	4	24	125	120	122	5	.259	.413
Sievers, Roy-Roy Edward (Squirrel)	49-53StLA 54-59WasA 60-61ChiA 62-64PhiN 64-65WasA	11-18-26	St. Louis, Mo.		R	R	6'1	204	1887	6387	945	1703	292	42	318	1147	841	920	14	.267	.475
Silvera, Al-Aaron Albert	55-56CinN	08-26-35	San Diego, Cal.	07-24-02	R	R	6'	180	14	7	3	1	0	0	0	2	0	1	0	.143	.143
Silvera, Charlie-Charles Anthony Ryan (Swede)	48-56NYA 57ChiN	10-13-24	San Francisco, Cal.		R	R	5'10	175	227	482	34	136	15	2	1	52	53	32	2	.282	.328
Simmons, Johnny-John Earl	46-47 played in B.A.A., 47 played in P.B.A., 49WasA	05-28-34	Birmingham, Ala.	07-07-02	R	R	5'11	192	62	93	12	20	0	0	0	5	11	6	0	.215	.215
Simpson, Harry-Harry Leon (Suitcase)	51-53,55CleA 55-57KCA 57-58NYA 58-59KCA 59ChiA 59PitN	12-03-25	Atlanta, Ga.	04-03-79	L	R	6'1	180	888	2829	343	752	101	41	73	381	271	429	17	.266	.408
Sisler, Dick-Richard Allan	46-47StLN 48-51PhiN 52CinN 52-53StLN M64-65CinN	11-02-20	St. Louis, Mo.		L	R	6'2	205	799	2606	302	720	118	28	55	360	226	253	6	.276	.406
Sisti, Sibby-Sebastian Daniel	39-42BosN 43-45MS 46-52BosN 53-54MilN	07-26-20	Buffalo, N.Y.	04-24-06	R	R	5'11	185	1016	2999	401	732	121	19	27	260	283	440	30	.244	.324
Skinner, Bob-Robert Ralph	54,56-63PitN 63-64CleN 64-66StLN M68-69PhiN M77SDN	10-03-31	La Jolla, Cal.		L	R	6'4	190	1381	4318	642	1198	197	58	103	531	485	646	67	.277	.421
Skizas, Lou-Louis Peter (The Nervous Greek)	56NYA 56-57KCA 58DetA 59ChiA	06-02-32	Chicago, Ill.		R	R	5'11	175	239	725	80	196	27	4	30	86	50	37	8	.270	.443
Slaughter, Enos-Enos Bradsher (Country)	38-42StLN 43-45MS 46-53StLN 54-55NYA 55-56KCA 56-59NYA 59MilN	04-27-16	Roxboro, N.C.	08-12-02	L	R	5'9	190	2380	7946	1247	2383	413	148	169	1304	1018	538	71	.300	.453
Small, Jim-James Arthur Patrick	55-57DetA 58KCA	03-08-37	Portland, Ore.		L	L	6'	180	108	141	22	38	6	2	0	10	10	22	0	.270	.340
Smalley, Roy-Roy Frederick Jr.	48-53ChiN 54MilN 55-58PhiN	06-09-26	Springfield, Mo.		R	R	6'3	190	872	2644	277	601	103	33	61	305	257	541	4	.227	.360
Smaza, Joe-Joseph Paul	46ChiA	07-03-23	Detroit, Mich.	05-30-79	R	R	5'11	175	2	5	2	1	0	0	0	0	0	0	0	.200	.200
Smith, Al-Alphonse Eugene (Fuzzy)	53-57CleA 58-62ChiA 63BalA 64CleA 64BosA	02-07-28	Kirkwood, Mo.	01-03-02	R	R	6'	196	1517	5357	843	1458	258	46	164	676	674	768	67	.272	.429
Smith, Bobby Gene-Bobby Gene	57-59StLN 60-61PhiN 62NYN 62CinN 62StLN 65CalA	05-28-34	Hood River, Ore.		R	R	5'11	190	476	962	101	234	35	5	13	96	55	154	5	.243	.331
Smith, Dick-Richard Harrison	51-55PitN	07-21-27	Blandburg, Pa.		R	R	5'8	185	70	186	17	25	2	2	0	11	30	22	0	.134	.167
Smith, Earl-Earl Calvin	55PitN	03-14-28	Sunnyside, Wash.		R	R	6'	185	5	16	1	1	0	0	0	0	4	2	0	.063	.063
Smith, Hal-Harold Raymond (Cura)	56-61StLN 62-64IL 65PitN	06-01-31	Barling, Ark.		R	R	5'10	195	570	1667	126	437	63	8	23	172	102	128	6	.258	.345
Smith, Hal-Harold Wayne	55-56BalA 56-59KCA 60-61PitN 62-63HouN 64CinN	12-07-30	West Frankfort, Ill.		R	R	6'	195	879	2682	269	715	148	10	58	323	196	361	7	.267	.394
Smith, Milt-Milton	55CinN	03-27-29	Columbus, Ga.	04-11-97	R	R	5'10	165	36	102	15	20	3	0	1	8	13	24	2	.196	.333
Smith, Paul-Paul Leslie	53PitN 55-56MS 57-58PitN 58ChiN	03-19-31	New Castle, Pa.		L	L	5'8	165	223	562	54	152	16	7	7	56	42	44	3	.270	.361
Snider, Duke-Edwin Donald (The Silver Fox)	47-57BknN 58-62LAN 63NYN 64SFN	09-19-26	Los Angeles, Cal.		L	R	6'	195	2143	7161	1259	2116	358	85	407	1333	971	1237	99	.295	.540
Snyder, Jerry-Gerald George	52-58WasA	07-21-29	Jenks, Okla.		R	R	6'	170	266	630	60	145	18	2	3	47	46	59	7	.230	.279
Sommers, Bill-William Dunn	50StLA	02-17-23	Brooklyn, N.Y.	09-22-00	R	R	6'	170	65	137	24	35	5	1	0	14	25	14	0	.255	.307
Souchock, Steve-Stephen (Bud)	46,48NYA 49ChiA 51-55DetA	03-19-19	Yatesboro, Pa.	07-28-02	R	R	6'2	203	473	1227	163	313	58	20	50	186	88	164	15	.255	.457
Speake, Bob-Robert Charles (Spook)	55,57ChiN 58-59SFN	08-22-30	Springfield, Mo.		L	L	6'1	178	305	761	110	170	26	10	31	104	80	158	8	.223	.406
Spencer, Daryl-Daryl Dean (Big Dee)	52-53NYN 54-55MS 56-57NYN 58-59SFN 60-61StLN 61-63LAN 63CinN	07-13-29	Wichita, Kans.		R	R	6'2	195	1098	3689	457	901	145	20	105	428	449	516	13	.244	.380
Stallcup, Virgil-Thomas Virgil (Red)	47-52CinN 52-53StLN	01-03-22	Ravensford, N.C.	05-02-89	R	R	6'3	185	587	2059	171	497	99	13	22	214	51	181	9	.241	.334
Stanky, Eddie-Edward Raymond (The Brat, Muggsy, The Mobile Muskrat)	43-44ChiN 44-47BknN 48-49BosN 50-51NYN 52-53,M52-55StLN M66-68ChiA M77TexA	09-03-16	Philadelphia, Pa.	06-06-99	L	R	5'8	170	1259	4301	811	1154	185	35	29	364	996	374	48	.268	.348
Stephens, Gene-Glen Eugene	52-53,55-60BosA 60-61BalA 61-62KCA 63-64ChiA	01-20-33	Gravette, Ark.		L	R	6'3	185	964	1913	283	460	78	15	37	207	233	322	27	.240	.355
Stephens, Vern-Vernon Daniel (Buster, Junior)	41-47StLA 48-52BosA 53ChiA 53StLA 54-55BalA 55ChiA	10-23-20	McAlister, N.M.	11-04-68	R	R	5'10	185	1720	6497	1001	1859	307	42	247	1174	692	685	25	.286	.460
Stephenson, Bobby-Robert Lloyd	55StLN	08-11-28	Blair, Okla.		R	R	6'	165	67	119	19	27	3	0	0	6	5	18	2	.243	.270
Stephenson, Joe-Joseph Chester	43NYN 44ChiN 45MS 47ChiA	06-30-21	Detroit, Mich.	09-20-01	R	R	6'2	185	29	67	8	12	1	0	0	4	2	15	1	.179	.194
Stevens, Chuck-Charles Augustus	41StLA 43-45MS 46,48StLA	07-10-18	Van Houten, N.M.		B	L	6'1	180	211	732	89	184	29	8	4	55	88	89	6	.251	.329
Stevens, Ed-Edward Lee (Big Ed)	45-47BknN 48-50PitN	01-12-25	Galveston, Tex.		L	R	6'1	190	375	1220	134	308	59	17	28	193	121	151	7	.252	.398
Stevens, R C-R C	58-60PitN 61WasA	07-22-34	Moultrie, Ga.		R	L	6'5	219	104	162	21	34	4	0	4	21	12	41	1	.210	.395
Stewart, Bill-William Wayne	55KCA	04-11-28	Bay City, Mich.		R	R	5'11	200	11	18	2	2	1	0	0	0	1	6	0	.111	.167
Stewart, Bud-Edward Perry	41-42PitN 43-44VR 44-45MS 48NYA 48-50WasA 51-54ChiA	06-15-16	Sacramento, Cal.	06-21-00	L	R	5'11	160	773	2041	288	547	96	32	32	260	252	157	29	.268	.393
Stirnweiss, Snuffy-George Henry	43-50NYA 50StLA 51-52CleA	10-26-18	New York, N.Y.	09-15-58	R	R	5'8	175	1028	3695	604	989	157	68	29	281	541	447	134	.268	.377
Streuli, Walt-Walter Herbert	54-56DetA	09-26-35	Memphis, Tenn.		R	R	6'2	195	6	12	1	3	2	0	0	2	3	2	0	.250	.417
Strickland, George-George Bevan (Bo)	50-52PitN 52-57CleA 58VR 59-60,M64,66CleA	01-10-26	New Orleans, La.		R	R	6'1	175	971	2824	305	633	84	27	36	284	362	453	12	.224	.317
Suder, Pete-Peter (Pecky)	41-43PhiA 44-45MS 46-54PhiA 55KCA	04-16-16	Aliquippa, Pa.		R	R	6'	175	1421	5085	469	1268	210	44	49	541	288	456	19	.249	.337
Sullivan, Russ-Russell Guy	51-53DetA	02-19-23	Fredericksburg, Va.		R	R	6'	196	45	150	16	40	4	2	3	12	18	11	1	.267	.447
Szekely, Joe-Joseph	53CinN	02-25-25	Cleveland, Ohio	10-16-95	R	R	5'11	180	5	13	0	1	0	0	0	0	3	0	0	.077	.077
Talbot, Dale-Robert Dale	06-06-27		Visalia, Cal.		R	R	6'	170	122	433	50	107	15	5	1	19	16	29	4	.247	.312
Tanner, Chuck-Charles William	55-57MilN 57-58ChiN 59-60CleA 61-62LAA M70-75ChiA M76OakA M77-85PitN M86-88AtlN	07-04-29	New Castle, Pa.		L	L	6'	185	396	885	98	231	39	5	21	105	82	93	2	.261	.388
Tappe, El-Elvin Walter	54-56,58,60,62,M61-62ChiN	05-21-27	Quincy, Ill.	10-10-98	R	R	5'11	180	145	304	20	63	10	0	0	17	29	25	0	.207	.240
Tappe, Ted-Theodore Nash	50-51CinN 55ChiN 56IL	02-02-31	Seattle, Wash.	02-13-04	L	R	6'3	185	34	58	13	15	2	0	5	12	12	12	0	.259	.552
Tasby, Willie-Willie James	58-60BalA 60BosA 61-62WasA 62-63CleA	01-08-33	Shreveport, La.		R	R	5'11	180	583	1868	246	467	61	10	46	174	201	327	12	.250	.367
Tate, Lee-Lee Willie (Skeeter)	58-59StLN	03-18-32	Black Rock, Ark.		R	R	5'10	165	51	94	9	14	3	1	0	5	10	10	0	.165	.259
Tatum, Tommy-VT	41BknN 42-45MS 47BknN 47CinN	07-16-19	Decatur, Tex.	11-07-89	R	R	6'	185	81	194	20	50	3	2	0	17	17	20	7	.258	.325
Taylor, Bennie-Benjamin Eugene	51StLA 52DetA 55MilN	09-30-27	Metropolis, Ill.	05-11-99	L	L	6'	195	52	121	16	28	2	1	0	16	6	31	1	.231	.339
Taylor, Bill-William Michael (Moose)	54-57NYN 57-58DetA	12-30-29	Alhambra, Cal.		R	R	6'4	212	149	173	17	41	8	0	7	26	5	39	0	.237	.405
Taylor, Fred-Frederick Rankin	50-52WasA	12-03-24	Zanesville, Ohio	01-06-02	R	R	6'3	201	22	47	5	9	0	0	0	4	6	3	0	.191	.234
Taylor, Joe-Joe Cephus (Cash)	54PhiA 57CinN 58StLN 58-59BalA	03-02-26	Chapman, Ala.	03-18-93	R	R	6'2	185	119	297	34	74	10	3	11	38	21	61	0	.249	.401
Taylor, Sammy-Samuel Douglas	58-62CinN 62-63NYN 63CinN 63CleA	02-27-33	Woodruff, S.C.		L	R	6'2	185	473	1263	124	309	47	9	16	147	122	181	3	.245	.358
Tebbetts, Birdie-George Robert	36-42DetA 43-45MS 46-47DetA 47-50BosA 51-52CleA M54-58CinN M61-62MilN M63-66CleA	11-10-12	Burlington, Vt.	03-24-99	R	R	5'11	190	1162	3704	357	1000	169	22	38	469	389	261	29	.270	.358

USE NAME - GIVEN NAMES (NICKNAMES) — TEAM BY YEAR	BIRTH DATE	BIRTH PLACE	DEATH DATE	B	T	HGT	WGT	G	AB	R	H	2B	3B	HR	RBI	BB	SO	SB	BA	SA
Teed, Dick-Richard Leroy 53BknN	03-08-26	Springfield, Mass.		R	R	5'11	180	1	1	0	0	0	0	0	0	0	1	0	.000	.000
Temple, Johnny-John Ellis 52-59CinN 60-61CleA 62BalA 62-63HouN 64CinN	08-08-28	Lexington, N.C.	01-09-94	R	R	5'11	175	1420	5218	720	1484	208	36	22	395	648	338	140	.284	.351
Tepsic, Joe-Joseph John 48BknN	09-18-23	Slovan, Pa.		R	R	5'9	170	15	5	2	0	0	0	0	0	1	1	0	.000	.000
Terwilliger, Wayne-Willard Wayne (Twig) 49-51ChiN 51BknN 53-54WasA 55-56NYN 59-60KCA	06-27-25	Clare, Mich.		R	R	5'11	165	666	2091	271	501	93	10	22	162	247	296	31	.240	.325
Testa, Nick-Nicholas 58SFN	06-29-28	New York, N.Y.		R	R	5'8	180	1	0	0	0	0	0	0	0	0	0	0	—	—
Tettelbach, Dick-Richard Morley (Tut) 55NYA 56-57WasA	06-26-29	New Haven, Conn.	01-26-95	R	R	6'	195	29	80	12	12	1	2	1	10	18	17	0	.150	.250
Thomas, Bud-John Tillman 51StLA	03-10-29	Sedalia, Mo.		R	R	6'	160	14	20	3	7	0	0	1	1	0	3	2	.350	.500
Thomas, Frank-Frank Joseph 51-58PittN 59CinN 60-61ChiN 61MilN 62-64NYN 64-65PhiN 65HouN 65MilN 66ChiN	06-11-29	Pittsburgh, Pa.		R	R	6'3	205	1766	6285	792	1671	262	31	286	962	484	894	15	.266	.454
Thomas, Kite-Keith Marshall 47 played in P.B.A. 52-53PhiA 53WasA		Kansas City, Kans.	01-07-95	R	R	6'1	195	137	223	35	52	9	3	7	32	34	40	0	.233	.395
Thomas, Leo-Leo Raymond (Tommy) 50,52StLA 52ChiA	07-26-23	Turlock, Cal.		R	R	5'11	178	95	269	32	57	11	1	1	27	43	25	2	.212	.271
Thomas, Valmy-Valmy 57NYN 58SFN 59PhiN 60BalA 61CleA	07-26-23	Santurce, P.R.		R	R	5'9	160	252	626	56	144	20	3	12	60	45	79	2	.230	.329
Thompson, Don-Donald Newlin 49BosN 51,53-54BknN	12-28-23	Swepsonville, N.C.		L	R	6'	185	217	307	52	67	8	0	1	19	31	32	4	.218	.254
Thompson, Hank-Henry Curtis 47StLA 49-56NYN	12-08-25	Oklahoma City, Okla.	09-30-69	L	R	5'9	174	933	3003	492	801	104	34	129	482	493	337	33	.267	.453
Thompson, Tim-Charles Lemoine 54BknN 56-57KCA 58DetA	03-01-24	Coalport, Pa.		L	R	5'11	190	187	517	49	123	24	2	8	47	39	52	2	.238	.338
Thomson, Bobby-Robert Brown (The Staten Island Scot) 46-53NYN 54-57NYN 57NYN 58-59ChiN 60BosA 60BalA	10-25-23	Glasgow, Scotland		R	R	6'2	185	1779	6305	903	1705	267	74	264	1026	559	804	38	.270	.462
Thorpe, Bob-Benjamin Robert 51-52BosA 53-54-MS 55-67BosA 57-60WasA 61LAA 61-62BalA 62-63YN	10-30-96	Caryville, Fla.		R	R	6'1	190	110	331	22	83	9	3	3	32	6	48	3	.251	.323
Throneberry, Faye-Maynard Faye 52BosA 53-54-MS 55-67BosA 57-60WasA 61LAA	06-22-31	Fisherville, Tenn.	04-26-99	R	R	5'11	185	521	1302	152	307	48	12	29	137	127	284	23	.236	.358
Throneberry, Marv-Marvin Eugene (Marvelous Marv) 55,58-59NYA 60-61KCA 61-62BalA 62-63YN	09-02-33	Collierville, Tenn.	06-23-94	L	L	6'1	195	480	1186	143	281	37	8	53	170	130	295	3	.237	.416
Thurman, Bob-Robert Burns 55-59CinN	05-14-17	Wichita, Kans.	10-31-98	L	L	6'1	205	334	663	106	163	18	11	35	106	62	112	1	.246	.465
Tipton, Joe-Joe Hicks 48CleA 49ChiA 50-52PhiA 52-53CleA 54WasA	02-18-22	McCaysville, Ga.	03-01-94	R	R	5'11	185	417	1117	116	264	36	5	29	125	186	142	3	.236	.355
Torgeson, Earl-Clifford Earl (The Earl of Snohomish) 47-52BosN 53-55PhiN 55-57DetA 57-61ChiA 61NYA	01-01-24	Snohomish, Wash.	11-08-90	L	L	6'3	190	1668	4969	848	1318	215	46	149	740	980	653	133	.265	.417
Torre, Frank-Frank Joseph 56-60MilN 62-63PhiN	12-30-31	Brooklyn, N.Y.		L	L	6'4	205	714	1482	150	404	78	15	13	179	155	64	4	.273	.372
Triandos, Gus-Gus 53-54NYA 55-62BalA 63DetA 64-65PhiN 65HouN	07-30-30	San Francisco, Cal.		R	R	6'3	215	1206	3907	389	954	147	6	167	608	440	636	1	.244	.413
Trouppe, Quincy-Quincy Thomas 52ChiA	12-25-12	Dublin, Ga.	08-10-93	B	R	6'2	225	6	10	1	1	0	0	0	0	1	3	0	.100	.100
Tucker, Thurman-Thurman Lowell (Joe E.) 42-44ChiA 45-MS 46-47ChiA 48-51CleA	09-26-17	Gordon, Tex.	05-07-93	L	L	5'10	165	701	2231	325	570	79	24	9	179	291	237	77	.255	.325
Turner, Earl-Earl Edwin 48,50PittN	05-06-23	Pittsfield, Mass.	10-20-99	R	R	5'9	170	42	75	10	18	4	0	0	5	4	13	1	.240	.360
Tuttle, Bill-William Robert 52,54-57DetA 58-61KCA 61-63MinA	07-04-29	Elwood, Ill.	07-27-98	R	R	6'	190	1270	4268	578	1105	149	47	67	443	480	416	38	.259	.363
Umphlett, Tommy-Thomas Mullen 53BosA 54-55WasA	05-12-30	Scotland Neck, N.C.		R	R	6'2	180	361	1160	108	285	45	8	6	111	75	107	7	.246	.314
Upright, Dixie-Roy T. (RT) 53StLA	05-30-26	Kannapolis, N.C.	11-13-86	L	L	6'	175	9	8	3	2	0	0	1	1	1	3	0	.250	.625
Upton, Tom-Thomas Herbert (Muscles) 50-51StLA 52ChiA	12-29-26	Esther, Mo.		R	R	6'	160	181	525	60	118	9	9	2	42	65	67	8	.225	.288
Usher, Bob-Robert Royce 46-47,50-51CinN 52ChiN 57CleA 57WasA	03-01-25	San Diego, Cal.		R	R	6'1	180	428	1101	133	259	41	4	18	102	90	136	9	.234	.329
Valdivielso, Jose-Jose Martinez [Lopez] (Joe) 55-56,59-60WasA 61MinA	05-22-34	Matanzas, Cuba		R	R	6'1	175	401	971	89	213	26	4	9	85	79	132	6	.219	.290
Valenzuela, Benny-Benjamin Beltran (Papalero) 58SFN	06-02-33	Los Mochis, Mexico		R	R	5'10	175	10	14	0	3	1	0	0	1	0	4	0	.214	.286
Valo, Elmer-Elmer William 40-43PhiA 44-45-MS 46-54PhiA 55-56KCA 56PhiN 57BknN 58LAN 59CleA 60NYA 60WasA 61MinA 61PhiN	03-05-21	Ribnik, Czechoslovakia	07-19-98	L	R	5'11	190	1806	5029	768	1420	228	73	58	601	942	284	110	.282	.391
Van Dusen, Fred-Frederick William 55PhiN	07-31-37	Queens, N.Y.		L	L	6'3	180	1	0	0	0	0	0	0	0	0	0	0	—	—
Van Noy, Jay-Jay Lowell 51StLN	11-04-28	Garland, Utah		R	R	6'1	200	6	7	1	0	0	0	0	0	1	6	0	.000	.000
Varner, Buck-Glen Gann 52WasA	01-25-31	Hixson, Tenn.	04-29-00	L	R	5'10	170	2	4	0	0	0	0	0	0	1	0	0	.000	.000
Veal, Coot-Orville Inman 58-60DetA 61WasA 62PittN 63DetA	07-09-32	Sandersville, Ga.		R	R	6'1	165	247	611	75	141	26	3	1	51	56	69	2	.231	.288
Verban, Emil-Emil Matthew (Dutch, The Antelope) 44-46StLN 46-48PhiN 48-50ChiN 50BosN	08-27-15	Lincoln, Ill.	06-08-68	R	R	5'11	165	853	2911	301	793	99	26	1	241	108	74	21	.272	.325
Verble, Gene-Gene Kermit (Satchel) 51,53WasA	06-29-28	Concord, N.C.		R	R	5'11	175	81	198	20	40	3	2	0	17	20	11	1	.202	.237
Verdi, Frank-Frank Michael 53NYA	06-02-26	Brooklyn, N.Y.		R	R	5'10	170	1	0	0	0	0	0	0	0	0	0	0	—	—
Vernon, Mickey-James Barton 39-43WasA 44-45-MS 46-48WasA 49-50CleA 50-55WasA 56-57BosA 58CleA 59MilN 60PittN M61-63WasA	04-22-18	Marcus Hook, Pa.		L	L	6'2	184	2409	8731	1196	2495	490	120	172	1311	935	869	137	.286	.428
Vico, George-George Steve (Sam) 48-49DetA	08-09-23	San Fernando, Cal.	01-14-94	L	R	6'4	200	211	663	65	166	28	11	12	76	60	56	2	.250	.380
Virdon, Bill-William Charles (Quail) 55-56StLN 56-65,68,M72-73PittN M74-75NYA M75-82HouN M83-84MonN	06-09-31	Hazel Park, Mich.		L	R	6'	185	1583	5980	735	1596	237	81	91	502	442	647	47	.267	.379
Virgil, Ozzie-Osvaldo Jose [Pichardo] 56-57NYN 58,60-61DetA 61KCA 62BalA 65PittN 66,69SFN	05-17-33	Montecristi, Dom. Rep.		R	R	6'1	174	324	753	75	174	19	7	14	73	34	91	6	.231	.331
Vollmer, Clyde-Clyde Frederick 42CinN 43-45-MS 46-48CinN 48-50WasA 50-53BosA 53-54WasA	09-24-21	Cincinnati, Ohio		R	R	6'	190	685	2021	283	508	77	10	69	339	243	328	7	.251	.402
Wade, Gale-Galeard Lee 55-56ChiN	01-20-29	Hollister, Mo.		L	R	6'1	185	19	45	5	6	1	0	1	1	5	9	0	.133	.222
Wahl, Kermit-Kermit Emerson 44-45,47CinN 50-51PhiA 51StLA	11-18-22	Columbia, S.D.	09-16-87	R	R	5'11	170	231	642	58	145	23	6	3	50	68	72	3	.226	.294
Waitkus, Eddie-Edward Stephen 41ChiN 42-45-MS 46-48ChiN 49-53PhiN 54-55BalA 55PhiN	09-04-19	Cambridge, Mass.	09-16-72	L	L	6'	180	1140	4254	528	1214	215	44	24	373	372	204	28	.285	.374
Wakefield, Dick-Richard Cummings 41,43-44DetA 45-MS 46-49DetA 50NYA 50ChiA 52NYN	05-06-21	Chicago, Ill.	08-26-85	L	R	6'4	210	638	2132	334	625	102	29	56	315	360	270	10	.293	.447
Walker, Harry-Harry William (The Hat) 40-43StLN 44-45-MS 46-47StLN 47-48PhiN 49ChiN 49CinN 50-51,55,M55StLN M65-67PittN M68-72HouN	10-22-16	Pascagoula, Miss.	08-08-99	L	R	6'2	175	807	2651	385	786	126	37	10	214	245	175	42	.296	.383
Walker, Rube-Albert Bluford 50ChiN 51-57BknN 58LAN	05-16-26	Lenoir, N.C.	12-12-92	L	R	6'	185	608	1585	114	360	69	3	57	192	150	213	3	.227	.341
Wallaesa, Jack-John 40,42PhiA 43-45-MS 46PhiA 47-48ChiA	08-31-19	Easton, Pa.	12-27-86	B	R	6'3	191	219	584	56	120	17	4	15	61	39	138	3	.205	.325
Walls, Lee-Ray Lee 52,56-57PittN 57-59ChiN 60CinN 60-61PhiN 62-64LAN	01-06-33	San Diego, Cal.	10-11-93	R	R	6'3	205	902	2558	331	670	88	31	66	284	245	470	21	.262	.398
Walters, Ken-Kenneth Rogers 60-61PhiN 63CinN	11-11-33	Fresno, Cal.		R	R	6'1	180	259	681	71	157	20	2	11	58	25	89	6	.231	.314
Ward, Preston-Preston Meyer 48BknN 50ChiN 51-52MS 53ChiN 53-56PittN 56-58CleA 58-59KCA	07-24-27	Columbia, Mo.		L	R	6'4	190	744	2067	219	522	83	15	50	262	231	315	7	.253	.380
Watlington, Neal-Julius Neal 53PhiA	12-25-22	Yanceyville, N.C.		L	R	6'	195	21	44	4	7	1	0	0	3	3	8	0	.159	.182
Webster, Ray-Raymond George 59CleA 60BosA	11-15-37	Grass Valley, Cal.		R	R	6'	175	47	77	11	15	2	1	2	11	6	7	1	.195	.325
Weigel, Ralph-Ralph Richard (Wig) 46CleA 48ChiA 49WasA	10-02-21	Coldwater, Ohio	04-15-92	R	R	6'	180	106	235	12	54	9	3	0	30	21	26	2	.230	.294
Wellman, Bob-Robert Joseph 48,50PhiN	07-15-25	Cincinnati, Ohio	12-20-94	R	R	6'4	210	15	25	2	7	0	1	1	1	3	5	0	.280	.480
Wells, Leo-Leo Donald 42ChiA 43-45-MS 46ChiA	07-18-17	Kansas City, Kans.	06-23-06	R	R	5'9	170	80	189	19	36	6	1	2	15	16	39	4	.190	.265
Wertz, Vic-Victor Woodrow 47-52DetA 52-53StLA 54BalA 54-58CleA 59-61BosA 61-63DetA 63MinA	02-09-25	York, Pa.	07-07-83	L	R	6'	195	1862	6099	867	1692	289	42	266	1178	828	842	9	.277	.469
Westlake, Jim-James Patrick 55PhiN	07-03-30	Sacramento, Cal.	01-03-03	L	L	6'1	190	1	1	0	0	0	0	0	0	0	1	0	.000	.000
Westlake, Wally-Waldon Thomas 47-51PittN 51-52StLN 52CinN 52-55CleA 55BalA 56PhiN	11-08-20	Gridley, Cal.		R	R	6'	195	958	3117	474	848	107	33	127	539	317	453	19	.272	.450
Westrum, Wes-Wesley Noreen 47-57NYN M65-67NYN M74-75SFN	11-28-22	Clearbrook, Minn.	05-28-02	R	R	5'11	190	919	2322	302	503	59	8	96	315	489	514	10	.217	.373
Wheeler, Don-Donald Wesley (Scotty) 49CinN	09-29-22	Minneapolis, Minn.	12-10-03	R	R	5'10	175	67	192	17	46	9	2	1	22	27	19	2	.240	.323
Whisenant, Pete-Thomas Peter 52BosN 55StLN 56CinN 57-60CinN 60CleA 60WasA 61MinA 61CinN	12-14-29	Asheville, N.C.	03-22-96	R	R	6'2	200	475	988	140	221	46	4	37	134	86	196	11	.224	.399
White, Charlie-Charles 54-55MilN	08-12-27	Kinston, N.C.	05-26-98	R	R	5'11	192	62	123	17	29	5	0	1	12	14	15	0	.236	.301
White, Don-Donald William 48-49PhiA	08-18-19	Everett, Wash.	06-15-87	R	R	6'1	195	143	422	41	98	20	2	1	38	33	28	2	.232	.296
White, Ed-Edward Perry 55CleA	04-06-26	Anniston, Ala.	09-28-82	R	R	6'2	200	3	4	0	2	0	0	0	0	0	1	0	.500	.500
White, Fuzz-Albert Eugene 40StLA 47NYN	06-27-16	Springfield, Mo.	04-24-03	L	R	6'	175	9	15	3	3	0	0	0	0	0	2	0	.200	.200
White, Sammy-Samuel Charles 51-59BosA 60VR 61MilN 62PhiN	07-07-27	Wenatchee, Wash.	08-05-91	R	R	6'3	195	1043	3502	324	916	167	20	66	421	218	381	14	.262	.377
Whitman, Dick-Dick Corwin 46-49BknN 50-51PhiN	11-09-20	Woodburn, Ore.	02-12-03	L	L	5'11	170	285	638	93	165	37	3	2	67	51	46	10	.259	.335
Whitman, Frank-Walter Franklin (Hooker) 46,48ChiA	08-15-24	Marengo, Ind.	02-06-94	R	R	6'	175	20	22	7	1	0	0	0	1	2	9	1	.045	.045
Wilber, Del-Delbert Quentin (Babe) 46-49StLN 51-52PhiN 52-54BosA M73TexA	02-24-19	Lincoln Park, Mich.	07-18-02	R	R	6'3	200	299	720	67	174	35	7	19	115	44	96	1	.242	.389
Wilhelm, Spider-Charles Ernest 53PhiA	05-23-29	Baltimore, Md.	10-20-92	R	R	5'9	170	7	7	1	2	1	0	0	1	1	0	0	.286	.429
Will, Bob-Robert Lee (Butch) 57-58,60-63ChiN	07-15-31	Irwin, Ill.		L	L	5'10	175	410	819	87	202	35	9	9	87	83	119	2	.247	.344
Williams, Davey-David Carlous 49,51-55NYN	11-02-27	Dallas, Tex.		R	R	5'10	160	517	1785	235	450	61	10	32	163	164	144	6	.252	.355
Williams, Dick-Richard Hirschfeld 51-54,56BknN 56-57BalA 57CleA 58BalA 59-60KCA 61-62BalA 63-64,M67-69BosA M71-73OakA M74-78CalA M77-81MonN M82-85SDN M86-88SeaA	05-07-29	St. Louis, Mo.		R	R	6'	190	1023	2959	358	768	157	12	70	331	227	392	12	.260	.392
Williams, Ted-Theodore Samuel (Thumper, The Splendid Splinter) 39-42BosA 43-45-MS 46-60BosA M69-71WasA M72TexA	08-30-18	San Diego, Cal.	07-05-02	L	R	6'3	205	2292	7706	1798	2654	525	71	521	1839	2021	709	24	.344	.634
Wilson, Archie-Archie Clifton 51-52NYA 52WasA 52BosA	11-25-23	Los Angeles, Cal.		R	R	5'11	175	51	140	9	31	5	3	0	17	7	14	0	.221	.300
Wilson, Artie-Arthur Lee 51NYN	10-28-20	Jefferson Co., Ala.		L	R	5'11	168	19	22	1	4	0	0	0	1	2	1	0	.182	.182
Wilson, Bill-William Donald 50ChiA 51-52MS 53-54ChiA 54PhiA 55KCA	11-06-28	Central City, Neb.		R	R	6'2	200	224	654	87	145	23	1	32	77	72	136	2	.222	.407
Wilson, Bob-Robert 58LAN	02-22-25	Dallas, Tex.	04-23-85	R	R	5'11	197	3	5	0	1	0	0	0	1	0	1	0	.200	.200
Wilson, George-George Washington (Teddy) 52ChiA 52-53,56NYN 56NYA	08-30-25	Cherryville, N.C.	10-29-74	L	R	6'1	190	145	209	15	40	9	1	3	19	14	32	0	.191	.273
Wilson, Grady-Grady Herbert 48PittN	11-23-22	Columbus, Ga.	07-23-03	R	R	5'11	170	12	10	1	1	0	0	0	0	0	4	0	.100	.200
Wilson, Neil-Sammy O'Neil 60SFN	06-14-35	Lexington, Tenn.		L	R	6'1	175	6	10	0	2	0	0	0	0	0	2	0	.200	.200
Wilson, Red-Robert James 51-54ChiA 54-60DetA 60CleA	03-07-29	Milwaukee, Wis.		R	R	6'	198	602	1765	206	455	84	8	24	189	215	163	25	.258	.355

SE NAME - GIVEN NAMES (NICKNAMES)	TEAM BY YEAR	BIRTH DATE	BIRTH PLACE	DEATH DATE	B	T	HGT	WGT	G	AB	R	H	2B	3B	HR	RBI	BB	SO	SB	BA	SA
Vinceniak, Ed-Edward Joseph	56-57ChiN	04-16-29	Chicago, Ill.		R	R	5'9	165	32	67	6	14	3	0	1	8	3	12	0	.209	.299
Wise, Casey-Kendall Cole	57ChiN 58-59MilN 60DetA	09-08-32	Lafayette, Ind.		B	R	6'	170	126	321	37	56	6	3	3	17	29	36	2	.174	.240
Witte, Jerry-Jerome Charles	46-47StLA	07-30-15	St. Louis, Mo.	04-27-02	R	R	6'1	190	52	172	11	28	4	1	4	16	11	40	0	.163	.267
Wood, Ken-Kenneth Lanier	48-51StLA 52BosA 52-53WasA	07-01-24	Lincolnton, N.C.		R	R	6'	200	342	995	110	223	52	7	34	143	102	141	1	.224	.393
Woodling, Gene-Eugene Richard	43CleA 44-45MS 46CleA 47PitN 49-54NYA 55BalA 55-57CleA 58-60BalA 61-62WasA 62NYN	08-16-22	Akron, Ohio	06-02-01	L	R	5'10	195	1796	5587	830	1585	257	63	147	830	921	477	29	.284	.431
Wooten, Earl-Earl Hazwell (Junior)	47-48WasA	01-16-24	Pelzer, S.C.	08-12-06	R	L	5'11	160	94	282	34	68	8	3	1	24	24	25	3	.241	.301
Workman, Hank-Henry Kilgariff	50NYA	02-05-26	Los Angeles, Cal.		L	R	6'1	185	2	5	1	1	0	0	0	0	0	1	0	.200	.200
Wright, Tom-Thomas Everette	48-51BosA 52StLA 52-53ChiA 54-56WasA	09-22-23	Shelby, N.C.		L	R	5'11	185	341	685	75	175	28	11	6	99	76	123	2	.255	.355
Wyrostek, Johnny-John Barney	42-43PitN 44-45MS 46-47PhiN 48-52CinN 52-54PhiN	07-12-19	Fairmont City, Ill.	12-12-86	L	R	6'2	180	1221	4240	525	1149	209	45	58	481	482	437	33	.271	.383
Yankowski, George-George Edward	42PhiA 43-46MS 49ChiA	11-19-22	Cambridge, Mass.		R	R	6'	180	18	31	0	5	2	0	0	4	0	4	0	.161	.226
Yewcic, Tom-Thomas (Kibby) 61-66 played in A.F.L.	57DetA	05-09-32	Conemaugh, Pa.		R	R	5'11	180	1	1	0	0	0	0	0	0	0	0	0	.000	.000
Yost, Eddie-Edward Frederick Joseph (The Walking Man)	44WasA 45MS 46-58WasA 59-60DetA 61-62LAA M63WasA	10-13-26	Brooklyn, N.Y.		R	R	5'10	180	2109	7346	1215	1863	337	56	139	683	1614	920	72	.254	.371
Young, Bobby-Robert George	48StLN 51-53StLA 54-55BalA 55-56CleA 58PhiN	11-22-25	Granite, Md.	01-28-85	L	R	6'1	175	687	2447	244	609	68	28	15	137	208	212	18	.249	.318
Young, Dick-Richard Ennis	51-52PhiN	06-03-28	Seattle, Wash.		L	R	5'11	175	20	77	10	18	6	0	0	2	4	9	1	.234	.312
Yvars, Sal-Salvador Anthony	Bats Both 52 47-53NYN 53-54StLN	02-20-24	New York, N.Y.		R	R	5'10	193	210	418	4	102	12	0	10	42	37	41	1	.244	.344
Zarilla, Al-Allen Lee (Zeke)	43-44StLA 45MS 46-49StLA 49-50BosA 51-52ChiA 52StLA 52-53BosA	05-01-19	Los Angeles, Cal.	08-28-96	L	R	5'11	185	1120	3535	507	975	186	43	61	456	415	382	33	.276	.405
Zauchin, Norm-Norbert Henry	51BosA 52-53MS 55-57BosA 58-59WasA	11-17-29	Royal Oak, Mich.	01-31-99	R	R	6'5	220	346	1038	134	242	28	2	50	159	137	226	5	.233	.408
Zernial, Gus-Gus Edward (Ozark Ike)	49-51ChiA 51-54PhiA 55-57KCA 58-59DetA	06-27-23	Beaumont, Tex.		R	R	6'2	210	1234	4131	572	1093	159	22	237	776	383	755	15	.265	.486
Zientara, Benny-Benedict Joseph	41CinN 42-45MS 46-48CinN	02-14-18	Chicago, Ill.	04-16-85	R	R	5'9	165	278	906	106	230	29	5	2	49	50	48	5	.254	.304
Zimmer, Don-Donald William	54-57BknN 58-59LAN 60-61ChiN 62NYN 62CinN 63LAN 63-65WasA M72-73SDN M76-80BosA M81-82TexA M88-91ChiN	01-17-31	Cincinnati, Ohio		R	R	5'9	175	1095	3283	353	773	130	22	91	352	246	678	45	.235	.372
Zupo, Frank-Frank Joseph (Noodles)	57-58,61BalA	08-29-39	San Francisco, Cal.	03-25-05	L	R	5'11	182	16	18	3	3	1	0	0	0	2	6	0	.167	.222

USE NAMES - GIVEN NAMES (NICKNAMES)	TEAM BY YEAR	BIRTH DATE	BIRTHPLACE	DEATH DATE	B	T	HGT	WGT	W	L	Pct.	SV	G	GS	CG	IP	H	BB	SO	ShO	ERA
Aber, Al-Albert Julius	50CleA 51-52MS 53CleA 53-57DetA 57KCA	07-31-27	Cleveland, Ohio	05-20-93	L	L	6'2	200	24	25	.490	14	168	30	7	390	398	160	169	0	4.18
Abernathie, Bill-William Edward	52CleA	01-30-29	Torrance, Cal.	02-19-06	L	L	5'10	190	0	0	—	0	2	0	0	4	11	9	1	0	13.50
Abernathy, Woody-Virgil Woodrow	46-47NYN	02-01-15	Forest City, N.C.	10-05-94	L	L	6'	170	1	1	.500	1	16	1	0	42	36	11	6	0	3.64
Acker, Tom-Thomas James (Shoulders)	56-59CinN	03-07-30	Paterson, N.J.		R	R	6'4	220	19	13	.594	8	153	23	5	381	365	150	256	1	4.13
Adams, Red-Charles Dwight	46ChiN	10-07-21	Parlier, Cal.		R	R	6'	185	0	1	.000	0	8	0	0	12	18	7	8	0	8.25
Adkins, Dewey-John Dewey	42-43WasA 49ChiN	05-11-18	Norcatur, Kans.	12-26-98	R	R	6'2	195	2	4	.333	0	38	6	1	98	114	50	47	0	5.69
Albanese, Joe-Joseph Peter	58WasA	06-26-33	New York, N.Y.	06-17-00	R	R	6'3	215	0	0	—	0	6	0	0	6	8	2	3	0	4.50
Albosta, Ed-Edward John (Rube)	41BknN 43-45MS 46PitN	10-27-18	Saginaw, Mich.	01-07-03	R	R	6'1	175	0	8	.000	0	19	8	0	53	52	43	24	0	6.11
Albrecht, Ed-Edward Arthur	49-50StLA	02-28-29	Affton, Mo.	12-29-79	R	R	5'10	165	1	1	.500	0	3	2	1	12	7	11	2	0	5.25
Alexander, Bob-Robert Somerville	55BalA 57CleA	08-07-22	Vancouver, Canada	04-07-93	R	R	6'2	205	1	1	.500	0	9	0	0	11	18	7	2	0	10.64
Aloma, Luis-Luis [Barba] (Witto)	50-53ChiA	06-19-23	Havana, Cuba	04-07-97	R	R	6'	195	18	3	.857	15	116	1	1	235	212	111	115	1	3.45
Amor, Vicente-Vicente [Alvarez]	55ChiN 57CinN	08-08-32	Havana, Cuba		R	R	6'3	182	1	3	.250	0	13	4	1	33	50	13	12	0	5.73
Anderson, Bob-Robert Carl	57-62ChiN 63DetA	09-29-35	East Chicago, Ind.		R	R	6'4	200	36	46	.439	13	246	93	15	841	858	319	502	1	4.26
Andre, John-John Edward (Long John)	55CinN	01-03-23	Brockton, Mass.	11-25-76	L	R	6'4	200	1	1	.000	1	22	3	0	45	45	28	19	0	5.80
Andrews, Hub-Hubert Carl	47-48NYN	08-31-22	Burbank, Okla.		R	R	6'	170	0	0	—	0	8	0	0	12	17	4	2	0	4.50
Antonelli, Johnny-John August	48-50BosN 51-52MS 53MilN 54-57NYN 58-60SFN 61CleA 61MilN	04-12-30	Rochester, N.Y.		L	L	6'1	185	126	110	.534	21	377	268	102	1992	1870	687	1162	25	3.34
Ardizoia, Rugger-Rinaldo Joseph	47NYA	11-20-19	Oleggio, Italy		R	R	5'11	180	0	0	—	0	1	0	0	2	4	1	0	0	9.00
Aries, Rudy-Rodolfo [Martinez]	59CinA	06-06-31	Mordoza, Cuba		L	L	5'10	165	2	0	1.000	2	34	0	0	44	49	20	28	0	4.09
Arroyo, Luis-Luis Enrique (Yo-Yo)	55StLN 56-57PitN 59CinN 60-63NYA	02-18-27	Penuelas, P.R.		L	L	5'8	178	40	32	.556	44	244	36	10	533	524	208	336	1	3.92
Atkins, Jim-James Curtis (Buddy)	50,52BosA	03-10-21	Birmingham, Ala.		L	R	6'3	205	0	1	.000	0	4	1	0	15	15	11	2	0	3.60
Avrea, Jim-James Epherium (Jay)	50CinN	07-06-20	Cleburne, Tex.	06-26-87	R	R	6'1	175	0	0	—	0	5	0	0	5	6	3	2	0	3.60
Ayers, Bill-William Oscar	47NYN	09-27-19	Newnan, Ga.	09-24-80	R	R	6'3	185	0	3	.000	1	13	4	0	35	46	14	22	0	8.23
Baczewski, Fred-Frederic John (Lefty)	53ChiN 53-55CinN	05-15-26	St. Paul, Minn.	11-14-76	L	L	6'2	185	17	10	.630	1	63	40	14	279	306	111	104	2	4.45
Bahr, Ed-Edson Garfield	46-47PitN	10-16-19	Rouleau, Canada		R	R	6'1	172	11	11	.500	0	46	25	8	219	210	95	69	0	3.37
Bailey, Jim-James Hopkins	59CinN	12-16-34	Strawberry Pl., Tenn.		B	L	6'2	210	0	1	.000	0	3	1	0	12	17	6	7	0	6.00
Bamberger, George-George Irvin	51-52NYN 59BalA M78-80MilA M82-83NYN M85-86MilA	08-01-25	Staten Island, N.Y.	04-04-04	R	R	6'	175	0	0	—	0	10	1	0	14	25	10	3	0	9.64
Bankhead, Dan-Daniel Robert	47,50-51BknN	05-03-20	Empire, Ala.	05-02-76	R	R	6'1	184	9	5	.643	4	52	13	2	153	161	110	111	1	6.53
Banta, Jack-Jackie Kay	45-50BknN	06-24-25	Hutchinson, Kans.		R	R	6'2	175	14	12	.538	5	69	19	3	204	176	113	116	1	3.79
Barclay, Curt-Curtis Cordell	57NYN 58-59SFN	08-22-31	Chicago, Ill.	03-25-85	R	R	6'3	210	10	9	.526	0	44	29	5	199	214	55	73	2	3.48
Barnes, Frank-Frank	57-58,60StLN	08-26-26	Longwood, Miss.		R	R	6'	185	1	3	.250	1	15	3	0	37	40	34	30	0	5.84
Barney, Rex-Rex Edward	43BknN 44-45MS 46-50BknN	12-19-24	Omaha, Neb.	08-12-97	R	R	6'3	185	35	31	.530	1	155	81	20	599	474	410	336	4	4.33
47 played in P.B.A.																					
Baumann, Frank-Frank Matt (The Beau)	55-59BosA 60-64ChiA 65ChiN	07-01-33	St. Louis, Mo.		L	L	6'	205	45	38	.542	13	244	78	19	798	856	300	384	4	4.11
Beeman, Charlie-Charles Alonzo	56-58BalA	12-25-34	Oakland, Cal.		R	R	5'11	195	3	3	.500	0	27	5	1	72	64	36	45	1	3.88
Beard, Ralph-Ralph William	54StLN	02-11-29	Cincinnati, Ohio	02-10-03	R	R	6'5	200	0	4	.000	0	13	10	0	58	62	28	17	0	3.72
Bearden, Gene-Henry Eugene	47-50CleA 50-51WasA 51DetA 52StLA 53ChiA	09-05-20	Lexa, Ark.	03-18-04	L	L	6'3	198	45	38	.542	1	193	84	29	789	791	435	259	7	3.96
Beers, Clarence-Clarence Scott	48StLN	12-09-18	El Dorado, Kans.	12-16-02	R	R	6'	175	0	0	—	0	1	0	0	1	3	1	0	0	9.00
Behrman, Hank-Henry Bernard	46-47BknN 47PitN 47-48BknN 49NYN	06-27-21	Brooklyn, N.Y.	01-20-87	R	R	5'11	174	24	17	.585	19	174	27	5	430	427	228	189	2	4.40
Bell, Bill-William Samuel (Ding Dong)	52PitN 53-54MS 55PitN	10-24-33	Goldsboro, N.C.	10-11-62	R	R	6'3	200	0	1	.000	0	5	1	0	17	16	14	4	0	4.24
Besana, Fred-Frederick Cyril	56BalA	04-05-31	Lincoln, Cal.		R	L	6'3	200	1	1	.500	0	7	2	0	18	22	14	7	0	5.04
Bessent, Don-Fred Donald (The Weasel)	55-57BknN 58LAN	03-13-31	Jacksonville, Fla.	07-07-90	R	R	6'	175	14	7	.667	12	108	2	1	210	196	88	118	0	3.34
Bevens, Bill-Floyd Clifford	44-47NYA	10-21-16	Hubbard, Ore.	10-26-91	R	R	6'3	210	40	36	.526	0	96	84	46	643	598	236	289	6	3.08
Bickford, Vern-Vernon Edgell	48-52BosN 53MilN 54BalA	08-27-20	Hellier, Ky.	05-06-60	R	R	6'	180	66	57	.537	2	182	149	73	1077	1040	467	450	9	3.71
Bicknell, Charlie-Charles Stephen (Bud)	48-49PhiN	07-27-28	Plainfield, N.J.		R	R	5'11	170	0	1	.000	0	30	1	0	54	61	34	9	0	6.83
Bilbrey, Jim-James Melvin	49StLA	04-20-24	Rickman, Tenn.	12-26-85	R	R	6'2	205	0	0	—	0	1	0	0	1	1	3	0	0	18.00
Birrer, Babe-Werner Joseph	55DetA 56BalA 58LAN	07-04-29	Buffalo, N.Y.		R	R	6'	195	4	3	.571	4	56	3	1	119	129	37	45	0	4.39
Biscan, Frank-Frank Stephen (Porky)	42StLA 43-45MS 46,48StLA	03-13-20	Mt. Olive, Ill.	05-22-59	L	L	5'11	190	7	9	.438	4	74	4	1	149	170	104	64	0	5.26
Bishop, Charlie-Charles Tuller	52-54PhiA 55KCA		Atlanta, Ga.	07-05-93	R	R	6'2	195	10	22	.313	3	69	37	6	295	307	168	121	1	5.31
Black, Bill-William Carroll (Bud)	52DetA 53-54MS 55-56DetA	07-09-32	St. Louis, Mo.	10-02-05	R	R	6'3	197	2	3	.400	0	10	5	1	32	36	18	14	1	4.22
Black, Joe-Joseph	52-55BknN 55-56CinN 57WasA	02-08-24	Plainfield, N.J.	05-17-02	R	R	6'2	220	30	12	.714	25	172	16	2	415	391	129	222	0	3.90
Blackburn, Jim-James Ray (Bones)	48,51CinN	06-19-24	Warsaw, Ky.	12-26-69	R	R	6'4	175	0	2	.000	0	18	0	0	36	46	16	11	0	5.50
Blackburn, Ron-Ronald Hamilton	58-59PitN	04-23-35	Mt. Airy, N.C.	04-29-98	R	R	6'	160	3	2	.600	4	64	2	0	108	111	42	50	0	3.50
Blackwell, Ewell-Ewell (The Whip)	42CinN 43-45MS 46-52CinN 52-53NYA 55KCA	10-23-22	Fresno, Cal.	10-29-96	R	R	6'6	195	82	78	.513	11	236	169	69	1322	1150	562	839	16	3.30
Blake, Ed-Edward James	51-53CinN 57KCA	02-23-25	E. St. Louis, Ill.		R	R	5'11	175	0	0	—	0	8	0	0	9	15	4	1	0	8.00
Blaylock, Bob-Robert Edward	56,59StLN	06-28-35	Chattanooga, Okla.		R	R	6'	185	1	7	.125	0	17	7	0	50	53	27	42	0	5.94
Blaylock, Gary-Gary Nelson	59StLN 59NYN	10-11-31	Clarkton, Mo.		R	R	6'	196	4	6	.400	2	41	13	3	126	147	58	81	0	4.79
Blemker, Ray-Raymond (Buddy)	60KCA	08-09-37	Huntingburg, Ind.	02-15-94	R	L	5'11	190	0	0	—	0	1	0	0	3	2	3	2	0	22.50
Blyzka, Mike-Michael John	53StLA 54BalA	12-25-28	Hamtramck, Mich.	10-13-04	R	R	6'	205	3	11	.214	1	70	9	2	180	193	107	58	0	5.60
Bokelmann, Dick-Richard Werner	51-53StLN	10-26-26	Arlington Hts., Ill.		R	R	6'	185	3	4	.429	3	34	7	0	68	73	38	27	0	4.90
Borland, Tom-Thomas Bruce (Spike)	60-61BosA	02-14-33	El Dorado, Kans.		L	L	6'3	172	0	4	.000	3	27	4	0	52	70	23	32	0	6.75
Bowman, Roger-Roger Clinton	49,51-52NYN 53,55PitN	08-18-27	Amsterdam, N.Y.	07-27-97	R	L	6'	175	2	11	.154	0	50	12	0	117	137	71	75	0	5.85
Boyer, Cloyd-Cloyd Victor (Junior)	49-52StLN 55KCA	09-01-27	Alba, Mo.		R	R	6'2	188	20	23	.465	2	112	48	13	394	393	218	198	3	4.75
Bradford, Bill-William D	56KCA	08-28-21	Choctaw, Ark.	08-22-00	R	R	6'2	180	0	0	—	0	1	0	0	2	2	1	0	0	9.00
Bradley, Fred-Fred Langdon	48-49ChiA	07-31-20	Parsons, Kans.		R	R	6'1	180	0	0	—	0	9	1	0	18	15	7	2	0	5.50
Brady, Jim-James Joseph (Diamond Jim)	58DetA	03-02-36	Jersey City, N.J.		L	L	6'2	185	0	0	—	0	6	0	0	6	15	11	3	0	30.00
Branca, Ralph-Ralph Theodore Joseph (Hawk)	44-53BknN 53-54DetA 54NYA 56BknN	01-06-26	Mt. Vernon, N.Y.		R	R	6'3	220	88	68	.564	19	322	188	71	1485	1372	663	829	12	3.79
Brazle, Al-Alpha Eugene (Cotton)	43StLN 44-45MS 46-54StLN	10-19-13	Loyal, Okla.	10-24-73	L	L	6'2	185	97	64	.602	60	441	117	47	1375	1387	492	554	7	3.31
Brecheen, Harry-Harry David (The Cat)	40,43-52StLN 53StLA	10-14-14	Broken Bow, Okla.	01-17-04	L	L	5'10	165	133	92	.591	18	318	240	125	1908	1731	536	901	25	2.91
Brewer, Tom-Thomas Austin	54-61BosA	09-03-31	Wadesboro, N.C.		R	R	6'	180	91	82	.526	3	241	217	75	1509	1478	669	733	13	4.00
Brickner, Ralph-Ralph Harold (Brick)	52BosA	05-02-25	Cincinnati, Ohio	05-09-94	R	R	6'3	215	3	1	.750	1	14	1	0	33	33	11	9	0	2.18
Briggs, Johnny-Jonathan Tift	56-58ChiN 59-60CleA 60KCA	01-24-34	Natoma, Cal.		R	R	5'10	175	9	11	.450	1	59	21	3	166	174	82	80	1	4.99
Brissie, Lou-Leland Victor	47-51PhiA 51-53CleA	06-05-24	Anderson, S.C.		L	L	6'4	210	44	48	.478	29	234	93	45	898	867	451	436	2	4.07
Brittin, Jack-John Albert	50-51PhiN	03-04-24	Athens, Ill.	01-05-94	R	R	5'11	175	0	0	—	0	6	0	0	8	7	9	6	0	6.75
Brodowski, Dick-Richard Stanley	52BosA 53-54MS 55BosA 56-57WasA 58-59CleA	07-26-32	Bayonne, N.J.		R	R	6'1	182	9	11	.450	5	72	15	5	216	212	124	85	0	4.75
Brosnan, Jim-James Patrick (Professor)	54,56-58ChiN 58-59StLN 59-63CinN 63ChiA	10-24-29	Cincinnati, Ohio		R	R	6'4	210	55	47	.539	67	385	47	7	832	790	312	507	2	3.54
Brown, Alton-Alton Leo (Deacon)	51WasA	04-16-25	Norfolk, Va.		R	R	6'2	195	0	0	—	0	7	0	0	12	14	12	7	0	9.00
Brown, Hal-Hector Harold (Skinny)	51-52ChiA 53-55BosA 55-62BalA 62NYA 63-64HouN	12-11-24	Greensboro, N.C.		R	R	6'2	185	85	92	.480	11	358	211	47	1680	1677	389	710	13	3.81
Brown, Norm-Norman Ladelle	43PhiA 44-45MS 46PhiA	02-01-19	Evergreen, N.C.	05-31-95	R	R	6'3	180	0	1	.000	0	5	0	0	14	13	6	4	0	3.21
Brown, Walter-Walter Irving	47StLA	04-23-15	Jamestown, N.Y.	02-03-91	R	R	5'11	175	1	0	1.000	1	19	0	0	46	50	28	10	0	4.89
Browning, Cal-Calvin Duane	60StLN	03-16-38	Burns Flat, Okla.		L	L	5'11	190	0	0	—	0	1	0	0	1	5	1	0	0	27.00
Bruner, Jack-Jack Raymond (Pappy)	49-50ChiA 50StLA	07-01-24	Waterloo, Iowa	06-24-03	R	R	6'1	185	2	4	.333	0	26	3	0	55	53	45	28	0	4.91
Budnick, Mike-Michael Joe	46-47NYN	09-15-19	Astoria, Ore.	12-02-99	R	R	6'1	200	2	3	.400	3	42	8	0	100	91	58	42	1	4.05
Buhl, Bob-Robert Ray	53-62MilN 62-66CinN 66-67PhiN	08-12-28	Saginaw, Mich.	02-16-01	R	R	6'2	185	166	132	.557	6	457	369	111	2587	2446	1105	1268	20	3.55
Bats Both 58-60,66																					
Burdette, Lew-Selva Lewis	50NYA 51-52BosN 53-63MilN 63-64StLN 64-65ChiN 65PhiN 66-67CalA	11-22-26	Nitro, W.Va.		R	R	6'2	190	203	144	.585	31	626	373	158	3068	3186	628	1074	33	3.66
Burkhart (Burkhardt), Ken-Kenneth William	45-48StLN 48-49CinN	11-18-16	Knoxville, Tenn.	12-29-04	R	R	6'	190	27	20	.574	7	148	41	18	519	546	165	181	6	3.85
Burnette, Wally-Wallace Harper	56-58KCA	06-20-29	Blairs, Va.	02-12-03	R	R	6'	178	14	21	.400	1	68	27	5	262	259	97	122	1	3.57
Burpo, George-George Harvie	46CinN		Jenkins, Ky.		R	L	6'	195	0	0	—	0	2	0	0	5	1	5	0	0	18.00
Burtschy, Moe-Edward Frank	50-51,54-56KCA	04-19-22	Cincinnati, Ohio	05-02-04	R	R	6'3	208	10	6	.625	4	90	1	0	185	178	126	97	0	4.72
Burwell, Dick-Richard Matthew	60-61ChiN	01-23-40	Alton, Ill.		R	R	6'1	190	0	0	—	0	5	1	0	11	11	11	1	0	6.43
Buxton, Ralph-Ralph Stanley (Buck)	38PhiA 49NYA	06-07-11	Weyburn, Canada	01-06-88	R	R	5'11	163	0	2	.000	2	19	0	0	36	34	21	23	0	4.25
Byerly, Bud-Eldred William	43-45StLN 50-52CinN 56-58WasA 58BosA 59-60SFN	10-26-20	Webster Groves, Mo.		R	R	6'	185	22	22	.500	14	237	17	4	492	519	167	209	0	3.70
Byrd, Harry-Harry Gladwin	50,52-53PhiA 54NYA 55BalA 55-56ChiA 57DetA	02-03-25	Darlington, S.C.	05-14-85	R	R	6'1	215	46	54	.460	2	187	108	33	827	890	355	381	4	4.35
Bats Both 55																					

USE NAMES - GIVEN NAMES (NICKNAMES)	TEAM BY YEAR	BIRTH DATE	BIRTHPLACE	DEATH DATE	B	T	HGT	WGT	W	L	Pct.	SV	G	GS	CG	IP	H	BB	SO	ShO	ERA
Byrne, Tommy-Thomas Joseph	43NYA 44-45MS 46-51NYA 51-52StLA 53ChiA 53WasA 54-57NYA	12-31-19	Baltimore, Md.		L	L	6'1	182	85	69	.552	12	281	170	65	1363	1138	1037	766	12	4.11
Cain, Bob-Robert Max (Sugar)	49-51ChiA 51DetA 52-53StLA 54ChiA	10-16-24	Longford, Kans.	04-08-97	L	L	6'	165	37	44	.457	8	140	89	27	629	618	316	249	3	4.49
Calvert, Paul-Paul Leo Emile	42-45CleA 49WasA 50-51DetA	10-06-17	Montreal, Canada	02-01-99	R	R	6'	175	9	22	.290	5	109	27	5	301	345	158	102	0	5.32
Candini, Milo-Milo Cain	43-44WasA 45MS 46-49WasA 50-51PhiN	08-03-17	Manteca, Cal.	03-17-98	R	R	6'	187	26	21	.553	8	174	37	13	538	530	250	183	5	3.91
Carden, John-John Bruton	46NYN	05-19-21	Killeen, Tex.	02-08-49	R	R	6'5	210	0	0	—	0	1	0	0	2	4	4	1	0	22.50
Carlson, Don-Donald Herbert	48ChiN 51-52PhiN	10-15-26	Chicago, Ill.		R	R	6'	180	2	4	.333	0	13	7	2	54	75	21	23	0	6.00
Cary, Scott-Scott Russell (Red)	47WasA	04-11-23	Kendallville, Ind.		L	L	5'11	168	3	1	.750	0	23	3	1	55	73	20	25	0	5.89
Casale, Jerry-Jerry Joseph	58-60BosA 61LAA 61-62DetA	09-27-33	Brooklyn, N.Y.		R	R	6'2	205	17	24	.415	1	96	49	10	371	376	204	207	3	5.07
Ceccarelli, Art-Arthur Edward (Chic)	55-56KCA 57BalA 59-60ChiN	04-02-30	New Haven, Conn.		R	L	6'	190	9	18	.333	0	79	42	8	307	309	147	166	3	5.04
Chakales, Bob-Robert Edward (Chick)	51-54CleA 54BalA 55ChiA 55-57WasA 57BosA	08-10-27	Asheville, N.C.		R	R	6'1	190	15	25	.375	10	171	23	3	420	445	225	187	1	4.54
Chambers, Cliff-Clifford Day (Lefty)	48ChiN 49-51PitN 51-53StLN	01-10-22	Portland, Ore.		L	L	6'3	208	48	53	.475	1	189	113	37	897	924	361	374	6	4.29
Chandler, Ed-Edward Oliver	47BknN	02-17-22	Pinson, Ala.	07-06-03	R	R	6'2	190	0	1	.000	1	15	1	0	30	31	12	8	0	6.30
Chesnes, Bob-Robert Vincent	48-50PitN	05-06-21	Oakland, Cal.	05-23-79	R	R	6'	180	24	22	.522	1	61	55	25	378	377	189	130	1	4.67
Chipman, Bob-Robert Howard (Mr. Chips)	41-44BknN 44-49ChiN 50-52BosN	10-11-18	Brooklyn, N.Y.	11-08-73	L	L	6'2	190	51	46	.526	14	293	87	29	880	889	386	322	7	3.72
Chittum, Nels-Nelson Boyd	58StLN 59-60BosA	03-25-33	Harrisonburg, Va.		R	R	6'1	180	3	1	.750	0	40	2	0	67	68	24	30	0	3.90
Choate, Don-Donald Leon	60SFN	07-02-38	Potosi, Mo.		R	R	6'	185	0	0	—	0	4	0	0	8	7	4	7	0	2.25
Church, Bubba-Emory Nicholas	50-52PhiN 52-53CinN 53-55ChiN	09-12-24	Birmingham, Ala.	09-17-01	R	R	6'	180	36	37	.493	4	147	95	32	713	738	277	274	7	4.10
Churn, Chuck-Clarence Nottingham	57PitN 58CleA 59LAN	02-01-30	Bridgetown, Va.		R	R	6'3	205	3	2	.600	3	25	0	0	48	49	19	32	0	5.06
Ciotte, Al-Alva Warren (Bozo)	57NYA 58WasA 58DetA 59CleA 61StLN 62HouN	12-23-29	Melvindale, Mich.	11-29-82	R	R	6'3	190	10	13	.435	4	102	16	0	260	280	119	149	0	4.36
Clark, Mike-Michael John	52-53StLN	02-12-22	Camden, N.J.	01-25-96	R	R	6'4	190	3	0	1.000	1	35	6	0	61	78	35	27	0	5.31
Clark, Phil-Philip James	58-59StLN	10-03-32	Albany, Ga.		R	R	6'3	210	0	2	.000	1	14	0	0	15	19	11	6	0	7.80
Clarke, Webbo-Vilbert Ernesto	55WasA	06-08-28	Colon, Panama	06-14-70	L	L	6'	165	0	0	—	0	7	2	0	21	17	14	9	0	4.71
Clevenger, Tex-Truman Eugene	54BosA 56-60WasA 61LAA 61-62NYA	07-09-32	Visalia, Cal.		R	R	6'1	185	36	37	.493	30	307	40	6	696	706	298	361	2	4.18
Cohen, Hy-Hyman	55ChiN	01-29-31	Brooklyn, N.Y.		R	R	6'5	215	0	0	—	0	7	0	0	17	28	10	4	0	7.94
Cole, Dave-David Bruce	51-52BosN 53MilN 54ChiN 55PhiN	08-29-30	Williamsport, Md.		R	R	6'2	180	6	18	.250	0	84	27	3	238	221	199	119	1	4.92
Coleman, Joe-Joseph Patrick	42PhiA 43-45MS 46-51,53PhiA 54-55BalA 55DetA	07-30-22	Medford, Mass.	04-09-97	R	R	6'2	200	52	76	.406	6	223	140	46	1133	1172	566	444	11	4.38
Coleman, Rip-Walter Gary	55-56NYA 57,59KCA 59-60BalA	07-31-31	Troy, N.Y.	05-14-04	L	L	6'2	185	7	25	.219	5	95	33	3	247	287	124	130	1	4.59
Collum, Jackie-Jack Dean	51-53StLN 53-55CinN 56StLN 57ChiN 57bknN 58LAN 62MinA 62CleA	06-21-27	Victor, Iowa		L	L	5'7	160	32	28	.533	12	171	37	11	464	480	173	171	2	4.15
Conley, Bob-Robert Burns	58PhiN	02-01-34	Mousie, Ky.	04-??-85	R	R	6'1	188	0	0	—	0	1	0	0	1	0	1	0	0	7.88
Conley, Gene-Donald Eugene	52BosN 54-58MilN 59-60PhiN 61-63BosA 52-53,58-61,62-64 played in N.B.A.	11-10-30	Muskogee, Okla.		R	R	6'8	225	91	96	.487	2	276	214	69	1589	1606	511	888	13	3.82
Connelly, Bill-William Wirt (Wild Bill)	45PhiA 50ChiA 50DetA 52-53NYN	06-29-25	Alberta, Va.	11-27-80	L	R	6'	175	2	0	.750	0	25	7	0	66	71	53	34	0	6.95
Constable, Jim-Jimmy Lee (Sheriff)	56-57NYN 58SFN 58CleA 58WasA 62MilN 63SFN	06-14-33	Jonesboro, Tenn.	09-04-02	B	L	6'1	185	3	4	.429	2	56	6	1	97	109	41	59	1	4.92
Consuegra, Sandy-Sandalio Simeon [Castello]	50-53WasA 53-56ChiA 56-57BalA 57NYN	09-03-20	Potrerillos, Cuba	11-16-05	R	R	5'11	165	51	32	.614	26	248	71	24	810	811	246	193	5	3.37
Cooper, Cal-Calvin Asa	48WasA	08-11-22	Great Falls, S.C.	07-04-94	R	R	6'2	180	0	0	—	0	1	0	0	1	5	1	0	0	45.00
Cooper, Pat-Orge Patterson (See B46-60)	46PhiA	11-26-17	Albemarle, N.C.	03-15-93	R	R	6'3	180	0	0	—	0	1	0	0	1	1	0	0	0	0.00
Corwin, Al-Elmer Nathan (Jingles)	51-55NYN	12-03-26	Newburgh, N.Y.	10-23-03	R	R	6'1	170	18	10	.643	5	117	22	6	290	289	156	142	2	3.97
Cox, Glenn-Glenn Melvin (Jingles)	55-58KCA	02-03-31	Montebello, Cal.		R	R	6'1	200	2	4	.200	0	16	5	0	43	50	35	17	0	6.49
Craddock, Walt-Walter Anderson	55-56,58KCA	03-25-32	Pax, W.Va.	07-06-80	R	L	6'	176	0	7	.000	0	29	5	0	61	68	40	39	0	6.49
Cress, Walker-Walker James (Foots)	48-49CinN	03-06-17	Ben Hur, Va.	04-21-96	R	R	6'5	205	0	1	.000	0	33	2	1	62	62	45	33	0	4.35
Crimian, Jack-John Melvin	51-52StLN 56KCA 57DetA	02-17-26	Philadelphia, Pa.		R	R	5'10	180	5	9	.357	8	74	7	0	160	177	65	69	0	6.35
Cristante, Leo-Dante Leo	51PhiN 55Det	12-10-26	Detroit, Mich.	08-24-77	R	R	6'1	195	1	2	.333	1	30	2	0	59	65	23	15	0	3.81
Crone, Ray-Raymond Hayes	54-57MilN 57NYN 58SFN	08-07-31	Memphis, Tenn.	10-11-94	R	R	6'2	185	30	30	.500	4	137	61	17	546	554	173	260	1	3.87
Cueller, Charlie-Jesus Patracis	50ChiA	09-24-17	Ybor City, Fla.	10-11-94	R	R	5'11	183	0	0	—	0	1	0	0	1	6	3	1	0	36.00
Currie, Bill-William Cleveland	55Was	11-29-28	Leary, Ga.		R	R	6'	175	0	0	—	0	2	0	0	4	7	2	2	0	13.50
Dahlke, Jerry-Jerome Alex (Joe)	56ChiN	06-08-30	Marathon, Wis.		R	R	6'	180	0	0	—	0	5	0	0	2	5	6	1	0	22.50
Daley, Buddy-Leavitt Leo	55-57CleA 58-61KCA 61-64NYA	10-07-32	Orange, Cal.		L	L	6'1	185	60	64	.484	10	248	116	36	966	998	351	549	3	4.03
Daniel, Chuck-Charles Edward	57DetA	09-17-33	Bluffton, Ark.		R	R	6'2	195	0	0	—	0	1	0	0	3	2	0	2	0	9.00
Darnell, Bob-Robert Jack	54,56BknN	11-06-30	Wewoka, Okla.	01-03-95	R	R	5'10	175	0	0	—	0	7	1	0	15	16	7	5	0	3.00
Davie, Jerry-Gerald Lee	59DetA	02-10-33	Detroit, Mich.		R	R	6'	180	2	2	.500	0	11	5	1	37	40	17	20	0	4.14
Davis, Bob-Robert Edward	56KCA	09-11-33	New York, N.Y.	12-22-01	R	R	6'	180	0	4	.000	0	63	76	34	50	0	5.71			
Davis, Jim-James Bennett	54-56ChiN 57StLN 57NYN	09-15-24	Red Bluff, Cal.	11-30-95	B	L	6'	180	24	26	.480	14	154	39	4	407	383	179	197	1	4.00
Deal, Cot-Ellis Fergason	47-48BosA 50,54StLN Bats Left 47-48	01-23-23	Arapaho, Okla.		R	R	6'	185	3	4	.429	1	45	2	0	90	111	48	34	0	6.50
Delock, Ike-Ivan Martin	52-53,55-63BosA 63BalA	11-11-29	Highland Pk., Mich.		R	R	5'11	175	84	75	.528	31	329	147	32	1237	1236	530	672	6	4.04
Dempsey, Con-Cornelius Francis	51PitN	09-16-22	San Francisco, Cal.	08-05-06	R	R	6'4	190	0	2	.000	0	3	2	0	7	11	4	3	0	9.00
Derrington, Jim-Charles James (Blackie)	56-57Chi	11-29-39	Compton, Cal.		L	L	6'3	190	0	2	.000	0	21	6	0	43	38	35	17	0	5.23
Deutsch, Mel-Melvin Elliott	46BosA	04-26-15	Caldwell, Tex.	11-18-01	R	R	6'4	180	0	2	—	0	4	0	0	5	4	5	1	0	6.00
Dickson, Murry-Murry Monroe	39-40,42-43StLN 44-45MS 46-48StLN 49-53PitN 54-56PhiN 56-57StLN 58KCA 58NYA 59KCA	08-21-16	Tracy, Mo.	09-21-89	R	R	5'10	170	172	181	.487	23	625	338	149	3053	3029	1058	1281	27	3.66
Ditmar, Art-Arthur John	54PhiA 55-56KCA 57-61NYA 61-62KCA	04-03-29	Winthrop, Mass.		R	R	6'2	195	72	77	.483	14	287	156	41	1267	1237	461	552	5	3.99
Dixon, Sonny-John Craig	53-54WasA 54PhiA 55KCA 56NYA	11-05-24	Charlotte, N.C.		B	R	6'2	205	11	18	.379	3	102	12	4	263	296	75	90	0	4.17
Dobernic, Jess-Andrew Joseph	39ChiA 48-49ChiN 49PitN	06-05-18	Mt.Olive, Ill.	07-16-98	R	R	5'10	170	7	3	.700	1	76	0	0	112	107	66	55	0	4.23
Dobson, Joe-Joseph Gordon (Burrhead)	39-40CleA 41-43BosA 44-45MS 46-50BosA 51-53ChiA 54BosA	01-20-17	Durant, Okla.	06-23-94	R	R	6'2	197	137	103	.571	18	414	273	112	2172	2048	851	992	22	3.62
Donnelly, Blix-Sylvester Urban	44-46StLN 46-50PhiN 51BosN	01-21-14	Olivia, Minn.	06-20-76	R	R	5'10	166	27	36	.429	12	190	75	27	691	659	306	296	7	3.49
Donnelly, Ed-Edward Vincent	59ChiN	12-10-32	Allen, Mich.		R	R	6'1	185	1	1	.500	0	14	18	9	6	0	3.21				
Donoso, Lino-Lino [Galata]	55-56PitN	09-23-22	Havana, Cuba	10-13-90	L	L	5'11	160	4	6	.400	1	28	9	3	97	108	36	39	0	5.20
Donovan, Dick-Richard Edward	50-52BosN 54DetA 55-60ChiA 61WasA 62-65CleA	12-07-27	Boston, Mass.	01-06-97	R	R	6'3	205	122	99	.552	9	345	273	101	2020	1988	495	880	25	3.67
Dorish, Harry-Harry (Fritz)	47-49BosA 50StLA 51-55ChiA 55-56BalA 56BosA	07-13-21	Swoyersville, Pa.	12-31-00	R	R	5'11	204	45	43	.511	44	323	40	13	835	850	301	332	2	3.83
Douglas, Whammy-Charles William	57PitN	02-17-35	Carrboro, N.C.		R	R	6'2	185	3	3	.500	0	11	8	0	47	48	30	28	0	3.26
Dozier, Buzz-William Joseph	47,49WasA	08-31-28	Waco, Tex.		R	R	6'	185	0	0	—	0	11	14	7	3	0	6.55				
Dreiseward, Clem-Clemens Johann (Steamboat)	44-46BosA 48StLA 48NYN	01-24-16	Old Monroe, Mo.	09-11-01	L	L	6'1	195	6	8	.429	2	46	10	3	141	160	39	39	0	4.53
Drews, Karl-Karl August	46-48NYA 48-49StLA 51-54PhiN 54CinN	02-22-20	Staten Island, N.Y.	08-13-63	R	R	6'4	192	44	53	.454	7	218	107	26	827	913	332	322	7	4.76
Drott, Dick-Richard Fred (Hummer)	57-61ChiN 62-63HouN	07-01-36	Cincinnati, Ohio	08-16-85	R	R	6'1	190	27	46	.370	0	176	104	14	687	626	405	460	5	4.78
Dubiel, Monk-Walter John	44-45NYA 48PhiN 49-52ChiN	02-12-18	Hartford, Conn.	10-23-69	R	R	6'	190	45	53	.459	11	187	97	41	808	854	349	289	3	3.87
Dunn, Jim-James William (Bill)	52PitN	02-25-31	Valdosta, Ga.	01-06-99	R	R	6'	185	0	0	—	0	4	0	0	3	2	0	1	0	3.60
Dusak, Erv-Ervin Frank (Four Sack) (See B46-60)	48,50-51StLN 51BosN	07-29-20	Chicago, Ill.	11-06-94	R	R	6'2	185	0	3	.000	1	23	3	0	54	51	44	26	0	5.33
Duser, Carl-Carl Robert	56,58KCA	07-22-32	Hazleton, Pa.		L	L	6'1	175	1	1	.500	0	8	0	0	19	13	5	5	0	7.88
Edelman, John-John Rogers	55MilN	07-27-35	Philadelphia, Pa.		R	R	6'3	185	0	0	—	0	6	0	0	7	8	7	1	0	10.50
Elliott, Glenn-Herbert Glenn (Lefty)	47-49BosN	11-11-19	Sapulpa, Okla.	07-27-69	B	L	5'11	175	5	4	.444	2	90	13	3	90	93	39	25	0	4.10
Elston, Don-Donald Ray	53ChiN 57BknN 57-64ChiN	04-06-29	Campbellstown, Ohio	01-02-95	R	R	6'	170	49	54	.476	63	450	15	2	755	702	327	519	0	3.70
Embree, Red-Charles Willard	41-42CleA 43VR 44-47CleA 48NYA 49StLA	08-30-17	El Monte, Cal.	09-24-96	R	R	6'	165	31	48	.392	1	141	90	29	707	653	330	286	1	3.72
Erautt, Eddie-Edward Lorenz Sebastian	47-51,53CinN 53ChiN	09-26-24	Portland, Ore.	10-06-76	R	R	5'11	185	15	23	.395	2	164	22	4	379	434	179	157	0	4.870
Erickson, Don-Don Lee	58PhiN	12-13-31	Springfield, Ill.		R	R	6'	175	0	0	—	0	12	0	0	11	9	4	2	0	4.50
Erickson, Hal-Harold James	53DetA	07-19-19	Portland, Ore.		R	R	6'5	230	0	1	.000	0	9	0	0	32	43	19	10	0	4.78
Erskine, Carl-Carl Daniel (Oisk)	48-57BknN 58-59LAN	12-13-26	Anderson, Ind.		R	R	5'10	165	122	78	.610	13	335	216	71	1719	1637	646	981	14	4.00
Estock, George-George John	51BosN	11-02-24	Stirling, N.J.		R	R	6'2	185	0	1	.000	0	17	0	0	60	56	37	11	0	4.35
Evans, Bill-William Lawrence	49ChiA 51BosA	03-25-19	Childress, Tex.		R	R	6'2	190	0	0	—	0	5	0	0	21	16	4	0	5.14	
Fagan, Everett-Everett Joseph	43PhiA 44-45MS 46PhiA	01-13-18	Pottersville, N.J.	02-16-83	R	R	6'2	195	2	7	.222	1	39	9	2	82	88	81	21	0	4.92
Fahr, Red-Gerald Warren	51CleA	02-24-24	Marmaduke, Ark.		R	R	6'5	185	0	0	—	0	1	0	0	1	5	3	0	0	4.50
Fannin, Cliff-Clifford Byrson (Mule)	45-52StLA	05-13-24	Louisa, Ky.	12-11-66	L	R	6'	170	34	51	.400	6	164	98	28	733	763	393	352	6	4.85
Fanovich, Frank-Frank Joseph (Lefty)	49CinN 53PhiA	01-11-22	New York, N.Y.		L	L	5'11	180	0	5	.000	0	55	4	0	105	106	65	64	0	5.49

USE NAMES - GIVEN NAMES (NICKNAMES)	TEAM BY YEAR	BIRTH DATE	BIRTHPLACE	DEATH DATE	B	T	HGT	WGT	W	L	Pct.	SV	G	GS	CG	IP	H	BB	SO	ShO	ERA
Faszholz, Jack-John Edward (Preacher)	53StLN	04-11-27	St. Louis, Mo.		R	R	6'3	205	0	0	—	0	4	1	0	12	16	1	7	0	6.75
Fear, Vern-Luvern Carl	52ChiN	08-21-24	Everly, Iowa	09-06-76	B	R	6'	170	0	0	—	0	8			9		3	4	0	7.88
Feller, Bob-Robert William Andrew (Rapid Robert)	36-41CleA 42-44MS 45-56CleA	11-03-18	Van Meter, Iowa		R	R	6'	185	266	162	.621	21	570	484	279	3828	3271	1764	2581	44	3.25
Ferens, Stan-Stanley (Lefty)	42,46StLA	03-05-15	Wendel, Pa.	10-07-94	B	L	5'11	170	5	13	.278	0	53	9	2	157	176	59	51	0	4.18
Ferrarese, Don-Donald Hugh (Midget)	55-57BalA 58-59CleA 60CinN 61-62PhiN 62StLN	06-19-29	Oakland, Cal.		R	L	5'9	170	19	36	.345	5	183	50	12	507	449	295	350	2	3.99
Ferrick, Tom-Thomas Jerome	41PhiA 42CleA 43-45MS 46CleA 46StLA 47-48WasA 49-50StLA 50-51NYA 51-52WasA	01-06-15	New York, N.Y.	10-15-96	R	R	6'2	220	40	40	.500	56	323	7	4	674	654	227	245	1	3.47
Ferriss, Boo-David Meadow	45-50BosA	12-05-21	Shaw, Miss.		L	R	6'2	208	65	30	.684	8	144	103	67	880	914	314	296	12	3.64
Fine, Tommy-Thomas Morgan	47BosA 50StLA	10-10-14	Cleburne, Tex.	01-10-05	B	R	6'	180	1	3	.250	0	23	7	1	73	94	44	16	0	6.78
Fischer, Bill-William Charles	56-58ChiA 58DetA 58-60WasA 60-61DetA 61-63KCA 64MinA	10-11-30	Wausau, Wis.		R	R	6'	195	45	58	.437	13	281	78	16	832	936	210	313	2	4.34
Fisher, Harry-Harry Deveraux (See B46-60)	52PitN	01-03-26	Newbury, Canada	09-20-81	L	R	6'	180	1	2	.333	0	8	3	0	18	17	13	5	0	7.00
Fisher, Maury-Maurice Wayne	55CinN	02-16-31	Uniondale, Ind.		R	R	6'5	210	0	0	—	0	3	0	0	3	5	2	1	0	6.00
Fitzgerald, John-John Francis	58SFN	09-15-33	Brooklyn, N.Y.		L	R	6'3	190	0	0	—	0	1	0	0	3	1	1	3	0	3.00
Flanigan, Ray-Raymond Arthur	46CleA	01-08-23	Morgantown, W.Va.	03-28-93	R	R	6'	190	0	1	.000	0	3	1	0	9	11	8	2	0	11.00
Flanigan, Tom-Thomas Anthony	54ChiA 58StLN	09-06-34	Cincinnati, Ohio		R	L	6'3	190	0	0	—	0	3	0	0	3	3	2	0	0	3.00
Fletcher, Van-Alfred Vanoide	55DetA	08-06-24	East Bend, N.C.		R	R	6'2	185	0	0	—	0	9	0	0	12	13	2	4	0	3.00
Flowers, Ben-Bennett	51,53BosA 55DetA 55-56StLN 56PhiN	06-15-27	Wilson, N.C.		R	R	6'4	200	3	7	.300	3	76	13	1	168	190	54	86	1	4.50
Fodge, Gene-Gene Arlan (Suds)	58CinN	06-13-31	South Bend, Ind.		R	R	6'	175	1	1	.500	0	16	6	1	40	47	11	15	0	4.73
Ford, Whitey-Edward Charles (The Chairman of the Board)	50NYA 51-52MS 53-67NYA	10-21-28	New York, N.Y.		L	L	5'10	178	236	106	.690	10	498	438	156	3171	2766	1086	1956	45	2.74
Fornieles, Mike-Jose Miguel [Torres]	52WasA 53-56ChiA 56-57BalA 57-63BosA 63MinA	01-18-32	Havana, Cuba	02-11-98	R	R	5'11	158	63	64	.496	55	432	76	20	1156	1165	421	576	4	3.96
Fowler, Art-John Arthur	54-57CinN 59LAN 61-64LAA	07-03-22	Converse, S.C.		R	R	5'11	180	54	51	.514	32	362	90	25	1025	1039	308	539	4	4.02
Fowler, Dick-Richard John	41-42PhiA 43-44MS 45-52PhiA	03-30-21	Toronto, Canada	05-22-72	R	R	6'4	215	66	79	.455	4	221	170	75	1304	1367	578	382	11	4.11
Fox, Howie-Howard Francis	44-46,48-51CinN 52PhiN 54BalA	03-01-21	Coburg, Ore.	10-09-55	R	R	6'3	210	43	72	.374	6	248	132	42	1108	1174	435	342	5	4.33
Foytack, Paul-Paul Eugene	53,55-63DetA 63-64LAA	11-16-30	Scranton, Pa.		R	R	6'1	180	86	87	.497	7	312	193	63	1499	1381	662	827	7	4.14
Freeman, Hersh-Hershell Baskin (Buster)	52-53,55BosA 55-58CinN 58ChiN	07-01-28	Gadsden, Ala.	01-17-04	R	R	6'3	220	30	16	.652	37	204	3	1	360	387	109	158	0	3.73
Freeman, Mark-Mark Price	59KCA 59NYA 60ChiN	12-07-30	Memphis, Tenn.	02-21-06	R	R	6'4	220	3	3	.500	1	34	9	1	88	82	38	55	0	5.52
Fricano, Marion John	52-54PhiA 55KCA	07-15-23	Brant, N.Y.	05-18-76	R	R	6'	170	15	23	.395	1	88	43	14	388	393	164	115	0	4.31
Friend, Bob-Robert Bartmess (Warrior)	51-65PitN 66NYA 66NYN	11-24-30	Lafayette, Ind.		R	R	6'	195	197	230	.461	11	602	497	163	3612	3772	894	1734	36	3.58
Froats, Bill-Willliam John	55DetA	10-20-30	New York, N.Y.	02-09-98	L	L	6'	180	0	0	—	0	1	0	0	2	0	2	0	0	0.00
Garber, Bob-Robert Mitchell	56PitN	09-10-28	Hunker, Pa.	06-07-99	R	R	6'1	190	0	0	—	0	2	0	0	4	3	3	3	0	2.25
Garcia, Mike-Edward Miguel (The Big Bear)	48-59CleA 60ChiA 61WasA	11-17-23	San Gabriel, Cal.	01-13-86	R	R	6'1	205	142	97	.594	23	428	281	111	2175	2148	719	1117	27	3.27
Garcia, Ramon-Ramon [Garcia]	48WasA	03-05-24	La Esperanza, Cuba		R	R	5'10	170	0	0	—	0	4	0	0	4	11	4	2	0	15.75
Garver, Ned-Ned Franklin	48-52StLA 52-56DetA 57-60KCA 61LAA	12-25-25	Ney, Ohio		R	R	5'10	185	129	157	.451	12	402	330	153	2477	2471	881	881	18	3.73
Gebrian, Pete-Peter (Gabe)	47ChiA	08-10-23	Bayonne, N.J.	05-06-05	R	R	6'	170	2	3	.400	1	27	4	0	66	61	33	17	0	4.50
Gettel, Al-Allen Jones	45-46NYA 47-48CleA 48-49ChiA 49WasA 51NYN 55StLN	09-17-17	Norfolk, Va.	04-08-05	R	R	6'3	200	38	45	.458	6	184	79	31	735	711	310	310	5	4.27
Giallombardo, Bob-Robert Paul	58LAN	05-20-37	Brooklyn, N.Y.		L	L	6'	175	1	1	.500	0	6	5	0	26	29	15	14	0	3.81
Giel, Paul-Paul Robert	54-55NYN 56-57MS 58SFN 59-60PitN 61MinN 61KCA	09-29-32	Winona, Minn.	05-22-02	R	R	5'11	185	11	9	.550	0	102	11	0	240	249	148	145	0	5.40
Giggie, Bob-Robert Thomas	59-60MilN 60,62KCA	08-13-33	Dorchester, Mass.		R	R	6'1	200	3	1	.750	1	30	2	0	57	70	32	32	0	5.21
Gillespie, Bob-Robert William (Bunch)	44DetA 47-48ChiA 50BosA	10-08-19	Columbus, Ohio	11-14-01	R	R	6'4	187	5	13	.278	0	58	23	2	202	223	102	59	0	5.08
Goetz, John-John Hardy	60CinN	10-24-37	Goetzville, Mich.		R	R	6'	185	0	0	—	0	4	0	0	6	10	4	4	0	13.50
Gomez, Ruben-Ruben [Colon]	53-57NYN 58SFN 59-60PhiN 62CleA 62MinA 67PhiN	07-13-27	Arroyo, P.R.	07-26-04	R	R	6'	170	76	86	.469	5	289	205	63	1453	1436	574	677	15	4.09
Gonzales(Gonzalez), Julio-Julio Enrique [Herrera]	49WasA	12-20-20	Rio Seco, Banes, Cuba	02-15-91	R	R	5'11	150	0	0	—	0	13	0	0	34	33	27	5	0	4.76
Gonzales, Vince-Wenceslao [O'Reilly]	55WasA	09-28-25	Quivican, Cuba	03-11-81	L	L	6'1	165	0	0	—	0	2	0	0	6	3	1	0	0	27.00
Goodwin, Jim-James Patrick	48ChiA	08-15-26	St. Louis, Mo.		L	L	6'1	170	0	0	—	0	8	1	0	10	9	12	3	0	9.00
Gorin, Charlie-Charles Perry	54-55MilN	02-06-28	Waco, Tex.		L	L	5'10	165	1	0	.000	0	7	0	0	10	6	9	12	0	3.60
Gorman, Tom-Thomas Aloysius	52-54NYA 55-59KCA	01-04-25	New York, N.Y.	12-26-92	R	R	6'1	195	36	36	.500	42	289	33	5	690	659	239	321	2	3.77
Grasmick, Lou-Louis Junior	48PhiN	09-11-24	Balitmore, Md.		R	R	6'	195	0	0	—	0	2	0	0	5	3	2	1	0	7.20
Gray, John-John Leonard	54PhiA 55KCA 57CleA 58PhiN	12-11-27	W. Palm Beach, Fla.		R	R	6'4	226	4	18	.182	0	48	24	6	169	172	142	75	1	6.18
Gray, Ted-Ted Glenn	46,48-54DetA 55ChiA 55CleA 55NYA 55BalA	12-31-24	Detroit, Mich.		B	L	5'11	175	59	74	.444	7	222	162	50	1133	1072	595	687	7	4.37
					Bats Right 46																
Greason, Willie-William Henry (Booster)	54StLN	09-03-24	Atlanta, Ga.		R	R	5'10	170	0	0	—	0	3	1	0	4	4	2	0	0	13.50
Green, Freddie-Fred Allen	59-61PitN 62WasA 64PitN	09-14-33	Titusville, N.J.	10-22-96	R	L	6'	190	9	7	.563	4	88	1	0	142	142	63	77	0	3.49
Greenwood, Bob-Robert Chandler (Greenie)	54-55PhiN	03-13-28	Cananea, Mexico	09-01-94	R	R	6'4	205	1	2	.333	0	12	4	0	39	35	18	9	0	3.92
Griffeth, Lee-Leon Clifford	46PhiN	05-20-25	Carmel, N.Y.		B	L	5'11	180	0	0	—	0	10	0	0	15	13	6	4	0	4.00
Griggs, Hal-Harold Lloyd	56-59WasA	08-24-28	Shannon, Ga.	05-10-05	R	R	6'	170	6	26	.188	3	105	45	8	348	372	209	172	1	5.48
Grim, Bob-Robert Anton	54-58NYA 58-59KCA 60CleA 60CinN 60StLN 62KCA	03-08-30	New York, N.Y.	10-23-96	R	R	6'1	175	61	41	.598	37	268	60	18	759	708	330	443	4	3.62
Grimsley, Ross-Ross Albert Sr. (Lefty)	51StLA	06-04-22	Americus, Kans.	02-06-94	L	L	6'	175	0	0	—	0	7	0	0	14	12	10	8	0	3.86
Grissom, Marv-Marvin Edward	46NYN 49DetA 52ChiA 53BosA 53-57NYN 58SFN 59StLN	03-31-18	Los Molinos, Cal.	09-19-05	R	R	6'3	205	47	45	.511	58	356	52	12	810	771	343	459	3	3.41
Grob, Connie-Conrad George	56WasA	11-09-32	Cross Plains, Wis.	09-28-97	L	R	6'	180	4	5	.444	0	37	1	0	79	121	26	27	0	7.86
Grodzicki, Johnny-John	41StLN 42-45MS 46-47StLN	02-26-17	Nanticoke, Pa.	05-02-98	R	R	6'1	200	2	2	.500	0	24	1	0	40	31	34	20	0	4.50
Gromek, Steve-Stephen Joseph	41-53CleA 53-57DetA	01-15-20	Hamtramck, Mich.	03-12-02	B	R	6'2	195	123	108	.532	23	447	225	92	2065	1940	630	904	15	3.41
					Bats Right 41-49																
Gross, Don-Donald John	55-57CinN 58-60PitN	06-30-31	Weidman, Mich.		L	L	5'11	186	20	22	.476	10	145	37	9	397	400	117	230	1	3.74
Grossman, Harley-Harley Joseph	52WasA	05-05-30	Evansville, Ind.	09-05-04	R	R	6'	170	0	0	—	0	1	0	0	0.1	0	1	0	0	54.00
Groth, Ernie-Ernest William	47-48CleA 49ChiA	05-03-22	Beaver Falls, Pa.	12-27-04	R	R	5'9	185	0	1	.000	0	6	0	0	7	3	6	2	0	5.14
Grunwald, Al-Alfred Henry (Stretch)	55PitN 59KCA	02-13-30	Los Angeles, Cal.		L	L	6'4	210	0	1	.000	0	9	1	0	19	25	18	11	0	6.63
Gumpert, Randy-Randall Pennington	36-38PhiA 43-45MS 46-48NYA 48-51ChiA 52BosA 52WasA	01-23-18	Monocacy, Pa.		R	R	6'3	200	51	59	.464	7	261	113	47	1052	1099	346	352	6	4.17
Habenicht, Bob-Robert Julius (Hobby)	51StLN 53StLA	02-13-26	St. Louis, Mo.	12-24-80	R	R	6'2	185	0	0	—	0	4	0	0	6	10	2	2	0	6.43
Hacker, Warren-Warren Louis	48-56ChiN 57CinN 57-58PhiN 61ChiA	11-21-24	Marissa, Ill.	05-22-02	R	R	6'1	185	62	89	.411	17	306	157	47	1283	1297	320	557	6	4.21
Haddix, Harvey-Harvey (The Kitten)	52-56StLN 56-57PhiN 58CinN 59-63PitN 64-65BalA	09-18-25	Medway, Ohio	01-08-94	L	L	5'9	170	136	113	.546	21	453	285	99	2235	2154	601	1575	20	3.63
Haefner, Mickey-Milton Arnold	43-49WasA 49-50ChiA 50BosN	10-09-12	Lenzburg, Ill.	01-03-95	L	L	5'8	160	78	91	.462	13	261	179	91	1467	1414	577	508	13	3.50
Hahn, Fred-Frederick Aloys	52StLN	02-16-29	Nyack, N.Y.		R	L	6'3	174	0	0	—	0	1	0	0	2	1	1	0	0	0.00
Hall, Bob-Robert Louis	49-50BosN 53PitN	12-22-23	Swissvale, Pa.	03-12-83	R	R	6'2	195	9	18	.333	1	89	27	8	276	307	146	133	1	5.41
Hall, Johnny-John Sylvester	48BknN	01-09-24	Muskogee, Okla.	01-17-95	R	R	6'2	170	0	0	—	0	3	0	0	4	4	2	2	0	6.75
Hamner, Granny-Granville Wilbur (See B46-60)	56-57PhiN 62KCA	04-26-27	Richmond, Va.	09-12-93	R	R	5'10	163	0	0	—	0	13	0	0	13	21	6	5	0	5.54
Hamner, Ralph-Ralph Conant (Bruz)	46ChiA 47-49ChiN	09-12-16	Gibsland, La.	05-22-01	R	R	6'3	165	8	20	.286	1	61	28	8	219	236	132	99	0	4.60
Hansen, Andy-Andrew Viggo (Swede)	44-45NYN 46MS 47-50NYN 51-53PhiN	11-12-24	Lake Worth, Fla.	02-02-02	R	R	6'3	185	23	30	.434	16	270	39	8	618	627	246	188	0	4.22
Hardy, Red-Francis Joseph	51NYN	01-06-23	Marmarth, N.D.	08-15-03	R	R	5'11	175	0	0	—	0	3	1	0	4	1	1	0	0	9.00
Harrington, Billy-Billy Womble	53PhiA 54MS 55-56KCA	10-03-27	Sanford, N.C.		R	R	5'11	160	5	5	.500	3	37	7	1	117	114	67	40	0	5.00
Harris, Bill-William Thomas (Billy)	57BknN 59LAN	12-03-31	Duguayville, Canada		L	R	5'8	187	0	1	.000	0	9	1	0	9	14	8	8	0	3.00
Harris, Charlie-Charles (Bubba)	48-49,51PhiA 51CleA	02-15-26	Sulligent, Ala.		R	R	6'4	204	6	6	.667	4	87	0	0	186	190	86	53	0	4.84
Harris, Mickey-Maurice Charles	40-41BosA 42-45MS 46-49BosA 49-52WasA 52CleA	01-30-17	New York, N.Y.	04-15-71	L	L	6'	195	59	71	.454	21	271	109	42	1051	1097	455	534	2	4.18
Harrison, Bob-Robert Lee	55-56BalA	09-22-30	St. Louis, Mo.		R	R	6'1	178	0	0	—	0	2	0	0	2	3	3	1	0	11.25
Harrist, Earl-Earl (Irish)	45CinN 47-48ChiA 48WasA 52StLA 53ChiA 53DetA	08-20-19	Dubach, La.	09-01-98	R	R	5'11	175	12	28	.300	10	132	24	2	383	391	193	162	0	4.34
Harshman, Jack-John Elvin (See B46-60)	52NYN 54-57ChiA 58-59BalA 59BosA 59-60CleA	07-12-27	San Diego, Cal.		L	L	6'2	189	69	65	.515	2	217	155	61	1168	1025	539	741	12	3.51
Hartung, Clint-Clinton Clarence (The Hondo Hurricane, Floppy) (See B46-60)	47-50NYN	08-10-22	Hondo, Tex.		R	R	6'5	210	29	29	.500	1	112	72	24	511	529	271	167	3	5.02
Hatten, Joe-Joseph Hilarian	46-51BknN 51-52CinN	11-07-16	Bancroft, Iowa	12-16-88	R	L	6'	176	65	49	.570	4	233	149	51	1087	1124	492	381	7	3.87
Haugstad, Phil-Phillip Donald	47-48,51BknN 52CinN	02-23-24	Black R. Falls, Wis.	10-21-98	R	R	6'2	165	1	1	.500	0	37	5	1	57	51	41	28	0	5.53
Hayden, Gene-Eugene Franklin (Lefty)	58CinN	04-14-35	San Francisco, Cal.		L	L	6'2	175	0	0	—	0	2	0	0	3	4	2	4	0	4.50
Haynes, Joe-Joseph Walton	39-40WasA 41-48ChiA 49-52WasA	09-21-17	Lincolnton, Ga.	01-07-67	R	R	6'2	190	76	82	.481	21	379	147	54	1580	1672	620	475	5	4.01
Heard, Jay-Jehosie	54BalA	01-17-20	Athens, Ga.	11-18-99	L	L	5'7	147	0	0	—	0	2	0	0	9	9	5	3	0	15.00
Hearn, Jim-James Tolbert	47-50StLN 50-56NYN 57-59PhiN	04-11-21	Atlanta, Ga.	06-10-98	R	R	6'3	205	109	89	.551	8	396	229	84	1704	1661	655	689	10	3.81

USE NAMES - GIVEN NAMES (NICKNAMES)	TEAM BY YEAR	BIRTH DATE	BIRTHPLACE	DEATH DATE	B	T	HGT	WGT	W	L	Pct.	SV	G	GS	CG	IP	H	BB	SO	ShO	ERA
Heintzelman, Ken-Kenneth Alphonse	37-42PitN 43-45MS 46-47PitN 47-52PhiN	10-14-15	Peruque, Mo.	08-14-00	R	L	5'11	185	77	98	.440	10	319	183	66	1502	1540	630	564	18	3.93
Heise, Jim-James James Edward	57WasA	10-02-32	Scottdale, Pa.		R	R	6'1	185	0	3	.000	0	8	2	0	19	25	16	8	0	8.05
Held, Mel-Melvin Nicholas (Country)	56BalA	04-12-29	Edon, Ohio		R	R	6'1	178	0	0	—	0	7	0	0	7	7	3	4	0	5.14
Herbert, Ray-Raymond Ernest	50-51DetA 52MS 53-54DetA 55,58-61KCA 61-64ChiA 65-66PhiN	12-15-29	Detroit, Mich.		R	R	5'11	185	104	107	.493	15	407	236	68	1883	2000	571	864	13	4.01
Hernandez, Evelio-Gregorio Evelio [Lopez]	56-57WasA	12-24-31	Guanabacoa, Cuba		R	R	6'1	180	1	1	.500	0	18	6	1	59	62	28	24	0	4.42
Hernandez, Rudy-Rudolph Albert [Fuentes]	60WasA 61WasA	12-10-31	Santiago, Dom. Rep.		R	R	6'3	185	4	2	.667	0	28	0	0	44	42	24	26	0	4.09
Herrera(Rodriguez), Tito-Procopio [Herrera] (Bobby)	51StLA	07-26-26	Nuevo Laredo, Mex.		R	R	6'	184	0	0	—	0	3	0	0	2	6	4	1	0	31.50
Herriage, Troy-William Troy (Dutch)	56KCA	12-20-30	Tipton, Okla.		R	R	6'1	170	1	13	.071	0	31	16	1	103	135	64	59	0	6.64
Herrin, Tom-Thomas Edward	54BosA	09-12-29	Shreveport, La.	11-29-99	R	R	6'3	190	1	2	.333	0	14	1	0	28	34	22	8	0	7.39
Hetki, Johnny-John Edward	45-48,50CinN 52StLA 53-54PitN	05-12-22	Leavenworth, Kans.		R	R	6'	202	18	26	.409	13	214	23	8	525	557	185	175	0	4.39
Hill, Dave-David Burnham	57KCA	11-11-37	New Orleans, La.		R	L	6'2	170	0	0	—	0	2	0	0	2	6	3	1	0	31.50
Hiller, Frank-Frank Walter (Dutch)	46,48-49NYA 50-51ChiN 52CinN 53NYN	07-13-20	Irvington, N.J.	01-08-87	R	R	6'	200	30	32	.484	4	138	60	22	533	553	158	197	5	4.42
Hillman, Dave-Darius Sutton	55-59ChiN 60-61BosA 62CinN 62NYN	09-14-27	Dungannon, Va.		R	R	5'11	168	21	37	.362	3	188	64	8	624	639	185	296	1	3.87
Hinrichs, Paul-Paul Edwin (Herky)	51BosA	08-31-25	Marengo, Iowa		R	R	6'	180	0	0	—	0	4	0	0	3	7	4	1	0	24.00
Hisner, Harley-Harley Parnell	51BosA	11-06-26	Maples, Ind.		R	R	6'1	185	0	1	.000	0	1	1	0	6	7	4	3	0	4.50
Hittle, Lloyd-Lloyd Eldon (Red)	49-50WasA	02-21-24	Lodi, Cal.		L	L	5'10	164	7	11	.389	0	47	13	4	152	183	74	41	2	4.44
Hobbie, Glen-Glen Frederick	57-64ChiN 64StLN	04-24-36	Witt, Ill.		R	R	6'2	195	62	81	.434	6	284	170	45	1263	1283	495	682	11	4.19
Hodkey, Eli-Aloysius Joseph	46PhiN	11-03-17	Lorain, Ohio	08-30-05	L	L	6'4	185	0	1	.000	0	4	0	0	4	9	5	0	0	13.50
Hoeft, Billy-William Frederick	52-59DetA 59BosA 59-62BalA 63SFN 64MilN 65-66ChiN 66SFN	05-17-32	Oshkosh, Wis.		L	L	6'3	195	97	101	.490	33	505	200	75	1848	1820	685	1140	17	3.94
Hogue, Bobby-Robert Clinton	45-51BosN 51StLA 51-52NYA 52StLA	04-05-21	Miami, Fla.	12-27-87	R	R	5'10	195	18	16	.529	17	172	3	0	327	336	142	108	0	3.96
Hogue, Cal-Calvin Grey	52-54PitN	10-24-27	Dayton, Ohio	08-05-05	R	R	6'	185	2	10	.167	0	25	16	5	114	109	96	51	0	4.89
Holcombe, Ken-Kenneth Edward	45NYA 48CinN 50-52ChiA 52StLA 53BosA	08-23-18	Burnsville, N.C.		R	R	5'11	185	18	32	.360	2	99	48	18	374	377	170	118	2	3.99
Holloman, Bob-Alva Lee	53StLA	03-07-23	Thomaston, Ga.	05-01-87	R	R	6'2	207	3	7	.300	0	22	10	1	65	69	50	25	1	5.26
Hood, Wally-Wallace James Jr.	49NYA	09-24-25	Los Angeles, Cal.	07-16-01	R	R	6'1	190	0	0	—	0	2	0	0	2	0	2	0	0	7.20
Hooper, Bob-Robert Nelson	50-52PhiA 53-54CleA 55CinN	05-30-22	Leamington, Canada	03-17-80	R	R	5'11	200	40	41	.494	25	194	57	16	620	640	280	196	0	4.80
Hoover, Dick-Richard Lloyd	52BosN	12-11-25	Columbus, Ohio	04-12-81	L	L	6'	170	0	0	—	0	2	0	0	5	8	3	0	0	7.20
Hopper, Jim-James McDaniel	46PitN	09-01-19	Charlotte, N.C.	01-23-82	R	R	6'1	175	0	1	.000	0	2	1	0	4	4	4	1	0	11.25
Hoskins, Dave-David Taylor	53-54CleA	08-03-25	Greenwood, Miss.	04-02-70	R	R	6'1	180	9	4	.692	1	40	8	3	140	131	48	64	0	3.79
Host, Gene-Eugene Earl (Twinkles, Slick)	56DetA 57KCA	01-01-33	Leeper, Pa.	10-20-98	B	L	5'11	190	0	2	.000	0	12	3	0	29	38	16	14	0	7.14
Houtteman, Art-Arthur Joseph	45-50DetA 51MS 52-53DetA 53-57CleA 57BalA	08-07-27	Detroit, Mich.	05-06-03	R	R	6'2	188	87	91	.489	20	325	181	78	1556	1646	516	639	14	4.14
Howard, Lee-Lee Vincent	46-47PitN	11-11-23	Staten Island, N.Y.		R	R	6'2	175	0	1	.000	0	5	2	1	16	18	9	8	0	2.25
Howe, Cal-Calvin Earl	52ChiN	11-27-24	Rock Falls, Ill.		L	L	6'3	230	0	0	—	0	1	0	0	1	2	1	0	0	0.00
Howell, Dixie-Millard	40CleA 49CinN 55-58ChiA	01-07-20	Harold, Ky.	03-18-60	L	R	6'2	210	19	15	.559	19	115	2	0	226	236	103	99	0	3.78
Hoyle, Tex-Roland Edison	52PhiA	07-17-21	Carbondale, Pa.	07-04-94	R	R	6'4	170	0	0	—	0	3	0	0	3	1	1	1	0	31.50
Hudson, Hal-Hal Campbell (Lefty)	52StLA 52-53ChiA	05-04-27	Grosse Point, Mich.		L	L	5'10	175	0	0	—	0	6	0	0	11	16	7	4	0	7.36
Hudson, Sid-Sidney Charles	40-42WasA 43-45MS 46-52WasA 52-54BosA	01-03-15	Coalfield, Tenn.		R	R	6'4	180	104	152	.406	13	380	279	123	2181	2384	835	734	11	4.28
Hughes, Jim-James Robert	52-56BknN 56ChiN 57ChiA	03-21-23	Chicago, Ill.	08-13-01	R	R	6'1	200	15	13	.536	39	172	1	0	297	278	152	165	0	3.82
Hughes, Tom-Thomas Edward	59StLN	09-13-34	Ancon, Canal Zone		L	R	6'2	180	0	0	—	0	2	0	0	4	9	2	2	0	15.75
Hughes, Tommy-Thomas Owen	41-42PhiN 43-45MS 46-47PhiN 48CinN	10-07-19	Wilkes-Barre, Pa.	11-28-90	R	R	6'1	190	31	56	.356	3	144	87	31	688	698	308	221	5	3.92
Hurd, Tom-Thomas Carr (Whitey)	54-55BosA	01-14-23	Danville, Va.	09-05-82	R	R	5'9	155	13	10	.565	11	99	0	0	187	177	97	96	0	3.93
Hutchinson, Fred-Frederick Charles (Big Bear) (See B46-60)	39-41DetA 42-45MS 46-53,M52-54DetA M56-58StLN M59-64CinN	08-12-19	Seattle, Wash.	11-12-64	L	R	6'2	190	95	71	.572	7	242	169	81	1465	1487	388	591	13	3.72
Hyde, Dick-Richard Elde	55,57-60WasA 61BalA	08-03-28	Hindsboro, Ill.	08-17-80	R	R	5'11	170	17	14	.548	23	169	2	0	298	273	137	144	0	3.56
Iott, Hooks-Clarence Eugene	41StLA 43-45MS 47StLA 47NYN	12-03-19	Mountain Grove, Mo.	08-17-80	B	L	6'2	200	3	9	.250	0	26	9	2	82	84	67	53	1	7.02
Jacobs, Tony-Anthony Robert	48ChiN 55StLN	08-05-25	Dixmoor, Ill.	12-21-80	R	R	5'9	150	0	0	—	0	2	0	0	4	1	3	1	0	11.25
Jansen, Larry-Lawrence Joseph	47-54NYN 56CinN	07-16-20	Verboort, Ore.		R	R	6'2	190	122	89	.578	10	291	237	107	1767	1751	410	842	17	3.58
Jeffcoat, Hal-Harold Bentley (See B46-60)	54-55ChiN 56-59CinN 59StLN	09-06-24	W. Columbia, S.C.		R	R	5'10	185	39	37	.513	25	245	51	13	697	772	257	239	1	4.22
Jester, Virgil-Virgil Milton	52BosN 53MilN	07-23-27	Denver, Colo.		R	R	5'11	188	3	5	.375	0	21	8	4	75	84	27	25	1	3.84
Johnson, Ben-Benjamin Franklin	59-60ChiN	05-16-31	Greenwood, S.C.		R	R	6'2	190	2	1	.667	1	21	2	0	46	56	15	15	0	3.91
Johnson, Chet-Chester Lillis (Chesty Chet)	46StLA	08-01-17	Redmond, Wash.	04-10-83	L	L	6'	175	0	0	—	0	5	3	0	18	20	13	8	0	5.00
Johnson, Connie-Clifford	53,55-56ChiA 56-58BalA	12-27-22	Stone Mountain, Ga.	11-28-04	R	R	6'4	200	40	39	.506	1	123	100	34	716	654	257	497	8	3.44
Johnson, Don-Donald Roy	47,50NYA 50-51StLA 51-52WasA 54ChiA 55BalA 56SFN	11-12-26	Portland, Ore.		R	R	6'3	200	27	28	.415	12	198	70	17	631	712	285	262	5	4.78
Johnson, Earl-Earl Douglas (Lefty)	40-41,46-50BosA 42-45MS 51DetA	04-02-19	Redmond, Wash.	12-03-94	L	L	6'3	190	40	32	.556	17	179	50	13	546	556	272	250	3	4.31
Johnson, Ernie-Ernest Thornwald	50,52BosN 53-58MilN 59BalA	06-16-24	Brattleboro, Vt.		R	R	6'3	195	40	23	.635	19	273	19	3	574	587	231	319	1	3.78
Johnson, Ken-Kenneth Wandersee (Hooks)	47-50StLN 50-51PhiN 52BosN	01-14-23	Topeka, Kans.	04-06-04	R	R	6'1	185	12	14	.462	0	74	34	8	269	251	195	147	4	4.58
Jolly, Dave-David (Gabby)	53-57MilN	10-14-24	Stony Point, N.C.	05-27-63	R	R	6'	185	16	14	.533	19	159	1	0	291	255	198	155	0	3.77
Jones, Gordon-Gordon Bassett	54-56StLN 57NYN 58-59SFN 60-61BalA 62KCA 64-65HouN	04-02-30	Portland, Ore.	04-25-94	R	R	6'	185	15	18	.455	12	171	21	4	379	405	120	232	2	4.16
Jones, Sam-Samuel (Toothpick, Sad Sam)	51-52CleA 55-56ChiN 57-58StLN 59-61SFN 62DetA 63StLN 64BalA	02-02-22	Stewartville, Ohio	11-05-71	R	R	6'4	205	102	101	.502	9	322	222	76	1644	1403	822	1376	17	3.59
Jones, Sheldon-Sheldon Leslie (Available)	46-51NYN 52BosN 53DetA	02-02-22	Tecumseh, Neb.	04-18-91	R	R	6'	180	54	57	.486	12	260	101	33	919	909	413	413	5	3.97
Jordan, Milt-Milton Mignot	53DetA	05-24-27	Mineral Sprs., Pa.	05-13-93	R	R	6'2	207	0	1	.000	0	8	1	0	17	26	5	4	0	5.82
Jordan, Niles-Niles Chapman	51PhiN 52CinN	12-01-25	Lyman, Wash.		L	L	5'11	180	4	3	.571	0	8	6	2	43	49	11	13	1	4.19
Judson, Howie-Howard Kolls	48-52ChiA 54CinN	02-16-26	Hebron, Ill.		R	R	6'1	195	17	37	.315	14	207	48	8	615	619	319	204	0	4.29
Kaiser, Don-Clyde Donald (Tiger)	55-57CinN	02-03-35	Byng, Okla.		R	R	6'5	195	6	15	.286	0	58	35	6	240	255	85	108	1	4.16
Karpel, Herb-Herbert (Lefty)	46NYA	12-27-17	Brooklyn, N.Y.	01-24-95	L	L	5'9	180	0	0	—	0	2	0	0	2	4	0	0	0	9.00
Keegan, Bob-Robert Charles (Smiley)	53-58ChiA	08-04-20	Rochester, N.Y.	06-20-01	R	R	6'2	207	40	36	.526	3	135	87	29	646	668	233	198	6	3.65
Kellner, Alex-Alexander Raymond	48-54PhiA 55-58KCA 58CinN 59StLN	08-26-24	Tuscon, Ariz.	05-03-96	R	L	6'	200	101	112	.474	5	321	250	99	1851	1925	747	816	9	4.41
Kellner, Walt-Walter Joseph	52-53PhiA	04-26-29	Tuscon, Ariz.	06-19-06	R	R	6'	180	0	0	—	0	2	0	0	6	9	4	2	0	6.43
Kelly, Bob-Robert Edward	51-53ChiN 53,58CinN 58CleA	10-04-27	Cleveland, Ohio		R	R	6'	180	12	18	.400	7	123	35	7	362	374	152	146	2	4.16
Kemmerer, Russ-Russell Paul (Rusty, Dutch)	54-55,57BosA 57-60WasA 60-62ChiA 62-63HouN	11-01-31	Pittsburgh, Pa.		R	R	6'2	198	43	59	.422	9	302	109	24	1066	1144	389	505	2	4.47
Kennedy, Bill-William Aulton (Lefty)	48CleA 48-51StLA 52ChiN 53BosA 56-57CinN	03-14-21	Carnesville, Ga.	04-09-83	L	L	6'2	200	15	28	.349	11	172	45	6	465	497	289	256	0	4.70
Kennedy, Bill-William Gorman	42WasA 43-45MS 46-47WasA	12-22-27	Alexandria, Va.	08-20-95	L	L	6'1	175	1	3	.250	0	31	4	1	64	71	44	23	0	6.75
Kennedy, Monte-Montia Calvin (Lefty)	46-53NYN	05-11-22	Amelia, Va.	03-01-97	L	L	6'2	185	42	55	.433	2	249	127	48	960	928	495	411	7	3.84
Keriazakos, Gus-Constantine Nicholas	50ChiA 54WasA 55KCA	07-28-31	West Orange, N.J.	05-04-96	R	R	6'3	187	2	5	.286	0	28	5	2	77	81	42	42	0	5.59
Kiely, Leo-Leo Patrick	51BosA 52-53MS 54-56,58-59BosA 60KCA	01-30-29	Hoboken, N.J.	01-18-84	L	L	6'	190	26	27	.491	29	209	39	4	523	562	189	212	1	3.37
Killeen, Evans-Evans Henry	59KCA	02-27-36	Brooklyn, N.Y.		R	R	6'	190	0	1	.000	0	6	0	0	6	4	4	1	0	4.50
Kinder, Ellis-Ellis Raymond (Old Folks)	46-47StLA 48-55BosA 56StLN 56-57ChiA	07-26-14	Atkins, Ark.	10-16-68	R	R	6'	195	102	71	.590	102	484	122	56	1480	1421	539	749	10	3.43
King, Clyde-Clyde Edward	44-45,47,48,51-53BknN 53CinN M69-70SFN M74-75AtlN M82NYA	05-23-24	Goldsboro, N.C.		B	R	6'1	183	32	25	.561	11	200	21	4	496	524	189	150	0	4.14
King, Nellie-Nelson Joseph	54-57PitN	03-15-28	Shenandoah, Pa.		R	R	6'6	185	7	5	.583	6	173	3	0	173	193	50	72	0	3.59
Kipp, Fred-Fred Leo	57BknN 58-59LAN 60NYA	10-01-31	Piqua, Kans.		L	L	6'4	200	6	7	.462	0	47	9	0	113	119	48	64	0	5.10
Kipper, Thornton-Thornton John	53-55PhiN	09-27-28	Bagley, Wis.		R	R	6'1	195	3	4	.429	1	55	3	0	100	128	46	35	0	5.22
Klieman, Eddie-Edward Frederick (Babe)	43-48CleA 49WasA 49ChiA 50PhiA	03-21-18	Norwood, Ohio	11-15-79	R	R	6'	190	26	28	.481	33	222	32	10	542	525	239	130	2	3.49
Klippstein, Johnny-John Calvin	50-54ChiN 55-58CinN 58-59LAN 60CleA 61WasA 62CinN 63-64PhiN 64-66MinA 67DetA	10-17-27	Washington, D.C.	10-10-03	R	R	6'1	185	101	118	.461	66	711	161	37	1970	1915	978	1158	6	4.24
Knerr, Lou-Wallace Luther	45-46PhiA 47WasA	08-21-21	Strasburg, Pa.	03-23-80	R	R	6'1	210	8	27	.229	0	73	38	11	287	330	149	104	0	5.05
Koecher, Dick-Richard Finlay (Highpockets)	46-48PhiN	03-30-26	Philadelphia, Pa.	09-28-97	R	R	6'5	196	0	4	.000	0	7	3	0	26	31	14	8	0	4.85
Konikowski, Alex-Alexander James (Whitey)	48,51NYN 52-53MS 54NYN	06-28-28	Throop, Pa.		R	R	6'	187	2	3	.400	0	35	1	0	49	58	29	20	0	6.98
Konstanty, Jim-Casimir James	44CinN 46BosN 48-54PhiN 54-56NYA 56StLN	03-02-17	Strykersville, N.Y.	06-11-76	R	R	6'2	202	66	48	.579	74	433	36	14	947	957	269	268	0	3.46
Koski, Bill-William John (T-Bone)	51PitN 52-54MS	06-02-32	Madera, Cal.		R	R	6'	190	0	2	.000	0	13	1	0	28	28	26	6	0	6.67
Koslo (Koslowski), Dave-George Bernard	41-42NYN 43-45MS 46-53NYN 54BalA 54-55MilN	03-31-20	Menasha, Wis.	12-02-75	R	R	5'11	185	92	107	.462	22	348	189	74	1592	1597	538	606	15	3.68
Kraly, Steve-Steve Charles (Lefty)	53NYA	04-18-29	Whiting, Ind.		L	L	5'10	152	0	0	—	0	8	0	0	25	19	16	8	0	3.24
Kramer, Jack-John Henry	39-41StLA 42WW 43-47StLA 48-49BosA 50-51NYN 51NYA	01-05-18	New Orleans, La.	05-18-95	R	R	6'2	190	95	103	.480	7	322	215	88	1638	1761	682	613	14	4.24

USE NAMES - GIVEN NAMES (NICKNAMES)	TEAM BY YEAR	BIRTH DATE	BIRTHPLACE	DEATH DATE	B	T	HGT	WGT	W	L	Pct.	SV	G	GS	CG	IP	H	BB	SO	ShO	ERA
Kretlow, Lou-Louis Henry	46,48-49DetA 50StLA 50-53ChiA 53StLA 54-55StLA 56KCA	06-27-21	Apache, Okla.		R	R	6'2	195	27	47	.365	1	199	104	22	786	781	522	450	3	4.87
Krieger, Kurt-Kurt Ferdinand (Dutch)	49,51StLN	09-16-26	Traisen, Austria	08-16-70	R	R	6'3	212	0	0	—	0	3	0	0	5	6	6	3	0	12.60
Kucab, Johnny-John Albert	50-52PhiA	12-17-19	Olyphant, Pa.	05-26-77	R	R	6'2	185	5	5	.500	6	59	3	2	152	169	51	48	0	4.44
Kucks, Johnny-John Charles	55-59NYA 59-60KCA	07-27-33	Hoboken, N.J.		R	R	6'3	190	54	56	.491	7	207	123	30	938	970	308	338	7	4.10
Kume, John-John Mike	05-19-26	Premier, W.Va.			R	R	6'	200	0	0	—	0	6	4	0	24	35	15	7	0	7.88
Kush, Emil-Emil Benedict	41-42ChiN 43-45MS 46-49ChiN	11-04-16	Chicago, Ill.	11-25-69	R	R	6'	185	21	12	.636	12	150	8	2	347	324	158	150	1	3.48
Kuzava, Bob-Robert LeRoy (Sarge)	46-47CleA 49-50ChiA 50-51WasA 51-54NYA 54-55BalA 55PhiN 57PitN 57StLN	05-28-23	Wyandotte, Mich.		B	L	6'2	202	49	44	.527	13	213	99	34	862	849	415	446	7	4.05
Labine, Clem-Clement Walter	50-57BknN 58-60LAN 60DetA 60-61PitN 62NYN	08-06-26	Lincoln, R.I.		R	R	6'	190	77	56	.579	96	513	38	7	1080	1043	396	551	2	3.63
Lade, Doyle-Doyle Marion (Porky)	46-50ChiN	08-15-21	Fairbury, Neb.	05-18-00					25	29	.463	3	126	64	20	537	583	221	178	2	4.39
						Bats Both 46-47															
LaMacchia, Al-Alfred Anthony	43,45-46StLA 46WasA	07-22-21	St. Louis, Mo.		R	R	5'10	190	2	2	.500	1	16	1	0	31	38	14	7	0	6.39
Lambert, Clay-Clayton Patrick	46-47CinN	03-26-17	Summit, Ill.	04-03-81	R	R	6'2	185	2	2	.500	1	26	4	2	59	60	26	21	0	5.34
Landrum, Joe-Joseph Butler	50BknN 51VR 52BknN	12-13-28	Columbia, S.C.		R	R	5'11	180	1	3	.250	1	16	5	2	45	58	11	22	0	5.60
Lane, Jerry-Jerald Hal	53WasA 54-55CinN	02-07-26	Ashland, N.Y.	07-24-88	R	R	6'	205	2	6	.250	1	31	2	0	79	84	25	33	0	4.44
Lanfranconi, Walt-Walter Oswald	41ChiN 42-45MS 47BosN	11-09-16	Barre, Vt.	08-18-86	R	R	5'7	155	4	5	.444	1	38	5	1	70	72	29	19	0	2.96
LaPalme, Paul-Paul Edmore	51-54PitN 55-56StLN 56CinN 56-57ChiA	12-14-23	Springfield, Mass.		L	L	5'10	185	24	45	.348	14	253	51	10	616	645	272	277	2	4.42
Larsen, Don-Don James	53BalA 54BalA 55-59NYA 60-61KCA 61ChiA 62-64SFN 64-65HouN 65BalA 67ChiN	08-07-29	Michigan City, Ind.		R	R	6'4	225	81	91	.471	23	412	171	44	1549	1442	725	849	11	3.78
Lary, Frank-Frank Strong (Mule, The Yankee Killer)	54-64DetA 64NYN 64MilN 65NYN 65ChiA	04-10-30	Northport, Ala.		R	R	5'11	185	128	116	.525	11	350	292	126	2162	2123	616	1099	21	3.49
Lasorda, Tommy-Thomas Charles	54-55BknN 56KCA M76-96LAN	09-22-27	Norristown, Pa.		L	L	5'10	175	0	4	.000	1	26	6	0	58	53	56	37	0	6.52
Law, Vern-Vernon Sanders (Deacon)	50-51PitN 52-53MS 54-67PitN	03-12-30	Meridian, Idaho		R	R	6'2	200	162	147	.524	13	483	364	119	2673	2833	597	1092	28	3.76
Lawrence, Brooks-Brooks Ulysses (Bull)	54-55StLN 56-60CinN	01-30-25	Springfield, Ohio	04-27-00	R	R	6'	205	69	62	.527	22	275	127	42	1041	1034	385	481	5	4.25
Lehman, Ken-Kenneth Karl	52,56-57BknN 57-58BalA 61PhiN	06-01-28	Seattle, Wash.		L	L	6'	180	14	10	.583	7	134	13	2	264	273	95	134	0	3.82
Lemon, Bob-Robert Granville (See B46-60)	46-58CleA M70-72KCA M77-78ChiA M78-79,81-82NYA	09-22-20	San Bernardino, Cal.	01-11-00	L	R	180	207	128	.618	22	460	350	188	2849	2559	1251	1277	31	3.23			
Lewandowski, Dan-Daniel William	51StLN	01-06-28	Buffalo, N.Y.	07-19-96	R	R	180	1	1	.000	0	2	0	0	1	3	1	1	0	9.00		
Liddle, Don-Donald Eugene	53MilN 54-56NYN 56StLN	05-25-25	Mt. Carmel, Ill.	06-05-00	L	L	5'10	165	28	18	.609	4	117	54	13	428	397	203	198	3	3.74
Linde, Lyman-Lyman Gilbert	47-48CleA	09-30-20	Beaver Dam, Wis.		R	R	5'11	185	0	0	—	0	4	0	0	11	12	5	0	0	6.55
Lindell, Johnny-John Harlan (See B46-60)	42NYA 45MS 53PitN 53PhiN	08-30-16	Greeley, Colo.	08-27-85	R	R	6'4	217	8	18	.308	1	55	28	15	252	247	161	146	1	4.46
Lint, Royce-Royce James	54StLN	01-01-21	Birmingham, Ala.	04-03-06	L	L	6'1	165	2	3	.400	0	30	4	1	70	75	30	36	1	4.89
LiPetri, Angelo-Michael Angelo	56,58PhiN	07-06-29	Brooklyn, N.Y.		R	R	6'1	180	0	0	—	0	10	0	0	15	13	3	9	0	5.40
Littlefield, Dick-Richard Bernard	50BosA 51ChiA 52DetA 52-53StLA 54BalA 54-56PitN 56StLN 56NYN 57ChiN 58MilN	03-18-26	Detroit, Mich.	11-20-97	L	L	6'	180	33	54	.379	4	243	83	16	761	750	413	495	2	4.72
Lively, Bud-Everett Adrian (Red)	47-49CinN	02-14-25	Birmingham, Ala.		R	R	6'	200	8	13	.381	1	79	27	6	249	230	127	94	2	4.16
Locke, Charlie-Charles Edward (Chuck)	55BalA	05-05-32	Malden, Mo.		R	R	5'11	185	0	0	—	0	2	0	0	3	1	1	0	0	0.00
Loes, Billy-William	50BknN 51MS 52-56BknN 56-59BalA 60-61SFN	12-13-29	Queens, N.Y.		R	R	6'1	180	80	63	.559	32	316	139	42	1190	1135	421	645	9	3.88
Lombardi, Vic-Victor Alvin	45-47BknN 48-50PitN	09-20-22	Reedley, Cal.	12-03-97	L	L	5'7	158	50	51	.495	16	223	100	42	945	919	418	340	5	3.68
Lombardo, Lou-Louis	48NYN	11-18-28	Carlstadt, N.J.	06-11-01	L	L	6'2	210	0	0	—	0	2	0	0	5	5	0	0	0	7.20
Lopat (Lopatynski), Ed-Edmund Walter (Steady Eddie)	44-47ChiA 48-55NYA 55BalA M63-64KCA	06-21-18	New York, N.Y.	06-15-92	L	L	5'10	185	166	112	.597	3	340	318	164	2439	2464	650	859	27	3.21
Lovenguth, Lynn-Lynn Richard	55PhiN 57StLN	11-29-22	Camden, N.Y.	09-29-00	L	R	5'10	170	0	2	.000	0	16	1	0	27	23	16	20	0	3.67
Lown, Turk-Omar Joseph	51-54,56-58ChiN 58CinN 58-62ChiA	05-30-24	Brooklyn, N.Y.		R	R	6'	185	55	61	.474	73	504	49	10	1031	978	590	574	1	4.12
Lumenti, Ralph-Ralph Anthony (Commuter)	57-59WasA	12-21-36	Milford, Mass.		L	L	6'3	185	1	3	.250	0	13	6	0	33	32	42	30	0	7.36
Luna, Memo-Guillermo Romero	54StLN	06-25-30	Mexico City, Mexico		L	L	6'	185	0	1	.000	0	1	1	0	1	2	1	0	0	18.00
Lyons, Al-Albert Harold	44NYA 45MS 46-47NYA 47PitN 48BosN	07-18-18	St. Joseph, Mo.	12-20-65	R	R	6'2	195	3	3	.500	2	39	1	0	100	125	59	46	0	6.30
Maas, Duke-Duane Frederick	55-57DetA 58KCA 58-61NYA	01-31-29	Utica, Mich.	12-07-76	R	R	5'10	170	45	44	.506	15	195	91	21	734	745	284	356	7	4.19
Mabe, Bob-Robert Lee	58StLN 59CinN 60BalA	10-08-29	Danville, Va.	01-09-05	R	R	5'11	165	7	11	.389	3	51	14	4	143	146	61	82	0	4.78
Macdonald, Bill-William Paul	50PitN 51-52MS 53PitN	03-28-29	Alameda, Cal.	05-04-91	R	R	5'11	185	8	11	.421	1	36	21	6	160	150	96	64	2	4.67
Mackinson, Johnny-John Joseph	53PhiA 55StLN	10-29-23	Orange, N.J.	10-17-89	R	R	5'10	160	0	1	.000	0	22	0	0	25	12	8	9	0	7.36
Madison, Dave-David Pledger	50NYA 51MS 52StLA 52-53DetA	02-01-21	Brooksville, Miss.	12-08-85	R	R	6'3	190	8	7	.533	2	74	6	0	158	173	103	70	0	5.70
Maglie, Sal-Salvatore Anthony (The Barber)	45NYN 46-49SM 50-55NYN 55-56CleA 56-57BknN 57-58NYA 58StLN	04-26-17	Niagara Falls, N.Y.	12-28-92	R	R	6'2	185	119	62	.657	14	303	232	93	1723	1591	562	862	25	3.15
Mahoney, Bob-Robert Paul	51ChiA 51-52StLA	06-20-28	LeRoy, Minn.	08-27-00	R	R	6'1	185	2	5	.286	0	36	4	0	91	99	50	34	0	4.95
Main, Woody-Forrest Harry	48,50,52-53PitN	02-12-22	Delano, Cal.	06-27-92	R	R	6'3	195	4	13	.235	2	79	11	2	204	210	84	107	0	5.16
Mallette, Mal-Malcolm Francis	50BknN	01-30-22	Syracuse, N.Y.	11-25-05	L	L	6'2	200	0	0	—	0	2	0	0	1	2	1	0	0	0.00
Malloy, Bob-Robert Paul	43-44CinN 45MS 46-47CinN 49StLA	05-28-18	Canonsburg, Pa.		R	R	5'11	185	4	7	.364	2	48	3	1	116	116	52	35	0	3.26
Manville, Dick-Richard Wesley	50BosN 52ChiN	12-25-26	Des Moines, Iowa		R	R	6'5	200	0	0	—	0	12	0	0	19	25	15	8	0	7.11
Marchildon, Phil-Philip Edward	40-42,45-49PhiA 43-44MS 50BosA	10-25-13	Penetanguishene, Canada	01-10-97	R	R	5'10	175	68	75	.476	2	185	162	82	1214	1084	684	481	6	3.93
Margoneri, Joe-Joseph Emanuel	56-57NYN	01-13-30	Somerset, Pa.		L	L	6'	185	7	7	.500	3	36	15	3	126	132	70	67	0	4.29
Markell (Makowsky), Duke-Harry Duquesne	51StLA	08-17-23	Paris, France	06-14-84	R	R	6'1	209	1	1	.500	0	5	2	1	21	25	20	10	0	6.43
Marlowe, Dick-Richard Burton	51-56DetA 56ChiA	06-27-29	Hickory, N.C.	12-30-68	R	R	6'2	185	13	15	.464	3	98	17	3	244	280	101	108	0	4.98
Marrero, Connie-Conrado Eugenio [Ramos]	50-54WasA	08-11-11	Sagua La Grande, Cuba		R	R	5'5	165	39	40	.494	3	118	94	51	735	736	249	297	7	3.67
Marshall, Cuddles-Clarence Westly	46,48-49NYA 50StLA	04-28-25	Ballingham, Wash.		R	R	6'3	200	7	7	.500	2	73	15	1	185	216	158	69	0	5.98
Martin, Barney-Barnes Robertson		03-03-23	Columbia, S.C.	10-30-97	R	R	5'11	170	0	0	—	0	1	0	0	2	3	1	1	0	9.00
Martin, Freddie-Fred Turner	46StLN 47-48SM 49-50StLN	06-27-15	Williams, Okla.	06-11-79	R	R	6'1	185	12	3	.800	9	57	10	5	162	181	58	68	0	3.78
Martin, Morris-Morris Webster	49BknN 51-54PhiA 54-56ChiA 56BalA 57-58StLN 58CleA 59CinN	09-03-22	Dixon, Mo.		L	L	6'	180	38	34	.528	15	250	42	8	604	607	251	245	1	3.76
Martin, Paul-Paul Charles	55PitN	03-10-32	Brownstown, Pa.		R	R	6'6	235	0	1	.000	0	7	0	0	7	13	17	3	0	14.14
Martin, Ray-Raymond Joseph	43BosN 44-46MS 47-48BosN	03-13-25	Norwood, Mass.		R	R	6'2	177	1	0	1.000	0	5	1	1	14	10	6	3	0	2.57
Martinez, Rogelio-Rogelio [Ulloa] (Limonar)	50WasA	11-05-18	Cidra, Cuba		R	R	180	0	1	.000	0	3	1	0	4	5	5	3	0	9.00		
Mason, Hank-Henry	58-60PhiN	06-19-31	Marshall, Mo.		R	R	6'	185	0	0	—	0	4	0	0	11	16	7	6	0	9.82
Masterson, Walt-Walter Edward	39-42WasA 43-44MS 45-49WasA 49-52BosA 52-53WasA 56DetA	06-22-20	Philadelphia, Pa.		R	R	6'2	189	78	100	.438	12	399	184	70	1648	1613	886	815	15	4.15
Matarazzo, Len-Leonard	52PhiA	09-12-28	New Castle, Pa.		R	R	6'4	195	0	0	—	0	1	0	0	1	1	0	0	0	0.00
Mathis, Carl-Carl Lynwood (Stubby)	60CleA 61WasA	06-13-36	Bechtelsville, Pa.		B	L	5'11	195	0	2	.000	0	11	3	0	29	36	12	20	0	7.14
Mauriello, Ralph-Ralph (Tami)	58LAN	08-25-34	Brooklyn, N.Y.		R	R	6'3	185	1	1	.500	0	12	10	0	18	18	11	12	0	4.50
Mayer, Ed-Edwin David	57-58ChiN	11-30-31	San Francisco, Cal.		L	L	6'2	185	2	2	.500	1	22	1	0	32	23	18	17	0	4.22
McAvoy, Tom-Thomas John	59WasA	08-12-36	Brooklyn, N.Y.		L	L	6'3	200	0	0	—	0	1	0	0	1	1	0	1	0	0.00
McCabe, Ralph-Ralph Herbert	46CleA	10-21-18	Napanee, Canada	05-03-74	R	R	6'4	195	0	1	.000	0	1	1	0	4	5	2	1	0	11.25
McCahan, Bill-William Glenn	46-47 played in N.B.L.	46-49PhiA	06-07-21	Philadelphia, Pa.	07-03-86	R	R	5'11	200	16	14	.533	0	57	40	17	291	297	145	76	2	3.84
McCall, Dutch-Robert Leonard	48CinN	12-15-20	Columbia, Tenn.	01-08-96	L	L	6'1	184	4	13	.235	0	30	20	5	151	158	85	89	0	4.83
McCall, Windy-John William	48-49BosA 50PitN 54-57NYN	07-18-25	San Francisco, Cal.		L	L	6'	180	11	15	.423	12	134	15	4	253	249	103	144	0	4.23
McDaniel, Von-Max Von	57-58StLN	04-18-39	Hollis, Okla.	08-29-95	R	R	6'2	180	7	5	.583	0	19	14	4	89	76	36	45	2	3.44
McDermott, Mickey-Maurice Joseph (See B46-60)	48-53BosA 54-55WasA 56NYA 57KCA 58DetA 61StLN 61KCA	08-29-28	Poughkeepsie, N.Y.	08-07-03	R	L	6'2	185	69	69	.500	14	291	156	54	1316	1161	838	757	11	3.91
McDevitt, Danny-Daniel Eugene	57BknN 58-60LAN 61NYA 61MinA 62KCA	11-18-32	New York, N.Y.		L	L	5'10	175	21	27	.438	1	155	60	13	456	461	264	303	4	4.40
McDonald, Jim-James LeRoy (Hot Rod)	50BosA 51StLA 52-54NYA 55BalA 56-58ChiA	05-17-27	Grants Pass, Ore.		R	R	5'10	192	24	27	.471	1	136	55	15	468	489	231	158	3	4.27
						Bats Both 50-51															
McGlothin, Pat-Ezra Mac	49-50BknN	10-20-20	Coalfield, Tenn.		R	R	6'	180	1	1	.500	0	8	0	0	18	18	6	13	0	5.50
McGowan, Mickey-Tullis Earl	48NYN	11-26-21	Dothan, Ala.	05-08-03	L	L	6'2	190	0	0	—	0	3	0	0	4	3	4	2	0	6.75
McIlwain, Stover-William Stover (Smokey)	57-58ChiA	09-22-39	Savannah, Ga.	01-15-66	R	R	6'4	195	0	0	—	0	2	0	0	3	1	4	1	0	1.80
McLeland, Wayne-Wayne Gaffney (Nubbin)	51-52DetA	08-29-24	Stockport, Iowa	05-09-04	R	R	185	0	1	.000	0	10	1	0	24	24	10	10	0	8.36		
McLish, Cal-Calvin Coolidge Julius Caesar Tuskahoma	44BknN 45MS 46BknN 47-48PitN 49,51ChiN 56-59CleA 60CinN 61ChiA 62-64PhiN	12-01-25	Anadarko, Okla.		R	R	6'1	200	92	92	.500	6	352	209	57	1609	1685	552	713	5	4.01
						Bats Right 44															
McMahan, Jack-Jack Wally	56PitN 56StLN	07-22-32	Hot Springs, Ark.		R	L	6'	175	2	1	.667	1	34	9	0	75	87	40	22	0	5.04
Mediinger, Irv-Irving John	49,51StLA	06-18-27	Chicago, Ill.	09-03-75	R	R	5'11	185	0	3	.000	0	14	1	0	14	21	15	9	0	13.50
Meers, Russ-Russell Harlan (Babe)	41ChiN 42-45MS 46-47ChiN	11-28-18	Tilton, Ill.	11-16-94	R	R	5'10	178	3	5	.375	0	43	6	1	83	76	48	35	0	4.01
Merritt, Lloyd-Lloyd Wesley	57StLN	04-08-33	St. Louis, Mo.		R	R	6'	190	1	2	.333	7	44	0	0	60	60	28	35	0	3.32
Meyer, Jack-John Robert	55-61PhiN	03-23-32	Philadelphia, Pa.	03-09-67	R	R	6'1	175	24	34	.414	21	202	56	7	455	385	244	375	0	3.92
Meyer, Russ-Russell Charles (The Mad Monk)	46-48ChiN 49-52PhiN 53-55BknN 56ChiN 56CinN 57BosA 59KCA	10-25-23	Peru, Ill.	11-16-97	B	R	6'1	175	94	73	.563	7	319	219	65	1531	1606	541	672	13	3.99
Mickens, Glenn-Glenn Roger	53BknN	07-26-30	Wilmer, Cal.		R	R	6'	175	0	1	.000	0	6	11	4	5	0	12.00					

USE NAMES - GIVEN NAMES (NICKNAMES)	TEAM BY YEAR	BIRTH DATE	BIRTHPLACE	DEATH DATE	B	T	HGT	WGT	W	L	Pct.	SV	G	GS	CG	IP	H	BB	SO	ShO	ERA
Miller, Bill-William Paul (Hooks)	52-54NYA 55Bal	07-26-27	Minersville, Pa.	07-01-03	L	L	5'11	180	6	9	.400	1	41	18	5	132	136	79	72	2	4.23
Miller, Bob-Robert Gerald	53-56DetA 62CinN 62NYN	07-15-35	Berwyn, Ill.		R	L	6'1	185	6	8	.429	1	86	8	1	189	206	92	75	0	4.71
Miller, Bob-Robert John	49-58PhiN	06-16-26	Detroit, Mich.		R	R	6'3	190	42	42	.500	15	261	69	23	821	889	247	263	6	3.97
Miller, Ox-John Anthony	43WasA 45,45-46StLA 47ChiN	05-04-15	Gause, Tex.		R	R	6'1	190	4	6	.400	1	24	10	4	91	123	33	27	0	6.43
Milliken, Bob-Robert Fogle (Bobo)	53-54BknN	08-25-26	Majorsville, W.Va.		R	R	6'	195	13	6	.684	4	61	13	3	181	152	60	90	0	3.58
Minarcin, Rudy-Rudolph Anthony (Buster)	55CinN 56-57BosA	03-25-30	N. Vandergrift, Pa.		R	R	6'	195	6	9	.400	3	70	13	3	171	169	89	70	1	4.63
Minner, Paul-Paul Edison (Lefty)	46,48-49BknN 50-56ChiN	07-30-23	New Wilmington, Pa.	03-28-06	L	L	6'5	200	69	84	.451	10	253	169	64	1311	1428	393	481	9	3.94
Minnick, Don-Donald Athey	57WasA	04-14-31	Lynchburg, Va.		R	R	6'3	195	0	1	.000	0	2	1	0	9	14	2	7	0	5.00
Mizell, Vinegar Bend-Wilmer David	52-53StLN 54-55MS 56-60StLN 60-62PitN 62NYN	08-13-30	Leakesville, Miss.	02-21-99	R	L	6'3	205	90	88	.506	0	268	230	61	1528	1434	680	918	15	3.85
Moford, Herb-Herbert	55StLN 58DetA59 BosA 62NYN	08-06-28	Brooksville, Ky.	12-03-05	R	R	6'1	175	5	13	.278	3	50	14	6	158	143	64	78	0	5.01
Moisan, Bill-William Joseph	53ChiN	07-30-25	Bradford, Mass.		R	R	6'1	170	0	0	—	0	3	0	0	5	5	2	1	0	5.40
Monahan, Rinty-Edward Francis	53PhiA	04-28-28	Brooklyn, N.Y.		R	R	6'	195	0	0	—	0	4	0	0	11	11	7	2	0	4.09
Monroe, Zack-Zachary Charles	58-59NYA	07-08-31	Peoria, Ill.		R	R	6'	198	4	2	.667	1	24	6	1	61	60	29	19	0	3.39
Monzant, Ray-Raymon Segundo [Espina]	54-57NYN 58SFN 59VR 60SFN	01-04-33	Maracaibo, Venez.	08-10-01	R	R	6'	160	16	21	.432	1	106	32	8	318	330	134	201	1	4.36
Moore, Ray-Raymond Leroy (Farmer)	52-53BknN 55-57BalA 58-60ChiA 60WasA 61-63MinA	06-01-26	Meadows, Md.	03-02-95	R	R	6'	200	63	59	.516	46	365	105	24	1073	935	560	612	5	4.06
Morehead, Seth-Seth Marvin (Moe)	57-59PhiN 59-60ChiN 61MilN	08-15-34	Houston, Tex.	01-17-06	L	L	6'	195	5	19	.208	5	132	24	3	318	357	110	184	0	4.81
Moreno, Julio-Julio [Gonzalez]	50-53WasA	01-28-21	Guines, Cuba	01-02-87	R	R	5'8	160	18	22	.450	2	73	45	14	336	349	157	119	0	4.26
Morgan, Tom-Thomas Stephen (Plowboy)	51-52NYA 53MS 54-56NYA 57KCA 58-60DetA 60WasA 61-63LAA	05-20-30	El Monte, Cal.	01-13-87	R	R	6'1	200	67	47	.588	64	443	61	18	1025	1040	300	364	7	3.60
Mossi, Don-Donald Louis (The Sphinx)	54-58CleA 59-63DetA 64ChiA 65KCA	01-11-29	St. Helena, Cal.		L	L	6'1	195	101	80	.558	50	460	165	55	1548	1493	385	932	8	3.43
Mossor, Earl-Earl Dalton	51BknN	07-21-25	Forbus, Tenn.	12-29-88	R	R	6'1	175	0	0	—	0	3	0	0	2	2	7	1	0	27.00
Moulder, Glen-Glen Hubert	46BknN 47StLA 48ChiA	09-28-17	Cleveland, Okla.	11-27-94	R	R	6'	180	7	8	.467	4	66	11	0	161	188	88	50	0	5.20
Mrozinski, Ron-Ronald Frank	54-55PhiN	09-16-30	White Haven, Pa.	10-19-05	R	L	5'11	160	1	3	.250	1	37	5	1	82	87	44	44	0	5.38
Mueller, Gordy-Joseph Gordon	50BosA	12-10-22	Baltimore, Md.		R	R	6'4	200	0	0	—	0	7			11	13		1	0	10.29
Muffett, Billy-Billy Arnold (Muff)	57-58StLN 59SFN 60-62BosA	09-21-30	Hammond, Ind.		R	R	6'1	198	16	23	.410	15	125	32	7	377	407	132	188	1	4.32
Muir, Joe-Joseph Allen	51-52PitN	11-26-22	Oriole, Md.	06-25-80	L	L	6'1	188	2	5	.286	0	21	6	1	52	53	25	22	0	5.19
Mulligan, Dick-Richard Charles	41WasA 42-45MS 46PhiN 46-47BosN	03-18-18	Swoyersville, Pa.	12-15-92	R	R	6'	167	3	3	.500	1	25	6	2	81	82	39	23	0	4.44
Munger, George-George David (Red)	43-44,46-52StLN 45MS 52,56PitN	10-04-18	Houston, Tex.	07-23-96	R	R	6'2	200	77	56	.579	12	273	161	54	1229	1243	500	564	13	3.83
Murff, Red-John Robert	56-57MilN	04-01-21	Burlington, Tex.		R	R	6'3	196	2	2	.500	3	26	2	0	50	56	18	31	0	4.68
Murray, Joe-Joseph Ambrose	50PhiA	11-11-20	Wilkes-Barre, Pa.	10-19-01	L	L	6'	165	0	0	—	0	8	2	0	30	34	21	8	0	5.70
Nagy, Steve-Stephen	47PitN 50WasA	05-28-19	Franklin, N.J.		R	R	5'9	174	3	8	.273	0	15	10	2	67	87	38	21	0	6.45
Naranjo, Cholly-Lazaro Ramon Gonzalo Couto	56PitN	11-25-34	Havana, Cuba		R	R	5'11	165	1	2	.333	0	17	3	2	34	37	17	26	0	4.50
Narleski, Ray-Raymond Edmond	54-58CleA 59DetA	11-25-28	Camden, N.J.		R	R	6'1	195	43	33	.566	58	266	52	17	701	606	335	454	1	3.61
Necciai, Ron-Ronald Andrew	52PitN 53MS	06-18-32	Gallatin, Pa.		R	R	6'5	185	1	6	.143	0	12	9	0	55	63	32	31	0	7.04
Negray, Ron-Ronald Alvin	52BknN 55-56PhiN 58LAN	02-26-30	Akron, Ohio		R	R	6'1	185	6	6	.500	2	66	15	2	163	170	57	81	0	4.03
Neiger, Al-Alvin Edward	60ChiN	03-26-39	Wilmington, Del.		L	L	6'	195	0	0	—	0	6	0	0	13	16	4	3	0	5.54
Nevel, Ernie-Ernie Wyre	50-51NYA 53CinN	08-17-19	Charleston, Mo.	07-10-88	R	R	5'11	180	1	1	.500	0	14	1	0	27	28	9	9	0	6.30
Newcombe, Don-Donald (Newk)	49-51BknN 52-53MS 54-57BknN 58LAN 58-60CinN 60CleA	06-14-26	Madison, N.J.		L	R	6'4	230	149	90	.623	7	344	294	136	2155	2102	490	1129	24	3.56
Newhouser, Hal-Harold (Prince Hal)	39-53DetA 54-55CleA	05-20-21	Detroit, Mich.	11-10-98	L	L	6'2	190	207	150	.580	26	488	374	212	2993	2674	1249	1796	33	3.06
Nichols, Chet-Chester Raymond Jr.	51BosN 52-53MS 54-56MilN 60-63BosA 64CinN	02-22-31	Providence, R.I.	03-27-95	B	L	6'1	180	34	36	.486	10	189	71	23	604	600	280	266	4	3.64
Nichols, Dolan-Dolan Levon (Nick)	58ChiN	02-28-30	Tishomingo, Miss.	11-20-89	R	R	6'	195	0	4	.000	1	24	0	0	41	46	16	9	0	5.05
Nixon, Willard-Willard Lee	50-58BosA	06-17-28	Taylorsville, Ga.	12-10-00	R	R	6'2	195	69	72	.489	3	225	177	51	1234	1277	530	616	9	4.39
Nuxhall, Joe-Joseph Henry	44,52-60CinN 61KCA 62LAA 62-66CinN	07-30-28	Hamilton, Ohio		R	R	6'3	215	135	117	.536	19	526	287	83	2304	2310	776	1372	20	3.90
O'Brien, Eddie-Edward Joseph (See B46-60)	56-58PitN	12-11-30	South Amboy, N.J.		R	R	5'9	165	1	0	1.000	0	5	1	1	16	16	4	11	0	3.38
O'Brien, Johnny-John Thomas (See B46-60)	56-58PitN	12-11-30	South Amboy, N.J.		R	R	5'9	171	1	3	.250	0	25	1	0	61	61	35	30	0	5.61
O'Donnell, George-George Dana	54PitN	05-27-29	Winchester, Ill.		R	R	6'3	175	3	9	.250	1	21	10	3	87	105	21	8	0	4.55
Oster, Bill-William Peter	54PhiA	01-02-33	New York, N.Y.		L	L	6'3	198	0	1	.000	0	16	1	0	16	19	12	5	0	6.19
Ostrowski, Joe-Joseph Paul (Professor)	48-50StLA 50-52NYA	05-16-19	West Wyoming, Pa.	01-03-03	R	L	5'7	170	23	25	.479	15	150	37	12	455	559	98	131	0	4.55
Overmire, Stubby-Frank W.	43-49DetA 50-51StLA 51NYA 52StLA	05-16-19	Moline, Ill.	03-03-77	R	L	5'7	170	58	67	.464	10	266	137	50	1130	1259	325	301	11	3.97
Page, Joe-Joseph Francis (Fireman)	44-50NYA 54PitN	10-28-17	Cherry Valley, Pa.	04-21-80	L	L	6'3	200	57	49	.538	76	285	45	14	790	727	421	519	3	3.53
Paige, Satchel-Leroy Robert (Satch)	48-49CleA 51-53StLA 65KCA	07-07-06	Mobile, Ala.	06-08-82	R	R	6'3	185	28	31	.475	32	179	26	7	476	429	180	288	4	3.29
Paine, Phil-Phillips Steere	51BosN 54-57MilN 58StLN	02-19-78	Cheppachet, R.I.	05-29-82	R	R	6'1	180	10	1	.909	1	95	0	0	149	144	80	101	0	3.38
Palica, Erv-Ervin Martin (Pavliecivich)	45,47-51BknN 52MS 53-54BknN 55-56BalA	02-09-28	Lomita, Cal.	05-29-82	R	R	6'1	190	41	55	.427	10	246	80	20	839	806	399	423	3	4.23
Palm, Mike-Richard Paul	48BosA	02-13-25	Boston, Mass.		R	R	6'3	190	0	0	—	0	3	0	0	3	6	5	1	0	6.00
Palmquist, Ed-Edwin Lee	60-61LAN 61MinA	06-10-33	Los Angeles, Cal.		R	R	6'3	185	1	3	.250	1	36	2	0	69	77	36	41	0	5.09
Papai, Al-Alfred Thomas	48StLN 49StLA 50BosA 50StLN 55ChiA	06-10-17	Divernon, Ill.	09-07-95	R	R	6'3	185	9	14	.391	4	88	18	8	240	281	138	70	0	5.36
Papish, Frank-Frank Richard (Pap)	45-48ChiA 49CleA 50PitN	10-21-17	Pueblo, Colo.	08-30-65	L	R	6'2	192	26	29	.473	9	149	64	18	580	541	319	255	3	3.58
Parnell, Mel-Melvin Lloyd (Dusty)	47-56BosA	06-13-22	New Orleans, La.		L	L	6'	180	123	75	.621	10	289	232	113	1752	1715	758	732	20	3.50
Pascual, Carlos-Carlos Alberto (Lus) (Big Potato)	50WasA	03-13-31	Havana, Cuba		R	R	5'7	180	1	1	.500	2	2	2	2	17	12	8	7	0	2.12
Pearce, Jim-James Madison	49-50,53WasA 54-55CinN	06-09-25	Zebulon, N.C.	07-17-05	R	R	6'6	190	3	4	.429	3	30	7	2	85	97	53	22	0	5.82
Penson, Paul-Paul Eugene	54PhiN	07-12-31	Kansas City, Kans.		R	R	6'	185	1	1	.500	0	5	3	0	16	14	14	3	0	4.50
Pepper, Laurin-Hugh McLaurin	54-57PitN	01-18-31	Vaughan, Miss.		R	R	5'11	190	2	8	.200	0	44	17	0	110	134	98	40	0	7.04
Perez, George-George Thomas	58PitN	12-29-37	San Fernando, Cal.		R	R	6'2	200	0	0	—	0	4	0	0	7	7	2	3	0	5.63
Perkovich, John-John Joseph	50ChiA	03-10-24	Chicago, Ill.	09-16-00	R	R	5'11	175	0	0	—	0	1	0	0	5	7	1	3	0	7.20
Perkowski, Harry-Harry Walter	47,49-54CinN 55ChiN	09-06-22	Dente, Va.		L	L	6'2	196	33	40	.452	5	184	76	24	698	719	324	296	4	4.37
Peterson, Kent-Kent Franklin	44CinN 45-46MS 47-51CinN 52-53PhiN	12-21-25	Goshen, Utah	04-27-95	R	L	5'10	170	13	38	.255	5	147	43	7	420	434	215	208	1	4.95
Pettit, Paul-George William Paul (Lefty)	51,53PitN	11-29-31	Los Angeles, Cal.		L	L	6'2	195	1	2	.333	0	12	5	0	31	35	21	14	0	7.26
Phillips, Taylor-William Taylor (Tay)	56-57MilN 58-59CinN 59-60PhiN 63ChiA	06-18-33	Atlanta, Ga.		L	L	5'11	185	16	22	.421	6	147	45	9	439	460	211	233	1	4.82
Picone, Mario-Mario Peter (Babe)	47,52,54NYN 54CinN	07-05-26	Brooklyn, N.Y.		R	R	5'11	180	0	2	.000	0	13	3	0	40	43	25	11	0	6.30
Pierce, Billy-Walter William	45,48DetA 49-61ChiA 62-64SFN	04-02-27	Detroit, Mich.		L	L	5'10	170	211	169	.555	32	585	432	193	3305	2989	1178	1999	38	3.27
Pieretti, Marino-Marino Paul (Chick)	45-48WasA 48-49ChiA 50CleA	09-23-20	Lucca, Italy	01-30-81	R	R	5'7	153	30	38	.441	8	194	68	21	673	713	321	188	4	4.53
Pierro, Bill-William Leonard (Wild Bill)	50PitN	04-15-26	Brooklyn, N.Y.	04-01-06	R	R	6'1	155	0	2	.000	0	12	3	0	29	33	28	13	0	10.55
Piktuzis, George-George Richard	56ChiN	01-03-32	Chicago, Ill.	11-28-93	R	L	6'2	200	0	0	—	0	2	0	0	5	6	2	1	0	7.20
Pillette, Duane-Duane Xavier (Dee)	49-50NYA 50-53StLA 54-55BalA 56PhiN	07-24-22	Detroit, Mich.	08-15-65	R	R	6'3	195	38	66	.365	2	188	119	34	904	985	391	305	4	4.40
Pitula, Stan-Stanley	57CleA	03-23-31	Hackensack, N.J.		R	R	5'10	195	2	2	.500	2	23	5	1	60	67	32	17	0	4.95
Poat, Ray-Raymond Willis	42-44CleA 45VR 47-49NYN 49PitN	12-19-17	Chicago, Ill.	04-29-90	R	R	6'2	200	22	30	.423	1	116	47	15	400	425	162	178	4	4.55
Podbielan, Bud-Clarence Anthony	49-52BknN 52-55,57CinN 59CleA	03-26-24	Curlew, Wash.	10-26-82	R	R	6'1	190	25	42	.373	3	172	76	20	641	693	245	242	2	4.49
Podres, Johnny-John Joseph	53-55BknN 56MS 57BknN 58-66LAN 66-67DetA 69SDN	09-30-32	Witherbee, N.Y.		L	L	5'11	180	148	116	.561	11	440	340	77	2265	2239	743	1435	24	3.67
Poholsky, Tom-Thomas George	50-51StLN 52-53MS 54-55StLN 57ChiN	08-26-29	Detroit, Mich.	01-16-01	R	R	6'3	205	31	52	.373	1	159	104	30	754	791	192	316	5	3.93
Polivka, Ken-Kenneth Lyle	47CinN	01-21-21	Chicago, Ill.	07-23-88	L	L	6'1	175	0	0	—	0	3	0	0	3	3	1	0	0	3.00
Pollet, Howie-Howard Joseph	41-43StLN 44-45MS 46-51StLN 51-53PitN 53-55ChiN 56ChiA 56PitN	06-26-21	New Orleans, La.	08-08-74	L	L	6'1	175	131	116	.530	20	403	278	116	2106	2096	745	934	20	3.51
Porterfield, Bob-Erwin Coolidge	48-51NYA 51-55WasA 56-58BosA 58-59PhiN 59ChiN 59PitN	08-10-23	Newport, Va.	04-28-80	R	R	6'	190	87	97	.473	9	318	193	92	1568	1571	552	572	23	3.79
Porto, Al-Alfred (Lefty)	48PhiN	06-27-26	Heilwood, Pa.		L	L	5'11	176	0	0	—	0	2	0	0	4	2	1	1	0	0.00
Portocarrero, Arnie-Arnold Mario	54PhiA 55-57KCA 58-60BalA 60PhiN	07-05-31	New York, N.Y.	06-21-86	R	R	6'3	200	38	57	.400	2	166	117	33	818	778	320	338	5	4.31
Possehl, Lou-Louis Thomas	46-48,51-52PhiN	04-12-26	Chicago, Ill.	10-07-97	R	R	6'2	185	2	5	.286	0				52	62	24	22	0	5.13
Prendergast, Jim-James Bartholomew	48BknN	08-23-17	Brooklyn, N.Y.	08-23-94	L	L	6'1	208	1	1	.500	0	10	2	0	17	30	15	6	0	10.06
Prasko, Joe-Joseph Edward (Little Joe)	51-54StLN 57-58DetA	10-07-28	Kansas City, Mo.		R	R	5'9	165	25	37	.403	5	128	61	15	492	511	188	202	4	4.59
Proctor, Jim-James Arthur	59DetA	09-09-35	Brandywine, Md.		R	R	6'	165	0	1	.000	0	2	1	0	3	8	3	0	0	15.00
Purkey, Bob-Robert Thomas	54-57PitN 58-64CinN 65StLN 66PitN	07-14-29	Pittsburgh, Pa.		R	R	6'	190	129	115	.529	9	386	276	92	2115	2170	510	793	13	3.79
Pyecha, John-John Nicholas	54ChiN	11-25-31	Aliquippa, Pa.		R	R	6'5	200	0	0	—	0	1	0	0	2	2	1	0	0	9.00
Qualters, Tom-Thomas Francis (Money Bags)	53PhiN 54DP 57-58PhiN 58ChiA	04-01-35	McKeesport, Pa.		R	R	6'	190	0	0	—	0	34	1	0	62	63	26	20	0	5.71
Queen, Mel-Melvin Joseph	42,44NYA 45MS 46-47NYA 47-52PitN	03-04-18	Maxwell, Pa.	04-04-82	R	R	6'	204	27	40	.403	1	146	77	15	556	567	329	328	3	5.10

USE NAMES - GIVEN NAMES (NICKNAMES) / TEAM BY YEAR	BIRTH DATE	BIRTHPLACE	DEATH DATE	B	T	HGT	WGT	W	L	Pct.	SV	G	GS	CG	IP	H	BB	SO	ShO	ERA
Quinn, Frank-Frank William 49-50BosA	11-27-27	Springfield, Mass.	01-11-93	R	R	6'2	180	0	0	—	0	9	0	0	24	20	10	4	0	3.38
Rabe, Charlie-Charles Henry 57-58CinN	05-06-32	Boyce, Tex.		L	L	6'1	180	0	4	.000	0	11	2	0	27	30	9	16	0	3.67
Raether, Hal-Harold Herman (Bud) 54PhiA 57KCA	10-10-32	Lake Mills, Wis.		R	R	6'1	185	0	0	—	0	2	0	0	4	3	4	0	0	6.75
Raffensberger, Ken-Kenneth David 39StLN 40-41ChiN 43-47PhiN 47-54CinN	08-08-17	York, Pa.	11-10-02	R	L	6'2	195	119	154	.436	16	396	282	133	2152	2257	449	806	31	3.60
Ramsdell, Willie-James Willard (Willie the Knuck) 47-48,50BknN 50-51CinN 52ChiN	04-04-16	Williamsburg, Kans.	10-08-69	R	R	5'11	165	24	39	.381	5	111	58	18	480	455	215	240	2	3.83
Raney (Raniszewski), Ribs-Frank Robert Donald 49-50StLA	02-26-23	Detroit, Mich.	07-07-03	R	R	6'4	190	1	3	.250	0	4	3	1	18	25	14	7	0	7.50
Raschi, Vic-Victor John Angelo (The Springfield Rifle) 46-53NYA 54-55StLN 55KCA	03-28-19	W. Springfield, Mass.	10-14-88	R	R	6'1	205	132	66	.667	3	269	255	106	1820	1666	727	944	26	3.72
Raydon, Curt-Curtis Lowell 58PitN	11-18-33	Bloomington, Ill.		R	R	6'4	190	8	4	.667	1	31	20	2	134	118	61	85	1	3.63
Reeder, Bill-William Edgar 49CinN	02-20-22	Dike, Tex.	03-12-01	R	R	6'5	205	1	1	.500	0	21	1	0	34	33	30	21	0	5.03
Reid, Earl-Earl Percy 46BosN	06-08-13	Bangor, Ala.	05-11-84	L	R	6'3	190	1	0	1.000	0	2	0	0	3	4	3	2	0	3.00
Renfroe, Marshall-Marshall Daniel 59SFN	05-25-36	Century, Fla.	12-10-70	L	L	6'	185	0	0	—	0	1	1	0	2	3	3	3	0	27.00
Reynolds, Allie-Allie Pierce (Superchief) 42-46CleA 47-54NYA	02-10-15	Bethany, Okla.	12-26-94	R	R	6'	195	182	107	.630	49	434	309	137	2492	2193	1261	1423	36	3.30
Richards, Duane-Duane Lee 60CinN	12-16-36	Spartanburg, Ind.		R	R	6'3	200	0	0	—	0	2	0	0	3	5	2	2	0	9.00
Ricketts, Dick-Richard James 55-58 played in N.B.A. 59StLN	12-04-33	Pottstown, Pa.	03-06-88	L	R	6'7	215	1	6	.143	0	12	9	0	56	68	30	25	0	5.79
Ridzik, Steve-Stephen George 50,52-55PhiN 55CinN 56-57NYN 58CleA 63-65WasA 66PhiN	04-29-29	Yonkers, N.Y.		R	R	5'11	170	39	38	.506	11	314	48	4	784	709	351	406	1	3.79
Roberts, Robin-Robin Evan 48-61PhiN 62-65BalA 65-66HouN 66ChiN	09-30-26	Springfield, Ill.		B	R	6'	190	286	245	.539	25	676	609	305	4689	4582	902	2357	45	3.41
Robinson, Humberto-Humberto Valentino 55-56,58MilN 59CleA 59-60PhiN	06-25-30	Colon, Panama		R	R	6'1	155	8	13	.381	4	102	7	2	214	189	90	114	0	3.24
Robinson, Jack-Jon Edward 49BosN	02-20-21	Orange, Mass.	03-02-00	R	R	6'	175	0	0	—	0	3	0	0	4	4	1	1	0	2.25
Rodriquez, Freddy-Fernando Pedro [Borrego] 58ChiN 59PhiN	04-29-28	Havana, Cuba		R	R	6'	180	0	0	—	0	5	0	0	5	5	6	0	0	9.00
Roe, Preacher-Elwin Charles 38StLN 44-47PitN 48-54BknN	02-26-15	Ash Flat, Ark.		R	L	6'2	170	127	84	.602	10	333	261	101	1916	1907	504	956	17	3.43
Roebuck, Ed-Edward Jack 55-57BknN 58,60-63LAN 63-64WasA 64-66PhiN	07-03-31	E. Millsboro, Pa.		R	R	6'2	185	52	31	.627	62	460	1	0	790	753	302	477	0	3.35
Rogovin, Saul-Saul Walter 49-51DetA 51-53ChiA 55BalA 55-57PhiN	03-24-22	Brooklyn, N.Y.	01-23-95	R	R	6'2	205	48	48	.500	2	150	121	43	885	888	308	388	9	4.06
Romano, Jim-James King 50BknN	04-06-27	Brooklyn, N.Y.	09-12-90	R	R	6'4	190	0	0	—	0	3	1	0	6	8	2	8	0	6.00
Romberger, Dutch-Allen Isaiah 54PhiA	05-26-27	Klingerstown, Pa.	05-26-83	R	R	6'	185	1	1	.500	0	10	0	0	16	28	12	6	0	11.25
Romonosky, John-John 53StLN 58-59WasA	07-07-29	Harrisburg, Ill.		R	R	6'2	195	3	4	.429	0	32	9	1	101	97	51	63	0	5.17
Ross, Bob-Floyd Robert 50-51WasA 52-53MS 56PhiN	11-02-28	Fullerton, Cal.		R	L	6'	165	0	2	.000	0	20	3	0	48	55	38	29	0	7.13
Ross, Cliff-Clifford Davis 54CinN	08-03-28	Philadelphia, Pa.	04-13-99	L	L	6'4	195	0	0	—	1	3	0	0	3	0	0	1	0	0.00
Rotblatt, Marv-Marvin 48,50-51ChiA	10-18-27	Chicago,Ill.		B	L	5'7	160	4	3	.571	2	35	4	0	75	74	51	30	0	4.80
Roy, Jean Pierre-Jean Pierre 46BknN	06-26-20	Montreal, Canada		B	R	5'10	160	0	0	—	0	3	0	0	6	5	5	6	0	10.50
Roy, Norm-Norman Brooks (Jumbo) 50BosN	11-15-28	Newton, Mass.		R	R	6'	200	4	3	.571	1	19	6	2	60	72	39	25	0	5.10
Rozek, Dick-Richard Louis 50-52CleA 53-54PhiA	03-27-27	Clear Rapids, Iowa	09-27-01	L	L	6'	190	1	0	1.000	0	33	4	0	65	65	55	26	0	4.57
Rush, Bob-Robert Ransom 48-57ChiN 58-60MilN 60ChiA	12-21-25	Battle Creek, Mich.		R	R	6'4	205	127	152	.455	8	417	321	118	2409	2327	789	1244	16	3.65
Rutherford, Johnny-John William (Doc) 52BknN	05-05-25	Belleville, Canada		L	R	5'10	170	7	7	.500	2	22	11	4	97	97	29	29	0	4.25
Sain, Johnny-John Franklin 42,46-51BosN 51-55NYA 55KCA	09-25-17	Havana, Ark.		R	R	6'2	200	139	116	.545	51	412	245	140	2125	2145	619	910	16	3.49
Sanchez, Raul-Raul Guadelupe [Rodriguez] 52WasA 57,60CinN	12-20-30	Marianao, Cuba		R	R	6'	150	5	3	.625	5	49	2	1	90	86	43	48	1	4.60
Sanford, Fred-John Frederick 43StLA 44-45MS 46-48StLA 49-51NYA 51WasA 51StLA	08-09-19	Garfield, Utah		B	R	6'	200	37	55	.402	6	164	98	26	744	768	391	285	3	4.45
Santiago, Jose-Jose Guillermo [Guzman] (Pants) 54-55CinN 56KCA	09-04-28	Coamo, P.R.		R	R	5'10	175	3	2	.600	0	27	5	0	57	57	33	29	0	4.58
Savage, Bob-John Robert 42PhiA 43-45MS 46-48PhiA 49StLA	12-01-21	Manchester, N.H.		R	R	6'2	180	16	27	.372	9	129	31	10	423	433	215	171	2	4.32
Savransky, Moe-Morris 54CinN	01-13-29	Cleveland, Ohio		L	L	5'11	175	0	0	—	0	16	0	0	24	23	8	7	0	4.88
Scantlebury, Pat-Patricio Athelstan 56CinN	11-11-17	Gatun, Canal Zone	05-24-91	L	L	6'	180	0	1	.000	0	6	2	0	19	24	5	10	0	6.63
Scarborough, Ray (Rae)-Ray Wilson 42-43WasA 44-45MS 46-50WasA 50ChiA 51-52BosA 52NYA 53DetA	07-23-17	Mt. Gilead, N.C.	07-01-82	R	R	6'	185	80	85	.485	12	318	168	59	1429	1487	611	564	9	4.13
Schacht, Sid-Sidney 50-51StLA 51BosN	02-03-18	Bogota, N.J.	03-30-91	R	R	5'11	170	0	2	.000	1	19	1	0	22	44	21	12	0	13.91
Schaeffer, Harry-Harry Edward (Lefty) 52NYA	06-23-24	Reading, Pa.		L	L	6'2	185	0	1	.000	0	5	2	0	17	18	18	15	0	5.29
Schaffernoth, Joe-Joseph Arthur 59-61ChiN 61CleA	08-06-37	Trenton, N.J.		R	R	6'4	195	3	8	.273	3	74	1	0	118	116	53	68	0	4.58
Schallock, Art-Arthur Lawrence 51-55NYA 55BalA	04-25-24	Mill Valley, Cal.		L	L	5'9	160	6	7	.462	1	58	14	3	169	199	91	77	0	4.05
Scheib, Carl-Carl Alvin 43-45PhiA 46MS 47-54PhiA 54StLN	01-01-27	Gratz, Pa.		R	R	6'1	204	45	65	.409	17	267	107	47	1072	1130	493	290	6	4.88
Schmidt, Willard-Willard Raymond 52-53,55-57StLN 58-59CinN	05-29-28	Hays, Kans.		R	R	6'1	187	31	29	.517	2	194	55	11	588	563	278	323	1	3.92
Schmitz, Johnny-John Albert (Bear Tracks) 41-42ChiN 43-45MS 46-51ChiN 51-52BknN 52NYA 52CinN 53NYA 53-55WasA 56BosA 56BalA	11-27-20	Wausau, Wis.		R	L	6'	170	93	114	.449	21	366	235	86	1813	1766	757	746	16	3.54
Schroll, Al-Albert Bringhurst 58BosA 59PhiN 59BosA 60ChiN 61MinN	03-22-33	New Orleans, La.	11-30-99	R	R	6'2	210	6	9	.400	0	35	13	3	118	121	64	63	0	5.34
Schultz, Bob-Robert Duffy 51-53ChiN 53PitN 55DetA	11-27-23	Louisville, Ky.	03-31-79	R	L	6'3	205	9	13	.409	4	65	19	3	182	179	125	67	0	5.19
Schultz, Mike-William Michael 47CinN	12-17-20	Syracuse, N.Y.	08-02-04	L	L	6'1	175	0	0	—	0	1	0	0	2	4	2	0	0	4.50
Schwamb, Blackie-Ralph Richard 48StLA	08-06-26	Los Angeles, Cal.	12-21-89	R	R	6'5	198	1	1	.500	0	12	5	0	32	44	21	7	0	8.44
Score, Herb-Herbert Jude 55-59CleA 60-62PhiN	06-07-33	Rosedale, N.Y.		L	L	6'2	185	55	46	.545	3	150	127	47	858	609	573	837	11	3.36
Semproch, Ray-Roman Anthony (Baby) 58-59PhiN 60DetA 61LAN	01-07-31	Cleveland, Ohio		R	R	5'11	180	19	21	.475	2	85	48	14	344	360	136	156	2	4.42
Sexauer, Elmer-Elmer George 48BknN	05-21-26	St. Louis Co., Mo.		R	R	6'4	220	0	0	—	0	2	0	0	4	6	3	3	0	9.00
Shantz, Bobby-Robert Clayton 49-54PhiA 55-56KCA 57-60NYA 61PitN 62HouN 62-64StLN 64ChiN 64PhiN	09-26-25	Pottstown, Pa.		R	L	5'6	139	119	99	.546	48	537	171	78	1936	1795	643	1072	15	3.38
Shea (O'Shea), Spec-Frank Joseph (The Naugatuck Nugget) 47-49,51NYA 52-55WasA	10-02-20	Naugatuck, Conn.	07-19-02	R	R	6'	200	56	46	.549	1	195	118	48	944	849	497	361	12	3.79
Shipley, Joe-Joseph Clark (Moses) 58-60SFN 63ChiA	05-09-35	Morristown, Tenn.		R	R	6'4	210	0	1	.000	0	29	1	0	44	48	35	23	0	5.93
Shore, Ray-Raymond Everett 46,48-49StLA	06-09-21	Cincinnati, Ohio	08-13-96	R	R	6'3	210	1	3	.250	0	31	4	0	62	70	67	26	0	8.27
Sima, Al-Albert 50-51,53WasA 54CinN 54PhiN	10-07-21	Mahwah, N.J.	08-17-93	R	R	6'2	190	11	21	.344	4	100	30	4	308	343	132	111	0	4.62
Simmons, Curt-Curtis Thomas 47-50PhiN 51MS 52-60PhiN 60-66StLN 66-67ChiN 67CalA	05-19-29	Egypt, Pa.		L	L	5'11	190	193	183	.513	5	569	462	163	3349	3313	1063	1697	36	3.54
Simpson, Duke-Thomas Leo 53ChiN	09-15-27	Columbus, Ohio		R	R	6'1	190	1	2	.333	0	30	1	0	45	60	25	21	0	8.00
Singleton, Elmer-Bert Elmer (Smoky) 45-46BosN 47-48PitN 50WasA 57-59ChiN	06-26-18	Ogden, Utah	01-05-96	R	R	6'2	174	11	17	.393	4	145	19	2	327	322	146	160	0	4.84
Sisler, Dave-David Michael 56-59BosA 59-60DetA 61WasA 62CinN	10-16-31	St. Louis, Mo.		R	R	6'4	200	38	44	.463	29	247	59	12	655	622	368	355	1	4.34
Skaugstad, Dave-David Wendell 57CinN	11-10-40	Algona, Iowa		L	L	6'1	180	0	0	—	0	2	0	0	6	4	6	4	0	1.50
Sleater, Lou-Louis Mortimer 50-52StLA 52WasA 55MilN 57-58DetA 58BalA	09-08-26	St. Louis, Mo.		L	L	5'10	185	12	18	.400	5	131	21	7	301	306	172	152	1	4.69
Sloat, Dwain-Dwain Clifford (Lefty) 48BknN 49CinN	12-01-18	Nokomis, Ill.	04-18-03	R	L	6'	168	0	1	.000	0	9	2	0	16	21	11	4	0	6.75
Smith, Bob-Robert Gilchrist 55BosA 57StLN 57-59PitN 59BosN	02-01-31	Woodsville, N.H.		L	L	6'1	190	4	9	.308	2	91	8	2	167	174	83	93	0	4.04
Smith, Frank-Frank Thomas 50-54CinN 55StLN 56CinN	04-04-28	Pierrepont Mr., N.Y.	09-24-05	R	R	6'3	190	35	33	.515	44	271	7	1	496	426	181	277	0	3.81
Smith, Riverboat-Robert Walkup 58BosA 59ChiN 59CleA	05-13-28	Clarence, Mo.	07-23-03	L	L	6'	185	4	4	.500	2	30	10	1	97	97	59	60	0	4.73
Snyder, Gene-Gene Walter 59LAN	03-31-31	York, Pa.	06-02-96	R	L	5'11	175	1	1	.500	0	11	2	0	26	32	20	20	0	5.54
Solis, Marcelino-Marcelino 58ChiN	07-19-30	Real de Catorce, Mex.	06-15-01	L	L	6'1	183	3	3	.500	0	15	4	0	52	74	20	15	0	6.06
Spahn, Warren-Warren Edward 42BosN 43-45MS 46-52BosN 53-64MilN 65NYN 65SFN	04-23-21	Buffalo, N.Y.	11-24-03	L	L	6'	175	363	245	.597	29	750	665	382	5244	4830	1434	2583	63	3.08
Spencer, George-George Elwell 50-55NYN 58,60DetA	07-07-26	Columbus, Ohio		R	R	6'1	215	16	10	.615	9	122	9	3	251	228	106	82	0	4.05
Spicer, Bob-Robert Oberton 55-56KCA	04-11-25	Richmond, Va.		R	R	5'10	173	0	0	—	0	5	0	0	5	15	5	2	0	27.00
Spooner, Karl-Karl Benjamin 54-55BknN	06-23-31	Oriskany Falls, N.Y.	04-10-84	R	L	6'	185	10	6	.625	2	31	16	4	117	86	47	105	3	3.08
Spragins, Homer-Homer Franklin 47PhiN	11-09-20	Grenada, Miss.	12-10-02	R	R	6'	190	0	0	—	0	4	0	0	5	3	3	3	0	7.20
Staley, Garry-Gerald Lee 47-54StLN 55CinN 55-56NYA 56-61ChiA 61KCA 61DetA	08-21-20	Brush Prairie, Wash.		R	R	6'	195	134	111	.547	61	640	186	58	1981	2070	529	727	9	3.70
Stanceau, Charley-Charles 41NYA 42-45MS 46NYA 46PhiN	01-09-16	Canton, Ohio	04-03-69	R	R	6'2	190	5	7	.417	0	39	13	1	122	135	79	47	0	4.94
Stanka, Joe-Joseph Donald 59ChiA	07-23-31	Hammon, Okla.		R	R	6'5	201	1	0	1.000	0	2	0	0	5	2	4	3	0	3.60
Starr, Dick-Richard Eugene 47-48NYA 49-51StLA 51WasA	03-02-21	Kittanning, Pa.		R	R	6'3	190	12	24	.333	2	93	45	7	344	390	198	120	2	5.26
Stephens, Bryan-Bryan Maris 47CleA 48StLA	07-14-20	Fayetteville, Ark.		R	R	6'4	190	8	16	.333	4	74	17	3	215	220	106	69	1	5.15
Stewart, Bunky-Veston Goff 52-56WasA	01-07-31	Jasper, N.C.		L	L	6'	154	5	11	.313	1	72	14	2	187	215	127	77	0	6.02
Stobbs, Chuck-Chuck Klein 47-51BosA 52ChiA 53-58WasA 58StLN 59-60WasA 61MinA	07-02-29	Wheeling, W.Va.		L	L	6'1	192	107	130	.451	19	459	238	65	1920	2003	753	897	7	4.29
Stone, Dean-Darrah Dean 53-57WasA 57BosA 59StLN 62HouN 62ChiA 63BalA	09-01-30	Moline, Ill.		L	L	6'4	195	29	39	.426	12	215	85	19	687	705	373	380	5	4.47
Stowe, Hal-Harold Rudolph (Rudy) 60NYA	08-29-37	Gastonia, N.C.		L	L	6'	170	0	0	—	0	1	0	0	1	1	1	0	0	9.00
Strahs, Dick-Richard Bernard 54ChiA	12-04-23	Evanston, Ill.	05-26-83	R	R	6'	192	0	0	—	0	6	0	0	14	16	8	6	0	5.79
Striker, Jake-Wilbur Scott 59CleA 60ChiA	10-23-33	New Washington, Ohio		L	L	6'2	200	1	0	1.000	0	3	1	1	11	13	5	6	0	3.27

USE NAMES - GIVEN NAMES (NICKNAMES)	TEAM BY YEAR	BIRTH DATE	BIRTHPLACE	DEATH DATE	B	T	HGT	WGT	W	L	Pct.	SV	G	GS	CG	IP	H	BB	SO	ShO	ERA
Stuart, Marlin-Marlin Henry	49-52DetA 52-53StLA 54BalA 54NYA	08-08-18	Paragould, Ark.	06-16-94	L	R	6'2	185	23	17	.575	15	196	31	7	486	544	256	185	0	4.65
Stuffel, Paul-Paul Herrington (Stu)	50,52-53PhiN	03-22-27	Canton, Ohio		R	R	6'2	185	0	1	1.000	0	7	1	0	11	9	12	6	0	5.73
Stump, Jim-James Gilbert	57,59DetA	02-10-32	Lansing, Mich.		R	R	6'	188	1	0	1.000	0	11	0	0	24	23	12	8	0	2.25
Sturdivant, Tom-Thomas Virgil (Snake)	55-59NYA 59KCA 60BosA 61WasA 61-63PitN 63DetA 63-64KCA 64NYN	04-28-30	Gordon, Kans.		L	R	6'	59	51	.536	17	335	101	22	1136	1029	449	704	7	3.75
Suchecki, Jim-James Joseph	50BosA 51StLA 52PitN	02-17-23	Chicago, Ill.	07-20-00	R	R	6'	200	0	6	.000	0	38	6	0	104	130	50	56	0	5.37
Sullivan, Frank-Franklin Leal	53-60BosA 61-62PhiN 62-63MinA	01-23-30	Hollywood, Cal.		R	R	6'7	225	97	100	.492	18	351	219	73	1732	1702	559	959	15	3.60
Sundin, Gordie-Gordon Vincent	56BalA	10-10-37	Minneapolis, Minn.		R	R	6'4	215	0	0	—	0	1	0	0	2	0	0	0	0	∞
Surkont, Max-Matthew Constantine	49ChiA 50-52BosN 53MilN 54-56PitN 56StLN 56-57NYN	06-16-22	Central Falls, R.I.	10-08-86	R	R	6'1	210	61	76	.445	8	236	149	53	1194	1209	481	571	7	4.38
Susce, George-George Daniel	55-58BosA 58-59DetA	09-13-31	Pittsburgh, Pa.		R	R	6'1	180	22	17	.564	3	117	36	8	410	407	170	177	1	4.41
Sutherland, Dizzy-Howard Alvin	49WasA	04-09-22	Washington, D.C.	08-26-79	L	L	6'	200	0	1	.000	0	1	1	0	1	2	6	0	0	45.00
Swanson, Red-Arthur Leonard	55-57PitN	10-15-36	Baton Rouge, La.		R	R	6'1	175	3	3	.500	2	42	8	1	87	91	42	34	0	4.86
Swartz, Bud-Sherwin Merle	47StLA	06-13-29	Tulsa, Okla.	06-24-91	L	L	6'2	180	0	0	—	0	5	0	0	5	9	7	1	0	7.20
Tate, Al-Alvin Walter	46PitN	07-01-18	Coleman, Okla.	05-08-93	R	R	6'	180	0	1	.000	0	2	1	1	9	8	7	2	0	5.00
Taylor, Harry-Harry Evans	57KCA	12-02-35	San Angelo, Tex.		R	R	6'	185	0	0	—	0	2	0	0	9	11	4	4	0	3.00
Taylor, Harry-James Harry	46-48BknN 50-52BosA	05-20-19	East Glenn, Ind.	11-05-00	R	R	6'1	190	19	21	.475	4	90	44	16	358	344	201	127	3	4.10
Taylor, Pete-Vernon Charles	52StLA	11-26-27	Severn, Md.	11-17-03	R	R	6'1	170	0	0	—	0	1	0	0	2	4	3	0	0	13.50
Templeton, Chuck-Charles Sherman	55-56BknN	06-01-32	Detroit, Mich.	10-09-97	R	L	6'3	210	0	2	.000	0	10	2	0	21	25	15	11	0	7.71
Thiel, Bert-Maynard Bert	52BosN	05-04-26	Marion, Wis.		R	R	5'10	185	1	1	.500	0	4	0	0	7	11	4	6	0	7.71
Thies, Jake-Vernon Arthur	54-55PitN	04-01-26	St. Louis, Mo.		R	R	5'11	170	3	10	.231	0	34	19	3	134	125	52	57	1	3.90
Thomas, Carl-Carl Leslie	60CleA	05-28-32	Minneapolis, Minn.		R	R	6'5	245	1	0	1.000	0	4	0	0	10	8	10	5	0	7.20
Thompson, Forrest-David Forrest	48-49WasA	03-03-18	Mooresville, N.C.	02-26-79	L	L	5'11	195	7	13	.350	4	55	14	1	147	156	63	48	0	3.92
Thompson, Jocko-John Samuel	48-51PhiN	01-17-17	Beverly, Mass.	02-03-88	L	L	6'	185	6	11	.353	1	41	21	5	167	151	83	81	2	4.26
Thorpe, Bob-Robert Joseph	55ChiN	01-12-35	San Diego, Cal.	03-17-60	R	R	6'1	170	0	0	—	0	2	0	0	3	4	0	0	0	3.00
Toenes, Hal-William Harrel	47WasA	10-08-17	Mobile, Ala.	06-28-04	R	R	5'11	175	0	1	.000	0	7	1	0	11	11	2	5	0	6.43
Tomanek, Dick-Richard Carl (Bones)	53-54,57-58CleA 58-59KCA	01-06-31	Avon Lake, Ohio		L	L	6'1	175	10	10	.500	7	106	11	4	231	231	112	166	0	4.95
Tomasic, Andy-Andrew John 42,46 played in N.F.L.	49NYN	12-10-19	Hokendauqua, Pa.		R	R	6'	175	0	1	.000	0	5	0	0	9	5	2	1	0	18.00
Tremel, Bill-William Leonard (Mumbles)	54-56CinN	07-04-29	Lilly, Pa.		R	R	5'11	180	4	2	.667	6	57	0	0	91	81	46	34	0	4.05
Trice, Bob-Robert Lee	53-54PhiA 55KCA	08-28-26	Newton, Ga.	09-16-88	R	R	6'3	190	9	9	.500	0	26	21	9	152	185	60	28	1	5.80
Trimble, Joe-Joseph Gerard	55BosA 57PitN	10-12-30	Providence, R.I.		R	R	6'1	190	0	2	.000	0	7	4	0	22	23	16	10	0	7.36
Trinkle, Ken-Kenneth Wayne	43NYN 44-45MS 46-48NYN 49PhiN	12-15-19	Paoli, Ind.	05-10-76	R	R	6'1	175	21	29	.420	21	216	19	3	436	442	208	130	0	3.74
Trosky (Trojovsky), Hal-Harold Arthur Jr. (Hoot)	58ChiA	09-29-36	Cleveland, Ohio		R	R	6'3	205	0	0	—	0	3	0	0	3	5	2	1	0	6.00
Trowbridge, Bob-Robert	56-59MilN 60KCA	06-27-30	Hudson, N.Y.	04-03-80	R	R	6'1	195	13	13	.500	5	116	25	4	330	324	156	201	1	3.95
Trucks, Virgil-Virgil Oliver (Fire)	41-43DetA 44MS 45-52DetA 53StLA 53-55ChiA 56DetA 57-58KCA 58NYA	04-26-17	Birmingham, Ala.		R	R	5'11	205	177	135	.567	30	517	328	124	2684	2416	1088	1534	33	3.38
Turley, Bob-Robert Lee (Bullet Bob)	51,53StLA 54BalA 55-62NYA 63LAA 63BosA	09-19-30	Troy, Ill.		R	R	6'2	215	101	85	.543	12	310	237	78	1711	1366	1068	1265	24	3.65
Upton, Bill-William Ray	54PhiA	06-18-29	Esther, Mo.	01-02-87	R	R	6'	167	0	0	—	0	2	0	0	5	6	1	2	0	1.80
Urban, Jack-Jack Elmer	57-58KCA 59StLN	12-05-28	Omaha, Neb.	06-26-06	R	R	5'8	155	15	15	.500	1	69	37	8	272	279	103	113	1	4.83
Valdes (Gutierrez), Rene-Rene Gutierrez [Valdes] (El Latigo)	57BknN	06-02-29	Guanabacoa, Cuba		R	R	6'3	175	1	1	.500	0	5	1	0	13	13	7	10	0	5.54
Valentine, Corky-Harold Lewis	54-55CinN	01-04-29	Troy, Ohio	01-21-05	R	R	6'1	203	14	12	.538	1	46	33	7	221	240	76	87	3	4.81
Valentinetti, Vito-Vito John	54ChiA 56-57ChiN 57CleA 58DetA 58-59WasA	09-16-28	W. New York, N.J.		R	R	6'	200	13	14	.481	3	108	15	3	257	266	122	94	0	4.73
Van Brabant, Ozzie-Camille Oscar	54PhiA 55KCA	09-28-26	Kingsville, Canada		R	R	6'1	165	0	2	.000	0	11	2	0	29	39	20	11	0	7.76
Van Cuyk, Chris-Christian Gerald	50-52BknN	01-03-27	Kimberly, Wis.	11-03-92	R	R	6'6	220	7	11	.389	4	44	26	5	160	170	63	103	0	5.18
Van Cuyk, Johnny-John Henry	47-49BknN	07-07-21	Little Chute, Wis		L	L	6'1	190	0	0	—	0	7	0	0	10	12	3	3	0	5.40
Varga, Andy-Andrew William	50-51ChiN	12-11-30	Chicago, Ill.	11-04-92	R	L	6'4	187	0	0	—	0	4	2	0	4	2	7	1	0	2.25
Vargas, Roberto-Robero Enrique [Velez]	55MilN	05-29-29	Santurce, P.R.		L	L	5'11	170	0	0	—	1	25	0	0	25	39	14	13	0	8.64
Voiselle, Bill-William Symmes (Big Bill, 96)	42-47NYN 47-49BosN 50ChiN	01-29-19	Greenwood, S.C.	01-31-05	R	R	6'4	200	74	84	.468	3	245	190	74	1373	1370	588	645	13	3.83
Wade, Ben-Benjamin Styron	48ChiN 52-54BknN 54StLN 55PitN	11-25-22	Morehead City, N.C.	12-02-02	R	R	6'3	195	19	17	.528	10	118	25	5	371	364	181	235	1	4.34
Wall, Murray-Murray Wesley (Tex)	50BosN 57-59BosA 59WasA 59BosA	09-19-26	Dallas, Tex.	10-08-71	R	R	6'3	190	13	14	.481	14	91	1	0	192	196	63	82	0	4.22
Walsh, Junior-James Gerald	46,48-51PitN	03-07-19	Newark, N.J.	11-12-90	R	R	5'11	190	4	10	.286	2	89	12	1	192	201	111	91	1	5.91
Waters, Fred-Fred Warren	55-56PitN	02-02-27	Benton, Miss.	08-28-89	L	L	5'11	185	2	2	.500	0	25	5	1	56	55	32	14	0	2.89
Waugh, Jim-James Elden	52-53PitN	11-25-33	Lancaster, Ohio		R	R	6'3	185	5	11	.313	1	46	18	2	142	169	88	41	0	6.46
Webb, Red-Samuel Henry	48-49NYN	09-25-24	Washington, D.C.	02-07-96	L	R	6'	175	3	2	.600	0	25	3	0	73	68	31	18	0	3.70
Wehmeier, Herm-Herman Ralph	45,47-54CinN 54-56PhiN 56-58StLN 58DetA	05-21-73	Cincinnati, Ohio	05-21-73	R	R	6'2	200	92	108	.460	9	361	240	79	1804	1806	852	794	9	4.79
Weik, Dick-Richard Henry (Legs)	48-50WasA 50CleA 51-52MS 53-54DetA	11-17-27	Waterloo, Iowa	04-21-91	R	R	6'3	184	6	22	.214	1	76	26	3	213	203	237	123	2	5.92
Welteroth, Dick-Richard John	48-50WasA	08-03-27	Williamsport, Pa.	10-15-05	R	R	5'11	165	4	6	.400	4	90	4	1	166	185	145	55	0	6.51
Werle, Bill-William George (Bugs)	49-52PitN 52StLN 53-54BosA	12-21-20	Oakland, Cal.		L	L	6'2	187	29	39	.426	15	185	60	18	666	770	194	283	2	4.69
Werley, George-George William	56BalA	09-08-38	St. Louis, Mo.		R	R	6'2	196	0	0	—	0	1	0	0	1	2	0	0	0	9.00
Wheat, Lee-Leroy William	54PhiA 55KCA	09-15-29	Edwardsville, Ill.		R	R	6'4	200	0	2	.000	0	11	0	0	30	46	12	8	0	6.90
White, Hal-Harold George	41-43DetA 44-45MS 46-52DetA 53StLA 53-54LN	03-18-19	Utica, N.Y.	04-21-01	L	R	5'10	165	46	54	.460	25	336	67	23	921	875	450	349	7	3.78
Widmar, Al-Albert Joseph	47BosA 48,50-51StLA 52ChiA	03-20-25	Cleveland, Ohio	10-15-05	R	R	6'3	195	13	30	.302	4	114	42	12	389	461	176	143	1	5.21
Wieand, Ted-Franklin Delano Roosevelt	58,60CinN	04-04-33	Walnutport, Pa.		R	R	6'2	195	0	1	.000	0	6	1	0	6	8	5	5	0	10.50
Wiesler, Bob-Robert George	51NYA 52MS 54-55NYA 56-58WasA	08-13-30	St. Louis, Mo.		B	L	6'3	195	7	19	.269	0	70	38	4	240	250	218	113	0	5.78
Wight, Bill-William Robert (Lefty)	46-47NYA 48-50CinA 51-52BosA 52-53DetA 53,55CleA 55-57BalA 58CinN 58StLN	04-12-22	Rio Vista, Cal.		L	L	6'1	190	77	99	.438	1	347	199	66	1532	1656	714	574	15	3.95
Wilks, Ted-Theodore (Cork)	44-51StLN 51-52PitN 52-53CleA	11-13-15	Fulton, N.Y.	08-21-89	R	R	5'9	195	59	30	.663	46	385	44	22	913	832	283	403	5	3.26
Williams, Don-Donald Fred	58-59PitN 62KCA	09-14-31	Floyd, Va.		R	R	6'	180	0	0	—	0	11	0	0	20	29	4	7	0	7.20
Willis, Jim-James Gladden	53-54CinN	03-20-27	Doyline, La.		L	R	6'3	210	2	2	.500	0	27	4	2	66	59	35	20	0	3.41
Willis, Les-Lester Evans (Wimpy, Lefty)	47CleA	01-17-08	Nacogdoches, Tex.	01-22-82	L	L	5'9	195	0	2	.000	1	22	2	0	44	58	24	10	0	3.48
Wilson, Duane-Duane Lewis	58BosA	06-29-34	Wichita, Kans.		R	R	6'1	185	0	0	—	0	2	0	0	6	10	7	3	0	6.00
Wilson, Jim-James Alger	45-46BosA 48StLA 49PhiA 51-52BosN 53-54MilN 55-56BalA 56-58ChiA	02-20-22	San Diego, Cal.	09-02-86	R	R	6'1	200	86	89	.491	9	257	217	75	1540	1479	608	692	19	4.01
Wilson, Maxie-Max	40PhiN 42-45MS 46WasA	06-03-16	Haw River, N.C.	01-02-77	L	L	5'7	160	0	1	.000	0	12	0	0	20	32	11	11	0	9.00
Witt, George-George Adrian (Red)	57-61PitN 62LAA 62HouN	11-09-33	Long Beach, Cal.		R	R	6'3	195	11	16	.407	0	66	38	5	229	225	127	156	3	4.32
Wojey, Pete-Peter Paul	54BknN 56-57DetA	12-01-19	Stowe, Pa.	04-23-91	R	R	5'11	185	1	1	.500	1	18	1	0	33	27	15	22	0	3.00
Wolfe, Ed-Edward Anthony	52PitN	01-02-28	Los Angeles, Cal.		R	R	6'3	185	0	0	—	0	4	7	5	1	0	0	6.75		
Wooldridge, Floyd-Floyd Lewis	55StLN	08-25-28	Jerico Springs, Mo.		R	R	6'1	185	1	2	.333	0	18	4	2	58	64	27	14	0	4.81
Wooten, Earl-Earl Haswell	48WasA	01-16-24	Pelzer, S.C.		R	L	5'11	160	0	0	—	0	1	0	0	2	2	2	1	0	9.00
Wright, Ed-Henderson Edward	45-48BosN 52PhiA	05-15-19	Dyersburg, Tenn.	11-19-95	R	R	6'1	180	25	16	.610	1	101	39	17	398	412	161	93	3	4.00
Wright, Mel-Melvin James	54-55StLN 60-61ChiN	05-11-28	Manilla, Ark.	05-16-83	R	R	6'3	210	2	4	.333	2	58	0	0	83	119	37	36	0	7.70
Wright, Roy-Roy Earl	56NYN	09-26-33	Buchtel, Ohio		R	R	6'2	170	0	1	.000	0	1	0	0	2	1	3	0	0	15.00
Wynn, Early-Early (Gus)	39,41-44WasA 45MS 46-48WasA 49-57CleA 58-62ChiA 63CleA	01-06-20	Hartford, Ala.	04-04-99					300	244	.551	15	691	612	290	4564	4291	1775	2334	49	3.54
					Bats Right 41-44																
Yochim, Len-Leonard Joseph	51,54PitN	10-16-28	New Orleans, La.		L	L	6'2	200	1	2	.333	0	12	3	0	29	40	19	12	0	7.45
Yochim, Ray-Raymond Austin Aloysius	48-49StLN	07-19-22	New Orleans, La.	01-26-02	R	R	6'	170	0	0	—	0	3	0	0	3	7	4	0	0	12.00
Yuhas, Eddie-John Edward	52-53StLN	08-05-24	Youngstown, Ohio	07-06-86	R	R	6'1	180	12	2	.857	9	56	2	0	100	93	35	39	0	2.88
Zick, Bob-Robert Goerge	54ChiN	08-03-27	Chicago, Ill.		R	R	6'	168	0	0	—	0	5	0	0	16	23	7	9	0	8.44
Zoldak, Sam-Samuel Walter (Sad Sam)	44-48StLA 48-50CleA 51-52PhiA	12-08-18	Brooklyn, N.Y.	08-25-66	L	L	5'11	185	43	53	.448	6	250	93	30	930	956	301	207	5	3.54
Zuverink, George-George	51-52CleA 54CinN 54-55DetA 55-59BalA	08-20-24	Holland, Mich.		R	R	6'4	205	32	36	.471	40	265	31	9	642	660	203	223	2	3.54

1961-1972
Unlocking the Floodgates

Until 1960, baseball had managed to preserve its limited franchise sanctuary of 16 teams since 1901, the year the American League first came into existence. Except for the slight intrusion of the Federal League in 1914-1915, the hallowed structure remained undisturbed through the season of 1960. But it could not survive Branch Rickey's plans for a third major circuit —the Continental League —the increasing reach of television, and jet travel shrinking the country, all of which led to the American League's expanding to ten teams in 1961. While the Washington Senators took advantage of the expansion by abandoning the attendance-starved capital city for the Minneapolis-St. Paul area and becoming the Minnesota Twins, a new team took residence in Washington, DC. The League's other entrant seeded their destinies in the increasingly popular west as the Los Angeles Angels. The two new teams also meant an increase in the regular season schedule to 162 games – a feat partly responsible for the New York Yankees' Roger Maris hitting a record 61 home runs – one more than his legendary teammate Babe Ruth poled in 1927.

The National League followed suit a year later by adding a team in Houston, Texas, and one in the city of New York, which had been jilted in 1958 by the exodus of the Giants and Dodgers. The Texas team began its career as the Houston Colts before changing its nickname to the Astros in 1965 – mostly to take advantage of the huge space complex, also located in Houston. New York's entry relied upon a newspaper contest for their nickname and simply called themselves the Mets – a name that later became synonymous with miracles, magic, and mayhem.

Although there was no further expansion until 1969, franchise movement continued to be popular as attendance figures became more important than the loyalty of one city. In 1966, the Milwaukee Braves moved to Atlanta after spending only 13 years in that mid-western city. Not unlike the Braves, the Athletics were also in search of a loyal following, and pulled up their stakes in Kansas City after a similar 13-year period to begin life anew in Oakland in time for the start of the 1968 season.

Then in 1969, with the demand for major league representation still on the rise, both leagues expanded their circuits to 12 teams. The National League used great imagination by placing one of their tenants across the border in Montreal and the other in San Diego. The American League placed one team in abandoned Kansas City and one in Seattle, with the latter being able to survive only one year before declaring bankruptcy and having to change owners and move to Milwaukee for the 1970 season. Two years later, the age-old cry of "first in the heart of America and last in the American League" became a phrase for history as the Washington Senators not only left the capital city to the politicians but their familiar nicknames as well when they journeyed to the Dallas suburb of Arlington to take up residence as the Texas Rangers.

Along with the expansion came a major innovation. Because of the great number of teams and the fact that a 12th place club could only have a negative effect on attendance, both leagues initiated divisional play, splitting their circuits into a six-team Western Division and a six-team Eastern Division. Although the same 162-game schedule remained intact, teams in the same league no longer played an equal number of games with each other team. The schedule now called for 18 games to be played with teams in the same division and 12 games with teams in the other division. Also, for the first time, a championship play-off series was established, with each divisional winner playing a best three-of-five games to decide the pennant winner.

Baseball's new look was also accompanied by a new generation of stadiums. In the National League, most clubs, with the exception of Montreal and Chicago, were playing in modern facilities which accommodated large crowds and ample parking. But while Montreal made plans for a new stadium, Chicago remained in Wrigley Field – a home the Cubs had enjoyed since 1916. In addition to retaining their sanctuary, which included an ivy-covered outfield and a greater intimacy between the fans and the players, the Cubs also remained the only club in the major leagues with no lights and consequently no night baseball.

By contrast, the American League did not keep up with the architectural pace. The only teams to build new stadiums were the California Angels, Oakland Athletics, and Minnesota Twins. But while they may have lacked the abundant parking and fancy scoreboards of the newer plants, the older ballparks like New York's Yankee Stadium, Boston's Fenway Park, Chicago's White Sox Park (formerly Comiskey Park), and Detroit's Tiger Stadium (formerly Briggs Stadium) dripped tradition and had the comfortable feel of familiar surroundings.

The new stadiums – the most famous of which was the enclosed, air-conditioned Astrodome in Houston – also brought with them synthetic grass and increased home run distances. But batting averages did not rise as home runs went down. The overriding reason for this was the pitcher, who began to take advantage of batters swinging for the fences on every pitch. The pitcher was able to reestablish himself with better control and training and mastery of a whole array of pitches, including the slider, knuckle ball, palm ball, and fork ball. The pitcher's reemergence could also be traced to the minor leagues, which not only helped the hurler sharpen his talents at an earlier age, but also allowed some to begin concentrating on relief pitching as a specialty unto itself. One result of better pitching was a lowering of the pitching mound by six inches in 1969 to give the hitter a better opportunity. Yet, even with this alteration, the pitcher remained dominant and plummeting batting averages were accompanied by an increase in strikeouts and shutouts.

Beyond the expansion, franchise shifts, and new role of the pitcher, was the establishment of black and Latin players who not only provided a return of daring on the basepaths – highlighted by Maury Wills' record-breaking feat – but also contributed to most of the long ball artistry of the period. In the years since the black athlete was allowed entry into the major leagues, three of the top four men attaining lifetime home run honors were Hank Aaron, Willie Mays, and Frank Robinson.

Stars of all backgrounds stocked the clubs which excelled over the period. The Yankees continued their domination of the A.L. with five straight pennants through 1964, finally collapsing into the second division for an extensive rebuilding. Moving into the power vacuum were the Baltimore Orioles, pennant winners in 1966, 1969, 1970, and 1971, centered around Frank and Brooks Robinson. In the N.L., the Dodgers built the speed of Wills and the pitching of Sandy Koufax and Don Drysdale into pennants in 1963, 1965, and 1966. The St. Louis Cardinals won in 1964, 1967, and 1968 behind Bob Gibson, Lou Brock, and Ken Boyer, and the Cincinnati Reds assembled a new powerhouse that was the class of the league in the early 1970's. Two unlikely Cinderella clubs captivated the nation with their championships – the 1967 Boston Red Sox and the Miracle Mets of 1969.

1961 Preserving History with an Asterisk

In 1892, as a result of the collapse of the American Association, the National League reluctantly expanded its membership to 12 teams. The union lasted through 1899, the year Baltimore, Louisville, Cleveland, and Washington were sliced from the circuit. In 1900, the National League enjoyed the status quo of former times when it had confined baseball to the major eastern cities. But, in 1901, when the fledgling American Association was born, it brought an end to the monopolistic harmony of eight teams. The American League arrived with money, determination, and enough National League talent to field another eight major league teams. After much feuding, franchise shake-ups and the like, both circuits settled down to ward off the intrusion of the Federal League, 1914-15, and two major World Wars.

But as television replaced radio, and jet travel made the going faster than trains or conventional prop airplanes, westward expansion was inevitable. The move of the Giants and Dodgers in 1958 to California did not lesson the necessity for growth, but rather increased it-with the result that, by the time the 1961 season got underway, the American League found itself with ten teams and a 162-game schedule. The new teams included the Los Angeles Angels and the Washington Senators, the last of which replaced the old Senators who were transplanted to the St. Paul-Minneapolis area under the name, Minnesota Twins. It was this expansion and the new 162-game schedule which provided baseball with the most exciting and controversial season in years, as the assault on the game's most precious single season's record was finally achieved.

On April 26, at Tiger Stadium, Paul Foytack's fastball got up too high, and Roger Maris launched his first circuit clout of the year into the right field stands. The next six months would see Maris chasing Babe Ruth's mark of 60 home runs in one season, clashing with a persistent press, and asterisks added to the record book by Commissioner Ford Frick. Along with Maris, teammate Mickey Mantle also got away to a fast start. Through May, Mantle had 14 home runs and Maris 12. By the end of July, Mantle had 39, Maris 40, and a buzz was universal in the baseball world. Mantle had been a star for years, and quote-hungry reporters did not bother him. For Maris, though, superstardom was new; the pressure of chasing Ruth's record and the unending pursuit of the press took a great toll on the right fielder, turning him surly and uncommunicative.

After Detroit had led the American League for the first half, the Yankees took charge after the All-Star break, and all interest turned from the pennant race to the M&M boys. The excitement was fueled by the first-time departure from the traditional 154-game schedule, with some writers and fans claiming that the extra eight games gave Maris an unfair advantage on the record. Commissioner Frick ended all doubt but not the clamor as he ruled, in July, that Ruth's record would fall only if broken in the first 154 games, and that if a new record was set in the final eight games, it would be entered in the record book with an asterisk along Ruth's treasured single-season mark.

With half the fans rooting for him and the other half rooting against his reaching the "sacred" mark of the Babe, and with the press making copy out of his every action, Maris suffered from the pressure but continued to belt home runs. By September 1, Maris had 51 home runs and Mantle had 48, but Mantle was starting to be hounded by little injuries and an infection, which put him out of action for part of September, ending his chance of surpassing Ruth. In the final game which matched Ruth's schedule, Maris hit #59 but could not get #60, thus assuring that the Babe's mark would stand. On September 26, Jack Fisher of Baltimore served up Maris' 60th in the 159th game of the season. In the season's finale, a Tracy Stallard pitch landed in Yankee Stadium's right field stands to give Maris a season's mark of 61 homers and a new record, or at least part of a new record. Mantle would up with 54 clouts to bring the duo's total to 115, eclipsing the two-man mark of 107 set by Ruth and Lou Gehrig in 1927.

With Maris and Mantle constant front page news, the Yankees' pennant drive took on a secondary aura. Finishing eight games ahead of the Tigers, new manager Ralph Houk used the long ball as his big weapon. In addition to Maris and Mantle, Moose Skowron, Yogi Berra, Elston Howard, and Johnny Blanchard all knocked over 20 home runs to set a new season's mark of 240 round trippers. Tony Kubek, Bobby Richardson, and Clete Boyer gave the infield an airtight look, and Houk made key changes by abandoning Casey Stengel's platooning policy. He moved aging Yogi

Berra to left field and installed Johnny Blanchard as Elston Howard's relief behind the plate. Whitey Ford got a chance to start every fourth day and thrived on the additional work, as he logged a 25-4 mark. Ralph Terry ended at 16-3, and Bill Stafford at 14-9, to round out the big three of the starting staff. Louis Arroyo, using his screwball to chalk up a spectacular season in relief, posted a league-leading 29 saves. The fireman's performance was such that it became routine to see Ford start and pitch seven innings and then watch Arroyo mop up the final six outs. The assault of the pitching and the tremendous hitting moved observers to place the 1961 squad in a class with the 1927 Yankees as the greatest clubs of all time.

Detroit's early season run on first place was sparked by the heavy hitting of Norm Cash, Al Kaline, and Rocky Colavito. Cash reached stardom by hitting a league-leading .361 with 41 home runs and 132 RBI's. Kaline remained consistent with a .324 mark, as Colavito hit 45 homers and drove in 140 Tigers. Frank Lary notched 23 victories to take second-place league runner up honors behind Ford, although his complete games far outdistanced the classy southpaw by a 22-11 margin.

Unlike the American -League, the National still had eight teams and still played a 154-game schedule. And, unlike the power-bludgeoned junior circuit, the more subdued senior league produced an upset pennant winner in the Cincinnati Reds. The Reds were generally figured as a second division club but led almost all the way under the direction of tough manager Fred Hutchinson. Rookie manager Al Dark kept his San Francisco Giants out front through May, but from June 15 to July 10, the Reds won 21 of 28 to create a five-game bulge over Willie Mays and Co. The Dodgers, hot in July, fought for the top spot until stumbling into a ten-game losing streak in Mid-August.

The heart of the Reds' attack came from Frank Robinson, who hit .323, hitting 37 home runs and driving in 124 runs. Vada Pinson hit .343 and Gordy Coleman, who became a full-time player, and Gene Freese, who was obtained from the White Sox, added fuel to the Rhinelander's fire by each belting 26 home runs. Oddly enough, Cincinnati bucked tradition by winning the pennant without a regular middle defense, as Don Blasingame and Elio Chacon shared second base, Eddie Kasko and Leo Cardenas split shortstop, and Jerry Zimmerman, Darrell Johnson, and Johnny Edwards combined to cover the catching duties. On the mound, Bob Purkey, Jim O'Toole, and winter-acquisition Joey Jay were ace starters, while Jim Brosnan and Bill Henry supplied top firefighting in their combined 32 saves.

Despite boasting of the league batting champion in Roberto Clemente, the Pirates fell off to sixth due to the sore arm of Vern Law, the off-season of Bob Friend, and the drop of 50 points in the batting average of Dick Groat, the 1960 league leader. Roy Face, although managing 17 saves to lead the league, lost twice as many as he won and posted a high 3.82 E..R.A.

In the Series it was no contest as the Yankees won the championships in five games. A Ford two-hitter gave New York game one, and home run power overwhelmed the Reds in game three, four, and five after a Joey Jay victory in game two. Even with Mantle hurt and Maris hitting .105, the Yankees outscored the Reds 27-13, due mostly to good hitting from Houk's reserves. In addition to Ruth suffering the eclipse of his home run record, a mark that was even more precious to the Babe also went. Ford, in winding up the Series with 32 scoreless innings, washed away the 29 2/3 consecutive zero frames once tossed by Ruth. The footnotes to baseball's explosive year included Willie Mays' four home runs in one game, Jim Gentile's record tying five grand-slams in one season, 18-year-old Lew Krausse's signing with the Athletics after his high school graduation and shutting out the Los Angeles Angles on three hits in his pro debut, and Leo Durocher's returning to uniform as a coach with the Dodgers to set off recurring rumors that he would replace stalwart Walter Alston as Dodger manager. There was also the arrival of Charley Finley who, in his first year as owner of the Athletics, fired his first manager and general manager, and the Chicago Cubs who went through the year with no manager but, rather, a rotating staff of head coaches. And while the All-Star Game played to its first tie, the Philadelphia Phillies set a record with 23 losses in a row. Finally, as the National League planned expansion in 1962 with a franchise in Houston and one in New York, 71-year-old Casey Stengel agreed to return to baseball after a year's retirement to pilot the New York entry.

NEW YORK — 1st 109-53 .673 — RALPH HOUK

NAME	G by Pos	B	AGE	G	AB	R	H	2B	3B	HR	RBI	BB	SO	SB	BA	SA
TOTALS			28	163	5559	827	1461	194	40	240	782	543	785	28	.263	.442
Bill Skowron	1B149	R	30	150	561	76	150	23	4	28	89	35	108	0	.267	.472
Bobby Richardson	2B161	R	25	162	662	80	173	17	5	3	49	30	23	9	.261	.316
Tony Kubek	SS145	L	24	153	617	84	170	38	6	8	46	27	60	1	.276	.395
Clete Boyer	3B141, SS12, OF1	R	24	148	504	61	113	19	5	11	55	63	83	1	.224	.347
Roger Maris	OF160	L	26	161	590	132	159	16	4	61	142	94	67	0	.269	.620
Mickey Mantle	OF150	R	29	153	514	132	163	16	6	54	128	126	112	12	.317	.687
Yogi Berra	OF87, C15	R	36	119	395	62	107	11	0	22	61	35	28	2	.271	.466
Elston Howard	C111, 1B9	R	32	129	446	64	155	17	5	21	77	28	65	0	.348	.549
Hector Lopez	OF72	R	31	93	243	27	54	7	2	3	22	24	38	1	.222	.305
Johnny Blanchard	C48, OF15	L	28	93	243	38	74	10	1	21	54	27	28	1	.305	.613
2 Bob Cerv	OF30, 1B3	R	35	57	118	17	32	5	1	6	20	12	17	1	.271	.483
2 Billy Gardner	3B33, 2B6	R	33	41	99	11	21	5	0	1	6	8	18	0	.212	.293
Joe DeMaestri	SS18, 2B5, 3B4	R	32	30	41	1	6	0	0	0	2	1	13	0	.146	.146
Jack Reed	OF27	R	28	28	13	4	2	0	0	0	1	1	1	0	.154	.154
2 Earl Torgeson	1B8	L	37	22	18	3	2	0	0	0	0	8	3	0	.111	.111
Jesse Gonder		L	25	15	12	2	4	1	0	0	3	3	1	0	.333	.417
1 Deron Johnson	3B8	R	22	13	19	1	2	0	0	0	0	0	5	0	.105	.105
1 Bob Hale	1B5	L	27	11	13	2	2	0	0	1	1	0	0	0	.154	.385

Tom Tresh 23 B 2-8, 1 Lee Thomas 25 L 1-2

NAME	T	AGE	W	L	PCT	SV	G	GS	CG	IP	H	BB	SO	SHO	ERA
		27	109	53	.673	39	163	163	47	1451	1288	542	866	14	3.46
Whitey Ford	L	32	25	4	.862	0	39	39	11	283	242	92	209	3	3.21
Ralph Terry	R	25	16	3	.842	0	31	27	9	188	162	42	86	2	3.16
Luis Arroyo	L	34	15	5	.750	29	65	0	0	119	83	49	87	0	2.19
Bill Stafford	R	21	14	9	.609	2	36	25	8	195	168	59	101	3	2.68
Jim Coates	R	28	11	5	.688	5	43	11	4	141	128	53	80	1	3.45
Rollie Sheldon	R	24	11	5	.688	0	35	21	6	163	149	55	84	2	3.59
2 Bud Daley	L	28	8	9	.471	0	23	17	7	130	127	51	83	0	3.95
Bob Turley (SA)	R	30	3	5	.375	0	15	12	1	72	74	51	48	0	5.75
Hal Reniff	R	22	2	0	1.000	2	25	0	0	45	31	31	21	0	2.60
1 Art Ditmar	R	32	2	3	.400	0	12	8	1	54	59	14	24	0	4.67
2 Tex Clevenger	R	28	1	1	.500	0	21	0	0	32	35	21	14	0	4.78
1 Danny McDevitt	L	28	1	2	.333	1	8	2	0	13	18	8	8	0	7.62
Al Downing	L	20	0	1	.000	0	5	1	0	9	7	12	12	0	8.00
1 Ryne Duren	R	32	0	1	—	0	4	0	0	5	2	4	7	0	5.40
1 Johnny James	R	27	0	0	—	1	1	0	0	1	2	0	2	0	0.00
Duke Maas	R	32	0	0	—	1	1	0	0	0.1	2	0	0	0	54.00

DETROIT — 2nd 101-61 .623 8 — BOB SCHEFFING

NAME	G by Pos	B	AGE	G	AB	R	H	2B	3B	HR	RBI	BB	SO	SB	BA	SA
TOTALS			27	163	5561	841	1481	215	53	180	779	673	867	98	.266	.421
Norm Cash	1B157	L	26	159	535	119	193	22	8	41	132	124	85	11	.361	.662
Jake Wood	2B162	R	24	162	663	96	171	17	14	11	69	58	141	30	.258	.376
Chico Fernandez	SS121, 3B8	R	29	133	435	41	108	15	4	3	40	36	45	8	.248	.322
Steve Boros (BC)	3B116	R	24	116	396	51	107	18	4	5	62	68	42	4	.270	.364
Al Kaline	OF147, 3B1	R	26	153	586	116	190	41	7	19	82	66	42	14	.324	.515
Bill Bruton	OF155	L	35	160	596	99	153	15	5	17	63	41	61	22	.257	.384
Rocky Colavito	OF161	R	27	163	583	129	169	30	2	45	140	113	75	1	.290	.580
Dick Brown	C91	R	26	93	308	32	82	12	2	16	45	22	57	0	.266	.474
Mike Roarke	C85	R	30	86	229	21	51	6	1	2	22	20	31	0	.223	.284
Dick McAuliffe	SS55, 3B22	L	21	80	285	36	73	12	4	6	33	24	39	2	.256	.389
Charlie Maxwell	OF25	L	34	79	131	11	30	4	2	5	18	20	24	0	.229	.405
Bubba Morton	OF30	R	29	77	108	26	31	5	1	2	19	9	25	3	.287	.407
Bobo Osborne	1B11, 3B8	L	25	71	93	8	20	7	0	2	13	20	15	1	.215	.355
2 Reno Bertoia	3B13, 2B7, SS1	R	26	24	46	6	10	1	0	1	4	3	8	2	.217	.304
1 Ozzie Virgil	3B9, C3, 2B1, SS1	R	28	20	30	1	4	0	0	0	1	1	5	0	.133	.233
Frank House	C14	L	31	17	22	3	5	1	0	0	3	0	3	0	.227	.364
1 George Thomas	OF2, SS1	R	23	17	6	2	0	0	0	0	0	0	0	0	.000	.000
1 Chuck Cottier	SS8, 2B2	R	25	10	7	2	2	0	0	0	0	1	2	0	.286	.286

George Alusik 26 R 2-14, 2 Vic Wertz 36 L 1-6, 1 Dick Gernert 32 R 1-5, Harry Chiti 28 R 1-12, Bill Freehan 19 R 4-10

NAME	T	AGE	W	L	PCT	SV	G	GS	CG	IP	H	BB	SO	SHO	ERA
		29	101	61	.623	30	163	163	62	1459	1404	469	836	12	3.55
Frank Lary	R	31	23	9	.719	0	36	36	22	275	252	66	146	4	3.24
Jim Bunning	R	29	17	11	.607	0	38	37	12	268	232	71	194	4	3.19
Don Mossi	L	32	15	7	.682	1	35	34	12	240	237	47	137	1	2.96
Paul Foytack	R	30	11	10	.524	0	32	30	6	170	152	56	89	0	3.92
Phil Regan	R	24	10	7	.588	2	32	16	8	120	134	41	46	0	5.25
Terry Fox	R	25	5	2	.714	12	39	0	0	57	42	16	32	0	1.42
2 Ron Kline	R	29	5	3	.625	0	10	8	3	58	53	17	27	1	2.73
1 Bill Fischer	R	30	3	2	.600	3	26	1	0	47	54	17	18	0	4.98
Howie Koplitz	R	23	2	0	1.000	0	4	1	1	12	16	4	9	0	2.25
Fred Gladding	R	25	1	0	1.000	0	8	0	0	16	18	11	11	0	3.38
Joe Grzenda	L	24	1	0	1.000	0	3	1	0	5	4	7	6	0	7.50
1 Jim Donohue	R	22	1	1	.500	1	14	0	0	20	23	15	20	0	3.60
3 Gerry Staley	R	40	1	1	.500	2	13	0	0	15	16	8	6	0	3.46
2 Hal Woodeshick	L	28	1	1	.500	0	18	2	0	18	25	17	13	0	8.00
Bob Bruce (IJ)	R	28	1	2	.333	0	11	0	0	24	31	10	19	0	4.40
2 Jerry Casale	R	27	0	0	—	0	6	0	0	12	9	7	3	0	5.25
Manny Montejo	R	27	0	0	—	0	12	0	0	14	9	8	9	0	3.94
Ron Nischwitz	L	24	0	0	.000	0	1	0	0	11	13	4	8	0	5.73

BALTIMORE — 3rd 95-67 .586 14 — PAUL RICHARDS 78-57 .578 — LUM HARRIS 17-10 .630

NAME	G by Pos	B	AGE	G	AB	R	H	2B	3B	HR	RBI	BB	SO	SB	BA	SA
TOTALS			27	163	5481	691	1393	227	36	149	638	581	902	39	.254	.390
Jim Gentile	1B144	L	27	148	486	96	147	25	2	46	141	96	106	1	.302	.646
Jerry Adair	2B107, SS27, 3B2	R	24	133	386	41	102	21	1	9	37	35	51	5	.264	.394
Ron Hansen	SS149, 2B7	R	23	155	533	51	132	13	2	12	51	66	96	1	.248	.347
Brooks Robinson	3B163, 2B2, SS1	R	24	163	668	89	192	38	7	7	61	47	57	1	.287	.397
Whitey Herzog	OF98	L	29	113	323	39	94	11	6	5	35	50	41	1	.291	.409
Jackie Brandt	OF136, 3B1	R	27	139	516	63	153	18	5	16	72	62	51	10	.297	.444
Russ Snyder	OF108	L	27	115	312	46	91	13	5	1	13	20	32	5	.292	.375
Gus Triandos	C114	R	30	115	397	35	97	21	0	17	63	44	60	0	.244	.426
Dick Williams	OF75, 1B20, 3B2	R	32	103	310	37	64	15	2	8	24	20	38	0	.206	.345
Dave Philley	1B1	B	41	99	144	13	36	9	2	1	23	10	24	2	.250	.361
Earl Robinson	OF82	R	24	96	222	37	59	12	3	8	30	31	54	4	.266	.455
Marv Breeding	2B80	R	27	90	244	32	51	8	0	1	16	14	33	5	.209	.254
Jim Busby	OF71	L	34	75	89	15	23	3	1	0	6	8	10	2	.258	.315
2 Marv Throneberry	OF15, 1B11	L	27	56	96	9	20	3	0	5	11	12	20	0	.208	.396
Hank Foiles (RJ)	C38	R	32	43	124	18	34	6	0	6	19	12	27	1	.274	.468
1 Gene Stephens	OF30	L	28	32	58	4	11	2	0	0	2	14	7	1	.190	.224
2 Clint Courtney	C16	L	34	22	45	3	12	2	0	0	4	10	3	0	.267	.311
2 Charlie Lau	C17	L	28	17	47	3	8	2	0	0	1	4	3	0	.170	.234
Walt Dropo	1B12	R	38	14	27	1	7	0	0	1	2	4	5	0	.259	.370
Frank Zupo	C4	L	21	5	4	1	2	1	0	0	0	1	0	0	.500	.750
Barry Shetrone	OF2	L	24	3	7	1	1	0	0	0	1	0	2	0	.143	.143

Boog Powell 19 L 1-13, 1 Chuck Essegian 29 R 0-1

NAME	T	AGE	W	L	PCT	SV	G	GS	CG	IP	H	BB	SO	SHO	ERA
		28	95	67	.586	33	163	163	54	1471	1226	617	926	21	3.22
Steve Barber	L	23	18	12	.600	1	37	34	14	248	194	130	150	8	3.34
Chuck Estrada	R	23	15	9	.625	0	33	31	6	212	159	132	160	1	3.69
Milt Pappas (AJ)	R	22	13	9	.591	1	26	23	11	178	134	78	89	4	3.03
Hal Brown	R	36	10	6	.625	1	27	23	6	167	153	33	61	3	3.18
Jack Fisher	R	22	10	13	.435	1	36	25	10	196	205	75	118	1	3.90
Hoyt Wilhelm	R	38	9	7	.563	18	51	1	0	110	89	41	87	0	2.29
Billy Hoeft	L	29	7	4	.636	3	35	12	3	138	106	55	100	1	2.02
Dick Hall	R	30	7	5	.583	4	29	13	4	122	102	30	92	2	3.10
Wes Stock	R	27	5	0	1.000	3	35	1	0	72	58	27	47	0	3.00
Dick Hyde	R	32	1	0	.333	1	15	0	0	21	18	13	15	0	5.57
Gordon Jones	R	31	0	0	—	1	9	0	0	5	5	1	4	0	5.40
Jim Lehew	R	23	0	0	—	0	2	0	0	6	6	0	1	0	4.50
John Papa	R	20	0	0	—	0	1	0	0	1	2	4	1	0	18.00

CHICAGO — 4th 86-76 .531 23 — AL LOPEZ

NAME	G by Pos	B	AGE	G	AB	R	H	2B	3B	HR	RBI	BB	SO	SB	BA	SA
TOTALS			30	163	5556	765	1475	216	46	138	704	550	612	100	.265	.395
Roy Sievers	1B132	R	34	141	492	76	145	26	6	27	92	61	62	1	.295	.537
Nellie Fox	2B159	L	33	159	606	67	152	11	5	2	51	59	12	2	.251	.295
Luis Aparicio	SS156	R	27	156	625	90	170	24	4	6	45	38	33	53	.272	.352
Al Smith	3B80, OF71	R	33	147	532	88	148	29	4	28	93	56	67	4	.278	.506
Floyd Robinson	OF106	L	25	132	432	69	134	20	7	11	59	52	32	7	.310	.465
Jim Landis	OF139	R	27	140	534	87	149	18	8	22	85	65	71	19	.283	.470
Minnie Minoso	OF147	R	38	152	540	91	151	28	3	14	82	67	46	9	.280	.420
Sherm Lollar	C107	R	36	116	337	38	95	10	1	7	41	37	22	1	.282	.380
J.C. Martin	1B60, 3B36	L	24	110	274	26	63	8	3	5	32	21	31	1	.230	.336
Cam Carreon	C71	R	23	78	229	32	62	5	1	4	27	21	24	0	.271	.354
Sammy Esposito	3B28, SS20, 2B11	R	29	63	94	12	16	5	0	1	6	12	21	0	.170	.255
2 Andy Carey	3B54	R	29	56	143	21	38	12	3	0	14	11	24	0	.266	.392
2 Al Pilarcik	OF17	L	30	47	62	9	11	0	1	0	6	10	7	0	.177	.242
Billy Goodman	3B7, 1B2, 2B1	L	35	41	51	4	13	0	0	0	7	6	5	0	.255	.392
2 Wes Covington	OF14	L	29	22	59	5	17	1	0	4	15	4	5	0	.288	.508
Bob Roselli	C10	R	29	22	38	2	10	3	0	0	5	5	11	0	.263	.342
1 Earl Torgeson	1B1	L	37	20	15	1	1	0	0	0	1	3	5	0	.067	.067
Mike Hershberger	OF13	R	21	15	55	9	17	3	0	0	3	2	6	1	.309	.364
1 Joe Ginsberg	C2	L	34	4	5	0	0	0	0	0	0	0	1	0	.000	.000

1 Ted Lepcio 30 R 0-2, Dean Look 23 R 0-6, 1 Jim Rivera 38 L 0-0

NAME	T	AGE	W	L	PCT	SV	G	GS	CG	IP	H	BB	SO	SHO	ERA
		33	86	76	.531	33	163	163	39	1449	1491	498	814	3	4.06
Juan Pizarro	L	24	14	7	.667	2	39	25	12	195	164	89	188	1	3.05
Billy Pierce	L	34	10	9	.526	3	39	28	5	180	190	54	106	1	3.80
Frank Baumann	L	28	10	13	.435	3	53	23	5	188	249	59	75	1	5.60
Cal McLish	R	35	10	13	.435	1	31	27	4	162	178	47	80	0	4.39
2 Ray Herbert	R	31	9	6	.600	0	21	20	4	138	142	36	50	0	4.04
Early Wynn (IL)	R	41	8	2	.800	0	17	16	5	110	88	47	64	0	3.52
2 Don Larsen	R	31	7	2	.778	2	25	0	0	74	64	29	53	0	4.14
Turk Lown	R	37	7	5	.583	11	59	0	0	101	87	35	50	0	2.76
Russ Kemmerer	R	29	3	3	.500	2	47	2	0	97	102	26	35	0	4.36
Warren Hacker	R	36	3	3	.500	8	42	0	0	57	73	13	32	0	3.79
1 Bob Shaw	R	28	3	4	.429	0	14	10	3	71	85	20	31	0	3.80
Herb Score	R	28	3	3	.333	0	8	5	1	24	25	13	11	0	6.75
Joe Horlen	R	23	1	3	.250	0	10	2	0	12	22	6	10	0	6.50
Gary Peters	R	24	0	1	—	0	1	0	0	2	6	3	2	0	1.80
Mike Degerick	R	18	0	0	—	0	3	0	0	4	4	3	4	0	4.50
Alan Brice	R	23	0	0	.000	0	2	0	0	2	1	3	2	0	5.00
1 Gerry Staley	R	40	0	0	—	0	18	0	0	15	17	5	5	0	5.00

CLEVELAND — 5th 78-83 .484 30.5 — JIMMY DYKES 77-83 .481 — MEL HARDER 1-0 1.000

NAME	G by Pos	B	AGE	G	AB	R	H	2B	3B	HR	RBI	BB	SO	SB	BA	SA
TOTALS			29	161	5609	737	1493	257	39	150	682	492	720	34	.266	.406
Vic Power	1B141, 2B7	R	33	147	563	64	151	34	4	5	63	38	16	4	.268	.369
Johnny Temple	2B129	R	32	129	518	73	143	17	2	3	30	61	36	9	.276	.347
Woodie Held	SS144	R	29	146	509	67	132	18	3	23	78	69	111	0	.267	.468
Bubba Phillips	3B143	R	31	143	546	64	144	23	1	18	72	29	61	1	.264	.408
Willie Kirkland	OF138	L	27	146	525	84	136	22	5	27	95	48	77	7	.259	.474
Jimmy Piersall	OF120	R	31	121	484	81	156	26	7	6	40	43	46	3	.322	.442
Tito Francona	OF138, 1B14	L	27	155	592	87	178	30	8	16	85	56	52	2	.301	.459
Johnny Romano	C141	R	26	142	509	70	153	29	1	21	80	61	60	0	.299	.483
Don Dillard	OF39	L	24	74	147	27	40	5	0	7	15	17	28	0	.272	.449
Mike de la Hoz	2B17, SS17, 3B16	R	22	61	173	20	45	10	0	3	23	7	10	0	.260	.370
3 Chuck Essegian	OF49	R	29	60	166	25	48	7	1	12	35	10	33	0	.289	.560
1 Bob Hale		R	27	42	36	0	6	0	0	0	0	4	3	0	.167	.167
2 Bob Nieman	OF12	R	34	39	65	2	23	6	0	2	10	7	4	1	.354	.538
Walt Bond	OF12	L	23	38	52	7	9	1	0	2	6	1	10	1	.173	.346
Valmy Thomas	C27	R	32	36	36	0	6	0	0	0	4	2	11	0	.209	.314
Jack Kubiszyn	3B8, SS7, 2B2	R	24	25	42	4	9	1	0	0	2	2	6	0	.214	.214
2 Ken Aspromonte	2B21	R	29	22	56	5	16	6	1	0	6	1	5	0	.229	.429
Ty Cline	OF12	L	22	21	43	9	9	3	0	0	0	1	6	1	.209	.302
Hal Jones	1B10	R	22	13	12	1	2	0	0	1	6	3	3	0	.171	.343
Al Luplow	OF5	L	22	5	18	0	1	0	0	0	0	1	4	0	.056	.056
Joe Morgan	OF2	L	30	4	10	1	2	0	0	0	2	0	6	0	.200	.200

NAME	T	AGE	W	L	PCT	SV	G	GS	CG	IP	H	BB	SO	SHO	ERA
		25	78	83	.484	23	161	161	35	1443	1426	599	801	12	4.15
Mudcat Grant	R	25	15	9	.625	0	35	35	11	245	207	109	146	3	3.86
Barry Latman	R	25	13	5	.722	0	45	18	4	177	163	54	108	2	4.02
Gary Bell	R	24	12	16	.429	0	34	34	11	228	214	100	163	2	4.11
Frank Funk	R	25	11	5	.688	11	56	0	0	92	79	31	64	0	3.33
Jim Perry	R	25	10	17	.370	0	35	26	8	224	238	87	90	1	4.70
Wynn Hawkins	R	25	4	4	.500	0	30	21	3	133	139	59	51	1	4.06
Bobby Locke	R	27	4	4	.500	2	37	6	1	95	112	40	37	0	4.55
Bob Allen	L	23	3	2	.600	3	48	0	0	82	96	40	42	0	3.73
Dick Stigman (EJ)	L	25	2	5	.286	0	22	6	1	79	65	25	48	0	4.64
Bill Dailey	R	26	1	0	1.000	0	12	0	0	19	16	6	7	0	0.95
1 Russ Heman	R	28	0	0	—	0	4	0	0	6	10	4	3	0	3.60
Steve Hamilton	L	27	0	0	—	0	2	0	0	5	1	3	5	0	3.00
Sam McDowell	L	18	0	0	.000	0	1	0	0	7	16	14	9	0	6.00
2 Joe Schaffernoth	R	23	0	0	.000	0	5	0	0	17	16	14	9	0	4.76
1 Johnny Antonelli	L	31	0	4	.000	0	11	5	0	48	68	18	23	0	6.56

BOSTON — 6th 76-86 .469 33 — PINKY HIGGINS

NAME	G by Pos	B	AGE	G	AB	R	H	2B	3B	HR	RBI	BB	SO	SB	BA	SA
TOTALS			28	163	5508	729	1401	251	37	112	682	647	847	56	.254	.374
Pete Runnels	1B113, 3B11, 2B7, SS1	L	33	143	360	49	114	20	3	3	38	46	32	5	.317	.414
Chuck Schilling	2B158	R	23	158	646	87	167	25	2	5	62	78	77	7	.259	.327
Don Buddin	SS109	R	27	115	339	58	89	22	3	6	42	72	45	0	.263	.398
Frank Malzone	3B149	R	31	151	590	74	157	21	4	14	87	44	49	1	.266	.386
Jackie Jensen	OF131	R	34	137	498	64	131	21	2	13	66	66	69	9	.263	.392
Gary Geiger	OF137	L	24	140	499	82	116	21	6	18	64	87	91	16	.232	.407
Carl Yastrzemski	OF147	L	21	148	583	71	155	31	6	11	80	50	96	6	.266	.396
Jim Pagliaroni	C108	R	23	120	376	50	91	17	0	16	58	55	74	1	.242	.415
1 Vic Wertz	1B86	L	36	99	317	33	83	16	2	11	60	38	43	0	.262	.414
Pumpsie Green (IL)	SS57, 2B7	B	27	88	219	33	57	12	3	6	27	42	32	4	.260	.425
Russ Nixon	C66	L	26	87	242	24	70	12	2	1	19	13	19	0	.289	.368
Carroll Hardy	OF76	R	28	85	281	46	74	20	2	3	36	26	53	4	.263	.381
Billy Harrell	3B10, SS7, 1B2	R	32	37	37	10	6	2	0	0	1	1	8	1	.162	.216
2 Joe Ginsberg	C6	L	34	19	24	1	6	0	0	0	5	0	2	0	.250	.250
Lu Clinton	OF13	R	23	17	51	4	13	2	1	0	3	2	10	0	.255	.333
Rip Repulski	OF4	R	32	15	25	2	7	1	0	0	1	1	5	0	.280	.320
Don Gile	1B6, C1	R	26	8	18	2	5	0	0	1	1	1	5	0	.278	.444

NAME	T	AGE	W	L	PCT	SV	G	GS	CG	IP	H	BB	SO	SHO	ERA
		28	76	86	.469	30	163	163	35	1443	1472	679	831	6	4.29
Don Schwall	R	25	15	7	.682	0	25	25	10	179	167	110	91	2	3.22
Bill Monbouquette	R	24	14	14	.500	0	32	32	12	236	233	100	161	1	3.39
Gene Conley	R	30	11	14	.440	1	33	30	6	200	229	65	113	2	4.91
Mike Fornieles	R	29	9	8	.529	15	57	2	1	119	121	54	70	0	4.69
Ike Delock	R	31	6	9	.400	0	28	28	3	156	185	52	80	1	4.90
Dave Hillman	R	33	3	2	.600	0	28	7	0	78	70	23	39	0	2.77
Chet Nichols (BH)	L	30	3	2	.600	0	22	5	2	52	40	26	20	0	3.62
Ted Wills	L	27	3	2	.600	0	20	0	0	24	19	11	15	0	5.85
Tom Brewer	R	29	3	2	.600	0	10	9	0	42	37	29	13	0	3.43
Billy Muffett	R	30	3	11	.214	2	38	11	2	113	130	36	47	0	5.65
Arnie Earley	L	28	2	4	.333	1	33	0	0	50	42	34	44	0	3.96
Galen Cisco	R	25	2	4	.333	0	17	8	0	52	67	28	26	0	6.75
Tracy Stallard	R	23	2	7	.222	2	43	14	1	133	110	96	109	0	4.87
Wilbur Wood	L	19	0	0	—	0	6	1	0	13	14	7	7	0	5.54
Tom Borland	L	28	0	0	—	0	1	0	0	1	3	0	0	0	18.00

MINNESOTA — 7th 70-90 .438 38 — COOKIE LAVAGETTO 23-36 .390   SAM MELE 47-54 .465

NAME	G by Pos	B	AGE	G	AB	R	H	2B	3B	HR	RBI	BB	SO	SB	BA	SA
TOTALS			28	161	5417	707	1353	215	40	167	665	597	840	47	.250	.397
Harmon Killebrew	1B119, 3B45, OF2	R	25	150	541	94	156	20	7	46	122	107	109	1	.288	.606
2 Billy Martin	2B105, SS1	R	33	108	374	44	92	15	5	6	36	13	42	3	.246	.361
Zoilo Versalles	SS129	R	21	129	510	65	143	25	5	7	53	25	61	16	.280	.390
1 Bill Tuttle	3B85, OF64, 2B2	R	31	113	370	38	91	12	3	5	38	43	41	1	.246	.335
Bob Allison	OF150, 1B18	R	26	159	556	83	136	21	3	29	105	103	100	2	.245	.450
Lenny Green	OF153	L	27	156	600	92	171	28	7	9	50	81	50	17	.285	.400
Jim Lemon	OF120	R	33	129	423	57	109	24	1	14	52	44	98	1	.258	.423
Earl Battey	C131	R	26	133	460	70	139	24	1	17	55	53	66	3	.302	.470
Jose Valdivielso	SS43, 2B15, 3B14	R	27	76	149	15	29	5	0	1	9	8	19	1	.195	.248
Dan Dobbek	OF48	L	26	72	125	12	21	3	1	4	14	13	18	1	.168	.304
Hal Naragon	C36	L	32	57	139	10	42	2	1	2	11	4	8	0	.302	.374
2 Julio Becquer	1B18, OF5, P1	L	29	57	84	13	20	1	2	5	18	2	12	0	.238	.476
2 Ted Lepcio	3B35, 2B22, SS6	R	30	47	112	11	19	3	1	7	19	8	31	1	.170	.402
1 Billy Gardner	2B41, 3B2	R	33	45	154	13	36	9	0	1	11	10	14	0	.234	.312
Joe Altobelli	OF25, 1B2	L	29	41	95	10	21	2	1	3	14	13	14	0	.221	.358
1 Reno Bertoia	3B32	R	26	35	104	17	22	2	0	1	8	20	12	0	.212	.260
Don Mincher	1B29	L	23	35	101	18	19	5	1	4	11	22	11	0	.188	.406
1 Elmer Valo	OF1	L	40	33	32	0	5	2	0	4	4	3	3	0	.156	.219

Ron Henry 24 R 4-28, Rich Rollins 23 R 5-17, Billy Consolo 26 R 0-5, 1 Pete Whisenant 31 R 0-6, Lamar Jacobs 24 R 2-8, Jim Snyder 28 R 0-5

NAME	T	AGE	W	L	PCT	SV	G	GS	CG	IP	H	BB	SO	SHO	ERA
		27	70	90	.438	23	161	161	49	1432	1415	570	914	14	4.28
Camilo Pascual	R	27	15	16	.484	0	35	33	15	252	205	100	221	8	3.46
Jack Kralick	L	26	13	11	.542	0	33	33	11	242	257	64	137	2	3.61
Pedro Ramos	R	26	11	20	.355	2	42	34	9	264	265	79	174	3	3.95
Jim Kaat	L	22	9	17	.346	0	36	29	8	201	188	82	122	1	3.90
Bill Pleis	L	23	4	2	.667	2	37	0	0	56	59	34	32	0	4.98
Ray Moore	R	35	4	4	.500	14	46	0	0	56	49	38	45	0	3.70
Al Schroll	R	29	4	4	.500	0	11	8	2	50	53	27	24	0	5.22
Don Lee	R	27	3	6	.333	3	37	10	4	115	93	35	65	0	3.52
Chuck Stobbs	L	31	2	3	.400	2	24	3	0	45	56	15	17	0	7.40
2 Danny McDevitt	L	28	1	0	1.000	0	16	1	0	27	20	19	15	0	2.33
1 Paul Giel	R	28	1	0	1.000	0	12	0	0	19	24	17	14	0	9.95
Lee Stange	R	24	1	1	.500	0	7	0	0	12	13	1	9	0	3.00
2 Ed Palmquist	R	28	1	1	.500	0	9	2	0	21	33	13	13	0	9.43
Berto Cueto	R	23	1	3	.250	0	7	5	0	21	27	6	5	0	7.29
Gary Dotter	L	18	0	0	—	0	2	0	0	1	6	4	2	0	9.00
Fred Bruckbauer	R	23	0	0	—	0	1	0	0	0	3	1	0	0	∞
2 Julio Becquer	L	29	0	0	—	0	1	0	0	1	2	2	0	0	27.00
Jerry Arrigo	L	20	0	1	.000	0	2	1	0	10	9	10	6	0	9.90
Ted Sadowski	R	25	0	2	.000	0	7	2	0	33	49	11	12	0	6.82

LOS ANGELES — 8th 70-91 .435 38.5 — BILL RIGNEY

NAME	G by Pos	B	AGE	G	AB	R	H	2B	3B	HR	RBI	BB	SO	SB	BA	SA
TOTALS			29	162	5424	744	1331	218	22	189	700	681	1068	37	.245	.398
Steve Bilko	1B86, OF3	R	32	114	294	49	82	16	1	20	59	58	81	1	.279	.544
1 Ken Aspromonte	2B62	R	29	66	238	29	53	10	0	2	15	23	21	0	.223	.290
2 Joe Koppe	SS88, 2B3, 3B1	R	30	91	338	46	85	12	2	5	40	45	77	3	.251	.343
Eddie Yost (BH)	3B67	R	34	76	213	29	43	4	0	3	15	50	48	0	.202	.263
Albie Pearson	OF113	L	26	144	427	92	123	21	3	7	41	96	40	11	.288	.400
Ken Hunt	OF134, 2B1	R	26	149	479	70	122	29	3	25	84	49	120	8	.255	.484
Leon Wagner	OF116	L	27	133	453	74	127	19	2	28	79	48	65	5	.280	.517
Earl Averill	C88, OF9, 2B1	R	29	115	323	56	86	9	0	21	59	62	70	1	.266	.489
2 Lee Thomas	OF86, 1B34	L	25	130	450	77	128	11	5	24	70	47	74	0	.284	.491
Ted Kluszewski	1B66	L	36	107	263	32	64	12	0	15	39	24	23	0	.243	.460
Rocky Bridges	2B58, SS25, 3B4	R	33	84	229	20	55	5	1	2	15	26	37	1	.240	.297
2 George Thomas	OF45, 3B38	R	23	79	282	39	79	12	1	13	59	21	66	3	.280	.468
Eddie Sadowski	C56	R	30	69	164	16	38	13	0	4	12	11	33	2	.232	.384
Gene Leek	3B49, SS7, OF1	R	24	57	199	16	45	9	1	5	20	7	54	0	.226	.357
Billy Moran	2B51, SS2	R	27	54	173	17	45	7	1	2	17	16	20	0	.260	.347
Del Rice	C30	R	38	44	83	11	20	4	0	4	11	20	19	0	.241	.434
Ken Hamlin	SS39	R	26	42	91	4	19	3	0	1	5	11	9	0	.209	.275
Tom Satriano	3B23, 2B10, SS1	L	20	35	96	15	19	5	1	1	8	12	16	2	.198	.302
Fritzie Brickell	OF15	R	26	21	49	3	6	0	0	0	3	6	9	0	.122	.122
1 Bob Cerv	OF15	R	35	18	57	3	9	3	0	2	6	1	8	0	.158	.316
Bob Rodgers	C14	B	22	16	56	8	18	2	0	1	6	2	13	1	.321	.464

Faye Throneberry 30 L 6-31, Jim Fregosi 19 R 6-27, 1 Julio Becquer 29 L 0-8, Chuck Tanner 31 L 1-8, Danny Ardell 20 L 1-4, Leo Burke 27 R 0-5, Lou Johnson 26 R 0-0

NAME	T	AGE	W	L	PCT	SV	G	GS	CG	IP	H	BB	SO	SHO	ERA
		28	70	91	.435	34	162	162	25	1438	1391	713	973	5	4.31
Ken McBride	R	25	12	15	.444	1	38	36	11	242	229	102	180	1	3.64
Ted Bowsfield	L	25	11	8	.579	2	41	21	4	157	154	63	88	1	3.73
Eli Grba	R	26	11	13	.458	2	40	30	8	212	197	114	105	0	4.25
Tom Morgan	R	31	8	2	.800	10	59	0	0	92	74	17	39	0	2.35
2 Ryne Duren	R	32	6	12	.333	2	40	14	1	99	87	75	108	1	5.18
Art Fowler	R	38	5	8	.385	11	53	3	0	89	68	29	78	0	3.64
2 Jim Donohue	R	22	4	4	.500	5	38	7	0	100	93	50	79	0	4.32
Ron Moeller	L	22	4	8	.333	0	33	18	1	113	122	83	87	1	5.81
Jack Spring	L	28	3	0	1.000	0	18	4	0	38	35	15	29	0	4.26
1 Ron Kline	R	29	5	8	.333	1	26	12	0	105	119	44	70	0	4.49
1 Tex Clevenger	R	28	2	1	.667	1	12	0	0	16	13	13	11	0	1.69
1 Jerry Casale	R	27	1	5	.167	1	13	7	0	43	52	25	35	0	6.49
2 Russ Heman	R	28	0	0	—	0	6	0	0	10	4	2	2	0	1.80
Ray Semproch	R	30	0	0	—	0	2	0	0	1	3	1	0	0	4.50
Bob Sprout	L	19	0	0	—	0	1	0	0	4	5	2	0	0	4.50
2 Johnny James	R	27	0	2	.000	0	36	3	0	71	66	54	41	0	5.32
Dean Chance	R	20	0	2	.000	0	5	4	0	18	33	5	11	0	7.00
Ned Garver	R	35	0	3	.000	0	12	2	0	29	40	16	9	0	5.59

KANSAS CITY — 9th(tie) 61-100 .379 47.5 — JOE GORDON 26-33 .441   HANK BAUER 35-67 .343

NAME	G by Pos	B	AGE	G	AB	R	H	2B	3B	HR	RBI	BB	SO	SB	BA	SA
TOTALS			27	162	5423	683	1342	216	47	90	632	580	772	58	.247	.354
Norm Siebern	1B109, OF47	L	27	153	560	68	166	36	5	18	98	82	91	2	.296	.475
Jerry Lumpe	2B147	L	28	148	569	81	167	29	9	3	54	48	39	1	.293	.392
Dick Howser	SS157	R	25	158	611	108	171	29	6	3	45	92	38	37	.280	.362
Wayne Causey	3B88, SS11, 2B9	L	24	104	312	37	86	14	1	8	49	37	28	0	.276	.404
2 Deron Johnson	OF59, 3B19, 1B3	R	22	83	283	31	61	11	3	8	42	14	44	0	.216	.360
2 Bobby Del Greco	OF73	R	28	74	239	34	55	14	1	5	21	30	31	1	.230	.360
Leo Posada	OF102	R	25	116	344	37	87	10	4	7	53	36	84	0	.253	.366
Haywood Sullivan	C88, 1B16, OF5	R	30	117	331	42	80	16	2	6	40	46	45	1	.242	.356
Joe Pignatano	C83, 3B2	R	31	92	243	31	59	10	3	4	22	36	42	2	.243	.358
Jay Hankins	OF65	L	25	76	173	23	32	10	3	4	6	38	42	2	.185	.272
2 Jim Rivera	OF43	L	38	64	141	20	34	3	4	1	16	10	24	6	.241	.340
2 Gene Stephens	OF54	L	28	62	183	22	38	6	1	4	26	16	27	2	.208	.317
Lou Klimchock	1B11, OF7, 3B6, 2B1	L	21	57	121	8	19	5	1	5	16	5	13	0	.215	.289
Hank Bauer	OF35	R	38	43	106	11	28	3	1	3	18	9	7	1	.264	.396
1 Marv Throneberry	1B30, OF10	L	27	40	130	17	31	3	0	4	11	20	32	0	.238	.408
1 Andy Carey	3B39	R	29	39	123	20	30	6	2	3	11	23	23	0	.244	.398
2 Reno Bertoia	3B29, 2B6	R	26	39	120	12	26	0	0	3	9	13	15	1	.242	.258
1 Al Pilarcik	OF21	L	30	35	60	9	12	1	1	0	5	9	6	1	.200	.250
1 Bob Boyd	1B8	L	41	20	26	2	6	2	0	0	5	2	1	0	.229	.271
1 Bill Tuttle	OF25	R	31	25	84	15	22	2	0	3	6	7	8	0	.262	.333
3 Wes Covington	OF12	L	29	17	44	3	7	0	0	1	6	4	7	0	.159	.227
Frank Cipriani	OF11	R	20	13	36	2	9	0	0	0	4	2	4	0	.250	.250
Charlie Shoemaker	2B	R	22	3	13	2	5	1	0	0	4	1	1	0	.385	.462

Gordon MacKenzie 23 R 3-24, 2 Ozzie Virgil 28 R 3-21, Bobby Prescott 30 R 1-12, Billy Bryan 22 L 3-19, 2 Chuck Essegian 29 R 2-6, Stan Johnson 24 L 0-3, 1 Clint Courtney 34 L 0-1

NAME	T	AGE	W	L	PCT	SV	G	GS	CG	IP	H	BB	SO	SHO	ERA
		28	61	100	.379	23	162	162	32	1415	1519	629	703	5	4.74
Norm Bass	R	22	11	11	.500	0	40	23	6	171	164	82	74	2	4.68
2 Bob Shaw	R	28	9	10	.474	0	26	24	6	150	165	58	60	0	4.32
Jim Archer	L	29	9	15	.375	2	39	27	6	205	204	60	110	2	3.20
Jerry Walker	R	22	8	14	.364	2	36	24	4	168	161	96	56	0	4.82
Joe Nuxhall	L	32	5	8	.385	1	37	13	1	128	135	65	81	0	5.30
1 Bud Daley	L	24	4	8	.333	1	16	10	2	64	84	22	36	0	4.92
Bill Kunkel	R	24	4	4	.429	1	58	2	0	89	103	32	46	0	5.16
1 Ray Herbert	R	31	3	6	.333	0	13	12	1	84	103	30	34	0	5.36
Dave Wickersham (XJ)	R	25	2	1	.667	2	17	0	0	21	25	5	10	0	5.14
Lew Krausse	R	18	2	5	.286	0	12	8	1	56	49	46	32	1	4.82
Ed Rakow	R	26	2	8	.200	1	45	11	1	125	131	49	81	0	4.75
1 Don Larsen	R	31	1	10	.091	6	45	4	0	90	86	44	53	0	4.90
2 Bill Fischer	R	30	1	1	.500	3	21	0	0	35	34	8	13	0	3.86
2 Gerry Staley	R	40	1	1	.500	2	23	0	0	37	40	10	16	0	3.60
2 Mickey McDermott	L	32	0	0	—	0	4	0	0	6	14	10	3	0	13.50
Ed Keegan	R	21	0	0	—	0	1	0	0	0	0	2	0	0	∞
John Wyatt	R	26	0	0	—	0	9	0	0	16	12	12	10	0	2.57
Dan Pfister	R	24	0	0	—	0	4	0	0	7	12	6	3	0	18.00
2 Paul Giel	R	28	0	2	.000	2	12	0	0	28	22	19	12	0	3.86
Bill Kirk	L	28	0	1	.000	0	3	1	0	8	9	5	1	0	31.50
1 Ken Johnson	R	28	0	0	—	0	6	1	0	9	11	7	4	0	12.00
2 Art Ditmar	R	32	0	5	.000	1	20	5	0	54	60	23	19	0	5.67

WASHINGTON — 9th(tie) 61-100 .379 47.5 — MICKEY VERNON

NAME	G by Pos	B	AGE	G	AB	R	H	2B	3B	HR	RBI	BB	SO	SB	BA	SA
TOTALS			29	161	5366	618	1307	217	44	119	578	558	917	81	.244	.367
Dale Long	1B95	L	35	123	377	52	94	20	4	17	49	39	41	0	.249	.459
2 Chuck Cottier	2B100	R	25	101	337	37	79	14	4	2	34	30	51	9	.234	.318
Coot Veal	SS63	R	28	69	218	21	44	10	0	0	8	19	29	1	.202	.248
Danny O'Connell	3B73, 2B61	R	34	138	493	61	128	30	1	3	37	77	62	15	.260	.331
Marty Keough	OF100, 1B10	L	27	135	390	57	97	18	9	9	34	32	60	12	.249	.410
Willie Tasby	OF139	R	28	141	494	54	124	13	2	17	63	58	94	4	.251	.396
Chuck Hinton	OF92	R	27	106	339	51	88	13	5	6	34	40	81	22	.260	.381
Gene Green	C79, OF21	R	28	110	364	52	102	16	3	18	62	35	65	0	.280	.489
Gene Woodling	OF90	L	38	110	342	39	107	16	1	10	57	50	24	1	.313	.471
Jim King	OF91, C1	L	28	110	263	43	71	12	1	11	46	38	45	1	.270	.449
Billy Klaus	3B51, SS18, 2B1, OF1	L	32	91	251	26	57	8	2	3	17	34	22	2	.227	.311
Pete Daley	C72	R	31	72	203	12	39	7	1	2	17	14	31	0	.192	.266
Harry Bright	3B40, C2, 2B1	R	31	72	183	20	44	6	0	4	17	13	26	0	.240	.339
Bob Johnson	SS57, 2B2, 3B2	R	25	61	224	27	66	13	5	4	28	11	33	4	.295	.442
Bud Zipfel	1B44	L	22	42	50	10	7	0	0	3	11	5	11	0	.140	.320
Jim Mahoney	SS31, 2B2	R	27	24	108	10	26	4	0	0	9	6	11	3	.241	.259
R C Stevens	1B25	R	26	24	31	5	4	1	0	1	6	5	11	1	.129	.258
Ken Retzer	C16	L	27	16	53	7	18	4	0	1	8	3	2	0	.340	.472

Joe Hicks 28 L 5-29, Ron Stillwell 21 R 2-16, Dutch Dotterer 29 R 5-19, Chet Boak 26 R 0-7, Eddie Brinkman 19 R 1-11

NAME	T	AGE	W	L	PCT	SV	G	GS	CG	IP	H	BB	SO	SHO	ERA
		30	61	100	.379	21	161	161	39	1425	1405	586	666	8	4.23
Bennie Daniels	R	29	12	11	.522	0	32	28	12	212	184	80	110	1	3.44
Dick Donovan	R	33	10	10	.500	3	33	23	11	169	138	35	62	2	2.40
Joe McClain	R	28	8	18	.308	1	33	29	7	212	221	48	76	2	3.86
Ed Hobaugh	R	27	7	9	.438	0	36	13	1	126	142	64	67	0	4.43
Marty Kutyna	R	28	6	3	.429	3	50	6	0	143	147	48	64	0	3.97
Pete Burnside	L	30	4	9	.308	2	33	16	4	113	106	51	56	2	4.54
1 Hal Woodeshick	L	28	4	3	.600	0	7	6	1	40	38	24	16	0	4.05
John Gabler	R	30	3	8	.273	4	29	9	0	93	104	37	33	0	4.84
Johnny Klippstein	R	33	2	9	.500	0	42	9	1	72	83	43	41	0	6.75
1 Tom Sturdivant	R	31	2	6	.250	0	15	11	0	60	55	40	39	1	4.61
Dave Sisler	R	29	2	8	.200	11	45	1	0	60	55	48	39	0	4.20
2 Claude Osteen	L	21	1	1	.500	0	9	0	0	14	10	5	8	0	2.60
2 Tom Cheney (SA)	R	26	1	2	.250	0	11	9	0	30	32	16	0	8.70
Roy Heiser	R	19	0	0	—	0	1	0	0	3	0	2	3	0	0.00
Mike Garcia	R	37	0	0	—	0	16	0	0	19	23	13	14	0	4.74
Rudy Hernandez	R	30	0	1	.000	3	17	0	0	23	28	9	14	0	4.74
Carl Mathias	L	23	0	2	.000	0	14	2	1	24	7	7	0	10.93
Carl Bouldin	R	21	0	1	.000	0	2	1	0	5	5	2	5	0	18.00
Hector Maestri	R	25	0	0	—	0	1	0	0	2	1	1	1	0	4.50

CINCINNATI 1st 93-61 .604 — FRED HUTCHINSON

NAME	G by Pos	B	AGE	G	AB	R	H	2B	3B	HR	RBI	BB	SO	SB	BA	SA
TOTALS			27	154	5243	710	1414	247	35	158	675	423	761	70	.270	.421
Gordy Coleman	1B150	L	26	150	520	63	149	27	4	26	87	45	67	1	.287	.504
2 Don Blasingame	2B116	L	29	123	450	59	100	18	4	1	21	39	38	4	.222	.287
Eddie Kasko	SS112,3B12,2B6	R	29	126	469	64	127	22	1	2	27	32	36	4	.271	.335
Gene Freese	3B151,2B1	R	27	152	575	78	159	27	4	26	87	27	78	8	.277	.466
Frank Robinson	OF150,3B1	R	25	153	545	117	176	32	7	37	124	71	64	22	.323	.611
Vada Pinson	OF153	L	22	154	607	101	208	34	8	16	87	39	63	23	.343	.504
Wally Post	OF81	R	31	99	282	44	83	16	3	20	57	22	61	0	.294	.585
Jerry Zimmerman	C76	R	26	76	204	8	42	5	0	0	10	11	21	1	.206	.230
Gus Bell	OF75	L	32	103	235	27	60	10	1	3	33	18	21	1	.255	.345
Jerry Lynch	OF44	L	30	96	181	33	57	13	2	13	50	27	25	0	.315	.624
Leo Cardenas	SS63	R	22	74	198	23	61	18	1	5	24	15	39	1	.308	.485
Elio Chacon	2B42,OF8	R	24	61	132	26	35	4	2	2	5	21	22	1	.265	.371
Johnny Edwards	C52	L	23	52	145	14	27	5	0	2	14	18	28	1	.186	.262
2 Dick Gernert	1B21	R	32	40	63	4	19	1	0	0	7	7	9	0	.302	.317
2 Bob Schmidt	C27	R	28	27	70	4	9	0	0	1	4	8	14	0	.129	.171
2 Pete Whisenant	OF12,3B1,C1	R	31	26	15	6	3	0	0	0	1	2	4	1	.200	.200
2 Darrell Johnson	C20	R	32	20	54	3	17	2	0	1	6	1	2	0	.315	.407
1 Ed Bailey	C12	L	30	12	43	4	13	4	0	0	3	5	1	0	.302	.395

Jim Baumer 30 R 3-24, Willie Jones 35 R 0-7, Joe Gaines 24 R 0-3, Cliff Cook 24 R 0-5, Harry Anderson 29 L 1-4, Hal Bevan 30 R 1-3

NAME	T	AGE	W	L	PCT	SV	G	GS	CG	IP	H	BB	SO	SHO	ERA
		26	93	61	.604	40	154	154	46	1370	1300	500	829	12	3.78
Joey Jay	R	25	21	10	.677	0	34	34	14	247	217	92	157	4	3.53
Jim O'Toole	L	24	19	9	.679	2	39	35	11	253	229	93	178	3	3.09
Bob Purkey	R	31	16	12	.571	1	36	34	13	246	245	51	116	1	3.73
Jim Brosnan	R	31	10	4	.714	16	53	0	0	80	77	18	40	0	3.04
Ken Hunt	R	22	9	10	.474	0	29	24	7	136	130	66	75	0	3.97
2 Ken Johnson	R	28	6	2	.750	1	15	11	3	83	72	22	42	1	3.25
Jim Maloney	R	21	6	7	.462	2	27	11	1	95	86	59	57	0	4.36
Bill Henry	L	33	2	1	.667	16	47	0	0	53	50	15	53	0	2.21
Howie Nunn (EJ)	R	25	2	1	.667	0	24	0	0	38	33	24	26	0	3.55
Sherman Jones	R	26	1	1	.500	2	24	2	0	55	51	27	32	0	4.42
Jay Hook	R	24	1	3	.250	0	22	5	0	63	83	22	30	0	7.71
1 Claude Osteen	L	21	0	0	—	0	1	0	0	0.1	0	1	1	0	0.00
Marshall Bridges	L	30	0	1	.000	0	13	0	0	21	26	11	17	0	7.71

LOS ANGELES 2nd 89-65 .578 4 — WALT ALSTON

NAME	G by Pos	B	AGE	G	AB	R	H	2B	3B	HR	RBI	BB	SO	SB	BA	SA
TOTALS			28	154	5189	735	1358	193	40	157	673	596	796	86	.262	.405
Norm Larker	1B86,OF1	L	30	97	282	29	76	16	1	5	38	24	22	0	.270	.387
Charlie Neal	2B104	R	30	108	341	40	80	16	1	10	48	30	49	3	.235	.346
Maury Wills	SS148	B	28	148	613	105	173	12	10	1	31	59	50	35	.282	.339
Jim Gilliam	3B74,2B71,OF11	B	32	144	439	74	107	26	3	4	32	79	34	8	.244	.344
Tommy Davis	OF86,3B59	R	22	132	460	60	128	13	2	15	58	32	53	10	.278	.413
Willie Davis	OF114	L	21	128	339	56	86	19	6	12	45	27	46	12	.254	.451
Wally Moon	OF133	L	31	134	463	79	152	26	3	17	88	89	79	7	.328	.505
Johnny Roseboro	C125	L	28	128	394	59	99	16	4	18	59	56	62	6	.251	.459
Ron Fairly	OF71,1B23	L	22	111	245	42	79	15	2	10	48	48	22	0	.322	.522
Gil Hodges	1B100	R	37	109	215	25	52	4	0	8	31	24	43	3	.242	.372
Frank Howard	OF65,1B7	R	24	92	267	36	79	10	2	15	45	21	50	0	.296	.517
Duke Snider (BE)	OF66	L	34	85	233	35	69	8	3	16	56	29	43	1	.296	.562
2 Daryl Spencer	3B57,SS3	R	31	60	189	27	46	7	0	8	27	20	35	0	.243	.407
Norm Sherry	C45	R	29	47	121	10	31	2	0	5	21	9	30	0	.256	.397
Bob Aspromonte	3B9,SS4,2B2	R	23	47	58	7	14	3	0	0	4	4	12	0	.241	.293
Don Drysdale	P40	R	24	40	83	6	16	1	0	5	12	6	24	0	.193	.386
Gordie Windhorn	OF17	R	27	34	33	10	8	2	1	2	6	4	9	0	.242	.545
1 Carl Warwick	OF12	R	24	19	11	2	1	0	0	0	1	2	3	0	.091	.091
1 Don Demeter	OF14	R	26	15	29	3	5	0	0	1	3	1	8	0	.172	.276
Doug Camilli	C12	R	24	13	30	3	4	1	0	0	1	4	9	0	.133	.433

1 Bob Lillis 31 R 1-9, 1 Charley Smith 23 R 6-24, Tim Harkness 23 L 4-8

NAME	T	AGE	W	L	PCT	SV	G	GS	CG	IP	H	BB	SO	SHO	ERA
		26	89	65	.578	35	154	154	40	1378	1346	544	1105	10	4.04
Johnny Podres	L	28	18	5	.783	0	32	29	6	183	192	51	124	1	3.74
Sandy Koufax	L	25	18	13	.581	1	42	35	15	256	212	96	269	2	3.52
Stan Williams	R	24	15	12	.556	0	41	35	6	235	213	108	205	2	3.91
Don Drysdale	R	24	13	10	.565	0	40	37	10	244	236	83	182	3	3.69
Ron Perranoski	L	25	7	5	.583	6	53	0	0	92	82	41	56	0	2.64
2 Dick Farrell	R	27	6	6	.500	10	50	0	0	89	107	43	80	0	5.06
Roger Craig	R	31	5	6	.455	2	40	14	2	113	130	52	63	0	6.13
Larry Sherry	R	25	4	4	.500	15	53	1	0	95	90	39	79	0	3.88
Ed Roebuck (SJ)	R	29	2	1	1.000	5	40	0	0	9	12	2	9	0	5.00
Jim Golden	R	25	1	1	.500	0	28	0	0	42	52	20	18	0	5.79
1 Ed Palmquist	R	28	0	0	—	0	5	0	0	9	10	7	5	0	6.00
Phil Ortega	R	21	0	0	—	0	4	2	1	13	10	2	15	0	5.54

SAN FRANCISCO 3rd 85-69 .552 8 — AL DARK

NAME	G by Pos	B	AGE	G	AB	R	H	2B	3B	HR	RBI	BB	SO	SB	BA	SA
TOTALS			26	155	5233	773	1379	219	32	183	709	506	764	79	.264	.423
Willie McCovey	1B84	L	23	106	328	59	89	12	3	18	50	37	60	1	.271	.491
Joey Amalfitano	2B95,3B6	R	27	109	384	64	98	11	4	2	33	24	59	7	.255	.320
Jose Pagan	SS132,OF4	R	26	134	434	38	110	15	2	5	46	31	45	6	.253	.332
Jim Davenport	3B132	R	27	137	436	64	121	28	4	12	65	45	65	4	.278	.449
Felipe Alou	OF122	R	26	132	415	59	120	19	0	18	52	26	41	0	.289	.465
Willie Mays	OF153	R	30	154	572	129	176	32	3	40	123	81	77	18	.308	.584
Harvey Kuenn	OF93,3B32,SS1	R	30	131	471	60	125	22	4	5	47	34	45	5	.265	.361
2 Ed Bailey	C103,OF1	L	30	107	340	39	81	9	1	13	51	42	41	1	.238	.385
Orlando Cepeda	1B81,OF80	R	23	152	585	105	182	28	4	46	142	39	91	12	.311	.609
Matty Alou	OF58	L	22	81	200	38	62	7	2	6	24	15	19	3	.310	.455
Chuck Hiller	2B67	L	26	70	240	38	57	12	1	2	12	32	30	4	.238	.321
Ed Bressoud	SS34,3B3,2B1	R	29	59	114	14	24	6	0	3	11	11	23	1	.211	.342
Hobie Landrith	C30	L	31	43	71	11	17	4	0	2	10	12	7	0	.239	.380
Ernie Bowman	2B13,SS12,3B7	R	23	38	38	10	8	0	2	0	1	3	6	0	.211	.316
Tom Haller	C25	L	24	30	62	5	9	1	0	2	6	8	23	0	.145	.258
John Orsino	C25	R	23	25	83	5	23	3	2	4	12	3	13	0	.277	.506

Jim Marshall 29 L 8-36, Bob Farley 23 L 2-20, 1 Don Blasingame 29 L 0-1, 1 Bob Schmidt 28 R 1-6

NAME	T	AGE	W	L	PCT	SV	G	GS	CG	IP	H	BB	SO	SHO	ERA
		27	85	69	.552	30	155	155	39	1388	1306	502	924	9	3.77
Stu Miller	R	33	14	5	.737	17	63	0	0	122	95	37	89	0	2.66
Jack Sanford	R	32	13	9	.591	0	38	33	6	217	203	87	112	0	4.23
Juan Marichal	R	23	13	10	.565	0	29	27	9	185	183	48	124	3	3.89
Mike McCormick	L	22	13	16	.448	0	40	35	13	250	235	75	163	3	3.20
Sam Jones	R	35	8	8	.500	1	37	17	2	128	134	57	105	0	4.50
Billy O'Dell	L	28	7	5	.583	2	46	14	4	130	132	33	110	1	3.60
Billy Loes	R	31	6	5	.545	0	26	18	3	115	114	39	55	1	4.23
Jim Duffalo	R	25	5	1	.833	1	24	4	1	62	59	32	37	0	4.21
Dick LeMay	L	22	3	3	.333	3	27	5	1	83	65	36	54	0	3.58
Bobby Bolin	R	22	2	2	.500	5	37	1	0	48	37	37	48	0	3.19
Dom Zanni	R	29	1	0	1.000	0	14	0	0	14	13	12	11	0	3.86
Eddie Fisher	R	24	0	2	.000	1	15	0	0	34	36	16	13	0	5.29

MILWAUKEE 4th 83-71 .539 10 — CHUCK DRESSEN 71-58 .550 BIRDIE TEBBETTS 12-13 .480

NAME	G by Pos	B	AGE	G	AB	R	H	2B	3B	HR	RBI	BB	SO	SB	BA	SA
TOTALS			28	155	5288	712	1365	199	34	188	662	534	880	70	.258	.415
Joe Adcock	1B148	R	33	152	562	77	160	20	0	35	108	59	94	2	.285	.507
Frank Bolling	2B148	R	29	148	585	86	153	16	4	15	56	57	62	2	.262	.379
Roy McMillan	SS154	R	31	154	505	64	111	16	0	7	48	61	86	2	.220	.293
Eddie Mathews	3B151	L	29	152	572	103	175	23	6	32	91	93	95	12	.306	.535
Lee Maye	OF96	L	26	110	373	68	101	11	5	14	41	36	50	10	.271	.440
Hank Aaron	OF154,3B2	R	27	155	603	115	197	39	10	34	120	56	64	21	.327	.594
2 Frank Thomas	OF109,1B11	R	32	124	423	58	120	13	3	25	67	29	70	2	.284	.506
Joe Torre	C112	R	20	113	406	40	113	21	4	10	42	28	60	2	.278	.424
Al Spangler	OF44	L	27	68	97	23	26	2	0	0	6	28	9	4	.268	.289
Felix Mantilla	SS19,2B10,OF10,3B6	R	26	93	183	23	39	5	0	5	10	16	23	1	.215	.388
Warren Spahn	P38	L	40	39	94	13	21	7	0	4	15	7	33	0	.223	.426
Gino Cimoli	OF31	R	31	37	117	12	23	5	0	3	4	11	15	1	.197	.316
2 Bob Boyd	1B3	L	41	36	41	3	10	0	0	0	5	0	4	0	.244	.244
John DeMerit	OF21	R	25	32	74	5	12	3	0	2	5	5	19	0	.162	.284
Mack Jones	OF26	R	22	28	104	13	24	3	2	0	12	12	24	4	.231	.298
1 Charlie Lau	C25	L	28	28	82	3	17	5	0	0	5	14	11	1	.207	.268
Sammy White	C20	R	33	21	63	1	14	1	0	1	9	2	8	0	.222	.286
Hawk Taylor	OF5,C1	R	22	22	26	1	5	1	1	0	3	3	4	1	.192	.308
1 Mel Roach	OF9,1B2	R	28	13	36	3	6	1	0	0	2	3	11	0	.167	.250

1 Johnny Logan 34 R 2-19, Del Crandall 31 R (SA) 6-30, Neil Chrisley 29 L 2-9, 1 Wes Covington 29 L 4-21, 1 Billy Martin 33 R 0-6, Phil Roof 20 R 0-0

NAME	T	AGE	W	L	PCT	SV	G	GS	CG	IP	H	BB	SO	SHO	ERA
		29	83	71	.539	16	155	155	57	1391	1357	493	652	8	3.90
Warren Spahn	L	40	21	13	.618	0	38	34	21	263	236	64	115	4	3.01
Lew Burdette	R	34	18	11	.621	0	40	36	14	272	295	33	92	3	4.00
Bob Buhl	R	32	9	10	.474	0	32	28	9	188	180	98	77	1	4.12
Tony Cloninger	R	20	7	2	.778	0	19	10	3	84	84	33	51	0	5.25
Don McMahon	R	31	6	4	.600	8	53	0	0	92	84	51	55	0	2.84
Don Nottebart	R	25	6	7	.462	3	38	11	2	126	117	48	66	0	4.07
Carl Willey	R	30	6	12	.333	0	35	22	4	160	147	65	91	0	3.83
Bob Hendley	L	22	5	7	.417	0	19	13	3	97	96	39	64	0	3.52
Ron Piche	R	26	2	2	.500	1	12	1	1	21	28	16	16	0	3.59
Claude Raymond	R	24	1	1	.500	0	13	0	0	20	22	9	13	0	4.05
Seth Morehead	L	26	1	1	.500	0	16	1	0	16	7	13	6	0	7.36
2 Johnny Antonelli	R	31	1	0	1.000	0	11	6	3	22	20	12	11	0	6.16
George Brunet (IL)	L	26	0	0	—	0	13	0	0	20	15	16	19	0	5.40
Chi Chi Olivo	R	35	0	0	—	0	2	0	0	4	8	3	1	0	18.00
Ken MacKenzie	L	27	0	1	.000	0	5	0	0	13	11	6	9	0	5.14
Moe Drabowsky	R	25	0	2	.000	0	10	0	0	25	26	18	25	0	4.68

ST. LOUIS 5th 80-74 .519 13 — SOLLY HEMUS 33-41 .446 JOHNNY KEANE 47-33 .588

NAME	G by Pos	B	AGE	G	AB	R	H	2B	3B	HR	RBI	BB	SO	SB	BA	SA
TOTALS			29	155	5307	703	1436	236	51	103	657	494	745	46	.271	.393
Bill White	1B151	L	27	153	591	69	169	28	11	20	90	64	84	8	.286	.472
Julian Javier (LJ)	2B113	R	24	113	445	58	124	14	3	2	41	30	51	11	.279	.337
Alex Grammas	SS65,2B18,3B3	R	35	89	170	23	36	10	1	0	21	19	21	0	.212	.282
Ken Boyer	3B153	R	30	153	589	109	194	26	11	24	95	68	91	6	.329	.533
Charlie James	OF90	R	23	108	349	43	89	19	2	4	44	15	59	2	.255	.355
Curt Flood	OF119	R	23	132	435	53	127	10	5	2	21	35	33	6	.322	.415
Stan Musial	OF103	L	40	123	372	46	107	22	4	15	70	52	35	0	.288	.489
Jimmie Schaffer	C68	R	24	68	153	15	39	7	1	0	16	9	29	0	.255	.392
Joe Cunningham	OF86,1B10	L	29	133	322	60	92	11	7	2	40	53	32	1	.286	.398
Don Taussig	OF87	R	29	98	188	27	54	14	5	2	25	16	34	2	.287	.447
2 Bob Lillis	SS56,2B24	R	31	86	230	24	50	4	0	0	21	7	13	2	.217	.235
Carl Sawatski	C60,OF1	L	33	86	174	23	52	8	0	10	33	25	17	0	.299	.517
Red Schoendienst	2B32	B	38	72	120	9	36	9	0	1	12	12	6	1	.300	.400
2 Carl Warwick	OF48	R	24	55	152	27	38	6	2	4	16	18	33	3	.250	.395
Hal Smith (IL)	C45	R	30	45	125	6	31	6	0	3	16	10	13	0	.248	.296
1 Daryl Spencer	SS37	R	32	32	130	19	33	4	0	6	22	13	17	1	.254	.377
Curt Simmons	P30	L	32	32	66	9	20	1	0	0	8	22	10	0	.303	.348
Jerry Buchek	SS31	R	19	22	15	2	2	0	0	0	2	2	4	0	.133	.133
Don Landrum	OF25,2B1	L	25	28	66	5	11	2	0	0	5	3	14	1	.167	.242
Gene Oliver	C15,OF1	R	25	24	45	8	12	1	0	3	8	3	7	0	.269	.538
Tim McCarver	C20	L	19	22	67	5	16	2	0	0	6	6	5	0	.239	.343
1 Walt Moryn	OF7	L	35	13	35	3	5	1	0	0	2	4	9	0	.143	.188
Julio Gotay	SS10	R	22	10	45	9	14	3	0	0	5	1	5	0	.244	.333

Ed Olivares 22 R 5-30, George Crowe 40 L 1-7, Chris Cannizzaro 23 R 1-2, 1 Bob Nieman 34 R 8-17, Doug Clemens 22 L 2-12

NAME	T	AGE	W	L	PCT	SV	G	GS	CG	IP	H	BB	SO	SHO	ERA
		27	80	74	.519	24	155	155	49	1369	1334	570	823	10	3.74
Ray Sadecki	L	20	14	10	.583	0	31	31	13	223	196	102	114	0	3.71
Larry Jackson (BJ)	R	30	14	11	.560	0	33	28	12	251	203	56	113	3	3.75
Bob Gibson	R	25	13	12	.520	1	35	27	10	211	186	119	166	2	3.24
Lindy McDaniel	R	25	10	6	.625	9	55	0	0	94	117	31	65	0	4.88
Curt Simmons	L	32	9	10	.474	0	30	29	6	196	203	64	99	2	3.12
Ernie Broglio	R	23	9	12	.429	0	29	26	7	175	166	75	113	2	4.11
Craig Anderson	R	23	4	3	.571	2	25	0	0	39	38	12	21	0	4.33
Ed Bauta	R	26	2	0	1.000	1	13	0	0	19	16	10	9	0	5.28
Al Cicotte	R	31	2	6	.250	1	29	7	0	75	83	34	51	0	5.28
1 Mickey McDermott	L	32	1	0	1.000	0	27	0	0	29	15	15	15	0	3.83
Ray Washburn	R	23	1	0	1.000	0	2	1	1	20	10	7	12	0	1.80
Bob Miller	R	22	1	3	.250	2	25	5	0	74	82	46	39	0	4.26
Bobby Tiefenauer	R	31	0	1	.000	1	10	0	0	22	26	6	13	0	6.75

PITTSBURGH 6th 75-79 .487 18 DANNY MURTAUGH

NAME	G by Pos	B	AGE	G	AB	R	H	2B	3B	HR	RBI	BB	SO	SB	BA	SA
TOTALS			29	154	5311	694	1448	232	57	128	646	428	721	26	.273	.410
Dick Stuart	1B132, OF1	R	28	138	532	83	160	28	8	35	117	34	121	0	.301	.581
Bill Mazeroski	2B152	R	24	152	558	71	148	21	2	13	59	26	55	2	.265	.380
Dick Groat	SS144, 3B1	R	30	148	596	71	164	25	6	6	55	40	44	0	.275	.367
Don Hoak	3B143	R	33	145	503	72	150	27	7	12	61	73	53	4	.298	.451
Roberto Clemente	OF144	R	26	146	572	100	201	30	10	23	89	35	59	4	.351	.559
Bill Virdon	OF145	L	30	146	599	81	156	22	8	9	58	49	45	5	.260	.369
Bob Skinner	OF97	L	29	119	381	61	102	20	3	12	42	51	49	1	.268	.360
Smoky Burgess	C92	L	34	100	323	37	98	17	3	12	52	30	16	1	.303	.486
Joe Christopher	OF55	R	25	76	186	25	49	7	3	0	14	18	24	6	.263	.333
Rocky Nelson	1B35	L	36	75	127	15	25	5	1	5	13	17	11	0	.197	.370
Hal Smith	C65	R	30	67	193	12	43	10	0	3	26	11	38	0	.223	.321
Dick Schofield	3B11, SS9, 2B5, OF3	B	26	60	78	16	15	2	1	0	2	10	19	0	.192	.244
2 Walt Moryn	OF11	L	35	40	65	6	13	1	0	3	9	2	10	0	.200	.354
2 Johnny Logan	3B7, SS6	R	34	27	52	5	12	4	0	0	5	4	8	0	.231	.308
Don Leppert	C21	R	29	22	60	6	16	2	1	3	5	1	11	0	.267	.483
1 Gino Cimoli	OF19	R	31	21	67	4	20	3	1	0	6	2	13	0	.299	.373

Donn Clendenon 25 R 11-35, Gene Baker 36 R 1-10, Bob Oldis 33 R 0-5, Roman Mejias 30 R 0-1

NAME	T	AGE	W	L	PCT	SV	G	GS	CG	IP	H	BB	SO	SHO	ERA
		30	75	79	.487	29	154	154	34	1362	1442	400	759	9	3.92
Bob Friend	R	30	14	19	.424	1	41	35	10	236	271	45	108	1	3.85
Joe Gibbon	L	26	13	10	.565	0	30	29	7	195	185	57	145	3	3.32
Harvey Haddix	L	35	10	6	.625	0	29	22	5	156	159	41	99	2	4.10
Vinegar Bend Mizell	L	30	7	10	.412	0	21	17	2	100	120	31	37	1	5.04
Bobby Shantz	L	35	6	3	.667	2	43	6	2	89	91	26	61	1	3.34
Roy Face	R	33	6	12	.333	17	62	0	0	92	94	10	55	0	3.82
2 Tom Sturdivant	R	31	5	2	.714	1	13	11	6	86	81	17	45	1	2.83
Clem Labine	R	34	4	1	.800	8	56	1	0	93	102	31	49	0	3.68
Al McBean	R	23	3	2	.600	0	27	2	0	74	72	42	49	0	3.77
Vern Law (SA)	R	31	3	4	.429	0	11	10	1	59	72	18	20	0	4.73
Earl Francis	R	24	2	8	.200	0	23	15	0	103	110	47	53	0	4.19
Al Jackson	L	25	1	0	1.000	0	3	1	1	24	20	4	15	0	3.38
Larry Foss	R	25	1	1	.500	0	3	3	0	15	15	11	9	0	6.00
Freddie Green	L	27	0	0	—	0	13	0	0	21	27	9	4	0	4.71
1 Tom Cheney	R	26	0	1	.000	0	1	1	0	4	4	1	4	0	∞
Jim Umbricht	R	30	0	0	—	0	1	0	0	3	5	2	1	0	3.00
George Witt (SA)	R	27	0	1	.000	0	9	1	0	16	17	5	6	0	6.19

CHICAGO 7th 64-90 .416 29 VEDIE HIMSL 10-21 .323 HARRY CRAFT 7-9 .438 EL TAPPE 42-54 .438 LOU KLEIN 5-6 .455

NAME	G by Pos	B	AGE	G	AB	R	H	2B	3B	HR	RBI	BB	SO	SB	BA	SA
TOTALS			28	156	5344	689	1364	238	51	176	650	539	1027	35	.255	.418
Ed Bouchee	1B107	L	28	112	319	49	79	12	6	38	58	77	1	.248	.417
Don Zimmer	2B116, 3B5, OF1	R	30	138	477	57	120	25	4	13	40	25	70	5	.252	.403
Ernie Banks	SS104, OF23, 1B7	R	30	138	511	75	142	22	4	29	80	54	75	1	.278	.507
Ron Santo	3B153	R	21	154	578	84	164	32	6	23	83	73	77	2	.284	.479
George Altman	OF130, 1B3	L	28	138	518	77	157	28	12	27	96	40	92	6	.303	.560
Al Heist	OF99	R	33	109	321	48	82	14	3	7	37	39	51	3	.255	.383
Billy Williams	OF135	L	23	146	529	75	147	20	7	25	86	45	70	6	.278	.484
Dick Bertell	C90	R	25	92	267	20	73	7	1	2	33	15	33	0	.273	.330
Richie Ashburn	OF76	L	34	109	307	49	79	7	4	0	19	55	27	7	.257	.306
Jerry Kindall	2B50, SS47	R	26	96	310	37	75	22	3	9	44	18	89	2	.242	.419
Sammy Taylor	C75	L	28	89	235	26	56	8	2	8	23	23	39	0	.238	.391
Bob Will	OF30, 1B1	L	29	86	113	9	29	9	0	8	15	19	15	0	.257	.336
Andre Rodgers	1B42, SS24, OF2, 2B1	R	26	73	214	27	57	17	0	6	23	25	54	1	.266	.430
Moe Thacker	C25	R	27	25	35	3	6	0	0	0	2	11	11	0	.171	.171
2 Mel Roach	1B7, 2B7	R	28	23	39	1	5	2	0	0	1	3	9	1	.128	.179
1 Frank Thomas	OF10, 1B6	R	32	15	50	7	13	2	0	2	6	2	8	0	.260	.420
Jim McAnany	OF1	R	24	11	10	1	3	1	0	0	1	0	3	0	.300	.400
Cuno Barragan (BN)	C10	R	29	10	28	3	6	0	0	1	2	2	7	0	.214	.321
Ken Hubbs	2B8	R	19	10	28	4	5	1	1	1	2	0	8	0	.179	.393
Moe Morhardt	1B7	L	24	7	18	3	5	0	0	0	4	1	3	0	.278	.278

Sammy Drake 26 B 0-5, George Freese 34 R 2-7, Danny Murphy 18 L 5-13, Lou Brock 22 L 1-11, Nelson Mathews 19 R 1-9

NAME	T	AGE	W	L	PCT	SV	G	GS	CG	IP	H	BB	SO	SHO	ERA
		26	64	90	.416	25	156	156	34	1385	1492	465	755	6	4.48
Don Cardwell	R	25	15	14	.517	0	39	38	13	259	243	88	156	3	3.82
Dick Ellsworth	L	21	10	11	.476	0	37	31	7	187	213	48	91	1	3.85
Jack Curtis	L	24	10	13	.435	0	31	27	6	180	220	51	57	0	4.90
Barney Schultz	R	34	7	6	.538	7	41	0	0	67	57	25	59	0	2.69
Bob Anderson	R	25	7	10	.412	8	57	12	1	152	162	56	96	0	4.26
Glen Hobbie	R	25	7	13	.350	2	36	29	7	199	207	54	103	2	4.25
Don Elston	R	32	6	7	.462	8	58	0	0	93	108	45	59	0	5.61
Dick Drott	R	25	1	4	.200	3	35	8	0	98	75	51	48	0	4.22
Jim Brewer	L	23	1	7	.125	0	36	11	0	87	116	21	57	0	5.79
Dick Burwell (MS)	R	21	0	0	—	0	4	0	0	4	6	4	0	0	9.00
Mel Wright	R	33	0	0	—	0	11	0	0	21	42	4	6	0	10.71
1 Joe Schaffernoth	R	23	0	4	.000	0	21	0	0	38	43	18	23	0	6.39

PHILADELPHIA 8th 47-107 .305 46 GENE MAUCH

NAME	G by Pos	B	AGE	G	AB	R	H	2B	3B	HR	RBI	BB	SO	SB	BA	SA
TOTALS			26	155	5213	584	1265	185	50	103	549	475	928	56	.243	.357
Pancho Herrera	1B115	R	27	126	400	56	103	17	2	13	51	55	120	5	.258	.408
Tony Taylor (RJ)	2B91, 3B3	R	25	106	400	47	100	17	3	2	26	29	51	11	.250	.323
Ruben Amaro	SS132, 1B3, 2B1	R	25	135	381	34	98	14	9	1	32	53	59	1	.257	.349
4 Charley Smith	3B94, SS14	R	23	112	411	43	102	13	4	9	47	23	76	3	.248	.365
2 Don Demeter	OF79, 1B22	R	26	106	382	54	98	18	4	20	68	19	74	2	.257	.482
Tony Gonzalez	OF118	L	24	126	426	58	118	16	8	12	58	49	66	15	.277	.437
Johnny Callison	OF124	L	22	138	455	74	121	20	11	9	47	69	76	10	.266	.418
Clay Dalrymple	C122	L	24	129	378	23	83	11	1	5	42	30	30	0	.220	.294
Bobby Malkmus	2B58, SS34, 3B25	R	29	121	342	39	79	8	2	7	31	20	43	1	.231	.327
Lee Walls	1B28, 3B26, OF18	R	28	91	261	32	73	6	4	8	30	19	48	2	.280	.425
Ken Walters	OF56, 1B5, 3B1	L	27	86	180	23	41	8	2	2	14	5	25	2	.228	.328
Bobby Gene Smith	OF47	R	27	79	174	16	44	7	0	2	18	15	32	0	.253	.328
4 Wes Covington	OF45	L	29	57	165	23	50	9	0	7	26	15	17	0	.303	.485
2 Elmer Valo	OF1	L	40	50	43	4	8	2	0	1	8	4	6	0	.186	.302
1 Bobby Del Greco	OF32, 2B1, 3B1	R	28	48	112	14	29	5	0	2	11	12	17	0	.259	.357
Choo Choo Coleman	C14	L	23	34	47	3	6	1	0	0	4	2	8	0	.128	.149
Jim Woods	3B15	R	21	23	48	6	11	3	0	2	9	4	15	0	.229	.417
1 Darrell Johnson	C21	R	32	21	61	4	14	1	0	0	3	8	7	0	.230	.246
George Williams	2B15	R	21	17	36	4	9	0	0	0	1	4	4	0	.250	.250
Bob Sadowski	3B14	R	24	16	54	4	7	0	0	0	4	7	1	0	.130	.130
Jimmie Coker	C11	R	25	11	25	3	10	1	0	1	5	0	4	0	.400	.560

Cal Neeman 32 R 7-31, Tony Curry 22 L 7-36, Al Kenders 24 R 4-23, 1 Joe Koppe 30 R 0-3

NAME	T	AGE	W	L	PCT	SV	G	GS	CG	IP	H	BB	SO	SHO	ERA
		28	47	107	.305	13	155	155	29	1383	1452	521	775	9	4.61
Art Mahaffey	R	23	11	19	.367	0	36	32	12	219	205	70	158	3	4.11
Chris Short	L	23	6	12	.333	1	39	16	1	127	157	71	80	0	5.95
John Buzhardt	R	24	6	18	.250	0	41	27	6	202	200	65	92	1	4.50
Jack Baldschun	R	24	5	3	.625	3	65	0	0	100	90	49	59	0	3.87
Jim Owens	R	27	5	10	.333	0	20	17	3	107	119	32	38	0	4.46
Don Ferrarese	L	32	5	12	.294	1	42	14	3	139	120	68	89	1	3.76
Frank Sullivan	R	31	3	16	.158	2	41	18	1	159	161	55	114	1	4.30
1 Dick Farrell	R	27	2	1	.667	6	49	0	0	10	16	6	10	0	6.30
Dallas Green	R	26	2	4	.333	1	42	10	1	128	160	47	51	1	4.85
Ken Lehman	L	33	1	1	.500	1	41	2	0	63	61	25	27	0	4.29
Robin Roberts (KJ)	R	34	1	10	.091	0	26	18	2	117	154	23	54	0	5.85
Jack Meyer	R	29	0	0	—	0	11	0	0	2	2	5	9	0	9.00
Paul Brown	R	20	0	1	.000	0	5	1	0	13	8	1	0	0	8.10

WORLD SERIES — NEW YORK (AL) 4 CINCINNATI (NL) 1

LINE SCORES

TEAM	1	2	3	4	5	6	7	8	9	10	11	12	R	H	E

Game 1 October 4 at New York

													R	H	E
CIN (NL)	0 0 0	0 0 0	0 0 0				0	2	0
NY (AL)	0 0 0	1 0 1	0 0 X				2	6	0

O'Toole, Brosnan (8) Ford

Game 2 October 5 at New York

										R	H	E
CIN	0 0 0	2 1 1	0 2 0	6	9	0
NY	0 0 0	2 0 0	0 0 0	2	4	3

Jay Terry, Arroyo (8)

Game 3 October 7 at Cincinnati

										R	H	E
NY	0 0 0	0 0 0	1 1 1	3	6	1
CIN	0 0 1	0 0 0	1 0 0	2	8	0

Stafford, Daley (7), Arroyo (8) Purkey

Game 4 October 8 at Cincinnati

										R	H	E
NY	0 0 0	1 1 2	3 0 0	7	11	0
CIN	0 0 0	0 0 0	0 0 0	0	5	1

Ford, Coates (6) O'Toole, Brosnan (6), Henry (9)

Game 5 October 9 at Cincinnati

										R	H	E
NY	5 1 0	5 0 2	0 0 0	13	15	1
CIN	0 0 3	0 2 0	0 0 0	5	11	3

Terry, Daley (3) Jay, Maloney (1), K. Johnson (2), Henry (3), Jones (4), Purkey (5), Brosnan (7), Hunt (9)

COMPOSITE BATTING

NAME	POS	G	AB	R	H	2B	3B	HR	RBI	BA
New York (AL)										
Totals		5	165	27	42	8	1	7	26	.255
Richardson	2B	5	23	2	9	1	0	0	0	.391
Kubek	SS	5	22	3	5	0	0	0	1	.227
Howard	C	5	20	5	5	3	0	1	1	.250
Maris	OF	5	19	4	2	1	0	1	2	.105
Skowron	1B	5	17	3	6	0	0	1	5	.353
Boyer	3B	5	15	0	4	2	0	0	3	.267
Berra	OF	4	11	2	3	0	0	1	3	.273
Blanchard	OF	4	10	4	4	1	0	2	3	.400
Lopez	OF	4	9	3	3	0	1	1	7	.333
Mantle	OF	2	6	0	1	0	0	0	0	.167
Ford	P	2	5	1	0	0	0	0	0	.000
Terry	P	2	3	0	0	0	0	0	0	.000
Stafford	P	1	2	0	0	0	0	0	1	.000
Daley	P	2	1	0	0	0	0	0	0	.000
Gardner	PH	1	1	0	0	0	0	0	0	.000
Coates	P	1	1	0	0	0	0	0	0	.000
Reed	OF	3	0	0	0	0	0	0	0	—
Arroyo	P	2	0	0	0	0	0	0	0	—
Cincinnati (NL)										
Totals		5	170	13	35	8	0	3	11	.206
Kasko	SS	5	22	1	7	0	0	0	0	.318
Pinson	OF	5	22	0	2	1	0	0	0	.091
Coleman	1B	5	20	2	5	1	0	0	2	.250
Post	OF	5	18	3	6	1	0	1	4	.333
Freese	3B	5	16	0	1	1	0	0	1	.063
Robinson	OF	5	15	3	3	2	0	1	4	.200
Chacon	2B	4	12	2	3	0	0	0	0	.250
Edwards	C	3	11	1	4	2	0	0	2	.364
Blasingame	2B	3	7	1	1	0	0	0	0	.143
D. Johnson	C	3	4	0	2	0	0	0	0	.500
Gernert	PH	4	4	0	0	0	0	0	0	.000
Jay	P	2	4	0	0	0	0	0	0	.000
Cardenas	PH	3	3	0	1	0	0	0	0	.333
Lynch	PH	3	3	0	0	0	0	0	0	.000
O'Toole	P	2	3	0	0	0	0	0	0	.000
Purkey	P	2	2	0	0	0	0	0	0	.000
Bell	PH	2	2	0	0	0	0	0	0	.000
Zimmerman	C	2	0	0	0	0	0	0	0	—
Brosnan	P	3	0	0	0	0	0	0	0	—
Henry	P	2	0	0	0	0	0	0	0	—
K. Johnson	P	2	0	0	0	0	0	0	0	—

Hunt P 0-0, Jones P 0-0, Maloney P 0-0

COMPOSITE PITCHING

NAME	G	IP	H	BB	SO	W	L	SV	ERA
New York (AL)									
Totals	5	45	35	8	27	4	1	1	1.60
Ford	2	14	6	1	7	2	0	0	0.00
Terry	2	9.1	12	2	7	0	1	0	4.82
Daley	2	7	5	0	3	1	0	0	0.00
Stafford	1	6.2	7	2	5	0	0	0	2.70
Arroyo	2	4	4	2	3	1	0	0	2.25
Coates	1	4	1	1	2	0	0	1	0.00
Cincinnati (NL)									
Totals	5	44	42	24	25	1	4	0	4.91
O'Toole	2	12	11	7	4	0	2	0	3.00
Purkey	2	11	6	3	5	0	1	0	1.64
Jay	2	9.2	8	6	6	1	1	0	5.59
Brosnan	3	6	9	4	5	0	0	0	7.50
Henry	2	2.1	4	2	3	0	0	0	19.29
Hunt	1	1	0	1	0	0	0	0	0.00
K. Johnson	1	0.2	0	0	0	0	0	0	0.00
Jones	1	0.2	4	1	1	0	0	0	27.00
Maloney	1	0.2	4	1	1	0	0	0	27.00

1962 Circulating into Second Place

After much struggle with the city fathers of Los Angeles, Walter O'Malley finally opened his baseball emporium, Dodger Stadium, for the start of the 1962 season. O'Malley's highly regarded team drew a record 2,755,184 fans into the park, while pacing the National League all summer behind the star performances of Maury Wills, Tommy Davis, and Don Drysdale. Of the trio, Wills proved the most exciting while en route to the league's MVP Award by committing the grandest theft act ever witnessed on major league turf—104 steals—to break the 1915 mark of the legendary Ty Cobb. Davis, by hitting .346 and knocking in 153 runs, captured two of the major batting categories while Drysdale won the coveted Cy Young Award on the strength of his 25 victories.

But all the individual glory could not make up for an unfortunate incident which took place on July 17, when ace southpaw Sandy Koufax was lost for the season with a circulatory ailment in his fingers. In the final 13 contests, the Dodgers could only win three, while the rival San Francisco Giants won seven to tie Los Angeles on the final day of the season.

In the first game of the play-offs, the Giants won easily behind Billy Pierce's 3-hit, 8-0 performance. The Dodgers came from behind to take the second game, 8-7, thus setting the stage for the showdown and evoking the memories of the 1951 play-offs. After eight innings, the Dodgers led 4-2. But the Giants crossed the plate four times in the ninth, with the winning run being walked across by Stan Williams.

The Giants stayed in contention all year with an attack centered on home run leader Willie Mays, and the slugging of Orlando Cepeda and Felipe Alou. Jack Sanford, by winning 16 games in a row and winding up with 24, led all the hurlers, which included Billy O'Dell's 19, Juan Marichal's 18, and 16 from the arm of the 35-year-old Pierce.

The Giant-Dodger pennant struggle partly overshadowed the league's expansion to ten teams, which brought Houston into the fold for the first time and a return of a National League team to New York in the unlikely name of the Mets. Led by Casey Stengel, also returning after his ouster by the Yankees, the Mets lost 120 games to set a modern record for futility.

In the American League, the fanfare took place before the final curtain. Cleveland, leading until the All-Star break, lost 19 of their next 24 games to drop into second division. While the Indians were faltering, the Los Angeles Angels and Minnesota Twins, the league's newest entries, were charging into contention. Although the joint efforts were commendable, both fell short. The Twins finished second on the strength of a strong batting attack, and the Angels third on the arms of their two colorful rookies, Dean Chance and Bo Belinsky.

As usual, the Yankees were on top when the season closed. Even in an off-year, New York mustered enough offense to win the pennant by five games. Mickey Mantle, although missing 39 games with injuries, also mustered enough of an attack, with his .321 batting and 30 home runs, to win the league's MVP Award. Roger Maris cooled off greatly from his record 1961 cloudburst and polled 33 homers, while Bobby Richardson turned in his best year with a .302 average. Rookie Tom Tresh filled in admirably at shortstop until Tony Kubek returned from the army in August, and Ralph Terry led all the Yankees and the league with his 23 victories.

On October 4, when the World Series got underway at Candlestick Park in San Francisco, the Giants and Yankees were meeting in the fall classic for the seventh time. The rivalry, which first began in 1921, saw the Giants take a commanding 2-0 lead before the Yankees came back to take the next four Series. Both clubs had not met since the Giants' memorable year of 1951, and events had changed sufficiently enough so that the once-prized championship, as well as the love of New York City itself, was no longer up for grabs.

In the opener Whitey Ford faced Billy O'Dell, and a homer by Clete Boyer in the seventh broke a 2-2 tie to give New York a final 6-2 victory and Ford his tenth win in Series play. Jack Sanford and Ralph Terry matched up the next day and the Giants, behind Chuck Hiller's double and Willie McCovey's home run, evened matters, 2-0, as Sanford held the Yankees to three hits. Both clubs traveled to New York for the third game which featured Billy Pierce and Bill Stafford. Much like the opener, the game remained tied until the seventh. This time for New York, Roger Maris came to the rescue with a single which scored two of the three runs collected in the inning in what turned out to be a 3-2 affair. Game four once again saw both clubs entering the seventh with identical scores, but the day belonged to the Giants in this go-around, or to be more precise, it was the possession of Chuck Hiller, who hit the first National League grand slam in Series play to once again even the contest.

Terry, who lost the second game to Sanford, returned to outpitch the Giants' ace right-hander, 5-3, behind a three-run homer by Tom Tresh. With the Yankees up, 3-2, both clubs returned West, but, a rain delay of three days made the final result nearly anticlimactic. When play resumed on October 15—five days since the last game—Pierce limited the Yankees to three hits in prolonging the seesaw battle another day. Finally, with Terry and Sanford hooking up for the third time, the Yankees won, 1-0, on a catch by Bobby Richardson of McCovey's line drive with two outs and two on in the ninth which gave a fitting end to a Series which did not seem to have an end.

WORLD SERIES — NEW YORK (AL) 4 SAN FRANCISCO (NL) 3

LINE SCORES

TEAM	1	2	3	4	5	6	7	8	9	10	11	12	R	H	E

Game 1 October 4 at San Francisco

													R	H	E
NY (AL)	2	0	0	0	0	0	1	2	1				6	11	0
SF (NL)	0	1	1	0	0	0	0	0	0				2	10	0

Ford   O'Dell, Larsen (8), Miller (9)

Game 2 October 5 at San Francisco

										R	H	E
NY	0	0	0	0	0	0	0	0	0	0	3	1
SF	1	0	0	0	0	0	1	0	X	2	6	0

Terry, Daley (8)   Sanford

Game 3 October 7 at New York

										R	H	E
SF	0	0	0	0	0	0	0	0	2	2	4	3
NY	0	0	0	0	0	0	3	0	X	3	5	1

Pierce, Larsen (7), Bolin (8)   Stafford

Game 4 October 8 at New York

										R	H	E
SF	0	2	0	0	0	0	4	0	1	7	9	1
NY	0	0	0	0	0	2	0	0	1	3	9	1

Marichal, Bolin (7),   Ford, Coates (7),
Larsen (6), O'Dell (7)   Bridges (7)

Game 5 October 10 at New York

										R	H	E
SF	0	0	1	0	1	0	0	0	1	3	8	2
NY	0	0	0	1	0	1	0	3	X	5	6	0

Sanford, Miller (8)   Terry

Game 6 October 15 at San Francisco

										R	H	E
NY	0	0	0	0	1	0	0	1	0	2	3	2
SF	0	0	0	3	2	0	0	0	X	5	10	1

Ford, Coates (5), Bridges (8)   Pierce

Game 7 October 16 at San Francisco

										R	H	E
NY	0	0	0	0	1	0	0	0	0	1	7	0
SF	0	0	0	0	0	0	0	0	0	0	4	1

Terry   Sanford, O'Dell (8)

COMPOSITE BATTING

NAME	POS	G	AB	R	H	2B	3B	HR	RBI	BA
New York (AL) Totals		7	221	20	44	6	1	3	17	.199
Kubek	SS	7	29	2	8	1	0	0	1	.276
Tresh	OF	7	28	5	9	1	0	1	4	.321
Richardson	2B	7	27	3	4	0	0	0	0	.148
Mantle	OF	7	25	2	3	1	0	0	0	.120
Maris	OF	7	23	4	4	1	0	1	5	.174
Boyer	3B	7	22	2	7	1	0	1	4	.318
Howard	C	6	21	1	3	1	0	0	1	.143
Skowron	1B	6	18	1	4	0	1	0	1	.222
Terry	P	3	8	0	1	0	0	0	0	.125
Ford	P	3	7	0	0	0	0	0	0	.000
Long	1B	2	5	0	1	0	0	0	1	.200
Stafford	P	1	3	0	0	0	0	0	0	.000
Berra	C	2	2	0	0	0	0	0	0	.000
Lopez	PH	2	2	0	0	0	0	0	0	.000
Blanchard	PH	1	1	0	0	0	0	0	0	.000
Coates	P	2	0	0	0	0	0	0	0	—
Bridges	P	2	0	0	0	0	0	0	0	—
Daley	P	1	0	0	0	0	0	0	0	—
San Francisco (NL) Totals		7	226	21	51	10	2	5	19	.226
Mays	OF	7	28	3	7	2	0	0	1	.250
Hiller	2B	7	26	4	7	3	0	1	5	.269
F. Alou	OF	7	26	2	7	1	1	0	1	.269
Davenport	3B	7	22	1	3	1	0	0	1	.136
Pagan	SS	7	19	2	7	0	0	1	2	.368
Cepeda	1B	5	19	1	3	1	0	0	2	.158
McCovey	1B-OF	4	15	2	3	0	1	1	1	.200
Haller	C	4	14	1	4	1	1	1	3	.286
Bailey	C	6	14	1	1	0	0	1	2	.071
M. Alou	OF	6	12	2	4	1	0	0	1	.333
Kuenn	OF	3	12	1	1	0	0	0	0	.083
Sanford	P	3	7	0	3	0	0	0	0	.429
Pierce	P	2	5	0	0	0	0	0	0	.000
O'Dell	P	3	3	0	1	0	0	0	0	.333
Marichal	P	1	2	0	0	0	0	0	0	.000
Bowman	SS	2	1	1	0	0	0	0	0	.000
Orsino	C	1	1	0	0	0	0	0	0	.000
Larsen	P	3	0	0	0	0	0	0	0	—
Miller	P	2	0	0	0	0	0	0	0	—
Bolin	P	2	0	0	0	0	0	0	0	—
Nieman	PH	1	0	0	0	0	0	0	0	—

COMPOSITE PITCHING

NAME	G	IP	H	BB	SO	W	L	SV	ERA
New York (AL) Totals	7	61	51	12	39	4	3	0	2.95
Terry	3	25	17	2	16	2	1	0	1.80
Ford	3	19.2	24	4	12	1	1	0	4.12
Stafford	1	9	4	2	5	1	0	0	2.00
Bridges	2	3.2	4	2	3	0	0	0	4.91
Coates	2	2.2	1	1	3	0	1	0	6.75
Daley	1	1	1	1	0	0	0	0	0.00
San Francisco (NL) Totals	7	61	44	21	39	3	4	1	2.66
Sanford	3	23.1	16	8	19	1	2	0	1.93
Pierce	2	15	8	2	5	1	1	0	2.40
O'Dell	3	12.1	12	3	9	0	1	1	4.38
Marichal	1	4	2	4	0	0	0	0	0.00
Bolin	2	2.2	4	2	2	0	0	0	6.75
Larsen	3	2.1	1	2	1	0	0	0	3.86
Miller	2	1.1	1	2	0	0	0	0	0.00

NEW YORK 1st 96-66 .593 — RALPH HOUK

NAME	G by Pos	B	AGE	G	AB	R	H	2B	3B	HR	RBI	BB	SO	SB	BA	SA
TOTALS			29	162	5644	817	1509	240	29	199	791	584	842	42	.267	.426
Bill Skowron	1B135	R	31	140	478	63	129	16	6	23	80	36	99	0	.270	.473
Bobby Richardson	2B161	R	26	161	692	99	209	38	5	8	59	37	24	11	.302	.406
Tom Tresh	SS111, OF43	B	24	157	622	94	178	26	5	20	93	67	74	4	.286	.441
Clete Boyer	3B157	R	25	158	566	85	154	24	1	18	68	51	106	3	.272	.413
Roger Maris	OF154	L	27	157	590	92	151	34	1	33	100	87	78	1	.256	.485
Mickey Mantle (KJ)	OF117	B	30	123	377	96	121	15	1	30	89	122	78	9	.321	.605
Hector Lopez	OF84, 2B1, 3B1	R	32	106	335	45	92	19	1	6	48	30	53	0	.275	.391
Elston Howard	C129	R	33	136	494	63	138	23	5	21	91	31	76	1	.279	.474
Johnny Blanchard	OF47, C15, 1B2	L	29	93	246	33	57	7	0	13	39	28	32	0	.232	.419
Jack Reed	OF75	R	29	88	43	17	13	2	1	0	4	4	7	2	.302	.465
Yogi Berra	C31, OF28	L	37	86	232	25	52	8	0	10	35	24	18	0	.224	.388
Phil Linz	SS21, 3B8, 2B5, OF2	R	23	71	129	28	37	8	0	1	14	6	17	5	.287	.372
Joe Pepitone	OF32, 1B16	L	21	63	138	14	33	3	2	7	17	3	21	1	.239	.442
Tony Kubek (MS)	SS35, OF6	L	25	45	169	28	53	6	1	4	17	12	17	2	.314	.432
1 Dale Long	1B31	L	36	41	94	12	28	4	0	4	17	18	9	1	.298	.468
1 Bob Cerv	OF3	R	36	14	17	1	2	1	0	0	0	2	3	0	.118	.176
1 Billy Gardner	3B1, 2B1	R	34	4	1	1	0	0	0	0	0	0	1	0	.000	.000
Jake Gibbs	3B1	R	23	2	2	0	2	0	0	0	0	0	0	0	—	—

NAME	T	AGE	W	L	PCT	SV	G	GS	CG	IP	H	BB	SO	SHO	ERA
TOTALS		28	96	66	.593	42	162	162	33	1470	1375	499	838	10	3.70
Ralph Terry	R	26	23	12	.657	2	43	39	14	299	257	57	176	3	3.19
Whitey Ford	L	33	17	8	.680	0	38	37	7	258	243	69	160	2	2.90
Bill Stafford	R	22	14	9	.609	0	35	33	7	213	188	77	109	2	3.68
Marshall Bridges	L	31	8	4	.667	18	52	0	0	72	49	48	66	0	3.13
Bud Daley	L	29	7	5	.583	4	43	6	0	105	105	21	55	0	3.60
Jim Coates	R	29	7	6	.538	6	50	6	0	118	119	50	67	0	4.42
Jim Bouton	R	23	7	7	.500	2	36	16	3	133	124	59	71	1	3.99
Rollie Sheldon	R	25	7	8	.467	1	34	16	2	118	136	28	54	0	5.49
Bob Turley	R	31	3	3	.500	1	24	8	0	69	68	47	42	0	4.57
Tex Clevenger	R	29	2	0	1.000	1	21	0	0	38	36	17	11	0	2.84
Luis Arroyo (SA)	L	35	1	3	.250	7	27	0	0	34	33	17	21	0	4.76
Jack Cullen	R	22	0	0	—	0	2	0	0	3	2	2	2	0	0.00
Hal Reniff	R	23	0	0	—	0	2	0	0	4	6	5	1	0	6.75
Al Downing	L	21	0	0	—	0	1	0	0	1	1	7	0	0	0.00
2 Hal Brown	R	37	0	1	.000	0	2	1	0	9	12	4	0	0	6.43

MINNESOTA 2nd 91-71 .562 5 — SAM MELE

NAME	G by Pos	B	AGE	G	AB	R	H	2B	3B	HR	RBI	BB	SO	SB	BA	SA
TOTALS			26	163	5561	798	1445	215	39	185	758	649	823	33	.260	.412
Vic Power	1B142, 2B2	R	34	144	611	80	177	28	2	16	63	22	35	7	.290	.421
Bernie Allen	2B158	L	23	159	573	79	154	27	4	12	64	62	82	0	.269	.403
Zoilo Versalles	SS160	R	22	160	568	69	137	18	3	17	67	37	71	5	.241	.373
Rich Rollins	3B159, SS1	R	24	159	624	96	186	23	5	16	96	75	61	3	.298	.428
Bob Allison	OF147	R	27	149	519	102	138	24	8	29	102	84	115	8	.266	.511
Lenny Green	OF156	L	28	158	619	97	168	33	3	14	63	88	36	8	.271	.402
Harmon Killebrew	OF151, 1B4	R	26	155	552	85	134	21	1	48	126	106	142	1	.243	.545
Earl Battey	C147	R	27	148	522	58	146	20	3	11	57	57	48	0	.280	.393
Bill Tuttle	OF104	R	32	110	123	21	26	4	1	3	13	19	14	1	.211	.285
Don Mincher	1B25	L	24	86	121	20	29	1	1	9	29	34	24	0	.240	.488
George Banks	OF17, 3B6	R	23	63	103	22	26	0	2	4	15	21	27	0	.252	.408
Johnny Goryl	2B4, SS1	R	28	37	26	6	5	0	1	2	2	2	6	0	.192	.500
Marty Martinez	SS11, 3B1	R	24	20	37	18	13	3	0	1	3	3	4	0	.167	.278
Jerry Zimmerman	C34	R	27	34	62	8	17	4	0	0	7	3	5	0	.274	.339
Hal Naragon	C9	L	33	24	35	1	8	1	0	0	3	1	0	0	.229	.257
Jim Lemon (SJ)	OF3	R	34	12	17	1	3	0	0	1	3	1	4	0	.176	.353
Jim Snyder	2B5, SS1	L	29	12	10	1	1	0	0	0	1	0	4	0	.100	.100
Tony Oliva	OF2	L	21	9	9	3	4	1	0	0	3	2	2	0	.444	.556

NAME	T	AGE	W	L	PCT	SV	G	GS	CG	IP	H	BB	SO	SHO	ERA
TOTALS		27	91	71	.562	27	163	163	53	1463	1400	493	948	11	3.89
Camilo Pascual	R	28	20	11	.645	0	34	33	18	258	236	59	206	5	3.31
Jim Kaat	L	23	18	14	.563	1	39	35	16	269	243	75	173	5	3.14
Dick Stigman	L	26	12	5	.706	3	40	15	6	143	122	64	116	0	3.65
Jack Kralick	R	27	12	11	.522	0	39	37	7	243	239	61	139	1	3.85
Ray Moore	R	36	8	3	.727	9	49	0	0	65	55	30	58	0	4.71
Joe Bonikowski	R	21	5	7	.417	2	30	13	3	100	95	38	45	0	3.87
2 Frank Sullivan	R	32	4	1	.800	5	21	0	0	33	33	13	10	0	3.27
1 Don Lee	R	28	3	3	.500	0	9	9	1	52	51	24	28	0	4.50
Bill Pleis	L	24	2	5	.286	3	21	4	0	45	46	14	31	0	4.40
Ted Sadowski	R	26	1	1	.500	0	19	0	0	34	37	11	15	0	5.03
2 Ruben Gomez	R	34	1	1	.500	0	6	2	1	19	17	11	6	0	4.74
Georges Maranda	R	30	1	3	.250	0	32	4	0	73	69	35	36	0	4.44
Jim Manning	R	18	0	0	—	0	5	1	0	7	14	1	3	0	5.14
Jerry Arrigo	L	21	0	0	—	0	1	0	0	1	1	1	1	0	18.00
Jim Roland	L	19	0	0	—	0	1	0	0	1	1	0	1	0	0.00
2 Jim Donohue	R	23	0	1	.000	0	6	1	0	12	16	3	10	0	7.20
1 Jackie Collum	L	35	0	0	—	0	3	0	0	15	29	1	5	0	11.40

LOS ANGELES 3rd 86-76 .531 10 — BILL RIGNEY

NAME	G by Pos	B	AGE	G	AB	R	H	2B	3B	HR	RBI	BB	SO	SB	BA	SA
TOTALS			27	162	5499	718	1377	232	35	137	667	602	917	46	.250	.380
Lee Thomas	1B90, OF74	L	26	160	583	88	169	21	2	26	104	55	74	6	.290	.467
Billy Moran	2B160	R	28	160	659	90	186	25	3	17	74	39	80	5	.282	.407
Joe Koppe	SS118, 2B5, 3B4	R	31	128	375	47	85	16	0	4	40	73	84	2	.227	.301
Felix Torres	3B123	R	30	127	451	44	117	19	4	11	74	24	78	0	.259	.392
George Thomas (MS)	OF51	R	24	56	181	13	43	10	2	4	12	21	37	0	.238	.381
Albie Pearson	OF160	L	27	160	614	115	160	29	6	5	42	95	36	15	.261	.352
Leon Wagner	OF156	L	28	160	612	96	164	21	5	37	107	50	87	7	.268	.500
Bob Rodgers	C150	B	23	155	565	65	146	34	6	6	61	45	68	1	.258	.372
Earl Averill	OF49, C6	R	30	92	187	21	41	9	0	4	22	43	47	0	.219	.332
Tom Burgess	1B35, OF2	L	34	87	143	17	28	7	1	2	13	36	20	2	.196	.301
Steve Bilko (LJ)	1B50	R	33	64	164	26	47	9	1	8	38	25	35	1	.287	.500
Jim Fregosi	SS52	R	20	58	175	15	51	3	4	3	23	18	27	2	.291	.406
Eddie Yost	3B28, 1B7	R	35	52	104	22	25	9	1	0	10	30	21	0	.240	.346
2 Gordie Windhorn	OF34	R	28	40	45	9	8	6	0	0	1	7	10	1	.178	.311
2 Billy Consolo	3B20, SS4, 2B1	R	27	28	20	4	2	0	0	0	3	5	11	2	.100	.100
Eddie Sadowski	C18	R	31	27	55	4	11	4	0	1	3	2	14	1	.200	.327
Leo Burke	OF12, 3B4, SS1	R	28	19	64	8	17	1	0	4	14	5	11	0	.266	.469
Ken Hunt (AJ-MS)	1B3	R	27	13	11	4	2	0	0	1	1	1	5	1	.182	.455
1 Marlan Coughtry	3B5, 2B2	L	27	11	22	0	4	0	0	0	2	0	6	0	.182	.182
Tom Satriano	3B5, 1B1	R	21	10	19	4	8	2	0	2	6	0	1	0	.421	.842
Gene Leek (MS)	3B4	R	25	7	14	0	2	0	0	0	0	1	6	0	.143	.143
Frank Leja	1B4	L	26	7	16	0	0	0	0	0	0	1	6	0	.000	.000
Chuck Tanner	OF2	L	32	7	8	0	1	0	0	0	0	0	3	0	.125	.125
Dick Simpson	OF4	R	18	6	8	1	2	1	0	0	1	2	3	0	.250	.375
Ed Kirkpatrick	C1	L	17	3	1	0	0	0	0	0	0	0	0	0	.000	.000

NAME	T	AGE	W	L	PCT	SV	G	GS	CG	IP	H	BB	SO	SHO	ERA
TOTALS		28	86	76	.531	47	162	162	23	1466	1412	616	858	15	3.70
Dean Chance	R	21	14	10	.583	8	50	24	6	207	195	66	127	2	2.96
Ken McBride (XJ)	R	26	11	5	.688	0	24	23	6	149	136	70	83	4	3.50
Bo Belinsky	L	25	10	11	.476	1	33	31	5	187	149	122	145	3	3.56
Ted Bowsfield	L	26	9	8	.529	1	34	25	1	139	154	40	52	0	4.40
2 Don Lee	R	28	8	8	.500	2	27	22	4	153	153	39	74	2	3.12
Eli Grba	R	27	8	9	.471	1	40	29	1	176	185	75	90	0	4.55
Tom Morgan	R	32	5	2	.714	9	48	0	0	59	53	19	29	2	2.90
Jack Spring	L	29	2	2	.667	6	57	0	0	65	66	30	31	0	4.02
Art Fowler	R	39	4	3	.571	5	48	0	0	77	67	25	38	0	2.81
Bob Botz	R	27	2	1	.667	2	35	0	0	63	71	11	24	0	3.43
Ryne Duren	R	33	2	9	.182	8	42	3	0	71	53	57	74	0	4.44
1 Jim Donohue	R	23	1	0	1.000	0	12	1	0	24	24	11	14	0	3.75
Julio Navarro	R	26	1	1	.500	0	15	0	0	15	20	4	11	0	4.80
1 George Witt	R	28	1	1	.500	0	10	0	0	15	15	5	10	0	8.10
1 Joe Nuxhall	L	33	0	0	—	0	4	1	0	6	11	3	4	0	10.80
Fred Newman	R	20	0	1	.000	0	4	0	0	8	6	3	3	0	10.50
Bobby Darwin	R	19	0	1	.000	0	1	0	0	1	3	4	1	0	12.00
Ron Moeller (MS) 23															

DETROIT 4th 85-76 .528 10.5 — BOB SCHEFFING

NAME	G by Pos	B	AGE	G	AB	R	H	2B	3B	HR	RBI	BB	SO	SB	BA	SA
TOTALS			28	161	5456	758	1352	191	36	209	719	651	894	69	.248	.411
Norm Cash	1B146, OF3	L	27	148	507	94	123	16	2	39	89	104	82	6	.243	.513
Jake Wood	2B90	R	25	111	367	68	83	10	5	8	30	33	69	24	.226	.346
Chico Fernandez	SS138, 3B2, 1B1	R	30	141	503	64	125	17	2	20	59	42	69	10	.249	.410
Steve Boros	3B105, 2B6	R	25	116	356	46	81	14	1	16	47	53	62	3	.228	.407
Al Kaline (BC)	OF100	R	27	100	398	78	121	16	6	29	94	47	39	4	.304	.593
Bill Bruton	OF145	L	36	147	561	90	156	27	5	16	74	55	67	14	.278	.430
Rocky Colavito	OF161	R	28	161	601	90	164	30	2	37	112	96	68	2	.273	.514
Dick Brown	C132	R	27	134	431	40	104	12	0	12	40	21	66	0	.241	.353
Dick McAuliffe	2B70, 3B49, SS16	L	22	139	471	50	124	20	5	12	63	64	76	4	.263	.403
Bubba Morton	OF62, 1B3	R	30	90	195	30	51	6	3	4	17	32	32	1	.262	.385
Vic Wertz	1B16	L	37	74	105	7	34	2	0	5	18	5	13	0	.324	.486
Bobo Osborne	3B13, 1B7, C1	L	26	64	74	12	17	1	0	0	7	16	25	0	.230	.243
Mike Roarke	C53	R	31	56	136	11	29	4	1	4	14	13	17	0	.213	.346
2 Bob Farley	1B6, OF6	L	24	36	50	9	8	2	0	1	4	14	10	0	.160	.260
2 Don Buddin	SS19, 2B5, 3B2	R	28	31	83	14	19	3	0	0	4	20	16	1	.229	.265
1 Charlie Maxwell	OF15, 1B1	L	35	30	67	5	13	2	0	1	9	8	10	0	.194	.269
Purnal Goldy	OF15	R	24	20	70	8	16	1	1	3	12	0	12	0	.229	.400
Frank Kostro	3B11	R	24	16	41	5	11	3	0	0	3	1	6	0	.268	.341
Reno Bertoia	2B1, SS1, 3B1	R	27	5	0	0	0	0	0	0	0	0	0	0	.000	.000
1 George Alusik		R	27	2	0	0	0	0	0	0	0	0	0	0	.000	.000

NAME	T	AGE	W	L	PCT	SV	G	GS	CG	IP	H	BB	SO	SHO	ERA
TOTALS		30	85	76	.528	35	161	161	46	1444	1452	503	873	8	3.81
Jim Bunning	R	30	19	10	.655	6	41	35	12	258	262	74	184	2	3.59
Hank Aguirre	L	31	16	8	.667	3	42	22	11	216	162	65	156	2	2.21
Phil Regan	R	25	11	9	.550	0	35	23	6	171	169	64	87	0	4.05
Don Mossi	L	33	11	13	.458	1	35	27	8	180	195	36	121	1	4.20
Paul Foytack	R	31	10	7	.588	0	29	21	5	144	145	86	63	1	4.38
Ron Nischwitz	L	25	4	4	.444	1	48	0	0	65	73	26	28	0	4.58
Howie Koplitz	R	24	3	1	1.000	0	6	1	0	38	54	10	16	0	5.21
Terry Fox	R	26	3	1	.750	16	44	0	0	58	48	16	23	0	1.71
Ron Kline	R	30	3	6	.333	2	36	4	1	77	88	28	47	0	4.32
Sam Jones	R	36	2	4	.333	1	30	6	1	81	77	35	73	0	3.65
Frank Lary (SA)	R	32	2	6	.250	0	17	14	2	80	98	21	41	1	5.74
Jerry Casale	R	28	1	2	.333	0	18	1	0	37	38	18	16	0	4.62
Fred Gladding	R	26	0	0	—	0	8	0	0	8	7	2	5	0	4.50
Bill Faul	R	22	0	0	—	0	2	0	0	2	4	3	2	0	27.00
Tom Fletcher	L	19	0	0	—	0	1	0	0	1	0	0	0	0	0.00
Bob Humphreys	R	26	0	1	.000	0	4	0	0	9	8	2	3	0	7.20
Doug Gallagher	L	22	0	0	—	0	7	2	0	25	31	15	14	0	4.68

CHICAGO 5th 85-77 .525 11 — AL LOPEZ

NAME	G by Pos	B	AGE	G	AB	R	H	2B	3B	HR	RBI	BB	SO	SB	BA	SA
TOTALS			30	162	5514	707	1415	250	56	92	662	620	674	76	.257	.372
Joe Cunningham	1B143, OF5	L	30	149	526	91	155	32	7	8	70	101	59	3	.295	.428
Nellie Fox	2B154	L	34	157	621	79	166	27	7	2	54	38	12	1	.267	.343
Luis Aparicio	SS152	R	28	153	581	72	140	23	5	7	40	32	36	31	.241	.334
Al Smith	3B105, OF39	R	34	142	511	62	149	23	8	16	82	57	60	3	.292	.462
Mike Hershberger	OF135	R	22	148	427	54	112	14	2	4	46	37	36	10	.262	.333
Jim Landis	OF144	R	28	149	534	82	122	16	5	15	61	80	105	19	.228	.375
Floyd Robinson	OF155	L	26	156	600	89	187	45	10	11	109	72	47	4	.312	.475
Cam Carreon	C93	R	24	106	313	31	80	19	1	4	37	33	37	1	.256	.361
Sherm Lollar (JJ)	C66	R	37	84	220	17	59	12	0	2	26	32	23	1	.268	.350
Bob Sadowski	3B16, 2B12	R	25	79	130	22	30	8	0	4	24	13	22	0	.231	.438
Sammy Esposito	3B41, SS20, 2B7	R	30	75	81	14	19	1	0	0	4	13	17	0	.235	.247
2 Charlie Maxwell	OF56, 1B6	L	35	69	206	30	61	8	3	9	43	34	32	0	.296	.495
Charley Smith	3B54	R	24	65	145	11	30	4	0	2	17	9	32	0	.207	.276
Bob Roselli	C20	R	30	35	64	4	12	3	1	1	6	13	15	1	.188	.313
2 Bob Farley	1B14	L	24	33	53	7	10	1	1	1	4	11	13	0	.189	.302
Deacon Jones	1B6	L	28	18	26	2	6	2	0	0	2	4	6	0	.231	.393
J.C. Martin	C6, 1B1, 3B1	L	25	18	26	2	2	0	0	0	0	2	4	0	.077	.077
Ramon Conde	3B7	R	27	14	16	0	0	0	0	0	0	1	3	0	.000	.000
Al Weis	SS4, 2B1, 3B1	B	24	7	12	2	1	0	0	0	1	2	3	1	.083	.083
Brian McCall	OF1	L	19	4	8	2	3	1	0	1	2	0	1	0	.375	1.125
Ken Berry	OF2	R	21	3	6	1	2	0	0	0	2	0	0	0	.333	.333
Dick Kenworthy	2B2	R	21	3	4	0	0	0	0	0	0	0	3	0	.000	.000

NAME	T	AGE	W	L	PCT	SV	G	GS	CG	IP	H	BB	SO	SHO	ERA
TOTALS		29	85	77	.525	28	162	162	50	1452	1380	537	821	13	3.73
Ray Herbert	R	32	20	9	.690	0	35	35	12	237	228	74	115	2	3.27
Juan Pizarro	L	25	12	14	.462	1	36	32	9	203	182	97	173	1	3.81
Eddie Fisher	R	25	9	5	.643	5	57	12	2	183	169	45	88	1	3.10
John Buzhardt	R	25	8	12	.400	0	28	25	8	152	156	59	64	2	4.20
Frank Baumann	L	29	7	6	.538	4	40	10	3	120	117	36	55	1	3.38
Joe Horlen (SA)	R	24	7	6	.538	0	20	19	5	109	108	43	63	1	4.87
Early Wynn	R	42	7	15	.318	0	27	26	11	168	171	56	91	3	4.45
Dom Zanni	R	30	5	4	.545	5	44	2	0	86	67	31	66	0	3.77
Turk Lown	R	38	4	2	.667	6	42	0	0	56	58	25	40	0	3.05
Mike Joyce	R	21	3	2	.600	0	25	1	0	43	40	14	9	0	3.35
1 Russ Kemmerer	R	31	1	0	1.000	0	5	0	0	10	10	2	5	0	3.60
2 Dean Stone	L	31	0	1	1.000	0	27	0	0	30	28	19	23	0	3.30
Dave DeBusschere	R	22	0	0	—	0	12	0	0	18	5	23	8	0	2.00
Herb Score	L	29	0	0	—	0	6	1	0	4	4	6	4	0	4.50
Verle Tiefenthaler	R	23	0	0	—	0	4	0	0	5	6	1	7	0	9.00
Mike Degerick	R	19	0	0	—	0	3	0	0	5	3	6	2	0	7.20
Frank Kreutzer	L	23	0	0	—	0	1	0	0	1	0	1	1	0	0.00
Gary Peters	L	25	0	0	—	0	5	0	0	5	8	1	4	0	6.00

CLEVELAND — 6th 80-82 .494 16 — MEL McGAHA

Batting

NAME	G by Pos	B	AGE	G	AB	R	H	2B	3B	HR	RBI	BB	SO	SB	BA	SA
TOTALS			27	162	5484	682	1341	202	22	180	644	502	939	35	.245	.388
Tito Francona	1B158	L	28	158	621	82	169	28	5	14	70	47	74	3	.272	.401
Jerry Kindall	2B154	R	27	154	530	51	123	21	1	13	55	45	107	4	.232	.349
Woodie Held	SS133, 3B5, OF1	R	30	139	466	55	116	12	2	19	58	73	107	5	.249	.406
Bubba Phillips	3B145, OF3, 2B1	R	32	148	562	53	145	26	0	10	54	20	55	4	.258	.358
Willie Kirkland	OF125	L	28	137	419	56	84	9	1	21	72	43	62	9	.200	.377
Ty Cline	OF107	L	23	118	375	53	93	15	5	2	28	28	50	5	.248	.331
Chuck Essegian	OF90	R	30	106	336	59	92	12	0	21	50	42	68	0	.274	.497
Johnny Romano	C130	R	27	135	459	71	120	19	3	25	81	73	64	0	.261	.479
Al Luplow	OF86	L	23	97	318	54	88	15	3	14	45	36	44	1	.277	.475
Don Dillard	OF50	L	25	95	134	22	40	5	1	5	14	11	25	0	.230	.356
2 Willie Tasby	OF66, 3B1	R	29	75	199	25	48	7	0	4	17	25	41	0	.241	.337
Gene Green	OF33, 1B2	R	29	66	143	16	40	4	1	11	28	8	21	0	.280	.552
Doc Edwards	C39	R	25	53	143	13	39	6	0	3	9	9	14	0	.273	.378
Jim Mahoney	SS23, 2B8, 3B1	R	28	41	74	12	18	4	0	3	5	3	14	0	.243	.419
Dick Donovan	P34	R	34	34	89	8	16	1	0	4	9	7	32	0	.180	.326
Jack Kubiszyn	SS18, 3B1	R	25	25	59	3	10	2	0	1	2	5	7	0	.169	.254
1 Ken Aspromonte	2B6, 3B3	R	30	20	28	4	4	2	0	0	1	6	5	0	.143	.214
Max Alvis	3B12	R	24	12	51	1	11	2	0	0	3	2	13	0	.216	.255
Walt Bond	OF12	L	24	12	50	10	19	3	0	6	17	4	9	1	.380	.800
Mike de la Hoz	2B2	R	23	12	12	0	1	0	0	0	0	0	3	0	.083	.083
Hal Jones	1B4	R	26	5	16	2	5	1	0	1	0	1	4	0	.313	.375

Tommie Agee 19 R 3-14, 3 Marlan Coughtry 27 L 1-2, 1 Bob Nieman 35 R 0-1

Pitching

NAME	T	AGE	W	L	PCT	SV	G	GS	CG	IP	H	BB	SO	SHO	ERA
		27	80	82	.494	31	162	162	45	1441	1410	594	780	12	4.14
Dick Donovan	R	34	20	10	.667	0	34	34	16	251	255	47	94	5	3.59
Jim Perry	R	26	12	12	.500	0	35	27	7	194	213	59	74	3	4.13
Gary Bell	R	25	10	9	.526	12	57	6	1	108	104	52	80	0	4.25
Pedro Ramos	R	27	10	12	.455	1	37	27	7	201	189	85	96	2	3.72
Barry Latman	R	26	8	13	.381	5	45	21	7	179	179	72	117	1	4.17
Mudcat Grant	R	26	7	10	.412	0	26	23	6	150	128	81	90	1	4.26
Sam McDowell	L	19	3	7	.300	1	25	13	0	88	81	70	70	0	6.03
Frank Funk	R	26	2	1	.667	6	47	0	0	81	62	32	49	0	3.22
Bill Dailey	R	27	2	2	.500	1	27	0	0	43	43	17	24	0	3.56
Ron Taylor	R	24	2	2	.500	0	8	4	1	33	36	13	15	0	6.00
Wynn Hawkins (MS)	R	26	1	0	1.000	0	3	0	0	9	9	1	0	0	6.75
Floyd Weaver	R	21	1	0	1.000	0	1	1	0	5	3	0	8	0	1.80
Bob Allen	L	24	1	1	.500	4	30	0	0	31	29	25	23	0	5.81
1 Ruben Gomez	R	34	1	2	.333	1	15	4	0	45	50	25	21	0	4.40
Dave Tyriver	R	24	0	0	—	0	4	0	0	11	10	7	7	0	4.09
2 Jackie Collum	L	35	0	0	—	0	1	0	0	1	4	0	1	0	18.00
1 Don Rudolph	L	30	0	0	—	0	1	0	0	0.1	0	1	0	0	0.00
Bob Hartman	L	24	0	1	.000	0	7	0	0	17	14	8	11	0	3.18

BALTIMORE — 7th 77-85 .475 19 — BILLY HITCHCOCK

Batting

NAME	G by Pos	B	AGE	G	AB	R	H	2B	3B	HR	RBI	BB	SO	SB	BA	SA
TOTALS			28	162	5491	652	1363	225	34	156	617	516	931	45	.248	.387
Jim Gentile	1B150	L	28	152	545	80	137	21	1	33	87	77	100	1	.251	.475
Marv Breeding	2B73, SS1, 3B1	R	28	95	240	27	59	10	1	2	18	8	41	2	.246	.321
Jerry Adair	SS113, 2B34, 3B1	R	25	139	538	67	153	29	4	11	48	27	77	7	.284	.414
Brooks Robinson	3B162, SS3, 2B2	R	25	162	634	77	192	29	9	23	86	42	70	3	.303	.486
Russ Snyder	OF121	L	28	139	416	47	127	19	4	9	40	17	46	7	.305	.435
Jackie Brandt	OF138, 3B2	R	28	143	505	76	129	29	5	19	75	55	64	9	.255	.446
Boog Powell	OF112, 1B1	L	20	124	400	44	97	13	2	15	53	38	79	1	.243	.398
Gus Triandos (BG)	C63	R	31	66	207	20	33	7	0	6	23	29	43	0	.159	.280
Whitey Herzog	OF70	L	30	99	263	34	70	13	1	7	35	41	36	2	.266	.403
Dave Nicholson	OF80	R	22	97	173	25	30	4	1	9	15	27	76	3	.173	.364
Dick Williams	OF29, 1B21, 3B4	R	33	82	178	20	44	7	1	1	18	14	26	0	.247	.315
Charlie Lau	C56	L	29	81	197	21	58	11	2	6	37	7	11	1	.294	.462
1 Johnny Temple	2B71	R	33	78	270	28	71	8	1	1	17	36	22	7	.263	.311
Ron Hansen (BG)	SS64	R	24	71	196	12	34	7	0	3	17	30	36	0	.173	.255
2 Hobie Landrith	C60	L	32	60	167	18	37	4	1	4	17	19	19	0	.222	.329
Milt Pappas	P35	R	23	35	69	5	6	1	0	4	8	1	41	0	.087	.275
Earl Robinson	OF17	R	25	29	63	12	18	3	1	1	8	10	8	2	.286	.413
Barry Shetrone	OF6	L	23	21	24	3	6	1	0	1	0	5	0	.250	.417
2 Marv Throneberry	OF2	L	28	9	9	1	0	0	0	0	0	0	0	0	.000	.000
Bob Saverine	2B7	R	21	8	21	2	5	0	0	0	3	1	3	0	.238	.333
Pete Ward	OF6	L	22	8	21	1	3	2	0	0	2	1	4	5	.143	.238
2 Darrell Johnson	C6	R	33	6	22	0	4	1	0	0	1	0	4	0	.182	.182

Mickey McGuire 21 R 0-4, Nate Smith 27 R 2-9, Andy Etchebarren 19 R 2-6, Ozzie Virgil 29 R 0-0

Pitching

NAME	T	AGE	W	L	PCT	SV	G	GS	CG	IP	H	BB	SO	SHO	ERA
		29	77	85	.475	33	162	162	32	1462	1373	549	898	8	3.69
Milt Pappas	R	23	12	10	.545	0	35	32	9	205	200	75	130	1	4.04
Robin Roberts	R	35	10	9	.526	0	27	25	6	191	176	41	102	2	2.78
Steve Barber (AJ)	R	24	9	6	.600	0	28	19	5	140	145	61	89	2	3.47
Chuck Estrada	R	24	9	17	.346	0	34	33	6	223	199	121	165	0	3.83
Jack Fisher (SJ)	R	23	7	9	.438	1	32	25	4	152	173	56	81	0	5.09
Hoyt Wilhelm	R	39	7	10	.412	15	52	0	0	93	64	34	90	1	1.94
1 Hal Brown	R	37	6	4	.600	1	22	11	0	86	88	21	25	0	4.08
Dick Hall	R	31	6	6	.500	6	43	6	1	118	102	19	71	0	2.29
Billy Hoeft	R	30	4	8	.333	7	57	4	0	114	103	43	73	0	4.58
Wes Stock	R	28	3	2	.600	3	53	0	0	65	50	36	34	0	4.43
Art Quirk	L	24	2	2	.500	0	7	5	0	27	36	18	18	0	6.00
Dave McNally	R	19	1	1	1.000	0	3	1	1	9	2	3	4	1	0.90
John Miller	R	21	1	1	.500	0	2	1	0	10	2	5	4	0	0.90
Jim Lehew	R	20	0	0	—	0	2	0	0	10	10	3	2	0	1.80
Bill Short	L	24	0	0	—	0	2	0	0	6	9	6	7	0	15.75
John Papa	R	21	0	0	—	0	2	0	0	1	4	4	1	0	27.00
Dick Luebke	L	27	0	1	.000	0	12	0	0	21	12	6	7	0	2.77

BOSTON — 8th 76-84 .475 19 — PINKY HIGGINS

Batting

NAME	G by Pos	B	AGE	G	AB	R	H	2B	3B	HR	RBI	BB	SO	SB	BA	SA
TOTALS			28	160	5530	707	1429	257	53	146	671	525	923	39	.258	.403
Pete Runnels	1B151	L	34	152	562	80	183	27	5	10	60	79	57	1	.326	.456
Chuck Schilling (BH)	2B118	R	24	119	413	48	95	17	1	7	35	29	48	1	.230	.327
Ed Bressoud	SS153	R	30	153	599	79	166	40	9	14	68	46	118	2	.277	.444
Frank Malzone	3B156	R	32	156	619	74	175	24	3	21	95	35	43	0	.283	.426
Lu Clinton	OF103	R	24	114	398	63	117	24	10	18	75	34	79	2	.294	.498
Gary Geiger	OF129	L	25	130	466	67	116	18	4	16	54	67	66	18	.249	.408
Carl Yastrzemski	OF160	L	22	160	646	99	191	43	6	19	94	66	82	7	.296	.469
Jim Pagliaroni	C73	R	24	90	260	39	67	14	0	11	37	36	55	2	.258	.438
Carroll Hardy	OF105	R	29	115	362	52	78	13	5	8	36	54	68	3	.215	.345
Bob Tillman	C66	R	25	81	249	28	57	6	4	14	38	19	65	0	.229	.454
Russ Nixon (AJ)	C38	R	27	65	151	11	42	7	2	1	19	8	14	0	.278	.371
Pumpsie Green	OF50, SS5	B	28	56	91	12	21	2	1	1	11	11	18	1	.231	.341
2 Billy Gardner	2B38, 3B7, SS4	R	34	53	199	22	54	9	2	2	12	10	39	0	.271	.337
Dave Philley	OF4	B	42	38	42	3	6	2	0	0	4	5	3	0	.143	.190
Don Gile	1B14	R	27	18	41	3	2	0	0	3	3	15	0	.049	.122

Pitching

NAME	T	AGE	W	L	PCT	SV	G	GS	CG	IP	H	BB	SO	SHO	ERA
		28	76	84	.475	40	160	160	70	1438	1416	632	923	12	4.22
Bill Monbouquette	R	25	15	13	.536	0	35	35	11	235	227	65	153	4	3.33
Gene Conley	R	31	15	14	.517	0	34	33	9	242	238	68	134	2	3.94
Earl Wilson	R	27	12	8	.600	0	31	28	4	191	163	111	137	1	3.91
Dick Radatz	R	25	9	6	.600	24	62	0	0	125	95	40	144	0	2.23
Don Schwall	R	26	9	15	.375	0	33	32	5	182	180	121	89	1	4.95
Arnie Earley	L	29	5	4	.444	0	38	3	0	68	76	46	59	0	5.82
Ike Delock	R	32	4	5	.444	0	17	13	4	86	89	24	49	2	3.77
1 Galen Cisco	R	26	4	7	.364	0	23	9	1	83	95	50	43	0	6.72
Mike Fornieles	R	30	3	6	.333	5	42	1	0	82	96	37	36	0	5.38
Chet Nichols	R	31	1	1	.500	3	29	1	0	57	61	22	33	0	3.00
Merlin Nippert	R	23	0	0	—	0	4	0	0	6	4	3	3	0	4.50
Wilbur Wood	L	20	0	0	—	0	6	0	0	6	8	4	3	0	3.38
Billy Muffett	R	31	0	0	—	0	1	0	0	4	6	2	3	0	9.00
Tracy Stallard	R	24	0	0	—	0	1	0	0	4	5	3	3	0	9.00
1 Ted Wills	L	28	0	0	—	0	2	0	0	1	0	1	1	0	∞
Bill MacLeod	L	20	0	1	.000	0	2	1	0	4	6	3	3	0	4.50
Pete Smith (MS)	R	22	0	1	.000	0	1	0	0	1	0	1	0	0	18.00
Hal Kolstad	R	27	0	2	.000	0	27	0	0	61	65	35	36	0	5.46

KANSAS CITY — 9th 72-90 .444 24 — HANK BAUER

Batting

NAME	G by Pos	B	AGE	G	AB	R	H	2B	3B	HR	RBI	BB	SO	SB	BA	SA
TOTALS			27	162	5576	745	1467	220	58	116	691	556	803	76	.263	.386
Norm Siebern	1B162	L	28	162	600	114	185	25	6	25	117	110	88	3	.308	.495
Jerry Lumpe	2B156, SS2	L	29	156	641	89	193	34	10	10	83	44	38	0	.301	.441
Dick Howser (BH)	SS72	R	26	83	286	53	69	8	3	6	34	38	37	19	.238	.350
Ed Charles	3B140, 2B2	R	27	147	535	81	154	24	7	17	74	54	70	20	.288	.454
Gino Cimoli	OF147	R	32	152	550	67	151	20	15	10	71	40	89	2	.275	.420
Bobby Del Greco	OF124	R	29	132	338	61	86	21	1	9	38	49	62	4	.254	.423
Manny Jimenez	OF122	L	23	139	459	44	148	24	2	11	69	31	54	0	.301	.428
Haywood Sullivan	C94, 1B1	R	31	95	274	33	68	7	2	4	29	31	54	1	.248	.332
Wayne Causey	SS51, 3B26, 2B9	R	25	117	305	40	77	14	1	4	38	41	30	2	.252	.344
Jose Tartabull	OF85	L	23	107	310	49	86	6	5	0	22	20	19	27	.277	.332
2 George Alusik	OF50, 1B1	R	27	90	209	29	57	10	1	11	35	16	29	1	.273	.488
Joe Azcue (JJ)	C70	R	22	72	223	18	51	9	1	2	25	17	27	1	.229	.305
3 Billy Consolo	SS48	R	27	54	154	11	37	4	2	0	16	23	33	1	.240	.292
Leo Posada	OF11	R	26	29	46	6	9	1	1	0	3	7	14	0	.196	.261
Billy Bryan	C22	L	23	25	74	5	11	2	1	2	7	5	32	0	.149	.284
Deron Johnson (MS)	1B2, 3B2, OF2	R	23	17	19	1	2	0	0	0	3	8	0	.105	.158
John Wojcik	OF12	L	20	16	43	8	13	4	0	0	1	4	9	3	.302	.395
1 Gordie Windhorn	OF7	R	28	14	19	1	3	0	1	0	1	0	3	0	.158	.211
Bill Kern	OF3	R	27	8	16	1	4	0	0	1	0	0	5	0	.250	.438
2 Marlan Coughtry	2B1	R	27	5	11	1	2	0	0	0	0	2	5	0	.182	.182

Charlie Shoemaker 22 L 2-11, Gene Stephens (LJ) 29 L 0-4, Hector Martinez 23 R 0-1

Pitching

NAME	T	AGE	W	L	PCT	SV	G	GS	CG	IP	H	BB	SO	SHO	ERA
		27	72	90	.444	33	162	162	32	1434	1450	655	825	4	4.79
Ed Rakow	R	27	14	17	.452	1	42	35	11	235	232	98	159	2	4.25
Dave Wickersham	R	26	11	4	.733	1	30	9	3	110	105	43	61	0	4.17
John Wyatt	R	27	10	7	.588	11	59	0	0	125	121	80	106	0	4.46
Diego Segui	R	24	8	5	.615	6	37	13	2	117	89	46	71	0	3.85
Jerry Walker	R	23	8	9	.471	0	31	21	3	143	165	78	57	1	5.92
Orlando Pena	R	28	6	4	.600	0	13	12	6	90	71	27	56	1	3.00
Bill Fischer	R	31	4	12	.250	2	34	16	5	128	150	8	38	0	3.94
Dan Pfister	R	25	4	14	.222	1	41	25	2	196	175	106	123	0	4.55
Gordon Jones	R	32	3	2	.600	8	21	0	0	33	31	14	20	0	4.86
Norm Bass	R	23	2	6	.250	0	22	10	0	75	96	46	33	0	6.12
2 Moe Drabowsky	R	26	1	0	1.000	0	10	3	0	28	29	10	19	0	5.14
Bob Giggie	R	28	1	1	.500	0	2	0	0	14	17	3	4	0	6.43
Bill Kunkel	R	25	0	0	—	0	4	0	0	5	3	0	3	0	3.38
1 Dan Osinski	R	28	0	0	—	0	2	0	0	4	9	4	2	0	16.20
Don Williams	R	30	0	0	—	0	2	1	0	13	13	2	6	0	13.50
Rupe Toppin	R	20	0	0	—	0	2	0	0	2	4	2	0	0	2.25
Fred Norman	L	19	0	0	—	0	1	0	0	3	4	2	2	0	6.23
Bob Grim	R	32	0	0	—	0	3	0	0	13	14	8	3	0	6.23
Jim Archer	L	29	0	0	—	0	12	1	0	22	31	13	13	0	6.55
Granny Hamner	R	35	0	0	—	0	3	0	0	5	11	3	5	0	9.32
Art Ditmar	R	33	0	3	.000	0	12	3	0	33	51	13	16	0	6.55
Danny McDevitt	L	29	0	3	.000	0	33	1	0	51	47	41	28	0	5.82

WASHINGTON — 10th 60-101 .373 35.5 — MICKEY VERNON

Batting

NAME	G by Pos	B	AGE	G	AB	R	H	2B	3B	HR	RBI	BB	SO	SB	BA	SA
TOTALS			29	162	5484	599	1370	206	38	132	566	466	789	99	.250	.373
Harry Bright	1B99, C3, 3B1	R	32	113	392	55	107	15	4	17	67	26	51	2	.273	.462
Chuck Cottier	2B134	R	26	136	443	50	107	14	6	6	40	44	57	14	.242	.341
Ken Hamlin	SS87, 2B2	R	27	98	292	29	74	10	0	3	22	22	22	7	.253	.325
Bob Johnson	3B72, SS50, 2B3, OF1	R	26	135	466	58	134	20	2	12	43	32	50	9	.288	.416
Jim King	OF101	L	29	132	333	39	81	15	0	11	35	55	37	4	.243	.387
Jimmy Piersall	OF132	R	32	135	471	38	115	20	4	4	31	39	53	12	.244	.329
Chuck Hinton	OF136, 2B12, SS1	R	28	151	542	73	168	25	6	17	75	47	66	28	.310	.472
Ken Retzer	C99	L	28	109	340	36	97	11	2	8	37	26	21	2	.285	.400
Joe Hicks	OF29	L	29	102	174	20	39	4	2	6	14	15	34	3	.224	.374
Bob Schmidt	C88	R	29	88	256	28	62	14	0	10	31	14	37	0	.242	.414
Danny O'Connell	3B41, 2B22	R	35	84	236	24	62	7	2	4	24	18	22	5	.263	.335
Johnny Schaive	3B49, 2B6	R	28	82	225	20	57	15	1	5	30	30	57	1	.253	.409
Don Lock	OF23	R	25	71	225	30	57	7	3	7	33	30	63	4	.253	.453
Bud Zipfel	1B26, OF23	L	23	68	184	21	44	6	1	5	21	17	43	1	.239	.370
1 Dale Long	1B51	L	36	67	191	17	48	4	0	4	24	18	22	2	.241	.346
Eddie Brinkman	SS38, 3B10	R	20	54	133	8	22	7	0	2	4	11	28	1	.165	.233
1 Gene Woodling	OF30	L	39	44	107	19	30	4	0	5	16	24	5	1	.280	.458
John Kennedy	SS9, 3B2	R	21	14	42	6	11	1	0	2	7	1	8	0	.262	.381
1 Willie Tasby	OF10	R	29	11	34	4	7	1	0	1	2	3	6	0	.206	.206
Ron Stillwell	2B6, SS1	R	22	6	22	5	6	2	0	0	5	1	3	0	.273	.273

Pitching

NAME	T	AGE	W	L	PCT	SV	G	GS	CG	IP	H	BB	SO	SHO	ERA
		28	60	101	.373	13	162	162	38	1445	1400	593	771	11	4.40
Dave Stenhouse	R	28	11	12	.478	0	34	26	9	197	169	90	123	2	3.65
2 Don Rudolph	L	30	8	10	.444	0	37	23	6	176	187	42	68	2	3.63
Claude Osteen	L	22	8	13	.381	1	28	22	7	150	140	47	59	2	3.66
Tom Cheney	R	27	7	9	.438	1	37	23	4	173	134	97	147	3	3.17
Bennie Daniels	R	30	7	16	.304	2	44	24	13	161	172	68	66	1	4.86
Marty Kutyna	R	30	6	5	.455	0	54	0	0	78	83	27	25	0	4.24
Pete Burnside	L	31	5	11	.313	2	40	20	6	150	152	51	74	0	4.44
Steve Hamilton	L	28	3	8	.273	1	41	10	1	107	103	36	83	0	3.79
Ed Hobaugh	R	28	2	4	.333	1	26	2	0	69	66	25	37	0	3.78
Jim Hannan	R	22	1	1	.333	4	27	3	0	49	56	49	39	0	3.31
Ray Rippelmeyer	R	28	1	2	.333	0	11	0	0	39	47	17	10	0	5.54
Carl Bouldin	R	23	1	2	.333	0	9	3	0	26	26	12	25	0	5.85
Freddie Green	L	28	0	1	.000	0	9	0	0	13	11	6	9	0	6.43
Bob Baird	L	23	0	2	.000	0	12	0	0	24	22	12	11	0	6.55
Jack Jenkins	R	19	0	1	.000	0	3	0	0	13	14	13	7	0	4.15
Joe McClain	R	29	0	4	.000	0	24	33	11	6	0	9.38

SAN FRANCISCO 1st 103-62 .624 — AL DARK (Defeated Los Angeles in playoff 2 games to 1)

NAME	G by Pos	B	AGE	G	AB	R	H	2B	3B	HR	RBI	BB	SO	SB	BA	SA
TOTALS			27	165	5588	878	1552	235	32	204	807	523	822	73	.278	.441
Orlando Cepeda	1B160, OF2	R	24	162	625	105	191	26	1	35	114	37	97	10	.306	.518
Chuck Hiller	2B161	L	27	161	602	94	166	22	2	3	48	55	49	5	.276	.334
Jose Pagan	SS164	R	27	164	580	73	150	25	6	7	57	47	77	13	.259	.359
Jim Davenport	3B141	R	28	144	485	83	144	25	5	14	58	45	76	2	.297	.456
Felipe Alou	OF150	R	27	154	561	96	177	30	3	25	98	33	66	10	.316	.513
Willie Mays	OF161	R	31	162	621	130	189	36	5	49	141	78	85	18	.304	.615
Harvey Kuenn	OF105, 3B30	R	31	130	487	73	148	23	6	10	68	49	37	3	.304	.454
Tom Haller	C91	L	25	99	272	53	71	13	1	18	55	51	59	1	.261	.515
Ed Bailey	C75	L	31	96	254	32	59	9	1	17	45	42	42	1	.232	.476
Willie McCovey	OF57, 1B17	L	24	91	229	41	67	6	1	20	54	29	35	1	.293	.590
Matty Alou	OF57	L	23	78	195	28	57	8	1	3	14	14	17	3	.292	.390
Manny Mota	OF27, 3B7, 2B3	R	24	47	74	9	13	1	0	0	9	7	8	3	.176	.189
Ernie Bowman	2B17, 3B11, SS10	R	24	46	42	9	8	1	0	1	4	1	10	0	.190	.286
2 Bob Nieman	OF3	R	35	30	30	1	9	2	0	1	3	1	9	0	.300	.467
Carl Boles	OF7	R	27	19	24	4	9	0	0	0	1	0	6	0	.375	.375
John Orsino	C16	R	24	18	48	4	13	2	0	0	4	5	11	0	.271	.313
1 Joe Pignatano	C7	R	32	7	5	2	1	0	0	0	0	0	4	0	.200	.200
Dick Phillips	1B1	L	30	5	3	1	0	0	0	0	0	1	1	0	.000	.000
Cap Peterson	SS2	R	19	4	6	1	1	0	0	0	1	1	1	0	.167	.167

NAME	T	AGE	W	L	PCT	SV	G	GS	CG	IP	H	BB	SO	SHO	ERA
		29	103	62	.624	39	165	165	62	1462	1399	503	886	10	3.79
Jack Sanford	R	33	24	7	.774	0	39	38	13	265	233	92	147	3	3.43
Billy O'Dell	L	29	19	14	.576	0	43	39	20	281	282	66	195	2	3.52
Juan Marichal	R	24	18	11	.621	1	37	36	18	263	233	90	153	3	3.35
Billy Pierce	L	35	16	6	.727	1	30	23	7	162	147	35	76	2	3.50
Bobby Bolin	R	23	7	3	.700	5	41	9	2	92	84	35	74	0	3.62
Don Larsen	R	32	5	4	.556	11	49	0	0	86	83	47	58	0	4.40
Mike McCormick (SA)	L	23	5	5	.500	0	28	15	1	99	112	45	42	0	5.36
Stu Miller	R	34	5	8	.385	19	59	0	0	107	107	42	78	0	4.12
Gaylord Perry	R	23	3	1	.750	0	13	7	1	43	54	14	20	0	5.23
Jim Duffalo	R	26	2	3	.333	2	34	2	0	42	42	23	29	0	3.64
Bob Garibaldi	R	20	0	0	—	1	9	0	0	12	13	5	9	0	5.25
Dick LeMay	L	23	0	1	.000	1	9	0	0	9	9	5	5	0	8.00

LOS ANGELES 2nd 102-63 .618 1 — WALT ALSTON (Defeated by San Francisco in playoff 2 games to 1)

NAME	G by Pos	B	AGE	G	AB	R	H	2B	3B	HR	RBI	BB	SO	SB	BA	SA
TOTALS			27	165	5628	842	1510	192	65	140	781	572	886	198	.268	.400
Ron Fairly	1B120, OF48	L	23	147	460	80	128	15	7	14	71	75	59	1	.278	.433
Jim Gilliam	2B113, 3B90, OF1	B	33	160	588	83	159	24	1	4	43	93	35	17	.270	.335
Maury Wills	SS165	B	29	165	695	130	208	13	10	6	48	51	57	104	.299	.373
Daryl Spencer	3B57, SS10	R	32	77	157	24	37	5	1	2	12	32	31	0	.236	.318
Frank Howard	OF131	R	25	141	493	80	146	25	6	31	119	39	108	1	.296	.560
Willie Davis	OF156	L	22	157	600	103	171	18	10	21	85	42	72	32	.285	.453
Tommy Davis	OF146, 3B39	R	23	163	665	120	230	27	9	27	153	33	65	18	.346	.535
Johnny Roseboro	C128	L	29	128	389	45	97	16	7	7	55	50	60	12	.249	.380
Larry Burright	2B109, SS1	R	24	115	249	35	51	6	5	4	30	21	67	4	.205	.317
Wally Moon	OF36, 1B32	L	32	95	244	36	59	9	1	4	31	30	33	5	.242	.336
Tim Harkness	1B59	L	24	92	62	9	16	2	0	2	7	10	20	1	.258	.387
Duke Snider	OF39	L	35	80	158	28	44	11	3	5	30	36	32	2	.278	.481
Lee Walls	OF17, 1B11, 3B4	R	29	60	109	9	29	3	1	0	17	10	21	1	.266	.312
Andy Carey	3B42	R	30	53	111	12	26	5	1	2	13	16	23	0	.234	.351
Doug Camilli	C39	R	25	45	88	16	25	5	2	4	22	12	21	0	.284	.523
Norm Sherry	C34	R	30	35	88	7	16	2	0	3	16	6	17	0	.182	.307
Dick Tracewski	SS4	R	27	15	2	3	0	0	0	0	0	0	2	0	.000	.000
Ken McMullen	OF2	R	20	6	11	4	3	0	0	0	0	0	3	0	.273	.273

NAME	T	AGE	W	L	PCT	SV	G	GS	CG	IP	H	BB	SO	SHO	ERA
		25	102	63	.618	46	165	165	44	1489	1386	588	1104	8	3.61
Don Drysdale	R	25	25	9	.735	1	43	41	19	314	272	78	232	2	2.84
Johnny Podres	L	29	15	13	.536	0	40	40	9	255	270	71	178	0	3.81
Sandy Koufax (RJ)	L	26	14	7	.667	1	28	26	11	184	134	57	216	2	2.54
Stan Williams	R	25	14	12	.538	1	40	28	4	186	184	98	108	1	4.45
Ed Roebuck	R	30	10	2	.833	9	64	0	0	119	102	54	72	0	3.10
Larry Sherry	R	26	7	3	.700	11	58	0	0	90	81	44	71	0	3.20
Joe Moeller	R	19	6	5	.545	1	19	15	1	86	87	58	46	0	5.23
Ron Perranoski	L	26	6	6	.500	20	70	0	0	107	103	36	68	0	2.86
Pete Richert	R	22	5	4	.556	0	19	12	1	81	77	45	75	0	3.89
Jack Smith	R	26	0	0	—	1	8	0	0	10	10	4	7	0	4.50
1 Willard Hunter	L	28	0	0	—	0	2	0	0	2	6	4	1	0	40.50
Phil Ortega	R	22	0	2	.000	1	24	0	0	54	60	39	30	0	6.83

CINCINNATI 3rd 98-64 .605 3.5 — FRED HUTCHINSON

NAME	G by Pos	B	AGE	G	AB	R	H	2B	3B	HR	RBI	BB	SO	SB	BA	SA
TOTALS			28	162	5645	802	1523	252	40	167	745	498	903	66	.270	.417
Gordy Coleman	1B128	L	27	136	476	73	132	13	1	28	86	36	68	2	.277	.485
Don Blasingame	2B137	L	30	141	494	77	139	9	7	2	35	63	44	4	.281	.340
Leo Cardenas	SS149	R	23	153	589	77	173	31	4	10	60	39	99	2	.294	.411
Eddie Kasko	3B114, SS21	R	30	134	533	74	148	26	2	4	41	35	44	3	.278	.356
Frank Robinson	OF161	R	26	162	609	134	208	51	2	39	136	76	62	18	.342	.624
Vada Pinson	OF152	L	23	155	619	107	181	31	7	23	100	45	96	26	.292	.477
Wally Post	OF90	R	32	109	285	43	75	13	3	17	62	32	67	1	.263	.498
Johnny Edwards	C130	L	24	133	452	47	115	28	5	8	50	45	70	1	.254	.392
Jerry Lynch	OF73	L	31	114	288	41	81	15	4	12	57	24	38	3	.281	.486
Marty Keough	OF71, 1B29	R	28	111	230	34	64	8	2	7	27	21	31	3	.278	.422
Joe Gaines	OF13	R	25	64	52	12	12	3	0	1	7	8	16	0	.231	.346
2 Don Zimmer	3B43, 2B17, SS1	R	31	63	192	16	48	7	2	2	16	14	30	1	.250	.359
Hank Foiles	C41	R	33	43	131	17	36	6	1	7	25	13	39	0	.275	.496
Cookie Rojas	2B30, 3B1	R	23	39	86	9	19	2	0	0	6	9	4	1	.221	.244
Don Pavletich	1B25, C2	R	23	34	63	7	14	3	0	1	7	8	18	0	.222	.317
Gene Freese (BN)	3B10	R	28	18	42	2	6	1	0	0	1	6	8	0	.143	.167
Rogelio Alvarez	1B13	R	24	14	28	1	6	0	0	0	2	1	10	0	.214	.214
Tommy Harper	3B6	R	21	6	23	1	4	1	0	0	2	6	1	.174	.174
1 Cliff Cook	3B4	R	25	6	5	0	0	0	0	0	0	0	2	0	.000	.000
Jesse Gonder		L	26	4	4	0	0	0	0	0	0	0	0	0	.000	.000
1 Darrell Johnson	C2	R	33	4	4	0	0	0	0	0	0	0	2	0	.000	.000

NAME	T	AGE	W	L	PCT	SV	G	GS	CG	IP	H	BB	SO	SHO	ERA
		29	98	64	.605	35	162	162	51	1461	1397	567	964	13	3.75
Bob Purkey	R	32	23	5	.821	0	37	37	18	288	260	64	141	2	2.81
Joey Jay	R	26	21	14	.600	0	39	37	16	273	269	100	155	4	3.76
Jim O'Toole	L	25	16	13	.552	0	36	34	11	252	222	87	170	3	3.50
Jim Maloney	R	22	9	7	.563	1	22	17	3	115	90	66	105	0	3.52
Johnny Klippstein	R	34	7	6	.538	4	40	7	0	109	113	64	67	0	4.46
2 Joe Nuxhall	L	33	5	0	1.000	1	12	9	1	66	59	25	57	0	2.45
Bill Henry	L	34	4	2	.667	11	40	0	0	37	40	20	35	0	4.62
Dave Sisler	R	30	4	3	.571	1	35	0	0	44	44	26	27	0	3.89
Jim Brosnan	R	32	4	4	.500	13	48	0	0	65	76	18	51	0	3.32
Sammy Ellis	R	21	2	2	.500	0	8	4	0	29	29	29	27	0	6.75
1 Moe Drabowsky	R	26	2	6	.250	1	23	10	1	83	84	31	56	0	4.99
John Tsitouris	R	26	1	0	1.000	0	4	2	1	21	13	7	7	1	0.86
1 Bob Miller	L	26	0	0	—	0	5	0	0	14	3	4	2	0	23.40
Howie Nunn	R	26	0	0	—	0	6	0	0	10	15	3	4	0	5.40
1 Dave Hillman	R	34	0	0	—	0	6	0	0	9	11	3	4	0	9.00
2 Ted Wills	L	28	0	2	.000	3	26	5	0	61	61	23	58	0	5.31

PITTSBURGH 4th 93-68 .578 8 — DANNY MURTAUGH

NAME	G by Pos	B	AGE	G	AB	R	H	2B	3B	HR	RBI	BB	SO	SB	BA	SA
TOTALS			30	161	5483	706	1468	240	65	108	655	432	836	50	.268	.394
Dick Stuart	1B101	R	29	114	394	52	90	11	4	16	64	32	94	0	.228	.398
Bill Mazeroski	2B159	R	25	159	572	55	155	24	9	14	81	37	47	0	.271	.418
Dick Groat	SS161	R	31	161	678	76	199	34	3	2	61	31	61	2	.294	.361
Don Hoak	3B116	R	34	121	411	63	99	14	8	5	48	49	49	4	.241	.350
Roberto Clemente	OF142	R	27	144	538	95	168	28	9	10	74	35	73	6	.312	.454
Bill Virdon	OF156	L	31	156	663	82	164	27	10	6	47	36	65	5	.247	.345
Bob Skinner	OF139	L	30	144	510	87	154	29	7	20	75	76	89	10	.302	.504
Smoky Burgess	C101	L	35	103	360	38	118	19	2	13	61	31	19	0	.328	.500
Howie Goss	OF66	R	27	89	111	19	27	6	0	2	10	9	36	5	.243	.351
Donn Clendenon	1B52, OF19	R	26	80	222	39	67	8	5	7	28	26	58	16	.302	.477
2 Jim Marshall	1B26	L	30	55	100	13	22	5	1	3	12	15	19	1	.220	.350
Dick Schofield	3B20, 2B2, SS1	B	27	54	104	19	30	3	2	0	10	17	22	0	.288	.375
Don Leppert	C44	R	30	45	139	14	37	6	1	3	18	12	21	0	.266	.388
Johnny Logan	3B19	R	35	44	80	7	24	3	0	1	12	7	6	0	.300	.375
Cal Neeman	C24	R	33	24	50	5	9	1	1	1	5	3	10	0	.180	.300
Bob Bailey	3B12	R	19	14	42	6	7	2	1	0	4	6	10	1	.167	.262
Willie Stargell	OF9	L	22	10	31	1	9	3	0	0	4	3	10	0	.290	.452
Orlando McFarlane	C8	R	24	8	23	1	2	0	0	0	1	1	4	0	.087	.087
Larry Elliot	OF3	L	24	8	10	2	3	0	0	0	1	1	4	0	.300	.300
Elmo Plaskett	C4	R	24	7	14	2	4	0	0	0	3	1	3	0	.286	.500
Coot Veal		R	29	1	1	1	0	0	0	0	0	0	0	0	.000	.000

NAME	T	AGE	W	L	PCT	SV	G	GS	CG	IP	H	BB	SO	SHO	ERA
		31	93	68	.578	41	161	161	40	1432	1433	466	897	13	3.38
Bob Friend	R	31	18	14	.563	1	39	36	13	262	280	53	144	5	3.06
Al McBean	R	24	15	10	.600	0	33	29	6	190	212	65	119	2	3.69
Vern Law	R	32	10	7	.588	0	23	20	7	139	156	27	73	1	3.95
Tom Sturdivant	R	32	9	5	.643	2	49	12	2	125	120	39	76	1	3.74
Harvey Haddix	L	36	9	6	.600	0	28	20	4	141	146	42	101	0	4.21
Earl Francis	R	25	9	8	.529	0	36	23	5	176	153	83	121	3	3.07
Roy Face	R	34	8	7	.533	28	63	0	0	91	74	18	45	0	1.88
Diomedes Olivo	L	43	5	1	.833	7	62	1	0	84	88	25	66	0	2.79
Jack Lamabe	R	25	3	1	.750	2	46	0	0	78	70	40	56	0	2.88
Joe Gibbon	L	27	3	4	.429	0	19	8	0	57	53	24	26	0	3.63
Bob Veale	L	26	2	2	.500	1	11	6	2	46	39	25	42	0	3.72
Bob Priddy	R	22	1	0	1.000	0	4	0	0	6	5	2	3	0	3.00
1 Vinegar Bend Mizell	L	31	1	1	.500	0	4	0	0	11	16	5	10	0	5.06
Tom Butters	R	24	0	0	—	0	4	0	0	6	6	6	10	0	1.50
Tommie Sisk	R	20	0	0	.000	0	4	0	0	13	18	8	6	0	4.00

MILWAUKEE 5th 86-76 .531 15.5 — BIRDIE TEBBETTS

NAME	G by Pos	B	AGE	G	AB	R	H	2B	3B	HR	RBI	BB	SO	SB	BA	SA
TOTALS			28	162	5458	730	1376	204	38	181	685	581	975	57	.252	.403
Joe Adcock	1B112	R	34	121	391	48	97	12	1	29	78	50	91	2	.248	.506
Frank Bolling	2B119	R	30	122	406	45	110	17	4	9	43	35	45	2	.271	.399
Roy McMillan	SS135	R	32	137	468	66	115	21	3	12	41	60	52	3	.246	.350
Eddie Mathews	3B140, 1B7	L	30	152	536	106	142	25	6	29	90	101	90	1	.265	.496
Mack Jones	OF91	L	23	93	331	51	85	17	4	10	36	44	100	5	.257	.450
Hank Aaron	OF153, 1B1	R	28	156	592	127	191	28	6	45	128	66	73	15	.323	.618
Lee Maye (IL)	OF94	L	27	99	349	40	85	10	0	10	41	25	58	9	.244	.358
Del Crandall	C90, 1B5	R	32	107	350	35	104	12	3	8	45	27	24	3	.297	.417
Tommie Aaron	1B110, OF42, 2B1, 3B1	R	22	141	334	54	77	20	2	8	38	41	58	6	.231	.374
Joe Torre	C63	R	21	80	220	23	62	8	1	5	26	24	24	1	.282	.395
2 Gus Bell	OF58	L	33	79	214	24	61	11	3	5	24	21	17	0	.285	.435
Amado Samuel	SS36, 2B28, 3B3	R	23	76	209	16	43	3	0	3	20	12	54	0	.206	.297
Lou Johnson	OF55	R	27	61	117	22	33	4	2	5	13	11	27	0	.282	.453
Howie Bedell	OF8	L	27	58	138	15	27	3	1	0	5	24	17	1	.196	.232
Denis Menke	2B20, 3B15, SS9, 1B2, OF1	R	21	50	146	12	28	6	1	3	16	16	38	0	.192	.308
2 Ken Aspromonte	2B12, 3B6	R	30	34	79	11	23	2	0	1	5	7	8	0	.291	.316
Bob Uecker	C24	R	27	33	64	5	16	2	0	0	7	6	15	0	.250	.328
Hawk Taylor (MS)	OF3	R	23	20	47	3	12	0	2	0	5	2	10	0	.255	.255
Mike Krsnich	OF3, 1B1, 3B1	R	30	11	12	0	1	0	0	0	0	1	2	0	.083	.167
Lou Klimchock		L	22	9	4	0	0	0	0	0	0	2	1	0	.000	.000
Ethan Blackaby	OF3	L	21	9	13	2	2	1	0	0	1	2	5	0	.154	.231

NAME	T	AGE	W	L	PCT	SV	G	GS	CG	IP	H	BB	SO	SHO	ERA
		27	86	76	.531	24	162	162	59	1435	1443	407	802	10	3.68
Warren Spahn	L	41	18	14	.563	0	34	34	22	269	248	55	118	0	3.04
Bob Shaw	R	29	15	9	.625	2	38	29	12	225	223	44	124	3	2.80
Bob Hendley	L	23	11	13	.458	1	35	29	7	200	188	59	112	2	3.60
Lew Burdette	R	35	10	9	.526	2	37	19	6	144	172	23	59	1	4.88
Tony Cloninger	R	21	8	3	.727	0	24	15	4	111	113	46	69	1	4.30
Claude Raymond	R	25	5	5	.500	1	30	6	0	43	37	15	40	0	2.72
2 Jack Curtis	L	25	4	4	.500	1	30	5	0	76	82	27	40	0	4.14
Ron Piche	R	27	3	2	.600	0	14	8	2	52	54	29	28	0	4.85
Denny Lemaster	L	23	3	4	.429	0	17	12	4	87	75	32	69	1	3.00
Cecil Butler	R	24	2	0	1.000	0	19	0	0	31	26	9	22	0	2.61
Don Nottebart	R	26	2	2	.500	0	19	0	0	64	64	20	35	0	3.23
Hank Fischer	R	22	1	4	.200	4	29	0	0	37	43	20	39	0	5.35
Carl Willey	R	31	2	5	.286	1	30	6	1	73	95	20	40	0	5.42
Jim Constable	L	29	1	0	.500	1	18	0	0	14	14	4	12	1	2.00
1 Don McMahon	R	32	0	0	—	1	9	0	0	6	4	4	6	0	6.00
1 Bob Buhl	R	33	0	0	—	0	2	0	0	2	6	1	1	0	22.50

ST. LOUIS — 6th 84-78 .519 17.5 — JOHNNY KEANE

NAME	G by Pos	B	AGE	G	AB	R	H	2B	3B	HR	RBI	BB	SO	SB	BA	SA
TOTALS			28	163	5643	774	1528	221	31	137	707	515	846	86	.271	.394
Bill White	1B146, OF27	L	28	159	614	93	199	31	3	20	102	58	69	9	.324	.482
Julian Javier	2B151, SS4	R	25	155	598	97	157	25	5	2	39	47	73	26	.263	.356
Julio Gotay	SS120, 2B8, OF2, 3B1	R	23	127	369	47	94	12	1	2	27	27	47	7	.255	.309
Ken Boyer	3B160	R	31	160	611	92	178	27	5	24	98	75	104	12	.291	.470
Charlie James	OF116	R	24	129	388	50	107	13	4	8	59	10	58	3	.276	.392
Curt Flood	OF151	R	24	151	635	99	188	30	5	12	70	42	57	8	.296	.416
Stan Musial		L	41	135	433	57	143	18	1	19	82	64	46	3	.330	.508
Gene Oliver	C98, OF8, 1B3	R	26	122	345	42	89	19	1	14	45	50	59	5	.258	.441
Red Schoendienst	2B21, 3B4	B	39	98	143	21	43	4	0	2	12	9	12		.301	.371
3 Bobby Gene Smith	OF80	B	28	91	130	13	30	9	0	0	12	7	14	1	.231	.300
Carl Sawatski	C70	L	34	85	222	26	56	9	1	13	42	36	38	0	.252	.477
Dal Maxvill	SS76, 3B1	R	23	79	189	20	42	3	1	1	18	17	39	1	.222	.265
Fred Whitfield	1B38	L	24	73	158	20	42	7	1	8	34	7	31		.266	.475
Jimmie Schaffer	C69	R	26	70	66	7	16	2	1	0	6	6	16	1	.242	.303
Doug Clemens	OF34	L	23	48	93	12	22	5	1	1	12	17	19	0	.237	.301
Minnie Minoso (BW)	OF27	R	39	39	97	14	19	5	0	1	10	7	17	4	.196	.278
1 Don Landrum	OF26	L	26	32	35	11	11	0	0	0	3	4	2	2	.314	.314
1 Alex Grammas	SS16, 2B2	R	36	21	18	0	2	0	0	0	1	1	6	0	.111	.111
1 Carl Warwick	OF10	R	25	13	23	4	8	0	0	1	3	1	4	2	.348	.478

Mike Shannon 22 R 2-15, Bob Burda 23 L 1-14, Gary Kolb 22 L 5-14, Hal Smith (IL) 31

NAME	T	AGE	W	L	PCT	SV	G	GS	CG	IP	H	BB	SO	SHO	ERA
		28	84	78	.519	25	163	163	53	1463	1394	517	914	17	3.55
Larry Jackson	R	31	16	11	.593	0	36	35	11	252	267	64	112	2	3.75
Bob Gibson	R	26	15	13	.536	1	32	30	15	234	174	95	208	5	2.85
Ernie Broglio	R	26	12	9	.571	0	34	30	11	222	193	93	132	4	3.00
Ray Washburn	R	24	12	9	.571	0	34	24	7	176	187	58	109	1	4.09
Curt Simmons	L	33	10	10	.500	0	31	22	9	154	167	32	74	4	3.51
Ray Sadecki	L	21	6	8	.429	1	22	17	4	102	121	43	50	1	5.56
2 Bobby Shantz	L	36	5	3	.625	4				58	45	20	47	0	2.17
Lindy McDaniel	R	26	3	10	.231	14	55	2	0	107	96	29	70	0	4.12
Bob Duliba	R	27	2	0	1.000	2	38	0	0	39	33	17	22	0	2.08
Ed Bauta	R	27	1	1	.500	2	20	0	0	32	28	21	25	0	5.06
1 Paul Toth	R	27	1	0	1.000	0	8	1	1	17	18	4	5	0	5.29
2 Don Ferrarese	R	33	1	4	.200	1	38	0	0	57	55	31	45	0	2.68
1 John Anderson	R	32	0	0	—	0	6	0	0	6	4	3	3	0	1.50
1 Bobby Locke	R	28	0	0	—	0	1	0	0	2	1	1	1	0	0.00
Harvey Branch	L	23	0	0	.000	0	1	1	0	5	5	2	0	0	5.40

PHILADELPHIA — 7th 81-80 .503 20 — GENE MAUCH

NAME	G by Pos	B	AGE	G	AB	R	H	2B	3B	HR	RBI	BB	SO	SB	BA	SA
TOTALS			27	161	5420	705	1410	199	39	142	658	531	923	79	.260	.390
Roy Sievers	1B130, OF7	R	35	144	477	61	125	19	5	21	80	56	80	2	.262	.455
Tony Taylor	2B150, SS2	R	26	152	625	87	162	21	5	7	43	68	82	20	.259	.342
Bobby Wine	SS89, 3B20	R	23	112	311	30	76	15	0	4	25	11	49	2	.244	.331
Don Demeter	3B105, OF63, 1B1	R	27	153	550	85	169	24	3	29	107	41	93	2	.307	.520
Johnny Callison	OF152	L	23	157	603	107	181	26	10	23	83	54	90	6	.300	.491
Tony Gonzalez (XJ)	OF114	L	25	118	437	76	132	16	4	20	63	40	82	17	.302	.494
Ted Savage	OF109	R	25	127	335	54	89	11	2	7	39	40	66	16	.266	.373
Clay Dalrymple	C119	L	25	123	370	40	102	13	3	11	54	70	32	1	.276	.416
Wes Covington	OF88	L	30	116	304	36	86	12	1	9	44	19	44	0	.283	.418
Frank Torre	1B76	L	30	108	168	13	52	8	2	0	20	24	6	1	.310	.381
Billy Klaus	3B53, SS30, 2B11	L	33	102	248	30	51	8	2	4	20	29	43	1	.206	.302
Ruben Amaro (MS)	SS78, 1B1	R	24	79	226	24	55	10	0	0	19	30	28	5	.243	.288
Mel Roach	3B26, 2B9, 1B4, OF3	R	29	65	105	9	20	4	0	0	8	5	19	0	.190	.229
Jacke Davis	OF26	R	26	48	75	9	16	0	1	1	6	4	20	1	.213	.280
Sammy White	C40	R	34	41	97	7	21	4	0	2	12	2	16	0	.216	.320
Bob Oldis	C30	R	34	34	80	7	21	3	1	0	7	6	6	0	.263	.313

1 Billy Consolo 27 R 2-5, John Herrnstein 24 L 1-5, Bobby Malkmus 30 R 1-5, Jimmie Coker (MS) 26 R 0-3

NAME	T	AGE	W	L	PCT	SV	G	GS	CG	IP	H	BB	SO	SHO	ERA
		26	81	80	.503	24	161	161	43	1427	1469	574	863	7	4.28
Art Mahaffey	R	24	19	14	.576	0	41	39	20	274	253	81	177	2	3.94
Jack Baldschun	R	25	12	7	.632	13	67	0	0	113	95	58	95	0	2.95
Cal McLish	R	36	11	5	.688	1	32	24	5	155	184	45	71	1	4.24
Chris Short	L	24	11	9	.550	3	47	12	4	142	149	56	91	0	3.42
Dennis Bennett	R	22	9	9	.500	3	31	24	7	175	144	68	149	2	3.81
Jack Hamilton	R	23	9	12	.429	2	41	26	4	182	185	107	101	1	5.09
Dallas Green	R	27	6	6	.500	1	37	10	2	129	145	43	58	0	3.84
Jim Owens	R	28	2	4	.333	0	23	12	1	70	90	33	21	0	6.30
2 Bobby Locke	R	28	1	0	1.000	0	5	0	0	16	16	10	9	0	5.63
Bill Smith	L	28	1	5	.167	0	24	5	0	50	59	10	26	0	4.32
John Boozer	R	22	0	0	—	0	4	0	0	9	10	6	5	0	5.85
Ed Keegan	R	22	0	0	—	0	4	0	0	8	5	5	0	0	5.25
1 Don Ferrarese	L	33	0	2	.000	0	9	0	0	18	19	5	9	0	7.71
1 Frank Sullivan	R	32	0	2	.000	0	19	0	0	38	41	12	12	0	6.26
Paul Brown (IL)	R	21	0	6	.000	1	23	9	0	74	73	29	29	0	5.91

HOUSTON — 8th 64-96 .400 36.5 — HARRY CRAFT

NAME	G by Pos	B	AGE	G	AB	R	H	2B	3B	HR	RBI	BB	SO	SB	BA	SA
TOTALS			30	161	5558	592	1370	170	47	105	549	493	806	42	.246	.351
Norm Larker	1B135, OF6	L	31	147	506	58	133	19	5	6	63	70	47	1	.263	.374
Joey Amalfitano	2B110, 3B5	R	28	117	380	44	90	12	5	1	27	45	43	4	.237	.303
Bob Lillis	SS99, 2B33, 3B9	R	32	129	457	38	114	12	4	1	30	28	23	7	.249	.300
Bob Aspromonte	3B142, SS11, 2B1	R	24	149	534	59	142	18	4	11	59	46	54	4	.266	.376
Roman Mejias	OF142	R	31	146	566	82	162	17	3	24	76	30	83	12	.286	.445
2 Carl Warwick	OF128	R	25	130	477	63	124	17	1	16	60	38	77	2	.260	.400
Al Spangler	OF121	L	28	129	418	51	119	10	9	5	35	70	46	7	.285	.388
Hal Smith	C92, 3B6, 1B2	R	31	109	345	32	81	14	0	12	35	24	55	0	.235	.380
Jim Pendleton	OF90, 1B8, 3B3, SS2	R	38	117	321	30	79	12	2	8	36	14	57	0	.246	.371
Billy Goodman	2B31, 3B17, 1B1	L	36	82	161	12	41	4	0	1	10	12	11	0	.255	.292
Merritt Ranew	C58	L	24	71	218	26	51	6	4	4	24	14	43	2	.234	.390
Pidge Browne	1B26	L	33	65	100	8	21	2	0	1	10	13	9	0	.210	.320
J C Hartman	SS48	R	28	51	148	11	33	5	0	0	5	4	16	1	.223	.257
1 Don Buddin	SS27, 3B9	R	28	40	80	10	13	4	1	2	10	17	17	0	.163	.313
2 Johnny Temple	2B26, 3B1	R	33	35	95	14	25	4	0	0	12	7	11	1	.263	.305
Jim Campbell	C25	R	25	27	86	6	19	4	0	3	6	3	23	0	.221	.372
Al Heist	OF23	R	34	27	72	4	16	1	0	0	3	3	9	0	.222	.236
2 Bob Cerv	OF6	R	36	19	31	2	7	0	0	2	3	2	10	0	.226	.419
Dave Roberts	OF12, 1B6	L	29	16	53	3	13	3	0	1	10	8	4	0	.245	.358
Don Taussig	OF4	R	30	16	25	1	5	0	0	1	1	2	11	0	.200	.320
Johnny Weekly	OF7	R	25	13	26	3	5	1	0	2	3	4	7	0	.192	.462

Jim Busby 35 R 2-11, Ernie Fazio 20 R 1-12, Dick Gernert 33 R 5-24, Ron Davis 20 R 3-14, George Williams 22 R 3-8

NAME	T	AGE	W	L	PCT	SV	G	GS	CG	IP	H	BB	SO	SHO	ERA
		29	64	96	.400	19	162	162	34	1454	1446	471	1047	9	3.83
Bob Bruce	R	29	10	9	.526	0	32	27	6	175	164	82	135	0	4.06
Dick Farrell	R	28	10	20	.333	4	43	29	11	242	210	55	203	2	3.01
Jim Golden	R	26	7	11	.389	1	37	18	5	153	163	50	88	2	4.06
Ken Johnson	R	29	7	16	.304	0	33	31	5	197	195	46	178	1	3.84
2 Russ Kemmerer	R	30	5	3	.625	3	20	0	0	68	72	15	23	0	4.10
2 Don McMahon	R	32	5	5	.500	8	51	0	0	77	53	33	69	0	1.52
Hal Woodeshick	L	29	5	16	.238	3	31	26	2	139	161	54	82	1	4.40
Jim Umbricht	R	31	4	0	1.000	2	34	0	0	67	51	17	55	0	2.01
1 Dean Stone	R	31	3	2	.600	5	17	2	2	52	61	20	31	2	4.50
Dave Giusti	R	22	3	3	.400	2	25	0	0	74	82	30	43	0	5.59
Bobby Tiefenauer	R	32	2	4	.333	1	43	0	0	85	91	21	60	0	4.34
George Brunet	R	27	2	4	.333	0	17	11	2	54	62	21	36	0	4.50
Dick Drott (SA)	R	26	1	0	1.000	0	6	1	0	13	9	10	7	0	7.62
1 Bobby Shantz	R	36	1	1	.500	0	3	3	1	21	15	5	14	0	1.29
2 John Anderson	R	32	0	0	—	0	10	0	0	18	26	3	6	0	5.00
Al Cicotte	R	34	0	0	—	0	5	1	0	8	5	3	1	0	3.60
2 George Witt	R	28	0	2	.000	0	8	2	0	15	20	9	10	0	7.20

CHICAGO — 9th 59-103 .364 42.5 — EL TAPPE 4-16 .200 LOU KLEIN 12-18 .400 CHARLIE METRO 43-69 .384

NAME	G by Pos	B	AGE	G	AB	R	H	2B	3B	HR	RBI	BB	SO	SB	BA	SA
TOTALS			25	162	5534	632	1398	196	56	126	600	504	1044	78	.253	.377
Ernie Banks	1B149, 3B3	R	31	154	610	87	164	20	6	37	104	30	71	5	.269	.503
Ken Hubbs	2B159	R	20	160	661	90	172	24	9	5	49	35	129	3	.260	.346
Andre Rodgers	SS133, 1B1	R	27	138	461	40	128	20	8	5	44	44	93	5	.278	.388
Ron Santo	3B157, SS8	R	22	162	604	44	137	20	4	17	83	65	94	4	.227	.358
George Altman	OF129, 1B16	L	29	147	534	74	170	27	5	22	74	62	89	19	.318	.511
Lou Brock	OF106	L	23	123	434	73	114	24	7	9	35	35	96	16	.263	.412
Billy Williams	OF159	L	24	159	618	94	184	22	8	22	91	70	72	9	.298	.466
Dick Bertell	C76	R	26	77	215	19	65	6	2	2	18	13	30	0	.302	.377
Bob Will	OF9	L	30	87	92	6	22	3	0	2	15	6	13	0	.239	.337
2 Don Landrum	OF59	L	26	83	238	29	67	5	2	1	15	30	31	9	.282	.332
Moe Thacker	C65	R	28	65	107	8	20	5	0	0	9	14	40	0	.187	.234
Jim McKnight	3B9, OF5, 2B2	R	26	60	85	6	19	0	1	0	5	2	13	0	.224	.247
Cuno Barragan	C55	R	30	58	134	11	27	6	0	1	12	21	28	0	.201	.261
El Tappe	C26	R	35	26	53	3	11	0	0	0	3	9	7	0	.208	.208
2 Alex Grammas	SS13, 2B3, 3B1	R	27	23	60	3	14	3	0	0	3	2	7	1	.233	.283
Elder White	SS15, 3B1	R	27	23	53	4	8	2	0	0	3	4	6	0	.151	.189
Moe Morhardt	1B5	L	25	18	16	1	2	0	0	0	1	1	6	0	.125	.125
Nelson Mathews	OF14	R	20	15	49	5	15	2	0	2	13	5	14	0	.306	.469
Danny Murphy	OF9	R	19	14	35	5	7	0	0	0	3	0	10	0	.200	.343
Billy Ott	OF7	R	21	13	28	4	4	0	0	1	2	2	10	0	.143	.250
2 Bobby Gene Smith	OF7	R	28	13	29	3	5	1	0	0	2	5	4	0	.172	.276

Daryl Robertson 26 R 2-19, 1 Sammy Taylor 29 L 2-15, Jim McAnany 25 R 0-6

NAME	T	AGE	W	L	PCT	SV	G	GS	CG	IP	H	BB	SO	SHO	ERA
		28	59	103	.364	26	162	162	29	1438	1509	601	783	4	4.54
2 Bob Buhl	R	33	12	13	.480	0	34	30	8	212	204	94	109	1	3.69
Cal Koonce	R	21	10	10	.500	0	35	30	3	191	200	86	84	1	3.96
Dick Ellsworth	L	22	9	20	.310	1	37	33	6	209	241	77	113	0	5.08
Don Cardwell	R	26	7	16	.304	4	41	29	6	196	205	60	104	1	4.91
Barney Schultz	R	35	5	5	.500	5	51	0	0	78	66	23	58	0	3.81
Glen Hobbie	R	26	5	14	.263	0	42	23	5	162	198	62	87	0	5.22
Don Elston	R	33	4	4	.333	8	57	0	0	66	57	32	37	0	2.45
2 Paul Toth	R	27	3	1	.750	0	6	4	1	34	29	11	11	0	4.24
Dave Gerard	R	25	3	2	.400	3	39	0	0	59	67	28	30	0	4.88
Bob Anderson	R	26	2	7	.222	4	57	4	0	108	111	60	82	0	5.00
Freddie Burdette	R	25	0	0	—	0	10	0	0	10	5	3	5	0	3.60
Jack Warner	R	21	0	0	—	0	9	0	0	10	13	6	7	0	7.71
George Gerberman	R	20	0	1	.000	0	1	1	0	8	5	2	4	0	1.80
Don Prince	R	24	0	0	—	0	1	0	0	1	0	1	1	0	0.00
Al Lary	R	33	0	0	—	0	15	0	0	34	42	15	18	0	7.15
Tony Balsamo	R	24	0	1	.000	0	18	0	0	29	34	20	27	0	6.52
Morrie Steevens	L	21	0	0	—	0	7	0	0	15	10	11	5	0	2.40
Jim Brewer	L	24	0	1	.000	0	17	0	0	18	18	16	9	0	3.50
1 Jack Curtis															

NEW YORK — 10th 40-120 .250 60.5 — CASEY STENGEL

NAME	G by Pos	B	AGE	G	AB	R	H	2B	3B	HR	RBI	BB	SO	SB	BA	SA
TOTALS			30	161	5492	617	1318	166	40	139	573	616	991	59	.240	.361
2 Marv Throneberry	1B97	L	28	116	357	29	87	11	3	16	49	34	83	1	.244	.426
Charlie Neal	2B85, SS39, 3B12	R	31	136	508	59	132	14	9	11	58	56	90	2	.260	.392
Elio Chacon	SS110, 2B2, 3B1	R	25	118	368	49	87	10	3	2	27	76	64	12	.236	.296
Felix Mantilla	3B95, SS25, 2B14	R	27	141	466	54	128	17	4	11	59	37	51	3	.275	.399
Richie Ashburn	OF97, 2B2	L	35	135	389	60	119	7	3	7	28	81	39	12	.306	.393
Jim Hickman	OF124	R	25	140	392	54	96	18	2	13	46	47	96	4	.245	.401
Frank Thomas	OF126, 1B11, 3B10	R	33	156	571	69	152	23	3	34	94	48	95	2	.266	.496
Chris Cannizzaro	C56, OF1	R	24	59	133	9	32	4	0	0	9	19	26	1	.241	.271
Rod Kanehl	2B62, 3B30, OF20, 1B3, SS2	R	28	133	351	52	87	10	2	4	23	36	48	8	.248	.322
Joe Christopher	OF94	R	26	119	271	25	66	10	2	6	32	35	42	11	.244	.362
2 Gene Woodling	OF48	L	39	81	190	18	52	8	2	4	25	24	22	0	.274	.405
2 Sammy Taylor	C50	L	29	68	158	12	35	4	2	3	20	23	17	0	.222	.329
Choo Choo Coleman	C44	L	24	55	152	24	38	7	2	6	17	11	24	2	.250	.441
Gil Hodges	1B47	R	38	54	127	15	32	1	0	9	17	15	21	0	.252	.472
Ed Bouchee	1B19	L	29	50	87	7	14	2	0	3	10	18	17	0	.161	.287
2 Cliff Cook	3B16, OF10	R	25	40	112	12	26	9	0	3	14	4	34	1	.232	.357
Rick Herrscher	1B10, 3B6, OF4, SS3	R	25	35	50	5	11	3	0	1	5	5	11	0	.220	.340
1 Gus Bell	OF26	L	33	30	101	8	15	2	0	0	6	7	11	0	.149	.198
2 Joe Pignatano	C25	R	32	27	56	2	13	2	0	0	2	11	10	0	.232	.268
Sammy Drake	2B10, 3B6	B	27	25	45	5	9	0	0	0	3	6	15	2	.200	.200
1 Hobie Landrith	C21	L	32	23	45	6	13	1	0	0	6	8	8	0	.289	.422
1 Jim Marshall	1B5, OF1	L	30	17	33	3	11	2	0	2	5	3	9	0	.344	.636
Harry Chiti	C14	R	29	15	41	2	8	2	0	0	3	1	8	0	.195	.220
1 Don Zimmer	3B14	R	31	14	16	3	1	0	0	0	0	3	10	0	.077	.096
John DeMerit	OF9	R	26	14	16	3	3	0	0	0	0	4	1	0	.188	.375

1 Bobby Gene Smith 28 R 3-22, Ed Kranepool 17 L 1-6, Joe Ginsberg 35 L 0-5

NAME	T	AGE	W	L	PCT	SV	G	GS	CG	IP	H	BB	SO	SHO	ERA
		27	40	120	.250	10	161	161	43	1430	1577	571	772	4	5.04
Roger Craig	R	32	10	24	.294	3	42	33	13	233	261	70	118	0	4.52
Jay Hook	R	25	8	19	.296	0	37	34	13	214	230	71	113	0	4.84
Al Jackson	L	26	8	20	.286	0	36	33	12	231	244	78	118	4	4.40
Ken MacKenzie	L	28	5	4	.556	1	42	0	0	80	87	34	51	0	4.95
Craig Anderson	R	24	3	17	.150	4	50	14	2	131	150	63	62	0	5.36
2 Bob Miller	R	23	2	2	.500	0	17	0	0	21	19	15	11	0	7.20
2 Galen Cisco	R	26	1	1	.500	0	4	1	0	19	15	11	13	0	3.32
Ray Daviault	R	28	1	5	.167	0	36	3	0	81	92	48	51	0	6.22
2 Willard Hunter	L	28	1	6	.143	0	27	6	1	63	67	34	40	0	5.57
Bob Miller	L	23	1	12	.077	0	33	21	1	144	146	62	91	0	4.88
2 Dave Hillman	R	34	0	0	—	0	16	0	0	16	21	4	8	0	6.19
Clem Labine	R	35	0	0	—	0	3	0	0	11	13	5	5	0	11.25
Herb Moford	R	33	0	1	.000	0	7	0	0	15	20	11	9	0	7.20
Larry Foss	R	26	0	1	.000	0	4	0	0	18	18	14	4	0	4.50
Bob Moorhead	R	24	0	2	.000	0	38	7	0	105	118	42	63	0	4.54
2 Vinegar Bend Mizell	R	31	0	2	.000	0	17	2	0	38	48	25	15	0	7.34
Sherman Jones	R	27	0	0	—	0	25	3	0	31	41	8	11	0	7.83

1963 Shutting Out the Ghost of Autumns Past

The year of 1963 included the expansion of the batter's strike zone, 43-year-old Early Wynn finally winning his 300th game, and the Mets' Roger Craig losing 18 games in a row. More important, though, was the coming of baseball's finest southpaw since Lefty Grove. Putting the talent and experience of nine major league campaigns together, the Dodgers' Sandy Koufax became the premier pitcher and gate attraction of the game. By using a dazzling fastball and a curve graceful enough to rival a prima ballerina, Koufax struck his way to 25 victories, a 1.88 E.R.A., and both the MVP and Cy Young Awards.

Koufax's performance was further intensified by his recovery from the 1962 finger ailment which had placed his career in doubt. While pitching the Dodgers steadily along the pennant road with the aid of Don Drysdale, a 19-game winner, and Ron Perranoski, the brilliant relief specialist who saved 21 games while winning 16 with a 1.67 E.R.A., the only real offensive help came from Tommy Davis, Frank Howard, and Maury Wills. Davis again won the batting title, while Howard provided the sole long-ball threat. Wills, although a good distance off from his 1962 stolen base mark, managed enough thefts and a .302 batting average to hamper the opposition.

Yet, before the Dodgers could claim the National League flag, they had to contend with the likes of Bill White, Dick Groat, Ken Boyer, and Stan Musial, the kingpins of the St. Louis Cardinals. Bouncing back from an eight-game losing streak right before the All-Star break, the Cards burned up the league in early September, winning 19 of 20 games to pull within one game of the Dodgers on September 16, when both clubs squared off for a three-game series at St. Louis.

Lefty Johnny Podres cooled off the Cards with a three hitter for a 3-1 Dodger win in the first game. Then Koufax took the stage and shut out the Cards on four hits for a 4-0 second-game triumph. In the final match, St. Louis led 5-1 after seven innings but a tiring Bob Gibson gave up three runs in the eighth and a home run to rookie Dick Nen in the ninth to send the game into extra innings. The Dodgers finally won 6-5 in 13 innings, sweeping the series and avoiding the embarrassment of a second straight late-season fold-up. The triple loss ended the Cards' dream of giving Stan Musial a World Series in his final year in uniform.

The Giants' strong bats kept them in the race until late August, but their pitching staff, weak outside of Juan Marichal, sabotaged any pennant hopes. The surprising Phillies came on strong at the end to capture fourth place, while the disappointing Reds finished fifth despite a fine rookie season by Pete Rose. At the bottom of the heap was the New York Mets, a horrendous team which drew 1,000,000 enthusiastic fans into the Polo Grounds. Managed by Casey Stengel, the Mets showcased fading stars like Duke Snider and Jimmy Piersall, and supported ace pitcher Roger Craig so sparingly that he lost 18 games in a row before he switched his uniform number to 13 and promptly won his first game in three months.

Despite serious injuries to Mickey Mantle and Roger Maris, the Yankees still managed the power to support a good pitching staff and win the American League flag by 10½ games over the Chicago White Sox. Mantle fractured his foot and then hurt his knee, and a bad back plagued Maris during the campaign, with the two sluggers appearing together in the starting lineup only 30 times all year. Manager Ralph Houk used Johnny Blanchard and Hector Lopez to take up the slack, and the duo responded with 30 combined home runs. While Joe Pepitone won the first base job in the spring and proceeded to confirm Houk's choice by belting 27 home runs, backstop Elston Howard won the MVP Award with a .287 performance spiced by 28 circuit blasts. The sound Yankee infield of Pepitone, Bobby Richardson, Tony Kubek, and Clete Boyer stayed healthy and supported the pitchers with air-tight defense. Veteran Whitey Ford paced the hurlers with 24 victories, surprising sophomore Jim Bouton won 21 games and Ralph Terry captured 17 wins. Al Downing, recalled in June, also helped to bolster the starting staff.

The Yankees' team battling effort was underscored by the absence of any pinstriper from the league leaders, as Boston's Carl Yastrzemski and Dick Stuart, respectively, won the batting and RBI titles, and the Twins' Harmon Killebrew the home run crown. Yankee pitcher ace Ford did lead the league in wins and winning percentage, and Chicago's Gary Peters, a failure in three previous big league trials, pleasantly surprised the White Sox by posting a league-low 2.33 E.R.A.

When the World Series dawned, it marked the eighth time the Yankees and Dodgers were getting together. In all but one previous attempt, the Dodgers had come up second best. Only the presence of Koufax, and the fact that the rematch was now a transcontinental affair, gave the Dodger rooters any hope that the jinx would finally be broken.

Game one in New York saw Koufax blow the Yankees apart with a record 15 strikeouts as ex-Yankee Moose Skowron made up for his poor season in the National League by driving in two runs. Johnny Podres continued the silencing of Bronx bats in the next game with a 4-1 victory finished by Perranoski and marked by a Skowron home run. Drysdale faced Bouton in a magnificent pitchers' battle in the opening of the Series in Los Angeles and came up on top of a 1-0 score. With their backs to the wall, the Yankees again faced Koufax in the fourth game and lost on a Frank Howard homer and a Pepitone error, 2-1.

It was all over, and the fans rejoiced in Brooklyn as well as Los Angeles. After the fanfare subsided, the Yankees promoted Houk to general manager and Yogi Berra to field boss, a move that would register its repercussions soon after one melodic tune would be played on a harmonica.

WORLD SERIES — LOS ANGELES (NL) 4 NEW YORK (AL) 0

LINE SCORES

TEAM	1	2	3	4	5	6	7	8	9	10	11	12	R	H	E
Game 1	**October 2 at New York**														
LA (NL)	0	4	1		0	0	0		0	0	0		5	9	0
NY (AL)	0	0	0		0	0	0		0	2	0		2	6	0
Koufax									Ford, Williams (6), Hamilton (9)						
Game 2	**October 3 at New York**														
LA	2	0	0		1	0	0		0	1	0		4	10	1
NY	0	0	0		0	0	0		0	0	1		1	7	0
Podres, Perranoski (9)									Downing, Terry (6), Reniff (9)						
Game 3	**October 5 at Los Angeles**														
NY	0	0	0		0	0	0		0	0	0		0	3	0
LA	1	0	0		0	0	0		0	0	X		1	4	1
Bouton, Reniff (8)									Drysdale						
Game 4	**October 6 at Los Angeles**														
NY	0	0	0		0	0	0		1	0	0		1	6	1
LA	0	0	0		0	1	0		1	0	X		2	2	1
Ford, Reniff (8)									Koufax						

COMPOSITE BATTING

NAME	POS	G	AB	R	H	2B	3B	HR	RBI	BA
Los Angeles (NL)										
Totals		4	117	12	25	3	2	3	12	.214
T. Davis	OF	4	15	0	6	0	2	0	2	.400
Wills	SS	4	15	1	2	0	0	0	0	.133
Roseboro	C	4	14	1	2	0	0	1	3	.143
Skowron	1B	4	13	2	5	0	0	1	3	.385
Gilliam	3B	4	13	3	2	0	0	0	0	.154
Tracewski	2B	4	13	1	2	0	0	0	0	.154
W. Davis	OF	4	12	2	2	2	0	0	3	.167
F. Howard	OF	3	10	2	3	1	0	1	1	.300
Koufax	P	2	6	0	0	0	0	0	0	.000
Podres	P	1	4	0	1	0	0	0	0	.250
Fairly	OF	4	1	0	0	0	0	0	0	.000
Drysdale	P	1	1	0	0	0	0	0	0	.000
Perranoski	P	1	0	0	0	0	0	0	0	—
New York (AL)										
Totals		4	129	4	22	3	0	2	4	.171
Kubek	SS	4	16	1	3	0	0	0	0	.188
E. Howard	C	4	15	0	5	0	0	0	0	.333
Tresh	OF	4	15	1	3	0	0	1	2	.200
Mantle	OF	4	15	1	2	0	0	1	1	.133
Richardson	2B	4	14	0	3	1	0	0	0	.214
Pepitone	1B	4	13	0	2	0	0	0	0	.154
Boyer	3B	4	13	0	1	0	0	0	0	.077
Lopez	OF	3	8	1	2	2	0	0	0	.250
Maris	OF	2	5	0	0	0	0	0	0	.000
Linz	PH	3	3	0	1	0	0	0	0	.333
Ford	P	2	3	0	0	0	0	0	0	.000
Blanchard	OF	1	3	0	0	0	0	0	0	.000
Bright	PH	2	2	0	0	0	0	0	0	.000
Bouton	P	1	2	0	0	0	0	0	0	.000
Downing	P	1	1	0	0	0	0	0	0	.000
Berra	PH	1	1	0	0	0	0	0	0	.000
Reniff	P	3	0	0	0	0	0	0	0	—
Williams	P	1	0	0	0	0	0	0	0	—
Hamilton	P	1	0	0	0	0	0	0	0	—
Terry	P	1	0	0	0	0	0	0	0	—

COMPOSITE PITCHING

NAME	G	IP	H	BB	SO	W	L	SV	ERA
Los Angeles (NL)									
Totals	4	36	22	5	37	4	0	1	1.00
Koufax	2	18	12	3	23	2	0	0	1.50
Drysdale	1	9	3	1	9	1	0	0	0.00
Podres	1	8.1	6	1	4	1	0	0	1.08
Perranoski	1	0.2	1	0	1	0	0	1	0.00
New York (AL)									
Totals	4	34	25	11	25	0	4	0	2.91
Ford	2	12	10	3	8	0	2	0	4.50
Bouton	1	7	4	5	4	0	1	0	1.29
Downing	1	5	7	1	6	0	1	0	5.40
Williams	1	3	1	0	5	0	0	0	0.00
Reniff	3	3	0	1	1	0	0	0	0.00
Terry	1	3	3	1	0	0	0	0	3.00
Hamilton	1	1	0	0	1	0	0	0	0.00

NEW YORK 1st 104-57 .646 — RALPH HOUK

NAME	G by Pos	B	AGE	G	AB	R	H	2B	3B	HR	RBI	BB	SO	SB	BA	SA
TOTALS			28	161	5506	714	1387	197	35	188	666	434	808	42	.252	.403
Joe Pepitone	1B143, OF16	L	22	157	580	79	157	16	3	27	89	23	63	3	.271	.448
Bobby Richardson	2B150	R	27	151	630	72	167	20	6	3	48	25	22	15	.265	.330
Tony Kubek	SS132, OF1	L	26	135	557	72	143	21	3	7	44	28	68	4	.257	.343
Clete Boyer	3B141, SS9, 2B1	R	26	152	557	59	140	20	3	12	54	33	91	4	.251	.363
Roger Maris	OF86	L	28	90	312	53	84	14	1	23	53	35	40	1	.269	.542
Tom Tresh	OF144	B	25	145	520	91	140	28	5	25	71	83	79	3	.269	.487
Hector Lopez	OF124, 3B1	R	33	130	433	54	108	13	4	14	52	35	71	1	.249	.395
Elston Howard	C132	R	34	135	487	75	140	21	6	28	85	35	68	0	.287	.528
Jack Reed	OF89	R	30	106	73	18	15	3	1	0	1	9	14	5	.205	.274
Johnny Blanchard	OF64	L	30	76	218	22	49	4	0	16	45	26	30	0	.225	.463
Phil Linz	SS22, 3B13, OF12, 2B6	R	24	72	186	22	50	9	0	2	12	15	18	1	.269	.349
Mickey Mantle (BF)	OF52	B	31	65	172	40	54	8	0	15	35	40	32	2	.314	.622
Yogi Berra	C35	L	38	64	147	20	43	6	0	8	28	15	17	1	.293	.497
2 Harry Bright	1B35, 3B12	R	33	60	157	15	37	7	0	7	23	13	31	0	.236	.414
Pedro Gonzalez	2B7	R	24	14	26	3	5	1	0	0	1	0	5	0	.192	.231
Dale Long	1B2	L	37	14	15	1	3	0	0	0	0	0	3	0	.200	.200
Jake Gibbs	C1	L	24	4	8	1	2	0	0	0	0	0	2	0	.250	.250

NAME	T	AGE	W	L	PCT	SV	G	GS	CG	IP	H	BB	SO	SHO	ERA
	L	27	104	57	.646	31	161	161	59	1449	1239	476	965	19	3.07
Whitey Ford	L	34	24	7	.774	1	38	37	13	269	240	56	189	3	2.74
Jim Bouton	R	24	21	7	.750	1	40	30	12	249	197	87	148	6	2.53
Ralph Terry	R	27	17	15	.531	1	40	37	18	268	246	39	114	3	3.22
Al Downing	L	22	13	5	.722	0	24	22	10	176	114	80	171	4	2.56
Stan Williams	R	26	9	8	.529	0	29	21	6	146	137	57	98	1	3.21
Steve Hamilton	L	29	5	1	.833	5	34	0	0	62	49	24	63	0	2.60
Hal Reniff	R	24	4	3	.571	18	48	0	0	89	63	42	56	0	2.63
Bill Stafford	R	23	4	8	.333	0	28	14	0	90	104	42	52	0	6.00
Bill Kunkel	R	26	3	2	.600	0	22	0	0	46	42	13	31	0	2.74
Marshall Bridges	L	32	2	1	1.000	1	23	0	0	33	27	30	35	0	3.82
Tom Metcalf	R	22	1	0	1.000	0	13	0	0	13	12	3	3	0	2.77
Luis Arroyo	L	36	1	1	.500	0	6	0	0	6	12	3	5	0	13.50
Bud Daley (SA)	L	30	0	0	—	0	6	0	0	1	2	1	0	0	0.00

CHICAGO 2nd 94-68 .580 10.5 — AL LOPEZ

NAME	G by Pos	B	AGE	G	AB	R	H	2B	3B	HR	RBI	BB	SO	SB	BA	SA
TOTALS			26	162	5508	683	1379	208	40	114	648	571	896	64	.250	.365
Tommy McCraw	1B97	L	22	102	280	38	71	11	3	6	33	21	46	15	.254	.379
Nellie Fox	2B134	L	35	137	539	54	140	19	0	2	42	24	17	0	.260	.306
Ron Hansen	SS144	R	25	144	482	55	109	17	2	13	67	78	74	1	.226	.351
Pete Ward	3B154, 2B1, SS1	L	23	157	600	80	177	34	6	22	84	52	77	7	.295	.482
Floyd Robinson	OF137	L	27	146	527	71	149	21	6	13	71	62	43	4	.283	.419
Jim Landis	OF124	R	29	133	396	56	89	6	6	13	45	47	75	4	.225	.369
Dave Nicholson	OF123	R	23	126	449	53	103	11	4	22	70	63	175	2	.229	.419
J.C. Martin	C98, 1B3, 3B1	L	26	105	259	25	53	11	1	5	28	26	35	0	.205	.313
Mike Hershberger	OF119	R	23	135	476	64	133	26	4	3	45	39	39	9	.279	.361
Cam Carreon	C92	R	25	101	270	28	74	10	1	2	35	23	32	1	.274	.341
Al Weis	2B48, SS27, 3B1	B	25	99	210	41	57	9	0	0	18	18	37	15	.271	.314
Charlie Maxwell	OF24, 1B17	L	36	71	130	17	30	4	2	3	17	31	27	0	.231	.362
Joe Cunningham (BC)	1B58	L	31	67	210	32	60	12	1	1	31	33	23	1	.286	.367
3 Jim Lemon	1B25	R	35	36	80	4	16	0	1	1	8	12	32	0	.200	.263
Sherm Lollar	C23, 1B2	R	38	35	73	4	17	4	0	0	6	8	7	0	.233	.288
Deacon Jones	1B1	L	29	17	16	4	3	0	1	1	2	2	7	0	.188	.500
Don Buford	3B9, 2B2	B	26	12	42	9	12	1	2	0	5	5	3	1	.286	.405
Gene Stephens	OF5	L	30	6	18	5	7	0	0	1	2	1	3	0	.389	.556
Ken Berry	OF2, 2B1	R	22	5	2	1	0	0	0	0	1	0	1	0	.200	.200
Charley Smith	SS1	R	25	4	7	0	2	0	1	0	0	1	0	0	.286	.571
Brian McCall	OF2	L	20	3	7	1	0	0	0	0	0	0	0	0	.000	.000
1 Sammy Esposito		R	31	1	0	0	0	0	0	0	0	0	0	0		

NAME	T	AGE	W	L	PCT	SV	G	GS	CG	IP	H	BB	SO	SHO	ERA
		29	94	68	.580	39	162	162	49	1469	1311	440	932	21	2.97
Gary Peters	L	26	19	8	.704	1	41	30	13	243	192	68	189	4	2.33
Juan Pizarro	L	26	16	8	.667	1	32	28	10	215	177	63	163	3	2.39
Ray Herbert	R	33	13	10	.565	0	33	33	14	225	230	35	105	7	3.24
Joe Horlen	R	25	11	7	.611	0	33	21	3	124	122	55	61	0	3.27
John Buzhardt (SA)	R	26	9	4	.692	0	19	18	6	126	100	31	59	3	2.43
Eddie Fisher	R	26	9	8	.529	0	33	15	2	121	114	28	67	1	3.94
Hoyt Wilhelm	R	40	5	8	.385	21	55	3	0	136	106	30	111	0	2.65
Dave DeBusschere	R	22	3	4	.429	0	24	10	1	84	80	34	53	1	3.11
2 Jim Brosnan	R	33	3	8	.273	14	45	0	0	73	71	22	40	0	2.84
Frank Baumann (AJ)	L	30	2	1	.667	1	24	0	0	50	52	17	31	0	3.06
Bruce Howard	R	20	2	1	.667	0	7	0	0	17	12	14	9	0	2.65
Fritz Ackley	R	26	1	0	1.000	0	2	0	0	13	7	7	13	0	2.08
Frank Kreutzer	L	24	1	0	1.000	0	4	2	0	13	7	1	6	0	1.80
Taylor Phillips	L	30	0	0	—	0	9	0	0	14	16	13	13	0	10.29
Mike Joyce	R	22	0	0	—	0	5	0	0	11	13	8	7	0	8.18
1 Dom Zanni	R	31	0	0	—	0	5	0	0	3	2	4	2	0	9.00
Fred Talbot	R	22	0	0	—	0	1	0	0	3	3	2	0	0	3.00
Joe Shipley	R	28	0	0	—	0	1	0	0	5	9	6	3	0	5.40

MINNESOTA 3rd 91-70 .565 13 — SAM MELE

NAME	G by Pos	B	AGE	G	AB	R	H	2B	3B	HR	RBI	BB	SO	SB	BA	SA
TOTALS			27	161	5531	767	1408	223	35	225	722	547	912	32	.255	.430
Vic Power	1B124, 2B18, 3B5	R	29	139	541	65	146	28	2	10	52	22	44	3	.270	.384
Bernie Allen	2B128	L	24	139	421	52	101	20	1	9	43	38	52	0	.240	.356
Zoilo Versalles	SS159	R	23	159	621	74	162	31	13	10	54	36	83	6	.261	.401
Rich Rollins	3B132, 2B1	R	25	136	531	75	163	23	1	16	61	36	59	2	.307	.444
Bob Allison	OF147	R	28	148	527	99	143	25	4	35	91	90	109	6	.271	.533
Jimmie Hall	OF143	L	25	156	497	88	129	21	5	33	80	63	101	3	.260	.521
Harmon Killebrew	OF137	R	27	142	515	88	133	18	0	45	96	72	105	0	.258	.555
Earl Battey	C146	R	28	147	508	64	145	17	1	26	84	61	75	0	.285	.476
Lenny Green	OF119	L	29	145	280	41	67	10	1	4	27	31	31	11	.239	.325
Don Mincher	1B60	L	25	82	225	41	58	8	0	17	42	30	51	0	.258	.520
Johnny Goryl	2B34, 3B11, SS7	R	29	64	150	29	43	5	3	9	24	15	29	0	.287	.540
Jerry Zimmerman	C39	R	28	39	56	3	13	1	0	0	3	2	8	0	.232	.250
2 Vic Wertz	1B6	L	38	35	44	3	6	0	0	3	7	6	5	0	.136	.341
George Banks	3B21	R	24	25	71	5	11	4	0	3	8	9	21	0	.155	.338
2 Wally Post	OF12	R	33	21	47	6	9	0	1	2	6	2	17	0	.191	.362
Bill Tuttle	OF14	R	33	16	3	0	0	0	0	0	1	0	0	0	.000	.000
Paul Ratliff	C7	L	19	10	21	2	4	1	0	1	3	2	7	0	.190	.381
Jay Ward	3B4, OF1	R	24	9	15	0	1	1	0	0	2	1	5	0	.067	.133
1 Jim Lemon	OF35	R	35	7	17	0	2	0	0	0	1	0	1	0	.118	.118
Tony Oliva	OF4	L	22	7	7	0	3	0	0	0	1	0	2	0	.429	.429
Julio Becquer		L	31														

NAME	T	AGE	W	L	PCT	SV	G	GS	CG	IP	H	BB	SO	SHO	ERA
		27	91	70	.565	30	161	161	58	1446	1322	459	941	13	3.28
Camilo Pascual	R	29	21	9	.700	0	31	31	18	248	205	81	202	3	2.47
Dick Stigman	L	27	15	15	.500	0	33	33	15	241	210	81	193	3	3.25
Lee Stange	R	26	12	5	.706	0	32	20	7	165	145	43	100	2	2.62
Jim Kaat	L	24	10	10	.500	1	31	27	7	178	195	38	105	1	4.20
2 Jim Perry	R	27	9	9	.500	1	35	25	5	168	167	57	65	1	3.75
Bill Pleis	L	25	6	3	.667	0	36	4	1	68	67	16	37	0	4.37
Bill Dailey	R	28	6	3	.667	21	66	0	0	109	80	19	72	0	1.98
Jim Roland	L	20	4	1	.800	0	10	7	2	49	32	27	34	1	2.57
Dwight Siebler	R	25	2	1	.667	0	7	5	2	39	25	12	22	0	2.77
Garry Roggenburk	L	23	2	4	.333	4	36	2	0	50	47	22	24	0	2.16
2 Mike Fornieles	R	31	1	1	.500	0	11	0	0	23	24	13	7	0	4.70
Jerry Arrigo	L	22	1	2	.333	0	5	1	0	16	12	4	13	0	2.81
Ray Moore	R	37	1	3	.250	2	31	1	0	39	50	17	38	0	6.92
1 Jack Kralick	L	28	1	4	.200	0	5	5	1	26	28	8	13	1	3.81
Fred Lasher	R	21	0	0	—	0	11	0	0	11	12	11	10	0	4.91
Don Williams	R	27	0	0	—	0	4	0	0	4	8	4	2	0	11.25
Gary Dotter	L	20	0	0	—	0	1	0	0	4	6	3	4	0	0.00
Frank Sullivan	R	33	0	1	.000	0	10	0	0	11	15	4	2	0	5.73

BALTIMORE 4th 86-76 .531 18.5 — BILLY HITCHCOCK

NAME	G by Pos	B	AGE	G	AB	R	H	2B	3B	HR	RBI	BB	SO	SB	BA	SA
TOTALS			27	162	5448	644	1359	207	32	146	609	469	940	97	.249	.380
Jim Gentile	1B143	L	29	145	496	65	123	16	1	24	72	76	101	1	.248	.429
Jerry Adair	2B103	R	26	109	382	34	87	21	3	6	30	9	51	3	.228	.346
Luis Aparicio	SS145	R	29	146	601	73	150	18	8	5	45	36	35	40	.250	.331
Brooks Robinson	3B160, SS1	R	26	161	589	67	148	26	4	11	67	46	84	2	.251	.365
Russ Snyder	OF130	L	29	142	429	51	110	21	2	7	36	40	48	18	.256	.384
Jackie Brandt	OF134, 3B1	R	29	142	451	49	112	16	5	15	61	34	85	4	.248	.404
Boog Powell	OF121, 1B23	L	21	140	491	67	130	22	2	25	82	49	87	1	.265	.470
John Orsino	C109, 1B3	R	25	116	379	53	103	18	1	19	56	38	53	2	.272	.475
Al Smith	OF97	R	35	120	368	45	100	17	1	10	39	32	74	9	.272	.405
Bob Saverine	OF59, 2B19, SS13	B	22	115	167	21	39	1	2	1	12	25	44	8	.234	.281
Bob Johnson	2B50, 1B8, SS7, 3B5	R	27	82	254	34	75	10	4	8	32	18	35	5	.295	.429
Joe Gaines	OF39	R	26	66	126	24	36	4	1	6	20	20	39	2	.286	.476
Dick Brown	C58	R	28	59	171	13	42	7	0	2	13	15	35	1	.246	.322
1 Charlie Lau	C8	L	30	29	48	4	9	2	0	0	6	1	5	0	.188	.229
Fred Valentine	OF10	B	28	26	41	5	11	1	0	0	5	2	7	1	.268	.293
Sam Bowens	OF13	R	24	15	48	8	16	3	1	1	9	4	5	1	.333	.500
1 Hobie Landrith	C1	L	33	2	1	0	0	0	0	0	0	0	1	0	.000	.000

NAME	T	AGE	W	L	PCT	SV	G	GS	CG	IP	H	BB	SO	SHO	ERA
		28	86	76	.531	43	162	162	35	1452	1353	507	913	8	3.45
Steve Barber	L	25	20	13	.606	0	39	36	11	259	253	92	180	2	2.75
Milt Pappas	R	24	16	9	.640	0	34	32	11	217	186	69	120	4	3.03
Robin Roberts	R	36	14	13	.519	0	35	35	9	251	230	40	124	2	3.33
Wes Stock	R	29	7	1	1.000	1	47	0	0	75	69	31	55	0	3.96
Dave McNally	L	20	7	8	.467	1	29	20	2	126	133	55	78	0	4.57
Mike McCormick	L	24	6	8	.429	0	25	21	2	136	132	66	75	0	4.30
Dick Hall	R	32	5	5	.500	12	47	3	0	112	91	16	74	0	2.97
Stu Miller	R	35	5	8	.385	27	71	0	0	112	93	53	114	0	2.25
Chuck Estrada (EJ)	R	25	3	2	.600	0	8	7	2	31	26	19	16	0	4.65
John Miller	R	22	1	0	1.000	0	3	2	0	17	12	14	16	0	3.18
Dean Stone	L	32	1	2	.333	1	17	0	0	23	16	12	5	0	5.21
3 Ike Delock	R	33	1	3	.250	0	5	1	0	25	25	16	11	0	5.40
Buster Narum	R	22	0	0	—	0	1	0	0	5	6	5	3	0	3.00
Herm Starrette	R	24	0	1	.000	0	18	0	0	26	26	7	13	0	3.46
2 George Brunet	L	28	0	1	.000	0	16	0	0	20	25	9	13	0	5.40
1 Pete Burnside	L	32	0	1	.000	0	7	0	0	11	12	6	6	0	5.14
Wally Bunker	R	18	0	0	—	0	1	0	0	4	10	3	1	0	13.50

CLEVELAND 5th (tie) 79-83 .488 25.5 — BIRDIE TEBBETTS

NAME	G by Pos	B	AGE	G	AB	R	H	2B	3B	HR	RBI	BB	SO	SB	BA	SA
TOTALS			27	162	5496	635	1314	214	29	169	592	469	1102	59	.239	.381
Fred Whitfield	1B92	L	25	109	346	44	87	17	3	21	54	24	61	0	.251	.500
Woodie Held	2B96, OF35, SS5, 3B3	R	31	133	416	61	103	19	4	17	61	61	96	2	.248	.435
Jerry Kindall	SS46, 2B37, 1B4	R	28	86	234	27	48	4	1	5	20	18	71	3	.205	.295
Max Alvis	3B158	R	25	158	602	81	165	32	7	22	67	36	109	4	.274	.460
Willie Kirkland	OF112	L	29	127	427	51	98	13	2	15	47	45	99	8	.230	.375
Vic Davalillo (BW)	OF89	L	26	90	370	44	108	18	5	7	36	16	41	3	.292	.424
Tito Francona	OF122, 1B11	L	29	142	500	57	114	29	0	10	41	47	77	9	.228	.346
2 Joe Azcue	C91	R	23	94	320	26	91	16	0	14	46	15	46	1	.284	.466
Al Luplow	OF85	L	24	100	295	34	69	6	2	7	27	33	62	4	.234	.339
Joe Adcock	1B78	R	35	97	283	28	71	7	1	13	49	30	53	1	.251	.420
Johnny Romano (BG)	C71, OF4	R	28	89	255	28	55	5	2	10	34	38	49	4	.216	.369
Larry Brown	SS46, 2B27	R	23	74	247	28	63	6	0	5	18	22	27	4	.255	.340
Mike de la Hoz	2B34, 3B6, SS2, OF2	R	24	67	150	15	40	10	0	5	25	9	29	0	.267	.433
Willie Tasby	OF37, 2B1	R	30	52	116	11	26	3	1	4	15	25	25	0	.224	.371
2 Dick Howser	SS44	R	27	49	162	25	40	5	0	1	10	22	18	9	.247	.296
Tony Martinez	SS41	R	23	43	141	10	22	4	0	0	8	5	18	1	.156	.184
1 Gene Green	OF18	R	30	43	78	4	16	3	0	2	11	4	21	0	.205	.321
1 Ellis Burton	OF16	B	26	31	62	6	12	1	0	1	4	2	11	0	.194	.387
Bob Chance	OF14	L	21	16	52	5	15	4	0	2	7	1	10	0	.288	.481
Tommie Agee	OF13	R	20	13	27	3	4	1	0	0	1	4	9	0	.148	.296
1 Doc Edwards	C10	R	26	10	31	6	8	1	0	2	4	0	8	0	.258	.323
1 Cal Neeman	C9	R	34	9	9	0	0	0	0	0	0	2	4	0	.000	.000
3 Sammy Taylor	C2	L	26	4	10	1	3	0	0	0	0	1	2	0	.300	.300
Jim Lawrence	C2	R	24	2	5	0	0	0	0	0	0	0	2	0	.000	—
Bob Lipski	C2	L	24	2	2	0	0	0	0	0	0	0	0	0	.000	.000

NAME	T	AGE	W	L	PCT	SV	G	GS	CG	IP	H	BB	SO	SHO	ERA
		29	79	83	.488	25	162	162	40	1469	1390	478	1018	14	3.79
2 Jack Kralick	L	28	13	9	.591	0	28	27	10	197	187	41	116	3	2.92
Mudcat Grant	R	27	13	14	.481	1	38	32	10	229	213	87	157	2	3.69
Dick Donovan	R	35	11	13	.458	0	30	30	7	206	211	28	84	3	4.24
Pedro Ramos	R	28	9	8	.529	0	36	22	5	185	156	41	169	0	3.11
Gary Bell	R	26	8	5	.615	5	58	7	0	119	91	52	98	0	2.95
Ted Abernathy	R	30	7	2	.778	12	43	0	0	59	54	29	47	0	2.90
Barry Latman	R	27	7	12	.368	2	38	21	4	149	146	52	133	2	4.95
Jerry Walker	R	24	6	6	.500	1	39	2	0	88	92	36	41	0	4.91
Sam McDowell	L	20	3	5	.375	0	14	12	3	65	43	63	41	1	4.85
Bob Allen	L	25	3	3	.500	2	43	0	0	56	58	29	51	0	4.66
Early Wynn	R	43	1	2	.333	1	20	5	1	55	50	15	29	0	2.29
1 Jim Perry	R	27	1	0	1.000	0	5	0	0	10	12	2	7	0	5.40
Jack Curtis	L	26	0	0	—	0	1	0	0	1	1	0	1	0	18.00
Gordon Seyfried	L	25	0	1	.000	0	4	0	0	14	17	13	8	0	1.29
Ron Nischwitz	L	26	0	2	.000	1	14	0	0	17	17	8	10	0	6.35
Tommy John	L	20	0	0	—	0	6	0	0	20	23	6	9	0	2.25

DETROIT — 5th (tie) 79-83 .488 25.5 — BOB SCHEFFING 24-36 .400   CHUCK DRESSEN 55-47 .539

NAME	G by Pos	B	AGE	G	AB	R	H	2B	3B	HR	RBI	BB	SO	SB	BA	SA
TOTALS			28	162	5500	700	1388	195	36	148	649	592	908	73	.252	.382
Norm Cash	1B142	L	28	147	493	67	133	19	1	26	79	89	76	2	.270	.471
Jake Wood (RJ)	2B81, 3B1	R	24	85	351	50	95	11	2	11	27	24	61	18	.271	.407
Dick McAuliffe	SS133, 2B15	L	23	150	568	77	149	18	6	13	61	64	75	11	.262	.384
Bubba Phillips	3B117, OF5	R	33	128	464	42	114	11	5	6	45	19	42	6	.246	.310
Al Kaline	OF140	R	28	145	551	89	172	24	3	27	101	54	48	6	.312	.514
Bill Bruton	OF138	L	37	145	524	84	134	21	8	8	48	59	70	14	.256	.372
Rocky Colavito	OF159	R	29	160	597	91	162	29	2	22	91	84	78	0	.271	.437
Gus Triandos	C90	R	32	106	327	28	78	13	0	14	41	32	67	0	.239	.407
Bill Freehan	C73, 1B19	R	21	100	300	37	73	12	2	9	36	39	56	2	.243	.387
Don Wert	3B47, 2B21, SS8	R	24	78	251	31	65	6	2	7	25	24	51	3	.259	.382
Gates Brown	OF16	L	24	55	82	16	22	3	1	2	14	8	13	2	.268	.402
George Smith	2B52	R	25	52	171	16	37	8	2	0	17	18	34	4	.216	.287
Whitey Herzog	1B7, OF4	L	31	52	53	5	8	2	1	0	7	11	17	0	.151	.226
2 George Thomas	OF40, 2B1	R	25	49	109	13	26	4	1	1	11	11	22	2	.239	.321
1 Frank Kostro	3B6, 1B3, OF3	R	25	31	52	4	12	1	0	0	9	3	15	0	.231	.250
Mike Roarke	C16	R	32	23	44	5	14	0	1	0	1	2	3	0	.318	.318
1 Chico Fernandez	SS14	R	31	15	49	3	7	1	0	0	2	6	11	0	.143	.163
Willie Horton	OF9	R	20	15	43	6	14	2	1	1	4	0	8	2	.326	.488
Coot Veal	SS12	R	30	15	32	5	7	0	0	0	4	0	6	0	.219	.219
Purnal Goldy	OF3	R	25	9	8	1	2	0	0	0	0	0	2	0	.250	.250
1 Bubba Morton	OF3	R	31	6	11	2	1	0	0	0	2	2	1	0	.091	.091
1 Vic Wertz		L	38	6	5	0	0	0	0	0	0	0	1	0	.000	.000
John Sullivan	C2	L	22	3	5	0	0	0	0	0	0	0	0	0	.000	.000

NAME	T	AGE	W	L	PCT	SV	G	GS	CG	IP	H	BB	SO	SHO	ERA
		28	79	83	.488	28	162	162	42	1456	1407	477	930	7	3.90
Phil Regan	R	26	15	9	.625	1	38	27	5	189	179	59	115	1	3.86
Hank Aguirre	L	32	14	15	.483	0	38	33	14	226	222	68	134	3	3.66
Jim Bunning	R	31	12	13	.480	1	39	35	6	248	245	69	196	2	3.88
Terry Fox	R	27	8	6	.571	11	46	0	0	80	81	20	35	0	3.60
Don Mossi	L	34	7	7	.500	2	24	16	3	123	110	17	68	0	3.73
Bill Faul	R	23	5	6	.455	1	28	10	2	97	93	48	64	0	4.64
Mickey Lolich	L	22	5	9	.357	0	33	18	4	144	145	56	103	0	3.56
Frank Lary	R	33	4	9	.308	0	16	14	6	107	107	26	46	0	3.28
Bob Anderson	R	27	3	1	.750	0	32	3	0	60	58	21	38	0	3.30
Denny McLain	R	19	2	1	.667	0	3	3	2	21	20	16	22	0	4.29
Willie Smith	L	24	1	0	1.000	2	11	2	0	22	24	13	16	0	4.50
Fred Gladding	R	27	1	1	.500	7	22	0	0	27	19	14	24	0	2.00
Alan Koch	R	25	1	1	.500	0	7	1	0	10	21	9	5	0	10.80
2 Tom Sturdivant	R	33	1	2	.333	2	28	0	0	55	43	24	36	0	3.76
Larry Foster	R	25	0	0	—	0	1	0	0	2	4	1	1	0	13.50
Dick Egan	L	21	0	0	.000	0	20	0	0	21	25	3	16	0	5.14
1 Paul Foytack	R	32	0	1	.000	1	9	0	0	18	18	8	7	0	8.50
Bob Dustal	R	27	0	0	.000	0	6	0	0	6	10	5	4	0	9.00

BOSTON — 7th 76-85 .472 28 — JOHNNY PESKY

NAME	G by Pos	B	AGE	G	AB	R	H	2B	3B	HR	RBI	BB	SO	SB	BA	SA
TOTALS			30	161	5575	666	1403	247	34	171	623	475	954	27	.252	.400
Dick Stuart	1B155	R	30	157	612	81	160	25	4	42	118	44	144	0	.261	.521
Chuck Schilling	2B143	R	25	146	576	63	135	25	4	8	40	41	72	3	.234	.319
Ed Bressoud	SS137	R	31	140	497	61	129	23	6	20	60	52	93	1	.260	.451
Frank Malzone	3B148	R	33	151	580	66	169	25	2	15	71	31	45	0	.291	.419
Lu Clinton	OF146	R	25	148	560	71	130	23	7	22	77	49	118	0	.232	.416
Gary Geiger	OF95, 1B6	L	26	121	399	67	105	13	5	16	46	63	63	9	.263	.441
Carl Yastrzemski	OF151	L	23	151	570	91	183	40	3	14	68	95	72	8	.321	.475
Bob Tillman	C95	R	26	96	307	24	69	10	2	8	32	34	64	0	.225	.349
Roman Mejias	OF86	R	32	111	357	43	81	18	0	11	39	14	36	4	.227	.370
Russ Nixon	C76	R	28	98	287	27	77	18	1	5	30	22	32	0	.268	.390
Dick Williams	3B17, 1B11, OF7	R	34	79	136	15	35	8	0	2	12	15	25	0	.257	.360
Felix Mantilla	SS27, OF11, 2B5	R	28	66	178	27	56	8	0	6	15	20	14	2	.315	.461
Billy Gardner	2B21, 3B21, 2B5	R	35	36	84	4	16	2	1	0	4	1	19	0	.190	.238
Jim Gosger	OF4	L	20	19	16	3	1	0	0	0	0	3	5	0	.063	.063
Rico Petrocelli	SS1	R	20	1	4	0	1	0	0	0	0	0	2	0	.250	.500

NAME	T	AGE	W	L	PCT	SV	G	GS	CG	IP	H	BB	SO	SHO	ERA
		26	76	85	.472	32	161	161	29	1450	1367	539	1009	7	3.97
Bill Monbouquette	R	26	20	10	.667	0	37	36	13	267	258	42	174	1	3.81
Dick Radatz	R	26	15	6	.714	25	66	0	0	132	94	51	162	0	1.98
Earl Wilson	R	28	11	16	.407	0	37	34	6	211	184	105	123	3	3.75
Dave Morehead	R	20	10	13	.435	0	29	29	6	175	137	99	136	3	3.81
Jack Lamabe	R	26	7	4	.636	6	65	2	0	151	139	46	93	0	3.16
Bob Heffner	R	24	4	9	.308	0	20	19	3	125	131	36	77	1	4.25
Gene Conley (SJ)	R	32	3	4	.429	0	9	9	0	41	51	21	14	0	6.59
Arnie Earley	L	30	3	7	.300	1	53	4	0	116	124	43	97	0	4.73
1 Ike Delock	R	33	1	2	.333	0	6	6	1	32	31	12	23	0	4.50
Chet Nichols	L	32	1	3	.250	0	21	7	0	53	61	24	27	0	4.75
2 Bob Turley (SA)	R	32	1	4	.200	0	11	7	0	41	42	28	35	0	6.15
1 Mike Fornieles	R	31	0	0	—	0	4	0	0	16	16	5	6	0	6.43
Pete Smith (MS)	R	23	0	0	—	0	1	0	0	15	14	9	6	0	3.60
Jerry Stephenson	R	19	0	0	—	0	1	0	0	2	3	2	1	0	9.00
Hal Kolstad	R	28	0	2	.000	0	11	0	0	22	26	10	11	0	13.09
Wilbur Wood	L	21	0	5	.000	0	25	7	0	65	67	13	28	0	3.74

KANSAS CITY — 8th 73-89 .451 31.5 — ED LOPAT

NAME	G by Pos	B	AGE	G	AB	R	H	2B	3B	HR	RBI	BB	SO	SB	BA	SA
TOTALS			28	162	5495	615	1356	225	38	95	582	529	829	47	.247	.353
Norm Siebern	1B131, OF16	L	29	152	558	80	151	25	2	16	83	79	82	1	.272	.410
Jerry Lumpe	2B155	L	30	157	595	75	161	26	7	5	59	58	44	3	.271	.363
Wayne Causey	SS135, 3B2	L	26	139	554	72	155	32	4	8	44	56	54	4	.280	.390
Ed Charles	3B158	R	28	158	603	82	161	28	2	15	79	50	79	15	.267	.395
Gino Cimoli	OF136	R	33	145	529	56	139	19	11	4	48	39	72	3	.263	.363
Bobby Del Greco	OF110, 3B2	R	30	121	306	40	65	7	1	8	29	40	52	1	.212	.320
Jose Tartabull	OF71	L	24	79	242	27	58	8	5	1	19	17	17	16	.240	.326
2 Doc Edwards	C63	R	26	71	240	16	60	12	0	6	35	11	23	0	.250	.375
Chuck Essegian	OF53	R	31	101	231	23	52	9	0	5	27	19	48	0	.225	.329
George Alusik (BW)	OF63	R	28	87	221	28	59	11	0	9	37	26	33	0	.267	.439
Ken Harrelson	1B34, OF28	R	21	79	226	16	52	10	1	6	23	23	58	1	.230	.363
2 Charlie Lau	C50	L	30	62	187	15	55	11	0	3	26	14	17	1	.294	.401
Manny Jimenez	OF40	L	24	60	157	12	44	9	0	0	15	16	14	0	.280	.338
Haywood Sullivan	C37	R	32	40	113	9	24	6	1	3	15	15	15	0	.212	.283
Tony LaRussa	SS14, 2B1	R	18	34	44	4	11	1	1	0	1	7	12	0	.250	.318
Billy Bryan	C24	L	24	24	65	11	11	1	1	3	7	9	22	0	.169	.354
John Wojcik	OF17	L	21	19	59	7	11	0	0	0	2	8	2	2	.186	.186
2 Sammy Esposito	2B7, SS4, 3B3	R	31	18	25	3	5	1	0	0	2	3	3	0	.200	.240
1 Dick Howser	SS10	R	27	15	41	4	8	0	0	0	1	7	3	0	.195	.195
Dick Green	SS6, 2B4	R	22	13	37	5	10	2	0	1	4	2	10	0	.270	.405
Jay Hankins	OF9	R	27	10	34	2	6	1	1	0	0	1	7	0	.176	.324
Tommie Reynolds	OF5	R	21	8	19	1	1	1	0	0	0	1	1	0	.053	.105
Hector Martinez	OF3	R	24	7	14	2	4	0	0	0	1	0	4	0	.286	.500
1 Joe Azcue	C1	R	23	2	4	0	0	0	0	0	0	0	0	0	.000	.000

NAME	T	AGE	W	L	PCT	SV	G	GS	CG	IP	H	BB	SO	SHO	ERA
		27	73	89	.451	29	162	162	35	1458	1417	540	887	11	3.92
Dave Wickersham	R	27	12	15	.444	1	38	34	4	238	244	79	118	1	4.08
Orlando Pena	R	29	12	20	.375	0	35	33	9	217	218	53	128	3	3.69
Bill Fischer	R	32	9	6	.600	3	45	2	0	96	86	29	34	0	3.56
Diego Segui	R	25	9	6	.600	0	38	23	4	167	173	73	116	1	3.77
Ed Rakow	R	28	9	10	.474	0	34	26	7	174	173	61	104	1	3.93
Moe Drabowsky	R	27	7	13	.350	0	26	22	9	174	135	64	109	2	3.05
John Wyatt	R	28	6	4	.600	21	63	0	0	92	83	43	81	0	3.13
Jose Santiago	R	22	1	0	1.000	0	7	0	0	7	8	2	6	0	9.00
Dan Pfister (EJ)	R	26	1	0	1.000	0	11	0	0	20	21	10	16	0	2.00
Pete Lovrich	R	20	1	1	.500	0	20	1	0	21	25	10	16	0	7.71
3 Tom Sturdivant	R	33	1	2	.333	0	17	3	0	53	47	17	26	0	3.74
Aurelio Monteagudo	R	19	0	0	—	0	1	0	0	2	2	1	3	0	2.57
Norm Bass	R	24	0	0	—	0	3	1	0	8	11	9	4	0	11.25
Bill Landis	L	20	0	0	—	0	2	0	0	2	1	3	0	0	0.00
Dave Thies	R	26	0	1	.000	0	9	0	0	12	9	6	7	0	4.68
Fred Norman	L	20	0	0	.000	0	1	0	0	6	7	2	6	0	12.00
John O'Donoghue	L	23	0	1	.000	0	1	0	0	8	9	0	1	0	1.50
3 Dale Willis	R	25	0	2	.000	0	45	0	0	45	46	25	47	0	5.00

LOS ANGELES — 9th 70-91 .435 34 — BILL RIGNEY

NAME	G by Pos	B	AGE	G	AB	R	H	2B	3B	HR	RBI	BB	SO	SB	BA	SA
TOTALS			27	161	5506	597	1378	208	38	95	551	448	916	43	.250	.354
Lee Thomas	1B104, OF43	L	26	149	528	52	116	12	6	9	55	53	82	6	.220	.316
Billy Moran	2B151	R	29	153	597	67	164	29	5	7	65	31	57	1	.275	.375
Jim Fregosi	SS151	R	21	154	592	83	170	29	12	9	50	36	104	2	.287	.422
Felix Torres	3B122, 1B2	R	31	138	463	40	121	32	1	4	50	30	73	1	.261	.361
Bob Perry	OF55	R	28	61	166	16	42	3	1	4	14	9	31	1	.253	.361
Albie Pearson	OF148	L	28	154	578	92	176	26	5	6	47	92	37	17	.304	.398
Leon Wagner	OF141	L	29	160	604	73	160	11	1	26	90	49	73	5	.291	.456
Bob Rodgers	C85	B	24	100	300	24	70	6	0	4	29	29	35	2	.233	.293
Bob Sadowski	OF25, 3B6, 2B4	L	26	88	144	12	36	6	0	1	22	15	34	2	.250	.313
Eddie Sadowski	C68	R	32	80	174	24	30	1	1	4	15	17	33	2	.172	.259
Joe Koppe	SS19, 3B18, 2B14, OF3	R	32	76	143	11	30	4	1	1	12	19	21	0	.210	.273
Charlie Dees	1B28	L	28	60	220	23	62	11	1	3	27	11	31	3	.307	.416
1 Ken Hunt	OF50	R	28	59	142	17	26	6	1	5	16	15	49	0	.183	.345
1 George Thomas	OF39, 3B10, 1B4	R	25	53	167	14	35	7	1	4	15	9	32	0	.210	.335
2 Frank Kostro	3B19, 1B5, OF3	R	25	43	99	6	22	2	1	1	9	6	17	0	.222	.323
2 Hank Foiles	C30	R	34	41	84	8	18	1	1	4	10	8	13	0	.214	.393
Ed Kirkpatrick	C14, OF10	L	18	34	77	4	15	5	0	2	7	6	19	1	.195	.338
Tom Satriano	3B13, C2, 1B1	R	22	33	50	1	9	2	0	0	3	7	14	0	.180	.200
3 Jimmy Piersall	OF18	R	33	20	52	4	16	1	0	0	6	5	11	0	.308	.327

NAME	T	AGE	W	L	PCT	SV	G	GS	CG	IP	H	BB	SO	SHO	ERA
		30	70	91	.435	31	161	161	30	1455	1317	578	889	13	3.52
Ken McBride	R	27	13	12	.520	0	36	36	11	251	198	82	147	2	3.26
Dean Chance	R	22	13	18	.419	3	45	35	6	248	229	90	168	2	3.19
Dan Osinski	R	29	8	8	.500	0	47	16	4	159	145	80	100	1	3.28
Don Lee	R	29	8	11	.421	1	40	22	3	154	148	51	89	2	3.68
Art Fowler	R	40	5	3	.625	10	57	0	0	89	70	19	53	0	2.43
2 Paul Foytack	R	32	5	5	.500	0	25	8	0	70	68	29	37	0	3.73
Julio Navarro	R	27	4	4	.444	12	57	0	0	90	75	32	53	0	2.90
Jack Spring	L	30	3	0	1.000	2	45	0	0	38	40	9	13	0	3.08
Mel Nelson	L	27	2	3	.400	1	36	3	0	53	55	32	41	0	5.26
1 Bob Turley	R	32	2	7	.222	0	19	12	3	87	71	51	70	0	3.31
Bo Belinsky	R	26	2	9	.182	0	13	13	2	77	78	35	60	0	5.73
Bob Duliba	R	28	1	1	.500	1	6	0	0	24	30	11	13	0	1.13
Mike Lee	R	22	1	1	.500	0	4	1	0	9	14	10	6	1	3.81
Aubrey Gatewood	R	24	1	1	.500	0	4	1	0	24	12	16	13	0	1.50
Eli Grba	R	28	1	2	.333	0	12	1	0	24	14	10	5	0	4.76
Fred Newman	R	21	1	5	.167	0	12	8	0	44	56	15	16	0	5.32
Tom Morgan	R	33	0	0	—	0	16	0	0	26	25	6	7	0	5.63
1 Ron Moeller	L	24	0	0	.000	0	4	0	0	6	9	7	5	0	6.00

WASHINGTON — 10th 56-106 .346 48.5 — MICKEY VERNON 14-26 .350   EDDIE YOST 0-1 .000   2 GIL HODGES 42-79 .347

NAME	G by Pos	B	AGE	G	AB	R	H	2B	3B	HR	RBI	BB	SO	SB	BA	SA
TOTALS			29	162	5446	578	1237	190	35	138	538	497	963	68	.227	.351
Bobo Osborne	1B81, 3B16	L	27	125	358	42	76	14	1	12	44	49	83	0	.212	.358
Chuck Cottier	2B85, SS24, 3B1	R	27	113	337	30	69	16	4	1	24	24	63	2	.205	.320
Eddie Brinkman	SS143	R	21	145	514	44	117	20	3	7	45	31	86	5	.228	.317
2 Don Zimmer	3B78, 2B2	R	32	83	298	37	74	12	1	13	44	18	57	3	.248	.426
2 Jim King	OF123	L	30	136	459	61	106	16	5	24	62	45	43	3	.231	.444
Don Lock	OF146	R	26	149	531	71	134	20	1	27	82	70	151	7	.252	.446
Chuck Hinton	OF125, 3B19, 1B6, SS2	R	29	150	566	80	152	20	12	15	55	64	79	25	.269	.426
Ken Retzer	C81	L	29	95	265	21	64	10	0	5	31	17	20	2	.242	.336
Dick Phillips	1B68, 2B5, 3B4	L	31	124	321	33	76	8	0	10	34	29	71	1	.237	.355
Minnie Minoso	OF74, 3B8	R	40	109	315	38	72	12	4	4	30	33	38	8	.229	.317
Don Leppert	C31	R	31	73	211	20	51	6	0	6	24	20	29	0	.237	.374
2 Don Blasingame	2B64	L	31	69	254	29	65	10	2	2	12	24	18	3	.256	.335
Tom Brown	OF16, 1B14	B	22	61	116	8	17	4	1	1	4	11	45	2	.147	.207
1 Marv Breeding	3B29, 2B22, SS2	R	29	58	197	20	54	7	2	1	14	7	21	1	.274	.345
2 Hobie Landrith	C37	L	33	42	103	6	18	3	2	1	9	15	9	0	.175	.233
John Kennedy	3B26, SS2	R	22	36	62	3	11	1	0	3	6	5	11	0	.177	.226
1 Jimmy Piersall	OF25	R	33	29	73	4	15	2	1	0	8	11	13	0	.205	.274
2 Cal Neeman	C12	R	34	14	18	1	1	0	0	0	1	3	6	0	.056	.056
Bob Schmidt	C6	R	30	9	14	1	2	0	0	0	2	0	5	0	.200	.267
1 Lou Klimchock	2B3	L	23	9	14	1	2	0	0	0	1	1	2	0	.143	.143
2 Ken Hunt	OF5	R	24	7	20	1	4	0	0	0	3	1	6	0	.200	.350
Johnny Schaive		R	29	3	0	0	0	0	0	0	0	0	0	0	.000	.000
Barry Shetrone		L	24	3	0	0	0	0	0	0	0	0	0	0	.000	.000

NAME	T	AGE	W	L	PCT	SV	G	GS	CG	IP	H	BB	SO	SHO	ERA
		29	56	106	.346	25	162	162	29	1447	1486	537	744	8	4.42
Claude Osteen	L	23	9	14	.391	0	40	29	8	212	222	60	109	2	3.35
Tom Cheney	R	28	8	9	.471	0	23	21	7	136	99	40	97	4	2.71
Don Rudolph	L	31	7	19	.269	1	37	26	4	174	189	36	70	0	4.55
Steve Ridzik	R	34	5	6	.455	1	20	10	0	90	82	35	47	0	4.80
Bennie Daniels	R	31	5	10	.333	1	35	24	6	169	163	58	88	1	4.37
Jim Duckworth	R	24	4	12	.250	0	37	15	2	121	131	67	66	0	6.02
Ron Kline	R	31	7	6	.273	17	62	1	0	94	85	30	49	0	2.78
Dave Stenhouse (EJ)	R	29	3	9	.250	0	16	16	2	87	90	45	47	1	4.55
2 Ron Moeller	L	24	1	0	1.000	0	3	0	0	24	31	10	10	0	6.38
2 Ed Roebuck	R	31	2	1	.667	4	26	0	0	53	63	29	25	0	3.32
Jim Hannan	R	23	2	2	.500	0	28	2	0	28	23	17	14	0	4.82
Carl Bouldin	R	23	2	5	.286	0	13	5	1	45	51	21	31	0	5.87
1 Jim Coates	R	30	2	4	.333	0	18	1	0	44	51	21	31	0	5.32
Art Quirk	L	25	1	0	1.000	0	4	1	0	14	10	5	4	0	4.29
Jim Bronstad	R	27	1	1	.250	0	10	1	0	57	66	22	22	0	5.68
Ed Hobaugh	R	23	0	0	—	0	5	0	0	12	16	6	10	0	6.19
2 Pete Burnside	R	32	0	0	—	0	7	0	0	67	84	24	23	0	6.18
1 Steve Hamilton	L	28	0	0	—	0	1	0	0	2	6	2	1	0	13.50
Jack Jenkins	R	20	0	1	.000	0	3	1	0	7	7	1	6	0	6.00
Bob Baird	L	21	0	3	.000	0	7	2	0	20	21	7	7	0	7.50

LOS ANGELES 1st 99-63 .611 WALT ALSTON

NAME	G by Pos	B	AGE	G	AB	R	H	2B	3B	HR	RBI	BB	SO	SB	BA	SA
TOTALS			27	163	5428	640	1361	178	34	110	584	453	867	124	.251	.357
Ron Fairly	1B119, OF45	L	24	152	490	62	133	21	0	12	77	58	69	5	.271	.388
Jim Gilliam	2B119, 3B55	B	34	148	525	77	148	27	4	6	49	60	28	19	.282	.383
Maury Wills	SS109, 3B33	B	30	134	527	83	159	19	3	0	34	44	48	40	.302	.349
Ken McMullen	3B71, 2B1, OF1	R	21	79	233	16	55	9	0	5	28	20	46	1	.236	.339
Frank Howard	OF111	R	26	123	417	58	114	16	1	28	64	33	116	1	.273	.518
Willie Davis	OF153	L	23	156	515	60	126	19	8	9	60	25	61	25	.245	.365
Tommy Davis	OF129, 3B40	R	24	146	556	69	181	19	3	16	88	29	59	15	.326	.457
Johnny Roseboro	C134	L	30	135	470	50	111	13	7	9	49	36	50	7	.236	.351
Wally Moon	OF96	L	33	122	343	41	90	13	2	8	48	45	43	5	.262	.382
Dick Tracewski	SS81, 2B23	R	28	104	217	23	49	2	1	1	10	19	39	2	.226	.258
Bill Skowron	1B66, 3B1	R	32	89	237	19	48	8	0	4	19	13	49	0	.203	.287
Nate Oliver	2B57, SS2	R	22	65	163	23	39	2	3	1	9	13	25	1	.239	.307
Lee Walls	OF18, 1B5, 3B2	R	30	64	86	12	20	1	0	3	11	7	25	0	.233	.349
Doug Camilli	C47	R	26	49	117	9	19	1	1	3	10	11	22	0	.162	.265
1 Don Zimmer	3B10, 2B1, SS1	R	32	22	23	4	5	1	0	1	2	3	10	0	.217	.391
Al Ferrara	OF11	R	23	21	44	2	7	0	0	1	1	6	9	0	.159	.227
2 Marv Breeding	2B17, SS1, 3B1	R	29	20	36	6	6	0	0	0	1	2	5	1	.167	.167
Dick Nen	1B5	L	23	7	8	1	1	0	0	1	1	3	3	0	.125	.500
1 Daryl Spencer	3B3	R	33	7	9	1	1	0	0	0	0	3	2	0	.111	.111

Roy Gleason 20 B 1-1, Derrell Griffith 19 L 0-2

NAME	T	AGE	W	L	PCT	SV	G	GS	CG	IP	H	BB	SO	SHO	ERA
		26	99	63	.611	29	163	163	51	1470	1329	402	1095	24	2.85
Sandy Koufax	L	27	25	5	.833	0	40	40	20	311	214	58	306	11	1.88
Don Drysdale	R	26	19	17	.528	0	42	42	17	315	287	57	251	3	2.63
Ron Perranoski	L	27	16	3	.842	21	69	0	0	129	112	43	75	0	1.67
Johnny Podres	L	30	14	12	.538	1	37	34	10	198	196	64	134	5	3.55
Bob Miller	R	24	10	8	.556	1	42	23	2	187	171	65	125	0	2.89
Pete Richert	L	23	5	3	.625	0	20	12	1	78	80	28	54	0	4.50
Dick Calmus	R	19	3	1	.750	0	21	1	0	44	52	16	25	0	2.66
Nick Willhite	L	22	2	3	.400	0	8	8	1	38	44	10	28	1	3.79
1 Ed Roebuck	R	31	2	4	.333	0	29	0	0	40	54	21	26	0	4.28
Larry Sherry	R	27	2	6	.250	3	36	3	0	80	82	24	47	0	3.71
Ken Rowe	R	29	1	1	.500	1	14	0	0	28	28	11	12	0	2.89
Dick Scott	R	30	0	0	—	2	9	0	0	12	11	1	6	0	6.75
Jack Smith	R	27	0	0	—	0	8	0	0	8	10	2	5	0	7.88
Phil Ortega	R	23	0	0	—	1	2	0	0	2	0	1	1	0	18.00

ST. LOUIS 2nd 93-69 .574 6 JOHNNY KEANE

NAME	G by Pos	B	AGE	G	AB	R	H	2B	3B	HR	RBI	BB	SO	SB	BA	SA
TOTALS			29	162	5678	747	1540	231	66	128	697	458	915	77	.271	.403
Bill White	1B162	L	29	162	658	106	200	28	8	27	109	59	100	10	.304	.491
Julian Javier	2B161	R	26	161	609	82	160	27	9	9	46	24	86	18	.263	.381
Dick Groat	SS158	R	32	158	631	85	201	43	11	6	73	56	58	3	.319	.450
Ken Boyer	3B159	R	32	159	617	86	176	28	2	24	111	70	90	1	.285	.454
George Altman	OF124	L	30	135	464	62	127	18	7	9	47	47	93	13	.274	.401
Curt Flood	OF158	R	25	158	662	112	200	34	9	5	63	42	57	17	.302	.403
Charlie James	OF101	R	25	115	347	34	93	14	2	10	45	10	64	2	.268	.406
Tim McCarver	C126	L	21	127	405	39	117	12	7	4	51	27	43	5	.289	.383
Stan Musial	OF96	L	42	124	337	34	86	10	2	12	58	35	43	2	.255	.404
Gary Kolb	OF58, 3B1, C1	L	23	75	96	23	26	1	5	3	10	22	26	2	.271	.479
1 Duke Carmel	OF38, 1B1	L	26	57	44	9	10	1	0	1	2	9	11	0	.227	.318
Carl Sawatski	C27	L	35	56	105	12	25	0	0	6	14	15	28	2	.238	.410
Dal Maxvill	SS24, 2B9, 3B3	R	24	53	51	12	12	2	0	0	3	6	11	0	.235	.275
Bob Gibson	P36	R	27	41	87	12	18	3	1	3	20	8	35	0	.207	.368
1 Gene Oliver	C35	R	27	39	102	10	23	4	0	6	18	13	19	0	.225	.441
Mike Shannon	OF26	R	23	32	6	3	8	0	0	1	2	0	6	0	.308	.423
1 Leo Burke	OF11, 3B5	R	29	30	49	6	10	2	1	1	5	4	12	0	.204	.347
Phil Gagliano	2B3, 3B1	R	21	10	5	1	2	0	0	0	1	1	1	0	.400	.400
Corky Withrow	OF2	R	25	6	1	0	0	0	0	0	0	0	2	0	.000	.000
Red Schoendienst		B	40	6	5	1	1	0	0	0	1	2	1	0	.200	.200
Doug Clemens	OF3	L	24	5	6	1	1	0	0	0	2	1	2	0	.167	.667
Jack Damaska	2B1, OF1	R	25	5	5	1	1	0	0	0	1	0	4	0	.200	.200
Jerry Buchek	SS1	R	21	3	4	0	1	0	0	0	0	1	2	0	.250	.250
Dave Ricketts	C3	B	27	3	4	0	1	0	0	0	0	2	1	0	.250	.250

Jeoff Long 21 R 1-5, Jim Beauchamp 23 R 0-3, Moe Thacker 29 R 0-4, Clyde Bloomfield 27 R 0-0, Hal Smith (IL) 32

NAME	T	AGE	W	L	PCT	SV	G	GS	CG	IP	H	BB	SO	SHO	ERA
		32	93	69	.574	32	162	162	49	1463	1329	463	978	17	3.32
Ernie Broglio	R	27	18	8	.692	0	39	35	11	250	202	90	145	5	2.99
Bob Gibson	R	27	18	9	.667	0	36	33	14	255	224	96	204	2	3.39
Curt Simmons	L	34	15	9	.625	0	32	32	11	233	209	48	127	6	2.47
Ray Sadecki	L	22	10	10	.500	1	36	28	4	193	198	78	136	1	4.10
Ron Taylor	R	25	9	7	.563	11	54	9	2	133	119	30	91	0	2.84
Bobby Shantz	L	37	6	4	.600	11	55	0	0	79	55	17	70	0	2.62
Ray Washburn	R	25	5	3	.625	0	11	11	4	64	50	14	47	2	3.09
1 Ed Bauta	R	28	3	4	.429	3	38	0	0	53	55	21	30	0	3.91
2 Lew Burdette	R	36	3	8	.273	2	21	14	3	98	106	16	45	0	3.77
2 Barney Schultz	R	36	2	0	1.000	1	24	0	0	35	36	8	26	0	3.60
Sam Jones	R	37	2	0	1.000	2	11	0	0	11	15	5	8	0	9.00
Harry Fanok	R	23	2	1	.667	1	12	0	0	26	24	21	25	0	5.19
2 Ken MacKenzie	L	29	0	0	—	0	4	0	0	4	7	3	4	0	4.00
Bob Humphreys	R	27	0	1	.000	0	11	0	0	11	11	7	6	0	4.91
Diomedes Olivo	L	44	0	5	.000	0	19	0	0	13	16	9	9	0	5.54

SAN FRANCISCO 3rd 88-74 .543 11 AL DARK

NAME	G by Pos	B	AGE	G	AB	R	H	2B	3B	HR	RBI	BB	SO	SB	BA	SA
TOTALS			29	162	5579	725	1442	206	35	197	680	441	889	55	.258	.414
Orlando Cepeda	1B150, OF3	R	25	156	579	100	183	33	4	34	97	37	70	8	.316	.563
Chuck Hiller	2B109	L	28	111	417	44	93	10	2	6	33	20	23	3	.223	.300
Jose Pagan	SS143, 2B1, OF1	R	28	148	483	46	113	12	1	6	39	26	67	0	.234	.300
Jim Davenport	3B127, 2B22, SS1	R	29	147	460	46	116	19	3	4	36	32	87	5	.252	.333
Felipe Alou	OF153	R	28	157	565	75	159	31	9	20	82	27	87	11	.281	.474
Willie Mays	OF157, SS, 1B1	R	32	157	596	115	187	32	7	38	103	66	83	8	.314	.582
Willie McCovey	OF135, 1B23	L	25	152	564	103	158	19	5	44	102	50	119	1	.280	.566
Ed Bailey	C88	L	32	105	308	41	81	8	0	21	68	50	64	0	.263	.494
Harvey Kuenn	OF64, 3B53	R	32	120	417	61	121	13	2	6	31	44	38	2	.290	.374
Tom Haller	C85, OF7	L	26	98	298	32	76	8	1	14	44	34	45	4	.255	.430
Ernie Bowman	SS40, 2B26, 3B12	R	25	81	125	10	23	3	0	0	4	0	15	1	.184	.208
Matty Alou	OF20	L	24	63	76	4	11	1	0	0	2	2	13	0	.145	.158
Joey Amalfitano	2B37, 3B7	R	29	54	137	11	24	3	0	1	7	12	18	2	.175	.219
Cap Peterson	2B8, 3B5, OF3, SS1	R	20	22	54	7	14	2	0	1	2	2	13	0	.259	.352
2 Norm Larker	1B11	L	32	19	14	0	1	0	0	0	0	5	3	0	.071	.071
Jesus Alou	OF12	R	21	16	24	3	6	1	0	0	5	0	3	0	.250	.292
Jose Cardenal	OF2	R	19	9	5	1	1	0	0	0	2	1	1	0	.200	.200
Jim Ray Hart (BS-PB)	3B7	R	21	7	20	1	4	1	0	0	1	0	5	0	.200	.250
Jimmie Coker	C2	R	27	4	5	0	1	0	0	0	0	0	2	0	.200	.200

NAME	T	AGE	W	L	PCT	SV	G	GS	CG	IP	H	BB	SO	SHO	ERA
		29	88	74	.543	30	162	162	46	1469	1380	464	954	9	3.35
Juan Marichal	R	25	25	8	.758	0	41	40	18	321	259	61	248	5	2.41
Jack Sanford	R	34	16	13	.552	0	42	42	11	284	273	76	158	0	3.52
Billy O'Dell	L	30	14	10	.583	1	36	33	10	222	218	70	116	3	3.16
Bobby Bolin	R	24	10	6	.625	7	47	12	2	137	128	57	134	0	3.28
Don Larsen	R	33	7	7	.500	3	46	0	0	62	46	30	44	0	3.05
Jack Fisher	R	24	6	10	.375	1	36	12	2	116	132	38	57	0	4.58
Jim Duffalo (HJ)	R	27	4	2	.667	2	34	5	2	75	56	37	55	0	2.88
Billy Pierce	L	36	3	11	.214	8	38	13	3	99	106	20	52	1	4.27
Billy Hoeft (SJ)	L	31	3	0	1.000	4	23	0	0	24	26	10	8	0	4.50
Gaylord Perry	R	24	1	6	.143	2	31	4	0	76	84	29	52	0	4.03
Al Stanek	L	19	0	0	—	0	11	0	0	13	10	12	5	0	4.85
Frank Linzy	R	22	0	0	—	1	7	0	0	22	10	14	0	0	4.76
John Pregenzer	R	27	0	0	—	1	9	0	0	8	6	9	5	0	5.00
Jim Constable	L	30	0	0	—	0	2	0	0	1	3	1	1	0	9.00
Ron Herbel	R	25	0	0	—	0	2	0	0	1	3	1	0	0	9.00
Bob Garibaldi	R	21	0	0	.000	0	8	0	0	8	4	1	6	0	1.13

PHILADELPHIA 4th 87-75 .537 12 GENE MAUCH

NAME	G by Pos	B	AGE	G	AB	R	H	2B	3B	HR	RBI	BB	SO	SB	BA	SA
TOTALS			28	162	5524	642	1390	228	54	126	599	403	955	56	.252	.381
Roy Sievers	1B126	R	36	138	450	46	108	19	2	19	82	43	72	0	.240	.418
Tony Taylor	2B149, 3B13	R	27	157	602	80	180	20	10	5	49	42	99	23	.281	.367
Bobby Wine	SS132, 3B8	R	24	142	418	29	90	14	3	6	44	14	83	1	.215	.306
Don Hoak	3B106	R	35	135	377	35	87	11	3	6	24	27	52	5	.231	.324
Johnny Callison	OF157	L	24	157	626	96	178	36	11	26	78	50	111	8	.284	.502
Tony Gonzalez	OF151	L	26	155	583	72	157	36	12	4	66	53	68	13	.306	.458
Wes Covington	OF101	L	31	119	353	46	107	24	1	17	64	26	56	1	.303	.521
Clay Dalrymple	C142	L	26	142	452	40	114	15	3	10	40	45	55	0	.252	.365
Don Demeter	OF119, 3B43, 1B26	R	28	154	515	63	133	20	2	22	83	31	93	1	.258	.433
Ruben Amaro	SS63, 3B45, 1B5	R	27	115	217	25	47	9	2	2	19	19	31	0	.217	.304
Frank Torre	1B56	L	31	92	112	8	28	7	2	1	10	11	7	0	.250	.375
Cookie Rojas	2B25, OF1	R	24	64	77	18	17	0	1	1	2	3	8	4	.221	.286
Bob Oldis	C43	R	35	47	85	8	19	3	0	0	8	3	5	0	.224	.259
Earl Averill	C20, OF8, 1B1, 3B1	R	31	47	71	8	19	2	0	3	8	9	14	0	.268	.423
2 Jim Lemon	OF18	R	35	31	59	6	16	2	0	2	6	4	18	0	.271	.407
Cal Emery	1B2	L	26	16	19	0	3	1	0	0	0	0	5	0	.158	.211
John Herrnstein	OF2, 1B1	R	25	15	12	1	2	1	0	0	1	0	5	0	.167	.417
Billy Klaus	SS5, 3B3	L	34	11	18	1	1	0	0	0	4	0	5	0	.056	.056
Dick Allen	OF7, 3B1	R	21	10	24	6	7	1	0	1	2	0	4	0	.292	.458
Wayne Graham	OF6	R	27	10	22	0	4	0	0	0	0	0	5	0	.182	.182
Mike Harrington		R	28	1	0	0	0	0	0	0	0	0	0	0		

NAME	T	AGE	W	L	PCT	SV	G	GS	CG	IP	H	BB	SO	SHO	ERA
		27	87	75	.537	31	162	162	45	1457	1262	553	1052	12	3.09
Ray Culp	R	21	14	11	.560	0	34	30	10	203	148	102	176	5	2.97
Cal McLish	R	37	13	11	.542	0	32	32	10	210	184	56	98	2	3.26
Jack Baldschun	R	26	11	7	.611	16	65	0	0	114	99	42	89	0	2.29
Dennis Bennett (BN)	L	23	9	5	.643	1	23	16	6	119	102	33	82	1	2.65
Chris Short	L	25	9	12	.429	3	38	27	6	198	185	69	160	3	2.95
Dallas Green	R	28	7	5	.583	2	40	14	4	120	134	38	68	0	3.23
Art Mahaffey	R	25	7	10	.412	0	26	22	6	149	143	48	97	1	3.99
Ryne Duren	R	34	6	2	.750	2	33	7	1	87	65	52	84	0	3.31
Johnny Klippstein	R	35	5	6	.455	8	49	1	0	112	80	46	86	0	1.93
John Boozer	R	23	3	4	.429	1	26	8	2	83	67	33	69	0	2.93
Jack Hamilton	R	24	1	6	.143	1	19	0	0	30	22	17	23	0	5.40
Marcelino Lopez	L	19	1	0	1.000	0	4	2	0	6	8	7	2	0	6.00
Bobby Locke	R	29	0	1	.000	1	9	0	0	11	15	5	5	0	5.73
Paul Brown	R	22	0	1	.000	0	6	2	0	15	15	5	11	0	4.20

CINCINNATI 5th 86-76 .531 13 FRED HUTCHINSON

NAME	G by Pos	B	AGE	G	AB	R	H	2B	3B	HR	RBI	BB	SO	SB	BA	SA
TOTALS			26	162	5416	648	1333	225	44	122	608	474	960	92	.246	.371
Gordy Coleman	1B107	L	28	123	365	38	90	20	2	14	59	29	51	1	.247	.427
Pete Rose	2B157, 3B1	B	22	157	623	101	170	25	9	6	41	55	72	13	.273	.371
Leo Cardenas	SS157	R	24	158	565	62	133	22	4	7	48	23	101	3	.235	.326
Gene Freese	3B62, OF1	R	29	66	217	20	53	9	1	6	26	17	42	4	.244	.378
Tommy Harper	OF118, 3B1	R	22	129	408	67	106	12	3	10	37	44	72	12	.260	.377
Vada Pinson	OF162	L	24	162	652	96	204	37	14	22	106	36	80	27	.313	.514
Frank Robinson	OF139, 1B1	R	27	140	482	79	125	19	3	21	91	81	69	26	.259	.442
Johnny Edwards	C148	L	25	148	495	46	128	19	4	11	67	45	93	1	.259	.380
Marty Keough	1B46, OF28	L	29	95	172	21	39	8	2	6	21	25	37	1	.227	.401
Eddie Kasko	3B48, SS15, 2B1	R	31	76	199	25	48	9	0	3	10	21	29	0	.241	.332
2 Bob Skinner	OF51	L	31	72	194	26	49	10	2	3	17	24	21	1	.253	.371
Don Pavletich	1B57, C13	R	24	71	183	18	38	11	0	5	18	17	12	0	.208	.350
Ken Walters	OF21, 1B1	R	32	50	155	21	37	7	0	1	23	31	37	1	.239	.303
2 Daryl Spencer	3B48	R	33	50	155	21	37	7	0	1	23	31	37	1	.239	.303
Charlie Neal	3B19, 2B1, SS1	R	32	34	64	2	10	1	0	0	4	5	15	0	.156	.172
1 Jesse Gonder	C7	L	27	26	43	4	10	2	0	3	10	2	6	0	.313	.656
1 Jerry Lynch	OF7	L	32	22	16	4	4	0	0	1	5	1	5	0	.250	.531
1 Don Blasingame	2B11, 3B2	L	31	15	31	3	5	1	0	0	1	5	2	0	.161	.226
2 Gene Green	C8	R	30	15	31	3	7	2	0	1	3	0	8	0	.226	.355
1 Wally Post	OF1	R	33	5	1	0	0	0	0	0	0	0	0	0	.000	.000

2 Sammy Taylor 30 L 0-6, 1 Hank Foiles 34 R 0-3, 1 Harry Bright 33 R 0-1

NAME	T	AGE	W	L	PCT	SV	G	GS	CG	IP	H	BB	SO	SHO	ERA
		30	86	76	.531	36	162	162	55	1440	1307	425	1048	22	3.29
Jim Maloney	R	23	23	7	.767	0	33	33	13	250	183	88	265	6	2.77
Jim O'Toole	L	26	17	14	.548	0	33	34	9	223	204	57	146	5	2.88
Joe Nuxhall	L	34	15	8	.652	2	29	29	14	217	194	39	169	2	2.61
John Tsitouris	R	27	12	8	.600	0	30	21	4	170	167	38	113	3	3.16
Joey Jay	R	27	7	18	.280	1	30	22	6	170	172	73	116	1	4.29
Bob Purkey	R	33	6	10	.375	0	21	21	4	137	143	33	55	0	3.55
Al Worthington	R	34	4	4	.500	10	50	0	0	81	75	31	55	0	3.00
2 Dom Zanni	R	31	1	1	.500	5	31	1	0	43	39	21	40	0	4.19
Bill Henry	L	35	1	3	.250	14	47	0	0	52	55	11	45	0	4.15
2 Jim Coates	R	30	0	0	—	0	9	0	0	16	21	7	11	0	5.63
1 Jim Brosnan	R	33	0	1	.000	4	19	3	0	42	42	24	29	0	7.20
Jim Owens	R	29	0	2	.000	4	19	3	0	42	42	24	29	0	5.36

MILWAUKEE — 6th 84-78 .519 15 — BOBBY BRAGAN

NAME	G by Pos	B	AGE	G	AB	R	H	2B	3B	HR	RBI	BB	SO	SB	BA	SA
TOTALS			28	163	5518	677	1345	204	39	139	624	525	954	75	.244	.370
2 Gene Oliver	1B55, OF35, C2	R	27	95	296	34	74	12	2	11	47	27	59	4	.250	.416
Frank Bolling	2B141	R	31	142	542	73	132	18	2	5	43	44	47	2	.244	.312
Roy McMillan	SS94	R	33	100	320	35	80	10	1	4	29	17	25	1	.250	.325
Eddie Mathews	3B121, OF42	L	31	158	547	82	144	19	4	23	84	124	119	0	.263	.453
Hank Aaron	OF161	R	29	161	631	121	201	29	4	44	130	78	94	31	.319	.586
Mack Jones	OF80	L	24	93	228	36	50	11	4	3	22	26	59	8	.219	.342
Lee Maye	OF111	L	28	124	442	67	120	22	7	11	34	36	52	14	.271	.428
Joe Torre	C105, 1B37, OF2	R	22	142	501	57	147	19	4	14	71	42	79	1	.293	.431
Denis Menke	SS82, 3B51, 2B22, 1B1, OF1	R	22	146	518	58	121	16	4	11	50	37	106	6	.234	.344
Del Crandall	C75, 1B7	R	33	86	259	18	52	4	0	3	28	18	22	1	.201	.251
Ty Cline	OF62	L	24	72	174	17	41	2	1	0	10	10	31	2	.236	.259
Tommie Aaron	1B45, OF14, 2B6, 3B1	R	23	72	135	6	27	6	1	1	15	11	27	0	.200	.281
Don Dillard	OF30	L	26	67	119	9	28	6	4	1	12	5	21	0	.235	.378
1 Norm Larker	1B42	L	32	64	147	15	26	6	0	1	14	24	24	0	.177	.238
Len Gabrielson	OF22, 1B16, 3B3	L	23	46	120	14	26	5	0	3	15	8	23	1	.217	.333
2 Lou Klimchock	1B12	L	23	24	46	6	9	1	0	0	1	0	12	0	.196	.217
Hawk Taylor (JJ)	OF8	R	24	16	29	1	2	0	0	0	0	1	12	0	.069	.069
2 Bubba Morton	OF9	R	31	15	28	1	5	0	0	0	1	2	3	0	.179	.179
Amado Samuel	SS7, 2B4	R	24	15	17	0	3	1	0	0	0	0	4	0	.176	.235

Bob Uecker 28 R 4-16, Woody Woodward 20 R 0-2, Gus Bell 34 L 1-3, Rico Carty 23 R 0-2

NAME	T	AGE	W	L	PCT	SV	G	GS	CG	IP	H	BB	SO	SHO	ERA
TOTALS		27	84	78	.519	25	163	163	56	1472	1327	489	924	18	3.26
Warren Spahn	L	42	23	7	.767	0	33	33	22	260	241	49	102	7	2.60
Denny Lemaster	L	24	11	14	.440	0	46	31	10	237	199	85	190	1	3.04
Bob Hendley	L	24	9	9	.500	3	41	24	7	169	153	64	105	3	3.94
Tony Cloninger	R	22	9	11	.450	1	41	18	4	145	131	63	100	2	3.79
Bob Shaw	R	30	7	11	.389	13	48	16	3	159	144	55	105	3	2.66
1 Lew Burdette	R	36	6	5	.545	0	15	13	4	84	71	24	28	1	3.64
Bob Sadowski	R	25	5	7	.417	0	19	8	1	117	99	30	72	1	2.62
Hank Fischer	R	23	4	3	.571	0	31	6	1	74	74	28	72	0	4.99
Claude Raymond	R	26	4	6	.400	5	45	0	0	53	57	27	44	0	5.43
Frank Funk	R	27	3	3	.500	2	25	0	0	44	42	13	19	0	2.66
Dan Schneider	L	20	1	0	1.000	0	30	3	0	44	36	20	19	0	3.07
Ron Piche	R	28	1	1	.500	0	37	1	0	53	53	25	40	0	3.40
Bobby Tiefenauer	R	33	1	1	.500	2	12	0	0	30	20	4	22	0	1.20
Wade Blasingame	L	19	0	0	—	0	3	0	0	7	2	6	0	0	12.00

CHICAGO — 7th 82-80 .506 17 — BOB KENNEDY

NAME	G by Pos	B	AGE	G	AB	R	H	2B	3B	HR	RBI	BB	SO	SB	BA	SA
TOTALS			26	162	5404	570	1286	205	44	127	530	439	1049	68	.238	.363
Ernie Banks	1B125	R	32	130	432	41	98	20	1	18	64	39	73	0	.227	.403
Ken Hubbs	2B152	R	21	154	566	54	133	19	3	8	47	39	93	3	.235	.322
Andre Rodgers	SS150	R	28	150	516	54	118	17	4	5	33	65	90	5	.229	.306
Ron Santo	3B162	R	23	162	630	79	187	29	6	25	99	42	92	6	.297	.481
Lou Brock	OF140	L	24	148	547	79	141	19	11	9	37	31	122	24	.258	.382
2 Ellis Burton	OF90	B	26	93	322	45	74	16	1	12	41	36	59	6	.230	.398
Billy Williams	OF160	L	25	161	612	87	175	36	9	25	95	68	78	7	.286	.497
Dick Bertell	C99	R	27	100	322	15	75	7	2	2	14	24	41	0	.233	.286
Don Landrum	OF57	R	27	84	227	27	55	4	1	1	10	13	42	6	.242	.282
Merritt Ranew	C37, 1B9	L	25	78	154	18	52	8	1	3	15	9	32	1	.338	.461
Nelson Mathews	OF46	R	21	61	155	12	24	3	2	4	10	16	48	3	.155	.277
Jimmie Schaffer	C54	R	27	57	142	17	34	7	0	7	19	11	35	0	.239	.437
Steve Boros	1B14, OF11	R	26	41	90	9	19	5	1	3	7	12	19	0	.211	.389
2 Leo Burke	2B10, 1B4	R	29	27	49	4	9	0	0	2	7	4	13	0	.184	.306
John Boccabella	1B24	R	22	24	74	7	14	4	1	5	6	21	0	.189	.311
Bob Will	1B1	R	31	23	23	0	4	0	0	0	1	4	0	.174	.174
Ken Aspromonte	2B7, 1B2	R	31	20	34	2	5	0	0	0	4	4	0	.147	.235
Alex Grammas	SS13	R	37	16	27	1	5	0	0	0	0	3	0	.185	.185
Billy Cowan	OF10	R	24	14	36	1	9	1	1	1	2	0	11	0	.250	.417
Jimmy Stewart	SS9, 2B1	B	24	13	37	1	11	2	0	1	1	7	1	.297	.351
Cuno Barragan	C1	R	31	1	1	0	0	0	0	0	0	0	0	.000	.000

NAME	T	AGE	W	L	PCT	SV	G	GS	CG	IP	H	BB	SO	SHO	ERA
TOTALS		29	82	80	.506	28	162	162	45	1457	1357	400	851	15	3.08
Dick Ellsworth	L	23	22	10	.688	0	37	37	19	291	223	75	185	4	2.10
Larry Jackson	R	32	14	18	.438	0	37	37	13	275	256	54	153	4	2.55
Lindy McDaniel	R	27	13	7	.650	22	57	0	0	88	82	27	75	0	2.86
Bob Buhl	R	34	11	14	.440	0	37	34	6	226	219	62	108	0	3.38
Glen Hobbie	R	27	7	10	.412	0	36	24	4	165	172	49	94	1	3.93
Paul Toth	R	28	5	9	.357	0	27	14	3	131	115	35	66	2	3.09
Don Elston	R	34	4	1	.800	4	51	0	0	70	57	21	41	0	2.83
Jim Brewer	L	25	3	2	.600	0	29	1	0	50	59	15	35	0	4.86
Cal Koonce	R	22	2	6	.250	0	21	13	0	73	75	32	44	0	4.56
1 Barney Schultz	R	36	1	0	1.000	2	15	0	0	27	25	9	18	0	3.67
Freddie Burdette	R	26	0	0	—	0	4	0	0	9	9	1	4	0	3.60
Phil Mudrock	L	26	0	0	—	0	1	0	0	1	2	0	0	0	9.00
Tom Baker	L	29	0	1	.000	0	10	1	0	18	20	7	14	0	3.00
Dick LeMay	L	24	0	1	.000	0	9	1	0	15	26	4	10	0	5.40
Jack Warner	R	24	0	0	—	0	11	0	0	23	21	8	7	0	2.74

PITTSBURGH — 8th 74-88 .457 25 — DANNY MURTAUGH

NAME	G by Pos	B	AGE	G	AB	R	H	2B	3B	HR	RBI	BB	SO	SB	BA	SA
TOTALS			28	162	5536	567	1385	181	49	108	523	454	940	57	.250	.359
Donn Clendenon	1B151	R	27	154	563	65	155	28	7	15	57	39	136	22	.275	.430
Bill Mazeroski	2B138	R	26	142	534	44	131	22	3	8	52	32	46	2	.245	.343
Dick Schofield	SS117, 2B20, 3B1	B	23	138	541	54	133	18	2	3	32	69	83	2	.246	.303
Bob Bailey	3B153, SS3	R	20	154	570	60	130	15	3	12	45	58	98	10	.228	.382
Roberto Clemente	OF151	R	28	152	600	77	192	23	8	17	76	31	64	12	.320	.470
Bill Virdon	OF142	L	32	142	554	54	150	22	6	8	53	43	55	1	.269	.374
Willie Stargell	OF65, 1B16	L	23	108	304	34	74	11	6	11	49	19	85	0	.243	.428
Jim Pagliaroni	C85	R	25	92	252	27	58	9	0	11	26	36	57	0	.230	.381
Smoky Burgess	C72	L	36	91	264	20	74	10	1	6	37	24	14	0	.280	.394
2 Jerry Lynch	OF64	L	32	88	237	26	63	6	3	10	36	22	28	0	.266	.443
Ted Savage (GJ)	OF47	R	26	85	149	22	29	2	1	5	14	34	31	4	.195	.322
Johnny Logan	SS44, 3B4	R	36	81	181	15	42	2	1	0	9	23	27	0	.232	.254
Manny Mota	OF37, 2B1	R	25	59	126	20	34	2	3	0	7	7	18	0	.270	.333
Ron Brand	C33, 2B2, 3B2	R	23	46	66	8	19	2	0	1	7	10	11	0	.288	.364
1 Bob Skinner	OF32	L	31	34	122	18	33	5	5	0	8	13	22	4	.270	.393
1 Gene Alley	3B7, 2B4, SS4	R	22	17	51	3	11	1	0	0	2	2	12	0	.216	.235
Elmo Plaskett	C5, 3B1	R	25	10	21	1	3	0	0	0	2	0	5	0	.143	.143

Julio Gotay 24 R 1-2, Larry Elliot 25 L 0-4

NAME	T	AGE	W	L	PCT	SV	G	GS	CG	IP	H	BB	SO	SHO	ERA
TOTALS		29	74	88	.457	33	162	162	34	1448	1350	457	900	16	3.10
Bob Friend	R	32	17	16	.515	0	39	38	12	269	236	44	144	4	2.34
Al McBean	R	25	13	3	.813	11	55	7	2	122	100	39	74	1	2.58
Don Cardwell	R	27	13	15	.464	0	33	32	7	214	195	52	112	2	3.07
Don Schwall	R	27	6	12	.333	0	33	24	3	168	158	74	86	2	3.32
Bob Veale	L	27	5	2	.714	3	34	7	3	78	59	40	68	2	1.04
Joe Gibbon	L	28	5	12	.294	1	37	22	5	147	147	54	110	0	3.31
Vern Law (VR)	R	33	4	5	.444	0	18	12	1	77	91	13	31	1	4.91
Earl Francis	R	26	4	6	.400	0	33	13	0	97	107	43	72	0	4.55
Harvey Haddix	L	37	3	3	.429	1	49	1	0	70	67	20	70	0	3.34
Roy Face	R	35	3	9	.250	16	56	0	0	70	75	19	41	0	3.21
Tommie Sisk	R	21	3	3	.250	1	57	4	1	108	85	45	73	0	2.92
Tom Butters	R	25	0	0	—	0	16	1	0	16	15	8	11	0	4.50
1 Tom Sturdivant	R	33	0	0	—	0	7	0	0	4	7	2	2	0	6.75
Tom Parsons	R	23	0	1	.000	0	4	1	0	13	24	6	11	0	9.00

HOUSTON — 9th 66-96 .407 33 — HARRY CRAFT

NAME	G by Pos	B	AGE	G	AB	R	H	2B	3B	HR	RBI	BB	SO	SB	BA	SA
TOTALS			27	162	5384	464	1184	170	39	62	420	456	938	39	.220	.301
Rusty Staub	1B109, OF49	L	19	150	513	43	115	17	4	6	45	59	58	0	.224	.308
Ernie Fazio	2B84, SS1, 3B1	R	21	102	228	31	42	10	3	2	5	27	70	4	.184	.281
Bob Lillis	SS124, 2B19, 3B6	R	33	147	469	31	93	13	1	1	19	15	35	3	.198	.237
Bob Aspromonte	3B131, 1B1	R	25	136	468	42	100	9	5	8	49	40	57	3	.214	.306
Carl Warwick	OF141, 1B2	R	26	150	528	49	134	19	5	7	47	49	70	3	.254	.348
Howie Goss	OF123	R	28	133	411	37	86	18	2	9	44	31	128	4	.209	.328
Al Spangler	OF113	L	29	120	430	52	121	25	4	4	27	50	38	5	.281	.386
John Bateman	C115	R	22	128	404	23	85	8	6	10	59	13	103	0	.210	.334
Pete Runnels	1B70, 2B36, 3B3	L	35	124	388	35	98	11	1	2	23	45	42	0	.253	.296
Johnny Temple	2B61, 3B29	R	34	100	322	22	85	12	1	1	17	24	21	7	.264	.317
Jim Wynn	OF53, SS21, 3B2	R	21	70	250	31	61	10	5	4	27	30	53	4	.244	.372
Jim Campbell	C42	R	26	55	158	9	35	3	0	4	19	10	40	0	.222	.316
J C Hartman	SS32	R	29	39	90	2	11	1	0	2	3	2	13	1	.122	.133
Johnny Weekly (JJ)	OF23	R	26	34	80	4	18	3	0	3	14	7	14	0	.225	.375
Brock Davis	OF14	L	19	34	55	7	11	2	0	1	4	4	10	0	.200	.291
Hal Smith	C11	R	32	31	58	1	14	2	0	0	4	4	15	0	.241	.276
Carroll Hardy	OF10	R	30	15	44	5	10	3	0	1	3	5	10	0	.227	.295
Glenn Vaughan	SS9, 3B1	R	18	9	30	1	5	0	0	0	3	6	6	0	.167	.167
Joe Morgan	2B7	L	19	8	20	5	4	0	1	0	3	5	1	.200	.350

Dave Adlesh 19 R 0-8, Mike White 24 R 2-7, Jerry Grote 20 R 1-5, Ivan Murrell 20 R 1-5, Aaron Pointer 21 R 1-5, John Paciorek 18 R 3-3, Sonny Jackson 18 L 0-3

NAME	T	AGE	W	L	PCT	SV	G	GS	CG	IP	H	BB	SO	SHO	ERA
TOTALS		30	66	96	.407	20	162	162	36	1450	1341	378	937	16	3.44
Dick Farrell	R	29	14	13	.519	1	34	26	12	202	161	35	141	0	3.03
Don Nottebart	R	27	11	8	.579	0	31	26	9	193	170	39	118	2	3.17
Hal Woodeshick	L	30	11	9	.550	10	55	0	0	114	75	42	94	0	1.97
Ken Johnson	R	30	11	17	.393	1	37	32	6	224	204	50	148	1	2.65
Bob Bruce	R	30	5	9	.357	0	30	25	1	170	162	60	123	1	3.60
Hal Brown	R	38	5	11	.313	0	26	20	6	141	137	8	68	3	3.32
Jim Umbricht	R	32	4	3	.571	0	35	3	0	76	52	21	48	0	2.61
Chris Zachary	R	19	2	2	.500	0	22	7	0	57	62	22	42	0	4.89
Dick Drott	R	27	2	12	.143	0	27	14	2	98	95	49	58	1	4.96
Don McMahon	R	33	1	5	.167	5	49	2	0	80	83	26	51	0	4.05
Russ Kemmerer	R	31	0	0	—	0	17	0	0	37	48	8	12	0	5.59
Larry Yellen	R	20	0	0	—	0	1	1	0	3	3	1	0	0	3.60
Joe Hoerner	L	26	0	0	—	0	1	0	0	1	0	0	1	0	0.00
Danny Coombs	L	21	0	0	—	0	2	0	0	0	1	5	0	0	27.00
Jim Dickson	R	26	0	0	—	0	13	0	0	13	15	7	7	0	6.00
Randy Cardinal	R	26	0	0	—	0	7	0	0	13	17	2	7	0	6.23
Jim Golden	R	27	0	0	—	0	8	0	0	13	16	8	8	0	6.00
Jay Dahl	L	17	0	1	.000	0	1	1	0	4	11	4	2	0	9.00
1 George Brunet	L	28	0	0	—	0	7	0	0	13	24	6	11	0	6.92

NEW YORK — 10th 51-111 .315 48 — CASEY STENGEL

NAME	G by Pos	B	AGE	G	AB	R	H	2B	3B	HR	RBI	BB	SO	SB	BA	SA
TOTALS			27	162	5336	501	1168	156	35	96	459	457	1078	41	.219	.315
Tim Harkness	1B106	L	25	123	375	35	79	12	3	10	42	46	79	4	.211	.339
Ron Hunt	2B142, 3B1	R	22	143	533	64	145	28	4	10	42	40	50	5	.272	.396
Al Moran	SS116, 3B1	R	24	119	331	26	64	5	2	1	23	36	60	3	.193	.230
1 Charlie Neal	3B66, SS, SS8	R	32	72	253	26	57	12	1	3	18	27	49	1	.225	.316
Duke Snider	OF106	L	36	129	354	44	80	8	3	14	45	56	74	0	.243	.401
Jim Hickman	OF82, 3B59	R	26	146	494	53	113	21	6	17	51	44	120	0	.229	.399
Frank Thomas	OF96, 1B15, 3B1	R	34	126	420	34	109	9	1	15	60	33	48	0	.260	.393
Choo Choo Coleman	C91, OF1	L	26	106	247	22	44	0	0	3	9	24	49	5	.178	.215
Rod Kanehl	OF58, 3B13, 2B12, 1B3	R	29	109	191	26	46	0	0	1	9	5	26	6	.241	.288
Ed Kranepool	1B55, OF6	L	18	86	273	22	57	12	2	2	14	18	50	0	.209	.289
Joe Christopher	OF45	R	27	64	149	19	33	5	1	1	8	13	21	1	.221	.289
Norm Sherry	C61	R	31	63	147	6	20	1	0	2	11	10	26	1	.136	.184
2 Chico Fernandez	SS45, 3B5, 2B3	R	31	58	145	12	29	4	0	9	30	9	30	3	.200	.262
Joe Hicks	OF41	L	30	56	159	16	36	6	1	3	22	7	31	0	.226	.371
Cliff Cook	OF21, 3B9, 1B5	R	26	50	106	6	15	3	0	2	16	12	37	0	.142	.236
2 Duke Carmel	OF21, 1B18	L	26	47	149	11	35	7	3	3	18	14	37	2	.235	.369
2 Jesse Gonder	C31	L	27	42	126	12	38	4	0	3	15	6	25	0	.302	.405
Larry Burright	SS19, 2B15, 3B1	R	25	41	100	9	22	1	0	1	8	2	25	1	.220	.260
2 Jimmy Piersall	OF38	R	33	40	124	13	24	4	0	1	8	18	11	2	.194	.266
Ted Schreiber	3B17, SS9, 2B3	R	24	39	50	1	8	1	0	0	1	4	10	0	.160	.160
1 Sammy Taylor	C13	L	30	22	33	1	5	2	0	0	3	3	5	0	.257	.314
Dick Smith	OF10, 1B2	R	24	20	42	4	10	0	0	0	3	1	10	0	.238	.238
Pumpsie Green	3B16	B	29	17	36	8	15	1	1	2	7	13	6	0	.278	.426
Chris Cannizzaro	C15	R	25	16	33	4	8	2	0	0	13	1	6	0	.242	.273

Marv Throneberry 29 L 2-14, 1 Gil Hodges 39 R 5-22, Cleon Jones 20 R 2-15

NAME	T	AGE	W	L	PCT	SV	G	GS	CG	IP	H	BB	SO	SHO	ERA
TOTALS		27	51	111	.315	12	162	162	42	1427	1452	529	806	5	4.12
Al Jackson	L	27	13	17	.433	1	37	34	11	227	237	84	142	0	3.96
Carl Willey	R	32	9	14	.391	0	30	28	7	183	149	69	101	4	3.10
Galen Cisco	R	27	7	15	.318	0	51	11	1	156	165	64	81	0	4.33
Tracy Stallard	R	25	6	17	.261	1	39	25	5	155	156	77	110	0	4.70
Roger Craig	R	33	5	22	.185	2	46	31	14	236	249	58	108	0	3.78
Jay Hook	R	26	4	14	.222	1	41	20	3	153	168	53	89	0	5.47
1 Ken MacKenzie	L	29	3	1	.750	3	34	0	0	63	62	13	41	0	4.97
Larry Bearnarth	R	21	3	8	.273	4	58	2	0	126	127	47	48	0	3.43
Grover Powell	L	22	1	1	.500	0	20	4	1	50	37	32	39	1	2.70
Don Rowe	L	27	0	0	—	0	26	1	0	55	59	21	27	0	4.25
2 Ed Bauta	R	27	0	0	—	0	19	0	0	22	19	13	10	0	5.11
Steve Dillon	L	20	0	0	—	0	3	0	0	6	6	9	3	0	9.00
Craig Anderson	R	25	0	2	.000	0	9	0	0	17	17	3	6	0	9.00

1964 Play It Again, Phil

Ralph Houk was rewarded for three straight pennants by being named general manager of the Yankees. In turn, Yogi Berra was rewarded for his 14 years of service and popularity by being named field boss. It was a move the Yankees soon regretted, as Berra proved more popular with the players than respected by them. The result was that in August, the Yankees found themselves in third place behind Baltimore and Chicago, playing sluggish ball and showing signs of never getting out of second gear. But oddly enough, the final challenge to Berra's authority provoked a new spirit via a shouting match between Berra and infielder Phil Linz. The incident took place on the team bus in mid-August over the issue whether or not Linz should play his harmonica. Berra thought not and quickly put an end to Linz's hopes for a second career. But suddenly, the apathy waned and the Yankee sun hung big and bright in the American League skies once again. Mickey Mantle returned from a leg injury in September to bolster the offense and Pedro Ramos was purchased from Cleveland to bolster a shaky bullpen. Mel Stottlemyre, recalled in August, came on to win nine games and, along with batters Joe Pepitone and Elston Howard and pitchers Whitey Ford and Jim Bouton, the Bronx Bombers were spurred on to a 22-6 September and a clinching of the pennant on the next-to-last day of the season.

The White Sox made their challenge with a host of good pitching. Gary Peters, Juan Pizarro, and Joe Horlen formed the Big Three which carried an offense boasting of only one power threat, Pete Ward. The Orioles attack packed a wallop in the form of the league's MVP, Brooks Robinson, and Boog Powell, the Bird's home run leader. Their hill staff featured 19-year-old Wally Bunker. Both clubs played well down the stretch but could not match the New York pace. Minnesota finished seventh, despite having the league's batting champ in rookie Tony Oliva and home run leader Harmon Killebrew.

The Los Angeles Angels just made the first division on the arm of Dean Chance, who won the Cy Young Award with 20 wins and a 1.65 E.R.A., and the fists of Bo Belinsky, who finished with nine victories before being suspended on August 14 for slugging a sportswriter.

In the National League, owner Gussie Busch showed his dissatisfaction with his St. Louis Cardinals' fifth-place occupancy by canning general manager Bing Devine on August 17, and rumors were rampant that manager Johnny Keane was next. But what was to come could not be seen yet, as two Devine acquisitions, outfielder Lou Brock and reliever Barney Schultz, led the Cards back into the pennant race.

The Phillies were leading the pack by 6½ games with two weeks remaining. It was enough of a lead to give Philadelphia printers the sign to ink up their presses for the first time in 14 years. But the imprint of Philadelphia on the World Series wasn't to be, as the Phillies dropped ten in a row to allow the Cards, Reds, and Giants to climb back into contention in the final week. When the dust finally settled, the Phillies and Reds found themselves staring at the pennant flag over Busch Stadium by a scant one-game margin.

The Cardinal cast was studded with starring performers. Brock joined the Cards from Chicago in June and hit a robust .348 the rest of the way. Ken Boyer led the league in RBI's and also won the MVP Award, while first baseman Bill White hit .303 and batted in 102 runs. Bob Gibson, Curt Simmons, and Ray Sadecki were outstanding starters for the Cards, and Barney Schultz was called up in August and provided top-notch relieving in the pennant drive.

The Reds finished second, despite losing their manager, Fred Hutchinson, who left the team in September with a cancer that would claim his life before another season would begin. Hutchinson's chief horses were outfielders Frank Robinson and Vada Pinson. The disappointed Phillies were spearheaded by Johnny Callison, rookie third baseman Dick Allen, and pitching ace Jim Bunning. The Dodgers fell back into sixth place with an anemic attack, while the Braves were fifth, despite five men chalking up 20 home run performances.

Roberto Clemente of the Pirates won the batting title with a .339 mark, while Willie Mays of the Giants led in home runs with 47. Larry Jackson of the lowly Cubs won 24 games to pace the loop in victories, and Sandy Koufax of Los Angeles had the lowest E.R.A. to complete the honor roll.

In the World Series, Tim McCarver and Bobby Richardson both hit .400 in leading their teams to three victories each in the first six games. In the decisive seventh game, Keane stayed with Gibson through three Yankee home runs and was rewarded with a 7-5 victory to bring the championship back to St. Louis for the first time since 1946.

It was not until the next day, however, that the fireworks began. While Keane was announcing his resignation, citing the Devine firing, and rumors of his own demise as reasons, the Yankees were revealing that Berra had been fired as manager because of his lack of control and communication with his players.

The musical chairs continued into the winter, as Berra rejoined his long-time mentor Casey Stengel with the New York Mets in the capacity of player-coach, while the Yankees turned right around and hired Keane to replace Berra at the helm of the Bronx Dynasty which, unknown to Keane and the world-at-large, was on its way to crumbling.

WORLD SERIES — ST. LOUIS (NL) 4 NEW YORK (AL) 3

LINE SCORES

TEAM	1	2	3	4	5	6	7	8	9	10	11	12	R	H	E

Game 1 October 7 at St. Louis

TEAM	1 2 3	4 5 6	7 8 9	R	H	E
NY (AL)	0 3 0	0 1 0	0 1 0	5	12	2
STL (NL)	1 1 0	0 0 4	0 3 X	9	12	0

Ford, Downing (6),   **Sadecki, Schultz (7)**
Sheldon (8), Mikkelsen (8)

Game 2 October 8 at St. Louis

TEAM	1 2 3	4 5 6	7 8 9	R	H	E
NY	0 0 0	1 0 1	2 0 4	8	12	0
STL	0 0 1	0 0 0	0 1 1	3	7	0

Stottlemyre   Gibson, Schultz (9),
                G. Richardson (9), Craig (9)

Game 3 October 10 at New York

TEAM	1 2 3	4 5 6	7 8 9	R	H	E
STL	0 0 0	0 1 0	0 0 0	1	6	0
NY	0 1 0	0 0 0	0 0 1	2	5	2

Simmons, Schultz (9)   **Bouton**

Game 4 October 11 at New York

TEAM	1 2 3	4 5 6	7 8 9	R	H	E
STL	0 0 0	0 0 4	0 0 0	4	6	1
NY	3 0 0	0 0 0	0 0 0	3	6	1

Sadecki, **Craig (1)**,   Downing, Mikkelsen (7),
Taylor (6)   Terry (8)

Game 5 October 12 at New York

TEAM	1 2 3	4 5 6	7 8 9	R	H	E
STL	0 0 0	0 2 0	0 0 3	5	10	1
NY	0 0 0	0 0 0	0 2 0	2	6	2

Gibson   Stottlemyre, Reniff (8),
          Mikkelsen (8)

Game 6 October 14 at St. Louis

TEAM	1 2 3	4 5 6	7 8 9	R	H	E
NY	0 0 0	0 1 2	0 5 0	8	10	0
STL	1 0 0	0 0 0	0 1 1	3	10	1

Bouton, Hamilton (9)   Simmons, Taylor (7), Schultz (8),
                        G. Richardson (8), Humphreys (9)

Game 7 October 15 at St. Louis

TEAM	1 2 3	4 5 6	7 8 9	R	H	E
NY	0 0 0	0 0 3	0 0 2	5	9	2
STL	0 0 0	3 3 0	1 0 X	7	10	1

Stottlemyre, Downing (5),   **Gibson**
Sheldon (5), Hamilton (7),
Mikkelsen (8)

COMPOSITE BATTING

NAME	POS	G	AB	R	H	2B	3B	HR	RBI	BA
St. Louis (NL)										
Totals		7	240	32	61	8	3	5	29	.254
Brock	OF	7	30	2	9	2	0	1	5	.300
Flood	OF	7	30	5	6	0	1	0	3	.200
Shannon	OF	7	28	6	6	0	0	1	2	.214
K. Boyer	3B	7	27	5	6	1	0	2	6	.222
White	1B	7	27	2	3	1	0	0	2	.111
Groat	SS	7	26	3	5	1	1	0	1	.192
McCarver	C	7	23	4	11	1	1	1	5	.478
Maxvill	2B	7	20	0	4	1	0	0	1	.200
Gibson	P	3	9	1	2	0	0	0	0	.222
Warwick	PH	5	4	2	3	0	0	0	0	.750
Simmons	P	2	4	0	2	0	0	0	1	.500
Skinner	PH	4	3	0	2	1	0	0	1	.667
James	PH	3	3	0	0	0	0	0	0	.000
Sadecki	P	2	2	0	1	0	0	0	1	.500
Buchek	2B	4	1	1	1	0	0	0	0	1.000
Schultz	P	4	1	0	0	0	0	0	0	.000
Craig	P	2	1	0	0	0	0	0	0	.000
Taylor	P	2	1	0	0	0	0	0	0	.000
Javier	2B	1	0	1	0	0	0	0	0	—
G. Richardson	P	2	0	0	0	0	0	0	0	—
Humphreys	P	1	0	0	0	0	0	0	0	—
New York (AL)										
Totals		7	239	33	60	11	0	10	33	.251
B. Richardson	2B	7	32	3	13	2	0	0	3	.406
Linz	SS	7	31	5	7	1	0	2	2	.226
Maris	OF	7	30	4	6	0	0	1	1	.200
Pepitone	1B	7	26	1	4	1	0	1	5	.154
Mantle	OF	7	24	8	8	2	0	3	8	.333
Howard	C	7	24	5	7	1	0	0	2	.292
C. Boyer	3B	7	24	4	5	1	0	1	3	.208
Tresh	OF	7	22	4	6	2	0	2	7	.273
Stottlemyre	P	3	8	0	1	0	0	0	0	.125
Bouton	P	2	7	0	1	0	0	0	1	.143
Blanchard	PH	4	4	0	1	1	0	0	0	.250
Lopez	OF	3	2	0	0	0	0	0	0	.000
Downing	P	3	2	0	0	0	0	0	0	.000
Ford	P	1	1	0	1	0	0	0	0	1.000
Gonzalez	3B	1	1	0	0	0	0	0	0	.000
Hegan	PH	3	1	0	0	0	0	0	0	.000
Mikkelsen	P	4	0	0	0	0	0	0	0	—
Sheldon	P	2	0	0	0	0	0	0	0	—
Hamilton	P	2	0	0	0	0	0	0	0	—
Terry	P	1	0	0	0	0	0	0	0	—
Reniff	P	1	0	0	0	0	0	0	0	—

COMPOSITE PITCHING

NAME	G	IP	H	BB	SO	W	L	SV	ERA
St. Louis (NL)									
Totals	7	63	60	25	54	4	3	2	4.29
Gibson	3	27	23	8	31	2	1	0	3.00
Simmons	2	14.1	11	3	8	0	1	0	2.51
Sadecki	2	6.1	12	5	2	1	0	0	8.53
Craig	2	5	2	3	9	1	0	0	0.00
Taylor	2	4.2	0	1	2	0	0	1	0.00
Schultz	4	4	9	3	1	0	1	1	18.00
Humphreys	1	1	0	0	1	0	0	0	0.00
G. Richardson	2	0.2	3	2	0	0	0	0	40.50
New York (AL)									
Totals	7	62	61	18	39	3	4	1	3.77
Stottlemyre	3	20	18	6	12	1	1	0	3.15
Bouton	2	17.1	15	5	7	2	0	0	1.56
Downing	3	7.2	9	2	5	0	1	0	8.22
Ford	1	5.1	8	1	4	0	1	0	8.44
Mikkelsen	4	4.2	4	2	4	0	1	0	5.79
Sheldon	2	2.2	2	2	0	0	0	0	0.00
Hamilton	2	2	3	0	2	0	0	0	4.50
Terry	1	2	2	0	3	0	0	0	0.00
Reniff	1	0.1	2	0	0	0	0	0	0.00

NEW YORK — 1st 99-63 .611 — YOGI BERRA

NAME	G by Pos	B	AGE	G	AB	R	H	2B	3B	HR	RBI	BB	SO	SB	BA	SA
TOTALS			29	164	5705	730	1442	208	35	162	688	520	976	54	.253	.387
Joe Pepitone	1B155, OF30	L	23	160	613	71	154	12	3	28	100	24	63	2	.251	.418
Bobby Richardson	2B157, SS1	R	28	159	679	90	181	25	4	4	50	28	36	11	.267	.333
Tony Kubek (XJ)	SS99	L	27	106	415	46	95	16	3	8	31	26	55	4	.229	.340
Clete Boyer	3B123, SS21	R	27	147	510	43	111	10	5	8	52	36	93	6	.218	.304
Roger Maris	OF137	L	29	141	513	86	144	12	2	26	71	62	78	3	.281	.464
Mickey Mantle	OF132	B	32	143	465	92	141	25	2	35	111	99	102	6	.303	.591
Tom Tresh	OF146	B	26	153	533	75	131	25	5	16	73	73	110	13	.246	.402
Elston Howard	C146	R	35	150	550	63	172	27	3	15	84	48	73	1	.313	.455
Hector Lopez	OF103, 3B1	R	34	127	285	34	74	9	3	10	34	24	54	1	.260	.418
Phil Linz	SS55, 3B41, 2B5, OF3	R	25	112	368	63	92	21	3	5	25	43	61	3	.250	.364
Pedro Gonzalez	1B31, OF20, 3B9, 2B6	R	25	80	112	18	31	8	1	0	5	7	22	3	.277	.366
Johnny Blanchard	C25, OF14, 1B3	L	31	77	161	18	41	8	0	7	28	24	24	1	.255	.435
Archie Moore	OF8, 1B7	L	22	31	23	4	4	2	0	0	1	2	9	0	.174	.261
Roger Repoz	OF9	L	23	11	1	1	0	0	0	0	0	0	1	0	.000	.000
Mike Hegan	1B2	L	21	5	5	0	0	0	0	0	0	0	2	0	.000	.000
Harry Bright	1B2	R	34	4	5	0	1	0	0	0	0	1	1	0	.200	.200
Jake Gibbs	C2	L	25	6	6	1	1	0	0	0	0	0	2	0	.167	.167
Elvio Jimenez	OF1	R	24	1	6	0	2	0	0	0	0	0	0	0	.333	.333

NAME	T	AGE	W	L	PCT	SV	G	GS	CG	IP	H	BB	SO	SHO	ERA
		27	99	63	.611	45	164	164	46	1507	1312	504	989	18	3.15
Jim Bouton	R	25	18	13	.581	0	38	37	11	271	227	60	125	4	3.02
Whitey Ford	L	35	17	6	.739	1	39	36	12	245	212	57	172	8	2.13
Al Downing	L	23	13	8	.619	2	37	35	11	244	201	120	217	1	3.47
Mel Stottlemyre	R	22	9	3	.750	0	13	12	5	96	77	35	49	2	2.06
Steve Hamilton	L	30	7	2	.778	3	30	3	1	60	55	15	49	0	3.50
Pete Mikkelsen	R	24	7	4	.636	12	50	0	0	86	79	41	63	0	3.56
Ralph Terry	R	28	7	11	.389	4	27	14	2	115	130	31	77	1	4.54
Hal Reniff	R	25	6	4	.600	9	41	0	0	69	47	30	38	0	3.13
Bill Stafford	R	24	5	0	1.000	4	31	1	0	61	50	22	39	0	2.66
Rollie Sheldon	R	27	5	2	.714	1	19	12	3	102	92	18	57	0	3.62
Bud Daley (SA)	L	31	3	2	.600	1	13	3	0	35	37	25	16	0	4.63
2 Pedro Ramos	R	29	1	0	1.000	8	13	0	0	22	13	0	21	0	1.25
Stan Williams	R	27	1	5	.167	0	21	10	1	82	76	38	54	0	3.84
1 Bob Meyer	L	24	0	3	.000	0	7	1	0	18	16	12	12	1	5.00

CHICAGO — 2nd 98-64 .605 1 — AL LOPEZ

NAME	G by Pos	B	AGE	G	AB	R	H	2B	3B	HR	RBI	BB	SO	SB	BA	SA
TOTALS			27	162	5491	642	1356	184	40	106	586	562	902	75	.247	.353
Tommy McCraw	1B84, OF36	L	23	125	368	47	96	11	5	6	36	32	65	15	.261	.367
Al Weis	2B116, SS9, OF2	B	26	133	328	36	81	4	4	2	23	22	41	22	.247	.302
Ron Hansen	SS158	R	26	158	575	85	150	20	3	20	68	73	73	1	.261	.419
Pete Ward	3B138	L	24	144	530	61	152	28	3	23	94	56	76	1	.282	.473
Mike Hershberger	OF134	R	24	141	452	55	104	15	3	2	31	48	47	8	.230	.290
Jim Landis	OF101	R	30	106	298	30	62	8	4	1	18	36	64	5	.208	.272
Floyd Robinson	OF138	L	28	141	525	83	158	39	3	11	59	70	41	9	.301	.408
J. C. Martin	C120	L	27	122	294	23	58	10	1	4	22	16	30	0	.197	.279
Don Buford	2B92, 3B37	B	27	135	442	62	116	14	6	4	30	46	62	12	.262	.348
Dave Nicholson	OF92	R	24	97	294	40	60	6	1	13	39	52	126	0	.204	.364
Gene Stephens	OF59	R	31	82	141	21	33	4	2	3	17	21	28	1	.234	.355
2 Bill Skowron	1B70	R	33	73	273	19	80	11	3	4	38	19	36	0	.293	.399
Jerry McNertney	C69	R	27	73	186	16	40	5	0	3	23	19	24	0	.215	.290
Gary Peters	P37	L	27	54	120	9	25	7	0	4	19	2	29	0	.208	.367
1 Joe Cunningham	1B33	L	32	40	108	13	27	7	0	0	10	14	15	0	.250	.315
Cam Carreon (SJ)	C34	R	26	37	95	12	26	5	0	0	4	7	13	0	.274	.326
Minnie Minoso	OF5	R	41	30	31	4	7	0	0	1	5	5	3	0	.226	.323
2 Jeoff Long	1B5, OF5	L	22	23	35	0	5	0	0	0	5	4	15	0	.143	.143
Ken Berry	OF12	R	23	12	32	4	12	1	0	1	4	5	5	1	.375	.500
2 Smoky Burgess		L	37	5	1	1	0	0	0	1	2	0	0	0	.200	.800
Marv Staehle		L	22	6	5	0	2	0	0	0	1	2	0	0	.400	.400
1 Charley Smith	3B2	R	26	2	7	1	1	0	0	1	0	4	0	0	.143	.429
Charlie Maxwell		L	37	2	2	0	0	0	0	0	0	0	0	0	.000	.000
Dick Kenworthy		R	23	2	2	0	0	0	0	0	0	0	0	0	.000	.000
Jim Hicks		R	24	2	0	0	0	0	0	0	0	0	0	0	.—	.—

NAME	T	AGE	W	L	PCT	SV	G	GS	CG	IP	H	BB	SO	SHO	ERA
		29	98	64	.605	45	162	162	44	1468	1216	401	955	20	2.72
Gary Peters	L	27	20	8	.714	0	37	36	11	274	217	104	205	3	2.50
Juan Pizarro	L	27	19	9	.679	0	33	33	11	239	193	55	162	4	2.56
Joe Horlen	R	26	13	9	.591	0	32	28	9	211	142	55	138	2	1.88
Hoyt Wilhelm	R	41	12	9	.571	27	73	0	0	131	94	30	95	0	1.99
John Buzhardt	R	27	10	8	.556	0	31	25	8	160	150	35	97	3	2.98
Eddie Fisher	R	27	6	3	.667	9	59	2	0	125	86	32	74	0	3.02
Ray Herbert (EJ)	R	34	6	7	.462	0	20	19	1	112	117	17	40	1	3.46
Fred Talbot	R	23	4	5	.444	0	17	12	3	75	83	20	34	2	3.72
Don Mossi	R	35	3	1	.750	7	34	0	0	40	37	7	36	0	2.93
1 Frank Kreutzer	L	25	3	1	.750	0	17	2	0	40	37	18	32	0	3.35
Bruce Howard	R	21	2	1	.667	0	3	3	1	22	10	8	17	1	0.82
Fritz Ackley	R	27	0	0	.—	0	2	0	0	6	10	4	6	0	9.00
Frank Baumann	L	30	0	0	.000	1	22	0	0	32	40	16	19	0	6.19
Dave DeBusschere (MS)		23													

BALTIMORE — 3rd 97-65 .599 2 — HANK BAUER

NAME	G by Pos	B	AGE	G	AB	R	H	2B	3B	HR	RBI	BB	SO	SB	BA	SA
TOTALS			27	163	5463	679	1357	229	20	162	632	537	1019	78	.248	.387
Norm Siebern	1B149	L	30	150	478	92	117	24	2	12	56	106	87	2	.245	.379
Jerry Adair	2B153	R	27	155	569	56	141	20	3	9	47	28	72	3	.248	.341
Luis Aparicio	SS145	R	30	146	578	93	154	20	3	10	37	49	51	57	.266	.363
Brooks Robinson	3B163	R	27	163	612	82	194	35	3	28	118	51	64	1	.317	.521
Sam Bowens	OF135	R	25	139	501	58	132	25	2	22	71	42	99	4	.263	.453
Jackie Brandt	OF134	R	30	137	523	66	127	25	1	13	47	45	104	1	.243	.369
Boog Powell	OF124, 1B5	L	22	134	424	74	123	17	0	39	99	76	91	0	.290	.606
Dick Brown	C84	R	29	88	230	24	59	6	0	8	32	12	45	2	.257	.387
Bob Johnson	SS18, 1B15, 2B15, 3B1, OF1	R	28	93	210	18	52	8	2	3	29	9	37	0	.248	.348
John Orsino	C66, 1B5	R	26	81	248	21	55	10	0	8	23	23	55	0	.222	.359
1 Willie Kirkland	OF58	L	30	66	150	14	30	5	0	3	22	17	26	3	.200	.293
2 Charlie Lau	C47	L	31	62	158	16	41	15	1	1	14	17	27	0	.259	.386
Russ Snyder (BN)	OF40	L	30	56	93	11	27	3	0	1	7	11	22	0	.290	.355
Bob Saverine	SS15, OF12	B	23	46	34	14	5	1	0	0	3	6	3	1	.147	.176
2 Gino Cimoli	OF35	R	34	38	58	6	8	3	2	0	3	2	13	0	.138	.259
Earl Robinson	OF34	R	27	37	121	11	33	5	1	3	10	7	24	1	.273	.405
1 Joe Gaines	OF5	R	27	16	26	2	4	0	0	1	2	3	7	0	.154	.269
3 Lenny Green	OF8	L	30	14	21	0	4	0	0	0	1	0	3	1	.190	.190
Paul Blair	OF6	R	20	8	1	0	0	0	0	0	0	0	1	0	.000	.000
Lou Jackson	OF1	R	28	4	8	0	3	0	0	0	0	0	1	0	.375	.375
Lou Piniella	OF	R	20	4	0	0	0	0	0	0	0	0	0	0	.000	.000

NAME	T	AGE	W	L	PCT	SV	G	GS	CG	IP	H	BB	SO	SHO	ERA
		28	97	65	.599	41	163	163	44	1459	1292	456	939	17	3.16
Wally Bunker	R	19	19	5	.792	0	29	29	12	214	161	62	96	1	2.69
Milt Pappas	R	25	16	7	.696	0	37	36	13	252	224	48	157	7	2.96
Robin Roberts	R	37	13	7	.650	0	31	31	8	204	203	52	109	4	2.91
Dick Hall	R	33	9	1	.900	7	45	0	0	88	58	16	52	0	1.84
Dave McNally	R	21	9	11	.450	0	30	23	5	159	157	51	88	3	3.68
Steve Barber	L	26	9	13	.409	1	36	26	4	157	144	81	118	0	3.84
Stu Miller	R	36	7	7	.500	23	66	0	0	97	77	34	87	0	3.06
Harvey Haddix	L	38	5	5	.500	10	49	0	0	90	68	23	90	0	2.30
Chuck Estrada (EJ)	R	26	3	2	.600	0	17	6	0	55	62	21	32	0	5.24
1 Wes Stock	R	30	2	0	1.000	0	14	0	0	21	17	8	14	0	3.80
Dave Vineyard	R	23	2	5	.286	0	19	6	1	54	57	27	50	0	4.17
Frank Bertaina	L	20	1	0	1.000	0	4	1	1	26	18	13	18	1	2.77
Ken Rowe	R	30	1	0	1.000	0	8	0	0	4	10	1	4	0	9.00
Herm Starrette	R	25	1	0	1.000	0	5	0	0	11	9	6	5	0	1.64
Sam Jones	R	38	0	0	.—	0	7	0	0	10	5	5	6	0	2.70
Mike McCormick	L	25	0	4	.000	0	4	2	0	17	21	8	13	0	5.29

DETROIT — 4th 85-77 .525 14 — CHUCK DRESSEN

NAME	G by Pos	B	AGE	G	AB	R	H	2B	3B	HR	RBI	BB	SO	SB	BA	SA
TOTALS			28	163	5513	699	1394	199	57	157	658	517	912	60	.253	.395
Norm Cash	1B137	L	29	144	479	63	123	15	5	23	83	70	66	2	.257	.443
Jerry Lumpe	2B158	L	31	158	624	75	160	21	6	6	46	50	61	2	.256	.338
Dick McAuliffe	SS160	L	24	162	557	85	154	18	7	24	66	77	96	8	.241	.427
Don Wert	3B142, SS4	R	25	148	525	63	135	18	5	9	55	50	74	3	.257	.362
Al Kaline	OF146	R	29	146	525	77	154	31	5	17	68	75	51	4	.293	.469
George Thomas	OF90, 3B1	R	26	105	308	39	88	15	2	12	44	18	53	4	.286	.464
Gates Brown	OF106	L	25	123	426	65	116	22	6	15	54	31	58	11	.272	.458
Bill Freehan	C141, 1B1	R	22	144	520	69	156	14	8	18	80	36	68	5	.300	.462
Don Demeter	OF88, 1B23	R	29	134	441	57	113	22	1	22	80	17	85	0	.256	.460
Bill Bruton	OF81	L	38	106	296	42	82	11	5	5	33	32	54	14	.277	.399
Jake Wood	1B11, 2B10, 3B6, OF1	R	27	64	125	11	29	2	2	1	7	4	34	0	.232	.304
Bubba Phillips	3B22, OF1	R	34	46	87	14	22	1	0	0	6	10	13	1	.253	.368
Mike Roarke	C27	R	33	29	42	4	9	1	0	0	7	10	10	0	.232	.244
Willie Horton	OF23	R	21	25	80	6	13	1	3	1	10	11	20	0	.163	.288
George Smith	2B3	R	26	5	7	1	2	0	0	0	2	1	4	1	.286	.286
Jim Northrup	OF2	L	24	5	12	1	1	0	0	0	1	0	3	1	.083	.167
Mickey Stanley	OF4	R	21	4	11	3	3	0	0	0	1	0	2	0	.273	.273
Bill Roman	1B2	L	25	3	8	1	3	0	0	1	2	1	2	0	.375	.750
John Sullivan	C2	L	23	4	0	0	0	0	0	0	0	0	0	0	.000	.000

NAME	T	AGE	W	L	PCT	SV	G	GS	CG	IP	H	BB	SO	SHO	ERA
		27	85	77	.525	35	163	163	35	1453	1343	536	993	11	3.84
Dave Wickersham	R	28	19	12	.613	1	40	36	11	254	224	81	164	1	3.44
Mickey Lolich	L	23	18	9	.667	2	44	33	12	232	196	64	192	6	3.26
Ed Rakow	R	29	8	9	.471	3	42	13	1	152	155	59	96	0	3.73
Fred Gladding	R	28	7	4	.636	7	42	0	0	67	57	27	59	0	3.09
Larry Sherry (FJ)	R	28	7	5	.583	11	38	0	0	66	52	37	58	0	3.68
Joe Sparma	R	22	5	6	.455	0	21	11	3	84	62	45	71	2	3.00
Phil Regan	R	27	5	10	.333	1	32	21	2	147	162	49	91	0	5.02
Hank Aguirre	L	33	5	10	.333	0	32	27	3	162	134	59	88	0	3.78
Terry Fox	R	28	4	3	.571	5	32	0	0	61	77	16	28	0	3.39
Denny McLain	R	20	4	5	.444	0	19	16	3	100	84	37	70	0	4.05
2 Julio Navarro	R	28	2	1	.667	2	26	0	0	41	40	16	36	0	3.95
Johnny Seale	L	25	0	0	1.000	0	10	6			4		5	0	3.60
Dick Egan	L	27	0	0	.—	0	23	0	0	34	33	17	21	0	4.50
1 Alan Koch	R	26	0	0	.—	0	4	0	0	5	6	3	1	0	6.75
Bill Faul	R	24	0	0	.—	0	2	0	0	5	5	2	1	0	10.80
Fritz Fisher	L	22	0	0	.—	0	1	0	0	0	2	1	0	0	108.00
Jack Hamilton	R	25	0	1	.000	0	8	0	0	15	24	10	6	0	8.40
1 Frank Lary	R	34	0	2	.000	0	4	0	0	6	11	2	5	0	7.00

LOS ANGELES — 5th 82-80 .506 17 — BILL RIGNEY

NAME	G by Pos	B	AGE	G	AB	R	H	2B	3B	HR	RBI	BB	SO	SB	BA	SA
TOTALS			27	162	5362	544	1297	186	27	102	508	472	920	49	.242	.344
Joe Adcock	1B105	R	36	118	366	39	98	13	0	21	64	48	61	0	.268	.475
Bobby Knoop	2B161	R	25	162	486	42	105	18	1	7	38	46	109	3	.216	.280
Jim Fregosi	SS137	R	22	147	505	86	140	22	9	18	72	72	87	8	.277	.463
Felix Torres	3B72, 1B3	R	32	100	277	25	64	10	0	6	38	13	56	1	.231	.397
1 Lu Clinton	OF86	R	26	91	306	30	76	18	0	9	38	31	40	3	.248	.395
Albie Pearson	OF66	L	29	107	265	34	59	7	1	3	16	35	22	6	.223	.272
Willie Smith	OF87, P15	L	25	118	359	46	108	14	6	11	51	8	39	7	.301	.465
Bob Rodgers	C146	B	25	148	514	38	125	18	3	4	54	40	71	4	.243	.313
Tom Satriano	3B38, 1B32, C25, SS2, 2B1	L	23	108	255	18	51	9	0	1	17	30	37	0	.200	.247
Jimmy Piersall	OF72	R	34	87	255	28	80	11	0	2	13	16	32	5	.314	.380
Ed Kirkpatrick	OF63	L	19	75	219	20	53	13	3	2	22	23	30	0	.242	.356
Bob Perry	OF62	R	29	70	221	19	61	8	1	3	16	14	52	1	.276	.362
2 Vic Power	1B48, 3B28, 2B5	R	36	68	221	17	55	6	1	0	18	5	13	0	.249	.317
Joe Koppe	SS31, 2B13, 3B3	R	33	54	113	10	29	6	0	1	13	13	15	0	.257	.310
1 Billy Moran	3B47, 2B1, SS1	R	30	50	198	26	53	10	1	1	13	3	25	1	.268	.328
1 Lee Thomas	OF47, 1B1	L	28	47	172	14	47	8	1	2	24	18	22	1	.273	.366
2 Lenny Green	OF23	R	30	39	120	14	33	7	2	2	4	10	8	2	.250	.375
Charlie Dees	1B12	L	29	26	26	3	2	0	0	0	1	6	0	0	.077	.115
Dick Simpson	OF16	R	20	21	50	11	7	1	0	1	4	8	15	2	.140	.280
Paul Schaal	2B9, 3B9	R	21	17	32	7	4	0	0	0	1	1	6	0	.125	.125
Rick Reichardt	OF11	R	21	11	37	0	6	0	1	0	1	1	12	1	.162	.162
Jack Hiatt	C3, 1B2	R	21	9	8	2	3	0	0	0	0	3	5	0	.375	.375
Hank Foiles	C	R	35	4	4	0	1	0	0	0	0	0	2	0	.250	.250

NAME	T	AGE	W	L	PCT	SV	G	GS	CG	IP	H	BB	SO	SHO	ERA
		27	82	80	.506	41	162	162	30	1451	1273	530	965	28	2.91
Dean Chance	R	23	20	9	.690	4	46	35	15	278	194	86	207	11	1.65
Fred Newman	R	22	13	10	.565	0	32	28	7	190	177	39	83	2	2.75
Bo Belinsky (ST)	L	27	9	8	.529	0	23	22	4	135	120	49	91	1	2.87
Bob Duliba	R	29	6	4	.600	9	58	0	0	73	80	22	33	0	3.58
Bob Lee	R	26	6	5	.545	19	64	5	0	137	87	58	111	0	1.51
Barry Latman	R	28	6	10	.375	2	40	18	2	138	128	52	81	1	3.85
Don Lee	R	30	5	4	.556	2	33	8	0	89	99	25	73	0	2.73
Ken McBride	R	28	4	13	.235	1	29	21	0	116	104	75	66	0	5.28
Dan Osinski	R	30	3	3	.500	3	47	4	1	93	87	39	88	1	3.48
Aubrey Gatewood	R	25	3	3	.500	0	15	7	0	50	59	12	25	0	2.25
Bill Kelso	R	22	1	0	1.000	0	10	1	0	24	19	9	21	1	2.25
George Brunet	L	31	1	0	1.000	0	10	7	0	42	38	25	36	0	3.64
1 Jack Spring	L	31	0	0	.—	0	5	0	0	6	6	3	1	0	3.00
2 Bob Meyer	L	25	0	2	.000	0	15	1	0	32	34	10	20	0	2.81
Willie Smith	L	25			.200	0	15	1							
1 Julio Navarro	R	33	0	0	.—	0	7	0	0	7	3	7	3	0	6.00
Paul Foytack	R	33	0	1	.000	0	7	2	0	17	19	5	11	0	6.00
Ed Sukla	R	21	0	1	.000	0	7	0	0	7	6	7	3	0	18.00
Art Fowler	R	41	0	0	.—	0	5	0	0	7	8	5	5	0	10.29

CLEVELAND — 6th (tie) 79-83 .488 20   GEORGE STRICKLAND 33-39 .458   BIRDIE TEBBETTS (IL) 46-44 .511

NAME	G by Pos	B	AGE	G	AB	R	H	2B	3B	HR	RBI	BB	SO	SB	BA	SA
TOTALS			27	164	5603	689	1386	208	22	164	640	500	1063	79	.247	.380
Bob Chance	1B81, OF31	R	23	120	390	45	109	16	1	14	75	40	101	3	.279	.433
Larry Brown	2B103, SS4	R	24	115	335	33	77	12	1	12	40	24	55	1	.230	.379
Dick Howser	SS162	R	28	162	637	101	163	23	4	3	52	76	39	20	.256	.379
Max Alvis (IL)	3B105	R	26	107	381	51	96	14	3	18	53	29	77	5	.252	.446
Tito Francona	OF69, 1B17	L	30	111	270	35	67	13	2	8	24	44	46	1	.248	.400
Vic Davalillo	OF143	R	27	150	577	64	156	26	2	6	51	34	77	21	.270	.354
Leon Wagner	OF163	L	30	163	641	94	162	19	2	31	100	56	121	14	.253	.434
Johnny Romano	C96, 1B1	R	29	106	352	46	85	18	1	19	47	51	83	2	.241	.460
Woodie Held	2B52, OF41, 3B30	R	32	118	364	50	86	13	0	18	49	43	88	1	.236	.420
Fred Whitfield	1B79	L	26	101	293	29	79	13	1	10	29	12	58	0	.270	.423
Chico Salmon	OF53, 2B32, 1B13	R	23	86	283	43	87	17	2	4	25	13	37	10	.307	.424
Joe Azcue	C76	R	24	83	271	20	74	9	1	4	34	16	38	0	.273	.358
2 Billy Moran	3B42, 2B15, 1B2	R	30	69	151	14	31	6	0	1	10	8	16	0	.205	.265
1 Al Smith	OF48, 3B1	R	36	61	136	15	22	1	1	4	9	8	32	1	.162	.272
1 Jerry Kindall	1B23	R	29	25	5	9	1	0	2	2	2	7	0	.360	.640	
Al Luplow	OF5	L	25	19	18	1	2	0	0	0	1	1	6	0	.111	.111
Tommie Agee	OF12	R	21	13	12	0	2	0	0	0	0	0	3	0	.167	.167
Paul Dicken		R	20	11	11	0	0	0	0	0	0	0	5	0	.000	.000
Tony Martinez	2B4, SS1	R	24	9	14	1	3	1	0	0	0	0	2	0	.214	.286
2 George Banks	OF3, 2B1, 3B1	R	25	9	17	6	5	1	0	2	3	6	6	0	.294	.706
Wally Post	OF2	R	34	5	8	1	0	0	0	0	0	1	4	0	.000	.000

Duke Sims 23 L 0-6, Vern Fuller (BS) 20 R 0-1

NAME	T	AGE	W	L	PCT	SV	G	GS	CG	IP	H	BB	SO	SHO	ERA
		28	79	83	.488	37	164	164	37	1488	1443	565	1162	16	3.75
Jack Kralick	L	29	12	7	.632	0	30	29	8	191	196	51	119	3	3.20
Sam McDowell	L	21	11	6	.647	1	31	24	6	173	148	100	177	2	2.71
Luis Tiant	R	23	10	4	.714	1	19	16	9	127	94	47	105	3	2.83
Gary Bell	R	27	8	6	.571	4	56	2	0	106	106	53	89	0	4.33
Sonny Siebert	R	27	7	9	.438	3	41	14	3	156	142	57	144	1	3.23
Dick Donovan	R	36	7	9	.438	2	30	23	5	158	181	29	83	0	4.56
1 Pedro Ramos	R	29	7	10	.412	0	36	19	3	133	144	26	98	1	5.14
Don McMahon	R	34	6	4	.600	16	37	0	0	101	67	52	92	0	2.41
2 Lee Stange	R	27	4	8	.333	0	23	14	0	92	98	31	78	0	4.12
1 Mudcat Grant	R	28	3	4	.429	0	13	9	1	62	82	25	43	0	5.95
Ted Abernathy	R	31	2	6	.250	11	53	0	0	73	66	46	57	0	4.32
Tommy John	L	21	2	9	.182	0	25	14	2	94	97	35	65	1	3.93
Tom Kelley	R	20	0	1	—	0	9	0	9	7	7	5	0	5.40	
Gordon Seyfried	L	26	0	0	—	0	2	0	0	2	6	4	0	0.00	
Jerry Walker	R	25	0	1	.000	0	10	9	4	5	4	0	4.50		

MINNESOTA — 6th (tie) 79-83 .488 20   SAM MELE

NAME	G by Pos	B	AGE	G	AB	R	H	2B	3B	HR	RBI	BB	SO	SB	BA	SA
TOTALS			26	163	5610	737	1413	227	46	221	707	553	1019	46	.252	.427
Bob Allison	1B93, OF61	R	29	149	492	90	141	27	4	32	86	92	99	10	.287	.553
Bernie Allen (NJ)	2B71	L	25	74	243	28	52	8	1	6	20	33	30	1	.214	.329
Zoilo Versalles	SS160	R	24	160	659	94	171	33	10	20	64	42	88	14	.259	.431
Rich Rollins	3B146	R	26	148	596	87	161	25	10	12	68	53	80	2	.270	.406
Tony Oliva	OF159	L	23	161	672	109	217	43	9	32	94	34	68	12	.323	.557
Jimmie Hall	OF137	L	26	149	510	61	144	20	3	25	75	44	112	5	.282	.480
Harmon Killebrew	OF157	R	28	158	577	95	156	11	1	49	111	93	135	0	.270	.548
Earl Battey	C125	R	29	131	405	33	110	17	1	12	52	51	49	1	.272	.407
Don Mincher	1B76	L	26	120	287	45	68	12	4	23	56	27	51	0	.237	.547
Jerry Zimmerman	C63	R	29	63	120	6	24	3	0	0	10	10	15	0	.200	.225
2 Jerry Kindall	2B51, SS7, 1B1	R	29	62	128	8	19	2	0	1	6	7	44	0	.148	.188
Frank Kostro	3B12, 2B7, OF2, 1B1	R	26	59	103	10	28	5	0	3	12	4	21	0	.272	.408
Johnny Goryl	2B28, 3B13	R	30	58	114	9	16	2	0	1	10	25	1	.140	.175	
Jim Snyder	2B25	R	31	26	71	3	11	2	0	0	9	4	11	0	.155	.225
1 Lenny Green	OF7	L	30	26	15	3	0	0	0	0	0	4	6	0	.000	.000
Ron Henry	C13	R	27	22	41	4	5	1	1	2	5	3	14	0	.122	.341
1 Vic Power	1B12, 2B11	R	36	19	45	6	10	2	0	0	1	1	3	0	.222	.267
Joe McCabe	C12	R	25	14	19	1	3	0	0	0	2	0	6	0	.158	.158
Jay Ward	2B9, OF3	R	25	12	31	4	7	2	0	0	2	4	6	13	0	.226	.290
Bill Bethea	2B7, SS3	R	22	10	30	4	5	1	0	0	2	6	4	0	.167	.200
Rich Reese	1B1	L	22	12	10	7	0	0	0	0	0	0	0	0	.000	.000
Clyde Bloomfield	2B3, SS2	R	28	7	7	1	1	0	0	0	0	1	2	0	.143	.143

Joe Nossek 23 R 0-1, 1 George Banks 25 R 0-1

NAME	T	AGE	W	L	PCT	SV	G	GS	CG	IP	H	BB	SO	SHO	ERA
		28	79	83	.488	29	163	163	47	1478	1361	545	1099	4	3.57
Jim Kaat	L	25	17	11	.607	1	36	34	13	243	231	60	171	0	3.22
Camilo Pascual	R	30	15	12	.556	0	36	36	14	267	245	98	213	1	3.30
2 Mudcat Grant	R	28	11	9	.550	1	26	23	10	166	162	36	75	1	2.82
Jerry Arrigo	L	23	7	4	.636	1	41	12	2	105	97	45	96	1	3.86
Jim Perry	R	28	6	3	.667	2	42	1	0	65	61	23	55	0	3.46
Dick Stigman	L	28	6	15	.286	0	32	29	5	190	160	70	159	1	4.03
2 Al Worthington	R	35	5	6	.455	14	41	0	0	72	47	28	59	0	1.38
Bill Pleis	L	26	4	1	.800	4	47	0	0	51	43	31	42	0	3.88
1 Lee Stange	R	27	3	6	.333	0	14	11	2	80	78	19	54	0	4.75
Dave Boswell	R	19	2	0	1.000	0	4	4	0	23	21	12	26	0	4.30
Jim Roland	L	21	2	6	.250	3	30	13	1	94	76	55	63	0	4.12
Bill Dailey (SA)	R	29	1	2	.333	0	14	0	0	15	23	17	6	0	8.40
Dwight Siebler	R	26	0	0	—	0	11	10	6	10	6	0	4.91		
Bill Whitby	R	20	0	0	—	0	1	0	0	3	3	2	0	9.00	
Gary Dotter	L	21	0	0	—	0	0	4	3	4	2	0	2.25		
Chuck Nieson	R	21	0	0	—	0	2	6	1	6	4	0	4.50		
Bill Fischer	R	33	1	0	1.000	0	8	0	0	7	16	3	8	0	7.71
Jerry Fosnow	L	23	0	1	.000	0	7	0	0	11	13	8	9	0	10.64
Garland Shifflett	R	29	0	0	—	0	9	0	0	18	22	7	8	0	4.50
2 Johnny Klippstein	R	36	0	4	.000	0	33	0	0	46	44	20	36	1	1.96

BOSTON — 8th 72-90 .444 27   JOHNNY PESKY 70-90 .438   BILLY HERMAN 2-0 1.000

NAME	G by Pos	B	AGE	G	AB	R	H	2B	3B	HR	RBI	BB	SO	SB	BA	SA
TOTALS			27	162	5513	688	1425	253	29	186	648	504	917	18	.258	.416
Dick Stuart	1B155	R	31	156	603	73	168	24	1	33	114	37	130	0	.279	.491
Dalton Jones	2B85, SS11, 3B1	L	20	118	374	37	86	16	4	6	39	22	38	6	.230	.342
Ed Bressoud	SS158	R	32	158	566	86	166	41	3	15	55	72	99	1	.293	.456
Frank Malzone	3B143	R	34	148	537	62	142	19	0	13	56	37	43	0	.264	.372
2 Lee Thomas	OF107, 1B1	L	28	107	401	44	103	19	2	13	42	34	29	2	.257	.411
Carl Yastrzemski	OF148, 3B2	L	24	151	567	77	164	29	9	15	67	75	90	6	.289	.451
Tony Conigliaro (BA)	OF106	R	19	111	404	69	117	21	2	24	52	35	78	2	.290	.530
Bob Tillman	C131	R	27	131	425	43	118	18	1	17	61	49	74	0	.278	.445
Felix Mantilla	OF48, 2B45, 3B7, SS6	R	29	133	425	69	123	20	1	30	64	41	46	0	.289	.553
Russ Nixon	C45	R	29	81	163	10	38	7	0	1	20	14	29	0	.233	.294
Roman Mejias	OF37	R	33	62	101	14	24	3	1	2	4	7	16	0	.238	.347
Dick Williams	1B21, 3B13, OF5	R	35	61	69	10	11	2	0	5	11	7	10	0	.159	.406
Earl Wilson	P33	R	29	54	73	19	15	4	0	5	13	9	22	0	.205	.466
Chuck Schilling	2B42	R	26	47	163	18	32	6	0	0	7	15	22	0	.196	.233
1 Lu Clinton	OF24, 1B8	R	26	37	120	15	31	4	3	3	6	9	33	1	.258	.417
Tony Horton	OF19, 1B8	R	19	36	126	9	29	5	0	1	8	2	10	0	.222	.286
2 Al Smith	3B10, OF8	R	36	29	51	10	11	4	0	2	7	13	10	0	.216	.412
Gary Geiger (IL)	OF4	L	27	5	13	3	5	0	1	0	1	2	2	0	.385	.538
Bob Guindon	OF1, 1B1	L	20	5	8	0	1	1	0	0	0	0	2	0	.125	.250
Mike Ryan	C1	R	23	1	3	0	1	0	0	0	0	0	0	0	.333	.333

NAME	T	AGE	W	L	PCT	SV	G	GS	CG	IP	H	BB	SO	SHO	ERA
		26	72	90	.444	38	162	162	21	1422	1464	571	1094	9	4.50
Dick Radatz	R	27	16	9	.640	29	79	0	0	157	103	58	181	0	2.29
Bill Monbouquette	R	27	13	14	.481	1	36	35	7	234	258	40	120	5	4.04
Earl Wilson	R	29	11	12	.478	0	33	31	5	202	213	73	166	0	4.50
Jack Lamabe	R	27	9	13	.409	1	39	25	3	177	235	57	109	0	5.90
Dave Morehead	R	21	8	15	.348	0	32	30	3	167	156	112	139	1	4.96
Bob Heffner	R	25	7	9	.438	6	55	10	1	159	152	44	112	1	4.08
Ed Connolly	L	24	4	11	.267	0	27	15	1	81	80	64	73	1	4.89
Bill Spanswick	L	25	2	3	.400	0	29	7	0	65	75	44	55	0	6.92
Arnie Earley (EJ)	L	31	1	1	.500	1	25	3	1	50	51	18	45	0	2.70
Jay Ritchie	R	27	1	1	.500	0	21	0	0	43	43	14	35	0	2.74
Dave Gray	R	21	0	0	—	0	13	0	0	13	18	20	17	0	9.00
1 Wilbur Wood	L	22	0	0	—	0	6	0	0	6	13	3	5	0	16.50
Pete Charton	R	21	0	2	.000	0	25	5	0	65	67	24	37	0	5.26

WASHINGTON — 9th 62-100 .383 37   GIL HODGES

NAME	G by Pos	B	AGE	G	AB	R	H	2B	3B	HR	RBI	BB	SO	SB	BA	SA
TOTALS			29	162	5396	578	1246	199	28	125	528	514	1124	47	.231	.348
1 Bill Skowron	1B66	R	33	73	262	28	71	10	0	13	41	11	56	0	.271	.458
Don Blasingame	2B135	L	32	143	506	56	135	17	2	1	34	40	44	8	.267	.314
Eddie Brinkman	SS125	R	22	130	447	54	100	20	3	4	34	26	99	3	.224	.336
John Kennedy	3B106, SS49, 2B2	R	23	148	482	55	111	16	4	7	35	29	119	3	.230	.324
Jim King	OF121	L	31	134	415	46	100	15	1	18	56	55	65	3	.241	.412
Don Lock	OF152	R	27	152	512	73	127	17	4	28	80	79	137	4	.248	.461
Chuck Hinton	OF131, 3B2	R	30	138	514	71	141	19	2	11	50	57	77	17	.274	.414
Mike Brumley	C132	L	25	136	426	36	104	19	2	3	35	40	53	1	.244	.312
Don Zimmer	3B87, OF4, C2, 2B1	R	33	121	341	38	84	16	2	12	38	27	94	1	.246	.411
Dick Phillips	1B61, 3B4	R	32	109	234	17	54	6	1	2	23	27	22	1	.231	.291
Fred Valentine	OF57	R	29	102	202	20	48	5	0	4	20	21	44	4	.226	.307
Chuck Cottier	2B53, 3B3, SS2	R	28	73	137	16	23	6	2	3	10	19	33	2	.168	.307
Ken Hunt	OF37	R	29	51	96	9	13	4	0	1	4	14	35	0	.135	.208
Don Leppert	C43	R	32	50	122	6	19	3	0	3	12	11	32	0	.156	.254
2 Joe Cunningham	1B41	L	32	49	126	15	27	4	0	1	7	23	10	0	.214	.246
2 Roy Sievers	1B15	R	37	33	58	5	10	1	2	0	5	9	14	0	.172	.397
2 Willie Kirkland	OF27	L	30	32	102	8	22	5	0	6	13	6	30	1	.216	.422
Ken Retzer	C13	R	30	17	32	1	3	0	0	0	3	6	4	0	.094	.094

NAME	T	AGE	W	L	PCT	SV	G	GS	CG	IP	H	BB	SO	SHO	ERA
		29	62	100	.383	26	162	162	27	1435	1417	505	794	5	3.98
Claude Osteen	L	24	15	13	.536	0	37	36	13	257	256	64	133	0	3.33
Ron Kline	R	32	10	7	.588	14	61	0	0	81	81	21	40	0	2.33
Buster Narum	R	23	9	15	.375	0	38	32	7	199	195	73	121	2	4.30
Bennie Daniels	R	32	8	10	.444	0	33	24	3	163	147	64	73	2	3.70
Steve Ridzik	R	35	5	5	.500	2	49	3	0	112	96	31	60	0	2.89
Jim Hannan	R	24	4	7	.364	3	49	7	0	106	100	45	67	0	4.08
2 Alan Koch	R	26	3	10	.231	0	32	14	1	114	110	43	67	0	4.89
2 Frank Kreutzer	L	25	2	6	.250	0	13	6	2	45	42	23	27	0	4.77
Dave Stenhouse (AJ)	R	30	2	7	.222	1	26	14	1	88	80	39	44	0	4.81
Don Loun	L	32	1	1	.500	0	2	1	1	13	13	3	1	1	2.08
Don Rudolph	L	32	1	3	.250	0	28	8	0	70	83	16	35	0	3.67
Tom Cheney (SA)	R	29	1	3	.250	1	15	6	1	49	45	13	25	0	3.67
Jim Duckworth (SA)	R	25	1	6	.143	3	30	2	0	56	52	25	56	0	4.34
Howie Koplitz	R	26	0	0	—	0	2	0	0	3	8	4	0	9.00	
Pete Craig	R	23	0	2	.000	0	3	1	0	8	7	4	0	40.50	
1 Ed Roebuck	R	32	0	0	—	0	28	0	0	35	35	9	14	0	5.14
Jim Bronstad	R	28	0	1	.000	0	17	0	0	30	37	11	25	0	5.70
Marshall Bridges	L	33	0	3	.000	0	17	0	0	30	28	17	12	0	5.40
Carl Bouldin	R	24	0	3	.000	0	25	5	0	25	30	11	12	0	5.40

KANSAS CITY — 10th 57-105 .352 42   ED LOPAT 17-35 .327   MEL McGAHA 40-70 .364

NAME	G by Pos	B	AGE	G	AB	R	H	2B	3B	HR	RBI	BB	SO	SB	BA	SA
TOTALS			27	163	5524	621	1321	216	29	166	594	485	1104	34	.239	.379
Jim Gentile	1B128	L	30	136	439	71	110	10	0	28	71	84	122	0	.251	.465
Dick Green	2B120	R	23	130	435	48	115	14	5	11	37	27	87	3	.264	.395
Wayne Causey	SS131, 2B17, 3B9	L	27	157	604	82	170	31	4	8	49	88	65	5	.281	.386
Ed Charles	3B147	R	29	150	537	62	142	19	12	16	63	64	92	12	.264	.379
Rocky Colavito	OF159	R	30	160	588	89	161	31	2	34	102	83	56	3	.274	.507
Nelson Mathews	OF154	R	22	157	573	58	137	27	5	14	60	43	143	2	.239	.377
Manny Jimenez	OF49	L	25	95	204	19	46	7	0	2	38	15	24	0	.225	.436
Doc Edwards	C79, 1B7	R	27	97	294	25	66	10	0	5	28	13	40	0	.224	.310
Jose Tartabull	OF59	L	25	104	100	19	20	2	0	0	3	5	12	4	.200	.220
George Alusik	OF44, 1B8	R	29	102	204	18	49	10	1	3	19	30	36	0	.240	.343
Billy Bryan	C65	L	25	93	220	19	53	9	2	13	36	16	69	0	.241	.477
Bert Campaneris	SS38, OF27, 3B6	R	22	67	269	14	69	14	3	4	22	15	41	10	.257	.375
Ken Harrelson	OF24, 1B15	R	22	49	139	15	27	5	0	7	12	13	34	0	.194	.381
1 Charlie Lau	C35	L	31	43	118	11	32	7	0	1	16	11	9	0	.271	.398
George Williams	2B20, SS2, 3B2, OF2	R	24	37	91	10	19	1	0	1	9	12	15	0	.209	.275
Tommie Reynolds	OF25, 3B3	R	22	29	76	11	19	1	0	1	4	5	20	0	.202	.277
Dave Duncan	C22	R	18	25	53	2	9	1	0	1	3	1	11	0	.170	.264
Rick Joseph	1B12, 3B3	R	24	16	45	3	10	1	0	1	3	6	12	0	.222	.289
Charlie Shoemaker	2B14	L	24	16	52	6	11	2	0	0	5	3	10	0	.212	.327
Larry Stahl	OF10	L	23	16	23	1	6	1	0	0	1	1	9	0	.261	.478
John Wojcik	OF6	L	22	11	22	1	3	0	0	0	0	1	5	0	.136	.136
1 Gino Cimoli	OF4	R	34	4	4	1	0	0	0	0	0	0	2	0	.000	.000

NAME	T	AGE	W	L	PCT	SV	G	GS	CG	IP	H	BB	SO	SHO	ERA
		27	57	105	.352	27	163	163	18	1456	1516	614	966	6	4.71
Orlando Pena	R	30	12	14	.462	0	40	32	5	219	231	73	184	0	4.44
John O'Donoghue	L	24	10	14	.417	0	39	32	2	174	202	65	79	1	4.92
John Wyatt	R	29	9	8	.529	20	81	0	0	128	111	52	74	0	3.59
Diego Segui	R	26	8	17	.320	0	40	35	5	217	219	94	155	2	4.56
2 Wes Stock	R	30	6	3	.667	5	50	0	0	93	69	34	101	0	1.94
Moe Drabowsky	R	28	5	13	.278	1	53	21	1	168	176	72	119	0	5.30
Ted Bowsfield	L	28	4	5	.444	0	23	7	1	92	119	35	45	1	4.08
Blue Moon Odom	R	19	1	4	.200	0	7	2	1	22	33	22	11	0	10.06
3 Bob Meyer	L	24	1	4	.200	0	9	7	2	42	37	33	30	0	3.86
Dan Pfister	R	27	0	6	.000	0	19	3	0	41	60	29	21	0	6.59
1 Tom Sturdivant	R	34	0	0	—	0	19	0	0	26	31	16	16	0	5.54
Vern Handrahan	R	25	0	1	.000	0	18	0	0	36	36	17	10	0	6.00
Jack Aker	R	23	0	1	.000	0	11	0	0	17	18	10	7	0	3.67
Ken Sanders	R	22	0	1	.000	0	7	0	0	12	13	17	8	0	4.71
Joe Grzenda	L	27	0	0	—	0	6	0	0	15	13	11	9	0	7.20
Lew Krausse	R	21	0	1	.000	0	5	4	0	23	23	11	14	0	4.90
Aurelio Monteagudo	R	21	0	0	—	0	14	0	0	21	17	10	10	0	5.14
Jose Santiago	R	23	0	0	—	0	34	0	0	84	84	53	64	0	4.71

ST. LOUIS — 1st 93-69 .574 — JOHNNY KEANE

NAME	G by Pos	B	AGE	G	AB	R	H	2B	3B	HR	RBI	BB	SO	SB	BA	SA
	TOTALS		27	162	5625	715	1531	240	53	109	654	427	925	73	.272	.392
Bill White	1B160	L	30	160	631	92	191	37	4	21	102	52	103	7	.303	.474
Julian Javier	2B154	R	27	155	535	66	129	19	5	12	65	30	82	1	.241	.363
Dick Groat	SS160	R	33	161	636	70	186	35	6	1	70	44	42	2	.292	.371
Ken Boyer	3B162	R	33	162	628	100	185	30	10	24	119	70	85	3	.295	.489
Mike Shannon	OF88	R	24	88	253	30	66	8	2	9	43	19	54	4	.261	.415
Curt Flood	OF162	R	26	162	679	97	211	25	3	5	46	43	53	4	.311	.378
2 Lou Brock	OF102	L	25	103	419	81	146	21	9	12	44	27	87	33	.348	.527
Tim McCarver	C137	L	22	143	465	53	134	19	3	9	52	40	44	2	.288	.400
Charlie James	OF60	R	26	88	233	24	52	9	1	5	17	11	58	0	.223	.335
Carl Warwick	OF49	R	27	88	158	14	41	7	1	3	15	11	30	2	.259	.373
2 Bob Skinner	OF31	L	32	55	118	10	32	5	0	1	16	11	20	0	.271	.339
Bob Uecker	C40	R	29	40	106	8	21	1	0	1	6	17	24	0	.198	.236
Johnny Lewis	OF36	L	24	40	94	10	22	2	2	2	7	13	23	2	.234	.362
Phil Gagliano	2B12, OF2, 1B1, 3B1	R	22	40	58	5	15	4	0	1	9	3	10	0	.259	.379
Dal Maxvill	2B15, SS13, 3B1, OF1	R	25	37	26	4	6	0	0	0	4	0	7	1	.231	.231
Jerry Buchek	SS20, 2B9, 3B1	R	22	35	30	7	6	0	0	2	0	1	3	11	.200	.333
1 Doug Clemens	OF22	L	25	33	78	8	16	4	3	1	9	6	16	0	.205	.372
1 Jeoff Long	OF4, 1B3	R	22	28	43	5	10	1	0	1	4	6	18	0	.233	.326
Ed Spiezio		R	22	12	12	0	4	0	0	0	0	0	1	0	.333	.333
Joe Morgan		L	33	3	3	0	0	0	0	0	0	0	2	0	.000	.000
Hal Smith (IL) 33																

NAME	T	AGE	W	L	PCT	SV	G	GS	CG	IP	H	BB	SO	SHO	ERA
		30	93	69	.574	38	162	162	47	1445	1405	410	877	10	3.43
Ray Sadecki	L	23	20	11	.645	1	37	32	9	220	232	60	119	2	3.68
Bob Gibson	R	28	19	12	.613	1	40	36	17	287	250	86	245	2	3.01
Curt Simmons	L	35	18	9	.667	0	34	34	12	244	233	49	104	3	3.43
Ron Taylor	R	26	8	4	.667	5	63	2	0	101	109	33	69	0	4.63
Roger Craig	R	34	7	9	.438	5	39	19	3	166	180	33	84	0	3.25
Mike Cuellar	L	27	5	5	.500	4	32	7	1	72	80	33	56	0	4.50
Gordie Richardson	L	24	4	2	.667	3	19	6	1	47	40	15	28	0	2.30
Ray Washburn (SA)	R	26	3	4	.429	2	15	10	0	60	60	17	28	0	4.05
1 Ernie Broglio	R	28	3	5	.375	0	11	11	3	69	65	26	36	1	3.52
Bob Humphreys	R	28	2	0	1.000	2	28	0	0	43	32	15	36	0	2.51
1 Lew Burdette	R	37	1	0	1.000	0	8	0	0	10	10	3	4	0	1.80
1 Glen Hobbie	R	28	1	2	.333	1	13	5	1	44	41	15	18	0	4.30
Barney Schultz	R	37	1	3	.250	14	30	0	0	49	35	11	29	0	1.65
1 Bobby Shantz	L	38	1	3	.250	0	16	0	0	17	14	7	12	0	3.18
Harry Fanok (SA)	R	24	0	0	—	0	4	0	0	8	5	10	5	0	5.63
Dave Bakenhaster	R	19	0	0	—	0	2	0	0	3	9	1	0	0	0.00
3 Jack Spring	L	31	0	0	—	0	3	0	0	3	8	1	0	0	3.00
Dave Dowling	L	21	0	0	—	0	1	0	0	2	1	0	0	0	0.00

CINCINNATI — 2nd (tie) 92-70 .568 1 — FRED HUTCHINSON (IL) 60-49 .550 DICK SISLER 32-21 .604

NAME	G by Pos	B	AGE	G	AB	R	H	2B	3B	HR	RBI	BB	SO	SB	BA	SA
	TOTALS		26	163	5561	660	1383	220	38	130	605	457	974	90	.249	.372
Deron Johnson	1B131, OF10, 3B1	R	25	140	477	63	130	24	4	21	79	37	98	4	.273	.472
Pete Rose	2B128	B	23	136	516	64	139	13	2	4	34	36	51	4	.269	.326
Leo Cardenas	SS163	R	25	163	597	61	150	32	2	9	69	41	110	4	.251	.357
Steve Boros	3B114	R	27	117	370	31	95	12	3	2	31	47	43	4	.257	.322
Frank Robinson	OF156	R	28	156	568	103	174	38	6	29	96	79	67	23	.306	.548
Vada Pinson	OF156	L	25	156	625	99	166	23	11	23	84	42	99	8	.266	.448
Tommy Harper	OF92, 3B2	R	23	102	317	42	77	5	2	4	22	39	56	24	.243	.309
Johnny Edwards	C120	L	26	126	423	47	119	23	1	7	55	34	65	1	.281	.390
Marty Keough	OF81, 1B4	L	30	109	276	29	71	9	1	9	28	22	58	1	.257	.395
Gordy Coleman	1B49	L	29	89	198	18	48	6	2	5	27	13	30	2	.242	.369
Chico Ruiz	3B49, 2B30	R	25	77	311	33	76	13	2	2	16	7	41	11	.244	.318
Mel Queen	OF20	L	22	48	95	7	19	2	0	2	4	4	19	0	.200	.284
1 Bobby Klaus	2B18, 3B11, SS3	R	26	40	93	10	17	5	1	2	6	4	13	1	.183	.323
Don Pavletich	C27, 1B1	R	25	34	91	12	22	4	0	5	11	10	17	0	.242	.451
Hal Smith	C20	R	33	32	66	6	8	1	0	3	6	3	12	0	.121	.136
1 Bob Skinner	OF12	L	32	25	59	6	13	3	0	1	5	4	12	0	.220	.424
Tony Perez	1B6	R	22	12	25	1	2	1	0	0	1	3	9	0	.080	.120
Jimmie Coker	C11	R	28	11	32	3	10	2	0	1	4	3	5	0	.313	.469
Johnny Temple		R	35	6	3	0	0	0	0	0	0	0	2	1	.000	.000
Tommy Helms		R	23	2	1	0	0	0	0	0	0	0	1	0	.000	.000

NAME	T	AGE	W	L	PCT	SV	G	GS	CG	IP	H	BB	SO	SHO	ERA
		29	92	70	.568	35	163	163	54	1467	1306	436	1122	14	3.07
Jim O'Toole	L	27	17	7	.708	0	30	30	9	220	194	51	145	3	2.66
Jim Maloney	R	24	15	10	.600	0	31	31	11	216	175	83	214	2	2.71
Bob Purkey	R	34	11	9	.550	1	34	25	9	196	181	49	78	2	3.03
Joey Jay	R	28	11	11	.500	2	34	23	10	183	167	36	134	0	3.39
Sammy Ellis	R	23	10	3	.769	14	52	1	0	122	101	28	125	0	2.58
Joe Nuxhall	L	35	9	8	.529	2	32	22	7	155	146	51	111	4	4.06
John Tsitouris	R	28	9	13	.409	2	37	24	6	175	178	75	146	1	3.81
Billy McCool	L	19	6	5	.545	7	40	3	0	89	66	29	87	0	2.43
Bill Henry	L	36	2	2	.500	6	37	0	0	52	31	12	28	0	0.87
1 Al Worthington	R	35	1	0	1.000	0	6	0	0	7	14	2	6	0	10.29
Jim Dickson	R	26	1	0	1.000	0	4	0	0	5	4	5	6	0	7.20
Chet Nichols	L	33	0	0	—	0	3	0	0	5	4	0	3	0	6.00
2 Ryne Duren	R	35	0	2	.000	1	26	0	0	44	41	15	39	0	2.86

PHILADELPHIA — 2nd (tie) 92-70 .568 1 — GENE MAUCH

NAME	G by Pos	B	AGE	G	AB	R	H	2B	3B	HR	RBI	BB	SO	SB	BA	SA
	TOTALS		27	162	5493	693	1415	241	51	130	649	440	924	30	.258	.391
John Herrnstein	OF69, 1B68	L	26	125	303	38	71	12	4	6	25	22	67	1	.234	.360
Tony Taylor	2B150	R	28	154	570	62	143	13	6	4	46	46	74	13	.251	.316
Bobby Wine	SS108, 3B18	R	25	126	283	28	60	8	3	4	34	21	54	3	.212	.304
Dick Allen	3B162	R	22	162	632	125	201	38	13	29	91	67	138	3	.318	.557
Johnny Callison	OF162	L	25	162	654	101	179	30	10	31	104	36	95	6	.274	.492
Tony Gonzalez	OF119	L	27	131	421	55	117	25	3	4	40	44	74	0	.278	.380
Wes Covington	OF108	L	32	129	339	37	95	18	0	13	58	38	50	0	.280	.448
Clay Dalrymple	C124	L	27	127	382	36	91	16	3	6	46	39	40	0	.238	.343
Ruben Amaro	SS79, 1B58, 2B3, 3B3, OF1	R	28	129	299	31	79	11	0	4	34	16	37	1	.264	.341
Cookie Rojas	OF70, 2B20, SS18, 3B1, C1	R	25	109	340	58	99	19	5	2	31	22	17	1	.291	.394
Gus Triandos	C64, 1B1	R	33	73	183	17	47	9	0	8	33	26	41	0	.250	.426
Johnny Briggs	OF19, 1B1	L	20	61	66	16	17	2	0	1	6	9	12	1	.258	.333
Danny Cater (BA)	OF39, 1B7, 3B1	R	24	60	152	13	45	9	1	1	13	7	15	1	.296	.388
1 Roy Sievers	1B33	R	37	49	120	7	22	3	1	4	16	13	20	0	.183	.325
Alex Johnson	OF35	R	21	43	109	7	33	7	1	4	18	6	26	1	.303	.495
2 Frank Thomas (BG)	1B36	R	35	39	143	20	42	11	0	7	26	5	12	0	.294	.517
3 Vic Power	1B17	R	36	18	48	1	10	4	0	0	3	2	3	0	.208	.292
Adolfo Phillips	OF4	R	22	13	13	4	3	0	0	0	1	1	3	0	.231	.231
Costen Shockley	1B9	L	22	11	35	4	8	0	0	1	6	3	6	0	.229	.314
Don Hoak		R	36	10	1	1	0	0	0	0	0	0	0	0	.000	.000
Pat Corrales		R	23	2	1	1	0	0	0	0	0	0	1	0	.000	.000

NAME	T	AGE	W	L	PCT	SV	G	GS	CG	IP	H	BB	SO	SHO	ERA
		26	92	70	.568	41	162	162	37	1461	1402	440	1009	17	3.36
Jim Bunning	R	32	19	8	.704	2	41	39	13	284	248	46	219	5	2.63
Chris Short	L	26	17	9	.654	2	42	31	12	221	174	51	181	4	2.20
Art Mahaffey	R	26	12	9	.571	0	34	29	2	157	161	82	80	2	4.53
Dennis Bennett	L	24	12	14	.462	1	41	32	7	208	222	58	125	2	3.68
Ray Culp (SA)	R	22	8	7	.533	0	30	19	3	135	139	56	96	1	4.13
Jack Baldschun	R	27	6	9	.400	21	71	0	0	118	111	40	96	0	3.13
2 Ed Roebuck	R	32	5	3	.625	12	60	0	0	77	55	25	42	0	2.22
Rick Wise	R	18	5	3	.625	0	25	8	0	69	78	25	39	0	4.04
John Boozer	R	24	3	4	.429	2	22	3	0	60	64	18	51	0	5.10
Dallas Green	R	29	2	1	.667	0	25	0	0	42	63	14	21	0	5.79
1 Johnny Klippstein	R	36	1	1	.500	1	11	0	0	22	13	8	18	0	4.09
3 Bobby Shantz	L	38	1	1	.500	0	14	0	0	32	23	6	18	0	2.25
Bobby Locke	R	30	0	0	—	0	9	0	0	19	21	6	11	0	2.84
Morrie Steevens	L	23	0	0	—	0	3	0	0	3	5	1	3	0	9.00
1 Ryne Duren	R	35	0	0	—	0	2	0	0	4	3	5	5	0	6.00
1 Gary Kroll	R	22	0	0	—	0	2	0	0	3	1	2	1	0	9.00
Dave Bennett	R	18	0	0	—	0	1	0	0	1	2	0	1	0	9.00
Cal McLish (SA)	R	38	0	1	.000	0	2	1	0	5	6	1	6	1	3.60

SAN FRANCISCO — 4th 90-72 .556 3 — AL DARK

NAME	G by Pos	B	AGE	G	AB	R	H	2B	3B	HR	RBI	BB	SO	SB	BA	SA
	TOTALS		28	162	5535	656	1360	185	38	165	608	505	900	64	.246	.382
Orlando Cepeda	1B139, OF1	R	26	142	529	75	161	27	2	31	97	43	83	9	.304	.539
Hal Lanier	2B98, SS3	R	21	98	383	40	105	16	3	2	28	5	44	2	.274	.347
Jose Pagan	SS132, OF8	R	29	134	367	33	82	10	1	1	28	35	66	5	.223	.264
Jim Ray Hart	3B149, OF6	R	22	153	566	71	162	15	6	31	81	47	94	5	.286	.498
Jesus Alou (LJ)	OF108	R	22	115	376	42	103	11	0	3	28	13	35	4	.274	.327
Willie Mays	OF155, 1B1, SS1, 3B1	R	33	157	578	121	171	21	9	47	111	82	72	19	.296	.607
Willie McCovey	OF83, 1B26	L	26	130	364	55	80	14	1	18	54	61	73	2	.220	.412
Tom Haller	C113, OF3	L	27	117	388	43	98	14	3	16	48	55	51	4	.253	.428
Jim Davenport	SS64, 3B41, 2B30	R	30	116	297	24	70	10	6	2	26	29	46	2	.236	.330
Harvey Kuenn	OF88, 1B11, 3B2	R	33	111	351	42	92	16	2	4	22	35	32	0	.262	.353
Matty Alou (BW)	OF80	L	25	110	250	28	66	4	2	1	14	11	25	5	.264	.308
Duke Snider	OF43	L	37	91	167	16	35	7	0	4	17	22	40	0	.210	.323
Chuck Hiller	2B60, 3B1	L	29	80	205	21	37	8	1	3	11	17	23	1	.180	.244
Del Crandall	C65	R	34	69	195	12	45	8	1	3	11	22	21	0	.231	.328
Cap Peterson	OF10, 1B2, 2B1, 3B1	R	21	66	74	8	15	1	1	1	8	3	20	0	.203	.284
Jose Cardenal	OF16	R	20	20	15	3	0	0	0	0	2	3	2	0	.000	.000
Gil Garrido	SS14	R	23	14	25	1	2	0	0	0	1	2	7	1	.080	.080
Randy Hundley	C2	R	22	3	1	1	0	0	0	0	0	0	1	0	.000	.000

NAME	T	AGE	W	L	PCT	SV	G	GS	CG	IP	H	BB	SO	SHO	ERA
		29	90	72	.556	30	162	162	48	1476	1348	480	1023	17	3.19
Juan Marichal	R	26	21	8	.724	0	33	33	22	269	241	52	206	4	2.48
Gaylord Perry	R	25	12	11	.522	5	44	19	5	206	179	43	155	2	2.75
Bob Hendley	R	25	10	11	.476	0	30	29	4	163	161	59	104	1	3.64
Ron Herbel	R	26	9	9	.500	1	40	22	7	161	162	61	98	2	3.07
Billy O'Dell	L	31	9	9	.500	3	36	8	1	85	82	35	54	0	5.40
Bob Shaw	R	31	7	6	.538	11	61	1	0	93	105	31	57	0	3.77
Bobby Bolin	R	25	6	6	.500	4	38	23	5	175	143	77	146	3	2.92
Jim Duffalo (BR)	R	28	5	1	.833	3	35	1	0	74	57	31	55	0	2.92
Jack Sanford (SJ)	R	35	5	7	.417	1	18	17	3	106	91	37	64	1	3.31
Billy Pierce	L	37	3	0	1.000	4	18	1	0	40	40	10	29	0	2.20
John Pregenzer	R	28	2	0	1.000	0	13	0	0	18	21	11	8	0	5.00
Masanori Murakami	L	20	1	0	1.000	1	9	0	0	15	8	1	15	0	1.80
Dick Estelle	L	22	1	2	.333	0	6	0	0	22	30	23	23	0	9.00
Ken MacKenzie	L	30	0	0	—	1	10	0	0	9	9	3	5	0	5.00
1 Don Larsen	R	34	0	1	.000	0	6	0	0	10	10	6	6	0	4.50

MILWAUKEE — 5th 88-74 .543 5 — BOBBY BRAGAN

NAME	G by Pos	B	AGE	G	AB	R	H	2B	3B	HR	RBI	BB	SO	SB	BA	SA
	TOTALS		28	162	5591	803	1522	274	32	159	755	486	825	53	.272	.418
Gene Oliver	1B76, C1	R	28	93	279	45	77	15	1	13	49	17	41	3	.276	.477
Frank Bolling	2B117	R	32	120	383	40	105	16	3	3	34	21	44	0	.199	.278
Denis Menke	SS141, 2B15, 3B6	R	23	151	505	79	143	29	5	20	65	68	77	4	.283	.479
Eddie Mathews	3B128, 1B2	L	32	141	502	83	171	19	1	23	74	85	100	2	.233	.412
Hank Aaron	OF139, 2B11	R	30	145	570	103	187	30	2	24	95	62	46	22	.328	.514
Lee Maye	OF135, 3B5	L	29	153	568	96	179	44	5	10	74	34	54	5	.304	.447
Rico Carty	OF121	R	24	133	455	72	150	28	4	22	88	43	78	1	.330	.554
Joe Torre	C96, 1B70	R	23	154	601	87	193	36	5	20	109	36	67	2	.321	.498
Felipe Alou (KJ)	OF92, 1B8	R	29	121	415	60	105	26	3	9	51	30	41	5	.253	.395
Ty Cline	OF54, 1B6	L	25	101	116	22	35	4	2	1	13	8	22	1	.302	.397
Ed Bailey	C80	L	33	98	277	31	70	11	1	5	34	34	39	2	.262	.362
Mike de la Hoz	2B25, 3B25, SS8	R	25	78	189	25	55	7	1	4	12	14	22	1	.291	.402
Woody Woodward	2B40, SS18, 3B7, 1B1	R	21	77	115	18	24	2	1	0	11	6	28	0	.209	.243
Gary Kolb	OF14, 3B7, 2B6, C2	L	24	36	64	7	12	1	0	0	2	6	10	1	.188	.203
1 Len Gabrielson	1B12, OF2	L	24	24	38	0	7	2	0	0	1	5	8	0	.184	.237
Sandy Alomar	SS19	R	20	19	53	1	9	2	0	0	3	1	6	1	.245	.264
Lou Klimchock	3B4, 2B2	L	24	10	21	3	7	2	0	1	3	0	2	0	.333	.429
Ethan Blackaby	OF3	L	24	9	12	4	1	0	0	0	0	3	5	0	.083	.083
2 Merritt Ranew	C3	L	26	9	17	1	2	0	0	0	1	0	6	0	.118	.118
1 Roy McMillan	SS8	R	34	8	13	1	4	1	0	0	3	1	4	0	.308	.308
Bill Southworth	3B2	R	18	3	7	1	2	0	0	0	0	0	3	0	.286	.714
Gus Bell		L	35	3	3	0	0	0	0	0	0	0	1	0	.000	.000
Phil Roof	C1	R	23	1	1	0	0	0	0	0	0	0	0	0	.000	.000

NAME	T	AGE	W	L	PCT	SV	G	GS	CG	IP	H	BB	SO	SHO	ERA
		29	88	74	.543	39	162	162	45	1435	1411	452	906	14	4.11
Tony Cloninger	R	23	19	14	.576	2	38	34	15	243	206	82	163	3	3.56
Denny Lemaster	L	25	17	11	.607	1	39	35	9	221	216	75	185	3	4.15
Hank Fischer	R	24	11	10	.524	2	37	28	9	168	177	39	99	5	4.02
Wade Blasingame	L	20	9	5	.643	2	28	17	3	111	113	51	70	1	4.23
Bob Sadowski	R	26	9	10	.474	5	41	18	3	167	159	56	96	0	4.10
Warren Spahn	L	43	6	13	.316	4	38	25	4	174	204	52	78	1	5.28
Billy Hoeft	L	32	6	3	.667	4	42	0	0	73	76	18	47	0	3.82
Bobby Tiefenauer	R	34	4	6	.400	13	43	0	0	73	61	18	48	0	3.21
Clay Carroll	R	23	2	0	1.000	1	11	0	0	20	15	3	17	0	1.80
Chi Chi Olivo	R	38	2	1	.667	5	30	0	0	60	55	21	45	0	3.75
Jack Smith	R	28	2	2	.500	0	22	0	0	31	28	11	19	0	3.77
3 Frank Lary	R	34	1	0	1.000	0	3	0	0	8	11	4	7	0	3.38
Arnie Umbach	R	21	1	0	1.000	0	4	0	0	8	11	4	7	0	4.50
Dan Schneider (XJ)	R	21	1	2	.333	0	36	0	0	38	36	13	14	0	5.50
Phil Niekro	R	25	0	0	—	0	10	0	0	15	15	7	4	0	4.80
Dave Eilers	R	27	0	0	—	0	9	0	0	11	11	0	9	0	4.50
Cecil Butler	R	23	0	0	—	0	2	0	0	3	6	2	3	0	9.00
Dick Kelley (AJ)	L	24	0	0	—	0	4	0	0	6	3	6	3	0	18.00
John Braun	R	24	0	0	—	0	1	0	0	1	2	0	1	0	9.00

LOS ANGELES 6th (tie) 80-82 .494 13 WALT ALSTON

NAME	G by Pos	B	AGE	G	AB	R	H	2B	3B	HR	RBI	BB	SO	SB	BA	SA
TOTALS			27	164	5499	614	1375	180	39	79	555	438	893	141	.250	.340
Ron Fairly	1B141	L	25	150	454	62	116	19	5	10	74	65	59	4	.256	.385
Nate Oliver	2B98, SS1	R	23	99	321	28	78	9	0	0	21	31	57	7	.243	.271
Maury Wills	SS149, 3B6	B	31	158	630	81	173	15	5	2	34	41	73	53	.275	.324
Jim Gilliam	3B86, 2B25, OF2	B	35	116	334	44	76	8	3	2	27	42	21	4	.228	.287
Frank Howard	OF122	R	27	134	433	60	98	13	2	24	69	51	113	1	.226	.432
Willie Davis	OF155	L	24	157	613	91	180	23	7	12	77	22	59	42	.294	.413
Tommy Davis	OF148	R	25	152	592	70	163	24	5	14	86	29	68	11	.275	.397
Johnny Roseboro	C128	L	31	134	414	42	119	24	1	3	45	44	61	3	.287	.372
Wes Parker	OF69, 1B31	B	24	124	214	29	55	7	1	3	10	14	45	5	.257	.341
Dick Tracewski	2B56, 3B30, SS19	R	29	106	304	31	75	13	4	1	26	31	61	3	.247	.326
Derrell Griffith	3B35, OF29	L	20	78	238	27	69	16	2	4	23	5	21	5	.290	.424
Wally Moon	OF23	L	34	68	118	8	26	2	1	2	9	12	22	1	.220	.305
Doug Camilli	C46	R	27	50	123	1	22	3	0	0	10	8	19	0	.179	.203
Lee Walls	OF6, C1	R	31	37	28	1	5	1	0	0	3	2	12	0	.179	.214
Johnny Werhas	3B28	R	26	29	83	6	16	2	1	0	8	13	12	0	.193	.241
Jeff Torborg	C27	R	22	28	43	4	10	1	1	0	4	3	8	0	.233	.302
Ken McMullen	1B13, 3B4, OF3	R	22	24	67	3	14	0	0	1	2	3	7	0	.209	.254
Bart Shirley	3B10, SS8	B	24	18	62	6	17	1	1	0	7	4	8	0	.274	.323
Willie Crawford	OF4	L	17	10	16	3	5	1	0	0	0	1	1	0	.313	.375

NAME	T	AGE	W	L	PCT	SV	G	GS	CG	IP	H	BB	SO	SHO	ERA
TOTALS		26	80	82	.494	27	164	164	47	1484	1289	458	1062	19	2.95
Sandy Koufax	L	28	19	5	.792	1	29	28	15	223	154	53	223	7	1.74
Don Drysdale	R	27	18	16	.529	0	40	40	21	321	242	68	237	5	2.19
Bob Miller	R	25	7	7	.500	9	74	2	0	138	115	63	94	0	2.61
Phil Ortega	R	24	7	9	.438	1	34	25	4	157	149	56	107	3	4.01
Joe Moeller	R	21	7	13	.350	0	27	24	1	145	153	31	97	0	4.22
Ron Perranoski	L	28	5	7	.417	14	72	0	0	125	128	46	79	0	3.10
Jim Brewer	R	26	4	3	.571	1	34	5	1	93	79	25	63	1	3.00
Larry Miller	L	27	4	8	.333	0	16	14	1	80	87	28	50	0	4.16
Howie Reed	R	27	3	4	.429	1	26	7	0	90	79	36	52	0	3.20
John Purdin	R	21	2	0	1.000	0	3	2	1	16	6	8	1	0	0.56
Pete Richert	R	24	2	3	.400	0	8	6	1	35	38	18	25	1	4.11
Nick Willhite	L	23	2	4	.333	0	10	7	2	44	43	13	24	0	3.68
Bill Singer	R	20	0	1	.000	0	2	0	0	14	11	12	3	0	3.21
Johnny Podres (EJ)	L	31	0	2	.000	0	3	5	3	0	0	0		0	15.00

PITTSBURGH 6th (tie) 80-82 .494 13 DANNY MURTAUGH

NAME	G by Pos	B	AGE	G	AB	R	H	2B	3B	HR	RBI	BB	SO	SB	BA	SA
TOTALS			27	162	5566	663	1469	225	54	121	630	408	970	39	.264	.389
Donn Clendenon	1B119	R	28	133	457	53	129	23	8	12	64	26	96	12	.282	.446
Bill Mazeroski	2B162	R	27	162	601	66	161	22	8	10	64	29	52	1	.268	.381
Dick Schofield	SS111	B	29	121	398	50	98	22	5	3	36	54	60	1	.246	.349
Bob Bailey	3B105, OF35, SS2	R	21	143	530	73	149	26	3	11	51	44	78	10	.281	.404
Roberto Clemente	OF154	R	29	155	622	95	211	40	7	12	87	51	87	5	.339	.484
Bill Virdon	OF134	L	33	145	473	59	115	11	3	3	27	30	48	1	.243	.298
Manny Mota	OF93, 2B1, C1	R	26	115	271	43	75	8	3	5	32	10	31	4	.277	.384
Jim Pagliaroni	C96	R	26	97	302	33	89	12	3	10	36	41	56	1	.295	.454
Willie Stargell	OF59, 1B50	L	24	117	421	53	115	19	7	21	78	17	92	1	.273	.501
Jerry Lynch	OF78	L	33	114	297	35	81	14	2	16	66	26	57	0	.273	.495
Gene Freese	3B72	R	30	99	289	33	65	13	2	9	40	19	45	1	.225	.377
Gene Alley	SS61, 3B3, 2B1	R	23	81	209	30	44	3	1	6	13	21	56	0	.211	.321
1 Smoky Burgess	C44	L	37	68	171	9	42	3	1	2	17	13	14	2	.246	.310
Orlando McFarlane	C35, OF1	R	26	37	78	5	19	5	0	1	4	2	27	0	.244	.308
Dave Wissman	OF10	L	23	16	27	2	4	0	0	0	0	1	9	1	.148	.148
Rex Johnston	OF8	R	27	14	7	1	0	0	0	0	0	3	0	0	.000	.000
Jerry May	C11	R	20	11	31	1	8	0	0	0	0	1	10	0	.258	.258
Julio Gotay	2S	R	25	3	2	1	1	0	0	0	0	1	0	0	.500	.500

NAME	T	AGE	W	L	PCT	SV	G	GS	CG	IP	H	BB	SO	SHO	ERA
TOTALS		28	80	82	.494	29	162	162	42	1444	1429	476	951	14	3.52
Bob Veale	L	28	18	12	.600	0	40	38	14	280	222	124	250	1	2.73
Bob Friend	R	33	13	18	.419	0	35	35	13	240	253	50	128	3	3.34
Vern Law	R	34	12	13	.480	0	35	29	7	192	203	32	93	5	3.61
Joe Gibbon	L	29	10	7	.588	0	28	24	3	147	145	54	97	0	3.67
Al McBean	R	26	8	3	.727	22	58	0	0	90	76	17	41	0	1.90
Steve Blass	R	22	5	8	.385	0	24	13	3	105	107	45	67	1	4.03
Don Schwall	R	28	4	3	.571	0	15	9	0	50	53	15	36	0	4.32
Roy Face	R	36	3	3	.500	4	55	0	0	80	82	27	63	0	5.18
Frank Bork	L	23	2	2	.500	2	33	2	0	42	51	11	31	0	4.07
Tom Butters	R	26	2	2	.500	0	28	4	0	64	52	37	58	0	2.39
Bob Priddy	R	24	1	2	.333	1	19	0	0	34	35	15	23	0	3.97
Don Cardwell (SJ)	R	28	1	2	.333	0	4	1	1	19	15	7	10	0	2.84
Tommie Sisk	R	22	1	4	.200	0	42	1	0	61	91	29	35	0	6.20
Freddie Green	L	30	0	0	—	0	7	0	0	9	11	1	4	0	1.29
John Gelnar	R	21	0	0	.000	0	3	0	0	9	11	1	4	0	5.00
Earl Francis	R	27	0	1	.000	0	2	1	0	7	11	6	6	0	9.00
2 Wilbur Wood	L	22	0	0	.000	0	3	2	1	17	16	11	7	0	3.71

CHICAGO 8th 76-86 .469 17 BOB KENNEDY

NAME	G by Pos	B	AGE	G	AB	R	H	2B	3B	HR	RBI	BB	SO	SB	BA	SA
TOTALS			27	162	5545	649	1391	239	50	145	609	499	1041	70	.251	.390
Ernie Banks	1B157	R	33	157	591	67	156	29	6	23	95	36	84	1	.264	.450
Joey Amalfitano	2B86, 1B1, SS1	R	30	100	324	51	78	19	6	4	27	40	42	2	.241	.373
Andre Rodgers	SS126	R	29	129	448	50	107	17	3	12	46	53	88	5	.239	.371
Ron Santo	3B161	R	24	161	592	94	185	33	13	30	114	86	96	3	.313	.564
2 Len Gabrielson	OF68, 1B8	L	24	89	272	27	67	11	2	5	23	19	37	3	.246	.357
Billy Cowan	OF134	R	25	139	497	52	120	16	4	19	50	18	128	12	.241	.404
Billy Williams	OF162	L	26	162	645	100	201	39	2	33	98	59	84	10	.312	.532
Dick Bertell	C110	R	28	112	353	29	84	11	3	4	35	33	67	2	.238	.320
Jimmy Stewart	2B61, SS45, OF4, 3B1	B	25	132	415	59	105	17	0	3	33	49	61	10	.253	.316
Leo Burke	OF18, 2B5, 3B4, 1B2, C1	R	30	59	103	11	27	3	1	1	14	7	31	0	.262	.340
Jimmie Schaffer (BH)	C43	R	28	54	122	9	25	6	1	2	9	17	17	2	.205	.320
2 Doug Clemens	OF40	L	25	54	140	23	39	10	2	2	12	18	22	0	.279	.421
1 Lou Brock	OF52	L	25	52	215	30	54	9	2	2	14	13	40	10	.251	.340
Ellis Burton	OF29	B	27	42	105	12	20	3	2	1	7	17	22	4	.190	.314
Vic Roznovsky	C26	L	25	35	76	2	15	1	0	0	2	5	18	0	.197	.211
Ron Campbell	2B26	R	24	26	92	7	25	6	1	1	10	1	21	0	.272	.391
Billy Ott	OF10	B	23	20	39	4	7	3	0	0	1	3	10	0	.179	.256
1 Merritt Ranew	C9	L	26	16	33	0	3	0	0	0	1	2	6	0	.091	.091
Don Landrum	OF1	L	28	11	11	2	0	0	0	0	0	0	4	0	.000	.000
John Boccabella	1B5, OF2	R	23	9	23	4	9	2	1	0	6	0	3	0	.391	.565
Don Kessinger	SS4	R	21	4	12	1	2	0	0	0	0	1	2	0	.167	.167

Paul Popovich 23 R 1-1, Ken Hubbs (DD) 22

NAME	T	AGE	W	L	PCT	SV	G	GS	CG	IP	H	BB	SO	SHO	ERA
TOTALS		30	76	86	.469	19	162	162	58	1445	1510	423	737	11	4.08
Larry Jackson	R	33	24	11	.686	0	40	38	19	298	265	58	148	3	3.14
Bob Buhl	R	35	15	14	.517	0	36	35	11	228	208	68	107	3	3.83
Dick Ellsworth	L	24	14	18	.438	0	37	36	16	257	267	71	148	1	3.75
2 Lew Burdette	R	37	9	9	.500	0	28	18	8	131	152	19	40	2	4.88
2 Ernie Broglio	R	28	4	7	.364	1	18	16	3	100	111	30	46	0	4.05
Cal Koonce	R	23	3	0	1.000	0	31	0	0	31	30	7	17	0	2.03
Sterling Slaughter	R	22	2	4	.333	0	15	1	0	52	64	32	32	0	5.71
Don Elston	R	35	2	5	.286	1	48	0	0	54	68	34	26	0	5.33
Freddie Burdette	R	27	1	0	1.000	0	20	0	0	20	17	10	4	0	3.15
Paul Jaeckel	R	22	1	0	1.000	1	4	0	0	8	4	3	2	0	0.00
Lindy McDaniel	R	28	1	7	.125	15	63	0	0	95	104	23	71	0	3.88
Wayne Schurr	R	26	0	0	—	0	26	0	0	48	57	11	29	0	3.75
Lee Gregory	L	26	0	0	—	0	11	0	0	18	23	5	8	0	3.50
2 Jack Spring	L	31	0	0	—	0	15	0	0	6	4	2	1	0	6.00
Jack Warner	R	23	0	0	—	0	9	0	0	12	4	6	3	0	3.00
Dick Scott	L	31	0	0	—	0	2	0	0	4	10	1	1	0	13.50
2 Bobby Shantz	L	38	0	1	.000	0	20	0	0	11	15	6	12	0	5.73
John Flavin	L	22	0	1	.000	0	2	0	0	5	4	4	4	0	8.18
Paul Toth	R	29	0	2	.000	0	4	0	0	11	16	5	6	0	8.18
1 Glen Hobbie	R	28	0	3	.000	0	8	4	0	27	39	10	14	0	8.00
Fred Norman	L	21	0	4	.000	0	8	5	0	33	34	21	20	0	6.47

HOUSTON 9th 66-96 .407 27 HARRY CRAFT 61-88 .409 LUM HARRIS 5-8 .385

NAME	G by Pos	B	AGE	G	AB	R	H	2B	3B	HR	RBI	BB	SO	SB	BA	SA
TOTALS			27	162	5303	495	1214	162	41	70	452	381	872	40	.229	.315
Walt Bond	1B76, OF71	L	26	148	543	63	138	16	7	20	85	38	90	2	.254	.420
Nellie Fox	2B115	L	36	133	442	45	117	12	6	0	28	27	13	0	.265	.319
Eddie Kasko	SS128, 3B2	R	32	133	448	45	109	16	1	0	22	37	52	4	.243	.283
Bob Aspromonte	3B155	R	26	157	553	51	155	20	3	12	69	35	54	6	.280	.392
2 Joe Gaines	OF81	R	27	89	307	37	78	9	7	7	34	27	69	8	.254	.397
Mike White	OF72, 2B10, 3B3	R	25	89	280	30	76	11	3	0	27	20	47	1	.271	.332
Al Spangler	OF127	L	30	135	449	51	110	18	5	4	38	41	43	7	.245	.334
Jerry Grote	C98	R	21	100	298	26	54	9	3	3	24	20	75	0	.181	.262
Bob Lillis	2B52, SS43, 3B12	R	34	109	332	31	89	11	2	0	17	11	10	4	.268	.313
Rusty Staub	1B49, OF38	L	20	89	292	26	63	10	2	8	35	21	31	1	.216	.346
John Bateman	C72	R	23	74	221	18	42	8	0	5	19	17	48	0	.190	.294
Jim Wynn	OF64	R	22	67	219	19	49	7	0	5	18	24	58	5	.224	.324
Dave Roberts	1B34, OF4	L	31	61	125	9	23	4	1	1	7	14	28	0	.184	.256
Carroll Hardy	OF41	R	31	46	157	14	29	1	1	2	12	8	30	0	.185	.242
Jim Beauchamp	OF15, 1B2	R	24	23	55	6	9	2	2	0	5	4	16	0	.164	.309
Pete Runnels	1B14	L	36	22	51	3	10	1	0	0	4	8	5	0	.196	.216
Joe Morgan	2B10	L	20	10	37	4	7	0	0	0	1	0	0	0	.189	.189
Ivan Murrell	OF5	R	21	10	14	1	2	1	0	0	1	0	6	0	.143	.214
Walt Williams	OF5	R	20	9	9	1	0	0	0	0	0	0	2	0	.000	.000
Sonny Jackson	SS7	L	19	9	23	3	8	0	0	0	1	2	3	1	.348	.391
Johnny Weekly	OF5	R	27	8	15	0	2	0	0	0	1	1	7	0	.133	.133
John Hoffman	C5	L	20	6	15	1	1	0	0	0	0	1	7	0	.067	.067
Dave Adlesh	C3	R	20	3	10	0	2	0	0	0	0	1	2	0	.200	.200

Steve Hertz 19 R 0-4, Brock Davis 20 L 0-3

NAME	T	AGE	W	L	PCT	SV	G	GS	CG	IP	H	BB	SO	SHO	ERA
TOTALS		32	66	96	.407	31	162	162	30	1428	1421	353	852	9	3.41
Bob Bruce	R	31	15	9	.625	0	35	29	9	202	191	33	135	4	2.76
Dick Farrell	R	30	11	9	.524	0	32	27	7	198	196	52	117	0	3.27
Ken Johnson	R	31	11	16	.407	0	35	35	7	218	209	44	117	1	3.63
Jim Owens	R	30	8	7	.533	6	48	11	0	118	115	32	88	0	3.28
Don Nottebart	R	28	6	11	.353	0	28	24	2	157	165	37	90	0	3.90
Claude Raymond	R	27	5	5	.500	0	38	0	0	80	64	22	56	1	2.81
2 Don Larsen	R	34	4	8	.333	1	30	10	2	103	92	20	58	1	2.27
Hal Brown	R	39	3	15	.167	1	27	21	3	132	154	26	53	0	3.95
Hal Woodeshick	L	31	2	9	.182	23	61	0	0	78	73	32	58	0	2.77
Danny Coombs (MS)	L	22	1	1	.500	0	13	1	0	21	27	10	14	0	5.06
Larry Yellen	R	21	0	0	—	0	14	3	1	21	27	11	9	0	6.86
Dave Giusti	R	24	0	0	.000	0	9	4	0	21	23	7	16	0	3.12
Joe Hoerner	R	27	0	0	—	0	11	0	0	11	13	4	6	0	4.91
Gordon Jones	R	34	0	1	.000	0	34	0	0	50	58	14	28	0	4.14
Larry Dierker	R	17	0	1	.000	0	3	1	0	12	11	3	6	0	2.00
Chris Zachary	R	20	0	2	.000	0	9	4	0	24	26	13	21	0	9.00
Don Bradey	R	29	0	2	.000	0	2	1	0	6	6	1	2	0	22.50

Jim Umbricht (DD) 33

NEW YORK 10th 53-109 .327 40 CASEY STENGEL

NAME	G by Pos	B	AGE	G	AB	R	H	2B	3B	HR	RBI	BB	SO	SB	BA	SA
TOTALS			27	163	5566	569	1372	195	31	103	527	353	932	36	.246	.348
Ed Kranepool	1B104, OF6	L	19	119	420	47	108	19	4	10	45	32	50	0	.257	.393
Ron Hunt	2B109, 3B12	R	23	127	475	59	144	19	6	6	42	29	30	6	.303	.406
2 Roy McMillan	SS111	R	34	113	379	30	80	8	2	1	25	14	16	3	.211	.251
2 Charley Smith	3B85, SS36, OF13	R	26	127	443	40	106	12	0	20	58	18	101	2	.239	.402
Joe Christopher	OF145	R	28	154	543	78	163	26	8	16	76	48	92	6	.300	.466
Jim Hickman	OF113, 3B1	R	27	139	409	48	105	14	1	11	57	36	90	0	.257	.377
George Altman	OF109	L	31	124	422	48	97	14	1	9	47	18	70	4	.230	.332
Jesse Gonder	C97	L	28	131	341	28	92	11	1	7	35	29	65	0	.270	.377
Rod Kanehl	2B34, OF25, 3B19, 1B2	R	30	98	254	29	59	7	1	1	11	7	18	3	.232	.280
Hawk Taylor	C45, OF16	R	25	92	225	20	54	8	0	4	23	8	33	0	.240	.329
Larry Elliot	OF63	L	26	92	222	27	51	8	0	9	22	28	55	1	.228	.384
1 Frank Thomas	OF31, 1B19, 3B2	R	35	60	197	19	50	6	1	3	19	10	29	1	.254	.340
Chris Cannizzaro	C53	R	26	60	161	11	51	10	0	0	16	16	25	0	.311	.372
2 Bobby Klaus	3B28, 2B25, SS5	R	26	55	209	25	51	13	1	2	11	25	30	1	.244	.340
Amado Samuel	SS34, 3B17, 2B3	R	26	55	147	13	36	5	1	0	14	4	20	2	.245	.293
Dick Smith	1B18, OF13	L	25	46	94	14	21	1	1	1	6	4	29	1	.223	.309
Tim Harkness (SJ)	1B32	L	26	39	117	11	33	7	2	2	18	18	16	1	.282	.368
Johnny Stephenson	3B14, OF8	L	23	37	57	2	9	1	0	0	3	1	18	0	.158	.211
Wayne Graham	3B11	R	28	20	22	1	2	0	0	0	0	5	5	0	.091	.091
Al Moran	SS15, 3B1	R	25	16	22	0	5	0	0	0	0	1	4	0	.227	.227
Larry Burright	2B3	R	25	3	7	0	0	0	0	0	0	0	3	0	.000	.000

NAME	T	AGE	W	L	PCT	SV	G	GS	CG	IP	H	BB	SO	SHO	ERA
TOTALS		26	53	109	.327	15	163	163	40	1439	1511	466	717	10	4.25
Al Jackson	L	28	11	16	.407	1	40	31	11	213	229	60	112	3	4.27
Jack Fisher	R	25	10	17	.370	0	40	34	8	228	256	56	115	1	4.22
Tracy Stallard	R	26	10	20	.333	0	36	34	10	226	213	73	118	2	3.79
Galen Cisco	R	28	6	19	.240	0	36	25	5	192	182	54	78	2	3.61
Larry Bearnarth	R	23	5	5	.500	3	44	1	0	78	79	38	31	0	4.15
Willard Hunter	L	30	3	5	.375	2	42	4	0	49	49	26	41	0	4.41
Bill Wakefield	R	23	3	5	.375	2	62	4	0	120	103	61	61	0	3.60
2 Frank Lary	R	34	2	3	.400	1	13	8	3	57	62	14	27	1	4.58
Ron Locke	L	22	1	2	.333	0	25	3	0	41	46	21	19	0	3.51
Tom Parsons	R	24	1	2	.333	0	11	4	0	52	55	16	31	0	4.26
Dennis Ribant	R	22	1	5	.167	1	11	1	0	58	65	19	35	1	5.12
2 Tom Sturdivant	R	34	0	0	—	0	16	0	0	29	37	17	18	0	5.90
Steve Dillon	L	21	0	0	—	0	3	0	0	4	7	6	3	0	9.00
2 Gary Kroll	R	22	0	0	1.000	0	5	0	0	19	15	13	24	0	4.09
Craig Anderson	R	26	0	1	.000	0	5	0	0	7	9	5	5	0	5.54
Jay Hook	R	27	0	1	.000	0	8	2	0	30	37	8	14	0	3.60
Carl Willey (BJ)	R	33	0	2	.000	0	5	3	0	28	30	15	8	0	3.60
Jerry Hinsley	R	20	0	2	.000	0	10	1	0	17	25	11	7	0	5.40
Ed Bauta	R	29	0	3	.000	1	27	0	0	45	61	21	20	0	6.47
Darrell Sutherland	R	22	0	3	.000	1	27	2	0	43	32	12	6	0	7.67

1965 An Appointment with Disaster

Johnny Keane came to New York with all the confidence of a man handpicked by Destiny for greatness. His journey to the city near the sea from the midlands of America had proven to be the coup of the previous year. What Keane had accomplished was simply to tell his Cardinal boss, Gussie Busch, where to get off. Keane spent the 1964 season with St. Louis and unexpectedly brought home the pennant despite seeing clouds every time he looked up into the sky which, oddly enough, resembled Busch's axe. Keane's patience with the Cardinals and himself proved the fulfillment of an age old fantasy: getting the last laugh on the boss. His decision to abandon Busch warmed the hearts of every working man in the country. Keane had further savored his personal triumph by beating Yogi Berra and the Yankees for the world's championship in 1964. Now, in 1965, he was on his way to pilot the Yankees—American League pennant winners since what seemed like time immemorial and the favorites to win an unprecedented sixth straight pennant. Such was not the case. Keane didn't know until it was too late that he had arrived just in time to preside over the collapse of an empire. The Bronx Bombers could never get untracked for Keane and skidded into sixth place, their lowest finish since 1925. Elston Howard's elbow, Mickey Mantle's shoulder, and Roger Maris' hand all kept them out of action for extended periods, and Jim Bouton was unable to win more than four games. Keane found himself replacing the star-studded cast of 1964 with the likes of Doc Edwards, Ray Barker, and Roger Repoz. Try as he may he could not prevent a resounding fall into the second division.

The Minnesota Twins captured 102 victories in picking up the fallen mantle of American League champion. Leading most of the way and ending with a seven-game margin over second-place Chicago, the Twins were powered by a heavy-hitting offense sparked by MVP Zoilo Versalles, batting champ Tony Oliva, and sluggers Harmon Killebrew, Jimmie Hall, Bob Allison, and Don Mincher. Killebrew started the year on first base, but was moved to third in June so that Mincher's bat could be fit into the lineup. Ace right-hander Camilo Pascual lost six weeks due to a torn muscle in his back, but Mudcat Grant came through with a league-pacing 21 wins to take up the slack. Jim Kaat and Jim Perry contributed 30 wins between them while reliever Al Worthington picked up ten victories and 21 saves.

The biggest story in the National League took place off the field. The directors of the Milwaukee Braves requested permission from the league to move to Atlanta, Georgia for the 1965 season. The league ruled that due to the year remaining on the Milwaukee stadium lease and due to threatened litigation on the part of the city of Milwaukee, the Braves had to remain in Milwaukee for 1965 but could move to Dixie in 1966. The lame-duck season turned into a much-publicized fiasco, with several crowds under 1,000 and an anemic season's attendance of 555,584. The decision to leave stirred some congressmen and generated much bitterness between the baseball establishment and the public over the wooing, using, and abandoning of the Wisconsin territory in the course of 13 years.

On the field, the bat of Juan Marichal made headlines—not for hitting baseballs, but for hitting the head of Johnny Roseboro. In an August 22 Dodger-Giant contest, words between Marichal and Roseboro led to Marichal's conking the catcher on the head with his bat. When tempers subsided, Marichal and the Giants found themselves on the short end of the stick. The ace right-hander received a fine of $1,750, a suspension of nine days, and was barred from accompanying the Giants on their final trip to Los Angeles—a move that would prove costly as the two clubs were in a torrid fight for the pennant. Marichal's suspension denied him at least one start down the all-important stretch drive.

The pennant race found the Dodgers, Giants, Pirates, and Reds all in contention as September began, with the two California teams pulling away during the month with winning streaks of 13 for the Dodgers and 14 for the Giants. The final outcome saw the Dodgers take the flag by two games over their Northern Californian rivals, as the temper outburst by Marichal came home to roost.

The Dodger attack was strictly popgun with a fantastic array of pitching. Maury Wills led the offense with a .286 mark and 94 stolen bases—which gave him the theft title for the sixth year in a row. Last in the league in home runs, the Dodger attack received a boost when 31-year-old Lou Johnson was recalled to play left field after Tommy Davis broke an ankle. Johnson hit 12 home runs to tie Jim Lefebvre for the club lead. But what the Dodgers lacked in power, they made up for in pitching as Sandy Koufax and Don Drysdale provided an unparalleled one-two mound punch, winning 49 games between them with machine-like regularity.

The presence of Drysdale and Koufax made the Dodgers heavy Series favorites, but the Twins stunned the baseball world by defeating Drysdale and Koufax in the first two games. Claude Osteen then came on in the third game and shut out the Twins, and Drysdale and Koufax returned to give the Dodgers a 3-2 Series lead before Mudcat Grant evened it up for Minny. In game seven, Dodger manager Walter Alston deliberated on which ace to start. He choose Koufax, ignoring the two days of rest between starts for his ace-lefty, and Sandy replied with his second shutout in succession, to wrap up the crown for Los Angeles.

The 1965 season, as all the others before it, was not without its footnotes to baseball history. Casey Stengel broke his hip on the eve of his 75th birthday, an injury which finally forced the Old Professor to retire, thus ending a long managerial career which included ten pennants with the Yankees and three-and-one-half years of fun with the Mets.

A free-agent draft was instituted to help equalize the distribution of talent and to cut down on large bonus outlays to untried green talent. A new commissioner was named in General William Eckert, a man who soon became known for his lack of public presence, and the Houston Astrodome had opened in the spring—baseball's first enclosed, air-conditioned stadium. The park was billed as the Eighth Wonder of the world, and whether it was mattered little, for it was at least enough of a conversation piece to triple Houston's attendance to 2,151,470.

WORLD SERIES — LOS ANGELES (NL) 4 MINNESOTA (AL) 3

LINE SCORES

TEAM	1	2	3	4	5	6	7	8	9	10	11	12	R	H	E
Game 1 October 6 at Minnesota															
LA (NL)	0	1	0	0	0	0	0	0	1				2	10	1
MIN (AL)	0	1	6	0	0	1	0	0	X				8	10	0
Drysdale, Reed (3), Brewer (5), Perronoski (7)						Grant									
Game 2 October 7 at Minnesota															
LA	0	0	0	0	0	0	1	0	0				1	7	3
MIN	0	0	0	0	0	2	1	2	X				5	9	0
Koufax, Perranoski (7), Miller (8)						Kaat									
Game 3 October 9 at Los Angeles															
MIN	0	0	0	0	0	0	0	0	0				0	5	0
LA	0	0	0	2	1	1	0	0	X				4	10	1
Pascual, Merritt (6), Klippstein (8)						Osteen									
Game 4 October 10 at Los Angeles															
MIN	0	0	0	1	0	1	0	0	0				2	5	2
LA	1	1	0	1	0	3	0	1	X				7	10	0
Grant, Worthington (6), Pleis (8)						Drysdale									
Game 5 October 11 at Los Angeles															
MIN	0	0	0	0	0	0	0	0	0				0	4	1
LA	2	0	2	1	0	0	2	0	X				7	14	0
Kaat, Boswell (3), Perry (6)						Koufax									
Game 6 October 13 at Minnesota															
LA	0	0	0	0	0	0	1	0	0				1	6	1
MIN	0	0	0	2	0	3	0	0	X				5	6	1
Osteen, Reed (6), Miller (8)						Grant									
Game 7 October 14 at Minnesota															
LA	0	0	0	2	0	0	0	0	0				2	7	0
MIN	0	0	0	0	0	0	0	0	0				0	3	1
Koufax						Kaat, Worthington (4), Klippstein (6), Merritt (7), Perry (9)									

COMPOSITE BATTING

NAME	POS	G	AB	R	H	2B	3B	HR	RBI	BA
Los Angeles (NL) Totals		7	234	24	64	10	1	5	21	.274
Wills	SS	7	30	3	11	3	0	0	3	.367
Fairly	OF	7	29	7	11	3	0	2	6	.379
Gilliam	3B	7	28	2	6	1	0	0	2	.214
Johnson	OF	7	27	3	8	2	0	2	4	.296
W. Davis	OF	7	26	3	6	0	0	0	0	.231
Parker	1B	7	23	3	7	0	1	1	2	.304
Roseboro	C	7	21	1	6	1	0	0	3	.286
Tracewski	2B	6	17	0	2	0	0	0	0	.118
Lefebvre	2B	3	10	2	4	0	0	0	0	.400
Koufax	P	3	9	0	1	0	0	0	1	.111
Drysdale	P	3	5	0	0	0	0	0	0	.000
Osteen	P	2	3	0	1	0	0	0	0	.333
Crawford	PH	2	2	0	1	0	0	0	0	.500
Moon	PH	2	2	0	0	0	0	0	0	.000
Kennedy	3B	4	1	0	0	0	0	0	0	.000
LeJohn	PH	1	1	0	0	0	0	0	0	.000
Reed	P	2	0	0	0	0	0	0	0	—
Perranoski	P	2	0	0	0	0	0	0	0	—
Miller	P	2	0	0	0	0	0	0	0	—
Brewer	P	1	0	0	0	0	0	0	0	—
Minnesota (AL) Totals		7	215	20	42	7	2	6	19	.195
Versalles	SS	7	28	3	8	1	1	1	4	.286
Oliva	OF	7	26	2	5	1	0	2	2	.192
Battey	C	7	25	1	3	0	1	0	2	.120
Mincher	1B	7	23	3	3	0	0	1	1	.130
Killebrew	3B	7	21	2	6	0	0	1	2	.286
Quilici	2B	7	20	2	4	2	0	0	1	.200
Nossek	OF	6	20	0	4	0	0	0	0	.200
Allison	OF	5	16	3	2	1	0	1	2	.125
Valdespino	OF	5	11	1	3	1	0	0	0	.273
Grant	P	3	8	3	2	1	0	1	3	.250
Hall	OF	7	7	0	1	0	0	0	0	.143
Kaat	P	3	6	0	1	0	0	0	2	.167
Rollins	PH	3	2	0	0	0	0	0	0	.000
Zimmerman	C	2	1	0	0	0	0	0	0	.000
Pascual	P	1	1	0	0	0	0	0	0	.000
Merritt	P	2	0	0	0	0	0	0	0	—
Klippstein	P	2	0	0	0	0	0	0	0	—
Worthington	P	2	0	0	0	0	0	0	0	—
Perry	P	2	0	0	0	0	0	0	0	—
Pleis P 0-0, Boswell P 0-0										

COMPOSITE PITCHING

NAME	G	IP	H	BB	SO	W	L	SV	ERA
Los Angeles (NL) Totals	7	60	42	19	54	4	3	0	2.10
Koufax	3	24	13	5	29	2	1	0	0.38
Osteen	2	14	9	5	4	1	1	0	0.64
Drysdale	2	11.2	12	3	15	1	1	0	3.86
Perranoski	2	3.2	3	4	1	0	0	0	7.36
Reed	2	3.1	2	2	4	0	0	0	8.10
Brewer	1	2	3	1	0	0	0	0	4.50
Miller	2	1.1	0	0	0	0	0	0	0.00
Minnesota (AL) Totals	7	60	64	13	31	3	4	0	3.15
Grant	3	23	22	2	12	2	1	0	2.74
Kaat	3	14.1	18	2	6	1	2	0	3.77
Pascual	1	5	8	1	0	0	1	0	5.40
Worthington	2	4	2	2	2	0	0	0	0.00
Perry	2	4	5	2	4	0	0	0	4.50
Merritt	2	3.1	2	0	1	0	0	0	2.70
Klippstein	2	2.2	2	2	3	0	0	0	0.00
Boswell	1	2.2	3	2	3	0	0	0	3.38
Pleis	1	1	2	0	0	0	0	0	9.00

MINNESOTA — 1st 102-60 .630 — SAM MELE

NAME	G by Pos	B	AGE	G	AB	R	H	2B	3B	HR	RBI	BB	SO	SB	BA	SA
TOTALS			27	162	5488	774	1396	257	42	150	711	554	969	92	.254	.399
Don Mincher	1B99, OF1	L	27	128	346	43	87	17	3	22	65	49	73	1	.251	.509
Jerry Kindall	2B106, 3B10, SS7	R	30	125	342	41	67	12	1	6	36	36	97	2	.196	.289
Zoilo Versalles	SS160	R	25	160	666	126	182	45	12	19	77	41	122	27	.273	.462
Rich Rollins	3B112, 2B16	R	27	140	469	59	117	22	1	5	32	37	54	4	.249	.333
Tony Oliva	OF147	L	24	149	576	107	185	40	5	16	98	55	64	19	.321	.491
Jimmie Hall	OF141	L	27	148	522	81	149	25	4	20	86	51	79	14	.285	.464
Bob Allison	OF122, 1B3	R	30	135	438	71	102	14	5	23	78	73	114	10	.233	.445
Earl Battey	C128	R	30	131	394	36	117	22	2	6	60	50	23	0	.297	.409
Harmon Killebrew (EJ)	1B72, 3B44, OF1	R	29	113	401	78	108	16	1	25	75	72	69	0	.269	.501
Sandy Valdespino	OF57	L	26	108	245	38	64	8	2	1	22	20	28	7	.261	.322
Joe Nossek	OF48, 3B9	R	24	87	170	19	37	9	0	2	16	7	22	2	.218	.306
Jerry Zimmerman	C82	R	30	83	154	8	33	1	1	1	11	12	23	0	.214	.253
Frank Quilici	2B52, SS4	R	26	56	149	16	31	5	1	0	7	15	33	1	.208	.255
Andy Kosco	OF14, 1B2	R	23	23	55	3	13	4	0	1	6	1	15	0	.236	.364
Frank Kostro	2B7, 3B6, OF2	R	27	20	31	2	5	2	0	0	1	4	5	0	.161	.226
Bernie Allen (KJ)	2B10, 3B1	L	26	19	39	2	9	2	0	0	6	6	8	0	.231	.282
Cesar Tovar	2B4, 3B2, OF2, SS1	R	24	18	25	3	5	1	0	0	2	2	3	2	.200	.240
Rich Reese	1B6, OF1	L	23	14	7	0	2	1	0	0	0	0	2	0	.286	.429
Ted Uhlaender	OF4	L	25	13	22	1	4	0	0	0	1	0	1	1	.182	.182
John Sevcik	C11	R	22	12	16	1	1	1	0	0	0	0	5	0	.063	.125

NAME	T	AGE	W	L	PCT	SV	G	GS	CG	IP	H	BB	SO	SHO	ERA
		28	102	60	.630	45	162	162	32	1457	1278	503	934	12	3.14
Mudcat Grant	R	29	21	7	.750	0	41	39	14	270	252	61	142	6	3.30
Jim Kaat	L	26	18	11	.621	2	45	42	7	264	267	63	154	2	2.83
Jim Perry	R	29	12	7	.632	0	36	19	4	168	142	47	88	2	2.63
Al Worthington	R	36	10	7	.588	21	62	0	0	80	57	41	59	0	2.14
Johnny Klippstein	R	37	9	3	.750	5	56	0	0	76	59	31	59	0	2.25
Camilo Pascual (XJ)	R	31	9	3	.750	0	27	27	5	156	126	63	96	1	3.35
Dave Boswell (IL)	R	20	6	5	.545	0	27	12	1	106	77	46	85	0	3.40
Jim Merritt	L	21	5	4	.556	2	16	9	1	77	68	20	61	0	3.16
Dick Stigman	L	29	4	2	.667	4	33	8	0	70	59	33	70	0	4.37
Bill Pleis	L	27	4	4	.500	4	41	2	0	51	49	27	33	0	3.00
Jerry Fosnow	L	24	3	3	.500	2	29	0	0	47	33	25	35	0	4.40
Garry Roggenburk	L	25	1	0	1.000	2	13	0	0	13	12	6	0		3.43
Dwight Siebler	R	27	0	0	—	0	7	1	0	15	11	11	15	0	4.20
Pete Cimino	R	22	0	0	—	0	1	0	0	0	0	0	0	0	0.00
Mel Nelson	L	29	0	4	.000	3	28	3	0	55	57	23	31	0	4.09

CHICAGO — 2nd 95-67 .586 7 — AL LOPEZ

NAME	G by Pos	B	AGE	G	AB	R	H	2B	3B	HR	RBI	BB	SO	SB	BA	SA
TOTALS			27	162	5509	647	1354	200	38	125	587	533	916	50	.246	.364
Bill Skowron	1B145	R	34	146	559	63	153	24	3	18	78	32	77	1	.274	.424
Don Buford	2B139, 3B41	B	28	155	586	93	166	22	5	10	47	67	76	17	.283	.389
Ron Hansen	SS161, 2B1	R	27	162	587	61	138	23	4	11	66	60	73	1	.235	.344
Pete Ward	3B134, 2B1	L	25	138	507	62	125	25	3	10	57	56	83	2	.247	.367
Floyd Robinson	OF153	R	29	156	577	70	153	16	6	14	66	76	51	4	.265	.385
Ken Berry	OF156	R	24	157	472	51	103	17	4	12	42	28	96	4	.218	.347
Danny Cater	OF127, 3B11, 1B3	R	25	142	514	74	139	18	4	14	55	33	65	3	.270	.403
Johnny Romano	C111, OF4, 1B2	R	30	122	356	39	86	11	0	18	48	59	74	0	.242	.424
Tommy McCraw	1B72, OF64	L	24	133	273	38	65	12	1	5	21	25	48	12	.238	.344
J. C. Martin	C112, 1B4, 3B2	L	28	119	230	21	60	12	0	2	21	24	29	2	.261	.339
Al Weis	2B74, SS7, 3B2, OF2	B	27	103	135	29	40	4	3	1	12	12	22	4	.296	.393
Smoky Burgess	C5	L	38	80	77	2	22	4	0	2	24	11	7	0	.286	.416
Dave Nicholson	OF36	R	25	54	85	11	13	2	1	2	12	9	40	0	.153	.271
1 Jimmie Schaffer	C14	R	29	17	31	2	6	3	1	0	1	3	4	0	.194	.355
2 Gene Freese	3B8	R	31	17	32	2	9	0	1	1	4	5	9	0	.281	.438
Jim Hicks	OF5	R	25	13	19	2	5	1	0	1	2	0	9	0	.263	.474
Bill Voss	OF10	L	21	11	33	4	6	0	1	0	3	3	5	0	.182	.333
Tommie Agee (BH)	OF9	R	22	10	19	2	3	1	0	0	3	2	6	0	.158	.211
Marv Staehle		L	23	7	7	0	3	0	0	0	2	0	0	0	.429	.429
Duane Josephson	C4	R	23	4	9	2	1	0	0	0	0	0	1	0	.111	.111
Dick Kenworthy		R	24	3	1	0	0	0	0	0	0	0	1	0	.000	.000
Bill Heath		L	26	1	1	0	0	0	0	0	0	0	0	0	.000	.000

NAME	T	AGE	W	L	PCT	SV	G	GS	CG	IP	H	BB	SO	SHO	ERA
		28	95	67	.586	53	162	162	21	1482	1261	460	946	14	2.99
Eddie Fisher	R	28	15	7	.682	24	82	0	0	165	118	43	90	0	2.40
Tommy John	L	22	14	7	.667	3	39	27	6	184	162	58	126	1	3.08
John Buzhardt	R	28	13	8	.619	1	32	30	4	189	167	56	108	1	3.00
Joe Horlen	R	27	13	13	.500	0	34	34	7	219	203	39	125	4	2.88
Gary Peters	L	28	10	12	.455	0	33	30	1	176	181	63	95	0	3.63
Bruce Howard	R	22	9	8	.529	0	30	22	1	148	123	72	120	1	3.47
Hoyt Wilhelm	R	42	7	7	.500	20	66	0	0	144	88	32	106	0	1.81
Juan Pizarro (SA)	L	28	6	3	.667	0	18	18	2	97	96	37	65	1	3.43
Bob Locker	R	27	5	2	.714	2	51	0	0	91	71	30	69	0	3.16
Ted Wills	L	31	2	0	1.000	1	15	0	0	19	17	14	12	0	2.84
2 Frank Lary	R	35	1	0	1.000	2	14	1	0	27	23	7	14	0	4.00
Greg Bollo	R	21	0	0	—	0	15	0	0	23	12	9	16	0	3.52

BALTIMORE — 3rd 94-68 .580 8 — HANK BAUER

NAME	G by Pos	B	AGE	G	AB	R	H	2B	3B	HR	RBI	BB	SO	SB	BA	SA
TOTALS			27	162	5450	641	1299	227	38	125	596	529	907	67	.238	.363
Boog Powell	1B78, OF71	L	23	144	472	54	117	20	2	17	72	71	93	1	.248	.407
Jerry Adair	2B157	R	28	157	582	51	151	26	3	7	66	35	65	6	.259	.351
Luis Aparicio	SS141	R	31	144	564	67	127	20	10	8	40	46	56	26	.225	.339
Brooks Robinson	3B143	R	28	144	559	81	166	25	2	18	80	47	47	3	.297	.445
Russ Snyder	OF106	L	31	132	345	49	93	11	2	1	29	27	38	3	.270	.322
Paul Blair	OF116	R	21	119	364	49	85	19	2	5	25	32	52	8	.234	.338
Curt Blefary	OF136	L	21	144	462	72	120	23	4	22	70	88	73	4	.260	.470
Dick Brown (IL)	C92	R	30	96	255	17	59	9	1	5	30	17	53	2	.231	.333
Norm Siebern	1B76	L	31	106	297	44	76	13	4	8	32	50	49	1	.256	.407
Jackie Brandt	OF84	R	31	96	243	35	59	17	0	8	24	21	40	1	.243	.412
Bob Johnson	1B34, SS23, 3B13, 2B5	R	29	87	273	36	66	13	2	5	27	15	34	1	.242	.359
Sam Bowens	OF68	R	26	84	203	16	33	4	1	7	20	10	41	7	.163	.296
John Orsino	C62, 1B5	R	27	77	232	30	54	10	2	9	28	23	51	1	.233	.409
Charlie Lau	C35	L	32	68	132	15	39	5	2	2	18	17	18	0	.295	.409
Dave Johnson	3B9, 2B3, SS2	R	22	20	47	5	8	3	0	0	1	6	3	0	.170	.234
Mark Belanger	SS4	R	21	11	3	1	1	0	0	0	0	0	0	0	.333	.333
2 Carl Warwick	OF3	R	28	9	14	3	0	0	0	0	0	3	2	0	.000	.000
Andy Etchebarren	C5	R	22	5	6	1	1	0	0	0	0	1	0	0	.167	.667

NAME	T	AGE	W	L	PCT	SV	G	GS	CG	IP	H	BB	SO	SHO	ERA
		29	94	68	.580	41	162	162	32	1478	1268	510	939	15	2.98
Steve Barber	L	27	15	10	.600	0	37	32	7	221	177	81	130	2	2.69
Stu Miller	R	37	14	7	.667	24	67	0	0	119	87	32	104	0	1.89
Milt Pappas	R	26	13	9	.591	0	34	34	9	221	192	52	127	3	2.61
Dave McNally	L	22	11	6	.647	0	35	29	6	199	163	73	116	2	2.85
Dick Hall	R	34	11	8	.579	12	48	0	0	94	84	11	79	0	3.06
Wally Bunker	R	20	10	8	.556	2	34	27	4	189	170	58	84	1	3.38
John Miller	R	24	6	4	.600	0	16	16	1	93	75	58	71	0	3.19
Jim Palmer	R	19	5	4	.556	1	27	6	0	92	75	56	75	0	3.72
1 Robin Roberts	R	38	5	7	.417	0	20	15	5	115	110	20	63	1	3.37
Harvey Haddix	L	39	2	3	.600	1	24	0	0	34	33	21	21	0	3.44
2 Don Larsen	R	35	1	2	.333	1	27	1	0	54	53	20	40	0	2.67
Ken Rowe	R	31	0	0	—	0	6	0	0	13	17	2	3	0	3.46
Ed Barnowski	R	19	0	0	—	0	4	3		7	6	6	2	0	2.25
Herm Starrette	R	26	0	0	—	0	9	0	0	9	8	3	1	0	1.00
Frank Bertaina	L	21	0	0	—	0	2	1	0	6	4	5	6	0	6.00
Darold Knowles	L	23	0	1	.000	0	5	1	0	15	14	10	12	0	9.00

DETROIT — 4th 89-73 .549 13 — BOB SWIFT 24-18 .571 / CHUCK DRESSEN 65-55 .542

NAME	G by Pos	B	AGE	G	AB	R	H	2B	3B	HR	RBI	BB	SO	SB	BA	SA
TOTALS			27	162	5368	680	1278	190	27	162	635	554	952	57	.238	.374
Norm Cash	1B139	L	30	142	467	79	124	23	1	30	82	77	62	6	.266	.512
Jerry Lumpe	2B139	L	32	145	502	72	129	15	4	4	39	56	34	7	.257	.323
Dick McAuliffe (BW)	SS112	L	25	113	404	61	105	13	6	15	54	49	62	6	.260	.433
Don Wert	3B161, SS3, 2B1	R	26	162	609	81	159	22	4	12	54	73	71	5	.261	.363
Al Kaline (BH)	OF112, 3B1	R	30	125	399	72	112	18	2	18	72	72	49	6	.281	.471
Don Demeter	OF82, 1B34	R	30	122	389	50	108	16	4	16	58	23	65	4	.278	.463
Willie Horton	OF141, 3B1	R	22	143	512	69	140	20	2	29	104	48	101	5	.273	.490
Bill Freehan	C129	R	23	130	431	45	101	15	0	10	43	39	63	4	.234	.339
Gates Brown	OF56	R	26	96	227	33	58	14	2	10	43	17	33	6	.256	.467
Ray Oyler	SS57, 2B11, 1B1, 3B1	R	26	82	194	22	36	6	0	5	13	21	61	1	.186	.294
Jim Northrup	OF54	L	25	80	219	20	45	12	3	2	16	12	50	1	.205	.315
George Thomas	OF59, 2B1	R	27	79	169	19	36	5	1	3	10	12	39	2	.213	.308
Jake Wood	2B20, 1B1, SS1, 3B1	R	28	58	104	12	30	3	0	2	7	10	19	3	.288	.375
John Sullivan	C29	L	24	34	86	5	23	0	0	2	11	9	13	0	.267	.337
George Smith	2B22, SS3, 3B3	R	27	32	53	6	5	0	0	1	1	3	16	0	.094	.151
Mickey Stanley	OF29	R	22	30	117	14	28	6	0	1	3	13	12	1	.239	.368
Jackie Moore	C20	R	26	21	53	2	5	0	0	0	2	6	12	0	.094	.094
Bill Roman	1B6	L	26	21	27	0	2	0	0	0	0	1	7	0	.074	.074
Wayne Redmond	OF2	R	19	4	4	1	0	0	0	0	0	1	0	0	.000	.000

NAME	T	AGE	W	L	PCT	SV	G	GS	CG	IP	H	BB	SO	SHO	ERA
		28	89	73	.549	31	162	162	45	1455	1283	509	1069	14	3.35
Denny McLain	R	21	16	6	.727	1	33	29	13	220	174	62	192	4	2.62
Mickey Lolich	L	24	15	9	.625	3	43	37	7	244	216	72	226	3	3.43
Hank Aguirre	L	34	14	10	.583	0	32	32	10	208	185	60	141	2	3.59
Joe Sparma	R	23	13	8	.619	0	30	28	6	167	142	75	127	0	3.18
Dave Wickersham	R	29	9	14	.391	0	34	27	8	195	179	61	109	3	3.78
Fred Gladding	R	29	6	2	.750	6	46	0	0	70	63	29	43	0	2.83
Terry Fox	R	29	6	4	.600	10	42	0	0	57	55	31	34	0	2.77
2 Orlando Pena	R	31	4	4	.400	0	39	0	0	57	54	20	55	0	2.53
Larry Sherry	R	29	3	6	.333	5	39	0	0	78	71	40	46	0	3.12
Ron Nischwitz	L	28	1	0	1.000	0	20	0	0	23	21	6	12	0	2.74
Jack Hamilton (JJ)	R	26	1	1	.500	0	4	1	0	4	3	6	4	0	15.75
Phil Regan	R	28	1	5	.167	0	16	7	1	52	57	20	37	0	5.02
Ed Rakow	R	30	0	0	—	0	13	1	0	13	14	11	10	0	6.23
John Hiller	L	22	0	0	—	0	6	0	0	7	5	3	4	0	12.00
Johnny Seale	L	26	0	0	—	0	5	1	0	7	3	8	2	0	0.00
Leo Marentette	R	24	0	0	—	0	3	0	0	5	2	1	3	0	0.00
Vern Holtgrave	L	22	0	0	—	0	1	0	0	2	3	1	0	0	6.00
Julio Navarro	R	29	0	2	.000	1	15	1	0	39	30	16	22	1	4.20

CLEVELAND — 5th 87-75 .537 15 — BIRDIE TEBBETTS

NAME	G by Pos	B	AGE	G	AB	R	H	2B	3B	HR	RBI	BB	SO	SB	BA	SA
TOTALS			27	162	5469	663	1367	198	21	156	615	506	857	109	.250	.379
Fred Whitfield	1B122	L	27	132	468	49	137	23	1	26	90	16	42	0	.293	.513
2 Pedro Gonzalez	2B112, OF3, 3B2	R	26	116	400	38	101	14	3	5	39	18	57	7	.253	.342
Larry Brown	SS95, 2B26	R	25	124	438	52	111	22	4	8	40	38	62	5	.253	.368
Max Alvis	3B156	R	27	159	604	88	149	24	2	21	61	47	121	12	.247	.397
Rocky Colavito	OF162	R	31	162	592	92	170	25	2	26	108	93	63	1	.287	.468
Vic Davalillo	OF134	L	28	142	505	67	152	19	1	5	40	35	50	26	.301	.372
Leon Wagner	OF134	L	31	149	517	91	152	18	4	28	79	60	52	2	.294	.495
Joe Azcue	C108	R	25	111	335	16	77	7	0	2	35	27	54	2	.230	.269
Chuck Hinton	OF72, 1B40, 2B23, 3B1	R	31	133	431	59	110	17	6	18	54	53	65	17	.255	.448
Dick Howser	SS73, 2B17	R	29	107	307	47	72	8	2	3	17	27	25	17	.235	.283
Chico Salmon	1B28, OF17, 2B5, 3B5	R	24	79	120	20	29	8	0	3	12	5	19	7	.242	.383
Al Luplow	OF6	L	25	53	45	3	6	2	0	0	4	3	14	0	.133	.244
Duke Sims	C40	R	24	48	118	9	21	0	0	6	15	15	33	0	.178	.331
2 Phil Roof	C41	R	24	43	52	3	9	1	0	1	5	6	13	0	.173	.192
Billy Moran	2B7, SS1	R	31	29	52	6	12	2	1	0	6	3	8	0	.231	.365
Cam Carreon	C19	R	27	19	52	6	12	2	1	0	3	4	6	0	.231	.365
3 Lu Clinton	OF9	R	27	12	34	2	6	1	1	0	3	2	5	0	.176	.294
1 Ray Barker	1B3	L	28	11	2	0	0	0	0	0	0	0	0	0	.000	.000
Bill Davis		L	23	10	10	0	3	0	0	0	0	1	4	0	.300	.400
George Banks	3B1	R	26	4	5	0	1	0	0	0	0	0	2	0	.200	.400
Richie Scheinblum		B	22	4	3	0	0	0	0	0	0	0	2	0	.000	.000
Tony Martinez		R	25	2	0	0	0	0	0	0	0	0	0	0	.000	.000
Ralph Gagliano		L	18	1	0	0	0	0	0	0	0	0	0	0	—	—

NAME	T	AGE	W	L	PCT	SV	G	GS	CG	IP	H	BB	SO	SHO	ERA
		28	87	75	.537	41	162	162	41	1458	1254	500	1156	13	3.30
Sam McDowell	L	22	17	11	.607	4	42	35	14	273	178	132	325	3	2.18
Sonny Siebert	R	28	16	8	.667	3	39	27	4	189	139	46	191	1	2.43
Ralph Terry	R	29	11	6	.647	0	39	26	6	166	154	23	84	2	3.69
Luis Tiant	R	24	11	11	.500	1	41	30	10	196	166	66	152	2	3.54
Lee Stange	R	28	8	4	.667	0	41	13	2	132	122	26	80	2	3.34
Gary Bell	R	28	6	5	.545	17	40	0	0	104	86	50	86	0	3.03
Jack Kralick	L	30	5	11	.313	0	30	16	1	86	106	21	34	0	4.92
Steve Hargan	R	22	4	3	.571	2	17	3	1	43	35	17	30	0	3.45
Don McMahon	R	35	3	3	.500	11	58	0	0	85	79	37	60	0	3.28
Tom Kelley	R	21	2	1	.667	0	4	1	0	13	11	9	20	0	2.40
Floyd Weaver	R	24	2	2	.500	1	32	1	0	61	61	24	37	0	5.46
Jack Spring	L	32	1	3	.333	0	19	0	0	20	24	6	13	0	3.68
Dick Donovan	R	37	1	3	.250	0	12	4	0	23	32	6	12	0	5.87
Mike Hedlund (JJ)	R	18	0	0	—	0	1	0	0	5	6	5	1	0	5.40
Stan Williams	R	28	0	0	—	0	8	0	0	14	11	5	11	0	6.75
3 Bobby Tiefenauer	R	35	0	5	.000	9	15	0	0	24	31	10	13	0	4.91

NEW YORK   6th 77-85 .475 25   JOHNNY KEANE

NAME	G by Pos	B	AGE	G	AB	R	H	2B	3B	HR	RBI	BB	SO	SB	BA	SA
TOTALS			29	162	5470	611	1286	196	31	149	576	489	951	35	.235	.364
Joe Pepitone	1B115, OF41	L	24	143	531	51	131	18	3	18	62	43	59	4	.247	.394
Bobby Richardson	2B158	R	29	160	664	76	164	28	2	6	47	37	39	7	.247	.322
Tony Kubek	SS93, OF3, 1B1	L	28	109	339	26	74	5	3	5	35	20	48	1	.218	.295
Clete Boyer	3B147, SS2	R	28	148	514	69	129	23	6	18	58	39	79	4	.251	.424
Hector Lopez	OF75, 1B2	R	35	111	283	25	74	12	2	7	39	26	61	0	.261	.392
Tom Tresh	OF154	B	27	156	602	94	168	29	6	26	74	59	92	5	.279	.477
Mickey Mantle (SJ)	OF108	B	33	122	361	44	92	12	1	19	46	73	76	4	.255	.452
Elston Howard (AJ)	C95, 1B5, OF1	R	36	110	391	38	91	15	1	9	45	24	65	0	.233	.345
Phil Linz	SS71, 3B4, OF4, 2B1	R	26	99	285	37	59	12	1	2	16	30	33	2	.207	.277
2 Ray Barker	1B61, 3B3	L	29	98	205	21	52	11	0	7	31	20	46	1	.254	.410
Ross Moschitto	OF89	R	20	96	27	12	5	0	0	1	3	0	12	0	.185	.296
Roger Repoz	OF69	L	24	79	218	34	48	7	4	12	28	25	57	1	.220	.454
Horace Clarke	3B17, 2B7, SS1	B	25	51	108	13	28	1	0	1	9	6	6	2	.259	.296
Roger Maris (LJ-HJ)	OF43	L	30	46	155	22	37	7	0	8	27	29	29	0	.239	.439
2 Doc Edwards	C43	R	28	45	100	3	19	3	0	1	9	13	14	1	.190	.250
Art Lopez	OF16	L	28	38	49	5	7	0	0	0	0	1	6	0	.143	.143
Jake Gibbs	C21	L	26	37	68	6	15	1	0	2	7	4	20	0	.221	.324
Bob Schmidt	C20	R	32	20	40	4	10	1	0	1	3	3	8	0	.250	.350
Roy White	OF10, 2B1	B	21	14	42	7	14	2	0	0	3	4	7	2	.333	.381
1 Johnny Blanchard	C12	L	32	12	34	1	5	1	0	1	3	1	7	0	.147	.265
Bobby Murcer	SS11	L	19	11	37	3	9	0	1	1	4	5	12	0	.243	.378

Archie Moore 23 L 7-17, 1 Pedro Gonzalez 26 R 2-5, Duke Carmel 28 L 0-8

NAME	T	AGE	W	L	PCT	SV	G	GS	CG	IP	H	BB	SO	SHO	ERA
		27	77	85	.475	31	162	162	41	1460	1337	511	1001	11	3.28
Mel Stottlemyre	R	23	20	9	.690	0	37	37	18	291	250	88	155	4	2.63
Whitey Ford	L	36	16	13	.552	0	37	36	9	244	241	50	162	2	3.25
Al Downing	L	24	12	14	.462	0	35	32	8	212	185	105	179	2	3.40
Pedro Ramos	R	30	5	5	.500	19	65	0	0	92	80	27	68	0	2.93
Pete Mikkelsen	R	25	4	9	.308	1	41	3	0	82	78	36	69	0	3.29
Jim Bouton	R	26	4	15	.211	0	30	25	2	151	158	60	97	0	4.83
Steve Hamilton	L	31	3	1	.750	5	46	1	0	58	47	16	51	1	1.40
Hal Reniff	R	26	3	4	.429	3	51	0	0	85	74	48	74	0	3.81
Jack Cullen	R	25	3	4	.429	0	12	9	2	59	59	21	25	1	3.57
Bill Stafford (SA)	R	25	3	8	.273	0	22	15	1	111	93	31	71	0	3.57
Rich Beck	R	24	2	1	.667	0	3	3	1	21	22	7	10	1	2.14
Gil Blanco	L	19	1	1	.500	0	17	1	0	20	16	12	14	0	4.05
2 Bobby Tiefenauer	R	35	1	1	.500	2	10	0	0	20	19	5	15	0	3.60
1 Rollie Sheldon	R	28	0	0	—	0	3	0	0	6	5	1	7	0	1.50
Jim Brenneman	R	24	0	0	—	0	3	0	0	5	3	2	6	0	18.00
Mike Jurewicz	L	19	0	0	—	0	2	0	0	2	5	1	2	0	9.00

CALIFORNIA   7th 75-87 .463 27   BILL RIGNEY

NAME	G by Pos	B	AGE	G	AB	R	H	2B	3B	HR	RBI	BB	SO	SB	BA	SA
TOTALS			25	162	5354	527	1279	200	36	92	486	443	973	107	.239	.341
Joe Adcock	1B97	R	37	122	349	30	84	14	0	14	47	37	74	2	.241	.401
Bobby Knoop	2B142	R	26	142	465	47	125	24	4	7	43	31	101	3	.269	.383
Jim Fregosi	SS160	R	23	161	602	66	167	19	7	15	64	54	107	13	.277	.407
Paul Schaal	3B153, 2B1	R	22	155	483	48	108	12	2	9	45	61	88	6	.224	.313
Albie Pearson	OF101	L	30	122	360	41	100	17	2	4	21	51	17	12	.278	.369
Jose Cardenal	OF129, 3B2, 2B1	R	21	134	512	54	128	23	2	11	57	27	72	37	.250	.367
Willie Smith	OF123, 1B2	L	26	136	459	52	120	14	9	14	57	32	60	9	.261	.423
Bob Rodgers	C128	B	26	132	411	33	86	14	3	1	32	35	61	4	.209	.265
Vic Power	1B107, 2B6, 3B2	R	37	124	197	11	51	7	1	1	20	5	13	2	.259	.320
1 Lu Clinton	OF73	R	27	89	222	29	54	12	3	1	8	23	37	2	.243	.338
Jimmy Piersall	OF41	R	35	53	112	10	30	5	2	2	12	5	15	2	.268	.402
2 Al Spangler	OF24	L	31	51	96	17	25	1	0	1	8	9	4	0	.260	.271
Tom Satriano	3B15, 2B12, C12, 1B3	L	24	47	79	8	13	2	0	1	4	10	10	1	.165	.228
Merritt Ranew	C24	L	27	41	91	12	19	4	0	1	10	7	22	0	.209	.286
Costen Shockley	1B31, OF1	L	23	40	107	5	20	2	0	2	17	9	16	0	.187	.262
Julio Gotay	2B23, 3B9, SS1	R	26	40	77	6	19	4	0	1	3	4	9	0	.247	.338
Bobby Gene Smith	OF15	R	31	23	57	1	13	9	0	0	5	2	10	0	.228	.281
Joe Koppe	2B10, SS4, 3B2	R	34	23	33	3	7	1	0	1	2	3	10	1	.212	.333
Rick Reichardt	OF20	R	22	20	75	8	20	4	0	1	6	5	12	1	.267	.360
Ed Kirkpatrick	OF19	L	20	19	73	8	19	5	0	3	8	3	19	0	.260	.452
Tom Egan	C16	R	19	18	38	3	10	0	1	0	1	3	12	0	.263	.316
Charlie Dees	1B6	L	30	12	32	1	5	0	0	0	1	1	8	1	.156	.156
1 Phil Roof	C9	R	24	9	22	1	3	0	0	0	0	1	6	0	.136	.136

Dick Simpson 21 R 6-27, Jackie Hernandez 24 R 2-6, Gino Cimoli 35 R 0-5

NAME	T	AGE	W	L	PCT	SV	G	GS	CG	IP	H	BB	SO	SHO	ERA
		25	75	87	.463	33	162	162	39	1442	1259	563	847	14	3.17
Dean Chance	R	24	15	10	.600	0	36	33	10	226	197	101	164	4	3.15
Marcelino Lopez	L	21	14	13	.519	1	35	32	8	215	185	82	122	1	2.93
Fred Newman	R	23	14	16	.467	0	36	36	10	261	225	64	109	2	2.93
Bob Lee	R	27	9	7	.563	23	69	0	0	131	95	42	89	0	1.92
George Brunet	L	30	9	11	.450	2	41	26	8	197	149	69	141	3	2.56
Aubrey Gatewood	R	26	4	5	.444	0	46	3	0	92	91	37	37	0	3.42
Rudy May	L	20	4	9	.308	0	30	19	2	124	111	78	76	1	3.92
Jim Coates	R	32	2	0	1.000	3	17	0	0	28	23	16	15	0	3.54
Ed Sukla	R	22	2	3	.400	3	25	0	0	32	32	10	15	0	4.50
Barry Latman	R	29	1	1	.500	0	18	0	0	32	36	16	18	0	2.81
2 Jack Sanford	R	36	1	2	.333	1	9	9	0	35	10	13	0		4.66
Dick Wantz (DD)	R	25	0	0	—	0	1	0	0	1	3	0	2	0	18.00
1 Don Lee	R	31	0	1	.000	0	15	0	0	21	21	6	9	0	6.43
Ron Piche	R	30	0	3	.000	0	14	1	0	20	20	12	14	0	6.75
Ken McBride (SA)	R	29	0	3	.000	0	4	3	0	22	24	14	11	0	6.14
Jim McGlothlin	R	21	0	0	—	0	3	0	0	9	9	4	9	0	3.50

WASHINGTON   8th 70-92 .432 32   GIL HODGES

NAME	G by Pos	B	AGE	G	AB	R	H	2B	3B	HR	RBI	BB	SO	SB	BA	SA
TOTALS			29	162	5374	591	1227	179	33	136	563	570	1125	30	.228	.350
Dick Nen	1B65	L	25	69	246	18	64	7	1	6	31	19	47	1	.260	.370
Don Blasingame	2B110	L	33	129	403	47	90	8	8	1	18	35	45	5	.223	.290
Eddie Brinkman	SS150	R	23	154	444	35	82	13	2	5	35	38	82	1	.185	.257
Ken McMullen	3B142, OF8, 1B1	R	23	160	555	75	146	18	6	18	54	47	90	2	.263	.414
Woodie Held	OF106, 3B5, 2B4, SS2	R	33	122	332	46	82	16	2	16	54	49	74	0	.247	.452
Don Lock	OF136	R	28	143	418	52	90	15	1	16	39	57	115	1	.215	.371
Frank Howard	OF138	R	28	149	516	53	149	22	6	21	84	55	112	0	.289	.477
Mike Brumley	C66	L	26	79	216	15	45	4	0	3	15	20	33	1	.208	.269
Willie Kirkland	OF92	L	31	123	312	38	72	9	1	14	54	19	65	3	.231	.401
Jim King	OF88	L	32	120	258	46	55	10	2	14	49	44	50	1	.213	.430
Ken Hamlin	2B77, SS47, 3B1	R	30	117	362	45	99	21	1	4	22	33	45	8	.273	.370
Don Zimmer	C33, 3B26, 2B12	R	34	95	226	20	45	6	0	2	17	26	59	2	.199	.252
Joe Cunningham	1B59	L	33	95	201	29	46	9	1	3	20	46	27	0	.229	.328
Doug Camilli	C59	R	28	75	193	13	37	6	1	3	16	16	34	0	.192	.280
Bob Chance	1B48, OF3	R	24	72	199	20	51	9	0	4	14	18	44	0	.256	.362
Joe McCabe	C11	R	26	14	27	1	5	0	0	1	5	4	13	1	.185	.296
Jim French	C13	L	23	13	37	4	11	0	0	1	7	9	5	1	.297	.378
Roy Sievers	1B7	R	38	12	21	3	4	1	0	0	4	3	2	0	.190	.238
Fred Valentine	OF11	B	30	12	29	6	7	0	0	2	4	7	0	3	.241	.241
Brant Alyea	1B3, OF1	R	24	8	13	3	3	0	0	2	6	1	4	0	.231	.692

Paul Casanova 23 R 4-13, Chuck Cottier 29 R 0-1

NAME	T	AGE	W	L	PCT	SV	G	GS	CG	IP	H	BB	SO	SHO	ERA
		29	70	92	.432	40	162	162	21	1436	1376	633	867	8	3.93
Pete Richert	L	25	15	12	.556	0	34	29	6	194	146	84	161	0	2.60
Phil Ortega	R	25	12	15	.444	0	35	29	4	180	176	97	88	2	5.10
Mike McCormick	L	26	8	8	.500	1	44	21	3	158	158	36	88	1	3.36
Ron Kline	R	33	7	6	.538	29	74	0	0	99	106	32	52	0	2.64
Steve Ridzik	R	36	6	4	.600	8	63	0	0	110	108	43	72	0	4.01
Bennie Daniels	R	33	5	13	.278	1	33	18	1	116	135	39	42	0	4.73
Howie Koplitz	R	27	4	1	.364	1	33	11	0	107	97	48	59	0	4.04
Buster Narum	R	24	4	12	.250	0	46	24	2	174	176	91	86	0	4.45
Joe Coleman	R	18	2	0	1.000	0	2	2	1	18	9	8	7	0	1.50
Jim Duckworth	R	26	2	2	.500	0	17	0	0	64	45	36	74	0	3.94
Frank Kreutzer	L	26	2	6	.250	0	33	14	2	85	73	54	65	1	4.34
2 Ryne Duren	R	36	1	1	.500	0	16	0	0	23	24	18	25	0	6.65
Jim Hannan	R	25	1	1	.500	0	15	1	0	18	18	6	5	1	4.80
Marshall Bridges	L	34	1	2	.333	0	40	0	0	57	62	25	39	0	2.68
Dallas Green	R	30	0	1	—	0	2	0	0	4	6	1	4	0	3.21
1 Nick Willhite	L	24	0	0	—	0	5	0	0	6	10	4	3	0	7.50
Barry Moore	L	24	0	0	—	0	1	0	0	2	1	1	1	0	0.00
Pete Craig	R	24	0	3	.000	0	2	0	0	7	8	4	5	0	8.36

Tom Cheney (VR) 30

BOSTON   9th 62-100 .383 40   BILLY HERMAN

NAME	G by Pos	B	AGE	G	AB	R	H	2B	3B	HR	RBI	BB	SO	SB	BA	SA
TOTALS			26	162	5487	669	1378	244	40	165	629	607	964	47	.251	.400
Lee Thomas	1B127, OF20	L	29	151	521	74	141	27	4	22	75	72	42	6	.271	.464
Felix Mantilla	2B123, OF27, 1B2	R	30	150	534	60	147	17	2	18	92	79	84	7	.275	.416
Rico Petrocelli	SS93	R	22	103	323	38	75	13	2	13	33	36	71	0	.232	.412
Frank Malzone	3B96	R	35	106	364	40	87	20	0	3	34	28	38	1	.239	.319
Tony Conigliaro	OF137	R	20	138	521	82	140	21	5	32	82	51	116	4	.269	.512
Lenny Green	OF95	L	31	119	373	69	103	24	6	7	24	48	43	8	.276	.429
Carl Yastrzemski	OF130	L	25	133	494	78	154	45	3	20	72	70	58	7	.312	.536
Bob Tillman	C106	R	28	111	368	20	79	10	3	6	35	40	69	0	.215	.307
Dalton Jones	3B81, 2B8	L	21	112	367	41	99	13	5	5	37	28	45	8	.270	.373
Ed Bressoud	SS86, 3B2, OF1	R	33	107	296	29	67	11	1	8	25	29	77	0	.226	.351
Jim Gosger	OF81	L	22	81	324	45	83	15	4	9	35	29	61	3	.256	.410
Chuck Schilling	2B41	R	27	71	171	14	41	3	2	3	9	13	17	0	.240	.333
Tony Horton	1B44	R	20	60	163	23	48	9	1	7	23	18	36	0	.294	.485
Russ Nixon	C38	L	30	59	137	11	37	5	1	0	11	6	23	0	.270	.321
Earl Wilson	P36	R	30	47	79	13	14	0	0	6	12	13	29	0	.177	.405
Mike Ryan	C33	R	23	33	107	7	17	0	1	3	9	5	19	0	.159	.262
Gary Geiger (IL-FS)	C28	L	28	24	45	5	9	3	0	1	2	13	10	3	.200	.333

Jerry Moses 18 R 1-4, Rudy Schlesinger 22 R 0-1

NAME	T	AGE	W	L	PCT	SV	G	GS	CG	IP	H	BB	SO	SHO	ERA
		27	62	100	.383	25	162	162	33	1439	1443	543	993	9	4.24
Earl Wilson	R	30	13	14	.481	0	36	36	8	231	221	77	164	1	3.97
Bill Monbouquette	R	28	10	18	.357	0	35	35	10	229	239	40	110	2	3.69
Dave Morehead	R	22	10	18	.357	0	34	33	5	193	157	113	163	2	4.06
Dick Radatz	R	28	9	11	.450	22	63	0	0	124	104	53	121	0	3.92
Jim Lonborg	R	23	9	17	.346	0	32	31	7	185	193	65	113	1	4.48
Dennis Bennett	L	25	5	7	.417	0	34	18	3	142	152	53	85	0	4.37
Bob Duliba	R	30	4	2	.667	1	39	0	0	64	60	22	27	0	3.80
Jay Ritchie	R	28	1	2	.333	2	44	0	0	71	83	26	55	0	3.17
Jerry Stephenson	R	21	1	5	.167	0	15	8	0	52	62	33	49	0	6.23
Arnie Earley	L	32	1	0	.000	0	57	0	0	74	79	29	47	0	3.65
Bob Heffner	R	26	0	2	.000	0	27	1	0	49	59	18	42	0	7.16
1 Jack Lamabe	R	28	0	0	—	0	14	0	0	25	34	14	17	0	8.28

KANSAS CITY   10th 59-103 .364 43   MEL McGAHA 5-21 .192   HAYWOOD SULLIVAN 54-82 .397

NAME	G by Pos	B	AGE	G	AB	R	H	2B	3B	HR	RBI	BB	SO	SB	BA	SA
TOTALS			25	162	5393	585	1294	186	59	110	546	521	1020	110	.240	.358
Ken Harrelson	1B125, OF4	R	23	150	483	61	115	17	3	23	66	66	112	9	.238	.429
Dick Green	2B126	R	24	133	474	64	110	15	1	15	55	50	110	0	.232	.363
Campaneris	SS109, OF39, 1B, 2B, 3B, C, P=1	R	23	144	578	67	156	23	12	6	42	41	71	51	.270	.382
Ed Charles	3B128, 2B1, SS1	R	32	134	480	55	129	19	7	8	56	44	72	13	.269	.388
Mike Hershberger	OF144	R	25	150	494	43	114	15	5	5	48	37	42	7	.231	.312
Jim Landis	OF108	R	31	118	364	46	87	15	1	3	36	57	84	8	.239	.310
Tommie Reynolds	OF83,3B1	R	23	90	270	34	64	11	2	3	36	26	41	9	.237	.311
Billy Bryan	C95	L	26	108	325	36	82	11	5	14	51	29	87	0	.252	.446
Wayne Causey	SS62, 2B45, 3B35	L	28	144	513	48	134	17	8	3	34	61	48	1	.261	.343
Rene Lachemann	C75	R	20	92	216	20	49	7	1	9	29	12	57	0	.227	.394
Santiago Rosario	1B31, OF3	L	25	81	85	8	20	3	0	2	6	10	20	1	.235	.341
Jose Tartabull	OF54	L	26	68	218	28	68	11	4	1	19	18	20	11	.312	.413
Nelson Mathews	OF57	R	23	67	184	17	39	7	7	2	15	24	49	1	.212	.359
2 Johnny Blanchard	OF20, C14	L	32	52	120	10	24	5	0	1	7	11	10	0	.200	.267
Skip Lockwood	3B7	R	18	37	33	4	4	0	0	0	2	7	11	0	.121	.121
1 Jim Gentile	1B35	L	31	38	118	14	29	5	0	10	29	16	26	0	.246	.542
Larry Stahl	OF21	L	24	28	81	9	16	2	1	4	14	5	16	1	.198	.395
1 Doc Edwards	C6	R	28	8	7	0	2	0	0	0	0	0	3	0	.150	.150
Randy Schwartz	1B2	R	21	6	7	0	2	0	0	0	0	2	5	0	.286	.286

2 Lu Clinton 27 R 0-1, John Sanders 19 0-0

NAME	T	AGE	W	L	PCT	SV	G	GS	CG	IP	H	BB	SO	SHO	ERA
		27	59	103	.364	32	162	162	18	1433	1399	574	882	7	4.24
2 Rollie Sheldon	R	28	10	8	.556	0	32	29	4	187	180	56	105	1	3.95
Fred Talbot	R	24	10	12	.455	0	39	33	2	198	188	86	117	1	4.14
John O'Donoghue	L	25	9	18	.333	0	34	30	4	178	183	66	82	1	3.94
Catfish Hunter	R	19	8	8	.500	2	32	20	3	133	124	46	82	2	4.26
Don Mossi	L	36	5	8	.385	7	51	0	0	55	59	20	41	0	3.76
Diego Segui	R	27	5	15	.250	0	40	25	5	163	166	67	119	1	4.64
Jack Aker	R	24	3	2	.571	3	34	0	0	51	45	18	26	0	3.18
Jim Dickson	R	27	3	2	.600	0	68	0	0	86	68	47	54	0	3.45
Lew Krausse	R	22	3	4	.333	0	7	5	0	29	25	9	22	0	5.04
John Wyatt	R	30	2	6	.250	18	65	0	0	89	78	53	70	0	3.24
Moe Drabowsky	R	29	1	5	.167	0	14	5	0	19	44	18	25	0	4.38
Ron Tompkins	R	22	1	0	—	0	10	0	0	10	9	14	8	0	3.48
Aurelio Monteagudo	R	21	1	0	—	0	5	2	0	10	13	6	6	0	3.86
Jose Santiago	R	24	0	0	—	0	1	0	0	1	4	2	2	0	9.00
Satchel Paige	R	58	0	0	—	0	1	0	0	3	1	0	1	0	0.00
Jess Hickman	L	25	0	0	—	0	5	0	0	8	8	16	6	0	6.00
Don Buschhorn (LJ)	R	19	0	0	—	0	1	0	0	3	6	4	0	0	4.35
Dick Joyce	L	21	0	1	.000	0	5	1	0	13	16	8	5	0	2.77
Paul Lindblad	R	24	0	0	—	0	2	0	0	5	3	2	1	0	11.57
Wes Stock	R	31	4	0	1.000	2	62	0	0	100	96	40	52	0	5.22
1 Orlando Pena	R	31	4	9	.400	0	35	42	13	24				0	6.94

Tom Harrison 20 R 0-0, Blue Moon Odom 20 R 0-0, Bert Campaneris 23 R 0-0

LOS ANGELES 1st 97-65 .599 — WALT ALSTON

NAME	G by Pos	B	AGE	G	AB	R	H	2B	3B	HR	RBI	BB	SO	SB	BA	SA
TOTALS			29	162	5425	608	1329	193	32	78	548	492	891	172	.245	.335
Wes Parker	1B154, OF1	B	25	154	542	80	129	24	7	8	51	75	95	13	.238	.352
Jim Lefebvre	2B156	B	22	157	544	57	136	21	4	12	69	71	92	3	.250	.369
Maury Wills	SS155	B	32	158	650	92	186	14	7	0	33	40	64	94	.286	.329
Jim Gilliam (RC)	3B80, OF22, 2B5	B	36	111	372	54	104	19	4	4	39	53	31	9	.280	.384
Ron Fairly	OF148, 1B13	L	26	158	555	73	152	28	1	9	70	76	72	2	.274	.377
Willie Davis	OF141	L	24	158	558	52	133	24	3	10	57	14	81	25	.238	.346
Lou Johnson	OF128	R	30	131	468	57	121	24	1	12	58	24	81	15	.259	.391
Johnny Roseboro	C131, 3B1	L	32	136	437	42	102	10	0	8	57	34	51	1	.233	.311
John Kennedy	3B95, SS5	R	24	104	105	12	18	3	0	1	5	8	33	1	.171	.229
Dick Tracewski	3B53, 2B14, SS7	R	30	78	186	17	40	6	0	1	20	25	30	2	.215	.263
Don Drysdale	P44	R	28	58	130	18	39	4	1	7	19	5	34	0	.300	.508
Jeff Torborg	C53	R	23	56	150	8	36	5	1	3	13	10	26	0	.240	.347
Wally Moon	OF23	L	35	53	89	6	18	3	0	1	11	13	22	2	.202	.270
Willie Crawford	OF8	L	18	52	27	10	4	0	0	0	2	6	2	2	.148	.148
Al Ferrara	OF27	R	26	41	81	5	17	2	1	1	10	9	20	0	.210	.296
Don LeJohn	3B26	R	31	34	78	2	20	2	0	0	7	5	13	0	.256	.282
Derrell Griffith	OF11	L	21	22	41	3	7	0	0	1	2	0	9	0	.171	.244
Tommy Davis (BN)	OF16	R	26	17	60	3	15	1	1	0	9	2	4	2	.250	.300
Dick Smith	OF9	R	26	10	6	0	0	0	0	0	1	0	3	0	.000	.000
Hec Valle	C6	R	24	9	13	4	4	0	0	0	2	2	3	0	.308	.308

Nate Oliver 24 R 1-1, Johnny Werhas 27 R 0-3

NAME	T	AGE	W	L	PCT	SV	G	GS	CG	IP	H	BB	SO	SHO	ERA
TOTALS		28	97	65	.599	34	162	162	58	1476	1223	425	1079	23	2.81
Sandy Koufax	L	29	26	8	.765	2	43	41	27	336	216	71	382	8	2.04
Don Drysdale	R	28	23	12	.657	0	44	42	20	308	270	66	210	7	2.78
Claude Osteen	L	25	15	15	.500	0	40	40	9	287	253	78	162	1	2.79
Howie Reed	R	28	7	5	.583	1	38	5	0	78	73	27	47	0	3.12
Johnny Podres	L	32	7	6	.538	1	27	22	2	134	126	39	63	1	3.43
Ron Perranoski	L	29	6	6	.500	17	59	0	0	105	85	40	53	0	2.23
Bob Miller	R	26	6	7	.462	9	61	1	0	103	82	26	77	0	2.97
Jim Brewer (EJ)	R	27	3	2	.600	2	19	2	0	49	33	28	31	0	1.84
John Purdin	R	22	2	1	.667	0	11	2	0	23	26	13	16	0	6.65
2 Nick Willhite	L	24	2	2	.500	1	15	6	0	42	47	22	28	0	5.36
Bill Singer	R	21	0	0	—	0	2	0	0	1	2	1	0	0	0.00
Mike Kekich	L	20	0	1	.000	0	5	1	0	10	13	9	9	0	9.90

SAN FRANCISCO 2nd 95-67 .586 2 — HERMAN FRANKS

NAME	G by Pos	B	AGE	G	AB	R	H	2B	3B	HR	RBI	BB	SO	SB	BA	SA
TOTALS			27	163	5495	682	1384	169	43	159	623	476	844	47	.252	.385
Willie McCovey	1B156	L	27	160	540	93	149	17	4	39	92	88	118	0	.276	.539
Hal Lanier	2B158, SS11	R	22	159	522	41	118	15	9	0	39	21	67	2	.226	.289
2 Dick Schofield	SS93	B	30	101	379	39	77	10	1	2	19	33	50	2	.203	.251
Jim Ray Hart	3B144, OF15	R	23	160	591	91	177	30	6	23	96	47	75	6	.299	.487
Jesus Alou	OF136	R	23	143	543	76	162	19	4	9	52	13	40	8	.298	.398
Willie Mays	OF151	R	34	157	558	118	177	21	3	52	112	76	71	9	.317	.645
Matty Alou	OF103, P1	L	26	117	324	37	75	12	2	2	18	17	28	10	.231	.299
Tom Haller	C133	L	28	134	422	40	106	4	3	16	49	47	67	0	.251	.389
Jim Davenport	3B39, SS37, 2B26	R	31	106	271	29	68	14	3	4	31	21	47	0	.251	.369
2 Len Gabrielson	OF77, 1B5	L	25	88	269	36	81	6	5	4	26	26	48	4	.301	.405
Cap Peterson	OF27	R	22	63	105	14	26	7	0	3	15	10	16	0	.248	.400
Ken Henderson	OF48	B	19	63	73	10	14	1	1	0	7	9	19	1	.192	.233
Jack Hiatt	C21, 1B7	R	22	40	67	5	19	4	0	1	7	12	14	0	.284	.388
Orlando Cepeda (KJ)	1B4, OF2	R	27	33	34	1	6	1	0	1	5	3	9	0	.176	.294
Bob Burda	1B11, OF1	L	26	31	27	0	3	0	0	0	5	5	6	0	.111	.111
Bob Schroder	2B4, 3B1	L	20	31	9	4	2	0	0	0	1	1	1	0	.222	.222
1 Jose Pagan	SS26	R	30	26	83	10	17	4	0	0	5	8	9	1	.205	.253
Tito Fuentes	SS18, 2B7, 3B1	R	21	26	72	12	15	1	0	0	5	5	14	0	.208	.222
1 Ed Bailey	C12, 1B2	L	34	24	28	1	3	0	0	0	3	6	7	0	.107	.107
1 Harvey Kuenn	OF14, 1B7	R	34	23	59	4	14	0	0	0	6	10	3	3	.237	.237
2 Dick Bertell	C22	R	29	22	48	1	9	1	0	0	3	7	5	0	.188	.208
1 Chuck Hiller	2B2	L	30	7	7	1	1	0	0	1	1	0	1	0	.143	.571
Randy Hundley	C6	R	23	6	15	0	1	0	0	0	0	0	4	0	.067	.067
Ollie Brown	OF4	R	21	6	10	0	2	1	0	0	0	0	3	0	.200	.300
Bob Barton	C2	R	23	4	7	1	4	0	0	0	1	0	0	0	.571	.571

NAME	T	AGE	W	L	PCT	SV	G	GS	CG	IP	H	BB	SO	SHO	ERA
TOTALS		30	95	67	.586	42	163	163	42	1465	1325	408	1060	17	3.20
Juan Marichal	R	27	22	13	.629	1	39	37	24	295	224	46	240	10	2.14
Bob Shaw	R	32	16	9	.640	2	43	33	6	235	213	53	148	1	2.64
Bobby Bolin	R	26	14	6	.700	2	45	13	2	163	125	56	135	0	2.76
Ron Herbel	R	27	12	9	.571	1	47	21	1	171	172	47	106	0	3.84
Frank Linzy	R	24	9	3	.750	21	57	0	0	82	76	23	35	0	1.43
Gaylord Perry	R	26	8	12	.400	1	47	26	6	196	194	70	170	0	4.18
Masanori Murakami	L	21	4	1	.800	8	45	1	0	74	57	22	85	0	3.77
1 Jack Sanford	R	36	4	5	.444	2	23	16	0	91	92	30	43	0	3.96
2 Warren Spahn	L	44	3	4	.429	0	16	11	3	72	70	21	34	0	3.38
2 Bill Henry	L	37	2	2	.500	4	35	0	0	42	40	8	35	0	3.64
Bob Priddy	R	25	1	0	1.000	1	6	0	0	15	7	13	8	0	1.80
1 Bob Hendley	L	26	0	0	—	0	8	2	0	15	27	13	8	0	12.60
Dick Estelle	L	23	0	0	—	0	6	1	0	11	12	6	6	0	4.09
Matty Alou	L	26	0	0	—	0	1	0	0	1	3	3	0	0	0.00
1 Jim Duffalo	R	29	0	1	.000	0	2	0	0	.1	2	1	2	0	27.00
Bill Hands	R	25	0	2	.000	0	2	0	0	6	13	6	5	0	16.50

PITTSBURGH 3rd 90-72 .556 7 — HARRY WALKER

NAME	G by Pos	B	AGE	G	AB	R	H	2B	3B	HR	RBI	BB	SO	SB	BA	SA
TOTALS			28	163	5686	675	1506	217	57	111	631	419	1008	51	.265	.382
Donn Clendenon	1B158, 3B1	R	29	162	612	89	184	32	14	14	96	48	128	9	.301	.467
Bill Mazeroski	2B127	R	28	130	494	52	134	17	1	6	54	18	34	2	.271	.346
Gene Alley	SS110, 2B40, 3B1	R	24	153	500	47	126	21	6	5	47	32	82	7	.252	.348
Bob Bailey	3B142, OF28	R	22	159	626	87	160	28	3	11	49	70	93	10	.256	.363
Roberto Clemente	OF145	R	30	152	589	91	194	21	14	10	65	43	78	8	.329	.463
Bill Virdon	OF128	L	34	135	481	58	134	22	5	4	24	30	49	4	.279	.370
Willie Stargell	OF137, 1B7	L	25	144	533	68	145	25	8	27	107	39	127	1	.272	.501
Jim Pagliaroni	C131	R	27	134	403	42	108	15	0	17	65	41	84	0	.268	.432
Manny Mota	OF95	R	27	121	294	47	82	7	6	4	29	22	32	2	.279	.384
Andre Rodgers	SS33, 3B15, 1B6, 2B1	R	30	75	178	17	51	12	0	2	25	18	28	2	.287	.388
Jerry Lynch	OF26	L	34	73	121	7	34	1	0	5	16	8	26	0	.281	.413
Del Crandall	C60	R	35	60	140	11	30	2	0	2	10	14	10	1	.214	.271
1 Gene Freese	3B19	R	31	43	80	6	21	4	0	0	8	6	18	0	.263	.313
2 Jose Pagan	3B15, SS7	R	30	42	38	6	9	1	0	0	1	1	7	1	.237	.263
Ozzie Virgil	C15, 3B7, 2B5	R	32	39	49	3	13	2	0	1	5	2	10	0	.265	.367
1 Dick Schofield	SS28	B	30	31	109	13	25	5	0	0	6	15	19	1	.229	.275
George Spriggs	OF1	L	24	9	2	5	1	0	0	0	0	0	0	2	.500	.500

Jerry May 21 R 1-2, Hal Smith 34 R 0-3, Bob Oliver 22 R 0-2

NAME	T	AGE	W	L	PCT	SV	G	GS	CG	IP	H	BB	SO	SHO	ERA
TOTALS		29	90	72	.556	27	163	163	49	1479	1324	469	882	17	3.01
Vern Law	R	35	17	9	.654	0	29	28	13	217	182	35	101	4	2.16
Bob Veale	L	29	17	12	.586	0	39	37	14	266	221	119	276	7	2.84
Don Cardwell	R	29	13	10	.565	0	37	34	12	240	214	59	107	2	3.19
Don Schwall	R	29	9	6	.600	4	43	1	0	77	77	30	55	0	2.92
Bob Friend	R	34	8	12	.400	0	34	34	8	222	221	47	74	2	3.24
Tommie Sisk	R	23	7	3	.700	0	38	12	1	111	103	50	66	1	3.41
Al McBean	R	27	6	6	.500	18	62	1	0	114	111	42	54	0	2.29
Roy Face (KJ)	R	37	5	2	.714	16	0	0	0	20	20	7	19	0	2.70
Joe Gibbon	L	30	4	9	.308	1	31	15	1	106	85	34	63	0	4.50
Frank Carpin	L	26	3	1	.750	4	39	0	0	40	35	24	27	0	3.15
Wilbur Wood	L	23	1	1	.500	0	34	1	0	51	44	16	29	0	3.18
Luke Walker	L	21	0	0	—	0	2	0	0	5	2	1	5	0	0.00
Tom Butters	R	27	0	1	.000	0	5	0	0	9	9	6	7	0	7.00

CINCINNATI 4th 89-73 .549 8 — DICK SISLER

NAME	G by Pos	B	AGE	G	AB	R	H	2B	3B	HR	RBI	BB	SO	SB	BA	SA
TOTALS			26	162	5658	825	1544	268	61	183	776	538	1003	82	.273	.439
Gordy Coleman	1B89	L	30	108	325	39	98	19	0	14	57	24	38	0	.302	.489
Pete Rose	2B162	B	24	162	670	117	209	35	11	11	81	69	76	8	.312	.446
Leo Cardenas	SS155	R	26	156	557	65	160	25	11	11	57	60	100	1	.287	.431
Deron Johnson	3B156	R	26	159	616	92	177	30	7	32	130	52	97	0	.287	.515
Frank Robinson	OF155	R	29	156	582	109	172	33	5	33	113	70	100	13	.296	.540
Vada Pinson	OF159	L	26	159	669	97	204	34	10	22	94	43	81	21	.305	.484
Tommy Harper	OF159, 3B2, 2B1	R	24	159	646	126	166	28	3	18	64	78	127	35	.257	.393
Johnny Edwards	C110	L	27	114	371	47	99	22	2	17	51	50	45	0	.267	.474
Tony Perez	1B93	R	23	104	281	40	73	14	4	12	47	21	67	0	.260	.466
Don Pavletich	C54, 1B9	R	26	68	191	25	61	11	4	8	32	23	27	1	.319	.513
Art Shamsky	OF18, 1B1	L	23	64	96	13	25	4	3	2	10	10	29	1	.260	.427
Marty Keough	1B32, OF4	L	31	62	43	14	5	0	0	3	3	14	0	.116	.116
Chico Ruiz (BL)	3B4, SS3	B	26	29	18	7	2	1	0	0	1	0	5	1	.111	.167
Charlie James	OF7	R	27	26	39	2	8	0	0	0	2	1	3	0	.205	.205
Jimmie Coker	C19	R	29	24	61	3	15	2	0	1	6	3	10	0	.246	.377
Tommy Helms	SS8, 3B2, 2B1	R	24	21	42	4	16	2	2	0	6	3	7	1	.381	.524

Mel Queen 23 L 0-3, Lee May 22 R 0-4, Steve Boros 28 R 0-0

NAME	T	AGE	W	L	PCT	SV	G	GS	CG	IP	H	BB	SO	SHO	ERA
TOTALS		28	89	73	.549	34	162	162	43	1457	1355	587	1113	9	3.89
Sammy Ellis	R	24	22	10	.688	2	44	39	15	264	222	104	183	2	3.78
Jim Maloney	R	25	20	9	.690	2	33	33	14	255	189	110	244	5	2.54
Joe Nuxhall	L	36	11	4	.733	2	32	16	5	149	142	31	117	1	3.44
Joey Jay	R	29	9	8	.529	1	37	24	4	156	150	63	102	1	4.21
Billy McCool	L	20	9	10	.474	21	62	2	0	105	93	47	120	0	4.29
John Tsitouris	R	29	6	9	.400	1	31	20	3	131	134	65	91	0	4.95
Ted Davidson	L	25	4	3	.571	1	24	1	0	69	57	17	54	0	2.22
Jim O'Toole	L	28	3	10	.231	1	29	22	2	128	154	47	71	0	5.91
1 Bill Henry	R	37	2	0	1.000	0	3	0	0	5	3	1	5	0	0.00
Jerry Arrigo	L	24	2	4	.333	2	37	5	0	54	75	30	43	0	6.17
Roger Craig	R	35	1	4	.200	2	40	0	0	64	74	25	30	0	3.66
Dom Zanni	R	33	0	0	—	0	3	0	0	10	5	5	10	0	1.38
Darrell Osteen	R	22	0	0	—	0	1	0	0	3	1	1	0	0	0.00
2 Jim Duffalo	R	29	0	1	.000	0	22	0	0	44	33	30	34	0	3.48
Bobby Locke	R	31	0	1	.000	0	7	0	0	17	24	8	6	0	5.82

MILWAUKEE 5th 86-76 .531 11 — BOBBY BRAGAN

NAME	G by Pos	B	AGE	G	AB	R	H	2B	3B	HR	RBI	BB	SO	SB	BA	SA
TOTALS			27	162	5542	708	1419	243	28	196	664	408	976	64	.256	.416
Gene Oliver	1B52, C64, OF1	R	29	122	392	56	106	20	0	21	58	36	61	5	.270	.482
Frank Bolling	2B147	R	33	148	535	55	141	26	3	7	50	24	61	4	.264	.363
Woody Woodward	SS107, 2B8	R	22	112	265	17	55	7	4	0	11	10	50	2	.208	.264
Eddie Mathews	3B153	L	33	156	546	77	137	23	0	32	95	73	110	1	.251	.469
Hank Aaron	OF148	R	31	150	570	109	181	40	1	32	89	60	81	24	.318	.560
Mack Jones	OF133	L	26	143	504	78	132	18	7	31	75	29	122	8	.262	.510
Felipe Alou	OF91, 1B69, 3B2, SS1	R	30	143	555	80	165	29	2	23	78	31	63	8	.297	.481
Joe Torre	C100, 1B49	R	24	148	523	68	152	21	1	27	80	61	79	0	.291	.489
Ty Cline	OF86, 1B5	L	26	123	220	27	42	5	3	0	16	16	50	2	.191	.241
Rico Carty	OF73	R	25	83	271	37	84	18	1	10	35	17	44	1	.310	.494
Mike de la Hoz	SS41, 3B22, 2B10, 1B1	R	26	81	176	15	45	3	2	2	11	8	21	0	.256	.330
Denis Menke (KJ)	SS54, 1B8, 3B4	R	24	71	181	16	44	13	1	4	18	18	28	1	.243	.392
Sandy Alomar	SS39, 2B19	B	21	67	108	16	26	1	1	0	8	4	12	12	.241	.269
Lou Klimchock	1B4	L	25	34	39	3	3	0	0	0	3	1	5	0	.077	.077
2 Jesse Gonder	C13	L	29	31	53	2	8	2	0	1	9	4	9	0	.151	.245
1 Gary Kolb	OF13	L	25	28	27	5	7	2	0	1	5	4	6	1	.259	.259
Don Dillard	OF1	L	28	20	19	1	3	2	0	0	1	1	6	0	.158	.316
2 Billy Cowan	OF10	R	26	19	45	5	10	1	0	1	2	0	11	0	.222	.311
1 Lee Maye	OF13	L	30	15	53	8	16	2	0	2	7	2	8	0	.302	.453
3 Frank Thomas	1B6, OF3	R	36	15	33	1	7	2	0	1	6	3	5	0	.212	.303
Johnny Blanchard	OF1	L	32	10	10	1	1	0	0	0	3	1	4	0	.100	.100
Tommie Aaron	1B6	R	25	10	16	1	3	1	0	0	1	1	1	0	.188	.188
3 Jim Beauchamp	1B2	R	23	4	5	0	0	0	0	0	0	0	2	0	.000	.000

NAME	T	AGE	W	L	PCT	SV	G	GS	CG	IP	H	BB	SO	SHO	ERA
TOTALS		27	86	76	.531	38	162	162	43	1448	1336	541	966	4	3.52
Tony Cloninger	R	24	24	11	.686	1	40	38	16	279	247	119	211	1	3.29
Wade Blasingame	L	21	16	10	.615	1	38	36	10	225	200	116	117	1	3.76
2 Ken Johnson	R	32	13	8	.619	2	29	26	8	180	165	37	123	1	3.20
Billy O'Dell	L	32	10	6	.625	18	62	1	0	111	87	30	78	0	2.19
Hank Fischer	R	25	8	9	.471	0	31	19	2	123	126	39	79	0	3.88
Denny Lemaster (SA)	R	26	7	13	.350	0	32	23	4	146	140	58	111	1	4.44
Bob Sadowski	R	27	5	3	.357	3	34	13	3	123	117	35	78	0	4.32
Phil Niekro	R	26	2	3	.400	4	41	0	0	75	73	26	49	0	2.88
Dick Kelley	L	25	1	1	.500	0	7	4	0	45	37	20	31	0	3.00
1 Dave Eilers	R	28	0	0	—	1	19	0	0	35	35	13	16	0	11.25
Clay Carroll	R	24	0	1	.000	1	19	1	0	35	35	13	16	0	4.37
Chi Chi Olivo	R	39	0	1	.000	3	12	0	0	18	12	5	11	0	1.38
1 Bobby Tiefenauer	R	35	0	1	.000	0	9	0	0	7	8	1	7	0	7.71
Dan Osinski	R	31	0	3	.000	6	61	0	0	83	81	40	54	0	2.82

1965 NATIONAL LEAGUE

PHILADELPHIA 6th 85-76 .528 11.5 GENE MAUCH

NAME	G by Pos	B	AGE	G	AB	R	H	2B	3B	HR	RBI	BB	SO	SB	BA	SA
TOTALS			27	162	5528	654	1380	205	53	144	608	494	1091	46	.250	.384
Dick Stuart	1B143, 3B1	R	32	149	538	53	126	19	1	28	95	39	136	1	.234	.429
Tony Taylor	2B86, 3B5	R	29	106	323	41	74	14	3	3	27	22	58	5	.229	.319
Bobby Wine	SS135, 1B4	R	26	139	394	31	90	8	1	5	33	31	69	0	.228	.292
Dick Allen	3B160, SS2	R	23	161	619	93	187	31	14	20	85	74	150	15	.302	.494
Johnny Callison	OF159	L	26	160	619	93	162	25	16	32	101	57	117	6	.262	.509
Tony Gonzalez	OF104	L	28	108	370	48	109	19	1	13	41	31	52	3	.295	.457
Alex Johnson	OF82	R	22	97	262	27	77	9	3	8	28	15	60	4	.294	.443
Clay Dalrymple	C102	L	28	103	301	14	64	5	5	4	23	34	37	0	.213	.302
Cookie Rojas	2B84, OF55, SS11, C2, 1B1	R	26	142	521	78	158	25	3	3	42	42	33	5	.303	.380
Ruben Amaro	1B60, SS60, 2B6	R	29	118	184	26	39	7	0	0	15	27	22	1	.212	.250
Wes Covington	OF64	L	33	101	235	27	58	10	1	15	45	26	47	0	.247	.489
Johnny Briggs	OF66	L	21	93	229	47	54	9	4	4	23	42	44	3	.236	.362
Pat Corrales	C62	R	24	63	174	16	39	8	1	2	15	25	42	0	.224	.316
John Herrnstein	1B18, OF14	L	27	63	85	8	17	2	0	1	5	2	18	0	.200	.259
Adolfo Phillips	OF32	R	23	41	87	14	20	4	0	3	5	5	34	3	.230	.379
1 Frank Thomas	OF12, 1B11, 3B1	R	36	35	77	7	20	4	0	1	7	4	10	0	.260	.351
1 Gus Triandos	C28	R	34	30	82	3	14	2	0	0	4	9	17	0	.171	.195
Bill Sorrell	3B1	L	24	10	13	2	5	0	0	1	2	2	1	0	.385	.615
Bobby Del Greco	OF4	R	32	8	4	1	0	0	0	0	0	0	1	0	.000	.000

NAME	T	AGE	W	L	PCT	SV	G	GS	CG	IP	H	BB	SO	SHO	ERA
		30	85	76	.528	21	162	162	50	1469	1426	466	1071	18	3.53
Jim Bunning	R	33	19	9	.679	0	39	39	15	291	253	62	268	7	2.60
Chris Short	L	27	18	11	.621	2	47	40	15	297	260	89	237	5	2.82
Ray Culp	R	23	14	10	.583	0	33	30	11	204	188	78	134	2	3.22
Gary Wagner	R	25	7	7	.500	7	59	0	0	105	87	49	91	0	3.00
Ed Roebuck	R	33	5	3	.625	3	44	0	0	50	55	15	29	0	3.42
Jack Baldschun	R	28	5	8	.385	6	65	0	0	99	102	42	91	0	3.82
Ray Herbert	R	35	5	8	.385	1	25	19	4	131	162	19	51	1	4.83
Bo Belinsky	L	28	4	9	.308	1	30	14	3	111	103	48	71	0	5.45
2 Lew Burdette	R	38	3	3	.500	0	19	9	1	71	95	17	23	1	5.45
Ferguson Jenkins	R	21	2	1	.667	1	7	0	0	12	7	2	10	0	2.25
Art Mahaffey	R	27	2	5	.286	0	22	9	1	71	82	32	52	0	6.21
Grant Jackson	L	22	1	1	.500	0	6	2	0	14	17	5	15	0	7.07
1 Ryne Duren	R	36	0	0	—	0	6	0	0	11	10	4	6	0	3.27
Morrie Steevens	L	24	0	0	.000	0	6	0	0	3	5	4	3	0	15.00

ST. LOUIS 7th 80-81 .497 16.5 RED SCHOENDIENST

NAME	G by Pos	B	AGE	G	AB	R	H	2B	3B	HR	RBI	BB	SO	SB	BA	SA
TOTALS			28	162	5579	707	1415	234	46	109	645	477	882	100	.254	.371
Bill White	1B144	L	31	148	543	82	157	26	3	24	73	63	86	3	.289	.481
Julian Javier (BG)	2B69	R	28	77	229	34	52	6	3	4	28	8	44	5	.227	.314
Dick Groat	SS148, 3B2	R	34	153	587	55	149	26	5	0	52	56	50	1	.254	.315
Ken Boyer	3B143	R	34	144	535	71	139	18	2	13	75	57	73	2	.260	.374
Mike Shannon	OF101, C4	R	25	124	244	32	54	17	3	3	25	28	46	2	.221	.352
Curt Flood	OF151	R	27	156	617	90	191	30	3	11	83	51	50	9	.310	.421
Lou Brock	OF153	L	26	155	631	107	182	35	8	16	69	45	116	63	.288	.445
Tim McCarver	C111	L	23	113	409	48	113	7	2	11	48	31	26	5	.276	.408
Phil Gagliano	2B57, OF25, 3B19	R	23	122	363	46	87	14	2	8	53	40	45	2	.240	.355
Tito Francona	OF34, 1B13	L	31	81	174	15	45	6	2	5	19	17	30	0	.259	.402
Bob Skinner	OF33	L	33	80	152	25	47	5	4	5	26	12	30	1	.309	.493
Dal Maxvill	2B49, SS23	R	26	68	89	10	12	2	0	0	10	7	15	0	.135	.202
Jerry Buchek	2B33, SS18, 3B1	R	23	55	166	17	41	8	3	3	21	13	46	1	.247	.386
Bob Uecker	C49	R	30	53	145	17	33	7	0	2	10	24	27	0	.228	.317
1 Carl Warwick	OF21, 1B4	R	28	50	77	3	12	2	1	0	6	4	18	1	.156	.208
Bob Gibson	P38	R	29	42	104	14	25	2	0	5	19	3	26	2	.240	.404
Ted Savage	OF20	R	28	30	63	7	10	3	0	1	4	6	9	1	.159	.254
Bobby Tolan	OF17	L	19	17	69	8	13	2	0	0	6	0	4	2	.188	.217
Dave Ricketts	C11	R	29	11	29	1	7	0	0	0	0	1	3	0	.241	.241
George Kernek	1B7	L	25	10	31	4	9	1	0	1	7	7	6	0	.290	.452
Ed Spiezio	3B3	R	23	10	18	0	3	0	0	0	5	1	4	0	.167	.167

NAME	T	AGE	W	L	PCT	SV	G	GS	CG	IP	H	BB	SO	SHO	ERA
		28	80	81	.497	35	162	162	40	1461	1414	467	916	11	3.77
Bob Gibson	R	29	20	12	.625	1	38	36	20	299	243	103	270	6	3.07
Tracy Stallard	R	27	11	8	.579	0	40	26	4	194	172	70	99	1	3.39
Bob Purkey	R	35	10	9	.526	2	32	17	3	124	148	33	39	1	5.81
Ray Washburn	R	27	9	11	.450	2	28	16	1	119	114	28	67	1	3.63
Curt Simmons	L	36	9	15	.375	0	34	32	5	203	229	54	96	0	4.08
Ray Sadecki	L	24	6	15	.286	1	36	24	1	173	192	64	122	0	5.20
Larry Jaster	L	21	1	0	1.000	0	4	3	3	28	21	7	10	0	1.61
2 Hal Woodeshick	L	32	3	3	.600	15	51	0	0	60	47	27	37	0	1.80
Nelson Briles	R	21	3	3	.500	4	37	2	0	82	79	26	52	0	3.51
1 Ron Taylor	R	27	2	1	.667	1	25	0	0	44	43	15	26	0	4.50
Barney Schultz	R	38	2	2	.500	2	34	0	0	42	39	11	38	0	3.86
Don Dennis	R	23	2	3	.400	6	41	0	0	55	47	16	29	0	2.29
Steve Carlton	L	20	0	0	—	0	15	2	0	25	27	8	21	0	2.52
Dennis Aust	R	24	0	0	—	0	7	0	0	7	6	2	7	0	5.14
Earl Francis	R	28	0	0	—	0	5	0	0	5	7	3	4	0	5.40

CHICAGO 8th 72-90 .444 25 BOB KENNEDY 24-32 .429 LOU KLEIN 48-58 .453

NAME	G by Pos	B	AGE	G	AB	R	H	2B	3B	HR	RBI	BB	SO	SB	BA	SA
TOTALS			27	164	5540	635	1316	202	33	134	590	532	948	65	.238	.358
Ernie Banks	1B162	R	34	163	612	79	162	25	3	28	106	55	64	3	.265	.453
Glenn Beckert	2B153	R	24	154	614	73	147	21	3	3	30	28	52	6	.239	.298
Don Kessinger	SS105	R	22	106	309	19	62	4	3	0	14	20	44	1	.201	.233
Ron Santo	3B164	R	25	164	608	88	173	30	4	33	101	88	109	3	.285	.510
Billy Williams	OF164	L	27	164	645	115	203	39	6	34	108	65	76	10	.315	.552
Don Landrum	OF115	L	29	131	425	60	96	20	4	6	34	30	84	14	.226	.334
Doug Clemens	OF105	L	26	128	340	36	75	11	0	4	26	38	53	5	.221	.288
Vic Roznovsky	C63	R	26	71	172	9	38	4	1	3	16	16	30	1	.221	.308
Jimmy Stewart	OF55, SS48	B	26	116	282	26	63	9	4	0	19	30	53	13	.223	.284
George Altman	OF45, 1B2	L	32	90	196	24	46	7	1	4	23	19	36	3	.235	.342
Joey Amalfitano	2B24, SS4	R	31	67	96	13	26	4	0	0	8	12	14	2	.271	.313
2 Ed Bailey	C54, 1B3	L	34	66	150	13	38	6	0	5	23	34	28	0	.253	.393
Chris Krug	C58	R	25	60	169	16	34	5	0	5	24	13	52	0	.201	.320
2 Harvey Kuenn	OF35, 1B1	R	34	54	120	11	26	5	0	0	6	22	13	1	.217	.258
Roberto Pena	SS50	R	28	51	170	17	37	5	1	2	12	16	19	1	.218	.294
1 Dick Bertell	C34	R	29	34	84	6	18	2	0	0	7	11	10	0	.214	.238
1 Len Gabrielson	OF14, 1B1	L	25	28	48	4	12	0	0	3	5	7	16	0	.250	.438
Harry Bright		R	35	27	25	1	7	1	0	0	4	0	8	0	.280	.320
Ellis Burton	OF12	B	28	17	40	6	7	1	0	0	4	1	10	1	.175	.200
Don Young	OF11	R	19	11	35	1	2	0	0	1	2	0	6	0	.057	.143

Leo Burke 31 R 2-10, John Boccabella 24 R 4-12, Byron Browne 22 R 0-6, Ron Campbell 25 R 0-2, Chuck Hartenstein 23 R 0-0

NAME	T	AGE	W	L	PCT	SV	G	GS	CG	IP	H	BB	SO	SHO	ERA
		29	72	90	.444	35	164	164	33	1472	1470	481	855	9	3.78
Dick Ellsworth	L	25	14	15	.483	1	36	34	8	222	227	57	130	0	3.81
Larry Jackson	R	34	14	21	.400	0	39	39	12	257	268	57	131	4	3.85
Bob Buhl	R	36	13	11	.542	0	32	31	2	184	207	57	92	0	4.40
Cal Koonce	R	24	7	9	.438	0	38	23	3	173	181	52	88	1	3.69
Bill Faul	R	25	6	6	.500	0	17	16	5	97	83	18	59	3	3.53
Lindy McDaniel	R	29	5	6	.455	2	71	0	0	129	115	47	92	0	2.58
2 Bob Hendley	L	26	4	4	.500	0	18	10	2	62	59	25	38	0	4.35
Ted Abernathy	R	32	4	6	.400	31	84	0	0	136	113	56	104	0	2.58
Bob Humphreys	R	29	2	0	1.000	0	41	0	0	66	59	27	38	0	3.14
Billy Hoeft	L	33	2	2	.500	1	29	2	1	51	41	20	44	0	2.22
Ernie Broglio	R	29	1	6	.143	0	26	6	0	51	63	46	22	0	6.88
Ken Holtzman	L	19	0		—	0	3	0	0	4	4	2	3	0	2.25
Jack Warner	R	24	0	1	.000	0	11	0	0	16	22	9	7	0	8.44
Frank Baumann	L	32	0	1	.000	0	2	0	0	3	4	6	2	0	6.75
1 Lew Burdette	R	38	0	2	.000	0	7	3	0	20	26	4	5	0	5.40

HOUSTON 9th 65-97 .401 32 LUM HARRIS

NAME	G by Pos	B	AGE	G	AB	R	H	2B	3B	HR	RBI	BB	SO	SB	BA	SA
TOTALS			27	162	5483	569	1299	188	42	97	523	502	877	90	.237	.340
Walt Bond	1B74, OF38	L	27	117	407	46	107	17	2	7	47	42	51	2	.263	.366
Joe Morgan	2B157	L	21	157	601	100	163	22	12	14	40	97	77	20	.271	.418
Bob Lillis	SS104, 3B9, 2B6	R	35	124	408	39	90	12	1	0	20	20	10	2	.221	.255
Bob Aspromonte	3B146, 1B6, SS4	R	27	152	578	53	152	15	2	5	52	38	54	2	.263	.322
Rusty Staub	OF112, 1B1	L	21	131	410	43	105	20	1	14	63	52	57	3	.256	.422
Jim Wynn	OF155	R	23	157	564	90	155	30	7	22	73	84	126	43	.275	.470
2 Lee Maye	OF103	L	30	108	415	38	104	17	7	3	36	20	37	1	.251	.347
Ron Brand	C102, 3B6, OF5	R	25	117	391	27	92	6	3	2	37	19	34	10	.235	.281
Joe Gaines	OF65	R	28	100	229	21	52	8	1	6	30	18	59	4	.227	.349
2 Jim Gentile	1B68	L	31	81	227	22	55	11	4	7	31	34	72	0	.242	.392
Eddie Kasko (KJ)	SS59, 3B2	R	33	68	215	18	53	7	1	1	10	11	20	1	.247	.302
John Bateman	C39	R	24	45	142	15	28	3	1	7	14	12	37	0	.197	.380
2 Al Spangler	OF33	L	31	38	112	18	24	1	1	1	7	14	8	1	.214	.268
2 Gus Triandos	C20	R	34	24	72	5	13	2	0	2	7	5	14	0	.181	.292
2 Jim Beauchamp	1B3	R	25	13	31	2	6	1	0	1	4	3	10	0	.189	.308
2 Frank Thomas	1B16, 3B2, OF1	R	36	23	58	7	10	2	0	3	9	5	8	0	.172	.362
Nellie Fox	2B46, 3B6	R	37	73	195	21	47	12	1	1	10	14	9	2	.241	.328
Chuck Harrison	1B12	R	24	15	45	2	9	3	0	0	5	3	14	0	.200	.356
David Adlesh	C13	R	22	15	43	1	6	3	0	0	1	2	12	0	.147	.209
Norm Miller	OF2	L	19	11	15	2	3	0	0	1	2	1	9	0	.200	.333
Sonny Jackson	SS8, 3B1	L	21	13	23	4	3	0	0	0	1	1	9	1	.130	.130

Mike White 26 R 0-9, Jim Mahoney 31 R 1-5, Gene Ratliff 19 R 0-4, John Hoffman 21 L 2-6

NAME	T	AGE	W	L	PCT	SV	G	GS	CG	IP	H	BB	SO	SHO	ERA
		28	65	97	.401	26	162	162	29	1461	1459	388	931	7	3.84
Dick Farrell	R	31	11	11	.500	1	33	29	8	208	202	35	122	3	3.50
Bob Bruce	R	32	9	18	.333	0	35	34	7	230	241	38	145	1	3.72
Dave Giusti	R	25	8	7	.533	3	38	13	4	131	132	46	92	1	4.33
Claude Raymond	R	28	7	4	.636	5	33	7	2	96	87	16	79	0	2.91
Larry Dierker	R	18	7	8	.467	0	26	19	1	147	135	37	109	0	3.49
2 Jim Owens	R	31	6	5	.545	8	50	0	0	71	64	29	53	0	3.30
2 Robin Roberts	R	38	5	7	.714	0	10	10	3	76	61	10	34	2	1.89
Don Nottebart	R	29	4	15	.211	0	29	25	3	158	166	55	77	0	4.67
1 Ken Johnson	R	32	2		.600	0	8	1	0	52	52	11	28	0	4.15
1 Hal Woodeshick	L	32	3	4	.429	3	27	0	0	37	36	18	22	0	3.09
2 Ron Taylor	R	27	1	5	.167	4	32	1	0	58	68	16	37	0	6.36
2 Don Lee	R	31	0	0	—	0	4	0	0	7	9	2	7	0	3.38
Bruce Von Hoff	R	22	0	0	—	0	2	0	0	3	4	2	3	0	3.00
Don Arlich	L	22	0	0	—	0	4	0	0	6	8	1	3	0	5.40
1 Don Larsen	R	35	0	0	—	0	1	0	0	3	2	1	1	0	0.00
Gordon Jones	R	35	0	0	—	0	4	0	0	4	6	1	3	0	3.86
Carroll Sembera	R	23	0	1	.000	0	4	1	0	11	13	4	9	0	4.79
Chris Zachary	R	21	0	0	—	0	4	0	0	7	14	5	3	0	4.09
2 Jack Lamabe	R	28	0	2	.000	0	12	0	0	13	17	3	8	0	4.15
Jim Ray	R	20	0	1	.000	0	2	0	0	8	11	6	7	0	10.13
Ken MacKenzie	L	31	0	0	—	0	7	0	0	37	46	6	26	0	3.89

NEW YORK 10th 50-112 .309 47 CASEY STENGEL 31-64 .326 WES WESTRUM 19-48 .284

NAME	G by Pos	B	AGE	G	AB	R	H	2B	3B	HR	RBI	BB	SO	SB	BA	SA
TOTALS			27	164	5441	495	1202	203	27	107	460	392	1129	28	.221	.327
Ed Kranepool	1B147	L	20	153	525	44	133	24	4	10	53	39	71	1	.253	.371
2 Chuck Hiller	2B80, OF4, 3B2	L	30	100	286	24	68	11	1	5	21	14	24	1	.238	.336
Roy McMillan	SS153	R	35	157	528	44	128	19	2	1	42	24	60	1	.242	.292
Charley Smith	3B131, SS6, 2B1	R	27	135	499	49	122	20	3	16	62	17	123	2	.244	.393
Johnny Lewis	OF142	L	25	148	477	64	117	15	3	15	45	59	117	4	.245	.384
Jim Hickman	OF91, 1B30, 3B14	R	28	141	369	32	87	14	2	10	27	30	76	3	.236	.407
Ron Swoboda	OF112	R	21	135	399	52	91	15	3	19	50	33	102	2	.228	.424
Chris Cannizzaro	C112	R	27	114	251	17	46	8	2	0	28	50	60	0	.183	.231
Joe Christopher	OF112	R	29	148	438	30	109	18	3	5	40	35	82	4	.249	.339
Bobby Klaus	2B72, SS28, 3B25	R	27	119	288	30	55	9	2	12	45	49	85	1	.191	.253
1 Billy Cowan	OF61, 2B2, SS1	R	26	82	156	16	28	8	3	2	9	7	45	1	.179	.314
Danny Napoleon	OF15, 3B7	R	23	69	97	5	14	1	1	0	8	2	23	0	.144	.175
Johnny Stephenson	C47, OF2, 1B1	L	24	62	121	9	26	3	0	1	6	11	19	0	.215	.355
Ron Hunt (SJ)	2B46, 3B6	R	24	57	196	21	47	12	1	1	10	14	9	2	.240	.327
1 Jesse Gonder	C31	L	28	57	153	10	37	6	0	2	21	7	19	0	.238	.327
2 Gary Kolb	OF29, 1B1, 3B1	L	25	50	90	6	15	2	1	1	8	9	15	3	.167	.222
Cleon Jones	OF30	R	22	30	74	6	11	2	0	0	1	2	18	1	.149	.203
Hawk Taylor	C15, 1B1	R	26	32	46	5	7	2	0	2	6	4	15	0	.152	.413
2 Jimmie Schaffer	C21	R	29	24	37	1	5	2	0	0	1	0	15	0	.135	.189
Bud Harrelson	SS18	R	21	19	37	2	5	0	0	0	1	1	6	1	.108	.189
Greg Goossen	C8	R	19	11	31	2	9	3	0	0	2	1	4	0	.290	.387
Kevin Collins (SJ)	3B7, SS3	L	18	11	23	3	4	2	0	0	1	2	1	0	.174	.217
Yogi Berra	C2	L	40	4	9	1	2	0	0	0	0	0	0	0	.222	.222

NAME	T	AGE	W	L	PCT	SV	G	GS	CG	IP	H	BB	SO	SHO	ERA
		26	50	112	.309	14	164	164	29	1455	1462	498	776	11	4.06
Al Jackson	L	29	8	20	.286	1	37	31	7	205	217	61	120	3	4.35
Jack Fisher	R	26	8	24	.250	1	43	36	10	254	252	68	116	0	3.93
Gary Kroll	R	23	6	6	.500	2	32	11	1	87	83	41	62	0	4.45
Galen Cisco	R	29	4	8	.333	3	32	11	1	112	119	51	54	1	4.50
1 Warren Spahn	L	44	4	12	.250	0	20	19	5	126	140	35	56	0	4.36
Darrell Sutherland	R	23	3	1	.750	0	18	2	0	48	33	17	16	0	2.81
Larry Bearnarth	R	23	3	5	.375	1	40	3	0	61	75	28	16	0	4.57
Jim Bethke	R	18	2	0	1.000	0	25	0	0	41	41	22	19	0	4.28
Dick Selma	R	21	1	6	.667	0	9	4	1	27	24	9	26	1	3.67
Gordie Richardson	L	25	2	2	.500	2	35	0	0	57	61	16	43	0	3.81
Tug McGraw	L	20	2	7	.222	1	37	9	1	98	88	48	57	0	3.31
2 Dave Eilers	R	29	1	4	.200	1	19	0	0	38	46	11	20	0	4.00
Carl Willey	R	34	1	2	.333	0	12	3	0	28	30	15	13	0	4.18
Dennis Ribant	R	23	1	3	.250	0	19	1	0	35	29	6	19	0	3.86
1 Frank Lary	R	35	1	3	.250	0	17	5	1	57	48	16	23	0	3.00
Larry Miller	L	28	1	4	.200	0	28	4	0	57	66	25	36	0	5.05
Tom Parsons	R	25	1	10	.091	1	17	11	1	91	108	17	58	1	4.65
Dennis Musgraves (E)	R	21	0	0	—	0	3	1	1	16	11	7	11	0	0.56
Bob Moorhead	R	27	0	1	.000	0	10	0	0	16	21	4	10	0	4.50
Rob Gardner	L	20	0	2	.000	0	5	4	0	28	31	7	18	0	3.21

1966 Heads You Win, Tails I Lose

Frank Robinson was a proven star. He had provided the muscle in the Cincinnati attack since first coming up to the majors in 1956. Milt Pappas was not a star, simply a good pitcher who had toiled with the Baltimore Orioles since 1957, never winning more than 16 games in one season. But Cincinnati was not happy with Robinson because of some off-field incidents and decided it was time for a trade. The Orioles were willing and made a clean swap, man for man, with Pappas for Robinson. The newspaper headlines generated much conversation. Cincinnati rooters screamed and Baltimore fans cheered. The Dodgers' Sandy Koufax was happy to see Robinson go, if only because of what his bat had done to the ace left-hander's E.R.A. When all the words were written and the throats hoarse, the consensus was that Baltimore got the best of it. Pappas defended himself and Cincinnati by saying that the trade could not be truly evaluated before several years had elapsed. Baltimore did not care what the years would prove because, by the time the 1966 season ended, it was clear they had it all.

Playing with a vengeance to prove the Cincinnati Reds wrong in trading him, the lean, confident Robinson used his first season in the American League to sweep the Triple Crown and the MVP Award, while leading the Orioles to an easy pennant victory—their first since coming to Baltimore in 1954.

After Cleveland held first place going into June, Hank Bauer's Birds flew into the lead and ran off a 13-game lead by the end of July, enough of a margin to allow the Orioles to coast home the rest of the way. Although Brooks Robinson and Boog Powell combined with the Cincinnati cast-off to give the Orioles three 100 RBI men and the league's best attack, the pitching staff was not without its problems. Dave McNally and Jim Palmer were healthy all year, but Steve Barber and Wally Bunker had to sit out parts of the season nursing bad arms. A very low total of complete games was compensated for by a standout veteran bullpen led by slow baller Stu Miller and knuckle baller Eddie Fisher.

The ascendance of the Orioles coincided with the complete collapse of the New York Yankees into last place. Maris and Mantle were no longer the feared threats they once were, Elston Howard was a mere shadow of his former self, Whitey Ford had problems in his shoulder and won only two games, and Tony Kubek was forced to retire before the season began because of a recurring back injury. In the course of two years, the club slipped from five straight pennants into an ignoble tenth-place finish. Manager Johnny Keane's dream of glory ended in May, as Ralph Houk left his general manager's chair to resume field director duties. At the season's end, Maris and Clete Boyer would be traded off, marking the start of a long rebuilding program for the once-masters of baseball, and Keane, troubled by his failure, would become the victim of a heart attack just as the new year got underway.

With Robinson sweeping the offensive awards, pitching leaderships went to Minnesota's Jim Kaat for the most victories and to Gary Peters of Chicago for the lowest earned run average.

The National League race was a close copy of the previous year with the Los Angeles Dodgers again nailing down the crown on the final day of the season to thwart season-long standout performances by the Giants and Pirates. In the spring, Dodger manager Walter Alston was not sure whether he would have his ace pitching duo of Sandy Koufax and Don Drysdale back in the fold. The two mound stars pulled a dramatic joint holdout, refusing to sign until both received the pacts they thought they deserved. As spring training was winding to an end, both finally signed—Koufax for $125,000 and Drysdale for $110,000.

The lack of spring training hardly hurt Koufax as he won 27 games and had a 1.73 E.R.A., both tops in the loop. But what the statistics didn't show, the arm did. As the year wound on, it was discovered that Koufax had arthritis in his pitching arm. The pain was such that only a combination of willpower and an increase in medication kept him on the mound. Further stress was placed on Koufax due to Drysdale's performance, which fell off to a mediocre 13-16 record and resulted in Koufax's having to pitch with little rest in the final game of the season to wrap up the pennant.

The Dodgers used the same formula as in 1965 to win the flag—many singles, much running, and good pitching. Maury Wills remained the inspirational leader at bat and in the field, and Jim Lefebvre and Lou Johnson came through with solid years with the bat. Tommy Davis made a partial comeback from his broken ankle by hitting .313 as a platoon left fielder. In addition to Koufax, Claude Osteen and rookie Don Sutton were solid starters, and Tiger-reject Phil Regan became the bullpen sensation of the year, earning the nickname "The Vulture" for his scavenger work in saving close games.

The Giants, sparked by Willie Mays, Willie McCovey, Juan Marichal, and Gaylord Perry fought the Dodgers to the end but finally lost out again. Harry Walker's Pirates used a blistering attack led by MVP Roberto Clemente and batting champ Matty Alou, to make a strong run to the top which ended three games back.

While the National League belonged to the Dodgers, the world's championship became the undisputed possession of Baltimore. The claim was made if for no other reason than the lack of Dodger run-power and the overabundance of Oriole shutout power.

The Dodgers tallied two early runs in the first game before Moe Drabowsky came out of the Birds' bullpen to pitch 6 2/3 innings of shutout relief in a 5-2 victory. The Dodgers never again would touch home, as Jim Palmer, Wally Bunker, and Dave McNally tossed shutouts in the next three games to blow the Dodgers into oblivion. Koufax appeared in the second game but could not keep up with center fielder Willie Davis' three successive errors in the fifth inning.

After the Series, the Dodgers traveled to Japan to play an exhibition slate. In the middle of the tour, Wills left the club without permission, prompting owner Walter O'Malley to trade him to the Pirates. In addition, Tommy Davis was traded to the Mets, and Koufax announced his retirement due to the arthritic elbow—marking the end to a phenomenal career in which, for his last five years, he compiled a 111-34 record, 1,444 strikeouts, and five straight E.R.A. titles.

WORLD SERIES — BALTIMORE (AL) 4 LOS ANGELES (NL) 0

LINE SCORES

TEAM	1	2	3	4	5	6	7	8	9	10	11	12	R	H	E

Game 1 October 5 at Los Angeles

BAL (AL)	3	1	0		1	0	0		0	0	0			5	9	0
LA (NL)	0	1	1		0	0	0		0	0	0			2	3	0

McNally, Drabowsky (3)   Drysdale, Moeller (3), R. Miller (5), Perranoski (8)

Game 2 October 6 at Los Angeles

BAL	0	0	0		0	3	1		0	2	0			6	8	0
LA	0	0	0		0	0	0		0	0	0			0	4	6

Palmer   Koufax, Perranoski (7), Regan (8), Brewer (9)

Game 3 October 8 at Baltimore

LA	0	0	0		0	0	0		0	0	0			0	6	0
BAL	0	0	0		0	1	0		0	0	X			1	3	0

Osteen, Regan (8)   Bunker

Game 4 October 9 at Baltimore

LA	0	0	0		0	0	0		0	0	0			0	4	0
BAL	0	0	0		1	0	0		0	0	X			1	4	0

Drysdale   McNally

COMPOSITE BATTING

NAME	POS	G	AB	R	H	2B	3B	HR	RBI	BA
Baltimore (AL)										
Totals		4	120	13	24	3	1	4	10	.200
Aparicio	SS	4	16	0	4	1	0	0	2	.250
Powell	1B	4	14	1	5	1	0	0	1	.357
F. Robinson	OF	4	14	4	4	0	1	2	3	.286
D. Johnson	2B	4	14	1	4	1	0	0	1	.286
B. Robinson	3B	4	14	2	3	0	0	1	1	.214
Blefary	OF	4	13	0	1	0	0	0	0	.077
Etchebarren	C	4	12	2	1	0	0	0	0	.083
Snyder	OF	3	6	1	1	0	0	1	1	.167
Blair	OF	4	6	2	1	0	0	1	1	.167
Palmer	P	1	4	0	0	0	0	0	0	.000
McNally	P	2	3	0	0	0	0	0	0	.000
Drabowsky	P	1	2	0	0	0	0	0	0	.000
Bunker	P	1	2	0	0	0	0	0	0	.000
Los Angeles (NL)										
Totals		4	120	2	17	3	0	1	2	.142
W. Davis	OF	4	16	0	1	0	0	0	0	.063
L. Johnson	OF	4	15	1	4	1	0	0	0	.267
Roseboro	C	4	14	0	1	0	0	0	0	.071
Parker	1B	4	13	0	3	2	0	0	0	.231
Wills	SS	4	13	0	1	0	0	0	0	.077
Lefebvre	2B	4	12	1	2	0	0	1	1	.167
T. Davis	OF	4	8	0	2	0	0	0	0	.250
Fairly	OF-1B	3	7	0	1	0	0	0	0	.143
Gilliam	3B	2	6	0	0	0	0	0	1	.000
Kennedy	3B	2	5	0	1	0	0	0	0	.200
Stuart	PH	2	2	0	0	0	0	0	0	.000
Drysdale	P	2	2	0	0	0	0	0	0	.000
Koufax	P	1	2	0	0	0	0	0	0	.000
Osteen	P	1	2	0	0	0	0	0	0	.000
Ferrara	PH	1	1	0	1	0	0	0	0	1.000
Covington	PH	1	1	0	0	0	0	0	0	.000
Barbieri	PH	1	1	0	0	0	0	0	0	.000
Perranoski	P	2	0	0	0	0	0	0	0	—
Regan	P	2	0	0	0	0	0	0	0	—
Moeller	P	1	0	0	0	0	0	0	0	—
R. Miller	P	1	0	0	0	0	0	0	0	—
Brewer	P	1	0	0	0	0	0	0	0	—
Oliver	PR	1	0	0	0	0	0	0	0	—

COMPOSITE PITCHING

NAME	G	IP	H	BB	SO	W	L	SV	ERA
Baltimore (AL)									
Totals	4	36	17	13	28	4	0	0	0.50
McNally	2	11.1	6	7	5	1	0	0	1.59
Palmer	1	9	4	3	6	1	0	0	0.00
Bunker	1	9	6	1	6	1	0	0	0.00
Drabowsky	1	6.2	1	2	11	1	0	0	0.00
Los Angeles (NL)									
Totals	4	34	24	11	17	0	4	0	2.65
Drysdale	2	10	8	3	6	0	2	0	4.50
Osteen	1	7	3	1	3	0	1	0	1.29
Koufax	1	6	6	2	2	0	1	0	1.50
Perranoski	2	3.1	4	1	2	0	0	0	5.40
R. Miller	1	3	2	1	1	0	0	0	0.00
Moeller	1	2	1	1	0	0	0	0	4.50
Regan	2	1.2	0	1	2	0	0	0	0.00
Brewer	1	1	0	1	1	0	0	0	0.00

BALTIMORE 1st 97-63 .606 HANK BAUER

NAME	G by Pos	B	AGE	G	AB	R	H	2B	3B	HR	RBI	BB	SO	SB	BA	SA
TOTALS			26	160	5529	755	1426	243	35	175	703	514	926	55	.258	.409
Boog Powell	1B136	L	24	140	491	78	141	18	0	34	109	67	125	0	.287	.532
Dave Johnson	2B126, SS33	R	23	131	501	47	129	20	3	7	56	31	64	2	.257	.351
Luis Aparicio	SS151	R	32	151	659	97	182	25	8	6	41	33	42	25	.276	.366
Brooks Robinson	3B157	R	29	157	620	91	167	35	2	23	100	56	36	2	.269	.444
Frank Robinson	OF151, 1B3	R	30	155	576	122	182	34	2	49	122	87	90	8	.316	.637
Paul Blair	OF27	R	22	133	303	35	84	20	2	6	33	15	36	5	.277	.416
Russ Snyder	OF104	L	32	117	373	66	114	21	5	3	41	38	37	2	.306	.413
Andy Etchebarren	C121	R	23	121	412	49	91	14	6	11	50	38	106	0	.221	.364
Curt Blefary	OF109, 1B20	L	22	131	419	73	107	14	3	23	64	73	56	1	.255	.468
Sam Bowens	OF68	R	27	89	243	26	51	9	1	6	20	17	52	1	.210	.329
Bob Johnson	2B20, 1B17, 3B3	R	30	71	157	13	34	5	0	1	10	12	24	0	.217	.268
Woodie Held	OF10, 2B5, SS3, 3B3	R	34	56	82	6	17	3	1	1	7	12	30	0	.207	.305
Vic Roznovsky	C34	L	27	41	97	4	23	5	0	1	10	9	11	0	.237	.320
Larry Haney	C20	R	23	20	56	3	9	1	0	1	3	1	15	0	.161	.232
Charlie Lau (EJ)		L	33	18	12	1	6	2	1	0	5	4	1	0	.500	.833
1 Jerry Adair	2B13	R	29	17	52	3	15	1	0	0	3	4	8	0	.288	.308
Mark Belanger	SS6	R	22	8	19	2	3	1	0	0	0	0	3	0	.158	.211
Mike Epstein	1B4	R	23	6	11	1	2	0	1	0	3	1	3	0	.182	.364
Cam Carreon	C3	R	28	4	9	2	2	2	0	0	2	3	2	0	.222	.444

NAME	T	AGE	W	L	PCT	SV	G	GS	CG	IP	H	BB	SO	SHO	ERA
TOTALS		27	97	63	.606	51	160	160	23	1466	1267	514	1070	13	3.32
Jim Palmer	R	20	15	10	.600	0	30	30	6	208	176	91	147	0	3.46
Dave McNally	R	23	13	6	.684	0	33	33	5	213	212	64	158	1	3.17
Steve Barber (AJ)	L	28	10	5	.667	0	25	22	5	133	104	69	91	3	2.30
Wally Bunker	R	21	10	6	.625	0	29	24	3	143	151	48	89	0	4.28
Stu Miller	R	38	9	4	.692	18	51	0	0	92	65	22	67	0	2.25
Eddie Watt	R	25	9	7	.563	4	43	13	1	146	123	44	102	0	3.82
Moe Drabowsky	R	30	6	0	1.000	7	44	0	0	96	62	29	98	0	2.81
Dick Hall	R	35	6	2	.750	7	32	0	0	66	59	8	44	0	3.95
2 Eddie Fisher	R	29	5	3	.625	13	44*	0	0	72	60	19	39	0	2.63
Gene Brabender	R	24	4	3	.571	2	31	1	0	71	57	29	62	0	3.55
John Miller	R	25	4	8	.333	0	23	16	0	101	92	58	81	0	4.72
Tom Phoebus	R	24	2	1	.667	0	3	3	2	22	16	6	17	2	1.23
1 Bill Short	L	28	2	3	.400	0	6	6	1	38	34	10	27	1	2.84
Frank Bertaina	L	22	2	5	.286	0	16	9	0	63	52	36	46	0	3.14
Ed Barnowski	R	20	0	0	—	0	3	0	0	3	1	2	3	0	3.00

*Fisher, also with Chicago, league leader in G with 67

MINNESOTA 2nd 89-73 .549 9 SAM MELE

NAME	G by Pos	B	AGE	G	AB	R	H	2B	3B	HR	RBI	BB	SO	SB	BA	SA
TOTALS			28	162	5390	663	1341	219	33	144	611	513	844	67	.249	.382
Don Mincher	1B130	L	28	139	431	53	108	30	0	14	62	58	68	3	.251	.418
Bernie Allen	2B89	L	27	101	319	34	76	18	1	5	30	26	40	2	.238	.348
Zoilo Versalles	SS135	R	26	137	543	73	135	20	6	7	36	40	85	10	.249	.346
Harmon Killebrew	3B107, 1B42, OF18	R	30	162	569	89	160	27	1	39	110	103	98	0	.281	.538
Tony Oliva	OF159	R	25	159	622	99	191	32	7	25	87	42	72	13	.307	.502
Ted Uhlaender	OF100	L	26	105	367	39	83	12	2	2	22	27	33	10	.226	.286
Jimmie Hall	OF103	L	28	120	356	52	85	7	4	20	47	33	66	1	.239	.449
Earl Battey	C113	R	31	115	364	30	93	12	1	4	34	43	30	4	.255	.327
Cesar Tovar	2B76, SS31, OF24	R	25	134	465	57	121	19	5	2	41	44	50	16	.260	.335
Rich Rollins	3B65, 2B2, OF1	R	28	90	269	30	66	7	1	10	40	13	34	0	.245	.390
Bob Allison	OF56	R	31	70	168	34	37	6	1	8	19	30	34	6	.220	.411
Jerry Zimmerman	C59	R	31	60	119	11	30	4	1	1	15	15	23	0	.252	.328
Andy Kosco	OF40, 1B5	R	24	57	158	11	35	5	0	2	13	7	31	0	.222	.291
Sandy Valdespino	OF23	L	27	52	108	11	19	1	1	2	9	4	24	2	.176	.259
Russ Nixon	C32	L	31	51	96	5	25	2	1	0	7	7	13	0	.260	.302
Ron Clark	3B1	R	22	5	1	1	1	0	0	0	0	1	0	0	1.000	1.000
1 Joe Nossek	OF2	R	25	4	0	0	0	0	0	0	0	0	0	0	.000	.000
George Mitterwald	C3	R	23	5	5	1	1	0	0	0	0	0	0	0	.200	.200
Rich Reese		L	24	3	2	0	0	0	0	0	0	0	0	2	.000	.000

NAME	T	AGE	W	L	PCT	SV	G	GS	CG	IP	H	BB	SO	SHO	ERA
TOTALS		29	89	73	.549	28	162	162	52	1439	1246	392	1015	11	3.13
Jim Kaat	L	27	25	13	.658	0	41	41	19	305	271	55	205	3	2.74
Mudcat Grant	R	30	13	13	.500	0	35	35	10	249	248	49	110	3	3.25
Dave Boswell	R	21	12	5	.706	0	28	21	8	169	120	65	173	1	3.14
Jim Perry	R	30	11	7	.611	0	33	25	8	184	149	53	122	1	2.54
Camilo Pascual (SA)	R	32	8	6	.571	0	21	19	2	103	113	30	56	0	4.89
Jim Merritt	L	22	7	14	.333	3	31	18	5	144	112	33	124	1	3.38
Al Worthington	R	37	6	3	.667	16	65	0	0	91	66	27	93	0	2.47
Dwight Siebler	R	28	2	2	.500	1	23	2	0	50	47	14	24	0	3.42
Pete Cimino	R	23	2	5	.286	4	35	0	0	65	65	30	57	0	2.91
Johnny Klippstein	R	38	1	1	.500	3	26	0	0	40	35	20	28	0	3.38
1 Garry Roggenburk	L	26	1	2	.333	1	12	0	0	12	14	10	3	0	6.00
Bill Pleis	L	28	1	2	.333	0	8	0	0	9	5	4	9	0	2.00
Ron Keller	R	23	0	0	—	0	1	0	0	5	7	1	1	0	5.40
Jim Roland	L	23	0	0	—	0	10	0	0	6	1	11		0	3.60
Jim Ollom	L	20	0	0	—	0	1	0	0	6	11	11		0	3.60

DETROIT 3rd 88-74 .543 10 CHUCK DRESSEN (DD) 16-10 .615 BOB SWIFT (IL-DD) 32-25 .561

NAME	G by Pos	B	AGE	G	AB	R	H	2B	3B	HR	RBI	BB	SO	SB	BA	SA
TOTALS			27	162	5507	719	1383	224	45	179	682	551	987	41	.251	.406
Norm Cash	1B158	L	31	160	603	98	168	18	3	32	93	66	91	2	.279	.478
Jerry Lumpe	2B95	L	33	113	385	30	89	14	3	1	26	24	44	0	.231	.291
Dick McAuliffe	SS105, 3B15	L	26	124	430	83	118	16	8	23	56	66	80	5	.274	.509
Don Wert	3B150	R	27	150	559	56	150	20	2	11	70	64	69	6	.268	.370
Jim Northrup	OF113	L	24	123	419	53	111	24	6	16	58	33	52	4	.265	.465
Al Kaline	OF136	R	31	142	479	85	138	29	1	29	88	81	66	5	.288	.534
Willie Horton	OF137	R	23	146	526	72	138	22	6	27	100	44	103	1	.262	.481
Bill Freehan	C132, 1B5	R	24	136	492	47	115	22	0	12	46	40	72	5	.234	.352
Jake Wood	2B52, 3B4, 1B2	R	29	98	230	39	58	9	3	2	27	28	48	4	.252	.343
Mickey Stanley (BH)	OF82	R	23	92	235	28	68	15	4	3	19	17	20	2	.289	.426
Gates Brown	OF43	L	27	88	169	27	45	5	1	7	27	18	19	3	.266	.432
Dick Tracewski	2B70, SS3	R	31	81	124	15	24	1	1	0	7	10	32	1	.194	.218
Ray Oyler	SS69	R	27	71	210	16	36	8	3	1	9	23	62	0	.171	.252
Orlando McFarlane	C33	R	28	49	138	16	35	7	0	5	13	9	46	0	.254	.413
1 Don Demeter	OF27, 1B4	R	31	32	99	12	21	5	0	5	12	3	19	1	.212	.414
2 Earl Wilson	P23	R	31	27	64	13	15	0	2	5	17	4	25	0	.234	.531
Don Pepper	1B1	L	22	4	2	0	0	0	0	0	0	0	0	1	.000	.000
Arlo Brunsberg	C2	L	25	2	3	1	1	1	0	0	0	0	0	0	.333	.667

FRANK SKAFF 40-39 .506

NAME	T	AGE	W	L	PCT	SV	G	GS	CG	IP	H	BB	SO	SHO	ERA
TOTALS		29	88	74	.543	38	162	162	36	1454	1356	520	1026	11	3.85
Denny McLain	R	22	20	14	.588	0	38	38	14	264	205	104	192	4	3.92
Mickey Lolich	L	25	14	14	.500	0	40	33	5	204	204	83	173	1	4.76
2 Earl Wilson	R	31	13	6	.684	0	23	23	8	163	126	38	133	2	2.60
Dave Wickersham	R	30	8	3	.727	1	38	14	3	141	139	54	93	0	3.19
Larry Sherry	R	30	8	5	.615	20	55	0	0	78	66	36	63	0	3.81
Bill Monbouquette	R	29	7	8	.467	0	30	14	2	103	120	22	61	1	4.72
Fred Gladding	R	30	5	1	1.000	2	51	0	0	74	62	29	57	0	3.28
Orlando Pena	R	32	4	2	.667	7	54	0	0	108	105	35	79	0	3.08
2 Johnny Podres	L	33	4	5	.444	4	36	13	2	108	106	34	53	1	3.42
Hank Aguirre	L	35	3	9	.250	0	30	14	2	104	104	26	50	0	3.81
Joe Sparma	R	24	2	7	.222	0	29	13	0	92	103	52	61	0	5.28
George Korince	R	20	0	0	—	0	3	3	0	3	3	1	2	0	0.00
Bill Graham	R	29	0	0	—	0	2	2	0	2	2	0	0	0	0.00
John Hiller	R	23	0	0	—	0	1	0	0	2	1	0	1	0	9.00
Julio Navarro	R	30	0	0	—	0	1	0	0	1	0	1	0	0	
1 Terry Fox	R	30	0	1	.000	0	10	0	0	10	9	2	6	0	6.30

CHICAGO 4th 83-79 .512 15 EDDIE STANKY

NAME	G by Pos	B	AGE	G	AB	R	H	2B	3B	HR	RBI	BB	SO	SB	BA	SA
TOTALS			28	162	5348	574	1235	193	40	87	524	476	872	153	.231	.331
Tommy McCraw	1B121, OF41	L	25	151	389	49	89	16	4	5	48	29	40	20	.229	.329
Al Weis	2B96, SS18	B	28	129	187	20	29	4	1	0	9	17	50	3	.155	.187
2 Jerry Adair	SS75, 2B50	R	29	105	370	27	90	18	2	4	36	17	44	3	.243	.335
Don Buford	3B133, 2B37, OF15	B	29	163	607	85	148	26	7	8	52	69	71	51	.244	.349
Floyd Robinson	OF113	L	30	127	342	44	81	11	2	5	35	44	32	8	.237	.325
Tommie Agee	OF159	R	23	160	629	98	172	27	8	22	86	41	127	44	.273	.447
Ken Berry	OF141	R	25	147	443	50	120	20	2	8	34	28	63	7	.271	.379
Johnny Romano	C102	R	31	122	329	33	76	12	0	15	47	58	72	0	.231	.404
Bill Skowron	1B98	R	35	120	337	27	84	15	2	6	29	26	45	1	.249	.359
Pete Ward (XJ)	OF59, 3B16, 1B5	L	26	84	251	22	55	7	1	3	28	24	49	3	.219	.291
Lee Elia	SS75	R	28	80	195	16	40	5	2	3	12	15	39	0	.205	.297
Smoky Burgess	C2	L	39	79	67	9	21	5	0	0	15	11	8	0	.313	.388
2 Wayne Causey	2B60, SS1, 3B1	L	29	78	164	23	40	8	2	0	13	24	13	2	.244	.317
J.C. Martin (BG)	C63	R	29	67	157	13	40	5	3	2	20	14	24	0	.255	.363
1 Gene Freese	3B34	R	32	48	106	8	22	3	0	3	10	8	20	2	.208	.311
Jerry McNertney	C37	R	29	44	59	3	13	0	0	1	7	6	1	0	.220	.220
Ron Hansen (XJ)	SS23	R	28	23	74	3	13	1	0	4	15	10	10	0	.176	.189
1 Danny Cater	OF18	R	26	21	60	3	11	1	1	0	4	0	10	3	.183	.233
Jim Hicks	OF10, 1B2	R	26	18	26	3	5	0	1	0	1	1	5	0	.192	.269
Buddy Bradford	OF9	R	21	14	28	3	4	0	0	0	2	0	8	0	.143	.143
Ed Stroud	OF11	L	26	12	36	3	6	2	0	0	1	2	6	3	.167	.222
Duane Josephson	C11	R	24	11	38	3	9	1	0	0	3	2	3	0	.237	.263
Dick Kenworthy	3B6	R	25	9	20	1	4	0	0	0	1	0	2	0	.200	.200
Marv Staehle	2B6	L	24	8	15	2	2	0	0	0	0	4	2	1	.133	.133
Deacon Jones		L	32	5	5	0	2	0	0	0	1	0	0	0	.400	.400
Bill Voss	OF1	L	22	2	5	0	0	0	0	0	0	0	1	0	.000	.000

NAME	T	AGE	W	L	PCT	SV	G	GS	CG	IP	H	BB	SO	SHO	ERA
TOTALS		29	83	79	.512	34	163	163	38	1475	1229	403	896	22	2.68
Tommy John	L	23	14	11	.560	0	34	33	10	223	195	57	138	5	2.62
Gary Peters	R	29	12	10	.545	0	30	27	11	205	156	45	129	4	1.98
Joe Horlen	R	28	10	13	.435	1	37	29	4	211	185	53	124	2	2.43
Bruce Howard	R	23	9	5	.643	0	27	21	4	149	110	44	85	2	2.30
Bob Locker	R	28	9	8	.529	12	56	0	0	95	73	23	70	0	2.46
Juan Pizarro	L	29	8	6	.571	3	34	9	1	89	91	39	42	0	3.74
Jack Lamabe	R	29	7	9	.438	0	34	17	3	121	116	35	67	2	3.94
John Buzhardt	R	30	6	11	.353	1	33	22	5	150	144	30	66	4	3.84
Hoyt Wilhelm (BG)	R	43	5	2	.714	6	46	0	0	81	50	17	61	0	1.67
Denny Higgins	R	26	1	0	1.000	5	42	0	0	93	66	33	86	0	2.52
Fred Klages	R	22	1	0	1.000	0	3	1	0	16	9	7	6	0	1.69
1 Eddie Fisher	R	29	1	3	.250	9	23*	0	0	35	27	17	18	0	2.31
Greg Bollo	R	22	0	1	.000	0	7	1	0	7	3	4	0	0	2.57

*Fisher, also with Baltimore, league leader in G with 67

CLEVELAND 5th 81-81 .500 17 BIRDIE TEBBETTS 66-57 .537 GEORGE STRICKLAND 15-24 .385

NAME	G by Pos	B	AGE	G	AB	R	H	2B	3B	HR	RBI	BB	SO	SB	BA	SA
TOTALS			29	162	5474	574	1300	156	25	155	536	450	914	53	.237	.360
Fred Whitfield	1B132	L	28	137	502	59	121	15	2	27	78	27	76	1	.241	.440
Pedro Gonzalez	2B104, 3B1, OF1	R	27	110	352	21	92	9	2	2	17	15	54	8	.233	.287
Larry Brown (FS)	SS90, 2B10	R	26	105	340	29	78	12	0	3	17	36	50	1	.229	.291
Max Alvis	3B157	R	28	151	596	67	146	22	3	17	55	50	98	4	.245	.378
Rocky Colavito	OF146	R	32	151	533	68	127	13	0	30	72	76	81	0	.238	.432
Vic Davalillo	OF108	L	29	121	344	42	86	6	4	3	19	24	37	8	.250	.317
Leon Wagner	OF139	L	32	150	549	70	153	20	0	23	66	46	69	5	.279	.441
Joe Azcue	C97	R	26	98	302	22	83	10	1	9	37	20	22	0	.275	.404
C. Salmon	SS61, 2B28, 1B24, OF10, 3B6	R	25	126	422	46	108	13	2	7	40	21	41	10	.256	.346
Chuck Hinton	OF104, 1B6, 2B2, C1	R	32	123	348	46	89	9	3	12	50	35	66	10	.256	.402
Jim Landis	OF61	R	32	85	158	23	35	5	1	3	14	20	26	2	.222	.323
Dick Howser	2B26, SS26	R	30	67	140	18	32	9	1	2	4	15	23	3	.229	.350
Duke Sims (XJ)	C48	L	25	52	133	12	35	2	0	5	19	14	31	0	.263	.444
Del Crandall	C49	R	36	50	108	10	25	2	0	4	14	9	21	0	.231	.361
2 Jim Gentile	1B9	L	32	33	47	2	6	1	0	2	5	6	18	0	.128	.277
Bill Davis	1B9	L	23	16	39	3	6	0	0	1	6	1	11	0	.158	.263
Tony Curry		L	27	19	16	4	4	0	0	0	3	0	4	0	.125	.125
Buddy Booker	C12	R	28	16	28	6	6	1	1	0	3	2	5	0	.214	.464
Jose Vidal	OF11	R	26	17	32	4	6	1	0	1	3	2	6	5	.188	.281
Tony Martinez	SS5, 2B4	R	26	17	17	2	5	0	0	0	2	7	6	1	.294	.294
Vern Fuller	2B16	R	22	16	47	7	11	2	0	1	7	6	6	0	.234	.447
George Banks		R	27	4	4	0	1	0	0	0	0	0	1	0	.250	.250
Paul Dicken		R	22	2	2	0	0	0	0	0	0	0	2	0	.000	.000

NAME	T	AGE	W	L	PCT	SV	G	GS	CG	IP	H	BB	SO	SHO	ERA
TOTALS		27	81	81	.500	28	162	162	49	1467	1260	489	1111	15	3.23
Sonny Siebert	R	29	16	8	.667	1	34	32	11	241	193	62	163	1	2.80
Gary Bell	R	29	14	15	.483	0	40	37	12	254	211	79	194	0	3.22
Steve Hargan	R	23	13	10	.565	0	38	21	7	192	173	45	132	3	2.48
Luis Tiant	R	25	12	11	.522	8	46	16	7	155	121	50	145	5	2.79
Sam McDowell (SA)	L	23	9	8	.529	3	35	28	8	194	130	102	225	1	2.88
John O'Donoghue	L	26	6	8	.429	0	32	13	2	108	109	23	49	0	3.83
Tom Kelley	R	22	6	4	.333	0	31	7	1	95	97	42	64	4	4.36
Jack Kralick	L	31	6	8	.429	0	27	4	0	68	69	20	31	0	3.84
Bob Allen	L	28	2	2	.500	5	36	0	0	51	56	13	33	0	4.24
1 Lee Stange	R	29	1	0	1.000	1	16	6	1	16	17	3	9	0	2.81
1 Don McMahon	R	36	1	1	.500	1	12	0	0	12	6	9	5	0	3.00
Bob Heffner	R	27	0	1	.000	0	15	0	0	15	21	8	7	0	3.46
George Culver	R	23	0	0	—	0	1	0	0	10	15	7	4	0	8.10
2 Dick Radatz	R	29	0	1	.000	10	39	0	0	57	49	34	49	0	4.58

CALIFORNIA — 6th 80-82 .494 18 — BILL RIGNEY

NAME	G by Pos	B	AGE	G	AB	R	H	2B	3B	HR	RBI	BB	SO	SB	BA	SA
TOTALS			26	162	5360	604	1244	179	54	122	562	525	1062	80	.232	.354
Norm Siebern	1B99	L	32	125	336	29	83	14	1	5	41	63	61	0	.247	.339
Bobby Knoop	2B161	R	27	161	590	54	137	18	11	17	72	43	144	1	.232	.386
Jim Fregosi	SS162,1B1	R	24	162	611	78	154	32	7	13	67	67	89	17	.252	.391
Paul Schaal	3B131	R	23	138	386	59	94	15	7	6	24	68	56	6	.244	.365
Ed Kirkpatrick	OF102, 1B3	L	21	117	312	31	60	7	4	9	44	51	67	7	.192	.327
Jose Cardenal	OF146	R	22	154	561	67	155	15	3	16	48	34	69	24	.276	.399
Rick Reichardt (IL)	OF87	R	23	89	319	48	92	5	4	16	44	27	61	8	.288	.460
Bob Rodgers	C133	R	27	133	454	45	107	20	3	7	48	29	57	3	.236	.339
Tom Satriano	C43, 1B36, 3B25, 2B4	R	25	103	226	16	54	5	3	0	24	27	32	3	.239	.288
Willie Smith	OF52	L	27	90	195	18	36	3	2	1	20	12	37	1	.185	.236
Joe Adcock	1B71	R	38	83	231	33	63	10	3	18	48	31	48	2	.273	.576
Frank Malzone	3B35	R	36	82	155	6	32	5	0	2	12	10	11	0	.206	.277
Jimmy Piersall	OF63	R	36	75	123	14	26	5	0	0	14	13	19	1	.211	.252
Jay Johnstone	OF61	R	20	61	254	35	67	12	4	3	17	11	36	3	.264	.378
Jackie Hernandez	3B11, 2B8, SS8, OF3	R	25	58	23	19	1	0	0	0	2	1	4	1	.043	.043
Jackie Warner	OF37	R	22	45	123	22	26	4	1	7	16	9	55	0	.211	.431
Bubba Morton	OF14	R	34	15	50	4	11	1	0	0	4	2	6	1	.220	.240
Chuck Vinson	1B11	L	22	13	22	3	4	2	0	1	6	5	9	0	.182	.409
Al Spangler	OF3	L	32	16	9	2	6	0	0	0	1	1	0	0	.667	.667

Willie Montanez 18 L 0-2, Tom Egan 20 R 0-11, Ed Bailey 35 L 0-3, Albie Pearson (XJ) 31 L 0-3

NAME	T	AGE	W	L	PCT	SV	G	GS	CG	IP	H	BB	SO	SHO	ERA
		29	80	82	.494	40	162	162	31	1457	1364	511	836	12	3.56
Jack Sanford	R	29	13	7	.650	5	50	6	0	108	108	27	54	0	3.83
George Brunet	R	31	13	13	.500	0	41	32	8	212	183	106	148	2	3.31
Dean Chance	R	25	12	11	.414	1	41	37	11	260	206	114	180	2	3.08
Lew Burdette	R	39	7	2	.778	5	54	0	0	80	80	12	27	0	3.38
Minnie Rojas	R	32	7	4	.636	10	47	2	0	84	83	15	37	0	2.89
Marcelino Lopez	L	22	7	14	.333	1	37	32	6	199	188	68	132	2	3.93
Bob Lee	R	28	5	4	.556	16	61	0	0	102	90	31	46	0	2.74
Fred Newman	R	24	4	7	.364	0	21	19	1	103	112	31	42	0	4.72
Clyde Wright	L	25	4	7	.364	0	20	13	3	91	92	25	37	1	3.76
Jim McGlothlin	R	22	3	1	.750	0	19	11	0	68	79	19	41	0	4.50
Jorge Rubio	R	21	2	1	.667	0	7	4	1	27	22	16	27	1	3.00
Ed Sukla	R	23	1	1	.500	1	12	0	0	17	18	6	8	0	6.35
Jim Coates	R	33	1	1	.500	0	9	4	1	32	32	10	16	1	3.94
Bill Kelso	R	26	1	1	.500	0	5	0	0	11	6	11	0	0	2.45
Dick Egan	L	29	0	0	—	0	14	0	0	14	17	6	11	0	4.50
Howie Reed	R	29	0	1	.000	1	19	1	0	43	39	15	17	0	2.93
Ramon Lopez	R	33	0	1	.000	0	4	1	0	7	4	4	2	0	5.14

Rudy May (SA) 21

KANSAS CITY — 7th 74-86 .463 23 — AL DARK

NAME	G by Pos	B	AGE	G	AB	R	H	2B	3B	HR	RBI	BB	SO	SB	BA	SA
TOTALS			26	160	5328	564	1259	212	56	70	509	421	982	132	.236	.337
1 Ken Harrelson	1B58, OF4	R	24	63	210	24	47	9	0	5	22	27	59	9	.224	.319
Dick Green	2B137, 3B2	R	24	140	507	58	127	24	3	9	62	27	101	6	.250	.363
Bert Campaneris	SS138	R	24	142	573	82	153	29	10	5	42	25	72	52	.267	.379
Ed Charles	3B104, 1B1, OF1	R	31	118	385	52	110	18	8	9	42	30	53	12	.286	.444
Mike Hershberger	OF143	R	26	146	538	55	136	27	7	2	57	47	37	13	.253	.340
2 Jim Gosger	OF77	L	23	88	272	34	61	14	1	5	27	37	53	5	.224	.338
Larry Stahl	OF94	L	25	119	312	37	78	11	5	3	34	17	63	5	.250	.365
Phil Roof	C123, 1B2	R	25	127	369	33	77	14	3	7	44	37	95	2	.209	.320
2 Danny Cater	1B53, 3B42, OF22	R	26	116	425	47	124	16	3	7	52	28	37	1	.292	.392
2 Roger Repoz	OF52, 1B45	R	25	101	319	40	69	10	3	11	34	44	80	3	.216	.370
2 Joe Nossek	OF78, 3B1	R	25	87	230	13	60	9	1	0	20	7	41	6	.261	.343
O. Chavarria	OF26, SS23,2B14, 1B8,3B5	R	25	86	191	26	46	10	2	2	10	18	43	3	.241	.325
1 Jose Tartabull	OF32	L	27	37	127	13	30	2	3	0	4	11	13	8	.236	.299
Tim Talton	C14, 1B9	L	27	53	53	8	18	3	1	2	6	1	5	0	.340	.547
Ken Suarez	C34	R	23	35	69	5	10	0	1	0	2	15	26	2	.145	.174
1 Billy Bryan	C21, 1B3	L	27	32	76	9	10	0	0	4	7	6	17	0	.132	.368
1 Wayne Causey	3B15, SS10	L	29	28	79	1	18	0	0	0	5	7	6	1	.228	.228
Ernie Fazio	2B10, SS4	R	24	27	34	3	7	0	0	0	2	4	10	1	.206	.265
Ron Stone	OF4, 1B3	L	23	26	22	2	6	1	0	0	0	2	1	0	.273	.318
Rick Monday	OF15	L	20	17	41	4	4	1	0	0	2	6	16	1	.098	.171
John Donaldson	2B9	L	23	15	30	4	4	0	1	0	3	4	1	0	.133	.133
Manny Jimenez	OF12	L	27	13	35	1	4	0	0	0	1	0	6	0	.114	.171
Sal Bando	3B7	R	22	11	24	1	7	1	1	0	1	1	3	0	.292	.417

2 Don Blasingame 34 L 3-19, Randy Schwartz 22 L 1-11, Rene Lachemann 21 R 1-5

NAME	T	AGE	W	L	PCT	SV	G	GS	CG	IP	H	BB	SO	SHO	ERA
		26	74	86	.463	47	160	160	19	1435	1281	630	854	11	3.55
Lew Krausse	R	23	14	9	.609	3	36	22	4	178	144	63	87	1	2.98
Jim Nash	R	21	12	1	.923	1	18	17	5	127	94	47	98	0	2.06
Catfish Hunter (IL)	R	20	9	11	.450	0	30	25	4	177	158	64	103	0	4.02
Jack Aker	R	25	8	4	.667	32	66	0	0	113	81	28	68	0	1.99
Blue Moon Odom	R	21	5	5	.500	0	14	14	4	90	70	53	47	2	2.50
Paul Lindblad	L	24	5	10	.333	1	38	14	0	121	138	37	69	0	4.17
1 Fred Talbot	R	25	4	4	.500	0	11	11	0	68	65	28	37	0	4.76
Chuck Dobson (SA)	R	22	4	6	.400	0	14	14	1	84	71	50	61	0	4.07
1 Rollie Sheldon	R	29	4	7	.364	0	14	13	1	69	73	26	26	1	3.13
2 Ken Sanders	R	24	3	4	.429	1	38	1	0	65	59	48	41	0	3.74
Wes Stock	R	32	2	2	.500	3	35	0	0	44	30	21	31	0	2.66
Gil Blanco	L	20	2	4	.333	0	11	8	0	38	31	36	21	0	4.74
Jim Dickson	R	28	1	0	1.000	1	24	1	0	37	37	23	20	0	5.35
1 Ralph Terry	R	30	1	5	.167	0	15	10	0	64	65	15	33	0	3.80
1 Aurelio Monteagudo	R	22	0	0	—	0	6	0	0	13	12	7	3	0	2.77
Jess Hickman	L	24	0	0	—	0	1	0	0	1	1	0	0	0	0.00
2 Guido Grilli	L	27	0	0	—	0	16	19	11	8	6	0	0	0	6.75
Vern Handrahan	R	27	0	1	.000	0	20	15	18	4	0	0	0	0	4.32
Bill Edgerton	L	24	0	1	.000	0	8	20	7	3	0	0	0	0	3.38
Joe Grzenda	R	29	0	2	.000	0	24	28	12	14	0	0	0	0	3.27
2 Jim Duckworth (SA)	R	27	0	2	.000	0	12	14	10	10	0	0	0	0	9.00
1 John Wyatt	R	31	0	3	.000	0	19	0	0	24	19	16	25	0	5.25
Bill Stafford	R	26	0	3	.000	0	9	40	42	12	31	0	0	0	4.95

WASHINGTON — 8th 71-88 .447 25.5 — GIL HODGES

NAME	G by Pos	B	AGE	G	AB	R	H	2B	3B	HR	RBI	BB	SO	SB	BA	SA
TOTALS			28	159	5318	557	1245	185	40	126	525	450	1069	53	.234	.355
Dick Nen	1B76	L	26	94	235	20	50	8	0	6	30	28	46	0	.213	.323
Bob Saverine	2B70, 3B26, SS11, OF9	B	25	120	406	54	102	10	4	5	24	29	62	4	.251	.333
Eddie Brinkman	SS158	R	24	158	582	42	133	18	9	7	48	29	105	7	.229	.326
Ken McMullen	3B141, 1B8, OF1	R	24	147	524	48	122	19	4	13	54	44	89	3	.233	.359
Fred Valentine	OF138, 1B2	B	31	146	508	77	140	29	7	16	59	51	63	22	.276	.455
Don Lock	OF129	R	29	138	386	52	90	13	1	16	48	57	126	2	.233	.394
Frank Howard	OF135	R	29	146	493	52	137	19	4	18	71	53	104	1	.278	.442
Paul Casanova	C119	R	24	122	429	45	109	16	5	13	44	14	78	1	.254	.406
Willie Kirkland	OF68	L	32	124	163	21	31	2	1	6	17	16	50	2	.190	.325
Jim King	OF85	L	33	117	310	41	77	14	2	10	30	38	41	4	.248	.403
2 Ken Harrelson	1B70	R	24	71	250	25	62	8	1	7	28	26	53	4	.248	.372
1 Don Blasingame	2B58, SS1	L	34	68	200	18	43	9	0	1	11	18	21	2	.215	.275
Ken Hamlin	2B50, 3B1	R	31	66	158	13	34	7	1	1	16	13	21	1	.215	.291
Doug Camilli (AJ)	C39	R	29	44	107	5	22	4	0	2	8	3	19	0	.206	.299
Bob Chance	1B13	L	25	37	57	1	10	3	0	0	4	2	5	0	.175	.281
Dick Phillips	1B5	L	34	25	37	3	6	0	0	0	4	2	5	1	.162	.162
Tim Cullen	3B8, 2B5	R	24	18	34	8	8	1	0	0	2	8	6	0	.235	.265
John Orsino (EJ)	1B5, C2	R	28	14	23	1	4	1	0	0	0	1	6	0	.174	.217
Hank Allen	OF9	R	26	6	31	3	12	1	1	0	4	0	5	0	.387	.484

Jim French (LJ) 24 L 5-24, Mike Brumley 27 L 2-18, Joe Cunningham 34 L 1-8

NAME	T	AGE	W	L	PCT	SV	G	GS	CG	IP	H	BB	SO	SHO	ERA
		28	71	88	.447	35	159	159	25	1419	1282	448	866	6	3.70
Pete Richert	L	26	14	14	.500	0	36	34	7	246	196	69	195	0	3.37
Phil Ortega	R	26	12	12	.500	0	33	31	5	197	158	53	121	1	3.93
Mike McCormick	L	27	11	14	.440	0	41	32	8	216	193	51	101	3	3.46
Bob Humphreys	R	30	7	3	.700	3	58	1	0	112	91	28	88	0	2.81
Ron Kline	R	34	6	4	.600	23	63	0	0	90	79	17	46	0	2.40
Dick Lines	L	27	5	2	.714	2	53	0	0	83	63	24	49	0	2.28
Casey Cox	R	24	5	5	.444	7	66	0	0	113	104	35	46	0	3.77
Barry Moore	L	23	3	3	.500	0	12	11	1	62	55	39	28	0	3.34
Diego Segui	R	28	3	7	.300	0	21	13	1	72	82	24	54	1	5.00
Jim Hannan	R	26	3	9	.250	0	30	18	2	114	125	59	68	0	4.26
Dick Bosman	R	22	3	9	.250	0	13	7	0	39	60	12	20	0	7.62
Joe Coleman	R	19	3	0	1.000	0	1	1	1	9	4	4	3	0	2.00
Dave Baldwin	R	28	1	0	1.000	1	14	0	0	7	8	1	4	0	3.86
Buster Narum	R	25	0	0	—	0	1	1	0	11	4	0	5	0	24.00
Alan Closter	L	23	0	0	—	0	1	0	0	0.1	1	2	0	0	0.00
Pete Craig	R	25	0	0	—	0	1	0	0	2	1	1	4	0	4.50
Howie Koplitz (SJ)	R	28	0	0	—	0	1	0	0	5	8	4	1	0	9.00
Tom Cheney	R	31	0	1	.000	0	4	1	0	4	6	3	6	0	5.40
1 Jim Duckworth	R	27	0	0	—	0	14	0	0	14	14	10	10	0	5.14
Frank Kreutzer	L	27	0	0	—	0	8	0	0	31	34	15	20	0	6.10

BOSTON — 9th 72-90 .444 26 — BILLY HERMAN 64-82 .438 — PETE RUNNELS 8-8 .500

NAME	G by Pos	B	AGE	G	AB	R	H	2B	3B	HR	RBI	BB	SO	SB	BA	SA
TOTALS			25	162	5498	655	1318	228	44	145	617	542	1020	35	.240	.376
George Scott	1B158, 3B5	R	22	162	601	73	147	18	7	27	90	65	152	4	.245	.433
George Smith	2B109, SS19	R	28	128	403	41	86	19	4	8	37	37	86	4	.213	.340
Rico Petrocelli	SS127, 3B5	R	23	139	522	58	124	20	1	18	59	41	99	1	.238	.383
Joe Foy	3B139, SS13	R	21	151	554	97	145	23	8	15	63	91	80	2	.262	.413
Tony Conigliaro	OF146	R	21	150	558	77	148	26	7	28	93	52	112	0	.265	.487
2 Don Demeter	OF57, 1B2	R	31	73	226	31	66	13	1	9	29	5	47	1	.292	.478
Carl Yastrzemski	OF158	L	26	160	594	81	165	39	2	16	80	84	60	8	.278	.431
Mike Ryan	C114	R	24	116	369	27	79	15	3	2	32	29	68	1	.214	.287
Dalton Jones	2B70, 3B3	L	22	115	252	26	59	11	5	4	23	17	26	0	.234	.365
Lenny Green	OF27	L	32	85	133	18	32	6	1	0	12	15	19	0	.241	.308
Bob Tillman	C72	R	29	78	204	12	47	8	0	3	24	22	35	0	.230	.314
George Thomas	OF48, 3B6, 1B2, C2	R	28	69	173	25	41	4	0	5	20	23	33	1	.237	.347
2 Jose Tartabull	OF47	L	27	68	195	28	54	7	4	0	11	6	11	11	.277	.354
Eddie Kasko (XJ)	SS20, 3B10, 2B8	R	34	58	136	11	29	7	0	1	12	15	19	1	.213	.287
1 Jim Gosger	OF32	L	23	40	126	16	32	4	0	5	17	15	20	0	.254	.405
Joe Christopher	OF2	R	30	12	13	1	1	0	0	0	0	4	4	0	.077	.077
Tony Horton	1B6	R	21	8	22	0	3	0	0	0	1	0	6	0	.136	.136
Reggie Smith	OF6	B	21	6	26	1	4	0	0	0	3	0	5	0	.154	.192
Mike Andrews	2B5	R	22	5	18	1	3	0	0	0	1	0	3	0	.167	.167

NAME	T	AGE	W	L	PCT	SV	G	GS	CG	IP	H	BB	SO	SHO	ERA
		28	72	90	.444	31	162	162	34	1464	1402	577	977	10	3.92
Jose Santiago	R	25	12	13	.480	2	35	28	7	172	155	58	119	1	3.66
Jim Lonborg	R	24	10	10	.500	2	45	23	3	182	173	55	131	1	3.86
2 Don McMahon	R	36	8	7	.533	9	49	0	0	78	65	38	57	0	2.65
Darrell Brandon	R	25	8	8	.500	2	40	17	5	158	129	70	101	2	3.30
2 Lee Stange	R	29	7	9	.438	2	28	19	8	153	140	43	77	2	3.35
1 Earl Wilson	R	31	5	5	.500	0	15	14	5	101	88	36	67	1	3.83
Dan Osinski	R	32	4	3	.571	2	44	1	0	67	68	28	44	0	3.63
Dennis Bennett (AJ)	L	26	3	3	.500	0	16	13	0	75	75	23	47	0	3.13
2 John Wyatt	R	31	3	4	.429	8	42	0	0	72	59	27	63	0	3.12
1 Ken Sanders	R	24	3	6	.333	2	24	0	0	47	38	28	33	0	3.83
Dick Stigman	L	30	2	1	.667	0	34	10	1	81	85	46	65	1	5.44
3 Hank Fischer	R	26	2	3	.400	0	15	5	1	31	35	11	26	0	2.90
Jerry Stephenson (SA)	R	22	2	5	.286	0	15	11	1	66	68	44	50	0	5.86
Bob Sadowski	R	28	1	1	.500	0	11	5	0	33	41	9	15	0	5.45
Dave Morehead	R	23	1	2	.333	0	12	5	1	28	31	7	20	0	5.46
2 Rollie Sheldon	R	29	1	6	.143	0	23	10	1	80	106	23	38	0	4.95
2 Bill Short	L	28	0	0	—	0	8	8	10	2	0	0	0	0	4.50
2 Garry Roggenburk	L	26	0	0	—	0	5	5	1	5	9	6	7	0	0.00
1 Guido Grilli	L	27	0	0	—	0	1	1	5	5	9	6	4	0	7.20
Pete Magrini	R	24	0	1	.000	0	4	1	0	4	2	9	1	0	9.82
1 Dick Radatz	R	29	0	2	.000	1	16	0	0	19	24	11	19	0	4.74

NEW YORK — 10th 70-89 .440 26.5 — JOHNNY KEANE 4-16 .200 — RALPH HOUK 66-73 .475

NAME	G by Pos	B	AGE	G	AB	R	H	2B	3B	HR	RBI	BB	SO	SB	BA	SA
TOTALS			29	160	5330	611	1254	182	36	162	569	485	817	49	.235	.374
Joe Pepitone	1B119, OF55	L	25	152	585	85	149	21	4	31	83	29	58	4	.255	.463
Bobby Richardson	2B147, 3B2	R	30	149	610	71	153	21	7	7	42	25	58	6	.251	.330
Horace Clarke	SS63, 2B16, 3B4	B	26	96	312	37	83	10	4	6	28	27	24	5	.266	.381
Clete Boyer	3B85, SS59	R	29	154	500	59	120	22	4	14	57	46	48	6	.240	.384
Roger Maris (KJ)	OF119	L	31	119	348	37	81	9	2	13	43	36	60	0	.233	.382
Mickey Mantle	OF97	B	34	108	333	40	96	12	1	23	56	57	76	1	.288	.538
Tom Tresh	OF84, 3B64	B	28	151	537	76	125	12	4	27	68	86	89	5	.233	.421
Elston Howard	C100, 1B13	R	37	126	410	38	105	19	2	6	35	37	65	0	.256	.356
Roy White	OF82, 2B2	B	22	115	316	39	71	13	2	7	20	37	43	14	.225	.345
Lu Clinton	OF63	R	28	80	159	18	35	10	2	5	21	16	27	0	.220	.403
Jake Gibbs (BG)	C54	L	27	62	182	19	47	4	0	3	20	19	16	5	.258	.341
Ray Barker	1B47	L	30	61	75	11	14	5	0	3	13	4	20	0	.187	.373
Hector Lopez	OF29	R	36	54	117	14	25	4	1	4	16	8	20	0	.214	.368
1 Roger Repoz	OF31	L	25	37	43	4	15	1	0	4	9	5	8	0	.349	.488
Steve Whitaker	OF31	L	23	27	69	5	16	2	1	3	12	5	15	3	.246	.493
2 Dick Schofield	SS19	B	31	25	65	15	12	2	0	1	5	15	8	0	.155	.190
2 Billy Bryan	C14, 1B3	L	27	27	69	5	15	2	0	4	5	5	19	0	.217	.420
1 Dick Schofield	SS18	B	31	25	65	15	12	2	0	1	5	15	8	0	.155	.190
Bobby Murcer	SS18	L	20	21	69	13	12	1	0	1	5	4	15	2	.174	.217
Ruben Amaro	SS3	R	30	14	23	0	5	0	0	0	2	7	3	0	.217	.217
Mike Hegan	1B13	L	23	13	39	7	8	2	1	0	2	7	11	0	.205	.256

Mike Ferraro 21 R 5-28, John Miller 22 R 2-23, Ross Moschitto (MS) 21

NAME	T	AGE	W	L	PCT	SV	G	GS	CG	IP	H	BB	SO	SHO	ERA
		28	70	89	.440	32	160	160	29	1416	1318	443	842	7	3.42
Fritz Peterson	L	24	12	11	.522	0	34	32	11	215	196	40	96	2	3.31
Mel Stottlemyre	R	24	12	20	.375	1	37	35	9	251	239	82	146	3	3.80
Al Downing	L	25	10	11	.476	0	30	30	1	200	178	79	152	0	3.56
Steve Hamilton	L	32	8	3	.727	3	44	3	0	90	69	22	57	1	3.00
Dooley Womack	R	26	7	3	.700	4	42	0	0	75	52	23	50	0	2.64
2 Fred Talbot	R	25	7	7	.500	0	23	19	3	124	123	45	48	0	4.14
Hal Reniff	R	27	3	7	.300	9	56	0	0	95	80	49	79	0	3.22
Jim Bouton (SA)	R	27	3	8	.273	1	24	19	3	120	117	38	65	0	2.70
Pedro Ramos	R	31	3	9	.250	13	52	1	0	90	98	18	58	0	3.73
Whitey Ford (SJ)	L	37	2	5	.286	0	22	9	0	73	79	24	43	0	2.47
Jack Cullen	R	26	1	0	1.000	0	3	1	0	13	11	5	7	0	0.00
Stan Bahnsen	R	21	0	0	—	0	4	2	0	18	13	7	9	0	3.52
1 Bob Friend	R	35	1	4	.200	0	12	8	0	45	61	9	22	0	4.80
Bill Henry	L	24	0	0	—	0	1	1	0	3	0	0	0	0	0.00

Rich Beck (MS) 25

LOS ANGELES 1st 95-67 .586 — WALT ALSTON

NAME	G by Pos	B	AGE	G	AB	R	H	2B	3B	HR	RBI	BB	SO	SB	BA	SA
TOTALS			29	162	5471	606	1399	201	27	108	565	430	830	94	.256	.362
Wes Parker	1B140, OF14	B	26	156	475	67	120	17	5	12	51	69	83	7	.253	.385
Jim Lefebvre	2B119, 3B40	B	23	152	544	69	149	23	3	24	74	48	72	1	.274	.460
Maury Wills	SS139, 3B4	B	33	143	594	60	162	14	2	1	39	34	60	38	.273	.308
John Kennedy	3B87, SS28, 2B15	R	25	125	274	15	55	9	2	3	24	10	64	1	.201	.281
Ron Fairly	OF98, 1B25	L	27	117	351	53	101	20	0	14	61	52	38	5	.288	.464
Willie Davis	OF152	R	26	153	624	74	177	31	6	11	61	15	68	21	.284	.405
Lou Johnson	OF148	R	31	152	526	71	143	23	2	17	73	21	75	8	.272	.414
Johnny Roseboro	C138	L	33	142	445	47	123	23	2	9	53	44	51	3	.276	.398
Tommy Davis	OF79, 3B2	R	27	100	313	27	98	11	1	3	27	16	36	3	.313	.383
Jim Gilliam	3B70, 1B2, 2B2	B	37	88	235	30	51	9	0	1	16	34	17	2	.217	.268
Nate Oliver	2B68, SS2, 3B1	R	25	80	119	17	23	2	0	0	3	13	17	3	.193	.210
Al Ferrara	OF32	R	26	63	115	15	31	4	0	5	23	9	35	0	.270	.435
Jeff Torborg	C45	R	24	46	120	4	27	3	0	1	13	10	23	0	.225	.275
Jim Barbieri	OF20	L	24	39	82	9	23	5	0	0	3	9	7	2	.280	.341
2 Dick Stuart	1B25	R	33	38	91	4	24	1	0	3	9	11	17	0	.264	.374
2 Wes Covington	OF2	L	34	37	33	1	4	0	1	1	6	6	5	0	.121	.273
Derrell Griffith	OF7	L	22	23	15	3	1	0	0	0	2	2	3	0	.067	.067
3 Dick Schofield	3B19, SS3	B	31	20	70	10	18	0	0	0	4	8	8	1	.257	.257
Bart Shirley	SS5	R	26	12	5	2	1	0	0	0	0	2	1	0	.200	.200

Willie Crawford 19 L 0-0, Tommy Hutton 20 L 0-2, Jim Campanis 22 R 0-1

NAME	T	AGE	W	L	PCT	SV	G	GS	CG	IP	H	BB	SO	SHO	ERA
TOTALS		27	95	67	.586	35	162	162	52	1458	1287	356	1084	20	2.62
Sandy Koufax	L	30	27	9	.750	0	41	41	27	323	241	77	317	5	1.73
Claude Osteen	L	26	17	14	.548	0	39	38	8	240	238	65	137	3	2.85
Phil Regan	R	29	14	1	.933	21	65	0	0	117	85	24	88	0	1.62
Don Drysdale	R	29	13	16	.448	0	40	40	11	274	279	45	177	3	3.42
Don Sutton	R	21	12	12	.500	0	37	35	6	226	192	52	209	2	2.99
Ron Perranoski	L	30	6	7	.462	7	55	0	0	82	82	31	50	0	3.18
Bob Miller	R	27	4	2	.667	5	46	0	0	84	70	23	59	0	2.79
Joe Moeller	R	23	2	4	.333	0	29	8	0	79	73	14	31	0	2.51
Nick Willhite	L	25	0	0	—	0	6	0	0	4	5	4	2	0	2.25
Bill Singer	R	22	0	0	—	0	3	0	0	4	4	2	1	0	0.00
1 Johnny Podres	L	33	0	0	—	0	1	0	0	2	2	1	1	0	0.00
1 Howie Reed	R	29	0	0	—	0	1	0	0	2	1	1	0	0	2.25
Jim Brewer (EJ)	L	30	0	2	.000	2	13	0	0	22	17	11	8	0	3.68

SAN FRANCISCO 2nd 93-68 .578 1.5 — HERMAN FRANKS

NAME	G by Pos	B	AGE	G	AB	R	H	2B	3B	HR	RBI	BB	SO	SB	BA	SA
TOTALS			26	161	5539	675	1373	195	31	181	627	414	860	29	.248	.392
Willie McCovey	1B145	L	28	150	502	85	148	26	6	36	96	76	100	2	.295	.586
Hal Lanier	2B112, SS41	R	23	149	459	37	106	14	2	3	37	16	49	1	.231	.290
Tito Fuentes	SS76, 2B60	R	22	133	541	63	141	21	3	9	40	9	57	6	.261	.360
Jim Ray Hart	3B139, OF17	R	22	156	578	88	165	23	4	33	93	48	75	2	.285	.510
Ollie Brown	OF114	R	22	115	348	32	81	7	1	7	33	33	66	2	.233	.319
Willie Mays	OF150	R	35	152	552	99	159	29	4	37	103	70	81	5	.288	.556
Jesus Alou	OF100	R	24	110	370	41	96	13	1	1	20	9	22	5	.259	.308
Tom Haller	C136, 1B4	L	29	142	471	74	113	19	2	27	67	53	74	1	.240	.461
Jim Davenport	SS58, 3B36, 2B21, 1B2	R	32	111	305	42	76	6	2	9	30	22	40	1	.249	.370
Len Gabrielson	OF67, 1B6	L	26	94	240	27	52	7	0	4	16	21	51	0	.217	.296
Cap Peterson	OF51, 1B2	R	23	89	190	13	45	6	1	2	19	11	32	2	.237	.311
Don Landrum	OF54	L	30	72	102	9	19	4	0	1	7	9	18	1	.186	.255
Bob Barton	C39	R	24	43	91	1	16	2	1	0	3	5	10	0	.176	.220
Ozzie Virgil	3B13, C13, 1B5, 2B2, OF2	R	33	42	89	7	19	2	0	2	9	4	12	1	.213	.303
Don Mason	2B9	R	21	42	25	8	3	0	0	1	0	2	2	0	.120	.240
Bob Burda	1B7, OF4	L	27	37	43	3	7	0	0	2	2	5	5	0	.163	.233
1 Orlando Cepeda	OF8, 1B6	R	28	19	49	5	14	2	0	3	15	4	11	0	.286	.510
Jack Hiatt	1B7	R	23	18	23	2	7	2	0	1	4	5	0	0	.304	.391
Frank Johnson	OF13	R	23	15	32	2	7	0	0	0	2	0	7	0	.219	.219
Dick Dietz	C6	R	24	13	23	1	1	0	0	0	0	2	9	0	.043	.043
Ken Henderson	OF10	B	20	11	29	4	9	1	1	1	2	3	6	0	.310	.517
1 Dick Schofield	SS8	B	31	11	16	4	1	0	0	0	1	2	3	0	.063	.063
Bob Schroder	SS9	L	21	10	33	4	8	0	0	0	2	0	1	0	.242	.242

Dick Bertell (LJ) 30

NAME	T	AGE	W	L	PCT	SV	G	GS	CG	IP	H	BB	SO	SHO	ERA
TOTALS		29	93	68	.578	27	161	161	52	1477	1370	359	973	14	3.24
Juan Marichal	R	28	25	6	.806	0	37	36	25	307	228	36	222	4	2.23
Gaylord Perry	R	27	21	8	.724	0	36	35	13	256	242	40	201	3	2.99
Bobby Bolin	R	27	11	10	.524	1	36	34	10	224	174	70	143	4	2.89
Lindy McDaniel	R	30	10	5	.667	6	64	0	0	122	103	35	93	0	2.66
Frank Linzy	R	25	7	7	.389	16	51	0	0	100	107	34	57	0	2.97
Bob Priddy	R	26	6	3	.667	1	38	3	0	91	88	28	51	0	3.96
Ron Herbel	R	28	5	4	.444	1	32	18	0	130	149	39	55	0	4.15
Joe Gibbon	L	31	4	6	.400	1	37	10	1	81	86	16	48	0	3.67
2 Ray Sadecki	R	25	3	7	.300	0	26	19	3	105	125	39	62	1	5.40
Bill Henry	L	38	1	1	.500	1	35	0	0	22	15	10	15	0	2.45
1 Bob Shaw	R	33	1	4	.200	0	13	6	0	32	45	7	21	0	6.19
Bob Garibaldi	R	24	0	0	—	0	1	0	0	1	0	0	0	0	0.00
Rich Robertson	R	21	0	0	—	0	2	0	0	3	2	2	0	0	9.00
2 Billy Hoeft	L	34	0	2	.000	0	4	0	0	4	3	4	3	0	6.75

Masanori Murakami (JL) 22

PITTSBURGH 3rd 92-70 .568 3 — HARRY WALKER

NAME	G by Pos	B	AGE	G	AB	R	H	2B	3B	HR	RBI	BB	SO	SB	BA	SA
TOTALS			28	162	5676	759	1586	238	66	158	715	405	1011	64	.279	.428
Donn Clendenon	1B152	R	30	155	571	80	171	22	10	28	98	52	142	8	.299	.520
Bill Mazeroski	2B162	R	29	162	621	56	163	22	7	16	82	31	62	4	.262	.398
Gene Alley	SS143	R	25	147	579	80	173	28	10	7	43	27	83	8	.299	.418
Bob Bailey	3B96, OF20	R	23	126	380	51	106	19	3	6	33	47	67	5	.279	.447
Roberto Clemente	OF154	R	31	154	638	105	202	31	11	29	119	46	109	7	.317	.536
Matty Alou	OF136	L	27	141	535	86	183	18	9	2	27	24	44	23	.342	.421
Willie Stargell	OF127, 1B15	L	26	140	485	84	153	30	0	33	102	48	109	2	.315	.581
Jim Pagliaroni	C118	R	28	123	374	37	88	20	0	11	49	50	71	0	.235	.377
Manny Mota	OF96, 3B4	R	28	116	322	54	107	16	7	5	46	25	28	7	.332	.472
Jose Pagan	3B83, SS18, 2B3, OF3	R	31	109	368	44	97	15	6	4	54	13	38	0	.264	.370
Jerry Lynch	OF4	L	35	64	56	5	12	1	0	1	6	4	10	0	.214	.286
Jesse Gonder	C52	L	30	59	160	13	36	3	1	7	16	12	39	0	.225	.388
Jerry May	C41	R	22	42	52	6	13	4	0	1	2	2	15	0	.250	.385
Andre Rodgers (LJ)	SS5, 3B3, OF3, 1B2	R	31	36	49	6	9	1	0	0	4	8	7	0	.184	.204
Gene Michael	SS8, 2B2, 3B1	B	28	30	33	9	5	2	1	0	2	3	6	0	.152	.273
Dave Roberts	1B2	L	33	14	16	3	2	1	0	0	0	0	7	0	.125	.188
George Spriggs	OF7	L	25	7	7	0	1	0	0	0	0	0	3	0	.143	.143
Don Bosch	OF1	B	23	3	7	1	0	0	0	0	0	0	0	0	.000	.000

NAME	T	AGE	W	L	PCT	SV	G	GS	CG	IP	H	BB	SO	SHO	ERA
TOTALS		30	92	70	.568	43	162	162	35	1463	1445	463	898	12	3.52
Bob Veale	L	30	16	12	.571	0	38	37	12	268	228	102	229	3	3.02
Vern Law (PJ)	R	36	12	8	.600	0	31	28	8	178	203	24	88	4	4.04
Woody Fryman	L	26	12	9	.571	1	36	28	9	182	182	47	105	3	3.81
Steve Blass	R	24	11	7	.611	0	34	25	1	156	173	46	76	0	3.87
Tommie Sisk	R	24	10	5	.667	1	34	23	4	150	146	52	60	1	4.14
Pete Mikkelsen	R	26	9	8	.529	14	71	0	0	126	106	51	76	0	3.07
Roy Face	R	38	6	8	.500	18	54	0	0	70	68	24	67	0	2.70
Don Cardwell	R	30	6	6	.500	1	32	14	1	102	112	27	60	0	4.59
Al McBean	R	28	4	4	.500	3	47	0	0	87	95	24	54	0	3.21
2 Billy O'Dell	L	33	3	2	.600	4	37	2	0	71	74	23	47	0	2.79
1 Don Schwall	R	30	3	2	.600	0	11	4	0	42	31	21	24	0	2.14
Jim Shellenback	R	22	0	0	—	0	2	0	0	3	3	0	0	0	9.00
Bob Purkey	R	36	0	1	.000	0	10	0	0	20	16	4	5	0	1.35
Luke Walker	L	22	0	1	.000	0	10	1	0	10	8	15	7	0	4.50

PHILADELPHIA 4th 87-75 .537 8 — GENE MAUCH

NAME	G by Pos	B	AGE	G	AB	R	H	2B	3B	HR	RBI	BB	SO	SB	BA	SA
TOTALS			29	162	5607	696	1448	224	49	117	628	510	969	56	.258	.378
Bill White	1B158	L	32	159	577	85	159	23	6	22	103	68	109	16	.276	.451
Cookie Rojas	2B106, OF56, SS2	R	27	156	626	77	168	18	1	6	55	35	46	4	.268	.329
Dick Groat	SS139, 3B20, 1B1	R	35	153	584	58	152	21	4	2	53	40	38	2	.260	.320
Dick Allen	3B91, OF47	R	24	141	524	112	166	25	10	40	110	68	136	10	.317	.632
Johnny Callison	OF154	L	27	155	612	93	169	40	7	11	55	56	83	6	.276	.418
Johnny Briggs (XJ)	OF69	L	22	81	255	43	72	13	5	10	23	41	55	3	.282	.490
Tony Gonzalez	OF121	L	29	132	384	53	110	24	4	6	40	26	60	2	.286	.406
Clay Dalrymple	C110	L	29	114	331	30	81	13	3	4	39	60	57	0	.245	.338
Tony Taylor	2B68, 3B52	R	30	125	434	47	105	14	8	5	40	31	56	8	.242	.346
2 Harvey Kuenn	OF31, 1B13, 3B1	R	35	86	159	15	47	9	0	0	15	10	10	0	.296	.352
Jackie Brandt	OF71	R	32	82	164	16	41	6	1	1	15	17	36	0	.250	.317
Doug Clemens	OF28, 1B1	L	27	79	121	10	31	1	0	1	15	16	25	1	.256	.289
Bob Uecker	C76	R	31	78	207	15	43	6	0	7	30	22	36	0	.208	.338
Bobby Wine (XJ)	SS40, OF2	R	27	46	89	8	21	5	0	6	13	3	25	0	.236	.472
Phil Linz	3B14, SS6, 2B3	R	27	40	70	4	14	3	0	0	4	2	14	0	.200	.243
Jimmie Schaffer	C6	R	30	8	15	2	2	1	0	1	4	1	7	0	.133	.400
1 John Herrnstein	OF2	L	28	4	10	0	1	0	0	0	1	0	1	0	.100	.100

Gary Sutherland 21 R 0-3, 1 Adolfo Phillips 24 R 0-3

NAME	T	AGE	W	L	PCT	SV	G	GS	CG	IP	H	BB	SO	SHO	ERA
TOTALS		29	87	75	.537	23	162	162	52	1460	1439	412	928	15	3.57
Chris Short	L	28	20	10	.667	0	42	39	19	272	257	68	177	4	3.54
Jim Bunning	R	34	19	14	.576	1	43	41	16	314	260	55	252	5	2.41
1 Larry Jackson	R	35	15	13	.536	0	35	33	12	247	243	58	107	5	2.99
Ray Culp	R	24	7	4	.636	1	34	12	1	111	106	53	100	0	5.03
Darold Knowles	L	24	6	5	.545	13	69	0	0	100	98	46	88	0	3.06
2 Bob Buhl	R	37	6	8	.429	1	32	18	1	132	156	39	59	0	4.77
Rick Wise	R	20	5	6	.455	0	22	13	3	99	100	24	58	0	3.73
2 Terry Fox	R	30	3	2	.600	4	36	0	0	44	57	17	22	0	4.50
Roger Craig	R	36	2	1	.667	1	14	0	0	23	5	13	13	0	5.48
Ray Herbert	R	36	2	5	.286	2	23	2	0	50	55	14	15	0	4.32
Joe Verbanic	R	23	1	1	.500	0	17	0	0	14	10	7	9	0	5.14
John Morris	L	24	1	1	.500	0	3	3	0	14	15	3	8	0	5.14
John Boozer	R	27	0	2	.000	0	2	0	0	2	5	2	2	0	7.20
Grant Jackson	L	23	0	0	—	0	2	0	0	2	4	2	2	0	4.50
Steve Ridzik	R	37	0	0	—	0	2	0	0	1	1	2	0	0	9.00
1 Ferguson Jenkins	R	22	0	1	.000	0	8	1	0	12	18	4	6	0	2.25
Gary Wagner	R	26	0	1	.000	0	6	0	0	8	8	5	4	0	4.50
Bo Belinsky	L	29	0	2	.000	0	7	0	0	15	14	5	8	0	3.00
Ed Roebuck	R	34	0	0	—	0	5	0	0	6	9	2	5	0	6.00

ATLANTA 5th 85-77 .525 10 — BOBBY BRAGAN 52-59 .468 / BILLY HITCHCOCK 33-18 .647

NAME	G by Pos	B	AGE	G	AB	R	H	2B	3B	HR	RBI	BB	SO	SB	BA	SA
TOTALS			29	163	5617	782	1476	220	32	207	734	512	913	59	.263	.424
Felipe Alou	1B90, OF79, 3B3, SS1	R	31	154	666	122	218	32	6	31	74	24	51	5	.327	.533
Woody Woodward	2B79, SS37	R	23	144	455	46	102	23	3	0	43	37	54	2	.264	.327
Denis Menke	SS106, 3B39, 1B7	R	25	138	454	55	114	20	4	15	60	71	87	0	.251	.412
Eddie Mathews	3B127	L	34	134	452	72	111	21	4	16	53	63	82	1	.250	.420
Hank Aaron	OF158, 2B2	R	32	158	603	117	168	23	1	44	127	76	96	21	.279	.539
Mack Jones (SJ)	OF112, 1B1	L	27	128	417	60	110	14	1	23	66	39	85	16	.264	.468
Rico Carty	OF126, C17, 1B2, 3B1	R	26	151	521	73	170	24	2	15	76	60	74	4	.326	.464
Joe Torre	C114, 1B36	R	25	148	546	83	172	20	3	36	101	60	61	0	.315	.560
Gary Geiger	OF49	L	29	78	126	23	33	5	3	4	10	21	29	0	.262	.444
Gene Oliver (NJ)	C48, 1B5, OF2	R	30	76	191	19	37	9	1	8	24	16	43	2	.194	.377
Frank Bolling	2B67	R	34	75	227	16	48	7	0	1	18	10	14	1	.211	.256
Mike de la Hoz	3B30, 2B8, SS1, 1B1	R	27	71	110	11	24	3	0	4	18	9	25	0	.218	.300
Tony Cloninger	P39	R	25	47	111	12	26	5	0	5	23	2	22	0	.234	.414
2 Ty Cline	OF19, 1B6	L	27	42	71	12	18	0	0	0	6	15	10	1	.254	.254
1 Lee Thomas	1B36	R	30	39	126	11	25	7	0	4	15	10	15	1	.198	.365
Felix Millan	2B25, SS5, 3B1	R	22	37	91	20	25	8	0	0	7	3	13	0	.275	.341
Sandy Alomar	2B21, SS5	R	22	31	44	4	4	1	0	0	3	6	7	0	.091	.114
3 John Herrnstein	OF5	L	28	18	18	2	4	0	0	0	1	2	7	0	.222	.222
1 Marty Keough	1B4, OF3	L	32	17	17	1	1	0	0	0	0	2	4	0	.059	.059
Lee Bales	2B7, 3B3	R	21	12	16	1	1	0	0	0	0	1	8	0	.063	.063
Bill Robinson	OF5	R	23	6	11	1	3	1	0	0	2	2	5	0	.273	.455
George Kopacz	1B2	L	23	4	3	0	0	0	0	0	0	0	0	0	.000	.000
Adrian Garrett	OF1	L	23	4	3	0	0	0	0	0	0	0	2	0	.000	.000
Eddie Sadowski	C3	R	35	3	9	1	1	0	0	0	0	1	3	0	.111	.111

NAME	T	AGE	W	L	PCT	SV	G	GS	CG	IP	H	BB	SO	SHO	ERA
TOTALS		29	85	77	.525	36	163	163	37	1469	1430	485	884	10	3.68
Ken Johnson	R	33	14	8	.636	0	32	31	11	216	213	46	105	2	3.29
Tony Cloninger	R	25	14	11	.560	1	39	38	11	258	253	116	178	1	4.12
Denny Lemaster	R	27	11	8	.579	0	37	27	10	171	170	41	139	3	3.74
Clay Carroll	R	25	8	7	.533	11	73	3	0	144	127	29	67	0	2.38
Dick Kelley	R	26	7	5	.583	0	20	13	2	81	75	21	50	2	3.22
Pat Jarvis	R	25	6	2	.750	0	10	9	3	62	46	12	41	1	2.32
Chi Chi Olivo	R	40	5	4	.556	7	46	0	0	66	59	19	41	0	4.23
Phil Niekro	R	27	4	3	.571	2	28	0	0	50	48	23	17	0	4.14
2 Ted Abernathy	R	33	4	4	.500	1	28	0	0	65	68	23	17	0	3.88
2 Don Schwall	R	30	3	3	.500	0	11	8	0	45	44	19	27	0	4.40
Wade Blasingame (AJ)	L	22	3	7	.300	0	15	9	0	58	65	33	46	0	5.29
1 Billy O'Dell	L	33	2	0	—	0	24	0	0	41	44	18	20	0	2.41
1 Hank Fischer	R	26	2	2	.500	0	14	8	0	48	55	14	22	0	3.94
Charlie Vaughan	L	18	1	0	1.000	0	1	1	0	8	5	2	3	0	2.57
Ron Reed	R	23	1	1	.500	0	2	2	0	14	10	1	8	0	2.25
Dan Schneider	L	24	0	1	.000	0	26	0	0	26	35	5	16	0	3.46
Cecil Upshaw	R	23	1	1	.500	0	14	0	0	18	23	9	11	0	4.15
Jay Ritchie	R	29	0	0	—	0	35	0	0	52	33	12	33	0	4.11
Herb Hippauf	R	24	0	1	.000	0	2	0	0	5	8	3	4	0	12.00
Arnie Umbach	R	23	0	0	—	0	22	0	0	41	40	18	24	0	3.07
2 Joey Jay	R	30	0	4	.000	0	4	0	0	39	36	20	19	0	7.80

ST. LOUIS 6th 83-79 .512 12   RED SCHOENDIENST

NAME	G by Pos	B	AGE	G	AB	R	H	2B	3B	HR	RBI	BB	SO	SB	BA	SA
TOTALS			27	162	5480	571	1377	196	61	108	533	345	977	144	.251	.368
2 Orlando Cepeda	1B120	R	28	123	452	65	137	24	0	17	58	34	68	9	.303	.469
Julian Javier	2B145	R	29	147	460	52	105	13	5	7	31	26	63	11	.228	.324
Dal Maxvill	SS128, 2B5, OF1	R	27	134	394	25	96	14	3	0	24	37	61	3	.244	.294
Charley Smith	3B107, SS1	R	28	116	391	34	104	13	4	10	43	22	81	0	.266	.396
Mike Shannon	OF129, C1	R	26	137	459	61	132	20	6	16	64	37	106	8	.288	.462
Curt Flood	OF159	R	28	160	626	64	167	24	5	10	78	26	50	14	.267	.364
Lou Brock	OF154	L	27	156	643	94	183	24	12	15	46	31	134	74	.285	.429
Tim McCarver	C148	L	24	150	543	50	149	19	13	12	68	36	38	9	.274	.424
Jerry Buchek	2B49, SS48, 3B4	R	24	100	284	23	67	10	4	4	25	23	71	0	.236	.342
Phil Gagliano	3B41, 1B8, OF5, 2B1	R	24	90	213	23	54	8	2	2	15	24	29	2	.254	.338
Tito Francona	1B30, OF9	L	32	83	156	14	33	4	1	4	17	7	27	0	.212	.327
Bob Skinner		L	34	49	45	2	7	1	0	1	5	2	17	0	.156	.244
Bobby Tolan	OF26, 1B1	L	20	43	93	10	16	5	1	6	6	15	1	.172	.280
Pat Corrales	C27	R	25	28	72	5	13	2	0	0	3	2	17	1	.181	.208
Ed Spiezio	3B19	R	24	26	73	4	16	5	1	2	10	5	11	1	.219	.397
Alex Johnson	OF22	R	23	25	86	7	16	0	1	2	6	5	18	1	.186	.279
George Kernek	1B16	L	26	20	50	5	12	0	1	0	1	6	9	1	.240	.280
Ted Savage	OF7	R	29	16	29	4	5	2	1	0	3	4	7	4	.172	.310
Jimy Williams (MS)	SS7, 2B3	R	22	13	11	1	3	0	0	0	1	1	5	0	.273	.273

NAME	T	AGE	W	L	PCT	SV	G	GS	CG	IP	H	BB	SO	SHO	ERA
		28	83	79	.512	32	162	162	47	1460	1345	448	892	19	3.11
Bob Gibson	R	30	21	12	.636	0	35	35	20	280	210	78	225	5	2.44
Al Jackson	L	30	13	15	.464	0	36	30	11	233	222	45	90	3	2.51
Larry Jaster	L	22	11	5	.688	0	26	21	6	152	124	45	92	5	3.26
Ray Washburn	R	28	11	9	.550	0	28	26	4	170	183	44	98	1	3.76
Joe Hoerner	L	29	5	1	.833	13	57	0	0	76	57	21	63	0	1.54
Don Dennis	R	24	4	2	.667	2	38	1	0	60	73	17	25	0	4.95
Nelson Briles	R	22	4	15	.211	6	49	17	0	154	162	54	100	0	3.21
Steve Carlton	L	21	3	3	.500	0	9	2	2	52	56	18	25	1	3.12
Hal Woodeshick	L	33	2	1	.667	4	59	0	0	70	57	23	30	0	1.93
Dick Hughes	R	28	2	1	.667	1	6	2	1	21	12	7	20	1	1.71
1 Ray Sadecki	R	25	2	1	.667	0	5	3	1	24	16	9	21	0	2.25
Jim Cosman	R	23	1	0	1.000	1	3	2	1	18	14	4	9	0	0.00
1 Curt Simmons	L	37	1	1	.500	0	10	5	1	33	35	14	14	0	4.64
Ron Piche	R	31	1	3	.250	0	20	0	0	25	21	18	24	0	4.32
Art Mahaffey	R	28	1	4	.200	1	12	5	0	35	37	21	19	0	6.43
Tracy Stallard	R	28	1	5	.167	1	20	7	0	52	65	25	35	0	5.71
Ron Willis	R	22	0	0	—	1	4	0	0	9	6	1	6	0	0.00
Dennis Aust	R	25	0	0	—	0	6	0	0	10	6	6	7	0	6.30

CINCINNATI 7th 76-84 .475 18   DON HEFFNER 37-46 .446   DAVE BRISTOL 39-38 .506

NAME	G by Pos	B	AGE	G	AB	R	H	2B	3B	HR	RBI	BB	SO	SB	BA	SA
TOTALS			26	160	5521	692	1434	232	33	149	651	394	877	70	.260	.395
Tony Perez	1B75	R	24	99	257	25	68	10	4	4	39	14	44	1	.265	.381
Pete Rose	2B140, 3B16	B	25	156	654	97	205	38	5	16	70	37	61	4	.313	.460
Leo Cardenas	SS160	R	27	160	568	59	145	25	4	20	81	45	87	9	.255	.419
Tommy Helms	3B113, 2B20	R	25	138	542	72	154	23	1	9	49	24	31	3	.284	.380
Tommy Harper	OF147	R	25	149	553	85	154	22	5	5	31	57	85	29	.278	.363
Vada Pinson	OF154	L	27	156	618	70	178	35	6	16	76	33	83	18	.288	.442
Deron Johnson	OF106, 1B71, 3B18	R	24	142	505	75	130	25	3	24	81	39	87	1	.257	.461
Johnny Edwards	C98	L	28	98	282	24	54	8	0	6	39	31	42	1	.191	.284
Art Shamsky	OF74	L	24	96	234	41	54	5	0	21	47	32	45	0	.231	.521
Dick Simpson	OF64	R	22	92	84	26	20	2	0	4	14	10	32	3	.238	.405
Gordy Coleman	1B65	R	31	91	227	20	57	7	0	5	37	16	45	2	.251	.348
Don Pavletich	C55, 1B10	R	27	83	235	29	69	13	2	12	38	18	37	1	.294	.519
Chico Ruiz	3B27, OF8, SS6	B	27	82	110	13	28	3	2	0	5		14	1	.255	.291
Mel Queen	OF32, P7	R	24	56	55	4	7	1	0	0	5	10	12	0	.127	.145
Jimmie Coker	C39, OF2	R	30	50	111	9	28	3	0	4	14	8	5	0	.252	.387
Lee May	1B16	R	23	25	75	14	25	5	0	2	10	0	14	0	.333	.507

NAME	T	AGE	W	L	PCT	SV	G	GS	CG	IP	H	BB	SO	SHO	ERA
		28	76	84	.475	35	160	160	28	1436	1408	490	1043	10	4.08
Jim Maloney	R	26	16	8	.667	0	32	32	10	225	174	90	216	5	2.80
Milt Pappas	R	27	12	11	.522	0	33	32	6	210	224	39	133	2	4.29
Sammy Ellis	R	25	12	19	.387	0	41	36	7	221	226	78	154	0	5.29
Billy McCool	L	21	8	8	.500	18	57	0	0	105	76	41	104	0	2.49
1 Joey Jay	R	30	6	2	.750	0	12	10	1	74	78	23	44	1	3.89
Joe Nuxhall (AJ)	R	37	6	8	.429	0	35	16	2	130	136	42	71	1	4.50
Don Nottebart	R	30	5	4	.556	11	59	1	0	111	97	43	69	0	3.08
Ted Davidson	L	26	5	4	.556	4	54	0	0	85	80	23	54	0	3.92
Jim O'Toole	L	29	5	7	.417	0	25	24	2	142	139	49	96	0	3.55
Jack Baldschun	R	29	1	5	.167	0	42	0	0	57	71	25	44	0	5.53
Mel Queen	R	24	0	0	—	1	7	0	0	7	11	6	9	0	6.43
Dom Zanni	R	34	0	0	—	1	7	0	0	5	7	5	3	0	0.00
1 Jerry Arrigo	R	25	0	0	—	0	3	0	0	5	6	3	5	0	5.14
John Tsitouris	R	30	0	0	—	1	3	1	0	1	3	1	0	0	18.00
Darrell Osteen	R	23	0	2	.000	0	13	0	0	15	26	9	17	0	12.00
2 Hank Fischer	R	26	0	3	.000	0	38	5	0	15	24	5	5	0	6.63

HOUSTON 8th 72-90 .444 23   GRADY HATTON

NAME	G by Pos	B	AGE	G	AB	R	H	2B	3B	HR	RBI	BB	SO	SB	BA	SA
TOTALS			26	163	5511	612	1405	203	35	112	570	491	885	90	.255	.365
Chuck Harrison	1B114	R	25	119	434	52	111	23	2	9	52	37	69	2	.256	.380
Joe Morgan (BK)	2B117	L	22	122	425	60	121	14	8	5	42	89	43	11	.285	.391
Sonny Jackson	SS150	R	21	150	596	80	174	16	8	1	25	42	53	49	.292	.334
Bob Aspromonte	3B149, 1B2, SS2	R	28	152	560	55	141	16	3	8	52	37	60	0	.252	.334
Rusty Staub	OF148, 1B1	R	22	153	554	60	155	28	3	13	81	58	61	2	.280	.412
Jim Wynn (EJ)	OF104	R	24	105	418	62	107	21	1	18	62	41	81	13	.256	.440
Lee Maye	OF97	L	31	115	358	38	103	12	4	9	36	20	26	4	.288	.419
John Bateman	C121	R	25	131	433	39	121	24	3	17	70	20	74	0	.279	.434
Dave Nicholson	OF90	R	26	100	280	36	69	8	4	10	31	46	92	1	.246	.411
Felix Mantilla	1B14, 3B14, 2B9, OF1	R	31	77	151	16	33	5	0	6	22	11	32	1	.219	.371
Bob Lillis	2B35, SS18, 3B6	R	36	68	164	14	38	6	0	0	11	7	4	1	.232	.268
Ron Brand	C25, 2B9, OF3, 3B1	R	26	56	123	12	30	2	0	0	9	9	13	0	.244	.260
Bill Heath	C37	L	27	55	123	12	37	6	0	1	8	9	11	1	.301	.350
1 Jim Gentile	1B43	L	32	49	144	16	35	4	1	7	18	21	39	0	.243	.444
Ron Davis	OF48	R	24	48	194	21	48	10	1	2	19	13	26	2	.247	.340
2 Gene Freese	3B4, 2B3, OF1	R	32	31	33	1	3	0	0	0	0	5	11	0	.091	.091
Nate Colbert		R	20	19	7	3	0	0	0	0	0	0	4	0	.000	.000
Aaron Pointer	OF11	R	24	11	26	5	9	1	0	1	5	5	6	1	.346	.500
Norm Miller	OF8, 3B2	L	20	11	34	1	5	0	0	0	3	2	8	0	.147	.235
Joe Gaines	OF3	R	29	11	13	4	1	1	0	0	0	2	1	0	.077	.154
Brock Davis	OF7	L	22	10	27	2	4	1	0	0	1	5	4	1	.148	.185

Greg Sims 20 B 1-6, Julio Gotay 27 R 0-5, Dave Adlesh 22 R 0-6, Bob Watson 20 R 0-1

NAME	T	AGE	W	L	PCT	SV	G	GS	CG	IP	H	BB	SO	SHO	ERA
		28	72	90	.444	26	163	163	34	1444	1468	391	929	13	3.76
Dave Giusti	R	26	15	14	.517	0	34	33	9	210	215	54	131	4	4.20
Mike Cuellar	L	29	12	10	.545	2	38	28	11	227	193	52	175	1	2.22
Larry Dierker	R	19	10	8	.556	0	29	28	8	187	173	45	108	2	3.18
Claude Raymond	R	29	7	5	.583	16	62	0	0	92	85	25	73	0	3.13
Dick Farrell	R	32	6	10	.375	2	32	21	3	153	167	28	101	0	4.59
Jim Owens	R	32	4	7	.364	2	40	0	0	50	53	17	32	0	4.68
1 Robin Roberts	R	39	3	5	.375	1	13	12	1	64	79	10	26	1	3.80
Chris Zachary	R	22	3	5	.375	0	10	6	0	55	44	32	37	0	3.44
Bob Bruce	R	33	3	13	.188	0	25	23	1	130	160	29	71	0	5.33
1 Don Lee	R	32	2	0	1.000	0	19	0	0	18	17	4	9	0	2.50
Ron Taylor (XJ)	R	28	2	3	.400	0	36	1	0	65	89	10	29	0	5.68
Barry Latman	R	30	2	7	.222	1	31	9	1	103	88	35	74	1	2.71
Frank Carpin	L	27	1	0	1.000	0	10	0	0	9	6	7	5	0	7.50
Don Wilson	R	21	1	0	1.000	0	2	2	0	9	5	2	9	0	3.00
Carroll Sembera	R	24	1	2	.333	1	24	0	0	33	36	16	21	0	3.00
Gary Kroll	R	24	0	0	—	0	10	0	0	24	26	11	22	0	3.75
2 Aurelio Monteagudo	R	22	0	0	—	1	9	0	0	15	14	11	7	0	4.80
Danny Coombs	L	24	0	1	.000	0	4	3	0	4	3	0	3	0	3.00
Jim Ray	R	21	0	0	—	0	1	0	0	1	4	1	1	0	∞
Don Arlich	L	23	0	1	.000	0	2	0	0	4	11	4	1	0	15.75

NEW YORK 9th 66-95 .410 28.5   WES WESTRUM

NAME	G by Pos	B	AGE	G	AB	R	H	2B	3B	HR	RBI	BB	SO	SB	BA	SA
TOTALS			28	161	5371	587	1286	187	35	98	534	446	992	55	.239	.342
Ed Kranepool	1B132, OF11	L	21	146	464	51	118	15	2	16	57	41	66	1	.254	.399
Ron Hunt	2B123, SS1, 3B1	R	25	132	479	63	138	19	2	3	33	41	34	8	.288	.355
Ed Bressoud	SS94, 3B32, 1B9, 2B7	R	34	133	405	48	91	15	4	10	49	47	107	2	.225	.360
Ken Boyer	3B130, 1B2	R	35	136	496	62	132	28	2	14	61	30	64	4	.266	.413
Al Luplow	OF101	L	27	111	334	31	84	9	1	7	31	38	46	2	.251	.347
Cleon Jones	OF129	R	23	139	495	74	136	16	4	8	57	30	62	16	.275	.372
Ron Swoboda	OF97	R	22	112	342	34	76	9	4	8	50	31	76	4	.222	.342
Jerry Grote	C115, 3B2	R	23	120	317	26	75	12	3	3	31	40	81	4	.237	.315
Chuck Hiller	2B45, 3B14, OF6	L	31	108	254	25	71	8	2	2	14	15	22	0	.280	.350
Billy Murphy	OF57	R	22	84	135	15	31	4	1	3	13	7	34	1	.230	.341
Roy McMillan	SS71	R	36	76	220	24	47	9	1	1	12	20	25	1	.214	.277
Larry Elliot	OF54	L	28	65	199	24	49	14	2	5	32	17	46	0	.246	.412
Johnny Lewis	OF49	L	26	65	166	21	32	6	1	5	20	21	43	2	.193	.331
Johnny Stephenson	C52, OF1	L	25	63	143	17	28	1	1	1	11	8	28	0	.196	.238
Jim Hickman (BW)	OF45, 1B17	R	29	58	160	15	38	7	0	4	16	13	34	2	.238	.356
Hawk Taylor	C29, 1B13	R	27	53	109	5	19	2	0	3	12	3	19	0	.174	.275
Bud Harrelson	SS29	B	22	33	99	20	22	2	4	0	4	13	21	7	.222	.323
1 Dick Stuart	1B23	R	33	31	87	7	19	4	0	6	13	9	26	0	.218	.356
Greg Goossen	C11	R	20	11	32	1	6	2	0	1	5	1	11	0	.188	.344
Danny Napoleon	OF10	L	24	12	19	2	4	2	0	0	0	1	10	0	.212	.273
Shaun Fitzmaurice	OF5	R	23	9	13	2	2	0	0	0	2	1	4	1	.154	.154
Choo Choo Coleman	C5	L	29	6	16	2	3	0	0	0	0	0	6	0	.188	.188
Lou Klimchock		L	26	6	5	0	0	0	0	0	0	0	0	0	.000	.000

NAME	T	AGE	W	L	PCT	SV	G	GS	CG	IP	H	BB	SO	SHO	ERA
		28	66	95	.410	22	161	161	37	1427	1497	521	773	9	4.17
Dennis Ribant	R	24	11	9	.550	3	39	26	10	188	184	40	84	1	3.21
2 Bob Shaw	R	33	11	10	.524	0	26	25	7	168	171	42	104	2	3.91
Jack Fisher	R	27	11	14	.440	0	38	33	10	230	229	54	127	2	3.68
Jack Hamilton	R	27	6	13	.316	13	57	13	3	149	138	86	93	1	3.93
2 Bob Friend	R	35	8	8	.385	1	22	12	2	86	101	16	30	1	4.40
Dick Selma	R	22	4	6	.400	1	30	7	0	81	84	39	58	0	4.22
Rob Gardner	L	20	4	8	.333	1	41	17	3	134	147	64	74	0	5.10
Bill Hepler	L	20	3	3	.500	0	37	3	0	69	71	51	25	0	3.52
2 Jerry Arrigo (RJ)	R	25	3	3	.500	0	17	5	0	43	47	16	28	0	3.77
Darrell Sutherland	R	24	2	0	1.000	1	31	0	0	44	60	25	23	0	4.91
Larry Bearnarth	R	24	2	3	.400	0	29	1	0	55	59	20	27	0	4.42
Tug McGraw (SA)	L	21	2	9	.182	0	15	12	1	62	72	25	34	0	5.37
Dave Eilers	R	29	1	1	.500	0	23	0	0	35	39	7	14	0	4.63
Dick Rusteck (SA)	L	24	1	2	.333	0	8	3	1	24	24	8	9	1	3.00
Dallas Green	R	31	1	0	—	1	5	0	0	15	20	7	11	0	5.40
2 Ralph Terry	R	30	1	0	.000	1	11	0	0	25	27	11	14	0	4.68
Nolan Ryan	R	19	1	1	.500	0	2	1	1	3	5	3	6	0	15.00
Gordie Richardson	L	26	0	0	—	0	19	0	0	24	24	6	15	0	9.00
Larry Miller	L	29	0	0	—	0	1	0	0	1	3	1	1	0	7.88

CHICAGO 10th 59-103 .364 36   LEO DUROCHER

NAME	G by Pos	B	AGE	G	AB	R	H	2B	3B	HR	RBI	BB	SO	SB	BA	SA
TOTALS			27	162	5592	644	1418	203	43	140	603	457	998	76	.254	.380
Ernie Banks	1B130, 3B8	R	35	141	511	52	139	23	7	15	75	29	59	0	.272	.432
Glenn Beckert	2B152, SS1	R	25	153	656	73	188	23	7	1	59	26	36	10	.287	.348
Don Kessinger	SS148	B	23	150	533	50	146	8	2	1	43	26	46	13	.274	.302
Ron Santo	3B152, SS8	R	26	155	561	93	175	21	8	30	94	95	78	4	.312	.538
Billy Williams	OF162	L	28	162	648	100	179	23	5	29	91	60	61	6	.276	.461
2 Adolfo Phillips	OF111	R	24	116	416	68	109	29	1	16	36	43	135	32	.262	.452
Byron Browne	OF114	R	23	120	419	46	102	15	7	16	51	40	143	3	.243	.427
Randy Hundley	C149	R	24	149	526	50	124	22	3	19	63	35	113	1	.236	.397
George Altman	OF42, 1B4	L	33	88	185	19	41	6	0	5	17	14	37	2	.222	.335
John Boccabella (EJ)	OF33, 1B30, C5	R	25	75	206	22	47	9	6	4	25	14	39	0	.228	.359
2 Lee Thomas	1B20, OF17	L	30	75	149	15	36	4	0	4	14	15	20	0	.242	.289
Jimmy Stewart	OF15, 2B8, SS2, 3B2	B	27	57	90	4	16	4	1	0	4	7	17	1	.178	.244
Joey Amalfitano	2B12, 3B3, SS2	R	32	57	45	3	8	6	2	0	4	3	10	0	.158	.211
1 Marty Keough	OF5	L	32	26	43	4	6	2	0	0	1	2	7	1	.231	.269
Ron Campbell	SS11, 3B7	R	24	25	26	2	5	1	0	0	4	5	4	1	.217	.233
Carl Warwick	OF10	R	29	21	13	0	3	0	0	0	0	2	1	0	.227	.227
Don Bryant	C10	R	24	21	28	1	6	2	0	0	5	1	8	0	.308	.385
Chris Krug	C10	R	26	11	28	1	6	0	0	0	2	0	6	0	.214	.250
1 John Herrnstein	1B4, OF1	L	28	11	11	0	2	0	0	0	0	0	2	0	.176	.176
1 Wes Covington	OF1	L	34	9	11	0	1	0	0	0	0	1	3	0	.091	.091
Bob Raudman	OF8	L	27	9	17	0	4	0	0	0	0	1	3	0	.241	.310
1 Ty Cline	OF5	L	26	8	17	0	6	1	0	0	2	0	1	1	.353	.353
Roberto Pena	SS5	R	29	6	17	1	3	0	0	0	1	0	2	0	.176	.294

Frank Thomas 37 R 0-5, 1 Harvey Kuenn 35 R 1-3, Paul Popovich 25 R 0-6

NAME	T	AGE	W	L	PCT	SV	G	GS	CG	IP	H	BB	SO	SHO	ERA
		28	59	103	.364	24	162	162	28	1458	1513	479	908	6	4.33
Ken Holtzman	L	20	11	16	.407	0	34	33	9	221	194	68	171	0	3.79
Bill Hands	R	26	8	13	.381	2	41	26	0	159	168	59	93	0	4.58
Dick Ellsworth	L	26	8	22	.267	0	38	37	9	269	321	51	144	0	3.98
2 Ferguson Jenkins	R	22	6	8	.429	5	60	12	2	182	147	51	148	1	3.31
Cal Koonce	R	25	5	5	.500	2	45	5	0	109	113	35	65	0	3.80
Bob Hendley	R	27	5	4	.444	7	43	6	0	90	98	39	65	0	3.90
1 Curt Simmons	L	37	4	7	.364	0	19	13	1	77	79	21	24	1	4.09
1 Don Lee (KJ)	R	32	2	1	.667	0	19	6	1	19	28	12	7	0	7.11
Arnie Earley	L	33	2	1	.667	0	13	0	0	13	18	12	12	0	3.50
2 Robin Roberts	R	39	2	3	.400	0	11	9	1	48	62	11	28	0	6.19
Ernie Broglio	R	30	2	6	.250	1	15	11	2	62	70	38	34	0	6.39
Dave Dowling	L	23	1	0	1.000	0	2	1	0	10	8	2	2	0	2.00
Chuck Estrada	R	28	1	1	.500	0	12	1	0	16	15	3	9	0	7.50
1 Billy Hoeft	L	34	1	2	.333	3	36	0	0	41	43	14	30	0	4.61
1 Ted Abernathy	R	33	1	3	.250	2	40	0	0	28	26	17	18	0	6.11
Bill Faul	R	26	1	4	.200	0	27	7	1	47	54	30	41	0	5.12
Chuck Hartenstein	R	24	0	1	.000	1	9	0	0	11	8	6	8	0	2.00
Fred Norman	L	23	0	1	.000	0	7	0	0	11	10	7	9	0	2.00
1 Bob Buhl	R	37	0	1	.000	0	5	0	0	6	13	7	1	0	18.00
Billy Connors	R	24	0	0	—	0	11	0	0	10	14	6	9	0	7.31
Len Church	L	24	0	0	—	0	4	1	0	10	10	7	9	0	7.50
1 Larry Jackson	R	35	0	0	—	0	2	1	0	14	14	4	6	0	13.50
Rich Nye	L	21	0	0	—	0	17	16	1	17	16	1	9	0	2.12

1967 The Fury at Fenway

They called it The Great Race, and through the final week the battle raged with the American League pennant at stake. Four teams fought, unable to shake off any of the others. The Boston Red Sox were the darlings of fans everywhere; rising up from ninth place in 1966, they were 100-to-one shots seeking The Impossible Dream. The Chicago White Sox had no batters as high as .250, but hung in the race on pitching, defense, and spirit. The Detroit Tigers were a strong team favored by the press to win it, and the Minnesota Twins came to life after manager Sam Mele was replaced in June by Cal Ermer. All four teams remained in the running into the final week, and the torrid chase set typewriters ablaze across the country.

Eddie Stanky's Hitless Wonders from Chicago were the first to drop out, losing a doubleheader to Kansas City on September 27, to end their hopes. Minnesota entered the final weekend one game up on Boston and Detroit. Rain caused the scheduling of back-to-back doubleheaders in Detroit with the California Angels, while the Twins came into Fenway Park to play two against the Red Sox. On Saturday, the Tigers split with the Angels, while an early Minnesota lead was lost after Jim Kaat had to leave the game with an injury, and Boston pounded Twin relievers for a 6-4 victory and a tie for the top. On Sunday, the capacity Boston crowd watched Jim Lonborg defeat Dean Chance to eliminate the Twins, while the Tigers won their first game to climb to a half-game behind the Red Sox. A Detroit victory would have ended the season in a tie, but all Boston—including the Red Sox—listened to their radios, and prayed as Detroit dropped the second game to the Angels 8-5. The Impossible Dream became a reality as Red Sox rooters floated in the celebration of their first pennant since 1946 behind freshman manager Dick Williams.

The story behind the Fenway Miracle rested on the bat, arm, and legs of Carl Yastrzemski, a good hitter with a touch of power, who spent the winter months lifting weights and the summer months converting hits into home runs and winning the coveted Triple Crown of batting and the league's MVP honors. Along with the advent of Boston's new superstar was the pitching of Jim Lonborg, who chalked up 22 wins after never having won more than 10, and the acquisition of Ken Harrelson, who finally made his way to the Red Sox after being made a free agent by the Kansas City A's owner Charley O. Finley. Harrelson called Finley "a menace to baseball" in the year's most famous off-the-field incident, which also included the suspension of pitcher Lew Krausse for misbehavior on the team plane and the firing of manager Al Dark.

What appeared to be a mediocre Red Sox squad responded to Yastrzemski's leadership with outstanding years by the cluster. George Scott and Rico Petrocelli shone in the infield, and Mike Andrews and Reggie Smith were stellar rookies. Catching was a problem until Elston Howard was obtained from New York in August. Tony Conigliaro was continuing his fine four year career until smashed in the face with a Jack Hamilton fastball that sidelined him for the season and left his eyesight in doubt. Infielder Jerry Adair was purchased from Chicago in June and proceeded to hit .291 and steady th infield. The parade of key acquisitions continued with Gary Bell, a ke starter who won 12 games for Boston after joining them in June. Jos Santiago posted a 12-4 mark with a hot September, and John Wya provided a solid relief hand. The collection of odds and ends and sta blended together to win perhaps the most thrilling pennant chase in history

The National League race proved to be a slaughter for the St. Loui Cardinals, as early challenges by the Giants and Cubs were beaten back Orlando Cepeda, acquired a year before from the Giants, turned in an MV performance with a .325 average, 25 homers, a league-leading 111 RBI' and proved to be the inspirational leader of the Cardinals. Curt Flood an Lou Brock also sparked the offense, while Bob Gibson led the mound staf until suffering a broken leg on July 15, as the result of a line drive off th bat of Roberto Clemente. The injury brought gloom over St. Louis, but th pitching staff took up the challenge, as young Steve Carlton won 14 games 29-year-old rookie Dick Hughes won 16, and Nelson Briles came out of th bullpen to win 14 games. During the time Gibson was out, the Cardinal racked up a 36-20 mark.

San Francisco finished second to St. Louis but was hampered by poo years from Willie Mays and Juan Marichal. Jim Ray Hart took on th Giants' run-producing leadership, and Mike McCormick won 22 games in a strong comeback from a sore arm to win the National League Cy Youn Award. Leo Durocher, in his second year as the Cubs manager, had his team in contention with an attack led by Ernie Banks, Ron Santo, and Bill Williams, and a hill staff aced by 20-game winner Ferguson Jenkins.

By the time the World Series got underway, there was still grea excitement in Boston. But the outcome, which was not to be Boston's, wa an anticlimactic matter after the torrid American League race. Th Cardinals and Red Sox split the first six games of the World Series with Jim Lonborg and Bob Gibson both winning two games. Game seven saw the two aces pitted against each other, with Lonborg pitching on two days rest and Gibson on three—a difference which was enough to have Lonborg pounde for seven runs in six innings, to give Gibson his third victory and th Cardinals their eighth Series title. Yastrzemski continued his inspirationa batting in the Series with a .400 mark, but Lou Brock outshined him with a .414 average, 12 hits, 8 runs, and a Series record seven stolen bases.

Although Boston's dream fell short by a single game, they at least ha the satisfaction of a pennant—something made possible in part by the temperament of Charley O. Finley. All Finley could muster out of a painfu season was another move for his team—this time to Oakland for the 1968 season— the city on the other side of the Golden Gate Bridge.

WORLD SERIES — ST. LOUIS (NL) 4 BOSTON (AL) 3

LINE SCORES

TEAM	1 2 3	4 5 6	7 8 9	10 11 12	R	H	E
Game 1 October 4 at Boston							
STL (NL)	0 0 1	0 0 0	1 0 0		2	10	0
BOS (AL)	0 0 1	0 0 0	0 0 0		1	6	0
B. Gibson			Santiago, Wyatt (8)				
Game 2 October 5 at Boston							
STL	0 0 0	0 0 0	0 0 0		0	1	1
BOS	0 0 0	1 0 1	3 0 X		5	9	0
Hughes, Willis (6), Lamabe (7)			Lonborg				
Hoerner (7), Lamabe (7)							
Game 3 October 7 at St. Louis							
BOS	0 0 0	0 0 1	1 0 0		2	7	1
STL	1 2 0	0 0 1	0 1 X		5	10	0
Bell, Waslewski (3),			Briles				
Stange (6), Osinski (8)							
Game 4 October 8 at St. Louis							
BOS	0 0 0	0 0 0	0 0 0		0	5	0
STL	4 0 2	0 0 0	0 0 X		6	9	0
Santiago, Bell (1), Stephenson (3),			B. Gibson				
Morehead (5), Brett (8)							
Game 5 October 9 at St. Louis							
BOS	0 0 1	0 0 0	0 0 2		3	6	1
STL	0 0 0	0 0 0	0 0 1		1	3	2
Lonborg			Carlton, Washburn (7),				
			Willis (9), Lamabe (9)				
Game 6 October 11 at Boston							
STL	0 0 2	0 0 0	2 0 0		4	8	0
BOS	0 1 0	3 0 0	4 0 X		8	12	1
Hughes, Willis (4),			Waslewski, Wyatt (6)				
Briles (5), Lamabe (7),			Bell (8)				
Hoerner (7), Jaster (7),							
Washbum (7), Woodshick (8)							
Game 7 October 12 at Boston							
STL	0 0 2	0 2 3	0 0 0		7	10	1
BOS	0 0 0	0 1 0	0 1 0		2	3	1
B. Gibson			Lonborg, Santiago (7),				
			Morehead (9), Osinski (9),				
			Brett (9)				

COMPOSITE BATTING

NAME	POS	G	AB	R	H	2B	3B	HR	RBI	BA
St. Louis (NL)										
Totals		7	229	25	51	11	2	5	24	.223
Brock	OF	7	29	8	12	2	1	1	3	.414
Cepeda	1B	7	29	1	3	2	0	0	1	.103
Flood	OF	7	28	2	5	1	0	0	3	.179
Maris	OF	7	26	3	10	1	0	1	7	.385
Javier	2B	7	25	2	9	3	0	1	4	.360
Shannon	3B	7	24	3	5	1	0	1	2	.208
McCarver	C	7	24	3	3	1	0	0	2	.125
Maxvill	SS	7	19	1	3	0	1	0	1	.158
B. Gibson	P	3	11	1	1	0	0	1	1	.091
Ricketts	PH	3	3	0	0	0	0	0	0	.000
Briles	P	2	3	0	0	0	0	0	0	.000
Hughes	P	2	3	0	0	0	0	0	0	.000
Tolan	PH	3	2	1	0	0	0	0	0	.000
Gagliano	PH	1	1	0	0	0	0	0	0	.000
Spiezio	PH	1	1	0	0	0	0	0	0	.000
Carlton	P	1	1	0	0	0	0	0	0	.000
Bressoud	SS	2	0	0	0	0	0	0	0	—
Lamabe P 0-0, Washburn P 0-0, Willis P 0-0, Hoerner P 0-0,										
Woodeshick P 0-0, Jaster P 0-0										
Boston (AL)										
Totals		7	222	21	48	6	1	8	19	.216
Scott	1B	7	26	3	6	1	1	0	3	.231
Yastrzemski	OF	7	25	4	10	2	0	3	5	.400
Smith	OF	7	24	3	6	1	0	2	3	.250
Petrocelli	SS	7	20	3	4	1	0	2	3	.200
Jones	3B	6	18	2	7	0	0	0	3	.389
Howard	C	7	18	0	2	0	0	0	1	.111
Adair	2B	5	16	0	2	0	0	0	1	.125
Foy	3B	6	15	2	2	1	0	0	1	.133
Andrews	2B	5	13	2	4	0	0	0	1	.308
Tartabull	OF	7	13	1	2	0	0	0	0	.154
Harrelson	OF	4	13	0	1	0	0	0	1	.077
Lonborg	P	3	9	0	0	0	0	0	0	.000
Siebern	OF	3	3	0	1	0	0	0	1	.333
Santiago	P	3	2	1	1	0	0	1	1	.500
Thomas	OF	2	2	0	0	0	0	0	0	.000
R. Gibson	C	2	2	0	0	0	0	0	0	.000
Ryan	C	2	2	0	0	0	0	0	0	.000
Waslewski	P	2	1	0	0	0	0	0	0	.000
Bell	P	3	0	0	0	0	0	0	0	—
Wyatt P 0-0, Morehead P 0-0, Osinski P 0-0, Brett P 0-0,										
Stephenson P 0-0, Stange P 0-0										

COMPOSITE PITCHING

NAME	G	IP	H	BB	SO	W	L	SV	ERA
St. Louis (NL)									
Totals	7	61	48	17	49	4	3	0	2.66
B. Gibson	3	27	14	5	26	3	0	0	1.00
Briles	2	11	7	1	4	1	0	0	1.64
Hughes	2	9	9	3	7	0	1	0	5.00
Carlton	1	6	3	2	5	0	1	0	0.00
Lamabe	3	2.2	5	0	4	0	1	0	6.75
Washburn	2	2.1	1	1	2	0	0	0	0.00
Woodeshick	1	1	1	0	0	0	0	0	0.00
Willis	3	1	2	4	1	0	0	0	27.00
Hoerner	2	0.2	4	1	0	0	0	0	40.50
Jaster	1	0.1	2	0	0	0	0	0	0.00
Boston (AL)									
Totals	7	61	51	17	30	3	4	1	3.39
Lonborg	3	24	14	2	11	2	1	0	2.63
Santiago	3	9.2	16	3	6	0	2	0	5.59
Waslewski	2	8.1	4	2	7	0	0	0	2.16
Bell	3	5.1	8	1	1	0	1	1	5.06
Wyatt	2	3.2	1	3	1	1	0	0	4.91
Morehead	2	3.1	0	4	3	0	0	0	0.00
Stange	1	2	3	0	0	0	0	0	0.00
Stephenson	1	2	3	1	0	0	0	0	9.00
Brett	2	1.1	0	1	1	0	0	0	0.00
Osinski	2	1.1	2	0	0	0	0	0	6.75

BOSTON 1st 92-70 .568 — DICK WILLIAMS

NAME	G by Pos	B	AGE	G	AB	R	H	2B	3B	HR	RBI	BB	SO	SB	BA	SA
TOTALS			25	162	5471	722	1394	216	39	158	666	522	1020	68	.255	.395
George Scott	1B152, 3B2	R	23	159	565	74	171	21	7	19	82	63	119	10	.303	.465
Mike Andrews	2B139, SS6	R	23	142	494	79	130	20	4	8	40	62	72	7	.263	.352
Rico Petrocelli	SS141	R	24	142	491	53	127	24	2	17	66	49	93	2	.259	.420
Joe Foy	3B118, OF1	R	24	130	446	70	112	22	4	16	49	46	87	8	.251	.426
Tony Conigliaro (IJ)	OF95	R	22	95	349	59	100	11	5	20	67	27	58	4	.287	.519
Reggie Smith	OF144, 2B6	B	22	158	565	78	139	24	6	15	61	57	95	16	.246	.389
Carl Yastrzemski	OF161	L	27	161	579	112	189	31	4	44	121	91	69	10	.326	.622
Mike Ryan	C79	R	25	79	226	21	45	4	2	2	27	26	42	2	.199	.261
Jose Tartabull	OF83	L	28	115	247	36	55	1	2	0	10	23	26	6	.223	.243
2 Jerry Adair	3B35, SS30, 2B23	R	30	89	316	41	92	13	1	3	26	13	35	1	.291	.367
Dalton Jones	3B30, 2B19, 1B1	L	23	89	159	18	46	6	2	3	25	11	23	0	.289	.409
George Thomas	OF43, 1B3, C1	R	29	65	89	10	19	2	0	1	6	3	23	0	.213	.270
Russ Gibson	C48	R	28	49	138	8	28	7	0	1	15	12	31	0	.203	.275
2 Elston Howard	C41	R	38	42	116	9	17	3	0	1	11	9	24	0	.147	.198
1 Norm Siebern	1B13, OF1	L	33	33	44	2	9	0	2	0	7	6	8	0	.205	.295
1 Bob Tillman	C26	R	30	30	64	4	12	1	0	1	4	3	18	0	.188	.250
1 Ken Harrelson	OF23, 1B1	R	25	23	80	9	16	4	1	3	14	5	12	1	.200	.388
1 Tony Horton	1B6	R	22	21	39	2	12	3	0	0	9	0	5	0	.308	.385
1 Don Demeter (IL)	OF12, 3B1	R	32	20	43	7	12	5	0	1	3	1	11	0	.279	.465

3 Jim Landis 33 R 1-7, Ken Poulsen 19 L 1-5

NAME		T	AGE	W	L	PCT	SV	G	GS	CG	IP	H	BB	SO	SHO	ERA
			28	92	70	.568	44	162	162	41	1459	1307	477	1010	9	3.36
Jim Lonborg		R	25	22	9	.710	0	39	39	15	273	228	83	246	2	3.16
Jose Santiago		R	26	12	4	.750	5	50	11	2	145	138	47	109	0	3.60
2 Gary Bell		R	30	12	8	.600	3	29	24	8	165	143	47	115	0	3.16
John Wyatt		R	32	10	7	.588	20	60	0	0	93	71	39	68	0	2.61
Lee Stange		R	30	8	10	.444	1	35	24	6	182	171	32	101	2	2.77
Dave Morehead		R	24	5	4	.556	0	10	9	1	48	48	22	41	0	4.31
Darrell Brandon		R	26	5	11	.313	3	39	19	2	158	147	59	96	0	4.16
1 Dennis Bennett		L	27	4	3	.571	0	13	11	4	70	72	22	34	1	3.86
Dan Osinski		R	33	3	1	.750	2	34	0	0	64	61	14	38	0	2.53
Jerry Stephenson		R	23	3	1	.750	1	8	6	0	40	32	16	24	0	3.83
Gary Waslewski		R	25	2	2	.500	0	12	8	0	42	34	20	20	0	3.21
Billy Rohr		L	21	2	3	.400	0	10	8	1	42	51	16	14	0	5.14
Bill Landis		L	24	1	0	1.000	0	18	1	0	26	24	11	23	0	5.19
Ken Fischer		R	27	1	2	.333	1	9	2	1	27	24	8	18	0	2.33
1 Don McMahon		R	37	1	2	.333	2	11	0	0	18	14	13	10	0	3.50
Sparky Lyle		L	22	1	2	.333	5	27	0	0	43	33	14	42	0	2.30
Ken Brett		L	18	0	0	—	0	1	0	0	2	4	4	4	0	4.50
Galen Cisco		R	31	0	0	.000	1	7	0	0	22	21	8	8	0	3.68

DETROIT 2nd (tie) 91-71 .562 1 — MAYO SMITH

NAME	G by Pos	B	AGE	G	AB	R	H	2B	3B	HR	RBI	BB	SO	SB	BA	SA
TOTALS			28	163	5410	683	1315	192	36	152	619	626	994	37	.243	.376
Norm Cash	1B146	L	32	152	488	64	118	16	5	22	72	81	100	3	.242	.430
Dick McAuliffe	2B145, SS43	L	27	153	557	92	133	16	7	22	65	105	118	6	.239	.411
Ray Oyler	SS146	R	28	148	367	33	76	14	2	1	29	37	91	0	.207	.264
Don Wert	3B140, SS1	R	28	142	534	60	137	23	2	6	40	44	59	1	.257	.341
Al Kaline (BG)	OF130	R	32	131	458	94	141	28	2	25	78	83	47	8	.308	.541
Jim Northrup	OF143	L	27	144	495	63	134	18	6	10	61	43	83	7	.271	.392
Willie Horton	OF110	R	24	122	401	47	110	20	3	19	67	36	95	0	.274	.481
Bill Freehan	C147, 1B11	R	25	155	517	66	146	23	1	20	74	73	71	1	.282	.447
Mickey Stanley	OF129, 1B8	R	24	145	333	38	70	7	3	7	24	29	46	9	.210	.312
Jerry Lumpe	2B54, 3B6	L	34	81	177	19	41	4	0	4	17	16	18	0	.232	.322
Dick Tracewski	SS44, 2B12, 3B10	R	32	74	107	19	30	4	2	1	9	8	20	1	.280	.383
Lenny Green	OF44	L	33	58	151	22	42	8	1	1	13	9	17	1	.278	.364
Earl Wilson	P39	R	32	52	108	8	20	2	0	4	15	8	39	0	.185	.315
Gates Brown (WJ)	OF20	L	28	51	91	17	17	1	1	2	9	13	15	0	.187	.286
Jim Price	C24	R	25	44	92	9	24	4	0	0	8	4	10	0	.261	.304
2 Eddie Mathews	3B21, 1B13	L	35	36	108	14	25	3	0	6	19	15	23	0	.231	.426
2 Jim Landis	OF12	R	33	23	48	4	10	4	0	0	4	7	12	0	.208	.333
2 Bill Heath	C7	L	28	20	32	0	4	0	0	0	4	1	4	0	.125	.125
1 Jake Wood	2B2, 1B2	R	30	14	20	2	1	1	0	0	1	0	7	1	.050	.100

Dave Campbell 25 R 0-2, Tom Matchick 23 L 1-6, Wayne Comer 23 R 1-3

NAME		T	AGE	W	L	PCT	SV	G	GS	CG	IP	H	BB	SO	SHO	ERA
			28	91	71	.562	40	163	163	46	1444	1230	472	1038	17	3.32
Earl Wilson		R	32	22	11	.667	0	39	38	12	264	216	92	184	0	3.27
Denny McLain		R	23	17	16	.515	0	37	37	10	235	209	73	161	3	3.79
Joe Sparma		R	25	16	9	.640	0	37	37	11	218	186	85	153	5	3.76
Mickey Lolich		L	26	14	13	.519	0	31	30	11	204	165	56	174	6	3.04
Fred Gladding		R	31	6	4	.600	12	42	1	0	77	62	19	64	0	1.99
John Hiller		L	24	4	3	.571	3	23	6	2	65	57	9	49	2	2.63
Dave Wickersham		R	31	4	5	.444	4	36	4	0	85	72	33	44	0	2.75
Johnny Podres		L	34	3	1	.750	1	21	8	0	63	58	11	34	0	3.86
Fred Lasher		R	25	2	1	.667	9	17	0	0	30	25	11	28	0	3.90
George Korince		R	21	1	0	1.000	0	9	0	0	14	10	11	11	0	5.14
Pat Dobson		R	25	1	2	.333	0	28	1	0	49	38	27	34	0	2.94
Mike Marshall		R	24	1	3	.250	10	37	0	0	59	51	20	41	0	1.98
Johnny Klippstein		R	39	0	0	—	2	7	0	0	6	1	4	9	0	5.14
1 Bill Monbouquette		R	30	0	0	—	0	5	0	0	4	0	0	2	0	0.00
Hank Aguirre		L	36	0	1	.000	0	31	1	0	41	34	17	33	0	2.41
1 Larry Sherry		R	31	0	1	.000	1	20	0	0	28	35	7	20	0	6.43
1 Orlando Pena		R	33	0	1	.000	0	2	0	0	2	5	0	2	0	13.50

MINNESOTA 2nd (tie) 91-71 .562 1 — SAM MELE 25-25 .500   CAL ERMER 66-46 .589

NAME	G by Pos	B	AGE	G	AB	R	H	2B	3B	HR	RBI	BB	SO	SB	BA	SA
TOTALS			28	164	5458	671	1309	216	48	131	619	512	976	55	.240	.369
Harmon Killebrew	1B160, 3B3	R	31	163	547	105	147	24	1	44	113	131	111	1	.269	.558
Rod Carew	2B134	L	21	137	514	66	150	22	7	8	51	37	91	5	.292	.409
Zoilo Versalles	SS159	R	27	160	581	63	116	16	7	6	50	33	113	5	.200	.282
Rich Rollins	3B97	R	29	109	339	31	83	11	2	6	39	27	58	1	.245	.342
Tony Oliva	OF146	L	26	146	557	76	161	34	6	17	83	44	61	11	.289	.463
Ted Uhlaender	OF118	L	27	133	415	41	107	19	7	6	49	13	45	4	.258	.381
Bob Allison	OF145	R	32	153	496	73	128	21	6	24	75	74	114	6	.258	.470
Jerry Zimmerman	C104	R	32	104	234	13	39	3	0	1	12	22	49	0	.167	.192
Cesar Tovar	OF74, 3B70, 2B36, SS9	R	26	164	649	98	173	32	7	6	47	46	51	19	.267	.365
Sandy Valdespino	OF65	L	28	99	99	16	16	2	0	1	3	5	22	3	.165	.216
Rich Reese	1B36, OF10	L	25	95	101	13	25	5	0	4	20	8	17	0	.248	.416
Russ Nixon	C69	L	32	74	170	16	40	6	1	1	22	18	29	0	.235	.300
Earl Battey	C41	R	32	48	109	6	18	3	1	0	8	13	24	0	.165	.211
Frank Kostro	OF3, 3B1	R	29	32	31	4	10	0	0	0	2	3	2	0	.323	.323
Jackie Hernandez	SS15, 3B13	R	26	29	28	1	4	0	0	0	3	1	10	0	.143	.143
Ron Clark (EJ)	3B16	R	24	20	60	7	10	3	1	2	11	4	9	0	.167	.350
Hank Izquierdo	C16	R	36	16	26	4	7	2	0	0	2	1	2	0	.269	.346
Walt Bond (DD)	OF3	L	29	10	16	4	5	1	0	1	5	3	1	0	.313	.563
Andy Kosco	OF7	R	25	9	28	4	4	1	0	1	5	2	6	0	.143	.179

Frank Quilici 28 R 2-19, Carroll Hardy 34 R 3-8, Graig Nettles 22 L 1-3, Pat Kelly (MS) 22 L 0-1

NAME		T	AGE	W	L	PCT	SV	G	GS	CG	IP	H	BB	SO	SHO	ERA
			28	91	71	.562	24	164	164	58	1461	1336	396	1089	18	3.14
Dean Chance		R	26	20	14	.588	1	41	39	18	284	244	68	220	5	2.73
Jim Kaat		L	28	16	13	.552	0	42	38	13	263	269	42	211	2	3.05
Dave Boswell		R	22	14	12	.538	0	37	32	11	223	162	107	204	3	3.27
Jim Merritt		L	23	13	7	.650	0	37	28	11	228	196	30	161	4	2.53
Jim Perry		R	31	8	7	.533	0	37	11	3	131	123	50	94	2	3.02
Al Worthington		R	38	8	9	.471	16	59	0	0	92	77	38	80	0	2.84
Ron Kline		R	35	7	1	.875	5	54	0	0	72	71	15	36	0	3.75
Mudcat Grant		R	31	5	6	.455	0	27	14	2	95	121	17	50	0	4.74
Dwight Siebler		R	29	0	0	—	0	2	0	0	0.1	3	0	0	0	54.00
Mel Nelson		L	31	0	0	—	0	1	0	0	1	3	0	1	0	9.00
Jim Roland		L	24	0	1	.000	2	25	0	0	34	33	17	16	0	3.00
Jim Ollom		L	22	0	1	.000	0	21	2	0	35	33	11	17	0	5.40

CHICAGO 4th 89-73 .549 3 — EDDIE STANKY

NAME	G by Pos	B	AGE	G	AB	R	H	2B	3B	HR	RBI	BB	SO	SB	BA	SA
TOTALS			28	162	5383	531	1209	181	34	89	491	480	849	124	.225	.320
Tommy McCraw	1B123, OF6	L	26	125	453	55	107	18	3	11	45	33	55	24	.236	.362
Wayne Causey	2B96, SS2	L	30	124	292	21	66	10	3	1	28	32	35	2	.226	.291
Ron Hansen	SS157	R	29	157	498	35	116	20	0	8	51	64	51	0	.233	.321
Don Buford	3B121, 2B51, OF1	B	30	156	535	61	129	10	9	4	32	65	51	34	.241	.316
Ken Berry	OF143	R	26	147	485	49	117	14	4	7	41	46	68	9	.241	.330
Tommie Agee	OF152	R	24	158	529	73	124	26	2	14	52	44	129	28	.234	.371
Pete Ward	OF89, 1B39, 3B22	L	27	146	467	49	109	16	2	18	62	61	109	3	.233	.392
J. C. Martin	C96, 1B1	L	30	101	252	22	59	12	1	4	22	30	41	4	.234	.341
Walt Williams	OF73	R	24	104	275	35	66	16	3	3	15	17	20	3	.240	.353
Smoky Burgess		L	40	77	60	2	8	2	0	1	11	14	8	0	.133	.250
Duane Josephson	C59	R	25	62	189	11	45	5	1	1	9	6	20	0	.238	.291
2 Rocky Colavito	OF58	R	33	60	190	20	42	4	1	3	29	25	10	1	.221	.300
2 Ken Boyer	3B33, 1B18	R	36	57	180	17	47	5	1	4	21	7	25	0	.261	.367
Jerry McNertney	C52	R	30	56	123	8	28	6	0	3	13	6	14	0	.228	.350
Dick Kenworthy	3B35	R	26	50	97	9	22	4	1	4	11	4	17	0	.227	.412
Al Weis (KJ)	2B32, SS13	B	29	50	53	9	13	2	0	0	4	1	9	2	.245	.283
Marv Staehle	2B17, SS5	L	25	32	54	1	6	1	0	0	1	4	8	1	.111	.130
1 Jerry Adair	2B27	R	30	28	98	6	20	4	0	0	4	0	9	4	.204	.245
Buddy Bradford	OF14	R	22	24	20	6	2	1	0	0	1	6	8	1	.100	.150
2 Jimmy Stewart	OF6, 2B5, SS2	B	28	24	18	5	3	0	0	0	1	1	5	0	.167	.167
2 Jim King	OF12	L	34	23	50	2	6	1	0	0	2	4	16	0	.120	.140
1 Ed Stroud	OF12	L	27	20	27	6	8	0	1	0	2	1	5	7	.296	.370
Bill Voss	OF11	L	23	13	22	4	2	0	0	0	0	1	6	0	.091	.091

2 Sandy Alomar 23 B 3-15, 1 Bill Skowron 36 R 0-8, Rich Morales 23 R 0-10, Ed Herrmann 20 L 2-3, Cotton Nash 24 R 0-3

NAME		T	AGE	W	L	PCT	SV	G	GS	CG	IP	H	BB	SO	SHO	ERA
			30	89	73	.549	39	162	162	36	1490	1197	465	927	24	2.45
Joe Horlen		R	29	19	7	.731	0	35	35	13	258	188	58	103	6	2.06
Gary Peters		L	30	16	11	.593	0	38	36	11	260	187	91	215	3	2.28
Tommy John		L	24	10	13	.435	0	31	29	9	178	143	47	110	6	2.48
Hoyt Wilhelm		R	44	8	3	.727	12	49	0	0	89	58	34	76	0	1.31
Bob Locker		R	29	7	5	.583	20	77	0	0	125	102	23	80	0	2.09
2 Don McMahon		R	37	5	0	1.000	3	32	0	0	52	47	27	74	0	1.66
Wilbur Wood		L	25	4	2	.667	4	51	0	0	95	95	28	47	0	2.46
Jim O'Toole (SJ)		L	30	4	3	.571	0	15	10	1	54	53	18	37	1	2.83
Fred Klages		R	23	4	4	.500	0	11	9	0	45	43	16	17	0	3.80
1 John Buzhardt		R	30	3	9	.250	0	30	17	3	89	100	37	33	0	3.94
Bruce Howard		R	23	3	10	.231	0	30	17	1	113	102	52	76	0	3.42
Cisco Carlos		R	26	2	0	1.000	0	8	7	1	42	23	9	27	1	0.86
Steve Jones		L	26	2	2	.500	0	11	3	0	26	21	12	17	0	4.15
1 Jack Lamabe		R	30	1	0	1.000	0	8	7	1	42	23	9	11	0	1.80
Denny Higgins (IJ)		R	27	1	2	.333	0	9	0	0	12	13	10	8	0	6.00
Roger Nelson		R	23	1	1	.500	0	6	1	0	14	8	5	8	1	1.29
Aurelio Monteagudo		R	23	0	1	.000	0	5	0	0	3	10	4	2	0	27.00

CALIFORNIA 5th 84-77 .522 7.5 — BILL RIGNEY

NAME	G by Pos	B	AGE	G	AB	R	H	2B	3B	HR	RBI	BB	SO	SB	BA	SA
TOTALS			27	163	5307	567	1265	170	37	114	524	453	1021	40	.238	.349
Don Mincher	1B142, OF1	L	29	147	487	81	133	23	4	25	76	69	69	0	.273	.487
Bobby Knoop	2B159	R	28	159	511	51	125	18	5	9	38	44	136	2	.245	.352
Jim Fregosi	SS151	R	25	151	590	75	171	23	6	9	56	49	77	9	.290	.395
Paul Schaal	3B88, SS2, 2B1	R	24	99	272	31	51	9	1	6	20	38	39	2	.188	.294
Jimmie Hall	OF120	L	29	129	401	54	100	18	3	16	55	42	65	4	.249	.404
Jose Cardenal	OF101	R	23	108	381	40	90	13	5	6	27	15	63	10	.236	.344
Rick Reichardt	OF138	R	24	146	498	56	132	14	2	17	69	35	90	5	.265	.404
Bob Rodgers	C134, OF1	B	28	139	429	29	94	13	4	6	41	34	55	1	.219	.305
Tom Satriano	3B38, C23, 2B15, 1B5	L	26	90	201	13	45	7	0	4	21	28	25	1	.224	.318
Bubba Morton	OF61	R	36	80	201	23	63	9	3	4	32	22	29	0	.313	.388
Jay Johnstone	OF63	L	21	79	230	18	48	7	1	2	10	5	37	3	.209	.274
2 Roger Repoz	OF63	L	26	74	176	25	44	9	5	5	20	19	37	2	.250	.398
2 Bill Skowron	1B32	R	36	62	123	8	27	5	1	1	10	4	18	0	.220	.276
2 Woodie Held	3B19, OF17, 2B3, 3B1	R	35	58	141	15	31	5	2	4	21	10	41	0	.220	.362
2 Johnny Werhas	3B30, 1B4, OF1	L	29	49	75	8	12	3	0	0	3	6	10	0	.160	.200
Aurelio Rodriguez	3B29	R	19	29	84	5	24	4	0	1	10	2	11	1	.238	.300
2 Hawk Taylor	C19	R	28	23	52	5	16	3	0	1	4	4	9	0	.308	.423
Orlando McFarlane	C6	R	29	12	31	2	7	1	0	0	4	5	7	0	.227	.227
1 Len Gabrielson	OF1	L	27	11	12	1	1	0	0	0	0	0	6	0	.083	.083

Ed Kirkpatrick 22 L 0-8, Don Wallace 26 L 0-6, Moose Stubing 29 L 0-5, Jimmy Piersall 37 R 0-3, Jim Hibbs 22 R 0-3, Tom Egan 21 R 0-1

NAME		T	AGE	W	L	PCT	SV	G	GS	CG	IP	H	BB	SO	SHO	ERA
			29	84	77	.522	46	161	161	19	1430	1246	525	892	14	3.19
Jim McGlothlin		R	23	12	8	.600	0	32	29	9	197	163	56	137	6	2.97
Minnie Rojas		R	33	12	9	.571	27	72	0	0	122	106	38	83	0	2.51
Rickey Clark		R	21	12	11	.522	0	32	30	1	174	144	69	81	1	2.59
George Brunet		L	32	11	19	.367	1	40	37	7	250	203	90	165	2	3.31
2 Jack Hamilton		R	28	6	6	.500	0	26	20	0	119	104	63	74	0	3.25
Bill Kelso		R	27	5	3	.625	11	69	1	0	112	85	63	91	0	2.97
Clyde Wright		L	26	5	5	.500	0	31	7	0	78	76	24	35	0	3.27
Jim Weaver		L	28	5	1	.833	0	13	2	0	36	26	9	20	0	2.70
Bobby Locke		R	32	3	0	1.000	3	19	4	1	19	14	7	3	0	2.37
1 Jack Sanford		R	38	3	2	.600	1	12	9	0	48	53	7	21	0	4.50
Pete Cimino		R	24	3	3	.500	1	46	1	0	88	73	31	80	0	3.27
2 Curt Simmons		L	38	2	1	.667	1	14	4	1	35	44	9	13	1	2.57
Lew Burdette		R	40	1	0	1.000	0	19	0	0	50	64	6	16	0	5.00
Fred Newman (SA)		R	25	1	1	.500	0	9	0	0	16	19	5	4	0	1.50
Jim Coates		R	34	1	2	.333	0	25	1	0	42	33	22	39	0	4.33
Ken Turner		R	23	1	3	.250	0	13	1	0	17	16	4	6	0	4.24
1 Nick Willhite		L	25	0	0	—	0	11	0	0	17	16	12	6	0	4.38
1 Marcelino Lopez		L	23	0	1	.000	0	9	1	0	11	6	6	9	0	9.00
Jorge Rubio		R	22	0	1	.000	0	3	0	0	3	3	4	3	0	9.00
Rudy May (SA)			22													

BALTIMORE 6th (tie) 76-85 .472 15.5 HANK BAUER

NAME	G by Pos	B	AGE	G	AB	R	H	2B	3B	HR	RBI	BB	SO	SB	BA	SA
TOTALS			27	161	5456	654	1312	215	44	138	624	531	1002	54	.240	.372
Boog Powell	1B114	L	25	125	415	53	97	14	1	13	55	55	94	1	.234	.366
Dave Johnson	2B144, 3B3	R	24	148	510	62	126	30	3	10	64	59	82	4	.247	.376
Luis Aparicio	SS131	R	33	134	546	55	127	22	5	4	31	29	44	18	.233	.313
Brooks Robinson	3B158	R	30	158	610	88	164	25	5	22	77	54	54	1	.269	.434
Frank Robinson (IJ)	OF126, 1B2	R	31	129	479	83	149	23	7	30	94	71	84	2	.311	.576
Paul Blair	OF146	R	23	151	552	72	162	27	12	11	64	50	68	8	.293	.446
Curt Blefary	OF103, 1B52	L	23	155	554	69	134	19	5	22	81	73	94	4	.242	.413
Andy Etchebarren	C110	R	24	112	330	29	71	13	0	7	35	38	80	1	.215	.318
Russ Snyder	OF69	L	33	108	275	40	65	8	2	4	23	32	48	5	.236	.324
Mark Belanger	SS38, 2B26, 3B2	R	23	69	184	19	32	5	0	1	10	12	46	6	.174	.217
Sam Bowens	OF32	R	28	62	120	13	22	2	1	5	12	11	43	3	.183	.342
Larry Haney	C57	R	24	58	164	13	44	11	0	3	20	6	28	1	.268	.390
Vic Roznovsky	C23	L	28	45	97	7	20	5	0	0	10	1	20	0	.206	.258
Dave May	OF19	L	23	36	85	12	20	1	1	1	7	6	13	0	.235	.306
Curt Motton	OF18	L	26	27	65	5	13	2	0	2	9	5	14	0	.200	.323
1 Woodie Held	2B9, 3B5, OF2	R	35	26	41	4	6	3	0	1	6	6	12	0	.146	.293
1 Charlie Lau		L	34	11	8	0	1	1	0	0	3	2	2	0	.125	.250
Mickey McGuire	2B4	R	26	10	17	2	4	0	0	0	2	0	2	0	.235	.235
1 Mike Epstein	1B3	R	24	9	13	0	2	0	0	0	0	1	5	0	.154	.154
1 Bob Johnson		R	31	4	3	1	1	0	0	0	0	0	0	0	.333	.333

NAME	T	AGE	W	L	PCT	SV	G	GS	CG	IP	H	BB	SO	SHO	ERA
TOTALS		27	76	85	.472	36	161	161	29	1457	1218	566	1034	17	3.32
Tom Phoebus	R	25	14	9	.609	0	33	33	7	208	177	114	179	4	3.33
Jim Hardin	R	23	8	3	.727	0	19	14	5	111	85	27	64	2	2.27
Moe Drabowsky	R	31	7	5	.583	12	43	0	0	95	66	25	96	0	1.61
Dave McNally	L	24	7	7	.500	0	24	22	3	119	134	39	70	1	4.54
2 Pete Richert	L	27	7	10	.412	2	26	19	5	132	107	41	90	1	3.00
Gene Brabender	R	25	4	6	.400	0	14	14	3	94	77	23	71	1	3.35
Bill Dillman	R	22	5	9	.357	0	32	15	2	124	115	33	69	1	4.35
2 Eddie Fisher	R	30	4	3	.571	1	46	0	0	90	82	26	53	0	3.60
1 Steve Barber	L	29	4	9	.308	0	15	15	1	75	47	61	48	1	4.08
Jim Palmer (SA)	R	21	3	1	.750	0	9	9	2	49	34	20	23	1	2.94
Eddie Watt	R	26	3	5	.375	9	49	0	0	104	67	37	93	0	2.25
Wally Bunker	R	22	3	7	.300	1	29	9	1	88	83	31	51	0	4.09
Stu Miller	R	39	3	10	.231	8	42	0	0	81	63	36	60	0	2.56
2 Marcelino Lopez (SA)	L	23	1	0	1.000	0	4	4	0	18	15	10	15	0	2.50
1 Frank Bertaina	L	23	1	1	.500	0	5	2	0	22	17	14	19	0	3.27
Dave Leonhard	R	26	0	0	—	0	3	2	0	14	11	6	9	0	3.21
John Miller	R	26	0	0	—	0	2	0	0	6	7	3	6	0	7.50
Tom Fisher	R	24	0	0	—	0	2	0	0	3	2	1	1	0	0.00
Paul Gilliford	L	22	0	0	—	0	3	0	0	3	6	1	2	0	12.00
2 John Buzhardt	R	30	0	1	.000	0	7	1	0	12	14	5	7	0	4.50
Mike Adamson	R	19	0	1	.000	0	2	1	0	10	9	12	6	0	8.10

WASHINGTON 6th (tie) 76-85 .472 15.5 GIL HODGES

NAME	G by Pos	B	AGE	G	AB	R	H	2B	3B	HR	RBI	BB	SO	SB	BA	SA
TOTALS			26	161	5441	550	1211	168	25	115	521	472	1037	53	.223	.326
2 Mike Epstein	1B80	L	24	96	284	32	65	7	4	9	29	38	74	1	.229	.377
Bernie Allen	2B75	L	28	87	254	13	49	5	1	3	18	18	43	1	.193	.256
Eddie Brinkman	SS109	R	25	109	320	21	60	9	2	1	18	24	58	1	.188	.238
Ken McMullen	3B145	R	25	146	563	73	138	22	2	16	67	46	84	5	.245	.377
Cap Peterson	OF101	R	24	122	405	35	97	17	2	8	46	32	61	0	.240	.351
Fred Valentine	OF136	B	32	151	457	52	107	19	1	11	44	56	70	17	.234	.346
Frank Howard	OF141, 1B4	R	30	149	519	71	133	20	2	36	89	60	155	0	.256	.511
Paul Casanova	C137	R	25	141	528	47	131	19	1	9	53	17	65	1	.248	.339
Tim Cullen	SS69, 2B46, 3B15, OF1	R	25	124	402	35	95	7	0	2	31	40	47	4	.236	.269
Hank Allen	OF99	R	26	116	292	34	68	8	4	3	17	13	53	3	.233	.318
Dick Nen	1B65, OF1	L	27	110	238	21	52	7	1	6	29	21	39	0	.218	.332
Bob Saverine	2B48, SS10, 3B8, OF2	B	26	89	233	22	55	13	0	0	8	17	34	8	.236	.292
2 Ed Stroud	OF79	L	27	87	204	36	41	5	3	1	10	25	29	8	.201	.270
1 Jim King	OF31, C1	L	34	47	100	10	21	2	1	2	12	15	13	1	.210	.300
Doug Camilli	C24	R	30	30	82	5	15	1	0	2	5	4	16	0	.183	.268
Bob Chance	1B10	R	26	27	42	5	9	2	0	0	3	7	13	0	.214	.476
1 Ken Harrelson	1B23	R	25	26	79	10	16	0	0	3	10	7	15	1	.203	.316
Frank Coggins	2B19	B	23	19	75	9	23	2	0	0	2	2	17	1	.307	.387
Jim French 25 L 1-16, John Orsino 29 R 0-1																

NAME	T	AGE	W	L	PCT	SV	G	GS	CG	IP	H	BB	SO	SHO	ERA
TOTALS		27	76	85	.472	39	161	161	24	1473	1334	495	878	14	3.38
Camilo Pascual	R	33	12	10	.545	0	28	27	5	165	147	43	106	1	3.27
Phil Ortega	R	27	10	10	.500	0	34	34	5	220	189	57	122	2	3.03
Joe Coleman	R	20	8	9	.471	0	28	22	3	134	154	47	77	0	4.63
Casey Cox	R	25	7	4	.636	1	54	0	0	73	67	21	32	0	2.96
Barry Moore	L	24	7	11	.389	0	27	26	3	144	127	71	74	1	3.75
Bob Humphreys	R	31	6	2	.750	4	48	2	0	106	93	41	54	0	4.16
2 Frank Bertaina	L	23	6	5	.545	0	18	17	4	96	90	37	67	4	2.91
Darold Knowles	L	25	6	8	.429	14	61	1	0	113	91	52	85	0	2.71
Dick Bosman	R	23	3	1	.750	0	7	7	2	51	38	10	25	1	1.76
Bob Priddy	R	27	3	7	.300	4	46	8	1	110	98	33	57	0	3.44
Dave Baldwin	R	29	2	4	.333	12	58	0	0	69	53	20	52	0	1.70
Dick Lines	L	28	2	5	.286	4	54	0	0	86	83	24	54	0	3.35
1 Pete Richert	R	27	2	6	.250	0	11	10	1	54	49	15	41	1	4.67
Buster Narum	R	26	1	0	1.000	0	2	1	0	8	4	8	0	—	3.00
Jim Hannan	R	27	1	1	.500	0	8	2	0	22	28	7	14	0	5.32
Dick Nold	R	24	0	2	.000	0	7	3	0	20	19	13	10	0	4.95

CLEVELAND 8th 75-87 .463 17 JOE ADCOCK

NAME	G by Pos	B	AGE	G	AB	R	H	2B	3B	HR	RBI	BB	SO	SB	BA	SA
TOTALS			28	162	5461	559	1282	213	35	131	514	413	984	53	.235	.359
2 Tony Horton	1B94	R	22	106	363	35	102	13	4	10	44	18	52	3	.281	.421
Vern Fuller	2B64, SS2	R	23	73	206	18	46	10	0	7	21	19	55	2	.223	.374
Larry Brown	SS150	R	27	152	485	38	110	16	2	5	37	53	62	4	.227	.311
Max Alvis	3B161	R	29	161	637	66	163	23	4	21	70	38	107	3	.256	.403
Chuck Hinton	OF136, 2B5	R	33	147	498	55	122	19	3	10	37	43	100	6	.245	.355
Vic Davalillo	OF125	L	30	139	359	47	103	17	5	2	22	10	30	6	.287	.379
Leon Wagner	OF117	L	33	135	433	56	105	15	1	15	54	37	76	0	.242	.386
Joe Azcue	C86	R	27	86	295	30	74	12	5	11	34	22	35	0	.251	.437
Lee Maye	OF77, 2B1	L	32	115	297	43	77	20	4	9	27	26	47	3	.259	.444
Fred Whitfield	1B66	L	29	100	257	24	56	10	0	9	31	25	45	3	.218	.362
C. Salmon	OF28, 1B24, 2B24, SS14, 3B6	R	26	90	203	19	46	13	1	2	19	13	29	10	.227	.320
Duke Sims	C85	L	26	88	272	25	55	8	2	12	37	30	64	3	.202	.379
Pedro Gonzalez	2B64, 1B4, 3B4, SS3	R	28	80	189	19	43	6	0	1	8	12	36	4	.228	.275
1 Rocky Colavito	OF50	R	33	63	191	10	46	9	0	5	21	24	31	2	.241	.366
2 Don Demeter	OF35, 3B1	R	32	51	121	15	25	4	0	5	12	6	16	0	.207	.364
Gus Gil	2B49, 1B1	R	27	51	96	11	11	4	0	0	5	9	18	0	.115	.156
Willie Smith	OF4, 1B3	L	28	21	32	0	7	2	0	0	2	1	10	0	.219	.281
3 Jim King	OF1	L	34	19	21	2	3	0	0	0	0	1	4	0	.143	.143
Richie Scheinblum	OF18	B	24	18	66	8	21	4	2	0	6	5	10	0	.318	.439
Jose Vidal	OF10	R	27	16	34	4	4	0	0	0	0	7	12	0	.118	.118
Ray Fosse	C7	R	20	7	16	0	1	0	0	0	0	0	5	0	.063	.063
Gordon Lund	SS2	R	26	3	8	1	2	1	0	0	0	1	1	0	.250	.375

NAME	T	AGE	W	L	PCT	SV	G	GS	CG	IP	H	BB	SO	SHO	ERA
TOTALS		27	75	87	.463	27	162	162	49	1478	1258	559	1189	14	3.25
Steve Hargan	R	24	14	13	.519	0	30	29	15	223	180	72	141	6	2.62
Sam McDowell	R	24	13	15	.464	0	37	37	10	236	201	123	236	1	3.85
Luis Tiant	R	26	12	9	.571	2	33	29	9	214	177	67	219	1	2.73
Sonny Siebert	R	30	10	12	.455	4	34	26	7	185	136	54	136	1	2.38
John O'Donoghue	R	27	8	9	.471	2	33	17	5	131	120	33	81	2	3.23
George Culver	R	23	7	3	.700	3	53	1	0	75	71	31	41	0	3.96
Stan Williams	R	30	6	4	.600	1	16	8	2	79	64	24	75	1	2.62
Ed Connolly	R	27	2	1	.667	0	15	4	0	49	63	34	45	0	7.53
Steve Bailey	R	25	2	5	.286	2	32	1	0	65	62	42	46	0	3.88
1 Gary Bell	R	30	1	5	.167	0	9	9	1	61	50	24	39	0	3.69
1 Dick Radatz	R	30	0	0	—	0	8	0	0	1	0	0	1	0	0.00
Tom Kelley (SA)	R	23	0	0	—	0	1	0	0	1	0	0	1	0	6.00
Bobby Tiefenauer	R	37	0	1	.000	0	5	0	0	10	9	6	6	0	0.82
Jack Kralick	L	32	0	2	.000	0	4	2	0	2	4	1	1	0	9.00
2 Orlando Pena	R	33	0	3	.000	5	48	1	0	88	67	22	72	0	3.38
Bob Allen	L	29	0	5	.000	5	47	0	0	54	49	25	50	0	3.00

NEW YORK 9th 72-90 .444 20 RALPH HOUK

NAME	G by Pos	B	AGE	G	AB	R	H	2B	3B	HR	RBI	BB	SO	SB	BA	SA
TOTALS			31	163	5443	522	1225	166	17	100	473	532	1043	63	.225	.317
Mickey Mantle	1B131	B	35	144	440	63	108	17	0	22	55	107	113	1	.245	.434
Horace Clarke	2B140	B	27	143	588	74	160	17	0	3	29	42	64	21	.272	.316
Ruben Amaro	SS123, 3B3, 1B2	R	31	130	417	31	93	12	0	1	17	43	49	3	.223	.259
Charley Smith	3B115	R	29	135	425	38	95	15	3	9	38	32	110	0	.224	.336
Steve Whitaker	OF114	L	24	143	441	37	107	12	3	11	50	23	89	2	.243	.358
Joe Pepitone	OF123, 1B6	L	26	133	501	45	126	18	3	13	64	34	62	1	.251	.377
Tom Tresh	OF118	B	29	130	448	45	98	23	3	14	53	50	86	5	.219	.377
Jake Gibbs	C99	L	28	116	374	33	87	7	1	4	25	28	57	7	.233	.289
Bill Robinson	OF102	R	24	116	342	31	67	6	1	7	29	28	56	2	.196	.281
John Kennedy	SS36, 3B34, 2B2	R	26	78	179	22	35	4	0	1	17	17	35	2	.196	.235
Roy White	OF36, 3B17	B	23	70	214	22	48	8	0	2	18	19	50	10	.224	.290
Mike Hegan (MS)	1B54, OF10	L	24	68	118	12	16	4	1	3	20	40	7	.136	.212
1 Elston Howard	C48, 1B1	R	38	66	199	13	39	6	0	3	17	12	36	0	.196	.271
Dick Howser (BW)	2B22, 3B12, SS3	R	31	63	149	18	40	6	0	0	10	25	15	1	.268	.309
2 Bob Tillman	C15	R	30	22	63	5	16	1	0	2	9	7	17	0	.254	.365
Jerry Kenney	SS18	L	21	20	58	4	18	2	0	1	5	8	23	2	.310	.397
Ray Barker	1B13	L	31	17	26	2	2	0	0	0	3	5	0	.077	.077
Billy Bryan	C1	L	28	16	12	1	2	0	0	1	2	5	3	0	.167	.417
Ross Moschitto	OF8	R	22	14	9	1	1	0	0	0	1	2	0	.111	.111
Frank Fernandez (MS)	C7, OF2	R	24	9	28	1	6	2	0	1	6	1	5	1	.214	.393
Tom Shopay	OF7	L	22	8	27	2	8	2	0	1	4	1	2	0	.296	.556
Frank Tepedino 19 L 2-5, Lu Clinton 29 R 2-4, Charlie Sands 19 L 0-1, Bobby Murcer (MS) 21																

NAME	T	AGE	W	L	PCT	SV	G	GS	CG	IP	H	BB	SO	SHO	ERA
TOTALS		27	72	90	.444	27	163	163	37	1481	1375	480	898	16	3.24
Mel Stottlemyre	R	25	15	15	.500	0	36	36	10	255	235	88	151	4	2.96
Al Downing	L	26	14	10	.583	0	31	28	10	202	158	61	171	4	2.63
Fritz Peterson	L	25	8	14	.364	0	36	30	6	181	179	43	102	1	3.48
2 Bill Monbouquette	R	30	6	5	.545	1	33	10	2	133	122	17	53	1	2.37
Fred Talbot	R	26	6	8	.429	0	29	22	2	139	132	54	61	0	4.21
2 Steve Barber	L	29	6	9	.400	0	17	17	3	98	103	54	70	1	4.05
Dooley Womack	R	28	5	6	.455	18	65	0	0	97	80	35	57	0	2.41
Joe Verbanic	R	24	4	3	.571	2	28	6	1	80	74	21	39	1	2.81
Thad Tillotson	R	26	3	9	.250	2	43	5	1	98	99	39	62	0	4.04
Steve Hamilton	L	33	2	4	.333	4	44	0	0	62	57	23	55	0	3.48
Whitey Ford	L	38	2	4	.333	0	7	7	2	44	40	9	21	1	1.64
Jim Bouton	R	28	1	0	1.000	0	17	1	0	44	47	18	31	0	4.70
Dale Roberts	L	25	0	0	—	0	2	0	0	1	6	0	0	0	9.00
Cecil Perkins	R	26	0	0	.000	0	2	0	0	4	4	1	1	0	9.00
1 Hal Reniff	R	28	0	2	.000	0	24	0	0	40	40	14	24	0	4.00
Rich Beck (MS) 26															

KANSAS CITY 10th 62-99 .385 29.5 AL DARK 52-69 .430 LUKE APPLING 10-30 .250

NAME	G by Pos	B	AGE	G	AB	R	H	2B	3B	HR	RBI	BB	SO	SB	BA	SA
TOTALS			25	161	5349	533	1244	212	50	69	481	452	1019	132	.233	.330
Ramon Webster	1B83, OF15	L	24	122	360	41	92	15	4	11	51	32	44	5	.256	.411
John Donaldson	2B101, SS15	L	24	105	377	27	104	15	5	0	28	37	39	6	.276	.345
Bert Campaneris	SS145	R	25	147	601	65	149	29	6	3	32	36	82	55	.248	.331
Dick Green	3B59, 2B50, 1B1, SS1	R	26	122	349	26	69	11	4	5	37	30	68	6	.198	.298
Mike Hershberger	OF130	R	27	142	480	55	122	25	1	1	49	38	40	10	.254	.317
Rick Monday	OF113	L	21	124	406	52	102	16	6	14	58	42	107	5	.251	.419
Jim Gosger	OF113	L	24	134	356	31	86	14	5	5	36	53	69	5	.242	.351
Phil Roof	C113	R	26	114	327	23	67	14	5	6	24	23	85	4	.205	.333
Danny Cater	3B56, OF55, 1B44	R	27	142	529	55	143	17	4	4	46	34	56	4	.270	.340
Joe Nossek	OF63	R	26	87	166	12	34	6	1	0	10	4	20	2	.205	.253
2 Ken Harrelson	1B45	R	25	61	174	23	53	11	0	6	30	17	17	8	.305	.471
Ted Kubiak	SS20, 2B10, 3B5	B	25	53	102	6	16	2	0	0	6	7	16	0	.157	.196
Sal Bando	3B44	R	23	47	130	11	25	4	0	2	6	16	24	1	.192	.246
Tim Talton	C22, 1B1	R	26	48	59	7	15	1	3	0	6	4	13	0	.254	.373
1 Roger Repoz	OF31	L	26	40	87	9	21	4	1	2	12	11	20	0	.241	.402
Ken Suarez	C36	R	23	38	87	9	23	3	0	0	7	16	1	.238	.413
Ossie Chavarria	2B17, 3B7, OF3, SS2	R	26	38	59	2	6	1	0	0	5	7	16	1	.102	.136
Reggie Jackson	OF34	L	21	35	118	13	21	4	0	1	6	10	46	1	.178	.305
Dave Duncan	C32	R	21	34	101	9	19	4	0	2	5	11	4	50	0	.188	.376
1 Ed Charles	3B18	R	33	24	61	5	15	2	0	1	12	13	1	.246	.262
Joe Rudi	1B9, OF6	R	20	19	43	4	8	2	0	1	5	2	9	0	.186	.233
Allan Lewis 25 B 1-6, Hoss Bowlin 26 R 1-5																

NAME	T	AGE	W	L	PCT	SV	G	GS	CG	IP	H	BB	SO	SHO	ERA
TOTALS		24	62	99	.385	34	161	161	26	1428	1265	558	990	10	3.68
Catfish Hunter	R	21	13	17	.433	0	35	35	13	260	209	84	196	5	2.80
Jim Nash	R	22	12	17	.414	0	37	34	8	222	200	87	186	2	3.77
Chuck Dobson	R	23	10	10	.500	0	32	29	4	198	172	75	110	1	3.68
Lew Krausse	R	24	7	17	.292	6	48	19	0	160	140	67	96	0	4.28
Paul Lindblad	L	25	5	8	.385	6	46	10	1	116	106	35	83	1	3.57
Tony Pierce	L	21	3	4	.429	7	49	6	0	98	79	30	61	0	3.03
Diego Segui	R	29	3	4	.429	1	36	3	0	70	62	31	52	0	3.09
Jack Aker	R	26	3	8	.273	12	57	0	0	88	87	32	65	0	4.30
Blue Moon Odom	R	22	3	3	.273	0	29	17	0	104	94	68	67	0	5.02
Bill Edgerton	L	25	1	0	1.000	0	29	0	0	11	9	8	6	0	2.25
Roberto Rodriguez	R	25	1	1	.500	2	15	0	0	40	42	14	23	0	3.60
2 Jack Sanford	R	38	1	2	.333	0	10	1	0	22	24	14	13	0	6.55
Bob Duliba	R	32	0	0	—	0	6	0	0	14	10	4	3	0	4.50
Wes Stock	R	33	0	0	—	0	10	0	0	6	12	6	3	0	18.00
Bill Stafford	R	28	0	1	.000	0	14	0	0	16	16	5	10	0	1.69
George Lauzerique	R	19	0	0	.000	0	1	1	0	6	11	6	10	0	2.25

ST. LOUIS 1st 101-60 .627 — RED SCHOENDIENST

NAME	G by Pos	B	AGE	G	AB	R	H	2B	3B	HR	RBI	BB	SO	SB	BA	SA
TOTALS			27	161	5566	695	1462	225	40	115	656	443	919	102	.263	.379
Orlando Cepeda	1B151	R	29	151	563	91	183	37	0	25	111	62	75	11	.325	.524
Julian Javier	2B138	R	30	140	520	68	146	16	3	14	64	25	92	6	.281	.404
Dal Maxvill	SS148, 2B7	R	28	152	476	37	108	14	4	1	41	48	66	2	.227	.279
Mike Shannon	3B122, OF6	R	27	130	482	53	118	18	3	12	77	37	89	2	.245	.369
Roger Maris	OF118	L	32	125	410	64	107	18	7	9	55	52	61	0	.261	.405
Curt Flood	OF126	R	29	134	514	68	172	24	1	5	50	37	46	2	.335	.414
Lou Brock	OF157	L	28	159	689	113	206	32	12	21	76	24	109	52	.299	.472
Tim McCarver	C130	L	25	138	471	68	139	26	3	14	69	54	32	6	.295	.452
Bobby Tolan	OF80, 1B13	L	21	110	265	35	67	7	3	6	32	19	43	12	.253	.370
Alex Johnson	OF57	R	24	81	175	20	39	9	2	1	12	9	26	6	.223	.314
Phil Gagliano	2B27, 3B25, 1B4, SS2	R	25	73	217	20	48	7	0	2	21	19	26	0	.221	.281
Ed Spiezio	3B19, OF7	R	25	55	105	9	22	2	0	3	10	7	18	2	.210	.314
Dave Ricketts	C21	R	32	52	99	11	27	8	0	1	14	4	7	0	.273	.384
Ed Bressoud	SS48, 3B1	R	35	52	67	8	9	1	1	1	7	9	18	1	.134	.224
Johnny Romano	C20	R	32	24	58	1	7	1	0	0	2	13	15	1	.121	.138
1 Ted Savage		B	30	8	8	1	1	0	0	0	0	1	2	0	.125	.125
Steve Huntz	2B2	B	21	3	6	1	1	0	0	0	0	1	2	1	.167	.167
Jimy Williams	SS1	R	23	1	2	0	0	0	0	0	0	0	0	0	.000	.000

NAME	T	AGE	W	L	PCT	SV	G	GS	CG	IP	H	BB	SO	SHO	ERA
TOTALS		28	101	60	.627	45	161	161	44	1465	1313	431	956	17	3.05
Dick Hughes	R	29	16	6	.727	3	37	27	12	222	164	48	161	3	2.68
Nelson Briles	R	23	14	5	.737	6	49	14	4	155	139	40	94	2	2.44
Steve Carlton	L	22	14	9	.609	1	30	28	11	193	173	62	168	2	2.98
Bob Gibson (BL)	R	31	13	7	.650	0	24	24	10	175	151	40	147	2	2.98
Ray Washburn	R	29	10	7	.588	0	27	27	3	186	190	42	98	1	3.53
Al Jackson	L	31	9	4	.692	1	38	11	1	107	117	29	43	1	3.95
Larry Jaster	L	23	9	7	.563	3	34	23	2	152	141	44	87	1	3.02
Ron Willis	R	24	6	5	.545	10	65	0	0	81	76	43	42	0	2.67
Joe Hoerner	L	30	4	4	.500	15	57	0	0	66	52	20	50	0	2.59
3 Jack Lamabe	R	30	3	4	.429	4	23	1	1	48	43	10	30	1	2.81
Hal Woodeshick	L	34	2	1	.667	2	36	0	0	42	41	28	20	0	5.14
Jim Cosman	R	24	1	0	1.000	0	10	5	0	11	21	24	11	0	3.19
Mike Torrez	R	20	0	1	.000	0	3	1	0	6	5	1	5	0	3.00

SAN FRANCISCO 2nd 91-71 .562 10.5 — HERMAN FRANKS

NAME	G by Pos	B	AGE	G	AB	R	H	2B	3B	HR	RBI	BB	SO	SB	BA	SA
TOTALS			27	162	5524	652	1354	201	39	140	604	520	978	22	.245	.372
Willie McCovey	1B127	L	29	135	456	73	126	17	4	31	91	71	110	3	.276	.535
Tito Fuentes	2B130, SS5	B	23	133	344	27	72	12	1	5	29	27	61	6	.209	.294
Hal Lanier	SS137, 2B34	R	24	151	525	37	112	16	3	0	42	16	61	2	.213	.255
Jim Ray Hart	3B89, OF72	R	25	158	578	98	167	26	4	29	99	77	100	1	.289	.509
Ollie Brown	OF115	R	23	120	412	44	110	12	1	13	53	25	65	0	.267	.396
Willie Mays	OF134	R	36	141	486	83	128	22	2	22	70	51	92	6	.263	.453
Jesus Alou	OF123	R	25	129	510	55	149	15	4	5	30	14	39	1	.292	.367
Tom Haller	C136, OF1	L	30	141	455	54	114	23	5	14	49	62	61	0	.251	.415
Jim Davenport	3B64, SS28, 2B12	R	33	124	295	42	81	10	3	5	30	39	50	1	.275	.380
Jack Hiatt	1B36, C3, OF2	R	24	73	153	24	42	6	0	6	26	27	37	0	.275	.431
Ken Henderson	OF52	B	21	65	179	15	34	3	0	4	14	19	52	0	.190	.274
2 Ty Cline	OF37	L	28	64	122	18	33	5	5	0	4	9	13	2	.270	.393
Bob Schroder	2B45, 3B4	L	22	62	135	20	31	4	0	0	7	15	15	1	.230	.259
Dick Dietz	C43	R	25	56	120	10	27	3	0	4	19	25	44	0	.225	.350
1 Norm Siebern	OF12	L	33	46	58	6	9	1	1	0	4	14	13	0	.155	.207
Bobby Etheridge	3B37	R	24	40	115	13	26	7	2	1	15	7	12	0	.226	.348
2 Dick Groat	SS24, 2B1	R	36	34	70	4	12	1	1	0	4	6	7	0	.171	.214
Cesar Gutierrez	SS15, 2B1	R	24	18	21	4	3	0	0	0	0	1	4	1	.143	.143
Bill Sorrell	OF5	R	26	18	17	1	3	1	0	0	1	3	2	0	.176	.235
Frank Johnson	OF3	R	24	8	10	3	3	0	0	0	1	0	2	0	.300	.300
Bob Barton	C7	R	25	7	19	0	4	0	0	0	1	3	0	1	.211	.211
Don Mason	2B2	R	22	4	2	0	0	0	0	0	0	0	0	0	.000	.000
Dave Marshall		L	24	2	0	0	0	0	0	0	0	0	0	0	—	—

NAME	T	AGE	W	L	PCT	SV	G	GS	CG	IP	H	BB	SO	SHO	ERA
TOTALS		30	91	71	.562	25	162	162	64	1474	1283	453	990	17	2.92
Mike McCormick	L	28	22	10	.688	0	35	34	14	262	220	81	150	5	2.85
Gaylord Perry	R	28	15	17	.469	1	39	37	18	293	231	84	230	3	2.61
Juan Marichal (LJ)	R	29	14	10	.583	0	26	26	18	202	195	42	166	2	2.76
Ray Sadecki	L	26	12	6	.667	0	35	24	10	188	165	58	145	2	2.78
Frank Linzy	R	26	7	7	.500	17	57	0	0	96	67	34	38	0	1.50
Joe Gibbon	L	32	2	2	.750	1	28	10	3	82	65	33	63	1	3.07
Bobby Bolin	R	28	6	8	.429	0	37	15	0	120	120	50	69	0	4.88
Ron Herbel	R	29	4	5	.444	1	42	11	1	126	125	35	52	1	3.07
Bill Henry	L	39	2	0	1.000	2	28	1	0	22	16	9	23	0	2.05
Lindy McDaniel	R	31	3	6	.250	3	41	3	0	73	69	24	48	0	3.70
Nestor Chavez	R	19	1	0	1.000	0	2	0	0	5	4	3	3	0	0.00
Rich Robertson	R	22	0	—		0	1	0	0	2	3	0	1	0	4.50
Ron Bryant	L	19	0	—		0	1	0	0	4	3	0	2	0	4.50

CHICAGO 3rd 87-74 .540 14 — LEO DUROCHER

NAME	G by Pos	B	AGE	G	AB	R	H	2B	3B	HR	RBI	BB	SO	SB	BA	SA
TOTALS			28	162	5463	702	1373	211	49	128	642	509	912	63	.251	.378
Ernie Banks	1B147	R	36	151	573	68	158	26	4	23	95	27	93	2	.276	.455
Glenn Beckert	2B144	R	26	146	597	91	167	32	3	5	40	30	25	10	.280	.369
Don Kessinger	SS143	B	24	145	580	61	134	10	7	0	42	33	80	6	.231	.272
Ron Santo	3B161	R	27	161	586	107	176	23	4	31	98	96	103	1	.300	.512
2 Ted Savage	OF86, 3B1	R	30	96	225	40	49	10	1	5	33	40	54	7	.218	.338
Adolfo Phillips	OF141	R	25	144	448	66	120	20	7	17	70	80	93	24	.268	.458
Billy Williams	OF162	L	29	162	634	92	176	21	12	28	84	68	67	0	.278	.481
Randy Hundley	C152	R	25	152	539	68	144	25	3	14	60	44	75	2	.267	.403
Lee Thomas	OF43, 1B10	L	31	77	191	16	42	4	1	2	23	15	22	1	.220	.283
Al Spangler	OF41	L	33	62	130	18	33	7	0	0	13	23	17	2	.254	.308
Clarence Jones	OF31, 1B13	L	24	53	135	13	34	7	0	2	16	14	33	0	.252	.348
Paul Popovich	SS31, 2B17, 3B2	B	26	49	159	18	34	4	0	0	2	9	12	0	.214	.239
Norm Gigon	2B12, OF4, 3B1	R	29	34	70	8	12	3	1	1	6	4	14	0	.171	.286
John Boccabella	OF9, 1B3, C1	R	26	25	35	0	6	1	1	0	8	3	7	0	.171	.257
Johnny Stephenson	C13	R	26	18	49	3	11	3	1	0	5	1	6	0	.224	.327
George Altman	OF4, 1B1	L	34	15	18	1	2	2	0	0	1	2	4	0	.111	.222
Byron Browne	OF8	R	24	10	19	3	3	2	0	0	2	4	5	1	.158	.263
Bob Raudman	OF8	L	25	8	26	0	4	0	0	0	1	1	4	0	.154	.154
1 Jimmy Stewart		B	28	6	6	1	1	0	0	0	1	0	0	0	.167	.167
Dick Bertell	C2	R	31	2	6	1	1	0	1	0	0	0	0	0	.167	.500
Joey Amalfitano		R	33	4	1	0	0	0	0	0	0	0	0	0	.000	.000
Joe Campbell	OF1	R	23	2	3	0	0	0	0	0	0	0	3	0	.000	.000

NAME	T	AGE	W	L	PCT	SV	G	GS	CG	IP	H	BB	SO	SHO	ERA
TOTALS		26	87	74	.540	28	162	162	47	1457	1352	463	888	7	3.48
Ferguson Jenkins	R	23	20	13	.606	0	38	38	20	289	230	83	236	3	2.80
Rich Nye	L	22	13	10	.565	0	35	30	7	205	179	52	119	0	3.20
Joe Niekro	R	22	10	7	.588	0	36	22	7	170	171	32	77	2	3.34
Ken Holtzman (MS)	L	21	9	0	1.000	0	12	12	3	93	76	44	62	0	2.52
Chuck Hartenstein	R	25	9	5	.643	10	45	0	0	73	74	17	20	0	3.08
Ray Culp	R	25	8	11	.421	0	30	22	4	153	138	59	111	1	3.88
Bill Hands	R	27	7	8	.467	6	49	11	3	150	134	48	84	1	2.46
1 Curt Simmons	L	38	3	3	.300	0	17	14	3	82	100	23	31	0	4.94
1 Bob Hendley	L	28	2	1	.667	1	7	0	0	12	17	3	10	0	6.75
1 Cal Koonce	R	26	2	2	.500	2	34	0	0	51	52	21	28	0	4.59
Bill Stoneman	R	23	2	4	.333	4	28	2	0	63	51	22	52	0	3.29
2 Dick Radatz	R	30	1	0	1.000	5	20	0	0	23	12	24	18	0	6.65
Jim Ellis	L	22	1	1	.500	0	8	1	0	17	20	9	8	0	3.18
1 Pete Mikkelsen	R	27	0	—		0	7	0	0	7	9	5	0	0	6.43
Don Larsen	R	37	0	—		0	3	0	0	4	5	2	1	0	9.00
Dick Calmus	R	23	0	—		0	1	0	0	4	3	1	0	0	9.00
Fred Norman	L	24	0	0	—	0	1	0	0	3	4	2	1	0	45.00
John Upham	L	25	0	1	.000	0	3	0	0	2	3	2	2	0	9.00
Rick James	R	19	0	1	.000	0	2	0	0	5	8	2	1	0	12.60
Rob Gardner	L	22	0	2	.000	0	18	5	0	32	33	6	16	0	3.94
2 Bob Shaw	R	34	0	2	.000	3	22	0	0	22	33	9	7	0	6.14

CINCINNATI 4th 87-75 .537 14.5 — DAVE BRISTOL

NAME	G by Pos	B	AGE	G	AB	R	H	2B	3B	HR	RBI	BB	SO	SB	BA	SA
TOTALS			27	162	5519	604	1366	251	54	109	560	372	969	92	.248	.372
Lee May	1B81, OF48	R	24	127	438	54	116	29	2	12	57	19	80	4	.265	.422
Tommy Helms	2B88, SS46	R	26	137	497	40	136	27	4	2	35	24	41	5	.274	.356
Leo Cardenas (BH)	SS108	R	28	108	379	30	97	14	3	2	21	34	77	4	.256	.325
Tony Perez	3B139, 1B18, 2B1	R	25	156	600	78	174	28	7	26	102	33	102	0	.290	.490
Tommy Harper (BW)	OF100	R	26	103	365	55	82	17	3	7	22	43	51	23	.225	.345
Vada Pinson	OF157	L	28	158	650	90	187	28	13	18	66	26	86	26	.288	.427
Pete Rose	OF123, 2B35	B	26	148	585	86	176	32	8	12	76	56	66	11	.301	.444
Johnny Edwards	C73	L	29	80	209	10	43	9	0	2	20	16	28	1	.206	.263
Deron Johnson	1B81, 3B24	R	28	108	361	39	81	18	1	13	53	22	104	0	.224	.388
Chico Ruiz	2B56, 3B13, SS11, OF5	B	28	105	250	32	55	12	4	0	13	11	35	9	.220	.300
Art Shamsky	OF40	L	25	76	147	6	29	3	1	3	13	15	34	0	.197	.293
Don Pavletich	C66, 1B6, 3B1	R	28	74	231	25	55	14	3	6	34	21	38	2	.238	.403
Floyd Robinson	OF39	L	31	55	130	19	31	6	2	1	14	14	14	3	.238	.338
Jimmie Coker	C34	R	31	45	97	8	18	2	1	2	4	4	20	0	.186	.289
Dick Simpson	OF26	R	23	44	54	8	14	3	0	1	6	7	11	0	.259	.370
Johnny Bench	C26	R	19	26	86	7	14	3	1	1	6	5	19	0	.163	.256
2 Jake Wood	OF2	R	30	16	17	1	2	0	0	0	1	1	3	0	.118	.118
Gordy Coleman	1B2	R	32	4	7	0	0	0	0	0	0	0	0	0	.000	.000
Len Boehmer	2B1	R	26	3	5	0	0	0	0	0	0	0	0	0	.000	.000

NAME	T	AGE	W	L	PCT	SV	G	GS	CG	IP	H	BB	SO	SHO	ERA
TOTALS		27	87	75	.537	39	162	162	34	1468	1328	498	1065	18	3.05
Milt Pappas	R	28	16	13	.552	0	34	32	5	218	218	38	129	3	3.34
Jim Maloney	R	27	15	11	.577	0	30	29	15	196	181	72	153	3	2.26
Gary Nolan	R	19	14	8	.636	0	33	32	8	227	193	62	206	5	2.58
Mel Queen	R	25	14	8	.636	0	31	24	6	196	155	52	154	2	2.76
Sammy Ellis	R	26	8	11	.421	0	32	27	8	176	197	67	80	1	3.84
Ted Abernathy	R	34	6	3	.667	28	70	0	0	106	63	41	88	0	1.27
Jerry Arrigo	L	26	6	6	.500	1	32	5	1	74	61	35	56	1	3.16
2 Bob Lee	R	29	3	3	.500	2	27	1	0	51	51	25	33	0	4.41
Billy McCool	L	22	3	7	.300	2	31	11	0	97	92	56	83	0	3.43
Ted Davidson (PB)	L	27	1	0	1.000	0	13	0	0	8	4	6	4	0	4.15
John Tsitouris	R	31	1	0	1.000	0	7	0	0	13	11	9	12	0	3.38
Jack Baldschun	R	30	0	—		0	13	0	0	13	9	12	6	0	4.15
Darrell Osteen	R	24	0	2	.000	0	8	0	0	9	13	6	6	0	6.43
Don Nottebart	R	31	0	3	.000	1	47	0	0	79	75	19	48	0	1.94

PHILADELPHIA 5th 82-80 .506 19.5 — GENE MAUCH

NAME	G by Pos	B	AGE	G	AB	R	H	2B	3B	HR	RBI	BB	SO	SB	BA	SA
TOTALS			28	162	5401	612	1306	221	47	103	553	545	1033	79	.242	.357
Bill White (FJ)	1B95	L	33	110	330	29	77	6	2	8	33	52	61	6	.250	.360
C. Rojas	2B137, OF9, C3, SS2, 3B1, P1	R	28	147	528	60	137	21	2	4	45	30	58	5	.259	.330
Bobby Wine	SS117	R	28	135	363	27	69	12	5	2	28	29	77	3	.190	.267
Dick Allen (NJ)	3B121, 2B1, SS1	R	25	122	463	89	142	31	10	23	77	75	117	20	.307	.566
Johnny Callison	OF147	L	28	149	556	63	145	30	5	14	64	55	63	6	.261	.408
Johnny Briggs	OF94	L	23	106	332	47	77	13	3	9	30	41	72	3	.232	.373
Tony Gonzalez	OF143	L	30	149	508	74	172	23	9	9	59	47	58	10	.339	.472
Clay Dalrymple	C97	L	30	101	268	12	46	7	1	3	21	36	49	1	.172	.239
Tony Taylor	1B58, 3B44, 2B42, SS3	R	31	132	462	55	110	16	6	2	34	42	74	10	.238	.312
Don Lock	OF97	R	30	112	313	44	79	13	1	14	51	43	98	9	.252	.435
Gary Sutherland	SS66, OF25	R	22	103	231	23	57	12	1	1	19	17	22	0	.247	.320
2 Gene Oliver	C79, 1B2	R	31	85	263	29	59	16	0	7	34	29	56	2	.224	.365
Doug Clemens	OF10	L	28	69	73	2	13	5	0	0	4	8	13	0	.178	.247
Billy Cowan	OF20, 2B1, 3B1	R	29	34	59	11	9	0	0	2	6	2	14	1	.153	.305
2 Chuck Hiller	2B6	L	32	27	53	4	16	3	0	0	3	4	6	0	.302	.326
1 Tito Francona	1B24, OF1	L	33	27	73	7	15	2	0	1	7	7	10	0	.205	.219
1 Phil Linz	SS7, 3B1	R	28	22	30	3	6	1	0	0	5	5	4	0	.222	.300
1 Bob Uecker	C17	R	32	18	35	3	6	2	0	0	3	7	9	0	.171	.229
Rick Joseph	1B13	R	27	17	22	0	4	0	0	0	1	0	3	0	.220	.341
1 Jackie Brandt	OF3	R	33	16	19	1	2	1	0	0	0	1	6	0	.105	.158
1 Dick Groat	SS6	R	36	10	26	3	3	0	0	0	1	1	4	0	.115	.115
Jimmie Schaffer	C1	R	31	6	1	0	0	0	0	0	0	0	1	0	.000	.000
Terry Harmon		R	23	3	0	0	0	0	0	0	0	0	0	0	—	—

NAME	T	AGE	W	L	PCT	SV	G	GS	CG	IP	H	BB	SO	SHO	ERA
TOTALS		30	82	80	.506	23	162	162	46	1454	1372	403	967	17	3.10
Jim Bunning	R	35	17	15	.531	0	40	40	16	302	241	73	253	6	2.29
Larry Jackson	R	36	13	15	.464	0	40	37	11	262	242	54	139	4	3.09
Rick Wise	R	21	11	11	.500	0	36	25	6	181	177	45	111	3	3.28
Dick Hall	R	36	10	8	.556	8	48	1	1	86	83	12	49	0	2.20
2 Dick Farrell	R	33	9	6	.600	12	50	1	0	92	76	15	68	0	2.05
Chris Short (KJ)	L	29	9	11	.450	1	29	26	8	199	163	74	142	2	2.40
Dick Ellsworth	L	27	6	7	.462	0	32	21	3	125	152	36	45	1	4.39
John Boozer	R	27	5	4	.556	2	71	0	0	75	86	24	48	0	4.08
Grant Jackson	L	24	2	3	.400	1	43	4	0	86	83	43	83	0	3.86
Dallas Green	R	32	0	0	—	0	15	0	0	15	25	6	12	0	9.00
Ruben Gomez	R	39	0	0	—	0	8	0	0	11	11	4	5	0	9.00
Pedro Ramos	R	32	0	0	—	0	8	0	0	13	17	1	9	0	16.20
Larry Loughlin	R	23	0	0	—	0	2	0	0	5	3	4	1	0	3.00
Bob Buhl	R	38	0	1	.000	0	6	0	0	16	20	6	3	0	12.00
Gary Wagner	R	27	0	1	.000	0	6	0	0	3	6	1	0	0	9.00
Dick Thoenen	R	28	0	0	—	0	1	0	0	1	1	1	1	0	0.00
Cookie Rojas	R	28	0	0	—	0	1	0	0	1	0	0	0	0	0.00

NAME	G by Pos	B	AGE	G	AB	R	H	2B	3B	HR	RBI	BB	SO	SB	BA	SA
PITTSBURGH 6th 81-81 .500 20.5			HARRY WALKER 42-42 .500				DANNY MURTAUGH 39-39 .500									
TOTALS			29	163	5724	679	1585	193	62	91	615	387	914	79	.277	.380
Donn Clendenon	1B123	R	31	131	478	46	119	15	2	13	56	34	107	4	.249	.370
Bill Mazeroski	2B163	R	30	163	639	62	167	25	3	9	77	30	55	1	.261	.352
Gene Alley	SS146	R	26	152	550	59	158	25	7	6	55	36	70	10	.287	.391
Maury Wills	3B144, SS2	B	34	149	616	92	186	12	9	3	45	31	44	29	.302	.365
Roberto Clemente	OF145	R	32	147	585	103	209	26	10	23	110	41	103	9	.357	.554
Matty Alou	OF134, 1B1	L	28	139	550	87	186	21	7	2	28	24	42	16	.338	.413
Willie Stargell	OF98, 1B37	L	27	134	462	54	125	18	6	20	73	67	103	1	.271	.465
Jerry May	C110	R	23	110	325	23	88	13	2	3	22	36	55	0	.271	.351
Manny Mota	OF99, 3B2	R	29	120	349	53	112	14	8	4	56	14	46	3	.321	.441
Jose Pagan	3B25, OF23, SS16, 2B2, C1	R	32	81	211	17	61	6	1	2	19	10	28	1	.289	.351
2 Al Luplow	OF25	L	28	55	103	13	19	1	0	1	8	6	14	1	.184	.223
Manny Jimenez	OF6	L	28	50	56	3	14	2	0	2	10	1	4	0	.250	.393
Andre Rodgers	1B9, 3B5, SS3, 2B2	R	32	47	61	8	14	3	0	2	4	8	18	1	.230	.377
Jim Pagliaroni (XJ)	C38	R	29	44	100	4	20	1	1	0	9	16	26	0	.200	.230
George Spriggs	OF13	L	26	38	57	14	10	1	1	0	5	6	20	3	.175	.228
Manny Sanguillen	C28	R	23	30	96	6	26	4	0	0	8	4	12	0	.271	.313
Jesse Gonder	C18	L	31	22	36	4	5	1	0	0	3	4	6	0	.139	.167
Bob Robertson	1B9	R	20	9	35	4	6	0	0	2	4	3	12	0	.171	.343

NAME	T	AGE	W	L	PCT	SV	G	GS	CG	IP	H	BB	SO	SHO	ERA
		30	81	81	.500	35	163	163	35	1458	1439	561	820	5	3.74
Bob Veale	L	31	16	8	.667	0	33	31	6	203	184	119	179	1	3.64
Tommie Sisk	R	25	13	13	.500	1	37	31	11	208	196	78	85	2	3.33
Dennis Ribant	R	25	9	8	.529	0	38	22	2	172	188	40	75	0	4.08
Juan Pizarro	L	30	8	10	.444	9	50	9	1	107	99	52	96	1	3.95
Al McBean	R	29	7	4	.636	4	51	8	5	131	118	43	54	0	2.54
Roy Face	R	39	7	5	.583	17	61	0	0	74	62	22	41	0	2.43
Steve Blass	R	25	6	8	.429	0	32	16	2	127	126	47	72	0	3.54
Billy O'Dell	L	34	5	6	.455	0	27	11	1	87	88	41	34	0	5.79
Woody Fryman	L	27	3	8	.273	1	28	18	3	113	121	44	74	1	4.06
Bruce Dal Canton	R	25	2	1	.667	0	8	2	1	24	19	10	13	0	1.88
Vern Law	R	37	2	6	.250	0	25	10	1	97	122	18	43	0	4.18
Bob Moose	R	19	1	0	1.000	0	2	2	1	15	14	4	7	0	3.60
Jim Shellenback	L	23	1	1	.500	0	2	1	1	23	23	12	11	0	2.74
1 Pete Mikkelsen	R	27	1	2	.333	2	32	0	0	56	50	19	30	0	4.34
Bill Short	L	29	0	0	—	0	9	0	0	2	1	1	1	0	4.50
John Gelnar	R	24	0	1	.000	0	10	1	0	19	30	11	5	0	8.05

NAME	G by Pos	B	AGE	G	AB	R	H	2B	3B	HR	RBI	BB	SO	SB	BA	SA
ATLANTA 7th 77-85 .475 24.5			BILLY HITCHCOCK 77-82 .484				KEN SILVESTRI 0-3 .000									
TOTALS			29	162	5450	631	1307	191	29	158	596	512	947	55	.240	.372
Felipe Alou	1B85, OF56	R	32	140	574	76	157	26	3	15	43	32	50	6	.274	.408
Woody Woodward	2B120, SS16	R	24	136	429	30	97	15	2	0	25	37	51	0	.226	.270
Denis Menke	SS124, 3B3	R	26	129	418	37	95	14	3	7	39	65	62	5	.227	.325
Clete Boyer	3B150, SS6	R	30	154	572	63	140	18	3	26	96	39	81	6	.245	.423
Hank Aaron	OF152, 2B1	R	33	155	600	113	184	37	3	39	109	63	97	17	.307	.573
Mack Jones	OF126	L	28	140	454	72	115	23	4	17	50	64	108	10	.253	.434
Rico Carty	OF112, 1B9	R	27	134	444	41	113	16	2	15	64	49	70	4	.255	.401
Joe Torre	C114, 1B23	R	26	135	477	67	132	18	1	20	68	49	75	2	.277	.444
2 Tito Francona	1B56, OF6	L	33	82	254	28	63	5	1	6	25	20	34	1	.248	.346
Mike de la Hoz	2B23, 3B22, SS1	R	28	74	143	10	29	3	0	3	14	4	14	1	.203	.287
Gary Geiger	OF38	L	30	69	117	17	19	1	1	1	5	20	35	1	.162	.214
2 Bob Uecker	C59	R	32	62	158	14	23	2	0	3	13	19	51	0	.146	.215
2 Charlie Lau	C34	L	34	52	45	3	9	1	0	0	4	9	2	0	.200	.289
Marty Martinez	SS25, 2B9, C3, 3B2, 1B1	B	25	44	73	14	21	2	1	0	5	11	11	1	.288	.342
Felix Millan	2B41	R	23	41	136	13	32	3	3	2	6	4	10	0	.235	.346
1 Gene Oliver	C14	R	31	17	51	8	10	2	0	3	6	0	5	0	.196	.412
Angel Hermoso	SS9, 2B2	R	20	11	26	3	8	0	0	0	0	2	4	1	.308	.308
Dave Nicholson	OF7	R	27	10	25	2	5	0	0	0	1	2	9	0	.200	.200
Mike Lum	OF6	L	21	9	10	2	2	0	0	0	1	1	1	0	.231	.231
Cito Gaston	OF7	R	23	9	25	1	3	0	1	0	1	0	5	1	.120	.200
1 Ty Cline (LJ) 28 L 0-8, Glen Clark 26 B 0-4, Jim Beauchamp 27 R 0-3																

NAME	T	AGE	W	L	PCT	SV	G	GS	CG	IP	H	BB	SO	SHO	ERA
		28	77	85	.475	32	162	162	35	1454	1377	449	862	5	3.47
Pat Jarvis	R	26	15	10	.600	0	32	30	7	194	195	62	118	1	3.66
Ken Johnson	R	34	13	9	.591	0	29	29	6	210	191	38	85	0	2.74
Phil Niekro	R	28	11	9	.550	9	46	20	10	207	164	55	129	1	1.87
Denny Lemaster	L	28	9	9	.500	0	31	31	8	215	184	72	148	2	3.35
Clay Carroll	R	26	6	12	.333	0	42	7	1	93	111	29	35	0	5.52
2 Claude Raymond	R	30	4	1	.800	5	28	0	0	34	33	11	14	0	2.65
Jay Ritchie	R	30	4	6	.400	2	52	0	0	82	75	29	57	0	3.18
Tony Cloninger (IL)	R	26	4	7	.364	0	16	16	1	77	85	31	55	0	5.14
Ed Rakow	R	32	3	2	.600	0	17	3	0	39	36	15	25	0	5.31
Cecil Upshaw	R	24	2	3	.400	8	30	0	0	45	42	8	31	0	2.60
Bob Bruce	R	34	3	4	.400	1	12	7	1	39	42	15	22	0	4.85
Dick Kelley	L	27	2	9	.182	2	33	9	1	98	88	42	75	1	3.77
1 Wade Blasingame	L	23	1	0	1.000	0	10	4	0	25	27	21	20	0	4.68
Ron Reed	R	24	1	1	.500	0	3	3	0	21	21	3	11	0	3.00
George Stone	L	20	0	1	.000	0	1	1	0	7	8	1	5	0	5.14
Don Schwall	R	31	0	0	—	0	1	0	0	1	0	1	1	0	0.00
Ramon Hernandez	L	26	0	2	.000	2	46	0	0	52	60	14	28	0	4.15
Jim Britton	R	23	0	2	.000	0	3	2	0	13	15	2	4	0	6.23

NAME	G by Pos	B	AGE	G	AB	R	H	2B	3B	HR	RBI	BB	SO	SB	BA	SA
LOS ANGELES 8th 73-89 .451 28.5			WALT ALSTON													
TOTALS			28	162	5456	519	1285	203	38	82	465	485	881	56	.236	.332
Wes Parker	1B112, OF18	B	27	139	413	56	102	16	5	5	31	65	83	10	.247	.346
Ron Hunt	2B90, 3B8	R	26	110	388	44	102	17	3	3	33	39	24	2	.263	.345
Gene Michael	SS83	R	29	98	223	20	45	3	1	0	7	11	30	1	.202	.224
Jim Lefebvre	3B92, 2B34, 1B5	B	24	136	494	51	129	18	5	8	50	44	64	1	.261	.366
Ron Fairly	OF97, 1B68	L	28	153	486	45	107	19	0	10	55	54	51	1	.220	.321
Willie Davis	OF138	L	27	143	569	65	146	27	9	6	41	29	65	20	.257	.367
Lou Johnson (BL)	OF91	R	32	104	330	39	89	14	1	11	41	24	52	4	.270	.418
Johnny Roseboro	C107	L	34	116	334	37	91	18	2	4	24	38	33	2	.272	.374
Al Ferrara	OF94	R	24	122	347	41	96	16	1	16	50	33	73	0	.277	.467
Bob Bailey	3B65, OF27, 1B4, SS1	R	24	116	322	21	73	8	2	4	28	40	50	5	.227	.301
2 Len Gabrielson	OF68	L	27	90	238	20	62	10	3	7	29	15	41	3	.261	.416
Dick Schofield	SS69, 2B4, 3B2	B	32	84	232	23	50	10	1	2	15	31	40	1	.216	.293
Nate Oliver	2B39, SS32, OF1	R	26	77	232	18	55	6	2	0	7	13	50	3	.237	.280
Jeff Torborg	C75	R	25	76	196	11	42	4	1	2	12	13	31	1	.214	.276
Jim Hickman	OF37, 1B2, 3B2, P1	R	30	65	98	7	16	1	0	1	10	14	28	1	.163	.245
Jim Campanis	C23	R	23	41	62	3	10	1	0	2	9	4	14	0	.161	.274
Luis Alcaraz	2B17	R	26	17	60	1	14	1	0	0	3	1	13	1	.233	.250
Tommy Dean	SS12	R	21	12	28	1	4	0	0	0	0	0	6	0	.143	.179
1 Johnny Werhas 29 R 1-7, Willie Crawford 20 L 1-4																

NAME	T	AGE	W	L	PCT	SV	G	GS	CG	IP	H	BB	SO	SHO	ERA
		28	73	89	.451	24	162	162	41	1473	1421	393	967	17	3.21
Claude Osteen	L	27	17	17	.500	0	39	39	14	288	298	52	152	5	3.22
Don Drysdale	R	30	13	16	.448	0	38	38	9	282	269	60	196	3	2.74
Bill Singer	R	23	12	8	.600	0	32	29	7	204	185	61	169	3	2.65
Don Sutton	R	22	11	15	.423	1	37	34	11	233	223	57	169	3	3.94
Ron Perranoski	R	31	6	7	.462	16	70	0	0	110	97	45	75	0	2.45
Phil Regan	R	30	6	9	.400	6	55	3	0	96	108	32	53	0	3.00
Jim Brewer	R	29	5	4	.556	1	30	11	0	101	78	31	74	0	2.67
Bob Miller	R	28	2	9	.182	0	52	4	0	86	88	27	32	0	4.29
Dick Egan	L	30	1	1	.500	0	32	0	0	32	34	15	20	0	6.19
Joe Moeller	R	24	0	0	—	0	6	0	0	7	8	1	2	0	9.00
1 Bob Lee	R	29	0	0	—	0	9	0	0	7	6	5	2	0	5.14
Bruce Brubaker	R	25	0	1	.000	0	1	1	0	3	8	4	0	0	27.00
Jim Hickman	R	26	0	0	—	0	1	0	0	2	4	0	0	0	4.50
Alan Foster	R	20	0	1	.000	0	3	2	0	17	10	3	15	0	2.12
John Duffie	R	21	0	2	.000	0	2	0	0	10	11	4	6	0	2.70
Sandy Koufax (RJ) 31																

NAME	G by Pos	B	AGE	G	AB	R	H	2B	3B	HR	RBI	BB	SO	SB	BA	SA
HOUSTON 9th 69-93 .426 32.5			GRADY HATTON													
TOTALS			26	162	5506	626	1372	259	46	93	581	537	934	88	.249	.364
1 Eddie Mathews	1B79, 3B24	L	35	101	328	39	78	13	2	10	38	48	65	2	.238	.381
Joe Morgan	2B130, OF1	L	23	133	494	73	136	27	11	6	42	81	51	29	.275	.411
Sonny Jackson	SS128	L	22	129	520	67	123	18	3	0	25	36	45	22	.237	.283
Bob Aspromonte	3B133	R	29	137	486	51	143	24	5	6	58	45	44	2	.294	.401
Rusty Staub	OF144	L	23	149	546	71	182	44	1	10	74	60	47	0	.333	.473
Jim Wynn	OF157	R	25	158	594	102	148	29	3	37	107	74	137	16	.249	.495
Ron Davis	OF80	R	25	94	285	31	73	19	1	7	38	17	48	5	.256	.404
John Bateman	C71	R	26	76	252	16	48	9	0	2	17	17	53	0	.190	.250
Ron Brand	C67, 2B1, OF1	R	27	84	215	22	52	8	1	0	18	23	17	4	.242	.288
Julio Gotay	2B30, SS20, 3B3	R	28	77	234	30	66	10	2	2	15	15	30	1	.282	.368
Chuck Harrison	1B59	R	26	70	177	13	43	7	3	2	26	13	30	0	.243	.350
Norm Miller (MS)	OF53	L	21	64	190	15	39	9	3	1	14	19	42	2	.205	.300
1 Jim Landis	OF44	R	33	50	143	19	36	11	1	1	14	20	35	2	.252	.364
Doug Rader	1B36, 3B7	R	22	47	162	24	54	10	4	2	26	7	31	0	.333	.481
2 Jackie Brandt	1B14, OF6, 3B1	R	33	41	89	7	21	4	1	2	15	8	9	0	.236	.337
Dave Adlesh	C31	R	23	39	94	4	17	1	0	1	4	11	28	0	.181	.223
Bob Lillis	SS23, 2B3, 3B2	R	37	82	82	3	20	1	0	0	5	1	8	0	.244	.256
Aaron Pointer	OF22	R	25	27	70	6	11	4	0	1	10	13	26	1	.157	.257
Lee Bales	2B6, SS1	R	22	19	27	4	3	0	0	0	2	8	7	1	.111	.111
Hal King	C11	L	23	15	44	2	11	1	0	2	6	3	12	0	.250	.364
Ivan Murrell	OF6	R	24	10	29	2	9	0	0	1	1	1	13	1	.310	.414
Bob Watson 21 R 3-14, 1 Bill Heath 28 L 1-11, Joe Herrera 25 R 1-4, Alonzo Harris 19 B 0-1																

NAME	T	AGE	W	L	PCT	SV	G	GS	CG	IP	H	BB	SO	SHO	ERA
		27	69	93	.426	21	162	162	36	1446	1444	485	1060	8	4.03
Mike Cuellar	L	30	16	11	.593	1	36	32	16	246	233	63	203	3	3.04
Dave Giusti	R	27	11	15	.423	1	37	33	8	222	231	58	157	1	4.18
Don Wilson	R	22	10	9	.526	0	31	28	7	184	141	69	159	3	2.79
Dave Eilers	R	30	6	4	.600	1	35	0	0	59	68	17	27	0	3.97
Larry Dierker (MS)	R	20	6	5	.545	0	15	15	5	99	95	25	68	0	3.36
2 Wade Blasingame	L	23	4	7	.364	0	15	14	0	77	91	27	46	0	5.96
Danny Coombs	L	25	3	0	1.000	0	9	2	0	24	21	9	23	0	3.38
Barry Latman	R	31	3	6	.333	2	39	1	0	78	73	34	70	0	4.50
Bo Belinsky	L	30	3	9	.250	0	27	18	0	115	112	54	80	0	4.70
Carroll Sembera	R	25	2	6	.250	3	45	0	0	60	66	19	40	0	4.80
1 Dick Farrell	R	33	1	0	1.000	0	3	0	0	7	6	3	3	0	4.50
Pat House	L	26	1	1	.500	0	9	0	0	11	9	3	10	0	4.50
Howie Reed	R	30	1	1	.500	1	7	0	0	10	10	3	9	0	3.50
2 Larry Sherry	R	31	1	2	.333	6	29	0	0	41	53	13	32	0	4.83
Chris Zachary	R	23	1	4	.200	0	36	4	1	68	70	28	44	0	5.29
Arnie Earley	L	34	0	0	—	0	6	0	0	6	8	5	3	0	36.00
3 John Buzhardt	R	30	0	0	—	0	1	0	0	2	0	0	0	0	0.00
Jim Owens	R	33	0	0	—	0	4	0	0	24	25	11	23	0	4.09
Dan Schneider	L	24	0	1	.000	0	17	0	0	24	24	11	20	0	5.25
Tom Dukes	R	24	0	2	.000	4	24	0	0	35	25	11	23	0	4.86
Bruce Von Hoff	R	23	0	4	.000	0	10	10	0	33	32	12	22	0	4.86
1 Claude Raymond	R	30	0	4	—	21	0	0	0	31	31	12	29	0	3.19

NAME	G by Pos	B	AGE	G	AB	R	H	2B	3B	HR	RBI	BB	SO	SB	BA	SA
NEW YORK 10th 61-101 .377 40.5			WES WESTRUM 57-94 .377				SALTY PARKER 4-7 .364									
TOTALS			27	162	5417	498	1288	178	23	83	461	362	981	58	.238	.325
Ed Kranepool	1B139	L	22	141	469	37	126	17	1	10	54	37	51	0	.269	.373
Jerry Buchek	2B95, 3B17, SS9	R	25	124	411	35	97	13	2	14	41	26	101	3	.236	.375
Bud Harrelson	SS149	R	23	151	540	59	137	16	4	1	28	48	64	12	.254	.304
2 Ed Charles	3B89	R	32	101	323	32	77	13	2	3	31	24	58	6	.238	.319
Ron Swoboda	OF108, 1B20	R	23	134	449	47	126	17	3	13	53	41	96	3	.281	.419
Cleon Jones	OF115	R	24	129	411	46	101	10	5	5	30	19	57	12	.246	.331
Tommy Davis	OF149, 1B1	R	28	154	577	72	174	32	0	16	73	31	71	0	.302	.440
Jerry Grote	C119	R	24	120	344	25	67	8	0	4	23	14	65	2	.195	.253
Tommie Reynolds	OF72, 3B5, C1	R	25	101	136	16	28	1	0	9	11	26	1	.206	.257	
2 Bob Johnson	2B39, 1B23, SS14, 3B1	R	30	90	230	26	80	8	3	5	27	12	29	1	.348	.474
Larry Stahl	OF43	L	26	71	155	9	37	5	0	1	18	8	25	2	.239	.290
John Sullivan	C57	L	26	65	147	4	32	5	0	0	18	10	23	0	.218	.252
1 Ken Boyer	3B44, 1B8	R	36	56	167	19	39	7	2	3	13	26	22	0	.235	.355
Don Bosch	OF39	B	24	44	93	7	13	0	2	0	9	9	29	1	.140	.161
1 Al Luplow	OF33	L	28	41	112	11	23	7	0	0	6	10	26	0	.205	.295
Greg Goossen	C27	R	21	37	69	2	11	1	0	2	9	8	19	0	.159	.174
1 Chuck Hiller (RJ)	2B14	L	32	25	54	0	5	3	0	0	0	3	4	0	.093	.148
2 Phil Linz	2B11, SS8, 3B1, OF1	R	28	22	41	2	7	0	0	0	1	2	7	1	.171	.171
Amos Otis	OF16, 3B1	R	20	19	59	6	13	0	0	0	1	2	13	0	.220	.254
Bob Heise	3B10	R	20	12	39	2	10	0	0	0	3	0	4	0	.256	.256
1 Sandy Alomar	SS10, 3B3, 2B2	R	23	22	62	6	16	0	0	0	2	5	3	3	.258	.258
Joe Moock	3B12	L	23	13	47	4	10	1	0	0	5	1	8	0	.213	.234
1 Hawk Taylor	C12	R	28	13	37	3	9	0	0	0	3	2	9	0	.243	.324
Johnny Lewis	OF10	L	27	9	17	2	2	0	0	0	0	1	7	0	.118	.147
Ken Boswell	2B6, 3B4	L	21	9	40	4	9	1	1	0	3	2	7	0	.225	.375
Bart Shirley 27 R 0-12, Kevin Collins 20 L 1-10																

NAME	T	AGE	W	L	PCT	SV	G	GS	CG	IP	H	BB	SO	SHO	ERA
		27	61	101	.377	19	162	162	36	1434	1369	536	893	10	3.73
Tom Seaver	R	22	16	13	.552	0	35	34	18	251	224	78	170	2	2.76
Jack Fisher	R	28	9	18	.333	0	39	30	7	220	251	64	117	1	4.70
Don Cardwell (EJ)	R	31	5	9	.357	0	26	16	3	118	112	39	71	3	3.58
Don Shaw (MS)	L	23	4	5	.444	3	40	0	0	73	60	23	44	0	3.00
Ron Taylor	R	29	4	6	.400	8	50	0	0	73	60	23	46	0	2.34
2 Hal Reniff	R	28	3	3	.500	4	29	0	0	43	42	23	21	0	3.35
2 Bob Hendley	L	28	2	5	.286	0	15	13	2	71	63	28	36	0	3.42
2 Cal Koonce	R	26	2	6	.250	5	46	5	0	45	45	7	24	1	2.80
1 Bob Shaw	R	34	3	9	.250	2	23	13	3	99	105	28	49	1	4.27
1 Jack Hamilton	R	28	2	0	1.000	1	17	1	0	31	24	16	22	0	3.77
Les Rohr	L	21	2	1	.667	0	3	3	0	13	9	13	15	0	2.12
Dick Selma	R	23	2	4	.333	2	38	4	0	81	71	36	52	0	2.78
2 Dennis Bennett	L	27	1	1	.500	0	26	0	0	37	28	17	16	0	5.19
Chuck Estrada	R	29	1	1	.500	2	28	0	0	28	28	17	15	0	9.41
Bill Graham	R	22	1	1	.500	0	2	2	0	14	11	5	9	0	2.67
Danny Frisella	R	21	1	6	.143	0	14	14	1	74	68	33	51	0	3.41
Bill Denehy	R	21	1	7	.125	0	15	9	1	50	49	29	35	0	4.67
Joe Grzenda	L	29	0	0	—	0	11	0	0	17	14	8	9	0	2.12
Billy Connors	R	25	0	0	—	0	11	0	0	7	16	5	6	0	6.23
Billy Wynne	R	23	0	1	.000	0	9	0	0	9	13	1	4	0	3.00
Jerry Hinsley	R	22	0	1	.000	0	3	0	0	3	4	3	1	0	3.60
Ralph Terry	R	31	0	1	.000	0	5	0	0	11	18	4	4	0	4.50
Al Schmelz	R	23	0	0	—	0	1	0	0	2	1	1	1	0	3.00
2 Nick Willhite	L	26	0	1	.000	0	4	0	0	9	11	4	4	0	9.00
Jerry Koosman	L	24	0	2	.000	0	9	3	1	22	23	19	13	0	6.14
2 Jack Lamabe	R	30	0	3	.000	0	16	2	0	24	24	7	13	0	3.94
Tug McGraw	L	22	0	3	.000	0	17	4	1	34	31	13	18	0	7.94

1968 The Revenge of '30

As batting had caught up with the pitcher in 1930, 1968 was to witness a [re]versal in what was best described as the Year of the Pitcher. The event was [ev]idenced by plummeting batting averages, a rise in low-scoring games, 335 [sh]utouts, and individual outstanding pitching performances. Denny McLain was [pe]rhaps the biggest story among the many pitchers who were headline news [du]ring the year. With national television present, the brash, cocky McLain [fa]stballed his way to his 30th victory on September 14, becoming the first hurler [to] achieve that mark since Dizzy Dean in 1934. Winning games with a steady [m]onotony during the season, Detroit's McLain wound up with 31 victories [ag]ainst 6 losses and both the MVP and Cy Young Awards.

The Tigers coasted into the American League championship with a margin [of] 12 games by playing consistent baseball all year. McLain acted as stopper par [ex]cellence, winning practically every fourth day to prevent any Detroit losing [st]reak as Mickey Lolich, the lefty counterpart to McLain, finished at 17-9. At [ba]t, veteran Al Kaline, Willie Horton, and Bill Freehan provided enough offense [fo]r the Tigers to lead the league in runs and home runs.

The rest of the teams spent the year chasing after Detroit. The Orioles, by [vi]rtue of staying a distant second all year, cost manager Hank Bauer his job during [th]e All-Star break. He was replaced by coach Earl Weaver. As with almost every [ot]her team, Baltimore's pitching far outshone lackluster hitting. Third-place [Cl]eveland also held a mediocre hand in terms of attack, but flashed a pair of aces [on] the mound. Sam McDowell cashed in on his great potential with an E.R.A. [of] 1.81 and the most strikeouts in the league, and Luis Tiant reversed the trend [of] his early mediocre career with a spectacular season, leading the league in E.R.A. [w]ith 1.60 and winning 21 games against 9 losses.

Carl Yastrzemski of Boston paced the league's batters in average, finishing [ju]st to end at .301 and spare the league the embarrassment of no .300 hitters. [F]rank Howard of last-place Washington developed into a mature power threat [b]y knocking 44 home runs to pace the loop. Ken Harrelson, the late-season [a]ddition to Boston's 1967 champions, spent the year in Fenway Park driving [in] 109 runs, tops in the league, to go with 35 home runs in a ballpark perfectly [pr]oportioned for his swing.

Bob Gibson piled up the honors in the National League as he led the Cardinals [to] a repeat pennant by nine games over San Francisco. Gibson's blistering 1.12 [w]as the best E.R.A. since the introduction of the lively ball in 1920 and his 13 [sh]utouts and 268 strikeouts paced the circuit. In winning 15 straight games and [pi]tching 28 complete games, Gibson compiled a season which won for him both [th]e MVP and Cy Young Awards. Pitching strength made up for a slumping [C]ardinal offense which witnessed bad years by Orlando Cepeda, Tim McCarver, [an]d Julian Javier. Curt Flood, Lou Brock, and Mike Shannon provided enough [ru]ns for the best pitching in the majors to win. Besides Gibson, Nelson Briles [an]d Steve Carlton lodged good years on the mound.

With Sandy Koufax retired, Don Drysdale claimed the Dodger pitching spotlight, and all baseball watched as Big D broke long-standing records in hurling six consecutive shutouts and 58 2/3 straight scoreless innings—2 2/3 more than notched by Walter Johnson in 1913. But good Dodger pitching could boost the club no higher than seventh place, due to a .230 team batting average.

The Year of the Pitcher is well exemplified by the Giant-Cardinal games of September 17-18. Gaylord Perry no-hit the Cards on the 17th, and the next night, Ray Washburn of St. Louis came back to throw a no-hitter at San Francisco. Earlier in the season, on July 9, in the first All-Star Game played at night, yawning fans watched as the National League squeaked by their foes, 1-0. The New York Mets and Houston Astros literally sent their audience to bed with a night contest on April 15, that took six hours and six minutes before being won by Houston in the bottom of the 24th, 1-0.

The Series was billed as a battle between Gibson and McLain, but McLain simply could not keep up with the Cardinals' ace. Gibson set a record by whiffing 17 Tigers in defeating McLain 4-0 in game one, and Denny was bombed out in a 10-1, fourth-game Gibson victory. The Cards took three of the first four games, but Mickey Lolich won his second in game five, and McLain finally made the victory column by defeating Washburn in game six.

Gibson seemed unbeatable in game seven as he and Lolich locked horns in a pitcher's duel through six innings. With two Tigers on base in the seventh, Jim Northrup lined a shot to center which Curt Flood misjudged into a triple, breaking Gibson's momentum and allowing the Tigers to go on to a decisive 4-1 victory. Although Norm Cash, Al Kaline, Willie Horton, and Jim Northrup had good games at bat for the Tigers, the spotlight fell on the triumphs of Lolich and Gibson and the failure of McLain.

In December, a minor bombshell was dropped when Commissioner William Eckert was fired by the club owners. Eckert's lack of decisive leadership and poor public image led the owners to seek a younger man to lead the game through the coming years of change. The man finally selected was 42-year-old Bowie Kuhn, a Wall Street attorney who would preside over baseball's first attempt at divisional play—a move prompted by both leagues expanding to twelve teams. Although the regular 162-game schedule would be kept intact, the new set up facilitated an uneven amount of games to be played. Each league was divided into two, six-team divisions, and while teams in the same division played each other 18 times, only 12 games were scheduled with each team in the other division. The new divisional play also added another exciting, but controversial feature. Whereas finishing first was once good enough to break open the champagne and prepare for the World Series, divisional winners now had to meet in a best, three-of-five championship series to decide the pennant winner.

WORLD SERIES — DETROIT (AL) 4 ST. LOUIS (NL) 3

LINE SCORES

TEAM	1	2	3	4	5	6	7	8	9	10	11	12	R	H	E

Game 1 October 2 at St. Louis
| DET (AL) | 0 | 0 | 0 | 0 | 0 | 0 | 0 | 0 | 0 | | | | 0 | 5 | 3 |
| STL (NL) | 0 | 0 | 0 | 3 | 0 | 0 | 1 | 0 | X | | | | 4 | 6 | 0 |

McLain, Dobson (6), McMahon (8)   Gibson

Game 2 October 3 at St. Louis
| DET | 0 | 1 | 1 | 0 | 0 | 3 | 1 | 0 | 2 | | | | 8 | 13 | 1 |
| STL | 0 | 0 | 0 | 0 | 0 | 1 | 0 | 0 | 0 | | | | 1 | 6 | 1 |

Lolich   Briles, Carlton (6), Willis (7), Hoerner (9)

Game 3 October 5 at Detroit
| STL | 0 | 0 | 0 | 0 | 4 | 0 | 3 | 0 | 0 | | | | 7 | 13 | 0 |
| DET | 0 | 0 | 2 | 0 | 1 | 0 | 0 | 0 | 0 | | | | 3 | 4 | 0 |

Washburn, Hoerner (6)   Wilson, Dobson (5), McMahon (6), Patterson (7), Hiller (8)

Game 4 October 6 at Detroit
| STL | 2 | 0 | 2 | 2 | 0 | 0 | 0 | 4 | 0 | | | | 10 | 13 | 0 |
| DET | 0 | 0 | 0 | 1 | 0 | 0 | 0 | 0 | 0 | | | | 1 | 5 | 4 |

Gibson   McLain, Sparma (3), Patterson (4), Lasher (6), Hiller (8), Dobson (8)

Game 5 October 7 at Detroit
| STL | 3 | 0 | 0 | 0 | 0 | 0 | 0 | 0 | 0 | | | | 3 | 9 | 0 |
| DET | 0 | 0 | 0 | 2 | 0 | 0 | 3 | 0 | X | | | | 5 | 9 | 1 |

Briles, Hoerner (7), Willis (7)   Lolich

Game 6 October 9 at St. Louis
| DET | 0 | 2 | 10 | 0 | 1 | 0 | 0 | 0 | 0 | | | | 13 | 12 | 1 |
| STL | 0 | 0 | 0 | 0 | 0 | 0 | 0 | 1 | 0 | | | | 1 | 9 | 1 |

McLain   Washburn, Jaster (3), Willis (3), Hughes (3), Carlton (4), Granger (7), Nelson (9)

Game 7 October 10 at St. Louis
| DET | 0 | 0 | 0 | 0 | 0 | 0 | 3 | 0 | 1 | | | | 4 | 8 | 1 |
| STL | 0 | 0 | 0 | 0 | 0 | 0 | 0 | 0 | 1 | | | | 1 | 5 | 0 |

Lolich   Gibson

COMPOSITE BATTING

NAME	POS	G	AB	R	H	2B	3B	HR	RBI	BA
Detroit (AL) Totals		7	231	34	56	4	3	8	33	.242
Kaline	OF	7	29	6	11	2	0	2	8	.379
Northrup	OF	7	28	4	7	0	1	2	8	.250
Stanley	SS-OF	7	28	4	6	0	1	0	0	.214
McAuliffe	2B	7	27	5	6	0	0	1	3	.222
Cash	1B	7	26	5	10	0	0	1	5	.385
Freehan	C	7	24	0	2	1	0	0	2	.083
Horton	OF	7	23	6	7	1	1	1	3	.304
Wert	3B	6	17	1	2	0	0	0	2	.118
Lolich	P	3	12	2	3	0	0	1	2	.250
McLain	P	3	6	0	0	0	0	0	0	.000
Mathews	3B	2	3	0	1	0	0	0	0	.333
Matchick	PH	3	3	0	0	0	0	0	0	.000
Price	PH	2	2	0	0	0	0	0	0	.000
Comer	PH	1	1	0	1	0	0	0	0	1.000
Brown	PH	1	1	0	0	0	0	0	0	.000
Wilson	P	1	1	0	0	0	0	0	0	.000
Oyler	SS	4	0	0	0	0	0	0	0	—
Tracewski	3B	2	0	1	0	0	0	0	0	—

Dobson P 0-0, Hiller P 0-0, McMahon P 0-0, Lasher P 0-0, Patterson P 0-0, Sparma P 0-0

NAME	POS	G	AB	R	H	2B	3B	HR	RBI	BA
St. Louis (NL) Totals		7	239	27	61	7	3	7	27	.255
Shannon	3B	7	29	3	8	1	0	1	4	.276
Brock	OF	7	28	6	13	3	1	2	5	.464
Flood	OF	7	28	4	8	1	0	0	2	.286
Cepeda	1B	7	28	2	7	0	0	2	6	.250
McCarver	C	7	27	3	9	0	2	1	4	.333
Javier	2B	7	27	1	9	1	0	0	3	.333
Maxvill	SS	7	22	1	0	0	0	0	0	.000
Maris	OF	6	19	5	3	1	0	0	1	.158
Gibson	P	3	8	2	1	0	0	1	2	.125
Davis	OF	2	7	0	0	0	0	0	0	.000
Briles	P	2	4	0	0	0	0	0	0	.000
Gagliano	PH	3	3	0	0	0	0	0	0	.000
Washburn	P	2	3	0	0	0	0	0	0	.000
Hoerner	P	3	2	0	1	0	0	0	0	.500
Ricketts	PH	1	1	0	1	0	0	0	0	1.000
Spiezio	PH	1	1	0	1	0	0	0	0	1.000
Edwards	PH	1	1	0	0	0	0	0	0	.000
Tolan	PH	1	1	0	0	0	0	0	0	.000

Schofield SS 0-0, Willis P 0-0, Carlton P 0-0, Granger P 0-0, Hughes P 0-0, Nelson P 0-0, Jaster P 0-0

COMPOSITE PITCHING

NAME	G	IP	H	BB	SO	W	L	SV	ERA
Detroit (AL) Totals	7	62	61	21	40	4	3	0	3.48
Lolich	3	27	20	6	21	3	0	0	1.67
McLain	3	16.2	18	4	13	1	2	0	3.24
Dobson	3	4.2	5	1	0	0	0	0	3.86
Wilson	1	4.1	4	6	3	0	1	0	6.23
Patterson	2	3	1	1	0	0	0	0	0.00
Lasher	1	2	1	0	1	0	0	0	0.00
Hiller	2	2	6	3	1	0	0	0	13.50
McMahon	2	2	4	0	1	0	0	0	13.50
Sparma	1	0.1	2	0	0	0	0	0	54.00

NAME	G	IP	H	BB	SO	W	L	SV	ERA
St. Louis (NL) Totals	7	62	56	27	59	3	4	1	4.65
Gibson	3	27	18	4	35	2	1	0	1.67
Briles	2	11.1	13	4	7	0	1	0	5.56
Washburn	2	7.1	7	7	6	1	1	0	9.82
Hoerner	3	4.2	5	5	3	0	1	1	3.86
Willis	3	4.1	2	4	3	0	0	0	8.31
Carlton	2	4	7	1	3	0	0	0	6.75
Granger	1	2	0	1	1	0	0	0	0.00
Nelson	1	1	0	0	1	0	0	0	0.00
Hughes	1	0.1	2	0	0	0	0	0	0.00
Jaster	1	0	2	1	0	0	0	0	—

DETROIT — 1st 103-59 .636 — MAYO SMITH

NAME	G by Pos	B	AGE	G	AB	R	H	2B	3B	HR	RBI	BB	SO	SB	BA	SA
TOTALS			28	164	5490	671	1292	190	39	185	640	521	964	26	.235	.385
Norm Cash	1B117	L	33	127	411	50	108	15	1	25	63	39	70	1	.263	.487
Dick McAuliffe	2B148, SS5	L	28	151	570	95	142	24	10	16	56	82	99	8	.249	.411
Ray Oyler	SS111	R	29	111	215	13	29	6	1	1	12	20	59	0	.135	.186
Don Wert	3B150	R	29	150	536	44	107	15	4	12	37	37	79	0	.200	.299
Jim Northrup	OF151	L	28	154	580	76	153	29	7	21	90	50	87	4	.264	.447
Mickey Stanley	OF130, 1B15, SS9, 2B1	R	25	153	583	88	151	16	6	11	60	42	57	4	.259	.364
Willie Horton	OF139	R	25	143	512	68	146	20	2	36	85	49	110	0	.285	.543
Bill Freehan	C138, 1B21, OF1	R	26	155	540	73	142	24	2	25	84	65	64	0	.263	.454
Al Kaline	OF74, 1B22	R	33	102	327	49	94	14	1	10	53	55	39	6	.287	.428
Dick Tracewski	SS51, 3B16, 2B14	R	33	90	212	30	33	3	1	4	15	24	51	3	.156	.236
Tom Matchick	SS59, 2B13, 1B6	L	24	80	227	18	46	6	2	3	14	10	46	0	.203	.286
Gates Brown	OF17, 1B1	L	29	67	92	15	34	7	2	6	15	12	4	0	.370	.685
Jim Price	C42	R	26	64	132	12	23	4	0	3	13	13	14	0	.174	.273
Wayne Comer	OF27, C1	R	24	48	48	8	6	0	1	1	3	2	7	0	.125	.229
Earl Wilson	P34	R	33	40	88	9	20	0	1	7	17	2	35	0	.227	.489
Eddie Mathews (XJ)	3B6, 1B6	L	36	31	52	4	11	0	0	3	8	5	12	0	.212	.385
Dave Campbell	2B5	R	26	9	8	1	1	0	0	1	2	1	3	0	.125	.500
Lenny Green	OF2	L	34	6	4	0	1	0	0	0	0	1	0	0	.250	.250
Bob Christian	1B1, OF1	R	22	3	3	0	1	1	0	0	0	0	0	0	.333	.667

NAME	T	AGE	W	L	PCT	SV	G	GS	CG	IP	H	BB	SO	SHO	ERA
TOTALS		28	103	59	.636	29	164	164	59	1490	1180	486	1115	19	2.71
Denny McLain	R	24	31	6	.838	0	41	41	28	336	241	63	280	6	1.96
Mickey Lolich	L	27	17	9	.654	0	39	32	8	220	178	65	197	4	3.19
Earl Wilson	R	33	13	12	.520	0	34	33	10	224	192	65	168	3	2.85
Joe Sparma	R	26	10	10	.500	0	34	31	7	182	169	77	110	1	3.71
John Hiller	L	25	9	6	.600	2	39	12	4	128	92	51	78	1	2.39
Fred Lasher	R	26	5	1	.833	5	34	0	0	49	37	22	32	0	3.31
Pat Dobson	R	26	5	8	.385	7	47	10	2	125	89	48	93	1	2.66
Jon Warden	L	21	4	1	.800	3	28	0	0	37	30	15	25	0	3.65
2 Don McMahon	R	38	3	7	.750	1	20	0	0	36	22	10	33	0	2.00
1 Dennis Ribant	R	26	2	2	.500	1	14	0	0	24	20	10	7	0	2.25
Daryl Patterson	R	24	2	3	.400	7	38	1	0	68	53	27	49	0	2.12
Les Cain	L	20	1	0	1.000	0	8	4	0	24	25	20	13	0	3.00
3 John Wyatt	R	33	1	0	1.000	2	22	0	0	30	26	11	25	0	2.40
2 Roy Face	R	40	0	0	—	0	2	0	0	1	2	1	1	0	0.00
Jim Rooker	R	25	0	0	—	0	2	0	0	5	4	1	4	0	3.60

BALTIMORE — 2nd 91-71 .562 12 — HANK BAUER 43-37 .538 — EARL WEAVER 48-34 .585

NAME	G by Pos	B	AGE	G	AB	R	H	2B	3B	HR	RBI	BB	SO	SB	BA	SA
TOTALS			27	162	5275	579	1187	215	28	133	534	570	1019	78	.225	.352
Boog Powell	1B149	L	26	154	550	60	137	21	1	22	85	73	97	7	.249	.411
Dave Johnson	2B127, SS34	R	25	145	504	50	122	24	4	9	56	44	80	7	.242	.359
Mark Belanger	SS145	R	24	145	472	40	98	13	0	2	21	40	114	10	.208	.248
Brooks Robinson	3B162	R	31	162	608	65	154	36	6	17	75	44	55	1	.253	.416
Frank Robinson	OF117, 1B3	R	32	130	421	69	113	27	1	15	52	73	84	11	.268	.444
Paul Blair	OF132, 3B1	R	24	141	441	48	89	22	1	7	38	37	60	4	.211	.318
Curt Blefary	OF92, C40, 1B12	L	24	137	451	50	90	8	1	15	39	65	66	6	.200	.322
Andy Etchebarren (BG)	C70	R	25	74	189	20	44	11	2	5	20	19	46	0	.233	.392
Don Buford	OF65, 2B58, 3B1	B	31	130	426	65	120	13	4	15	46	57	46	27	.282	.437
Dave May	OF61	L	24	84	152	15	29	6	3	0	7	9	29	3	.191	.270
Curt Motton	OF54	R	27	83	217	27	43	7	0	8	25	31	43	1	.198	.341
Ellie Hendricks	C53	L	27	79	183	19	37	8	1	7	23	19	51	0	.202	.372
2 Fred Valentine	OF26	B	33	47	91	9	17	3	2	2	5	7	20	0	.187	.330
Larry Haney	C32	R	25	38	89	5	21	3	1	1	5	0	19	0	.236	.326
Merv Rettenmund	OF23	R	25	31	64	10	19	5	0	2	7	18	20	1	.297	.469
Chico Fernandez	SS7, 2B4	R	29	24	18	0	2	0	0	0	0	1	3	0	.111	.111
Mike Fiore	1B5, OF1	L	23	6	17	2	1	0	0	0	0	4	4	0	.059	.059
Bobby Floyd	SS4	R	24	5	9	0	1	0	0	0	0	1	2	0	.111	.222

NAME	T	AGE	W	L	PCT	SV	G	GS	CG	IP	H	BB	SO	SHO	ERA
TOTALS		27	91	71	.562	31	162	162	53	1451	1111	502	1044	16	2.66
Dave McNally	L	25	22	10	.688	0	35	35	18	273	175	55	202	5	1.95
Jim Hardin	R	24	18	13	.581	0	35	35	16	244	188	70	160	2	2.51
Tom Phoebus	R	26	15	15	.500	0	36	36	9	241	186	105	193	3	2.61
Dave Leonhard	R	27	7	7	.500	1	28	18	5	126	95	57	61	2	3.14
Pete Richert (MS)	L	28	6	3	.667	6	36	0	0	62	51	12	47	0	3.48
Gene Brabender	R	26	6	7	.462	3	37	15	3	125	116	48	92	2	3.31
Eddie Watt	R	27	5	5	.500	11	59	0	0	83	63	35	72	0	2.28
Roger Nelson	R	24	4	3	.571	1	19	6	0	71	49	26	70	0	2.41
Moe Drabowsky	R	32	4	4	.500	7	45	0	0	61	35	25	46	0	1.92
Wally Bunker	R	23	2	1	.667	0	18	10	2	71	59	14	44	1	2.41
John Morris	L	26	2	0	1.000	0	19	0	0	32	19	17	22	0	2.53
John O'Donoghue	L	28	0	0	—	2	16	0	0	22	34	7	11	0	6.14
Fred Beene	R	25	0	0	—	0	1	0	0	1	2	1	1	0	9.00
Mike Adamson	R	20	0	2	.000	0	2	2	0	8	9	4	4	0	9.00
1 Bruce Howard	R	25	0	0	—	0	10	5	0	31	30	26	19	0	3.77
Jim Palmer (SA) 22															

CLEVELAND — 3rd 86-75 .534 16.5 — AL DARK

NAME	G by Pos	B	AGE	G	AB	R	H	2B	3B	HR	RBI	BB	SO	SB	BA	SA
TOTALS			28	162	5416	516	1266	210	36	75	476	427	858	115	.234	.327
Tony Horton	1B128	R	23	133	477	57	119	29	3	14	59	34	56	3	.249	.411
Vern Fuller	2B73, 3B23, SS4	R	24	97	244	14	59	8	2	0	18	24	49	2	.242	.291
Larry Brown	SS154	R	28	154	495	43	116	18	3	6	35	43	46	1	.234	.319
Max Alvis	3B128	R	30	131	452	38	101	17	3	8	37	41	91	5	.223	.327
Tommy Harper	OF115, 2B2	R	27	130	235	26	51	15	2	6	26	26	56	11	.217	.374
Jose Cardenal	OF153	R	24	157	583	78	150	27	7	7	44	39	74	40	.257	.353
Lee Maye	OF80, 1B1	L	33	109	299	20	84	13	2	4	26	15	24	0	.281	.378
Joe Azcue	C97	R	28	115	357	23	100	10	0	4	42	28	33	1	.280	.342
Duke Sims	C84, 1B31, OF4	L	27	122	361	48	90	21	0	11	44	62	68	1	.249	.399
C. Salmon	2B45, 3B18, SS15, OF13, 1B11	R	27	103	276	24	59	8	1	3	12	12	30	7	.214	.283
Dave Nelson	2B59, SS14	R	24	88	189	26	44	4	5	0	19	17	35	23	.233	.307
2 Russ Snyder	OF54, 1B1	L	34	68	217	30	61	8	2	2	23	25	21	1	.281	.364
2 Lou Johnson	OF57	R	33	65	202	25	52	11	1	5	23	9	24	6	.257	.396
2 Jimmie Hall	OF29	L	30	53	111	4	22	4	0	1	8	10	19	1	.198	.261
1 Vic Davalillo	OF49	L	31	51	180	15	43	2	3	2	13	3	19	8	.239	.317
Billy Harris	2B27, 3B10, SS1	R	24	38	94	10	20	5	1	0	3	8	22	2	.213	.287
1 Leon Wagner	OF10	L	34	38	49	5	9	4	0	0	6	6	6	0	.184	.265
1 Jose Vidal	OF26, 1B1	R	28	37	54	5	9	0	0	2	5	2	15	3	.167	.278
1 Willie Smith	1B7, P2, OF1	L	29	33	42	1	6	2	0	0	5	3	14	0	.143	.190
Richie Scheinblum	OF16	B	25	19	55	3	12	5	0	0	5	5	8	0	.218	.309
Ken Suarez	C12, 2B1, 3B1, OF1	R	25	17	10	1	1	0	0	0	1	0	1	0	.100	.100
Lou Klimchock	3B4, 1B1, 2B1	L	28	11	15	0	2	0	0	0	1	0	3	0	.133	.133
Lou Piniella	OF2	R	24	6	5	1	0	0	0	0	1	0	0	0	.000	.000
Eddie Leon	SS6	R	22	6	1	0	0	0	0	0	0	0	1	0	.000	.000
Russ Nagelson		L	23	5	3	0	1	0	0	0	0	2	1	0	.333	.333
Ray Fosse	C1	R	21	1											—	—

NAME	T	AGE	W	L	PCT	SV	G	GS	CG	IP	H	BB	SO	SHO	ERA
TOTALS		27	86	75	.534	32	162	162	48	1464	1087	540	1157	23	2.66
Luis Tiant	R	27	21	9	.700	0	34	32	19	258	152	73	264	9	1.60
Sam McDowell	L	25	15	14	.517	0	38	37	11	269	181	110	283	3	1.81
Stan Williams	R	31	13	11	.542	9	44	24	6	194	163	51	147	2	2.51
Sonny Siebert	R	31	12	10	.545	0	31	30	8	206	145	88	146	4	2.97
Steve Hargan	R	25	8	15	.348	0	32	27	4	158	139	81	78	2	4.16
2 Vicente Romo	R	25	5	3	.625	12	40	1	0	83	43	32	54	0	1.63
Mike Paul	L	23	5	8	.385	0	36	7	0	92	72	35	87	0	3.91
Eddie Fisher	R	31	4	2	.667	4	54	0	0	95	87	17	42	0	2.84
Hal Kurtz	R	24	1	0	1.000	0	38	0	0	38	37	15	16	0	5.21
Billy Rohr	L	23	1	0	1.000	1	17	0	0	18	18	10	5	0	7.00
Horacio Pina	R	23	1	1	.500	2	12	3	0	31	24	15	24	0	1.74
Rob Gardner	L	23	0	0	—	0	5	0	0	3	5	2	6	0	9.00
Mike Hedlund	R	21	0	0	—	0	3	0	0	3	6	4	2	0	9.00
Darrell Sutherland	R	26	0	0	—	0	3	0	0	6	4	2	0	0	9.00
1 Willie Smith	R	29	0	0	—	0	2	0	0	3	6	3	2	0	3.60
Steve Bailey	R	26	0	1	.000	0	3	0	0	3	5	3	0	0	3.60
Tommy Gramly	R	23	0	0	—	0	1	0	0	3	1	2	1	0	3.00
Tom Kelley (EJ) 24															

BOSTON — 4th 86-76 .531 17 — DICK WILLIAMS

NAME	G by Pos	B	AGE	G	AB	R	H	2B	3B	HR	RBI	BB	SO	SB	BA	SA
TOTALS			27	162	5303	614	1253	207	17	125	558	582	974	76	.236	.352
George Scott	1B112, 3B6	R	24	124	350	23	60	14	0	3	25	26	88	3	.171	.237
Mike Andrews	2B139, SS4, 3B1	R	24	147	536	77	145	22	1	7	45	81	57	3	.271	.354
Rico Petrocelli	SS117, 1B1	R	25	123	406	41	95	17	2	12	46	51	73	0	.234	.374
Joe Foy	3B147, OF3	R	25	150	515	65	116	18	2	10	60	84	91	26	.225	.326
Ken Harrelson	OF132, 1B19	R	26	150	535	79	147	17	4	35	109	69	90	2	.275	.518
Reggie Smith	OF155	B	23	155	558	78	148	37	5	15	69	64	77	22	.265	.430
Carl Yastrzemski	OF155, 1B3	L	28	157	539	90	162	32	2	23	74	119	90	13	.301	.495
Russ Gibson	C74, 1B1	R	29	76	231	15	52	11	1	3	20	8	38	1	.225	.320
Dalton Jones	1B56, 2B26, 3B8	L	24	111	354	38	83	13	0	5	29	17	53	1	.234	.314
Jerry Adair	SS46, 2B12, 3B7, 1B1	R	31	74	208	18	45	10	0	2	12	9	28	0	.216	.250
Jose Tartabull (GJ)	OF43	L	29	72	139	24	39	6	0	0	6	8	5	2	.281	.324
Elston Howard	C68	R	39	71	203	22	49	4	0	5	18	22	45	1	.241	.335
Joe Lahoud	OF25	L	21	29	78	5	15	1	0	1	6	16	16	0	.192	.244
Russ Nixon	C27	L	33	29	85	1	13	2	0	0	6	7	13	0	.153	.176
Norm Siebern	1B2, OF2	L	34	27	30	0	2	0	0	0	0	6	7	0	.067	.067
2 Floyd Robinson	OF10	L	32	23	24	1	3	0	0	0	2	3	4	1	.125	.125
1 Gene Oliver	C10, OF1	R	32	16	35	2	5	0	0	1	4	4	12	0	.143	.143
George Thomas	OF9	R	30	12	10	3	2	1	0	0	1	1	3	1	.200	.500
Luis Alvarado	SS11	R	19	11	46	4	6	2	0	1	1	1	11	0	.130	.174
Jerry Moses	C6	R	21	6	6	0	2	0	0	0	1	0	3	0	.333	.667
Tony Conigliaro (IL) 23																

NAME	T	AGE	W	L	PCT	SV	G	GS	CG	IP	H	BB	SO	SHO	ERA
TOTALS		27	86	76	.531	31	162	162	55	1447	1303	523	972	17	3.33
Ray Culp	R	26	16	6	.727	0	35	30	11	216	166	82	190	6	2.92
Dick Ellsworth	L	28	16	7	.696	0	31	28	10	196	196	37	106	1	3.03
Gary Bell	R	31	11	11	.500	1	35	27	9	199	177	68	103	3	3.12
Jose Santiago (EJ)	R	27	9	4	.692	0	18	18	7	124	96	42	86	2	2.25
Sparky Lyle	R	23	6	1	.857	11	49	0	0	66	67	14	52	0	2.73
2 Juan Pizarro	L	31	6	8	.429	2	19	12	6	108	97	44	84	0	3.58
Jim Lonborg (KJ)	R	26	6	10	.375	0	23	17	4	113	89	59	73	1	4.30
Lee Stange	R	31	5	5	.500	12	50	2	1	103	89	25	53	0	3.93
Gary Waslewski	R	26	4	7	.364	2	34	11	2	105	108	40	59	0	3.69
Bill Landis (MS)	L	25	3	3	.500	3	38	1	0	68	61	40	59	1	3.15
Jerry Stephenson	R	24	2	3	.400	0	23	7	2	69	81	42	51	0	5.61
1 John Wyatt	R	33	1	2	.333	0	11	0	0	11	9	11	6	0	4.09
Dave Morehead	R	25	1	4	.200	0	9	3	0	55	52	27	40	0	2.45
Darrell Brandon	R	27	0	0	—	0	13	0	0	19	19	9	10	0	6.23
Garry Roggenburk (SA)	L	28	0	0	—	0	2	0	0	4	4	2	4	0	2.25
Fred Wenz	R	26	0	0	—	0	2	0	0	3	1	2	3	0	2.25

NEW YORK — 5th 83-79 .512 20 — RALPH HOUK

NAME	G by Pos	B	AGE	G	AB	R	H	2B	3B	HR	RBI	BB	SO	SB	BA	SA
TOTALS			28	164	5310	536	1137	154	34	109	501	566	958	90	.214	.318
Mickey Mantle	1B131	B	36	144	435	57	103	14	1	18	54	106	97	6	.237	.398
Horace Clarke	2B139	B	28	148	579	52	133	16	1	2	23	26	46	20	.230	.254
Tom Tresh	SS119, OF27	B	30	152	507	60	99	18	3	11	52	76	97	10	.195	.308
Bobby Cox	3B132	R	27	135	437	33	100	15	1	7	41	41	85	2	.229	.316
Bill Robinson	OF98	R	25	107	342	34	82	16	7	6	40	24	55	8	.240	.380
Joe Pepitone	OF92, 1B12	L	27	108	380	41	93	9	3	15	56	37	45	8	.245	.403
Roy White	OF154	B	24	159	577	89	154	20	7	17	62	73	50	20	.267	.414
Jake Gibbs	C121	L	29	124	423	31	90	12	3	3	29	27	67	9	.213	.277
Andy Kosco	OF95, 1B28	R	26	131	466	47	112	19	1	15	59	16	72	0	.240	.382
Dick Howser	2B29, 3B2, SS1	R	32	85	150	24	23	2	1	0	3	35	17	0	.153	.180
Gene Michael	SS43, P1	R	30	61	116	8	23	3	0	1	8	2	23	3	.198	.250
Frank Fernandez	C45, OF4	R	25	51	135	15	23	6	1	7	30	35	50	1	.170	.385
Ruben Amaro	SS23, 1B22	R	32	47	41	3	5	1	0	0	1	4	12	0	.122	.146
Charley Smith (KJ)	3B13	R	30	46	70	2	16	1	0	1	7	1	16	0	.229	.357
2 Rocky Colavito	OF28, P1	R	34	39	91	13	20	2	2	3	13	14	17	0	.220	.451
Steve Whitaker	OF14	L	25	28	60	3	7	2	0	0	3	4	19	0	.117	.150
Mike Ferraro	3B22	R	23	23	87	5	14	0	1	0	7	1	18	0	.161	.184
Ellie Rodriguez	C9	R	22	9	24	1	5	0	0	0	2	1	0	0	.208	.208
Tony Solaita	1B1	L	21	1	1	0	0	0	0	0	0	0	1	0	.000	.000
Bobby Murcer (MS) 22, Jerry Kenney (MS) 23																

NAME	T	AGE	W	L	PCT	SV	G	GS	CG	IP	H	BB	SO	SHO	ERA
TOTALS		28	83	79	.512	27	164	164	45	1467	1308	424	831	14	2.79
Mel Stottlemyre	R	26	21	12	.636	0	36	36	19	279	243	65	140	6	2.45
Stan Bahnsen	R	23	17	12	.586	0	37	34	10	267	216	68	162	1	2.06
Fritz Peterson	R	26	12	11	.522	0	36	27	6	212	187	29	115	2	2.63
Steve Barber	L	30	6	5	.545	0	29	19	3	128	127	64	87	1	3.23
Joe Verbanic	R	25	6	7	.462	4	40	11	2	97	104	41	40	1	3.15
1 Bill Monbouquette	R	31	5	7	.417	0	17	11	2	89	92	13	32	0	4.45
2 Lindy McDaniel	R	32	4	1	.800	10	24	0	0	51	30	12	43	0	1.76
Al Downing (SJ)	L	27	3	3	.500	0	15	1	1	61	54	20	40	0	3.54
Dooley Womack	R	28	3	7	.300	2	45	0	0	62	53	29	27	0	3.19
Steve Hamilton	L	34	2	2	.500	11	40	0	0	51	37	13	42	0	2.12
2 Rocky Colavito	R	34	1	0	1.000	0	1	0	0	1	0	0	1	0	0.00
Thad Tillotson	R	28	0	1	.000	0	10	1	0	20	21	9	11	0	4.50
Jim Bouton	R	29	1	1	.500	0	12	1	0	44	49	9	24	0	3.68
Fred Talbot	R	27	1	1	.500	0	11	3	0	28	20	17	15	0	3.36
John Cumberland	L	21	0	0	—	0	1	0	0	7	8	6	5	0	9.00
Gene Michael	R	30	0	0	—	0	1	0	0	2	2	1	0	0	0.00
2 John Wyatt	R	33	0	2	.000	0	7	0	0	8	9	6	5	0	2.25

OAKLAND 6th 82-80 .506 21 BOB KENNEDY

NAME	G by Pos	B	AGE	G	AB	R	H	2B	3B	HR	RBI	BB	SO	SB	BA	SA
TOTALS			25	163	5406	569	1300	192	40	94	522	472	1022	147	.240	.343
Danny Cater	1B121, OF20, 2B1	R	28	147	504	53	146	28	3	6	62	35	43	8	.290	.393
John Donaldson	2B98, 3B5, SS1	L	25	127	363	37	80	9	2	2	27	45	44	5	.220	.273
Bert Campaneris	SS155, OF3	R	26	159	642	87	177	25	9	4	38	50	69	62	.276	.361
Sal Bando	3B162, OF1	R	24	162	605	67	152	25	5	9	67	51	78	13	.251	.354
Reggie Jackson	OF151	L	22	154	553	82	138	13	6	29	74	50	171	14	.250	.452
Rick Monday	OF144	L	22	148	482	56	132	24	7	8	49	72	143	14	.274	.402
Mike Hershberger	OF90	R	28	99	246	23	67	9	2	5	32	21	22	8	.272	.386
Dave Duncan	C79	R	22	82	246	15	47	4	0	7	28	25	68	1	.191	.293
Jim Gosger	OF64	L	25	88	150	7	27	1	1	0	5	17	21	4	.180	.200
Dick Green	2B61, 3B1, C1	R	27	76	202	19	47	6	0	6	18	21	41	3	.233	.351
Joe Rudi	OF56	R	26	68	181	10	32	5	1	1	12	12	32	1	.177	.232
Jim Pagliaroni (BW)	C63	R	30	66	199	19	49	4	0	6	20	24	42	0	.246	.357
Ramon Webster	1B55	L	25	66	196	17	42	11	1	3	23	12	24	3	.214	.327
1 Floyd Robinson	OF18	L	32	53	81	5	20	5	0	1	14	4	10	0	.247	.346
Ted Kubiak (MS)	2B24, SS12	B	26	48	120	10	30	5	2	0	8	8	18	1	.250	.325
Catfish Hunter	P36	R	22	39	82	9	19	3	0	1	8	0	19	0	.232	.305
Joe Keough	OF29, 1B1	R	22	34	98	7	21	2	1	2	18	8	11	1	.214	.316
Phil Roof (AJ)	C32	R	27	34	64	5	12	0	0	1	2	2	15	1	.188	.234
Rene Lachemann	C16	R	23	19	60	3	9	1	0	0	4	1	11	0	.150	.167

Allan Lewis 26 B 1-4, Tony LaRussa 23 R 1-3

NAME	T	AGE	W	L	PCT	SV	G	GS	CG	IP	H	BB	SO	SHO	ERA
		24	82	80	.506	29	163	163	45	1456	1220	505	997	18	2.94
Blue Moon Odom	R	23	16	10	.615	0	32	31	9	231	179	98	143	4	2.45
Catfish Hunter	R	22	13	13	.500	0	36	34	11	234	210	69	172	5	3.35
Jim Nash	R	23	13	13	.500	0	34	33	12	229	185	55	169	6	2.28
Chuck Dobson	R	24	12	14	.462	0	34	34	11	225	197	80	168	3	3.00
Lew Krausse	R	25	10	11	.476	4	36	25	2	185	147	62	105	0	3.11
Diego Segui	R	30	6	5	.545	6	52	0	0	83	51	32	72	0	2.39
Paul Lindblad	L	26	4	3	.571	2	47	1	0	56	51	14	42	0	2.41
Jack Aker	R	27	4	4	.500	11	64	0	0	75	72	33	44	0	4.08
Ed Sprague	R	22	3	4	.429	4	47	1	0	69	51	34	34	0	3.26
Tony Pierce	L	22	1	2	.333	1	17	3	0	33	39	10	16	0	3.82
Warren Bogle	L	21	0	0	—	0	16	1	0	23	26	8	26	0	4.30
Rollie Fingers	R	21	0	0	—	0	1	0	0	1	4	1	0	0	36.00
George Lauzerique	R	20	0	0	—	0	1	0	0	1	1	1	0	0	0.00
Ken Sanders	R	26	0	1	.000	0	11				8	6	0		3.27

MINNESOTA 7th 79-83 .488 24 CAL ERMER

NAME	G by Pos	B	AGE	G	AB	R	H	2B	3B	HR	RBI	BB	SO	SB	BA	SA
TOTALS			28	162	5373	562	1274	207	41	105	522	445	966	98	.237	.350
Rich Reese	1B87, OF15	L	26	126	332	40	86	15	2	4	28	18	36	3	.259	.352
Rod Carew	2B117, SS4	L	22	127	461	46	126	27	2	1	42	26	71	12	.273	.347
Jackie Hernandez	SS79, 1B1	R	27	83	199	13	35	3	0	2	17	9	52	5	.176	.221
Tovar	OF78, 3B75, SS35, 2B18, 1B, C, P=1	R	27	157	613	89	167	31	6	6	47	34	41	35	.272	.372
Tony Oliva	OF126	L	27	128	470	54	136	24	5	18	68	45	61	10	.289	.477
Ted Uhlaender	OF129	L	28	140	488	52	138	21	5	7	52	28	46	16	.283	.389
Bob Allison	OF117, 1B17	R	33	145	469	63	116	16	8	22	52	52	98	9	.247	.456
Johnny Roseboro	C117	L	35	135	380	31	82	12	0	8	39	46	57	2	.216	.311
Ron Clark	3B52, SS43, 2B10	R	25	104	227	14	42	5	1	1	13	16	44	3	.185	.229
Harmon Killebrew (GJ)	1B77, 3B11	R	32	100	295	40	62	7	2	17	40	70	70	0	.210	.420
Frank Quilici	2B48, 3B40, SS6, 1B1	R	29	97	229	22	56	11	4	1	22	21	45	0	.245	.341
Rich Rollins	3B56	R	30	93	203	14	49	5	0	6	30	10	34	3	.241	.355
Jim Holt	OF38, 1B1	L	24	70	106	9	22	2	1	0	9	6	20	1	.208	.245
Frank Kostro	OF24, 1B5	R	30	63	108	9	26	4	1	0	9	6	20	0	.241	.296
Bruce Look	C41	L	25	59	118	7	29	4	0	0	9	24	20	0	.246	.280
Rick Renick	SS40	R	24	42	97	16	21	5	2	3	13	9	42	0	.216	.402
Jerry Zimmerman	C24	R	33	24	45	3	5	1	0	0	2	3	10	0	.111	.133
Graig Nettles	OF16, 3B5, 1B3	L	23	22	76	13	17	2	1	5	8	7	20	0	.224	.474
Pat Kelly	OF10	L	23	12	35	2	4	2	0	1	2	3	10	1	.114	.257
George Mitterwald	C10	R	23	11	34	1	7	1	0	1	6	3	8	0	.206	.235

NAME	T	AGE	W	L	PCT	SV	G	GS	CG	IP	H	BB	SO	SHO	ERA
		29	79	83	.488	29	162	162	46	1433	1224	414	996	14	2.89
Dean Chance	R	27	16	16	.500	1	43	39	15	292	224	63	234	6	2.53
Jim Kaat (SA)	L	29	14	12	.538	0	33	29	9	208	192	40	130	2	2.94
Jim Merritt	L	24	12	16	.429	1	38	34	11	238	207	52	181	1	3.25
Dave Boswell	R	23	10	13	.435	0	34	28	7	190	148	87	143	2	3.32
Jim Perry	R	32	8	6	.571	1	32	18	3	139	113	26	69	2	2.27
Ron Perranoski	L	32	8	7	.533	6	66	0	0	87	86	38	65	0	3.10
Jim Roland	L	25	4	1	.800	0	28	4	1	62	55	24	36	0	3.48
Al Worthington	L	39	4	5	.444	18	54	0	0	76	67	32	57	0	2.72
Tom Hall	L	20	2	1	.667	0	8	4	0	30	27	12	18	0	2.40
Buzz Stephen	R	23	1	1	.500	0	2	2	0	11	11	7	4	0	4.91
Cesar Tovar	R	27	0	0	—	1	1	0	0	1	0	1	0	0	0.00
Ron Keller (MS)	R	25	0	0	.000	0	7	1	0	16	18	4	11	0	2.81
Danny Morris	R	22	0	1	.000	0	3	2	0	11	11	4	6	0	1.64
Bob Miller	R	29	0	0	.000	2	45	0	0	72	65	24	41	0	2.75

CALIFORNIA 8th (tie) 67-95 .414 36 BILL RIGNEY

NAME	G by Pos	B	AGE	G	AB	R	H	2B	3B	HR	RBI	BB	SO	SB	BA	SA
TOTALS			28	162	5331	498	1209	170	33	83	453	447	1080	62	.227	.318
Don Mincher	1B113	L	30	120	399	35	94	12	1	13	48	43	65	0	.236	.368
Bobby Knoop	2B151	R	29	152	494	48	123	20	4	3	39	35	128	3	.249	.324
Jim Fregosi	SS159	R	26	159	614	77	150	21	13	9	49	60	101	9	.244	.365
Aurelio Rodriguez (IL)	3B70, 2B2	R	20	76	223	14	54	10	1	1	16	7	36	0	.242	.309
Roger Repoz	OF114	L	27	133	375	30	90	8	1	13	54	38	83	8	.240	.371
2 Vic Davalillo	OF86	L	31	69	339	34	101	15	4	1	18	15	34	17	.298	.375
Rick Reichardt	OF148	R	25	151	534	62	136	20	3	21	73	42	118	8	.255	.421
Bob Rodgers	C87	R	29	91	258	13	49	6	0	1	14	16	48	2	.190	.225
Chuck Hinton	1B48, OF37, 3B13, 2B9	R	34	116	267	28	52	10	3	7	23	24	61	3	.195	.333
Tom Satriano	C85, 2B14, 3B11, 1B1	R	27	111	297	20	75	9	0	8	35	37	44	0	.253	.364
Ed Kirkpatrick	OF45, C4, 1B2	L	23	89	161	23	37	4	0	1	15	25	32	1	.230	.273
Bubba Morton	OF50, 3B1	R	36	81	163	13	44	6	0	1	14	18	22	0	.270	.325
Paul Schaal (FS)	3B58	R	25	60	219	22	46	7	1	2	16	29	25	1	.210	.279
1 Jimmie Hall	OF39	L	30	48	126	15	27	3	0	1	8	16	19	1	.214	.262
Jay Johnstone	OF29	L	22	41	115	11	30	4	1	0	5	7	15	0	.261	.313
1 Woodie Held	2B5, 3B5, SS5, OF3	R	36	33	45	4	5	1	0	0	5	5	15	0	.111	.133
Chuck Cottier	3B27, 2B4	R	32	33	67	2	13	4	1	0	1	2	15	0	.194	.284
Jim Spencer	1B19	L	20	19	68	2	13	1	0	0	5	3	10	0	.191	.206
Orlando McFarlane (LJ)	C9	R	30	18	31	1	9	0	0		2	0	9	0	.290	.290
Jarvis Tatum	OF11	R	21	17	51	7	9	1	0		2	3	6		.176	.196
Bobby Trevino	OF11	R	22	17	40	1	9	1	0	0	3	3		0	.225	.250
Tom Egan	C14	R	22	16	43	2	5	1	0	1	4	2	15	0	.116	.209

Winston Llenas 24 R 5-39, 2 Wayne Causey 31 L 0-11

NAME	T	AGE	W	L	PCT	SV	G	GS	CG	IP	H	BB	SO	SHO	ERA
		27	67	95	.414	31	162	162	29	1437	1234	519	869	11	3.43
George Brunet	L	33	13	17	.433	0	39	36	8	245	191	68	132	5	2.87
Clyde Wright	R	27	10	6	.625	3	41	13	2	126	123	44	71	1	3.93
Jim McGlothlin	R	24	10	15	.400	3	40	32	8	208	187	60	135	0	3.55
Sammy Ellis	R	27	9	10	.474	2	42	24	3	164	150	56	93	0	3.95
Tom Murphy	R	22	5	6	.455	0	15	15	3	99	67	28	56	0	2.18
Andy Messersmith	R	22	4	2	.667	4	28	3	2	81	44	35	74	1	2.22
Minnie Rojas (SA)	R	34	4	3	.571	6	38	0	0	55	55	15	33	0	4.25
Marty Pattin	R	25	4	4	.500	3	52	4	1	84	67	37	66	0	2.79
Jack Hamilton	R	29	3	1	.750	2	21	2	1	38	34	15	18	0	3.32
Bobby Locke	R	34	3	2	.600	2	29	0	0	36	51	13	21	0	6.50
Tom Burgmeier	L	24	1	4	.200	5	56	2	0	73	65	24	33	0	4.32
Bill Harrelson	R	22	1	6	.143	0	10	5	1	34	28	26	22	0	5.03
Rickey Clark (IL)	R	22	1	11	.083	0	21	17	0	94	74	54	60	0	3.54
Bob Heffner	R	29	0	0	—	0	5	0	0	9	7	4	2	0	2.25
Pete Cimino	R	25	0	0	—	0	7	0	0	7	4	2	7	0	2.57
Larry Sherry	R	32	0	0	—	0	4	0	0	8	9	7	5	0	6.00
Steve Kealey	R	21	0	1	.000	0	9	0	0	23	18	12	10	0	2.70
Jim Weaver	L	29	0	0	—	0	14	0	0	23	22	10	8	0	2.35
Dennis Bennett	L	28	0	5	.000	1	16	7	1	48	46	17	31	0	3.56

CHICAGO 8th (tie) 67-95 .414 36 EDDIE STANKY 34-45 .430 LES MOSS 12-24 .333 AL LOPEZ 21-26 .447

NAME	G by Pos	B	AGE	G	AB	R	H	2B	3B	HR	RBI	BB	SO	SB	BA	SA
TOTALS			28	162	5405	463	1233	169	33	71	431	397	840	90	.228	.311
Tommy McCraw	1B135	L	27	136	477	51	112	16	12	9	44	36	58	20	.235	.379
Sandy Alomar	2B99, 3B27, SS9, OF1	B	24	133	363	41	92	4	2	0	12	20	42	5	.253	.287
Luis Aparicio	SS154	R	34	157	622	55	164	24	4	4	36	33	43	17	.264	.334
Pete Ward	3B77, 1B31, OF22	L	28	123	399	43	86	15	0	15	50	76	85	4	.216	.366
Buddy Bradford	OF99	R	23	103	281	32	61	11	0	5	24	23	67	8	.217	.310
Ken Berry	OF151	R	27	153	504	49	127	21	2	7	32	25	64	6	.252	.343
Tommy Davis	OF116, 1B6	R	29	132	456	30	122	5	3	8	50	16	48	4	.268	.344
Duane Josephson	C122	R	26	128	434	35	107	16	6	4	45	18	52	2	.247	.353
Jerry McNertney	C64, 1B1	R	31	74	169	18	37	4	1	3	18	16	29	0	.219	.308
1 Tim Cullen	2B71	R	26	72	155	16	31	7	0	2	13	15	23	0	.200	.284
2 Leon Wagner	OF46	L	34	69	162	14	46	8	0	1	18	21	31	2	.284	.352
Walt Williams	OF34	R	24	63	133	6	32	6	0	1	4	17		0	.241	.308
Bill Voss (BY)	OF55	L	24	61	167	14	26	2	1	2	15	16	34	5	.156	.216
1 Wayne Causey	2B41	L	31	59	100	8	18	2	0	0	7	14	7	0	.180	.200
Dick Kenworthy	3B38	R	27	58	122	2	27	5	2	0	5	4	21	0	.221	.238
2 Ron Hansen	3B29, SS7, 2B2	R	30	40	87	7	20	3	0	1	8	6	22	0	.230	.299
2 Woodie Held	OF33, 3B5, 2B1	R	36	40	54	5	9	1	0	0	5	5	14	0	.167	.185
1 Russ Snyder	OF22	L	34	38	57	2	11	2	0	0	5	4	6	0	.134	.195
Bill Melton	3B33	R	22	34	109	5	29	8	0	3	16	10	32	1	.266	.394
Gail Hopkins	1B7	L	25	29	37	4	8	2	0	0	3	4	6	0	.216	.270
Carlos May	OF17	L	24	17	67	4	12	3	0	1	3	3	15	0	.179	.194

Rich Morales 24 R 5-29, 1 Ken Boyer 37 R 3-24, Buddy Booker 26 L 0-5

NAME	T	AGE	W	L	PCT	SV	G	GS	CG	IP	H	BB	SO	SHO	ERA
		30	67	95	.414	40	162	162	20	1468	1290	451	834	11	2.75
Wilbur Wood	L	26	13	12	.520	16	88	2	0	159	179	33	74	0	1.87
Joe Horlen	R	30	12	14	.462	0	35	35	4	224	197	70	102	1	2.37
Tommy John (SJ)	L	25	10	5	.667	0	25	25	5	177	135	49	117	1	1.98
Jack Fisher	R	29	8	13	.381	0	35	28	2	181	176	48	80	0	2.98
Bob Locker	R	30	6	6	.500	10	70	0	0	90	78	27	62	0	2.30
Hoyt Wilhelm	R	45	4	4	.500	12	72	0	0	94	69	24	72	0	1.72
Gary Peters	L	31	4	13	.235	1	31	25	6	163	146	60	110	1	3.75
Cisco Carlos	R	27	4	14	.222	0	29	21	0	122	121	37	57	0	3.91
Bob Priddy	R	28	3	11	.214	0	35	11	2	114	106	41	66	0	3.63
1 Don McMahon	R	38	3	1	.667	0	25	0	0	46	31	20	32	0	1.96
Jerry Nyman	L	25	2	1	.667	0	4		0	38	16	27	1		2.03
Fred Rath	R	24	0	0	—	0	11	0	0	13	8	4	2	0	1.64
Billy Wynne	R	24	0	1	.000	0	4	1	0	10	4	4	2	0	4.50
Danny Lazar	L	24	0	0	—	0	13	1	0	31	42	17	11	0	6.03
2 Dennis Ribant	R	26													

WASHINGTON 10th 65-96 .404 37.5 JIM LEMON

NAME	G by Pos	B	AGE	G	AB	R	H	2B	3B	HR	RBI	BB	SO	SB	BA	SA
TOTALS			27	161	5400	524	1208	160	37	124	489	454	960	29	.224	.336
Mike Epstein	1B110	L	25	123	385	40	90	8	2	13	33	48	91	1	.234	.366
Bernie Allen	2B110, 3B2	L	29	120	373	31	90	12	4	6	40	28	35	2	.241	.343
1 Ron Hansen	SS81, 3B5	R	30	86	275	28	51	12	0	8	28	35	49	0	.185	.316
Ken McMullen	3B145, SS11	R	26	151	557	66	138	11	2	20	62	63	66	1	.248	.382
Ed Stroud	OF84	L	28	105	306	41	73	10	4	2	23	20	50	9	.239	.330
Del Unser	OF156, 1B1	L	23	156	635	66	146	16	4	1	30	46	66	11	.230	.277
Frank Howard	OF107, 1B55	R	31	158	598	79	164	28	3	44	106	54	141	0	.274	.552
Paul Casanova	C92	R	26	96	322	19	63	6	0	4	21	7	52	0	.196	.252
Cap Peterson	OF53	R	25	94	226	20	46	8	1	3	18	18	31	2	.204	.288
Eddie Brinkman	SS74, 2B2, OF1	R	26	77	193	12	36	3	0	0	9	19	31	0	.187	.202
Gary Holman	1B33, OF10	L	24	75	85	10	25	5	0	1	5	5	19	2	.294	.376
Hank Allen	OF25, 3B16, 2B11	R	27	68	128	16	27	4	0	0	8	4	21	0	.219	.289
Frank Coggins	2B52	B	23	57	68	7	12	1	0	0	6	10	12	3	.175	.221
Jim French	C53	R	26	59	165	9	32	5	0	1	10	19	24	1	.194	.242
Sam Bowens	OF27	R	29	57	115	14	22	4	0	4	15	7	24	1	.191	.330
Brant Alyea	OF39	R	27	53	150	18	40	11	0	6	23	10	35	0	.267	.473
2 Tim Cullen	SS33, 2B16, 3B10	R	26	47	114	9	21	2	1	3	16	7	12	0	.272	.368
Billy Bryan	C28	L	29	40	108	12	22	8	0	4	14	12	27	0	.204	.315
1 Fred Valentine	OF27, 1B2	B	33	26	52	3	8	1	0	1	6	3	13	1	.154	.347
Dick Billings	OF8, 3B4	R	25	12	33	1	6	1	0	0	3	1	6	0	.182	.303

Gene Martin 21 L 4-11, Doug Camilli (RC) 31

NAME	T	AGE	W	L	PCT	SV	G	GS	CG	IP	H	BB	SO	SHO	ERA
		27	65	96	.404	28	161	161	26	1440	1402	517	826	11	3.64
Camilo Pascual	R	34	13	12	.520	0	31	31	8	201	181	59	111	4	2.69
Joe Coleman	R	21	12	16	.429	0	33	33	12	223	212	51	139	2	3.27
Jim Hannan	R	28	10	6	.625	0	25	22	4	140	147	50	75	1	3.02
Frank Bertaina	L	24	7	13	.350	0	27	23	1	127	133	69	81	0	4.68
Bob Humphreys	R	32	5	7	.417	2	56	0	0	80	78	30	56	0	3.68
Phil Ortega	R	28	5	12	.294	0	31	16	1	116	115	62	57	1	4.97
Denny Higgins	L	28	4	4	.500	13	59	0	0	101	81	66	66	0	3.24
Barry Moore	L	25	4	4	.500	0	32	18	0	118	116	42	56	0	3.36
Dick Bosman	R	24	2	9	.182	1	46	10	0	139	139	35	63	0	3.69
Darold Knowles (MS)	L	26	1	0	—	0	32	0	0	41	38	12	37	0	2.20
Steve Jones	L	26	1	4	.200	1	44	0	0	49	63	23	45	0	5.73
2 Bruce Howard	R	25	1	2	.333	1	7		0	25	23	10	6	0	5.33
Bill Haywood	R	31	0	0	—	0	23	0	0	42	41	12	10	0	4.70
Bill Denehy	R	22	0	3	.000	0	3	2	0	9	13	9	9	0	9.00
Jim Miles	R	22	0	0	—	0	4	0	0	4	5	4	0	0	13.50
Casey Cox	R	27	0	0	—	0	4	0	0	7	7	1	4	0	2.25
Jerry Schoen	R	21	0	1	—	0	4	0	0	8	9	6	5	0	6.75
Dave Baldwin	R	30	0	2	.000	4	42	0	0	40	18	24	34	0	4.07

ST. LOUIS 1st 97-65 .599 — RED SCHOENDIENST

NAME	G by Pos	B	AGE	G	AB	R	H	2B	3B	HR	RBI	BB	SO	SB	BA	SA
TOTALS			29	162	5561	583	1383	227	48	73	539	378	897	110	.249	.346
Orlando Cepeda	1B154	R	30	157	600	71	149	26	2	16	73	43	96	8	.248	.378
Julian Javier	2B139	R	31	139	519	54	135	25	4	4	52	24	61	10	.260	.347
Dal Maxvill	SS151	R	29	151	459	51	116	8	5	1	24	52	71	0	.253	.298
Mike Shannon	3B156	R	28	156	576	62	153	29	2	15	79	37	114	1	.266	.401
Roger Maris	OF84	L	33	100	310	25	79	18	2	5	45	24	38	0	.255	.374
Curt Flood	OF149	R	30	150	618	71	186	17	4	5	60	33	58	11	.301	.366
Lou Brock	OF156	L	29	159	660	92	184	46	14	6	51	46	124	62	.279	.418
Tim McCarver	C109	L	26	128	434	35	110	15	6	5	48	26	31	4	.253	.350
Bobby Tolan	OF67, 1B9	L	22	92	278	28	64	12	1	5	17	13	42	9	.230	.335
Johnny Edwards	C54	L	30	85	230	14	55	9	1	3	29	16	20	1	.239	.326
Dick Schofield	SS43, 2B23	B	33	69	127	14	28	7	1	1	8	13	31	1	.220	.315
Phil Gagliano	2B17, 3B10, OF5	R	26		105	13	24	4	2	0	13	7	12	0	.229	.305
2 Ron Davis	OF25	R	26	33	79	11	14	4	2	0	5	5	17	1	.177	.278
Ed Spiezio	OF11, 3B2	R	26	29	51	1	8	0	0	2	3	5	6	1	.157	.157
1 Dick Simpson	OF22	R	24	26	56	11	13	0	0	3	8	8	21	0	.232	.393
Dave Ricketts	C1	R	32	20	22	1	3	0	0	0	1	0	3	0	.136	.136
Joe Hague	OF3, 1B2	L	24	7	17	2	4	0	0	1	1	2	2	0	.235	.412
Floyd Wicker		L	24	5	4	2	2	0	0	0	0	0	0	0	.500	.500
Ted Simmons	C2	B	18	2	3	0	1	0	0	0	0	0	1	1	.333	.333

NAME	T	AGE	W	L	PCT	SV	G	GS	CG	IP	H	BB	SO	SHO	ERA
		27	97	65	.599	32	162	162	63	1479	1282	375	971	30	2.49
Bob Gibson	R	32	22	9	.710	0	34	34	28	305	198	62	268	13	1.12
Nelson Briles	R	24	19	11	.633	0	33	33	13	244	251	55	141	4	2.80
Ray Washburn	R	30	14	8	.636	0	31	30	8	215	191	47	124	4	2.26
Steve Carlton	L	23	13	11	.542	0	34	33	10	232	214	61	162	5	2.99
Larry Jaster	L	24	9	13	.409	0	31	21	3	154	153	38	70	1	3.51
Joe Hoerner	L	31	8	2	.800	17	47	0	0	49	34	12	42	0	1.47
Wayne Granger	R	24	4	2	.667	4	34	0	0	44	40	12	22	0	2.25
Mel Nelson	L	32	2	1	.667	1	18	4	1	53	49	9	16	0	2.89
Mike Torrez	R	21	2	1	.667	0	3	1	0	19	20	12	6	0	2.84
Dick Hughes (SA)	R	30	2	2	.500	4	25	5	0	64	45	21	49	0	3.52
Ron Willis	R	24	2	3	.400	4	48	0	0	64	50	28	39	0	3.38
2 Pete Mikkelsen	R	28	0	0	—	2	13	0	0	16	10	7	8	0	1.13
1 Hal Gilson	L	26	0	2	.000	2	13	0	0	22	27	11	19	0	4.50

SAN FRANCISCO 2nd 88-74 .543 9 — HERMAN FRANKS

NAME	G by Pos	B	AGE	G	AB	R	H	2B	3B	HR	RBI	BB	SO	SB	BA	SA
TOTALS			27	163	5441	599	1301	162	33	108	566	508	904	50	.239	.341
Willie McCovey	1B146	L	30	148	523	81	153	16	4	36	105	72	71	4	.293	.545
Ron Hunt	2B147	R	27	148	529	79	132	19	4	1	20	78	41	6	.250	.297
Hal Lanier	SS150	B	25	151	486	37	100	14	1	0	27	12	57	2	.206	.239
Jim Davenport	3B82, SS17, 2B1	R	34	113	272	27	61	1	1	1	17	26	32	0	.224	.246
Bobby Bonds	OF80	R	22	81	307	55	78	10	5	9	35	38	64	16	.254	.407
Willie Mays	OF142, 1B1	R	37	148	498	84	144	20	5	23	79	67	81	12	.289	.488
Jesus Alou	OF105	R	26	120	419	26	110	15	4	0	39	9	23	1	.263	.317
Dick Dietz	C90	R	26	98	301	21	82	14	2	6	38	34	68	1	.272	.392
Jim Ray Hart	3B72, OF65	R	26	136	480	67	124	14	3	23	78	46	74	3	.258	.444
Ty Cline	OF70, 1B24	L	26	116	291	37	65	6	3	1	28	11	26	0	.223	.275
Jack Hiatt	C58, 1B10	R	25	90	224	14	52	10	2	4	34	41	61	0	.232	.348
Dave Marshall	OF50	L	25	76	174	17	46	5	1	1	16	20	37	2	.264	.322
Frank Johnson	3B36, OF8, SS5, 2B3	R	25	67	174	11	33	2	0	1	7	12	23	1	.190	.218
Bob Barton	C45	R	26	46	92	4	24	2	0	0	5	7	18	0	.261	.283
Ollie Brown	OF35	R	24	40	95	7	22	4	0	0	11	3	23	1	.232	.274
Nate Oliver (IL)	2B14, SS13, 3B1	R	27	36	73	3	13	2	0	0	1	1	13	0	.178	.205
Bob Schroder	2B12, SS4, 3B2	L	23	35	44	5	7	1	1	0	2	7	3	0	.159	.227
Don Mason	2B5, SS4, 3B2	L	23	10	19	3	3	0	0	0	1	1	4	1	.158	.158
Ken Henderson	OF2	L	22	3	3	1	1	0	0	0	0	0	2	1	.333	.333

NAME	T	AGE	W	L	PCT	SV	G	GS	CG	IP	H	BB	SO	SHO	ERA
		29	88	74	.543	16	163	163	77	1469	1302	344	942	20	2.71
Juan Marichal	R	30	26	9	.743	0	38	38	30	326	295	46	218	5	2.43
Gaylord Perry	R	29	16	15	.516	1	39	38	19	291	240	59	173	3	2.44
Mike McCormick	L	29	12	14	.462	1	38	28	9	198	196	49	121	2	3.59
Ray Sadecki	L	27	12	18	.400	0	38	36	13	254	225	70	206	6	2.91
Bobby Bolin	R	29	10	5	.667	0	34	19	6	177	128	46	126	3	1.98
Frank Linzy	R	27	9	8	.529	12	57	0	0	95	76	27	36	0	2.08
Rich Robertson	R	23	2	1	1.000	0	3	1	0	9	9	3	8	0	6.00
Joe Gibbon	L	33	1	2	.333	1	29	0	0	40	33	19	22	0	1.58
Ron Herbel	R	30	0	0	—	0	28	2	0	43	55	15	18	0	3.35
1 Lindy McDaniel	R	32	0	0	—	0	12	0	0	19	30	5	9	0	7.58
2 Bill Monbouquette	R	31	0	1	.000	1	7	0	0	12	11	2	5	0	3.75
1 Bill Henry	L	40	0	0	—	0	7	1	0	5	4	3	4	0	5.40

CHICAGO 3rd 84-78 .519 13 — LEO DUROCHER

NAME	G by Pos	B	AGE	G	AB	R	H	2B	3B	HR	RBI	BB	SO	SB	BA	SA
TOTALS			30	163	5458	612	1319	203	43	130	576	415	854	41	.242	.366
Ernie Banks	1B147	R	37	150	552	71	136	27	0	32	83	27	67	2	.246	.469
Glenn Beckert	2B155	R	27	155	643	98	189	28	4	4	37	31	20	8	.294	.369
Don Kessinger	SS159	B	25	160	655	63	157	14	7	1	32	38	86	9	.240	.287
Ron Santo	3B162	R	28	162	577	86	142	17	3	26	98	96	106	3	.246	.421
Jim Hickman	OF66	R	31	75	188	22	42	6	3	5	23	13	48	1	.223	.367
Adolfo Phillips	OF141	R	26	143	439	49	106	20	5	13	33	47	90	9	.241	.399
Billy Williams	OF163	L	30	163	642	71	185	30	8	30	98	48	63	4	.288	.500
Randy Hundley	C160	R	26	160	553	41	125	18	4	7	65	39	69	1	.226	.311
Al Spangler	OF48	L	34	88	177	21	48	9	3	2	18	20	24	0	.271	.390
Dick Nen	1B52	L	28	81	94	8	17	1	1	2	16	6	17	0	.181	.277
1 Lou Johnson	OF57	R	33	62	205	14	50	14	3	1	14	6	23	3	.244	.356
Jose Arcia	OF17, 2B10, SS7, 3B1	R	24	59	84	15	16	4	0	1	8	3	24	0	.190	.274
2 Willie Smith	OF38, 1B4, P1	R	29	55	142	13	39	8	2	5	25	12	33	0	.275	.465
Lee Elia	SS2, 3B1, 2B1	R	30	15	17	1	3	0	0	0	3	0	4	0	.176	.176
John Upham	OF2, P2	L	26	13	10	0	2	0	0	0	0	1	2	0	.200	.200
Gene Oliver	1B2, OF1, C1	R	32	8	11	1	4	0	0	1	3	2	0	.364	.364
John Boccabella	C4, OF1	R	27	7	14	0	1	0	0	0	0	2	2	0	.071	.071
Randy Bobb	C7	R	20	7	8	0	1	0	0	0	0	1	2	0	.125	.125
Jimmy McMath	OF3	L	18	6	14	0	2	0	0	0	2	0	6	0	.143	.143
Clarence Jones	1B1	L	25	5	2	0	0	0	0	0	0	2	1	0	.000	.000
John Felske	C3	R	26	4	2	0	0	0	0	0	0	0	1	0	.000	.000
Vic LaRose	2B2, SS2	R	23	4	2	0	0	0	0	0	0	1	0	0	.000	.000
1 Ted Savage	OF2	R	31	3	8	0	2	0	0	0	0	0	2	0	.250	.250
Bill Plummer	C1	R	21	2	2	0	0	0	0	0	0	0	2	0	.000	.000
Johnny Stephenson		L	27	1	2	0	0	0	0	0	0	0	0	0	.000	.000

NAME	T	AGE	W	L	PCT	SV	G	GS	CG	IP	H	BB	SO	SHO	ERA
		26	84	78	.519	32	163	163	46	1454	1399	392	894	12	3.41
Ferguson Jenkins	R	24	20	15	.571	0	40	40	20	308	255	65	260	3	2.63
Bill Hands	R	24	16	10	.615	0	38	34	11	259	221	36	148	4	2.88
Joe Niekro	R	23	14	10	.583	2	34	29	2	177	204	59	65	1	4.32
Ken Holtzman	L	22	11	14	.440	1	34	32	6	215	201	76	151	3	3.35
2 Phil Regan	R	31	10	5	.667	25*	68	0	0	127	109	24	60	0	2.20
Rich Nye	L	23	7	12	.368	1	27	20	6	133	145	34	74	1	3.79
Jack Lamabe	R	31	3	2	.600	1	42	0	0	61	68	24	30	0	4.28
Chuck Hartenstein	R	26	2	4	.333	1	20	0	0	36	41	11	17	0	4.50
Gary Ross	R	20	1	1	.500	0	13	5	1	41	44	25	31	0	4.17
Ramon Hernandez	L	27	0	0	—	0	9	0	0	14	0	3	9	0	9.00
1 Pete Mikkelsen	R	28	0	0	—	0	3	0	0	5	7	1	5	0	7.20
John Upham	L	26	0	0	—	0	3	0	0	7	2	1	2	0	4.50
Jophery Brown	R	23	0	0	—	0	1	0	0	2	2	1	0	0	4.50
2 Willie Smith	L	29	0	0	—	0	1	0	0	2	4	1	0	0	4.50
Bill Stoneman	R	24	0	1	.000	0	18	0	0	29	35	14	18	0	5.59
Bobby Tiefenauer	R	38	0	1	.000	1	9	0	0	13	20	2	9	0	6.23
Darcy Fast	L	21	0	0	—	1	3	0	0	8	8	6	10	0	5.40
Archie Reynolds	R	24	0	0	—	0	3	1	0	13	14	7	6	0	6.92
Frank Reberger	R	24	0	0	—	0	1	0	0	3	1	2	0	0	9.00

* Regan, also with Los Angeles, league leader in SV with 25

CINCINNATI 4th 83-79 .512 14 — DAVE BRISTOL

NAME	G by Pos	B	AGE	G	AB	R	H	2B	3B	HR	RBI	BB	SO	SB	BA	SA
TOTALS			27	163	5767	690	1573	281	36	106	638	379	938	59	.273	.389
Lee May	1B122, OF33	R	27	146	559	78	162	32	1	22	80	34	100	4	.290	.469
Tommy Helms	2B127, SS2, 3B1	R	27	127	507	35	146	28	2	2	47	12	27	5	.288	.363
Leo Cardenas	SS136	R	29	137	452	45	106	13	2	7	41	36	83	2	.235	.319
Tony Perez	3B160	R	26	160	625	93	176	25	7	18	92	51	92	3	.282	.430
Pete Rose	OF148, 2B3, 1B1	B	27	149	626	94	210	42	6	10	49	56	76	3	.335	.470
Vada Pinson	OF123	L	29	130	499	60	135	29	6	5	48	32	59	11	.271	.406
Alex Johnson	OF140	R	25	149	603	79	188	32	6	2	58	26	71	16	.312	.395
Johnny Bench	C154	R	20	154	564	67	155	40	2	15	82	31	96	1	.275	.433
Mack Jones	OF60	L	29	103	234	40	59	9	1	10	34	28	46	2	.252	.427
Fred Whitfield	1B41	L	30	87	171	15	44	8	0	6	32	9	46	0	.257	.409
Chico Ruiz	2B34, 1B16, 3B5, SS3	B	29	85	139	15	36	2	1	0	9	12	18	4	.259	.288
2 Woody Woodward	SS41, 2B9, 1B1	R	25	56	119	13	29	2	0	0	10	7	23	1	.244	.261
Don Pavletich (EJ)	1B22, C5	R	29	46	98	11	28	3	1	2	11	8	23	0	.286	.398
Jim Beauchamp	OF13, 1B1	R	28	31	57	10	15	2	0	2	14	4	19	0	.263	.404
Pat Corrales	C20	R	27	20	56	3	15	1	0	0	4	6	20	0	.268	.339
Hal McRae	2B16	R	22	17	51	1	10	1	0	0	2	4	14	1	.196	.216
1 Bob Johnson	SS2, 1B1	R	32	16	15	2	4	0	0	0	1	0	2	1	.267	.267
Jimmie Schaffer	C2	R	32	4	6	1	1	0	0	0	0	0	1	0	.167	.167

NAME	T	AGE	W	L	PCT	SV	G	GS	CG	IP	H	BB	SO	SHO	ERA
		27	83	79	.512	38	163	163	24	1490	1399	573	963	16	3.56
Jim Maloney	R	28	16	10	.615	0	33	32	8	207	183	80	181	5	3.61
Jerry Arrigo	L	27	12	10	.545	0	36	31	5	205	181	77	140	1	3.34
George Culver	R	24	11	16	.407	2	42	35	5	226	229	84	114	2	3.23
Ted Abernathy	R	35	10	7	.588	13	78	0	0	135	111	55	64	0	2.47
Gary Nolan	R	20	9	4	.692	0	23	22	4	150	105	49	111	2	2.40
2 Clay Carroll	R	27	7	7	.500	17	58	1	0	122	102	32	61	0	2.29
Bill Kelso	R	28	4	1	.800	1	35	0	0	54	56	15	39	0	4.00
2 Tony Cloninger	R	27	4	7	.571	0	17	17	2	91	81	48	65	2	4.05
Billy McCool (WJ)	L	23	4	3	.429	2	30	4	0	51	59	41	30	4	4.94
Jay Ritchie	R	31	2	3	.400	0	28	0	0	57	68	13	32	0	4.58
Bob Lee	R	30	2	3	.400	3	44	1	0	65	73	37	34	0	5.12
1 Milt Pappas	R	29	2	5	.286	0	15	11	0	63	70	10	43	0	5.57
1 Ted Davidson	L	28	1	0	1.000	0	23	0	0	22	13	11	16	0	7.14
Dan McGinn	L	24	0	0	—	0	14	0	0	12	13	11	6	0	5.25
Mel Queen (SJ)	R	26	0	1	.000	0	4	0	0	18	24	6	20	0	6.00
John Tsitouris	R	32	0	3	.000	0	3	3	0	13	18	8	6	0	6.92

ATLANTA 5th 81-81 .500 16 — LUM HARRIS

NAME	G by Pos	B	AGE	G	AB	R	H	2B	3B	HR	RBI	BB	SO	SB	BA	SA
TOTALS			29	163	5552	514	1399	179	31	80	480	414	782	83	.252	.339
Deron Johnson (BH)	1B97, 3B21	R	29	146	555	57	133	21	1	8	33	33	79	0	.208	.316
Felix Millan	2B145	R	24	149	570	49	165	22	2	1	33	22	26	6	.289	.340
Sonny Jackson (GJ)	SS99	R	23	105	358	37	81	8	2	1	19	25	35	16	.226	.287
Clete Boyer (HJ)	3B69	R	31	71	273	19	62	7	2	4	17	16	32	2	.227	.311
Hank Aaron	OF151, 1B14	R	34	160	606	84	174	33	4	29	86	64	62	28	.287	.498
Felipe Alou	OF158	R	33	160	662	72	210	37	5	11	57	48	56	12	.317	.438
Mike Lum	OF95	L	22	122	232	22	52	7	3	3	21	14	35	3	.224	.319
Joe Torre (BY)	C92, 1B29	R	27	115	424	45	115	11	2	10	55	34	72	1	.271	.377
Tito Francona	OF65, 1B33	L	34	122	346	32	99	13	1	2	47	51	45	3	.286	.347
Marty Martinez	SS54, 3B37, 2B16, C14	B	26	113	356	34	82	5	3	0	12	29	28	6	.230	.261
Tommie Aaron	OF62, 1B28, 3B1	R	28	98	283	21	69	10	3	1	25	21	37	3	.244	.311
Bob Tillman	C75	R	31	86	236	16	52	4	0	5	20	16	55	1	.220	.301
Mike Page	OF20	L	32	59	187	15	49	5	1	0	11	10	20	2	.262	.299
Sandy Valdespino	OF20	L	29	36	86	8	20	1	0	0	4	10	14	0	.233	.279
Gil Garrido	SS17	R	27	18	53	5	11	0	0	0	2	1	5	0	.208	.208
3 Wayne Causey	2B6, 3B2, SS2	L	31	16	12	1	3	0	0	0	1	0	3	0	.108	.243
1 Woody Woodward	SS6, 3B2, 2B1	R	25	12	24	2	4	1	0	0	1	4	6	1	.167	.208
Ralph Garr		R	22	11	7	1	2	0	0	0	0	0	1	0	.286	.286
Walt Hriniak	C9	L	25	9	26	4	9	1	0	0	4	3	5	0	.346	.346
Dusty Baker	OF3	R	19	6	4	0	1	0	0	0	0	0	1	0	.400	.400
Rico Carty (IL) 28																

NAME	T	AGE	W	L	PCT	SV	G	GS	CG	IP	H	BB	SO	SHO	ERA
		27	81	81	.500	29	163	163	44	1475	1326	362	871	16	2.92
Pat Jarvis	R	27	16	12	.571	0	34	34	14	256	202	50	157	1	2.60
Phil Niekro	R	29	14	12	.538	2	37	34	15	257	228	45	140	5	2.59
Ron Reed	R	25	11	10	.524	0	35	34	15	202	189	49	111	3	3.34
2 Milt Pappas	R	29	10	8	.556	0	22	19	3	121	111	22	75	1	2.38
Cecil Upshaw	R	25	8	7	.533	13	52	0	0	117	98	24	74	0	2.46
George Stone	L	21	7	4	.636	0	17	7	0	75	63	19	52	0	2.76
Ken Johnson	R	35	5	8	.385	0	31	16	1	135	145	25	57	0	3.47
Jim Britton	R	24	4	4	.400	3	34	9	2	90	81	34	61	2	3.10
Claude Raymond	R	31	5	6	.375	10	36	0	0	60	56	18	37	0	2.85
Dick Kelley	L	27	2	4	.333	1	31	11	1	98	86	45	73	1	2.76
1 Tony Cloninger	R	27	2	2	.250	0	13	9	1	49	42	28	26	0	4.89
Rick Kester	R	21	0	0	—	0	4	0	0	7	10	4	3	0	6.00
2 Ted Davidson	L	28	0	0	—	0	7	0	0	10	14	4	5	0	6.43
Skip Guinn	L	24	0	0	—	0	5	0	0	7	10	4	3	0	3.60
Stu Miller	R	40	0	0	—	0	2	0	0	2	5	6	1	0	36.00
1 Clay Carroll	R	27	0	0	—	0	3	0	0	22	26	6	10	0	4.91
Al Santorini	R	20	0	0	—	0	1	0	0	3	3	0	0	0	0.00

PITTSBURGH 6th 80-82 .494 17 — LARRY SHEPARD

NAME	G by Pos	B	AGE	G	AB	R	H	2B	3B	HR	RBI	BB	SO	SB	BA	SA
TOTALS			30	163	5569	583	1404	180	44	80	538	422	953	130	.252	.343
Donn Clendenon	1B155	R	32	158	584	63	150	20	6	17	87	47	163	10	.257	.399
Bill Mazeroski	2B142	R	31	143	506	36	127	18	2	3	42	38	38	3	.251	.312
Gene Alley	SS109,2B24	R	27	133	474	48	116	20	2	4	39	39	78	13	.245	.321
Maury Wills	3B141,SS10	B	35	153	627	76	174	12	6	0	31	45	57	52	.278	.316
Roberto Clemente	OF131	R	33	132	502	74	146	18	12	18	57	51	77	2	.291	.482
Matty Alou	OF144	L	29	146	558	59	185	28	4	0	52	27	36	18	.332	.396
Willie Stargell	OF113,1B13	L	28	128	435	57	103	15	1	24	67	47	105	5	.237	.441
Jerry May	C135	R	24	137	416	26	91	15	2	1	33	41	80	0	.219	.272
Manny Mota	OF92,2B1,3B1	R	30	111	331	35	93	10	2	1	33	20	19	4	.281	.332
Jose Pagan	3B30,OF19,SS8,2B2,1B1	R	33	80	163	24	36	7	1	4	21	11	32	2	.221	.350
Gary Kolb	OF25,C10,3B4,2B1	L	28	74	119	16	26	4	1	2	6	11	17	2	.218	.319
Manny Jiminez	OF5	L	29	66	66	7	20	1	1	1	11	6	15	0	.303	.394
Freddie Patek (BW)	SS52,3B1	R	23	61	208	31	53	4	2	2	18	12	37	18	.255	.322
Carl Taylor	C29,OF2	R	24	44	71	5	15	1	0	0	7	10	10	1	.211	.225
Chris Cannizzaro	C25	R	25	35	58	5	14	2	2	1	7	9	13	0	.241	.397
Chuck Hiller	2B2	R	33	11	13	2	5	1	0	0	1	0	0	0	.385	.462
Bill Virdon	OF4	L	37	6	3	1	1	0	0	1	0	2	0	0	.333	.333
Al Oliver	OF1	L	21	4	8	1	1	0	0	0	0	0	2	0	.125	.125
Richie Hebner		L	20	2	1	0	0	0	0	0	0	0	0	0	.000	.000
Bob Robertson (IL) 21																

NAME	T	AGE	W	L	PCT	SV	G	GS	CG	IP	H	BB	SO	SHO	ERA
		29	80	82	.494	30	163	163	42	1487	1322	485	897	19	2.74
Steve Blass	R	26	18	6	.750	0	33	31	12	220	191	57	132	7	2.13
Bob Veale	L	32	13	14	.481	0	36	33	13	245	187	94	171	4	2.06
Ron Kline	R	36	12	5	.706	7	56	0	0	113	94	31	48	0	1.67
Al McBean	R	30	9	12	.429	0	36	28	9	198	204	63	100	2	3.59
Bob Moose	R	20	8	12	.400	3	38	22	3	171	186	41	126	3	2.74
Dock Ellis	R	23	6	5	.545	0	26	10	2	104	82	38	52	0	2.51
Tommie Sisk	R	26	5	5	.500	1	33	11	3	96	101	35	41	0	3.28
Jim Bunning	R	36	4	14	.222	0	27	26	3	160	168	48	95	1	3.88
1 Roy Face	R	40	2	4	.333	13	43	0	0	52	46	7	34	0	2.60
Dave Wickersham	R	32	1	0	1.000	1	11	0	0	21	21	13	9	0	3.43
Bruce Dal Canton	R	26	1	1	.500	2	17	0	0	17	7	6	8	0	2.12
1 Juan Pizarro	L	31	1	1	.500	0	10	0	0	11	14	10	6	0	3.27
2 Bill Henry	L	40	0	0	—	0	10	0	0	17	29	3	9	0	7.94
Luke Walker (IL)	L	24	0	3	.000	3	39	2	0	62	42	39	66	0	2.03

LOS ANGELES 7th (tie) 76-86 .469 21 — WALT ALSTON

NAME	G by Pos	B	AGE	G	AB	R	H	2B	3B	HR	RBI	BB	SO	SB	BA	SA
TOTALS			28	162	5354	470	1234	202	36	67	434	439	980	57	.230	.319
Wes Parker	1B114,OF28	B	28	135	468	42	112	22	2	3	27	49	87	4	.239	.314
Paul Popovich	2B89,SS45,3B7	B	27	134	418	35	97	8	1	2	25	29	37	1	.232	.270
Zoilo Versalles	SS119	R	28	122	403	29	79	16	3	2	24	26	84	6	.196	.266
Bob Bailey	3B90,SS1,OF1	R	25	105	322	24	73	9	3	8	39	38	69	1	.227	.348
Ron Fairly	OF105,1B36	L	29	141	441	32	103	15	1	4	43	41	61	0	.234	.299
Willie Davis	OF158	L	28	160	643	86	161	24	10	7	31	31	88	36	.250	.351
Len Gabrielson	OF86	L	28	108	304	38	82	16	1	10	35	32	47	1	.270	.428
Tom Haller	C139	L	31	144	474	37	135	27	5	4	53	46	76	1	.285	.388
Jim Fairey	OF63	L	23	99	156	17	31	3	3	1	10	9	32	1	.199	.276
Jim Lefebvre (WJ)	2B62,3B16,OF5,1B3	B	25	84	286	23	69	12	1	5	31	26	55	0	.241	.343
2 Ken Boyer	3B34,1B32	R	37	83	221	20	60	7	2	6	41	16	34	2	.271	.403
Willie Crawford	OF48	L	21	61	175	25	44	12	1	4	14	20	64	1	.251	.400
2 Ted Savage	OF39	R	31	61	126	7	26	6	1	2	7	10	20	1	.206	.317
Luis Alcaraz	2B20,3B13,SS1	R	27	41	106	4	16	1	0	2	5	9	23	1	.151	.217
1 Rocky Colavito	OF33	R	34	40	113	8	23	3	0	3	11	15	18	0	.204	.310
Bart Shirley	SS21,2B18	R	28	39	83	6	15	3	0	0	4	10	13	0	.181	.217
Jeff Torborg	C37	R	26	37	93	2	15	2	0	0	4	6	10	0	.161	.183
Bill Sudakis	3B24	B	22	24	87	11	24	4	2	3	12	15	14	1	.276	.471
Cleo James	OF2	R	27	10	10	2	2	1	0	0	1	0	4	0	.200	.300
Jim Campanis	C4	R	24	4	11	0	1	0	0	0	0	1	3	0	.091	.091
Al Ferrara (BN)	OF2	R	28	2	7	0	1	0	0	0	0	0	1	0	.143	.143

NAME	T	AGE	W	L	PCT	SV	G	GS	CG	IP	H	BB	SO	SHO	ERA
		28	76	86	.469	31	162	162	38	1449	1293	414	994	23	2.74
Don Drysdale	R	31	14	12	.538	0	31	31	12	239	201	56	155	8	2.15
Bill Singer	R	24	13	17	.433	0	37	36	12	256	227	78	227	6	2.88
Claude Osteen	L	28	12	18	.400	0	39	36	5	254	267	54	119	3	3.08
Don Sutton	R	23	11	15	.423	1	35	27	7	208	179	59	162	2	2.60
Jim Brewer	R	30	8	3	.727	14	54	0	0	76	59	33	75	0	2.49
Mudcat Grant	R	32	6	4	.600	3	37	4	1	95	77	19	35	0	2.08
Jack Billingham	R	25	3	0	1.000	8	50	1	0	71	54	30	46	0	2.15
1 Phil Regan	R	31	2	0	1.000	0*	5	0	0	9	7	3	3	0	3.38
John Purdin	R	25	2	3	.400	3	35	1	0	56	42	21	38	0	3.05
Mike Kekich	L	23	2	10	.167	0	25	20	1	115	116	46	84	1	3.91
Alan Foster (SJ)	R	21	1	1	.500	3	3	0	0	16	11	2	10	0	1.69
Joe Moeller	R	25	1	1	.500	0	3	3	0	16	17	2	11	0	5.06
Hank Aguirre	L	37	1	2	.333	1	25	0	0	39	32	13	25	0	0.69
1 Vicente Romo	R	25	0	0	—	0	1	0	0	1	0	1	0	0	0.00

*Regan, also with Chicago, league leader in SV with 25

PHILADELPHIA 7th (tie) 76-86 .469 21 — GENE MAUCH 27-27 .500 GEORGE MYATT 1-0 1.000 BOB SKINNER 48-59 .449

NAME	G by Pos	B	AGE	G	AB	R	H	2B	3B	HR	RBI	BB	SO	SB	BA	SA
TOTALS			29	162	5372	543	1253	178	30	100	505	462	1003	58	.233	.333
Bill White	1B111	L	34	127	385	34	92	16	2	9	40	39	79	0	.239	.361
Cookie Rojas	2B150,C1	R	29	152	621	53	144	19	0	9	48	16	55	4	.232	.306
Roberto Pena	SS133	R	31	138	500	56	130	13	2	1	38	34	63	3	.260	.300
Tony Taylor	3B138,2B5,1B1	R	32	145	547	59	137	20	2	3	38	39	60	22	.250	.311
Johnny Callison	OF109	L	29	121	398	46	97	18	4	14	40	42	70	4	.244	.415
Tony Gonzalez	OF117	L	31	121	416	45	110	13	4	3	38	40	42	6	.264	.337
Dick Allen	OF139,3B10	R	26	152	521	87	137	17	9	33	90	74	161	7	.263	.520
Mike Ryan	C96	R	26	96	296	12	53	6	1	1	15	15	59	0	.179	.216
Johnny Briggs	OF65,1B36	L	24	110	338	36	86	13	1	7	31	58	72	8	.254	.361
Don Lock	OF78	R	31	99	248	27	52	7	2	8	34	26	64	3	.210	.351
Clay Dalrymple	C80	L	31	85	241	19	50	9	1	3	26	22	57	1	.207	.290
Gary Sutherland	2B17,3B10,SS10,OF7	R	23	67	138	16	38	7	0	0	15	8	15	0	.275	.326
Rick Joseph	1B30,3B14,OF1	R	28	66	155	20	34	5	0	3	12	16	35	0	.219	.310
Doug Clemens	OF17	L	29	29	57	6	12	1	1	2	8	7	13	0	.211	.368
Bobby Wine (XJ)	SS25,3B1	R	29	27	71	5	12	3	0	2	7	6	17	0	.169	.296
John Sullivan	C8	L	27	18	18	0	4	0	0	0	1	0	4	0	.222	.222
Howie Bedell		L	32	9	7	0	1	0	0	0	1	0	1	0	.143	.143
Larry Hisle	OF6	R	21	11	11	1	4	1	0	0	1	1	4	0	.364	.455
Don Money	SS4	R	21	9	13	1	3	1	0	0	1	2	2	0	.231	.385

NAME	T	AGE	W	L	PCT	SV	G	GS	CG	IP	H	BB	SO	SHO	ERA
		29	76	86	.469	27	162	162	42	1448	1416	421	935	12	3.36
Chris Short	L	30	19	13	.594	1	42	36	9	270	236	81	202	2	2.93
Larry Jackson	R	37	13	17	.433	0	34	34	12	244	229	60	127	2	2.77
Woody Fryman	L	28	12	14	.462	0	34	32	10	214	198	64	151	5	2.78
Rick Wise	R	22	9	15	.375	0	30	30	7	182	210	37	97	1	4.55
Dick Hall	R	37	4	1	.800	0	32	0	0	46	53	5	31	0	4.89
Jeff James	R	26	4	4	.500	0	29	13	1	116	112	46	83	1	4.27
Jerry Johnson	R	24	4	4	.500	0	16	11	2	81	82	29	40	0	3.22
Gary Wagner	R	28	4	4	.500	8	44	0	0	78	69	31	43	0	3.00
Dick Farrell	R	34	4	6	.400	12	54	0	0	83	83	32	57	0	3.47
John Boozer	R	28	2	2	.500	5	38	0	0	69	76	15	49	0	3.65
Grant Jackson	L	25	1	0	.143	1	33	6	1	61	59	20	49	0	2.95
Paul Brown	R	27	0	1	.000	0	2	0	0	4	6	1	4	0	9.00
Larry Colton	R	26	0	0	—	0	1	0	0	2	3	0	2	0	4.50

NEW YORK 9th 73-89 .451 24 — GIL HODGES

NAME	G by Pos	B	AGE	G	AB	R	H	2B	3B	HR	RBI	BB	SO	SB	BA	SA
TOTALS			26	163	5503	473	1252	178	30	81	434	379	1203	72	.228	.315
Ed Kranepool	1B113,OF2	L	23	127	373	29	86	13	1	3	20	19	39	0	.231	.295
Ken Boswell (BG)	2B69	L	22	75	284	37	74	7	2	4	11	16	27	1	.261	.342
Bud Harrelson	SS106	B	24	111	402	38	88	7	3	0	14	29	68	4	.219	.251
Ed Charles	3B106,1B2	R	33	117	369	41	102	11	1	15	53	28	57	5	.276	.434
Ron Swoboda	OF125	R	24	132	450	46	109	14	6	11	59	52	113	8	.242	.373
Tommie Agee	OF127	R	25	132	368	30	80	12	3	5	17	15	103	13	.217	.307
Cleon Jones	OF139	R	25	147	509	63	151	29	4	14	55	31	98	23	.297	.452
Jerry Grote	C115	R	25	124	404	29	114	18	3	7	31	44	81	1	.282	.349
Art Shamsky	OF82,1B17	L	26	116	345	30	82	4	4	12	48	21	58	1	.238	.406
Al Weis	SS59,2B29,3B2	B	30	90	274	15	47	6	0	1	14	21	63	3	.172	.204
Phil Linz	2B71	R	29	78	258	19	54	7	0	0	17	10	41	1	.209	.236
J.C. Martin	C53,1B14	L	31	79	244	20	55	9	2	3	31	21	31	1	.225	.316
Jerry Buchek	3B37,2B12,OF9	R	26	92	192	8	35	4	0	4	18	17	52	0	.182	.219
Kevin Collins	3B40,2B6,SS1	L	21	58	154	12	31	5	2	1	13	7	37	0	.201	.279
Larry Stahl	OF47,1B9	L	27	94	167	13	42	3	2	3	10	21	38	3	.235	.344
Don Bosch	OF33	B	25	50	111	14	19	1	0	3	7	9	33	0	.171	.261
Greg Goossen	1B31,C1	R	22	38	106	4	22	7	0	2	10	6	21	0	.208	.274
Mike Jorgensen	1B4	L	19	8	14	0	2	1	0	0	0	0	5	0	.143	.214
Bob Heise	SS6,2B1	R	21	7	23	1	5	0	0	0	1	1	1	0	.217	.217
Duffy Dyer	C1	R	22	3	3	0	1	0	0	0	0	0	1	0	.333	.333

NAME	T	AGE	W	L	PCT	SV	G	GS	CG	IP	H	BB	SO	SHO	ERA
		27	73	89	.451	32	163	163	45	1483	1250	430	1014	25	2.72
Jerry Koosman	L	25	19	12	.613	0	35	34	17	264	221	69	178	7	2.08
Tom Seaver	R	23	16	12	.571	0	36	35	14	278	224	48	205	5	2.20
Dick Selma	R	24	9	10	.474	0	33	23	4	170	148	54	117	3	2.75
Don Cardwell	R	32	7	13	.350	1	29	25	5	180	156	50	82	1	2.95
Cal Koonce	R	27	6	4	.600	11	55	2	0	97	80	32	50	0	2.41
Nolan Ryan (HJ)	R	21	6	9	.400	0	21	18	3	134	93	75	133	0	3.09
Jim McAndrew	R	24	4	7	.364	0	12	12	2	79	66	17	46	1	2.28
Al Jackson	L	32	3	7	.300	3	25	9	0	93	88	17	59	0	3.63
Danny Frisella	R	22	2	4	.333	2	19	4	0	51	53	17	47	0	3.60
Ron Taylor	R	30	1	5	.167	13	58	0	0	77	64	18	49	0	2.69
Don Shaw	L	24	0	0	—	2	9	0	0	14	21	7	8	0	9.00
Billy Connors	R	26	0	1	.000	0	9	0	0	14	14	7	5	0	4.50
Les Rohr	L	22	0	0	—	0	3	1	0	6	9	7	5	0	4.50
Bill Short	L	31	0	1	.000	0	24	0	0	24	14	24	0		4.80

HOUSTON 10th 72-90 .444 25 — GRADY HATTON 23-38 .377 HARRY WALKER 49-52 .485

NAME	G by Pos	B	AGE	G	AB	R	H	2B	3B	HR	RBI	BB	SO	SB	BA	SA
TOTALS			26	162	5336	510	1233	205	28	66	473	479	988	44	.231	.317
Rusty Staub	1B147,OF15	L	24	161	591	54	172	37	1	6	72	73	57	2	.291	.387
Denis Menke	2B119,SS35,1B5,3B4	R	27	150	542	56	135	23	6	6	56	64	81	5	.249	.347
Hector Torres	SS127,2B1	R	22	128	466	44	104	11	1	1	24	18	64	2	.223	.258
Doug Rader	3B86,1B5	R	23	98	333	42	89	16	4	6	43	31	51	2	.267	.393
Norm Miller	OF74	L	22	79	257	35	61	18	2	6	28	22	48	6	.237	.393
1 Ron Davis	OF52	R	26	52	217	22	46	10	1	2	12	13	48	0	.212	.281
Jim Wynn	OF153	R	26	156	542	85	146	23	5	26	67	90	131	11	.269	.474
John Bateman	C108	R	27	111	350	28	87	19	0	4	33	23	46	1	.249	.337
Bob Aspromonte	3B75,OF36,SS1,1B1	R	30	124	409	26	92	9	1	4	46	35	57	1	.225	.264
Lee Thomas	OF48,1B8,3B1	L	32	92	201	14	39	4	0	1	11	14	22	2	.194	.229
Julio Gotay	2B48,3B1	R	29	75	165	9	41	3	0	4	8	4	21	1	.248	.285
2 Dick Simpson	OF49	R	24	59	177	25	33	7	2	3	11	20	61	4	.186	.299
Bob Watson (NJ)	OF40	R	22	45	140	13	32	7	0	0	8	13	32	1	.229	.321
Ron Brand	C29,3B1,OF1	R	28	43	81	7	15	1	0	0	4	9	11	1	.160	.185
Dave Adlesh	C36	R	24	40	104	3	19	1	1	0	7	16	27	0	.183	.212
Ivan Murrell	OF15	R	23	32	59	3	6	1	0	1	4	2	12	0	.102	.153
Joe Herrera	OF17,2B7	R	25	27	50	2	12	1	0	0	4	1	12	0	.240	.280
Hal King	C19	L	24	27	55	4	8	2	1	0	7	16	10	0	.145	.218
Nate Colbert	OF11,1B5	R	22	52	55	4	15	2	0	1	3	1	11	0	.151	.170
Leon McFadden	SS16	R	21	26	47	4	13	1	0	0	6	6	10	1	.277	.298
Joe Morgan (KJ)	2B5,OF1	L	24	10	20	6	5	0	0	0	1	4	6	0	.250	.250
Byron Browne	OF2	R	25	10	13	0	3	0	0	0	1	4	6	0	.231	.231
John Mayberry	1B2	L	19	4	4	0	0	0	0	0	0	0	0	0	.000	.000
Danny Walton		R	20	1	0	0	0	0	0	0	0	0	0	0	.000	.000

NAME	T	AGE	W	L	PCT	SV	G	GS	CG	IP	H	BB	SO	SHO	ERA
		26	72	90	.444	23	162	162	50	1447	1362	479	1021	12	3.26
Don Wilson	R	23	13	16	.448	0	33	30	9	209	187	70	175	3	3.27
Larry Dierker	R	21	12	15	.444	0	32	32	10	234	206	89	161	1	3.31
Dave Giusti	R	28	11	14	.440	1	37	34	12	251	226	67	186	2	3.19
Denny Lemaster	L	29	10	15	.400	0	33	32	7	224	231	72	146	2	2.81
Mike Cuellar	L	31	8	11	.421	1	28	24	11	171	152	45	133	2	2.74
Danny Coombs	L	26	4	3	.571	2	40	4	2	84	73	35	37	3	3.11
John Buzhardt	R	31	4	4	.500	8	40	4	0	78	94	17	29	0	3.26
Steve Shea	R	25	4	4	.500	6	30	0	0	53	62	28	37	0	2.67
Tom Dukes	R	26	3	5	.375	2	58	0	0	86	78	39	42	0	2.73
Jim Ray	R	23	3	4	.400	1	41	2	1	81	65	25	71	0	2.67
Pat House	L	24	1	0	1.000	0	19	0	0	16	18	6	16	0	7.88
Wade Blasingame (BG)	L	24	1	2	.333	1	22	0	0	36	45	10	22	0	4.75
Fred Gladding (EJ)	R	32	0	0	—	0	7	0	0	4	2	3	2	0	15.75
2 Hal Gilson	L	24	0	0	—	0	4	0	0	8	13	1	6	0	6.75
Carroll Sembera (JJ) 26															

1969 The Miracle at Flushing Meadows

Professional baseball's centennial year began with the expansion of both leagues to 12 teams and the introduction of division play in both leagues, as Montreal and San Diego joined the National League and Seattle and Kansas City the American League. Because pitchers had become overly dominant in the game, the pitcher's mound was lowered and the strike zone shrunk to spruce up the batting. Other news items included Ken Harrelson, who created an uproar by refusing to report after Boston traded him to Cleveland, and only did so after a significant pay raise; Donn Clendenon, who refused to be traded to Houston by Montreal and wound up in New York; Mickey Mantle, who could no longer fight injury and age and called it quits before the season opened; and Ted Williams, who returned to uniform as the manager of the Washington Senators. None of these events, including the firing at season's end of Billy Martin of the Western Division champion Minnesota Twins, or the bankruptcy of the Seattle Pilots, could equal the biggest surprise in baseball's long history-the miracle of the amazing Mets!

The Mets, born and nurtured in mediocrity, had never risen above ninth place since entering the National League in 1962, and a loss on opening day to the newly-minted Montreal Expos only seemed to confirm another season of futility. But manager Gil Hodges had a vision and a plan which he patiently put in motion, the result of which found the Mets trailing only the Cubs in the National League's Eastern Division as summer dawned. The first real sign of what was to come arrived in early July when the Mets took two of three games from Chicago at Shea Stadium—one of the contests being a near-perfect performance by right-hander Tom Seaver, who lost his bid for immortality with one out in the ninth inning to outfielder Jimmy Qualls. Then, in Chicago the next week, light-hitting Al Weis swatted two homers in two games as the Mets again took two parts of a three-game set.

A slump in early August seemed to end all hopes of a miracle as the Mets dropped to 9½ games back. But they then again caught fire. With Tommie Agee, Cleon Jones, and Bud Harrelson starring day after day, and Hodges skillfully platooning at every other position, the one-time doormat rushed to within 2½ games of the slumping Cubs on September 8, when the Bruins came into New York for two games. With momentum on their side, the Mets swept both games, moved into first place on September 10, and kept winning until they had amassed 100 victories and the division title.

The Mets' pitching staff boasted of young aces Seaver and Jerry Koosman, relief bulwark Tug McGraw, and strong arms up and down a deep staff. In contrast, the Atlanta Braves copped the Western Division crown in a close race with the San Francisco Giants and MVP Willie McCovey by wielding a powerful attack featuring Hank Aaron, Orlando Cepeda, and Rico Carty, but the favored Braves fell before the Mets' steamroller, three games to none in the championship playoff.

The Baltimore Orioles began a string of American League championships by taking the Eastern crown and then icing the Minnesota Twins for the American League title. Harmon Killebrew of the Twins took the MVP Award, but a good case could have been made for Frank Robinson, or Boog Powell, stars of the Orioles. Mike Cuellar won 23 games after joining the Birds in an off-season trade, Jim Palmer chalked up 16 victories after two injury-plagued seasons, and Dave McNally won his first 15 decisions on the way to a 20-win season.

After dropping the first game to Cuellar, the Mets' machine rolled on with four straight wins via unbelievable catches by Agee in the third game and Ron Swoboda in the fourth game to become the unlikeliest champions in baseball history. In addition to Swoboda and the gremlins who haunted the Orioles, the winning play of the game came in the tenth inning when J.C. Martin bunted and was hit in the wrist by Pete Richert's throw to score Rod Gaspar from second after the ball ricocheted into short right field. What was not definitely known until evening was the newspaper photograph which showed Martin running in fair territory for which he should have been declared out by umpire Shag Crawford. Yet it was the final game which best showed the winks that fate was constantly tossing the Mets' direction. Trailing 3-0 in the sixth inning, Cleon Jones was awarded first base when shoe polish on the ball revealed he had been struck on the foot. Donn Clendenon then promptly drilled a homer over the left-field wall. Al Weis tied it up in the seventh with his first and only Shea Stadium home run, and in the eighth inning the two winning runs scored on doubles by Jones and Swoboda and two Baltimore errors. As the screaming continued long into the night, it was certain that the 5-3 victory climaxed a meteoric rise which had absolutely no worlds left to conquer.

1969 AMERICAN LEAGUE

EAST DIVISION

NAME	G by Pos	B	AGE	G	AB	R	H	2B	3B	HR	RBI	BB	SO	SB	BA	SA
BALTIMORE	1st 109-53 .673		EARL WEAVER													
TOTALS			28	162	5518	779	1465	234	29	175	722	634	806	82	.265	.414
Boog Powell	1B144	L	27	152	533	83	162	25	0	37	121	72	76	1	.304	.559
Dave Johnson	2B142, SS2	R	26	142	511	52	143	34	1	7	57	57	52	3	.280	.391
Mark Belanger	SS148	R	25	150	530	76	152	17	4	2	50	53	54	14	.287	.345
Brooks Robinson	3B156	R	32	156	598	73	140	21	3	23	84	56	55	2	.234	.395
Frank Robinson	OF134, 1B19	R	33	148	539	111	166	19	5	32	100	88	62	9	.308	.540
Paul Blair	OF150	R	25	150	625	102	178	32	5	26	76	40	72	20	.285	.477
Don Buford	OF128, 2B10, 3B6	B	32	144	554	99	161	31	3	11	64	96	62	19	.291	.417
Ellie Hendricks	C87, 1B4	L	28	105	295	36	72	5	0	12	38	39	44	0	.244	.383
Merv Rettenmund	OF78	R	26	95	190	27	47	10	3	4	25	28	28	6	.247	.395
Dave May	OF40	L	25	78	120	8	29	3	0	3	10	9	23	2	.242	.367
Andy Etchebarren	C72	R	26	73	217	29	54	9	2	3	26	28	42	1	.249	.350
Curt Motton	OF20	R	28	56	89	15	27	6	0	6	21	13	10	3	.303	.573
Chico Salmon	1B17, 2B9, SS9, 3B3, OF1	R	28	52	91	18	27	5	0	3	12	10	22	0	.297	.451
Bobby Floyd	2B15, SS15, SS8, 3B9	R	25	39	84	7	17	4	0	0	1	6	17	0	.202	.250
Clay Dalrymple	C30	L	32	37	80	8	19	1	1	3	6	13	8	0	.238	.388
Terry Crowley	1B3, OF2	L	22	7	18	2	6	0	0	0	3	1	4	0	.333	.333
DETROIT	2nd 90-72 .556 19		MAYO SMITH													
TOTALS			29	162	5441	701	1316	188	29	182	649	578	922	35	.242	.387
Norm Cash	1B134	L	34	142	483	81	135	15	4	22	74	63	80	2	.280	.464
Dick McAuliffe (KJ)	2B72	L	29	74	271	49	71	10	5	11	33	47	41	2	.262	.458
2 Tom Tresh	SS77, OF11, 3B1	B	31	94	331	46	74	13	1	13	37	39	47	2	.224	.387
Don Wert	3B129	R	30	132	423	46	95	11	4	14	50	49	60	3	.225	.355
Al Kaline	OF118, 1B9	R	34	131	456	74	124	17	0	21	69	54	61	1	.272	.447
Jim Northrup	OF143	L	29	148	543	79	160	31	5	25	66	52	83	4	.295	.508
Willie Horton	OF136	R	26	141	508	66	133	17	1	28	91	52	93	3	.262	.465
Bill Freehan	C120, 1B20	R	27	143	489	61	128	16	3	16	49	53	55	1	.262	.405
Mickey Stanley	OF101, SS59, 1B4	R	26	149	592	73	139	28	1	16	70	52	56	8	.235	.367
Tom Matchick	2B47, 3B27, SS6, 1B2	L	25	94	298	25	72	11	2	0	32	15	51	3	.242	.292
Jim Price	C51	R	27	72	192	21	45	8	0	9	28	18	20	0	.234	.417
Ike Brown	2B45, 3B12, OF3, SS1	R	27	70	170	24	39	4	3	5	12	26	43	2	.229	.376
Dick Tracewski	SS41, 2B13, 3B6	R	34	66	79	10	11	2	0	0	4	15	20	3	.139	.165
Gates Brown	OF14	L	30	60	93	13	19	1	2	1	6	5	17	0	.204	.290
Dave Campbell	1B13, 2B5, 3B1	R	27	32	39	4	4	1	0	0	2	4	15	0	.103	.128
2 Cesar Gutierrez 26 R 12-49, 1 Ron Woods 26 R 4-15, Wayne Redmond 23 R 0-3																
BOSTON	3rd 87-75 .537 22		DICK WILLIAMS 82-71 .536				EDDIE POPOWSKI 5-4 .556									
TOTALS			26	162	5494	743	1381	234	37	197	701	658	923	41	.251	.415
Dalton Jones	1B81, 3B9, 2B1	L	25	111	336	50	74	18	3	3	33	39	36	1	.220	.318
Mike Andrews	2B120	R	25	121	464	79	136	26	2	15	59	71	53	1	.293	.455
Rico Petrocelli	SS153, 3B1	R	26	154	535	92	159	32	2	40	97	98	68	3	.297	.589
George Scott	3B109, 1B53	R	25	152	549	63	139	14	5	16	52	61	74	4	.253	.384
Tony Conigliaro	OF137	R	24	141	506	57	129	21	3	20	82	48	111	2	.255	.427
Reggie Smith	OF139	B	24	143	543	87	168	29	7	25	93	54	67	7	.309	.527
Carl Yastrzemski	OF143, 1B22	L	29	162	603	96	154	28	2	40	111	101	91	15	.255	.507
Russ Gibson	C83	R	30	85	287	21	72	9	1	3	27	15	25	1	.251	.321
Joe Lahoud	OF66, 1B1	L	22	101	218	32	41	5	0	9	21	40	48	2	.188	.335
Syd O'Brien	3B53, SS15, 2B12	R	25	100	263	47	64	10	5	9	29	15	37	2	.243	.422
Dick Schofield	2B37, SS11, 3B9, OF5	B	34	94	226	30	58	9	3	2	20	29	44	0	.257	.350
Jerry Moses	C36	R	22	53	135	13	41	4	1	4	17	5	23	0	.304	.474
2 Don Lock	OF28, 1B4	R	32	58	58	4	13	2	0	4	9	13	16	0	.224	.293
2 Tom Satriano	C44	L	28	47	127	9	24	2	0	0	11	22	12	0	.189	.205
Billy Conigliaro	OF24	R	21	32	80	14	23	6	2	1	7	4	18	1	.288	.563
George Thomas (KJ)	OF12, 1B10, 3B1, C1	R	31	59	51	9	18	3	1	0	5	8	9	0	.353	.451
2 Joe Azcue	C19	R	29	19	51	7	13	1	0	0	6	3	10	0	.216	.255
1 Ken Harrelson	1B10	R	27	10	46	6	17	3	1	1	5	4	9	0	.217	.435
Luis Alvarado 20 R 0-5, Carlton Fisk 21 R 0-5, Tony Muser 21 L 1-9																

EAST DIVISION

NAME	T	AGE	W	L	PCT	SV	G	GS	CG	IP	H	BB	SO	SHO	ERA
		28	109	53	.673	36	162	162	50	1474	1194	498	897	20	2.83
Mike Cuellar	L	32	23	11	.676	0	39	39	18	291	213	79	182	5	2.38
Dave McNally	L	26	20	7	.741	0	41	40	11	269	232	84	166	4	3.21
Jim Palmer (XJ)	R	23	16	4	.800	0	26	23	11	181	131	64	123	6	2.34
Tom Phoebus	R	27	14	7	.667	0	35	33	6	202	180	87	117	2	3.52
Dave Leonhard	R	28	7	4	.636	1	37	3	1	94	78	38	37	1	2.49
Pete Richert	L	29	7	4	.636	12	44	0	0	57	42	14	54	0	2.21
Jim Hardin	R	25	6	7	.462	1	30	20	3	138	128	43	64	1	3.59
Dick Hall	R	38	5	2	.714	6	39	0	0	66	49	9	31	0	1.91
Eddie Watt	R	28	5	2	.714	16	56	0	0	71	49	26	46	0	1.65
Marcelino Lopez	L	25	5	3	.625	0	27	4	0	69	65	34	57	0	4.43
Al Severinsen	R	24	1	1	.500	0	12	0	0	20	14	10	13	0	2.25
Fred Beene	R	26	0	0	—	0	2	0	0	3	2	1	0	0	0.00
2 Frank Bertaina	L	25	0	0	—	0	3	0	0	6	1	3	5	0	0.00
Mike Adamson	R	21	0	0	.000	0	6	0	0	8	10	6	2	0	4.50
		28	90	72	.556	28	162	162	55	1455	1250	586	1032	20	3.31
Danny McLain	R	25	24	9	.727	0	42	41	23	325	288	67	181	9	2.80
Mickey Lolich	L	28	19	11	.633	1	37	36	15	281	214	122	271	1	3.14
Earl Wilson	R	34	12	10	.545	0	35	35	5	215	209	69	150	1	3.31
Mike Kilkenny	L	24	8	6	.571	2	39	15	6	128	99	63	97	4	3.38
Joe Sparma	R	27	6	8	.429	0	23	16	3	93	78	77	41	2	4.74
Pat Dobson	R	27	5	10	.333	9	49	9	1	105	100	39	64	0	3.60
Tom Timmermann	R	29	4	3	.571	1	31	1	1	56	50	26	42	0	2.73
John Hiller	L	26	4	4	.500	4	40	8	1	99	97	44	74	1	4.00
1 Don McMahon	R	39	3	5	.375	11	34	0	0	37	25	18	38	0	3.89
Fred Lasher	R	27	2	1	.667	0	32	0	0	44	34	22	26	0	3.07
1 Dick Radatz	R	32	2	2	.500	0	11	0	0	19	14	5	18	0	3.32
Fred Scherman	L	24	1	0	1.000	0	4	0	0	4	6	0	3	0	6.75
Norm McRae	R	21	0	0	—	0	3	0	0	3	2	1	3	0	6.00
Bob Reed	R	24	0	1	.000	0	8	1	0	15	9	8	9	0	1.80
Gary Taylor	R	23	0	1	.000	0	7	0	0	10	10	6	3	0	5.40
Daryl Patterson (MS)	R	25	0	0	.000	0	18	0	0	22	15	19	12	0	4.08
Jon Warden (SJ) 22															
		27	87	75	.537	41	162	162	30	1467	1423	685	935	7	3.92
Ray Culp (SA)	R	27	17	8	.680	0	32	32	9	227	195	79	172	2	3.81
2 Sonny Siebert	R	32	14	10	.583	5	43	22	2	163	151	68	127	0	3.81
Mike Nagy	R	21	12	2	.857	0	33	28	7	197	183	106	84	1	3.11
Sparky Lyle	L	24	8	3	.727	17	71	0	0	103	91	48	93	0	2.53
2 Vicente Romo	R	26	7	9	.438	11	52	11	4	127	116	50	89	1	3.19
Jim Lonborg	R	27	7	11	.389	0	29	23	4	144	148	65	100	0	4.50
Lee Stange	R	32	6	9	.400	3	41	15	2	137	137	56	59	0	3.68
Bill Landis	L	26	5	5	.500	1	45	5	0	82	82	40	50	0	5.27
Ray Jarvis	R	23	5	6	.455	1	29	12	2	100	105	43	36	0	4.77
Ken Brett	R	20	2	3	.400	0	8	6	0	39	41	22	23	0	5.31
Mike Garman	R	19	1	0	1.000	0	4	2	0	13	13	10	10	0	4.50
Fred Wenz	R	27	1	0	1.000	0	11	0	0	15	13	11	15	0	5.73
Bill Lee	L	22	1	0	1.000	1	20	0	0	52	56	28	45	0	4.50
1 Dick Ellsworth	L	29	0	0	—	0	1	1	0	16	14	4	4	0	6.19
Jose Santiago (EJ)	R	29	0	0	—	1	10	6	0	28	24	17	22	0	3.75
3 Ron Kline	R	37	0	0	—	0	17	0	0	17	24	17	7	0	4.76
1 Juan Pizarro	L	32	0	0	.000	0	3	0	0	14	15	6	9	0	6.00
1 Garry Roggenburk (VR)	L	29	0	0	—	0	10	0	0	13	16	6	8	0	8.10

EAST DIVISION

WASHINGTON — 4th 86-76 .531 23 — TED WILLIAMS

NAME	G by Pos	B	AGE	G	AB	R	H	2B	3B	HR	RBI	BB	SO	SB	BA	SA
TOTALS			28	162	5447	694	1365	171	40	148	640	630	900	52	.251	.378
Mike Epstein	1B118	L	26	131	403	73	112	18	1	30	85	85	99	2	.278	.551
Bernie Allen	2B110, 3B6	L	30	122	365	33	90	17	4	9	45	50	35	5	.247	.389
Eddie Brinkman	SS150	R	27	151	576	71	153	18	5	2	43	50	42	1	.266	.325
Ken McMullen	3B154	R	27	158	562	83	153	25	2	19	87	70	103	4	.272	.425
Hank Allen	OF91, 3B6, 2B3	R	28	109	271	42	75	9	3	1	17	13	28	12	.277	.343
Del Unser	OF149	L	24	153	581	69	166	19	8	7	57	58	54	8	.286	.382
Frank Howard	OF114, 1B70	R	32	161	592	111	175	17	2	48	111	102	96	1	.296	.574
Paul Casanova	C122	R	27	124	379	26	82	9	2	4	37	18	52	0	.216	.282
Ed Stroud	OF85	L	29	123	206	35	52	5	6	4	29	30	33	12	.252	.393
Tim Cullen	2B105, SS9, 3B1	R	27	119	249	22	52	7	0	1	15	14	27	1	.209	.249
Brant Alyea	OF69, 1B3	R	28	104	237	29	59	4	0	11	40	34	67	1	.249	.405
2 Lee Maye	OF65	L	34	71	238	41	69	9	3	9	26	20	25	1	.290	.466
Jim French	C63	L	27	63	158	14	29	6	3	2	13	41	15	1	.184	.297
Gary Holman	1B11, OF3	L	25	41	31	1	5	1	0	0	2	4	7	0	.161	.194
Sam Bowens	OF30	R	30	33	57	6	11	1	0	0	4	5	14	1	.193	.211
2 Zoilo Versalles	SS13, 2B6, 3B5	R	29	31	75	9	20	2	1	0	6	3	13	1	.267	.320
Dick Billings	OF6, 3B1	R	26	27	37	3	5	0	0	0	0	0	6	0	.135	.135
Dick Smith	OF9	R	21	28	28	2	3	0	0	0	0	4	7	1	.107	.107

Doug Camilli (RC) 32 R 1-3, Toby Harrah 20 R 0-1

NAME	T	AGE	W	L	PCT	SV	G	GS	CG	IP	H	BB	SO	SHO	ERA
		27	86	76	.531	41	162	162	28	1447	1310	656	835	10	3.49
Dick Bosman	R	25	14	5	.737	1	31	26	5	193	156	39	99	2	2.19
Casey Cox	R	27	12	7	.632	0	52	13	4	172	161	64	73	0	2.77
Joe Coleman	R	22	12	13	.480	1	40	36	12	248	222	100	182	4	3.27
Denny Higgins	R	29	10	9	.526	16	55	0	0	85	79	56	71	0	3.49
Darold Knowles (MS)	L	27	9	2	.818	13	53	0	0	84	73	31	59	0	2.25
Barry Moore	R	27	8	8	.529	0	31	25	4	134	123	67	61	1	4.30
Jim Hannan	R	29	7	6	.538	0	35	28	1	158	138	91	72	1	3.65
2 Jim Shellenback	R	25	4	7	.364	1	30	11	2	85	87	48	50	0	4.02
Bob Humphreys	R	33	3	3	.500	7	47	0	0	80	69	38	43	0	3.04
Dave Baldwin	R	31	2	4	.333	4	43	0	0	67	57	34	51	0	4.03
1 Camilo Pascual	R	35	2	5	.286	0	14	13	0	55	49	38	34	0	6.87
2 Cisco Carlos	R	28	1	1	.500	0	14	5	0	36	43	23	25	0	4.50
1 Frank Bertaina	L	25	1	3	.250	1	14	5	0	36	43	23	26	0	6.50
Frank Kreutzer	L	30	0	0	—	0	4	0	0	12	8	4	4	0	4.50
Jim Miles	R	25	0	0	.000	0	10	1	0	20	19	15	15	0	6.30
Jan Dukes	L	23	0	2	.000	0	8	0	0	11	8	4	3	0	2.45

NEW YORK — 5th 80-81 .497 28.5 — RALPH HOUK

NAME	G by Pos	B	AGE	G	AB	R	H	2B	3B	HR	RBI	BB	SO	SB	BA	SA
TOTALS			27	162	5308	562	1247	210	44	94	521	565	840	119	.235	.344
Joe Pepitone	1B132	L	28	135	513	49	124	16	3	27	70	30	42	8	.242	.442
Horace Clarke	2B156	B	29	156	641	82	183	26	7	4	48	53	41	33	.285	.367
Gene Michael	SS118	R	31	119	412	41	112	24	4	2	31	43	56	7	.272	.364
Jerry Kenney	3B83, OF31, SS10	L	24	130	447	49	115	14	2	3	34	48	36	25	.257	.311
Bobby Murcer	OF118, 3B31	L	23	152	564	82	146	24	4	26	82	50	103	7	.259	.454
Bill Robinson	OF62, 1B1	R	26	87	222	23	38	11	2	3	21	16	39	1	.171	.279
Roy White	OF126	B	25	130	448	55	130	30	5	7	74	81	51	18	.290	.426
Jake Gibbs	C66	L	30	71	219	18	49	9	2	0	18	23	30	1	.224	.283
Frank Fernandez	C65, OF14	R	26	89	229	34	51	6	1	12	29	65	68	1	.223	.415
Bobby Cox	3B56, 2B6	R	28	85	191	17	41	7	1	2	17	34	41	0	.215	.293
2 Jimmie Hall	OF50, 1B7	L	31	80	212	21	50	8	5	3	26	19	34	3	.236	.363
2 Ron Woods	OF67	R	26	72	171	18	30	5	2	1	7	22	29	2	.175	.246
1 Tom Tresh	SS41	B	31	45	143	13	26	5	2	1	9	17	23	2	.182	.266
Len Boehmer	1B21, 3B8, 2B1, SS1	R	28	45	108	5	19	4	0	0	7	8	10	0	.176	.213
1 Billy Cowan	OF14	R	30	32	48	5	8	0	0	1	3	3	9	0	.167	.229
Jim Lyttle	OF28	L	23	28	83	7	15	4	0	0	4	4	19	1	.181	.229
Tom Shopay	OF11	L	23	28	48	2	4	1	0	0	4	6	9	1	.083	.125
Thurman Munson	C25	R	22	26	86	6	22	1	2	1	9	10	10	1	.256	.349
Johnny Ellis	C15	R	20	22	62	2	18	4	0	1	8	1	11	0	.290	.403
Frank Tepedino	OF13	L	21	13	39	6	9	0	0	0	4	4	4	1	.231	.231
Dave McDonald	1B7	L	26	9	23	0	5	1	0	0	2	5	5	0	.217	.261

1 Dick Simpson 25 R 3-11, Ron Blomberg 20 L 3-6, 1 Nate Oliver 28 R 0-1

NAME	T	AGE	W	L	PCT	SV	G	GS	CG	IP	H	BB	SO	SHO	ERA
		27	80	81	.497	20	162	162	53	1441	1258	522	801	13	3.23
Mel Stottlemyre	R	27	20	14	.588	0	39	39	24	303	267	97	113	3	2.82
Fritz Peterson	L	27	17	16	.515	0	37	37	16	272	228	43	150	4	2.55
Stan Bahnsen	R	24	9	16	.360	1	40	33	5	221	222	90	130	2	3.83
2 Jack Aker	R	28	8	4	.667	11	38	0	0	66	51	22	40	0	2.05
Al Downing	L	28	7	5	.583	0	30	15	5	131	117	49	85	1	3.37
Bill Burbach	R	21	6	8	.429	0	31	24	2	141	112	102	82	1	3.64
Lindy McDaniel	R	33	5	6	.455	5	51	0	0	84	84	23	60	0	3.54
Mike Kekich	L	24	4	6	.400	1	28	13	1	105	91	49	66	0	4.54
Steve Hamilton	L	35	3	4	.429	2	38	0	0	57	39	21	39	0	3.32
2 Ken Johnson	R	36	1	2	.333	0	12	0	0	26	19	11	21	0	3.46
John Cumberland	L	22	0	0	—	0	3	2	0	12	6	5	6	0	4.50
Ron Klimkowski	R	24	0	1	.000	0	3	0	0	14	6	5	0	0	0.64
1 Don Nottebart	R	33	0	0	—	2	9	0	0	24	20	8	12	0	4.50
1 Fred Talbot	R	28	0	0	—	0	8	0	0	12	13	6	7	0	5.25

Joe Verbanic (SA) 26

CLEVELAND — 6th 62-99 .385 46.5 — AL DARK

NAME	G by Pos	B	AGE	G	AB	R	H	2B	3B	HR	RBI	BB	SO	SB	BA	SA
TOTALS			27	161	5365	573	1272	173	24	119	534	535	906	85	.237	.345
Tony Horton	1B157	R	24	159	625	77	174	25	4	27	93	37	91	3	.278	.461
Vern Fuller	2B102, 3B7	R	25	108	254	25	60	11	4	2	22	20	53	2	.236	.335
Larry Brown	SS101, 3B29, 2B5	R	29	132	469	48	112	10	2	4	24	44	43	5	.239	.294
Max Alvis (KJ)	3B58, SS1	R	31	66	191	13	43	6	0	1	15	14	26	1	.225	.272
2 Ken Harrelson	OF144, 1B16	R	27	149	519	83	115	13	4	27	84	95	96	17	.222	.418
Jose Cardenal	OF142, 3B5	R	25	146	557	75	143	26	3	11	45	49	58	36	.257	.373
Russ Snyder	OF84	L	35	122	266	26	66	10	0	2	24	25	33	3	.248	.308
Duke Sims	C102, OF3, 1B1	L	28	114	326	40	77	8	0	18	45	66	80	1	.236	.426
Richie Scheinblum	OF50	B	26	102	199	13	37	5	1	1	13	19	30	0	.186	.236
Chuck Hinton	OF40, 3B14	R	35	94	121	18	31	3	2	3	19	8	22	2	.256	.388
Lou Klimchock	3B56, 2B21, C1	L	29	90	258	26	74	13	2	6	26	18	14	0	.287	.422
Cap Peterson	OF30, 3B4	R	26	76	110	8	25	3	0	1	14	24	18	0	.227	.300
2 Zoilo Versalles	2B46, 3B30, SS3	R	29	72	217	21	49	11	1	1	13	21	41	3	.226	.300
Eddie Leon	SS64	R	22	64	213	20	51	6	0	3	19	19	37	2	.239	.310
Frank Baker	OF46	L	25	52	172	21	44	5	3	3	15	14	34	2	.256	.372
Dave Nelson (LJ)	2B33, OF2	R	25	52	123	11	25	0	0	0	6	9	26	4	.203	.203
1 Lee Maye	OF28	L	34	43	108	9	27	5	0	1	15	8	15	0	.250	.324
Ray Fosse	C37	R	22	37	116	11	20	3	0	2	9	8	29	1	.172	.250
Ken Suarez	C36	R	26	36	85	7	25	5	0	1	9	15	12	1	.294	.388
Russ Nagelson	OF3, 1B1	L	24	12	17	1	6	0	0	0	0	3	1	0	.353	.353
1 Joe Azcue	C6	R	29	7	24	1	7	2	0	0	1	4	5	0	.292	.417

Lou Camilli 22 B 0-14, 1 Jimmie Hall 31 L 0-10, Jack Heidemann 19 R 0-3

NAME	T	AGE	W	L	PCT	SV	G	GS	CG	IP	H	BB	SO	SHO	ERA
		27	62	99	.385	22	161	161	35	1437	1330	681	1000	7	3.94
Sam McDowell	L	26	18	14	.563	1	39	38	18	285	222	102	279	4	2.94
Luis Tiant	R	28	9	20	.310	0	38	37	9	250	229	129	156	1	3.71
2 Dick Ellsworth	L	29	6	9	.400	0	34	22	3	135	162	40	48	1	4.13
Stan Williams	R	32	6	14	.300	12	61	15	3	178	155	67	139	0	3.94
Mike Paul	L	24	5	10	.333	2	47	12	0	117	104	54	98	0	3.62
Steve Hargan	R	26	5	14	.263	0	32	23	1	144	145	81	76	1	5.69
Horacio Pina	R	24	4	2	.667	1	31	4	0	47	44	27	32	0	5.17
2 Juan Pizarro	L	32	3	3	.500	4	48	4	1	83	67	49	44	0	3.14
Ron Law	R	23	3	4	.429	1	35	1	0	52	68	34	29	0	5.02
Phil Hennigan	R	23	2	1	.667	0	16	0	0	16	14	4	10	0	3.38
1 Vicente Romo	R	26	1	1	.500	0	8	0	0	7	3	7	2	0	2.25
Gary Kroll	R	27	0	0	—	0	19	0	0	24	16	22	28	0	4.13
1 Sonny Siebert	R	32	0	1	.000	0	2	2	0	14	10	8	6	0	3.21
Gary Boyd	R	22	0	0	.000	0	3	0	0	11	8	14	9	0	9.00
Larry Burchart (JJ)	R	23	0	0	.000	0	29	0	0	42	42	24	26	0	4.29
1 Jack Hamilton	R	30	0	1	.000	0	20	0	0	37	37	23	13	0	4.35

WEST DIVISION

MINNESOTA — 1st 97-65 .599 — BILLY MARTIN

NAME	G by Pos	B	AGE	G	AB	R	H	2B	3B	HR	RBI	BB	SO	SB	BA	SA
TOTALS			29	162	5677	790	1520	246	32	163	733	599	906	115	.268	.408
Rich Reese	1B117, OF5	L	27	132	419	52	135	24	4	16	69	23	57	1	.322	.513
Rod Carew	2B118	L	23	123	458	79	152	30	4	8	56	37	72	19	.332	.467
Leo Cardenas	SS160	R	30	160	578	67	162	24	4	10	70	66	96	5	.280	.388
Harmon Killebrew	3B105, 1B80	R	33	162	555	106	153	20	2	49	140	145	84	8	.276	.584
Tony Oliva	OF152	L	28	153	637	97	197	39	4	24	101	45	66	10	.309	.496
Cesar Tovar	OF113, 2B41, 3B20	B	28	158	535	99	154	25	5	11	52	37	37	45	.288	.415
Ted Uhlaender	OF150	L	29	152	554	93	151	19	2	8	62	44	52	15	.273	.356
Johnny Roseboro	C111	L	36	115	361	39	95	12	0	3	32	39	44	1	.263	.321
Frank Quilici	3B84, 2B36, SS1	R	30	128	144	19	25	3	1	2	12	12	22	2	.174	.250
Graig Nettles	OF54, 3B21	L	24	96	225	27	50	9	2	7	26	32	47	1	.222	.373
Charlie Manuel	OF46	L	25	83	164	14	34	6	0	2	24	28	33	1	.207	.280
Bob Allison	OF58, 1B3	R	34	81	189	18	43	8	2	8	30	27	39	2	.228	.418
Rick Renick	3B30, OF10, SS6	R	25	71	139	21	34	9	0	5	17	12	32	0	.245	.374
George Mitterwald	C63, OF1	R	24	69	187	18	48	6	5	3	17	17	47	0	.257	.380
Tom Tischinski	C32	R	24	37	47	2	9	0	0	0	2	4	9	0	.191	.191
Jim Holt	OF5, 1B1	L	25	15	14	0	5	1	0	0	2	1	1	0	.357	.571

Herm Hill 23 L 0-2, Cotton Nash 26 R 2-9, Rick Dempsey 19 R 3-6, Frank Kostro 31 R 0-2, 1 Ron Clark 26 R 1-8

NAME	T	AGE	W	L	PCT	SV	G	GS	CG	IP	H	BB	SO	SHO	ERA
		29	97	65	.599	43	162	162	41	1498	1388	524	906	8	3.24
Jim Perry	R	33	20	6	.769	0	46	36	12	262	244	66	153	3	2.82
Dave Boswell	R	24	20	12	.625	0	39	38	10	256	215	99	190	0	3.23
Jim Kaat	L	30	14	13	.519	1	40	32	10	242	252	75	139	0	3.50
Ron Perranoski	L	33	9	10	.474	31	75	0	0	120	85	52	62	0	2.10
Tom Hall	L	21	8	7	.533	0	31	18	5	141	129	50	92	2	3.32
Dick Woodson	R	24	7	5	.583	1	44	10	2	110	99	49	66	0	3.68
Dean Chance (SA)	R	28	5	4	.556	0	20	15	1	88	76	35	50	0	2.97
Bob Miller	R	30	5	5	.500	3	48	11	1	119	118	32	57	0	3.03
Joe Grzenda	L	32	4	1	.800	3	40	0	0	49	52	17	24	0	3.86
Al Worthington (VR)	R	40	4	1	.800	3	46	0	0	65	65	20	51	0	4.57
Jerry Crider	R	27	1	0	1.000	1	21	1	0	29	31	15	16	0	4.86
Charley Walters	R	22	0	0	—	0	6	0	0	7	6	4	2	0	5.14
Bill Zepp	R	22	0	0	—	0	5	0	0	5	6	3	1	0	7.20
2 Darrell Brandon	R	28	0	0	—	0	5	0	0	6	6	4	3	0	3.00
Danny Morris	L	23	0	1	.000	0	5	1	0	9	9	8	8	0	5.40

OAKLAND — 2nd 88-74 .543 9 — HANK BAUER 80-69 .537 — JOHN McNAMARA 8-5 .615

NAME	G by Pos	B	AGE	G	AB	R	H	2B	3B	HR	RBI	BB	SO	SB	BA	SA
TOTALS			27	162	5614	740	1400	210	28	148	680	617	953	100	.249	.376
Danny Cater	1B132, OF20, 2B4	R	29	162	584	64	153	24	2	10	76	28	40	1	.262	.361
Dick Green	2B131	R	28	136	483	61	133	25	6	12	64	53	94	2	.275	.427
Bert Campaneris	SS125	R	27	135	547	71	142	15	2	2	30	62	62	62	.260	.305
Sal Bando	3B162	R	25	162	609	106	171	25	3	31	113	111	82	1	.281	.484
Reggie Jackson	OF150	L	23	152	549	123	151	36	3	47	118	114	142	13	.275	.608
Rick Monday (BW)	OF119	L	23	122	399	57	108	17	4	12	54	70	100	12	.271	.424
Tommie Reynolds (SJ)	OF89	R	27	107	315	51	81	10	2	2	19	34	29	1	.257	.308
Phil Roof	C106	R	28	106	247	19	58	6	1	7	19	32	55	1	.235	.291
Ted Kubiak	SS42, 2B33	B	27	92	305	38	76	9	1	2	27	25	35	2	.249	.305
Jose Tartabull	OF63	L	30	75	266	28	71	11	1	0	11	9	12	5	.267	.316
Ramon Webster	1B13	L	26	64	77	5	20	0	1	3	13	12	8	0	.260	.325
Dave Duncan	C56	R	23	58	127	11	16	3	0	2	19	41	0	0	.126	.220
2 Larry Haney	C53	R	26	53	86	4	13	4	0	2	12	7	19	0	.151	.267
Mike Hershberger (SJ)	OF35	R	29	51	129	11	26	2	1	0	10	10	15	1	.202	.240
2 Bob Johnson	1B7, 2B2	R	33	51	67	5	23	1	0	0	5	4	8	0	.343	.403
Blue Moon Odom (EJ)	P32	R	24	41	45	7	12	0	1	0	5	4	9	0	.266	.506
Lew Krausse	P43	R	26	43	48	7	8	1	0	1	6	4	22	0	.167	.438
Joe Rudi	OF18, 1B11	R	22	35	122	10	23	4	0	2	12	11	10	0	.341	.541
2 Tito Francona	1B19, OF1	L	35	32	65	6	19	1	1	0	6	6	6	0	.292	.431
Bobby Brooks	OF21	R	23	29	79	13	19	5	0	3	10	20	24	0	.241	.418
Gene Tenace	C13	R	22	16	38	6	7	0	0	1	2	8	5	0	.158	.237
1 Jim Pagliaroni (BG)	C7	R	31	14	27	1	4	1	0	0	1	3	6	0	.148	.296
1 John Donaldson (BT)	2B1	L	26	13	13	1	1	0	0	0	0	2	4	1	.077	.077

Bill McNulty 22 R 0-17, Tony LaRussa 24 R 0-8, 1 Joe Nossek 28 R 0-6, Allen Lewis 27 B 0-1

NAME	T	AGE	W	L	PCT	SV	G	GS	CG	IP	H	BB	SO	SHO	ERA
		24	88	74	.543	36	162	162	42	1481	1356	586	887	14	3.71
Blue Moon Odom (EJ)	R	24	15	6	.714	0	32	32	10	231	179	112	150	3	2.92
Chuck Dobson	R	25	15	13	.536	0	35	35	11	235	244	80	137	1	3.87
Catfish Hunter	R	23	12	15	.444	0	38	35	10	247	210	85	150	3	3.35
Paul Lindblad	L	27	9	6	.600	0	60	0	0	78	72	33	64	0	4.15
Jim Nash (SJ)	R	24	8	8	.500	0	26	19	3	115	112	30	75	1	3.68
Lew Krausse	R	26	5	7	.417	0	43	16	4	140	134	48	85	2	4.44
Rollie Fingers	R	22	6	7	.462	12	60	8	0	119	116	41	61	1	3.71
Jim Roland	L	26	5	1	.833	12	39	3	2	86	59	46	48	0	2.20
Marcel Lachemann	R	28	4	1	.800	2	28	4	3	43	19	16	30	0	3.98
George Lauzerique	R	21	3	4	.429	0	19	8	1	61	58	27	39	0	4.72
Vida Blue	L	19	1	1	.500	1	12	4	0	42	49	18	24	0	6.64
2 Juan Pizarro	L	32	1	1	.500	1	5	1	0	11	11	5	6	0	2.25
Ed Sprague	R	23	1	1	.500	2	14	0	0	31	31	20	9	0	4.50
3 Fred Talbot	R	28	0	1	.000	0	12	2	0	19	24	7	20	0	5.21
John Wyatt	R	34	0	0	—	0	8	0	0	8	9	6	6	0	5.63

CALIFORNIA — 3rd 71-91 .438 26   BILL RIGNEY 11-28 .282   LEFTY PHILLIPS 60-63 .488

NAME	G by Pos	B	AGE	G	AB	R	H	2B	3B	HR	RBI	BB	SO	SB	BA	SA
TOTALS			26	163	5316	528	1221	151	29	88	480	516	929	54	.230	.319
Jim Spencer	1B107	L	21	113	386	39	98	14	3	10	31	26	53	1	.254	.383
2 Sandy Alomar	2B134	B	25	134	559	60	140	14	3	1	30	36	48	18	.250	.281
Jim Fregosi	SS160	R	27	161	580	78	151	22	6	12	47	93	86	9	.260	.381
Aurelio Rodriguez	3B159	R	21	159	561	47	130	17	2	7	47	32	88	5	.232	.307
Bill Voss	OF111, 1B2	L	25	133	349	33	91	11	4	2	40	35	40	5	.261	.332
Jay Johnstone	OF144	L	23	148	540	64	146	20	5	10	59	38	75	3	.270	.381
Rick Reichardt	OF136, 1B3	R	26	137	493	60	125	11	4	13	68	43	100	1	.254	.371
3 Joe Azcue	C80	R	29	80	248	15	54	6	0	1	19	27	28	0	.218	.254
Roger Repoz	OF48, 1B31	B	28	103	219	25	36	1	1	8	19	32	52	1	.164	.288
Bubba Morton	OF49, 1B1	R	37	87	172	18	42	10	1	7	32	28	29	2	.244	.436
Lou Johnson	OF44	R	34	67	133	10	27	8	0	0	9	10	19	5	.203	.263
Tom Egan (BY)	C46	R	23	46	120	7	17	1	0	5	16	17	41	0	.142	.275
1 Tom Satriano	C36, 1B5, 2B2	L	28	41	108	5	28	2	0	1	16	18	15	0	.259	.306
2 Jim Hicks	OF10, 1B8	R	29	37	48	4	4	0	0	3	8	13	16	1	.083	.271
Winston Llenas	3B9	R	25	34	47	4	8	2	0	0	4	2	10	0	.170	.213
1 Vic Davalillo	OF22, 1B3	L	32	33	71	10	11	1	1	0	1	6	5	3	.155	.197
2 Billy Cowan	OF13, 1B6	R	30	28	56	10	17	1	0	4	10	3	9	0	.304	.536
1 Bobby Knoop	2B27	R	30	27	71	5	14	1	0	1	6	13	16	1	.197	.254
Dick Stuart	1B13	R	36	22	71	5	17	1	0	3	13	5	21	0	.239	.394

Bob Rodgers 30 B 9-46, Ruben Amaro 33 R 6-27, Randy Brown 24 L 4-25, Jarvis Tatum 22 R 7-22, Marty Perez 23 R 3-13, Bob Chance 28 L 1-7, Chuck Cottier 33 R 0-2

NAME	T	AGE	W	L	PCT	SV	G	GS	CG	IP	H	BB	SO	SHO	ERA
		28	71	91	.438	39	163	163	25	1438	1294	517	885	9	3.54
Andy Messersmith	R	23	16	11	.593	2	40	33	10	250	169	100	211	2	2.52
Rudy May	L	24	10	13	.435	2	43	25	4	180	142	66	133	0	3.45
Tom Murphy	R	23	10	16	.385	0	36	35	4	216	213	69	100	4	4.21
Jim McGlothlin	R	25	8	16	.333	0	37	35	4	201	188	58	96	1	3.18
Ken Tatum	L	34	7	2	.778	22	45	0	0	86	51	39	65	0	1.36
1 George Brunet	L	34	8	8	.500	0	19	19	2	101	98	39	56	2	3.83
1 Hoyt Wilhelm	R	46	5	7	.417	10	44	0	0	66	48	18	53	0	2.45
Eddie Fisher	R	32	3	2	.600	2	52	1	0	97	100	28	47	0	3.62
Steve Kealey	R	22	2	1	1.000	0	15	3	1	37	48	13	17	1	3.89
Pedro Borbon	R	22	2	3	.400	0	22	0	0	41	55	11	20	0	6.15
Vern Geishert	R	23	1	1	.500	0	11	5	0	31	32	7	18	0	4.65
Clyde Wright	L	28	1	8	.111	0	37	5	0	64	66	30	31	0	4.08
Rickey Clark	R	23	0	1	—	0	6	0	0	10	12	7	6	0	5.40
Phil Ortega (BJ)	R	29	0	0	—	0	3	0	0	13	7	4	1	0	10.13
Wally Wolf	R	27	0	0	—	0	2	0	0	2	5	3	0	0	13.50
Lloyd Allen	R	19	0	1	.000	0	4	1	0	5	10	5	5	0	5.40
Tom Bradley	R	22	0	0	—	0	2	0	0	2	1	1	2	0	27.00
2 Bob Priddy	R	29	0	0	.000	0	15	0	0	26	24	7	15	0	4.85
Greg Washburn	R	22	0	2	.000	0	5	4	0	21	21	5	4	0	8.18

KANSAS CITY — 4th 69-93 .426 28   JOE GORDON

NAME	G by Pos	B	AGE	G	AB	R	H	2B	3B	HR	RBI	BB	SO	SB	BA	SA
TOTALS			25	163	5462	586	1311	179	32	98	538	532	901	129	.240	.338
Mike Fiore	1B91, OF13	L	24	107	339	53	93	14	1	12	35	84	63	4	.274	.428
Jerry Adair	2B109, SS8, 3B1	R	32	126	432	29	108	9	1	5	48	20	36	1	.250	.310
Jackie Hernandez	SS144	R	28	145	504	54	112	14	2	4	40	38	111	17	.222	.282
Joe Foy	3B113, 1B16, OF16, SS5, 2B3	R	26	145	519	72	136	19	2	11	71	74	75	37	.262	.370
Bob Oliver	OF98, 1B24, 3B8	R	26	118	394	43	100	8	4	13	43	21	74	5	.254	.393
Pat Kelly	OF107	L	24	112	417	61	110	20	4	8	32	49	70	40	.264	.388
Lou Piniella	OF129	R	25	135	493	43	139	21	6	11	68	33	56	2	.282	.416
Ellie Rodriguez	C90	R	23	95	267	27	63	10	0	2	20	31	26	3	.236	.296
Ed Kirkpatrick	OF82, C8, 1B2, 3B2, 2B1	L	24	120	315	40	81	11	4	14	49	43	42	3	.257	.451
Juan Rios	2B46, SS32, 3B4	R	23	87	196	20	44	5	1	1	17	6	19	1	.224	.276
Chuck Harrison	1B55	R	28	75	213	18	47	5	1	5	18	16	20	1	.221	.296
Buck Martinez (RL)	C55, OF1	R	20	72	205	14	47	6	1	4	23	8	25	0	.229	.327
Joe Keough	OF49, 1B1	L	22	70	166	17	31	2	0	7	13	13	35	5	.187	.199
Hawk Taylor	OF18, C6	R	30	64	89	7	24	5	0	3	21	6	18	0	.270	.427
Paul Schaal	3B49, 2B6, SS6	R	26	61	205	22	54	6	1	1	13	25	27	2	.263	.307
Jim Rooker	P28	L	26	34	57	7	16	3	0	4	8	1	19	0	.281	.544
Jim Campanis	C26	R	25	30	83	4	13	5	0	0	5	5	19	0	.157	.217
Luis Alcaraz	2B19, 3B2, SS1	R	28	22	79	15	20	2	1	5	12	9	18	5	.253	.342

George Spriggs 28 L 4-29, Scott Northey 22 R 16-61, Dennis Paepke 24 R 3-27, Fred Rico 24 R 6-26, Fran Healy 22 R 4-10, Billy Harris 25 L 2-7

NAME	T	AGE	W	L	PCT	SV	G	GS	CG	IP	H	BB	SO	SHO	ERA
		26	69	93	.426	25	163	163	42	1465	1357	560	894	10	3.72
Wally Bunker	R	24	12	11	.522	2	35	31	10	223	198	62	130	1	3.23
Moe Drabowsky	R	33	11	9	.550	11	52	0	0	98	80	30	76	0	2.94
Dick Drago	R	24	11	13	.458	1	41	26	10	201	190	65	108	2	3.76
Bill Butler	L	22	9	10	.474	0	34	29	5	194	174	91	156	4	3.90
Roger Nelson	R	25	7	13	.350	0	29	29	8	193	170	65	82	1	3.31
Jim Rooker	L	26	4	16	.200	0	29	22	8	158	136	73	108	1	3.76
Tom Burgmeier	L	25	3	1	.750	0	31	0	0	54	67	21	23	0	4.17
Mike Hedlund	R	22	6	8	.333	2	34	16	1	125	123	40	74	0	3.24
Steve Jones	L	28	2	3	.400	0	20	4	0	45	45	24	31	0	4.20
Dave Morehead	R	26	2	3	.400	0	33	0	0	38	28	28	32	0	5.73
Dave Wickersham	R	33	2	3	.400	5	34	0	0	50	58	14	27	0	3.96
Galen Cisco	R	32	1	1	.500	1	15	0	0	22	17	15	18	0	3.68
Al Fitzmorris	R	23	1	1	.500	0	7	0	0	11	9	4	9	0	4.09
Don O'Riley	R	24	1	0	1.000	0	18	0	0	32	35	15	10	0	7.04
Jerry Cram	R	21	0	1	.000	0	3	0	0	17	16	6	10	0	3.18
Chris Zachary	R	25	0	1	.000	0	18	0	0	27	37	6	8	0	8.00

CHICAGO — 5th 68-94 .420 29   AL LOPEZ 8-9 .471   DON GUTTERIDGE 60-85 .414

NAME	G by Pos	B	AGE	G	AB	R	H	2B	3B	HR	RBI	BB	SO	SB	BA	SA
TOTALS			27	162	5450	625	1346	210	27	112	585	552	844	54	.247	.357
Gail Hopkins	1B101	L	26	124	373	52	99	14	3	8	46	50	66	2	.265	.381
2 Bobby Knoop	2B104	R	30	104	345	34	79	14	1	6	45	35	68	2	.229	.328
Luis Aparicio	SS154	R	35	156	599	77	168	24	5	5	51	66	29	24	.280	.362
Bill Melton	3B148, OF11	R	23	157	556	67	142	26	3	23	87	56	106	1	.255	.433
Walt Williams	OF111	R	25	135	471	59	143	22	1	3	32	26	33	6	.304	.374
Ken Berry	OF120	R	28	130	297	35	69	12	2	4	18	24	50	1	.232	.327
Carlos May (HJ)	OF100	L	21	100	367	62	103	18	2	18	62	58	66	1	.281	.488
Ed Herrmann	C92	R	22	102	290	31	67	8	0	8	31	30	55	0	.231	.341
Pete Ward	1B25, 3B21, OF9	L	29	105	199	22	49	7	0	6	32	33	38	0	.246	.372
Buddy Bradford (GJ)	OF88	R	24	93	273	36	70	8	2	11	27	34	75	5	.256	.421
Tommy McCraw (KJ)	1B44, OF41	L	28	93	240	21	62	12	2	2	25	21	34	5	.258	.350
Ron Hansen	2B26, 1B21, SS8, 3B7	R	31	85	185	15	48	8	1	2	22	18	25	2	.259	.335
Don Pavletich	C51, 1B13	R	30	73	188	26	46	12	0	6	33	28	45	0	.245	.404
Woodie Held	OF18, SS3, 3B3, 2B1	R	37	56	63	9	9	2	0	1	6	6	13	0	.143	.317
Rich Morales	2B38, SS13, 3B1	R	26	55	121	12	26	0	1	0	6	7	18	1	.215	.231
Duane Josephson (AJ)	C47	R	27	52	162	19	39	4	2	1	20	13	17	0	.241	.321
Bob Christian	OF38	R	23	39	129	11	38	4	3	1	16	10	19	3	.217	.318
Angel Bravo	OF25	L	26	27	90	10	26	4	2	1	4	5	9	2	.289	.411
1 Sandy Alomar	2B22	B	25	26	85	5	19	4	1	0	3	5	6	2	.224	.294

Bob Spence 23 L 4-26, Chuck Brinkman 24 R 1-15, Doug Adams 26 L 3-14, Jose Ortiz 22 R 3-11

NAME	T	AGE	W	L	PCT	SV	G	GS	CG	IP	H	BB	SO	SHO	ERA
		28	68	94	.420	25	162	162	29	1438	1470	564	810	10	4.21
Joe Horlen	R	31	16	14	.533	0	36	35	7	236	237	77	121	2	3.78
Wilbur Wood	L	27	10	11	.476	15	76	0	0	120	113	40	73	0	3.00
Gary Peters	L	32	10	15	.400	0	36	32	7	219	238	78	140	3	4.52
Tommy John	R	26	9	11	.450	0	33	33	6	232	230	90	128	2	3.26
Billy Wynne	R	25	7	7	.500	0	20	20	6	129	143	50	67	1	4.05
Dan Osinski	R	35	5	5	.500	2	51	0	0	61	56	23	27	0	3.54
1 Cisco Carlos	R	28	4	3	.571	0	25	4	0	49	52	23	23	0	5.69
Jerry Nyman	L	26	4	4	.500	0	20	10	2	65	58	39	40	1	5.26
Danny Murphy	R	26	2	1	.667	4	17	0	0	31	28	10	16	0	2.03
1 Bob Locker	R	31	2	3	.400	4	17	0	0	26	6	15	0	6.55
Bart Johnson	R	19	1	3	.250	0	9	4	0	22	22	6	15	0	5.73
Paul Edmondson (DD)	R	26	1	6	.143	0	14	13	1	88	72	39	46	0	3.68
2 Gary Bell	R	32	0	0	—	0	23	0	0	39	48	23	26	0	6.23
Danny Lazar	L	25	0	0	—	0	6	0	0	11	11	9	6	0	6.43
1 Bob Priddy	R	29	0	0	—	0	8	0	0	10	12	5	6	0	4.50
Denny O'Toole	R	20	0	0	.000	0	19	0	0	40	35	14	23	0	6.08
Don Secrist (BH)	L	25	0	1	.000	0	19	0	0	17	17	15	8	0	7.50
Fred Rath	R	25	0	0	—	1	6	0	0	8	10	2	5	0	9.00
Sammy Ellis	R	28	0	0	.000	0	10	0	0	29	42	16	15	0	5.90
2 Jack Hamilton	R	30	0	0	.000	0	8	0	0	12	23	7	5	0	12.00

SEATTLE — 6th 64-98 .395 33   JOE SCHULTZ

NAME	G by Pos	B	AGE	G	AB	R	H	2B	3B	HR	RBI	BB	SO	SB	BA	SA
TOTALS			28	163	5444	639	1276	179	27	125	583	626	1015	167	.234	.346
Don Mincher	1B122	L	31	140	427	53	105	14	0	25	78	78	69	10	.246	.454
2 John Donaldson	2B90, 3B2, SS1	L	26	95	338	22	79	8	3	1	19	36	36	6	.234	.284
Ray Oyler	SS106	R	30	106	255	24	42	5	0	7	22	31	80	1	.165	.267
Tommy Harper	3B59, 2B59, OF26	R	28	148	537	78	126	10	2	9	41	95	90	73	.235	.311
Steve Hovley	OF84	R	24	91	329	41	91	14	3	0	20	30	34	10	.277	.365
Wayne Comer	OF139, 3B1, C1	R	25	147	481	88	118	18	1	15	54	82	79	18	.245	.380
2 Tommy Davis	OF112, 1B1	R	30	123	454	52	123	29	1	6	80	30	46	19	.271	.379
Jerry McNertney	C122	R	32	128	410	39	99	18	1	8	55	29	63	1	.241	.349
Mike Hegan	OF64, 1B19	L	26	95	267	54	78	9	6	8	37	62	61	6	.292	.461
Gus Gil	3B38, 2B18, SS12	R	29	92	221	20	49	7	0	0	17	16	28	2	.222	.253
Steve Whitaker	OF39	L	26	69	116	15	29	4	3	4	14	14	28	1	.250	.440
John Kennedy (RJ)	SS33, 3B23	R	28	61	128	18	30	3	1	4	14	14	25	4	.234	.367
Rich Rollins (KJ)	3B47, SS1	R	31	58	187	15	42	5	1	4	21	7	19	2	.225	.316
2 Ron Clark	SS38, 3B15, 2B5, 1B1	R	26	57	163	9	32	5	0	1	9	14	34	2	.196	.227
Merritt Ranew	C13, OF3, 3B1	L	31	54	81	11	20	4	0	1	10	14	14	0	.247	.272
2 Jim Pagliaroni	C29, 1B2, OF1	R	31	40	110	10	19	4	5	3	16	21	16	0	.264	.455
Greg Goossen	1B31, OF2	R	23	52	139	19	43	5	1	10	24	14	29	1	.309	.597
1 Jim Gosger	OF39	L	26	39	55	4	6	7	2	5	1	4	15	11	1	.176	.333
2 Dick Simpson	OF17	R	25	26	51	8	9	2	1	1	4	11	19	0	.176	.353
Danny Walton	OF23	R	21	23	92	12	20	7	0	2	11	6	21	0	.217	.370
1 Larry Haney	C20	R	26	22	63	3	16	5	0	0	6	12	11	1	.254	.407
Gordon Lund	SS17, 2B1, 3B1	R	28	20	21	1	3	0	0	0	1	1	5	0	.143	.143
Fred Stanley	SS15, 2B1	B	21	17	43	2	12	1	0	0	1	6	12	1	.279	.372

Jose Vidal 29 R 5-26, 2 Sandy Valdespino 30 L 8-38, Freddy Velazquez 31 R 2-16, Mike Ferraro 24 R 0-4, Billy Williams 36 L 0-10

NAME	T	AGE	W	L	PCT	SV	G	GS	CG	IP	H	BB	SO	SHO	ERA
		28	64	98	.395	33	163	163	21	1464	1490	653	963	6	4.35
Gene Brabender	R	27	13	14	.481	0	40	29	7	202	193	103	139	1	4.37
Diego Segui	R	31	12	6	.667	12	66	8	2	142	127	61	113	0	3.36
Marty Pattin	R	26	7	12	.368	0	34	27	2	159	166	71	126	1	5.60
2 Fred Talbot	R	28	5	8	.385	0	25	16	1	115	125	41	67	1	4.15
Steve Barber (SA)	L	31	4	7	.364	0	25	16	0	86	99	48	69	0	4.81
2 Bob Locker	R	31	3	3	.500	6	51	0	0	78	69	26	46	0	2.19
John Gelnar	R	26	3	10	.231	3	40	10	1	109	103	26	69	0	3.30
Mike Marshall	R	26	3	10	.231	0	20	14	3	88	99	35	47	1	5.11
2 Jim Bouton	R	29	2	1	.667	1	57	1	0	92	77	38	68	0	3.91
2 Dooley Womack	R	29	2	2	.500	6	55	0	0	70	58	37	43	0	2.57
John O'Donoghue	L	29	2	2	.500	0	55	0	0	74	28	17	44	0	2.96
2 Garry Roggenburk	L	29	2	2	.500	1	24	27	11	11	0	4.50
2 George Brunet	L	34	2	5	.286	0	12	11	0	61	70	37	0	5.34
1 Gary Bell	R	32	2	6	.250	2	13	11	1	61	76	34	30	1	4.72
Dick Baney	R	22	1	0	1.000	0	7	2	0	18	22	9	8	0	3.79
Mickey Fuentes (DD)	R	20	1	3	.250	0	8	4	0	26	29	16	14	0	5.19
John Morris	L	27	0	0	—	0	20	0	0	28	29	16	19	0	6.23
Gary Timberlake (MS)	L	20	0	0	—	0	2	2	0	7	9	7	3	0	7.50
Jerry Stephenson	R	25	0	0	—	0	6	0	0	14	14	8	9	0	5.79
Dick Bates	R	22	0	0	—	0	1	0	0	2	2	5	0	22.50
1 Darrell Brandon	R	28	0	3	.000	1	18	1	0	15	16	10	9	0	8.40
Skip Lockwood	R	22	0	1	.000	0	8	0	0	33	24	16	19	0	3.52
Bill Edgerton	L	27	0	0	—	0	1	0	0	2	5	2	2	0	13.50
1 Jack Aker	R	28	0	0	—	0	15	0	0	17	25	10	12	0	7.41
Bob Meyer	L	29	0	0	—	1	33	30	10	17	0	3.28

AMERICAN LEAGUE CHAMPIONSHIP — BALTIMORE (EAST) 3   MINNESOTA (WEST) 0

LINE SCORES

TEAM	1	2	3	4	5	6	7	8	9	10	11	12	R	H	E
Game 1 October 4 at Baltimore															
MIN	0	0	0	1	0	0	2	0	0	0	0	0	3	4	2
BAL	0	0	0	1	1	0	0	0	1	0	0	1	4	10	1

Perry, Perranoski (9)   Cuellar, Richert (9), Watt (10), Lopez (12), Hall (12)

TEAM	1	2	3	4	5	6	7	8	9	10	11	R	H	E
Game 2 October 5 at Baltimore														
MIN	0	0	0	0	0	0	0	0	0	0	0	0	3	1
BAL	0	0	0	0	0	0	0	0	1			1	8	0

Boswell, Perranoski (11)   McNally

TEAM	1	2	3	4	5	6	7	8	9	R	H	E
Game 3 October 6 at Minnesota												
BAL	0	3	0	2	0	1	0	2	3	11	18	0
MIN	1	0	0	0	1	0	0	0	0	2	10	2

Palmer   Miller, Woodson (2), Hall (4), Worthington (5), Grzenda (6), Chance (7), Perranoski (9)

COMPOSITE BATTING

NAME	POS	G	AB	R	H	2B	3B	HR	RBI	BA
Baltimore Totals		3	123	16	36	8	1	4	15	.293
Blair	OF	3	15	1	6	2	0	1	6	.400
Belanger	SS	3	15	4	4	0	1	0	0	.267
B. Robinson	3B	3	14	1	7	1	0	0	0	.500
Buford	OF	3	14	3	4	1	0	0	0	.286
Powell	1B	3	13	2	5	0	0	2	5	.385
Johnson	2B	3	13	4	3	0	0	0	0	.231
F. Robinson	OF	3	12	1	4	1	0	1	3	.333
Hendricks	C	3	8	0	2	0	0	0	1	.250

Etchebarren C 0-4, Motton PH 1-2, May PH 0-1, Salmon PH 0-1, Rettenmund PH 0-0

NAME	POS	G	AB	R	H	2B	3B	HR	RBI	BA
Minnesota Totals		3	110	5	17	3	1	1	5	.155
Carew	2B	3	14	0	1	0	0	0	0	.071
Oliva	OF	3	13	1	5	3	0	0	1	.385
Cardenas	SS	3	13	0	2	0	0	0	0	.154
Tovar	OF	3	13	0	1	0	0	0	0	.077
Reese	1B	3	12	0	2	0	0	1	2	.167
Killebrew	3B	3	8	1	1	0	0	0	1	.125
Allison	OF	2	8	0	0	0	0	0	0	.000

Mitterwald C 1-7, Uhlaender OF 1-6, Roseboro C 1-5, Nettles PH 1-1, Renick PH 0-1, Manuel PH 0-0

COMPOSITE PITCHING

NAME	G	IP	H	BB	SO	W	L	SV	ERA
Baltimore Totals	3	32	17	12	27	3	0	0	1.13
McNally	1	11	3	5	11	1	0	0	0.00
Palmer	1	9	10	2	4	1	0	0	2.00
Cuellar	1	8	3	1	7	0	0	0	2.25
Watt	1	1	0	2	1	0	0	0	0.00
Richert	1	1	0	0	2	0	0	0	0.00
D. Hall	1	0.2	0	1	1	1	0	0	0.00
Lopez	1	0.1	1	1	1	0	0	0	0.00
Minnesota Totals	3	31.1	36	13	14	0	3	0	4.02
Boswell	1	10.2	7	7	4	0	1	0	0.84
Perry	1	8	7	2	4	0	1	0	3.38
Perranoski	3	4.2	8	2	3	0	0	0	5.79
Chance	1	2	2	0	2	0	0	0	13.50
Miller	1	1.2	5	0	0	0	1	0	5.40

Worthington 1G, Woodson 1G, Grzenda 1G, T. Hall 1G

NATIONAL LEAGUE CHAMPIONSHIP — NEW YORK (EAST) 3   ATLANTA (WEST) 0

LINE SCORES

TEAM	1	2	3	4	5	6	7	8	9	10	11	12	R	H	E
Game 1		October 4 at Atlanta													
NY	0	2	0	2	0	0	0	5	0				9	10	1
ATL	0	1	2	0	1	0	1	0	0				5	10	2

Seaver, Taylor (8)   Niekro, Upshaw (9)

Game 2		October 5 at Atlanta													
NY	1	3	2	2	1	0	2	0	0				11	13	1
ATL	0	0	0	1	5	0	0	0	0				6	9	3

Koosman, Taylor (5),   Reed, Doyle (2), Pappas (3),
McGraw (7)   Britton (6), Upshaw (6),
                           Neibauer (9)

Game 3		October 6 at New York													
ATL	2	0	0	0	2	0	0	0	0				4	8	1
NY	0	0	1	2	3	1	0	0	X				7	14	0

Jarvis, Stone (5),   Gentry, Ryan (3)
Upshaw (6)

COMPOSITE BATTING

NAME	POS	G	AB	R	H	2B	3B	HR	RBI	BA
New York										
Totals		3	113	27	37	8	1	6	24	.327
Jones	OF	3	14	4	6	2	0	1	4	.429
Agee	OF	3	14	4	5	1	0	2	4	.357
Shamsky	OF	3	13	3	7	0	0	0	1	.538
Garrett	3B	3	13	3	5	2	0	1	3	.385
Boswell	2B	3	12	4	4	0	0	2	5	.333
Kranepool	1B	3	12	2	3	1	0	0	1	.250
Grote	C	3	12	3	2	1	0	0	0	.167
Harrelson	SS	3	11	2	2	1	1	0	3	.182
Martin	PH	2	2	0	1	0	0	0	2	.500
Weis	2B	3	1	1	0	0	0	0	0	.000
Gaspar	OF	3	0	0	0	0	0	0	0	—
Atlanta										
Totals		3	106	15	27	9	0	5	15	.255
H. Aaron	OF	3	14	3	5	2	0	3	7	.357
Gonzalez	OF	3	14	4	5	1	0	1	2	.357
Millan	2B	3	12	2	4	1	0	0	0	.333
Cepeda	1B	3	11	2	5	2	0	1	3	.455
Didier	C	3	11	0	0	0	0	0	0	.000
Carty	OF	3	10	4	3	2	0	0	0	.300
Garrido	SS	3	10	0	2	0	0	0	0	.200
Boyer	3B	3	9	0	1	0	0	0	3	.111
Aspromonte	PH	3	3	0	0	0	0	0	0	.000
Lum	OF	2	2	0	1	0	0	0	1	1.000
T.Aaron	PH	1	1	0	0	0	0	0	0	.000

Alou PH 0-1, Jackson SS 0-0, Tillman C 0-0

COMPOSITE PITCHING

NAME	G	IP	H	BB	SO	W	L	SV	ERA
New York									
Totals	3	27	27	11	20	3	0	2	5.00
Ryan	1	7	3	2	7	1	0	0	2.57
Seaver	1	7	8	3	2	1	0	0	6.43
Koosman	1	4.2	7	4	5	1	0	0	11.57
Taylor	2	3.1	3	0	4	0	0	1	0.00
McGraw	1	3	1	1	1	0	0	1	0.00
Gentry	1	2	5	1	1	0	0	0	9.00
Atlanta									
Totals	3	26	37	10	25	0	3	0	6.92
Niekro	1	8	9	4	4	0	1	0	4.50
Upshaw	3	6.1	5	1	4	0	0	0	2.84
Jarvis	1	4.1	10	4	6	0	1	0	12.46
Pappas	1	2.1	4	0	4	0	0	0	11.57
Reed	1	1.2	5	3	3	0	1	0	21.60
Doyle	1	1	0	0	1	0	0	0	0.00
Neibauer	1	1	0	1	0	0	0	0	0.00
Stone	1	1	2	0	0	0	0	0	9.00
Britton	1	0.1	1	0	0	0	0	0	0.00

EAST DIVISION

NEW YORK — 1st 100-62 .617 — GIL HODGES

NAME	G by Pos	B	AGE	G	AB	R	H	2B	3B	HR	RBI	BB	SO	SB	BA	SA
TOTALS			27	162	5427	632	1311	184	41	109	598	527	1089	66	.242	.351
Ed Kranepool	1B106, OF2	L	24	112	353	36	84	9	2	11	49	37	32	3	.238	.368
Ken Boswell	2B96	L	23	102	362	48	101	14	7	3	32	36	47	7	.279	.381
Bud Harrelson	SS119	B	25	123	395	42	98	11	6	0	24	54	54	1	.248	.306
Wayne Garrett	3B72, 2B47, SS9	L	21	124	400	38	87	11	3	1	39	40	75	4	.218	.268
Ron Swoboda	OF97	R	25	109	327	38	77	10	2	9	52	43	90	1	.235	.361
Tommie Agee	OF146	R	26	149	565	97	153	23	4	26	76	59	137	12	.271	.464
Cleon Jones	OF122, 1B15	R	26	137	483	92	164	25	4	12	75	64	60	16	.340	.482
Jerry Grote	C112	R	26	113	365	38	92	12	3	6	40	32	59	2	.252	.351
Rod Gaspar	OF91	B	23	118	215	26	49	6	1	1	14	25	19	7	.228	.279
Al Weis	SS52, 2B43, 3B1	B	31	103	247	20	53	9	2	2	23	15	51	3	.215	.291
Art Shamsky (XJ)	OF78, 1B9	L	27	100	303	42	91	9	3	14	47	36	32	1	.300	.488
2 Donn Clendenon	1B58, OF7	R	33	72	202	31	51	5	0	12	37	19	62	3	.252	.455
J.C. Martin	C48, 1B2	L	32	66	177	12	37	5	4	4	21	12	32	0	.209	.316
Bobby Pfeil	3B49, 2B11, OF1	R	25	62	211	20	49	9	0	0	10	7	27	2	.232	.275
Ed Charles	3B52	R	34	61	169	21	35	8	1	3	18	18	31	4	.207	.320
Amos Otis	OF35, 3B3	R	22	48	93	6	14	3	1	0	4	6	27	1	.151	.204
Duffy Dyer	C19	R	23	29	74	5	19	3	1	3	12	4	22	0	.257	.446

1 Kevin Collins 22 L 6-40, 2 Jim Gosger 26 L 2-15, Bob Heise 22 R 3-10

CHICAGO — 2nd 92-70 .568 8 — LEO DUROCHER

NAME	G by Pos	B	AGE	G	AB	R	H	2B	3B	HR	RBI	BB	SO	SB	BA	SA
TOTALS			30	163	5530	720	1400	215	40	142	671	559	928	30	.253	.384
Ernie Banks	1B153	R	38	155	565	60	143	19	2	23	106	42	101	0	.253	.416
Glenn Beckert (BG)	2B129	R	28	131	543	69	158	22	1	1	37	24	24	6	.291	.341
Don Kessinger	SS157	B	26	158	664	109	181	38	6	4	53	61	70	11	.273	.366
Ron Santo	3B160	R	29	160	575	97	166	18	4	29	123	96	97	1	.289	.485
Jim Hickman	OF125	R	32	134	338	38	80	11	2	21	54	47	74	2	.237	.467
Don Young	OF100	R	23	101	272	36	65	12	3	6	27	38	74	1	.239	.371
Billy Williams	OF159	L	31	163	642	103	188	33	10	21	95	61	61	9	.293	.474
Randy Hundley	C151	R	27	151	522	67	133	15	1	18	64	61	90	2	.255	.381
Willie Smith	OF33, 1B24	L	30	103	195	21	48	9	1	9	25	25	49	1	.246	.441
Al Spangler	OF58	L	35	82	213	23	45	8	1	4	23	21	16	0	.211	.315
2 Paul Popovich	2B25, SS7, 3B6, OF1	B	28	60	154	26	48	9	1	0	14	18	14	0	.312	.370
Nate Oliver	2B13	R	28	44	49	4	7	3	0	1	4	4	10	0	.159	.295
Jim Qualls (SJ)	OF35, 2B4	B	22	43	120	12	30	5	3	0	14	2	24	1	.250	.342
1 Adolfo Phillips	OF25	R	27	28	49	5	11	3	0	1	7	16	15	1	.224	.327
Bill Heath	C9	L	30	27	32	1	5	0	1	0	1	2	4	0	.156	.219
Ken Rudolph	C11, OF3	R	22	27	34	7	7	1	0	0	6	6	11	0	.206	.324
Oscar Gamble	OF24	L	19	24	71	6	16	1	1	1	5	5	10	2	.225	.310
Gene Oliver	C6	R	33	23	27	0	6	3	0	0	1	9	9	0	.222	.333

3 Jimmie Hall 31 L 5-24, Rick Bladt 22 R 2-13, Manny Jimenez 30 L 1-6, John Hairston 24 R 1-4, Charlie Smith 31 R 0-2, Randy Bobb 21 R 0-2

PITTSBURGH — 3rd 88-74 .543 12 — LARRY SHEPARD 84-73 .535   ALEX GRAMMAS 4-1 .800

NAME	G by Pos	B	AGE	G	AB	R	H	2B	3B	HR	RBI	BB	SO	SB	BA	SA
TOTALS			27	162	5626	725	1557	220	52	119	651	454	944	74	.277	.398
Al Oliver	1B106, OF21	L	22	129	463	55	132	19	2	17	70	21	38	8	.285	.445
Bill Mazeroski (LJ)	2B65	R	32	67	227	13	52	7	1	3	25	22	16	1	.229	.308
Freddie Patek	SS146	R	24	147	460	48	110	9	1	5	32	53	86	15	.239	.296
Richie Hebner	3B124, 1B1	L	21	129	459	72	138	23	4	8	47	53	53	4	.301	.420
Roberto Clemente	OF135	R	34	138	507	87	175	20	12	19	91	56	73	4	.345	.544
Matty Alou	OF162	L	30	162	698	105	231	41	6	1	48	42	46	22	.331	.411
Willie Stargell	OF116, 1B23	L	29	145	522	89	160	31	6	29	92	61	120	1	.307	.556
Manny Sanguillen	C113	R	25	129	459	62	139	21	6	5	57	12	48	8	.303	.407
Jose Pagan	3B44, OF23, 2B1	R	34	108	274	29	78	11	4	9	42	17	46	1	.285	.453
Carl Taylor	OF36, 1B24	R	25	104	221	30	77	10	1	4	33	31	36	2	.348	.452
Gene Alley (SJ)	2B53, SS25, 3B5	R	28	82	285	28	70	3	2	8	32	19	48	4	.246	.354
Jose Martinez	2B42, SS20, 3B5, OF2	R	26	77	168	20	45	6	0	1	16	9	32	1	.268	.321
Jerry May (SJ)	C52	R	25	62	190	21	44	9	0	7	23	9	23	1	.232	.384
Ron Davis	OF51	R	27	62	64	10	15	1	0	0	4	7	14	0	.234	.281
Bob Robertson	1B26	R	22	32	96	7	20	4	1	1	9	3	31	0	.208	.302
Gary Kolb	C7	L	29	29	37	4	3	0	0	0	3	2	14	0	.081	.108
Johnnie Jeter	OF20	R	24	29	29	7	9	1	1	0	1	6	15	1	.310	.517
Dave Cash	2B17	R	21	18	61	8	17	3	1	0	4	5	9	2	.279	.361
Angel Mangual	OF3	R	22	6	4	1	1	0	0	0	0	0	1	0	.250	.500

ST. LOUIS — 4th 87-75 .537 13 — RED SCHOENDIENST

NAME	G by Pos	B	AGE	G	AB	R	H	2B	3B	HR	RBI	BB	SO	SB	BA	SA
TOTALS			30	162	5536	595	1403	228	44	90	561	503	876	87	.253	.359
Joe Torre	1B144, C17	R	28	159	602	72	174	29	6	18	101	66	85	0	.289	.447
Julian Javier	2B141	R	32	143	493	59	139	28	2	10	42	40	74	8	.282	.408
Dal Maxvill	SS131	R	30	132	372	27	65	10	2	0	32	44	52	1	.175	.228
Mike Shannon	3B149	R	29	150	551	51	140	15	5	12	55	49	63	4	.254	.365
Vada Pinson (BW)	OF124	L	30	132	495	58	126	22	6	10	70	35	63	4	.255	.384
Curt Flood	OF152	R	31	153	606	80	173	31	3	4	57	40	57	9	.285	.366
Lou Brock	OF157	L	30	157	655	97	195	33	10	12	47	50	115	53	.298	.434
Tim McCarver	C136	L	27	138	515	46	134	27	5	7	51	49	26	1	.260	.365
Steve Huntz	SS52, 2B12, 3B6	B	23	71	139	13	27	4	0	3	13	27	34	0	.194	.288
2 Vic Davalillo	OF23, P2	L	33	63	98	15	26	8	0	1	10	6	15	0	.265	.357
Phil Gagliano	2B20, 1B9, 3B9, OF2	R	27	62	128	7	29	5	0	0	14	14	12	0	.227	.266
Bill White	1B15	L	35	49	57	7	12	1	0	1	5	4	9	1	.211	.298
Joe Hague	OF17, 1B9	L	25	40	100	12	17	3	0	0	5	12	23	0	.170	.270
Dave Ricketts	C11	R	33	30	44	2	12	5	0	0	7	5	3	0	.273	.395
Byron Browne	OF16	R	26	23	53	9	12	5	0	1	7	11	14	0	.226	.321
1 Jim Hicks	OF16	R	29	21	33	3	6	0	0	1	2	2	10	0	.182	.314
1 Bob Johnson	3B4, 1B1	R	33	19	29	1	6	0	0	0	2	3	4	0	.207	.310
1 Jerry DaVanon	SS16	R	23	16	40	3	12	0	0	0	3	4	6	0	.300	.450

Leron Lee 21 L 5-23, Tom Coulter 24 B 6-19, Ted Simmons 19 B 3-14, 2 Joe Nossek 28 R 1-5, Boots Day 21 L 0-6

NEW YORK PITCHING

NAME	T	AGE	W	L	PCT	SV	G	GS	CG	IP	H	BB	SO	SHO	ERA
		26	100	62	.617	35	162	162	51	1468	1217	517	1012	28	2.99
Tom Seaver	R	24	25	7	.781	0	36	35	18	273	202	82	208	5	2.21
Jerry Koosman	L	26	17	9	.654	0	32	32	16	241	187	68	180	6	2.28
Gary Gentry	R	22	13	12	.520	0	35	35	6	234	192	81	154	3	3.42
Tug McGraw	L	24	9	3	.750	12	42	4	1	100	89	47	92	0	2.25
Ron Taylor	R	31	9	4	.692	13	59	0	0	76	61	24	42	0	2.72
Don Cardwell	R	33	8	10	.444	0	30	21	4	152	145	47	60	0	3.02
Cal Koonce	R	28	6	3	.667	7	40	0	0	83	85	42	48	0	4.99
Nolan Ryan (GJ)	R	22	6	3	.667	1	25	10	2	89	60	53	92	0	3.54
Jim McAndrew	R	25	6	7	.462	0	27	21	4	135	112	44	90	2	3.47
Jack DiLauro	L	26	1	4	.200	1	23	4	0	64	50	18	27	0	2.39
Danny Frisella	R	23	0	1	—	0	3	0	0	5	8	3	2	0	7.20
Jesse Hudson	L	21	0	0	—	0	1	0	0	4	3	2	1	0	4.50
1 Al Jackson	L	33	0	0	—	0	9	0	0	11	18	4	10	0	10.64
Bob Johnson	R	26	0	0	—	0	2	0	0	2	1	1	1	0	0.00
Les Rohr	L	23	0	0	—	0	1	0	0	1	5	1	0	0	27.00

CHICAGO PITCHING

NAME	T	AGE	W	L	PCT	SV	G	GS	CG	IP	H	BB	SO	SHO	ERA
		29	92	70	.568	27	163	163	58	1454	1366	475	1017	22	3.34
Ferguson Jenkins	R	25	21	15	.583	1	43	42	23	311	284	71	273	7	3.21
Bill Hands	R	29	20	14	.588	0	41	41	18	300	268	73	181	3	2.49
Ken Holtzman	L	23	17	13	.567	0	39	39	12	261	248	93	176	6	3.59
Phil Regan	R	32	12	6	.667	17	71	0	0	112	120	35	56	0	3.70
2 Dick Selma	R	25	10	8	.556	1	36	25	4	169	137	72	161	2	3.62
Ted Abernathy	R	36	4	3	.571	3	56	0	0	85	75	42	55	0	3.18
Rich Nye	L	24	3	5	.375	3	34	5	1	69	72	21	39	0	5.09
Hank Aguirre	L	38	1	0	1.000	1	41	0	0	45	45	12	19	0	2.60
Jim Colborn	R	23	1	0	1.000	0	5	1	0	15	15	9	4	0	3.00
Joe Decker	R	22	1	0	1.000	0	4	1	0	12	10	6	13	0	4.50
2 Don Nottebart	R	33	1	1	.500	0	16	0	0	18	28	7	8	0	7.00
3 Ken Johnson	R	36	1	2	.333	1	9	2	0	19	17	13	18	0	2.84
Alec Distaso	R	20	0	0	—	0	2	0	0	5	6	1	1	0	3.60
1 Gary Ross	R	21	0	0	—	0	2	0	0	2	5	1	0	0	13.50
Dave Lemonds	L	20	0	0	.000	0	1	0	0	5	5	4	3	0	3.60
1 Joe Niekro	R	24	0	1	.000	0	4	0	0	19	24	6	7	0	3.76
Archie Reynolds	R	23	0	0	—	0	2	0	0	7	11	7	4	0	2.57

Darcy Fast (MS) 22

PITTSBURGH PITCHING

NAME	T	AGE	W	L	PCT	SV	G	GS	CG	IP	H	BB	SO	SHO	ERA
		29	88	74	.543	33	162	162	39	1446	1348	553	1124	9	3.61
Steve Blass	R	27	16	10	.615	2	38	32	9	210	207	86	147	0	4.46
Bob Moose	R	21	14	3	.824	4	44	19	6	170	149	62	165	1	2.91
Bob Veale	L	33	13	14	.481	0	34	34	9	226	232	91	213	1	3.23
Dock Ellis	R	24	11	17	.393	0	35	33	4	219	206	76	173	2	3.58
1 Jim Bunning	R	37	10	9	.526	0	25	25	4	156	147	49	124	0	3.81
Bruce Dal Canton	R	27	8	2	.800	5	57	0	0	86	79	49	56	0	3.35
2 Joe Gibbon	L	34	5	1	.833	9	56	0	0	51	38	17	35	0	1.94
Chuck Hartenstein	R	27	5	4	.556	10	56	0	0	96	84	27	44	0	3.94
Luke Walker	L	25	4	6	.400	0	31	3	1	119	98	57	96	1	3.63
Lou Marone	L	23	1	1	.500	0	29	0	0	35	24	13	25	0	2.57
1 Ron Kline	L	25	0	0	—	3	20	0	0	17	14	4	7	0	5.81
1 Jim Shellenback	L	25	0	0	—	0	2	2	0	14	13	6	10	0	3.18
Gene Garber	R	21	0	0	—	0	3	0	0	5	6	1	4	0	5.40
Frank Brosseau	R	24	0	0	—	0	2	0	0	2	1	5	3	0	9.00
1 Pedro Ramos	R	34	0	0	—	0	6	0	0	8	8	4	6	0	6.00
Bo Belinsky	L	32	0	3	.000	0	8	3	0	18	17	14	15	0	4.50

ST. LOUIS PITCHING

NAME	T	AGE	W	L	PCT	SV	G	GS	CG	IP	H	BB	SO	SHO	ERA
		28	87	75	.537	26	162	162	63	1460	1289	511	1004	12	2.94
Bob Gibson	R	33	20	13	.606	0	35	35	28	314	251	95	269	4	2.18
Steve Carlton	L	24	17	11	.607	0	31	31	12	236	185	93	210	2	2.17
Nelson Briles	R	25	15	11	.536	0	36	33	10	228	218	63	126	3	3.51
Mike Torrez	R	22	10	4	.714	0	24	15	3	108	96	62	61	0	3.58
2 Mudcat Grant	R	33	7	5	.583	7	30	4	1	63	60	22	35	0	4.14
Chuck Taylor	R	27	7	5	.583	0	27	13	5	127	108	30	62	1	2.55
Dave Giusti	R	29	3	7	.300	0	22	12	2	100	96	37	62	1	3.60
Ray Washburn	R	31	3	8	.273	1	28	16	2	132	133	49	80	0	3.07
Joe Hoerner	L	32	2	3	.400	15	45	0	0	53	44	19	35	0	2.89
Sal Campisi	R	26	1	0	1.000	1	7	0	0	9	6	3	9	0	0.90
Jerry Reuss	L	20	1	0	1.000	0	1	0	0	7	7	1	6	0	0.00
1 Ron Willis	R	25	1	2	.333	0	26	0	0	31	26	19	23	0	4.22
Tom Hilgendorf	L	26	0	0	—	0	1	1	0	4	2	2	1	0	1.50
Jim Ellis	L	24	0	0	—	0	1	0	0	5	3	0	1	0	1.80
2 Vic Davalillo	L	33	0	0	—	0	2	0	0	4	0	0	0	0	□
Reggie Cleveland	R	21	0	0	—	0	2	0	0	3	6	4	2	0	9.00
1 Dennis Ribant	R	27	0	0	—	0	2	0	0	5	12	1	4	0	18.00
Santiago Guzman	R	19	0	0	—	0	1	0	0	5	6	3	5	0	5.14
Mel Nelson	L	33	0	0	—	0	5	0	0	4	4	1	2	0	12.60
1 Gary Waslewski	R	27	0	2	.000	0	12	0	0	19	21	9	16	0	3.86

Dick Hughes (SA) 31

PHILADELPHIA 5th 63-99 .389 37 — BOB SKINNER 44-64 — GEORGE MYATT 19-35 .352

NAME	G by Pos	B	AGE	G	AB	R	H	2B	3B	HR	RBI	BB	SO	SB	BA	SA
TOTALS			27	162	5408	645	1304	227	35	137	593	549	1130	73	.241	.372
Dick Allen (ST)	1B117	R	27	118	438	79	126	23	3	32	89	64	144	2	.288	.573
Cookie Rojas	2B95, OF2	R	30	110	391	35	89	11	4	4	30	23	28	1	.228	.292
Don Money	SS126	R	22	127	450	41	103	22	2	6	42	43	83	1	.229	.327
Tony Taylor	3B71, 2B57, 1B10	R	33	138	557	68	146	24	5	3	42	42	62	19	.262	.339
Johnny Callison	OF129	L	30	134	495	66	131	29	5	16	64	49	73	2	.265	.440
Larry Hisle (BG)	OF140	R	22	145	482	75	128	23	5	20	56	48	152	18	.266	.459
Johnny Briggs	OF108, 1B2	L	25	124	361	51	86	20	3	12	46	64	78	9	.238	.410
Mike Ryan	C132	R	27	133	446	41	91	17	2	12	44	30	66	1	.204	.332
Deron Johnson	OF72, 3B50, 1B18	R	30	138	475	51	121	19	4	17	80	60	111	4	.255	.419
Ron Stone	OF69	L	26	103	222	22	53	7	1	2	20	29	28	3	.239	.293
Rick Joseph	3B58, 1B17, 2B1	R	29	99	264	35	72	15	0	6	37	22	57	2	.273	.398
Terry Harmon	SS38, 2B19, 3B2	R	25	87	201	25	48	8	1	0	16	22	31	1	.239	.289
Dave Watkins	C54, OF5, 1B2	R	25	69	148	17	26	2	1	4	12	22	53	2	.176	.284
Rich Barry	OF9	R	28	20	32	4	6	1	0	0	0	5	6	0	.188	.219
Gene Stone	1B5	L	25	18	28	4	6	0	1	0	0	4	9	0	.214	.286
Scott Reid	OF5	R	22	13	19	5	4	0	0	0	0	7	5	1	.211	.211
Vic Roznovsky	C2	L	30	13	13	0	3	0	0	0	1	1	4	0	.231	.231
1 Don Lock	OF1	L	32	4	4	0	0	0	0	0	0	0	1	0	.000	.000
Leroy Reams		L	25	1	1	0	0	0	0	0	0	0	1		.000	.000

NAME	T	AGE	W	L	PCT	SV	G	GS	CG	IP	H	BB	SO	SHO	ERA
		26	63	99	.389	21	162	162	47	1434	1494	570	921	14	4.14
Rick Wise	R	23	15	13	.536	0	33	31	14	220	215	61	144	4	3.23
Grant Jackson	L	26	14	18	.438	1	38	35	13	253	237	92	180	4	3.34
Woody Fryman	R	29	12	15	.444	0	36	35	10	228	243	89	150	1	4.42
Jerry Johnson	R	25	6	13	.316	1	33	21	4	147	151	57	82	2	4.29
Billy Champion	R	21	5	10	.333	1	23	20	4	117	130	63	70	2	5.00
Dick Farrell	R	35	3	4	.429	3	46	0	0	74	92	27	40	0	4.01
Jeff James	R	27	2	2	.500	0	6	5	1	32	34	11	21	0	5.34
Billy Wilson (AJ)	R	26	2	5	.286	6	37	0	0	62	53	36	48	0	3.34
Lowell Palmer	R	21	2	8	.200	0	26	9	1	90	91	47	68	1	5.20
John Boozer	R	29	1	2	.333	6	46	2	0	82	91	36	47	0	4.28
Al Raffo	R	27	1	3	.250	1	45	0	0	72	81	25	38	0	4.13
Lou Peraza	R	26	0	0	—	0	9	0	0	9	12	2	7	0	6.00
Chris Short (XJ)	R	31	0	0	—	0	2	2	0	10	11	4	5	0	7.20
Barry Lersch	R	24	0	3	.000	0	10	0	0	18	20	10	13	0	7.00
1 Gary Wagner	R	29	0	0	—	0	9	1	31	7	8			0	8.05

MONTREAL 6th 52-110 .321 48 — GENE MAUCH

NAME	G by Pos	B	AGE	G	AB	R	H	2B	3B	HR	RBI	BB	SO	SB	BA	SA
TOTALS			28	162	5419	582	1300	202	33	125	542	529	962	52	.240	.359
Bob Bailey (BN)	1B85, OF12, 3B1	R	26	111	358	46	95	16	6	9	53	40	76	3	.265	.419
Gary Sutherland	2B139, SS15, OF1	R	24	141	544	63	130	26	1	3	35	37	31	5	.239	.307
Bobby Wine	SS118, 1B1, 3B1	R	30	121	370	23	74	8	1	3	25	28	49	0	.200	.251
Coco Laboy	3B156	R	29	157	562	53	145	25	1	18	83	40	96	0	.258	.409
Rusty Staub	OF156	L	25	158	549	89	166	26	5	29	79	110	61	3	.302	.526
2 Adolfo Phillips (IL)	OF53	R	27	58	199	25	43	4	4	4	7	19	62	6	.216	.337
Mack Jones	OF129	L	30	135	455	73	123	23	5	22	79	67	110	6	.270	.488
Ron Brand	C84, OF2	R	29	103	287	19	74	12	0	0	20	30	19	2	.258	.300
Ty Cline	OF41, 1B17	L	30	101	209	26	50	5	3	2	12	32	22	4	.239	.321
John Bateman (RJ)	C66	R	28	74	235	16	49	4	0	8	19	12	44	0	.209	.328
2 Ron Fairly (HJ)	1B52, OF21	L	30	70	253	35	73	13	4	12	39	28	22	1	.289	.514
1 Kevin Collins	2B20, 3B16	L	22	52	96	5	23	5	1	2	12	8	16	0	.240	.375
Don Bosch (KJ)	OF32	B	26	49	112	13	20	5	0	1	4	8	20	1	.179	.250
Maury Wills	SS46, 2B1	R	36	47	189	23	42	3	0	0	8	20	11	15	.222	.238
Joe Herrera	OF31, 2B2, 3B1	R	27	47	126	7	36	5	0	2	12	3	14	1	.286	.373
Floyd Wicker	OF11	L	25	41	39	2	4	0	0	2	2	0	13	0	.103	.103
John Boccabella	C32	R	28	40	86	4	9	2	0	1	6	6	30	1	.105	.163
1 Donn Clendenon	1B24, OF11	R	33	38	129	14	31	6	1	4	14	6	32	2	.240	.349
1 Manny Mota	OF22	R	31	31	89	6	28	1	0	0	6	11	1	3	.315	.348
Angel Hermoso	2B18, SS6	R	22	28	74	6	12	0	0	0	5	3	10	3	.162	.162
Jim Fairey	OF13	L	24	20	49	6	14	1	0	1	6	1	7	1	.286	.367
Marv Staehle	2B4	L	27	6	17	4	7	2	0	1	1	2	4	0	.412	.706
Garry Jestadt	SS1	R	22	6	6	1	0	0	0	0	1	0	0	0	.000	.000
Don Hahn	OF3	R	20	9	9	1	0	0	0	0	0	0	5	0	.111	.111

NAME	T	AGE	W	L	PCT	SV	G	GS	CG	IP	H	BB	SO	SHO	ERA
		28	52	110	.321	21	162	162	26	1426	1429	702	973	8	4.33
Bill Stoneman	R	25	11	19	.367	0	42	36	8	236	233	123	185	5	4.39
Dan McGinn	L	25	7	10	.412	6	74	1	0	132	123	65	112	0	3.95
Howie Reed	R	32	6	7	.462	1	31	15	2	106	119	50	59	1	4.84
Steve Renko	R	24	6	7	.462	0	18	15	4	103	94	50	68	0	4.02
Mike Wegener	R	22	5	14	.263	0	32	26	4	166	150	96	124	1	4.39
Jerry Robertson	R	25	5	16	.238	1	38	27	3	180	186	81	133	0	3.95
Roy Face	R	41	4	2	.667	5	44	0	0	59	62	15	34	0	3.97
2 Gary Waslewski	L	25	2	5	.286	1	35	1	0	66	61	37	45	0	5.18
Don Shaw	L	25	2	2	.500	3	35	1	0	45	55	18	27	0	4.09
2 Claude Raymond	R	32	2	3	.333	1	15	0	0	22	23	8	11	0	4.09
1 Mudcat Grant	R	33	1	6	.143	0	11	10	1	51	64	14	20	0	4.76
Larry Jaster	L	25	1	4	.143	0	24	11	1	77	95	28	39	0	5.49
Steve Shea	R	26	0	0	—	0	10	0	0	16	18	8	11	0	2.81
Leo Marentette	R	28	0	0	—	0	5	0	0	5	9	1	4	0	7.20
Bob Reynolds	R	22	0	0	—	1	0	1	0	3	2	2	0		27.00
Carroll Sembera	R	27	0	2	.000	2	23	0	0	33	28	24	15	0	3.55
Carl Morton	R	25	0	0	—	1	8	0	0	29	29	18	16	0	4.66
2 Dick Radatz	R	32	0	4	.000	2	22	0	0	35	32	18	32	0	5.66

WEST DIVISION

ATLANTA 1st 93-69 .574 — LUM HARRIS

NAME	G by Pos	B	AGE	G	AB	R	H	2B	3B	HR	RBI	BB	SO	SB	BA	SA
TOTALS			29	162	5460	691	1411	195	22	141	640	485	665	59	.258	.380
Orlando Cepeda	1B153	R	31	154	573	74	147	28	2	22	88	55	76	12	.257	.428
Felix Millan	2B162	R	25	162	652	98	174	23	5	6	57	34	35	14	.267	.345
Sonny Jackson (LJ)	SS97	L	24	98	318	41	76	3	5	1	27	35	33	12	.239	.289
Clete Boyer	3B141	R	32	144	496	57	124	16	1	14	57	55	87	3	.250	.371
Hank Aaron	OF144, 1B4	R	35	147	547	100	164	30	3	44	97	87	47	9	.300	.607
Felipe Alou	OF116	R	34	123	476	54	134	13	1	5	32	23	23	4	.282	.345
2 Tony Gonzalez	OF82	L	32	89	320	51	94	15	2	10	50	27	22	3	.294	.447
Bob Didier	C114	B	20	114	352	30	90	16	1	0	32	34	39	1	.256	.307
Mike Lum	OF89	L	23	121	168	20	45	8	0	1	22	16	18	0	.268	.333
Rico Carty	OF79	R	29	104	304	47	104	15	4	16	58	32	26	0	.342	.549
Gil Garrido	SS81	R	28	82	227	18	50	5	1	0	10	16	11	0	.220	.251
Bob Aspromonte	OF24, 3B23, SS18, 2B2	R	31	82	198	16	50	8	1	3	24	13	19	0	.253	.348
Bob Tillman	C69	R	32	69	190	18	37	5	0	12	29	18	47	0	.195	.411
1 Tito Francona	OF15, 1B7	L	35	51	88	5	26	1	0	2	22	13	10	0	.295	.375
Tommie Aaron	OF16, 1B6	R	29	69	60	13	15	2	0	1	5	6	9	0	.250	.333
Ralph Garr	OF7	L	23	22	27	6	6	1	0	0	1	1	2	2	.222	.259
Darrell Evans	3B6	L	22	12	26	3	6	0	0	0	1	3	6	0	.231	.231
1 Walt Hriniak (BG)	C6	L	26	7	7	0	1	0	0	0	0	1	1	0	.143	.143
Oscar Brown	OF3	R	23	7	4	2	1	0	0	0	0	0	1	0	.250	.250
Dusty Baker	OF3	R	20	3	7	0	0	0	0	0	0	0	2	0	.000	.000
Jim Breazeale	1B1	L	19	3	1	1	1	0	0	0	0	0	2	0	.000	.000

NAME	T	AGE	W	L	PCT	SV	G	GS	CG	IP	H	BB	SO	SHO	ERA
		27	93	69	.574	42	162	162	38	1445	1334	438	893	7	3.53
Phil Niekro	R	30	23	13	.639	1	40	35	21	284	235	57	193	4	2.57
Ron Reed	R	26	18	10	.643	0	36	33	7	241	227	56	160	1	3.47
George Stone	L	23	13	10	.565	3	36	20	3	165	166	48	102	0	3.65
Pat Jarvis	R	28	13	11	.542	0	37	33	4	217	204	73	123	1	4.44
Jim Britton	R	25	7	5	.583	1	24	13	2	88	69	49	60	1	3.78
Cecil Upshaw	R	26	6	4	.600	27	62	0	0	105	102	29	57	0	2.91
Milt Pappas	R	30	6	10	.375	0	26	24	1	144	149	44	72	0	3.63
Paul Doyle	L	29	2	0	1.000	4	36	0	0	39	31	16	25	0	2.08
2 Hoyt Wilhelm	R	46	2	0	1.000	4	8	0	0	12	5	4	14	0	0.75
1 Claude Raymond	R	32	2	1	.500	1	33	0	0	48	56	13	15	0	5.25
Gary Neibauer	R	24	1	2	.333	0	29	0	0	58	42	31	42	0	3.88
Larry Maxie	R	28	0	0	—	0	2	0	0	3	1	1	0		3.00
Rick Kester	R	22	0	1	.000	0	2	0	0	5	2	3	0		13.50
Mike McQueen	L	18	0	0	—	0	2	0	0	5	3	4	5	0	3.00
3 Bob Priddy	R	29	0	0	—	0	1	0	0	2	1	0	1	0	18.00
Charlie Vaughan	L	21	0	0	—	0	1	0	0	1	1	2	1	0	18.00
1 Ken Johnson	R	36	0	0	.000	0	2	0	0	9	32	9	20	0	4.97
Garry Hill	R	22	0	0	—	0	2	0	0	2	6	2	1	0	18.00

SAN FRANCISCO 2nd 90-72 .556 3 — CLYDE KING

NAME	G by Pos	B	AGE	G	AB	R	H	2B	3B	HR	RBI	BB	SO	SB	BA	SA
TOTALS			28	162	5474	713	1325	187	28	136	657	711	1054	71	.242	.361
Willie McCovey	1B148	L	31	149	491	101	157	26	2	45	126	121	66	0	.320	.656
Ron Hunt	2B125, 3B1	R	28	128	478	72	125	23	3	4	41	51	47	9	.262	.341
Hal Lanier	SS150	R	26	150	495	37	113	9	1	0	35	25	68	0	.228	.251
Jim Davenport	3B104, 1B1, SS1, OF1	R	35	112	303	20	73	10	1	2	42	29	37	0	.241	.300
Bobby Bonds	OF155	R	23	158	622	120	161	25	6	32	90	81	187	45	.259	.473
Willie Mays	OF108, 1B1	R	38	117	403	64	114	17	3	13	58	49	71	6	.283	.437
Ken Henderson (LJ)	OF111, 3B3	B	23	113	374	42	84	14	4	6	44	42	64	6	.225	.332
Dick Dietz	C73	R	27	79	244	28	56	8	1	11	35	53	53	0	.230	.406
Dave Marshall	OF87	L	26	110	267	32	62	7	1	2	33	40	68	1	.232	.288
Don Mason	2B51, 3B21, SS7	R	24	104	250	43	57	4	2	0	13	36	29	1	.228	.284
Bob Burda	1B45, OF19	L	30	97	161	20	37	8	0	6	27	21	12	0	.230	.391
Jim Ray Hart	OF68, 3B3	R	27	95	236	27	60	9	0	3	26	28	49	0	.254	.331
Jack Hiatt (FJ)	C60, 1B3	R	26	69	194	18	38	4	0	4	34	48	58	0	.196	.325
Tito Fuentes	3B36, SS36, 2B6	B	25	67	183	28	54	5	3	1	14	15	25	2	.295	.366
Bobby Etheridge	3B39, SS1	R	26	56	131	13	34	9	1	0	10	19	26	0	.260	.351
Bob Barton	C49	R	27	49	106	5	18	2	0	1	9	9	19	0	.170	.189
Johnny Stephenson	C9, 3B1	L	28	22	27	2	6	2	0	0	3	4	4	0	.222	.296
1 Cesar Gutierrez	3B7, SS4	R	26	15	23	4	5	1	0	0	0	2	1	0	.217	.261
Leon Wagner	OF1	L	35	11	12	0	4	1	0	0	4	0	3	0	.333	.333
George Foster	OF8	R	20	9	10	2	4	0	0	0	2	1	5	0	.400	.400
Frank Johnson	OF7	R	26	7	10	2	1	0	0	0	0	1	4	0	.100	.100
John Harrell	C2	R	21	2	4	1	2	0	0	0	2	0	0	0	.500	.500
Ozzie Virgil		R	31	1	1	0	0	0	0	0	0	0	0	0	.000	.000

NAME	T	AGE	W	L	PCT	SV	G	GS	CG	IP	H	BB	SO	SHO	ERA
		29	90	72	.556	17	162	162	71	1474	1381	461	906	15	3.25
Juan Marichal	R	31	21	11	.656	0	37	36	27	300	244	54	205	8	2.10
Gaylord Perry	R	30	19	14	.576	0	40	39	26	325	290	91	233	3	2.49
Frank Linzy	R	28	14	9	.609	11	58	0	0	116	129	38	62	0	3.65
Mike McCormick	L	30	11	9	.550	0	32	28	9	197	175	77	76	0	3.34
Bobby Bolin	R	30	7	7	.500	0	30	22	2	146	149	49	102	0	4.44
Ray Sadecki	L	28	5	8	.385	0	29	17	4	138	137	53	104	3	4.24
Ron Herbel	R	31	4	1	.800	1	37	4	0	87	92	33	34	0	4.03
Ron Bryant	L	21	3	4	.571	1	16	8	0	58	60	25	30	0	4.34
2 Don McMahon	R	39	3	1	.750	2	13	0	0	24	13	9	21	0	3.00
1 Joe Gibbon	L	34	3	1	.750	2	16	0	0	15	13	9		0	3.60
Rich Robertson	R	24	3	2	.250	0	17	7	1	44	53	21	20	1	5.52
Mike Davison	L	23	0	0	—	0	11	0	0	10	8	4	5	0	4.50
Bob Garibaldi	R	27	0	0	—	0	2	0	0	5	4	2	3	0	1.80
2 Ron Kline	R	37	0	0	—	0	20	0	0	32	34	9	13	0	4.09

CINCINNATI 3rd 89-73 .549 4 — DAVE BRISTOL

NAME	G by Pos	B	AGE	G	AB	R	H	2B	3B	HR	RBI	BB	SO	SB	BA	SA
TOTALS			26	163	5634	798	1558	224	42	171	750	474	1042	79	.277	.422
Lee May	1B156, OF7	R	26	158	607	85	169	32	3	38	110	45	142	5	.278	.529
Tommy Helms	2B125, SS4	R	28	126	480	38	129	18	1	1	40	18	33	4	.269	.317
Woody Woodward	SS93, 2B2	R	26	97	241	36	63	12	0	0	15	24	40	3	.261	.311
Tony Perez	3B160	R	27	160	629	103	185	31	2	37	122	63	131	4	.294	.526
Pete Rose	OF156, 2B2	B	28	156	627	120	218	33	11	16	82	88	65	7	.348	.512
Bobby Tolan	OF150	L	23	152	637	104	194	25	10	21	93	27	92	26	.305	.474
Alex Johnson	OF132	R	26	139	523	86	165	18	4	17	88	25	69	11	.315	.463
Johnny Bench	C147	R	21	148	532	83	156	23	1	26	90	49	86	6	.293	.487
Jimmy Stewart	OF66, 2B18, 3B6, SS1	B	30	121	221	26	56	7	4	0	22	26	41	5	.253	.339
Darrel Chaney	SS91	B	21	93	209	21	40	5	2	4	15	24	75	1	.191	.234
Chico Ruiz	2B39, SS29, 3B7, 1B2, OF1	R	30	88	196	19	48	4	0	3	13	14	22	8	.245	.276
Fred Whitfield	1B14	L	31	74	74	7	11	3	0	2	13	6	18	0	.149	.189
Ted Savage	OF42, 3B1	R	32	68	110	20	25	5	0	3	12	24	27	6	.227	.345
Jim Beauchamp	OF9, 1B3	R	29	43	60	8	15	1	0	1	6	5	13	0	.250	.317
Pat Corrales	C3	R	27	30	10	1	4	0	0	0	3	3	0	0	.264	.375
Danny Breeden	C3	R	27	8	8	0	1	0	0	0	0	0	3	0	.125	.125

Mike de la Hoz 30 R 0-1, Bernie Carbo 21 L 0-3, Clyde Mashore 24 R 0-1, Hal McRae (BL) 23

NAME	T	AGE	W	L	PCT	SV	G	GS	CG	IP	H	BB	SO	SHO	ERA
		28	89	73	.549	44	163	163	23	1465	1478	611	818	11	4.11
Jim Merritt	L	25	17	9	.654	0	42	36	8	251	269	61	144	1	4.37
Jim Maloney (FJ)	R	29	12	5	.706	0	30	27	6	179	135	86	102	3	2.77
Clay Carroll	R	28	12	6	.667	7	71	4	0	151	149	78	90	0	3.52
Tony Cloninger	R	28	11	17	.393	0	35	34	6	190	184	103	103	2	5.02
Wayne Granger	R	25	9	6	.600	27	90	0	0	145	143	40	60	0	2.79
Gary Nolan (SA)	R	21	8	8	.500	0	16	5	2	109	102	40	83	1	3.55
George Culver (IL)	R	25	7	6	.417	4	32	13	0	101	117	52	58	0	4.28
2 Pedro Ramos	R	34	4	3	.571	2	38	6	0	66	73	24	40	0	5.18
Jack Fisher	R	30	4	4	.500	1	34	15	0	113	137	30	55	0	5.50
Jerry Arrigo	L	28	4	7	.364	0	20	16	1	91	99	48	63	0	4.15
2 Al Jackson	L	33	1	0	1.000	0	33	0	0	27	17	16		0	5.33
Mel Queen	R	26	0	2	.000	1	8	4	0	34	37	17	16	0	5.03
Jose Pena	R	26	0	0	—	0	9	0	0	14	15	8	12	0	5.63
John Noriega	R	22	0	0	—	0	6	0	0	5	5	7	4	0	18.00
2 Camilo Pascual	R	35	0	0	—	0	4	0	0	14	14	4	9	0	5.79
2 Dennis Ribant	R	27	0	0	—	0	6	0	0	5	5	1	1	0	1.13
Bill Short	L	31	0	0	—	0	3	0	0	5	5	0	4	0	18.00

LOS ANGELES — 4th 85-77 .525 8 — WALT ALSTON

NAME	G by Pos	B	AGE	G	AB	R	H	2B	3B	HR	RBI	BB	SO	SB	BA	SA
TOTALS			27	162	5532	645	1405	185	52	97	584	484	823	80	.254	.359
Wes Parker (IL)	1B128, OF2	B	29	132	471	76	131	23	4	13	68	56	46	4	.278	.427
Ted Sizemore	2B118, SS46, OF1	R	24	159	590	69	160	20	5	4	46	45	40	4	.271	.342
2 Maury Wills	SS104	B	36	104	434	57	129	7	8	4	39	39	40	25	.297	.378
Bill Sudakis	3B121	B	23	132	462	50	108	17	5	14	53	40	94	3	.234	.383
Andy Kosco	OF109, 1B3	R	27	120	424	51	105	13	2	19	74	21	66	0	.248	.422
Willie Davis	OF125	L	29	129	498	66	155	23	8	11	59	33	39	24	.311	.456
Willie Crawford	OF113	L	22	129	389	64	96	17	5	11	41	49	85	4	.247	.401
Tom Haller	C132	L	31	132	445	46	117	18	3	6	39	48	58	0	.263	.357
Bill Russell	OF86	R	20	98	212	35	48	6	2	5	15	22	45	4	.226	.344
Jim Lefebvre	3B44, 2B37, 1B6	B	26	95	275	29	65	15	2	4	44	48	37	2	.236	.349
2 Manny Mota	OF80	R	31	85	294	35	95	6	4	3	30	26	25	5	.323	.401
Len Gabrielson	OF47, 1B2	L	29	83	178	13	48	5	1	3	18	12	25	1	.270	.326
Jeff Torborg	C50	R	27	51	124	7	23	4	0	0	7	9	17	1	.185	.218
Billy Grabarkewitz	SS18, 3B6, 2B3	R	23	34	65	4	6	1	1	0	5	4	19	1	.092	.138
1 Ron Fairly (HJ)	1B12, OF10	L	30	30	64	3	14	3	2	0	8	9	6	0	.219	.328
Paul Popovich	2B23, SS3	B	28	28	50	5	10	0	0	0	4	1	4	0	.200	.200
John Miller	OF6, 1B5, 3B2, 2B1	R	23	26	38	3	8	1	0	1	1	2	9	0	.211	.316
Ken Boyer	1B4	R	38	25	34	0	7	2	0	0	4	2	7	0	.206	.265
Tommy Hutton	1B16	L	23	14	48	2	13	0	0	0	4	3	7	0	.271	.271

Bob Stinson 23 B 3-8, Von Joshua 21 L 2-8, Bill Buckner 19 L 0-1, Bobby Valentine 19 R 0-0, Steve Garvey 20 R 1-3

NAME	T	AGE	W	L	PCT	SV	G	GS	CG	IP	H	BB	SO	SHO	ERA
		27	85	77	.525	31	162	162	47	1457	1324	420	975	20	3.08
Bill Singer	R	25	20	12	.625	1	41	40	16	316	244	74	247	2	2.34
Claude Osteen	L	29	20	15	.571	0	41	41	16	321	293	74	183	1	2.66
Don Sutton	R	24	17	18	.486	0	41	41	11	293	269	91	217	4	3.47
Pete Mikkelsen	R	29	7	5	.583	4	48	0	0	81	57	30	51	0	2.78
Jim Brewer	R	31	7	6	.538	20	59	0	0	88	71	41	92	0	2.56
Don Drysdale (SJ)	R	32	5	4	.556	0	12	12	1	63	71	13	24	1	4.43
2 Jim Bunning	R	37	3	1	.750	0	9	1	0	56	65	10	33	0	3.38
Alan Foster	R	22	3	9	.250	0	24	15	2	103	119	29	59	2	4.37
2 Al McBean	R	31	2	6	.250	4	31	0	0	48	46	21	26	0	3.94
Joe Moeller	R	26	1	0	1.000	0	23	4	0	51	54	13	25	0	3.35
John Purdin	R	26	0	0	—	0	9	0	0	16	19	12	6	0	6.19
Bobby Darwin	R	26	0	0	—	0	4	0	0	4	5	0	9	0	9.00
Jack Jenkins	R	26	0	0	—	0	1	0	0	1	0	1	1	0	0.00
Ray Lamb	R	24	0	1	.000	0	10	0	0	15	12	7	11	0	1.80

HOUSTON — 5th 81-81 .500 12 — HARRY WALKER

NAME	G by Pos	B	AGE	G	AB	R	H	2B	3B	HR	RBI	BB	SO	SB	BA	SA
TOTALS			26	162	5348	676	1284	208	40	104	618	699	972	101	.240	.352
Curt Blefary	1B152, OF1	L	25	155	542	66	137	26	7	12	67	77	79	8	.253	.393
Joe Morgan	2B132, OF14	L	25	147	535	94	146	18	5	15	43	110	74	49	.236	.372
Denis Menke	SS131, 2B23, 1B9, 3B1	R	28	154	553	72	149	25	5	10	90	87	87	2	.269	.387
Doug Rader	3B154, 1B4	R	24	155	569	62	140	25	3	11	83	62	103	1	.246	.359
Norm Miller	OF114	L	23	119	409	58	108	21	4	4	50	47	77	4	.264	.364
Jim Wynn	OF149	R	27	149	495	113	133	17	1	33	87	148	142	23	.269	.507
Jesus Alou (CN)	OF112	R	27	115	452	49	112	19	4	5	34	15	30	4	.248	.341
Johnny Edwards	C151	L	31	151	496	52	115	20	6	6	50	53	69	2	.232	.333
Gary Geiger	OF65	L	32	93	125	19	28	4	1	0	16	24	34	2	.224	.272
M. Martinez	OF21, SS17, 3B15, C7, 2B1, P1	B	27	78	198	14	61	5	4	0	15	10	21	0	.308	.374
Julio Gotay	2B16, 3B1	R	30	46	81	7	21	5	0	0	9	7	13	2	.259	.321
Leon McFadden	OF17, SS8	R	23	45	74	3	13	2	0	3	4	9	13	1	.176	.203
1 Sandy Valdespino (CN)	OF29	L	30	41	119	17	29	4	0	0	12	15	19	2	.244	.277
Hector Torres (CN)	SS22	R	23	34	69	5	11	1	0	1	8	2	12	0	.159	.217
Don Bryant	C28	R	27	31	59	2	11	1	0	1	6	4	13	0	.186	.254
2 Tommy Davis	OF21	R	30	24	79	2	19	3	0	1	9	8	9	1	.241	.316
Bob Watson	OF6, 1B5, C1	R	23	20	40	3	11	3	0	0	3	6	5	0	.275	.350

Cesar Geronimo 21 L 2-8, Keith Lampard 23 L 3-12, John Mayberry 20 L 0-4

NAME	T	AGE	W	L	PCT	SV	G	GS	CG	IP	H	BB	SO	SHO	ERA
		26	81	81	.500	34	162	162	52	1436	1347	547	1221	11	3.60
Larry Dierker	R	22	20	13	.606	0	39	37	20	305	240	72	232	4	2.33
Don Wilson	R	24	16	12	.571	0	34	34	13	225	210	97	235	1	4.00
Denny Lemaster	L	30	13	17	.433	1	38	37	11	245	232	72	173	1	3.16
Tom Griffin	R	21	11	10	.524	0	31	31	6	188	156	93	200	3	3.54
Jim Ray	R	24	8	2	.800	0	40	13	0	115	105	48	115	0	3.91
Jack Billingham	R	26	6	7	.462	2	52	4	1	83	92	29	71	0	4.23
Fred Gladding	R	33	4	8	.333	29	57	0	0	73	83	27	40	0	4.19
1 Dooley Womack	R	29	2	1	.667	0	30	0	0	51	49	20	32	0	3.53
Skip Guinn	L	24	1	2	.333	0	28	0	0	27	34	21	33	0	6.67
Bob Watkins	R	21	0	0	—	0	3	0	0	13	13	11	0	0	5.06
Bill Henry	L	41	0	0	—	0	5	0	0	6	2	2	2	0	0.00
2 Ron Willis	R	25	0	0	—	0	3	0	0	3	2	0	2	0	9.00
Scipio Spinks	R	21	0	0	—	0	1	0	0	1	1	4	0	0	0.00
Marty Martinez			0	0	—	0	1	0	0	1	1	1	0	0	0.00
Danny Coombs	L	27	0	1	.000	0	8	2	0	18	15	8	6	0	6.75
Dan Schneider	L	26	0	1	.000	0	7	0	0	7	16	5	3	0	14.14
2 Jim Bouton	R	30	0	2	.000	1	16	1	1	31	32	12	32	0	4.06
Wade Blasingame	L	25	0	5	.000	1	26	5	0	52	66	33	16	0	5.37

SAN DIEGO — 6th 52-110 .321 41 — PRESTON GOMEZ

NAME	G by Pos	B	AGE	G	AB	R	H	2B	3B	HR	RBI	BB	SO	SB	BA	SA
TOTALS			26	162	5357	468	1203	180	42	99	431	423	1143	45	.225	.329
Nate Colbert	1B134	R	23	139	483	64	123	20	9	24	66	45	123	6	.255	.482
Jose Arcia	2B68, SS37, 3B8, OF4, 1B1	R	25	120	302	35	65	11	3	0	10	14	47	14	.215	.272
Tommy Dean	SS97, 2B2	R	25	101	273	14	48	9	2	2	9	27	54	0	.176	.245
Ed Spiezio	3B98, OF1	R	27	121	355	29	83	9	0	13	43	38	64	1	.234	.369
Ollie Brown	OF148	R	25	151	568	76	150	17	3	20	61	44	97	10	.264	.412
Cito Gaston	OF113	R	25	129	391	20	90	11	7	2	28	24	117	4	.230	.309
Al Ferrara	OF96	R	29	138	366	39	95	22	1	14	56	45	69	0	.260	.440
Chris Cannizzaro	C132	R	31	134	418	23	92	14	3	4	33	42	81	0	.220	.297
Roberto Pena	SS65, 2B33, 3B27, 1B12	R	32	139	472	44	118	16	3	4	30	21	63	0	.250	.322
Ivan Murrell	OF72, 1B2	R	26	111	247	19	63	10	6	3	25	11	65	3	.255	.381
Larry Stahl	OF37, 1B13	L	28	95	162	10	32	6	3	3	10	17	31	3	.198	.315
Van Kelly	3B49, 2B10	L	23	73	209	16	51	7	1	3	15	12	24	0	.244	.330
John Sipin (XJ)	2B60	R	22	68	229	22	51	12	2	2	9	8	44	2	.223	.319
1 Tony Gonzalez	OF49	L	26	53	182	17	41	4	0	2	8	19	24	1	.225	.280
2 Walt Hriniak	C19	L	26	31	66	4	15	0	0	0	1	8	11	0	.227	.227
Bill Davis	1B14	L	27	31	57	1	10	1	0	0	3	3	18	0	.175	.193
1 Jerry DaVanon	2B15, SS7	R	23	24	59	4	8	1	0	0	3	3	12	0	.136	.153
Jerry Morales	OF19	R	20	19	41	5	8	2	0	1	6	5	7	0	.195	.317
Sonny Ruberto	C15	R	23	19	21	3	3	0	0	0	1	1	5	0	.143	.143
Ron Slocum	2B4, 3B4, SS1	R	22	13	24	6	7	1	0	1	5	5	5	0	.292	.458
Jim Williams	OF6	R	22	13	25	4	7	1	0	0	2	1	9	0	.280	.320
Fred Kendall	C9	R	20	10	26	2	4	0	0	0	1	2	4	0	.154	.154
Frankie Libran	SS9	R	21	10	10	0	1	1	0	0	0	0	4	0	.100	.200
Chris Krug	C7	R	29	8	17	0	1	0	0	0	0	1	5	0	.059	.059
Rafael Robles	SS6	R	21	6	10	0	1	0	0	0	0	0	1	0	.100	.100

NAME	T	AGE	W	L	PCT	SV	G	GS	CG	IP	H	BB	SO	SHO	ERA
		26	52	110	.321	25	162	162	16	1422	1454	592	764	9	4.24
Al Santorini	R	21	8	14	.364	0	32	30	2	185	194	73	111	1	3.94
2 Joe Niekro	R	24	8	17	.320	0	37	31	8	202	213	45	55	3	3.70
Jack Baldschun	R	32	7	2	.778	1	61	0	0	77	80	29	67	0	4.79
Clay Kirby	R	21	7	20	.259	0	35	35	2	216	204	100	113	0	3.79
Johnny Podres	L	36	5	6	.455	0	17	9	1	65	66	28	17	0	4.29
Dick Kelley	L	29	4	8	.333	0	27	23	1	136	113	61	96	1	3.57
Billy McCool	L	25	3	5	.375	7	54	0	0	59	59	42	35	0	4.27
2 Gary Ross	R	21	3	12	.200	2	46	7	0	110	104	56	58	0	4.17
1 Dick Selma	R	25	2	2	.500	0	4	3	1	22	19	9	20	0	4.09
Tommie Sisk	R	27	2	13	.133	6	53	13	1	143	160	48	59	0	4.78
Tom Dukes	R	26	1	0	1.000	1	13	0	0	22	26	10	15	0	7.36
Frank Reberger	R	25	1	2	.333	6	67	0	0	88	83	41	65	0	3.58
Mike Corkins	R	23	1	3	.250	0	7	6	0	28	17	8	13	0	8.47
Leon Everitt	R	22	0	1	—	0	6	0	0	16	18	12	11	0	7.88
Steve Arlin	R	23	0	1	.000	0	5	5	0	11	13	9	9	0	9.00
1 Al McBean	R	31	0	0	—	0	1	0	0	7	10	2	1	0	5.14
Dave Roberts	L	24	0	3	.000	1	22	5	0	49	65	19	19	0	4.78

WORLD SERIES — NEW YORK (NL) 4 BALTIMORE (AL) 1

LINE SCORES

TEAM	1	2	3	4	5	6	7	8	9	10	11	12	R	H	E

Game 1 — October 11 at Baltimore

	1	2	3	4	5	6	7	8	9	R	H	E
NY (NL)	0	0	0	0	0	0	1	0	0	1	6	1
BAL (AL)	1	0	0	3	0	0	0	0	X	4	6	0

Seaver, Cardwell (6), Taylor (7) — Cuellar

Game 2 — October 12 at Baltimore

	1	2	3	4	5	6	7	8	9	R	H	E
NY	0	0	0	1	0	0	0	0	1	2	6	0
BAL	0	0	0	0	0	1	0	0	0	1	2	0

Koosman, Taylor (9) — McNally

Game 3 — October 14 at New York

	1	2	3	4	5	6	7	8	9	R	H	E
BAL	0	0	0	0	0	0	0	0	0	0	4	1
NY	1	2	0	0	0	1	0	1	X	5	6	0

Palmer, Leonhard (7) — Gentry, Ryan (7)

Game 4 — October 15 at New York

	1	2	3	4	5	6	7	8	9	10	R	H	E
BAL	0	0	0	0	0	0	0	0	1	0	1	6	1
NY	0	1	0	0	0	0	0	0	0	1	2	10	1

Cuellar, Watt (8), Hall (10), Richert (10) — Seaver

Game 5 — October 16 at New York

	1	2	3	4	5	6	7	8	9	R	H	E
BAL	0	0	3	0	0	0	0	0	0	3	5	2
NY	0	0	0	0	0	2	1	2	X	5	7	0

McNally, Watt (8) — Koosman

COMPOSITE BATTING

NAME	POS	G	AB	R	H	2B	3B	HR	RBI	BA
New York (NL) Totals		5	159	15	35	8	0	6	13	.220
Grote	C	5	19	1	4	2	0	0	1	.211
Jones	OF	5	19	2	3	1	0	0	0	.158
Agee	OF	5	18	1	3	0	0	1	1	.167
Harrelson	SS	5	17	1	3	0	0	0	0	.176
Swoboda	OF	4	15	1	6	1	0	0	0	.400
Charles	3B	4	15	1	2	1	0	0	0	.133
Clendenon	1B	4	14	4	5	0	0	3	4	.357
Weis	2B	5	11	1	5	0	0	1	3	.455
Koosman	P	2	7	0	1	0	0	0	0	.143
Shamsky	OF	3	6	0	0	0	0	0	0	.000
Kranepool	1B	1	4	1	1	0	0	0	1	.250
Seaver	P	2	4	0	0	0	0	0	0	.000
Boswell	2B	1	3	1	1	0	0	0	0	.333
Gentry	P	1	3	0	1	0	0	0	0	.333
Gaspar	OF	3	2	1	0	0	0	0	0	.000
Garrett	3B	2	1	0	0	0	0	0	0	.000
Dyer	PH	1	1	0	0	0	0	0	0	—
Martin	PH	1	1	0	0	0	0	0	0	—
Taylor	P	2	0	0	0	0	0	0	0	—
Cardwell	P	1	0	0	0	0	0	0	0	—
Ryan	P	1	0	0	0	0	0	0	0	—
Baltimore (AL) Totals		5	157	9	23	1	0	3	9	.146
Blair	OF	5	20	1	2	0	0	0	0	.100
Buford	OF	5	20	1	2	0	0	0	0	.100
Powell	1B	5	19	0	5	0	0	0	0	.263
B. Robinson	3B	5	19	0	1	0	0	0	0	.053
F. Robinson	OF	5	16	2	3	0	0	1	1	.188
Johnson	2B	5	16	0	1	0	0	0	1	.063
Belanger	SS	5	15	2	3	0	0	0	0	.200
Hendricks	C	5	13	0	1	0	0	0	0	.100
Etchebarren	C	2	6	0	0	0	0	0	0	.000
Cuellar	P	2	5	0	2	0	0	0	0	.400
McNally	P	2	5	1	1	0	0	1	2	.200
Dalrymple	PH	2	2	0	2	0	0	0	0	1.000
Palmer	P	1	2	0	0	0	0	0	0	.000
May	PH	2	2	0	0	0	0	0	0	.000
Motton	PH	2	2	0	0	0	0	0	0	.000
Salmon	PR	2	0	0	0	0	0	0	0	—
Rettenmund	PR	1	0	0	0	0	0	0	0	—
Watt	P	2	0	0	0	0	0	0	0	—

Hall P 0-0, Leonhard P 0-0, Richert P 0-0

COMPOSITE PITCHING

NAME	G	IP	H	BB	SO	W	L	SV	ERA
New York (NL) Totals	5	45	23	15	28	4	1	2	1.80
Koosman	2	17.2	7	4	9	2	0	0	2.04
Seaver	2	15	12	3	9	1	1	0	3.00
Gentry	1	6.2	3	5	4	1	0	0	0.00
Taylor	2	2.1	0	3	0	0	0	1	0.00
Ryan	1	2.1	1	2	3	0	0	1	0.00
Cardwell	1	1	0	1	0	0	0	0	0.00
Baltimore (AL) Totals	5	43	35	15	35	1	4	0	2.72
Cuellar	2	16	13	4	13	1	0	0	1.13
McNally	2	16	11	5	13	1	0	0	2.81
Palmer	1	6	5	4	5	0	1	0	6.00
Watt	2	3	4	0	3	0	1	0	3.00
Leonhard	1	2	1	1	1	0	0	0	4.50
Hall	1	1	1	1	2	0	0	0	—
Richert	1	0	0	1	0	0	0	0	—

1970 Damned If You Do

After winning the Cy Young Award in the American League two years in a row, Denny McLain lost it all: his money, his good name, and his fastball. Commissioner Bowie Kuhn suspended the fun-loving right-hander in February for a number of incidents which besmirched baseball's reputation for uprightness. Specifically, McLain had become involved with underworld gamblers during the 1967 season, going as far as to provide monetary backing for a bookmaking operation. Previously known for his 31-win season, his egotistical conduct, and his off-season organ playing, McLain had become the center of numerous tales concerning his sorry financial state when Kuhn sentenced him to a rather light suspension ending on July 1.

The Tigers hoped to start a pennant drive upon McLain's return, and a SRO crowd packed Tiger Stadium on July 1, to see the arrogant hurler take the mound against the Yankees. McLain, though, was knocked out in the sixth inning, and a 3-5 record through August gave stark evidence to the fact that his fastball had lost its old zip during the months of turmoil. When he doused two local reporters with buckets of ice water in the Detroit clubhouse, McLain was slapped with a week's suspension by the Tigers. To cap an infamous season, Kuhn again suspended McLain on September 9, for the duration of the season for carrying a pistol in violation of the probationary conditions set by the commissioner. At the season's end, the Tigers hastily unloaded Denny in a large trade with the Washington Senators.

While McLain was being called in Kuhn's chambers, Curt Flood was presenting his antitrust suit against baseball before New York City's Federal Court. When Flood was traded by St. Louis to Philadelphia during the winter, he refused to report and filed suit against baseball's reserve clause which bound a player forever to whatever team held his contract. Flood wanted the right to sign with the team of his choice. The New York court gave Flood a negative and, while his attorneys prepared to make an appeal, he sat out the season. In a final irony, Flood joined McLain as a member of the Senators after they acquired his "reserve" from the

Phillies and after he was assured that the move would not hurt his case.

Kuhn was forced to cope with other problems during the year. Baseball had to navigate through treacherous legal waters when the bankrupt Seattle franchise was shifted to Milwaukee four days before the season's opening. Houston pitcher Jim Bouton published *Ball Four*, a diary which revealed some of the hidden personal aspects of major league baseball. Kuhn duly censored Bouton, who by autumn had become a television sportscaster. Finally, a one-day strike by major league umpires during the play-offs was settled by the commissioner.

By comparison, action on the field could not equal the off-field headlines as the Cincinnati Reds used a torrid first half, and the Pittsburgh Pirates a final spurt, to each win their divisional titles. Freshman manager Sparky Anderson guided a Cincinnati lineup including MVP Johnny Bench, Pete Rose, Lee May, Tony Perez, and Bobby Tolan to a pennant, despite injuries to several key pitchers. The Pirates also boasted of a powerful attack but dropped the championship series to Cincinnati in three straight games.

The Baltimore Orioles and Minnesota Twins repeated as division leaders in the American League, and the Birds duplicated their three-game sweep of the Twins in the play-off. The Orioles overwhelmed their opposition, using MVP Boog Powell, Brooks Robinson, and Frank Robinson to amass runs, and 20-game winners Mike Cuellar, Dave McNally, and Jim Palmer to shut the opposition out. Despite injuries to Rod Carew, Dave Boswell, and Luis Tiant, the Twins repeated under new manager Bill Rigney with fine performances from Harmon Killebrew, Tony Oliva, and Cy Young winner Jim Perry.

By the time the World Series got around, baseball's foundation was a bit shaken. But, with Brooks Robinson starring both afield and at bat, and the Orioles avenging their 1969 Series loss by knocking off the Reds handily in five games, there was little doubt about professional baseball's endurance at the start of its second century.

1970 AMERICAN LEAGUE — EAST DIVISION

NAME	G by Pos	B	AGE	G	AB	R	H	2B	3B	HR	RBI	BB	SO	SB	BA	SA
BALTIMORE 1st 108-54 .667			EARL WEAVER													
TOTALS			29	162	5545	792	1424	213	25	179	748	717	952	84	.257	.401
Boog Powell	1B145	L	28	154	526	82	156	28	0	35	114	104	80	1	.297	.549
Dave Johnson	2B149, SS2	R	27	149	530	68	149	27	1	10	53	66	68	2	.281	.392
Mark Belanger	SS143	R	26	145	459	53	100	6	5	1	36	52	65	13	.218	.259
Brooks Robinson	3B156	R	33	158	608	84	168	31	4	18	94	53	53	1	.276	.429
Frank Robinson	OF120, 1B7	R	34	132	471	88	144	24	1	25	78	69	70	2	.306	.520
Paul Blair (BC)	OF128, 3B1	R	26	133	480	79	128	24	2	18	65	56	93	24	.267	.438
Don Buford	OF130, 2B3, 3B3	B	33	144	504	99	137	15	2	17	66	109	55	16	.272	.411
Ellie Hendricks	C95	L	29	106	322	32	78	9	0	12	41	33	44	1	.242	.382
Merv Rettenmund	OF93	R	27	106	338	60	109	17	2	18	58	38	59	13	.322	.544
Terry Crowley	OF27, 1B23	L	23	83	152	25	39	5	0	5	20	35	26	2	.257	.388
Andy Etchebarren	C76	R	27	78	230	19	56	10	1	4	28	21	41	4	.243	.348
Chico Salmon	SS33, 2B12, 3B11, 1B2	R	29	63	172	19	43	4	0	7	22	8	30	2	.250	.395
Curt Motton	OF21	R	29	52	84	16	19	3	1	3	19	18	20	1	.226	.393
1 Dave May	OF9	L	25	31	6	6	0	1	1	6	4	4	4	0	.194	.355
Clay Dalrymple (BN)	C11	L	33	13	32	4	7	1	0	1	3	7	4	0	.219	.344
Bobby Grich	SS20, 2B9, 3B1	R	21	30	95	11	20	1	3	0	8	9	21	1	.211	.284
Don Baylor	OF6	R	21	8	17	4	4	0	0	0	4	2	3	1	.235	.235
Johnny Oates	C4	L	24	5	18	2	5	0	1	0	2	2	0	0	.278	.389
1 Bobby Floyd	SS2, 2B1	R	26	3	2	0	0	0	0	0	0	0	2	0	.000	.000
Roger Freed	1B3, OF1	R	24	4	13	0	2	1	0	0	1	3	4	0	.154	.154
NEW YORK 2nd 93-69 .574 15			RALPH HOUK													
TOTALS			26	163	5492	680	1381	208	41	111	627	588	808	105	.251	.365
Danny Cater	1B131, 3B42, OF7	R	30	155	582	64	175	26	5	6	76	34	44	4	.301	.393
Horace Clarke	2B157	B	30	158	686	81	172	24	2	4	46	35	35	23	.251	.309
Gene Michael	SS123, 3B4, 2B3	B	32	134	435	42	93	10	1	2	38	50	93	3	.214	.255
Jerry Kenney	3B135, 2B2	L	25	140	404	46	78	10	7	4	35	52	44	20	.193	.282
Curt Blefary	OF79, 1B6	L	26	99	269	34	57	6	0	9	37	43	37	1	.212	.335
Bobby Murcer	OF155	L	24	159	581	95	146	23	3	23	78	87	100	15	.251	.420
Roy White	OF161	B	26	162	609	109	180	30	6	22	94	95	66	24	.296	.473
Thurman Munson	C125	R	23	132	453	59	137	25	4	6	53	57	56	5	.302	.415
Ron Woods	OF78	R	27	95	225	30	51	5	3	8	27	33	35	4	.227	.382
Jim Lyttle	OF70	L	24	87	126	20	39	7	1	3	14	10	26	3	.310	.452
Johnny Ellis	1B53, 3B5, C2	R	21	78	226	24	56	12	1	7	29	18	47	0	.248	.403
Pete Ward	1B13	L	30	66	77	5	20	2	2	1	18	9	17	0	.260	.377
Ron Hansen	SS15, 3B11, 2B1	R	32	52	91	13	27	4	0	4	14	19	9	0	.297	.473
Jake Gibbs	C44	L	31	49	153	23	46	9	2	8	26	7	14	2	.301	.542
Frank Baker	SS35	L	23	35	117	6	27	4	1	0	11	14	26	1	.231	.282
Frank Tepedino	1B1, OF1	L	22	16	19	2	6	2	0	0	2	1	3	0	.316	.421
Bobby Mitchell	OF7	R	26	10	22	1	5	2	0	0	4	2	3	0	.227	.318
BOSTON 3rd 87-75 .537 21			EDDIE KASKO													
TOTALS			25	162	5535	786	1450	252	28	203	743	594	855	50	.262	.428
Carl Yastrzemski	1B94, OF69	L	30	161	566	125	186	29	0	40	102	128	66	23	.329	.592
Mike Andrews	2B148	R	26	151	589	91	148	28	1	17	65	81	63	2	.253	.390
Rico Petrocelli	SS141, 3B18	R	27	157	583	82	152	31	3	29	103	67	82	1	.261	.473
George Scott (BH)	3B68, 1B59	R	26	127	480	50	142	24	5	16	63	44	95	4	.296	.467
Tony Conigliaro	OF146	R	25	146	560	89	149	21	1	36	116	43	93	4	.266	.498
Reggie Smith	OF145	B	25	147	580	109	176	32	7	22	74	51	60	10	.303	.497
Billy Conigliaro	OF108	R	22	114	398	59	108	16	3	18	58	35	73	3	.271	.462
Jerry Moses	C88, OF1	R	23	92	315	26	83	18	1	6	35	21	45	1	.263	.384
Dick Schofield	2B15, 3B15, SS3	B	35	76	139	16	26	1	2	1	14	21	26	0	.187	.245
Luis Alvarado	3B29, SS27	R	21	59	183	19	41	11	0	1	9	9	30	1	.224	.301
Tom Satriano	C51	L	29	59	165	21	39	9	1	3	13	21	23	1	.236	.358
2 John Kennedy	3B33, 2B1	R	29	43	129	15	33	7	1	4	17	6	14	0	.256	.419
2 Mike Fiore	1B17, OF2	L	25	41	50	5	7	0	0	1	4	8	6	0	.140	.140
George Thomas (RC)	OF26, 3B6	R	32	38	99	13	34	8	0	2	13	6	10	0	.343	.485
Don Pavletich	1B16, C10	R	31	32	65	4	9	1	0	2	9	10	15	1	.138	.185
Mike Derrick	OF2, 1B1	R	26	24	33	3	7	1	0	0	1	6	3	0	.212	.242
Bob Montgomery	C22	R	26	22	78	8	14	2	0	1	4	6	20	0	.179	.244
Joe Lahoud	OF13	L	23	17	49	6	12	1	0	2	6	12	12	0	.245	.388
Carmen Fanzone	3B5	R	28	10	15	0	3	0	0	0	2	2	5	0	.200	.267
1 Tom Matchick	3B2, 2B1, SS1	L	26	10	14	2	1	0	0	0	0	1	2	0	.071	.071

NAME	T	AGE	W	L	PCT	SV	G	GS	CG	IP	H	BB	SO	SHO	ERA
		29	108	54	.667	31	162	162	60	1479	1317	469	941	12	3.15
Mike Cuellar	L	33	24	8	.750	0	40	40	21	298	273	69	190	4	3.47
Dave McNally	L	27	24	9	.727	0	40	40	16	296	277	78	185	1	3.22
Jim Palmer	R	24	20	10	.667	0	39	39	17	305	263	100	199	5	2.71
Dick Hall	R	39	10	5	.667	3	32	0	0	61	51	6	30	0	3.10
Pete Richert	L	30	7	2	.778	13	50	0	0	55	36	24	66	0	1.96
Eddie Watt	R	29	7	7	.500	12	53	0	0	55	44	29	33	0	3.27
Jim Hardin	R	26	6	5	.545	1	36	19	3	145	150	26	78	2	3.54
Tom Phoebus	R	28	5	5	.500	0	27	21	3	135	106	62	72	0	3.07
2 Moe Drabowsky	R	34	4	2	.667	1	21	0	0	33	30	15	21	0	3.82
Marcelino Lopez	L	26	1	1	.500	0	25	3	0	61	47	37	49	0	2.07
Dave Leonhard	R	29	0	0	—	1	23	0	0	28	32	18	14	0	5.14
Fred Beene	R	27	0	0	—	0	4	0	0	6	8	5	4	0	6.00
		28	93	69	.574	49	163	163	36	1472	1386	451	777	6	3.24
Fritz Peterson	L	28	20	11	.645	0	39	37	8	260	247	40	127	2	2.91
Mel Stottlemyre	R	28	15	13	.536	0	37	37	14	271	262	84	126	0	3.09
Stan Bahnsen	R	25	14	11	.560	0	36	35	6	233	227	75	116	2	3.32
Lindy McDaniel	R	34	9	5	.643	29	62	0	0	112	88	23	81	0	2.01
Mike Kekich (LJ)	L	25	6	6	.500	0	26	14	1	99	103	55	63	0	4.82
Steve Kline	R	22	6	6	.500	0	16	15	5	100	99	24	49	0	3.42
Ron Klimkowski	R	25	6	7	.462	1	45	3	1	98	80	33	40	1	2.66
Jack Aker	R	29	4	2	.667	16	41	0	0	70	57	20	36	0	2.06
1 Steve Hamilton	L	36	4	3	.571	3	35	0	0	45	36	16	33	0	2.80
1 John Cumberland	L	23	3	4	.429	0	15	8	1	64	62	15	38	0	3.94
1 Mike McCormick	L	31	2	0	1.000	0	9	4	0	21	26	13	12	0	6.00
2 Gary Waslewski	R	28	2	2	.500	0	26	5	0	55	42	27	27	0	3.11
Rob Gardner	L	25	1	1	.500	0	7	4	0	36	20	12	8	0	5.14
Joe Verbanic	R	27	1	0	1.000	0	7	0	0	16	16	4	6	0	4.50
Gary Jones	L	25	0	0	—	0	3	0	0	2	3	1	2	0	0.00
Loyd Colson	R	22	0	0	—	0	1	0	0	2	3	1	2	0	4.50
Bill Burbach	R	22	0	1	.000	0	4	4	0	17	23	14	9	0	10.06
		28	87	75	.537	44	162	162	38	1446	1391	594	1003	8	3.87
Ray Culp	R	28	17	14	.548	0	33	33	15	251	211	91	197	1	3.05
Gary Peters	L	33	16	11	.593	0	34	34	10	222	221	83	155	4	4.05
Sonny Siebert	R	33	15	8	.652	0	33	34	10	223	207	60	142	2	3.43
Ken Brett	L	21	8	9	.471	2	41	14	1	139	118	79	155	0	4.08
Vicente Romo	R	27	7	3	.700	6	48	10	0	108	115	43	71	0	4.08
Mike Nagy	R	22	6	5	.545	0	23	20	4	129	138	64	56	0	4.47
Jim Lonborg (SJ)	R	28	4	1	.800	0	9	4	1	34	33	9	21	0	3.18
Gary Wagner	R	30	3	1	.750	7	38	0	0	40	36	19	20	0	3.38
2 Cal Koonce	R	29	3	4	.429	2	23	8	1	76	64	29	37	0	3.55
2 Bobby Bolin	R	31	2	0	1.000	5	21	1	0	37	30	16	38	0	3.04
Bill Lee (MS)	L	23	2	2	.500	1	11	5	0	26	24	10	19	0	4.62
1 Lee Stange	R	33	2	2	.500	3	20	0	0	37	34	12	14	0	5.67
Roger Moret	L	20	1	0	1.000	0	1	1	0	9	5	3	5	0	3.38
Sparky Lyle	L	25	1	7	.125	20	63	0	0	67	62	34	51	0	3.90
Dick Mills	R	24	0	0	—	0	2	0	0	2	4	3	1	0	13.50
John Curtis	L	22	0	0	—	0	1	0	0	9	3	5	6	0	3.94
Ray Jarvis	R	23	0	0	—	0	2	0	0	24	29	10	23	0	5.25
Ed Phillips	R	25	0	0	—	0	18	0	0	11	18	8	8	0	10.64
Jose Santiago (EJ)	R	29	0	2	.000	0	4	0	0	24	21	12	12	0	8.05
3 Chuck Hartenstein	R	28	0	3	.000	1	19	0	0	21	12	12	10	0	8.05

DETROIT 4th 79-83 .488 29 MAYO SMITH

NAME	G by Pos	B	AGE	G	AB	R	H	2B	3B	HR	RBI	BB	SO	SB	BA	SA
TOTALS			29	162	5377	666	1282	207	38	148	619	656	825	29	.238	.374
Norm Cash	1B114	L	35	130	370	58	96	18	2	15	53	72	58	0	.259	.441
Dick McAuliffe	2B127, SS15, 3B12	L	30	146	530	73	124	21	1	12	50	101	62	5	.234	.345
Cesar Gutierrez	SS135	R	27	135	415	40	101	11	6	0	22	18	39	4	.243	.299
Don Wert	3B117, 2B2	R	31	128	363	34	79	13	0	6	33	44	56	1	.218	.303
Al Kaline	OF91, 1B52	R	35	131	467	64	130	24	4	16	71	77	49	2	.278	.457
Mickey Stanley	OF132, 1B9	R	27	142	568	83	143	21	11	13	47	45	56	10	.252	.396
Jim Northrup	OF136	L	30	139	504	71	132	21	3	24	80	58	68	3	.262	.458
Bill Freehan (XJ)	C114	R	28	117	395	44	95	17	3	16	52	52	48	0	.241	.420
Elliott Maddox	3B40, OF37, SS19, 2B1	R	22	109	258	30	64	13	4	3	24	30	42	2	.248	.364
Willie Horton (NJ)	OF96	R	27	96	371	53	113	18	2	17	69	28	43	0	.305	.501
Dalton Jones	2B35, 3B18, 1B10	L	26	89	191	29	42	7	0	6	21	33	33	1	.220	.351
Gates Brown	OF26	L	31	81	124	18	28	3	0	3	24	20	14	1	.226	.323
Ike Brown	2B23, OF4, 3B1	R	28	56	94	17	27	5	0	4	15	13	26	0	.287	.468
Jim Price	C38	R	28	52	132	12	24	4	0	5	15	21	23	0	.182	.326
Ken Szotkiewicz (KJ)	SS44	L	23	47	84	9	9	1	0	3	9	12	29	0	.107	.226
2 Russ Nagelson	OF4, 1B1	L	25	28	32	5	6	0	0	0	2	5	6	0	.188	.188
Kevin Collins	1B1	L	23	25	24	2	5	1	0	1	3	1	10	0	.208	.375
Gene Lamont	C15	R	23	15	44	3	13	3	1	1	4	2	9	0	.295	.477
Tim Hosley	C4	R	23	7	12	1	2	0	1	0	1	2	5	0	.167	.417

NAME	T	AGE	W	L	PCT	SV	G	GS	CG	IP	H	BB	SO	SHO	ERA
		26	79	83	.488	39	162	162	33	1447	1443	623	1045	9	4.09
Mickey Lolich	L	29	14	19	.424	0	40	39	13	273	272	109	230	3	3.79
Les Cain	L	22	12	7	.632	0	29	29	5	181	167	98	156	0	3.83
Joe Niekro	R	25	12	13	.480	0	38	34	6	213	221	72	101	2	4.06
Daryl Patterson	R	26	7	1	.875	2	43	0	0	78	81	39	55	0	4.85
Mike Kilkenny	L	25	7	6	.538	0	36	21	3	129	147	70	105	0	5.16
John Hiller	L	27	6	6	.500	3	47	5	1	104	82	46	89	1	3.03
Tom Timmermann	R	30	6	7	.462	27	61	0	0	85	90	34	49	0	4.13
Fred Scherman	L	25	4	4	.500	1	48	0	0	70	61	28	49	0	3.21
1 Earl Wilson	R	35	4	6	.400	0	18	16	4	96	87	32	74	1	4.41
Denny McLain (SL)	R	26	3	5	.375	0	14	14	1	91	100	28	52	0	4.65
Bob Reed	R	25	2	4	.333	2	16	4	0	46	54	14	26	0	4.89
Dennis Saunders	R	21	1	1	.500	0	8	0	0	14	16	5	8	0	3.21
1 Fred Lasher	R	28	1	3	.250	3	12	0	0	19	30	15	15	0	5.00
Norm McRae	R	22	0	0	—	0	19	0	0	31	26	25	16	0	2.90
Jerry Robertson	R	26	0	0	—	0	11	0	0	15	19	5	11	0	3.60
Lerrin LaGrow	R	21	0	0	.000	0	10	0	0	12	16	6	7	0	7.50

CLEVELAND 5th 76-86 .469 32 AL DARK

NAME	G by Pos	B	AGE	G	AB	R	H	2B	3B	HR	RBI	BB	SO	SB	BA	SA
TOTALS			26	162	5463	649	1358	197	23	183	617	503	909	25	.249	.394
Tony Horton (IL)	1B112	R	25	115	413	48	111	19	3	17	59	30	54	3	.269	.453
Eddie Leon	2B141, SS23, 3B6	R	23	152	549	58	136	20	4	10	56	47	89	1	.248	.353
Jack Heidemann	SS132	R	20	133	445	44	94	14	2	6	37	34	88	2	.211	.292
Graig Nettles	3B154, OF3	L	25	157	549	81	129	13	1	26	62	81	77	3	.235	.404
Vada Pinson	OF141, 1B7	L	31	148	574	74	164	28	6	24	82	28	69	7	.286	.481
Ted Uhlaender	OF134	L	30	141	473	56	127	21	2	11	46	39	44	3	.268	.391
Roy Foster	OF131	R	24	139	477	66	128	26	0	23	60	54	75	3	.268	.468
Ray Fosse	C120	R	23	120	450	62	138	17	1	18	61	39	55	1	.307	.469
Duke Sims	C39, OF36, 1B29	L	29	110	345	46	91	12	0	23	56	46	59	0	.264	.499
Chuck Hinton	1B40, OF35, C4, 2B3, 3B2	R	36	107	195	24	62	4	0	9	25	25	34	0	.318	.477
2 Buddy Bradford	OF64, 3B1	R	25	75	163	25	32	6	1	7	23	21	43	0	.196	.374
Larry Brown	SS27, 3B17, 2B16	R	30	72	155	17	40	5	2	0	15	20	14	1	.258	.316
2 Rich Rollins	3B5	R	32	42	43	6	10	0	0	2	4	3	5	0	.233	.372
Lou Klimchock	1B5, 2B5	L	30	41	56	5	9	0	0	1	3	2	9	0	.161	.214
Vern Fuller	2B16, 3B4, 1B1	R	26	29	33	3	6	2	0	1	1	3	4	0	.182	.333
Ted Ford	OF12	R	23	26	46	5	8	1	0	1	1	6	13	0	.174	.261
John Lowenstein	2B10, 3B2, OF2, SS1	R	23	17	43	5	11	3	1	0	6	1	11	0	.256	.442
Ken Harrelson (BL)	1B13	R	28	17	39	3	11	1	0	1	6	4	6	0	.282	.385
1 Russ Nagelson	OF4	L	25	17	24	3	3	1	0	1	2	3	9	0	.125	.292
Lou Camilli	SS3, 2B2, 3B1	B	23	16	15	0	0	0	0	0	0	6	0	0	.000	.000

NAME	T	AGE	W	L	PCT	SV	G	GS	CG	IP	H	BB	SO	SHO	ERA
		26	76	86	.469	35	162	162	34	1451	1333	689	1076	8	3.91
Sam McDowell	L	27	20	12	.625	0	39	39	19	305	236	131	304	1	2.92
Steve Hargan (SA)	R	27	11	3	.786	0	23	19	8	143	101	53	72	1	2.90
1 Dean Chance	R	29	8	8	.529	4	45	19	1	155	172	59	109	1	4.24
Phil Hennigan	R	24	6	3	.667	3	42	0	0	72	69	44	43	0	4.00
Rich Hand	R	21	6	13	.316	3	35	25	3	160	132	69	110	1	3.83
Denny Higgins	R	30	4	6	.400	11	58	0	0	90	82	54	82	0	4.00
Steve Dunning	R	21	4	4	.308	0	19	17	0	94	93	54	77	0	4.98
1 Dick Ellsworth	L	30	3	3	.500	2	29	1	0	44	49	14	13	0	4.50
1 Barry Moore	R	27	3	5	.375	0	13	12	0	70	70	46	35	0	4.24
1 Bob Miller	R	31	2	2	.500	1	15	3	0	35	35	15	15	0	4.18
Rick Austin	L	23	2	5	.286	3	31	8	1	68	74	26	53	1	4.76
Mike Paul	L	25	2	8	.200	0	30	15	1	88	91	45	70	0	4.81
Steve Mingori	L	26	1	0	1.000	1	21	0	0	20	17	12	16	0	2.70
Vince Colbert	R	24	1	1	.500	2	23	0	0	31	37	16	17	0	7.26
Jim Rittwage	R	25	1	1	.500	0	8	3	1	26	18	21	16	0	4.15
2 Fred Lasher	R	28	1	7	.125	5	43	1	0	58	57	30	44	0	4.03

WASHINGTON 6th 70-92 .432 38 TED WILLIAMS

NAME	G by Pos	B	AGE	G	AB	R	H	2B	3B	HR	RBI	BB	SO	SB	BA	SA
TOTALS			29	162	5460	626	1302	184	28	138	583	635	989	72	.238	.358
Mike Epstein	1B122	L	27	140	430	55	110	15	3	20	56	73	117	2	.256	.444
Tim Cullen	2B112, SS6	R	28	123	262	22	56	10	2	1	31	31	38	3	.214	.279
Eddie Brinkman	SS157	R	28	158	625	63	164	17	2	1	40	60	41	8	.262	.301
2 Aurelio Rodriguez	3B136, SS7	R	22	142	547	64	135	31	5	19	76	37	81	15	.247	.426
Ed Stroud	OF118	L	30	129	433	69	115	11	5	3	32	40	79	29	.266	.349
Del Unser	OF103	L	25	119	322	37	83	11	1	1	30	30	29	1	.258	.326
Frank Howard	OF120, 1B48	R	33	161	566	90	160	15	1	44	126	132	125	1	.283	.546
Paul Casanova	C100	R	28	104	328	25	75	17	3	6	30	10	47	0	.229	.354
2 Rick Reichardt	OF79, 3B1	R	27	107	277	42	70	14	2	15	46	29	69	2	.253	.480
Bernie Allen	2B80, 3B12	L	31	104	261	31	61	7	1	8	29	43	21	0	.234	.360
1 Lee Maye	OF68, 3B1	L	35	96	255	28	67	12	1	7	30	21	32	4	.263	.400
2 Wayne Comer	OF58, 3B1	R	26	77	129	21	30	4	0	0	8	22	16	4	.233	.264
Jim French	C62, OF1	L	28	69	166	20	35	3	1	1	13	38	23	0	.211	.259
Tommy Grieve	OF39	R	22	47	116	12	23	5	1	3	10	14	38	0	.198	.336
Dave Nelson	2B33	R	26	47	107	5	17	1	0	0	4	7	24	2	.159	.168
Johnny Roseboro	C30	L	37	46	86	7	20	4	0	1	6	18	10	1	.233	.314
1 Hank Allen	OF17	R	29	22	38	3	8	2	0	0	5	9	0		.211	.263
2 Greg Goossen	OF5, 1B2	R	24	21	36	2	8	3	0	0	1	2	9	0	.222	.306
1 Ken McMullen	3B15	R	28	15	59	5	12	2	0	1	2	5	4	0	.203	.237
Dick Billings	C8	R	27	11	24	3	6	2	0	0	4	0	5	0	.250	.458

Jeff Burroughs 19 R 2-12, Dick Nen 30 L 1-5, Larry Biittner 24 L 0-2

NAME	T	AGE	W	L	PCT	SV	G	GS	CG	IP	H	BB	SO	SHO	ERA
		28	70	92	.432	40	162	162	20	1458	1375	611	823	11	3.80
Dick Bosman	R	26	16	12	.571	0	36	34	7	231	212	71	134	3	3.00
Jim Hannan	R	30	9	11	.450	0	42	17	1	128	119	54	61	1	4.01
1 George Brunet	L	35	8	6	.571	0	24	20	2	118	124	48	67	1	4.42
Joe Coleman	R	23	8	12	.400	0	39	29	6	219	190	89	152	1	3.58
Casey Cox	R	28	8	12	.400	1	37	30	1	192	211	44	68	0	4.45
Jim Shellenback	L	26	6	7	.462	0	39	14	2	117	107	51	57	1	3.69
Horacio Pina	R	25	5	3	.625	6	61	0	0	71	66	35	41	0	2.79
Joe Grzenda	L	33	3	6	.333	6	49	3	0	85	86	34	38	0	4.98
Jackie Brown	R	27	2	2	.500	0	24	5	1	57	49	37	47	0	3.95
Bill Gogolewski	R	22	2	2	.500	0	8	5	0	34	33	25	19	0	4.76
Darold Knowles	L	28	2	14	.125	27	71	0	0	119	100	58	71	0	2.04
Dick Such	R	25	1	5	.167	0	21	6	0	50	48	45	41	0	7.56
Cisco Carlos	R	29	0	0	—	0	5	0	0	6	3	4	2	0	1.50
Jan Dukes	L	24	0	0	—	0	5	0	0	7	4	6	1	0	2.57
1 Bob Humphreys	R	34	0	0	—	0	8	0	0	7	4	9	5	0	1.29
Pedro Ramos	R	35	0	0	—	0	8	0	0	8	10	4	10	0	7.88
Denny Riddleberger	L	24	0	0	—	0	8	0	0	9	7	2	5	0	1.00

WEST DIVISION

MINNESOTA 1st 98-64 .605 BILL RIGNEY

NAME	G by Pos	B	AGE	G	AB	R	H	2B	3B	HR	RBI	BB	SO	SB	BA	SA
TOTALS			28	162	5483	744	1438	230	41	153	694	501	905	57	.262	.403
Rich Reese	1B146	L	28	153	463	62	131	15	5	10	56	48	70	5	.261	.391
Rod Carew (KJ)	2B45, 1B1	L	24	51	191	27	70	12	3	4	28	11	28	4	.366	.524
Leo Cardenas	SS160	R	31	160	580	67	145	34	4	11	65	42	101	2	.247	.374
Harmon Killebrew	3B138, 1B28	R	34	157	527	96	143	20	1	41	113	128	84	0	.271	.546
Tony Oliva	OF157	R	29	157	628	96	204	36	7	23	107	38	67	5	.325	.514
Cesar Tovar	OF151, 2B3, 3B4	R	29	161	650	120	195	36	13	10	54	52	47	30	.300	.442
Jim Holt	OF130, 1B2	L	26	142	319	37	85	9	3	3	40	17	32	3	.266	.342
George Mitterwald	C117	R	25	117	369	36	82	12	2	15	46	34	84	1	.222	.388
Frank Quilici	2B73, 3B27, SS1	R	31	111	141	19	32	3	0	2	12	15	16	0	.227	.291
Danny Thompson	2B81, 3B37, SS6	R	23	96	302	25	66	9	0	2	22	7	39	0	.219	.248
Brant Alyea	OF75	R	29	94	258	34	75	12	1	16	61	28	51	3	.291	.531
Rick Renick	3B30, OF25, SS1	R	26	81	179	20	41	8	0	7	25	22	29	0	.229	.391
Paul Ratliff	C53	L	26	69	149	19	40	7	2	5	22	15	51	0	.268	.443
Charlie Manuel	OF11	L	26	59	64	4	12	0	0	1	7	6	17	0	.188	.234
Bob Allison	OF17, 1B7	R	35	47	52	5	15	5	0	1	9	14	20	1	.208	.319
Herm Hill (DD)	OF14	R	24	27	22	8	2	0	0	0	2	6	0		.091	.091
Tom Tischinski	C22	R	25	24	46	6	9	2	0	0	2	0	9	0	.196	.261
Minnie Mendoza	3B5, 2B4	R	36	16	16	2	3	0	0	0	2	0	1	0	.188	.188
Jim Nettles	OF11	L	23	13	20	3	5	1	0	0	0	1	5	0	.250	.250

Steve Brye 21 R 2-11, Rick Dempsey 20 R 0-7, Cotton Nash 27 R 1-4

NAME	T	AGE	W	L	PCT	SV	G	GS	CG	IP	H	BB	SO	SHO	ERA
		27	98	64	.605	58	162	162	26	1448	1329	486	940	12	3.23
Jim Perry	R	34	24	12	.667	0	40	40	13	279	258	57	168	4	3.03
Jim Kaat	L	31	14	10	.583	0	45	34	4	230	244	58	120	1	3.56
Tom Hall	L	22	11	6	.647	4	52	11	1	155	94	66	184	0	2.55
Stan Williams	R	33	10	1	.909	15	68	0	0	113	85	32	76	0	1.99
Bert Blyleven	R	19	10	9	.526	0	27	25	5	164	143	47	135	1	3.18
Bill Zepp	R	23	9	4	.692	2	43	20	1	151	154	51	64	1	3.22
Luis Tiant (BS)	R	29	7	3	.700	0	18	17	2	93	84	41	50	1	3.39
Ron Perranoski	L	34	7	8	.467	34	67	0	0	111	108	42	55	0	2.43
Dave Boswell (XJ)	R	25	3	7	.300	0	18	15	0	69	80	44	45	0	6.39
Hal Haydel	R	25	2	1	1.000	0	9	0	0	9	7	4	4	0	3.00
Dick Woodson	R	25	2	1	.333	1	19	0	0	31	29	19	22	0	3.77
Steve Barber	L	32	0	1	.000	0	18	0	0	27	26	18	14	0	4.67
Pete Hamm	R	22	0	0	—	0	1	0	0	16	17	7	3	0	5.63

OAKLAND 2nd 89-73 .549 9 JOHN McNAMARA

NAME	G by Pos	B	AGE	G	AB	R	H	2B	3B	HR	RBI	BB	SO	SB	BA	SA
TOTALS			28	162	5376	678	1338	208	24	171	630	584	977	131	.249	.392
Don Mincher	1B137	L	32	140	464	60	118	18	0	27	74	56	71	5	.246	.460
Dick Green	2B127, 3B5, C1	R	29	135	384	34	73	7	0	4	29	38	73	1	.190	.240
Bert Campaneris	SS143	R	28	147	603	97	168	28	4	22	64	36	73	42	.279	.448
Sal Bando	3B152	R	26	155	502	93	132	20	2	20	75	118	88	6	.263	.430
Reggie Jackson	OF142	L	24	149	426	57	101	21	2	23	66	75	135	26	.237	.458
Rick Monday	OF109	L	24	112	376	63	109	19	7	10	37	59	98	17	.290	.457
Felipe Alou	OF145, 1B1	R	35	154	575	70	156	25	3	8	55	32	31	10	.271	.367
Frank Fernandez	C76, OF1	R	27	94	252	30	54	5	0	15	44	40	76	1	.214	.413
Joe Rudi	OF63, 1B28	R	23	106	350	40	108	23	2	11	42	16	61	3	.309	.480
Dave Duncan	C73	R	24	86	232	21	60	7	0	10	29	22	38	0	.259	.414
2 Steve Hovley	OF42	L	25	72	100	8	20	4	1	0	6	5	11	9	.200	.200
2 Tommy Davis	OF45, 1B8	R	31	66	200	17	58	9	1	2	27	8	18	2	.290	.360
Tony LaRussa	2B44	R	25	52	106	6	21	4	1	0	6	15	19	0	.198	.255
John Donaldson	2B21, SS6, 3B1	L	27	41	89	4	22	2	1	1	11	9	6	1	.247	.326
Gene Tenace	C30	R	23	38	105	19	32	6	0	7	20	23	30	0	.305	.562
1 Tito Francona	1B6, OF1	L	36	32	33	2	8	0	0	0	6	6	3	0	.242	.333
Bob Johnson	3B6, 1B1	R	24	31	23	2	4	2	0	0	3	1	7	0	.174	.261
Jose Tartabull	OF6	L	31	24	13	1	3	1	0	0	1	0	1	0	.231	.385
Allan Lewis	OF2	R	29	21	8	8	2	0	0	0	1	0	0	7	.250	.625
Jim Driscoll	2B7, SS7	L	26	21	52	2	10	0	2	0	5	2	9	0	.192	.250
1 Roberto Pena	SS12, 3B5	R	33	19	54	4	15	1	0	0	3	1	7	0	.259	.278
Bobby Brooks	OF5	L	24	9	18	2	6	3	0	0	2	1	7	0	.333	.722
Larry Haney	C1	R	27	2	1	0	0	0	0	0	0	0	0	0	.000	.000

NAME	T	AGE	W	L	PCT	SV	G	GS	CG	IP	H	BB	SO	SHO	ERA
		28	89	73	.549	40	162	162	33	1443	1253	542	858	15	3.30
Catfish Hunter	R	24	18	14	.563	0	40	40	9	262	253	74	178	1	3.81
Chuck Dobson	R	26	16	15	.516	0	42	40	13	267	230	92	149	5	3.74
Diego Segui	R	32	10	10	.500	2	47	19	3	162	130	68	95	2	2.56
Blue Moon Odom (EJ)	R	25	9	6	.600	0	39	29	4	156	128	100	88	1	3.81
Paul Lindblad	L	29	8	2	.800	3	62	0	0	63	52	28	42	0	2.72
Rollie Fingers	R	23	7	9	.438	2	45	19	1	148	137	48	79	0	3.65
1 Mudcat Grant	R	34	6	2	.750	24	72	0	0	123	104	30	54	0	1.83
1 Al Downing	L	29	3	3	.500	0	41	10	0	94	89	37	66	0	3.34
Marcel Lachemann	R	29	3	3	.500	4	58	0	0	58	58	18	39	0	2.79
2 Bob Locker	R	32	3	3	.500	4	38	0	0	56	49	19	33	0	2.89
Jim Roland (KJ)	R	27	3	2	.600	4	32	0	0	58	49	20	33	0	2.72
Vida Blue	L	20	2	0	1.000	0	6	6	3	39	20	12	35	2	2.08
Darrell Osteen (MS)	R	27	1	0	1.000	0	4	0	0	6	10	9	3	0	6.00
1 Roberto Rodriguez	R	30	0	0	—	0	6	0	0	12	10	3	6	0	3.00
Dooley Womack	R	30	0	1	.000	0	3	0	0	1	3	1	0	0	15.00
Fred Talbot	R	29	0	1	.000	0	10	0	0	9	10	4	6	0	9.00

CALIFORNIA — 3rd 86-76 .531 12 — LEFTY PHILLIPS

NAME	G by Pos	B	AGE	G	AB	R	H	2B	3B	HR	RBI	BB	SO	SB	BA	SA
TOTALS			26	162	5532	631	1391	197	40	114	598	447	922	69	.251	.363
Jim Spencer	1B142	L	22	146	511	61	140	20	4	12	68	24	61	0	.274	.399
Sandy Alomar	2B153, SS10, 3B1	B	26	162	672	82	169	18	4	2	36	49	65	35	.251	.293
Jim Fregosi	SS150, 1B6	R	28	158	601	95	167	33	5	22	82	69	92	0	.278	.459
Ken McMullen	3B122	R	28	124	422	50	98	9	3	14	61	59	81	1	.232	.367
Roger Repoz	OF110, 1B18	L	29	137	407	50	97	17	6	18	47	45	90	4	.238	.442
Jay Johnstone	OF100	L	24	119	320	34	76	10	5	11	39	24	53	1	.238	.403
Alex Johnson	OF156	R	27	156	614	85	202	26	6	14	86	35	68	17	.329	.459
Joe Azcue	C112	R	30	114	351	19	85	13	1	2	25	24	40	0	.242	.302
Bill Voss (BW)	OF55	L	26	80	181	21	44	3	3	3	30	23	18	2	.243	.348
Tom Egan	C79	R	24	79	210	14	50	6	0	4	20	14	67	0	.238	.324
Jarvis Tatum	OF58	R	23	75	181	28	43	7	0	0	9	17	35	1	.238	.276
Billy Cowan	OF27, 1B14, 3B2	R	31	68	134	20	37	9	1	5	25	11	29	0	.276	.470
Chico Ruiz	3B27, 2B3, SS3, 1B2, C1	B	31	68	107	10	26	3	1	0	12	7	16	3	.243	.290
Tommie Reynolds	OF32, 3B1	R	28	59	120	11	30	3	1	1	6	6	10	1	.250	.317
2 Tony Gonzalez	OF24	L	33	26	92	9	28	2	0	1	12	2	11	1	.304	.359
Doug Griffin	2B11, 3B8	R	23	18	55	2	7	1	0	0	4	6	5	0	.127	.145
1 Aurelio Rodriguez	3B17	R	22	17	63	6	17	2	2	0	7	0	8	0	.270	.365

Mickey Rivers 21 L 8-25, Ray Oyler 31 R 2-24, Tommy Silverio 24 L 0-15, 1 Rick Reichardt 27 R 1-6, Jim Hicks 30 R 1-4, Randy Brown 25 L 0-4, Marty Perez 24 R 0-3

NAME	T	AGE	W	L	PCT	SV	G	GS	CG	IP	H	BB	SO	SHO	ERA
		26	86	76	.531	49	162	162	21	1462	1280	559	922	10	3.48
Clyde Wright	L	29	22	12	.647	0	39	39	7	261	226	88	110	2	2.83
Tom Murphy	R	24	16	13	.552	0	39	38	5	227	223	81	99	2	4.24
Andy Messersmith (VJ)	R	24	11	10	.524	5	37	26	6	195	144	78	162	1	3.00
Ken Tatum	R	26	7	4	.636	17	62	0	0	89	68	26	50	0	2.93
Rudy May	L	25	7	13	.350	0	38	34	2	209	190	81	164	2	4.00
Greg Garrett	L	23	5	6	.455	0	32	7	0	75	48	44	53	0	2.64
Dave LaRoche	L	22	4	1	.800	4	50	0	0	50	41	21	44	0	3.42
Eddie Fisher	R	33	4	4	.500	8	67	2	0	130	117	35	74	0	3.05
1 Joe Doyle	R	30	3	1	.750	5	40	0	0	42	43	21	34	0	5.14
Mel Queen	R	28	3	6	.333	0	34	3	0	60	58	28	44	0	4.20
Tom Bradley	R	23	2	5	.286	0	17	11	1	70	71	33	53	1	4.11
Steve Kealey	R	23	1	0	1.000	1	17	0	0	22	19	6	14	0	4.09
Lloyd Allen	R	20	1	1	.500	3	8	2	0	24	23	11	12	0	2.63
Wally Wolf	R	28	0	0	—	0	5	0	0	5	5	4	3	0	5.40
Terry Cox	R	21	0	0	—	0	2	0	0	4	0	3	6	0	4.50
Harvey Shank	R	23	0	0	—	0	1	0	0	2	2	1	0	0	9.00

KANSAS CITY — 4th (tie) 65-97 .401 33 — CHARLIE METRO 19-33 .365 — BOB LEMON 46-64 .418

NAME	G by Pos	B	AGE	G	AB	R	H	2B	3B	HR	RBI	BB	SO	SB	BA	SA
TOTALS			27	162	5503	611	1341	202	41	97	572	514	958	97	.244	.348
Bob Oliver	1B115, 3B46	R	27	160	612	83	159	24	6	27	99	42	126	3	.260	.451
2 Cookie Rojas	2B97	R	31	98	384	36	100	13	3	2	28	20	29	3	.260	.326
Jackie Hernandez	SS77	R	29	83	238	14	55	4	1	2	15	14	50	1	.231	.282
Paul Schaal	3B97, SS10, 2B6	R	27	124	380	50	102	12	3	5	35	43	39	7	.268	.355
Pat Kelly	OF118	L	25	136	452	56	106	16	1	6	38	76	105	34	.235	.314
Amos Otis	OF159	R	23	159	620	91	176	36	9	11	58	68	67	33	.284	.424
Lou Piniella	OF139, 1B1	R	26	144	542	54	163	24	5	11	88	35	42	3	.301	.424
Ed Kirkpatrick	C89, OF19, 1B16	L	25	134	424	59	97	17	2	18	62	55	65	4	.229	.406
Ellie Rodriguez	C75	R	24	80	231	25	52	8	2	1	15	27	35	2	.225	.290
Rich Severson	SS50, 2B25	R	25	77	240	22	60	11	1	1	22	16	33	0	.250	.317
Joe Keough (BL)	OF34, 1B18	L	24	57	183	28	59	6	2	4	21	23	18	1	.322	.443
Bill Sorrell	3B29, OF4, 1B3	R	29	57	135	12	36	2	0	4	14	10	13	1	.267	.370
Hawk Taylor	C3, 1B1	R	31	57	55	3	9	3	0	1	6	6	16	0	.164	.218
2 Tom Matchick	SS43, 2B10, 3B1	L	26	55	158	11	31	3	2	0	11	5	23	0	.196	.241
George Spriggs	OF36	L	29	51	130	12	27	3	2	1	7	14	32	4	.208	.292
Luis Alcaraz	2B31	R	29	35	120	10	20	5	1	1	14	4	13	0	.167	.250
Jim Campanis	C13, OF1	R	26	31	54	6	7	0	0	2	4	4	14	0	.130	.241
1 Mike Fiore	1B20	L	25	25	72	6	13	2	0	0	4	13	24	1	.181	.208
2 Bobby Floyd	SS8, 3B6	R	26	14	43	5	14	4	0	0	3	4	5	0	.326	.419

Jerry Adair 33 R 4-27, Buck Martinez (MS) 21 R 1-9

NAME	T	AGE	W	L	PCT	SV	G	GS	CG	IP	H	BB	SO	SHO	ERA
		27	65	97	.401	25	162	162	31	1464	1346	641	915	11	3.78
Jim Rooker	L	27	10	15	.400	1	38	29	6	204	190	102	117	3	3.53
3 Ted Abernathy	R	37	9	3	.750	12	36	0	0	56	41	38	49	0	2.57
Dick Drago	R	25	9	15	.375	0	35	34	7	240	239	72	127	1	3.75
Al Fitzmorris	R	24	8	5	.615	1	43	11	2	118	112	52	47	0	4.42
Bob Johnson	R	27	8	13	.381	4	40	26	10	214	178	82	206	1	3.07
Tom Burgmeier	L	26	6	6	.500	7	41	0	0	68	59	23	43	0	3.18
Bill Butler	L	23	4	12	.250	0	25	25	2	141	117	87	75	1	3.77
Dave Morehead	R	27	3	5	.375	1	28	17	1	122	121	62	69	0	3.61
Mike Hedlund (IL)	R	23	2	3	.400	0	9	3	0	15	18	7	5	0	7.20
Wally Bunker (SJ)	R	25	2	11	.154	0	24	15	2	122	109	50	59	1	4.20
Aurelio Monteagudo	R	26	1	1	.500	0	21	0	0	27	32	9	18	0	3.00
Jim York	R	22	1	1	.500	0	8	5	2	6	8	3	3	0	3.38
1 Moe Drabowsky	R	34	1	2	.333	2	24	0	0	36	28	12	38	0	5.26
Ken Wright	R	23	1	2	.333	1	47	0	0	53	49	29	30	0	5.26
Don O'Riley	R	23	0	0	—	0	23	0	0	26	16	15	10	0	5.48
Paul Splittorff	L	23	0	0	.000	0	9	0	0	9	16	15	10	0	7.00
Roger Nelson (SA)	R	26	0	0	.000	0	9	0	0	9	10	3	10	0	10.00

MILWAUKEE — 4th (tie) 65-97 .401 33 — DAVE BRISTOL

NAME	G by Pos	B	AGE	G	AB	R	H	2B	3B	HR	RBI	BB	SO	SB	BA	SA
TOTALS			29	163	5395	613	1305	202	24	126	571	592	985	91	.242	.358
Mike Hegan	1B139, OF8	L	27	148	476	70	116	21	2	11	52	67	116	9	.244	.366
Ted Kubiak	2B91, SS73	B	28	158	546	63	136	9	6	4	41	72	51	4	.252	.313
2 Roberto Pena	SS99, 2B15, 1B7	R	33	121	416	36	99	19	1	3	42	25	45	3	.238	.310
Tommy Harper	3B128, 2B22, OF13	R	29	154	604	104	179	35	4	31	82	77	107	38	.296	.522
Russ Snyder	OF106	L	36	124	276	34	64	11	0	4	31	16	40	1	.232	.315
2 Dave May	OF99	L	26	100	342	36	82	8	1	7	31	34	56	8	.240	.330
Danny Walton	OF114	R	22	117	397	52	102	20	1	17	66	51	126	2	.257	.441
Phil Roof	C107, 1B1	R	29	110	321	39	73	7	1	9	37	32	72	0	.227	.377
Ted Savage	OF82, 1B1	R	33	114	276	43	77	10	5	12	50	57	44	10	.279	.482
Jerry McNertney	C94, 1B13	R	33	111	296	27	72	11	1	6	22	22	33	1	.243	.348
2 Bob Burda	OF64, 1B7	L	31	78	222	19	55	9	0	4	20	16	17	1	.248	.342
Gus Gil	2B38, 3B14	R	30	64	119	12	22	4	0	1	12	12	21	1	.185	.244
Max Alvis	3B6	R	32	62	115	16	21	2	0	3	12	5	20	1	.183	.278
2 Tito Francona	1B13	L	36	52	65	4	15	3	0	0	6	5	5	0	.231	.277
Mike Hershberger (SJ)	OF35	R	30	49	98	7	23	5	0	1	6	10	8	1	.235	.316
Bernie Smith	OF39	R	28	44	76	8	21	5	0	1	6	11	12	1	.276	.382
1 Steve Hovley	OF38	L	25	40	135	17	38	9	0	0	16	17	11	5	.281	.348
2 Hank Allen	OF14, 2B5, 1B4	R	29	28	61	4	14	4	0	0	5	2	9	0	.230	.295
1 John Kennedy	2B16, 3B5, SS4, 1B1	R	29	25	55	8	14	2	0	2	5	6	9	0	.255	.400
1 Greg Goossen	1B15	R	24	21	43	2	11	3	0	3	10	12	9	0	.255	.383
Floyd Wicker	OF12	L	26	15	41	3	8	1	0	1	2	5	9	0	.195	.293

1 Rich Rollins 32 R 5-25, Pete Koegel 22 R 2-8, 1 Wayne Comer 26 R 1-17, Sandy Valdespino 31 L 0-9, Fred Stanley 22 B 0-0

NAME	T	AGE	W	L	PCT	SV	G	GS	CG	IP	H	BB	SO	SHO	ERA
		29	65	97	.401	27	163	163	31	1447	1397	587	895	2	4.21
Marty Pattin	R	27	14	12	.538	0	37	29	11	233	204	71	161	0	3.40
Lew Krausse	R	27	13	18	.419	0	37	35	8	216	235	67	130	1	4.75
Gene Brabender	R	28	6	15	.286	1	29	21	2	129	127	79	76	0	6.00
Ken Sanders	R	28	5	2	.714	13	50	0	0	92	64	25	64	0	1.76
1 Bobby Bolin	R	31	5	11	.313	1	32	20	3	132	131	67	81	0	4.91
Skip Lockwood	R	23	5	12	.294	0	27	26	3	174	173	79	93	1	4.29
John Gelnar	R	27	4	3	.571	4	53	0	0	92	98	23	48	0	4.21
John Morris (IL)	L	28	4	3	.571	0	20	9	2	73	70	22	40	0	3.95
1 John O'Donoghue	L	30	2	1	1.000	0	25	0	0	23	29	9	13	0	5.09
Dave Baldwin	R	32	2	1	.667	1	28	0	0	35	28	20	26	0	2.57
2 Bob Humphreys	R	34	2	4	.333	3	23	1	0	46	37	12	26	0	3.13
2 Al Downing	L	29	2	10	.167	0	17	16	1	94	79	59	53	0	3.35
George Lauzerique	R	22	1	2	.333	0	11	4	1	35	41	14	24	0	6.94
2 Dick Ellsworth	L	30	0	0	—	0	14	0	0	16	11	3	9	0	1.69
Wayne Twitchell	R	22	0	0	—	0	2	0	0	2	1	1	0	0	9.00
Bruce Brubaker	R	28	0	0	—	0	2	0	0	2	4	1	0	0	9.00
1 Bob Locker	R	32	0	1	.000	1	28	0	0	37	16	19	28	0	3.38
Bob Meyer	R	30	0	1	.000	0	10	0	0	18	24	12	20	0	6.50
Ray Peters	R	23	0	2	.000	0	2	2	0	2	7	5	1	0	31.50

CHICAGO — 6th 56-106 .346 42 — DON GUTTERIDGE 49-87 .360 — BILL ADAIR 4-6 .400 — CHUCK TANNER 3-13 .188

NAME	G by Pos	B	AGE	G	AB	R	H	2B	3B	HR	RBI	BB	SO	SB	BA	SA
TOTALS			28	162	5514	633	1394	192	20	123	587	477	872	53	.253	.362
Gail Hopkins	1B77, C8	L	27	116	287	32	82	8	1	6	29	29	28	0	.286	.383
Bobby Knoop	2B126	R	31	130	402	34	92	13	2	5	36	34	79	0	.229	.308
Luis Aparicio	SS146	R	36	146	552	86	173	29	3	5	43	53	34	8	.313	.404
Bill Melton	3B70, OF71	R	24	141	514	74	135	15	1	33	96	56	107	2	.263	.488
Walt Williams	OF79	R	26	110	315	43	79	18	1	3	15	19	30	3	.251	.343
Ken Berry	OF138	R	29	141	463	45	128	12	2	7	40	33	61	6	.276	.378
Carlos May	OF141, 1B7	L	22	150	555	83	158	28	4	12	68	79	96	12	.285	.414
Duane Josephson (BG)	C84	R	28	96	285	28	90	12	2	4	41	24	28	0	.316	.407
Tommy McCraw	1B59, OF49	L	29	129	332	39	73	12	3	1	21	50	12	22	.220	.319
Syd O'Brien	3B68, 2B43, SS5	R	26	121	441	48	109	13	2	8	44	22	62	1	.247	.340
Ed Herrmann	C88	L	23	96	297	42	84	9	0	19	52	31	41	0	.283	.505
Rich Morales	SS24, 3B20, 2B12	R	26	112	224	18	36	2	0	1	9	17	41	1	.161	.205
John Matias	OF22, 1B18	L	24	58	117	7	22	1	1	2	10	8	16	0	.188	.266
Bob Spence	1B37	R	24	46	130	11	29	4	0	1	15	14	32	0	.223	.362
Rich McKinney	3B23, SS11	R	23	43	119	12	20	5	1	0	6	8	23	0	.168	.311
Ossie Blanco	1B22, OF1	R	24	34	66	4	13	0	0	0	1	4	13	0	.197	.197
1 Buddy Bradford	OF27	R	25	32	91	8	17	3	0	2	10	10	30	1	.187	.286
Jose Ortiz	OF8	R	23	15	24	4	8	1	0	0	0	6	4	1	.333	.375
Bob Christian	OF4	R	24	7	15	2	4	0	0	0	1	1	0	0	.267	.467

Chuck Brinkman 25 R 5-20, Art Kusnyer 24 R 1-10, 2 Lee Maye 35 L 1-6

NAME	T	AGE	W	L	PCT	SV	G	GS	CG	IP	H	BB	SO	SHO	ERA
		28	56	106	.346	30	162	162	20	1430	1554	556	762	6	4.54
Tommy John	L	27	12	17	.414	0	37	37	10	269	253	101	138	3	3.28
Jerry Janeski	R	24	10	17	.370	0	35	35	4	206	247	63	79	1	4.76
Wilbur Wood	L	28	9	13	.409	21	77	0	0	122	118	36	85	0	2.80
Joe Horlen (KJ)	R	32	6	16	.273	0	28	26	4	172	198	41	77	0	4.87
2 Bob Miller	R	31	4	6	.400	0	15	12	0	70	88	33	36	0	5.01
Jerry Crider	R	28	4	7	.364	4	32	8	0	91	101	34	40	0	4.45
Bart Johnson	R	20	4	4	.500	3	18	5	2	90	92	46	71	1	4.80
Danny Murphy	R	27	2	3	.400	5	51	0	0	81	82	49	53	0	5.67
2 Lee Stange	R	33	1	0	1.000	0	16	0	0	22	28	5	14	0	5.32
Tommie Sisk	R	28	1	1	.500	0	13	0	0	37	13	16	6	0	5.45
Floyd Weaver	R	26	1	3	.250	3	31	3	0	62	52	31	51	0	4.35
Billy Wynne	R	26	1	4	.200	0	23	8	0	44	54	22	19	0	5.32
Jim Magnuson	R	23	1	5	.167	0	6	0	0	45	46	16	20	0	4.80
Don Secrist	L	26	0	0	—	0	12	0	0	19	12	9	6	0	5.40
Don Eddy	R	23	0	0	—	0	12	0	0	12	9	9	8	0	2.25
Denny O'Toole	R	21	0	0	—	0	4	0	0	9	3	3	3	0	3.00
2 Steve Hamilton	L	36	0	0	—	0	3	0	0	4	8	1	6	0	6.00
Gene Rounsaville	R	25	0	1	.000	0	8	0	0	13	24	12	12	0	10.50
Jerry Arrigo (SJ)	L	29	0	0	.000	0	3	0	0	13	24	9	12	0	13.15
2 Barry Moore	R	27	0	0	.000	0	20	0	0	71	85	34	34	0	6.34

Rich Moloney 20 R 0-0

AMERICAN LEAGUE CHAMPIONSHIP — BALTIMORE (EAST) 3 MINNESOTA (WEST) 0

LINE SCORES

TEAM	1	2	3	4	5	6	7	8	9	10	11	12	R	H	E
Game 1 — October 3 at Minnesota															
BAL	0	2	0	7	0	1	0	0	0				10	13	0
MIN	1	1	0	1	3	0	0	0	0				6	11	2

Cuellar, D. Hall (5) — Perry, Zepp (4), Woodson (5), Williams (6), Perranoski (9)

TEAM	1	2	3	4	5	6	7	8	9	R	H	E
Game 2 — October 4 at Minnesota												
BAL	1	0	2	1	0	0	0	0	7	11	13	0
MIN	0	0	0	3	0	0	0	3	0	3	6	2

McNally — T. Hall, Zepp (4), Williams (5), Perranoski (8), Tiant (9)

TEAM	1	2	3	4	5	6	7	8	9	R	H	E
Game 3 — October 5 at Baltimore												
MIN	0	0	0	0	1	0	0	0	0	1	7	2
BAL	1	1	3	0	0	0	1	0	X	6	10	0

Kaat, Blyleven (3), T. Hall (5), Perry (7) — Palmer

COMPOSITE BATTING

NAME	POS	G	AB	R	H	2B	3B	HR	RBI	BA
Baltimore Totals		3	109	27	36	7	0	6	24	.330
Powell	1B	3	14	2	6	2	0	1	6	.429
Blair	OF	3	13	0	1	0	0	0	0	.077
B. Robinson	3B	3	12	3	7	2	0	0	1	.583
Belanger	SS	3	12	5	4	0	0	0	0	.333
Johnson	2B	3	11	4	4	0	0	2	4	.364
F. Robinson	OF	3	10	3	2	0	0	1	2	.200
Etchebarren	C	3	9	0	1	0	0	0	1	.111
Buford	OF	3	7	3	3	1	0	1	2	.429
Hendricks	C	1	5	2	2	0	0	0	0	.400
Rettenmund	OF	1	3	1	1	0	0	0	1	.333
Minnesota Totals		3	101	10	24	4	3	1	10	.238
Tovar	OF-2B	3	13	2	5	0	1	0	1	.385
Oliva	OF	3	12	2	6	2	0	0	1	.500
Killebrew	3B-1B	3	11	2	3	0	0	1	2	.273
Cardenas	SS	3	11	2	2	0	0	0	0	.182
Mitterwald	C	3	8	0	4	2	0	0	2	.500
Thompson	2B	2	8	0	1	0	0	0	0	.125
Reese	1B	2	7	0	1	0	0	0	0	.143
Alyea	OF	3	7	1	0	0	0	0	0	.000

Renick 3B 1-5, Holt OF 0-5, Ratliff C 1-4, Allison PH 0-2, Quilici 2B 0-2, Carew PH 0-2, Manuel PH 0-1

COMPOSITE PITCHING

NAME	G	IP	H	BB	SO	W	L	SV	ERA
Baltimore Totals	3	27	24	9	22	3	0	0	3.33
McNally	1	9	6	5	5	1	0	0	3.00
Palmer	1	9	7	3	12	1	0	0	1.00
Cuellar	1	4.1	10	1	2	1	0	0	12.46
D. Hall	1	4.2	1	0	3	1	0	0	0.00
Minnesota Totals	3	26	36	12	19	0	3	0	7.62
Williams	2	6	2	1	0	0	0	0	0.00
T. Hall	2	5.1	6	4	6	0	1	0	6.75
Perry	2	5.1	10	1	3	0	1	0	13.50
Perranoski	2	2.1	5	1	3	0	0	0	19.29
Blyleven	1	2	6	2	4	0	0	0	9.00
Kaat	1	2	6	2	1	0	1	0	9.00

Zepp 2G, Woodson 1G, Tiant 1G

NATIONAL LEAGUE CHAMPIONSHIP — CINCINNATI (WEST) 3 PITTSBURGH (EAST) 0

LINE SCORES

TEAM	1	2	3		4	5	6		7	8	9		10 11 12	R	H	E
Game 1			October 3 at Pittsburgh													
CIN	0	0	0		0	0	0		0	0	3			3	9	0
PIT	0	0	0		0	0	0		0	0	0			0	8	0

Nolan, Carroll (10)   Ellis, Gibbon (10)

Game 2			October 4 at Pittsburgh													
CIN	0	0	1		0	1	0		0	1	0			3	8	1
PIT	0	0	0		0	0	1		0	0	0			1	5	2

Merritt, Carroll (6), Gullett (6)   Walker, Giusti (8)

Game 3			October 5 at Cincinnati													
PIT	1	0	0		0	1	0		0	0	0			2	10	0
CIN	2	0	0		0	0	0		0	1	X			3	5	0

Moose, Gibbon (8), Cloninger (6), Giusti (8)   Wilcox (6), Granger (9), Gullett (9)

COMPOSITE BATTING

NAME	POS	G	AB	R	H	2B	3B	HR	RBI	BA
Cincinnati Totals		3	100	9	22	3	1	3	8	.220
Rose	OF	3	13	1	3	0	0	1		.231
Tolan	OF	3	12	3	5	0	0	1	2	.417
Perez	3B-1B	3	12	1	4	2	0	1	2	.333
May	1B	3	12	0	2	1	0	0	2	.167
Helms	2B	3	11	0	3	0	0	0		.273
Woodward	SS-3B	3	10	0	1	0	0	0		.100
Bench	C	3	9	2	2	0	0	1	1	.222
Carbo	OF	2	6	0	0	0	0	0		.000
McRae	OF	2	4	0	0	0	0	0		.000
Stewart	OF	2	2	0	0	0	0	0		.000
Cline	OF	2	1	2	1	0	1	0		1.000
Bravo	PH	1	1	0	0	0	0	0		.000
Concepcion	SS	3	0	0	0	0	0	0		—
Pittsburgh Totals		3	102	3	23	6	0	3		.225
Clemente	OF	3	14	1	3	0	0	0	1	.214
Stargell	OF	3	12	0	6	1	0	0	1	.500
Alou	OF	3	12	1	3	1	0	0		.250
Sanguillen	C	3	12	0	2	0	0	0	1	.167
Oliver	1B	2	8	0	2	0	0	0	1	.250
Cash	2B	2	8	1	1	0	0	0		.125
Alley	SS	2	7	0	0	0	0	0		.000
Hebner	3B	2	6	0	4	2	0	0	1	.667
Robertson	1B	2	5	0	1	0	0	0		.200
Pagan	3B	1	3	0	1	0	0	0		.333

Patek SS 0-3, Jeter OF 0-2, Mazeroski 2B 0-2

COMPOSITE PITCHING

NAME	G	IP	H	BB	SO	W	L	SV	ERA
Cincinnati Totals	3	28	23	12	19	3	0	3	0.96
Nolan	1	9	8	4	6	1	0	0	0.00
Merritt	1	5.1	3	0	2	1	0	0	1.69
Cloninger	1	5	7	4	1	0	0	0	3.60
Gullett	2	3.2	1	2	3	0	0	2	0.00
Wilcox	1	3	1	2	5	1	0	0	0.00
Carroll	2	1.1	2	0	1	0	0	1	0.00
Granger	1	0.2	1	0	1	0	0	0	0.00
Pittsburgh Totals	3	27	22	8	12	0	3	0	2.67
Ellis	1	9.2	9	4	1	0	1	0	2.79
Moose	1	7.2	4	2	4	0	1	0	3.52
Walker	1	7	5	1	5	0	1	0	1.29
Giusti	2	2.1	3	1	1	0	0	0	3.86
Gibbon	2	0.1	1	0	1	0	0	0	0.00

EAST DIVISION

PITTSBURGH   1st 89-73 .549   DANNY MURTAUGH

NAME	G by Pos	B	AGE	G	AB	R	H	2B	3B	HR	RBI	BB	SO	SB	BA	SA
TOTALS			28	162	5637	729	1522	235	70	130	676	444	871	66	.270	.406
Bob Robertson	1B99, 3B5, OF3	R	23	117	390	69	112	19	4	27	82	51	98	4	.287	.564
Bill Mazeroski	2B102	R	33	112	367	29	84	14	0	7	39	27	40	2	.229	.324
Gene Alley	SS108, 2B8, 3B2	R	29	121	426	46	104	16	5	8	41	31	70	7	.244	.362
Richie Hebner	3B117	L	22	120	420	60	122	24	8	11	46	42	48	2	.290	.464
Roberto Clemente	OF104	R	35	108	412	65	145	22	10	14	60	38	66	3	.352	.556
Matty Alou	OF153	L	31	155	677	97	201	21	8	1	47	30	18	19	.297	.356
Willie Stargell	OF125, 1B1	L	30	136	474	70	125	18	3	31	85	44	119	0	.264	.511
Manny Sanguillen	C125	R	26	128	486	63	158	19	7	5	61	17	45	2	.325	.444
Al Oliver	OF80, 1B77	L	23	151	551	63	149	33	5	12	83	35	35	1	.270	.414
Jose Pagan	3B53, OF4, 1B1, 2B1	R	35	89	230	21	61	14	1	7	29	20	24	1	.265	.426
Johnnie Jeter	OF56	R	25	85	126	27	30	3	2	2	12	13	34	9	.238	.341
Freddie Patek	SS65	R	25	84	237	42	58	10	5	1	19	29	46	8	.245	.342
Dave Cash	2B55	R	22	64	210	30	66	7	6	1	28	17	25	5	.314	.419
Jerry May	C45	R	26	51	139	13	29	4	2	1	16	21	25	0	.209	.288
Gene Clines	OF7	R	23	31	37	4	15	2	0	0	3	2	5	2	.405	.459
Jose Martinez	3B7, 2B4, SS1	R	27	19	20	1	1	0	0	0	1	5	3	0	.050	.050
Dave Ricketts	C7	B	34	14	11	0	2	0	0	0	1	1	3	0	.182	.182
George Kopacz	1B3	L	27	10	16	1	3	0	0	0	0	5	0	.188	.188
Milt May		L	19	5	4	1	2	1	0	0	2	0	0	0	.500	.750

CHICAGO   2nd 84-78 .519 5   LEO DUROCHER

NAME	G by Pos	B	AGE	G	AB	R	H	2B	3B	HR	RBI	BB	SO	SB	BA	SA
TOTALS			30	162	5491	806	1424	228	44	179	761	607	844	39	.259	.415
Ernie Banks	1B62	R	39	72	222	25	56	6	2	12	44	20	33	0	.252	.459
Glenn Beckert	2B138, OF1	R	29	143	591	99	170	15	6	3	36	32	22	4	.288	.349
Don Kessinger	SS154	B	27	154	631	100	168	21	14	1	39	66	59	12	.266	.349
Ron Santo	3B152, OF1	R	30	154	555	83	148	30	4	26	114	92	108	0	.267	.476
Johnny Callison	OF144	L	31	147	477	65	126	23	2	19	68	60	93	0	.264	.440
Jim Hickman	OF79, 1B74	R	33	149	514	102	162	33	4	32	115	93	99	0	.315	.582
Billy Williams	OF160	L	32	161	636	137	205	34	4	42	129	72	65	7	.322	.586
Randy Hundley	C73	R	28	73	250	13	61	5	0	7	36	16	52	0	.244	.348
Cleo James	OF90	R	29	100	176	33	37	7	2	3	14	17	24	5	.210	.324
Willie Smith	1B43, OF1	L	31	87	167	15	36	9	1	5	24	11	32	2	.216	.371
Paul Popovich	2B22, SS17, 3B16	B	29	78	186	22	47	9	1	4	20	18	18	0	.253	.355
2 Jack Hiatt	C63, 1B2	R	27	66	178	19	43	12	1	2	22	31	48	0	.242	.354
2 Joe Pepitone	OF56, 1B13	L	29	56	213	38	57	9	2	12	44	15	15	0	.268	.498
J.C. Martin	C36, 1B3	L	33	40	77	11	12	1	0	1	4	2	15	0	.156	.208
1 Jimmie Hall	OF8	L	32	28	32	2	3	1	0	0	4	4	12	0	.094	.125
2 Phil Gagliano	2B16, 1B1, 3B1	R	28	26	40	5	6	0	0	0	3	3	0	.150	.150
Al Spangler	OF6	L	36	21	14	2	2	1	0	0	1	3	3	0	.143	.429
Ken Rudolph	C16	R	23	20	40	1	4	1	0	1	2	3	0	.100	.225
3 Tommy Davis	OF10	R	31	11	42	4	11	2	0	1	5	1	6	0	.262	.452

1 Boots Day 22 L 2-8, Terry Hughes 21 R 1-3, Brock Davis 26 L 0-3, Adrian Garrett 27 L 0-3, Roger Metzger 22 L 0-2, Roe Skidmore 24 R 1-1

NEW YORK   3rd 83-79 .512 6   GIL HODGES

NAME	G by Pos	B	AGE	G	AB	R	H	2B	3B	HR	RBI	BB	SO	SB	BA	SA
TOTALS			27	162	5443	695	1358	211	42	120	640	684	1062	118	.249	.370
Donn Clendenon	1B100	R	34	121	396	65	114	18	3	22	97	39	91	4	.288	.515
Ken Boswell	2B101	L	24	105	351	32	89	13	2	5	44	41	32	5	.254	.345
Bud Harrelson	SS156	B	26	157	564	72	137	18	8	1	42	95	74	23	.243	.309
Joe Foy	3B97	R	27	99	322	39	76	12	0	6	37	68	58	22	.236	.329
Ron Swoboda	OF100	R	26	115	245	29	57	6	2	9	40	40	72	0	.233	.392
Tommie Agee	OF130	R	27	153	636	107	182	30	7	24	75	55	156	31	.286	.469
Cleon Jones	OF130	R	27	134	506	71	140	25	8	10	63	50	87	5	.277	.417
Jerry Grote	C125	R	27	126	415	38	106	14	1	2	34	30	39	2	.255	.308
Art Shamsky	OF58, 1B56	L	28	122	403	48	118	19	2	11	49	49	33	1	.293	.432
Wayne Garrett	3B70, 2B45, SS1	L	22	114	366	74	93	17	4	12	45	81	60	5	.254	.421
Dave Marshall	OF43	L	27	92	189	21	46	10	1	6	29	17	43	4	.243	.402
Mike Jorgensen	1B50, OF10	L	21	76	87	15	17	3	1	4	10	23	21	0	.195	.356
Al Weis	2B44, SS15	R	32	75	121	20	25	1	1	1	11	7	21	1	.207	.306
Ken Singleton	OF51	B	23	69	198	22	52	8	0	5	26	30	48	1	.263	.379
Duffy Dyer	C57	R	24	59	148	8	31	4	0	2	12	21	32	1	.209	.307
Ed Kranepool	1B25	L	25	43	47	2	8	1	0	0	3	4	8	0	.170	.170

Tim Foli 19 R 4-11, Rod Gaspar 24 B 0-14, Ted Martinez 22 R 1-16, Lee Stanton 24 R 1-4

ST. LOUIS   4th 76-86 .469 13   RED SCHOENDIENST

NAME	G by Pos	B	AGE	G	AB	R	H	2B	3B	HR	RBI	BB	SO	SB	BA	SA
TOTALS			28	162	5689	744	1497	218	51	113	688	569	961	117	.263	.379
Dick Allen (LJ)	1B79, 3B38, OF3	R	28	122	459	88	128	17	5	34	101	71	118	5	.279	.560
Julian Javier	2B137	R	33	139	513	62	129	16	3	2	42	24	70	6	.251	.306
Dal Maxvill	SS136, 2B22	R	31	152	399	35	80	5	2	0	28	51	56	0	.201	.223
Joe Torre	3B73, C90, 1B1	R	29	161	624	89	203	27	9	21	100	70	91	2	.325	.498
Leron Lee	OF77	L	22	121	264	28	60	13	1	7	24	5	56	5	.227	.352
Jose Cardenal	OF134	R	26	148	552	73	162	32	6	10	74	45	70	26	.293	.428
Lou Brock	OF152	L	31	155	664	114	202	29	5	13	57	60	99	51	.304	.422
Ted Simmons (MS)	C79	B	20	82	284	29	69	8	2	4	24	37	37	2	.243	.317
Joe Hague	1B82, OF52	L	26	139	451	58	122	16	4	14	68	63	87	2	.271	.417
Vic Davalillo	OF54	L	33	111	183	29	57	14	3	1	19	11	18	4	.311	.437
Carl Taylor	OF46, 1B15, 3B1	R	26	104	245	29	61	12	2	4	45	41	30	5	.249	.388
Milt Ramirez	SS59, 2B1	R	20	76	82	7	16	2	1	0	4	13	20	1	.195	.244
Mike Shannon (IL)	3B51	R	30	55	174	18	37	9	0	2	16	20	31	0	.213	.287
2 Jim Beauchamp	OF10, 1B6	R	30	44	68	8	15	2	0	1	6	8	20	0	.221	.294
Bob Gibson	P34	R	34	40	109	14	33	7	0	2	19	3	25	0	.303	.404
Ed Crosby	SS35, 3B2, 2B1	B	21	38	95	9	24	4	0	0	2	6	14	0	.253	.337
2 Cookie Rojas	2B10, OF3, SS2	R	31	32	57	1	6	1	0	0	2	5	8	0	.105	.123
Luis Melendez	OF18	R	21	20	71	11	21	5	1	1	5	4	11	3	.296	.437
1 Phil Gagliano	3B6, 1B3, 2B2	R	28	18	22	4	5	0	0	0	1	2	5	0	.227	.227

Jim Campbell 27 L 3-13, Jim Kennedy 23 L 3-24, Jerry DaVanon 24 R 2-18, Jose Cruz 22 L 6-17
Joe Nossek 29 R 0-1, Jorge Roque 20 R 0-1, Bart Zeller 28 R 0-0

PITTSBURGH pitching

NAME	T	AGE	W	L	PCT	SV	G	GS	CG	IP	H	BB	SO	SHO	ERA
		28	89	73	.549	43	162	162	36	1454	1386	625	990	13	3.70
Luke Walker	L	26	15	6	.714	3	42	19	5	163	129	89	124	3	3.04
Dock Ellis	R	25	13	10	.565	0	30	30	9	202	194	87	128	4	3.21
Bob Moose (SA)	R	22	11	10	.524	0	28	27	9	190	186	64	119	2	3.98
Steve Blass (EJ)	R	28	10	12	.455	0	31	31	6	197	187	73	120	1	3.52
Bob Veale	L	34	10	15	.400	0	34	32	5	202	189	94	178	1	3.92
Dave Giusti	R	30	9	3	.750	26	64	1	0	103	98	39	85	0	3.06
Bruce Dal Canton	R	22	9	4	.692	1	41	6	1	85	94	39	53	0	4.55
Jim Nelson	R	22	4	2	.667	0	15	10	1	68	64	38	42	1	3.44
Orlando Pena	R	36	2	1	.667	2	23	0	0	38	38	7	25	0	4.74
2 Mudcat Grant	R	34	2	1	.667	0	8	0	0	11	9	8	6	0	2.25
Dick Colpaert	R	26	1	0	1.000	3	8	0	0	11	9	8	6	0	5.73
1 Chuck Hartenstein	R	28	1	1	.500	7	17	0	0	24	25	8	14	0	4.50
George Brunet	L	35	1	1	.500	0	12	1	0	17	19	9	17	0	2.65
Fred Cambria	R	22	1	3	.333	0	6	5	0	33	37	12	14	0	3.55
2 Al McBean	R	32	0	0	—	1	7	0	0	10	13	7	3	0	8.10
Ed Acosta	R	26	0	0	—	1	3	0	0	3	5	2	1	0	12.00
Lou Marone	L	24	0	0	—	0	4	0	0	4	3	1	0	0	4.50
Joe Gibbon	L	35	0	0	—	5	41	0	0	41	44	24	26	0	4.83
John Lamb	L	23	0	1	.000	3	23	0	0	32	23	13	24	0	2.81
Gene Garber	R	23	0	0	—	0	14	0	0	22	22	11	7	0	5.32

CHICAGO pitching

NAME	T	AGE	W	L	PCT	SV	G	GS	CG	IP	H	BB	SO	SHO	ERA
		28	84	78	.519	25	162	162	59	1435	1402	475	1000	9	3.76
Ferguson Jenkins	R	26	22	16	.579	0	40	39	24	313	265	60	274	3	3.39
Bill Hands	R	30	18	15	.545	1	39	38	12	265	278	76	170	2	3.70
Ken Holtzman	L	24	17	11	.607	0	39	38	15	288	271	94	202	1	3.34
2 Milt Pappas	R	31	10	8	.556	0	21	20	6	145	135	36	80	2	2.87
Phil Regan	R	33	5	9	.357	12	54	0	0	76	81	32	31	0	4.74
Hank Aguirre	L	39	5	3	.625	0	17	0	0	14	13	9	11	0	4.50
Jim Colborn	R	24	3	1	.750	4	34	5	0	73	68	23	50	0	3.58
3 Roberto Rodriguez	R	26	3	2	.600	2	26	0	0	43	50	15	46	0	5.86
Joe Decker	R	23	2	7	.222	0	24	17	1	109	108	56	79	0	4.62
Larry Gura	L	22	1	3	.250	0	20	3	1	38	35	23	21	0	3.79
Juan Pizarro	L	33	0	0	—	1	12	0	0	16	16	9	14	0	4.50
1 Ted Abernathy	R	37	0	0	—	1	11	0	0	9	9	5	2	0	2.00
3 Bob Miller	R	31	0	0	—	0	4	0	0	6	9	3	4	0	9.00
Jim Cosman	R	27	0	0	—	0	1	0	0	1	3	1	0	0	27.00
1 Steve Barber	L	32	0	1	.000	0	5	0	0	6	10	6	3	0	9.00
2 Hoyt Wilhelm	R	47	0	1	.000	0	3	0	0	4	3	1	9	0	6.00
Jimmy Dunegan	R	22	0	0	—	0	7	0	0	13	13	12	9	0	4.85
Archie Reynolds	R	24	0	0	—	0	5	0	0	17	17	9	9	0	6.60

NEW YORK pitching

NAME	T	AGE	W	L	PCT	SV	G	GS	CG	IP	H	BB	SO	SHO	ERA
		26	83	79	.512	32	162	162	47	1460	1260	575	1064	10	3.45
Tom Seaver	R	25	18	12	.600	0	37	36	19	291	230	83	283	2	2.81
Jerry Koosman (EJ)	L	27	12	7	.632	0	30	29	5	212	189	71	118	1	3.14
Jim McAndrew	R	26	10	14	.417	2	32	27	9	188	166	38	111	3	3.57
Gary Gentry	R	23	9	9	.500	1	32	29	5	188	155	86	134	2	3.69
Danny Frisella	R	24	8	3	.727	9	30	1	0	66	49	34	54	0	3.00
Ray Sadecki	L	29	8	4	.667	0	28	24	3	139	134	52	89	0	3.88
Nolan Ryan	R	23	7	11	.389	1	27	19	5	132	86	97	125	2	3.41
Ron Taylor	R	32	5	4	.556	13	57	0	0	66	65	16	28	0	3.95
Tug McGraw	L	25	4	6	.400	10	57	0	0	91	77	49	81	0	3.26
2 Ron Herbel	R	32	2	2	.500	1	12*		0	13	14	2	8	0	1.38
1 Dean Chance	R	29	0	1	.000	0	3	0	0	2	6	3	0	0	13.50
1 Don Cardwell	R	34	0	2	.000	0	6	1	0	25	31	6	8	0	6.48
Rich Folkers	L	24	0	0	—	0	16	1	0	29	36	25	15	0	6.52
1 Cal Koonce	R	29	0	0	—	0	13	0	0	22	25	14	10	0	3.27

* Herbel, also with San Diego, league leader in G with 76

ST. LOUIS pitching

NAME	T	AGE	W	L	PCT	SV	G	GS	CG	IP	H	BB	SO	SHO	ERA
		26	76	86	.469	20	162	162	51	1476	1483	632	960	11	4.05
Bob Gibson	R	34	23	7	.767	0	34	34	23	294	262	88	274	3	3.12
Steve Carlton	L	25	10	19	.345	0	34	33	13	254	239	109	193	2	3.72
Mike Torrez	R	23	8	10	.444	0	30	20	5	179	168	93	100	1	4.22
Jerry Reuss	L	21	7	8	.467	0	20	15	4	127	132	49	74	2	4.11
Chuck Taylor	R	28	7	5	.583	8	56	7	1	124	116	31	64	1	3.12
Nelson Briles	R	26	6	7	.462	0	30	19	1	107	120	36	59	1	6.22
1 George Culver	R	26	3	5	.375	0	11	7	2	57	64	24	23	0	4.58
2 Frank Linzy	R	29	3	1	.750	9	47	0	0	61	66	23	19	0	3.69
1 Jerry Johnson	R	26	2	1	.667	0	16	4	1	19	22	7	12	0	3.27
Al Hrabosky	L	20	2	1	.667	0	16	1	0	19	22	12	12	0	4.74
Sal Campisi	R	28	2	2	.500	3	32	0	0	53	37	26	29	0	2.94
2 Ted Abernathy	R	37	1	0	1.000	1	15	0	0	22	26	12	10	0	3.00
Santiago Guzman	R	20	1	0	1.000	0	2	0	0	9	5	4	5	0	5.00
Harry Parker	R	22	0	0	—	0	6	1	0	13	17	5	12	0	3.27
Frank Bertaina	L	26	0	0	—	0	7	0	0	7	13	8	4	0	3.19
2 Chuck Hartenstein	R	28	0	0	—	0	11	0	0	13	24	5	5	0	9.00
1 Rich Nye	L	26	0	0	—	0	3	0	0	4	2	3	4	0	4.50
2 Fred Norman	L	27	0	0	—	0	4	0	0	8	6	5	7	0	6.75
Bob Chlupsa	R	24	0	0	—	0	18	0	0	22	16	16	14	0	6.14
Billy McCool	L	25	0	0	—	0	9	0	0	20	16	13	13	0	6.75
Tom Hilgendorf	L	28	0	0	—	0	23	0	0	36	31	18	22	0	3.86
Reggie Cleveland	R	22	0	0	—	0	16	1	0	26	31	18	22	0	7.62

PHILADELPHIA 5th 73-88 .453 15.5 — FRANK LUCCHESI

Batting

NAME	G by Pos	B	AGE	G	AB	R	H	2B	3B	HR	RBI	BB	SO	SB	BA	SA
TOTALS			26	161	5456	594	1299	224	58	101	553	519	1066	72	.238	.356
Deron Johnson	1B154, 3B3	R	31	159	574	66	147	28	3	27	93	72	132	0	.256	.456
Denny Doyle	2B103	L	26	112	413	43	86	10	7	2	16	33	64	6	.208	.281
Larry Bowa	SS143, 2B1	B	24	145	547	50	137	17	6	0	34	21	48	24	.250	.303
Don Money (IJ)	3B119, SS2	R	23	120	447	66	132	25	4	14	66	43	68	4	.295	.462
Ron Stone	OF99, 1B6	R	27	123	321	30	84	12	5	3	39	38	45	5	.262	.386
Larry Hisle	OF121	R	23	126	405	52	83	22	4	10	44	53	139	5	.205	.353
Johnny Briggs (LJ)	OF95	L	26	110	341	43	92	15	7	9	47	39	65	5	.270	.434
Tim McCarver (BH)	C44	L	28	44	164	16	47	11	1	4	14	14	10	2	.287	.439
Tony Taylor	2B59, 3B38, OF18, SS1	R	34	124	439	74	132	26	9	9	55	50	67	9	.301	.462
Byron Browne	OF88	R	27	104	270	29	67	17	2	10	36	33	72	1	.248	.437
Oscar Gamble	OF74	L	20	88	275	31	72	12	4	1	19	27	37	5	.262	.345
Terry Harmon	SS35, 2B14, 3B2	R	26	71	129	16	32	2	4	0	7	12	22	6	.248	.326
Rick Joseph	OF12, 1B10, 3B9	R	30	71	119	7	27	2	1	3	10	6	28	0	.227	.336
Jim Hutto	OF22, 1B12, C5, 3B1	R	22	57	92	7	17	2	0	3	12	5	20	0	.185	.304
Mike Compton	C40	R	25	47	110	8	18	0	1	1	7	9	22	0	.164	.209
Mike Ryan (BH)	C46	R	28	46	134	14	24	8	0	2	11	16	24	0	.179	.284
Doc Edwards	C34	R	33	35	78	5	21	0	0	0	6	4	10	0	.269	.269
Scott Reid	OF18	L	23	25	49	5	6	1	0	0	1	11	22	0	.122	.143
Del Bates	C20	L	30	22	60	1	8	2	0	0	1	6	15	0	.133	.167
Willie Montanez	OF10, 1B5	L	22	18	25	3	6	0	0	0	3	1	4	0	.240	.240
Joe Lis	OF9	R	23	13	37	1	7	2	0	1	4	5	11	0	.189	.324
Sammy Parrilla	OF3	R	27	11	16	0	2	1	0	0	0	1	6	0	.125	.188
Greg Luzinski	1B3	R	19	8	12	0	2	0	0	0	0	3	5	0	.167	.167

John Vukovich 22 R 1-8, Curt Flood (HO) 32

Pitching

NAME	T	AGE	W	L	PCT	SV	G	GS	CG	IP	H	BB	SO	SHO	ERA
TOTALS		28	73	88	.453	36	161	161	24	1461	1483	538	1047	8	4.17
Rick Wise	R	24	13	14	.481	0	35	34	5	220	253	65	113	1	4.17
Jim Bunning	R	38	10	15	.400	0	34	34	8	219	233	56	147	0	4.11
Joe Hoerner	L	33	9	5	.643	9	44	0	0	58	53	20	39	0	2.64
Chris Short	L	32	9	16	.360	1	36	34	7	199	211	66	133	2	4.30
Woody Fryman (SA)	L	30	8	6	.571	0	27	20	4	128	122	43	97	3	4.08
Dick Selma	R	26	8	9	.471	22	73	0	0	134	108	59	153	0	2.75
Barry Lersch	R	25	6	3	.667	3	42	11	3	138	119	47	92	0	3.26
Grant Jackson	L	27	5	15	.250	0	32	23	1	150	170	61	104	0	5.28
Fred Wenz	R	28	2	0	1.000	1	22	0	0	30	27	13	24	0	4.50
Billy Wilson	R	27	1	0	1.000	0	37	0	0	58	57	33	41	0	4.81
Mike Jackson	R	24	1	1	.500	0	5	0	0	6	6	4	4	0	1.50
Lowell Palmer	R	22	1	2	.333	0	38	5	0	102	98	55	85	0	5.47
Ken Reynolds	L	23	0	0	—	0	4	0	0	2	3	4	1	0	0.00
Bill Laxton	L	22	0	0	—	0	2	0	0	2	2	2	2	0	13.50
Billy Champion	R	22	0	2	.000	0	7	1	0	14	21	10	12	0	9.00

MONTREAL 6th 73-89 .451 16 — GENE MAUCH

Batting

NAME	G by Pos	B	AGE	G	AB	R	H	2B	3B	HR	RBI	BB	SO	SB	BA	SA
TOTALS			27	161	5411	687	1284	211	35	136	646	659	972	65	.237	.365
Ron Fairly (BF)	1B118, OF4	L	31	119	385	54	111	19	0	15	61	72	64	10	.288	.455
Gary Sutherland	2B97, SS15, 3B1	R	25	159	359	37	74	10	0	3	26	31	22	2	.206	.259
Bobby Wine	SS159	R	31	159	501	40	116	21	3	3	51	39	94	0	.232	.303
Coco Laboy	3B132, 2B3	R	30	137	432	37	86	26	1	5	32	31	81	0	.199	.299
Rusty Staub	OF160	L	26	160	569	98	156	23	7	30	94	112	93	12	.274	.497
Adolfo Phillips	OF75	R	28	92	214	36	51	6	3	6	21	36	51	7	.238	.379
Mack Jones	OF87	L	31	108	271	51	65	11	3	14	32	59	61	5	.240	.458
John Bateman	C137	R	29	139	520	51	123	21	5	15	68	28	75	8	.237	.383
Bob Bailey	3B48, OF44, 1B18	R	27	131	352	77	101	19	3	28	84	72	70	5	.287	.597
Marv Staehle	2B91, SS1	L	28	104	321	41	70	9	1	0	26	39	21	1	.218	.252
Jim Fairey	OF59	L	25	92	211	35	51	9	3	3	25	14	38	1	.242	.355
Jim Gosger	OF71, 1B19	L	27	91	274	38	72	11	2	5	37	35	55	3	.263	.372
Don Hahn	OF61	R	21	82	149	22	38	8	0	0	8	27	27	4	.255	.309
Ron Brand	SS19, 3B12, C9, OF5, 2B3	R	30	72	126	10	30	2	3	0	9	9	16	2	.238	.302
John Boccabella	1B33, C24, 3B1	R	29	61	145	18	39	3	1	5	17	11	24	0	.269	.407
2 Boots Day	OF35	L	22	41	108	14	29	4	0	0	5	6	18	3	.269	.306
1 Jack Hiatt	C12, 1B2	R	27	43	43	4	14	2	0	0	7	14	14	0	.326	.372
Clyde Mashore	OF10	R	25	13	25	2	4	0	0	1	3	4	11	0	.160	.280
Fred Whitfield	1B4	L	32	4	15	0	1	0	0	0	0	1	3	0	.067	.067

Jim Qualls 23 B 1-9, 1 Ty Cline (IL) 31 L 1-2, Angel Hermoso 23 R 0-1, Joe Herrera 28 R 0-1

Pitching

NAME	T	AGE	W	L	PCT	SV	G	GS	CG	IP	H	BB	SO	SHO	ERA
TOTALS		27	73	89	.451	32	162	162	29	1439	1434	716	914	10	4.50
Carl Morton	R	26	18	11	.621	0	43	37	10	285	281	125	154	4	3.60
Steve Renko	R	25	13	11	.542	1	41	33	7	223	203	104	142	1	4.32
Dan McGinn	L	26	7	10	.412	0	52	19	3	131	154	78	83	2	5.43
Bill Stoneman	R	26	7	15	.318	0	40	30	5	208	209	109	176	3	4.59
Howie Reed	R	33	6	5	.545	5	57	1	0	89	81	40	42	0	3.13
Claude Raymond	R	33	6	7	.462	23	59	0	0	83	76	27	68	0	4.45
John Strohmayer	R	23	3	1	.750	0	42	0	0	76	85	39	74	0	4.86
2 Rich Nye	L	25	3	2	.600	0	8	6	2	46	47	20	21	0	4.11
Mike Wegener (EJ)	R	23	3	6	.333	0	25	16	1	104	100	56	35	0	5.28
2 Mike Marshall	R	27	3	7	.300	3	24	5	0	65	56	29	38	0	3.46
Bill Dillman	R	25	2	4	.400	1	18	0	0	31	28	18	17	0	5.23
2 John O'Donoghue	L	30	2	3	.400	0	9	3	0	22	20	11	6	0	5.32
Carroll Sembera	R	28	0	0	—	0	7	0	0	14	11	6	9	0	18.00
Ken Johnson	R	37	0	0	—	0	3	0	0	6	9	1	4	0	7.50
1 Gary Waslewski	R	28	0	2	.000	0	15	0	0	25	23	15	19	0	5.04
Balor Moore	L	19	0	2	.000	0	6	2	0	10	14	8	6	0	7.20
Joe Sparma	R	28	0	0	—	0	9	6	1	29	34	25	23	0	7.14

WEST DIVISION

CINCINNATI 1st 102-60 .630 — SPARKY ANDERSON

Batting

NAME	G by Pos	B	AGE	G	AB	R	H	2B	3B	HR	RBI	BB	SO	SB	BA	SA
TOTALS			25	162	5540	775	1498	253	45	191	726	547	984	115	.270	.436
Lee May	1B153	R	27	153	605	78	153	34	2	34	94	38	125	1	.253	.464
Tommy Helms	2B148, SS12	R	29	150	575	42	136	21	1	1	45	21	33	2	.237	.282
Dave Concepcion	SS93, 2B3	R	22	101	265	38	69	11	3	1	25	24	45	10	.260	.317
Tony Perez	3B153, 1B8	R	28	158	587	107	186	28	6	40	129	83	134	8	.317	.589
Pete Rose	OF159	B	29	159	649	120	205	37	9	15	52	73	64	12	.316	.470
Bobby Tolan	OF150	L	24	152	589	112	186	34	6	16	80	62	94	57	.316	.475
Bernie Carbo	OF119	L	22	125	365	54	113	19	3	21	63	94	77	10	.310	.551
Johnny Bench	C139, OF24, 1B12, 3B1	R	22	158	605	97	177	35	4	45	148	54	102	5	.293	.587
Jimmy Stewart	OF48, 2B18, 3B9, 1B1, C1	B	31	101	105	15	28	3	1	1	4	12	20	1	.267	.343
Woody Woodward	SS77, 3B20, 2B10, 1B2	R	27	100	264	23	59	8	3	1	14	20	21	1	.223	.288
Hal McRae	OF46, 3B6, 2B1	R	24	70	165	18	41	6	1	8	23	15	23	0	.248	.442
Angel Bravo	OF22	R	27	65	65	10	18	1	1	0	3	9	13	0	.277	.323
Darrel Chaney	SS30, 2B18, 3B3	B	22	57	95	7	22	3	0	1	4	3	16	1	.232	.295
2 Ty Cline (IL)	OF20, 1B2	L	31	48	63	13	17	7	1	0	8	12	11	1	.270	.413
Pat Corrales	C42	R	29	43	106	9	25	5	1	1	10	8	22	0	.236	.330
Frank Duffy	SS5	R	23	6	11	1	2	2	0	0	0	1	2	1	.182	.364
Jay Ward	3B2, 2B1, 1B1	R	31	6	3	0	0	0	0	0	0	0	2	0	.000	.000
Bill Plummer	C4	R	23	4	8	0	1	0	0	0	0	0	2	0	.125	.125

Pitching

NAME	T	AGE	W	L	PCT	SV	G	GS	CG	IP	H	BB	SO	SHO	ERA
TOTALS		26	102	60	.630	60	162	162	32	1445	1370	592	843	15	3.69
Jim Merritt (EJ)	L	26	20	12	.625	0	35	35	12	234	248	53	136	1	4.08
Gary Nolan	R	22	18	7	.720	0	37	37	4	251	226	96	181	2	3.26
Wayne Simpson (SJ)	R	21	14	3	.824	0	26	26	10	176	125	81	119	2	3.02
Jim McGlothlin	R	26	14	10	.583	0	35	34	5	211	192	86	97	3	3.58
Clay Carroll	R	29	9	4	.692	16	65	0	0	104	104	27	63	0	2.60
Tony Cloninger	R	29	9	7	.563	1	30	18	0	148	136	78	56	0	3.83
Wayne Granger	R	26	6	5	.545	35	67	0	0	85	79	27	38	0	2.65
Don Gullett	L	19	5	2	.714	6	44	2	0	78	54	44	76	0	2.42
Ray Washburn	R	32	4	4	.500	0	35	3	0	66	90	48	37	0	6.95
Milt Wilcox	R	20	3	1	.750	0	5	2	1	22	19	7	13	1	2.45
John Noriega	R	26	0	0	—	0	0	0	0	18	25	10	6	0	8.00
Bo Belinsky	L	33	0	0	—	0	3	0	0	8	13	6	6	0	9.00
Jim Maloney (LJ)	R	30	0	1	.000	0	7	3	0	17	26	15	7	0	11.12
Pedro Borbon	R	23	0	2	.000	0	12	1	0	17	15	8	7	0	6.88
Mel Behney (MS)	L	22	0	0	—	0	2	0	0	10	15	8	2	0	4.50

LOS ANGELES 2nd 87-74 .540 14.5 — WALT ALSTON

Batting

NAME	G by Pos	B	AGE	G	AB	R	H	2B	3B	HR	RBI	BB	SO	SB	BA	SA
TOTALS			28	162	5606	749	1515	233	67	87	695	541	841	138	.270	.382
Wes Parker	1B161	B	30	161	614	84	196	47	4	10	111	79	70	4	.319	.458
Ted Sizemore (LJ)	2B86, OF9, SS2	R	25	96	340	40	104	10	1	4	34	34	19	5	.306	.350
Maury Wills	SS126, 3B4	B	37	132	522	77	141	19	3	0	34	50	34	28	.270	.318
Billy Grabarkewitz	3B97, SS50, 2B20	R	24	156	529	92	153	20	8	17	84	95	149	19	.289	.454
Willie Crawford	OF94	L	23	109	299	48	70	8	6	8	40	33	68	4	.234	.381
Willie Davis	OF143	L	30	146	593	92	181	23	16	8	93	29	54	38	.305	.438
Manny Mota	OF111, 3B1	R	32	124	417	63	127	12	6	3	37	47	37	11	.305	.384
Tom Haller	C106	L	33	112	325	47	93	16	6	10	47	32	35	3	.286	.465
Jim Lefebvre	2B70, 3B21, 1B1	B	27	109	314	33	79	15	1	4	44	29	42	1	.252	.344
Bill Sudakis	C38, 3B37, OF25, 1B1	B	24	94	269	37	71	11	0	14	44	35	46	4	.264	.461
Bill Russell	OF79, SS1	R	21	81	278	30	71	11	0	0	28	16	28	9	.259	.363
Andy Kosco	OF58, 1B1	R	28	74	224	21	51	12	0	8	27	1	40	1	.228	.388
Von Joshua	OF41	L	22	72	109	23	29	1	3	1	8	6	24	2	.266	.358
Jeff Torborg	C63	R	28	64	134	11	31	8	0	1	17	14	15	1	.231	.313
Len Gabrielson	OF2, 1B1	L	30	43	42	1	8	0	0	0	6	1	15	0	.190	.238
Steve Garvey	3B27, 2B1	R	21	34	93	8	25	5	0	1	6	6	17	1	.269	.355
Bill Buckner	OF20, 1B1	L	20	28	68	6	13	3	1	0	4	3	6	1	.191	.265
Tom Paciorek	OF3	R	23	8	9	2	2	1	0	0	0	0	3	0	.222	.333
Gary Moore	OF5, 1B1	R	25	7	8	2									.188	.438

Joe Ferguson 23 R 1-4, Bob Stinson 24 B 0-3

Pitching

NAME	T	AGE	W	L	PCT	SV	G	GS	CG	IP	H	BB	SO	SHO	ERA
TOTALS		27	87	74	.540	42	161	161	37	1459	1394	496	880	17	3.82
Claude Osteen	L	30	16	14	.533	0	37	37	11	259	280	52	114	4	3.82
Don Sutton	R	25	15	13	.536	0	38	38	10	260	251	78	201	4	4.08
Alan Foster	R	23	10	13	.435	0	33	33	7	199	200	81	83	1	4.25
Bill Singer (IL)	R	26	8	5	.615	0	16	16	5	106	79	32	93	3	3.14
Jim Brewer	L	32	7	6	.538	24	58	0	0	89	66	33	91	0	3.13
Sandy Vance	R	23	7	5	.500	0	20	18	2	115	109	37	45	0	3.13
Joe Moeller	R	27	7	9	.438	4	31	19	2	135	131	43	63	1	3.93
Ray Lamb	R	25	6	1	.857	0	35	0	0	57	59	27	32	0	3.79
Pete Mikkelsen (IL)	R	30	4	2	.667	6	33	0	0	62	48	20	47	0	2.76
Jose Pena	R	27	4	3	.571	2	29	12	0	57	51	29	31	0	4.42
1 Fred Norman	L	27	2	0	1.000	1	30	0	0	62	65	33	47	0	5.23
Mike Strahler	R	23	1	1	.500	0	6	0	0	19	13	10	11	0	1.42
Camilo Pascual	R	36	0	0	—	0	10	0	0	14	12	5	6	0	2.57
Charlie Hough	R	22	0	0	—	0	8	0	0	17	11	8	5	0	5.29
Jerry Stephenson	R	26	0	0	—	0	2	0	0	7	11	5	6	0	9.00
1 Al McBean	R	32	0	0	—	0	4	0	0	4	5	4	2	0	4.50

SAN FRANCISCO 3rd 86-76 .531 16 — CLYDE KING 19-23 .452 / CHARLIE FOX 67-53 .558

Batting

NAME	G by Pos	B	AGE	G	AB	R	H	2B	3B	HR	RBI	BB	SO	SB	BA	SA
TOTALS			28	162	5578	831	1460	257	35	165	773	729	1005	83	.262	.409
Willie McCovey	1B146	L	32	152	495	98	143	39	2	39	126	137	75	0	.289	.612
Ron Hunt	2B85, 3B16	R	29	117	367	70	103	17	1	6	41	44	29	1	.281	.381
Hal Lanier	SS130, 2B4, 1B2	R	27	134	438	33	101	13	1	2	41	21	41	1	.231	.279
Alan Gallagher	3B91	R	24	109	282	31	75	13	2	2	28	30	37	2	.266	.376
Bobby Bonds	OF157	R	24	157	663	134	200	36	10	26	78	77	189	48	.302	.504
Willie Mays	OF129, 1B5	R	39	139	478	94	139	15	2	28	83	79	90	5	.291	.506
Ken Henderson	OF146	B	24	148	554	104	163	35	3	17	80	88	78	20	.294	.460
Dick Dietz	C139	R	28	148	493	82	148	36	2	22	107	109	106	0	.300	.515
Tito Fuentes	2B78, SS36, 3B24	R	26	123	435	49	116	13	7	2	32	36	52	4	.267	.343
Jim Ray Hart	3B56, OF8	R	28	76	255	30	72	12	1	8	37	30	29	0	.282	.431
Frank Johnson	OF33, 1B27	R	27	67	161	25	44	1	2	3	31	19	18	1	.273	.360
Bob Heise	SS33, 2B28, 3B2	R	23	61	154	15	36	5	1	1	22	5	18	0	.234	.299
Bob Taylor	OF26, C1	L	26	63	84	14	16	2	0	2	10	12	13	0	.190	.262
Don Mason		R			36	4	5								.139	.139
1 Bob Burda	1B8, OF1	L	31	28	23	1	6	0	0	0	3	0	5	0	.261	.261
Russ Gibson	C23	R	31	24	69	3	16	6	0	0	6	7	12	0	.232	.319
Johnny Stephenson	C9, OF1	L	29	23	43	3	3	0	0	0	3	4	8	0	.070	.093
Jim Davenport	3B10	R	36	22	21	3									.143	.270
Steve Whitaker	OF9	R	27	16	27	3	3	1	0	0	2	2	14	0	.111	.148
George Foster	OF8	R	21	9	6	1	2	0	0	0	2	1	6	0	.333	.333
Bernie Williams	OF6	R	21	7	16	2	5	2	0	0	2	0	1	1	.313	.438
Ed Goodson	1B2	L	22	7	11	1	3	0	0	0	1	0	2	0	.273	.273

Pitching

NAME	T	AGE	W	L	PCT	SV	G	GS	CG	IP	H	BB	SO	SHO	ERA
TOTALS		28	86	76	.531	30	162	162	50	1458	1514	604	931	7	4.50
Gaylord Perry	R	31	23	13	.639	0	41	41	23	329	292	84	214	5	3.20
Juan Marichal (IL)	R	32	12	10	.545	0	34	33	14	243	269	48	123	1	4.11
Don McMahon	R	40	4	6	.400	19	61	0	0	94	70	45	74	0	2.97
Rich Robertson	R	25	8	9	.471	1	41	26	6	184	199	96	121	0	4.84
Frank Reberger	R	26	4	8	.467	2	45	18	3	152	178	94	117	0	5.57
Skip Pitlock	L	22	5	5	.500	0	18	15	1	87	92	48	56	0	4.66
Ron Bryant	L	22	5	8	.385	0	34	11	1	96	103	38	66	0	4.78
2 Jerry Johnson	R	26	3	4	.429	3	33	4	0	65	67	38	44	0	4.29
1 Mike McCormick	L	31	3	4	.429	2	23	11	1	78	86	30	37	0	6.23
Mike Davison	L	24	3	0	.375	1	31	0	0	36	46	22	21	0	6.50
2 John Cumberland	L	23	1	0	1.000	0	7	1	0	20	20	6	15	0	0.82
1 Frank Linzy	R	29	2	1	.667	1	20	0	0	26	33	11	16	0	6.92
Don Carrithers	R	21	1	1	.667	0	11	3	0	14	14	14	10	0	7.36
Jim Johnson	R	24	1	0	1.000	0	7	0	0	10	9	6	6	0	7.71
Miguel Puente	R	18	1	0	1.000	0	7	0	0	11	14	10	8	0	8.05
Bill Faul	R	30	0	0	—	0	9	0	0	15	16	6	9	0	7.20

HOUSTON — 4th 79-83 .488 23 — HARRY WALKER

NAME	G by Pos	B	AGE	G	AB	R	H	2B	3B	HR	RBI	BB	SO	SB	BA	SA
TOTALS			27	162	5574	744	1446	250	47	129	694	598	911	114	.259	.391
Bob Watson	1B83, C6, OF1	R	24	97	327	48	89	19	2	11	61	24	59	1	.272	.443
Joe Morgan	2B142	L	26	144	548	102	147	28	9	8	52	102	55	42	.268	.396
Denis Menke	SS133,2B21,1B5,3B5,OF3	R	29	154	562	82	171	26	6	13	92	82	80	6	.304	.441
Doug Rader	3B154,1B1	R	25	156	576	90	145	25	3	25	87	57	102	3	.252	.436
Jesus Alou	OF108	R	28	117	458	59	140	27	4	1	44	21	15	3	.306	.384
Cesar Cedeno	OF90	R	19	90	355	46	110	21	4	7	42	15	57	17	.310	.451
Jim Wynn	OF151	R	28	157	554	82	156	32	4	27	88	106	96	24	.282	.493
Johnny Edwards	C139	R	32	140	458	46	101	16	4	7	49	51	63	1	.221	.319
Norm Miller	OF72, C1	L	24	90	226	29	54	9	0	4	29	41	33	3	.239	.332
1 Joe Pepitone	1B50, OF28	L	29	75	279	44	70	9	5	14	35	18	28	5	.251	.470
Marty Martinez	SS29, 3B10, C6, 2B4	B	28	75	150	12	33	3	0	0	12	9	22	0	.220	.240
1 Tommy Davis	OF53	R	31	57	213	24	60	12	3	2	30	7	25	4	.282	.399
Keith Lampard	OF16, 1B2	L	23	52	72	8	17	8	1	0	5	5	24	0	.236	.375
John Mayberry	1B45	L	21	50	148	23	32	3	2	5	14	21	33	1	.216	.365
Cesar Geronimo	OF26	L	22	47	37	5	9	0	0	2	2	5	7	0	.243	.243
Larry Howard	C26, 1B2, OF1	R	25	31	88	11	27	6	0	2	16	10	23	0	.307	.443
Hector Torres	SS22, 2B6	R	24	31	65	6	16	1	2	0	5	6	8	0	.246	.323
1 Jim Beauchamp	OF16	R	30	31	26	3	5	0	0	1	4	3	7	0	.192	.308
Don Bryant	C13	R	28	15	24	2	5	0	0	0	3	1	8	0	.208	.208
Gary Geiger	OF2	L	33	5	4	0	1	0	0	0	0	0	0	0	.250	.250
Leon McFadden		R	26	2	0	0	0								—	—

NAME	T	AGE	W	L	PCT	SV	G	GS	CG	IP	H	BB	SO	SHO	ERA
TOTALS		27	79	83	.488	35	162	162	36	1456	1491	577	942	6	4.23
Larry Dierker	R	23	16	12	.571	1	37	36	17	270	263	82	191	2	3.87
Jack Billingham	R	27	13	9	.591	0	46	24	8	188	190	63	134	2	3.97
Don Wilson	R	25	11	6	.647	0	29	27	3	184	188	66	94	0	3.91
Fred Gladding	R	34	7	4	.636	18	63	0	0	71	64	24	46	0	4.06
Denny Lemaster	L	31	7	12	.368	3	39	21	3	162	169	65	103	0	4.56
Jim Ray	R	25	6	3	.667	5	52	2	0	105	97	49	67	0	3.26
Ron Cook	R	22	4	4	.500	2	41	7	0	82	80	42	50	0	3.73
Jim Bouton	R	31	4	6	.400	0	29	6	1	73	94	33	49	0	5.42
2 George Culver	R	26	3	3	.500	3	32	0	0	45	44	21	31	0	3.20
Wade Blasingame	L	26	3	3	.500	0	13	13	1	78	76	23	55	0	3.46
Tom Griffin	R	22	3	13	.188	0	23	20	2	111	118	72	72	1	5.76
Ken Forsch	R	23	1	2	.333	0	4	4	1	24	28	5	13	0	5.63
Jack DiLauro	L	27	1	3	.250	3	42	0	0	34	34	17	23	0	4.24
Buddy Harris	R	21	0	0	—	0	2	0	0	6	2	6	6	0	6.00
Scipio Spinks	R	22	0	1	.000	0	5	2	0	14	17	9	6	0	9.64
1 Mike Marshall	R	27	0	1	.000	0	4	0	0	5	8	4	5	0	9.00
Dan Osinski	R	36	0	1	.000	0	4	0	0	4	5	2	1	0	9.00

ATLANTA — 5th 76-86 .469 26 — LUM HARRIS

NAME	G by Pos	B	AGE	G	AB	R	H	2B	3B	HR	RBI	BB	SO	SB	BA	SA
TOTALS			29	162	5546	736	1495	215	24	160	692	522	736	58	.270	.404
Orlando Cepeda	1B148	R	32	148	567	87	173	33	0	34	111	47	75	6	.305	.543
Felix Millan	2B142	R	26	142	590	100	183	25	5	2	37	35	23	16	.310	.380
Sonny Jackson	SS87	R	25	103	328	60	85	14	3	0	20	24	27	11	.259	.320
Clete Boyer	3B126, SS5	R	33	134	475	44	117	14	1	16	62	41	71	2	.246	.381
Hank Aaron	OF125,1B11	R	36	150	516	103	154	26	1	38	118	74	63	9	.298	.574
1 Tony Gonzalez	OF119	L	33	123	430	57	114	18	2	7	55	46	45	3	.265	.365
Rico Carty	OF133	R	30	136	478	84	175	23	3	25	101	77	46	1	.366	.584
Bob Tillman	C70	R	33	71	223	19	53	5	0	11	30	20	66	0	.238	.408
Mike Lum	OF98	L	24	123	291	25	74	17	2	7	28	17	43	3	.254	.399
Gil Garrido	SS80, 2B26	R	29	101	367	38	97	9	4	1	19	15	16	0	.264	.308
Hal King	C62	L	26	89	204	29	53	8	0	11	30	32	41	1	.260	.461
Bob Aspromonte	3B30, SS4, 1B1, OF1	R	32	62	127	5	27	3	0	7	13	13	13	0	.213	.236
Bob Didier	C57	B	21	57	168	9	25	2	1	0	7	12	11	1	.149	.173
Tommie Aaron	1B16, OF12	L	30	44	63	3	13	2	0	2	7	3	10	0	.206	.333
2 Jimmie Hall	OF28	L	32	39	47	7	10	2	0	2	4	2	14	0	.213	.383
Ralph Garr	OF21	L	24	37	96	18	27	3	0	1	7	5	12	5	.281	.313
Oscar Brown	OF25	R	24	28	47	6	18	2	1	1	7	7	5	0	.383	.532
Dusty Baker	OF11	R	21	24	13	2	4	3	0	0	0	4	4	0	.292	.292
Darrell Evans	3B12	L	23	12	44	4	14	1	1	0	5	3	4	1	.318	.386
Earl Williams	1B4, 3B3	R	21	10	19	4	7	4	0	0	5	3	4	0	.368	.579

NAME	T	AGE	W	L	PCT	SV	G	GS	CG	IP	H	BB	SO	SHO	ERA
TOTALS		29	76	86	.469	24	162	162	45	1431	1451	478	960	9	4.33
Pat Jarvis	R	29	16	16	.500	0	36	34	11	254	240	72	173	1	3.61
Jim Nash	R	26	13	9	.591	0	34	33	6	212	211	90	153	2	4.08
Phil Niekro	R	31	12	18	.400	0	34	32	10	230	222	68	168	3	4.27
George Stone	L	23	11	11	.500	0	35	30	9	207	218	50	131	2	3.87
Ron Reed (BC)	R	27	7	10	.412	0	21	18	6	135	140	39	68	0	4.40
Hoyt Wilhelm	R	47	4	6	.400	13	50	0	0	78	69	39	67	0	3.12
Bob Priddy	R	30	5	5	.500	8	41	0	0	73	75	24	32	0	5.42
2 Don Cardwell	R	34	2	1	.667	0	16	2	1	23	31	13	16	1	9.00
1 Milt Pappas	R	31	2	2	.500	0	11	3	1	36	44	7	25	0	6.00
Larry Jaster	L	26	1	1	.500	0	14	0	0	22	33	8	9	0	6.95
Mike McQueen	L	19	1	5	.167	0	22	8	1	66	67	31	54	0	5.59
Julio Navarro	R	34	0	0	—	0	17	0	0	26	24	1	21	0	4.15
Rich Kester	R	23	0	0	—	0	15	0	0	32	36	19	20	0	5.63
Ron Kline	R	38	0	0	—	0	6	0	0	9	6	3	2	0	7.50
Aubrey Gatewood	R	31	0	0	—	0	2	0	0	4	2	0	0	0	4.50
2 Steve Barber	L	32	0	1	.000	0	2	0	0	15	17	5	11	0	4.80
Gary Neibauer	R	25	0	3	.000	0	5	2	0	13	11	8	9	0	4.85
Cecil Upshaw (RJ)		27													
Jim Britton (EJ)		26													

SAN DIEGO — 6th 63-99 .389 39 — PRESTON GOMEZ

NAME	G by Pos	B	AGE	G	AB	R	H	2B	3B	HR	RBI	BB	SO	SB	BA	SA
TOTALS			27	162	5494	681	1353	208	36	172	629	500	1164	60	.246	.391
Nate Colbert	1B153, 3B1	R	24	156	572	84	148	17	6	38	86	56	150	3	.259	.509
Dave Campbell	2B153	R	28	154	581	71	127	28	2	12	40	40	115	18	.219	.336
Tommy Dean (BG)	SS55	R	26	81	158	18	35	5	1	2	13	11	29	2	.222	.304
Ed Spiezio	3B93	R	28	110	316	45	90	18	1	12	42	43	42	2	.285	.462
Ollie Brown	OF137	R	26	139	534	79	156	34	1	23	89	34	78	5	.292	.489
Cito Gaston	OF142	R	26	146	584	92	186	26	9	29	93	41	142	4	.318	.543
Al Ferrara	OF96	R	30	138	372	44	103	15	4	13	51	46	63	0	.277	.444
Chris Cannizzaro	C110	R	32	111	341	27	95	13	3	5	42	48	49	2	.279	.378
Ivan Murrell	OF101, 1B1	R	27	125	347	43	85	9	3	12	35	17	93	9	.245	.392
Jose Arcia	SS67, 2B20, 3B9, OF7	R	26	114	229	28	51	9	3	0	17	12	36	3	.223	.288
Steve Huntz	SS57, 3B51	B	24	106	352	54	77	8	0	11	37	66	69	0	.219	.335
Ramon Webster	1B15, OF1	L	27	95	116	12	30	3	0	2	11	11	12	1	.259	.336
Bob Barton	C59	R	28	61	188	15	41	6	1	4	16	15	37	1	.218	.314
Ron Slocum	C19, SS17, 3B11, 2B9	R	24	60	71	8	10	2	2	1	11	8	24	0	.141	.268
Larry Stahl	OF20	L	29	52	66	5	12	2	0	0	3	14	12	2	.182	.212
Van Kelly	3B27, 2B1	L	24	38	89	9	15	3	0	1	9	15	21	0	.169	.236
Jerry Morales	OF26	R	21	28	58	6	9	1	1	1	4	3	11	0	.155	.241
Rafael Robles	SS23	R	22	23	89	5	19	1	0	0	3	5	11	3	.213	.225
Dave Robinson	OF13	B	24	15	38	5	12	2	0	2	8	5	12	0	.316	.526
Jim Williams	OF6	R	23	11	14	4	4	0	0	0	1	1	3	0	.286	.286
Fred Kendall	C2, OF1, 1B1	R	21	4	2	0	0	0	0	0	0	0	1	0	.000	.000

NAME	T	AGE	W	L	PCT	SV	G	GS	CG	IP	H	BB	SO	SHO	ERA
TOTALS		26	63	99	.389	32	162	162	24	1440	1483	611	886	9	4.36
Pat Dobson	R	28	14	15	.483	0	40	34	8	251	257	78	185	1	3.76
Danny Coombs	L	28	10	14	.417	0	35	27	5	188	185	76	105	1	3.30
Clay Kirby	R	22	10	16	.385	0	36	34	6	215	198	120	154	1	4.52
Dave Roberts	L	25	8	14	.364	0	43	21	3	182	182	43	102	2	3.81
1 Ron Herbel	R	32	7	5	.583	9	64*	0	0	111	114	39	53	0	4.95
Mike Corkins	R	24	4	5	.455	0	24	18	1	111	109	79	75	0	4.62
Ron Willis	R	26	2	2	.500	4	42	0	0	56	53	28	20	0	4.02
Gary Ross	R	22	2	3	.400	1	33	2	0	62	72	36	39	0	5.23
Jack Baldschun	R	33	1	0	1.000	0	12	0	0	13	24	4	12	0	10.38
Steve Arlin	R	24	1	0	1.000	0	2	1	1	13	11	8	3	1	2.77
Tom Dukes (BR)	R	27	1	6	.143	10	53	0	0	69	62	25	56	0	4.04
2 Earl Wilson	R	35	1	6	.143	0	15	9	0	65	82	19	29	0	4.85
Al Santorini	R	22	1	8	.111	1	21	12	0	76	91	43	41	0	6.04
2 Roberto Rodriguez	R	26	0	0	—	3	10	0	0	16	26	5	8	0	6.75
2 Paul Doyle	L	30	0	2	.000	0	7	0	0	7	8	6	2	0	6.43
Jerry Nyman	L	27	0	2	.000	0	2	2	0	5	8	2	1	0	16.20
Dick Kelley (SJ)		30													

* Herbel, also with New York, league leader in G with 76

WORLD SERIES — BALTIMORE (AL) 4 CINCINNATI (NL) 1

LINE SCORES

TEAM	1	2	3	4	5	6	7	8	9	10	11	12	R	H	E

Game 1 — October 10 at Cincinnati

													R	H	E
BAL (AL)	0	0	0	2	1	0	1	0	0				4	7	2
CIN (NL)	1	0	2	0	0	0	0	0	0				3	5	0

Palmer, Richert (9)   Nolan, Carroll (7)

Game 2 — October 11 at Cincinnati

													R	H	E
BAL	0	0	0	1	5	0	0	0	0				6	10	2
CIN	3	0	1	0	0	1	0	0	0				5	7	0

Cuellar, Phoebus (3), Drabowsky (5), Lopez (7), Hall (7)   McGlothlin, Wilcox (5), Carroll (5), Gullett (8)

Game 3 — October 13 at Baltimore

													R	H	E
CIN	0	1	0	0	0	0	2	0	0				3	9	0
BAL	2	0	1	0	1	4	1	0	X				9	10	1

Cloninger, Granger (6), Gullett (7)   McNally

Game 4 — October 14 at Baltimore

													R	H	E
CIN	0	1	1	0	1	0	0	3	0				6	8	3
BAL	0	1	3	0	0	1	0	0	0				5	8	0

Nolan, Gullett (3), Carroll (6)   Palmer, Watt (8), Drabowsky (9)

Game 5 — October 15 at Baltimore

													R	H	E
CIN	3	0	0	0	0	0	0	0	0				3	6	0
BAL	2	2	2	0	1	0	0	2	X				9	15	0

Merritt, Granger (2), Wilcox (3), Cloninger (5), Washburn (7), Carroll (8)   Cuellar

COMPOSITE BATTING

Baltimore (AL)

NAME	POS	G	AB	R	H	2B	3B	HR	RBI	BA
Totals		5	171	33	50	7	0	10	32	.292
F. Robinson	OF	5	22	5	6	0	0	2	4	.273
B. Robinson	3B	5	21	5	9	2	0	2	6	.429
Blair	OF	5	19	5	9	1	0	0	3	.474
Belanger	SS	5	19	0	2	0	0	0	1	.105
Powell	1B	5	17	6	5	0	0	2	5	.294
Johnson	2B	5	16	2	5	2	0	0	2	.313
Buford	OF	4	15	3	4	0	0	1	1	.267
Hendricks	C	5	11	1	4	1	0	1	4	.364
Etchebarren	C	2	7	1	1	0	0	0	0	.143
Palmer	P	2	7	1	1	0	0	0	0	.143
Rettenmund	OF	2	5	2	2	0	0	0	2	.400
McNally	P	1	4	1	1	0	0	1	4	.250
Cuellar	P	2	4	0	0	0	0	0	0	.000
Salmon	PH	1	1	1	1	0	0	0	0	1.000
Crowley	PH	2	1	0	0	0	0	0	0	.000
Drabowsky	P	2	1	0	0	0	0	0	0	.000
Hall	P	1	1	0	0	0	0	0	0	.000
Lopez	P	1	0	0	0	0	0	0	0	—

Phoebus P 0-0, Richert P 0-0, Watt P 0-0

Cincinnati (NL)

NAME	POS	G	AB	R	H	2B	3B	HR	RBI	BA
Totals		5	164	20	35	6	1	5	20	.213
Rose	OF	5	20	2	5	1	0	1	2	.250
Bench	C	5	19	3	4	1	0	1	3	.211
Tolan	OF	5	19	5	4	1	0	1	1	.211
May	1B	5	18	6	7	2	0	2	8	.389
Helms	2B	5	18	1	4	0	0	0	1	.222
Perez	3B	5	18	2	1	1	0	0	2	.056
McRae	OF	3	11	1	5	2	0	0	3	.455
Concepcion	SS	3	9	0	3	0	0	0	1	.333
Carbo	OF	3	8	0	0	0	0	0	0	.000
Woodward	SS	4	5	0	1	0	0	0	0	.200
Cline	PH	3	3	0	1	0	0	0	0	.333
Nolan	P	2	3	0	0	0	0	0	0	.000
Bravo	PH	2	2	0	0	0	0	0	0	.000
Stewart	PH	2	2	0	0	0	0	0	0	.000
Cloninger	P	2	2	0	0	0	0	0	0	.000
McGlothlin	P	1	2	0	0	0	0	0	0	.000
Chaney	SS	3	1	0	0	0	0	0	0	.000
Corrales	PH	1	1	0	0	0	0	0	0	.000
Carroll	P	4	1	0	0	0	0	0	0	.000
Gullett	P	2	0	0	0	0	0	0	0	—

Merritt P 0-1, Granger P 0-0, Wilcox P 0-0, Washburn P 0-0

COMPOSITE PITCHING

Baltimore (AL)

NAME	G	IP	H	BB	SO	W	L	SV	ERA
Totals	5	45	35	15	23	4	1	2	3.40
Palmer	2	15.2	11	9	9	1	0	0	4.60
Cuellar	2	11.1	10	2	5	1	0	0	3.18
McNally	1	9	9	2	5	1	0	0	3.00
Drabowsky	2	3.1	2	1	1	0	0	0	2.70
Hall	1	2.1	0	1	0	0	0	1	0.00
Phoebus	1	1.2	1	0	0	0	0	0	0.00
Watt	1	1	1	2	1	3	0	1	9.00
Lopez	1	0.1	1	0	0	0	0	0	0.00
Richert	1	0.1	1	0	0	0	0	0	0.00

Cincinnati (NL)

NAME	G	IP	H	BB	SO	W	L	SV	ERA
Totals	5	43	50	20	33	1	4	0	6.70
Nolan	2	9.1	9	3	9	0	1	0	7.71
Carroll	4	9	5	0	11	1	0	0	0.00
Cloninger	2	7.1	10	5	4	0	1	0	7.36
Gullett	2	6.2	5	4	4	0	0	0	1.35
McGlothlin	1	4.1	6	2	2	0	0	0	8.31
Wilcox	2	2	3	2	0	0	0	0	9.00
Granger	2	1.1	7	1	1	0	1	0	33.75
Merritt	1	1.2	3	1	0	0	1	0	21.60
Washburn	1	1.1	2	2	0	0	0	0	13.50

1971 Fast and Blue and Wait 'Til Next Year

In the dying days of the 1970 season, a 21-year-old southpaw with a blazing fastball gave advance notice of his stardom by pitching a no-hitter. The pitcher was Oakland's Vida Blue. By winning nine of his first ten decisions, he began the 1971 season in spectacular fashion to become a major drawing card in the American League. Despite a second-half slump due to pressure, Blue finished with a 24-8 record and pocketed the MVP and the Cy Young Awards, despite the 25-win season of Detroit's Mickey Lolich. Blue's arrival in Oakland further strengthened owner Charley Finley's squad with home-grown talent as hitting stars Reggie Jackson and Sal Bando and ace right-hander Catfish Hunter teamed up with the talented Blue to lead the Athletics to an easy win in the Western Division.

The California Angels, expected to contend strongly, finished fourth in a whirlpool of dissension and controversy. Alex Johnson, the eye of the Angel's storm, was fined and benched several times by manager Lefty Phillips for not hustling, and the surly outfielder, on poor terms with all his teammates, was finally suspended for the season on June 26. California's other woe was Tony Conigliaro, obtained from Boston, who retired on July 11, due to deteriorating eyesight suffered in a 1967 beaning.

The Orioles repeated as Eastern Division leaders by waltzing to a 12-game lead over runner-up Detroit. By winning their final 11 games, the Birds finished with over 100 wins for the third straight year. The pitching staff flashed four 20-win aces in Mike Cuellar, Dave McNally, Jim Palmer, and newcomer Pat Dobson, while sluggers Frank Robinson, Brooks Robinson, and Boog Powell were joined by Merv Rettenmund as batting stars in the Baltimore lineup. The other big story in the East was the Washington Senators; Denny McLain flopped to a 10-22 mark, Curt Flood jumped the team after only 13 games while his antitrust suit was pending before the Supreme Court, and owner Bob Short added the coup de grace by moving the financially-troubled club to Arlington, Texas, (a Dallas suburb) after the conclusion of the season. The post-season championship play-off resulted in a third-consecutive sweep by the Orioles.

Unlike the junior circuit, the National League witnessed close races. In the West, there was a tooth-and-nail fight between the rival Giants and Dodgers. San Francisco jumped out to a 10 ½ game lead by the end of May and, as late as September 5, held an 8 ½ game bulge over Los Angeles. But when Willie McCovey injured his knee, the Giants fell into a hitting slump and went into a tailspin, dropping 16 of their last 24 tilts. By September 14, the Dodgers had melted the lead to only one game—a slim lead that the Giants' pitching aces, Juan Marichal and Gaylord Perry, protected over the last two weeks of the season. With a bad knee troubling McCovey, and 40-year-old Willie Mays tiring after a good start, most of the offense generated by the Giants down the stretch came from the bat of young Bobby Bonds.

The Pittsburgh Pirates again won in the East by staving off a late season threat from the St. Louis Cardinals and MVP Joe Torre. The Pirates' potent offense boasted of sluggers Roberto Clemente, Willie Stargell, Manny Sanguillen, Al Oliver, and Bob Robertson and a deep pitching staff headed by Dock Ellis and Steve Blass.

The Bucs defeated the Giants in four games to win the National League pennant, and then came back from two opening losses to defeat the favored Orioles in seven games in the World Series. The talent-laden Pirates had a myriad of heroes, but the standout performers were Roberto Clemente, a .414 swinger, and pitcher Steve Blass, whose two wins included a clutch seventh-game four-hitter.

1971 AMERICAN LEAGUE — EAST DIVISION

BALTIMORE — 1st 101-57 .639 — EARL WEAVER

NAME	G by Pos	B	AGE	G	AB	R	H	2B	3B	HR	RBI	BB	SO	SB	BA	SA
TOTALS			30	158	5303	742	1382	207	25	158	702	672	844	66	.261	.398
Boog Powell	1B124	L	29	128	418	59	107	19	0	22	92	82	64	1	.256	.459
Dave Johnson	2B140	R	28	142	510	67	144	26	1	18	72	51	55	3	.282	.443
Mark Belanger	SS149	R	27	150	500	67	133	19	4	0	35	73	48	10	.266	.320
Brooks Robinson	3B156	R	34	156	589	67	160	21	1	20	92	63	50	0	.272	.413
Merv Rettenmund	OF134	R	28	141	491	81	156	23	4	11	75	87	60	15	.318	.448
Paul Blair	OF138	R	27	141	516	75	135	24	8	10	44	32	94	14	.262	.397
Don Buford	OF115	B	34	122	449	99	130	19	4	19	54	89	62	15	.290	.477
Ellie Hendricks	C90,1B3	L	30	101	316	33	79	14	1	9	42	39	38	0	.250	.386
Frank Robinson	OF92,1B37	R	35	133	455	82	128	16	2	28	99	72	62	3	.281	.510
Andy Etchebarren	C70	R	28	70	222	21	60	18	2	9	29	16	40	1	.270	.428
Tom Shopay (NJ)	OF13	L	26	47	74	10	19	2	0	0	5	3	7	2	.257	.284
Chico Salmon	1B9,2B9,3B6,SS5	R	30	42	84	11	15	1	0	2	7	3	21	0	.179	.262
Jerry DaVanon	2B20,SS11,3B3,1B1	R	25	38	81	14	19	5	0	4	4	12	20	0	.235	.296
Curt Motton	OF16	R	30	38	53	13	10	1	0	4	8	10	12	0	.189	.434
Clay Dalrymple	C18	L	34	23	49	6	10	1	0	1	6	16	13	0	.204	.286
Terry Crowley	OF6,1B2	L	24	18	23	2	4	0	0	0	1	3	4	0	.174	.174
Bobby Grich	SS5,2B2	R	22	7	30	7	9	0	0	1	6	5	8	1	.300	.400
Don Baylor	OF1	R	22	1	2	0	0	0	0	0	0	1	2	1	.000	.000

NAME	T	AGE	W	L	PCT	SV	G	GS	CG	IP	H	BB	SO	SHO	ERA
TOTALS		30	101	57	.639	22	158	158	71	1415	1257	416	793	15	2.99
Dave McNally (SA)	L	28	21	5	.808	0	30	30	11	224	188	58	91	1	2.89
Pat Dobson	R	29	20	8	.714	1	38	37	18	282	248	63	187	4	2.90
Mike Cuellar	L	34	20	9	.690	0	38	38	21	292	250	78	124	4	3.08
Jim Palmer	R	25	20	9	.690	0	37	37	20	282	231	106	184	3	2.68
Dick Hall	R	40	6	6	.500	1	27	0	0	43	52	11	26	0	5.02
Grant Jackson	L	28	4	3	.571	0	29	9	0	78	72	20	51	0	3.12
Eddie Watt (BH)	R	30	3	1	.750	11	35	0	0	40	39	8	26	0	1.80
Pete Richert	L	31	3	5	.375	4	35	0	0	36	26	22	35	0	3.50
Dave Leonhard	R	30	2	3	.400	1	12	6	1	54	51	19	18	1	4.32
2 Dave Boswell	R	26	1	2	.333	0	15	1	0	25	32	15	14	0	4.32
Tom Dukes	R	28	1	5	.167	4	28	0	0	38	40	8	30	0	3.55
1 Jim Hardin	R	27	0	0	—	0	6	0	0	6	12	3	3	0	4.50
Orlando Pena	R	37	0	1	.000	0	15	0	0	16	15	5	4	0	.296

DETROIT — 2nd 91-71 .562 12 — BILLY MARTIN

NAME	G by Pos	B	AGE	G	AB	R	H	2B	3B	HR	RBI	BB	SO	SB	BA	SA
TOTALS			31	162	5502	701	1399	214	38	179	652	540	854	35	.254	.405
Norm Cash	1B131	L	36	135	452	72	128	10	3	32	91	59	86	1	.283	.531
Dick McAuliffe	2B123,SS7	L	31	128	477	67	99	16	6	18	57	53	67	4	.208	.379
Eddie Brinkman	SS159	R	29	159	527	40	120	18	2	1	37	44	54	1	.228	.275
Aurelio Rodriguez	3B153,SS1	R	23	154	604	68	153	30	7	15	39	27	93	4	.253	.401
Al Kaline	OF129,1B5	R	36	133	405	69	119	19	2	15	54	82	57	4	.294	.462
Mickey Stanley	OF139	R	28	139	401	43	117	14	5	7	41	24	44	1	.292	.404
Willie Horton (IJ)	OF118	R	28	119	450	64	130	25	1	22	72	37	75	1	.289	.496
Bill Freehan	C144,OF1	R	29	148	516	57	143	26	4	21	71	54	48	2	.277	.465
Jim Northrup	OF108,1B32	L	31	136	459	72	124	27	2	16	71	60	43	7	.270	.442
Dalton Jones	OF16,3B13,1B3,2B1	L	27	83	138	15	35	5	0	5	11	9	21	1	.254	.399
Gates Brown	OF56	L	32	82	195	37	66	2	3	11	29	21	17	4	.338	.549
Ike Brown	1B17,OF9,2B8,3B4,SS1	R	29	59	110	20	28	1	0	8	19	19	25	0	.255	.482
2 Tony Taylor	2B51,3B3	R	35	55	181	27	52	10	2	3	19	12	11	5	.287	.414
Cesar Gutierrez	SS14,3B5,2B2	R	28	38	37	4	7	0	0	0	0	3	0	0	.189	.189
Kevin Collins	3B4,OF2,2B1	L	24	35	41	6	11	2	1	1	4	0	12	0	.268	.439
Jim Price (LJ)	C25	R	29	29	54	4	13	2	0	1	7	6	3	0	.241	.333
Marvin Lane	OF6	R	21	8	14	0	2	0	0	0	1	1	4	0	.143	.143
Tim Hosley	C4,1B1	R	24	7	16	2	3	0	0	2	6	1	5	0	.188	.563
Gene Lamont	C7	L	24	7	15	2	1	0	0	0	0	1	5	0	.067	.067
John Young	1B1	R	22	2	4	1	2	1	0	0	1	0	0	0	.500	.750

NAME	T	AGE	W	L	PCT	SV	G	GS	CG	IP	H	BB	SO	SHO	ERA
TOTALS		27	91	71	.562	32	162	162	53	1468	1355	609	1000	11	3.63
Mickey Lolich	L	30	25	14	.641	0	45	45	29	376	336	92	308	4	2.92
Joe Coleman	R	24	20	9	.690	0	39	38	16	286	241	96	236	3	3.15
Fred Scherman	L	26	11	6	.647	20	69	1	1	113	91	49	46	0	2.71
Les Cain (SJ)	L	23	10	9	.526	0	26	26	3	145	121	91	118	1	4.34
Tom Timmermann	R	31	7	6	.538	4	52	2	0	84	82	37	51	0	3.86
Joe Niekro	R	26	6	7	.462	1	31	15	0	122	136	49	43	0	4.50
Mike Kilkenny (IL)	R	26	4	5	.444	1	30	11	2	86	83	44	47	0	5.02
Dean Chance	R	30	4	6	.400	0	31	14	0	90	91	50	64	0	3.50
Bill Gilbreth	L	23	2	1	.667	0	9	5	2	30	28	21	14	0	4.80
1 Jim Hannan	R	31	1	0	1.000	0	11	7	7	7	1			0	3.27
Bill Zepp	R	24	1	1	.500	2	16	4	0	32	41	17	15	0	5.06
Chuck Seelbach	R	24	1	1	.500	0	6	4	1	6	7	1		0	13.50
1 Dave Boswell	R	26	0	0	—	0	2			4	6	7	1	0	6.75
Jim Foor	R	22	0	0	—	0	2			3	6			0	18.00
1 Daryl Patterson	R	27	0	0	.000	0	12	0	0	9	14	6	5	0	5.00
2 Ron Perranoski	R	35	0	1	.000	2	11	0	0	18	16	3	8	0	2.50
Jack Whillock	R	28	0	2	.000	1	7	0	0	8	10	2	6	0	5.63
Bill Denehy	R	25	0	3	.000	1	31	1	0	49	47	28	27	0	4.22
John Hiller (IL) 28															

BOSTON — 3rd 85-77 .525 18 — EDDIE KASKO

NAME	G by Pos	B	AGE	G	AB	R	H	2B	3B	HR	RBI	BB	SO	SB	BA	SA
TOTALS			28	162	5401	691	1360	246	28	161	650	552	871	51	.252	.397
George Scott	1B143	R	27	146	537	72	141	16	4	24	78	41	102	0	.263	.441
Doug Griffin (XJ)	2B124	R	24	125	483	51	118	23	2	3	27	31	45	11	.244	.319
Luis Aparicio	SS121	R	37	125	491	56	114	23	0	4	45	35	43	6	.232	.303
Rico Petrocelli	3B156	R	28	158	553	82	139	24	4	28	89	91	108	2	.251	.461
Billy Conigliaro	OF100	R	23	101	351	42	92	26	1	11	33	25	68	3	.262	.436
Reggie Smith	OF159	R	26	159	618	85	175	33	2	30	96	63	82	11	.283	.489
Carl Yastrzemski	OF146	L	31	148	508	75	129	21	2	15	70	106	60	8	.254	.392
Duane Josephson	C87	R	29	91	306	38	75	14	1	10	39	22	22	5	.245	.395
Joe Lahoud	OF69	L	24	107	256	39	55	9	3	14	32	40	45	2	.215	.438
John Kennedy	2B37,SS33,3B5	R	30	74	272	41	75	12	5	5	22	14	42	1	.276	.412
Bob Montgomery	C66	R	27	67	205	19	49	11	2	2	24	16	43	1	.239	.341
Mike Fiore	1B12	L	26	51	62	9	11	2	0	1	6	12	14	0	.177	.258
Phil Gagliano	OF11,2B7,3B4	R	29	47	68	11	22	5	0	0	13	11	5	0	.324	.397
Sonny Siebert	P32	R	34	32	79	10	21	3	0	2	15	1	20	0	.266	.532
Juan Beniquez	SS15	R	21	16	57	8	17	2	0	0	4	3	4	1	.298	.333
Rick Miller	OF14	L	23	15	33	9	11	2	0	0	7	8	6	0	.333	.576
Carlton Fisk	C14	R	23	14	48	7	15	2	1	2	6	1	10	0	.313	.521
Cecil Cooper	1B11	L	21	14	25	3	8	1	0	1	3	5	6	0	.310	.452
Don Pavletich	C8	R	32	14	27	5	7	1	0	1	3	5	5	0	.259	.407
Ben Oglivie	OF11	L	22	14	29	2	6	0	0	1	2	1	6	0	.263	.342
1 George Thomas	OF5	R	33	9	13	0	1	0	0	0	0	1	4	0	.077	.077
Buddy Hunter	2B6	R	23	9	9	2	2	0	0	0	0	2	1	0	.222	.333

NAME	T	AGE	W	L	PCT	SV	G	GS	CG	IP	H	BB	SO	SHO	ERA
TOTALS		29	85	77	.525	35	162	162	44	1443	1424	535	871	11	3.80
Sonny Siebert	R	34	16	10	.615	0	32	32	12	235	220	60	131	4	2.91
Gary Peters	L	34	14	11	.560	1	34	32	9	214	241	70	100	1	4.37
Ray Culp	R	29	14	16	.467	0	35	35	12	242	236	67	151	3	3.61
Jim Lonborg (SJ)	R	29	10	7	.588	0	27	26	5	168	167	67	100	1	4.13
Bill Lee	L	24	9	2	.818	2	47	3	0	102	102	46	74	0	2.74
Sparky Lyle	L	26	6	4	.600	16	50	0	0	52	52	37	37	2	2.77
Bobby Bolin	R	32	5	3	.625	6	52	0	0	70	57	34	51	0	4.24
Roger Moret	L	21	4	3	.571	0	13	7	4	71	50	40	47	1	2.92
John Curtis	L	23	2	2	.500	0	6	3	1	26	30	16	19	0	3.12
Ken Tatum	R	27	2	4	.333	5	34	0	0	54	50	25	21	0	4.17
Mike Garman	R	21	1	1	.500	0	3	1	0	19	15	9	6	0	3.79
Mike Nagy	R	23	1	1	.250	0	12	7	0	38	46	20	19	0	6.63
Luis Tiant	R	30	1	7	.125	0	21	10	1	72	73	32	59	0	4.88
Cal Koonce	R	30	0	1	.000	0	13	1	0	21	22	11	9	0	5.57
Ken Brett	L	22	0	1	.000	1	29	2	0	59	57	35	57	0	5.34
Ray Jarvis (AJ) 25															

NEW YORK — 4th 82-80 .506 21 — RALPH HOUK

NAME	G by Pos	B	AGE	G	AB	R	H	2B	3B	HR	RBI	BB	SO	SB	BA	SA
TOTALS			28	162	5413	648	1377	195	43	97	607	581	717	75	.254	.360
Danny Cater	1B78, 3B52	R	31	121	428	39	118	16	5	4	50	19	25	0	.276	.364
Horace Clarke	2B156	B	31	159	625	76	156	23	7	2	41	64	43	17	.250	.318
Gene Michael	SS136	R	33	139	456	36	102	15	0	3	35	48	64	3	.224	.276
Jerry Kenney	3B109, SS5, 1B1	B	26	120	325	50	85	10	3	0	20	56	38	5	.262	.311
2 Felipe Alou	OF80, 1B42	R	36	131	461	52	133	20	6	8	69	32	24	5	.289	.410
Bobby Murcer	OF143	L	25	146	529	94	175	25	6	25	94	91	60	14	.331	.543
Roy White	OF145	B	27	147	524	86	153	22	7	19	84	86	66	14	.292	.469
Thurman Munson	C117, OF1	R	24	125	451	71	113	15	4	10	42	52	65	6	.251	.368
Johnny Ellis	1B65, C2	R	22	83	238	16	58	12	1	3	34	23	42	0	.244	.340
Jake Gibbs	C51	L	32	70	206	23	45	9	0	5	21	12	23	1	.218	.335
Ron Blomberg	OF57	L	22	64	199	30	64	6	2	7	31	14	23	2	.322	.477
Ron Hansen	3B30, 2B9, SS3	R	33	61	145	6	30	3	0	2	20	9	27	0	.207	.269
2 Ron Swoboda	OF47	R	27	54	138	17	36	2	1	2	20	27	35	0	.261	.333
Jim Lyttle	OF29	L	25	49	86	7	17	5	0	1	7	8	18	0	.198	.291
Frank Baker	SS38	L	24	43	79	9	11	2	0	0	2	16	22	3	.139	.165
1 Ron Woods	OF9	R	28	25	32	4	8	1	0	1	2	4	2	0	.250	.375
1 Curt Blefary	OF6, 1B4	L	27	21	36	4	7	1	0	1	2	3	5	0	.194	.306
Rusty Torres	OF5	B	22	9	26	5	10	3	0	2	3	0	8	0	.385	.731

2 Danny Walton 23 R 2-14, 1 Frank Tepedino 23 L 0-6, Len Boehmer 30 R 0-5

NAME	T	AGE	W	L	PCT	SV	G	GS	CG	IP	H	BB	SO	SHO	ERA
TOTALS		28	82*	80	.506	12	162	162	67	1452	1382	423	707	15	3.43
Mel Stottlemyre	R	29	16	12	.571	0	35	35	19	270	234	69	132	7	2.87
Fritz Peterson	L	29	15	13	.536	1	37	35	16	274	269	42	139	4	3.05
Stan Bahnsen	R	26	14	12	.538	0	36	34	14	242	221	72	110	3	3.35
Steve Kline	L	23	12	13	.480	0	31	30	15	222	206	37	81	1	2.96
Mike Kekich	L	26	10	9	.526	0	37	24	3	170	167	82	93	0	4.08
Lindy McDaniel	R	35	5	10	.333	4	44	0	0	70	82	24	59	0	5.01
Jack Aker	R	30	4	4	.500	4	41	0	0	56	48	26	24	0	2.57
Roger Hambright	R	22	3	1	.750	2	18	1	0	27	22	10	14	0	4.33
Alan Closter	L	28	2	2	.500	0	14	1	0	28	33	13	22	0	5.14
Gary Jones	L	26	0	0	—	0	12	0	0	14	19	7	10	0	9.00
Terry Ley	L	24	0	0	—	0	6	0	0	9	9	9	7	0	5.00
2 Rob Gardner	L	26	0	0	—	0	1	0	0	2	3	0	3	0	3.00
Gary Waslewski	R	29	0	1	.000	1	24	0	0	36	28	16	17	0	3.25
Bill Burbach	R	23	0	1	.000	0	2	2	0	6	5	3	1	0	12.00
2 Jim Hardin (SJ)	R		0	2	.000	0	12	3	0	28	35	9	14	0	5.08

*1 win by forfeit

WASHINGTON — 5th 63-96 .396 38.5 — TED WILLIAMS

NAME	G by Pos	B	AGE	G	AB	R	H	2B	3B	HR	RBI	BB	SO	SB	BA	SA
TOTALS			27	159	5290	537	1219	189	30	86	501	575	956	68	.230	.326
2 Don Mincher	1B88	L	33	100	323	35	94	15	1	10	45	53	52	2	.291	.437
Tim Cullen	2B78, SS62	R	29	125	403	34	77	13	4	2	26	33	47	2	.191	.258
Toby Harrah	SS116, 3B7	R	22	127	383	45	88	11	3	2	22	40	47	10	.230	.290
Dave Nelson	3B84, 2B1	R	27	85	329	47	92	11	3	5	33	23	29	17	.280	.377
Elliott Maddox	OF103, 3B12	R	23	128	258	38	56	8	2	1	18	51	42	3	.217	.275
Del Unser	OF151	L	26	153	581	63	148	19	6	9	41	59	68	11	.255	.355
Frank Howard	OF100, 1B68	R	34	153	549	60	153	25	2	26	83	77	121	0	.279	.474
Paul Casanova	C83	R	29	94	311	19	63	9	1	5	26	14	52	0	.203	.286
Tommy McCraw	OF60, 1B30	L	30	122	207	33	44	6	4	7	25	19	38	3	.213	.382
Dick Billings	C62, OF32, 3B2	R	28	116	349	32	86	14	0	6	48	21	54	2	.246	.338
Bernie Allen	2B41, 3B34	L	32	97	229	18	61	11	1	4	22	33	27	2	.266	.376
Lenny Randle	2B66	R	22	75	215	27	47	11	0	2	13	24	56	1	.219	.298
Larry Biittner	OF41, 1B3	L	25	66	171	12	44	4	1	0	16	16	20	1	.257	.292
Jeff Burroughs	OF50	R	20	59	181	20	42	9	0	5	25	22	55	1	.232	.365
Joe Foy	3B37, 2B3, SS1	R	28	41	128	12	30	8	0	0	11	27	14	1	.234	.297
Richie Scheinblum	OF13	B	28	27	49	5	7	3	0	1	4	4	10	1	.143	.204
1 Mike Epstein	1B24	L	28	24	85	6	21	1	1	1	9	12	31	1	.247	.318
Don Wert	SS7, 3B7, 2B1	R	32	20	40	2	2	1	0	0	4	5	10	0	.050	.075
2 Frank Fernandez	OF6, C1	R	28	18	30	0	3	0	0	0	4	4	10	0	.100	.100
Jim French	C14	L	29	14	41	6	6	2	0	0	4	7	7	0	.146	.195
Curt Flood	OF10	R	33	13	35	4	7	0	0	0	2	5	2	0	.200	.200

Tom Ragland 25 R 4-23, Jim Mason 20 L 3-9, Dick Stelmaszek 22 L 0-9, Bill Fahey 21 L 0-8

NAME	T	AGE	W	L	PCT	SV	G	GS	CG	IP	H	BB	SO	SHO	ERA
TOTALS		26	63	96*	.396	26	159	159	30	1419	1376	554	762	10	3.70
Dick Bosman	R	27	12	16	.429	0	35	35	7	237	245	71	113	1	3.72
Denny McLain	R	27	10	22	.313	0	33	32	9	217	233	72	103	3	4.27
2 Paul Lindblad	L	29	6	4	.600	4	43	0	0	84	58	29	50	0	2.57
Bill Gogolewski	R	23	6	5	.545	0	27	17	4	124	112	39	70	1	2.76
Joe Grzenda	L	34	5	2	.714	5	46	0	0	70	54	17	56	0	1.93
Casey Cox	R	29	5	7	.417	7	54	11	0	124	131	40	43	0	3.99
Pete Broberg	R	21	5	9	.357	0	18	18	7	125	104	53	89	1	3.46
Denny Riddleberger	L	25	3	1	.750	1	57	0	0	70	67	32	56	0	3.21
Jackie Brown	R	27	3	4	.429	0	14	9	4	47	60	27	21	0	5.94
Jim Shellenback	L	27	3	11	.214	0	40	15	3	120	123	49	47	1	3.53
1 Darold Knowles	R	29	2	2	.500	2	12	0	0	15	17	6	16	0	3.60
Horacio Pina	R	26	1	1	.500	2	56	0	0	58	47	31	38	0	3.57
Jerry Janeski	R	25	1	5	.167	1	23	10	0	62	72	34	19	0	4.94
Mike Thompson	R	21	1	6	.143	0	16	12	0	67	53	54	41	0	4.84

*1 loss by forfeit

CLEVELAND — 6th 60-102 .370 43 — AL DARK 42-61 .408 JOHNNY LIPON 18-41 .305

NAME	G by Pos	B	AGE	G	AB	R	H	2B	3B	HR	RBI	BB	SO	SB	BA	SA
TOTALS			26	162	5467	543	1303	200	20	109	507	467	868	57	.238	.342
Chris Chambliss	1B108	L	22	111	415	49	114	20	4	9	48	40	83	2	.275	.407
Eddie Leon	2B107, SS24	R	24	131	429	35	112	12	2	4	35	34	69	3	.261	.326
Jack Heidemann (KJ)	SS81	R	21	81	240	16	50	7	0	0	9	12	46	1	.208	.238
Graig Nettles	3B158	R	26	158	598	78	156	18	1	28	86	82	56	7	.261	.435
Vada Pinson	OF141, 1B3	L	32	146	566	60	149	23	4	11	35	21	73	25	.263	.376
Ted Uhlaender	OF131	R	31	141	500	54	144	20	3	2	47	38	44	3	.288	.352
Roy Foster	OF107	R	25	125	396	51	97	21	1	18	45	35	84	6	.245	.439
Ray Fosse	C126, 1B4	R	24	133	486	53	134	21	1	12	62	36	62	4	.276	.397
Chuck Hinton	1B20, OF20, C5	R	37	88	147	13	33	7	0	5	14	20	34	0	.224	.374
Gomer Hodge	1B3, 3B3, 2B2	B	27	80	83	3	17	3	0	1	9	4	19	0	.205	.277
Ted Ford	OF55	R	24	74	196	15	38	6	0	2	14	9	34	2	.194	.255
Frank Baker	OF51	L	27	73	181	18	38	12	1	2	13	12	34	1	.210	.304
Fred Stanley	SS55, 2B3	R	23	60	129	14	29	4	0	2	12	27	25	1	.225	.302
John Lowenstein (LJ)	2B29, OF18, SS3	L	24	58	140	15	26	5	0	9	16	28	1		.186	.307
Kurt Bevacqua	2B36, OF5, 3B3, SS2	R	24	55	137	9	28	3	1	3	13	4	28	0	.204	.307
Ken Harrelson	1B40, OF7	R	29	52	161	20	32	2	0	5	14	24	28	1	.199	.304
Ken Suarez	C48	R	28	50	123	10	25	7	0	1	9	18	15	0	.203	.285
Lou Camilli	SS23, 2B16	B	24	39	81	5	16	2	0	0	8	10	30	0	.198	.222
1 Buddy Bradford	OF18	R	26	20	38	4	6	2	0	1	3	6	10	0	.158	.263

1 Larry Brown 31 R 11-50, Jim Clark 24 3-18, Tony Horton (IL) 26

NAME	T	AGE	W	L	PCT	SV	G	GS	CG	IP	H	BB	SO	SHO	ERA
TOTALS		25	60	102	.370	32	162	162	21	1440	1352	770	937	7	4.28
Sam McDowell	L	28	13	17	.433	1	35	31	8	215	160	153	192	2	3.39
Alan Foster	R	24	8	12	.400	0	36	26	3	182	158	82	97	0	4.15
Steve Dunning	R	22	8	14	.364	1	31	29	3	184	173	109	132	1	4.50
Vince Colbert	R	25	7	6	.538	2	50	10	2	143	140	71	74	0	3.97
Ray Lamb	R	26	6	12	.333	1	43	21	3	158	147	69	91	1	3.36
Ed Farmer	R	21	5	4	.556	4	43	4	0	79	77	41	48	0	4.33
Phil Hennigan	R	25	4	3	.571	14	57	0	0	82	80	51	69	0	4.94
Camilo Pascual (AJ)	R	37	2	2	.500	0	23	1	0	23	17	11	20	0	3.13
Rich Hand (AJ)	R	22	2	6	.250	0	15	12	0	61	74	38	26	0	5.75
Mike Paul	L	26	2	2	.222	0	17	12	1	62	78	14	33	0	5.95
Steve Mingori	L	27	1	2	.333	4	54	0	0	57	31	24	45	0	1.42
Mark Ballinger	R	22	1	1	.333	0	18	0	0	35	30	13	25	0	4.63
Steve Hargan (BN)	R	28	1	13	.071	0	37	16	1	113	138	56	52	0	6.21
Rick Austin	L	24	0	1	—	1	23	0	0	23	25	20	20	0	5.09
Bob Kaiser	R	21	0	0	—	0	1	0	0	8	3	4	4	0	4.50
Chuck Machemehl	R	25	0	2	.000	3	14	0	0	18	16	15	9	0	6.50

WEST DIVISION

OAKLAND — 1st 101-60 .627 — DICK WILLIAMS

NAME	G by Pos	B	AGE	G	AB	R	H	2B	3B	HR	RBI	BB	SO	SB	BA	SA
TOTALS			27	161	5494	691	1383	195	25	160	642	542	1018	80	.252	.384
2 Mike Epstein	1B96	L	28	104	329	43	77	13	0	18	51	62	71	0	.234	.438
Dick Green	2B143, SS1	R	30	144	475	58	116	14	1	12	49	51	83	1	.244	.354
Bert Campaneris	SS133	R	29	134	569	80	143	18	4	5	47	29	64	34	.251	.323
Sal Bando	3B153	R	27	153	538	75	146	23	1	24	94	86	55	3	.271	.452
Reggie Jackson	OF145	R	25	150	567	87	157	29	3	32	80	63	161	16	.277	.508
Rick Monday	OF111	L	25	116	355	53	87	9	3	18	56	49	93	6	.245	.439
Joe Rudi	OF121, 1B5	R	24	127	513	56	137	23	4	10	52	24	58	3	.267	.386
Dave Duncan	C102	R	25	103	363	39	92	13	1	15	40	28	77	1	.253	.419
Angel Mangual	OF81	R	24	94	287	32	82	8	1	4	30	17	27	1	.286	.362
Tommy Davis	1B35, OF16, 2B3, 3B2	R	32	79	219	26	71	8	1	3	42	15	19	7	.324	.411
2 Larry Brown	SS31, 2B23, 3B10	R	31	70	189	14	37	2	1	1	9	7	19	1	.196	.233
Gene Tenace	C52, OF1	R	24	65	179	26	49	7	0	7	25	29	34	2	.274	.430
2 Mike Hegan	1B47, OF2	L	28	65	55	5	13	2	0	3	5	13	0	.236	.291	
2 Curt Blefary	OF14, C14, 3B5, 2B2	L	27	50	101	15	22	2	0	5	12	15	15	0	.218	.386
George Hendrick	OF36	R	21	42	114	8	27	1	0	6	14	5	28	0	.237	.289
Catfish Hunter	P37	R	25	38	103	14	36	1	1	1	12	2	11	0	.350	.408
1 Don Mincher	1B27	L	33	28	92	9	22	6	1	2	8	20	14	1	.239	.391
Steve Hovley	OF11	R	26	24	27	3	3	2	0	0	0	6	5	0	.111	.185
1 Tony LaRussa	2B7, SS4, 3B2	R	26	23	9	1	0	0	0	0	0	3	4	0	.000	.000
Dwain Anderson	SS10, 2B5, 3B1	R	23	16	37	3	10	3	0	0	2	3	5	0	.270	.378
Adrian Garrett	OF5	L	28	14	21	1	3	0	0	1	2	1	6	0	.143	.286

1 Felipe Alou 36 R 2-8, 13 Frank Fernandez 28 R 1-9, 2 Ramon Webster 28 L 0-5, Ron Clark 28 R 0-1

NAME	T	AGE	W	L	PCT	SV	G	GS	CG	IP	H	BB	SO	SHO	ERA
TOTALS		28	101	60	.627	36	161	161	57	1469	1229	501	999	18	3.05
Vida Blue	L	21	24	8	.750	0	39	39	24	312	209	88	301	8	1.82
Catfish Hunter	R	25	21	11	.656	0	37	37	16	274	225	80	181	4	2.96
Chuck Dobson (EJ)	R	27	15	5	.750	0	30	30	7	189	185	71	100	1	3.81
Diego Segui	R	33	10	8	.556	0	26	21	5	146	122	63	81	0	3.14
Blue Moon Odom (EJ)	R	26	10	12	.455	0	25	25	3	141	147	71	69	1	4.28
Bob Locker	R	33	7	2	.778	6	47	0	0	72	68	19	46	0	2.88
2 Darold Knowles	L	29	5	4	.556	4	43	0	0	53	40	16	40	0	3.57
Rollie Fingers	R	24	4	6	.400	17	48	8	2	129	94	30	98	1	3.00
Ron Klimkowski	R	26	2	2	.500	2	26	0	0	45	37	23	25	0	3.40
2 Mudcat Grant	R	35	1	1	.000	3	15	0	0	27	25	6	13	0	2.00
1 Paul Lindblad	L	29	1	0	1.000	0	16		18	2	4	3	0		3.94
Jim Roland	L	28	1	3	.250	1	31	0	0	45	34	19	30	0	3.20
1 Rob Gardner	L	26	0	0	—	0	4	0	0	6	5	4	7	0	2.25
2 Daryl Patterson	R	27	0	0	—	0	6	0	0	6	7	4	5	0	7.50
Marcel Lachemann	R	30	0	0	—	0	1	0	0	0.1	0	1	0	0	54.00
Jim Panther	R	26	0	2	.000	0	6	1	0	10	15	4	5	0	10.50

KANSAS CITY — 2nd 85-76 .528 16 — BOB LEMON

NAME	G by Pos	B	AGE	G	AB	R	H	2B	3B	HR	RBI	BB	SO	SB	BA	SA
TOTALS			27	161	5295	603	1323	225	40	80	573	490	819	130	.250	.353
Gail Hopkins	1B83	L	28	103	295	35	82	16	1	9	47	37	13	0	.278	.431
Cookie Rojas (BN)	2B111, SS2, OF1	R	32	115	414	56	124	22	6	2	59	39	35	8	.300	.406
Freddie Patek	SS147	R	26	147	591	86	158	21	11	6	36	44	80	49	.267	.371
Paul Schaal	3B161	R	28	161	548	80	150	31	6	11	63	103	51	7	.274	.412
Joe Keough	OF100	L	25	110	351	34	87	14	2	3	30	35	60	4	.248	.325
Amos Otis	OF144	R	24	147	555	80	167	26	4	15	79	40	74	52	.301	.443
Lou Piniella (BG)	OF115	R	27	126	448	43	125	21	5	3	51	21	43	5	.279	.368
Jerry May (BG)	C71	R	27	71	218	16	55	13	1	0	24	27	37	0	.252	.344
Bob Oliver	1B68, OF48, 3B2	R	28	128	373	35	91	12	2	8	52	14	88	0	.244	.351
Ed Kirkpatrick	OF61, C59	L	26	127	365	46	80	12	1	9	46	48	60	3	.219	.332
Bobby Knoop	2B52, 3B1	R	32	72	161	14	33	8	1	1	15	15	36	1	.205	.286
Dennis Paepke	C32, OF17	R	26	60	152	11	31	4	0	2	20	14	28	0	.204	.283
Chuck Harrison	1B39	R	30	49	143	9	31	4	0	2	21	11	19	0	.217	.287
Bobby Floyd	SS15, 2B8, 3B1	R	22	41	66	8	13	0	1	0	3	7	15	0	.197	.197
Buck Martinez	C21	R	22	22	46	3	7	3	0	0	2	1	13	0	.152	.196
Carl Taylor	OF12	R	27	20	39	3	7	0	0	0	4	6	9	0	.179	.179
2 Ted Savage	OF9	R	34	19	29	2	5	0	0	1	2	5	9	2	.172	.172
Sandy Valdespino	OF15	L	32	18	63	10	20	3	0	1	5	2	15	2	.317	.508
Rich Severson	2B6, SS6, 3B1	R	26	16	30	4	9	1	0	0	3	0	8	0	.300	.433

NAME	T	AGE	W	L	PCT	SV	G	GS	CG	IP	H	BB	SO	SHO	ERA
TOTALS		27	85	76	.528	44	161	161	34	1420	1301	496	775	15	3.25
Dick Drago	R	26	17	11	.607	0	35	34	15	241	251	46	109	4	2.99
Mike Hedlund	R	24	15	8	.652	0	32	30	7	206	168	72	76	1	2.71
Tom Burgmeier	L	27	9	7	.563	17	67	0	0	88	71	30	44	0	1.74
Bruce Dal Canton	R	29	8	6	.571	0	25	22	6	141	144	44	58	0	3.45
Paul Splittorff	L	24	8	9	.471	0	22	22	6	144	129	35	80	3	2.69
Al Fitzmorris	R	25	7	5	.583	0	34	16	2	127	112	55	53	1	4.18
Jim York	R	23	5	5	.500	3	53	0	0	93	70	44	103	0	2.90
Ted Abernathy	R	38	4	5	.400	23	63	0	0	81	60	50	55	0	2.56
Monty Montgomery	L	24	1	0	1.000	0	3	1	0	10	12	9	2	0	2.14
Ken Wright (SJ)	R	24	3	6	.333	1	21	12	1	78	66	47	56	1	3.69
Wally Bunker	R	26	2	3	.400	0	7	5	0	43	51	9	13	0	5.06
Jim Rooker	L	28	2	7	.222	0	20	7	1	54	59	24	31	1	5.33
Lance Clemons	L	23	1	0	1.000	0	5	0	0	11	11	7	5	0	4.13
Bill Butler (EJ)	L	24	1	4	.333	0	14	6	1	44	45	18	32	0	3.48
Mike McCormick	L	32	0	0	—	0	14	0	0	15	14	5	9	0	9.00
Roger Nelson	R	27	0	0	—	0	13	1	0	34	35	5	29	0	5.29

CHICAGO — 3rd 79-83 .488 22.5 — CHUCK TANNER

NAME	G by Pos	B	AGE	G	AB	R	H	2B	3B	HR	RBI	BB	SO	SB	BA	SA
	TOTALS		25	162	5382	617	1346	185	30	138	568	562	870	83	.250	.373
Carlos May	1B130, OF9	L	23	141	500	64	147	21	7	7	70	62	61	16	.294	.406
Mike Andrews (BW)	2B76, 1B25	R	27	109	330	45	93	16	0	12	47	67	36	3	.282	.439
Luis Alvarado	SS71, 2B16	R	22	99	264	22	57	14	1	0	8	11	34	1	.216	.277
Bill Melton	3B148	R	25	150	543	72	146	18	2	33	86	61	87	3	.269	.492
Walt Williams	OF90, 3B1	R	27	114	361	43	106	17	3	8	35	24	27	5	.294	.424
Jay Johnstone	OF119	L	25	124	388	53	101	14	1	16	40	38	50	10	.260	.425
Rick Reichardt	OF128, 1B9	R	28	138	496	53	138	14	2	19	62	37	90	5	.278	.425
Ed Herrmann	C97	L	24	101	294	32	63	6	0	11	35	44	48	2	.214	.347
Rich McKinney	2B67, OF25, 3B5	R	24	114	369	35	100	11	2	8	46	35	37	0	.271	.377
Lee Richard	SS68, OF16	R	22	87	260	38	60	7	3	2	17	20	46	8	.231	.304
Tom Egan	C77, 1B1	R	25	85	251	29	60	11	1	10	34	26	94	1	.239	.410
Rich Morales	SS57, 3B18, 2B3, OF1	R	27	84	185	19	45	8	0	2	14	22	26	2	.243	.319
Mike Hershberger	OF59	R	31	74	177	22	46	9	0	2	15	30	23	6	.260	.339
Pat Kelly	OF61	L	26	67	213	32	62	6	3	3	22	36	29	14	.291	.390
Ed Stroud	OF44	L	31	53	141	19	25	3	4	3	0	2	11	20	4	.177	.248
Steve Huntz	2B14, SS7, 3B6	B	25	35	86	10	18	3	1	2	6	7	9	1	.209	.337

Lee Maye (SJ) 36 L 9-44, Bob Spence 25 L 4-27, Chuck Brinkman 26 R 4-20, Tony Muser 23 L 5-16, Ken Hottman 23 R 2-16, Ron Lolich 24 R 1-8

NAME		T	AGE	W	L	PCT	SV	G	GS	CG	IP	H	BB	SO	SHO	ERA
			25	79	83	.488	32	162	162	46	1450	1348	468	976	19	3.12
Wilbur Wood		L	29	22	13	.629	1	44	42	22	334	272	62	210	7	1.91
Tom Bradley		R	24	15	15	.500	2	45	39	7	286	273	74	206	6	2.96
Tommy John		L	28	13	16	.448	0	38	35	10	229	244	58	131	3	3.62
Bart Johnson		R	21	12	10	.545	14	53	16	4	178	148	111	153	0	2.93
Joe Horlen (KJ)		R	33	8	9	.471	2	34	18	3	137	150	30	82	0	4.27
Rich Hinton		L	24	3	4	.429	0	18	7	0	45	45	25	19	0	4.50
Steve Kealey		R	24	2	2	.500	6	54	1	0	77	69	26	50	0	3.86
Terry Forster		L	19	2	3	.400	1	45	3	0	50	46	23	48	0	3.96
Jim Magnuson		L	24	1	1	.500	0	15	4	0	30	30	16	11	0	4.50
Vicente Romo		R	28	1	7	.125	5	45	2	0	72	52	37	48	0	3.38
Pat Jacquez		R	24	0	0		0	2	0	0	4	2	1	4	0	4.50
Denny O'Toole		R	22	0	0		1	2	0	0	2	2	1	1	0	4.50
Stan Perzanowski		R	20	0	1	.000	0	2	1	0	6	14	3	5	0	12.00
Don Eddy		L	24	0	2	.000	1	22	0	0	23	19	19	14	0	2.35

CALIFORNIA — 4th 76-86 .469 25.5 — LEFTY PHILLIPS

NAME	G by Pos	B	AGE	G	AB	R	H	2B	3B	HR	RBI	BB	SO	SB	BA	SA
	TOTALS		28	162	5495	511	1271	213	18	96	476	441	827	72	.231	.329
Jim Spencer	1B145	L	23	148	510	50	121	21	2	18	59	48	63	0	.237	.392
Sandy Alomar	2B137, SS28	B	27	162	689	77	179	24	3	4	42	41	60	39	.260	.321
Jim Fregosi (FJ)	SS74, 1B18, OF7	R	29	107	347	31	81	15	1	5	33	39	61	2	.233	.329
Ken McMullen	3B158	R	29	160	593	63	148	19	2	21	68	53	74	1	.250	.395
Roger Repoz	OF97, 1B13	L	30	113	297	39	59	11	1	13	41	60	69	3	.199	.374
Ken Berry	OF101	R	30	111	298	29	66	17	0	3	21	18	33	3	.221	.309
Tony Gonzalez	OF88	L	34	111	314	32	77	9	2	3	38	28	28	0	.245	.315
Johnny Stephenson	C88	L	30	98	279	24	61	17	0	3	25	22	21	0	.219	.312
Syd O'Brien	SS52, 2B7, 3B6, 1B1, OF1	R	27	90	251	25	50	8	1	5	21	15	33	0	.199	.299
Mickey Rivers (MS)	OF76	L	22	79	268	31	71	12	2	1	12	19	38	13	.265	.336
Tony Conigliaro (IJ)	OF72	R	26	74	266	23	59	16	0	4	15	32	53	2	.222	.335
Billy Cowan	OF40, 1B5	R	32	74	174	12	48	8	0	4	20	7	41	1	.276	.391
Jerry Moses	C63, OF1	R	24	69	181	12	41	8	2	4	15	14	34	0	.227	.359
Alex Johnson (ST)	OF61	R	28	65	242	19	63	8	0	2	21	15	34	5	.260	.318
Jeff Torborg (BG)	C49	R	29	55	123	6	25	5	0	0	5	3	6	0	.203	.244
Tommie Reynolds	OF26, 3B1	R	29	45	86	4	16	3	0	2	8	9	6	1	.186	.291
Chico Ruiz	C63, OF1	R	33	31	19	4	5	0	0	0	2	7	1	3	.263	.263
Bruce Christensen	SS24	L	23	29	63	4	17	1	0	0	7	5	2	0	.270	.286

Billy Parker 24 R 16-70, Art Kusnyer 25 R 2-13, Tommy Silverio 25 L 1-3, Rudy Meoli 20 L 0-3, Joe Azcue (HO) 31

NAME		T	AGE	W	L	PCT	SV	G	GS	CG	IP	H	BB	SO	SHO	ERA
			26	76	86	.469	32	162	162	39	1481	1246	607	904	11	3.10
Andy Messersmith		R	25	20	13	.606	0	38	38	14	277	224	121	179	4	2.99
Clyde Wright		L	30	16	17	.485	0	37	37	10	277	225	82	135	2	2.99
Rudy May (BW)		L	26	11	12	.478	0	32	31	7	208	160	87	156	2	3.03
Eddie Fisher		R	34	10	8	.556	3	57	3	0	119	92	50	82	0	2.72
Tom Murphy		R	25	6	17	.261	0	37	36	7	243	228	82	89	0	3.78
Dave LaRoche		L	23	5	1	.833	9	56	0	0	72	55	27	63	0	2.50
Lloyd Allen		R	21	4	6	.400	15	54	1	0	94	75	40	72	0	2.49
Rickey Clark		R	25	2	1	.667	1	11	7	1	44	36	28	31	1	2.86
Mel Queen		R	29	2	2	.500	4	44	0	0	66	49	29	53	0	1.77
Billy Wynne		R	27	0	0		0	3	0	0	4	6	2	6	0	4.50
Fred Lasher		R	29	0	0		0	3	0	0	5	9	1	0	0	36.00
Jim Maloney (GJ)		R	31	0	3	.000	0	13	4	0	30	35	24	13	0	5.10
Archie Reynolds		R	25	0	3	.000	0	15	1	0	27	32	18	15	0	4.67
Andy Hassler		L	19	0	1	.000	0	4	1	0	19	25	15	13	0	3.79

MINNESOTA — 5th 74-86 .463 26.5 — BILL RIGNEY

NAME	G by Pos	B	AGE	G	AB	R	H	2B	3B	HR	RBI	BB	SO	SB	BA	SA
	TOTALS		28	160	5414	654	1406	197	31	116	618	512	846	66	.260	.372
Harmon Killebrew	1B90, 3B64	R	35	147	500	61	127	19	1	28	119	114	96	3	.254	.464
Rod Carew	2B142, 3B2	L	25	147	577	88	177	16	10	2	48	45	81	6	.307	.380
Leo Cardenas	SS153	R	32	153	554	59	146	25	4	18	75	51	69	3	.264	.421
Steve Braun	3B73, 2B28, SS10, OF2	L	23	128	343	51	87	12	2	5	35	48	50	8	.254	.344
Tony Oliva (KJ)	OF121	L	30	126	487	73	164	30	3	22	81	25	44	4	.337	.546
Cesar Tovar	OF154, 3B7, 2B2	R	30	157	657	94	204	29	3	1	45	45	39	18	.311	.368
Jim Holt	OF106, 1B3	L	27	126	340	35	88	11	3	1	29	35	25	5	.259	.318
George Mitterwald	C120	R	26	125	388	38	97	13	1	13	44	39	104	3	.250	.389
Rich Reese	1B95, OF9	L	29	120	329	40	72	8	3	10	39	20	35	7	.219	.353
Brant Alyea	OF48	R	30	79	168	13	28	4	0	2	15	24	38	1	.167	.241
Jim Nettles	OF62	L	24	70	168	17	42	5	1	6	24	19	24	3	.250	.399
Danny Thompson (AJ)	3B17, 2B3, SS1	R	24	48	57	10	15	2	0	0	7	7	12	0	.263	.298
2 Phil Roof	C29	R	30	31	87	6	21	4	0	1	6	8	18	0	.241	.287
Steve Brye	OF28	R	22	28	107	10	24	1	0	3	11	7	15	3	.224	.318
Rick Renick (KJ)	3B7, OF7	R	27	27	45	4	10	2	0	1	5	5	14	0	.222	.333
2 George Thomas	OF11, 1B1, 3B1	R	33	23	30	4	8	0	0	0	3	4	8	0	.267	.300

Eric Soderholm 22 R 10-64, 1 Paul Ratliff 27 L 7-44, Paul Powell 23 R 5-31, Tom Tischinski 26 R 3-23, Charlie Manuel 27 L 2-16, Rick Dempsey 21 R 4-13

NAME		T	AGE	W	L	PCT	SV	G	GS	CG	IP	H	BB	SO	SHO	ERA
			27	74	86	.463	25	160	160	43	1417	1384	529	895	9	3.81
Jim Perry		R	35	17	17	.500	1	40	39	8	270	263	102	126	0	4.23
Bert Blyleven		R	20	16	15	.516	0	38	38	17	278	267	59	224	5	2.82
Jim Kaat		L	32	13	14	.481	0	39	38	15	260	275	47	137	4	3.32
Ray Corbin		R	22	8	11	.421	3	52	11	2	140	141	70	83	0	4.11
Hal Haydel		R	26	4	2	.667	1	31	0	0	40	33	20	29	0	4.15
1 Stan Williams		R	34	4	5	.444	4	46	1	0	78	63	44	47	0	4.15
Tom Hall		L	23	4	7	.364	9	48	11	0	130	104	58	137	0	3.32
Pete Hamm		R	23	2	4	.333	0	13	8	1	44	55	18	16	0	6.75
Steve Luebber		R	21	2	5	.286	1	18	12	0	68	73	37	35	0	5.03
Steve Barber		L	23	1	0	1.000	0	4	2	0	12	8	13	4	0	6.00
Jim Strickland		L	25	1	0	1.000	0	24	0	0	31	20	18	21	0	1.45
Bob Gebhard		R	28	1	2	.333	0	17	0	0	18	17	11	13	0	3.00
1 Ron Perranoski		L	35	1	4	.200	5	36	0	0	43	60	24	21	0	6.70
Sal Campisi		R	28	0	1	.000	0	6	0	0	6	5	4	2	0	4.50

MILWAUKEE — 6th 69-92 .429 32 — DAVE BRISTOL

NAME	G by Pos	B	AGE	G	AB	R	H	2B	3B	HR	RBI	BB	SO	SB	BA	SA
	TOTALS		27	161	5185	534	1188	160	23	104	496	543	924	82	.229	.329
2 Johnny Briggs	1B60, OF65	L	27	125	375	51	99	11	1	21	59	71	79	1	.264	.467
Ron Theobald	2B111, SS1, 3B1	R	27	126	388	50	107	12	2	1	23	38	39	11	.276	.325
Rick Auerbach	SS78	R	21	79	236	22	49	10	0	1	9	20	40	3	.203	.258
Tommy Harper	3B70, OF90, 2B1	R	30	152	585	79	151	26	3	14	52	65	92	25	.258	.385
Bill Voss	OF79	L	27	97	275	31	69	4	0	10	30	24	45	2	.251	.375
Dave May	OF142	L	27	144	501	74	139	20	3	16	65	50	59	15	.277	.425
2 Jose Cardenal	OF52	R	27	53	198	20	51	10	0	3	32	13	20	9	.258	.354
Ellie Rodriguez	C114	R	25	115	319	28	67	10	1	3	30	41	51	1	.210	.257
Roberto Pena	1B50, 3B37, SS23, 2B1	R	34	113	274	17	65	9	3	3	28	15	37	2	.237	.325
Andy Kosco	OF45, 1B29, 3B12	R	29	98	264	27	60	6	2	10	39	24	57	1	.227	.379
1 Ted Kubiak	2B48, SS39	B	29	89	260	26	59	6	5	3	17	41	31	0	.227	.323
2 Bob Heise	SS51, 3B11, 2B3, OF1	R	24	68	189	10	48	7	0	0	11	9	14	2	.254	.291
1 Frank Tepedino	1B28	L	23	53	106	11	21	1	0	2	7	4	17	2	.198	.264
1 Mike Hegan	1B45	L	28	46	122	19	27	1	4	11	26	19	21	1	.221	.369
Tom Matchick	3B41, 2B1	L	27	42	114	6	25	2	1	0	10	8	28	0	.219	.254
1 Phil Roof	C39	R	30	41	114	6	22	1	0	2	10	8	24	0	.193	.254
Rob Ellis	3B19, OF15	R	20	36	111	9	22	2	0	0	6	12	24	2	.198	.216
Bobby Mitchell	OF19	R	27	35	55	7	10	1	1	2	6	6	18	0	.182	.345
1 Danny Walton	OF19, 3B1	R	23	30	69	5	14	3	1	1	9	7	22	0	.203	.333
Al Yates	OF12	R	26	24	47	5	13	2	0	1	4	2	9	1	.277	.383
2 Paul Ratliff	C13	L	27	23	47	3	8	0	0	2	3	6	11	0	.171	.415
2 Dick Schofield	3B12, SS4, 2B2	B	36	23	28	4	3	2	0	0	1	6	4	0	.107	.179

Darrell Porter 19 L 15-70, Bernie Smith 29 R 5-36, Gus Gil 31 R 5-32, 1 Ted Savage 34 R 3-17, 1 Floyd Wicker 27 L 1-8, 1 Pete Koegel 23 R 0-3

NAME		T	AGE	W	L	PCT	SV	G	GS	CG	IP	H	BB	SO	SHO	ERA
			27	69	92	.429	32	161	161	32	1416	1303	569	795	23	3.38
Marty Pattin		R	28	14	14	.500	0	36	36	9	265	225	73	169	5	3.12
Bill Parsons		R	22	13	17	.433	0	36	35	12	245	219	93	139	4	3.20
Jim Slaton		R	21	10	8	.556	0	26	23	5	148	140	71	63	4	3.77
Skip Lockwood		R	24	10	15	.400	0	33	32	5	208	191	91	115	1	3.33
Lew Krausse		R	28	8	12	.400	0	43	22	1	180	164	62	92	0	2.95
Ken Sanders		R	29	7	12	.368	31	83	0	0	136	111	34	80	0	1.92
Jerry Bell		R	23	2	1	.667	0	8	0	0	15	10	9	8	0	3.00
John Morris (AJ)		L	29	2	2	.500	1	43	1	0	68	69	27	42	0	3.71
Marcelino Lopez		L	27	2	7	.222	0	31	11	0	68	64	60	42	0	4.63
2 Jim Hannan		R	31	1	1	.500	0	21	1	0	32	38	21	17	0	5.06
Larry Bearnarth		R	29	0	0		0	3	0	0	3	10	2	2	0	18.00
John Gelnar		R	28	0	0		0	2	0	0	3	5	4	1	0	18.00
Floyd Weaver		R	30	0	1	.000	0	9	0	0	27	33	18	12	0	7.33
Dick Ellsworth		L	31	0	1	.000	0	11	0	0	15	22	7	10	0	4.80
2 Bob Reynolds		R	24	0	1	.000	0	3	0	0	4	3	4	0	0	4.50

AMERICAN LEAGUE CHAMPIONSHIP — BALTIMORE (EAST) 3   OAKLAND (WEST) 0

LINE SCORES

TEAM	1	2	3	4	5	6	7	8	9	10	11	12	R	H	E

Game 1   October 3 at Baltimore

													R	H	E
OAK	0	2	0	1	0	0	0	0	0				3	9	0
BAL	0	0	0	1	0	0	4	0	x				5	7	1

Blue, Fingers (8)   McNally, Watt (8)

Game 2   October 4 at Baltimore

													R	H	E
OAK	0	0	0		1	0	0		0	0	0		1	6	0
BAL	0	1	1		0	0	0		1	2	x		5	7	0

Hunter   Cuellar

Game 3   October 5 at Oakland

													R	H	E
BAL	1	0	0		0	2	0		2	0	0		5	12	0
OAK	0	0	1		0	0	1		0	1	0		3	7	0

Palmer   Segui, Fingers (5), Knowles (7), Locker (7), Grant (8)

COMPOSITE BATTING

NAME	POS	G	AB	R	H	2B	3B	HR	RBI	BA
Baltimore										
Totals		3	95	15	26	7	1	4	14	.274
F. Robinson	OF	3	12	2	1	1	0	0	1	.083
B. Robinson	3B	3	11	2	4	1	0	1	3	.364
Johnson	2B	3	10	2	3	2	0	0	0	.300
Powell	1B	3	10	4	3	0	0	2	3	.300
Blair	OF	3	9	1	3	0	0	0	2	.333
Belanger	SS	3	8	1	2	0	0	0	1	.250
Rettenmund	OF	3	8	0	2	1	0	0	1	.250
Buford	OF	3	7	3	3	1	0	1	0	.429
Hendricks	C	2	4	1	2	0	1	0	2	.500

Etchebarren C 0-5, Motton PH 1-1

NAME	POS	G	AB	R	H	2B	3B	HR	RBI	BA
Oakland										
Totals		3	96	7	22	8	1	3	7	.229
Jackson	OF	3	12	2	4	1	0	2	2	.333
Campaneris	SS	3	12	0	2	1	0	0	1	.167
Mangual	OF	3	12	1	2	1	0	0	0	.167
Bando	3B	3	11	3	4	2	0	1	1	.364
Davis	1B	3	8	0	3	0	0	0	0	.375
Green	2B	3	7	0	2	1	0	0	1	.286
Rudi	OF	2	7	0	1	1	0	0	0	.143
Duncan	C	2	6	0	0	0	0	0	0	.000

Epstein 1B 1-5, Monday OF 0-3, Tenace C 0-3, Blefary PH 0-1, Hegan PH 0-1

COMPOSITE PITCHING

NAME	G	IP	H	BB	SO	W	L	SV	ERA
Baltimore									
Totals	3	27	22	5	16	3	0	1	2.33
Cuellar	1	9	6	1	2	1	0	0	1.00
Palmer	1	9	7	3	8	1	0	0	3.00
McNally	1	7	7	1	5	1	0	0	3.86
Watt	1	2	2	0	1	0	0	1	0.00

NAME	G	IP	H	BB	SO	W	L	SV	ERA
Oakland									
Totals	3	25	26	13	22	0	3	0	5.40
Hunter	1	8	7	2	6	0	1	0	5.63
Blue	1	7	7	2	8	0	1	0	6.43
Segui	1	4.2	6	6	4	0	0	0	5.79
Fingers	2	2.1	4	2	2	0	0	0	7.71
Grant	1	2	2	1	2	0	0	0	0.00
Locker	1	0.2	0	0	0	0	0	0	0.00
Knowles	1	0.1	1	0	0	0	0	0	0.00

NATIONAL LEAGUE CHAMPIONSHIP — PITTSBURGH (EAST) 3   SAN FRANCISCO (WEST) 1

LINE SCORES

TEAM	1	2	3	4	5	6	7	8	9	10	11	12	R	H	E
Game 1 October 2 at San Francisco															
PIT	0	0	2	0	0	0	2	0	0				4	9	0
SF	0	0	1	0	4	0	0	0	x				5	7	2

Blass, Moose (6), Giusti (8)   Perry

Game 2 October 3 at San Francisco															
PIT	0	1	0	2	1	0	4	0	1				9	15	0
SF	1	1	0	0	0	0	0	0	2				4	9	0

Ellis, Miller (6),   Cumberland, Barr (4)
Giusti (9)   McMahon (5), Carrithers (7),
                           Bryant (7), Hamilton (9)

Game 3 October 5 at Pittsburgh															
SF	0	0	0	0	0	1	0	0	0				1	5	2
PIT	0	1	0	0	0	0	0	1	x				2	4	1

Marichal   Johnson, Giusti (9)

Game 4 October 6 at Pittsburgh															
SF	1	4	0	0	0	0	0	0	0				5	10	0
PIT	2	3	0	0	0	4	0	0	x				9	11	2

Perry, Johnson (6),   Blass, Kison (3), Giusti (9)
McMahon (8)

COMPOSITE BATTING

NAME	POS	G	AB	R	H	2B	3B	HR	RBI	BA
Pittsburgh										
Cash	2B	4	19	5	8	2	0	0	1	.421
Clemente	OF	4	18	2	6	0	0	0	4	.333
Hebner	3B	4	17	3	5	1	0	1	4	.294
Robertson	1B	4	16	5	7	1	0	4	6	.438
Sanguillen	C	4	15	1	4	0	0	0	1	.267
Stargell	OF	4	14	1	0	0	0	0	0	.000
Hernandez	SS	4	13	2	3	0	0	0	0	.231
Oliver	OF	4	12	2	3	0	0	1	5	.250
Clines	OF	1	3	1	1	0	0	0	1	.333
Alley	SS	1	2	1	1	0	0	0	0	.500
Davalillo	PH	2	2	0	0	0	0	0	0	.000

Mazeroski PH 1-1, May PH 0-1, Pagan 3B 0-1

NAME	POS	G	AB	R	H	2B	3B	HR	RBI	BA
San Francisco										
Fuentes	2B	4	16	4	5	1	0	1	2	.313
Henderson	OF	4	16	3	5	1	0	0	2	.313
Mays	OF	4	15	2	4	2	0	1	3	.267
Dietz	C	4	15	0	1	0	0	0	1	.067
McCovey	1B	4	14	2	6	0	0	2	6	.429
Speier	SS	4	14	4	5	1	0	1	1	.357
Gallagher	3B	4	10	0	1	0	0	0	0	.100
Klingman	OF	4	9	0	1	0	0	0	0	.111
Bonds	OF	3	8	0	2	0	0	0	0	.250

Hart 3B 0-5, Lanier 3B 0-1, Duffy PH 0-1, Rosario PR 0-0

COMPOSITE PITCHING

NAME	G	IP	H	BB	SO	W	L	SV	ERA
Pittsburgh									
B. Johnson	1	8	5	3	7	1	0	0	0.00
Blass	2	7	14	2	11	0	1	0	11.57
Giusti	4	5.1	2	2	3	0	0	3	0.00
Ellis	1	5	6	4	1	0	0	0	3.60
Kison	1	4.2	2	1	3	1	0	0	0.00
Miller	1	3	3	3	0	0	0	0	6.00
Moose	1	2	0	0	0	0	0	0	0.00

NAME	G	IP	H	BB	SO	W	L	SV	ERA
San Francisco									
Perry	2	14.2	19	3	11	1	1	0	6.14
Marichal	1	8	4	6	0	1	0	0	2.25
McMahon	2	3	0	0	4	0	0	0	0.00
Cumberland	1	3	7	0	4	0	1	0	9.00
Bryant	1	2	1	1	2	0	0	0	4.50
J. Johnson	2	1.1	1	1	2	0	0	0	13.50
Barr	1	1	3	0	1	0	0	0	9.00
Hamilton	1	1	1	3	0	0	0	0	9.00
Carrithers	1	0	3	0	1	0	0	0	—

EAST DIVISION

PITTSBURGH   1st 97-65   .599   DANNY MURTAUGH

NAME	G by Pos	B	AGE	G	AB	R	H	2B	3B	HR	RBI	BB	SO	SB	BA	SA
TOTALS			28	162	5674	788	1555	223	61	154	744	469	919	65	.274	.416
Bob Robertson	1B126	R	24	131	469	65	127	18	2	26	72	60	101	1	.271	.484
Dave Cash	2B105, 3B24, SS3	R	23	123	478	79	138	17	4	2	34	35	43	13	.289	.354
Gene Alley	SS108, 3B1	R	30	114	348	38	79	8	7	6	36	35	43	9	.227	.342
Richie Hebner	3B108	L	23	112	388	50	105	17	8	17	67	32	68	2	.271	.487
Roberto Clemente	OF124	R	36	132	522	82	178	29	8	13	86	26	65	1	.341	.502
Al Oliver	OF116, 1B25	L	24	143	529	69	149	31	7	14	64	27	72	4	.282	.446
Willie Stargell	OF138	L	31	141	511	104	151	26	6	48	125	83	154	0	.295	.628
Manny Sanguillen	C135	R	27	138	533	60	170	26	5	7	81	19	32	6	.319	.426
Vic Davalillo	OF61, 1B16	L	34	99	295	48	84	14	6	1	33	11	31	0	.285	.383
Gene Clines	OF74	R	24	97	273	52	84	12	4	1	24	22	36	15	.308	.392
Jackie Hernandez	SS75, 3B9	R	30	88	233	30	48	7	3	3	26	17	45	0	.206	.300
Bill Mazeroski	2B46, 3B7	R	34	70	193	17	49	7	1	1	16	15	8	0	.254	.295
Jose Pagan (BA)	3B41, OF3, 1B2	R	36	57	158	16	38	1	0	5	15	16	25	0	.241	.342
Rennie Stennett	2B36	R	20	50	153	24	54	5	4	1	15	7	9	1	.353	.458
Milt May	C31	L	21	49	126	15	35	1	0	6	25	9	16	0	.278	.429
Charlie Sands	C3	L	23	28	25	4	5	2	0	1	5	7	6	0	.200	.400
Richie Zisk	OF6	R	22	7	15	2	3	1	0	1	2	4	7	0	.200	.467

2 Carl Taylor 27 R 2-12, Rimp Lanier 22 L 0-4, Frank Taveras 21 R 0-0

ST. LOUIS   2nd 90-72   .556   7   RED SCHOENDIENST

NAME	G by Pos	B	AGE	G	AB	R	H	2B	3B	HR	RBI	BB	SO	SB	BA	SA
TOTALS			28	163	5610	739	1542	225	54	95	686	543	786	124	.275	.385
Joe Hague	1B91, OF36	L	27	129	380	49	86	9	3	16	54	58	69	0	.226	.392
Ted Sizemore	2B93, SS39, OF15, 3B1	R	26	135	478	53	126	14	5	3	42	42	26	4	.264	.333
Dal Maxvill	SS140	R	32	152	421	61	80	10	1	0	24	43	45	1	.225	.258
Joe Torre	3B161	R	30	161	634	97	230	34	8	24	137	63	70	4	.363	.555
Matty Alou	OF94, 1B57	L	32	149	609	85	192	28	6	7	74	34	27	19	.315	.415
Jose Cruz	OF83	L	23	83	292	46	80	13	2	9	27	49	35	6	.274	.425
Lou Brock	OF157	L	32	157	640	126	200	37	7	7	61	76	107	64	.313	.425
Ted Simmons	C130	B	21	133	510	64	155	32	4	7	77	36	50	1	.304	.424
Julian Javier	2B80, 3B1	R	34	90	259	32	67	6	4	3	28	9	33	5	.259	.347
1 Jose Cardenal	OF83	R	27	89	301	37	73	12	4	7	48	29	35	12	.243	.379
Luis Melendez	OF66	R	21	88	173	25	39	3	1	0	11	24	29	2	.225	.254
Jim Beauchamp	1B44, OF1	R	31	77	162	24	38	8	3	2	16	9	26	3	.235	.358
Bob Burda	1B13, OF1	L	32	65	71	6	21	0	0	1	12	10	11	0	.296	.338
Jerry McNertney	C36	R	34	56	128	15	37	4	2	4	22	12	14	0	.289	.445
1 Dick Schofield	SS17, 2B13, 3B3	B	36	54	60	7	13	2	0	0	6	10	9	0	.217	.300
2 Ted Kubiak	SS17, 2B14	B	29	52	72	8	18	3	2	1	10	11	12	1	.250	.389
1 Leron Lee	OF8	L	23	25	28	4	5	1	0	0	3	3	8	0	.179	.321

Bob Stinson 25 B 4-19, Milt Ramirez 21 R 3-11, Jorge Roque 21 R 3-10

CHICAGO   3rd (tie) 83-79   .512   14   LEO DUROCHER

NAME	G by Pos	B	AGE	G	AB	R	H	2B	3B	HR	RBI	BB	SO	SB	BA	SA
TOTALS			31	5438	637	1401	202	34	128	603	527	772	44	.258	.378	
Joe Pepitone (EJ)	1B95, OF23	L	30	115	427	50	131	19	4	16	61	24	41	1	.307	.482
Glenn Beckert (RJ)	2B129	R	30	131	530	80	181	18	5	2	42	24	24	3	.342	.409
Don Kessinger	SS154	B	28	155	617	77	159	18	6	2	38	52	54	15	.258	.316
Ron Santo	3B149, OF4	R	31	154	555	77	148	22	1	21	88	79	95	4	.267	.423
Johnny Callison	OF89	L	32	103	290	27	61	12	4	8	38	36	55	2	.210	.341
Brock Davis	OF93	L	27	106	301	22	77	9	5	0	28	35	34	6	.256	.312
Billy Williams	OF154	L	33	157	594	86	179	27	5	28	93	77	44	7	.301	.505
2 Chris Cannizzaro	C70	R	33	71	197	18	42	8	1	5	23	28	24	0	.213	.340
Jim Hickman	OF69, 1B44	R	34	117	383	50	98	13	2	19	60	50	61	0	.256	.449
Paul Popovich	2B40, 3B16, SS1	B	30	89	226	24	49	7	1	2	20	16	17	0	.217	.310
Cleo James	OF48, 3B2	R	22	91	150	25	43	7	0	2	13	10	16	6	.287	.373
J.C. Martin	C43, OF1	L	34	47	125	10	33	6	0	1	10	16	16	1	.264	.352
Ferguson Jenkins	P39	R	27	39	115	13	28	7	1	6	20	7	40	0	.243	.478
Ernie Banks (KJ)	1B20	R	40	39	83	4	16	2	0	3	6	6	14	0	.193	.325
Jose Ortiz	OF30	R	24	36	88	10	26	7	0	3	4	6	10	2	.295	.398
Hector Torres	SS18, 2B4	R	25	31	58	4	13	3	0	0	3	4	10	0	.224	.276
Danny Breeden	C25	R	29	25	65	3	10	1	0	0	5	4	9	0	.154	.169
Ken Rudolph	C25	R	24	25	76	5	15	3	0	1	7	6	20	0	.197	.237
Hal Breeden	1B8	L	27	23	36	1	5	1	0	1	2	3	7	0	.139	.250
4 Frank Fernandez (BG)	C16	R	28	17	41	11	7	4	0	1	4	17	15	0	.171	.488
Carmen Fanzone	OF6, 3B3, 1B2	R	29	12	43	5	8	2	0	2	7	1	9	0	.186	.372

Gene Hiser 22 L 6-29, Randy Hundley (KJ) 29 R 3-11, Billy North 23 R 6-16, Al Spangler 37 L 2-5, 1 Garry Jestadt 24 R 0-3, 3 Ramon Webster 28 L 5-16, Pat Bourque 24 L 7-37

NEW YORK   3rd (tie) 83-79   .512   14   GIL HODGES

NAME	G by Pos	B	AGE	G	AB	R	H	2B	3B	HR	RBI	BB	SO	SB	BA	SA
TOTALS			27	5477	588	1365	203	29	98	546	547	958	89	.249	.351	
Ed Kranepool	1B108, OF11	L	26	122	421	61	118	20	4	14	58	38	30	0	.280	.447
Ken Boswell	2B109	L	25	116	392	46	107	20	1	5	40	36	31	5	.273	.347
Bud Harrelson	SS140	B	27	142	547	55	138	16	6	0	32	53	59	28	.252	.303
Bob Aspromonte	3B97	R	33	104	342	21	77	9	1	5	33	29	25	0	.225	.301
Ken Singleton	OF96	B	24	115	298	34	73	5	0	13	46	61	64	0	.245	.393
Tommie Agee	OF107	R	28	113	425	58	121	19	4	14	50	50	84	28	.285	.428
Cleon Jones	OF132	R	28	136	505	63	161	24	4	14	69	49	73	6	.319	.473
Jerry Grote	C122	R	28	125	403	35	109	25	0	2	35	40	47	1	.270	.347
Dave Marshall	OF64	L	28	100	214	28	51	9	3	3	21	26	54	1	.238	.332
Don Hahn	OF80	R	22	98	178	16	42	6	1	1	11	21	32	0	.236	.292
Tim Foli	2B58, 3B36, SS12, OF1	R	20	97	288	32	65	12	2	0	21	11	41	0	.226	.316
Donn Clendenon	1B72	R	35	88	263	29	65	10	0	11	37	22	78	0	.247	.411
Art Shamsky (XJ)	OF38, 1B1	L	29	68	135	13	25	6	1	3	15	20	18	1	.185	.370
Duffy Dyer	C53	R	25	59	169	13	39	18	1	4	45	1	42	1	.231	.320
Wayne Garrett (MS)	3B53, 2B9	L	23	56	192	20	43	2	0	1	9	26	28	2	.224	.260
Mike Jorgensen	OF31, 1B1	L	23	45	118	16	26	1	0	1	11	24	21	1	.220	.297
Ted Martinez	SS23, 2B13, 3B3, OF1	R	23	40	104	12	30	5	2	0	4	22	1	.288	.384

Lee Stanton 25 R 4-21, John Milner 21 L 3-18, Al Weis 33 R 0-11, Frank Estrada 23 R 1-2

PITTSBURGH (pitching)

NAME	T	AGE	W	L	PCT	SV	G	GS	CG	IP	H	BB	SO	SHO	ERA
		28	97	65	.599	48	162	162	43	1461	1426	470	813	15	3.31
Dock Ellis	R	26	19	9	.679	0	31	31	11	227	207	63	137	2	3.05
Steve Blass	R	29	15	8	.652	0	33	33	12	240	226	68	136	5	2.85
Bob Moose	R	23	11	7	.611	1	30	18	3	140	169	35	68	4	4.11
Luke Walker	L	27	10	8	.556	0	28	24	4	160	157	53	86	2	3.54
Bob Johnson	R	28	9	10	.474	0	31	27	7	175	170	55	101	1	3.45
Nelson Briles	R	27	8	4	.667	1	37	14	4	136	131	35	76	2	3.04
Bob Veale	L	35	6	0	1.000	1	37	0	0	46	59	24	40	0	7.04
Bruce Kison	R	21	6	5	.545	0	18	13	2	95	93	36	60	1	3.41
1 Mudcat Grant	R	35	5	3	.625	7	42	0	0	86	79	31	55	0	2.93
Dave Giusti	R	31	5	6	.455	30	58	0	0	89	79	31	55	0	2.93
Jim Nelson	R	23	2	2	.500	0	17	2	0	35	37	26	11	0	2.31
3 Bob Miller	R	32	1	2	.333	3	16	0	0	28	20	13	13	0	1.29
John Lamb (FS)	R	24	0	0	—	0	2	0	0	3	1	1	0	0	0.00
Frank Brosseau	R	26	0	0	—	0	1	0	0	2	1	0	0	0	0.00
Ramon Hernandez	L	30	1	0	1.000	4	11	0	0	12	5	2	7	0	0.75

ST. LOUIS (pitching)

NAME	T	AGE	W	L	PCT	SV	G	GS	CG	IP	H	BB	SO	SHO	ERA
		28	90	72	.556	12	163	163	56	1482	1576	911	911	14	3.85
Steve Carlton	L	26	20	9	.690	0	37	36	18	273	275	98	172	4	3.56
Bob Gibson	R	35	16	13	.552	0	31	31	20	246	215	76	185	5	3.04
Jerry Reuss	L	22	14	14	.500	0	36	35	7	211	228	109	131	2	4.78
Reggie Cleveland	R	23	12	12	.500	0	34	34	10	222	238	53	148	2	4.01
Don Shaw	L	27	7	2	.778	2	45	0	0	51	51	31	19	0	2.65
Moe Drabowsky	R	35	6	1	.857	9	51	0	0	60	45	33	49	0	3.45
Frank Linzy	R	30	4	3	.571	6	50	0	0	59	49	27	24	0	2.14
2 Stan Williams	R	34	3	0	1.000	0	10	0	0	13	13	2	9	0	1.38
Chuck Taylor	R	29	3	1	.750	3	43	1	0	71	72	25	46	0	3.55
Denny Higgins	R	24	3	10	.231	0	23	12	1	90	114	26	48	1	5.30
1 Al Santorini	R	23	1	0	1.000	0	9	0	0	9	4	1	2	0	3.86
1 Mike Torrez	R	24	1	2	.333	0	9	6	0	36	41	30	8	0	6.00
1 Fred Norman	L	28	0	0	—	0	2	1	0	8	11	2	5	0	11.25
3 Daryl Patterson	R	27	0	1	.000	1	13	2	0	20	15	11	4	0	4.33
Rudy Arroyo	L	26	0	0	—	0	5	0	0	9	12	8	5	0	5.25
George Brunet	L	36	0	1	.000	0	7	0	0	9	12	7	4	0	6.00
2 Al Jackson	L	35	0	1	.000	0	2	0	0	6	5	3	0	0	3.00

1 Bob Reynolds 24 R 0-0, Harry Parker 23 R 0-0, Santiago Guzman 21 R 0-0, Bob Chlupsa 25 R 0-0
Al Hrabosky (MS) 21 L 0-0, Mike Jackson 25 L 0-0

CHICAGO (pitching)

NAME	T	AGE	W	L	PCT	SV	G	GS	CG	IP	H	BB	SO	SHO	ERA
		28	83	79	.512	13	162	162	75	1444	1458	411	900	17	3.61
Ferguson Jenkins	R	27	24	13	.649	0	39	39	30	325	304	37	263	3	2.77
Milt Pappas	R	32	17	14	.548	0	35	35	14	261	279	62	99	5	3.52
Bill Hands	R	31	12	18	.400	0	36	35	14	242	248	50	128	1	3.42
Ken Holtzman	L	25	9	15	.375	0	30	29	9	195	213	64	143	3	4.48
Juan Pizarro	L	34	7	6	.538	0	16	14	6	101	78	40	67	3	3.48
Phil Regan	R	34	5	5	.500	6	48	0	0	73	84	33	28	0	3.95
Joe Decker	R	24	3	2	.600	0	21	4	0	46	62	25	37	0	4.70
Burt Hooton	R	22	2	1	.667	0	3	3	3	21	13	8	15	1	2.14
Bill Bonham	R	22	1	6	.143	0	33	6	1	60	63	36	41	0	4.65
Earl Stephenson	L	23	1	0	1.000	1	24	0	0	54	44	11	11	0	4.50
Ray Newman	L	26	1	2	.333	2	30	0	0	38	30	17	35	0	3.55
Larry Gura	L	23	1	0	1.000	0	5	0	0	3	4	1	2	0	6.00
1 Bob Miller	R	32	0	1	.000	0	2	0	0	7	10	1	2	0	5.14
Jim Colborn	R	25	1	0	1.000	0	14	0	0	31	38	21	20	0	7.20
Ron Tompkins	R	27	0	0	—	0	3	0	0	40	31	21	20	0	4.05

NEW YORK (pitching)

NAME	T	AGE	W	L	PCT	SV	G	GS	CG	IP	H	BB	SO	SHO	ERA
		27	83	79	.512	22	162	162	42	1466	1227	529	1157	13	2.99
Tom Seaver	R	26	20	10	.667	0	36	35	21	286	210	61	289	4	1.76
Gary Gentry	R	24	12	11	.522	0	32	31	8	203	167	82	155	3	3.24
Tug McGraw	L	26	11	4	.733	8	51	1	0	111	73	41	109	3	1.70
Nolan Ryan	R	24	10	14	.417	0	30	26	3	152	125	116	137	0	3.97
Danny Frisella	R	25	8	5	.615	12	53	0	0	91	76	30	93	0	1.98
Ray Sadecki	L	30	7	7	.500	0	34	20	5	163	139	44	120	2	2.93
Jerry Koosman (VJ)	L	28	6	11	.353	0	26	24	4	166	160	51	96	0	3.04
Charlie Williams	R	23	5	6	.455	0	31	9	1	90	92	41	53	0	4.80
Ron Taylor	R	33	2	2	.500	2	45	0	0	69	71	11	32	0	3.65
Jim McAndrew	R	27	1	4	.286	0	24	10	0	90	78	32	42	0	4.40
Don Rose	R	24	0	1	.000	0	1	1	0	4	3	0	1	0	0.00
Buzz Capra	R	23	0	1	.000	0	5	1	0	12	12	11	6	0	5.06
Jon Matlack	L	21	0	3	.000	0	7	5	0	37	31	15	24	0	4.14

MONTREAL — 5th 71-90 .441 25.5 — GENE MAUCH

NAME	G by Pos	B	AGE	G	AB	R	H	2B	3B	HR	RBI	BB	SO	SB	BA	SA
TOTALS			28	162	5335	622	1312	197	29	88	567	543	800	51	.246	.343
Ron Fairly	1B135, OF10	L	32	146	447	58	115	23	0	13	71	81	65	1	.257	.396
Ron Hunt	2B133, 3B19	R	30	152	520	89	145	20	3	5	38	58	41	0	.279	.358
Bobby Wine (BW)	SS119	R	32	119	340	25	68	9	0	1	16	25	46	0	.200	.235
Bob Bailey	3B120, OF51, 1B9	R	28	157	545	65	137	21	4	14	83	97	105	13	.251	.382
Rusty Staub	OF162	L	27	162	599	94	186	34	6	19	97	74	42	9	.311	.482
Boots Day	OF120	L	23	127	371	53	105	10	2	4	33	33	39	9	.283	.353
Jim Fairey	OF58	L	26	92	200	19	49	8	1	1	19	12	23	1	.245	.310
John Bateman	C137	R	30	139	492	34	119	17	3	10	56	19	87	1	.242	.350
Gary Sutherland	2B56, SS46, OF4, 3B2	R	26	111	304	25	78	7	2	4	26	18	12	3	.257	.332
Coco Laboy	3B65, 2B2	R	31	76	151	10	38	4	0	1	14	11	19	0	.252	.298
John Boccabella	1B37, C37, 3B2	R	30	74	177	15	39	11	0	3	15	14	26	0	.220	.333
Clyde Mashore	OF47, 3B1	R	26	66	114	20	22	5	0	1	7	10	22	1	.193	.263
2 Ron Woods	OF45	R	28	51	138	26	41	7	3	1	17	19	18	0	.297	.413
Jim Gosger	OF23, 1B6	L	28	51	102	7	16	2	2	0	8	9	17	1	.157	.216
Stan Swanson	OF38	L	27	49	106	14	26	3	0	2	11	10	13	1	.245	.330
Ron Brand	SS22, 3B4, OF4, 2B1, C1	R	31	47	56	3	12	0	0	0	1	3	5	1	.214	.214
Mack Jones	OF27	L	32	43	91	11	15	3	0	3	9	15	24	1	.165	.297
1 Ron Swoboda	OF26	R	27	39	75	7	19	4	3	0	6	11	16	0	.253	.387
Dave McDonald	1B8, OF1	L	28	24	39	3	4	2	0	1	4	4	14	0	.103	.231
Rich Hacker	SS16	B	23	16	33	2	4	1	0	0	2	3	12	0	.121	.152
Terry Humphrey	C9	R	21	9	26	1	5	1	0	0	1	0	1	0	.192	.231

NAME	T	AGE	W	L	PCT	SV	G	GS	CG	IP	H	BB	SO	SHO	ERA
TOTALS		28	71	90	.441	25	162	162	49	1434	1418	658	829	8	4.12
Bill Stoneman	R	27	17	16	.515	0	39	39	20	295	243	146	251	3	3.14
Steve Renko	R	26	15	14	.517	0	40	37	9	276	256	135	129	3	3.75
Ernie McAnally	R	24	11	12	.478	0	31	25	8	178	150	87	98	2	3.89
Carl Morton	R	27	10	18	.357	1	36	35	9	214	252	83	84	0	4.79
John Strohmayer	R	24	7	5	.583	1	27	14	2	114	124	31	56	0	4.34
Mike Marshall	R	28	5	8	.385	23	66	0	0	111	100	50	85	0	4.30
Jim Britton (EJ)	R	27	2	3	.400	0	16	6	0	46	49	27	23	0	5.67
Howie Reed	R	34	2	3	.400	0	43	0	0	57	66	24	25	0	4.26
Dan McGinn	L	27	1	4	.200	0	28	6	1	71	74	42	40	0	5.96
Claude Raymond	R	34	1	7	.125	0	37	0	0	54	81	25	29	0	4.67
John O'Donoghue	L	31	0	0	—	0	13	0	0	17	19	7	7	0	4.76
2 Mike Torrez	R	24	0	0	—	0	1	0	0	3	4	1	2	0	0.00

PHILADELPHIA — 6th 67-95 .414 30 — FRANK LUCCHESI

NAME	G by Pos	B	AGE	G	AB	R	H	2B	3B	HR	RBI	BB	SO	SB	BA	SA
TOTALS			26	162	5538	558	1289	209	35	123	522	499	1031	63	.233	.350
Deron Johnson	1B136, 3B22	R	32	158	582	74	154	29	0	34	95	72	146	0	.265	.490
Denny Doyle (NJ)	2B91	L	27	95	342	34	79	12	1	3	24	19	31	4	.231	.298
Larry Bowa	SS157	B	25	159	650	74	162	18	5	0	25	36	61	28	.249	.292
John Vukovich	3B74	R	23	74	217	11	36	5	0	0	14	12	34	2	.166	.189
Roger Freed	OF106, C1	R	25	118	348	23	77	12	1	6	37	44	86	0	.221	.313
Willie Montanez	OF158, 1B9	L	23	158	599	78	153	27	6	30	99	67	105	4	.255	.471
Oscar Gamble	OF80	L	21	92	280	24	62	11	1	6	23	21	35	5	.221	.332
Tim McCarver	C125	L	29	134	474	51	132	20	5	8	46	43	26	5	.278	.392
Don Money	3B68, OF40, 2B20	R	24	121	439	40	98	22	8	7	38	31	80	4	.223	.358
Ron Stone	OF51, 1B3	L	28	95	185	16	42	8	1	2	23	25	36	2	.227	.314
Terry Harmon	2B58, SS9, 3B3, 1B2	R	27	79	221	27	45	4	2	0	12	20	45	3	.204	.240
Joe Lis	OF35	R	24	59	123	16	26	6	0	6	10	16	43	0	.211	.407
Byron Browne (LJ)	OF30	R	28	58	68	5	14	3	0	3	5	8	23	0	.206	.382
B. Pfeil	3B15, C4, OF3, 1B1, 2B1, SS1	R	27	44	70	5	19	3	0	2	9	6	9	1	.271	.400
Mike Ryan	C43	R	29	43	134	9	22	5	1	3	6	10	32	1	.164	.284
Rick Wise	P38	R	25	39	97	14	23	2	1	6	15	3	34	0	.237	.464
1 Tony Taylor	2B14, 3B11, 1B2	R	35	36	107	9	25	2	1	1	5	9	12	1	.234	.299
Larry Hisle	OF27	R	24	36	76	7	15	3	0	0	3	6	22	1	.197	.237
Greg Luzinski	1B28	R	20	28	100	13	30	8	0	3	15	12	32	2	.300	.470
Mike Anderson	OF26	R	20	26	89	11	22	5	1	2	5	13	28	0	.247	.393
2 Pete Koegel	C7, OF1	R	23	12	26	1	6	1	0	0	3	2	7	0	.231	.269
1 Johnny Briggs	OF8	L	27	10	22	3	4	1	0	0	3	6	2	0	.182	.227

NAME	T	AGE	W	L	PCT	SV	G	GS	CG	IP	H	BB	SO	SHO	ERA
TOTALS		29	67	95	.414	25	162	162	31	1471	1396	525	838	10	3.71
Rick Wise	R	25	17	14	.548	0	38	38	17	272	261	70	155	4	2.88
Woody Fryman	L	31	10	7	.588	2	37	17	3	149	133	46	104	2	3.38
Chris Short	L	33	7	14	.333	1	31	26	5	173	182	63	95	2	3.85
Darrell Brandon	R	30	6	6	.500	4	52	0	0	83	81	47	44	0	3.90
Ken Reynolds	L	24	5	9	.357	0	35	25	2	162	163	82	81	1	4.50
Jim Bunning	R	39	5	12	.294	1	29	16	1	110	126	37	58	0	5.48
Barry Lersch	R	26	5	14	.263	0	38	30	3	214	203	50	113	0	3.79
Joe Hoerner	L	34	4	5	.444	9	49	0	0	73	57	21	57	0	1.97
Billy Wilson	R	28	4	6	.400	7	38	0	0	59	39	22	40	0	3.05
Billy Champion	R	23	3	5	.375	0	37	9	0	109	100	48	49	0	4.38
Wayne Twitchell	R	23	1	0	1.000	0	6	1	0	16	8	10	15	0	0.00
Lowell Palmer	R	23	0	0	—	0	3	1	0	15	13	13	6	0	6.00
Manny Muniz	R	23	0	0	.000	0	1	0	0	1	0	9	8	0	7.20
Dick Selma (AJ)	R	27	0	2	.000	1	9	0	0	25	21	8	15	0	3.24

WEST DIVISION

SAN FRANCISCO — 1st 90-72 .556 — CHARLIE FOX

NAME	G by Pos	B	AGE	G	AB	R	H	2B	3B	HR	RBI	BB	SO	SB	BA	SA
TOTALS			28	162	5461	706	1348	224	36	140	653	654	1042	101	.247	.378
Willie McCovey (KJ)	1B95	L	33	105	329	45	91	13	0	18	70	64	57	0	.277	.480
Tito Fuentes	2B152	B	27	152	630	63	172	28	4	5	52	18	46	12	.273	.356
Chris Speier	SS156	R	21	157	601	74	141	17	6	8	46	56	90	4	.235	.323
Alan Gallagher	3B128	R	25	136	429	47	119	18	5	5	57	40	57	2	.277	.378
Bobby Bonds	OF154	R	25	155	619	110	178	32	4	33	102	62	137	26	.288	.512
Willie Mays	OF84, 1B48	R	40	136	417	82	113	24	5	18	61	112	123	23	.271	.482
Ken Henderson	OF138, 1B1	B	25	141	504	80	133	26	6	15	65	84	76	18	.264	.429
Dick Dietz	C135	R	29	142	453	58	114	19	0	19	72	97	86	1	.252	.419
Hal Lanier	3B83, 2B13, SS8, 1B3	R	28	109	206	21	48	8	0	1	13	15	26	0	.233	.286
Jimmy Rosario	OF67	R	27	92	192	26	43	6	1	0	13	33	35	7	.224	.266
Fran Healy	C22	R	24	47	93	10	26	3	0	2	11	15	24	1	.280	.376
Dave Kingman	1B20, OF14	R	22	41	115	17	32	10	2	6	24	9	35	5	.278	.557
1 George Foster	OF30	R	22	36	105	11	28	5	0	3	8	6	27	0	.267	.400
Bernie Williams	OF27	R	22	35	73	8	13	1	0	1	5	12	24	1	.178	.233
Frank Johnson	1B9, OF4	R	28	32	49	4	4	1	0	0	5	3	9	0	.082	.102
Jim Ray Hart	3B3, OF3	R	29	31	39	5	10	0	0	2	5	6	8	0	.256	.410
Russ Gibson	C22	R	32	25	57	2	11	1	1	1	7	2	13	0	.193	.298
2 Frank Duffy	SS6, 2B1, 3B1	R	24	21	28	4	5	0	0	0	0	0	10	0	.179	.179
Ed Goodson	1B14	L	23	20	42	4	8	1	0	0	1	2	4	0	.190	.214
1 Bob Heise	SS3, 2B1, 3B1	R	24	13	11	2	0	0	0	0	0	0	1	0	.000	.000

2 Floyd Wicker 27 L 3-21, Chris Arnold 23 R 3-13, Jim Howarth 24 L 3-13, Dave Rader 22 L 0-4

NAME	T	AGE	W	L	PCT	SV	G	GS	CG	IP	H	BB	SO	SHO	ERA
TOTALS		28	90	72	.556	30	162	162	45	1455	1324	471	831	14	3.32
Juan Marichal	R	33	18	11	.621	0	37	37	18	279	244	56	159	4	2.94
Gaylord Perry	R	32	16	12	.571	0	37	37	14	280	255	67	158	2	2.76
Jerry Johnson	R	27	12	9	.571	18	67	0	0	109	93	48	85	0	2.97
Don McMahon	R	41	10	6	.625	4	61	0	0	82	73	37	71	0	4.06
John Cumberland	L	24	9	6	.600	2	45	21	5	185	153	55	65	2	2.92
Ron Bryant (SA)	L	23	7	10	.412	0	27	22	3	140	146	49	79	2	3.79
Don Carrithers	R	21	5	3	.625	1	22	12	2	80	77	37	41	1	4.05
Steve Stone	R	23	5	9	.357	0	24	19	2	111	110	55	63	2	4.14
Frank Reberger (RJ)	R	27	3	0	1.000	0	13	7	0	44	37	19	21	0	3.89
Steve Hamilton	L	37	2	2	.500	4	39	0	0	45	29	11	38	0	3.00
Rich Robertson	R	26	2	2	.500	1	23	6	1	61	66	31	32	0	4.57
Jim Barr	R	23	1	1	.500	0	17	0	0	35	33	5	16	0	3.60
Jim Willoughby	R	22	0	1	.000	0	4	1	0	8	13	3	3	0	9.00

LOS ANGELES — 2nd 89-73 .549 1 — WALT ALSTON

NAME	G by Pos	B	AGE	G	AB	R	H	2B	3B	HR	RBI	BB	SO	SB	BA	SA
TOTALS			28	162	5523	663	1469	213	38	95	631	489	755	76	.266	.370
Wes Parker	1B148, OF18	B	28	157	533	69	146	24	1	6	62	63	63	6	.274	.356
Jim Lefebvre	2B102, 3B7	B	28	119	388	40	95	14	2	12	68	39	55	0	.245	.384
Maury Wills	SS144, 3B4	B	38	149	601	73	169	14	3	3	44	40	44	15	.281	.329
Steve Garvey (BH)	3B79	R	22	81	225	27	51	12	1	7	26	21	33	1	.227	.382
Willie Crawford	OF97	L	24	114	342	64	96	16	6	9	40	28	49	5	.281	.442
Willie Davis	OF157	L	31	158	641	84	198	33	10	10	74	23	47	20	.309	.438
Dick Allen	OF60, 3B67, 1B28	R	29	155	549	82	162	24	1	23	90	93	113	8	.295	.468
Duke Sims	C74	L	30	90	230	23	63	7	2	6	33	39	40	0	.274	.400
Bill Buckner	OF86, 1B11	L	21	108	358	37	99	15	1	5	41	11	18	4	.277	.366
Bobby Valentine	SS37, 3B23, 2B21, OF11, 1B2	R	21	101	281	32	70	12	1	2	25	15	20	5	.249	.310
Manny Mota	OF80	R	33	91	269	24	84	13	5	0	34	20	20	4	.312	.398
Bill Russell	2B41, OF40, SS6	R	22	91	211	29	48	7	4	2	15	11	39	6	.227	.327
Tom Haller	C67	L	34	84	202	23	54	5	0	5	32	25	30	1	.267	.366
Billy Grabarkewitz (AJ)	2B13, 3B10, SS1	R	25	44	71	9	16	5	0	0	6	19	16	1	.225	.296
Bill Sudakis (KJ)	C19, 3B3, 1B1, OF1	B	25	41	83	10	16	3	0	2	7	12	12	0	.193	.337
Joe Ferguson	C35	R	24	36	102	13	22	3	0	2	7	12	15	1	.216	.304

Bobby Darwin 28 R 5-20, Von Joshua 23 L 0-7, Tom Paciorek 24 R 1-2, Ron Cey 23 R 0-2

NAME	T	AGE	W	L	PCT	SV	G	GS	CG	IP	H	BB	SO	SHO	ERA
TOTALS		28	89	73	.549	33	162	162	48	1450	1363	399	853	18	3.23
Al Downing	L	30	20	9	.690	0	37	36	12	262	245	84	136	5	2.68
Don Sutton	R	26	17	12	.586	0	38	37	12	265	231	55	194	4	2.55
Claude Osteen	L	31	14	11	.560	0	38	38	11	259	262	63	109	4	3.51
Bill Singer	R	27	10	17	.370	0	31	31	8	203	195	71	144	1	4.17
Pete Mikkelsen	R	31	8	6	.615	5	41	0	0	74	67	17	46	0	3.65
Jim Brewer	L	33	6	5	.545	22	55	0	0	81	55	24	66	0	1.89
Doyle Alexander	R	20	6	6	.500	0	17	12	4	92	105	18	30	0	3.82
Jose Pena	R	28	2	1	.667	0	10	3	0	43	32	18	44	0	3.56
Sandy Vance	R	24	2	1	.667	0	10	3	0	26	38	9	11	0	6.92
Bob O'Brien	R	22	2	1	.500	0	14	4	1	42	42	13	15	1	3.00
Joe Moeller	R	28	2	4	.333	1	28	1	0	66	72	12	32	0	3.82
Mike Strahler	R	24	0	0	—	0	13	0	0	13	8	7	0	0	2.77
Charlie Hough	R	23	0	0	—	0	4	3	0	4	4	1	5	0	4.50
2 Hoyt Wilhelm	R	48	0	1	.000	0	3	0	0	4	6	4	15	0	1.00

ATLANTA — 3rd 82-80 .506 8 — LUM HARRIS

NAME	G by Pos	B	AGE	G	AB	R	H	2B	3B	HR	RBI	BB	SO	SB	BA	SA
TOTALS			27	162	5575	643	1434	192	30	153	597	434	747	57	.257	.385
Hank Aaron	1B71, OF60	R	37	139	495	95	162	22	3	47	118	71	58	1	.327	.669
Felix Millan	2B141	R	27	143	577	65	167	20	8	2	45	37	22	11	.289	.362
Marty Perez	SS126, 2B1	R	25	130	410	28	93	15	3	4	32	25	44	1	.227	.307
Darrell Evans	3B72, OF3	B	24	89	260	42	63	11	1	12	38	39	54	2	.242	.431
Mike Lum	OF125, 1B1	L	25	145	454	56	122	14	1	13	55	47	43	0	.269	.390
Sonny Jackson	OF145	L	26	149	547	58	141	20	5	2	25	35	45	7	.258	.324
Ralph Garr	OF153	L	25	154	639	101	219	24	6	9	44	30	68	30	.343	.441
Earl Williams	C72, 3B42, 1B31	R	22	145	497	64	129	14	1	33	87	42	80	0	.260	.491
Hal King	C60	R	27	86	198	14	41	9	0	9	19	29	43	0	.207	.328
Gil Garrido	SS32, 3B28, 2B18	R	30	79	125	8	27	3	0	0	12	15	12	0	.216	.240
Orlando Cepeda (KJ)	1B63	R	33	71	250	31	69	10	1	14	44	22	29	1	.276	.492
Zoilo Versalles	3B30, SS24, 2B1	R	31	66	194	21	37	11	0	5	22	11	40	2	.191	.325
Bob Didier	C50	B	22	51	155	9	34	4	1	0	6	6	11	0	.219	.258
Clete Boyer	3B25, SS1	R	34	30	98	10	24	4	1	0	6	9	8	1	.245	.439
Dusty Baker	OF18	R	22	29	62	4	14	2	0	2	5	4	14	0	.226	.355
Oscar Brown	OF15	R	25	27	43	4	9	4	0	0	5	3	6	0	.209	.302
Tommie Aaron	1B11, 3B7	R	31	25	53	4	12	2	0	0	5	5	6	0	.226	.264
Marv Staehle	2B7, 3B1	L	29	22	36	5	4	0	0	0	1	4	5	0	.111	.111
Jim Breazeale	1B4	L	21	11	14	1	1	0	0	0	1	0	4	0	.190	.333

Leo Foster 20 R 0-10, 2 Tony LaRussa 26 R 2-7, Rico Carty (KJ) 31

NAME	T	AGE	W	L	PCT	SV	G	GS	CG	IP	H	BB	SO	SHO	ERA
TOTALS		28	82	80	.506	31	162	162	40	1475	1529	485	823	11	3.75
Phil Niekro	R	32	15	14	.517	2	42	36	18	269	248	70	173	4	2.98
Ron Reed	R	28	13	14	.481	0	32	32	8	222	221	54	129	1	3.73
Cecil Upshaw	R	28	11	6	.647	17	49	0	0	82	95	28	56	0	3.51
Tom Kelley	R	27	9	5	.643	0	28	20	5	143	140	69	68	0	2.96
Jim Nash	R	26	9	7	.563	2	32	19	2	133	166	50	65	0	4.94
George Stone	L	24	6	8	.429	0	27	24	3	173	186	35	110	2	3.59
Pat Jarvis	R	30	6	14	.300	1	35	23	3	162	162	51	68	3	4.11
Mike McQueen (SA)	L	20	4	1	.800	1	7	3	0	56	47	23	38	0	3.54
Bob Priddy	R	31	4	9	.308	1	40	0	0	64	71	44	36	0	4.22
Steve Barber	L	33	4	5	.750	2	39	5	0	75	92	25	40	0	4.80
Tom House	L	24	1	0	1.000	0	11	1	0	21	20	3	11	0	3.00
Gary Neibauer	R	26	1	0	1.000	0	21	1	0	29	14	16	9	0	4.40
1 Hoyt Wilhelm	R	48	0	0	—	0	3	0	0	2	3	1	6	0	18.00
Ron Herbel	R	33	0	0	.000	1	25	0	0	52	61	23	22	0	5.19

CINCINNATI 4th (tie) 79-83 .488 11 — SPARKY ANDERSON

NAME	G by Pos	B	AGE	G	AB	R	H	2B	3B	HR	RBI	BB	SO	SB	BA	SA
TOTALS			26	162	5414	586	1306	203	28	138	542	438	907	59	.241	.366
Lee May	1B143	R	28	147	553	85	154	17	3	39	98	42	135	3	.278	.532
Tommy Helms	2B149	R	30	150	547	40	141	26	4	3	52	26	33	3	.258	.325
Dave Concepcion	SS112, 2B10, 3B7, OF5	R	23	130	327	24	67	4	1	20	18	51	9	.205	.251
Tony Perez	3B148, 1B44	R	29	158	609	72	164	22	3	25	91	51	120	4	.269	.438
Pete Rose	OF158	B	30	160	632	86	192	27	4	13	44	68	50	13	.304	.421
2 George Foster	OF102	R	22	104	368	39	86	18	4	10	50	23	93	7	.234	.386
Bernie Carbo	OF58	L	23	106	310	33	68	20	1	5	20	54	56	2	.219	.339
Johnny Bench	C141, 1B12, OF12, 3B3	R	23	149	562	80	134	19	2	27	61	49	83	2	.238	.423
Woody Woodward	SS85, 3B63, 2B9	R	28	136	273	22	66	9	1	0	18	27	28	4	.242	.282
Hal McRae	OF91	R	25	99	337	39	89	24	2	9	34	11	35	3	.264	.427
Jimmy Stewart	OF19, 3B9, 2B6	B	32	80	82	7	19	2	2	0	9	9	12	3	.232	.305
2 Buddy Bradford	OF66	R	26	79	100	17	20	3	0	2	12	14	23	4	.200	.290
Ty Cline	OF28, 1B2	L	32	69	97	12	19	1	0	1	8	18	16	2	.196	.206
Pat Corrales	C39	R	30	40	94	6	17	2	0	0	6	6	17	0	.181	.202
2 Al Ferrara	OF5	R	31	32	33	2	6	0	0	1	5	3	10	0	.182	.273
Willie Smith	1B10	L	32	31	55	3	9	2	0	1	4	3	9	0	.164	.255
1 Frank Duffy	SS10	R	24	13	16	0	3	1	0	0	1	1	2	0	.188	.250
Darrel Chaney	SS7, 2B1, 3B1	B	23	10	24	2	3	0	0	0	1	1	3	0	.125	.125

Bill Plummer 24 R 0-19, 1 Angel Bravo 28 L 1-5, Bobby Tolan (FJ) 25

NAME	T	AGE	W	L	PCT	SV	G	GS	CG	IP	H	BB	SO	SHO	ERA
		26	79	83	.488	38	162	162	27	1444	1298	501	750	11	3.35
Don Gullett	L	20	16	6	.727	0	35	31	4	218	196	64	107	3	2.64
Gary Nolan	R	23	12	15	.444	0	35	35	9	245	208	59	146	0	3.16
Clay Carroll	R	30	10	4	.714	15	61	0	0	94	78	42	64	0	2.49
Ross Grimsley	R	21	10	7	.588	0	26	26	6	161	151	43	67	3	3.58
Jim McGlothlin	R	27	8	12	.400	0	30	26	6	171	151	47	93	0	3.21
Wayne Granger	R	27	7	6	.538	11	70	0	0	100	94	28	51	0	3.33
Joe Gibbon	L	36	5	6	.455	11	50	0	0	64	54	32	34	0	2.95
Wayne Simpson	R	22	4	7	.364	0	22	21	1	117	106	77	61	0	4.77
Tony Cloninger	R	30	3	6	.333	0	28	8	1	97	79	49	51	1	3.90
Milt Wilcox	R	21	2	2	.500	1	18	3	0	43	43	17	21	0	3.35
Ed Sprague	R	25	1	0	1.000	7	0	0	0	11	8	1	7	0	0.00
Jim Merritt	R	27	1	11	.083	0	28	11	0	107	115	31	38	0	4.37
Pedro Borbon	R	24	0	0	—	0	4	3	1	4	6	4	0	0	4.50
Steve Blateric	R	27	0	0		0	2	0	0	5	3	1	6	0	12.00
Greg Garrett	L	24	0	1	.000	0	2	1	0	9	7	10	2	0	1.00

HOUSTON 4th (tie) 79-83 .488 11 — HARRY WALKER

NAME	G by Pos	B	AGE	G	AB	R	H	2B	3B	HR	RBI	BB	SO	SB	BA	SA
TOTALS			27	162	5492	585	1319	230	52	71	547	478	888	101	.240	.340
Denis Menke	1B101, 3B32, SS17, 2B5	R	30	146	475	57	117	26	1	1	43	59	48	4	.246	.320
Joe Morgan	2B157	L	27	160	583	87	149	27	11	13	56	88	52	40	.256	.407
Roger Metzger	SS148	B	23	150	562	64	132	14	11	0	26	44	50	15	.235	.299
Doug Rader	3B135	R	26	135	484	51	118	21	4	12	56	40	112	5	.244	.378
Jim Wynn	OF116	R	29	123	404	38	82	16	0	7	45	55	82	6	.203	.295
Cesar Cedeno	OF157, 1B2	R	20	161	611	85	161	40	6	10	81	25	102	20	.264	.398
Jesus Alou	OF109	R	29	122	433	41	121	21	4	2	40	13	17	3	.279	.360
Johnny Edwards (HJ)	C104	L	33	106	317	30	74	13	4	1	23	26	38	1	.233	.309
Bob Watson	OF87, 1B45	R	25	129	468	49	135	17	3	9	67	41	56	0	.288	.395
Cesar Geronimo	OF64	L	23	94	82	13	18	2	1	1	6	5	31	2	.220	.329
Jack Hiatt (BZ)	C65, 1B1	R	28	69	174	16	48	8	1	1	16	35	39	0	.276	.351
Rich Chiles	OF27	L	21	67	119	12	27	5	1	2	15	6	20	1	.227	.336
John Mayberry	1B37	L	22	46	137	16	25	0	1	7	14	13	32	0	.182	.350
Norm Miller (BW)	OF20, C1	L	25	74	74	5	19	5	0	2	10	5	13	0	.257	.405
Marty Martinez	2B9, SS7, 1B4, 3B3	B	29	32	62	4	16	3	1	0	4	3	6	1	.258	.339
Larry Howard	C22	R	26	24	64	6	15	3	0	2	14	3	17	0	.234	.375
Ray Busse	SS5, 3B3	R	22	10	34	2	5	1	0	0	2	1	13	0	.147	.235

Derrel Thomas 20 B 0-5, Jay Schlueter 21 R 1-3

NAME	T	AGE	W	L	PCT	SV	G	GS	CG	IP	H	BB	SO	SHO	ERA
		27	79	83	.488	25	162	162	43	1471	1318	475	914	10	3.13
Don Wilson	R	26	16	10	.615	0	35	34	18	268	195	79	180	3	2.45
Larry Dierker (EJ)	R	24	12	6	.667	0	24	24	6	159	150	33	91	2	2.72
Jim Ray	R	26	10	4	.714	3	47	1	0	98	72	31	46	0	2.11
Jack Billingham	R	28	10	16	.385	0	33	24	6	228	205	68	139	3	3.39
Wade Blasingame	L	27	9	11	.450	0	30	28	2	158	177	45	93	0	4.61
Ken Forsch	R	24	8	8	.500	0	33	23	7	188	162	53	131	2	2.54
George Culver	R	27	5	8	.385	7	59	0	0	95	89	38	57	0	2.65
Fred Gladding	R	35	4	4	.444	12	48	0	0	51	51	22	17	0	2.12
J.R. Richard	R	21	2	1	.667	0	4	4	1	21	17	16	29	0	3.43
Scipio Spinks	R	23	1	0	1.000	0	5	3	1	29	22	13	26	0	3.72
Bill Greif	R	21	1	1	.500	0	7	3	0	16	18	8	14	0	5.06
Buddy Harris	R	22	1	1	.500	0	20	0	0	31	33	16	21	0	6.39
Skip Guinn	L	26	0	0		1	0	0	0	3	3	3	3	0	6.00
Larry Yount	R	21	0	0		0	1	0	0	0	0	0	0	0	∞
Denny Lemaster	L	32	0	2	.000	0	42	0	0	60	59	22	28	0	3.45
Ron Cook (SA)	R	23	0	4	.000	0	26	0	0	26	23	8	10	0	4.85
Tom Griffin	R	23	0	6	.000	0	10	6	0	38	44	20	29	0	4.74

SAN DIEGO 6th 61-100 .379 28.5 — PRESTON GOMEZ

NAME	G by Pos	B	AGE	G	AB	R	H	2B	3B	HR	RBI	BB	SO	SB	BA	SA
TOTALS			27	161	5366	486	1250	184	31	96	447	438	966	70	.233	.332
Nate Colbert	1B153	R	25	156	565	81	149	25	3	27	84	63	119	5	.264	.462
Don Mason	2B90, 3B3	R	26	113	344	43	73	12	1	2	11	27	35	6	.212	.270
Enzo Hernandez	SS143	R	22	143	549	58	122	9	3	0	12	34	66	21	.222	.250
Ed Spiezio (KJ)	3B91, OF1	R	29	97	308	16	71	10	1	7	36	22	50	6	.231	.338
Ollie Brown	OF134	R	27	145	484	36	132	16	0	9	55	52	74	3	.273	.362
Cito Gaston	OF133	R	27	141	518	57	118	13	9	1	61	24	121	1	.228	.386
Larry Stahl	OF75, 1B7	L	30	114	308	27	78	13	4	8	36	59	59	4	.253	.399
Bob Barton	C119	R	29	121	376	23	94	17	2	5	23	35	49	0	.250	.346
D. Campbell (LJ)	2B69,3B40,SS4,1B2,OF2	R	29	108	365	38	83	14	2	7	29	37	75	9	.227	.334
Ivan Murrell	OF72	R	28	103	255	23	60	6	3	7	24	7	60	5	.235	.365
2 Leron Lee	OF68	L	23	79	256	29	70	20	2	4	21	18	45	4	.273	.414
2 Garry Jestadt	3B49, 2B23, SS1	R	24	75	189	17	55	13	0	1	13	11	24	1	.291	.360
2 Angel Bravo	OF9	L	28	52	58	6	9	2	0	0	6	8	12	0	.155	.190
Fred Kendall	C39, 1B1, 3B1	R	22	49	111	2	19	1	0	1	7	16	1	0	.171	.207
Tommy Dean	SS28, 3B11, 2B1	R	25	41	70	2	8	0	0	0	1	4	13	1	.114	.114
1 Chris Cannizzaro	C19	R	33	21	63	2	12	1	0	1	8	11	10	0	.190	.254
Johnnie Jeter	OF17	R	26	18	75	8	24	4	0	1	3	2	16	2	.320	.413
1 Al Ferrara	OF2	R	31	17	17	0	2	1	0	0	2	5	5	0	.118	.176
Rod Gaspar	OF2	R	25	16	17	1	2	0	0	0	0	3	3	0	.118	.118
Jerry Morales	OF7	R	22	12	17	1	2	0	0	0	1	2	1	1	.118	.118
1 Ramon Webster		L	28	10	8	0	1	0	0	0	0	0	1	0	.125	.125
Ron Slocum	3B6	R	25	7	18	1	0	0	0	0	0	0	8	0	.000	.000
Dave Robinson		B	25	7	6	0	0	0	0	0	0	0	3	0	.000	.000
Mike Ivie	C6	R	18	6	17	0	8	0	0	0	3	1	1	0	.471	.471

NAME	T	AGE	W	L	PCT	SV	G	GS	CG	IP	H	BB	SO	SHO	ERA
		27	61	100	.379	17	161	161	47	1438	1351	559	923	10	3.22
Clay Kirby	R	23	15	13	.536	0	38	36	13	267	213	103	231	2	2.83
Dave Roberts	R	26	14	17	.452	0	37	34	14	270	238	61	135	2	2.10
2 Steve Arlin	R	25	9	19	.321	0	36	34	10	228	211	103	156	4	3.47
2 Bob Miller	R	32	3	7	.300	2	38	0	0	64	53	26	36	0	1.41
Ed Acosta	R	27	3	3	.500	0	8	6	3	46	43	7	16	1	2.74
Tom Phoebus	R	29	3	11	.214	0	29	21	2	133	144	64	80	0	4.47
2 Fred Norman	L	28	3	12	.200	0	20	18	5	127	114	56	77	0	3.33
Dick Kelley	L	31	2	3	.400	2	48	1	0	60	52	23	42	0	3.45
Al Severinsen	R	26	2	5	.286	8	59	0	0	70	77	30	31	0	3.47
Mike Caldwell	R	22	1	0	1.000	0	7	0	0	7	4	3	5	0	0.00
Gary Ross	R	23	1	3	.250	0	19	1	0	44	45	17	13	0	3.00
Danny Coombs	L	29	1	6	.143	0	19	7	0	58	81	25	37	0	6.21
Mike Corkins	R	25	0	0	—	0	8	0	0	13	14	6	16	0	3.46
Jay Franklin	R	18	0	1	.000	0	3	1	0	6	4	5	3	0	6.00
1 Al Santorini	R	23	0	2	.000	0	18	3	0	38	43	11	21	0	3.79
Bill Laxton	L	23	0	2	.000	0	8	3	0	28	32	26	23	0	6.75

WORLD SERIES — PITTSBURGH(NL) 4 BALTIMORE (AL) 3

LINE SCORES

TEAM	1 2 3	4 5 6	7 8 9	10 11 12	R	H	E

Game 1 October 9 at Baltimore

PIT	0 3 0	0 0 0	0 0 0	·	3	3	0
BAL(AL)	0 1 3	0 1 0	0 0 x	·	5	10	3

Ellis, Moose (3), Miller (7)   McNally

Game 2 October 11 at Baltimore

PIT	0 0 0	0 0 0	0 3 0		3	8	1
BAL	0 1 0	3 6 1	0 0 x		11	14	1

B. Johnson, Kison (4), Moose (4), Veale (5), Miller (6), Giusti (8)   Palmer, Hall (9)

Game 3 October 12 at Pittsburgh

BAL	0 0 0	0 0 0	1 0 0		1	3	3
PIT	1 0 0	0 0 1	3 0 x		5	7	0

Cuellar, Dukes (7), Watt (8)   Blass

Game 4 October 13 at Pittsburgh

BAL	3 0 0	0 0 0	0 0 0		3	4	1
PIT	2 0 1	0 0 0	1 0 x		4	14	0

Dobson, Jackson (6), Watt (7), Richert (8)   Walker, Kison (1), Giusti (8)

Game 5 October 14 at Pittsburgh

BAL	0 0 0	0 0 0	0 0 0		0	2	1
PIT	0 2 1	0 1 0	0 0 x		4	9	0

McNally, Leonhard (5), Dukes (6)   Briles

Game 6 October 16 at Baltimore

PIT	0 1 1	0 0 0	0 0 0	0	2	9	1
BAL	0 0 0	1 0 0	1 0 0	1	3	8	0

Moose, B. Johnson (6), Giusti (7), Miller (10)   Palmer, Dobson (10), McNally (10)

Game 7 October 17 at Baltimore

PIT	0 0 0	1 0 0	0 1 0		2	6	1
BAL	0 0 0	0 0 0	0 1 0		1	4	0

Blass   Cuellar, Dobson (9), McNally (9)

COMPOSITE BATTING

NAME	POS	G	AB	R	H	2B	3B	HR	RBI	BA
Pittsburgh (NL)										
Totals		7	238	23	56	9	2	5	21	.235
Cash	2B	7	30	2	4	1	0	0	0	.133
Clemente	OF	7	29	3	12	2	1	2	4	.414
Sanguillen	C	7	29	3	11	0	0	0	1	.379
Robertson	1B	7	25	4	6	0	0	2	5	.240
Stargell	OF	7	24	3	5	0	0	0	1	.208
Oliver	OF	5	19	1	4	2	0	0	2	.211
Hernandez	SS	7	18	2	4	0	0	0	0	.222
Pagan	3B	4	15	0	4	2	0	0	2	.267
Hebner	3B	3	12	2	2	0	0	0	1	.167
Clines	OF	3	11	2	1	0	0	0	0	.091
Blass	P	2	4	0	1	0	0	0	0	.250
Davalillo	OF	3	3	1	1	0	0	0	0	.333
B. Johnson	P	2	3	0	0	0	0	0	0	.000
May	PH	2	2	0	1	0	0	0	0	.500
Briles	P	1	2	0	1	0	0	0	0	.500
Alley	SS	2	2	0	0	0	0	0	0	.000
Kison	P	2	2	0	0	0	0	0	0	.000
Moose	P	3	2	0	0	0	0	0	0	.000
Mazeroski	PH	1	1	0	0	0	0	0	0	.000
Sands	PH	1	1	0	0	0	0	0	0	.000
Ellis	P	1	1	0	0	0	0	0	0	.000

Giusti P 0-0, Miller P 0-0, Veale P 0-0, Walker P 0-0

NAME	POS	G	AB	R	H	2B	3B	HR	RBI	BA
Baltimore (AL)										
Totals		7	219	24	45	3		5	22	.205
Rettenmund	OF	7	27	3	5	0	0	0	4	.185
D. Johnson	2B	7	27	1	4	0	0	0	3	.148
Powell	1B	7	27	3	3	0	0	0	0	.111
F. Robinson	OF	7	25	5	7	0	0	2	2	.280
Buford	OF	6	23	3	6	1	0	2	4	.261
B. Robinson	3B	7	22	2	7	0	0	0	5	.318
Belanger	SS	7	21	4	5	0	0	0	0	.238
Hendricks	C	6	19	3	5	1	0	1	1	.263
Blair	OF	4	9	2	3	0	0	0	0	.333
Shopay	PH	5	4	0	0	0	0	0	0	.000
McNally	P	2	4	0	0	0	0	0	0	.000
Palmer	P	2	4	0	0	0	0	0	0	.000
Cuellar	P	2	3	0	0	0	0	0	0	.000
Etchebarren	C	2	2	0	0	0	0	0	0	.000
Dobson	P	3	2	0	0	0	0	0	0	.000
Dukes	P	2	1	0	0	0	0	0	0	.000
Watt	P	2	0	0	0	0	0	0	0	—

Hall P 0-0, Jackson P 0-0, Leonhard P 0-0, Richert P 0-0

COMPOSITE PITCHING

NAME	G	IP	H	BB	SO	W	L	SV	ERA
Pittsburgh (NL)									
Totals	7	61.2	45	20	35	4	3	1	3.50
Blass	2	18	7	4	13	2	0	0	1.00
Moose	3	9.2	12	2	7	0	0	0	6.52
Briles	1	9	2	2	1	1	0	0	0.00
Kison	2	6.1	1	3	1	1	0	0	0.00
Giusti	3	5.1	3	2	4	0	0	1	0.00
B. Johnson	2	5	5	3	3	0	1	0	9.00
Miller	3	4.2	7	1	2	0	0	0	3.86
Ellis	1	2.1	4	1	1	0	1	0	15.43
Veale	1	0.2	1	3	1	0	0	0	13.50
Walker	1	0.2	3	1	0	0	0	0	40.50
Baltimore (AL)									
Totals	7	61	56	26	47	3	4	1	2.66
Palmer	2	17	15	9	15	1	0	0	2.65
Cuellar	2	14	11	6	10	0	2	0	3.86
McNally	4	13.2	10	5	12	2	1	0	1.98
Dobson	3	6.2	13	4	6	0	0	0	4.05
Dukes	2	4	2	1	6	0	0	0	0.00
Watt	2	2.1	4	0	1	0	1	1	3.86
Hall	1	1	1	0	0	0	0	0	0.00
Leonhard	1	1	1	0	0	0	0	0	0.00
Jackson	1	0.2	3	1	0	0	0	0	0.00
Richert	1	0.2	0	0	0	0	0	0	0.00

1972 Tragedy, Protest, and Finley's Moustache Brigade

Near the final day of the regular season, Pittsburgh's Roberto Clemente got his 3,000th hit. On the final day of the year, he was flying with supplies en route from his native Puerto Rico to lead a mercy mission for the earthquake victims of Managua, Nicaragua. The plane, considered unsafe, never arrived. The superstar's death ended a year which had begun with another tragedy—the death of New York Mets' manager Gil Hodges, who died of a heart attack in spring training. The news of the tragedy came at a time when the ballplayers from spring training camps all around the country walked off the diamond in protest of several issues—the main one being the conditions of their pension plan. As major league players' representative Marvin Miller negotiated with the owners and their representatives, all baseball activity remained frozen. When a settlement was finally reached, 13 days and 86 games were scratched from the regular season. The players, although winning versus the owners, lost when the Supreme Court finally ruled against Curt Flood's 1970 reserve clause lawsuit.

During the season, which was to include big winter trades, the trading of aging superstar Willie Mays to the Mets, and the continuing saga of Denny McLain going from the majors to the minors and the majors again, the moustache became the symbol of success. And no one wore it more stylishly than the Oakland Athletics. With half of A's owner Charley O. Finley's team sporting moustaches, as well as manager Dick Williams, the squad made it to their first pennant since 1931. Even with Vida Blue holding out well into the season and never reaching top form, Oakland outlasted a threat from the surprising Chicago White Sox, while flashing the best pitching staff in the West with Catfish Hunter and Ken Holtzman leading the starters and Rollie Fingers acing the bullpen. Reggie Jackson, Sal Bando, Joe Rudi, and Mike Epstein provided the sock in the lineup, and Bert Campaneris spark-plugged the attack by heisting 52 bases.

In the American League East, the Tigers, Orioles, Red Sox, and Yankees all stayed within a postage stamp of the top into September. But Detroit and Boston—locked in a virtual tie—were the only contenders remaining in the final days of the season. The Tigers finally clinched the crown by knocking off the Red Sox in two of three games before a cheering Detroit crowd. Personalities dominated each of the four squads in the late going: Al Kaline and his hot late season bat, former heart attack victim John Hiller's fine comeback in Detroit, Luis Tiant by his totally unexpected spectacular hurling in Boston, Bobby Murcer's home run bat in New York, and Frank Robinson, who was traded to the Dodgers during the winter and was conspicuous by his absence in Baltimore. In the play-offs, the Tigers bowed to the A's in a thrilling five-game series.

Rod Carew of the Twins became the first American League batting champion not to hit any home runs and Chicago's Dick Allen won the home run and RBI crown and the MVP Award in his first season in the junior circuit. Another A.L. newcomer, Cleveland's Gaylord Perry, edged Detroit's Mickey Lolich and Chicago's Wilbur Wood for the Cy Young Award.

The National League produced no pennant suspense, as Pittsburgh and Cincinnati clearly outclassed their competition. While the Pirates were returning to the Eastern title for the third straight year, Cincinnati was back for Western honors after a one-year interruption on the return to form of MVP Johnny Bench, the hustling of Pete Rose, and the speed of former Houston star Joe Morgan. The individual highlight of the year, though, came from Steve Carlton, the winner of 27 games and the Cy Young Award while playing on a Philadelphia team that wound up with the worst record in the National League. An exciting play-off between the two champions ended with Cincinnati scoring the deciding run in the bottom of the ninth on a wild pitch by Pittsburgh's Bob Moose. Nate Colbert of San Diego had 111 RBI's, knocking in nearly 23 % of his team's runs, an all-time record.

The World Series produced six one-run games. After the A's jumped out to a three-to-one edge in games, the Reds battled back and knotted the count before Oakland walked away victorious in a 3-2 seventh game triumph. The unlikely Series hero was Oakland's Gene Tenace, a second-string catcher during the season who drove in nine runs and tied a Series record with four home runs.

1972 AMERICAN LEAGUE — EAST DIVISION

DETROIT 1st 86-70 .551 — BILLY MARTIN

NAME	G by Pos	B	AGE	G	AB	R	H	2B	3B	HR	RBI	BB	SO	SB	BA	SA
	TOTALS		32	156	5099	558	1206	179	32	122	531	483	793	17	.237	.356
Norm Cash	1B134	L	37	137	440	51	114	16	0	22	61	50	64	0	.259	.445
Dick McAuliffe	2B116, SS3, 3B1	L	32	122	408	47	98	16	3	8	30	59	59	0	.240	.353
Eddie Brinkman	SS156	R	30	156	516	42	105	19	1	6	49	38	51	0	.203	.279
Aurelio Rodriguez	3B153, SS2	R	24	153	601	65	142	23	5	13	56	28	104	2	.236	.356
Jim Northrup	OF127, 1B2	L	32	134	426	40	111	15	2	8	42	38	47	4	.261	.362
Mickey Stanley	OF139	R	29	142	435	45	102	16	6	14	55	29	49	1	.234	.395
Willie Horton	OF98	R	29	108	333	44	77	9	5	11	36	27	47	0	.231	.387
Bill Freehan	C105 1B1	R	30	111	374	51	98	18	2	10	56	48	51	0	.262	.401
Al Kaline (LJ)	OF84, 1B11	R	37	106	278	46	87	11	2	10	32	28	33	1	.313	.475
Gates Brown	OF72	L	33	103	252	33	58	5	0	10	31	26	28	3	.230	.369
Tony Taylor	2B67, 3B8, 1B1	R	36	78	228	33	69	12	4	1	20	14	34	5	.303	.404
Tom Haller	C36	L	35	59	121	7	25	5	2	2	13	15	14	0	.207	.331
Ike Brown	OF22, 1B13, 2B3, SS1, 3B1	R	30	51	84	12	21	3	0	2	10	17	23	1	.250	.357
2 Duke Sims	C25, OF4	L	31	38	98	11	31	4	0	4	19	19	18	0	.316	.480
Paul Jata	1B12, OF10, C1	R	22	32	74	8	17	2	0	0	3	7	14	0	.230	.257
Wayne Comer	OF17	R	28	27	9	1	1	0	0	0	1	0	1	0	.111	.111
2 Frank Howard	1B10, OF1	R	35	14	33	1	8	1	0	1	7	4	8	0	.242	.364
John Knox	2B4	L	23	14	13	1	1	0	0	0	0	1	2	0	.077	.154

1 Dalton Jones 28 L 0-7, Marvin Lane 22 R 0-6, Ike Blessitt 22 R 0-5, John Gamble 24 R 0-3,
Joe Staton 24 L 0-2, Gene Lamont 25 L 0-0

NAME	T	AGE	W	L	PCT	SV	G	GS	CG	IP	H	BB	SO	SHO	ERA
		28	86	70	.551	33	156	156	46	1388	1212	465	952	11	2.96
Mickey Lolich	L	31	22	14	.611	0	41	41	23	327	282	74	250	4	2.50
Joe Coleman	R	25	19	14	.576	0	40	39	9	280	216	110	222	3	2.80
2 Woody Fryman	L	32	10	3	.769	0	16	14	6	114	93	31	72	1	2.05
Chuck Seelbach	R	24	9	8	.529	14	61	3	0	112	96	39	76	0	2.89
Tom Timmermann	R	32	8	10	.444	0	34	25	3	150	121	41	88	2	2.88
Fred Scherman	L	27	7	3	.700	12	57	3	0	94	91	53	53	0	3.64
Bill Slayback	R	24	5	6	.455	0	23	13	3	82	74	25	65	1	3.18
Joe Niekro (PJ)	R	27	3	2	.600	1	18	7	1	47	62	8	24	0	3.83
Jim Foor	L	23	1	0	1.000	0	7	0	0	4	6	6	2	0	13.50
Chris Zachary	R	28	1	1	.500	1	25	1	0	38	27	15	21	0	1.42
John Hiller (IL)	L	29	1	2	.333	3	24	3	1	44	39	13	26	0	2.05
Bob Strampe	R	22	0	0	—	0	7	0	0	5	6	7	4	0	10.80
Bill Gilbreth	L	24	0	0	—	0	2	0	0	5	10	4	2	0	16.20
1 Mike Kilkenny	L	27	0	0	—	0	1	0	0	1	1	0	0	0	9.00
Don Leshnock	R	25	0	0	—	0	1	0	0	1	2	0	2	0	0.00
1 Ron Perranoski	L	36	0	1	.000	0	17	0	0	19	23	8	10	0	7.58
Lerrin LaGrow	R	23	0	1	.000	2	16	0	0	27	22	6	9	0	1.33
Phil Meeler	R	23	0	1	.000	0	7	0	0	8	14	7	4	0	4.50
Fred Holdsworth	R	20	0	1	.000	0	2	2	0	7	13	2	5	0	12.86
Les Cain	L	24	0	3	.000	0	5	5	0	24	18	16	16	0	3.75

BOSTON 2nd 85-70 .548 .5 — EDDIE KASKO

NAME	G by Pos	B	AGE	G	AB	R	H	2B	3B	HR	RBI	BB	SO	SB	BA	SA
	TOTALS		29	155	5208	640	1289	229	34	124	594	522	858	66	.248	.376
Danny Cater	1B90	R	32	92	317	32	75	17	1	8	39	15	33	0	.237	.372
Doug Griffin	2B129	R	25	129	470	43	122	12	1	2	35	45	48	9	.260	.302
Luis Aparicio (BG)	SS109	R	38	110	436	47	112	26	3	3	39	26	28	3	.257	.351
Rico Petrocelli	3B146	R	29	147	521	62	125	15	2	15	75	78	91	0	.240	.363
Reggie Smith	OF129	R	27	131	467	75	126	25	4	21	74	68	63	15	.270	.475
Tommy Harper	OF144	R	31	144	556	92	141	29	2	14	49	67	104	25	.254	.388
Carl Yastrzemski (KJ)	OF83, 1B42	L	32	125	455	70	120	18	2	12	68	67	44	5	.264	.391
Carlton Fisk	C131	R	24	131	457	74	134	28	9	22	61	52	83	5	.293	.538
Ben Oglivie	OF65	L	23	94	253	27	61	10	2	8	30	18	61	1	.241	.391
Rick Miller	OF75	L	24	89	98	13	21	4	1	3	15	11	27	0	.214	.367
John Kennedy	2B32, SS27, 3B11	R	31	71	212	22	52	11	1	2	22	18	40	1	.245	.335
Phil Gagliano	OF12, 3B5, 2B4, 1B2	R	30	52	82	9	21	4	1	0	10	10	13	1	.256	.329
Bob Burda	1B15, OF1	L	33	45	73	4	12	1	0	2	9	8	11	0	.164	.260
Juan Beniquez	SS27	R	22	33	99	10	24	4	1	1	8	7	11	2	.242	.333
Duane Josephson (IL)	1B16, C6	R	30	26	82	11	22	1	0	2	7	4	11	0	.268	.378
Bob Montgomery	C22	R	28	24	77	7	22	1	0	2	3	3	17	0	.286	.377
Dwight Evans	OF17	R	20	18	57	2	15	3	1	1	6	7	13	0	.263	.404
2 Andy Kosco	OF12	R	30	17	47	5	10	2	1	3	6	2	9	0	.213	.489

Cecil Cooper 22 L 0-5, Bob Gallagher 23 L 0-5, Vic Correll 26 R 2-4

NAME	T	AGE	W	L	PCT	SV	G	GS	CG	IP	H	BB	SO	SHO	ERA
		29	85	70	.548	25	155	155	48	1383	1309	512	918	20	3.47
Marty Pattin	R	29	17	13	.567	0	38	35	13	253	232	65	168	4	3.24
Luis Tiant	R	31	15	6	.714	3	43	19	12	179	128	65	123	6	1.91
Sonny Siebert	R	35	12	12	.500	0	32	30	7	196	204	59	123	3	3.80
John Curtis	L	24	11	8	.579	0	26	21	8	154	161	50	106	3	3.74
Lynn McGlothen	R	22	8	7	.533	0	22	22	4	145	135	59	112	1	3.41
Bill Lee	L	25	7	4	.636	5	47	0	0	84	75	32	43	0	3.21
Ray Culp (SJ)	R	30	5	8	.385	0	16	16	4	105	104	53	52	1	4.46
Don Newhauser	R	24	4	2	.667	4	31	0	0	37	30	25	27	0	2.43
Gary Peters	L	35	3	3	.500	1	33	4	0	85	91	38	67	0	4.34
2 Bob Veale	L	36	2	0	1.000	2	6	0	0	8	2	3	10	0	0.00
Lew Krausse	R	29	1	3	.250	1	24	7	0	61	74	28	35	0	6.34
Roger Moret	L	22	0	0	—	0	3	0	0	5	5	6	4	0	3.60
Stan Williams	R	35	0	0	—	0	3	0	0	4	5	1	3	0	6.75
Mike Nagy	R	24	0	0	—	0	1	0	0	3	2	0	2	0	9.00
Bobby Bolin	R	33	0	1	.000	5	21	0	0	31	24	11	27	0	2.90
Mike Garman	R	22	0	1	.000	0	3	1	0	3	4	2	1	0	12.00
Ken Tatum (LJ)	R	28	0	2	.000	4	29	0	0	29	32	15	15	0	3.10

BALTIMORE 3rd 80-74 .519 5 — EARL WEAVER

NAME	G by Pos	B	AGE	G	AB	R	H	2B	3B	HR	RBI	BB	SO	SB	BA	SA
	TOTALS		28	154	5028	519	1153	193	29	100	483	507	935	78	.229	.339
Boog Powell	1B133	L	30	140	465	53	117	20	1	21	81	65	92	4	.252	.434
Dave Johnson	2B116	R	29	118	376	31	83	22	3	5	32	52	68	1	.221	.335
Mark Belanger	SS105	R	28	113	285	36	53	9	1	2	16	18	53	6	.186	.246
Brooks Robinson	3B152	R	35	153	556	48	139	23	2	8	64	43	45	1	.250	.342
Merv Rettenmund	OF98	R	29	102	301	40	70	10	2	6	21	41	37	6	.233	.339
Paul Blair	OF139	R	28	142	477	47	111	20	8	8	49	25	78	7	.233	.358
Don Buford	OF105	B	35	125	408	46	84	6	2	5	22	69	83	8	.206	.267
Johnny Oates	C82	L	26	85	253	20	66	12	1	4	21	28	31	5	.261	.364
Bobby Grich	SS81, 2B45, 1B16, 3B8	R	23	133	460	66	128	21	3	12	50	53	96	13	.278	.415
Don Baylor	OF84, 1B9	R	23	102	320	33	81	13	3	11	38	29	50	24	.253	.416
Terry Crowley	OF68, 1B15	L	25	97	247	30	57	10	0	11	39	32	32	0	.231	.405
Andy Etchebarren	C70	R	29	71	188	13	38	6	1	2	21	17	43	0	.202	.277
Tom Shopay	OF3	L	27	49	40	3	9	0	0	2	5	5	12	0	.225	.325
1 Ellie Hendricks	C28	L	31	33	84	6	13	4	0	0	4	10	8	0	.155	.202
2 Tommy Davis	OF18, 1B3	R	33	26	82	9	21	3	0	0	6	6	18	2	.256	.293
Chico Salmon	1B2, 3B1	R	31	21	16	1	1	0	0	0	0	0	1	0	.063	.125
Rich Coggins	OF13	L	21	16	39	5	13	4	0	0	1	1	6	1	.333	.436

Al Bumbry 25 L 4-11, Tom Matchick 28 L 2-9, Sergio Robles 26 R 1-5, Enos Cabell 22 R 0-5

NAME	T	AGE	W	L	PCT	SV	G	GS	CG	IP	H	BB	SO	SHO	ERA
		28	80	74	.519	21	154	154	62	1372	1116	395	788	20	2.53
Jim Palmer	R	26	21	10	.677	0	36	36	18	274	219	70	184	3	2.07
Mike Cuellar	L	35	18	12	.600	0	35	35	17	248	197	71	132	4	2.58
Pat Dobson	R	30	16	18	.471	0	38	36	13	268	220	69	161	3	2.65
Dave McNally	R	29	13	17	.433	0	36	36	12	241	220	68	120	6	2.95
Doyle Alexander	R	21	6	8	.429	2	35	9	2	106	78	30	49	2	2.45
Roric Harrison	R	25	3	4	.429	4	39	2	0	94	68	34	62	0	2.30
Eddie Watt	R	31	3	4	.400	7	38	0	0	46	30	20	23	0	2.15
Grant Jackson	L	29	1	1	.500	8	32	0	0	39	32	9	34	0	2.63
Dave Leonhard	R	31	0	0	—	0	14	0	0	21	20	12	7	0	4.50
Bob Reynolds	R	25	0	0	—	0	8	1	0	10	8	7	5	0	1.80
Mickey Scott	L	24	0	0	—	0	15	0	0	23	23	5	11	0	2.74

NEW YORK   4th 79-76   .510   6.5   RALPH HOUK

NAME	G by Pos	B	AGE	G	AB	R	H	2B	3B	HR	RBI	BB	SO	SB	BA	SA
TOTALS			29	155	5168	557	1288	201	24	103	526	491	689	71	.249	.357
Ron Blomberg	1B95	L	23	107	299	36	80	22	1	14	49	38	26	0	.268	.488
Horace Clarke	2B143	B	32	147	547	65	132	20	2	3	37	56	44	10	.241	.302
Gene Michael	SS121	R	34	126	391	29	91	7	4	1	32	32	45	4	.233	.279
Celerino Sanchez	3B68	R	28	71	250	18	62	9	0	0	22	12	30	0	.248	.304
Johnny Callison	OF74	L	33	92	275	28	71	10	0	9	34	18	34	3	.258	.393
Bobby Murcer	OF151	R	26	153	585	102	171	30	7	33	96	63	67	11	.292	.537
Roy White	OF155	B	28	155	556	76	150	29	0	10	54	99	59	23	.270	.376
Thurman Munson	C132	R	25	140	511	54	143	16	3	7	46	47	58	6	.280	.364
Felipe Alou	1B95, OF15	R	37	120	324	33	90	18	1	6	37	22	27	1	.278	.395
Bernie Allen	3B44, 2B20	L	33	84	220	26	50	9	0	9	21	23	42	0	.227	.391
Rusty Torres	OF62	B	23	80	199	15	42	7	0	3	13	18	44	0	.211	.291
Ron Swoboda	OF35, 1B2	R	28	63	113	9	28	8	0	1	12	17	29	0	.248	.345
Hal Lanier	3B47, SS9, 2B3	R	29	60	103	5	22	3	0	0	6	2	13	1	.214	.243
Johnny Ellis	C25, 1B8	R	23	52	136	13	40	5	1	5	25	8	22	0	.294	.456
Jerry Kenney	SS45, 3B1	R	27	50	119	16	25	2	0	0	7	16	13	3	.210	.227
Rich McKinney	3B33	R	25	37	121	10	26	2	0	1	7	7	13	1	.215	.256
Charlie Spikes	OF9	R	21	14	34	2	5	1	0	0	3	1	13	0	.147	.176
Frank Tepedino		L	24	8	8	0	0	0	0	0	0	0	1	0	.000	.000

NAME	T	AGE	W	L	PCT	SV	G	GS	CG	IP	H	BB	SO	SHO	ERA
TOTALS		29	79	76	.510	39	155	155	35	1373	1306	419	625	19	3.05
Fritz Peterson	R	30	17	15	.531	0	35	35	12	250	270	44	100	3	3.24
Steve Kline	R	24	16	9	.640	0	32	32	11	236	210	44	58	4	2.40
Mel Stottlemyre	R	30	14	18	.438	0	36	36	9	260	250	85	110	7	3.22
Mike Kekich	L	27	10	13	.435	0	29	28	2	175	172	76	78	0	3.70
Sparky Lyle	L	27	9	5	.643	35	59	0	0	108	84	29	75	0	1.92
Rob Gardner	L	27	8	5	.615	0	20	14	1	97	91	28	58	0	3.06
Lindy McDaniel	R	36	3	1	.750	0	37	0	0	68	54	25	47	0	2.25
1 Rich Hinton	L	25	1	0	1.000	0	7	1	0	17	20	8	13	0	4.76
Fred Beene	R	29	1	3	.250	3	29	1	0	58	55	24	37	0	2.33
Jack Aker	R	31	0	0	—	0	4	0	0	6	5	3	1	0	3.00
Steve Blateric	R	28	0	0	—		1	0	0	4	2	2	4	0	0.00
Alan Closter	L	29	0	0	—	0	2	1	0	4	2	4	2	0	13.50
Doc Medich	R	23	0	0	—	0	2								∞
1 Jim Roland	L	29	0	1	.000	0	16	0	0	25	27	16	13	0	5.04
2 Wade Blasingame	L	28	0	1	.000	0	12	1	0	17	14	11	7	0	4.24
2 Casey Cox	R	30	0	1	.000	0	5	1	0	12	13	3	4	0	4.50
Larry Gowell	R	25	0	1	.000	0	1	1	0	7	3	2	7	0	1.29
Ron Klimkowski	R	27	0	1	.000	1	16	2	0	31	32	15	11	0	4.06

CLEVELAND   5th 72-84   .462   14   KEN ASPROMONTE

NAME	G by Pos	B	AGE	G	AB	R	H	2B	3B	HR	RBI	BB	SO	SB	BA	SA
TOTALS			25	156	5207	472	1220	187	18	91	440	420	762	49	.234	.330
Chris Chambliss (LJ)	1B119	L	23	121	466	51	136	27	2	6	44	26	63	3	.292	.397
Jack Brohamer	2B132, 3B1	L	22	136	527	49	123	13	2	5	35	27	46	3	.233	.294
Frank Duffy	SS126	R	25	130	385	23	92	16	4	3	27	31	54	6	.239	.325
Graig Nettles	3B150	L	27	150	557	65	141	28	0	17	70	57	50	2	.253	.395
Buddy Bell	OF123, 3B6	R	20	132	466	49	119	21	1	9	36	34	29	5	.255	.363
Del Unser	OF119	L	27	132	383	29	91	12	0	1	17	28	46	5	.238	.277
Alex Johnson	OF95	R	29	108	356	31	85	10	1	8	37	22	40	6	.239	.340
Ray Fosse	C124, 1B3	R	25	134	457	42	110	20	1	10	41	45	46	3	.241	.354
Tommy McCraw	OF84, 1B38	R	31	129	391	43	101	13	5	7	33	41	47	12	.258	.371
Eddie Leon	2B36, SS35	R	25	89	225	14	45	2	1	4	16	20	47	0	.200	.271
Roy Foster	OF45	R	26	73	143	19	32	4	0	4	13	21	23	0	.224	.336
John Lowenstein	OF58, 1B2	L	25	68	151	16	32	8	1	6	21	20	43	2	.212	.397
Jerry Moses	C39, 1B3	R	25	52	141	9	31	3	0	4	14	11	29	0	.220	.326
Lou Camilli	SS8, 2B2	B	25	39	41	2	6	2	0	0	3	3	8	0	.146	.195
Ron Lolich	OF22	R	25	24	80	4	15	1	0	2	8	4	20	0	.188	.275
Kurt Bevacqua	OF11, 3B1	R	25	15	35	2	4	1	0	0	3	3	6	0	.114	.200

Jack Heidemann 22 R 3-20, 1 Fred Stanley 24 R 2-12, Adolpho Phillips 30 R 0-7, Larry Johnson 21 R 1-2

NAME	T	AGE	W	L	PCT	SV	G	GS	CG	IP	H	BB	SO	SHO	ERA
TOTALS		26	72	84	.462	24	156	156	47	1410	1232	534	846	13	2.92
Gaylord Perry	R	33	24	16	.600	1	41	40	29	343	253	82	234	5	1.92
Dick Tidrow	R	25	14	15	.483	0	39	34	10	237	200	70	123	3	2.77
Milt Wilcox	R	22	7	14	.333	0	32	27	4	156	145	72	90	2	3.40
Steve Dunning	R	23	6	4	.600	0	16	16	1	105	98	43	52	0	3.26
Phil Hennigan (SJ)	R	26	5	3	.625	5	38	1	0	67	54	18	44	0	2.69
Ray Lamb	R	27	5	6	.455	0	34	9	0	108	101	29	64	0	3.08
4 Mike Kilkenny	L	27	4	1	.800	1	22	7	1	58	51	39	44	0	3.41
Tom Hilgendorf	L	30	3	1	.750	0	19	5	1	47	51	21	25	0	2.68
Ed Farmer	R	22	2	5	.286	7	46	1	0	61	51	27	33	0	4.43
Denny Riddleberger	L	26	1	3	.250	0	38	0	0	54	54	22	34	0	2.50
Vince Colbert	R	26	1	7	.125	0	22	11	1	75	74	38	36	1	4.56
Bill Butler	L	25	0	0	—	0	6	2	0	12	9	10	6	0	1.50
Marcelino Lopez	L	28	0	0	—	0	8	0	1	8	10	1	5	0	5.63
2 Lowell Palmer	R	24	0	0	—	0	2	2	0	2	2	3	4	0	4.50
Steve Hargan	R	29	0	3	.000	0	11	2	0	20	23	15	10	0	5.85
Steve Mingori	L	28	0	0	—	10	41	0	0	57	67	36	47	0	3.95

MILWAUKEE   6th 65-91   .417   21   DAVE BRISTOL 10-20 .333   ROY McMILLAN 1-1 .500   DEL CRANDALL 54-70 .435

NAME	G by Pos	B	AGE	G	AB	R	H	2B	3B	HR	RBI	BB	SO	SB	BA	SA
TOTALS			26	156	5124	493	1204	167	22	88	461	472	868	64	.235	.328
George Scott	1B139, 3B23	R	28	152	578	71	154	24	4	20	88	43	130	16	.266	.426
Ron Theobald	2B113	B	28	125	391	45	86	11	0	1	19	68	38	0	.220	.256
Rick Auerbach	SS153	R	22	153	554	50	121	16	3	2	30	43	62	24	.218	.269
Mike Ferraro	3B115, SS1	R	27	124	381	19	97	18	1	2	30	17	41	0	.255	.323
Joe Lahoud	OF97	L	25	111	316	35	75	9	3	12	34	45	54	3	.237	.399
Dave May	OF138	L	28	143	500	49	119	20	2	9	45	47	56	11	.238	.340
Johnny Briggs	OF106, 1B28	L	28	135	418	58	111	14	1	21	65	54	67	1	.266	.455
Ellie Rodriguez	C114	R	25	116	355	31	101	14	2	2	35	52	43	1	.285	.352
Bob Heise	2B49, 3B24, SS9	R	25	95	271	23	72	10	1	0	12	12	14	1	.266	.310
Brock Davis	OF43	R	28	95	154	17	49	2	0	0	12	12	23	6	.318	.331
Tommie Reynolds	OF41, 1B1, 3B1	R	30	72	130	13	26	5	1	2	13	10	25	0	.200	.300
3 Ollie Brown	OF56, 3B1	R	28	66	179	21	50	8	0	3	25	17	24	0	.279	.374
Billy Conigliaro (VR)	OF50	R	24	52	191	22	44	6	2	7	16	8	54	1	.230	.393
John Felske	C23, 1B8	R	30	37	80	6	11	3	0	1	5	3	13	0	.138	.213
2 Syd O'Brien	3B9, 2B7	R	28	31	58	5	12	2	0	1	5	2	13	0	.207	.293
1 Bill Voss	OF11	L	28	27	36	1	3	1	0	0	3	5	4	0	.083	.111
2 Ron Clark	2B11, 3B10	R	28	22	54	8	10	1	1	2	5	5	11	0	.185	.352
Paul Ratliff	C13	L	28	22	42	1	3	0	0	1	4	2	23	0	.071	.143
Darrell Porter	C18	L	20	18	56	6	7	1	0	1	2	5	21	0	.125	.196

2 Joe Azcue 32 R 2-14, 1 Curt Motton 31 R 1-6

NAME	T	AGE	W	L	PCT	SV	G	GS	CG	IP	H	BB	SO	SHO	ERA
TOTALS		26	65	91	.417	32	156	156	37	1392	1289	486	740	14	3.45
Jim Lonborg	R	30	14	12	.538	1	33	30	11	223	197	76	143	2	2.83
Bill Parsons	R	23	13	13	.500	0	33	30	10	214	194	68	111	2	3.91
Skip Lockwood	R	25	8	15	.348	0	29	27	5	170	148	71	106	3	3.60
Jim Colborn	R	26	7	7	.500	0	39	12	4	148	135	43	97	1	3.10
Ken Brett (XJ)	L	23	7	12	.368	0	26	22	2	133	121	49	74	1	4.53
Jerry Bell (XJ)	R	24	5	1	.833	0	25	3	0	71	50	33	20	0	1.65
Earl Stephenson	L	24	3	5	.375	0	35	8	1	80	79	33	33	0	3.26
Gary Ryerson	L	24	3	8	.273	0	21	14	4	102	119	21	45	1	3.62
Frank Linzy	R	31	2	2	.500	12	47	0	0	77	70	27	24	0	3.04
Ken Sanders	R	30	2	9	.182	17	62	0	0	92	88	31	51	0	3.13
2 Chuck Taylor	R	30	0	1	.000	1	5	0	0	12	8	3	5	0	1.50
Ray Newman	L	27	0	0	—	0	7	0	0	4	2	1	0	0	0.00
Jim Slaton	R	22	1	6	.143	0	9	8	0	44	50	21	17	0	5.52
Archie Reynolds	R	26	1	0	1.000	0	5	2	0	19	26	8	13	0	7.11

WEST DIVISION

OAKLAND   1st 93-62   .600   DICK WILLIAMS

NAME	G by Pos	B	AGE	G	AB	R	H	2B	3B	HR	RBI	BB	SO	SB	BA	SA
TOTALS			25	155	5200	604	1248	195	29	134	565	463	886	87	.240	.366
Mike Epstein	1B137	L	29	138	455	63	123	18	2	26	70	68	68	0	.270	.490
Tim Cullen	2B65, 3B4, SS1	R	30	72	142	10	37	8	1	0	15	5	17	0	.261	.331
Bert Campaneris	SS148	R	30	149	625	85	150	25	4	8	32	32	88	52	.240	.325
Sal Bando	3B151, 2B1	R	28	152	535	64	126	20	3	15	77	78	55	3	.236	.368
Angel Mangual	OF74	R	25	91	272	19	67	13	2	5	32	14	48	0	.246	.364
Reggie Jackson	OF135	R	25	135	499	72	132	25	2	25	75	59	125	9	.265	.473
Joe Rudi	OF147, 3B1	R	25	147	593	94	181	32	9	19	75	37	62	3	.305	.486
Dave Duncan	C113	R	26	121	403	39	88	13	0	19	59	34	68	0	.218	.392
Mike Hegan	1B64, OF3	L	29	98	79	13	26	3	1	1	5	7	20	1	.329	.430
Gene Tenace	C49, OF9, 1B7, 2B2, 3B2	R	25	82	227	22	51	5	3	5	32	24	42	0	.225	.339
George Hendrick	OF41	R	22	58	121	10	22	1	1	4	15	3	22	3	.182	.306
2 Ted Kubiak	2B49, 3B1	B	30	91	94	14	17	4	1	0	5	9	11	0	.181	.245
2 Larry Brown (XJ)	2B46, 3B1	R	32	47	142	11	26	2	0	0	13	8	13	0	.183	.197
2 Don Mincher	1B11	L	34	47	54	2	8	1	0	0	5	10	16	0	.148	.167
2 Bill Voss	OF34	L	28	40	97	10	22	5	1	1	5	9	16	0	.227	.340
2 Matty Alou	OF32, 1B1	L	33	32	121	11	34	5	1	0	16	11	12	2	.281	.347
2 Dal Maxvill	2B24, SS4	R	33	27	36	2	9	1	0	0	3	4	8	0	.250	.278
Dick Green (XJ)	2B26	R	31	26	42	1	12	1	1	0	5	5	8	0	.286	.357
2 Marty Martinez	2B17, SS6, 3B1	B	30	24	40	3	5	0	0	0	4	3	4	1	.125	.125
Gonzalo Marquez	1B2	L	26	23	21	2	8	2	0	0	3	3	4	1	.381	.381
Allen Lewis	OF6	R	30	24	10	5	2	1	0	0	2	0	1	8	.200	.300
1 Brant Alyea	OF8	R	31	20	31	3	6	1	1	0	4	0	9	0	.194	.323
2 Ollie Brown	OF16	R	28	20	54	5	13	1	0	1	4	6	14	1	.241	.315
Bobby Brooks	OF11	R	28	16	39	4	7	0	0	1	2	4	18	0	.179	.179
1 Ron Clark	2B11, 3B3	R	29	14	15	4	4	0	0	0	2	2	4	0	.267	.400

1 Curt Blefary 28 L 5-11, Bill McNulty 25 L 1-10, Adrian Garrett 29 L 0-11, 2 Art Shamsky 30 L 0-7,
1 Dwain Anderson 24 R 0-7, Larry Haney 29 R 0-4, 2 Orlando Cepeda (KJ) 34 R 0-3

NAME	T	AGE	W	L	PCT	SV	G	GS	CG	IP	H	BB	SO	SHO	ERA
TOTALS		28	93	62	.600	43	155	155	42	1418	1170	418	862	23	2.58
Catfish Hunter	R	26	21	7	.750	0	38	37	16	295	200	70	191	5	2.04
Ken Holtzman	L	26	19	11	.633	0	39	37	16	265	232	52	134	4	2.51
Blue Moon Odom	R	27	15	6	.714	0	31	30	4	194	164	87	86	2	2.51
Rollie Fingers	R	25	11	9	.550	21	65	0	0	111	85	32	113	0	2.51
Bob Locker	R	34	6	1	.857	10	56	0	0	78	69	16	47	0	2.65
Dave Hamilton	L	24	6	6	.500	0	25	14	1	101	94	31	55	0	2.94
Vida Blue (HO)	L	22	6	10	.375	0	25	23	5	151	117	48	111	4	2.80
Darold Knowles	L	30	5	1	.833	11	54	0	0	66	49	37	36	0	1.36
Joe Horlen	R	34	3	4	.429	1	32	6	0	84	74	20	58	0	3.00
1 Denny McLain	R	28	1	2	.333	0	5	5	0	22	32	8	6	0	6.14
2 Jim Roland	L	29	0	0	—	0	5	0	0	7	4	4	1	0	4.50
2 Mike Kilkenny	L	27	0	0	—	0	2	0	0	0	0	0	0	0	0.00
2 Diego Segui	R	34	0	1	.000	0	23			25		7	11		3.52
2 Don Shaw	L	27	0	0	—		3			12		8	8	0	18.00
Gary Waslewski	R	30	0	0	—	0	3	1	0	12	8	8	6	0	2.00
Chuck Dobson (EJ) 28															

CHICAGO   2nd 87-67   .565   5.5   CHUCK TANNER

NAME	G by Pos	B	AGE	G	AB	R	H	2B	3B	HR	RBI	BB	SO	SB	BA	SA
TOTALS			27	154	5083	566	1208	170	28	108	528	511	991	100	.238	.346
Dick Allen	1B143, 3B2	R	30	148	506	90	156	28	5	37	113	99	126	19	.308	.603
Mike Andrews	2B145, 1B5	R	28	148	505	58	111	18	0	7	50	70	78	2	.220	.297
Rich Morales	SS86, 2B16, 3B14	R	28	110	287	24	59	7	1	2	20	19	49	2	.206	.258
Ed Spiezio	3B74	R	30	74	277	20	66	10	1	2	33	13	43	0	.238	.303
Pat Kelly	OF109	L	27	119	402	57	119	14	7	5	24	55	69	32	.261	.368
Rick Reichardt	OF90	R	29	101	291	31	73	14	4	8	43	28	63	2	.251	.409
Carlos May	OF145, 1B5	L	24	148	523	83	161	26	3	12	68	79	70	23	.308	.438
Ed Herrmann	C112	L	25	116	354	23	88	9	0	10	40	43	37	0	.249	.359
Jay Johnstone	OF97	L	26	113	261	27	49	9	0	4	17	25	42	2	.188	.268
Luis Alvarado	SS81, 2B16, 3B2	R	23	103	254	30	54	9	1	2	19	13	36	2	.213	.283
Walt Williams	OF57, 1B1	R	29	77	221	22	55	7	1	2	19	11	19	2	.249	.317
Bill Melton (XJ)	3B56	R	26	57	208	22	51	5	0	7	30	23	31	1	.245	.370
Jorge Orta	SS18, 2B14, 3B9	L	21	51	124	20	25	1	1	1	5	3	23	0	.202	.315
Tom Egan	C46	R	26	50	141	8	27	5	0	3	9	4	48	0	.191	.255
Jim Lyttle	OF21	L	26	44	61	6	17	1	2	0	5	1	12	0	.279	.426
Tony Muser	1B29, OF1	L	24	44	61	6	17	1	2	0	5	1	12	0	.279	.426
Buddy Bradford	OF28	R	27	35	48	13	13	2	0	2	8	7	15	4	.271	.458
Chuck Brinkman	C33	R	27	35	52	1	7	1	0	0	4	3	15	0	.135	.135

Lee Richard 23 R 7-29, Rudy Hernandez 20 R 4-21, Hank Allen 31 R 3-21, Jim Qualls 25 B 0-10, Hugh Yancy 22 R 1-9

NAME	T	AGE	W	L	PCT	SV	G	GS	CG	IP	H	BB	SO	SHO	ERA
TOTALS		25	87	67	.565	42	154	154	36	1385	1269	431	936	14	3.12
Wilbur Wood	L	30	24	17	.585	0	49	49	20	377	325	74	193	8	2.51
Stan Bahnsen	R	27	21	16	.568	0	43	41	5	252	263	73	157	1	3.61
Tom Bradley	R	25	15	14	.517	0	40	40	11	260	225	65	209	2	2.98
Goose Gossage	R	20	7	1	.875	2	36	0	0	80	72	44	57	0	4.28
Terry Forster	L	20	6	5	.545	29	62	0	0	100	75	44	104	0	2.25
Dave Lemonds	L	23	4	7	.364	0	31	18	0	95	87	38	69	0	2.94
Cy Acosta	R	25	3	0	1.000	5	26	0	0	48	37	15	28	0	1.54
Vicente Romo (SA)	R	29	3	0	1.000	1	28	0	0	52	47	18	46	0	3.29
Steve Kealey	R	29	1	2	.600	4	40	0	0	57	50	12	37	0	3.32
Ken Frailing	L	24	1	0	1.000	0	3	0	0	3	3	1	1	0	3.00
2 Moe Drabowsky	R	36	0	1	.000	2	19	0	0	27	29	12	17	0	2.57
Jim Geddes	R	23	0	1	.000	0	5	0	0	10	12	10	3	0	7.20
Dan Neumeier	R	24	0	0	—	0	4	0	0	4	7	9	3	0	9.00
Denny O'Toole	R	24	0	0	—	0	9	0	0	8	8	5	6	0	5.40
2 Eddie Fisher	R	35	0	1	.000	1	6	0	0	22	31	9	10	0	4.50
2 Phil Regan	R	35	0	0	—	0	14	0	0	14	18	11	6	0	4.15
Bart Johnson (KJ)	R	22	0	3	.000	0	5	5	0	14	18	13	9	0	9.00

MINNESOTA — 3rd 77-77 .500 15.5 — BILL RIGNEY 36-34 .514 — FRANK QUILICI 41-43 .488

NAME	G by Pos	B	AGE	G	AB	R	H	2B	3B	HR	RBI	BB	SO	SB	BA	SA
TOTALS			27	154	5234	537	1277	182	31	93	506	478	905	53	.244	.344
Harmon Killebrew	1B130	R	36	139	433	53	100	13	2	26	74	94	91	0	.231	.450
Rod Carew	2B139	L	26	142	535	61	170	21	6	0	51	43	60	12	.318	.379
Danny Thompson	SS144	R	28	143	573	54	158	22	6	4	48	34	57	1	.276	.336
Eric Soderholm	3B79	R	23	93	287	28	54	10	0	13	39	19	48	3	.188	.359
Cesar Tovar	OF139	R	31	141	548	86	145	20	6	2	31	39	39	21	.265	.334
Bobby Darwin	OF142	R	29	145	513	48	137	20	2	22	80	38	145	2	.267	.442
Steve Brye	OF93	R	23	100	253	18	61	9	3	0	12	17	38	3	.241	.300
Glenn Borgmann	C56	R	22	56	175	11	41	4	0	3	14	25	25	0	.234	.309
Rich Reese	1B98, OF13	L	30	132	197	23	43	3	2	5	26	25	27	0	.218	.330
Steve Braun	3B74, 2B20, SS11, OF2	L	24	121	402	40	116	21	0	2	50	45	38	4	.289	.356
Jim Nettles	OF78, 1B1	L	25	102	235	28	48	5	2	4	15	32	52	4	.204	.294
George Mitterwald	C61	R	27	64	163	12	30	4	1	1	8	9	37	0	.184	.270
Charlie Manuel	OF28	L	28	63	122	6	25	5	0	1	6	4	16	0	.205	.270
Phil Roof	C61	R	31	61	146	16	30	11	1	3	12	6	27	0	.205	.356
Rick Renick	OF21, 1B6, 3B4, SS1	R	28	55	93	10	16	2	0	4	8	15	25	0	.172	.323
Dan Monzon	2B13, 3B5, SS3, OF1	R	26	55	55	13	15	1	0	0	5	8	12	1	.273	.291

Rick Dempsey 22 R 8-40, Tony Oliva (KJ) 31 L 9-28, Jim Holt 28 L 12-27, Mike Adams 23 R 2-6, Bucky Guth 24 R 0-3

NAME	T	AGE	W	L	PCT	SV	G	GS	CG	IP	H	BB	SO	SHO	ERA
		26	77	77	.500	34	154	154	37	1399	1188	444	838	17	2.84
Bert Blyleven	R	21	17	17	.500	0	39	38	11	287	247	69	228	3	2.73
Dick Woodson	R	27	14	14	.500	0	36	36	9	252	193	101	150	3	2.71
Jim Perry	R	36	13	16	.448	0	35	35	5	218	191	60	85	2	3.34
Jim Kaat (BW)	L	33	10	2	.833	0	15	15	5	113	94	20	64	0	2.07
Ray Corbin	R	23	8	9	.471	0	31	19	5	162	135	53	83	3	2.61
Dave LaRoche	L	24	5	7	.417	10	62	0	0	95	72	39	79	0	2.84
Wayne Granger	R	28	4	6	.400	19	63	0	0	90	83	28	45	0	3.00
Jim Strickland	L	26	3	1	.750	3	25	0	0	36	28	19	30	0	2.50
Dave Goltz	R	23	3	3	.500	1	15	11	2	91	75	26	38	0	2.67
Steve Luebber	R	22	0	0	—	0	2	0	0	3	2	1	0	0	0.00
Tom Norton (EJ)	R	22	0	1	.000	0	21	0	0	32	31	14	22	0	2.81
Bob Gebhard	R	29	0	1	.000	0	21	0	0	21	36	13	13	0	8.57

KANSAS CITY — 4th 76-78 .494 16.5 — BOB LEMON

NAME	G by Pos	B	AGE	G	AB	R	H	2B	3B	HR	RBI	BB	SO	SB	BA	SA
TOTALS			28	154	5167	580	1317	220	26	78	547	534	711	85	.255	.353
John Mayberry	1B146	L	23	149	503	65	150	24	3	25	100	78	74	0	.298	.507
Cookie Rojas	2B131, 3B6, SS2	R	33	137	487	49	127	25	0	3	53	11	35	2	.261	.331
Freddie Patek	SS136	R	27	136	518	59	110	25	4	0	32	47	64	33	.212	.276
Paul Schaal	3B123, SS1	R	29	127	435	47	99	19	3	6	41	61	59	1	.228	.326
Richie Scheinblum	OF119	B	29	134	450	60	135	21	4	8	66	58	40	0	.300	.418
Amos Otis	OF137	R	25	143	540	75	158	28	2	11	54	50	59	26	.293	.413
Lou Piniella	OF150	R	28	151	574	65	179	33	4	11	72	34	59	7	.312	.441
Ed Kirkpatrick	C108, 1B1	L	27	113	364	43	100	15	1	9	43	51	50	3	.275	.396
Steve Hovley	OF68	L	27	105	196	24	53	1	3	0	14	24	29	3	.270	.352
Carl Taylor	C21, OF7, 1B6, 3B5	R	28	63	113	17	30	2	1	0	11	17	16	4	.265	.301
Bobby Floyd	3B30, SS29, 2B2	R	28	61	134	9	24	3	0	0	5	5	29	1	.179	.201
Jerry May	C41	R	28	53	116	10	22	5	1	1	14	13	13	0	.190	.276
Joe Keough	OF16	L	26	56	64	8	14	2	0	0	5	8	7	2	.219	.250
Gail Hopkins	1B13, 3B1	L	29	53	71	1	15	2	0	0	5	7	4	0	.211	.239
Bobby Knoop	2B33, 3B4	R	33	44	97	8	23	5	0	0	7	9	16	0	.237	.289

1 Bob Oliver 29 R 17-63, Ron Hansen 34 R 4-30, Jim Wohlford 21 R 6-25, Dennis Paepke 27 R 0-6

NAME	T	AGE	W	L	PCT	SV	G	GS	CG	IP	H	BB	SO	SHO	ERA
		28	76	78	.494	29	154	154	44	1381	1293	405	801	16	3.24
Paul Splittorff	L	25	12	12	.500	0	35	33	12	216	189	67	140	2	3.13
Dick Drago	R	27	12	17	.414	0	34	33	11	239	230	51	135	2	3.01
Roger Nelson (SJ)	R	28	11	6	.647	3	34	19	10	173	120	31	120	6	2.08
Tom Burgmeier	R	28	6	2	.750	9	51	0	0	55	67	33	18	0	4.25
Bruce Dal Canton	R	30	6	6	.500	2	35	16	1	132	135	29	75	0	3.41
Jim Rooker	L	29	5	7	.417	0	29	16	1	113	119	41	52	0	4.38
Mike Hedlund	R	25	5	7	.417	0	18	10	4	72	78	24	44	2	4.78
2 Tom Murphy	R	26	4	4	.500	1	18	9	1	79	77	16	34	1	3.09
Steve Busby	R	22	1	1	.750	0	5	3	0	40	28	8	31	0	1.58
Monty Montgomery	R	25	3	3	.500	0	9	8	1	56	55	17	24	1	3.05
Ted Abernathy	R	39	1	3	.429	5	45	0	0	58	44	19	28	0	1.71
Norm Angelini	L	24	2	1	.667	2	21	0	0	16	13	12	16	0	2.25
Al Fitzmorris	R	26	2	5	.286	3	38	2	0	101	99	28	51	0	3.74
Mike Jackson	L	26	1	2	.333	0	7	3	0	20	24	14	15	0	6.30
Ken Wright	R	25	1	2	.333	4	17	0	0	18	15	15	18	0	6.00

CALIFORNIA — 5th 75-80 .484 18 — DEL RICE

NAME	G by Pos	B	AGE	G	AB	R	H	2B	3B	HR	RBI	BB	SO	SB	BA	SA
TOTALS			28	155	5165	454	1249	171	26	78	420	358	850	57	.242	.330
2 Bob Oliver	1B127, OF8	R	29	134	509	47	137	20	4	19	70	27	97	4	.269	.436
Sandy Alomar	2B154, SS4	B	28	155	616	65	146	20	3	1	47	55	20	20	.239	.287
Leo Cardenas	SS150	R	33	150	551	25	123	11	2	6	42	35	73	1	.223	.283
Ken McMullen	3B137	R	30	137	472	36	127	18	1	9	34	48	59	1	.269	.369
Lee Stanton	OF124	R	26	127	402	44	101	15	3	12	39	42	100	2	.251	.393
Ken Berry	OF116	R	31	119	401	41	118	15	3	5	39	35	47	5	.289	.377
Vada Pinson	OF134, 1B1	L	33	136	484	56	133	24	7	7	49	30	54	17	.275	.376
Art Kusnyer	C63	R	26	64	179	13	37	2	1	2	13	16	33	0	.207	.263
Jim Spencer	1B35, OF3	L	24	82	212	13	47	5	0	1	14	12	25	0	.222	.259
Johnny Stephenson	C56	L	31	66	146	14	40	3	1	2	17	11	8	0	.274	.349
Jeff Torborg (IL)	C58	R	30	59	153	5	32	6	0	3	14	21	8	0	.209	.229
Mickey Rivers	OF48	L	23	58	159	18	34	4	2	0	8	8	26	4	.214	.277
1 Andy Kosco	OF36	R	30	49	142	15	34	4	2	6	13	5	23	1	.239	.423
Winston Llenas	3B10, 2B2, OF2	R	28	44	64	3	17	3	0	0	7	3	8	0	.266	.313
2 Curt Motton	OF9	R	31	42	39	6	7	1	0	0	5	12	0	0	.154	.179
Billy Parker	3B21, 2B9, OF5, SS1	R	25	36	80	11	17	2	0	2	10	7	17	0	.213	.313
1 Syd O'Brien	3B8, SS4, 2B3, 1B1	R	28	36	39	10	7	2	1	1	5	8	10	0	.179	.308

2 Jack Hiatt 29 R 13-45, Doug Howard 24 R 10-38, Chris Coletta 27 L 9-30, Tommy Silverio 26 L 2-12, Roger Repoz 31 L 1-3, Billy Cowan 33 R 0-3, 1 Joe Azcue 32 R 0-2

NAME	T	AGE	W	L	PCT	SV	G	GS	CG	IP	H	BB	SO	SHO	ERA
		28	75	80	.484	16	155	155	57	1378	1109	620	1000	18	3.06
Nolan Ryan	R	25	19	16	.543	0	39	39	20	284	166	157	329	9	2.28
Clyde Wright	L	31	18	11	.621	0	35	35	15	251	229	80	87	2	2.98
Rudy May	L	27	12	11	.522	1	35	30	10	205	162	82	169	3	2.94
Andy Messersmith (RJ)	R	26	8	11	.421	2	25	21	10	170	125	68	142	3	2.81
2 Steve Barber	L	34	4	4	.500	2	34	3	0	58	37	30	34	0	2.02
1 Eddie Fisher	R	35	4	5	.444	4	43	1	0	81	73	31	32	0	3.78
Rickey Clark	R	22	3	7	.300	1	26	15	2	110	105	55	61	0	4.50
Lloyd Allen	R	22	3	8	.273	5	42	6	0	85	76	55	53	0	3.49
Dave Sells	R	25	2	0	1.000	0	10	0	0	16	11	5	2	0	2.81
Don Rose	R	25	1	4	.200	0	16	4	0	43	49	19	39	0	4.19
Mel Queen	R	30	0	0	—	0	17	0	0	31	31	19	19	0	4.35
1 Tom Murphy	R	26	0	0	—	0	10	0	0	13	8	2	5	0	5.40
Dick Lange	R	23	0	0	—	0	4	0	0	10	8	4	5	0	4.50
Paul Doyle	L	32	0	0	—	0	1	0	0					0	0.00
Alan Foster	R	25	0	0	.000	0	13	0	0	13	12	6	11	0	4.85
Tom Dukes (EJ)	R	29	0	0	.000	0	11	0	0	11	11	0	6	0	1.64

TEXAS — 6th 54-100 .351 38.5 — TED WILLIAMS

NAME	G by Pos	B	AGE	G	AB	R	H	2B	3B	HR	RBI	BB	SO	SB	BA	SA
TOTALS			26	154	5029	461	1092	166	17	56	424	503	926	126	.217	.290
1 Frank Howard	1B66, OF21	R	35	95	287	28	70	9	0	9	31	42	55	1	.244	.369
Lenny Randle	2B65, SS4, OF2	B	23	74	249	23	48	13	0	2	21	13	51	4	.193	.269
Toby Harrah (IL)	SS106	R	23	116	374	47	97	14	3	1	31	34	31	16	.259	.321
Dave Nelson	3B119, OF15	R	28	145	499	68	113	16	3	2	28	67	81	51	.226	.283
Ted Ford	OF119	R	25	129	429	43	101	19	1	14	50	37	80	4	.235	.382
Joe Lovitto	OF103	R	21	117	330	23	74	9	1	1	19	37	54	13	.224	.267
Elliott Maddox (BH)		R	24	98	294	40	74	7	2	0	10	49	53	20	.252	.289
Dick Billings	C92, OF41, 3B5, 1B1	R	29	133	469	41	119	25	1	5	58	29	71	1	.254	.322
Larry Biittner	1B65, OF65	L	26	137	382	34	99	18	1	3	31	29	37	1	.259	.335
2 Dalton Jones	3B23, 2B17, 1B7, OF2	L	28	72	153	14	24	4	0	1	19	10	31	1	.159	.252
Tommy Grieve	OF49	R	24	64	142	12	29	2	1	3	14	11	39	1	.204	.296
1 Don Mincher	1B59	L	34	61	191	23	45	10	0	6	39	46	23	2	.236	.382
Vic Harris	2B58, SS1	R	22	61	186	8	26	5	0	1	12	25	35	0	.140	.177
Hal King	C38	L	28	50	122	12	22	5	0	4	12	25	35	0	.180	.320
Jim Mason	SS32, 3B10	L	21	46	147	10	29	9	0	0	10	9	39	0	.197	.218
1 Ted Kubiak	2B25, SS15, 3B1	B	30	46	116	5	26	3	0	0	9	12	12	0	.224	.250
Bill Fahey	C39	L	22	39	119	8	20	4	0	1	9	12	23	1	.168	.210
3 Marty Martinez	SS5, 3B4, 2B1	B	30	26	41	3	6	1	1	0	4	1	3	0	.146	.220

Tom Ragland 26 R 10-58, Ken Suarez 29 R 5-33, Jeff Burroughs (XJ) 21 R 12-65, Jim Driscoll 28 L 0-18

NAME	T	AGE	W	L	PCT	SV	G	GS	CG	IP	H	BB	SO	SHO	ERA
		26	54	100	.351	34	154	154	11	1375	1258	613	868	8	3.53
Rich Hand	R	23	10	14	.417	0	30	28	2	171	139	103	109	1	3.32
Mike Paul	L	27	8	9	.471	1	49	20	2	162	149	52	108	1	2.17
Dick Bosman	R	28	8	10	.444	0	29	29	1	173	183	48	105	1	3.64
Paul Lindblad	L	30	5	8	.385	9	66	0	0	100	95	29	51	0	2.61
Jim Panther	R	27	5	9	.357	0	58	4	0	94	101	46	44	0	4.12
Pete Broberg	R	22	5	12	.294	1	39	25	3	176	153	85	133	2	4.30
Bill Gogolewski	R	24	4	11	.267	2	36	21	2	151	136	58	95	1	4.23
1 Casey Cox	R	30	3	5	.375	4	35	3	0	65	73	26	27	0	4.43
Jim Shellenback	L	28	2	4	.333	1	22	6	0	57	46	16	30	0	3.47
Horacio Pina	R	27	2	7	.222	15	60	0	0	76	61	43	60	0	3.20
Don Stanhouse (EJ)	R	21	2	9	.182	0	24	16	1	105	83	73	78	0	3.77
Steve Lawson	L	21	0	0	—	0	13	0	0	16	13	10	13	0	2.81
3 Jim Roland	L	34	0	0	—	0	13	0	0					0	9.00
Jan Dukes	R	26	0	0	—	0	4	0	0	11	10	4	4	0	4.50
2 Rich Hinton	L	25	0	0	.000	0	11	0	0	11	14	6	9	0	2.45
Jerry Janeski	R	26	0	1	.000	0	13	1	1	7	13	11	7	0	2.77

AMERICAN LEAGUE CHAMPIONSHIP —OAKLAND (WEST) 3 DETROIT (EAST) 2

LINE SCORES

TEAM	1	2	3	4	5	6	7	8	9	10	11	12	R	H	E

Game 1 October 7 at Oakland
| DET | 0 | 1 | 0 | 0 | 0 | 0 | 0 | 0 | 1 | | | | 2 | 6 | 2 |
| OAK | 0 | 0 | 1 | 0 | 0 | 0 | 0 | 2 | x | | | | 3 | 10 | 1 |

Lolich, Seelbach (11)   Hunter, Blue (9), **Fingers** (9)

Game 2 October 8 at Oakland
| DET | 0 | 0 | 0 | 0 | 0 | 0 | 0 | 0 | 0 | | | | 0 | 3 | 1 |
| OAK | 1 | 0 | 0 | 0 | 4 | 0 | 0 | 0 | x | | | | 5 | 8 | 0 |

Fryman, Zachary (5), Scherman (5), LaGrow (6), Hiller (7)   **Odom**

Game 3 October 10 at Detroit
| OAK | 0 | 0 | 0 | 0 | 0 | 0 | 0 | 0 | 0 | | | | 0 | 7 | 0 |
| DET | 0 | 0 | 0 | 2 | 0 | 0 | 0 | 1 | X | | | | 3 | 8 | 1 |

Holtzman, Fingers (5), Blue (6), Locker (7)   **Coleman**

Game 4 October 11 at Detroit
| OAK | 0 | 0 | 0 | 0 | 0 | 0 | 1 | 0 | 0 | 2 | | | 3 | 9 | 2 |
| DET | 0 | 0 | 1 | 0 | 0 | 0 | 0 | 0 | 0 | 3 | | | 4 | 10 | 1 |

Hunter, Fingers (8), Blue (9), Locker (10), **Horlen** (10), Hamilton (10)   Lolich, Seelbach (10), **Hiller** (10)

Game 5 October 12 at Detroit
| OAK | 0 | 1 | 0 | 0 | 0 | 0 | 0 | 0 | 0 | | | | 2 | 4 | 0 |
| DET | 1 | 0 | 0 | 0 | 0 | 0 | 0 | 0 | 0 | | | | 1 | 5 | 2 |

Odom, Blue (6)   Fryman, Hiller (9)

COMPOSITE BATTING

Oakland
NAME	POS	G	AB	R	H	2B	3B	HR	RBI	BA
Totals		5	170	13	38	8	0	1	10	.224
Alou	OF	5	21	2	8	4	0	0	2	.381
Rudi	OF	5	20	1	5	1	0	0	0	.250
Bando	3B	5	20	1	4	0	0	0	0	.200
Jackson	OF	5	18	1	5	1	0	0	2	.278
Tenace	C-2B	5	17	1	1	0	0	0	1	.059
Epstein	1B	5	16	1	3	0	0	0	0	.188
Green	2B	5	8	0	1	0	0	0	0	.125
Maxvill	SS-2B	5	8	0	1	0	0	0	0	.125
Campaneris	SS	5	7	3	3	0	0	0	0	.429
Hendrick	OF	5	7	2	1	0	0	0	0	.143
Kubiak	2B-SS	4	4	0	2	0	0	0	0	.500
Marquez	PH	3	3	0	2	0	0	0	0	.667
Mangual	PH	3	3	0	0	0	0	0	0	.000
Duncan	C	2								.000

Odom P-PR 1-4, Cullen SS 0-1, Mincher PH 0-1, Hegan 1B 0-1

Detroit
NAME	POS	G	AB	R	H	2B	3B	HR	RBI	BA
Totals		5	162	10	32	6	4	1	10	.198
McAuliffe	SS-2B	5	20	3	4	0	0	1	1	.200
Kaline	OF	5	19	3	5	1	0	0	1	.263
Rodriguez	3B	5	16	0	0	0	0	0	0	.000
Cash	1B	5	15	1	4	0	0	0	0	.267
Taylor	2B	5	15	0	2	0	0	0	1	.133
Northrop	OF	5	14	0	5	0	0	0	1	.357
Sims	C-OF	4	14	0	3	2	0	0	0	.214
Freehan	C	5	14	0	3	0	0	0	3	.250
Horton	OF	5	10	0	1	0	0	0	0	.100
Stanley	OF	4								.333

Brinkman SS 1-4, I. Brown 1B 1-2, G. Brown PH 0-2, Haller PH 0-1, Knox PR 0-0, Niekro PR 0-0

COMPOSITE PITCHING

Oakland
NAME	G	IP	H	BB	SO	W	L	SV	ERA
Totals	5	46	32	13	25	3	2	1	1.76
Hunter	2	15.1	10	5	9	0	0	0	1.17
Odom	2	14	5	2	5	2	0	0	0.00
Blue	4	5.1	4	1	5	0	0	0	0.00
Fingers	3	5.1	4	1	3	1	0	0	1.69
Holtzman	1	4	4	2	2	0	1	0	4.50
Locker	2	2	4	0	0	0	1	0	13.50
Hamilton	1	0	1	0	0	0	0	0	—
Horlen	1	0	1	0	0	0	0	1	∞

Detroit
NAME	G	IP	H	BB	SO	W	L	SV	ERA
Totals	5	46.1	38	12	35	2	3	0	2.14
Lolich	2	19	14	5	10	0	1	0	1.42
Fryman	2	12.1	11	2	8	0	2	0	3.65
Coleman	1	9	7	3	14	1	0	0	0.00
Hiller	3	3.1	4	1	2	0	0	0	0.00
LaGrow	1								
Seelbach	2	1	4	0	1	0	0	0	18.00
Scherman	1	0.2	1	0	1	0	0	0	∞
Zachary	1	0	1	0	0	0	0	0	∞

NATIONAL LEAGUE CHAMPIONSHIP — CINCINNATI (WEST) 3　PITTSBURGH (EAST) 2

LINE SCORES

TEAM	1	2	3	4	5	6	7	8	9	10	11	12	R	H	E

Game 1 October 7 at Pittsburgh

CIN	1	0	0	0	0	0	0	0	0				1	8	0
PIT	3	0	0	0	2	0	0	0	x				5	6	0

Gullett, Borbon (7)　**Blass**, R. Hernandez (9)

Game 2 October 8 at Pittsburgh

CIN	4	0	0	0	0	0	0	1	0				5	8	1
PIT	1	0	0	1	1	1	0	0	0				3	7	1

Billingham, Hall (5)　**Moose**, Johnson (1), Kison (6), R. Hernandez (7), Giusti (9)

Game 3 October 9 at Cincinnati

PIT	0	0	0	0	1	0	1	1	0				3	7	0
CIN	0	0	2	0	0	0	0	0	0				2	8	1

Briles, Kison (7)　Nolan, Borbon (7), **Carroll** (7), Giusti (8)　McGlothlin (9)

Game 4 October 10 at Cincinnati

PIT	0	0	0	0	0	0	1	0	0				1	2	3
CIN	1	0	0	2	0	2	2	0	x				7	11	1

Ellis, Johnson (6), **Grimsley**　Walker (7), Miller (8)

Game 5 October 11 at Cincinnati

PIT	0	2	0	1	0	0	0	0	0				3	8	0
CIN	0	0	1	0	1	0	0	0	2				4	7	1

Blass, R. Hernandez (8), Giusti (9), Moose (9)　Gullett, Borbon (4), Hall (6), **Carroll** (9)

COMPOSITE BATTING

NAME	POS	G	AB	R	H	2B	3B	HR	RBI	BA
Cincinnati										
Totals		5	166	19	42	9	2	4	16	.253
Tolan	OF	5	21	3	5	1	1	0	4	.238
Rose	OF	5	20	1	9	4	0	0	0	.450
Perez	1B	5	20	0	4	1	0	0	2	.200
Geronimo	OF	5	20	2	2	0	0	1	1	.100
Morgan	2B	5	19	5	5	0	0	2	3	.263
Bench	C	5	18	3	6	1	1	1	2	.333
Menke	3B	5	16	1	4	1	0	0	0	.250
Chaney	SS	5	16	3	3	0	0	0	1	.188
Uhlaender	PH	2	2	0	1	0	0	0	0	.500
Concepcion	SS	3	2	0	0	0	0	0	0	.000

Hague PH 0-1, McRae PH 0-0, Foster PR 0-0

NAME	POS	G	AB	R	H	2B	3B	HR	RBI	BA
Pittsburgh										
Totals		5	158	15	30	6	1	3	14	.190
Stennett	OF-2B	5	21	2	6	0	0	0	1	.286
Oliver	OF	5	20	3	5	2	1	1	3	.250
Cash	2B	5	19	0	4	0	0	0	3	.211
Clemente	OF	5	17	1	4	1	0	1	2	.235
Sanguillen	C	5	16	4	5	1	0	1	2	.313
Hebner	3B	5	16	2	3	1	0	0	1	.188
Stargell	1B-OF	5	16	1	1	0	0	0	0	.063
Alley	SS	5	16	1	0	0	0	0	0	.000
May	C	1	2	0	1	0	0	0	0	.500
Mazeroski	PH	2	2	1	1	0	0	0	0	.500

Clines PH-PR 0-2, Davalillo PH 0-0, Robertson 1B 0-0, Ellis P-PR 0-1

COMPOSITE PITCHING

NAME	G	IP	H	BB	SO	W	L	SV	ERA
Cincinnati									
Totals	5	44	30	9	27	3	2	0	3.07
Grimsley	1	9	2	0	5	1	0	0	1.00
Gullett	2	9	12	0	5	0	1	0	8.00
Hall	2	7.1	3	8	1	0	0	1	1.23
Nolan	1	6	4	1	4	0	0	0	1.50
Billingham	1	4.2	5	2	4	0	0	0	3.86
Borbon	3	4.1	2	0	1	0	0	0	2.08
Carroll	2	2.2	2	3	0	1	1	0	3.38
McGlothin	1	1	0	0	1	0	0	0	0.00

NAME	G	IP	H	BB	SO	W	L	SV	ERA
Pittsburgh									
Totals	5	43.2	42	10	28	2	3	2	3.30
Blass	2	15.2	12	6	5	1	0	0	1.72
Briles	1	6	6	1	3	0	0	0	3.00
Johnson	2	6	4	2	7	0	0	0	3.00
Ellis	1	5	5	1	3	0	1	0	0.00
R. Hernandez	3	3.1	1	0	3	0	0	1	2.70
Giusti	3	2.2	5	0	3	0	1	1	6.75
Kison	2	2.1	1	0	3	1	0	0	0.00
Miller	1	1	3	0	0	0	0	0	18.00
Walker	1	1	3	0	1	0	0	0	18.00
Moose	2	0.2	5	0	0	0	1	0	54.00

EAST DIVISION

NAME	G by Pos	B	AGE	G	AB	R	H	2B	3B	HR	RBI	BB	SO	SB	BA	SA
PITTSBURGH 1st 96-59 .619									BILL VIRDON							
TOTALS			28	155	5490	691	1505	251	47	110	654	404	871	49	.274	.397
Willie Stargell	1B101, OF32	L	32	138	495	75	145	28	2	33	112	65	129	1	.293	.558
Dave Cash	2B97	R	24	99	425	58	120	22	4	3	30	22	31	9	.282	.374
Gene Alley	SS114, 3B4	R	31	119	347	30	86	12	2	3	36	38	52	4	.248	.320
Richie Hebner	3B121	L	24	124	427	63	128	24	4	19	72	52	54	0	.300	.508
Roberto Clemente (NJ, DD)	OF94	R	37	102	378	68	118	19	7	10	60	29	49	0	.312	.479
Al Oliver	OF138, 1B3	L	25	140	565	88	176	27	4	12	89	34	44	2	.312	.437
Vic Davalillo	OF97, 1B8	L	35	117	368	59	117	19	2	4	28	26	44	14	.318	.413
Manny Sanguillen	C127, OF2	R	28	136	520	55	155	18	8	7	71	21	38	1	.298	.404
Bob Robertson	1B89, OF23, 3B11	R	25	115	306	25	59	11	0	12	41	41	84	1	.193	.346
Rennie Stennett	2B49, OF41, SS6	R	21	109	370	43	106	14	5	3	30	9	41	5	.286	.378
Gene Clines	OF83	R	25	107	311	52	104	15	6	0	17	16	47	12	.334	.421
Jackie Hernandez	SS68, 3B4	R	31	72	176	12	33	7	1	1	14	9	43	1	.188	.256
Milt May	C33	L	21	57	139	12	39	10	0	0	14	10	13	0	.281	.353
Jose Pagan	3B32, OF2	R	37	53	127	11	32	9	0	3	8	5	17	0	.252	.394
Bill Mazeroski (XJ)	2B15, 3B3	R	35	34	64	3	12	4	0	0	3	2	9	0	.188	.250

Richie Zisk 23 R 7-37, Chuck Goggin 26 B 2-7, Frank Taveras 22 R 0-3, Fernando Gonzalez 22 R 0-2, Charlie Sands 24 L 0-1

NAME	T	AGE	W	L	PCT	SV	G	GS	CG	IP	H	BB	SO	SHO	ERA
		28	96	59	.619	48	155	155	39	1414	1282	433	838	15	2.81
Steve Blass	R	30	19	8	.704	0	33	32	11	250	227	84	117	2	2.48
Dock Ellis	R	27	15	7	.682	0	25	25	4	163	156	33	96	1	2.71
Nelson Briles	R	28	14	11	.560	0	28	27	9	196	185	43	120	2	3.08
Bob Moose	R	24	13	10	.565	1	31	30	6	226	213	47	144	3	2.91
Bruce Kison	R	22	9	7	.563	3	32	18	6	152	123	69	102	1	3.26
Dave Giusti	R	32	7	4	.636	22	54	0	0	75	59	20	54	0	1.92
Ramon Hernandez	L	31	5	0	1.000	14	53	0	0	70	50	22	47	0	1.67
Bob Miller	R	33	5	2	.714	3	36	0	0	54	54	24	18	0	2.67
Bob Johnson	R	29	4	4	.500	3	31	11	1	116	98	46	79	0	2.95
Luke Walker (XJ)	L	28	4	6	.400	2	26	12	2	93	98	34	48	0	3.39
Jim McKee	R	25	1	0	1.000	1	4	0	0	12	8	4	8	0	3.00
1 Bob Veale	L	36	0	0	—	5	0	0	0	9	10	7	6	0	6.00
Gene Garber	R	24	0	0	—	0	4	0	0	5	7	3	3	0	7.50

NAME	G by Pos	B	AGE	G	AB	R	H	2B	3B	HR	RBI	BB	SO	SB	BA	SA
CHICAGO 2nd 85-70 .548 11								1 LEO DUROCHER 46-44 .511			WHITEY LOCKMAN 39-26 .600					
TOTALS			31	156	5247	685	1346	206	40	133	634	565	815	69	.257	.387
Jim Hickman	1B77, OF27	R	35	115	368	65	100	15	2	17	64	52	64	3	.272	.462
Glenn Beckert	2B118	R	31	120	474	51	100	22	3	4	43	23	17	2	.270	.344
Don Kessinger	SS146	B	29	149	577	77	158	20	6	1	39	67	44	8	.274	.334
Ron Santo (BW)	3B129, 2B3, SS1, OF1	R	32	133	464	68	140	25	5	17	74	69	75	1	.302	.487
Jose Cardenal	OF137	R	28	143	533	96	155	24	6	17	70	55	58	25	.291	.454
Rick Monday	OF134	L	26	138	434	68	100	25	5	11	42	78	102	14	.249	.399
Billy Williams	OF144, 1B5	L	34	150	574	95	191	34	6	37	122	62	59	3	.333	.606
Randy Hundley	C113	R	30	114	357	23	78	12	0	5	30	22	62	1	.218	.294
C. Fanzone	3B36, 1B21, 2B13, SS1, OF1	R	30	86	222	26	50	11	0	8	42	35	45	2	.225	.383
Joe Pepitone (VR)	1B66	L	31	66	214	23	56	5	0	8	21	13	22	1	.262	.397
Billy North	OF48	B	24	66	127	22	23	2	0	4	13	33	33	6	.181	.244
Paul Popovich (IL)	2B36, SS8, 3B1	B	31	58	129	8	25	3	2	1	11	12	8	0	.194	.271
Ken Rudolph	C41	R	25	42	106	10	25	1	1	2	9	6	14	1	.236	.321
Gene Hiser	OF15	L	23	32	46	2	9	0	0	0	1	7	5	1	.196	.196
J.C. Martin (EJ)	C17	L	35	25	50	3	12	1	0	0	7	6	9	1	.240	.300
2 Ellie Hendricks	C16	L	31	17	43	7	5	1	0	2	6	7	13	0	.116	.302

Pat Bourque 25 L 7-27, 1 Tommy Davis 33 R 7-26, 1 Art Shamsky 30 L 2-16, Dave Rosello 22 R 3-12, Al Montreuil 28 R 1-11, Jim Tyrone 23 R 0-8, Pete LaCock 20 L 3-6, Frank Fernandez 29 R 0-3, Frank Coggins 28 B 0-1, Chris Ward 23 L 0-1

NAME	T	AGE	W	L	PCT	SV	G	GS	CG	IP	H	BB	SO	SHO	ERA
		29	85	70	.548	32	156	156	54	1399	1329	421	824	19	3.22
Ferguson Jenkins	R	28	20	12	.625	0	36	36	23	289	253	62	184	5	3.21
Milt Pappas	R	33	17	7	.708	0	29	28	10	195	187	29	80	3	2.77
Bill Hands	R	32	11	8	.579	0	32	28	6	189	168	47	96	3	3.00
Burt Hooton	R	22	11	14	.440	0	33	31	9	218	201	81	132	3	2.81
Rick Reuschel	R	23	10	8	.556	0	21	18	5	129	127	29	87	4	2.93
2 Jack Aker	R	31	6	6	.500	17	48	0	0	67	65	23	36	0	2.96
Juan Pizarro	L	35	4	5	.444	1	16	7	1	59	66	32	24	0	3.97
2 Tom Phoebus	R	30	3	3	.500	6	37	1	0	83	76	45	59	0	3.80
Steve Hamilton	L	38	1	0	1.000	0	17	0	0	17	24	8	13	0	4.76
Joe Decker	R	25	1	0	1.000	0	5	1	0	13	9	4	7	0	2.08
Bill Bonham	R	24	1	0	.500	4	19	0	0	58	56	25	49	0	3.10
Larry Gura	L	24	0	0	—	0	7	0	0	12	11	3	13	0	3.75
Clint Compton	L	21	0	0	—	0	1	0	0	2	2	2	0	0	9.00
1 Phil Regan	R	35	0	1	.000	1	6	0	0	6	6	3	2	0	2.25
Dan McGinn	R	28	0	0	.000	0	18	0	0	63	78	24	42	0	5.86

NAME	G by Pos	B	AGE	G	AB	R	H	2B	3B	HR	RBI	BB	SO	SB	BA	SA
NEW YORK 3rd 83-73 .532 13.5								GIL HODGES (DD) 47			YOGI BERRA 83-73 .532					
TOTALS			28	156	5135	528	1154	171	31	105	490	589	990	41	.225	.332
Ed Kranepool	1B108, OF1	L	27	122	327	28	88	15	1	8	34	34	35	1	.269	.394
Ken Boswell	2B94	L	26	100	355	35	75	9	1	9	33	32	35	2	.211	.318
Bud Harrelson (XJ)	SS115	B	28	115	418	53	90	10	4	1	24	58	57	12	.215	.266
Jim Fregosi	3B85, SS6, 1B3	R	30	101	340	31	79	15	4	5	32	38	71	0	.232	.344
John Milner	OF109	L	22	117	362	52	86	12	2	17	38	51	74	2	.238	.423
Tommie Agee	OF84, 1B20	R	29	106	375	39	92	15	1	5	52	30	83	1	.245	.379
Cleon Jones	OF84, 1B20	R	29	106	375	39	92	15	1	5	52	30	83	1	.245	.379
Duffy Dyer	C91, OF1	R	26	94	325	33	75	17	3	8	36	28	71	0	.231	.375
Wayne Garrett	3B82, 2B22	L	24	111	298	41	69	3	2	9	29	70	58	3	.232	.315
Ted Martinez	2B47, SS42, OF15, 3B2	R	24	103	330	22	74	5	5	1	19	12	49	7	.224	.279
Dave Marshall	OF42	L	29	72	156	21	39	5	0	4	11	22	28	3	.250	.359
2 Willie Mays	OF49, 1B11	R	41	69	195	27	52	9	1	8	19	43	43	1	.267	.446
Rusty Staub (BH)	OF65	L	28	66	239	32	70	11	0	9	38	31	13	0	.293	.452
Jerry Grote	C59, 3B3, OF1	R	29	64	205	15	43	5	1	3	21	26	27	1	.210	.288
Jim Beauchamp	1B35, OF5	R	32	58	120	10	29	1	0	3	12	6	23	1	.242	.375
Dave Schneck	OF33	L	23	37	87	7	23	3	2	3	10	10	26	0	.187	.437
Lute Barnes	2B14, SS6	R	25	24	72	5	17	4	0	0	6	6	4	0	.236	.319

Bill Sudakis (KJ) 26 B 7-49, Don Hahn 23 R 6-37, Joe Nolan 21 L 0-10

NAME	T	AGE	W	L	PCT	SV	G	GS	CG	IP	H	BB	SO	SHO	ERA
		27	83	73	.532	41	156	156	32	1415	1263	486	1059	12	3.26
Tom Seaver	R	27	21	12	.636	0	35	35	13	262	215	77	249	3	2.92
Jon Matlack	L	22	15	10	.600	0	34	32	8	244	215	71	169	4	2.32
Jim McAndrew	R	28	11	8	.579	1	28	23	4	161	133	38	81	0	2.80
Jerry Koosman	L	29	11	12	.478	1	34	24	4	163	155	52	147	1	4.14
Tug McGraw	R	27	8	6	.571	27	54	0	0	106	71	40	92	0	1.70
Gary Gentry	R	25	7	10	.412	0	32	26	3	164	153	75	120	0	4.01
Danny Frisella	R	26	5	8	.385	9	39	0	0	67	63	20	46	0	3.36
Buzz Capra	R	24	3	2	.600	0	14	6	0	53	50	27	45	0	4.58
Ray Sadecki	L	31	2	1	.667	0	2	0	0	76	73	31	38	0	3.08
1 Chuck Taylor	R	30	1	0	1.000	2	20	0	0	31	44	9	9	0	5.52
Hank Webb	R	22	0	0	—	0	3	0	0	12	11	8	5	0	4.50
Tommy Moore	R	23	0	1	—	0	3	0	0	12	12	1	5	0	5.00
Bob Rauch	R	23	0	0	1.000	0	11	5	0	27	34	15	20	0	6.90
Brent Strom	R	23	0	1	—	0	11	0	0	30	34	15	20	0	6.90

NAME	G by Pos	B	AGE	G	AB	R	H	2B	3B	HR	RBI	BB	SO	SB	BA	SA
ST. LOUIS 4th 75-81 .481 21.5								RED SCHOENDIENST								
TOTALS			27	156	5326	568	1383	214	42	70	518	437	793	104	.260	.355
1 Matty Alou	1B66, OF39	L	33	108	404	46	127	17	2	3	31	24	23	11	.314	.389
Ted Sizemore	2B111	R	27	120	439	53	116	17	2	3	38	37	36	8	.264	.335
1 Dal Maxvill	SS95, 2B11	R	33	105	276	22	61	6	1	1	23	31	47	0	.221	.261
Joe Torre	3B117, 1B27	R	31	149	544	71	157	26	6	11	81	54	64	3	.289	.419
2 Bernie Carbo	OF92, 3B1	L	24	99	302	42	78	13	1	7	34	57	56	0	.258	.377
Jose Cruz	OF102	L	24	117	332	33	78	14	4	2	23	36	54	9	.235	.319
Lou Brock	OF149	L	33	153	621	81	193	26	8	3	42	47	93	63	.311	.393
Ted Simmons	C135, 1B15	B	22	152	594	70	180	36	6	16	96	29	57	1	.303	.465
Luis Melendez	OF105	R	22	118	332	32	79	11	3	5	28	33	44	5	.238	.334
Ed Crosby	SS43, 2B38, 3B14	L	23	101	276	27	60	9	1	0	19	18	27	1	.217	.257
Donn Clendenon	1B36	R	36	61	136	13	26	4	0	4	9	17	37	1	.191	.309
1 Dwain Anderson	SS43, 3B13, 2B1	R	24	57	135	12	36	4	1	0	9	14	23	0	.267	.333
Jerry McNertney	C10	R	35	39	48	3	10	1	0	0	8	3	7	0	.208	.313
Bob Gibson	P34	R	36	34	103	12	20	5	1	0	12	4	25	0	.194	.398
Jorge Roque	OF24	R	22	27	76	7	10	1	0	1	1	9	17	0	.104	.209
1 Joe Hague	1B22, OF3	L	28	27	76	8	18	7	0	2	11	17	19	0	.237	.447
Mick Kelleher	SS23	R	24	27	68	7	18	3	0	0	5	5	6	0	.265	.309
Skip Jutze	C17	R	26	21	71	11	17	3	1	0	6	5	16	0	.239	.268
Ken Reitz	3B20	R	21	21	61	3	22	1	0	0	4	1	4	0	.361	.410
1 Mike Fiore	1B6, OF1	L	27	17	10	1	1	0	0	0	1	5	4	0	.100	.100
Bill Stein	3B4, OF4	R	24	14	35	2	11	2	0	0	5	1	5	1	.314	.543
Mike Tyson	2B11, SS2	B	22	13	37	1	7	0	1	0	1	0	5	0	.189	.216

3 Bill Voss 28 L 4-15, Ron Allen 28 B 1-11, 1 Marty Martinez 30 B 3-7, 2 Brant Alyea 31 R 3-19

NAME	T	AGE	W	L	PCT	SV	G	GS	CG	IP	H	BB	SO	SHO	ERA
		30	75	81	.481	13	156	156	64	1400	1290	531	912	13	3.42
Bob Gibson	R	36	19	11	.633	0	34	34	23	278	226	88	208	4	2.46
Rick Wise	R	26	16	16	.500	0	35	35	20	269	250	71	142	2	3.11
Reggie Cleveland	R	24	14	15	.483	0	33	33	11	231	229	60	153	3	3.94
Al Santorini	R	24	8	11	.421	0	30	19	3	134	136	46	72	3	4.10
Scipio Spinks (KJ)	R	24	5	5	.500	0	16	16	6	118	96	59	93	0	2.67
2 Diego Segui	R	34	3	1	.750	9	33	0	0	58	42	22	35	0	3.05
Don Durham	R	23	2	7	.222	0	10	8	1	48	47	22	35	0	4.31
Joe Grzenda	L	34	1	0	1.000	3	33	0	0	35	46	17	15	0	5.66
Charlie Hudson	L	22	1	0	1.000	0	12	0	0	12	18	11	8	0	5.25
Rich Folkers	L	25	1	0	1.000	0	13	0	0	36	27	15	36	0	3.46
Al Hrabosky	L	22	1	0	1.000	0	11	0	0	16	9	11	10	0	5.06
1 Moe Drabowsky	R	36	1	1	.500	2	30	0	0	56	39	24	42	0	2.57
2 John Cumberland	L	24	1	0	.500	0	14	1	0	22	23	7	6	0	6.55
Denny Higgins	R	23	1	1	.333	1	15	0	0	24	22	19	15	0	3.91
Jim Bibby	R	27	1	3	.250	0	16	8	0	63	49	39	53	0	3.38
Santiago Guzman	R	23	0	0	—	0	4	0	0	4	3	0	4	0	4.50
Tim Plodinec	R	25	0	0	—	0	1	0	0	0	0	0	0	0	27.00
Ray Bare	R	23	0	0	—	0	1	0	0	3	2	3	2	0	0.53
1 Don Shaw	L	28	0	0	—	1	7	0	0	9	10	5	3	0	10.80
Lance Clemons	L	24	0	0	—	0	8	0	0	12	21	12	6	0	10.80
Tony Cloninger	R	31	0	0	—	0	11	0	0	26	29	19	11	0	5.19
1 Lowell Palmer	R	24	0	0	—	0	15	0	0	35	30	26	25	0	3.86

MONTREAL — 5th 70-86 .449 26.5 — GENE MAUCH

NAME	G by Pos	B	AGE	G	AB	R	H	2B	3B	HR	RBI	BB	SO	SB	BA	SA
TOTALS			27	156	5156	513	1205	156	22	91	462	474	828	68	.234	.325
Mike Jorgensen	1B76, OF28	L	23	113	372	48	86	12	3	13	47	53	75	12	.231	.384
Ron Hunt	2B122, 3B5	R	31	129	443	56	112	20	0	0	18	51	29	9	.253	.298
Tim Foli	SS148, 2B1	R	21	149	540	45	130	12	2	2	35	25	43	11	.241	.281
Bob Bailey	3B134, OF5, 1B3	R	29	143	489	55	114	15	4	16	57	59	112	6	.233	.368
Ron Fairly	OF70, 1B68	L	33	140	446	51	124	15	1	17	68	46	45	3	.278	.430
Boots Day	OF117	L	24	128	386	32	90	7	4	0	30	29	44	3	.233	.272
Ken Singleton	OF137	B	25	142	507	77	139	23	2	14	50	70	99	5	.274	.410
Terry Humphrey (LJ)	C65	R	22	69	215	13	40	8	0	1	9	16	38	4	.186	.237
Ron Woods	OF73	R	29	97	221	21	57	5	1	10	31	22	33	3	.258	.425
Clyde Mashore	OF74	R	27	93	176	23	40	7	1	3	23	14	41	6	.227	.330
Jim Fairey	OF37	L	27	86	141	9	33	7	0	1	15	10	21	1	.234	.305
John Boccabella	C73, 1B7, 3B1	R	31	83	207	14	47	8	1	1	10	9	29	1	.227	.290
Hector Torres	2B60, SS16, OF2, 3B1, P1	R	26	83	181	14	28	4	1	2	7	13	26	0	.155	.221
2 Tim McCarver	C45, OF14, 3B6	L	30	77	239	19	60	5	1	5	20	19	14	4	.251	.343
Hal Breeden	1B26, OF1	L	28	42	87	6	20	2	0	3	10	7	15	0	.230	.356
Bobby Wine	3B21, SS4, 2B1	R	33	34	18	2	4	1	0	0	0	0	2	0	.222	.278
Coco Laboy (KJ)	3B24, 2B3, SS2	R	32	28	69	6	18	2	0	3	14	10	16	0	.261	.420
1 John Bateman	C7	R	31	18	29	0	7	1	0	0	3	3	4	0	.241	.276
Pepe Mangual	OF3	R	20	8	11	2	3	0	0	0	0	1	5	0	.273	.273

NAME	T	AGE	W	L	PCT	SV	G	GS	CG	IP	H	BB	SO	SHO	ERA
TOTALS		25	70	86	.449	23	156	156	39	1401	1281	579	888	11	3.59
Mike Torrez	R	25	16	12	.571	0	34	33	13	243	215	103	112	0	3.33
Mike Marshall	R	29	14	8	.636	18	65	0	0	116	82	47	95	0	1.78
Bill Stoneman	R	28	12	14	.462	0	36	35	13	251	213	102	171	4	3.98
Balor Moore	L	21	9	9	.500	0	22	22	6	148	122	59	161	3	3.47
Carl Morton	R	28	7	13	.350	0	27	27	3	172	170	53	51	1	3.92
Ernie McAnally	R	25	6	15	.286	0	29	27	4	170	165	71	102	2	3.81
Denny Lemaster	L	33	2	1	1.000	0	13	0	0	20	28	6	13	0	7.65
Tom Walker	R	23	2	2	.500	3	46	0	0	75	71	22	42	0	2.88
John Strohmayer	R	25	1	2	.333	3	48	0	0	77	73	31	50	0	3.51
Steve Renko	R	27	1	10	.091	0	30	12	0	97	96	67	66	0	5.20
Hector Torres	R	26	0	0	—	0	1	0	0	1	5	0	0	0	18.00
Joe Gilbert	L	20	0	1	.000	0	22	0	0	33	41	18	25	0	8.45

PHILADELPHIA — 6th 59-97 .378 37.5 — FRANK LUCCHESI 26-50 .342 — PAUL OWENS 33-47 .413

NAME	G by Pos	B	AGE	G	AB	R	H	2B	3B	HR	RBI	BB	SO	SB	BA	SA
TOTALS			27	156	5248	503	1240	200	36	98	469	487	930	42	.236	.344
Tommy Hutton	1B87, OF48	L	26	134	381	40	99	16	2	4	38	56	24	5	.260	.344
Denny Doyle	2B119	L	28	123	442	33	110	14	2	1	26	31	33	6	.249	.296
Larry Bowa	SS150	B	26	152	579	67	145	11	13	1	31	32	51	17	.250	.320
Don Money	3B151, SS2	R	25	152	536	54	119	16	2	15	52	41	92	5	.222	.343
Bill Robinson	OF72	R	29	82	188	19	45	9	1	8	21	5	30	2	.239	.426
Willie Montanez	OF130, 1B14	L	24	147	531	60	131	39	3	13	64	58	108	1	.247	.405
Greg Luzinski	OF145, 1B2	R	21	150	563	66	158	33	5	18	68	42	114	0	.281	.453
2 John Bateman	C80	R	31	82	122	10	56	9	0	3	17	8	39	0	.222	.294
Deron Johnson (LJ)	1B62	R	33	96	230	19	49	4	1	9	31	26	69	0	.213	.357
Oscar Gamble	OF35, 1B1	L	22	74	135	17	32	5	2	1	13	19	26	3	.237	.326
Terry Harmon	2B50, SS15, 3B5	R	28	73	218	35	62	8	2	2	13	29	28	3	.284	.367
Roger Freed	OF46	R	26	73	129	10	29	4	0	6	18	23	39	0	.225	.395
Joe Lis	1B30, OF14	R	25	62	140	13	34	6	0	6	18	30	34	0	.243	.414
Mike Ryan	C46	R	30	46	106	6	19	4	0	2	10	10	25	0	.179	.274
1 Tim McCarver	C40	L	30	45	152	14	36	8	0	2	14	17	15	1	.237	.329
Ron Stone	OF15	L	29	41	54	3	9	0	1	0	3	9	11	0	.167	.204
Pete Koegel	1B8, C5, 3B4, OF1	R	24	41	49	3	7	2	0	1	6	1	16	0	.143	.184
Mike Anderson	OF35	R	21	36	103	8	20	5	1	2	5	19	36	1	.194	.320
Byron Browne	OF39	R	29	21	21	2	4	0	0	0	0	1	8	0	.190	.190
Bob Boone	C14	R	24	16	51	4	14	1	0	1	4	5	11	0	.275	.353
Mike Schmidt	3B11, 2B1	R	22	13	34	2	7	0	1	1	3	5	15	0	.206	.294
Craig Robinson	SS4	R	23	5	15	0	3	1	0	0	0	1	2	0	.200	.267

NAME	T	AGE	W	L	PCT	SV	G	GS	CG	IP	H	BB	SO	SHO	ERA
TOTALS		28	59	97	.378	15	156	156	43	1400	1318	536	927	13	3.66
Steve Carlton	L	27	27	10	.730	0	41	41	30	346	257	87	310	8	1.98
Darrell Brandon	R	31	7	7	.500	2	42	6	0	104	106	46	67	0	3.46
Wayne Twitchell	R	24	5	9	.357	1	49	15	1	140	138	56	112	1	4.05
Barry Lersch (IL)	R	27	4	6	.400	0	36	8	3	101	86	33	48	1	3.03
1 Woody Fryman	L	32	4	10	.286	1	23	17	3	120	131	39	69	2	4.35
Billy Champion	R	24	4	14	.222	0	30	22	2	133	155	54	54	0	5.08
Dick Selma	R	28	2	9	.182	3	46	10	1	99	91	73	58	0	5.55
Ken Reynolds	L	25	2	15	.118	0	33	23	2	154	149	60	87	0	4.27
Billy Wilson (XJ)	R	29	1	1	.500	0	23	0	0	30	26	11	18	0	3.30
Chris Short (XJ)	L	34	1	1	.500	1	19	0	0	23	24	8	20	0	3.91
Dave Downs	R	20	1	1	.500	0	4	4	1	23	25	3	5	1	2.74
Mac Scarce	L	23	1	2	.333	4	31	0	0	37	30	20	40	0	3.41
Bob Terlecki	R	27	0	0	—	0	13	0	0	16	10	5	6	0	4.85
Joe Hoerner	L	35	0	2	.000	3	15	0	0	22	21	5	12	0	2.05
2 Gary Neibauer	R	27	0	2	.000	0	9	2	0	19	17	14	7	0	5.21
2 Jim Nash (SJ)	R	27	0	8	.000	0	9	8	0	37	46	17	15	0	6.32

WEST DIVISION

CINCINNATI — 1st 95-59 .617 — SPARKY ANDERSON

NAME	G by Pos	B	AGE	G	AB	R	H	2B	3B	HR	RBI	BB	SO	SB	BA	SA
TOTALS			27	154	5241	707	1317	214	44	124	650	606	914	140	.251	.380
Tony Perez	1B136	R	30	136	515	64	146	33	7	21	90	55	121	4	.283	.497
Joe Morgan	2B149	L	28	149	552	122	161	23	4	16	73	115	44	58	.292	.435
Dave Concepcion	SS114, 3B9, 2B1	R	24	119	378	40	79	13	2	2	29	32	65	13	.209	.270
Denis Menke	3B130, 1B11	R	31	140	447	41	104	19	2	9	50	58	76	0	.233	.345
Cesar Geronimo	OF106	L	24	120	255	32	70	9	7	4	29	24	64	2	.275	.412
Bobby Tolan	OF149	L	26	149	604	88	171	28	5	8	82	44	88	42	.283	.386
Pete Rose	OF154	B	31	154	645	107	198	31	11	6	57	73	46	10	.307	.417
Johnny Bench	C129, OF17, 1B7, 3B4	R	24	147	538	87	145	22	2	40	125	100	84	6	.270	.541
Darrel Chaney	SS64, 2B12, 3B10	B	24	83	196	29	49	7	2	2	19	29	28	1	.250	.337
Ted Uhlaender	OF27	L	32	73	113	9	18	3	0	0	6	13	11	0	.159	.186
2 Joe Hague	1B22, OF19	L	28	69	138	17	34	7	1	4	20	20	18	1	.246	.399
Hal McRae	OF12, 3B11	R	26	61	97	9	27	5	0	5	26	2	10	0	.278	.474
George Foster	OF47	R	23	59	145	15	29	4	1	2	12	5	44	2	.200	.283
Julian Javier	3B19, 2B5, 1B1	R	35	44	91	3	19	2	0	2	12	6	11	1	.209	.297
Bill Plummer (FJ)	C36, 1B1, 3B1	R	25	38	102	8	19	4	0	2	9	4	20	0	.186	.284
1 Bernie Carbo	OF4	R	24	19	21	2	3	0	0	0	0	0	5	0	.143	.143
Sonny Ruberto	C2	R	26	3	0	0	0	0	0	0	0	0	0	0	.000	.000
1 Pat Corrales	C2	R	31	2	1	0	0	0	0	0	0	0	2	0	.000	.000

NAME	T	AGE	W	L	PCT	SV	G	GS	CG	IP	H	BB	SO	SHO	ERA
TOTALS		25	95	59	.617	60	154	154	25	1413	1313	435	806	15	3.21
Gary Nolan	R	24	15	5	.750	0	25	25	6	176	147	30	90	2	1.99
Ross Grimsley	L	22	14	8	.636	1	30	28	4	198	194	50	79	1	3.05
Jack Billingham	R	29	12	12	.500	1	36	31	8	218	197	64	137	4	3.18
Tom Hall	L	24	10	1	.909	8	47	7	1	124	77	56	134	1	2.61
Jim McGlothlin	R	28	9	8	.529	0	31	21	3	145	165	49	69	1	3.91
Don Gullett	L	21	9	10	.474	2	31	16	2	135	127	43	96	0	3.93
Pedro Borbon	R	25	8	3	.727	11	62	2	0	122	115	32	48	0	3.17
Wayne Simpson	R	23	8	5	.615	0	24	22	1	130	124	49	70	0	4.15
Clay Carroll	R	31	6	4	.600	37	65	0	0	96	89	32	51	0	2.25
Ed Sprague	R	26	3	3	.500	0	33	1	0	57	55	26	25	0	4.11
Jim Merritt	L	28	1	0	1.000	0	4	1	0	8	13	2	4	0	4.50
1 Joe Gibbon	L	37	0	0	—	0	2	0	0	0.1	3	1	1	0	54.00
Dave Tomlin	L	23	0	0	—	0	3	0	0	1	1	1	0	0	9.00

HOUSTON — 2nd 84-69 .549 10.5 — HARRY WALKER 67-54 .554 — SALTY PARKER 1-0 1.000 — 2 LEO DUROCHER 16-15 .516

NAME	G by Pos	B	AGE	G	AB	R	H	2B	3B	HR	RBI	BB	SO	SB	BA	SA
TOTALS			28	153	5267	708	1359	233	38	134	660	524	907	111	.258	.393
Lee May	1B146	R	29	148	592	87	168	31	2	29	98	52	145	3	.284	.490
Tommy Helms	2B139	R	31	139	518	45	134	20	5	5	60	24	27	4	.259	.346
Roger Metzger	SS153	B	24	153	641	84	142	12	3	2	38	60	71	23	.222	.259
Doug Rader	3B152	R	27	152	553	70	131	24	7	22	90	57	120	1	.237	.425
Jim Wynn	OF144	R	30	145	542	117	148	29	3	24	90	103	99	17	.273	.470
Cesar Cedeno	OF137	R	21	139	559	103	179	39	8	22	82	56	62	55	.320	.537
Bob Watson	OF143, 1B2	R	26	147	548	74	171	27	4	16	86	53	83	1	.312	.464
Johnny Edwards	C105	L	34	108	332	33	89	16	2	5	40	50	39	2	.268	.373
Jimmy Stewart	OF11, 1B9, SS8, 3B2	B	33	68	96	14	21	5	2	0	9	6	9	0	.219	.313
Norm Miller	OF26	L	26	67	107	18	26	4	0	4	13	13	23	1	.243	.393
Larry Howard	C53, OF1	R	27	54	157	16	35	7	0	2	13	17	30	0	.223	.306
Jesus Alou	OF23	R	30	52	93	8	29	4	1	0	11	7	5	0	.312	.376
Bob Fenwick	2B17, SS4, 3B2	B	25	36	50	7	9	3	0	0	4	3	13	0	.180	.240
Bob Stinson	C12, OF3	B	26	27	35	3	6	1	0	0	2	1	6	0	.171	.200
1 Jack Hiatt	C10	R	29	10	25	2	5	3	0	0	0	5	5	0	.200	.320
Rich Chiles	OF2	L	22	9	11	0	3	1	0	0	2	1	1	0	.273	.364
Gary Sutherland	2B1, 3B1	R	27	8	8	0	1	0	0	0	1	0	2	0	.125	.125
Cliff Johnson	C1	R	24	5	4	0	1	0	0	0	0	0	2	0	.250	.250

NAME	T	AGE	W	L	PCT	SV	G	GS	CG	IP	H	BB	SO	SHO	ERA
TOTALS		27	84	69	.549	31	153	153	38	1385	1340	498	971	14	3.77
Larry Dierker	R	25	15	8	.652	0	31	31	12	215	209	51	115	5	3.39
Don Wilson	R	27	15	10	.600	0	33	33	13	228	196	66	172	3	2.68
Dave Roberts	L	27	12	7	.632	2	35	28	7	192	227	57	111	3	4.50
Jim Ray	R	27	10	9	.526	8	54	0	0	90	77	44	50	0	4.30
Jerry Reuss	L	23	9	13	.409	1	33	30	4	192	177	83	174	1	4.17
George Culver	R	28	6	2	.750	2	45	0	0	97	73	43	82	0	3.06
Ken Forsch	R	25	6	8	.429	0	30	24	1	156	163	62	113	0	3.92
Tom Griffin	R	24	4	4	.556	3	39	5	1	94	92	38	83	1	3.26
Fred Gladding	R	36	5	6	.455	14	42	0	0	49	38	12	18	0	2.78
J. R. Richard	R	22	1	0	1.000	0	4	1	0	6	10	8	3	0	13.50
1 Wade Blasingame	L	28	0	0	—	0	10	0	0	9	10	9	0	0	9.00
2 Joe Gibbon	L	37	0	0	—	0	7	0	0	13	5	4	0	0	10.29
Jim York	R	24	0	1	.000	1	26	0	0	36	45	18	25	0	5.25
Mike Cosgrove	L	21	0	0	—	0	14	0	0	16	16	3	7	0	4.50

LOS ANGELES — 3rd 85-70 .548 10.5 — WALT ALSTON

NAME	G by Pos	B	AGE	G	AB	R	H	2B	3B	HR	RBI	BB	SO	SB	BA	SA
TOTALS			28	155	5270	584	1349	178	39	98	543	480	786	82	.256	.360
Wes Parker	1B120, OF5	B	24	130	427	45	119	14	3	4	59	62	43	3	.279	.354
Lee Lacy (KJ)	2B58	R	24	60	243	34	63	7	3	0	12	19	37	5	.259	.313
Bill Russell	SS121, OF6	R	23	129	434	47	118	19	5	4	34	34	64	14	.272	.366
Steve Garvey	3B85, 1B3	R	23	96	294	36	79	14	2	9	30	19	36	4	.269	.422
Frank Robinson	OF95	R	36	103	342	41	86	6	1	19	59	55	76	2	.251	.442
Willie Davis	OF146	L	32	149	615	81	178	22	7	19	79	27	61	20	.289	.441
Manny Mota	OF99	R	34	118	371	57	120	16	5	4	48	27	15	4	.323	.434
Chris Cannizzaro	C72	R	34	73	200	14	48	6	0	2	18	31	38	0	.240	.300
Bobby Valentine	2B49, 3B39, OF16, SS10	R	22	119	391	42	107	11	2	3	32	27	33	5	.274	.335
Bill Buckner	OF61, 1B35	L	22	105	383	47	122	14	3	5	37	17	13	10	.319	.414
Willie Crawford	OF74	L	25	96	243	28	61	7	3	8	27	35	55	4	.251	.403
Maury Wills	SS31, 3B26	B	39	71	132	16	17	3	0	0	4	11	12	3	.129	.167
Jim Lefebvre	2B33, 3B11	B	30	70	169	11	34	4	0	2	24	17	30	0	.201	.337
Billy Grabarkewitz (SJ)	3B24, 2B19, SS2	R	26	53	144	17	24	4	0	6	16	18	53	3	.167	.278
1 Duke Sims	C48	L	31	51	151	7	29	7	0	5	18	21	40	0	.192	.278
Steve Yeager	C35	R	23	35	106	18	29	5	1	3	15	16	26	0	.274	.406
Dick Dietz (BH)	C22	R	30	27	56	4	9	1	0	1	6	14	11	2	.161	.232
Tom Paciorek	1B6, OF6	R	25	11	47	4	12	1	0	0	5	1	11	1	.255	.404
Ron Cey	3B11	L	24	11	37	3	10	1	0	1	7	7	10	0	.270	.378
Davey Lopes	2B11	R	27	11	42	6	9	4	0	0	2	6	7	4	.214	.310
Terry McDermott	1B7	R	21	9	23	2	3	0	0	0	2	0	4	0	.130	.130
Joe Ferguson	C7, OF2	R	25	8	24	2	7	3	0	0	2	2	6	0	.292	.542

NAME	T	AGE	W	L	PCT	SV	G	GS	CG	IP	H	BB	SO	SHO	ERA
TOTALS		32	85	70	.548	29	155	155	50	1403	1196	429	856	23	2.78
Claude Osteen	L	32	20	11	.645	0	33	33	14	252	232	69	100	4	2.64
Don Sutton	R	32	19	9	.679	0	33	33	18	273	186	63	207	9	2.08
Tommy John	L	29	11	5	.688	0	29	29	4	187	172	40	117	1	2.89
Al Downing	L	31	9	9	.500	0	31	30	7	203	196	67	117	4	2.97
Jim Brewer	L	34	8	7	.533	17	51	0	0	78	41	25	69	0	1.27
Bill Singer	R	28	6	16	.273	0	26	25	4	169	148	60	101	3	3.67
Pete Mikkelsen	R	32	5	5	.500	5	33	0	0	58	65	23	41	0	4.03
2 Ron Parranoski	R	36	2	0	1.000	0	17	0	0	7	19	8	5	0	2.65
Doug Rau	L	23	2	2	.500	0	7	2	0	30	31	11	19	0	2.18
Pete Richert	R	32	3	3	.400	4	30	0	0	52	42	18	38	0	2.25
Mike Strahler	R	25	1	0	.333	0	19	2	1	47	42	22	25	0	3.26
Jose Pena	R	29	0	0	—	0	7	1	0	7	13	6	4	0	9.00
Charlie Hough	R	24	0	0	—	0	2	0	0	3	3	1	0	0	3.00
Hoyt Wilhelm	R	49	0	1	.000	1	16	0	0	25	20	15	9	0	4.68

NAME	G by Pos	B	AGE	G	AB	R	H	2B	3B	HR	RBI	BB	SO	SB	BA	SA
ATLANTA 4th 70-84 .455 25	LUM HARRIS 47-57 .452	EDDIE MATHEWS 23-27 .460														
TOTALS			27	155	5278	628	1363	186	17	144	593	532	770	47	.258	.382
Hank Aaron	1B109, OF15	R	38	129	449	75	119	10	0	34	77	92	55	4	.265	.514
Felix Millan	2B120	R	28	125	498	46	128	19	3	1	38	23	28	6	.257	.313
Marty Perez	SS141	R	26	141	479	33	109	13	1	1	28	30	55	0	.228	.265
Darrell Evans	3B123	L	25	125	418	67	106	12	0	19	71	90	58	4	.254	.419
Ralph Garr	OF131	L	26	134	554	87	180	22	9	12	53	25	41	25	.325	.504
Dusty Baker	OF123	R	23	127	446	62	143	27	2	17	76	45	68	4	.321	.504
Rico Carty (LJ)	OF78	R	32	86	271	31	75	12	2	6	29	44	33	0	.277	.402
Earl Williams	C116, 3B21, 1B20	R	23	151	565	72	146	24	2	28	87	62	118	0	.258	.457
Mike Lum	OF109, 1B2	L	26	123	369	40	84	14	2	9	38	50	52	1	.228	.350
Oscar Brown	OF59	R	26	76	164	19	37	5	1	3	16	4	29	0	.226	.323
Sonny Jackson (NJ)	SS17, OF10, 3B6	L	27	60	126	20	30	6	3	0	8	7	9	1	.238	.333
Jim Breazeale	1B16, 3B1	L	22	52	85	10	21	2	0	5	17	6	12	0	.247	.447
Paul Casanova	C43	R	30	49	136	8	28	3	0	2	10	4	28	0	.206	.272
Gil Garrido	2B21, SS10, 3B3	R	31	40	75	11	20	1	0	0	7	11	6	1	.267	.320
Larvell Blanks	2B18, SS4, 3B2	R	22	33	85	10	28	5	0	1	7	7	12	0	.329	.424
1 Orlando Cepeda (KJ)	1B22	R	34	28	84	6	25	3	0	4	9	7	17	0	.298	.476
Rod Gilbreath	2B7, 3B4	R	19	18	38	2	9	1	0	1	4	2	10	1	.237	.263
Bob Didier	C11	B	23	13	40	5	12	2	1	0	5	2	4	0	.300	.400
Rowland Office	OF1	L	19	5	5	2	2	0	0	0	0	1	0		.400	.400

Gary Thomasson 20 L 9-27, Russ Gibson 33 R 2-12, Jimmy Rosario 28 B 0-2

NAME	T	AGE	W	L	PCT	SV	G	GS	CG	IP	H	BB	SO	SHO	ERA
		28	70	84	.455	27	155	155	40	1377	1412	512	732	4	4.27
Phil Niekro	R	33	16	12	.571	0	38	34	17	282	254	53	164	1	3.06
Pat Jarvis	R	31	11	7	.611	2	37	6	0	99	94	44	56	0	4.09
Ron Reed	R	29	11	15	.423	0	31	30	11	213	222	60	111	1	3.93
George Stone	L	25	6	11	.353	1	31	16	2	111	143	44	63	1	5.51
Jim Hardin	R	28	5	2	.714	2	26	9	1	80	93	24	25	0	4.39
Tom Kelley	R	28	5	7	.417	0	27	14	2	116	122	65	59	1	4.58
Ron Schueler	R	24	5	8	.385	2	37	18	3	145	122	60	96	0	3.66
Cecil Upshaw	R	29	3	5	.375	13	54	0	0	54	50	19	23	0	3.67
2 Denny McLain	R	28	3	5	.375	1	15	8	2	54	60	18	21	0	6.50
Jimmy Freeman	L	21	2	2	.500	0	6	6	1	36	40	22	18	0	6.00
1 Jim Nash	R	27	1	1	.500	0	11	4	0	31	35	25	10	0	5.52
Larry Jaster	L	28	1	1	.500	0	5	1	0	12	12	8	6	0	5.25
1 Gary Neibauer	R	27	0	0	—	0	17	0	0	17	27	6	8	0	7.41
1 Steve Barber	L	34	0	0	—	0	5	0	0	16	18	6	6	0	5.63
Tom House	L	25	0	0	—	0	8	0	0	9	7	6	7	0	3.00
Mike McQueen (AJ)	L	21	0	5	.000	1	23	7	1	78	79	44	40	0	4.62

NAME	G by Pos	B	AGE	G	AB	R	H	2B	3B	HR	RBI	BB	SO	SB	BA	SA
SAN FRANCISCO 5th 69-86 .445 26.5	CHARLIE FOX															
TOTALS			26	155	5245	662	1281	211	36	150	600	480	964	123	.244	.384
Willie McCovey (BA)	1B74	L	34	81	263	30	56	8	0	14	35	38	45	0	.213	.403
Tito Fuentes	2B152	R	28	152	572	64	151	33	6	7	53	39	56	16	.264	.379
Chris Speier	SS150	R	22	150	562	74	151	25	2	15	71	82	92	9	.269	.400
Alan Gallagher	3B69	R	26	82	233	19	52	3	1	2	18	33	39	2	.223	.270
Bobby Bonds	OF153	R	26	153	626	118	162	29	5	26	80	60	137	44	.259	.446
Garry Maddox	OF121	R	22	125	458	62	122	26	7	12	58	14	97	13	.266	.432
Ken Henderson	OF123	B	26	130	439	60	113	21	2	18	51	38	66	14	.257	.437
Dave Rader	C127	L	23	133	459	44	119	14	1	6	41	29	31	1	.259	.333
Dave Kingman	3B59, 1B56, OF22	R	23	135	472	65	106	17	4	29	83	51	140	16	.225	.462
Jim Howarth	OF25, 1B4	L	25	74	119	16	28	4			7	16	18	3	.235	.294
Ed Goodson (KJ)	1B42	L	24	58	150	15	42	1	1	6	30	8	12	0	.280	.420
Chris Arnold	3B17, 2B7, SS4	R	24	51	84	8	19	3	1	1	4	2	12	0	.226	.321
Bernie Williams	OF15	R	23	46	68	12	13	3	1	3	9	7	22	0	.191	.397
Fran Healy	C43	R	25	45	99	12	15	4	0	1	8	13	24	0	.152	.222
Damie Blanco	3B19, SS8, 2B3	R	30	39	20	5	7	1	0	0	2	4	3	2	.350	.400
Jim Ray Hart	3B20	R	30	24	79	10	24	5	0	5	18	6	10	0	.304	.557
Gary Matthews	OF19	R	21	20	62	11	18	1	1	4	14	7	13	0	.290	.532
1 Willie Mays	OF14	R	41	19	49	8	9	2	0	0	3	17	5	3	.184	.224

NAME	T	AGE	W	L	PCT	SV	G	GS	CG	IP	H	BB	SO	SHO	ERA
		28	69	86	.445	23	155	155	44	1386	1309	507	771	8	3.69
Ron Bryant	R	24	14	7	.667	0	35	28	11	214	176	77	107	4	2.90
Sam McDowell (SJ)	L	29	10	8	.556	0	28	25	4	164	155	86	122	0	4.34
Jerry Johnson	R	28	8	6	.571	8	48	0	0	73	73	40	57	0	4.44
Jim Barr	R	24	8	10	.444	2	44	18	8	179	166	41	86	2	2.87
Jim Willoughby	R	23	6	4	.600	0	11	11	7	88	72	14	40	0	2.35
Steve Stone	R	24	6	8	.429	0	27	16	4	124	97	49	85	1	2.98
Juan Marichal	R	34	6	16	.273	0	25	24	6	165	176	46	72	0	3.71
Don Carrithers	R	22	4	8	.333	1	25	14	2	90	108	42	42	0	5.80
Don McMahon	R	42	3	3	.500	3	44	0	0	63	46	21	45	0	3.71
Frank Reberger	R	28	3	4	.429	0	20	11	2	99	97	37	52	0	4.00
Randy Moffitt	R	23	1	5	.167	4	40	0	0	71	72	30	37	0	3.68
John Morris	L	30	0	0	—	0	7	0	0	6	9	2	5	0	4.50
Elias Sosa	R	22	0	0	.000	1	6	0	0	16	10	12	10	0	2.25
Charlie Williams	R	24	0	2	.000	0	3	2	0	9	14	3	3	0	9.00
1 John Cumberland	L	25	0	4	.000	0	9	6	0	25	38	7	8	0	8.64

NAME	G by Pos	B	AGE	G	AB	R	H	2B	3B	HR	RBI	BB	SO	SB	BA	SA
SAN DIEGO 6th 58-95 .379 36.5	PRESTON GOMEZ 4-7 .364	DON ZIMMER 54-88 .380														
TOTALS			25	153	5213	488	1181	168	38	102	452	407	976	78	.227	.332
Nate Colbert	1B150	R	26	151	563	87	141	27	2	38	111	70	127	15	.250	.508
Derrel Thomas	2B83, SS49, OF3	B	21	130	500	48	115	15	5	5	36	41	73	9	.230	.310
Enzo Hernandez	SS107, OF3	R	23	114	329	33	64	11	2	1	15	22	25	24	.195	.249
Dave Roberts	3B84, 2B20, SS3, C1	R	28	100	418	38	102	17	0	5	33	18	64	7	.244	.321
Cito Gaston (NJ)	OF94	R	28	111	379	30	102	14	0	7	44	22	76	0	.269	.361
Johnnie Jeter	OF91	R	27	110	326	25	72	4	3	7	21	8	92	11	.221	.316
Leron Lee (BG)	OF96	L	24	101	370	50	111	23	7	12	47	29	58	2	.300	.497
Fred Kendall	C82, 1B1	R	23	91	273	18	59	3	4	6	18	11	42	0	.216	.322
Jerry Morales	OF96, 3B4	R	23	115	347	38	83	15	7	4	18	35	54	4	.239	.357
Larry Stahl	OF76, 1B1	L	31	107	297	31	67	9	3	7	20	31	67	1	.226	.347
Garry Jestadt	2B48, 3B25, SS3	R	25	92	256	15	63	5	1	6	22	13	21	0	.246	.344
2 Curt Blefary	C12, 1B6, 3B3, OF3	L	28	74	102	10	20	3	0	3	9	19	18	0	.196	.314
2 Pat Corrales	C43	R	31	44	119	6	23	0	0		6	11	26	0	.193	.193
2 Fred Stanley	2B21, SS17, 3B4	R	24	39	85	15	17	2	0	1	9	14	19	1	.200	.224
Dave Campbell	3B31, 2B1	R	30	33	100	6	24	5	0	0	3	11	12	0	.240	.290
Bob Barton	C29	R	30	29	88	1	17	1	0	0	9	2	19	2	.193	.205
1 Ollie Brown	OF17	R	28	23	70	3	12	2	0	0	3	5	9	0	.171	.200
1 Ed Spiezio	3B5	R	30	20	29	2	4	2	0	0	4	1	6	1	.138	.207
Rafael Robles	SS15, 3B1	R	24	18	24	1	4	0	0	0	0	3	0		.167	.167
Randy Elliott	OF13	R	21	14	49	5	10	3	1	0	6	2	11	0	.204	.306
Dave Hilton	3B13	R	21	13	47	2	10	2	1	0	5	3	5	1	.213	.298
Joe Goddard	C12	L	21	11	35	4	7	2	0	0	5	2	9	0	.200	.257

Johnny Grubb 23 L 7-21, Don Mason 27 L 2-11, Ivan Murrell 29 R 1-7, 2 Mike Fiore 27 L 0-6

NAME	T	AGE	W	L	PCT	SV	G	GS	CG	IP	H	BB	SO	SHO	ERA
		25	58	95	.379	19	153	153	39	1404	1350	618	960	17	3.78
Clay Kirby	R	24	12	14	.462	0	34	34	9	239	197	116	175	2	3.13
Steve Arlin	R	26	10	21	.323	0	38	37	12	250	217	122	159	3	3.60
Fred Norman	L	29	9	11	.450	2	42	28	10	212	195	88	167	6	3.44
Mike Caldwell	L	23	7	11	.389	2	42	20	4	164	183	49	102	2	4.01
Mike Corkins	R	26	6	9	.400	4	47	9	2	140	125	62	108	1	3.54
Bill Greif	R	22	5	16	.238	2	34	22	2	125	143	47	91	1	5.62
Gary Ross	R	24	4	3	.571	3	60	0	0	92	87	49	46	0	2.45
Ed Acosta	R	28	3	6	.333	0	46	2	0	89	105	30	53	0	4.45
Mark Schaeffer	L	24	2	0	1.000	1	41	0	0	41	52	28	25	0	4.61
3 Mike Kilkenny	L	27	0	0	—	0	5	0	0	4	7	3	5	0	9.00
Ron Taylor	R	34	0	1	.000	0	4	0	0	4	9	2	4	0	12.60
Ralph Garcia	R	23	0	0	—	0	3	0	0	5	4	3	3	0	1.80
Al Severinsen	R	27	0	1	.000	1	17	0	0	21	13	7	9	0	2.57
1 Tom Phoebus	R	30	0	1	.000	0	8	0	0	8	8	4	6	0	7.50
Steve Simpson	R	23	0	2	.000	2	9	0	0	11	10	8	9	0	4.91

Jay Franklin (JJ) 19

WORLD SERIES — OAKLAND (AL) 4   CINCINNATI (NL) 3

LINE SCORES

TEAM	1	2	3	4	5	6	7	8	9	10	11	12	R	H	E
Game 1 October 14 at Cincinnati															
OAK(AL)	0	2	0	0	1	0	0	0	0				3	4	0
CIN(NL)	0	1	0	1	0	0	0	0	0				2	7	0

Holtzman, Fingers (6), Blue (7), **Nolan**, Borbon (7), Carroll (8)

	1	2	3	4	5	6	7	8	9				R	H	E
Game 2 October 15 at Cincinnati															
OAK	0	1	1	0	0	0	0	0	0				2	9	2
CIN	0	0	0	0	0	0	0	0	1				1	6	0

Hunter, Fingers (9), **Grimsley**, Borbon (6), Hall (8)

	1	2	3	4	5	6	7	8	9				R	H	E
Game 3 October 18 at Oakland															
CIN	0	0	0	0	0	0	1	0	0				1	4	2
OAK	0	0	0	0	0	0	0	0	0				0	3	2

Billingham, Carroll (9), **Odom**, Blue (8), Fingers (8)

	1	2	3	4	5	6	7	8	9				R	H	E
Game 4 October 19 at Oakland															
CIN	0	0	0	0	0	0	0	2	0				2	7	1
OAK	0	0	0	0	0	0	0	0	2				3	10	1

Gullett, Borbon (8), **Carroll** (9), Holtzman, Blue (8), **Fingers** (9)

	1	2	3	4	5	6	7	8	9				R	H	E
Game 5 October 20 at Oakland															
CIN	1	0	0	1	1	0	0	1	1				5	8	0
OAK	0	3	0	1	0	0	0	0	0				4	7	2

McGlothlin, Borbon (4), Hall (5), Carroll (7), **Grimsley** (8), Billingham (9), Hunter, **Fingers** (5), Hamilton (9)

	1	2	3	4	5	6	7	8	9				R	H	E
Game 6 October 21 at Cincinnati															
OAK	0	0	0	0	1	0	0	0	0				1	7	1
CIN	0	0	0	1	1	1	5	0	x				8	10	0

Blue, Locker (6), Hamilton (7), Horlen (7), **Nolan**, Grimsley (5), Borbon (6), Hall (7)

	1	2	3	4	5	6	7	8	9				R	H	E
Game 7 October 22 at Cincinnati															
OAK	1	0	0	0	0	2	0	0	0				3	6	1
CIN	0	1	0	0	1	0	0	0	0				2	4	2

Odom, **Hunter** (5), Holtzman (8), Fingers (8), Billingham, **Borbon** (6), Carroll (6), Grimsley (7), Hall (8)

COMPOSITE BATTING

NAME	POS	G	AB	R	H	2B	3B	HR	RBI	BA
Oakland (AL)										
Totals		7	220	16	46	4	0	5	16	.209
Campaneris	SS	7	28	1	5	0	0	0	0	.179
Bando	3B	7	26	2	7	1	0	0	1	.269
Rudi	OF	7	25	1	6	0	0	1	1	.240
Alou	OF	7	24	0	1	0	0	0	0	.042
Tenace	C-1B	7	23	5	8	1	0	4	9	.348
Green	2B	7	18	0	6	2	0	0	1	.333
Epstein	1B	7	16	1	0	0	0	0	0	.000
Hendrick	OF	5	15	3	2	0	0	0	0	.133
Mangual	OF	4	10	1	3	0	0	0	0	.300
Marquez	PH	5	5	0	3	0	0	0	0	.600
Hegan	1B	6	5	0	1	0	0	0	0	.200
Duncan	C	3	5	0	1	0	0	0	0	.200
Hunter	P	3	5	0	1	0	0	0	0	.200
Holtzman	P	3	4	0	0	0	0	0	0	.000
Odom	P-PR	4	4	0	0	0	0	0	0	.000
Kubiak	2B	4	3	0	1	0	0	0	0	.333
Mincher	PH	3	1	0	1	0	0	0	1	1.000
Fingers	P	6	1	0	0	0	0	0	0	.000
Blue	P	4	1	0	0	0	0	0	0	.000
Lewis	PR	6	0	1	0	0	0	0	0	—

Hamilton P 0-0, Horlen P 0-0, Locker P 0-0

NAME	POS	G	AB	R	H	2B	3B	HR	RBI	BA
Cincinnati (NL)										
Totals		7	220	21	46	8	1	3	21	.209
Rose	OF	7	28	1	6	0	0	1	2	.214
Tolan	OF	7	26	4	7	1	0	0	6	.269
Morgan	2B	7	24	4	3	2	0	0	1	.125
Menke	3B	7	24	1	2	0	0	1	3	.083
Perez	1B	7	23	3	10	2	0	0	2	.435
Bench	C	7	23	4	6	1	0	1	1	.261
Geronimo	OF	7	19	1	3	0	0	0	0	.158
Concepcion	SS	6	13	2	4	1	0	0	2	.308
McRae	OF	5	9	1	4	1	0	0	2	.444
Chaney	SS	4	7	0	0	0	0	0	0	.000
Billingham	P	3	5	0	0	0	0	0	0	.000
Uhlaender	PH	4	4	0	1	0	0	0	0	.250
Hague	OF	3	3	0	0	0	0	0	0	.000
Nolan	P	2	3	0	0	0	0	0	0	.000
Javier	PH	4	2	0	0	0	0	0	0	.000
Grimsley	P	4	2	0	0	0	0	0	0	.000
Hall	P	4	1	0	0	0	0	0	0	.000
Gullett	P	1	1	0	0	0	0	0	0	.000
McGlothlin	P	1	1	0	0	0	0	0	0	.000

Foster OF 0-0, Carroll P 0-0, Borbon P 0-0

COMPOSITE PITCHING

NAME	G	IP	H	BB	SO	W	L	SV	ERA
Oakland (AL)									
Totals	7	62	46	27	46	4	3	3	3.05
Hunter	3	16	12	6	11	2	0	0	2.81
Holtzman	3	12.2	11	3	4	1	0	0	2.13
Odom	2	11.1	5	6	13	1	0	1	1.59
Fingers	6	10.1	4	4	11	1	1	2	1.74
Blue	4	8.2	8	5	5	0	1	1	4.15
Hamilton	2	1.1	3	1	1	0	0	0	27.00
Horlen	1	1.1	2	1	0	0	0	0	6.75
Locker	1	.1	1	0	0	0	0	0	0.00
Cincinnati (NL)									
Totals	7	62.1	46	21	37	3	4	3	2.17
Billingham	3	13.2	6	4	11	1	0	1	0.00
Nolan	2	10.2	7	3	6	0	1	0	3.38
Hall	4	8.1	6	7	7	0	0	1	0.00
Borbon	6	7	7	4	0	1	0	0	3.86
Grimsley	4	7	7	3	2	1	0	0	2.57
Gullett	1	7	6	2	4	0	0	0	1.29
Carroll	5	5.2	4	3	0	1		1	1.59
McGlothlin	1	3	3	2	3	0	0	0	12.00

USE NAME - GIVEN NAMES (NICKNAMES) / TEAM BY YEAR	BIRTH DATE	BIRTH PLACE	DEATH DATE	B	T	HGT	WGT	G	AB	R	H	2B	3B	HR	RBI	BB	SO	SB	BA	SA
Aaron, Hank-Henry Louis (Hammerin Hank) 54-65MilN 66-74AtlN 75-76MilA	02-05-34	Mobile, Ala.		R	R	6'	180	3298	12364	2174	3771	624	98	755	2297	1402	1383	240	.305	.555
Aaron, Tommie-Tommie Lee 62-63,65MilN 68-71AtlN	08-05-39	Mobile, Ala.	08-16-84	R	R	6'	200	437	944	102	216	42	6	13	94	86	145	9	.229	.327
Adair, Jerry-Kenneth Jerry 58-66BalA 66-67ChiA 67-68BosA 69-70KCA	12-17-36	Sand Springs, Okla.	05-31-87	R	R	6'	180	1165	4019	378	1022	163	19	57	366	208	499	29	.254	.347
Adams, Doug-Harold Douglas 69ChiA	01-27-43	Blue River, Wis.		L	R	6'3	195	8	14	1	3	0	0	0	1	1	3	0	.214	.214
Adlesh, Dave-David George 63-68HouN	07-15-43	Long Beach, Cal.		R	R	6'	187	106	256	9	43	3	1	1	11	18	80	0	.168	.199
Agee, Tommie-Tommie Lee 62-64CleA 65-67ChiA 68-72NYN 73HouN 73StLN	08-09-42	Magnolia, Ala.	01-22-01	R	R	5'11	190	1129	3912	558	999	170	27	130	433	342	918	167	.255	.412
Alcaraz, Luis-Angel Luis [Acosta] 67-68LAN 69-70KCA	06-20-41	Humacao, P.R.		R	R	5'9	165	115	345	30	70	9	2	4	29	21	58	2	.192	.260
Allen, Bernie-Bernard Keith 62-66MinA 67-71WasA 72-73NYA 73MonN	04-16-39	East Liverpool, Ohio		L	R	6'	180	1139	3404	357	815	140	21	73	351	370	424	13	.239	.357
Allen, Dick-Richard Anthony 63-69PhiN 70StLN 71LAN 72-74ChiA 75-76PhiN 77OakA	03-08-42	Wampum, Pa.		R	R	5'11	187	1749	6332	1099	1848	320	79	351	1119	894	1556	133	.292	.534
Allen, Hank-Harold Andrew 66-70WasA 70MilA 72-73ChiA	07-23-40	Wampum, Pa.		R	R	6'	190	389	881	104	212	27	9	6	57	49	128	15	.241	.312
Allen, Ron-Ronald Frederick 72StLN	12-23-43	Wampum, Pa.		B	R	6'3	210	7	11	2	1	0	0	1	1	3	5	0	.091	.364
Alley, Gene-Leonard Eugene 63-73PitN	07-10-40	Richmond, Va.		R	R	5'10	160	1195	3927	442	999	140	44	55	342	300	622	63	.254	.354
Allison, Bob-William Robert 58-60WasA 61-70MinA	07-11-34	Raytown, Mo.	04-09-95	R	R	6'2	220	1541	5032	811	1281	216	53	256	796	795	1033	84	.255	.471
Alomar, Sandy-Santos [Conde] 64-65MilN 67-71ChiN 67-69ChiA 69-74CalA 74-76NYA 77-78TexA	10-19-43	Salinas, P.R.		B	R	5'9	155	1481	4760	558	1168	126	19	13	282	302	482	227	.245	.288
Bats Right 65-66, part of 64																				
Alou (Rojas), Felipe-Felipe Rojas [Alou] 58-63SFN 64-65MilN 66-69AtlN 70-71OakA 71-73NYA 73MonN 74MilA M92-01MonN M03-06SFN	05-12-35	Haina, Dom. Rep.		R	R	6'1	195	2082	7339	985	2101	359	49	206	852	423	706	107	.286	.433
Alou (Rojas), Jesus-Jesus Maria Rojas [Alou] (Jay) 63-68SFN 69-73HouN 73-74OakA 75NYN 78-79HouN	03-24-42	Haina, Dom. Rep.		R	R	6'2	190	1380	4345	448	1216	170	26	32	377	138	267	31	.280	.353
Alou (Rojas), Matty-Mateo Rojas [Alou] 60-65SFN 66-70PitN 71-72StLN 72OakA 73NYA 73StLN 74SDN	12-22-38	Haina, Dom. Rep.		L	L	5'9	160	1667	5789	780	1777	236	50	31	427	311	377	156	.307	.381
Altman, George-George Lee 59-62ChiN 63StLN 64NYN 65-67ChiN	03-20-33	Goldsboro, N.C.		L	R	6'4	200	991	3091	409	832	132	34	101	403	268	572	52	.269	.432
Alusik, George-George Joseph (Turk, Glider) 58,61-62DetA 62-64KCA	02-11-35	Ashley, Pa.		R	R	6'3	180	298	652	75	167	31	2	23	93	73	103	1	.256	.416
Alvarado, Luis-Luis Cesar [Martinez] (Pimba, The Frito Bandito) 68-70BosA 71-74ChiA 74StLN 74CleA 76StLN 77DetA 77NYN	01-15-49	Lajas, P.R.	03-20-01	R	R	5'9	162	463	1160	116	248	43	4	5	84	49	160	11	.214	.271
Alvarez, Rogelio-Rogelio [Hernandez] (Gorrego) 60,62CinN	04-18-38	Pinar Del Rio, Cuba		R	R	5'11	183	37	37	2	7	0	0	0	2	1	13	0	.189	.189
Alvis, Max-Roy-Maxwell 62-69CleA 70MilA	02-02-38	Jasper, Tex.		R	R	5'11	185	1013	3629	421	895	142	22	111	373	262	662	43	.247	.390
Alyea, Brant-Garrabrant Ryerson 65,68-69WasA 70-71MinA 72OakA 72StLN 72OakA	12-08-40	Passaic, N.J.		R	R	6'3	215	371	866	100	214	33	2	38	148	10	210	5	.247	.421
Amalfitano, Joey-John Joseph 54-55NYN 60-61SFN 62HouN 63SFN 64-67ChiN M79-81ChiN	01-23-34	San Pedro, Cal.		R	R	5'11	175	643	1715	248	418	67	19	9	123	185	224	19	.244	.321
Amaro, Ruben-Ruben [Mora] 58StLN 60-65PhiN 66-68NYA 69CalA	01-06-36	Veracruz, Mexico		R	R	5'11	170	940	2155	211	505	75	13	6	156	227	280	11	.234	.292
Anderson, Dwain-Swain Cleaven (D) 71-72OakA 72-73StLN 73SD 74CleA	11-04-47	Oakland, Cal.		R	R	6'	180	149	306	33	62	6	2	1	14	32	70	2	.203	.245
Andrews, Mike-Michael Jay 66-70BosA 71-73ChiA 73OakA	07-09-43	Los Angeles, Cal.		R	R	6'3	195	893	3116	441	803	140	4	66	316	458	390	19	.258	.369
Aparicio, Luis-Luis Ernesto [Monteil] (Little Louie) 56-62ChiA 63-67BalA 68-70ChiA 71-73BosA	04-29-34	Maracaibo, Venezuela		R	R	5'9	160	2601	10230	1335	2677	394	92	83	791	736	742	506	.262	.343
Arcia, Jose-Jose Raimundo [Ortel] (Flako) 68ChiN 69-70SDN	08-22-43	Havana, Cuba		R	R	6'3	170	293	615	78	132	24	6	1	35	29	107	17	.215	.278
Ardell, Danny-Daniel Miers 61LAA	05-27-41	Seattle, Wash.		L	R	6'2	190	7	4	1	1	0	0	0	1	2	0		.250	.250
Aspromonte, Bob-Robert Thomas 56BknN 60-61LAN 62-68HouN 6-70AtlN 71NYN	06-19-38	Brooklyn, N.Y.		R	R	6'2	190	1324	4369	386	1103	135	26	60	457	333	459	19	.252	.336
Averill, Earl-Earl Douglass 56,58CleA 59-60ChiN 60-61LAA 62CalN 63PhiN	09-09-31	Cleveland, Ohio		R	R	5'10	200	449	1031	137	249	41	0	44	159	162	220	3	.242	.409
Azcue, Joe-Jose Joaquin [Lopez] 60CinN 62-63KCA 63-69CleA 69BosA 69-70CalA 71HO 72CalA 72MilA	08-18-39	Cienfuegos, Cuba		R	R	6'	195	909	2828	201	712	94	9	50	304	207	344	5	.252	.344
Bailey, Bob-Robert Sherwood 62-66PitN 67-68LAN 69-75MonN 76-77CinN 77-78BosA	10-13-42	Long Beach, Cal.		R	R	6'	185	1931	6082	772	1564	234	43	189	773	852	1126	85	.257	.403
Baker, Frank-Frank 69,71CleA	01-11-44	Bartow, Fla.		L	R	5'10	188	125	353	39	82	17	4	4	38	26	68	3	.232	.337
Baker, Frank-Frank Watts 70-71NYA 73-74BalA	10-29-46	Meridan, Miss.		L	R	6'2	185	146	288	28	55	8	3	1	24	40	60	4	.191	.250
Bales, Lee-Wesley Owen 66AtlN 67HouN	12-04-44	Los Angeles, Cal.		B	R	5'10	165	43	43	4	4	0	0	0	2	8	12	1	.093	.093
Banks, Ernie-Ernest 53-71ChiN	01-31-31	Dallas, Tex.		R	R	6'1	180	2528	9421	1305	2583	407	90	512	1636	763	1236	50	.274	.500
Banks, George-George Edward 62-64MinA 64-66CleA	09-24-38	Pacelot Mills, S.C.	03-01-85	R	R	5'11	185	106	201	33	44	6	2	9	27	37	59	0	.219	.403
Barbieri, Jim-James Patrick 66LAN	09-15-41	Schenectady, N.Y.		R	R	5'7	155	39	82	9	23	5	0	0	3	9	7	2	.280	.341
Barker, Ray-Raymond Herrell (Buddy) 60BalA 65ClkeA 65-67NYA	03-12-36	Martinsburg, W.Va.		L	R	6'	192	318	384	34	68	16	0	10	44	29	76	1	.214	.358
Barnes, Lute-Luther Owen 72-73NYN	04-28-47	Forest City, Iowa		R	R	5'10	162	27	74	7	18	2	2	0	7	6	5	0	.243	.324
Barragan,Cuno-Facundo Anthony 61-63ChiN	06-20-32	Sacramento, Cal.		R	R	5'11	180	69	163	14	33	6	1	1	14	23	36	0	.202	.270
Barry, Rich-Richard Donovan 69PhiN	09-12-40	Berkeley, Cal.		R	R	6'4	205	20	32	4	6	1	0	0	0	5	6	0	.188	.219
Barton, Bob-Robert Wilbur 65-69SFN 70-72SDN 73CinN 74SDN	07-30-41	Norwood, Ohio		R	R	6'	185	393	1049	54	237	31	3	9	66	87	168	3	.226	.287
Bateman, John-John Alvin 63-68HouN 69-72MonN 72PhiN	07-21-40	Killeen, Tex.	12-03-96	R	R	6'3	215	1017	3330	250	765	123	18	81	375	172	610	10	.230	.350
Bates, Del-Delbert Oakley (Butch) 70PhiN	06-12-40	Seattle, Wash.		L	R	6'3	210	22	60	1	8	2	0	0	6	6	15	0	.133	.167
Battey, Earl-Earl Jesse 55-59ChiA 60WasA 61-67MinA	01-05-35	Los Angeles, Cal.	11-15-03	R	R	6'1	215	1141	3586	393	969	150	17	104	449	421	470	13	.270	.409
Baumer, Jim-James Sloan 49ChiA 61CinN	01-29-31	Tulsa, Okla.	07-08-96	R	R	6'2	185	18	34	2	7	1	1	0	2	2	10	0	.206	.294
Beauchamp, Jim-James Edward 63StLN 64-65HouN 65MilN 67AtlN 68-69CinN 70HouN 70-71StLN 72-73NYN	08-21-39	Vinita, Okla.		R	R	6'2	205	393	661	79	153	18	4	14	90	54	150	6	.231	.334
Beckert, Glenn-Glenn Alfred 65-73ChiN 74-75SDN	12-10-40	Pittsburgh, Pa.		R	R	6'1	190	1320	5208	685	1473	196	31	22	360	260	243	49	.283	.345
Bedell, Howie-Howard William 62MilN 68PhiN	09-25-35	Clearfield, Pa.		L	R	6'1	185	67	145	15	28	1	2	0	3	12	22	1	.193	.228
Berry, Ken-Allan Kent 62-70ChiA 71-73CalA 74MilA 75CleA	05-10-41	Kansas City, Mo.		R	R	6'	185	1383	4136	422	1053	150	23	58	343	298	569	45	.255	.390
Bertell, Dick-Richard George 60-65ChiN 65SFN 66KJ 67ChiN	11-21-35	Oak Park, Ill.	12-20-99	R	R	6'	185	444	1310	91	327	34	9	10	112	106	188	2	.250	.312
Bethea, Bill-William Lamar (Spot) 64MinA	01-01-42	Houston, Tex.		R	R	6'	175	10	30	4	5	1	0	0	2	4	2	0	.167	.200
Billings, Dick-Richard Arlin (Rich) 68-71WasA 72-74TexA 74-75StLN	12-04-42	Detroit, Mich.		R	R	6'1	195	400	1231	101	280	44	1	16	142	87	207	6	.227	.304
Blackaby, Ethan-Ethan Allen 62,64MilN	07-24-40	Cincinnati, Ohio		L	L	5'11	190	15	25	0	3	1	0	0	0	1	6	0	.120	.160
Blair, Paul-Paul L.D. (Motormouth) 64-76BalA 77-79NYA 79CinN 80NYA	02-01-44	Cushing, Okla.		R	R	6'	170	1947	6042	776	1513	282	55	134	620	449	877	171	.250	.382
Bats Both part of 71																				
Blanchard, Johnny-John Edwin 55,59-65NYA 65KCA65MilN	02-26-33	Minneapolis, Minn.		L	R	6'1	198	516	1193	137	285	36	2	67	200	136	163	2	.239	.455
Blanco, Ossie-Oswaldo Carlos [Diaz] 70ChiA 74CleA	09-08-45	Carcas, Venezuela		R	R	6'	185	52	102	5	20	0	0	0	9	10	18	0	.196	.196
Blefary, Curt-Curtis Leroy 65-68BalA 69HouN 70-71NYA 71-72OakA 72SDN	07-05-43	Brooklyn, N.Y.	01-28-01	L	R	6'2	200	974	2947	394	699	104	20	112	382	456	444	24	.247	.400
Blessitt, Ike-Isaiah 72DetA	09-03-49	Detroit, Mich.		R	R	5'10	185	4	5	0	0	0	0	0	0	0	0	0	.000	.000
Bloomfield, Clyde-Clyde Stalcup (Bud) 63StLN 64MinA	01-05-36	Oklahoma City, Okla.		R	R	5'11	175	8	7	1	1	0	0	0	0	0	0	0	.143	.143
Bobb, Randy-Mark Randall 68-69ChiN	01-01-48	Los Angeles, Cal.	06-13-82	R	R	6'1	195	10	10	0	1	0	0	0	0	1	3	0	.100	.100
Boccabella, John-John Dominic 63-68ChiN 69-73MonN 74SFN	06-29-41	San Francisco, Cal.		R	R	6'1	195	551	1462	117	320	56	5	26	148	96	246	3	.219	.317
Boehmer, Len-Leonard Joseph Stephen 67CinN 69-71NYA	06-28-41	Flinthill, Mo.		R	R	6'1	192	50	116	5	19	4	0	0	7	8	10	0	.163	.198
Boles, Carl-Carl Theodore 62SFN	10-31-34	Center Point, Ark.		R	R	5'11	185	19	24	4	9	1	0	0	1	0	6	0	.375	.375
Bond, Walt-Walter Franklin 60-62CleA 64-65HouN 67MinA	10-19-37	Denmark, Tenn.	09-14-67	L	R	6'7	228	365	1199	149	307	40	11	41	179	106	175	10	.256	.410
Booker, Buddy-Richard Lee 66CleA 68ChiA	05-28-42	Lynchburg, Va.		R	R	5'10	170	23	33	6	6	1	0	2	5	3	8	0	.182	.394
Boros, Steve-Stephen 57-58,61-62DetA 63ChiN 64-65CinN M83-84OakA M86SDN	09-03-36	Flint, Mich.		R	R	6'	185	422	1255	141	308	50	7	26	149	181	174	11	.245	.359
Bosch, Don-Donald John 66PitN 67-68NYN 69MonN	07-15-42	San Francisco, Cal.		B	R	5'10	165	146	318	34	52	6	1	4	13	22	77	4	.164	.226
Boswell, Ken-Kenneth George 67-74NYN 75-77HouN	02-23-46	Austin, Tex.		L	R	6'	170	930	2517	266	625	91	19	31	244	240	239	27	.248	.337
Bowens, Sam-Samuel Edward 63-67BalA 68-69WasA	03-23-39	Wilmington, N.C.	03-28-03	R	R	6'1	188	479	1287	141	287	48	6	45	143	100	293	25	.223	.375
Bowlin, Hoss-Lois Weldon 67KCA	12-10-40	Peragould, Ark.		L	L	5'9	155	2	5	1	1	0	0	0	0	1	0	0	.200	.200
Bowman, Ernie-Ernest Ferrell 61-63SFN	07-28-37	Johnson City, Tenn.		R	R	5'10	160	165	205	29	39	4	1	0	10	12	33	3	.190	.244
Boyer, Clete-Cletus LeRoy 55-57StLN 59-66NYA 67-71AtlN	02-08-37	Cassville, Mo.		R	R	6'	180	1725	5780	645	1396	200	33	162	654	470	931	41	.242	.372
Boyer, Ken-Kenton Lloyd 55-65StLN 66-67NYN 67-68ChiA 68-69LAN M78-80StLN	05-20-31	Liberty, Mo.	09-07-82	R	R	6'2	200	2034	7455	1104	2143	318	68	282	1141	713	1017	105	.287	.462
Bradford, Buddy-Charles William 66-70ChiA 70-71CleA 71CinN 72-75ChiA 75StLN 76ChiA	07-25-44	Mobile, Ala.		R	R	5'11	190	697	1603	224	363	50	8	52	175	184	411	36	.226	.348
Brand, Ron-Ronald George 63PitN 65-68HouN 69-71MonN	01-01-40	Los Angeles, Cal.		R	R	5'7	170	568	1368	108	322	34	7	3	106	112	126	20	.238	.282
Brandt, Jackie-John George (Flakey) 56StLN 56NYN 57MS 58-59SFN 60-65BalA 66-67PhiN 67HouN	04-28-34	Omaha, Neb.		R	R	5'11	175	1221	3895	540	1020	175	37	112	485	351	574	45	.262	.416
Bravo, Angel-Angel Alfonso [Urdaneta] 69ChiN 70-71CinN 71SDN	08-04-42	Maracaibo, Venezuela		L	L	5'8	155	149	218	26	54	7	3	1	12	20	31	2	.248	.321
Breazeale, Jim-James Leo 69,71-72AtlN 73BN 78ChiA	10-03-49	Houston, Tex.		L	R	6'2	210	89	179	20	40	5	0	9	33	16	25	0	.223	.402
Breeden, Danny-Danny Richard 69CinN	06-27-42	Albany, Ark.		R	R	6'	185	28	73	3	11	1	0	0	5	2	19	0	.151	.164
Breeding, Marv-Marvin Eugene 60-62BalA 63WasA 63LAN	03-08-34	Decatur, Ala.		R	R	6'	175	415	1268	154	317	50	5	7	92	66	180	19	.250	.314
Bressoud, Ed-Edward Francis 56-57NYN 58-61 SFN 62-65BosA 66NYN 67StLN	05-02-32	Los Angeles, Cal.		R	R	6'1	180	1186	3672	443	903	184	40	94	365	359	723	9	.252	.401
Brickell, Fritzie-Fritz Darrell 58-59NYA 61LAA	03-19-35	Wichita, Kans.	10-15-65	R	R	5'5	157	41	88	7	16	1	1	0	5	7	9	0	.182	.227
Briggs, Johnny-John Edward 64-71PhiN 71-75MilA 75MinA	03-10-44	Patterson, N.J.		L	L	6'	200	1366	4117	601	1041	170	43	139	507	663	785	64	.253	.416
Bright, Harry-Harry James 58-60PitN 61-62WasA 63CinN 63-64NYA 65ChiN	09-22-29	Kansas City, Mo.	03-13-00	R	R	6'	190	336	839	99	214	31	4	25	126	65	133	2	.255	.416
Brinkman, Chuck-Charles Ernest 69-74ChiA 74PhiN	09-16-44	Cincinnati, Ohio		R	R	6'2	195	148	267	22	46	11	0	1	23	23	60	0	.172	.210
Brinkman, Eddie-Edwin Albert 61-70WasA 71-74DetA 75StLN 75TexA 75NYA	12-08-41	Cincinnati, Ohio		R	R	6'	180	1845	6045	550	1355	201	38	60	461	444	845	30	.224	.300
Brock, Lou-Louis Clark 61-64ChiN 64-79StLN	06-18-39	El Dorado, Ark.		L	L	5'11	170	2616	10332	1610	3023	486	141	149	900	761	1730	938	.293	.410
Brooks, Bobby-Robert (Hammer) 69-70,72OakA 73CalA	11-01-45	Los Angeles, Cal.	10-11-94	R	R	5'9	175	55	143	19	33	6	0	6	20	29	42	0	.231	.378

USE NAME - GIVEN NAMES (NICKNAMES)	TEAM BY YEAR	BIRTH DATE	BIRTH PLACE	DEATH DATE	B	T	HGT	WGT	G	AB	R	H	2B	3B	HR	RBI	BB	SO	SB	BA	SA
Brown, Dick-Richard Ernest	57-59CleA 60ChiA 61-62DetA 63-65BalA	01-17-35	Shinnston, W.Va.	04-17-70	R	R	6'2	190	636	1866	175	475	62	3	62	223	119	356	7	.244	.380
Brown, Gates-William James	63-75DetA	05-02-39	Crestline, Ohio		L	R	5'11	230	1051	2262	330	582	78	19	84	322	242	275	30	.257	.420
Brown, Ike-Isaac	69-74DetA	04-13-42	Memphis, Tenn.	05-17-01	R	R	6'1	195	280	536	85	137	15	4	20	65	90	130	3	.256	.410
Brown, Larry-Larry Leslie	63-71CleA 71-72OakA 73BalA 74TexA	03-01-40	Shinnston, W.Va.		R	R	5'10	170	1129	3449	331	803	108	13	47	254	317	414	22	.233	.313
Brown, Ollie-Ollie Lee (Downtown)	65-67SFN 69-72SDN 72OakA 72-73MilA 74HouN 74-77PhiN	02-11-44	Tuscaloosa, Ala.		R	R	6'2	200	1221	3642	404	964	144	11	102	454	314	616	30	.265	.394
Brown, Oscar-Oscar Lee	69-73AtlN	02-08-46	Long Beach, Cal.		R	R	6'	175	160	316	34	77	14	2	4	28	17	55	0	.244	.339
Brown, Randy-Edwin Randolph	69-70CalA		Leesburg, Fla.		L	R	5'7	170	18	29	3	4	1	0	0	0	6	1	0	.138	.172
Brown, Tom-Thomas William	64-69 played in N.F.L. 63WasA	12-12-40	Laureldale, Pa.		B	L	6'1	190	61	116	8	17	4	0	1	4	11	45	2	.147	.207
Browne, Byron-Byron Ellis (By)	65-67ChiN 68HouN 69StlN 70-72PhiN	12-27-42	St. Joseph, Mo.		R	R	6'2	200	349	869	94	205	37	10	30	102	101	273	5	.236	.405
Browne, Pidge-Prentice Almont	62HouN	03-21-29	Peekskill, N.Y.	06-03-97	L	L	6'	190	65	100	8	21	4	2	1	10	13	9	0	.210	.320
Brumley, Mike-Tony Mike	64-66WasA	07-10-38	Granite, Okla.		L	R	5'10	195	224	660	52	151	24	2	5	50	60	89	2	.229	.294
Brunsburg, Arlo-Arlo Adolph	66DetA	08-15-40	Fertile, Minn.		R	R	6'	195	2	3	1	1	1	0	0	0	0	0	0	.333	.667
Bryan, Billy-William Ronald	61-66KCA 66-67NYA 68WasA	12-04-38	Morgan, Ga.		R	R	6'4	210	374	968	86	209	32	9	41	125	91	283	0	.216	.395
Bryant, Don-Donald Ray	66ChiN 69-70HouN	07-13-41	Jasper, Fla.		R	R	6'5	210	59	109	6	24	3	0	4	13	6	25	1	.220	.275
Buchek, Jerry-Gerald Peter	61,63-66StlN 67-68NYN	05-09-42	St. Louis, Mo.		R	R	5'11	185	421	1177	96	259	35	11	22	108	75	312	5	.220	.325
Buford, Don-Donald Alvin	63-67ChiA 68-72BalA	02-02-37	Linden,Tex.		B	R	5'7	160	1286	4553	718	1203	157	44	93	418	672	575	200	.264	.379
Burda, Bob-Edward Robert	62StlN 65-66,69-70SFN 70MilA 71StlN 72BosA	07-16-38	St. Louis, Mo.		L	L	6'	180	388	634	53	142	21	0	13	78	70	65	2	.224	.319
Burgess, Tom-Thomas Roland (Tim)	54StlN 62LAA	09-01-27	London, Canada		L	L	6'	180	104	164	19	29	8	1	2	14	39	29	2	.177	.274
Burright, Larry-Larry Allen (Possum)	62LAN 63-64NYN	07-10-37	Roseville, Ill.		R	R	5'11	170	159	356	44	73	8	6	4	33	29	92	5	.205	.295
Burton, Ellis-Ellis Narrington	58,60StlN 63CleA 63-65ChiN	08-12-36	Los Angeles, Cal.		B	R	5'11	160	215	556	79	120	24	4	17	59	65	117	11	.216	.365
Callison, Johnny-John Wesley	58-59ChiA 60-69PhiN 70-71ChiN 72-73NYA	03-12-39	Qualls, Okla.		L	R	5'10	180	1886	6652	956	1757	321	89	226	840	650	1064	74	.264	.441
Camilli, Doug-Douglas Joseph	60-64LAN 65-67WasA 68RC 69WasA	09-22-36	Philadelphia, Pa.		R	R	5'11	195	313	767	56	153	22	4	18	80	56	146	0	.199	.309
Camilli, Lou-Louis Steven	69-72CleA	09-24-46	El Paso, Tex.		R	R	5'10	175	107	151	7	22	4	0	0	3	13	23	0	.146	.172
Campaneris (Campaneria), Bert-Dagoberto [Blanco] (Campy)	64-67KCA 68-78OakA 77-79TexA 79-81CalA 83NYA	03-09-42	Pueblo Nuevo, Cuba		R	R	5'10	160	2328	8684	1181	2249	313	86	79	646	618	1142	649	.259	.342
Campanis, Jim-James Alexander	66-68LAN 69-70KCA 73PitN	02-09-44	New York, N.Y.		R	R	6'	195	113	217	13	32	6	0	4	9	19	49	0	.147	.230
Campbell, Dave-David Wilson	67-69DetA 70-73SDN 73StlN 73-74HouN	01-14-42	Manistee, Mich.		R	R	6'1	180	428	1252	128	267	54	4	20	89	102	254	29	.213	.311
Campbell, Jim-James Robert	70StlN	01-10-43	Hartsville, S.C.		L	R	6'2	205	13	13	0	3	0	0	0	1	0	3	0	.231	.231
Campbell, Jim-James Robert	62-63HouN	06-24-37	Palo Alto, Cal.		R	R	6'	190	82	244	15	54	7	0	7	25	16	63	0	.221	.336
Campbell, Joe-Joseph Earl	67ChiN	08-28-38	Louisville, Ky.		R	R	6'1	175	1	3	0	0	0	0	0	0	0	3	0	.000	.000
Campbell, Ron-Ronald Thomas	64-66ChiN	04-05-40	Chattanooga, Tenn.		R	R	6'1	180	52	154	11	38	7	1	1	14	7	26	1	.247	.325
Cannizzaro, Chris-Christopher John	60-61StlN 62-65NYN 68PitN 69-71SDN 71ChiN 72-73LAN 74SDN	05-03-38	Oakland, Cal.		R	R	6'	190	740	1950	132	458	66	12	18	169	241	354	3	.235	.309
Cardenal (Domec), Jose-Jose Rosario [Cardenal]	63-64SFN 65-67CalA 68-69CleA 70-71StlN 71MilA 72-77ChiN 78-79PhiN 79-80NYN 80KCA	10-07-43	Mantanzas, Cuba		R	R	5'10	150	2017	6964	936	1913	333	46	138	775	608	807	329	.275	.395
Cardenas, Leo-Leonardo Lazaro [Alfonso] (Chico)	60-68CinN 69-71MinA 72CalA 73CleA 74-75TexA	12-17-38	Mantanzas, Cuba		R	R	5'11	160	1941	6707	662	1725	255	49	118	689	522	1135	39	.257	.367
Carmel, Duke-Leon James	59-60,63StlN 63NYN 65NYA	04-23-37	New York, N.Y.		L	L	6'3	202	124	227	22	48	7	3	4	23	27	60	3	.211	.322
Carreon, Cam-Camilo [Garcia]	59-64ChiA 65CleA 66BalA	08-06-37	Colton, Cal.	09-02-87	R	R	6'1	198	354	986	113	260	43	4	11	114	97	117	3	.264	.349
Carty, Rico-Ricardo Adolfo Jacobo	63-65MilN 66-67AtlN 68IL 69-70AtlN 71KJ 72AtlN 73TexA 73ChiN 73OakA 74-77CleA 78TorA 78OakA 79TorA	09-01-39	San Pedro de Marcoris, Dom. Rep.		R	R	6'4	200	1651	5606	712	1677	278	17	204	890	642	663	21	.299	.464
Casanova, Paul-Paulino [Ortiz]	65-71WasA 72-74AtlN	12-31-41	Colon, Cuba		R	R	6'4	200	859	2786	214	627	87	12	50	252	101	430	2	.225	.319
Cash, Norm-Norman Dalton	58-60ChiA 60-74DetA	11-10-34	Justiceburg, Tex.	10-12-86	L	L	6'	190	2089	6705	1046	1820	241	41	377	1103	1043	1091	43	.271	.488
Cater, Danny-Danny Anderson	64PhiN 65-66KCA 66-67KCA 68-69OakA 70-71NYA 72-74BosA 75StlN	02-25-40	Austin, Tex.		R	R	6'	185	1289	4451	491	1229	191	29	66	519	254	406	26	.276	.377
Causey, Wayne-James Wayne	55-57BalA 61-66KCA 66-68ChiA 68CalA 68AtlN	12-28-36	Ruston, La.		L	R	5'10	175	1105	3244	357	819	130	26	35	285	390	341	12	.252	.341
Cepeda, Orlando-Orlando Manuel [Penne] (The Baby Bull, Cha-Cha)	58-66SFN 66-68StlN 69-72AtlN 72OakA 73BosA 74KCA	09-17-37	Ponce, P.R.		R	R	6'2	210	2124	7927	1131	2351	417	27	379	1365	588	1169	142	.297	.499
Chacon, Elio-Elio [Rodriguez]	60-61CinN 62NYN	10-26-36	Caracas, Venezuela	04-24-92	R	R	5'10	170	228	616	89	143	15	5	4	39	111	109	20	.232	.292
Chance, Bob-Robert	63-64CleA 65-67WasA 69CalA	09-09-40	Statesboro, Ga.		L	R	6'2	217	277	747	76	195	34	1	24	112	68	195	3	.261	.406
Charles, Ed-Edwin Douglas (The Gilder)	62-67KCA 67-69NYN	04-29-35	Daytona Beach, Fla.		R	R	5'10	170	1005	3482	438	917	147	30	86	421	332	525	86	.263	.397
Chavarria, Ossie-Odvaldo [Quijano]	66-67KCA	08-05-40	Colon, Panama		R	R	5'11	160	124	250	28	52	12	0	2	14	25	59	4	.208	.280
Christensen, Bruce-Bruce Ray	71CalA	02-22-48	Madison, Wis.		R	R	5'11	160	29	63	4	17	1	0	0	3	6	5	0	.270	.286
Christian, Bob-Robert Charles	68DetA 69-70ChiA	10-17-45	Chicago, Ill.	02-20-74	R	R	5'10	180	54	147	14	33	5	0	4	19	11	23	3	.224	.340
Christopher, Joe-Joseph O'Neal	59-61PitN 62-65NYN 66BosA	12-13-35	Frederiksted, V.I.		R	R	5'10	175	638	1667	224	434	68	17	29	173	157	277	29	.260	.374
Cipriani, Frank-Frank Dominick	61KCA	04-14-41	Buffalo, N.Y.		R	R	6'	180	13	36	2	9	0	0	0	2	2	4	0	.250	.250
Clark, Glen-Glen Ester	67AtlN	03-07-41	Austin, Tex.		B	R	6'	190	4	4	0	0	0	0	0	0	0	1	0	.000	.000
Clark, Jim-James Edward	71CleA	04-30-47	Kansas City, Kans.		R	R	6'1	190	13	18	2	3	0	1	0	0	2	7	0	.167	.278
Clark, Ron-Ronald Bruce	66-69MinA 69SeaA 71-72OakA 72MilA 75PhiN	01-14-43	Fort Worth, Tex.		R	R	5'11	175	230	530	40	100	16	3	5	43	41	98	4	.189	.258
Clarke, Horace-Horace Meredith (Hoss)	65-74NYA 74SDN	06-02-40	Frederickstedt, V.I.		B	R	5'9	175	1272	4813	548	1230	150	23	27	304	365	362	151	.256	.313
Clemens, Doug-Douglas Horace	60-64StlN 64-65ChiN 66-68PhiN	06-09-39	Leesport, Pa.		L	R	6'	180	452	920	99	211	34	7	12	88	114	166	6	.229	.321
Clemente (Walker), Roberto-Roberto [Walker]	55-72PitN	08-18-34	Carolina, P.R.	12-31-72	R	R	5'11	180	2433	9454	1416	3000	440	166	240	1305	621	1230	83	.317	.475
Clendenon, Donn-Donn Alvin (Clink)	61-68PitN 69MonN 69-71NYN 72StlN	07-15-35	Neosho, Mo.		R	R	6'4	210	1362	4648	594	1273	192	57	159	682	379	1140	90	.274	.442
Cline, Ty-Tyrone Alexander	60-62CleA 63-65MilN 66ChiN 66-67AtlN 67-68SFN 69-70MonN 70-71CinN	06-15-39	Hampton, S.C.		L	L	6'	170	892	1834	251	437	53	25	6	125	153	262	22	.238	.304
Clinton, Lu-Lucien Louis	60-64BosA 64LAA 65CalA 65KCA 65CleA 66-67NYA	10-13-37	Ponca City, Okla.	12-06-97	R	R	6'1	185	691	2153	270	532	112	31	65	269	188	418	12	.247	.418
Coggins, Frank-Franklin (Swish)	67-68WasA 72ChiN	05-22-44	Griffen, Ga.		B	R	6'2	180	87	247	25	53	9	1	1	15	12	50	2	.215	.271
Coker, Jimmie-Jimmie Goodwin	58-62PhiN 63SFN 64-67CinN	03-28-36	Holly Mill, S.C.	10-29-91	R	R	5'11	200	233	592	44	137	15	4	16	70	55	99	1	.231	.351
Colavito, Rocky-Rocco Domenico	55-59CleA 60-63DetA 64KCA 65-67CleA 67ChiA 68LAN 68NYA	08-10-33	Bronx, N.Y.		R	R	6'3	195	1841	6503	971	1730	283	21	374	1159	951	880	19	.266	.489
Colbert, Nate-Nathan	66,68HouN 69-74SDN 75DetA 75-76MonN 76OakA	04-09-46	St. Louis, Mo.		R	R	6'2	210	1004	3422	481	833	141	25	173	520	383	902	52	.243	.451
Coleman, Choo-Choo-Clarence	61PhiN 62-63,66NYN	08-25-37	Orlando, Fla.		L	R	5'9	165	201	462	51	91	8	2	9	30	37	85	7	.197	.294
Coleman, Gordy-Gordon Calvin	59CleA 60-67CinN	07-05-34	Rockville, Md.	03-12-94	L	R	6'3	208	773	2384	282	650	102	11	98	387	177	333	9	.273	.448
Coletta, Chris-Christopher Michael	72CalA	08-02-44	Brooklyn, N.Y.		R	R	5'11	185	14	30	5	9	1	0	0	7	1	4	0	.300	.433
Collins, Kevin-Kevin Michael (Casey)	65,67-69NYN 69MonN 70-71DetA	08-04-46	Springfield, Mass.		L	R	6'2	190	201	388	30	81	17	4	6	34	20	97	1	.209	.320
Comer, Wayne-Harry Wayne	67-68DetA 69SeaA 70MilA 70WasA 72DetA	02-03-44	Shenandoah, Va.		R	R	5'10	175	316	687	119	157	22	2	16	67	106	106	22	.229	.336
Compton, Mike-Michael Lynn	70PhiN	08-15-44	Stamford, Conn.		R	R	5'10	180	47	110	8	18	0	1	1	9	9	22	0	.164	.209
Conde, Ramon-Ramon Luis [Roman] (Witto)	62ChiA	12-29-34	Juana Diaz, P.R.		R	R	5'8	172	14	16	0	0	0	0	0	0	1	3	0	.000	.000
Conigliaro, Billy-William Michael	69-71BosA 72MilA 73OakA	08-15-47	Revere, Mass.		R	R	6'	178	347	1130	142	284	56	10	40	128	86	244	9	.256	.429
Conigliaro, Tony-Anthony Richard	64-67BosA 68IJ 69-70BosA 71CalA 72-74IJ 75BosA	01-07-45	Revere, Mass.	02-24-90	R	R	6'3	190	876	3221	464	849	139	23	166	516	287	629	20	.264	.476
Cook, Cliff-Raymond Clifford	59-62CinN 62-63NYN	08-20-36	Dallas, Tex.		R	R	6'	185	193	383	38	80	17	3	7	35	26	136	2	.201	.312
Corrales, Pat-Patrick	64-65PhiN 66StlN 68-72CinN 72-73SDN M79-80TexA M82-83PhiN M83-87CleA	03-20-41	Los Angeles, Cal.		R	R	6'	195	300	737	63	166	28	3	4	54	75	167	1	.216	.276
Cottier, Chuck-CharlesKeith	59-60MilN 61DetA 61-65WasA 68-69CalA M84-86SeaA	01-08-36	Delta, Colo.		R	R	5'10	175	580	1584	168	348	63	17	19	127	137	248	28	.220	.317
Coughtry, Marlan-James Marlan	60BosA 62LAA 62KCA 62CleA	09-11-34	Hollywood, Cal.		R	R	6'1	170	35	54	5	10	0	0	0	4	10	18	0	.185	.185
Coulter, Tom-Thomas Lee (Chip)	69StlN	06-05-45	Steubenville, Ohio		R	R	5'10	172	6	19	9	6	1	0	0	0	4	1	0	.316	.474
Covington, Wes-John Wesley	56-61MilN 61ChiA 61KCA 61-65PhiN 66ChiN 66LAN	03-27-32	Laurinburg, N.C.		L	R	6'1	205	1075	2978	355	832	128	17	131	499	247	414	7	.279	.466
Cowan, Billy-Billy Rolland	63-64ChiN 65NYN 65MilN 67PhiN 69NYA 69-72CalA	08-28-38	Calhoun City, Miss.		R	R	6'	190	493	1190	131	281	44	8	40	125	50	297	17	.236	.387
Cox, Bobby-Robert Joseph	68-69NYA M80-81AtlN M82-85TorA M90-06AtlN	05-21-41	Tulsa, Okla.		R	R	5'11	180	220	628	50	141	22	2	9	58	75	126	3	.225	.309
Crawford, Willie-Willie Murphy	64-75LAN 76StlN 77HouN 77OakA	09-07-46	Los Angeles, Cal.	08-27-04	L	L	6'1	197	1210	3435	507	921	152	35	86	419	431	664	47	.268	.408
Cullen, Tim-Timothy Leo (The Worm)	66-67WasA 68ChiA 68-71WasA 72OakA	02-16-42	San Francisco, Cal.		R	R	5'11	185	700	1761	155	387	57	9	9	134	147	219	10	.220	.278
Dalrymple, Clay-Clayton Errol	60-68PhiN 69-71BalA	12-03-36	Chico, Cal.		L	R	6'	190	1079	3042	243	710	98	23	55	327	387	403	3	.233	.335
Damaska, Jack-Jack Lloyd	63StlN	08-21-37	Beaver Falls, Pa.		R	R	5'11	168	5	5	1	1	0	0	0	1	0	4	0	.200	.200
Davalillo, Vic-Victor Jose [Romero]	63-68CleA 68-69CalA 69-70StlN 71-73PitN 73-74OakA 77-80LAN	07-31-36	Cabimas, Venezuela		L	L	5'7	150	1458	4017	509	1122	160	37	36	329	212	422	125	.279	.364
Davenport, Jim-James Houston	58-70SFN M85SFN	08-17-33	Siluria, Ala.		R	R	5'11	185	1501	4427	552	1142	177	37	77	456	382	673	16	.258	.367
Davis, Bill-Arthur Willard	65-66CleA 69SDN	08-06-42	Graceland, Minn.		L	L	6'7	222	64	105	3	19	2	0	1	5	14	28	0	.181	.238
Davis, Brock-Bryshear Barnett	63-64,66HouN 70-71ChiN 72MilA	10-19-43	Oakland, Cal.		L	L	5'10	160	242	543	48	141	12	5	3	43	57	73	7	.260	.306
Davis, Jacke-Jack Sylvester	62PhiN	08-28-36	Carthage, Tex.		R	R	5'11	190	46	110	15	23	5	0	1	10	11	17	1	.213	.280
Davis, Ron-Ronald Everette	62,66-68HouN 68StlN 69PitN	10-21-41	Roanoke Rapids, N.C.	09-05-92	R	R	6'	175	295	853	96	199	44	6	10	79	56	160	9	.233	.334
Davis, Tommy-Herman Thomas	59-66LAN 67NYN 68ChiA 69SeaA 69-70HouN 70OakA 70ChiN 71OakA 72ChiN 72-75BalA 76CalA 76KCA	03-21-39	Brooklyn, N.Y.		R	R	6'2	195	1999	7223	811	2121	272	35	153	1052	381	754	136	.294	.405
Davis, Willie-William Henry	60-73LAN 74MonN 75TexA 75StlN 76SDN 77-78JL 79CalA	04-15-40	Mineral Springs, Ark.		L	L	6'2	185	2429	9174	1217	2561	395	138	182	1053	418	1977	398	.279	.412
Day, Boots-Charles Frederick	69StlN 70ChiN 70-74MonN	08-31-47	Ilion, N.Y.		L	L	5'9	165	471	1151	146	295	45	8	15	98	95	141	15	.256	.342
Dean, Tommy-Tommy Douglas	67LAN 69-71SDN	08-30-45	Luka, Miss.		R	R	6'	165	215	529	35	95	15	3	4	32	42	105	3	.180	.242
Dees, Charlie-Charles Henry	63-64LAA 65CalA	06-24-35	Birmingham, Ala.		L	L	6'1	173	98	260	27	69	12	1	3	25	24	40	0	.265	.354
de la Hoz, Mike-Miguel Angel [Piloto]	60-63CleA 64-65MilN 66-67AtlN 69CinN	10-02-38	Havana, Cuba		R	R	5'11	173	494	1114	116	280	42	5	25	115	56	150	2	.251	.365
Del Greco, Bobby-Robert George	52,56PitN 56StlN 57ChiC 57-58NYA 60-61PhiN 61-63KCA 65PhiN	04-07-33	Pittsburgh, Pa.		R	R	5'10	185	731	1982	271	454	95	11	42	169	271	372	16	.229	.352

USE NAME - GIVEN NAMES (NICKNAMES)	TEAM BY YEAR	BIRTH DATE	BIRTH PLACE	DEATH DATE	B	T	HGT	WGT	G	AB	R	H	2B	3B	HR	RBI	BB	SO	SB	BA	SA
DeMerit, John-John Stephen (Thumper)	57-59,61MilN 62NYN	01-08-36	West Bend, Wis.		R	R	6'1	195	93	132	21	23	3	0	3	7	8	33	1	.174	.265
Demeter, Don-Donald Lee	56BknN 58-61LAN 61-63PhiN 64-66DetA 66-67BosA 67CleA	06-25-35	Oklahoma City, Okla.		R	R	6'4	190	1109	3443	467	912	147	17	163	563	180	658	22	.265	.459
Derrick, Mike-James Michael	70BosA	09-19-43	Columbia, S.C.		L	R	6'	190	24	33	3	7	1	0	0	5	0	11	0	.212	.242
Dicken, Paul-Paul Franklin	64,66CleA	10-02-43	Deland, Fla.		R	R	6'5	195	13	13	0	0	0	0	0	0	0	6	0	.000	.000
Didier, Bob-Robert Daniel	69-72AtlN 73DetA 74BosA	02-16-49	Hattiesburg, Miss.		R	R	6'	190	247	751	56	172	25	4	0	51	59	72	2	.229	.273
Dietz, Dick-Richard Allen (Mule)	66-71SFN 72LAN 73AtlN	09-18-41	Crawfordsville, Ind.	06-27-05	R	R	6'1	195	646	1829	226	478	89	6	66	301	381	402	4	.261	.461
Dillard, Don-David Donald	59-62CleA 63,65MilN	01-08-37	Greenville, S.C.		L	R	6'1	200	272	476	59	116	16	5	14	47	32	85	0	.244	.387
Donaldson, John-John David	66-67KCA 68-69OakA 69SeaA 70,74OakA	05-05-43	Charlotte, N.C.		L	R	5'11	160	405	1225	96	292	35	11	4	86	132	133	19	.238	.295
Drake, Sammy-Samuel Harrison	60-61ChiN 62NYN	10-07-34	Little Rock, Ark.		B	R	5'11	175	53	72	8	11	0	0	0	7	8	17	0	.153	.153
Driscoll, Jim-James Bernard (J.D.)	70OakA 72TexA	05-14-44	Medford, Mass.		L	R	5'11	175	36	70	2	10	0	0	1	2	4	18	0	.143	.186
Duncan, Dave-David Edwin	64,67KCA 68-72OakA 73-74CleA 75-76BalA	09-26-45	Dallas, Tex.		R	R	6'2	195	929	2885	274	617	79	4	109	341	252	677	5	.214	.357
Edwards, Doc-Howard Rodney	62-63CleA 63-65KCA 65NYA 70PhiN M87-88CleA	12-10-36	Red Jacket, W.Va.		R	R	6'2	215	317	906	69	216	33	0	15	87	53	109	1	.238	.325
Edwards, Johnny-John Alban	61-67CinN 68StLN 69-74HouN	06-10-38	Columbus, Ohio		L	R	6'4	220	1470	4577	430	1106	202	32	81	524	465	635	15	.242	.353
Egan, Tom-Thomas Patrick	65-70CalA 71-72ChiA 74-75CalA	06-09-46	Los Angeles, Cal.		R	R	6'2	218	373	979	74	196	25	3	22	91	80	336	1	.200	.299
			Bats Both 75, part of 74																		
Elia, Lee-Lee Constantine	66ChiA M82-83ChiN M87-88PhiN	07-16-37	Philadelphia, Pa.		R	R	5'11	184	95	212	17	43	5	2	3	25	15	45	0	.203	.288
Elliot, Larry-Lawrence Lee	62-63PitN 64,66NYN	03-05-38	San Diego, Cal.		L	L	6'2	200	157	437	53	103	22	2	15	56	45	105	1	.236	.398
Emery, Cal-Calvin Wayne	63PhiN	06-28-37	Centre Hall, Pa.		L	L	6'2	205	16	19	0	3	1	0	0	0	0	2	0	.158	.211
Epstein, Mike-Michael Peter	66-67BalA 67-71WasA 71-72OakA 73TexA 73-74CalA	04-04-43	Bronx, N.Y.		L	L	6'3	230	907	2854	362	695	93	16	130	380	448	645	7	.244	.424
Essegian, Chuck-Charles Abraham	58PhiN 59StLN 59-60LAN 61BalA 61KCA 61-62CleA 63KCA	08-09-31	Boston, Mass.		R	R	5'11	200	404	1018	139	260	45	4	47	150	97	233	0	.255	.446
Estrada, Frank-Francisco [Soto]	71NYN	02-12-48	Navajoa, Mexico		R	R	5'8	185	1	2	0	1	0	0	0	0	0	0	0	.500	.500
Etchebarren, Andy-Andrew Auguste	62,65-75BalA 75-77CalA 78MilA	06-20-43	Whittier, Cal.		R	R	6'1	195	948	2618	245	615	101	17	49	309	246	529	13	.235	.343
Etheridge, Bobby-Bobby Lamar (Luke)	67,69SFN	11-25-42	Greenville, Miss.		R	R	5'9	170	96	246	26	60	16	2	2	25	26	38	0	.244	.350
Fairey, Jim-James Burke	68LAN 69-72MonN 73LAN	09-22-44	Orangeburg, S.C.		L	L	5'10	190	399	766	86	180	28	7	7	75	47	122	6	.235	.317
Fairly, Ron-Ronald Ray	58-69LAN 69-74MonN 75-76StLN 76OakA 77TorA 78CalA	07-12-38	Macon, Ga.		L	L	5'10	180	2442	7184	931	1913	307	33	215	1044	1052	877	35	.266	.408
Fanzone, Carmen-Carmen Ronald	70BosA 71-74ChiN	08-30-41	Detroit, Mich.		R	R	6'	200	237	588	66	132	27	0	20	94	74	119	3	.224	.342
Farley, Bob-Robert Jacob	61SFN 62ChiA 62DetA	11-15-37	Watsontown, Pa.		L	L	6'2	200	84	123	19	20	3	1	2	9	30	28	0	.163	.252
Fazio, Ernie-Ernest Joseph	62-63HouA 66KCA	01-25-42	Oakland, Cal.		R	R	5'7	165	141	274	37	50	10	4	2	8	33	85	5	.182	.270
Felske, John-John Frederick (Big John)	68ChiN 72-73MilA M85-87PhiN	05-30-42	Chicago, Ill.		R	R	6'3	195	54	104	7	14	3	1	1	9	9	35	0	.135	.212
Fenwick, Bob-Robert Richard (Bloop)	72HouN 73StLN	12-10-46	Okinawa, Ryukyu Is.		R	R	5'8	165	41	56	7	10	3	0	0	5	3	15	0	.179	.232
Fernandez, Chico-Lorenzo Marto [Mosquera]	68BalA	04-23-39	Havana, Cuba		R	R	5'10	160	24	18	0	2	0	0	0	0	1	9	1	.111	.111
Fernandez, Frank-Frank	67-69NYA 70-71OakA 71WasA 71-72CinN	04-16-43	Staten Island, N.Y.		R	R	6'1	185	285	727	92	145	21	2	39	116	164	231	4	.199	.395
Ferrara, Al-Alfred John (The Bull)	63,65-68LAN 69-71SDN 71CinN	12-22-39	Brooklyn, N.Y.		R	R	6'1	210	574	1382	148	358	60	7	51	198	156	286	0	.259	.423
Ferraro, Mike-Michael Dennis	66,68NYA 69SeaA 72MilA M83CleA M86KCA	08-14-44	Kingston, N.Y.		R	R	5'11	175	162	500	28	116	18	2	2	30	23	61	0	.232	.268
Fiore, Mike-Michael Garry Angelo	68BalA 69-70KCA 70-71BosA 72StLN 72SDN	11-01-44	Brooklyn, N.Y.		L	L	6'	175	254	556	75	126	18	1	13	50	124	115	5	.227	.333
Fitzmaurice, Shaun-Shaun Earle	66NYN	08-25-42	Worcester, Mass.		R	R	6'	180	9	13	2	2	0	0	0	0	2	6	1	.154	.154
Flood, Curt-Curtis Charles	56-57CinN 58-69StLN 70HO 71WasA	01-18-38	Houston, Tex.	01-20-97	R	R	5'9	165	1759	6357	851	1861	271	44	85	636	444	609	88	.293	.389
Floyd, Bobby-Robert Nathan	68-70BalA 70-74KCA	02-21-43	Hawthorne, Cal.		R	R	6'1	180	214	425	40	93	18	1	0	26	28	99	2	.219	.266
Ford, Ted-Theodore Henry	70-71CleA 72TexA 73CleA	02-07-47	Vineland, N.J.		R	R	5'10	180	240	711	66	156	26	2	17	68	51	134	7	.219	.333
Foster, Roy-Roy	70-72CleA	07-29-45	Bixby, Okla.		R	R	6'	185	337	1016	136	257	51	4	45	118	110	146	9	.253	.438
Foy, Joe-Joseph Anthony	66-68BosA 69KCA 70NYN 71WasA	02-21-43	New York, N.Y.	10-12-89	R	R	6'	215	716	2484	355	615	102	16	58	291	390	405	99	.248	.372
Francona, Tito-John Patsy	56-57BalA 58ChiA 58DetA 59-64CleA 65-66StLN 67PhiN 67-69AtlN 69-70OakA 70MilA	11-04-33	Aliquippa, Pa.		L	L	5'11	190	1719	5121	650	1395	224	34	125	656	544	694	46	.272	.403
Freehan, Bill-William Ashley	61,63-76DetA	11-29-41	Detroit, Mich.		R	R	6'3	208	1774	6073	706	1591	241	35	200	758	626	753	24	.262	.412
Fregosi, Jim-James Louis	61-64LAA 65-71CalA 72-73NYN 73-77TexA 77-78PitN M78-81CalA M86-88ChiA M91-96PhiN M99-00TorA	04-04-42	San Francisco, Cal.		R	R	6'2	190	1902	6523	844	1726	264	78	151	706	715	1097	76	.265	.398
French, Jim-Richard James	65-71WasA	08-13-41	Warren, Ohio		L	R	5'8	185	234	607	53	119	17	4	5	51	121	78	3	.196	.262
Fuentes, Tito-Rigoberto [Peat]	65-67,69-74SFN 75-76SDN 77DetA 78OakA	01-04-44	Havana, Cuba		B	R	5'11	180	1499	5566	610	1491	211	46	45	438	298	561	80	.268	.347
			Bats Right 65-67, part of 70																		
Fuller, Vern-Vernon Gordon	64,66-70CleA	03-01-44	Menomonie, Wis.		R	R	5'10	170	325	785	67	182	33	4	14	65	73	172	6	.232	.338
Gabrielson, Len-Leonard Gary	60-64MilN 64-65ChiN 65-66SFN 67CalA 67-70LAN	02-14-40	Oakland, Cal.		L	R	6'4	215	708	1764	178	446	64	12	37	176	145	315	20	.253	.366
Gagliano, Phil-Philip Joseph	63-70StLN 70ChiN 71-72BosA 73-74CinN	12-27-41	Memphis, Tenn.		R	R	6'1	185	702	1411	150	336	50	7	14	159	163	184	5	.238	.313
Gagliano, Ralph-Ralph Michael	65CleA	10-18-46	Memphis, Tenn.		L	R	5'11	170	1	0	0	0	0	0	0	0	0	0	0	—	—
Gaines, Joe-Arnesta Joe	60-62CinN 63-64BalA 64-66HouN	11-22-36	Bryan, Tex.		R	R	6'	190	362	771	104	186	25	9	21	95	81	197	14	.241	.379
Gallagher, Alan-Alan Mitchell Edward George Patrick Henry (Dirty Al)	70-73SFN 73CalA	10-19-45	San Francisco, Cal.		R	R	6'	185	442	1264	114	333	42	9	11	130	138	164	7	.263	.337
Gamble, John-John Robert	72-73DetA	03-28-42	Reno, Nev.		R	R	5'10	165	13	3	1	0	0	0	0	0	0	0	0	.000	.000
Garrido, Gil-Gil Gonzalo	64SFN 68-72AtlN	06-26-41	Panama, Panama		R	R	5'9	160	334	872	81	207	14	5	1	51	61	54	2	.237	.268
Gaspar, Rod-Rodney Earl	69-70NYN 71-74SDN	04-03-46	Long Beach, Cal.		B	L	5'11	165	178	260	35	54	6	1	1	17	33	29	8	.208	.250
Geiger, Gary-Gary Merle	58CleA 59-65BosA 66-67AtlN 69-70HouN	04-04-37	Sand Ridge, Ill.	04-24-96	L	R	6'	168	954	2569	388	633	91	29	77	283	341	466	62	.246	.394
Gentile, Jim-James Edward (Diamond Jim)	57-58BknN 58LAN 60-63BalA 64-65KCA 65-68HouN 66CleA	06-03-34	San Francisco, Cal.		L	L	6'4	210	936	2922	434	759	113	6	179	549	475	663	3	.260	.486
Gibbs, Jake-Jerry Dean	62-71NYA	11-07-38	Grenada, Miss.		L	R	6'1	185	538	1639	157	382	53	8	25	146	120	230	28	.233	.321
Gibson, Russ-John Russell	67-69BosA 70-72SFN	05-06-39	Fall River, Mass.		R	R	6'1	195	264	794	49	181	34	4	8	78	44	123	2	.228	.311
Gigon, Norm-Norman Phillip	67ChiN	05-12-38	Teaneck, N.J.		R	R	6'	195	34	70	8	12	3	1	1	6	4	14	0	.171	.286
Gil, Gus-Thomas Gustavo [Guillen]	67CleA 69SeaA 70-71MilA	04-19-40	Caracas, Venezuela		R	R	5'10	180	221	468	46	87	16	0	1	37	56	63	5	.186	.239
Gleason, Roy-Roy William	63LAN	04-09-43	Melrose Park, Ill.		B	R	6'5	220	8	1	3	1	1	0	0	0	0	0	0	1.000	2.000
Goddard, Joe-Joseph Harold	72SDN	07-23-50	Beckley, W.Va.		R	R	6'	182	12	35	0	7	2	0	0	2	5	9	0	.200	.257
Goldy, Purnal-Purnal William	62-63DetA	11-28-37	Camden, N.J.		R	R	6'5	200	29	78	9	18	1	1	3	12	0	16	0	.231	.385
Gonder, Jesse-Jesse Lemar	60-61NYA 62-63CinN 63-65NYN 65MilN 66-67PitN	01-20-36	Monticello, Ark.	11-14-04	L	R	5'10	190	395	876	73	220	28	2	26	94	72	184	1	.251	.377
Gonzalez, Pedro-Pedro [Olivares]	63-65NYA 65-67CleA	12-12-38	San Pedro de Macoris, D.R.		R	R	6'	175	407	1084	99	264	39	6	8	70	52	176	22	.244	.313
Gonzalez, Tony-Andrew Antonio [Gonzalez]	60CinN 60-68PhiN 70-71CalN 69SDN 70-71AtlN 71CalA	08-28-36	Central Canagua, Cuba		L	R	5'9	178	1559	5195	690	1485	238	57	103	615	467	706	79	.286	.413
Goosen, Greg-Gregory Bryant	65-68NYN 69SeaA 70MilA 70WasA	12-14-45	Los Angeles, Cal.		R	R	6'1	210	193	460	33	111	24	1	13	44	42	112	1	.241	.383
Goryl, Johnny-John Albert	57-59ChiN 62-64,M80-81MinA	10-21-33	Cumberland, R.I.		R	R	5'10	175	276	595	79	134	19	10	16	48	64	106	2	.225	.371
Gosger, Jim-James Charles	63,65-66BosA 66-67KCA 68OakA 69SeaA 69NYN 70-71MonN 73-74NYN	11-06-42	Port Huron, Mich.		L	L	5'11	185	705	1815	197	411	67	16	30	177	217	316	25	.226	.334
Goss, Howie-Howard Wayne	62PitN 63HouN	11-01-34	Wewoka, Okla.	07-31-96	R	R	6'4	204	222	522	56	113	24	2	11	54	40	164	9	.216	.333
Gotay, Julio-Julio Enrique [Sanchez]	60-62StLN 63-64PitN 65CalA 66-69HouN	06-09-39	Fajardo, P.R.		R	R	6'	180	389	988	106	257	38	3	6	70	61	127	12	.260	.323
Grabarkewitz, Billy-Billy Cordell	69-72LAN 73CalA 73-74PhiN 74ChiN 75OakA	01-18-46	Lockhart, Tex.		R	R	5'10	175	466	1161	189	274	41	12	28	141	202	321	33	.236	.264
Graham, Wayne-Wayne Leon	63PhiN 64NYN	04-06-36	Yoakum, Tex.		R	R	6'	200	30	55	2	7	1	0	0	3	6	10	0	.127	.145
Green, Dick-Richard Larry	63-67KCA 68-74OakA	04-21-41	Sioux City, Iowa		R	R	5'10	180	1288	4007	427	960	139	23	80	422	345	785	26	.240	.347
Green, Gene-Gene Leroy	57-59StLN 60BalA 61WasA 62-63CleA 63CinN	06-26-33	Los Angeles, Cal.	05-23-81	R	R	6'2	200	408	1151	130	307	49	7	46	160	89	185	2	.267	.448
Green, Lenny-Leonard Charles	57-59BalA 59-60WasA 61-64MinA 64LAA 64BalA 65-66BosA 67-68DetA	01-06-34	Detroit, Mich.		L	L	5'11	175	1136	2956	461	788	138	27	47	253	368	260	78	.267	.379
Griffith, Derrell-Robert Derrell	63-66LAN	12-14-43	Anadarko, Okla.		R	R	6'	180	124	296	33	77	16	2	5	27	7	33	5	.260	.378
Groat, Dick-Richard Morrow	52PitN 53-54MS 55-62PitN 63-65StLN	11-04-30	Wilkinsburg, Pa.		R	R	5'11	180	1929	7484	829	2138	352	67	39	707	490	512	14	.286	.366
52-53 played in N.B.A.																					
Grote, Jerry-Gerald Wayne	63-64HouN 66-77NYN 77-78LAN 79-80VR 81KCA 81LAN	10-06-42	San Antonio, Tex.		R	R	5'10	185	1421	4339	352	1092	160	22	39	404	399	600	15	.252	.326
Guindon, Bob-Robert Joseph	64BosA	09-04-43	Brookline, Mass.		L	L	6'2	185	5	8	0	1	0	0	0	0	0	0	0	.125	.125
Guth, Bucky-Charles Henry	72MinA	08-18-47	Baltimore, Md.		R	R	6'	180	3	3	1	0	0	0	0	0	2	0	0	.000	.000
Gutierrez, Cesar-Cesar Dario (Cocoa)	67,69SFN 69-71DetA	01-26-43	Coro, Venezuela	01-22-05	R	R	5'9	155	223	545	61	128	13	6	0	26	30	51	7	.235	.281
Hacker, Rich-Richard Warren	71MonN	10-06-47	Belleville, Ill.		B	R	6'	170	16	33	2	4	1	0	0	0	2	3	0	.121	.151
Hague, Joe-Joe Clarence	68-72StLN 72-73CinN	04-25-44	Huntington, W.Va.	11-05-94	L	L	6'	195	430	1195	141	286	41	10	40	163	177	222	4	.239	.391
Hahn, Don-Donald Antone	69-70MonN 71-74NYN 75PhiN 75StLN 75SDN	11-16-48	San Francisco, Cal.		R	R	6'1	185	454	997	104	235	38	4	7	74	122	158	11	.236	.302
Hariston, Johnny-John Louis	69ChiN	08-21-44	Birmingham, Ala.		R	R	6'2	180	4	8	1	2	0	0	0	1	0	3	0	.250	.250
Hall, Jimmie-Jimmie Randolph	63-66MinA 67-68CalA 68-69CleA 69NYA 69,69KCA 70-71ChiN 71ChiA	03-17-38	Mount Holly, N.C.		L	R	6'	175	968	2848	387	724	100	24	121	391	287	529	38	.254	.458
Haller, Tom-Thomas Frank	61-67SFN 68-71LAN 72DetA	06-23-37	Lockport, Ill.	11-26-04	L	R	6'4	205	1294	3935	461	1011	153	31	134	504	477	593	14	.257	.414
Hamlin, Ken-Kenneth Lee	57,59PitN 60KCA 61LAA 62,65-66WasA	05-18-35	Detroit, Mich.		R	R	5'10	170	468	1340	143	323	53	4	18	89	125	146	17	.241	.311
Haney, Larry-Wallace Larry	66-68BalA 69SeaA 69-70,72-73OakA 73StLN 74-76OakA 77-78MilA	11-19-42	Charlottesville, Va.		R	R	6'2	195	480	919	68	198	30	1	12	73	44	175	3	.215	.289
Hankins, Jay-Jay Nelson	61,63KCA	11-07-35	St. Louis Co, Mo.		R	R	5'7	170	86	207	25	38	6	0	3	10	21	32	1	.184	.280
Hansen, Ron-Ronald Lavern	58-62BalA 63-67ChiA 68WasA 68-69ChiA 70-71NYA 72KCA	04-05-38	Oxford, Neb.		R	R	6'3	200	1384	4311	446	1007	156	17	106	501	551	643	5	.234	.351

USE NAME - GIVEN NAMES (NICKNAMES)	TEAM BY YEAR	BIRTH DATE	BIRTH PLACE	DEATH DATE	B	T	HGT	WGT	G	AB	R	H	2B	3B	HR	RBI	BB	SO	SB	BA	SA
Hardy, Carroll-Carroll William 56 played in N.F.L.	58-60CleA 60-62BosA 63-64HouN 67MinA	05-18-33	Sturgis, S.D.		R	R	6'	190	433	1117	172	251	47	10	17	113	120	222	13	.225	.330
Harkness, Tim-Thomas William	61-62LAN 63-64NYN	12-23-37	Lachine, Canada		L	L	6'2	182	259	562	59	132	18	4	14	61	58	118	7	.235	.356
Harmon, Terry-Terry Walter	67,69-77PhiN	04-12-44	Toledo, Ohio		R	R	6'2	180	547	1152	164	262	31	12	4	72	117	175	17	.233	.292
Harper, Tommy-Tommy	62-67CinN 68SeaA 69SeaA 70-71MilA 72-74BosA 75CalA 75OakA 76BalA	10-14-40	Oak Grove, La.		R	R	5'9	165	1810	6269	972	1609	256	36	146	567	753	1080	408	.257	.359
Harrell, John-John Robert	69SFN	11-27-47	Long Beach, Cal.		R	R	6'2	190	2	6	0	3	0	0	0	2	2	1	0	.500	.500
Harrelson, Bud-Darrel McKinley	65-77NYN 78-79PhiN 80TexA M90-91NYN	06-06-44	Niles, Cal.		B	R	5'11	160	1533	4744	539	1120	136	45	7	287	633	653	127	.236	.288
			Bats Right 65, part of 75																		
Harrelson, Ken-Kenneth Smith (Hawk)	63-66KCA 66-67WasA 67KCA 67-69BosA 69-71CleA	09-04-41	Woodruff, S.C.		R	R	6'2	190	900	2941	374	703	94	14	131	421	382	577	53	.239	.414
Harrington, Mickey-Charles Michael	63PhiN	10-08-34	Hattiesburg, Miss.		R	R	6'4	205	1	0	0	0	0	0	0	0	0	0	0	——	——
Harris, Alonzo-Alonzo (Candy)	67HouN	09-17-47	Selma, Ala.		B	R	6'	160	6	1	0	0	0	0	0	0	0	1	0	.000	.000
Harris, Billy-James William	68CleA 69KCA	11-24-43	Hamlet, N.C.		L	R	6'	175	43	101	11	22	6	1	0	3	8	3	2	.218	.297
Harrison, Chuck-Charles William	65-67HouN 69,71KCA	04-25-41	Abilene, Tex.		R	R	5'10	210	328	1012	94	241	43	6	17	126	85	147	3	.238	.343
Hart, Jim Ray-James Ray	63-73SFN 73-74NYA	10-30-41	Hookerton, N.C.		R	R	5'11	190	1125	3783	518	1052	148	29	170	578	380	573	17	.278	.467
Hartman, J.C.-J.C.	62-63HouN	04-15-34	Cottonton, Ala.		R	R	6'	175	90	238	13	44	8	6	0	8	6	29	2	.185	.210
Heath, Bill-William Chris	65ChiA 66-67HouN 67DetA 69ChiN	03-10-39	Yuba City, Cal.		L	R	5'8	175	112	199	13	47	6	1	0	13	26	22	1	.236	.276
Hegan, Mike-James Michael	64,66-67NYA 67-68,71-73OakA 73-74NYA 74-77MilA	07-21-42	Cleveland, Ohio		L	L	6'1	188	965	2080	281	504	73	18	53	229	311	489	28	.242	.371
Heidemann, Jack-Jack Seale	69-72,74CleA 74StLN 75-76NYN 76-77MilA 74StLN 74CalA 75-76BosA 77KCA	07-11-49	Brenham, Tex.		R	R	6'	175	426	1093	94	231	27	4	9	75	78	203	5	.211	.268
Heise, Bob-Robert Lowell	67-69NYN 70-71SFN 71-73MilA	05-12-47	San Antonio, Tex.		R	R	6'	175	499	1144	104	283	43	3	1	86	47	77	3	.247	.293
Heist, Al-Alfred Michael	60-61ChiN 62HouN	10-05-27	Brooklyn, N.Y.		R	R	6'2	185	177	495	63	126	20	6	6	46	52	72	6	.255	.368
Held, Woody-Woodson George	54,57NYA 57-58KCA 58-64CleA 65WasA 66-67BalA 67-68CalA 68-69ChiA	03-25-32	Sacramento, Cal.		R	R	5'10	180	1390	4019	524	963	150	22	179	559	508	944	14	.240	.421
Helms, Tommy-Tommy Van	64-71CinN 72-75HouN 76-77PittN 77BosA	05-05-41	Charlotte, N.C.		R	R	5'10	170	1435	4997	414	1342	223	21	34	477	231	301	33	.269	.342
Hendricks, Ellie-Elrod Jerome	68-72BalA 72ChiN 73-76BalA 76-77NYA 78-79BalA	12-22-40	Charlotte Amalie, V.I.	12-21-05	L	R	6'1	195	711	1888	205	415	66	7	62	230	229	319	1	.220	.361
Henry, Ron-Ronald Baxter	61,64MinN	08-07-36	Chester, Pa.		R	R	6'1	180	42	69	5	9	1	1	2	8	4	24	0	.130	.261
Hermoso, Angel-Angel Remigio (Remy)	67AtlN 69-70MonN 74CleA 75KJ	10-01-46	Caracas, Venezuela		R	R	5'9	155	91	223	25	47	3	1	0	8	14	21	6	.211	.233
Hernandez, Jackie-Jacinto [Zulueta]	65-66CalA 67-68MinA 69-70KCA 71-73PittN	09-11-40	Central Tinguaro, Cuba		R	R	6'	170	618	1480	153	308	37	9	12	121	93	324	25	.208	.270
Hernandez, Rudy-Rodolfo [Acosta]	72ChiA	10-18-51	Empalme, Mexico		R	R	5'8	150	8	21	0	4	0	0	0	1	0	3	0	.190	.190
Herrera, Joe-Jose Concepcion [Ontiveros] (Loco)	67-68HouN 69-70MonN	04-08-42	San Lorenzo, Venezuela		R	R	5'9	175	80	231	16	61	10	0	2	20	7	28	1	.264	.333
Herrnstein, John-John Elliott	62-66PhiN 66ChiN 66AtlN	03-31-38	Hampton, Va.		L	L	6'3	215	239	450	52	99	14	4	8	34	29	115	1	.220	.322
Herrscher, Rick-Richard Franklin	62NYN	11-03-36	St. Louis, Mo.		R	R	6'2	187	35	50	5	11	3	0	1	6	5	11	0	.220	.340
Hershberger, Mike-Norman Michael	61-64ChiA 65-67KCA 68-69OakA 70MilA 71ChiA	10-09-39	Massillon, Ohio		R	R	5'10	180	1150	3572	398	900	150	22	26	344	319	311	74	.252	.328
Hertz, Steve-Stephen Allan	64HouN	02-26-45	Fairfield, Ohio		R	R	6'	195	5	4	2	0	0	0	0	0	0	0	0	.000	.000
Hiatt, Jack-Jack E.	64LAA 65-69SFN 70MonN 70ChiN 71-72HouN 72CalA	07-27-42	Bakersfield, Cal.		R	R	6'2	190	483	1142	110	287	51	5	22	154	224	295	0	.251	.363
Hibbs, Jim-James Kerr	67CalA	09-10-44	Klamath Falls, Ore.		R	R	6'	190	3	3	0	0	0	0	0	2	0	1	0	.000	.000
Hickman, Jim-James Lucius	62-66NYN 67LAN 68-73ChiN 74StLN	05-10-37	Henning, Tenn.		R	R	6'3	195	1421	3974	518	1002	163	25	159	560	491	832	17	.252	.426
Hicks, Jim-James Edward	64-66ChiA 69StLN 69-70CalA	05-18-40	East Chicago, Ind.		R	R	6'2	205	93	141	16	23	1	3	5	14	18	48	0	.163	.319
Hicks, Joe-William Joseph	59-60ChiA 61-62WasA 63NYN	04-07-33	Ivy, Va.		L	R	6'	180	212	416	41	92	11	3	12	39	29	73	3	.221	.349
Hill, Herm-Herman Alexander	69-70MinA	10-12-45	Tuskegee, Ala.	12-01-70	L	R	6'2	190	43	24	12	2	0	0	0	0	0	7	1	.083	.083
Hiller, Chuck-Charles Joseph (Iron Hands)	61-65SFN 65-67NYN 67PhiN 68PittN	10-01-34	Johnsburg, Ill.	10-20-04	L	R	5'11	170	704	2121	253	516	76	9	20	152	157	187	14	.243	.316
Hinton, Chuck-Charles Edward	61-64WasA 65-67CleA 68CalA 69-71CleA	05-03-34	Rocky Mount, N.C.		R	R	6'1	180	1353	3968	518	1048	152	47	113	443	416	685	130	.264	.412
Hodge, Gomer-Harold Morris	71CleA	04-03-44	Rutherfordton, N.C.		B	R	6'2	190	80	83	3	17	3	0	1	9	4	19	0	.205	.277
Hoffman, John-John Edward (Pork Chop)	64-65HouN	10-31-43	Aberdeen, S.D.	12-27-01	R	R	6'	190	8	21	2	3	0	0	0	1	1	10	0	.143	.143
Holman, Gary-Gary Richard	68-69WasA	01-25-44	Long Beach, Cal.		L	L	6'	200	116	116	11	30	6	1	0	9	17	22	0	.259	.328
Holt, Jim-James William	68-74MinA 74-76OakA	05-27-44	Graham, N.C.		L	R	6'	195	707	1616	174	428	64	10	19	177	93	166	8	.265	.352
Hopkins, Gail-Gail Eason	68-70ChiA 71-73KCA 74LAN	02-19-43	Tulsa, Okla.		L	R	5'10	198	514	1219	142	324	47	6	25	145	160	63	6	.266	.376
Horton, Tony-Anthony Darrin	64-67BosA 67-70CleA 71IL	12-06-44	Santa Monica, Cal.		R	R	6'3	210	636	2228	251	597	102	15	76	297	140	319	12	.268	.430
Horton, Willie-Willie Wattison	63-77DetA 77TexA 78CleA 78OakA 78TorA 78-80SeaA	10-18-42	Arno, Va.		R	R	5'11	210	2028	7298	873	1993	284	40	325	1163	620	1313	20	.273	.457
Hottman, Ken-Kenneth Roger	71ChiA	12-07-48	Stockton, Cal.		R	R	5'11	200	6	16	1	2	0	0	0	0	1	2	0	.125	.125
Hovley, Steve-Stephen Eugene (Orbie)	69SeaA 70MilA 70-71OakA 72-73KCA	12-18-44	Ventura, Cal.		L	L	5'9	180	436	1019	122	263	39	5	8	88	116	128	29	.258	.330
Howard, Elston-Elston Gene (Ellie)	55-67NYA 67-68BosA	02-23-29	St. Louis, Mo.	12-14-80	R	R	6'2	200	1605	5363	619	1471	218	15	167	762	373	786	9	.274	.427
Howard, Frank-Frank Oliver (Hondo, The Capital Punisher)	58-64LAN 65-71WasA 72TexA 72-74DetA M81SDN M83NYN	08-08-36	Columbus, Ohio		R	R	6'7	275	1895	6488	864	1774	245	35	382	1119	782	1460	8	.273	.499
Howard, Larry-Lawrence Rayford	70-73HouN 73AtlN	06-06-45	Columbus, Ohio		R	R	6'2	205	133	365	36	86	19	0	6	47	37	85	0	.236	.337
Howarth, Jim-James Eugene	71-74SFN	05-07-47	Biloxi, Miss.		L	L	5'11	180	152	226	27	49	6	1	1	16	26	29	4	.217	.265
Howser, Dick-Richard Dalton	61-63KCA 63-66CleA 67-68,M78,M80NYA M81-86KCA	05-14-36	Miami, Fla.	06-17-87	R	R	5'8	155	789	2483	398	617	90	17	16	165	367	186	105	.248	.318
Hriniak, Walt-Walter John	68-69AtlN 69SDN	05-22-43	Natick, Mass.		L	R	5'11	180	47	99	4	25	0	0	0	4	10	15	0	.253	.253
Hubbs, Ken-Kenneth Douglas	61-63ChiN	12-23-41	Riverside, Cal.	02-13-64	R	R	6'2	175	324	1255	148	310	44	13	6	98	74	230	11	.247	.336
Hundley, Randy-Cecil Randolph	64-65SFN 66-73ChiN 74MinA 75SDN 76-77ChiN	06-01-42	Martinsville, Va.		R	R	5'11	170	1061	3442	311	813	118	13	82	381	271	565	12	.236	.350
Hunt, Ken-Kenneth Lawrence	07-13-34	Grand Forks, N.D.		06-08-97	R	R	6'3	205	310	782	107	177	42	4	33	111	85	222	9	.226	.417
Hunt, Ron-Ronald Kenneth	63-66NYN 67LAN 68-70SFN 71-74MonN 74StLN	02-23-41	St. Louis, Mo.		R	R	6'	186	1483	5235	745	1429	223	23	39	370	555	382	65	.273	.347
Huntz, Steve-Steven Michael	67,69StLN 70SDN 71ChiA 75SDN	12-03-45	Cleveland, Ohio		B	R	6'1	204	237	636	81	131	19	1	16	60	108	122	1	.206	.314
Hutto, Jim-James Neamon	70PhiN 75BalA	10-17-47	Norfolk, Va.		R	R	6'	190	61	97	7	17	2	0	3	12	5	22	0	.175	.289
Izquierdo, Hank-Enrique Roberto [Valdez]	67MinA	03-20-31	Matanzas, Cuba		R	R	5'11	175	16	26	4	7	2	0	0	2	1	2	0	.269	.346
Jackson, Sonny-Roland Thomas	63-67HouN 68-74AtlN	07-09-44	Washington, D.C.		L	R	5'9	155	936	3055	396	767	81	28	7	162	250	265	126	.251	.303
Jacobs, Lamar-Lamar Gary (Jake)	06-09-37	Youngstown, Ohio	60MinA	61MinA	R	R	6'	175	10	10	0	2	0	0	0	0	0	3	0	.200	.200
James, Charles Wesley	60-64StLN 65CinN	12-22-37	St. Louis, Mo.		R	R	6'1	195	510	1406	158	358	56	9	29	172	48	260	7	.255	.369
James, Cleo-Cleo Joel	68LAN 70-71,73ChiN	08-31-40	Clarksdale, Miss.		R	R	5'10	176	208	381	69	87	15	2	5	27	28	52	16	.228	.318
Jata, Paul-Paul	72DetA	09-04-49	Queens, N.Y.		R	R	6'1	195	32	74	8	17	2	0	1	7	3	14	0	.230	.257
Javier, Julian-Manuel Julian [Liranzo] (Hoolie, The Phantom)	60-71StLN 72CinN	08-09-36	San Francisco de Mac., D.R.		R	R	6'1	175	1622	5722	722	1469	216	55	78	506	314	812	135	.257	.355
Jestadt, Garry-Garry Arthur	69MonN 71ChiN 71-72SDN	03-19-47	Chicago, Ill.		R	R	6'2	188	176	454	33	118	18	1	6	36	24	45	1	.260	.344
Jeter, Johnnie-Johnnie James	69-70PittN 71-72SDN 73ChiA 74ClA	10-24-44	East Point, La.		R	R	6'1	186	336	873	108	213	27	10	18	69	46	237	28	.244	.360
Jimenez, Elvio-Felix Elvio [Rivera]	64NYA	01-06-40	San Pedro de Macoris, D.R.		R	R	5'9	170	1	6	0	2	0	0	0	0	0	0	0	.333	.333
Jimenez, Manny-Manuel Emilio [Rivera]	62-64,66KCA 67-68PittN 69ChiN	11-19-38	San Pedro de Macoris, D.R.		L	R	6'1	190	429	1003	90	273	43	4	26	144	75	97	0	.272	.401
Johnson, Alex-Alexander	64-65PhiN 66-67StLN 68-69CinN 70-71CalA 72CleA 73-74TexA 74-75NYA 76DetA	12-07-42	Helena, Ark.		R	R	6'	205	1322	4623	550	1331	180	33	78	525	244	626	103	.288	.392
Johnson, Bob-Robert Wallace	60KCA 61-62WasA 63-67BalA 67NYN 68CinN 68StLN 69-70OakA	03-04-36	Omaha, Neb.		R	R	5'10	180	874	2307	254	628	88	11	44	230	156	291	24	.272	.377
Johnson, Dave-David Allen (known as Davey as Mgr)	65-72BalA 73-75AtlN 76JL 77-78PhiN 78ChiN M84-90NYN M95-97CinN M96-97BalA M99-00LAN	01-30-43	Orlando, Fla.		R	R	6'	180	1435	4797	564	1252	242	18	136	609	559	675	33	.261	.404
Johnson, Deron-Deron Roger	60-61NYA 61-62KCA 64-67CinN 68AtlN 69-73PhiN 73-74OakA 74MilA 74BosA 75CinN 75-76BosA	07-17-38	San Diego, Cal.	04-23-92	R	R	6'2	205	1765	5941	706	1447	247	33	245	923	585	1318	11	.244	.420
Johnson, Frank-Frank Herbert	66-71SFN	07-22-42	El Paso, Tex.		R	R	6'1	165	196	436	47	92	9	4	5	43	37	60	2	.211	.257
Johnson, Lou-Louis Brown (Slick, Sweet Lou)	60ChiN 61LAA 62MilL 65-67LAN 68ChiN 68CleA 69CalA	09-22-34	Lexington, Ky.		R	R	5'11	170	677	2049	244	529	97	14	48	232	110	320	50	.258	.389
Johnston, Rex-Rex David 60 played in N.F.L.	64PittN	11-08-36	Colton, Cal.		B	R	6'2	202	14	7	1	0	0	0	0	0	3	0	0	.000	.000
Jones, Clarence-Clarence Woodrow	61-68ChiN	11-07-42	Zanesville, Ohio		L	R	6'2	205	58	137	13	31	5	1	2	16	16	34	0	.248	.343
Jones, Cleon-Cleon Joseph	63,65-75NYN 76ChiA	08-04-42	Plateau, Ala.		R	L	6'	190	1213	4263	565	1195	183	33	93	524	360	702	91	.281	.404
Jones, Dalton-James Dalton	64-69BosA 70-72DetA 72TexA	12-10-43	McComb, Miss.		L	R	6'1	180	907	2329	268	547	91	19	41	237	191	309	21	.235	.343
Jones, Deacon-Grover William	62-63,66ChiA	04-18-34	White Plains, N.Y.		L	R	5'10	190	40	49	5	14	2	1	1	10	6	4	0	.286	.429
Jones, Hal-Harold Marion	61-62CleA	04-09-36	Louisiana, Mo.		L	L	6'2	194	11	51	4	11	5	1	0	6	3	16	0	.216	.353
Jones, Mack-Mack F. (Mack the Knife)	61-63,65MilN 66-67AtlN 68CinN 69-71MonN	11-06-38	Atlanta, Ga.		L	R	6'1	180	1002	3091	485	778	132	31	133	415	383	756	65	.252	.444
Joseph, Rick-Ricardo Emelindo [Harrigan]	64KCA 67-70PhiN	08-24-39	San Pedro de Macoris, D.R.	09-08-79	R	R	6'1	192	270	663	76	161	26	1	13	65	51	141	2	.243	.358
Josephson, Duane-Duane Charles	65-70ChiA 71-72BosA 73IL	06-03-42	New Hampton, Iowa	01-30-97	R	R	6'	190	470	1505	147	388	58	12	23	164	92	174	2	.258	.358
Kaline, Al-Albert William	53-74DetA	12-19-34	Baltimore, Md.		R	R	6'1	180	2834	10116	1622	3007	498	75	399	1583	1277	1020	137	.297	.480
Kanehl, Rod-Roderick Edwin (Hot Rod)	62-64NYN	04-01-34	Wichita, Kans.	12-14-04	R	R	6'1	180	340	796	103	192	22	3	6	47	35	80	17	.241	.300
Kasko, Eddie-Edward Michael	57-58StLN 59-63CinN 64-65HouN 66,M70-73BosA	06-27-32	Linden, N.J.		R	R	6'1	180	1077	3546	411	935	146	13	22	261	265	353	31	.264	.331
Kelly, Van-Van Howard	69-70SDN	03-18-46	Charlotte, N.C.		L	R	5'11	180	171	298	26	66	10	1	2	24	27	45	0	.221	.302
Kenders, Al-Albert Daniel George	61PhiN	04-04-37	Barrington, N.J.		R	R	6'	185	10	23	0	4	1	0	0	1	1	5	0	.174	.217
Kennedy, Jim-James Earl	70StLN	11-01-46	Tulsa, Okla.		R	R	5'9	160	12	24	1	3	1	0	0	2	1	2	0	.125	.125

USE NAME - GIVEN NAMES (NICKNAMES)	TEAM BY YEAR	BIRTH DATE	BIRTH PLACE	DEATH DATE	B	T	HGT	WGT	G	AB	R	H	2B	3B	HR	RBI	BB	SO	SB	BA	SA
Kennedy, John-John Edward	62-64WasA 65-66LAN 67NYA 69SeaA 70MilA 70-74BosA	05-09-41	Chicago, Ill.		R	R	6'	185	856	2110	237	475	77	17	32	185	142	461	0	.225	.323
Kennedy, Jerry-Gerald Tennyson	67NYA 68MS 69-72NYA 73CleA	06-30-45	St. Louis, Mo.		L	R	6'1	170	465	1369	165	325	38	13	7	103	184	139	59	.237	.299
Kenworthy, Dick-Richard Lee	62,64-68ChiA	04-01-41	Red Oak, Iowa		R	R	5'9	170	125	251	12	54	6	1	4	13	10	42	0	.215	.295
Keough, Joe-Joseph William	68OakA 69-72KCA 73ChiA	01-07-43	Pomona, Cal.		L	L	6'	185	332	863	95	212	26	5	9	81	87	75	9	.246	.319
Keough, Marty-Richard Martin	56-60BosA 60CleA 61WasA 62-65CinN 66AtlN 66ChiN	04-14-34	Oakland, Cal.		L	L	6'	180	841	1796	256	434	71	23	43	176	164	318	26	.242	.379
Kern, Bill-William George	62KCA	02-28-35	Coplay, Pa.		R	R	6'2	184	8	16	1	4	0	0	1	1	0	3	0	.250	.438
Kernek, George-George Boyd	65-66StlN	01-12-40	Holdenville, Okla.		L	L	6'3	190	30	81	11	21	3	2	0	6	6	13	1	.259	.346
Kessinger, Don-Donald Eulon	64-75ChiN 76-77StlN 77-79,M79ChiA	07-17-42	Forrest City, Ark.		B	R	6'1	170	2078	7651	899	1931	254	80	14	527	684	759	100	.252	.312
Bats Right 64-65																					
Killebrew, Harmon-Harmon Clayton (Killer)	54-60WasA 61-74MinA 75KCA	06-29-36	Payette, Idaho		R	R	6'	210	2435	8147	1283	2086	290	24	573	1584	1559	1699	19	.256	.509
Kindall, Jerry-Gerald Donald	56-58,60,61ChiN 62-64CleA 64-65MinA	05-27-35	St. Paul, Minn.		R	R	6'2	175	742	2057	211	439	83	9	44	198	145	535	17	.213	.327
Bats Both part of 60																					
King, Hal-Harold	67-68HouN 70-71AtlN 72TexA 73-74CinN	02-01-44	Oviedo, Fla.		R	R	6'1	200	322	683	67	146	26	3	24	82	104	158	0	.214	.366
King, Jim-James Hubert	55-56ChiN 57StlN 58SFN 61-67WasA 67ChiA 67CleA	08-27-32	Elkins, Ark.		L	R	6'1	190	1125	2918	374	699	112	19	117	401	363	401	23	.240	.411
Kirkland, Willie-Willie Charles	58-60SFN 61-63CleA 64BalA 64-66WasA	02-17-34	Siluria, Ala.		L	R	6'1	206	1149	3494	443	837	134	29	148	509	323	648	52	.240	.422
Kirkpatrick, Ed-Edgar Leon	62-64LAA 65-68CalA 69-73KCA 74-77PitN 77TexA 77MilA	10-08-44	Spokane, Wash.		L	R	5'11	195	1311	3467	411	824	143	18	85	424	456	518	34	.238	.363
Klaus, Bobby-Robert Francis	64CinN 64-65NYN	12-27-37	Spring Grove, Ill.		R	R	5'10	170	215	590	65	123	25	4	6	29	74	92	5	.208	.295
Klimchock, Lou-Louis Stephen	58-61KCA 62MilN 63WasA 63-65MilN 66NYN 68-70CleA	10-15-39	Hostetter, Pa.		L	R	5'11	180	318	669	64	155	21	3	13	69	31	71	0	.232	.330
Knoop, Bobby-Robert Frank	64LAA 65-69CalA 69-70ChiA 71-72KCA	10-18-38	Sioux City, Iowa		R	R	6'1	180	1153	3622	337	856	129	29	56	331	305	833	16	.236	.334
Koegel, Pete-Peter John (Jolly)	70-71MilA 71-72PhiN	07-31-47	Mineola, N.Y.		R	R	6'6	230	62	86	6	15	3	0	1	5	11	28	0	.174	.244
Kolb, Gary-Gary Alan	60,62-63StlN 64-65MilN 65NYN 68-69PitN	03-13-40	Rock Falls, Ill.		R	R	6'	194	293	450	63	94	9	6	6	29	46	104	10	.209	.296
Kopacz, George-George Felix (Sonny)	66AtlN 70PitN	02-26-41	Chicago, Ill.		L	L	6'1	195	16	25	2	3	0	0	0	0	1	10	0	.120	.120
Koppe (Kopchia), Joe-Joseph	58MilN 59-61PhiN 61-64LAA 65CalA	05-19-30	Detroit, Mich.		R	R	5'10	165	578	1606	202	379	61	12	19	141	209	345	16	.236	.324
Kosco, Andy-Andrew John	65-67MinA 68NYA 69-70LAN 71MilA 72CalA 72BosA 73-74CinN	10-05-41	Youngstown, Ohio		R	R	6'3	205	668	1963	204	464	75	8	73	267	99	351	5	.236	.394
Kostro, Frank-Frank Jerry	62-63DetA 63LAA 64-65,67-69MinA	08-04-37	Windber, Pa.		R	R	6'2	190	266	467	40	114	17	2	5	37	33	85	0	.244	.321
Kranepool, Ed-Edward Emil	62-79NYN	11-08-44	Bronx, N.Y.		L	L	6'3	205	1853	5436	536	1418	225	25	118	614	454	581	15	.261	.377
Krsnich, Mike-Michael	60,62MilN	09-24-31	West Allis, Wis.		R	R	6'1	190	15	21	0	4	2	0	0	1	0	5	0	.190	.286
Krug, Chris-Everett Ben	65-66ChiN 69SDN	12-25-39	Los Angeles, Cal.		R	R	6'4	200	79	214	17	41	6	0	5	25	15	66	0	.192	.290
Kubek, Tony-Anthony Christopher	57-65NYA	10-12-36	Milwaukee, Wis.		L	R	6'3	190	1092	4167	522	1109	178	30	57	373	217	441	29	.266	.364
Kubiak, Ted-Theodore Rodger	67KCA 68-69OakA 70-71MilA 71StlN 72TexA 72-75OakA 75-76SDN	05-12-42	New Brunswick, N.J.		B	R	6'	175	977	2447	238	565	61	21	13	202	271	272	13	.231	.289
Kubiszyn, Jack-John Henry	61-62CleA	12-19-36	Buffalo, N.Y.		R	R	5'11	170	50	101	7	19	2	0	1	2	7	12	0	.188	.238
Laboy, Coco-Jose Alberto [Guilbe]	69-73MonN	07-03-39	Ponce, P.R.		R	R	5'10	170	420	1247	108	291	62	2	28	166	97	220	0	.233	.354
Lachemann, Rene-Rene George	65-66KCA 68OakA M81-82SeaA M84MilA M93-96FlaN M02ChiN	05-04-45	Los Angeles, Cal.		R	R	6'	198	118	281	23	59	9	1	9	33	13	69	0	.210	.345
Lamont, Gene-Gene William	70-72,74-75DetA M92-95ChiA M97-00PitN	12-25-46	Rockford, Ill.		L	R	6'1	195	87	159	15	37	8	1	4	17	9	35	1	.233	.371
Lampard, Keith-Christopher Keith	69-70HouN	12-20-45	Warrington, England		L	R	6'2	195	62	84	10	20	8	1	1	7	5	27	0	.238	.393
Landis, Jim-James Henry	57-64ChiA 65CalA 66CleA 67HouN 67DetA 67BosA	03-09-34	Fresno, Cal.		R	R	6'1	180	1346	4288	625	1061	169	50	93	467	588	767	139	.247	.375
Landrum, Don-Donald LeRoy	57PhiN 60-62StlN 62-65ChiN 66SFN	02-16-36	Santa Rosa, Cal.		L	R	6'	180	456	1160	151	272	36	8	12	75	104	200	36	.234	.310
Lanier, Hal-Harold Clifton	64-71SFN 72-73NYA M86-88HouN	07-04-42	Denton, N.C.	01-09-03	R	R	6'2	186	1196	3703	297	843	111	20	8	273	136	436	11	.228	.275
Bats Both 68-70, part of 67																					
Lanier, Rimp-Lorenzo	71PitN	10-19-48	Tuskegee, Ala.		R	L	5'8	150	6	4	0	0	0	0	0	0	0	1	0	.000	.000
LaRose, Vic-Victor Raymond	68CinN	12-23-44	Los Angeles, Cal.		R	R	5'11	180	4	2	0	0	0	0	0	0	0	0	0	.000	.000
LaRussa, Tony-Anthony	63KCA 68-71OakA 71AtlN 73ChiN M79-86ChiA M86-95OakA M96-06StlN	10-04-44	Tampa, Fla.		R	R	6'	180	132	176	15	35	5	2	0	7	23	37	0	.199	.239
Lau, Charlie-Charles Richard	56,58-59DetA 60-61MilN 61-63BalA 63-64KCA 64-67BalA 67AtlN	04-12-33	Romulus, Mich.	03-18-84	L	R	6'	190	527	1170	105	298	63	9	16	140	109	150	3	.255	.387
Lawrence, Jim-James Ross	63CleA	02-12-39	Hamilton, Canada		L	R	6'1	185	2	0	0	0	0	0	0	0	0	0	0	——	——
Lee, Leron-Leron	69-71StlN 71-73SDN 74-75CleA 75-76LAN	03-04-48	Bakersfield, Cal.		R	R	6'1	196	614	1617	173	404	83	13	31	152	133	315	19	.250	.375
Leek, Gene-Eugene Harold	59CleA 61-62LAA	07-15-36	San Diego, Cal.		R	R	6'	185	77	249	23	55	12	1	6	25	9	67	0	.221	.349
Lefebvre, Jim-James Kenneth (Frenchy)	65-72LAN M89-91SeaA M92-93ChiN M99MilN	01-07-43	Hawthorne, Cal.		B	R	6'	180	922	3014	313	756	126	18	74	404	322	447	8	.251	.378
LeJohn, Don-Donald Everett	65LAN	05-13-34	Daisytown, Pa.	02-25-05	R	R	5'10	175	34	78	2	20	2	0	0	7	5	13	0	.256	.282
Leon, Eddie-Eduardo Antonio	68-72CleA 73-74ChiA 75NYA	08-11-46	Tucson, Ariz.		R	R	6'	175	601	1862	165	440	51	10	24	159	156	358	7	.236	.313
Leppert, Don-Donald George	61-62PitN 63-64WasA	10-19-31	Indianapolis, Ind.		R	R	6'2	220	190	532	46	122	22	2	15	59	44	93	0	.229	.344
Lewis, Allan-Allan Sydney	67KCA 68-70,72-73OakA	12-12-41	Colon, Panama		B	R	6'	170	156	29	47	6	1	0	1	3	1	4	44	.207	.345
Lewis, Johnny-Johnny Joe	64StlN 65-67NYN	08-10-39	Greenville, Ala.		L	R	6'	189	266	771	97	175	24	6	22	74	95	194	8	.227	.359
Libran, Frankie-Francisco [Rosas]	69SDN	05-06-48	Mayaguez, P.R.		R	R	6'	168	10	10	1	1	0	0	0	1	1	2	0	.100	.200
Lillis, Bob-Robert Perry (Flea)	58-61LAN 61StlN 62-67,M82-85HouN	06-02-30	Altadena, Cal.		R	R	5'11	160	817	2328	198	549	68	9	3	137	99	116	23	.236	.277
Linz, Phil-Phillip Francis (Supersub)	62-65NYA 66-67PhiN 67-68NYN	06-04-39	Baltimore, Md.		R	R	6'1	180	519	1372	185	322	64	4	11	96	112	195	13	.235	.311
Lipske, Bob-Robert Peter	63CleA	07-07-38	Scranton, Pa.		R	R	6'1	180	2	1	0	0	0	0	0	0	0	0	0	.000	.000
Llenas, Winston-Winston Enriquillo [Davila] (Chilote)	68-69,72-75CalA	09-23-43	Santiago, Dom. Rep.		R	R	5'10	170	300	531	50	122	17	0	3	61	38	69	0	.230	.279
Lock, Don-Don Wilson	62-66WasA 67-68PhiN 69BosA	07-27-36	Wichita, Kans.		R	R	6'2	205	921	2695	359	642	92	12	122	373	373	776	30	.238	.417
Lockwood, Skip-Claude Edward (See P73-_)	65KCA 69SeaA 70-73MilA 74CalA 75-79NYN 80BosA	08-17-46	Roslindale, Mass.		R	R	6'1	195	468	260	15	40	4	0	3	11	18	66	0	.154	.204
Lolich, Ron-Ronald John	71ChiA 72-73CleA	09-19-46	Portland, Ore.		R	R	6'1	195	87	228	20	48	9	2	4	23	11	49	0	.211	.303
Long, Jeoff-Jeoffrey Keith	63-64StlN 64ChiA	10-09-41	Covington, Ky.		L	R	6'1	200	56	83	5	16	1	0	1	9	10	34	0	.193	.241
Look, Bruce-Bruce Michael	68MinA	06-09-43	Lansing, Mich.		L	R	5'11	183	59	118	7	29	4	0	0	9	20	24	0	.246	.280
Look, Dean-Dean Zachary 62 played in A.F.L.	61ChiA	07-23-37	Lansing, Mich.		R	R	5'11	185	3	6	0	0	0	0	0	0	1	1	0	.000	.000
Lopez, Art-Arturo [Rodriguez]	65NYA	05-08-37	Mayaguez, P.R.		L	L	5'9	170	38	49	5	7	0	0	0	1	6	6	1	.143	.143
Lumpe, Jerry-Jerry Dean	58-59NYA 59-63KCA 64-67DetA	06-02-33	Lincoln, Mo.		L	R	6'2	185	1371	4912	620	1314	190	52	47	454	428	411	20	.268	.355
Lund, Gordon-Gordon Thomas	67CleA 69SeaA	02-23-41	Iron Mountain, Mich.		R	R	5'11	170	23	46	5	12	1	0	0	1	5	9	1	.261	.283
Luplow, Al-Alvin David	61-65CleA 66-67NYN 67PitN	03-13-39	Saginaw, Mich.		L	R	5'10	185	481	1243	147	292	34	6	33	125	127	213	8	.235	.352
Lyttle, Jim-James Lawrence	69-71NYA 72ChiA 73-76MonN 76LAN	05-20-46	Hamilton, Ohio		L	R	6'	185	391	710	71	176	37	5	9	70	61	139	4	.248	.352
MacKenzie, Gordon-Henry Gordon	61KCA	07-09-37	St. Petersburg, Fla.		R	R	5'11	175	11	24	1	3	0	0	0	1	6	9	0	.125	.142
Mahoney, Jim-James Thomas (Moe)	59BosA 61WasA 62CleA 65HouN	05-26-34	Englewood, N.J.		R	R	6'	175	120	210	32	48	4	1	4	15	11	47	1	.229	.314
Malkmus, Bobby-Robert Edward	57MilN 58-59WasA 60-64PhiN	07-04-31	Newark, N.J.		R	R	5'9	175	268	572	69	123	15	5	8	46	38	90	3	.215	.301
Malzone, Frank-Frank James (Lamela)	55-65BosA 66CalA	02-28-30	Bronx, N.Y.		R	R	5'10	180	1441	5428	647	1486	239	21	133	728	337	434	14	.274	.399
Mantilla, Felix-Felix [Lamela]	56-61MilN 62NYN 63-65BosA 66HouN	07-29-34	Isabela, P.R.		R	R	6'	170	969	2707	360	707	97	10	89	330	256	352	27	.261	.403
Manuel, Charlie-Charles Fuqua (Chuck)	69-72MinA 74-75LAN M00-02CleA M05-06PhiN	01-04-44	Northfork, W.Va.		L	R	6'4	200	242	384	25	76	12	0	4	43	40	77	1	.198	.260
Maris(Maras), Roger-Roger Eugene	57-58CleA 58-59KCA 60-66NYA 67-68StlN	09-10-34	Fargo, N.D.	12-14-85	L	R	6'	200	1463	5101	826	1325	195	42	275	850	652	733	21	.260	.476
Marshall, Dave-David Lewis	67-69SFN 70-72NYN 73SDN	01-14-43	Artesia, Cal.		L	R	6'1	192	491	1049	123	258	41	4	16	114	133	239	13	.246	.338
Martin, Gene-Thomas Eugene	68WasA	01-12-47	Americus, Ga.		R	R	6'	190	9	11	1	4	1	0	1	1	1	4	0	.364	.727
Martin, J.C.-Joseph Clifton	59-67ChiA 68-69NYN 70-72ChiN	12-13-36	Axton, Va.		L	R	6'2	188	908	2189	189	487	82	12	32	230	201	299	9	.222	.315
Martinez, Hector-Rodolfo Hector	62-63KCA	05-11-39	Las Villas, Cuba	12- -99	R	R	5'10	160	7	15	2	4	0	0	1	2	0	2	0	.267	.467
Martinez, Jose-Jose [Azcuiz]	69-70PitN	07-26-42	Cardenas, Cuba		R	R	6'	178	96	188	21	46	6	0	1	16	10	37	1	.245	.293
Martinez, Marty-Orlando [Oliva]	62MinA 67-68AtlN 69-71HouN 72StlN 72OakA 72TexA M88SeaA	08-23-41	Batabano, Cuba		R	R	6'	175	436	945	97	230	19	11	0	57	70	107	7	.243	.297
Bats Right 62																					
Martinez, Tony-Gabriel Antonio [Diaz]	63-66CleA	03-18-40	Perico, Cuba	08-24-91	R	R	5'10	165	73	175	13	30	5	0	0	10	6	26	2	.171	.200
Mashore, Clyde-Clyde Wayne	69CinN 70-73MonN	05-29-45	Concord, Cal.		R	R	6'	190	241	419	58	87	15	1	8	47	43	102	11	.208	.305
Mason, Don-Donald Stetson	66-70SFN 71-73SDN	12-20-44	Boston, Mass.		R	R	5'11	160	336	696	102	143	16	3	3	27	70	80	8	.205	.250
Matchick, Tom-John Thomas	67-69DetA 70BosA 70KCA 71MilA 72BalA	09-07-43	Hazelton, Pa.		L	R	5'11	180	292	626	63	178	21	6	4	60	34	148	6	.215	.270
Mathews, Nelson-Nelson Elmer	60-63ChiN 64-65KCA	07-21-41	Columbia, Ill.		R	R	6'4	195	306	978	93	218	39	14	22	98	88	248	8	.223	.359
Matias, John-John Roy (Gido)	70ChiA	08-15-44	Honolulu, Hawaii		L	L	5'11	180	58	117	7	22	4	0	1	6	5	22	1	.188	.256
Maxvill, Dal-Charles Dallan	62-72StlN 72-73OakA 73-74PitN 74-75OakA	02-18-39	Granite City, Ill.		R	R	5'11	157	1423	3443	302	748	79	24	6	252	370	538	7	.217	.259
May, Jerry-Jerry Lee	64-70PitN 71-73KCA 73NYN	12-14-43	Staunton, Va.	06-30-96	R	R	6'2	200	556	1527	120	357	63	10	15	130	157	293	1	.234	.318
Maye, Lee-Arthur Lee	59-65MilN 65-66HouN 67-69CleA 69-70WasA 70-71ChiA	12-11-34	Tuscaloosa, Ala.	07-17-02	L	R	6'2	190	1298	4048	533	1109	190	39	94	419	282	481	59	.274	.410
Mays, Willie-Willie Howard (Say Hey)	51-52NYN 53MS 54-57NYN 58-72NYN 72-73NYN	05-06-31	Westfield, Ala.		R	R	5'11	180	2992	10881	2062	3283	523	140	660	1903	1463	1526	338	.302	.557
Mazeroski, Bill-William Stanley (Maz)	56-72PitN	09-05-36	Wheeling, W.Va.		R	R	5'11	187	2163	7755	769	2016	294	62	138	853	447	706	27	.260	.367
McAuliffe, Dick-Richard John	60-73DetA 74-75BosA	11-29-39	Hartford, Conn.		L	R	5'11	176	1763	6185	888	1530	231	71	197	697	882	974	63	.247	.403
McCabe, Joe-Joseph Robert	64MinA 65WasA	08-27-38	Indianapolis, Ind.		R	R	6'	190	28	46	2	8	1	0	0	2	6	11	0	.174	.239
McCall, Brian-Brian Allen (Bam)	62-63ChiA	01-25-43	Kentfield, Cal.		L	L	5'10	170	7	15	3	3	0	0	2	4	1	2	0	.200	.600
McCarver, Tim-James Timothy	59-69StlN 70-72PhiN 72MonN 73-74StlN 74-75BosA 75-80PhiN	10-16-41	Memphis, Tenn.		L	R	6'1	193	1909	5529	590	1501	242	57	97	645	548	422	61	.271	.388
McCovey, Willie-Willie Lee (Stretch)	59-73SFN 74-76SDN 76OakA 77-80SFN	01-10-38	Mobile, Ala.		L	L	6'4	215	2588	8197	1229	2211	353	46	521	1555	1345	1550	26	.270	.515
McCraw, Tommy-Tommy Lee	63-70ChiA 71WasA 72CleA 73-74CalA 74-75CleA	11-21-40	Malvern, Ark.		L	L	6'	183	1468	3956	484	972	150	42	75	404	332	544	143	.246	.362

USE NAME - GIVEN NAMES (NICKNAMES)	TEAM BY YEAR	BIRTH DATE	BIRTH PLACE	DEATH DATE	B	T	HGT	WGT	G	AB	R	H	2B	3B	HR	RBI	BB	SO	SB	BA	SA
McDermott, Terry-Terrence Michael	72LAN	03-20-51	Rockville Centre, N.Y.		R	R	6'4	205	9	23	2	3	0	0	0	0	2	8	0	.130	.130
McDonald, Dave-David Bruce	69NYA 71MonN	05-20-43	New Albany, Ind.		L	R	6'2	215	33	62	3	9	3	0	1	6	6	19	0	.145	.242
McFadden, Leon-Leon	68-70HouN	04-26-44	Little Rock, Ark.		R	R	6'2	195	62	121	5	26	3	0	0	4	10	19	2	.215	.240
McFarlane, Orlando-Orlando deJesus [Quesada]	62,64PitN 66DetA 67-68CalA	06-28-38	Oriente, Cuba		R	R	6'	180	124	292	22	70	12	0	5	20	20	93	0	.240	.332
McGuire, Mickey-McAdolfus	62,67BalA	01-18-41	Dayton, Ohio		R	R	5'10	170	16	21	2	4	0	0	0	2	0	2	0	.190	.190
McKnight, Jim-James Arthur	60,62ChiN	07-01-36	Bee Branch, Ark.	04-24-94	R	R	6'1	185	83	91	6	21	0	1	0	6	2	14	0	.231	.253
McMath, Jimmy-Jimmy Lee (Mac)	68ChiN	10-49	Tuscaloosa, Ala.		L	L	6'1	195	3	14	0	2	0	0	0	2	0	6	0	.143	.143
McMullen, Ken-Kenneth Lee	62-64LAN 65-70WasA 70-72CalA 73-75LAN 76OakA 77MilA	06-01-42	Oxnard, Cal.		R	R	6'3	190	1583	5131	568	1273	172	26	156	606	510	815	20	.248	.383
McNertney, Jerry-Gerald Edward	64,66-68ChiA 69SeaA 70MilA 71-72StLN 73PitN	08-07-36	Boone, Iowa		R	R	6'1	190	590	1423	128	337	51	6	27	163	119	199	3	.237	.338
McNulty, Bill-William Francis	69,72OakA	08-29-46	Sacramento, Cal.		R	R	6'4	205	9	27	0	1	0	0	0	0	2	11	0	.037	.037
Mejias, Roman-Roman [Gomez]	55,57-61PitN 62HouN 63-64BosA	08-09-30	Abreus, Cuba		R	R	6'	185	627	1768	212	449	57	12	54	202	89	238	20	.254	.391
Mendoza, Minnie-Cristobal Rigoberto [Carreras]	70MinA		Ceiba del Agua, Cuba		R	R	6'	160	16	2	3	0	0	0	0	2	0	1	0	.188	.188
Menke, Denis-Denis John	62-65MilN 66-67AtlN 68-71HouN 72-73CinN 74HouN	07-21-40	Bancroft, Iowa		R	R	6'	185	1598	5071	605	1270	225	40	101	606	698	853	35	.250	.370
Michael, Gene-Eugene Richard (The Stick)	66PitN 67LAN 68-74NYA 75DetA M81,82NYA M86-87ChiN	06-02-38	Kent, Ohio		B	R	6'2	183	973	2806	249	642	86	12	15	226	234	421	22	.229	.284
Millan, Felix-Felix Bernardo [Martinez] (The Cat)	66-72AtlN 73-77NYN	08-21-43	Yabucoa, P.R.		R	R	5'11	172	1480	5791	699	1617	229	38	22	403	318	242	67	.279	.343
Miller, John-John Allen	66NYA 69ChiN		Alhambra, Cal.		R	R	5'11	195	32	61	4	10	1	0	2	3	2	18	0	.164	.279
Miller, Norm-Norman Calvin	65-73HouN 73-74AtlN	02-05-46	Los Angeles, Cal.		L	R	5'10	185	540	1364	166	325	68	10	24	159	160	265	16	.238	.356
Mincher, Don-Donald Ray	60WasA 61-66MinA 67-68CalA 69SeaA 70-71OakA 71WasA 72TexA 72OakA	06-04-38	Huntsville, Ala.		L	R	6'3	205	1400	4026	530	1003	176	16	200	643	606	668	24	.249	.450
Montreuil, Al-Allan Arthur	72ChiN	08-23-43	New Orleans, La.		R	R	5'4	158	5	11	0	1	0	0	0	0	1	4	0	.091	.091
Moock, Joe-Joseph Geoffrey	67NYN	03-12-44	Plaquemine, La.		L	L	5'11	180	13	40	2	9	1	0	0	5	0	7	2	.225	.275
Moore, Archie-Archie Francis	64-65NYA	08-30-41	Upper Darby, Pa.		L	L	6'2	190	40	40	5	11	4	0	1	5	6	13	0	.275	.450
Moore, Gary-Gary Douglas	70LAN	02-24-45	Tulsa, Okla.		R	L	5'10	190	7	16	2	3	0	2	0	0	0	1	1	.188	.438
Moore, Jackie-Jackie Spencer	65DetA M84-86OakA	02-19-39	Jay, Fla.		R	R	6'	180	21	53	2	5	0	0	0	2	6	12	0	.094	.094
Morales, Rich-Richard Angelo	67-73ChiA 73-74SDN	09-20-43	San Francisco, Cal.		R	R	5'11	170	480	1053	81	205	26	3	6	64	95	159	7	.195	.242
Moran, Al-Richard Alan	63-64NYN	12-05-38	Detroit, Mich.		R	R	6'1	190	135	353	28	69	5	2	1	27	38	62	3	.195	.229
Moran, Bill-William Nelson	58-59CleA 61-64LAA 64-65CleA	11-27-33	Montgomery, Ala.		R	R	5'11	185	634	2076	242	545	88	10	28	202	133	218	10	.263	.355
Morhardt, Moe-Meredith Goodwin	61-62MinN	01-16-37	Manchester, Conn.		L	L	6'1	185	25	34	4	7	0	0	0	3	5	13	0	.206	.206
Morton, Bubba-Wycliffe Nathaniel	61-63DetA 63MilN 67-69CalA	12-13-31	Washington, D.C.	01-14-06	R	R	5'10	175	451	928	117	248	37	8	14	128	111	143	7	.267	.370
Moschitto, Ross-Ross Allen	65NYA 66MS 67NYA	02-15-45	Fresno, Cal.		R	R	6'2	175	110	36	13	6	0	0	1	3	1	14	0	.167	.250
Moses, Jerry-Gerald Braheen	65,68-70BosA 71CalA 72CleA 73NYA 74DetA 75SDN 75ChiA	08-09-46	Yazoo City, Miss.		R	R	6'3	210	386	1072	89	269	48	8	25	109	63	184	1	.251	.381
Mota, Manny-Manuel Rafael [Geronimo]	62SFN 63-68PitN 69MonN 69-80,82LAN	02-18-38	Santa Domingo, Dom. Rep.		R	R	5'10	170	1536	3779	496	1149	125	52	31	438	289	320	50	.304	.389
Motton, Curt-Curtell Howard	67-71BalA 72MilA 72CalA 73-74BalA	09-24-40	Darnell, La.		R	R	5'8	170	316	567	85	121	20	1	25	89	86	116	5	.213	.384
Murphy, Billy-William Eugene	66NYN	05-07-44	Pineville, La.		R	R	6'1	190	84	135	15	31	4	1	3	13	7	34	1	.230	.341
Murphy, Danny-Daniel Francis (See P61-72)	60-62ChiN 69-70ChiA	08-23-42	Beverly, Mass.		L	R	5'11	185	117	130	18	23	5	1	4	13	11	29	0	.177	.323
Murrell, Ivan-Ivan Augustus [Peters]	63-64,67-68HouN 69-73SDN 74AtlN	04-24-43	Almirante, Panama		R	R	6'2	195	564	1306	126	308	41	15	33	123	44	342	20	.236	.366
Nagelson, Russ-Russell Charles (Rusty)	68-70CleA 70DetA	09-19-44	Cincinnati, Ohio		L	R	6'	205	62	76	9	16	1	0	1	4	13	20	0	.211	.263
Napoleon, Danny-Daniel	65-66NYN	01-11-42	Claysburg, Pa.	04-26-03	R	R	5'11	190	80	130	7	21	3	1	0	9	9	30	0	.162	.200
Nash, Cotton-Charles Francis 64-65 played in N.B.A. 67-68 played in A.B.A.	67ChiA 69-70MinA	07-24-42	Jersey City, N.J.		R	R	6'8	220	13	16	2	3	0	0	0	2	3	3	0	.188	.188
Nen, Dick-Richard LeRoy	63LAN 65-67WasA 68ChiN 70WasA	09-24-39	South Gate, Cal.		L	L	6'2	205	367	826	70	185	23	3	21	107	77	152	1	.224	.335
Nettles, Jim-James William	70-72MinA 73JL 79KCA 81OakA	03-02-47	San Diego, Cal.		L	L	6'1	190	240	587	68	129	15	4	16	57	70	109	10	.220	.341
Nicholson, Dave-David Lawrence	60,62BalA 63-65ChiA 66HouN 67AtlN	08-29-39	St. Louis, Mo.		R	R	6'2	215	538	1419	184	301	32	12	61	179	219	573	6	.212	.381
Nixon, Russ-Russell Eugene	57-60CleA 60-65BosA 66-67MinA 68BosA M82-83ChiN M88-90AtlN	02-19-35	Cleves, Ohio		L	R	6'1	195	906	2504	215	670	115	19	27	266	154	279	0	.268	.361
Northey, Scott-Scott Richard	69KCA	10-15-46	Philadelphia, Pa.		R	R	6'	175	20	61	11	16	2	2	1	7	7	19	6	.262	.410
Northrup, Jim-James Thomas	64-70DetA 74MonN 74-75BalA	11-24-39	Breckenridge, Mich.		L	R	6'3	190	1392	4692	603	1254	218	42	153	610	449	635	39	.267	.429
Nossek, Joe-Joseph Rudolph	64-66MinA 66-67KCA 69OakA 69-70StLN	11-08-40	Cleveland, Ohio		R	R	6'	178	295	579	47	132	25	4	3	53	19	72	8	.228	.301
O'Brien, Syd-Sydney Lloyd	69BosA 70ChiA 71-72CalA 72MilA	02-18-44	Compton, Cal.		R	R	6'1	185	378	1052	135	242	35	8	24	100	60	155	5	.230	.347
Oldis, Bob-Robert Carl	53-55WasA 60-61PitN 62-63PhiN	01-05-28	Preston, Iowa		R	R	6'1	185	135	236	20	56	6	0	1	22	20	22	0	.237	.275
Oliva, Tony-Pedro [Lopez]	62-76MinA	07-20-40	Pinar del Rio, Cuba		L	R	6'2	190	1676	6301	870	1917	329	46	220	947	448	645	86	.304	.476
Olivares, Ed-Edward [Balzac]	60-61StLN	11-05-38	Mayaguez, P.R.		R	R	5'11	180	24	35	2	5	0	0	0	1	0	7	1	.143	.143
Oliver, Bob-Robert Lee	65PitN 69-72KCA 72-74BalA 75NYA	02-08-43	Shreveport, La.		R	R	6'3	205	847	2914	293	745	102	19	94	419	156	562	17	.256	.400
Oliver, Gene-Eugene George	59,61-63StLN 63-65MilN 66-67AtlN 67PhiN 68BosA 68-69ChiN	03-22-36	Moline, Ill.		R	R	6'2	225	786	2216	268	546	111	5	93	320	215	420	24	.246	.427
Oliver, Nate-Nathaniel (Pee Wee)	63-67LAN 68SFN 69NYA 69ChiN	12-13-40	St. Petersburg, Fla.		R	R	5'10	160	410	954	107	216	24	5	2	45	72	172	17	.226	.268
Orsino, John-John Joseph (Horse)	61-62SFN 63-65BalA 66-67WasA	04-22-38	Teaneck, N.J.		R	R	6'3	215	332	1014	114	252	44	5	40	123	92	191	3	.249	.420
Ortiz, Jose-Jose Luis [Irizarry] (Polilla)	69-70ChiA 71ChiN	06-25-47	Ponce, P.R.		R	R	5'9	155	67	123	14	37	4	1	0	6	7	12	3	.301	.390
Osborne, Bobo-Lawrence Sidney	57-59,61-62DetA 63WasA	10-12-35	Chattahoochie, Ga.		L	R	6'1	205	359	763	93	157	30	2	17	86	104	171	2	.206	.317
Ott, Billy-William Joseph	62,64ChiN	11-23-40	New York, N.Y.		B	R	6'1	180	32	67	7	11	3	0	1	3	5	20	0	.164	.224
Oyler, Ray-Raymond Francis	65-68DetA 69SeaA 70CalA	08-04-38	Indianapolis, Ind.	01-26-81	R	R	5'11	170	542	1265	110	221	39	6	15	86	135	359	2	.175	.251
Paciorek, John-John Francis	63HouN	02-11-45	Detroit, Mich.		R	R	6'2	200	1	3	4	3	0	0	0	3	2	0	0	1.000	1.000
Paepke, Dennis-Dennis Ray	69,71-72,74KCA	04-17-45	Long Beach, Cal.		R	R	6'4	202	80	197	13	36	7	0	2	14	12	36	0	.183	.249
Pagan, Jose-Jose Antonio [Rodriguez]	59-65SFN 65-75PitN 73PhiN	05-03-35	Barceloneta, P.R.		R	R	5'9	170	1326	3689	387	922	138	26	52	372	244	510	46	.250	.344
Page, Mike-Michael Randy	68AtlN	07-12-40	Woodruff, S.C.		L	R	6'2	210	20	28	1	5	0	0	0	1	0	4	0	.179	.179
Pagliaroni, Jim-James Vinvent (Pag)	55BosA 56-57MS 60-62BosA 63-67PitN 68-69OakA 69SeaA	12-08-37	Dearborn, Mich.		R	R	6'4	210	849	2465	269	622	98	7	90	326	330	494	4	.252	.407
Parker, Billy-William David (Wee Willie)	71-73CalA	01-14-47	Haynesville, Ala.	02-09-03	R	R	5'8	168	94	252	29	56	4	2	3	21	19	60	1	.222	.290
Parker, Wes-Maurice Wesley	64-72LAN	11-13-39	Evanston, Ill.		B	L	6'1	180	1288	4157	548	1110	194	32	64	470	532	615	60	.267	.375
Parrilla, Sammy-Samuel [Monge]	70PhiN	06-12-43	Santurce, P.R.	02-09-94	R	R	5'11	200	11	16	0	2	1	0	0	1	4	6	0	.125	.188
Pavletich, Don-Donald Stephen	57CinN 58MS 59,62-68CinN 69ChiA 70-71BosA	07-13-38	Milwaukee, Wis.		R	R	5'11	213	536	1373	163	349	73	8	46	193	148	237	5	.254	.420
Pearson, Albie-Albert Gregory	58-59WasA 59-60BalA 61-66CalA 65-66CalA	09-12-34	Alhambra, Cal.		L	L	5'5	140	988	3077	485	831	130	24	28	214	477	195	77	.270	.355
Pena (Zapata), Roberto-Roberto Cesar Zapata [Pena]	65-66ChiN 68PhiN 69SDN 70OakA 70-71MilA	04-17-37	Santo Domingo, Dom. Rep.	07-23-82	R	R	5'8	175	587	1907	174	467	65	10	13	154	114	235	10	.245	.310
Pepitone, Joe-Joseph Anthony (Pepi)	62-69NYA 70HouN 70-73ChiN 73AtlN	10-09-40	Brooklyn, N.Y.		L	L	6'2	195	1397	5097	606	1315	158	35	219	721	302	526	41	.258	.432
Pepper, Don-Donald Hoyte	66DetA	10-08-43	Saratoga Springs, N.Y.		L	L	6'4	215	4	3	0	0	0	0	0	0	1	0	0	.000	.000
Perry, Bob-Melvin Gray	63-64LAA	09-14-34	New Bern, N.C.		R	R	6'2	180	131	387	35	103	17	1	6	30	23	83	2	.266	.382
Peterson, Cap-Charles Andrew	62-66SFN 67-68WasA 69CleA	08-15-42	Tacoma, Wash.	05-17-80	R	R	6'2	195	536	1170	106	269	44	5	19	122	101	195	4	.230	.325
Petrocelli, Rico-Americo Peter	63,65-76BosA	06-27-43	Brooklyn, N.Y.		R	R	6'	185	1553	5390	653	1352	237	22	210	773	661	926	10	.251	.420
Pfiel, Bobby-Robert Raymond	69NYN 71PhiN	11-13-43	Passaic, N.J.		R	R	6'1	180	106	281	25	68	12	0	2	19	13	36	1	.242	.306
Phillips, Adolfo-Adolfo Emelio [Lopez]	64-66PhiN 66-69ChiN 69MonN 72CleA	12-16-41	Bethania, Panama		R	R	6'1	175	649	1875	270	463	86	21	59	173	251	485	82	.247	.410
Phillips, Dick-Richard Eugene	62SFN 63-64,66WasA	11-24-31	Racine, Wis.	03-29-98	L	R	6'	185	263	595	54	136	14	1	12	60	59	63	2	.229	.316
Pinson, Vada-Vada Edward	58-68CinN 69tLN 70-71CleA 72-73CalA 74-75KCA	08-11-38	Memphis, Tenn.	10-21-95	L	L	5'11	180	2469	9645	1366	2757	485	127	256	1170	574	1196	305	.286	.442
Plaskett, Elmo-Elmo Alexander	62-63PitN	06-27-38	Fredericksted, V.I.	11-02-98	R	R	5'10	195	17	35	3	7	0	0	1	5	1	8	0	.200	.266
Pointer, Aaron-Aaron Elton (Hawk)	63,66-67HouN	04-19-42	Little Rock, Ark.		R	R	6'2	185	40	101	11	21	5	0	0	3	15	33	2	.208	.317
Popovich, Paul-Paul Edward	64,66-67ChiN 68-69LAN 69-73ChiN 74-75PitN	08-18-40	Flemington, W.Va.		B	R	5'11	175	682	1732	176	403	42	9	14	134	127	151	4	.233	.292
Posada, Leo-Leopoldo Jesus [Hernandez] (Popy)	60-62KCA Bats Right 64,66-67	04-15-36	Havana, Cuba		R	R	5'11	155	155	426	51	109	11	7	8	58	46	105	1	.256	.371
Poulsen, Ken-Ken Sterling	67BosA	08-04-47	Van Nuys, Cal.		R	R	6'1	190	5	7	0	2	0	0	0	0	0	4	0	.286	.400
Powell, Boog-John Wesley	61-74BalA 75-76CleA 77LAN	08-17-41	Lakeland, Fla.		L	R	6'4	250	2042	6681	889	1776	270	11	339	1187	1001	1226	20	.266	.462
Prescott, Bobby-Goerge Bertrand	61KCA	03-27-31	Colon, Panama		R	R	6'1	180	10	12	0	1	0	0	0	1	0	6	0	.083	.083
Price, Jim-Jimmie William	67-71DetA	10-13-41	Harrisburg, Pa.		R	R	6'	192	261	602	58	129	22	0	18	71	62	70	0	.214	.341
Qualls, Jim-James Robert	69ChiN 70MonN 72ChiA	10-09-46	Exeter, Cal.		B	R	5'10	158	63	139	13	31	6	3	0	10	2	16	2	.223	.309
Queen, Mel-Melvin Douglas (See P61-72)	64-69CinN 70-72CalA 72OakA	03-26-42	Johnson, City, N.Y.		R	R	6'1	190	269	274	20	49	7	0	5	25	21	50	0	.179	.226
Quillici, Frank Ralph [Guido]	65,67-70,M72-75MinA	05-11-39	Chicago, Ill.		R	R	5'11	175	405	682	78	146	23	6	5	53	66	120	2	.214	.287
Rader, Doug-Douglas Lee (The Red Rooster)	67-75HouN 76-77SDN 77TorA M83-84TexA M86ChiA M89-91CalA	07-30-44	Chicago, Ill.		R	R	6'2	208	1465	5186	613	1302	245	39	155	722	528	1055	37	.251	.403
Ragland, Tom-Thomas	71WasA 72TexA 73CalA	06-16-46	Talladega, Ala.		R	R	5'10	160	120	264	20	61	9	1	0	14	13	47	2	.231	.273
Ramirez, Milt-Milton [Barbosa] (Ramrod)	70-71StLN 79OakA	04-02-50	Mauaguez, P.R.		R	R	5'10	150	94	152	14	28	3	2	0	6	13	46	0	.184	.230
Ranew, Merritt-Merritt Thomas	62HouN 63-64ChiN 64MilN 65CalA 69SeaA	05-10-38	Albany, Ga.		L	R	5'11	175	269	594	63	147	20	7	11	54	42	120	3	.247	.352
Ratliff, Gene-Kelly Eugene	65HouN	09-28-45	Chicago, Ill.		R	R	6'5	185	1	4	0	0	0	0	0	0	0	1	0	.000	.000
Ratliff, Paul-Paul Hawthorne	63,70-71MinA 71-72MilA	01-23-44	San Diego, Cal.		B	R	6'2	190	145	297	28	61	10	2	12	42	28	119	0	.205	.374
Raudman, Bob-Robert Joyce (Shorty)	66-67ChiN	03-14-42	Erie, Pa.		L	L	5'9	190	16	55	1	11	2	0	0	3	2	6	1	.200	.236

USE NAME - GIVEN NAMES (NICKNAMES)	TEAM BY YEAR	BIRTH DATE	BIRTH PLACE	DEATH DATE	B	T	HGT	WGT	G	AB	R	H	2B	3B	HR	RBI	BB	SO	SB	BA	SA
Reams, Leroy-Leroy (Cat)	69PhiN	08-11-43	Wabbaseka, Ark.		L	R	6'2	190	1	1	0	0	0	0	0	0	0	1	0	.000	.000
Redmond, Wayne-Howard Wayne	65,69DetA	01-25-45	Athens, Ala.		R	R	5'10	165	9	7	1	0	0	0	0	0	1	3	0	.000	.000
Reed, Jack-John Burwell	61-63NYA	02-02-33	Silver City, Miss.		R	R	6'1	185	222	129	39	30	5	2	1	6	14	22	7	.233	.326
Reese, Rich-Richard Benjamin	64-72MinA 73DetA 73MinA	09-29-41	Leipsic, Ohio		L	L	6'3	185	866	2020	248	512	73	17	52	245	158	270	16	.253	.384
Reichardt, Rick-Frederic Carl	64LAA 65-70CalA 70WasA 71-73ChiA 73-74KCA	03-16-43	Madison, Wis.		R	R	6'3	215	997	3307	391	864	109	24	116	445	263	672	40	.261	.414
Reid, Scott-Scott Donald	69-70PhiN	01-07-47	Chicago, Ill.		L	R	6'1	195	38	68	10	10	1	0	0	1	18	27	0	.147	.162
Renick, Rick-Warren Richard	68-72MinA	03-16-44	London, Ohio		R	R	6'	188	276	553	71	122	20	2	20	71	63	142	1	.221	.373
Repoz, Roger-Roger Allen	64-66NYA 66-67KCA 67-72CalA	08-03-40	Bellingham, Wash.		L	L	6'3	190	831	2145	257	480	73	19	82	260	280	499	26	.224	.390
Retzer, Ken-Kenneth Leo	61-64WasA	04-30-34	Wood River, Ill.		L	R	6'	185	237	690	65	182	25	2	14	72	52	50	5	.264	.367
Reynolds, Tommie-Tommie D	63-65KCA 67NYN 69OakA 70-71CalA 72MilA	08-15-41	Arizona, La.		Bats Both part of 67 R	R	6'2	190	513	1170	141	265	35	5	12	87	117	166	12	.226	.296
Richardson, Bobby-Robert Clinton	55-66NYA	08-19-35	Sumter, S.C.		R	R	5'9	170	1412	5386	643	1432	196	37	34	390	262	243	73	.266	.335
Ricketts, Dave-David William	63,65,67-69StLN 70PitN	07-12-35	Pottstown, Pa.		B	R	6'2	190	130	213	15	53	9	0	1	20	10	13	0	.249	.305
Rico, Fred-Alfredo [Cruz] (Rock)	69KCA	07-04-44	Jerome, Ariz.		R	R	5'10	190	12	26	2	6	2	0	0	2	9	10	0	.231	.308
Rios, Juan-Juan Onofre (Velez) [Rios]	69KCA	07-14-45	Mayaguez, P.R.	08-28-95	R	R	6'3	188	87	196	20	44	5	1	1	5	7	19	1	.224	.276
Roarke, Mike-Michael Thomas	61-64DetA	11-08-30	West Warwick, R.I.		R	R	6'2	195	194	491	41	113	11	2	6	44	45	61	0	.230	.297
Roberts, Dave-David Leonard	62,64HouN 66PitN	06-30-33	Panama, Panama		L	L	6'	172	91	194	15	38	8	1	2	17	22	43	0	.196	.278
Robertson, Daryl-Daryl Martin	62CinN	01-05-36	Cripple Creek, Colo.		R	R	6'	184	9	19	0	2	0	0	0	2	2	10	0	.105	.105
Robinson, Brooks-Brooks Calbert (The Vacumn Cleaner)	55-77BalA	05-18-37	Little Rock, Ark.		R	R	6'1	190	2896	10654	1232	2848	482	68	268	1357	860	990	28	.267	.401
Robinson, Dave-David Tanner	70-71SDN	05-22-46	Minneapolis, Minn.		B	L	6'1	186	22	44	5	12	2	0	2	6	6	7	2	.273	.455
Robinson, Earl-Earl John	58LAN 61-62,64BalA	11-03-36	New Orleans, La.		R	R	6'1	190	170	421	63	113	20	5	12	44	47	92	7	.268	.425
Robinson, Floyd-Floyd Andrew	60-66ChiA 67CinN 68OakA 68BosA	05-09-36	Prescott, Ariz.		L	R	5'9	175	1012	3284	458	929	140	36	67	426	408	282	42	.283	.409
Robinson, Frank-Frank (The Judge)	56-65CinN 66-71BalA 72LAN 73-74CalA 74-76,M75-77CleA M81-84SFN M88-91BalA M02-04MonN M05-06WasN	08-31-35	Beaumont, Tex.		R	R	6'1	190	2808	10006	1829	2943	528	72	586	1812	1420	1532	204	.294	.537
Robles, Rafael-Rafael Radames [Natera] (Orlando)	69-70,72SDN	10-20-47	Ingenio Quisquaya, D. R.	08-13-98	R	R	5'9	170	47	133	7	25	1	0	0	3	6	17	4	.188	.195
Rodgers, Andre-Kenneth Andre Ian (Andy)	57NYN 58-60SFN 61-64ChiN 65-67PitN	12-02-34	Nassau, Bahamas	12-13-04	R	R	6'3	195	854	2521	268	628	112	23	45	245	290	507	22	.249	.365
Rodgers,Bob-Robert Leroy (known as Buck as Mgr.)	61-64LAA 65-69CalA M80-82MilA M85-91MonN M91-94CalA	08-16-38	Delaware, Ohio		B	R	6'2	190	932	3033	259	704	114	18	31	288	234	409	17	.232	.312
Rodriguez, Ellie-Eliseo [Delgado]	68NYA 69-70KCA 71-73MilA 74-75CalA 76LAN 77BC	05-24-46	Fajardo, P.R.		R	R	5'11	185	775	2173	220	533	76	6	16	203	332	291	17	.245	.308
Rojas, Cookie-Octavio Victor [Rivas]	62CinN 63-69PhiN 70StLN 70-77KCA M88CalA M96FlaN	03-06-39	Havana, Cuba		R	R	5'10	165	1822	6309	714	1660	254	25	54	593	396	489	74	.263	.337
Rollins, Rich-Richard John (Red)	61-68MinA 69SeaA 70MilA 70CleA	04-16-38	Mt. Pleasant, Pa.		R	R	5'10	185	1002	3303	419	887	125	20	77	399	266	410	17	.269	.388
Roman, Bill-William Anthony	64-65DetA	10-11-38	Detroit, Mich.		L	L	6'4	190	24	35	2	5	0	0	1	2	9	4	0	.143	.229
Romano, Johnny-John Anthony (Honey)	58-59ChiA 60-64CleA 65-66ChiA 67StLN	08-23-34	Hoboken, N.J.		R	R	5'11	205	905	2767	355	706	112	10	129	417	414	485	7	.255	.443
Roof, Phil-Philip Anthony	61,64MilN 65CalA 65CleA 66-67KCA 68-69OakA 70-71MilA 71-76MinA 76ChiA 77TorA	03-05-41	Paducah, Ky.		R	R	6'3	200	857	2151	190	463	69	13	43	210	184	504	1	.215	.319
Roque, Jorge-Jorge [Vargas]	70-72StLN 73MonN	04-28-50	Ponce, P.R.		R	R	5'10	185	65	139	14	19	4	1	2	12	10	40	4	.137	.223
Rosario, Jimmy-Angel Ramon [Ferrer]	71-72SFN 75JL 76MilA	05-05-44	Bayamon, P.R.		B	R	5'11	170	114	231	31	50	6	1	1	18	36	43	8	.216	.264
Rosario, Santiago-Santiago	65KCA	07-25-39	Guayanilla, P.R.		L	L	5'11	165	81	85	8	20	3	0	2	8	6	16	0	.235	.341
Roseboro, Johnny-John Junior	57BknN 58-67LAN 68-69MinA 70WasA	05-13-33	Ashland, Ohio	08-16-02	L	R	5'11	195	1585	4847	512	1206	190	44	104	548	547	677	67	.249	.371
Roselli, Bob-Robert Edward	55-56,58MilN 61-62ChiA	12-10-31	San Francisco, Cal.		R	R	5'11	185	68	114	8	25	7	1	2	10	12	31	1	.219	.351
Roznovsky, Vic-Victor Joseph	64-65ChiN 66-67BalA 69PhiN	10-19-38	Shiner, Tex.		L	R	6'	180	205	455	22	99	15	1	4	38	32	83	1	.218	.284
Ruberto, Sonny-John Edward	69SDN 72CinN	01-02-46	Staten Island, N.Y.		R	R	5'11	175	21	24	3	3	0	0	0	1	8	0	0	.125	.125
Ruiz (Sablon), Chico-Hiraldo Sablon [Ruiz]	64-69CinN 70-71CalA	12-05-38	Santo Domingo, Cuba	02-09-72	B	R	6'	170	565	1150	133	276	37	10	2	69	58	164	34	.240	.295
Ryan, Mike-Michael James	64-67BosA 68-73PhiN 74PitN	11-25-41	Haverhill, Mass.		R	R	6'2	210	636	1920	146	370	60	12	28	161	152	370	4	.193	.280
Sadowski, Bob-Robert Frank (Sid)	60StLN 61PhiN 62ChiA 63LAA	01-15-37	St. Louis, Mo.		L	R	6'	175	184	329	38	73	9	3	7	46	33	63	3	.222	.331
Sadowski, Eddie-Edward Roman	60BosA 61-63LAA 66AtlN	01-19-31	Pittsburgh, Pa.	11-06-93	R	R	5'11	175	217	495	55	100	20	1	12	39	39	94	5	.202	.319
Salmon, Chico-Ruthford Eduardo	64-68CleA 69-72BalA	12-03-40	Colon, Panama	09-17-00	R	R	5'10	160	658	1667	202	415	70	6	31	149	89	233	46	.249	.354
Samuel, Amado-Amado Ruperto	62-63MilN 64NYN	12-06-38	San Pedro de Mac., D.R.		R	R	6'1	170	144	368	23	79	18	0	3	25	16	82	0	.215	.288
Sanchez, Celerino-Celerino [Perez]	72-73NYA	02-03-44	El Guayabal, Mexico	05-01-92	R	R	5'11	190	105	314	30	76	11	3	1	31	14	42	1	.242	.306
Sanders, John-John Frank	65KCA	11-20-45	Grand Island, Neb.		R	R	6'2	200	1	0	0	0	0	0	0	0	0	0	0	.000	.000
Santo, Ron-Ronald Edward	60-73ChiN 74ChiA	02-25-40	Seattle, Wash.		R	R	6'	194	2243	8143	1138	2254	365	67	342	1331	1108	1343	35	.277	.464
Satriano, Tom-Thomas Victor Nicholas (Satch)	61-64LAA 65-69CalA 69-70BosA	08-28-40	Pittsburgh, Pa.		B	R	6'1	185	674	1623	130	365	53	5	21	157	214	225	7	.225	.303
Savage, Ted-Theodore Ephesian	62PhiN 63PitN 65-67StLN 67-68ChiN 68LAN 69CinN 70-71MilA 71KCA	02-21-37	Venice, Ill.		R	R	6'1	185	642	1375	202	321	51	11	34	163	200	272	49	.233	.361
Saverine, Bob-Robert Paul (Rabbit)	59,62-64BalA 66-67WasA	06-02-41	Norwalk, Conn.		B	R	5'10	160	379	861	114	206	27	6	6	47	73	149	23	.239	.305
Schaal, Paul-Paul	64LAA 65-68CalA 69-74KCA 74CalA	03-03-43	Pittsburgh, Pa.		R	R	5'11	185	1128	3555	436	869	132	26	57	323	516	466	43	.244	.344
Schaffer, Jimmie-Jimmie Ronald	61-62StLN 63-64ChiN 65ChiA 65NYN 66-67PhiN 68CinN	04-05-36	Limeport, Pa.		R	R	5'9	185	314	574	53	128	28	3	11	56	49	127	3	.223	.340
Schaive, Johnny-John Edward	58-60,62-63WasA	02-25-34	Springfield, Ill.		R	R	5'8	175	114	323	25	75	18	1	5	40	50	72	4	.232	.350
Scheinblum, Richie-Richard Alan	65,67-69CleA 71WasA 72KCA 73CinN 73-74CalA 74KCA 74StLN	11-05-42	New York, N.Y.		B	R	6'1	180	462	1218	131	320	52	9	13	127	149	135	0	.263	.352
Schilling, Chuck-Charles Thomas	61-65BosA	10-25-37	Brooklyn, N.Y.		R	R	5'10	170	541	1969	230	470	76	5	23	146	176	236	11	.239	.317
Schlesinger, Rudy-William Cordes	65BosA	11-05-42	Cincinnati, Ohio		R	R	6'2	175	1	1	0	0	0	0	0	0	0	0	0	.000	.000
Schlueter, Jay-Jay D. (Slushy)	71HouN	03-08-49	Phoenix, Ariz.		R	R	6'	185	7	3	1	1	0	0	0	0	1	0	1	.333	.333
Schofield, Dick-John Richard (Ducky)	53-58StLN 58-65PitN 65-66SFN 66NYA 66-67LAN 68StLN 69-70BosA 71StLN 71MilA	01-07-35	Springfield, Ill.		B	R	5'9	163	1321	3083	394	699	113	20	21	211	390	526	12	.227	.319
Schreiber, Ted-Theodore Henry	63NYN	07-11-38	Brooklyn, N.Y.		R	R	5'11	175	39	50	1	8	0	0	0	2	4	14	0	.160	.160
Schroder, Bob-Robert James	65-68SFN	12-30-44	Ridgefield, N.J.		R	R	6'	175	138	221	29	48	5	1	0	12	23	21	1	.217	.249
Schwartz, Randy-Douglas Randall	65-66KCA	02-09-44	Los Angeles, Cal.		L	L	6'3	230	16	18	0	3	0	0	0	2	1	7	0	.167	.167
Scott, George-George Charles (The Boomer)	66-71BosA 72-76MilA 77-79BosA 79KCA 79NYA	02-23-44	Greenville, Miss.		R	R	6'2	215	2034	7433	957	1992	306	60	271	1051	699	1418	69	.268	.435
Sevcik, John-John Joseph	65MinA	07-11-42	Oak Park, Ill.		R	R	6'2	205	12	16	1	1	0	0	0	0	1	5	0	.063	.125
Severson, Rich-Richard Allen	70-71KCA	01-18-45	Artesia, Cal.		R	R	6'	174	93	270	26	69	11	3	1	23	19	38	0	.256	.330
Shamsky, Art-Arthur Louis	65-67CinN 68-71NYN 72ChiN 72OakA	10-14-41	St. Louis, Mo.		L	L	6'1	180	665	1686	194	426	60	15	68	233	188	254	5	.253	.427
Shannon, Mike-Thomas Michael (Moonman)	62-70StLN	07-15-39	St. Louis, Mo.		R	R	6'3	195	882	2780	313	710	116	23	68	367	224	525	19	.255	.387
Sherry, Norm-Norman Burt	59-62LAN 63NYN M76-77CalA	07-16-31	New York, N.Y.		R	R	5'11	180	194	497	45	107	9	1	18	69	37	102	1	.215	.346
Shirley, Bart-Barton Arvin	64,66LAN 67NYN 68LAN	01-04-40	Corpus Christi, Tex.		R	R	5'10	183	75	162	15	33	4	1	0	11	14	28	0	.204	.241
Shockley, Costen-John Costen	64PhiN 65CalA	02-08-42	Georgetown, Del.		L	L	6'2	200	51	142	9	28	2	0	3	19	11	24	0	.197	.275
Shoemaker, Charlie-Charles Landis	61-62,64KCA	08-10-39	Los Angeles, Cal.	05-31-90	L	R	5'10	155	28	89	12	23	4	2	0	4	2	13	0	.258	.348
Shopay, Tom-Thomas Michael	67-69NYA 71-72,75,77BalA	02-21-45	Bristol, Conn.		L	R	5'9	160	253	309	40	62	7	1	3	20	26	51	11	.201	.259
Siebern, Norm-Norman Leroy	56,58-59NYA 60-63KCA 64-65BalA 66CalA 67SFN 67-68BosA	07-26-33	St. Louis, Mo.		L	R	6'2	205	1406	4481	662	1217	206	38	132	636	708	749	18	.272	.423
Silverio, Tommy-Thomas Roberto [Veloz]		10-14-45	Santiago, Dom. Rep.		L	L	5'10	170	31	30	2	3	0	0	0	0	2	8	0	.100	.100
Simpson, Dick-Richard Charles	62-64LAA 65CalA 66-67CinN 68StLN 68HouN 69NYA 69SeaA	07-28-43	Washington, D.C.		R	R	6'4	176	288	518	94	107	19	2	15	56	64	174	10	.207	.338
Sims, Duke-Duane B.	64-70CleA 71-72LAN 72-73DetA 73-74NYA 74TexA	06-05-41	Salt Lake City, Utah		L	R	6'2	210	843	2422	263	580	80	6	100	310	338	483	6	.239	.401
Sims, Greg-Gregory Emmett	66HouN	06-28-46	San Francisco, Cal.		B	R	6'	190	7	6	1	1	0	0	0	0	0	1	0	.167	.167
Sipin, John-John White	69SDN	07-07-46	Watsonville, Cal.		R	R	5'11	175	68	229	22	51	12	2	2	9	18	44	2	.223	.319
Skidmore, Roe-Robert Roe (Cotton)	70ChiN	10-30-45	Decatur, Ill.		R	L	6'3	210	1	1	0	1	0	0	0	1	0	0	0	1.000	1.000
Skowron, Bill-William Joseph (Moose)	54-62NYA 63LAN 64WasA 64-67ChiA 67CalA	12-18-30	Chicago, Ill.		R	R	5'11	195	1658	5547	681	1566	243	53	211	888	383	870	16	.282	.459
Slocum, Ron-Ronald Reece	69-71SDN	07-02-45	Modesto, Cal.		B	R	6'2	185	80	113	15	17	3	2	6	16	8	37	0	.150	.265
Smith, Bernie-Calvin Bernard	70-71MilA	09-04-45	Ponchatoula, La.		R	R	5'8	164	59	112	9	26	2	1	2	9	13	23	5	.232	.339
Smith, Charley-Charles William	60-61BalA 61PhiN 62-64ChiA 64-65NYN 66StLN 67-68NYA 69ChiN	09-15-37	Charleston, N.C.	11-29-94	R	R	6'1	176	771	2484	228	594	83	18	69	281	130	565	7	.239	.390
Smith, Dick-Richard Arthur	63-64NYN 65LAN	05-17-39	Lebanon, Ore.		R	R	6'2	205	76	142	18	31	4	0	0	7	6	42	9	.218	.289
Smith, Dick-Richard Kelly	65-66KCA	05-05-44	Lincolnton, N.C.		R	R	6'5	200	21	28	3	3	0	0	0	0	2	10	0	.107	.107
Smith, George-George Cornelius	63-65DetA 68BosA	07-07-37	St. Petersburg, Fla.	06-15-87	R	R	5'10	170	217	634	64	130	27	6	9	57	59	142	9	.205	.309
Smith, Nate-Nathaniel Beverly	62BalA	04-26-35	Chicago, Ill.		R	R	5'11	170	1	0	0	0	0	0	0	0	0	0	0	.222	.333
Smith, Willie-Willie (Wonderful Willie) (See P61-72)	63DetA 64LAA 65-66CalA 67-68CleA 68-70ChiN 71CinN	02-11-39	Anniston, Ala.	01-16-06	L	L	6'	192	691	1654	171	410	63	11	46	211	107	284	20	.248	.395
Snyder, Jim-James Robert	61,64MinA M88SeaA	08-15-32	Dearborn, Mich.		R	R	6'1	180	41	86	4	12	2	0	1	6	4	12	0	.140	.198
Snyder, Russ-Russell Henry	59-60KCA 61-70BalA 70ChiA 70CleA 70MilA	06-22-34	Oak, Neb.		L	R	6'1	190	1365	3631	488	984	150	29	42	319	294	438	58	.271	.370
Sorrell, Bill-William	65PhiN 67SFN 70KCA	10-14-40	Morehead, Ky.		R	R	6'	190	85	165	15	44	9	0	5	17	15	16	1	.267	.376

USE NAME - GIVEN NAMES (NICKNAMES)	TEAM BY YEAR	BIRTH DATE	BIRTH PLACE	DEATH DATE	B	T	HGT	WGT	G	AB	R	H	2B	3B	HR	RBI	BB	SO	SB	BA	SA
Southworth, Bill-William Frederick	64MilN	11-10-45	Madison, Wis.		R	R	6'2	205	3	7	2	2	0	0	1	2	0	3	0	.286	.714
Spangler, Al-Albert Donald	59-61MilN 62-65HouN 65-66CalA 67-61ChiN	07-08-33	Philadelphia, Pa.		L	L	6'	175	912	2267	307	594	87	26	21	175	295	234	37	.262	.351
Spence, Bob-John Robert	68-71ChiA	02-10-46	San Diego, Cal.		R	R	6'4	215	72	183	13	37	5	1	4	19	16	47	0	.202	.306
Spiezio, Ed-Edward Wayne	64-68StLN 69-72ChiN	10-31-41	Joliet, Ill.		R	R	5'11	175	554	1544	126	367	56	4	39	174	135	245	16	.238	.355
Spriggs, George-George Herman	65-67PitN 69-70KCA	05-22-41	Jewell, Md.		L	R	5'11	175	130	225	35	43	5	5	1	12	23	63	9	.191	.271
Staehle, Marv-Marvin Gustave	64-67ChiA 69-70MonN 71AtlN	03-13-42	Oak Park, Ill.		L	R	5'10	165	185	455	53	94	12	1	1	33	54	35	4	.207	.244
Stahl, Larry-Larry Floyd	64-66KCA 67-68NYN 69-72SDN 73CinN	06-29-41	Bellville, Ill.		L	L	6'	180	730	1721	167	400	58	19	36	163	142	357	22	.232	.351
Stanley, Mickey-Mitchell Jack	64-78DetA	07-20-42	Grand Rapids, Mich.		R	R	6'1	190	1516	5022	641	1243	201	48	117	500	371	564	44	.248	.377
Stargell, Willie-Wilver Dornel	62-82PitN	03-06-40	Earlsboro, Okla.	04-09-01	L	L	6'3	225	2360	7927	1195	2232	423	55	475	1540	937	1936	17	.282	.529
Stephenson, Johnny-John Herman	64-66NYN 67-68ChiN 69-70SFN 71-73CalA	04-13-41	South Portsmouth, Ky.		L	R	5'11	180	451	989	83	214	37	3	12	93	63	118	0	.216	.296
Stewart, Jimmy-James Franklin	63-67ChiN 67ChiA 69-71CinN 72-73HouN	06-11-39	Opelika, Ala.		B	R	6'	165	777	1420	164	336	45	14	8	112	139	218	38	.237	.305
Stillwell, Ron-Ronald Roy	61-62WasA	12-03-39	Los Angeles, Cal.		R	R	5'11	165	14	38	8	8	1	0	0	3	3	6	0	.211	.237
Stone, Gene-Eugene Daniel	69PhiN	01-16-44	Pacoima, Cal.		L	L	5'11	190	18	28	4	6	1	0	0	0	4	9	0	.214	.286
Stone, Ron-Harry Ronald	66KCA 69-72PhiN	09-09-42	Corning, Cal.		L	L	6'2	195	388	804	73	194	28	8	6	89	101	122	11	.241	.318
Stroud, Ed-Edwin Marvin (The Creeper)	66-67ChiA 67-70WasA 71ChiA	10-31-39	Lapine, Ala.		B	R	5'11	175	529	1353	209	320	37	28	14	100	129	224	72	.237	.336
Stuart, Dick-Richard Lee (Dr. Strangeglove)	58-62PitN 63-64BosA 65PhiN 66NYN 66LaaN 67-68JL 69CalA	11-07-32	San Francisco, Cal.	12-15-02	R	R	6'4	212	1112	3997	506	1055	157	30	228	743	301	957	2	.264	.489
Stubing, Moose-Lawrence George	67CalA M88CalA	03-11-38	Bronx, N.Y.		L	L	6'3	220	5	5	0	0	0	0	0	0	0	4	0	.000	.000
Suarez, Ken-Kenneth Raymond	66-67KCA 68-69,71CleA 72-73TexA	04-12-43	Tampa, Fla.		R	R	5'9	175	295	661	57	150	29	1	5	60	99	97	4	.227	.297
Sudakis, Bill-William Paul (Suds)	68-71LAN 72NYN 73TexA 74NYA 75CalA 75CleA	03-27-46	Joliet, Ill.		B	R	6'1	190	530	1548	177	362	56	7	59	214	172	313	9	.234	.393
Sullivan, Haywood-Haywood Cooper	55,57BosA 58JJ 59-60BosA 61-63,M65KCA	12-15-30	Donalsonville, Ga.	02-12-03	R	R	6'4	215	312	851	94	192	30	5	13	87	109	140	2	.226	.318
Sullivan, John-John Peter	63-65DetA 67NYN 68PhiN	01-03-41	Somerville, N.J.		L	R	6'	195	116	259	9	59	5	0	2	18	19	45	0	.228	.270
Sutherland, Gary-Gary Lynn (Suds)	66-68PhiN 69-71MonN 72-73HouN 74-76DetA 76MilA 77SDN 78StLN	09-27-44	Glendale, Cal.		R	R	6'	185	1031	3104	306	754	109	10	24	239	207	219	11	.243	.306
Swanson, Stan-Stanley Lawrence	71MonN	05-19-44	Yuba City, Cal.		R	R	5'10	175	49	106	14	26	3	0	2	11	10	13	1	.245	.330
Swoboda, Ron-Ronald Alan (Rocky)	65-70NYN 71MonN 71-73NYA	06-30-44	Baltimore, Md.		R	R	6'2	205	928	2581	285	624	87	24	73	344	299	647	20	.242	.379
Szotkiewicz, Ken-Kenneth John (Sock)	70DetA	02-25-47	Wilmington, Del.		L	R	6'	170	47	84	9	9	1	0	3	9	12	29	0	.107	.226
Talton, Tim-Marion Lee	66-67KCA	01-14-39	Pikeville, N.C.		R	R	6'3	200	83	112	15	33	6	2	2	11	8	18	0	.295	.438
Tartabull, Jose-Jose Guzman [Milages]	62-66KCA 66-68BosA 69-70OakA	12-17-38	Cienfuegos, Cuba		L	L	5'11	165	749	1857	247	484	56	24	2	107	115	136	81	.261	.320
Tatum, Jarvis-Jarvis	68-70CalA	10-11-46	Fresno, Cal.	01-06-03	R	R	6'	185	102	254	37	59	8	0	0	8	17	50	1	.232	.264
Taussig, Don-Donald Franklin	58SFN 61StLN 62HouN	02-19-32	New York, N.Y.		R	R	6'	180	153	263	38	69	14	5	4	30	21	53	2	.262	.399
Taylor, Bob-Robert Lee (T-Bone)	70SFN	03-20-44	Leland, Miss.		L	R	5'9	182	63	84	12	16	0	0	2	10	12	13	0	.190	.262
Taylor, Carl-Carl Means	68-69PitN 70StLN 71KCA 71PitN 72-73KCA	01-20-44	Sarasota, Fla.		R	R	6'2	200	411	846	113	225	31	6	10	115	136	130	12	.266	.352
Taylor, Hawk-Robert Dale	57-58,61-63MilN 64-67NYN 67CalA 69-70KCA	04-03-39	Metropolis, Ill.		R	R	6'2	195	394	724	56	158	24	2	16	82	61	146	0	.218	.319
Taylor, Tony-Antonio Nemesio [Sanchez]	58-60CinN 60-71PhiN 71-73DetA 74-76PhiN	12-19-35	Central Alara, Cuba		R	R	5'9	180	2195	7680	1005	2007	298	86	75	598	613	1083	234	.261	.352
Tepedino, Frank-Frank Ronald	67,69-71NYA 71MilA 72NYA 73-75AtlN	11-23-47	Brooklyn, N.Y.		L	L	5'11	190	265	507	50	122	13	1	6	58	33	61	4	.241	.306
Thacker, Moe-Morris Benton	58,60-62ChiN 63StLN	05-21-34	Louisville, Ky.	11-13-97	R	R	6'3	205	158	260	20	46	7	0	2	20	40	81	1	.177	.227
Theobold, Ron-Ron Merle	71-72MilA	07-28-44	Oakland, Cal.		R	R	5'8	165	251	779	94	193	23	2	2	42	106	77	11	.248	.290
Thomas, George-George Edward	57-58,61DetA 61-63LAA 63-65DetA 66-71BosA 71MinA	11-29-37	Minneapolis, Minn.		R	R	6'3	190	680	1688	203	430	71	9	46	202	138	343	13	.255	.389
Thomas, Lee-James Leroy	61NYA 61-64LAA 64-65BosA 66AtlN 66-67ChiN 68HouN	02-05-36	Peoria, Ill.		L	L	6'2	195	1027	3324	405	847	111	22	106	428	332	397	25	.255	.397
Tillman, Bob-John Robert	62-67BosA 67NYA 68-70AtlN	03-24-37	Nashville, Tenn.	06-21-00	R	R	6'4	205	775	2329	189	540	68	10	79	282	228	510	1	.232	.371
Tischinski, Tom-Thomas Arthur	69-71MinA	07-12-44	Kansas City, Mo.		R	R	5'10	190	82	116	8	21	2	0	1	6	18	18	0	.181	.224
Tolan, Bobby-Robert	65-68StLN 69-70CinN 71FJ 72-73CinN 74-75SDN 76-77PhiN 77PitN 78JL 79SDN	11-19-45	Los Angeles, Cal.		L	L	5'11	180	1282	4238	572	1121	173	34	86	497	258	587	193	.265	.382
Torborg, Jeff-Jeffrey Allen	64-70LAN 71-73CalA M77-79CleA M89-91ChiA M92-93NYN M01MonN M02-03FlaN	11-26-41	Plainfield, N.J.		R	R	6'	195	574	1391	78	297	42	3	8	101	103	189	3	.214	.265
Torre, Joe-Joseph Paul	60-65MilN 66-68AtlN 69-74StLN 75-77,M77-81NYN M82-84AtlN M90-95StLN M96-06NYA	07-18-40	Brooklyn, N.Y.		R	R	6'2	212	2209	7874	996	2342	344	59	252	1185	779	1094	23	.297	.452
Torres, Felix-Felix [Sanchez]	62-64LAA	05-01-32	Ponce, P.R.		R	R	5'11	182	365	1191	109	302	61	5	27	153	71	202	2	.254	.281
Torres, Hector-Hector Epitacio [Marroquin]	68-70HouN 71ChiN 72MonN 73HouN 75-76SDN 77TorA	09-16-45	Monterrey, Mexico		R	R	6'	175	622	1738	148	375	46	7	18	115	104	229	7	.216	.281
Tovar (Perez), Cesar-Cesar Leonardo [Tovar] (Pepi)	65-72MinA 73PhiN 74-75TexA 75-76OakA 76NYA	07-03-40	Caracas, Venezuela	07-14-94	R	R	5'9	155	1488	5569	834	1546	253	55	46	435	413	410	226	.278	.368
Tracewski, Dick-Richard Joseph	62-65LAN 66-69,M79DetA	02-03-35	Eynon, Pa.		R	R	5'11	170	614	1231	148	262	31	6	8	91	134	253	15	.213	.272
Tresh, Tom-Thomas Michael	61-69NYA 69ChiN	09-20-37	Detroit, Mich.		B	R	6'1	185	1192	4251	595	1041	179	34	153	530	550	698	45	.245	.411
Trevino, Bobby-Carlos [Castro]	68CalA	08-15-45	Monterrey, Mexico		R	R	6'2	185	17	40	1	9	1	0	0	1	2	9	0	.225	.250
Uecker, Bob-Robert George	62-63MilN 64-65StLN 66-67PhiN 67AtlN	01-26-35	Milwaukee, Wis.		R	R	6'1	190	297	731	65	146	22	0	14	74	96	167	0	.200	.287
Uhlaender, Ted-Theodore Otto	65-69MinA 70-71CleA 72CinN	10-01-39	Chicago Heights, Ill.		L	R	6'	190	898	2932	343	772	114	21	36	285	202	277	52	.263	.353
Valdespino, Sandy-Hilario [Borroto]	65-67MinA 68AtlN 69HouN 69SeaA 70MilA 71KCA	01-14-39	San Jose de las Lajas, Cuba		L	L	5'8	170	382	765	96	176	23	3	7	67	57	129	14	.230	.295
Valentine, Fred-Fred Lee (Squeaky)	59,63BalA 64-68WasA 68BalA	01-09-35	Clarksdale, Miss.		B	R	6'	190	533	1458	180	360	56	10	36	138	156	228	47	.247	.373
Valle, Hector-Hector Jose	65LAN	10-27-40	Vega Baja, P.R.		B	R	5'9	180	9	13	1	4	0	0	0	2	0	5	0	.308	.308
Vaughn, Glenn-Glenn Edward (Sparky)	63HouN	02-16-44	Compton, Cal.	12-18-04	B	R	5'11	170	9	30	1	5	0	0	0	0	2	5	0	.167	.167
Versalles, Zoilo-Zoilo Casanova [Rodriguez] (Zorro)	59-60WasA 61-67MinA 68LAN 69CleA 69WasA 71AtlN	12-18-39	Havana, Cuba	06-09-95	R	R	5'10	165	1400	5141	650	1246	230	63	95	471	318	810	97	.242	.367
Vidal, Jose-Jose [Nicholas] (Papito)	66-68CleA 69SeaA	04-03-40	Batey Lechugas, D. R.		R	R	6'	190	88	146	20	24	1	2	3	10	18	46	4	.164	.260
Vinson, Chuck-Charles Anthony	66CalA	01-05-44	Washington, D.C.		R	R	6'3	207	13	22	3	4	2	0	1	0	5	9	0	.182	.409
Voss, Bill-William Edward	65-68ChiA 69-70CalA 70-71MilA 72OakA 72StLN	10-31-43	Glendale, Cal.		L	L	6'2	160	475	1177	119	267	29	10	19	127	117	167	13	.227	.317
Wagner, Leon-Leon Lamar (Daddy Wags)	58-59SFN 60StLN 61-63LAA 64-68CleA 68ChiA 69SFN	05-13-34	Chattanooga, Tenn.	01-03-04	L	R	6'1	195	1352	4426	636	1202	150	15	211	669	435	656	54	.272	.455
Wallace, Don-Donald Allen	67CalA	08-25-40	Sapulpa, Okla.		L	R	5'8	165	23	6	2	0	0	0	0	0	0	2	0	.000	.000
Walton, Danny-Daniel James	68HouN 69SeaA 70-71MilA 71NYA 73,75MinA 76LaaN 77HouN 78JL 80TexA	07-14-47	Los Angeles, Cal.		R	R	6'	195	297	779	69	174	27	4	28	107	88	240	4	.223	.376
	Bats Both 75-80																				
Ward, Jay-Jay Francis	63-64MinA 66JL 70CinN	09-09-38	Brookfield, Mo.		R	R	6'1	190	27	49	4	8	0	0	0	4	6	19	0	.163	.224
Ward, Pete-Peter Thomas	62BalA 63-69ChiA 70NYA	07-26-39	Montreal, Canada		L	R	6'1	190	973	3060	345	776	136	17	98	427	371	539	20	.254	.405
Warner, Jackie-Jon Joseph	66CalA	08-01-43	Monrovia, Cal.		R	R	6'	180	45	123	22	26	4	1	7	16	9	55	0	.211	.431
Warwick, Carl-Carl Wayne	61LAN 61-62StLN 62-63HouN 64-65StLN 65BalA 66ChiN	02-27-37	Dallas, Tex.		R	L	5'10	170	530	1462	168	363	51	10	31	149	127	241	13	.248	.360
Watkins, Dave-David Roger	69PhiN	03-15-44	Owensboro, Ky.		R	R	5'10	185	69	148	17	26	2	1	4	12	12	53	2	.176	.284
Webster, Ramon-Ramon Alberto	67KCA 68-69OakA 70-71SDN 71OakA 71ChiN	08-31-42	Colon, Panama		L	L	6'	185	380	778	76	190	31	6	17	98	70	94	0	.244	.365
Weekly, Johnny-Johnny	62-64HouN	06-14-37	Waterproof, La.	11-24-74	R	R	6'1	200	53	121	7	25	4	0	5	19	15	21	0	.207	.364
Weis, Al-Albert John	62-67ChiA 68-71NYN	04-02-38	Franklin Square, N.Y.		B	R	6'	160	800	1578	195	346	45	11	7	115	117	299	55	.219	.275
	Bats Right 69-71																				
Werhas, Johnny-John Charles (Peaches)	64-65,67LAN 67CalA	02-07-38	Highland Park, Mich.		R	R	6'2	200	89	168	15	29	3	2	2	14	24	34	0	.173	.260
Wert, Don-Donald Ralph	63-70DetA 71WasA	07-29-38	Strasburg, Pa.		R	R	5'10	180	1110	3840	417	929	129	15	77	366	389	529	22	.242	.343
Whitaker, Steve-Steve Edward	66-68NYA 69SeaA 70SFN	05-07-43	Tacoma, Wash.		L	L	6'1	180	266	758	73	174	20	6	24	85	54	174	4	.230	.367
White, Bill-William DeKova	56NYN 57MS 58SFN 59-65StLN 66-68PhiN 69StLN	01-28-34	Lakewood, Fla.		L	L	6'	195	1673	5972	843	1706	278	65	202	870	596	927	103	.286	.455
White, Elder-Elder Lafayette	62ChiN	12-23-34	Colerain, N.C.		R	R	5'11	165	23	53	8	8	2	0	0	1	8	11	3	.151	.189
White, Mike-Joyner Michael	63-65HouN	12-18-38	Detroit, Mich.		R	R	5'8	160	100	296	30	78	11	3	0	27	21	49	1	.264	.321
White, Roy-Roy Hilton	65-79NYA	12-27-43	Los Angeles, Cal.		B	R	5'11	170	1881	6650	964	1803	300	51	160	758	934	708	233	.271	.404
	Bats Right 65																				
Whitfield, Fred-Fred Dwight	62StLN 63-67CleA 68-69CinN 70MonN	01-07-38	Vandiver, Ala.		L	L	6'1	190	817	2284	242	578	93	8	108	356	139	371	7	.253	.443
Wicker, Floyd-Floyd Euliss	68StLN 69MonN 70-71MilA 71SFN	09-12-43	Burlington, N.C.		L	R	6'2	175	81	113	10	18	1	0	3	6	7	33	0	.159	.195
Williams, Bernie-Bernard	70-72SFN 74SDN	10-08-48	Akaneda, Cal.		R	R	6'1	180	102	172	23	35	5	2	1	12	21	53	2	.192	.308
Williams, Billy-Billy Leo	59-74ChiN 75-76OakA	06-15-38	Whistler, Ala.		L	R	6'1	175	2488	9350	1410	2711	434	88	426	1475	1045	1046	90	.290	.492
Williams, Billy-William	69SeaA	06-13-33	Newberry, S.C.		R	R	6'3	195	4	10	1	0	0	0	0	0	0	2	0	.000	.000
Williams, George-George	61PhiN 62HouN 64KCA	10-23-39	Detroit, Mich.		R	R	5'11	165	59	135	15	31	7	0	0	9	20	25	0	.230	.281
Williams, Jim-James Alfred	69-70SDN	04-29-47	Zachary, La.		R	R	6'3	190	24	39	8	11	1	0	1	4	2	14	1	.282	.308
Williams, Jimy-James Francis	66-67StLN M86-88TorA M97-01BosA M02-04HouN	10-04-43	Santa Maria, Cal.		R	R	5'10	170	14	13	1	3	1	0	0	1	0	5	0	.231	.231
Williams, Walt-Walter Allen (No Neck)	64HouN 67-72ChiA 73CleA 74-75NYA	12-19-43	Brownwood, Tex.		R	R	5'6	180	842	2373	284	640	106	11	33	173	126	211	34	.270	.365
Wills, Maury-Maurice Morning	59-66LAN 67-68PitN 69MonN 69-72LAN M80-81SeaA	10-02-32	Washington, D.C.		B	R	5'11	170	1942	7588	1067	2134	177	71	20	458	552	684	586	.281	.331
Windhorn, Gordie-Gordon Ray	59NYA 61LAN 62KCA 62LAA	12-19-33	Maywood, Ill.		R	R	6'1	195	108	20	19	1	1	1	1	19	11	1	.176	.333
Wine, Bobby-Robert Paul	60,62-68PhiN 69-72MonN M85AtlN	09-17-38	New York, N.Y.		R	R	6'1	187	1164	3172	249	682	104	15	30	268	214	538	7	.215	.286

USE NAME - GIVEN NAMES (NICKNAMES)	TEAM BY YEAR	BIRTH DATE	BIRTH PLACE	DEATH DATE	B	T	HGT	WGT	G	AB	R	H	2B	3B	HR	RBI	BB	SO	SB	BA	SA
Wissman, Dave-David Alvin	64PitN	02-17-41	Greenfield, Miss.		L	R	6'2	178	16	27	2	4	0	0	0	0	1	9	0	.148	.148
Withrow, Corky-Raymond Wallace	63StLN	11-28-37	High Coal, W.Va.		R	R	6'3	197	6	9	0	0	0	0	0	1	0	2	0	.000	.000
Wojcik, John-John Joseph	62-64KCA	04-06-42	Olean, N.Y.		L	R	6'	175	41	124	16	27	4	0	0	11	23	20	5	.218	.250
Wood, Jake-Jacob	61-67DetA 67CinN	06-22-37	Elizabeth, N.J.		R	R	6'1	170	608	1877	279	469	53	26	35	168	159	362	79	.250	.362
Woods, Jim-James Jerome (Woody)	57ChiN 60-61PhiN	09-17-39	Chicago, Ill.		R	R	6'	175	36	82	11	17	3	0	3	12	7	28	0	.207	.354
Woods, Ron-Ronald Lawrence	69DetA 69-71NYA 71-74MonN	02-01-43	Hamilton, Ohio		R	R	5'10	168	582	1247	162	290	34	12	26	130	175	171	27	.233	.342
Woodward, Woody-William Frederick	63-65MilN 66-68AtlN 68-71CinN	09-23-42	Miami, Fla.		R	R	6'2	185	880	2187	208	517	79	14	1	148	169	301	14	.236	.287
Wynn, Jim-James Sherman (The Toy Cannon)	63-73HouN 74-75LAN 76AtlN 77NYA 77MilA	03-12-42	Hamilton, Ohio		R	R	5'9	170	1920	6653	1105	1665	285	39	291	964	1224	1427	225	.250	.436
Yastrzemski, Carl-Carl Michael (Yaz)	61-83BosA	08-22-39	Southampton, N.Y.		L	R	6'	185	3308	11988	1816	3419	646	59	452	1844	1845	1393	168	.285	.462
Yates, Al-Albert Arthur (Bunny)	71MilA	04-26-45	Jersey City, N.J.		R	R	6'3	210	24	47	5	13	2	0	1	4	3	7	1	.277	.383
Young, Don-Donald Wayne	65,69ChiN	10-18-45	Houston, Tex.		R	R	6'2	185	112	307	37	67	12	3	7	29	38	85	1	.218	.345
Young, John-John Thomas	71DetA	02-09-49	Los Angeles, Cal.		L	L	6'3	215	2	4	1	2	1	0	0	1	0	0	0	.500	.750
Zeller, Bart-Barton Wallace	70StLN	07-22-41	Chicago Heights, Ill.		R	R	6'1	190	1	0	0	0	0	0	0	0	0	0	0	—	—
Zimmerman, Jerry-Gerald Robert	61CinN 62-68MinA	09-21-41	Omaha, Neb.	09-09-98	R	R	6'2	185	483	994	60	203	22	2	3	72	78	154	1	.204	.239
Zipfel, Bud-Marion Sylvester	61-62WasA	11-18-38	Belleville, Ill.		L	R	6'3	200	118	354	38	78	11	6	10	39	32	92	2	.220	.370

USE NAMES - GIVEN NAMES (NICKNAMES)	TEAM BY YEAR	BIRTH DATE	BIRTHPLACE	DEATH DATE	B	T	HGT	WGT	W	L	Pct.	SV	G	GS	CG	IP	H	BB	SO	ShO	ERA
Abernathy, Ted-Theodore Wade	55-57,60WasA 63-64CleA 65-66ChiN 66AtlN 67-68CinN 69-70ChiN 70StLN 70-72KCA	03-06-33	Stanley, N.C.	12-16-04	R	R	6'4	215	63	69	.477	148	681	34	7	1148	1010	592	765	2	3.46
Ackley, Fritz-Florian Frederick	63-64ChiA	04-10-37	Hayward, Wis.	05-22-02	L	R	6'1	202	1	0	1.000	0	5	4	0	19	17	11	17	0	4.26
Acosta, Ed-Eduardo Elixbet [Montenegro] (Coca-Cola)	70PitN 71-72SDN	03-09-44	Boquete, Panama		B	R	6'5	223	6	9	.400	1	57	8	3	138	153	39	70	1	4.04
Adamson, Mike-John Michael	67-69BalA	09-13-47	San Diego, Cal.		R Bats Right 70	R	6'2	190	0	4	.000	0	11	4	0	26	28	22	14	0	7.27
Aguirre, Hank-Hank John	55-57CleA 58-67DetA 68LAN 69-70ChiN	01-31-31	Azusa, Cal.	09-05-94	R	L	6'4	205	75	72	.510	33	447	149	44	1376	1216	479	856	9	3.24
Aker, Jack-Jackie Deland (Chief)	64-67KCA 68OakA 69SeaA 69-72NYA 72-73ChiN 74AtlN 74NYN	07-13-40	Tulare, Cal.		R Bats Both 65-70	R	6'2	190	47	45	.511	123	495	0	0	746	679	274	404	0	3.28
Allen, Bob-Robert Gray	61-63,66-67CleA	10-23-37	Tatum, Tex.		R	R	6'2	185	7	12	.368	19	204	0	0	274	288	132	199	0	4.11
Allen, Lloyd-Lloyd Cecil	69-73CalA 73-74TexA 74-75ChiA	05-08-50	Merced, Cal.		R	R	6'1	185	8	25	.242	22	159	19	0	297	291	196	194	0	4.70
Anderson, Craig-Norman Craig	61StLN 62-64NYN	07-01-38	Washington, D.C.		R	R	6'2	205	7	23	.233	5	82	17	2	192	226	81	94	0	5.11
Anderson, John-John Charles	58PhiN 60BalA 62StLN 62HouN	11-23-29	St. Paul, Minn.	12-20-98	R	R	6'1	190	0	0	—	1	24	1	0	45	64	14	19	0	6.40
Angelini, Norm-Norman Stanley	72-73KCA	09-24-47	San Francisco, Cal.		L	L	5'11	180	2	1	.667	3	28	0	0	20	15	19	19	0	2.70
Archer, Jim-James William	61-62KCA	05-25-32	Max Meadows, Va.		R	L	6'	190	9	16	.360	5	57	28	9	233	244	70	122	2	3.94
Arlich, Don-Donald Louis	65-66HouN	02-15-43	Wayne, Mich.		L	L	6'2	185	0	1	.000	0	8	1	0	10	16	5	1	0	8.10
Arlin, Steve-Stephen Ralph	69-74SDN 74CleA	09-25-45	Seattle, Wash.		R	R	6'3	195	34	67	.337	1	141	123	32	790	792	373	463	11	4.32
Arrigo, Jerry-Gerald William	61-64MinA 65-66CinN 66NYN 67-69CinN 70ChiA	06-12-41	Chicago, Ill.		L	L	6'1	195	35	40	.467	3	194	80	9	620	605	291	433	3	4.14
Arroyo, Rudy-Rudolph (Yo-Yo)	71StLN	06-19-41	New York, N.Y.		R	L	6'2	190	0	1	1.000	0	9	0	0	12	18	5	5	0	5.25
Aust, Dennis-Dennsi Kay	65-68StLN	11-25-40	Tecumseh, Neb.		R	R	5'11	180	0	1	.000	2	15	0	0	17	18	8	14	0	5.82
Austin, Rick-Rick Gerald	70-71CleA 74JL 75-76MilA	10-27-46	Seattle, Wash.		R	L	6'4	200	4	8	.333	5	89	8	1	136	141	78	106	1	4.63
Bailey, Steve-Steven John	67-68CleA	02-12-42	Bronx, N.Y.		R	R	6'1	194	2	6	.250	2	34	2	0	70	66	44	47	0	3.86
Baird, Bob-Robert Allen	62-63WasA	01-16-42	Knoxville, Tenn.	04-11-74	L	L	6'1	195	0	4	.000	0	8	6	0	23	25	15	10	0	7.04
Bakenhaster, Dave-David Lee	64StLN	03-05-45	Columbus, Ohio		R	R	5'10	168	0	0	—	0	2	0	0	3	9	1	0	0	6.00
Baker, Tom-Thomas Henry	63ChiN	05-06-34	Port Townsend, Wash.	03-09-80	L	L	6'	195	0	1	.000	0	10	1	0	18	20	7	14	0	3.00
Baldschun, Jack-Jack Edward	61-65PhiN 66-67CinN 69-70SDN	10-16-36	Greenville, Ohio		R	R	6'	190	48	41	.539	60	457	0	0	704	687	298	555	0	3.69
Baldwin, Dave-David George	66-69WasA 70MilA 73ChiN	03-30-38	Tuscon, Ala.		R	R	6'2	205	6	11	.353	22	176	0	0	225	190	89	164	0	3.08
Ballinger, Mark-Mark Alan	71CleA	01-31-49	Glendale, Cal.		R	R	6'6	205	1	2	.333	1	18	0	0	35	30	13	25	0	4.63
Balsamo, Tony-Anthony Fred	62ChiN	11-21-37	Brooklyn, N.Y.		R	R	6'2	185	0	1	.000	0	18	0	0	29	34	20	27	0	6.52
Barber, Steve-Stephen David	60-67BalA 67-68NYA 69SeaA 70ChiN 70-72AtlN 72-73CalA 74SFN	02-22-38	Takoma Park, Md.		L	L	6'	200	121	106	.533	13	466	272	59	1998	1818	950	1309	21	3.36
Barber, Steve-Stephen Lee	70-71MinA	03-13-48	Grand Rapids, Mich.		R	R	6'1	190	1	0	1.000	2	22	2	0	39	34	31	18	0	5.08
Barnowski, Ed-Edward Anthony	65-66BalA	08-23-45	Scranton, Pa.		R	R	6'2	200	0	0	—	0	6	0	0	7	7	8	8	0	2.57
Bass, Norm-Norman Delaney 64 played in A.F.L.	61-63KCA	01-21-39	Laurel, Miss.		R	R	6'3	205	13	17	.433	2	65	34	6	254	271	137	111	2	5.31
Bates, Dick-Charles Richard	69SeaA	10-07-45	McArthur, Ohio		R	R	6'1	190	0	0	—	0	1	0	0	2	3	3	3	0	22.50
Bauta, Ed-Eduardo [Galvez]	60-63StLN 63-64NYN	01-06-35	Florida, Cuba		R	R	6'3	200	6	6	.500	11	97	0	0	149	148	70	89	0	4.35
Bearnarth, Larry-Lawrence Donald	63-66NYN 71MilA	09-11-41	New York, N.Y.	01-01-00	R	R	6'2	203	13	21	.382	8	173	7	0	323	350	135	124	0	4.12
Beck, Rich-Richard Henry	65NYA 66-67MS	01-21-41	Pasco, Wash.		B	R	6'3	190	2	1	.667	0	3	3	1	21	22	7	10	1	2.14
Beene, Fred-Freddy Ray	68-70BalA 72-74NYA 74-75CleA	11-24-42	Angleton, Tex.		R Bats Right 68	R	6'	150	12	7	.632	8	112	6	0	289	274	111	156	0	3.61
Behney, Mel-Melvin Brian	70CinN	09-02-47	Newark, N.J.		L	L	6'2	180	0	2	.000	0	5	0	0	10	15	8	2	0	4.50
Belinsky, Bo-Robert	62-64LAA 65-66PhiN 67HouN 69PitN 70CinN	12-07-36	New York, N.Y.	11-23-01	L	L	6'2	190	28	51	.354	2	146	102	14	665	603	333	476	0	4.10
Bell, Gary-Gary	58-67CleA 67-68BosA 69SeaA 69ChiA	11-17-36	San Antonio, Tex.		R	R	6'1	196	121	117	.508	51	519	233	71	2015	1794	842	1378	9	3.68
Bennett, Dave-David Hans	64PhiN	11-07-45	Berkeley, Cal.		R	R	6'5	195	0	0	—	0	1	0	0	1	2	0	1	0	9.00
Bennett, Dennis-Dennis John	62-64PhiN 65-67NYN 68CalA	10-05-39	Oakland, Cal.		L	L	6'3	205	43	47	.478	6	182	127	28	863	850	281	572	6	3.69
Bertaina, Frank-Frank Louis	64-67BalA 67-69WasA 69BalA 70StLN	04-14-44	San Francisco, Cal.		L	L	6'	185	19	29	.396	0	99	66	6	412	399	214	280	5	3.84
Bethke, Jim-James Charles	65NYN	11-05-46	Falls City, Neb.		R	R	6'3	185	2	0	1.000	0	25	0	0	40	41	22	19	0	4.28
Blanco, Gil-Gilbert Henry	65NYA 66KCA	12-15-45	Phoenix, Ariz.		L	L	6'5	205	3	5	.375	0	28	9	0	58	47	48	35	0	4.50
Blasingame, Wade-Wade Allen	63-65MilN 66-67AtlN 67-72HouN 72NYA	11-22-43	Deming, N.M.		L	L	6'1	190	46	51	.474	5	222	128	16	864	891	372	512	2	4.52
Blass, Steve-Stephen Robert	64,66-74PitN	04-18-42	Canaan, Conn.		R	R	6'1	175	103	76	.575	2	282	231	57	1599	1558	597	896	16	3.62
Blateric, Steve-Stephen Lawrence	71CinN 72NYA 75CleA	03-20-44	Denver, Colo.		R	R	6'3	200	0	0	—	0	5	0	0	11	16	1	13	0	5.73
Bogle, Warren-Warren Frederick	68OakA	10-19-46	Passaic, N.J.		L	L	6'4	220	0	0	—	0	16	1	0	23	26	8	26	0	4.30
Bolin, Bobby-Bobby Donald	61-69SFN 70MilA 70-73BosA	01-29-39	Hickory Grove, S.C.		R	R	6'4	210	88	75	.540	50	495	164	32	1576	1364	597	1175	10	3.40
Bollo, Greg-Gregory Gene	65-66ChiA	11-16-43	Detroit, Mich.		R	R	6'4	183	0	1	.000	0	18	1	0	30	19	12	20	0	3.30
Bonikowski, Joe-Joseph Peter	62MinA	01-16-41	Philadelphia, Pa.		R	R	6'	175	5	7	.417	2	30	13	3	100	95	38	45	0	3.87
Boozer, John-John Morgan	62-64,66-69PhiN	07-06-39	Columbia, S.C.	01-24-86	R	R	6'3	205	14	16	.467	15	171	22	3	394	414	139	282	0	4.09
Bork, Frank-Frank Bernard	64PitN	07-13-40	Buffalo, N.Y.		R	L	6'2	175	2	2	.500	2	33	2	0	42	51	11	31	0	3.83
Bosman, Dick-Richard Allen	66-71WasA 72-73TexA 73-75CleA 75-76OakA	02-17-44	Kenosha, Wis.		R	R	6'2	200	82	85	.491	2	306	229	37	1590	1594	412	757	10	3.67
Boswell, Dave-David Wilson	64-70MinA 71DetA 71BalA	01-20-45	Baltimore, Md.		R	R	6'3	185	68	56	.548	6	205	151	37	1065	858	481	882	6	3.52
Botz, Bob-Robert Allen (Butterball)	62LAA	04-28-35	Milwaukee, Wis.		B	R	5'11	170	2	1	.667	2	35	0	0	63	71	11	24	0	3.43
Bouldin, Carl-Carl Edward	61-64WasA	09-17-39	Germantown, Ky.		R	R	6'2	185	3	8	.273	0	27	10	1	71	96	30	36	0	6.21
Bouton, Jim-James Alan (Bulldog)	62-68NYA 69SeaA 69-70HouN 78AtlN	03-08-39	Newark, N.J.		R Bats Left 61	R	6'	185	62	63	.496	6	304	144	34	1237	1131	435	720	11	3.58
Bowsfield, Ted-Edward Oliver	58-60BosA 60CleA 61-62LAA 63-64KCA	01-10-36	Vernon, Canada		R	L	6'1	190	37	39	.487	6	215	86	12	663	699	259	326	4	4.34
Boyd, Gary-Gary Lee	69CleA	08-22-46	Pasadena, Cal.		R	R	6'4	200	0	2	.000	0	11	8	1	14	9	9	6	0	9.00
Brabender, Gene-Eugene Mathew (Bender)	66-68BalA 69SeaA 70MilA	08-16-41	Madison, Wis.	12-27-96	R	R	6'5	225	35	43	.449	6	151	80	15	621	570	282	440	4	4.25
Bradey, Don-Donald Eugene	64HouN	10-04-34	Charlotte, N.C.		R	R	5'9	180	0	2	.000	0	2	2	0	6	3	2	0	0	22.50
Bradley, Tom-Thomas William (Fry)	69-70CalA 71-72ChiA 73-75SFN	03-16-47	Asheville, N.C.		R	R	6'3	185	55	61	.474	2	183	151	27	1018	999	311	691	10	3.72
Branch, Harvey-Harvey Alfred	62StLN	02-08-39	Memphis, Tenn.		R	R	6'1	175	0	1	.000	0	5	5	2	11	5	5	2	0	5.40
Brandon, Darrell-Darrell G. (Bucky)	66-69BosA 69SeaA 69MinA 71-73PhiN	07-08-40	Nacogdoches, Tex.		R	R	6'2	200	28	37	.431	13	228	43	7	590	556	275	354	2	4.04
Braun, John-John Paul	64MilN	12-26-39	Madison, Wis.		R	R	6'5	218	0	0	—	0	1	0	0	2	3	2	1	0	4.50
Branneman, Jim-James LeRoy	65NYA	02-13-41	San Diego, Cal.	03-10-94	R	R	6'2	180	0	0	—	0	3	0	0	2	1	1	0	0	18.00
Brewer, Jim-James Thomas	60-63ChiN 64-75LAN 75-76CalA	11-17-37	Merced, Cal.	11-16-87	L	L	6'1	195	69	65	.515	132	584	15	1	1041	898	360	810	1	3.07
Brice, Alan-Alan Healey	61ChiA	10-01-37	New York, N.Y.		R	R	6'5	215	0	1	.000	0	3	0	0	3	4	3	0	0	0.00
Bridges, Marshall-Marshall (Sheriff)	59-60StLN 60-61CinN 62-63NYA 64-65WasA	06-02-31	Jackson, Miss.	09-03-90	L Bats Both 59-61	L	6'2	195	23	15	.605	25	206	5	1	346	315	191	302	0	3.75
Briles, Nelson-Nelson Kelley (Nellie)	65-70StLN 71-72PitN 74-75KCA 76-77TexA 77-78BalA	08-05-43	Dorris, Cal.	02-13-05	R	R	5'11	195	129	112	.535	22	452	279	58	2112	2141	547	1163	17	3.43
Britton, Jim-James Alan	67-69AtlN 70EJ 71MonN	03-24-44	N. Tonawanda, N.Y.		R	R	6'5	225	13	16	.448	4	70	34	2	237	214	112	148	3	3.99
Broglio, Ernie-Ernest Gilbert	59-64StLN 64-66ChiN	08-27-35	Berkeley, Cal.		R	R	6'2	200	77	74	.510	2	259	184	52	1337	1216	587	849	18	3.74
Bronstad, Jim-James Warren	59NYA 63-64WasA	06-22-36	Fort Worth, Tex.		R	R	6'2	196	3	11	.125	0	45	3	0	93	110	37	45	0	5.52
Brosseau, Frank-Franklin Lee	69,71PitN	07-31-44	Drayton, N.D.		R	R	6'2	200	0	0	—	0	4	0	0	3	2	2	6	0	4.50
Brown, Jophery-Jophery Clifford	68ChiN	01-22-45	Grambling, La.		L	R	6'2	190	0	0	—	0	1	0	0	2	2	1	0	0	4.50
Brown, Paul-Paul Dwayne	61-63,68PhiN	06-18-41	Fort Smith, Ark.		R	R	6'1	190	0	8	.000	0	36	12	0	93	108	47	45	0	6.00
Brubaker, Bruce-Bruce Ellsworth	67LAN 70MilA	12-29-41	Harrisburg, Pa.		R	R	6'1	198	0	0	—	0	5	1	0	11	13	5	11	0	15.00
Bruce, Bob-Robert James	59-61DetA 62-66HouN 67AtlN	05-16-33	Detroit, Mich.		R	R	6'3	210	49	71	.408	1	219	167	26	1123	1146	340	733	6	3.85
Bruckbauer, Fred-Frederick John	61MinA	05-27-38	New Ulm, Minn.		R	R	6'1	185	0	0	—	0	1	0	0	3	1	1	0	0	∞
Brunet, George-George Stuart (Lefty)	56-57,59-60KCA 60-61MilN 62-63HouN 63BalA 64LAA 65-69CalA 69SeaA 70WasA 70PitN 71StLN	06-08-35	Houghton, Mich.	10-25-91	R	L	6'1	200	69	93	.426	7	324	213	39	1431	1303	581	921	15	3.62
Bryant, Ron-Ronald Raymond (Bear)	67,69-74SFN 75StLN	11-12-47	Redlands, Cal.		B	L	6'1	195	57	56	.504	1	205	132	23	918	890	379	509	6	4.02
Bunker, Wally-Wallace Edward	63-68BalA 69-71KCA	01-25-45	Seattle, Wash.		R	R	6'2	197	60	52	.536	5	206	152	34	1086	976	334	569	5	3.51
Bunning, Jim-James Paul David	55-63DetA 64-67PhiN 68-69PitN 69LAN 70-71PhiN	10-23-31	Southgate, Ky.		R	R	6'3	200	224	184	.549	16	591	519	151	3759	3433	1000	2855	40	3.27
Burbach, Bill-William David	69-71NYA	08-22-47	Dickeyville, Wis.		R	R	6'4	215	6	11	.353	0	37	28	2	161	141	116	95	1	4.47
Burchart, Larry-Larry Wayne (Turk)	69CleA	02-08-46	Tulsa, Okla.		R	R	6'2	205	0	2	.000	4	42	0	0	42	24	26	24	0	4.29
Burdette, Freddie-Freddie Thomason	62-64ChiN	09-15-36	Moultrie, Ga.		R	R	6'2	170	1	0	1.000	0	30	0	0	35	27	20	10	0	3.34
Burnside, Pete-Peter Willits	55,57NYN 58SFN 59-60DetA 61-62WasA 63BalA 63WasA	07-02-30	Evanston, Ill.		R	L	6'2	180	19	36	.345	7	196	64	14	589	607	230	203	4	4.79
Buschhorn, Don-Donald Lee	65KCA	04-29-46	Independence, Mo.		R	R	6'	190	0	0	—	0	3	0	0	3	6	8	0	0	4.35
Butler, Bill-William Franklin	69-71KCA 72CleA 74-75,77MinA	06-28-47	Hyattsville, Md.		L	L	6'2	210	23	35	.397	4	134	86	10	593	555	312	408	0	4.30
Butler, Cecil-Cecil Dean	62,64MilN	10-23-37	Dallas, Ga.		R	R	6'4	195	2	0	1.000	0	11	2	1	35	33	9	24	0	3.34
Butters, Tom-Thomas Arden	62-65PitN	04-08-38	Delaware, Ohio		R	R	6'2	195	3	4	.400	7	43	5	0	95	81	56	85	0	3.13
Buzhardt, John-John William	58-59ChiN 60-61PhiN 62-67ChiA 67BalA 67-68HouN	08-15-36	Prosperity, S.C.		R	R	6'2	195	71	96	.425	7	326	200	44	1489	1425	457	678	15	3.67

USE NAMES - GIVEN NAMES (NICKNAMES)	TEAM BY YEAR	BIRTH DATE	BIRTHPLACE	DEATH DATE	B	T	HGT	WGT	W	L	Pct.	SV	G	GS	CG	IP	H	BB	SO	ShO	ERA
Cain, Les-Leslie	68,70-72DetA	01-13-48	San Luis Obispo, Cal.		L	L	6'1	200	23	19	.548	0	68	64	8	374	331	225	303	1	3.97
Calmus, Dick-Richard Lee	63LAN 67ChiN	01-07-44	Los Angeles, Cal.		R	R	6'4	187	3	1	.750	0	22	2	0	48	37	16	26	0	3.19
Cambria, Fred-Frederick Dennis	70PitN	01-22-48	Queens, N.Y.		R	R	6'2	195	1	2	.333	0	6	5	0	33	37	12	14	0	3.55
Campisi, Sal-Salvatore John	69-70StLN 71MinA	08-11-42	Brooklyn, N.Y.		R	R	6'2	210	3	2	.600	4	50	0	0	63	62	47	35	0	2.71
Cardinal, Randy-Conrad Seth	63HouN	03-30-42	Brooklyn, N.Y.		R	R	6'1	190	0	1	.000	0	6	1	0	13	15	7	7	0	6.23
Cardwell, Don-Donald Eugene	57-60PhiN 60-62ChiN 63-66PitN 67-70NYN 70AtlN	12-07-35	Winston-Salem, N.C.		R	R	6'4	210	102	138	.425	7	410	301	72	2122	2009	671	1211	17	3.92
Carlos, Cisco-Francisco Manuel	67-69ChiA 69-70WasA	09-17-40	Monrovia, Cal.		R	R	6'3	205	11	18	.379	0	73	36	1	237	222	79	119	1	3.72
Carpin, Frank-Frank Dominic	65PitN 66HouN	09-14-38	Brooklyn, N.Y.		L	L	5'10	172	4	1	.800	4	49	0	0	46	44	30	29	0	3.72
Carroll, Clay-Clay Palmer (Hawk, Sheriff)	64-65MilN 66-68AtlN 68-75CinN 76-77ChiA 77StLN 78PitN	05-02-41	Clanton, Ala.		R	R	6'1	205	96	73	.568	143	731	28	1	1353	1296	442	681	0	2.94
Chance, Dean-Wilmer Dean	61-64LAA 65-66CalA 67-69MinN 70CleA 70NYN 71DetA	06-01-41	Wooster, Ohio		R	R	6'3	204	128	115	.527	23	406	294	83	2148	1864	739	1534	33	2.92
Chartron, Pete-Frank Lane	64BosN	12-21-42	Jackson, Tenn.		R	R	6'2	190	0	2	.000	0	25	5	0	65	67	24	37	0	5.26
Chavez, Nestor-Nestor Isais [Silva]	67SFN	07-06-47	Chacao, Venezuela	03-16-69	R	R	6'	170	1	0	1.000	0	2	0	0	5	4	3	3	0	0.00
Cheney, Tom-Thomas Edgar	57StLN 58MS 59StLN 60-61PitN 61-64WasA 66VR 66WasA	10-14-34	Morgan, Ga.	11-01-01	R	R	5'11	170	19	29	.396	2	115	71	13	466	382	245	345	8	3.77
Chlupsa, Bob-Robert Joseph	70-71StLN	09-16-45	New York, N.Y.		R	R	6'7	220	0	2	.000	0	15	0	0	18	29	9	11	0	9.00
Church, Len-Leonard	66ChiN	03-21-42	Chicago, Ill.	04-22-88	B	R	6'	190	0	1	.000	0	4	0	0	6	10	7	3	0	7.50
Cimino, Pete-Peter William	65-66MinA 67-68CalA	10-17-42	Philadelphia, Pa.		R	R	6'2	195	5	8	.385	2	86	1	0	161	133	65	139	0	3.97
Cisco, Galen-Galen Bernard	61-62BosA 62-65NYN 67BosA 69KCA	03-07-36	St. Marys, Ohio		R	R	6'	200	25	56	.309	5	192	78	9	658	681	281	325	3	4.57
Clark, Rickey-Rickey Charles	67-69,71-72CalA	03-21-46	Mt. Clemens, Mich.		R	R	6'2	170	19	32	.373	2	96	70	4	432	371	213	236	2	3.38
Clemons, Lance-Lance Levis	71KCA 72StLN 74BosN	07-06-47	Philadelphia, Pa.		L	L	6'2	210	2	1	.667	0	19	4	0	35	42	21	23	0	6.17
Cloninger, Tony-Tony Lee	61-65MilN 66-68AtlN 68-71CinN 72StLN	08-13-40	Lincoln Co., N.C.		R	R	6'	210	113	97	.538	6	352	247	63	1768	1643	798	1120	13	4.07
Closter, Alan-Alan Edward	66WasA 71-72NYA 73AtlN	06-15-43	Creighton, Neb.		L	L	6'2	190	2	2	.500	0	21	1	0	34	43	23	26	0	6.88
Coates, Jim-James Alton	56,59-62NYA 63WasA 63CinN 65-67CalA	08-04-32	Farnham, Va.		R	R	6'4	192	43	22	.662	18	247	46	13	683	650	286	396	4	4.01
Colbert, Vince-Vincent Norman	70-72CleA	12-20-45	Washington, D.C.		R	R	6'4	200	9	14	.391	4	95	21	3	249	255	125	127	1	4.55
Coleman, Joe-Joseph Howard	65-70WasA 71-76DetA 76ChiN 77-78OakA 78TorA 79SFN 79PitN	02-03-47	Boston, Mass.		R	R	6'3	195	142	135	.513	7	484	340	94	2571	2416	1003	1728	18	3.69
Colpaert, Dick-Richard Charles	70PitN	01-03-44	Fraser, Mich.		R	R	5'10	175	1	0	1.000	0	8	0	0	11	9	8	6	0	5.73
Colson, Loyd-Loyd Albert	70NYA	11-04-47	Wellington, Tex.		R	R	6'1	190	0	0	—	0	1	0	0	2	3	0	3	0	4.50
Colton, Larry-Lawrence Robert	68PhiN	06-08-42	Los Angeles, Cal.		L	R	6'3	200	0	0	—	0	1	0	0	2	1	2	0	0	4.50
Compton, Clint-Robert Clinton	72ChiN	11-01-50	Montgomery, Ala.		L	L	5'11	170	0	0	—	0	1	0	0	2	2	2	0	0	9.00
Connolly, Ed-Edward Joseph, Jr.	64BosA 67CleA	12-02-39	Brooklyn, N.Y.	07-01-98	L	L	6'1	190	6	12	.333	0	42	19	1	130	143	91	118	1	5.88
Connors, Billy-William Joseph	66ChiN 67-68NYN	11-02-41	Schenectady, N.Y.		R	R	6'1	185	0	2	.000	0	26	1	0	43	49	19	24	0	7.53
Cook, Ron-Ronald Wayne	70-71HouN	07-11-47	Jefferson, Tex.		L	L	6'1	190	4	8	.333	2	46	11	0	108	103	50	60	0	4.00
Coombs, Danny-Daniel Bernard	63-69HouN 70-71SDN	03-23-42	Lincoln, Me.		R	L	6'4	200	19	27	.413	2	144	52	2	393	433	162	249	1	4.08
Corkins, Mike-Michael Patrick	69-74SDN	05-25-46	Riverside, Cal.		R	R	6'1	195	19	28	.404	9	157	44	5	459	458	248	335	1	4.39
Cosman, Jim-James Henry	66-67StLN 70ChiN	02-19-43	Brockport, N.Y.		R	R	6'4	210	2	0	1.000	0	12	6	1	41	26	27	16	1	3.07
Cox, Casey-Joseph Casey	66-71WasA 72TexA 72-73NYA	07-03-41	Long Beach, Cal.		R	R	6'5	200	39	42	.481	20	380	59	5	762	772	234	297	0	3.70
Cox, Terry-Terry Lee	70CalA	03-30-49	Odessa, Tex.		R	R	6'5	235	0	0	—	0	3	0	0	2	4	0	3	0	4.50
Craig, Pete-Peter Joel	64-66WasA	07-10-40	LaSalle, Canada		R	R	6'5	220	0	3	.000	0	6	4	0	18	28	13	3	0	11.50
Craig, Roger-Roger Lee	55-57BknN 58-61LAN 62-63NYN 64StLN 65CinN 66PhiN M78-79SDN M85-92SFN	02-17-30	Durham, N.C.		R	R	6'4	200	74	98	.430	19	368	186	58	1537	1528	522	803	7	3.82
Crider, Jerry-Jerry Stephen	69MinA 70ChiA	09-02-41	Sioux Falls, S.D.		R	R	6'1	185	3	7	.417	1	53	9	0	120	132	49	56	0	4.50
Cuellar, Mike-Miguel Angel [Santana]	59CinN 64StLN 65-68HouN 69-76BalA 77CalA	05-08-37	Las Villas, Cuba		L	L	5'11	175	185	130	.587	11	453	379	172	2807	2538	822	1632	36	3.14
Cueto, Bert-Dagoberto [Concepcion]	61MinA	08-14-37	San Luis, Cuba		R	R	6'4	170	1	3	.250	0	7	5	0	21	27	10	5	0	7.29
Cullen, Jack-John Patrick	62,65-66NYA	10-06-39	Newark, N.J.		R	R	5'11	170	4	4	.500	1	19	9	2	73	72	28	34	1	3.08
Culp, Ray-Raymond Leonard	63-66PhiN 67ChiN 68-73BosA	08-06-41	Elgin, Tex.		R	R	6'	200	122	101	.547	1	322	268	80	1897	1677	752	1411	22	3.58
Culver, George-George Raymond	66-67CleA 68-69CinN 70StLN 70-72HouN 73LAN 73-74PhiN	07-08-43	Salinas, Cal.		R	R	6'2	195	48	49	.495	23	335	57	7	789	793	352	451	2	3.62
Cumberland, John-John Sheldon	68-70NYA 70-72SFN 72StLN 74CalA	05-10-47	Westbrook, Me.		R	L	6'	195	15	16	.484	2	110	36	6	335	312	103	137	2	3.81
Curtis, Jack-Jack Patrick	61-62ChiN 62MilN 63CleA	01-11-37	Rhodhiss, N.C.		L	L	5'10	175	14	19	.424	2	69	35	6	279	328	89	108	0	4.84
Dahl, Jay-Jay Steven	63HouN	12-06-45	San Bernardino, Cal.	06-20-65	B	L	6'2	180	0	1	.000	0	1	1	0	3	7	0	0	0	15.00
Dailey, Bill-William Garland	61-62CleA 63-64MinN	05-13-35	Arlington, Va.		R	R	6'3	180	10	7	.588	22	119	0	0	186	162	59	109	0	2.76
Dal Canton, Bruce-John Bruce	67-70PitN 71-75KCA 75-76AtlN 77ChiA	06-15-42	California, Pa.		R	R	6'2	205	51	49	.510	19	316	83	15	930	894	391	485	2	3.68
Daniels, Bennie-Bennie	57-60PitN 61-65WasA	06-17-32	Tuscaloosa, Ala.		R	R	6'1	205	45	76	.372	5	230	139	26	997	1004	383	471	5	4.44
Darwin, Bobby-Arthur Bobby Lee (See B73-_)	62LAA 69LAN	02-16-43	Los Angeles, Cal.		R	R	6'2	200	0	1	.000	0	4	1	0	7	12	9	6	0	10.29
Daviault, Ray-Raymond Joseph	62NYN	05-27-34	Montreal, Canada		R	R	6'1	170	1	5	.167	0	36	3	0	81	92	48	51	0	6.22
Davidson, Ted-Thomas Eugene	65-68CinN 68AtlN	10-04-39	Las Vegas, Nev.		L	R	6'2	192	11	7	.611	5	114	1	0	195	189	54	124	0	3.69
Davison, Mike-Michael Lynn	69-70SFN	08-04-45	Galesburg, Ill.		L	L	6'1	190	3	5	.375	1	32	0	0	38	48	22	23	0	6.39
DeBusschere, Dave-David Albert (62-74 played in N.B.A.)	62-63ChiA 64MS	10-16-40	Detroit, Mich.	05-14-03	R	R	6'6	225	3	4	.429	0	36	10	1	102	85	57	61	1	2.91
Degerick, Mike-Michael Arthur	61-62ChiA	04-01-43	New York, N.Y.		R	R	6'2	178	0	0	—	0	3	0	0	3	2	1	0	0	3.00
Denehy, Bill-William Francis	67NYN 68WasA 71DetA	03-31-46	Middletown, Conn.		B	R	6'3	200	1	10	.091	1	49	9	0	105	102	61	63	0	4.54
Bats Left 71																					
Dennis, Don-Donald Ray	65-66StLN	03-02-42	Uniontown, Kans.		R	R	6'2	190	6	5	.545	7	79	1	0	115	120	33	54	0	3.68
Dickson, Jim-James Edward	63HouN 64CinN 65-66KCA	04-20-38	Portland, Ore.		R	R	6'1	185	5	3	.625	5	109	1	0	143	135	77	86	0	4.34
Dierker, Larry-Lawrence Edward	64-76HouN 77StLN M97-01HouN	09-22-46	Hollywood, Cal.		R	R	6'4	215	139	123	.531	1	356	329	106	2334	2130	711	1493	25	3.30
DiLauro, Jack-Jack Edward	69NYN 70HouN	05-03-43	Akron, Ohio		B	L	6'2	185	2	7	.222	4	65	4	0	98	84	35	50	0	3.03
Dillman, Bill-William Howard	67BalA 70MonN	05-25-45	Trenton, N.J.		R	R	6'2	180	7	12	.368	3	50	15	2	155	143	51	86	1	4.53
Dillon, Steve-Stephen Edward	63-64NYN	03-20-43	Bronx, N.Y.		L	L	5'10	160	0	0	—	0	3	0	0	5	7	2	3	0	9.00
Distaso, Alec-Alec John	69ChiN	12-23-48	Los Angeles, Cal.		R	R	6'2	200	0	0	—	0	2	0	0	5	6	1	1	0	3.60
Dobson, Chuck-Charles Thomas	66-67KCA 68-71OakA 72EJ 73OakA 74-75CalA	01-10-44	Kansas City, Mo.		R	R	6'4	200	74	69	.517	0	202	190	49	1258	1174	476	758	11	3.78
Donohue, Jim-James Thomas	61DetA 61-62LAA 62MinN	10-31-38	St. Louis, Mo.		R	R	6'4	190	6	8	.429	7	70	9	0	156	152	82	116	0	4.27
Dotter, Gary-Gary Richard	61,63-64MinA	08-07-42	St. Louis, Mo.		L	R	6'1	180	0	0	—	0	7	0	0	12	9	7	10	0	5.25
Dowling, Dave-David Barclay	64StLN 66ChiN	08-23-42	Baton Rouge, La.		R	L	6'2	180	1	0	1.000	0	2	1	1	10	12	0	3	0	1.80
Downing, Al-Alphonso Erwin	61-69NYA 70OakA 70MilA 71-77LAN	06-28-41	Trenton, N.J.		R	L	5'11	180	123	107	.535	3	405	317	73	2269	1946	933	1639	24	3.22
Downs, Dave-David Ralph	72PhiN 73SA	06-21-52	Logan, Utah		R	R	6'6	220	1	1	.500	0	4	4	1	23	25	3	5	1	2.74
Doyle, Paul-Paul Sinnott	69AtlN 70CalA 70SDN 72CalA	10-02-39	Philadelphia, Pa.		L	L	5'11	172	5	3	.625	11	87	0	0	90	85	46	65	0	3.80
Drabowsky, Moe-Myron Walter	56-60ChiN 58-60MilN 62CinN 62-65KCA 66-68BalA 69-70KCA 70BalA 71-72StLN 72ChiA	07-21-35	Ozanna, Poland	06-10-06	R	R	6'3	190	88	105	.456	55	589	154	33	1640	1441	702	1162	6	3.71
Drysdale, Don-Donald Scott (Big D)	56-57BknN 58-69LAN	07-23-36	Van Nuys, Cal.	07-03-93	R	R	6'5	215	209	166	.557	6	518	465	167	3422	3084	855	2486	49	2.95
Duckworth, Jim-James Raymond	63-66WasA 66KCA	05-24-39	National City, Cal.		R	R	6'4	190	4	15	.211	4	97	29	2	267	256	148	220	0	5.26
Duffalo, Jim-James Francis	61-65SFN 65CinN	11-25-35	Helvetia, Pa.		R	R	6'1	180	15	8	.652	6	141	14	2	298	248	155	210	0	3.38
Duffie, John-John Brown	67LAN	10-04-45	Greenwood, S.C.		R	R	6'2	210	0	2	.000	0	2	2	0	10	11	4	6	0	2.70
Dukes, Jan-Noble Jan	69-70WasA 72TexA	08-16-45	Cheyenne, Wyo.		L	L	5'11	180	0	2	.000	2	16	0	0	20	15	10	7	0	2.70
Dukes, Tom-Thomas Earl	67-68HouN 69-70SDN 71BalA 72CalA	08-31-42	Knoxville, Tenn.		R	R	6'2	200	5	16	.238	21	161	0	0	217	226	82	169	0	4.35
Duliba, Bob-Robert John	59-60,62StLN 63-64LAA 65BosA 67KCA	01-09-35	Glen Lyon, Pa.		R	R	5'10	180	17	12	.586	14	176	0	0	258	257	96	129	0	3.45
Dunegan, Jimmy-James William	70ChiN	08-06-47	Burlington, Iowa		R	R	6'1	205	0	0	—	0	7	0	0	13	13	12	3	0	4.85
Duren, Ryne-Rinold George	54BalA 57KCA 58-61NYA 61-62LAA 63-64PhiN 64CinN 65PhiN 65WasA	02-22-29	Cazenovia, Wis.		R	R	6'2	194	27	44	.380	57	311	32	2	590	443	392	630	3	3.83
Durham, Don-Donald Gary	72StLN 73TexA	03-21-49	Yosemite, Ky.		R	R	6'	170	2	11	.154	2	25	12	1	88	91	45	58	0	5.83
Dustel, Bob-Robert Andrew	63DetA	09-28-35	Sayreville, N.J.		R	R	6'	172	0	1	.000	0	6	1	0	5	4	4	7	0	9.00
Earley, Arnie-Arnold Carl	60-65BosA 66ChiN 67HouN	09-04-33	Lincoln Park, Mich.	09-29-99	L	L	6'1	195	12	20	.375	14	223	10	1	381	400	184	310	0	4.49
Eddy, Don-Donald Eugene	70-71ChiA	05-02-46	Mason City, Iowa		R	L	5'11	180	0	0	—	3	29	0	0	35	29	25	23	0	2.31
Edgarton, Bill-William Albert	66-67KCA 69SeaA	08-16-41	South Bend, Ind.		L	L	6'2	185	1	2	.333	0	20	3	0	31	30	11	6	0	4.95
Edmondson, Paul-Paul Michael	69ChiA	02-12-43	Kansas City, Kans.	02-13-70	R	R	6'5	195	1	6	.143	0	14	13	1	88	72	39	46	0	3.68
Egan, Dick-Richard Wallis	63-64DetA 66CalA 67LAN	03-24-37	Berkeley, Cal.		L	L	6'4	193	1	2	.333	2	74	0	0	101	109	41	68	0	5.17
Eilers, Dave-David Louis	64-65MilN 65-66NYN 67HouN	12-03-36	Oldenberg, Tex.		R	R	5'11	188	8	6	.571	3	81	0	0	124	146	29	52	0	4.43
Ellis, Jim-James Russell	67ChiN 69StLN	03-25-45	Tulare, Cal.		R	L	6'2	185	1	1	.500	0	10	2	0	22	27	12	8	0	2.86
Ellis, Sammy-Samuel Joseph	62,64-66CinN 68CalA 69ChiA	02-11-41	Youngstown, Ohio		R	R	6'1	182	63	58	.521	18	229	140	35	1004	967	378	677	3	4.15
Ellsworth, Dick-Richard Clark	58,60-66ChiN 67PhiN 68-69BosA 69-70CleA 70-71MilA	03-22-40	Lusk, Wyo.		L	L	6'3	195	115	137	.456	5	407	310	87	2156	2274	595	1140	9	3.72

USE NAMES - GIVEN NAMES (NICKNAMES)	TEAM BY YEAR	BIRTH DATE	BIRTHPLACE	DEATH DATE	B	T	HGT	WGT	W	L	Pct.	SV	G	GS	CG	IP	H	BB	SO	ShO	ERA
Estelle, Dick-Richard Henry	64-65SFN	01-18-42	Lakewood, N.J.		B	L	6'2	170	1	2	.333	0	12	7	0	53	51	31	29	0	3.23
Estrada, Chuck-Charles Leonard	60-64BalA 66ChiN 67NYN	02-15-38	San Luis Obispo, Cal.		R	R	6'1	185	50	44	.532	2	146	105	24	764	652	416	535	2	4.08
Everitt, Leon-Edward Leon (Lash)	69SDN	01-12-47	Marshall, Tex.		B	R	6'2	190	0	1	.000	0	5	0	0	16	18	12	11	0	7.88
Face, Roy-Elroy Leon	53,55-68PitN 68DetA 69MonN	02-20-28	Stephentown, N.Y.		B	R	5'8	155	104	95	.523	193	848	27	6	1375	1347	362	877	0	3.48
Bats Right 53-59																					
Fanok, Harry-Harry Michael (The Flame Thrower)		05-11-40	Whippany, N.J.		B	R	6'	185	2	1	.667	1	16	0	0	34	29	24	35	0	5.29
Farrell, Dick-Richard Joseph (Turk)	56-61PhiN 61LAN 62-67HouN 67-69PhiN	04-08-34	Boston, Mass.	06-11-77	R	R	6'4	215	106	111	.488	83	590	134	41	1704	1628	468	1177	5	3.45
Fast, Darcy-Darcy Rae	68ChiN 69MS	03-10-47	Dallas, Ore.		L	L	6'3	195	0	0	.000	0	6	1	0	10	8	8	10	0	5.40
Faul, Bill-William Alvan	62-64DetA 65-66ChiN 70SFN	04-21-40	Cincinnati, Ohio	02-21-02	R	R	5'10	184	12	16	.429	2	71	33	8	262	247	95	164	3	4.71
Fischer, Hank-Henry William (Bulldog)	62-65MilN 66AtlN 66CinN 66-67BosA	01-11-40	Yonkers, N.Y.		R	R	6'	190	30	39	.435	7	168	77	14	546	587	174	369	5	4.24
Fisher, Eddie-Eddie Gene	59-61SFN 62-66ChiA 66-67BalA 68CleA 69-72HouN 72-73ChiA 73StLN	07-16-36	Shreveport, La.		R	R	6'2	200	85	70	.548	81	690	63	7	1541	1398	438	812	2	3.40
Fisher, Fritz-Frederick Brown	64DetA	11-28-41	Adrian, Mich.		L	L	6'1	180	0	0	—	0	1	0	0	1	2	2	1	0	108.00
Fisher, Jack-John Howard (Fat Jack)	59-62BalA 63SFN 64-67NYN 68ChiA 69CinN	03-04-39	Frostburg, Md.		R	R	6'2	225	86	139	.382	9	400	265	62	1977	2061	605	1017	9	4.06
Fisher, Tom-Thomas Gene	67BalA	04-04-43	Cleveland, Ohio		R	R	6'	180	0	0	—	0	2	0	0	3	2	2	1	0	0.00
Flavin, John-John Thomas	64ChiN	05-07-42	Albany, Cal.		L	L	6'2	208	0	1	.000	0	5	1	0	5	11	3	5	0	12.60
Fletcher, Tom-Thomas Wayne	62DetA	06-28-42	Elmira, N.Y.		B	L	6'	170	0	0	—	0	1	0	0	2	2	2	1	0	0.00
Foor, Jim-James Emerson	71-72DetA 73PitN	01-13-49	St. Louis, Mo.		L	L	6'2	185	1	0	1.000	0	13	6	0	10	11	5	5	0	12.00
Fosnow, Jerry-Gerald Eugene	64-65MinA	09-21-40	Deshler, Ohio		R	L	6'4	195	3	4	.429	2	36	0	0	58	46	33	44	0	5.59
Foss, Larry-Larry Curtis	61PitN 62NYN	04-18-36	Castleton, Kans.		R	R	6'2	187	1	2	.333	0	8	4	0	27	32	18	12	0	5.33
Foster, Alan-Alan Benton	67-70LAN 71CleA 72CalA 73-74StLN 75-76SDN	12-08-46	Pasadena, Cal.		R	R	6'	180	48	63	.432	0	217	148	26	1028	988	383	501	6	3.73
Foster, Larry-Larry Lynn	63DetA	12-24-37	Lansing, Mich.		R	L	6'	185	0	0	—	0	1	0	0	2	4	1	1	0	13.50
Fox, Terry-Terrence Edward	60MilN 61-66DetA 66PhiN	07-31-35	Chicago, Ill.		R	R	6'	175	29	19	.604	59	248	0	0	396	379	124	185	0	3.00
Francis, Earl-Earl Coleman	60-64PitN 65StLN	07-14-36	Slab Fork, W.Va.	07-03-02	R	R	6'2	210	16	23	.410	0	103	52	5	405	398	181	263	1	3.78
Franklin, Jay-John William	71SDN 72JJ	03-16-53	Arlington, Va.		R	R	6'3	200	0	1	.000	0	3	1	0	6	5	4	4	0	6.00
Freeman, Jimmy-Jimmy Lee	72-73AtlN	06-29-51	Carlsbad, N.M.		L	L	6'4	180	2	4	.333	1	19	11	1	73	90	47	38	0	6.90
Frisella, Danny-Daniel Vincent	67-72NYN 73-74AtlN 75SDN 76StLN 76MilA	03-04-46	San Francisco, Cal.	01-01-77	R	R	6'	190	34	40	.459	57	351	17	0	611	529	286	471	3	3.32
Fuentes, Mickey-Miguel [Pinet]	69SeaA	05-10-49	Loiza Aldea, P.R.	01-29-70	R	R	6'	160	1	3	.250	0	8	4	1	26	29	16	14	0	5.19
Funk, Frank-Franklin Ray	60-62CleA 63MilN	08-30-35	Washington, D.C.		R	R	6'	180	20	17	.541	18	137	0	0	249	210	85	150	0	3.00
Gables, John-John Richard (Gabe)	59-60NYA 61WasA	10-02-30	Kansas City, Mo.		B	R	6'2	170	7	12	.368	2	53	14	0	164	171	79	63	0	4.39
Gallagher, Doug-Douglas Eugene	62DetA	02-21-40	Fremont, Ohio		R	L	6'3	205	0	4	.000	0	9	2	0	25	31	15	14	0	4.68
Gardner, Rob-Richard Frank	65-66NYN 67ChiN 68CleA 70NYA 71OakA 71-72NYA 73OakA 73MilA	12-19-44	Binghamton, N.Y.		R	L	6'1	185	14	18	.438	2	109	42	4	332	345	133	193	0	4.34
Garibaldi, Bob-Robert Roy	62-63,66,69SFN	03-03-42	Stockton, Cal.		L	R	6'4	210	0	2	.000	2	15	1	0	26	28	11	14	0	3.12
Garrett, Greg-Gregory	70CalA 71CinN	03-12-47	Atascadero, Cal.	06-07-03	B	L	6'	210	5	7	.417	0	34	8	0	84	55	54	55	0	2.46
Gatewood, Aubrey-Aubrey Lee	63-64LAA 65CalA 70AtlN	11-17-38	Little Rock, Ark.		R	R	6'1	170	8	9	.471	2	68	13	1	178	166	67	75	0	2.78
Gebhard, Bob-Robert Henry	71-72MinA 74MonN	01-03-43	Lamberton, Minn.		R	R	6'2	210	1	3	.250	1	31	0	0	41	58	24	26	0	5.93
Geishert, Vern-Vernon William	69CalA	01-10-46	Madison, Wis.		R	R	6'2	215	1	1	.500	0	11	3	0	31	32	7	18	0	4.65
Gelnar, John-John Richard	64,67PitN 69SeaA 70-71MilA	06-25-43	Granite, Okla.		R	R	6'2	185	7	14	.333	7	111	11	0	230	245	62	126	0	4.19
Gentry, Gary-Gary Edward	69-72NYN 73-75AtlN	10-06-46	Phoenix, Ariz.		R	R	6'1	180	46	49	.484	2	157	138	25	903	770	369	615	8	3.56
Gerard, Dave-David Frederick	62ChiN	08-06-36	New York, N.Y.	10-10-01	R	R	6'2	205	2	3	.400	3	39	0	0	59	67	28	30	0	4.88
Gerberman, George-George Alois	62ChiN	03-08-42	El Campo, Tex.		R	R	6'6	180	0	1	.000	1	1	0	0	3	5	1	1	0	1.80
Gibbon, Joe-Joseph Charles	60-65PitN 66-69SFN 69-70PitN 71-72CinN 72HouN	04-10-35	Hickory, Miss.		R	L	6'4	210	61	65	.484	32	419	127	20	1119	1053	414	743	4	3.52
Bats Both 67-68																					
Gibson, Bob-Pack Robert (Gibby)	59-75StLN	11-19-35	Omaha, Neb.		R	R	6'1	190	251	174	.591	6	528	482	255	3885	3279	1336	3117	56	2.91
Gilbreth, Bill-William Freeman	71-72DetA 74CalA	09-03-47	Abilene, Tex.		L	L	6'	190	2	1	.667	0	14	5	2	36	40	26	16	0	6.75
Gilliford, Paul-Paul Gant (Gorilla)	67BalA	01-12-45	Bryn Mawr, Pa.		R	L	5'11	210	0	0	—	0	2	0	0	3	6	1	2	0	12.00
Gilson, Hal-Harold (Lefty)	68StLN 68HouN	02-09-42	Los Angeles, Cal.		R	L	6'5	195	0	2	.000	2	15	0	0	25	34	12	20	0	5.04
Giusti, Dave-David John	62,64-68HouN 69StLN 70-76PitN 77OakA 77ChiN	11-27-39	Seneca Falls, N.Y.		R	R	5'11	195	100	93	.518	145	668	133	16	1718	1654	570	1103	3	3.60
Gladding, Fred-Fred Earl	61-67DetA 68-73HouN	06-28-36	Flat Rock, Mich.		L	R	6'1	225	48	34	.588	109	450	1	0	600	566	223	394	0	3.13
Gogolewski, Bill-William Joseph (Go-Go)	70-71WasA 72-73TexA 74CleA 75ChiA	10-26-47	Oshkosh, Wis.		L	R	6'4	205	15	24	.385	10	144	44	6	502	496	200	301	2	4.02
Golden, Jim-James Edward	60-61LAN 62-63HouN	03-20-36	Eldon, Mo.		L	R	6'	175	9	13	.409	0	69	20	5	208	233	76	115	2	4.54
Gowell, Larry-Lawrence Clyde	72NYA	05-02-47	Lewiston, Me.		R	R	6'2	190	0	1	.000	0	2	1	0	7	3	2	7	0	1.29
Graham, Bill-William Albert	66DetA 67NYN	01-21-37	Flemingsburg, Ky.		R	R	6'3	217	1	2	.333	0	8	3	0	29	22	11	16	0	2.48
Gramley, Tommy-Bert Thomas	68CleA	04-19-45	Dallas, Tex.		R	R	6'	175	0	1	.000	0	3	0	0	3	2	1	1	0	3.00
Granger, Wayne-Wayne Allen	68StLN 69-71CinN 72MinA 73StLN 73NYA 74ChiA 75HouN 76MonN	03-15-44	Springfield, Mass.		R	R	6'2	165	35	35	.500	108	451	0	0	640	632	201	303	0	3.14
Grant, Mudcat-James Timothy	58-64CleA 64-67MinA 68LAN 69MonN 69StLN 70OakA 70-71PitN 71OakA	08-13-35	Lacoochee, Fla.		R	R	6'1	186	145	119	.549	53	571	293	89	2441	2292	849	1267	18	3.63
Gray, Dave-David Alexander	64BosA	01-07-43	Ogden, Utah		R	R	6'1	190	0	0	—	0	13	0	0	13	18	20	17	0	9.00
Grba, Eli-Eli	59-60NYA 61-63LAA	08-09-34	Chicago, Ill.		R	R	6'2	210	28	33	.459	4	135	75	10	536	513	284	255	0	4.48
Green, Dallas-George Dallas	60-64PhiN 65WasA 66NYN 67,M79-81PhiN M89NYA M93-96NYN	08-04-34	Newport, Del.		L	R	6'5	210	20	22	.476	4	185	46	12	562	647	197	268	2	4.26
Gregory, Lee-Grover LeRoy	64ChiN	06-02-38	Bakersfield, Cal.		L	L	6'1	180	0	0	—	0	11	0	0	18	23	5	8	0	3.50
Grilli, Guido-Guido John	66BosA 66KCA	01-09-39	Memphis, Tenn.		L	L	6'	188	0	2	.000	1	22	0	0	22	24	20	12	0	7.20
Grzenda, Joe-Joseph Charles	61DetA 64,66KCA 67NYN 69MinA 70-71WasA 72StlN	06-08-37	Scranton, Pa.		R	L	6'2	180	14	13	.519	14	219	3	0	309	323	120	173	0	3.99
Guinn, Skip-Drannon Eugene	68AtlN 70-71HouN	10-25-44	St. Charles, Mo.		R	L	5'10	180	1	2	.333	1	35	0	0	37	38	27	40	0	5.35
Guzman(Donovan), Santiago-Santiago Donovan [Guzman]	69-72StLN	07-25-49	San Pedro de Mac., D.R.		R	R	6'	180	1	2	.333	0	12	5	1	32	30	18	29	0	4.50
Hall, Dick-Richard Wallace (Turkey Neck) (See B46-60)	55-57PitN 58VR 59PitN 60KCA 61-66BalA 67-68PhiN 69-71BalA	09-27-30	St. Louis, Mo.		R	R	6'6	205	93	75	.554	68	495	74	20	1259	1152	236	741	3	3.32
Hall, Tom-Tom Edward (The Blade)	68-71MinA 72-75CinN 75-76NYN 76-77KCA	11-23-47	Thomasville, N.C.		L	L	6'	158	52	33	.612	32	358	63	7	854	656	382	797	3	3.27
Hambright, Roger-Roger Dee	71NYA	03-26-49	Sunnyside, Wash.		R	R	5'10	180	3	1	.750	3	18	0	0	27	22	10	14	0	4.33
Hamilton, Jack-Jack Edwin (Hairbreadth Harry)	62-63PhiN 64-65DetA 66-67NYN 67-68CalA 69CleA 69ChiA	12-25-38	Burlington, Iowa		R	R	6'	205	32	40	.444	20	218	65	8	612	597	348	357	2	4.53
Hamilton, Steve-Steve Absher (58-60 played in N.B.A.)	61CleA 62-63WasA 63-70NYA 70ChiA 71SFN 72ChiN	11-30-33	Columbia, Ky.	12-02-97	L	L	6'7	200	40	31	.563	42	421	17	3	662	556	214	531	1	3.06
Hamm, Pete-Peter Whitfield	70-71MinA	09-21-47	Buffalo, N.Y.		R	R	6'5	215	2	6	.250	0	23	8	1	60	72	25	19	0	6.43
Hand, Rich-Richard Allen	70-71CleA 72-73TexA 73CalA	07-10-48	Bellevue, Wash.		R	R	6'1	195	24	39	.381	4	104	78	6	486	452	250	278	1	4.00
Handrahan, Vern-James Vernon	64,66KCA	11-27-38	Charlottetown, Canada		R	R	6'2	185	0	2	.000	0	34	2	0	61	53	40	36	0	5.31
Hands, Bill-William Alfred	65SFN 66-72ChiN 73-74MinA 74-75TexA	05-06-40	Hackensack, N.J.		R	R	6'2	195	111	110	.502	4	374	260	72	1951	1895	492	1128	17	3.35
Hannan, Jim-James John	62-70WasA 71DetA 71MilA	01-07-40	Jersey City, N.J.		R	R	6'3	205	41	48	.461	7	276	101	9	822	807	406	438	4	3.88
Hardin, Jim-James Warren	67-71BalA 71NYA 72AtlN	08-06-43	Morris Chapel, Tenn.	03-09-91	R	R	6'	190	43	32	.573	4	164	100	28	752	691	202	408	7	3.18
Hargan, Steve-Steven Lowell	65-72CleA 74-76TexA 77ToraA 77TexA 77CleA	09-08-42	Fort Wayne, Ind.		R	R	6'3	175	87	107	.448	4	354	215	56	1631	1593	614	891	17	3.92
Harrelson, Bill-William Charles	68CalA	11-17-45	Tahlequah, Okla.		B	R	6'5	215	1	6	.143	0	10	5	1	34	28	26	22	0	5.03
Harris, Buddy-Walter Francis	70-71HouN	12-05-48	Philadelphia, Pa.		R	R	6'7	250	1	1	.500	0	22	0	0	37	39	16	23	0	6.32
Harrison, Tom-Thomas James	65KCA	11-18-45	Trail, Canada		R	R	6'3	200	0	0	.000	0	1	2	1	9	6	8	1	0	9.00
Hartenstein, Chuck-Charles Oscar (Twiggy)	65-68ChiN 69-70PitN 70StLN 70BosA 77TorA	05-26-42	Seguin, Tex.		R	R	5'11	165	17	19	.472	23	187	0	0	297	317	89	135	0	4.52
Hartman, Bob-Robert Lewis	59MilN 62CleA	08-28-37	Kenosha, Wis.		R	L	5'11	185	0	0	.000	0	11	2	0	19	20	10	12	0	5.21
Hawkins, Wynn-Wynn Firth (Hawk)	60-62CleA	02-20-36	East Palestine, Ohio		R	R	6'2	190	12	13	.480	1	48	34	6	203	216	99	90	1	4.17
Haydel, Hal-John Harold	70-71MinA	07-09-44	Houma, La.		R	R	6'	190	3	0	.750	1	35	0	0	49	40	24	33	0	4.04
Haywood, Bill-William Kiernan	68WasA	04-21-37	Colon, Panama		R	R	6'3	205	0	0	—	0	14	0	0	23	27	12	10	0	4.70
Hedlund, Mike-Michael David (Red)	65,68CleA 69-72KCA	08-11-46	Dallas, Tex.		R	R	6'2	195	25	24	.510	2	113	62	9	466	440	167	211	3	3.55
Bats Right 65,72																					
Heffner, Bob-Robert Frederic (Butch)	63-65BosA 66CleA 68CalA	09-13-38	Allentown, Pa.		R	R	6'4	200	11	21	.344	8	114	31	5	354	360	107	241	2	4.50
Heiser, Roy-Leroy Barton	61WasA	06-22-42	Baltimore, Md.		R	R	6'	190	0	0	—	0	6	0	0	6	6	9	1	0	6.00
Heman, Russ-Russell Frederick	61CleA 61LAA	04-30-39	Olive, Cal.		R	R	6'	180	0	0	—	0	20	0	0	12	10	10	6	0	2.70
Hendley, Bob-Charles Robert	61-63MilN 64-65SFN 65-67ChiN 67NYN	04-30-39	Macon, Ga.		R	L	6'2	195	48	52	.480	12	216	126	25	879	864	329	522	6	3.97
Hennigan, Phil-Phillip Winston	69-72CleA 73NYN	04-10-46	Jasper, Tex.		R	R	6'	185	17	14	.548	26	176	2	0	280	267	133	188	0	4.27
Henry, Bill-William Francis	66NYA	02-15-42	Long Beach, Cal.		R	R	6'	180	0	0	—	0	2	0	0	2	1	1	0	0	9.00
Henry, Bill-William Rodman	52-55BosA 58-59ChiN 60-65CinN 65-68SFN 68PitN 68HouN	10-15-27	Alice, Tex.		L	L	6'2	187	46	50	.479	90	527	44	12	914	842	296	621	2	3.26
Hepler, Bill-William Lewis	66NYN	09-25-45	Covington, Va.		L	L	6'	160	3	3	.500	0	37	6	0	69	71	51	25	0	3.52
Herbel, Ron-Ronald Samuel	63-69SFN 70SDN 70NYN 71NYA 71-76PitN	01-16-38	Denver, Colo.	01-20-00	R	R	6'1	195	42	37	.532	16	331	79	11	895	945	285	447	3	3.82
Hernandez, Ramon-Ramon [Gonzalez]	67AtlN 68ChiN 71-76PitN 76-77ChiN 77BosA	08-31-40	Carolina, P.R.		B	L	5'11	180	23	15	.605	46	337	0	0	432	399	135	255	0	3.02

USE NAMES - GIVEN NAMES (NICKNAMES)	TEAM BY YEAR	BIRTH DATE	BIRTHPLACE	DEATH DATE	B	T	HGT	WGT	W	L	Pct.	SV	G	GS	CG	IP	H	BB	SO	ShO	ERA
Hickman, Jess-Jesse Owens	65-66KCA	02-18-40	Lacompte, La.		R	R	6'2	186	0	1	.000	0	13	0	0	16	9	9	16	0	5.63
Higgins, Denny-Dennis Dean	66-67ChiA 68-69WasA 70CleA 71-72StLN	08-04-39	Jefferson City, Mo.		R	R	6'3	190	22	23	.489	46	241	2	0	410	346	223	339	0	3.42
Hilgendorf, Tom-Thomas Eugene	69-70StLN 72-74CleA 75PhiN	03-10-42	Clinton, Iowa		B	L	6'1	187	19	14	.576	14	184	6	2	314	302	127	173	0	3.04
Hill, Garry-Garry Alton	69AtlN	11-03-46	Rutherfordton, N.C.		R	R	6'2	195	0	1	.000	0	1	1	0	2	6	1	2	0	18.00
Hinsley, Jery-Jerry Dean	64,67NYN	04-09-45	Hugo, Okla.		R	R	5'11	165	0	2	.000	0	11	2	0	20	27	11	14	0	7.20
Hippauf, Herb-Herbert August	66AtlN	05-09-39	New York, N.Y.		R	L	6'	180	0	1	.000	0	3	0	0	3	6	1	1	0	12.00
Hobaugh, Ed-Edward Russell	61-63WasA	06-27-34	Kittanning, Pa.		R	R	6'	175	9	10	.474	1	61	21	3	211	228	95	115	0	4.35
Hoerner, Joe-Joseph Walter	63-64HouN 66-69StLN 70-72PhiN 72-73AtlN 73-74KCA 75PhiN 76TexA 77CinN	11-12-36	Dubuque, Iowa	10-04-96	R	L	6'1	200	39	34	.534	99	493	0	0	563	519	181	412	0	2.99
Holtgrave, Vern-Lavern George (Woody)	65DetA	10-18-42	Aviston, Ill.		R	R	6'1	183	0	0	—	0	1	0	0	3	4	2	2	0	6.00
Holtzman, Ken-Kenneth Dale	65-71ChiN 72-75OakA 76BalA 76-78NYA 78-79ChiN	11-03-45	St. Louis, Mo.		R	L	6'2	190	174	150	.537	3	451	410	127	2867	2787	910	1601	31	3.49
Hook, Jay-James Wesley	57-61CinN 62-64NYN	11-18-36	Waukegan, Ill.		L	R	6'2	185	29	62	.319	1	160	112	30	754	808	275	394	2	5.22
Horlen, Joe-Joel Edward	61-71ChiA 72OakA	08-14-37	San Antonio, Tex.		R	R	6'	170	116	117	.498	4	361	290	59	2003	1829	554	1065	18	3.11
House, Pat-Patrick Lory	67-68HouN	09-01-40	Boise, Idaho		L	L	6'3	185	2	1	.667	1	24	0	0	20	24	6	8	0	7.20
Howard, Bruce-Bruce Ernest	63-67ChiA 68BalA 68WasA	03-23-43	Salisbury, Md.		B	R	6'2	180	26	31	.456	1	120	75	7	529	449	239	349	4	3.18
Hudson, Jesse-Jesse James	69NYN	07-22-48	Mansfield, La.		R	L	6'2	170	0	0	—	0	1	0	0	2	2	3	2	0	4.50
Hughes, Dick-Richard Henry	66-68StLN 69SA	02-13-38	Stephens, Ark.		R	R	6'3	195	20	9	.690	8	68	34	13	307	221	76	230	4	2.79
Humphreys, Bob-Robert William	62DetA 63-64StLN 65CinN 66-70WasA 70MilA	06-18-35	Covington, Va.		R	R	5'10	170	27	21	.563	20	319	4	0	568	482	219	364	0	3.34
Hunt, Ken-Kenneth Raymond	61CinN	12-14-38	Ogden, Utah		R	R	6'	200	9	10	.474	0	29	22	4	136	130	66	75	0	3.97
Hunter, Catfish-James Augustus	65-67KCA 68-74OakA 75-79NYA	04-08-46	Hertford, N.C.	09-09-99	R	R	6'	200	224	166	.574	1	500	476	181	3449	2958	954	2012	42	3.26
Hunter, Willard-Willard Mitchell (Hawk)	62LAN 62,64NYN	03-18-34	Newark, N.J.		R	L	6'2	180	4	9	.308	5	69	6	1	114	127	47	63	0	5.68
Jackson, Al-Alvin Neill	59,61PitN 62-65NYN 66-67StLN 68-69NYN 69CinN	12-25-35	Waco, Tex.		L	L	5'10	170	67	99	.404	10	302	184	54	1389	1449	407	738	14	3.98
Jackson, Larry-Lawrence Curtis	55-62StLN 63-66ChiN 66-68PhiN	06-02-31	Nampa, Idaho	08-28-90	R	R	6'1	190	194	183	.515	20	558	429	149	3262	3206	824	1709	37	3.40
Jackson, Mike-Michael Warren	70PhiN 71StLN 72-73KCA 73CleA	03-27-46	Paterson, N.J.		L	L	6'3	197	2	3	.400	0	23	3	0	50	57	39	33	0	5.76
Jacquez, Pat-Patrick Thomas (Wahoo)	71ChiA	04-23-47	Stockton, Cal.		R	R	6'	200	0	0	—	0	2	0	0	2	4	2	1	0	4.50
Jaeckel, Paul-Paul Henry (Jake)	64ChiN	04-01-42	East Los Angeles, Cal.		R	R	5'10	170	1	0	1.000	1	4	0	0	8	4	3	2	0	0.00
James, Jeff-Jeffrey Lynn (Jesse)	68-69PhiN	09-29-41	Indianapolis, Ind.	05-07-06	R	R	6'3	195	6	6	.500	1	35	18	2	148	148	60	104	1	4.50
James, Johnny-John Phillip	58,60-61NYA 61LAA	07-23-33	Bonners Ferry, Idaho		L	R	5'10	160	5	3	.625	2	66	3	0	119	107	84	73	0	4.76
James, Rick-Richard Lee	67CinN	10-11-47	Sheffield, Ala.		R	R	6'2	205	0	1	.000	0	3	1	0	5	9	2	2	0	12.60
Janeski, Jerry-Gerald Joseph	70ChiA 71WasA 72TexA	04-18-46	Pasadena, Cal.		R	R	6'4	205	11	23	.324	1	62	46	4	281	330	104	105	1	4.71
Jarvis, Pat-Robert Patrick	66-72AtlN 73MonN	03-18-41	Carlyle, Ill.		R	R	5'10	180	85	73	.538	3	249	169	42	1283	1180	380	755	8	3.58
Jarvis, Ray-Raymond Arnold	69-70BosA 71AJ	05-10-46	Providence, R.I.		R	R	6'2	198	5	7	.417	1	44	12	2	116	122	57	44	0	4.66
Jaster, Larry-Larry Edward	65-68StLN 69MonN 70,72AtlN	01-13-44	Midland, Mich.		L	L	6'3	190	35	33	.515	3	138	80	15	597	579	178	313	7	3.65
Jay, Joey-Joseph Richard	53-55,57-60MilN 61-66CinN 66AtlN	08-15-35	Middletown, Conn.		B	R	6'4	228	99	91	.521	7	310	203	63	1546	1460	607	999	16	3.77
Bats Right 53																					
Jenkins, Jack-Warren Washington	62-63WasA 69LAN	12-22-42	Covington, Va.	06-18-02	R	R	6'2	205	0	3	.000	0	8	3	1	26	28	19	16	0	4.87
Johnson, Bob-Robert Dale	69NYN 70KCA 71-73PitN 74CleA 77AtlN	03-04-43	Aurora, Ill.		R	R	6'4	220	28	34	.452	12	183	76	18	693	644	269	507	2	3.48
Johnson, Jim-James Brian	70SFN	11-03-45	Muskegon, Mich.	12-06-87	L	L	6'	180	1	0	1.000	0	3	0	0	7	8	5	2	0	7.71
Johnson, Ken-Kennth Travis	58-61KCA 61CinN 62-65HouN 65MilN 66-69AtlN 69NYA 69ChiA 70MonN	06-16-33	West Palm Beach, Fla.		R	R	6'4	210	91	106	.462	9	334	231	50	1736	1670	413	1042	7	3.46
Jones, Gary-Gary Howell	70-71NYA	06-12-45	Huntington Park, Cal.		L	L	6'	190	0	0	—	0	14	0	0	16	22	8	12	0	7.87
Jones, Sherman-Sherman Jarvis (Roadblock)	60SFN 61CinN 62NYN	02-10-35	Winton, N.C.		L	R	6'4	205	2	6	.250	3	48	5	0	110	119	46	53	0	4.75
Jones, Steve-Steven Howell	67ChiA 68WasA 69KCA	04-22-41	Huntington Park, Cal.		L	L	5'10	175	5	7	.417	0	38	7	0	80	74	43	59	0	4.50
Joyce, Dick-Richard Edward		11-18-43	Portland, Me.		L	L	6'5	225	0	1	.000	0	5	3	0	13	12	4	7	0	2.77
Joyce, Mike-Michael Lewis	62-63ChiA	02-12-41	Detroit, Mich.		R	R	6'2	193	2	1	.667	2	31	1	0	54	53	22	16	0	4.33
Jurewicz, Mike-Michael Allen	65NYA	09-20-45	Buffalo, N.Y.		B	L	6'3	205	0	0	—	0	2	0	0	2	5	1	2	0	9.00
Kaat, Jim-James Lee	59-60WasA 61-73MinA 73-75ChiA 76-79PhiN 79-80NYA 80-83StLN	11-07-38	Zeeland, Mich.		L	L	6'4	215	283	237	.544	18	898	625	180	4530	4620	1083	2461	31	3.45
Kaiser, Bob-Robert Thomas (Chisel)	71CleA	04-29-50	Cincinnati, Ohio		B	L	5'10	175	0	0	—	0	5	0	0	6	8	3	4	0	4.50
Kealey, Steve-Steven William	68-70CalA 71ChiA	05-13-47	Torrance, Cal.		R	R	6'2	195	8	5	.615	11	139	4	1	214	219	69	126	1	4.29
Keegan, Ed-Edward Charles	59PhiN 61KCA 62PhiN	07-08-39	Camden, N.J.		R	R	6'3	165	0	3	.000	1	13	3	0	23	31	23	11	0	9.00
Kekich, Mike-Michael Dennis	65, 68LAN 69-73NYA 73CleA 74JL 75TexA 77SeaA	04-02-45	San Diego, Cal.		R	L	6'2	200	39	51	.433	6	235	112	8	860	875	442	497	1	4.59
Keller, Ron-Ronald Lee	66,68MinA	06-03-43	Indianapolis, Ind.		R	R	6'2	200	0	1	.000	0	9	1	0	21	25	5	12	0	3.43
Kelley, Dick-Richard Anthony	64-65ChiN 66-68AtlN 69SDN 70SJ,71SDN	01-08-40	Brighton, Mass.	12-11-91	R	L	6'	185	18	30	.375	5	188	61	5	520	453	215	369	5	3.39
Kelley, Tom-Thomas Henry	64-67CleA 68SJ 71-73AtlN	01-05-44	Manchester, Conn.		R	R	6'1	190	20	22	.476	0	104	45	9	408	400	207	234	1	3.75
Kelso, Bill-William Eugene	64LAA 66-67CalA 68CinN	02-19-40	Kansas City, Mo.		R	R	6'4	215	12	5	.706	12	119	2	1	201	171	93	162	1	3.13
Kester, Rick-Richard Lee	68-70AtlN	07-07-46	Iola, Kans.		R	R	6'1	190	0	0	—	0	21	0	0	40	49	22	31	0	6.08
Kilkenny, Mike-Michael David	69-72DetA 72OakA 72SDN 72-73CleA	04-11-45	Bradford, Canada		R	L	6'3	175	23	18	.561	4	139	54	12	409	387	224	301	4	4.44
Kirby, Clay-Clayton Laws	69-73SDN 74-75CinN 76MonN	06-25-48	Washington, D.C.	10-11-91	R	R	6'3	185	75	104	.419	4	261	239	42	1548	1430	713	1061	8	3.84
Bats Both part of 76																					
Kirk, Bill-William Partlemore	61KCA	07-19-35	Coatesville, Pa.		L	L	6'	165	0	0	—	0	1	1	0	3	6	1	3	0	12.00
Klagas, Fred-Frederick Albert Anthony	66-67ChiA	10-31-43	Ambridge, Pa.		R	R	6'2	185	5	4	.556	0	14	12	0	61	52	23	23	0	3.25
Klimkowski, Ron-Ronald Bernard	69-70NYA 71OakA 72NYA	03-01-45	Jersey City, N.J.		R	R	6'2	190	8	12	.400	4	90	6	1	188	155	76	79	1	2.92
Kline, Ron-Ronald Lee	52PitN 53-54MS 55-59PitN 60AtlN 61LAA 61-62DetA 63-66WasA 67MinA 68-69PitN 69SFN 69BosA 70AtlN	03-09-32	Callery, Pa.	06-22-02	R	R	6'3	205	114	144	.442	108	736	203	44	2078	2113	731	989	8	3.75
Kline, Steve-Steven Jack	70-74NYA 74CleA 75EJ 77AtlN	10-06-47	Wenatchee, Wash.		R	R	6'3	205	43	45	.489	1	129	105	34	749	708	184	240	6	3.27
Knowles, Darold-Darold Duane	65BalA 66PhiN 67-71WasA 71-74OakA 75-76ChiN 77TexA 78MonN 79-80StLN	12-09-41	Brunswick, Mo.		L	L	6'	185	66	74	.471	143	765	8	1	1092	1006	480	681	1	3.12
Koch, Alan-Alan Goodman	63-64DetA 64WasA	03-25-38	Decatur, Ala.		R	R	6'4	195	4	11	.267	0	42	15	1	128	137	55	73	0	5.41
Kolstad, Hal-Harold Everette	62-63BosA	06-01-35	Rice Lake, Wis.		R	R	5'9	190	0	4	.000	2	34	2	0	72	81	41	42	0	6.63
Koonce, Cal-Calvin Lee	62-67ChiN 67-70NYN 70-71BosA	11-18-40	Fayetteville, N.C.	10-28-93	R	R	6'2	190	47	49	.490	24	334	90	9	972	972	368	504	3	3.78
Koplitz, Howie-Howard Dean	61-62DetA 64-66WasA	05-04-38	Oshkosh, Wis.		R	R	5'10	190	9	7	.563	1	54	19	2	176	187	80	87	0	4.19
Korince, George-George Eugene (Moose)	66-67DetA	01-10-46	Ottawa, Canada		R	R	6'3	210	1	0	1.000	0	11	0	0	17	11	14	13	0	4.24
Koufax, Sandy-Sanford	55-57BknN 58-66LAN 67RJ	12-30-35	Brooklyn, N.Y.		R	L	6'2	205	165	87	.655	9	397	314	137	2325	1754	817	2396	40	2.76
Kralick, Jack-John Francis	59-60WasA 61-63MinA 63-67CleA	06-01-35	Youngstown, Ohio		L	L	6'2	180	67	65	.508	1	235	169	45	1218	1238	318	668	12	3.56
Krausse, Lew-Lewis Bernard Jr.	61,64-67KCA 68-69OakA 70-71MilA 72BosA 73StLN 74AtlN	04-25-43	Media, Pa.		R	R	6'	185	68	91	.428	21	321	167	21	1285	1205	493	721	5	4.00
Kreutzer, Frank-Franklin James	62-64ChiA 64-66,69WasA	02-07-39	Buffalo, N.Y.		R	L	6'1	175	8	18	.308	1	78	32	2	210	194	109	151	1	4.41
Kroll, Gary-Gary Melvin	64PhiN 64-65NYN 68HouN 69CleN	07-18-41	Culver City, Cal.		R	R	6'6	220	6	7	.462	1	71	13	1	160	147	91	138	0	4.22
Kunkel, Bill-William Gustave James	61-62KCA 63NYA	07-07-36	Hoboken, N.J.	05-04-85	R	R	6'1	185	6	6	.500	4	89	2	0	143	153	49	83	0	4.28
Kurtz, Hal-Harold James (Bud)	68CleA	08-20-43	Washington, D.C.		R	R	6'3	205	1	0	1.000	1	28	0	0	38	37	15	16	0	5.21
Kutyna, Marty-Marion James	59-60KCA 61-62WasA	11-14-32	Philadelphia, Pa.		R	R	6'	190	14	16	.467	8	159	6	0	290	301	108	110	0	3.88
Lachemann, Marcel-Marcel Ernest	69-71OakA M94-96CalA	06-13-41	Los Angeles, Cal.		R	R	6'1	185	7	4	.636	5	70	0	0	101	103	38	55	0	3.48
Lambe, Jack-John Alexander	62PitN 63-65BosA 65HouN 66-67ChiA 67NYN 67StLN 68CinN	10-03-36	Farmingdale, N.Y.		R	R	6'1	198	33	41	.446	15	285	49	7	710	753	238	434	3	4.25
Lamb, John-John Andrew	70-71,73PhiN	07-20-46	Sharon, Conn.		R	R	6'1	180	0	2	.000	4	47	0	0	66	63	24	36	0	4.09
Lamb, Ray-Raymond Richard	69-70LAN 71-73CleA	12-28-44	Glendale, Cal.		R	R	6'1	170	20	23	.465	4	154	31	3	424	417	174	258	1	3.54
Landis, Bill-William Henry	63KCA 67-69BosA	10-08-42	Hanford, Cal.		L	L	6'2	185	9	8	.529	4	102	7	0	170	158	91	135	0	4.45
Lary, Al-Alfred Allen	54-55,62CinN	09-26-28	Northport, Ala.	07-10-01	R	R	6'2	185	0	1	.000	0	14	0	0	40	45	22	22	0	6.53
Lasher, Fred-Frederick Walter	63MinA 67-70DetA 70CleA 71CalA	08-19-41	Poughkeepsie, N.Y.		R	R	6'5	190	11	13	.458	22	151	1	0	202	179	110	148	0	3.88
Latman, Barry-Arnold Barry	57-59ChiA 60-63CleA 64LAA 65CalA 66-67HouN	05-21-36	Los Angeles, Cal.		R	R	6'3	210	59	68	.465	16	344	134	28	1219	1130	489	829	10	3.91
Lauzerique, George-George Albert	67KCA 68-69OakA 70MilA	07-22-47	Havana, Cuba		R	R	6'1	180	4	8	.333	0	34	14	2	113	110	48	73	0	5.02
Law, Ron-Ronald David	69CleA	03-14-46	Hamilton, Canada		R	R	6'1	178	3	4	.290	9	35	1	0	52	68	34	29	0	5.02
Lawson, Steve-Steven George	72TexA	12-28-50	Oakland, Cal.		R	L	6'2	190	0	0	—	0	11	0	0	14	10	13	12	0	2.61
Lazar, Danny-John Dan	68-69ChiA	11-14-43	East Chicago, Ind.		L	L	6'1	190	0	0	—	0	17	4	0	34	35	15	20	0	5.56
Lee, Bob-Robert Dean (Horse)	64LAA 65-66CalA 67LAN 67-68CinN	11-26-37	Ottumwa, Iowa		R	R	6'3	235	25	23	.521	63	269	7	0	492	402	196	315	0	2.71
Lee, Don-Donald Edward	57-58DetA 60WasA 61-62MinA 62-64LAA 65CalA 65-66HouN 66ChiN	02-26-34	Globe, Ariz.		R	R	6'4	205	40	44	.476	11	244	97	13	888	827	281	467	3	3.61
Lee, Mike-Michael Randall	60CleA 63LAA	05-19-41	Bell, Cal.		L	L	6'5	220	1	1	.500	0	13	4	0	35	36	25	17	0	3.34

USE NAMES - GIVEN NAMES (NICKNAMES)	TEAM BY YEAR	BIRTH DATE	BIRTHPLACE	DEATH DATE	B	T	HGT	WGT	W	L	Pct.	SV	G	GS	CG	IP	H	BB	SO	ShO	ERA
Lehew, Jim-James Anthony	61-62BalA	08-19-37	Baltimore, Md.		R	R	6'	185	0	0		0	8	0	0	12	11	3	2	0	1.50
Lemaster, Denn-Denver Clayton	62-65MilN 66-67AtlN 68-71HouN 72MonN	02-25-39	Corona, Cal.		R	L	6'1	182	90	105	.462	8	357	249	66	1788	1703	600	1305	14	3.58
LeMay, Dick-Richard Paul	61-62SFN 63ChiN	08-28-38	Cincinnati, Ohio		L	L	6'3	190	3	8	.273	4	45	6	1	107	100	49	69	0	4.21
Lemonds, Dave-David Lee	69ChiN 72ChiA 73AJ	07-05-48	Charlotte, N.C.		L	L	6'1	180	4	8	.333	0	33	19	0	100	92	43	69	0	2.97
Leonhard, Dave-David Paul	67-72BalA	01-22-41	Arlington, Va.		R	R	5'11	170	16	14	.533	5	117	29	7	336	287	150	146	4	3.16
Lersch, Barry-Barry Lee	69-73PhiN 74StLN	09-07-44	Denver, Colo.		B	R	6'	175	18	32	.360	6	169	53	9	570	536	172	317	1	3.82
			Bats Left 73-74																		
Leshnock, Don-Donald Lee	72DetA	11-25-46	Youngstown, Ohio		R	L	6'3	195	0	0		0	1	0	0	1	2	0	2	0	0.00
Ley, Terry-Terrence Richard	71NYA	02-21-47	Portland, Ore.		L	L	6'	195	0	0		0	6	0	0	9	9	9	7	0	5.00
Lindblad, Paul-Paul Aaron	65-67KCA 68-71OakA 71WasA 72TexA 73-76OakA 77-78TexA 78NYA	08-09-41	Chanute, Kans.	01-01-06	L	L	6'1	185	68	63	.519	64	655	32	1	1214	1157	384	671	1	3.28
Lines, Dick-Richard George	66-67WasA	08-17-38	Montreal, Canada		R	L	6'1	175	7	7	.500	6	107	0	0	169	146	48	103	0	2.82
Linzy, Frank-Frank Alfred	63,65-70SFN 70-71StLN 72-73MilA 74PhiN	09-15-40	Fort Gibson, Okla.		R	R	6'1	195	62	57	.521	111	516	2	0	817	790	282	358	0	2.85
Locke, Bobby-Lawrence Donald	59-61CleA 62StLN 62-64PhiN 65CinN 67-68CalA	03-03-34	Rowe's Run, Pa.		R	R	5'11	185	16	15	.516	10	165	23	2	416	432	165	194	2	4.02
Locke, Ron-Ronald Thomas	64NYN	04-04-42	Wakefield, R.I.		R	L	5'11	168	1	2	.333	0	25	3	0	41	46	22	17	0	3.51
Locker, Bob-Robert Awtry	65-69ChiA 69SeaA 70MilN 70-72OakA 73ChiN 74EJ 75ChiN	03-15-38	George, Iowa		B	R	6'3	200	57	39	.594	95	576	0	0	878	776	257	577	0	2.76
			Bats Right 65-67																		
Lolich, Mickey-Michael Stephen	63-75DetA 76NYN 77VR 78-79SDN	09-12-40	Portland, Ore.		B	L	6'	210	217	191	.532	11	586	496	195	3640	3366	1099	2832	41	3.44
			Bats Right 76,78																		
Lonborg, Jim-James Reynold	65-71BosA 72MilA 73-79PhiN	04-16-42	Santa Maria, Cal.		R	R	6'5	210	157	137	.534	4	425	368	90	2464	2400	823	1475	15	3.86
Lopez, Marcelino-Marcelino Pons [Lito]	63PhiN 65-67CalA 67,69-70BalA 71MilA 72CleA	09-23-43	Havana, Cuba	11-29-01	R	L	6'3	205	31	40	.437	2	171	93	14	653	591	317	426	3	3.62
Lopez, Ramon-Jose Ramon [Hevia]	66CalA	05-26-33	Las Villas, Cuba	09-04-82	R	R	6'	175	0	1	.000	0	7	4	0	7	4	4	2	0	5.14
Loughlin, Larry-Larry John	67PhiN	08-16-41	Tacoma, Wash.	01-26-99	L	L	6'1	190	0	0		0	3	0	0	5	9	4	5	0	16.20
Loun, Don-Donald Nelson	64WasA	11-09-40	Frederick, Md.		L	L	6'2	185	1	1	.500	0	2	2	1	13	13	3	3	1	2.08
Lovrich, Pete-Peter	63KCA 64-65MS	10-16-42	Blue Island, ill.		R	R	6'4	200	1	1	.500	0	20	1	0	21	25	10	16	0	7.71
Luebke, Dick-Richard Raymond	62BalA	04-08-35	Chicago, Ill.	12-04-74	R	L	6'4	200	0	1	.000	0	10	0	0	13	12	6	7	0	2.77
Machemehl, Chuck-Charles Walker	71CleA	04-20-46	Branham, Tex.		R	R	6'4	215	0	2	.000	3	14	0	0	18	16	15	9	0	6.50
MacKenzie, Ken-Kenneth Purvis	60-61MilN 62-63NYN 63StLN 64SFN 65HouN	03-10-34	Gore Bay, Canada		R	L	6'	185	8	10	.444	5	129	1	0	207	231	63	142	0	4.83
MacLeod, Bill-William Daniel	62BosA	05-13-42	Gloucester, Mass.		L	L	6'2	190	0	0		0	2	0	0	2	4	1	2	0	4.50
Maestri, Hector-Hector Anibal [Garcia]	60-61WasA	04-19-35	Havana, Cuba		R	R	5'10	158	0	1	.000	0	2	1	0	8	7	3	3	0	1.13
Magnuson, Jim-James Robert	70-71ChiA 73NYA	08-18-46	Marinette, Wis.	05-30-91	R	L	6'2	195	2	7	.222	0	36	10	0	102	113	41	40	0	4.59
Magrini, Pete-Peter Alexander	66BosA	06-08-42	San Francisco, Cal.		R	R	6'	195	0	1	.000	0	3	1	0	7	8	8	3	0	10.29
Mahaffey, Art-Arthur	60-65PhiN 66StLN	06-04-38	Cincinnati, Ohio		R	R	6'2	200	59	64	.480	1	185	148	46	998	959	368	639	9	4.18
Maloney, Jim-James William	60-70CinN 71CalN	06-02-40	Fresno, Cal.		L	R	6'2	200	134	84	.615	2	302	262	74	1849	1518	810	1605	30	3.19
Manning, Jim-James Benjamin	62MinA	07-21-43	L'Anse, Mich.		R	R	6'1	195	0	0	—	0	1	1	0	14	1	3	0	0	5.14
Maranda, Georges-Georges Henri	60SFN 62MinN	01-15-32	Levis, Canada	07-14-00	R	R	6'2	195	2	7	.222	0	49	8	0	124	119	65	64	0	4.50
Marentette, Leo-Leo John	65DetA 69MonN	02-18-41	Detroit, Mich.		R	R	6'2	200	0	0	—	0	5	0	0	8	10	2	7	0	4.50
Marichal, Juan-Juan Antonio [Sanchez]	60-73SFN 74BosA 75LAN	10-20-37	Laguna Verde, D.R.		R	R	6'	190	243	142	.631	2	471	457	244	3506	3153	709	2303	52	2.89
Marone, Lou-Louis Stephen	69-70PitN	12-03-45	San Diego, Cal.		R	R	5'10	195	1	1	.500	3	30	0	0	37	26	13	25	0	2.68
Maxie, Larry-Larry Hans	69AtlN	10-10-40	Upland, Cal.		R	R	6'4	220	0	0	—	0	3	1	1	1	1	1	1	0	3.00
McAnally, Ernie-Ernest Lee	71-74MonN	08-15-46	Mt. Pleasant, Tex.		R	R	6'1	195	30	49	.380	0	112	97	21	624	599	268	351	6	4.02
McAndrew, Jim-James Clement	68-73NYN 74SDN	01-11-44	Lost Nation, Iowa		R	R	6'2	185	37	53	.411	4	161	110	20	771	712	213	424	6	3.65
McBean, Al-Alvin O'Neal	61-68PitN 69SDN 69-70LAN 70PitN	05-15-38	Charlotte Amalie, V.I.		R	R	5'11	175	67	50	.573	63	409	76	22	1072	1058	365	575	5	3.13
McBride, Ken-Kenneth Faye	59-60ChiA 61-64LAA 65CalA	08-12-35	Huntsville, Ala.		R	R	6'1	195	40	50	.444	2	151	122	28	808	717	363	503	7	3.79
McClain, Joe-Joe Fred	61-62WasA	05-05-33	Johnson City, Tenn.		R	R	6'	183	8	22	.267	1	43	33	7	236	254	59	82	2	4.42
McCool, Billy-William John	64-68CinN 69SDN 70StLN	07-14-44	Batesville, Ind.		R	L	6'2	200	32	42	.432	58	528	465	272	471	0	3.60
McCormick, Mike-Michael Francis	56-57NYN 58-62SFN 63-64BalA 65-66WasA 67-70SFN 70NYA 71KCA	09-29-38	Pasadena, Cal.		L	L	6'2	195	134	128	.511	12	484	333	91	2381	2281	795	1321	23	3.73
McDaniel, Lindy-Lyndall Dale	55-62StLN 63-65ChiN 66-68SFN 68-73NYA 74-75KCA	12-13-35	Hollis, Okla.		R	R	6'3	195	141	119	.542	172	987	74	18	2140	2099	623	1361	2	3.45
McDowell, Sam-Samuel Edward Thomas (Sudden Sam)	61-71CleA 72-73SFN 73-74NYA 75PitN	09-21-42	Pittsburgh, Pa.		L	L	6'5	215	141	134	.513	14	425	346	103	2492	1948	1312	2453	23	3.17
McGinn, Dan-Daniel Michael	68CinN 69-71MonN 72CinN	11-29-43	Omaha, Neb.		L	L	6'	200	15	30	.333	10	210	28	4	409	442	225	293	2	5.11
McGlothlin, Jim-James Milton (Red)	65-69CalN 70-73CinN 73ChiA	10-06-43	Los Angeles, Cal.	12-23-75	R	R	6'1	185	67	77	.465	3	256	201	36	1300	1247	418	709	11	3.61
McLain, Denny-Dennis Dale	63-70DetA 71WasA 72-73AtlN 72AtlN	03-29-44	Chicago, Ill.		R	R	6'1	185	131	91	.590	2	280	264	105	1885	1646	548	1282	29	3.39
McMahon, Don-Donald John	57-62MilN 62-63HouN 64-66CleA 66-67BosA 67-68ChiA 68-69DetA 69-74SFN	01-04-30	Brooklyn, N.Y.	07-22-87	R	R	6'2	215	90	68	.570	153	874	2	0	1312	1054	579	1003	0	2.96
McNally, Dave-David Arthur	62-74BalA 75MonN	10-31-42	Billings, Mont.	12-01-02	R	L	5'11	195	184	119	.607	2	424	396	120	2730	2488	826	1512	33	3.24
McQueen, Mike-Michael Robert	69-72AtlN 73BP 74CinN	08-30-50	Oklahoma City, Okla.		L	L	6'	188	5	11	.313	3	73	19	2	218	212	112	140	0	4.67
McRae, Norm-Norman	69-70DetA	09-26-47	Elizabeth, N.J.	07-25-03	R	R	6'2	200	0	0	—	0	22	0	0	34	28	26	19	0	3.18
Meeler, Phil-Charles Phillip	72DetA	07-03-48	South Boston, Va.		R	R	6'5	225	0	1	.000	0	7	0	0	8	10	7	5	0	4.50
Merritt, Jim-James Joseph	65-68MinA 69-72CinN 73-75TexA	12-09-43	Altadena, Cal.		L	L	6'2	180	81	86	.485	7	297	192	56	1484	1468	322	932	5	3.65
Metcalf, Tom-Thomas John	63NYA	07-16-40	Amherst, Wis.		R	R	6'2	174	1	0	.000	0	8	0	0	13	12	8	3	0	2.77
Meyer, Bob-Robert Bernard	64NYA 64LAA 64KCA 69SeaA 70MilA	08-30-39	Toldeo, Ohio		R	L	6'2	195	2	12	.143	0	38	18	3	129	132	80	92	0	4.40
Mikkelsen, Pete-Peter James	64-65NYA 66-67PitN 67-68ChiN 68StLN 69-72LAN	10-25-39	Staten Island, N.Y.		R	R	6'2	210	45	40	.529	49	364	3	0	653	576	250	436	0	3.38
Miles, Jim-James Charlie	68-69WasA	08-08-43	Grenada, Miss.		R	R	6'2	210	0	1	.000	0	13	1	0	24	27	17	20	0	7.50
Miller (Gemeinweisser), Bob-Robert Lane	57,59-61StLN 62NYN 63-67LAN 68-69MinA 70CleA 70ChiN 70-71ChiN 71SDN 71-72PitN 73DetA 73SDN 73-74NYN	02-18-39	St. Louis, Mo.	08-06-93	R	R	6'1	190	69	81	.460	52	694	99	7	1552	1487	608	895	0	3.37
Miller, John-John Ernest	62-63,65-67BalA	05-30-41	Baltimore, Md.		R	R	6'2	210	12	14	.462	0	46	35	1	227	188	138	178	0	3.89
Miller, Larry-Larry Don	64LAN 65-66NYN	09-19-37	Topeka, Kans.		L	L	6'1	195	5	14	.263	0	48	20	1	145	162	57	93	0	4.72
Miller, Stu-Stuart Leonard	53-54,56StLN 56PhiN 57NYN 58-62SFN 63-67BalA 68AtlN	12-26-27	Northampton, Mass.		R	R	5'11	165	105	103	.505	154	704	93	24	1694	1522	600	1164	5	3.24
Mills, Dick-Richard Allen	70BosA	01-29-45	Boston, Mass.		R	R	6'3	200	0	0		0	2	0	0	4	6	3	3	0	2.25
Moeller, Joe-Joseph Douglas	62,64,66-71LAN	02-15-43	Blue Island, Ill.		R	R	6'5	192	26	36	.419	7	166	74	4	583	596	176	307	1	4.01
Moeller, Ron-Ronald Ralph (The Kid)	56,58BalA 61LAA 62MS 63LAA 63WasA	10-13-38	Cincinnati, Ohio		L	L	6'	180	4	9	.400	0	52	22	1	153	174	100	104	1	5.76
Moloney, Rich-Richard Henry	70ChiA	06-07-50	Brookline, Mass.		R	R	6'3	195	0	0		0	1	0	0	1	2	0	1	0	0.00
Monbouquette, Bill-William Charles (Mombo)	58-65BosA 66-67DetA 67-68NYA 68SFN	08-11-36	Medford, Mass.		R	R	5'11	195	114	112	.504	3	343	263	78	1962	1995	462	1122	18	3.68
Monteagudo, Aurelio-Aurelio Fautino [Cintra]	63-66KCA 66HouN 67ChiA 70KCA 73CalA	11-19-43	Caibarien, Cuba	11-10-90	R	R	5'11	185	3	7	.300	4	72	7	0	131	122	62	58	0	5.08
Montejo, Manny-Manuel [Bofill] (Pete)	61DetA	10-16-35	Caibarien, Cuba		R	R	5'11	166	0	0		0	12	0	0	16	13	6	15	0	3.94
Montgomery, Monty-Monty Bryson	71-72KCA	09-01-46	Albermarle, N.C.		R	R	6'3	205	6	3	.667	0	12	10	1	77	71	20	36	1	2.81
Moore, Barry-Robert Barry	65-69WasA 70CleA 70ChiA	04-03-43	Statesville, N.C.		L	L	6'1	190	26	37	.413	3	140	99	8	600	577	300	278	1	4.15
Moorhead, Bob-Charles Robert	62,65NYN	01-23-38	Chambersburg, Pa.	12-03-86	R	R	6'2	208	0	3	.000	0	47	7	0	119	134	47	68	0	4.54
Moose, Bob-Robert Ralph	67-76PitN	10-09-47	Export, Pa.	10-09-76	R	R	6'	200	76	71	.517	19	289	160	35	1305	1308	387	827	13	3.50
Morehead, Dave-David Michael (Moe)	63-68BosA 69-70KCA	09-05-42	San Diego, Cal.		R	R	6'1	195	40	64	.385	1	177	134	19	821	730	463	627	6	4.14
Morris, Danny-Danny Walker	68-69MinA	06-11-46	Greenville, Ky.		R	R	6'1	200	0	2	.000	0	6	3	0	16	16	8	7	0	2.81
Morris, John-John Wallace	66PhiN 68BalA 69SeaA 70-71MilS 72-74SFN	08-23-41	Lewes, Del.		L	R	6'2	200	11	7	.611	2	132	10	2	233	227	86	137	0	3.94
Mudrock, Phil-Phillip Ray	63ChiN	06-12-37	Louisville, Colo.		R	R	6'2	198	0	0		0	1	0	0	5	9	3	0	0	9.00
Muniz, Manny-Manuel [Rodriguez]	71PhiN	12-31-47	Caguas, P.R.		R	R	5'11	190	0	0		0	1	0	0	10	9	5	9	0	7.20
Murakami, Masanori-Masanori (Mashi)	64-65SFN 66JL	05-06-44	Otauki, Japan		L	L	6'	180	5	1	.833	9	54	1	0	89	65	23	100	0	3.44
Murphy, Danny-Daniel Francis (See B61-72)	69-70ChiA	08-23-42	Beverly, Mass.		R	R	5'11	185	4	4	.500	0	112	110	59	58	0	4.66
Musgraves, Dennis-Dennis Eugene	65NYN	12-25-43	Indianapolis, Ind.		R	R	6'4	188	0	0	—	0	6	1	0	18	11	7	11	0	0.56
Nagy, Mike-Michael Timothy	69-72BosA 73StLN 74HouN	03-25-48	Bronx, N.Y.		R	R	6'1	195	20	13	.606	0	76	42	8	420	431	210	170	1	4.14
Narum, Buster-Leslie Ferdinand	63BalA 64-67WasA	12-02-40	Philadelphia, Pa.	05-17-04	R	R	6'1	194	14	27	.341	0	96	58	9	397	398	177	220	2	4.44
Nash, Jim-James Edwin (Jumbo)	66-67KCA 68-69OakA 70-72AtlN 72PhiN	02-09-45	Hawthorne, Nev.		R	R	6'5	225	68	64	.515	4	201	167	36	1107	1050	401	771	11	3.59
Navarro, Julio-Julio [Ventura] (Whiplash)	62-64LAA 64-66DetA 70AtlN	01-09-36	Vieques, P.R.		R	R	6'	190	7	9	.438	17	130	2	0	211	191	70	151	0	3.67
Neibauer, Gary-Gary Wayne	69-72AtlN 72PhiN 73AtlN	10-29-44	Billings, Mont.		R	R	6'3	200	4	8	.333	0	149	135	87	81	0	4.77
Nelson, Jim-James Lorin	70-71PitN	07-04-47	Birmingham, Ala.	08-22-04	R	R	6'	182	6	4	.600	0	32	12	1	103	91	64	53	1	3.06
Nelson, Mel-Melvin Frederick	60StLN 63LAA 65,67MinA 68-69StLN	05-30-36	San Diego, Cal.		R	L	6'	185	4	10	.286	5	93	11	0	174	184	69	98	0	4.40

USE NAMES - GIVEN NAMES (NICKNAMES)	TEAM BY YEAR	BIRTH DATE	BIRTHPLACE	DEATH DATE	B	T	HGT	WGT	W	L	Pct.	SV	G	GS	CG	IP	H	BB	SO	ShO	ERA
Nelson, Roger-Roger Eugene (Spider)	67ChiA 68BalA 69-72KCA 73-74CinN 766KCA	06-07-44	Altadena, Cal.		R	R	6'3	200	29	32	.475	5	135	77	20	636	516	190	371	7	3.06
Neumeier, Dan-Daniel George	72ChiA	03-09-48	Shawano, Wis.		R	R	6'5	230	0	0	—	0	3	0	0	3	2	3	0	0	9.00
Newman, Fred-Frederick William	62-64LAA 65-67CalA	02-21-42	Boston, Mass.	06-24-87	R	R	6'3	210	33	39	.458	0	108	93	18	610	589	154	254	4	3.41
Newman, Ray-Raymond Francis	71ChiN 72-73MonN	06-20-45	Evansville, Ind.		L	L	6'5	215	3	3	.500	4	45	0	0	63	53	24	46	0	3.00
Nieson, Chuck-Charles Bassett	64MinA	09-24-42	Hanford, Cal.		R	R	6'2	185	0	0	—	0	2	0	0	2	1	1	5	0	4.50
Nippert, Merlin-Merlin Lee	62BosA	09-01-38	Mangum, Okla.		R	R	6'1	175	0	0	—	0	4	0	0	6	4	4	3	0	4.50
Nischwitz, Ron-Ronald Lee	61-62DetA 63CleA 65DetA	07-01-37	Dayton, Ohio		B	L	6'3	205	5	8	.385	2	88	1	0	116	124	48	58	0	4.19
Nolan, Gary-Gary Lynn	67-73CinN 74SJ 75-77CinN 77CalA	05-27-48	Herlong, Cal.		R	R	6'3	197	110	70	.611	0	250	247	45	1675	1505	413	1039	14	3.08
Nold, Dick-Richard Louis	67WasA	05-04-43	San Francisco, Cal.		R	R	6'2	190	0	2	.000	0	7	3	0	20	19	13	10	0	4.95
Noriega, John-John Alan	69-70CinN	12-20-43	Ogden, Utah	09-29-01	R	R	6'4	185	0	0	—	0	13	0	0	26	37	13	10	0	7.27
Norton, Tom-Thomas John	72MinA	04-26-50	Elyria, Ohio		R	R	6'2	200	0	1	.000	0	21	0	0	32	31	14	22	0	2.81
Nottebart, Don-Donald Edward	60-62MilN 63-65HouN 66-67CinN 69NYA 69ChiN	01-23-36	West Newton, Mass.		R	R	6'1	195	36	51	.414	21	296	89	16	927	902	283	525	2	3.66
Nunn, Howie-Howard Ralph	59StLN 61-62CinN	10-18-35	Westfield, N.C.		R	R	6'	185	4	3	.571	0	46	0	0	69	73	42	50	0	5.09
Nye, Rich-Richard Raymond	66-69ChiN 70StLN 70MonN	08-04-44	Oakland, Cal.		L	L	6'4	185	26	31	.456	4	113	63	16	478	472	140	267	1	3.71
Nyman, Jerry-Gerald Smith	68-69ChiA 70SDN	11-23-42	Logan, Utah		L	L	5'10	165	6	7	.462	0	30	19	3	110	104	57	69	1	4.58
O'Brien, Bob-Robert Allen	71LAN	04-23-49	Pittsburgh, Pa.		L	L	5'10	172	2	2	.500	2	14	4	1	42	42	13	15	1	3.00
O'Dell, Billy-William Oliver (Digger)	54BalA 54MS 56-59BalA 60-64SFN 65MilA 66AtlN 66-67PitN	02-10-33	Whitmire, S.C.		B	L	5'11	170	105	100	.512	48	479	199	63	1816	1697	556	1133	13	3.30
Odom, Blue Moon-Johnny Lee	64-67KCA 68-75OakA 75CleA 75AtlA 76ChiA	05-29-45	Macon, Ga.		R	R	6'	178	84	85	.497	1	295	229	40	1507	1362	788	857	15	3.70
O'Donoghue, John-John Eugene	63-65CleA 68-67CleA 68BalA 69SeaA 70MilA 70-71CinN	10-07-39	Kansas City, Mo.		R	L	6'4	210	39	55	.415	10	257	96	13	751	780	260	377	4	4.07
Olivo, Chi Chi-Federico Emilio [Maldonado]	61,64-65MilN 66AtlN	03-18-26	Guayubin, Dom. Rep.	02-03-77	R	R	6'2	217	7	6	.538	12	96	0	0	141	129	50	98	0	3.96
Olivo, Diomedes-Diomedes Antonio [Maldonado] (Guayubin)	60,62PitN 63StLN	01-22-19	Guayubin, Dom. Rep.	02-15-77	L	L	6'1	195	6	6	.455	7	86	1	0	107	112	39	85	0	3.11
Ollom, Jim-James Donald	66-67MinA	07-08-45	Snohomish, Wash.		R	L	6'4	210	0	1	.000	0	24	3	0	45	39	12	28	0	5.00
O'Riley, Don-Donald Lee	69-70KCA	03-12-45	Topeka, Kans.	05-02-97	R	R	6'3	205	1	1	.500	1	27	2	0	46	58	24	23	0	6.26
Ortega, Phil-Filomeno Coronado	60-64LAN 65-68WasA 69CalA	10-07-39	Gilbert, Ariz.		R	R	6'2	185	46	62	.426	2	204	141	20	952	884	378	549	9	4.42
Osinski, Dan-Daniel	62KCA 62-64LAA 65MilN 66-67BosA 69ChiN 70HouN	11-17-33	Chicago, Ill.		R	R	6'1	190	29	28	.509	18	324	21	5	590	566	264	400	2	3.34
Osteen, Claude-Claude Wilson	57,59-61CinN 61-64WasA 65-73LAN 74HouN 74StLN 75ChiA	08-09-39	Caney Springs, Tenn.		L	L	5'11	170	196	195	.501	1	541	488	140	3459	3471	940	1612	40	3.30
Osteen, Darrell-Milton Darrell	65-67CinN 70OakA	02-14-43	Oklahoma City, Okla.		R	R	6'1	175	1	4	.200	3	29	1	0	38	47	29	34	0	8.05
O'Toole, Denny-Dennis Joseph	69-73ChiA	03-13-49	Chicago, Ill.		R	R	6'3	195	0	0	—	0	15	0	0	30	43	10	22	0	5.10
O'Toole, Jim-James Jerome	58-66CinN 67ChiA	01-10-37	Chicago, Ill.		B	L	6'	200	98	84	.538	4	270	238	58	1615	1545	546	1039	18	3.57
Owens, Jim-James Philip (Bear)	55-56PhiN 57MS 58-62PhiN 63CinN 64-67HouN	01-16-34	Gifford, Pa.		R	R	5'11	195	42	68	.382	21	286	103	21	886	932	340	516	1	4.31
Palmer, Lowell-Lowell Raymond	69-71PhiN 72CleA 72SDN	08-18-47	Sacramento, Cal.		R	R	6'1	195	5	18	.217	0	106	25	2	317	302	202	239	1	5.28
Panther, Jim-James Edward	70OakA 72TexA 73AtlN	03-01-45	Burlington, Iowa		R	R	6'1	195	7	13	.350	2	85	4	0	131	156	60	66	0	5.22
Papa, John-John Paul	61-62BalA	12-05-40	Bridgeport, Conn.		R	R	5'11	190	0	0	—	0	3	0	0	2	5	4	3	0	22.50
Pappas(Pappastediodis), Milt-Milton Stephen (Miltiades Stergios)	57-65BalA 66-68CinN 68-70AtlN 70-73ChiN	05-11-39	Detroit, Mich.		R	R	6'3	205	209	164	.560	4	520	465	129	3186	3046	858	1728	43	3.40
Parsons, Bill-William Raymond	71-73MilA 74OakA	08-17-48	Riverside, Cal.		R	R	6'6	200	29	36	.446	0	93	82	22	521	473	231	282	6	3.89
Parsons, Tom-Thomas Anthony (Long Tom)	63PitN 64-65NYN	09-13-39	Lakeville, Conn.		R	R	6'7	210	2	13	.133	1	40	14	2	114	135	25	70	1	4.74
Pascual, Camilo-Camilo Alberto [Lus] (Little Potato)	54-60WasA 61-66MinA 67-69WasA 69CinN 70LAN 71CleA	01-20-34	Havana, Cuba		R	R	5'11	185	174	170	.506	10	529	404	132	2930	2703	1069	2167	36	3.63
Patterson, Daryl-Daryl Alan	68-71DetA 71OakA 71StLN 74PitN	11-21-43	Coalinga, Cal.		L	R	6'4	192	11	9	.550	11	142	3	0	231	223	119	142	0	4.09
Paul, Mike-Michael George	68-71DetA 72-73TexA 73-74ChiN	04-18-45	Detroit, Mich.		L	L	6'	175	27	48	.360	8	228	77	5	627	619	246	452	1	3.92
Pena, Jose-Jose [Gutierrez] (Paluche)	69CinN 70-72LAN	12-03-42	Ciudad Juarez, Mex.		R	R	6'2	190	7	4	.636	5	61	0	0	112	106	58	82	0	4.98
Pena, Orlando-Orlando Gregorio [Guevara]	58-60CinN 62-65KCA 65-67DetA 67CleA 70PitN 71,73BalA 73-74StLN 74-75CalA	11-17-33	Victoria de las Tunes, Cuba		R	R	5'11	170	56	77	.421	40	427	93	21	1203	1175	352	818	4	3.70
Peraza, Luis-Luis [Rios]	69PhiN	08-17-45	Rio Piedras, P.R.		R	R	5'11	185	0	0	—	0	9	1	2	7	0	6.00			
Perkins, Cecil-Cecil Boyce	67NYA	12-01-40	Baltimore, Md.		R	R	6'	175	0	1	.000	0	2	1	0	5	6	2	1	0	9.00
Perranoski(Perzanowski), Ron-Ronald Peter	61-67LAN 68-71MinA 71-72DetA 72LAN 73CalA	04-01-36	Paterson, N.J.		L	L	6'	185	79	74	.516	179	737	1	0	1176	1097	468	687	0	2.79
Perry, Jim-James Evan	59-63CleA 63-72MinA 73DetA 74-75CleA 75OakA	10-30-35	Williamston, N.C.		B	R	6'4	200	215	174	.563	10	630	447	109	3287	3127	998	1576	32	3.45
Peters, Gary-Gary Charles	59-69ChiA 70-72BosA	04-21-37	Grove City, Pa.		L	L	6'2	200	124	103	.546	5	359	286	79	2081	1894	706	1420	23	3.25
Peters, Ray-Raymond James	70MilA	08-27-48	Buffalo, N.Y.		R	R	6'6	220	0	2	.000	0	2	2	0	7	5	1	0	0	31.50
Peterson, Fritz (Fred Ingels)-Fritz Fred	66-74NYA 74-76CleA 76TexA	02-08-42	Chicago, Ill.		R	L	6'	190	133	131	.504	1	355	330	90	2217	2217	426	1015	20	3.30
Pfister, Dan-Daniel Albin	61-64KCA	10-20-36	Plainfield, N.J.		R	R	6'	187	6	19	.240	1	65	29	2	248	238	142	156	0	4.87
Phillips, Ed-Norman Edwin	70BosA	09-20-44	Ardmore, Okla.		R	R	6'2	198	0	2	.000	0	18	0	0	24	29	10	23	0	5.25
Phoebus, Tom-Thomas Harold	66-70BalA 71-72SDN 72ChiN	04-07-42	Baltimore, Md.		R	R	5'8	185	56	52	.519	4	201	149	29	1030	888	489	725	11	3.33
Piche, Ron-Ronald Jacques	60-63MilN 65CalA 66StLN	05-22-35	Verdun, Canada		R	R	5'11	165	10	16	.385	12	134	11	3	221	216	123	157	0	4.19
Pierce, Tony-Tony Michael	67KCA 68OakA	01-29-46	Brunswick, Ga.		R	L	6'1	190	4	6	.400	8	66	9	0	131	118	40	77	0	3.23
Pina, Horacio-Horacio [Garcia]	68-69CleA 70-71WasA 72TexA 73OakA 74ChiN 74CalA 78PitN	03-12-45	Matamoros , Mexico		R	R	6'2	177	23	23	.500	38	314	7	0	432	358	216	278	0	3.25
Pizzaro, Juan-Juan Ramon [Cordova]	57-60MilN 61-66ChiA 67-68PitN 68-69BosA 69CleA 69OakA 70-73ChiN 73HouN 74PitN	02-07-37	Santurce, P.R.		L	L	5'11	185	131	105	.555	28	488	245	79	2035	1807	888	1522	17	3.43
Pleis, Bill-William	61-66MinA	08-05-37	St. Louis, Mo.		L	L	5'10	175	21	16	.568	13	190	10	1	280	269	126	184	0	4.00
Plodinec, Tim-Timothy Alfred	72StLN	01-27-47	Aliquippa, Pa.		R	R	6'4	200	0	0	—	0	1	0	0	.1	3	0	0	0	27.00
Powell, Grover-Grover David	63NYN	10-10-40	Sayre, Pa.	05-21-85	L	L	5'10	175	1	1	.500	0	20	4	1	50	37	32	39	1	2.70
Pregenzer, John-John Arthur	63-64SFN	08-02-35	Burlington, Wis.		R	R	6'5	220	2	0	1.000	1	19	0	0	27	29	19	13	0	5.00
Priddy, Bob-Robert Simpson	62,64PitN 65-66SFN 67WasA 68-69ChiA 69CalA 69-71AtlN	12-10-39	Pittsburgh, Pa.		R	R	6'1	200	24	38	.387	18	249	29	3	535	518	198	294	0	4.00
Prince, Don-Donald Mark	62ChiN	04-05-38	Clarkton, N.C.		R	R	6'4	200	0	0	—	0	1	0	0	1	0	1	0	0	0.00
Puente, Miguel-Miguel Antonio [Aguilar]	70SFN	05-08-48	San Luis Potosi, Mexico		R	R	6'	165	1	3	.250	0	6	4	1	19	25	11	14	0	8.05
Purdin, John-John Nolan	64-65,68-69LAN	07-16-42	Lynx, Ohio		R	R	6'2	185	6	4	.600	2	58	5	1	111	93	52	68	1	3.89
Queen, Mel-Melvin Douglas (See B61-72)	66-69CinN 70-72CalA	03-26-42	Johnson City, N.Y.		L	R	6'1	190	20	17	.541	14	140	33	6	390	336	143	306	2	3.14
Quirk, Art-Arthur Lincoln	62BalA 63WasA	04-11-38	Providence, R.I.		R	L	5'11	170	3	2	.600	0	14	8	0	48	59	26	30	0	5.25
Radatz, Dick-Richard Raymond (The Monster)	62-66BosA 66-67CleA 67ChiN 69DetA 69MonN	04-02-37	Detroit, Mich.	03-16-05	R	R	6'6	235	52	43	.547	122	381	0	0	694	532	296	745	0	3.13
Raffo, Al-Albert Martin	69PhiN	11-27-41	San Francisco, Cal.		R	R	6'5	210	1	3	.250	1	45	0	0	72	81	25	38	0	4.13
Rakow, Ed-Edward Charles (Rock)	60LAN 61-63KCA 64-65DetA 67AtlN	05-30-35	Pittsburgh, Pa.	08-26-00	B	R	5'11	178	36	47	.434	5	195	90	20	760	771	304	484	3	4.33
	Bats Right 60-61																				
Ramos, Pedro-Pedro [Guerra] (Pete)	55-60WasA 61MinA 62-64CleA 64-66NYA67 PhiN 69PitN 69CinN 70WasA	04-28-35	Piner del Rio, Cuba		B	R		175	117	160	.442	55	582	268	73	2355	2364	724	1305	13	4.08
	Bats Right 55-59, 62-64																				
Rath, Fred-Frederick Helsher Sr.	68-69ChiA	09-01-43	Little Rock, Ark.		R	R	6'3	200	0	0	—	2	8	0	0	23	19	11	7	0	4.70
Rauch, Bob-Robert John	72NYN	06-16-49	Brookings, S.D.		R	R	6'4	205	0	1	.000	1	19	0	0	27	27	21	23	0	5.00
Ray, Jim-James Francis (Sting)	65-66,68-73HouN 74DetA	12-01-44	Rock Hill, S.C.		R	R	6'1	194	43	30	.589	25	308	20	1	618	541	271	407	0	3.61
Raymond, Claude-Joseph Claude Marc (Frenchy)	59ChiA 61-63MilN 64-67HouN 67-69AtlN 69-71MonN	05-07-37	St. Jean, Canada		R	R	5'10	180	46	53	.465	83	449	7	2	720	711	225	497	0	3.66
Reberger, Frank-Frank Beall (Crane)	68ChiN 69SDN 70-72SFN	06-07-44	Caldwell, Idaho		L	R	6'5	210	14	15	.483	9	148	37	5	389	404	197	258	0	4.51
Reed, Bob-Robert Edward	01-12-45		Boston, Mass.		R	R	5'10	175	2	4	.333	1	24	5	0	61	63	22	35	0	4.13
Reed, Howie-Howard Dean	58-60KCA 64-66LAN 66CalA 67HouN 69-71MonN	12-21-36	Dallas, Tex.	12-07-84	R	R	6'1	200	26	29	.473	9	229	35	3	516	510	208	268	1	3.72
Regan, Phil-Phillip Raymond (The Vulture)	60-65DetA 66-68LAN 68-72ChiN 72ChiA M95BalA	04-06-37	Otsego, Mich.		R	R	6'3	200	96	81	.542	92	551	105	20	1373	1392	447	743	1	3.83
Reniff, Hal-Harold Eugene (Porkie)	61-67NYA 67NYN	07-02-38	Warren, Ohio	09-07-04	R	R	6'	215	21	23	.477	45	276	0	0	470	383	242	314	0	3.27
Reynolds, Archie-Arhcie Edward	68-70ChiN 71CalA 72MilA	07-03-46	Glendale, Cal.		R	R	6'2	205	0	8	.000	0	36	7	0	81	100	49	47	0	5.78
Reynolds, Ken-Kenneth Lee	70-72PhiN 73MilA 75StLN 76SDN	01-04-47	Trevose, Pa.		L	L	6'	186	7	29	.194	0	103	51	4	374	370	196	197	1	4.48
Ribant, Dennis-Dennis Joseph	64-66NYN 67PitN 68DetA 68ChiA 69StLN 69CinN	09-20-41	Detroit, Mich.		R	R	5'11	175	24	29	.453	9	149	56	13	519	536	126	241	2	3.87
Richardson, Gordie-Gordon Clark	64StLN 65-66NYN	07-19-39	Colquitt, Ga.		R	L	6'	185	6	6	.500	4	69	7	1	118	105	37	86	0	4.04
Richert, Pete-Peter Gerard	62-64LAN 65-67WasA 67-71BalA 72-73LAN 74StLN 74PhiN	10-29-39	Floral Park, N.Y.		L	L	6'	180	80	73	.523	51	429	122	12	1166	959	424	925	3	3.19
Riddleberger, Denny-Dennis Michael	70-71WasA 72CleA	11-22-45	Clinton Forge, Va.		R	L	6'3	197	4	4	.500	7	103	0	0	133	119	56	95	0	2.77

USE NAMES - GIVEN NAMES (NICKNAMES) / TEAM BY YEAR	BIRTH DATE	BIRTHPLACE	DEATH DATE	B	T	HGT	WGT	W	L	Pct.	SV	G	GS	CG	IP	H	BB	SO	ShO	ERA
Ripplemayer, Ray-Raymond Roy — 62WasA	07-09-33	Valmeyer, Ill.		R	R	6'4	200	1	2	.333	0	18	1	0	39	47	17	17	0	5.54
Ritchie, Jay-Jay Seay — 64-65BosA 66-67AtlN 68CinN	11-20-36	Salisbury, N.C.		R	R	6'4	190	8	13	.381	8	167	2	0	291	301	94	212	0	3.49
Rittwage, Jim-James Michael William — 70CleA	10-23-44	Cleveland, Ohio		R	R	6'3	190	1	1	.500	0	8	3	1	26	18	21	16	0	4.15
Roberts, Dale-Dale (Mountain Man) — 67NYA	04-12-42	Owenton, Ky.		R	L	6'4	180	0	0	—	0	2	0	0	2	3	2	0	0	9.00
Robertson, Jerry-Jerry Lee — 69MonN 70DetA	10-13-43	Winchester, Kans.	03-24-96	B	R	6'2	205	5	16	.238	1	49	27	3	195	205	86	144	0	3.92
Robertson, Rich-Richard Paul — 66-71SFN	10-14-44	Albany, Cal.		R	R	6'2	210	13	14	.481	2	86	40	8	302	333	153	184	1	4.95
Rodriguez, Roberto-Roberto [Munoz] (Bobby) — 67KCA 70OakA 70SDN 70ChiN	11-29-43	Caracas, Venezuela		R	R	6'3	185	4	3	.571	7	57	5	0	112	128	37	91	0	4.82
Roggenburk, Garry-Garry Earl — 63,65-66MinA 66,68-69BosA 69SeaA	04-16-40	Cleveland, Ohio		L	L	6'6	205	6	9	.400	7	79	6	1	126	132	64	56	0	3.64
Rohr, Billy-William Joseph — 67BosA 68CleA	07-01-45	San Diego, Cal.		L	L	6'3	170	3	3	.500	1	27	8	2	60	61	32	21	1	5.70
Rohr, Les-Leslie Norvin — 67-69NYN	03-05-46	Lowestoft, England		L	L	6'5	205	2	3	.400	0	6	4	0	24	27	17	20	0	3.75
Rojas, Minnie-Minervo Alejandro [Landin] — 66-68CalA	11-26-33	Remedios, Cuba	03-23-02	R	R	6'1	188	23	16	.590	43	157	2	0	261	244	66	153	0	3.00
Roland, Jim-James Ivan — 62-64,66-68MinA 69-72OakA 72NYA 72TexA	12-14-42	Franklin, N.C.		L	L	6'3	185	19	17	.528	9	216	29	6	450	357	229	272	1	3.22
Romo, Vicente-Vicente [Navarro] (Huevo) — 68LAN 68-69CleA 69-70BosA 71-72ChiA 73-74SDN 82LAN	04-12-43	Santa Rosalia, Mexico		R	R	6'1	185	32	33	.492	52	335	32	4	646	569	280	416	1	3.36
Rose, Don-Donald Gary — 71NYN 72CalA 74SFN	03-19-47	Covina, Cal.		R	R	6'3	195	1	4	.200	0	19	4	0	46	55	20	40	0	4.11
Rounsaville, Gene-Virl Gene — 70ChiA	09-27-44	Konawa, Okla.		R	R	6'3	205	0	1	.000	0	8	0	0	6	10	2	3	0	10.50
Rowe, Don-Donald Howard — 63NYN	04-03-36	Brawley, Cal.	10-15-05	L	L	6'	180	0	0	—	0	26	1	0	55	59	21	27	0	4.25
Rowe, Ken-Kenneth Darrell — 63LAN 64-65BalA	12-31-33	Ferndale, Mich.		R	R	6'2	205	2	1	.667	1	26	0	0	45	55	14	19	0	3.60
Rubio, Jorge-Jorge Jesus [Chavez] — 66-67CalA	04-23-45	Mexicali, Mexico		R	R	6'3	200	3	3	.400	1	10	7	1	42	40	25	31	1	3.21
Rudolph, Don-Frederick Donald — 57-59ChiA 59CinN 62CleA 62-64WasA	08-16-31	Baltimore, Md.	09-12-68	R	L	5'11	195	18	32	.360	3	124	57	10	450	485	102	182	2	4.00
Rusteck, Dick-Richard Frank — 66NYN	07-12-40	Chicago, Ill.		R	L	6'1	175	1	2	.333	0	8	3	1	24	24	8	9	1	3.00
Ryerson, Gary-Gary Lawrence — 72-73MilA	06-17-48	Los Angeles, Cal.		R	L	6'1	180	3	9	.250	0	29	18	4	125	151	28	55	1	4.39
Sadecki, Ray-Raymond Michael — 60-66StlN 66-69SFN 70-74NYN 75StlN 75AtlN 75-76KCA 76MilA 77NYN	12-26-40	Kansas City, Kans.		L	L	5'11	185	135	131	.508	7	563	328	85	2500	2456	922	1614	20	3.78
Sadowski, Bob-Robert F. — 63-65MilN 66BosA	02-19-38	Pittsburgh, Pa.		R	R	6'2	195	20	27	.426	8	115	54	13	440	416	130	257	1	3.87
Sadowski, Ted-Theodore — 60WasA 61-62MinA	04-01-36	Pittsburgh, Pa.	07-18-93	R	R	6'1	190	2	3	.400	1	43	2	0	84	103	31	39	0	5.79
Sanders, Ken-Kenneth George — 64KCA 66BosA 66KCA 68OakA 70-72MilA 73MinA 73-74CleA 74CalA 75-76NYN 76KCA	07-08-41	St. Louis, Mo.		R	R	5'11	180	29	45	.392	86	408	1	0	657	564	258	360	0	2.97
Sanford, Jack-John Stanley — 56-58PhiN 59-65SFN 65-67CalA 67KCA	05-18-29	Wellesley Hills, Mass.	03-07-00	R	R	6'	185	137	101	.576	11	388	293	76	2047	1907	737	1182	14	3.69
Santiago, Jose-Jose Rafael [Alfonso] — 63-65KCA 66-70BosA	08-15-40	Juana Diaz, P.R.		R	R	6'	185	34	29	.540	8	163	65	16	556	518	200	404	3	3.74
Santorini, Al-Alan Joel — 68AtlN 69-71SDN 71-73StlN	05-19-48	Irvington, N.J.		R	R	6'	190	17	38	.309	3	127	70	5	494	533	194	268	4	4.23
Saunders, Dennis-Dennis James (Buttons) — 70DetA	01-04-49	Alhambra, Cal.		R	R	6'3	200	1	1	.500	1	8	0	0	14	16	5	8	0	3.21
Schaeffer, Mark-Mark Phillip — 72SDN	06-05-48	Santa Monica, Cal.		L	L	6'6	220	2	0	1.000	3	41	0	0	41	52	28	25	0	4.61
Scherman, Fred-Frederick John — 69-73DetA 74-75HouN 75-76MonN	07-25-44	Dayton, Ohio		L	L	6'1	195	33	26	.559	39	346	11	1	537	522	245	297	0	3.66
Schmelz, Al-Alan George — 67NYN	11-12-43	Whittier, Cal.		R	R	6'4	210	0	0	—	0	3	0	0	3	4	1	2	0	3.00
Schneider, Dan-Daniel Louis — 63-64MilN 66AtlN 67,69HouN	08-29-42	Evansville, Ind.		L	L	6'3	170	2	5	.286	2	117	8	0	166	185	70	86	0	4.72
Schoen, Jerry-Gerald Thomas — 68WasA	01-15-47	New Orleans, La.		R	R	6'3	215	0	1	.000	0	1	1	0	4	6	1	1	0	6.75
Schultz, Barney-George Warren — 55StlN 59DetA 61-63ChiN 63-65StlN	08-15-26	Beverly, N.J.		R	R	6'2	200	20	20	.500	35	227	0	0	347	303	116	264	0	3.63
Schurr, Wayne-Wayne Allen — 64ChiN	08-06-37	Garrett, Ind.		R	R	6'4	185	0	0	—	0	26	0	0	48	57	11	29	0	3.75
Schwall, Don-Donald Bernard — 61-62BosA 63-66PitN 66-67AtlN	03-02-36	Wilkes-Barre, Pa.		R	R	6'6	200	49	48	.505	4	172	103	18	744	710	391	408	5	3.71
Scott, Dick-Richard Lewis — 63LAN 64ChiN	03-15-33	Portsmouth, N.H.		R	L	6'2	200	0	0	—	0	12	0	0	16	27	4	7	0	8.44
Seale, Johnny-Johnny Ray (The Durango Kid) — 64-65DetA	11-14-38	Edgewater, Colo.		L	L	5'10	155	1	0	1.000	0	8	0	0	13	13	6	8	0	5.54
Secrist, Don-Donald Lavern — 69-70ChiA	02-26-44	Seattle, Wash.		L	L	6'2	195	0	1	.000	0	28	0	0	55	54	26	32	0	5.89
Segui, Diego-Diego Pablo [Gonzalez] — 62-65KCA 66WasA 67KCA 68OakA 69SeaA 70-72OakA 73StlN 74-75BosA 77SeaA	08-17-37	Holguin, Cuba		R	R	6'	190	92	111	.453	71	639	171	28	1808	1656	786	1298	7	3.81
Selma, Dick-Richard Jay — 65-68NYN 69SDN 69ChiN 70-73PhiN 74CalA 74MilA — Bats Both part of 66	11-04-43	Santa Ana, Cal.	08-29-01	R	R	5'11	160	42	54	.438	31	307	76	11	841	734	381	681	6	3.62
Sembera, Carroll-Carroll William — 65-67HouN 68JJ 69-70MonN	07-26-41	Shiner, Tex.	06-15-05	R	R	6'	160	3	11	.214	2	99	1	0	140	149	73	94	0	4.69
Severinsen, Al-Albert Henry — 69BalA 71-72SDN	11-09-44	Brooklyn, N.Y.		R	R	6'3	220	3	7	.300	9	88	0	0	111	104	47	53	0	3.08
Seyfried, Gordon-Gordon Clay — 63-64CleA	07-04-37	Long Beach, Cal.		R	R	6'	185	0	0	—	0	5	1	0	13	13	3	1	0	0.90
Shank, Harvey-Harvey Tillman — 70CalA	07-29-46	Toronto, Canada		R	R	6'4	220	0	0	—	0	1	0	0	3	2	2	1	0	0.00
Shaw, Bob-Robert John — 57-58DetA 58-61ChiA 61CleA 62-63MilN 64-66SFN 66-67NYN 67ChiN	06-29-33	Bronx, N.Y.		R	R	6'2	195	108	98	.524	32	430	223	55	1779	1837	511	880	14	3.52
Shaw, Don-Donald Wellington — 67-68NYN 69MonN 71-72StlN 72OakA	02-23-44	Pittsburgh, Pa.		L	L	6'	185	13	14	.481	6	138	1	0	188	166	101	123	0	4.02
Shea, Steve-Steven Francis — 68HouN 69MonN	12-05-52	Worchester, Mass.		R	R	6'3	215	4	4	.500	4	60	0	0	51	45	19	26	0	3.18
Sheldon, Rollie-Roland Frank — 61-62,64-65NYA 65-66KCA 66BosA	12-17-36	Putnam, Conn.		R	R	6'4	190	38	36	.514	2	160	101	17	725	741	207	371	4	4.08
Shellenback, Jim-James Philip — 66-67,69PitN 69-71WasA 72-74TexA 77MinA	11-18-43	Riverside, Cal.		L	L	6'2	200	16	30	.348	2	165	48	8	455	443	200	222	2	3.80
Sherry, Larry-Lawrence — 58-63LAN 64-67DetA 67HouN 68CalA	07-25-35	Los Angeles, Cal.		R	R	6'2	200	53	44	.546	82	416	16	2	799	747	374	606	1	3.67
Shifflett, Garland-Garland Jessie (Duck) — 57WasA 64MinA	03-28-35	Elkton, Va.		R	R	5'10	165	0	2	.000	1	16	1	0	26	28	17	10	0	6.23
Short, Bill-William Ross — 60NYA 62,66BalA 66BosA 67PitN 68NYN 69CinN	11-27-37	Kingston, N.Y.		L	L	5'9	170	5	11	.313	2	73	16	3	131	130	64	71	1	4.74
Short, Chris-Christopher Joseph — 59-72PhiN 73MilA — Bats Both 70-71	09-19-37	Milford, Del.	08-01-91	L	L	6'4	213	135	132	.506	18	501	308	88	2324	2215	806	1629	24	3.43
Siebert, Sonny-Wilfred Charles — 64-69CleA 69-73BosA 73TexA 74StlN 75SDN 75OakA	01-14-37	St. Mary, Mo.		R	R	6'3	205	140	114	.551	16	399	307	67	2152	1919	692	1512	21	3.21
Siebler, Dwight-Dwight Leroy — 63-67MinA	08-05-37	Columbus, Neb.		R	R	6'2	184	4	3	.571	1	48	6	2	118	97	44	71	0	3.43
Simpson, Steve-Steven Edward — 72SDN	08-30-48	St. Joseph, Mo.	11-02-89	R	R	6'2	205	0	2	.000	2	9	0	0	11	10	7	6	0	4.91
Singer, Bill-William Robert (The Singer Throwing Machine) — 64-72LAN 73-75CalA 76TexA 76MinA 77TorA 78XJ	04-24-44	Los Angeles, Cal.		R	R	6'4	200	118	127	.482	2	322	308	94	2174	1952	781	1515	24	3.39
Sisk, Tommie-Tommie Wayne — 62-68PitN 69SDN 70ChiA	04-12-42	Ardmore, Okla.		R	R	6'3	195	40	49	.449	10	316	99	19	928	937	358	441	4	3.92
Slaughter, Sterling-Sterling Feore (Stu) — 64ChiN	11-18-41	Danville, Ill.		R	R	5'11	165	2	3	.333	0	20	6	1	52	64	32	32	0	5.71
Smith, Bill-William Garland — 58-59ChiA 62PhiN	06-08-34	Washington, D.C.	03-30-97	L	L	6'	190	1	6	.143	0	32	6	0	68	82	17	34	0	4.24
Smith, Jack-Jack Hatfield — 62-63LAN 64MilN	11-15-35	Pikeville, Ky.		R	R	6'	185	2	2	.500	1	34	0	0	49	48	17	31	0	4.59
Smith, Pete-Peter Luke — 62-63BosA	03-19-40	Natick, Mass.		R	R	6'	190	0	1	.000	0	7	0	0	19	19	8	7	0	6.63
Smith, Willie-Willie (Wonderful Willie) (See B61-72) — 63DetA 64LAA 68CleA 68CalA	02-11-39	Anniston, Ala.	01-16-06	L	L	6'	182	2	4	.333	0	29	3	0	62	60	24	39	0	3.05
Spanswick, Bill-William Henry — 64BosA	07-08-38	Springfield, Mass.		L	L	6'3	195	2	3	.400	0	29	7	0	65	75	44	55	0	6.92
Sparma, Joe-Joseph Blase — 64-69DetA 70MonN	02-04-42	Massillon, Ohio	05-14-86	R	R	6'1	194	52	52	.500	0	183	142	31	865	774	436	586	10	3.94
Spinks, Scipio-Scipio Ronald — 69-71HouN 72-73StlN	07-12-47	Chicago, Ill.		R	R	6'2	190	7	11	.389	0	35	29	7	202	175	107	154	0	3.70
Spring, Jack-Jack Russell — 55PhiN 57BosA 58WasA 61-64LAA 64ChiN 64StlN 65CleA	03-11-33	Spokane, Wash.		R	L	6'1	185	12	5	.706	4	155	5	0	186	195	78	86	0	4.26
Sprout, Bob-Robert Samuel — 61LAA	12-05-41	Florin, Pa.		L	L	6'	165	0	0	—	0	1	0	0	4	4	3	2	0	4.50
Stafford, Bill-William Charles — 60-65NYA 66-67KCA	08-13-39	Catskill, N.Y.	09-19-01	R	R	6'1	188	43	40	.518	9	186	104	18	786	707	270	449	6	3.52
Stallard, Tracy-Evan Tracy — 60-62BosA 63-64NYN 65-66StlN	08-31-37	Coeburn, Va.		R	R	6'5	204	30	57	.345	4	183	104	21	765	716	343	477	3	4.16
Stanek, Al-Albert Wilfred (Lefty) — 63SFN	12-24-43	Springfield, Mass.		L	L	5'11	190	0	0	—	0	11	0	0	13	10	12	5	0	4.85
Stange, Lee-Albert Lee — 61-64MinA 64-66CleA 66-70BosA 70ChiA	10-27-36	Chicago, Ill.		R	R	5'10	170	62	61	.504	21	359	115	32	1216	1172	344	718	3	3.56
Starrette, Herm-Herman Paul — 63-65BalA	11-20-38	Statesville, N.C.		R	R	6'	175	1	1	.500	1	27	0	0	46	43	16	21	0	2.54
Steevens, Morrie-Morris Dale — 62ChiN 64-65PhiN	10-07-40	Salem, Ill.		L	L	6'2	185	0	2	.000	0	21	0	0	20	16	11	13	0	4.29
Stenhouse, Dave-David Rotchford — 62-64WasA	09-12-33	Westerly, R.I.		R	R	6'	195	16	28	.364	1	76	56	12	372	339	174	214	3	4.14
Stephan, Buzz-Louis Roberts — 68MinA	07-13-44	Porterville, Cal.		R	R	6'4	205	1	1	.500	0	2	2	0	11	11	7	4	0	4.91
Stephenson, Earl-Chester Earl — 71ChiN 72MilA 77-78BalA	07-31-47	Benson, N.C.		L	L	6'3	190	4	5	.444	1	54	8	1	113	118	49	50	0	3.58
Stephenson, Jerry-Jerry Joseph — 63,65-68BosA 69SeaA 70LAN	10-06-43	Detroit, Mich.		L	R	6'2	195	8	19	.296	1	67	33	3	239	265	145	184	0	5.69
Stigman, Dick-Richard Lewis — 60-61CleA 62-65BosA	01-24-36	Nimrod, Minn.		R	L	6'3	200	46	54	.460	16	235	117	30	923	819	406	755	5	4.03
Stock, Wes-Wesley Gay — 59-64BalA 64-67KCA	04-10-34	Longview, Wash.		R	R	6'2	185	27	13	.675	22	321	5	0	518	434	215	365	0	3.60
Stone, George-George Heard — 67-72AtlN 73-75NYN	07-09-46	Ruston, La.		L	L	6'3	210	60	57	.513	4	203	145	24	1020	1119	270	590	5	3.89
Stoneman, Bill-William Hambly — 67-68ChiN 69-73MonN 74CalA	04-07-44	Oak Park, Ill.		R	R	5'10	170	54	85	.388	0	245	170	46	1238	1182	602	934	15	4.08
Stottlemyre, Mel-Melvin Leon — 64-74NYA	11-13-41	Hazleton, Mo.		R	R	6'1	195	164	139	.541	1	360	356	152	2662	2435	809	1257	40	2.97
Strahler, Mike-Michael Wayne — 70-72LAN 73DetA	03-14-47	Chicago, Ill.		R	R	6'4	185	9	8	.429	1	53	13	2	159	149	79	80	0	3.57
Strampe, Bob-Robert Edwin — 72DetA	06-13-50	Janesville, Wis.		B	R	6'1	185	0	0	—	0	7	0	0	5	6	7	4	0	10.80
Strohmayer, John-John Emery — 70-73MonN 73-74NYN	10-13-46	Belle Fourche, S.D.		R	R	6'	190	11	9	.550	4	127	12	2	313	329	128	200	0	4.46
Such, Dick-Richard Stanley — 70WasA	10-15-44	Sanford, N.C.		R	R	6'4	200	1	5	.167	0	21	6	0	50	48	45	41	0	7.56
Sukla(Suckla), Ed-Edward Anthony — 64LAA 65-66CalA	03-03-43	Long Beach, Cal.		R	R	5'11	170	3	5	.375	4	52	1	0	52	52	26	41	0	5.19
Sutherland, Darrell-Darrell Wayne — 64-66NYN	11-14-41	Glendale, Cal.		R	R	6'2	185	3	4	.429	0	73	1	0	122	131	58	50	0	4.80
Talbot, Fred-Fred Lealand — 63-64ChiA 65-66KCA 66-69NYA 69SeaA 69-70OakA	06-28-41	Washington, D.C.		R	R	6'2	200	38	56	.404	2	195	126	12	854	844	334	449	4	4.12
Tatum, Ken-Kenneth Ray — 69-70CalA 71-73BosA 74ChiA	04-25-44	Alexandria, La.		R	R	6'2	205	16	12	.571	52	176	2	0	283	230	117	156	0	2.93

USE NAMES - GIVEN NAMES (NICKNAMES)	TEAM BY YEAR	BIRTH DATE	BIRTHPLACE	DEATH DATE	B	T	HGT	WGT	W	L	Pct.	SV	G	GS	CG	IP	H	BB	SO	ShO	ERA
Taylor, Chuck-Charles Gilbert	69-71StLN 72NYN 72MilA 73-76MonN	04-18-42	Murfreesboro, Tenn.		R	R	6'2	195	28	20	.583	31	305	21	6	607	576	162	282	2	3.07
Taylor, Gary-Gary William	69DetA	10-19-45	Detroit, Mich.		R	R	6'2	190	0	1	.000	0	7	0	0	10	10	6	3	0	5.40
Taylor, Ron-Ronald Wesley	62CleA 63-65StLN 65-66HouN 67-71NYN 72SDN	12-13-37	Toronto, Canada		R	R	6'1	195	45	43	.511	72	491	17	3	799	794	209	464	0	3.93
Terlecki, Bob-Robert Joseph	72PhiN	02-14-45	Trenton, N.J.		R	R	5'9	183	0	0	—	0	9	0	0	13	16	10	5	0	4.85
Terry, Ralph-Ralph Willard	56-57NYA 57-59KCA 59-64NYA 65CleA 66KCA 66-67NYN	01-09-36	Big Cabin, Okla.		R	R	6'3	195	107	99	.519	11	338	257	75	1850	1748	448	1000	20	3.62
Thies, Dave-David Robert	63KCA	03-21-37	Minneapolis, Minn.		R	R	6'4	205	0	1	.000	0	9	2	0	25	26	12	9	0	4.68
Thoenen, Dick-Richard Crispin	67PhiN	01-09-44	Mexico, Mo.		R	R	6'6	215	0	0	—	0	1	0	0	1	2	0	0	0	9.00
Tiant, Luis-Luis Clemente [Vega]	64-69CleA 70MinA 71-78BosA 79-80NYA 81PitN 82CalA	11-23-40	Marianao, Cuba		R	R	6'	195	229	172	.571	15	573	484	187	3486	3075	1104	2416	49	3.30
Tiefenauer, Bobby-Bobby Gene	52,55StLN 60CleA 61StLN 62HouN 63-65MilN 65NYA 65,67CleA 68ChiN	10-10-29	Desloge, Mo.	06-13-00	R	R	6'2	185	9	25	.265	23	179	0	0	316	312	87	204	0	3.84
Tiefenthaler, Verle-Verle Matthew	62CalA	07-11-37	Breda, Iowa		L	R	6'1	190	0	0	—	0	3	0	0	4	6	7	1	0	9.00
Tillotson, Thad-Thaddeus Asa	67-68NYA	12-20-40	Merced, Cal.		R	R	6'2	195	4	9	.308	2	50	5	1	108	110	46	63	0	4.08
Timberlake, Gary-Gary Dale	69SeaA	08-09-48	Laconia, ind.		R	L	6'2	205	0	0	—	0	2	2	0	6	7	9	4	0	7.50
Timmermann, Tom-Thomas Henry	69-73DetA 73-74CleA	05-12-40	Breese, Ill.		R	R	6'4	215	35	35	.500	36	228	44	8	548	508	208	315	2	3.78
Tompkins, Ron-Ronald Everett (Stretch)	65KCA 71ChiA	11-27-44	San Diego, Cal.		R	R	6'4	198	0	2	.000	3	40	1	0	50	40	24	24	0	3.96
Toppin, Rube-Ruperto	62KCA	12-07-41	Panama, Panama		R	R	6'1	185	0	0	—	0	2	0	0	2	1	5	1	0	13.50
Toth, Paul-Paul Louis	62StLN 62-64ChiN	06-30-35	McRoberts, Ky.	03-20-99	R	R	6'1	192	9	12	.429	0	43	21	5	193	177	54	82	2	3.78
Tsitouris, John-John Philip	57DetA 58-60KCA 62-68CinN	05-04-36	Monroe, N.C.		R	R	6'	175	34	38	.472	3	149	84	18	662	653	260	432	5	4.13
Turner, Ken-Kenneth Charles	67CalA	08-17-43	Framingham, Mass.		R	L	6'2	190	1	2	.333	0	13	1	0	17	16	4	6	0	4.24
Tyriver, Dave-David Burton	62CleA	10-31-37	Oshkosh, Wis.	10-28-88	R	R	6'	175	0	0	—	0	4	0	0	11	10	7	7	0	4.09
Umbach, Arnie-Arnold William	64MilN 66AtlN	12-06-42	Williamsburg, Va.		R	R	6'1	180	1	2	.333	0	23	4	0	49	51	22	30	0	3.12
Umbricht, Jim-James	59-61PitN 62-63HouN	09-17-30	Chicago, Ill.	04-08-64	R	R	6'4	215	9	5	.643	3	88	7	0	194	155	71	133	0	3.06
Upham, John-John Leslie	67-68CinN	12-29-41	Windsor, Canada		L	L	6'	180	0	1	.000	0	7	0	0	8	6	5	4	0	5.63
Upshaw, Cecil-Cecil Lee	66-69AtlN 70PitN 71-73AtlN 73HouN 74CleA 74NYA 75ChiA	10-22-42	Spearsville, La.	02-07-95	R	R	6'6	205	34	36	.486	86	348	0	0	563	545	177	323	0	3.13
Vance, Sandy-Gene Covington	70-71LAN	01-05-47	Lamar, Colo.		R	R	6'	180	9	8	.529	0	30	21	2	141	147	46	56	0	3.83
Vaughan, Charlie-Charles Wayne	66,69AtlN	10-06-47	Mercedes, Tex.		R	L	6'1	185	1	0	1.000	0	3	2	0	9	6	7	7	0	4.50
Veale, Bob-Robert Andrew	62-72PitN 72-74BosA	10-28-35	Birmingham, Ala.		B	L	6'6	218	120	95	.558	21	397	255	78	1926	1684	858	1703	20	3.07
Verbanic, Joe-Joseph Michael	66PhiN 67-68NYA 69SeaA 70NYA	04-24-43	Washington, Pa.		R	R	6'	165	12	11	.522	6	92	17	3	207	210	84	94	2	3.26
Vineyard, Dave-David Kent	64BalA	02-25-41	Clay, W.Va.		R	R	6'3	165	2	5	.286	0	19	6	1	54	57	27	50	0	4.17
Von Hoff, Bruce-Bruce Frederick	65,67HouN	11-17-43	Oakland, Cal.		R	R	6'	187	0	3	.000	0	13	10	0	53	55	30	23	0	5.09
Wagner, Gary-Gary Edward	65-69PhiN 69-70BosA	06-28-40	Bridgeport, Ill.		R	R	6'4	190	15	19	.441	22	162	4	0	266	250	126	174	0	3.72
Wakefield, Bill-William Sumner	64NYN	05-24-41	Kansas City, Mo.		R	R	6'	175	3	5	.375	2	62	4	0	120	103	61	61	0	3.60
Walker, Jerry-Jerry Allen	57-60BalA 61-62KCA 63-64CleA	02-12-39	Ada, Okla.		B R Bats Right 63-64		6'1	195	37	44	.457	13	190	90	16	747	734	341	326	4	4.36
Walker, Luke-James Luke	65-66,68-73PitN 74DetA	09-02-43	DeKalb, Tex.		L	L	6'2	200	45	47	.489	7	243	100	16	826	703	408	558	7	3.64
Walters, Charlie-Charles Leonard	69MinA	02-21-47	Minneapolis, Minn.		R	R	6'4	190	0	0	—	0	6	0	0	7	6	3	2	0	5.14
Wantz, Dick-Richard Carter	65CalA	04-11-40	South Gate, Cal.	05-14-65	R	R	6'5	175	0	0	—	0	1	0	0	1	3	0	2	0	18.00
Warden, Jon-Jonathan Edgar (Warbler)	68DetA 69SJ	10-01-46	Columbus, Ohio		B	L	6'	205	4	1	.800	3	28	0	0	37	30	15	25	0	3.66
Warner, Jack-Jack Dyer	62-65ChiN	07-12-40	Brandywine, W.Va.		R	R	5'11	190	0	2	.000	0	33	0	0	55	64	21	23	0	5.07
Washburn, Greg-Gregory James	69CalA	12-03-46	Coal City, Ill.		R	R	6'	190	0	2	.000	0	8	2	0	11	21	1	4	0	8.18
Washburn, Ray-Ray Clark	61-69StLN 70CinN	05-11-38	Pasco, Wash.		R	R	6'2	200	72	64	.529	5	239	166	25	1208	1208	354	700	10	3.54
Waslewski, Gary-Gary Lee	67-68BosA 69StLN 69-70MonN 70-71NYA 72OakA	07-21-41	Meriden, Conn.		R	R	6'4	195	11	26	.297	5	152	42	5	411	368	197	229	1	3.44
Watkins, Bob-Robert Cecil	69MinA	03-12-48	San Francisco, Cal.		R	R	6'	190	0	0	—	0	5	0	0	16	13	13	11	0	5.06
Watt, Eddie-Eddie Dean	66-73BalA 74PhiN 75ChiN	04-04-41	Lamoni, Iowa		R	R	5'10	190	38	36	.514	80	411	13	1	660	530	254	462	0	2.90
Weaver, Floyd-David Floyd	62,65CleA 70ChiA 71MilA	05-12-41	Ben Franklin, Tex.		R	R	6'4	195	4	5	.444	1	85	5	0	155	149	73	108	0	5.23
Weaver, Jim-James Brian (Fluff)	67-68CalA	02-19-39	Lancaster, Pa.		L	L	6'	178	3	1	.750	1	27	2	0	53	48	19	28	8	2.55
Wegener, Mike-Michael Denis	69-70MonN	10-08-46	Denver, Colo.		R	R	6'4	215	8	20	.286	0	57	42	5	270	250	152	159	1	4.73
Wenz, Fred-Frederick Charles (Fireball)	68-69BosA 70PhiN	08-26-41	Bound Brook, N.J.		R	R	6'3	214	3	0	1.000	1	31	0	0	42	36	25	38	0	4.71
Whillock, Jack-Jack Franklin	71DetA	11-04-42	Searcy, Ark.		R	R	6'3	195	0	2	.000	0	7	0	0	8	10	2	6	0	5.63
Whitby, Bill-William Edward	64MinA	07-29-43	Crewe, Va.		R	R	6'1	190	0	0	—	0	4	0	0	6	8	1	2	0	9.00
Wickersham, Dave-David Clifford	60-63KCA 64-67DetA 68PitN 69KCA	09-27-35	Erie, Pa.		R	R	6'3	195	68	57	.544	18	228	124	29	1123	1071	384	638	5	3.66
Wilhelm, Hoyt-James Hoyt	52-56NYN 57StLN 57-58CleA 58-62BalA 63-68ChiA 69CalA 69-70AtlN 70ChiN 71AtlN 71-72LAN	07-26-22	Huntersville, N.C.	08-23-02	R	R	6'	190	143	122	.540	227	1070	52	20	2253	1757	778	1610	5	2.52
Willey, Carl-Carlton Francis	58-62MilN 63-65NYN	06-06-31	Cherryfield, Me.		R	R	6'	175	38	58	.396	1	199	117	28	876	830	326	493	11	3.76
Willhite, Nick-Jon Nicholas	63-64LAN 65WasA 65-66LAN 67CalA 67MinN	01-27-41	Tulsa, Okla.		L	L	6'2	195	6	12	.333	1	58	29	3	182	195	75	118	1	4.55
Williams, Don-Donald Reid (Dino)	63MinA	09-02-35	Los Angeles, Cal.	12-20-91	R	R	6'5	218	0	0	—	0	3	0	0	4	8	6	2	0	11.25
Williams, Stan-Stanley Wilson	58-62LAN 63-64NYA 65,67-69CleA 70-71MinA 71StLN 72BosA	09-14-36	Enfield, N.H.		R	R	6'5	230	109	94	.537	43	482	208	42	1763	1527	748	1305	11	3.48
Willis, Dale-Dale Jerome	63KCA	05-29-38	Calhoun, Ga.		R	R	5'11	165	0	2	.000	1	25	0	0	45	46	25	47	0	5.00
Willis, Ron-Ronald Earl	66-69StLN 69HouN 70SDN	07-12-43	Willisville, Tenn.	11-21-77	R	R	6'2	185	11	12	.478	19	188	0	0	239	209	119	128	0	3.31
Wills, Ted-Theodore Carl	59-62BosA 62CinN 65ChiA	02-09-34	Fresno, Cal.		L	L	6'2	200	8	11	.421	5	83	13	2	186	210	97	133	0	5.52
Wilson, Billy-William Harlan	69-70PhiN	09-21-42	Pomeroy, Ohio	08-11-93	R	R	6'2	200	9	15	.375	17	179	0	0	258	229	131	171	0	4.22
Wilson, Don-Donald Edward	66-74HouN	02-12-45	Monroe, La.	01-05-75	R	R	6'3	205	104	92	.531	2	266	245	78	1748	1479	640	1283	20	3.15
Wilson, Earl-Earl (Earl Lawrence)-Robert Earl	59-60,62-66BosA 66-70DetA 70SDN	10-02-34	Ponchatoula, La.	04-23-05	R	R	6'3	216	121	109	.526	0	338	310	69	2052	1863	796	1452	13	3.69
Wolf, Wally-Walter Beck	69-70CalA	01-05-42	Los Angeles, Cal.		R	R	6'	190	0	0	—	0	6	0	0	7	6	7	7	0	7.71
Womack, Dooley-Horace Guy	66-68NYA 69HouN 69SeaA 70OakA	08-25-39	Columbia, S.C.		L	R	6'	170	19	18	.514	24	193	1	0	302	253	111	177	0	2.95
Wood, Wilbur-Wilbur Forrester	61-64BosA 64-65PitN 67-78ChiA	10-22-41	Cambridge, Mass.		L	L	6'	190	164	156	.513	57	651	297	114	2684	2582	724	1411	24	3.24
Woodeshick, Hal-Harold Joseph	58DetA 58CleA 59-61WasA 61DetA 62-65HouN 65-67StLN	08-24-32	Wilkes-Barre, Pa.		R	L	6'3	200	44	62	.415	61	427	62	7	847	816	389	484	1	3.56
Woodson, Dick-Richard Lee	69-70,72-74MinA 74NYA	03-30-45	Oelwein, Iowa		R	R	6'5	205	34	32	.515	2	137	76	15	589	522	253	315	5	3.47
Worthington, Al-Allan Fulton (Red)	53-54,56-57NYN 58-59SFN 60BosA 60ChiA 63-64CinN 64-69MinA	02-05-29	Birmingham, Ala.		R	R	6'2	205	75	82	.478	110	602	69	11	1245	1130	527	834	3	3.39
Wright, Clyde-Clyde	66-73CalA 74MilA 75TexA	02-20-41	Jefferson City, Tenn.		R	L	6'1	195	100	111	.474	3	329	235	67	1729	1679	550	667	9	3.50
Wright, Ken-Kenneth Warren	70-73KCA 74NYA	09-04-46	Pensacola, Fla.		R	R	6'2	230	11	15	.423	8	113	24	2	236	195	180	181	1	4.54
Wyatt, John-John Thomas	61-66KCA 66-68BosA 68NYA 68DetA 69OakA	04-19-35	Chicago, Ill.	04-06-98	R	R	5'11	205	42	44	.488	103	435	9	0	686	600	346	540	0	3.48
Wynne, Billy-Billy Vernon	67NYN 68-70ChiA 71CalA	07-31-43	Williamston, N.C.		L	R	6'3	205	8	11	.421	0	42	30	6	188	217	78	97	1	4.31
Yellen, Larry-Lawrence Allen	63-64HouN	01-04-43	Brooklyn, N.Y.		R	R	5'11	190	0	0	—	0	14	2	0	26	34	11	12	0	6.23
Yount, Larry-Lawrence King	71HouN	02-15-50	Houston, Tex.		R	R	6'3	195	0	0	—	0	1	0	0	0	0	0	0	0	—
Zachary, Chris-William Christopher	63-67HouN 69KCA 71StLN 72DetA 73PitN	02-19-44	Knoxville, Tenn.	04-19-03	L	R	6'2	200	10	29	.256	2	108	40	1	321	344	122	184	1	4.51
Zanni, Dom-Dominick Thomas	58-59,61SFN 62-63ChiA 63,65-66CinN	03-01-32	Bronx, N.Y.		R	R	5'11	180	9	6	.600	10	111	3	0	182	155	85	148	0	3.81
Zepp, Bill-William Clinton	69-70MinA 71DetA	07-22-46	Detroit, Mich.		R	R	6'2	185	10	5	.667	4	63	24	1	188	201	72	81	1	3.64

1973-2006

1973 O, Charley O.

In a season which saw Hank Aaron come within one of Babe Ruth's lifetime home run record, Nolan Ryan go beyond Sandy Koufax's single-season strikeout record, and the American League offer a rule which dramatically changed the style of play in the junior circuit, the unpredictable New York Mets stole the whole show with their late-season theatrics. If the Mets had any rival for showmanship and fanfare, it wasn't a team but an individual in Charley O. Finley, owner of the Oakland Athletics. While the Mets earned their half of the twin billing in baseball's 1973 extravaganza by proving the best of the worst in the National League's Eastern Division, Finley arrived on the balanced strength of the A's, who proved the class of the American League West.

In reaching the second World Series in their short history, the Mets waited until September before awakening to the fact that winning was an important part of baseball. Yet, in all fairness to the Amazing Nine from Flushing Meadows, several key injuries threw their balance out of wack. Shortstop Bud Harrelson, the secret to the infield, catcher Jerry Grote, and left fielder Cleon Jones all sat out at least one month with injuries and Willie Mays, who finally said good-bye to baseball after 21 years, played only 66 games as a result of injuries and age. While the Mets were suffering their woes, the senior circuit race went on as usual. But in all respects neither the race nor the finish had anything commonplace about it.

The St. Louis Cardinals started out in dismal fashion and soon found themselves in the cellar. The Pittsburgh Pirates entered the season without superstar Roberto Clemente, the victim of a tragic plane accident on December 31, 1972, and tried to fill the vacant spot in right field with the bat of catcher Manny Sanguillen— a move which kept the Pirates away from the top until they finally sent Sanguillen behind the plate. And while the Phillies were experiencing shock with the drastic reversal of form in Steve Carlton, the 1972 Cy Young winner, Montreal had found some consistency due to the development of Ken Singleton and the super endurance of relief specialist Mike Marshall. The Cubs, once again trying for Eastern honors, and using the experience of an aging ball club, soon found themselves in the top spot as the All-Star game approached.

However, by the time the morning of August 17 arrived, St. Louis was magically transplanted in first place by three games over the Pirates and the Cubs were in fourth, 5½ back. Montreal was seemingly in the midst of a miracle with third-place occupancy and the Mets in last, 7½ off the leader. Yet neither the scramble, nor the race, was over yet, and by early September every team, including the Mets, still had a shot at the top. Then, as the Mets regulars began to return and the victories became consistent, a critical blow came to the Cardinals when their ace righty, Bob Gibson, injured his leg and was shelved until the last weekend of the season. By September 20, Pittsburgh had taken over the lead with the Cubs in fifth, four games off the pace. Only the Phillies, then 9½ back, could be counted out. Finally on the 27th, the Mets found themselves in first and Montreal in fifth by a scant 4½ games.

During the last weekend of the regular season, Pittsburgh finally eliminated Montreal, and St. Louis beat back Philadelphia to still have a chance depending upon the outcome of the Mets-Cubs series in Chicago. Rainouts had caused the Mets to play four games in two days with the Cubs as well as force the regular season a day past its regular schedule when the Mets could only split the first two to give St. Louis, Pittsburgh and even Chicago a chance. The sky was still heavy with clouds when the Mets and Cubs took to the field on October 1st, but Jon Matlack, pitching a strong two-hit shutout, gave the Mets the first game and the Eastern Division title.

For the Mets, in coming out of the mediocre rubble to post the lowest winning percentage of any pennant winner in baseball history, the credit belonged to Cy Young winner Tom Seaver, who won 19 games in posting a league-low 2.08 E.R.A., Tug McGraw, who recovered from early season lethargy to save 25 games and start the phrase, "You Gotta Believe", Jon Matlack, who won 14 games and lost a lot of tough decisions and Felix Millan, who came over from the Braves to hit .290 to keep the Mets in contention. For manager Yogi Berra, the victory couldn't have been sweeter as it quickly transformed him from inept to hero as he became the only manager besides Joe McCarthy to win pennants in both leagues.

In the National League West the furor ended early. After the Dodgers, led by several promising youngsters, gained the lead in the first half of the season, the Cincinnati Reds came on behind the MVP performance of Pete Rose, who collected 230 hits, the slugging of Tony Perez, who hit .314 with 27 home runs and 101 RBI's, Johnny Bench, who hit 25 home runs after successfully going through a winter lung operation, and Joe Morgan. Third-place San Francisco had to settle for the growing maturity of Bobby Bonds, who hit 39 home runs, and the arrival of pitcher Ron Bryant, who won a league high 24 games without the help of a single shutout. For the Braves, there was a lot of home run hitting and little pitching— all facts which were mostly obscured by Hank Aaron's drive toward Babe Ruth's lifetime home run record of 714. Aaron, who finished fourth in the league with 40 home runs, went into the last game of the season with a chance to tie the record.

But with the commissioner Bowie Kuhn in attendance, as well as a lot of the press, Aaron could only manage three singles and finish the year with 713 home runs. Teammate Dave Johnson, who came over from the Orioles and who never hit more than 18 home runs in the American League, surprised many by belting 43 home runs to eclipse the second baseman's home run mark set by the legendary Rogers Hornsby. Third baseman Darrell Evans finished between the two with 41 round-trippers to give Atlanta the top three spots behind league-leader Willie Stargell of Pittsburgh.

In the American League the season began with the innovation of a new rule which allowed the manager to name a "designated hitter" to bat throughout the game for the pitcher, and the move, which was designed to bolster the action, instead produced a record twelve 20-game winners. Armed with the best of this new breed, the Orioles began a resurgence which gave them the Eastern title by eight games over the Red Sox. For Baltimore, Tommy Davis found enough success in the designated hitter spot to hit .293 and Orlando Cepeda, signed by the Red Sox after Oakland released him, took top power honors for designated hitters with 20 home runs. Baltimore's return to the top was also sparked by the superb play of rookies, Al Bumbry and Rich Coggins, and the stellar pitching of Jim Palmer, who posted a 22-9 season with a league-low 2.40 E.R.A. to win the Cy Young Award. For third-place Detroit, who managed to stay in the race until the Orioles started their late-season winning skein, there was some consolation in John Hiller's 38 saves—a major league record.

Over in the Western Division, the White Sox began the season by throwing knuckle-baller Wilbur Wood so often that it seemed he would have no trouble posting 40 victories. But as things turned out Wood finished at 24-20 and Chicago in fifth, 17 games back. Whatever chance Chicago might have had was lost when Dick Allen, the highest paid player in baseball, broke his leg in mid-season and was sidelined for the year. Oakland, on the other hand, had no costly injuries until late in the year, and managed to again take the Western title, this time by six games over oncoming Kansas City. Led by MVP Reggie Jackson, the A's managed their return on the arms of the division's best mound staff which consisted of starters Catfish Hunter, Ken Holtzman, and Vida Blue, and ace reliever Rollie Fingers. Also included in manager Dick Williams' star-studded cast was shortstop Bert Campaneris, third baseman Sal Bando, first baseman Gene Tenace, and young center fielder Billy North. For the California Angels, who finished fourth, the only satisfaction came in Nolan Ryan, who hurled two no-hitters and burned his way past 383 batters to set a new major league strikeout record.

In the American League championship play-off series, Oakland and Baltimore played out the five game string before the A's emerged victorious with a 3-0 performance from Hunter. In the National League series, the frenzy of the Mets' fans nearly put a premature end to play. The fans' hysteria was ignited by a fight between Rose and Harrelson in the third game. But after order had been restored, the fans' anger continued and when Rose returned to his left field position, he was bombarded by whatever objects the fans could find to throw. Finally Rose, in an effort to save himself from injury, marched off the field. He was followed by the other Reds and only after Willie Mays, Tom Seaver, and a few other Mets went out to left field to plead with the fans did they begin to settle down. Although the hostilities continued throughout the series, the Mets, behind Tom Seaver and Tug McGraw, posted a win in the fifth game to give New York the National League pennant.

By the time the World Series started Met fans were already exhausted from all the fanfare which led up to the fall classic. But their fatigue quickly diminished and their fears began when Oakland got off to an opening game extra inning victory. In the second game, the Series again went beyond the ninth frame, but this time the Mets emerged the winner. As the see-saw Series continued the Mets pitching completely cut off the A's home run power. However, the A's battled the Mets despite their failure to hit a single home run, and when Reggie Jackson's three clutch hits beat Seaver in the sixth game, the Series went into a crucial seventh game showdown. With singles hitter Bert Campaneris and Reggie Jackson both hitting two-run home runs in the third inning, Oakland routed Matlack and came away with a 5-2 victory and their second straight world's championship.

Although the Series had its usual excitement and great moments of play, they were matters which became overshadowed by Finley's off the field maneuvers when, in the second game reserve second baseman Mike Andrews came in and committed two errors to give the Mets a victory. After the game Finley put Andrews on the disabled list and the Oakland players and the press screamed bloody murder. Andrews was restored to the active roster for the next game on orders of Commissioner Kuhn and he received a standing ovation, even from Finley, when he came out of the dugout to pinch hit. But for all the final victory, Finley lost his manager, Dick Williams, who publicly announced his displeasure with Finley's interference, and left the team after the series was over.

BALTIMORE — 1st 97-65 .599 — EARL WEAVER

NAME	G by Pos	B	AGE	G	AB	R	H	2B	3B	HR	RBI	BB	SO	SB	BA	SA
TOTALS			28	162	5537	754	1474	229	48	119	692	648	752	146	.266	.389
Boog Powell	1B111	L	31	114	370	52	98	13	1	11	54	85	64	0	.265	.395
Bobby Grich	2B162	R	24	162	581	82	146	29	7	12	50	107	91	17	.251	.387
Mark Belanger	SS154	R	29	154	470	60	106	15	1	0	27	49	54	13	.226	.262
Brooks Robinson	3B154	R	36	155	549	53	141	17	2	9	72	55	50	2	.257	.344
Don Baylor	OF110, 1B6, DH1	R	24	118	405	64	116	20	4	11	51	35	48	32	.286	.437
Paul Blair	OF144, DH1	R	29	146	500	73	140	25	3	10	64	43	72	18	.280	.402
Rich Coggins	OF101, DH1	L	22	110	389	54	124	19	9	7	41	28	24	17	.319	.468
Earl Williams	C95, 1B42, DH2	R	24	132	459	58	109	18	1	22	83	66	107	0	.237	.425
Tommy Davis	DH127, 1B4	R	34	137	552	53	169	20	3	7	89	30	56	11	.306	.391
Al Bumbry	OF86, DH7	L	26	110	356	73	120	15	11	7	34	34	49	23	.337	.500
Merv Rettenmund	OF90	R	30	95	321	59	84	17	2	9	44	57	38	11	.262	.411
Andy Etchebarren	C51	R	30	54	152	16	39	9	1	2	13	12	21	1	.257	.368
Terry Crowley	DH23, OF10, 1B7	L	26	54	131	16	27	4	0	3	15	16	14	0	.206	.305
Frank Baker	SS32, 2B7, 1B1, 3B1	L	26	44	63	10	12	1	2	1	11	7	7	0	.190	.317
Ellie Hendricks (BN)	C38, DH1	L	32	41	101	9	18	5	1	3	15	10	22	0	.178	.337
Enos Cabell	1B23, 3B1	R	23	32	47	12	10	2	0	1	3	3	7	1	.213	.319
Larry Brown	3B15, 2B1	R	33	17	28	4	7	0	0	1	5	5	4	0	.250	.357
Doug DeCinces	3B8, 2B2, SS1	R	22	10	18	2	2	0	0	0	3	1	5	0	.111	.111
Jim Fuller	OF5, 1B2, DH1	R	22	9	26	2	3	0	0	2	4	1	17	0	.115	.346
Sergio Robles	C8	R	27	8	13	0	1	0	0	0	0	0	3	1	.077	.077
Curt Motton	OF1, DH1	R	32	5	6	2	2	0	0	1	4	1	1	0	.333	.833

NAME	T	AGE	W	L	PCT	SV	G	GS	CG	IP	H	BB	SO	SHO	ERA
		28	97	65	.599	26	162	162	67	1462	1297	475	715	14	3.07
Jim Palmer	R	27	22	9	.710	1	38	37	19	296	225	113	158	6	2.40
Mike Cuellar	R	36	18	13	.581	0	38	38	17	267	265	84	140	2	3.27
Dave McNally	R	30	17	17	.500	0	38	38	17	266	247	81	87	4	3.21
Doyle Alexander (EJ)	R	22	12	8	.600	0	29	26	10	175	169	52	63	0	3.86
Grant Jackson	L	30	8	0	1.000	9	45	0	0	80	54	24	47	0	1.91
Bob Reynolds	R	26	7	5	.583	9	42	1	0	111	88	31	77	0	1.95
Jesse Jefferson	R	24	6	5	.545	0	18	15	3	101	104	46	52	0	4.10
Don Hood	L	23	3	2	.600	1	8	4	1	32	31	6	18	1	3.94
Eddie Watt	R	32	3	4	.429	5	30	0	0	71	62	21	38	0	3.30
1 Orlando Pena	R	39	1	1	.500	1	11	2	0	45	36	8	23	0	4.00
1 Mickey Scott	L	25	0	0	—	0	4	0	0	2	2	2	2	0	4.50
Wayne Garland	R	22	0	1	.000	0	4	1	0	16	14	7	10	0	3.94

BOSTON — 2nd 89-73 .549 8 — EDDIE KASKO 88-73 .547 — EDDIE POPOWSKI 1-0 1.000

NAME	G by Pos	B	AGE	G	AB	R	H	2B	3B	HR	RBI	BB	SO	SB	BA	SA
TOTALS			29	162	5513	738	1472	235	30	147	692	581	799	114	.267	.401
Carl Yastrzemski	1B107, 3B31, OF14	L	33	152	540	82	160	25	4	19	95	105	58	9	.296	.463
Doug Griffin (BH)	2B113	R	26	113	396	43	101	14	5	1	33	21	42	7	.255	.323
Luis Aparicio	SS132	R	39	132	499	56	135	17	1	0	49	43	33	13	.271	.309
Rico Petrocelli (EJ)	3B99	R	30	100	356	44	87	13	1	13	45	47	64	0	.244	.396
Reggie Smith	OF104, DH8, 1B1	B	28	115	423	79	128	23	2	21	69	68	49	3	.303	.515
Tommy Harper	OF143, DH1	R	32	147	566	92	159	23	3	17	71	61	93	54	.281	.422
Rick Miller	OF137	L	25	143	441	65	115	17	7	6	43	51	59	12	.261	.372
Carlton Fisk	C131, DH3	R	25	135	508	65	125	21	0	26	71	37	99	7	.246	.441
Orlando Cepeda	DH142	R	35	142	550	51	159	25	0	20	86	50	81	0	.289	.444
Dwight Evans	OF113, DH2	R	21	119	282	46	63	13	1	10	32	40	52	5	.223	.383
John Kennedy	2B31, 3B24, DH9	R	32	67	155	17	28	9	1	1	16	12	45	0	.181	.271
Mike Guerrero	SS46, 2B24	R	23	66	219	19	51	5	2	0	11	10	21	2	.233	.274
Danny Cater	1B37, 3B21, OF4	R	33	63	195	30	61	12	0	1	24	10	12	0	.313	.390
Ben Oglivie	OF32, DH13	L	24	58	147	16	32	9	1	2	9	9	32	1	.218	.333
Bob Montgomery	C33	R	29	34	128	18	41	6	2	7	25	7	36	0	.320	.563
Cecil Cooper	1B29	R	23	30	101	12	24	2	0	3	11	7	12	1	.238	.347
Buddy Hunter	3B3, 2B2, DH1	R	25	13	7	3	3	1	0	0	2	3	1	0	.429	.571
Duane Josephson (IL) 31																

NAME	T	AGE	W	L	PCT	SV	G	GS	CG	IP	H	BB	SO	SHO	ERA
		30	89	73	.549	33	162	162	67	1440	1417	499	808	10	3.65
Luis Tiant	R	32	20	13	.606	0	35	35	23	272	217	78	206	0	3.34
Bill Lee	L	26	17	11	.607	1	38	33	18	285	275	76	120	1	2.75
Marty Pattin	R	30	15	15	.500	1	34	30	11	219	238	69	119	2	4.32
Roger Moret (KJ)	L	23	13	2	.867	3	30	15	5	156	138	67	90	2	3.17
John Curtis	L	25	13	13	.500	0	35	30	10	221	225	83	101	4	3.58
Dick Pole	R	22	3	2	.600	0	12	7	0	55	70	18	24	0	5.56
Bobby Bolin	R	34	3	4	.429	15	39	0	0	53	45	13	31	0	2.72
Bob Veale	L	37	2	3	.400	1	32	0	0	36	37	12	25	0	3.50
Ray Culp (SJ)	R	31	2	6	.250	0	10	9	0	50	46	32	32	0	4.50
Lynn McGlothen (KJ)	R	23	1	2	.333	0	3	3	0	23	39	8	16	0	8.22
Mike Garman	R	23	0	0	—	0	12	0	0	22	32	15	9	0	5.32
Don Newhauser (XJ)	R	25	0	0	—	1	9	0	0	12	9	13	8	0	0.00
Ken Tatum	R	29	0	0	—	0	7	0	0	9	12	9	3	0	6.21
Craig Skok	L	25	0	1	.000	0	11	0	0	29	35	11	22	0	6.21
1 Sonny Siebert	R	36	0	0	—	0	1	1	0	5	5	2	5	0	9.00

DETROIT — 3rd 85-77 .525 12 — BILLY MARTIN 71-63 .530 — JOE SCHULTZ 14-14 .500

NAME	G by Pos	B	AGE	G	AB	R	H	2B	3B	HR	RBI	BB	SO	SB	BA	SA
TOTALS			32	162	5508	642	1400	213	32	157	592	509	722	28	.254	.390
Norm Cash	1B114, DH3	L	38	121	363	51	95	19	0	19	40	47	73	1	.262	.471
Dick McAuliffe	2B102, SS2, DH1	L	33	106	343	39	94	18	1	12	44	49	52	0	.274	.437
Eddie Brinkman	SS162	R	31	162	515	55	122	16	4	7	40	34	79	0	.237	.324
Aurelio Rodriguez	3B160, SS1	R	25	160	555	46	123	27	3	9	58	31	85	3	.222	.330
Jim Northrup	OF116	L	33	119	404	55	124	14	7	12	44	38	41	4	.307	.465
Mickey Stanley	OF157	R	30	157	602	81	147	23	5	17	57	48	65	0	.244	.384
Willie Horton	OF107, DH1	R	30	111	411	42	130	19	3	17	53	23	57	1	.316	.501
Bill Freehan	C98, 1B7, DH1	R	31	110	380	33	89	10	1	6	29	40	30	0	.234	.313
Gates Brown	DH119, OF2	L	34	125	377	48	89	11	1	12	50	52	41	1	.236	.366
Al Kaline	OF63, 1B36	R	38	91	310	40	79	13	0	10	45	29	28	4	.255	.394
Dick Sharon	OF91	R	23	91	178	20	43	9	0	7	16	10	31	2	.242	.410
Frank Howard	DH76, 1B2	R	36	85	227	26	58	9	1	12	29	24	28	0	.256	.463
Tony Taylor	2B72, 1B6, 3B4, DH2, OF1	R	37	84	275	35	63	9	3	5	24	17	29	9	.229	.338
Duke Sims	C68, OF6	L	32	80	252	31	61	10	0	8	30	30	36	1	.242	.377
1 Rich Reese	1B37, OF21	L	31	59	160	14	22	4	0	2	4	7	17	0	.137	.206
Ike Brown	1B21, OF12, 3B2, DH2	R	31	42	76	12	22	2	1	1	9	15	13	0	.289	.382
Tom Veryzer	SS18	R	20	18	20	1	6	0	1	0	2	2	4	0	.300	.400
Ron Cash	OF7, 3B6	L	23	14	39	8	16	1	1	0	6	5	5	0	.410	.487
John Knox	2B9	L	24	13	32	1	9	1	0	0	3	3	1	1	.281	.313
Joe Staton	1B5	L	25	9	17	2	4	1	0	0	0	1	4	0	.235	.235
Bob Didier	C7	R	24	7	22	3	10	1	0	0	4	2	1	0	.455	.500
John Gamble		R	25	7	0	1	0	0	0	0	0	0	0	0	—	—
Marvin Lane	OF4	R	23	6	8	2	2	1	0	0	1	0	4	0	.250	.625

NAME	T	AGE	W	L	PCT	SV	G	GS	CG	IP	H	BB	SO	SHO	ERA
		30	85	77	.525	46	162	162	39	1448	1468	493	911	11	3.90
Joe Coleman	R	26	23	15	.605	0	40	40	13	288	283	93	202	2	3.53
Mickey Lolich	L	32	16	15	.516	0	42	42	17	309	315	79	214	3	3.82
Jim Perry	R	37	14	13	.519	0	35	34	7	203	225	55	66	1	4.03
John Hiller	L	30	10	5	.667	38	65	0	0	125	89	39	124	0	1.44
Woody Fryman	L	33	6	13	.316	0	34	29	1	170	200	64	119	0	5.35
2 Bob Miller	R	34	6	4	.667	1	22	0	0	42	34	22	23	0	3.43
Mike Strahler	R	26	4	5	.444	0	22	11	1	80	84	39	37	0	4.39
2 Ed Farmer	R	23	3	0	1.000	2	24	0	0	45	52	27	28	0	5.00
Fred Scherman	L	28	2	2	.500	1	34	0	0	62	59	30	28	0	4.21
Chuck Seelbach (SJ)	R	25	1	0	1.000	0	5	0	0	7	7	2	2	0	3.86
1 Tom Timmermann	R	33	1	1	.500	1	17	1	0	39	39	11	21	0	3.69
Lerrin LaGrow (SA)	R	24	1	5	.167	3	21	3	0	54	54	23	33	0	4.33
Gary Ignasiak	L	23	0	0	—	0	3	0	0	5	3	4	0	0	3.60
Bill Slayback	R	25	0	0	—	0	5	1	0	11	9	5	8	0	4.50
Dave Lemanczyk	R	22	0	0	—	0	4	0	0	2	5	5	2	0	13.50
Fred Holdsworth	R	21	0	1	.000	0	5	1	0	13	16	6	9	0	6.60

NEW YORK — 4th 80-82 .494 17 — RALPH HOUK

NAME	G by Pos	B	AGE	G	AB	R	H	2B	3B	HR	RBI	BB	SO	SB	BA	SA
TOTALS			30	162	5492	641	1435	212	17	131	616	489	680	47	.261	.378
1 Felipe Alou	1B67, OF22	R	38	93	280	25	66	12	0	4	27	9	25	0	.236	.321
Horace Clarke	2B147	B	33	148	590	60	155	21	0	2	35	47	48	11	.263	.308
Gene Michael	SS129	R	35	129	418	30	94	11	1	3	47	26	51	1	.225	.278
Graig Nettles	3B157, DH2	L	28	160	552	65	129	18	0	22	81	78	76	0	.234	.386
1 Matty Alou	OF85, 1B40, DH1	L	34	123	497	59	147	22	1	2	28	30	43	5	.296	.366
Bobby Murcer	OF160	L	27	160	616	83	187	29	2	22	95	50	67	6	.304	.464
Roy White	OF162	B	29	162	639	88	157	22	3	18	60	78	81	16	.246	.374
Thurman Munson	C142, DH1	R	26	147	519	80	156	29	4	20	74	48	64	4	.301	.487
2 Jim Ray Hart	DH106	R	31	114	339	29	86	13	2	13	52	36	45	0	.254	.419
Ron Blomberg	DH55, 1B41	L	24	100	301	45	99	13	1	12	57	34	25	0	.329	.498
Johnny Callison	OF32, DH10	L	34	45	136	10	24	4	0	1	10	4	24	1	.176	.228
2 Mike Hegan	1B30	L	30	37	131	12	36	3	2	6	14	7	34	0	.275	.466
Hal Lanier	SS26, 2B8, 3B1	R	30	35	86	9	18	3	0	0	5	3	8	0	.209	.244
Ron Swoboda	OF29, DH4	R	29	35	63	6	5	0	0	1	2	4	18	0	.116	.186
Celerino Sanchez	3B11, DH11, SS2, OF2	R	29	34	64	12	14	3	0	0	7	3	12	1	.219	.313
Fred Stanley	SS21, 2B3	R	25	26	66	6	14	0	1	1	5	7	16	0	.212	.288
Otto Velez	OF23	R	22	23	77	9	15	4	0	2	7	15	24	0	.195	.325
Jerry Moses	C17, DH1	R	26	21	59	15	15	2	0	0	3	4	5	0	.254	.288
1 Bernie Allen	2B13, DH2	L	34	17	57	5	13	3	0	0	4	4	5	0	.228	.281
Rick Dempsey	C5	R	23	6	11	0	2	0	0	0	1	1	1	0	.182	.182
2 Duke Sims	DH2, C1	L	32	4	9	1	3	0	0	0	0	0	2	0	.333	.667

NAME	T	AGE	W	L	PCT	SV	G	GS	CG	IP	H	BB	SO	SHO	ERA
		30	80	82	.494	39	162	162	47	1428	1379	457	708	16	3.34
Mel Stottlemyre	R	31	16	16	.500	0	38	38	19	273	259	79	95	4	3.07
Doc Medich	R	24	14	9	.609	0	34	32	11	235	217	74	145	3	2.95
Lindy McDaniel	R	37	12	6	.667	10	47	3	1	160	148	49	93	0	2.87
2 Pat Dobson	R	31	9	8	.529	0	22	21	6	142	150	34	70	1	4.18
Fritz Peterson	R	31	8	15	.348	0	31	31	6	188	207	49	59	0	3.96
Fred Beene	R	30	6	0	1.000	1	19	4	0	91	67	27	49	0	1.68
2 Sam McDowell	L	30	5	8	.385	0	16	15	2	96	73	64	75	1	3.94
Sparky Lyle	L	28	5	9	.357	27	51	0	0	82	66	18	63	0	2.52
Steve Kline (EJ)	R	25	4	7	.364	0	14	13	2	74	76	31	19	1	4.01
1 Mike Kekich	L	28	1	1	.500	0	5	4	0	15	20	14	4	0	9.00
Dave Pagan	R	23	0	0	—	0	13	0	0	13	11	9	6	0	2.77
Casey Cox	R	31	0	0	—	0	3	0	0	3	5	1	0	0	6.00
Tom Buskey	R	27	0	0	1.000	1	8	0	0	18	18	4	8	0	5.29
Jim Magnuson	L	26	0	0	—	0	4	0	0	27	38	9	4	0	4.33
2 Wayne Granger	R	29	0	0	.000	0	7	0	0	15	19	3	10	0	1.80

MILWAUKEE — 5th 74-88 .457 23 — DEL CRANDALL

NAME	G by Pos	B	AGE	G	AB	R	H	2B	3B	HR	RBI	BB	SO	SB	BA	SA
TOTALS			26	162	5526	708	1399	229	40	145	669	563	977	110	.253	.388
George Scott	1B157, DH1	R	29	158	604	98	185	30	4	24	107	61	94	9	.306	.488
Pete Garcia	2B160	R	23	160	580	67	142	32	5	15	54	40	119	11	.245	.395
Tim Johnson	SS135	L	23	136	465	39	99	10	2	0	32	29	93	6	.213	.243
Don Money	3B124, SS21	R	26	145	590	57	155	28	2	11	61	53	53	22	.263	.401
Bob Coluccio	OF108, DH11	R	21	124	438	65	98	21	8	15	58	54	92	13	.224	.411
Dave May	OF152, DH2	L	29	156	624	94	169	28	4	25	93	44	76	5	.303	.473
Johnny Briggs	OF137, DH1	L	29	142	488	78	120	20	7	18	57	87	83	15	.246	.426
Darrell Porter	C90, DH1	L	21	117	350	50	89	19	2	16	67	57	85	5	.254	.457
Ollie Brown	DH82, OF4	R	29	97	296	28	83	10	1	7	32	33	53	4	.280	.392
Joe Lahoud	DH41, OF40	L	26	96	225	29	46	9	0	5	26	27	36	5	.204	.311
Ellie Rodriguez	C75, DH14	R	27	94	290	30	78	8	1	0	30	41	28	4	.269	.303
Gorman Thomas	OF50, DH3, 3B1	R	22	59	155	16	29	7	1	2	11	14	61	5	.187	.284
Bob Vukovich	3B40, 1B13, 3B5	R	25	55	128	10	16	3	0	2	4	4	41	0	.125	.195
Bob Heise	SS29, 3B9, 1B4, 2B4, DH2	R	26	49	98	8	20	2	0	0	4	4	1	0	.204	.224
Bobby Mitchell	OF20, DH19	L	18	33	84	8	23	2	0	3	8	6	15	0	.274	.405
Wilbur Howard	OF12, DH1	B	24	16	39	3	8	0	0	0	2	10	0		.205	.205
John Felske	C7, 1B6	R	31	13	22	1	5	1	0	0	2	1	4	0	.227	.273
Charlie Moore	C8	R	20	8	27	0	7	1	0	0	4	2	0		.185	.259
Rick Auerbach	SS2	R	23	6	10	2	1	0	0	0	0	3	0		.100	.200

NAME	T	AGE	W	L	PCT	SV	G	GS	CG	IP	H	BB	SO	SHO	ERA
		26	74	88	.457	28	162	162	50	1454	1476	623	671	11	3.98
Jim Colborn	R	27	20	12	.625	1	43	36	22	314	297	87	135	4	3.18
Jim Slaton	R	23	13	15	.464	0	38	38	13	276	266	99	134	3	3.72
Eduardo Rodriguez	R	21	9	7	.563	5	36	7	1	76	71	47	49	0	3.32
Jerry Bell	R	25	9	9	.500	1	31	25	8	184	185	70	57	0	3.96
Skip Lockwood	R	26	5	12	.294	0	37	15	3	155	164	59	87	0	3.89
Chris Short	L	35	3	5	.375	2	42	7	0	72	86	44	44	0	5.13
Billy Champion	R	25	3	6	.385	1	37	13	6	136	139	62	67	3	3.71
Bill Parsons	R	24	3	6	.333	0	20	17	0	60	59	67	30	0	6.75
Ray Newman	L	27	1	1	.667	1	9	0	0	8	10	6	6	0	2.60
Carlos Velazquez	R	25	2	2	.500	2	18	0	0	38	46	10	12	0	2.60
Frank Linzy	R	32	2	6	.250	13	42	1	0	63	68	21	21	0	3.57
2 Rob Gardner	L	28	1	1	.500	1	10	0	0	13	17	13	5	0	9.69
Gary Ryerson	L	23	1	4	.200	0	7	4	0	30	38	17	13	0	7.83
3 Ed Sprague	R	27	0	1	.000	0	8	1	0	25	37	10	14	3	9.00
Kevin Kobel	L	19	0	1	.000	0	5	1	0	11	14	3	9	0	7.71
Ken Reynolds	L	26	0	0	.000	0	7	0	0	5	11	5	10	0	7.71

CLEVELAND   6th 71-91 .438 26   KEN ASPROMONTE

NAME	G by Pos	B	AGE	G	AB	R	H	2B	3B	HR	RBI	BB	SO	SB	BA	SA
TOTALS			25	162	5592	680	1429	205	29	158	636	471	793	60	.256	.387
Chris Chambliss	1B154	L	24	155	572	70	156	30	2	11	53	58	76	4	.273	.390
Jack Brohamer	2B97	L	23	102	300	29	66	12	1	4	29	32	23	0	.220	.307
Frank Duffy (SJ)	SS115	R	26	116	361	34	95	16	4	8	50	25	41	6	.263	.396
Buddy Bell	3B154, OF2	R	21	156	631	86	169	23	7	14	59	49	47	7	.268	.393
Rusty Torres	OF114	B	24	122	312	31	64	8	1	7	28	50	62	6	.205	.304
George Hendrick (BW)	OF110	R	23	113	440	64	118	18	0	21	61	25	71	7	.268	.452
Charlie Spikes	OF111, DH26	R	22	140	506	68	120	12	3	23	73	45	103	5	.237	.409
Dave Duncan (BW)	C86, DH9	R	27	95	344	43	80	11	1	17	43	35	86	3	.233	.419
Oscar Gamble	DH70, OF37	L	23	113	390	56	104	11	3	20	44	34	37	3	.267	.404
Johnny Ellis	C72, DH38, 1B12	R	24	127	437	59	118	12	2	14	68	46	57	0	.270	.403
Walt Williams	OF61, DH26	R	30	104	350	43	101	15	1	8	38	14	29	9	.289	.406
J. Lowenstein	OF51, 2B25, 3B8, DH4, 1B1	L	26	98	305	42	89	16	1	6	40	23	41	5	.292	.410
Leo Cardenas	SS67, 3B5	R	34	72	195	9	42	4	0	0	12	13	42	1	.215	.236
Tom Ragland	2B65, SS2	R	27	67	183	16	47	7	1	0	12	8	31	2	.257	.306
Ron Lolich	OF32, DH12	R	26	61	140	16	32	7	0	2	15	7	27	0	.229	.321
Tommy Smith	OF13	L	24	14	41	6	10	2	0	2	3	1	2	1	.244	.439
Ted Ford	OF10	R	26	11	40	3	9	1	0	1	3	2	7	1	.225	.275
Alan Ashby	C11	B	21	11	29	4	5	1	0	1	3	2	11	0	.172	.310
Jerry Kenney	2B5	L	28	5	16	0	4	1	0	0	2	2	0	0	.250	.375

NAME	T	AGE	W	L	PCT	SV	G	GS	CG	IP	H	BB	SO	SHO	ERA
		28	71	91	.438	21	162	162	55	1465	1532	602	883	9	4.58
Gaylord Perry	R	34	19	19	.500	0	41	41	29	344	315	115	238	7	3.38
Dick Tidrow	R	26	14	16	.467	0	42	40	13	275	289	95	138	2	4.42
2 Tom Timmermann	R	33	8	7	.533	2	29	15	4	124	117	54	62	0	4.93
Milt Wilcox (FJ)	R	23	8	10	.444	0	26	19	4	134	143	68	82	0	5.84
2 Ken Sanders	R	31	5	1	.833	5	15	0	0	27	18	9	14	0	1.67
Tom Hilgendorf	L	31	5	3	.625	6	48	1	1	95	87	36	58	0	3.13
Jerry Johnson	R	29	5	6	.455	5	39	1	0	60	70	39	45	0	6.15
Ray Lamb	R	28	3	3	.500	2	32	1	0	86	98	42	60	0	4.60
Brent Strom (EJ)	L	24	2	10	.167	0	27	18	2	123	134	47	91	0	4.61
2 Mike Kekich	R	28	1	4	.200	0	16	6	0	50	73	35	26	0	7.02
2 Dick Bosman	R	29	1	8	.111	0	22	17	2	97	130	29	41	0	6.22
1 Steve Mingori	L	29	0	0	—	0	5	0	0	12	10	10	4	0	6.00
Mike Kilkenny	L	28	0	0	—	0	5	0	0	2	5	5	3	0	22.50
2 Mike Jackson	R	28	0	0	—	0	1	1	0	1	1	0	1	0	0.00
1 Ed Farmer	R	23	0	2	.000	1	16	0	0	17	25	5	10	0	4.76
1 Steve Dunning	R	24	0	2	.000	0	4	3	0	18	17	13	10	0	6.50

WEST DIVISION

OAKLAND   1st 94-68 .580   DICK WILLIAMS

NAME	G by Pos	B	AGE	G	AB	R	H	2B	3B	HR	RBI	BB	SO	SB	BA	SA
TOTALS			28	162	5507	758	1431	216	28	147	714	595	919	128	.260	.389
Gene Tenace	1B134, C33, DH3, 2B1	R	26	160	510	83	132	18	2	24	84	101	94	2	.259	.443
Dick Green	2B133, SS1, 3B1	R	32	133	332	33	87	17	0	3	42	21	63	0	.262	.340
Bert Campaneris	SS149	R	31	151	601	89	150	17	6	4	46	50	79	34	.250	.318
Sal Bando	3B159, DH3	R	29	162	592	97	170	32	3	29	98	82	84	4	.287	.498
Reggie Jackson	OF145, DH3	L	27	151	539	99	158	28	2	32	117	76	111	22	.293	.531
Billy North	OF138, DH6	B	25	146	554	98	158	10	5	5	34	78	89	53	.285	.348
Joe Rudi	OF117, 1B1, DH1	R	26	120	437	53	118	25	1	12	66	30	72	0	.270	.414
Ray Fosse	C141, DH2	R	26	143	492	37	126	23	2	7	52	25	62	2	.256	.354
2 Deron Johnson	DH107, 1B23	R	34	131	464	61	114	14	2	19	81	59	116	0	.246	.407
Ted Kubiak	2B83, SS26,3B2	B	31	106	182	15	40	6	1	3	17	12	19	1	.220	.313
1 Mike Hegan	1B56, OF3, DH3	L	31	75	71	8	13	2	0	1	5	5	17	0	.183	.254
Angel Mangual	OF50, DH14, 1B2, 2B1	R	26	74	192	20	43	4	1	3	13	8	34	1	.224	.302
Billy Conigliaro (KJ)	OF40, DH6	R	25	48	110	5	22	2	2	0	14	9	26	1	.200	.255
Rich McKinney	3B17, 2B7, DH6, OF3	R	26	48	65	9	16	3	0	1	7	7	4	0	.246	.338
2 Vic Davalillo	OF19, 1B8, DH2	L	36	38	64	5	12	1	0	0	4	3	4	0	.188	.203
2 Jesus Alou	OF21, DH6	R	31	36	108	10	33	3	0	1	11	2	6	0	.306	.361
Allen Lewis	DH6, OF1	B	31	35	0	16	0	0	0	0	0	0	0	7	—	—
1 Dal Maxvill	SS18, 2B11, 3B1	R	34	29	19	0	4	0	0	0	1	1	3	0	.211	.211
2 Pat Bourque	DH15, 1B5	L	26	23	42	8	8	4	1	2	9	15	10	0	.190	.476
Jay Johnstone	OF7, DH4, 2B2	L	27	23	28	1	3	1	0	0	3	2	4	0	.107	.143
1 Gonzalo Marquez	2B2, 1B1, OF1, DH1	L	27	23	25	1	6	1	0	0	2	0	4	0	.240	.240
2 Mike Andrews	2B9, DH2	R	29	18	21	1	4	1	0	0	3	1	0	0	.190	.238
Manny Trillo	2B16	R	22	17	12	0	3	2	0	0	3	0	4	0	.250	.417
Tim Hosley	C13	R	26	13	14	3	3	0	0	0	2	2	3	0	.214	.214
Phil Garner	3B9	R	24	9	5	0	0	0	0	0	0	0	3	0	.000	.000
3 Rico Carty	DH2	R	33	7	8	1	2	1	0	1	2	1	0	0	.250	.750
1 Jose Morales	DH3	R	28	6	14	0	4	1	0	0	1	1	5	0	.286	.357
1 Larry Haney	C2	R	30	3	2	0	1	0	0	0	0	0	0	0	.500	.500

NAME	T	AGE	W	L	PCT	SV	G	GS	CG	IP	H	BB	SO	SHO	ERA
		27	94	68	.580	41	162	162	46	1457	1311	494	797	16	3.29
Catfish Hunter (BG)	R	27	21	5	.808	0	36	36	11	256	222	69	124	3	3.34
Ken Holtzman	R	27	21	13	.618	0	40	40	16	297	275	66	157	4	2.97
Vida Blue	L	23	20	9	.690	0	37	37	13	264	214	105	158	4	3.27
Rollie Fingers	R	26	7	8	.467	22	62	2	0	127	107	39	110	0	1.91
Horacio Pina	R	28	6	3	.667	8	47	0	0	88	58	34	41	0	2.76
Dave Hamilton	L	25	6	4	.600	0	16	11	1	70	74	24	34	0	4.37
Darold Knowles	L	31	6	8	.429	9	52	5	1	99	87	49	46	1	3.09
Blue Moon Odom	R	28	5	12	.294	0	30	24	3	150	153	67	83	0	4.50
Glenn Abbott	R	22	1	0	1.000	0	3	1	1	19	16	7	6	0	3.79
Paul Lindblad	L	31	1	5	.167	2	36	3	0	78	89	28	33	0	3.69
1 Rob Gardner	L	28	0	0	—	0	7	0	0	9	10	4	2	0	5.14
Chuck Dobson	R	29	0	0	.000	0	1	1	0	2	6	2	3	0	9.00

KANSAS CITY   2nd 88-74 .543 6   JACK McKEON

NAME	G by Pos	B	AGE	G	AB	R	H	2B	3B	HR	RBI	BB	SO	SB	BA	SA
TOTALS			28	162	5508	755	1440	239	40	114	703	644	696	105	.261	.381
John Mayberry	1B149, DH1	L	24	152	510	87	142	20	2	26	100	122	79	3	.278	.478
Cookie Rojas	2B137	R	34	139	551	78	152	29	3	6	69	37	38	18	.276	.372
Freddie Patek	SS135	R	28	135	501	82	117	19	5	5	45	54	63	36	.234	.321
Paul Schaal	3B121	R	30	121	396	61	114	14	3	8	42	63	45	5	.288	.399
Ed Kirkpatrick	OF108, C14, DH8	L	28	126	429	61	113	24	3	6	45	46	48	3	.263	.375
Amos Otis	OF135, DH14	R	26	148	583	89	175	21	4	26	93	47	67	13	.300	.484
Lou Piniella	OF128, DH9	R	29	144	513	53	128	28	1	9	69	30	65	5	.250	.361
Fran Healy	C92, DH1	R	26	95	279	25	77	13	2	6	34	31	56	3	.276	.409
Hal McRae	DH37, OF64, 3B2	R	27	106	338	36	79	18	3	9	50	34	38	2	.234	.385
Steve Hovley	OF79, DH15	L	28	104	232	29	59	8	1	2	24	33	34	6	.254	.323
K. Bevacqua	3B40, 2B16, DH16, OF10, 1B9	R	26	99	276	39	71	8	3	2	40	25	42	2	.257	.330
Gail Hopkins	DH36, 1B10	R	30	74	138	17	34	6	1	2	16	29	15	1	.246	.348
Carl Taylor	C63, 1B2, DH1	R	29	69	145	18	33	6	0	1	16	32	20	2	.228	.283
Frank White	SS37, 2B11	R	22	51	139	20	31	6	1	0	5	8	23	3	.223	.281
Bobby Floyd	2B25, SS24	R	29	51	78	10	26	3	1	0	8	4	14	1	.333	.397
Jim Wohlford	DH19, OF13	R	22	45	109	21	29	1	3	2	10	11	12	1	.266	.385
2 Rick Reichardt	DH31, OF7	R	30	41	127	15	28	5	2	3	17	11	28	0	.220	.362
Tom Poquette	OF20	L	21	21	28	4	6	1	0	0	3	0	4	0	.214	.250
Buck Martinez	C14	R	24	14	32	2	8	1	0	1	6	4	5	0	.250	.375
George Brett	3B13	R	20	13	40	2	5	2	0	0	0	0	5	0	.125	.175
1 Jerry May	C11	R	29	11	30	4	4	1	1	0	2	3	5	0	.133	.233
Frank Ortenzio	1B7, DH1	R	22	9	25	1	7	2	0	0	6	2	6	0	.280	.480
Keith Marshall	OF8	R	21	8	9	0	2	0	0	0	0	0	2	0	.222	.333

NAME	T	AGE	W	L	PCT	SV	G	GS	CG	IP	H	BB	SO	SHO	ERA
		27	88	74	.543	41	162	162	40	1449	1521	617	790	7	4.19
Paul Splittorff	L	26	20	11	.645	0	38	38	12	262	279	78	110	3	3.98
Steve Busby	R	23	16	15	.516	0	37	37	7	238	246	105	174	1	4.24
Dick Drago	R	28	12	14	.462	0	37	33	10	213	252	76	98	1	4.23
Gene Garber	R	25	9	9	.500	11	48	4	3	153	164	49	60	0	4.24
Al Fitzmorris	R	27	8	3	.727	0	15	13	3	89	88	25	26	1	2.83
Ken Wright	R	26	6	5	.545	0	25	12	1	81	60	82	75	0	4.89
Bruce Dal Canton	R	31	4	3	.571	0	32	3	1	97	108	46	38	0	4.82
Doug Bird	R	23	4	4	.500	20	54	0	0	102	81	30	83	0	3.00
2 Steve Mingori	L	29	3	3	.500	1	19	1	0	56	59	23	46	0	3.05
Wayne Simpson	R	24	3	4	.429	0	16	10	1	60	66	35	29	0	5.70
2 Joe Hoerner	L	36	2	0	1.000	4	22	0	0	19	28	13	15	0	5.21
Mark Littell	R	20	1	3	.250	0	8	7	1	38	44	23	16	0	5.68
1 Mike Jackson	L	27	0	0	—	0	9	0	0	22	25	20	13	0	6.95
Norm Angelini	L	25	0	0	—	1	6	0	0	9	13	4	4	0	4.50
Tom Burgmeier	L	29	0	0	—	0	2	0	0	10	13	4	4	0	5.40
Barry Raziano	R	26	0	0	—	0	2	0	0	6	1	0	0	0	5.40

MINNESOTA   3rd 81-81 .500 13   FRANK QUILICI

NAME	G by Pos	B	AGE	G	AB	R	H	2B	3B	HR	RBI	BB	SO	SB	BA	SA
TOTALS			28	162	5625	738	1521	240	44	120	688	598	954	87	.270	.393
Joe Lis	1B96, DH1	R	26	103	253	37	62	10	2	9	25	28	66	0	.245	.403
Rod Carew	2B147	L	27	149	580	98	203	30	11	6	62	62	55	41	.350	.471
Danny Thompson	SS95, 3B1, DH1	R	26	99	347	29	78	13	2	1	36	16	41	1	.225	.282
Steve Braun (KJ)	3B102, OF6	R	25	115	361	46	102	18	5	6	42	74	48	4	.283	.438
Larry Hisle	OF143	R	26	143	545	88	148	25	6	15	64	64	128	11	.272	.422
Bobby Darwin	OF140, DH1	R	30	145	560	69	141	20	2	18	90	46	137	5	.252	.391
Jim Holt	OF102, 1B33	L	28	132	441	52	131	25	3	11	58	29	43	0	.297	.442
George Mitterwald	C122, DH3	R	28	125	432	50	112	15	0	16	64	39	111	3	.259	.405
Tony Oliva	DH142	L	32	146	571	63	166	20	0	16	92	45	44	2	.291	.410
Jerry Terrell	SS81, 3B30, 2B14, OF1, DH1	R	26	124	438	43	116	15	2	1	32	21	56	13	.265	.315
Steve Brye	OF87, DH1	R	24	92	278	39	73	9	5	6	33	35	43	3	.263	.396
Harmon Killebrew (KJ)	1B57, DH9	R	37	69	248	29	60	9	1	5	32	41	59	0	.242	.347
Mike Adams	OF24, DH2	R	24	55	66	21	14	2	0	3	6	17	18	2	.212	.379
Phil Roof	C47	R	32	47	117	10	23	4	1	1	15	13	27	0	.197	.274
Dan Monzon	2B17, 3B14, OF1	R	26	37	76	10	17	1	1	1	4	11	19	1	.224	.263
Danny Walton	OF18, DH11, 3B1	R	25	37	96	13	17	1	1	4	8	17	28	0	.177	.333
Eric Soderholm	3B33, SS1	R	24	35	111	22	33	7	2	1	9	21	16	1	.297	.423
2 Rich Reese	1B17	L	31	22	23	7	4	1	0	0	3	6	6	0	.174	.435
Craig Kusick	1B11, OF2, DH2	R	24	15	48	4	12	2	0	0	9	6	14	0	.250	.292
Glenn Borgmann	C12	R	23	12	34	7	9	1	0	0	6	6	10	0	.265	.324

NAME	T	AGE	W	L	PCT	SV	G	GS	CG	IP	H	BB	SO	SHO	ERA
		27	81	81	.500	34	162	162	48	1452	1443	519	879	18	3.77
Bert Blyleven	R	22	20	17	.541	0	40	40	25	325	296	67	258	9	2.52
1 Jim Kaat	L	34	11	12	.478	0	29	28	7	182	206	39	93	2	4.40
Dick Woodson (SA)	R	28	10	8	.556	0	23	23	4	141	137	58	63	3	3.96
Joe Decker	R	26	10	10	.500	0	29	24	6	170	167	88	109	3	4.18
Ray Corbin	R	24	8	5	.615	14	51	7	1	148	124	60	83	0	3.04
Bill Hands	R	33	7	10	.412	2	39	15	3	142	138	41	78	1	3.49
Dave Goltz	R	24	6	4	.600	1	32	10	1	106	138	32	65	0	5.26
Dan Fife	R	23	3	2	.600	0	10	7	1	52	54	29	18	0	4.33
Bill Campbell	R	24	3	3	.500	7	28	2	0	92	100	42	58	0	3.12
1 Ken Sanders	R	31	2	4	.333	8	27	0	0	44	53	21	19	0	6.14
Vic Albury	L	26	1	0	1.000	0	14	0	0	23	13	19	13	0	2.74
Jim Strickland	L	27	0	1	.000	0	5	1	0	5	11	5	6	0	12.60
Eddie Bane	L	21	0	5	.000	2	23	6	0	60	62	30	42	0	4.95

CALIFORNIA — 4th 79-83 .488 15 — BOBBY WINKLES

NAME	G by Pos	B	AGE	G	AB	R	H	2B	3B	HR	RBI	BB	SO	SB	BA	SA
TOTALS		30	162	5505	629	1395	183	29	93	595	509	816	59	.253	.348	
2 Mike Epstein	1B86	L	30	91	312	30	67	8	2	8	32	34	54	1	.215	.330
Sandy Alomar	2B110, SS31	B	29	136	470	45	112	7	1	0	28	34	44	25	.238	.257
Rudy Meoli	SS95, 3B13, 2B8	L	22	120	305	36	68	12	1	2	23	31	38	2	.223	.289
2 Alan Gallagher	3B98, 2B1, SS1	R	27	110	311	16	85	6	1	0	26	35	31	1	.273	.299
Lee Stanton	OF107	R	27	119	306	41	72	9	4	8	34	27	88	3	.235	.356
Ken Berry	OF129	R	32	136	415	48	108	11	2	3	36	26	40	1	.284	.342
Vada Pinson	OF120	L	34	124	466	56	121	14	6	8	57	20	55	5	.260	.360
Jeff Torborg (BG)	C102	R	31	102	255	20	56	7	0	1	18	21	32	0	.220	.259
Frank Robinson	DH127, OF17	R	37	147	534	85	142	29	0	30	97	82	93	1	.266	.489
Bob Oliver	3B49, OF47, 1B32, DH12	R	30	151	544	51	144	24	1	18	89	33	100	1	.265	.412
Tommy McCraw	OF34, 1B25, DH8	L	32	99	264	25	70	7	0	3	24	30	42	3	.265	.326
Winston Llenas	2B20, 3B11, OF, DH4	R	29	78	130	16	35	1	0	1	25	10	16	0	.269	.300
2 Richie Scheinblum	OF54, DH7	B	30	77	229	28	75	10	2	3	21	35	27	0	.328	.428
1 B. Grabarkewitz	2B18, 3B12, DH5, SS1, OF1	R	29	61	129	27	21	6	1	3	9	27	28	2	.163	.295
Johnny Stephenson	C56	L	32	60	122	9	30	5	0	1	9	7	7	0	.246	.311
Art Kusnyer	C41	R	27	41	64	5	8	2	0	0	3	2	12	0	.125	.156
Jerry DaVanon	SS14, 2B12, 3B7	R	27	41	49	6	12	3	0	0	2	3	9	1	.245	.306
Billy Parker	2B32, SS3, DH1	R	26	38	102	14	23	2	1	0	7	8	23	0	.225	.265
Bobby Valentine (BL)	SS25, OF8	R	23	32	126	12	38	5	2	1	13	5	9	6	.302	.397
Mickey Rivers	OF29	L	24	30	129	26	45	6	4	0	16	8	11	8	.349	.457
1 Jim Spencer	1B26, DH2	L	25	29	87	10	21	4	2	2	11	9	9	0	.241	.402
Dave Chalk	SS22	R	24	24	69	14	16	2	0	0	6	9	13	0	.232	.261
2 Dick Stelmaszek	C22	L	24	22	26	2	4	1	0	0	3	6	7	0	.154	.192
Charlie Sands	C10	L	25	17	33	5	9	2	1	1	5	5	10	0	.273	.485
Doug Howard	OF6, 1B1, 3B1	R	25	8	21	2	2	0	0	0	1	1	6	0	.095	.095
Bobby Brooks	OF1	R	27	4	7	0	1	0	0	0	0	0	2	0	.143	.143

NAME	T	AGE	W	L	PCT	SV	G	GS	CG	IP	H	BB	SO	SHO	ERA
		28	79	83	.488	19	162	162	72	1456	1351	614	1010	13	3.53
Nolan Ryan	R	26	21	16	.568	1	41	39	26	326	238	162	383	4	2.87
Bill Singer	R	29	20	14	.588	0	40	40	19	316	280	130	241	2	3.22
Clyde Wright	R	32	11	19	.367	0	37	36	13	257	273	76	65	1	3.68
Dave Sells	R	26	7	2	.778	10	51	0	0	68	72	35	25	0	3.71
Rudy May	L	28	7	17	.292	0	34	28	10	185	177	80	134	4	4.38
2 Rich Hand	R	24	4	3	.571	0	16	6	0	55	58	21	19	0	3.60
Steve Barber	L	35	3	2	.600	4	50	1	0	89	90	32	58	0	3.54
Dick Lange	R	24	2	1	.667	0	17	4	1	53	61	21	27	0	4.42
Aurelio Monteagudo	R	29	2	1	.667	3	15	0	0	30	23	16	8	0	4.20
Frank Tanana	L	19	2	2	.500	0	4	4	2	26	20	8	22	1	3.12
1 Lloyd Allen	R	23	0	1	.000	1	5	0	0	9	15	5	4	0	10.00
Terry Wilshusen	R	24	0	0	—	0	1	0	0	0.1	0	2	0	0	81.00
Ron Perranoski (SJ)	L	37	0	2	.000	0	8	0	0	11	11	7	5	0	4.09
Andy Hassler	L	21	0	4	.000	0	7	4	1	32	33	19	19	0	3.66

CHICAGO — 5th 77-85 .475 17 — CHUCK TANNER

NAME	G by Pos	B	AGE	G	AB	R	H	2B	3B	HR	RBI	BB	SO	SB	BA	SA
TOTALS		26	162	5475	652	1400	228	38	111	598	537	952	83	.256	.372	
Dick Allen (BL)	1B67, 2B, DH1	R	31	72	250	39	79	20	3	16	41	33	51	7	.316	.612
Jorge Orta	2B122, SS1	L	22	128	425	46	113	9	10	6	40	37	87	8	.266	.376
Eddie Leon	SS122, 2B3	R	26	127	399	37	91	10	3	3	30	34	103	1	.228	.291
Bill Melton	3B151, DH1	R	27	152	560	83	155	29	1	20	87	75	66	4	.277	.439
Pat Kelly	OF141, DH1	L	28	144	550	77	154	24	5	1	44	65	91	22	.280	.347
Johnnie Jeter	OF72, DH3	R	28	89	300	38	72	14	4	7	26	9	74	4	.240	.383
Bill Sharp	OF70, DH1	L	25	77	196	23	54	8	3	4	22	9	22	3	.276	.408
Ed Herrmann	C114, DH2	L	26	119	379	42	85	17	1	10	39	31	55	2	.224	.354
Carlos May	DH75, OF70, 1B2	L	25	149	553	62	148	20	0	20	96	53	73	8	.268	.412
Tony Muser	1B89, OF, DH1, OF2	L	25	109	309	38	88	14	3	4	30	33	36	6	.285	.388
Luis Alvarado	2B45, SS18, 3B10, DH1	R	24	80	203	21	47	7	2	0	20	4	30	6	.232	.286
Ken Henderson (KJ)	OF44, DH26	B	28	73	262	32	68	13	0	6	32	27	49	3	.260	.378
Chuck Brinkman	C63	R	28	63	139	13	26	6	0	1	10	11	37	0	.187	.252
Jerry Hairston	OF33, 1B19, DH8	B	26	60	210	25	57	11	1	0	23	33	30	0	.271	.333
Buddy Bradford (SJ)	OF51	R	28	53	168	24	40	3	1	8	15	17	43	4	.238	.411
1 Mike Andrews	DH30, 1B9, 2B6, 3B5	R	29	52	159	10	32	9	0	10	23	28	29	0	.201	.358
1 Rick Reichardt	OF37, DH6	R	30	46	153	15	42	8	1	3	16	8	29	2	.275	.399
Bucky Dent	SS36, 2B3, 3B1	R	21	40	117	17	29	2	0	0	10	10	18	2	.248	.265
Brian Downing (KJ)	OF13, C11, 3B8, DH1	R	22	34	73	5	13	1	0	2	4	10	17	0	.178	.274
Hank Allen	3B9, 1B8, OF5, 2B1, C1	R	32	28	39	2	4	2	0	0	1	0	6	0	.150	.200
Sam Ewing	1B4	L	24	11	20	1	3	1	0	0	0	1	1	0	.000	.000
1 Rich Morales	3B5, 2B2	R	29	7	4	1	0	0	0	0	0	1	1	0	.000	.000
Pete Varney	C5	R	24	5	4	0	0	0	0	0	0	0	0	0	.000	.000
Joe Keough		L	27	5	1	0	0	0	0	0	0	0	1	0	.000	.000

NAME	T	AGE	W	L	PCT	SV	G	GS	CG	IP	H	BB	SO	SHO	ERA
		26	77	85	.475	35	162	162	48	1456	1484	574	848	15	3.86
Wilbur Wood	L	31	24	20	.545	0	49	48	21	359	381	91	199	4	3.46
Stan Bahnsen	R	28	18	21	.462	0	42	42	14	282	290	117	120	4	3.57
Cy Acosta	R	26	10	6	.625	18	48	0	0	97	66	39	60	0	2.23
1 Eddie Fisher	R	36	6	7	.462	0	26	16	2	111	135	38	57	0	4.86
Terry Forster	L	21	6	11	.353	16	51	12	4	173	174	78	120	0	3.23
Steve Stone	R	25	6	11	.353	1	36	22	3	176	163	82	138	0	4.24
2 Jim Kaat	L	34	4	1	.800	0	7	3	4	43	44	4	16	1	4.20
Bart Johnson	R	23	3	3	.500	0	22	9	0	81	76	40	56	0	4.11
Ken Frailing	R	25	0	0	—	0	10	0	0	18	18	7	15	0	2.00
Steve Kealey (SA)	R	26	0	0	—	0	11	0	0	11	23	7	4	0	15.55
Jim Geddes	R	24	0	0	—	0	1	1	0	16	14	14	7	0	2.81
Denny O'Toole	R	24	0	0	—	0	16	0	0	16	23	6	3	0	5.63
Dave Baldwin	R	35	0	0	—	0	3	0	0	3	5	3	2	0	3.60
2 Jim McGlothlin	R	29	0	1	.000	0	5	1	0	18	13	13	14	0	4.00
Goose Gossage	R	21	0	4	.000	0	20	4	1	50	57	37	33	0	7.38
Dave Lemonds (AJ)		24													

TEXAS — 6th 57-105 .352 37 — WHITEY HERZOG 47-91 .341 — DEL WILBER 1-0 1.000 — 2 BILLY MARTIN 9-14 .391

NAME	G by Pos	B	AGE	G	AB	R	H	2B	3B	HR	RBI	BB	SO	SB	BA	SA
TOTALS		27	162	5488	619	1397	195	29	110	574	503	791	91	.255	.361	
2 Jim Spencer	1B99, DH1	L	25	122	352	35	94	12	3	4	43	34	41	0	.267	.352
Dave Nelson	2B140	R	29	142	576	71	165	24	4	7	48	34	78	43	.286	.378
Jim Mason	SS74, 2B19, 3B1	L	22	92	238	23	49	7	2	3	19	23	48	0	.206	.290
Toby Harrah (BG)	SS76, 3B52	R	24	118	461	64	120	16	1	10	50	46	49	10	.260	.364
Elliott Maddox (SJ)	OF89, 3B7, DH5	R	24	100	172	24	41	1	0	1	17	29	28	5	.238	.262
Vic Harris	OF113, 3B25, 2B18	R	23	152	555	71	138	14	7	8	44	55	81	13	.249	.342
Jeff Burroughs	OF148, 1B3, DH1	R	22	151	526	71	147	17	1	30	85	67	88	0	.279	.487
Ken Suarez	C90	R	30	93	278	25	69	11	0	1	27	33	16	1	.248	.299
Alex Johnson	DH116, OF41	R	30	158	624	62	179	26	3	8	68	32	82	10	.287	.377
1 Rico Carty	OF53, DH31	R	33	86	306	24	71	12	0	3	33	36	39	2	.232	.301
Larry Biittner	OF57, 1B20, DH3	L	27	83	258	19	65	8	0	1	22	20	21	1	.252	.310
Bill Sudakis	3B29, 1B24, C9, DH8, OF2	B	27	82	235	32	60	11	0	15	43	23	53	0	.255	.494
Dick Billings (BG)	C72, OF4, 1B3, DH2	R	30	81	280	17	50	11	0	3	32	20	43	1	.179	.250
Tommy Grieve	OF59, DH1	R	25	66	123	22	38	6	0	7	21	7	25	1	.309	.528
2 Jim Fregosi	3B34, 1B10, SS6	R	31	45	157	25	42	6	2	6	16	12	31	0	.268	.446
Pete Mackanin	SS33, 3B10	R	21	44	90	3	9	2	0	1	4	2	26	0	.100	.122
1 Mike Epstein	1B25	L	30	27	85	9	16	3	0	1	6	14	19	0	.188	.259
Joe Lovitto	3B20, OF3	R	22	26	44	3	6	1	0	0	6	1	9	1	.136	.159
Bill Madlock	3B21	R	22	21	77	16	27	5	3	1	5	7	9	3	.351	.532
Lenny Randle	2B5, OF2	B	24	20	29	3	6	1	1	1	2	2	4	0	.207	.414
1 Dick Stelmaszek	C7	L	24	7	9	0	1	0	0	0	0	2	1	0	.111	.111
Don Castle	DH3	R	23	4	13	0	4	1	0	0	3	0	1	0	.308	.385

NAME	T	AGE	W	L	PCT	SV	G	GS	CG	IP	H	BB	SO	SHO	ERA
		25	57	105	.352	27	162	162	35	1430	1514	680	831	10	4.64
2 Jim Bibby	R	28	9	10	.474	1	26	23	11	180	121	106	155	2	3.25
2 Sonny Siebert (SJ)	R	36	7	11	.389	2	25	20	1	120	120	37	76	1	3.97
1 Mike Paul	L	28	5	4	.556	2	36	10	1	87	104	36	49	0	4.97
Jackie Brown	R	30	5	5	.500	2	25	3	2	67	82	25	45	1	3.90
Pete Broberg	R	23	5	9	.357	0	22	20	6	119	130	66	57	1	5.60
Jim Merritt	L	29	5	13	.278	1	35	19	8	160	191	34	65	1	4.05
Charlie Hudson (RJ)	R	23	4	2	.667	1	25	4	1	62	59	31	34	1	4.65
David Clyde	L	18	4	8	.333	0	18	18	0	93	106	54	74	0	5.03
Bill Gogolewski	R	25	3	6	.333	6	49	1	0	124	139	48	77	0	4.21
1 Rich Hand	R	24	3	4	.333	1	28	7	1	42	49	19	14	0	5.36
Steve Foucault (BJ)	R	23	2	4	.333	8	21	1	0	56	54	31	28	0	3.86
1 Dick Bosman	R	29	2	6	.286	0	7	7	1	40	42	17	14	0	4.28
2 Steve Dunning	R	24	2	6	.250	2	28	12	2	94	101	52	38	0	5.36
Rick Henninger	R	25	1	0	1.000	0	6	2	0	23	23	11	6	0	2.74
Don Stanhouse	R	22	1	7	.125	1	21	5	1	70	70	44	42	0	4.76
Jim Shellenback	L	21	0	0	—	0	4	0	0	9	9	6	6	0	9.00
Rick Waits	L	24	0	0	—	0	2	0	0	5	6	3	2	0	9.00
Jim Kremmel	L	24	0	0	.000	0	23	0	0	40	49	23	23	0	7.65
Don Durham	R	24	0	0	—	0	8	0	0	40	58	39	25	0	9.22
2 Lloyd Allen	R	23	0	0	.000	1	23	5	0	41	58	39	25	0	9.22

AMERICAN LEAGUE CHAMPIONSHIP — OAKLAND (WEST) 3 BALTIMORE (EAST) 2

LINE SCORES

TEAM	1 2 3	4 5 6	7 8 9	10 11 12	R	H	E
Game 1 October 6 at Baltimore							
OAK	000	000	000		0	5	1
BAL	400	000	11X		6	12	0

Blue, Pina (1), Odom (3), Fingers (8) — **Palmer**

TEAM	1 2 3	4 5 6	7 8 9	R	H	E
Game 2 October 7 at Baltimore						
OAK	100	002	021	6	9	0
BAL	100	001	010	3	8	0

Hunter, Fingers (8) — McNally, Reynolds (8), Jackson (9)

TEAM	1 2 3	4 5 6	7 8 9	10 11	R	H	E
Game 3 October 9 at Oakland							
BAL	010	000	000	0 0	1	3	0
OAK	000	000	010	1	2	4	3

Cuellar — **Holtzman**

TEAM	1 2 3	4 5 6	7 8 9	R	H	E
Game 4 October 10 at Oakland						
BAL	000	000	410	5	8	0
OAK	030	001	000	4	7	0

Palmer, Reynolds (2), **Watt** (7), Jackson (7) — Blue, **Fingers** (7)

TEAM	1 2 3	4 5 6	7 8 9	R	H	E
Game 5 October 11 at Oakland						
BAL	000	000	000	0	5	2
OAK	001	200	00x	3	7	0

Alexander, Palmer (4) — **Hunter**

COMPOSITE BATTING

NAME	POS	G	AB	R	H	2B	3B	HR	RBI	BA
Oakland Totals		5	160	15	32	5	1	5	15	.200
Campaneris	SS	5	21	3	7	1	0	0	2	.333
Jackson	OF	5	21	1	3	0	0	0	3	.143
Rudi	OF	5	18	1	4	0	0	1	3	.222
Bando	3B	5	18	2	3	0	0	1	3	.167
Tenace	1B-C	5	17	3	4	1	0	0	0	.235
Green	2B	5	13	0	1	0	0	0	1	.077
Fosse	C	5	11	2	1	0	0	0	3	.091
Johnson	DH	4	10	0	1	0	0	0	0	.100
Mangual	OF	3	9	1	1	0	0	0	0	.111
Davalillo	1B-OF	4	8	2	5	0	0	0	1	.625
Alou	DH-PH	4	3	0	1	0	0	0	0	.333

Conigliaro OF 0-4, Kubiak 2B 0-2, Andrews DH-1B 0-1, Bourque DH 0-1, Lewis PR 0-0

NAME	POS	G	AB	R	H	2B	3B	HR	RBI	BA
Baltimore Totals		5	171	15	36	7	0	3	15	.211
Davis	DH	5	21	1	6	1	0	0	2	.286
Grich	2B	5	20	1	2	0	0	1	1	.100
Robinson	3B	5	20	1	5	0	0	2	2	.250
Williams	1B-C	5	18	2	5	2	0	0	4	.278
Blair	OF	5	18	1	3	1	0	0	1	.167
Belanger	SS	5	16	0	2	0	0	0	1	.125
Etchebarren	C	4	14	1	5	0	0	0	4	.357
Baylor	OF	5	11	1	3	0	0	0	0	.273
Rettenmund	OF	5	11	0	1	0	0	0	0	.091
Coggins	OF	5	9	1	4	1	0	0	1	.444
Bumbry	OF	2	1	0	0	0	0	0	0	.000

Powell 1B 0-4, Crowley OF 0-2, Baker SS 0-0, Brown 3B 0-0, Hood PR 0-0

COMPOSITE PITCHING

NAME	G	IP	H	BB	SO	W	L	SV	ERA
Oakland Totals	5	46	36	16	25	3	2	1	2.74
Hunter	2	16.1	5	6	2	0	0		1.65
Holtzman	1	11	3	1	7	1	0	0	0.82
Blue	2	7	8	5	3	0	1	0	10.29
Odom	1	5	6	2	4	0	0	0	1.80
Fingers	3	4.2	4	2	4	0	1	1	1.93
Pina	1	2	3	1	1	0	0	0	0.00

NAME	G	IP	H	BB	SO	W	L	SV	ERA
Baltimore Totals	5	45	32	17	39	2	3	0	2.80
Palmer	3	14.2	11	8	15	1	0	0	1.84
Cuellar	1	10	4	3	11	0	1	0	1.80
McNally	1	7.2	7	2	7	0	1	0	5.87
Reynolds	2	5.2	5	3	5	0	0	0	3.18
Alexander	1	3.2	5	1	3	0	0	0	4.91
Jackson	1	2	0	0	0	0	0	0	0.00
Watt	1	.1	0	0	0	0	1	0	9.00

NATIONAL LEAGUE CHAMPIONSHIP — NEW YORK (EAST) 3 CINCINNATI (WEST) 2

LINE SCORES

TEAM	1 2 3	4 5 6	7 8 9	10 11 12	R	H	E
Game 1 October 6 at Cincinnati							
NY	0 1 0	0 0 0	0 0 0		1	3	0
CIN	0 0 0	0 0 0	0 1 1		2	6	0

Seaver   Billingham, Hall (9), **Borbon** (9)

Game 2 October 7 at Cincinnati							
NY	0 0 0	1 0 0	0 0 4		5	7	0
CIN	0 0 0	0 0 0	0 0 0		0	2	0

Matlack   Gullett, Carroll (6), Hall (9), Borbon (9)

Game 3 October 8 at New York							
CIN	0 0 2	0 0 0	0 0 0		2	8	1
NY	1 5 1	2 0 0	0 0 x		9	11	1

Grimsley, Hall (2), Tomlin (3),   Koosman
Nelson (4), Borbon (7)

Game 4 October 9 at New York							
CIN	0 0 0	0 0 0	1 0 0	0 0 1	2	8	0
NY	0 0 1	0 0 0	0 0 0	0 0 0	1	3	2

Norman, Gullett (6),   Stone, McGraw (7),
Carroll (10), Borbon (12)   **Parker** (12)

Game 5 October 10 at New York							
CIN	0 0 1	0 1 0	0 0 0		2	7	1
NY	2 0 0	0 4 1	0 0 x		7	13	1

Billingham, Gullett (5), Carroll (5),   **Seaver**, McGraw (9)
Grimsley (7)

COMPOSITE BATTING

NAME	POS	G	AB	R	H	2B	3B	HR	RBI	BA
New York Totals		5	168	23	37	5	0	3	22	.220
Garrett	3B	5	23	1	2	1	0	0	1	.087
Jones	OF	5	20	3	6	2	0	0	3	.300
Millan	2B	5	19	5	6	0	0	0	2	.316
Grote	C	5	19	2	4	0	0	0	2	.211
Harrelson	SS	5	18	1	3	0	0	0	2	.167
Hahn	OF	5	17	2	4	1	0	0	0	.235
Milner	1B	5	17	2	3	0	0	0	0	.176
Staub	OF	4	15	4	3	0	0	3	5	.200
Seaver	P	2	6	1	2	0	0	0	0	.333

Koosman P 2-4, Mays OF 1-3, Kranepool OF 1-2, Matlack P 0-2,
Boswell PH 0-1, McGraw P 0-1, Stone P 0-1, Parker P 0-0

NAME	POS	G	AB	R	H	2B	3B	HR	RBI	BA
Cincinnati Totals		5	167	8	31	6	0	5	8	.186
Perez	1B	5	22	1	2	0	0	0	1	.091
Rose	OF	5	21	3	8	1	0	2	2	.381
Morgan	2B	5	20	1	2	1	0	0	2	.100
Bench	C	5	19	1	5	2	0	1	1	.263
Geronimo	OF	4	15	0	1	0	0	0	0	.067
Driessen	3B	4	12	0	2	1	0	1	0	.167
Kosco	OF	3	10	3	3	0	0	2	2	.300
Menke	SS-3B	3	9	1	2	0	0	0	1	.222
Chaney	SS	5	9	0	0	0	0	0	1	.000

Griffey OF 1-7, Armbrister OF 1-6, Stahl PH 2-4, Gagliano PH 0-3, Billingham P 0-3,
Crosby SS 1-2, King PH 1-2, Gullett P 0-1, Nelson P 0-1, Norman P 0-1, Borbon P 0-0,
Carroll P 0-0, Hall P 0-0, Grimsley P 0-0, Tomlin P 0-0

COMPOSITE PITCHING

NAME	G	IP	H	BB	SO	W	L	SV	ERA
New York Totals	5	47.1	31	13	42	3	2	1	1.33
Seaver	2	16.2	13	5	17	1	0	0	1.62
Matlack	1	9	2	3	9	1	0	0	0.00
Koosman	1	9	8	0	9	1	0	0	2.00
Stone	1	6.2	3	2	4	0	0	0	1.35
McGraw	2	5	4	3	3	0	0	1	0.00
Parker	1	1	1	0	0	0	1	0	9.00

NAME	G	IP	H	BB	SO	W	L	SV	ERA
Cincinnati Totals	5	46	37	19	28	2	3	1	4.50
Billingham	2	12	9	4	9	0	1	0	4.50
Gullett	3	9	4	3	6	0	1	0	2.00
Carroll	3	7	5	2	3	1	0	0	1.29
Norman	1	5	1	3	3	0	0	0	1.80
Borbon	4	4.2	3	2	3	1	0	1	0.00
Grimsley	2	3.2	7	2	5	0	1	0	12.27
Nelson	1	2.1	0	1	0	0	0	0	0.00
Tomlin	1	1.2	5	1	0	0	0	0	16.20
Hall	3	0.2	3	1	1	0	0	0	67.50

EAST DIVISION

NEW YORK 1st 82-79 .509 YOGI BERRA

NAME	G by Pos	B	AGE	G	AB	R	H	2B	3B	HR	RBI	BB	SO	SB	BA	SA
TOTALS			28	161	5457	608	1345	198	24	85	553	540	805	27	.246	.338
John Milner (LJ)	1B95, OF29	L	23	129	451	69	108	12	3	23	72	62	84	1	.239	.432
Felix Millan	2B153	R	29	153	638	82	185	23	4	3	37	35	22	2	.290	.353
Bud Harrelson (BH)	SS103	B	29	106	356	35	92	12	3	0	20	48	49	5	.258	.309
Wayne Garrett	3B130, SS9, OF8	L	25	140	504	76	129	20	3	16	58	72	74	6	.256	.403
Rusty Staub	OF152	L	29	152	585	77	163	36	1	15	76	74	52	1	.279	.421
Don Hahn	OF87	R	24	93	262	22	60	10	0	2	21	22	43	2	.229	.290
Cleon Jones (WJ)	OF92	R	30	92	339	48	88	13	0	11	48	24	51	1	.260	.395
Jerry Grote (BA)	C81, 3B2	R	30	84	285	17	73	10	2	1	32	13	23	0	.256	.316
Ed Kranepool	1B51, OF32	L	28	100	284	28	68	12	2	1	35	30	28	1	.239	.306
Ted Martinez	SS44, OF21, 3B14, 2B5	R	25	92	263	34	67	11	0	1	14	13	38	3	.255	.308
Ken Boswell	3B17, 2B3	L	27	76	110	12	25	2	1	1	14	12	11	0	.227	.318
Duffy Dyer	C60	R	27	70	189	9	35	6	1	1	9	13	40	0	.185	.243
Willie Mays	OF45, 1B17	R	42	66	209	24	44	10	0	6	25	27	47	1	.211	.344
Jim Beauchamp	1B11	R	33	50	61	5	17	1	1	0	14	7	11	1	.279	.328
Ron Hodges	C40	L	24	45	127	5	33	2	0	1	14	7	11	1	.260	.299
1 Jim Fregosi	SS17, 3B17, 1B3, OF1	R	31	45	124	7	29	4	1	0	18	11	19	1	.234	.282
George Theodore (PJ)	OF33, 1B4	R	26	45	116	14	30	4	0	1	15	10	13	1	.259	.319
Jim Gosger	OF35	L	30	38	92	9	22	2	0	0	9	16	16	0	.239	.261

Dave Schneck 24 L 7-36, Rich Chiles 23 L 3-25, 2 Jerry May 29 R 2-8, Brian Ostrosser 24 L 0-5, Lute Barnes 26 R 1-2, Greg Harts 23 L 1-2

NAME	T	AGE	W	L	PCT	SV	G	GS	CG	IP	H	BB	SO	SHO	ERA
		27	82	79	.509	40	161	161	47	1465	1345	490	1027	15	3.26
Tom Seaver	R	28	19	10	.655	0	36	36	18	290	219	64	251	3	2.08
Jerry Koosman	L	30	14	15	.483	0	35	35	12	263	234	76	156	3	2.84
Jon Matlack	L	23	14	16	.467	0	34	34	14	242	210	99	205	3	3.20
George Stone	L	26	12	3	.800	1	27	20	2	148	157	31	77	0	2.80
Harry Parker	R	25	8	4	.667	5	38	9	0	97	79	36	63	0	3.34
Ray Sadecki	L	32	5	4	.556	1	31	11	1	117	109	41	87	0	3.38
Tug McGraw	L	28	5	6	.455	25	60	2	0	119	106	55	81	0	3.86
Jim McAndrew	R	29	3	8	.273	1	23	12	0	80	109	31	38	0	5.40
Buzz Capra	R	25	2	7	.222	4	24	0	0	48	38	35	0	3.86
2 John Strohmayer	R	26	0	1			6	0	0	10	13	4	5	0	8.10
Hank Webb	R	23	0	0			1	0	0	1	2	1	0	0	T
Bob Apodaca	R	23	0	0			1	0	0	2	0	1	0	0	T
3 Bob Miller	R	34	0	0			1	0	0	1	3	0	1	0	12.00
Tommy Moore	R	24	1	0	.000		3	0	0	6	3	1	0	0	9.00
Craig Swan	R	22	0	1	.000		3	1	0	4	10	2	4	0	9.00
Phil Hennigan	R	27	0	0			30	0	0	43	50	16	22	0	4.98

ST. LOUIS 2nd 81-81 .500 1.5 RED SCHOENDIENST

NAME	G by Pos	B	AGE	G	AB	R	H	2B	3B	HR	RBI	BB	SO	SB	BA	SA
TOTALS			27	162	5478	643	1418	240	35	75	592	531	796	100	.259	.357
Joe Torre	1B114, 3B58	R	32	141	519	67	149	17	2	13	69	65	78	2	.287	.403
Ted Sizemore	2B139, 3B3	R	28	142	521	69	147	22	1	1	54	60	34	6	.282	.334
Mike Tyson	SS128, 2B16	R	23	144	469	48	114	15	4	1	33	23	66	2	.243	.299
Ken Reitz	3B135, SS2	R	22	147	426	40	100	20	2	6	42	9	25	0	.235	.333
Luis Melendez	OF95	R	23	121	341	39	91	18	1	2	35	27	50	2	.267	.343
Jose Cruz	OF118	L	25	132	406	51	92	15	5	10	57	51	66	5	.227	.391
Lou Brock	OF159	L	34	160	650	110	193	29	8	7	63	71	112	70	.297	.398
Ted Simmons	C153, 1B6, OF2	B	23	161	619	62	192	36	2	13	91	61	47	2	.310	.438
Tim McCarver	1B77, C11	L	31	130	331	30	88	16	4	3	49	36	31	0	.266	.366
Bernie Carbo	OF94	L	25	111	308	42	88	18	0	8	40	58	52	2	.286	.422
Mick Kelleher	SS42	R	25	43	38	4	7	2	0	0	4	2	11	0	.184	.237
Bake McBride	OF17	L	24	44	63	9	19	3	0	0	5	4	11	0	.302	.349
Bill Stein	OF10, 1B2, 3B1	R	26	32	55	4	12	2	0	0	7	1	8	0	.218	.255
Jim Dwyer	OF20	L	23	28	57	7	11	1	1	0	5	11	10	0	.193	.246
2 Tommie Agee	OF19	R	30	26	62	8	11	3	1	0	7	5	13	1	.177	.403
1 Ray Busse	SS23	R	24	24	70	3	10	3	0	1	4	4	23	0	.143	.343

Tom Heintzelman 26 R 9-29, 1 Ed Crosby 24 L 5-39, 1 Dwain Anderson 25 R 2-17, 2 Dave Campbell 31 R 0-21,
2 Matty Alou 34 L 3-11, Terry Hughes 24 R 3-14, Heity Cruz 20 R 0-11, Bob Fenwick 26 R 1-6, Tommy Cruz 22 L 0-0,
2 Larry Haney 30 R 0-1, Marc Hill 21 R 0-3

NAME	T	AGE	W	L	PCT	SV	G	GS	CG	IP	H	BB	SO	SHO	ERA
		29	81	81	.500	36	162	162	42	1461	1366	486	867	14	3.25
Rick Wise	R	27	16	12	.571	0	35	34	14	259	259	59	144	5	3.37
Reggie Cleveland	R	25	14	10	.583	0	32	32	6	224	211	61	122	3	3.01
Alan Foster	R	26	13	9	.591	0	35	29	6	204	195	63	106	2	3.13
Bob Gibson (KJ)	R	37	12	10	.545	0	25	25	13	195	159	57	142	1	2.77
Diego Segui	R	35	7	6	.538	17	65	0	0	100	78	53	93	0	2.79
2 Orlando Pena	R	39	4	4	.500	6	42	0	0	62	60	14	38	0	2.18
Rich Folkers	L	26	4	4	.500	3	34	9	1	82	74	34	44	0	3.62
Tom Murphy	R	27	3	7	.300	0	19	13	2	89	89	22	42	0	3.74
2 Eddie Fisher	R	36	2	1	.667	0	7	0	0	7	1	1	0	0	1.29
Al Hrabosky	L	23	2	4	.333	5	44	0	0	56	45	21	57	0	2.09
1 Wayne Granger	R	29	2	4	.333	5	33	0	0	47	51	21	14	0	4.21
John Andrews	L	24	1	1	.500	0	16	6	1	47	56	21	20	0	4.50
Scipio Spinks (SJ)	R	25	1	5	.167	0	8	8	0	39	39	25	25	0	4.85
2 Ed Sprague	R	27	0	1		0	8	0	0	8	8	4	2	0	2.25
Al Santorini	R	25	0	0		0	4	0	0	5	2	3	2	0	5.63
Mike Thompson	R	23	0	0		0	7	1	0	16	22	11	5	0	7.31
Lew Krausse	R	30	0	0		0	3	0	0	3	4	2	0	0	9.00
Mike Nagy	R	25	0	0	.000	0	7	0	0	41	44	15	14	0	4.17
1 Jim Bibby	R	28	0	0	.000	0	3	0	0	16	19	17	12	0	9.56

PITTSBURGH 3rd 80-82 .494 2.5 BILL VIRDON 67-69 .493 DANNY MURTAUGH 13-13 .500

NAME	G by Pos	B	AGE	G	AB	R	H	2B	3B	HR	RBI	BB	SO	SB	BA	SA
TOTALS			27	162	5489	704	1465	257	44	154	664	432	842	23	.261	.405
Bob Robertson	1B107	R	26	119	397	43	95	16	0	14	40	55	77	0	.239	.385
Dave Cash	2B92, 3B17	R	25	116	436	59	118	21	2	2	31	38	36	2	.271	.342
2 Dal Maxvill	SS74	R	34	74	217	19	41	4	3	0	17	22	44	0	.189	.235
Richie Hebner	3B139	L	25	144	509	73	138	28	1	25	74	56	60	0	.271	.477
Richie Zisk	OF84	R	24	103	333	44	108	23	1	10	54	21	63	0	.324	.526
Al Oliver	OF109, 1B50	L	26	158	654	90	191	38	7	20	99	22	52	6	.292	.463
Willie Stargell	OF142	L	33	148	522	106	156	43	3	44	119	80	129	0	.299	.646
Manny Sanguillen	C89, OF59	R	29	149	640	66	166	26	7	12	65	17	29	2	.282	.411
Rennie Stennett	2B84, SS43, OF5	R	22	128	466	45	113	9	3	10	55	16	63	0	.242	.358
Gene Clines (NJ)	OF77	R	26	110	304	42	80	11	3	1	23	26	36	8	.263	.329
Milt May	C79	L	22	101	283	29	76	8	1	7	34	26	26	0	.269	.378
Gene Alley	SS49, 3B8	R	32	76	158	25	32	3	2	6	20	28	21	1	.203	.285
1 Vic Davalillo	1B10, OF10	L	36	59	83	9	15	1	0	1	3	2	7	0	.181	.229
Dave Parker	OF39	L	22	54	139	17	40	9	1	4	14	2	27	1	.288	.453
Jackie Hernandez	SS49	R	32	54	73	8	13	1	2	0	4	4	12	0	.247	.315
Fernando Gonzalez	3B5	R	23	37	49	4	11	0	0	1	4	2	6	1	.224	.327

Dave Augustine 23 R 2-7, Jerry McNertney 36 R 1-4, Jim Campanis 29 R 1-6, 1 Chuck Goggin 27 B 1-1

NAME	T	AGE	W	L	PCT	SV	G	GS	CG	IP	H	BB	SO	SHO	ERA
		29	80	82	.494	44	162	162	26	1451	1426	564	839	11	3.73
Nelson Briles	R	29	14	13	.519	0	33	33	7	219	201	51	94	1	2.84
Bob Moose	R	25	12	13	.480	0	33	29	6	201	219	70	111	3	3.54
Dock Ellis (EJ)	R	28	12	14	.462	0	28	28	3	192	176	55	122	1	3.05
Jim Rooker	L	30	10	6	.625	1	41	18	6	170	143	52	122	3	2.86
Dave Giusti	R	33	9	2	.818	20	67	0	0	99	98	34	68	0	2.36
Luke Walker	L	29	7	12	.368	1	37	18	2	122	129	66	74	1	4.65
Bob Johnson	R	30	4	2	.667	4	52	2	0	92	98	34	68	0	3.62
Ramon Hernandez	L	32	4	5	.444	11	59	0	0	90	71	25	64	0	2.40
Bruce Kison (SA)	R	23	3	0	1.000	0	10	7	1	47	42	21	27	0	3.09
Steve Blass	R	31	3	9	.250	0	23	18	1	89	109	84	27	0	9.81
John Morlan	R	25	2	2	.500	0	10	7	1	41	42	23	23	0	3.95
Jim Foor	L	24	0	0		1	6	0	0	9	8	4	6	0	6.00
John Lamb	L	27	0	0		0	10	0	0	30	30	10	11	0	6.00
Jim McKee	R	26	0	1	.000	0	15	0	0	27	31	11	13	0	5.00
Tom Dettore	R	26	0	1	.000	1	13	0	0	23	33	14	13	0	5.87
Chris Zachary	R	29	0	1	.000	0	10	1	0	16	13	6	7	0	9.00

MONTREAL 4th 79-83 .488 3.5 GENE MAUCH

NAME	G by Pos	B	AGE	G	AB	R	H	2B	3B	HR	RBI	BB	SO	SB	BA	SA
TOTALS			28	162	5369	668	1345	190	23	125	613	695	777	77	.251	.364
Mike Jorgensen	1B123, OF11	L	24	138	413	49	95	16	2	9	47	64	49	16	.230	.344
Ron Hunt (KJ)	2B102, 3B14	R	32	113	401	61	124	14	0	1	18	52	19	10	.309	.344
Tim Foli (BJ)	SS123, 2B, OF1	R	22	126	458	37	110	11	0	2	36	19	40	8	.240	.277
Bob Bailey	3B146, OF2	R	30	151	513	77	140	25	4	26	86	88	99	5	.273	.489
Ken Singleton	OF161	B	26	162	560	100	169	26	4	23	103	123	91	2	.302	.479
Ron Woods	OF114	R	30	133	318	45	73	11	3	3	36	32	48	12	.230	.311
Ron Fairly	OF121, 1B5	L	34	143	413	70	123	13	1	17	49	86	33	0	.298	.458
John Boccabella	C117, 1B1	R	32	118	425	25	94	13	0	7	46	26	57	1	.233	.318
Hal Breeden	1B66	L	29	105	258	36	71	10	6	15	43	29	45	0	.275	.535
Boots Day	OF51	L	25	101	207	36	57	7	0	4	23	29	16	5	.275	.367
Pepe Frias	SS46, 2B4, 3B6, OF1	R	24	100	258	24	59	5	2	1	16	12	45	1	.231	.284
Clyde Mashore (IL)	OF44, 2B1	R	28	67	103	12	21	5	1	4	15	13	31	0	.204	.388
Larry Lintz	2B34, SS15	B	23	59	116	13	27	0	3	0	7	18	22	12	.233	.284
Jim Lyttle	OF36	L	27	49	116	12	30	4	1	2	11	9	14	0	.259	.362
Bob Stinson	C35, 1B1	B	27	48	116	14	35	8	0	1	16	13	20	3	.302	.397
Terry Humphrey	C35	R	23	43	90	15	15	4	0	0	7	7	14	0	.167	.222
Pepe Mangual	OF22	R	21	33	62	7	11	2	1	0	1	5	17	7	.177	.387

Jorge Roque 23 R 9-61, Coco Laboy 33 R 4-33, 2 Felipe Alou 38 R 10-48, 2 Bernie Allen 34 L 9-50, Tony Scott 21 B 0-1
Jim Cox 23 R 2-15, Barry Foote 21 R 4-6, 2 Jose Morales 28 R 2-5, Curt Brown 27 R 0-4

NAME	T	AGE	W	L	PCT	SV	G	GS	CG	IP	H	BB	SO	SHO	ERA
		26	79	83	.488	38	162	162	26	1452	1356	681	866	6	3.71
Steve Renko	R	28	15	11	.577	0	36	34	9	250	201	108	164	0	2.81
Mike Marshall	R	30	14	11	.560	31	92	0	0	179	163	75	124	0	2.66
Steve Rogers	R	23	10	5	.667	0	17	17	7	134	93	49	64	3	1.54
Mike Torrez	R	26	9	12	.429	0	35	34	3	208	207	115	90	1	4.46
Tom Walker	R	24	7	5	.583	4	54	0	0	92	95	42	68	0	3.62
Ernie McAnally	R	26	9	7	.438	0	27	24	4	147	158	54	72	0	4.04
Balor Moore	L	22	7	16	.304	0	35	32	3	176	151	109	151	4	4.50
Bill Stoneman (SJ)	R	29	4	8	.333	1	29	17	0	97	120	55	48	0	6.77
Chuck Taylor	R	31	2	0	1.000	7	27	0	0	20	17	3	18	0	1.80
Pat Jarvis (VJ)	R	32	2	1	.667	0	20	4	0	37	44	9	23	0	3.23
2 Mickey Scott	L	26	1	3	.333	2	28	0	0	44	48	11	21	0	5.25
Joe Gilbert	R	26	1	1	.500	2	27	0	0	42	39	24	30	0	4.97
Craig Caskey	R	23	0	0		0	14	0	0	14	15	14	9	0	5.79
John Montague	R	25	0	0	.000	0	5	1	0	21	22	8	9	0	3.38
John Strohmayer	R	26	0	0	.000	0	5	0	0	34	40	16	16	0	5.14

CHICAGO 5th 77-84 .478 5 WHITEY LOCKMAN

NAME	G by Pos	B	AGE	G	AB	R	H	2B	3B	HR	RBI	BB	SO	SB	BA	SA
TOTALS			31	161	5363	614	1322	201	21	117	570	575	855	65	.247	.357
Jim Hickman	1B51, OF13	R	36	92	201	27	49	1	2	3	20	42	42	1	.244	.338
Glenn Beckert (FJ)	2B88	R	32	114	372	38	95	13	0	2	29	30	15	0	.255	.290
Don Kessinger	SS158	B	30	160	577	52	151	22	3	0	43	57	44	6	.262	.310
Ron Santo	3B146	R	33	149	536	65	143	29	2	20	77	63	97	1	.267	.440
Jose Cardenal	OF142	R	29	145	522	80	158	33	2	11	68	58	62	19	.303	.437
Rick Monday	OF148	L	27	149	554	93	148	24	5	26	56	92	124	5	.267	.469
Billy Williams	OF138, 1B16	L	35	156	576	72	166	22	2	20	86	76	72	4	.288	.438
Randy Hundley	C122	R	31	124	368	35	83	11	1	10	43	30	51	5	.226	.342
Gene Hiser	OF64	L	24	100	109	15	19	3	0	1	6	11	17	4	.174	.229
Paul Popovich	2B84, SS9, 3B1	B	32	99	280	24	66	6	3	2	24	18	27	3	.236	.300
Carmen Fanzone	3B25, 1B24, OF6	R	31	64	150	22	41	7	0	6	22	20	38	1	.273	.440
Ken Rudolph	C64	R	26	64	170	12	35	8	1	2	17	7	25	1	.206	.300
1 Pat Bourque	1B38	L	25	57	139	11	29	6	0	7	20	16	21	1	.209	.403
Cleo James	OF22	R	32	44	45	9	5	0	0	0	6	1	6	5	.111	.111
Adrian Garrett	OF7, C6	L	30	36	54	7	12	0	0	3	8	4	18	1	.222	.389
1 Joe Pepitone	1B28	L	32	31	112	16	30	3	0	3	18	8	6	3	.268	.375
2 Rico Carty	OF19	R	33	22	70	4	15	0	0	1	6	6	10	0	.214	.257
2 Gonzalo Marquez	1B18	L	27	19	58	5	13	2	0	1	4	3	4	0	.224	.310
Andre Thornton	1B9	R	23	17	35	3	7	3	0	0	2	2	7	0	.200	.286
Dave Rosello	2B13, SS1	R	23	16	38	4	10	2	0	0	2	2	4	2	.263	.316

Matt Alexander 26 B 1-5, Pete LaCock 21 L 4-16, Tom Lundstedt 24 B 0-5, Tony LaRussa 28 R 0-0

NAME	T	AGE	W	L	PCT	SV	G	GS	CG	IP	H	BB	SO	SHO	ERA
		27	77	84	.478	40	161	161	27	1438	1471	438	885	13	3.66
Rick Reuschel	R	24	14	15	.483	0	36	36	7	237	244	62	168	3	3.00
Ferguson Jenkins	R	29	14	16	.467	0	38	38	7	271	267	57	170	2	3.89
Burt Hooton	R	23	14	17	.452	0	42	34	9	240	248	73	134	2	3.68
Bob Locker	R	35	10	6	.625	18	63	0	0	106	96	42	76	0	2.55
Bill Bonham	R	24	7	5	.583	6	44	15	3	152	126	64	121	0	3.02
Milt Pappas	R	34	7	12	.368	0	30	29	1	162	192	40	48	1	4.28
Dave LaRoche	L	25	4	1	.800	4	45	0	0	54	55	29	34	0	5.83
Jack Aker	R	32	4	5	.444	12	47	0	0	64	76	23	25	0	4.08
Larry Gura	L	25	2	4	.333	0	21	7	0	65	79	11	43	0	4.85
Ray Burris	R	22	1	1	.500	0	31	1	0	65	65	27	57	0	2.91
2 Mike Paul	L	28	0	1	.000	0	11	1	0	18	17	9	6	0	3.50
1 Juan Pizarro	L	36	0	1	.000	0	2	0	0	4	6	1	3	0	11.25

PHILADELPHIA 6th 71-91 .438 11.5 DANNY OZARK

NAME	G by Pos	B	AGE	G	AB	R	H	2B	3B	HR	RBI	BB	SO	SB	BA	SA
TOTALS			26	162	5546	642	1381	218	29	134	592	476	979	51	.249	.371
Willie Montanez	1B99, OF51	L	25	146	552	69	145	16	5	11	65	46	80	2	.263	.370
Denny Doyle	2B114	L	29	116	370	45	101	9	3	3	26	31	32	1	.273	.338
Larry Bowa (BL)	SS122	B	27	122	446	42	94	11	3	0	23	24	31	10	.211	.249
Mike Schmidt	3B125, 2B4, 1B2, SS2	R	23	132	367	43	72	11	0	18	52	62	136	1	.196	.373
Bill Robinson	OF113, 3B14	R	30	124	452	62	130	32	1	25	65	27	91	5	.288	.529
Del Unser	OF132	L	28	136	440	64	127	20	4	11	52	47	55	5	.289	.427
Greg Luzinski	OF159	R	22	161	610	76	174	26	4	29	97	51	135	3	.285	.484
Bob Boone	C145	R	25	145	521	42	136	20	2	10	61	41	36	1	.261	.365
Tommy Hutton	1B71	L	27	106	247	31	65	11	0	5	29	32	31	3	.263	.368
Cesar Tovar (KJ)	3B46, OF24, 2B22	R	32	97	328	49	88	18	4	1	21	29	35	6	.268	.357
Mike Anderson (JJ)	OF67	R	22	87	193	32	49	9	1	9	28	19	53	0	.254	.451
Terry Harmon	2B43, SS19, 3B1	R	29	72	148	17	31	3	0	0	8	13	14	1	.209	.230
Mike Rogodzinski	OF16	L	25	66	80	13	19	3	0	2	7	12	19	0	.238	.350
Craig Robinson	SS42, 2B4	R	24	46	146	11	33	7	0	0	9	0	25	1	.226	.274
Jose Pagan	3B16, 1B5, OF2, 2B1	R	38	46	78	4	16	5	0	1	6	1	15	0	.205	.269
Ken Brett	P31	R	24	37	80	6	20	5	0	4	16	4	11	0	.250	.463
Mike Ryan	C27	R	31	28	69	7	16	1	2	1	5	6	19	0	.232	.348
2 Billy Grabarkewitz	2B20, 3B3, OF1	R	27	25	66	12	19	2	0	2	7	12	18	1	.288	.409
1 Deron Johnson	1B10	R	34	12	36	3	6	2	0	1	5	5	10	0	.167	.306
Jim Essian	C1	R	22	2	3	0	0	0	0	0	0	0	1	0	.000	.000
Larry Cox	C1	R	25	1	1	0	0	0	0	0	0	0	0	0	—	—

NAME	T	AGE	W	L	PCT	SV	G	GS	CG	IP	H	BB	SO	SHO	ERA
		27	71	91	.438	22	162	162	49	1447	1435	632	919	11	3.99
Wayne Twitchell	R	25	13	9	.591	0	34	28	10	223	172	99	169	5	2.50
Ken Brett	L	24	13	9	.591	0	25	25	10	212	206	74	111	1	3.44
Jim Lonborg	R	31	13	16	.448	0	38	30	6	199	218	80	106	0	4.88
Steve Carlton	L	28	13	20	.394	0	40	40	18	293	293	113	223	3	3.90
Dick Ruthven (IL)	R	22	6	9	.400	1	25	23	3	128	125	75	98	1	4.22
2 George Culver	R	29	3	1	.750	0	14	0	0	19	26	15	7	0	4.74
Barry Lersch	R	28	3	6	.333	1	42	4	0	98	105	27	51	0	4.41
Darrell Brandon	R	32	2	4	.333	2	36	0	0	56	54	25	25	0	5.46
Mike Wallace	L	22	1	1	.500	1	20	3	1	33	38	15	20	0	3.82
Dick Selma	R	29	1	1	.500	0	6	0	0	8	6	5	4	0	5.63
Billy Wilson	R	30	1	3	.250	4	44	0	0	49	54	29	24	0	6.61
Larry Christenson	R	19	1	4	.200	0	10	9	1	34	53	20	11	0	6.62
Mac Scarce	L	24	1	8	.111	12	52	0	0	71	54	47	57	0	2.41
Ron Diorio	R	26	0	0	—	1	23	0	0	19	18	6	11	0	2.37
Dave Wallace	R	25	0	0	—	0	4	0	0	4	13	2	2	0	20.25

Dave Downs (SA) 21

WEST DIVISION

CINCINNATI 1st 99-63 .611 SPARKY ANDERSON

NAME	G by Pos	B	AGE	G	AB	R	H	2B	3B	HR	RBI	BB	SO	SB	BA	SA
TOTALS			27	162	5505	741	1398	232	34	137	686	639	947	148	.254	.383
Tony Perez	1B151	R	31	151	564	73	177	33	3	27	101	74	117	3	.314	.527
Joe Morgan	2B154	L	29	157	576	116	167	35	2	26	82	111	61	67	.290	.493
Dave Concepcion (BN)	SS88, OF2	R	25	89	328	39	94	18	3	8	46	21	55	22	.287	.433
Denis Menke	3B123, SS7, 2B5, 1B1	R	32	139	241	38	46	10	0	3	26	69	53	1	.191	.270
Bobby Tolan	OF120	L	27	129	457	42	94	14	2	9	51	27	68	15	.206	.304
Cesar Geronimo	OF130	L	25	139	324	35	68	14	3	4	33	23	74	5	.210	.309
Pete Rose	OF159	B	32	160	680	115	230	36	8	5	64	65	42	10	.338	.437
Johnny Bench	C134, OF23, 1B4, 3B1	R	25	152	557	83	141	17	3	25	104	83	83	4	.253	.429
Darrel Chaney	SS75, 2B14, 3B12	B	25	105	227	27	41	7	1	0	14	26	50	4	.181	.220
Dan Driessen	3B87, 1B35, OF1	L	21	102	366	49	110	15	2	4	47	24	37	8	.301	.385
Larry Stahl	OF29, 1B2	L	32	76	111	17	25	2	2	2	12	14	34	1	.225	.333
Phil Gagliano	3B7, 2B4, 1B1, 3B5	R	31	63	69	8	20	2	0	0	7	13	16	0	.290	.319
Bill Plummer	C42, 3B5	R	26	50	119	8	18	3	0	2	11	8	26	1	.151	.227
Andy Kosco	OF36, 1B1	R	31	47	118	17	33	7	0	9	21	13	26	0	.280	.568
2 Ed Crosby	SS29, 2B5	L	24	36	51	4	11	1	1	0	5	7	12	0	.216	.275
Hal King	C9	L	29	35	43	5	8	0	0	4	10	6	10	0	.186	.465
1 Gene Locklear	OF5	L	23	29	26	6	5	0	0	0	1	2	6	0	.192	.192
1 Richie Scheinblum	OF19	B	30	29	54	5	12	2	0	1	8	10	4	0	.222	.315
Ken Griffey	OF21	L	23	25	86	19	33	5	1	3	14	6	10	4	.384	.570
Joe Hague	OF5, 1B4	L	29	19	33	2	5	2	0	0	1	5	5	1	.152	.212
Ed Armbrister	OF14	R	24	18	37	5	8	3	1	1	5	2	8	0	.216	.432
George Foster	OF13	R	24	17	39	6	11	3	0	4	9	4	7	0	.282	.667
Bob Barton	C2	R	31	5	2	0	0	0	0	0	0	1	0	0	.000	.000

NAME	T	AGE	W	L	PCT	SV	G	GS	CG	IP	H	BB	SO	SHO	ERA
		27	99	63	.611	43	162	162	33	1473	1389	518	801	17	3.40
Jack Billingham	R	30	19	10	.655	0	40	40	16	293	257	95	155	7	3.04
Don Gullett	L	22	18	8	.692	2	45	30	7	228	198	69	153	4	3.51
Ross Grimsley	L	23	13	10	.565	1	38	36	8	242	245	68	90	1	3.24
2 Fred Norman	L	30	12	6	.667	0	24	24	7	166	136	72	112	3	3.31
Pedro Borbon	R	26	11	4	.733	14	80	0	0	121	137	35	60	0	2.16
Tom Hall	L	25	8	5	.615	8	54	7	0	104	74	48	96	0	3.46
Clay Carroll	R	32	8	8	.500	14	53	5	0	93	111	34	41	0	3.68
Roger Nelson (EJ)	R	29	3	2	.600	0	14	8	1	55	49	24	17	0	3.44
1 Jim McGlothlin	R	29	3	3	.500	0	24	9	0	63	91	23	18	0	6.71
Dick Baney	R	26	2	1	.667	2	11	0	0	31	26	6	17	0	2.90
Dave Tomlin	L	24	1	2	.333	1	16	0	0	28	24	15	20	0	4.82
1 Ed Sprague	R	27	1	3	.250	1	28	0	0	39	35	22	19	0	5.08
Gary Nolan (SA)	R	25	1	0	1.000	0	2	0	1	10	6	7	3	0	3.60

LOS ANGELES 2nd 95-66 .590 3.5 WALT ALSTON

NAME	G by Pos	B	AGE	G	AB	R	H	2B	3B	HR	RBI	BB	SO	SB	BA	SA
TOTALS			27	162	5604	675	1473	219	29	110	623	497	795	109	.263	.371
Bill Buckner	1B93, OF48	L	23	140	575	68	158	20	0	8	46	17	34	12	.275	.337
Davey Lopes	2B135, OF5, SS2, 3B1	R	28	142	535	77	147	13	5	6	37	62	77	36	.275	.351
Bill Russell	SS162	R	24	162	615	55	163	26	3	4	56	34	63	15	.265	.337
Ron Cey	3B146	R	25	152	507	60	124	18	4	15	80	74	77	1	.245	.385
Willie Crawford	OF138	L	26	145	457	75	135	26	4	14	66	78	91	12	.295	.453
Willie Davis	OF146	L	33	152	599	82	171	29	9	16	77	29	62	17	.285	.444
Manny Mota	OF74	R	35	89	293	30	92	11	2	0	23	26	12	5	.314	.365
Joe Ferguson	C122, OF20	R	26	136	487	84	128	26	0	25	88	87	81	1	.263	.470
Steve Garvey	1B76, OF10	R	24	114	349	37	106	17	3	8	50	11	42	0	.304	.438
Tom Paciorek	OF77, 1B4	R	26	96	195	26	51	8	0	5	18	11	35	3	.262	.379
Von Joshua (BW)	OF46	L	25	75	159	19	40	4	1	2	17	8	29	7	.252	.327
Lee Lacy	2B41	R	25	57	135	14	28	2	0	2	8	15	34	1	.207	.222
Steve Yeager	C50	R	24	54	134	18	34	5	0	2	10	15	33	1	.254	.336
Ken McMullen (XJ)	3B24	R	31	42	85	6	21	5	0	1	6	8	13	0	.247	.482
Chris Cannizzaro	C13	R	35	17	21	0	4	0	0	0	3	2	3	0	.190	.190
Jerry Royster	3B6, 2B1	R	20	19	1	4	0	0	0	2	0	5	1	.211	.211
Jim Fairey		L	28	10	9	1	2	0	0	0	1	3	0	.222	.222

Orlando Alvarez 21 R 1-4, Paul Powell 25 R 0-1

NAME	T	AGE	W	L	PCT	SV	G	GS	CG	IP	H	BB	SO	SHO	ERA
		30	95	66	.590	38	162	162	45	1491	1270	461	961	15	3.00
Don Sutton	R	28	18	10	.643	0	33	33	14	256	196	56	200	3	2.43
Tommy John	L	30	16	7	.696	0	36	31	4	218	202	50	116	2	3.10
Claude Osteen	L	33	16	11	.593	0	33	33	12	237	227	61	86	3	3.30
Andy Messersmith	R	27	14	10	.583	0	33	33	10	250	196	77	177	3	2.70
Al Downing	L	32	9	9	.500	0	30	28	5	193	155	68	124	2	3.31
Jim Brewer	R	35	8	7	.533	20	56	0	0	72	58	25	56	0	3.00
Charlie Hough	R	25	4	2	.667	5	37	0	0	72	52	45	70	0	2.75
Doug Rau	L	24	2	2	.500	0	31	3	0	64	64	28	51	0	3.94
1 George Culver	R	29	1	0	1.000	3	19	0	0	42	45	21	23	0	3.00
Pete Richert	L	33	3	3	.500	7	39	0	0	51	44	19	31	0	3.18
Geoff Zahn	L	27	1	0	1.000	0	6	1	0	13	5	2	9	0	1.38
Greg Shanahan	R	25	0	0	—	1	7	0	0	16	14	6	11	0	3.38
Eddie Solomon	R	22	0	0	—	0	6	0	0	6	10	4	6	0	7.50
Greg Heydeman	R	21	0	0	—	0	4	0	0	6	6	4	2	0	4.50

SAN FRANCISCO 3rd 88-74 .543 11 CHARLIE FOX

NAME	G by Pos	B	AGE	G	AB	R	H	2B	3B	HR	RBI	BB	SO	SB	BA	SA
TOTALS			25	162	5537	739	1452	212	52	161	684	590	913	112	.262	.407
Willie McCovey	1B117	L	35	130	383	52	102	14	3	29	75	105	78	1	.266	.546
Tito Fuentes	2B160, 3B1	R	29	160	656	78	182	25	5	6	63	45	62	12	.277	.358
Chris Speier	SS150, 2B1	R	23	153	542	58	135	11	4	11	71	66	69	4	.249	.356
Ed Goodson	3B93	L	25	102	384	37	116	20	1	12	53	15	44	0	.302	.453
Bobby Bonds	OF158	R	27	160	643	131	182	34	4	39	96	87	148	43	.283	.530
Garry Maddox	OF140	R	23	144	587	81	187	30	10	11	76	24	73	24	.319	.460
Gary Matthews	OF145	R	22	148	540	74	162	22	10	12	58	58	83	17	.300	.444
Dave Rader	C148	L	24	148	462	59	106	15	4	9	41	63	52	0	.229	.338
Dave Kingman	3B60, 1B46, P2	R	24	112	305	54	62	10	1	24	55	41	122	8	.203	.479
Gary Thomasson	1B47, OF43	L	21	112	235	35	67	10	4	4	30	22	43	2	.285	.413
Jim Howarth	OF33,1B1	L	26	65	90	8	18	1	1	0	7	8	22	0	.200	.233
Mike Phillips	3B28, SS20, 2B7	L	22	63	104	18	25	3	0	0	6	4	30	0	.240	.375
Chris Arnold	C9, 2B1, 3B1	R	25	49	54	7	16	2	0	1	3	8	11	0	.296	.389
Mike Sadek	C35	R	27	39	66	6	11	1	0	0	4	6	11	0	.167	.212
Damie Blanco	3B7, SS5, 2B3	R	31	28	12	4	0	0	0	0	0	0	5	0	.000	.000
Steve Ontiveros	1B5, OF1	L	21	24	33	3	8	2	0	0	4	6	3	0	.242	.333
Bruce Miller	3B4, 2B3. SS1	R	26	12	21	1	3	0	0	0	2	3	6	0	.143	.143
1 Alan Gallagher	3B5	R	26	12	9	1	2	0	0	0	1	1	0	0	.222	.222
1 Jim Ray Hart		R	31	5	2	0	0	0	0	0	0	0	1	0	.000	.000

NAME	T	AGE	W	L	PCT	SV	G	GS	CG	IP	H	BB	SO	SHO	ERA
		28	88	74	.543	44	162	162	33	1452	1442	485	787	8	3.79
Ron Bryant	L	25	24	12	.667	0	41	39	8	270	240	115	143	0	3.53
Tom Bradley	R	26	13	12	.520	0	35	34	6	224	212	69	136	1	3.90
Juan Marichal	R	35	11	15	.423	0	34	32	9	207	231	37	87	2	3.83
Jim Barr	R	25	11	17	.393	2	41	33	8	231	240	49	88	3	3.82
Elias Sosa	R	23	10	4	.714	18	71	1	0	107	95	41	70	0	3.28
Don McMahon (RC)	R	43	4	0	1.000	6	22	0	0	36	21	20	30	0	1.50
Randy Moffitt	R	24	4	5	.444	14	60	0	0	100	86	31	65	0	2.43
Jim Willoughby	R	24	4	5	.444	1	39	12	1	123	138	37	60	1	4.68
Charlie Williams	R	25	3	0	1.000	0	12	2	0	23	32	7	11	0	6.65
John Morris (BG)	L	31	1	0	1.000	6	12	0	0	6	12	3	3	0	9.00
John D'Acquisto	R	21	1	1	.500	0	3	2	0	28	23	19	29	0	3.54
Don Carrithers	R	23	1	1	.500	1	25	3	0	58	64	35	36	0	4.81
1 Sam McDowell	L	30	2	3	.333	3	18	3	0	40	45	29	35	0	4.50
Dave Kingman	R	24	0	0	—	0	2	0	0	4	3	6	4	0	9.00

HOUSTON — 4th 82-80 .506 17 — LEO DUROCHER

NAME	G by Pos	B	AGE	G	AB	R	H	2B	3B	HR	RBI	BB	SO	SB	BA	SA
TOTALS			29	162	5532	681	1391	216	35	134	634	469	962	92	.251	.376
Lee May	1B144	R	30	148	545	65	147	24	3	28	105	34	122	1	.270	.479
Tommy Helms	2B145	R	32	146	543	44	156	28	2	4	61	32	21	1	.287	.368
Roger Metzger	SS149	B	25	154	580	67	145	11	14	1	35	39	70	10	.250	.322
Doug Rader	3B152	R	28	154	574	79	146	26	0	21	89	46	97	4	.254	.409
Bob Watson	OF142, 1B26, C3	R	27	158	573	97	179	24	3	16	94	45	73	1	.312	.449
Cesar Cedeno	OF136	R	22	139	525	86	168	35	2	25	70	41	79	56	.320	.537
Jim Wynn	OF133	R	31	139	481	90	106	14	5	20	55	91	102	14	.220	.395
Skip Jutze	C86	R	27	90	278	18	62	6	0	0	18	19	37	0	.223	.245
1 Tommie Agee	OF67	R	30	83	204	30	48	5	2	8	15	16	55	2	.235	.397
Johnny Edwards (IL)	C76	L	35	79	250	24	61	10	2	5	27	19	23	1	.244	.360
Bob Gallagher	OF42, 1B1	L	24	71	148	16	39	3	1	2	10	3	27	0	.264	.338
Jimmy Stewart	3B8, OF3, 2B1	B	34	61	68	6	13	0	0	0	3	9	12	0	.191	.191
Hector Torres	SS22, 2B13	R	27	38	66	3	6	1	0	0	2	7	13	0	.091	.106
1 Jesus Alou	OF14	R	31	28	55	7	13	2	0	1	8	1	6	0	.236	.327
1 Larry Howard	C20	R	28	20	48	3	8	3	0	0	4	5	12	0	.167	.229
Gary Sutherland	2B14, SS1	R	28	16	54	8	14	5	0	0	3	3	5	0	.259	.352
2 Ray Busse	SS5, 3B3	R	24	15	17	1	1	0	0	0	0	1	12	0	.059	.059
Greg Gross	OF9	L	20	14	39	5	9	2	1	0	1	4	4	2	.231	.333
Rafael Batista	1B8	R	27	12	15	2	4	0	0	0	2	1	6	0	.267	.267
3 Dave Campbell	3B5, 1B2, OF1	R	31	9	15	1	4	2	0	0	2	0	4	0	.267	.400
Cliff Johnson	1B5	R	25	7	20	6	6	2	0	2	6	6	1	0	.300	.700

Mike Easler 22 L 0-7, 1 Norm Miller (XJ) 27 L 0-3, Otis Thornton 28 R 0-3

NAME	T	AGE	W	L	PCT	SV	G	GS	CG	IP	H	BB	SO	SHO	ERA
TOTALS		28	82	80	.506	26	162	162	45	1461	1389	575	907	14	3.75
Dave Roberts	L	28	17	11	.607	0	39	36	12	249	264	62	119	6	2.86
Jerry Reuss	R	24	16	13	.552	0	41	40	12	279	271	117	177	3	3.74
Don Wilson	R	28	11	16	.407	2	37	32	10	239	187	92	149	3	3.20
Ken Forsch	R	26	9	12	.429	4	46	26	5	201	197	74	149	0	4.21
J.R. Richard	R	23	6	2	.750	0	16	10	2	72	54	38	75	1	4.00
Jim Ray	R	28	6	4	.600	4	42	0	0	69	65	38	25	0	4.43
Tom Griffin (VJ)	R	25	4	6	.400	0	25	12	4	100	83	46	69	0	4.14
Jim York	R	25	3	4	.429	6	41	0	0	53	46	29	22	0	4.42
Fred Gladding	R	37	2	1	.667	1	16	0	0	16	18	4	9	0	4.50
2 Juan Pizarro	R	36	2	2	.500	0	15	1	0	23	28	11	10	0	6.65
2 Cecil Upshaw	R	30	2	3	.400	1	35	0	0	38	38	15	21	0	4.50
Jim Crawford	L	22	2	4	.333	1	48	0	0	70	69	33	56	0	4.50
Larry Dierker (RJ,SJ)	R	26	1	1	.500	0	14	3	0	27	27	13	18	0	4.33
Mike Cosgrove	L	22	1	1	.500	0	13	0	0	11	11	8	2	0	1.80
Doug Konieczny	R	21	0	1	.000	0	2	2	0	13	12	4	6	0	5.54

ATLANTA — 5th 76-85 .472 22.5 — EDDIE MATHEWS

NAME	G by Pos	B	AGE	G	AB	R	H	2B	3B	HR	RBI	BB	SO	SB	BA	SA
TOTALS			29	162	5631	799	1497	219	34	206	758	608	870	84	.266	.427
Mike Lum	1B84, OF64	L	27	138	513	74	151	26	6	16	82	41	89	2	.294	.462
Dave Johnson	2B156	R	30	157	559	84	151	25	0	43	99	81	93	5	.270	.546
Marty Perez	SS139	R	27	141	501	66	125	15	5	8	57	49	66	2	.250	.347
Darrell Evans	3B146, 1B20	L	26	161	595	114	167	25	8	41	104	124	104	6	.281	.556
Hank Aaron	OF105	R	39	120	392	84	118	12	1	40	96	68	51	1	.301	.643
Dusty Baker	OF156	R	24	159	604	101	174	29	4	21	99	67	72	24	.288	.454
Ralph Garr	OF148	L	27	148	668	94	200	32	6	11	55	22	64	35	.299	.415
Johnny Oates (KJ)	C86	L	27	93	322	27	80	6	0	4	27	22	31	1	.248	.304
Sonny Jackson	OF56, SS36	L	28	117	206	29	43	5	2	0	12	22	13	6	.209	.252
Dick Dietz	1B36, C20	R	31	83	139	22	41	8	1	3	24	49	25	0	.295	.432
Paul Casanova	C78	R	31	82	236	18	51	7	0	7	18	11	36	0	.216	.335
Frank Tepedino	1B58	L	25	74	148	20	45	5	0	4	29	13	21	0	.304	.419
2 Chuck Goggin	2B19, OF6, SS5, C1	B	27	64	90	18	26	5	0	0	9	9	19	2	.289	.344
Rod Gilbreath	3B22	R	20	29	74	10	21	2	1	0	2	6	10	2	.284	.338
Oscar Brown (JJ)	OF13	R	27	22	58	3	12	3	0	0	3	0	10	0	.207	.259
Larvell Blanks	3B3, 2B2, SS2	R	23	17	18	1	4	0	0	0	0	1	3	0	.222	.222
Freddy Velazquez	C11	R	35	15	23	2	8	1	0	0	3	1	3	0	.348	.391
Jack Pierce	1B5	L	24	11	20	1	1	0	0	0	1	1	5	0	.050	.050

2 Norm Miller (XJ) 27 L 3-8, 2 Larry Howard 28 R 1-8, Leo Foster 22 R 1-6, 2 Joe Pepitone 32 L 4-11

NAME	T	AGE	W	L	PCT	SV	G	GS	CG	IP	H	BB	SO	SHO	ERA
TOTALS		28	76	85	.472	35	162	162	34	1462	1467	575	803	9	4.25
Carl Morton	R	29	15	10	.600	0	38	37	10	256	254	70	112	4	3.41
Phil Niekro	R	34	13	10	.565	4	42	30	9	245	214	89	131	1	3.31
Roric Harrison	R	26	11	8	.579	5	38	22	3	177	161	98	130	0	4.17
Ron Schueler	R	25	8	7	.533	2	39	20	4	186	179	66	124	2	3.87
Tom House	L	26	4	2	.667	4	52	0	0	67	58	31	42	0	4.70
Gary Gentry (EJ)	R	26	4	6	.400	1	16	14	3	87	74	35	42	0	3.41
Ron Reed (AJ)	R	30	4	11	.267	1	20	19	2	116	133	31	64	0	4.42
1 Pat Dobson	R	31	3	7	.300	0	12	10	1	58	73	19	23	1	4.97
Gary Neibauer	R	28	2	1	.667	0	16	1	0	21	24	19	9	0	7.29
1 Joe Hoerner (KJ)	L	36	2	2	.500	2	20	0	0	13	17	4	10	0	6.23
Max Leon	R	23	2	2	.500	0	12	1	1	27	30	9	18	0	5.33
Adrian Devine	R	21	2	3	.400	1	24	0	0	32	45	12	15	0	6.47
Jim Panther	R	28	2	3	.400	0	23	0	0	31	45	9	8	0	7.55
Joe Niekro	R	28	2	4	.333	2	20	4	0	24	23	11	12	0	4.13
Danny Frisella (SJ)	R	27	1	2	.333	8	42	0	0	45	40	23	27	0	4.20
Wenty Ford	R	26	1	1	.333	0	4	2	1	16	17	4	9	0	5.63

Tom Kelley 29 R 0-1, 1 Cecil Upshaw 30 R 0-1, Dave Cheadle 21 L 0-1,
Jimmy Freeman 22 L 0-2, Alan Closter 30 L 0-0
Mike McQueen (PB) 22

SAN DIEGO — 6th 60-102 .370 39 — DON ZIMMER

NAME	G by Pos	B	AGE	G	AB	R	H	2B	3B	HR	RBI	BB	SO	SB	BA	SA
TOTALS			26	162	5457	548	1330	198	26	112	516	401	966	88	.244	.351
Nate Colbert	1B144	R	27	145	529	73	143	25	2	22	80	54	146	9	.270	.450
2 Rich Morales	2B79, SS10	R	29	90	244	9	40	6	1	0	16	27	36	0	.164	.197
Derrel Thomas	SS74, 2B47	B	22	113	404	41	91	7	1	0	34	34	52	15	.238	.290
Dave Roberts	3B111, 2B12	R	22	127	479	56	137	20	3	21	64	17	83	11	.286	.472
Jerry Morales	OF100	R	24	122	388	47	109	23	2	9	34	27	55	6	.281	.420
Johnny Grubb	OF102, 3B2	L	24	113	389	52	121	20	3	8	37	37	50	9	.311	.445
Cito Gaston	OF119	R	29	133	476	51	119	18	4	16	57	20	88	0	.250	.405
Fred Kendall	C138	R	24	145	507	39	143	22	3	10	59	30	35	3	.282	.396
Leron Lee	OF84	L	25	118	333	36	79	7	3	3	30	33	61	4	.237	.297
Ivan Murrell	OF37, 1B24	R	30	93	210	23	48	13	1	9	21	2	52	2	.229	.429
Enzo Hernandez (NJ)	SS67	R	24	70	247	26	55	2	1	0	17	14	15	2	.223	.239
Dave Hilton	3B47, 2B23	R	22	70	234	21	46	9	0	5	16	19	35	2	.197	.299
2 Gene Locklear	OF37	L	23	67	154	20	37	6	1	3	25	6	20	1	.240	.351
Dave Winfield	OF36, 1B1	R	21	56	141	9	39	4	1	3	12	12	19	0	.277	.383
2 Dwain Anderson	SS39, 3B6	R	25	53	107	11	13	4	1	0	3	14	29	2	.121	.121
Dave Marshall	OF8	L	30	39	49	4	14	5	0	0	4	7	6	0	.286	.388
1 Dave Campbell	2B27, 1B3, 3B2	R	31	33	98	2	22	3	0	0	7	15	1	0	.224	.255
Pat Corrales	C28	R	32	29	72	7	15	2	1	0	3	6	10	0	.208	.264
Don Mason	2B1	R	28	8	8	0	0	0	0	0	0	2	0	0	.000	.000
Bob Davis	C5	R	21	5	11	1	1	0	0	0	0	0	5	0	.091	.091

NAME	T	AGE	W	L	PCT	SV	G	GS	CG	IP	H	BB	SO	SHO	ERA
TOTALS		26	60	102	.370	23	162	162	34	1430	1461	548	845	10	4.16
Steve Arlin	R	27	11	14	.440	0	34	27	7	180	196	72	98	3	5.10
Bill Greif	R	23	10	17	.370	1	36	31	9	199	181	62	120	3	3.21
Clay Kirby (SA)	R	25	8	18	.308	0	34	31	4	192	214	66	129	2	4.78
Randy Jones	L	23	7	6	.538	0	20	19	6	140	129	37	77	1	3.15
Rich Troedson	L	23	7	9	.438	1	50	18	2	152	167	59	81	0	4.26
Mike Corkins	R	27	5	8	.385	2	47	11	2	122	130	61	82	0	4.50
Mike Caldwell	L	24	5	14	.263	10	55	13	3	149	146	53	86	1	3.74
Gary Ross	R	25	4	4	.500	0	58	0	0	76	93	33	44	0	5.45
Vicente Romo	R	30	2	3	.400	7	49	1	0	88	85	46	51	0	3.68
1 Fred Norman	L	30	1	7	.125	0	12	11	1	74	72	29	49	0	4.26
Frank Snook	R	24	0	2	.000	1	18	0	0	27	19	18	13	0	3.67
1 Bob Miller	R	34	0	1		1	18	0	0	31	29	12	15	0	4.06

WORLD SERIES — OAKLAND (AL) 4 NEW YORK (NL) 3

LINE SCORES

TEAM	1 2 3	4 5 6	7 8 9	10 11 12	R	H	E

Game 1 October 13 at Oakland
NY(NL) 0 0 0 | 1 0 0 | 0 0 0 | | 1 7 2
OAK(AL) 0 0 2 | 0 0 0 | 0 0 X | | 2 4 0
Matlack, McGraw (7) — **Holtzman**, Fingers (6), Knowles (9)

Game 2 October 14 at Oakland
NY 0 1 1 | 0 0 4 | 0 0 0 | 0 0 4 | 10 15 1
OAK 2 1 0 | 1 0 2 | 0 0 2 | 0 0 0 | 7 13 5
Koosman, Sadecki (3), Parker (5), **McGraw** (6), Stone (12) — Blue, Pina (6), Knowles (6), Odom (8), **Fingers** (10), Lindblad (12)

Game 3 October 16 at New York
OAK 0 0 0 | 0 0 1 | 0 1 0 | 0 1 | 3 10 1
NY 2 0 0 | 0 0 0 | 0 0 0 | 0 0 | 2 10 2
Hunter, Knowles (7), **Lindblad** (9), Fingers (11) — Seaver, Sadecki (9), McGraw (9), **Parker** (11)

Game 4 October 17 at New York
OAK 0 0 0 | 1 0 0 | 0 0 0 | | 1 5 1
NY 3 0 0 | 0 0 0 | 0 0 x | | 6 13 1
Holtzman, Odom (1), Knowles (4), Pina (5), Lindblad (8) — **Matlack**, Sadecki (9)

Game 5 October 18 at New York
OAK 0 0 0 | 0 0 0 | 0 0 0 | | 0 3 1
NY 0 1 0 | 0 0 1 | 0 0 x | | 2 7 1
Blue, Knowles (6), Fingers (7) — **Koosman**, McGraw (7)

Game 6 October 20 at Oakland
NY 0 0 0 | 0 0 0 | 0 1 0 | | 1 6 2
OAK 1 0 1 | 0 0 0 | 0 1 x | | 3 7 0
Seaver, McGraw (8) — **Hunter**, Knowles (8), Fingers (8)

Game 7 October 21 at Oakland
NY 0 0 0 | 0 0 1 | 0 0 1 | | 2 8 1
OAK 0 0 4 | 0 0 0 | 0 0 x | | 5 9 1
Matlack, Parker (3), Sadecki (5), Stone (7) — **Holtzman**, Fingers (6), Knowles (9)

COMPOSITE BATTING

Oakland (AL)

NAME	POS	G	AB	R	H	2B	3B	HR	RBI	BA
Totals		7	241	21	51	12	3	2	20	.212
Campaneris	SS	7	31	6	9	0	1	1	3	.290
Jackson	OF	7	29	3	9	3	1		6	.310
Rudi	OF	7	27	3	9	2	0		4	.333
Bando	3B	7	26	5	6	1	1	0	1	.231
Alou	OF	7	19	0	3	1	0	0		.158
Fosse	C	7	19	0	3	1	0	0		.158
Tenace	1B-C	7	19	3	3	1	0	0		.158
Green	2B	7	16	0	1	0	0	0		.063
Davalillo	OF-1B	6	11	0	1	0	0	0		.091
Johnson	1B	6	10	0	3	1	0	0		.300
Mangual	OF	5	6	0	0	0	0	0		.000
Hunter	P	2	5	0	0	0	0	0		.000
Blue	P	2	4	0	0	0	0	0		.000
Holtzman	P	3	3	2	2	1	0	0		.667
Fingers	P	6	3	0	1	0	0	0		.333
Kubiak	2B	3	3	1	0	0	0	0		.000
Conigliaro	PH	3	3	0	0	0	0	0		.000
Andrews	2B	2	3	0	0	0	0	0		.000
Bourque	1B	2	2	0	1	0	0	0		.500
Odom	P-PR	3	1	0	0	0	0	0		.000
Lindblad	P	2	0	0	0	0	0	0		.000

Knowles P 0-0, Lewis PR 0-0, Pina P 0-0

New York (NL)

NAME	POS	G	AB	R	H	2B	3B	HR	RBI	BA
Totals		7	261	24	66	7	2	4	16	.253
Millan	2B	7	32	3	6	1	1	0	1	.188
Grote	C	7	30	2	8	1	0		1	.267
Garrett	3B	7	30	4	5	0	0	2	1	.167
Hahn	OF	7	29	2	7	0	0	0		.241
Jones	OF	7	28	5	8	2	0	0		.286
Milner	1B	7	27	2	8	1	0	0		.296
Staub	OF	7	26	1	11	2	0	1	6	.423
Harrelson	SS	7	24	2	6	1	0	0		.250
Mays	OF	7	24	2	6	0	0	0		.286
Seaver	P	2	5	0	0	0	0	0		.000
Beauchamp	PH	4	4	0	0	0	0	0		.000
Matlack	P	3	4	0	1	0	0	0		.250
Koosman	P	3	4	0	0	0	0	0		.000
Boswell	PH	3	3	1	3	0	0	0		1.000
McGraw	P	5	3	1	1	0	0	0		.333
Kranepool	OF	3	3	0	0	0	0	0		.000
Theodore	OF	4	0	0	0	0	0	0		.000

Sadecki P 0-0, Parker P 0-0, Martinez PR 0-0, Stone P 0-0, Hodges PH 0-0

COMPOSITE PITCHING

Oakland (AL)

NAME	G	IP	H	BB	SO	W	L	SV	ERA
Totals	7	66	66	26	36	4	3	4	2.32
Fingers	6	13.2	13	4	8	0	1	2	0.66
Hunter	2	13.1	11	4	6	1	0	0	2.03
Blue	2	11	10	8	0	1	0		4.91
Hotzman	3	10.2	13	5	6	2	1	0	4.22
Knowles	7	6.1	4	5	0	0	0	2	0.00
Odom	2	4.2	5	2	2	0	0	0	3.86
Lindblad	3	3.1	4	1	1	0	0	0	0.00
Pina	2	3	6	2	0	0	0	0	0.00

New York (NL)

NAME	G	IP	H	BB	SO	W	L	SV	ERA
Totals	7	65	51	28	62	3	4	3	2.22
Matlack	3	16.2	10	5	11	1	2	0	2.16
Seaver	2	15	13	3	18	0	1	0	2.40
McGraw	5	13.2	8	9	14	1	0	1	2.63
Koosman	2	8.2	9	7	8	1	0	0	3.12
Sadecki	4	4.2	5	1	6	0	0	1	1.93
Parker	3	3.1	2	2	3	0	0	0	0.00
Stone	2	4	1	3	4	1	0	1	0.00

1974 Aaron in April, Oakland in October

History was made as the season began—Hank Aaron broke Babe Ruth's home run record. Aaron's feat came on the night of April 8th, when he hit home run no. 715 off of the Los Angeles Dodgers' Al Downing. The "shot" from Atlanta's stadium finally put to rest the controversy which began when Braves' owner, Bill Bartholomay, opted to save the history-making feat for Atlanta by benching Aaron in the three-game opener at Cincinnati. Commissioner Bowie Kuhn stepped in and ordered Aaron to play. He did. In his first at bat he slammed home run no. 714 off of Jack Billingham to tie Ruth's lifetime total. Of course, no other home runs were hit at Cincinnati, and the durable Aaron returned home to end the most publicized chase in baseball history at 9:07 Eastern Standard Time before a standing-room-only crowd of 53,775.

With the home run question settled, baseball returned to its divisional races. In the American League West, Oakland, despite losing manager Dick Williams after their 1973 World Series triumph, took their fourth straight divisional title, this one under the reins of Al Dark. In Dark's second turn at the helm under owner Charles O. Finley, the race was taken by five games over the improving Texas Rangers, who were helped by the acquisition of Ferguson Jenkins and the development of young Jeff Burroughs, who won the league's MVP honors. For the A's, Catfish Hunter won 25 games and Rollie Fingers chalked up 18 saves in 76 appearances. Reggie Jackson led the offense with 29 home runs, but lost the power title to Dick Allen, who finished with 32 homers despite "retiring" from the White Sox on September 14th. Two other footnotes to the A's season included the debuts of Claudell and Herb Washington, who were related by name only. Claudell, 19 years old, finished the season at .285 with only a year-and-a-half baseball experience. Herb became the game's first full-time pinch runner owing to his ability as a world class sprinter. Without any professional baseball experience, he went on to steal 29 bases in 45 attempts.

In the A.L. East, Baltimore won 28 of their last 34 games to beat the greatly improved New York Yankees by two games. After beating the Yankees in a three-game series in early September to take a half-game lead, the Orioles went on their stretch drive, which included 15 one-run victories. Other A.L. highlights included Al Kaline's 3000th hit, and Nolan Ryan's third no-hitter.

In the N.L. West, the Dodgers ruled the roost on newly acquired Mike Marshall's arm, which was strong enough to chalk up a record 106 relief appearances and win the Cy Young Award, and the bat of Steve Garvey, which produced a .312 average and 111 runs batted in, good enough to earn him MVP honors. In the East, the St. Louis Cardinals seemed to have everything with Lou Brock stealing a record 118 bases, and newly-acquired Reggie Smith driving in 100 runs, to go with Ted Simmons' 103. But the Cards could not overcome a disappointing starting staff, which featured Bob Gibson's fall to an 11-13 record in a season which saw him achieve the unique goal of recording his 3000th strikeout to join the immortal Walter Johnson in that category. As a result of the Redbirds' poor front line pitching, the Pittsburgh Pirates, led by the bats of Willie Stargell, Al Oliver, and Richie Zisk, and the arms of Jim Rooker and Jerry Reuss, won the division by a game-and-a-half.

In the playoffs, Oakland took Baltimore in four games and the Dodgers eliminated the Pirates in four games. For the World Series it was a question of Los Angeles' youth against Oakland's experience. Experience prevailed as the A's won their third straight crown, 4 games to 1.

1974 AMERICAN LEAGUE — EAST DIVISION

NAME	G by Pos	B	AGE	G	AB	R	H	2B	3B	HR	RBI	BB	SO	SB	BA	SA
BALTIMORE 1st 91-71 .562	EARL WEAVER		28	162	5535	659	1418	226	27	116	608	509	770	145	.256	.370
Boog Powell	1B102,DH1	L	32	110	344	37	91	13	1	12	45	52	58	0	.265	.413
Bobby Grich	2B160	R	25	160	582	92	153	29	6	19	82	90	117	17	.263	.431
Mark Belanger	SS155	R	30	155	493	54	111	14	4	5	36	51	69	17	.225	.300
Brooks Robinson	3B153	R	37	153	553	46	159	27	0	7	59	56	47	2	.288	.374
Rich Coggins	OF105	L	23	113	411	53	100	13	3	4	32	29	31	26	.243	.319
Paul Blair	OF151	R	30	151	552	77	144	27	4	17	62	43	59	27	.261	.417
Don Baylor	OF129,1B8,DH1	R	25	137	489	66	133	22	1	10	59	43	56	29	.272	.382
Earl Williams	C75,1B47,DH1	R	25	118	413	47	105	16	0	14	52	40	79	0	.254	.395
Tommy Davis	DH155	R	35	158	626	67	181	20	1	11	84	34	49	6	.289	.377
Al Bumbry	OF67,DH7	L	27	94	270	35	63	10	3	1	19	21	46	12	.233	.304
Enos Cabell 1B28,OF22,3B19,2B1,DH1		R	24	80	174	24	42	4	2	3	17	7	29	5	.241	.339
Ellie Hendricks	C54,1B1,DH1	L	33	66	159	18	33	8	2	3	17	15	25	0	.208	.340
Jim Fuller	OF59,1B4,DH2	R	23	64	189	17	42	11	0	7	28	6	88	1	.222	.392
Andy Etchebarren	C60	R	31	62	180	13	40	8	0	2	15	6	26	1	.222	.300
Frank Baker	SS17,2B3,3B1	L	27	24	29	3	5	1	0	0	3	5	0	.172	.207
Mike Reinbach	OF3,DH3	R	24	12	20	2	5	1	0	0	2	2	5	0	.250	.300
2 Bob Oliver	1B4,DH1	R	31	9	20	1	3	2	0	0	4	0	5	1	.150	.250
3 Jim Northrup	OF6,DH1	L	34	8	7	2	4	0	0	1	3	2	1	0	.571	1.000

Tim Nordbrook 24 R 4-15, Curt Motton 33 R 0-8, Doug DeCinces 23 R 0-1

NEW YORK 2nd 89-73 .549 2	BILL VIRDON		28	162	5524	671	1451	220	30	101	637	515	690	53	.263	.368
2 Chris Chambliss	1B106	L	25	110	400	38	97	16	3	6	43	23	43	0	.243	.343
2 Sandy Alomar	2B76	B	30	76	279	35	75	8	0	1	27	14	25	6	.269	.308
Jim Mason	SS152	L	23	152	440	41	110	18	6	5	37	35	87	1	.250	.352
Graig Nettles	3B154,SS1	L	29	155	566	74	139	21	1	22	75	59	75	1	.246	.403
Bobby Murcer	OF156	L	28	156	606	69	166	25	4	10	88	57	59	14	.274	.378
Elliott Maddox	OF135,2B2,3B1	R	26	137	466	75	141	26	2	3	45	69	48	6	.303	.386
Lou Piniella	OF130,DH6,1B1	R	30	140	518	71	158	26	0	9	70	32	58	1	.305	.407
Thurman Munson	C137,DH4	R	27	144	517	64	135	19	2	13	60	44	66	2	.261	.381
Ron Blomberg	DH58,OF19	L	25	90	264	39	82	11	2	10	48	29	33	2	.311	.481
Roy White	OF136	B	30	136	473	68	130	19	8	7	43	67	44	15	.275	.393
Bill Sudakis	DH39,1B33,3B3,C1	B	28	89	259	26	60	8	0	7	39	25	48	0	.232	.344
Gene Michael	2B45,SS39,3B2	B	36	81	177	19	46	9	1	1	13	14	24	1	.260	.311
2 Fernando Gonzalez	2B42,3B7,SS3	R	24	51	121	11	26	5	1	1	7	7	7	0	.215	.298
Rick Dempsey	C31,OF2,DH1	R	24	43	109	12	26	3	0	2	12	8	7	1	.239	.321
Walt Williams	OF24,DH3	R	30	43	53	5	6	0	0	0	3	1	10	1	.113	.113
Fred Stanley	SS19,2B15	R	26	33	38	2	7	0	0	0	3	3	2	1	.184	.184
Otto Velez	1B21,OF3,3B2	R	23	27	67	9	14	1	1	2	10	15	24	0	.209	.343
1 Horace Clarke	2B20,DH1	B	34	24	47	3	11	1	0	0	1	4	5	1	.234	.255
1 Mike Hegan	1B17	L	31	18	53	3	12	2	0	2	9	5	9	1	.226	.377
2 Alex Johnson	DH4,OF1	R	31	10	28	3	6	1	0	2	0	3	0	.214	.357

Jim Ray Hart 32 R 1-19, 1 Duke Sims 33 L 2-15, Larry Murray 21 B 0-1, Terry Whitfield 21 L 1-5, Jim Deidel 25 R 0-2

BOSTON 3rd 84-78 .519 7	DARRELL JOHNSON		27	162	5499	696	1449	236	31	109	658	569	811	104	.264	.377
Carl Yastrzemski	1B84,OF63,DH4	L	34	148	515	93	155	25	2	15	79	104	48	12	.301	.445
Doug Griffin (PB)	2B91,SS1	R	27	93	312	35	83	12	4	0	33	28	21	2	.266	.330
Mike Guerrero	SS93	R	24	93	284	19	70	6	2	0	23	13	22	3	.246	.282
Rico Petrocelli	3B116,DH9	R	31	129	454	53	121	23	1	15	76	48	74	1	.267	.421
Dwight Evans	OF122,DH7	R	22	133	463	60	130	19	8	10	70	38	77	4	.281	.421
Juan Beniquez	OF97,DH4	R	24	106	389	60	104	14	3	5	33	25	61	19	.267	.357
Bernie Carbo	OF87,DH15	L	26	117	338	40	84	20	0	12	61	58	90	4	.249	.414
Carlton Fisk (KJ)	C50,DH2	R	26	52	187	36	56	12	1	11	26	24	23	5	.299	.551
Tommy Harper	OF61,DH51	R	33	118	443	66	105	15	3	5	24	46	65	28	.237	.318
Cecil Cooper	1B74,DH41	L	24	121	414	55	114	24	1	8	43	32	74	2	.275	.396
Rick Burleson	SS88,2B31,3B2	R	23	114	384	36	109	22	0	4	44	21	34	3	.284	.372
Rick Miller	OF105	L	26	114	280	41	73	8	1	5	22	37	47	13	.261	.350
Dick McAuliffe	2B53,3B40,SS3,DH3	L	34	100	272	32	57	13	1	5	24	39	40	2	.210	.320
Bob Montgomery	C79,DH5	R	30	88	254	26	64	10	0	4	38	13	50	3	.252	.350
Danny Cater	1B23,DH14	R	34	56	126	14	31	5	0	5	20	10	13	1	.246	.405
Tim Blackwell	C44	B	21	44	122	9	16	1	0	0	6	10	24	1	.246	.270
Terry Hughes	3B36,DH1	R	25	41	69	5	14	2	0	1	6	6	13	0	.203	.275
Jim Rice	DH16,OF3	R	21	24	67	6	18	2	1	1	13	4	12	0	.269	.373
Fred Lynn	OF12,DH1	L	22	15	43	5	18	2	2	2	10	6	6	0	.419	.698
3 Deron Johnson	DH8	R	35	11	25	3	3	0	1	1	1	0	3	0	.120	.120

2 Tim McCarver 32 L 7-28, John Kennedy 33 R 2-15, Bob Didier 25 B 1-14, Chuck Goggin 28 B 0-1

Pitchers

NAME	T	AGE	W	L	PCT	SV	G	GS	CG	IP	H	BB	SO	SHO	ERA
BALTIMORE		27	91	71	.562	25	162	162	57	1474	1393	480	701	16	3.27
Mike Cuellar	L	37	22	10	.688	0	38	38	20	269	253	86	106	5	3.11
Ross Grimsley	L	24	18	13	.581	1	40	39	17	296	287	76	158	4	3.07
Dave McNally	L	31	16	10	.615	1	39	37	13	259	260	81	111	4	3.58
Bob Reynolds	R	27	7	5	.583	7	54	0	0	69	75	14	43	0	2.74
Jim Palmer (SA)	R	28	7	12	.368	0	26	26	5	179	176	69	84	2	3.27
Grant Jackson	L	31	6	4	.600	12	49	0	0	67	48	22	56	0	2.55
Doyle Alexander	R	23	6	9	.400	0	30	12	2	114	127	43	40	0	4.03
Wayne Garland	R	23	5	5	.500	1	20	6	0	91	68	26	40	0	2.97
Dave Johnson	R	25	2	2	.500	2	11	0	0	15	17	5	6	0	3.00
Jesse Jefferson	R	25	1	0	1.000	1	20	2	0	57	55	38	31	0	4.42
Don Hood	L	24	1	1	.500	1	20	2	0	57	47	20	26	0	3.47

NEW YORK		28	89	73	.549	24	162	162	53	1455	1402	528	829	13	3.31
Pat Dobson	R	32	19	15	.559	0	39	39	12	281	282	75	157	2	3.07
Doc Medich	R	25	19	15	.559	0	38	38	17	280	275	91	154	4	3.60
2 Dick Tidrow	R	27	11	9	.550	1	33	25	5	191	205	53	100	0	3.86
Sparky Lyle	L	29	9	3	.750	15	66	0	0	114	93	43	89	0	1.66
2 Rudy May (SJ)	L	29	8	4	.667	0	17	15	8	114	75	48	90	2	2.29
2 Mike Wallace	L	23	6	0	1.000	0	23	1	0	52	42	35	34	0	2.42
Mel Stottlemyre (SJ)	R	32	6	7	.462	0	16	15	6	113	119	37	40	0	3.58
Larry Gura	L	26	5	1	.833	0	8	8	3	56	54	12	17	2	2.41
2 Steve Kline	R	26	2	2	.500	0	4	4	0	26	26	5	6	0	3.46
2 Dick Woodson	R	29	1	2	.333	0	8	3	0	28	34	12	12	0	5.79
Dave Pagan	R	24	1	3	.250	0	16	6	1	49	49	28	39	0	5.14
2 Cecil Upshaw	R	31	1	5	.167	6	36	0	0	60	53	24	37	0	3.00
Sam McDowell (XJ-J)	L	31	1	6	.143	0	13	7	0	48	42	41	33	0	4.69
Tippy Martinez	L	24	0	1		0	10	0	0	13	14	9	14	0	4.15
1 Fred Beene	R	31	0	0		0	9	0	0	10	9	2	10	0	2.70
1 Fritz Peterson	L	32	0	0		0	3	1	0	8	13	2	5	0	4.50
Ken Wright	R	27	0	0		0	4	0	0	5	7	2	0	0	3.00
Rick Sawyer	R	26	0	0		0	3	1	0	6	5	3	3	0	13.50
1 Tom Buskey	R	27	0	1	.000	2	10	0	0	6	10	1	3	0	6.00

BOSTON		29	84	78	.519	18	162	162	71	1455	1462	463	751	12	3.72
Luis Tiant	R	33	22	13	.629	0	38	38	25	311	281	82	176	7	2.92
Bill Lee	L	27	17	15	.531	0	38	37	16	282	320	67	95	1	3.51
Reggie Cleveland	R	26	12	14	.462	0	41	27	10	221	234	69	103	0	4.32
Roger Moret	L	24	9	10	.474	2	31	21	10	173	158	79	111	1	3.75
Dick Drago	R	29	7	10	.412	3	33	18	8	176	165	56	90	0	3.48
Diego Segui	R	36	6	8	.429	10	58	0	0	108	106	49	76	0	4.00
Juan Marichal (XJ)	R	36	5	1	.833	0	11	9	0	57	61	14	21	0	4.89
Rick Wise (SJ)	R	28	3	4	.429	0	9	9	1	49	47	16	25	0	3.86
Steve Barr	L	22	1	0	1.000	0	2	1	1	7	6	3	0	0	4.00
Lance Clemons	L	26	1	0	1.000	0	6	0	0	8	4	1	0	0	10.50
Dick Pole	R	23	1	1	.500	1	15	2	0	45	55	13	32	0	4.20
Bob Veale	L	38	0	1	.000	1	13	0	0	13	14	16	15	0	5.54
Don Newhauser	R	26	0	0		0	5	0	0	5	9	8	4	1	9.00

CLEVELAND 4th 77-85 .475 14   KEN ASPROMONTE

NAME	G by Pos	B	AGE	G	AB	R	H	2B	3B	HR	RBI	BB	SO	SB	BA	SA
TOTALS			25	162	5474	662	1395	201	19	131	616	432	756	79	.255	.370
Johnny Ellis (BF)	1B69,C42,DH21	R	25	128	477	58	136	23	6	10	64	32	53	1	.285	.421
Jack Brohamer	2B99	L	24	101	315	33	85	11	1	2	30	26	22	1	.270	.330
Frank Duffy	SS158	R	27	158	549	62	128	18	0	8	48	30	64	7	.233	.310
Buddy Bell (KJ)	3B115,DH1	R	22	116	423	51	111	19	1	7	46	35	29	1	.262	.352
Charlie Spikes	OF154	R	23	155	568	63	154	23	1	22	80	34	100	10	.271	.431
George Hendrick	OF133,DH1	R	24	139	495	65	138	21	1	19	67	33	73	6	.279	.444
John Lowenstein	OF100,3B12,1B12,2B4	L	27	140	508	65	123	14	2	8	48	53	85	36	.242	.325
Dave Duncan	C134,1B3,DH1	R	28	136	425	45	85	11	0	16	46	42	91	0	.200	.341
Oscar Gamble	DH115,OF13	L	24	135	454	74	132	16	4	19	59	48	51	5	.291	.469
Rusty Torres	OF94,DH1	B	25	108	150	19	28	2	0	3	12	13	24	2	.187	.260
Leron Lee	OF62,DH1	L	26	79	232	18	54	13	0	5	25	15	42	3	.233	.353
3 Luis Alvarado	2B46,SS7DH3	R	25	61	114	12	25	2	0	0	12	6	14	1	.219	.237
2 Joe Lis	1B31,3B9,DH9,OF1	R	27	57	109	15	22	3	0	6	16	14	30	1	.202	.394
Angel Hermoso (KJ)	2B45	R	27	48	122	15	27	3	1	0	5	7	7	2	.221	.262
2 Tommy McCraw	1B38,DH2,OF1	L	33	45	112	17	34	8	0	3	17	5	11	0	.304	.455
Ed Crosby	3B18,SS13,2B3	R	25	37	86	11	18	3	0	0	6	6	12	0	.209	.244
Rico Carty	DH14,1B8	R	34	33	91	6	33	5	0	1	16	5	9	0	.363	.451
Tommy Smith (BA)	OF17,DH1	R	25	23	31	4	3	1	0	0	0	2	7	0	.097	.129
Ossie Blanco	1B16,DH1	R	28	18	36	1	7	0	0	0	2	7	4	0	.194	.194
1 Chris Chambliss	1B17	L	25	17	67	8	22	4	0	0	7	5	5	0	.328	.388
1 Frank Robinson	DH11,1B4	R	38	15	50	6	10	1	1	2	5	10	10	0	.200	.380

Duane Kuiper 24 L 11-22, Johnnie Jeter 29 R 6-17, 1 Jack Heidemann 24 R 1-11, Alan Ashby 22 B 1-7 , Dwain Anderson 26 R 1-3. Larry Johnson 23 R 0-0

NAME	T	AGE	W	L	PCT	SV	G	GS	CG	IP	H	BB	SO	SHO	ERA
		30	77	85	.475	27	162	162	45	1446	1419	479	650	9	3.80
Gaylord Perry	R	35	21	13	.618	0	37	37	28	322	230	99	216	4	2.52
Jim Perry	R	38	17	12	.586	0	36	36	8	252	242	64	71	3	2.96
2 Fritz Peterson	L	32	9	14	.391	0	29	29	3	153	187	37	52	0	4.35
Dick Bosman	R	30	7	5	.583	0	25	18	2	127	126	29	56	1	4.11
Tom Hilgendorf	L	32	4	3	.571	3	35	0	0	48	58	17	23	0	4.88
2 Fred Beene	R	31	4	4	.500	2	32	0	0	73	68	26	35	0	4.93
Bob Johnson	R	31	3	4	.429	1	14	10	0	72	75	37	36	0	4.38
2 Steve Kline (EJ)	R	26	3	8	.273	0	16	11	1	71	70	31	17	0	5.07
Milt Wilcox	R	24	2	2	.500	4	41	2	1	71	74	24	33	0	4.69
Steve Arlin	R	28	2	5	.286	0	11	10	1	44	59	22	20	0	6.55
2 Tom Buskey	R	27	2	6	.250	17	51	0	0	93	93	33	40	0	3.19
Bruce Ellingsen	L	25	1	1	.500	0	16	2	0	42	45	17	16	0	3.21
Tom Timmermann	R	34	1	1	.500	0	4	0	0	10	9	5	2	0	5.40
1 Dick Tidrow	R	27	1	3	.250	0	4	4	0	19	21	13	8	0	7.11
Bill Gogolewski	R	26	0	0	—	0	5	0	0	14	15	2	3	0	4.50
Jim Kern	R	25	0	1	.000	0	4	3	1	15	16	14	11	0	4.80
1 Ken Sanders	R	32	0	1	.000	0	8	0	0	11	21	5	4	0	9.82
1 Cecil Upshaw	R	31	0	0	—	0	7	0	0	8	10	4	7	0	3.38

*1 loss by forfeit

MILWAUKEE 5th 76-86 .469 15   DEL CRANDALL

NAME	G by Pos	B	AGE	G	AB	R	H	2B	3B	HR	RBI	BB	SO	SB	BA	SA
TOTALS			27	162	5472	647	1335	228	49	120	612	500	909	106	.244	.369
George Scott	1B148,DH9	R	30	158	604	74	170	36	2	17	82	59	90	9	.281	.432
Pete Garcia	2B140	R	24	141	452	46	90	15	4	3	54	26	67	8	.199	.330
Robin Yount	SS107	R	18	107	344	48	86	14	5	3	26	12	46	7	.250	.346
Don Money	3B157,2B1,DH1	R	27	159	629	85	178	32	3	15	65	62	80	19	.283	.415
Dave May	OF121,DH8	L	30	135	477	56	108	15	1	10	42	28	73	4	.226	.325
Bob Coluccio	OF131,DH2	R	22	138	394	42	88	13	4	6	31	43	61	15	.223	.322
Johnny Briggs	OF149,DH2	L	30	154	554	72	140	30	8	17	73	71	102	9	.253	.428
Darrell Porter	C117,DH9	L	22	131	432	59	104	15	4	12	56	50	88	8	.241	.377
Bobby Mitchell	DH53,OF26	L	30	88	173	27	42	6	5	2	20	18	46	7	.243	.387
Ken Berry	OF82,DH13	R	33	98	267	21	64	9	2	1	24	18	26	3	.240	.300
Tim Johnson	SS64,2B26,3B1,OF1,DH1	L	24	93	245	25	60	7	0	0	25	11	48	4	.245	.331
2 Mike Hegan	DH37,1B7,OF17	L	31	89	190	21	45	7	1	7	32	33	34	0	.237	.395
Charlie Moore	C61,DH6	R	21	72	204	17	50	10	4	0	19	21	34	3	.245	.333
Bob Hansen	DH18,1B3	L	26	58	88	8	26	4	1	2	9	3	16	2	.295	.432
2 Deron Johnson	DH46,1B2	R	35	49	152	14	23	3	0	6	18	21	41	1	.151	.289
John Vukovich	3B12,SS12,2B11,1B4	R	26	38	80	5	15	1	0	3	11	1	16	2	.188	.313
Rob Ellis	OF11,DH9,3B1	R	23	22	48	4	14	2	0	0	4	1	8	1	.292	.333
Gorman Thomas	OF13,DH2	R	23	17	46	10	12	4	0	2	11	8	15	4	.261	.478

Sixto Lezcano 20 R 13-54, Bobby Sheldon 23 L 2-17, Jack Lind 28 B 4-17, Felipe Alou 39 R 0-3

NAME	T	AGE	W	L	PCT	SV	G	GS	CG	IP	H	BB	SO	SHO	ERA
		26	76	86	.469	24	162	162	43	1458	1476	493	621	11	3.76
Jim Slaton	R	24	13	16	.448	0	40	35	10	250	255	102	126	3	3.92
Billy Champion	R	26	11	4	.733	0	31	23	2	162	168	49	60	0	3.61
Tom Murphy	R	28	10	10	.500	20	70	0	0	123	97	51	47	0	1.90
Jim Colborn (GJ)	R	28	10	13	.435	0	33	31	10	224	230	60	83	1	4.06
Clyde Wright	L	33	9	20	.310	0	38	32	15	232	264	54	64	0	4.42
Ed Sprague (KJ)	R	28	7	2	.778	0	20	10	3	94	94	31	57	0	2.39
Eduardo Rodriguez	R	22	7	4	.636	4	43	6	0	112	97	51	58	0	3.62
Kevin Kobel	L	20	6	14	.300	0	34	24	3	169	166	54	74	2	3.99
Bill Travers	L	21	2	3	.400	0	23	1	0	53	59	30	31	0	4.92
Jerry Bell	R	26	1	1	1.000	0	5	0	0	14	17	5	4	0	2.57
Bill Castro	R	20	0	0	—	0	18	0	0	18	19	5	10	0	4.50
Larry Anderson	R	21	0	0	—	0	2	0	0	2	1	2	0	0	4.50
Roger Miller	R	19	0	0	—	0	2	0	0	2	3	1	2	0	13.50
2 Dick Selma	R	30	0	0	—	0	5	0	0	5	6	5	1	0	22.50

DETROIT 6th 72-90 .444 19   RALPH HOUK

NAME	G by Pos	B	AGE	G	AB	R	H	2B	3B	HR	RBI	BB	SO	SB	BA	SA
TOTALS			30	162	5568	620	1375	200	35	131	579	436	784	67	.247	.366
Bill Freehan	1B65,C63,DH1	R	32	130	445	58	132	17	5	18	60	42	44	2	.297	.479
Gary Sutherland	2B147,SS10,3B4	R	29	149	619	60	157	20	1	5	49	26	37	1	.254	.313
Eddie Brinkman	SS151,3B2	R	32	153	502	55	111	15	3	14	54	29	71	2	.221	.347
Aurelio Rodriguez	3B159	R	26	159	571	54	127	23	5	5	49	36	70	2	.222	.306
1 Jim Northrup	OF97	L	34	97	376	41	89	12	1	11	42	36	46	0	.237	.362
Mickey Stanley (BH)	OF91,1B12,2B1	R	31	99	394	40	87	13	2	8	34	26	63	5	.221	.325
Willie Horton (KJ)	OF64,DH1	R	31	72	238	32	71	8	1	15	47	21	36	0	.298	.529
Jerry Moses	C74	R	27	74	198	19	47	6	3	4	19	11	38	0	.237	.359
Al Kaline	DH146	R	39	147	558	71	146	28	2	13	64	65	75	2	.262	.389
Ben Oglivie	OF63,1B10,DH4	L	25	92	252	28	68	11	3	4	29	34	38	12	.270	.385
Gates Brown	DH13	L	35	73	99	7	24	2	0	4	17	10	15	0	.242	.384
Dick Sharon	OF56	R	24	60	129	12	28	4	0	2	10	14	29	4	.217	.295
Gene Lamont	C60	L	27	60	92	4	20	4	0	3	7	8	19	0	.217	.359
Ron LeFlore	OF59	R	26	59	254	37	66	8	1	2	13	13	58	23	.260	.323
John Knox	2B33,DH2,3B1	L	25	55	88	11	27	1	1	0	6	6	13	5	.307	.341
Norm Cash	1B44	L	39	53	149	11	34	3	2	7	12	19	30	1	.228	.416
Marvin Lane	OF46,DH1	R	24	50	103	16	24	4	1	2	9	19	24	2	.233	.350
Jim Nettles	OF41	L	27	43	141	20	32	5	1	6	17	15	26	3	.227	.404
Reggie Sanders	1B25,DH1	R	24	26	99	12	27	7	0	3	10	5	20	1	.273	.434
Tom Veryzer	SS20	R	21	22	55	4	13	2	0	2	9	5	8	1	.236	.382
Ron Cash (IL)	1B15,3B4	R	24	20	62	6	14	2	0	0	5	0	11	0	.226	.258
Leon Roberts	OF17	R	23	17	63	5	17	3	2	0	7	3	10	0	.270	.381

Dan Meyer 21 L 10-50, John Wockenfuss 25 R 4-29, Ike Brown 32 R 0-2

NAME	T	AGE	W	L	PCT	SV	G	GS	CG	IP	H	BB	SO	SHO	ERA
		29	72	90	.444	15	162	162	54	1456	1443	621	869	7	4.16
John Hiller	L	31	17	14	.548	13	59	0	0	150	127	62	134	0	2.64
Mickey Lolich	L	33	16	21	.432	0	41	41	27	308	310	78	202	3	4.15
Joe Coleman	R	27	14	12	.538	0	41	41	11	286	272	158	177	2	4.31
Lerrin LaGrow	R	25	8	19	.296	0	37	34	11	216	245	80	85	0	4.31
Woody Fryman	L	34	6	9	.400	0	27	22	4	142	120	67	92	1	4.31
Luke Walker (YJ)	L	30	5	5	.500	0	28	9	0	92	100	54	52	0	4.99
Vern Ruhle	R	23	2	0	1.000	0	5	3	1	33	35	6	10	0	2.73
Dave Lemanczyk	R	23	2	1	.667	0	22	3	0	79	79	44	52	0	3.99
Bill Slayback	R	26	1	3	.250	0	16	4	0	55	57	26	23	0	4.75
Jim Ray	R	29	1	3	.250	2	28	0	0	52	49	29	26	0	4.50
Chuck Seelbach	R	26	0	0	—	0	4	0	0	8	3	0	3	0	4.50
Fred Holdsworth	R	22	0	3	.000	0	8	5	0	36	40	14	16	0	4.25

WEST DIVISION

OAKLAND 1st 90-72 .556   AL DARK

NAME	G by Pos	B	AGE	G	AB	R	H	2B	3B	HR	RBI	BB	SO	SB	BA	SA
TOTALS			28	162	5331	689	1315	205	37	132	637	568	876	164	.247	.373
Gene Tenace	1B106,C79,2B3	R	27	158	484	71	102	17	1	26	73	110	105	2	.211	.411
Dick Green	2B100	R	33	100	287	20	61	8	2	2	22	22	50	2	.213	.275
Bert Campaneris	SS133,DH1	R	32	134	527	77	153	18	4	2	41	47	81	34	.290	.366
Sal Bando	3B141,DH3	R	30	146	498	84	121	21	2	22	103	86	79	2	.243	.426
Reggie Jackson	OF127,DH19	L	28	148	506	90	146	25	1	29	93	86	105	25	.289	.514
Billy North	OF138,DH8	B	26	149	543	79	141	20	5	4	33	69	86	54	.260	.357
Joe Rudi	OF140,1B27,DH1	R	27	158	593	73	174	39	4	22	99	34	92	2	.293	.484
Ray Fosse (XJ)	C68,DH1	R	27	69	204	20	40	8	3	4	23	11	31	1	.196	.324
1 Deron Johnson	DH23	R	35	50	174	16	34	1	2	7	23	11	37	1	.195	.345
Angel Mangual	OF74,DH37,3B1	R	27	115	365	37	85	14	4	9	43	17	59	3	.233	.367
Ted Kubiak	2B71,SS19,3B14,DH1	B	32	99	220	22	46	3	0	0	18	18	15	1	.209	.223
Jesus Alou	DH41,OF25	R	32	96	220	13	59	8	0	2	15	5	9	0	.268	.332
Herb Washington		R	22	92	0	29	0	0	0	0	0	0	0	29	—	—
Larry Haney	C73,3B3,1B2	R	31	76	121	12	20	4	0	2	3	3	18	1	.165	.248
Claudell Washington	DH38,OF32	L	19	73	221	16	63	10	5	0	19	13	44	6	.285	.376
1 Pat Bourque	1B39,DH8	L	27	73	96	6	12	1	0	6	16	15	20	0	.229	.302
2 Dal Maxvill	2B30,SS29,3B1	R	35	60	52	3	10	0	0	0	3	8	10	0	.192	.192
2 Jim Holt	1B17,DH3	L	30	30	42	1	6	0	0	0	1	0	9	0	.143	.143
Phil Garner	3B19,SS8,2B3,DH2	R	25	30	28	4	5	1	0	0	1	4	5	0	.179	.214
Manny Trillo (LJ)	2B21	R	23	21	33	3	7	1	0	0	3	1	9	0	.152	.212

Gaylen Pitts 28 R 10-41, Champ Summers 28 L 3-24, Vic Davalillo 37 L 4-23, John Donaldson 31 L 2-15, Tim Hosley 27 R 2-7, Rich McKinney 27 R 1-7

NAME	T	AGE	W	L	PCT	SV	G	GS	CG	IP	H	BB	SO	SHO	ERA
		28	90	72	.556	28	162	162	33	1440	1322	430	755	12	2.95
Catfish Hunter	R	28	25	12	.676	0	41	41	23	318	268	46	143	6	2.49
Ken Holtzman	L	28	19	17	.528	0	39	38	9	255	273	51	117	3	3.07
Vida Blue	L	24	17	15	.531	0	40	40	12	282	246	98	174	1	3.26
Rollie Fingers	R	27	9	5	.643	18	76	0	0	119	104	29	95	0	2.65
Dave Hamilton	L	26	7	4	.636	0	29	18	1	117	104	48	69	1	3.15
Glenn Abbott	R	23	5	7	.417	0	19	17	3	96	89	34	38	0	3.00
Paul Lindblad	L	32	4	4	.500	6	45	2	0	101	85	30	46	0	2.05
Darold Knowles	L	32	3	3	.500	4	45	1	0	53	61	35	18	0	4.25
Blue Moon Odom	R	29	1	5	.167	1	34	5	1	87	85	52	52	0	3.83
Leon Hooten	R	26	0	0	—	0	6	0	0	8	6	4	1	0	3.38
Bill Parsons	R	26	0	0	—	0	2	1	0	1	3	5	0	0	0.00

Bob Locker (EJ) 36

TEXAS 2nd 84-76 .525 5   BILLY MARTIN

NAME	G by Pos	B	AGE	G	AB	R	H	2B	3B	HR	RBI	BB	SO	SB	BA	SA
TOTALS			27	161	5449	690	1482	198	39	99	643	508	710	113	.272	.377
Mike Hargrove	1B91,DH32,OF6	L	24	131	415	57	134	18	6	4	66	49	42	0	.323	.424
Dave Nelson (BZ)	2B120,DH1	R	30	121	474	71	112	13	4	3	42	34	72	25	.236	.287
Toby Harrah	SS158,3B3	R	25	161	573	79	149	23	2	21	74	50	65	15	.260	.417
Lenny Randle	3B89,2B40,OF21,DH2,SS1	B	25	151	520	65	157	17	4	1	49	29	63	26	.302	.356
Cesar Tovar	OF135,DH3	R	33	138	562	78	164	24	6	4	58	47	33	13	.292	.377
Joe Lovitto	OF107,1B5	R	23	113	283	27	63	9	3	2	26	25	36	6	.223	.297
Jeff Burroughs	OF150,1B2,DH1	R	23	152	554	84	167	33	2	25	118	91	104	2	.301	.504
Jim Sundberg	C132	R	23	132	368	45	91	13	3	3	36	62	61	2	.247	.323
Jim Spencer	1B60,DH54	L	26	118	352	36	98	11	4	7	44	22	71	1	.278	.392
1 Alex Johnson	OF81,DH32	R	31	114	453	57	132	14	4	1	41	28	59	20	.291	.362
Tommy Grieve	DH40,OF38,1B1	R	26	84	159	16	40	10	4	9	32	20	48	0	.255	.429
Jim Fregosi	1B47,3B32	R	32	78	230	31	60	13	0	12	34	22	41	0	.261	.439
Larry Brown	3B47,2B8,SS1	R	34	54	76	10	15	2	0	0	3	10	9	0	.197	.224
2 Duke Sims	C30,DH2,OF1	L	33	39	106	17	22	6	0	4	13	14	20	1	.208	.292
Leo Cardenas	3B21,SS10,DH4	R	36	38	81	8	18	1	1	2	11	4	18	1	.272	.384

Roy Howell 20 L 11-44,1 Dick Billings 31 R 7-31, Bill Fahey 24 L 4-16, Mike Cubbage 23 L 0-15, Tom Robson 28 R 3-13, Pete Mackanin 22 R 1-6, Bobby Jones 24 L 0-5, Dave Moates 26 L 0-0

NAME	T	AGE	W	L	PCT	SV	G	GS	CG	IP	H	BB	SO	SHO	ERA
		27	84*	76	.525	12	161	161	62	1434	1423	449	871	16	3.82
Ferguson Jenkins	R	30	25	12	.676	0	41	41	29	328	286	45	225	6	2.83
Jim Bibby	R	29	19	19	.500	0	41	41	11	264	255	113	149	5	4.74
Jackie Brown	R	31	13	12	.520	0	35	26	9	217	219	74	134	2	3.57
Steve Hargan	R	31	12	9	.571	0	37	27	8	187	202	48	98	2	3.95
Steve Foucault	R	24	8	9	.471	12	69	0	0	144	123	40	106	0	2.25
David Clyde	L	19	3	9	.250	0	28	21	4	117	129	47	52	0	4.38
2 Bill Hands	R	34	2	0	1.000	0	7	2	1	14	11	3	4	1	1.93
Don Stanhouse	R	23	1	2	.333	0	21	3	0	47	38	17	26	0	4.94
Jim Merritt (SA)	L	30	1	0	1.000	0	26	1	0	33	46	18	16	0	4.09
Jim Shellenback	L	30	0	0	—	0	12	0	0	14	22	6	8	0	5.76
Stan Thomas	R	24	0	0	—	0	12	0	0	14	22	6	4	0	6.43
Jeff Terpko	R	23	0	0	—	0	4	0	0	12	15	5	6	0	6.55
Steve Dunning	R	25	0	0	—	0	3	1	0	12	22	13	15	0	22.50
1 Lloyd Allen	L	24	0	0	—	0	12	0	0	10	19	18	10	0	8.07
Pete Broberg	R	24	0	0	—	0	12	0	0	29	29	13	15	0	8.07

* 1 win by forfeit

Batting

NAME	G by Pos	B	AGE	G	AB	R	H	2B	3B	HR	RBI	BB	SO	SB	BA	SA
MINNESOTA 3rd 82-80 .506 8																FRANK QUILICI
TOTALS			28	163	5632	673	1530	190	37	111	632	520	791	74	.272	.378
Craig Kusick	1B75	R	25	76	201	36	48	7	1	8	26	35	56	0	.239	.403
Rod Carew	2B148	L	28	153	599	86	218	30	5	3	55	74	49	38	.364	.446
Danny Thompson (LJ)	SS88,3B5,DH1	R	27	97	264	25	66	6	1	4	25	22	29	1	.250	.326
Eric Soderholm	3B130,SS1	R	25	141	464	63	128	18	3	10	51	48	68	7	.276	.392
Larry Hisle	OF137	R	27	143	510	68	146	20	7	19	79	48	112	12	.286	.465
Steve Brye	OF129	R	25	135	488	52	138	32	1	2	41	22	54	5	.283	.365
Bobby Darwin	OF142	R	31	155	575	67	152	13	7	25	94	37	127	1	.264	.442
Glenn Borgmann	C128	R	24	128	345	33	87	8	1	3	45	39	44	2	.252	.307
Tony Oliva	DH112	L	33	127	459	43	131	16	2	13	57	27	31	0	.285	.414
Steve Braun	OF108,3B17	L	26	129	453	53	127	12	1	8	40	56	51	4	.280	.364
Harmon Killebrew	DH57,1B33	R	38	122	333	28	74	7	0	13	54	45	61	0	.222	.360
J. Terrell	SS34,2B26,3B21,DH12,OF3,1B2	B	27	116	229	43	56	4	6	0	19	11	27	3	.245	.314
Luis Gomez	SS74,2B2,DH1	R	22	82	168	18	35	1	0	0	3	12	16	2	.208	.214
1 Jim Holt	1B67,OF5	L	30	79	197	24	50	11	0	0	16	14	16	0	.254	.310
Phil Roof	C44	R	33	44	97	10	19	1	0	2	13	6	24	0	.196	.268
Randy Hundley (KJ)	C28	R	32	32	88	2	17	2	0	0	5	4	12	0	.193	.216
Pat Bourque 27 L 14-64, Sergio Ferrer 23 B 16-57, 1 Joe Lis 27 R 8-41																
CHICAGO 4th 80-80 .500 9																CHUCK TANNER
TOTALS			27	163	5577	684	1492	225	23	135	633	519	858	64	.268	.389
Dick Allen (VR)	1B125,DH1,2B1	R	32	128	462	84	139	23	1	32	88	57	89	7	.301	.563
Jorge Orta	2B123,DH10,SS3	L	23	139	525	73	166	31	2	10	67	40	88	9	.316	.440
Bucky Dent	SS154	R	22	154	496	55	136	15	3	5	45	28	48	3	.274	.347
Bill Melton	3B123,DH11	R	28	136	495	63	120	17	0	21	63	59	60	3	.242	.404
Bill Sharp	OF99	L	24	100	320	45	81	13	2	4	24	25	37	0	.253	.344
Ken Henderson	OF162	B	28	162	602	76	176	35	5	20	95	66	112	12	.292	.467
Carlos May	OF129,DH13	L	26	149	551	66	137	19	2	8	58	46	76	8	.249	.334
Ed Herrmann	C107	L	27	107	367	32	95	13	1	10	39	16	49	1	.259	.381
Pat Kelly	DH67,OF53	L	29	122	424	60	119	16	3	4	21	46	58	18	.281	.361
Ron Santo	DH47,2B39,3B8,1B3,SS1	R	34	117	375	29	83	12	1	5	41	37	72	0	.221	.299
Brian Downing	C63,OF39,DH9	R	23	108	293	41	66	12	1	10	39	51	72	0	.225	.375
Tony Muser	1B80,DH13	L	26	103	206	16	60	5	1	1	18	12	24	1	.291	.340
Jerry Hairston (LJ)	OF22,DH10	B	22	45	109	8	25	7	0	0	8	13	18	1	.229	.294
Buddy Bradford (BC)	OF32,DH1	R	29	39	96	16	32	2	0	5	10	13	11	1	.333	.510
Lee Richard	3B12,SS6,DH5,2B3,OF1	R	25	32	67	5	11	1	0	0	1	5	8	1	.164	.179
Eddie Leon	SS21,2B7,3B2,DH1	R	27	31	46	1	5	1	0	0	2	5	7	0	.109	.130
Bill Stein	3B11,DH2	R	27	13	43	5	12	1	0	0	5	7	8	0	.279	.302
Lamar Johnson 23 R 10-29, Pete Varney 25 R 7-28, Nyls Nyman 20 L 9-14, 1 Chuck Brinkman 29 R 2-14, 1 Luis Alvarado 25 R 1-10, Hugh Yancy 24 R 0-0																
KANSAS CITY 5th 77-85 .475 13																JACK McKEON
TOTALS			27	162	5582	667	1448	232	42	89	623	550	768	146	.259	.364
John Mayberry	1B106,DH16	L	25	126	427	63	100	13	1	22	69	77	72	4	.234	.424
Cookie Rojas	2B141	R	35	144	542	52	147	13	4	5	48	20	43	8	.271	.339
Freddie Patek	SS149	R	29	149	537	72	121	18	6	3	38	77	69	33	.225	.298
George Brett	3B132,SS1	L	21	133	457	49	129	21	5	2	47	21	38	8	.282	.363
Jim Wohlford	OF138,DH1	R	23	143	501	55	136	16	7	2	44	39	74	16	.271	.343
Amos Otis	OF143,DH2	R	27	146	552	87	157	31	9	12	73	58	67	18	.284	.438
Vada Pinson	OF110,DH2,1B1	L	35	115	406	46	112	24	2	6	41	21	45	21	.276	.374
Fran Healy	C138	R	28	139	445	59	112	24	2	9	53	62	73	16	.252	.375
Hal McRae	DH90,OF56,3B1	R	28	148	539	71	167	36	4	15	88	54	66	11	.310	.475
Al Cowens	OF102,DH4,3B2	R	22	110	269	26	65	7	1	5	25	23	38	5	.242	.286
Frank White	2B50,SS29,3B16,DH3	R	23	99	204	19	45	6	3	1	18	6	33	5	.221	.294
Tony Solaita	1B65,DH14,OF1	L	27	96	239	31	64	12	0	7	30	35	70	0	.268	.406
Buck Martinez	C38	R	25	43	107	10	23	3	1	1	8	14	19	0	.215	.290
2 Kurt Bevacqua	1B14, 3B13,2B7,DH3,SS2	R	27	39	90	10	19	0	0	0	3	9	20	1	.211	.211
2 Richie Scheinblum	DH17,OF2	B	31	36	83	7	15	2	0	0	2	8	8	0	.181	.205
Orlando Cepeda	DH26	R	36	33	107	3	23	5	0	1	18	9	16	1	.215	.290
1 Paul Schaal 31 R 6-34, 1 Fernando Gonzalez 24 R 3-21, Dennis Paepke 29 R 2-12, Bobby Floyd 30 R 1-9, Rick Reichardt 31 R 1-1																
CALIFORNIA 6th 68-94 .420 22												BOBBY WINKLES 30-44 .405	WHITEY HERZOG 2-2 .500		DICK WILLIAMS 36-48 .429
TOTALS			25	163	5401	618	1372	203	41	95	550	509	801	119	.254	.356
John Doherty	1B70,DH2	L	22	74	223	20	57	14	1	3	26	9	13	2	.256	.368
Denny Doyle	2B146,SS2	L	30	147	514	41	133	19	2	1	34	25	49	6	.260	.311
Dave Chalk	SS99,3B38	R	23	133	465	44	117	9	3	5	31	30	57	10	.252	.316
2 Paul Schaal	3B51	R	31	53	165	10	41	5	0	2	20	18	27	2	.248	.315
Lee Stanton (BH)	OF114	R	28	118	415	48	111	21	2	11	44	62	107	10	.267	.407
Mickey Rivers (BH)	OF116	L	25	118	466	69	133	19	11	3	31	39	47	30	.285	.393
Joe Lahoud	OF106,DH10	L	27	132	325	46	88	16	3	13	44	47	57	4	.271	.458
Ellie Rodriguez	C137,DH1	R	28	140	395	48	100	20	0	7	36	69	56	4	.253	.357
1 Frank Robinson	DH123,OF1	R	38	129	427	75	107	26	2	20	63	75	85	5	.251	.461
Bobby Valentine	OF62,SS36,3B15,DH10,2B1	R	24	117	371	39	97	10	3	3	39	25	25	8	.261	.329
1 Bob Oliver	1B57,3B46,OF4,DH1	R	31	110	359	22	89	9	1	8	55	16	51	2	.248	.345
Winston Llenas (KJ)	OF32,2B15,DH10,3B2	R	30	72	138	16	36	6	0	2	17	11	19	0	.261	.348
Bruce Bochte	OF39,1B24	L	23	57	196	24	53	4	1	5	26	18	23	6	.270	.378
Morris Nettles	OF54	L	22	56	175	27	48	4	0	0	16	18	20	20	.274	.297
1 Tommy McCraw	1B29,OF12,DH3	L	33	56	119	21	34	8	0	3	17	12	13	1	.286	.429
1 Sandy Alomar	SS19,2B15,3B5,OF1	B	30	46	54	12	12	0	1	0	2	8	2	2	.222	.259
Tom Egan	C41	R	27	43	94	4	11	0	0	0	4	10	40	0	.117	.117
Charlie Sands	DH1,C5	L	26	43	83	6	16	2	0	4	13	23	17	0	.193	.361
Rudy Meoli	3B20,SS8,2B1,1B1	L	23	36	90	9	22	2	0	3	8	10	22	4	.244	.267
Orlando Ramirez	SS31	R	22	31	86	4	14	0	0	0	7	6	15	2	.163	.163
2 Bob Heise	2B17,3B6,SS3	R	27	29	75	7	20	1	0	0	4	6	10	0	.267	.360
Mike Epstein 31 L 10-62, John Balaz 23 R 10-42, Doug Howard 26 R 9-39, 1 Richie Scheinblum 31 B 4-26																

Pitching

NAME	T	AGE	W	L	PCT	SV	G	GS	CG	IP	H	BB	SO	SHO	ERA
		27	82	80	.506	29	163	163	43	1455	1436	513	934	11	3.64
Bert Blyleven	R	23	17	17	.500	0	37	37	19	281	244	77	249	3	2.66
Joe Decker	R	27	16	14	.533	0	37	37	11	249	234	97	158	1	3.29
Dave Goltz	R	25	10	10	.500	1	28	24	5	174	192	45	89	1	3.26
Bill Campbell	R	25	8	7	.533	19	63	0	0	120	109	55	89	0	2.63
Vic Albury	L	27	8	9	.471	0	32	22	4	164	159	80	85	1	4.12
Ray Corbin	R	25	7	6	.538	0	29	15	1	112	133	40	50	0	5.30
Tom Burgmeier	L	30	5	3	.625	4	50	0	0	92	92	26	34	0	4.50
1 Bill Hands	R	34	4	5	.444	3	35	10	0	115	130	25	74	0	4.48
Bill Butler	L	27	4	6	.400	1	26	12	2	99	91	56	79	0	4.09
Tom Johnson	R	23	2	0	1.000	1	4	0	0	9	6	7	4	0	0.00
1 Dick Woodson	R	29	1	1	.500	0	5	4	0	27	30	4	12	0	4.33
Dan Fife	R	24	0	1	.000	0	2	1	0	5	5	3	5	0	16.20
Jim Hughes	R	22	0	2	.000	0	2	2	1	10	8	4	8	0	5.40
		27	80	80	.500	29	163	163	55	1466	1470	548	826	11	3.94
Jim Kaat	L	35	21	13	.618	0	42	39	15	277	263	63	142	3	2.92
Wilbur Wood	L	32	20	19	.513	0	42	42	22	320	305	80	169	1	3.60
Stan Bahnsen	R	29	12	15	.444	0	38	35	10	216	230	110	102	1	4.71
Bart Johnson	R	24	10	4	.714	0	18	18	4	122	105	32	76	2	2.73
Terry Forster	L	22	7	8	.467	24	59	1	0	134	120	48	105	0	3.63
Goose Gossage (UJ)	R	22	4	6	.400	1	39	3	0	89	92	47	64	0	4.15
Skip Pitlock	L	26	3	3	.500	1	40	5	0	106	103	55	68	0	4.42
Joe Henderson	R	27	1	0	1.000	0	5	0	0	15	21	11	12	0	8.40
Bill Moran	R	23	1	3	.250	0	15	5	0	46	57	23	17	0	4.70
Jack Kucek	R	21	1	4	.200	0	9	7	0	38	48	21	25	0	5.21
Ken Tatum	R	30	0	0	—	0	10	1	0	21	23	9	5	0	4.71
Wayne Granger	R	30	0	0	—	0	8	0	0	16	3	4	7	0	7.88
Stan Perzanowski	R	23	0	0	—	0	2	1	0	2	9	2	2	0	22.50
Francisco Barrios	R	21	0	0	—	0	2	0	0	2	7	2	2	0	27.00
Jim Otten	R	23	0	1	.000	0	5	1	0	16	17	12	11	0	5.63
2 Lloyd Allen	R	24	0	1	.000	0	4	1	0	7	12	11	5	0	10.29
Cy Acosta (IJ)	R	27	0	0	—	3	17	0	0	46	43	18	19	0	3.72
		30	77	85	.475	17	162	162	54	1472	1477	482	731	13	3.51
Steve Busby	R	24	22	14	.611	0	38	38	20	292	284	92	198	3	3.39
Al Fitzmorris	R	28	13	6	.684	1	34	27	9	190	189	63	53	4	2.79
Pul Splittorff	L	27	13	19	.406	0	36	36	8	226	252	75	90	1	4.10
Bruce Dal Canton	R	32	8	10	.444	0	31	22	9	175	175	82	96	2	3.14
Doug Bird	R	24	7	6	.538	10	55	1	1	92	100	27	62	0	2.74
Nelson Briles (KJ)	R	30	5	7	.417	0	18	17	3	103	117	21	41	0	4.02
Marty Pattin	R	31	3	7	.300	0	25	11	2	117	121	28	50	0	4.00
Steve Mingori	L	30	3	3	.500	3	36	0	0	67	53	23	43	0	2.82
Joe Hoerner	L	37	2	3	.400	2	30	0	0	35	32	12	24	0	3.86
1 Gene Garber	R	26	1	1	.333	1	17	0	0	28	35	13	14	0	4.82
Lindy McDaniel	R	38	1	4	.200	1	38	5	2	107	109	24	47	0	3.45
Aurelio Lopez	R	25	0	0	—	0	11	0	0	16	21	10	5	0	5.63
Dennis Leonard	R	23	0	0	.000	0	4	0	0	22	28	12	8	0	5.32
		25	68	94	.420	12	163	163	64	1439	1339	649	986	13	3.52
Nolan Ryan	R	27	22	16	.579	0	42	41	26	333	221	202	367	3	2.89
Frank Tanana	L	20	14	19	.424	0	39	35	12	269	262	77	180	4	3.11
Bill Singer (XJ)	R	30	7	4	.636	0	14	14	8	109	102	43	77	0	2.97
Andy Hassler	L	23	7	11	.389	1	23	22	10	162	132	79	76	2	2.61
Dick Lange	R	25	3	8	.273	0	21	18	1	114	111	47	57	0	3.79
Luis Quintana	L	22	2	1	.667	0	18	0	0	23	17	14	11	0	4.59
1 Dick Selma	R	30	2	2	.500	1	19	0	0	23	18	13	16	0	5.09
Dave Sells	R	27	3	3	.400	2	20	0	0	48	31	16	18	0	3.69
Chuck Dobson	R	30	2	3	.400	0	9	8	2	30	39	13	16	0	5.70
Skip Lockwood	R	27	2	5	.286	1	37	2	0	81	81	32	39	0	4.33
Ed Figueroa	R	25	2	8	.200	0	25	12	5	105	119	36	49	1	3.69
Barry Raziano	R	26	2	1	.333	1	13	0	0	17	15	8	9	0	6.35
2 Horacio Pina	R	29	1	2	.333	0	11	0	0	12	9	3	6	0	2.25
Bill Stoneman	R	30	1	3	.250	0	13	11	0	59	78	31	33	0	6.10
2 Ken Sanders	R	32	0	0	—	0	10	0	0	10	14	3	4	0	2.70
2 Orlando Pena	R	40	0	0	—	0	5	0	0	5	10	1	6	0	9.00
Don Kirkwood	R	24	0	0	—	0	1	0	0	1	1	0	1	0	18.00
Bill Gilbreth	R	26	0	0	—	0	4	0	0	4	5	3	0	0	9.00
1 Rudy May	L	29	0	1	.000	0	9	2	0	22	30	14	12	0	2.70
John Cumberland	L	27	0	0	.000	0	7	0	0	22	24	10	12	0	3.68

AMERICAN LEAGUE CHAMPIONSHIP —OAKLAND (WEST) 3   BALTIMORE (EAST) 1

LINE SCORES

TEAM	1	2	3	4	5	6	7	8	9	10	11	12	R	H	E
Game 1 October 5 at Oakland															
BAL	1	0	0	1	4	0	0	0	0				6	10	0
OAK	0	0	1	0	1	0	0	0	1				3	9	0
Cuellar, Grimsley (9) Hunter, Odom (5), Fingers (9)															
Game 2 October 6 at Oakland															
BAL	0	0	0	0	0	0	0	0	0				0	5	2
OAK	0	0	1	0	1	0	3	0	x				5	8	0
McNally, Garland (6), Reynolds (7), Jackson (8) Holtzman															
Game 3 October 8 at Baltimore															
OAK	0	0	0	1	0	0	0	0	0				1	4	2
BAL	0	0	0	0	0	0	0	0	0				0	2	1
Blue Palmer															
Game 4 October 9 at Baltimore															
OAK	0	0	0	0	1	0	1	0	0				2	1	0
BAL	0	0	0	0	0	1	0	0	0				1	5	1
Hunter, Fingers (8) Cuellar, Grimsley (5)															

COMPOSITE BATTING

NAME	POS	G	AB	R	H	2B	3B	HR	RBI	BA
Oakland Totals		4	120	11	22	4	1	3	11	.183
Campaneris	SS	4	17	0	3	1	0	0	3	.176
North	CF	4	16	3	1	1	0	0	0	.063
Bando	3B	4	13	4	3	0	0	2	1	.231
Rudi	LF	4	13	0	2	0	0	1	2	.154
Fosse	C	4	12	1	4	0	0	0	3	.333
Jackson	DH-RF	4	12	0	2	1	0	0	1	.167
C. Washington	RF	4	11	3	3	1	0	0	0	.273
Tenace	1B	4	11	1	0	0	0	0	0	.000
Green	2B	4	9	0	1	0	0	0	0	.111
Mangual DH 1-4, Alou PH 1-1, Maxvill 2B 0-1, Holt 1B 0-0, H. Washington PR 0-0, Odom P-PR 0-0, Trillo PR 0-0										
Baltimore Totals		4	124	7	22	3	7	1	7	.177
Grich	2B	4	16	1	4	1	0	1	2	.250
Davis	DH	4	15	0	4	0	0	0	0	.267
Baylor	LF	4	15	0	4	0	0	0	0	.267
Blair	CF	4	14	3	4	1	0	0	1	.286
Robinson	3B	4	12	0	1	0	0	0	0	.083
Coggins	RF	4	13	0	0	0	0	0	0	.000
Belanger	SS	4	13	0	3	0	1	0	0	.231
Powell	1B	4	8	0	1	0	0	0	0	.125
Hendricks	C	4	6	0	1	0	0	0	0	.167
Etchebarren C 2-6, Williams 1B 0-6, Cabell RF 1-4, Bumbry PH-PR 0-0, Motton PH 0-1, Baker SS 0-0, Palmer P-PR 0-0										

COMPOSITE PITCHING

NAME	G	IP	H	BB	SO	W	L	SV	ERA
Oakland Totals	4	36	22	5	20	3	1	1	1.75
Hunter	2	11.2	11	2	6	1	1	0	4.63
Blue	1	9	2	7	1	1	0	0	0.00
Holtzman	1	9	5	2	3	1	0	0	0.00
Odom	1	3.1	1	1	3	0	0	0	0.00
Fingers	2	3	3	1	3	0	0	1	3.00
Baltimore Totals	4	35	22	22	16	1	3	0	1.80
Cuellar	2	12.2	9	13	6	1	1	0	2.84
Palmer	1	9	4	1	4	0	1	0	1.00
McNally	1	5.2	6	2	2	0	1	0	1.59
Grimsley	2	5.1	4	3	2	0	0	0	1.69
Reynolds	1	1.1	0	3	1	0	0	0	0.00
Garland	1	1	0	0	1	0	0	0	0.00
Jackson	1	0	0	1	0	0	0	0	0.00

NATIONAL LEAGUE CHAMPIONSHIP — LOS ANGELES (WEST) 3 PITTSBURGH (EAST) 1

LINE SCORES

TEAM	1 2 3	4 5 6	7 8 9	10 11 12	R	H	E

Game 1 October 5 at Pittsburgh

| LA | 0 1 0 | 0 0 0 | 0 0 2 | | 3 | 9 | 2 |
| PIT | 0 0 0 | 0 0 0 | 0 0 0 | | 0 | 4 | 0 |

Sutton   Reuss, Giusti(8)

Game 2 October 6 at Pittsburgh

| LA | 1 0 0 | 1 0 0 | 0 3 0 | | 5 | 12 | 0 |
| PIT | 0 0 0 | 0 0 0 | 2 0 0 | | 2 | 8 | 3 |

Messersmith, Marshall (8)   Rooker, Giusti (8),
                             Demery (8), Hernandez (8)

Game 3 October 8 at Los Angeles

| PIT | 5 0 2 | 0 0 0 | 0 0 0 | | 7 | 10 | 0 |
| LA | 0 0 0 | 0 0 0 | 0 0 0 | | 0 | 4 | 5 |

Kison, Hernandez(7)   Rau, Hough(1), Downing (4),
                       Solomon (8)

Game 4 October 9 at Los Angeles

| PIT | 0 0 0 | 0 0 0 | 1 0 0 | | 1 | 3 | 1 |
| LA | 1 0 2 | 0 2 2 | 2 3 X | | 12 | 12 | 0 |

Reuss, Brett (3), Demery (6), Sutton, Marshall (9)
Giusti (7), Pizarro (8)

COMPOSITE BATTING

NAME	POS	G	AB	R	H	2B	3B	HR	RBI	BA
Los Angeles Totals		4	138	20	37	8	1	3	19	.268
Garvey	1B	4	18	4	7	1	0	2	5	.389
Russell	SS	4	18	1	7	0	0	0	3	.389
Buckner	LF	4	18	0	3	1	0	0	0	.167
Cey	3B	4	16	2	5	3	0	1	1	.313
Lopes	2B	4	15	4	4	0	1	0	1	.267
Ferguson	RF-C	4	13	3	3	0	0	0	2	.231
Wynn	CF	4	10	4	2	2	0	0	3	.200
Yeager	C	3	9	1	0	0	0	0	0	.000
Sutton	P	2	7	0	2	0	0	0	0	.286
Crawford	RF	4	4	1	1	0	0	0	0	.250
Mota	LF	3	3	0	1	0	0	0	0	.333
Messersmith	P	1	3	0	0	0	0	0	0	.000

Paciorek RF 1-1, Auerbach PH 1-1, McMullen PH 0-1, Downing P 0-1, Joshua PH 0-0, Lacy PR 0-0, Marshall P 0-0, Hough P 0-0, Solomon P 0-0, Rau P 0-0

NAME	POS	G	AB	R	H	2B	3B	HR	RBI	BA
Pittsburgh Totals		4	129	10	25	1	0	3	10	.194
Sanguillen	C	4	16	0	4	1	0	0	0	.250
Stennett	2B	4	16	1	1	0	0	0	0	.063
Stargell	LF	4	15	3	6	0	0	2	4	.400
Oliver	CF	4	14	1	2	0	0	0	1	.143
Hebner	3B	4	13	1	3	0	0	1	4	.231
Zisk	RF	3	10	1	3	0	0	0	0	.300
Kirkpatrick	1B	3	9	0	0	0	0	0	0	.000
Parker	RF	3	8	0	1	0	0	0	0	.125
Popovich	SS	3	5	1	3	0	0	0	0	.600
Mendoza	SS	3	5	0	1	0	0	0	0	.200
Robertson	1B	1	5	1	0	0	0	0	0	.000

Kison P 0-3, Rooker P 1-2, Reuss P 0-2, Clines LF-RF 0-1, Howe PH 0-1, Hernandez P 0-1, Brett P 0-1, Taveras SS 0-2, Giusti P 0-0, Demery P 0-0, Pizarro P 0-0

COMPOSITE PITCHING

NAME	G	IP	H	BB	SO	W	L	SV	ERA
Los Angeles Totals	4	36	25	8	17	3	1	0	2.00
Sutton	2	17	7	2	13	2	0	0	0.53
Messersmith	1	7	8	3	0	0	0	0	2.57
Downing	1	4	1	1	0	0	0	0	0.00
Marshall	2	3	0	0	1	0	0	0	0.00
Hough	1	2.1	4	0	2	0	0	0	7.71
Solomon	1	2	2	1	1	0	0	0	0.00
Rau	1	.2	3	1	0	0	1	0	45.00

NAME	G	IP	H	BB	SO	W	L	SV	ERA
Pittsburgh Totals	4	35	37	30	16	1	3	0	5.14
Reuss	2	9.2	7	8	3	0	2	0	3.72
Rooker	1	7	6	5	4	0	0	0	2.57
Kison	1	6.2	6	5	1	0	0	0	0.00
Hernandez	2	4	3	1	2	0	0	0	0.00
Giusti	3	3.1	13	5	1	1	0	1	21.60
Brett	1	2.1	3	2	1	0	0	0	7.71
Demery	2	1	3	2	0	0	0	0	36.00
Pizarro	1	.2	0	1	0	0	0	0	0.00

EAST DIVISION

NAME	G by Pos	B	AGE	G	AB	R	H	2B	3B	HR	RBI	BB	SO	SB	BA	SA
PITTSBURGH 1st 88-74 .543 DANNY MURTAUGH			27	162	5702	751	1560	238	46	114	692	514	828	55	.274	.391
TOTALS																
Bob Robertson	1B63	R	27	91	236	25	54	11	0	16	48	33	48	0	.229	.479
Rennie Stennett	2B154, OF2	R	23	157	673	84	196	29	3	7	56	32	51	8	.291	.374
Frank Taveras	SS124	R	24	126	333	33	82	4	2	0	26	25	41	13	.246	.270
Richie Hebner	3B141	L	26	146	550	97	160	21	6	18	68	60	53	0	.291	.449
Richie Zisk	OF141	R	25	149	536	75	168	30	4	17	100	65	91	1	.313	.476
Al Oliver	OF98,1B49	L	27	147	617	96	198	38	12	11	85	33	58	10	.321	.475
Willie Stargell	OF135,1B1	L	34	140	508	90	153	37	4	25	96	87	106	0	.301	.537
Manny Sanguillen	C151	R	30	151	596	77	171	21	4	7	68	21	27	2	.287	.371
Ed Kirkpatrick	1B59,OF14,C6	L	29	116	271	32	67	9	0	6	38	51	30	1	.247	.347
Gene Clines	OF78	R	27	107	276	29	62	5	1	0	14	30	40	14	.225	.250
Mario Mendoza	SS87	R	23	91	163	10	36	3	2	0	15	8	18	1	.221	.252
Dave Parker (LJ)	OF49,1B6	L	23	73	220	27	62	10	3	4	29	10	53	3	.282	.409
Paul Popovich	2B12,SS10	B	33	59	83	9	18	2	1	0	5	9	11	0	.217	.265
Art Howe	3B20,SS2	R	27	29	74	10	18	4	1	1	5	9	13	0	.243	.365
1 Kurt Bevacqua	3B8,OF1	R	27	18	35	1	4	1	0	0	0	4	6	0	.114	.143
Dave Augustine	OF11	R	24	18	22	3	4	0	0	0	0	0	5	0	.182	.182

Mike Ryan 32 R 3-30, 1 Dal Maxvill 35 R 4 -22, 2 Chuck Brinkman 29 R 1-7, Ken Macha 23 R 3-5, Ed Ott 22 L 0-5, Miguel Dilone 19 B 0-2

NAME	T	AGE	W	L	PCT	SV	G	GS	CG	IP	H	BB	SO	SHO	ERA
		28	88	74	.543	17	162	162	51	1466	1428	543	721	9	3.49
Jerry Reuss	L	25	16	11	.593	0	35	35	14	260	259	101	105	1	3.50
Jim Rooker	L	31	15	11	.577	0	33	33	15	263	228	83	139	1	2.77
Ken Brett (EJ)	R	25	13	9	.591	0	27	27	10	191	192	52	96	3	3.30
Dock Ellis (BH)	R	29	12	9	.571	0	26	26	9	177	163	41	91	0	3.15
Bruce Kison	R	24	9	8	.529	2	40	16	1	129	123	57	71	0	3.49
Dave Giusti	R	34	7	5	.583	12	64	2	0	106	101	40	53	0	3.31
Larry Demery	R	21	6	6	.500	0	19	15	2	95	95	51	51	0	4.26
Ramon Hernandez	L	33	5	2	.714	2	58	0	0	69	68	18	33	0	2.74
Daryl Patterson	R	30	2	1	.667	1	14	0	0	21	33	9	7	0	7.29
Juan Pizarro	L	37	1	1	.500	0	7	2	0	24	20	11	7	0	1.88
Kent Tekulve	R	27	1	1	.500	0	8	0	0	9	12	5	6	0	6.00
Bob Moose (IL)	R	26	1	5	.167	0	7	6	0	36	59	7	15	0	7.50
Steve Blass	R	32	0	1		0	1	0	0	5	5	7	2	0	9.00
Juan Jimenez	R	25	0	0		0	1	0	0	1	1	2	1	0	6.75
Jim Minshall	R	26	0	1		0	4	0	0	4	1	2	3	0	6.00
Jim Sadowski	R	22	0	1		0	3	0	0	7	9	1	6	0	6.00
John Morlan	R	26	0	3	.000	1	39	0	0	65	54	48	38	0	4.29

NAME	G by Pos	B	AGE	G	AB	R	H	2B	3B	HR	RBI	BB	SO	SB	BA	SA
ST. LOUIS 2nd 86-75 .534 1.5 RED SCHOENDIENST			28	161	5620	617	1492	216	46	83	610	531	752	172	.265	.365
TOTALS																
Joe Torre	1B139,3B18	R	33	147	529	59	149	28	1	11	70	69	88	1	.282	.401
Ted Sizemore	2B128,SS1,OF1	R	29	129	504	68	126	17	0	2	47	70	37	8	.250	.296
Mike Tyson	SS143,2B12	R	24	151	422	35	94	14	5	3	37	22	70	4	.223	.287
Ken Reitz	3B151,SS2,2B1	R	23	154	579	48	157	28	2	7	54	23	63	0	.271	.363
Reggie Smith	OF132,1B1	B	29	143	517	79	160	26	4	23	100	71	70	4	.309	.528
Bake McBride	OF144	L	25	150	559	81	173	19	5	6	56	43	57	30	.309	.394
Lou Brock	OF152	L	35	153	635	105	194	25	7	3	48	61	88	118	.306	.381
Ted Simmons	C141,1B12	B	24	152	599	66	163	33	6	20	103	47	35	0	.272	.447
Jose Cruz	OF53,1B1	L	26	107	161	24	42	4	3	5	20	20	27	4	.261	.416
Luis Melendez	OF46,SS1	R	24	83	124	15	24	4	3	0	8	11	9	2	.218	.298
1 Tim McCarver	C21,1B6	L	32	74	106	13	23	0	1	1	14	6	10	0	.217	.234
Jim Dwyer	OF25,1B3	L	24	74	86	13	24	1	0	2	11	11	16	0	.279	.360
Jim Hickman	1B14,3B1	R	37	50	92	8	24	5	0	1	14	8	17	0	.261	.367
2 Jack Heidemann	SS45,3B1	R	24	47	70	8	19	4	0	0	5	5	10	1	.271	.386
Tom Heintzelman	2B28,3B2,SS11	R	27	38	74	9	17	3	0	0	5	4	5	0	.230	.324

Jerry DaVanon 28 R 6-40, 2 Luis Alvarado 25 R 5-36, Keith Hernandez 20 L 10-34, 2 Ron Hunt 33 R 4-23, Marc Hill 22 R 5-21, Danny Godby 27 R 2-13, Larry Herndon 20 R 1-1,1 Bob Heise 27 R 1-7, 3 Richie Scheinblum 31 B 2-6, Dick Billings 31 R 1-5, Stan Papi 23 R 1-4, Jerry Mumphrey 21 B 0-2

NAME	T	AGE	W	L	PCT	SV	G	GS	CG	IP	H	BB	SO	SHO	ERA
		29	86	75	.534	37	161	161	37	1473	1399	616	794	13	3.48
Lynn McGlothen	R	24	16	12	.571	0	31	31	8	237	212	89	142	3	2.70
Bob Gibson	R	38	11	13	.458	0	33	33	9	240	236	104	129	1	3.83
John Curtis	L	26	10	14	.417	1	33	29	5	195	199	83	89	2	3.78
Al Hrabosky	L	24	8	1	.889	9	65	0	0	88	71	38	82	0	2.97
Sonny Siebert (EJ)	R	37	8	8	.500	0	28	20	5	134	150	51	68	3	3.83
Mike Garman	R	24	7	2	.778	6	64	0	0	82	66	27	45	0	2.63
Bob Forsch	R	24	7	4	.636	0	19	14	5	100	84	34	39	2	2.97
Alan Foster	R	27	7	10	.412	0	31	25	5	162	167	61	78	1	3.89
Rich Folkers	L	27	6	2	.750	2	55	0	0	90	65	38	57	0	3.00
1 Orlando Pena	R	40	5	2	.714	1	42	0	0	45	45	20	23	0	2.60
Ray Bare	R	25	1	2	.333	1	13	3	0	24	25	9	6	0	6.00
1 Pete Richert	L	34	0	1	—	0	13	0	0	11	10	11	4	0	2.45
John Denny	R	21	0	1		0	1	1	0	3	2	4	1	0	0.00
Barry Lersch	R	29	0	1		0	4	0	0	7	9	6	3	0	54.00
2 Claude Osteen	L	34	0	0	.000	0	8	4	0	38	37	15	25	0	4.30
1 Mike Thompson	R	24	0	0		0	19	4	0	19	37	35	15	0	5.68

NAME	G by Pos	B	AGE	G	AB	R	H	2B	3B	HR	RBI	BB	SO	SB	BA	SA
PHILADELPHIA 3rd 80-82 .494 8 DANNY OZARK			27	162	5494	676	1434	233	50	95	636	469	822	115	.261	.373
TOTALS																
Willie Montanez	1B137,OF1	L	26	143	527	56	160	33	1	7	79	32	57	0	.304	.410
Dave Cash	2B162	R	26	162	687	89	206	26	11	2	58	46	33	20	.300	.378
Larry Bowa	SS162	B	28	162	669	97	184	19	10	1	36	23	52	39	.275	.338
Mike Schmidt	3B162	R	24	162	568	108	160	28	7	36	116	106	138	23	.282	.546
Mike Anderson	OF133,1B1	R	23	145	395	35	99	22	2	5	34	37	75	2	.251	.354
Del Unser	OF135	L	29	143	454	72	120	18	5	11	60	42	56	2	.264	.399
Greg Luzinski (KJ)	OF82	R	23	85	302	29	82	7	1	7	48	29	76	1	.272	.394
Bob Boone	C146	R	26	146	488	41	118	24	3	3	52	35	29	3	.242	.322
Bill Robinson	OF87	R	31	100	280	32	66	14	1	5	29	17	61	5	.236	.346
Tommy Hutton	1B39,OF33	L	28	99	208	32	50	14	4	3	30	13	22	1	.240	.356
Jay Johnstone	OF59	L	28	64	200	30	59	10	4	6	30	24	28	1	.295	.475
Tony Taylor	1B7,3B5,2B4	R	38	82	64	5	21	4	1	1	8	9	8	1	.328	.484
2 Ollie Brown	OF33	R	30	43	99	11	24	5	1	3	6	6	20	0	.242	.455
1 Billy Grabarkewitz	OF5,3B1	R	28	34	30	7	4	0	0	2	5	10	5	2	.133	.233
Larry Cox (KJ)	C29	R	26	30	53	5	9	2	0	0	4	4	8	0	.170	.208
Terry Harmon	SS7,2B5	R	30	27	15	5	2	1	0	0	1	3	3	1	.133	.133
Alan Bannister	OF8,SS2	R	23	26	25	4	3	1	1	0	2	0	3	2	.120	.240
Jim Essian	C15,1B1,3B1	R	23	17	20	1	2	0	0	0	1	4	5	0	.100	.150

Mike Rogodzinski 26 L 1-15, Jerry Martin 25 R 3-14, John Stearns 22 R 1-2

NAME	T	AGE	W	L	PCT	SV	G	GS	CG	IP	H	BB	SO	SHO	ERA
		29	80	82	.494	19	162	162	46	1447	1394	682	892	4	3.91
Jim Lonborg	R	32	17	13	.567	0	39	39	16	283	280	70	121	3	3.21
Steve Carlton	L	29	16	13	.552	0	39	39	17	291	249	136	240	1	3.22
Ron Schueler	R	26	11	16	.407	1	44	27	5	203	202	98	109	0	3.72
Dick Ruthven	R	23	9	13	.409	0	35	35	6	213	182	116	153	0	4.01
Wayne Twitchell (KJ)	R	26	4	9	.400	0	25	18	2	112	122	65	72	0	5.22
2 Gene Garber	R	26	4	0	1.000	4	34	0	0	48	39	31	27	0	2.06
Frank Linzy	R	33	3	2	.600	0	22	0	0	37	7	12	10	0	3.24
Mac Scarce	L	25	3	8	.273	5	58	0	0	70	72	35	50	0	5.01
2 Pete Richert (AJ)	L	34	2	1	.667	0	11	0	0	12	12	7	9	0	2.25
Ed Farmer	R	24	1	0	1.000	0	14	3	0	31	41	27	20	0	8.42
Jesus Hernaiz	R	22	1	3	.400	1	27	1	0	41	53	25	16	0	5.93
George Culver	R	30	1	0	1.000	0	14	0	0	22	22	16	16	0	6.55
Tom Underwood	R	21	1	0	1.000	0	3	2	0	13	15	5	8	0	4.85
1 Mike Wallace	L	23	1	0	1.000	0	4	0	0	9	9	4	3	0	5.83
Eddie Watt	R	33	1	1	.500	2	42	0	0	38	39	26	23	0	4.03
Larry Christenson	R	20	1	1	.500	0	2	10	1	20	23	15	18	0	4.30
Ron Diorio	R	25	0	0		0	2	0	0	9	8	3	6	0	18.00
Erskine Thomason	R	25	0	0		0	1	0	0	1	1	0	1	0	0.00
Dave Wallace	R	26	0	0	.000	0	7	0	0	5	5	7	2	0	9.00

NAME	G by Pos	B	AGE	G	AB	R	H	2B	3B	HR	RBI	BB	SO	SB	BA	SA
MONTREAL 4th 79-82 .491 8.5 GENE MAUCH			28	161	5343	662	1355	201	29	86	610	652	812	124	.254	.350
TOTALS																
Mike Jorgensen	1B91,OF29	L	25	131	287	45	89	16	1	11	59	70	39	3	.310	.488
Jim Cox (BH)	2B72	R	24	77	236	29	52	9	1	2	26	23	36	2	.220	.292
Tim Foli	SS120,3B1	R	23	121	441	41	112	15	0	0	39	28	27	2	.254	.290
1 Ron Hunt	3B75,2B31,SS1	R	33	115	403	66	108	15	0	0	26	68	31	21	.268	.305
Ken Singleton	OF143	B	27	148	511	68	141	18	2	9	74	93	84	5	.276	.376
Willie Davis	OF151	L	34	153	611	86	180	27	9	12	89	27	66	25	.295	.427
Bob Bailey	OF78,3B68	R	31	152	599	69	142	20	2	20	73	100	107	4	.280	.446
Barry Foote	C122	R	22	125	420	44	110	23	4	11	60	35	74	2	.262	.414
Larry Lintz	2B67,SS31,3B1	B	24	113	319	60	76	10	1	0	15	48	50	50	.238	.276
Ron Fairly	1B67,OF20	L	35	101	282	35	69	9	1	12	43	57	28	2	.245	.411
Ron Woods	OF61	R	31	90	127	15	26	7	0	4	17	20	17	5	.205	.228
Hal Breeden	1B56	L	30	79	190	14	47	13	0	2	24	11	47	0	.247	.347
Pepe Frias	SS30,3B27,2B15,OF3	R	25	75	112	12	24	1	1	0	7	6	10	1	.214	.241
Boots Day	OF16	L	26	52	35	6	6	0	0	0	1	5	8	1	.185	.185
Bob Stinson (BT)	C29	B	28	38	87	4	15	2	0	0	5	16	11	0	.172	.230
Larry Parrish	3B24	R	20	25	89	10	18	2	0	0	5	6	16	1	.202	.303
Pepe Mangual	OF22	R	22	23	61	10	19	4	1	1	8	4	15	3	.311	.361
2 Jim Northrup	OF13	L	34	21	54	3	13	3	1	0	8	4	7	0	.241	.370
Terry Humphrey	C17	R	24	20	52	3	10	1	0	0	3	6	8	0	.192	.250

Gary Carter 20 R 11-27, Jose Morales 29 R 7-26, Larry Biittner 28 L 7-26, Warren Cromartie 20 L 3-17, Jerry White 21 B 4-10, Jim Lyttle 28 L 3-9, Tony Scott 22 B 2-7, Pat Scanlon 21 L 1-4

NAME	T	AGE	W	L	PCT	SV	G	GS	CG	IP	H	BB	SO	SHO	ERA
		25	79	82	.491	27	161	161	35	1429	1340	544	822	13	3.60
Mike Torrez	R	27	15	8	.652	0	32	30	6	186	184	84	92	1	3.58
Steve Rogers	R	24	15	22	.405	0	38	38	11	254	255	80	154	1	4.46
Steve Renko	R	29	12	16	.429	0	37	35	8	228	222	81	138	1	4.03
Dennis Blair	R	20	11	7	.611	0	22	22	4	146	113	72	76	1	3.27
Chuck Taylor	R	32	6	2	.750	11	61	0	0	108	101	25	43	0	2.17
Ernie McAnally	R	26	6	13	.316	0	25	21	5	129	126	56	79	2	4.47
Don Carrithers	R	24	5	2	.714	1	22	9	0	60	56	17	31	0	3.00
Tom Walker	R	26	5	5	.444	2	33	6	1	92	86	28	70	0	3.82
John Montague	R	26	3	4	.429	3	46	1	0	83	73	38	43	0	3.14
Don DeMola	R	22	3	1	.750	1	25	0	0	53	46	21	47	0	3.10
Dale Murray	R	24	1	1	.500	10	32	0	0	70	66	33	31	0	1.03
Bob Gebhard	R	31	0	0	—	0	2	0	0	4	8	4	4	0	4.50
Terry Enyart	L	24	0	0		0	2	0	0	3	6	3	1	0	13.50
Balor Moore	L	23	0	0	.000	0	4	1	0	13	15	16	11	0	3.86

NEW YORK — 5th 71-91 .438 17 — YOGI BERRA

NAME	G by Pos	B	AGE	G	AB	R	H	2B	3B	HR	RBI	BB	SO	SB	BA	SA
TOTALS			28	162	5468	572	1286	183	22	96	538	597	735	43	.235	.329
John Milner	1B133	L	24	137	507	70	128	19	0	20	63	66	77	10	.252	.408
Felix Millan	2B134	R	30	136	518	50	139	15	2	1	33	31	14	5	.268	.311
Bud Harrelson (BH)	SS97	B	30	106	331	48	75	10	0	1	13	71	39	9	.227	.266
Wayne Garrett	3B144,SS9	L	26	151	522	55	117	14	3	13	53	89	96	4	.224	.337
Rusty Staub	OF147	L	30	151	561	65	145	22	2	19	78	77	39	2	.258	.406
Don Hahn	OF106	R	25	110	323	34	81	14	1	4	28	37	34	2	.251	.337
Cleon Jones (KJ)	OF120	R	31	124	461	62	130	23	1	13	60	38	79	3	.282	.421
Jerry Grote (HJ)	C94	R	31	97	319	25	82	8	1	5	36	33	33	0	.257	.338
Ted Martinez	SS75,3B12,2B11,OF10	R	26	116	334	32	73	15	7	2	43	14	40	3	.219	.323
Ken Boswell	2B28,3B20,OF7	L	28	96	222	19	48	6	1	2	15	18	19	0	.216	.279
Ed Kranepool	OF33,1B24	L	29	94	217	20	65	11	1	4	24	18	14	1	.300	.415
Dave Schneck	OF84	L	25	93	254	23	52	11	1	5	25	16	43	4	.205	.315
Duffy Dyer	C45	R	28	63	142	14	30	1	1	0	10	18	15	0	.211	.232
George Theodore	1B14,OF12	R	27	60	76	7	12	1	0	1	1	8	14	0	.158	.211
Ron Hodges	C44	L	25	59	136	16	30	4	0	4	14	19	11	0	.221	.338
Jim Gosger	OF24	L	31	26	33	3	3	0	0	0	0	3	2	0	.091	.091
Benny Ayala	OF20	R	23	23	68	9	16	1	0	2	8	7	17	0	.235	.338
Brock Pemberton	1B4	B	20	11	22	0	4	0	0	0	3	0	3	0	.182	.182
Bruce Boisclair	OF5	L	21	7	12	0	3	1	0	0	1	1	4	0	.250	.333
Rich Puig	2B3,3B1	R	21	4	10	0	0	0	0	0	0	1	2	0	.000	.000
Ike Hampton	C1	R	21	4	5	0	0	0	0	0	0	0	0	0	.000	.000

NAME	T	AGE	W	L	PCT	SV	G	GS	CG	IP	H	BB	SO	SHO	ERA
		29	71	91	.438	14	162	162	46	1470	1433	504	908	15	3.42
Jerry Koosman	L	31	15	11	.577	0	35	35	13	265	258	85	188	3	3.36
Jon Matlack	L	24	13	15	.464	0	34	34	14	265	221	76	195	7	2.41
Tom Seaver	R	29	11	11	.500	0	32	32	12	236	199	75	201	5	3.20
Ray Sadecki	L	33	8	8	.500	0	34	10	3	103	107	35	46	1	3.41
Bob Apodaca	R	24	6	6	.500	3	35	8	1	103	92	42	54	0	3.50
Tug McGraw (SJ)	L	29	6	11	.353	3	41	4	1	89	96	32	54	1	4.15
Harry Parker	R	26	4	12	.250	4	40	16	1	131	145	46	58	0	3.92
2 Jack Aker (XJ)	R	33	2	1	.667	2	24	0	0	41	33	14	18	0	3.51
Bob Miller	R	35	2	2	.500	2	58	0	0	78	89	39	35	0	3.58
George Stone (SJ)	L	27	2	7	.222	0	15	13	1	77	103	21	29	0	5.03
Randy Sterling	R	23	1	1	.500	0	3	2	0	9	3	2	5	0	5.00
Craig Swan (EJ)	R	23	1	3	.250	0	7	5	0	30	28	21	10	0	4.50
Nino Espinosa	R	20	0	0	—	0	1	0	0	9	12	0	2	0	5.00
John Strohmayer	R	27	0	0	—	0	1	0	0	1	1	0	0	0	0.00
Jerry Cram	R	26	0	1	.000	0	10	0	0	22	22	4	8	0	1.64
Hank Webb	R	24	0	0	.000	0	3	2	0	15	10	8	4	0	7.20

CHICAGO — 6th 66-96 .407 22 — WHITEY LOCKMAN 41-52 .441 — JIM MARSHALL 25-44 .362

NAME	G by Pos	B	AGE	G	AB	R	H	2B	3B	HR	RBI	BB	SO	SB	BA	SA
TOTALS			28	162	5574	669	1397	221	42	110	610	621	857	78	.251	.365
Billy Williams	1B65,OF43	L	36	117	404	55	113	22	0	16	68	67	44	4	.280	.453
Vic Harris (KJ)	2B56	R	24	62	200	18	39	6	3	0	11	29	26	9	.195	.255
Don Kessinger	SS150	R	31	153	599	83	155	20	7	1	42	62	54	7	.259	.321
Bill Madlock (NJ)	3B121	R	23	128	453	65	142	21	5	9	54	42	39	11	.313	.442
Jose Cardenal	OF137	R	30	143	542	75	159	35	3	13	72	56	67	23	.293	.441
Rick Monday	OF139	L	28	142	538	84	158	19	7	20	58	70	94	7	.294	.467
Jerry Morales	OF143	R	25	151	534	70	146	21	7	15	82	46	63	2	.273	.423
Steve Swisher	C90	R	22	90	280	21	60	5	0	5	27	37	63	0	.214	.286
Andre Thornton	1B90,3B1	R	24	107	303	41	79	16	4	10	46	48	50	2	.261	.439
Chris Ward	OF22,1B6	L	25	92	137	8	28	4	0	1	15	18	13	0	.204	.255
George Mitterwald	C68	R	29	78	215	17	54	7	0	7	28	18	42	1	.251	.381
Carmen Fanzone	3B35,2B10,1B7,OF1	R	32	65	158	13	30	6	0	4	22	15	27	0	.190	.304
Dave Rosello	2B49,SS12	R	24	62	148	9	30	7	0	0	10	10	28	1	.203	.250
Jim Tyrone	OF32,3B1	R	25	57	81	19	15	0	1	3	3	6	8	1	.185	.321
2 Billy Grabarkewitz	2B45,SS7,3B6	R	28	53	125	21	31	3	2	1	12	21	28	1	.248	.328
Matt Alexander	3B19,OF4,2B2	B	27	45	54	15	11	2	1	0	6	12	12	8	.204	.278
Rob Sperring	2B35,SS8	R	24	42	107	9	22	3	0	1	5	9	28	1	.206	.262
Pete LaCock	OF22,1B11	L	22	35	110	9	20	4	1	1	8	12	16	0	.182	.264
Dick Stelmaszek	C16	L	25	25	44	2	10	2	0	1	7	1	10	6 0	.227	.341
Ron Dunn	2B21,3B6	R	24	23	68	6	20	7	0	2	15	12	8	0	.294	.485
Tom Lundstedt	C22	R	25	22	32	1	3	0	0	0	0	5	7	0	.094	.094
Gene Hiser	OF8	L	25	17	17	2	4	1	0	0	3	4	3	0	.235	.294
Gonzalo Marquez	1B1	L	28	11	11	1	0	0	0	0	0	1	2	0	.000	.000
Adrian Garrett	C3,1B1,OF1	L	31	10	8	0	0	0	0	0	0	1	1	0	.000	.000

NAME	T	AGE	W	L	PCT	SV	G	GS	CG	IP	H	BB	SO	SHO	ERA
		26	66	96	.407	26	162	162	23	1466	1593	576	895	6	4.28
Rick Reuschel	R	25	13	12	.520	0	41	38	8	241	262	83	160	2	4.29
Bill Bonham	R	25	11	22	.333	1	44	36	10	243	246	109	191	2	3.85
Steve Stone	R	26	8	6	.571	0	38	23	1	170	185	64	90	0	4.13
Burt Hooton	R	24	7	11	.389	1	48	21	3	176	214	51	94	1	4.81
Ken Frailing	L	26	6	9	.400	1	55	16	1	125	150	43	71	0	3.89
Dave LaRoche	L	26	5	6	.455	5	49	4	0	92	103	47	49	0	4.79
Jim Todd	R	26	4	2	.667	3	43	6	0	88	82	41	42	0	3.89
1 Horacio Pina	R	29	3	4	.429	4	43	0	0	47	49	28	32	0	4.02
Ray Burris	R	23	3	5	.375	1	40	9	0	75	76	40	40	0	6.60
Tom Dettore	R	26	3	5	.375	0	16	9	0	65	64	31	43	0	4.15
Oscar Zamora	R	29	3	9	.250	10	56	0	0	84	82	19	38	0	3.11
Mike Paul	L	29	0	0	.000	0	2	0	0	1	4	1	1	0	36.00
Jim Kremmel	L	25	0	0	.000	0	23	0	0	31	37	18	22	0	5.23
Herb Hutson (JJ)	R	24	0	0	.000	0	20	2	0	29	24	15	22	0	3.41

WEST DIVISION

LOS ANGELES — 1st 102-60 .630 — WALT ALSTON

NAME	G by Pos	B	AGE	G	AB	R	H	2B	3B	HR	RBI	BB	SO	SB	BA	SA
TOTALS			27	162	5557	798	1511	231	34	139	744	597	820	149	.272	.401
Steve Garvey	1B156	R	25	158	642	95	200	32	3	21	111	31	66	5	.312	.469
Davey Lopes	2B143	R	29	145	530	95	141	26	3	10	35	66	71	59	.266	.383
Bill Russell	SS160,OF1	R	25	160	553	61	149	18	6	5	65	53	53	14	.269	.351
Ron Cey	3B158	R	26	159	577	88	151	20	2	18	97	76	80	1	.262	.397
Willie Crawford	OF133	L	27	139	468	73	138	23	4	11	61	64	88	7	.295	.432
Jim Wynn	OF148	R	32	150	535	104	145	17	4	32	108	108	104	18	.271	.497
Bill Buckner	OF137,1B6	L	24	145	580	83	182	30	3	7	58	30	24	31	.314	.412
Steve Yeager	C93	R	25	94	316	41	84	16	1	12	41	32	77	2	.266	.437
Joe Ferguson	C82,OF32	R	27	111	349	54	88	14	1	16	57	75	73	2	.252	.436
Tom Paciorek	OF77,1B1	R	27	85	175	23	42	8	6	1	24	10	32	1	.240	.371
Von Joshua	OF35	L	26	81	124	11	29	5	1	1	16	7	17	3	.234	.315
Manny Mota	OF3	R	36	66	57	5	16	2	0	0	16	5	4	0	.281	.316
Lee Lacy	2B34,3B1	R	26	48	78	13	22	6	0	0	2	8	14	2	.282	.359
Rick Auerbach	SS19,2B16,3B3	R	24	45	73	12	25	0	0	1	6	8	9	4	.342	.384
Ken McMullen (VR)	3B7,2B3	R	32	44	60	5	15	1	0	3	12	12	12	0	.250	.417
Gail Hopkins	C2,1B2	L	31	15	18	1	4	0	0	0	3	0	2	0	.222	.222
Jerry Royster	3B1,2B1,OF1	R	21	6	0	2	0	0	0	0	0	0	0	0	—	—
John Hale	OF3	L	20	4	4	0	1	0	0	0	0	0	1	0	1.000	1.250

Charlie Manuel 30 L 1-3, Ivan DeJesus 21 R 1-3, Orlando Alvarez 22 R 0-1, Kevin Pasley 20 R 0-0

NAME	T	AGE	W	L	PCT	SV	G	GS	CG	IP	H	BB	SO	SHO	ERA
		30	102	60	.630	23	162	162	33	1465	1272	464	943	19	2.97
Andy Messersmith	R	28	20	6	.769	0	39	39	13	292	227	94	221	3	2.59
Don Sutton	R	29	19	9	.679	0	40	40	10	276	241	80	179	5	3.23
Mike Marshall	R	31	15	12	.556	21	106	0	0	208	191	56	143	0	2.42
Tommy John (EJ)	L	31	13	3	.813	0	22	22	5	153	133	42	78	3	2.59
Doug Rau	L	25	13	11	.542	0	36	35	3	198	191	70	126	1	3.73
Charlie Hough	R	26	9	4	.692	1	49	0	0	96	65	63	63	0	3.75
Al Downing	L	33	5	6	.455	0	21	16	1	98	94	45	63	1	3.67
Jim Brewer (XJ)	L	36	4	4	.500	0	24	0	0	39	29	10	26	0	2.54
Geoff Zahn	L	28	3	5	.375	0	21	10	1	80	78	16	33	0	2.03
Rick Rhoden	R	21	1	0	1.000	0	4	0	0	9	5	4	7	0	2.00
Greg Shanahan	R	26	0	0	—	0	7	0	0	7	5	2	3	0	3.86
Eddie Solomon	R	23	0	0	—	0	4	0	0	6	5	2	1	0	1.50
Rex Hudson	R	20	0	0	—	0	1	0	0	2	6	1	0	0	22.50

CINCINNATI — 2nd 98-64 .605 4 — SPARKY ANDERSON

NAME	G by Pos	B	AGE	G	AB	R	H	2B	3B	HR	RBI	BB	SO	SB	BA	SA
TOTALS			27	163	5535	776	1437	271	35	135	714	693	940	146	.260	.394
Tony Perez	1B157	R	32	158	596	81	158	28	2	28	101	61	112	1	.265	.460
Joe Morgan	2B142	L	30	149	512	107	150	31	3	22	67	120	69	58	.293	.494
Dave Concepcion	SS160,OF1	R	26	160	594	70	167	25	1	14	82	44	79	41	.281	.397
Dan Driessen	3B126,1B47,OF3	L	22	150	470	63	132	23	6	7	56	48	62	10	.281	.400
George Foster	OF98	R	25	106	276	31	73	18	0	7	41	30	52	3	.264	.406
Cesar Geronimo	OF145	L	26	150	474	73	133	17	8	7	54	46	96	9	.281	.395
Pete Rose	OF163	B	33	163	652	110	185	45	7	3	51	106	54	2	.284	.388
Johnny Bench	C137,3B36,1B5	R	26	160	621	108	174	38	2	33	129	80	90	5	.280	.507
Darrel Chaney	3B81,2B38,SS12	L	26	117	135	27	27	6	1	2	16	26	33	1	.200	.304
Ken Griffey	OF70	L	24	88	227	24	57	9	5	2	19	27	43	9	.251	.361
Terry Crowley	OF22,1B7	L	27	84	125	11	30	12	0	1	20	10	16	1	.240	.360
Merv Rettenmund	OF69	R	31	80	208	30	45	6	0	6	28	37	39	5	.216	.332
Bill Plummer	C49,3B1	R	27	50	120	7	27	7	0	2	10	6	21	1	.225	.333
Phil Gagliano	2B2,3B1,1B1	R	32	46	31	2	2	0	0	0	0	15	7	0	.065	.065
Andy Kosco (XJ)	3B8,OF1	R	32	33	37	3	7	2	0	0	5	7	8	0	.189	.243
Junior Kennedy	2B17,3B5	R	23	22	19	2	3	0	0	0	0	6	4	0	.158	.158
Hal King	C5	L	30	20	17	1	3	1	0	0	3	3	4	0	.176	.235
Ray Knight	3B14	R	21	14	11	1	2	1	0	0	2	0	3	0	.182	.273
Ed Armbrister	OF4	R	25	14	7	1	2	0	0	0	1	1	1	0	.286	.286
Roger Freed	1B1	R	28	6	6	1	2	1	0	0	0	1	1	0	.333	.833

NAME	T	AGE	W	L	PCT	SV	G	GS	CG	IP	H	BB	SO	SHO	ERA
		27	98	64	.605	27	163	163	34	1466	1364	536	875	11	3.41
Jack Billingham	R	31	19	11	.633	0	36	35	8	212	233	64	103	3	3.95
Don Gullett	L	23	17	11	.607	0	36	35	10	243	201	88	183	3	3.04
Fred Norman	L	31	13	12	.520	0	35	26	8	186	170	68	141	2	3.15
Clay Carroll	R	33	12	5	.706	6	57	3	0	101	96	30	46	0	2.14
Clay Kirby	R	26	12	9	.571	0	36	35	7	231	210	91	160	1	3.27
Pedro Borbon	R	27	10	7	.588	14	73	0	0	139	132	32	53	0	3.24
Tom Carroll	R	21	4	3	.571	0	16	13	0	78	68	44	37	0	3.69
Roger Nelson (SJ)	R	30	4	4	.500	1	14	12	1	85	67	35	42	0	3.39
Tom Hall	L	26	3	1	.750	2	40	1	0	64	54	30	48	0	4.08
Will McEnaney	L	22	3	1	.667	2	24	0	0	27	24	9	13	0	4.33
Dick Baney	R	27	1	0	1.000	1	22	1	0	41	51	17	12	0	5.49
Pat Darcy	R	24	1	0	1.000	0	3	1	0	11	12	6	4	0	3.00
Rawly Eastwick	R	23	1	0	—	0	18	0	0	18	12	5	14	0	2.00
Mike McQueen	L	23	0	1	—	0	9	0	0	13	17	11	5	0	5.40
Pat Osburn	L	25	0	0	—	0	6	1	0	9	14	4	4	0	8.00
Gary Nolan (SJ) 26															

ATLANTA — 3rd 88-74 .543 14 — EDDIE MATHEWS 50-49 .505 — CLYDE KING 38-25 .603

NAME	G by Pos	B	AGE	G	AB	R	H	2B	3B	HR	RBI	BB	SO	SB	BA	SA
TOTALS			28	163	5533	661	1375	202	37	120	599	571	772	72	.249	.363
Dave Johnson	1B73,2B71	R	31	136	454	56	114	18	0	15	62	75	59	1	.251	.390
Marty Perez	2B102,SS14,3B6	R	28	127	447	51	116	20	5	2	34	35	51	2	.260	.340
Craig Robinson	SS142	R	25	145	452	52	104	4	6	0	29	30	57	11	.230	.265
Darrell Evans	3B160	L	27	160	571	99	137	21	3	25	79	126	88	4	.240	.419
Ralph Garr	OF139	L	28	143	606	87	214	24	17	11	54	28	52	26	.353	.503
Dusty Baker	OF148	R	25	149	574	80	147	35	0	20	69	71	87	18	.256	.422
Hank Aaron	OF89	R	40	112	340	47	91	16	0	20	69	39	29	1	.268	.491
Johnny Oates	C91	L	28	100	294	22	65	10	0	1	21	23	24	2	.223	.268
Rowland Office	OF119	L	21	131	248	20	61	16	1	3	31	16	30	5	.246	.355
Mike Lum (BY)	1B60,OF50	L	28	106	361	50	84	11	2	11	50	45	49	0	.233	.366
Frank Tepedino	1B46	L	26	78	169	11	39	5	1	0	16	9	13	1	.231	.272
Vic Correll	C59	R	28	73	202	20	48	5	1	4	29	21	38	0	.238	.381
Ivan Murrell	OF32,1B13	R	31	73	133	13	31	5	1	5	20	5	35	0	.233	.436
Leo Foster	SS43,2B10,3B3,OF1	R	23	72	112	16	22	1	2	0	4	5	11	0	.196	.241
Paul Casanova	C33	R	32	42	164	7	23	4	0	2	11	2	24	0	.140	.201
Norm Miller	OF4	L	28	42	41	4	7	1	0	0	0	3	12	0	.171	.268

Jack Pierce 25 L 1-9, Larvell Blanks 24 R 2-8, Sonny Jackson 29 L 3-7, Rod Gilbreath 21 R 2-6, John Fuller 24 L 1-3

NAME	T	AGE	W	L	PCT	SV	G	GS	CG	IP	H	BB	SO	SHO	ERA
		29	88	74	.543	22	163	163	46	1474	1343	488	772	21	3.05
Phil Niekro	R	35	20	13	.606	1	41	39	18	302	249	88	195	6	2.38
Buzz Capra	R	26	16	8	.667	1	39	27	11	217	163	84	137	5	2.28
Carl Morton	R	30	16	12	.571	0	38	38	7	275	293	89	113	1	3.14
Ron Reed (BH)	R	31	16	11	.476	0	38	28	6	186	171	41	78	2	3.39
Tom House	L	27	6	2	.750	11	56	0	0	103	74	27	64	0	1.92
Roric Harrison (KJ)	R	27	6	6	.500	0	20	20	3	126	148	49	46	0	4.71
Lew Krausse	R	31	4	3	.571	0	29	4	0	67	65	32	27	0	4.16
Max Leon	R	24	4	7	.364	3	34	2	1	75	84	14	38	1	3.56
Joe Niekro	R	29	3	2	.600	0	27	2	0	43	36	18	31	0	3.56
Danny Frisella	R	28	4	4	.429	6	36	1	0	42	37	28	27	0	5.14
Mike Beard	L	24	1	0	—	0	9	1	0	9	9	4	1	0	3.00
Gary Gentry (EJ)	R	27	1	1	.500	0	4	4	0	17	24	6	7	0	1.29
2 Mike Thompson	R	24	0	1	—	0	4	1	0	9	14	9	2	0	4.50
Jamie Easterly	L	21	0	2	—	0	6	0	0	6	10	4	4	0	15.00
1 Jack Aker	R	33	0	0	1.000	0	1	0	0	17	17	7	7	0	3.71

HOUSTON — 4th 81-81 .500 21 — PRESTON GOMEZ

NAME	G by Pos	B	AGE	G	AB	R	H	2B	3B	HR	RBI	BB	SO	SB	BA	SA
TOTALS			27	162	5489	653	1441	222	41	110	603	471	864	108	.263	.378
Lee May	1B145	R	31	152	556	59	149	26	0	24	85	17	97	1	.268	.444
Tommy Helms	2B133	R	33	137	452	32	126	21	1	5	50	23	27	5	.279	.363
Roger Metzger	SS143	B	26	143	572	66	145	18	10	0	30	37	73	9	.253	.320
Doug Rader	3B152	R	29	152	533	61	137	27	3	17	78	60	131	7	.257	.415
Greg Gross	OF151	L	21	156	589	78	185	21	8	0	36	76	39	12	.314	.377
Cesar Cedeno	OF157	R	23	160	610	95	164	29	5	26	102	64	103	57	.269	.461
Bob Watson	OF140,1B35	R	28	150	524	69	156	19	4	11	67	60	61	3	.298	.412
Milt May	C116	L	23	127	405	47	117	17	4	7	54	39	33	0	.289	.402
Larry Milbourne	2B87,SS8,OF4	B	23	112	136	31	38	2	1	0	9	10	14	6	.279	.309
Bob Gallagher	OF62,1B4	L	25	102	87	13	15	2	0	0	3	12	23	1	.172	.195
Cliff Johnson	C28,1B21	R	26	83	171	26	39	4	1	10	29	33	45	0	.228	.439
Wilbur Howard	OF50	B	25	64	111	19	24	4	0	2	5	5	18	4	.216	.306
Johnny Edwards	C32	L	36	50	117	8	26	7	1	1	10	11	12	1	.222	.325
Dave Campbell (HJ)	2B9,1B6,3B2,OF1	R	32	35	23	4	2	1	0	0	2	1	8	1	.087	.130
Denis Menke	1B12,3B7,2B3,SS2	R	33	30	29	2	3	1	0	0	1	4	10	0	.103	.138
1 Ollie Brown	OF20	R	30	27	69	8	15	1	0	3	6	4	15	0	.217	.362
Mick Kelleher	SS18	R	26	19	57	4	9	0	0	0	2	5	10	1	.158	.158
Ray Busse	3B8	R	25	19	34	3	7	1	0	0	3	3	12	0	.206	.235
Mike Easler		L	23	15	15	0	1	0	0	0	0	0	5	0	.067	.067
Skip Jutze	C7	R	28	8	13	0	3	0	0	0	1	1	1	0	.231	.231

NAME	T	AGE	W	L	PCT	SV	G	GS	CG	IP	H	BB	SO	SHO	ERA
		28	81	81	.500	18	162	162	36	1451	1396	601	738	18	3.46
Tom Griffin	R	26	14	10	.583	0	34	34	8	211	202	89	110	3	3.54
Larry Dierker	R	27	11	10	.524	0	33	33	7	224	189	82	150	3	2.89
Don Wilson	R	29	11	13	.458	0	33	27	5	205	170	100	112	4	3.07
Dave Roberts	L	29	10	12	.455	1	34	30	8	204	216	65	72	2	3.40
1 Claude Osteen	L	34	9	9	.500	0	23	21	7	138	158	47	45	2	3.72
Ken Forsch	R	27	8	7	.533	10	70	0	0	103	98	37	48	0	2.80
Mike Cosgrove	L	23	7	3	.700	2	45	0	0	90	76	39	47	0	3.50
Jerry Johnson	R	30	2	1	.667	0	34	0	0	45	47	24	32	0	4.80
Jim York	R	26	2	2	.500	1	28	0	0	38	48	19	15	0	3.32
J.R. Richard	R	24	2	3	.400	0	15	9	0	65	58	36	42	0	4.15
Fred Scherman	L	29	2	5	.286	4	53	0	0	61	67	26	35	0	4.13
Paul Siebert	L	21	1	1	.500	0	5	5	1	25	21	11	10	1	3.60
Mike Nagy	R	26	1	1	.500	0	9	0	0	13	17	5	5	0	8.31
Ramon de los Santos	L	25	1	1	.500	0	12	0	0	12	11	9	7	0	2.25
Doug Konieczny	R	23	0	3	.000	0	6	3	0	16	18	12	8	0	7.88

SAN FRANCISCO — 5th 72-90 .444 30 — CHARLIE FOX 34-42 .447 — WES WESTRUM 38-48 .442

NAME	G by Pos	B	AGE	G	AB	R	H	2B	3B	HR	RBI	BB	SO	SB	BA	SA
TOTALS			25	162	5482	634	1380	228	38	93	568	548	869	107	.252	.358
Dave Kingman	1B91,3B21,OF2	R	25	121	350	41	78	18	2	18	55	37	125	8	.223	.440
Tito Fuentes	2B103	B	30	108	390	33	97	15	2	0	22	22	32	7	.249	.297
Chris Speier	SS135,2B4	R	24	141	501	55	125	19	5	9	53	62	64	3	.250	.361
Steve Ontiveros	3B75,1B19,OF2	B	22	120	343	45	91	15	1	4	33	57	41	0	.265	.350
Bobby Bonds	OF148	R	28	150	567	97	145	22	8	21	71	95	134	41	.256	.434
Garry Maddox	OF131	R	24	135	538	74	153	31	3	8	50	29	64	21	.284	.398
Gary Matthews	OF151	R	23	154	561	87	161	27	6	16	82	70	69	11	.287	.442
Dave Rader	C109	L	25	113	323	26	94	16	2	1	26	31	21	1	.291	.362
Gary Thomasson	OF76,1B15	L	22	120	315	41	77	14	3	2	29	38	56	7	.244	.327
Mike Phillips	3B34,2B30,SS23	B	23	100	283	19	62	6	1	2	20	14	37	4	.219	.269
Ed Goodson	1B73,3B8	L	26	98	298	25	81	15	0	6	48	18	22	1	.272	.383
Chris Arnold	2B31,3B7,SS1	R	26	78	174	22	42	7	3	1	26	15	27	1	.241	.333
Bruce Miller	3B41,SS13,2B9	R	27	73	198	19	55	7	1	0	16	11	15	1	.278	.323
Ken Rudolph	C56	R	27	57	158	11	41	3	0	0	10	21	15	0	.259	.278
John Boccabella	C26	R	33	29	80	6	11	3	0	0	5	3	6	0	.138	.175
Glenn Redmon	2B4	R	26	7	17	0	4	3	0	0	4	1	3	0	.235	.412
Jim Howarth	OF1	R	27	6	4	0	0	0	0	0	0	0	0	0	.000	.000
Damie Blanco		R	25	2	2	0	0	0	0	0	0	0	1	0	.000	.000

NAME	T	AGE	W	L	PCT	SV	G	GS	CG	IP	H	BB	SO	SHO	ERA
		26	72	90	.444	25	162	162	27	1439	1409	559	756	11	3.78
Mike Caldwell	L	25	14	5	.737	0	31	27	6	189	176	63	83	2	2.95
Jim Barr	R	26	13	9	.591	2	44	27	11	240	223	47	84	5	2.74
John D'Acquisto	R	22	12	14	.462	0	38	36	5	215	182	124	167	1	3.77
Elias Sosa	R	24	9	7	.563	6	68	0	0	101	94	45	48	0	3.48
Tom Bradley	R	27	8	11	.421	0	30	21	2	134	152	52	72	0	5.17
Randy Moffitt	R	25	5	7	.417	15	61	1	0	102	99	29	49	0	4.50
John Montefusco	R	24	3	2	.600	0	7	5	1	39	41	19	34	1	4.85
Ron Bryant (UJ)	R	26	3	15	.167	0	41	23	0	127	142	68	75	0	5.60
Butch Metzger	R	22	1	0	1.000	0	10	0	0	13	11	12	5	0	3.46
John Morris	L	32	1	1	.500	1	17	0	0	21	17	4	9	0	3.00
Charlie Williams	R	26	1	3	.250	0	39	7	0	100	93	31	48	0	2.79
Jim Willoughby	R	25	1	4	.200	0	18	4	0	41	51	9	12	0	4.61
Ed Halicki	R	23	1	8	.111	0	16	11	2	74	84	31	40	0	4.26
Don McMahon (RC)	R	44	0	0	—	0	12	0	0	12	13	2	3	0	3.00
Don Rose	R	27	0	0	—	0	2	0	0	5	4	0	1	0	9.00
Steve Barber	L	36	0	1	.000	0	13	0	0	14	13	12	13	0	5.14
Gary Lavelle	L	25	0	1	.000	0	10	0	0	17	14	10	12	0	2.12

SAN DIEGO — 6th 60-102 .370 42 — JOHN McNAMARA

NAME	G by Pos	B	AGE	G	AB	R	H	2B	3B	HR	RBI	BB	SO	SB	BA	SA
TOTALS			27	162	5415	541	1239	196	27	99	506	564	900	85	.229	.330
Willie McCovey	1B104	L	36	128	344	53	87	19	1	22	63	96	76	1	.253	.506
Derrel Thomas	2B104,3B22,OF20,SS5	B	23	141	523	48	129	24	6	3	41	51	58	7	.247	.333
Enzo Hernandez	SS145	R	25	147	512	55	119	19	2	0	34	38	36	37	.232	.277
Dave Roberts	3B103,SS3,OF1	R	23	113	318	26	53	10	1	5	18	32	69	2	.167	.252
Dave Winfield	OF131	R	22	145	498	57	132	18	4	20	75	40	96	9	.265	.438
Johnny Grubb	OF122,3B2	L	25	140	444	53	127	20	4	8	42	46	47	4	.286	.403
Bobby Tolan (KJ)	OF88	L	28	95	357	45	95	16	1	8	40	20	41	7	.266	.384
Fred Kendall	C133	R	25	141	424	32	98	15	2	8	45	49	33	0	.231	.333
Nate Colbert	1B79,OF48	R	28	119	368	53	76	16	0	14	54	62	108	10	.207	.364
Cito Gaston	OF63	R	30	106	267	19	57	11	0	6	33	16	51	0	.213	.322
Dave Hilton	3B55,2B15	R	23	74	217	17	52	8	2	1	12	13	28	3	.240	.309
Glenn Beckert(NJ)	2B36,3B1	R	33	64	172	11	44	1	0	0	7	11	8	0	.256	.262
Rich Morales	SS29,2B18,3B6,1B1	R	30	54	61	8	12	3	0	1	5	3	6	0	.197	.295
Matty Alou	OF13,1B2	L	35	48	81	8	16	3	0	0	3	5	6	1	.198	.235
2 Horace Clarke	2B21	B	34	42	90	5	17	1	0	0	4	4	8	1	.189	.200
Gene Locklear	OF12	L	24	39	74	7	20	3	2	1	9	4	12	0	.270	.405
Rod Gaspar	OF8,1B2	B	28	33	14	4	3	0	0	0	1	4	3	0	.214	.214
Bob Barton (BG)	C29	R	32	30	81	4	19	1	0	0	7	13	19	0	.235	.247
Chris Cannizzaro	C26	R	36	26	60	2	11	1	0	0	4	6	11	0	.183	.200
Jerry Turner	OF13	L	20	17	48	4	14	1	0	0	2	3	5	2	.292	.313
Bill Almon	SS14	R	21	16	38	4	12	1	0	0	3	2	9	1	.316	.342
Bernie Williams	OF3	R	25	14	15	1	2	0	0	0	0	0	6	0	.133	.133
John Scott	OF8	R	25	14	15	3	1	0	0	0	2	0	4	1	.067	.067
Randy Elliott	OF11,1B1	R	23	13	33	5	7	1	0	0	3	2	10	0	.212	.333
Mike Ivie	1B11	R	21	12	34	1	3	0	0	0	3	2	9	0	.088	.176

NAME	T	AGE	W	L	PCT	SV	G	GS	CG	IP	H	BB	SO	SHO	ERA
		25	60	102	.370	19	162	162	25	1446	1536	715	855	7	4.58
Larry Hardy	R	26	9	4	.692	2	76	1	0	102	129	44	57	0	4.68
Dan Spillner	R	22	9	11	.450	0	30	25	5	148	153	70	95	2	4.01
Dave Freisleben	R	22	9	14	.391	0	33	31	6	212	194	112	130	2	3.65
Bill Greif	L	24	9	19	.321	4	33	35	7	226	244	95	137	1	4.66
Randy Jones	L	24	8	22	.267	2	40	34	4	208	217	78	124	1	4.46
Vicente Romo	R	31	5	5	.500	9	54	0	0	71	78	37	26	0	4.56
Dave Tomlin	L	25	2	0	1.000	1	47	0	0	58	59	30	29	0	4.34
Rusty Gerhardt	L	23	2	1	.667	1	23	1	0	36	44	17	22	0	7.00
Mike Corkins (SA)	R	28	2	2	.500	0	25	2	0	56	53	32	41	0	4.82
Lowell Palmer	R	26	2	5	.286	0	22	8	1	73	68	59	52	0	5.67
Rich Troedson	L	24	1	1	.500	1	15	1	0	19	24	8	11	0	8.53
Jim McAndrew	R	30	1	4	.200	0	15	5	1	42	48	13	16	0	5.57
1 Steve Arlin	R	28	1	7	.125	1	16	12	1	64	85	37	18	0	5.91
Gary Ross	R	26	0	0	—	0	9	0	0	18	23	6	11	0	4.50
Ralph Garcia	R	25	0	0	—	0	8	0	0	10	15	7	9	0	6.30
Bill Laxton	L	26	0	1	.000	0	30	1	0	45	37	38	40	0	4.00
Mike Johnson	R	23	0	0	.000	0	10	5	0	21	29	15	15	0	4.71
Joe McIntosh	R	22	0	0	.000	0	10	5	0	37	36	17	22	0	3.65

WORLD SERIES — OAKLAND (AL) 4 LOS ANGELES (NL) 1

LINE SCORES

TEAM	1	2	3	4	5	6	7	8	9	10	11	12	R	H	E

Game 1 October 12 at Los Angeles
| OAK(AL) | 0 | 1 | 0 | 0 | 1 | 0 | 0 | 1 | 0 | | | | 3 | 6 | 2 |
| LA(NL) | 0 | 0 | 0 | 0 | 1 | 0 | 0 | 0 | 1 | | | | 2 | 11 | 1 |

Holtzman, Fingers (5), Hunter(9) Messersmith, Marshall (9)

Game 2 October 13 at Los Angeles
| OAK | 0 | 0 | 0 | 0 | 0 | 0 | 0 | 0 | 2 | | | | 2 | 6 | 0 |
| LA | 0 | 1 | 0 | 0 | 0 | 2 | 0 | 0 | x | | | | 3 | 6 | 1 |

Blue, Odom (8) Sutton, Marshall (9)

Game 3 October 15 at Oakland
| LA | 0 | 0 | 0 | 0 | 0 | 0 | 0 | 1 | 1 | | | | 2 | 7 | 2 |
| OAK | 0 | 0 | 2 | 1 | 0 | 0 | 0 | 0 | x | | | | 3 | 5 | 2 |

Downing, Brewer (4), Hough (5), Marshall (7) Hunter, Fingers (8)

Game 4 October 16 at Oakland
| LA | 0 | 0 | 0 | 2 | 0 | 0 | 0 | 0 | 0 | | | | 2 | 7 | 1 |
| OAK | 0 | 0 | 1 | 0 | 0 | 4 | 0 | 0 | x | | | | 5 | 7 | 0 |

Messersmith, Marshall (7) Holtzman, Fingers (8)

Game 5 October 17 at Oakland
| LA | 0 | 0 | 0 | 0 | 0 | 2 | 0 | 0 | 0 | | | | 2 | 5 | 1 |
| OAK | 1 | 1 | 0 | 0 | 0 | 0 | 1 | 0 | x | | | | 3 | 6 | 1 |

Sutton, Marshall (6) Blue, Odom (7), Fingers (8)

COMPOSITE BATTING

NAME	POS	G	AB	R	H	2B	3B	HR	RBI	BA
Oakland (AL) Totals		5	142	16	30	4	0	4	14	.211
Rudi	LF-1B	5	18	1	6	0	0	1	4	.333
Campaneris	SS	5	17	1	6	2	0	0	2	.353
North	CF	5	17	3	1	0	0	0	0	.059
Bando	3B	5	16	3	1	0	0	0	1	.063
Jackson	RF	5	14	3	4	1	0	1	1	.286
Fosse	C	5	14	1	2	0	0	0	1	.143
Green	2B	5	13	1	0	0	0	0	0	.000
Tenace	1B	5	9	0	2	0	0	0	0	.222
C. Washington	RF-CF-LF	5	7	1	4	0	0	0	0	.571
Holtzman	P	2	4	2	2	1	0	0	1	.500
Blue	P	2	4	0	0	0	0	0	0	.000
Holt	1B	4	3	0	2	0	0	0	0	.667
Fingers	P	4	2	0	0	0	0	0	0	.000
Hunter	P	2	2	0	0	0	0	0	0	.000
Alou	PH	1	1	0	0	0	0	0	0	.000
Mangual	PH	1	1	0	0	0	0	0	0	.000
H. Washington	PR	3	0	0	0	0	0	0	0	—
Haney	C	2	0	0	0	0	0	0	0	—
Maxvill	2B	2	0	0	0	0	0	0	0	—
Odom	P	2	0	0	0	0	0	0	0	—
Los Angeles (NL) Totals		5	158	11	36	4	0	4	10	.228
Garvey	1B	5	21	2	8	4	0	0	0	.381
Buckner	LF	5	20	1	5	1	0	1	1	.250
Russell	SS	5	18	0	4	0	0	0	2	.222
Lopes	2B	5	18	2	2	0	1	0	1	.111
Cey	3B	5	17	1	3	0	0	0	1	.176
Wynn	CF	5	16	1	3	1	0	1	2	.188
Ferguson	RF-C	5	16	2	2	0	0	1	2	.125
Yeager	C	4	11	0	4	1	0	0	3	.364
Crawford	RF	3	6	1	2	0	0	0	0	.333
Messersmith	P	2	4	0	2	0	0	0	0	.500
Joshua	PH	3	4	0	0	0	0	0	0	.000
Sutton	P	2	3	0	0	0	0	0	0	.000
Paciorek	PH-PR	2	2	0	1	0	0	0	0	.500
Lacy	PH	1	1	0	0	0	0	0	0	.000
Downing	P	1	0	0	0	0	0	0	0	—
Marshall	PR	1	0	0	0	0	0	0	0	—
Auerbach	PR	1	0	0	0	0	0	0	0	—
Brewer	P	1	0	0	0	0	0	0	0	—
Hough	P	1	0	0	0	0	0	0	0	—

COMPOSITE PITCHING

NAME	G	IP	H	BB	SO	W	L	SV	ERA
Oakland (AL) Totals	5	44	36	16	32	4	1	3	2.05
Blue	2	13.2	10	7	9	0	1	0	3.29
Holtzman	2	12	13	4	10	1	0	0	1.50
Fingers	4	9.1	8	2	6	1	0	2	1.93
Hunter	2	7.2	5	2	5	1	0	1	1.17
Odom	2	1.1	0	1	2	1	0	0	0.00
Los Angeles (NL) Totals	5	42	30	16	42	1	4	1	2.79
Messersmith	2	14	11	7	12	0	2	0	4.50
Sutton	2	13	9	3	12	1	0	0	2.77
Marshall	5	9	6	1	10	0	1	1	1.00
Downing	1	3.2	4	3	0	0	1	0	2.45
Hough	1	2	0	1	4	0	0	0	0.00
Brewer	1	.1	0	0	1	0	0	0	0.00

1975 Coming Up Red

As a result of a contract dispute with Oakland owner Charles O. Finley, Catfish Hunter was made a free agent—a move which precipitated "the most celebrated auction in baseball history". The New York Yankees got Hunter for a package which cost them over $3 million. That deal, and the trade of Bobby Murcer to the Giants for Bobby Bonds, was enough to make New York a pre-season pick along with Baltimore to win the American League East. But the team taken lightly, the Boston Red Sox, came up with two sensational rookie finds and beat out the Orioles, who didn't get into high gear until the end of the season, and the Yankees, who suffered a rash of injuries. Of the two rookies—Fred Lynn and Jim Rice—Lynn took most of the headlines by playing a flawless centerfield, hitting .331 with 21 homers and 105 runs batted in, and becoming the first man to win both the MVP and rookie-of-the-year awards. Rice, although suffering a broken wrist in late September, finished with a .309 average, 22 homers, and 102 runs batted in.

In the A.L. West, the A's seemed ripe to be overthrown without Hunter, but despite the gap in the pitching rotation and Sal Bando's poor season, the A's once again captured the Western title handily by beating back a late challenge from the Kansas City Royals. To supplement the familiar faces on the Oakland roster, Claudell Washington blossomed into a dangerous hitter and Billy Williams came over from the National League to provide power as the designated hitter.

In the N.L. East, the winner was also familiar as the Pittsburgh Pirates held off the Phillies to capture the title for the fifth time in six years. The Bucs had a balanced squad, highlighted by a seven-for-seven day at the plate by second baseman Rennie Stennett. In the West, Cincinnati put together a 41-9 record in late May to pull away from the injury-ridden defending champs, the Los Angeles Dodgers. The Reds' devastating attack—which won the division by 20 games—featured the hitting of Joe Morgan, Pete Rose, Tony Perez, and Johnny Bench, while Don Gullett spearheaded a mound staff that was their deepest in recent history.

The Reds continued their domination in the playoffs by taking Pittsburgh in three straight for their third pennant in six years. Oakland, also favored to win their fourth straight pennant, was surprised and embarrassed by Boston, which easily won the playoffs in three straight.

In the World Series, favorite Cincinnati was looking for their first title since 1940. Boston also suffered a drought by not winning a Series since 1918. The Red Sox were not expected to provide much of a challenge, but they kept their season-long performance intact in a Series which proved the most exciting in years and produced a folk hero for Boston in pitcher Luis Tiant. The clubs battled back and forth, with the Reds winning three of the first five games—one on a disputed extra innings interference call. The sixth game crammed a heaping portion of drama into twelve innings, with superb fielding plays by George Foster and Dwight Evans and a three-run pinch homer by Bernie Carbo paving the way for Carlton Fisk's game-winning homer in the bottom of the twelfth for a 7-6 Boston victory. The seventh game, watched by an estimated 71 million TV viewers, saw the Reds triumph in the ninth inning on a bloop single by Joe Morgan for 4-3 win.

Beyond the Series, there were many other events which made up the year: Rod Carew won his fourth straight A.L. batting title, Frank Robinson led the Cleveland Indians as the first black manager in major league history, Nolan Ryan notched his fourth no-hitter, Juan Marichal, Mel Stottlemyre, and Bob Gibson called it quits, and Hank Aaron moved to Milwaukee as a DH, where he hit 12 homers to run his career total to 745. Death also took its toll and counted Houston pitcher Don Wilson and the game's most colorful character — Casey Stengel.

1975 AMERICAN LEAGUE — EAST DIVISION

BOSTON — 1st 95-65 .594 — DARRELL JOHNSON

NAME	G by Pos	B	AGE	G	AB	R	H	2B	3B	HR	RBI	BB	SO	SB	BA	SA
TOTALS			27	160	5448	796	1500	284	44	134	756	565	741	66	.275	.417
Carl Yastrzemski	1B140,OF8,DH2	L	35	149	543	91	146	30	1	14	60	87	67	8	.269	.405
2 Denny Doyle	2B84,3B6,SS2	L	31	89	310	50	96	21	2	4	36	14	11	5	.310	.429
Rick Burleson	SS158	R	24	158	580	66	146	25	1	6	62	45	44	8	.252	.329
Rico Petrocelli	3B113,DH1	R	32	115	402	31	96	15	1	7	59	41	66	0	.239	.333
Dwight Evans	OF115,DH7	R	23	128	412	61	113	24	6	13	56	47	60	3	.274	.456
Fred Lynn	OF144	L	23	145	528	103	175	47	7	21	105	62	90	10	.331	.566
Jim Rice	OF90,DH54	R	22	144	564	92	174	29	4	22	102	36	122	10	.309	.491
Carlton Fisk (BA)	C71,DH6	R	27	79	263	47	87	14	4	10	52	27	32	4	.331	.529
Cecil Cooper	DH54,1B35	L	25	106	305	49	95	17	6	14	44	19	33	1	.311	.544
Bernie Carbo	OF85,DH13	L	27	107	319	64	82	21	3	15	50	83	69	2	.257	.483
Doug Griffin	2B99,SS1	R	28	100	287	21	69	6	0	1	29	18	29	2	.240	.272
Juan Beniquez	OF44,DH20,3B14	R	25	78	254	43	74	14	4	2	17	25	26	7	.291	.402
Rick Miller	OF65	L	27	77	108	21	21	2	1	0	15	21	20	3	.194	.231
Bob Heise	3B45,2B14,SS4,1B1	R	28	63	126	12	27	3	0	0	21	4	6	0	.214	.238
Bob Montgomery	C53,1B6,DH3	R	31	62	195	16	44	10	1	2	26	4	37	1	.226	.318
Tim Blackwell	C57,DH2	B	22	59	132	15	26	3	2	0	6	19	13	0	.197	.250
Tony Conigliaro (GJ)	DH15	R	30	21	57	8	7	1	0	2	9	8	9	1	.123	.246
1 Tim McCarver	C7,1B1	L	33	12	21	1	8	2	1	0	3	1	3	0	.381	.571
Dick McAuliffe (VR)	3B7	L	35	7	15	0	2	0	0	0	1	1	2	0	.133	.133
2 Deron Johnson	1B2,DH1	R	36	3	10	2	6	0	0	1	3	2	0	0	.600	.900

Steve Dillard 24 R 2-5, Andy Merchant 24 L 2-4, Butch Hobson 23 R 1-4, Kim Andrew 21 R 1-2, Buddy Hunter 27 R 0-1

NAME	T	AGE	W	L	PCT	SV	G	GS	CG	IP	H	BB	SO	SHO	ERA
		29	95	65	.594	31	160	160	62	1437	1463	490	720	11	3.98
Rick Wise	R	29	19	12	.613	0	35	35	17	255	262	72	141	1	3.95
Luis Tiant	R	34	18	14	.563	0	35	35	18	260	262	72	142	2	4.02
Bill Lee	L	28	17	9	.654	0	41	34	17	260	274	69	78	4	3.95
Roger Moret	L	25	14	3	.824	1	36	16	4	145	132	76	80	1	3.60
Reggie Cleveland	R	27	13	9	.591	0	31	20	3	171	173	52	78	1	4.42
Jim Willoughby	R	26	5	2	.714	8	24	0	0	48	46	16	29	0	3.56
Dick Pole (BY)	R	24	4	6	.400	0	18	11	2	90	102	32	42	1	4.40
Dick Drago	R	30	2	2	.500	15	40	2	0	73	69	31	43	0	3.82
Diego Segui	R	37	2	5	.286	6	33	1	1	71	71	43	45	0	4.82
Jim Burton	L	25	1	2	.333	1	29	4	0	53	58	19	39	0	2.89
Rick Kreuger	L	26	0	0	—	0	2	0	0	4	3	1	1	0	4.50
Steve Barr	L	23	0	1	.000	0	3	2	0	7	11	7	2	0	2.57

BALTIMORE — 2nd 90-69 .566 4.5 — EARL WEAVER

NAME	G by Pos	B	AGE	G	AB	R	H	2B	3B	HR	RBI	BB	SO	SB	BA	SA
TOTALS			31	159	5474	682	1382	224	33	124	635	580	834	104	.252	.373
Lee May	1B144,DH2	R	32	146	580	67	152	28	4	20	99	36	91	1	.262	.424
Bobby Grich	2B150	R	26	150	524	81	136	26	4	13	57	107	88	14	.260	.399
Mark Belanger	SS152	R	31	152	442	44	100	11	1	3	27	36	53	16	.226	.276
Brooks Robinson	3B143	R	38	144	482	50	97	15	1	6	53	44	33	0	.201	.274
Ken Singleton	OF155	B	28	155	586	88	176	37	4	15	55	118	82	1	.300	.454
Paul Blair	OF138,DH1,1B1	R	31	140	440	51	96	13	4	5	31	25	82	17	.218	.300
Don Baylor	OF135,DH7,1B2	R	26	145	524	79	148	21	6	25	76	53	64	32	.282	.489
Dave Duncan	C95	R	29	96	307	30	63	7	0	12	41	16	82	0	.205	.345
Tommy Davis	DH111	R	36	116	460	43	130	14	1	6	57	23	52	2	.283	.357
Al Bumbry	DH48,OF39,3B1	L	28	114	349	47	94	19	4	2	32	32	81	16	.269	.364
Ellie Hendricks	C83	L	34	85	223	24	48	8	2	8	38	34	40	0	.215	.377
Jim Northrup	OF58,DH3	L	35	84	194	27	53	13	0	5	29	22	22	0	.273	.418
Doug DeCinces	3B34,SS13,2B11,1B2	R	24	61	167	20	42	6	3	4	23	13	32	0	.251	.395
Tim Nordbrook	SS37,2B3	R	25	40	34	6	4	1	0	0	0	7	7	0	.118	.147
Tom Shopay	OF13,DH3,C1	L	30	40	31	4	5	1	0	0	2	4	7	3	.161	.194
1 Andy Etchebarren (BE)	C7	R	32	8	20	0	4	1	0	0	3	0	5	0	.200	.250

Royle Stillman 24 L 6-14, Bob Bailor 23 R 1-7, Jim Hutto 27 R 0-5, Larry Harlow 23 L 1-3

NAME	T	AGE	W	L	PCT	SV	G	GS	CG	IP	H	BB	SO	SHO	ERA
		29	90	69	.566	21	159	159	70	1451	1285	500	717	19	3.17
Jim Palmer	R	29	23	11	.676	1	39	38	25	323	253	80	193	10	2.09
Mike Torrez	R	28	20	9	.690	0	36	36	16	271	238	133	119	2	3.06
Mike Cuellar	L	38	14	12	.538	0	36	36	17	256	229	84	105	5	3.66
Ross Grimsley	L	25	10	13	.435	0	35	32	8	197	210	47	89	1	4.07
Doyle Alexander	R	24	8	8	.500	1	32	11	3	133	127	47	46	1	3.05
Dyar Miller	R	29	6	3	.667	8	30	0	0	46	32	16	33	0	2.74
Grant Jackson	L	32	4	3	.571	7	41	0	0	48	42	21	39	0	3.38
Paul Mitchell	R	24	3	0	1.000	0	11	4	1	57	41	19	31	0	3.63
Wayne Garland	R	24	2	5	.286	4	29	1	0	87	80	31	46	0	3.72
Mike Flanagan	L	23	0	1	.000	0	2	1	0	10	9	6	7	0	2.70
Dave Johnson	R	26	0	1	.000	0	6	0	0	9	8	7	4	0	4.00
1 Bob Reynolds	R	26	0	1	.000	0	7	0	0	5	8	1	1	0	9.00
1 Jesse Jefferson	R	26	0	2	.000	0	3	0	0	8	4	5	4	0	2.25

NEW YORK — 3rd 83-77 .519 12 — BILL VIRDON 53-51 .510 — 2 BILLY MARTIN 30-26 .536

NAME	G by Pos	B	AGE	G	AB	R	H	2B	3B	HR	RBI	BB	SO	SB	BA	SA
TOTALS			29	160	5415	681	1430	230	39	110	642	486	710	102	.264	.382
Chris Chambliss	1B147	L	26	150	562	66	171	38	4	9	72	29	50	0	.304	.434
Sandy Alomar	2B150,SS1	B	31	151	489	61	117	18	4	2	39	26	58	24	.239	.305
Fred Stanley	SS83,2B33,3B1	R	27	117	252	34	56	5	1	0	15	21	27	3	.222	.250
Graig Nettles	3B157	L	30	157	581	71	155	24	4	21	91	54	88	1	.267	.430
Bobby Bonds	OF129,DH12	R	29	145	529	93	143	26	3	32	85	89	137	30	.270	.512
Elliott Maddox (KJ)	OF55,2B1	R	27	55	218	36	67	10	3	1	23	21	24	9	.307	.394
Roy White	OF135,1B7,DH2	B	31	148	556	81	161	32	5	12	59	72	50	16	.290	.430
Thurman Munson	C130,DH22,1B2,OF2,3B1	R	28	157	597	83	190	24	3	12	102	45	52	3	.318	.429
Ron Blomberg	DH27,OF1	L	26	34	106	18	27	8	2	4	17	13	10	0	.255	.481
Jim Mason	SS93,2B1	L	24	94	223	17	34	3	2	2	16	22	49	1	.152	.211
Walt Williams	OF31,DH17,2B6	R	31	82	185	27	52	5	1	5	16	8	23	0	.281	.400
Ed Herrmann	DH35,C24	L	28	80	200	16	51	9	2	6	30	16	22	0	.255	.410
Lou Piniella (IL)	OF46,DH12	R	31	74	199	7	39	4	1	0	22	16	22	0	.196	.226
Rick Dempsey	C19,DH18,OF8,3B1	R	25	71	145	18	38	8	0	1	11	21	15	0	.262	.338
Alex Johnson	DH28,OF7	R	32	52	119	15	31	5	1	2	15	7	21	2	.261	.345
Rick Bladt	OF51	R	28	52	117	13	26	3	1	1	11	11	16	2	.222	.291
2 Rich Coggins	OF36,DH9	L	24	51	107	7	24	1	0	0	7	6	16	3	.224	.270
3 Eddie Brinkman	SS39,3B3,2B3	R	33	44	63	2	11	4	0	0	3	6	9	0	.174	.270
Terry Whitfield	OF25,DH1	L	22	28	81	9	23	5	1	1	7	1	17	1	.272	.395
Bob Oliver	1B8,DH3,3B1	R	32	18	38	3	5	1	0	1	4	1	5	0	.132	.158

Kerry Dineen 23 L 8-22, Dave Bergman 22 L 0-17, Otto Velez 24 R 2-8, Larry Murray 22 B 0-1, Eddie Leon 28 R 0-0

NAME	T	AGE	W	L	PCT	SV	G	GS	CG	IP	H	BB	SO	SHO	ERA
		29	83	77	.519	20	160	160	70	1424	1325	502	809	11	3.29
Catfish Hunter	R	29	23	14	.622	0	39	39	30	328	248	83	177	7	2.58
Doc Medich	R	26	16	16	.500	0	38	37	15	272	271	72	132	2	3.51
Rudy May	L	30	14	12	.538	0	32	31	13	212	179	99	145	1	3.06
Pat Dobson	R	33	11	14	.440	0	33	30	7	208	205	83	129	1	4.07
Larry Gura	L	27	7	8	.467	0	26	20	5	151	173	41	65	0	3.52
Dick Tidrow	R	28	6	3	.667	5	37	0	0	69	65	31	38	0	3.13
Sparky Lyle	L	30	5	7	.417	6	49	0	0	89	94	36	65	0	3.13
Tippy Martinez	L	25	1	2	.333	8	23	2	0	37	27	32	20	0	2.68
Dave Pagan	R	25	0	0	—	1	13	0	0	31	30	13	18	0	4.06
Rick Sawyer	R	27	0	0	—	0	4	0	0	6	7	3	3	0	3.00
1 Mike Wallace	L	24	0	1	.000	1	16	0	0	16	15	9	15	0	15.50
Ron Guidry	L	24	0	1	.000	0	10	0	0	16	15	9	15	0	3.38

CLEVELAND 4th 79-80 .497 15.5 FRANK ROBINSON

NAME	G by Pos	B	AGE	G	AB	R	H	2B	3B	HR	RBI	BB	SO	SB	BA	SA
TOTALS			26	159	5404	688	1409	201	25	153	643	525	667	106	.261	.392
Boog Powell	1B121,DH5	L	33	134	435	64	129	18	0	27	86	59	72	1	.297	.524
Duane Kuiper	2B87,DH1	R	25	90	346	42	101	11	1	0	25	30	26	19	.292	.329
Frank Duffy	SS145	R	28	146	482	44	117	22	2	1	47	27	60	10	.243	.303
Buddy Bell	3B153	R	23	153	553	66	150	20	4	10	59	51	72	6	.271	.376
George Hendrick	OF143	R	25	145	561	82	145	21	2	24	86	40	78	6	.258	.431
Rick Manning	OF118,DH1	L	20	120	480	69	137	16	5	3	35	44	62	19	.285	.358
Charlie Spikes	OF103,DH2	R	24	111	345	41	79	13	3	11	33	30	51	7	.229	.380
Alan Ashby	C87,1B2,DH1,3B1	B	25	90	254	32	57	10	1	5	32	30	42	3	.224	.331
Rico Carty	DH72,1B26,OF12	R	35	118	383	57	118	19	1	18	64	45	31	2	.308	.504
Oscar Gamble	OF82,DH29	L	25	121	348	60	91	16	3	15	45	53	39	11	.261	.454
Johnny Ellis	C84,DH3,1B2	R	26	92	296	22	68	11	1	7	32	14	33	0	.230	.345
Johny Lowenstein	OF36,DH31,3B8,2B2	L	28	91	265	37	64	5	1	12	33	28	28	15	.242	.404
Jack Brohamer (PJ)	2B66	L	25	69	217	15	53	5	0	6	16	14	14	2	.244	.350
Ed Crosby	SS30,2B19,3B13	L	26	61	128	12	30	3	0	0	7	13	14	0	.234	.258
Frank Robinson (SJ)	DH42	R	39	49	118	19	28	5	0	9	24	29	15	0	.237	.508
Ken Berry	OF18,DH5	R	34	55	40	6	8	1	0	0	1	1	7	0	.200	.225
Tommy McCraw	1B16,OF3	L	34	23	51	7	14	1	1	2	5	7	7	4	.275	.451
2 Bill Sudakis	1B12,C6	R	29	40	46	4	9	0	0	1	3	4	7	0	.196	.261

1 Leron Lee 27 L 3-23, Joe Lis 28 R 4-13, Rick Cerone 21 R 3-12, Tommy Smith 26 L 1-8, Angel Hermoso (KJ) 28

NAME	T	AGE	W	L	PCT	SV	G	GS	CG	IP	H	BB	SO	SHO	ERA
TOTALS		28	79	80	.497	33	159	159	37	1435	1395	599	800	6	3.84
Fritz Peterson (HJ)	L	33	14	8	.636	0	25	25	6	146	154	40	47	2	3.95
Dennis Eckersley	R	20	13	7	.650	2	34	24	6	187	147	90	152	2	2.60
2 Roric Harrison	R	28	7	7	.500	0	19	19	4	126	137	46	52	0	4.79
Eric Raich	R	23	7	8	.467	0	18	17	2	93	118	31	34	0	5.52
Rick Waits	L	23	6	2	.750	1	16	7	3	70	57	25	34	0	2.96
1 Gaylord Perry	R	36	6	9	.400	0	15	15	5	122	120	34	85	1	3.54
Don Hood	L	25	6	10	.375	0	29	19	2	135	136	57	51	0	4.40
Dave LaRoche	L	27	5	3	.625	17	61	0	0	82	61	57	94	0	2.20
Tom Buskey (XJ)	R	28	5	3	.625	7	50	0	0	77	69	29	29	0	2.57
2 Jim Bibby	R	30	5	9	.357	1	24	12	2	113	99	50	62	0	3.20
Fred Beene (SJ)	R	32	1	1	1.000	1	19	1	0	47	53	25	20	0	6.89
2 Blue Moon Odom	R	30	1	1	1.000	0	3	1	0	10	4	8	0	1	2.70
2 Jackie Brown	R	32	1	2	.333	1	25	3	1	69	72	29	41	0	4.28
Jim Kern	R	26	1	2	.333	0	13	7	0	72	60	45	55	0	3.75
1 Jim Perry	R	39	1	6	.143	0	8	6	0	38	48	18	11	0	6.63
Jim Strickland	L	29	0	0	—	1	4	0	0	5	4	2	3	0	1.80
Larry Andersen	R	22	0	0	.000	0	3	0	0	6	4	2	4	0	4.50
1 Dick Bosman	R	31	0	2	.000	0	6	2	0	29	33	8	11	0	4.03
2 Bob Reynolds	R	28	0	0	.000	0	2	0	0	10	11	5	5	0	4.50
Steve Kline (EJ) 27															

MILWAUKEE 5th 68-94 .420 28 DEL CRANDALL 67-94 .416 HARVEY KUENN 1-0 1.000

NAME	G by Pos	B	AGE	G	AB	R	H	2B	3B	HR	RBI	BB	SO	SB	BA	SA
TOTALS			27	162	5378	675	1343	242	34	146	632	553	922	65	.250	.389
George Scott	1B144,DH12,3B5	R	31	158	617	86	176	26	4	36	109	51	97	6	.285	.515
Pete Garcia (XJ)	2B94,DH1	R	25	98	302	40	68	15	2	6	38	18	59	12	.225	.348
Robin Yount	SS145	R	19	147	558	67	149	28	2	8	52	33	69	12	.267	.367
Don Money (GJ)	3B99,SS7	R	28	109	405	58	112	16	1	15	43	31	51	7	.277	.432
Sixto Lezcano	OF129,DH2	R	21	134	429	55	106	19	3	11	43	46	93	5	.247	.382
1 Bill Sharp	OF124	L	25	125	373	37	95	27	3	1	34	19	26	0	.255	.351
Gorman Thomas	OF113,DH6	R	24	121	240	34	43	12	2	10	28	31	84	4	.179	.371
Darrell Porter	C124,DH2	L	23	130	409	66	95	12	5	18	60	89	77	2	.232	.418
Hank Aaron	DH128,OF3	R	41	137	465	45	109	16	2	12	60	70	51	0	.234	.355
Kurt Bevacqua	3B60,2B32,SS5,1B3,DH1	R	28	104	258	30	59	14	0	2	24	26	45	3	.229	.306
Bobby Mitchell	OF72,DH11	R	31	93	229	39	57	14	3	9	41	25	69	3	.249	.454
Mike Hegan	1B42,1B7,DH5	L	32	93	203	19	51	11	0	5	22	31	42	1	.251	.379
Charlie Moore	C47,OF22,DH1	R	22	73	241	26	70	20	1	1	29	17	31	1	.290	.394
2 Bobby Darwin (BH)	OF43,DH9	R	32	55	186	19	46	6	2	8	23	11	54	4	.247	.430
Bobby Sheldon	2B44,DH6	L	24	53	181	17	52	3	0	0	14	13	14	0	.287	.337
T. Johnson (EJ)	2B11,3B11,SS10,DH3,1B2	R	22	35	85	6	12	1	0	0	2	6	17	3	.141	.153
1 Johnny Briggs (NJ)	OF21,DH1	L	31	28	74	12	22	1	0	3	5	20	13	0	.297	.432
1 Bob Coluccio	OF22	R	23	22	62	8	12	0	1	1	5	11	15	1	.194	.274
Tommy Bianco	3B7,1B5,DH2	R	22	17	34	6	6	1	0	0	3	1	6	0	.176	.206

Jack Lind 29 B 1-20, Rob Ellis 24 R 2-7

NAME	T	AGE	W	L	PCT	SV	G	GS	CG	IP	H	BB	SO	SHO	ERA
TOTALS		25	68	94	.420	34	162	162	36	1432	1496	624	643	10	4.34
Pete Broberg	R	25	14	16	.467	0	38	32	7	220	219	106	100	2	4.13
Jim Colborn	R	29	11	13	.458	2	36	29	8	206	215	65	79	1	4.28
Jim Slaton	R	25	11	18	.379	0	37	33	10	217	238	90	119	3	4.52
Eduardo Rodriguez (SJ)	R	23	7	0	1.000	3	43	1	0	88	77	44	65	0	3.48
Billy Champion (AJ)	R	27	6	6	.500	0	27	13	3	110	125	55	40	1	5.89
Bill Travers	L	22	6	11	.353	1	28	25	5	136	130	60	57	0	4.30
Bill Castro (EJ)	R	21	3	2	.600	1	18	5	0	75	78	17	25	0	2.52
Tom Hausman (XJ)	R	22	3	6	.333	0	29	9	1	112	110	47	46	0	4.10
Jerry Augustine	L	22	2	0	1.000	0	5	3	1	27	26	12	8	0	3.00
Rick Austin	L	28	2	3	.400	1	32	0	0	40	32	32	30	0	4.05
Larry Anderson	R	22	1	0	1.000	0	8	1	1	30	36	6	13	1	5.10
Ed Sprague (KJ)	R	29	1	1	.125	1	18	11	0	67	81	40	21	0	4.70
Tom Murphy (SJ)	R	29	1	9	.100	20	52	0	0	72	85	27	32	0	4.63
Pat Osburn	L	26	0	1	.000	0	6	1	0	12	19	9	1	0	5.25
Lafayette Currence	L	23	0	2	.000	0	8	1	0	19	25	14	7	0	7.58

DETROIT 6th 57-102 .358 37.5 RALPH HOUK

NAME	G by Pos	B	AGE	G	AB	R	H	2B	3B	HR	RBI	BB	SO	SB	BA	SA
TOTALS			27	162	5366	570	1338	171	39	125	546	383	872	63	.249	.366
Jack Pierce	1B49	L	26	53	170	19	40	6	1	8	22	20	40	0	.235	.424
Gary Sutherland	2B160	R	30	129	503	51	130	12	3	6	39	45	41	0	.258	.330
Tom Veryzer	SS128	R	22	128	404	37	102	13	1	5	48	23	76	2	.252	.327
Aurelio Rodriguez	3B151	R	27	151	507	47	124	20	6	13	60	30	63	1	.245	.385
Leon Roberts	OF127,DH1	R	24	129	447	51	115	17	5	10	38	36	94	3	.257	.385
Ron LeFlore	OF134	R	26	136	550	66	142	13	6	8	37	33	139	28	.258	.347
Ben Oglivie	OF86,1B5	L	26	100	332	45	95	14	1	9	36	16	62	11	.286	.416
Bill Freehan	C113,1B5	R	33	120	427	42	105	17	3	14	47	32	56	2	.246	.398
Willie Horton	DH159	R	32	159	615	62	169	13	1	25	92	44	109	1	.275	.421
Dan Meyer	OF74,1B46	L	22	122	470	56	111	17	3	8	47	26	25	8	.236	.336
Gene Michael	SS44,2B7,3B4	B	37	56	145	15	31	2	0	1	13	18	28	0	.214	.290
Mickey Stanley (RJ)	OF28,1B14,3B7,DH1	R	32	52	164	26	42	7	3	3	19	15	27	1	.256	.390
Gates Brown	DH...	L	36	47	35	1	6	2	0	1	3	9	6	0	.171	.314
1 Nate Colbert	1B44,DH1	R	29	45	156	16	23	4	2	4	18	17	52	0	.147	.276
John Knox	2B23,3B3,DH3	L	26	43	86	8	23	1	0	0	2	10	9	1	.267	.279
John Wockenfuss	C34	R	26	35	118	15	27	6	3	4	13	10	15	0	.229	.432
Billy Baldwin	OF25,DH1	L	24	30	95	8	21	3	0	4	8	5	14	2	.221	.379
Terry Humphrey (SJ)	C18	R	25	18	41	0	10	0	0	0	0	1	2	0	.244	.244
Art James	OF11	L	22	11	40	2	9	2	0	0	1	1	3	1	.225	.275

Bob Molinaro 25 L 5-19, Jerry Manuel 21 B 1-18, Chuck Scrivener 27 R 4-16, Gene Lamont 28 L 3-8

NAME	T	AGE	W	L	PCT	SV	G	GS	CG	IP	H	BB	SO	SHO	ERA
TOTALS		28	57	102	.358	17	159	159	52	1396	1496	533	787	10	4.27
Mickey Lolich	L	34	12	18	.400	0	32	32	19	241	260	64	139	1	3.77
Vern Ruhle	R	24	11	12	.478	0	32	31	8	190	199	65	67	3	4.03
Joe Coleman	R	28	10	18	.357	0	31	31	6	201	234	85	125	1	5.55
Ray Bare	R	26	8	13	.381	0	29	21	6	151	174	47	71	1	4.47
Lerrin LaGrow	R	26	7	14	.333	0	32	26	7	164	183	66	75	2	4.39
Tom Walker	R	26	3	4	.273	0	36	9	1	115	116	40	60	0	4.46
Fernando Arroyo	R	23	2	1	.667	0	14	2	1	53	56	22	25	0	4.58
John Hiller (AJ)	L	32	2	3	.400	14	36	0	0	71	52	36	87	0	2.15
Dave Lemanczyk (SJ)	R	24	2	7	.222	0	26	4	1	109	120	46	67	0	4.46
Ike Brookens	R	25	0	0	—	0	10	0	0	11	5	8	9	0	5.40
Tom Makowski	L	24	0	0	—	0	9	0	0	10	9	3	6	0	5.00
Steve Grilli	R	26	0	0	—	0	7	0	0	7	3	6	1	0	1.29
2 Bob Reynolds	R	28	0	2	.000	3	21	0	0	35	40	14	26	0	4.63
Ed Glynn	L	22	0	0	.000	0	3	0	0	15	11	8	4	0	4.20
Gene Pentz	R	22	0	4	.000	0	13	0	0	27	20	21			3.24

WEST DIVISION

OAKLAND 1st 98-64 .605 AL DARK

NAME	G by Pos	B	AGE	G	AB	R	H	2B	3B	HR	RBI	BB	SO	SB	BA	SA
TOTALS			29	162	5415	758	1376	220	33	151	703	609	846	183	.254	.391
Joe Rudi (RJ)	1B91,OF44,DH2	R	28	126	468	66	130	26	6	21	75	40	56	2	.278	.494
Phil Garner	2B160,SS1	R	26	160	488	46	120	21	5	6	54	30	65	4	.246	.346
Bert Campaneris	SS137	R	33	137	509	69	135	15	3	4	46	50	71	24	.265	.330
Sal Bando	3B160	R	31	160	562	64	129	24	1	15	78	87	80	7	.230	.356
Reggie Jackson	OF147,DH9	R	29	157	593	91	150	39	3	36	104	67	133	17	.253	.511
Billy North	OF138,DH1	B	27	140	524	74	143	17	5	1	43	81	80	30	.273	.330
Claudell Washington	OF148	L	20	148	590	86	182	24	7	10	77	32	80	40	.308	.424
Gene Tenace	C125,1B68,DH1	R	28	158	498	83	127	17	0	29	87	106	127	7	.255	.464
Billy Williams	DH145,1B7	L	37	155	520	68	127	20	1	23	81	76	68	0	.244	.419
Jim Holt	1B52,DH4,OF2,C1	L	31	102	123	7	27	3	0	2	16	11	11	0	.220	.293
2 Ted Martinez	SS45,2B31,3B14	R	27	86	87	7	15	0	0	0	3	2	9	1	.172	.172
Ray Fosse	C82,1B1,2B1	R	28	82	136	14	19	3	2	0	12	8	19	0	.140	.191
Don Hopkins	OF5	S	25	82	6	25	1	0	0	0	0	0	0	21	.167	.167
Matt Alexander (IJ)	DH17,OF11,2B3,3B2	B	28	63	10	16	1	0	0	0	0	1	1	17	.100	.100
Angel Mangual	OF39,DH15	R	28	62	109	13	24	3	0	3	6	3	18	0	.220	.275
Larry Haney	C43,3B4	R	32	42	26	3	5	0	0	0	2	1	4	0	.192	.308
2 Tommy Harper	1B16,OF9,DH3,3B2	R	34	34	69	11	22	4	0	3	7	5	9	4	.319	.464
1 Ted Kubiak	3B7,SS7,2B6	B	33	30	28	2	7	1	0	0	3	2	5	0	.250	.286
2 Cesar Tovar	DH7,2B4,DH4,3B3,SS1	R	34	19	26	5	6	1	0	0	3	3	3	4	.231	.269

Dal Maxvill 36 R 2-10, Denny Walling 21 L 1-8, Rich McKinney 28 L 1-7, Charlie Chant 20 L 0-5, Gaylen Pitts 29 R 1-3, Charlie Sands 27 L 1-2, Billy Grabarkewitz 29 R 0-2, Herb Washington 23 R 0-0, Tommy Sandt 24 R 0-0

NAME	T	AGE	W	L	PCT	SV	G	GS	CG	IP	H	BB	SO	SHO	ERA
TOTALS		30	98	64	.605	44	162	162	36	1448	1267	523	784	10	3.27
Vida Blue	L	25	22	11	.667	1	39	38	13	278	243	99	189	2	3.01
Ken Holtzman	L	29	18	14	.563	0	39	38	13	266	217	108	122	2	3.15
2 Dick Bosman	R	31	11	4	.733	0	22	21	2	123	112	24	42	0	3.51
Rollie Fingers	R	28	10	6	.625	24	75	0	0	127	95	33	115	0	2.98
Paul Lindblad	L	33	9	1	.900	7	68	0	0	122	105	43	58	0	2.73
Jim Todd	R	28	8	3	.727	12	58	0	0	122	104	33	50	0	2.29
2 Stan Bahnsen	R	30	6	7	.462	0	21	16	2	100	88	37	49	0	3.24
Glenn Abbott	R	24	5	5	.500	0	30	15	3	114	109	50	51	1	4.26
2 Sonny Siebert (GJ)	R	38	4	4	.500	0	17	13	0	61	60	31	44	0	3.69
2 Jim Perry	R	39	3	4	.429	0	15	11	2	68	61	26	33	1	4.63
Mike Norris (EJ)	R	20	1	1	.500	0	11	4	0	36	42	18	20	0	4.00
1 Dave Hamilton	L	27	1	0	1.000	0	11	0	0	36	42	18	20	0	4.00
Craig Mitchell	R	21	0	1	1.000	0	1	1	0	4	1	0	0	0	11.25
1 Blue Moon Odom	R	30	0	0	.000	0	7	2	0	11	19	11	4	0	12.27

KANSAS CITY 2nd 91-71 .562 7 JACK McKEON 50-46 .521 WHITEY HERZOG 41-25 .621

NAME	G by Pos	B	AGE	G	AB	R	H	2B	3B	HR	RBI	BB	SO	SB	BA	SA
TOTALS			29	162	5491	710	1431	263	58	118	667	591	675	155	.261	.394
John Mayberry	1B131,DH27	L	26	156	554	95	161	38	1	34	106	119	73	5	.291	.547
Cookie Rojas	2B117,DH1	R	36	109	406	34	103	18	2	2	37	23	27	4	.254	.323
Freddie Patek	SS136,DH1	R	30	136	483	58	110	14	5	5	46	65	32	32	.228	.308
George Brett	3B159,SS1	L	22	159	634	84	195	35	13	11	89	46	49	13	.308	.456
Al Cowens	OF113,DH2	R	23	120	328	44	91	13	8	4	42	28	36	12	.277	.402
Amos Otis	OF130	R	28	132	470	87	116	26	4	9	46	66	48	39	.247	.385
Hal McRae	OF114,DH12,3B1	R	29	128	480	58	147	38	6	5	71	47	47	11	.306	.442
Buck Martinez	C79	R	26	80	226	15	51	9	2	3	23	21	28	1	.226	.327
Harmon Killebrew	DH92,1B5	R	39	106	312	25	62	13	0	14	44	54	70	1	.199	.375
Jim Wohlford	OF102,DH4	R	24	116	353	46	90	10	2	0	34	37	12		.255	.312
Frank White	2B67,SS42,3B4,DH2,C1	R	24	111	304	43	76	10	2	7	36	20	39	11	.250	.365
Vada Pinson	OF82,DH5,1B4	L	36	103	319	38	71	14	5	4	22	10	52	5	.223	.335
Tony Solaita	DH37,1B35	L	28	93	231	35	60	10	0	16	44	39	79	0	.260	.515
Bob Stinson	C59,OF1,1B1,2B1,DH1	B	29	63	147	18	39	9	1	5	18	14	19	1	.265	.361
Fran Healy (SJ)	C51,DH4	R	28	56	188	16	48	8	2	1	18	14	19	4	.255	.335
Rodney Scott	DH22,2B9,SS8	B	22	48	15	13	1	0	0	0	2	1	3	6	.067	.067
Jamie Quirk	OF10,3B2,DH1	L	20	14	39	2	10	1	0	0	5	2	6	0	.256	.308
Gary Martz	OF1	R	24	9	1	0	0	0	0	0	0	0	0	1	.000	.000

NAME	T	AGE	W	L	PCT	SV	G	GS	CG	IP	H	BB	SO	SHO	ERA
TOTALS		29	91	71	.562	25	162	162	52	1457	1422	498	815	11	3.47
Steve Busby	R	29	18	12	.600	0	34	34	18	260	233	81	160	3	3.08
Al Fitzmorris	R	29	16	12	.571	0	35	35	11	242	239	76	78	3	3.57
Dennis Leonard	R	24	15	7	.682	0	32	30	8	212	212	90	146	0	3.78
Marty Pattin	R	32	10	10	.500	5	44	15	5	177	173	45	69	1	3.25
Doug Bird	R	25	9	6	.600	11	54	4	0	105	100	40	81	0	3.26
Paul Splittorff	L	28	9	10	.474	1	35	23	6	159	156	56	76	3	3.17
Nelson Briles (EJ)	R	31	6	6	.500	2	24	16	3	112	127	25	73	0	4.26
Lindy McDaniel (IL)	R	39	5	1	.833	1	40	0	0	78	81	24	40	0	4.15
Bob McClure	L	23	0	0	1.000	0	4	0	0	14	14	10			3.00
3 Ray Sadecki	L	34	1	0	1.000	0	2	0	0	6	9	3	3	0	3.00
Mark Littell	R	22	1	2	.333	0	7	1	1	15	15	19			3.42
George Throop	R	24	0	0	—	0	2	0	0	7	4	4		0	4.00
1 Bruce Dal Canton	R	33	0	0	.000	0	9	0	0	23	7	5	9	0	15.00
Steve Mingori (IL)	L	31	0	3	.000	2	36	0	0	50	42	20	25	0	2.52

TEXAS — 3rd 79-83 .488 19 — BILLY MARTIN 44-51 .463 / FRANK LUCCHESI 35-32 .522

NAME	G by Pos	B	AGE	G	AB	R	H	2B	3B	HR	RBI	BB	SO	SB	BA	SA
	TOTALS		27	162	5599	714	1431	208	17	134	675	613	863	102	.256	.371
Jim Spencer	1B99,DH25	L	27	132	403	50	107	18	1	11	47	35	43	0	.266	.397
L. Randle	2B79,OF66,3B17,DH3,SS1,C1	B	26	156	601	85	166	24	7	4	57	57	80	15	.276	.359
Toby Harrah	SS118,3B28,2B1	R	26	151	522	81	153	24	1	20	93	98	71	23	.293	.458
Roy Howell	3B115,DH5	R	21	125	383	43	96	15	2	10	51	39	79	2	.251	.379
Jeff Burroughs	OF148,DH3	R	24	152	585	81	132	20	0	29	94	79	155	4	.226	.409
Dave Moates	OF51,DH1	L	27	54	175	21	48	9	3	1	14	13	15	9	.274	.377
Mike Hargrove	OF96,1B48,DH12	L	25	145	519	82	157	22	2	11	62	79	66	4	.303	.416
Jim Sundberg	C155	R	24	155	472	45	94	9	0	6	36	51	77	3	.199	.258
1 Cesar Tovar	DH66,OF31,2B1	R	34	102	427	53	110	16	0	3	28	27	25	16	.258	.316
Tommy Grieve	OF63,DH45	R	27	118	369	46	102	17	1	14	61	22	74	0	.276	.442
Roy Smalley	SS59,2B19,C1	B	22	78	250	27	57	8	0	3	33	30	42	4	.228	.296
Jim Fregosi	1B54,DH13,3B4	R	33	77	191	25	50	5	0	7	33	20	39	0	.262	.398
Mike Cubbage	2B37,3B3,DH2	L	24	58	143	12	32	6	0	4	21	18	14	0	.224	.350
Leo Cardenas	3B43,SS5,2B3	R	36	55	102	15	24	2	0	1	5	14	12	0	.235	.284
Joe Lovitto (VJ)	OF38,1B2,DH2,C1	B	24	50	106	17	22	3	0	1	8	13	16	2	.208	.264
1 Willie Davis	OF42	L	35	42	169	16	42	8	2	5	17	4	25	13	.249	.408
Dave Nelson (NJ)	2B23,DH1	R	31	28	80	9	17	1	0	0	5	8	12	4	.213	.300

Bill Fahey (BH) 25 L 11-37, Tom Robson 29 R 7-35, Ron Pruitt 23 R 3-17, Bobby Jones 25 L 1-11, 2 Eddie Brinkman 33 R 0-2

NAME	T	AGE	W	L	PCT	SV	G	GS	CG	IP	H	BB	SO	SHO	ERA
		30	79	83	.488	17	162	162	60	1466	1456	518	792	16	3.86
Ferguson Jenkins	R	31	17	18	.486	0	37	37	22	270	261	56	157	4	3.93
2 Gaylord Perry	R	36	12	8	.600	0	22	22	15	184	157	36	148	4	3.03
Steve Hargan	R	32	9	10	.474	0	33	26	8	189	203	62	93	1	3.81
Steve Foucault	R	25	8	7	.533	16	59	0	0	107	96	55	56	0	4.12
Jim Umbarger	L	22	8	7	.533	2	56	12	3	131	134	59	50	2	4.12
Bill Hands (XJ)	R	35	6	7	.462	0	18	18	4	110	118	28	67	1	4.01
1 Jackie Brown	R	32	5	5	.500	1	17	7	2	70	70	35	35	1	4.09
Stan Thomas	R	25	4	4	.500	3	46	1	0	81	72	34	46	0	3.11
Clyde Wright	L	34	4	6	.400	0	25	14	1	93	105	47	32	0	4.45
Stan Perzanowski	R	24	3	3	.500	0	12	8	1	66	59	25	26	0	3.00
1 Jim Bibby	R	30	2	6	.250	0	12	12	4	68	73	28	31	1	5.03
Mike Bacsik	R	23	1	2	.333	0	7	3	0	27	28	9	13	0	3.67
Mike Kekich	L	30	1	1	.500	2	23	0	0	31	33	21	19	0	3.77
Jim Merritt (LJ)	L	31	0	0	—	0	5	0	0	4	3	2	1	0	2.25
Jim Gideon	R	21	0	0	—	0	1	1	0	6	7	5	2	0	7.50
David Clyde	L	20	0	0	.000	1	1	0	0	7	6	6	2	0	2.57
2 Tommy Moore	R	26	0	2	.000	0	12	0	0	21	31	12	15	0	8.14

MINNESOTA — 4th 76-83 .478 20.5 — FRANK QUILICI

NAME	G by Pos	B	AGE	G	AB	R	H	2B	3B	HR	RBI	BB	SO	SB	BA	SA
	TOTALS		28	159	5514	724	1497	215	28	121	669	563	746	81	.271	.386
2 Johnny Briggs	1B49,OF35,DH2	L	31	87	264	44	61	9	2	9	39	60	41	6	.231	.360
Rod Carew	2B123,1B14,DH2	L	29	143	535	89	192	24	4	14	80	64	40	35	.359	.497
Danny Thompson	SS100,3B2,3B7,2B1	R	28	112	355	25	96	11	2	5	37	18	30	0	.270	.355
Eric Soderholm (KJ)	3B113,DH3	R	26	117	419	62	120	17	2	11	58	53	66	1	.286	.415
Larry Hisle (EJ)	OF58,DH14	R	28	80	255	37	80	9	2	11	51	27	39	17	.314	.494
Dan Ford	OF120,DH3	R	23	130	440	72	123	21	1	15	59	30	79	6	.280	.434
Lyman Bostock (BN)	OF92,DH1	L	24	98	369	52	104	21	5	0	29	28	42	2	.282	.366
Glenn Borgmann	C125	R	25	125	352	34	73	15	2	2	33	47	59	0	.207	.278
Tony Oliva	DH120	L	34	131	455	46	123	10	0	13	58	41	45	0	.270	.378
Steve Braun	OF106,1B9,DH9,3B2,2B1	L	27	136	453	70	137	18	3	11	45	66	55	0	.302	.428
J. Terrell	SS41,2B39,1B15,3B12,OF6,DH2	R	28	108	385	48	110	16	2	1	36	19	27	4	.286	.345
Luis Gomez	SS70,DH7,2B6,DH1	R	23	89	72	7	10	0	0	0	5	4	12	0	.139	.139
Steve Brye (BH)	OF72,DH6	R	26	86	246	41	62	13	1	9	34	21	37	2	.252	.423
Phil Roof (LJ)	C63	R	34	63	126	18	38	2	0	7	21	9	28	0	.302	.484
Craig Kusick	1B51	R	26	57	156	14	37	8	0	6	27	21	23	0	.237	.404
Tom Kelly	1B43,OF2	L	24	49	127	11	23	5	0	1	11	15	22	0	.181	.244
1 Bobby Darwin	OF27,DH19	R	32	48	169	26	37	6	0	5	18	18	44	2	.219	.343
Danny Walton	1B7,DH6,C2	R	27	42	63	4	11	2	0	1	6	4	18	0	.175	.254
Dave McKay	3B33	R	25	33	125	8	32	2	1	2	16	6	14	1	.256	.352

Sergio Ferrer 24 B 20-81, Mike Poepping 24 R 5-37, Tom Lundstedt 26 B 3-28

NAME	T	AGE	W	L	PCT	SV	G	GS	CG	IP	H	BB	SO	SHO	ERA
		26	76	83	.478	22	159	159	57	1423	1381	617	846	7	4.05
Jim Hughes	R	23	16	14	.533	0	37	34	12	250	241	127	130	2	3.82
Bert Blyleven	R	24	15	10	.600	0	35	35	20	276	219	84	233	3	3.00
Dave Goltz	R	26	14	14	.500	0	32	32	15	243	235	72	128	1	3.67
Vic Albury	L	28	6	7	.462	1	32	15	2	135	115	97	72	0	4.53
Bill Butler	L	28	5	4	.556	0	23	8	1	82	100	35	55	0	5.93
Ray Corbin (EJ)	R	26	5	7	.417	0	18	11	3	90	105	38	49	0	5.10
Tom Burgmeier	L	31	5	8	.385	11	46	0	0	76	76	23	41	0	3.08
Bill Campbell	R	26	4	6	.400	5	47	7	2	121	119	46	76	1	3.79
Eddie Bane	L	23	3	1	.750	0	4	4	0	28	28	15	14	0	2.89
Tom Johnson	R	24	3	1	.750	0	18	0	0	39	40	21	17	0	4.15
Mark Wiley	R	27	1	3	.250	2	15	3	1	39	50	13	15	0	6.00
Joe Decker (IL)	R	28	1	3	.250	0	10	7	1	26	25	36	8	0	8.65
Mike Pazik	L	25	0	4	.000	0	5	3	0	20	28	10	8	0	8.10

CHICAGO — 5th 75-86 .466 22.5 — CHUCK TANNER

NAME	G by Pos	B	AGE	G	AB	R	H	2B	3B	HR	RBI	BB	SO	SB	BA	SA
	TOTALS		26	161	5490	655	1400	209	38	94	604	611	800	101	.255	.358
Carlos May	1B63,OF46,DH19	L	26	128	454	55	123	19	2	8	53	67	46	12	.271	.374
Jorge Orta	2B135,DH2	L	24	140	542	64	165	26	10	11	83	48	67	16	.304	.450
Bucky Dent	SS157	R	23	157	602	52	159	29	4	3	58	36	48	2	.264	.341
Bill Melton	3B138,DH11	R	29	149	512	62	123	16	0	15	70	78	106	5	.240	.338
Pat Kelly	OF115,DH14	L	30	133	471	73	129	21	7	9	45	58	69	18	.274	.406
Ken Henderson	OF137,DH1	B	29	140	513	65	129	20	3	9	53	74	65	5	.251	.355
Nyls Nyman	OF94,DH4	L	21	106	327	36	74	6	3	2	28	11	34	10	.226	.281
Brian Downing	C137,DH1	R	24	138	420	58	101	12	1	7	41	76	75	3	.240	.324
1 Deron Johnson	DH93,1B55	R	36	148	555	66	129	25	1	18	72	48	117	0	.232	.378
Bill Stein	2B28,3B24,DH18,OF1	R	28	76	226	23	61	7	1	3	21	18	32	2	.270	.350
Jerry Hairston	OF59,DH8	B	23	69	219	26	62	8	0	5	23	46	23	1	.283	.320
2 Bob Coluccio (NJ)	OF59,DH1	R	23	61	161	22	33	4	2	4	13	13	34	4	.205	.329
1 Tony Muser	1B41	L	27	43	111	11	27	3	0	0	6	7	8	2	.243	.270
Lee Richard	3B12,SS9,2B5,DH5	R	26	43	45	11	9	0	1	0	5	4	7	2	.200	.244
Pete Varney	C34,DH2	R	26	36	107	12	29	5	1	2	16	14	17	0	.271	.393
1 Buddy Bradford	OF18,DH4	R	30	25	58	8	9	3	1	2	5	3	8	22	.155	.345
Mike Squires	1B20	L	23	20	65	5	15	0	0	0	4	8	5	2	.231	.231
1 Bill Sharp	OF14	L	25	18	35	1	7	0	0	0	0	2	1	0	.200	.200

Chet Lemon 20 R 9-35, Lamar Johnson 24 R 6-30, 2 Jerry Moses 28 R 1-2

NAME	T	AGE	W	L	PCT	SV	G	GS	CG	IP	H	BB	SO	SHO	ERA
		29	75	86	.466	39	161	161	34	1452	1489	655	799	7	3.93
Jim Kaat	L	36	20	14	.588	0	43	41	32	321	71	142	1	3.11	
Wilbur Wood	L	33	16	20	.444	0	43	43	14	291	309	92	140	2	4.11
Goose Gossage	R	23	9	8	.529	26	62	0	0	142	99	70	130	0	1.84
Claude Osteen	L	35	7	16	.304	0	37	37	5	204	237	92	63	0	4.37
2 Dave Hamilton	L	27	6	5	.545	6	30	1	0	70	63	29	51	0	2.83
2 Jesse Jefferson	R	26	5	9	.357	0	22	21	1	108	100	94	67	0	5.08
1 Stan Bahnsen	R	30	4	6	.400	0	12	12	2	67	78	40	31	0	6.04
Danny Osborn	R	29	3	0	1.000	0	24	0	0	58	57	37	38	0	4.50
Terry Forster (EJ)	L	23	3	3	.500	4	17	1	0	37	30	24	32	0	2.19
Rich Hinton	L	28	1	1	.500	0	15	0	0	37	41	15	30	0	4.86
Cecil Upshaw	R	32	1	1	.500	1	29	0	0	47	49	21	22	0	3.26
Bill Gogolewski (XJ)	R	27	0	1	.000	2	19	0	0	55	61	28	37	0	5.24
Jim Otten	R	24	0	1	.000	0	2	2	0	4	7	3	0	0	7.20
Jack Kucek	R	22	0	0	—	0	2	2	0	12	14	7	6	0	4.50
Chris Knapp	R	21	0	0	—	0	1	1	0	2	2	0	1	0	4.50
Tim Stoddard	R	22	0	0	—	0	1	1	0	1	2	0	0	0	9.00
Skip Pitlock	L	27	0	0	—	0	2	0	0	4	7	3	4	0	4.50
Pete Vuckovich	R	22	0	1	.000	0	4	0	0	10	17	7	5	0	13.50
Ken Kravec	L	23	0	1	.000	0	2	1	0	4	1	6	1	0	6.75
Lloyd Allen	R	25	0	2	.000	0	3	0	0	5	8	8	5	0	12.60

Bart Johnson (XJ) 25

CALIFORNIA — 6th 72-89 .447 25.5 — DICK WILLIAMS

NAME	G by Pos	B	AGE	G	AB	R	H	2B	3B	HR	RBI	BB	SO	SB	BA	SA
	TOTALS		26	161	5377	628	1324	195	41	55	572	593	811	220	.246	.328
Bruce Bochte (BG)	1B105,DH1	L	24	107	375	41	107	19	3	3	46	45	43	3	.285	.373
Jerry Remy	2B147	L	22	147	569	82	147	17	5	1	46	45	55	34	.258	.311
Mike Miley	SS70	B	22	70	224	17	39	3	2	4	26	16	54	0	.174	.259
Dave Chalk	3B149	R	24	149	513	59	140	24	2	3	56	66	49	6	.273	.345
Lee Stanton	OF131,DH1	R	29	137	440	67	115	20	3	14	82	52	85	18	.261	.436
Mickey Rivers	OF152,DH1	L	26	155	616	70	175	17	13	1	53	43	42	70	.284	.359
Dave Collins	OF75,DH12	B	22	93	319	41	85	13	4	3	29	36	55	24	.266	.361
Ellie Rodriguez (NJ)	C90	R	29	90	226	20	53	6	0	3	27	49	37	2	.235	.301
1 Tommy Harper	DH57,1B19,OF9	R	34	89	285	40	68	10	1	3	31	38	51	19	.239	.312
Morris Nettles	OF90,DH6	L	23	112	294	50	68	11	0	3	26	57	22	31	.231	.269
Joe Lahoud (XJ)	DH35,OF29	L	28	76	192	21	41	6	2	6	33	48	33	2	.214	.359
Rudy Meoli	SS28,3B15,2B11,DH3	L	24	70	126	12	27	4	1	0	6	15	20	3	.214	.262
Billy Smith	SS50,1B6,DH4,3B2	B	21	59	143	10	29	5	1	0	14	11	30	1	.203	.252
Winston Llenas	2B12,OF10,1B6,DH6,3B3	R	31	56	113	6	21	4	0	0	11	10	11	1	.186	.221
John Balaz	OF27,DH11	L	24	45	120	10	29	8	1	1	10	5	25	0	.242	.350
Orlando Ramirez	SS40	R	23	44	100	10	24	4	0	0	4	11	22	9	.240	.300
2 Adrian Garrett	DH23,1B10,OF2,C1	L	32	37	107	17	28	5	0	8	18	14	28	1	.262	.477
2 Andy Etchebarren (BG)	C31	R	32	31	100	10	28	4	1	3	17	14	19	1	.280	.390
Ike Hampton	C28,SS2,3B1	R	23	31	66	8	10	3	0	4	7	19	0	.152	.197	
John Doherty	1B26,DH1	R	23	30	94	7	19	4	0	1	11	2	11	1	.202	.266

Tom Egan 29 B 16-70, 1 Bill Sudakis 29 B 7-58, 1Bobby Valentine 25 R 16-57, Bob Allietta (BG) 23 R 8-45, Ron Jackson 22 R 9-39, Dan Briggs 22 L 7-31, Paul Dade 23 R 6-30, 1 Denny Doyle 31 L 1-15, Danny Goodwin 21 L 1-10

NAME	T	AGE	W	L	PCT	SV	G	GS	CG	IP	H	BB	SO	SHO	ERA
		27	72	89	.447	16	161	161	59	1453	1386	613	975	19	3.89
Frank Tanana	L	21	16	9	.640	0	34	33	16	257	211	73	269	5	2.63
Ed Figueroa	R	26	16	13	.552	0	33	32	16	245	213	84	139	2	2.90
Nolan Ryan (EJ)	R	28	14	12	.538	0	28	28	10	198	152	132	186	5	3.45
Bill Singer	R	31	7	15	.318	1	29	27	8	179	171	81	78	0	4.98
Don Kirkwood	R	25	6	5	.545	7	44	2	0	84	85	28	49	0	3.31
Mickey Scott	L	27	4	2	.667	1	50	0	0	68	59	18	31	0	3.31
Dick Lange	R	26	4	6	.400	1	30	8	1	102	119	53	45	0	5.21
Andy Hassler	L	23	3	12	.200	0	30	18	6	133	158	53	82	1	5.95
2 Jim Brewer	L	37	1	0	1.000	5	33	0	0	38	11	22	0	1.80	
Joe Pactwa	L	27	1	0	1.000	0	3	16	23	11	10	2	0	3.94	
1 Dave Sells	R	28	0	0	—	0	9	0	0	14	9	4	5	0	6.75
Steve Blateric	R	31	0	1	.000	0	9	1	0	9	4	1	6	0	4.00
Charlie Hudson	R	27	0	1	.000	3	15	0	0	35	37	14	16	0	5.40
Gary Ross	R	27	0	1	.000	0	5	0	0	5	5	1	4	0	5.40
Chuck Dobson	R	31	0	2	.000	0	7	2	0	28	30	13	14	0	6.75
Sid Monge	L	24	0	2	.000	0	7	4	0	24	22	12	13	0	4.13
Orlando Pena	R	41	0	0	—	0	7	0	0	13	13	4	8	0	2.08
Luis Quintana	L	24	0	2	.000	0	10	0	0	18	13	14	9	0	6.43
Chuck Hockenbery	R	24	0	5	.000	1	16	4	0	41	48	19	15	0	5.27

AMERICAN LEAGUE CHAMPIONSHIP — BOSTON (EAST) 3   OAKLAND (WEST) 0

LINE SCORES

TEAM	1	2	3		4	5	6		7	8	9		10	11	12		R	H	E
Game 1 October 4 at Boston																			
OAK	0	0	0		0	0	0		0	1	0						1	3	4
BOS	2	0	0		0	5	0		X								7	8	3

Holtzman, Todd (7), Lindblad (7),   **Tiant**
Bosman (7), Abbott (8)

Game 2 October 5 at Boston																			
OAK	2	0	0		1	0	0		0	0	0						2	10	0
BOS	0	0	0		3	0	1		1	1	x						6	12	0

Blue, Todd (4),   Cleveland, **Moret** (6),
Fingers (5)   Drago (7)

Game 3 October 7 at Oakland																			
BOS	0	0	0		1	3	0		0	1	0						5	11	1
OAK	0	0	0		0	0	1		0	2	0						3	6	2

Wise, Drago (8)   Holtzman, Todd (5),
Lindblad (5)

COMPOSITE BATTING

NAME	POS	G	AB	R	H	2B	3B	HR	RBI	BA
Boston										
Totals		3	98	18	31	8	0	2	14	.316
Fisk	C	3	12	4	5	1	0	1		.417
Beniquez	DH	3	12	2	3				1	.250
Petrocelli	3B	3	12	1	2	0	0	1		.167
Yastrzemski	LF	3	11	4	5	2	0		1	.455
Lynn	CF	3	11	1	4	0	0		3	.364
Doyle	2B	3	11	3	3					.273
Cooper	1B	3	10	0	4				2	.400
Evans	RF	3	10	1	1					.100
Burleson	SS	3	9	2	4	2	0		4	.444
Oakland										
Totals		3	98	7	19	6	0	1	7	.194
Bando	3B	3	12	1	6	2	0	0	2	.500
Jackson	RF	3	12	1	5	1	0	1	2	.417
Rudi	1B-LF	3	12	1	3	2	0	0	0	.250
C. Washington	LF-DH	3	12	2	3	1	0	0	1	.250
Campaneris	SS	3	11	0	0					.000
North	CF	3	9	1	0					.000
Tenace	C-1B	3	7	0	0					.000
Williams	DH	3	5	0	0					.000
Garner	2B	3	5	0	0					.000

Holt 1B 1-3, Tovar 2B 1-2, Fosse C 0-2, Martinez 2B 0-0, Hopkins DH 0-0, Harper PH 0-0

COMPOSITE PITCHING

NAME	G	IP	H	BB	SO	W	L	SV	ERA
Boston									
Totals	3	27	19	9	14	3	0	2	1.67
Tiant	1	9	3	8	1	0	0	0	0.00
Wise	1	7.1	6	3	2	1	0	0	2.45
Cleveland	1	5	7	1	2	0	0	0	5.40
Drago	2	4.2	1	1	4	0	0	2	0.00
Moret	1	1	1	1	1	0	0	0	0.00
Oakland									
Totals	3	25	31	3	12	0	3	0	4.32
Holtzman	2	11	12	1	7	0	2	0	4.09
Lindblad	2	4.2	5	1	1	0	0	0	0.00
Fingers	1	4	5	0	1	0	0	0	6.75
Blue	1	3	5	0	2	0	1	0	9.00
Abbott	1	1	2	0	1	0	0	0	9.00
Todd	3	1	0	1	0	0	0	0	0.00
Bosman	1	0.1	0	0	0	0	0	0	0.00

NATIONAL LEAGUE CHAMPIONSHIP — CINCINNATI (WEST) 3 PITTSBURGH (EAST) 0

LINE SCORES

TEAM	1	2	3	4	5	6	7	8	9	10	11	12	R	H	E

Game 1 October 4 at Cincinnati

| PIT | 0 2 0 | 0 0 0 | 0 0 1 | | 3 8 0 |
| CIN | 0 1 3 | 0 4 0 | 0 0 x | | 8 11 0 |

Reuss, Brett (3), Demery (5), Ellis (7)   Gullett

Game 2 October 5 at Cincinnati

| PIT | 0 0 0 | 1 0 0 | 0 0 0 | | 1 5 0 |
| CIN | 2 0 0 | 1 0 x | | | 6 12 1 |

Rooker, Tekulve (5), **Norman**, Eastwick (7)
Brett (6), Kison (7)

Game 3 October 7 at Pittsburgh

| CIN | 0 1 0 | 0 0 0 | 0 2 0 | 2 | 5 6 0 |
| PIT | 0 0 0 | 0 0 1 | 0 0 0 | 0 | 3 7 2 |

Nolan, C.Carroll (7),   Candelaria, Giusti (8)
McEnaney (8), **Eastwick** (9), Hernandez (10), Tekulve (10)
Borbon (10)

COMPOSITE BATTING

NAME	POS	G	AB	R	H	2B	3B	HR	RBI	BA
Cincinnati										
Totals		3	102	19	29	4	0	4	18	.284
Rose	3B	3	14	3	5	0	0	1	2	.357
Bench	C	3	13	1	1	0	0	0	0	.077
Perez	1B	3	12	5	5	0	0	4	4	.417
Griffey	RF	3	12	3	4	1	0	0	4	.333
Concepcion	SS	3	11	2	5	0	0	0	0	.455
Foster	LF	3	11	3	4	0	0	0	0	.364
Morgan	2B	3	11	2	3	3	0	0	1	.273
Geronimo	CF	3	10	0	0	0	0	0	0	.000
Gullett	P	1	4	1	2	0	0	1	3	.500
Nolan	P	1	2	0	1	0	0	0	0	.500

Rettenmund PH 0-1, Norman P 0-1, Crowley PH 0-0, Armbrister PH 0-0

NAME	POS	G	AB	R	H	2B	3B	HR	RBI	BA
Pittsburgh										
Totals		3	101	7	20	3	0	1	7	.198
Stennett	2B-SS	3	14	0	3	0	0	0	0	.214
Hebner	3B	3	12	2	4	1	0	0	2	.333
Sanguillen	C	3	12	0	2	0	0	0	0	.167
Oliver	CF	3	11	1	2	0	0	0	2	.182
Stargell	1B	3	11	1	2	1	0	0	0	.182
Zisk	LF	3	10	0	5	1	0	0	1	.500
Parker	RF	3	10	2	0	0	0	0	0	.000
Taveras	SS	3	7	0	1	0	0	0	0	.143
Candelaria	P	1	3	0	0	0	0	0	0	.000
Robertson	1B	3	2	0	1	0	0	0	0	.500
Randolph	2B	2	1	0	0	0	0	0	0	.000

Kirkpatrick PH 0-2, Robinson PH 0-2, Reynolds SS 0-1, Rooker P 0-1, Reuss P 0-1, Dyer PH 0-0

COMPOSITE PITCHING

NAME	G	IP	H	BB	SO	W	L	SV	ERA
Cincinnati									
Totals	3	28	20	10	18	3	0	2	2.25
Gullett	1	9	8	2	5	1	0	0	3.00
Norman	1	6	4	5	4	1	0	0	1.50
Nolan	1	6	5	0	5	0	0	0	3.00
Eastwick	2	3.2	2	1	1	1	0	1	0.00
McEnaney	1	1.1	1	0	1	0	0	0	9.00
Borbon	1	1	0	1	1	0	0	1	0.00
C. Carroll	1	1	0	1	1	0	0	0	0.00

NAME	G	IP	H	BB	SO	W	L	SV	ERA
Pittsburgh									
Totals	3	26	29	9	28	0	3	0	6.58
Candelaria	1	7.2	3	2	14	0	0	0	3.38
Rooker	1	4	7	0	5	0	1	0	9.00
Reuss	1	2.2	4	4	1	0	1	0	12.00
Brett	2	2.1	1	0	1	0	0	0	0.00
Ellis	1	2	2	0	2	0	0	0	18.00
Kison	1	2	2	1	1	0	0	0	4.50
Demery	1	2	4	1	1	0	0	0	18.00
Tekulve	2	1.1	3	1	2	0	0	0	9.00
Giusti	1	1.1	0	0	1	0	0	0	0.00
Hernandez	1	0.2	3	0	0	0	0	1	18.00

EAST DIVISION

NAME	G by Pos	B	AGE	G	AB	R	H	2B	3B	HR	RBI	BB	SO	SB	BA	SA
PITTSBURGH 1st 92-69 .571			DANNY MURTAUGH													
TOTALS			28	161	5489	712	1444	255	47	138	669	468	832	49	.263	.402
Willie Stargell (BR)	1B122	L	35	124	461	71	136	32	2	22	90	58	109	0	.295	.516
Rennie Stennett	2B144	R	24	148	616	89	176	25	7	7	62	33	42	5	.286	.383
Frank Taveras	SS132	R	25	134	378	44	80	9	4	0	23	37	63	17	.212	.257
Richie Hebner	3B126	L	27	128	472	65	116	16	4	15	57	43	48	0	.246	.392
Dave Parker	OF141	L	24	148	558	75	172	35	10	25	101	38	89	8	.308	.541
Al Oliver	OF153,1B4	L	28	155	628	90	176	39	8	18	84	25	73	4	.280	.454
Richie Zisk	OF140	R	26	147	504	69	146	27	3	20	75	68	109	0	.290	.474
Manny Sanguillen	C132	R	31	133	481	60	158	24	4	9	58	48	31	5	.328	.451
Bill Robinson	OF57	R	32	92	200	26	56	12	6	6	33	11	36	3	.280	.450
Ed Kirkpatrick	1B28,OF14	L	28	89	144	15	34	5	0	5	16	18	22	1	.236	.375
Bob Robertson	1B27	R	28	75	124	17	34	4	0	6	18	23	25	0	.274	.452
Art Howe	3B42,SS3	R	28	63	146	13	25	9	0	1	10	15	15	1	.171	.253
Mario Mendoza	SS53,3B1	R	24	56	50	8	9	1	0	0	3	2	17	0	.180	.200
Duffy Dyer	C36	R	29	48	132	8	30	5	2	3	16	6	30	0	.227	.364
Craig Reynolds	SS30	L	22	31	76	8	17	3	0	0	4	6	5	0	.224	.263
Willie Randolph	2B14,3B1	R	20	30	61	9	10	1	0	0	3	7	6	1	.164	.180
Paul Popovich	2B8,SS8	B	34	25	40	5	8	1	0	0	1	3	2	0	.200	.225

Omar Moreno 22 L 1-6, Miguel Dilone 20 B 0-6, Ed Ott 23 L 1-5

NAME	T	AGE	W	L	PCT	SV	G	GS	CG	IP	H	BB	SO	SHO	ERA
		28	92	69	.571	31	161	161	43	1437	1302	551	768	14	3.01
Jerry Reuss	L	26	18	11	.621	0	32	32	15	237	224	78	131	6	2.54
Jim Rooker	L	32	13	11	.542	0	28	28	7	197	177	76	102	1	2.97
Bruce Kison	R	25	12	11	.522	0	33	29	6	192	160	92	89	0	3.23
Ken Brett (EJ)	L	26	9	5	.643	0	23	16	4	118	110	43	47	1	3.36
John Candelaria	L	21	8	6	.571	0	18	18	4	121	95	36	95	1	2.75
Dock Ellis	R	30	8	9	.471	0	27	24	5	140	163	43	69	2	3.79
Ramon Hernandez	L	34	7	2	.778	5	46	0	0	64	62	28	43	0	2.95
Larry Demery	R	22	7	5	.583	4	45	3	1	115	95	43	59	0	2.90
Dave Giusti	R	35	5	4	.556	17	61	0	0	92	79	42	38	0	2.93
Sam McDowell	L	32	2	1	.667	0	14	1	0	35	30	20	29	0	2.83
Bob Moose (RJ)	R	27	2	2	.500	0	23	5	1	68	63	25	34	0	3.71
Kent Tekulve	R	28	1	2	.333	5	34	0	0	56	43	23	28	0	2.25
Odell Jones	R	22	0	0	—	0	3	1	0	2	1	0	2	0	0.00
Jim Minshall	R	27	0	0	—	0	2	0	0	3	1	4	2	0	9.00

NAME	G by Pos	B	AGE	G	AB	R	H	2B	3B	HR	RBI	BB	SO	SB	BA	SA
PHILADELPHIA 2nd 86-76 .531 6.5			DANNY OZARK													
TOTALS			27	162	5592	735	1506	283	42	125	687	610	960	126	.269	.402
2 Dick Allen	1B113	R	33	119	416	54	97	21	3	12	62	58	109	11	.233	.385
Dave Cash	2B162	R	27	162	699	111	213	40	3	4	57	56	34	13	.305	.388
Larry Bowa (BG)	SS135	B	29	136	583	79	178	18	9	2	38	24	24	24	.305	.377
Mike Schmidt	3B151,SS10	R	25	158	562	93	140	34	3	38	95	101	180	29	.249	.523
Jay Johnstone	OF101	L	29	122	350	50	115	19	2	7	54	42	39	7	.329	.454
2 Garry Maddox (BK)	OF97	R	25	99	374	50	109	25	8	4	46	36	54	24	.291	.433
Greg Luzinski	OF159	R	24	161	596	85	179	35	3	34	120	89	151	3	.300	.540
Bob Boone	C92,3B3	R	27	97	289	28	71	14	2	2	20	32	14	1	.246	.329
Mike Anderson	OF105,1B3	R	24	115	247	24	64	10	3	4	28	17	66	1	.259	.372
Tommy Hutton	1B71,OF12	L	29	113	165	24	41	6	0	3	24	17	20	0	.248	.339
2 Johnny Oates	C82	L	29	90	269	28	77	14	0	1	25	33	29	1	.286	.349
Ollie Brown	OF63	R	31	84	145	19	44	12	0	6	26	15	29	1	.303	.510
Tony Taylor	3B16,1B4,2B3	R	39	79	103	13	35	5	1	1	17	17	18	3	.340	.437
Jerry Martin	OF49	R	26	57	113	15	24	7	1	2	11	11	16	2	.212	.345
Terry Harmon	SS25,2B7,3B1	R	31	48	72	14	13	1	2	0	5	9	13	0	.181	.250
2 Tim McCarver	C10,1B1	L	33	47	59	6	15	2	0	1	7	14	7	2	.254	.339
Alan Bannister	OF18,SS1,2B1	R	23	24	61	10	16	3	1	0	5	3	16	2	.262	.344
1 Willie Montanez	1B21	L	27	21	84	9	24	4	0	2	16	4	12	1	.286	.452

Mike Rogodzinski 27 L 5-19, Larry Cox 27 R 1-5,1 Don Hahn 26 R 0-5, Jim Essian 24 R 1-1, Larry Fritz 26 L 0-1, Ron Clark 32 R 0-1

NAME	T	AGE	W	L	PCT	SV	G	GS	CG	IP	H	BB	SO	SHO	ERA
		29	86	76	.531	30	162	162	33	1455	1353	546	897	11	3.82
Steve Carlton	L	30	15	14	.517	0	37	37	14	255	217	104	192	3	3.56
Tom Underwood	L	21	14	13	.519	0	35	35	7	219	221	84	123	2	4.15
Larry Christenson	R	21	11	6	.647	1	29	26	5	172	149	45	88	2	3.66
Gene Garber	R	27	10	12	.455	14	71	0	0	110	104	27	69	0	3.60
Tug McGraw	L	30	9	6	.600	14	56	0	0	103	84	36	55	0	2.97
Jim Lonborg (GJ)	R	33	8	6	.571	0	27	26	6	159	161	45	72	2	4.13
Tom Hilgendorf	L	33	7	3	.700	0	53	0	0	97	81	38	52	0	2.13
Wayne Twitchell	R	27	5	10	.333	0	36	20	0	134	132	78	101	0	4.43
Ron Schueler	R	27	4	4	.500	0	46	6	1	93	88	40	69	0	5.23
Dick Ruthven	R	24	2	2	.500	0	11	7	0	41	37	22	26	0	4.17
Wayne Simpson	R	26	1	0	1.000	0	7	5	0	31	31	11	19	0	3.19
Joe Hoerner (FJ)	L	38	0	0	—	0	25	0	0	21	26	8	20	0	2.57
Cy Acosta	R	28	0	0	—	0	7	0	0	8	4	4	6	0	6.00
Randy Lerch	L	20	0	1	—	0	3	0	0	7	8	4	1	0	6.43
2 John Montague	R	27	0	0	—	0	3	0	0	7	8	4	1	0	9.00

NAME	G by Pos	B	AGE	G	AB	R	H	2B	3B	HR	RBI	BB	SO	SB	BA	SA
NEW YORK 3rd(tie) 82-80 .506 10.5			YOGI BERRA 56-53 .514 ROY McMILLAN 26-27 .491													
TOTALS			28	162	5587	646	1430	217	34	101	604	501	805	32	.256	.361
Ed Kranepool	1B82,OF4	L	30	106	325	42	105	16	0	4	43	27	21	1	.323	.409
Felix Millan	2B162	R	31	162	676	81	191	37	2	1	56	36	28	1	.283	.348
2 Mike Phillips	SS115,2B1	L	24	116	383	31	98	10	7	1	28	25	47	3	.256	.320
Wayne Garrett	3B94,SS3,2B1	L	27	107	274	49	73	8	3	6	34	50	45	3	.266	.383
Rusty Staub	OF153	L	31	155	574	93	162	30	4	19	105	77	55	2	.282	.448
Del Unser	OF144	L	30	147	531	65	156	18	2	10	53	37	76	4	.294	.392
Dave Kingman	OF71,1B58,3B12	R	26	134	502	65	116	22	1	36	88	34	153	7	.231	.494
Jerry Grote	C111	R	32	119	386	28	114	14	5	2	39	38	23	0	.295	.373
Joe Torre	3B83,1B24	R	34	114	361	33	89	16	3	6	35	35	55	0	.247	.357
John Milner	OF31,1B29	L	25	91	220	24	42	11	0	7	29	33	22	1	.191	.336
Gene Clines	OF60	R	28	82	203	25	46	6	3	0	10	11	21	4	.227	.286
Jesus Alou	OF20	R	33	62	102	8	27	3	0	0	11	4	5	0	.265	.294
Jack Heidemann	SS44,3B4,2B1	R	25	61	145	12	31	4	2	1	16	17	28	1	.214	.290
John Stearns	C54	R	23	59	169	25	32	3	1	0	17	17	15	4	.189	.284
Mike Vail	OF36	R	23	38	162	17	49	8	1	0	17	8	30	4	.302	.420
Bud Harrelson (KJ)	SS34	B	31	34	73	5	16	2	0	0	3	12	13	0	.219	.247
Cleon Jones (KJ)	OF12	R	32	21	50	2	11	1	0	0	7	4	6	0	.240	.260

Ron Hodges 26 L 7-34, Roy Staiger 25 R 3-19, Bob Gallagher 26 L 2-15, Brock Pemberton 21 B 0-2

NAME	T	AGE	W	L	PCT	SV	G	GS	CG	IP	H	BB	SO	SHO	ERA
		27	82	80	.506	31	162	162	40	1466	1344	580	989	14	3.39
Tom Seaver	R	30	22	9	.710	0	36	36	15	280	217	88	243	5	2.38
Jon Matlack	L	25	16	12	.571	0	37	32	8	229	224	58	154	3	3.38
Jerry Koosman	L	32	14	13	.519	2	36	34	11	240	234	98	173	4	3.41
Hank Webb	R	25	7	6	.538	0	29	15	3	115	102	62	38	1	4.07
Randy Tate	R	22	5	13	.278	0	26	23	2	138	121	86	99	0	4.43
2 Tom Hall	R	27	4	3	.571	1	34	0	0	51	48	18	48	0	4.72
George Stone (SJ)	L	28	3	3	.500	0	13	11	1	57	75	21	21	0	5.05
Bob Apodaca (BZ)	R	25	3	4	.429	13	46	0	0	85	66	28	45	0	1.48
Rick Baldwin	R	22	3	5	.375	6	54	0	0	97	97	34	54	0	3.34
1 Harry Parker (SJ)	R	27	2	3	.400	2	18	3	0	37	19	22	0	0	4.37
Ken Sanders	R	33	1	1	.500	5	29	0	0	43	31	14	8	0	2.30
Skip Lockwood	R	28	1	3	.250	2	24	0	0	38	23	25	61	0	1.50
Craig Swan	R	24	1	3	.250	0	6	3	0	31	38	13	19	0	6.39
Jerry Cram	R	28	0	0	—	0	6	0	0	7	2	4	2	0	5.40
Mac Scarce	L	26	0	1	—	0	5	0	0	5	7	4	6	0	—
Nino Espinosa	R	21	0	1	.000	0	1	1	0	7	8	4	4	0	18.00

NAME	G by Pos	B	AGE	G	AB	R	H	2B	3B	HR	RBI	BB	SO	SB	BA	SA
ST. LOUIS 3rd(tie) 82-80 .506 10.5			RED SCHOENDIENST													
TOTALS			28	163	5597	662	1527	239	46	81	619	444	649	116	.273	.375
Reggie Smith	OF69,1B66,3B1	B	30	135	477	67	144	26	3	19	76	63	59	9	.302	.488
Ted Sizemore	2B153	R	30	153	562	56	135	23	1	0	49	45	37	1	.240	.301
Mike Tyson	SS95,2B24,3B5	R	25	122	368	45	98	16	3	2	37	24	39	5	.266	.342
Ken Reitz	3B160	R	24	161	592	43	159	25	1	5	63	22	54	1	.269	.340
2 Willie Davis	OF89	L	35	98	350	41	102	19	6	6	50	14	27	10	.291	.431
Bake McBride (SJ)	OF107	L	26	116	413	70	124	10	5	5	36	34	52	26	.300	.404
Lou Brock	OF128	L	36	136	528	78	163	27	6	3	47	38	64	56	.309	.400
Ted Simmons	C154,1B2,OF2	B	25	157	581	80	193	32	3	18	100	63	35	1	.332	.491
Luis Melendez	OF89	R	25	110	291	33	77	8	5	2	27	16	25	3	.265	.347
Ron Fairly	1B56,OF20	L	36	107	229	30	69	13	2	7	37	45	26	0	.301	.467
Keith Hernandez	1B56	L	21	64	188	20	47	11	2	3	20	17	26	0	.250	.362
Mike Guerrero	SS64	R	25	64	184	17	44	9	0	1	10	7	29	2	.239	.304
2 Buddy Bradford	OF25	R	30	50	81	12	22	5	1	4	14	9	20	3	.272	.432
Ken Rudolph	C31	R	28	44	80	5	16	2	0	0	5	3	10	0	.200	.263
1 Eddie Brinkman	SS24	R	33	28	75	6	18	4	0	1	11	10	13	0	.240	.333
Heity Cruz	3B12,OF6	R	22	28	48	4	7	2	0	0	4	6	9	0	.146	.271
Danny Cater	1B12	R	35	22	46	3	13	3	0	0	5	2	3	0	.283	.348
1 Jim Dwyer	OF9	L	25	31	31	4	6	1	0	0	1	5	6	0	.194	.226

Doug Howard 27 R 6-29, 1 Ted Martinez 27 R 4-21, 2 Larry Lintz 25 B 5-18, Jerry Mumphrey 22 B 6-16, 2 Don Hahn 26 R 1-8, Mick Kelleher 27 R 0-4, Dick Billings 32 R 0-3

NAME	T	AGE	W	L	PCT	SV	G	GS	CG	IP	H	BB	SO	SHO	ERA
		27	82	80	.506	36	163	163	33	1455	1452	571	824	13	3.57
Bob Forsch	R	25	15	10	.600	0	34	34	7	230	213	70	108	4	2.86
Lynn McGlothen	R	25	15	13	.536	0	35	34	9	239	231	97	146	2	3.92
Al Hrabosky	L	25	13	3	.813	22	65	0	0	97	72	33	82	0	1.67
John Denny	R	22	10	7	.588	0	25	24	3	136	149	51	72	2	3.97
2 Ron Reed	R	32	9	8	.529	0	24	24	7	176	181	37	99	2	3.22
John Curtis	L	27	8	9	.471	1	39	18	4	147	151	65	67	0	3.43
Eric Rasmussen	R	23	5	5	.500	0	14	13	2	81	68	20	59	1	3.78
Mike Garman	R	25	2	5	.273	10	66	0	0	79	73	48	48	0	2.39
Bob Gibson	R	39	3	10	.231	2	22	14	1	109	120	62	60	0	5.04
1 Ray Sadecki	L	34	1	0	1.000	0	10	0	0	11	13	7	8	0	3.27
1 Tommy Moore	R	27	0	0	—	0	9	0	0	19	15	12	6	0	3.79
2 Mike Wallace	L	24	0	0	—	0	7	0	0	19	15	13	4	0	2.00
Mike Barlow	R	27	0	0	—	0	4	0	0	8	7	6	5	0	4.50
Ryan Kurosaki	R	23	0	0	—	0	7	0	0	13	19	4	6	0	7.62
Greg Terlecky	R	23	0	0	—	0	20	0	0	30	38	12	13	0	4.50
2 Harry Parker	R	27	0	0	—	0	9	0	0	13	11	10	13	0	6.16
2 Ken Reynolds	L	28	0	0	—	0	11	0	0	17	12	11	7	0	1.59
Ron Bryant	L	27	0	0	—	0	14	0	0	22	28	19	7	0	16.00
1 Elias Sosa	R	25	0	0	—	0	27	0	0	22	14	15	15	0	4.00

CHICAGO 5th(tie) 75-87 .463 17.5   JIM MARSHALL

NAME	G by Pos	B	AGE	G	AB	R	H	2B	3B	HR	RBI	BB	SO	SB	BA	SA
	TOTALS		27	162	5470	712	1419	229	41	95	645	650	802	67	.259	.368
Andre Thornton (BW)	1B113,3B2	R	25	120	372	70	109	21	4	18	60	88	63	3	.293	.516
Manny Trillo	2B153,SS1	R	24	154	545	55	135	12	2	7	70	45	78	1	.248	.316
Don Kessinger	SS140,3B13	B	32	154	601	77	146	26	10	0	46	68	47	4	.243	.319
Bill Madlock	3B128	R	24	130	514	77	182	29	7	7	64	42	34	9	.354	.479
Jose Cardenal	OF151	R	31	154	574	85	182	30	2	9	68	77	50	34	.317	.423
Rick Monday	OF131	L	29	136	491	89	131	29	4	17	60	83	95	8	.267	.446
Jerry Morales	OF151	R	26	153	578	62	156	21	0	12	91	50	65	3	.270	.369
Steve Swisher	C93	R	23	93	254	20	54	16	2	1	22	30	57	1	.213	.303
Pete LaCock	1B53,OF26	L	23	106	249	30	57	8	1	6	30	37	27	0	.229	.341
George Mitterwald	C59,1B10	R	30	84	200	19	44	4	3	5	26	19	42	0	.220	.345
Champ Summers	OF18	L	29	76	91	14	21	5	1	1	16	10	13	6	.231	.341
Rob Sperring	3B22,2B17,SS16,OF8	R	25	65	144	25	30	4	1	1	9	16	31	0	.208	.271
Tim Hosley	C53	R	28	62	141	22	36	7	0	6	20	27	25	1	.255	.433
Vic Harris	OF11,3B7,2B5	B	25	51	56	6	10	0	0	0	5	6	7	0	.179	.179
Gene Hiser	OF18,1B1	L	26	45	62	11	15	3	0	0	6	11	7	0	.242	.290
Ron Dunn	3B11,OF2,2B1	R	25	32	44	2	7	3	0	1	6	6	17	0	.159	.295
Dave Rosello	SS19	R	25	19	58	7	15	2	0	1	8	9	8	0	.259	.345
Joe Wallis	OF15	B	23	16	56	9	16	2	2	1	4	5	14	2	.286	.446
1 Adrian Garrett	1B4	L	32	16	21	1	2	0	0	1	6	1	8	0	.095	.238
Jim Tyrone	OF8	R	26	11	22	0	5	0	1	0	3	1	4	1	.227	.318

NAME		T	AGE	W	L	PCT	SV	G	GS	CG	IP	H	BB	SO	SHO	ERA
			28	75	87	.463	33	162	162	27	1444	1587	551	850	8	4.49
Ray Burris		R	24	15	10	.600	0	36	35	8	238	259	73	108	2	4.12
Bill Bonham		R	26	13	15	.464	0	38	36	7	229	254	109	165	2	4.72
Steve Stone		R	27	12	8	.600	0	33	32	6	214	198	80	139	1	3.95
Rick Reuschel		R	26	11	17	.393	1	38	37	6	234	244	67	155	0	3.73
Darold Knowles		L	33	6	9	.400	15	58	0	0	88	107	36	63	0	5.83
Oscar Zamora (XJ)		R	30	5	2	.714	10	52	0	0	71	84	15	28	0	5.07
Tom Dettore		R	27	5	4	.556	0	36	5	0	85	88	31	46	0	5.40
Buddy Schultz		L	24	2	0	1.000	0	6	0	0	6	5	4	6	0	6.00
Ken Frailing		L	27	2	5	.286	1	41	0	0	53	61	26	39	0	5.43
2 Geoff Zahn (SJ)		L	29	2	7	.222	1	16	10	0	63	67	26	21	0	4.43
Ken Crosby		R	27	1	0	1.000	0	9	0	0	8	10	7	6	0	3.38
Paul Reuschel		R	28	1	3	.250	5	28	0	0	36	44	13	12	0	3.50
Donnie Moore		R	21	0	0	—	0	9	12	4	8	9	4	8	0	4.00
Eddie Solomon		R	24	0	0	—	0	6	0	0	7	6	3	1	0	1.29
Milt Wilcox		R	25	0	1	.000	0	38	50	17	21	0				5.68
Bob Locker		R	37	0	1	.000	0	22	0	0	33	38	16	14	0	4.91
Eddie Watt		R	34	0	1	.000	0	6	0	0	6	14	8	6	0	13.50
1 Burt Hooton		R	25	0	2	.000	0	3	3	0	11	8	4	5	0	8.18
Willie Prall		L	25	0	2	.000	0	3	3	0	15	21	8	7	0	8.40

MONTREAL 5th(tie) 75-87 .463 17.5   GENE MAUCH

NAME	G by Pos	B	AGE	G	AB	R	H	2B	3B	HR	RBI	BB	SO	SB	BA	SA
	TOTALS		25	162	5518	601	1346	216	31	98	542	579	954	108	.244	.348
Mike Jorgensen	1B133,OF6	L	26	144	445	58	116	18	0	18	67	79	75	3	.261	.422
Pete Mackanin	2B127,SS1,3B1	R	23	130	448	59	101	19	6	12	44	31	99	11	.225	.375
Tim Foli	SS151,2B1	R	24	152	572	64	136	25	2	1	29	36	49	13	.238	.294
Larry Parrish	3B143,2B1,SS1	R	21	145	532	50	146	32	5	10	65	28	74	4	.274	.410
Gary Carter	OF92,C66,3B1	R	21	144	503	58	136	20	1	17	68	72	83	5	.270	.416
Pepe Mangual	OF138	R	23	140	514	84	126	16	2	9	45	74	115	33	.245	.337
Larry Biittner	OF93	L	29	121	346	34	109	13	5	3	28	34	33	2	.315	.408
Barry Foote	C115	R	23	118	387	25	75	16	1	7	30	17	48	0	.194	.295
Bob Bailey (BH)	OF61,3B3	R	32	106	227	23	62	5	0	5	30	46	38	4	.273	.361
Jose Morales	1B27,OF6,C5	R	30	93	163	18	49	6	1	2	24	14	21	0	.301	.387
Tony Scott	OF71	B	23	92	143	19	26	4	2	0	11	12	38	5	.182	.238
2 Jim Dwyer	OF52	L	25	60	175	22	50	7	1	3	20	23	30	4	.286	.389
Pat Scanlon	3B28,1B1	L	22	60	109	5	20	3	1	2	15	17	25	0	.183	.284
Pepe Frias (BZ)	SS29,3B11,2B7	R	26	51	64	4	8	2	0	0	4	3	13	0	.125	.156
1 Larry Lintz	2B39,SS2	B	25	46	132	18	26	0	0	0	3	23	18	17	.197	.197
Jim Lyttle	OF16	L	29	44	55	7	15	4	0	0	6	13	6	0	.273	.345
Jerry White	OF30	B	22	39	97	14	29	7	1	2	7	10	7	5	.299	.423
2 Nate Colbert	1B22	R	29	38	81	10	14	4	1	4	11	5	31	0	.173	.395
Hal Breeden	1B12	L	31	34	37	4	5	2	0	0	1	7	5	0	.135	.189
1 Rich Coggins (IL)	OF10	L	24	13	37	1	10	3	1	0	4	1	7	0	.270	.405
Ellis Valentine	OF11	R	20	12	33	2	12	6	0	0	3	2	4	0	.364	.576
Jim Cox	2B8	R	25	11	27	1	7	1	0	1	5	1	2	1	.259	.407

Bombo Rivera 22 R 1-9, Larry Johnson 24 R 1-3, Stan Papi (IL) 24

NAME		T	AGE	W	L	PCT	SV	G	GS	CG	IP	H	BB	SO	SHO	ERA
			27	75	87	.463	25	162	162	30	1480	1448	665	831	12	3.72
Dale Murray (IL)		R	25	15	8	.652	9	63	0	0	111	134	39	43	0	3.97
Steve Rogers		R	25	11	12	.478	3	35	35	12	252	248	88	137	3	3.29
Woody Fryman		L	35	9	12	.429	3	38	20	7	157	141	68	118	3	3.32
Dan Warthen		L	22	8	6	.571	3	40	18	2	168	130	87	128	0	3.11
Dennis Blair		R	21	8	15	.348	0	30	27	1	163	150	106	82	0	3.81
Steve Renko		R	30	6	12	.333	1	31	25	3	170	175	76	99	1	4.08
Don Carrithers (SJ)		R	25	5	3	.625	0	19	14	5	101	90	38	37	2	3.30
2 Fred Scherman		L	30	4	3	.571	0	34	0	0	76	84	41	43	0	3.55
Don DeMola		R	22	4	7	.364	1	60	0	0	98	92	42	63	0	4.13
Dave McNally (VR)		L	32	3	6	.333	0	12	12	0	77	86	36	36	0	5.26
Chuck Taylor		R	33	2	2	.500	6	54	0	0	74	72	24	29	0	3.53
Don Stanhouse		R	24	0	0	—	0	4	3	0	13	19	11	5	0	8.31
Chip Lang		R	22	0	0	—	0	1	1	0	2	1	2	1	0	9.00
1 John Montague		R	27	0	1	.000	2	12	0	0	18	23	6	6	0	5.50

WEST DIVISION

CINCINNATI 1st 108-54 .667   SPARKY ANDERSON

NAME	G by Pos	B	AGE	G	AB	R	H	2B	3B	HR	RBI	BB	SO	SB	BA	SA
	TOTALS		28	162	5581	840	1515	278	37	124	779	691	916	168	.271	.401
Tony Perez	1B132	R	33	137	511	74	144	28	3	20	109	54	101	1	.282	.466
Joe Morgan	2B142	L	31	146	498	107	163	27	6	17	94	132	52	67	.327	.508
Dave Concepcion	SS130,3B6	R	27	140	507	62	139	23	1	5	49	39	51	33	.274	.353
Pete Rose	3B137,OF35	B	34	162	662	112	210	47	4	7	74	89	50	0	.317	.432
Ken Griffey	OF119	L	25	132	463	95	141	15	9	4	46	67	67	16	.305	.402
Cesar Geronimo	OF148	L	27	148	501	69	129	25	5	6	53	48	97	13	.257	.363
George Foster	OF125,1B1	R	26	134	463	71	139	24	4	23	78	40	73	2	.300	.518
Johnny Bench	C121,OF19,1B9	R	27	142	530	83	150	39	1	28	110	65	108	11	.283	.519
Merv Rettenmund	OF61,3B1	R	32	93	188	24	45	6	1	2	19	35	22	5	.239	.314
Doug Flynn	3B40,2B30,SS17	R	24	89	127	17	34	7	0	1	20	11	13	3	.268	.346
Dan Driessen	1B41,OF29	L	23	88	210	38	59	8	1	7	38	35	30	10	.281	.429
Darrel Chaney	SS34,2B23,3B13	B	27	71	160	18	35	6	0	2	26	14	38	3	.219	.294
Terry Crowley	OF4,1B4	L	28	66	71	8	19	6	0	1	11	7	6	0	.268	.394
Bill Plummer	C63	R	28	65	159	17	29	7	0	1	19	24	28	1	.182	.245
Ed Armbrister	OF19	R	26	59	65	9	12	1	0	0	2	5	19	3	.185	.200
John Vukovich	3B31	R	27	31	38	4	8	1	0	0	2	1	6	0	.211	.289
Don Werner	C7	R	22	7	8	0	1	0	0	0	1	0	3	0	.125	.125

NAME		T	AGE	W	L	PCT	SV	G	GS	CG	IP	H	BB	SO	SHO	ERA
			28	108	54	.667	50	162	162	22	1459	1422	487	663	8	3.37
Don Gullett (BG)		L	24	15	4	.789	0	22	22	8	160	127	56	98	3	2.42
Gary Nolan		R	27	15	9	.625	0	32	32	5	211	202	29	74	1	3.16
Jack Billingham		R	32	15	10	.600	0	33	32	5	208	222	76	79	0	4.11
Fred Norman		L	32	12	4	.750	0	34	26	2	188	163	84	119	0	3.73
Pat Darcy		R	25	11	5	.688	1	27	22	1	131	134	59	46	0	3.57
Clay Kirby		R	27	10	6	.625	0	26	19	1	111	113	54	48	0	4.70
Pedro Borbon		R	28	9	5	.643	5	67	0	0	125	145	21	29	0	2.95
Clay Carroll		R	34	7	5	.583	7	56	2	0	96	93	32	44	0	2.63
Will McEnaney		L	23	5	2	.714	15	70	0	0	91	92	23	48	0	2.47
Rawly Eastwick		R	24	5	3	.625	22	58	0	0	90	77	25	61	0	2.60
Tom Carroll		R	22	4	1	.800	0	12	7	0	47	52	26	14	0	4.98
1 Tom Hall		L	27	0	0	—	0	2	0	0	2	2	3	3	0	0.00

LOS ANGELES 2nd 88-74 .543 20   WALT ALSTON

NAME	G by Pos	B	AGE	G	AB	R	H	2B	3B	HR	RBI	BB	SO	SB	BA	SA
	TOTALS		27	162	5453	648	1355	217	31	118	606	611	825	138	.248	.365
Steve Garvey	1B160	R	26	160	659	85	210	38	6	18	95	33	66	11	.319	.476
Davey Lopes	2B137,OF24,SS14	R	30	155	618	108	162	24	6	8	41	91	93	77	.262	.359
Bill Russell (BH-KJ)	SS83	R	26	84	252	24	52	9	2	0	14	23	28	5	.206	.258
Ron Cey	3B158	R	27	158	566	72	160	29	2	25	101	78	74	5	.283	.473
Willie Crawford	OF113	L	28	124	373	46	98	15	2	9	46	49	43	5	.263	.386
Jim Wynn	OF120	R	33	130	412	80	102	16	0	18	58	110	77	0	.248	.417
Bill Buckner (NJ)	OF72	L	25	92	288	30	70	11	2	6	31	17	15	8	.243	.358
Steve Yeager	C135	R	26	135	452	34	103	16	1	12	54	40	75	2	.228	.347
Lee Lacy	2B43,OF43,SS1	R	27	101	306	44	96	11	5	7	40	22	29	5	.314	.451
Rick Auerbach (NJ)	SS81,2B1,3B1	R	25	85	170	18	38	9	0	0	12	18	22	3	.224	.276
John Hale	OF68	L	21	71	204	20	43	7	0	6	22	26	51	1	.211	.333
Joe Ferguson (BW)	C35,OF34,2B1	R	28	66	202	15	42	2	1	5	23	35	47	2	.208	.302
Ivan DeJesus	SS63	R	22	63	87	10	16	2	1	0	1	11	15	1	.184	.230
Tom Paciorek	OF54	R	28	62	145	14	28	8	0	1	5	11	29	4	.193	.269
Henry Cruz	OF5	R	23	52	93	8	25	1	0	0	10	5	7	6	.266	.319
Manny Mota	OF5	R	37	52	49	3	13	1	0	0	5	1	0	0	.265	.286
2 Leron Lee	OF4	L	27	48	43	2	11	4	0	0	3	9	6	0	.256	.349
Ken McMullen	3B11,1B3	R	33	39	46	4	11	1	1	2	14	7	12	0	.239	.435
Jerry Royster	OF7,2B4,3B3,SS1	R	22	13	36	2	9	2	1	0	1	1	5	2	.250	.361

Charlie Manuel 31 L 2-15, Paul Powell 27 R 2-10, Joe Simpson 23 L 2-6, Orlando Alvarez 23 R 0-4

NAME		T	AGE	W	L	PCT	SV	G	GS	CG	IP	H	BB	SO	SHO	ERA
			29	88	74	.543	21	162	162	51	1470	1215	448	894	18	2.92
Andy Messersmith		R	29	19	14	.576	1	42	40	19	322	244	96	213	7	2.29
2 Burt Hooton		R	25	18	7	.720	0	31	30	12	224	172	64	148	4	2.81
Don Sutton		R	30	16	13	.552	0	35	35	11	254	202	62	175	4	2.87
Doug Rau		L	26	15	9	.625	0	38	38	8	258	227	61	151	2	3.10
Mike Marshall (VJ)		R	32	9	14	.391	13	57	0	0	109	98	39	64	0	3.30
1 Jim Brewer		L	37	3	1	.750	2	21	0	0	33	44	12	11	0	5.18
Rick Rhoden		R	22	3	3	.500	0	26	11	1	99	94	32	40	0	3.09
Charlie Hough		R	27	3	7	.300	4	38	0	0	61	43	34	34	0	2.95
Al Downing		L	34	2	1	.667	1	22	6	0	75	59	28	39	0	2.88
Dennis Lewallyn		R	21	0	0	—	0	1	1	0	5	3	0	5	0	0.00
Stan Wall		L	24	0	1	.000	0	10	0	0	14	12	7	6	0	1.69
1 Geoff Zahn		L	29	0	1	.000	0	1	1	0	2	7	1	1	0	9.00
Juan Marichal		R	37	0	1	.000	0	2	2	0	6	11	5	1	0	13.50
2 Dave Sells		R	28	0	2	.000	0	9	0	0	7	6	3	1	0	3.86

Tommy John (EJ) 32

SAN FRANCISCO 3rd 80-81 .497 27.5   WES WESTRUM

NAME	G by Pos	B	AGE	G	AB	R	H	2B	3B	HR	RBI	BB	SO	SB	BA	SA
	TOTALS		25	161	5447	659	1412	235	45	84	606	604	775	99	.259	.365
2 Willie Montanez	1B134	L	27	135	518	52	158	26	2	8	85	45	50	5	.305	.409
Derrel Thomas	2B141,OF1	B	24	144	540	99	144	21	9	6	48	57	56	28	.276	.381
Chris Speier	SS136,3B1	R	25	148	487	60	132	36	5	10	69	70	50	4	.271	.415
Steve Ontiveros	3B89,OF8,1B4	B	23	108	325	21	94	16	0	3	31	55	44	2	.289	.366
Bobby Murcer	OF144	L	29	147	526	80	157	29	4	11	91	91	45	9	.298	.432
Von Joshua	OF117	L	27	129	500	75	161	25	10	7	43	32	75	20	.322	.448
Gary Matthews (BG)	OF113	R	24	116	425	67	119	23	3	12	58	65	53	13	.280	.431
Dave Rader	C94	L	26	98	292	39	85	15	0	5	31	32	30	1	.291	.394
Gary Thomasson	OF74,1B17	L	23	114	326	44	74	12	3	7	32	37	48	9	.227	.347
Bruce Miller	3B68,2B21,SS6	R	28	99	309	22	74	13	1	1	31	15	26	0	.239	.288
Marc Hill	C60,3B1	R	23	72	182	14	39	4	0	5	23	25	27	0	.214	.319
Glenn Adams	OF25	L	27	61	90	10	27	5	2	0	15	11	25	1	.300	.478
Mike Sadek	C38	R	29	42	106	14	25	4	0	1	9	14	14	1	.236	.321
Jake Brown	OF27	R	27	41	43	6	9	3	0	0	3	5	6	5	.209	.279
1 Ed Goodson	1B16,3B13	L	27	39	121	10	25	7	0	2	16	9	7	0	.207	.289
Chris Arnold	2B4,OF4	R	27	29	41	5	8	0	0	0	1	6	4	0	.195	.195
2 Craig Robinson	SS12,2B9	R	26	29	29	4	2	0	0	0	1	0	6	0	.069	.103
Johnnie LeMaster	SS22	R	21	22	74	4	14	4	0	2	5	3	13	4	.189	.324
1 Garry Maddox	OF13	R	25	17	52	4	7	0	1	0	5	1	6	5	.135	.212
1 Mike Phillips	2B6,3B6,1B2	L	24	31	67	10	13	2	0	0	3	3	6	3	.194	.194

Jack Clark 19 R 4-17, Horace Speed 23 R 2-15, Gary Alexander 22 R 0-3

NAME		T	AGE	W	L	PCT	SV	G	GS	CG	IP	H	BB	SO	SHO	ERA
			25	80	81	.497	24	161	161	37	1433	1406	612	856	9	3.74
John Montefusco		R	25	15	9	.625	0	35	34	10	244	210	86	215	4	2.88
Jim Barr		R	27	13	14	.481	0	35	33	12	244	244	58	77	2	3.06
Pete Falcone		L	21	12	11	.522	0	34	32	3	190	171	111	131	1	4.17
Ed Halicki		R	24	9	13	.409	0	24	23	7	160	143	59	153	2	3.49
Mike Caldwell		L	26	7	13	.350	1	38	21	4	163	194	48	57	0	4.80
Gary Lavelle		L	26	5	7	.417	8	65	0	0	82	80	48	51	0	2.35
Charlie Williams		R	27	5	3	.625	3	55	0	0	98	94	66	45	0	3.48
Randy Moffitt		R	26	4	5	.444	11	55	0	0	74	73	32	39	0	3.89
Dave Heaverlo		R	24	3	1	.750	0	64	0	0	64	62	31	35	0	2.39
Tom Bradley		R	28	2	3	.400	0	13	6	0	42	57	18	13	0	6.00
John D'Acquisto (EJ)	R	23	2	4	.333	0	10	6	0	28	39	34	22	0	10.29
Rob Dressler		R	21	1	0	1.000	0	3	1	1	16	11	2	9	0	1.13
Greg Minton		R	23	1	1	.500	0	11	2	0	17	19	11	6	0	6.88
Tommy Toms		R	23	0	0	—	0	10	0	0	10	12	6	8	0	6.30
1 Ron Bryant (VR)		R	27													

SAN DIEGO — 4th 71-91 .438 37 — JOHN McNAMARA

NAME	G by Pos	B	AGE	G	AB	R	H	2B	3B	HR	RBI	BB	SO	SB	BA	SA
TOTALS			28	162	5429	552	1324	215	22	78	505	506	754	85	.244	.335
Willie McCovey	1B115	L	37	122	413	43	104	17	0	23	68	57	80	1	.252	.460
Tito Fuentes	2B142	B	31	146	565	57	158	21	3	4	43	25	51	4	.280	.349
Enzo Hernandez	SS111	R	26	116	344	37	75	12	2	0	19	26	25	20	.218	.265
2 Ted Kubiak	3B64,2B11,1B1	B	33	87	196	13	44	5	0	0	14	24	18	3	.224	.250
Dave Winfield	OF138	R	23	143	509	74	136	20	2	15	76	69	82	23	.267	.403
Johnny Grubb	OF139	L	26	144	553	72	149	36	2	4	38	59	59	2	.269	.363
Bobby Tolan	OF120,1B27	L	29	147	506	58	129	19	4	5	43	28	45	11	.255	.338
Fred Kendall	C85	R	26	103	286	16	57	17	2	1	0	24	26	28	0	.199	.248
Hector Torres	SS75,3B42,2B16	R	29	112	352	31	91	12	0	5	26	22	32	2	.259	.335
Mike Ivie	1B78,3B61,C1	R	22	111	377	36	94	16	2	8	46	20	63	4	.249	.366
Gene Locklear	OF57	L	25	100	237	31	76	11	1	5	27	22	26	4	.321	.439
Dick Sharon	OF57	R	25	91	160	14	31	7	0	4	20	26	35	0	.194	.313
Randy Hundley	C51	R	33	74	180	7	37	5	1	2	14	19	29	0	.206	.278
Bob Davis	C43	R	23	43	128	6	30	3	2	0	7	11	31	0	.234	.289
3 Don Hahn	OF26	R	26	34	26	7	6	1	2	0	3	10	2	1	.231	.423
Dave Roberts	3B30,2B5	R	24	33	113	7	32	2	0	2	12	13	19	1	.283	.354
John Scott	OF1	R	23	25	9	6	0	0	0	0	0	0	2	2	.000	.000
Steve Huntz	3B16,2B2	B	29	22	53	3	8	4	0	0	4	7	8	0	.151	.226
1 Jerry Moses	C5	R	28	13	19	1	3	2	0	0	1	2	3	0	.158	.263
Jerry Turner	OF4	L	21	11	22	1	6	0	0	0	0	0	2	1	.273	.273
Glenn Beckert (NJ)	3B4	R	34	9	16	2	6	1	0	0	1	0	1	0	.375	.438
2 Bobby Valentine	OF4	R	25	7	15	1	2	1	0	0	1	4	0	1	.133	.333

Bill Almon 22 R 4-10, Dave Hilton (IL) 24 R 0-8

NAME	T	AGE	W	L	PCT	SV	G	GS	CG	IP	H	BB	SO	SHO	ERA
		26	71	91	.438	20	162	162	40	1463	1494	521	713	12	3.48
Randy Jones	L	25	20	12	.625	0	37	36	18	285	242	56	103	6	2.24
Brent Strom (EJ)	L	26	8	8	.500	0	18	16	6	120	103	33	56	2	2.55
Joe McIntosh	R	23	8	15	.348	0	37	28	4	183	195	60	71	1	3.69
Rich Folkers	R	28	6	11	.353	0	45	15	4	142	155	59	87	0	4.18
Dan Spillner	R	23	5	13	.278	1	37	25	3	167	194	63	104	0	4.26
Dave Freisleben	R	23	5	14	.263	0	36	27	4	181	206	82	77	1	4.28
Dave Tomlin	L	26	4	2	.667	1	67	0	0	83	87	31	48	0	3.25
Bill Greif	R	25	4	6	.400	9	59	1	0	72	74	38	43	0	3.88
Alan Foster (SJ)	R	28	3	1	.750	0	17	4	1	45	41	21	20	0	2.40
Jerry Johnson	R	33	3	1	.750	0	21	0	0	54	60	31	18	0	5.17
1 Sonny Siebert	R	38	3	2	.600	0	6	6	0	27	37	10	10	0	4.33
Butch Metzger	R	23	1	0	1.000	4	4	0	0	5	6	4	6	0	7.20
Danny Frisella	R	29	1	6	.143	9	65	0	0	98	86	51	67	0	3.12
Larry Hardy	R	27	0	0	—	0	3	0	0	3	8	2	3	0	12.00

ATLANTA — 5th 67-94 .416 40.5 — CLYDE KING 58-76 .433 — CONNIE RYAN 9-18 .333

NAME	G by Pos	B	AGE	G	AB	R	H	2B	3B	HR	RBI	BB	SO	SB	BA	SA
TOTALS			26	161	5424	583	1323	179	28	107	541	543	759	55	.244	.346
Earl Williams	1B90,C11	R	26	111	383	42	92	13	0	11	50	34	66	0	.240	.360
Marty Perez (BG)	2B116,SS7	R	29	120	461	50	127	14	2	3	34	37	44	2	.275	.328
Larvell Blanks	SS129,2B12	R	25	141	471	49	110	13	4	3	38	37	43	4	.234	.293
Darrell Evans	3B156,1B5	L	28	156	567	82	138	22	2	22	73	105	106	12	.243	.406
Rowland Office	OF107	L	22	126	355	30	103	14	1	3	30	23	41	2	.290	.361
Dusty Baker	OF136	R	26	142	494	63	129	18	2	19	72	67	57	12	.261	.421
Ralph Garr	OF148	L	29	151	625	74	174	26	11	6	31	44	50	14	.278	.384
Vic Correll	C97	R	29	103	325	37	70	12	1	11	39	42	66	0	.215	.360
Mike Lum	1B60,OF38	L	29	124	364	32	83	8	2	8	36	39	38	2	.228	.327
Rod Gilbreath	2B52,3B10,SS1	R	22	90	202	24	49	3	1	2	16	24	26	5	.243	.297
Dave May	OF53	L	31	82	203	28	56	8	0	12	40	25	27	1	.276	.493
Biff Pocoroba	C62	R	21	67	188	15	48	7	1	1	22	20	11	0	.255	.319
Cito Gaston	OF35,1B1	R	31	64	141	17	34	4	0	6	15	17	33	1	.241	.397
2 Ed Goodson	1B13,3B1	L	27	47	76	5	16	2	0	1	4	2	11	0	.211	.276
Rob Belloir	SS38,2B1	R	26	43	105	11	23	2	1	0	9	7	8	0	.219	.257
Bob Beall	1B8	B	27	20	31	2	7	2	0	0	5	8	5	0	.226	.290
1 Craig Robinson	SS7	R	26	10	17	1	1	0	0	0	0	0	5	0	.059	.059
1 Johnny Oates	C8	L	29	8	18	0	4	1	0	0	1	0	4	0	.222	.278

Frank Tepedino 27 L 0-7, Joe Nolan 24 L 1-4, Dave Johnson 32 (JL) R 1-1, 1 Dick Allen (RR) 33

NAME	T	AGE	W	L	PCT	SV	G	GS	CG	IP	H	BB	SO	SHO	ERA
		29	67	94	.416	24	161	161	32	1430	1543	519	669	4	3.91
Carl Morton	R	31	17	16	.515	0	39	39	11	278	302	82	78	2	3.50
Phil Niekro	R	36	15	15	.500	0	39	37	13	276	285	72	144	1	3.20
Tom House	L	28	7	7	.500	11	58	0	0	79	79	36	36	0	3.19
Mike Beard	L	25	4	0	1.000	0	34	2	0	70	71	28	27	0	3.21
1 Ron Reed	R	32	4	4	.444	0	10	10	1	75	93	16	40	0	4.20
Buzz Capra (SJ)	R	27	4	7	.364	0	12	12	5	78	77	28	35	0	4.27
1 Roric Harrison	R	28	3	4	.429	1	15	7	2	55	58	19	22	0	4.75
Max Leon	R	25	2	1	.667	6	50	1	0	85	90	33	53	0	4.13
2 Elias Sosa	R	25	2	2	.500	2	43	0	0	62	70	29	31	0	4.50
2 Ray Sadecki	L	34	2	3	.400	1	25	5	0	66	73	21	24	0	4.23
2 Bruce Dal Canton	R	33	2	7	.222	3	26	9	0	67	63	24	34	0	3.36
Jamie Easterly	L	22	2	9	.182	0	21	13	0	69	73	42	34	0	4.96
Adrian Devine	R	23	1	0	1.000	1	16	1	0	18	16	13	9	0	4.50
Gary Gentry	R	28	1	0	1.000	0	7	2	0	20	25	8	10	0	4.95
3 Blue Moon Odom	R	30	1	7	.125	0	15	10	0	56	78	28	30	0	7.07
Preston Hanna	R	20	0	0	—	0	4	0	0	5	4	6	3	0	1.50
Pablo Torrealba	L	29	0	1	.000	0	6	0	0	15	13	6	10	0	1.29
Frank LaCorte	R	23	0	3	.000	0	6	4	0	14	13	6	10	0	5.14
Mike Thompson	R	25	0	6	.000	0	16	10	0	52	60	32	42	0	4.67

HOUSTON — 6th 64-97 .398 43.5 — PRESTON GOMEZ 47-80 .370 — BILL VIRDON 17-17 .500

NAME	G by Pos	B	AGE	G	AB	R	H	2B	3B	HR	RBI	BB	SO	SB	BA	SA
TOTALS			26	162	5515	664	1401	218	54	84	606	523	762	133	.254	.359
Bob Watson	1B118,OF9	R	29	132	485	67	157	27	1	18	85	40	50	3	.324	.495
Rob Andrews	2B94,SS6	R	22	103	277	29	66	5	4	0	19	31	34	12	.238	.285
Roger Metzger	SS126	B	27	127	450	54	102	7	9	2	26	41	39	4	.227	.296
Doug Rader	3B124,SS2	R	30	129	448	41	100	23	2	12	48	42	101	5	.223	.364
Wilbur Howard	OF95	B	26	121	392	62	111	16	8	0	21	21	67	32	.283	.365
Cesar Cedeno (RJ)	OF131	R	24	131	500	93	144	31	3	13	63	62	50	50	.288	.440
Greg Gross	OF121	L	22	132	483	67	142	16	14	0	41	63	37	2	.294	.364
Milt May	C102	L	24	111	386	29	93	15	1	4	52	26	41	1	.241	.316
Cliff Johnson	1B47,C41,OF1	R	27	122	340	52	94	16	1	20	65	46	64	1	.276	.506
Jose Cruz	OF94	L	27	120	315	44	81	15	2	9	49	52	44	6	.257	.403
Enos Cabell	OF67,1B25,3B22	R	25	117	348	43	92	17	6	2	43	18	53	12	.264	.365
Ken Boswell	2B31,3B23	L	29	86	178	16	43	8	2	0	21	30	19	0	.242	.309
Larry Milbourne	2B43,SS22	R	24	73	151	17	32	1	2	1	9	6	14	1	.212	.265
Tommy Helms	2B42,3B3,SS1	R	34	64	135	7	28	2	0	0	14	10	8	0	.207	.222
Skip Jutze	C47	R	29	51	93	9	21	2	0	0	6	2	4	1	.226	.247
Jerry DaVanon	SS21,2B9,3B3	R	29	32	97	15	27	4	2	1	10	16	7	2	.278	.392
Art Gardner	OF8	L	22	13	31	3	6	0	0	0	3	2	8	1	.194	.194
Rafael Batista		L	29	10	10	0	3	0	0	0	1	0	0	0	.300	.400

Mike Easler 24 L 0-5, Jesus de la Rosa 21 R 1-3

NAME	T	AGE	W	L	PCT	SV	G	GS	CG	IP	H	BB	SO	SHO	ERA
		27	64	97	.398	25	162	162	39	1458	1436	679	839	6	4.04
Larry Dierker	R	28	14	16	.467	0	34	34	14	232	225	91	127	2	4.00
J.R. Richard	R	25	12	10	.545	0	33	31	7	203	178	138	176	1	4.39
Dave Roberts	L	30	8	14	.364	1	32	27	7	198	182	73	101	0	4.27
Joe Niekro	R	30	6	4	.600	4	40	4	1	88	79	39	54	1	3.07
Doug Konieczny	R	23	6	13	.316	0	32	29	4	171	184	87	89	1	4.47
Jim York	R	27	4	4	.500	0	19	4	0	47	43	25	17	0	3.83
Ken Forsch (NJ)	R	28	4	8	.333	2	34	9	2	109	114	30	54	0	3.22
Jim Crawford	L	24	3	5	.375	4	44	2	0	87	92	37	37	0	3.62
Tom Griffin (HJ)	R	27	2	2	.273	0	17	13	3	79	89	46	56	1	5.35
Wayne Granger	R	31	2	5	.286	5	55	0	0	74	76	23	30	0	3.65
Mike Cosgrove	L	24	2	3	.333	5	32	3	1	71	62	37	32	0	3.64
Jose Sosa	R	22	1	3	.250	1	25	1	0	47	51	23	31	0	4.02
1 Fred Scherman	L	30	1	0	1.000	0	16	0	0	16	21	4	13	0	5.06
Paul Siebert	L	23	0	2	.000	2	7	2	0	18	20	6	6	0	3.00
Mike Stanton	R	22	0	2	.000	1	7	0	0	17	20	16	16	0	7.41

WORLD SERIES — CINCINNATI (NL) 4 BOSTON (AL) 3

LINE SCORES

TEAM	1 2 3	4 5 6	7 8 9	10 11 12	R	H	E

Game 1 October 11 at Boston

CIN (NL)	0 0 0	0 0 0	0 0 0		0	5	0
BOS (AL)	0 0 0	0 0 0	6 0 x		6	12	0

Gullett, Carroll (7), McEnaney (7) — Tiant

Game 2 October 12 at Boston

CIN	0 0 0	1 0 0	0 0 2		3	7	1
BOS	1 0 0	0 0 1	0 0 0		2	7	0

Billingham, Borbon (6), McEnaney (7), Eastwick (9) — Lee, Drago (9)

Game 3 October 14 at Cincinnati

BOS	0 1 0	0 0 1	1 0 2	0	5	10	2
CIN	0 0 0	2 3 0	0 0 0	1	6	7	0

Wise, Burton (5), Cleveland (5), Willoughby (7), Moret (10) — Nolan, Darcy (5) Carroll (7), McEnaney (7), Eastwick (9)

Game 4 October 15 at Cincinnati

BOS	0 0 0	5 0 0	0 0 0		5	11	1
CIN	2 0 0	2 0 0	0 0 0		4	9	1

Tiant — Norman, Borbon (4), Carroll (7), Eastwick (7)

Game 5 October 16 at Cincinnati

BOS	1 0 0	0 0 0	0 0 1		2	5	0
CIN	0 0 0	1 1 3	0 1 x		6	8	0

Cleveland, Willoughby (6), Pole (8), Segui (9) — Gullett, Eastwick (9)

Game 6 October 21 at Boston

CIN	0 0 0	0 3 0	2 1 0	0 0 0	6	14	0
BOS	3 0 0	0 0 3	0 0 1	0 0 1	7	10	1

Nolan, Norman (3), Billingham (3), Carroll (5), Borbon (6), Eastwick (8), McEnaney (9), Darcy (10) — Tiant, Moret (8), Drago (9), Wise (12)

Game 7 October 22 at Boston

CIN	0 0 0	0 0 2	1 0 1		4	9	0
BOS	0 0 3	0 0 0	0 0 0		3	5	2

Gullett, Billingham (6), Carroll (7), McEnaney (9) — Lee, Moret (7), Willoughby (7), Burton (9), Cleveland (9)

COMPOSITE BATTING

NAME	POS	G	AB	R	H	2B	3B	HR	RBI	BA
Cincinnati (NL)										
Totals		7	244	29	59	9	3	7	29	.242
Foster	LF	7	29	1	8	0	0	0	7	.276
Bench	C	7	29	5	6	2	0	1	4	.207
Perez	1B	7	28	4	5	0	0	3	7	.179
Concepcion	SS	7	28	3	5	1	0	1	4	.179
Rose	3B	7	27	3	10	1	1	0	2	.370
Morgan	2B	7	27	4	7	1	0	0	3	.259
Griffey	RF	7	26	4	7	3	1	0	4	.269
Geronimo	CF	7	25	3	7	0	1	2	3	.280
Gullett	P	7	7	1	2	0	0	0	2	.286
Rettenmund	PH	3	3	0	0	0	0	0	0	.000
Crowley	PH	3	2	0	1	0	0	0	0	.500
Billingham	P	3	2	0	0	0	0	0	0	.000
Chaney	PH	2	2	0	0	0	0	0	0	.000
Driessen	PH	3	2	0	0	0	0	0	0	.000
McEnaney	P	5	1	0	1	0	0	0	1	1.000
Armbrister	PH	4	1	0	0	0	0	0	0	.000
Eastwick	P	5	1	0	0	0	0	0	0	.000
Borbon	P	2	1	0	0	0	0	0	0	.000
Nolan	P	2	1	0	0	0	0	0	0	.000
Norman	P	2	1	0	0	0	0	0	0	.000

Darcy P 0-1, C. Carroll P 0-0

NAME	POS	G	AB	R	H	2B	3B	HR	RBI	BA
Boston (AL)										
Totals		7	239	30	60	7	2	6	30	.251
Doyle	2B	7	30	3	8	1	1	0	4	.267
Yastrzemski	LF-1B	7	29	7	9	0	0	0	4	.310
Petrocelli	3B	7	26	3	8	0	0	0	4	.308
Lynn	CF	7	25	3	7	1	0	1	5	.280
Fisk	C	7	25	5	6	0	0	0	4	.240
Evans	RF	7	24	3	7	1	1	1	5	.292
Burleson	SS	7	24	3	7	1	0	0	2	.292
Cooper	1B	7	19	0	1	1	0	0	0	.053
Beniquez	LF	3	8	0	1	0	0	0	0	.125
Tiant	P	3	8	1	2	0	0	0	0	.250
Carbo	LF	4	7	3	3	0	0	2	4	.429
Lee	P	2	6	0	1	0	0	0	0	.167
Miller	LF	3	2	0	0	0	0	0	0	.000
Cleveland	P	2	1	0	0	0	0	0	0	.000
Wise	P	2	1	0	0	0	0	0	0	.000
Griffin	PH	1	1	0	0	0	0	0	0	.000
Montgomery	PH	1	1	0	0	0	0	0	0	.000

Moret P 0-0, Willoughby P 0-0, Drago P 0-0, Burton P 0-0, Segui P 0-0, Pole P 0-0

COMPOSITE PITCHING

NAME	G	IP	H	BB	SO	W	L	SV	ERA
Cincinnati (NL)									
Totals	7	65	60	30	40	4	3	2	3.88
Gullett	3	18.2	19	10	15	1	1	0	4.34
Billingham	3	9	8	5	7	0	0	0	1.00
Eastwick	5	8	6	3	4	2	0	1	2.25
McEnaney	5	6.2	3	2	5	0	0	1	2.70
Nolan	2	6	6	1	2	0	0	0	6.00
C. Carroll	5	5.2	4	2	3	1	0	0	3.18
Norman	2	3	4	1	1	0	1	0	9.00
Darcy	2	4	3	2	1	0	1	0	4.50
Borbon	3	3	3	1	0	0	0	0	6.00

NAME	G	IP	H	BB	SO	W	L	SV	ERA
Boston (AL)									
Totals	7	65.1	59	25	30	3	4	0	3.86
Tiant	3	25	25	8	12	2	0	0	3.60
Lee	2	14.1	12	3	7	0	0	0	3.14
Cleveland	3	6.2	7	3	5	0	1	0	6.75
Willoughby	3	6.1	3	0	2	1	0	0	0.00
Wise	2	5.1	6	2	1	1	0	0	8.44
Drago	3	4	3	1	1	0	1	0	2.25
Moret	1	1	0	0	0	0	0	0	0.00
Segui	1	1	0	0	0	0	0	0	0.00
Burton	1	0	2	2	0	0	1	0	9.00
Pole	1	0	1	0	0	0	0	0	∞

1976 100 Years Later

Before the season got underway, pitchers Andy Messersmith and Dave McNally were declared "free agents", a move which came about when both men decided to play out the 1975 season without a contract. Because of the ruling, made by arbitrator Peter Seitz in December, the players of all the clubs found themselves locked out in spring training by the owners. Although commissioner Bowie Kuhn stepped in time to get major league's baseball's 100th season underway, the game would never be the same. Messersmith, who had played for the Dodgers, found himself in an Atlanta uniform after the start of play, but not before rejecting a supposed "close deal" from New York Yankees' owner George Steinbrenner. McNally decided to retire.

When the season began Mike Schmidt led Philadelphia with four consecutive home runs against Chicago in a ten-inning 18-16 slugfest, and the Yankees returned to the Bronx to re-open the newly renovated Yankee Stadium after a two-year hiatus at Shea Stadium. While the season was settling down headlines were made by an agreement between the owners and the baseball players' association which gave players the right to be traded after five years and free agents after six, thus ending the court battles which began with the Seitz decision.

While the bad taste of the off-the-field dramatics left the fans disheartened, the magic of the game was saved by the debut of a 21-year old pitcher from Massachusetts, who took the mound for Detroit and instantly started to talk to baseballs, show open affection to his infielders after a good play, and flap his arms on the mound, the last of which, when coupled with his curly blonde hair, earned Mark Fidrych the nickname, "Big Bird". As Fidrych was capturing the public's attention, further trouble brewed off the field when Oakland owner Charles O. Finley attempted to unload three of his stars — Rollie Fingers, Vida Blue, and Joe Rudi — for three-and-a-half million dollars. Blue was headed to New York and Fingers and Rudi to Boston. But Kuhn stopped the sale because it would be detrimental to the game and Finley ran to his lawyers, who would not get a court ruling until the following year.

In the wars on the field Cincinnati, led by Joe Morgan's second consecutive MVP performance, had little trouble in nailing down their second straight National League pennant by easily beating Philadelphia 3-0 in the playoffs. In the American League finals, the cast was completely new with the revamped Yankees barely edging out the Kansas City Royals in the five-game set. For New York, it was their first pennant since 1964. Catcher Thurman Munson was the team's anchor and received MVP honors for his efforts.

In the World Series, which was to be a question of the Yankees' pitching and speed vs. the Reds' offense and the arm of catcher Johnny Bench, it became a matter of Cincinnati's brilliant defense and their surprising relief pitching—all of which was enough to embarrass the Yankees in a four-game sweep. As the Reds enjoyed the distinction of becoming the first National League team in 54 years to win back-to-back honors, Hank Aaron called an end to his playing days with an all-time high of 755 home runs, and Walt Alston, who had guided the Dodgers for 23 years, decided to "call it a day" as he returned home to Venice, Ohio.

For the 1977 season, which promised to be a little quieter, the American League added new teams in Seattle and Toronto. For the owners, the new season would be a case of wallet bending as 23 top players prepared to offer their services on the "new" open market.

1976 AMERICAN LEAGUE — EAST DIVISION

NEW YORK — 1st 97-62 .610 — BILLY MARTIN

NAME	G by Pos	B	AGE	G	AB	R	H	2B	3B	HR	RBI	BB	SO	SB	BA	SA
TOTALS			28	159	5555	730	1496	231	36	120	682	470	616	163	.269	.389
Chris Chambliss	1B155,DH1	L	27	156	641	79	188	32	6	17	96	27	80	1	.293	.441
Willie Randolph	2B124	R	21	125	430	59	115	15	4	1	40	58	39	37	.267	.328
Fred Stanley	SS110,2B3	R	28	110	260	32	62	2	2	1	20	34	29	1	.238	.273
Graig Nettles	3B158,SS1	L	31	158	583	88	148	29	2	32	93	62	94	11	.254	.475
Oscar Gamble	OF104,DH1	L	26	110	340	43	79	13	1	17	57	38	38	5	.232	.426
Mickey Rivers	OF136	L	27	137	590	95	184	31	8	8	67	13	51	43	.312	.432
Roy White	OF156	B	32	156	626	104	179	29	3	14	65	83	52	31	.286	.409
Thurman Munson	C121,DH21,OF11	R	29	152	616	79	186	27	1	17	105	29	38	14	.302	.432
2 Carlos May	DH71,OF7,1B1	L	28	87	288	38	80	11	2	3	40	34	32	1	.278	.361
Lou Piniella	OF49,DH38	R	32	100	327	36	92	16	6	3	38	18	34	0	.281	.394
Jim Mason	SS93	L	25	93	217	17	39	7	1	1	14	9	37	0	.180	.235
S. Alomar	2B38,DH9,SS6,3B3,1B1,OF1	B	32	67	163	20	39	4	0	1	10	13	12	12	.239	.282
Otto Velez	OF24,1B8,DH5,3B1	R	25	49	94	11	25	6	0	2	10	23	26	0	.266	.394
2 Fran Healy	C31,DH9	R	29	46	120	10	32	3	0	0	9	9	17	3	.267	.292
2 Ellie Hendricks	C18	L	35	26	53	6	12	1	0	3	5	3	10	0	.226	.415
1 Rick Dempsey	C9,OF4	R	26	21	42	1	5	0	0	0	5	5	4	0	.119	.119
Elliott Maddox (KJ)	OF13,DH2	R	28	18	46	4	10	2	0	0	3	4	3	0	.217	.261

2 Cesar Tovar 35 R 6-39, 2 Gene Locklear 26 L 7-32, Juan Bernhardt 22 R 4-21, Larry Murray 23 B 1-10,
Kerry Dineen 24 L 2-7, 1 Rich Coggins 25 L 1-4, Mickey Klutts 21 R 0-3, Ron Blomberg (SJ) 27 L 0-2, Terry Whitfield 23 L 0-0

NAME	T	AGE	W	L	PCT	SV	G	GS	CG	IP	H	BB	SO	SHO	ERA
		30	97	62	.610	37	159	159	62	1455	1300	448	674	15	3.19
Ed Figueroa	R	27	19	10	.655	0	34	34	14	257	237	94	119	4	3.01
Catfish Hunter	R	30	17	15	.531	0	36	36	21	299	268	68	173	2	3.52
Dock Ellis	R	31	17	8	.680	0	32	32	8	212	195	76	65	1	3.18
2 Doyle Alexander	R	25	10	5	.667	0	19	19	5	137	114	39	41	2	3.28
2 Ken Holtzman	L	30	9	7	.563	0	21	21	10	149	165	35	41	2	4.17
Sparky Lyle	L	31	7	8	.467	23	64	0	0	104	82	42	61	0	2.25
2 Grant Jackson	L	33	6	0	1.000	1	21	2	1	59	38	16	25	1	1.68
1 Rudy May	R	31	4	3	.571	0	11	11	2	68	49	28	38	1	3.57
Dick Tidrow	R	29	4	5	.444	10	47	2	0	92	80	24	65	0	2.64
1 Tippy Martinez	L	26	2	0	1.000	2	11	0	0	28	18	14	14	0	1.93
Jim York	R	28	1	0	1.000	0	3	0	0	10	14	4	6	0	5.40
1 Dave Pagan	R	26	1	1	.500	0	7	2	1	24	18	4	13	0	2.25
Ron Guidry	L	25	0	0	—	0	7	0	0	16	20	4	12	0	5.63
1 Ken Brett	L	27	0	0	—	1	2	0	0	2	1	0	1	0	0.00

BALTIMORE — 2nd 88-74 .543 10.5 — EARL WEAVER

NAME	G by Pos	B	AGE	G	AB	R	H	2B	3B	HR	RBI	BB	SO	SB	BA	SA
TOTALS			29	162	5457	619	1326	213	28	119	576	519	883	150	.243	.358
Tony Muser	1B109,OF12,DH10	L	28	136	326	25	74	7	1	1	30	21	34	1	.227	.264
Bobby Grich	2B140,3B2,DH2	R	27	144	518	93	138	31	4	13	54	86	99	14	.266	.417
Mark Belanger	SS153	R	31	153	522	66	141	22	2	1	40	51	64	27	.270	.326
D. DeCinces	3B109,2B17,1B11,SS2,DH1	R	25	129	440	36	103	17	2	11	42	49	68	6	.234	.357
Reggie Jackson	OF121,DH11	L	30	134	498	84	138	27	2	27	91	54	108	28	.277	.502
Paul Blair	OF139,DH1	R	32	145	375	29	74	16	0	3	16	22	49	15	.197	.264
Ken Singleton	OF134,DH19	B	29	154	544	62	151	25	2	13	70	79	76	2	.278	.403
Dave Duncan	C93	R	30	93	284	20	58	7	0	4	17	25	56	0	.204	.271
Lee May	1B94,DH52	R	33	148	530	61	137	17	4	25	109	41	104	4	.258	.447
Al Bumbry	OF116,DH10	L	29	133	450	71	113	15	7	9	36	43	76	42	.251	.376
Andres Mora	DH34,OF31	R	21	73	220	18	48	11	0	6	25	13	49	1	.218	.350
Brooks Robinson	3B71	R	39	71	218	16	46	8	2	3	11	8	24	0	.211	.307
2 Rick Dempsey	C58,OF3	R	26	59	174	11	37	2	0	0	10	13	17	1	.213	.224
Tommy Harper	DH27,1B1,OF1	R	35	46	77	8	18	5	0	1	7	10	16	4	.234	.338
2 Terry Crowley	DH17,1B1	L	29	33	61	5	15	1	0	0	5	7	11	0	.246	.262
1 Ellie Hendricks	C27	L	35	28	79	2	11	1	0	1	4	7	13	0	.139	.190
1 Tim Nordbrook	2B14,SS12	R	26	27	22	4	5	0	0	0	3	3	5	0	.227	.227
Royle Stillman	DH5,1B2	L	25	20	22	0	2	0	0	0	1	3	4	1	.091	.091
Tom Shopay	OF11,C1	L	31	14	20	4	4	2	0	0	1	3	1	0	.200	.200

Rich Dauer 23 R 4-39, Kiko Garcia 22 R 7-32, Bob Bailor (SJ) 24 R 2-6

NAME	T	AGE	W	L	PCT	SV	G	GS	CG	IP	H	BB	SO	SHO	ERA
		28	88	74	.543	23	162	162	59	1469	1396	489	678	16	3.32
Jim Palmer	R	30	22	13	.629	0	40	40	23	315	255	84	159	6	2.51
Wayne Garland	R	25	20	7	.741	1	38	25	14	232	224	64	113	4	2.68
2 Rudy May	R	31	11	7	.611	0	24	21	5	152	156	42	71	1	3.79
Ross Grimsley	L	26	8	7	.533	0	28	19	2	137	143	35	41	0	3.94
1 Ken Holtzman	L	30	5	4	.556	0	13	13	6	98	100	35	25	1	2.85
Fred Holdsworth	R	24	4	1	.800	2	16	0	0	40	24	13	24	0	2.03
Mike Cuellar	L	39	4	13	.235	1	26	19	2	107	129	50	32	1	4.96
2 Tippy Martinez	L	26	3	1	.750	8	28	0	0	42	32	28	31	0	2.57
1 Doyle Alexander	R	25	3	4	.429	0	11	6	2	64	58	24	17	1	3.52
Mike Flanagan	L	24	3	5	.375	0	20	10	4	85	83	33	56	0	4.13
Dyar Miller	R	30	2	4	.333	7	49	0	0	89	79	36	37	0	2.93
1 Grant Jackson	L	33	1	1	.500	3	13	0	0	19	19	9	14	0	5.21
Dennis Martinez	R	21	1	2	.333	0	4	2	1	28	23	8	18	0	2.57
2 Dave Pagan	R	26	1	4	.200	1	25	5	0	47	54	23	34	0	5.94
Scott McGregor	L	22	0	0	—	0	2	0	0	15	17	5	6	0	3.60

Dave Johnson 27 (BW)

BOSTON — 3rd 83-79 .512 15.5 — DARRELL JOHNSON 41-45 .477 — DON ZIMMER 42-34 .553

NAME	G by Pos	B	AGE	G	AB	R	H	2B	3B	HR	RBI	BB	SO	SB	BA	SA
TOTALS			27	162	5511	716	1448	257	53	134	664	500	832	95	.263	.402
Carl Yastrzemski	1B94,OF51,DH10	L	36	155	546	71	146	23	2	21	102	80	67	5	.267	.432
Denny Doyle	2B112	L	32	117	432	51	108	15	5	0	26	22	39	6	.250	.308
Rick Burleson	SS152	R	25	152	540	75	157	27	1	7	42	60	37	14	.291	.383
Butch Hobson	3B76	R	24	76	269	34	63	7	5	8	34	15	62	0	.234	.387
Dwight Evans	OF145, DH1	R	24	146	501	61	121	34	5	17	62	57	92	6	.242	.431
Fred Lynn	OF128,DH5	L	24	132	507	76	159	32	8	10	65	48	67	14	.314	.467
Jim Rice	OF98,DH54	R	23	153	581	75	164	25	8	25	85	28	123	8	.282	.482
Carlton Fisk	C133,DH1	R	28	134	487	76	124	17	5	17	58	56	71	12	.255	.415
Cecil Cooper	1B66,DH53	L	26	123	451	66	127	22	6	15	78	16	62	7	.282	.457
Rick Miller	OF82,DH4	L	28	105	269	40	76	15	3	0	27	34	47	11	.283	.361
Rico Petrocelli	3B73,2B5,DH4,SS1,1B1	R	33	85	240	17	51	7	1	3	24	34	36	0	.213	.288
Steve Dillard	3B18,2B17,SS12,DH7	R	25	57	167	22	46	14	0	1	15	17	20	6	.275	.377
Doug Griffin	2B44,DH2	R	29	49	127	14	24	2	0	0	4	9	14	2	.189	.205
2 Bobby Darwin	OF17,DH16	R	33	43	106	9	19	5	2	3	13	2	35	1	.179	.349
Bob Heise	3B22,SS9,2B1	R	29	32	56	5	15	2	0	0	5	1	2	0	.268	.304
Bob Montgomery	C30,DH1	R	32	31	93	10	23	3	1	3	13	5	20	0	.247	.398
1 Bernie Carbo	DH15,OF1	L	28	17	55	5	13	4	0	2	6	11	8	1	.236	.418
Deron Johnson	DH9,1B5	R	37	15	38	3	5	1	1	0	6	5	11	0	.132	.211
Jack Baker	1B8,DH1	R	26	12	23	1	3	0	0	1	3	0	9	0	.130	.261
Ernie Whitt	C8	L	24	8	18	4	4	2	0	1	3	2	5	0	.222	.500
Andy Merchant	C1	L	25	3	2	0	0	0	0	0	2	1	0	0	.000	.000

NAME	T	AGE	W	L	PCT	SV	G	GS	CG	IP	H	BB	SO	SHO	ERA
		29	83	79	.512	27	162	162	49	1458	1495	409	673	13	3.52
Luis Tiant	R	35	21	12	.636	0	38	38	19	279	274	64	131	3	3.06
Rick Wise	R	30	14	11	.560	0	34	34	11	224	218	48	93	4	3.54
Ferguson Jenkins (FJ)	R	32	12	11	.522	0	30	29	12	209	201	43	142	2	3.27
Reggie Cleveland	R	28	10	9	.526	2	41	14	3	170	159	61	76	0	3.07
Dick Pole	R	25	6	5	.545	0	31	15	1	121	131	48	49	0	4.31
Rick Jones	L	21	5	3	.625	0	24	14	1	104	133	26	45	0	3.38
Bill Lee (SJ)	L	29	5	7	.417	3	24	14	1	96	124	28	29	0	5.63
2 Tom Murphy	R	30	4	5	.444	8	37	0	0	81	91	25	32	0	3.44
Jim Willoughby	R	27	3	12	.200	10	54	0	0	99	94	31	37	0	2.82
Rick Kreuger	L	27	2	1	.667	0	8	4	1	31	31	16	12	0	4.06
Tom House (KJ)	L	29	1	3	.250	4	36	0	0	44	39	19	27	0	4.30

447

Batting

NAME	G by Pos	B	AGE	G	AB	R	H	2B	3B	HR	RBI	BB	SO	SB	BA	SA
CLEVELAND 4th 81-78 .509 16 **FRANK ROBINSON**			27	159	5412	615	1423	189	38	85	567	479	631	75	.263	.359
TOTALS																
Boog Powell	1B89	L	34	95	293	29	63	9	0	9	33	41	43	1	.215	.338
Duane Kuiper	2B128,1B5,DH2	L	26	135	506	47	133	13	6	0	37	30	42	10	.263	.312
Frank Duffy	SS132	R	29	133	392	38	83	11	2	2	30	29	50	10	.212	.265
Buddy Bell	3B158,1B2	R	24	159	604	75	170	26	2	7	60	44	49	3	.281	.366
Charlie Spikes	OF98,DH2	R	25	101	334	34	79	11	5	3	31	23	50	5	.237	.326
Rick Manning	OF136	L	21	138	552	73	161	24	7	6	43	41	75	16	.292	.393
George Hendrick	OF146,DH3	R	26	149	551	72	146	20	3	25	81	51	82	4	.265	.448
Alan Ashby	C86,1B2,3B1	L	24	89	247	26	59	5	1	4	32	27	49	0	.239	.316
Rico Carty	DH137,1B12,OF1	R	36	152	552	67	171	34	0	13	83	67	45	1	.310	.442
Larvell Blanks	SS56,2B46,DH3,3B2	R	26	104	328	45	92	8	7	5	41	30	31	1	.280	.393
John Lowenstein	OF61,DH11,1B9	L	29	93	229	33	47	8	2	2	14	25	35	11	.205	.284
Ray Fosse	C85,1B3,DH1	R	29	90	276	26	83	9	1	2	30	20	20	1	.301	.362
Tommy Smith	OF50,DH2	L	27	55	164	17	42	3	1	2	12	8	8	8	.256	.323
Ron Pruitt	OF26,3B6,C6,DH4,1B1	R	24	47	86	7	23	1	1	0	5	16	8	2	.267	.302
Doug Howard	1B32,DH4,OF2	R	28	39	90	7	19	4	0	0	13	3	13	1	.211	.256
Frank Robinson	DH18,1B2,OF1	R	40	36	67	5	15	0	0	3	10	11	12	0	.224	.358
Orlando Gonzalez	1B15,OF7,DH2	L	24	28	68	5	17	2	0	0	4	5	7	1	.250	.279
Joe Lis	1B17,DH1	R	29	20	51	4	16	1	0	2	7	8	10	1	.314	.451

Rick Cerone 22 R 2-16, Alfredo Griffin 18 B 1-4, Ed Crosby 27 L 1-2

NAME	G by Pos	B	AGE	G	AB	R	H	2B	3B	HR	RBI	BB	SO	SB	BA	SA
DETROIT 5th 74-87 .460 24 **RALPH HOUK**			28	161	5441	609	1401	207	38	101	566	450	730	107	.257	.365
TOTALS																
Jason Thompson	1B117	L	21	123	412	45	90	12	1	17	54	68	72	2	.218	.376
2 Pete Garcia	2B77	R	26	77	227	21	45	10	2	3	20	9	40	2	.198	.300
Tom Veryzer (NJ)	SS97	R	23	97	354	31	83	8	2	1	25	21	44	1	.234	.277
Aurelio Rodriguez (NJ)	3B128	R	28	128	480	40	115	13	2	8	50	19	61	0	.240	.325
Rusty Staub	OF126,DH36	L	32	161	589	73	176	28	3	15	96	83	49	3	.299	.433
Ron LeFlore	OF132,DH1	R	28	135	544	93	172	23	8	4	39	51	111	58	.316	.410
Alex Johnson	OF90,DH19	R	33	125	429	41	115	15	2	6	45	19	44	14	.268	.354
Bill Freehan	C61,DH3,1B2	R	34	71	237	22	64	10	1	5	27	12	27	0	.270	.384
Willie Horton (FJ)	DH105	R	33	114	401	40	105	17	0	14	56	49	63	0	.262	.409
Ben Oglivie	OF64,1B9,DH1	L	27	115	305	36	87	12	3	15	47	11	44	9	.285	.492
Dan Meyer	OF47,1B19,DH1	L	23	105	294	37	74	8	4	2	16	17	22	10	.252	.327
M.Stanley	OF38,1B17,3B11,SS3,2B2,DH2	R	33	84	214	34	55	17	1	4	29	14	19	2	.257	.402
Chuck Scrivener	2B43,SS37,3B5	R	28	80	222	28	49	7	1	2	16	19	34	1	.221	.288
Bruce Kimm	C61,DH2	R	25	63	152	13	40	8	0	1	6	15	20	4	.263	.336
John Wockenfuss	C59	R	27	60	144	18	32	7	2	3	10	17	14	0	.222	.361
Jerry Manuel	2B47,SS4,DH1	B	22	54	43	4	6	1	0	0	2	3	9	1	.140	.163
1 Gary Sutherland	2B42	R	31	42	117	10	24	5	2	0	6	7	12	0	.205	.282
Mark Wagner	SS39	R	22	39	115	9	30	3	0	1	12	8	13	0	.261	.330
Phil Mankowski	3B23	L	23	24	85	9	23	2	1	1	4	4	8	0	.271	.353

Marvin Lane 26 R 9-48, Milt May (BN) 25 L 7-25, Art James (FJ) 23

NAME	G by Pos	B	AGE	G	AB	R	H	2B	3B	HR	RBI	BB	SO	SB	BA	SA
MILWAUKEE 6th 66-95 .410 32 **ALEX GRAMMAS**			27	161	5396	570	1326	170	38	88	536	511	909	62	.246	.340
TOTALS																
George Scott	1B155	R	32	156	606	73	166	21	5	18	77	53	118	0	.274	.414
Tim Johnson	2B100,3B17,1B1,SS1	L	26	105	273	25	75	4	3	0	14	19	32	4	.275	.311
Robin Yount	SS161,OF1	R	20	161	638	59	161	19	3	2	54	38	69	16	.252	.301
Don Money	3B103,DH10,SS1	R	29	117	439	51	117	18	4	12	62	47	50	6	.267	.408
Sixto Lezcano	OF142,DH3	R	22	145	513	53	146	19	5	7	56	51	112	14	.285	.382
Gorman Thomas (SJ)	OF94,3B1,DH1	R	25	99	227	27	45	9	2	8	36	31	67	2	.198	.361
Von Joshua	OF105,DH1	L	28	107	423	44	113	13	5	5	28	18	58	8	.267	.357
Darrell Porter	C111,DH2	L	24	119	389	43	81	14	1	5	32	51	61	2	.208	.288
Hank Aaron	DH74,OF1	R	42	85	271	22	62	8	0	10	35	35	38	0	.229	.369
Charlie Moore	C49,OF28,DH2,3B1	R	23	87	241	33	46	7	4	3	16	43	45	1	.191	.290
Mike Hegan	DH40,OF20,1B10	L	33	80	218	30	54	4	3	5	31	25	54	0	.248	.362
Bill Sharp	OF56,DH7	L	28	78	180	16	44	4	0	0	11	10	15	1	.244	.267
2 Bernie Carbo	OF33,DH24	L	28	69	183	20	43	7	0	3	15	33	55	1	.235	.322
2 Jack Heidemann	3B40,2B24,DH1	R	26	69	146	11	32	1	0	2	10	7	24	1	.219	.267
2 Gary Sutherland	2B45,DH8,1B2	R	31	59	115	9	25	2	0	1	9	8	7	0	.217	.261
1 Pete Garcia	2B39	R	26	41	106	12	23	7	1	1	9	4	23	2	.217	.330
Danny Thomas	OF32	R	25	32	105	13	29	5	1	4	15	14	28	1	.276	.457
Jim Gantner	3B24,DH2	L	23	26	69	6	17	1	0	0	7	6	11	1	.246	.261
1 Bobby Darwin	OF21,DH1	R	33	25	73	6	18	3	1	1	5	6	16	0	.247	.356
Bob Hansen	DH14,1B1	L	28	24	61	4	10	4	0	0	1	3	9	0	.164	.180

Steve Bowling 24 R 7-42, Jimmy Rosario 32 B 7-37, Art Kusnyer 30 R 4-34, Kurt Bevacqua 29 R 1-7

WEST DIVISION

NAME	G by Pos	B	AGE	G	AB	R	H	2B	3B	HR	RBI	BB	SO	SB	BA	SA
KANSAS CITY 1st 90-72 .556 **WHITEY HERZOG**			27	162	5540	713	1490	259	57	65	656	484	650	218	.269	.371
TOTALS																
John Mayberry	1B160,DH2	L	27	161	594	76	138	22	2	13	95	82	73	3	.232	.342
Frank White	2B130,SS37	R	25	152	446	39	102	17	6	2	46	19	42	20	.229	.307
Freddie Patek	SS143,DH1	R	31	144	432	58	104	19	3	1	43	50	63	51	.241	.306
George Brett	3B157,SS4	L	23	159	645	94	215	34	14	7	67	49	36	21	.333	.462
Al Cowens	OF148,DH1	R	24	152	581	91	154	23	6	3	59	26	50	23	.265	.341
Amos Otis	OF152	R	29	153	592	93	165	40	2	18	86	55	100	26	.279	.444
Tom Poquette	OF98,DH2	L	24	104	344	43	104	18	10	2	34	29	31	6	.302	.430
Buck Martinez	C94	R	27	95	267	24	61	13	3	5	34	16	45	0	.228	.356
Hal McRae	DH117,OF31	R	30	149	527	75	175	34	5	8	73	64	43	22	.332	.461
Jim Wohlford	OF93,DH3,2B1	R	25	107	293	47	73	10	2	1	24	29	24	22	.249	.307
Bob Stinson	C79	B	30	79	209	26	55	7	1	2	25	25	29	1	.263	.335
Dave Nelson	2B46,DH22,1B3	R	32	78	153	24	36	4	2	1	17	14	26	15	.235	.307
Jamie Quirk	DH19,SS12,3B11,1B2	L	21	64	114	11	28	6	0	0	15	2	22	0	.246	.325
Cookie Rojas	2B40,DH9,3B6,1B1	R	37	63	132	11	32	6	0	0	16	8	6	5	.242	.288
1 Tony Solaita	DH14,1B5	L	31	68	68	4	16	4	0	0	9	8	17	0	.235	.294
Ruppert Jones	OF17,DH14	L	21	28	51	9	11	1	1	1	3	3	16	0	.216	.333
John Wathan (BH)	C23,1B3	R	26	27	42	5	12	1	0	0	5	2	5	2	.286	.310
Willie Wilson	OF6	R	20	12	6	0	1	0	0	0	0	0	1	2	.167	.167
1 Fran Healy	C6,DH1	R	29	8	24	2	3	0	0	0	1	4	10	2	.125	.125
2 Tommy Davis	DH3	R	37	3	19	1	5	0	0	0	1	0	0	0	.263	.263

NAME	G by Pos	B	AGE	G	AB	R	H	2B	3B	HR	RBI	BB	SO	SB	BA	SA
OAKLAND 2nd 87-74 .540 2.5 **CHUCK TANNER**			30	161	5353	686	1319	208	33	113	625	592	818	341	.246	.361
TOTALS																
Gene Tenace (KJ)	1B70,C65,DH2	R	29	128	417	64	104	19	1	22	66	81	91	5	.249	.458
Phil Garner	2B159	R	27	159	555	54	145	29	12	8	74	36	71	35	.261	.400
Bert Campaneris	SS149	R	34	149	536	67	137	14	1	1	52	63	80	54	.256	.291
Sal Bando	3B155,SS5,DH2	R	32	158	550	75	132	18	2	27	84	76	74	20	.240	.427
Claudell Washington	OF126,DH4	L	21	134	490	65	126	20	6	5	53	30	90	37	.257	.353
Billy North	OF144,DH8	B	28	154	590	91	163	20	5	2	31	73	95	75	.276	.337
Joe Rudi	OF126,1B2,DH2	R	29	130	500	54	135	32	3	13	94	41	71	6	.270	.424
Larry Haney	C87	R	33	98	177	12	40	7	0	0	10	13	26	0	.226	.237
Billy Williams	DH106,OF1	L	38	120	351	36	74	12	0	11	41	58	44	4	.211	.339
Don Baylor	OF76,1B69,DH23	R	27	157	595	85	147	25	1	15	68	58	72	52	.247	.368
Ken McMullen	3B35,1B26,DH23,OF5,2B1	R	34	98	186	20	41	6	2	5	23	22	33	1	.220	.355
Larry Lintz	DH19,2B5,OF3	B	26	68	1	21	0	0	0	0	0	0	0	31	.000	.000
Matt Alexander	OF23,DH19	B	29	61	30	16	1	0	0	0	0	3	4	20	.033	.033
Jeff Newman	C43	R	27	43	77	8	15	3	0	1	6	2	19	0	.195	.247
Tommy Sandt	SS29,2B9,3B2	R	25	41	67	6	14	1	0	0	3	2	9	0	.209	.224
2 Tim Hosley	C37	R	29	34	45	3	8	1	0	2	10	5	8	0	.164	.355
1 Cesar Tovar (BW)	OF20,DH4	R	35	29	45	1	8	1	0	0	3	6	4	3	.178	.178
2 Ron Fairly	1B15	L	37	15	11	0	3	0	0	1	1	3	1	0	.273	.545

2 Willie McCovey 38 L 5-24, Wayne Gross 24 L 4-18, Angel Mangual 29 R 2-12, Denny Walling 22 L 3-11, Gary Woods 21 R 1-8,
Jim Holt 32 L 2-7, 2 Nate Colbert 30 R 0-5, Dan Hopkins 24 L 0-0

Pitching

NAME	T	AGE	W	L	PCT	SV	G	GS	CG	IP	H	BB	SO	SHO	ERA
(CLEVELAND)		28	81	78	.509	46	159	159	30	1432	1361	533	928	17	3.47
Pat Dobson	R	34	16	12	.571	0	35	35	6	217	226	65	117	0	3.48
Dennis Eckersley	R	21	13	12	.520	1	36	30	9	199	155	78	200	3	3.44
Jim Bibby	R	31	13	7	.650	1	34	21	4	163	162	56	84	3	3.20
Jim Kern	R	27	10	7	.588	15	50	2	0	118	91	50	111	0	2.36
Jackie Brown	R	33	9	11	.450	0	32	27	5	180	193	55	104	2	4.25
Rick Waits	L	24	7	9	.438	0	26	22	4	124	143	54	65	2	3.99
Tom Buskey (XJ)	R	29	5	4	.556	1	39	0	0	94	88	34	32	0	3.64
Stan Thomas	R	26	4	4	.500	6	37	7	2	106	88	41	54	0	2.29
Don Hood	L	26	3	5	.375	1	33	6	0	78	89	41	32	0	4.85
Dave LaRoche	L	28	1	4	.200	21	61	0	0	96	57	49	104	0	2.25
Harry Parker	R	28	0	0	—	0	3	0	0	7	3	0	5	0	0.00
Eric Raich	R	25	0	0	—	0	1	0	0	3	7	0	1	0	15.00
1 Fritz Peterson	L	34	0	3	.000	0	9	9	0	47	59	10	19	0	5.55

NAME	T	AGE	W	L	PCT	SV	G	GS	CG	IP	H	BB	SO	SHO	ERA
(DETROIT)		27	74	87	.460	20	161	161	55	1431	1426	550	738	12	3.87
Mark Fidrych	R	21	19	9	.679	0	31	29	24	250	217	53	97	4	2.34
Dave Roberts	R	31	16	17	.485	0	36	36	18	252	254	63	79	4	4.00
John Hiller	L	33	12	8	.600	13	56	1	1	121	93	67	117	1	2.38
Vern Ruhle	R	25	9	12	.429	0	32	32	5	200	227	59	88	1	3.92
Ray Bare	R	27	7	8	.467	0	30	21	3	134	157	51	59	2	4.63
Dave Lemanczyk	R	25	4	6	.400	0	20	10	1	81	86	34	51	0	5.11
Steve Grilli	R	27	3	1	.750	3	36	0	0	66	63	41	36	0	4.64
1 Joe Coleman	R	29	2	5	.286	0	12	12	1	67	80	34	38	0	4.84
Ed Glynn	L	23	1	3	.250	0	5	4	1	24	22	20	17	0	6.00
Jim Crawford	L	25	1	8	.111	2	32	5	1	109	115	43	68	0	4.54
Bill Laxton	L	28	0	3	.000	2	26	3	0	95	77	51	74	0	4.07
Frank MacCormack	R	21	0	5	.000	0	9	8	0	33	33	34	14	0	5.73

NAME	T	AGE	W	L	PCT	SV	G	GS	CG	IP	H	BB	SO	SHO	ERA
(MILWAUKEE)		27	66	95	.410	27	161	161	45	1435	1406	567	677	10	3.64
Bill Travers	L	23	15	16	.484	0	34	34	15	240	211	95	120	3	2.81
Jim Slaton	R	26	14	15	.483	0	38	38	12	293	287	94	138	2	3.44
Jerry Augustine	L	23	9	12	.429	0	39	24	5	172	167	56	59	3	3.30
Jim Colborn	R	30	9	15	.375	0	32	32	7	226	232	54	101	0	3.72
2 Danny Frisella (DD)	R	30	5	2	.714	9	32	0	0	49	30	34	43	0	2.76
Eduardo Rodriguez	R	24	5	13	.278	8	45	12	3	136	124	65	77	0	3.64
Bill Castro	R	22	4	6	.400	8	39	0	0	70	70	19	23	0	3.47
2 Ray Sadecki	L	35	2	0	1.000	1	36	0	0	37	38	20	27	0	4.38
Gary Beare	R	23	2	3	.400	0	6	5	2	41	43	15	32	0	3.29
Pete Broberg	R	26	1	7	.125	0	20	11	1	92	99	72	28	0	4.99
Rick Austin	R	29	0	0	—	0	5	0	0	5	10	3	5	0	5.40
Tom Hausman	R	23	0	0	—	0	3	0	0	3	3	1	1	0	6.00
1 Tom Murphy	R	30	0	1	.000	1	15	0	0	18	25	9	7	0	7.50
Billy Champion	R	28	0	1	.000	0	10	3	0	24	35	13	8	0	7.13
Moose Haas	R	20	0	1	.000	0	4	2	0	16	12	12	9	0	3.94
Kevin Kobel	L	22	0	1	.000	0	4	0	0	4	6	3	1	0	11.25
Ed Sprague (KJ)	R	30	0	2	.000	2	8	0	0	8	14	3	0	0	6.75

NAME	T	AGE	W	L	PCT	SV	G	GS	CG	IP	H	BB	SO	SHO	ERA
(KANSAS CITY)		28	90	72	.556	35	162	162	41	1472	1356	493	735	12	3.21
Dennis Leonard	R	25	17	10	.630	0	35	34	16	259	247	70	150	2	3.51
Al Fitzmorris	R	30	15	11	.577	0	35	33	8	220	227	56	80	2	3.07
Doug Bird	R	26	12	10	.545	2	39	27	2	198	191	31	107	1	3.36
Paul Splittorff (RJ)	L	29	11	8	.579	0	26	23	5	159	169	59	59	1	3.96
Mark Littell	R	23	8	4	.667	16	60	1	0	104	68	60	92	0	2.08
Marty Pattin	R	33	8	14	.364	5	44	15	4	141	114	38	65	1	2.49
Steve Mingori	L	32	5	5	.500	10	55	0	0	85	73	25	38	0	2.33
2 Andy Hassler	L	24	5	6	.455	0	19	14	4	100	89	39	45	1	2.88
Larry Gura (JJ)	L	28	4	0	1.000	1	20	2	1	63	47	20	22	1	2.29
Steve Busby (SJ)	R	26	3	3	.500	0	13	13	1	72	58	49	29	0	4.38
Tom Bruno	R	23	1	0	1.000	0	12	0	0	17	20	9	11	0	6.88
2 Tom Hall	L	28	1	1	.500	1	31	0	0	30	28	18	25	0	4.50
Bob McClure	L	24	0	0	—	0	4	0	0	4	2	1	2	0	9.00
Jerry Cram	R	28	0	0	—	0	4	0	0	4	6	2	2	0	6.75
Roger Nelson	R	32	0	0	—	0	9	0	0	9	8	4	5	0	2.00
1 Ray Sadecki	L	35	0	0	—	0	4	0	0	4	3	2	1	0	2.25
2 Ken Sanders	R	34	0	0	—	0	3	0	0	5	7	3	1	0	3.60

NAME	T	AGE	W	L	PCT	SV	G	GS	CG	IP	H	BB	SO	SHO	ERA
(OAKLAND)		28	87	74	.540	29	161	161	39	1459	1412	415	711	15	3.26
Vida Blue	L	26	18	13	.581	0	37	37	20	298	268	63	166	6	2.35
Mike Torrez	R	29	16	12	.571	0	39	39	13	266	231	87	115	4	2.50
Rollie Fingers	R	29	13	11	.542	20	70	0	0	135	118	40	113	0	2.47
Paul Mitchell	R	25	9	7	.563	0	26	26	4	142	169	30	67	1	4.25
Stan Bahnsen	R	31	8	7	.533	0	35	14	1	143	124	43	82	1	3.34
Jim Todd	R	28	7	8	.467	4	49	0	0	83	87	34	22	0	3.80
Paul Lindblad	L	34	6	5	.545	5	65	0	0	115	111	24	37	0	3.05
Dick Bosman	R	32	4	2	.667	0	27	15	0	112	118	19	34	0	4.10
Mike Norris	R	21	4	5	.444	0	24	19	1	96	91	56	44	1	4.78
Glenn Abbott	R	25	2	2	.333	0	19	10	0	62	87	16	27	0	5.52
Chris Batton	R	21	0	0	—	0	4	0	0	6	3	3	1	0	9.00
Craig Mitchell	R	22	0	0	—	0	3	0	0	3	4	4	0	0	3.00

WEST DIVISION

Batting

NAME	G by Pos	B	AGE	G	AB	R	H	2B	3B	HR	RBI	BB	SO	SB	BA	SA
MINNESOTA 3rd 85-77 .525 5							**GENE MAUCH**									
TOTALS			26	162	5574	743	1526	222	51	81	691	550	714	146	.274	.375
Rod Carew	1B152,2B7	L	30	156	605	97	200	29	12	9	90	67	52	49	.331	.463
Bob Randall	2B153	R	28	153	475	55	127	19	4	1	28	28	38	3	.267	.328
2 Roy Smalley	SS103	B	23	103	384	46	104	16	3	2	36	47	79	0	.271	.344
3 Mike Cubbage	3B99,2B2,DH2	L	25	104	342	40	89	19	5	3	49	42	37	1	.260	.371
Dan Ford	OF139,DH3	R	24	145	514	87	137	24	7	20	86	36	118	17	.267	.457
Lyman Bostock	OF124	L	25	128	474	75	153	19	5	4	60	33	37	12	.323	.430
Larry Hisle	OF	R	29	155	581	81	158	19	5	14	96	56	93	31	.272	.394
Butch Wynegar	C137,DH15	B	20	149	534	58	139	21	2	10	69	79	63	0	.260	.363
Craig Kusick	DH79,1B23	R	27	109	266	33	69	13	0	11	36	35	44	5	.259	.432
Steve Braun	DH71,OF32,3B16	L	28	122	417	73	120	12	3	3	61	67	43	12	.288	.353
J. Terrell	2B31,3B26,SS16,DH12,OF6	R	29	89	171	29	42	3	1	0	8	9	15	11	.246	.275
Steve Brye	OF78,DH3	R	27	87	258	33	68	11	0	2	23	13	31	1	.264	.329
Tony Oliva	DH32	L	37	67	123	3	26	3	0	1	16	2	13	0	.211	.260
Dave McKay	3B41,SS2,DH1	R	26	45	138	4	28	2	0	0	8	9	27	1	.203	.217
Luis Gomez	SS24,2B8,3B4,OF1,DH1	R	24	38	57	5	11	1	0	0	3	3	3	1	.193	.211
1 Danny Thompson	SS34	R	29	34	124	9	29	4	0	0	6	3	8	1	.234	.266
Glenn Borgmann	C24	R	26	24	65	10	16	3	0	1	6	4	19	7	1	.246	.338
1 Phil Roof	C12,DH1	R	35	18	46	1	10	3	0	0	4	2	6	0	.217	.283
Eric Soderholm (KJ) 27																

NAME		T	AGE	W	L	PCT	SV	G	GS	CG	IP	H	BB	SO	SHO	ERA
			27	85	77	.525	23	162	162	29	1459	1421	610	762	11	3.69
Bill Campbell		R	27	17	5	.773	20	78	0	0	168	145	62	115	0	3.00
Dave Goltz		R	27	14	14	.500	0	36	35	13	249	239	91	133	4	3.36
2 Bill Singer		R	32	9	9	.500	0	26	26	5	172	177	69	63	3	3.77
Jim Hughes		R	24	9	14	.391	0	37	26	3	177	190	73	67	0	4.98
Tom Burgmeier		L	32	8	1	.889	1	57	0	0	115	95	29	45	0	2.50
Pete Redfern		R	21	8	8	.500	0	23	17	1	118	105	63	74	1	3.51
Steve Luebber		R	26	4	5	.444	2	38	12	1	119	109	62	45	1	4.01
1 Bert Blyleven		R	25	4	5	.444	0	12	12	4	95	101	35	75	0	3.13
Eddie Bane		L	24	4	7	.364	0	17	15	1	79	92	39	24	0	5.13
Vic Albury (FJ)		L	29	3	1	.750	0	23	0	0	50	51	24	23	0	3.60
Tom Johnson		R	25	3	1	.750	0	18	1	0	48	44	8	37	0	2.63
Joe Decker		R	29	2	7	.222	1	13	12	0	58	60	51	35	0	5.28
Mike Pazik		L	26	0	0	—	0	5	0	0	9	13	4	6	0	7.00

NAME	G by Pos	B	AGE	G	AB	R	H	2B	3B	HR	RBI	BB	SO	SB	BA	SA
CALIFORNIA 4th(tie) 76-86 .469 14							**DICK WILLIAMS 39-57 .406**			**NORM SHERRY 37-29 .561**					
TOTALS			27	162	5385	550	1265	210	23	63	511	534	812	126	.235	.318
2 Tony Solaita	1B54,DH7	L	29	63	215	25	58	9	0	9	33	34	44	1	.270	.437
Jerry Remy	2B133,DH5	L	23	143	502	64	132	14	3	0	28	38	43	35	.263	.301
Dave Chalk	SS103,3B49	R	25	142	438	39	95	14	1	0	33	49	62	0	.217	.253
Ron Jackson	3B114,2B7,DH6,OF4	R	23	127	410	44	93	18	3	8	40	30	58	5	.227	.344
Bobby Bonds (HJ)	OF98,DH1	R	30	99	378	48	100	13	2	10	54	41	90	30	.265	.386
Rusty Torres	OF105,DH6,3B1	B	27	120	264	37	54	16	3	6	27	36	39	4	.205	.356
Bruce Bochte	OF86,1B59,DH1	L	25	146	466	53	120	17	1	2	49	64	53	4	.258	.311
Andy Etchebarren	C102	R	33	103	247	15	56	9	1	3	26	15	18	1	.227	.271
1 Tommy Davis	DH54,1B1	R	37	72	219	16	58	4	0	3	26	15	18	1	.265	.329
Bill Melton	DH51,1B30,3B21	R	30	118	341	31	71	17	3	6	42	44	53	2	.208	.328
Dave Collins	OF71,DH22	B	23	99	365	45	96	12	1	4	28	40	55	32	.263	.334
Lee Stanton	OF79,DH4	R	30	93	231	12	44	13	1	2	25	24	71	2	.190	.281
Mike Guerrero	2B41,SS41,DH7	R	26	83	268	24	76	12	0	1	18	7	12	0	.284	.340
Bobby Jones	OF62,DH2	L	26	78	166	22	35	6	0	6	17	14	30	3	.211	.355
Dan Briggs	1B44,OF40,DH1	L	23	77	248	19	53	13	2	1	14	13	47	0	.214	.294
Terry Humphrey	C71	R	26	71	196	17	48	10	1	1	19	13	30	1	.245	.311
1 Joe Lahoud	OF26,DH3	L	29	42	96	9	17	4	0	4	18	16	0	1	.177	.219
Orlando Ramirez	SS30	R	24	37	70	3	14	1	0	0	2	6	11	3	.200	.214
Mike Easler 25 L 13-54, Adrian Garrett 33 L 6-48, 1 Ed Herrmann 29 L 8-46, Orlando Alvarez 23 R 7-42, Mike Miley 23 B 7-38,																
Carlos Lopez 27 R 0-10, Paul Dade 24 R 1-9, Billy Smith 22 B 3-8, 2 Tim Nordbrook 26 R 0-8, Ike Hampton 24 B 0-2																

NAME		T	AGE	W	L	PCT	SV	G	GS	CG	IP	H	BB	SO	SHO	ERA
			26	76	86	.469	17	162	162	64	1477	1323	553	992	15	3.36
Frank Tanana		L	22	19	10	.655	0	34	34	23	288	212	73	261	2	2.44
Nolan Ryan		R	29	17	18	.486	0	39	39	21	284	193	183	327	7	3.36
Gary Ross		R	28	8	16	.333	0	34	31	7	225	224	58	100	2	3.00
Paul Hartzell		R	22	7	4	.636	2	37	15	7	166	166	43	51	2	2.77
Dick Drago		R	31	7	8	.467	6	43	0	0	79	80	31	43	0	4.44
Sid Monge		L	25	5	6	.462	2	32	13	2	118	108	49	53	0	3.36
Don Kirkwood		R	26	6	12	.333	0	28	26	4	158	167	57	78	0	4.61
Mickey Scott (ZJ)		L	28	3	0	1.000	1	33	0	0	39	47	12	10	0	3.26
Jim Brewer (EJ)		L	38	3	1	.750	2	13	0	0	20	26	6	16	0	2.70
1 Steve Dunning		R	27	0	0	—	0	4	0	0	9	6	4	7	0	7.50
Gary Wheelock		R	24	0	0	—	0	2	0	0	2	6	1	2	0	27.00
John Verhoeven		R	23	0	2	.000	1	21	0	0	37	35	14	23	0	3.41
Mike Overy		R	25	0	0	—	0	7	3	0	8	8	4	1	0	6.43
1 Andy Hassler		L	24	0	0	—	0	14	4	0	47	50	17	16	0	5.17

NAME	G by Pos	B	AGE	G	AB	R	H	2B	3B	HR	RBI	BB	SO	SB	BA	SA
TEXAS 4th(tie) 76-86 .469 14							**FRANK LUCCHESI**									
TOTALS			26	162	5555	616	1390	213	26	80	574	568	809	87	.250	.341
Mike Hargrove	1B141,DH5	L	26	151	541	80	155	30	1	7	58	97	64	2	.287	.384
Lenny Randle	2B113,OF30,3B2,DH1	B	27	142	539	53	121	11	6	1	51	46	63	30	.224	.273
Toby Harrah	SS146,3B5,DH1	R	27	155	584	64	152	21	1	15	67	91	59	6	.260	.377
Roy Howell	3B130,DH8	L	22	140	491	55	124	28	2	8	37	51	94	2	.253	.367
Jeff Burroughs	OF155,DH3	R	25	158	604	71	143	22	2	18	86	69	93	0	.237	.369
Juan Beniquez	OF141,2B1	R	26	145	478	49	122	14	4	0	33	39	56	17	.255	.301
Gene Clines	OF103,DH10	R	29	116	446	52	123	12	3	0	38	16	59	11	.276	.316
Jim Sundberg	C140	R	25	140	448	33	102	24	2	3	34	37	61	0	.228	.310
Tommy Grieve	DH96,OF52	R	28	149	546	57	139	23	4	20	81	55	119	4	.255	.418
Dave Moates	OF66,DH7	L	28	85	137	21	33	7	1	0	13	11	18	6	.241	.307
2 Danny Thompson	3B39,2B14,SS10,DH1	R	29	64	196	12	42	3	1	1	13	13	19	2	.214	.245
Jim Fregosi	1B26,DH18,3B5	R	34	58	133	17	31	7	0	2	12	23	33	2	.233	.331
1 Roy Smalley	2B38,SS5	B	23	41	129	15	29	2	0	1	8	29	27	2	.225	.264
2 Joe Lahoud	DH22,OF5	L	29	38	89	10	20	3	1	1	5	10	16	1	.225	.315
Bill Fahey	C38	L	26	32	80	9	20	2	1	0	7	3	6	0	.250	.313
1 Mike Cubbage 25 L 7-32, Johnny Ellis (BL) 27 R 13-31, Ken Pape 24 R 5-23, Doug Ault 26 R 6-20, Greg Pryor 26 R 3-8																

NAME		T	AGE	W	L	PCT	SV	G	GS	CG	IP	H	BB	SO	SHO	ERA
			29	76	86	.469	15	162	162	63	1472	1464	461	773	15	3.45
Gaylord Perry		R	37	15	14	.517	0	32	32	21	250	232	52	143	2	3.24
Nelson Briles		R	32	11	9	.550	1	32	31	7	210	224	47	98	1	3.11
Jim Umbarger		L	23	10	12	.455	0	30	30	10	197	208	54	105	3	3.15
2 Bert Blyleven		R	25	9	11	.450	0	24	24	14	202	182	46	144	6	2.76
Steve Foucault		R	26	8	8	.500	5	46	0	0	76	68	25	41	0	3.32
Steve Hargan		R	33	8	8	.500	1	35	8	2	124	127	38	63	1	3.32
1 Bill Singer		R	32	4	1	.800	0	10	10	2	65	56	27	34	1	3.46
Mike Bacsik		L	24	3	2	.600	0	23	0	0	55	66	26	21	0	4.25
Jeff Terpko		R	25	3	3	.500	0	53	0	0	53	42	29	24	0	2.38
Steve Barr		L	24	2	6	.250	0	20	10	3	68	70	44	27	0	5.56
2 Fritz Peterson (SJ)		L	34	1	0	1.000	0	3	2	0	15	21	7	4	0	3.60
Len Barker		R	20	1	0	1.000	0	13	1	0	15	7	6	7	1	2.40
Tommy Boggs		R	20	1	7	.125	0	13	13	3	90	87	34	36	0	3.50
Stan Perzanowski		R	22	1	0	—	0	12	0	0	20	4	6	0	0	4.50
Craig Skok		L	28	0	1	.000	0	5	0	0	13	3	5	1	0	12.60
Joe Hoerner		L	39	0	0	—	0	41	0	0	35	41	19	15	0	5.14

NAME	G by Pos	B	AGE	G	AB	R	H	2B	3B	HR	RBI	BB	SO	SB	BA	SA
CHICAGO 6th 64-97 .398 25.5							**PAUL RICHARDS**									
TOTALS			26	161	5532	586	1410	209	46	73	538	471	739	120	.255	.349
Jim Spencer	1B143,DH2	L	28	150	518	53	131	13	2	14	70	49	52	6	.253	.367
Jack Brohamer	2B117,3B1	L	26	119	354	33	89	12	2	7	40	44	28	1	.251	.356
Bucky Dent	SS158	R	24	158	562	44	138	18	4	2	52	43	45	3	.246	.302
Kevin Bell	3B67,DH1	R	20	68	230	24	57	7	6	5	20	18	56	2	.248	.396
Ralph Garr	OF125,DH6	L	30	136	527	63	158	22	6	4	36	17	41	14	.300	.387
Chet Lemon	OF131	R	21	132	451	46	111	15	5	4	38	28	65	13	.246	.328
Jorge Orta	OF77,3B49,DH31	L	25	158	636	74	174	29	8	14	72	38	77	24	.274	.410
Brian Downing	C93,DH11	R	25	104	317	38	81	14	0	3	30	40	55	1	.256	.328
Pat Kelly	DH63,OF26	L	31	107	311	42	79	20	3	5	34	45	45	15	.254	.386
B. Stein	2B58,3B58,OF1,SS1,3B1	R	29	117	392	32	105	15	2	4	36	22	67	4	.268	.347
Lamar Johnson	DH35,1B34,OF1	R	25	82	222	29	71	11	1	4	33	19	37	2	.320	.432
Jim Essian	C77,1B2,3B1	R	25	78	199	20	49	7	0	0	21	23	28	2	.246	.281
Alan Bannister	OF43,SS14,2B4,DH4,3B1	R	24	73	145	19	36	6	0	0	8	14	21	12	.248	.317
Buddy Bradford	OF48,DH3	R	31	55	160	20	35	5	2	6	14	17	36	6	.219	.350
Jerry Hairston	OF40	R	24	44	119	20	27	2	0	1	10	24	19	1	.227	.277
2 Rich Coggins	OF26,DH1	L	25	32	96	4	15	2	0	0	5	6	15	3	.156	.177
Wayne Nordhagen	OF10,DH6,C5	R	27	22	53	6	10	2	0	0	5	4	12	0	.189	.226
1 Carlos May	DH10,OF9	L	28	20	63	7	11	0	2	0	5	4	12	0	.175	.206
1 Pete Varney 27 R 10-41, Sam Ewing 27 L 9-41, Cleon Jones 33 R 8-40, Hugh Yancy 26 R 1-10, 2 Phil Roof 35 R 1-9,																
Nyls Nyman 22 L 2-15, Minnie Minoso 53 R 1-8, George Enright 22 R 0-1																

NAME		T	AGE	W	L	PCT	SV	G	GS	CG	IP	H	BB	SO	SHO	ERA
			26	64	97	.398	22	161	161	54	1448	1460	600	802	10	4.25
2 Ken Brett		L	27	10	12	.455	1	27	26	16	201	171	76	91	1	3.31
Bart Johnson		R	26	9	16	.360	1	32	32	8	211	231	62	91	3	4.73
Goose Gossage		R	24	9	17	.346	1	31	29	15	224	214	90	135	0	3.94
Pete Vuckovich		R	23	7	4	.636	0	33	7	1	110	122	60	62	0	4.66
Dave Hamilton		L	28	6	6	.500	10	45	1	0	90	81	45	62	0	3.60
Francisco Barrios		R	23	5	9	.357	3	35	14	6	142	136	66	81	0	4.31
Wilbur Wood (BK)		L	34	4	3	.571	0	7	5	6	56	51	11	31	1	2.25
Clay Carroll (BG)		R	35	4	4	.500	6	29	0	0	77	67	24	38	0	2.57
Chris Knapp		R	22	3	1	.750	0	11	6	1	52	54	32	41	0	4.85
Blue Moon Odom		R	31	2	2	.500	0	4	4	0	28	31	20	18	0	5.79
Jesse Jefferson		R	27	2	5	.286	0	19	9	0	62	86	42	30	0	8.56
Terry Forster		L	24	2	12	.143	1	29	16	1	111	126	41	70	0	4.38
Ken Kravec		L	24	1	5	.167	0	11	8	1	60	49	32	38	0	4.86
Jim Otten		R	25	0	0	—	0	4	3	0	20	22	9	4	0	4.50
Jack Kucek		R	23	0	0	—	0	5	0	0	10	13	9	6	0	9.00
Larry Monroe		R	20	0	1	.000	0	22	23	13	9	6	8	4	0	4.09

AMERICAN LEAGUE CHAMPIONSHIP — NEW YORK (EAST) 3 KANSAS CITY (WEST) 2

LINE SCORES

TEAM	1	2	3	4	5	6	7	8	9	10	11	12	R	H	E
Game 1 October 9 at Kansas City															
NY	2	0	0	0	0	0	0	0	2				4	12	0
KC	0	0	0	0	0	0	0	1	0				1	5	2
Hunter						Gura, Littell (9)									
Game 2 October 10 at Kansas City															
NY	0	1	2	0	0	0	0	0	0				3	12	5
KC	0	0	2	0	0	2	0	3	x				7	9	0
Figueroa, Tidrow (6)					Leonard, Splittorff (3), Mingori (9)										
Game 3 October 12 at New York															
KC	3	0	0	0	0	0	0	0	0				3	6	0
NY	0	0	2	0	3	0	0	0	x				5	9	0
Hassler, Pattin (6), Hall (6), Ellis, Lyle (9) Mingori, Littell (6)															
Game 4 October 13 at New York															
KC	0	3	0	2	0	1	0	1	0				7	9	1
NY	0	2	0	0	0	2	1	0	x				4	11	0
Gura, Bird (3), Mingori (7)					Hunter, Tidrow (4), Jackson (7)										
Game 5 October 14 at New York															
KC	2	1	0	0	0	0	0	3	0				6	11	1
NY	2	0	2	0	0	0	0	0	1				7	11	1
Leonard, Splittorff (1), Pattin (4), Hassler (5), Littell (7)					Figueroa, Jackson (8), Tidrow (9)										

COMPOSITE BATTING

NAME	POS	G	AB	R	H	2B	3B	HR	RBI	BA
New York Totals	C	5	174	23	55	13	2	4	21	.316
Munson	C	5	23	3	10	2	0	0	2	.435
Rivers	CF	5	23	5	8	1	0	0	0	.348
Chambliss	1B	5	21	5	11	1	1	2	8	.524
White	LF	5	17	4	5	3	0	0	3	.294
Nettles	3B	5	17	4	4	2	0	1	1	.235
Randolph	2B	5	17	2	2	0	1	0	0	.118
Stanley	SS	5	15	1	5	2	0	0	3	.333
Piniella	DH-PH	4	11	3	3	0	0	0	2	.273
May	DH-PH	5	10	1	2	0	0	0	0	.200
Maddox	RF	3	9	0	2	1	0	0	2	.222
Gamble	RF-PH	3	4	1	1	0	0	0	0	.250
Alomar PH-PR 0-1, Hendricks PH 1-1, Velez PH 0-0, Mason SS 0-0, Guidry PR 0-0										
Kansas City Totals		5	162	24	40	6	4	2	24	.247
Cowens	CF-RF	5	21	3	4	0	1	0	0	.190
Brett	3B	5	18	4	8	1	1	1	5	.444
Patek	SS	5	18	2	7	1	1	0	4	.389
Mayberry	1B	5	18	4	4	0	0	1	3	.222
McRae	DH-RF	5	17	2	2	0	0	0	1	.118
Poquette	RF-LF	4	16	3	4	2	0	0	4	.188
Martinez	C	5	15	0	5	0	0	0	0	.333
Wohlford	LF-PH	5	11	1	2	0	0	0	0	.182
Rojas	2B-PH	5	6	1	2	0	0	0	1	.333
White	2B-PH	5	8	1	1	0	0	0	0	.125
Quirk	DH-PH	4	7	1	1	0	0	0	1	.143
Nelson PH-DH 0-2, Otis CF 0-1, Stinson PH-C 0-1, Wathan C 0-0										

COMPOSITE PITCHING

NAME	G	IP	H	BB	SO	W	L	SV	ERA
New York Totals	5	44	40	11	18	3	2	1	4.70
Figueroa	2	12.1	14	2	5	0	1	0	5.84
Hunter	2	12	10	1	4	1	1	0	4.50
Ellis	1	8	6	2	5	1	0	0	3.38
Tidrow	3	7.1	6	4	1	1	0	0	3.68
Jackson	2	3.1	4	1	3	0	0	0	8.10
Lyle	1	1	0	1	0	0	0	0	0.00
Kansas City Totals	5	43	55	16	15	2	3	1	4.40
Gura	2	10.2	18	1	4	0	1	0	4.22
Splittorff	2	9.1	7	2	3	0	0	0	1.93
Hassler	2	7.1	8	6	4	0	0	0	6.14
Bird	1	4.2	4	0	1	0	0	0	1.93
Littell	3	4.2	4	2	0	1	0	0	1.93
Mingori	4	4	7	0	1	0	0	0	0.00
Leonard	2	2.1	4	2	1	0	1	0	19.29
Pattin	2	.1	0	1	0	0	0	0	27.00
Hall	1	.1	3	2	1	0	0	0	0.00

NATIONAL LEAGUE CHAMPIONSHIP — CINCINNATI (WEST) 3 PHILADELPHIA (EAST) 0

LINE SCORES

TEAM	1	2	3	4	5	6	7	8	9	10	11	12	R	H	E

Game 1 October 9 at Philadelphia

CIN 0 0 1 0 0 2 0 3 0 6 10 0
PHI 1 0 0 0 0 0 0 2 0 3 6 1
Gullett, Eastwick (9) Carlton, McGraw (8)

Game 2 October 10 at Philadelphia

CIN 0 0 0 0 0 4 2 0 0 6 6 0
PHI 0 1 0 0 1 0 0 0 0 2 10 1
Zachry, Borbon(6) Lonborg, Garber (6), McGraw (7), Reed (7)

Game 3 October 12 at Cincinnati

PHI 0 0 0 1 0 0 2 2 1 6 11 0
CIN 0 0 0 0 0 0 4 0 3 7 9 2
Kaat,Reed (7), Garber (9), Nolan, Sarmiento (6),
Underwood (9) Borbon (7), Eastwick (8)

COMPOSITE BATTING

NAME	POS	G	AB	R	H	2B	3B	HR	RBI	BA
Cincinnati										
Totals		3	99	19	25	5	3	3	17	.253
Rose	3B	3	14	3	6	2	1	0	2	.429
Griffey	RF	3	13	2	5	0	1	0	2	.385
Bench	C	3	12	3	4	1	0	1	1	.333
Foster	LF	3	12	2	2	0	0	2	4	.167
Geronimo	CF	3	11	0	2	0	1	0	2	.182
Concepcion	SS	3	10	4	2	1	0	0	0	.200
Perez	1B	3	10	1	2	0	0	0	0	.200
Morgan	2B	3	7	2	0	0	0	0	0	.000
Gullett	P	1	1	1	0	0	0	3	1	.500

Borbon P 0-2, Driessen PH 0-1, Lum PH 0-1, Sarmiento P 0-1,
Armbrister PH 0-0, Eastwick P 0-0, Zachry P 0-1, Flynn 2B 0-0, Nolan P 0-0

NAME	POS	G	AB	R	H	2B	3B	HR	RBI	BA
Philadelphia										
Totals		3	100	11	27	8	1	1	11	.270
Cash	2B	3	13	1	4	1	0	0	1	.308
Schmidt	3B	3	13	1	4	2	0	0	2	.308
Maddox	CF	3	13	2	3	1	0	0	1	.231
Luzinski	LF	3	11	2	3	2	0	1	3	.273
Johnstone	RF-PH	3	9	1	7	1	1	0	2	.778
Allen	1B	3	9	1	2	0	0	0	0	.222
Bowa	SS	3	8	1	1	0	0	0	1	.125
Boone	C	3	7	0	2	1	0	0	0	.286
McCarver	C-PH	2	4	0	0	0	0	0	0	.000

Kaat P 1-2, Brown RF 0-2, Carlton P 0-2, Tolan LF-1B-PH 0-2,
Hutton PH 0-1, Lonborg P 0-1, Martin LF-PH 0-1, Oates C 0-1,
Reed P 0-1, Garber P 0-0, Harmon PR 0-0, McGraw P 0-0, Underwood 0-0

COMPOSITE PITCHING

NAME	G	IP	H	BB	SO	W	L	SV	ERA
Cincinnati									
Totals		3	27	27	12	9	3	0	1	3.33
Gullett	1	8	2	3	4	1	0	0	1.13
Nolan	1	5.2	6	2	1	0	0	0	1.59
Zachry	1	5	6	3	3	1	0	0	3.60
Borbon	2	4.1	4	1	0	0	0	1	0.00
Eastwick	2	3	7	2	1	1	0	0	12.00
Sarmiento	1	1	2	1	0	0	0	0	18.00

NAME	G	IP	H	BB	SO	W	L	SV	ERA
Philadelphia									
Totals		3	26.1	25	15	16	0	3	0	5.13
Carlton	1	7	8	5	6	0	1	0	5.14
Kaat	1	6	2	2	1	0	0	0	3.00
Lonborg	1	5.1	2	2	2	0	1	0	1.69
Reed	2	4.2	6	2	2	0	0	0	7.71
McGraw	2	2.1	4	1	5	0	0	0	11.57
Garber	1	.2	2	1	0	0	1	0	13.50
Underwood	1	.1	1	2	0	0	0	0	0.00

EAST DIVISION

NAME	G by Pos	B	AGE	G	AB	R	H	2B	3B	HR	RBI	BB	SO	SB	BA	SA
PHILADELPHIA 1st 101-61 .623	DANNY OZARK															
TOTALS			29	162	5528	770	1505	259	45	110	708	542	793	127	.272	.395
Dick Allen (SJ)	1B85	R	34	85	298	52	80	16	1	15	49	37	63	11	.268	.480
Dave Cash	2B158	R	28	160	666	92	189	14	12	1	56	54	13	10	.284	.345
Larry Bowa	SS156	B	30	156	624	71	155	15	9	0	49	32	31	30	.248	.301
Mike Schmidt	3B160	R	26	160	584	112	153	31	4	38	107	100	149	14	.262	.524
Jay Johnstone	OF122,1B6	L	30	129	440	62	140	38	4	5	53	31	39	5	.318	.457
Garry Maddox	OF144	R	26	146	531	75	175	37	6	6	68	42	59	29	.330	.456
Greg Luzinski	OF144	R	25	149	533	74	162	28	1	21	95	50	107	1	.304	.478
Bob Boone	C108,1B4	R	28	121	361	40	98	18	2	4	54	45	44	2	.271	.366
Jerry Martin	OF110,1B1	R	27	130	121	30	30	7	0	2	15	7	28	3	.248	.355
Bobby Tolan	1B50,OF35	L	30	110	272	32	71	7	0	5	35	7	39	10	.261	.342
Tommy Hutton	1B72,OF1	L	30	95	124	15	25	5	1	1	13	27	11	1	.202	.282
Ollie Brown	OF75	R	32	92	209	30	53	10	1	5	30	33	33	2	.254	.383
Tim McCarver	C41,1B2	L	34	90	155	26	43	11	2	3	29	35	14	2	.277	.432
Terry Harmon	SS19,2B13,3B5	R	32	42	61	12	18	4	1	0	6	3	10	3	.295	.393
Johnny Oates (BC)	C33	L	30	37	99	10	25	2	0	0	8	8	12	0	.253	.273
Tony Taylor (EJ)	2B2,3B1	R	40	26	23	2	6	1	0	0	3	1	7	0	.261	.304
Rick Bosetti	OF6	R	22	13	18	6	5	1	0	0	1	3	3	.278	.333

Fred Andrews 24 R 4-6, Tim Blackwell 23 B 2-8, John Vukovich 28 R 1-8, Bill Nahorodny 22 R 1-5

NAME	T	AGE	W	L	PCT	SV	G	GS	CG	IP	H	BB	SO	SHO	ERA
		29	101	61	.623	44	162	162	34	1459	1377	397	918	9	3.08
Steve Carlton	L	31	20	7	.741	0	35	35	13	253	224	72	195	2	3.13
Jim Lonborg	R	34	18	10	.643	1	33	32	8	222	210	50	118	1	3.08
Larry Christenson	R	22	13	8	.619	0	32	29	2	169	199	42	54	0	3.67
Jim Kaat	R	37	12	14	.462	0	38	35	7	228	241	32	83	1	3.47
Tom Underwood	R	22	10	5	.667	2	33	25	3	156	154	63	94	0	3.52
Gene Garber	R	28	9	3	.750	11	59	0	0	93	78	30	92	0	2.81
Ron Reed	R	33	8	7	.533	14	59	4	1	128	88	32	96	0	2.46
Tug McGraw	L	31	7	6	.538	11	58	0	0	97	81	42	76	0	2.51
Wayne Twitchell	R	28	3	1	.750	1	26	2	0	62	55	18	47	0	1.74
Ron Schueler	R	28	1	1	.500	1	35	0	0	50	44	16	43	0	2.88
Randy Lerch	L	21	0	—		1	3	0	0	3	0	1	0	0	3.00

NAME	G by Pos	B	AGE	G	AB	R	H	2B	3B	HR	RBI	BB	SO	SB	BA	SA
PITTSBURGH 2nd 92-70 .568 9	DANNY MURTAUGH (DD)															
TOTALS			29	162	5604	708	1499	249	56	110	660	433	807	130	.267	.391
Willie Stargell	1B111	L	36	117	428	54	110	20	3	20	65	50	101	2	.257	.458
Rennie Stennett	2B157,SS4	R	25	157	654	59	168	31	9	2	60	19	32	18	.257	.341
Frank Taveras	SS141	R	28	144	519	76	134	8	6	0	24	44	79	58	.258	.297
Richie Hebner	3B126	L	28	132	434	60	108	21	3	8	51	47	39	1	.249	.366
Dave Parker	OF134	L	25	138	537	82	168	28	10	13	90	30	80	19	.313	.475
Al Oliver	OF106,1B3	L	29	121	443	62	143	22	5	12	61	26	29	6	.323	.476
Richie Zisk	OF152	R	27	155	581	91	168	35	2	21	89	52	96	1	.289	.465
Manny Sanguillen	C111	R	32	114	389	52	113	16	6	2	36	28	12	2	.290	.378
Bill Robinson	OF78,3B37,1B3	R	33	122	393	55	119	22	3	21	64	16	73	2	.303	.534
Ed Kirkpatrick	1B25,OF9,3B1	L	31	83	146	14	34	9	0	16	14	6	1	1	.233	.295
Duffy Dyer	C58	R	30	69	184	12	41	8	0	3	9	29	35	0	.223	.315
Tommy Helms	3B22,2B11,SS1	R	35	62	87	10	24	5	1	0	13	10	5	0	.276	.391
Bob Robertson	1B29	R	29	61	129	10	28	5	1	2	25	16	23	0	.217	.318
Mario Mendoza	SS45,3B2,2B1	R	25	50	92	6	17	5	0	0	12	4	15	0	.185	.239
Omar Moreno	OF42	L	23	48	122	24	33	4	1	2	12	16	24	15	.270	.369
Ed Ott (BH)	C8	L	24	27	39	12	12	4	1	0	5	5	6	0	.308	.359

Miguel Dilone 21 B 4-17, Tony Armas 22 R 2-6, Craig Reynolds 23 L 1-4

NAME	T	AGE	W	L	PCT	SV	G	GS	CG	IP	H	BB	SO	SHO	ERA
		29	92	70	.568	35	162	162	45	1466	1402	460	762	12	3.36
John Candelaria	L	22	16	7	.696	1	32	31	11	220	173	60	138	4	3.15
Jim Rooker	L	33	15	8	.652	1	30	29	10	199	201	72	92	1	3.35
Bruce Kison	R	26	14	9	.609	1	31	29	6	193	180	52	98	1	3.08
Jerry Reuss	L	27	14	9	.609	2	31	29	11	209	209	51	108	3	3.53
Larry Demery	R	23	10	7	.588	2	36	15	4	145	123	58	72	1	3.17
Doc Medich	R	27	8	11	.421	0	29	26	3	179	193	48	86	0	3.52
Kent Tekulve	R	29	5	3	.625	9	64	0	0	103	91	25	68	0	2.45
Dave Giusti (LJ)	R	36	5	4	.556	6	40	0	0	58	59	27	24	0	4.34
Bob Moose (DD)	R	28	3	9	.250	10	53	2	0	88	100	32	38	0	3.68
Ramon Hernandez	L	35	2	2	.500	3	37	0	0	43	42	16	17	0	3.56
Rick Langford	R	24	0	1	.000	0	12	1	0	23	27	14	17	0	6.26
Doug Bair	R	26	0	—		0	4	0	0	6	4	1	4	0	6.00

NAME	G by Pos	B	AGE	G	AB	R	H	2B	3B	HR	RBI	BB	SO	SB	BA	SA
NEW YORK 3rd 86-76 .531 15	JOE FRAZIER															
TOTALS			29	162	5415	615	1334	198	34	102	560	561	797	66	.246	.352
Ed Kranepool	1B86,OF31	L	31	123	415	47	121	17	1	10	49	35	38	1	.292	.410
Felix Millan	2B136	R	32	139	531	55	150	21	2	1	35	41	19	2	.282	.343
Bud Harrelson	SS117	B	32	118	359	34	84	12	4	1	26	63	56	9	.234	.298
Roy Staiger	3B93,SS1	R	25	95	304	23	67	8	1	2	26	25	35	2	.220	.273
Dave Kingman	OF111,1B16	R	27	123	474	70	113	14	1	37	86	28	135	7	.238	.506
1 Del Unser	OF77	L	31	77	276	28	63	13	2	5	25	18	40	4	.228	.344
John Milner	OF112,1B12	L	26	127	443	56	120	25	4	15	78	65	59	0	.271	.447
Jerry Grote	C95,OF2	R	33	101	330	30	90	18	2	2	28	38	19	1	.272	.365
Joe Torre	1B78,3B4	R	35	114	310	36	95	10	3	5	31	21	35	1	.306	.406
Bruce Boisclair	OF87	L	23	110	286	42	82	13	3	2	13	28	55	9	.287	.374
Mike Phillips	SS53,2B19,3B10	L	25	87	262	30	67	9	4	5	25	25	29	2	.256	.363
1 Wayne Garrett	3B64,2B10,SS1	L	28	80	251	36	56	8	1	4	26	52	26	7	.223	.311
Leon Brown	OF43	R	26	64	70	11	15	3	0	0	4	2	14	3	.214	.257
Ron Hodges	C52	L	27	56	155	21	35	6	0	4	24	17	16	2	.226	.342
Mike Vail	OF35	R	24	53	143	8	31	5	1	0	9	6	16	0	.217	.266
2 Pepe Mangual	OF38	R	24	41	102	16	19	5	2	1	9	10	32	7	.186	.304
John Stearns	C30	R	24	32	103	13	27	2	0	2	10	16	11	1	.262	.379
Lee Mazzilli	OF23	B	21	24	77	9	15	2	0	1	7	14	10	5	.195	.299
Leo Foster	3B9,SS7,2B3	R	25	24	72	9	15	2	2	1	6	3	12	1	.203	.333

Benny Ayala 25 R 3-26, 2 Jim Dwyer 26 L 2-13, Billy Baldwin 25 L 6-22, 1 Jack Heidemann 26 R 1-12, Jay Kleven 26 R 1-5

NAME	T	AGE	W	L	PCT	SV	G	GS	CG	IP	H	BB	SO	SHO	ERA
		29	86	76	.531	25	162	162	53	1449	1248	419	1025	18	2.94
Jerry Koosman	L	33	21	10	.677	0	34	32	17	247	205	66	200	3	2.70
Jon Matlack	L	26	17	10	.630	0	35	35	16	262	236	57	153	6	2.95
Tom Seaver	R	31	14	11	.560	0	35	34	13	271	211	77	235	5	2.59
Skip Lockwood	R	29	10	7	.588	19	56	0	0	94	62	34	108	0	2.68
Mickey Lolich	L	35	8	13	.381	0	31	30	5	193	184	52	120	2	3.22
Craig Swan	R	25	6	9	.400	0	23	22	2	132	129	44	83	1	3.55
Nino Espinosa	R	22	4	4	.500	0	12	8	1	42	41	13	30	0	3.64
Bob Apodaca	R	26	3	7	.300	5	43	3	0	90	71	29	45	0	2.80
Bobby Myrick	R	23	1	1	.500	0	21	1	0	28	34	13	11	0	3.21
1 Tom Hall	L	28	1	1	.500	0	31	0	0	47	42	15	5	0	5.40
1 Ken Sanders	R	34	1	3	.333	1	31	0	0	47	39	12	16	0	2.87
Hank Webb	R	26	0	1	.000	0	16	0	0	16	17	7	7	0	4.50
Rick Baldwin	R	23	0	1	.000	0	23	0	0	23	14	10	9	0	2.35

NAME	G by Pos	B	AGE	G	AB	R	H	2B	3B	HR	RBI	BB	SO	SB	BA	SA
CHICAGO 4th 75-87 .463 26	JIM MARSHALL															
TOTALS			27	162	5519	611	1386	216	24	105	559	490	834	74	.251	.356
Pete LaCock	1B54,OF19	L	24	106	244	34	54	9	2	8	28	42	37	1	.221	.373
Manny Trillo	2B156,SS1	R	25	158	582	42	139	24	3	4	59	53	70	17	.239	.311
Mick Kelleher	SS101,3B22,2B5	R	28	124	337	28	77	12	1	0	23	28	17	2	.228	.270
Bill Madlock	3B142	R	25	142	514	68	174	36	1	15	84	54	50	15	.339	.500
Jerry Morales	OF136	R	27	140	537	66	147	19	0	16	67	44	49	3	.274	.395
Rick Monday	OF103,1B32	L	30	137	534	107	145	20	5	32	77	60	125	5	.272	.507
Jose Cardenal	OF128	R	32	136	521	64	156	25	2	8	47	32	39	23	.299	.401
Steve Swisher	C107	R	24	109	377	25	89	13	3	5	42	20	82	2	.236	.326
Joe Wallis	OF90	L	24	121	338	51	86	11	9	5	28	36	53	10	.254	.361
George Mitterwald	C64,1B25	R	31	101	303	30	61	9	1	5	28	26	63	0	.215	.287
Dave Rosello	SS86,2B31	R	26	91	227	26	55	7	1	3	21	16	44	3	.242	.304
Champ Summers	OF26,1B10,C1	L	30	73	126	16	26	6	1	3	16	14	33	1	.206	.294
2 Larry Biittner	OF78	L	30	78	192	24	47	14	3	0	24	9	13	3	.245	.323
Rob Sperring	3B20,SS15,2B4,OF3	R	26	93	83	9	24	2	0	0	8	8	13	1	.258	.292
Wayne Tyrone	OF7,1B5,3B5	R	26	30	69	8	17	0	0	2	14	4	14	0	.246	.333
1 Andre Thornton	1B25	R	26	27	85	6	17	4	0	2	10	14	20	1	.200	.341
Mike Adams	OF4,3B3,2B1	R	27	35	29	1	4	0	0	0	2	5	6	0	.138	.207

Jerry Tabb 24 L 7-24, Randy Hundley (ZJ) 34 R 3-18, Ed Putman 22 R 3-7, 1 Tim Hosley 29 R 0-1

NAME	T	AGE	W	L	PCT	SV	G	GS	CG	IP	H	BB	SO	SHO	ERA
		28	75	87	.463	33	162	162	27	1471	1511	490	850	12	3.93
Ray Burris	R	25	15	13	.536	0	37	36	10	249	251	70	112	4	3.11
Rick Reuschel	R	27	14	12	.538	0	38	37	9	260	260	64	146	2	3.46
Bill Bonham	R	27	9	13	.409	0	32	31	3	196	215	96	110	0	4.27
2 Steve Renko	R	31	8	11	.421	0	28	27	4	163	164	43	112	1	3.87
Bruce Sutter	R	23	6	3	.667	10	52	0	0	83	63	26	73	0	2.71
Oscar Zamora	R	31	5	3	.625	3	40	2	0	75	70	17	27	0	5.24
Darold Knowles	L	34	5	7	.417	9	58	0	0	72	64	22	39	0	2.88
Paul Reuschel	R	29	4	2	.667	3	50	2	0	89	94	33	55	0	4.55
Steve Stone (SJ)	R	28	3	6	.333	0	17	15	1	75	70	35	33	1	4.08
Mike Garman	R	26	2	4	.333	6	47	0	0	79	79	35	37	0	4.97
2 Joe Coleman	R	29	2	8	.200	4	39	4	0	79	79	35	66	0	4.10
Buddy Schultz	L	25	1	1	.500	0	16	1	0	35	35	14	26	0	4.37
Ken Frailing	L	28	0	1	.000	0	15	1	0	19	20	5	10	0	2.37
Ken Crosby	R	28	0	1	.000	0	5	1	0	9	12	4	5	0	12.00
2 Ramon Hernandez	L	35	0	0		0	3	0	0	4	4	4	0	0	0.00
Mike Krukow	R	24	0	0		0	1	0	0	8	8	3	3	0	0.00
Tom Dettore	R	28	0	0		0	3	1	0	6	11	4	0	0	10.29
Geoff Zahn	L	30	0	0		0	3	1	0	4	11	4	1	0	11.25

ST. LOUIS 5th 72-90 .444 29 RED SCHOENDIENST

NAME	G by Pos	B	AGE	G	AB	R	H	2B	3B	HR	RBI	BB	SO	SB	BA	SA
TOTALS			27	162	5516	629	1432	243	57	63	584	512	860	123	.260	.359
Keith Hernandez	1B110	L	22	129	374	54	108	21	5	7	46	49	53	4	.289	.428
Mike Tyson (LJ,BG)	2B74	R	26	76	245	26	70	12	9	3	28	16	34	1	.286	.445
Don Kessinger	SS113,2B31,3B2	B	33	145	502	55	120	22	6	1	40	61	51	3	.239	.313
Heity Cruz	3B148	R	23	151	526	54	120	17	1	13	71	42	119	1	.228	.338
Willie Crawford	OF107	L	27	129	392	49	119	17	5	9	50	37	53	2	.304	.441
Bake McBride (KJ)	OF66	L	27	72	272	40	91	13	4	3	24	18	28	10	.335	.445
Lou Brock	OF123	L	37	133	498	73	150	24	5	4	67	35	75	56	.301	.394
Ted Simmons	C113,1B30,OF7,3B2	B	26	150	546	60	159	35	3	5	75	73	35	0	.291	.394
Jerry Mumphrey	OF94	B	23	112	384	51	99	15	5	1	26	37	53	22	.258	.331
Vic Harris	2B37,OF35,3B12,SS1	B	26	97	259	21	59	12	3	1	19	16	55	1	.228	.309
Mike Anderson	OF58,1B5	R	25	86	199	17	58	8	1	1	12	26	30	1	.291	.357
1 Ron Fairly	1B27	L	37	73	110	13	29	4	0	0	21	23	12	0	.264	.300
1 Joe Ferguson	C48,OF14	R	29	71	189	22	38	8	4	4	21	32	40	4	.201	.349
Lee Richard	2B26,SS12,3B1	R	27	66	91	12	16	4	2	0	5	4	9	1	.176	.264
Garry Templeton	SS53	R	20	53	213	32	62	8	2	1	17	7	33	11	.291	.362
1 Reggie Smith	1B17,OF16,3B13	B	31	47	170	20	37	7	1	8	23	14	28	1	.218	.412
Ken Rudolph	C14	R	29	27	50	1	8	3	0	0	5	1	7	0	.160	.220
Luis Alvarado	2B16	R	27	16	42	5	13	2	1	0	4	2	6	0	.286	.310

1 Luis Melendez 26 R 3-24, Sammy Mejias 24 R 3-21, Mike Potter 25 R 0-16, Charlie Chant 24 R 2-14, John Tamargo 24 B 3-10, Doug Clarey 22 R 1-4

NAME	T	AGE	W	L	PCT	SV	G	GS	CG	IP	H	BB	SO	SHO	ERA
		26	72	90	.444	26	162	162	35	1454	1416	581	731	15	3.60
Lynn McGlothen	R	26	13	15	.464	0	33	32	10	205	209	68	106	4	3.91
Pete Falcone	L	22	12	16	.429	0	32	32	9	212	173	93	138	2	3.23
John Denny	R	23	11	9	.550	0	30	30	8	207	189	74	74	3	2.52
Al Hrabosky	L	26	8	6	.571	13	68	0	0	95	89	39	73	0	3.32
Bob Forsch	R	26	8	10	.444	0	33	32	2	194	209	71	76	0	3.94
John Curtis	L	28	6	11	.353	1	37	15	3	134	139	65	52	1	4.50
Eric Rasmussen	R	24	6	12	.333	0	43	17	2	150	139	54	76	1	3.54
Mike Wallace	L	25	2	2	.600	2	49	0	0	66	66	39	40	0	4.09
Mike Proly	R	25	1	0	1.000	0	14	0	0	17	21	6	4	0	3.71
Doug Capilla	L	24	1	0	1.000	0	7	0	0	8	8	4	5	0	5.63
Eddie Solomon	R	25	1	1	.500	0	26	2	0	37	45	16	19	0	4.86
Tom Walker	R	27	1	2	.333	3	10	0	0	20	22	3	11	0	4.05
2 Bill Greif	R	26	1	5	.167	6	47	0	0	55	60	26	32	0	4.09
1 Danny Frisella	R	30	0	1	.000	1	18	0	0	23	19	13	11	0	3.91
Steve Waterbury	R	24	0	0	—	0	5	0	0	6	7	3	4	0	6.00
Lerrin LaGrow	R	27	0	1	.000	0	8	2	1	24	21	7	10	0	1.50

MONTREAL 6th 55-107 .340 46 KARL KUEHL 43-85 .336 CHARLIE FOX 12-22 .353

NAME	G by Pos	B	AGE	G	AB	R	H	2B	3B	HR	RBI	BB	SO	SB	BA	SA
TOTALS			25	162	5428	531	1275	224	32	94	507	433	841	86	.235	.340
Mike Jorgensen	1B81,OF41	L	27	125	343	36	87	13	0	6	23	53	48	7	.254	.344
Pete Mackanin	2B100,3B8,SS3,OF1	R	24	114	380	36	85	15	2	8	33	15	66	6	.224	.337
Tim Foli	SS146,3B1	R	25	149	546	41	144	36	1	6	54	16	33	6	.264	.366
Larry Parrish	3B153	R	22	154	543	65	126	28	5	11	61	41	91	2	.232	.363
Ellis Valentine	OF88	R	21	94	305	36	85	15	2	7	39	30	51	14	.279	.410
Jerry White	OF92	B	23	114	278	32	68	11	1	2	21	27	31	15	.245	.313
Barry Foote	C96,3B2,1B1	R	24	105	350	32	82	12	2	7	27	17	32	2	.234	.340
Jose Morales	1B21,C12	R	31	104	158	12	50	11	0	4	37	3	20	0	.316	.462
Gary Carter (BG)	C60,OF36	R	22	91	311	31	68	8	2	6	38	30	43	0	.219	.309
Pepe Frias	2B35,SS35,3B4,OF1	B	27	76	113	7	28	5	0	0	8	4	14	1	.248	.292
2 Andre Thornton	1B43,OF11	R	26	69	183	20	35	5	2	9	24	28	32	2	.191	.388
Bombo Rivera	OF56	R	23	68	185	22	51	11	4	2	19	13	32	1	.276	.411
1 Pepe Mangual	OF62	R	24	66	215	34	56	9	1	3	16	50	49	17	.260	.353
1 Earl Williams	1B47,C13	R	27	61	190	17	45	10	2	8	29	14	32	0	.237	.437
1 Wayne Garrett	2B54,3B2	L	28	59	177	15	43	4	1	2	11	30	20	2	.243	.311
1 Jim Dwyer	OF19	L	26	50	92	7	17	3	1	0	5	11	10	1	.185	.239
1 Jim Lyttle	OF29	L	30	42	85	6	23	4	1	1	8	7	13	0	.271	.376
Warren Cromartie	OF20	L	22	33	81	8	17	1	0	0	2	1	5	1	.210	.222
Gary Roenicke	OF25	R	21	29	90	9	20	3	1	1	5	4	18	0	.222	.344
Andre Dawson	OF24	R	21	24	85	9	20	4	1	0	7	5	13	1	.235	.306
1 Nate Colbert	OF7,1B6	R	30	14	40	5	8	2	0	0	4	9	16	1	.200	.400

1 Larry Biittner 30 L 6-32, Jim Cox 26 R 5-29, Pat Scanlon 23 L 5-27, Roger Freed 30 R 3-15, Rodney Scott 22 B 4-10, Larry Johnson 25 R 2-13

NAME	T	AGE	W	L	PCT	SV	G	GS	CG	IP	H	BB	SO	SHO	ERA
		28	55	107	.340	21	162	162	26	1440	1442	659	783	10	3.99
Woody Fryman	L	36	13	13	.500	2	34	32	4	216	218	76	123	2	3.38
Don Stanhouse	R	25	9	12	.429	1	34	26	8	184	182	92	79	1	3.77
Steve Rogers (BG)	R	26	7	17	.292	1	33	32	8	230	212	69	150	4	3.21
Don Carrithers	R	26	6	12	.333	0	34	19	2	140	153	78	71	0	4.44
Dale Murray	R	26	4	9	.308	13	81	0	0	113	117	37	35	0	3.27
Gerald Hannahs	L	23	2	0	1.000	0	3	3	0	16	20	12	10	0	6.75
Fred Scherman	L	31	2	2	.500	1	31	0	0	40	42	14	18	0	4.95
Chuck Taylor	R	34	2	3	.400	0	31	0	0	40	38	13	14	0	4.50
Joe Kerrigan	R	21	2	6	.250	1	38	0	0	57	63	23	22	0	3.79
2 Steve Dunning	R	27	2	6	.250	0	32	7	1	91	93	33	72	0	4.15
Dan Warthen	L	23	2	10	.167	0	23	16	2	90	76	66	67	1	5.30
Wayne Granger	R	32	1	0	1.000	2	27	0	0	32	32	16	16	0	3.66
Larry Landreth	R	21	1	2	.333	0	3	3	0	11	13	10	7	0	4.09
Chip Lang	R	23	1	3	.250	0	29	0	0	62	56	34	30	0	4.21
Clay Kirby	R	28	1	8	.111	0	22	15	0	79	81	63	51	0	5.70
Bill Atkinson	R	21	0	0	—	0	4	0	0	5	3	1	4	0	0.00
1 Steve Renko	R	31	0	1	.000	0	2	2	0	8	7	8	1	0	11.25
Joe Keener	R	23	0	0	.000	0	2	2	0	4	7	3	1	0	5.54
Dennis Blair	R	22	0	0	.000	0	1	1	0	16	21	11	9	0	3.94
Don DeMola (AJ) 23															

WEST DIVISION

CINCINNATI 1st 102-60 .630 SPARKY ANDERSON

NAME	G by Pos	B	AGE	G	AB	R	H	2B	3B	HR	RBI	BB	SO	SB	BA	SA
TOTALS			29	162	5702	857	1599	271	63	141	802	681	902	210	.280	.424
Tony Perez	-1B136	R	34	139	527	77	137	32	6	19	91	50	88	10	.260	.452
Joe Morgan	2B133	L	32	141	472	113	151	30	5	27	111	114	41	60	.320	.576
Dave Concepcion	SS150	R	28	152	576	74	162	28	7	9	69	49	68	21	.281	.401
Pete Rose	3B159,OF1	B	35	162	665	130	215	42	6	10	63	86	54	9	.323	.450
Ken Griffey	OF144	L	26	148	562	111	189	28	9	6	74	62	65	34	.336	.450
Cesar Geronimo	OF146	L	28	149	486	59	149	24	11	2	49	56	95	22	.307	.414
George Foster	OF142,1B1	R	27	144	562	86	172	21	9	29	121	52	99	17	.306	.530
Johnny Bench	C128,OF5,1B1	R	28	135	465	62	109	24	1	16	74	81	95	13	.234	.394
Dan Driessen	1B40,OF20	L	24	98	219	32	54	11	1	7	44	43	32	14	.247	.402
Doug Flynn	2B55,3B23,SS20	R	25	93	219	20	62	5	2	1	20	10	24	2	.283	.338
Mike Lum	OF38	L	30	84	136	15	31	5	1	3	20	22	24	0	.228	.346
Ed Armbrister	OF32	R	27	73	78	20	23	3	2	2	9	6	22	7	.295	.462
Bob Bailey	OF31,3B10	R	33	69	124	17	37	6	1	6	23	16	26	0	.298	.508
Bill Plummer	C54	R	29	56	153	16	38	6	1	4	19	14	36	0	.248	.359
Joel Youngblood	OF9,3B6,2B1,C1	R	24	55	57	8	11	1	1	0	1	2	8	1	.193	.246
Don Werner	C3	R	23	3	4	0	2	1	0	0	1	0	2	0	.500	.750

NAME	T	AGE	W	L	PCT	SV	G	GS	CG	IP	H	BB	SO	SHO	ERA
		27	102	60	.630	45	162	162	33	1471	1436	491	790	12	3.51
Gary Nolan	R	28	15	9	.625	0	34	34	7	239	232	27	113	1	3.46
Pat Zachry	R	24	14	7	.667	0	38	28	6	204	170	83	143	1	2.74
Fred Norman	L	33	12	7	.632	0	33	24	8	180	153	70	126	3	3.10
Jack Billingham	R	33	12	10	.545	1	34	29	5	177	190	62	76	2	4.32
Don Gullett (SJ)	L	25	11	3	.786	1	23	20	4	126	119	48	64	0	3.00
Santo Alcala	R	23	11	4	.733	0	30	21	3	132	131	67	67	1	4.70
Rawly Eastwick	R	25	11	5	.688	26	71	0	0	108	93	27	70	0	2.08
Manny Sarmiento	R	20	5	1	.833	0	22	0	0	44	36	12	20	0	2.05
Pedro Borbon	R	29	4	3	.571	8	69	1	0	121	135	31	53	0	3.35
Joe Henderson	R	29	2	0	1.000	0	11	9	7					0	0.00
Pat Darcy	R	26	2	3	.400	2	11	4	0	39	41	22	15	0	6.23
Will McEnaney	L	24	2	6	.250	7	55	0	0	72	97	23	28	0	4.88
Rich Hinton	L	29	1	2	.333	0	12	1	0	18	30	11	8	0	7.50

LOS ANGELES 2nd 92-70 .568 10 WALT ALSTON 90-68 .570 TOMMY LASORDA 2-2 .500

NAME	G by Pos	B	AGE	G	AB	R	H	2B	3B	HR	RBI	BB	SO	SB	BA	SA
TOTALS			28	162	5472	608	1371	200	34	91	561	486	744	104	.251	.349
Steve Garvey	1B162	R	27	162	631	85	200	37	4	13	80	50	69	19	.317	.450
Davey Lopes	2B100,OF19	R	31	117	427	72	103	17	4	4	20	56	49	63	.241	.342
Bill Russell	SS149	R	27	149	554	53	152	17	3	5	65	21	46	15	.274	.343
Ron Cey	3B144	R	28	145	502	69	139	18	3	23	80	89	74	0	.277	.462
2 Reggie Smith	OF58,3B1	B	31	65	225	35	63	8	4	10	26	18	42	2	.280	.484
Dusty Baker	OF106	R	27	112	384	36	93	13	0	4	39	31	54	2	.242	.307
Bill Buckner	OF153,1B1	L	26	154	642	76	193	28	4	7	60	26	28	28	.301	.389
Steve Yeager	C115	R	27	117	359	42	77	11	3	11	50	30	84	3	.214	.354
Ted Sizemore	2B71,3B3,C2	R	31	84	266	18	64	8	1	0	18	15	22	2	.241	.278
Ed Goodson	3B16,1B3,OF7,2B1	L	28	83	118	8	27	4	0	3	17	6	18	0	.229	.339
1 Joe Ferguson	OF39,C17	R	29	54	185	24	41	7	0	6	18	25	41	2	.222	.357
2 Lee Lacy	OF37,3B3,2B2	R	28	53	158	17	42	7	1	0	14	16	13	1	.266	.323
Manny Mota	OF6	R	38	50	52	1	15	3	0	0	13	7	5	0	.288	.346
Henry Cruz	OF23	L	24	49	88	8	16	2	1	4	14	9	10	0	.182	.364
John Hale	OF37	R	22	44	91	4	14	2	1	0	8	16	14	0	.154	.198
Ellie Rodriguez	C33	R	30	36	66	10	14	0	0	0	9	1	12	0	.212	.212
Rick Auerbach	SS12,3B8,2B7	R	26	36	47	7	6	1	0	0	1	6	6	0	.128	.128
Glenn Burke	OF20	R	23	25	46	9	11	2	0	0	2	0	6	3	.239	.283
2 Jim Lyttle	OF18	L	30	23	68	3	15	3	0	0	5	8	12	0	.221	.265
Kevin Pasley	C23	R	22	23	52	4	12	2	0	0	2	3	7	0	.231	.269
Leron Lee	OF10	L	28	23	45	1	6	1	0	0	2	6	6	0	.133	.178
Ivan DeJesus	SS13,3B7	R	23	22	41	4	7	2	1	0	2	4	9	0	.171	.268

Joe Simpson 24 L 4-30, Danny Walton 28 B 2-15, Sergio Robles 30 R 0-3

NAME	T	AGE	W	L	PCT	SV	G	GS	CG	IP	H	BB	SO	SHO	ERA
		29	92	70	.568	28	162	162	47	1471	1330	479	747	17	3.02
Don Sutton	R	31	21	10	.677	0	35	34	15	268	231	82	161	4	3.06
Doug Rau	L	27	16	12	.571	0	34	32	8	231	221	69	98	3	2.57
Rick Rhoden	R	23	12	3	.800	0	27	26	10	181	165	53	77	3	2.98
Charlie Hough	R	28	12	8	.600	18	77	0	0	143	102	77	81	0	2.20
Burt Hooton	R	26	11	15	.423	0	33	33	8	227	203	60	116	4	3.25
Tommy John	R	33	10	10	.500	0	31	31	6	207	207	61	91	2	3.09
1 Mike Marshall	R	33	4	3	.571	8	30	0	0	63	64	25	39	0	4.43
Stan Wall	R	25	2	2	.500	1	31	0	0	50	50	15	27	0	3.60
2 Elias Sosa	R	26	2	4	.333	1	24	0	0	34	30	12	20	0	3.44
Dennis Lewallyn	R	22	1	1	.500	0	7	1	0	17	12	6	4	0	2.12
Al Downing	L	35	1	2	.333	0	17	3	0	47	43	18	30	0	3.83
Rick Sutcliffe	R	20	0	1	.000	0	2	1	0	3	1	3	0	0	0.00

HOUSTON 3rd 80-82 .494 22 BILL VIRDON

NAME	G by Pos	B	AGE	G	AB	R	H	2B	3B	HR	RBI	BB	SO	SB	BA	SA
TOTALS			27	162	5464	625	1401	195	50	66	571	530	719	150	.256	.347
Bob Watson	1B155	R	30	157	585	76	183	31	3	16	102	62	64	3	.313	.458
Rob Andrews	2B107,SS3	R	23	109	410	42	105	8	5	0	23	33	27	7	.256	.300
Roger Metzger	SS150,2B2	B	28	152	481	37	101	13	8	0	29	52	63	1	.210	.270
Enos Cabell	3B143,1B3	R	26	144	586	85	160	13	7	2	43	29	79	35	.273	.329
Greg Gross	OF115	L	23	128	426	52	122	12	3	0	27	64	39	2	.286	.329
Cesar Cedeno	OF146	R	25	150	575	89	171	26	5	18	83	55	57	58	.297	.454
Jose Cruz	OF125	L	28	133	439	49	133	21	5	4	61	53	46	28	.303	.441
2 Ed Herrmann	C79	L	29	79	265	14	54	8	0	3	25	22	40	0	.204	.268
Cliff Johnson	C66,OF20,1B16	R	28	108	318	36	72	21	2	10	49	62	59	0	.226	.399
Wilbur Howard	OF63,2B2	B	27	94	191	26	42	7	2	1	18	7	28	7	.220	.293
Ken Boswell	3B16,2B3,OF1	L	30	91	126	12	33	8	1	0	16	20	9	1	.262	.341
Leon Roberts	OF60	R	25	87	235	31	68	11	0	8	19	15	43	1	.289	.443
Jerry DaVanon	2B17,SS17,3B9	R	30	74	107	19	31	3	3	2	7	14	19	0	.290	.402
Larry Milbourne	2B32	R	25	59	145	22	34	7	0	0	7	14	10	6	.248	.276
Skip Jutze	C42	R	29	52	92	7	14	2	0	0	6	4	15	0	.152	.196
Art Howe	3B8,2B2	R	29	21	29	4	4	0	0	0	6	1	5	0	.138	.172
Alex Taveras	SS7,2B7	R	20	14	46	3	10	0	0	0	2	1	14	1	.217	.217
Al Javier	OF7	R	22	8	24	1	5	0	0	0	2	1	3	0	.208	.208
Rich Chiles	OF1	L	26	5	4	1	2	1	0	0	0	1	0	0	.500	.750

NAME	T	AGE	W	L	PCT	SV	G	GS	CG	IP	H	BB	SO	SHO	ERA
		26	80	82	.494	29	162	162	42	1444	1349	662	780	17	3.56
J.R. Richard	R	26	20	15	.571	0	39	39	14	291	221	151	214	3	2.75
Larry Dierker	R	29	13	14	.481	0	28	28	7	188	171	72	112	4	3.69
Joaquin Andujar	R	23	9	10	.474	0	28	25	9	172	163	75	59	4	3.61
1 Tom Griffin	R	28	5	3	.625	0	20	7	0	61	44	37	33	0	6.00
Dan Larson	R	21	5	5	.385	0	13	13	5	92	81	28	42	0	3.03
Ken Forsch	R	29	4	5	.571	19	52	0	0	92	76	26	49	0	2.15
Bo McLaughlin	R	22	5	1	.444	1	17	11	4	79	71	17	32	2	2.85
Joe Niekro	R	31	4	8	.333	0	36	13	0	118	107	56	77	0	3.36
Mark Lemongello	R	20	3	1	.750	0	4	4	1	29	26	7	9	0	2.79
Joe Sambito	L	23	2	1	.600	1	20	1	0	27	26	6	19	0	3.57
Gene Pentz (JJ)	R	23	3	0	.500	5	40	0	0	64	62	31	36	0	2.95
Mike Cosgrove	L	25	1	4	.429	0	22	16	1	90	106	58	34	1	5.50
Gil Rondon	R	22	2	2	.500	0	19	7	2	54	70	39	21	0	5.67
Mike Barlow	R	27	0	2	.000	0	11	0	0	22	34	10	10	0	4.50
Larry Hardy	R	28	0	0	—	0	15	0	0	22	34	10	10	0	6.95
Jose Sosa	R	25	1	2	.333	2	16	0	0	16	6	5	0	6.75
Paul Siebert	L	23	0	2	.000	0	29	18	10	5	3.12
Joe McIntosh (SJ) 24															

SAN FRANCISCO 4th 74-88 .457 28 BILL RIGNEY

NAME	G by Pos	B	AGE	G	AB	R	H	2B	3B	HR	RBI	BB	SO	SB	BA	SA
	TOTALS		26	162	5452	595	1340	211	37	85	552	518	778	88	.246	.345
2 Darrell Evans	1B83,3B5	L	29	92	257	42	57	9	1	10	36	42	38	6	.222	.381
2 Marty Perez	2B89,SS5	R	30	93	332	37	86	13	1	2	26	30	28	1	.259	.322
Chris Speier	SS135,2B7,3B5,1B1	R	25	145	495	51	112	18	4	3	40	60	52	2	.226	.297
Ken Reitz	3B155,SS1	R	25	155	577	40	154	21	1	5	66	24	48	5	.267	.333
Bobby Murcer	OF146	L	30	147	533	73	138	20	2	23	90	84	78	12	.259	.433
Larry Herndon	OF110	R	22	115	337	42	97	11	3	2	23	23	45	12	.288	.356
Gary Matthews	OF156	R	25	156	587	79	164	28	4	20	84	75	94	12	.279	.443
Dave Rader	C81	L	27	88	255	25	67	15	0	1	22	27	21	2	.263	.333
Gary Thomasson (NJ)	OF54,1B39	L	24	103	328	45	85	20	5	8	38	30	45	8	.259	.424
Derrel Thomas (LJ)	2B69,OF2,SS1,3B1	B	25	81	272	38	63	5	4	2	19	29	26	10	.232	.301
Glenn Adams	OF6	L	28	69	74	2	18	4	0	0	3	1	12	1	.243	.297
1 Willie Montanez	1B58	L	28	60	230	22	71	15	2	2	20	15	15	2	.309	.417
Chris Arnold	2B8,3B4,1B1,SS1	R	28	60	69	4	15	0	1	0	5	6	16	0	.217	.246
Steve Ontiveros	3B7,OF7,1B4	B	24	59	74	8	13	3	0	0	5	6	11	0	.176	.216
Mike Sadek	C51	R	30	55	93	8	19	2	0	0	7	11	10	0	.204	.226
Marc Hill	C49,1B1	R	24	54	131	11	24	5	0	3	15	10	19	0	.183	.290
1 Von Joshua	OF35	L	28	42	156	13	41	5	2	0	2	4	20	1	.263	.321
Johnnie LeMaster	SS31	R	22	33	100	9	21	3	2	0	9	2	21	2	.210	.280
Jack Clark	OF26	R	20	26	102	14	23	6	2	2	10	8	18	6	.225	.382
Gary Alexander	C23	R	23	23	73	12	13	1	1	2	7	10	16	1	.178	.301
1 Craig Robinson	2B7,3B2,SS1	R	27	15	13	4	4	1	0	0	2	3	4	0	.308	.385
Bruce Miller	2B8,3B2	R	29	12	25	1	4	1	0	0	2	2	5	0	.160	.200

NAME	T	AGE	W	L	PCT	SV	G	GS	CG	IP	H	BB	SO	SHO	ERA
		26	74	88	.457	31	162	162	27	1462	1464	518	746	18	3.53
John Montefusco	R	26	16	14	.533	0	37	36	11	253	224	74	172	6	2.85
Jim Barr	R	28	15	12	.556	0	37	37	8	252	260	60	75	3	2.89
Ed Halicki	R	25	12	14	.462	0	32	31	8	186	171	61	130	4	3.63
Gary Lavelle	L	27	10	6	.625	12	65	0	0	110	102	52	71	0	2.70
Randy Moffitt	R	27	6	6	.500	14	58	0	0	103	92	35	50	0	2.27
Dave Heaverlo	R	25	4	4	.500	1	61	0	0	75	85	15	40	0	4.44
John D'Acquisto	R	24	3	8	.273	0	28	19	0	106	93	102	53	0	5.35
Rob Dressler	R	22	3	10	.231	0	25	19	0	108	125	35	33	0	4.42
Charlie Williams	R	28	2	0	1.000	1	48	2	0	85	80	39	34	0	2.96
Frank Riccelli	L	23	1	1	.500	0	4	3	0	16	16	5	11	0	5.63
Bob Knepper	L	22	1	2	.333	0	4	4	0	25	26	7	11	0	3.24
Mike Caldwell	L	27	1	7	.125	2	50	0	0	107	145	20	55	0	4.88
Tommy Toms	R	24	0	1	.000	1	9	0	0	9	13	1	4	0	6.00
Greg Minton	R	24	0	3	.000	0	10	2	0	26	32	12	7	0	4.85

SAN DIEGO 5th 73-89 .451 29 JOHN McNAMARA

NAME	G by Pos	B	AGE	G	AB	R	H	2B	3B	HR	RBI	BB	SO	SB	BA	SA
	TOTALS		29	162	5369	570	1327	216	37	64	528	488	716	92	.247	.337
Mike Ivie	1B135,3B2,C2	R	23	140	405	51	118	19	5	7	70	30	41	6	.291	.415
Tito Fuentes	2B127	B	32	135	520	48	137	18	0	2	36	18	38	5	.263	.310
Enzo Hernandez	SS101	R	27	113	340	31	87	13	3	1	24	32	16	12	.256	.321
Doug Rader	3B137	R	31	139	471	45	121	22	4	9	55	55	102	3	.257	.388
Dave Winfield	OF134	R	24	137	492	81	139	26	4	13	69	65	78	26	.283	.431
Willie Davis	OF128	L	36	141	493	61	132	18	10	5	46	19	34	14	.268	.375
Johnny Grubb (NJ)	OF98,1B9,3B3	L	27	109	384	54	109	22	1	5	27	65	53	1	.284	.385
Fred Kendall	C146	R	27	146	456	30	112	17	0	2	39	36	42	1	.246	.296
Jerry Turner	OF74	L	22	105	281	41	75	16	5	5	37	32	38	12	.267	.413
Ted Kubiak	3B27,2B25,SS6,1B1	B	34	96	212	16	50	5	2	0	26	25	28	0	.236	.278
Merv Rettenmund	OF43	R	33	86	140	16	32	7	0	2	11	29	23	4	.229	.321
Hector Torres	SS63,3B4,2B3	R	30	74	215	8	42	6	0	4	15	16	31	2	.195	.279
2 Luis Melendez	OF60	R	26	72	119	15	29	5	0	0	5	3	12	1	.244	.286
1 Willie McCovey	1B51	L	38	71	202	20	41	9	0	7	36	21	39	0	.203	.351
Bob Davis	C47	R	24	51	83	7	17	0	1	0	5	5	13	0	.205	.229
1 Gene Locklear	OF11	L	26	43	67	9	15	3	0	0	4	8	15	0	.224	.269
Bobby Valentine	OF10,1B4	R	26	15	49	3	18	4	0	0	4	6	2	0	.367	.449
Bill Almon	SS14	R	23	14	57	6	14	3	0	1	6	2	9	3	.246	.351
Mike Champion	2B11	R	21	11	38	4	9	2	0	1	2	1	3	0	.237	.368
Tucker Ashford	3B1	R	21	4	5	0	3	1	0	0	1	0	1	2	.600	.800

NAME	T	AGE	W	L	PCT	SV	G	GS	CG	IP	H	BB	SO	SHO	ERA
		27	73	89	.451	31	162	162	47	1432	1368	543	652	11	3.65
Randy Jones	L	26	22	14	.611	0	40	40	25	315	274	50	93	5	2.74
Brent Strom	L	27	12	16	.429	0	36	33	8	211	188	73	103	1	3.28
Butch Metzger	R	24	11	4	.733	16	77	0	0	123	119	52	89	0	2.93
Dave Freisleben	R	24	10	13	.435	1	34	24	6	172	163	66	81	3	3.51
Rick Sawyer	R	28	5	3	.625	0	13	11	4	82	84	38	33	2	2.52
2 Tom Griffin	R	28	4	3	.571	0	11	11	2	70	56	42	36	0	2.96
Alan Foster	R	29	3	6	.333	0	26	11	2	87	75	35	22	0	3.21
Rich Folkers	L	29	2	3	.400	1	33	3	0	60	67	25	26	0	5.25
Dan Spillner (XJ)	R	24	2	11	.154	0	32	14	0	107	120	55	57	0	5.05
Jerry Johnson	R	32	1	3	.250	0	24	1	0	39	39	26	27	0	5.31
1 Bill Greif	R	26	1	3	.250	0	5	5	0	22	27	11	5	0	8.18
Mike Dupree	R	23	0	0	—	0	12	0	0	16	18	7	5	0	9.00
Dave Tomlin	L	27	0	1	.000	1	49	1	0	73	62	20	43	0	2.84
Bob Owchinko	L	21	0	0	—	0	2	1	0	4	11	3	4	0	18.00
Ken Reynolds	L	—	0	0	—	1	19	2	0	32	38	29	18	0	6.47
Dave Wehrmeister	R	23	0	4	.000	0	7	4	0	19	27	11	10	0	7.58

ATLANTA 6th 70-92 .432 32 DAVE BRISTOL

NAME	G by Pos	B	AGE	G	AB	R	H	2B	3B	HR	RBI	BB	SO	SB	BA	SA
	TOTALS		27	162	5345	620	1309	170	30	82	586	589	811	74	.245	.334
2 Willie Montanez	1B103	L	28	103	420	52	135	14	0	9	64	21	32	0	.321	.419
Rod Gilbreath	2B104,3B7,SS1	R	23	116	383	57	96	11	8	1	32	42	36	7	.251	.329
Darrel Chaney	SS151,2B1,3B1	B	28	153	496	42	125	20	8	1	50	54	92	5	.252	.331
Jerry Royster	3B148,SS2	R	23	149	533	65	132	13	1	5	46	52	92	24	.248	.304
Ken Henderson	OF122	B	30	133	435	52	114	19	0	13	61	62	68	5	.262	.395
Rowland Office (KJ)	OF92	L	23	99	359	51	101	17	4	3	34	37	49	2	.281	.368
Jim Wynn	OF138	R	34	148	449	75	93	19	1	17	66	127	111	16	.207	.367
Biff Pocoroba (KJ)	C54	B	22	54	174	16	42	7	0	0	14	19	12	1	.241	.282
Tom Paciorek	OF84,1B12,3B1	R	29	111	324	39	94	10	4	4	36	19	57	2	.290	.383
Dave May	OF60	L	32	105	214	27	46	5	3	3	23	26	31	5	.215	.308
Vic Correll	C65	R	30	69	200	26	45	6	2	5	16	21	37	0	.225	.350
Cito Gaston	OF28,1B2	R	32	69	134	15	39	4	0	4	25	11	33	1	.291	.410
1 Earl Williams	C38,1B17	R	27	61	184	18	39	3	0	9	26	19	33	0	.212	.375
1 Lee Lacy	2B44,OF5,3B1	R	28	50	180	25	49	4	2	3	20	6	22	2	.272	.367
1 Darrell Evans	1B36,3B7	L	29	44	139	11	24	0	1	0	10	30	33	3	.173	.194
1 Marty Perez	2B18,SS17,3B2	R	30	31	96	12	24	4	0	1	6	8	9	0	.250	.323
Rob Belloir	SS12,3B10,2B5	R	27	30	60	5	12	2	0	0	5	7	10	0	.200	.233
Junior Moore	3B6,2B1,OF1	R	23	20	26	1	7	1	0	0	2	2	6	0	.269	.308
Dale Murphy	C19	R	20	19	65	3	17	6	0	0	9	7	9	0	.262	.354
2 Craig Robinson	2B5,SS2,3B1	R	27	15	17	4	4	0	0	0	3	5	2	0	.235	.235
Brian Asselstine	OF9	L	23	20	33	2	7	0	0	1	1	5	3	0	.212	.303
1 Terry Crowley		L	29	7	6	0	0	0	0	0	0	0	0	0	.000	.000
2 Pete Varney	C5	R	27	5	10	0	1	0	0	0	0	1	5	0	.100	.100
Mike Eden	2B2	B	27	5	5	0	0	0	0	0	0	1	1	0	.000	.000
Pat Rockett	SS2	R	21	4	5	0	1	0	0	0	0	0	0	0	.200	.200

NAME	T	AGE	W	L	PCT	SV	G	GS	CG	IP	H	BB	SO	SHO	ERA
		29	70	92	.432	27	162	162	33	1438	1435	564	818	13	3.86
Phil Niekro	R	37	17	11	.607	0	38	37	10	271	249	101	173	2	3.29
Dick Ruthven	R	25	14	17	.452	0	36	36	8	240	255	90	142	4	4.20
Andy Messersmith (LJ)	R	30	11	11	.500	1	29	28	12	207	166	74	135	3	3.04
Adrian Devine (NJ)	R	24	5	6	.455	9	48	1	0	73	72	26	48	0	3.21
1 Elias Sosa	R	26	4	4	.500	3	21	0	0	35	41	13	32	0	5.40
Carl Morton	R	32	4	9	.308	0	26	24	1	140	172	45	42	1	4.18
Bruce Dal Canton	R	34	3	5	.375	1	42	1	0	73	67	42	36	0	3.58
Roger Moret (SJ)	R	26	3	5	.375	1	27	12	1	77	84	27	30	0	5.03
Frank LaCorte	R	24	3	12	.200	0	19	17	1	105	97	53	79	0	4.71
2 Mike Marshall (KJ)	R	33	2	1	.667	6	24	0	0	37	35	14	17	0	3.16
Max Leon (KJ-NJ)	R	26	2	4	.333	3	30	0	0	36	32	15	16	0	2.75
Al Autry	R	24	1	0	1.000	0	1	1	0	5	4	3	3	0	5.40
Jamie Easterly	L	23	1	1	.500	0	4	4	0	22	23	13	11	0	4.91
Preston Hanna	R	21	0	0	—	0	5	0	0	8	11	4	3	0	4.50
Rick Camp	R	23	0	1	.000	0	11	0	0	11	13	2	6	0	6.55
Buzz Capra (SJ)	R	28	0	0	—	0	5	0	0	9	9	6	4	0	9.00
Pablo Torrealba	L	28	0	2	.000	1	36	0	0	53	67	22	33	0	3.57
Mike Beard	L	26	0	0	—	1	30	0	0	34	38	14	8	0	4.24

WORLD SERIES — CINCINNATI (NL) 4 NEW YORK (AL) 0

LINE SCORES

TEAM	1	2	3		4	5	6		7	8	9		10	11	12		R	H	E

Game 1 October 16 at Cincinnati

	1	2	3	4	5	6	7	8	9	R	H	E
NY (AL)	0	1	0	0	0	0	0	0	0	1	5	1
CIN (NL)	1	0	1	0	0	1	2	0	X	5	10	1

Alexander, Lyle (7)   Gullett, Borbon (8)

Game 2 October 17 at Cincinnati

	1	2	3	4	5	6	7	8	9	R	H	E
NY	0	0	0	1	0	0	2	0	0	3	9	1
CIN	0	3	0	0	0	0	0	0	1	4	10	0

Hunter   Norman, Billingham (7)

Game 3 October 19 at New York

	1	2	3	4	5	6	7	8	9	R	H	E
CIN	0	3	0	1	0	0	2	0	0	6	13	2
NY	0	0	0	1	0	0	1	0	0	2	8	0

Zachry, McEnaney (7)   Ellis, Jackson (4), Tidrow (8)

Game 4 October 21 at New York

	1	2	3	4	5	6	7	8	9	R	H	E
CIN	0	0	0	3	0	0	0	0	4	7	9	2
NY	1	0	0	0	1	0	0	0	0	2	8	0

Nolan, McEnaney (7)   Figueroa, Tidrow (9), Lyle (9)

COMPOSITE BATTING

Cincinnati (NL)

NAME	POS	G	AB	R	H	2B	3B	HR	RBI	BA
Totals		4	134	22	42	10	3	4	21	.313
Griffey	RF	4	17	2	1	0	0	0	0	.059
Perez	1B	4	16	1	5	1	0	0	2	.313
Rose	3B	4	16	3	3	1	0	0	1	.188
Bench	C	4	15	4	8	1	1	2	6	.533
Morgan	2B	4	15	3	5	1	1	1	2	.333
Foster	LF	4	14	2	6	1	0	1	4	.429
Concepcion	SS	4	14	1	5	1	0	0	3	.357
Driessen	DH	4	14	4	5	2	0	1	1	.357
Geronimo	CF	4	13	3	4	2	0	0	1	.308

New York (AL)

NAME	POS	G	AB	R	H	2B	3B	HR	RBI	BA
Totals		4	135	8	30	3	1	1	8	.222
Rivers	CF	4	18	1	3	0	0	0	0	.167
Munson	C	4	17	2	9	0	0	0	2	.529
Chambliss	1B	4	16	1	5	1	0	0	3	.313
White	LF	4	15	0	2	0	0	0	0	.133
Randolph	2B	4	14	1	1	0	0	0	0	.071
Nettles	3B	4	12	0	3	0	0	0	1	.250
Piniella	DH-RF-PH	4	9	1	3	1	0	0	0	.333
May	PH-DH	4	9	0	0	0	0	0	0	.000
Gamble	PH-RF	4	8	0	1	0	0	0	0	.125
Stanley	SS	4	6	1	1	0	0	0	0	.167
Maddox	RF-DH	4	5	0	1	0	0	0	0	.200
Velez	PH	3	3	0	0	0	0	0	0	.000
Hendricks	PH	2	2	0	0	0	0	0	0	.000
Mason	SS	3	1	1	1	0	0	0	0	1.000

COMPOSITE PITCHING

Cincinnati (NL)

NAME	G	IP	H	BB	SO	W	L	SV	ERA
Totals	4	36	30	12	16	4	0	2	2.00
Gullett	1	7.1	5	3	4	1	0	0	1.23
Nolan	1	6.2	8	1	1	1	0	0	2.70
Zachry	1	6.2	6	5	6	1	0	0	2.70
Norman	1	6.1	9	2	2	0	0	0	4.26
McEnaney	2	4.2	2	1	2	0	0	2	0.00
Billingham	1	2.2	0	0	1	0	0	0	0.00
Borbon	1	1.2	0	0	0	0	0	0	0.00

New York (AL)

NAME	G	IP	H	BB	SO	W	L	SV	ERA
Totals	4	34.2	42	12	16	0	4	0	5.45
Hunter	1	8.2	10	4	5	0	1	0	3.12
Figueroa	1	6	9	2	1	0	1	0	5.63
Alexander	1	6	9	2	1	0	1	0	7.50
Jackson	1	3.2	4	0	3	0	0	0	4.91
Ellis	1	3.1	7	1	0	0	1	0	10.80
Lyle	2	2.2	1	1	3	0	0	0	7.71
Tidrow	2	2.1	5	1	1	0	0	0	7.71

1977 All That Money Can Buy

George Steinbrenner opened his wallet and gave the New York Yankees that same awesome look they wore through the 1950's and early 1960's. With over 20 free agents testing the new market for their services, Steinbrenner signed two plums in power-hitting Reggie Jackson and lefty pitcher Don Gullett. The Yanks had plenty of holdover stars such as Thurman Munson, Mickey Rivers, Catfish Hunter, Sparky Lyle, Graig Nettles, and Willie Randolph, and when they acquired shortstop Bucky Dent from the White Sox just before the start of the season, the New Yorkers truly could field an All-Star at every position.

But the juggernaut bogged down at the start of the season. A line drive struck Hunter on the foot on opening day and put him on the disabled list for a month; Catfish never regained his proper form all season. Rumors of dissension circled the team, and the press several times carried reports of manager Billy Martin's imminent firing. Martin did almost engage in a fistfight with Jackson in the Yankee dugout in full view of national television, and he was fined $2,500 for criticizing management. But he held on to his job by leading the Yanks to a strong stretch drive to the A.L. East title, helped by a surprise 16-7 season from young southpaw Ron Guidry. The torrid Yankee finish just edged out the Boston Red Sox, who hit 213 home runs but swung to extremes with a nine game losing streak in July and an eleven game winning streak in August, and the Baltimore Orioles, surprise contenders after losing a lot of talent in the free agent draft.

In the A.L. West, the Kansas City Royals had an easier time, winning the crown by eight games behind George Brett, Hal McRae, Al Cowens, and Dennis Leonard. The second-place Texas Rangers made headlines with their managerial situation. Frank Lucchesi was punched out by player Lenny Randle during a spring training disagreement, then was fired in mid-season. Eddie Stanky took over, was with the club one night, and then decided that he missed his family and went home. Coach Connie Ryan managed for a few days until Billy Hunter could be hired to lead the team to a strong second half. The California Angels hoped to contend after signing Joe Rudi, Bobby Grich, and Don Baylor as free agents, but they finished a weak fifth. The Oakland A's finished dead last, wiped out by free agent desertions. A feature of the division was the batting of Minnesota's Rod Carew, who flirted with .400 for most of the summer before settling for a .388 average.

In the N.L., the Philadelphia Phillies prevailed in the East by the sheer weight of excellence, overcoming a fast start by the Chicago Cubs, whose owner, Phil Wrigley, died in April. Pittsburgh was hurt by injuries to Rennie Stennett and Willie Stargell, St. Louis had a minor rebellion over a ban on facial hair during a season in which Lou Brock broke Ty Cobb's all-time base-stealing record, and the Mets suffered from internal turmoil which led to the trading of Dave Kingman and Tom Seaver. The Cincinnati Reds profited by obtaining Seaver, but could not catch the Los Angeles Dodgers, who ran away from the pack with 17 victories in the first 20 games, four 30-home run hitters, and a likable new manager in Tommy Lasorda.

The Dodgers took on the Yankees in the World Series, with the Yankees triumphing in six games behind the pitching of Guidry and Mike Torrez and Jackson's three homers in game six, a fitting close to a season in which a record 3,644 homers were hit and a record 39 million fans attended games.

1977 AMERICAN LEAGUE — EAST DIVISION

Name	G by Pos	B	AGE	G	AB	R	H	2B	3B	HR	RBI	BB	SO	SB	BA	SA
NEW YORK	1st 100-62 .617		BILLY MARTIN													
	TOTALS		29	162	5605	831	1576	267	47	184	784	533	681	93	.281	.444
Chris Chambliss	1B157	L	28	157	600	90	172	32	6	17	90	45	73	4	.287	.445
Willie Randolph	2B147	R	22	147	551	91	151	28	11	4	40	64	53	13	.274	.387
Bucky Dent	SS158	R	25	158	477	54	118	18	4	8	49	39	28	1	.247	.352
Graig Nettles	3B156, DH1	L	32	158	589	99	150	23	4	37	107	68	79	2	.255	.496
Reggie Jackson	OF127,DH18	L	31	146	525	93	150	39	2	32	110	74	129	17	.286	.550
Mickey Rivers	OF136, DH1	L	28	138	565	79	184	18	5	12	69	18	45	22	.326	.439
Roy White	OF135,DH4	B	33	143	519	72	139	25	2	14	52	75	58	18	.268	.405
Thurman Munson	C136, DH10	R	30	149	595	85	183	28	5	18	100	39	55	5	.308	.462
Carlos May	DH53, OF4	L	29	65	181	21	41	7	1	2	16	17	24	0	.227	.309
Lou Piniella	OF51, DH43, 1B1	R	33	103	339	47	112	19	3	12	45	20	31	2	.330	.510
Paul Blair	OF79, DH1	R	33	83	164	20	43	4	3	4	25	9	16	3	.262	.396
Cliff Johnson	DH25, C15, 1B11	R	29	56	142	24	42	8	0	12	31	20	23	0	.296	.606
Fred Stanley	SS42, 3B3, 2B2	R	29	48	46	6	12	0	0	1	7	8	6	1	.261	.326
Jim Wynn	DH15, OF8	R	35	30	77	7	11	2	1	1	3	15	16	1	.143	.234
Fran Healy	C26	R	30	27	67	10	15	5	0	0	7	6	13	1	.224	.299
George Zeber	2B21, 3B2, SS2, DH1	B	26	25	65	8	21	3	0	3	10	9	11	0	.323	.508
Dell Alston	DH10, OF2	L	24	22	40	10	13	4	0	1	4	3	4	3	.325	.500
Ellie Hendricks	C6	L	36	10	11	1	3	1	0	1	5	0	2	0	.273	.636
Dave Kingman	DH6	R	28	8	24	5	6	2	0	4	7	2	13	0	.250	.833
Mickey Klutts (BH)	3B4, SS1	R	22	5	15	3	4	1	0	1	4	2	1	0	.267	.533
Dave Bergman	OF3, 1B2	L	24	5	4	1	1	0	0	0	1	0	0	0	.250	.250
Gene Locklear	OF1	L	27	1	5	1	3	0	0	0	2	0	0	0	.600	.600
Marty Perez	3B1	R	31	1	4	0	2	0	0	0	0	0	1	0	.500	.500
Ron Blomberg (KJ)28																

NAME		T	AGE	W	L	PCT	SV	G	GS	CG	IP	H	BB	SO	SHO	ERA
			29	100	62	.617	34	162	162	52	1449	1395	486	758	16	3.61
Ron Guidry		L	26	16	7	.696	1	31	25	9	211	174	65	176	5	2.82
Ed Figueroa		R	28	16	11	.593	0	32	32	12	239	228	75	104	2	3.58
Don Gullett (SJ)		L	26	14	4	.778	0	22	22	7	158	137	69	116	1	3.59
2 Mike Torrez		R	30	14	12	.538	0	31	31	15	217	212	75	90	2	3.82
Sparky Lyle		L	32	13	5	.722	26	72	0	0	137	131	33	68	0	2.17
Dick Tidrow		R	30	11	4	.733	5	49	7	0	151	143	41	83	0	3.16
Catfish Hunter (FJ)		R	31	9	9	.500	0	22	22	8	143	137	47	52	1	4.72
Ken Holtzman		L	31	2	3	.400	0	18	11	0	72	105	24	14	0	5.75
Ken Clay		R	23	2	3	.400	1	21	3	0	56	53	24	20	0	4.34
2 Stan Thomas		R	27	1	0	1.000	0	3	0	0	6	7	4	1	0	7.50
1 Dock Ellis		R	32	1	1	.500	0	3	3	1	20	18	8	5	0	1.83
Gil Patterson (SJ)		R	21	1	2	.333	1	10	6	0	33	38	20	29	0	5.40
Larry McCall		R	24	0	1	.000	0	2	0	0	6	12	1	0	0	7.50

Name	G by Pos	B	AGE	G	AB	R	H	2B	3B	HR	RBI	BB	SO	SB	BA	SA
BALTIMORE	2nd(tie) 97-64 .602 2.5		EARL WEAVER													
	TOTALS		27	161	5494	719	1433	231	25	148	677	560	945	90	.261	.393
Lee May	1B110, DH39	R	34	150	585	75	148	16	2	27	99	38	119	2	.253	.426
Billy Smith	2B104, SS5, 1B2, 3B1	B	23	149	367	44	79	12	2	5	29	33	71	3	.215	.300
Mark Belanger	SS142	R	33	144	402	39	83	13	4	2	30	43	68	15	.206	.274
Doug DeCinces	3B148, 2B1, 1B1, DH1	R	26	150	522	63	135	28	3	19	69	64	86	8	.259	.433
Ken Singleton	OF150, DH1	B	30	152	536	90	176	24	0	24	99	107	101	0	.328	.507
Al Bumbry (LJ)	OF130	L	30	133	518	74	164	31	3	4	41	45	88	19	.317	.411
Pat Kelly	OF109, DH1	L	32	120	360	50	92	13	0	10	49	53	75	25	.256	.375
Rick Dempsey (BH)	C91	R	27	91	270	27	61	7	4	3	34	34	34	2	.226	.315
Eddie Murray	DH111, 1B42, OF3	B	21	160	611	81	173	29	2	27	88	48	104	0	.283	.470
Tony Muser	1B77, OF11, DH1	L	29	120	118	14	27	6	0	0	7	13	16	1	.229	.280
Rich Dauer	2B83, 3B9, DH2	R	24	96	304	38	74	15	1	5	25	20	28	1	.243	.349
Dave Skaggs	C80	R	26	80	216	22	62	9	1	1	24	20	34	0	.287	.352
Andres Mora	OF57, DH5, 3B1	R	22	77	233	32	57	8	2	13	44	5	53	0	.245	.464
Tom Shopay	OF52, DH2	L	32	67	69	15	13	3	0	1	4	8	7	3	.188	.275
Kiko Garcia	SS61, 2B2	R	23	65	131	20	29	6	0	2	10	6	31	2	.221	.313
Elliott Maddox (KJ)	OF45, 3B1	R	29	49	107	14	28	7	0	2	9	13	9	2	.262	.383
Larry Harlow	OF38	L	25	46	48	4	10	0	1	0	5	5	8	6	.208	.250
Mike Dimmel	OF23	R	22	25	5	8	0	0	0	0	0	1	1	0	1.000	.000
Brooks Robinson (VR)	3B15	R	40	24	47	3	7	2	0	1	4	4	4	0	.149	.255
Terry Crowley	DH2, 1B1	L	30	18	22	3	8	1	0	1	3	6	3	0	.364	.545
Ken Rudolph	C11	R	30	11	14	2	4	1	0	0	2	0	4	0	.286	.357
Dave Criscione	C7	R	25	7	9	1	3	0	0	1	0	0	1	0	.333	.667

Name		T	AGE	W	L	PCT	SV	G	GS	CG	IP	H	BB	SO	SHO	ERA
			27	97	64	.602	23	161	161	65	1451	1414	494	737	11	3.74
Jim Palmer		R	31	20	11	.645	0	39	39	22	319	263	99	193	3	2.91
Rudy May		L	32	18	14	.563	0	37	37	11	252	243	78	105	4	3.61
Mike Flanagan		L	25	15	10	.600	1	36	33	15	235	235	70	149	2	3.64
Dennis Martinez		R	22	14	7	.667	4	42	13	5	167	157	64	107	0	4.10
Ross Grimsley		L	27	14	10	.583	0	34	34	11	218	230	74	53	2	3.96
2 Dick Drago		R	32	6	3	.667	3	36	0	0	40	49	15	20	0	3.60
Tippy Martinez		L	27	5	1	.833	9	41	0	0	50	47	27	29	0	2.70
Scott McGregor		L	23	3	5	.375	4	29	5	1	114	119	30	55	0	4.42
1 Dyar Miller		R	31	2	2	.500	1	12	0	0	22	25	10	9	0	5.73
Tony Chevez		R	23	0	0	—	0	4	0	0	8	10	8	7	0	12.38
Mike Parrott		R	22	0	0	—	0	3	0	0	4	4	2	2	0	2.25
2 Nelson Briles		R	33	0	1	—	1	9	0	0	4	5	0	2	0	6.75
Earl Stephenson		L	29	0	0	—	0	1	0	0	3	5	2	0	0	9.00
Randy Miller		R	24	0	0	—	0	1	0	0	1	4	0	0	0	27.00
Ed Farmer		R	27	0	0	—	0	1	0	0	1	1	0	0	0	∞
1 Fred Holdsworth (SJ)		R	25	0	1	.000	0	12	0	0	14	17	16	4	0	6.43

BOSTON 2nd(tie) 97-64 .602 2.5 DON ZIMMER

Name	G by Pos	B	AGE	G	AB	R	H	2B	3B	HR	RBI	BB	SO	SB	BA	SA
TOTALS			29	161	5510	859	1551	258	56	213	828	528	905	66	.281	.465
George Scott	1B157	R	33	157	584	103	157	26	5	33	95	57	112	1	.269	.500
Denny Doyle	2B137	L	33	137	455	54	109	13	6	2	49	29	50	2	.240	.308
Rick Burleson	SS154	R	26	154	663	80	194	36	7	3	52	47	69	13	.293	.382
Butch Hobson	3B159	R	25	159	593	77	157	33	5	30	112	27	162	5	.265	.489
Dwight Evans (KJ)	OF63,DH6	R	25	73	230	39	66	9	2	14	36	28	58	4	.287	.526
Fred Lynn	OF125,DH1	L	25	129	497	81	129	29	5	18	76	51	63	2	.260	.447
Carl Yastrzemski	OF140,1B7,DH6	L	37	150	558	99	165	27	3	28	102	73	40	11	.296	.505
Carlton Fisk	C151	R	29	152	536	106	169	26	3	26	102	75	85	7	.315	.521
Jim Rice	DH116,OF44	R	24	160	644	104	206	29	15	39	114	53	120	5	.320	.593
Bernie Carbo	OF67,DH7	L	29	86	228	36	66	6	1	15	34	47	72	1	.289	.522
Rick Miller (BG)	OF79,DH1	L	29	86	189	34	48	9	3	0	24	22	30	11	.254	.333
Steve Dillard	2B45,SS9,DH6	R	26	66	141	22	34	7	0	1	13	7	13	4	.241	.312
2 Tommy Helms	DH13,3B2,2B1	R	36	21	59	5	16	2	0	1	5	4	4	0	.271	.356
Bob Montgomery	C15	R	33	17	40	6	12	2	0	2	7	4	9	0	.300	.500
Ted Cox	DH13	R	22	13	58	11	21	3	1	1	6	3	6	0	.362	.500
Dave Coleman	OF9	R	26	11	12	1	0	0	0	0	0	1	3	0	.000	.000
Doug Griffin	2B3	R	30	5	6	0	0	0	0	0	0	0	0	0	.000	.000
1 Bobby Darwin	DH2,OF1	R	34	4	9	1	2	1	0	0	1	0	4	0	.222	.333
Sam Bowen	OF3	R	24	3	2	0	0	0	0	0	0	0	2	0	.000	.000
Jack Baker	1B1	R	27	2	3	0	0	0	0	0	0	0	0	0	.000	.000
2 Bob Bailey		R	34	2	2	0	0	0	0	0	0	0	0	0	.000	.000
Bo Diaz	C2	R	24	2	1	0	0	0	0	0	0	0	0	0	.000	.000
Ramon Aviles	2B1	R	25	1	0	0	0	0	0	0	0	0	0	0	—	—

NAME	T	AGE	W	L	PCT	SV	G	GS	CG	IP	H	BB	SO	SHO	ERA
		29	97	64	.602	40	161	161	40	1428	1555	378	758	13	4.11
Bill Campbell	R	28	13	9	.591	31	69	0	0	140	112	60	114	0	2.96
Luis Tiant	R	36	12	8	.600	0	32	32	3	189	210	51	124	3	4.52
Rick Wise	R	31	11	5	.688	0	26	20	4	128	151	28	85	2	4.78
Reggie Cleveland	R	29	11	8	.579	2	36	27	9	190	211	43	85	1	4.26
Mike Paxton	R	23	10	5	.667	0	29	12	2	108	134	25	58	1	3.83
Ferguson Jenkins	R	33	10	10	.500	0	28	28	11	193	190	36	105	1	3.68
Bill Lee	L	30	9	5	.643	1	27	16	4	128	155	29	31	0	4.43
Bob Stanley	R	22	8	7	.533	3	41	13	3	151	176	43	44	1	3.99
Jim Willoughby (BN)	R	28	6	2	.750	2	31	0	0	55	54	18	33	0	4.91
Don Aase	R	22	6	2	.750	0	13	13	4	92	85	19	49	2	3.13
1 Tom House	L	30	1	0	1.000	0	8	0	0	8	15	6	6	0	12.38
Jim Burton	L	27	0	0	—	0	1	0	0	3	2	1	3	0	0.00
1 Tom Murphy	R	31	0	1	.000	0	16	0	0	31	44	12	13	0	6.68
2 Ramon Hernandez	L	36	0	1	.000	1	12	0	0	13	14	7	8	0	5.54
Rick Kreuger	L	28	0	0	.000	0	1	0	0	2	0	0	0	0	∞

DETROIT 4th 74-88 .457 26 RALPH HOUK

Name	G by Pos	B	AGE	G	AB	R	H	2B	3B	HR	RBI	BB	SO	SB	BA	SA
TOTALS			28	162	5604	714	1480	228	45	166	676	452	764	60	.264	.410
Jason Thompson	1B158	L	22	158	585	87	158	24	5	31	105	73	91	0	.270	.487
Tito Fuentes	2B151,DH1	B	33	151	615	83	190	19	10	5	51	38	61	4	.309	.397
Tom Veryzer	SS124	R	24	125	350	31	69	12	1	2	28	16	44	0	.197	.254
Aurelio Rodriguez (NJ)	3B95,SS1	R	29	96	306	30	67	14	1	10	32	16	36	1	.219	.369
Ben Oglivie	OF125,DH2	L	28	132	450	63	118	24	2	21	61	40	80	9	.262	.464
Ron LeFlore	OF152	R	29	154	652	100	212	30	10	16	57	37	121	39	.325	.475
Steve Kemp	OF148	L	22	151	552	75	142	29	4	18	88	71	93	3	.257	.422
Milt May	C111	L	26	115	397	32	99	9	3	12	46	26	31	0	.249	.378
Rusty Staub	DH156	L	33	158	623	84	173	34	3	22	101	59	47	1	.278	.448
Phil Mankowski	3B85,2B11	L	24	94	286	21	79	7	3	3	27	16	41	1	.276	.353
Mickey Stanley	OF57,1B3,SS3,DH2	R	34	75	222	30	51	9	1	8	23	18	30	0	.230	.387
Chuck Scrivener	SS50,2B8,3B3	R	29	61	72	10	6	0	0	0	2	5	9	0	.083	.083
Tim Corcoran	OF18,DH3	L	24	55	103	13	29	3	0	3	15	6	9	0	.282	.398
John Wockenfuss	C37,OF9,DH3	R	28	53	164	26	45	8	1	9	25	14	18	0	.274	.500
Mark Wagner	SS21,2B1	R	23	22	48	4	7	0	1	1	3	4	12	0	.146	.250
Alan Trammell	SS19	R	19	19	43	6	8	0	0	0	0	4	12	0	.186	.186
Bob Adams	1B2,C1	R	25	15	24	2	6	1	0	2	6	2	5	0	.250	.542
Bruce Kimm	C12,DH2	R	26	14	25	2	2	1	0	0	1	0	4	0	.080	.120
Lance Parrish	C12	R	21	12	46	10	9	2	0	3	7	5	12	0	.196	.435
Lou Whitaker	2B9	L	20	11	32	5	8	1	0	0	2	4	6	2	.250	.281
1 Bob Molinaro		L	24	7	4	0	1	1	0	0	0	0	2	0	.250	.500
2 Luis Alvarado	3B2	R	28	2	1	0	0	0	0	0	0	0	0	0	.000	.000
1 Willie Horton	OF1	R	34	1	4	0	1	0	0	0	0	0	0	0	.250	.250

NAME	T	AGE	W	L	PCT	SV	G	GS	CG	IP	H	BB	SO	SHO	ERA
		26	74	88	.457	23	162	162	44	1457	1526	470	784	3	4.13
Dave Rozema	R	20	15	7	.682	0	28	28	16	218	222	34	92	1	3.10
John Hiller	L	34	8	14	.364	7	45	8	3	124	120	61	115	0	3.56
Fernando Arroyo	R	25	8	18	.308	0	38	28	8	209	227	52	60	1	4.18
Steve Foucault	R	27	7	7	.500	13	44	0	0	74	64	17	58	0	3.16
Jim Crawford	L	26	7	8	.467	1	37	7	0	126	156	50	91	0	4.79
Milt Wilcox	R	27	6	2	.750	0	20	13	1	106	96	37	82	0	3.65
Mark Fidrych (KJ-SJ)	R	22	6	4	.600	0	11	11	7	81	82	12	42	1	2.89
Bob Sykes	L	22	5	7	.417	0	32	20	3	133	141	50	58	0	4.40
1 Dave Roberts	L	32	4	10	.286	0	22	22	5	129	143	41	46	0	5.16
Vern Ruhle (SJ)	R	26	3	5	.375	0	14	10	0	66	83	15	27	0	5.73
Ed Glynn	L	24	2	1	.667	0	8	3	0	27	36	12	13	0	5.33
Bruce Taylor	R	24	1	0	1.000	2	19	0	0	29	23	10	19	0	3.41
Jack Morris (SJ)	R	22	1	1	.500	0	7	6	1	46	38	23	28	0	3.72
Steve Grilli	R	28	1	1	.333	0	30	0	0	73	71	49	49	0	4.81
Ray Bare	R	28	0	2	.000	0	5	4	0	14	24	7	4	0	12.86

CLEVELAND 5th 71-90 .441 28.5 FRANK ROBINSON 26-31 .456 JEFF TORBORG 45-59 .433

Name	G by Pos	B	AGE	G	AB	R	H	2B	3B	HR	RBI	BB	SO	SB	BA	SA
TOTALS			27	161	5491	676	1476	221	46	100	631	531	688	87	.269	.380
Andre Thornton	1B117, DH9	R	27	131	433	77	114	20	5	28	70	70	82	3	.263	.527
Duane Kuiper	2B148	L	27	148	610	62	169	15	8	1	50	37	55	11	.277	.333
Frank Duffy	SS121	R	30	122	334	30	67	13	2	4	31	21	47	3	.201	.287
Buddy Bell (KJ)	3B118, OF11	R	25	129	479	64	140	23	4	11	64	45	63	1	.292	.426
Jim Norris	OF124, 1B3	L	28	133	440	59	119	23	6	2	37	64	57	26	.270	.364
Rick Manning (XJ)	OF68	R	22	68	252	33	57	7	3	5	18	21	35	9	.226	.337
1 Bruce Bochte	OF76, 1B36, DH1	L	26	112	392	52	119	19	1	5	43	40	38	3	.304	.395
Fred Kendall	C102, DH1	R	28	103	317	18	79	13	1	3	39	16	27	0	.249	.325
Rico Carty	DH123, 1B2	R	37	127	461	50	129	23	1	15	80	56	51	1	.280	.432
Paul Dade	OF99, 3B26, DH7, 2B1	R	25	134	461	65	134	15	3	3	45	32	58	16	.291	.356
Larvell Blanks	SS66, 3B18, 2B12, DH6	R	27	105	322	43	92	10	4	6	38	19	37	3	.286	.398
John Lowenstein	OF39, DH19, 1B1	L	30	81	149	24	36	6	1	4	12	21	29	1	.242	.376
1 Ray Fosse	C77, 1B1, DH1	R	30	78	238	25	63	7	1	6	27	7	26	0	.265	.378
Ron Pruitt	OF69, C4, DH4, 3B1	R	25	78	219	29	63	10	2	2	32	28	22	2	.288	.379
Bill Melton	1B15, DH14, 3B13	R	31	50	133	17	32	11	0	0	14	17	21	1	.241	.323
Johnny Grubb (SJ-BH)	OF28, DH4	L	28	34	93	8	28	3	2	0	14	19	18	0	.301	.462
Charlie Spikes	OF27, DH2	R	26	32	95	13	22	2	0	3	11	11	17	0	.232	.347
Alfredo Griffin	SS13, DH2	B	19	14	41	5	6	1	0	0	3	3	6	2	.146	.171
Dave Oliver	2B7	R	26	7	22	2	7	0	1	0	3	4	0	0	.318	.409

NAME	T	AGE	W	L	PCT	SV	G	GS	CG	IP	H	BB	SO	SHO	ERA
		28	71	90	.441	30	161	161	45	1452	1441	550	876	8	4.10
Dennis Eckersley	R	22	14	13	.519	0	33	33	12	247	214	54	191	3	3.53
Wayne Garland	R	26	13	19	.406	0	38	38	21	283	281	88	118	1	3.50
Jim Bibby	R	32	12	13	.480	2	37	30	9	207	197	73	141	2	3.57
Rick Waits	L	25	9	7	.563	2	37	16	1	135	132	64	62	0	4.00
Jim Kern	R	28	8	10	.444	18	60	0	0	92	85	47	91	0	3.42
Al Fitzmorris	R	31	6	10	.375	0	29	21	1	133	164	53	54	0	5.41
Pat Dobson	R	35	3	12	.200	1	33	17	0	133	155	65	81	0	6.16
Don Hood	L	27	2	1	.667	0	41	5	1	105	87	49	62	0	3.00
1 Dave LaRoche	L	29	2	2	.500	4	13	0	0	19	15	7	18	0	5.21
Cardell Camper	R	24	1	0	1.000	0	3	1	0	9	7	4	9	0	4.00
2 Sid Monge	L	26	1	2	.333	3	33	0	0	39	47	27	25	0	6.23
Tom Buskey	R	30	0	0	—	0	21	0	0	34	45	8	15	0	5.29
2 Bill Laxton	L	29	0	0	—	0	2	0	0	2	2	4	4	0	4.50
Larry Andersen	R	24	0	0	.000	0	11	0	0	14	10	9	8	0	3.21

MILWAUKEE 6th 67-95 .414 33 ALEX GRAMMAS

Name	G by Pos	B	AGE	G	AB	R	H	2B	3B	HR	RBI	BB	SO	SB	BA	SA
TOTALS			26	162	5517	639	1425	255	46	125	598	443	862	85	.258	.389
Cecil Cooper	1B148, DH10	L	27	160	643	86	193	31	7	20	78	28	110	13	.300	.463
Don Money	2B116, OF23, 3B15, DH7	R	30	152	570	86	159	28	3	25	83	57	70	8	.279	.470
Robin Yount	SS153	R	21	154	605	66	174	34	4	4	49	41	80	16	.288	.377
Sal Bando	3B135, DH24, 2B1, SS1	R	33	159	580	65	145	27	3	17	82	75	89	4	.250	.395
Sixto Lezcano (BH)	OF108	R	23	109	400	50	109	25	4	21	49	52	78	6	.273	.503
Von Joshua	OF140	L	29	144	536	58	140	25	7	9	49	21	74	12	.261	.384
Jim Wohlford	OF125, 2B1, DH1	R	24	129	391	41	97	16	3	2	36	21	49	17	.248	.320
Charlie Moore	C137	R	24	138	375	42	93	15	6	5	45	31	39	1	.248	.360
Jamie Quirk	DH53, OF10, 3B8	L	22	93	221	16	48	14	1	3	13	8	47	0	.217	.330
Steve Brye	OF83, DH6	R	28	94	241	27	60	14	3	7	28	16	39	1	.249	.419
Ken McMullen	DH29, 1B11, 3B7	R	35	63	136	15	31	7	1	5	19	15	33	0	.228	.404
Larry Haney	C63	R	34	63	127	7	29	2	0	0	15	5	30	0	.228	.244
Lenn Sakata	2B53	R	23	53	154	13	25	2	0	2	12	9	22	1	.162	.214
2 Jim Wynn	OF17, DH15	R	35	36	117	10	23	3	1	0	10	17	31	3	.197	.299
Mike Hegan	OF8, DH7, 1B6	L	34	35	53	8	9	3	0	1	2	3	10	0	.170	.283
Bobby Sheldon	DH17, 2B5	R	26	31	66	9	13	4	1	0	3	6	9	0	.203	.297
Tim Johnson (PJ)	2B10, SS6, 3B4, DH4, OF1	L	27	30	33	5	2	1	0	0	2	5	5	1	.061	.091
3 Ed Kirkpatrick	OF22, DH3, 3B1	L	32	29	77	8	21	4	0	0	6	10	8	0	.273	.325
Danny Thomas	OF9, DH9	L	23	22	70	11	19	3	2	2	11	8	11	0	.271	.457
Dick Davis	OF12, DH6	R	23	22	51	7	14	2	0	0	6	2	15	0	.275	.314
Jim Gantner	3B14	L	24	14	47	4	14	1	0	1	2	1	3	2	.298	.383
Ed Romero	SS10	R	19	10	25	4	7	1	0	0	2	3	5	0	.280	.320
Jack Heidemann	DH3, 2B1	R	27	5	1	0	0	0	0	0	0	1	0	0	.000	.000

NAME	T	AGE	W	L	PCT	SV	G	GS	CG	IP	H	BB	SO	SHO	ERA
		24	67	95	.414	25	162	162	38	1431	1461	566	719	6	4.32
Jerry Augustine	L	24	12	18	.400	0	33	33	10	209	222	72	68	1	4.48
Moose Haas	R	21	10	12	.455	0	32	32	6	198	195	84	113	0	4.32
Jim Slaton	R	27	10	14	.417	0	32	31	7	221	223	77	104	1	3.58
Bill Castro	R	23	8	6	.571	13	51	0	0	69	76	23	28	0	4.17
Lary Sorensen	R	21	7	10	.412	0	23	20	9	142	147	36	57	0	4.37
Eduardo Rodriguez	R	25	6	8	.455	4	42	5	1	143	126	56	104	1	4.34
2 Mike Caldwell	L	28	5	8	.385	0	21	12	2	94	101	36	38	0	4.60
Bill Travers (EJ)	L	24	4	12	.250	0	19	19	2	122	140	57	49	1	5.24
Gary Beare	R	24	3	3	.500	0	17	6	0	59	63	38	32	0	6.41
Bob McClure	L	25	2	1	.667	6	68	0	0	71	64	34	57	0	2.54
Barry Cort (SJ)	R	21	1	1	.500	0	7	3	1	24	25	9	17	0	3.38
Rich Folkers	L	30	1	1	.000	0	9	0	0	6	7	4	6	0	4.50
Sam Hinds	R	23	0	3	.000	2	29	1	0	72	72	40	46	0	4.75

TORONTO 7th 54-107 .335 45.5 ROY HARTSFIELD

Name	G by Pos	B	AGE	G	AB	R	H	2B	3B	HR	RBI	BB	SO	SB	BA	SA
	TOTALS		27	161	5418	605	1367	230	41	100	553	499	819	65	.252	.365
Doug Ault	1B122, DH4	R	27	129	445	44	109	22	3	11	64	39	68	4	.245	.382
Steve Staggs	2B72	R	26	72	290	37	75	11	6	2	28	36	38	5	.259	.359
Hector Torres	SS68, 2B23, 3B2	R	31	91	266	33	64	7	3	5	26	16	33	1	.241	.346
2 Roy Howell (HJ)	3B87, DH8	R	23	96	364	41	115	17	1	10	44	42	76	4	.316	.451
Otto Velez	OF79, DH28	R	26	120	360	50	92	19	3	16	62	65	87	4	.256	.453
Bob Bailor (RJ)	OF63, SS53, DH7	R	25	122	496	62	154	21	5	5	32	17	26	15	.310	.403
Al Woods	OF115, DH4	L	23	122	440	58	125	17	4	6	35	36	38	8	.284	.382
Alan Ashby	C124	B	25	124	396	25	83	16	3	2	29	50	51	0	.210	.280
Ron Fairly	DH58, 1B40, OF33	L	38	132	458	60	128	24	2	19	64	58	58	0	.279	.465
Sam Ewing	OF46, DH27, 1B2	L	27	97	244	24	70	8	2	4	34	19	42	1	.287	.385
2 Doug Rader	3B45, DH34, 1B7, OF1	R	32	96	313	47	75	18	2	13	40	38	65	2	.240	.435
Dave McKay	2B40, 3B32, SS20, DH2	R	27	95	274	18	54	4	3	3	22	7	51	2	.197	.266
Steve Bowling	OF87	R	25	89	194	19	40	8	1	1	13	37	42	2	.206	.273
John Scott	OF67, DH4	R	25	79	233	26	56	9	0	2	15	8	39	10	.240	.305
Gary Woods	OF60	R	22	60	227	21	49	9	1	0	17	7	38	5	.216	.264
Pete Garcia	2B34, DH4	R	27	41	130	10	27	10	1	0	9	5	21	0	.208	.300
Rick Cerone (RJ)	C31	R	23	31	100	7	20	4	0	1	10	6	12	0	.200	.270
2 Tim Nordbrook	SS24	R	27	24	63	9	11	0	1	0	1	4	11	1	.175	.206
Ernie Whitt (FJ)	C14	L	25	23	41	4	7	3	0	0	6	2	12	0	.171	.244
1 Jim Mason	SS22	L	26	22	79	10	13	3	0	0	2	7	10	1	.165	.203
Phil Roof (KJ)	C3	R	36	3	5	0	0	0	0	0	0	0	1	0	.000	.000

NAME	T	AGE	W	L	PCT	SV	G	GS	CG	IP	H	BB	SO	SHO	ERA
		26	54	107	.335	20	161	161	40	1428	1538	623	771	3	4.57
Dave Lemanczyk	R	26	13	16	.448	0	34	34	11	252	278	87	105	0	4.25
Jerry Garvin	L	21	10	18	.357	0	34	34	12	245	247	85	127	1	4.19
Jesse Jefferson	R	28	9	17	.346	0	33	33	8	217	224	83	114	0	4.31
Pete Vuckovich	R	24	7	7	.500	8	53	8	3	148	143	59	123	1	3.47
Jim Clancy	R	21	4	9	.308	0	13	13	4	77	80	47	44	1	5.03
2 Tom Murphy	R	31	2	1	.667	2	19	1	0	52	63	18	26	0	3.63
Jerry Johnson	R	33	2	4	.333	5	43	0	0	86	91	54	54	0	4.60
Mike Willis	L	26	2	6	.250	5	43	3	0	107	105	38	59	0	3.95
Bill Singer (SJ-XJ)	R	33	2	8	.200	0	13	12	0	60	71	39	33	0	6.75
Jeff Byrd	R	20	2	13	.133	0	17	17	1	87	98	68	40	0	6.21
1 Steve Hargan	R	34	1	3	.250	0	6	5	1	29	36	14	11	0	5.26
Dennis DeBarr	L	24	0	1	.000	0	14	0	0	21	29	8	10	0	6.00
Tom Bruno	R	24	0	1	.000	0	12	0	0	18	30	13	9	0	8.00
Mike Darr	R	21	0	1	.000	1	1	1	0	1	4	1	4	0	45.00
Chuck Hartenstein (BG)	R	35	0	2	.000	1	13	0	0	27	40	6	15	0	6.67

WEST DIVISION

KANSAS CITY 1st 102-60 .630 WHITEY HERZOG

Name	G by Pos	B	AGE	G	AB	R	H	2B	3B	HR	RBI	BB	SO	SB	BA	SA
	TOTALS		27	162	5594	822	1549	299	77	146	773	522	687	170	.277	.436
John Mayberry	1B145, DH8	L	28	153	543	73	125	22	1	23	82	83	86	1	.230	.401
Frank White	2B152, SS4	R	26	152	474	59	116	21	5	5	50	25	67	23	.245	.342
Freddie Patek	SS154	R	32	154	497	72	130	26	6	5	60	41	84	53	.262	.368
George Brett	3B135, DH3, SS1	L	24	139	564	105	176	32	13	22	88	55	24	14	.312	.532
Al Cowens	OF159, DH1	R	25	162	606	98	189	32	14	23	112	41	64	16	.312	.525
Amos Otis	OF140	R	30	142	478	85	120	20	8	17	78	71	88	23	.251	.433
Tom Poquette	OF96	L	25	106	342	43	100	23	6	2	33	19	21	1	.292	.412
Darrell Porter	C125, DH1	L	25	130	425	61	117	21	5	16	60	53	70	1	.275	.452
Hal McRae	DH16, OF46, DH16	R	31	162	641	104	191	54	11	21	92	59	43	18	.298	.515
Joe Zdeb	OF93, DH4, 3B1	R	24	105	195	26	58	5	2	2	23	16	23	6	.297	.374
Pete LaCock	1B29, DH26, OF12	L	25	88	218	25	66	12	1	3	29	15	25	2	.303	.408
Cookie Rojas	3B31, 2B16, DH6	R	38	64	156	8	39	9	1	0	18	4	17	1	.250	.321
John Wathan	C35, 1B5, DH2	R	27	55	119	18	39	5	3	2	21	5	8	2	.328	.471
Bob Heise	2B21, SS21, 3B12, 1B1	R	30	54	62	11	16	2	1	0	5	2	8	0	.258	.323
Joe Lahoud	OF15, DH4	L	30	34	65	8	17	5	0	2	8	11	16	1	.262	.431
Buck Martinez	C28	R	28	29	80	3	18	4	0	1	9	3	12	0	.225	.313
Dave Nelson (LJ-GJ)	2B11, DH7	R	33	27	48	8	9	3	1	0	4	7	11	1	.188	.292
Willie Wilson	OF9, DH2	B	21	13	34	10	11	2	0	0	1	1	8	6	.324	.382
U.L. Washington	SS9	B	23	10	20	4	4	1	0	0	1	5	4	1	.200	.350
Clint Hurdle	OF9	L	19	9	26	5	8	0	0	2	7	2	7	0	.308	.538

NAME	T	AGE	W	L	PCT	SV	G	GS	CG	IP	H	BB	SO	SHO	ERA
		29	102	60	.630	42	162	162	41	1461	1377	499	850	15	3.52
Dennis Leonard	R	26	20	12	.625	1	38	37	21	293	246	79	244	5	3.04
Jim Colborn	R	31	18	14	.563	0	36	35	6	239	233	81	103	1	3.62
Paul Splittorff	L	30	16	6	.727	0	37	37	6	229	243	83	99	2	3.69
Doug Bird	R	27	11	4	.733	14	53	5	0	118	120	29	83	0	3.89
Marty Pattin	R	34	10	3	.769	0	31	10	4	128	115	37	55	0	3.59
Andy Hassler (KJ)	L	25	9	6	.600	0	29	27	3	156	166	75	83	1	4.21
Mark Littell	R	24	8	4	.667	12	48	5	0	105	73	55	106	0	3.60
Larry Gura	L	29	8	5	.615	10	52	6	1	106	108	28	46	1	3.14
Steve Mingori	L	33	2	4	.333	4	43	0	0	64	59	19	19	0	3.09
Tom Hall	L	29	0	0	—	0	3	0	0	8	4	6	10	0	3.38
George Throop	R	26	0	0	—	1	4	0	0	5	1	4	1	0	3.60
Randy McGilberry	R	23	0	1	.000	0	3	0	0	7	1	1	0	0	5.14
Gary Lance	R	28	0	1	.000	0	4	0	0	4	4	3	2	0	4.50
Steve Busby (SJ) 27															

TEXAS 2nd 94-68 .580 8 FRANK LUCCHESI 31-31 .500 EDDIE STANKY 1-0 1.000 CONNIE RYAN 2-4 .333 BILLY HUNTER 60-33 .645

Name	G by Pos	B	AGE	G	AB	R	H	2B	3B	HR	RBI	BB	SO	SB	BA	SA
	TOTALS		29	162	5541	767	1497	265	39	135	704	596	904	154	.270	.405
Mike Hargrove	1B152	L	27	153	525	98	160	28	4	18	69	103	59	2	.305	.476
Bump Wills	2B150, SS2, 1B1, DH1	B	24	152	541	87	155	28	6	9	62	65	96	28	.287	.410
Bert Campaneris	SS149	R	35	150	552	77	140	19	7	5	46	47	86	27	.254	.341
Toby Harrah	3B159, SS1	R	28	159	539	90	142	25	5	27	87	109	73	27	.263	.479
Dave May	OF111, DH5	L	33	120	340	46	82	14	1	7	42	32	43	4	.241	.350
Juan Beniquez	OF123	R	27	123	424	56	114	19	6	10	50	43	43	26	.269	.413
Claudell Washington	OF127, DH1	L	22	129	521	63	148	31	2	12	68	25	112	21	.284	.420
Jim Sundberg	C149	R	26	149	453	61	132	20	3	6	65	53	77	3	.291	.389
2 Willie Horton	DH128, OF10	R	34	139	519	55	150	23	3	15	75	42	117	2	.289	.432
Tommy Grieve (BH)	OF60, DH13	R	29	79	236	24	53	9	0	7	30	13	57	1	.225	.352
Ken Henderson (LJ, VJ)	OF65, DH3	B	31	75	244	23	63	14	0	5	23	18	37	2	.258	.377
Sandy Alomar	DH26, 2B18, SS6, OF5, 1B4, 3B1	B	33	69	83	21	22	3	0	1	11	8	13	4	.265	.337
Johnny Ellis	C16, DH15, 1B8	R	28	49	119	7	28	7	0	4	15	8	26	0	.235	.395
Kurt Bevacqua	OF14, 3B11, 2B5, 1B5, DH3	R	30	39	96	13	32	7	2	5	28	6	13	0	.333	.604
Bill Fahey	C34	L	27	37	68	3	15	4	0	0	5	3	5	0	.221	.279
2 Jim Mason	SS32, 3B1, DH1	L	26	36	55	9	12	3	0	1	7	6	10	0	.218	.327
Lew Beasley	OF18, SS1, DH1	L	28	25	32	5	7	1	0	0	3	2	1	1	.219	.250
Keith Smith	OF22	R	24	23	67	13	16	4	0	2	6	4	7	2	.239	.388
2 Ed Kirkpatrick	OF6, DH5, 1B3, C1	L	32	20	48	2	9	1	0	0	4	11	2	1	.188	.208
Eddie Miller	DH3, OF2	B	20	17	6	7	2	0	0	0	1	4	3	3	.333	.333
1 Jim Fregosi (KJ)	1B5, DH3	R	35	13	28	4	7	1	0	1	3	4	6	0	.250	.393
Pat Putnam	1B7, DH3	L	23	11	26	3	8	4	0	0	3	1	4	0	.308	.462
1 Roy Howell	OF2, DH2, 3B1, 1B1	L	23	7	17	0	0	0	0	0	0	2	4	0	.000	.000
Gary Gray	OF1	R	24	1	2	0	0	0	0	0	0	0	0	0	.000	.000
1 Lenny Randle (ST) 28																

NAME	T	AGE	W	L	PCT	SV	G	GS	CG	IP	H	BB	SO	SHO	ERA
		30	94	68	.580	31	162	162	49	1472	1412	471	864	17	3.56
Doyle Alexander	R	26	17	11	.607	0	34	34	12	237	221	82	82	1	3.65
Gaylord Perry	R	38	15	12	.556	0	34	34	13	238	239	56	177	4	3.37
Bert Blyleven	R	26	14	12	.538	0	30	30	15	235	181	69	182	5	2.72
Adrian Devine	R	25	11	6	.647	15	56	2	0	106	102	31	67	0	3.57
3 Dock Ellis	R	32	10	6	.625	1	23	22	7	167	158	42	90	1	2.91
1 Nelson Briles	R	33	6	4	.600	1	28	15	2	108	114	30	57	1	4.08
Darold Knowles	L	35	5	2	.714	4	42	0	0	50	50	23	14	0	3.24
Len Barker	R	21	4	1	.800	1	15	3	0	47	36	24	51	0	2.68
Paul Lindblad	L	35	4	5	.444	4	42	1	0	99	103	29	46	0	4.18
Roger Moret (SJ)		27	3	3	.500	4	18	8	2	72	59	38	39	0	3.75
2 Mike Marshall (KJ)	R	34	2	2	.500	1	12	0	0	18	13	9	7	0	3.75
2 Steve Hargan	R	34	1	0	1.000	0	6	1	0	12	12	5	10	0	9.00
John Poloni	R	23	1	0	1.000	0	2	1	1	9	6	4	5	0	6.43
2 Jim Umbarger	L	24	1	1	.500	0	3	2	0	13	14	4	5	0	5.54
Mike Wallace	L	26	0	0	—	0	4	0	0	10	12	10	2	0	7.88
Bobby Cuellar	R	24	0	0	—	0	4	0	0	7	4	2	3	0	1.29
Mike Bacsik	R	25	0	0	—	0	1	0	0	4	10	2	1	0	22.50
Tommy Boggs	R	21	0	3	.000	0	4	4	0	12	15	10	6	0	6.00

CHICAGO 3rd 90-72 .556 12 BOB LEMON

Name	G by Pos	B	AGE	G	AB	R	H	2B	3B	HR	RBI	BB	SO	SB	BA	SA
	TOTALS		27	162	5633	844	1568	254	52	192	809	559	666	42	.278	.444
Jim Spencer	1B125	L	29	128	470	56	116	16	1	18	69	36	50	1	.247	.400
Jorge Orta	2B139	L	26	144	564	71	159	27	8	11	84	46	49	4	.282	.417
Alan Bannister	SS133, 2B3, OF3	R	25	139	560	87	154	20	3	3	57	54	49	4	.275	.338
Eric Soderholm	3B126, DH3	R	28	130	460	77	129	20	3	25	67	47	47	2	.280	.500
Richie Zisk	OF109, DH28	R	28	141	531	78	154	17	6	30	101	55	98	0	.290	.514
Chet Lemon	OF149	R	22	150	553	99	151	38	4	19	67	52	88	8	.273	.459
Ralph Garr	OF126, DH2	L	31	134	543	74	163	29	7	10	54	27	44	12	.300	.435
Jim Essian	C111, 3B2	R	26	114	322	50	88	18	2	10	44	52	35	1	.273	.435
Oscar Gamble	DH79, OF4	L	27	137	408	75	121	22	2	31	83	54	54	1	.297	.588
Lamar Johnson	DH68, 1B45	R	26	118	374	52	113	12	5	18	65	24	53	1	.302	.505
Brian Downing	C61, OF3, DH2	R	26	69	169	28	48	4	2	4	25	34	21	1	.284	.402
Jack Brohamer	3B38, 2B16, DH1	L	27	59	152	26	39	10	3	2	20	21	8	0	.257	.401
Royle Stillman	OF26, DH13, 1B1	L	26	56	119	18	25	7	1	3	13	17	21	2	.210	.361
Wayne Nordhagen	OF46, C3, DH2	R	28	52	124	16	39	7	3	4	22	2	12	1	.315	.516
2 Don Kessinger	SS21, 2B13, 3B9	B	34	39	119	12	28	3	2	0	11	13	7	2	.235	.294
Bob Coluccio	OF19	L	25	20	37	4	10	0	0	0	7	6	2	2	.270	.270
Henry Cruz	OF9	L	25	16	21	3	6	0	0	2	3	6	2	0	.286	.571
1 Tim Nordbrook	SS11, DH2, 3B1, 2B1	R	27	15	20	2	5	0	0	0	1	7	4	1	.250	.250
1 Jerry Hairston	OF11	B	25	13	26	3	8	2	0	0	4	5	7	1	.308	.385
Kevin Bell (KJ)	SS5, 3B4, DH1	R	21	9	28	4	5	1	0	1	3	4	5	0	.179	.321
Bill Nahorodny	C7	R	23	7	23	3	6	1	0	0	1	0	6	0	.261	.435
John Flannery	SS4, 3B1, DH1	R	20	5	11	0	1	0	0	0	0	1	1	0	.000	.000
Tommy Cruz	OF2	R	25	3	4	0	0	0	0	0	0	0	0	0	.000	.000
Mike Squires	1B1	L	25	3	1	0	0	0	0	0	0	0	0	0	.000	.000
2 Bob Molinaro		L	27	3	2	1	1	0	0	0	0	1	0	1	.500	.500
Nyls Nyman		L	23	1	1	0	0	0	0	0	0	0	0	0	.000	.000

NAME	T	AGE	W	L	PCT	SV	G	GS	CG	IP	H	BB	SO	SHO	ERA
		27	90	72	.556	40	162	162	34	1445	1557	516	842	3	4.25
Steve Stone	R	29	15	12	.556	0	31	31	8	207	228	80	124	0	4.52
Francisco Barrios	R	24	14	7	.667	0	33	31	9	231	241	58	119	0	4.13
Chris Knapp	R	23	12	7	.632	0	27	26	4	148	166	61	103	0	4.81
Ken Kravec	R	25	11	8	.579	0	26	25	6	167	161	57	125	1	4.10
Lerrin LaGrow	R	28	7	3	.700	25	66	0	0	99	81	35	63	0	2.45
Wilbur Wood (KJ)	L	35	7	8	.467	0	24	18	5	123	139	50	42	1	4.98
1 Ken Brett	L	28	6	4	.600	0	13	13	2	83	101	15	39	0	4.99
2 Steve Renko	R	32	5	0	1.000	0	8	8	0	53	55	17	36	0	3.63
Dave Hamilton	L	29	4	5	.444	9	55	0	0	77	71	33	45	0	3.63
Bart Johnson	R	27	4	5	.444	2	29	4	0	92	114	38	46	0	4.01
2 Don Kirkwood	R	27	1	1	.500	0	10	0	0	40	49	10	24	0	5.18
Randy Wiles	L	25	1	1	.500	0	3	0	0	3	6	1	0	0	9.00
Dave Frost	R	24	1	1	.500	0	4	3	0	30	3	15	0	0	3.60
2 Clay Carroll	R	36	1	1	.250	6	33	0	0	11	14	4	4	0	4.91
Larry Anderson	R	24	1	3	.250	0	4	4	0	30	2	3	0	0	1.80
2 John Verhoeven	R	24	0	1	.000	1	9	0	0	10	9	2	3	0	5.57
Silvio Martinez	R	21	0	1	.000	0	1	0	0	3	6	2	1	0	6.00
Jack Kucek	R	24	0	1	.000	0	3	3	1	35	35	10	25	0	3.60
Bruce Dal Canton (EJ)	R	35	0	2	.000	0	17	0	0	24	20	13	9	0	3.75

Name	G by Pos	B	AGE	G	AB	R	H	2B	3B	HR	RBI	BB	SO	SB	BA	SA
MINNESOTA 4th 84-77 .522 17.5	GENE MAUCH															
TOTALS			27	161	5639	867	1588	273	60	123	804	563	754	105	.282	.417
Rod Carew	1B151, 2B4, DH1	L	31	155	616	128	239	38	16	14	100	69	55	23	.388	.570
Bob Randall (KJ)	2B101, 3B1, 1B1, DH1	R	29	103	306	36	73	13	2	0	22	15	25	1	.239	.294
Roy Smalley	SS150	B	24	150	584	93	135	21	5	6	56	74	89	5	.231	.315
Mike Cubbage	3B126, DH1	R	26	129	417	60	110	16	5	9	55	37	49	1	.264	.391
Dan Ford	OF137, DH3	R	25	144	453	66	121	25	7	11	60	41	79	6	.267	.426
Lyman Bostock	OF149	L	26	153	593	104	199	36	12	14	90	51	59	16	.336	.508
Larry Hisle	OF134, DH6	R	30	141	546	95	165	36	3	28	119	56	106	21	.302	.533
Butch Wynegar	C142, 3B1	B	21	144	532	76	139	22	3	10	79	68	61	2	.261	.370
Craig Kusick	DH85, 1B23	R	28	115	268	34	68	12	0	12	45	49	60	3	.254	.433
Rich Chiles	DH61, OF22	L	27	108	261	31	69	16	1	3	36	23	17	0	.264	.368
Glenn Adams (BW)	DH47, OF44	L	29	95	269	32	91	17	0	6	49	18	30	0	.338	.468
Jerry Terrell	3B59, 2B14, DH9, SS7, 1B1, OF1	R	30	93	214	32	48	6	0	1	20	11	21	10	.224	.266
Rob Wilfong	2B66, DH1	L	23	73	171	22	42	1	1	1	13	17	26	10	.246	.281
Bob Gorinski	OF37, DH9	R	25	54	118	14	23	4	1	3	22	5	29	1	.195	.322
Willie Norwood	OF28, DH6	R	26	39	83	15	19	3	0	3	9	6	17	6	.229	.373
Luis Gomez	2B19, SS7, 3B4, DH2, OF1	R	25	32	65	6	16	4	2	0	11	4	9	0	.246	.369
Glenn Borgmann (KJ)	C17	R	27	17	43	12	11	1	0	2	7	11	9	0	.256	.419
Terry Bulling	C10, DH3	R	24	15	32	2	5	1	0	0	5	5	5	0	.156	.188
Sam Perlozzo	2B10, 3B1	R	26	10	24	6	7	0	2	0	0	2	3	0	.292	.458
Randy Bass	DH6	L	23	9	19	0	2	0	0	0	0	0	5	0	.105	.105
Larry Wolfe	3B8	R	24	8	25	3	6	1	0	0	6	1	0	0	.240	.280

NAME	T	AGE	W	L	PCT	SV	G	GS	CG	IP	H	BB	SO	SHO	ERA
TOTALS		27	84	77	.522	25	161	161	35	1442	1546	507	737	4	4.36
Dave Goltz	R	28	20	11	.645	0	39	39	19	303	284	91	186	2	3.36
Tom Johnson	R	26	16	7	.696	15	71	0	0	147	152	47	87	0	3.12
Geoff Zahn	L	31	12	14	.462	0	34	32	7	198	234	66	88	1	4.68
Paul Thormodsgard	R	23	11	15	.423	0	37	37	8	218	236	65	94	1	4.62
Ron Schueler	R	29	8	7	.533	3	52	7	0	135	131	61	77	0	4.40
Tom Burgmeier	L	33	6	4	.600	7	61	0	0	97	113	33	35	0	5.19
Pete Redfern	R	22	6	9	.400	0	30	28	1	137	164	66	73	0	5.19
Jeff Holly	L	24	3	4	.400	0	18	5	0	48	57	12	32	0	6.94
Dave Johnson	R	28	2	5	.286	0	30	6	0	73	86	23	33	0	4.56
Mike Pazik (AA)	L	27	1	0	1.000	0	3	3	0	18	18	6	6	0	2.50
Gary Serum	R	20	0	0	—	0	3	0	0	23	22	10	14	0	4.30
Jim Shellenback	L	33	0	0	—	0	5	0	0	6	10	5	3	0	7.50
Jim Hughes	R	25	0	0	—	0	2	0	0	4	4	1	1	0	2.25
Don Carrithers (AA)	R	27	0	1	.000	0	7	0	0	14	16	6	3	0	7.07
Bill Butler	L	30	0	1	.000	0	6	4	0	21	19	15	5	0	6.86

Name	G by Pos	B	AGE	G	AB	R	H	2B	3B	HR	RBI	BB	SO	SB	BA	SA
CALIFORNIA 5th 74-88 .457 28	NORM SHERRY 39-42 .481 DAVE GARCIA 35-46 .432															
TOTALS			26	162	5410	675	1380	233	40	131	636	542	880	159	.255	.386
Tony Solaita	1B91, DH6	L	30	116	324	40	78	15	0	14	53	56	77	1	.241	.417
Jerry Remy	2B152, SS1	L	24	154	575	74	145	19	10	4	44	59	59	41	.252	.341
Bobby Grich (XJ)	SS52	R	28	52	181	24	44	6	0	7	23	37	40	6	.243	.392
Dave Chalk	3B141, 2B7, SS4	R	26	144	519	58	144	27	2	3	45	52	69	12	.277	.355
Bobby Bonds	OF140, DH18	R	31	158	592	103	156	23	9	37	115	74	141	41	.264	.520
Gil Flores	OF85, DH8	R	24	104	342	41	95	19	4	1	26	23	39	12	.278	.365
Joe Rudi (BG)	OF61, DH3	R	30	64	242	48	64	13	2	13	53	22	48	1	.264	.496
Terry Humphrey	C123	R	27	123	304	17	69	11	0	2	34	21	58	1	.227	.283
Don Baylor	OF77, DH61, 1B18	R	28	154	561	87	141	27	0	25	75	62	76	26	.251	.433
Ron Jackson	1B43, 3B30, DH20, OF3, SS1	R	24	106	292	38	71	15	2	8	28	24	42	3	.243	.390
Mike Guerrero (HJ)	SS31, DH19, 2B12	R	27	86	244	17	69	8	2	1	28	4	16	0	.283	.344
Andy Etchebarren	C80	R	34	80	114	11	29	2	0	1	14	12	19	0	.254	.307
Rance Mulliniks	SS77	R	21	78	271	36	73	13	2	3	21	23	36	1	.269	.365
Dan Briggs	1B45, OF13	L	24	59	74	6	12	2	0	1	4	8	14	0	.162	.230
Thad Bosley (LJ)	OF55	L	20	58	212	19	63	10	2	0	19	16	32	5	.297	.363
Rusty Torres (HJ)	OF9	B	28	58	77	9	12	1	1	3	10	10	16	1	.156	.312
Ike Hampton	C47, DH2	R	25	52	44	5	13	1	0	3	9	2	10	0	.295	.523
Willie Aikens	1B13, DH1	L	22	42	91	5	18	4	0	0	6	10	23	1	.198	.242
Danny Goodwin	DH23	L	23	35	91	5	19	6	1	1	8	5	19	0	.209	.330
1 Bruce Bochte	OF24, DH1	L	26	25	100	12	29	4	0	2	8	7	4	3	.290	.390
Orlando Ramirez (RJ)	2B5, SS3, DH1	R	25	25	13	6	1	0	0	0	0	0	3	1	.077	.077
Ken Landreaux	OF22	L	22	23	76	6	19	5	1	0	5	5	5	1	.250	.342
Bobby Jones	DH6	L	27	14	17	3	3	0	0	0	1	4	5	0	.176	.353
2 Carlos May	1B3, DH1	L	29	11	18	0	6	0	0	0	1	5	1	0	.333	.333
3 Dave Kingman	1B8, OF2	R	28	10	36	4	7	2	0	1	4	1	16	0	.194	.417

NAME	T	AGE	W	L	PCT	SV	G	GS	CG	IP	H	BB	SO	SHO	ERA
TOTALS		28	74	88	.457	26	162	162	53	1438	1383	572	965	13	3.72
Nolan Ryan	R	30	19	16	.543	0	37	37	22	299	198	204	341	4	2.77
Frank Tanana	L	23	15	9	.625	0	31	31	20	241	201	61	205	7	2.54
Paul Hartzell	R	23	8	12	.400	4	41	23	6	189	200	38	79	0	3.57
2 Ken Brett	L	28	7	10	.412	0	21	21	5	142	157	38	41	0	4.25
2 Dave LaRoche	L	29	6	5	.545	13	46	0	0	81	64	37	61	0	3.11
Wayne Simpson	R	28	6	12	.333	0	27	23	0	122	154	62	55	0	5.83
Mike Barlow	R	29	4	2	.667	1	20	1	0	59	53	27	25	0	4.58
2 Dyar Miller	R	29	4	4	.500	4	41	0	0	92	81	30	49	0	3.03
John Caneira	R	24	2	2	.500	0	4	4	1	29	27	16	17	0	4.03
Gary Ross (SJ)	R	29	2	4	.333	0	14	12	0	58	83	11	30	0	5.59
1 Don Kirkwood	R	27	1	0	1.000	1	13	0	0	18	20	9	10	0	5.00
Fred Kuhaulua	L	24	1	0	—	0	6	1	0	15	7	3	0	0	16.50
2 Tom Walker	R	28	0	0	—	0	5	0	0	6	11	3	1	0	9.00
1 Dick Drago	R	32	0	1	.000	2	13	0	0	21	29	3	15	0	3.00
1 Sid Monge	L	24	0	1	.000	1	4	0	0	12	14	6	4	0	3.00
Mike Cuellar	L	40	0	1	.000	0	2	0	0	7	13	6	1	0	21.00
Mickey Scott	L	29	0	1	.000	0	7	3	0	23	28	10	14	0	5.63
Balor Moore	R	25	0	0	—	0	7	0	0	19	19	6	11	0	3.91
1 John Verhoeven	R	24	0	2	.000	0	5	0	0	5	4	3	5	0	5.40
2 Gary Nolan (SJ)	R	29	0	3	.000	0	5	5	0	18	31	2	4	0	9.00

Name	G by Pos	B	AGE	G	AB	R	H	2B	3B	HR	RBI	BB	SO	SB	BA	SA
SEATTLE 6th 64-98 .395 38	DARRELL JOHNSON															
TOTALS			26	162	5460	624	1398	218	33	133	589	426	769	110	.256	.381
Dan Meyer	1B159	L	24	159	582	75	159	24	4	22	90	43	51	11	.273	.442
Jose Baez	2B77, DH3, 3B1	R	23	91	305	39	79	14	1	1	17	19	20	6	.259	.321
Craig Reynolds	SS134	L	24	135	424	41	104	12	3	4	28	15	23	6	.248	.319
Bill Stein	3B147, DH3, SS2	R	30	151	556	53	144	26	5	13	67	29	79	3	.259	.394
Lee Stanton	OF91, DH33	R	31	158	454	56	125	24	1	27	90	42	115	0	.275	.511
Ruppert Jones	OF155, DH4	L	22	160	597	85	157	26	8	24	76	55	120	13	.263	.454
Steve Braun	OF100, DH32, 3B1	L	29	139	451	51	106	19	1	5	31	80	59	8	.235	.315
Bob Stinson	C99, DH4	B	32	124	344	34	93	20	4	5	38	43	54	7	.270	.395
Juan Bernhardt (LJ)	DH54, 3B21, 1B8	R	23	89	305	32	74	9	2	7	30	5	26	1	.243	.354
Dave Collins	OF73, DH40	B	24	120	402	46	96	9	3	5	28	33	66	25	.239	.313
Carlos Lopez (BW)	OF90, DH2	R	28	99	297	39	84	18	1	8	34	14	61	16	.283	.431
Larry Milbourne	2B41, SS40, 3B1, DH1	B	26	86	242	24	53	10	0	2	21	6	22	9	.219	.285
Julio Cruz	2B54, DH1	B	22	60	199	25	51	3	1	1	7	24	29	15	.256	.296
Skip Jutze	C40	R	31	42	109	10	24	2	0	3	15	7	12	0	.220	.321
Larry Cox	C35	R	29	35	93	6	23	6	0	2	6	10	12	1	.247	.376
Tommy Smith	OF14	R	28	21	27	1	7	1	0	0	4	0	4	0	.259	.370
Jimmy Sexton	SS12	R	25	14	37	5	8	1	1	1	3	2	6	1	.216	.378
Luis Delgado	OF13	R	23	13	22	4	4	0	0	0	3	0	8	0	.182	.182
2 Ray Fosse	C8, DH2	R	30	11	34	3	12	3	0	0	5	1	2	0	.353	.441
Joe Lis	1B4, C1	R	30	9	13	1	3	0	0	0	1	2	6	0	.231	.231
2 Kevin Pasley	C4	R	23	4	13	1	5	0	0	0	2	2	1	0	.385	.385
Tommy McMillan	SS2	R	25	2	5	0	0	0	0	0	0	0	1	0	.000	.000

NAME	T	AGE	W	L	PCT	SV	G	GS	CG	IP	H	BB	SO	SHO	ERA
TOTALS		29	64	98	.395	31	162	162	18	1433	1508	578	785	1	4.83
Glenn Abbott	R	26	12	13	.480	0	36	34	7	204	212	56	100	0	4.48
Enrique Romo	R	29	8	10	.444	16	58	3	0	114	93	39	105	0	2.84
John Montague	R	29	8	12	.400	4	47	15	2	182	193	75	98	0	4.30
Dick Pole (VJ)	R	26	7	12	.368	0	25	24	3	122	127	57	51	0	5.16
Gary Wheelock (EJ)	R	25	6	9	.400	0	17	17	2	88	94	26	47	0	4.91
Mike Kekich (SJ)	L	32	5	4	.556	3	41	2	0	90	90	51	55	0	5.60
2 Tom House (SJ)	L	30	4	5	.444	1	26	11	1	89	94	19	39	0	3.94
1 Bill Laxton (SA)	L	29	3	2	.600	3	43	0	0	73	62	39	49	0	4.93
2 Paul Mitchell	R	28	2	6	.250	0	13	9	1	58	74	25	14	0	6.05
2 Doc Medich	R	28	2	0	1.000	0	3	3	1	22	26	4	3	0	3.68
Tommy Moore	R	28	1	1	.667	0	14	1	0	33	36	21	13	0	4.91
1 Stan Thomas (SJ)	R	27	2	6	.250	0	13	9	1	66	86	23	14	0	6.14
1 Dave Pagan	L	22	1	1	.500	2	14	0	0	42	47	37	16	0	5.14
Rick Jones (EJ)	L	22	0	0	—	0	3	3	0	14	12	4	2	0	3.86
Frank MacCormack	R	22	0	1	.000	0	3	0	0	5	4	4	1	0	36.00
Byron McLaughlin	R	21	0	0	—	0	1	0	0	3	0	4	1	0	3.00
Rick Honeycutt	L	23	0	1	.000	0	10	3	0	29	26	11	17	0	4.34
Steve Burke	R	23	0	0	—	0	6	0	0	16	12	7	6	0	2.81
Greg Erardi	R	23	0	1	.000	0	9	2	0	12	16	6	5	0	6.00
Bob Galasso	R	25	0	6	.000	0	11	7	0	35	57	8	21	0	9.00
Diego Segui	R	39	0	7	.000	2	40	7	0	111	108	43	91	0	5.69

Name	G by Pos	B	AGE	G	AB	R	H	2B	3B	HR	RBI	BB	SO	SB	BA	SA
OAKLAND 7th 63-98 .391 38.5	JACK McKEON 26-27 .491 BOBBY WINKLES 37-71 .343															
TOTALS			28	161	5358	605	1284	176	37	117	548	516	910	176	.240	.352
Dick Allen (ST-VR)	1B50, DH1	R	35	54	171	19	41	4	0	5	31	24	38	1	.240	.351
2 Marty Perez	2B105, 3B12, SS4	R	31	118	373	32	86	14	5	2	23	29	65	1	.231	.311
Rob Picciolo	SS148	R	24	148	419	35	84	12	3	2	22	9	55	5	.200	.258
Wayne Gross	3B145, DH1	L	25	146	445	66	113	21	1	22	63	86	84	5	.233	.416
Jim Tyrone	OF81, DH4, 1B1, SS1	R	28	96	294	32	72	11	1	5	26	25	62	3	.245	.340
Billy North (BG)	OF52, DH1	B	29	58	184	32	48	3	1	0	13	36	26	17	.261	.326
Mitchell Page	OF133, DH8	L	25	145	501	85	154	28	8	21	75	78	95	42	.307	.521
Manny Sanguillen	C77, DH58, OF9, 1B7	R	33	152	571	42	157	17	5	6	58	22	35	2	.275	.354
Earl Williams (BW)	DH45, C36, 1B29	R	28	100	348	39	84	13	0	13	38	18	58	2	.241	.391
Rodney Scott	2B71, SS70, 3B5, OF1, DH1	B	23	133	364	56	95	4	4	0	20	43	50	33	.261	.294
Tony Armas (GJ)	OF112, SS1	R	23	118	363	26	87	8	2	13	53	20	99	1	.240	.380
Jeff Newman	C94, P1	R	28	94	162	17	36	9	0	4	15	4	22	0	.222	.352
Larry Murray	OF78, DH3, SS1	B	24	90	162	19	29	5	2	1	9	17	36	12	.179	.253
Matt Alexander	OF31, SS12, DH12, 2B4, 3B1	R	30	90	42	24	10	1	0	2	4	6	26	26	.238	.262
Rich McKinney	1B32, DH18, 3B7, OF5, 2B3	R	30	86	198	13	35	7	0	6	21	16	43	0	.177	.303
2 Mike Jorgensen (BW)	1B48, OF20, DH2	L	28	66	203	18	50	9	1	8	32	25	44	3	.246	.394
Sheldon Mallory (BW)	OF45, DH17, 1B4	B	24	64	126	19	27	3	1	0	5	11	18	12	.214	.262
2 Willie Crawford	OF22, DH18	L	30	59	136	7	25	7	1	2	16	18	20	1	.184	.272
Jerry Tabb	1B36, DH5	L	25	41	115	14	24	7	0	2	11	11	22	0	.209	.368
Larry Lintz	2B28, DH5, SS2, 3B1	B	27	41	30	11	4	0	0	0	0	8	13	13	.133	.167
Tim Hosley	C19, DH12, 1B3	R	30	39	78	5	15	0	0	1	10	16	13	0	.192	.231
Mark Williams	OF1	L	23	3	3	0	0	0	0	0	0	0	0	0	.000	.000

NAME	T	AGE	W	L	PCT	SV	G	GS	CG	IP	H	BB	SO	SHO	ERA
TOTALS		28	63	98	.391	26	161	161	32	1437	1459	560	788	4	4.04
Vida Blue	L	27	14	19	.424	0	38	38	16	280	284	86	157	1	3.83
1 Doc Medich (EJ)	R	28	10	6	.625	0	26	25	1	148	155	49	74	0	4.68
Rick Langford	R	25	8	19	.296	0	37	31	6	208	223	73	141	1	4.02
Bob Lacey	L	24	8	9	.429	7	64	0	0	122	100	43	69	0	3.02
Joe Coleman	R	30	4	4	.500	2	43	12	2	128	114	49	55	0	2.95
Doug Bair	R	27	4	6	.400	8	45	0	0	83	78	57	68	0	3.47
Pablo Torrealba	L	29	4	6	.400	2	41	10	3	117	127	38	51	0	2.62
1 Mike Torrez	R	30	3	1	.750	0	4	4	3	36	23	11	12	0	4.50
1 Dave Giusti	R	37	3	3	.500	6	40	0	0	60	54	20	28	0	3.00
Mike Norris	R	22	2	7	.222	0	16	12	1	77	77	31	35	1	4.79
Steve Dunning	R	28	1	0	1.000	0	3	1	0	18	17	10	4	0	4.00
1 Stan Bahnsen	R	32	1	2	.333	1	11	2	0	43	39	22	23	0	6.14
Matt Keough	R	21	1	3	.250	0	7	6	0	43	39	22	23	0	4.81
1 Jim Umbarger	R	24	1	3	.167	1	12	1	0	36	28	14	11	0	6.55
2 Dock Ellis	R	32	1	5	.167	0	12	8	0	26	35	14	11	0	9.69
Steve McCatty	R	23	0	0	—	0	1	0	0	16	17	6	9	0	5.14
Jeff Newman	R	28	0	0	—	0	1	0	0	1	1	0	0	0	0.00
Craig Mitchell	R	23	0	1	.000	0	3	0	0	14	14	7	5	0	7.50
1 Paul Mitchell	R	26	0	1	—	0	4	0	0	14	21	7	5	0	10.29

LINE SCORES

Team	1	2	3	4	5	6	7	8	9	10	11		R	H	E

AMERICAN LEAGUE CHAMPIONSHIPS: NEW YORK (EAST) 3 KANSAS CITY (WEST) 2

Game 1 October 5 at New York
KC 2 2 2 0 0 0 0 1 0   7 9 0
NY 0 0 2 0 0 0 0 0 0   2 9 0
Splittorff, Bird (9) **Gullett**, Tidrow (3), Lyle (9)

Game 2 October 6 at New York
KC 0 0 1 0 0 1 0 0 0   2 3 1
NY 0 0 0 0 2 3 0 1 x   6 10 1
Hassler, Littell (6), **Guidry**
Mingori (8)

Game 3 October 7 at Kansas City
NY 0 0 0 1 0 0 0 1   2 4 1
KC 0 1 1 0 1 2 1 0 x   6 12 2
Torrez, Lyle (6) **Leonard**

Game 4 October 8 at Kansas City
NY 1 2 1 0 0 1 0 0 1   6 13 0
KC 0 0 2 2 0 0 0 0 0   4 8 2
Figueroa, Tidrow (4), Gura, Pattin (3), Mingori (9),
Lyle (4) Bird (9)

Game 5 October 9 at Kansas City
NY 0 0 1 0 0 0 0 1 3   5 10 0
KC 2 0 1 0 0 0 0 0 0   3 10 1
Guidry, Torrez (3), Splittorff, Bird (8),
Lyle (8) Mingori (8), Leonard (9),
 Gura (9), Littell (9)

NATIONAL LEAGUE CHAMPIONSHIPS: LOS ANGELES (WEST) 3 PHILADELPHIA (EAST) 1

Game 1 October 4 at Los Angeles
PHI 2 0 0 0 2 1 0 0 2   7 9 0
LA   0 0 0 0 1 0 4 0 0   5 9 2
Carlton, **Garber** (7), John, Garman (5), Hough (6),
McGraw (8) Sosa (8)

Game 2 October 5 at Los Angeles
PHI 0 0 1 0 0 0 0 0 0   1 9 1
LA   0 0 1 4 0 1 1 0 x   7 9 1
Lonborg, Reed (5), **Sutton**
Brusstar (7)

Game 3 October 7 at Philadelphia
LA   0 2 0 0 1 0 0 0 3   6 12 2
PHI 0 3 0 0 0 0 0 2 0   5 6 2
Hooten, Rhoden (2), Rau (7), Christenson, Brusstar (4),
Sosa (8), **Rautzhen** (8), Reed (5), **Garber** (7)
Garman (9)

Game 4 October 8 at Philadelphia
LA   0 2 0 0 2 0 0 0 0   4 5 0
PHI 0 0 0 1 0 0 0 0 0   1 7 0
John **Carlton**, Reed (6), McGraw (7),
 Gerber (9)

WORLD SERIES — NEW YORK (AL) 4 LOS ANGELES (NL) 2

Game 1 October 11 at New York
LA (NL) 2 0 0 0 0 0 0 0 1 0 0 0   3 6 0
NY (AL) 1 0 0 0 0 1 0 1 0 0 0 1   4 11 0
Sutton, Rautzhan (8), Gullett, **Lyle** (9)
Sosa (8), Garman (9),
Rhoden (12)

Game 2 October 12 at New York
LA 2 1 2 0 0 0 0 0 1   6 9 0
NY 0 0 0 1 0 0 0 0 0   1 5 0
Hooton **Hunter**, Tidrow (3), Clay (6),
 Lyle (9)

Game 3 October 14 at Los Angeles
NY 3 0 0 1 1 0 0 0 0   5 10 0
LA 0 0 3 0 0 0 0 0 0   3 7 1
Torrez **John**, Hough (7)

Game 4 October 15 at Los Angeles
NY 0 3 0 0 0 1 0 0 0   4 7 0
LA 0 0 2 0 0 0 0 0 0   2 4 0
Guidry **Rau**, Rhoden (2), Garman (9)

Game 5 October 16 at Los Angeles
NY 0 0 0 0 0 2 2 0 0   4 9 2
LA 1 0 0 4 3 2 0 0 x   10 13 0
Gullett, Clay (5), **Sutton**
Tidrow (6), Hunter (7)

Game 6 October 18 at New York
LA 2 0 1 0 0 0 0 0 1   4 9 0
NY 0 2 0 3 2 0 0 1 X   8 8 1
Hooton, Sosa (4), Rau (5), **Torrez**
Hough (7)

COMPOSITE BATTING

New York

NAME	POS	G	AB	R	H	2B	3B	HR	RBI	BA
Totals		5	175	21	46	12	0	2	17	.263
Rivers	CF	5	23	5	9	2	0	0	2	.391
Piniella	LF-RF-DH	5	21	1	7	3	0	0	2	.333
Munson	C	5	21	3	6	1	0	1	5	.286
Nettles	3B	5	20	1	3	0	0	0	1	.150
Randolph	2B	5	18	4	5	1	0	0	2	.278
Chambliss	1B	5	17	0	1	0	0	0	0	.059
Jackson	RF-PH-DH	5	16	1	2	0	0	0	0	.125
Johnson	DH-PH	5	15	2	6	2	0	1	2	.400
Dent	SS	5	14	3	3	1	0	0	2	.214
Blair	RF-PH-DH	3	5	1	2	0	0	0	0	.400
White	PH-LF-PR-DH	4	5	2	2	2	0	0	0	.400
Stanley	SS	2	0	0	0	0	0	0	0	—

Kansas City

NAME	POS	G	AB	R	H	2B	3B	HR	RBI	BA
Totals		5	163	22	42	9	3	3	21	.258
Brett	3B	5	20	2	6	0	2	0	2	.300
Cowens	RF-CF	5	19	2	5	0	0	1	5	.263
McRae	DH-LF	5	18	6	8	3	0	1	2	.444
Patek	SS	5	18	4	7	3	1	0	5	.389
White	2B	5	18	1	5	1	0	0	5	.278
Otis	CF-PH	5	16	1	2	1	0	0	2	.125
Porter	C-PH	5	15	3	5	0	0	0	0	.333
Mayberry	1B	4	12	1	2	1	0	1	3	.167
Zdeb	LF-PH	4	9	0	0	0	0	0	0	.000
Poquette	RF	2	6	0	1	0	0	0	0	.167
Wathen	1B-PH-C-DH	4	6	0	0	0	0	0	0	.000
Rojas	DH	1	4	0	1	0	0	0	0	.250
LaCock	PH-1B	4	1	0	0	0	0	0	0	.000
Lahoud	DH	1	1	2	0	0	0	0	0	.000

Los Angeles

NAME	POS	G	AB	R	H	2B	3B	HR	RBI	BA
Totals		4	133	22	35	6	1	3	20	.263
Russell	SS	4	18	3	5	1	0	0	2	.278
Lopes	2B	4	17	2	4	0	0	0	3	.235
Smith	RF	4	16	2	3	0	1	0	1	.188
Baker	LF	4	14	4	5	1	0	2	8	.357
Cey	3B	4	13	4	4	1	0	1	6	.308
Garvey	1B	4	13	2	4	0	0	0	0	.308
Yeager	C	4	13	1	3	0	0	0	2	.231
Burke	CF	4	7	0	0	0	0	0	0	.000
Monday	CF-PH	3	7	1	2	0	0	0	0	.286
John	P	2	5	0	1	0	0	0	0	.200
Sutton	P	1	3	0	0	0	0	0	0	.000

Devalillo PH 1-1, Hooton P 1-1, Lacy PH 1-1, Mota PH 1-1, Sosa P 0-1, Goodson PH 0-1, Rhoden P 0-1, Garman P 0-0, Grote C-PH 0-0, Hough P 0-0, Rau P 0-0, Rautzhan P 0-0

Philadelphia

NAME	POS	G	AB	R	H	2B	3B	HR	RBI	BA
Totals		4	138	14	31	3	0	2	12	.225
McBride	CF-RF	4	18	2	4	0	0	1	2	.222
Bowa	SS	4	17	2	2	0	0	0	0	.118
Schmidt	3B	4	16	2	1	0	0	0	1	.063
Hebner	1B-PH	4	14	2	5	2	0	0	0	.357
Luzinski	LF	4	14	4	4	1	0	1	2	.286
Sizemore	2B	4	13	1	3	0	0	0	0	.231
Boone	C	4	10	1	4	0	0	0	0	.400
Maddox	CF	2	7	1	3	0	0	0	2	.429
McCarver	C-PH	3	6	1	1	0	0	0	0	.167
Johnstone	RF-PH	2	5	0	1	0	0	0	0	.200
Johnson	1B	2	4	0	1	0	0	0	0	.250
Martin	RF-PR	3	4	0	0	0	0	0	0	.000
Carlton	P	2	4	0	2	0	0	0	1	.500
Hutton	1B-PH	3	3	0	0	0	0	0	0	.000
Brown	PH	2	2	0	0	0	0	0	0	.000

Lonborg P 0-1, Garber P 0-0, Reed P 0-0, Brusstar P 0-0, McGraw P 0-0, Christenson P 0-0

World Series — New York

NAME	POS	G	AB	R	H	2B	3B	HR	RBI	BA
Totals		6	205	26	50	10	0	8	25	.244
Rivers	CF	6	27	1	6	2	0	0	1	.222
Munson	C	6	25	4	8	2	0	1	3	.320
Randolph	2B	6	25	5	4	2	0	1	1	.160
Chambliss	1B	6	24	4	7	2	0	1	4	.292
Piniella	LF	6	22	1	6	0	0	0	3	.273
Nettles	3B	6	21	1	4	1	0	0	2	.190
Jackson	RF	6	20	10	9	1	0	5	8	.450
Dent	SS	6	19	0	5	0	0	0	2	.263
Torrez	P	2	6	0	0	0	0	0	0	.000
Blair	RF-PH	4	4	0	1	0	0	0	1	.250
White	PH	2	4	0	0	0	0	0	0	.000
Zeber	PH	2	2	0	0	0	0	0	0	.000
Gullett	P	2	2	0	0	0	0	0	0	.000
Lyle	P	2	2	0	0	0	0	0	0	.000
Guidry	P	1	2	0	0	0	0	0	0	.000

Johnson PH-C 0-1, Tidrow P 0-1, Clay P 0-0, Hunter P 0-0, Stanley SS 0-0

World Series — Los Angeles

NAME	POS	G	AB	R	H	2B	3B	HR	RBI	BA
Totals		6	208	28	48	5	3	9	28	.231
Russell	SS	6	26	3	4	0	1	0	2	.154
Baker	LF	6	24	4	7	0	0	1	5	.292
Garvey	1B	6	24	5	9	1	1	1	3	.375
Lopes	2B	6	24	3	4	0	1	1	2	.167
Smith	RF-CF	6	22	7	6	1	0	3	5	.273
Cey	3B	6	21	2	4	1	0	1	3	.190
Yeager	C	6	19	2	6	1	0	2	5	.316
Monday	CF	4	12	0	2	0	0	0	0	.167
Lacy	PH-RF	4	7	1	3	0	0	0	0	.429
Sutton	P	2	6	0	3	0	0	0	0	.000
Burke	CF	3	5	0	0	0	0	0	0	.000
Hooton	P	2	5	0	0	0	0	0	0	.000
Davalillo	PH	3	3	0	1	0	0	0	0	.333
Mota	PH	3	3	0	0	0	0	0	0	.000
Rhoden	P	2	2	1	1	1	0	0	0	.500
John	P	1	1	0	0	0	0	0	0	.000
Goodson	PH	1	1	0	0	0	0	0	0	.000
Grote	C	1	1	0	0	0	0	0	0	.000
Oates	PH-C	1	1	0	0	0	0	0	0	.000

Garman P 0-0, Hough P 0-0, Rau P 0-0, Sosa P 0-0, Rautzhan P 0-0
Landestoy PR 0-0

COMPOSITE PITCHING

New York

NAME	G	IP	H	BB	SO	W	L	SV	ERA
Totals	5	44	42	15	22	3	2	0	4.50
Guidry	2	11.1	9	3	8	1	0	0	3.97
Torrez	2	11	11	5	5	0	1	0	4.09
Lyle	4	9.1	7	0	3	2	0	0	0.96
Tidrow	2	7	6	3	3	0	0	0	3.86
Figueroa	1	3.1	5	2	3	0	0	0	10.80
Gullett	1	2	4	2	0	0	1	0	18.00

Kansas City

NAME	G	IP	H	BB	SO	W	L	SV	ERA
Totals	5	44	46	9	16	2	3	0	3.27
Splittorff	2	15	14	3	4	1	0	0	2.40
Leonard	2	9	5	2	4	1	1	0	3.00
Pattin	1	6	6	0	0	0	0	0	1.50
Hassler	1	5.2	5	0	3	0	1	0	4.76
Littell	2	3	5	3	1	0	0	0	3.00
Bird	3	2	4	1	0	0	0	0	0.00
Gura	2	2	7	1	2	0	1	0	18.00
Mingori	3	1.1	0	0	1	0	0	0	0.00

Los Angeles

NAME	G	IP	H	BB	SO	W	L	SV	ERA
Totals	4	36	31	11	21	3	1	1	2.25
John	2	13.2	11	5	11	1	0	0	0.65
Sutton	1	9	9	4	1	0	0	0	1.00
Rhoden	1	4.1	2	2	0	0	0	0	0.00
Sosa	2	2.2	5	0	0	1	0	0	10.13
Hough	1	2	2	0	3	0	0	0	4.50
Hooton	1	1.2	2	4	1	0	0	0	16.20
Garman	2	1.1	0	1	0	0	0	1	0.00
Rau	1	1	0	0	1	0	0	0	0.00
Rautzhan	1	0.1	0	0	1	0	0	0	0.00

Philadelphia

NAME	G	IP	H	BB	SO	W	L	SV	ERA
Totals	4	35	35	14	22	1	3	1	5.40
Carlton	2	11.2	13	8	6	0	1	0	6.94
Garber	3	5.1	4	0	3	1	1	0	3.38
Reed	3	5	3	2	5	0	0	0	1.80
Lonborg	1	4	5	1	1	0	1	0	11.25
Christenson	1	3.1	7	0	2	0	0	0	8.10
McGraw	2	3	1	2	3	0	0	1	0.00
Brusstar	2	2.2	1	1	2	0	0	0	3.38

World Series — New York

NAME	G	IP	H	BB	SO	W	L	SV	ERA
Totals	6	56	48	16	36	4	2	0	4.02
Torrez	2	18	16	5	15	2	0	0	2.50
Gullett	2	12.2	13	7	10	1	0	0	6.39
Guidry	1	9	4	3	7	1	0	0	2.00
Lyle	3	4.2	2	0	2	1	0	0	1.93
Hunter	2	4.1	6	0	1	0	1	0	10.38
Clay	2	3.2	2	1	0	0	0	0	2.45
Tidrow	2	3.2	5	0	1	0	1	0	4.91

World Series — Los Angeles

NAME	G	IP	H	BB	SO	W	L	SV	ERA
Totals	6	55	50	11	37	2	4	0	4.09
Sutton	2	16	17	1	6	1	0	0	3.94
Hooton	2	12	8	2	9	1	0	0	3.75
Rhoden	2	7	4	1	5	0	1	0	2.57
John	1	6	9	3	7	1	0	0	6.00
Hough	2	5	3	0	5	0	0	0	1.80
Garman	2	4	1	1	2	0	0	0	0.00
Rau	2	2.1	4	0	1	0	1	0	11.57
Sosa	2	2.1	3	1	1	0	1	0	11.57
Rautzhan	1	.1	0	2	0	0	0	0	0.00

Name	G by Pos	B	AGE	G	AB	R	H	2B	3B	HR	RBI	BB	SO	SB	BA	SA
PHILADELPHIA 1st 101-61 .623	DANNY OZARK															
TOTALS			29	162	5546	847	1548	266	56	186	795	573	806	**135**	.279	.448
Richie Hebner	1B103,3B13,2B1	L	29	118	397	67	113	17	4	18	62	61	46	7	.285	.484
Ted Sizemore	2B152	R	32	152	519	64	146	20	4	0	47	52	40	8	.281	.355
Larry Bowa	SS154	B	31	154	624	93	175	19	3	4	41	32	32	32	.280	.340
Mike Schmidt	3B149,SS2,2B1	R	27	154	544	114	149	27	11	38	101	104	122	15	.274	.574
Jay Johnstone	OF91,1B19	L	31	112	363	64	103	18	4	15	59	38	38	3	.284	.479
Garry Maddox	OF138	R	27	139	571	85	167	27	10	14	74	24	58	22	.292	.448
Greg Luzinski	OF148	R	26	149	554	99	171	35	3	39	130	80	**140**	3	.309	.594
Bob Boone	C131,3B2	R	29	132	440	55	125	26	4	11	66	42	54	5	.284	.436
Jerry Martin	OF106,1B1	R	28	116	215	34	56	16	3	6	28	18	42	6	.260	.447
Tommy Hutton	1B73,OF9	L	31	107	81	12	25	3	0	2	11	12	10	1	.309	.420
Tim McCarver	C42,1B3	L	35	93	169	28	54	13	2	6	30	28	11	3	.320	.527
2 Bake McBride	OF73	L	28	85	280	55	95	20	5	11	41	25	25	27	.339	.564
Dave Johnson	1B43,2B9,3B6	R	34	78	156	23	50	9	1	8	36	23	20	1	.321	.545
Ollie Brown	OF21	R	33	53	70	5	17	3	1	1	13	4	14	1	.243	.357
Terry Harmon	2B28,SS16,3B3	R	33	46	60	13	11	1	0	2	5	6	9	0	.183	.300
2 Barry Foote	C17	R	25	18	32	3	7	1	0	1	3	3	6	0	.219	.344
1 Bobby Tolan	1B5	L	31	15	16	1	2	0	0	0	1	1	4	0	.125	.125
1 Dane Iorg	1B9	L	27	12	30	3	5	1	0	0	2	1	3	0	.167	.200
Fred Andrews	2B7	R	25	12	23	3	4	0	1	0	2	1	5	1	.174	.261
Mike Buskey	SS6	R	28	6	7	1	2	0	0	0	1	0	1	0	.286	.571
Jim Morrison	3B5	R	24	5	7	3	3	0	0	0	1	1	1	0	.429	.429
John Vukovich		R	29	2	2	0	0	0	0	0	0	0	0	0	.000	.000
1 Tim Blackwell	C1	B	24	1	0	1	0	0	0	0	0	0	0	0	—	—

NAME	T	AGE	W	L	PCT	SV	G	GS	CG	IP	H	BB	SO	SHO	ERA
		30	**101**	61	.623	47	162	162	31	1456	1451	482	856	7	3.71
Steve Carlton	L	32	**23**	10	.697	0	36	36	17	283	229	89	198	2	2.64
Larry Christenson	R	23	19	6	.760	0	34	34	5	219	229	69	118	1	4.07
Jim Lonborg (SJ)	R	35	11	4	.733	0	25	25	4	158	157	50	76	1	4.10
Randy Lerch	L	22	10	6	.625	0	32	28	3	169	207	75	81	0	5.06
Gene Garber	R	29	8	6	.571	19	64	0	0	103	82	23	78	0	2.36
Warren Brusstar	R	25	7	2	.778	3	46	0	0	71	64	24	46	0	2.66
Tug McGraw (EJ)	L	32	7	3	.700	9	45	0	0	79	62	24	58	0	2.62
Ron Reed	R	34	7	5	.583	15	60	3	0	124	101	37	84	0	2.74
Jim Kaat	L	38	6	11	.353	0	35	27	2	160	211	40	55	0	5.40
1 Tom Underwood	R	23	3	2	.600	1	14	0	0	33	44	18	20	0	5.18
Manny Seoane	R	22	0	0	—	0	2	1	0	6	11	3	4	0	6.00
2 Dan Warthen	L	24	0	1	.000	0	3	0	0	4	4	5	1	0	0.00
1 Wayne Twitchell	R	29	0	5	.000	0	12	8	0	46	50	25	37	0	4.50

Name	G by Pos	B	AGE	G	AB	R	H	2B	3B	HR	RBI	BB	SO	SB	BA	SA
PITTSBURGH 2nd 96-66 .593 5	CHUCK TANNER															
TOTALS			29	162	5662	734	1550	278	57	133	678	474	878	**260**	.274	.413
Willie Stargell	1B55	L	37	63	186	29	51	12	0	13	35	31	55	0	.274	.548
Rennie Stennett (LJ)	2B113	R	26	116	453	53	152	20	4	5	51	29	24	28	.336	.430
Frank Taveras	SS146	R	27	147	544	72	137	20	10	1	29	38	71	70	.252	.331
Phil Garner	3B107,2B50,SS12	R	28	153	585	99	152	35	10	17	77	55	65	32	.260	.441
Dave Parker	OF158,2B1	L	26	159	637	107	215	44	8	21	88	58	107	17	.338	.531
Omar Moreno	OF147	L	24	150	492	69	118	19	9	7	34	38	102	53	.240	.358
Al Oliver	OF148	L	30	154	568	75	175	29	6	19	82	40	38	13	.308	.481
Ed Ott	C90	L	24	104	311	40	82	14	3	7	38	32	41	7	.264	.395
Bill Robinson	1B86,OF43,3B17	R	34	137	507	74	154	32	1	26	104	25	92	12	.304	.525
Duffy Dyer	C93	R	31	94	270	27	65	11	1	3	19	54	49	6	.241	.322
Fernando Gonzalez	3B37,OF16,2B6,SS2	B	27	80	181	17	50	10	0	4	27	13	21	3	.276	.398
Mario Mendoza	SS45,3B19,P1	R	26	70	81	5	16	3	0	0	4	3	10	0	.198	.235
2 Jerry Hairston	OF14,2B1	R	25	51	52	5	10	2	0	2	6	6	10	0	.192	.346
2 Bobby Tolan	1B20,OF2	L	31	49	74	7	15	4	0	2	9	4	10	1	.203	.338
2 Jim Fregosi	1B15,3B1	R	35	36	56	10	16	1	1	3	16	13	10	2	.286	.500
Ken Macha	3B17,1B11,OF4	R	26	35	95	2	26	4	0	0	11	6	17	1	.274	.316
Miguel Dilone (RJ)	OF17	B	22	29	44	5	6	0	0	0	0	2	3	12	.136	.136
1 Ed Kirkpatrick	1B10,OF2,3B1	L	32	21	28	5	4	2	0	1	4	8	6	1	.143	.321
Dale Berra	3B14	R	20	17	40	0	7	1	0	0	3	1	8	0	.175	.200
1 Tommy Helms		R	36	15	12	0	0	0	0	0	0	0	3	0	.000	.000
Mike Easler	OF4	L	26	10	18	3	8	2	0	1	5	0	1	0	.444	.722
Mike Edwards	2B4	R	24	7	6	1	0	0	0	0	0	1	2	0	.000	.000
Bob Robertson (XJ) 30																

NAME	T	AGE	W	L	PCT	SV	G	GS	CG	IP	H	BB	SO	SHO	ERA
		27	96	66	.593	39	162	162	25	**1482**	1406	485	890	15	3.61
John Candelaria	L	23	20	5	**.800**	0	33	33	6	231	197	50	133	1	**2.34**
Jim Rooker	L	34	14	9	.609	0	30	30	7	204	196	64	89	2	3.09
Goose Gossage	R	25	11	9	.550	26	72	0	0	133	78	49	151	0	1.62
Kent Tekulve	R	30	10	1	.909	7	72	0	0	103	89	33	59	0	3.06
Jerry Reuss	L	28	10	13	.435	0	33	33	8	208	225	71	116	2	4.11
Bruce Kison	R	27	9	10	.474	0	33	32	3	193	209	55	122	1	4.90
Terry Forster	L	25	6	4	.600	1	33	6	0	87	90	32	58	0	4.45
Larry Demery	R	24	6	5	.545	1	39	8	0	90	100	47	35	0	5.10
Grant Jackson	L	34	5	3	.625	4	49	2	0	91	81	39	41	0	3.86
Odell Jones	R	24	3	7	.300	0	34	15	1	108	118	31	66	0	5.08
Ed Whitson	R	22	1	0	1.000	0	5	2	0	16	11	9	10	0	3.38
Tim Jones	R	23	1	0	1.000	0	3	1	0	14	3	5	0	0	0.00
Al Holland	L	24	0	0	—	0	2	0	0	2	4	1	1	0	9.00
2 Dave Pagan	R	27	0	0	—	0	1	0	0	3	1	0	4	0	0.00
Mario Mendoza	R	26	0	0	—	0	1	0	0	3	2	0	0	0	13.50

Name	G by Pos	B	AGE	G	AB	R	H	2B	3B	HR	RBI	BB	SO	SB	BA	SA
ST. LOUIS 3rd 83-79 .512 18	VERN RAPP															
TOTALS			26	162	5527	737	1490	252	56	96	686	489	823	134	.270	.388
Keith Hernandez	1B158	L	23	161	560	90	163	41	4	15	91	79	88	7	.291	.459
Mike Tyson	2B135	R	27	138	418	42	103	15	2	7	57	30	48	3	.246	.342
Garry Templeton	SS151	B	21	153	621	94	200	19	**18**	8	79	15	70	28	.322	.449
Ken Reitz	3B157	R	27	157	587	58	153	36	1	17	79	19	74	2	.261	.412
Heity Cruz	OF106,3B2	R	24	118	339	50	80	19	2	6	42	46	56	4	.236	.357
Tony Scott (KJ)	OF89	S	25	95	292	38	85	16	3	3	41	33	48	13	.291	.397
Lou Brock	OF130	L	38	141	489	69	133	22	6	2	46	30	74	35	.272	.354
Ted Simmons	C143,OF1	B	27	150	516	82	164	25	3	21	95	79	37	2	.318	.500
Jerry Mumphrey	OF133	B	24	145	463	73	133	20	10	2	38	47	70	22	.287	.387
Mike Anderson	OF77	R	26	94	154	18	34	4	1	4	17	14	31	2	.221	.338
Dave Rader	C38	L	28	66	114	15	30	7	1	1	16	9	10	1	.263	.368
1 Don Kessinger	SS26,2B24,3B4	B	34	59	134	14	32	4	0	0	7	14	26	0	.239	.269
Roger Freed	1B18,OF6	R	31	49	83	10	33	2	5	2	11	11	9	0	.398	.627
2 Mike Phillips	2B31,SS5,3B5	L	26	48	87	17	21	3	2	0	9	9	13	1	.241	.322
1 Bake McBride	OF33	L	28	43	122	21	32	5	1	4	20	7	19	9	.262	.418
Rick Bosetti	OF35	R	23	41	69	12	16	0	0	3	6	11	4	.232	.232	
1 Dane Iorg	OF7	L	27	30	32	2	10	1	0	0	4	5	4	0	.313	.344
1 Joel Youngblood	OF11,3B6	R	25	25	27	1	5	2	0	0	1	3	5	0	.185	.259
Jim Dwyer	OF12	L	27	13	31	3	7	1	0	0	2	4	5	0	.226	.258
Ken Oberkfell	2B6	L	21	9	9	1	1	0	0	0	1	0	3	0	.111	.111
Jerry DaVanon	2B5	R	31	9	9	0	0	0	0	0	0	0	1	0	.000	.000
Taylor Duncan	3B5	R	24	8	12	2	4	0	0	0	2	1	1	0	.333	.583
Mike Potter	OF1	R	26	5	7	0	0	0	0	0	0	0	2	0	.000	.000
John Tamargo	C1	B	25	4	4	0	0	0	0	0	0	0	0	0	.000	.000
Benny Ayala	OF1	R	26	1	3	0	1	0	0	0	0	0	1	0	.333	.333

NAME	T	AGE	W	L	PCT	SV	G	GS	CG	IP	H	BB	SO	SHO	ERA
		26	83	79	.512	31	162	162	26	1446	1420	532	768	10	3.81
Bob Forsch	R	27	20	7	.741	0	35	35	8	217	210	69	95	2	3.48
Eric Rasmussen	R	25	11	17	.393	0	34	34	11	233	223	63	120	3	3.48
John Denny (LJ)	R	24	8	8	.500	0	26	26	3	150	165	62	60	1	4.50
John Urrea	R	22	7	6	.538	4	41	12	2	140	126	35	81	1	3.15
Buddy Schultz	L	26	6	1	.857	1	40	3	0	85	76	24	66	0	2.33
Al Hrabosky	L	27	6	5	.545	10	65	0	0	86	82	41	68	0	4.40
2 Tom Underwood	R	23	6	9	.400	0	19	17	1	100	104	57	66	0	4.95
Butch Metzger	R	25	4	2	.667	7	58	0	0	93	78	38	48	0	3.10
1 Clay Carroll	R	36	4	4	.500	4	51	1	0	90	77	24	34	0	2.50
Pete Falcone	R	23	4	8	.333	1	27	22	1	124	130	61	75	1	5.44
2 Rawly Eastwick	R	26	3	7	.300	4	41	1	0	54	74	21	30	0	4.67
Johnny Sutton	R	24	2	1	.667	0	14	0	0	24	28	9	9	0	2.63
Larry Dierker (BN-SJ)	R	30	2	6	.250	0	11	9	0	39	40	16	6	0	4.62
1 John D'Acquisto (LJ)	R	25	0	0	—	0	3	2	0	8	5	10	9	0	4.50
1 Doug Capilla	L	25	0	0	—	0	2	2	1	2	1	1	0	0	18.00

Name	G by Pos	B	AGE	G	AB	R	H	2B	3B	HR	RBI	BB	SO	SB	BA	SA
CHICAGO 4th 81-81 .500 20	HERMAN FRANKS															
TOTALS			28	162	5604	692	1489	271	37	111	649	534	796	64	.266	.387
Bill Buckner (NJ)	1B99	L	27	122	426	40	121	27	0	11	60	21	23	7	.284	.425
Manny Trillo	2B149	R	26	152	504	51	141	18	5	7	57	44	58	3	.280	.377
Ivan DeJesus	SS154	R	24	155	624	91	166	31	7	3	40	56	90	24	.266	.353
Steve Ontiveros	3B155	R	26	156	546	54	163	32	3	10	68	81	69	3	.299	.423
Bobby Murcer	OF150,2B1,SS1	L	31	154	554	90	147	18	3	27	89	80	77	16	.265	.455
Jerry Morales	OF128	R	28	136	490	56	142	34	5	11	69	43	75	0	.290	.447
Jose Cardenal (KJ)	OF62,2B1,SS1	R	33	100	226	33	54	12	1	3	18	28	30	5	.239	.341
George Mitterwald	C109,1B1	R	32	110	349	40	83	22	0	9	43	28	69	3	.238	.378
Larry Biittner	1B80,OF52,P1	L	31	138	493	74	147	28	1	12	62	35	36	2	.298	.432
Greg Gross	OF71	L	24	115	239	43	77	10	4	5	32	33	19	0	.322	.460
Gene Clines	OF63	R	30	101	239	27	70	12	2	3	41	25	25	1	.293	.397
Steve Swisher	C72	R	25	74	205	21	39	7	0	5	15	9	47	0	.190	.298
Mick Kelleher (BG)	2B40,SS14,3B1	R	29	63	122	14	28	5	2	0	11	9	12	0	.230	.303
Dave Rosello	3B21,SS10,2B3	R	27	56	82	18	18	2	1	1	9	12	12	0	.220	.305
Joe Wallis (BG)	OF35	B	25	56	80	14	20	3	0	2	8	16	25	0	.250	.363
2 Bobby Darwin	OF1	R	34	11	12	2	2	1	0	0	2	2	6	0	.167	.250
Mike Gordon	C8	B	23	8	23	0	1	0	0	0	0	2	8	0	.043	.043
Mike Sember	2B1	R	24	3	4	1	1	0	0	0	0	1	0	0	.250	.250
Randy Hundley (RC)	C2	R	35	3	4	0	0	0	0	0	0	0	1	0	.000	.000
Mike Adams	OF2	R	28	2	4	0	0	0	0	0	0	0	1	0	.000	.000

NAME	T	AGE	W	L	PCT	SV	G	GS	CG	IP	H	BB	SO	SHO	ERA
		28	81	81	.500	44	162	162	16	1468	1500	489	**942**	10	4.01
Rick Reuschel	R	28	20	10	.667	1	39	37	8	252	233	74	166	4	2.79
Ray Burris	R	26	14	16	.467	0	39	39	5	221	270	67	105	1	4.72
Bill Bonham	R	28	10	13	.435	0	34	34	1	215	207	82	134	0	4.35
Willie Hernandez	L	22	8	7	.533	4	67	1	0	110	94	28	78	0	3.03
Mike Krukow	R	25	8	14	.364	0	34	33	1	172	195	61	106	1	4.40
Bruce Sutter (XJ)	R	24	7	3	.700	31	62	0	0	107	69	23	129	0	1.35
Paul Reuschel	R	30	5	6	.455	4	69	0	0	107	105	40	62	0	4.37
1 Steve Renko (IL)	R	32	2	2	.500	1	13	8	0	51	51	21	34	0	4.59
Jim Todd	R	29	1	1	.500	0	20	0	0	31	47	19	17	0	9.00
2 Dave Roberts	L	32	1	1	.500	1	17	6	1	53	55	12	23	0	3.23
Pete Broberg	R	27	1	2	.333	0	22	0	0	36	34	18	20	0	4.75
1 Ramon Hernandez	L	36	0	0	—	1	6	0	0	8	11	3	4	0	7.88
Larry Biittner	L	31	0	0	—	0	1	0	0	1	1	3	0	0	54.00
2 Dave Giusti	R	37	0	0	—	1	20	0	0	25	30	14	15	0	6.12
Dennis Lamp	R	24	0	0	—	0	11	3	0	30	43	8	12	0	6.30
Ken Frailing (SJ) 29																

EAST DIVISION

MONTREAL — 5th 75-87 .463 26 — DICK WILLIAMS

Name	G by Pos	B	AGE	G	AB	R	H	2B	3B	HR	RBI	BB	SO	SB	BA	SA
TOTALS			26	162	5675	665	1474	294	50	138	622	478	877	88	.260	.402
Tony Perez	1B148	R	35	154	559	71	158	32	6	19	91	63	111	4	.283	.463
Dave Cash	2B153	R	29	153	650	91	188	42	7	0	43	52	33	21	.289	.375
2 Chris Speier	SS138	R	27	139	531	58	125	30	6	5	38	67	78	1	.235	.343
Larry Parrish	3B115	R	23	123	402	50	99	19	2	11	46	37	71	2	.246	.386
Ellis Valentine (LJ)	OF126	R	22	127	508	63	149	28	2	25	76	30	58	13	.293	.504
Andre Dawson	OF136	R	22	139	525	64	148	26	9	19	65	34	93	21	.282	.474
Warren Cromartie	OF155	L	23	155	620	64	175	41	7	5	50	33	40	10	.282	.395
Gary Carter	C146,OF1	R	23	154	522	86	148	29	2	31	84	58	103	5	.284	.525
Del Unser	OF72,1B27	L	32	113	289	33	79	14	1	12	40	33	41	2	.273	.453
Sammy Mejias	OF56	R	25	74	101	14	23	4	1	3	8	2	17	1	.228	.376
Wayne Garrett (NJ)	3B49,2B1	L	29	68	159	17	43	6	1	2	22	30	18	2	.270	.358
Jose Morales	C8,1B8	R	32	65	74	3	15	4	1	1	9	5	12	0	.203	.324
Pete Mackanin	2B9,SS8,3B5,OF4	R	25	55	85	9	19	2	2	1	6	4	17	3	.224	.329
Pepe Frias	2B16,SS14,3B1	R	28	53	70	10	18	1	0	0	5	0	10	1	.257	.271
1 Mike Jorgensen	1B5	L	28	19	20	3	4	1	0	0	0	3	4	0	.200	.250
2 Tim Blackwell	C14	B	24	16	22	3	2	1	0	0	0	2	7	0	.091	.136
Jerry White	OF8	B	24	16	21	4	4	0	0	0	1	1	3	1	.190	.190
1 Barry Foote	C13	R	25	15	49	4	12	3	1	2	8	4	10	0	.245	.469
1 Tim Foli	SS13	R	26	13	57	2	10	5	1	0	3	0	4	0	.175	.298
Stan Papi	3B10,SS2,2B1	R	26	13	43	5	10	2	1	0	4	1	9	1	.233	.326

NAME	T	AGE	W	L	PCT	SV	G	GS	CG	IP	H	BB	SO	SHO	ERA
		27	75	87	.463	33	162	162	31	1481	1426	579	856	11	4.01
Steve Rogers	R	27	17	16	.515	0	40	40	17	302	272	81	206	4	3.10
Don Stanhouse	R	26	10	10	.500	10	47	16	1	158	147	84	89	1	3.42
Jackie Brown	R	34	9	12	.429	0	42	25	6	186	189	71	89	2	4.50
2 Stan Bahnsen	R	32	8	9	.471	2	23	22	3	127	142	38	58	1	4.82
Bill Atkinson	R	22	7	2	.778	7	55	0	0	83	72	29	56	0	3.36
2 Wayne Twitchell	R	29	6	5	.545	0	22	22	2	139	116	49	93	0	4.21
2 Fred Holdsworth	R	25	3	3	.500	0	14	6	0	42	35	18	21	0	3.21
Will McEnaney	L	25	3	5	.375	3	69	0	0	87	92	22	38	0	3.93
Joe Kerrigan	R	22	3	5	.375	11	66	0	0	89	80	33	43	0	3.24
Dan Schatzeder	L	22	2	1	.667	0	6	3	1	22	16	13	14	1	2.45
1 Dan Warthen	L	24	2	3	.400	0	12	6	1	35	33	38	26	0	7.97
2 Santo Alcala	R	24	2	6	.250	2	31	10	0	102	104	47	64	0	4.68
1 Tom Walker	R	28	1	1	.500	0	11	0	0	19	15	7	10	0	4.74
Hal Dues	R	22	1	1	.500	0	6	4	0	23	26	9	9	0	4.30
Gerald Hannahs	L	24	1	5	.167	0	8	7	0	37	43	17	21	0	4.86
Jeff Terpko	R	26	0	1	.000	0	13	0	0	21	28	15	14	0	5.57
Larry Landreth	R	22	0	2	.000	0	4	1	0	9	16	6	6	0	10.00

NEW YORK — 6th 64-98 .395 37 — JOE FRAZIER 15-30 .333 — JOE TORRE 49-68 .419

Name	G by Pos	B	AGE	G	AB	R	H	2B	3B	HR	RBI	BB	SO	SB	BA	SA
TOTALS			27	162	5410	587	1319	227	30	88	525	529	887	98	.244	.346
John Milner	1B87,OF22	L	27	131	388	43	99	20	3	12	57	61	55	6	.255	.415
Felix Millan (BC)	2B89	R	33	91	314	40	78	11	2	2	21	18	9	1	.248	.315
Bud Harrelson (BH)	SS98	R	33	107	269	25	48	6	2	1	12	27	28	5	.178	.227
2 Lenny Randle	3B110,2B20,OF6,SS1	B	28	136	513	78	156	22	7	5	27	65	70	33	.304	.404
Mike Vail	OF85	R	25	108	279	29	73	12	1	8	35	19	58	0	.262	.398
Lee Mazzilli	OF156	B	22	159	537	66	134	24	3	6	46	72	72	22	.250	.339
Steve Henderson	OF97	R	24	99	350	67	104	16	6	12	65	43	79	6	.297	.480
John Stearns	C127,1B6	R	25	139	431	52	108	25	1	12	55	77	76	9	.251	.397
Bruce Boisclair	OF91,1B9	L	24	127	307	41	90	21	1	4	44	31	57	6	.293	.407
Ed Kranepool	OF42,1B41	L	32	108	281	28	79	17	0	10	40	23	20	1	.281	.484
2 Doug Flynn	SS65,2B29,3B2	R	26	90	282	14	54	6	1	0	14	11	23	1	.191	.220
2 Joel Youngblood	2B33,OF22,3B10	R	25	70	182	16	46	11	1	0	11	13	40	1	.253	.324
Ron Hodges	C27	L	28	66	117	6	31	4	0	1	9	9	17	0	.265	.325
1 Dave Kingman	OF45,1B17	R	28	58	211	22	44	7	0	9	28	13	66	3	.209	.370
1 Jerry Grote	C28,3B11	R	34	42	115	8	31	3	1	0	7	9	12	0	.270	.313
2 Bobby Valentine (NJ)	1B15,SS14,3B4	R	27	42	83	8	11	1	0	1	3	6	9	0	.133	.181
Roy Staiger	3B36,SS1	R	27	40	123	16	31	9	0	2	11	4	20	1	.252	.374
1 Mike Phillips	SS24,3B9,2B4	L	26	38	86	5	18	2	1	1	3	2	15	0	.209	.291
Leo Foster	2B20,SS8,3B2	R	26	36	75	6	17	3	0	0	6	5	14	3	.227	.267
Joe Torre	1B16,3B1	R	36	26	51	2	9	3	0	1	9	2	10	0	.176	.294
Luis Rosado	1B7,C1	R	21	9	24	1	5	1	0	0	3	1	3	0	.208	.250
Pepe Mangual	OF4	R	25	8	7	1	1	0	0	0	2	1	4	1	.143	.143
Dan Norman	OF6	R	22	7	16	2	4	1	0	0	4	2	5	0	.250	.313
1 Luis Alvarado	2B1	R	28	1	2	0	0	0	0	0	0	0	1	0	.000	.000

NAME	T	AGE	W	L	PCT	SV	G	GS	CG	IP	H	BB	SO	SHO	ERA
		26	64	98	.395	28	162	162	27	1434	1378	490	911	12	3.77
Nino Espinosa	R	23	10	13	.435	0	32	29	7	200	188	55	105	1	3.42
Craig Swan	R	26	9	10	.474	0	26	24	2	147	153	56	71	1	4.22
Jerry Koosman	R	34	8	20	.286	0	32	32	6	227	195	81	192	1	3.49
1 Tom Seaver	R	32	7	3	.700	0	13	13	5	96	79	28	72	3*	3.00
2 Pat Zachry	R	25	7	6	.538	0	19	19	2	120	129	48	63	1	3.75
Jon Matlack (AJ)	L	27	7	15	.318	0	26	26	5	169	175	43	123	3	4.21
Skip Lockwood	R	30	4	8	.333	20	63	0	0	104	87	31	84	0	3.38
Bob Apodaca	R	27	4	8	.333	5	59	0	0	84	83	30	53	0	3.43
Jackson Todd	R	25	3	6	.333	0	19	10	0	72	78	20	39	0	4.75
2 Paul Siebert	L	24	2	1	.667	0	25	0	0	28	27	13	20	0	3.86
Bobby Myrick	L	24	2	2	.500	2	44	4	0	87	86	33	49	0	3.62
Rick Baldwin	R	24	1	3	.333	1	40	0	0	63	62	31	23	0	4.43
Johnny Pacella	R	20	0	0	—	0	3	0	0	4	2	1	0	0	0.00
Ray Sadecki	L	36	0	0	.000	0	1	0	0	7	6	1	3	0	6.00
3 Doc Medich	R	28	0	0	.000	0	1	0	0	5	6	3	1	0	3.86
Roy Lee Jackson	R	23	0	2	.000	0	4	4	0	24	25	15	13	0	6.00

* Seaver, also with Cincinnati, league leader in ShO with 7

WEST DIVISION

LOS ANGELES — 1st 98-64 .605 — TOMMY LASORDA

Name	G by Pos	B	AGE	G	AB	R	H	2B	3B	HR	RBI	BB	SO	SB	BA	SA
TOTALS			29	162	5589	769	1484	223	28	191	729	588	896	114	.266	.418
Steve Garvey	1B160	R	28	162	646	91	192	25	3	33	115	38	90	9	.297	.498
Davey Lopes	2B130	R	32	134	502	85	142	19	5	11	53	73	69	47	.283	.406
Bill Russell	SS153	R	29	153	634	84	176	28	6	4	51	24	43	16	.278	.360
Ron Cey	3B153	R	29	153	564	77	136	22	3	30	110	93	106	3	.241	.450
Reggie Smith	OF140	B	32	148	488	104	150	27	4	32	87	104	76	7	.307	.576
Rick Monday	OF115,1B3	L	31	118	392	47	90	13	1	15	48	60	109	1	.230	.383
Dusty Baker	OF152	R	28	153	533	86	155	26	1	30	86	58	89	2	.291	.512
Steve Yeager	C123	R	28	125	387	53	99	21	2	16	55	43	84	1	.256	.444
Glenn Burke	OF74	R	24	83	169	16	43	8	0	1	13	5	22	13	.254	.320
John Hale	OF73	L	23	79	108	10	26	4	1	2	11	5	28	2	.241	.352
Lee Lacy (RJ)	OF32,2B22,3B12	R	29	75	169	28	45	7	0	6	21	10	21	4	.266	.414
Ted Martinez (KJ)	2B27,SS13,3B12	R	29	67	137	21	41	6	1	1	10	2	20	3	.299	.380
Ed Goodson	1B13,3B4	L	29	61	66	3	11	1	0	1	5	3	10	0	.167	.227
Johnny Oates	C56	L	31	60	156	18	42	4	0	3	11	11	11	1	.269	.353
Boog Powell	1B4	L	35	50	41	0	10	0	0	1	5	12	9	0	.244	.244
Manny Mota	OF1	R	39	49	38	5	15	1	0	1	4	10	0	1	.395	.500
Joe Simpson	OF28,1B1	L	25	29	23	2	4	0	0	0	1	2	6	1	.174	.174
Vic Davalillo	OF12	L	40	24	48	3	15	2	0	0	4	0	6	0	.313	.354
2 Jerry Grote	C16,3B2	R	34	18	27	3	7	0	0	0	4	2	5	0	.259	.259
Rafael Landestoy	2B8,SS3	R	24	15	18	6	5	0	0	0	3	2	2	1	.278	.278
Jeff Leonard	OF10	R	21	11	10	1	3	0	1	0	2	1	4	0	.300	.500
Ron Washington	SS10	R	25	10	19	4	7	0	0	0	1	0	1	0	.368	.368
1 Kevin Pasley	C2	R	23	2	3	1	1	0	0	0	0	0	0	0	.333	.333
Ellie Rodriguez (BC)31																

NAME	T	AGE	W	L	PCT	SV	G	GS	CG	IP	H	BB	SO	SHO	ERA
		28	98	64	.605	39	162	162	34	1475	1393	438	930	13	3.22
Tommy John	L	34	20	7	.741	0	31	31	11	220	225	50	123	3	2.78
Rick Rhoden	R	24	16	10	.615	0	31	31	4	216	223	63	122	1	3.75
Don Sutton	R	32	14	8	.636	0	33	33	9	240	207	69	150	3	3.19
Doug Rau	L	28	14	8	.636	0	32	32	4	212	232	49	126	2	3.44
Burt Hooton	R	27	12	7	.632	1	32	31	6	223	184	60	153	2	2.62
Charlie Hough	R	29	6	12	.333	22	70	0	0	127	98	70	105	0	3.33
Lance Rautzhan	L	24	4	1	.800	2	25	0	0	21	25	7	13	0	4.29
Mike Garman	R	27	4	4	.500	12	49	0	0	63	60	22	29	0	2.71
Dennis Lewallyn	R	23	3	1	.750	1	5	1	0	17	22	4	8	0	4.24
Elias Sosa	R	27	2	2	.500	1	44	0	0	64	42	12	47	0	1.97
Stan Wall	L	26	2	3	.400	0	25	0	0	32	36	13	22	0	5.34
Bobby Castillo	R	22	1	0	1.000	0	6	1	0	11	12	2	7	0	4.09
Hank Webb	R	27	0	0	—	0	8	5	1	2	2	0	2.25		
Al Downing (GJ)	L	36	0	1	.000	0	12	2	0	22	16	23	10	0	6.75

CINCINNATI — 2nd 88-74 .543 10 — SPARKY ANDERSON

Name	G by Pos	B	AGE	G	AB	R	H	2B	3B	HR	RBI	BB	SO	SB	BA	SA
TOTALS			30	162	5524	802	1513	269	42	181	750	600	911	170	.274	.436
Dan Driessen	1B148	L	25	151	536	75	161	31	4	17	91	64	85	31	.300	.468
Joe Morgan	2B151	L	33	153	521	113	150	21	6	22	78	117	58	49	.288	.478
Dave Concepcion	SS156	R	29	156	572	59	155	26	3	8	64	46	77	29	.271	.369
Pete Rose	3B161	B	36	162	655	95	204	38	7	9	64	66	42	16	.311	.432
Ken Griffey	OF147	L	27	154	585	117	186	35	8	12	57	69	84	17	.318	.467
Cesar Geronimo	OF147	L	29	149	492	54	131	22	4	10	52	35	89	10	.266	.388
George Foster	OF158	R	28	158	615	124	197	31	2	52	149	61	107	6	.320	.631
Johnny Bench	C135,OF8,1B4,3B1	R	29	142	494	67	136	34	2	31	109	58	95	2	.275	.540
Mike Lum	1B8,OF24	L	31	81	125	14	20	1	0	5	16	9	33	2	.160	.288
Ray Knight	3B37,2B17,OF5,SS3	R	24	80	92	8	24	5	1	1	13	9	16	1	.261	.370
Ed Armbrister	OF27	R	28	65	78	12	20	4	3	1	5	10	21	5	.256	.423
Champ Summers	OF16,3B1	L	31	59	76	11	13	4	0	3	6	6	16	0	.171	.342
Bill Plummer	C50	R	30	51	117	10	16	5	0	1	17	14	34	1	.137	.205
2 Bob Bailey	1B19,OF3	R	34	49	79	9	20	2	1	2	11	12	10	1	.253	.380
1 Doug Flynn	3B25,2B9,SS4	R	26	36	32	0	8	1	0	0	3	0	5	0	.250	.344
Rick Auerbach	2B9,SS12	R	27	33	45	5	7	2	0	0	4	2	3	0	.156	.200
Don Werner	C10	R	24	10	23	4	4	2	0	0	4	2	3	0	.174	.435

NAME	T	AGE	W	L	PCT	SV	G	GS	CG	IP	H	BB	SO	SHO	ERA
		29	88	74	.543	32	162	162	33	1437	1469	544	868	12	4.22
2 Tom Seaver	R	32	14	3	.824	0	20	20	14	165	120	38	124	4*	2.35
Fred Norman	R	34	14	13	.519	0	35	34	8	221	200	98	160	1	3.38
Pedro Borbon	R	30	10	5	.667	18	73	0	0	127	131	24	48	0	3.19
Jack Billingham	R	34	10	10	.500	0	36	23	3	162	195	56	76	2	5.22
Dale Murray	R	27	7	7	.500	4	61	1	0	102	125	46	42	0	4.94
2 Doug Capilla	L	25	7	8	.467	0	22	16	1	106	94	59	74	0	4.52
Paul Moskau	R	23	6	6	.500	0	20	19	2	108	116	40	71	2	4.00
Woody Fryman(VR)	L	37	5	5	.500	1	17	12	0	75	83	45	57	0	5.40
1 Gary Nolan (JL)	R	29	4	1	.800	0	8	8	0	39	53	12	28	0	4.85
Tom Hume	R	24	3	3	.500	0	14	5	0	43	54	17	22	0	7.12
1 Pat Zachry	R	25	3	7	.300	0	12	12	3	75	78	29	36	0	5.04
Rawly Eastwick	R	26	2	2	.500	7	23	0	0	40	48	17	40	0	2.93
Mario Soto	R	20	2	6	.250	0	12	10	2	61	60	26	44	1	5.31
1 Santo Alcala	R	24	1	1	.500	0	7	2	0						
Manny Sarmiento	R	21	0	0	—	1	24	0	0	40	28	11	23	0	2.48
1 Mike Caldwell	L	28	0	0	—	0	14	0	0	25	8	11		0	3.96
Joe Hoerner	L	40	0	0	—	0	6	0	0	9	9	1	8	0	3.00
Angel Torres	R	23	0	0	—	0	5	0	0	5	12	2	5	0	12.00
Dan Dumoulin	R	23	0	0		0	2	0	0	5	13	1	3	0	14.40
Joe Henderson	R	30	0	2	.000	0	9	1	0	17	26	7	6	0	12.00

* Seaver, also with New York, league leader in ShO with 7

HOUSTON 3rd 81-81 .500 17 BILL VIRDON

Name	G by Pos	B	AGE	G	AB	R	H	2B	3B	HR	RBI	BB	SO	SB	BA	SA
TOTALS			27	162	5530	680	1405	263	60	114	638	515	839	187	.254	.385
Bob Watson	1B146	R	31	151	554	77	160	38	6	22	110	57	69	5	.289	.498
Art Howe (VJ)	2B96,3B19,SS11	R	30	125	413	44	109	23	7	8	58	41	60	0	.264	.412
Roger Metzger (BL)	SS96,2B1	B	29	97	269	24	50	9	6	0	16	32	24	2	.186	.264
Enos Cabell	3B144,1B8,SS1	R	27	150	625	101	176	36	7	16	68	27	55	42	.282	.438
Jose Cruz	OF155	L	29	157	579	87	173	31	10	17	87	69	67	44	.299	.475
Cesar Cedeno	OF137	R	26	141	530	92	148	36	8	14	71	47	50	61	.279	.457
Terry Puhl	OF59	L	20	60	229	40	69	13	5	0	10	30	31	10	.301	.402
Joe Ferguson	C122,1B1	R	30	132	421	59	108	21	3	16	61	85	79	6	.257	.435
Julio Gonzalez	SS63,2B45	R	24	110	383	34	94	18	3	1	27	19	45	3	.245	.316
Wilbur Howard	OF62,2B4	B	28	87	187	22	48	6	0	2	13	5	30	11	.257	.321
Ken Boswell	2B26,3B2	L	31	72	97	7	21	1	1	0	12	10	12	0	.216	.247
Art Gardner	OF26	L	24	66	65	7	10	0	0	0	3	3	15	0	.154	.154
Rob Sperring	SS22,2B20,3B11	R	27	58	129	6	24	3	0	1	9	12	23	0	.186	.233
Ed Herrmann	C49	L	30	56	158	7	46	7	0	1	17	15	18	1	.291	.354
1 Cliff Johnson	OF34,1B10	R	29	51	144	22	43	8	0	10	23	23	30	0	.299	.563
1 Willie Crawford	OF30	L	30	42	114	14	29	3	0	2	18	16	10	0	.254	.333
Jim Fuller	OF27,1B1	R	26	34	100	5	16	6	0	2	9	10	45	0	.160	.280
Leon Roberts	OF9	R	26	19	27	1	2	0	0	0	2	1	8	0	.074	.074
Danny Walton	1B5	R	29	13	21	0	4	0	0	0	1	0	5	0	.190	.190
Mike Fischlin	SS12	R	21	13	15	0	3	0	0	0	0	0	2	0	.200	.200
Joe Cannon	OF3	L	23	9	17	3	2	2	0	0	1	0	5	1	.118	.235
Craig Cacek	1B6	R	22	7	20	0	1	0	0	0	1	1	3	0	.050	.050
Denny Walling	OF5	L	23	6	21	1	6	0	1	0	6	2	4	0	.286	.381
Luis Pujols	C6	R	21	6	15	0	1	0	0	0	0	0	3	0	.067	.067

NAME	T	AGE	W	L	PCT	SV	G	GS	CG	IP	H	BB	SO	SHO	ERA
		25	81	81	.500	28	162	162	37	1466	1384	545	871	11	3.54
J.R. Richard	R	27	18	12	.600	0	36	36	13	267	212	104	214	3	2.97
Joe Niekro	R	32	13	8	.619	5	44	14	9	181	155	64	101	3	3.03
Joaquin Andujar (LJ)	R	24	11	8	.579	0	26	25	4	159	149	64	69	1	3.68
Mark Lemongello	R	21	9	14	.391	0	34	30	5	215	237	52	83	0	3.47
Floyd Bannister (EJ)	L	22	8	9	.471	0	24	23	4	143	138	68	112	1	4.03
Gene Pentz	R	24	5	2	.714	2	41	4	0	87	76	44	51	0	3.83
Joe Sambito	L	25	5	5	.500	7	54	1	0	89	77	24	67	0	2.33
Ken Forsch	R	30	5	8	.385	8	42	5	0	86	80	28	45	0	2.72
Bo McLaughlin	R	23	4	7	.364	5	46	6	0	85	81	34	59	0	4.24
Tom Dixon	R	22	1	0	1.000	0	9	4	1	30	40	7	15	0	3.30
Doug Konieczny	R	25	1	1	.500	0	4	4	0	21	26	8	7	0	6.00
Dan Larson	R	22	1	7	.125	0	32	10	1	98	108	45	44	0	5.79
Roy Thomas	R	24	0	1	—	0	4	0	0	6	5	3	4	0	3.00

SAN FRANCISCO 4th 75-87 .463 23 JOE ALTOBELLI

Name	G by Pos	B	AGE	G	AB	R	H	2B	3B	HR	RBI	BB	SO	SB	BA	SA
TOTALS			27	162	5497	673	1392	227	41	134	624	568	842	90	.253	.383
Willie McCovey	1B136	L	39	141	478	54	134	21	0	28	86	67	106	3	.280	.500
Rob Andrews	2B115	R	24	127	436	60	115	11	3	0	25	56	33	5	.264	.303
2 Tim Foli (BR)	SS102,3B1,2B1,OF1	R	26	104	368	30	84	17	3	4	27	11	16	2	.228	.323
Bill Madlock	3B126,2B6	R	26	140	533	70	161	28	1	12	46	43	33	13	.302	.426
Jack Clark	OF114	R	21	136	413	64	104	17	4	13	51	49	73	12	.252	.407
Derrel Thomas	OF78,2B27,SS26,3B6,1B3	B	26	148	506	75	135	13	10	8	44	46	70	15	.267	.379
Gary Thomasson	OF113,1B31	L	25	145	446	63	114	24	6	17	71	75	102	16	.256	.451
Marc Hill	C102	R	25	108	320	28	80	10	0	9	50	34	34	0	.250	.366
Darrell Evans	OF81,1B41,3B35	L	30	144	461	64	117	18	3	17	72	69	50	9	.254	.416
Terry Whitfield	OF84	L	24	114	326	41	93	21	3	7	36	20	46	2	.285	.433
Randy Elliott	OF46	R	26	73	167	17	40	5	1	7	26	8	24	0	.240	.407
Vic Harris	2B27,SS11,3B9,OF3	B	27	69	165	28	43	12	0	2	14	19	36	2	.261	.370
Johnnie LeMaster	SS54,3B2	R	23	68	134	13	20	5	1	0	8	13	27	2	.149	.201
Mike Sadek	C57	R	31	61	126	12	29	7	0	1	15	12	5	2	.230	.310
Gary Alexander	C33,OF1	R	24	51	119	17	36	4	2	5	20	20	33	3	.303	.496
Larry Herndon (KJ,JT)	OF44	R	23	49	109	13	26	4	3	1	5	5	20	4	.239	.358
1 Ken Rudolph	C11	R	27	15	15	1	3	0	0	0	1	0	3	0	.200	.200
Skip James	1B9	L	27	10	15	3	4	1	0	0	3	2	3	0	.267	.333
1 Chris Speier	SS5	R	27	8	17	1	3	1	0	0	0	0	3	0	.176	.235
Tom Heintzelman		R	30	2	2	0	0	0	0	0	0	0	0	0	.000	.000

NAME	T	AGE	W	L	PCT	SV	G	GS	CG	IP	H	BB	SO	SHO	ERA
		27	75	87	.463	33	162	162	27	1459	1501	529	854	10	3.75
Ed Halicki	R	26	16	12	.571	0	37	37	7	258	241	70	168	2	3.31
Jim Barr	R	29	12	16	.429	0	38	38	6	234	286	56	97	2	4.77
Bob Knepper	R	23	11	9	.550	0	27	27	6	166	151	72	100	2	3.36
Gary Lavelle	L	28	7	7	.500	20	73	0	0	118	106	37	93	0	2.06
John Montefusco (NJ)	R	27	7	12	.368	0	26	25	4	157	170	46	110	0	3.50
Charlie Williams	R	29	6	5	.545	0	55	8	1	119	116	60	41	0	4.01
Dave Heaverlo	R	26	5	1	.833	1	56	0	0	99	92	21	58	0	2.55
Randy Moffitt	R	28	4	9	.308	11	64	0	0	88	91	39	68	0	3.58
John Curtis	L	29	3	3	.500	1	43	9	1	77	95	48	47	1	5.49
Lynn McGlothen (SJ)	R	27	2	9	.182	0	21	15	2	80	94	52	42	0	5.63
Greg Minton	R	25	1	1	.500	0	2	0	0	14	4	5	4	0	4.50
Terry Cornutt	R	24	1	2	.333	0	28	0	0	44	38	22	23	0	3.89
Tommy Toms	R	25	0	1	.000	0	4	0	0	4	7	2	2	0	2.25

SAN DIEGO 5th 69-93 .426 29 JOHN McNAMARA 20-28 .417 BOB SKINNER 1-0 1.000 AL DARK 48-65 .430

Name	G by Pos	B	AGE	G	AB	R	H	2B	3B	HR	RBI	BB	SO	SB	BA	SA
TOTALS			25	162	5602	692	1397	245	49	120	652	602	1057	133	.249	.375
Mike Ivie	1B105,3B25	R	24	134	489	66	133	29	2	9	66	39	57	3	.272	.395
Mike Champion	2B149	R	22	150	507	35	116	14	6	1	43	27	85	3	.229	.286
Bill Almon	SS155	R	24	155	613	75	160	18	11	2	43	37	114	20	.261	.336
Tucker Ashford	3B74,SS10,2B4	R	22	81	249	25	54	18	0	3	24	9	55	2	.217	.325
Dave Winfield	OF156	R	25	157	615	104	169	29	7	25	92	58	75	16	.275	.467
George Hendrick	OF142	R	27	152	541	75	168	25	2	23	81	61	74	11	.311	.492
Gene Richards	OF109,1B32	L	23	146	525	79	152	16	11	5	32	60	80	56	.290	.390
Gene Tenace	C99,1B36,3B14	R	30	147	437	66	102	24	4	15	61	125	119	5	.233	.410
Jerry Turner	OF69	L	23	118	289	43	71	16	1	10	48	31	43	12	.246	.412
Merv Rettenmund	OF27,3B1	R	34	107	126	23	36	6	1	4	17	33	28	1	.286	.444
Dave Roberts	C63,3B2,2B2,SS1	R	26	82	186	15	41	14	1	1	23	11	32	2	.220	.323
Gary Sutherland	2B21,3B20,1B4	R	32	80	103	5	25	3	0	1	11	7	15	0	.243	.301
2 Dave Kingman	OF28,1B13,3B2	R	28	56	168	16	40	9	0	11	39	12	48	2	.238	.488
1 Doug Rader	3B51	R	32	52	170	19	46	8	3	5	27	33	40	0	.271	.441
Bob Davis	C46	R	25	48	94	9	17	2	0	1	10	5	24	0	.181	.234
Pat Scanlon	2B15,3B11,OF1	L	24	47	79	9	15	3	0	1	11	12	20	0	.190	.266
1 Bobby Valentine	3B10,SS10,1B1	R	27	44	67	5	12	3	0	1	10	7	10	0	.179	.269
Luis Melendez (AJ)	OF2	R	27	8	3	1	0	0	0	0	0	1	1	0	.000	.000
Enzo Hernandez (XJ)	SS7	R	28	7	3	1	0	0	0	0	0	0	3	0	.000	.000
Brian Greer		R	18	1	1	0	0	0	0	0	0	0	1	0	.000	.000

NAME	T	AGE	W	L	PCT	SV	G	GS	CG	IP	H	BB	SO	SHO	ERA
		26	69	93	.426	44	162	162	6	1466	1556	673	827	5	4.43
Bob Shirley	L	23	12	18	.400	0	39	35	1	214	215	100	146	0	3.70
Bob Owchinko	L	22	9	12	.429	0	30	28	3	170	191	67	101	2	4.45
Rollie Fingers	R	30	8	9	.471	35	78	0	0	132	123	36	113	0	3.00
Dan Spillner	R	25	7	6	.538	6	76	0	0	123	130	60	74	0	3.73
Rick Sawyer	R	29	7	6	.538	0	56	9	0	111	136	55	45	0	5.84
Dave Freisleben	R	25	7	9	.438	0	33	23	1	139	140	71	72	0	4.60
Tom Griffin	R	29	7	9	.400	0	38	20	0	151	144	88	79	0	4.47
Randy Jones (AJ)	L	27	6	12	.333	0	27	25	1	147	173	36	44	0	4.59
Dave Tomlin	L	28	4	4	.500	3	76	0	0	102	98	32	55	0	3.00
Vic Bernal	R	23	1	1	.500	0	15	0	0	20	23	9	6	0	5.40
2 John D'Acquisto	R	25	1	2	.333	0	17	12	0	44	49	47	45	0	6.95
Dave Wehrmeister	R	24	1	3	.250	0	30	6	0	70	81	44	32	0	6.04
1 Butch Metzger	R	25	0	0	—	0	17	1	0	23	27	12	6	0	5.48
1 Paul Siebert	L	24	0	1	—	0	4	0	0	4	3	4	1	0	2.25
Brent Strom (AJ)	L	28	0	2	.000	0	8	3	0	17	23	12	8	0	12.18

ATLANTA 6th 61-101 .377 37 DAVE BRISTOL 8-21 .276 TED TURNER 0-1 1.000 VERN BENSON 1-0 1.000 DAVE BRISTOL 52-79 .397

Name	G by Pos	B	AGE	G	AB	R	H	2B	3B	HR	RBI	BB	SO	SB	BA	SA
TOTALS			25	162	5534	678	1404	218	20	139	638	537	876	82	.254	.376
Willie Montanez (GJ)	1B134	L	29	136	544	70	156	31	1	20	68	35	60	1	.287	.458
Rod Gilbreath	2B122,3B1	R	24	128	407	47	99	15	2	8	43	45	79	3	.243	.349
Pat Rockett (EJ)	SS84	R	22	93	264	27	67	10	0	1	24	27	32	1	.254	.303
Junior Moore	3B104,2B1	R	24	112	361	41	94	9	3	5	34	33	29	4	.260	.343
Jeff Burroughs	OF154	R	26	154	579	91	157	19	1	41	114	86	126	4	.271	.520
Rowland Office	OF104,1B1	L	24	124	428	42	103	13	1	5	39	23	58	2	.241	.311
Gary Matthews	OF145	R	26	148	555	89	157	25	5	17	64	67	90	22	.283	.438
Biff Pocoroba	C100	L	23	113	321	46	93	24	1	8	44	57	27	3	.290	.445
Jerry Royster	3B56,SS51,2B38,OF1	R	24	140	445	64	96	10	2	6	28	38	67	28	.216	.288
Barry Bonnell	OF75,3B32	R	23	100	360	41	108	11	0	1	45	17	52	7	.300	.339
Brian Asselstine	OF35	R	23	83	124	12	26	6	0	4	17	9	10	1	.210	.355
Darrel Chaney (FJ)	SS41,2B24	B	29	74	209	22	42	7	2	3	15	17	44	0	.201	.297
Tom Paciorek	1B32,OF9,3B1	R	30	72	155	20	37	8	0	3	15	6	46	1	.239	.348
Joe Nolan	C19	R	26	62	82	13	23	3	0	3	9	13	12	1	.280	.427
Cito Gaston	OF9,1B5	R	33	56	85	6	23	3	0	1	21	5	19	1	.271	.424
Vic Correll	C49	R	31	54	144	16	30	7	0	7	16	22	33	2	.208	.403
Craig Robinson	SS33	R	28	27	29	4	6	1	0	0	1	1	6	0	.207	.241
Dale Murphy	C18	R	21	18	76	5	24	8	1	2	14	0	19	0	.316	.526
Rob Belloir	SS3	R	28	6	1	2	0	0	0	0	1	0	3	0	.000	.000
Larry Whisenton		L	20	4	4	0	0	0	0	0	0	1	1	0	.250	.250

NAME	T	AGE	W	L	PCT	SV	G	GS	CG	IP	H	BB	SO	SHO	ERA
		28	61	101	.377	31	162	162	28	1445	1581	701	915	5	4.85
Phil Niekro	R	38	16	20	.444	0	44	43	20	330	315	164	262	2	4.04
Dick Ruthven (FJ)	R	26	7	13	.350	0	25	23	6	151	158	62	89	0	4.23
Rick Camp (SJ)	R	24	6	3	.667	10	54	0	0	79	89	47	51	0	3.99
Eddie Solomon	R	26	6	6	.500	0	18	16	0	89	110	34	54	0	4.55
Buzz Capra	R	29	6	11	.353	0	45	16	0	139	142	80	100	0	5.37
Andy Messersmith (EJ)	R	31	5	4	.556	0	16	16	1	102	101	39	69	0	4.41
Max Leon (ST)	R	27	4	4	.500	1	31	9	0	82	89	25	44	0	3.95
Don Collins	L	24	3	9	.250	2	40	6	0	71	82	41	27	0	5.07
Jamie Easterly (EJ)	L	24	2	4	.333	1	22	5	0	59	72	30	37	0	6.10
Preston Hanna	R	22	2	6	.250	1	17	9	1	60	69	34	37	0	4.95
1 Mike Marshall	R	34	1	1	1.000	0	6			12	12	2	6	0	9.00
Duane Theiss	R	23	1	1	.500	0	17	0	0	21	26	16	7	0	6.49
Mickey Mahler	L	24	1	2	.333	0	5	5	0	23	31	9	14	0	6.26
Frank LaCorte	R	25	1	8	.111	0	14	7	0	37	67	29	28	0	11.68
Steve Kline	R	29	0	0	—	1	16	0	0	20	21	12	10	0	6.75
Mike Davey	L	25	0	0	—	0	16	0	0	16	19	7	10	0	5.06
Mike Beard	L	27	0	0	—	0	2	0	0	5	14	2	1	0	9.00
Joey McLaughlin	R	20	0	0	—	0	3	0	0	3	3	0	1	0	3.00
Larry Bradford	L	27	0	0	—	0	3	3	0	3	3	0	1	0	3.00
Bob Johnson	R	30	0	3	.000	1	22	14	1	55	54	26	48	0	9.36
3 Steve Hargan	R	34	0	3	.000	0	16	16	1	37	49	16	18	0	6.81
Dave Campbell	R	25	0	6	.000	13	65	0	0	89	78	33	42	0	3.03

1978 A Fold For All Seasons

In the heat of July, people were comparing the Boston Red Sox with the greatest teams in baseball history. The Sox fielded a lineup with plenty of batting muscle, with the powerful Jim Rice especially terrorizing pitchers. With the addition of Jerry Remy and Dennis Eckersley in trades and Mike Torrez as a free agent, the Bosox had their best defense and pitching in years. By mid-July, they were cruising atop the A.L. East with a 10-game lead over the Milwaukee Brewers.

Back in fourth place were the defending champion New York Yankees, a team in big trouble. Although Ron Guidry was almost untouchable and free agent Goose Gossage excelled in the bullpen, injuries had decimated the pitching staff. Manager Billy Martin had taken to juggling his lineup, making Thurman Munson his right fielder and demoting Reggie Jackson to a part-time designated hitter. On July 17, after a loss which dropped the Yanks 14 games behind Boston, Martin suspended Jackson for five games for disobeying one of his signals. One week later, Martin made some remarks to the press uncomplimentary to Jackson and owner George Steinbrenner. Under pressure, Martin resigned and was replaced by Bob Lemon, who had been fired as manager of the White Sox only three weeks earlier.

When Lemon took over on July 24 New York was 10 ½ games behind the Red Sox. In August, however, the champions began winning under Lemon's relaxed regime. After being written off as a has-been earlier in the season, Catfish Hunter sparked the comeback by pitching strong baseball over the last two months. The Red Sox, meanwhile, had lost their luster and were struggling. Under the New York charge, the Bosox began to wilt. When the Yanks came to Fenway Park on September 7 for a four-game series, the Sox had lost five of their last seven games, the Yanks had won 12 of their last 14, and the Boston lead had shrunk to four games. The Yankees left Boston tied for first place by massacring the Red Sox 15-3, 13-2, 7-0, and 7-4. By the time the Red Sox came to Yankee Stadium on September 15 for three games, the Yanks led by 1½ games. New York won the first two before Boston ended the skid by taking the third. The Red Sox then came back strong over the final two weeks to tie the Yanks on the final day of the season. In a one-game playoff in Boston, the Sox took a 2-0 lead into the seventh inning, but a three-run

homer by Bucky Dent put New York ahead and on the way to a 5-4 victory. Many experts said that the two best teams in baseball had met that day in the playoff.

Of course, teams in the other divisions disputed that. The Kansas City Royals won the A.L. West title for the third year running, relying on strong pitching and timely hitting. The closest challengers were the Texas Rangers, who were loaded with talent but never jelled into a consistent team, and the California Angels, whose good young team was devastated on September 23 when Lyman Bostock, the star outfielder they had signed as a free agent, was murdered in Gary, Indiana.

In the N.L., both division champions repeated. The Phillies captured the East title once again despite a late season rush by the Pirates. In the West, the Dodgers survived challenges by the Reds and Giants to take first place. Although strong in all positions, the Dodgers played their best ball only after Steve Garvey and Don Sutton had a clubhouse scuffle on August 20. The Reds came up short despite a heroic season by Pete Rose. Early in May, he chalked up his 3,000th career base hit, and during the height of summer, he commanded the attention of the entire sports world with a hitting streak that challenged Joe DiMaggio's record. Beginning on June 14, Rose's streak set a new modern N.L. record of 38 on July 25, beat George Sisler's mark of 41 on July 29, and tied Willie Keeler's string of 44 for the second longest history in history before being snapped in Atlanta on August 1.

After 3-1 triumphs in the league playoffs, the Yankees and Dodgers squared off in a rematch of last year's World Series. The Dodgers swept the first two games in Los Angeles, capping the second with a dramatic strikeout of Reggie Jackson by rookie reliever Bob Welch. When the clubs went to New York, third baseman Graig Nettles turned in four great plays in game three to get the Yankees into the victory column. The New Yorkers swept the remaining two games in Yankee Stadium, then won the Series with a sixth game triumph that was iced by Jackson's long homer off Welch. Although Jackson led the Yanks in RBI's, the batting leaders of the club were singles-hitters Bucky Dent and Brian Doyle, whose barrages hurt the Dodgers that much more for being unexpected.

1978 AMERICAN LEAGUE — EAST DIVISION

Name	G by Pos	B	AGE	G	AB	R	H	2B	3B	HR	RBI	BB	SO	SB	BA	SA
NEW YORK	**1st 100-63 .613**															BILLY MARTIN 52-42 .553 DICK HOWSER 0-1 .000 2 BOB LEMON 48-20 .706 (Defeated Boston in a 1 game playoff)
TOTALS			30	163	5583	735	1489	228	38	125	693	505	695	98	.267	.388
Chris Chambliss	1B155, DH7	L	29	162	625	81	171	26	3	12	90	41	60	2	.274	.382
Willie Randolph (KJ)	2B134	R	23	134	499	87	139	18	6	3	42	82	51	36	.279	.357
Bucky Dent (LJ)	SS123	R	26	123	379	40	92	11	1	5	40	23	24	3	.243	.317
Graig Nettles	3B159, SS2	L	33	159	587	81	162	23	2	27	93	59	69	1	.276	.460
Reggie Jackson	OF104, DH35	L	32	139	511	82	140	13	5	27	97	58	133	14	.274	.477
Mickey Rivers	OF138	L	29	141	559	78	148	25	8	11	48	29	51	25	.265	.397
Lou Piniella	OF103, DH23	R	34	130	472	67	148	34	5	6	69	34	36	3	.314	.445
Thurman Munson	C125, DH14, OF13	R	31	154	617	73	183	27	1	6	71	35	70	2	.297	.373
Cliff Johnson	DH39, C22, 1B1	R	30	76	174	20	32	9	1	6	19	30	32	0	.184	.351
Roy White	OF74, DH23	B	34	103	346	44	93	13	3	8	43	42	35	10	.269	.393
Fred Stanley	SS71, 2B11, 3B4	R	30	81	160	14	35	7	0	1	9	25	31	0	.219	.281
Paul Blair	OF64, 2B5, SS4, 3B3	R	34	75	125	10	22	5	0	2	13	9	17	1	.176	.264
Jim Spencer	DH35, 1B15	L	30	71	150	14	34	9	1	7	24	15	32	0	.227	.440
Gary Thomasson	OF50, DH1	L	26	55	116	20	32	4	1	3	20	13	22	0	.276	.405
Brian Doyle	2B29, SS7, 3B5	L	24	39	52	6	10	0	1	0	6	4	10	0	.192	.192
Jay Johnstone	OF22, DH5	L	32	36	65	6	17	0	1	1	6	4	10	0	.262	.308
Mike Heath	C33	R	23	33	92	6	21	3	1	0	8	4	9	0	.228	.283
Damaso Garcia	2B16, SS3	R	23	18	41	5	8	0	0	1	2	6	1	.195	.195
George Zeber	2B1	B	27	3	6	0	0	0	0	0	0	0	0	0	.000	.000
Dell Alston		L	25	3	3	0	0	0	0	0	0	0	2	0	.000	.000
Denny Sherrill	DH1, 3B1	R	22	2	1	1	0	0	0	0	0	0	0	0	.000	.000
Mickey Klutts (BG)	3B1	R	23	1	2	1	2	1	0	0	0	0	0	0	1.000	1.500
Bran Healy (ZJ)	C1	R	31	1	1	0	0	0	0	0	0	0	1	0	.000	.000
Domingo Ramos	SS1	R	20	1	0	0	0	0	0	0	0	0	0	0	—	—

NAME	T	AGE	W	L	PCT	SV	G	GS	CG	IP	H	BB	SO	SHO	ERA
		28	100	63	.613	36	163	163	39	1461	1321	478	817	16	3.18
Ron Guidry	L	27	25	3	.893	0	35	35	16	274	187	72	248	9	1.74
Ed Figueroa	R	29	20	9	.690	0	35	35	12	253	233	77	92	2	2.99
Catfish Hunter (SJ)	R	32	12	6	.667	0	21	20	5	118	98	35	56	1	3.58
Goose Gossage	R	26	10	11	.476	27	63	0	0	134	87	59	122	0	2.01
Sparky Lyle	L	33	9	3	.750	9	59	0	0	112	116	33	33	0	3.46
Dick Tidrow	R	31	7	11	.389	0	31	25	4	185	191	53	73	0	3.84
Jim Beattie	R	23	6	9	.400	0	25	22	0	128	123	51	65	0	3.73
Don Gullett (SJ)	L	27	4	2	.667	0	8	8	2	45	46	20	28	0	3.60
Ken Clay (TJ)	R	24	3	4	.429	0	28	6	0	76	89	21	32	0	4.26
1 Rawly Eastwick	R	27	2	1	.667	0	8	0	0	25	22	4	13	0	3.24
1 Ken Holtzman	L	32	1	0	1.000	0	5	3	0	18	21	9	3	0	4.00
Larry McCall	R	25	1	1	.500	0	5	1	0	16	20	6	7	0	5.63
Bob Kammeyer	R	27	0	0	—	0	7	0	0	22	24	6	11	0	5.73
2 Paul Lindblad	L	36	0	0	—	0	7	1	0	18	21	8	9	0	4.50
Dave Rajsich	L	26	0	0	—	0	4	2	0	13	16	6	9	0	4.15
Ron Davis	R	22	0	0	—	0	4	0	0	2	3	3	0	0	13.50
Andy Messersmith (SJ)	R	32	0	3	.000	0	6	5	0	22	24	15	16	0	5.73

Name	G by Pos	B	AGE	G	AB	R	H	2B	3B	HR	RBI	BB	SO	SB	BA	SA
BOSTON	**2nd 99-64 .607 1**															DON ZIMMER (Defeated by New York in a 1 game playoff)
TOTALS			28	163	5587	796	1493	270	46	172	738	582	835	74	.267	.424
George Scott (XJ-BG)	1B113, DH7	R	34	120	412	51	96	16	4	12	54	44	86	1	.233	.389
Jerry Remy	2B140, DH4, SS1	L	25	148	583	87	162	24	6	2	44	40	55	30	.278	.350
Rick Burleson	SS144	R	27	145	626	75	155	32	5	5	49	40	51	8	.248	.339
Butch Hobson	3B133, DH14	R	26	147	512	65	128	26	2	17	80	50	122	1	.250	.408
Dwight Evans	OF142, DH4	R	26	147	497	75	123	24	2	24	63	65	119	8	.247	.449
Fred Lynn	OF149	L	26	150	541	75	161	33	3	22	82	75	50	3	.298	.492
Carl Yastrzemski	OF71, 1B50, DH27	L	38	144	523	70	145	21	2	17	81	76	44	4	.277	.423
Carlton Fisk	C154, OF1, DH1	R	30	157	571	94	162	39	5	20	88	71	83	7	.284	.475
Jim Rice	OF114, DH49	R	25	163	677	121	213	25	15	46	139	58	126	7	.315	.600
Jack Brohamer	3B30, DH25, 2B23	L	28	81	244	34	57	14	1	1	25	25	13	1	.234	.311
Frank Duffy	3B22, SS21, 2B12, DH6	R	31	64	104	12	27	5	0	0	4	6	11	1	.260	.308
Bob Bailey	DH34, 3B1, OF1	R	35	43	94	12	18	3	0	4	9	19	19	2	.191	.351
Garry Hancock	OF19, DH13	L	24	38	80	10	18	3	0	4	1	1	12	0	.225	.263
Fred Kendall	1B13, C5, DH1	R	29	20	41	3	8	1	0	0	4	1	8	0	.195	.220
Ernie Carbo (NJ)	OF9, DH8	L	30	17	46	7	12	3	0	1	6	8	1	0	.261	.391
Bob Montgomery	C10	R	34	10	29	2	7	1	1	0	5	2	12	0	.241	.345
Sam Bowen	OF4	R	25	6	7	3	1	0	0	1	1	1	2	0	.143	.571

NAME	T	AGE	W	L	PCT	SV	G	GS	CG	IP	H	BB	SO	SHO	ERA
		29	99	64	.607	26	163	163	57	1473	1530	464	706	15	3.54
Dennis Eckersley	R	23	20	8	.714	0	35	35	16	268	258	71	162	3	2.99
Mike Torrez	R	31	16	13	.552	0	36	36	15	250	272	99	120	2	3.96
Bob Stanley	R	23	15	2	.882	10	52	3	0	142	142	34	38	0	2.60
Luis Tiant	R	37	13	8	.619	0	32	31	12	212	185	57	114	5	3.31
Bill Lee	L	31	10	10	.500	0	28	24	8	177	198	59	44	1	3.46
Jim Wright	R	27	8	4	.667	0	24	16	5	116	122	24	56	3	3.57
Bill Campbell (EJ)	R	29	7	5	.583	4	29	0	0	51	62	17	47	0	3.88
Dick Drago	R	33	4	4	.500	7	37	1	0	77	71	32	42	0	3.04
Tom Burgmeier	L	34	2	1	.667	4	35	1	0	61	74	23	24	0	4.43
2 Andy Hassler	L	26	2	1	.667	1	13	2	0	30	38	13	23	0	3.00
Allen Ripley	R	25	2	5	.286	0	15	11	1	73	92	22	26	0	5.55
John LaRose	L	26	0	0	—	0	1	0	0	2	3	0	1	0	22.50
1 Reggie Cleveland	R	30	0	1	.000	0	5	0	0	9	13	4	6	0	0.00
Bobby Sprowl	L	22	0	2	.000	0	3	2	0	13	12	10	10	0	6.23

MILWAUKEE — 3rd 93-69 .574 6.5 — GEORGE BAMBERGER

Name	G by Pos	B	AGE	G	AB	R	H	2B	3B	HR	RBI	BB	SO	SB	BA	SA
TOTALS			27	162	5536	804	1530	265	38	173	762	520	805	95	.276	.432
Cecil Cooper (LJ)	1B84, DH19	L	28	107	407	60	127	23	4	13	54	32	72	3	.312	.474
Paul Molitor	2B91, SS31, DH2, 3B1	R	21	125	521	73	142	26	4	6	45	19	54	30	.273	.372
Robin Yount (NJ)	SS125	R	22	127	502	66	147	23	9	9	71	24	43	16	.293	.428
Sal Bando	3B134, DH12, 1B5	R	34	152	540	85	154	20	6	17	78	72	52	3	.285	.439
Sixto Lezcano	OF127, DH3	R	24	132	442	67	129	21	4	15	61	64	83	3	.292	.459
Gorman Thomas	OF137	R	27	137	452	70	111	24	1	32	86	73	133	4	.246	.515
Ben Oglivie	OF89, DH27, 1B11	L	29	128	469	71	142	29	4	18	72	52	69	11	.303	.497
Charlie Moore	C95	R	25	96	268	30	72	7	1	5	31	12	24	1	.269	.358
Larry Hisle	OF87, DH51	R	31	142	520	96	151	24	0	34	115	67	90	10	.290	.533
Don Money	1B61, 2B36, 3B25, DH15, SS2	R	31	137	518	88	152	30	2	14	54	48	70	3	.293	.440
Buck Martinez	C89	R	29	89	256	26	56	10	1	1	20	14	42	1	.219	.277
Dick Davis	DH34, OF28	R	24	69	218	28	54	10	1	5	26	7	23	2	.248	.372
Jim Wohlford	OF35, DH4	R	27	46	118	16	35	7	2	1	19	6	10	3	.297	.415
Jim Gantner	2B21, 3B15, SS1, 1B1	L	25	43	97	14	21	1	0	1	8	5	10	2	.216	.258
2 Dave May	OF16, DH8	L	34	39	77	9	15	4	0	2	11	9	10	0	.195	.325
Lenn Sakata	2B29	R	24	30	78	8	15	4	0	0	3	8	11	1	.192	.244
Tony Muser	1B12	L	30	15	30	0	4	1	1	0	5	3	5	0	.133	.233
Jeff Yurak	OF1	B	24	5	5	0	0	0	0	0	0	0	1	0	.000	.000
Andy Etchebarren (EJ)	C4	R	35	4	5	1	2	1	0	0	2	1	2	0	.400	.600
Larry Haney	C4	R	35	4	5	1	1	0	0	0	1	0	1	0	.200	.200
1 Tim Johnson	SS2	R	28	3	3	1	0	0	0	0	0	0	2	0	.000	.000
2 Tim Nordbrook (KJ)	SS2	R	28	2	5	0	0	0	0	0	0	1	1	0	.000	.000

Ray Fosse (KJ) 31

NAME	T	AGE	W	L	PCT	SV	G	GS	CG	IP	H	BB	SO	SHO	ERA
TOTALS		25	93	69	.574	24	162	162	62	1436	1442	398	577	19	3.65
Mike Caldwell	L	29	22	9	.710	1	37	34	23	293	258	54	131	6	2.37
Lary Sorensen	R	22	18	12	.600	1	37	36	17	281	277	50	78	3	3.20
Jerry Augustine	R	25	13	12	.520	0	35	30	9	188	204	61	59	2	4.55
Bill Travers (EJ)	L	25	12	11	.522	0	28	28	8	176	184	58	66	3	4.40
Andy Replogle	R	24	9	5	.643	0	32	18	3	149	177	47	41	2	3.93
Bill Castro	R	24	5	4	.556	8	42	0	0	50	43	14	17	0	1.80
Eduardo Rodriguez	R	26	5	5	.500	2	32	8	0	105	107	26	51	0	3.94
Randy Stein	R	25	3	2	.600	1	31	1	0	73	78	39	42	0	5.30
Moose Haas (EJ)	R	22	2	3	.400	1	7	6	2	31	33	8	32	0	6.10
Bob McClure	L	26	2	6	.250	9	44	0	0	65	53	30	47	0	3.74
Willie Mueller	R	21	1	0	1.000	0	5	0	0	13	16	6	6	0	6.23
Ed Farmer	R	28	1	0	1.000	0	11	7	4	11	7	4	6	0	0.82
Mark Bomback	R	25	0	0	—	0	2	1	0	2	5	1	1	0	13.50

BALTIMORE — 4th 90-71 .559 9 — EARL WEAVER

Name	G by Pos	B	AGE	G	AB	R	H	2B	3B	HR	RBI	BB	SO	SB	BA	SA
TOTALS			28	161	5422	659	1397	248	19	154	612	552	864	75	.258	.396
Eddie Murray	1B157, 3B3, DH1	R	22	161	610	85	174	32	3	27	95	70	97	6	.285	.480
Rich Dauer	2B87, 3B52, DH1	R	25	133	459	57	121	23	0	6	46	26	22	0	.264	.353
Mark Belanger	SS134	R	34	133	348	39	74	13	0	0	16	40	55	6	.213	.250
Doug DeCinces	3B130, 2B12	R	27	142	511	72	146	37	1	28	80	46	81	7	.286	.526
Ken Singleton	OF140, DH5	B	31	149	502	67	147	21	2	20	81	98	94	0	.293	.462
Larry Harlow	OF138, P1	L	26	147	460	67	112	25	1	8	26	55	72	14	.243	.354
Al Bumbry (BL)	OF28	L	31	33	114	21	27	5	2	2	6	17	15	5	.237	.368
Rick Dempsey	C135	R	28	136	441	41	114	25	0	6	32	48	54	7	.259	.356
Lee May	DH140, 1B4	R	35	148	556	56	137	16	1	25	80	31	110	5	.246	.414
Carlos Lopez	OF114, DH1	R	29	129	193	21	46	6	0	4	20	9	34	5	.238	.332
Pat Kelly	OF80, DH2	L	33	100	274	38	75	12	1	11	40	34	58	10	.274	.445
Billy Smith (VJ)	2B83, SS2	B	24	85	288	37	69	12	2	5	30	27	40	3	.260	.339
Kiko Garcia	SS74, 2B3	R	24	79	186	17	49	6	4	0	13	7	43	7	.263	.339
Andres Mora	OF69, DH1	R	23	76	229	21	49	8	0	8	14	13	47	0	.214	.354
Terry Crowley	DH17, OF2, 1B1	L	31	62	95	9	24	2	0	0	12	8	12	0	.253	.274
Mike Anderson	OF47	R	27	53	32	2	3	0	1	0	3	3	10	0	.094	.156
Dave Skaggs	C35	R	27	36	86	6	13	1	1	0	7	5	9	0	.151	.186
Gary Roenicke	OF20	R	23	27	58	5	15	3	0	3	15	8	3	0	.259	.466
Ellie Hendricks (RC)	C6, DH1, P1	L	37	13	18	4	6	1	0	1	3	3	0	0	.333	.556
Mike Dimmel	OF7	R	23	9	0	2	0	0	0	0	0	0	0	0	—	—

NAME	T	AGE	W	L	PCT	SV	G	GS	CG	IP	H	BB	SO	SHO	ERA
TOTALS		27	90	71	.559	33	161	161	65	1429	1340	509	754	16	3.56
Jim Palmer	R	32	21	12	.636	0	38	38	19	296	246	97	138	6	2.46
Mike Flanagan	L	26	19	15	.559	0	40	40	17	281	271	87	167	2	4.04
Dennis Martinez	R	23	16	11	.593	0	40	38	15	276	257	93	142	2	3.52
Scott McGregor	L	24	15	13	.536	1	35	32	13	233	217	47	94	4	3.32
Don Stanhouse	R	27	6	9	.400	24	56	0	0	75	60	52	42	0	2.88
Nelson Briles (LJ)	R	34	4	4	.500	0	16	8	1	54	58	21	30	0	4.67
Joe Kerrigan	R	23	3	1	.750	3	26	2	0	72	75	36	41	0	4.75
Tippy Martinez	L	28	3	3	.500	5	42	0	0	69	77	40	57	0	4.83
Dave Ford	R	21	1	0	1.000	0	3	2	1	15	10	2	5	0	0.00
John Flinn	R	23	1	0	1.000	0	13	0	0	16	24	13	8	0	7.88
Sammy Stewart	R	23	1	1	.500	0	2	2	0	11	10	3	11	0	3.27
Earl Stephenson	L	30	0	0	—	0	2	0	0	10	10	5	4	0	2.70
Ellie Hendricks	R	37	0	0	—	0	1	0	0	1	1	0	0	0	0.00
Larry Harlow	L	26	0	0	—	0	1	0	0	2	4	1	0	0	45.00
Tim Stoddard	R	25	0	1	.000	0	8	0	0	18	22	8	14	0	6.00

DETROIT — 5th 86-76 .531 13.5 — RALPH HOUK

Name	G by Pos	B	AGE	G	AB	R	H	2B	3B	HR	RBI	BB	SO	SB	BA	SA
TOTALS			26	162	5601	714	1520	218	34	129	666	563	695	90	.271	.392
Jason Thompson	1B151	L	23	153	589	79	169	25	3	26	96	74	96	0	.287	.472
Lou Whitaker	2B136, DH2	L	21	139	484	71	138	12	7	3	58	61	65	7	.285	.357
Alan Trammell	SS139	R	20	139	448	49	120	14	6	2	34	45	56	3	.268	.339
Aurelio Rodriguez	3B131	R	30	134	385	40	102	25	2	7	43	19	37	0	.265	.395
Tim Corcoran	OF109, DH1	L	25	116	324	37	86	13	1	1	27	24	27	3	.265	.321
Ron LeFlore	OF155	R	30	155	666	126	198	30	3	12	62	65	104	68	.297	.405
Steve Kemp	OF157	L	23	159	582	75	161	18	4	15	79	97	87	2	.277	.399
Milt May	C94	L	28	97	352	24	88	9	0	10	37	27	26	0	.250	.361
Rusty Staub	DH162	L	34	162	642	75	175	30	1	24	121	76	35	3	.273	.435
Phil Mankowski	3B80, DH1	L	25	88	222	28	61	8	0	4	20	22	28	2	.275	.365
Lance Parrish	C79	R	22	85	288	37	63	11	3	14	41	11	71	0	.219	.424
John Wockenfuss	OF60, DH2	R	29	71	187	23	53	5	0	7	22	21	14	0	.283	.422
Steve Dillard	2B41, DH4	R	27	56	130	21	29	5	2	0	7	6	11	1	.223	.292
Mickey Stanley	OF34, 1B12	R	35	53	151	15	40	9	0	3	8	9	19	0	.265	.384
Mark Wagner	SS35, 2B4	R	24	39	109	10	26	1	2	0	6	3	11	1	.239	.284
Charlie Spikes	OF9	R	27	10	28	1	7	1	0	0	2	1	6	0	.250	.286
Dave Stegman	OF7	R	24	8	14	3	4	2	0	1	3	1	2	0	.286	.643

NAME	T	AGE	W	L	PCT	SV	G	GS	CG	IP	H	BB	SO	SHO	ERA
TOTALS		27	86	76	.531	21	162	162	60	1456	1441	503	684	12	3.64
Jim Slaton	R	27	17	11	.607	0	35	34	11	234	235	85	92	2	4.12
Jack Billingham	R	35	15	8	.652	0	30	30	10	202	218	65	59	4	3.88
Milt Wilcox	R	28	13	12	.520	0	29	27	16	215	208	68	132	2	3.77
John Hiller	L	35	9	4	.692	15	51	0	0	92	64	35	74	0	2.35
Dave Rozema	R	21	9	12	.429	0	28	28	11	209	205	41	57	2	3.14
Bob Sykes (NJ)	L	23	6	6	.500	2	22	10	3	94	99	34	58	2	3.93
Kip Young	R	23	6	7	.462	0	14	13	7	106	94	30	49	0	2.80
Jack Morris	R	23	3	5	.375	0	28	7	0	106	107	49	48	0	4.33
Mark Fidrych (SJ)	R	23	2	0	1.000	0	3	3	2	22	17	5	10	0	2.45
Jim Crawford	R	27	2	3	.400	0	39	0	0	39	45	19	24	0	4.38
1 Steve Foucault	R	28	2	4	.333	4	24	0	0	37	48	21	18	0	4.57
Steve Baker	R	21	2	4	.333	0	15	10	0	63	66	42	39	0	4.57
Ed Glynn	L	25	0	0	—	0	10	0	0	15	11	4	9	0	3.00
Dave Tobik	R	25	0	0	—	0	2	0	0	12	12	3	11	0	3.75
Fernando Arroyo (KJ)	R	26	0	0	—	0	2	0	0	4	8	1	0	0	9.00
Sheldon Burnside	L	23	0	0	—	0	1	0	0	4	4	2	3	0	9.00
Bruce Taylor	R	25	0	0	—	0	1	0	0	1	0	1	0	0	0.00

CLEVELAND — 6th 69-90 .434 29 — JEFF TORBORG

Name	G by Pos	B	AGE	G	AB	R	H	2B	3B	HR	RBI	BB	SO	SB	BA	SA
TOTALS			27	159	5365	639	1400	223	45	106	596	488	698	64	.261	.379
Andre Thornton	1B145	R	28	145	508	97	133	22	4	33	105	93	72	4	.262	.516
Duane Kuiper	2B149	L	28	149	547	52	155	18	6	0	43	19	35	4	.283	.338
Tom Veryzer	SS129	R	25	130	421	48	114	18	4	1	32	13	36	1	.271	.340
Buddy Bell	3B139, DH1	R	26	142	556	71	157	27	8	6	62	39	43	1	.282	.392
Paul Dade	OF81, DH9	R	26	93	307	37	78	12	1	3	20	34	45	12	.254	.329
Rick Manning	OF144	L	23	148	566	65	149	27	3	3	50	38	62	12	.263	.337
1 Johnny Grubb	OF110	L	29	113	378	54	100	16	6	14	61	59	60	5	.265	.450
2 Gary Alexander	C66, DH25	R	25	90	324	39	76	14	3	17	62	35	100	0	.235	.454
2 Bernie Carbo	DH49, OF4	L	30	60	174	21	50	8	0	4	16	20	31	1	.287	.402
Jim Norris	OF78, DH15, 1B6	L	29	113	315	41	89	14	5	2	27	42	20	12	.283	.378
Ted Cox	OF38, 3B20, DH12, 1B7, SS1	R	23	82	227	14	53	7	0	1	19	16	30	0	.233	.278
Ron Pruitt	C48, OF16, DH5, 3B2	R	26	71	187	17	44	6	1	6	17	16	20	2	.235	.374
Larvell Blanks	SS43, 2B17, 3B3, DH1	R	28	70	193	19	49	10	0	2	20	10	16	0	.254	.337
Horace Speed (FJ)	OF61, DH3	R	26	70	106	13	24	4	1	0	4	14	31	2	.226	.283
1 Willie Horton	DH48	R	35	50	169	15	42	7	0	5	22	15	25	3	.249	.379
Bo Diaz (BN)	C44	R	25	44	127	12	30	4	0	2	11	4	17	0	.236	.315
Wayne Cage	DH20, 1B11	L	26	36	98	11	24	6	1	4	13	9	28	1	.245	.449
Ron Hassey	C24	L	25	25	74	5	15	0	0	2	9	7	4	0	.203	.284
Dan Briggs	OF15	L	25	15	49	4	8	0	1	1	1	4	9	0	.163	.265
1 Mike Vail	OF9, DH1	R	26	14	34	2	8	2	1	0	2	0	9	1	.235	.353
Alfredo Griffin	SS2	B	20	5	4	1	2	1	0	0	2	1	0	0	.500	.750
Larry Lintz		B	28	3	0	1	0	0	0	0	0	0	0	0	—	—

NAME	T	AGE	W	L	PCT	SV	G	GS	CG	IP	H	BB	SO	SHO	ERA
TOTALS		27	69	90	.434	28	159	159	36	1407	1397	568	739	6	3.97
Rick Waits	L	26	13	15	.464	0	34	33	15	230	206	86	97	2	3.21
Mike Paxton	R	24	12	11	.522	1	33	27	5	191	199	63	96	2	3.86
Jim Kern	R	29	10	10	.500	13	58	0	0	99	77	58	95	0	3.09
Rick Wise	R	32	9	19	.321	0	33	31	9	212	226	59	106	1	4.33
David Clyde	L	23	8	11	.421	0	28	25	5	153	166	60	83	0	4.29
Don Hood	L	29	5	6	.455	0	36	19	1	155	166	77	73	0	4.47
Sid Monge	L	27	4	3	.571	4	48	2	0	85	71	51	54	0	2.75
2 Dan Spillner	R	27	3	3	.750	3	36	0	0	56	54	21	48	0	3.70
Wayne Garland (SJ)	R	27	2	3	.400	0	4	4	3	30	43	16	13	0	7.80
2 Paul Reuschel	R	31	2	4	.333	0	18	5	1	90	95	22	24	0	3.10
1 Dave Freisleben	R	26	1	4	.200	0	12	10	0	44	52	31	19	0	7.16
Rick Kreuger	L	29	0	0	—	0	6	0	0	3	7	0	4	0	4.00
1 Al Fitzmorris (ZJ)	R	32	0	1	.000	0	7	0	0	14	19	7	5	0	6.43
1 Dennis Kinney	L	26	0	2	.000	5	18	0	0	39	37	14	19	0	4.35

Pat Dobson 36 (XJ)

TORONTO 7th 59-102 .366 40 — ROY HARTSFIELD

Name	G by Pos	B	AGE	G	AB	R	H	2B	3B	HR	RBI	BB	SO	SB	BA	SA
TOTALS			27	161	5430	590	1358	217	39	98	551	448	645	28	.250	.359
John Mayberry	1B139, DH7	L	29	152	515	51	129	15	2	22	70	60	57	1	.250	.416
Dave McKay	2B140, SS3, 3B2, DH1	B	28	145	504	59	120	20	8	7	45	20	91	4	.238	.351
Luis Gomez	SS153	R	26	153	413	39	92	7	3	0	32	34	41	2	.223	.254
Roy Howell	3B131, OF5, DH1	L	24	140	551	67	149	28	3	8	61	44	78	0	.270	.376
Bob Bailor	OF125, 3B28, SS4	R	26	154	621	74	164	29	7	1	52	38	21	5	.264	.338
Rick Bosetti	OF135	R	24	136	568	61	147	25	5	5	42	30	65	6	.259	.347
Otto Velez	OF74, DH9, 1B1	R	27	91	248	29	66	14	2	9	38	45	41	1	.266	.448
Rick Cerone	C84, DH2	R	24	88	282	25	63	8	2	3	20	23	32	0	.223	.298
1 Rico Carty	DH101	R	38	104	387	51	110	16	0	20	68	36	41	1	.284	.481
Willie Upshaw	OF52, DH18, 1B10	L	21	95	224	26	53	8	2	1	17	21	35	4	.237	.304
Alan Ashby	C81	B	26	81	264	27	69	15	0	9	29	28	32	1	.261	.420
2 Tim Johnson	SS49, 2B13	L	28	68	79	9	19	2	0	0	3	8	16	0	.241	.266
1 Tommy Hutton	OF55, 1B9	L	32	64	173	19	44	9	0	2	9	19	11	1	.254	.341
Al Woods	OF60	L	24	62	220	19	53	12	3	3	25	11	23	1	.241	.364
Doug Ault	1B25, OF7, DH5	R	28	54	104	10	25	1	1	3	7	17	14	0	.240	.356
Sam Ewing	DH9, OF3	L	29	40	56	3	10	0	0	2	9	5	9	0	.179	.286
3 Willie Horton	DH30	R	35	33	122	12	25	6	0	3	19	4	29	0	.205	.328
Garth Iorg	2B18	R	23	19	49	3	8	0	0	0	3	3	4	0	.163	.163
Gary Woods	OF6	R	23	8	19	1	3	1	0	0	0	1	1	1	.158	.211
1 Tim Nordbrook	SS7	R	28	7	0	1	0	0	0	0	0	0	0	0	—	—
Butch Alberts	DH4	R	28	6	18	1	5	1	0	0	0	0	2	0	.278	.333
Brian Milner	C2	L	18	2	9	3	4	0	1	0	2	0	1	0	.444	.667
Ernie Whitt	C1	L	26	2	4	0	0	0	0	0	0	0	1	1	.000	.000

NAME	T	AGE	W	L	PCT	SV	G	GS	CG	IP	H	BB	SO	SHO	ERA
		26	59	102	.366	23	161	161	35	1429	1529	614	758	5	4.54
Jim Clancy	R	22	10	12	.455	0	31	30	7	194	199	91	106	0	4.08
Victor Cruz	R	20	7	3	.700	9	32	0	0	47	28	35	51	0	1.72
Jesse Jefferson	R	29	7	16	.304	0	31	30	9	212	214	86	97	2	4.37
Tom Murphy	R	32	6	9	.400	7	50	0	0	94	87	37	36	0	3.93
Balor Moore	L	27	6	9	.400	0	37	18	2	144	165	54	75	0	4.94
Tom Underwood	L	24	6	14	.300	0	31	30	7	198	201	87	139	1	4.09
Don Kirkwood (AJ)	R	28	4	5	.444	0	16	9	3	68	76	25	29	0	4.24
Jerry Garvin	L	22	4	12	.250	0	26	22	3	145	189	48	67	0	5.52
Dave Lemanczyk	R	27	4	14	.222	0	29	20	3	137	170	65	62	0	6.24
Mike Willis	L	23	3	7	.300	7	44	2	1	101	104	39	52	0	4.54
2 Joe Coleman	R	31	2	0	1.000	0	31	0	0	61	67	30	28	0	4.57
Dave Wallace	R	30	0	0	—	0	6	0	0	14	12	11	7	0	3.86
2 Mark Wiley	R	30	0	0	—	0	2	0	0	3	3	1	2	0	6.00
Tom Buskey	R	31	0	1	.000	2	8	0	0	13	14	5	7	0	3.46
Bill Singer (XJ) 34															

WEST DIVISION

KANSAS CITY 1st 92-70 .568 — WHITEY HERZOG

Name	G by Pos	B	AGE	G	AB	R	H	2B	3B	HR	RBI	BB	SO	SB	BA	SA
TOTALS			27	162	5474	743	1469	305	59	98	695	498	644	216	.268	.399
Pete LaCock	1B106	L	26	118	322	44	95	21	2	5	48	21	27	1	.295	.419
Frank White	2B140	R	27	143	461	66	127	24	6	7	50	26	59	13	.275	.399
Freddie Patek	SS137	R	33	138	440	54	109	23	1	2	46	42	56	38	.248	.318
George Brett	3B128, SS1	L	25	128	510	79	150	45	8	9	62	39	35	23	.294	.467
Al Cowens (KJ)	OF127, 3B5, DH2	R	26	132	485	63	133	24	8	5	63	31	54	14	.274	.388
Amos Otis	OF136, DH1	R	31	141	486	74	145	30	7	22	96	66	54	32	.298	.525
Clint Hurdle	OF78, 1B52, DH1, 3B1	L	20	133	417	48	110	25	5	7	56	56	84	1	.264	.398
Darrell Porter	C145, DH4	L	26	150	520	77	138	27	6	18	78	75	75	0	.265	.444
Hal McRae	DH153, OF3	R	32	156	623	90	170	39	5	16	72	51	62	17	.273	.429
Willie Wilson	OF112, DH6	B	22	127	198	43	43	8	2	0	16	16	33	46	.217	.278
Tom Poquette	OF63, DH1	L	26	80	204	16	44	9	2	4	30	14	9	2	.216	.338
Jerry Terrell	2B31, 3B25, SS11, 1B5	R	31	133	133	14	27	1	0	0	8	4	13	8	.203	.211
U. L. Washington	SS49, 2B19, DH1	B	24	69	129	10	34	2	1	0	9	10	20	12	.264	.295
John Wathan	1B47, C21	R	28	67	190	19	57	10	1	2	28	3	12	2	.300	.395
2 Steve Braun	OF33, 3B11	L	30	64	137	16	36	10	1	0	14	28	16	3	.263	.350
Joe Zdeb	OF52, 3B1, 2B1, DH1	R	25	60	127	18	32	2	3	0	11	7	18	3	.252	.315
Jamie Quirk	3B10, SS2, DH1	L	23	17	29	3	6	2	0	0	2	5	4	0	.207	.276
Joe Lahoud	OF1, DH1	L	31	13	16	0	2	0	0	0	0	0	1	0	.125	.125
Art Kusnyer	C9	R	32	9	13	1	3	1	0	1	2	2	4	0	.231	.538
Luis Silverio	OF6, DH2	R	21	8	11	7	6	2	1	0	3	2	3	1	.545	.909
Dave Cripe	3B5	R	27	7	13	1	2	0	0	0	1	0	2	0	.154	.154
Jim Gaudet	C3	R	23	3	3	0	0	0	0	0	0	0	0	0	.000	.000
Randy Bass		L	24	2	2	0	0	0	0	0	0	0	0	0	.000	.000

NAME	T	AGE	W	L	PCT	SV	G	GS	CG	IP	H	BB	SO	SHO	ERA
		29	92	70	.568	33	162	162	53	1439	1350	478	657	14	3.44
Dennis Leonard	R	27	21	17	.553	0	40	40	20	295	283	78	183	4	3.33
Paul Splittorff	L	31	19	13	.594	0	39	38	13	262	244	60	76	2	3.40
Larry Gura	L	30	16	4	.800	0	35	26	8	222	183	60	81	2	2.72
Rich Gale	R	24	14	8	.636	0	31	30	9	192	171	100	88	3	3.09
Al Hrabosky	L	28	8	7	.533	20	58	0	0	75	52	35	60	0	2.88
Doug Bird	R	28	6	6	.500	1	40	6	0	99	110	31	48	0	5.27
Marty Pattin	R	35	3	3	.500	4	32	5	2	79	72	25	30	0	3.30
Steve Busby	R	28	1	0	1.000	0	7	5	0	21	24	15	10	0	7.71
George Throop	R	27	1	0	1.000	0	3	0	0	3	2	3	2	0	0.00
1 Jim Colborn	R	32	1	2	.333	0	3	0	0	28	31	12	8	0	4.82
Steve Mingori	L	34	1	1	.500	7	45	0	0	69	64	16	28	2	2.74
1 Andy Hassler (RJ)	L	26	1	2	.200	0	11	9	1	58	76	24	26	0	4.34
2 Steve Foucault	R	28	0	0	—	0	3	0	0	7	9	4	2	0	4.50
Randy McGilberry	R	24	0	0	—	0	18	0	0	26	27	18	12	0	4.15
Bill Paschall	R	24	0	1	.000	1	2	0	0	8	6	5	0	0	3.38

CALIFORNIA 2nd(tie) 87-75 .537 5 — DAVE GARCIA 25-20 .556 — JIM FREGOSI 62-55 .530

Name	G by Pos	B	AGE	G	AB	R	H	2B	3B	HR	RBI	BB	SO	SB	BA	SA
TOTALS			28	162	5472	691	1417	226	28	108	646	539	682	86	.259	.370
Ron Jackson (BW)	1B75, 3B31, OF1, DH1	R	25	105	387	49	115	18	4	6	57	16	31	2	.297	.421
Bobby Grich	2B144	R	29	144	487	68	122	16	2	6	42	75	83	4	.251	.329
Dave Chalk	SS97, 2B29, 3B22, DH1	R	27	135	470	42	119	12	0	1	34	38	34	5	.253	.285
Carney Lansford (RJ)	3B117, SS2, DH1	R	21	121	453	63	133	23	2	8	52	31	67	20	.294	.406
Lyman Bostock (DD)	OF146, DH1	L	27	147	568	74	168	24	4	5	71	59	36	15	.296	.379
Rick Miller	OF129	L	30	132	475	66	125	25	4	1	37	54	70	3	.263	.339
Joe Rudi (LJ)	OF111, DH11, 1B10	R	31	133	497	58	127	27	1	17	79	28	82	2	.256	.416
Brian Downing	C128, DH2	R	27	133	412	42	105	15	0	7	46	52	47	3	.255	.342
Don Baylor	DH102, OF39, 1B17	R	29	158	591	103	151	26	0	34	99	56	71	22	.255	.472
Ken Landreaux	OF83, DH1	L	23	93	260	37	58	7	5	5	23	20	20	7	.223	.346
Ron Fairly	1B78, DH5	L	39	91	235	23	51	5	0	10	40	25	31	0	.217	.366
Tony Solaita	DH18, 1B11	L	31	60	94	10	21	3	0	1	14	16	25	0	.223	.287
Terry Humphrey	C52, 3B1, 2B1	R	28	53	114	11	25	4	1	1	9	6	12	0	.219	.298
Rance Mulliniks	SS47, DH1	L	22	50	119	6	22	3	1	1	6	8	23	2	.185	.252
Merv Rettenmund	OF22, DH18	R	35	50	108	16	29	5	1	1	14	30	13	0	.269	.361
Jim Anderson	SS47, 2B1	R	21	48	108	6	21	7	0	0	7	11	16	0	.194	.259
Danny Goodwin	DH15	R	24	20	58	9	16	5	0	2	10	10	13	0	.276	.466
Ike Hampton	C13, DH4, 1B1	R	26	19	14	2	3	0	1	1	4	2	7	1	.214	.571
Dave Machemer	2B5, 3B3, SS1	R	27	10	11	2	3	1	0	0	3	2	3	0	.273	.455

NAME	T	AGE	W	L	PCT	SV	G	GS	CG	IP	H	BB	SO	SHO	ERA
		27	87	75	.537	33	162	162	44	1456	1382	599	892	13	3.65
Frank Tanana	L	24	18	12	.600	0	33	33	10	239	239	60	137	4	3.65
Chris Knapp (JT)	R	24	14	8	.636	0	30	29	6	188	178	67	126	0	4.21
Don Aase	R	23	11	8	.579	0	29	29	6	179	185	80	93	1	4.02
Dave LaRoche	L	30	10	9	.526	25	59	0	0	96	73	48	70	0	2.81
Nolan Ryan (LJ)	R	31	10	13	.435	0	31	31	14	235	183	148	260	3	3.71
Dyar Miller (JJ)	R	32	6	2	.750	1	41	0	0	85	85	41	34	0	2.65
Paul Hartzell	R	24	6	10	.375	6	54	12	5	157	168	41	55	0	3.44
Dave Frost	R	25	5	4	.556	0	11	10	2	80	71	24	30	1	2.59
Tom Griffin	R	30	3	4	.429	0	24	4	0	56	63	31	35	0	4.02
Ken Brett	L	29	3	5	.375	1	31	10	1	100	100	42	43	1	4.95
2 Al Fitzmorris	R	32	1	0	1.000	0	9	2	0	32	26	14	8	0	1.69
John Caneira	R	25	0	0	—	0	2	2	0	8	9	1	2	0	6.75
Mike Barlow	R	30	0	0	—	0	5	0	0	2	3	0	1	0	4.50

TEXAS 2nd(tie) 87-75 .537 5 — BILLY HUNTER 86-75 .534 — PAT CORRALES 1-0 1.000

Name	G by Pos	B	AGE	G	AB	R	H	2B	3B	HR	RBI	BB	SO	SB	BA	SA
TOTALS			30	162	5347	692	1353	216	36	132	650	624	779	196	.253	.381
Mike Hargrove	1B140, DH4	L	28	146	494	63	124	24	1	7	40	107	47	2	.251	.346
Bump Wills	2B156	B	25	157	539	78	135	17	4	9	57	63	91	52	.250	.347
Bert Campaneris	SS89, DH4	R	36	98	269	30	50	15	3	1	17	20	36	22	.186	.238
Toby Harrah	3B91, SS49	R	29	139	450	56	103	17	3	12	59	83	66	31	.229	.360
2 Bobby Bonds (BH)	OF111, DH18	R	32	130	475	85	126	15	4	29	82	69	110	41	.265	.497
Juan Beniquez (BH)	OF126	R	27	127	473	61	123	17	3	11	50	20	59	10	.260	.378
Al Oliver (VJ)	OF107, DH26	L	31	133	525	65	170	35	5	14	89	31	41	8	.324	.490
Jim Sundberg	C148, DH1	R	27	149	518	54	144	23	6	6	58	64	70	2	.278	.380
Richie Zisk	OF90, DH49	R	29	140	511	68	134	19	1	22	85	58	76	3	.262	.432
Mike Jorgensen	1B78, OF9, DH1	L	29	96	97	20	19	3	0	1	9	18	10	3	.196	.258
Kurt Bevacqua	3B49, DH16, 2B13, 1B1	R	31	90	248	21	55	12	0	6	30	18	31	1	.222	.343
John Lowenstein	3B25, DH21, OF16	L	31	77	176	28	39	8	3	5	21	37	29	16	.222	.386
Bobby Thompson	OF52, DH3	B	24	64	120	23	27	3	2	12	9	26	7		.225	.350
Jim Mason	SS42, 3B11, 2B1, DH1	R	27	55	105	10	20	4	0	0	3	5	17	0	.190	.229
Johnny Ellis	C22, DH7	R	30	34	94	7	23	4	1	1	17	6	20	0	.245	.383
Sandy Alomar	1B9, 2B6, 3B3, DH3, SS2	B	34	24	29	3	6	1	0	0	1	0	5	0	.207	.241
Nelson Norman	SS18, 3B6	R	20	23	34	1	9	2	0	0	1	0	5	0	.265	.324
2 Johnny Grubb	OF13, DH3	L	29	21	23	8	13	3	0	1	6	11	5	1	.394	.576
Pat Putnam	DH12, 1B4	L	24	20	46	4	7	1	0	2	2	5	6	0	.152	.239
Gary Gray	DH11	R	25	17	50	4	12	1	0	2	6	1	12	1	.240	.380
1 Claudell Washington (NJ)	OF7, DH4	L	23	12	42	1	7	0	0	0	1	0	12	0	.167	.167
Billy Sample	DH3, OF2	R	23	8	15	2	7	2	0	0	3	0	3	0	.467	.600
LaRue Washington	2B2, DH1	R	24	3	3	0	0	0	0	0	0	0	1	0	.000	.000
Greg Mahlberg	C1	R	25	1	1	0	0	0	0	0	0	0	0	0	.000	.000
1 Dave May (SJ) 34																

NAME	T	AGE	W	L	PCT	SV	G	GS	CG	IP	H	BB	SO	SHO	ERA
		29	87	75	.537	25	162	162	54	1456	1431	421	776	12	3.36
Ferguson Jenkins	R	34	18	8	.692	0	34	30	16	249	228	41	157	4	3.04
Jon Matlack	L	28	15	13	.536	1	35	33	18	270	252	51	157	2	2.27
Steve Comer	R	24	11	8	.688	2	30	11	3	117	107	37	65	2	2.31
Dock Ellis (GJ)	R	33	9	7	.563	0	22	22	3	141	131	46	45	0	4.21
Doc Medich	R	29	9	8	.529	2	28	22	6	171	166	52	71	2	3.74
Doyle Alexander	R	27	9	10	.474	0	31	28	7	191	198	71	81	1	3.86
2 Reggie Cleveland	R	30	5	7	.417	12	53	0	0	76	76	23	46	0	3.08
Jim Umbarger	L	25	5	8	.385	1	32	9	1	98	116	36	60	0	4.87
Paul Mirabella	L	24	3	2	.600	1	10	4	0	28	30	17	23	0	5.79
Danny Darwin	R	22	1	0	1.000	0	3	1	0	3	1	1	8	0	4.00
1 Paul Lindblad	L	36	1	1	.500	2	18	0	0	40	41	15	25	0	3.60
Len Barker	R	22	1	5	.167	1	29	0	0	52	63	29	33	0	4.85
Roger Moret (IL)	L	28	0	1	.000	1	7	2	0	15	23	2	5	0	4.80

MINNESOTA 4th 73-89 .451 19 GENE MAUCH

Name	G by Pos	B	AGE	G	AB	R	H	2B	3B	HR	RBI	BB	SO	SB	BA	SA
TOTALS			27	162	5522	666	1472	259	47	82	621	604	684	99	.267	.375
Rod Carew	1B148, 2B4, OF1	L	32	152	564	85	188	26	10	5	70	78	62	27	.333	.441
Bob Randall	2B116, 3B2, DH1	R	30	119	330	36	89	11	3	0	21	24	22	5	.270	.321
Roy Smalley	SS157	B	25	158	586	80	160	31	3	19	77	85	70	4	.273	.433
Mike Cubbage	3B115, 2B5	L	27	125	394	40	111	12	7	7	57	40	44	1	.282	.401
Hosken Powell	OF117	L	23	121	381	55	94	20	2	3	31	45	31	11	.247	.333
Dan Ford	OF149, DH1	R	26	151	592	78	162	36	10	11	82	48	88	7	.274	.424
Willie Norwood	OF115, DH6	R	27	115	428	56	109	22	3	8	46	28	64	25	.255	.376
Butch Wynegar	C131, 3B1	B	22	135	454	36	104	22	1	4	45	47	42	1	.229	.308
Glenn Adams	DH110, OF5	L	30	116	310	29	80	18	1	7	35	17	32	0	.258	.390
Bombo Rivera	OF94, DH1	R	25	101	251	35	68	8	2	3	23	35	47	5	.271	.355
Jose Morales	DH77, C1, 1B1, OF1	R	33	101	242	22	76	13	1	2	38	20	35	0	.314	.401
Rob Wilfong (BH)		L	24	92	199	23	53	8	0	1	11	19	27	8	.266	.322
Larry Wolfe	3B81, SS7	L	25	88	235	25	55	10	1	3	25	36	27	0	.234	.323
Rich Chiles	OF61, DH8	L	28	87	198	22	53	12	0	1	22	20	25	1	.268	.343
Craig Kusick	DH35, 1B27, OF9	R	29	77	191	23	33	3	2	4	20	37	38	3	.173	.272
Glenn Borgmann	C46, DH1	R	28	49	123	16	26	4	1	3	15	18	17	0	.211	.333
Dave Edwards	OF15	R	24	15	44	7	11	3	0	1	8	3	7	1	.250	.386

NAME	T	AGE	W	L	PCT	SV	G	GS	CG	IP	H	BB	SO	SHO	ERA
		27	73	89	.451	26	162	162	48	1460	1468	520	703	9	3.69
Dave Goltz (VJ-RJ)	R	29	15	10	.600	0	29	29	13	220	209	67	116	2	2.50
Roger Erickson	R	21	14	13	.519	0	37	37	14	266	268	79	121	0	3.96
Geoff Zahn	L	32	14	14	.500	0	35	35	12	252	260	81	106	1	3.04
Mike Marshall	R	35	10	12	.455	21	54	0	0	99	80	37	56	0	2.45
Gary Serum	R	21	9	9	.500	1	34	23	6	184	188	44	80	1	4.11
Darrell Jackson	L	22	4	6	.400	0	19	15	1	92	89	48	54	1	4.50
Stan Perzanowski	R	27	2	7	.222	1	13	7	1	57	59	26	31	0	5.21
Greg Thayer	R	28	1	1	.500	0	20	0	0	45	40	30	30	0	3.80
Mac Scarce	L	29	1	1	.500	0	17	0	0	32	35	15	17	0	3.94
Jeff Holly	L	25	1	1	.500	0	15	1	0	35	28	18	12	0	3.60
Tom Johnson (SJ)	R	27	1	4	.200	3	18	0	0	33	42	17	21	0	5.45
Paul Thormodsgard	R	24	1	6	.143	0	12	12	1	66	81	17	23	0	5.05
Johnny Sutton	R	25	0	0	—	0	17	0	0	44	46	15	18	0	3.48
Roric Harrison	R	31	0	1	.000	0	9	0	0	12	18	11	7	0	7.50
Dave Johnson	R	29	0	2	.000	0	6	1	0	12	15	9	7	0	7.50
Pete Redfern	R	23	0	2	.000	0	10	10	0	10	10	6	4	0	6.30

CHICAGO 5th 71-90 .441 20.5   1 BOB LEMON 34-40 .459   LARRY DOBY 37-50 .425

Name	G by Pos	B	AGE	G	AB	R	H	2B	3B	HR	RBI	BB	SO	SB	BA	SA
TOTALS			27	161	5393	634	1423	221	41	106	595	409	625	83	.264	.379
Lamar Johnson	1B108, DH36	R	27	148	498	52	136	23	2	8	72	43	46	6	.273	.376
Jorge Orta	2B114, DH2	L	27	117	420	45	115	19	2	13	53	42	39	1	.274	.421
Don Kessinger	SS123, 2B9	B	35	131	431	35	110	18	1	1	31	36	34	2	.255	.309
Eric Soderholm	3B128, DH1, 2B1	R	25	143	457	57	118	17	1	20	67	39	44	2	.258	.431
2 Claudell Washington (NJ)	OF82, DH1	L	23	86	314	33	83	16	5	6	31	12	57	5	.264	.404
Chet Lemon (GJ)	OF95, DH10	R	23	105	357	51	107	24	6	13	55	39	46	5	.300	.510
Ralph Garr	OF109, DH9	L	32	118	443	67	122	18	9	3	29	24	41	7	.275	.377
Bill Nahorodny	C104, 1B4, DH1	R	25	107	347	29	82	11	2	8	35	23	52	1	.236	.349
Ron Blomberg	DH36, 1B7	L	29	61	156	16	36	7	0	5	22	11	17	0	.231	.372
Bob Molinaro	OF62, DH32	L	28	105	286	39	75	5	5	6	27	19	12	22	.262	.378
Greg Pryor	2B35, SS28, 3B20	R	28	82	222	27	58	11	0	2	15	11	18	3	.261	.338
Wayne Nordhagen (IL)	OF36, DH16, C12	R	29	68	206	28	62	16	0	5	35	5	18	0	.301	.451
Thad Bosley (GJ)	OF64	L	21	66	219	25	59	5	1	2	13	13	32	12	.269	.329
Kevin Bell (WJ)	3B52, DH1	R	22	54	68	9	13	0	0	2	5	5	13	0	.191	.279
Henry Cruz	OF40, DH1	L	26	53	77	13	17	2	1	2	10	8	11	0	.221	.351
Alan Bannister (SJ)	DH19, OF15, SS8, 2B2	R	24	49	107	16	24	3	2	0	8	11	12	3	.224	.290
Mike Colbern	C47, DH1	R	23	48	141	11	38	5	1	2	20	1	36	0	.270	.362
Mike Squires	1B45	L	26	46	150	25	42	9	2	0	19	16	21	4	.280	.367
Tom Spencer	OF27, DH2	R	27	29	65	3	12	1	0	0	4	2	9	0	.185	.200
1 Bobby Bonds	OF22, DH3	R	32	26	90	8	25	4	0	2	8	10	10	6	.278	.389
Jim Breazeale	1B19, DH4	L	28	25	72	8	15	3	0	3	13	8	10	0	.208	.375
Junior Moore	DH12, 3B6, OF5	R	25	24	65	8	19	0	0	0	6	4	7	1	.292	.323
Harry Chappas	SS20	B	20	20	75	11	20	1	0	0	6	6	11	1	.267	.280
Rusty Torres	OF14	B	29	16	44	7	14	3	0	3	6	6	7	0	.318	.591
Marv Foley	C10	L	24	11	34	3	12	0	0	0	6	4	0	0	.353	.353
Mike Eden	SS5, 2B4	B	29	10	17	1	2	0	0	0	0	0	4	0	.118	.118
Joe Gates	2B8	B	23	8	24	6	6	0	0	0	1	4	6	1	.250	.250
Larry Johnson	C2, DH1	R	27	3	8	0	1	0	0	0	0	1	2	0	.125	.125

NAME	T	AGE	W	L	PCT	SV	G	GS	CG	IP	H	BB	SO	SHO	ERA
		30	71	90	.441	33	161	161	38	1409	1380	586	710	9	4.21
Steve Stone	R	30	12	12	.500	0	30	30	6	212	196	84	118	1	4.37
Ken Kravec	L	26	11	16	.407	0	30	30	7	203	188	95	154	2	4.08
Wilbur Wood	L	36	10	10	.500	0	28	27	4	168	187	74	69	0	5.20
Francisco Barrios	R	25	9	15	.375	0	33	32	9	196	180	85	79	2	4.04
Lerrin LaGrow	R	29	6	5	.545	16	52	0	0	88	85	38	41	0	4.40
Mike Proly (BG)	R	27	5	2	.714	1	14	6	2	66	63	12	19	0	2.73
Steve Trout	L	20	3	0	1.000	0	4	3	1	22	19	11	11	0	4.09
Rich Wortham	L	24	3	2	.600	0	8	8	2	59	59	23	25	0	3.05
Ron Schueler	R	30	3	5	.375	0	30	7	0	82	76	39	39	0	4.28
Ross Baumgarten	L	23	2	2	.500	0	7	4	1	23	29	9	15	1	5.87
Jack Kucek	R	25	2	3	.400	1	10	5	3	52	42	27	30	0	5.29
Pablo Torrealba (IL)	L	30	2	4	.333	1	25	3	1	57	69	39	23	1	4.74
Rich Hinton	R	31	2	6	.250	1	29	4	2	81	78	28	48	0	4.00
Jim Willoughby	R	29	1	6	.143	13	59	0	0	93	95	19	36	0	3.87
Britt Burns	L	19	0	0	—	0	2	2	0	8	14	3	3	0	12.38

OAKLAND 6th 69-93 .426 23   BOBBY WINKLES 24-15 .615   JACK McKEON 45-78 .366

Name	G by Pos	B	AGE	G	AB	R	H	2B	3B	HR	RBI	BB	SO	SB	BA	SA
TOTALS			26	162	5321	532	1304	200	31	100	492	433	800	144	.245	.351
Dave Revering	1B138, DH3	L	25	152	521	49	141	21	3	16	46	26	55	0	.271	.415
Mike Edwards	2B133, SS9, DH4	R	25	142	414	48	113	16	2	1	23	16	32	27	.273	.329
Mike Guerrero	SS142	R	28	143	505	27	139	18	4	3	38	15	35	0	.275	.345
Wayne Gross	3B106, 1B15	L	26	118	285	18	57	10	2	7	23	40	63	0	.200	.323
Tony Armas (KJ)	OF85, DH3	R	24	91	239	17	51	6	1	2	13	10	62	1	.213	.272
2 Joe Wallis	OF80, DH1	B	26	85	279	28	66	16	1	6	26	24	42	1	.237	.366
Mitchell Page	OF114, DH33	L	26	147	516	62	147	25	4	17	70	53	95	23	.285	.459
Jim Essian	C119, 1B3, DH1, 2B1	R	27	126	278	21	62	9	1	3	26	44	22	1	.223	.295
2 Rico Carty	DH41	R	38	41	141	19	39	5	1	11	31	21	16	0	.277	.560
Miguel Dilone	OF99, DH11, 3B3	B	23	135	258	34	59	8	0	1	14	23	30	50	.229	.271
Jeff Newman	C61, 1B36, DH2	R	29	105	268	25	64	7	1	9	32	16	40	1	.239	.373
Taylor Duncan	3B84, 2B11, DH7, SS1	R	25	104	319	25	82	15	2	2	37	19	38	1	.257	.335
Rob Picciolo	SS41, 2B19, 3B13	R	25	78	93	16	21	1	0	2	7	2	13	1	.226	.301
Glenn Burke (ZJ)	OF67, DH2, 1B1	R	25	78	200	19	47	6	1	1	14	10	26	15	.235	.290
Dwayne Murphy	OF45, DH5	L	23	60	52	15	10	2	0	0	5	7	14	0	.192	.231
1 Gary Alexander	DH45, OF6, C1,1B1	R	25	58	174	18	36	6	1	10	22	24	66	0	.207	.425
2 Dell Alston	OF50, 1B9, DH3	L	25	58	173	17	36	2	0	1	10	10	21	11	.208	.237
1 Gary Thomasson	OF44, 1B5	L	26	47	154	17	31	4	1	5	16	15	44	4	.201	.338
Steve Staggs	2B40, 3B2, DH2, SS2	R	27	47	78	10	19	2	2	0	9	19	17	2	.244	.321
Darrell Woodard	2B14, 3B1, DH1	R	21	33	9	10	0	0	0	0	0	1	3	.000	.000
2 Willie Horton	DH27, OF1	R	35	32	102	11	32	8	0	3	19	9	15	0	.314	.480
Bruce Robinson	C28	L	24	28	84	5	21	3	1	0	8	3	8	0	.250	.310
1 Billy North	OF17	B	30	24	52	5	11	4	0	0	5	9	13	3	.212	.288
Marty Perez	3B11, SS3, 2B1	R	32	16	12	1	0	0	0	0	0	5	0	0	.000	.000
Mike Adams	2B6, 3B3, DH3	R	29	15	15	5	3	1	0	0	1	2	6	0	.200	.267
Tito Fuentes	2B13	R	34	13	43	5	6	1	0	0	2	1	6	0	.140	.163
Tim Hosley	C6, DH1	R	31	13	23	1	7	2	0	0	3	6	4	0	.304	.391
Jerry Tabb	1B2, DH2	L	26	12	9	1	1	0	0	0	0	0	5	0	.111	.111
Larry Murray	OF6	B	25	11	12	1	1	0	0	0	0	0	2	0	.083	.083
Scott Meyer	C7	R	20	8	9	1	1	0	0	0	0	2	2	0	.111	.222
Mark Budaska	OF2	B	25	4	8	0	2	1	0	0	0	0	3	0	.250	.500
2 Mickey Klutts (BG) 23																

NAME	T	AGE	W	L	PCT	SV	G	GS	CG	IP	H	BB	SO	SHO	ERA
		26	69	93	.426	29	162	162	26	1433	1401	582	750	11	3.62
John Henry Johnson	L	21	11	10	.524	0	33	30	7	186	164	82	91	2	3.39
Pete Broberg	R	28	10	12	.455	0	35	26	2	166	174	65	94	0	4.61
Elias Sosa	R	28	8	2	.800	14	68	0	0	109	106	44	61	0	2.64
Bob Lacey	L	24	8	9	.471	5	74	0	0	120	126	35	60	0	3.00
Matt Keough	R	22	8	15	.348	0	32	32	6	197	178	85	108	0	3.24
Rick Langford	R	26	7	13	.350	0	37	24	4	176	169	56	92	2	3.43
Steve Renko	R	33	6	12	.333	0	27	25	3	151	152	67	89	1	4.29
Alan Wirth	R	21	5	6	.455	0	16	14	2	81	72	34	31	1	3.44
1 Joe Coleman	R	31	3	0	1.000	0	10	0	0	21	12	4	4	0	1.35
Dave Heaverlo	R	27	3		.333	10	69	0	0	130	141	41	71	0	3.25
Steve McCatty	R	24	0		—	0	20			26	9	10	0		4.50
Craig Minetto	L	24	0	4			4	0	0	12	13	7	3	0	3.75
Tim Conroy	L	18	0		—	0	4	1	0	7	7	3	1	0	7.20
Mike Morgan	R	18	0	3	.000	0	3	1	0	7	9	2	0	0	7.50
Mike Norris	R	23	0	5	.000	0	14	5	1	49	46	35	36	0	5.51

SEATTLE 7th 56-104 .350 35 DARRELL JOHNSON

Name	G by Pos	B	AGE	G	AB	R	H	2B	3B	HR	RBI	BB	SO	SB	BA	SA
TOTALS			27	160	5358	614	1327	229	37	97	571	522	702	123	.248	.359
Dan Meyer (VJ)	1B121, OF2, DH1	L	25	123	444	38	101	18	1	8	56	24	39	7	.227	.327
Julio Cruz	2B141, SS5, DH1	B	23	147	550	77	129	14	1	1	26	69	66	59	.235	.268
Craig Reynolds	SS146	R	25	148	548	57	160	16	7	5	44	36	45	9	.292	.374
Bill Stein	3B111, DH1	R	31	141	403	41	105	24	4	4	37	37	56	1	.261	.370
Leon Roberts	OF128, DH2	R	27	134	472	78	142	21	7	22	92	41	52	6	.301	.515
Ruppert Jones (IL)	OF128	L	23	129	472	48	111	24	3	6	46	55	85	22	.235	.337
Bruce Bochte	OF91, DH43, 1B1	L	27	140	486	58	128	25	3	11	55	80	47	3	.263	.395
Bob Stinson	C123, DH1	B	32	124	364	46	94	14	3	11	55	45	42	2	.258	.404
Lee Stanton	DH59, OF30	R	32	93	302	24	55	11	0	3	24	34	80	1	.182	.248
John Hale	OF98, DH2	L	24	107	211	24	36	8	0	4	22	34	64	3	.171	.265
Larry Milbourne	3B32, SS23, 2B15, DH10	B	27	93	234	31	53	6	2	2	20	9	25	5	.226	.295
2 Tom Paciorek	OF54, DH12, 1B3	R	31	70	251	32	75	20	3	4	30	15	39	2	.299	.450
Bob Robertson (XJ)	DH29, 1B18	R	31	64	174	17	40	8	2	8	28	24	39	0	.230	.420
Juan Bernhardt	1B25, 3B22, DH1	R	24	54	165	13	38	9	0	2	14	9	10	1	.230	.321
Bill Plummer	C40	R	31	41	93	6	20	5	0	2	7	12	19	0	.215	.333
1 Steve Braun	DH14, OF4	L	30	32	74	11	17	3	1	2	15	9	15	0	.230	.405
Kevin Pasley	C25	R	24	25	54	3	13	1	0	0	6	4	9	0	.241	.389
Jose Baez	2B14, 3B3, DH1	R	24	23	50	8	8	0	0	0	2	6	6	1	.160	.200
Charlie Beamon	DH6, 1B2	L	24	10	11	2	2	1	0	0	1	0	0	0	.182	.182

NAME	T	AGE	W	L	PCT	SV	G	GS	CG	IP	H	BB	SO	SHO	ERA
		27	56	104	.350	20	160	160	28	1419	1540	567	630	4	4.67
Enrique Romo	R	30	11	7	.611	10	56	0	0	107	88	39	62	0	3.70
Paul Mitchell	R	27	8	14	.364	0	29	29	4	168	173	79	75	2	4.18
Glenn Abbott	R	27	7	15	.318	0	29	28	6	155	191	44	67	1	5.28
Tom House	R	31	5	4	.556	0	34	9	3	116	130	35	29	0	4.68
Rick Honeycutt (EJ)	R	24	5	11	.313	0	26	24	4	134	150	49	50	1	4.90
Byron McLaughlin	R	22	4	8	.333	0	20	17	4	107	97	39	87	0	4.37
Shane Rawley	L	22	4	9	.308	4	12	11	1	111	114	51	66	0	4.14
Dick Pole	R	27	4	11	.267	0	21	18	2	99	122	41	41	0	6.45
Jim Todd	R	30	3	4	.429	3	49	2	0	107	113	61	37	0	3.87
2 Jim Colborn	R	32	3	10	.231	0	20	19	3	114	125	38	26	0	5.37
John Montague (PJ)	R	30	1	3	.250	2	19	0	0	44	52	24	14	0	6.14
Mike Parrott (SJ)	R	23	1	5	.167	1	27	10	0	82	108	32	41	0	5.53
Tom Brown	R	23	0	0	—	0	3	0	0	5	4	1	0	0	
Steve Burke (JJ)	R	30	0	0	.000	0	18	0	0	49	46	24	16	0	3.49
Rick Jones	L	23	0	2	.000	0	7	2	1	12	17	7	11	0	6.00

LINE SCORES

Team	1	2	3	4	5	6	7	8	9	10	11		R	H	E

AMERICAN LEAGUE CHAMPIONSHIPS: NEW YORK (EAST) 3 KANSAS CITY (WEST) 1

Game 1   October 3 at Kansas City

	1	2	3	4	5	6	7	8	9		R	H	E
NY	0	1	1	0	2	0	0	3	0		7	16	0
KC	0	0	0	0	0	1	0	0	0		1	2	2

Beattie, Clay (6)   Leonard, Mingori (5), Hrabosky (8), Bird (9)

Game 2   October 4 at Kansas City

	1	2	3	4	5	6	7	8	9		R	H	E
NY	0	0	0	0	0	0	2	2	0		4	12	1
KC	1	4	0	0	0	0	3	2	x		10	16	1

Figueroa, Tidrow (2),   Gura, Pattin (7), Lyle (7)   Hrabosky (8)

Game 3   October 6 at New York

	1	2	3	4	5	6	7	8	9		R	H	E
KC	1	0	1	0	1	0	0	2	0		5	10	1
NY	0	1	0	2	0	1	0	2	x		6	10	0

Splittorff, Bird (8),   Hunter, Gossage (7) Hrabosky (8)

Game 4   October 7 at New York

	1	2	3	4	5	6	7	8	9		R	H	E
KC	1	0	0	0	0	0	0	0	0		1	7	0
NY	0	1	0	0	0	1	0	0	x		2	4	0

Leonard   Guidry, Gossage (9)

NATIONAL LEAGUE CHAMPIONSHIPS: LOS ANGELES (WEST) 3 PHILADELPHIA (EAST) 1

Game 1   October 4 at Philadelphia

	1	2	3	4	5	6	7	8	9		R	H	E
LA	0	0	4	2	1	1	0	0	1		9	13	1
PHI	0	1	0	0	3	0	0	0	1		5	12	1

Hooton, Welch (5)   Christenson, Brusstar (5), Eastwick (6), McGraw (7)

Game 2   October 5 at Philadelphia

	1	2	3	4	5	6	7	8	9		R	H	E
LA	0	0	0	1	2	0	1	0	0		4	8	0
PHI	0	0	0	0	0	0	0	0	0		0	4	0

John   Ruthven, Brusstar (5), Reed (7), McGraw (9)

Game 3   October 6 at Los Angeles

	1	2	3	4	5	6	7	8	9		R	H	E
PHI	0	4	0	0	0	3	1	0	1		9	11	1
LA	0	1	2	0	0	0	0	1	0		4	8	2

Carlton   Sutton, Rautzhan (6), Hough (8)

Game 4   October 7 at Los Angeles

	1	2	3	4	5	6	7	8	9	10		R	H	E
PHI	0	0	2	0	0	0	1	0	0	0		3	8	2
LA	0	1	0	1	0	0	1	0	0	1		4	13	0

Lerch, Brusstar (6),   Rau, Rhoden (6), Forster (10) Reed (7), McGraw (9)

WORLD SERIES — NEW YORK (AL) 4 LOS ANGELES (NL) 2

Game 1   October 10 at Los Angeles

	1	2	3	4	5	6	7	8	9		R	H	E
NY	0	0	0	0	0	0	3	2	0		5	9	1
LA	0	3	0	3	1	0	3	1	x		11	15	2

Figueroa, Clay (2),   John, Forster (8) Lindblad (5), Tidrow (7)

Game 2   October 11 at Los Angeles

	1	2	3	4	5	6	7	8	9		R	H	E
NY	0	0	2	0	0	0	1	0	0		3	11	0
LA	0	0	0	1	0	3	0	0	x		4	7	0

Hunter, Gossage (7)   Hooton, Forster (7), Welch (9)

Game 3   October 13 at New York

	1	2	3	4	5	6	7	8	9		R	H	E
LA	0	0	1	0	0	0	0	0	0		1	8	0
NY	1	1	0	0	0	0	3	0	x		5	10	0

Sutton, Rautzhan (7),   Guidry Hough (8)

Game 4   October 14 at New York

	1	2	3	4	5	6	7	8	9		R	H	E
LA	0	0	0	3	0	0	0	0	0		3	6	1
NY	0	0	0	0	0	2	0	1	1		4	9	0

John, Forster (8),   Figueroa, Tidrow (6), Welch (8)   Gossage (9)

Game 5   October 15 at New York

	1	2	3	4	5	6	7	8	9		R	H	E
LA	1	0	1	0	0	0	0	0	0		2	9	3
NY	0	0	4	3	0	0	4	1	X		12	18	0

Hooton, Rautzhan (3),   Beattie Hough (4)

Game 6   October 17 at Los Angeles

	1	2	3	4	5	6	7	8	9		R	H	E
NY	0	3	0	0	0	0	2	2	0		7	11	0
LA	1	0	1	0	0	0	0	0	0		2	7	1

Hunter, Gossage (8)   Sutton, Welch (6), Rau (8)

COMPOSITE BATTING

NAME	POS	G	AB	R	H	2B	3B	HR	RBI	BA
New York		4	140	19	42	3	1	5	18	.300
Munson	C	4	18	2	5	1	0	1	2	.278
Piniella	RF	4	17	2	4	0	0	0	0	.235
White	LF-DH	4	16	5	5	1	0	1	1	.313
Chambliss	1B	4	15	1	6	0	0	0	2	.400
Nettles	3B	4	15	3	5	0	1	1	2	.333
Dent	SS	4	15	0	3	0	0	0	4	.200
Jackson	DH-RF	4	13	5	6	1	0	2	6	.462
Rivers	CF	4	11	0	5	0	0	0	0	.455
Doyle	2B	3	7	0	2	0	0	0	1	.286
Blair	CF-2B-PH-PR	4	6	1	0	0	0	0	0	.000
Stanley	2B	2	5	0	1	0	0	0	0	.200
Johnson	PH	1	1	0	0	0	0	0	0	.000
Thomasson	LF-PH-CF	3	1	0	0	0	0	0	0	.000
Kansas City		4	133	17	35	6	3	4	16	.263
Brett	3B	4	18	7	7	1	1	3	3	.389
Cowens	RF	4	15	2	2	0	0	0	1	.133
Otis	CF	4	14	2	6	2	0	0	1	.429
Porter	CF	4	14	1	5	1	0	0	3	.357
McRae	DH	4	14	0	3	0	0	0	2	.214
White	2B	4	13	1	3	0	0	0	2	.231
Patek	SS	4	13	2	1	0	1	0	2	.077
LaCock	1B-PH	4	11	4	4	2	1	0	1	.364
Hurdle	LF-PH	4	8	1	3	0	1	0	1	.375
Braun	LF-PH	2	5	0	0	0	0	0	0	.000
Wilson	LF-PR	3	4	0	1	0	0	0	0	.250
Wathan	1B	1	3	0	0	0	0	0	0	.000
Poquette	PH	1	1	0	0	0	0	0	0	.000
Los Angeles		4	147	21	42	8	3	8	21	.286
Garvey	1B	4	18	6	7	1	1	4	7	.389
Lopes	2B	4	18	3	7	1	1	2	5	.389
Russell	SS	4	17	1	7	1	0	0	2	.412
Cey	3B	4	16	4	5	1	0	1	3	.313
Smith	RF	4	16	2	3	1	0	0	1	.188
Baker	LF	4	15	1	7	2	0	0	1	.467
Yeager	C	4	13	2	3	0	0	1	2	.231
Monday	CF-PH	3	10	2	2	0	1	0	0	.200
North	CF	4	8	0	0	0	0	0	0	.000
John	P	1	3	0	0	0	0	0	0	.000
Ferguson	PH	2	2	0	0	0	0	0	0	.000
Lacy	PH	2	2	0	0	0	0	0	0	.000

Hooton P 0-2, Sutton P 0-2, Welch P 0-2, Mota PH 1-1, Rau P 0-1, Rhoden P 0-1, Forster P 0-0, Grote C 0-0, Hough P 0-0, Rautzhan P 0-0

NAME	POS	G	AB	R	H	2B	3B	HR	RBI	BA
Philadelphia		4	140	17	35	3	2	5	16	.250
Maddox	CF	4	19	1	5	0	0	0	2	.263
Bowa	SS	4	18	2	6	0	0	0	0	.333
Luzinski	LF	4	16	3	6	0	1	2	3	.375
Schmidt	3B	4	15	1	3	2	0	0	1	.200
Sizemore	2B	4	13	3	5	0	1	0	1	.385
Boone	C	3	11	0	2	0	0	0	0	.182
Martin	RF-PH	4	9	1	2	1	0	1	2	.222
McBride	RF-PH	3	9	2	2	0	0	1	1	.222
Hebner	1B-PH	3	9	0	1	0	0	0	1	.111
Cardenal	1B-PH	2	6	0	1	0	0	0	0	.167
Carlton	P	1	4	2	2	0	0	1	4	.500
McCarver	C-PH	2	4	2	0	0	0	0	0	.000

Lerch P 0-2, Christenson P 0-1, Foote PH 0-1, Gonzalez PH 0-1, Morrison PH 0-1, Ruthven P 0-1, Brusstar P 0-0, Eastwick P 0-0, McGraw P 0-0, Reed P 0-0

NAME	POS	G	AB	R	H	2B	3B	HR	RBI	BA
New York		6	222	36	68	8	0	3	34	.306
Munson	C	6	25	5	8	3	0	0	7	.320
Piniella	RF	6	25	3	7	0	0	0	4	.280
Nettles	3B	6	25	2	4	0	0	0	1	.160
Dent	SS	6	24	3	10	1	0	0	7	.417
White	LF	6	24	9	8	0	0	1	4	.333
Jackson	DH	6	23	2	9	1	0	2	8	.391
Rivers	CF-PH	5	18	2	6	0	0	0	1	.333
Doyle	2B	6	16	4	7	1	0	0	2	.438
Spencer	1B-PH	4	12	3	2	0	0	0	0	.167
Chambliss	1B	3	11	1	2	0	0	0	0	.182
Blair	CF-PH-PR	6	8	2	3	1	0	0	0	.375
Stanley	2B	4	5	0	1	0	0	0	0	.200
Thomasson	CF-LF	3	4	0	1	0	0	0	0	.250
Johnson	PH	2	2	0	0	0	0	0	0	.000

Gossage P 0-0, Figueroa P 0-0, Hunter P 0-0, Johnstone RF 0-0, Tidrow P 0-0, Heath C 0-0, Beattie P 0-0, Clay P 0-0, Guidry P 0-0, Lindblad P 0-0

NAME	POS	G	AB	R	H	2B	3B	HR	RBI	BA
Los Angeles		6	199	23	52	8	0	6	22	.261
Russell	SS	6	26	1	11	2	0	0	2	.423
Lopes	2B	6	26	7	8	0	0	3	7	.308
Smith	RF	6	25	3	5	0	0	1	5	.200
Garvey	1B	6	24	1	5	0	0	0	1	.208
Cey	3B	6	21	2	6	0	0	1	4	.286
Baker	LF	6	21	2	5	0	0	1	4	.238
Lacy	DH	4	14	0	2	0	0	0	1	.143
Yeager	C	5	13	2	3	1	0	0	4	.231
Monday	CF-DH	5	13	2	2	1	0	0	0	.154
North	CF-PH	4	8	0	1	0	0	0	0	.125
Ferguson	C	2	4	1	2	2	0	0	0	.500
Davalillo	PH-DH	3	3	0	1	0	0	0	0	.333
Oates	PH-C	1	1	0	1	0	0	0	0	1.000

Forster P 0-0, Welch P 0-0, Grote C 0-0, Hooton P 0-0, Hough P 0-0, John P 0-0, Rautzhan P 0-0, Sutton P 0-0, Mota PH 0-0, Rau P 0-0

COMPOSITE PITCHING

NAME	G	IP	H	BB	SO	W	L	SV	ERA
New York	4	35	35	14	21	3	1	2	3.86
Guidry	1	8	7	1	7	1	0	0	1.12
Hunter	1	6	7	3	5	0	0	0	4.50
Tidrow	1	5.2	8	2	4	0	0	0	4.76
Beattie	1	5.1	2	5	3	1	0	0	1.69
Gossage	2	4	3	0	1	0	0	1	4.50
Clay	1	3.2	0	3	2	0	0	1	0.00
Lyle	1	1.1	3	0	0	0	0	0	13.50
Figueroa	1	1	5	0	0	0	1	0	27.00
Kansas City	4	34	42	7	18	1	3	0	4.76
Leonard	2	12	13	2	11	0	2	0	3.75
Splittorff	1	7.1	9	0	2	0	0	0	4.91
Gura	1	6.1	8	2	2	1	0	0	2.84
Mingori	1	3.2	5	3	0	0	0	0	7.36
Hrabosky	3	3	3	0	2	0	0	0	0.00
Pattin	1	0.2	2	0	0	0	0	0	27.00
Bird	2	1	2	0	1	0	1	0	9.00
Los Angeles	4	37	35	9	21	3	1	0	3.41
John	1	9	4	2	4	1	0	0	0.00
Sutton	1	5.2	7	2	0	0	1	0	6.35
Rau	1	5	5	2	1	0	0	0	3.60
Hooton	1	4.2	10	5	0	0	0	0	7.71
Welch	1	4.1	2	0	5	1	0	0	2.08
Rhoden	1	4	2	1	3	0	0	0	2.25
Hough	1	2	1	0	1	0	0	0	4.50
Rautzhan	1	1.1	3	2	0	0	0	0	6.75
Forster	1	1	1	0	2	1	0	0	0.00
Philadelphia	4	36.2	42	9	22	1	3	0	4.66
Carlton	1	9	8	2	8	1	0	0	4.00
McGraw	3	5.2	3	5	5	0	1	0	1.59
Lerch	1	5.1	7	0	0	0	0	0	5.06
Ruthven	1	4.2	6	0	3	0	1	0	5.79
Christenson	1	4.1	7	1	3	0	1	0	12.46
Reed	2	4	6	0	2	0	0	0	2.25
Brusstar	3	2.2	1	1	0	0	0	0	0.00
Eastwick	1	1	3	0	1	0	0	0	9.00

NAME	G	IP	H	BB	SO	W	L	SV	ERA
New York	6	53	52	20	31	4	2	0	3.74
Hunter	2	13	13	1	5	1	1	0	4.15
Guidry	1	9	8	7	4	1	0	0	1.00
Beattie	1	9	9	4	8	1	0	0	2.00
Figueroa	2	6.2	9	5	2	0	1	0	8.10
Gossage	3	6	1	1	4	1	0	0	0.00
Tidrow	2	4.2	4	0	5	0	0	0	1.93
Clay	2	2.1	4	2	2	0	0	0	11.57
Lindblad	1	2.1	4	0	1	0	0	0	11.57
Los Angeles	6	52.2	68	16	40	2	4	1	5.47
John	2	14.2	14	4	6	1	0	0	3.07
Sutton	2	12	17	4	8	0	2	0	7.50
Hooton	2	8.1	13	3	6	1	1	0	6.48
Hough	2	5.1	10	2	5	0	0	0	8.44
Welch	3	4.1	4	2	6	0	1	1	6.23
Forster	3	4	5	1	6	0	0	0	0.00
Rau	1	2	1	0	3	0	0	0	0.00
Rautzhan	2	2	4	0	0	0	0	0	13.50

1978 NATIONAL LEAGUE — EAST DIVISION

PHILADELPHIA 1st 90-72 .556 — DANNY OZARK

Name	G by Pos	B	AGE	G	AB	R	H	2B	3B	HR	RBI	BB	SO	SB	BA	SA
TOTALS			30	162	5448	708	1404	248	32	133	661	552	866	152	.258	.388
Richie Hebner	1B117, 3B19, 2B1	L	30	137	435	61	123	22	3	17	71	53	58	4	.283	.464
Ted Sizemore (BH)	2B107	R	33	108	351	38	77	12	0	0	25	25	29	8	.219	.254
Larry Bowa	SS156	B	32	156	654	78	192	31	5	3	43	24	40	27	.294	.370
Mike Schmidt	3B139, SS1	R	28	145	513	93	129	27	2	21	78	91	103	19	.251	.435
Bake McBride	OF119	L	29	122	472	68	127	20	4	10	49	28	68	10	.269	.392
Garry Maddox	OF154	R	28	155	598	62	172	34	3	11	68	39	89	33	.288	.410
Greg Luzinski	OF154	R	27	155	540	85	143	32	2	35	101	100	135	8	.265	.526
Bob Boone	C129, 1B3, OF1	R	30	132	435	48	123	18	4	12	62	46	37	2	.283	.425
Jerry Martin	OF112	R	29	128	266	40	72	13	4	9	36	28	65	9	.271	.451
Tim McCarver	C34, 1B11	L	36	90	146	18	36	9	1	1	14	28	24	2	.247	.342
Jose Cardenal	1B50, OF13	R	34	87	201	27	50	12	0	4	33	23	16	2	.249	.368
Bud Harrelson	2B43, SS15	B	34	71	103	16	22	1	0	0	9	18	21	5	.214	.223
Jim Morrison	2B31, 3B3, OF1	R	25	53	108	12	17	1	1	3	10	10	21	1	.157	.269
1 Dave Johnson	2B15, 3B9, 1B7	R	35	44	89	14	17	2	0	2	14	10	19	0	.191	.281
Barry Foote	C31	R	26	39	57	4	9	0	0	1	4	1	11	0	.158	.211
1 Jay Johnstone	1B8, OF7	L	32	35	56	3	10	2	0	0	4	6	9	0	.179	.214
Orlando Gonzalez	OF11, 1B3	L	26	26	26	1	5	0	0	0	1	0	4	0	.192	.192
Lonnie Smith	OF11	R	22	17	4	6	0	0	0	0	0	0	3	4	.000	.000
Pete Mackanin	3B1, 1B1	R	26	5	8	0	2	0	0	0	1	0	4	0	.250	.250
Kerry Dineen	OF1	L	26	5	8	0	2	1	0	0	1	0	0	0	.250	.375
Todd Cruz	SS2	R	22	3	4	0	2	0	0	0	2	0	1	0	.500	.500
Keith Moreland	C1	R	24	1	2	0	0	0	0	0	0	0	0	0	.000	.000

NAME	T	AGE	W	L	PCT	SV	G	GS	CG	IP	H	BB	SO	SHO	ERA
TOTALS		30	90	72	.556	29	162	162	38	1436	1343	393	813	9	3.33
Steve Carlton	L	33	16	13	.552	0	34	34	12	247	228	63	161	3	2.84
2 Dick Ruthven	R	27	13	5	.722	0	20	20	9	151	136	28	75	2	2.98
Larry Christenson	R	24	13	14	.481	0	33	33	9	228	209	47	131	3	3.24
Randy Lerch	L	23	11	8	.579	0	33	28	5	184	183	70	96	0	3.96
Jim Kaat	L	39	8	5	.615	0	26	24	2	140	150	32	48	1	4.11
Tug McGraw	L	33	8	7	.533	9	55	1	0	90	82	23	63	0	3.20
Jim Lonborg	R	36	8	10	.444	0	22	22	1	114	132	45	48	0	5.21
Warren Brusstar	R	26	6	3	.667	0	58	0	0	89	74	30	60	0	2.33
Ron Reed	R	35	3	4	.429	17	66	0	0	109	87	23	85	0	2.23
2 Rawly Eastwick	R	27	2	1	.667	2	22	0	0	40	31	18	14	0	4.05
1 Gene Garber	R	30	2	1	.667	3	22	0	0	39	26	11	24	0	1.38
Horacio Pina	R	33	0	0	—	0	2	0	0	2	0	1	4	0	0.00
Danny Boitano	R	25	0	0	—	0	1	0	0	1	1	0	1	0	0.00
Dan Larson	R	23	0	1	.000	0	1	0	0	1	1	1	2	0	9.00
Kevin Saucier	L	21	0	0	—	0	2	0	0	4	1	2	1	0	18.00

PITTSBURGH 2nd 88-73 .547 1.5 — CHUCK TANNER

Name	G by Pos	B	AGE	G	AB	R	H	2B	3B	HR	RBI	BB	SO	SB	BA	SA
TOTALS			28	161	5406	684	1390	239	54	115	631	480	874	213	.257	.385
Willie Stargell	1B112	L	38	122	390	60	115	18	2	28	97	50	93	3	.295	.567
Rennie Stennett (LJ)	2B80, 3B6	R	27	106	333	30	81	9	2	3	35	13	22	2	.243	.309
Frank Taveras	SS157	R	28	157	654	81	182	31	9	0	38	29	60	46	.278	.353
Phil Garner	3B81, 2B81, SS4	R	29	154	528	66	138	25	9	10	66	66	71	27	.261	.400
Dave Parker	OF147	L	27	148	581	102	194	32	12	30	117	57	92	20	.334	.585
Omar Moreno	OF152	L	25		515	95	121	15	7	2	33	81	104	71	.235	.303
Bill Robinson	OF127, 3B29, 1B3	R	35	136	499	70	123	36	2	14	80	35	105	14	.246	.411
Ed Ott	C97, OF4	L	26	112	379	49	102	18	4	9	38	27	56	4	.269	.409
John Milner	OF69, 1B28	L	28	108	295	39	80	17	0	6	38	34	25	5	.271	.390
Manny Sanguillen	1B40, C18	R	34	85	220	15	58	5	1	3	16	9	10	2	.264	.336
Steve Brye	OF47	R	29	66	115	16	27	7	0	1	9	11	10	2	.235	.322
Duffy Dyer	C55	R	32	58	175	7	37	8	1	0	13	18	32	2	.211	.269
Mario Mendoza	2B21, 3B18, SS14	R	27	57	55	5	12	1	0	1	3	2	9	3	.218	.291
Dale Berra	3B55, SS2	R	21	56	135	16	28	2	0	6	14	13	20	3	.207	.356
Ken Macha	3B21	R	27	29	52	5	11	1	1	0	5	12	10	2	.212	.269
Jim Fregosi (RM)	3B5, 1B2, 2B1	R	36	20	20	3	4	1	0	0	1	6	8	0	.200	.250
1 Fernando Gonzalez	2B4, 3B3	R	28	9	21	2	4	1	0	0	0	1	3	0	.190	.238
Matt Alexander		B	31	7	0	2	0	0	0	0	0	0	0	4	—	—
Doe Boyland	1B1	L	23	6	8	1	2	0	0	0	1	0	1	0	.250	.250
3 Dave May		L	34	5	4	0	0	0	0	0	0	1	1	1	.000	.000
Steve Nicosia	C1	R	22	3	5	0	0	0	0	0	0	0	0	0	.000	.000
Alberto Lois	OF2	R	22	3	4	0	1	0	1	0	0	0	0	0	.250	.750
2 Cito Gaston	OF1	R	34	2	2	1	1	0	0	0	0	0	0	0	.500	.500

NAME	T	AGE	W	L	PCT	SV	G	GS	CG	IP	H	BB	SO	SHO	ERA
TOTALS		29	88	73	.547	44	161	161	30	1445	1366	499	880	13	3.41
Don Robinson	R	21	14	6	.700	1	35	32	9	228	203	57	135	1	3.47
Bert Blyleven	R	27	14	10	.583	0	34	34	11	244	217	66	182	4	3.02
John Candelaria	L	24	12	11	.522	1	30	29	3	189	191	49	94	1	3.24
Jim Rooker	R	35	9	11	.450	0	28	28	1	163	160	81	74	0	4.25
Kent Tekulve	R	31	8	7	.533	31	91	0	0	135	115	55	77	0	2.33
Jim Bibby	R	33	8	7	.533	1	34	14	3	107	100	39	72	2	3.53
Grant Jackson	L	35	7	5	.583	5	60	0	0	77	89	32	45	0	3.27
Bruce Kison (RJ)	R	28	6	6	.500	0	28	11	0	96	81	39	62	0	3.19
Ed Whitson	R	23	5	6	.455	4	43	0	0	74	66	37	64	0	3.28
Jerry Reuss	L	29	3	2	.600	0	23	12	3	83	97	23	42	1	4.88
Odell Jones	R	25	2	0	1.000	0	3	1	0	9	7	4	10	0	2.00
Will McEnaney	L	26	0	0	—	0	9	0	0	15	2	6	0	0	10.00
Clay Carroll	R	37	0	0	—	0	2	0	0	4	2	0	0	0	2.25
2 Dave Hamilton	L	30	0	2	.000	1	16	0	0	26	23	12	15	0	3.46
Larry Demery 25 (SJ)															

CHICAGO 3rd 79-83 .488 11 — HERMAN FRANKS

Name	G by Pos	B	AGE	G	AB	R	H	2B	3B	HR	RBI	BB	SO	SB	BA	SA
TOTALS			28	162	5532	664	1461	224	48	72	612	562	746	110	.264	.361
Bill Buckner	1B105	L	28	117	446	47	144	26	1	5	74	18	17	7	.323	.419
Manny Trillo	2B149	R	27	152	552	53	144	17	5	4	55	50	67	0	.261	.332
Ivan DeJesus	SS160	R	25	160	619	104	172	24	7	3	35	74	78	41	.278	.354
Steve Ontiveros (SJ)	3B77, 1B1	B	26	82	278	34	67	14	4	1	22	34	33	0	.243	.333
Bobby Murcer	OF138	L	32	146	499	66	140	22	6	9	64	80	57	14	.281	.403
Greg Gross	OF111	L	25	124	347	34	92	12	7	1	39	33	19	3	.265	.349
Dave Kingman (LJ)	OF100, 1B6	R	29	119	395	65	105	17	4	28	79	39	111	3	.266	.542
Dave Rader	C114	L	29	116	305	29	62	13	3	3	36	34	26	1	.203	.295
Larry Biittner	1B62, OF29	L	32	120	343	32	88	15	1	4	50	23	37	0	.257	.341
Gene Clines	OF66	R	31	109	229	31	59	10	2	0	17	21	28	4	.258	.319
Rodney Scott	3B59, OF10, 2B6, SS6	B	24	78	227	41	64	5	1	0	15	43	41	27	.282	.313
2 Mike Vail	OF45, 3B1	R	26	74	180	15	60	6	2	4	33	3	24	0	.333	.456
Mick Kelleher	3B37, 2B17, SS10	R	30	68	95	8	24	1	0	0	6	7	11	4	.253	.263
2 Jerry White	OF54	B	25	59	136	22	37	6	0	1	10	23	16	4	.272	.338
Larry Cox (RJ)	C58	R	30	59	121	10	34	5	0	2	18	12	16	0	.281	.372
Tim Blackwell	C49	B	25	49	103	8	23	3	0	0	7	23	17	0	.223	.252
Rudy Meoli	2B6, 3B5	L	27	47	29	10	3	0	1	0	2	6	4	1	.103	.172
1 Heity Cruz	OF14, 3B7	R	25	30	78	8	18	5	0	2	9	3	6	0	.237	.382
1 Joe Wallis	OF25	B	26	28	55	7	17	2	1	1	6	5	13	0	.309	.436
2 Dave Johnson	3B12	R	35	24	49	5	15	1	1	2	6	5	9	0	.306	.490
Scot Thompson	OF5, 1B2	L	22	19	36	7	15	3	0	0	2	4	6	0	.417	.500
Ed Putman	3B8, 1B3, C2	R	24	17	25	2	5	0	0	0	3	4	6	0	.200	.200
Mike Sember	3B7, SS1	R	25	9	3	2	1	0	0	0	0	2	0	0	.333	.333
Mike Gordon	C4	B	24	4	5	0	1	0	0	0	1	2	0	0	.200	.200
Karl Pagel		L	23	2	0	0	0	0	0	0	0	0	0	0	.000	.000

NAME	T	AGE	W	L	PCT	SV	G	GS	CG	IP	H	BB	SO	SHO	ERA
TOTALS		27	79	83	.488	38	162	162	24	1455	1475	539	768	7	4.05
Rick Reuschel	R	29	14	15	.483	0	35	35	9	243	235	54	115	1	3.41
Mike Krukow	R	26	9	3	.750	0	27	20	3	138	125	53	81	1	3.91
Donnie Moore	R	24	9	7	.563	4	71	1	0	103	117	31	50	0	4.11
Willie Hernandez	L	23	8	2	.800	3	54	0	0	60	57	35	38	0	3.75
Bruce Sutter	R	25	8	10	.444	27	64	0	0	99	82	34	106	0	3.18
Ray Burris	R	27	7	13	.350	1	40	32	4	199	210	79	94	1	4.75
Dennis Lamp	R	25	7	15	.318	0	37	36	6	224	221	56	73	3	3.29
Dave Roberts	L	33	6	8	.429	1	35	20	2	142	159	56	54	1	5.26
2 Lynn McGlothen	R	28	5	3	.625	0	49	1	0	80	77	39	60	0	3.04
1 Paul Reuschel (EJ)	R	31	2	0	1.000	0	16	0	0	28	29	13	13	0	5.14
1 Woody Fryman	L	38	2	4	.333	0	13	9	0	56	64	37	28	0	5.14
Dave Geisel	L	23	1	0	1.000	0	18	1	0	23	27	11	15	0	4.30
Manny Seoane	R	23	1	0	1.000	0	7	1	0	8	11	6	5	0	5.63
2 Ken Holtzman	L	32	0	3	.000	2	23	6	0	53	61	35	36	0	6.11

MONTREAL 4th 76-86 .469 14 — DICK WILLIAMS

Name	G by Pos	B	AGE	G	AB	R	H	2B	3B	HR	RBI	BB	SO	SB	BA	SA
TOTALS			27	162	5530	633	1404	269	31	121	589	396	881	80	.254	.379
Tony Perez	1B145	R	36	148	544	63	158	38	3	14	78	38	104	2	.290	.469
Dave Cash	2B159	R	30	159	658	66	166	26	3	3	43	37	29	12	.252	.315
Chris Speier	SS148	R	28	150	501	47	126	18	3	5	51	60	75	1	.251	.329
Larry Parrish	3B139	R	24	144	520	68	144	39	4	15	70	32	103	2	.277	.454
Ellis Valentine	OF146	R	23	151	570	75	165	35	2	25	76	35	88	13	.289	.480
Andre Dawson	OF153	R	23	157	609	84	154	24	8	25	72	30	128	28	.253	.442
Warren Cromartie	OF158, 1B4	L	24	159	607	77	180	32	6	10	56	33	60	8	.297	.418
Gary Carter	C152, 1B1	R	24	157	533	76	136	27	1	20	72	62	70	10	.255	.422
Del Unser	1B64, OF33	L	33	130	179	16	35	5	0	2	15	24	29	2	.196	.257
Pepe Frias	2B61, SS3	R	29	73	15	5	4	2	1	0	5	0	3	0	.267	.533
Stan Papi	SS22, 3B15, 2B5	R	27	67	152	15	35	11	0	0	11	10	28	0	.230	.303
Sammy Mejias	OF52, P1	R	26	67	56	9	13	1	0	0	6	2	5	0	.232	.250
1 Wayne Garrett	3B13	L	30	49	69	6	12	0	1	0	5	8	10	0	.174	.217
2 Tommy Hutton	1B17, OF5	L	32	39	59	4	12	3	0	0	5	10	5	0	.203	.254
2 Ed Herrmann	C12	L	31	19	40	1	7	1	0	2	3	1	4	0	.175	.300
1 Jerry White	OF9	B	25	18	10	2	2	0	0	0	1	0	2	0	.200	.200
Bob Reece	C9	R	27	11	11	1	2	1	0	0	0	0	6	0	.182	.273
Jerry Fry	C4	R	22	4	9	1	0	0	0	0	0	1	1	0	.000	.000
Bobby Ramos	C1	R	22	2	4	0	0	0	0	0	0	0	1	0	.000	.000

NAME	T	AGE	W	L	PCT	SV	G	GS	CG	IP	H	BB	SO	SHO	ERA
TOTALS		29	76	86	.469	32	162	162	42	1446	1332	572	740	13	3.42
Ross Grimsley	R	28	20	11	.645	0	36	36	19	263	237	87	84	3	3.05
Steve Rogers (EJ)	R	28	13	10	.565	1	30	29	11	219	186	64	126	1	2.47
Rudy May (BF)	L	33	8	10	.444	0	27	23	4	144	141	42	87	1	3.88
Dan Schatzeder	L	23	7	7	.500	0	29	18	2	144	108	68	69	0	3.06
Hal Dues	R	23	5	6	.455	1	25	12	1	99	85	42	36	0	2.36
2 Woody Fryman	L	38	5	7	.417	1	19	17	4	95	93	37	53	3	3.60
Scott Sanderson	R	21	4	2	.667	0	10	9	1	61	52	21	50	1	2.51
2 Mike Garman	R	28	4	6	.400	13	47	0	0	61	54	31	23	0	4.43
Wayne Twitchell	R	30	4	12	.250	0	33	15	0	112	121	71	69	0	5.38
Darold Knowles	L	36	3	3	.500	6	60	0	0	72	63	30	34	0	2.38
Bill Atkinson	R	23	2	2	.500	3	29	0	0	42	45	28	32	0	4.40
Stan Bahnsen (SJ)	R	33	1	5	.167	7	44	1	0	75	74	31	44	0	3.84
Fred Holdsworth (SA)	R	26	0	0	—	0	9	0	0	16	8	3	7	0	7.00
Sammy Mejias	R	26													
David Palmer	R	20	0	0	—	0	3	1	0	10	9	2	0		2.70
Randy Miller	R	23	0	0	—	0	1			7	2	1	1	0	10.29
Bob James	R	19	0	1	.000	0	2			5	7	4	0		9.00
Gerry Pirtle	R	30	0	0	—	0	19			26	33	23	14	0	5.88

ST. LOUIS 5th 69-93 .426 21   VERN RAPP 6-11 .353   JACK KROL 1-1 .500   KEN BOYER 62-81 .434

Name	G by Pos	B	AGE	G	AB	R	H	2B	3B	HR	RBI	BB	SO	SB	BA	SA
TOTALS			28	162	5415	600	1351	263	44	79	568	420	713	97	.249	.358
Keith Hernandez	1B158	L	24	159	542	90	138	32	4	11	64	82	68	13	.255	.389
Mike Tyson	2B124	R	28	125	377	26	88	16	0	3	26	24	41	2	.233	.300
Garry Templeton	SS155	B	22	155	647	82	181	31	13	2	47	22	87	34	.280	.377
Ken Reitz	3B150	R	27	150	540	41	133	26	2	10	75	23	61	1	.246	.357
Jerry Morales	OF126	R	29	130	457	44	109	19	8	4	46	33	44	4	.239	.341
2 George Hendrick	OF101	R	28	102	382	55	110	27	1	17	67	28	44	1	.288	.497
Lou Brock	OF79	L	39	92	298	31	66	9	0	0	12	17	29	17	.221	.252
Ted Simmons	C134, OF23	B	28	152	516	71	148	40	5	22	80	77	39	1	.287	.512
Jerry Mumphrey	OF116	B	25	125	367	41	96	13	4	2	37	30	40	14	.262	.335
Tony Scott	OF77	R	26	96	219	28	50	5	2	1	14	14	41	5	.228	.283
Mike Phillips	2B55, SS10, 3B1	L	27	76	164	14	44	8	1	1	28	13	25	0	.268	.348
Roger Freed	1B15, OF6	R	32	52	92	3	22	6	0	2	20	8	17	1	.239	.370
Steve Swisher	C42	R	26	45	115	11	32	5	1	1	10	8	14	1	.278	.365
Dane Iorg	OF25	L	28	35	85	6	23	4	1	0	4	4	10	0	.271	.341
1 Jim Dwyer	OF22	L	28	34	65	8	14	3	0	1	4	9	3	1	.215	.308
2 Wayne Garrett	3B19	L	30	33	63	11	21	4	0	1	10	11	16	1	.333	.444
Ken Oberkfell	2B17, 3B4	L	22	24	50	7	6	1	0	0	3	1	0		.120	.140
Mike Ramsey	SS4	B	24	12	5	4	1	0	0	0	0	0	1	0	.200	.200
Terry Kennedy	C10	L	22	10	29	0	5	0	0	0	2	4	3	0	.172	.172
Gary Sutherland	2B1	R	33	10	6	1	1	0	0	0	0	0	0	0	.167	.167
Jim Lentine	OF3	R	23	8	11	1	2	0	0	0	1	0	1	0	.182	.182
1 John Tamargo	C1	R	26	6	6	0	0	0	0	0	0	0	0	0	.000	.000
Bob Coluccio	OF2	R	26	5	3	0	0	0	0	0	0	0	1	2	.000	.000

NAME	T	AGE	W	L	PCT	SV	G	GS	CG	IP	H	BB	SO	SHO	ERA
		25	69	93	.426	22	162	162	32	1438	1300	600	859	13	3.58
John Denny	R	25	14	11	.560	0	33	33	11	234	200	74	103	2	2.96
Pete Vuckovich	R	25	12	12	.500	1	45	23	6	198	187	59	149	2	2.55
Bob Forsch	R	28	11	17	.393	0	34	34	7	234	240	57	114	3	3.69
Silvio Martinez	R	22	9	8	.529	0	22	22	5	138	114	71	45	2	3.65
Aurelio Lopez	R	29	4	2	.667	0	25	4	0	65	52	32	46	0	4.29
Tom Bruno	R	25	4	3	.571	1	18	3	0	50	38	17	33	0	1.98
Mark Littell	R	25	4	8	.333	11	72	0	0	106	80	59	130	0	2.80
John Urrea	R	23	4	9	.308	0	27	12	1	99	108	47	61	0	5.36
Buddy Schultz	L	27	2	4	.333	6	62	0	0	83	68	36	70	0	3.80
1 Eric Rasmussen	R	26	2	5	.286	0	10	10	2	60	61	20	32	1	4.20
Pete Falcone	L	24	2	7	.222	0	19	14	0	75	94	48	28	0	5.76
Roy Thomas	R	25	1	1	.500	3	16	1	0	28	21	16	16	0	3.86
1 Dave Hamilton	L	30	0	0	—	0	13	0	0	14	16	6	8	0	6.43
Rob Dressler	R	24	0	1	.000	0	3	2	0	13	12	4	4	0	2.08
Dan O'Brien	R	24	0	2	.000	0	7	2	0	18	22	8	12	0	4.50
George Frazier	R	23	0	3	.000	0	14	0	0	22	22	6	8	0	4.09

NEW YORK 6th 66-96 .407 24   JOE TORRE

Name	G by Pos	B	AGE	G	AB	R	H	2B	3B	HR	RBI	BB	SO	SB	BA	SA
TOTALS			27	162	5433	607	1332	227	47	86	561	549	829	100	.245	.352
Willie Montanez	1B158	L	30	159	609	66	156	32	0	17	96	60	92	9	.256	.392
Doug Flynn	2B128, SS60	R	27	156	532	37	126	12	8	0	39	30	50	3	.237	.289
Tim Foli (KJ)	SS112	R	27	113	413	37	106	21	1	1	27	14	30	2	.257	.320
Lenny Randle	3B124, 2B5	B	29	132	437	53	102	16	8	2	35	64	57	14	.233	.320
Elliott Maddox	OF79, 3B43, 1B1	R	30	119	389	43	100	18	2	2	39	71	38	2	.257	.329
Lee Mazzilli	OF144	B	23	148	542	78	148	28	5	16	61	69	82	20	.273	.432
Steve Henderson	OF155	R	25	157	587	83	156	30	9	10	65	60	109	13	.266	.399
John Stearns	C141, 3B1	R	26	143	477	65	126	24	1	15	73	70	57	25	.264	.413
Joel Youngblood	OF50, 2B39, 3B9, SS1	R	26	113	266	40	67	12	8	7	30	16	39	4	.252	.436
Bruce Boisclair	OF69, 1B1	L	25	107	214	24	48	7	1	4	15	23	43	3	.224	.322
Bobby Valentine	2B45, 3B9	R	28	69	160	17	43	7	0	1	18	19	18	1	.269	.331
Ed Kranepool	OF12, 1B3	L	33	66	81	7	17	2	0	3	19	8	12	0	.210	.346
Tommy Grieve	OF26, 1B2	R	30	54	101	5	21	3	0	2	8	9	23	0	.208	.297
Ron Hodges	C30	L	29	47	102	4	26	4	1	0	7	10	11	1	.255	.314
Sergio Ferrer	SS29, 2B3, 3B2	B	27	37	33	8	7	0	1	0	1	4	7	1	.212	.273
Dan Norman	OF18	R	23	19	64	7	17	0	1	4	10	2	14	1	.266	.484
Gil Flores	OF8	R	25	11	29	8	8	0	1	0	1	3	5	1	.276	.345
1 Ken Henderson (EJ)	OF7	B	32	17	22	2	5	2	0	1	4	4	4	0	.227	.455
Alex Trevino	C5, 3B1	R	20	6	12	3	3	0	0	0	0	1	2	0	.250	.250
Butch Benton	C1	R	20	4	4	1	2	0	0	0	2	0	0	0	.500	.500

NAME	T	AGE	W	L	PCT	SV	G	GS	CG	IP	H	BB	SO	SHO	ERA
		27	66	96	.407	26	162	162	21	1455	1447	531	775	7	3.87
Nino Espinosa	R	24	11	15	.423	0	32	32	6	204	230	75	76	1	4.72
Pat Zachry (BF)	R	26	10	6	.625	0	21	21	5	138	120	60	78	2	3.33
Craig Swan	R	27	9	6	.600	0	29	28	5	207	164	58	125	1	2.43
2 Dale Murray	R	28	8	5	.615	9	53	0	0	86	85	36	37	0	3.66
Skip Lockwood	R	31	7	13	.350	15	57	0	0	91	78	31	73	0	3.56
Kevin Kobel	L	24	6	9	.455	0	32	11	1	108	95	30	51	0	2.92
Mardie Cornejo	R	26	4	2	.667	3	25	0	0	37	37	14	17	0	2.43
Mike Bruhert	R	27	4	11	.267	0	27	22	1	134	171	34	56	1	4.77
Tom Hausman	R	25	3	3	.500	0	10	10	0	52	58	9	16	0	4.67
Jerry Koosman	L	35	3	15	.167	2	38	32	3	235	221	84	160	0	3.75
Butch Metzger	R	26	1	3	.250	0	25	0	0	37	48	22	21	0	6.57
Dwight Bernard	R	26	1	4	.200	0	30	1	0	48	54	27	26	0	4.31
Roy Lee Jackson	R	24	0	0	—	0	4	2	0	13	21	6	6	0	9.00
Paul Siebert	L	25	0	2	.000	1	27	0	0	28	30	21	12	0	5.14
Juan Berenguer	R	23	0	2	.000	0	5	3	0	13	17	11	8	0	8.31
Bobby Myrick	L	25	0	3	.000	0	17	0	0	25	18	13	13	0	3.24
Bob Apodaca 28 (EJ)															

WEST DIVISION

LOS ANGELES 1st 95-67 .586   TOMMY LASORDA

Name	G by Pos	B	AGE	G	AB	R	H	2B	3B	HR	RBI	BB	SO	SB	BA	SA
TOTALS			30	162	5437	727	1435	251	27	149	686	610	818	137	.264	.402
Steve Garvey	1B162	R	29	162	639	89	202	36	9	21	113	40	70	10	.316	.499
Davey Lopes	2B147, OF2	R	33	151	587	93	163	29	4	17	36	71	70	45	.278	.421
Bill Russell	SS155	R	29	155	625	72	179	32	4	3	46	30	34	10	.286	.365
Ron Cey	3B158	R	30	159	555	84	150	20	0	23	84	96	96	2	.270	.452
Reggie Smith	OF126	B	33	128	447	82	132	27	2	29	93	70	90	12	.295	.559
2 Billy North	OF103	B	30	110	304	54	71	10	0	0	10	65	48	27	.234	.266
Dusty Baker	OF145	R	29	149	522	62	137	24	1	11	66	47	66	12	.262	.375
Steve Yeager (VJ)	C91	R	29	94	228	19	44	7	0	4	23	36	41	0	.193	.276
Rick Monday	OF103, 1B1	L	32	119	342	54	87	14	1	19	57	49	100	2	.254	.468
Lee Lacy	OF44, 2B24, 3B9, SS1	R	30	103	245	29	64	16	4	13	40	27	30	7	.261	.518
Vic Davalillo	OF25, 1B1	L	41	75	77	15	24	1	1	1	11	3	7	2	.312	.390
2 Joe Ferguson	C62, OF3	R	31	67	198	20	47	11	0	7	28	34	41	1	.237	.399
Ted Martinez	SS17, 3B16, 2B10	R	30	54	55	13	14	1	0	1	5	4	14	3	.255	.327
Jerry Grote (BW)	C32, 3B7	R	35	41	70	5	19	5	0	0	9	10	5	0	.271	.343
Johnny Oates	C24	L	32	40	75	6	23	1	0	0	6	8	3	0	.307	.320
Manny Mota		R	40	37	33	2	10	1	0	0	6	3	4	0	.303	.333
1 Glenn Burke	OF15	R	25	16	19	2	4	0	0	0	2	0	4	1	.211	.211
Rudy Law	OF6	L	21	11	12	2	3	0	0	0	1	1	2	3	.250	.250
Joe Simpson	OF10	L	26	10	5	1	2	0	0	0	1	0	2	0	.400	.400
Myron White	OF4	L	20	7	4	1	2	0	0	0	1	0	0	0	.500	.500
Pedro Guerrero	1B4	R	22	5	8	3	5	0	0	0	1	0	0	0	.625	.875
Enzo Hernandez	SS2	R	29	4	3	0	0	0	0	0	0	0	0	0	.000	.000
Brad Gulden	C3	L	22	3	4	0	0	0	0	0	0	0	2	0	.000	.000

NAME	T	AGE	W	L	PCT	SV	G	GS	CG	IP	H	BB	SO	SHO	ERA
		28	95	67	.586	38	162	162	46	1440	1362	440	800	16	3.12
Burt Hooton	R	28	19	10	.655	0	32	32	10	236	196	61	104	3	2.71
Tommy John	L	35	17	10	.630	1	33	30	7	213	230	53	124	0	3.30
Doug Rau	L	29	15	9	.625	0	30	30	7	199	219	68	95	2	3.26
Don Sutton	R	33	15	11	.577	0	34	34	12	238	228	54	154	2	3.55
Rick Rhoden	R	25	10	8	.556	0	30	23	13	165	160	51	79	3	3.65
Bob Welch	R	21	7	4	.636	3	23	13	4	111	92	26	66	3	2.03
Terry Forster	R	26	5	4	.556	22	47	0	0	65	56	23	46	0	1.94
Charlie Hough	R	30	5	5	.500	7	55	0	0	93	69	48	66	0	3.29
Lance Rautzhan	L	25	2	1	.667	4	43	0	0	61	61	19	25	0	2.95
Rick Sutcliffe	R	22	0	0	—	0	2	0	0	2	2	1	0	0	0.00
Dave Stewart	R	21	0	0	—	0	1	0	0	2	1	0	1	0	0.00
Dennis Lewallyn	R	24	0	0	—	0	1	0	0	2	2	0	0	0	0.00
Gerald Hannahs	L	25	0	0	—	0	1	0	0	3	5	4	3	0	9.00
1 Mike Garman	R	28	0	0	.000	0	10	0	0	16	15	3	5	0	4.50
Bobby Castillo	R	23	0	0	.000	0	14	0	0	34	28	33	30	0	3.97

CINCINNATI 2nd 92-69 .571 2.5   SPARKY ANDERSON

Name	G by Pos	B	AGE	G	AB	R	H	2B	3B	HR	RBI	BB	SO	SB	BA	SA
TOTALS			30	161	5392	710	1378	270	32	136	668	636	899	137	.256	.393
Dan Driessen	1B151	L	26	153	624	68	131	23	3	16	70	75	79	28	.250	.397
Joe Morgan	2B124	L	34	132	441	68	104	27	0	13	75	79	40	19	.236	.412
Dave Concepcion	SS152	R	30	153	565	75	170	33	4	6	67	51	83	23	.301	.405
Pete Rose	3B156, OF7, 1B2	B	37	159	655	103	198	51	3	7	52	62	30	13	.302	.421
Ken Griffey	OF154	L	28	158	614	90	177	35	8	10	63	54	70	23	.288	.417
Cesar Geronimo	OF115	L	30	122	296	28	67	15	1	5	27	43	67	8	.226	.334
George Foster	OF157	R	29	158	604	97	170	29	7	40	120	70	138	4	.281	.546
Johnny Bench (XJ)	C107, 1B11, OF2	R	30	120	393	52	102	17	1	23	73	50	83	4	.260	.483
Dave Collins	OF24	B	25	102	102	13	22	1	0	0	7	15	18	7	.216	.225
Junior Kennedy	2B71, 3B4	R	27	89	157	22	40	2	2	0	11	31	28	4	.255	.293
Mike Lum	OF43, 1B7	L	32	86	146	15	39	7	1	6	23	22	18	0	.267	.452
Ray Knight	3B60, 2B4, OF3, SS1, 1B1	R	25	83	65	7	13	3	0	1	4	3	13	0	.200	.292
2 Ken Henderson	OF38	B	32	64	144	10	24	6	1	3	19	23	32	1	.167	.285
Rick Auerbach	SS26, 2B10, 3B3	R	28	63	55	17	18	6	0	2	5	7	12	1	.327	.545
Vic Correll	C52	R	32	52	105	9	25	7	0	1	6	8	17	0	.238	.333
Don Werner	C49	R	25	50	113	7	17	2	0	1	11	14	30	1	.150	.186
Champ Summers	OF12	L	32	13	35	4	9	2	0	1	3	7	4	2	.257	.400
Arturo DeFreitas	1B6	R	25	9	19	1	4	1	0	0	2	1	4	0	.211	.421
Ron Oester	SS6	B	22	6	8	1	3	1	0	0	1	0	1	0	.375	.375
Mike Grace	3B2	R	22	5	4	0	0	0	0	0	0	0	0	0	.000	.000
Harry Spilman		L	24	3	4	0	1	0	0	0	0	0	2	0	.250	.250

NAME	T	AGE	W	L	PCT	SV	G	GS	CG	IP	H	BB	SO	SHO	ERA
		28	92	69	.571	46	161	161	16	1448	1437	567	908	10	3.81
Tom Seaver	R	33	16	14	.533	0	36	36	8	260	218	89	226	1	2.87
Bill Bonham (EJ)	R	29	11	5	.688	0	23	23	1	140	151	50	83	0	3.54
Fred Norman	L	35	11	9	.550	1	36	31	0	177	173	82	111	0	3.71
Dave Tomlin	L	29	9	1	.900	4	57	0	0	62	88	30	32	0	5.81
Manny Sarmiento	R	22	9	7	.563	5	63	4	0	127	109	54	72	0	4.39
Pedro Borbon	R	31	8	2	.800	4	62	0	0	99	102	27	35	0	5.00
Tom Hume	R	25	8	11	.421	1	42	23	3	174	198	50	90	0	4.14
Doug Bair	R	28	7	6	.538	28	70	0	0	100	87	38	91	0	1.98
Paul Moskau	R	24	4	6	.600	1	26	25	2	145	139	57	88	1	3.97
Mike LaCoss	R	22	4	8	.333	0	16	15	2	96	104	46	31	1	4.50
Mario Soto	R	21	1	0	1.000	0	3	0	0	18	13	13	13	0	2.50
Dan Dumoulin	R	24	1	0	1.000	0	3	0	0	7	3	2	0	0	1.80
1 Dale Murray	R	28	1	1	.500	2	15	0	0	33	34	17	25	0	4.09
Doug Capilla	L	26	0	1	.000	0	6	0	0	11	14	11	9	0	9.82

SAN FRANCISCO 3rd 89-73 .549 6   JOE ALTOBELLI

Name	G by Pos	B	AGE	G	AB	R	H	2B	3B	HR	RBI	BB	SO	SB	BA	SA
TOTALS			27	162	5364	613	1331	240	41	117	576	554	814	87	.248	.374
Willie McCovey	1B97	L	40	108	351	32	80	19	2	12	64	36	57	1	.228	.396
Bill Madlock	2B114, 1B3	R	27	122	447	76	138	26	3	15	44	48	39	16	.309	.481
Johnnie LeMaster	SS96, 2B2	R	24	101	272	23	64	18	3	1	14	21	45	6	.235	.335
Darrell Evans	3B155	R	31	159	547	82	133	24	2	20	78	105	64	4	.243	.404
Jack Clark	OF152	R	22	156	592	90	181	46	8	25	98	50	72	15	.306	.537
Larry Herndon	OF149	L	24	151	471	52	122	15	9	1	32	35	71	13	.259	.335
Terry Whitfield	OF140	L	25	149	488	70	141	20	2	10	32	33	69	5	.289	.400
Marc Hill	C116, 1B2	R	26	117	358	20	87	15	1	3	36	45	39	1	.243	.316
Mike Ivie	1B76, OF22	R	25	117	318	34	98	14	3	11	55	27	45	3	.308	.475
2 Heity Cruz	OF53, 3B14	R	25	79	197	19	44	8	1	6	24	21	39	0	.223	.365
Rob Andrews	2B62, SS1	R	25	79	177	21	39	3	3	1	11	20	18	5	.220	.288
2 Roger Metzger	SS74	B	30	75	235	17	61	6	1	0	17	12	17	8	.260	.294
2 Jim Dwyer	OF36, 1B29	L	28	73	173	22	39	9	2	5	22	28	29	6	.225	.387
Vic Harris	SS22, 2B10, OF6	B	28	53	100	8	15	4	0	1	11	11	24	0	.150	.220
Skip James	1B27	L	28	41	21	5	2	1	0	0	3	4	5	1	.095	.143
Mike Sadek (BJ)	C37	R	32	40	109	15	26	3	0	2	9	10	11	1	.239	.321
2 John Tamargo	C31	B	26	36	92	6	22	4	1	1	8	18	7	1	.239	.337
Tom Heintzelman	2B5, 3B3, 1B2	R	31	27	35	2	8	1	0	2	6	2	5	0	.229	.429
Art Gardner		L	25	7	3	2	0	0	0	0	0	0	2	0	.000	.000
Dennis Littlejohn	C2	R	23	4	0	0	0	0	0	0	0	0	0	0		

NAME	T	AGE	W	L	PCT	SV	G	GS	CG	IP	H	BB	SO	SHO	ERA
		28	89	73	.549	29	162	162	42	1455	1377	453	840	17	3.30
Vida Blue	L	28	18	10	.643	0	35	35	9	258	233	70	171	4	2.79
Bob Knepper	L	24	17	11	.607	0	36	35	16	260	218	85	147	6	2.63
Gary Lavelle	L	29	13	10	.565	14	67	0	0	98	96	44	63	0	3.31
John Montefusco	R	28	11	9	.550	0	36	36	3	239	233	68	177	0	3.80
Ed Halicki (UJ)	R	27	9	10	.474	1	29	28	9	199	166	45	105	4	2.85
Randy Moffitt	R	29	8	4	.667	12	70	0	0	82	79	33	52	0	3.29
Jim Barr	R	30	8	11	.421	1	32	25	5	163	180	35	44	2	3.53
John Curtis	L	30	1	3	.571	1	46	0	0	63	60	29	38	0	3.71
Charlie Williams	R	30	1	3	.250	0	25	1	0	48	60	28	22	0	5.44
1 Lynn McGlothen	R	28	0	0	—	0	5	1	0	13	15	4	9	0	4.85
Ed Plank	R	26	0	0	—	0	5	0	0	7	6	2	1	0	3.86
Terry Cornutt	R	25	0	0	—	0	1	0	0	3	1	0	0	0	0.00
Greg Minton	R	26	0	1	.000	0	11	0	0	16	22	8	6	0	7.88
Phil Nastu	L	23	0	1	.000	0	3	1	0	8	8	2	5	0	5.63

SAN DIEGO 4th 84-78 .519 11   ROGER CRAIG

Name	G by Pos	B	AGE	G	AB	R	H	2B	3B	HR	RBI	BB	SO	SB	BA	SA
TOTALS			26	162	5360	591	1349	208	42	75	542	536	848	152	.252	.348
Gene Tenace	1B80, C71, 3B1	R	31	142	401	60	90	18	4	16	61	101	98	6	.224	.409
2 Fernando Gonzalez	2B94	R	28	101	320	27	80	10	2	2	29	18	32	1	.250	.313
Ozzie Smith	SS159	B	23	159	590	69	152	17	6	1	46	47	43	40	.258	.312
Bill Almon	3B114, SS15, 2B7	R	25	138	405	39	102	19	2	0	21	33	74	17	.252	.309
Oscar Gamble	OF107	L	28	126	375	46	103	15	3	7	47	51	45	1	.275	.387
Dave Winfield	OF154, 1B2	R	26	158	587	88	181	30	5	24	97	55	81	21	.308	.499
Gene Richards	OF124, 1B26	L	24	154	555	90	171	26	12	4	45	64	80	37	.308	.420
Rick Sweet	C76	B	25	88	226	15	50	8	0	1	11	27	22	1	.221	.270
Derrel Thomas	OF77, 2B40, 3B26, 1B14	B	27	128	352	36	80	10	2	3	26	35	37	11	.227	.293
Jerry Turner	OF58	L	24	106	225	28	63	9	1	8	37	21	32	6	.280	.434
Tucker Ashford	3B32, 2B18, 1B14	R	23	75	155	11	38	11	0	3	26	14	31	1	.245	.374
Broderick Perkins	1B59	L	23	62	217	14	52	14	1	2	33	5	29	4	.240	.341
Don Reynolds	OF25	R	25	57	87	8	22	2	0	0	10	15	14	1	.253	.276
Dave Roberts	C41, 1B8, OF2	R	27	54	97	7	21	4	1	1	7	12	25	0	.216	.309
Chuck Baker	2B24, SS12	R	24	48	58		12	1	0	0	3	2	15	0	.207	.224
1 George Hendrick	OF33	R	28	36	111	9	27	4	0	3	8	12	16	1	.243	.360
Mike Champion	2B20, 3B4	R	23	32	53	3	12	0	2	0	4	5	13	0	.226	.302
Barry Evans	3B24	R	21	24	90	7	24	1	1	0	4	4	10	0	.267	.300
Bob Davis	C16	R	26	19	40	3	8	1	0	0	2	1	5	0	.200	.225
Jim Beswick	OF6	R	20	17	20	2	1	0	0	0	0	1	7	0	.050	.050
Jim Wilhelm	OF10	R	25	10	19	2	7	2	0	0	4	0	2	1	.368	.474
Tony Castillo	C5	R	21	5	8	0	1	0	0	0	0	1	0	0	.125	.125

NAME	T	AGE	W	L	PCT	SV	G	GS	CG	IP	H	BB	SO	SHO	ERA
		28	84	78	.519	55	162	162	21	1434	1385	483	744	10	3.28
Gaylord Perry	R	39	21	6	.778	0	37	37	5	261	241	66	154	2	2.72
Randy Jones	L	28	13	14	.481	0	37	36	7	253	263	64	71	2	2.88
2 Eric Rasmussen	R	26	12	10	.545	0	27	24	3	146	154	43	59	2	4.07
Bob Owchinko	L	23	10	13	.435	0	36	33	4	202	198	78	94	1	3.56
Bob Shirley	L	24	8	11	.421	5	50	20	2	166	164	61	102	0	3.69
Rollie Fingers	R	31	6	13	.316	37	67	0	0	107	84	29	72	0	2.52
Mark Lee	R	25	5	1	.833	2	56	0	0	85	74	36	31	0	3.28
John D'Acquisto	R	26	4	3	.571	10	45	3	0	93	60	56	104	0	2.13
Mickey Lolich (KJ)	L	37	2	1	.667	1	20	2	0	35	30	11	13	0	1.54
1 Dan Spillner	R	26	1	0	1.000	0	17	0	0	26	32	7	16	0	4.50
1 Mark Wiley	R	30	1	0	1.000	0	4	1	0	8	11	1	1	0	5.63
Dave Wehrmeister	R	25	1	0	1.000	0	3	0	0	7	8	5	2	0	6.43
Juan Eichelberger	R	24	0	0	—	0	3	0	0	3	4	2	2	0	12.00
2 Dennis Kinney	L	26	0	1	.000	0	7	0	0	7	6	4	2	0	6.43
Steve Mura	R	23	0	2	.000	0	5	2	0	15	16	5	5	0	11.25
1 Dave Freisleben	R	26	0	3	.000	1	12	4	0	27	41	15	16	0	6.00

HOUSTON 5th 74-88 .457 21   BILL VIRDON

Name	G by Pos	B	AGE	G	AB	R	H	2B	3B	HR	RBI	BB	SO	SB	BA	SA
TOTALS			26	162	5458	605	1408	231	45	70	557	434	743	178	.258	.355
Bob Watson	1B128	R	32	139	461	51	133	25	4	14	79	51	57	3	.289	.451
Art Howe (BG)	2B107, 3B11, 1B1	R	31	119	420	46	123	33	4	7	55	34	41	2	.293	.436
Rafael Landestoy	SS50, OF3, 2B2	B	25	59	218	18	58	5	1	0	9	8	23	7	.266	.298
Enos Cabell	3B153, 1B14, SS1	R	28	162	660	92	195	31	8	7	71	22	80	33	.295	.398
Jose Cruz	OF152, 1B2	L	30	153	565	79	178	34	9	10	83	57	57	37	.315	.460
Cesar Cedeno (KJ)	OF50	R	27	50	192	31	54	8	2	7	23	15	24	23	.281	.453
Terry Puhl	OF148	L	21	149	585	87	169	25	6	3	35	48	46	32	.289	.368
Luis Pujols	C55, 1B1	R	22	56	153	11	20	8	1	1	11	12	45	0	.131	.216
Denny Walling	OF78	L	24	120	247	30	62	11	3	3	36	30	24	9	.251	.356
Dave Bergman	1B66, OF29	L	25	104	186	15	43	5	1	0	12	39	32	2	.231	.269
Jimmy Sexton	SS58, 3B8, 2B3	R	26	88	141	17	29	3	2	2	6	13	28	16	.206	.298
Wilbur Howard	OF38, C3, 2B1	B	29	84	148	17	34	4	1	1	13	5	22	6	.230	.291
Julio Gonzalez	2B54, SS17, 3B4	R	25	78	223	24	52	3	1	1	16	8	31	6	.233	.269
Jesus Alou	OF28	R	36	77	139	7	45	5	1	2	19	6	5	0	.324	.417
Bruce Bochy	C53	R	23	54	154	8	41	8	0	3	15	11	35	0	.266	.377
1 Joe Ferguson	C51	R	31	51	150	20	31	5	0	7	22	37	30	0	.207	.380
1 Roger Metzger	SS42, 3B1	B	30	45	123	11	27	4	1	0	6	12	9	0	.220	.268
Mike Fischlin	SS41	R	22	44	86	3	10	1	0	0	4	4	9	1	.116	.128
Reggie Baldwin	C14	R	23	38	67	5	17	5	0	1	11	3	3	0	.254	.373
Keith Drumright	2B17	L	23	17	55	5	9	0	0	0	2	3	4	0	.164	.164
1 Ed Herrmann	C14	L	31	16	36	1	4	1	0	0	3	0	3	0	.111	.139
Jim Obradovich	1B3	R	28	10	17	3	3	0	1	0	1	0	3	0	.176	.294
Jeff Leonard	OF8	R	22	8	26	2	10	2	0	0	4	1	2	1	.385	.462
Joe Cannon	OF5	L	24	8	18	1	4	0	0	0	1	0	1	0	.222	.222

NAME	T	AGE	W	L	PCT	SV	G	GS	CG	IP	H	BB	SO	SHO	ERA
		26	74	88	.457	23	162	162	48	1440	1328	578	930	17	3.63
J.R. Richard	R	28	18	11	.621	0	36	36	16	275	192	141	303	3	3.11
Joe Niekro	R	33	14	14	.500	0	35	29	10	203	190	73	97	1	3.86
Ken Forsch	R	31	10	6	.625	7	52	6	4	133	136	37	71	2	2.71
Mark Lemongello	R	22	9	14	.391	1	33	30	9	210	204	66	77	1	3.94
Tom Dixon	R	23	7	11	.389	1	30	19	3	140	140	40	66	2	3.99
Joaquin Andujar	R	25	5	7	.417	1	35	13	2	111	88	58	55	0	3.41
Joe Sambito	L	26	4	9	.308	11	62	0	0	88	85	32	96	0	3.07
Vern Ruhle	R	27	3	3	.500	0	13	10	2	68	57	20	27	2	2.12
Floyd Bannister	L	23	3	9	.250	0	28	16	2	110	120	63	94	2	4.83
Rick Williams	R	25	1	2	.333	0	17	1	0	35	43	10	17	0	4.63
Gene Pentz (XJ)	R	25	0	0	—	0	10	0	0	15	12	13	8	0	6.00
Oscar Zamora	R	33	0	0	—	0	10	0	0	15	20	7	6	0	7.20
Frank Riccelli	L	25	0	0	—	0	2	0	0	3	1	0	1	0	0.00
Bo McLaughlin	R	24	0	1	.000	2	12	1	0	23	30	16	10	0	5.09
Dan Warthen	L	25	0	1	.000	0	5	1	0	11	10	2	2	0	4.09

ATLANTA 6th 69-93 .426 26   BOBBY COX

Name	G by Pos	B	AGE	G	AB	R	H	2B	3B	HR	RBI	BB	SO	SB	BA	SA
TOTALS			25	162	5381	600	1313	191	39	123	558	550	874	90	.244	.363
Dale Murphy	1B129, C21	R	22	151	530	66	120	14	3	23	79	42	145	11	.226	.394
Glenn Hubbard (EJ)	2B44	R	20	44	163	15	42	4	0	2	13	10	20	2	.258	.319
Jerry Royster	2B75, SS60, 3B1	R	25	140	529	67	137	17	4	3	35	56	49	27	.259	.333
Bob Horner	3B89	R	20	89	323	50	86	17	1	23	63	24	42	0	.266	.539
Gary Matthews (SJ)	OF127	R	27	129	474	75	135	20	5	18	62	61	92	8	.285	.462
Rowland Office	OF136	L	25	146	404	40	101	13	1	9	40	22	52	8	.250	.354
Jeff Burroughs	OF146	R	27	153	488	72	147	30	6	23	77	117	92	1	.301	.529
Biff Pocoroba (SJ)	C79	B	24	92	289	21	70	8	0	6	34	29	14	0	.242	.332
Barry Bonnell	OF105, 3B15	R	24	117	304	36	73	13	3	1	16	20	30	12	.240	.306
Rod Gilbreath	3B62, 2B39	R	26	116	326	22	80	13	3	3	31	26	51	7	.245	.331
Bob Beall	1B40, OF8	B	30	108	185	29	45	8	0	1	16	36	27	4	.243	.303
Joe Nolan	C61	L	27	95	213	22	49	7	3	4	22	34	28	3	.230	.347
Darrel Chaney	SS77, 3B8, 2B1	B	30	89	245	27	55	9	1	3	20	25	48	1	.224	.306
1 Cito Gaston	OF29, 1B4	R	34	60	118	5	27	1	0	1	9	3	20	0	.229	.263
Pat Rockett	SS51	R	23	55	142	6	22	4	0	1	13	12	11	1	.141	.155
Brian Asselstine (BL)	OF35	L	24	39	103	11	28	3	3	2	13	11	16	2	.272	.417
Bruce Benedict	C22	R	22	22	52	3	13	2	0	0	1	6	6	0	.250	.288
Chico Ruiz	2B14, 3B1	R	26	18	46	3	13	3	0	0	2	2	4	0	.283	.348
Jerry Maddox	3B5	R	24	7	14	1	3	0	0	0	1	2	1	0	.214	.214
Eddie Miller	OF5	R	21	6	21	5	3	1	0	0	2	0	4	3	.143	.190
Larry Whisenton	OF4	L	21	6	16	1	3	1	0	0	1	2	1	0	.188	.250
1 Tom Paciorek		R	31	5	9	2	3	0	0	0	0	1	0	0	.333	.333
Rob Belloir	SS1, 3B1	R	29	2	1	0	0	0	0	0	0	0	0	0	1.000	2.000
Hank Small	1B1	R	24	1	1	0	1	0	0	0	0	0	0	0	.000	.000

NAME	T	AGE	W	L	PCT	SV	G	GS	CG	IP	H	BB	SO	SHO	ERA
		27	69	93	.426	32	162	162	29	1440	1404	624	848	12	4.08
Phil Niekro	R	39	19	18	.514	1	44	42	22	334	295	102	248	4	2.88
Larry McWilliams	L	24	9	3	.750	0	15	15	3	99	84	35	42	1	2.82
Preston Hanna	R	23	7	13	.350	0	29	28	0	140	132	93	90	0	5.14
Adrian Devine (EJ)	R	26	5	4	.556	3	31	6	0	65	84	25	26	0	5.95
Dave Campbell	R	26	4	4	.500	1	53	0	0	69	67	49	45	0	4.83
2 Gene Garber	R	30	4	4	.500	22	43	0	0	78	58	13	61	0	2.54
Buddy Solomon (KJ)	R	27	4	6	.400	2	37	8	0	106	98	50	64	0	4.08
Mickey Mahler	L	26	4	11	.267	0	34	21	1	135	130	66	92	0	4.67
Craig Skok	L	29	3	2	.600	2	43	0	0	62	64	27	28	0	4.35
Jamie Easterly	L	25	3	6	.333	1	37	8	0	78	91	45	42	0	5.65
Rick Camp	R	25	2	4	.333	0	42	4	0	74	99	32	23	0	3.77
1 Dick Ruthven	R	27	2	6	.250	0	13	13	2	81	78	28	45	1	4.11
Tommy Boggs	R	22	2	8	.200	0	16	12	1	59	80	26	21	1	6.71
Jim Bouton	R	39	1	3	.250	0	5	5	1	29	25	11	10	0	4.97
Max Leon	R	28	0	0	—	0	5	0	0	6	6	4	1	0	6.00
Duane Theiss	R	24	0	0	—	0	3	0	0	3	3	0	1	0	1.50
Mike Davey	L	26	0	0	—	0	3	0	0	6	8	4	5	0	4.67
Frank LaCorte	R	26	0	1	.000	0	2	2	0	15	9	4	7	0	3.60

1979 The Older They Get...

Once upon a time when all of baseball used real grass a Detroit Tiger outfielder by the name of Ty Cobb made newspaper headlines when he signed a one-year contract for $10,000. Some sixty odd years later newspaper headlines were written again when another player signed a contract which called for a cool million dollars a season plus. The player to pull the feat-considered an all-time high-was Pete Rose who, at age 37, came from the Cincinnati Reds to the Philadelphia Phillies in a free agent deal which made Rose an instant millionaire.

Although Rose managed to hit .331 and wind up behind Co-M.V.P. Keith Hernandez of St. Louis for National League batting honors, the Phillies were unable to finish in the first division of the N.L. East, instead lugging home a poor fourth with a .519 winning percentage. While the Phillies were wishing the season from memory their counterparts from across the state, Pittsburgh, enjoyed a better summer by winning the N.L. East by a slight edge over the Montreal Expos and then sweeping the Championship Playoffs from the Reds before staging a dramatic come-from-behind victory in the World Series.

The Pirates were led by the veteran slugger Willie Stargell who shared the league's M.V.P. honors with Hernandez by posting 32 home runs, 82 R.B.I.'s and a .281 batting mark. The 39-year-old Stargell spearheaded a potent attack which featured Dave Parker's 25 home runs. Bill Robinson and John Milner who platooned in left field and contributed 40 homers and 135 R.B.I.'s, and centerfielder Omar Moreno, who hit .282 and chalked up a league leading 77 stolen bases. Although John Candelaria was the club leader with only 14 wins a strong bullpen saved the Pirates, led by Kent Tekulve's 31 saves and 10 wins. If anything, the Bucs benefited most from deals which brought shortstop Tim Foli from the Mets and Bill Madlock from San Francisco which, with the presence of Phil Garner at second, made the infield into a tight cohesive unit.

In the American League, the Yankees began the year by losing star reliever Goose Gossage for two months with a finger injury as a result of a locker room fight in April with teammate Cliff Johnson. Then, on August 2, the news that captain Thurman Munson had died while flying his private plane left them stunned. They were also plagued by former New Yorker Sparky Lyle who wrote a best-seller and got everyone angry by putting all his out-of-school tales on paper. But more than Lyle, the Yankees were plagued by Baltimore, who left the defending world champions in fourth place while winning by a comfortable margin of eight games over Milwaukee and 11 1/2 over Boston.

Baltimore, in winning their first pennant since 1971, were led by Cy Young winner Mike Flanagan who posted a 23-9 record and Ken Singleton, whose 35 home runs and .295 batting average were enough to earn him runner-up honors in the M.V.P. voting. The key ingredient for manager Earl Weaver's surprising Orioles, however, was the return to center of Al Bumbry.

In the A.L. West, California surprised Kansas City by winning their first title in the club's 19-year franchise, but didn't have enough to get by Baltimore in the playoffs as they salvaged one game in the best three-out-of-five series. The Angels were led by the M.V.P. Don Baylor, who hit 36 homers to go along with a .296 batting average and 139 R.B.I.'s. While injuries cost Rod Carew his ninth batting title, he was able to provide California the needed punch for the Western crown along with Bobby Grich, Al Cowens, Carney Lansford and Brian Downing.

In the World Series, the Pirates entered the fifth game down 3-1 and facing extinction when they magically called upon that "extra" resource and pulled out the next three in a row, clinching the championship in game seven behind Stargell's third homer of the series which capped a .400 performance good enough to get him the series M.V.P. honors.

As a historic footnote to the season, St. Louis outfielder Lou Brock called it quits after registering an all-time high of 938 stolen bases to go along with his more than 3,000 hits.

1979 AMERICAN LEAGUE — EAST DIVISION

BALTIMORE 1st 102-57 .642 EARL WEAVER

Name	G by Pos	B	AGE	G	AB	R	H	2B	3B	HR	RBI	BB	SO	SB	BA	SA
TOTALS			29	159	5371	757	1401	258	24	181	717	608	847	99	.261	.419
Eddie Murray	1B157, DH2	B	23	159	606	90	179	30	2	25	99	72	78	10	.295	.475
Rich Dauer	2B103, 3B44	R	26	142	479	63	123	20	0	9	61	36	36	0	.257	.355
Kiko Garcia	SS113, 2B25, OF2, 3B2	R	25	126	417	54	103	15	9	5	24	32	87	11	.247	.362
Doug DeCinces (XJ)	3B120	R	28	120	422	67	97	27	1	16	61	54	68	5	.230	.412
Ken Singleton	OF143, DH16	B	32	159	570	93	168	29	1	35	111	109	118	3	.295	.533
Al Bumbry	OF146	L	32	148	569	80	162	29	1	7	49	43	74	37	.285	.376
Gary Roenicke	OF130, DH2	R	24	133	376	60	98	16	1	25	64	61	74	1	.261	.508
Rick Dempsey	C124	R	29	124	368	48	88	23	0	6	41	38	37	0	.239	.351
Lee May	DH117, 1B2	R	36	124	456	59	116	15	0	19	69	28	100	1	.254	.412
Mark Belanger (BG)	SS98	R	35	101	198	28	33	6	2	0	9	29	33	5	.167	.217
John Lowenstein (NJ)	OF72, DH3, 1B1, 3B1	L	32	97	197	33	50	8	2	11	34	30	37	16	.254	.482
Pat Kelly	OF24, DH18	L	34	68	153	25	44	11	0	9	25	20	25	4	.288	.536
Billy Smith	2B63, SS5	B	25	68	189	18	47	9	4	6	33	15	33	1	.249	.434
Dave Skaggs	C63	R	28	63	137	9	34	8	0	1	14	13	14	0	.248	.328
Terry Crowley	DH15, 1B2	L	32	61	63	8	20	5	1	1	8	14	13	0	.317	.476
Benny Ayala	OF24, DH10	R	28	42	86	15	22	5	0	6	13	6	9	0	.256	.523
1 Larry Harlow	OF31, DH1	L	27	38	41	5	11	1	0	0	1	7	4	1	.268	.293
Wayne Krenchicki	3B7, 2B6	L	24	16	21	1	4	1	0	0	0	0	0	0	.190	.238
Mark Corey	OF11, DH1	R	23	13	13	1	2	0	0	0	1	0	4	1	.154	.154
Bob Molinaro	OF5	L	29	8	6	0	0	0	0	0	0	0	3	1	.000	.000
Tom Chism	1B4	L	24	6	3	0	0	0	0	0	0	0	0	0	.000	.000
Ellie Hendricks (RC)	C1	L	38	1	1	0	0	0	0	0	0	0	0	0	.000	.000

NAME	T	AGE	W	L	PCT	SV	G	GS	CG	IP	H	BB	SO	SHO	ERA
		27	102	57	.642	30	159	159	52	1434	1279	467	786	12	3.26
Mike Flanagan	L	27	23	9	.719	0	39	38	16	266	245	70	190	5	3.08
Dennis Martinez	R	24	15	16	.484	0	40	39	18	292	279	78	132	3	3.67
Scott McGregor	L	25	13	6	.684	0	27	23	7	175	165	23	81	2	3.34
Steve Stone	R	31	11	7	.611	0	32	32	3	186	173	73	96	0	3.77
Tippy Martinez	L	29	10	3	.769	3	39	0	0	78	59	31	61	0	2.88
Jim Palmer (EJ)	R	33	10	6	.625	0	23	22	7	156	144	43	67	0	3.29
Sammy Stewart	R	24	8	5	.615	1	31	3	1	118	96	71	71	0	3.51
Don Stanhouse	R	28	7	3	.700	21	52	0	0	73	49	51	34	0	2.84
Tim Stoddard (UJ)	R	26	3	1	.750	3	29	0	0	58	44	19	47	0	1.71
Dave Ford	R	22	2	1	.667	2	9	2	0	30	23	7	7	0	2.10
John Flinn	R	24	0	0	—	0	4	0	0	3	2	1	0	0	0.00
Jeff Rineer	L	23	0	0	—	0	1	0	0	1	0	1	0	0	0.00

MILWAUKEE 2nd 95-66 .590 8 GEORGE BAMBERGER

Name	G by Pos	B	AGE	G	AB	R	H	2B	3B	HR	RBI	BB	SO	SB	BA	SA
TOTALS			28	161	5536	807	1552	291	41	185	766	549	745	100	.280	.448
Cecil Cooper	1B135, DH15	L	29	150	590	83	182	44	1	24	106	56	77	15	.308	.508
Paul Molitor	2B122, SS10, DH8	R	22	140	584	88	188	27	16	9	62	48	48	33	.322	.469
Robin Yount	SS149	R	23	149	577	72	154	26	5	8	51	35	52	11	.267	.371
Sal Bando	3B109, DH19, 1B4, 2B1, P1	R	35	130	476	57	117	14	3	9	43	57	42	2	.246	.345
Sixto Lezcano	OF135, DH1	R	28	138	473	84	152	29	3	28	101	77	74	4	.321	.573
Gorman Thomas	OF152, DH4	R	28	156	557	97	136	29	0	45	123	98	175	1	.244	.539
Ben Oglivie	OF120, DH13, 1B9	L	30	139	514	88	145	30	4	29	81	48	56	12	.282	.525
Charlie Moore	C106	R	26	111	337	45	101	16	2	5	38	29	32	8	.300	.404
Dick Davis	DH53, OF35	R	25	91	335	51	89	13	1	12	41	16	46	3	.266	.418
Don Money (LJ)	DH33, 3B26, 1B19, 2B16	R	32	92	350	52	83	20	1	6	38	40	47	1	.237	.351
Jim Gantner	3B42, 2B22, SS3, P1	L	26	70	208	29	59	10	3	2	22	16	17	3	.284	.389
Buck Martinez	C68, P1	R	30	69	196	17	53	8	0	4	26	8	25	0	.270	.372
Jim Wohlford	OF55, DH5	R	28	63	175	19	46	13	1	1	17	8	28	6	.263	.366
Larry Hisle (SJ)	DH15, OF10	R	32	26	96	18	27	7	0	3	14	11	19	1	.281	.448
Ray Fosse	C13, DH5, 1B1	R	32	19	52	6	12	3	1	0	2	2	6	0	.231	.327
Lenn Sakata	2B4	R	25	4	14	1	7	2	0	1	4	0	1	0	.500	.643
Tim Nordbrook	SS2	R	29	2	2	0	1	0	0	0	0	0	1	0	.500	.500

NAME	T	AGE	W	L	PCT	SV	G	GS	CG	IP	H	BB	SO	SHO	ERA
		27	95	66	.590	23	161	161	61	1440	1563	381	580	12	4.03
Mike Caldwell	L	30	16	6	.727	0	30	30	16	235	252	39	89	4	3.29
Jim Slaton	R	29	15	9	.625	0	32	31	12	213	229	54	80	3	3.63
Lary Sorensen	R	23	15	14	.517	0	34	34	16	235	250	42	63	2	3.98
Bill Travers	R	26	14	8	.636	0	30	27	9	187	196	45	74	2	3.90
Moose Haas	R	23	11	11	.500	0	29	28	8	185	198	59	95	1	4.77
Jerry Augustine	L	26	9	6	.600	5	43	2	0	86	95	30	41	0	3.45
Bob McClure	L	27	5	2	.714	5	36	0	0	51	53	24	37	0	3.88
Bill Castro	R	25	3	1	.750	6	39	0	0	44	40	13	10	0	2.05
Bob Galasso	R	27	3	1	.750	3	31	0	0	51	64	26	28	0	4.41
2 Paul Mitchell	R	28	3	3	.500	0	18	8	0	75	81	10	32	0	5.76
Reggie Cleveland	R	31	1	5	.167	4	29	1	0	55	77	23	22	0	6.71
Danny Boitano	R	26	0	0	—	0	6	0	0	6	6	3	5	0	1.50
Andy Replogle	R	26	0	0	—	0	8	0	0	13	2	2	1	0	5.63
Sal Bando	R	35	0	0	—	0	0	0	0	3	3	1	0	0	9.00
Jim Gantner	R	26	0	0	—	0	0	0	0	1	1	1	0	0	9.00
2 Lance Rautzhan	L	26	0	0	—	0	3	0	0	3	10	1	0	0	9.00
Buck Martinez	R	30	0	0	—	0	0	0	0	1	1	1	0	0	9.00

BOSTON — 3rd 91-69 .569 11.5 — DON ZIMMER

Name	G by Pos	B	AGE	G	AB	R	H	2B	3B	HR	RBI	BB	SO	SB	BA	SA
TOTALS			29	160	5538	841	1567	310	34	194	785	512	708	60	.283	.456
2 Bob Watson	1B58, DH26	R	33	84	312	48	105	19	4	13	53	29	33	3	.337	.548
Jerry Remy (KJ)	2B76	L	26	80	306	49	91	11	2	0	29	26	25	14	.297	.346
Rick Burleson	SS153	R	28	153	627	93	174	32	5	5	60	35	54	9	.278	.368
Butch Hobson	3B142, 2B1	R	27	146	528	74	138	28	4	28	93	30	78	3	.261	.496
Dwight Evans	OF149	R	27	152	489	69	134	24	1	21	58	69	76	6	.274	.456
Fred Lynn	OF143, DH1	L	27	147	531	116	177	42	1	39	122	82	79	2	.333	.637
Jim Rice	OF125, DH33	R	26	158	619	117	201	39	6	39	130	57	97	9	.325	.596
Carlton Fisk (EJ)	C39, DH42, OF1	R	31	91	320	49	87	23	2	10	42	10	38	3	.272	.450
Carl Yastrzemski	DH56, 1B51, OF36	L	39	147	518	69	140	28	1	21	87	62	46	3	.270	.450
Gary Allenson	C104, 3B3	R	24	108	241	27	49	10	2	3	22	20	42	1	.203	.299
Jim Dwyer	1B25, OF19, DH4	L	29	76	113	19	30	7	0	2	14	17	9	3	.265	.381
Jack Brohamer (KJ)	2B36, 3B22	L	29	64	192	25	51	7	1	1	11	15	15	0	.266	.328
2 Tom Poquette	OF43, DH4	L	27	63	154	14	51	9	0	2	23	8	7	2	.331	.429
Stan Papi (KJ)	2B26, SS21, DH1	R	28	50	117	9	22	4	0	1	6	5	20	0	.188	.282
Larry Wolfe	2B27, 3B9, SS2, 1B1, C1, DH1	R	26	47	78	12	19	4	0	3	15	17	21	0	.244	.410
1 George Scott	1B41	R	35	45	156	18	35	9	1	4	23	17	22	0	.224	.372
Mike O'Berry	C43	R	25	43	59	8	10	1	0	1	4	5	16	0	.169	.237
Bob Montgomery (EJ)	C31	R	35	32	86	13	30	4	1	0	7	4	24	1	.349	.419
2 Ted Sizemore	2B26, C2	R	34	26	88	12	23	7	0	1	6	4	5	1	.261	.375
Frank Duffy	2B3, 1B1	R	32	6	3	0	0	0	0	0	0	0	1	0	.000	.000

NAME	T	AGE	W	L	PCT	SV	G	GS	CG	IP	H	BB	SO	SHO	ERA
TOTALS		29	91	69	.569	29	160	160	47	1431	1487	463	731	11	4.03
Dennis Eckersley	R	24	17	10	.630	0	33	33	17	247	234	59	150	2	2.99
Bob Stanley	R	24	16	12	.571	1	40	30	9	217	250	44	56	4	3.98
Mike Torrez	R	32	16	13	.552	0	36	36	12	252	254	121	125	1	4.50
Steve Renko	R	34	11	9	.550	0	27	27	4	171	174	53	99	1	4.11
Dick Drago	R	34	10	6	.625	13	53	1	0	89	85	21	67	0	3.03
Chuck Rainey (SJ)	R	24	8	5	.615	1	20	16	4	104	97	41	41	1	3.81
Allen Ripley	R	26	3	1	.750	1	16	3	0	65	77	25	34	0	5.12
Tom Burgmeier	L	35	3	2	.600	4	44	0	0	89	89	16	60	0	2.73
Bill Campbell	R	30	3	4	.429	9	41	0	0	55	55	23	25	0	4.25
Jim Wright (SJ)	R	28	1	0	1.000	0	11	1	0	23	19	7	15	0	5.09
Win Remmerswaal	R	25	1	0	1.000	0	8	0	0	20	26	12	16	0	7.20
1 Andy Hassler	L	27	1	2	.333	0	8	0	0	15	23	7	7	0	9.00
John Tudor	L	25	1	2	.333	0	6	6	1	28	39	9	11	0	6.43
Joel Finch	R	22	0	3	.000	0	15	7	0	57	65	25	25	0	4.89

NEW YORK — 4th 89-71 .556 13.5 — BOB LEMON 34-31 .523 — BILLY MARTIN 55-40 .679

Name	G by Pos	B	AGE	G	AB	R	H	2B	3B	HR	RBI	BB	SO	SB	BA	SA
TOTALS			31	160	5421	734	1443	226	40	150	694	509	590	65	.266	.406
Chris Chambliss	1B134, DH16	L	30	149	554	61	155	27	3	18	63	34	53	3	.280	.437
Willie Randolph	2B153	R	24	153	574	98	155	15	13	5	61	95	39	33	.270	.368
Bucky Dent	SS141	R	27	141	431	47	99	14	2	2	32	37	30	0	.230	.285
Graig Nettles	3B144	L	34	145	521	71	132	15	1	20	73	59	53	1	.253	.401
Reggie Jackson (LJ)	OF125, DH3	L	33	131	465	78	138	24	2	29	89	65	107	9	.297	.544
1 Mickey Rivers	OF69, DH1	L	30	74	286	37	82	18	5	3	25	13	21	3	.287	.416
Lou Piniella	OF112, DH16	R	35	130	461	49	137	22	2	11	69	17	31	3	.297	.425
Thurman Munson (DD)*	C88, DH5, 1B3	R	32	97	382	42	110	18	3	3	39	32	37	1	.288	.374
Jim Spencer	DH71, 1B26	L	31	106	295	60	85	15	3	23	53	38	25	0	.288	.593
Roy White	DH29, OF27	B	35	81	205	24	44	6	0	3	27	23	21	2	.215	.288
2 Bobby Murcer	OF70	L	33	74	264	42	72	12	0	8	33	25	32	1	.273	.409
Juan Beniquez (GJ)	OF60, 3B3	R	29	62	142	19	36	6	1	4	17	9	17	3	.254	.394
Jerry Narron	C56, DH1	L	23	61	123	17	21	3	1	4	18	9	26	0	.171	.309
Fred Stanley	SS31, 3B16, 2B8, OF1, 1B1	R	31	57	100	9	20	1	0	2	14	5	11	0	.200	.270
Brad Gulden	C40	L	23	40	92	10	15	4	0	0	6	9	16	0	.163	.207
2 Oscar Gamble	OF27, DH6	L	29	36	113	21	44	4	1	11	32	13	13	0	.389	.735
2 Bobby Brown	OF27, DH1	B	25	30	68	7	17	3	0	2	6	3	17	2	.250	.324
1 Cliff Johnson	DH22, C4	R	31	28	64	11	17	6	0	2	6	10	7	0	.266	.453
1 Jay Johnstone	OF19, DH3	L	33	23	48	7	10	1	0	1	7	2	7	1	.208	.292
Lenny Randle	OF11, DH2	B	30	20	39	2	7	0	0	0	3	3	2	0	.179	.179
Brian Doyle	2B13, 3B6	L	25	20	32	2	4	2	0	0	5	3	1	0	.125	.188
Darryl Jones	DH15, OF2	R	28	18	47	6	12	5	1	0	6	2	7	0	.255	.404
3 George Scott	DH15, 1B1	R	35	16	44	9	14	3	1	1	6	2	7	1	.318	.500
Damaso Garcia	SS10, 3B1	R	24	11	38	3	10	1	0	0	4	0	2	2	.263	.289
Bruce Robinson	C6	L	25	6	12	0	2	0	0	0	2	1	0	0	.167	.167
Roy Staiger	3B4	R	29	4	11	1	3	1	0	0	1	1	0	0	.273	.364
Dennis Werth	1B1	R	26	3	4	1	1	0	0	0	0	0	1	0	.250	.250
1 Paul Blair	OF2	R	35	2	5	0	1	0	0	0	0	0	1	0	.200	.200

*Munson was killed in an airplane accident - Aug. 2

NAME	T	AGE	W	L	PCT	SV	G	GS	CG	IP	H	BB	SO	SHO	ERA
TOTALS		30	89	71	.556	37	160	160	43	1432	1446	455	731	10	3.83
Tommy John	L	36	21	9	.700	0	37	36	17	276	268	65	111	3	2.97
Ron Guidry	L	28	18	8	.692	0	33	30	15	236	203	71	201	2	2.78
Ron Davis	R	23	14	2	.875	9	44	0	0	85	84	28	43	0	2.86
Luis Tiant	R	38	13	8	.619	0	30	30	5	196	190	53	104	1	3.90
Goose Gossage (RJ)	R	27	5	3	.625	18	36	0	0	58	48	19	41	0	2.64
Ed Figueroa (EJ)	R	30	4	6	.400	0	16	16	4	105	109	35	42	1	4.11
2 Don Hood	L	29	3	1	.750	1	27	6	0	67	62	30	22	0	3.09
Jim Beattie (HJ)	R	24	3	6	.333	0	15	13	1	76	85	41	32	1	5.21
1 Dick Tidrow	R	32	2	1	.667	2	14	0	0	23	38	4	7	0	7.83
2 Jim Kaat	L	40	2	3	.400	2	40	1	0	58	64	14	23	0	3.88
Catfish Hunter	R	33	2	9	.182	0	19	19	1	105	128	34	34	0	5.31
2 Ray Burris	R	28	1	3	.250	0	15	0	0	28	40	10	19	0	6.11
Ken Clay	R	25	1	7	.125	2	32	5	0	78	88	25	28	0	5.42
Mike Griffin	R	22	0	1	—	0	4	0	0	4	5	2	6	0	4.50
Roger Slagle	R	25	0	0	—	0	1	0	0	2	0	0	2	0	0.00
Rick Anderson	R	25	0	0	—	0	4	0	0	4	5	1	4	0	4.50
Bob Kammeyer	R	28	0	1	—	0	1	0	0	0	7	6	1	0	∞
Dave Righetti	L	20	0	1	.000	0	3	3	0	17	10	10	13	0	3.71
Paul Mirabella	L	25	0	4	.000	1	10	1	0	14	16	11	4	0	9.00
Don Gullett (SJ) 28															

DETROIT — 5th 85-76 .528 18 — LES MOSS 27-26 .509 — DICK TRACEWSKI 2-0 1.000 — SPARKY ANDERSON 56-50 .528

Name	G by Pos	B	AGE	G	AB	R	H	2B	3B	HR	RBI	BB	SO	SB	BA	SA
TOTALS			27	160	5375	770	1446	221	35	164	729	575	814	176	.269	.415
Jason Thompson	1B140, DH2	L	24	145	492	58	121	16	1	20	79	70	90	2	.246	.404
Lou Whitaker	2B126	L	22	127	423	75	121	14	8	3	42	78	66	20	.286	.378
Alan Trammell	SS142	R	21	142	460	68	127	11	4	6	50	43	55	17	.276	.357
Aurelio Rodriguez	3B106, 1B1	R	31	106	343	27	87	18	0	5	36	11	40	0	.254	.350
Jerry Morales	OF119, DH7	R	30	129	440	50	93	23	1	14	56	30	56	10	.211	.364
Ron LeFlore	OF113, DH34	R	31	148	600	110	180	22	10	9	57	52	95	78	.300	.415
Steve Kemp	OF120, DH11	L	24	134	490	88	156	26	3	26	105	68	70	5	.318	.543
Lance Parrish	C142	R	23	143	493	65	136	26	3	19	65	49	105	6	.276	.456
1 Rusty Staub (HO)	DH66	L	35	68	246	32	58	12	1	9	40	32	18	1	.236	.402
Lynn Jones	OF84, DH6	R	26	95	213	33	63	8	0	4	26	17	22	9	.296	.390
John Wockenfuss	1B31, C20, DH18, OF6	R	30	87	231	27	61	9	1	15	46	18	40	2	.264	.506
2 Champ Summers	OF69, DH10, 1B4	L	33	90	246	47	77	12	1	20	51	40	33	7	.313	.614
Mark Wagner	SS41, 2B29, 3B2, DH1	R	25	75	146	16	40	3	0	1	13	16	25	3	.274	.315
Tom Brookens	3B42, 2B19, DH1	R	25	60	190	23	50	5	2	4	21	11	40	10	.263	.374
Phil Mankowski (BG)	3B36, DH1	L	26	42	99	11	22	4	0	0	8	10	16	0	.222	.263
Al Greene	DH15, OF6	L	24	29	59	9	8	1	0	3	6	6	15	0	.136	.305
Ed Putman	C16, 1B5	R	25	21	39	4	9	3	0	2	4	4	12	0	.231	.462
Dave Machemer	2B11, OF1, DH1	R	28	19	26	8	5	1	0	0	2	3	2	1	.192	.231
Tim Corcoran	OF9, 1B5, DH2	L	26	18	22	4	5	0	0	0	6	4	2	1	.227	.273
Dave Stegman	OF12	R	25	12	31	6	6	0	0	0	1	1	9	1	.194	.484
Rickey Peters	3B3, DH3, 2B2, OF1	B	23	12	19	3	5	0	0	0	2	1	3	0	.263	.263
Kirk Gibson	OF10	L	22	12	38	3	9	3	0	1	4	1	3	0	.237	.395
Dan Gonzales	OF3, DH1	L	25	7	18	1	4	1	0	0	2	0	5	0	.222	.278
1 Milt May	C5	L	28	5	11	1	3	0	0	0	2	2	0	0	.273	.455

NAME	T	AGE	W	L	PCT	SV	G	GS	CG	IP	H	BB	SO	SHO	ERA
TOTALS		27	85	76	.528	37	160	160	25	1423	1429	547	802	5	4.27
Jack Morris	R	24	17	7	.708	0	27	27	9	198	179	59	113	1	3.27
Milt Wilcox	R	29	12	10	.545	0	33	29	7	196	201	73	109	0	4.36
Aurelio Lopez	R	30	10	5	.667	21	61	0	0	127	95	51	106	0	2.41
Jack Billingham	R	36	10	7	.588	3	35	19	2	158	163	60	59	0	3.30
Pat Underwood	L	22	6	4	.600	0	27	15	1	122	128	29	83	0	4.57
Dan Petry	R	20	6	5	.545	0	15	15	2	98	90	33	43	0	3.95
Dave Rozema (SJ)	R	22	4	4	.500	0	16	16	4	97	101	30	33	1	3.53
John Hiller (SJ)	L	36	4	7	.364	9	43	0	0	79	83	55	46	0	5.24
Mike Chris	L	21	3	3	.500	0	13	8	0	39	46	21	31	0	6.92
Bruce Robbins	L	19	3	3	.500	0	10	8	0	46	45	21	22	0	3.91
Dave Tobik	R	26	3	5	.375	3	37	0	0	69	59	25	48	0	4.30
Kip Young	R	24	2	2	.500	0	13	7	0	44	60	11	22	0	6.34
Sheldon Burnside	L	24	1	1	.500	0	10	2	0	21	28	8	13	0	6.43
Fernando Arroyo	R	27	1	1	.500	0	8	1	0	18	27	3	5	0	8.25
Bruce Taylor	R	24	1	1	.333	0	10	0	0	19	16	7	8	0	4.74
Steve Baker	R	22	1	7	.125	1	21	12	0	84	97	51	54	0	6.10
Mark Fidrych (SJ)	R	24	0	3	.000	0	4	4	0	15	23	9	5	0	10.20

One win by forfeit

CLEVELAND — 6th 81-80 .503 22 — JEFF TORBORG 43-52 .453 — DAVE GARCIA 38-28 .576

Name	G by Pos	B	AGE	G	AB	R	H	2B	3B	HR	RBI	BB	SO	SB	BA	SA
TOTALS			28	161	5376	760	1388	206	29	138	707	657	786	143	.258	.384
Andre Thornton	1B130, DH13	R	29	143	515	89	120	31	1	26	93	90	93	5	.233	.449
Duane Kuiper	2B140	L	26	140	479	46	122	9	5	0	39	37	27	4	.255	.294
Tom Veryzer	SS148	R	26	149	449	41	99	9	3	0	34	34	54	2	.220	.254
Toby Harrah	3B127, DH4	R	30	149	527	99	147	25	1	20	77	89	60	20	.279	.444
Bobby Bonds	OF116, DH29	R	33	146	538	93	148	24	1	25	85	74	135	34	.275	.463
Rick Manning (LJ)	OF141, DH1	L	24	144	560	67	145	12	2	3	51	55	48	30	.259	.304
2 Mike Hargrove	OF65, 1B28, DH7	L	29	100	338	60	110	21	4	10	56	63	40	2	.325	.500
Gary Alexander	C91, DH13, OF2	R	26	110	358	54	82	9	2	15	54	46	100	4	.229	.391
2 Cliff Johnson	DH62, C1	R	31	72	240	37	65	10	0	18	61	24	39	2	.271	.538
Jim Norris	OF93, DH13	L	30	124	353	50	87	15	6	3	30	44	35	15	.246	.348
Ted Cox	3B52, OF16, 2B4, DH1	R	24	78	189	17	40	6	0	4	22	14	27	2	.212	.307
Ron Hassey	C68, 1B2, DH4	L	26	75	223	20	64	14	0	4	32	19	19	1	.287	.404
Ron Pruitt	OF29, DH14, C11, 3B3	R	27	64	166	23	47	7	0	2	21	19	21	2	.283	.361
Dave Rosello	2B33, 3B14, SS11	R	29	59	107	20	26	6	1	3	14	15	20	1	.243	.402
Dell Alston	OF30, DH7	L	26	54	62	10	18	0	2	1	12	10	10	4	.290	.403
1 Paul Dade	OF37, DH4, 3B2	R	27	44	170	22	48	4	1	3	18	12	22	12	.282	.371
Wayne Cage	DH9, 1B7	L	27	29	56	6	13	2	0	1	6	5	16	0	.232	.321
Horace Speed	OF16, DH4	R	27	26	14	6	2	0	0	0	1	3	7	2	.143	.143
Bo Diaz (BG)	C15	R	26	15	32	2	5	1	0	0	5	0	9	0	.156	.219

NAME	T	AGE	W	L	PCT	SV	G	GS	CG	IP	H	BB	SO	SHO	ERA
TOTALS		27	81	80	.503	32	161	161	21	1432	1502	570	781	7	4.57
Rick Waits	L	27	16	13	.552	0	34	34	8	231	230	91	91	3	4.44
Rick Wise	R	33	15	10	.600	0	34	34	9	232	229	68	108	2	3.72
Sid Monge	L	28	12	10	.545	19	76	0	0	131	96	64	108	0	2.40
Dan Spillner	R	27	9	5	.643	1	49	13	3	158	153	64	97	0	4.61
Mike Paxton	R	25	8	8	.500	0	33	24	3	160	210	52	70	0	5.91
Len Barker	R	23	6	6	.500	0	29	19	2	137	146	70	93	0	4.93
Wayne Garland (SJ)	R	28	4	10	.286	0	18	14	2	95	120	34	40	0	5.87
David Clyde (IL-XJ)	L	24	3	4	.429	0	9	8	1	46	50	13	17	0	5.91
Victor Cruz	R	21	3	9	.250	10	61	0	0	79	70	44	63	0	4.22
Paul Reuschel (SJ)	R	32	2	1	.667	1	17	1	0	45	73	11	22	0	8.00
Eric Wilkins (EJ)	R	22	2	4	.333	0	16	14	0	70	77	38	52	0	4.37
1 Don Hood	R	29	1	0	1.000	1	13	0	0	22	13	14	7	0	3.68
Larry Andersen	R	26	0	0	—	0	5	0	0	5	4	6	1	0	7.41
Sandy Wihtol	R	24	0	0	—	0	5	0	0	11	10	3	6	0	3.27

Name	G by Pos	B	AGE	G	AB	R	H	2B	3B	HR	RBI	BB	SO	SB	BA	SA
TORONTO	**7th 53-109 .327 50.5**				**ROY HARTSFIELD**											
TOTALS			27	162	5423	613	1362	253	34	95	562	448	663	75	.251	.363
John Mayberry	1B135	L	30	137	464	61	127	22	1	21	74	69	60	1	.274	.461
Danny Ainge (RL)	2B86, DH1	R	20	87	308	26	73	7	1	2	19	12	58	1	.237	.286
Alfredo Griffin	SS153	B	21	153	624	81	179	22	10	2	31	40	59	21	.287	.364
Roy Howell	3B133, DH4	L	25	138	511	60	126	28	4	15	72	42	91	1	.247	.405
Bob Bailor	OF118, 3B9, DH1	R	27	130	414	50	95	11	5	1	38	36	27	14	.229	.287
Rick Bosetti	OF162	R	25	162	619	59	161	35	2	8	65	22	70	13	.260	.362
Al Woods	OF127, DH2	L	25	132	436	57	121	24	4	5	36	40	28	6	.278	.385
Rick Cerone	C136	R	25	136	469	47	112	27	4	7	61	37	40	1	.239	.358
Rico Carty	DH129	R	39	132	461	48	118	26	0	12	55	46	45	3	.256	.390
Otto Velez	OF73, DH9, 1B6	R	28	99	274	45	79	21	0	15	48	46	45	0	.288	.529
Joe Cannon	OF50	L	25	61	142	14	30	1	1	1	5	1	34	12	.211	.254
Luis Gomez	3B22, 2B20, SS15	R	27	59	163	11	39	7	0	0	11	6	17	1	.239	.282
Dave McKay	2B46, 3B2	B	29	47	156	19	34	9	0	0	12	7	19	1	.218	.276
Tim Johnson	2B25, 3B9, 1B7	L	29	43	86	6	16	2	1	0	6	8	15	0	.186	.233
2 Tony Solaita	DH26, 1B6	L	32	36	102	14	27	8	1	2	13	17	16	0	.265	.422
Bob Davis	C32	R	27	32	89	6	11	2	0	1	8	6	15	0	.124	.180
2 Craig Kusick	1B20, DH1, P1	R	30	24	54	3	11	1	0	2	7	7	7	0	.204	.333
Ted Wilborn	OF7, DH4	B	20	22	12	3	0	0	0	0	0	0	1	7	.000	.000
Bob Robertson	1B9, DH4	R	32	15	29	1	3	0	0	1	1	3	9	0	.103	.207
1 Bobby Brown	OF4	B	25	4	10	1	0	0	0	0	0	0	2	1	.000	.000
Pedro Hernandez		R	20	3	1	0	0	0	0	0	0	0	0	0	—	—

NAME		T	AGE	W	L	PCT	SV	G	GS	CG	IP	H	BB	SO	SHO	ERA
			26	53	109	.327	11	162	162	44	1417	1537	594	613	7	4.82
Tom Underwood		L	25	9	16	.360	0	33	32	12	227	213	95	127	1	3.69
Dave Stieb		R	21	8	8	.500	0	18	18	7	129	139	48	52	1	4.33
Dave Lemanczyk (XJ)		R	28	8	10	.444	0	22	20	11	143	137	45	63	3	3.71
Tom Buskey (LJ)		R	32	6	10	.375	7	44	0	0	79	74	25	44	0	3.42
Phil Huffman		R	21	6	18	.250	0	31	31	2	173	220	68	56	1	5.77
Balor Moore		L	28	5	7	.417	0	34	16	5	139	135	79	51	0	4.86
Butch Edge		R	22	3	4	.429	0	9	9	1	52	60	24	19	0	5.19
Dave Freisleben		R	27	2	3	.400	3	42	2	0	91	101	53	35	0	4.95
Jim Clancy (FJ)		R	23	2	7	.222	0	12	11	2	64	65	31	33	0	5.48
Jesse Jefferson		R	30	2	10	.167	1	34	10	2	116	150	45	43	0	5.51
Tom Murphy		R	33	1	2	.333	1	10	0	0	18	23	8	6	0	5.50
Mark Lemongello		R	23	1	9	.100	0	18	10	2	83	97	34	40	0	6.29
2 Dyar Miller		R	33	0	0	—	0	10	0	0	15	27	5	7	0	10.80
Craig Kusick		R	30	0	0	—	0	1	0	0	4	3	0	0	0	4.50
Steve Grilli		R	30	0	0	—	0	1	0	0	2	1	0	1	0	0.00
Steve Luebber		R	29	0	0	—	0	1	0	0	1	1	0	0	0	∞
Jackson Todd		R	27	0	1	.000	0	12	1	0	32	40	7	14	0	5.91
Jerry Garvin (AJ)		L	23	0	1	.000	0	8	1	0	23	15	10	14	0	2.74
Mike Willis		L	28	0	3	.000	0	17	1	0	27	35	16	8	0	8.33

WEST DIVISION

CALIFORNIA	1st 88-74 .543				JIM FREGOSI											
TOTALS			29	162	5550	866	1563	242	43	164	808	589	843	100	.282	.429
Rod Carew (RJ)	1B103, DH6	L	33	110	409	78	130	15	3	3	44	73	46	18	.318	.391
Bobby Grich (XJ)	2B153	R	30	153	534	78	157	30	5	30	101	59	84	1	.294	.537
2 Bert Campaneris	SS82, DH1	R	37	85	239	27	56	4	4	0	15	19	32	12	.234	.285
Carney Lansford	3B157	R	22	157	654	114	188	30	5	19	79	39	115	20	.287	.436
Dan Ford	OF141	R	27	142	569	100	165	26	5	21	101	40	86	8	.290	.464
Rick Miller (BH)	OF117, DH2	L	31	120	427	60	125	15	5	2	28	50	69	5	.293	.365
Joe Rudi (BW)	OF80, 1B5, DH3	R	32	90	330	35	80	11	3	11	61	24	61	0	.242	.394
Brian Downing	C129, DH18	R	28	148	509	87	166	27	3	12	75	77	57	3	.326	.462
Don Baylor	DH65, OF97, 1B1	R	30	162	628	120	186	33	3	36	139	71	51	22	.296	.530
Willie Aikens	1B55, DH51	L	24	116	379	59	106	18	0	21	81	61	79	1	.280	.493
Jim Anderson	SS82, 3B10, 2B6, C3	R	22	96	234	33	58	13	1	3	23	17	31	3	.248	.350
2 Larry Harlow	OF58	L	27	62	159	22	37	8	2	0	14	25	34	1	.233	.308
Willie Davis	OF7, DH6	L	39	43	56	9	14	2	1	0	4	4	7	1	.250	.321
Tom Donohue	C38	R	26	38	107	13	24	3	1	3	14	3	29	2	.224	.355
Merv Rettenmund	DH17, OF9	R	36	35	76	7	20	2	0	1	10	11	14	1	.263	.329
Dickie Thon	2B24, SS8, 3B1, DH1	R	21	35	56	6	19	3	0	0	5	5	10	0	.339	.393
Rance Mulliniks	SS22	L	23	22	68	7	10	0	0	1	8	4	14	0	.147	.191
Bobby Clark	OF19	R	24	19	54	8	16	2	2	1	5	5	11	1	.296	.463
Orlando Ramirez	SS10, DH1	R	27	13	12	1	0	0	0	0	0	1	6	1	.000	.000
Terry Humphrey (SJ)	C9	R	29	9	17	2	1	0	0	0	0	0	5	0	.059	.059
2 Ralph Garr	DH6	L	33	6	24	0	3	0	0	0	0	0	3	0	.125	.125
Ike Hampton	1B2	B	27	4	5	0	2	0	0	0	1	0	1	0	.400	.400
John Harris	1B1	L	24	1	2	0	0	0	0	0	0	0	0	0	.000	.000
Brian Harper	DH1	R	19	1	2	0	0	0	0	0	0	0	1	0	.000	.000
1 Dave Chalk (KJ) 28																

		R	28	88	74	.543	33	162	162	46	1436	1463	573	820	9	4.34
Dave Frost		R	26	16	10	.615	1	36	33	12	239	226	77	107	2	3.58
Nolan Ryan		R	32	16	14	.533	0	34	34	17	223	169	114	223	5	3.59
Mark Clear		R	23	11	5	.688	14	52	0	0	109	87	68	98	0	3.63
Jim Barr		R	31	10	12	.455	0	36	25	5	197	217	55	69	0	4.20
Don Aase		R	24	9	10	.474	2	37	28	7	185	200	77	96	1	4.82
Frank Tanana (SJ)		L	25	7	5	.583	0	18	17	2	90	93	25	46	1	3.90
Dave LaRoche		L	31	7	11	.389	10	53	1	0	86	107	32	59	0	5.55
Chris Knapp (XJ)		R	25	5	5	.500	0	20	18	3	98	109	35	36	0	5.51
2 John Montague		R	31	2	0	1.000	6	14	0	0	18	16	9	6	0	5.00
Ralph Botting		L	24	2	0	1.000	1	3	3	0	30	46	15	22	0	8.70
Mike Barlow (NJ)		R	31	1	1	.500	0	35	0	0	86	106	30	33	0	5.13
Steve Eddy		R	21	1	1	.500	0	7	4	0	32	36	20	7	0	4.78
1 Dyar Miller		R	33	1	0	1.000	0	14	1	0	35	44	13	16	0	3.34
Bob Ferris		R	24	0	0	—	0	2	0	0	6	5	3	2	0	1.50
Dave Schuler		L	25	0	0	—	0	1	0	0	2	2	0	0	0	0.00

KANSAS CITY	2nd 85-77 .525 3				WHITEY HERZOG											
TOTALS			28	162	5653	851	1596	286	79	116	791	528	675	207	.282	.422
Pete LaCock	1B108, DH16	L	27	132	408	54	113	25	4	3	56	37	26	2	.277	.380
Frank White (BG)	2B125	R	28	127	467	73	124	26	4	10	48	25	54	28	.266	.403
Freddie Patek (NJ)	SS104	R	34	106	306	30	77	17	0	5	37	16	42	11	.252	.317
George Brett	3B149, 1B8, DH1	L	26	154	645	119	212	42	20	23	107	51	36	17	.329	.563
Al Cowens	OF134, DH1	R	27	136	516	69	152	18	7	9	73	40	44	10	.295	.444
Amos Otis	OF146, DH4	R	32	151	577	100	170	28	2	18	90	68	92	30	.295	.444
Willie Wilson	OF152, DH2	B	23	154	588	113	185	18	13	6	49	28	92	83	.315	.420
Darrell Porter	C141, DH15	L	27	157	533	101	155	23	10	20	112	121	65	3	.291	.484
Hal McRae	DH100	R	33	101	393	55	113	32	4	10	74	38	46	5	.288	.466
U.L. Washington	SS50, 2B46, DH3, 3B1	B	25	101	268	32	68	12	5	2	25	20	44	10	.254	.358
John Wathan	1B49, C23, DH11, OF3	R	29	90	199	26	41	7	3	2	28	7	24	2	.206	.302
Clint Hurdle	OF50, DH16, 3B1	L	21	59	171	16	41	10	3	3	30	28	24	0	.240	.386
Steve Braun (FJ)	OF18, DH11, 3B2	L	31	58	116	15	31	2	0	4	10	22	11	0	.267	.388
Todd Cruz	SS48, 3B9	R	23	55	118	9	24	7	0	2	15	3	19	0	.203	.314
Jamie Quirk	C9, DH9, SS5, 3B1	L	24	51	79	8	24	6	1	1	5	5	13	0	.304	.443
2 George Scott	1B41, DH2, 3B1	R	35	44	146	19	39	8	2	1	20	12	32	1	.267	.370
Jerry Terrell (BG)	3B19, 2B7, DH2, SS1, P1	R	32	31	40	5	12	3	0	1	2	1	1	1	.300	.450
1 Tom Poquette	OF10	L	27	21	26	1	5	0	0	0	3	1	4	0	.192	.192
Joe Zdeb	OF9	R	26	15	23	3	4	1	1	0	2	4	1	1	.174	.304
Jim Nettles	OF8, 1B1	L	32	11	23	0	2	0	0	0	1	3	2	0	.087	.087
German Barranca	3B1, 2B1, DH1	L	22	5	5	3	3	1	0	0	0	0	3	.600	.800
Jim Gaudet	C3	R	24	3	6	0	1	0	0	0	0	0	3	0	.167	.167

			29	85	77	.525	27	162	162	42	1448	1477	536	640	7	4.45
Paul Splittorff		L	32	15	17	.469	0	36	35	11	240	248	77	77	0	4.24
Dennis Leonard (EJ)		R	28	14	12	.538	0	32	32	12	236	226	56	126	5	4.08
Larry Gura		L	31	13	12	.520	0	39	33	7	234	226	73	85	1	4.46
Al Hrabosky		L	29	9	4	.692	11	58	0	0	65	67	41	39	0	3.74
Rich Gale		R	25	9	10	.474	0	34	31	2	182	197	99	103	1	5.64
Steve Busby		R	29	6	6	.500	0	22	12	4	94	71	64	45	0	3.64
Marty Pattin (NJ)		R	36	5	2	.714	3	31	7	1	94	109	21	41	0	4.60
Eduardo Rodriguez (LJ)		R	27	4	1	.800	2	29	1	1	74	79	34	26	0	4.86
Craig Chamberlain		R	22	4	4	.500	0	10	10	4	70	68	18	30	0	3.73
Dan Quisenberry		R	26	3	2	.600	5	32	0	0	40	42	7	13	0	3.15
Steve Mingori (SJ)		L	35	3	3	.500	1	30	1	0	47	69	17	18	0	5.74
Gary Christenson		L	26	0	0	—	0	9	1	0	16	12	2	4	0	3.27
Craig Eaton		R	24	0	0	—	0	5	0	0	10	8	3	4	0	2.70
1 George Throop		R	28	0	0	—	0	3	0	0	3	7	5	1	0	12.00
Jerry Terrell		R	32	0	0	—	0	1	0	0	3	5	1	0	0	6.00
Bill Paschall		R	25	0	1	.000	0	7	0	0	14	18	5	3	0	6.43
Renie Martin		R	23	0	3	.000	5	25	2	0	35	32	14	25	0	5.14

TEXAS	3rd 83-79 .512 5				PAT CORRALES											
TOTALS			28	162	5562	750	1549	252	26	140	718	461	607	79	.278	.409
Pat Putnam	1B96, DH32	R	25	139	426	57	118	19	2	18	64	23	50	1	.277	.458
Bump Wills	2B146	B	26	146	543	90	148	21	3	5	46	53	58	35	.273	.360
Nelson Norman	SS142, 2B1	B	21	147	343	36	76	9	3	0	21	19	41	4	.222	.265
Buddy Bell	3B147, SS33	R	27	162	670	89	200	42	3	18	101	30	45	5	.299	.451
Richie Zisk	OF134, DH3	R	30	144	503	69	132	21	1	18	64	57	75	1	.262	.416
2 Mickey Rivers	OF57	L	30	58	247	35	74	9	3	6	25	9	18	7	.300	.433
Al Oliver	OF119, DH10	L	32	136	492	69	159	28	4	12	76	34	34	4	.323	.470
Jim Sundberg	C150	R	28	150	495	50	136	23	4	5	64	51	51	3	.275	.368
Johnny Ellis	DH62, 1B30, C7	R	30	111	316	33	90	12	0	12	61	15	55	2	.285	.437
Billy Sample	OF103, DH9	R	24	128	325	60	95	21	2	5	35	37	28	8	.292	.415
Johnny Grubb (BG)	OF82	L	30	102	289	42	79	14	0	10	37	34	44	2	.273	.426
Mike Jorgensen (YJ)	1B60, OF20, DH2	L	30	90	157	21	35	7	0	6	16	14	29	0	.223	.382
Larvell Blanks (JJ)	SS49, 2B16, DH1	R	29	68	120	13	24	5	0	1	15	11	9	0	.200	.267
1 Oscar Gamble (BF)	DH37, OF21	L	29	64	161	27	54	6	0	8	32	37	15	2	.335	.522
2 Eric Soderholm	3B37, DH14, 1B2	R	30	63	147	15	40	4	0	4	19	12	9	0	.272	.395
D. Roberts	C14, OF11, 2B8, 1B6, DH4, 3B1	R	28	44	84	12	23	2	1	3	14	7	17	1	.262	.417
2 Willie Montanez	1B19, DH17	L	31	38	144	19	46	6	0	8	24	8	14	0	.319	.528
LaRue Washington	OF13, 3B1, DH1	R	25	25	18	5	5	0	0	0	0	2	1	4	.278	.278
Gary Gray	DH13	R	26	16	42	4	10	0	0	0	1	2	8	1	.238	.238
2 Dave Chalk	SS3, DH2, 2B1	R	28	9	20	5	5	0	0	0	1	2	0	0	.250	.250
1 Bert Campaneris	SS8	R	37	8	9	2	1	0	0	0	0	0	1	0	.111	.111
Greg Mahlberg	C7	R	26	7	17	2	2	1	0	0	1	2	4	0	.118	.294
Gary Holle	1B1	R	24	5	6	0	1	0	0	0	0	1	0	0	.167	.333

			28	83	79	.512	42	162	162	26	1437	1371	532	773	10	3.86
Steve Comer		R	25	17	12	.586	0	36	36	6	242	230	84	86	1	3.68
Ferguson Jenkins		R	35	16	14	.533	0	37	37	10	259	252	81	164	3	4.07
Jim Kern		R	30	13	5	.722	29	71	0	0	143	99	62	136	0	1.57
Doc Medich		R	30	10	7	.588	0	29	19	4	149	156	49	58	1	4.17
Jon Matlack (EJ)		L	29	5	4	.556	0	13	13	2	85	98	15	35	0	4.13
Doyle Alexander (XJ)		R	28	5	7	.417	0	23	18	0	113	114	69	50	0	4.46
Sparky Lyle		L	34	5	8	.385	13	67	0	0	95	78	28	48	0	3.13
Danny Darwin		R	23	4	4	.500	0	20	6	1	78	50	30	58	0	4.04
1 Ed Farmer		R	29	2	0	1.000	0	11	2	0	33	30	19	25	0	4.36
2 John Henry Johnson		L	22	2	6	.250	0	17	12	1	82	79	36	46	0	4.94
Larry McCall		R	26	1	0	1.000	0	2	1	0	8	7	3	5	0	4.50
Dave Rajsich		L	27	1	3	.250	0	27	3	0	54	56	18	32	0	3.50
Brian Allard		R	21	1	3	.250	0	4	3	0	33	36	13	14	0	4.36
1 Dock Ellis		R	34	1	5	.167	0	10	9	0	47	64	16	10	0	5.94
Bob Babcock		R	26	0	0	—	0	4	0	0	5	7	7	6	0	10.80
Jerry Don Gleaton		L	21	0	0	—	0	7	0	0	10	15	2	2	0	6.30

MINNESOTA — 4th 82-80 .506 6 — GENE MAUCH

Name	G by Pos	B	AGE	G	AB	R	H	2B	3B	HR	RBI	BB	SO	SB	BA	SA
TOTALS			27	162	5544	764	1544	256	46	112	714	526	693	66	.278	.402
Ron Jackson	1B157, SS1, 3B1, OF1	R	26	159	583	85	158	40	5	14	68	51	59	5	.271	.429
Rob Wilfong	2B133, OF3	L	25	140	419	71	131	22	6	9	59	29	54	11	.313	.458
Roy Smalley	SS161, 1B1	B	26	162	621	94	168	28	3	24	95	80	80	2	.271	.441
John Castino	3B143, SS5	R	24	148	393	49	112	13	6	5	52	27	72	5	.285	.397
Hosken Powell (BW)	OF93, DH5	L	24	104	338	49	99	17	3	2	36	33	25	5	.293	.379
Ken Landreaux	OF147	L	24	151	564	81	172	27	5	15	83	37	57	10	.305	.450
Bombo Rivera	OF105, DH2	R	26	112	263	37	74	13	5	2	31	17	40	5	.281	.392
Butch Wynegar	C146, DH2	B	23	149	504	74	136	20	0	7	57	74	36	2	.270	.351
Jose Morales	DH77, 1B1	R	34	92	191	21	51	5	1	2	27	14	27	0	.267	.335
Glenn Adams	DH55, OF53	L	31	119	326	34	98	13	1	8	50	25	27	2	.301	.420
Dave Edwards	OF86, DH3	R	25	96	229	42	57	8	0	8	35	24	45	4	.249	.389
Willie Norwood	OF71, DH14	R	28	96	270	32	67	13	3	6	30	20	51	9	.248	.385
Mike Cubbage (XJ)	3B63, DH21, 2B1, 1B1	L	28	94	243	26	67	10	1	2	23	39	26	1	.276	.350
Bob Randall	2B71, 3B7, SS1	R	31	80	199	25	49	7	0	0	14	15	17	2	.246	.281
Danny Goodwin	DH51, 1B8	L	25	58	159	22	46	8	5	5	27	11	23	0	.289	.497
Rick Sofield	OF35	L	22	35	93	8	25	5	0	0	12	12	27	2	.301	.355
Glenn Borgmann	C31	R	29	31	70	4	14	3	0	0	8	12	11	1	.200	.243
1 Craig Kusick	DH12, 1B8	R	30	24	54	8	13	4	0	3	6	3	11	0	.241	.481
Gary Ward	OF5, DH3	R	25	10	14	2	4	0	0	0	1	3	1	0	.286	.286
Jesus Vega	DH3	R	23	4	7	0	0	0	0	0	0	0	2	0	.000	.000
Dan Graham	DH1	L	24	2	4	0	0	0	0	0	0	0	0	0	.000	.000

NAME	T	AGE	W	L	PCT	SV	G	GS	CG	IP	H	BB	SO	SHO	ERA
TOTALS		28	82	80	.506	33	162	162	31	1444	1590	452	721	6	4.13
Jerry Koosman	L	36	20	13	.606	0	37	36	10	264	268	83	157	2	3.38
Dave Goltz	R	30	14	13	.519	0	38	35	12	251	282	69	132	1	4.16
Geoff Zahn (SJ)	L	33	13	7	.650	0	26	24	4	169	181	41	58	0	3.57
Mike Marshall	R	36	10	15	.400	32	90	1	0	143	132	48	81	0	2.64
Pete Redfern	R	24	7	3	.700	1	40	6	0	108	106	35	85	0	3.50
Paul Hartzell	R	25	6	10	.375	0	28	26	4	163	193	44	44	0	5.36
Mike Bacsik	R	27	4	2	.667	0	31	0	0	66	61	29	33	0	4.36
Darrell Jackson	L	23	4	4	.500	0	24	8	1	69	89	26	43	0	4.30
Roger Erickson	R	22	3	10	.231	0	24	21	0	123	154	48	47	0	5.63
Gary Serum	R	22	1	3	.250	0	20	5	0	64	93	20	31	0	6.61
1 Ken Brett	L	30	0	0	—	0	9	0	0	13	16	6	3	0	4.85
Jeff Holly	L	26	0	0	—	0	6	0	0	6	10	3	5	0	7.50
Kevin Stanfield	R	23	0	0	—	0	3	0	0	3	2	0	0	0	6.00
Paul Thormodsgard	R	25	0	0	—	0	1	0	0	1	3	0	1	0	9.00
Terry Felton	R	21	0	0	—	0	1	0	0	2	0	0	1	0	0.00

CHICAGO — 5th 73-87 .456 14 — DON KESSINGER 46-60 .434 — TONY LaRUSSA 27-27 .500

Name	G by Pos	B	AGE	G	AB	R	H	2B	3B	HR	RBI	BB	SO	SB	BA	SA
TOTALS			27	159	5463	730	1505	290	33	127	680	454	668	97	.275	.410
Lamar Johnson	1B94, DH37	R	28	133	479	60	148	29	1	12	74	41	56	0	.309	.449
Alan Bannister	2B65, OF47, 3B12, DH9, 1B1	R	27	136	506	71	144	28	8	2	55	43	40	22	.285	.383
Greg Pryor	SS119, 3B22, 2B25	R	29	143	476	60	131	23	3	3	34	25	41	3	.275	.355
Kevin Bell (SJ)	3B68, SS2	R	24	70	200	20	49	8	1	4	22	15	43	2	.245	.355
Claudell Washington	OF122, DH3	L	24	131	471	79	132	33	5	13	66	28	93	19	.280	.454
Chet Lemon	OF147, DH1	R	24	148	556	79	177	44	2	17	86	56	68	7	.318	.496
1 Ralph Garr	OF67, DH17	L	33	102	307	34	86	10	2	9	39	17	19	2	.280	.414
2 Milt May (SJ)	C65	L	28	65	202	23	51	13	0	7	28	14	27	0	.252	.421
Jorge Orta	DH62, 2B41	L	28	113	325	49	85	18	3	11	46	44	33	1	.262	.437
Mike Squires	1B110, OF1	L	27	122	295	44	78	10	1	2	22	22	9	15	.264	.325
Rusty Torres	OF85	B	30	90	170	26	43	5	0	8	24	23	37	1	.253	.424
Junior Moore	OF61, DH10, 2B2	R	26	88	201	24	53	8	2	1	23	12	20	0	.264	.328
Wayne Nordhagen	DH47, OF12, C5, P2	R	30	78	193	20	54	15	0	7	25	13	22	0	.280	.466
Jim Morrison	2B48, 3B29	R	26	67	240	38	66	14	0	14	35	15	48	11	.275	.508
Bill Nahorodny (KJ)	C60, DH3	R	25	65	179	20	46	10	0	6	29	18	23	0	.257	.413
1 Eric Soderholm	3B56	R	30	56	210	31	53	8	2	6	34	19	19	0	.252	.395
1 Don Kessinger (VR)*	SS54, 1B1, 2B1	B	36	56	110	14	22	6	0	1	7	10	12	1	.200	.282
Thad Bosley	OF28, DH1	L	26	56	77	13	24	1	1	1	8	9	14	4	.312	.390
Marv Foley	C33	L	25	34	97	6	24	3	0	2	10	7	5	0	.247	.340
Mike Colbern (EJ)	C32	R	24	32	83	5	20	5	1	0	8	4	25	0	.241	.325
Harry Chappas	SS23	R	21	26	59	9	17	1	0	0	4	5	5	1	.288	.356
Joe Gates	2B8, 3B1, OF1	B	24	16	16	1	1	0	1	0	1	2	3	1	.063	.188
Rusty Kuntz	OF5	R	24	5	11	0	1	0	0	0	0	2	6	0	.091	.091

*Kessinger retired as a player when he resigned as a manager

NAME	T	AGE	W	L	PCT	SV	G	GS	CG	IP	H	BB	SO	SHO	ERA
TOTALS		26	73	87	.456	37	159	159	28	1409	1365	618	675	9	4.10
Ken Kravec	L	27	15	13	.536	1	36	35	10	250	208	111	132	3	3.74
Rich Wortham	L	25	14	14	.500	0	34	33	5	204	195	100	119	0	4.90
Ross Baumgarten	L	24	13	8	.619	0	28	28	4	191	175	83	72	3	3.60
Steve Trout	L	21	11	8	.579	4	34	18	6	155	165	59	76	2	3.89
Francisco Barrios (SJ)	R	26	8	3	.727	0	15	15	2	95	88	33	28	0	3.60
2 Ed Farmer	R	29	3	7	.300	14	42	3	0	81	66	34	48	0	2.44
Mike Proly (EJ)	R	28	3	8	.273	9	38	6	0	88	89	40	32	0	3.89
Rich Dotson	R	20	2	0	1.000	0	5	5	1	24	28	6	13	1	3.75
Randy Scarbery	R	27	2	8	.200	4	45	5	0	101	102	34	45	0	4.63
Fred Howard	R	22	1	5	.167	0	28	4	0	68	73	32	36	0	3.57
1 Rich Hinton	L	32	1	1	.333	2	16	2	0	42	57	8	27	0	6.00
Britt Burns	L	20	0	0	—	0	6	0	0	5	10	1	2	0	5.40
Gil Rondon	R	25	0	0	—	0	4	0	0	10	11	6	3	0	3.60
Pablo Torrealba	L	31	0	0	—	0	3	0	0	6	5	2	1	0	1.50
LaMarr Hoyt	R	24	0	0	—	0	2	0	0	5	4	1	1	0	9.00
Wayne Nordhagen	R	30	0	0	—	0	2	0	0	2	4	1	0	0	9.00
Mark Esser	R	23	0	0	—	0	2	0	0	2	4	1	0	0	13.50
1 Jack Kucek	R	26	0	0	—	0	1	0	0	3	0	0	0	0	0.00
Dewey Robinson	R	22	0	0	1.000	0	11	0	0	14	11	9	5	0	6.43
Ron Schueler (RC-NJ)	R	31	0	0	1.000	0	8	0	0	20	19	13	6	0	7.20
1 Lerrin LaGrow	R	30	0	3	.000	1	11	2	0	18	27	16	9	0	9.00
Guy Hoffman	L	22	0	5	.000	0	24	0	0	30	30	23	18	0	5.40

One loss by forfeit

SEATTLE — 6th 67-95 .414 21 — DARRELL JOHNSON

Name	G by Pos	B	AGE	G	AB	R	H	2B	3B	HR	RBI	BB	SO	SB	BA	SA
TOTALS			29	162	5544	711	1490	250	52	132	676	515	725	126	.269	.404
Bruce Bochte	1B147	L	28	150	554	81	175	38	6	16	100	67	64	2	.316	.493
Julio Cruz (RJ)	2B107	B	24	107	414	70	112	16	2	1	29	62	61	49	.271	.326
Mario Mendoza	SS148	R	28	148	373	26	74	10	3	1	29	9	62	3	.198	.249
Dan Meyer	3B101, OF31, 1B15	L	26	144	525	72	146	21	7	20	74	29	35	11	.278	.459
Joe Simpson	OF105, DH3	L	27	120	265	29	75	11	0	2	27	11	21	6	.283	.347
Ruppert Jones	OF161	L	24	162	622	109	166	29	9	21	78	85	78	33	.267	.444
Leon Roberts	OF136, DH1	R	28	140	450	61	122	24	6	15	54	56	64	3	.271	.451
Larry Cox	C99	R	31	100	293	32	63	11	4	3	36	22	39	2	.215	.314
Willie Horton	DH162	R	36	162	646	77	180	19	5	29	106	42	112	1	.279	.458
Larry Milbourne	SS65, 2B49, 3B11	B	28	123	356	40	99	13	4	2	26	19	20	5	.278	.354
Tom Paciorek	OF75, 1B15	R	32	103	310	38	89	23	4	6	42	28	62	6	.287	.445
Bob Stinson	C91	R	33	95	247	19	60	8	0	6	28	33	38	1	.243	.348
Bill Stein (VJ)	3B67, 2B17, SS3	R	32	88	250	28	62	9	2	7	27	17	28	1	.248	.384
B. Valentine	SS29, OF15, 2B4, 3B4, C2, DH1	R	26	82	98	9	27	6	0	0	7	22	5	1	.276	.337
John Haie	OF42, DH2	L	25	54	63	6	14	3	0	2	7	12	26	0	.222	.365
Charlie Beamon	1B7, DH5, OF2	L	25	27	25	5	5	1	0	0	0	1	5	1	.200	.240
Rodney Craig	OF15	L	21	16	52	9	20	8	1	0	6	1	5	1	.385	.577
Juan Bernhardt		R	25	1	1	0	0	0	0	0	0	0	0	0	1.000	1.000

NAME	T	AGE	W	L	PCT	SV	G	GS	CG	IP	H	BB	SO	SHO	ERA
TOTALS		26	67	95	.414	26	162	162	37	1438	1567	571	736	7	4.58
Mike Parrott	R	24	14	12	.538	0	38	30	13	229	231	86	127	2	3.77
Rick Honeycutt	L	25	11	12	.478	0	33	28	8	194	201	67	83	1	4.04
Floyd Bannister	L	24	10	15	.400	0	30	30	6	182	185	68	115	2	4.05
Byron McLaughlin	R	23	7	7	.500	14	47	7	1	124	114	60	74	0	4.21
1 John Montague	R	31	6	4	.600	1	41	1	0	116	125	47	60	0	5.59
Shane Rawley (BH)	L	23	5	6	.357	11	48	3	0	84	88	40	48	0	3.86
Glenn Abbott (EJ)	R	28	4	10	.288	0	23	19	3	117	138	38	25	0	5.15
Rob Dressler	R	25	3	6	.600	0	21	14	2	104	134	22	36	0	4.93
Odell Jones	R	26	3	11	.214	0	25	19	3	119	151	58	72	0	6.05
Randy Stein	R	26	2	3	.400	0	23	1	0	41	48	27	39	0	5.93
Rafael Vasquez	R	21	1	0	1.000	0	16	0	0	16	23	9	9	0	5.06
1 Paul Mitchell	R	28	1	4	.200	0	10	6	1	37	46	15	18	0	4.38
Jim Lewis	R	23	0	0	—	0	2	0	0	10	1	0	0	0	18.00
Joe Decker	R	32	0	1	.000	0	9	0	0	27	27	14	12	0	4.33
Roy Branch	R	25	0	1	.000	0	4	1	0	12	7	6	0		8.18
2 Rich Hinton	L	32	0	0	.000	0	3	0	0	20	23	5	7	0	5.40
2 Wayne Twitchell	R	31	0	0	.000	0	2	0	0	14	11	10	5	0	5.14

OAKLAND — 7th 54-108 .333 34 — JIM MARSHALL

Name	G by Pos	B	AGE	G	AB	R	H	2B	3B	HR	RBI	BB	SO	SB	BA	SA
TOTALS			26	162	5348	573	1276	188	32	108	541	482	751	104	.239	.346
Dave Revering	1B104, DH18	L	26	125	472	63	136	25	5	19	77	34	65	1	.288	.483
Mike Edwards	2B113, SS3, DH2	R	26	122	400	35	93	12	2	1	23	15	37	10	.233	.280
Rob Picciolo	SS105, 2B6, 3B4, OF1	R	26	115	348	37	88	16	2	2	27	3	45	2	.253	.328
Wayne Gross	3B120, 1B18, OF2	L	27	138	442	54	99	19	1	14	50	72	62	4	.224	.387
Tony Armas (SJ)	OF80	R	25	80	278	29	69	9	3	11	34	16	67	1	.248	.421
1 Dwayne Murphy (RJ)	OF118	L	24	121	388	57	99	10	4	11	40	80	68	15	.255	.387
Rickey Henderson	OF88	R	20	89	351	49	96	13	3	1	26	34	39	33	.274	.336
Jeff Newman	C81, 1B46, 3B7, DH7	R	30	143	516	53	119	17	2	22	71	27	88	2	.231	.399
Mitchell Page	DH126, OF4	L	27	133	478	51	118	18	1	9	42	52	93	17	.247	.335
Larry Murray	OF90, 2B3	B	26	105	226	25	42	11	2	2	20	28	34	6	.186	.279
Jim Essian	C70, 3B10, 1B4, OF4, DH3	R	28	98	313	34	76	16	0	8	40	25	29	1	.243	.371
Mike Heath	OF46, C22, 3B1, DH3	R	24	74	258	19	66	8	0	3	27	17	18	1	.256	.322
3 Dave Chalk	2B37, 3B16, SS16	R	28	66	212	15	47	6	0	2	13	29	14	2	.222	.278
Mike Guerrero	SS43	R	29	46	166	12	38	5	0	0	13	10	10	0	.229	.259
Derek Bryant (JJ)	OF33, DH2	R	27	30	106	8	19	5	0	0	13	10	10	0	.179	.217
1 Miguel Dilone	OF25	R	24	30	91	15	17	7	1	0	4	7	6	8	.187	.275
Mickey Klutts (BG)	SS10, 2B8, 3B6, DH2	R	24	73	3	14	2	1	1	4	7	20	0	.192	.288
Joe Wallis (SJ)	OF23	L	27	23	74	3	4	2	1	1	6	5	20	0	.141	.205
Glenn Burke (VR)	OF23	R	26	23	89	4	19	4	0	0	4	10	3	0	.213	.258
Milt Ramirez	3B12, 2B11, SS8	R	29	28	62	4	10	1	4	0	3	5	8	0	.161	.210

NAME	T	AGE	W	L	PCT	SV	G	GS	CG	IP	H	BB	SO	SHO	ERA
TOTALS		26	54	108	.333	20	162	162	41	1429	1606	654	726	4	4.74
Rick Langford	R	27	12	16	.429	0	34	29	14	219	233	57	101	1	4.27
Steve McCatty	R	25	11	12	.478	0	31	23	8	186	207	80	87	0	4.21
Brian Kingman	R	24	8	7	.533	0	18	17	5	113	113	33	58	1	4.30
Mike Norris (HJ)	R	24	5	8	.385	0	29	18	3	146	146	94	96	0	4.81
Dave Heaverlo	R	28	4	11	.267	9	62	0	0	86	97	42	40	0	4.08
Dave Hamilton	L	31	3	4	.429	5	40	7	1	83	80	43	52	0	3.69
Jim Todd	R	31	2	5	.286	2	51	0	0	81	108	51	26	0	6.56
1 John Henry Johnson	L	22	2	8	.200	0	14	13	1	85	89	36	50	0	4.34
Mike Morgan	R	19	2	10	.167	0	13	13	2	77	102	50	17	0	5.96
Matt Keough	R	23	2	17	.105	0	30	28	7	177	220	78	95	1	5.03
Alan Wirth	R	23	1	0	1.000	0	9	1	0	14	22	13	6	0	6.00
Bob Lacey (NJ)	L	25	1	5	.167	4	42	0	0	48	66	24	33	0	5.81
Craig Minetto	L	25	1	5	.167	0	36	13	0	118	131	58	64	0	5.57

LINE SCORES

Team	1	2	3	4	5	6	7	8	9	10	11		R	H	E

AMERICAN LEAGUE CHAMPIONSHIPS: BALTIMORE (EAST) 3   CALIFORNIA (WEST) 1

Game 1   October 3 at Baltimore

| CAL | 1 0 1 0 0 1 0 0 0 0 0 | 3 7 1 |
| BAL | 0 0 2 1 0 0 0 0 0 3 | 6 6 0 |

Ryan, Montague (8)   Palmer, **Stanhouse** (10)

Game 2   October 4 at Baltimore

| CAL | 1 0 0 0 0 0 1 3 2 | 8 10 1 |
| BAL | 4 4 1 0 0 0 0 0 X | 9 11 1 |

Frost, Clear (2), Aase (8)   **Flanagan**, Stanhouse (8)

Game 3   October 5 at California

| BAL | 0 0 0 1 0 0 1 1 0 0 | 3 8 3 |
| CAL | 1 0 0 1 0 0 0 0 2 | 4 9 0 |

D. Martinez, Stanhouse (9)   Tanana, **Aase** (6)

Game 4   October 6 at California

| BAL | 0 0 2 1 0 0 5 0 0 | 8 12 1 |
| CAL | 0 0 0 0 0 0 0 0 0 | 0 6 0 |

McGregor   Knapp, LaRoche (3), Frost (4), Montague (7), Barlow (9)

NATIONAL LEAGUE CHAMPIONSHIPS: PITTSBURGH (EAST) 3   CINCINNATI (WEST) 0

Game 1 October 2 at Cincinnati

| PIT | 0 0 2 0 0 0 0 0 0 0 0 3 | 5 10 0 |
| CIN | 0 0 0 2 0 0 0 0 0 0 0 | 2 7 0 |

Candelaria, Romo (8), Tekulve (8), **Jackson** (10), D. Robinson (11)   Seaver, **Hume** (9), Tomlin (11)

Game 2 October 3 at Cincinnati

| PIT | 0 0 0 1 1 0 0 0 1 | 3 11 0 |
| CIN | 0 1 0 0 0 0 0 1 0 | 2 8 0 |

Bibby, Jackson (8), Romo (8), Tekulve (8), Roberts (9), **D. Robinson** (9)   Pastore, Tomlin (8), Hume (8), **Bair** (10)

Game 3 October 5 at Pittsburgh

| CIN | 0 0 0 0 0 1 0 0 0 | 1 8 1 |
| PIT | 1 1 2 2 0 0 0 1 X | 7 7 0 |

LaCoss, Norman (2), Leibrandt (4), Soto (5), Tomlin (7), Hume (8)   **Blyleven**

WORLD SERIES — PITTSBURGH (NL) 4 BALTIMORE (AL) 3

Game 1 October 10 at Baltimore

| PIT | 0 0 0 1 0 2 0 1 0 | 4 11 3 |
| BAL | 5 0 0 0 0 0 0 0 X | 5 6 3 |

Kison, Rooker (1), Romo (5), D. Robinson (6), Jackson (8)   **Flanagan**

Game 2 October 11 at Baltimore

| PIT | 0 2 0 0 0 0 0 0 1 | 3 11 2 |
| BAL | 0 1 0 0 0 1 0 0 0 | 2 6 1 |

Blyleven, **D. Robinson** (7), Tekulve (9)   Palmer, T. Martinez (8), **Stanhouse** (9)

Game 3 October 12 at Pittsburgh

| BAL | 0 0 2 5 0 0 1 0 0 | 8 13 0 |
| PIT | 1 2 0 0 0 1 0 0 0 | 4 9 2 |

McGregor   Candelaria, Romo (4), Jackson (7), Tekulve (8)

Game 4 October 13 at Pittsburgh

| BAL | 0 0 3 0 0 0 0 6 0 | 9 12 0 |
| PIT | 4 0 0 1 1 0 0 0 0 | 6 17 1 |

D. Martinez, Stewart (2), Stone (5), **Stoddard** (7)   Bibby, Jackson (6), D. Robinson (8), **Tekulve** (8)

Game 5 October 14 at Pittsburgh

| BAL | 0 0 0 0 1 0 0 0 0 | 1 6 2 |
| PIT | 0 0 0 0 0 2 3 X | 7 13 1 |

Flanagan, Stoddard (7), T. Martinez (7), Stanhouse (8)   Rooker, **Blyleven** (6)

Game 6 October 16 at Baltimore

| PIT | 0 0 0 0 0 0 2 2 0 | 4 10 0 |
| BAL | 0 0 0 0 0 0 0 0 0 | 0 7 1 |

Candelaria, Tekulve (7)   Palmer, Stoddard (9)

Game 7 October 17 at Baltimore

| PIT | 0 0 0 0 0 2 0 0 2 | 4 10 0 |
| BAL | 0 0 1 0 0 0 0 0 0 | 1 4 2 |

Bibby, D. Robinson (5), **Jackson** (5), **McGregor**, Stoddard (9), Flanagan (9), Tekulve (8)   Stanhouse (9), T. Martinez (9), D. Martinez (9)

COMPOSITE BATTING

NAME	POS	G	AB	R	H	2B	3B	HR	RBI	BA
Baltimore										
TOTALS		4	133	26	37	5	1	3	25	.278
Singleton	RF	4	16	4	6	2	0	0	2	.375
Bumbry	CF	4	16	5	4	0	1	0	0	.250
DeCinces	3B	4	13	4	4	1	0	0	0	.308
Murray	1B	4	12	3	5	0	0	1	5	.417
Dauer	2B	4	11	0	2	0	0	0	0	.182
Kelly	DH-LF	3	11	3	4	0	0	1	4	.364
Garcia	SS	3	11	1	3	0	0	0	2	.273
Dempsey	C	3	10	3	4	2	0	0	0	.400
May	DH	2	7	0	1	0	0	0	1	.143
Lowenstein	LF-PH	4	6	2	1	0	0	0	1	.167
Belanger	SS-PR	3	5	0	1	0	0	0	0	.200
Roenicke	LF-PH	2	5	1	1	0	0	0	0	.200
Skaggs	C	1	4	0	0	0	0	0	0	.000
Smith	2B	1	4	0	0	0	0	0	0	.000
Crowley	PH	2	2	0	1	0	0	0	1	.500
California										
TOTALS		4	137	15	32	7	0	3	14	.234
Carew	1B	4	17	4	7	3	0	0	1	.412
Ford	RF	4	17	2	5	1	0	2	4	.294
Lansford	3B	4	17	2	5	0	0	0	3	.294
Miller	CF	4	16	2	4	0	0	0	0	.250
Baylor	DH-LF	4	16	2	3	0	0	1	2	.188
Downing	C	4	15	1	3	0	0	0	1	.200
Grich	2B	4	13	0	2	1	0	0	1	.154
Anderson	SS	4	11	0	1	0	0	0	0	.091
Harlow	LF-PH	3	8	0	1	0	0	0	1	.125
Clark	LF	1	3	0	0	0	0	0	0	.000
Davis	PH	2	2	1	1	0	0	0	0	.500
Rettenmund	PH-DH	2	2	0	0	0	0	0	0	.000
Campaneris	SS	1	0	0	0	0	0	0	0	—
Thon	PR-SS	1	0	1	0	0	0	0	0	—
Pittsburgh										
TOTALS		3	105	15	28	3	2	4	14	.267
Ott	C	3	13	0	3	0	0	0	0	.231
Garner	2B-SS	3	12	4	5	0	1	1	1	.417
Foli	SS	3	12	1	4	1	0	0	0	.333
Parker	RF	3	12	2	4	0	0	0	3	.333
Madlock	3B	3	12	1	3	0	0	1	2	.250
Moreno	CF	3	12	3	3	0	1	0	0	.250
Stargell	1B	3	11	2	5	2	0	2	6	.455
Milner	LF	3	9	0	0	0	0	0	0	.000
B. Robinson	3B	3	4	0	0	0	0	0	0	.000
Blyleven	P	3	3	1	1	0	0	0	0	.333
Candelaria P 0-3, Easler PH 0-1, Jackson P 0-1, Tekulve P 0-1, Stennett 2B 0-0, Alexander PR 0-0, Bibby P 0-0, Roberts P 0-0, D. Robinson P 0-0, Romo P 0-0										
Cincinnati										
TOTALS		3	107	5	23	4	1	2	5	.215
Concepcion	SS	3	14	1	6	1	0	0	0	.429
Collins	RF	3	14	0	5	1	0	0	1	.357
Knight	3B	3	14	0	4	1	0	0	0	.286
Bench	C	3	12	1	3	0	1	1	1	.250
Driessen	1B	3	12	1	1	0	0	0	0	.083
Morgan	2B	3	11	0	0	0	0	0	0	.000
Foster	LF	3	10	1	2	0	0	1	2	.200
Geronimo	CF	2	7	0	1	0	0	0	0	.143
Cruz	CF-PH	2	5	1	1	0	0	0	0	.200
Auerbach PH 0-2, Seaver P 0-2, Spilman PH 0-2, Hume P 0-1, Norman P 0-1, Tomlin P 0-0, Bair P 0-0, LaCoss P 0-0, Leibrandt P 0-0, Pastore P 0-0, Soto P 0-0										
Pittsburgh										
TOTALS		7	251	32	81	18	1	3	32	.323
Moreno	CF	7	33	4	11	2	0	3	3	.333
Stargell	1B	7	30	7	12	4	0	3	7	.400
Foli	SS	7	30	6	10	1	1	0	3	.333
Parker	RF	7	29	2	10	3	0	0	4	.345
Garner	2B	7	24	4	12	4	0	0	5	.500
Madlock	3B	7	24	2	9	1	0	0	3	.375
B. Robinson	LF-PH	7	19	2	5	1	0	0	3	.263
Nicosia	C	4	16	1	1	0	0	0	0	.063
Ott	C	3	12	2	4	1	0	0	3	.333
Milner	LF	3	9	2	3	1	0	0	1	.333
Lacy	PH	4	4	0	1	0	0	0	0	.250
Bibby	P	2	4	0	0	0	0	0	0	.000
Sanguillen	PH	3	3	0	1	0	0	0	1	.333
Blyleven	P	2	3	0	0	0	0	0	0	.000
Candelaria	P	2	3	0	1	0	0	0	0	.333
Tekulve P 0-2, Rooker P 0-2, Easler 0-1, Stennett PH 1-1, Jackson P 0-1, Romo P 0-1, D. Robinson P 0-0, Kison P 0-0, Alexander PR-LF 0-0										
Baltimore										
TOTALS		7	233	26	54	10	1	4	23	.232
Singleton	RF	7	28	1	10	1	0	0	3	.357
Murray	1B	7	26	3	4	1	0	1	2	.154
DeCinces	3B	7	25	2	5	0	0	1	3	.200
Dempsey	C-PR	7	21	3	6	2	0	0	0	.286
Bumbry	CF-PH	7	21	3	3	0	0	0	1	.143
Garcia	SS	6	20	4	8	2	1	0	6	.400
Dauer	2B-PH	6	17	2	5	1	0	1	1	.294
Roenicke	LF-CF-PH	6	16	4	2	0	0	1	1	.125
Lowenstein	LF-PH	6	13	2	3	1	0	0	3	.231
Smith	2B-PH	4	7	1	2	0	0	0	0	.286
Ayala	LF-PH	4	6	1	2	0	0	1	2	.333
Belanger	SS-PR	3	5	0	0	0	0	0	0	.000
Flanagan	P	3	5	0	0	0	0	0	0	.000
Kelly	PH	5	4	0	1	0	0	0	1	.250
Crowley	PH	5	4	0	1	0	0	0	0	.250
McGregor	P	2	4	1	0	0	0	0	0	.000
Palmer	P	2	4	0	0	0	0	0	0	.000
Skaggs	C	2	3	1	1	0	0	0	0	.333
May PH 0-1, Stoddard P 1-1, Stewart P 0-1, T. Martinez P 0-0, Stanhouse P 0-0, D. Martinez P 0-0, Stone P 0-0										

COMPOSITE PITCHING

NAME	G	IP	H	BB	SO	W	L	SV	ERA
Baltimore									
TOTALS	4	36.1	32	7	13	3	1	0	2.97
McGregor	1	9	6	1	4	1	0	0	0.00
Palmer	1	9	7	2	3	0	0	0	3.00
D. Martinez	2	8.1	8	0	4	0	0	0	3.24
Flanagan	1	7	6	1	2	1	0	0	5.14
Stanhouse	3	3	5	3	0	1	1	0	6.00
California									
TOTALS	4	35.2	37	18	24	1	3	0	5.80
Ryan	1	7	4	3	8	0	0	0	1.29
Clear	1	5.2	4	2	3	0	0	0	4.76
Aase	2	5	4	2	6	1	0	0	1.80
Tanana	1	5	6	3	2	0	0	0	3.60
Frost	2	4.1	8	5	1	0	1	0	18.69
Montague	2	4	4	2	2	0	1	0	9.00
Knapp	1	2.1	5	1	0	0	1	0	7.71
LaRoche	1	1.1	2	1	1	0	0	0	6.75
Barlow	1	1	0	1	0	0	0	0	0.00
Pittsburgh									
TOTALS	3	30	23	11	26	3	0	1	1.50
Blyleven	1	9	8	0	9	1	0	0	1.00
Bibby	1	7	4	4	5	0	0	0	1.29
Candelaria	1	7	5	1	4	0	0	0	2.57
Tekulve	2	2.2	2	2	2	0	0	0	3.38
Jackson	2	2	1	1	2	1	0	0	0.00
D. Robinson	2	2	0	3	1	1	0	1	0.00
Romo	2	0.1	3	1	0	0	0	0	0.00
Roberts	1	0	0	0	0	0	0	0	—
Cincinnati									
TOTALS	3	29	28	13	13	0	3	0	4.34
Seaver	1	8	5	2	5	0	0	0	2.25
Pastore	1	7	7	3	1	0	0	0	2.57
Hume	3	4	6	0	2	0	1	0	6.75
Tomlin	3	3	3	2	3	0	0	0	0.00
Soto	1	2	0	0	1	0	0	0	0.00
Norman	1	2	4	1	1	0	0	0	18.00
LaCoss	1	1.2	4	0	0	0	1	0	10.80
Bair	1	1	2	1	0	0	1	0	9.00
Leibrandt	1	0.1	0	1	0	0	0	0	0.00
Pittsburgh									
TOTALS	7	62	54	26	41	4	3	3	3.19
Bibby	2	10.1	10	2	10	0	0	0	2.61
Blyleven	2	10	8	3	4	1	0	0	1.80
Tekulve	5	9.1	4	3	10	0	1	3	2.89
Candelaria	2	9	14	2	4	1	1	0	5.00
Rooker	2	8.2	5	3	4	0	0	0	1.04
D. Robinson	4	5	6	3	5	1	0	0	5.40
Romo	2	4.2	5	3	4	0	0	0	3.86
Jackson	4	4.2	1	2	2	1	0	0	0.00
Kison	1	0.1	3	2	0	0	1	0	108.00
Baltimore									
TOTALS	7	62	81	16	35	3	4	0	4.35
McGregor	2	17	16	2	8	1	1	0	3.18
Flanagan	3	15	18	2	13	1	1	0	3.00
Palmer	2	15	18	5	8	0	0	0	3.60
Stoddard	4	5	6	1	3	1	0	0	5.40
Stewart	1	2.2	4	1	0	0	0	0	9.00
Stone	1	2	4	2	2	0	0	0	9.00
D. Martinez	2	2	6	2	0	0	0	0	18.00
Stanhouse	3	2	6	3	0	0	1	0	13.50
T. Martinez	3	1.1	3	0	1	0	0	0	6.75

PITTSBURGH 1st 98-64 .605 — CHUCK TANNER

Name	G by Pos	B	AGE	G	AB	R	H	2B	3B	HR	RBI	BB	SO	SB	BA	SA
TOTALS			30	163	5561	775	1541	264	52	148	710	483	855	180	.272	.416
Willie Stargell	1B113	L	39	126	424	60	119	19	0	32	82	47	105	0	.281	.552
Rennie Stennett	2B102	R	28	108	319	31	76	13	2	0	24	24	25	1	.238	.292
2 Tim Foli	SS132	R	28	133	525	70	153	23	1	0	65	28	14	6	.291	.345
2 Bill Madlock	3B85	R	28	85	311	48	102	17	3	7	44	34	22	21	.328	.469
Dave Parker	OF158	L	28	158	622	109	193	45	7	25	94	67	101	20	.310	.526
Omar Moreno	OF162	L	26	162	695	110	196	21	12	8	69	51	104	77	.282	.381
Bill Robinson	OF125, 1B28, 3B3	R	36	148	421	59	111	17	6	24	75	24	81	13	.264	.504
Ed Ott	C116	L	27	117	403	49	110	20	2	7	51	26	62	0	.273	.385
Phil Garner	2B83, 3B78, SS14	R	30	150	549	76	161	32	8	11	59	55	74	17	.293	.441
John Milner	OF64, 1B48	L	29	128	326	52	90	9	4	16	60	53	37	3	.276	.475
Lee Lacy	OF41, 2B5	R	31	84	182	17	45	9	3	5	15	22	36	6	.247	.412
Steve Nicosia	C65	R	23	70	191	22	55	16	0	4	13	23	17	0	.288	.435
Manny Sanguillen	C8, 1B5	R	35	56	74	8	17	5	2	0	4	2	5	0	.230	.351
Mike Easler	OF4	L	28	55	54	8	15	1	1	2	11	8	13	0	.278	.444
Dale Berra	SS22, 3B22	R	22	44	123	11	26	5	0	3	15	11	17	0	.211	.325
Matt Alexander	OF11, SS1	R	32	44	13	16	7	0	1	0	1	0	0	13	.538	.692
1 Frank Taveras	SS11	R	29	11	45	4	11	3	0	1	0	0	2	2	.244	.311
Alberto Lois		R	23	11	0	6	0	0	0	0	0	0	0	0	—	—
Doe Boyland		L	24	4	3	0	0	0	0	0	0	0	2	0	.000	.000
Gary Hargis		R	22	1	0	0	0	0	0	0	0	0	0	0	—	—

NAME	T	AGE	W	L	PCT	SV	G	GS	CG	IP	H	BB	SO	SHO	ERA
		30	98	64	.605	52	163	163	24	1493	1424	504	904	7	3.41
John Candelaria	L	25	14	9	.609	0	33	30	8	207	201	41	101	0	3.22
Bruce Kison	R	29	13	7	.650	0	33	25	3	172	157	45	105	1	3.19
Jim Bibby	R	34	12	4	.750	0	34	17	4	138	110	47	103	1	2.80
Bert Blyleven	R	28	12	5	.706	0	37	37	4	237	238	92	172	0	3.61
Enrique Romo	R	31	10	5	.667	5	84	0	0	129	122	43	106	0	3.00
Kent Tekulve	R	32	10	8	.556	31	94	0	0	134	109	49	75	0	2.75
Grant Jackson	L	36	8	5	.615	14	72	0	0	82	67	35	39	0	2.96
Don Robinson	R	22	8	8	.500	0	29	25	4	161	171	52	96	0	3.86
2 Dave Roberts	L	34	5	2	.714	1	21	3	0	39	47	12	15	0	3.23
Jim Rooker	L	36	4	7	.364	0	19	17	1	104	106	39	44	0	4.59
1 Ed Whitson	R	24	2	3	.400	1	19	7	0	58	53	36	31	0	4.34
2 Joe Coleman	R	32	0	0	—	0	10	0	0	21	29	9	14	0	6.00
3 Dock Ellis	R	34	0	0	—	0	3	1	0	7	9	7	2	0	2.57
Rick Rhoden (SJ)	R	26	0	1	.000	0	1	1	0	5	5	2	2	0	7.20

MONTREAL 2nd 95-65 .594 2 — DICK WILLIAMS

Name	G by Pos	B	AGE	G	AB	R	H	2B	3B	HR	RBI	BB	SO	SB	BA	SA
TOTALS			27	160	5465	701	1445	273	42	143	651	432	890	121	.264	.408
Tony Perez	1B129	R	37	132	489	58	132	29	4	13	73	38	82	2	.270	.425
Rodney Scott	2B113, SS39	B	25	151	562	69	134	12	5	3	42	66	82	39	.238	.294
Chris Speier	SS112	R	29	113	344	31	78	13	1	7	26	43	45	0	.227	.331
Larry Parrish	3B153	R	25	153	544	83	167	39	2	30	82	41	101	5	.307	.551
Ellis Valentine	OF144	R	24	146	548	73	151	29	3	21	82	22	74	11	.276	.454
Andre Dawson	OF153	R	24	155	639	90	176	24	12	25	92	27	115	35	.275	.468
Warren Cromartie	OF158	L	25	158	659	84	181	46	5	6	46	38	78	6	.275	.396
Gary Carter	C138	R	25	141	505	74	143	26	5	22	75	40	62	3	.283	.485
Jerry White	OF43	B	26	88	138	30	41	7	1	3	18	21	23	8	.297	.428
Tommy Hutton	1B25, OF9	L	33	86	83	14	21	2	1	1	13	10	7	0	.253	.337
Dave Cash	2B47	R	31	76	187	24	60	11	1	2	19	12	12	7	.321	.422
Jim Mason	SS33, 3B6	R	29	40	71	3	13	5	1	0	6	7	16	0	.183	.282
2 Rusty Staub	1B22, OF1	L	35	38	86	9	23	3	0	3	14	14	10	0	.267	.407
1 Tony Solaita	1B13	L	32	29	42	5	12	4	0	1	7	11	16	0	.286	.452
Duffy Dyer	C27	R	33	28	74	4	18	6	0	1	8	9	17	0	.243	.365
Ken Macha	3B13, 1B2, OF2, C1	R	28	25	36	8	10	3	1	0	4	2	9	0	.278	.417
Tony Bernazard	2B14	B	22	22	40	11	12	2	0	1	8	15	12	1	.300	.425
2 John Tamargo	C4	B	27	12	21	0	8	2	0	0	5	3	3	0	.381	.476
Tim Raines		B	19	6	0	3	0	0	0	0	0	0	0	2	—	—
Randy Bass	1B1	L	25	1	1	0	0	0	0	0	0	0	0	0	.000	.000

NAME	T	AGE	W	L	PCT	SV	G	GS	CG	IP	H	BB	SO	SHO	ERA
		29	95	65	.594	39	160	160	33	1447	1379	450	813	18	3.14
Bill Lee	L	32	16	10	.615	0	33	33	6	222	230	46	59	3	3.04
Steve Rogers	R	29	13	12	.520	0	37	37	13	249	232	78	143	5	3.00
David Palmer	R	21	10	2	.833	2	36	11	2	123	110	30	72	1	2.63
Rudy May	L	34	10	3	.769	0	33	7	2	94	88	31	67	1	2.30
Dan Schatzeder	L	24	10	5	.667	1	32	21	3	162	136	59	106	0	2.83
Ross Grimsley	L	29	10	9	.526	0	32	27	2	151	199	41	42	0	5.36
Scott Sanderson	R	22	9	8	.529	1	34	24	5	168	148	54	138	3	3.43
Elias Sosa	R	29	8	7	.533	18	62	0	0	97	77	37	59	0	1.95
Stan Bahnsen	R	34	3	1	.750	5	55	0	0	94	80	42	71	0	3.16
Woody Fryman	L	39	3	6	.333	10	44	0	0	58	52	22	44	0	2.79
Bill Atkinson	R	24	2	0	1.000	1	10	0	0	14	9	4	7	0	1.93
2 Dale Murray	R	29	1	2	.333	1	9	0	0	13	14	3	4	0	13.50
Bob James	R	20	0	0	—	0	2	0	0	2	3	1	0		13.50
Bill Gullickson	R	20	0	0	—	0	1	0	0	1	2	0	0	0	0.00

ST. LOUIS 3rd 86-76 .531 12 — KEN BOYER

Name	G by Pos	B	AGE	G	AB	R	H	2B	3B	HR	RBI	BB	SO	SB	BA	SA
TOTALS			27	163	5734	731	1594	279	63	100	685	460	838	116	.278	.401
Keith Hernandez	1B160	L	25	161	610	116	210	48	11	11	105	80	78	11	.344	.513
Ken Oberkfell	2B117, 3B37, SS2	L	23	135	369	53	111	19	5	1	35	57	35	4	.301	.388
Garry Templeton	SS150	B	23	154	672	105	211	32	19	9	62	18	91	26	.314	.458
Ken Reitz	3B158	R	28	159	605	42	162	41	2	8	73	25	85	1	.268	.382
George Hendrick	OF138	R	29	140	493	67	148	27	1	16	75	49	62	2	.300	.456
Tony Scott	OF151	B	27	153	587	69	152	22	10	6	68	34	92	37	.259	.361
Lou Brock	OF98	L	40	120	405	56	123	15	4	5	38	23	43	21	.304	.398
Ted Simmons (BW)	C122	B	29	123	448	68	127	22	0	26	87	61	34	0	.283	.507
Jerry Mumphrey	OF114	B	26	124	339	53	100	10	3	3	32	26	39	8	.295	.369
Dane Iorg	OF39, 1B10	L	29	79	179	12	52	11	1	1	21	12	28	1	.291	.380
Mike Tyson (KJ)	2B71	R	29	75	190	18	42	8	2	5	20	13	28	2	.221	.363
Bernie Carbo	OF17	L	31	52	64	6	18	1	0	3	12	10	22	1	.281	.438
Mike Phillips	SS25, 2B16, 3B1	L	28	44	97	10	22	3	1	1	6	10	9	0	.227	.309
Steve Swisher	C33	R	27	38	73	4	11	1	1	1	3	6	17	0	.151	.233
Terry Kennedy	C32	L	23	33	109	11	31	7	0	2	17	8	20	0	.284	.404
Roger Freed	1B1	R	33	34	31	2	8	2	0	2	8	5	8	0	.258	.516
Tommy Herr	2B6	B	23	14	10	4	2	0	0	0	1	2	2	1	.200	.200
Jim Lentine	OF8	R	24	11	23	2	9	1	0	0	1	3	6	0	.391	.435
Tommy Grieve	OF5	R	31	9	15	1	3	1	0	0	0	4	1	0	.200	.267
Keith Smith	OF5	R	26	6	13	1	3	0	0	0	0	0	1	0	.231	.231
Mike Dimmel	OF5	R	24	6	3	1	1	0	0	0	0	0	0	0	.333	.333

NAME	T	AGE	W	L	PCT	SV	G	GS	CG	IP	H	BB	SO	SHO	ERA
		27	86	76	.531	25	163	163	38	1487	1449	501	788	10	3.72
Silvio Martinez	R	23	15	8	.652	0	32	29	7	207	204	67	102	2	3.26
Pete Vuckovich	R	26	15	10	.600	0	34	32	9	233	229	64	145	0	3.59
Bob Forsch	R	29	11	11	.500	0	33	32	7	219	215	52	92	1	3.82
John Fulgham	R	23	10	6	.625	0	20	19	10	146	123	26	75	2	2.53
Mark Littell	R	26	9	4	.692	13	63	0	0	82	60	39	67	0	2.20
John Denny	R	26	8	11	.421	0	31	31	5	206	206	100	99	2	4.85
Buddy Schultz (SJ)	L	28	4	3	.571	3	31	0	0	42	40	14	38	0	4.50
Bob Sykes (SJ)	L	24	4	3	.571	0	13	11	0	67	88	34	35	0	6.18
Roy Thomas	R	26	3	4	.429	1	26	6	0	77	66	24	44	0	2.92
Tom Bruno	R	26	2	3	.400	0	27	1	0	38	37	22	27	0	4.26
George Frazier	R	24	2	4	.333	0	25	0	0	32	35	12	14	0	4.50
Darold Knowles	L	37	2	5	.286	6	48	0	0	49	54	17	22	0	4.04
Dan O'Brien	R	25	1	1	.500	0	6	0	0	11	21	3	5	0	8.18
John Urrea	R	24	0	0	—	0	2	0	0	11	13	9	5	0	4.09
Kim Seaman	L	22	0	0	—	0	3	0	0	2	2	3	0	0	0.00
Will McEnaney	L	27	0	3	.000	2	45	0	0	64	60	16	15	0	2.95

PHILADELPHIA 4th 84-78 .519 14 — DANNY OZARK 65-67 .492 — DALLAS GREEN 19-11 .633

Name	G by Pos	B	AGE	G	AB	R	H	2B	3B	HR	RBI	BB	SO	SB	BA	SA
TOTALS			30	163	5463	683	1453	250	53	119	641	602	764	128	.266	.396
Pete Rose	1B159, 3B5, 2B1	B	38	163	628	90	208	40	5	4	59	95	32	20	.331	.430
Manny Trillo (BA)	2B118	R	28	118	431	40	112	22	1	6	42	20	59	4	.260	.357
Larry Bowa	SS146	B	33	147	539	74	130	17	11	0	31	61	32	20	.241	.314
Mike Schmidt	3B157, SS2	R	29	160	541	109	137	25	4	45	114	120	115	9	.253	.564
Bake McBride	OF147	L	30	151	582	82	163	16	12	12	60	41	77	25	.280	.411
Garry Maddox	OF140	R	29	148	548	70	154	28	6	13	61	17	71	26	.281	.425
Greg Luzinski	OF125	R	28	137	452	47	114	23	1	18	81	56	103	3	.252	.427
Bob Boone (KJ)	C117, 3B2	R	31	119	398	38	114	21	3	9	58	49	33	1	.286	.422
Greg Gross	OF73	L	26	111	174	21	58	6	3	0	15	29	5	5	.333	.402
Del Unser	OF30, 1B22	L	34	95	141	26	42	8	0	6	29	14	23	2	.298	.482
Tim McCarver	C31, OF1	L	37	79	137	13	33	5	1	1	12	19	12	2	.241	.314
Mike Anderson	OF70, P1	R	28	79	78	12	18	4	0	1	2	13	14	3	.231	.321
Bud Harrelson (VR)	2B25, SS17, 3B9, OF1	B	35	53	71	7	20	6	0	0	1	5	6	3	.282	.366
Dave Rader	C25	L	30	31	54	3	11	1	1	1	5	6	7	0	.204	.315
Rudy Meoli	SS16, 2B15, 3B1	L	28	30	73	2	13	4	1	0	4	9	15	2	.178	.260
1 Jose Cardenal	OF12, 1B1	R	35	29	48	4	10	2	0	0	9	8	1	2	.208	.271
Ramon Aviles	2B27	R	27	27	61	7	17	2	2	0	6	2	8	0	.279	.311
Lonnie Smith	OF11	R	23	17	30	4	5	2	0	0	3	4	5	2	.167	.233
Keith Moreland	C13	R	25	14	48	3	18	5	0	0	7	2	5	0	.375	.521
Pete Mackanin (AJ)	3B2, 2B2, SS2	R	27	13	9	2	1	0	1	0	0	2	1	0	.111	.444
John Poff	OF4, 1B1	L	26	12	19	2	2	1	0	0	1	0	6	0	.105	.158
John Vukovich	3B7, 2B3	R	31	10	31	0	6	0	0	0	1	1	6	0	.200	.267

NAME	T	AGE	W	L	PCT	SV	G	GS	CG	IP	H	BB	SO	SHO	ERA
		29	84	78	.519	29	163	163	33	1441	1455	477	787	14	4.16
Steve Carlton	L	34	18	11	.621	0	35	35	13	251	202	89	213	4	3.62
Nino Espinosa	R	25	14	12	.538	0	33	33	8	212	211	65	88	3	3.65
Ron Reed	R	36	13	8	.619	5	61	0	0	102	110	32	58	0	4.15
Randy Lerch	L	24	10	13	.435	0	37	35	6	214	228	60	92	1	3.74
Dick Ruthven (EJ)	R	28	7	5	.583	0	20	20	3	122	121	37	58	2	4.28
Larry Christenson (BC)	R	25	5	10	.333	0	19	17	2	106	118	30	53	0	4.50
Tug McGraw	L	34	4	3	.571	16	65	1	0	84	83	29	57	0	5.14
Dickie Noles	R	22	3	4	.429	0	14	14	0	90	80	38	42	0	3.80
Rawly Eastwick	R	28	3	6	.333	6	51	0	0	83	90	25	47	0	4.88
Doug Bird	R	29	2	0	1.000	0	32	1	1	61	73	16	33	0	5.16
Warren Brusstar (SJ)	R	27	1	0	1.000	1	13	0	0	14	8	4	3	0	7.07
2 Jack Kucek	R	26	1	0	1.000	0	4	0	0	4	6	1	2	0	9.00
1 Jim Kaat	L	40	1	0	1.000	0	4	0	0	4	6	1	2	0	4.50
Dan Larson	R	24	1	1	.500	0	3	1	0	19	17	9	9	0	4.26
Kevin Saucier	L	22	1	4	.200	1	29	2	0	62	68	33	21	0	4.21
Mike Anderson	R	28	0	0	—	0	1	0	0	1	1	0	0	0	0.00
Jim Lonborg	R	37	0	0	—	0	1	0	0	7	14	4	7	0	11.57

CHICAGO   5th 80-82 .494 18   HERMAN FRANKS 78-77 .503   JOEY AMALFITANO 2-5 .286

Name	G by Pos	B	AGE	G	AB	R	H	2B	3B	HR	RBI	BB	SO	SB	BA	SA
TOTALS			29	162	5550	706	1494	250	43	135	663	478	762	73	.269	.403
Bill Buckner	1B140	L	29	149	591	72	168	34	7	14	66	30	28	1	.284	.437
1 Ted Sizemore	2B96	R	34	98	330	36	82	17	0	2	24	32	25	1	.248	.318
Ivan DeJesus	SS160	R	26	160	636	92	180	26	10	5	52	59	82	24	.283	.379
Steve Ontiveros	3B142, 1B1	R	27	152	519	58	148	28	2	4	57	58	68	0	.285	.370
Scot Thompson	OF100	L	23	128	346	36	100	13	5	2	29	17	37	4	.289	.373
Jerry Martin	OF144	R	30	150	534	74	145	34	3	19	73	38	85	2	.272	.453
Dave Kingman	OF139	R	30	145	532	97	153	19	5	48	115	45	131	4	.288	.613
Barry Foote	C129	R	27	132	429	47	109	26	0	16	56	34	49	5	.254	.427
Larry Biittner	OF44, 1B32	L	33	111	272	35	79	13	3	3	50	21	23	1	.290	.393
Steve Dillard	2B60, 3B9	R	28	89	166	31	47	6	1	5	24	17	24	1	.283	.422
Mike Vail	OF39, 3B2	R	27	87	179	28	60	8	2	7	35	14	27	0	.335	.520
Mick Kelleher	3B32, 2B29, SS14	R	31	73	142	14	36	4	1	0	10	7	9	2	.254	.296
Tim Blackwell	C63	B	26	63	122	8	20	3	1	0	12	32	25	0	.164	.205
2 Ken Henderson	OF23	R	33	62	81	11	19	2	0	2	8	15	16	0	.235	.333
1 Bobby Murcer	OF54	L	33	58	190	22	49	4	1	7	22	36	20	2	.258	.400
2 Miguel Dilone	OF22	B	24	43	36	14	11	0	0	0	1	2	5	15	.306	.306
1 Sammy Mejias	OF23	R	27	31	11	4	2	0	0	0	0	2	5	0	.182	.182
Steve Macko	2B10, 3B4	R	24	19	40	2	9	1	0	0	3	4	8	0	.225	.250
Gene Clines (RC)		R	32	10	10	0	2	0	0	0	0	0	1	0	.200	.200
Bruce Kimm	C9	R	28	9	11	0	1	0	0	0	0	0	0	0	.091	.091
Kurt Seibert	2B1	B	23	7	2	2	0	0	0	0	0	0	1	0	.000	.000
Steve Davis	2B2, 3B1	R	25	3	4	0	0	0	0	0	0	0	1	0	.000	.000
Karl Pagel	1B		24	1	1	0	0	0	0	0	0	0	0	0	.000	.000

NAME	T	AGE	W	L	PCT	SV	G	GS	CG	IP	H	BB	SO	SHO	ERA
		27	80	82	.494	44	162	162	20	1447	1500	521	933	11	3.88
Rick Reuschel	R	30	18	12	.600	0	36	36	5	239	251	75	125	1	3.62
Lynn McGlothen	R	29	13	14	.481	2	42	29	6	212	236	55	147	1	4.12
2 Dick Tidrow	R	32	11	5	.688	4	63	0	0	103	86	42	68	0	2.71
Dennis Lamp	R	26	11	10	.524	0	38	32	6	200	223	46	86	1	3.51
Mike Krukow	R	27	9	9	.500	0	38	28	0	165	172	81	119	0	4.20
Bruce Sutter	R	26	6	6	.500	37	62	0	0	101	67	32	110	0	2.23
Ken Holtzman (XJ)	L	33	6	9	.400	0	23	20	3	118	133	53	44	2	4.58
Willie Hernandez	L	24	4	4	.500	0	51	2	0	79	85	39	53	0	5.01
Donnie Moore	R	25	4	4	.500	1	39	1	0	73	95	25	43	0	5.18
Bill Caudill	R	22	1	7	.125	0	29	12	0	90	89	41	104	0	4.80
1 Ray Burris	R	28	0	0	—	0	14	0	0	22	23	15	14	0	6.14
Dave Geisel	L	24	0	0	—	0	7	0	0	15	10	4	5	0	0.60
2 Doug Capilla	L	27	0	1	.000	0	13	1	0	17	14	7	10	0	2.65
George Riley	L	22	0	1	.000	1	4	1	0	13	16	6	5	0	5.54

NEW YORK   6th 63-99 .389 35   JOE TORRE

Name	G by Pos	B	AGE	G	AB	R	H	2B	3B	HR	RBI	BB	SO	SB	BA	SA
TOTALS			28	163	5591	593	1399	255	41	74	558	498	817	135	.250	.350
1 Willie Montanez	1B108	L	31	109	410	36	96	19	0	5	47	25	48	0	.234	.317
Doug Flynn	2B148,	R	28	157	555	35	135	19	5	4	61	17	46	0	.243	.317
2 Frank Taveras	SS153	R	29	153	635	89	167	26	9	1	33	33	72	42	.263	.337
Richie Hebner	3B134, 1B6	R	31	136	473	54	127	25	2	10	79	59	59	5	.268	.436
Joel Youngblood	OF147, 2B13, 3B12	R	27	158	590	90	162	37	5	16	60	60	84	18	.275	.436
Lee Mazzilli	OF143, 1B15	B	24	158	597	78	181	34	4	15	79	93	74	34	.303	.449
Steve Henderson (NJ)	OF94	R	26	98	350	42	107	16	8	5	39	38	58	13	.306	.440
John Stearns	C121, 1B16, 3B11, OF6	R	27	155	538	58	131	29	2	9	66	52	57	15	.243	.355
Elliott Maddox (NJ-LJ)	OF65, 3B11	R	31	86	224	21	60	13	0	1	12	20	27	3	.268	.339
Ed Kranepool	OF8, 1B29	L	34	82	155	7	36	5	0	2	17	13	18	0	.232	.303
Alex Trevino	C36, 3B27, 2B8	R	21	79	207	24	56	11	1	0	20	20	27	2	.271	.333
Gil Flores	OF32	R	26	70	93	9	18	1	1	1	10	8	17	2	.194	.258
Ron Hodges	C22	L	30	59	86	4	14	4	0	0	5	19	16	0	.163	.209
Bruce Boisclair (BW)	OF24, 1B1	L	26	59	98	7	18	5	1	0	4	3	20	0	.184	.255
Dan Norman	OF33	R	24	44	110	9	27	3	1	3	11	10	26	2	.245	.373
Kelvin Chapman	2B22, 3B1	R	23	35	80	7	12	1	2	0	4	5	15	0	.150	.213
Sergio Ferrer	3B12, SS5, 2B4	B	28	32	7	1	0	0	0	0	0	2	0	0	.000	.000
2 Jose Cardenal (BH)	OF9, 1B2	R	35	11	37	8	11	4	0	2	4	6	1	1	.297	.568
1 Tim Foli	SS3	R	28	3	7	0	0	0	0	0	0	0	0	0	.000	.000

NAME	T	AGE	W	L	PCT	SV	G	GS	CG	IP	H	BB	SO	SHO	ERA
		27	63	99	.389	36	163	163	16	1483	1486	607	819	10	3.84
Craig Swan	R	28	14	13	.519	0	35	35	10	251	241	57	145	3	3.30
Kevin Kobel (NJ)	L	25	6	8	.429	0	30	27	1	162	169	46	67	1	3.50
Neil Allen (VJ)	R	21	6	10	.375	8	50	5	0	99	100	47	65	0	3.55
Pete Falcone	L	25	6	14	.300	0	33	31	1	184	194	76	113	1	4.16
Pat Zachry (AJ)	R	27	5	1	.833	0	7	7	1	43	44	21	17	0	3.56
1 Wayne Twitchell	R	31	5	3	.625	0	33	2	0	64	55	55	44	0	5.20
2 Andy Hassler	L	24	4	4	.444	4	29	8	1	80	74	42	53	0	3.71
1 Dale Murray	R	29	4	8	.333	4	58	0	0	97	105	52	37	0	4.82
2 Dock Ellis	R	34	3	7	.300	0	17	14	1	85	110	34	41	0	6.04
Skip Lockwood (SJ)	R	32	2	5	.286	9	27	0	0	42	33	14	42	0	1.50
Tom Hausman	R	26	2	6	.250	2	29	10	1	79	66	19	33	0	2.73
Roy Lee Jackson	R	25	1	0	1.000	0	8	0	0	16	11	5	10	0	2.25
Juan Berenguer	R	24	1	1	.500	0	5	5	0	31	28	12	25	0	2.90
Jesse Orosco	L	22	1	2	.333	0	18	2	0	35	33	22	22	0	4.89
Jeff Reardon	R	23	1	2	.333	2	18	0	0	21	12	9	10	0	1.71
Mike Scott	R	24	1	3	.250	0	18	9	0	52	59	20	21	0	5.37
Ed Glynn	L	26	1	4	.200	7	46	0	0	60	57	40	32	0	3.00
3 Ray Burris (BW)	R	28	0	0	—	0	4	4	0	22	21	6	10	0	3.27
Johnny Pacella	R	22	0	2	.000	0	3	3	0	16	16	4	12	0	4.50
Dwight Bernard	R	27	0	3	.000	2	18	1	0	44	59	26	20	0	4.70
Bob Apodaca 29 (EJ)															
Bobby Myrick 26 (SA)															

WEST DIVISION

CINCINNATI   1st 90-71 .559   JOHN McNAMARA

Name	G by Pos	B	AGE	G	AB	R	H	2B	3B	HR	RBI	BB	SO	SB	BA	SA
TOTALS			29	161	5477	731	1445	266	31	132	686	614	902	99	.264	.396
Dan Driessen	1B143	L	27	150	515	72	129	24	3	18	75	62	77	11	.250	.414
Joe Morgan	2B121	L	35	127	436	70	109	26	1	9	32	93	45	28	.250	.376
Dave Concepcion	SS148	R	31	149	590	91	166	25	3	16	84	64	73	19	.281	.415
Ray Knight	3B149	R	26	150	551	64	175	37	4	10	79	38	57	4	.318	.454
Ken Griffey (KJ)	OF93	L	29	95	380	62	120	27	4	8	32	36	39	12	.316	.471
Cesar Geronimo	OF118	L	31	123	356	38	85	17	4	4	38	37	56	1	.239	.343
George Foster (LJ)	OF116	R	30	121	440	68	133	18	3	30	98	59	105	0	.302	.561
Johnny Bench	C126, 1B2	R	31	130	464	73	128	19	0	22	80	67	73	4	.276	.459
Dave Collins	OF91, 1B10	B	26	122	396	59	126	16	4	3	35	27	48	16	.318	.402
Junior Kennedy	2B59, SS5, 3B8	R	28	83	220	29	60	7	0	1	17	28	31	4	.273	.318
2 Paul Blair	OF67	R	35	75	140	7	21	4	1	2	15	11	27	0	.150	.236
2 Heity Cruz	OF69	R	26	74	182	24	44	10	2	4	27	31	39	0	.242	.385
Rick Auerbach	3B18, SS16, 2B3	R	29	62	100	17	21	8	1	1	12	14	19	0	.210	.340
Vic Correll	C47	R	33	43	113	14	31	12	0	1	15	14	26	0	.233	.346
Harry Spilman	1B12, 3B4	L	24	43	56	7	12	3	0	0	5	7	5	0	.214	.268
1 Champ Summers	OF13, 1B6	L	33	27	60	10	12	2	1	1	11	13	15	0	.200	.317
Arturo DeFreitas	1B6, OF1	R	26	23	34	2	7	2	0	0	2	0	10	0	.206	.265
1 Ken Henderson (FJ)	OF2	B	33	10	13	1	3	1	0	0	2	0	2	0	.231	.308
2 Sammy Mejias	OF5	B	27	9	2	1	1	0	0	0	0	0	0	1	.500	.500
Rafael Santo Domingo		B	23	7	6	0	1	0	0	0	0	0	1	3	.167	.167
Ron Oester	SS2	B	23	5	1	0	0	0	0	0	0	0	0	0	.000	.000

NAME	T	AGE	W	L	PCT	SV	G	GS	CG	IP	H	BB	SO	SHO	ERA
		28	90	71	.559	40	161	161	27	1440	1415	485	773	10	3.58
Tom Seaver	R	34	16	6	.727	0	32	32	9	215	187	61	131	5	3.14
Mike LaCoss	R	23	14	8	.636	0	35	32	6	206	202	79	73	1	3.50
Doug Bair	R	29	11	7	.611	16	65	0	0	94	93	51	86	0	4.31
Fred Norman	L	36	11	13	.458	0	34	31	5	195	193	57	95	0	3.65
Tom Hume	R	26	10	9	.526	17	57	12	2	163	162	53	80	0	2.76
Bill Bonham (SJ)	R	30	7	5	.583	0	29	29	2	176	173	60	78	0	3.78
Frank Pastore	R	21	6	7	.462	4	30	9	2	95	102	23	63	1	4.26
Paul Moskau	R	25	5	4	.556	0	21	15	1	106	107	51	58	0	3.91
Mario Soto (XJ)	R	22	3	2	.600	0	25	0	0	37	33	30	32	0	5.35
Dave Tomlin	L	30	2	2	.500	1	53	0	0	58	59	18	30	0	2.64
1 Pedro Borbon	R	32	2	2	.500	2	30	0	0	45	48	8	23	0	3.40
1 Doug Capilla	L	27	1	0	1.000	0	3	0	0	6	7	5	0	0	9.00
Charlie Leibrandt	R	22	0	0	—	0	3	0	0	4	4	2	1	0	0.00
Manny Sarmiento	R	23	0	4	.000	0	23	0	0	39	47	7	23	0	4.62

HOUSTON   2nd 89-73 .549 1.5   BILL VIRDON

Name	G by Pos	B	AGE	G	AB	R	H	2B	3B	HR	RBI	BB	SO	SB	BA	SA
TOTALS			27	162	5394	583	1382	224	52	49	542	461	745	190	.256	.344
Cesar Cedeno	1B91, OF40	R	28	132	470	57	123	27	4	6	54	64	52	30	.262	.374
Art Howe (LJ)	2B68, 3B59, 1B3	R	32	118	355	32	88	15	2	6	33	36	37	3	.248	.352
Craig Reynolds	SS143	L	26	146	555	63	147	20	9	0	39	21	49	12	.265	.333
Enos Cabell	3B132, 1B51	R	29	155	603	60	164	30	5	6	67	21	68	37	.272	.368
Jeff Leonard	OF123	R	23	134	411	47	119	15	5	0	47	46	68	23	.290	.350
Terry Puhl	OF152	L	22	157	600	87	172	22	4	8	49	58	46	30	.287	.387
Jose Cruz	OF156	L	31	157	558	73	161	33	7	9	72	72	66	36	.289	.421
Alan Ashby (BG)	C105	B	27	108	336	25	68	15	2	2	35	26	70	0	.202	.277
Rafael Landestoy	2B114, SS3	B	26	129	282	33	76	9	6	0	30	29	24	13	.270	.344
Denny Walling	OF42	L	25	82	147	21	48	8	4	3	31	17	21	3	.327	.497
Julio Gonzalez	2B32, SS21, 3B9	R	26	68	181	16	45	5	2	0	10	5	14	2	.249	.298
Bruce Bochy	C55	R	24	56	122	11	28	4	0	1	6	13	25	0	.217	.271
Jimmy Sexton	SS11, 3B4, 2B2	R	27	52	43	8	9	0	0	0	1	7	7	1	.209	.209
1 Bob Watson	OF6, 1B4	R	33	84	163	15	39	4	0	3	18	16	23	0	.239	.319
Jesus Alou	OF6, 1B1	R	37	42	43	3	11	4	0	0	10	6	1	0	.256	.349
Luis Pujols	C28	R	26	75	171	7	39	5	1	0	14	8	40	0	.227	.275
Danny Heep	OF2	L	21	14	14	0	2	1	0	0	1	1	2	0	.143	.143
Reggie Baldwin	C3, 1B1	R	24	14	20	0	4	1	0	0	1	0	6	0	.200	.250
Dave Bergman	1B4	L	26	13	15	4	6	1	0	0	4	4	5	0	.400	.600
Alan Knicely	C3, 3B1	R	24	7	6	0	4	2	0	0	2	1	6	0	.667	.833
Tom Wiedenbauer	OF3	R	20	4	6	0	4									

NAME	T	AGE	W	L	PCT	SV	G	GS	CG	IP	H	BB	SO	SHO	ERA
		27	89	73	.549	31	162	162	55	1448	1278	504	854	19	3.20
Joe Niekro	R	34	21	11	.656	0	38	38	11	264	221	107	119	5	3.00
J.R. Richard	R	29	18	13	.581	0	38	38	19	292	220	98	313	4	2.71
Joaquin Andujar	R	26	12	12	.500	4	46	23	8	194	168	88	77	0	3.43
Ken Forsch (AJ)	R	32	11	6	.647	0	26	24	10	178	155	35	58	2	3.03
Joe Sambito	L	27	8	7	.533	22	63	0	0	91	80	23	83	0	1.78
Rick Williams	R	26	4	7	.364	0	31	16	2	121	122	30	37	2	3.27
Bert Roberge (EJ)	R	24	3	0	1.000	4	26	0	0	32	20	17	13	0	1.69
Randy Niemann	R	23	3	2	.600	1	26	7	3	67	68	22	24	2	3.76
Frank Riccelli (EJ)	R	26	2	2	.500	0	11	2	0	22	22	18	20	0	4.09
Vern Ruhle	R	28	2	6	.250	0	13	10	2	66	64	8	33	2	4.09
2 George Throop	R	28	1	0	1.000	0	14	0	0	22	23	11	15	0	3.27
Pete Ladd	R	22	1	1	.500	0	10	0	0	12	8	8	6	0	3.00
Tom Dixon (SJ-BW)	R	24	1	3	.333	0	19	1	0	26	39	15	9	0	6.58
2 Frank LaCorte	R	27	1	3	.333	0	12	3	0	27	21	10	24	0	5.00
1 Bo McLaughlin	R	24	1	3	.333	0	12	3	0	16	22	4	12	0	5.63
Gary Wilson	R	24	0	0	—	0	6	0	0	7	15	6	6	0	12.86
Gordy Pladson	R	23	0	1	.000	0	4	0	0	8	12	2	3	0	4.50
Bobby Sprowl	L	23	0	1	.000	0	3	0	0	3	4	4	3	0	0.00
Mike Mendoza	R	23	0	0	—	0	2	0	0	6	6	0	0	0	0.00

Name	G by Pos	B	AGE	G	AB	R	H	2B	3B	HR	RBI	BB	SO	SB	BA	SA

LOS ANGELES 3rd 79-83 .488 11.5 TOMMY LASORDA

Name	G by Pos	B	AGE	G	AB	R	H	2B	3B	HR	RBI	BB	SO	SB	BA	SA
TOTALS			31	162	5490	739	1443	220	24	183	713	556	834	106	.263	.412
Steve Garvey	1B162	R	30	162	648	92	204	32	1	28	110	37	59	3	.315	.497
Davey Lopes	2B152	L	34	153	582	109	154	20	6	28	73	97	88	44	.265	.464
Bill Russell	SS150	R	30	153	627	72	170	26	4	7	56	24	43	6	.271	.359
Ron Cey	3B150	R	31	150	487	77	137	20	1	28	81	86	85	3	.281	.499
Reggie Smith	OF82	B	34	68	234	41	64	13	1	10	32	31	50	6	.274	.466
Derrel Thomas	OF119, 3B18, 2B5, SS3, 1B1	B	28	141	406	47	104	15	4	5	44	41	49	18	.256	.350
Dusty Baker	OF150	R	30	151	554	86	152	29	1	23	88	56	70	11	.274	.455
Steve Yeager	C103	R	30	105	310	33	67	9	2	13	41	29	68	1	.216	.384
Joe Ferguson	C67, OF52	R	32	122	363	54	95	14	0	20	69	70	68	1	.262	.466
Gary Thomasson	OF100, 1B1	L	27	115	315	39	78	11	1	14	45	43	70	4	.248	.422
Von Joshua	OF46	L	31	94	142	22	40	7	1	3	14	7	23	1	.282	.408
Ted Martinez	3B23, SS21, 2B18	R	31	81	112	19	30	5	1	0	2	4	16	3	.268	.330
Manny Mota	OF1	R	41	47	42	1	15	0	0	0	3	3	4	0	.357	.357
Mickey Hatcher	OF19, 3B17	R	24	33	93	9	25	4	1	1	5	7	12	1	.269	.366
Vic Davalillo	OF3	L	42	29	27	2	7	1	0	0	2	2	0	0	.259	.296
Johnny Oates	C20	L	33	26	46	4	6	2	0	0	2	4	1	0	.130	.174
Pedro Guerrero	OF12, 1B8, 3B3	R	23	25	62	7	15	2	0	2	9	1	14	2	.242	.371
Rick Monday (FJ)	OF10	L	33	12	33	2	10	0	0	0	5	5	6	0	.303	.303

NAME		T	AGE	W	L	PCT	SV	G	GS	CG	IP	H	BB	SO	SHO	ERA
			27	79	83	.488	34	162	162	30	1444	1425	555	811	6	3.83
Rick Sutcliffe		R	23	17	10	.630	0	39	30	5	242	217	97	117	1	3.46
Don Sutton		R	34	12	15	.444	1	33	32	6	226	201	61	146	1	3.82
Burt Hooton		R	29	11	10	.524	0	29	29	12	212	191	63	129	1	2.97
Charlie Hough		R	31	7	5	.583	0	42	14	0	151	152	66	76	0	4.77
Jerry Reuss		L	30	7	14	.333	3	39	21	4	160	178	60	83	1	3.54
2 Lerrin LaGrow (SJ)		R	30	5	1	.833	4	31	0	0	37	38	18	22	0	3.41
Bob Welch (SA)		R	22	5	6	.455	5	25	12	1	81	82	32	64	0	4.00
Dave Patterson		R	22	4	1	.800	6	36	0	0	53	62	22	34	0	5.26
2 Ken Brett		L	30	4	3	.571	2	30	0	0	47	52	12	13	0	3.45
Bobby Castillo		R	24	2	0	1.000	7	19	0	0	24	26	13	25	0	1.13
Andy Messersmith (AJ)		R	33	2	4	.333	0	11	11	1	62	55	34	26	0	4.94
Joe Beckwith		R	24	1	2	.333	2	17	0	0	37	42	15	28	0	4.38
Terry Forster (EJ)		L	27	1	2	.333	2	17	0	0	16	18	11	8	0	5.63
Doug Rau (SJ)		L	30	1	5	.167	0	11	11	1	56	73	22	28	1	5.30
Dennis Lewallyn		R	25	0	0	.000	0	7	0	0	12	19	5	1	0	5.25
1 Lance Rautzhan		L	26	0	2	.000	1	12	0	0	10	9	11	5	0	7.20
Gerald Hannahs		L	26	0	2	.000	1	4	2	0	16	10	13	6	0	3.38

SAN FRANCISCO 4th 71-91 .438 19.5 JOE ALTOBELLI 61-79 .436 DAVE BRISTOL 10-12 .455

Name	G by Pos	B	AGE	G	AB	R	H	2B	3B	HR	RBI	BB	SO	SB	BA	SA
TOTALS			28	162	5395	672	1328	192	36	125	616	580	925	140	.246	.365
Willie McCovey	1B89	L	41	117	353	34	88	9	0	15	57	36	70	0	.249	.402
Joe Strain	2B67, 3B1	R	25	67	257	27	62	8	1	1	12	13	21	8	.241	.292
Johnnie LeMaster	SS106	R	25	108	343	42	87	11	2	3	29	23	55	9	.254	.324
Darrell Evans	3B159	L	32	160	562	68	142	23	2	17	70	91	80	6	.253	.391
Jack Clark	OF140, 1B4	R	23	143	527	84	144	25	2	26	86	63	95	11	.273	.476
Billy North	OF130	B	31	142	460	87	119	15	4	5	30	96	84	58	.259	.341
Terry Whitfield	OF106	L	26	133	394	52	113	20	4	5	44	36	47	5	.287	.396
Marc Hill (BW)	C58, 1B1	R	27	63	169	20	35	3	0	3	15	26	25	0	.207	.278
Mike Ivie	1B98, OF24, 3B4, 2B1	R	26	133	402	58	115	18	3	27	89	47	80	5	.286	.547
Larry Herndon	OF122	R	25	132	354	35	91	14	5	7	36	29	70	8	.257	.384
Roger Metzger	SS78, 2B10, 3B1	B	31	94	259	24	65	7	8	0	31	23	31	11	.251	.340
Rob Andrews	2B53, 3B3	R	26	75	154	22	40	3	0	2	9	14	19	11	.260	.318
1 Bill Madlock	2B63, 1B5	R	28	69	249	37	65	9	2	7	41	18	19	11	.261	.398
Dennis Littlejohn	C63	R	24	63	193	15	38	6	1	1	13	21	46	0	.197	.254
Mike Sadek	C60, OF1	L	33	63	126	14	30	5	0	1	11	15	24	1	.238	.302
Max Venable	OF25	L	22	55	85	12	14	1	1	0	3	10	18	3	.165	.200
Greg Johnston	OF17	L	24	42	74	5	15	2	0	1	7	2	17	0	.203	.270
1 John Tamargo	C17	B	27	30	60	7	12	3	0	2	6	4	8	0	.200	.350
1 Heity Cruz	OF6, 3B2	R	26	16	25	2	3	0	0	0	1	3	7	0	.120	.120
Bob Kearney	C1	R	22	2	0	0	0	0	0	0	0	0	1	0	—	—

NAME		T	AGE	W	L	PCT	SV	G	GS	CG	IP	H	BB	SO	SHO	ERA
			29	71	91	.438	34	162	162	25	1436	1484	577	880	6	4.16
Vida Blue		L	29	14	14	.500	0	34	34	10	237	246	111	138	0	5.01
John Curtis		L	31	10	9	.526	0	27	18	3	121	121	42	85	2	4.17
Bob Knepper		L	25	9	12	.429	0	34	34	6	207	241	77	123	2	4.65
Gary Lavelle		L	30	7	9	.438	20	70	0	0	97	86	42	80	0	2.51
Tom Griffin		R	31	5	6	.455	2	59	3	0	94	83	46	82	0	3.93
Ed Halicki (IL)		R	28	5	8	.385	0	33	19	3	126	134	47	81	1	4.57
2 Ed Whitson		R	24	5	8	.385	0	18	17	2	100	98	39	62	0	3.96
Greg Minton (KJ)		R	27	4	3	.571	4	46	0	0	80	59	27	33	0	1.80
2 Pedro Borbon		R	32	4	3	.571	3	30	0	0	46	56	13	26	0	4.89
Phil Nastu		L	24	3	4	.429	0	25	14	1	100	105	41	47	0	4.32
John Montefusco (AJ)		R	29	3	8	.273	0	22	22	0	137	145	51	76	0	3.94
Randy Moffitt (SJ)		R	30	2	5	.286	2	28	0	0	35	53	14	16	0	7.71
1 Joe Coleman		R	32	0	—		0	5	0	0	4	3	2	0	0	0.00
Ed Plank		R	27	0	—		0	4	0	0	4	4	2	1	0	6.75
Al Holland		L	26	0	—		0	3	0	0	7	3	5	7	0	0.00
1 Dave Roberts		L	34	0	2	.000	3	26	1	0	42	42	18	23	0	2.57

SAN DIEGO 5th 68-93 .422 22 ROGER CRAIG

Name	G by Pos	B	AGE	G	AB	R	H	2B	3B	HR	RBI	BB	SO	SB	BA	SA
TOTALS			28	161	5446	603	1316	193	53	93	559	534	770	100	.242	.348
Gene Tenace	1B72, C94	R	32	151	463	61	122	16	4	20	67	105	106	2	.263	.445
Fernando Gonzalez	2B103, 3B3	R	29	114	323	22	70	13	2	9	34	18	34	0	.217	.359
Ozzie Smith	SS155	B	24	156	587	77	124	18	6	0	27	37	37	28	.211	.262
2 Paul Dade	3B70, OF4	R	27	76	283	38	78	19	2	1	19	14	48	13	.276	.367
Dave Winfield	OF157	R	27	159	597	97	184	27	10	34	118	85	71	15	.308	.558
Gene Richards	OF132	L	25	150	545	77	152	17	9	4	41	47	62	24	.279	.365
Jerry Turner	OF115	L	25	138	448	55	111	23	2	9	61	34	58	4	.248	.368
Bill Fahey	C68	L	29	73	209	14	60	8	1	3	19	21	17	1	.287	.378
Kurt Bevacqua	3B64, 2B16, 1B8, OF8	R	32	114	297	23	75	12	4	1	34	38	25	2	.253	.330
Dan Briggs	1B50, OF44	L	26	104	227	34	47	4	3	8	30	18	45	2	.207	.357
Bill Almon	2B61, SS25, OF1	R	26	100	198	20	45	3	0	1	8	21	48	6	.227	.258
2 Jay Johnstone	OF45, 1B22	L	33	75	201	10	59	8	2	0	32	18	21	1	.294	.353
Broderick Perkins	1B28	L	24	57	87	8	23	0	0	0	8	8	12	0	.264	.264
Barry Evans	3B53, SS2, 2B1	R	22	56	162	9	35	5	0	1	14	5	16	0	.216	.265
1 Mike Hargrove	1B37	L	29	52	125	15	24	5	0	0	8	25	15	0	.192	.232
Fred Kendall	C40, 1B2	R	30	46	102	8	17	2	0	1	6	11	7	0	.167	.216
Jim Wilhelm	OF30	R	26	39	103	8	25	4	3	0	8	2	12	1	.243	.340
Don Reynolds	OF14	L	26	30	45	6	10	1	2	0	6	7	6	0	.222	.333
Tim Flannery	2B22	L	21	22	65	2	10	0	1	0	4	4	5	0	.154	.185
Bobby Tolan	1B5, OF1	L	33	22	21	2	4	0	1	0	2	0	2	0	.190	.286
Brian Greer	OF4	R	20	4	3	0	0	0	0	0	0	0	1	0	.000	.000
Sam Perlozzo	2B2	R	28	2	2	0	0	0	0	0	0	0	0	0	.000	.000

NAME		T	AGE	W	L	PCT	SV	G	GS	CG	IP	H	BB	SO	SHO	ERA
			29	68	93	.422	25	161	161	29	1453	1438	513	779	7	3.69
Gaylord Perry (JT)		R	40	12	11	.522	0	32	32	10	233	225	67	140	0	3.05
Randy Jones		L	29	11	12	.478	0	39	39	6	263	257	64	112	0	3.63
Rollie Fingers (EJ)		R	32	9	9	.500	13	54	0	0	84	91	37	65	0	4.50
John D'Acquisto		R	27	9	13	.409	2	51	11	1	134	140	86	97	1	4.90
Bob Shirley		L	25	8	16	.333	0	49	25	4	205	196	59	117	1	3.38
Eric Rasmussen		R	27	6	9	.400	3	45	20	5	157	142	42	54	3	3.27
Bob Owchinko		L	24	6	12	.333	0	42	20	2	149	144	55	66	0	3.74
Steve Mura (EJ)		R	24	4	4	.500	2	38	5	0	73	57	37	59	0	3.08
Mark Lee		R	26	2	4	.333	5	46	1	0	65	88	25	25	0	4.29
Juan Eichelberger		R	25	1	1	.500	0	3	3	1	21	15	11	12	0	3.43
Dennis Kinney		L	27	0	—		0	13	0	0	18	17	8	11	0	3.50
Tom Tellmann		R	25	0	0		0	3	0	0	3	7	0	1	0	15.00
Mickey Lolich		L	38	0	2	.000	0	27	5	0	49	59	22	20	0	4.78

ATLANTA 6th 66-94 .413 23.5 BOBBY COX

Name	G by Pos	B	AGE	G	AB	R	H	2B	3B	HR	RBI	BB	SO	SB	BA	SA
TOTALS			26	160	5422	669	1389	220	28	126	626	490	818	98	.256	.377
Dale Murphy (KJ)	1B76, C27	R	23	104	384	53	106	7	2	21	57	38	67	6	.276	.469
Jerry Royster	2B77, 3B80	R	26	154	601	103	164	25	6	3	51	62	59	35	.273	.349
Pepe Frias	SS137	R	30	140	475	41	123	18	4	1	44	20	36	3	.259	.320
Bob Horner (NJ)	3B82, 1B45	R	21	121	487	66	153	15	1	33	98	22	77	0	.314	.552
Gary Matthews	OF156	R	28	156	631	97	192	34	5	27	90	60	75	18	.304	.502
Rowland Office	OF97	L	26	124	277	35	69	14	2	2	37	27	33	5	.249	.336
Jeff Burroughs	OF110	R	28	116	397	49	89	14	1	11	47	73	75	2	.224	.348
Bruce Benedict	C76	R	23	76	204	14	46	11	0	0	15	33	18	1	.225	.279
Barry Bonnell	OF124, 3B1	R	25	127	375	47	97	20	3	12	45	26	55	8	.259	.424
Mike Lum	1B51, OF3	L	33	111	217	27	54	6	0	6	27	18	34	0	.249	.359
Glenn Hubbard	2B91	R	21	97	325	34	75	12	0	3	29	27	43	4	.231	.295
Joe Nolan	C74	L	28	89	230	28	57	9	3	4	21	27	28	1	.248	.365
Charlie Spikes	OF15	R	28	66	93	12	26	8	0	3	17	6	23	0	.280	.462
Darrel Chaney	SS39, 2B5, 3B4, C1	B	31	63	117	15	19	5	0	0	10	19	34	2	.162	.205
Biff Pocoroba (SJ)	C7	B	25	28	38	6	12	4	0	0	4	7	0	1	.316	.421
Eddie Miller	OF27	B	22	27	113	12	35	1	0	0	5	5	24	15	.310	.319
Bob Beall	1B3	B	31	17	15	1	2	2	0	0	1	3	4	0	.133	.267
Larry Whisenton	OF13	L	22	13	37	3	9	2	1	0	3	6	9	1	.243	.351
Jim Wessinger	2B2	R	23	10	7	2	0	0	0	0	0	1	1	0	.000	.000
Brian Asselstine (LJ)	OF1	L	25	8	10	1	1	0	0	0	0	0	5	0	.100	.100
Mike Macha	3B3	R	25	6	13	2	2	0	0	0	1	1	0	0	.154	.154

NAME		T	AGE	W	L	PCT	SV	G	GS	CG	IP	H	BB	SO	SHO	ERA
			28	66	94	.413	34	160	160	32	1408	1496	494	779	3	4.18
Phil Niekro		R	40	21	20	.512	0	44	44	23	342	311	113	208	1	3.39
Rick Matula		R	25	8	10	.444	0	28	23	3	171	193	64	67	0	4.16
Buddy Solomon		R	28	7	14	.333	0	31	30	4	186	184	51	96	0	4.21
Tony Brizzolara		R	22	6	9	.400	0	20	19	2	107	133	33	64	0	5.30
Gene Garber		R	31	6	16	.273	25	68	0	0	106	121	24	56	0	4.33
Joey McLaughlin		R	22	5	3	.625	5	37	0	0	69	54	34	40	0	2.48
Mickey Mahler		L	26	5	11	.313	0	26	18	1	100	123	47	71	0	5.85
Larry McWilliams (EJ)		L	25	3	2	.600	0	13	13	1	66	69	22	32	0	5.59
Larry Bradford		L	29	1	0	1.000	2	21	0	0	19	11	10	11	0	0.95
2 Bo McLaughlin		R	25	1	1	.500	0	37	1	0	50	63	16	45	0	4.86
Preston Hanna (AJ)		R	24	1	1	.500	0	4	4	0	24	27	15	15	0	3.00
Adrian Devine		R	27	1	2	.333	0	40	0	0	67	84	25	22	0	3.22
Craig Skok		L	30	1	3	.250	2	44	0	0	54	58	17	30	0	4.00
Rick Mahler		R	25	0	0		0	15	0	0	22	28	11	12	0	6.14
1 Frank LaCorte		R	27	0	—		0	3	0	0	8	9	5	6	0	7.88
Jamie Easterly		L	26	0	0		0	3	0	0	3	3	1	0	0	12.00
Tommy Boggs		R	23	0	2	.000	0	3	3	0	13	21	4	1	0	6.23

1980
Anything Worth Waiting For...

When the dust of the season finally settled it proved a teasing reality which few who followed the National pastime could easily accept. Standing alone atop the baseball world was one of the National League's early tenants-the Philadelphia Phillies who, after a century and then some of near misses, choking in the clutch, and come from behind victories, finally discovered the missing inch to complete the dream of every franchise, namely winning the World Series.

For the Phillies to realize their rainbow it took a combination of talent and events which began with rookie manager Dallas Green and finished with Tug McGraw's theatrical relief appearance. Sandwiched in between were Cy Young Award winner Steve Carlton's 24 wins, M.V.P. Mike Schmidt's 48 home runs, Pete Rose's hustling tactics, and the most dramatic pre-World Series play in many a summer.

For the Phillies to reach the World Series' door it took a home run by Schmidt over Montreal in the next to the last regular season game. After winning the N.L. East the Phillies had to wait on the N.L. West winner. And wait they did. In the final series of the year Houston marched into Los Angeles with a three game lead only to find themselves dropping all three and having to play an extra game to decide the title. Although Houston, midway, lost the services of pitching ace J.R. Richard due to a crippling blood clot in his neck, they were able to wrest strikeout king Nolan Ryan from the free agent pool for an estimated million per season contract. Then, finally, with the help of first baseman Art Howe's R.B.I.'s and Joe Niekro's 6-hit 20th victory, the Astros were able to bear Los Angeles, 7-1, to reach the championship playoffs.

After Carlton laid the jubilant Astros to rest, 3-1, in the first game, the five game series went to extra innings in every other game in what is considered the most exciting playoff series ever staged. But in the fifth game Ryan could not hold onto a 5-2 lead in the eighth inning and the Phillies, with one in the tenth, secured their first pennant since the 1950 Whiz Kids.

In the American League, owner George Steinbrenner did enough maneuvering to bring his New York Yankee club back to the front with the aid of Reggie Jackson's 41 home runs, catcher Rick Cerone's .77 average and clutch hitting, and veteran Tommy John's 22 wins. But New York could not overcome ace Ron Guidry's off-again, on-again season of 17 victories and rookie manager Dick Howser's questionable field decision, nor the potent Kansas City Royals, who finally made it to the altar by embarrassingly sweeping the New Yorkers in three straight games in the championship playoffs.

After making early shambles of the A.L. West, the attention focused on third baseman George Brett and his run at the elusive .400 batting mark. Throughout the summer and into the final stanza of play Brett sported a plus .400 average, only to be overtaken by small injuries and the haunting pressure of the media to finish at .390, the highest major league batting average since Ted Williams hit .406 for the Boston Red Sox in 1941.

It took Philadelphia six games to beat the Royals and win the title. Catcher Bob Boone contributed with a .412 average and Schmidt hit .381 with two home runs to win the Series M.V.P. award. Carlton chalked up two victories, in game two and in the finale, while McGraw saved the day by making his fourth Series appearance in the last game and holding the Royals in check after coming on in the eighth inning for a 4-1 victory.

For the Royals, who figured to go all the way after beating the Yankees, they were hurt by Brett's bout with hemorrhoids which almost kept him out of play, and Willie Wilson's disappointing sub-.200 Series after batting .326 during regular season play.

The human interest story of the season belonged to San Francisco and shortstop Roger Metzger, who tried to return after losing four fingers in an off-season accident, but failed in the comeback with a .074 average.

After the season headlines were made by San Diego's slugger Dave Winfield, who entered the free agent draft and got a record million and a half dollar contract per season from the New York Yankees.

EAST DIVISION

1980 AMERICAN LEAGUE

Name	G by Pos	B	AGE	G	AB	R	H	2B	3B	HR	RBI	BB	SO	SB	BA	SA
NEW YORK 1st 103-59 .636	**DICK HOWSER**															
TOTALS			31	162	5553	820	1484	239	34	189	772	643	739	86	.267	.425
Bob Watson	1B104, DH21	R	34	130	469	62	144	25	3	13	68	48	56	2	.307	.456
Willie Randolph	2B138	R	25	138	513	99	151	23	7	7	46	119	45	30	.294	.407
Bucky Dent	SS141	R	28	141	489	57	128	26	2	5	52	48	37	1	.262	.354
Craig Nettles (IL)	3B88, SS1	L	35	89	324	52	79	14	0	16	45	42	42	0	.244	.435
Reggie Jackson	OF94, DH46	L	34	143	514	94	154	22	4	41	111	83	122	1	.300	.597
Ruppert Jones (IL-SJ)	OF82	L	25	83	328	38	73	11	3	9	42	34	50	18	.223	.357
Lou Piniella	OF104, DH7	R	36	116	321	39	92	18	0	2	27	29	20	0	.287	.361
Rick Cerone	C147	R	26	147	519	70	144	30	4	14	85	32	56	1	.277	.432
Eric Soderholm	DH51, 3B37	R	31	95	275	38	79	13	1	11	35	27	25	0	.287	.462
Bobby Brown	OF131, DH1	B	26	137	412	65	107	12	5	14	47	29	82	27	.260	.415
Bobby Murcer	OF59, DH33	L	34	100	297	41	80	9	1	13	57	34	28	2	.269	.438
Jim Spencer	1B75, DH1	L	32	97	259	38	61	9	0	13	43	30	44	1	.236	.421
Oscar Gamble (BT)	OF49, DH20	L	30	89	194	40	54	10	2	14	50	28	21	2	.278	.567
Joe Lefebvre	OF71	L	24	74	150	26	34	1	1	8	21	27	30	0	.227	.407
Aurelio Rodriguez	3B49, 2B6	R	32	52	164	14	36	6	1	3	14	7	35	0	.220	.335
Fred Stanley	SS19, 2B17, 3B12	R	32	49	86	13	18	3	0	0	5	5	5	0	.209	.244
Dennis Werth	1B12, OF8, DH8, C1, 3B1	R	27	39	65	15	20	3	0	3	12	12	19	0	.308	.492
Johnny Oates	C39	L	34	39	64	6	12	3	0	1	3	2	3	1	.188	.281
Brian Doyle	2B20, SS12, 3B2	L	26	34	75	8	13	1	0	1	5	6	7	1	.173	.227
Paul Blair (RC)	OF12	R	36	12	2	2	0	0	0	0	0	0	0	0	.000	.000
Ted Wilborn	C3	B	21	8	8	2	2	0	0	0	1	0	1	0	.250	.250
Bruce Robinson	1B2, DH1	L	26	4	5	0	0	0	0	0	0	0	4	0	.000	.000
Marshall Brant	SS2, 2B1	R	24	3	4	0	1	0	0	0	0	0	3	0	.000	.000
Denny Sherrill	2B2	R	24	3	4	0	1	0	0	0	0	0	0	0	.250	.250
Roger Holt	2B2	B	24	2	6	0	1	0	0	0	1	1	2	0	.167	.167
Brad Gulden	C2	L	24	2	3	1	1	0	0	0	1	2	0	0	.333	1.333

NAME	T	AGE	W	L	PCT	SV	G	GS	CG	IP	H	BB	SO	SHO	ERA
		31	103	59	.636	50	162	162	29	1464	1433	463	845	15	3.58
Tommy John	L	37	22	9	.710	0	36	36	16	265	270	56	78	6	3.43
Ron Guidry	L	29	17	10	.630	1	37	29	5	220	215	80	166	3	3.56
Rudy May	L	35	15	5	.750	3	41	17	3	175	144	39	133	1	2.47
Tom Underwood	L	26	13	9	.591	2	38	27	2	187	163	66	116	2	3.66
Ron Davis	R	24	9	3	.750	7	53	0	0	131	121	32	65	0	2.95
Luis Tiant (LJ)	R	39	8	9	.471	0	25	25	3	136	139	50	84	0	4.90
Goose Gossage	R	28	6	2	.750	33	64	0	0	99	74	37	103	0	2.27
2 Gaylord Perry	R	41	4	4	.500	0	10	8	0	51	65	18	28	0	4.41
Doug Bird	R	30	3	0	1.000	1	22	1	0	51	47	14	17	0	2.65
1 Ed Figueroa	R	31	3	3	.500	1	15	9	0	58	90	24	16	0	6.98
Mike Griffin	R	23	2	4	.333	0	13	9	0	54	64	23	25	0	4.83
Tim Lollar	L	24	1	0	1.000	2	14	1	0	32	33	20	13	0	3.38
1 Jim Keat	L	41	0	1	.000	0	4	0	0	5	8	4	1	0	7.20
Don Gullett 29 (SJ)															

Name	G by Pos	B	AGE	G	AB	R	H	2B	3B	HR	RBI	BB	SO	SB	BA	SA
BALTIMORE 2nd 100-62 .617 3	**EARL WEAVER**															
TOTALS			30	162	5585	805	1523	258	29	156	751	587	766	111	.273	.413
Edie Murray	1B154, DH1	B	24	158	621	100	186	36	2	32	116	54	71	7	.300	.519
Rich Dauer	2B137, 3B35	R	27	152	557	71	158	32	0	2	63	46	19	3	.284	.352
Mark Belanger	SS109	R	36	113	268	37	61	7	3	0	22	12	25	6	.228	.276
Doug DeCinces	3B142, 1B1	R	29	145	489	64	122	23	2	16	64	49	83	11	.249	.403
Ken Singleton	DH151, DH5	B	33	158	583	85	177	28	3	24	104	92	94	0	.304	.485
Al Bumbry	OF160	L	33	160	645	118	205	29	9	9	53	78	75	44	.318	.433
Gary Roenicke (BW)	OF113	R	25	118	297	40	71	13	0	10	28	41	49	2	.239	.384
Rick Dempsey	C112, OF6, 1B2, DH1	R	30	119	362	51	95	26	3	9	40	36	45	3	.262	.425
Terry Crowley	DH65, 1B3	L	33	92	233	33	67	8	0	12	50	29	21	0	.288	.476
Kiko Garcia	SS96, 2B27, OF1	R	26	111	311	27	62	8	0	1	27	24	57	8	.199	.235
John Lowenstein (PJ)	OF91, DH3	L	33	104	196	38	61	8	0	4	27	32	29	7	.311	.413
Pat Kelly	OF36, DH30	L	35	89	200	38	52	10	1	3	26	34	54	16	.260	.365
Dan Graham	C73, 3B9, DH2, OF1	L	25	86	266	32	74	7	1	15	54	14	40	0	.278	.481
Lee May	DH58, 1B7	R	37	78	222	20	54	10	2	7	31	15	53	2	.243	.401
Benny Ayala	DH41, OF19	R	29	76	170	28	45	8	1	10	33	19	21	1	.265	.500
Lenn Sakata	2B34, SS4, DH1	R	26	43	83	12	16	3	2	1	9	6	10	2	.193	.313
Mark Corey	OF34	R	24	36	36	7	10	2	0	1	2	5	7	0	.278	.417
Wayne Kranchicki	SS6, 2B1, DH1	L	25	9	14	1	2	0	0	0	1	0	5	0	.143	.143
Floyd Rayford	3B4, 2B1, DH1	R	22	8	18	1	4	0	0	0	1	0	5	0	.222	.222
Drungo Hazewood	OF3	R	20	6	5	1	0	0	0	0	0	0	4	0	.000	.000
Bob Bonner	SS3	R	23	4	4	1	0	0	0	0	0	0	0	0	.000	.000
Dave Skaggs	C2	R	29	2	5	0	1	0	0	0	0	0	0	0	.200	.200

NAME	T	AGE	W	L	PCT	SV	G	GS	CG	IP	H	BB	SO	SHO	ERA
		28	100	62	.617	41	162	162	42	1460	1438	507	789	10	3.64
Steve Stone	R	32	25	7	.781	0	37	37	9	251	224	101	149	1	3.23
Scott McGregor	L	26	20	8	.714	0	36	36	12	252	254	58	119	4	3.32
Jim Palmer	R	34	16	10	.615	0	34	33	4	224	238	74	109	0	3.98
Mike Flanagan	L	28	16	13	.552	0	37	37	12	251	278	71	128	2	4.12
Sammy Stewart (SJ)	R	25	7	7	.500	0	33	3	2	119	103	60	78	0	3.55
Dennis Martinez (SJ)	R	25	6	4	.600	1	25	12	2	100	103	44	42	0	3.96
Tim Stoddard	R	27	5	3	.625	26	64	0	0	86	72	38	64	0	2.51
Tippy Martinez	L	30	4	4	.500	10	53	0	0	81	69	34	68	0	3.00
Dave Ford	R	23	1	3	.250	1	25	3	1	70	66	13	22	0	4.24
Joe Kerrigan	R	25	0	0		0	3	0	0	2	3	0	1	0	4.50
Mike Boddicker	R	22	0	0	.000	0	1	1	0	7	6	5	4	0	6.43
Paul Hartzell	R	26	0	2	.000	0	6	0	0	18	22	9	5	0	6.50

MILWAUKEE 3rd 86-76 .531 17 BUCK RODGERS 26-21 .553 GEORGE BAMBERGER (IL) 47-45 .511 BUCK RODGERS 13-10 .565

Name	G by Pos	B	AGE	G	AB	R	H	2B	3B	HR	RBI	BB	SO	SB	BA	SA
TOTALS			29	162	5653	811	1555	298	36	203	774	455	745	131	.275	.448
Cecil Cooper	1B142, DH11	L	30	153	622	96	219	33	4	25	122	39	42	17	.352	.539
Paul Molitor (VJ)	2B91, SS12, DH7, 3B1	R	23	111	450	81	137	29	2	9	37	48	48	34	.304	.438
Robin Yount	SS133, DH9	R	24	143	611	121	179	49	10	23	87	26	67	20	.293	.519
Don Money (KJ)	3B55, 1B14, DH14, 2B2	R	33	86	289	39	74	17	1	17	46	40	36	0	.256	.498
Sixto Lezcano (BW)	OF108, DH4	R	26	112	411	51	94	19	3	18	55	39	75	1	.229	.421
Gorman Thomas	OF160, DH2	R	29	162	628	78	150	26	3	38	105	58	170	8	.239	.471
Ben Oglivie	OF152, DH4	L	31	156	592	94	180	26	2	41	118	54	71	11	.304	.563
Charlie Moore	C105	R	27	111	320	42	93	13	2	2	30	24	28	10	.291	.363
Dick Davis	DH63, OF38	R	26	106	365	50	99	26	2	4	30	11	43	5	.271	.386
Jim Gantner	3B69, 2B66, SS1	L	27	132	415	47	117	21	3	4	40	30	29	11	.282	.376
Sal Bando	3B57, DH15, 1B7	R	36	78	254	28	50	12	1	5	31	29	35	1	.197	.311
Buck Martinez	C76	R	31	76	219	16	49	9	0	3	17	12	33	1	.224	.306
Mark Brouhard	DH21, OF12, 1B10	R	24	45	125	17	29	6	0	5	16	7	24	1	.232	.400
Ed Romero	SS22, 2B15, 3B3	R	22	42	104	20	27	7	0	1	10	9	11	2	.260	.356
Vic Harris	OF31, 3B2, 2B1	B	30	34	89	8	19	4	1	1	7	12	13	4	.213	.315
John Poff	OF7, DH7, 1B3	L	27	19	68	7	17	1	2	1	7	3	7	0	.250	.368
Larry Hisle (SJ)	DH17	R	33	17	60	16	17	0	0	6	16	14	7	1	.283	.583
Ned Yost	C15	R	25	15	31	0	5	0	0	0	0	0	6	0	.161	.161

NAME	T	AGE	W	L	PCT	SV	G	GS	CG	IP	H	BB	SO	SHO	ERA
	R	27	86	76	.531	30	162	162	48	1450	1530	420	575	14	3.71
Moose Haas	R	24	16	15	.516	0	33	33	14	252	246	56	146	3	3.11
Mike Caldwell	L	31	13	11	.542	0	34	33	11	225	248	56	74	2	4.04
Bill Travers	L	27	12	6	.667	0	29	25	7	154	147	47	62	1	3.92
Lary Sorensen	R	24	12	10	.545	0	35	29	8	196	242	45	54	2	3.67
Reggie Cleveland	R	32	11	9	.550	4	45	13	5	154	150	49	54	2	3.54
Paul Mitchell	R	29	5	5	.500	1	17	11	1	89	92	15	29	1	3.54
Bob McClure	L	28	5	8	.385	10	52	5	2	91	83	37	47	1	3.07
Jerry Augustine	L	27	4	3	.571	2	39	1	0	70	83	36	22	0	4.50
John Flinn	R	25	2	1	.667	2	20	1	0	37	31	20	15	0	3.89
Buster Keeton	R	22	2	2	.500	0	5	5	0	28	35	9	8	0	4.82
Bill Castro	R	26	2	4	.333	8	56	0	0	84	89	17	32	0	2.79
Dave LaPoint	L	20	1	0	1.000	1	5	3	0	15	17	13	5	0	6.00
Jim Slaton (SJ)	R	30	1	1	.500	0	3	3	0	16	17	5	4	0	4.50
Fred Holdsworth	R	28	0	0	—	0	9	0	0	20	24	9	12	0	4.50
Danny Boitano	R	27	0	1	.000	0	11	0	0	18	26	6	11	0	8.00

BOSTON 4th 83-77 .519 19 DON ZIMMER 82-73 .529 JOHNNY PESKY 1-4 .200

Name	G by Pos	B	AGE	G	AB	R	H	2B	3B	HR	RBI	BB	SO	SB	BA	SA
TOTALS			30	160	5603	757	1588	297	36	162	717	475	720	79	.283	.436
Tony Perez	1B137, DH13	R	38	151	585	73	161	31	3	25	105	41	93	1	.275	.467
Jerry Remy (KJ)	2B60, OF1	L	27	63	230	24	72	7	2	0	9	10	14	14	.313	.361
Rick Burleson	SS155	R	29	155	644	89	179	29	2	8	51	62	51	12	.278	.366
Glenn Hoffman	3B110, SS5, 2B2	R	21	114	312	37	89	15	4	4	42	19	41	2	.285	.397
Dwight Evans	OF144, DH2	R	28	148	463	72	123	37	5	18	60	64	98	3	.266	.484
Fred Lynn (BT)	OF110	L	28	110	415	67	125	32	3	12	61	58	39	12	.301	.480
Jim Rice (BW)	OF109, DH15	R	27	124	504	81	148	22	6	24	86	30	87	8	.294	.504
Carlton Fisk	C115, OF5, DH5, 3B3, 1B3	R	32	131	478	73	138	25	3	18	62	36	62	11	.289	.467
Carl Yastrzemski (BR)	DH49, OF39, 1B16	L	40	105	364	49	100	21	1	15	50	44	38	0	.275	.462
Dave Stapleton	2B94, 1B8, OF6, DH3, 3B2	R	26	106	449	61	144	33	5	7	45	13	32	3	.321	.463
Butch Hobson (SJ)	3B57, DH36	R	28	93	324	35	74	6	0	11	39	25	69	1	.228	.349
Jim Dwyer	OF65, DH12, 1B9	L	30	93	260	41	74	11	1	9	38	28	23	3	.285	.438
Dave Rader	C34, DH9	L	31	50	137	14	45	11	0	3	17	14	12	1	.328	.474
Garry Hancock	OF27, DH12	L	26	46	115	9	33	6	0	4	19	3	11	0	.287	.443
Gary Allenson	C24, DH6, 3B5	R	25	36	70	9	25	6	0	0	10	13	11	2	.357	.443
1 Jack Brohamer	3B13, 2B4, DH3	L	30	21	57	5	18	2	0	1	6	4	3	0	.316	.404
Chico Walker	2B11, DH7	B	22	11	19	3	4	1	0	0	4	0	5	0	.211	.263
Larry Wolfe	3B14, DH4	R	27	18	23	3	3	1	0	1	4	0	5	0	.130	.304
Reid Nichols	OF9, DH1	R	21	12	36	5	8	0	1	0	3	3	8	0	.222	.278
Rich Gedman	DH4, C2	L	20	9	24	2	5	0	0	0	1	0	5	0	.208	.208
Ted Sizemore	2B8	R	35	9	23	1	5	1	0	0	0	0	4	0	.217	.261
Julio Valdez	SS8	R	24	8	19	4	5	1	0	1	4	0	5	2	.263	.474
Sam Bowen	OF6	R	27	7	13	0	2	0	0	0	0	0	2	3	.154	.154
1 Stan Papi	3B1	R	29	1	0	0	0	0	0	0	0	0	0	0	—	—
Tom Poquette 28 (SJ)																

NAME	T	AGE	W	L	PCT	SV	G	GS	CG	IP	H	BB	SO	SHO	ERA
	R	30	83	77	.519	43	160	160	30	1441	1557	481	696	8	4.38
Dennis Eckersley (XJ)	R	25	12	14	.462	0	30	30	8	198	188	44	121	0	4.27
Bob Stanley	R	25	10	8	.556	14	52	17	5	175	186	52	71	1	3.39
Steve Renko	R	35	9	9	.500	0	32	23	1	165	180	56	90	0	4.20
Mike Torrez	R	33	9	16	.360	0	36	32	6	207	256	75	97	1	5.09
Chuck Rainey (EJ)	R	25	8	3	.727	0	16	13	2	87	92	41	43	1	4.86
John Tudor	L	26	8	5	.615	0	16	13	5	92	81	31	45	0	3.03
Dick Drago	R	35	7	7	.500	3	43	7	1	133	127	44	63	0	4.13
Tom Burgmeier	L	36	4	4	.556	24	62	0	0	99	87	20	54	0	2.00
Bill Campbell (SJ)	R	31	4	0	1.000	1	23	0	0	41	44	22	17	0	4.83
Skip Lockwood	R	33	3	1	.750	2	24	1	0	46	61	17	11	0	5.25
Steve Crawford	R	22	2	0	1.000	0	6	4	2	32	41	8	10	0	3.66
Win Remmerswaal	R	26	2	1	.667	0	14	0	0	35	39	9	20	0	4.63
Bruce Hurst	L	22	2	2	.500	0	12	7	0	31	39	16	16	0	9.00
Bob Ojeda	L	22	1	1	.500	0	7	7	0	26	39	14	12	0	6.92
2 Jack Billingham	R	37	1	3	.250	0	7			24	45	12	4	0	11.25
Luis Aponte	R	27	0	0	—	0	4	0	0	7	6	2	1	0	1.29
Keith MacWhorter	R	24	0	3	.000	0	14	2	0	42	46	18	21	0	5.57

DETROIT 5th 84-78 .519 19 SPARKY ANDERSON

Name	G by Pos	B	AGE	G	AB	R	H	2B	3B	HR	RBI	BB	SO	SB	BA	SA
TOTALS			27	163	5648	830	1543	232	53	143	767	645	844	75	.273	.409
Richie Hebner (FJ)	1B61, 3B32, DH5	L	32	104	341	48	99	10	7	12	82	38	45	0	.290	.466
Lou Whitaker	2B143	L	23	145	477	68	111	19	1	1	45	73	79	8	.233	.283
Alan Trammell	SS144	R	22	146	560	107	168	21	5	9	65	69	63	12	.300	.404
Tom Brookens	3B138, 2B9, SS1, DH1	R	26	151	509	64	140	25	9	10	66	32	71	13	.275	.418
2 Al Cowens	OF107, DH2	R	28	108	403	58	113	15	3	5	42	37	40	5	.280	.370
Kirk Gibson (WJ)	OF49, DH1	L	23	51	175	23	46	9	1	9	16	10	45	4	.263	.440
Steve Kemp	OF109, DH46	L	25	135	508	88	149	23	3	21	101	69	64	6	.293	.474
Lance Parrish	C121, DH16, 1B5, OF5	R	24	144	553	79	158	34	6	24	82	31	109	6	.286	.499
Champ Summers	DH64, OF47, 1B1	L	34	120	347	61	103	19	1	17	60	52	52	4	.297	.504
Rickey Peters	OF109, DH11	B	24	133	477	79	139	19	7	2	42	54	48	13	.291	.373
John Wockenfuss	1B52, DH28, C25, OF23	R	31	126	372	56	102	13	2	16	65	68	64	1	.274	.449
Tim Corcoran	1B48, OF18, DH5	L	27	84	153	20	44	7	1	3	18	22	10	0	.288	.405
2 Jim Lentine	OF57, DH2	R	26	65	161	19	42	8	1	1	17	28	30	2	.261	.342
Dave Stegman	OF57, DH2	R	26	65	130	12	23	5	0	2	9	14	23	1	.177	.262
Duffy Dyer	C37, DH10	R	34	48	108	11	20	1	0	4	11	13	34	0	.185	.306
2 Stan Papi	2B31, 3B11, SS5, 1B1	R	29	46	114	12	27	3	0	4	17	5	24	0	.237	.412
Mark Wagner	SS28, 2B6	R	26	45	72	5	17	1	0	0	3	7	11	0	.236	.250
1 Jason Thompson	1B36	L	25	36	126	10	27	5	0	4	20	13	26	0	.214	.349
Lynn Jones (KJ)	OF17, DH1	R	27	30	55	9	14	2	2	0	6	10	5	1	.255	.364
Dan Gonzales	OF1, DH1	L	26	2	7	1	1	0	0	0	0	0	1	0	.143	.143

NAME	T	AGE	W	L	PCT	SV	G	GS	CG	IP	H	BB	SO	SHO	ERA
	R	25	84	78	.519	30	163	163	40	1467	1505	558	741	9	4.25
Jack Morris	R	25	16	15	.516	0	36	36	11	250	252	87	112	2	4.18
Aurelio Lopez	R	31	13	6	.684	21	67	1	0	124	125	45	97	0	3.77
Milt Wilcox	R	30	13	11	.542	0	32	31	13	199	201	68	97	1	4.48
Dan Schatzeder	L	25	11	13	.458	0	32	28	9	193	178	58	94	2	4.01
Dan Petry	R	21	10	9	.526	0	27	25	4	165	156	83	88	3	3.93
Dave Rozema	R	23	6	9	.400	4	42	13	2	145	152	49	49	1	3.91
Bruce Robbins	L	20	4	2	.667	0	15	6	0	52	60	28	23	0	6.58
Roger Weaver (SJ)	R	25	3	4	.429	0	19	6	0	64	56	34	42	0	4.08
Pat Underwood	L	23	3	6	.333	5	49	7	0	113	121	35	60	0	3.58
Mark Fidrych	R	25	2	3	.400	0	9	9	1	44	58	20	16	0	5.73
Dave Tobik	R	27	1	0	1.000	0	17	0	0	61	61	21	34	0	3.98
John Hiller (VR)	L	37	1	0	1.000	0	11	0	0	31	38	14	18	0	4.35
Jerry Ujdur	R	23	1	0	1.000	0	2	1	0	21	36	10	8	0	7.71
1 Jack Billingham	R	37	0	0	—	0	7	1	0	11	6	3	0	7.71	

CLEVELAND 6th 79-81 .494 23 DAVE GARCIA

Name	G by Pos	B	AGE	G	AB	R	H	2B	3B	HR	RBI	BB	SO	SB	BA	SA
TOTALS			28	160	5470	738	1517	221	40	89	692	617	625	118	.277	.381
Mike Hargrove	1B160	L	30	160	589	86	179	22	2	11	85	111	36	4	.304	.404
Duane Kuiper (KJ)	2B42	L	30	42	149	10	42	5	0	0	9	13	8	0	.282	.315
Tom Veryzer (SJ)	SS108	R	27	109	358	28	97	12	0	2	28	10	25	0	.271	.321
Toby Harrah	3B156, DH3, SS2	R	31	160	561	100	150	22	4	11	72	98	60	17	.267	.380
Jorge Orta	OF120, DH7	L	29	129	481	78	140	18	3	10	64	71	44	6	.291	.403
Rick Manning	OF139	L	25	140	471	55	110	17	4	5	52	63	66	12	.234	.306
Miguel Dilone	OF118, DH11	R	25	132	528	82	180	30	9	0	40	28	45	61	.341	.432
Ron Hassey	C113, DH7, 1B2	L	27	130	390	43	124	18	6	8	65	49	51	0	.318	.446
Joe Charboneau	OF67, DH57	R	25	131	453	76	131	17	2	23	87	49	70	2	.289	.488
Jerry Dybzinski	SS73, 2B29, 3B4, DH2	R	24	114	248	32	57	11	1	1	23	13	35	4	.230	.294
2 Alan Bannister	2B41, OF40, 3B3, SS2	B	27	81	262	41	86	17	4	1	32	28	25	9	.328	.435
Bo Diaz	C75	R	27	76	207	15	47	11	2	3	32	7	27	1	.227	.343
Gary Alexander	DH40, C13, OF2	R	27	76	178	22	40	7	1	5	31	17	52	0	.225	.360
Dave Rosello	2B43, 3B22, SS3, DH1	R	30	71	117	16	29	3	0	2	12	9	19	0	.248	.325
1 Cliff Johnson	DH45	R	32	54	174	25	40	3	1	6	28	25	30	0	.230	.362
2 Jack Brohamer	2B47, DH1	L	30	53	142	13	32	5	1	1	15	14	6	0	.225	.296
Dell Alston	OF26, DH6	L	27	52	54	11	12	1	2	0	9	5	7	2	.222	.315
Gary Gray	DH9, 1B6, OF6	R	27	28	54	4	8	1	0	2	8	3	13	0	.148	.278
1 Ron Pruitt	OF6, 3B2, DH2	R	28	23	36	1	11	1	0	0	4	6	5	0	.306	.333
Andres Mora	OF3	R	25	9	18	0	2	0	0	0	0	0	5	0	.111	.111
Andre Thornton 30 (KJ)																

NAME	T	AGE	W	L	PCT	SV	G	GS	CG	IP	H	BB	SO	SHO	ERA
	R	26	79	81	.494	32	160	160	35	1428	1519	552	843	8	4.68
Len Barker	R	24	19	12	.613	0	36	36	8	246	237	92	187	1	4.17
Dan Spillner	R	28	16	11	.593	0	34	30	7	194	225	74	100	1	5.29
Rick Waits	L	28	13	14	.481	0	33	33	9	224	231	82	109	2	4.46
John Denny (FJ)	R	27	8	6	.571	0	16	16	4	109	116	47	59	1	4.38
Victor Cruz	R	22	6	7	.462	12	55	0	0	86	71	27	88	0	3.45
Wayne Garland	R	29	6	9	.400	0	25	20	4	150	163	48	55	1	4.62
2 Ross Grimsley	L	30	4	5	.444	0	14	11	2	75	103	24	18	0	6.72
Sid Monge	L	29	3	5	.375	14	67	0	0	94	80	40	61	0	3.54
Bob Owchinko	L	25	2	9	.182	0	29	14	1	114	138	47	66	1	5.29
Sandy Wihtol	R	25	1	0	1.000	1	17	0	0	35	35	14	20	0	3.60
Mike Stanton	R	27	1	3	.250	5	51	0	0	86	89	44	74	0	5.44
Mike Paxton	R	26	0	0	—	0	6	0	0	8	13	6	6	0	12.38
Don Collins	R	27	0	0	—	0	9	0	0	6	7	0	0	0	7.50

TORONTO — 7th 67-95 .414 36 — BOBBY MATTICK

Name	G by Pos	B	AGE	G	AB	R	H	2B	3B	HR	RBI	BB	SO	SB	BA	SA
TOTALS			26	162	5571	624	1398	249	53	126	580	448	813	67	.251	.383
John Mayberry	1B136, DH8	L	31	149	501	62	124	19	2	30	82	77	80	0	.248	.473
Damaso Garcia	2B138, DH1	R	25	140	543	50	151	30	7	4	46	12	55	13	.278	.381
Alfredo Griffin	SS155	B	22	155	653	63	166	26	15	2	41	24	58	18	.254	.349
Roy Howell	3B138, DH2	L	26	142	528	51	142	28	9	10	57	50	92	0	.269	.413
Lloyd Moseby	OF104, DH6	L	20	114	389	44	89	24	1	9	46	25	85	4	.229	.365
Rick Bosetti (BA)	OF51	R	26	53	188	24	40	7	1	4	18	15	29	4	.213	.324
Al Woods	OF88, DH13	L	26	109	373	54	112	18	2	15	47	37	35	4	.300	.480
Ernie Whitt	C105	L	28	106	295	23	70	12	2	6	34	22	30	1	.237	.353
Otto Velez (BY)	DH97, 1B3	R	29	104	357	54	96	12	3	20	62	54	86	0	.269	.487
Barry Bonnell	OF122, DH3	R	26	130	463	55	124	22	4	13	56	37	59	3	.268	.417
Bob Bailor	OF98, SS12, 3B11, P3, 2B1, DH1	R	28	117	347	44	82	14	2	1	16	36	33	12	.236	.297
Bob Davis	C89	R	28	91	218	18	47	11	0	4	19	12	25	0	.216	.321
Garth Iorg	2B32, 3B20, OF14, 1B11, DH2, SS1	R	25	80	222	24	55	10	1	2	14	12	39	2	.248	.329
Joe Cannon	OF33, DH1	L	26	70	50	16	4	0	0	0	4	0	14	2	.080	.080
Doug Ault	1B32, DH21, OF1	R	30	64	144	12	28	5	1	3	15	14	23	0	.194	.306
Danny Ainge (RL)	OF29, 3B3, DH2, 2B1	R	21	38	111	11	27	6	1	0	4	2	29	3	.243	.364
2 Steve Braun	DH13, 3B1	L	32	37	55	4	15	2	0	1	9	8	5	0	.273	.344
Willie Upshaw	1B14, DH12, OF1	L	23	34	61	10	13	3	1	1	5	6	14	1	.213	.344
Paul Hodgson	OF11, DH3	R	20	20	41	5	9	1	0	1	5	3	12	0	.220	.341
Domingo Ramos	2B2, SS2, DH1	R	22	5	16	0	2	0	0	0	0	2	5	0	.125	.125
Mike Macha	3B2, C1	R	26	5	8	0	0	0	0	0	0	0	4	0	.000	.000
Pat Kelly	C3	R	24	3	7	0	2	0	0	0	0	0	0	0	.286	.286

NAME	T	AGE	W	L	PCT	SV	G	GS	CG	IP	H	BB	SO	SHO	ERA
		27	67	95	.414	23	162	162	39	1466	1523	635	705	9	4.19
Jim Clancy	R	24	13	16	.448	0	34	34	15	251	217	128	152	2	3.30
Dave Stieb	R	22	12	15	.444	0	34	32	14	243	232	83	108	4	3.70
Joey McLaughlin	R	23	6	9	.400	4	55	10	0	136	159	53	70	0	4.50
Jackson Todd	R	28	5	12	.294	0	12	12	4	85	90	30	44	0	4.02
Paul Mirabella	L	26	5	12	.294	0	33	22	3	131	151	66	53	1	4.33
Jerry Garvin	L	24	4	7	.364	8	61	0	0	83	70	27	52	0	2.28
Jesse Jefferson	R	31	4	13	.235	0	29	18	2	122	130	52	53	2	5.46
Mike Barlow	R	32	3	1	.750	5	40	1	0	55	57	21	19	0	4.09
Tom Buskey	R	33	3	1	.750	0	33	0	0	67	68	26	34	0	4.43
Luis Leal	R	23	3	4	.429	0	13	10	1	60	72	31	26	0	4.50
Jack Kucek	R	27	3	8	.273	1	23	12	0	68	83	41	35	0	6.75
Mike Willis	L	29	2	1	.667	3	20	0	0	26	25	11	14	0	1.73
1 Dave Lemanczyk	R	29	2	5	.286	0	10	8	0	43	57	15	10	0	5.44
Ken Schrom	R	25	1	0	1.000	0	17	0	0	31	32	19	13	0	5.23
Balor Moore	L	29	1	1	.500	1	31	0	0	65	76	31	22	0	5.26
Bob Bailor	R	28	0	0	—	0	3	0	0	2	4	1	0	0	9.00

WEST DIVISION

KANSAS CITY — 1st 97-65 .599 — JIM FREY

Name	G by Pos	B	AGE	G	AB	R	H	2B	3B	HR	RBI	BB	SO	SB	BA	SA
TOTALS			28	162	5714	809	1633	266	59	115	766	508	709	185	.286	.413
Willie Aikens	1B138, DH13	L	25	151	543	70	151	24	0	20	98	64	88	1	.278	.433
Frank White	2B153	R	26	154	560	70	148	23	4	7	60	19	69	19	.264	.357
U.L. Washington	SS152	B	26	153	549	79	150	16	11	6	53	53	78	20	.273	.375
George Brett (FJ)	3B112, 1B1	L	27	117	449	87	175	33	9	24	118	58	22	15	.390	.664
Clint Hurdle	OF126	L	22	130	395	50	116	31	2	10	60	34	61	0	.294	.458
Amos Otis (RJ)	OF105	R	33	107	394	56	99	16	3	10	53	39	70	16	.251	.383
Willie Wilson	OF159	B	24	161	705	133	230	28	15	3	49	28	81	79	.326	.421
Darrell Porter (IL)	C81, DH34	L	28	118	418	51	104	14	2	7	51	69	50	1	.249	.342
Hal McRae	DH110, OF9	R	34	124	489	73	145	39	5	14	83	29	56	10	.297	.483
John Wathan	C77, OF35, 1B12	R	30	126	453	57	138	14	7	6	58	50	42	17	.305	.406
Pete LaCock	1B86, OF29	L	28	114	156	14	32	6	0	1	18	17	10	1	.205	.263
Dave Chalk	3B33, 2B17, DH6, SS1	R	29	69	167	19	42	10	1	1	20	18	27	1	.251	.341
Jamie Quirk	3B28, C15, OF7, 1B1, DH1	L	25	62	163	13	45	5	0	5	21	7	24	3	.276	.399
Rusty Torres	OF40, DH1	R	31	51	72	10	12	0	0	0	3	8	7	1	.167	.167
Rance Mulliniks	SS18, 2B14	L	24	36	54	4	14	3	0	0	6	7	10	0	.259	.315
2 Jose Cardenal	OF23	R	36	25	53	8	18	2	0	0	5	3	3	0	.340	.377
Jerry Terrell	OF7, 2B3, 1B3, DH1, P1	R	33	23	16	4	1	0	0	0	1	0	1	0	.063	.063
Bobby Detherage	OF20	R	25	20	26	2	8	2	0	1	7	1	4	1	.308	.500
1 Steve Braun	OF5, DH1	L	32	14	23	0	1	0	0	0	1	2	2	0	.043	.043
Onix Concepcion	SS6	R	22	12	15	1	2	0	0	0	0	0	5	0	.133	.133
Manny Castillo	3B3, DH2, 2B1	R	23	7	10	1	2	0	0	0	0	0	0	0	.200	.200
German Barranca		L	23	7	3	0	0	0	0	0	0	0	0	1	—	—
Ken Phelps	1B2	L	25	3	4	0	0	0	0	0	0	0	0	0	.000	.000

NAME	T	AGE	W	L	PCT	SV	G	GS	CG	IP	H	BB	SO	SHO	ERA
		29	97	65	.599	42	162	162	37	1459	1496	465	614	10	3.83
Dennis Leonard	R	29	20	11	.645	0	38	38	9	280	271	80	155	3	3.79
Larry Gura	L	32	18	10	.643	0	36	36	16	283	272	76	113	4	2.96
Paul Splittorff	L	33	14	11	.560	0	34	33	4	204	236	43	53	0	4.15
Rich Gale	R	26	13	9	.591	1	32	28	6	191	169	78	97	1	3.91
Dan Quisenberry	R	27	12	7	.632	33	75	0	0	128	129	27	37	0	3.09
Renie Martin	R	24	10	10	.500	2	32	20	2	137	133	70	68	0	4.40
Marty Pattin	R	37	4	0	1.000	4	37	0	0	89	97	23	40	0	3.64
Gary Christenson	L	27	3	0	1.000	1	24	0	0	31	35	18	16	0	5.23
Jeff Twitty	L	22	2	1	.667	0	13	0	0	22	33	7	9	0	6.14
Steve Busby	R	30	1	3	.250	0	11	6	0	42	59	19	12	0	6.21
Ken Brett	L	31	1	0	—	1	9	0	0	13	8	5	4	0	0.00
Jerry Terrell	R	33	0	0	—	0	5	0	0	1	1	1	0	0	0.00
Rawly Eastwick	R	29	0	0	.000	0	14	0	0	22	37	8	5	0	5.32
Craig Chamberlain	R	23	0	1	.000	0	3	1	0	9	10	5	3	0	7.00
Mike Jones	L	20	0	1	.000	0	3	1	0	5	6	5	2	0	10.80

OAKLAND — 2nd 83-79 .512 14 — BILLY MARTIN

Name	G by Pos	B	AGE	G	AB	R	H	2B	3B	HR	RBI	BB	SO	SB	BA	SA
TOTALS			27	162	5495	686	1424	212	35	137	635	506	824	175	.259	.385
Dave Revering	1B95, DH5	L	27	106	376	48	109	21	5	15	62	32	37	1	.290	.492
Dave McKay	2B62, 3B54, SS10	B	30	123	295	29	72	16	2	9	29	10	57	1	.244	.315
Mike Guerrero	SS116	R	30	116	381	32	91	16	2	2	23	19	32	3	.239	.307
Wayne Gross	3B99, 1B10, DH1	L	28	113	366	45	103	18	3	14	61	44	39	5	.281	.467
Tony Armas	OF158	R	26	158	628	87	175	18	8	35	109	29	128	5	.279	.500
Dwayne Murphy	OF158	L	25	159	573	86	157	18	2	13	68	102	96	26	.274	.380
Rickey Henderson	OF157, DH1	R	21	158	591	111	179	22	4	9	53	117	54	100	.303	.399
Jim Essian	C68, DH11, 1B1	R	29	87	285	19	66	11	0	5	29	30	18	1	.232	.323
Mitchell Page	DH101	L	28	110	348	58	85	14	0	17	51	35	87	14	.244	.443
Jeff Newman	1B60, C55, DH9, 3B2, 2B1	R	31	127	438	37	102	19	1	15	56	25	81	3	.233	.384
Rob Picciolo	SS49, 2B47, OF1	R	27	95	271	32	65	9	2	5	18	2	63	1	.240	.343
Mike Heath	C47, DH31, OF8	R	25	92	305	27	74	10	2	1	33	16	28	3	.243	.298
Mickey Klutts (LJ)	3B62, SS8, 2B7, DH1	R	24	59	169	20	36	3	0	0	9	14	23	0	.213	.231
Jeff Cox	2B58	R	24	59	169	20	36	3	0	0	9	14	23	8	.213	.231
Mike Davis	OF18, 1B7, DH6	L	21	51	95	11	20	2	1	1	8	7	14	2	.211	.284
Mike Edwards	2B23, DH5, OF1	R	27	46	59	10	14	0	0	0	1	9	8	0	.237	.237
Orlando Gonzalez	1B11, DH8, OF2	L	28	25	70	10	17	0	0	0	9	1	6	0	.243	.243
Randy Elliott	DH11	R	29	14	39	4	5	3	0	0	1	0	13	0	.128	.205
Ray Cosey		L	24	9	9	1	1	0	0	0	0	0	0	0	.111	.111
Glenn Burke	27 (KJ)															

NAME	T	AGE	W	L	PCT	SV	G	GS	CG	IP	H	BB	SO	SHO	ERA
		26	83	79	.512	13	162	162	94	1472	1347	521	769	9	3.46
Mike Norris	R	25	22	9	.710	0	33	33	24	284	215	83	180	1	2.54
Rick Langford	R	28	19	12	.613	0	35	33	28	290	276	64	102	2	3.26
Matt Keough	R	24	16	13	.552	0	34	32	20	250	218	94	121	2	2.92
Steve McCatty	R	26	14	14	.500	0	33	31	11	222	202	99	114	1	3.85
Brian Kingman	R	25	8	20	.286	0	32	30	10	211	209	82	116	1	3.84
Bob Lacey	L	26	3	2	.600	6	47	1	0	80	68	21	45	1	2.93
Jeff Jones	R	23	1	3	.250	5	35	0	0	44	32	26	34	0	2.86
Rick Lysander	R	27	0	0	—	0	5	0	0	14	24	4	5	0	7.71
Ernie Camacho	R	25	0	0	—	0	5	0	0	12	10	5	9	0	6.75
Mark Souza	L	25	0	0	—	0	5	0	0	7	5	5	2	0	7.71
Alan Wirth	R	23	0	1	.000	0	2	0	0	3	4	0	1	0	4.50
Rich Bordi	R	21	0	1	.000	1	3	0	0	4	4	5	3	0	4.50
Dave Beard	R	20	0	1	.000	0	13	0	0	30	44	28	23	0	3.38
Craig Minetto	L	23	0	3	.000	0	11	8	1	11	8	11	7	0	7.88
Dave Hamilton	L	32	0	3	.000	0	21	0	0	30	44	28	23	0	11.40

MINNESOTA — 3rd 77-84 .478 19.5 — GENE MAUCH 54-71 .432   JOHNNY GORYL 23-13 .639

Name	G by Pos	B	AGE	G	AB	R	H	2B	3B	HR	RBI	BB	SO	SB	BA	SA
TOTALS			27	161	5530	670	1468	252	46	99	634	436	703	62	.265	.381
Ron Jackson	1B119, OF15, 3B2, DH1	R	27	131	396	48	105	29	3	5	42	28	41	1	.265	.391
Rob Wilfong	2B120, OF6	L	26	131	416	55	103	16	5	8	45	34	61	10	.248	.368
Roy Smalley	SS125, 1B3, DH3	B	27	133	486	64	135	24	1	12	63	65	63	3	.278	.405
John Castino	3B138, SS18	R	25	150	546	67	165	17	7	13	64	29	67	7	.302	.430
Hosken Powell	OF129	L	25	137	485	58	127	17	5	6	35	32	46	14	.262	.355
Ken Landreaux	OF120, DH6	L	25	129	484	56	136	23	11	7	62	39	42	8	.281	.417
Rick Sofield	OF126, DH2	L	23	131	417	52	103	18	4	9	49	24	92	4	.247	.374
Butch Wynegar	C142, DH1	B	24	146	486	61	124	18	3	5	57	63	36	1	.255	.335
Jose Morales	DH86, 1B2, C2	R	35	97	241	36	73	17	2	8	52	22	19	0	.303	.490
Pete Mackanin	2B71, SS30, DH5, 1B4, 3B3	R	29	108	319	31	85	18	0	4	35	14	34	6	.266	.361
Mike Cubbage	1B72, 3B32, 2B1, DH1	L	29	103	285	29	70	9	0	8	42	23	37	0	.246	.361
Glenn Adams	DH81, OF12	L	32	99	262	32	75	11	2	6	38	15	26	2	.286	.412
Dave Edwards	OF72, DH3	R	26	81	200	26	50	9	1	2	20	12	51	2	.250	.335
Danny Goodwin	DH38, 1B13	R	26	55	115	12	23	5	0	1	11	17	32	0	.200	.270
Bombo Rivera (BK)	OF37, DH1	R	27	44	113	13	25	7	0	3	10	4	20	0	.221	.363
Sal Butera	C32, DH2	R	27	34	85	4	23	1	0	0	3	5	8	0	.271	.282
Willie Norwood	OF17, DH9	R	29	34	73	6	12	2	0	1	3	2	13	1	.164	.233
Greg Johnston	OF14	L	25	14	27	3	5	3	0	0	1	2	4	0	.185	.296
Gary Ward	OF12	R	26	13	41	11	19	6	2	1	10	3	6	0	.463	.780
Jesus Vega	DH9, 1B2	R	24	12	30	3	5	0	0	0	3	1	7	0	.167	.167
Bob Randall	3B4, 2B1	R	32	5	15	2	3	1	0	0	1	0	0	0	.200	.267
Lenny Faedo	SS5	R	20	5	8	1	2	0	0	0	0	0	0	0	.250	.375

NAME	T	AGE	W	L	PCT	SV	G	GS	CG	IP	H	BB	SO	SHO	ERA
		28	77	84	.478	30	161	161	35	1451	1502	468	744	9	3.93
Jerry Koosman	L	37	16	13	.552	2	38	34	8	243	252	69	149	0	4.04
Geoff Zahn	L	34	14	18	.438	0	38	35	13	233	273	66	96	5	4.40
Darrell Jackson	L	24	9	9	.500	1	32	25	1	172	161	69	90	0	3.87
Doug Corbett	R	27	8	6	.571	23	73	0	0	136	102	42	89	0	1.99
Pete Redfern (EJ)	R	25	7	7	.500	2	23	16	2	105	117	33	73	0	4.54
Roger Erickson	R	23	7	13	.350	0	32	27	7	191	198	56	97	0	3.25
Al Williams	R	26	6	2	.750	1	18	9	3	77	73	30	35	0	3.51
Fernando Arroyo	R	28	5	6	.500	0	21	11	1	92	97	32	27	1	4.70
John Verhoeven	R	27	3	3	.500	0	44	0	0	100	109	29	42	0	3.96
Mike Marshall	R	37	1	3	.250	0	18	0	0	49	42	12	13	0	6.19
Mike Kinnunen	L	22	0	0	—	0	21	0	0	25	29	9	8	0	5.04
Mike Bacsik	R	28	0	0	—	0	10	0	0	23	26	11	9	0	4.30
Bob Veselic	R	24	0	0	—	0	5	4	0	18	20	5	14	0	4.50
Terry Felton	R	22	0	3	.000	0	5	4	0	18	20	9	14	0	7.00

TEXAS — 4th 76-85 .472 20.5 — PAT CORRALES

Name	G by Pos	B	AGE	G	AB	R	H	2B	3B	HR	RBI	BB	SO	SB	BA	SA
TOTALS			30	163	5690	756	1616	263	27	124	720	480	589	91	.284	.405
Pat Putnam	1B137, 3B1, DH1	L	26	147	410	42	108	16	2	13	55	36	49	0	.263	.407
Bump Wills	2B144	B	27	146	578	102	152	31	5	5	58	51	71	34	.263	.360
Bud Harrelson (LJ)	SS87, 2B2	B	36	87	180	26	49	6	0	1	9	29	23	4	.272	.322
Buddy Bell	3B120, SS3	R	28	129	490	76	161	24	4	17	83	40	39	3	.329	.498
Johnny Grubb	OF77, DH8	L	31	110	274	40	76	12	1	9	32	42	35	2	.277	.427
Mickey Rivers	OF141, DH4	L	31	147	630	96	210	32	6	7	60	20	34	18	.333	.437
Al Oliver	OF157, DH4, 1B1	L	33	163	656	96	209	43	3	19	117	39	47	5	.319	.480
Jim Sundberg	C151	R	29	151	505	59	138	24	1	10	63	64	67	2	.273	.384
Richie Zisk	DH86, OF37	R	31	135	448	48	130	17	1	19	77	39	72	0	.290	.460
Jim Norris	OF82, 1B10, DH1	L	31	119	174	23	43	5	0	0	16	23	16	6	.247	.276
1 Pepe Frias	SS106, 3B7, 2B2	R	31	116	227	27	55	5	1	0	14	0	23	5	.242	.273
Rusty Staub (BG)	DH57, 1B30, OF14	L	36	109	340	42	102	23	2	9	55	39	18	1	.300	.459
Dave Roberts	3B37, SS33, C22, OF5, 1B4, 2B4	R	29	101	235	27	56	4	0	10	30	13	38	0	.238	.383
Billy Sample	OF72, DH4	R	25	99	204	29	53	10	4	4	19	18	15	8	.260	.368
Johnny Ellis	1B39, DH21, C3	R	31	73	182	12	43	9	1	1	23	14	23	3	.236	.313
Mike Richardt	2B20, DH1	R	22	22	71	2	16	2	0	0	8	1	7	0	.225	.254
Nelson Norman	SS17	B	22	17	32	4	7	0	0	0	1	1	1	0	.219	.219
Odie Davis	SS13, 3B1	R	24	17	8	0	1	0	0	0	0	0	2	1	.125	.125
Tucker Ashford	3B12, SS2	R	25	15	32	2	4	0	0	0	3	3	3	0	.125	.125
Danny Walton	DH1	R	32	10	10	2	2	0	0	0	1	3	5	0	.200	.200
Mike Hart	OF2	B	28	5	4	1	1	0	0	0	0	1	1	0	.250	.250
2 Rick Auerbach 30 (RR)																

NAME	T	AGE	W	L	PCT	SV	G	GS	CG	IP	H	BB	SO	SHO	ERA
		31	76	85	.472	25	163	163	35	1452	1561	519	890	6	4.02
Doc Medich	R	31	14	11	.560	0	34	32	6	204	230	56	91	0	3.93
Danny Darwin	R	24	13	4	.765	8	53	2	0	110	98	50	104	0	2.62
Ferguson Jenkins(SD)	R	36	12	12	.500	0	29	29	12	198	190	52	129	0	3.77
Jon Matlack	L	30	10	10	.500	1	35	34	8	235	265	48	142	1	3.68
1 Gaylord Perry	R	41	6	9	.400	0	24	24	6	155	159	46	107	2	3.43
1 Sparky Lyle	L	35	3	2	.600	8	49	0	0	81	97	28	43	0	4.67
John Butcher	R	23	3	3	.500	0	6	6	1	35	34	13	27	0	4.11
Jim Kern (SJ)	R	31	3	11	.214	2	38	1	0	63	65	45	40	0	4.86
Dave Rajsich	L	28	2	1	.667	2	24	1	0	48	56	22	35	0	6.00
John Henry Johnson	L	23	2	2	.500	4	33	0	0	39	27	15	44	0	2.31
2 Charlie Hough	R	32	2	2	.500	0	16	2	2	61	54	37	47	1	3.98
Ken Clay	R	26	2	3	.400	0	8	8	0	43	43	29	17	0	4.60
Steve Comer (SJ)	R	26	2	4	.333	0	12	11	0	42	65	22	9	0	7.93
Adrian Devine (SJ)	R	28	1	1	.500	0	13	0	0	28	49	9	8	0	4.82
Bob Babcock	R	30	1	2	.333	0	19	0	0	23	20	8	15	0	4.70
Jerry Don Gleaton	L	22	0	0	—	0	5	0	0	7	5	4	2	0	2.57
Don Kainer	R	24	0	0	—	0	4	3	0	20	22	9	10	0	1.80
Dennis Lewallyn	R	26	0	0	—	0	4	0	0	6	7	4	1	0	7.50
Brian Allard	R	22	0	1	.000	0	5	2	0	14	13	10	10	0	5.79
2 Ed Figueroa	R	31	0	7	.000	0	8	8	0	40	62	12	9	0	5.85

CHICAGO — 5th 70-90 .438 26 — TONY LaRUSSA

Name	G by Pos	B	AGE	G	AB	R	H	2B	3B	HR	RBI	BB	SO	SB	BA	SA
TOTALS			27	162	5444	587	1408	255	38	91	547	399	670	68	.259	.370
Mike Squires	1B114, C2	L	28	131	343	38	97	11	3	2	33	33	24	8	.283	.350
Jim Morrison	2B161, SS1, DH1	R	27	162	604	66	171	40	4	15	57	36	74	9	.283	.424
2 Todd Cruz	SS90	R	24	90	293	23	68	11	1	2	18	9	54	2	.232	.297
Kevin Bell	3B83, SS3, DH3	R	24	92	191	16	34	5	2	1	11	29	37	0	.178	.241
Harold Baines	OF137, DH1	L	21	141	491	55	125	23	6	13	49	19	65	2	.255	.405
Chet Lemon	OF139, DH6, 2B1	R	25	147	514	76	150	32	6	11	51	71	56	6	.292	.442
Wayne Nordhagen	OF74, DH32	R	32	123	415	45	115	22	4	15	50	10	45	0	.277	.458
Bruce Kimm	C98	R	29	100	251	20	61	10	1	0	19	17	26	1	.243	.291
Lamar Johnson	1B80, DH66	R	29	147	541	51	150	26	3	13	81	47	53	2	.277	.409
Greg Pryor	SS76, 3B41, 2B5, DH1	R	30	122	338	32	81	18	4	1	29	12	35	2	.240	.325
Bob Molinaro	OF49, DH47	L	30	119	344	48	100	16	4	5	36	26	29	18	.291	.404
Thad Bosley (WJ)	OF52	L	23	70	147	12	33	2	0	2	14	10	27	3	.224	.279
Marv Foley	C64, 1B3	L	26	68	137	14	29	5	0	4	15	9	22	0	.212	.336
1 Alan Bannister	OF23, 3B17	B	26	45	130	16	25	6	0	0	9	12	16	5	.192	.238
Junior Moore	3B34, DH2, 1B1	R	27	45	121	9	31	4	1	1	10	7	11	0	.256	.331
Rusty Kuntz	OF34	R	25	36	62	5	14	4	0	0	3	5	13	1	.226	.290
Leo Sutherland	OF23	L	22	34	89	9	23	3	0	0	5	1	11	4	.258	.292
2 Ron Pruitt	OF11, DH7, C5, 3B3, 1B1	R	28	33	70	8	21	2	0	2	11	8	7	0	.300	.414
1 Claudell Washington	OF23, DH2	L	25	32	90	15	26	4	2	1	12	5	19	4	.289	.411
Glenn Borgmann	C32	R	30	32	87	10	19	2	0	1	14	14	9	0	.218	.310
Harry Chappas	SS19, DH2, 2B1	B	22	26	50	6	8	2	0	0	4	2	4	10	.160	.200
Fran Mullins	3B21	R	23	21	62	9	12	4	0	0	3	9	8	0	.194	.258
Ricky Seilheimer	C21	L	19	21	52	4	11	3	1	1	3	4	15	1	.212	.365
Randy Johnson	DH4, 1B1, OF1	L	21	12	20	0	4	0	0	0	3	2	4	0	.200	.200
Minnie Minoso		R	57	2	2	0	0	0	0	0	0	0	0	0	.000	.000

NAME	T	AGE	W	L	PCT	SV	G	GS	CG	IP	H	BB	SO	SHO	ERA
		25	70	90	.438	42	162	162	32	1435	1434	563	724	12	3.92
Britt Burns	L	21	15	13	.536	0	34	32	11	238	213	63	133	1	2.84
Rich Dotson	R	21	12	10	.545	0	33	32	8	198	185	87	109	0	4.27
LaMarr Hoyt	R	25	9	3	.750	0	24	13	3	112	123	41	55	1	4.58
Steve Trout	L	22	9	16	.360	0	32	30	7	200	229	49	89	2	3.69
Ed Farmer	R	30	7	9	.438	30	64	0	0	100	92	56	54	0	3.33
Mike Proly	R	29	5	10	.333	8	62	3	0	147	136	58	56	0	3.06
Rich Wortham	L	26	4	7	.364	1	41	10	0	92	102	58	45	0	5.97
Ken Kravec	L	28	3	6	.333	0	20	15	0	82	100	44	37	0	6.91
Ross Baumgarten(SJ)	L	25	2	12	.143	0	24	23	3	136	127	52	66	1	3.44
Guy Hoffman	L	23	1	0	1.000	1	23	1	0	38	38	17	24	0	2.61
Dewey Robinson	R	25	1	1	.500	0	15	0	0	35	26	16	28	0	3.09
Francisco Barrios(SJ)	R	27	1	1	.500	0	3	3	0	16	21	8	2	0	5.06
Randy Scarbery	R	28	1	2	.333	2	15	0	0	29	24	7	18	0	4.03
Nardi Contreras	R	28	0	0	—	0	8	0	0	14	18	7	8	0	5.79

CALIFORNIA — 6th 65-95 .406 31 — JIM FREGOSI

Name	G by Pos	B	AGE	G	AB	R	H	2B	3B	HR	RBI	BB	SO	SB	BA	SA
TOTALS			29	160	5443	698	1442	236	32	106	655	539	889	91	.265	.378
Rod Carew	1B103, DH32	L	34	144	540	74	179	34	7	3	59	59	38	23	.331	.437
Bobby Grich	2B146, 1B3	R	31	150	498	60	135	22	2	14	62	84	108	3	.271	.408
Freddie Patek	SS81	R	35	86	273	41	72	10	5	5	34	15	26	7	.264	.392
Carney Lansford	3B150	R	23	151	602	87	157	27	3	15	80	50	93	14	.261	.390
Dan Ford (KJ)	OF45, DH15	R	28	65	226	22	63	11	0	7	26	19	45	0	.279	.420
Rick Miller	OF118	L	32	129	412	52	113	16	3	1	38	48	71	7	.274	.337
Joe Rudi (LJ)	OF90, 1B6, DH3	R	33	104	372	42	88	17	1	16	53	17	84	1	.237	.417
Brian Downing (BN)	C16, DH13	R	29	30	93	5	27	2	0	2	25	12	12	0	.290	.419
Don Baylor (BW-BT)	OF54, DH36	R	31	90	340	39	85	12	2	5	51	24	32	6	.250	.341
Larry Harlow	OF94, 1B1, DH1	L	28	109	301	47	83	13	4	4	27	48	61	3	.276	.385
2 Jason Thompson	1B47, DH45	L	25	102	312	59	99	14	0	17	70	70	60	2	.317	.526
Tom Donohue	C84	R	27	84	219	18	41	4	1	2	14	7	63	5	.188	.243
Dickie Thon	SS22, 2B21, DH15, 3B10, 1B1	R	22	80	267	32	68	12	0	0	15	10	28	7	.255	.315
Bobby Clark	OF77	R	25	78	261	26	60	10	1	5	23	11	42	0	.230	.333
Bert Campaneris	SS64, DH2, 2B8	R	38	77	210	32	53	8	1	2	18	14	33	10	.252	.329
Stan Cliburn	C54	R	23	54	56	7	10	2	0	2	6	3	9	0	.179	.321
Dan Whitmer	C48	R	24	48	87	8	21	3	0	0	7	4	21	1	.241	.276
1 Al Cowens	OF30, DH1	R	28	34	119	11	27	5	0	1	17	12	21	1	.227	.294
2 Dave Skaggs (BN)	C24	R	29	24	66	7	13	0	0	1	9	9	13	0	.197	.242
Gil Kubski	OF20	L	25	22	63	11	16	3	0	0	6	6	10	1	.254	.302
Ralph Garr	DH8, OF2	L	34	21	42	5	8	1	0	0	3	4	6	0	.190	.214
John Harris	1B10, OF3	L	25	19	41	8	12	5	0	2	7	7	4	0	.293	.561
1 Todd Cruz	SS12, 3B4, 2B1, OF1	R	24	18	40	5	11	3	0	1	5	5	8	0	.275	.425
Merv Rettenmund (RC)	DH1	R	37	2	4	0	1	0	0	0	0	1	1	0	.250	.250

NAME	T	AGE	W	L	PCT	SV	G	GS	CG	IP	H	BB	SO	SHO	ERA
		28	65	95	.406	30	160	160	22	1428	1548	529	725	6	4.52
Mark Clear	R	24	11	11	.500	9	58	0	0	106	82	65	105	0	3.31
Frank Tanana	L	26	11	12	.478	0	32	31	7	204	223	45	113	0	4.15
Don Aase	R	25	8	13	.381	2	40	21	5	175	193	66	74	1	4.06
Freddie Martinez	R	23	7	9	.438	0	30	23	4	149	150	59	57	1	4.53
2 Andy Hassler	L	28	5	1	.833	10	41	0	0	83	67	37	75	0	2.49
John Montague	R	32	4	2	.667	3	37	0	0	74	97	21	22	0	5.11
Dave Frost (XJ)	R	27	4	8	.333	0	15	15	2	78	97	21	28	0	5.31
2 Ed Halicki (UJ)	R	29	3	1	.750	0	10	6	0	35	39	11	16	0	4.89
Dave LaRoche	L	32	3	5	.375	4	52	9	1	128	122	39	89	0	4.08
Bruce Kison (EJ)	R	30	3	6	.333	0	13	13	2	73	73	32	28	1	4.93
2 Dave Lemanczyk	R	29	2	4	.333	0	21	2	0	67	81	27	19	0	4.30
Chris Knapp	R	26	2	11	.154	1	32	20	1	117	133	51	46	0	6.15
Jim Dorsey	R	24	1	2	.333	0	4	4	0	16	25	8	8	0	9.00
Jim Barr (SJ)	R	32	1	4	.200	1	24	7	0	68	90	23	22	0	5.56
Dave Schuler	L	26	0	1	.000	0	8	0	0	13	13	7	9	0	3.46
Bob Ferris	L	25	0	2	.000	0	5	3	0	15	23	9	4	0	6.00
Ralph Botting	L	25	0	3	.000	0	6	6	0	28	40	13	12	0	5.88

SEATTLE — 7th 59-103 .364 38 — DARRELL JOHNSON 39-65 .375 — MAURY WILLS 20-38 .345

Name	G by Pos	B	AGE	G	AB	R	H	2B	3B	HR	RBI	BB	SO	SB	BA	SA
TOTALS			29	163	5489	610	1359	211	35	104	564	483	727	116	.248	.356
Bruce Bochte	1B133, DH11	L	29	148	520	62	156	34	4	13	78	72	81	2	.300	.456
Julio Cruz	2B115, DH3	B	25	119	422	66	88	9	2	2	16	59	49	45	.209	.258
Mario Mendoza	SS114	R	29	114	277	27	68	6	3	2	14	16	42	3	.245	.310
Ted Cox	3B80	R	25	83	247	17	60	7	0	2	23	19	25	0	.243	.304
Leon Roberts	OF104, DH4	R	29	119	374	48	94	18	3	10	33	43	59	6	.251	.396
Juan Beniquez (SJ)	OF65, DH1	R	30	70	237	28	54	10	0	6	21	17	25	2	.228	.346
Dan Meyer	OF123, DH7, 3B5, 1B4	L	27	146	531	56	146	25	6	11	71	31	42	8	.275	.407
Larry Cox	C104	R	32	105	243	18	49	9	0	6	21	17	25	1	.202	.292
Willie Horton (HJ)	DH92	R	37	97	335	32	74	10	1	8	36	39	70	0	.221	.328
Joe Simpson	OF119, 1B3	L	28	129	365	42	91	15	3	3	34	28	43	17	.249	.332
Tom Paciorek	OF60, 1B36, DH23	R	33	126	418	44	114	19	1	15	59	17	67	3	.273	.431
Jim Anderson	SS65, 3B33, DH5, 2B2, C1	R	23	116	317	46	72	7	0	8	30	27	39	2	.227	.325
Larry Milbourne	2B38, SS34, DH5, 3B6	B	29	106	258	31	68	6	6	0	26	19	13	7	.264	.333
Rodney Craig	OF63	B	22	70	240	30	57	15	1	3	20	17	35	3	.238	.346
Bill Stein (XJ)	3B34, 2B14, 1B8, DH5	R	33	67	198	16	53	5	2	5	27	16	25	1	.268	.379
Bob Stinson	C45	B	34	48	107	6	23	2	0	1	8	5	19	0	.215	.262
Jerry Narron	C39, DH1	L	24	48	107	7	21	3	0	4	18	13	18	0	.196	.336
Reggie Walton	OF17, DH11	R	27	31	83	8	23	6	0	2	9	3	10	2	.277	.422
2 Marc Hill	C29	R	28	29	70	8	16	2	1	0	9	3	10	0	.229	.371
Dave Edler	3B28	R	23	28	89	11	20	1	0	3	8	4	16	0	.225	.337
Kim Allen	2B15, OF4, SS1	R	27	23	51	9	12	3	0	0	3	6	3	10	.235	.294

NAME	T	AGE	W	L	PCT	SV	G	GS	CG	IP	H	BB	SO	SHO	ERA
		26	59	103	.364	26	163	163	31	1457	1565	540	703	7	4.38
Glenn Abbott	R	29	12	12	.500	0	31	31	7	215	228	49	78	2	4.10
Rick Honeycutt	L	26	10	17	.370	0	30	30	9	203	221	60	79	1	3.95
Floyd Bannister	L	25	9	13	.409	0	32	32	8	218	200	66	155	0	3.47
Shane Rawley	L	24	7	7	.500	13	59	0	0	114	103	63	68	0	3.32
Dave Heaverlo	R	29	6	3	.667	4	60	0	0	79	75	35	42	0	3.87
Jim Beattie	R	25	5	15	.250	0	33	29	3	187	205	98	67	0	4.86
Rob Dressler	R	26	4	10	.286	0	30	14	3	149	161	33	50	0	3.99
Byron McLaughlin	R	24	3	6	.333	2	45	4	0	91	124	50	41	0	6.82
2 Dave Roberts (GJ)	L	35	2	3	.400	3	37	4	0	80	86	27	47	0	4.39
Mike Parrott (GJ)	R	25	1	16	.059	3	27	16	1	94	136	42	53	0	7.28
Rick Anderson	R	26	0	1	.000	0	5	2	0	10	8	10	7	0	3.60
Gary Wheelock (SJ)	R	28	0	0	—	0	1	0	0	3	4	1	1	0	6.00
Manny Sarmiento	R	24	0	1	.000	0	9	0	0	15	14	6	15	0	3.60

LINE SCORES

Team	1	2	3	4	5	6	7	8	9	10	11		R	H	E

AMERICAN LEAGUE CHAMPIONSHIPS: KANSAS CITY (WEST) 3   NEW YORK (EAST) 0

Game 1 October 8 at Kansas City
```
NY  0 2 0 0 0 0 0 0 0    2 10 1
KC  0 2 2 0 0 0 1 2 X    7 10 0
Guidry, Davis (4),       Gura
Underwood (8)
```

Game 2 October 9 at Kansas City
```
NY  0 0 0 0 0 2 0 0 0    2 8 0
KC  0 0 3 0 0 0 0 0 X    3 6 0
May              Leonard, Quisenberry (9)
```

Game 3 October 10 at New York
```
KC  0 0 0 0 1 0 3 0 0    4 12 1
NY  0 0 0 0 0 2 0 0 0    2 8 0
Splittorff, Quisenberry (6)   John, Gossage (7),
                              Underwood (8)
```

NATIONAL LEAGUE CHAMPIONSHIPS: PHILADELPHIA (EAST) 3   HOUSTON (WEST) 2

Game 1 October 7 at Philadelphia
```
HOU  0 0 1 0 0 0 0 0 0   1 7 0
PHI  0 0 0 0 0 2 1 0 X   3 8 1
Forsch            Carlton, McGraw (8)
```

Game 2 October 8 at Philadelphia
```
HOU  0 0 1 0 0 0 1 1 0 4   7 8 1
PHI  0 0 0 2 0 0 0 1 0 1   4 14 2
Ryan, Sambito (7), Smith (7),   Ruthven, McGraw (8), Reed (9),
LaCorte (9), Andujar (10)       Saucier (10)
```

Game 3 October 10 at Houston
```
PHI  0 0 0 0 0 0 0 0 0 0 0   0 7 1
HOU  0 0 0 0 0 0 0 0 0 0 1   1 6 1
Christenson, Noles (7),     Niekro, Smith (11)
McGraw (8)
```

Game 4 October 11 at Houston
```
PHI  0 0 0 0 0 0 3 0 2   5 13 0
HOU  0 0 0 1 1 0 0 1 0   3 5 1
Carlton, Noles (6),     Ruhle, Smith (8),
Saucier (7), Reed (7),  Sambito (8)
Brusstar (8), McGraw (10)
```

Game 5 October 12 at Houston
```
PHI  0 2 0 0 0 0 5 0 1   8 13 2
HOU  1 0 0 0 0 1 3 2 0   7 14 0
Bystrom, Brusstar (6),     Ryan, Sambito (8),
Christenson (7), Reed (7), Forsch (8), LaCorte (9)
McGraw (8), Ruthven (9)
```

WORLD SERIES — PHILADELPHIA (NL) 4   KANSAS CITY (AL) 2

Game 1 October 14 at Philadelphia
```
KC   0 2 2 0 0 0 0 2 0   6 9 1
PHI  0 0 5 1 1 0 0 0 X   7 11 0
Leonard, Martin (4),     Walk, McGraw (8)
Quisenberry (8)
```

Game 2 October 15 at Philadelphia
```
KC   0 0 0 0 0 1 3 0 0   4 11 0
PHI  0 0 0 0 2 0 0 4 X   6 8 1
Gura, Quisenberry (7)    Carlton, Reed (9)
```

Game 3 October 17 at Kansas City
```
PHI  0 1 0 0 1 0 0 1 0 0   3 14 0
KC   1 0 0 1 0 0 1 0 0 1   4 11 0
Ruthven, McGraw (10)     Gale, Martin (5),
                         Quisenberry (8)
```

Game 4 October 18 at Kansas City
```
PHI  0 1 0 0 0 0 1 1 0   3 10 1
KC   4 1 0 0 0 0 0 0 X   5 10 2
Christenson, Noles (1),  Leonard, Quisenberry (8)
Saucier (6), Brusstar (6)
```

Game 5 October 19 at Kansas City
```
PHI  0 0 0 2 0 0 0 0 2   4 7 0
KC   0 0 0 0 1 2 0 0 0   3 12 2
Bystrom, Reed (6),       Gura, Quisenberry (7)
McGraw (7)
```

Game 6 October 21 at Philadelphia
```
KC   0 0 0 0 0 0 0 1 0   1 7 2
PHI  0 0 2 0 1 1 0 0 X   4 9 0
Gale, Martin (3),        Carlton, McGraw (8)
Splittorff (5), Pattin (7),
Quisenberry (8)
```

COMPOSITE BATTING

Kansas City

NAME	POS	G	AB	R	H	2B	3B	HR	RBI	BA
TOTALS		3	97	14	28	6	1	3	14	.289
Wilson	LF	3	13	2	4	2	1	0	4	.308
Otis	CF	3	12	4	4	1	0	0	0	.333
White	2B	3	11	3	6	1	0	1	3	.545
Aikens	1B	3	11	0	4	0	0	0	0	.364
Washington	SS	3	11	1	4	0	0	0	1	.364
Brett	3B	3	11	3	3	1	0	2	4	.273
McRae	DH	3	10	0	2	0	0	0	0	.200
Porter	C	3	10	2	1	0	0	0	0	.100
Wathan	RF-PH	3	6	1	0	0	0	0	0	.000
Hurdle	RF	3	2	0	0	0	0	0	0	.000
LaCock	1B	1	0	0	0	0	0	0	0	—

New York

NAME	POS	G	AB	R	H	2B	3B	HR	RBI	BA
TOTALS		3	102	6	26	7	1	3	5	.255
Randolph	2B	3	13	0	5	2	0	0	1	.385
Watson	1B	3	12	0	6	3	1	0	0	.500
Cerone	C	3	12	1	4	0	0	1	2	.333
Jackson	RF	3	11	1	3	1	0	0	0	.273
Dent	SS	3	11	0	2	0	0	0	0	.182
Brown	CF	3	10	1	0	0	0	0	0	.000
Rodriguez	3B	2	6	0	2	1	0	0	0	.333
Nettles	3B-PH	2	6	1	1	0	0	1	1	.167
Soderholm	DH	2	6	0	1	0	0	0	0	.167
Gamble	LF-PH-DH	2	5	1	1	0	0	0	0	.200
Piniella	LF-PH-DH	2	5	1	1	0	0	0	1	.200
Murcer	DH	1	4	0	0	0	0	0	0	.000
Spencer	PH	1	1	0	0	0	0	0	0	.000
Lefebvre	LF	1	1	0	0	0	0	0	0	—

Philadelphia

NAME	POS	G	AB	R	H	2B	3B	HR	RBI	BA
TOTALS		5	190	20	55	8	1	1	19	.289
Schmidt	3B	5	24	1	5	1	0	0	1	.208
Trillo	2B	5	21	1	8	2	1	0	4	.381
McBride	RF	5	21	0	5	0	0	0	2	.238
Rose	1B	5	20	3	8	0	0	0	2	.400
Maddox	CF	5	20	2	6	1	0	0	3	.300
Bowa	SS	5	19	2	6	0	0	0	0	.316
Boone	C	5	18	1	4	0	0	0	2	.222
Luzinski	LF-PH	5	17	3	5	2	0	1	4	.294
Smith	LF-PR	3	5	2	3	0	0	0	0	.600
Unser	RF-LF-PH	5	5	2	2	1	0	0	1	.400
Gross	LF-PH	4	4	2	3	0	0	0	1	.750
Carlton	P	2	4	0	0	0	0	0	0	.000
Vukovich	LF-PH	4	3	0	0	0	0	0	0	.000

Christenson P 0-2, Ruthven P 0-2, Bystrom P 0-2, McGraw P 0-1, Brusstar P 0-1, Moreland C-PH 0-1, Aviles PR 0-0, Reed P 0-0, Saucier P 0-0, Noles P 0-0

Houston

NAME	POS	G	AB	R	H	2B	3B	HR	RBI	BA
TOTALS		5	172	19	40	7	5	0	18	.233
Cabell	3B	5	21	5	5	1	0	0	0	.238
Puhl	CF-RF-PH	5	19	4	10	2	0	0	3	.526
Cruz	LF	5	15	3	6	1	1	0	4	.400
Howe	1B-PH	5	15	0	3	1	1	0	2	.200
Morgan	2B	4	13	1	2	1	1	0	0	.154
Reynolds	SS	4	13	2	2	1	0	0	0	.154
Cedeno	CF	3	11	1	2	0	0	0	1	.182
Pujols	C	4	10	1	1	0	1	0	0	.100
Landestoy	2B-SS-PR	5	9	3	2	0	0	0	2	.222
Walling	RF-1B-PH	3	9	2	1	0	0	0	2	.111
Woods	RF-PH	4	8	0	2	0	0	0	1	.250
Ashby	C-PH	2	8	0	1	0	0	0	0	.125
Ryan	P	4	4	0	0	0	0	0	0	.000
Bergman	1B-PR	4	3	0	1	0	1	0	2	.333
Leonard	PH-RF	3	3	0	0	0	0	0	0	.000
Ruhle	P	1	3	0	0	0	0	0	0	.000
Niekro	P	1	3	0	0	0	0	0	0	.000
Forsch	P	2	2	0	2	0	0	0	0	1.000

LaCorte P 0-1, Bochy C 0-1, Heep PH 0-1, Sambito P 0-0, Andujar P 0-0, Smith P 0-0

Philadelphia (World Series)

NAME	POS	G	AB	R	H	2B	3B	HR	RBI	BA
TOTALS		6	201	27	59	13	0	3	26	.294
Bowa	SS	6	24	3	9	1	0	0	2	.375
McBride	RF	6	23	3	7	1	0	1	5	.304
Rose	1B	6	23	2	6	1	0	0	1	.261
Trillo	2B	6	23	4	5	2	0	0	2	.217
Maddox	CF	6	22	1	5	2	0	0	1	.227
Schmidt	3B	6	21	6	8	1	0	2	7	.381
Smith	LF-DH-PR	6	19	2	5	1	0	0	1	.263
Boone	C	6	17	3	7	2	0	0	4	.412
Moreland	DH	3	12	1	4	0	0	0	1	.333
Luzinski	DH-LF	3	9	0	0	0	0	0	0	.000
Unser	PH-CF-LF	3	6	2	3	2	0	0	2	.500
Gross	PH-LF	4	2	0	0	0	0	0	0	.000

Kansas City (World Series)

NAME	POS	G	AB	R	H	2B	3B	HR	RBI	BA
TOTALS		6	207	23	60	9	2	8	22	.290
Wilson	LF	6	26	3	4	1	0	0	0	.154
White	2B	6	25	4	2	0	0	0	0	.080
Brett	3B	6	24	3	9	2	1	1	3	.375
McRae	DH	6	24	3	9	3	0	1	3	.375
Otis	CF	6	23	4	11	2	0	3	7	.478
Washington	SS	6	22	1	6	0	0	0	2	.273
Aikens	1B	6	20	5	8	0	1	4	8	.400
Porter	C-PH	5	14	1	2	0	0	0	1	.143
Hurdle	RF	4	12	1	5	1	0	0	4	.417
Cardenal	RF-PH	4	10	0	2	0	0	0	0	.200
Wathan	PH-RF-C	3	7	1	2	0	0	0	1	.286
Concepcion	PR	3	0	0	0	0	0	0	0	—
Chalk	3B	1	0	1	0	0	0	0	0	—
LaCock	1B	1	0	0	0	0	0	0	0	—

COMPOSITE PITCHING

Kansas City

NAME	G	IP	H	BB	SO	W	L	SV	ERA
TOTALS	3	27	26	6	16	3	0	1	1.67
Gura	1	9	10	1	4	1	0	0	2.00
Leonard	1	8	7	1	8	1	0	0	2.25
Splittorff	1	5.1	5	2	3	0	0	0	1.69
Quisenberry	2	4.2	4	2	1	1	0	1	0.00

New York

NAME	G	IP	H	BB	SO	W	L	SV	ERA
TOTALS	3	25	28	9	15	0	3	0	4.32
May	1	8	6	3	4	0	1	0	3.38
John	1	6.2	8	1	3	0	0	0	2.70
Davis	1	4	3	1	3	0	0	0	2.25
Underwood	2	3	3	0	3	0	0	0	0.00
Guidry	1	3	5	4	2	0	1	0	12.00
Gossage	1	0.1	3	0	0	0	0	1	54.00

Philadelphia

NAME	G	IP	H	BB	SO	W	L	SV	ERA
TOTALS	5	49.1	40	31	19	3	2	2	3.28
Carlton	2	12.1	11	8	6	1	0	0	2.19
Ruthven	2	9	3	5	4	1	0	0	2.00
McGraw	5	8	8	4	5	0	1	2	4.50
Christenson	2	6.2	5	5	2	0	0	0	4.05
Bystrom	2	5.1	7	2	1	0	0	0	1.69
Noles	2	2.1	3	0	1	0	0	0	0.00
Brusstar	2	2.2	1	1	0	1	0	0	3.38
Reed	3	2	3	1	1	0	0	1	18.00
Saucier	2	0.2	1	2	0	1	0	0	0.00

Houston

NAME	G	IP	H	BB	SO	W	L	SV	ERA
TOTALS	5	49	55	13	37	2	3	1	3.49
Ryan	2	13.1	16	3	14	0	0	0	5.40
Niekro	1	10	6	1	2	0	0	0	0.00
Forsch	2	8.2	10	1	6	0	1	0	4.15
Ruhle	1	7	8	1	3	0	0	0	3.86
Sambito	3	3.2	4	2	6	0	1	0	4.91
LaCorte	2	3	7	2	2	1	1	0	3.00
Smith	3	2.1	4	2	4	1	0	0	3.86
Andujar	1	1	0	1	0	0	0	1	0.00

Philadelphia (World Series)

NAME	G	IP	H	BB	SO	W	L	SV	ERA
TOTALS	6	53.2	60	26	49	4	2	3	3.69
Carlton	2	15	14	9	17	2	0	0	2.40
Ruthven	1	9	9	0	7	0	0	0	3.00
McGraw	4	7.2	5	8	10	1	1	2	1.17
Walk	1	7	8	3	4	0	0	0	7.71
Bystrom	1	5	10	1	4	0	0	0	5.40
Noles	1	4.2	5	2	6	0	0	0	1.93
Brusstar	1	2.1	0	1	0	0	0	0	0.00
Reed	2	2	2	0	2	0	0	1	0.00
Saucier	1	0.2	2	2	0	0	0	0	0.00
Christenson	1	0.1	5	1	0	0	0	0	108.00

Kansas City (World Series)

NAME	G	IP	H	BB	SO	W	L	SV	ERA
TOTALS	6	52	59	15	17	2	4	1	4.15
Gura	2	12.1	8	3	4	0	0	0	2.19
Leonard	2	10.2	15	2	5	1	1	0	6.75
Quisenberry	6	10.1	10	3	0	1	2	1	5.23
Martin	3	9.2	11	3	2	0	1	0	2.79
Gale	2	6.1	11	4	0	1	0	0	4.26
Splittorff	1	1.2	4	0	2	0	0	0	5.40
Pattin	1	1	0	0	2	0	0	0	0.00

PHILADELPHIA 1st 91-71 .562   DALLAS GREEN

Name	G by Pos	B	AGE	G	AB	R	H	2B	3B	HR	RBI	BB	SO	SB	BA	SA
TOTALS			31	162	5625	728	1517	272	54	117	674	472	708	140	.270	.400
Pete Rose	1B162	B	39	162	655	95	185	42	1	1	64	66	33	12	.282	.354
Manny Trillo	2B140	R	29	141	531	68	155	25	9	7	43	32	46	8	.292	.412
Larry Bowa	SS147	B	34	147	540	57	144	16	4	2	39	24	28	21	.267	.322
Mike Schmidt	3B149	R	30	150	548	104	157	25	8	48	121	89	119	12	.286	.624
Bake McBride	OF133	L	31	137	554	68	171	33	10	9	87	26	58	13	.309	.453
Garry Maddox	OF143	R	30	143	549	59	142	31	3	11	73	18	52	25	.259	.386
Greg Luzinski (KJ)	OF105	R	29	106	368	44	84	19	1	19	56	60	100	3	.228	.440
Bob Boone	C138	R	32	141	480	34	110	23	1	9	55	48	41	3	.229	.338
Greg Gross	OF91, 1B1	L	27	127	154	19	37	7	2	0	12	24	7	1	.240	.312
Lonnie Smith	OF82	R	24	100	298	69	101	14	4	3	20	26	48	33	.339	.443
Del Unser	1B31, OF23	L	35	96	110	15	29	6	4	0	10	10	21	0	.264	.391
George Vukovich	OF28	L	24	78	58	6	13	1	1	0	8	6	9	0	.224	.276
Keith Moreland	C39, 3B4, OF2	R	26	62	159	13	50	8	0	4	29	8	14	3	.314	.440
Ramon Aviles	SS29, 2B15	R	28	51	101	12	28	6	0	2	9	10	9	0	.277	.396
John Vukovich	3B34, 2B9, SS5, 1B1	R	32	49	62	4	10	1	1	0	5	2	7	0	.161	.210
Luis Aguayo	2B14, SS5	R	21	20	47	7	13	1	2	1	8	2	3	1	.277	.447
Jay Loviglio	2B1	R	24	16	5	7	0	0	0	0	0	0	1	0	1.000	1.000
Bob Dernier	OF3	R	23	10	7	5	4	0	0	0	1	1	0	3	.571	.571
Tim McCarver	1B2	L	38	6	5	2	1	1	0	0	2	1	0	0	.200	.400
Orlando Isales	OF2	R	20	3	5	1	2	0	1	0	3	1	0	0	.400	.800
Don McCormack	C2	R	24	2	1	0	1	0	0	0	0	0	0	0	01.000	1.000
Ozzie Virgil	C1	R	23	1	5	0	1	0	0	0	0	0	1	0	.200	.400

NAME	T	AGE	W	L	PCT	SV	G	GS	CG	IP	H	BB	SO	SHO	ERA
TOTALS		29	91	71	.562	40	162	162	25	1480	1419	530	889	8	3.43
Steve Carlton	L	35	24	9	.727	0	38	38	13	304	243	90	286	3	2.34
Dick Ruthven	R	29	17	10	.630	0	33	33	6	223	241	74	86	1	3.55
Bob Walk	R	23	11	7	.611	0	27	27	2	152	163	71	94	0	4.56
Ron Reed	R	37	7	5	.583	9	55	0	0	91	88	30	54	0	4.05
Kevin Saucier (AJ)	L	23	7	3	.700	0	40	0	0	50	50	20	25	0	3.42
Marty Bystrom	R	21	5	0	1.000	0	6	5	1	36	26	9	21	1	1.50
Larry Christenson(EJ)	R	26	5	1	.833	0	14	14	0	74	62	27	49	0	4.01
Tug McGraw	L	35	5	4	.556	20	57	0	0	92	62	23	75	0	1.47
Randy Lerch	L	25	4	14	.222	0	30	22	2	150	178	55	57	0	5.16
Nino Espinosa (SJ)	R	26	3	5	.375	0	12	12	1	76	73	19	13	0	3.79
Warren Brusstar (SJ)	R	28	2	2	.500	0	26	0	0	39	42	13	21	0	3.69
Dickie Noles	R	23	1	4	.200	6	48	3	0	81	80	42	57	0	3.89
2 Sparky Lyle	L	35	0	0	—	2	10	0	0	14	11	6	6	0	1.93
Scott Munninghoff	R	21	0	0	—	0	4	0	0	6	8	5	2	0	4.50
Mark Davis	L	19	0	0	—	0	2	1	0	7	4	5	5	0	2.57
Lerrin LaGrow	R	31	0	2	.000	3	25	0	0	39	42	17	21	0	4.15
Dan Larson	R	25	0	5	.000	0	12	7	0	46	46	24	17	0	3.13

MONTREAL 2nd 90-72 .556 1   DICK WILLIAMS

Name	G by Pos	B	AGE	G	AB	R	H	2B	3B	HR	RBI	BB	SO	SB	BA	SA
TOTALS			27	162	5465	694	1407	250	61	114	647	547	865	237	.257	.388
Warren Cromartie	1B158, OF2	L	26	162	597	74	172	33	5	14	70	51	64	8	.288	.430
Rodney Scott	2B129, SS21	B	26	154	567	84	127	13	13	0	46	70	75	63	.224	.293
Chris Speier	SS127, 3B1	R	30	128	388	35	103	14	4	1	32	52	38	0	.265	.330
Larry Parrish (WJ)	3B124	R	26	126	452	55	115	27	3	15	72	36	80	2	.254	.427
Ellis Valentine (BY-LJ)	OF83	R	25	86	311	40	98	22	2	13	67	25	44	5	.315	.524
Andre Dawson	OF147	R	25	151	577	96	178	41	7	17	87	44	69	34	.308	.492
Ron LeFlore	OF130	R	32	139	521	95	134	21	11	4	39	62	99	97	.257	.363
Gary Carter	C149	R	26	154	549	76	145	25	5	29	101	58	78	3	.264	.486
Rowland Office	OF97	L	27	116	292	36	78	13	4	6	30	36	39	3	.267	.401
Jerry White	OF84	R	27	110	214	22	56	9	3	7	23	30	37	3	.262	.430
Tony Bernazard	2B39,SS22	B	23	82	183	26	41	7	1	5	18	17	41	9	.224	.355
Tommy Hutton	1B7, OF4, P1	L	34	62	55	2	12	2	0	0	5	4	10	0	.218	.255
Ken Macha	3B33, 1B2, OF1, C1	R	29	49	107	10	31	5	1	1	8	11	17	0	.290	.383
John Tamargo (RJ)	C12	B	28	37	51	4	14	3	0	1	13	6	5	0	.275	.392
Bob Pate	OF18	R	26	23	39	3	10	2	0	0	5	3	6	0	.256	.308
Brad Mills	3B18	L	23	21	60	1	18	0	0	0	8	5	6	0	.300	.317
1 Bill Almon	SS12, 2B1	R	27	18	38	2	10	1	1	0	3	1	5	0	.263	.342
Tim Raines	2B7, OF1	B	20	15	20	5	1	0	0	0	0	6	3	5	.050	.050
2 Willie Montanez	1B4	L	32	14	19	1	4	0	0	0	1	3	1	0	.211	.211
Bobby Ramos	C12	R	24	13	32	5	5	2	0	0	2	5	5	0	.156	.219
Jerry Manuel	SS7	R	26	7	6	0	0	0	0	0	0	0	2	0	.000	.000
Tim Wallach	OF3, 1B1	R	22	5	11	1	2	1	0	0	2	1	5	0	.182	.455

NAME	T	AGE	W	L	PCT	SV	G	GS	CG	IP	H	BB	SO	SHO	ERA
TOTALS		32	90	72	.556	36	162	162	33	1457	1447	460	823	15	3.48
Steve Rogers	R	30	16	11	.593	0	37	37	14	281	247	85	147	4	2.98
Scott Sanderson	R	23	16	11	.593	0	33	33	7	211	206	56	125	3	3.11
Bill Gullickson	R	21	10	5	.667	0	24	19	5	141	127	50	120	2	3.00
Elias Sosa	R	30	9	6	.600	9	67	0	0	94	104	19	58	0	3.06
David Palmer (AJ)	R	22	8	6	.571	0	24	19	3	130	124	30	73	1	2.98
Woody Fryman	L	40	7	4	.636	17	61	0	0	80	61	30	59	0	2.25
Charlie Lea	R	23	7	5	.583	0	21	19	0	104	103	55	56	0	3.72
Stan Bahnsen	R	35	7	6	.538	4	57	0	0	91	80	33	48	0	3.07
Fred Norman	L	37	4	4	.500	4	48	8	2	98	96	40	58	0	4.13
Bill Lee (PJ)	L	33	4	6	.400	0	24	18	2	118	156	22	34	0	4.96
1 Ross Grimsley	L	30	2	4	.333	0	11	7	0	41	61	12	11	0	6.37
Steve Ratzer	R	26	0	0	—	0	1	1	0	4	2	1	1	0	11.25
Tommy Hutton	L	34	0	0	—	0	1	0	0	3	1	1	0	0	27.00
Dale Murray	R	30	0	1	.000	0	16	0	0	29	39	12	16	0	6.21
Hal Dues	R	25	0	0	—	0	6	1	0	12	17	4	2	0	6.75
2 John D'Acquisto	R	28	0	2	.000	2	11	0	0	21	14	9	15	0	2.14

PITTSBURGH 3rd 83-79 .512 8   CHUCK TANNER

Name	G by Pos	B	AGE	G	AB	R	H	2B	3B	HR	RBI	BB	SO	SB	BA	SA
TOTALS			30	162	5517	666	1469	249	38	116	626	452	760	209	.266	.388
Willie Stargell (KJ)	1B54	L	40	67	202	28	53	10	1	11	38	26	52	0	.282	.485
Phil Garner	2B151, SS1	R	31	151	548	62	142	27	6	5	58	46	53	32	.259	.358
Tim Foli	SS125	R	29	127	495	61	131	22	0	3	38	19	23	11	.265	.327
Bill Madlock	3B127, 1B12	R	29	137	494	62	137	22	4	10	53	45	33	16	.277	.399
Dave Parker	OF130	L	29	139	518	71	153	31	1	17	79	25	69	10	.295	.458
Omar Moreno	OF162	L	27	162	676	87	168	20	13	2	36	57	101	96	.249	.325
Mike Easler	OF119	L	29	132	393	66	133	27	3	21	74	43	65	5	.338	.583
Ed Ott	C117, OF3	L	28	120	392	35	102	14	0	8	41	33	47	1	.260	.357
John Milner	1B70, OF11	L	30	114	238	31	58	6	0	8	34	52	29	2	.244	.370
Lee Lacy	OF88, 3B3	R	32	109	278	45	93	20	4	7	33	28	33	18	.335	.511
Bill Robinson	1B49, OF41	R	37	100	272	28	78	10	1	12	36	15	45	1	.287	.463
Dale Berra	3B48, SS45, 2B4	R	23	93	245	21	54	8	2	6	31	16	52	2	.220	.343
Steve Nicosia	C58	R	24	60	176	16	38	8	0	1	22	19	16	0	.216	.278
Manny Sanguillen	1B5	R	36	47	48	2	12	3	0	0	2	3	1	0	.250	.313
Matt Alexander	OF4, 2B1	R	33	37	3	13	1	0	0	0	0	0	0	10	.333	.667
Vance Law	2B11, SS8, 3B1	R	23	25	74	11	17	2	2	0	3	3	7	2	.230	.311
2 Kurt Bevacqua	3B9, 1B2	R	33	22	43	1	7	1	0	0	4	6	7	0	.163	.186
Tony Pena	C6	R	23	8	21	1	9	1	1	0	1	0	4	0	.429	.571
2 Bernie Carbo		L	32	7	6	0	2	0	0	0	1	1	1	0	.333	.333
Bob Beall		B	32	3	1	0	0	0	0	0	0	0	0	0	.000	.000

NAME	T	AGE	W	L	PCT	SV	G	GS	CG	IP	H	BB	SO	SHO	ERA
TOTALS		30	83	79	.512	43	162	162	25	1458	1422	451	832	8	3.58
Jim Bibby	R	35	19	6	.760	0	35	34	6	238	210	88	144	1	3.33
John Candelaria	L	26	11	14	.440	1	35	34	7	233	246	50	97	0	4.02
Grant Jackson	L	37	8	4	.667	9	61	0	0	71	71	20	31	0	2.92
Kent Tekulve	R	33	8	12	.400	21	78	0	0	93	96	40	47	0	3.39
Bert Blyleven	R	29	8	13	.381	0	34	32	5	217	219	59	168	2	3.82
Eddie Solomon	R	29	7	3	.700	0	26	12	2	100	96	37	35	0	2.70
Rick Rhoden	R	27	7	5	.583	0	20	19	2	127	133	40	70	0	3.83
Don Robinson	R	23	7	10	.412	1	29	24	3	160	157	45	103	2	3.99
Enrique Romo	R	32	5	5	.500	11	74	0	0	124	117	28	82	0	3.27
Jim Rooker (SJ)	L	37	2	2	.500	0	4	4	0	18	16	12	8	0	3.50
2 Jesse Jefferson	R	31	1	0	1.000	0	1	1	0	7	3	2	4	0	1.29
1 Andy Hassler	L	28	0	0	—	0	6	0	0	12	9	4	4	0	3.75
Mickey Mahler	L	27	0	0	—	0	2	0	0	4	3	1	0		63.00
Mark Lee	R	27	0	0	—	0	6	0	0	6	5	3	2	0	4.50
Pascual Perez	R	23	0	1	.000	0	2	0	0	12	15	2	7	0	3.75
1 Dave Roberts	L	35	0	0	—	0	20	0	0	38	23	17	28	1	4.50
Rod Scurry	L	24	0	0	—	0	20	0	0	10	8	8	9	0	2.13

ST. LOUIS 4th 74-88 .457 17   KEN BOYER 18-33 .353 JACK KROL 0-1 .000 WHITEY HERZOG 38-35 .521 RED SCHOENDIENST 18-19 .486

Name	G by Pos	B	AGE	G	AB	R	H	2B	3B	HR	RBI	BB	SO	SB	BA	SA
TOTALS			27	162	5608	738	1541	300	49	101	688	451	781	117	.275	.400
Keith Hernandez	1B157	L	26	159	595	111	191	39	8	16	99	86	73	14	.321	.494
Ken Oberkfell (KJ)	2B101, 3B16	L	24	116	422	58	128	27	6	3	46	51	23	4	.303	.417
Garry Templeton (BG)	SS115	B	24	118	504	83	161	19	9	4	43	18	43	31	.319	.417
Ken Reitz	3B150	R	29	151	523	39	141	33	0	8	58	22	44	0	.270	.379
George Hendrick	OF149	R	30	150	572	73	173	33	2	25	109	32	67	6	.302	.498
Tony Scott	OF134	B	28	143	415	51	104	19	3	0	28	35	68	22	.251	.311
Bobby Bonds	OF70	R	34	86	231	37	47	5	3	5	24	33	74	15	.203	.316
Ted Simmons	C129, OF5	B	30	145	495	84	150	33	2	21	98	59	45	1	.303	.505
Dane Iorg	OF63, 1B5, 3B1	L	30	105	251	33	76	23	1	3	36	20	34	1	.303	.438
Leon Durham	OF78, 1B8	L	22	96	303	42	82	15	4	8	42	18	55	8	.271	.426
Terry Kennedy	C41, OF28	L	24	84	248	28	63	12	3	4	34	28	34	0	.254	.375
Tommy Herr	2B58, SS14	B	24	76	222	29	55	12	5	0	15	16	21	9	.248	.347
Mike Phillips	SS37, 2B9, 3B8	L	30	63	128	13	30	5	0	0	7	8	17	0	.234	.273
Mike Ramsey	2B24, SS20, 3B8	B	26	59	126	11	33	4	1	0	7	4	15	0	.262	.341
Tito Landrum	OF29	R	25	35	77	6	19	2	0	6	6	11	9	2	.247	.325
Bob Forsch	P31	R	30	32	78	11	23	5	0	3	10	2	18	1	.295	.474
Keith Smith	OF7	R	24	31	3	4	1	0	0	2	1	6	0	.129	.161
Steve Swisher	C8	R	28	18	24	2	6	1	0	0	1	7	1	0	.250	.292
1 Bernie Carbo		L	32	14	11	0	2	0	0	0	1	3	6	0	.182	.182
1 Jim Lentine	OF6	R	25	9	10	1	1	0	0	0	1	0	2	0	.100	.100
Joe DeSa	1B1, OF1	L	20	7	11	0	3	1	0	0	1	0	1	0	.273	.273
Ty Waller	3B5	R	23	5	12	1	1	0	0	0	1	1	5	0	.083	.083

NAME	T	AGE	W	L	PCT	SV	G	GS	CG	IP	H	BB	SO	SHO	ERA
TOTALS		28	74	88	.457	27	162	162	34	1447	1454	495	664	9	3.93
Pete Vuckovich	R	27	12	9	.571	1	32	30	7	222	203	68	132	3	3.41
Bob Forsch	R	30	11	10	.524	0	31	31	8	215	225	33	87	0	3.77
2 Jim Kaat	L	41	8	7	.533	4	49	14	6	130	140	33	36	1	3.81
Bob Sykes	L	25	6	10	.375	0	27	19	4	126	134	54	50	3	4.64
John Littlefield	R	26	5	5	.500	9	52	0	0	66	71	20	22	0	3.14
Silvio Martinez (EJ)	R	24	5	10	.333	0	25	20	2	120	127	48	39	0	4.80
John Urrea	R	25	4	1	.800	3	30	1	0	65	57	41	36	0	3.46
Don Hood	L	30	4	6	.400	0	33	8	1	82	90	34	35	0	3.63
John Fulgham (SJ)	R	24	4	4	.500	0	15	14	4	85	66	32	48	1	3.39
Andy Rincon	R	21	3	1	.750	0	4	4	1	31	23	7	22	0	2.61
Kim Seaman	L	23	3	3	.500	4	26	0	0	24	16	13	10	0	3.38
Roy Thomas	R	27	2	3	.400	0	24	5	0	55	59	25	22	0	4.75
John Martin	L	24	2	3	.400	0	9	5	1	42	39	9	23	0	4.29
Pedro Borbon	R	33	1	0	1.000	1	10	0	0	19	17	10	4	0	7.50
Donnie Moore	R	26	1	1	.500	0	11	0	0	22	25	5	10	0	6.14
Jeff Little	L	23	1	1	.500	0	12	0	0	16	11	9	7	0	3.79
Al Olmsted	L	23	1	1	.500	0	5	5	1	35	32	14	14	0	2.83
George Frazier	R	25	1	4	.200	3	25	4	0	23	24	7	11	0	2.74
Darold Knowles	L	38	1	1	.500	0	2	0	0	2	1	1	1	0	9.00
Mark Littell (EJ)	R	27	0	0	—	0	11	0	0	7	11	7	0		2.20
Jim Otten	R	29	0	0	—	0	5	0	0	31	4	0	55	71	5.56
Buddy Schultz 29 (SJ)															

EAST DIVISION

NEW YORK — 5th 67-95 .414 24 — JOE TORRE

Name	G by Pos	B	AGE	G	AB	R	H	2B	3B	HR	RBI	BB	SO	SB	BA	SA
TOTALS			28	162	5478	611	1407	218	41	61	554	501	840	158	.257	.345
Lee Mazzilli	1B92, OF66	B	25	152	578	82	162	31	4	16	76	82	92	41	.280	.431
Doug Flynn (BW)	2B128	R	29	128	443	46	113	9	8	0	24	22	20	2	.255	.312
Frank Taveras	SS140	R	30	141	562	65	157	27	0	0	25	23	64	32	.279	.327
Elliott Maddox	3B115, OF4, 1B2	R	32	130	411	35	101	16	1	4	34	52	44	1	.246	.319
Claudell Washington	OF70	L	25	79	284	38	78	16	4	10	42	20	63	14	.275	.465
Joel Youngblood	OF121, 3B21, 2B6	R	28	146	514	58	142	26	2	8	69	52	69	14	.276	.381
Steve Henderson	OF136	R	27	143	513	75	149	17	8	8	58	62	90	23	.290	.402
John Stearns (BG)	C74, 1B16, 3B1	R	28	91	319	42	91	25	1	0	45	33	24	7	.285	.370
Mike Jorgensen	1B72, OF31	L	31	119	321	43	82	11	0	7	43	46	55	0	.255	.355
Alex Trevino	C86, 3B14, 2B1	R	22	106	355	26	91	11	2	0	37	13	41	0	.256	.299
Jerry Morales	OF63	R	31	94	193	19	49	7	1	3	30	13	31	2	.254	.347
Dan Norman	OF19	R	25	69	92	5	17	1	1	2	9	6	14	5	.185	.283
2 Bill Almon	SS22, 2B18, 3B9	R	27	48	112	13	19	3	2	0	4	8	27	2	.170	.232
Jose Moreno	2B4, 3B4	R	22	37	46	6	9	2	1	0	3	3	12	1	.196	.413
Ron Hodges (SJ)	C9	L	31	36	42	4	10	2	0	0	5	10	13	1	.238	.286
Mookie Wilson	OF26	B	24	27	105	16	26	5	3	0	4	12	19	7	.248	.352
Wally Backman	2B20, SS8	B	20	27	93	12	30	1	1	0	9	11	14	2	.323	.355
1 Jose Cardenal	OF6, 1B5	R	36	26	42	4	7	1	0	0	4	6	4	0	.167	.190
Hubie Brooks	3B23	R	23	24	81	8	25	2	1	1	10	5	9	1	.309	.395
Mario Ramirez	SS7, 2B4, 3B3	R	22	18	24	2	5	0	0	0	0	2	4	0	.208	.208
Butch Benton	C8	R	22	12	21	0	1	0	0	0	0	0	7	0	.048	.048
Phil Mankowski (SJ-IL)	3B3	L	27	8	12	1	2	1	0	0	1	2	4	0	.167	.250
Luis Rosado	1B1	R	24	2	4	0	0	0	0	0	0	0	1	0	.000	.000

NAME	T	AGE	W	L	PCT	SV	G	GS	CG	IP	H	BB	SO	SHO	ERA
	R	27	67	95	.414	33	162	162	17	1451	1473	510	886	9	3.85
Mark Bomback	R	27	10	8	.556	0	36	25	2	163	191	49	68	1	4.09
Jeff Reardon	R	24	8	7	.533	6	61	0	0	110	96	47	101	0	2.62
Neil Allen	R	22	7	10	.412	22	59	0	0	97	87	40	79	0	3.71
Pete Falcone	L	26	7	10	.412	1	37	23	1	157	163	58	109	0	4.53
Ray Burris (BG)	R	29	7	13	.350	0	29	29	1	170	181	54	83	0	4.02
Tom Hausman	R	27	6	5	.545	5	40	5	0	122	125	36	53	0	3.98
Pat Zachry (AJ)	R	28	6	10	.375	0	28	26	7	165	145	58	88	3	3.00
Craig Swan (SJ)	R	29	5	9	.357	0	21	21	4	128	117	30	79	1	3.59
Ed Glynn	L	27	3	3	.500	1	38	0	0	52	49	23	32	0	4.15
Johnny Pacella	R	23	3	4	.429	0	32	15	0	84	89	59	68	0	5.14
Mike Scott	R	25	1	1	.500	0	6	6	1	29	40	8	13	1	4.34
Ed Lynch	R	24	1	1	.500	0	5	4	0	19	24	5	9	0	5.21
Dyar Miller	R	34	1	2	.333	1	31	0	0	42	37	11	28	0	1.93
Kevin Kobel	L	26	1	4	.200	0	14	1	0	24	36	11	8	0	7.13
Roy Lee Jackson	R	26	1	7	.125	1	24	8	1	71	78	20	58	0	4.18
Scott Holman	R	21	0	0	.——	0	4	0	0	7	6	1	3	0	1.29
Juan Berenguer	R	25	0	1	.000	0	6	0	0	9	9	7	0	0	6.00

CHICAGO — 6th 64-98 .395 27 — PRESTON GOMEZ 38-52 .422 — JOEY AMALFITANO 26-46 .361

Name	G by Pos	B	AGE	G	AB	R	H	2B	3B	HR	RBI	BB	SO	SB	BA	SA
TOTALS			28	162	5619	614	1411	251	35	107	578	471	912	93	.251	.365
Bill Buckner	1B94, OF50	L	30	145	578	69	187	41	3	10	68	30	18	1	.324	.457
Mike Tyson	2B117	B	30	123	341	34	91	19	3	3	23	15	61	1	.267	.337
Ivan DeJesus	SS156	R	27	157	618	78	160	26	3	3	33	60	81	44	.259	.325
Lenny Randle	3B111, 2B17, OF6	R	31	130	489	67	135	19	6	5	39	50	55	19	.276	.370
Mike Vail	OF77	R	28	114	312	30	93	17	2	6	47	14	77	2	.298	.423
Jerry Martin	OF129	R	31	141	494	57	112	22	2	23	73	38	107	8	.227	.419
Dave Kingman (SJ)	OF61, 1B2	R	31	81	255	31	71	8	0	18	57	21	44	2	.278	.522
Tim Blackwell	C103	B	27	103	320	24	87	16	4	5	30	41	62	0	.272	.394
Larry Biittner	1B41, OF38	L	34	127	273	21	68	12	2	1	34	18	33	1	.249	.319
Jesus Figueroa	OF57	L	25	115	198	20	50	5	0	1	11	14	16	2	.253	.293
Mick Kelleher	2B57, 3B31, SS17	R	32	105	96	12	14	1	1	0	4	9	17	1	.146	.177
Scot Thompson (CN)	OF66, 1B12	L	24	102	226	26	48	10	1	2	13	28	31	6	.212	.292
Steve Dillard	3B51, 2B38, SS2	R	29	100	244	31	55	8	1	4	27	20	54	2	.225	.316
2 Cliff Johnson	1B46, OF3, C1	R	32	68	196	28	48	8	0	10	34	29	35	0	.235	.429
Barry Foote (XJ)	C55	R	28	63	202	16	48	13	1	6	28	13	18	1	.238	.401
Ken Henderson (KJ)	OF22	B	34	44	82	7	16	3	0	2	9	17	19	0	.195	.305
Jim Tracy	OF39	L	24	42	88	15	18	4	1	3	12	11	29	1	.205	.375
Carlos Lezcano	OF31, 1B1	R	23	42	122	12	31	3	3	3	13	13	37	2	.254	.402
Steve Ontiveros (JL)	3B24	B	28	31	77	7	16	3	0	1	3	14	17	0	.208	.286
Mike O'Berry	C19	R	26	19	48	7	10	1	0	0	5	5	13	0	.208	.229
Steve Macko (KJ)	SS3, 3B2, 2B1	R	25	6	20	2	6	2	0	0	2	0	5	0	.300	.400
Bill Hayes	C3	R	22	4	9	0	2	1	0	0	0	3	0	0	.222	.333

NAME	T	AGE	W	L	PCT	SV	G	GS	CG	IP	H	BB	SO	SHO	ERA
	R	27	64	98	.395	35	162	162	13	1479	1525	589	923	6	3.89
Lynn McGlothen	R	30	12	14	.462	0	39	27	2	182	211	64	119	2	4.80
Rick Reuschel	R	31	11	13	.458	0	38	38	6	257	281	76	140	0	3.40
Dennis Lamp	R	27	10	14	.417	0	41	37	2	203	259	82	83	1	5.19
Mike Krukow	R	28	10	15	.400	0	34	34	3	205	200	80	130	0	4.39
Dick Tidrow	R	33	6	5	.545	6	84	0	0	116	97	53	97	0	2.79
Bruce Sutter	R	27	5	8	.385	28	60	0	0	102	90	34	76	0	2.65
Bill Caudill	R	23	4	6	.400	1	72	2	0	128	100	59	112	0	2.18
Lee Smith	R	22	2	0	1.000	0	18	0	0	22	21	14	17	0	2.86
Doug Capilla	L	28	2	3	.400	0	39	11	0	90	82	51	51	0	4.10
Randy Martz	R	24	2	2	.500	0	8	3	0	30	28	11	5	0	2.10
Willie Hernandez	L	25	1	9	.100	0	53	7	0	108	115	45	75	0	4.42
George Riley	L	23	0	0	.000	0	22	0	0	36	41	20	18	0	5.75

WEST DIVISION

HOUSTON — 1st 93-70 .571 — BILL VIRDON (Defeated Los Angeles in a 1 game playoff)

Name	G by Pos	B	AGE	G	AB	R	H	2B	3B	HR	RBI	BB	SO	SB	BA	SA
TOTALS			28	163	5566	637	1455	231	67	75	599	540	755	194	.261	.367
Art Howe	1B77, 3B25, SS5, 2B3	R	33	110	321	34	91	12	5	10	46	34	29	1	.283	.445
Joe Morgan	2B130	L	36	141	461	66	112	17	5	11	49	93	47	24	.243	.373
Craig Reynolds	SS135	L	27	137	381	34	86	9	6	3	28	20	39	2	.226	.304
Enos Cabell	3B150, 1B1	R	30	152	604	69	167	23	8	2	55	26	84	21	.276	.351
Terry Puhl	OF135	L	24	141	535	75	151	24	5	13	55	60	52	27	.282	.410
Cesar Cedeno	OF136	R	29	137	499	71	154	32	8	10	73	66	72	48	.309	.465
Jose Cruz	OF158	L	32	160	612	79	185	29	7	11	91	60	66	36	.302	.426
Alan Ashby	C114	B	28	116	352	30	90	19	2	3	48	35	40	0	.256	.347
Rafael Landestoy	2B94, SS65, 3B3	B	27	149	393	42	97	13	8	1	27	31	37	23	.247	.328
Denny Walling	1B63, OF19	L	26	100	284	30	85	6	5	3	29	35	26	4	.299	.387
Dave Bergman	1B59, OF5	L	27	90	78	12	20	6	1	0	3	10	10	1	.256	.359
Jeff Leonard	OF56, 1B11	R	24	88	216	29	46	7	5	3	20	19	46	4	.213	.333
Luis Pujols	C75, 3B1	R	24	78	221	15	44	6	1	0	20	13	29	0	.199	.235
Julio Gonzalez	SS16, 3B11, 2B2	R	27	40	52	5	6	1	0	0	1	1	8	1	.115	.135
Danny Heep	1B22	L	22	33	87	6	24	8	0	0	6	8	9	0	.276	.368
Bruce Bochy	C10, 1B1	R	25	22	22	0	4	1	0	0	0	5	7	0	.182	.227
Gary Woods	OF14	R	25	19	53	8	20	5	0	2	15	2	9	1	.377	.585
Scott Loucks	OF4	R	23	8	3	4	1	0	0	0	0	0	0	2	.333	.333
Mike Fischlin	SS1	R	24	1	1	0	0	0	0	0	0	0	0	0	.000	.000
Alan Knicely		R	25	1	0	0	0	0	0	0	0	0	0	0	.000	.000

NAME	T	AGE	W	L	PCT	SV	G	GS	CG	IP	H	BB	SO	SHO	ERA
	R	29	93	70	.571	41	163	163	31	1483	1367	466	929	18	3.10
Joe Niekro	R	35	20	12	.625	0	37	36	11	256	268	79	127	2	3.55
Vern Ruhle	R	29	12	4	.750	0	28	22	6	159	148	29	55	2	2.38
Ken Forsch	R	33	12	13	.480	0	32	32	6	222	230	41	84	3	3.20
Nolan Ryan	R	33	11	10	.524	0	35	35	4	234	205	98	200	2	3.35
J.R. Richard(IL-stroke)	R	30	10	4	.714	0	17	17	4	114	65	40	119	4	1.89
Joe Sambito	L	28	8	4	.667	17	64	0	0	90	65	22	75	0	2.20
Frank LaCorte	R	28	8	5	.615	11	55	0	0	83	61	43	66	0	2.82
Dave Smith	R	25	7	5	.583	10	57	0	0	103	90	32	85	0	1.92
Joaquin Andujar	R	27	3	8	.273	2	35	14	0	122	132	43	75	0	3.91
Bert Roberge	R	25	2	0	1.000	0	14	0	0	24	24	10	9	0	6.00
Bobby Sprowl	L	24	0	0	.——	0	1	0	0	2	1	0	1	0	0.00
Randy Niemann	L	24	0	1	.000	1	22	1	0	33	44	12	18	0	5.45
Gordy Pladson	R	23	0	4	.000	1	12	6	0	41	38	16	13	0	4.39

LOS ANGELES — 2nd 92-71 .564 1 — TOMMY LASORDA (Defeated by Houston in a 1 game playoff)

Name	G by Pos	B	AGE	G	AB	R	H	2B	3B	HR	RBI	BB	SO	SB	BA	SA
TOTALS			31	163	5568	663	1462	209	24	148	638	492	846	123	.263	.388
Steve Garvey	1B162	R	31	163	658	78	200	27	1	26	106	36	67	6	.304	.467
Davey Lopes	2B140	R	31	141	553	79	139	15	3	10	49	58	71	23	.251	.384
Bill Russell (BG)	SS129	R	31	130	466	43	123	23	2	3	34	18	44	13	.264	.341
Ron Cey	3B157	R	32	157	551	81	140	25	0	28	77	69	92	2	.254	.452
Reggie Smith (SJ)	OF84	B	35	92	311	47	100	13	0	15	55	41	63	4	.322	.508
Rudy Law	OF106	L	23	128	388	55	101	5	4	1	23	23	27	40	.260	.302
Dusty Baker	OF151	R	31	153	579	80	170	26	4	29	97	43	66	12	.294	.503
Steve Yeager	C95	R	31	96	227	20	48	8	0	4	20	20	54	2	.211	.273
Derrel Thomas	OF52, SS49, 2B18, C5, 3B4	B	29	117	297	32	79	18	3	1	22	26	48	7	.266	.357
Jay Johnstone	OF61	L	34	109	251	31	77	15	2	2	20	24	29	1	.307	.406
Rick Monday	OF50	L	34	96	194	35	52	7	1	10	25	28	49	2	.268	.469
Gary Thomasson	OF31, 1B1	R	28	80	111	6	24	6	1	1	12	17	26	0	.216	.270
Joe Ferguson (XJ)	C66, OF1	R	33	77	172	20	41	3	2	9	29	38	46	2	.238	.436
Pedro Guerrero (KJ)	OF40, 2B12, 3B3, 1B2	R	24	75	183	27	59	9	1	7	31	12	31	2	.322	.497
Mickey Hatcher	OF25, 3B18	R	25	57	84	4	19	2	0	1	5	2	12	0	.226	.286
Mike Scioscia	C54	L	21	54	134	8	34	5	1	1	8	12	9	1	.254	.321
Jack Perconte	2B9	L	25	14	17	2	4	1	0	0	1	2	3	1	.235	.235
2 Pepe Frias	SS11	R	31	14	9	3	3	0	0	0	0	0	3	0	.333	.333
Bobby Mitchell	OF8	L	25	9	3	1	1	0	0	0	0	0	2	0	.333	.333
Gary Weiss		B	24	9	1	0	0	0	0	0	0	0	0	0	.000	.000
Manny Mota (RC)		R	42	7	7	0	3	0	0	0	0	0	0	0	.429	.429
Vic Davalillo	1B1	L	43	7	6	1	1	0	0	0	0	0	1	0	.167	.167

NAME	T	AGE	W	L	PCT	SV	G	GS	CG	IP	H	BB	SO	SHO	ERA
	L	31	92	71	.564	42	163	163	24	1473	1358	480	835	19	3.25
Jerry Reuss	L	31	18	6	.750	3	37	29	10	229	193	40	111	6	2.52
Burt Hooton	R	30	14	8	.636	0	34	33	4	207	194	64	118	2	3.65
Bob Welch	R	23	14	9	.609	0	32	32	3	214	190	79	141	2	3.28
Don Sutton	R	35	13	5	.722	1	32	31	4	212	163	47	128	2	2.21
Bobby Castillo	R	25	8	6	.571	5	61	0	0	98	70	45	60	0	2.78
Steve Howe	L	22	7	9	.438	17	59	0	0	85	83	22	39	0	2.65
Dave Goltz	R	31	7	11	.389	1	35	27	2	171	198	59	91	0	4.32
Joe Beckwith	R	25	3	3	.500	0	38	0	0	60	60	23	40	0	1.95
Rick Sutcliffe	R	24	3	9	.250	5	42	10	1	110	122	55	59	1	5.56
Fernando Valenzuela	L	19	2	0	1.000	1	10	0	0	18	8	5	16	0	0.00
Don Stanhouse (XJ)	R	29	2	2	.500	7	21	0	0	25	30	16	5	0	5.04
Terry Forster (EJ)	L	28	0	0	.——	0	9	0	0	12	10	4	2	0	3.00
1 Charlie Hough	R	32	1	3	.250	1	19	1	0	32	37	21	25	0	5.83

Doug Rau 31 (SJ)

CINCINNATI 3rd 89-73 .549 3.5 — JOHN McNAMARA

Name	G by Pos	B	AGE	G	AB	R	H	2B	3B	HR	RBI	BB	SO	SB	BA	SA
TOTALS			29	163	5516	707	1445	256	45	113	668	537	852	156	.262	.386
Dan Driessen	1B151	L	28	154	524	81	139	36	1	14	74	93	68	19	.265	.418
Junior Kennedy	2B103	R	29	104	337	31	88	16	3	1	34	36	34	3	.261	.335
Dave Concepcion	SS155, 2B1	R	32	156	622	72	162	31	8	5	77	37	107	12	.260	.360
Ray Knight	3B162	R	27	162	618	71	163	39	7	14	78	36	62	1	.264	.417
Ken Griffey	OF138	L	30	146	544	89	160	28	10	13	85	62	77	23	.294	.454
Dave Collins	OF141	B	27	144	551	94	167	20	4	3	35	53	68	79	.303	.370
George Foster	OF141	R	31	144	528	79	144	21	5	25	93	75	99	1	.273	.473
Johnny Bench	C105	R	32	114	360	52	90	12	0	24	68	41	64	4	.250	.483
Cesar Geronimo	OF86	L	32	103	145	16	37	5	0	2	9	14	24	2	.255	.331
Ron Oester	2B79, SS17, 3B3	B	24	100	303	40	84	16	2	2	20	26	44	6	.277	.363
Sammy Mejias	OF67	R	28	71	108	16	30	5	1	1	10	6	13	4	.278	.370
Harry Spilman	1B18, OF2, 3B1, C1	L	25	65	101	14	27	4	0	4	19	9	19	0	.267	.426
2 Joe Nolan	C51	L	29	53	154	14	48	7	0	3	24	13	8	0	.312	.416
Heity Cruz	OF29	R	27	52	75	5	16	4	1	1	5	8	16	0	.213	.333
Don Werner	C24	R	27	24	64	2	11	2	0	0	5	7	10	1	.172	.203
1 Rick Auerbach	SS3, 3B3, 2B1	R	30	24	33	5	11	1	1	1	4	3	5	0	.333	.515
Paul Householder	OF14	B	21	20	45	3	11	1	1	0	7	1	13	1	.244	.311
Vic Correll (LJ)	C10	R	34	10	19	1	8	1	0	0	3	0	2	0	.421	.474
Eddie Milner		L	25	6	3	1	0	0	0	0	0	0	0	0	.000	.000

NAME	T	AGE	W	L	PCT	SV	G	GS	CG	IP	H	BB	SO	SHO	ERA
		26	89	73	.549	37	163	163	30	1459	1404	506	833	12	3.85
Frank Pastore (RJ)	R	22	13	7	.650	0	27	27	9	185	161	42	110	2	3.26
Mario Soto	R	23	10	8	.556	4	53	12	3	190	126	84	182	1	3.08
Tom Seaver (SJ)	R	35	10	8	.556	0	26	26	5	168	140	59	101	1	3.64
Charlie Leibrandt	L	23	10	9	.526	0	36	27	5	174	200	54	62	2	4.24
Mike LaCoss	R	24	10	12	.455	0	34	29	4	169	207	68	59	2	4.63
Paul Moskau	R	26	9	7	.563	2	33	19	2	153	147	41	94	1	4.00
Tom Hume	R	27	9	10	.474	25	78	0	0	137	121	38	68	0	2.56
Joe Price	L	23	7	3	.700	0	24	13	2	111	95	37	44	0	3.57
Dave Tomlin	L	31	3	0	1.000	0	27	0	0	26	38	11	6	0	5.54
Doug Bair	R	30	3	6	.333	6	61	0	0	85	91	39	62	0	4.24
Bill Bonham (SJ)	R	31	2	1	.667	0	4	4	0	19	21	5	13	0	4.74
Bruce Berenyi	R	25	2	2	.500	0	6	6	0	28	34	23	19	0	7.71
Sheldon Burnside	L	25	1	0	1.000	0	7	0	0	5	6	1	2	0	1.80
Jay Howell	R	24	0	0	—	0	5	0	0	3	8	1	0	0	15.00
Geoff Combe	R	24	0	0	—	0	4	0	0	7	9	4	10	0	10.29

ATLANTA 4th 81-80 .503 11 — BOBBY COX

Name	G by Pos	B	AGE	G	AB	R	H	2B	3B	HR	RBI	BB	SO	SB	BA	SA
TOTALS			26	161	5402	630	1352	226	22	144	597	434	899	73	.250	.380
Chris Chambliss	1B158	L	31	158	602	83	170	37	2	18	72	49	73	7	.282	.440
Glenn Hubbard	2B117	R	22	117	431	55	107	21	3	9	43	49	69	7	.248	.374
Luis Gomez	SS119	R	28	121	278	18	53	6	0	0	24	17	27	0	.191	.212
Bob Horner	3B121, 1B	R	22	124	463	81	124	14	1	35	89	27	50	3	.268	.529
Gary Matthews	OF143	R	29	155	571	79	159	17	3	19	75	42	93	11	.278	.419
Dale Murphy	OF154, 1B	R	24	156	569	98	160	27	2	33	89	59	133	9	.281	.510
Jeff Burroughs	OF73	R	29	99	278	35	73	14	0	13	51	35	57	1	.263	.453
Bruce Benedict	C120	R	24	120	359	18	91	14	1	2	34	28	36	3	.253	.315
Jerry Royster	2B49, 3B48, OF41	R	27	123	392	42	95	17	5	1	20	37	48	22	.242	.319
Mike Lum	OF19, 1B10	L	34	93	83	7	17	3	0	0	5	18	19	0	.205	.241
Larvell Blanks	SS56, 3B43, 2B1	R	30	88	221	23	45	6	0	2	12	16	27	1	.204	.258
Brian Asselstine (KJ)	OF61	L	26	87	218	18	62	13	1	3	25	11	37	1	.284	.394
Biff Pocoroba (AJ)	C10	B	26	70	83	7	22	4	0	0	8	11	11	1	.265	.386
Bill Nahorodny	C54, 1B1	R	26	59	157	14	38	12	0	5	18	8	21	0	.242	.414
Rafael Ramirez	SS46	R	22	50	165	17	44	6	1	2	11	2	33	2	.267	.352
Charlie Spikes	OF7	R	29	41	36	6	10	1	0	0	2	3	18	0	.278	.306
Chico Ruiz	3B16, SS4, 2B2	R	28	25	26	3	8	2	1	0	2	3	7	0	.308	.462
Terry Harper	OF18	R	24	21	54	3	10	2	1	0	3	6	5	2	.185	.259
Gary Cooper	OF13	R	23	21	2	3	0	0	0	0	0	0	1	0	.000	.000
1 Joe Nolan	C6	L	29	17	22	2	6	1	0	0	2	2	4	0	.273	.318
Eddie Miller	OF9	B	23	11	19	3	3	0	0	0	0	0	5	1	.158	.158

NAME	T	AGE	W	L	PCT	SV	G	GS	CG	IP	H	BB	SO	SHO	ERA
		29	81	80	.503	37	161	161	29	1428	1397	454	696	9	3.77
Phil Niekro	R	41	15	18	.455	1	40	38	11	275	256	85	176	3	3.63
Doyle Alexander	R	29	14	11	.560	0	35	35	7	232	227	74	114	1	4.19
Tommy Boggs	R	24	12	9	.571	0	32	26	4	192	180	46	84	3	3.42
Rick Matula	R	26	11	13	.458	0	33	30	3	177	195	60	62	1	4.58
Larry McWilliams	L	26	9	14	.391	0	30	30	4	164	188	39	77	1	4.94
Rick Camp	R	27	6	4	.600	22	77	0	0	108	92	29	33	0	1.92
Gene Garber	R	32	5	5	.500	7	68	0	0	82	95	24	51	0	3.84
Al Hrabosky	L	30	4	2	.667	3	45	0	0	60	50	31	31	0	3.60
Larry Bradford	L	30	3	4	.429	4	56	0	0	55	49	22	32	0	2.45
Preston Hanna	R	25	2	0	1.000	0	32	2	0	79	63	44	35	0	3.19
Rick Mahler	R	26	0	0	—	0	2	0	0	2	1	0	1	0	2.25

SAN FRANCISCO 5th 75-86 .466 17 — DAVE BRISTOL

Name	G by Pos	B	AGE	G	AB	R	H	2B	3B	HR	RBI	BB	SO	SB	BA	SA
TOTALS			27	161	5368	573	1310	199	44	80	539	509	840	100	.244	.342
Mike Ivie (IL-VR)	1B72	R	27	79	286	21	69	16	1	4	25	19	40	1	.241	.346
Rennie Stennett	2B111	R	29	120	397	34	97	13	2	2	37	22	31	4	.244	.302
Johnnie LeMaster	SS134	R	26	135	405	33	87	16	6	3	31	25	57	6	.215	.306
Darrell Evans	3B140, 1B14	L	33	154	556	69	147	23	0	20	78	83	65	17	.264	.414
Jack Clark (BH)	OF124	R	24	127	437	77	124	20	8	22	82	74	52	2	.284	.517
Billy North	OF115	B	32	128	415	73	104	12	1	1	19	81	78	45	.251	.292
Larry Herndon	OF122	R	26	139	493	54	127	17	11	8	49	19	91	8	.258	.385
Milt May	C103	L	29	111	358	27	93	16	2	6	50	25	40	0	.260	.366
Terry Whitfield	OF95	L	27	118	321	38	95	18	2	4	26	20	44	4	.296	.396
Jim Wohlford	OF49, 3B1	R	29	91	193	17	54	6	4	1	24	13	23	1	.280	.368
Joe Strain (SJ)	2B42, 3B6, SS1	R	26	77	189	26	54	6	0	0	16	10	10	1	.286	.317
Mike Sadek	C59	R	34	64	151	14	38	4	1	1	16	27	18	0	.252	.311
Max Venable	OF40	L	23	64	138	13	37	5	0	0	10	15	22	8	.268	.304
Joe Pettini	SS42, 3B18, 2B8	R	25	63	190	19	44	3	1	1	9	17	33	5	.232	.274
Rich Murray (RJ)	1B53	R	22	52	159	19	42	8	2	4	24	11	48	2	.216	.340
Willie McCovey (VR)	1B27	L	42	48	113	8	23	8	0	1	16	13	23	0	.204	.301
Roger Metzger	SS13, 2B1	B	32	28	27	5	2	0	0	0	3	2	4	0	.074	.074
Guy Sularz	2B21, 3B5	R	24	25	65	3	16	1	1	0	3	9	6	1	.246	.292
1 Marc Hill	C14	R	28	17	41	1	7	2	0	0	3	7	7	0	.171	.220
Dennis Littlejohn	C10	R	25	13	29	2	7	1	0	0	2	1	7	0	.241	.276
Chris Bourjos	OF6	R	24	13	22	4	5	1	0	1	2	2	7	0	.227	.409

NAME	T	AGE	W	L	PCT	SV	G	GS	CG	IP	H	BB	SO	SHO	ERA
		28	75	86	.466	35	161	161	27	1448	1446	492	811	10	3.46
Vida Blue (XJ)	L	30	14	10	.583	0	31	31	10	224	202	61	129	3	2.97
Ed Whitson	R	25	11	13	.458	0	34	34	6	212	222	56	90	2	3.10
Allen Ripley	R	27	9	10	.474	0	23	20	2	113	119	36	65	0	4.14
Bob Knepper	L	26	9	16	.360	0	35	33	8	215	242	61	103	1	4.10
Gary Lavelle	R	31	6	8	.429	9	62	0	0	100	106	36	66	0	3.42
Tom Griffin	R	32	5	1	.833	0	42	4	0	108	80	49	79	0	2.75
Al Holland	L	27	5	3	.625	7	54	0	0	82	71	34	65	0	1.76
Greg Minton	R	28	4	6	.400	19	68	0	0	91	81	34	42	0	2.47
Alan Hargesheimer	R	23	4	4	.500	0	15	13	0	75	82	32	40	0	4.32
John Montefusco (VJ)	R	30	4	8	.333	0	22	17	1	113	120	39	61	0	4.38
Bill Bordley	L	22	3	1	.750	0	5	5	1	31	34	21	11	0	4.65
Mike Rowland	R	27	1	1	.500	0	19	0	0	27	20	8	8	0	2.33
Randy Moffitt (IL)	R	31	1	1	.500	0	13	0	0	17	18	4	10	0	4.76
1 Ed Halicki	R	29	0	0	—	0	4	2	0	25	29	10	14	0	5.40
Phil Nastu	L	25	0	0	—	0	6	0	0	6	10	5	1	0	6.00
Fred Breining	R	24	0	0	—	0	6	0	0	7	8	4	3	0	5.14
Jeff Stember	R	22	0	0	—	0	1	1	0	3	4	3	0	0	3.00

SAN DIEGO 6th 73-89 .451 19.5 — JERRY COLEMAN

Name	G by Pos	B	AGE	G	AB	R	H	2B	3B	HR	RBI	BB	SO	SB	BA	SA
TOTALS			28	163	5540	591	1410	195	43	67	546	563	791	239	.255	.342
1 Willie Montanez	1B124	L	32	128	481	39	132	12	4	6	63	38	52	3	.274	.353
Dave Cash	2B123	R	32	130	397	25	90	14	1	1	23	35	21	6	.227	.280
Ozzie Smith	SS158	R	25	158	609	67	140	18	5	0	35	71	49	57	.230	.276
Aurelio Rodriguez	3B88, SS2	R	32	89	175	7	35	7	2	2	13	6	26	1	.200	.297
Dave Winfield	OF159	R	28	162	558	89	154	25	6	20	87	79	83	23	.276	.450
Jerry Mumphrey	OF153	B	27	160	564	61	168	24	3	4	59	49	90	52	.298	.372
Gene Richards	OF156	L	26	158	642	91	193	26	8	4	41	61	73	61	.301	.385
Gene Tenace	C104, 1B19	R	33	133	316	46	70	11	1	17	50	92	63	4	.222	.424
Tim Flannery	2B53, 3B41	L	22	95	292	15	70	12	0	0	25	18	30	2	.240	.281
Bill Fahey	C85	R	30	93	241	18	62	4	0	1	22	21	16	2	.257	.286
Jerry Turner (BH)	OF34	L	26	85	153	22	44	5	0	3	18	10	18	8	.288	.379
Barry Evans	3B43, 2B19, SS4, 1B1	R	23	73	125	11	29	3	2	1	14	17	21	1	.232	.312
Paul Dade	3B21, OF8, 2B1	R	28	68	53	17	10	0	0	0	3	12	10	4	.189	.189
1 Kurt Bevacqua	3B13, OF4, 2B2, 1B1	R	33	62	71	4	19	6	1	0	12	6	1	1	.268	.380
Von Joshua	OF12, 1B2	L	32	53	63	8	15	2	1	2	7	5	15	0	.238	.397
Luis Salazar	3B42, OF4	R	24	44	169	28	57	4	7	1	25	9	25	11	.337	.462
Broderick Perkins	1B20, OF10	L	25	43	100	18	37	9	0	2	14	11	10	2	.370	.520
Craig Stimac	C11, 3B2	R	25	20	50	5	11	2	0	0	7	1	6	0	.220	.260
Randy Bass	1B15	L	26	19	49	5	14	0	1	1	8	7	7	0	.286	.510
Fred Kendall	C14, 1B1	R	31	19	24	2	7	0	0	0	2	0	4	0	.292	.292
Chuck Baker	SS8	R	27	9	22	0	3	1	0	0	3	1	8	0	.136	.182

NAME	T	AGE	W	L	PCT	SV	G	GS	CG	IP	H	BB	SO	SHO	ERA
		29	73	89	.451	39	163	163	19	1466	1474	536	728	9	3.65
Rollie Fingers	R	33	11	9	.550	23	66	0	0	103	101	32	69	0	2.80
Bob Shirley	L	26	11	12	.478	7	59	12	3	137	143	54	67	0	3.55
John Curtis	L	32	10	8	.556	0	30	27	6	187	184	67	71	0	3.51
Steve Mura	R	25	8	7	.533	2	37	23	3	169	149	86	109	1	3.67
Rick Wise (VJ)	R	34	6	8	.429	0	27	27	1	154	172	37	59	0	3.68
Gary Lucas	L	25	5	8	.385	3	48	18	0	150	138	43	85	0	3.24
Randy Jones (V-J-SJ)	L	30	5	13	.278	0	24	24	4	154	165	29	53	3	3.92
Juan Eichelberger(IL)	R	26	4	2	.667	0	15	13	0	89	73	55	43	3	3.64
Dennis Kinney	L	28	4	4	.400	1	50	0	0	83	79	37	40	0	4.23
Eric Rasmussen	R	28	4	11	.267	1	40	14	0	111	130	33	50	0	4.38
Tom Tellmann	R	26	3	0	1.000	1	22	2	0	22	23	8	9	0	1.64
1 John D'Acquisto	R	28	2	3	.400	1	39	0	0	67	67	36	44	0	3.76
Mike Armstrong	R	26	0	0	—	0	11	0	0	14	16	13	14	0	5.79
Dennis Blair	R	26	0	1	.000	0	5	1	0	14	18	3	11	0	6.43
George Stablein	R	22	0	0	—	0	4	2	0	12	16	3	4	0	3.00

1981
The Sixteenth Man

Perhaps more than any other baseball season in history—save the scandal of 1919—the summer of 1981 will be remembered far beyond any statistic which could be squeezed between the first and final out of any ball game. As things turned out, the event of reference was really a non-event as the cry of "Play Ball" was hushed from every major league diamond in the land for a period of seven weeks and a day.

The silence and locked turnstiles were the results of a strike by the Major League Baseball Players Association and the inventory of the aftermath included the loss of 713 games and an estimated ninety-eight million dollars in player's salaries and ticket, broadcast, and concession revenues. More than money, however, was the interruption of the Great American Summer Ballet for the first time since major league baseball set up shop in the summer of 1876.

In a summer which frustrated the aging stars trying to rise a notch higher in the lifetime standings, and the younger players losing the needed time of a full schedule to hone their talents, there was a split season, an extra round of playoff games, and anger and bitterness from the players and fans alike. Although the strike, which began on June 12, was called by the players, the credit for the crisis was attributed to the owners, who sought to win back what they had previously lost at the bargaining table and in the courts on the issue of the free-agent draft. What the owners wanted was compensation for losing a player to the draft. The compensation—considered to be a crippling penalty by the players—was the loss of a man from the middle of the roster (the sixteenth man) to be assigned to the team from which the free agent came. To the players it was a totally unacceptable concept. After fighting for years to obtain free-agent status the players were not about to give up what amounted to an erosion of their victory.

The owners had thoughtfully taken out strike insurance with Lloyds of London and fittingly enough, called an end to the clamor as the insurance ran out. The players had won their point, but the damage was irrevocable. The season's schedule had been sheared by one-third and the owners' intervention to salvage the season brought as much confusion as the strike itself.

When it became evident that the strike would be lasting enough to make it impossible to complete the regulation season intact, a split season was served up. The pre-strike standings were treated as "total" and the teams who were leading their divisions were declared the "first-half" winners. The four teams would then compete in a best three-of-five playoff series against the team which won the second half. If the same team happened to win the second season then the opponent would be the team which finished second in the second half.

At best, it was a formula that gave baseball an unprecedented avalanche of asterisks. It also turned out to be one which left the Cincinnati Reds, holder of the season 's best won and lost record, out of the playoffs. When the strike came the Reds were in second place, a half game behind the Los Angeles Dodgers in the Western Division of the National League. When Houston won the second half it gave Cincinnati the greatest reason to scream "foul play". For the fans of Cincinnati, as in many other cities throughout the country, the split season had robbed the game of its continuity and to a greater extent diluted the tradition the tradition of the national habit.

While the Astros had enjoyed the brief fruits of their victory and the joy of Nolan Ryan throwing an unprecedented fifth no-hitter, they nevertheless fell to the Dodgers, three games to two, in the mini playoffs. The Dodgers nearly saved the game from its chagrin on the left arm of 20-year old Fernando Valenzuela's incredible screwball. The pudgy Mexican southpaw, unable to speak a trace of English, began his official rookie season with a shutout and then notched seven more victories (four of which were shutouts) before being dealt his first loss. Although the league managed to catch up with him, his league-leading 180 strikeouts, 13-7 record, and 2.48 earned run average were enough to prompt Dodger manager Tommy Lasorda to thank the heavens and not the Mexican League for his coming.

In the National League East the first half went to the Phillies and the second half to Montreal although St. Louis had the best combined record. In the end, in the cold at Montreal, the Expos were able to nail down their first division flag only to fall victim to the Dodgers in the championship series behind the heroic eighth-inning homer of Steve Garvey, which tied the series at two games each, and on the final day when Rick Monday hit a ninth inning homer to bring the Dodgers the flag.

For the Phillies, winner of the World Series a year before, their only consolation was in Pete Rose, who broke Stan Musial's National League hit mark (3630) on the day the season resumed.

In the American League Western Division Billy Martin got his Oakland charges off to an 18-2 effort behind a daring running game, amongst other tactics to have the press dub his style, "Billy Ball". The A's played well enough to win the first leg of the season. In the second half Kansas City managed to restore some of last season's grandeur to win the division. But they could not get past Oakland in the mini-playoffs, losing in three straight games. Even George Brett, who managed .390 the year before, could only muster a respectable .314 average.

Over in the Eastern division the Yankees were able to hold together to find themselves two games over Baltimore at strike time. But in the second half the league's eventual Cy Young winner, Rollie Fingers, came out of the bullpen again and again to lead the Milwaukee Brewers to a second half victory behind 28 saves and an incredible 1.04 earned run average.

In the playoffs preceding the playoffs, the Yankees Graig Nettles was unreal at third base, and Goose Gossage was somewhere beyond unreal out of the bullpen to win the first two games of the series. Milwaukee recovered to take back two games but could not best the Yankees in the finale behind the combination of Ron Guidry, rookie Dave Righetti, and Gossage.

A fight at the victory party between Reggie Jackson and Nettles helped only to sell more newspapers as the Yankees easily ended the reign of "Billy Ball" with a clean sweep of the championship series.

The final embarrassment season came at World Series time when George Steinbrenner, owner of the New York Yankees, held a press conference in which he apologized to the people of New York for the poor showing of the Yankees in the World Series. Steinbrenner, who had Bob Lemon holding the managerial reins after firing Gene Michael in September, did congratulate the Dodgers on their victory but the dying echo of his controlled tirade had all the conviction of a Yankee loss and not a Dodger victory.

During the heat of play, which saw the Dodgers snap back from a two-game deficit, Steinbrenner got a broken hand as a result of a fight with a fan in an elevator at the hotel in L.A. But it was not enough to incite his disgruntled troops to victory in the final game at Yankee Stadium, which easily went to the Dodgers, 9-2, behind Burt Hooten's knuckle curve ball.

In a way, the madness continued into the off-season when Frank Robinson and Henry Aaron were elected into the Hall of Fame. Robinson was satisfied enough, but that Aaron, baseball's all-time home run champion, was not elected unanimously, caused many a head to shake.

And the final sadness came in January when Red Smith, dean of American sportswriters, died in his home of a heart attack.

NEW YORK

1st 34-22 .607 —
6th 25-26 .490 5
— 59-48 .551 —
GENE MICHAEL 48-34 .585   BOB LEMON 11-14 .440

Name	G by Pos	B	AGE	G	AB	R	H	2B	3B	HR	RBI	BB	SO	SB	BA	SA
TOTALS			31	107	3529	421	889	148	22	100	403	391	434	47	.252	.391
Bob Watson (GJ)	1B50, DH6	R	35	59	156	15	33	3	3	6	12	24	17	0	.212	.385
Willie Randolph	2B93	R	26	93	357	59	83	14	3	2	24	57	24	14	.232	.305
Bucky Dent	SS73	R	29	73	227	20	54	11	0	7	27	19	17	0	.238	.379
Graig Nettles	3B97, DH4	L	36	103	349	46	85	7	1	15	46	47	49	0	.244	.398
Reggie Jackson	OF61, DH33	L	35	94	334	33	79	17	1	15	54	46	82	0	.237	.428
Jerry Mumphrey	OF79	B	28	80	319	49	98	11	5	6	32	24	27	14	.307	.429
Dave Winfield	OF102, DH1	R	29	105	388	52	114	25	1	13	68	43	41	11	.294	.464
Rick Cerone (BG)	C69	R	27	71	234	23	57	13	2	2	21	12	24	0	.244	.342
Bobby Murcer	DH33	L	35	50	117	14	31	6	0	6	24	12	15	0	.265	.470
Oscar Gamble	OF43, DH33	L	31	80	189	24	45	8	0	10	27	35	23	0	.238	.439
Larry Milbourne	SS39, 2B14, 3B3, DH3	B	30	61	163	24	51	7	2	1	12	9	14	2	.313	.399
Lou Piniella	OF36, DH19	R	37	60	159	16	44	9	0	5	18	13	9	0	.277	.428
2 Dave Revering	1B44	L	28	45	119	8	28	4	1	2	7	11	20	0	.235	.336
2 Barry Foote	C34, DH4, 1B1	R	29	40	125	12	26	4	0	6	10	8	21	0	.208	.384
Dennis Werth (GJ)	1B19, OF8, DH4, C3	R	28	34	55	7	6	1	0	0	1	12	12	1	.109	.127
Bobby Brown	OF29, DH2	B	27	31	62	5	14	1	0	0	6	5	15	4	.226	.242
Aurelio Rodriguez	3B20, 2B3, DH2, 1B1	R	33	27	52	4	18	2	0	2	8	2	10	0	.346	.500
1 Jim Spencer	1B25	L	33	25	63	6	9	2	0	2	4	9	7	0	.143	.270
Johnny Oates	C10	L	35	10	26	4	5	1	0	0	0	0	2	0	.192	.231
Andre Robertson	SS8, 2B3	R	23	10	19	1	5	1	0	0	0	0	3	1	.263	.316
2 Mike Patterson	OF4	L	23	9	2	2	0	2	0	0	0	0	0	0	.222	.667
Steve Balboni	1B3, DH1	R	24	4	7	2	2	1	1	0	2	1	4	0	.286	.714
Tucker Ashford	2B2	R	26	3	0	0	0	0	0	0	0	0	0	0	—	—
Bruce Robinson 27 (SJ)																
Eric Soderholm 32 (KJ)																

NAME	T	AGE	W	L	PCT	SV	G	GS	CG	IP	H	BB	SO	SHO	ERA
		30	59	48	.551	30	107	107	16	948	827	287	606	13	2.90
Ron Guidry	L	30	11	5	.688	0	23	21	0	127	100	26	104	0	2.76
Tommy John (RJ)	L	38	9	8	.529	0	20	20	7	140	135	39	50	0	2.64
Dave Righetti	L	22	8	4	.667	0	15	15	2	105	75	38	89	0	2.06
Rudy May	L	36	6	11	.353	1	27	22	4	148	137	41	79	0	4.14
1 Doug Bird	R	31	5	1	.833	0	17	4	0	53	58	16	28	0	2.72
Dave LaRoche	L	33	4	1	.800	0	26	1	0	47	38	16	24	0	2.49
2 Rick Reuschel	R	32	4	4	.500	0	12	11	3	71	75	10	22	0	2.66
Ron Davis	R	25	4	5	.444	6	43	0	0	73	47	25	83	0	2.71
Gene Nelson	R	20	3	1	.750	0	8	7	0	39	40	23	16	0	4.85
Goose Gossage	R	29	3	2	.600	20	32	0	0	47	22	14	48	0	0.77
Bill Castro	R	27	1	1	.500	0	11	0	0	19	26	5	4	0	3.79
1 Tom Underwood	L	27	1	4	.200	0	9	6	0	33	32	13	29	0	4.36
Dave Wehmeister	R	28	0	0	—	0	5	0	0	7	6	7	7	0	5.14
Andy McGaffigan	R	24	0	0	—	0	2	0	0	7	5	3	2	0	2.57
1 Mike Griffin	R	24	0	0	—	0	2	0	0	4	5	0	4	0	2.25
George Frazier	R	26	0	1	.000	3	16	0	0	28	26	11	17	0	1.61

MILWAUKEE

3rd 31-25 .554 3
1st 31-22 .585 —
— 62-47 .569 —
BUCK RODGERS

Name	G by Pos	B	AGE	G	AB	R	H	2B	3B	HR	RBI	BB	SO	SB	BA	SA
TOTAL			29	109	3743	493	961	173	20	96	475	300	461	39	.257	.391
Cecil Cooper	1B101, DH5	L	31	106	416	70	133	35	1	12	60	28	30	5	.320	.495
Jim Gantner	2B107	R	28	107	352	35	94	14	1	2	33	29	29	3	.267	.330
Robin Yount	SS93, DH3	R	25	96	377	50	103	15	5	10	49	22	37	4	.273	.419
Don Money	3B56, DH2, 1B1	R	34	60	185	17	40	7	0	2	14	19	27	0	.216	.286
Gorman Thomas	OF97, DH6	R	30	103	363	54	94	22	0	21	65	50	85	4	.259	.493
Paul Molitor (NJ)	OF47, DH16	R	24	64	251	45	67	11	0	2	19	25	29	10	.267	.335
Ben Oglivie	OF101, DH16	L	32	107	400	53	97	15	2	14	72	37	49	2	.243	.395
Ted Simmons	C75, DH22, 1B4	B	31	100	380	45	92	13	3	14	61	23	32	0	.216	.376
Larry Hisle (SJ)	DH24	R	34	87	11	20	4	0	4	11	6	17	0	.230	.414	
Roy Howell	3B53, DH13, 1B3, OF1	L	27	76	244	37	58	13	1	6	33	23	39	0	.238	.373
Mark Brouhard	OF51, DH7	R	25	60	186	19	51	6	3	2	20	7	41	1	.274	.371
Charlie Moore	C34, OF8, DH6	R	28	48	156	16	47	8	3	1	9	12	13	1	.301	.410
Ed Romero	SS22, 2B18, 3B3	R	23	44	91	6	18	3	0	1	10	4	9	0	.198	.264
Thad Bosley	OF37, DH1	L	28	42	105	11	24	2	0	0	3	6	13	2	.229	.248
Marshall Edwards	OF36, DH1	L	28	40	58	10	14	1	1	0	4	0	2	6	.241	.293
Sal Bando	3B15, 1B9, DH2	R	37	32	65	10	13	4	0	2	9	6	3	1	.200	.354
Ned Yost	C16	R	26	18	27	4	6	0	0	3	3	3	6	0	.222	.556

NAME	T	AGE	W	L	PCT	SV	G	GS	CG	IP	H	BB	SO	SHO	ERA
		29	62	47	.569	35	109	109	11	986	994	352	448	4	3.91
Pete Vuckovich	R	28	14	4	.778	0	24	23	2	150	137	57	84	1	3.54
Moose Haas	R	25	11	7	.611	0	24	22	5	137	146	40	64	0	4.47
Mike Caldwell	L	32	11	9	.550	0	24	23	3	144	151	38	41	0	3.94
Randy Lerch	L	26	7	9	.438	0	23	18	1	111	134	43	53	0	4.30
Rollie Fingers	R	34	6	3	.667	28	47	0	0	78	55	13	61	0	1.04
Jim Slaton	R	31	5	7	.417	0	24	21	0	117	120	50	47	0	4.38
Jamie Easterly	L	28	3	3	.500	4	44	0	0	62	46	34	31	0	3.19
Jerry Augustine	L	28	2	2	.500	2	27	2	0	61	75	18	26	0	4.28
Reggie Cleveland	R	33	2	3	.400	1	35	0	0	65	57	30	18	0	5.12
Buster Keeton	R	23	1	0	1.000	0	17	0	0	35	47	11	9	0	5.14
Dwight Bernard	R	29	1	1	.500	0	6	0	0	5	6	1	1	0	3.60
Bob McClure (SJ)	L	29	0	0	—	0	4	0	0	8	7	4	6	0	3.38
Chuck Porter	R	25	0	0	—	0	3	0	0	4	4	1	4	0	4.50
Donnie Moore	R	27	0	0	—	0	3	0	0	4	4	4	3	0	6.75
Frank DiPino	L	24	0	0	—	0	3	0	0	3	3	3	0	0	0.00
Willie Mueller	R	24	0	0	—	0	1	0	0	2	1	1	3	0	4.50

BALTIMORE

2nd 31-23 .574 2
4th 28-23 .549 2
— 59-46 .562 —
EARL WEAVER

Name	G by Pos	B	AGE	G	AB	R	H	2B	3B	HR	RBI	BB	SO	SB	BA	SA
TOTALS			31	105	3516	429	883	165	11	88	408	404	454	41	.251	.379
Eddie Murray	1B99	B	25	99	378	57	111	21	2	22	78	40	43	2	.294	.534
Rich Dauer	2B95, 3B4	R	28	96	369	41	97	27	0	4	38	27	18	0	.263	.369
Mark Belanger	SS63	R	37	64	139	9	23	3	2	1	10	12	25	2	.165	.237
Doug DeCinces	3B100, 1B1, OF1	R	30	100	346	49	91	23	2	13	55	41	32	0	.263	.454
Ken Singleton	OF72, DH30	B	34	103	363	48	101	16	1	13	49	61	59	0	.278	.419
Al Bumbry	OF101	L	34	101	392	61	107	18	2	1	27	51	31	22	.273	.337
Gary Roenicke	OF83	R	26	85	219	31	59	16	0	3	20	23	29	1	.269	.384
Rick Dempsey	C90, DH1	R	31	92	251	24	54	10	1	6	15	32	36	0	.215	.335
Terry Crowley	DH42, 1B4	L	34	68	134	12	33	4	0	4	25	29	12	0	.246	.381
John Lowenstein	OF73, DH4	L	34	83	189	19	47	7	0	6	20	22	32	7	.249	.381
Jim Dwyer	OF59, 1B3, DH1	L	31	68	134	16	30	0	1	3	10	20	19	0	.224	.306
Lenn Sakata	SS42, 2B20	R	27	61	150	19	34	4	0	5	15	11	18	4	.227	.353
Dan Graham	C40, DH6, 3B4	L	26	55	142	7	25	3	0	2	11	13	32	0	.176	.239
Benny Ayala	DH27, OF4	R	30	44	86	12	24	2	0	3	13	11	9	0	.279	.407
Jose Morales	DH22, 1B3	R	36	38	86	6	21	3	0	2	14	3	13	0	.244	.349
Wayne Krenchicki	SS16, 2B7, DH1	L	26	33	56	7	12	4	0	0	6	4	9	0	.214	.286
Cal Ripken	SS12, 3B6	R	20	23	39	1	5	0	0	0	2	1	8	0	.128	.128
Bob Bonner	SS9	R	24	10	27	6	8	2	0	0	2	1	4	1	.296	.370
Mark Corey	OF9	R	25	10	8	2	0	0	0	0	0	0	2	0	.000	.000
John Shelby	OF4	B	23	7	2	2	0	0	0	0	0	0	1	0	.000	.000
Willie Royster	C4	R	23	7	4	0	0	0	0	0	0	0	2	0	.000	.000
Dallas Williams	OF1	L	23	2	0	1	0	0	0	0	0	0	0	0	.500	.500

NAME	T	AGE	W	L	PCT	SV	G	GS	CG	IP	H	BB	SO	SHO	ERA
		29	59	46	.562	23	105	105	25	940	923	347	489	10	3.70
Dennis Martinez	R	26	14	5	.737	0	25	24	9	179	173	62	88	2	3.32
Scott McGregor	L	27	13	5	.722	0	24	22	8	160	167	40	82	3	3.26
Mike Flanagan (EJ)	L	29	9	6	.600	0	20	20	3	116	108	37	72	2	4.19
Jim Palmer	R	35	7	8	.467	0	22	22	5	127	117	46	35	0	3.76
Tim Stoddard	R	28	4	2	.667	7	31	0	0	37	38	18	32	0	3.89
Steve Stone (EJ)	R	33	4	7	.364	0	15	12	0	63	63	27	30	0	4.57
Sammy Stewart	R	26	4	8	.333	4	29	3	0	112	89	57	57	0	2.33
Tippy Martinez	L	31	3	3	.500	11	37	0	0	59	48	32	50	0	2.90
Dave Ford	R	24	1	2	.333	0	15	2	0	40	61	10	12	0	6.53
Jeff Schneider	L	28	0	0	—	1	11	0	0	24	27	12	17	0	4.88
Steve Luebber	R	31	0	0	—	0	7	0	0	17	26	4	12	0	7.41
Mike Boddicker	R	23	0	0	—	0	2	0	0	6	6	2	2	0	4.50

DETROIT

4th 31-26 .544 3.5
(tie) 2nd 29-23 .558 1.5
— 60-49 .550 —
SPARKY ANDERSON

Name	G by Pos	B	AGE	G	AB	R	H	2B	3B	HR	RBI	BB	SO	SB	BA	SA
TOTALS			28	109	3600	427	922	148	29	65	403	404	500	61	.256	.368
Richie Hebner	1B61, DH11	L	33	78	226	19	51	8	2	5	28	27	28	1	.226	.345
Lou Whitaker	2B108	L	24	109	335	48	88	14	4	5	36	40	42	5	.263	.373
Alan Trammell	SS105	R	23	105	392	52	101	15	3	2	31	49	31	10	.258	.327
Tom Brookens	3B71	R	27	71	239	19	58	10	1	4	25	14	43	5	.243	.343
Kirk Gibson	OF67, DH9	L	24	83	290	41	95	11	3	9	40	18	64	17	.328	.479
Al Cowens	OF83	R	29	85	253	27	66	11	4	1	18	22	36	3	.261	.348
Steve Kemp	OF92, SH12	L	26	105	372	52	103	18	4	9	49	70	48	9	.277	.419
Lance Parrish	C90, DH5	R	25	96	348	39	85	18	2	10	46	34	52	2	.244	.394
Champ Summers	DH37, OF6	L	35	64	165	16	42	8	0	3	21	19	35	1	.255	.358
Lynn Jones	OF60, DH4	R	28	71	174	19	45	5	0	2	19	18	10	1	.259	.322
John Wockenfuss	DH39, 1B25, C5, OF1	R	32	70	172	20	37	4	0	9	25	28	22	0	.215	.395
Rickey Peters	OF38, DH19	B	25	63	207	26	53	7	3	0	15	29	28	1	.256	.319
Mick Kelleher	3B39, 2B11, SS9	R	33	61	77	10	17	0	0	0	6	7	10	0	.221	.273
Rick Leach	1B32, OF15, DH2	L	24	54	83	9	16	3	1	1	11	16	15	0	.193	.289
Stan Papi	3B32, DH3, 1B1, 2B1, OF1	R	30	40	93	8	19	3	1	3	12	3	18	1	.204	.344
2 Ron Jackson	1B29	R	28	31	95	12	27	6	0	1	9	4	4	4	.254	.421
Bill Fahey (WJ)	C27	L	31	27	67	5	17	2	0	1	9	2	4	0	.254	.328
Darrell Brown	OF6, DH4	B	25	16	4	4	1	0	0	0	0	1	1	0	.250	.250
Marty Castillo	3B4, OF1, C1	R	24	6	8	1	1	0	0	0	0	1	1	0	.125	.125
Duffy Dyer	C2	R	35	4	8	1	1	0	0	0	0	0	3	0	.125	.125

NAME	T	AGE	W	L	PCT	SV	G	GS	CG	IP	H	BB	SO	SHO	ERA
		27	60	49	.550	22	109	109	33	969	840	373	476	13	3.53
Jack Morris	R	26	14	7	.667	0	25	25	15	198	153	78	97	1	3.05
Milt Wilcox	R	31	12	9	.571	0	24	24	8	166	152	52	79	1	3.04
Dan Petry	R	22	10	9	.526	0	23	22	7	141	115	57	79	2	3.00
Dan Schatzeder	L	26	6	6	.429	0	17	14	1	71	74	29	20	0	6.08
Aurelio Lopez	R	32	5	2	.714	3	29	3	0	82	70	31	53	0	3.62
Dave Rozema	R	24	5	5	.500	3	28	9	2	104	99	25	46	2	3.63
Kevin Saucier	L	24	4	2	.667	13	38	0	0	49	26	21	23	0	1.65
Dave Tobik	R	28	4	2	.500	1	27	0	0	60	47	33	32	0	2.70
George Capuzzello	L	27	1	1	.500	1	18	3	0	34	28	18	19	0	3.44
Howard Bailey	L	23	1	4	.200	0	9	5	0	37	45	13	17	0	7.30
Dennis Kinney	L	29	0	0	—	0	4	0	0	6	4	6	1	0	9.00
Larry Rothschild	R	27	0	0	—	1	2	0	0	4	4	6	1	0	6.43
Jerry Ujdur	R	24	0	0	—	0	4	0	0	14	19	5	5	0	6.43
Dave Rucker	L	23	0	0	—	0	4	0	0	4	3	1	2	0	6.75

BOSTON — 5th 30-26 .536 4 / (tie) 2nd 29-23 .558 1.5 / — 59-49 .546 —   RALPH HOUK

Name	G by Pos	B	AGE	G	AB	R	H	2B	3B	HR	RBI	BB	SO	SB	BA	SA
TOTALS			29	108	3820	519	1052	168	17	90	492	378	520	32	.275	.399
Tony Perez	1B56, DH23	R	29	84	306	35	77	11	3	9	39	27	66	0	.252	.395
Jerry Remy	2B87	L	28	88	358	55	110	14	3	0	31	36	30	9	.307	.338
Glenn Hoffman	SS78, 3B1	R	22	78	242	28	56	10	0	1	20	12	25	0	.231	.285
Carney Lansford	3B86, DH16	R	24	102	399	61	134	23	3	4	52	34	28	15	.336	.439
Dwight Evans	OF108	R	29	108	412	84	122	19	4	22	71	85	85	3	.296	.522
Rick Miller	OF95	L	33	97	316	38	92	17	2	2	33	28	36	3	.291	.377
Jim Rice	OF108	R	28	108	451	51	128	18	1	17	62	34	76	2	.284	.441
Rich Gedman	C59	L	21	62	205	22	59	15	0	5	26	9	31	0	.288	.434
Carl Yastrzemski	DH48, 1B39	L	41	91	338	36	83	14	1	7	53	49	28	0	.246	.355
Dave Stapleton	SS33, 3B25, 2B23, 1B12, DH3	R	27	93	355	45	101	17	1	10	42	21	22	0	.285	.423
Joe Rudi	DH21, 1B5, OF1	R	34	49	122	14	22	3	0	6	24	8	29	0	.180	.352
Gary Allenson (LJ)	C47	R	26	47	139	23	31	8	0	5	25	23	33	0	.233	.388
Reid Nichols	OF27, DH7, 3B	R	22	39	48	13	9	0	1	0	3	2	6	0	.188	.229
Garry Hancock	OF8, DH4	L	27	26	45	4	7	3	0	0	3	2	4	0	.156	.222
Julio Valdez	SS17	B	25	17	23	1	5	0	0	0	3	0	2	0	.217	.217
Dave Schmidt	C15	R	24	15	42	6	10	1	0	2	3	7	17	0	.238	.405
Chico Walker	2B5	B	23	6	17	3	6	0	0	0	2	1	2	0	.353	.353
1 Tom Poquette	OF2	L	29	3	2	0	0	0	0	0	0	0	0	0	.000	.000
John Lickert	C1	R	21	1	0	0	0	0	0	0	0	0	0	0	—	—

NAME	T	AGE	W	L	PCT	SV	G	GS	CG	IP	H	BB	SO	SHO	ERA
TOTALS		29	59	49	.546	24	108	108	19	987	983	354	536	4	3.81
Mike Torrez	R	34	10	3	.769	0	22	22	2	127	130	51	54	0	3.69
Bob Stanley	R	26	10	8	.556	0	35	1	0	99	110	38	28	0	3.62
Dennis Eckersley	R	26	9	8	.529	0	23	23	8	154	160	35	79	2	4.27
Mark Clear	R	25	8	3	.727	9	34	0	0	77	69	51	82	0	4.09
Bob Ojeda	L	23	6	2	.750	0	10	10	2	66	50	25	28	0	3.14
John Tudor	L	27	4	3	.571	1	18	11	2	79	74	28	44	0	4.56
Tom Burgmeier	L	37	4	6	.444	6	32	0	0	60	61	17	35	0	2.85
Frank Tanana	L	27	4	10	.286	0	24	23	5	141	142	43	78	2	4.02
Bruce Hurst	L	23	2	0	1.000	0	5	5	0	23	23	12	11	0	4.30
Luis Aponte	R	28	1	1	.500	1	7	0	0	16	11	3	11	0	0.56
Bill Campbell	R	32	1	1	.500	7	30	0	0	48	45	20	37	0	3.19
Chuck Rainey	R	26	1	0	1.000	0	11	2	0	40	39	13	20	0	2.70
Steve Crawford	R	23	0	5	.000	0	14	11	0	58	69	18	29	0	4.79

CLEVELAND — 6th 26-24 .520 5 / 5th 26-27 .491 5 / — 52-51 .505 —   DAVE GARCIA

Name	G by Pos	B	AGE	G	AB	R	H	2B	3B	HR	RBI	BB	SO	SB	BA	SA
TOTALS			28	103	3507	431	922	150	21	29	397	343	379	119	.263	.351
Mike Hargrove	1B88, DH4	L	31	94	322	43	102	21	0	2	49	60	16	5	.317	.401
Duane Kuiper	2B72	L	31	72	206	15	53	6	0	0	14	8	13	1	.257	.286
Tom Veryzer	SS75	R	28	75	221	13	54	4	0	0	14	10	10	1	.244	.262
Toby Harrah	3B101, SS3, DH1	R	32	103	361	64	105	12	4	5	44	57	44	12	.291	.388
Jorge Orta	OF86	L	30	88	338	50	92	14	3	5	34	21	43	4	.272	.376
Rick Manning	OF103	L	26	103	360	47	88	15	3	4	33	40	57	25	.244	.336
Miguel Dilone	OF56, DH11	B	26	72	269	33	78	5	5	0	19	18	28	29	.290	.346
Bo Diaz	C51, DH3	R	28	63	182	25	57	19	0	7	38	13	23	2	.313	.533
Andre Thornton	DH53, 1B11	R	31	69	226	22	54	12	0	6	30	23	37	0	.239	.372
Alan Bannister	OF35, 2B30, 1B2, SS1	R	29	68	232	36	61	11	1	1	17	16	19	16	.263	.332
Ron Hassey	C56, 1B5, DH1	L	28	61	190	8	44	4	0	1	25	17	11	0	.232	.268
Joe Charboneau	OF27, DH14	R	26	48	138	14	29	7	1	4	18	7	22	1	.210	.362
Pat Kelly	DH18, OF8	L	36	48	75	8	16	4	0	1	16	14	9	2	.213	.307
Jerry Dybzinski	SS34, 2B3, 3B3, DH1	R	25	48	57	10	17	0	0	0	6	5	8	7	.298	.298
Von Hayes	DH21, OF13, 3B5	L	22	43	109	21	28	8	2	1	17	14	10	8	.257	.394
Dave Rosello	2B26, 3B8, SS4, DH4	R	31	43	84	11	20	4	0	1	7	7	12	0	.238	.321
Larry Littleton	OF24	R	27	26	23	2	0	0	0	0	1	3	6	0	.000	.000
Mike Fischlin	SS19, 2B1	R	25	22	43	3	10	1	0	0	5	3	6	3	.233	.256
Chris Bando	C15, DH2	B	25	21	47	3	10	3	0	0	6	2	7	0	.213	.277
Karl Pagel	1B6, DH1	L	26	14	15	3	4	0	2	1	4	4	1	0	.267	.733
Ron Pruitt	OF3, C1, DH1	R	29	5	9	0	0	0	0	0	0	1	2	0	.000	.000

NAME	T	AGE	W	L	PCT	SV	G	GS	CG	IP	H	BB	SO	SHO	ERA
TOTALS		28	52	51	.505	13	103	103	33	931	989	311	569	10	3.88
Bert Blyleven	R	30	11	7	.611	0	20	20	9	159	145	40	107	1	2.89
John Denny	R	29	10	6	.625	0	19	19	6	146	139	66	94	3	3.14
Len Barker	R	25	8	7	.533	0	22	22	9	154	150	46	127	3	3.92
Rick Waits	L	29	8	10	.444	0	22	21	5	126	173	44	51	1	4.93
Dan Spillner	R	29	4	4	.500	7	32	5	1	97	86	39	59	0	3.15
Mike Stanton	R	28	3	3	.500	2	24	0	0	43	43	18	44	0	4.40
Sid Monge	L	30	3	5	.375	4	31	0	0	58	58	21	41	0	4.34
Wayne Garland	R	30	3	7	.300	0	12	10	2	56	89	14	15	1	5.79
Tom Brennan	R	28	2	2	.500	0	7	1	0	48	49	14	15	0	3.19
1 Bob Lacey	L	27	0	0	—	0	14	0	0	21	36	3	11	0	7.71
Dennis Lewellyn	R	27	0	0	—	0	5	0	0	13	16	2	11	0	5.54
Ed Glynn	L	28	0	0	—	0	9	0	0	13	6	3	6	0	1.13
Ross Grimsley 31 (VJ)															

TORONTO — 7th 16-42 .276 19 / 7th 21-27 .438 7.5 / — 37-69 .349 —   BOBBY MATTICK

Name	G by Pos	B	AGE	G	AB	R	H	2B	3B	HR	RBI	BB	SO	SB	BA	SA
TOTAL			26	106	3521	329	797	137	23	61	314	284	556	66	.226	.330
John Mayberry	1B80, DH10	L	32	94	290	34	72	6	1	17	43	44	45	1	.248	.452
Damaso Garcia	2B62, DH1	R	26	64	250	24	63	8	1	1	13	9	32	13	.252	.304
Alfredo Griffin	SS97, 3B4, 2B1	B	23	101	388	30	81	19	6	0	21	17	38	8	.209	.289
Danny Ainge	3B77, SS6, OF4, 2B2, DH1	R	22	86	246	20	46	6	2	0	14	23	41	8	.187	.228
Barry Bonnell	OF66	R	27	66	227	21	50	7	4	4	28	12	25	4	.220	.339
Lloyd Moseby	OF100	L	21	100	378	36	88	16	2	9	43	24	86	11	.233	.357
Al Woods	OF77, DH1	L	27	85	288	20	71	15	0	1	21	19	31	3	.247	.309
Ernie Whitt	C72	L	29	74	195	16	46	9	1	1	16	20	30	5	.236	.297
Otto Velez	DH74, 1B1	R	30	80	240	32	51	9	2	11	28	55	60	0	.213	.404
Garth Iorg	2B46, 3B14, SS2, 1B1, DH1	R	26	70	215	17	52	11	0	0	10	7	31	2	.242	.293
Willie Upshaw	DH15, 1B14, OF14	L	24	61	111	15	19	3	1	4	10	11	16	2	.171	.324
George Bell	OF44, DH8	R	21	60	163	19	38	2	1	5	12	5	27	3	.233	.350
Buck Martinez	C45	R	32	45	128	6	29	8	1	4	21	11	16	1	.227	.398
Ken Macha	3B19, 1B16, DH2, C1	R	30	37	85	4	17	2	0	0	6	8	15	1	.200	.224
Greg Wells	1B22, DH3	R	27	32	73	7	18	5	0	0	5	5	12	0	.247	.315
Jesse Barfield	OF25	R	21	25	95	7	22	3	2	2	9	4	19	4	.232	.368
1 Rick Bosetti	OF19, DH1	R	27	25	47	5	11	2	0	0	4	2	6	2	.234	.277
Ted Cox	3B14, 1B1, DH1	R	26	16	50	6	15	4	0	2	9	5	10	0	.300	.500
Fred Manrique	SS11, 3B2, DH1	R	20	14	14	2	2	0	0	0	1	0	12	0	.143	.143
Charlie Beamon	DH4, 1B1	L	27	8	15	1	3	1	0	0	3	0	6	2	.200	.267
Dan Whitmer	C7	R	25	7	9	0	1	0	0	0	0	0	2	0	.111	.222

NAME	T	AGE	W	L	PCT	SV	G	GS	CG	IP	H	BB	SO	SHO	ERA
TOTALS		26	37	69	.349	18	106	106	20	953	908	377	451	4	3.81
Dave Stieb	R	23	11	10	.524	0	25	25	11	184	148	61	89	2	3.18
Luis Leal	R	24	7	13	.350	1	29	19	3	130	127	44	71	0	3.67
Jim Clancy	R	25	6	12	.333	0	22	22	2	125	126	64	56	0	4.90
Mark Bomback	R	28	5	5	.500	0	20	11	0	90	84	35	33	0	3.90
Jackson Todd	R	29	2	7	.222	0	21	13	3	98	94	31	41	0	3.95
2 Juan Berenguer	R	26	2	*9	.182	0	12	11	1	71	62	35	29	0	4.31
Dale Murray	R	31	1	0	1.000	0	11	0	0	15	12	5	12	0	1.20
Roy Lee Jackson	R	27	1	1	.333	7	39	0	0	62	65	25	27	0	2.61
Jerry Garvin	L	25	1	2	.333	0	35	0	0	53	46	23	25	0	3.40
Joey McLaughlin	R	24	1	5	.167	10	40	0	0	60	55	21	38	0	2.85
Mike Barlow	R	33	0	0	—	0	12	0	0	15	22	6	5	0	4.20
Paul Mirabella	L	27	0	0	—	0	8	1	0	15	16	7	9	0	7.20
2 Nino Espinosa	R	27	0	0	—	0	1	0	0	1	0	0	2	0	9.00
Mike Willis	L	30	0	4	.000	0	20	0	0	35	43	20	16	0	5.91

* Berenguer, Also with Kansas City, league leader in L with 13

LINE SCORES

TEAM 1 2 3   4 5 6   7 8 9 10 11   R H E

EAST DIVISIONAL SERIES: NEW YORK 3 MILWAUKEE 2

Game 1   October 7 at Milwaukee
```
NY   0 0 0  4 0 0  0 0 1         5 13 1
MIL  0 1 1  0 1 0  0 0 0         3  8 3
```
Guidry, **Davis** (5)   Haas, Bernard (4), McClure (5)
Gossage (8)   Slaton (6), Fingers (8)

Game 2   October 8 at Milwaukee
```
NY   0 0 0  1 0 0  0 0 2         3  7 0
MIL  0 0 0  0 0 0  0 0 0         0  7 0
```
Righetti, Davis (7),   **Caldwell**, Slaton (9)
Gossage (7)

Game 3   October 9 at New York
```
MIL  0 0 0  0 0 0  3 2 0         5  9 0
NY   0 0 0  1 0 0  2 0 0         3  8 2
```
Lerch, **Fingers** (7)   **John**, May (8)

Game 4   October 10 at New York
```
MIL  0 0 0  2 0 0  0 0 0         2  4 2
NY   0 0 0  0 0 1  0 0 0         1  5 0
```
Vuckovich, Easterly (6),   **Reuschel**, Davis (7)
Slaton (7), McClure (8), Fingers (9)

Game 5   October 11 at New York
```
MIL  0 1 1  0 0 0  1 0 0         3  8 0
NY   0 4 0  0 1 2  X             7 13 0
```
Haas, Caldwell (4),   Guidry, **Righetti** (5),
Bernard (4), McClure (6), Gossage (8)
Slaton (7), Easterly (8),
Vuckovich (8)

COMPOSITE BATTING

NAME	POS	G	AB	R	H	2B	3B	HR	RBI	BA
New York										
TOTALS		5	171	19	46	8	0	6	18	.269
Mumphrey	CF	5	21	1	2	0	0	0	0	.095
Winfield	LF	5	20	2	7	3	0	0	0	.350
Jackson	RF	5	20	4	6	0	0	2	4	.300
Randolph	2B	5	19	4	6	1	0	0	0	.316
Milbourne	SS	5	19	4	6	1	0	0	0	.316
Cerone	C	5	18	1	6	2	0	1	5	.333
Nettles	3B	5	17	1	1	0	0	0	1	.059
Watson	1B	5	16	2	7	0	0	0	1	.438
Piniella	PH-DH	4	10	1	2	1	0	0	3	.200
Gamble	PH-DH	4	9	2	5	1	0	2	3	.556
Murcer	PH	2	1	0	0	0	0	0	0	.000
Revering	1B	2	1	0	0	0	0	0	0	.000
Brown	PR	1	0	0	0	0	0	0	0	.000
Foote	PH	1	0	0	0	0	0	0	0	.000
Milwaukee										
TOTALS		5	162	13	36	6	1	3	13	.222
Molitor	CF-RF	2	20	2	5	0	0	0	0	.250
Yount	SS	5	19	4	6	0	0	0	0	.316
Simmons	C	5	19	1	4	1	0	1	4	.211
Cooper	1B	5	18	1	4	1	0	0	0	.222
Oglivie	LF	5	18	0	3	0	0	0	1	.167
Bando	3B	5	17	1	5	3	0	0	0	.294
Thomas	CF-DH	5	17	2	2	0	0	1	1	.118
Gantner	2B	5	14	1	2	0	0	0	0	.143
Moore	RF-DH	4	9	1	2	0	0	0	2	.222
Howell	PH-DH	5	5	0	2	0	0	0	0	.400
Money	2B-PH-DH	2	5	0	0	0	0	0	0	.000
Romero	2B	2	2	1	1	0	0	0	0	.500
Edwards	CF-RF-PR	2	1	0	0	0	0	0	0	.000
Bosley	PR-DH	1	0	0	0	0	0	0	0	.000

COMPOSITE PITCHING

NAME	G	IP	H	BB	SO	W	L	SV	ERA
New York									
TOTALS	5	45	36	13	39	3	2	3	2.60
Righetti	2	9	8	3	13	2	0	0	1.00
Guidry	2	8.1	11	3	8	0	0	0	5.40
John	1	7	8	2	0	0	1	0	6.43
Gossage	3	6.2	3	2	8	0	0	3	0.00
Davis	3	6	1	2	6	1	0	0	0.00
Reuschel	1	6	4	1	3	0	1	0	3.00
May	1	2	1	0	1	0	0	0	0.00
Milwaukee									
TOTALS	5	44	46	9	22	2	3	1	3.48
Caldwell	2	8	9	0	4	0	1	0	4.32
Haas	2	6.2	13	1	1	0	2	0	9.45
Lerch	1	6	3	4	3	0	0	0	1.50
Slaton	4	6	6	0	0	3	0	0	0.00
Vuckovich	2	5.1	2	3	4	1	0	0	3.86
Fingers	3	4.2	7	1	5	1	0	1	3.86
McClure	3	3.1	4	0	2	0	0	0	0.00
Bernard	2	2.1	0	0	3	0	0	0	0.00
Easterly	2	1	2	0	1	0	0	0	6.75

OAKLAND — 1st 37-23 .617 / 2nd 27-22 .551 1 / 64-45 .587 —   BILLY MARTIN

Name	G by Pos	B	AGE	G	AB	R	H	2B	3B	HR	RBI	BB	SO	SB	BA	SA
TOTALS			29	109	3677	458	910	119	26	104	430	342	647	98	.247	.379
2 Jim Spencer	1B48	L	33	54	171	14	35	6	0	2	9	10	20	1	.205	.275
Shooty Babitt	2B52	R	22	54	156	10	40	1	3	0	14	13	13	6	.258	.301
Rob Picciolo	SS82	R	28	82	179	23	48	5	3	4	13	5	22	0	.268	.397
Wayne Gross	3B73, 1B2, DH1	L	29	82	243	29	50	7	1	10	13	34	28	2	.206	.386
Tony Armas	OF109	R	27	109	440	51	115	24	3	22	76	19	115	5	.261	.480
Dwayne Murphy	OF106, DH1	L	26	107	390	58	98	10	3	15	60	73	94	10	.251	.408
Rickey Henderson	OF107	R	22	108	423	89	135	18	7	6	35	64	68	56	.319	.437
Mike Heath	C78, OF6	R	26	84	301	26	71	7	1	8	30	13	36	3	.236	.346
Cliff Johnson	DH68, 1B9	R	33	84	273	40	71	8	0	17	59	28	60	5	.260	.476
Dave McKay	3B43, 2B38, SS7	R	31	79	224	25	59	11	1	4	21	16	43	4	.263	.375
Jeff Newman	C37, 1B30	R	32	68	216	17	50	12	0	3	15	9	28	0	.231	.329
Fred Stanley	SS62, 2B6	R	33	66	145	15	28	4	0	0	7	15	23	2	.193	.221
Mitchell Page	DH29	L	29	34	92	9	13	1	0	4	13	7	29	2	.141	.283
1 Dave Revering	1B29, DH2	L	28	31	87	12	20	1	1	2	10	11	12	0	.230	.333
Keith Drumright	2B19, DH5	L	26	31	86	8	25	1	1	0	11	4	4	0	.291	.326
Tim Hosley (RC)	DH4, 1B1	R	34	18	21	2	2	0	0	1	5	2	5	0	.095	.238
Brian Doyle	2B17	L	27	17	40	2	5	0	0	0	3	1	2	0	.125	.125
Mike Davis	DH3, OF2, 1B1	L	22	17	20	0	1	1	0	0	0	2	4	0	.050	.100
Mickey Klutts (KJ)	3B14	R	26	15	46	9	17	0	0	5	11	2	9	0	.370	.696
Kelvin Moore	1B13	R	23	14	47	5	12	0	1	1	3	5	15	1	.255	.362
1 Mike Patterson	OF5, DH2	L	23	12	23	4	8	1	1	0	1	2	5	0	.348	.478
Mark Budaska	DH9	L	28	9	32	3	5	1	0	0	2	4	10	0	.156	.188
2 Rick Bosetti	OF5, DH2	R	27	9	19	4	2	0	0	0	1	3	3	0	.105	.105
Jimmy Sexton	3B1, DH1	R	29	7	3	3	0	0	0	0	0	0	3	2	.000	.000
Jeff Cox	2B1	R	25	2	0	0	0	0	0	0	0	0	0	0	—	—
Jim Nettles	OF1	L	34	1	0	0	0	0	0	0	0	0	0	0	—	—
Bob Kearney	C1	R	24	1	0	0	0	0	0	0	0	0	0	0	—	—

NAME	T	AGE	W	L	PCT	SV	G	GS	CG	IP	H	BB	SO	SHO	ERA
TOTALS		26	64	45	.587	10	109	109	60	993	883	370	505	11	3.30
Steve McCatty	R	27	14	7	.667	0	22	22	16	186	140	61	91	4	2.32
Mike Norris	R	26	12	9	.571	0	23	23	12	173	145	63	78	2	3.75
Rick Langford	R	29	12	10	.545	0	24	24	18	195	190	58	84	2	3.00
Matt Keough	R	25	10	6	.625	0	19	19	10	140	125	45	60	2	3.41
Jeff Jones	R	24	4	1	.800	3	33	0	0	61	51	40	43	0	3.39
Bob Owchinko	L	26	4	3	.571	2	29	0	0	39	34	19	26	0	3.23
2 Tom Underwood	L	27	3	2	.600	1	16	5	1	51	37	25	46	0	3.18
Brian Kingman	R	26	3	6	.333	0	18	15	3	100	112	32	52	1	3.96
Dave Heaverlo	R	30	1	0	1.000	0	6	0	0	6	7	3	2	0	1.50
Dave Beard	R	21	1	1	.500	1	8	0	0	13	9	4	15	0	2.77
Bo McLaughlin (BY)	R	27	0	0	—	1	11	0	0	12	17	9	3	0	11.25
Craig Minetto	L	27	0	0	—	0	8	0	0	7	7	4	4	0	2.57
Ed Figueroa	R	32	0	0	—	0	2	1	0	8	8	6	1	0	5.63
Rich Bordi	R	22	0	0	—	0	2	0	0	2	1	1	0	0	0.00

KANSAS CITY — 5th 20-30 .400 12 / 1st 30-23 .566 — / 50-53 .485 —   JIM FREY 30-40 .429   DICK HOWSER 20-13 .606

Name	G by Pos	B	AGE	G	AB	R	H	2B	3B	HR	RBI	BB	SO	SB	BA	SA
TOTALS			29	103	3560	397	952	169	29	61	381	301	419	100	.267	.383
Willie Aikens	1B99	L	26	101	349	45	93	16	0	17	53	62	47	0	.266	.458
Frank White	2B93	R	30	94	364	35	91	17	1	9	38	19	50	4	.250	.376
U.L. Washington	SS98	R	27	96	339	40	77	19	1	2	29	41	43	10	.227	.307
George Brett	3B88	L	28	89	347	42	109	27	7	6	43	27	23	14	.314	.484
Clint Hurdle (XJ)	OF28	L	23	28	78	12	25	3	1	4	15	13	10	0	.329	.553
Amos Otis	OF57, DH1	R	34	99	372	49	100	22	3	9	57	31	59	16	.269	.417
Willie Wilson	OF102	B	25	102	439	54	133	10	7	1	32	18	42	34	.303	.364
John Wathan	C73, OF16, 1B1	R	31	89	301	24	76	9	3	1	19	19	23	11	.252	.312
Hal McRae	DH97, OF4	R	35	101	389	38	106	23	2	7	36	34	33	2	.272	.396
Cesar Geronimo	OF57	L	33	59	118	14	29	0	2	3	13	11	16	6	.246	.331
Jamie Quirk	C22, 3B8, 2B1, OF1	L	26	46	100	8	25	7	0	0	10	6	17	0	.250	.320
Darryl Motley	OF39	R	21	42	125	15	29	4	0	2	8	7	15	1	.232	.312
Dave Chalk	3B14, 2B10, SS1	R	30	27	49	2	11	3	0	0	5	4	2	0	.224	.286
Lee May	1B8, DH4	R	38	26	55	3	16	3	0	0	8	3	14	0	.291	.345
Rance Mulliniks	2B10, SS7, 3B5	L	25	24	44	6	10	3	0	0	5	5	2	0	.227	.295
1 Jerry Grote	C22	R	38	22	56	4	17	3	1	1	9	3	2	1	.304	.446
Ken Phelps	DH4, 1B2	L	26	21	22	1	3	0	0	1	1	13	13	0	.136	.227
Danny Garcia	OF6, 1B2	R	27	12	14	4	2	0	0	0	0	0	2	0	.143	.143
Tim Ireland	1B4	B	28	4	0	1	0	0	0	0	0	0	0	0	—	—
Pat Sheridan	OF3	L	23	3	1	0	0	0	0	0	0	0	1	0	.000	.000
Onix Concepcion	SS1	R	23	2	0	0	0	0	0	0	0	0	0	0	—	—
Greg Keatley	C2	R	27	2	0	0	0	0	0	0	0	0	0	0	—	—

NAME	T	AGE	W	L	PCT	SV	G	GS	CG	IP	H	BB	SO	SHO	ERA
TOTALS		29	50	53	.485	24	103	103	24	922	909	273	404	8	3.56
Dennis Leonard	R	30	13	11	.542	0	26	26	9	202	202	41	107	2	2.99
Larry Gura	L	33	11	8	.579	0	23	23	12	172	139	35	61	2	2.72
Mike Jones	L	21	6	3	.667	0	12	11	0	76	74	28	29	0	3.20
Rich Gale	R	27	6	6	.500	0	19	15	2	102	107	38	47	0	5.38
Paul Splittorff	L	34	5	5	.500	0	21	15	1	99	111	23	48	0	4.36
Renie Martin	R	25	4	5	.444	4	29	0	0	62	55	29	25	0	2.76
Jim Wright	R	26	2	3	.400	0	17	4	0	52	57	21	27	0	3.46
Ken Brett	L	32	1	1	.500	2	22	0	0	32	35	14	7	0	4.22
Atlee Hammaker	L	23	1	3	.250	0	10	6	0	39	44	12	11	0	5.54
Dan Quisenberry	R	28	1	4	.200	18	40	0	0	62	59	15	20	0	1.74
Bill Paschall	R	27	0	0	—	0	1	0	0	4	4	1	2	0	4.50
Jeff Shattinger	R	25	0	0	—	0	1	0	0	3	2	1	1	0	0.00
1 Juan Berenguer	R	26	0	*4	.000	0	8	3	0	20	22	16	20	0	8.55

*Berenguer. also with Toronto, league leader in L with 13

TEXAS — 2nd 33-22 .600 1.5 / 3rd 24-26 .480 4.5 / 57-48 .543 —   DON ZIMMER

Name	G by Pos	B	AGE	G	AB	R	H	2B	3B	HR	RBI	BB	SO	SB	BA	SA
TOTALS			30	105	3581	452	968	178	15	49	418	295	396	46	.270	.369
Pat Putnam	1B94, OF3	L	27	95	297	33	79	17	2	8	35	17	38	4	.266	.418
Bump Wills	2B101, DH1	B	28	102	410	51	103	13	2	2	41	32	49	12	.251	.307
Mario Mendoza	SS88	R	30	88	229	18	53	6	1	0	22	7	25	2	.231	.266
Buddy Bell	3B96, SS1	R	29	97	360	44	106	16	1	10	64	42	30	3	.294	.428
Leon Roberts	OF71	R	30	72	233	26	65	17	2	4	31	25	38	3	.279	.421
Mickey Rivers	OF97	L	32	99	399	62	114	21	2	3	26	24	31	9	.286	.371
Billy Sample (BW)	OF64	R	26	66	230	36	65	16	0	3	25	17	21	4	.283	.391
Jim Sundberg	C98, OF2	R	30	102	339	42	94	17	2	3	28	50	48	2	.277	.366
Al Oliver	DH101, 1B1	L	34	102	421	53	130	29	1	4	55	24	28	3	.309	.411
Johnny Grubb	OF58	L	32	67	199	26	46	9	1	3	26	23	25	0	.231	.332
Bill Stein	1B20, OF8, 3B7, 2B3, SS1	R	34	53	115	21	38	6	0	2	22	7	15	1	.330	.435
Mark Wagner	SS43, 2B4, 3B2	R	27	50	85	15	22	4	1	1	14	8	13	1	.259	.365
2 Tom Poquette	OF18	L	29	30	64	2	10	1	0	0	7	5	1	0	.156	.172
Johnny Ellis	1B18, DH1	R	32	23	58	2	8	3	0	1	7	5	10	0	.138	.241
Wayne Tolleson	3B6, SS2	B	25	14	24	6	4	0	0	0	1	1	5	2	.167	.167
Dan Duran	OF7, 1B1	L	24	13	16	1	4	0	0	0	1	0	1	0	.250	.250
Bobby Jones	OF10	L	31	10	34	4	9	1	0	3	7	1	7	0	.265	.559
Rick Lisi	OF8	R	23	9	16	6	5	0	0	0	1	4	0	0	.313	.313
Nelson Norman	SS5	B	23	7	13	1	3	1	0	0	2	1	2	0	.231	.308
Bobby Johnson	C5, 1B1	R	21	6	18	2	5	0	0	2	4	1	3	0	.278	.611
Larry Cox	C5	R	33	5	13	0	3	1	0	0	0	0	4	0	.231	.308
Don Werner	DH2	R	28	2	8	1	2	0	0	0	0	0	2	0	.250	.250

NAME	T	AGE	W	L	PCT	SV	G	GS	CG	IP	H	BB	SO	SHO	ERA
TOTALS		30	57	48	.543	18	105	105	23	940	851	322	488	13	3.40
Rick Honeycutt	L	27	11	6	.647	0	20	20	8	128	120	17	40	2	3.30
Doc Medich	R	32	10	6	.625	0	20	20	4	143	136	33	65	4	3.08
Danny Darwin	R	27	9	9	.500	0	22	22	6	146	115	57	98	2	3.64
Steve Comer	R	27	8	2	.800	0	36	1	0	77	70	31	22	0	2.57
Ferguson Jenkins	R	37	5	8	.385	0	19	16	1	106	122	40	63	0	4.50
Charlie Hough	R	33	4	1	.800	1	21	5	2	82	61	31	69	0	2.96
Jon Matlack	L	31	4	7	.364	0	17	16	1	104	101	41	43	1	4.15
John Henry Johnson	L	24	3	1	.750	0	24	0	0	24	19	6	8	0	2.63
Bob Babcock	R	31	1	1	.500	0	16	0	0	29	21	16	18	0	2.17
Jim Kern (SJ)	R	32	1	2	.333	6	23	0	0	30	21	22	20	0	2.70
John Butcher	R	24	1	2	.333	0	5	3	1	28	18	8	19	1	1.61
2 Bob Lacey	L	27	0	0	—	0	14	1	0	32	31	11	13	0	3.09
Dave Schmidt	R	24	0	1	.000	1	14	1	0	17	13	3	7	0	4.50
Mark Mercer	R	27	0	1	.000	0	7	0	0	8	7	7	8	0	4.50
Len Whitehouse	L	23	0	0	—	0	2	0	0	3	8	2	2	0	18.00

CHICAGO — 3rd 31-22 .585 2.5 / 6th 23-30 .434 7 / 54-52 .509 —   TONY LaRUSSA

Name	G by Pos	B	AGE	G	AB	R	H	2B	3B	HR	RBI	BB	SO	SB	BA	SA
TOTALS			29	106	3615	476	982	135	27	76	438	322	518	86	.272	.387
Mike Squires	1B88, OF1	L	29	92	294	35	78	9	0	0	25	22	17	7	.265	.296
Tony Bernazard	2B105, DH1	B	24	106	384	53	106	14	4	6	34	54	66	4	.276	.380
Bill Almon	SS103	R	28	103	349	46	105	10	2	4	41	21	60	16	.301	.375
Jim Morrison	3B87, 2B1, DH1	R	28	90	290	27	68	11	3	10	41	12	39	3	.234	.372
Harold Baines	OF80, DH1	L	22	80	280	42	80	11	7	10	41	12	41	6	.286	.482
Chet Lemon	OF94	R	26	94	328	50	99	23	6	9	50	33	48	5	.302	.491
Ron LeFlore	OF82	R	33	82	337	46	83	10	4	0	24	28	70	36	.244	.300
Carlton Fisk	C92, 1B1, 3B1, OF1	R	33	96	338	44	89	12	0	7	45	38	37	3	.263	.361
Greg Luzinski	DH103	R	30	104	378	55	100	15	1	21	62	68	80	0	.265	.476
Rusty Kuntz	OF51, DH5	R	26	67	55	15	14	2	0	0	5	11	10	1	.255	.291
Wayne Nordhagen	OF60	R	32	65	208	19	64	8	1	6	33	10	25	0	.308	.442
Greg Pryor	3B27, SS13, 2B5	R	31	47	76	4	17	5	0	0	6	6	8	0	.224	.237
Bob Molinaro	DH4, OF2	L	31	47	42	7	11	1	1	0	9	8	1	1	.262	.405
Lamar Johnson	1B36, DH2	R	30	41	134	10	37	7	0	1	15	5	14	0	.276	.351
Jim Essian	C25, 3B2	R	30	27	52	6	16	3	0	0	5	4	5	0	.308	.346
Mark Hill	C14, 1B1, 3B1	R	29	16	6	0	0	0	0	0	0	4	0	0	.000	.000
Jay Loviglio	3B4, 2B3, DH2	B	25	14	15	5	4	0	0	0	1	1	3	2	.267	.267
Leo Sutherland	OF7	L	23	13	12	1	2	0	0	0	2	0	1	0	.167	.167
2 Jerry Turner	OF1	L	27	10	12	1	2	0	0	0	0	2	0	0	.167	.167
Jerry Hairston	OF7	B	29	9	25	5	7	1	0	1	6	2	4	0	.280	.440
Todd Cruz 25 (XJ)																

NAME	T	AGE	W	L	PCT	SV	G	GS	CG	IP	H	BB	SO	SHO	ERA
TOTALS		25	54	52	.509	23	106	106	20	941	891	336	529	8	3.47
Britt Burns	L	22	10	6	.625	0	24	23	5	157	139	49	108	1	2.64
LaMarr Hoyt	R	26	9	3	.750	10	43	1	0	91	80	28	60	0	3.56
Rich Dotson	R	22	9	8	.529	0	24	24	5	141	145	49	73	4	3.77
Steve Trout	L	23	8	7	.533	0	20	18	3	125	122	38	54	0	3.46
Dennis Lamp	R	28	7	6	.538	0	27	10	3	127	103	43	71	0	2.41
Ross Baumgarten	L	26	5	9	.357	0	19	19	2	102	101	40	52	1	4.06
Ed Farmer	R	31	3	3	.500	10	42	0	0	53	53	34	42	0	4.58
Dewey Robinson	R	26	1	0	1.000	0	4	0	0	4	5	3	2	0	4.50
2 Francisco Barrios (SJ)	R	28	1	3	.250	0	8	5	0	36	45	14	12	0	4.00
2 Jerry Kossman	L	38	1	*4	.200	0	8	3	1	27	27	7	21	0	3.33
Lynn McGlothen	R	31	0	0	—	0	11	0	0	22	14	7	12	0	4.09
Juan Agosto	L	23	0	0	—	0	2	0	0	4	5	2	1	0	4.50
Reggie Patterson	R	23	0	1	.000	0	7	1	0	7	14	6	2	0	14.14
Kevin Hickey	L	24	0	2	.000	3	41	0	0	44	38	18	17	0	3.68

*Kossman, also with Minnesota, league leader in L with 13

Name	G by Pos	B	AGE	G	AB	R	H	2B	3B	HR	RBI	BB	SO	SB	BA	SA
CALIFORNIA	4th 31-29 .517 6															
	7th 20-30 .400 8.5															
	— 51-59 .484 —															
	TOTALS		31	110	3688	476	944	134	16	97	439	393	571	44	.256	.380
Rod Carew	1B90, DH2	L	35	93	364	57	111	17	1	2	21	45	45	16	.305	.380
Bobby Grich	2B100	R	32	100	352	56	107	14	2	22	61	40	71	2	.304	.543
Rick Burleson	SS109	R	30	109	430	53	126	17	1	5	33	42	38	1	.293	.372
Butch Hobson	3B83, DH2	R	29	85	268	27	63	7	4	4	36	35	60	1	.235	.336
Dan Ford	OF97	R	29	97	375	53	104	14	1	15	48	23	71	2	.277	.440
Fred Lynn	OF69	L	29	76	256	28	56	8	1	5	31	38	42	1	.219	.316
Brian Downing	OF56, DH5	R	30	93	317	47	79	14	0	9	41	46	35	1	.249	.379
Ed Ott	C72	L	29	75	258	20	56	8	1	2	22	17	42	2	.217	.279
Don Baylor	DH97, 1B4, OF1	R	32	103	377	52	90	18	1	17	66	42	51	3	.239	.427
Juan Beniquez	OF55, DH1	R	31	58	166	18	30	5	0	3	13	15	16	2	.181	.265
Bert Campaneris	3B45, SS3, 2B2	R	39	55	82	11	21	2	1	1	10	5	10	5	.256	.341
Larry Harlow	OF39	L	29	43	62	13	17	1	0	0	4	16	25	1	.207	.220
John Harris	1B11, OF10, DH1	L	26	36	77	5	19	3	0	3	9	3	11	0	.247	.403
Bobby Clark (LJ)	OF34	R	26	34	88	12	22	2	1	4	19	7	18	0	.250	.432
Freddie Patek	2B16, 3B7, SS3	R	36	27	47	3	11	1	1	0	5	1	5	1	.234	.298
Daryl Sconiers	1B12, DH3	L	22	15	52	6	14	1	1	1	7	1	10	0	.269	.385
2 Joe Ferguson	C8, OF4	R	34	12	30	5	7	1	0	1	5	9	8	0	.233	.367
Tom Brunansky	OF11	R	20	11	33	7	5	0	0	3	6	8	10	1	.152	.424
Steve Lubratich	3B6	R	26	7	21	2	3	1	0	0	1	0	2	0	.143	.190
Brian Harper	OF2, DH1	R	21	4	11	1	3	0	0	0	1	0	1	0	.273	.273
Bob Davis	C1	R	29	1	2	0	0	0	0	0	0	0	0	0	.000	.000
SEATTLE	6th 21-36 .368 14.5															
	5th 23-29 .442 6.5															
	— 44-65 .404 —															
	TOTALS		28	110	3780	426	950	148	13	89	406	329	553	100	.251	.368
Bruce Bochte	1B82, OF14, DH1	L	30	99	335	39	87	16	0	6	30	47	53	1	.260	.361
Julio Cruz	2B92, SS1	B	26	94	352	57	90	12	3	2	24	39	40	43	.256	.324
Jim Anderson	SS68, 3B2	R	24	70	162	12	33	7	0	2	19	17	29	3	.204	.284
Lenny Randle	3B59, 2B21, OF5, SS3	B	32	82	273	22	63	9	1	4	25	17	22	11	.231	.315
Jeff Burroughs	OF87, DH1	R	30	89	319	32	81	13	1	10	41	41	64	0	.254	.395
Joe Simpson	OF88	L	29	91	288	32	64	11	3	2	30	15	41	12	.222	.302
Tom Paciorek	OF103	R	34	104	405	50	132	28	2	14	66	35	50	13	.326	.509
Jerry Narron	C65	L	25	76	203	13	45	5	0	3	17	16	35	0	.222	.291
Richie Zisk	DH93	R	32	94	357	42	111	12	1	16	43	28	63	0	.311	.485
Dan Meyer	3B49, OF14, 1B3, DH3	L	28	83	252	26	66	10	1	3	22	10	16	4	.262	.345
Gary Gray	1B34, DH15, OF4	R	28	69	208	27	51	7	1	13	31	4	44	2	.245	.476
Terry Bulling	C62	R	28	62	154	15	38	3	0	2	15	21	20	0	.247	.305
Dave Henderson	OF58	R	22	59	126	17	21	3	0	6	13	16	24	1	.167	.333
Rick Auerbach (BG)	SS38	R	31	38	84	12	13	3	0	1	6	4	15	1	.155	.226
Casey Parsons	OF24, 1B1	L	27	36	22	6	5	1	0	1	4	5	4	0	.227	.409
Paul Serna	SS23, 2B7	R	22	30	94	11	24	2	0	4	9	3	11	2	.255	.404
Dave Edler	3B26, SS1	R	24	29	78	7	11	3	0	1	5	11	13	3	.141	.179
Kim Allen	2B2, OF2, DH2	R	28	19	3	1	0	0	0	0	0	2	2	1	.000	.000
Vance McHenry	SS13, DH1	R	24	15	18	3	4	0	0	0	2	1	1	0	.222	.222
Dan Firova	C13	R	24	13	3	0	0	0	0	0	0	1	1	0	.000	.000
Jim Maler	1B5, DH2	R	22	12	23	1	8	1	0	0	2	2	1	1	.348	.391
Reggie Walton (LJ)	OF4, DH1	R	28	12	6	1	0	0	0	0	0	1	2	0	.000	.000
Brad Gulden	C6	L	25	8	16	0	3	2	0	0	1	0	2	0	.188	.313
MINNESOTA	7th 17-39 .304 18															
	5th 24-29 .453 6.5															
	— 41-68 .376 —															
	TOTALS		27	110	3676	378	884	147	36	47	359	275	497	34	.240	.338
1 Ron Jackson	1B36, OF7, DH6, DH3	R	28	54	175	17	46	9	0	4	28	10	15	2	.263	.383
Rob Wilfong	2B93	L	27	93	305	32	75	11	3	3	19	29	43	2	.246	.331
Roy Smalley (XJ)	SS37, DH15, 1B1	B	28	56	167	24	44	7	1	7	22	31	24	0	.263	.443
John Castino	3B93, 2B4	R	26	101	381	41	102	13	9	6	36	18	52	4	.268	.396
Dave Engle	OF76, 3B1, DH1	R	24	82	248	29	64	14	4	5	32	13	37	0	.258	.407
Mickey Hatcher	OF91, 1B7, 3B2, DH1	R	26	99	377	36	96	23	2	3	37	15	29	3	.255	.350
Gary Ward	OF80, DH2	R	27	85	295	42	78	7	6	3	29	28	48	5	.264	.359
Butch Wynegar (EJ)	C37, DH9	B	25	47	150	11	37	5	0	0	10	17	9	0	.247	.280
Glenn Adams	DH62	L	33	72	220	13	46	10	0	2	24	20	20	0	.209	.282
Hosken Powell	OF64, DH8	L	26	80	264	30	63	11	3	2	25	17	31	7	.239	.326
Pete Mackanin	2B31, SS28, 1B10, DH6, 3B4	R	29	77	225	21	52	7	1	4	18	7	40	1	.231	.324
Sal Butera	C59, 1B1, DH1	R	28	62	167	13	40	7	1	0	18	22	14	0	.240	.293
Danny Goodwin	1B40, DH5, OF1	L	27	59	151	18	34	6	1	2	17	16	32	3	.225	.318
Rick Sofield	OF34	L	24	41	102	9	18	2	0	0	6	3	22	3	.176	.196
Chuck Baker	SS31, 2B3, 3B1, DH1	R	28	40	66	6	12	0	3	0	6	1	8	0	.182	.273
Ron Washington	SS26, OF2	R	29	28	84	8	19	3	1	0	5	4	14	4	.226	.286
Kent Hrbek	1B13, DH8	L	21	24	67	5	16	5	0	1	7	5	9	0	.239	.358
Tim Corcoran	1B16, DH3	L	28	22	51	4	9	3	0	0	4	6	7	0	.176	.235
Ray Smith (BW)	C15	R	25	15	40	4	8	1	0	1	1	3	0	0	.200	.300
Tim Laudner	C12, DH2	R	23	14	43	4	7	1	2	0	5	3	17	0	.163	.349
Lenny Faedo	SS12	R	21	12	41	3	8	1	0	0	6	1	5	1	.195	.244
Gary Gaetti	3B8, DH1	R	22	9	25	4	5	0	0	2	3	0	6	0	.192	.423
Mark Funderburk	OF6, DH1	R	24	8	15	2	3	1	0	0	3	0	2	0	.200	.267
Greg Johnston	OF6	L	26	7	16	2	2	0	0	0	0	0	3	0	.125	.125

NAME	T	AGE	W	L	PCT	SV	G	GS	CG	IP	H	BB	SO	SHO	ERA
		30	51	59	.464	19	110	110	27	971	958	323	426	8	3.70
Ken Forsch	R	34	11	7	.611	0	20	20	10	153	143	27	55	4	2.88
Geoff Zahn	L	35	10	11	.476	0	25	25	9	161	181	43	52	0	4.42
Steve Renko	R	36	8	4	.667	1	22	15	0	102	93	42	50	0	3.44
Mike Witt	R	20	8	9	.471	0	22	21	7	129	123	47	75	1	3.28
Andy Hassler	L	29	4	3	.571	5	42	0	0	76	72	33	44	0	3.20
Don Aase	R	26	4	4	.500	11	39	0	0	65	56	24	38	0	2.35
Jesse Jefferson	R	32	2	4	.333	0	26	5	0	77	80	24	27	0	3.62
Bruce Kison (EJ)	R	31	1	1	.500	0	11	4	0	44	40	14	19	0	3.48
Doug Rau (SJ)	L	32	1	2	.333	0	3	3	0	10	14	4	3	0	9.00
Angel Moreno	L	26	1	3	.250	0	8	4	1	31	27	14	12	0	2.90
Dave Frost (SJ)	R	28	1	8	.111	0	12	9	0	47	44	19	16	0	5.55
John D'Acquisto	R	29	0	0	—	0	6	0	0	19	26	12	8	0	10.89
Mickey Mahler	L	28	0	0	—	0	4	0	0	6	1	2	5	0	0.00
Freddie Martinez	R	24	0	0	—	0	2	0	0	4	3	3	1	0	3.00
Bill Travers (SJ)	L	28	0	1	.000	0	4	4	0	10	14	4	5	0	8.10
Luis Sanchez	R	27	0	2	.000	2	17	0	0	34	39	11	13	0	2.91
		27	44	65	.404	23	110	110	10	997	1039	360	478	5	4.23
Floyd Bannister	L	26	9	9	.500	0	21	20	5	121	128	39	85	2	4.46
Shane Rawley	L	25	4	6	.400	8	46	0	0	68	64	38	35	0	3.97
Dick Drago	R	36	4	6	.400	5	39	0	0	54	71	15	27	0	5.50
Jerry Don Gleaton	R	23	4	7	.364	0	20	13	1	85	88	38	31	0	4.76
Glenn Abbott	R	30	4	9	.308	0	22	20	1	130	127	28	35	0	3.95
Jim Beattie	R	26	3	2	.600	1	13	9	0	67	59	18	36	0	2.96
Brian Allard (EJ)	R	23	3	2	.600	0	7	7	1	48	48	8	20	0	3.75
Larry Andersen	R	28	3	3	.500	5	41	0	0	68	57	18	40	0	2.65
Mike Parrott	R	26	3	6	.333	1	24	12	0	85	102	28	43	0	5.08
Bob Stoddard	R	24	2	1	.667	0	5	5	1	35	35	9	22	0	2.57
Bryan Clark	L	24	2	5	.286	2	29	9	1	93	92	55	52	0	4.35
Ken Clay	R	27	2	7	.222	0	22	14	0	101	116	42	32	0	4.63
Bob Galasso (EJ)	R	29	1	1	.500	1	13	1	0	32	32	13	14	0	4.78
Bud Black	L	24	0	0	—	0	2	0	0	1	2	3	0	0	0.00
Randy Stein	R	28	0	1	.000	0	5	0	0	9	18	8	6	0	11.00
		28	41	68	.376	22	110	110	13	979	1021	376	500	6	3.98
Pete Redfern	R	26	9	8	.529	0	24	23	3	142	140	52	77	0	4.06
Fernando Arroyo	R	29	7	10	.412	0	23	19	2	128	144	34	39	0	3.94
Al Williams	R	27	6	10	.375	0	23	22	4	150	160	52	76	0	4.08
Jack O'Connor	L	23	3	2	.600	0	28	0	0	35	46	30	16	0	5.91
Darrell Jackson (IL)	L	25	4	5	.500	0	14	5	0	33	35	19	26	0	4.36
Brad Havens	L	21	3	6	.333	0	14	12	1	78	76	24	43	1	3.58
Roger Erickson (BG)	R	24	3	8	.273	0	14	14	1	91	93	31	44	0	3.86
1 Jerry Koosman	L	38	3	*9	.250	5	19	13	2	94	98	34	55	1	4.21
Doug Corbett	R	28	2	6	.250	17	54	0	0	88	80	34	60	0	2.56
Bob Veselic	R	25	1	1	.500	0	5	0	0	23	22	13	13	0	3.13
Don Cooper	R	25	1	5	.167	0	27	2	0	59	61	32	33	0	4.27
John Verhoeven	R	28	0	0	—	0	25	0	0	52	57	14	16	0	3.98
Jack Hobbs	L	24	0	0	—	0	4	0	0	6	5	6	1	0	3.00
Terry Felton	R	23	0	0	—	0	1	0	0	4	2	1	1	0	54.00

*Koosman, also with Chicago, league leader in L with 13

LINE SCORES

TEAM	1	2	3		4	5	6		7	8	9	10	11		R	H	E

WEST DIVISIONAL SERIES: OAKLAND 3   KANSAS CITY 0

Game 1   October 6 at Kansas City

OAK	0 0 0	3 0 0	0 1 0		4	8	2
KC	0 0 0	0 0 0	0 0 0		0	4	1

Norris   Leonard, Martin (9)

Game 2   October 7 at Kansas City

OAK	1 0 0	0 0 0	0 1 0		2	10	1
KC	0 0 0	0 1 0	0 0 0		1	6	0

McCatty   Jones, Quisenberry (9)

Game 3   October 9 at Oakland

KC	0 0 0	1 0 0	0 0 0		1	10	3
OAK	1 0 1	2 0 0	0 0 X		4	8	0

Gura, Martin (4)   Langford, Underwood (8) Beard (8)

COMPOSITE BATTING

NAME	POS	G	AB	R	H	2B	3B	HR	RBI	BA
Oakland										
TOTALS		3	99	10	25	5	0	3	9	.253
Armas	RF	3	11	1	6	2	0	0	3	.545
Murphy	CF	3	11	4	6	1	0	1	2	.545
McKay	2B	3	11	0	3	0	0	1	1	.273
Henderson	LF	3	11	3	2	0	0	0	0	.182
Heath	C	3	8	0	0	0	0	0	0	.000
Moore	1B	2	8	0	0	0	0	0	0	.000
Johnson	DH	2	7	0	2	1	0	0	0	.286
Klutts	3B	2	7	0	1	0	0	0	0	.143
Gross	3B-DH	2	5	1	2	0	0	1	3	.400

Stanley SS 0-6, Drumright DH1-4, Spencer 1B 1-4, Picciolo SS 1-3, Newman C 0-3, Bosetti RF-PR 0-0

NAME	POS	G	AB	R	H	2B	3B	HR	RBI	BA
Kansas City										
TOTALS		3	98	2	20	0	0	0	2	.204
Wilson	LF	3	13	0	4	0	0	0	1	.308
Brett	3B	3	12	0	2	0	0	0	0	.167
Otis	CF	3	12	0	0	0	0	0	1	.000
Hurdle	RF	3	11	0	3	0	0	0	0	.273
White	2B	3	11	1	2	0	0	0	0	.182
McRae	DH	3	11	0	1	0	0	0	0	.091
Wathan	C	3	10	1	3	0	0	0	0	.300
Aikens	1B	3	9	0	3	0	0	0	0	.333
Washington	SS	3	9	0	2	0	0	0	0	.222

Geronimo PR 0-0, May 1B 0-0

COMPOSITE PITCHING

NAME	G	IP	H	BB	SO	W	L	SV	ERA
Oakland									
TOTALS	3	27	20	7	11	3	0	1	0.67
Norris	1	9	4	3	2	1	0	0	0.00
McCatty	1	9	6	4	3	1	0	0	1.00
Langford	1	7.1	10	0	3	1	0	0	1.23
Beard	1	1.1	0	0	2	0	0	1	0.00
Underwood	1	1	0	0	1	0	0	0	0.00
Kansas City									
TOTALS	3	26	25	6	10	0	3	0	2.08
Leonard	1	8	7	1	3	0	1	0	1.13
Jones	1	8	9	0	2	0	1	0	2.25
Martin	2	5.1	1	2	2	0	0	0	0.00
Gura	1	3.2	7	3	3	0	1	0	7.36
Quisenberry	1	1	1	0	0	0	0	0	0.00

MONTREAL

3rd 30-25 .545 4
1st 30-23 .566 —
— 60-48 .556 —
DICK WILLIAMS 44-37 .543   JIM FANNING 16-11 .593

Name	G by Pos	B	AGE	G	AB	R	H	2B	3B	HR	RBI	BB	SO	SB	BA	SA
TOTALS			26	108	3591	443	883	146	28	81	407	368	498	138	.246	.270
Warren Cromartie	1B62, OF38	L	27	99	358	41	109	19	2	6	42	39	27	2	.304	.419
Rodney Scott	2B93	B	27	95	336	43	69	9	3	0	26	50	35	30	.205	.250
Chris Speier	SS96	R	31	96	307	33	69	10	2	2	25	38	29	1	.225	.290
Larry Parrish	3B95	R	27	97	349	41	85	19	3	8	44	28	73	0	.244	.384
Tim Wallach	OF35, 1B16, 3B15	R	23	71	212	19	50	9	1	4	13	15	37	0	.236	.344
Andre Dawson	OF103	R	26	103	394	71	119	21	3	24	64	35	50	26	.302	.553
Tim Raines	OF81, 2B1	B	21	88	313	61	95	13	7	5	37	45	31	71	.304	.438
Gary Carter	C100, 1B1	R	27	100	374	48	94	20	2	16	68	35	35	1	.251	.444
Jerry White	OF39	B	28	59	119	11	26	5	1	3	11	13	17	5	.318	.353
Terry Francona	OF26, 1B1	L	22	34	95	11	26	0	1	1	8	5	6	1	.274	.326
2 Mike Phillips	SS26, 2B6	L	30	34	55	5	12	2	0	0	4	5	15	0	.218	.255
Tommy Hutton	1B9, OF2	L	35	31	29	1	3	0	0	0	2	2	1	0	.103	.103
2 John Milner	1B21	L	31	31	76	6	18	5	0	3	9	12	6	0	.237	.421
Jerry Manuel (KJ)	2B23, SS2	B	27	27	55	10	11	5	0	3	10	6	11	0	.200	.455
Bobby Ramos	C23	R	25	26	41	4	8	1	0	1	3	3	5	0	.195	.293
Rowland Office (BN)	OF15	L	28	26	40	4	7	0	0	0	4	6	0		.175	.175
1 Willie Montanez	1B16	L	33	26	62	6	11	0	1	0	5	4	9	0	.177	.210
1 Ellis Valentine	OF21	R	26	22	76	8	16	3	0	1	15	6	11	0	.211	.368
Brad Mills	3B7, 2B2	L	24	17	21	3	5	1	0	0	1	2	1	0	.238	.286
Wallace Johnson	2B1	B	24	11	9	1	2	0	1	0	3	1	1	1	.222	.444
Dan Briggs	1B3, OF3	L	28	9	11	0	1	0	0	0	0	0	3	0	.091	.091
Bob Pate	OF5	R	27	8	6	0	2	0	0	0	0	1	0	0	.333	.333
Chris Smith	2B1	B	23	7	7	0	0	0	0	0	0	0	2	0	.000	.000
Dave Hastetler	1B2	R	25	5	6	1	3	0	0	1	0	2	0		.500	1.000
Pat Rooney	OF2	R	23	4	5	0	0	0	0	0	0	0	3	0	.000	.000
Tony Johnson	OF1	R	25	2	1	0	0	0	0	0	0	0	0	0	.000	.000
Mike Gates	2B1	L	24	1	2	1	1	0	1	0	1	0	1		.500	1.500
Tom Wieghaus	C1	R	24	1	1	0	0	0	0	0	0	0	0	0	.000	.000

NAME	T	AGE	W	L	PCT	SV	G	GS	CG	IP	H	BB	SO	SHO	ERA
TOTALS		30	60	48	.556	23	108	108	20	975	902	268	520	12	3.30
Steve Rogers	R	31	12	8	.600	0	22	22	7	161	149	41	87	3	3.41
Scott Sanderson	R	24	9	7	.563	0	22	22	1	137	122	31	77	1	2.96
Ray Burris	R	30	9	7	.563	0	22	21	4	136	117	41	52	0	3.04
Bill Gullickson	R	22	7	9	.438	0	22	22	3	157	142	34	115	2	2.81
Woody Fryman	L	41	5	3	.625	7	35	0	0	43	38	14	25	0	1.88
Charlie Lea	R	24	5	4	.556	0	16	11	2	64	63	26	31	2	4.64
Bill Lee	L	34	5	6	.455	6	31	7	0	89	90	14	34	0	2.93
2 Jeff Reardon	R	25	2	0	1.000	6	25	0	0	43	21	9	21	0	1.29
Stan Bahnsen	R	36	2	1	.667	1	25	3	0	49	45	24	28	0	4.96
2 Grant Jackson	L	38	1	0	1.000	0	10	0	0	11	14	9	4	0	7.36
Bryn Smith	R	25	1	0	1.000	0	7	0	0	13	14	3	9	0	2.77
Steve Ratzer	R	27	1	1	.500	0	12	0	0	17	23	7	4	0	6.35
Elias Sosa	R	31	1	2	.333	3	32	0	0	39	46	8	18	0	3.69
Tom Gorman	L	23	0	0	—	0	9	0	0	15	12	6	13	0	4.20
Rick Engle	L	24	0	0	—	0	1	0	0	2	6	1	2	0	18.00
David Palmer 23 (EJ)															

PHILADELPHIA

1st 34-21 .618 —
3rd 25-27 .481 4.5
— 59-48 .551 —
DALLAS GREEN

Name	G by Pos	B	AGE	G	AB	R	H	2B	3B	HR	RBI	BB	SO	SB	BA	SA
TOTALS			31	107	3665	491	1002	165	25	69	453	372	432	103	.273	.389
Pete Rose	1B107	B	40	107	431	73	140	18	5	0	33	46	26	4	.325	.390
Manny Trillo	2B94	R	30	94	349	37	100	14	3	6	36	26	37	0	.287	.395
Larry Bowa	SS102	B	35	103	360	34	102	14	3	0	31	26	17	16	.283	.339
Mike Schmidt	3B101	R	31	102	354	78	112	19	2	31	91	73	71	12	.316	.644
Bake McBride	OF56	L	32	58	221	26	60	17	1	2	21	11	25	5	.271	.385
Garry Maddox	OF94	R	31	94	323	37	85	7	1	5	40	17	42	9	.263	.337
Gary Matthews	OF100	R	30	121	359	62	108	21	3	9	67	59	42	15	.301	.451
Bob Boone	C75	R	33	76	227	19	48	7	0	4	24	22	16	2	.211	.295
Greg Gross	OF55	L	28	83	102	14	23	6	1	0	7	15	5	2	.225	.304
Lonnie Smith	OF51	R	25	62	176	40	57	14	3	2	11	18	14	21	.324	.472
Del Unser	1B18, OF16	L	36	62	59	5	9	3	0	0	6	13	9	0	.153	.203
Keith Moreland	C50, 3B7, 1B2, OF2	R	27	61	196	16	50	7	0	6	37	15	13	1	.255	.383
Dick Davis	OF32	R	27	45	96	12	32	6	1	2	19	8	13	1	.333	.479
Luis Aguayo	2B21, SS21, 3B3	R	22	45	84	11	18	4	0	1	7	6	15	1	.214	.298
Ramon Aviles	2B20, 3B13, SS5	R	29	38	28	2	6	1	0	0	3	3	5	0	.214	.250
George Vukovich	OF9	L	25	20	26	5	10	0	0	1	4	1	0	1	.385	.500
Len Matuszek	1B1, 3B1	L	26	13	11	1	3	1	0	0	1	3	1	0	.273	.364
Ryne Sandberg	SS5, 3B1	R	21	13	6	2	1	0	0	0	0	0	1	0	.167	.167
John Vukovich	3B9, 1B1, 2B1	R	33	11	1	0	0	0	0	0	0	0	0	0	.000	.000
Bob Dernier	OF5	R	24	10	4	0	3	0	0	0	0	0	2	2	.750	.750
Ozzie Virgil	C1	R	24	6	6	0	0	0	0	0	0	0	2	0	.000	.000
Don McCormack	C3	R	25	3	4	0	1	0	0	0	0	0	1	0	.250	.250

NAME	T	AGE	W	L	PCT	SV	G	GS	CG	IP	H	BB	SO	SHO	ERA
TOTALS		33	59	48	.551	23	107	107	19	960	967	347	580	5	4.05
Steve Carlton	L	36	13	4	.765	0	24	24	10	190	152	62	179	1	2.42
Dick Ruthven	R	30	12	7	.632	0	23	22	5	147	162	54	80	0	5.14
Sparky Lyle	L	36	9	6	.600	2	48	0	0	75	85	33	29	0	4.44
Ron Reed	R	38	5	3	.625	8	39	0	0	61	54	17	40	0	3.10
Marty Bystrom	R	22	4	3	.571	0	9	9	1	54	55	16	24	0	3.33
Larry Christianson (GJ)	R	27	4	7	.364	1	20	15	0	107	108	30	70	0	3.53
Dan Larson	R	26	3	0	1.000	0	5	4	1	28	27	15	15	0	4.18
Mike Proly	R	30	2	1	.667	2	35	2	0	63	66	19	19	0	3.86
Dickie Noles	R	24	2	2	.500	0	13	8	0	58	57	23	34	0	4.19
Tug McGraw	L	36	2	4	.333	10	34	0	0	44	35	14	26	0	2.66
1 Nino Espinosa	R	27	2	5	.286	0	14	14	2	74	98	24	22	0	6.08
Mark Davis	L	20	1	4	.200	0	9	6	0	43	49	24	29	0	7.74
Warren Brusstar	R	29	0	1	.000	0	14	0	0	12	12	10	8	0	4.50
Jerry Reed	R	25	0	1	.000	0	4	0	0	5	7	6	5	0	7.20

ST. LOUIS

2nd 30-20 .600 1.5
2nd 29-23 .558 4.5
— 59-43 .578 —
WHITEY HERZOG

Name	G by Pos	B	AGE	G	AB	R	H	2B	3B	HR	RBI	BB	SO	SB	BA	SA
TOTALS			28	103	3537	464	936	158	45	50	431	379	495	88	.265	.377
Keith Hernandez	1B98, OF3	L	27	103	376	65	115	27	4	8	48	61	45	12	.306	.463
Tommy Herr	2B103	B	25	103	411	50	110	14	9	0	46	39	30	23	.268	.345
Garry Templeton	SS76	B	25	80	333	47	96	16	8	1	33	14	55	8	.288	.393
Ken Oberkfell	3B102, SS1	L	25	102	376	43	110	12	6	2	45	37	28	6	.293	.372
Sixto Lezcano	OF65	R	27	72	214	26	57	8	2	5	28	40	40	1	.266	.393
George Hendrick	OF101	R	31	101	394	67	112	19	3	18	61	41	44	4	.284	.485
Dane Iorg	OF57, 1B8, 3B2	L	31	75	217	23	71	11	2	2	39	7	9	2	.327	.424
Darrell Porter (SJ)	C52	L	29	61	174	22	39	10	2	6	31	39	32	1	.224	.408
Tito Landrum	OF67	R	26	81	119	13	31	5	4	0	10	6	14	4	.291	.370
Gene Tenace	C38, 1B7	R	34	58	129	26	30	7	0	5	22	38	26	0	.233	.403
Mike Ramsey (BH)	SS35, 3B5, OF1	B	27	47	124	19	32	3	0	0	9	8	16	4	.258	.282
1 Tony Scott	OF44	B	29	45	176	21	40	5	2	2	17	5	22	10	.227	.313
Steve Braun	OF12, 3B1	L	33	44	46	9	9	2	1	0	2	15	7	1	.196	.283
Orlando Sanchez	C18	R	24	27	49	5	14	2	1	0	6	2	6	1	.286	.367
Gene Roof	OF20	B	23	23	60	11	18	6	0	0	3	2	16	5	.300	.400
David Green	OF18	R	20	21	34	6	5	1	0	0	2	6	5	0	.147	.176
Glenn Brummer	C19	R	26	21	30	2	6	1	0	0	2	0	3	0	.200	.233
Julio Gonzalez	SS5, 2B4, 3B2	R	28	20	22	2	7	1	0	1	3	1	3	0	.318	.500
1 Neil Fiala		L	24	3	3	0	0	0	0	0	0	0	1	0	.000	.000

NAME	T	AGE	W	L	PCT	SV	G	GS	CG	IP	H	BB	SO	SHO	ERA
TOTALS		29	59	43	.578	33	103	103	11	943	902	290	388	5	3.63
Bob Forsch	R	31	10	5	.667	0	20	20	1	124	106	29	41	0	3.19
John Martin	L	25	8	5	.615	0	17	15	4	103	85	26	36	0	3.41
Lary Sorensen	R	25	7	7	.500	0	23	23	3	140	149	26	52	1	3.28
2 Joaquin Andujar	L	28	6	1	.857	0	11	8	1	55	56	11	19	0	3.76
Bob Shirley	L	27	6	4	.600	1	28	11	1	79	78	34	35	0	4.10
Jim Kaat	L	42	6	6	.500	4	41	1	0	53	60	17	8	0	3.40
Andy Rincon (BA)	R	22	3	1	.750	0	5	5	1	36	27	5	13	1	1.75
Bruce Sutter	R	28	3	5	.375	25	48	0	0	82	64	24	57	0	2.63
Bob Sykes	L	26	2	0	1.000	0	22	1	0	37	37	18	14	0	4.62
2 Doug Bair	R	31	2	0	1.000	1	10	0	0	16	13	2	14	0	3.38
Silvio Martinez	R	25	2	5	.286	0	18	16	0	97	95	39	34	0	3.99
Jim Otten (AJ)	R	30	1	0	1.000	0	24	0	0	36	44	20	20	0	5.25
1 Joe Edelen	R	25	1	0	1.000	0	13	0	0	17	29	3	10	0	9.53
Dave LaPoint	L	21	1	0	1.000	0	3	2	0	11	12	4	4	0	4.09
Mark Littell (EJ)	R	28	1	3	.250	2	28	1	0	41	36	31	22	0	4.39
Luis DeLeon	R	22	0	0	—	0	10	0	0	15	11	3	8	0	2.40
John Fulgham 25 (SJ)															

PITTSBURGH

4th 25-23 .521 5.5
6th 21-33 .389 9.5
— 46-56 .451 —
CHUCK TANNER

Name	G by Pos	B	AGE	G	AB	R	H	2B	3B	HR	RBI	BB	SO	SB	BA	SA
TOTALS			28	103	3576	407	920	176	30	56	384	278	494	122	.257	.369
Jason Thompson	1B78	L	26	86	223	36	55	15	0	15	42	59	49	9	.242	.502
1 Phil Garner	2B50	R	32	56	181	22	46	6	2	1	20	21	21	4	.254	.326
Tim Foli	SS81	R	30	86	316	32	78	12	2	0	20	17	10	7	.247	.297
Bill Madlock	3B79	R	30	82	279	35	95	23	1	6	45	34	17	18	.341	.495
Dave Parker	OF60	L	30	67	240	29	62	14	3	9	48	9	25	6	.258	.454
Omar Moreno	OF103	L	28	103	434	62	120	18	8	1	35	26	75	39	.276	.362
Mike Easler	OF90	L	30	95	349	43	97	18	5	7	42	24	45	4	.286	.431
Tony Pena	C64	R	24	66	210	16	63	9	1	2	17	8	23	1	.300	.381
Dale Berra	3B42, SS30, 2B18	R	24	81	232	21	56	8	2	2	27	17	34	11	.241	.319
Lee Lacy	OF63, 3B1	R	33	78	213	31	57	11	4	2	10	11	29	24	.268	.385
Steve Nicosia	C52	R	25	54	169	21	39	10	1	2	18	13	10	3	.231	.337
Bill Robinson (LJ)	1B23, OF7, 3B1	R	38	39	88	8	19	3	0	2	8	5	18	1	.216	.318
Willie Stargell	1B9	L	41	38	60	2	17	4	0	0	9	13	8	0	.283	.350
1 John Milner	1B8, OF8	L	31	34	59	6	14	1	0	2	9	5	9	0	.237	.356
Johnny Ray	2B31	B	24	31	102	10	25	11	0	0	6	6	9	0	.245	.353
Vance Law	2B19, 1B11, SS7, 3B2	R	24	40	67	1	9	0	1	2	3	2	15	1	.134	.164
2 Willie Montanez	1B11	L	33	19	38	3	10	0	1	0	2	0	4	0	.263	.342
Kurt Bevacqua	2B4, 3B2	R	34	29	27	2	7	1	0	1	4	4	6	0	.259	.407
Gary Alexander	1B9, OF8	R	28	21	47	6	10	4	1	1	6	3	12	0	.213	.404
Matt Alexander	OF6	B	34	15	11	5	4	1	0	0	1	3	0		.364	.364
Doe Boyland		L	26	11	8	0	0	0	0	0	0	0	1	3	.000	.000

NAME	T	AGE	W	L	PCT	SV	G	GS	CG	IP	H	BB	SO	SHO	ERA
TOTALS		29	46	56	.451	29	103	103	11	942	953	346	492	5	3.56
Rick Rhoden	R	28	9	4	.692	0	21	21	4	136	147	53	76	2	3.90
Eddie Solomon	R	30	8	6	.571	1	22	17	2	127	133	27	38	0	3.12
Jm Bibby	R	26	6	3	.667	0	14	14	2	94	79	26	48	2	2.49
Kent Tekulve	R	34	5	5	.500	3	45	0	0	65	61	17	34	0	2.49
Rod Scurry	L	25	5	5	.500	3	27	7	0	74	74	40	65	0	3.77
Odell Jones	R	28	4	5	.444	0	13	8	0	54	51	23	30	0	3.33
John Candelaria (AJ)	L	27	2	2	.500	0	6	6	0	41	42	11	14	0	3.51
Luis Tiant	R	40	2	5	.286	0	9	9	1	57	54	19	32	0	3.95
Pascual Perez	R	24	2	7	.222	0	17	13	2	86	92	34	46	0	3.98
1 Grant Jackson	L	38	1	1	.500	1	22	0	0	34	33	15	28	0	2.65
Bob Long	R	26	1	2	.333	0	5	3	0	20	23	10	8	0	2.53
Enrique Romo	R	33	1	3	.250	9	33	0	0	42	47	18	23	0	4.50
Ernie Camacho	R	25	0	1	.000	0	5	0	0	3	3	5	3	0	4.91
Mark Lee	R	28	0	3	.000	2	12	0	0	20	17	15	9	0	2.70
Don Robinson (SJ)	R	24	0	3	.000	2	16	2	0	38	47	23	17	0	5.92

NEW YORK

Name	G by Pos	B	AGE	G	AB	R	H	2B	3B	HR	RBI	BB	SO	SB	BA	SA
NEW YORK	5th 17-34 .333 15															
	4th 24-28 .462 5.5															
	— 41-62 .398 —															
TOTALS				30	105	3493	348	868	136	35	57	325	304	603	103	.248	.356
Dave Kingman	1B56, OF48	R	32	100	353	40	78	11	3	22	59	55	105	6	.221	.456
Doug Flynn	2B100, SS5	R	30	105	325	24	72	12	4	1	20	11	19	1	.222	.292
Frank Taveras	SS79	R	31	84	283	30	65	11	3	0	11	12	36	16	.230	.290
Hubie Brooks	3B93, OF3, SS1	R	24	96	358	34	110	21	2	4	38	23	65	9	.307	.411
Joel Youngblood (KJ)	OF41	R	29	43	143	16	50	10	2	4	25	12	19	2	.350	.531
Mookie Wilson	OF80	B	25	92	328	49	89	8	8	3	14	20	59	24	.271	.372
Lee Mazzilli	OF89	B	26	95	324	36	74	14	5	6	34	46	53	17	.228	.358
John Stearns	C66, 1B9, 3B4	R	29	80	273	25	74	12	1	1	24	24	17	12	.271	.333
Mike Jorgensen	1B40, OF19	L	32	86	122	8	25	5	2	3	15	12	24	4	.205	.352
Rusty Staub	1B41	L	37	70	161	9	51	9	0	5	21	22	12	1	.317	.466
Mike Cubbage	3B12	L	30	67	80	9	17	2	2	1	4	9	15	0	.213	.325
Alex Trevino	C45, 2B4, OF2, 3B1	R	23	56	149	17	39	2	0	0	10	13	19	3	.262	.275
Bob Bailor	SS22, 2B13, OF13, 3B1	R	29	51	81	11	23	3	1	0	8	8	11	2	.284	.346
2 Ellis Valentine	OF47	R	26	48	169	15	35	8	1	5	21	5	38	0	.207	.355
Ron Hodges	C7	L	32	35	43	5	13	2	0	1	6	5	8	1	.302	.419
Ron Gardenhire	SS18, 2B6, 3B1	R	23	27	48	2	13	1	0	0	3	5	9	2	.271	.292
Wally Backman	2B11, 3B1	B	21	26	36	5	10	2	0	0	4	7	1	0	.278	.333
Mike Howard	OF14	R	23	14	24	4	4	1	0	0	3	4	6	2	.167	.208
Brian Giles	2B2, SS2	R	21	9	7	0	0	0	0	0	0	0	3	0	.000	.000

NAME	T	AGE	W	L	PCT	SV	G	GS	CG	IP	H	BB	SO	SHO	ERA
		28	41	62	.398	24	105	105	7	926	906	336	490	3	3.55
Neil Allen	R	23	7	6	.538	18	43	0	0	67	64	26	50	0	2.96
Pat Zachry	R	29	7	14	.333	0	24	24	3	139	151	56	76	0	4.14
Pete Falcone	L	27	5	3	.625	1	35	9	3	95	84	36	56	1	2.56
Mike Scott	R	26	5	10	.333	0	23	23	1	136	130	34	54	0	3.90
Ed Lynch	R	25	4	5	.444	0	17	13	0	80	79	21	27	0	2.93
Mike Marshall	R	38	3	2	.600	0	20	0	0	31	26	28	8	0	2.61
Greg Harris	R	25	3	5	.375	1	16	14	0	69	65	28	54	0	4.43
Danny Boitano	R	28	2	1	.667	0	15	0	0	16	21	5	8	0	5.63
Ray Searage	L	26	1	0	1.000	1	26	0	0	37	34	17	16	0	3.65
Dyar Miller	R	35	1	0	1.000	0	23	0	0	38	49	15	22	0	3.32
1 Jeff Reardon	R	25	1	0	1.000	2	18	0	0	29	27	12	28	0	3.41
Terry Leach	R	27	1	1	.500	0	21	1	0	35	26	12	16	0	2.57
Randy Jones (NJ)	L	31	1	8	.111	0	13	12	0	59	65	38	14	0	4.88
Charlie Puleo	R	26	0	0	—	0	4	1	0	8	8	8	8	0	0.00
Tim Leary (EJ)	R	22	0	0	—	0	1	1	0	2	0	1	3	0	0.00
Tom Hausman (EJ)	R	28	0	1	.000	0	20	0	0	33	28	7	13	0	2.18
Jesse Orosco	L	24	0	1	.000	0	8	0	0	17	31	6	18	0	1.59
Craig Swan (BR, SJ)	R	30	0	2	.000	0	5	3	0	14	10	1	9	0	3.21
Dave Roberts	L	36	0	3	.000	0	7	4	0	15	26	5	10	0	9.60

CHICAGO

Name	G by Pos	B	AGE	G	AB	R	H	2B	3B	HR	RBI	BB	SO	SB	BA	SA
CHICAGO	8th 15-37 .288 17.5															
	5th 23-28 .451 6															
	— 38-65 .369 —															
TOTALS				29	106	3546	370	838	138	29	57	348	342	611	72	.236	.340
Bill Buckner	1B105	L	31	106	421	45	131	35	3	10	75	26	16	5	.311	.480
Pat Tabler	2B35	R	23	35	101	11	19	3	1	1	5	13	26	0	.188	.267
Ivan DeJesus	SS106	R	28	106	403	49	78	8	4	0	13	46	61	21	.194	.233
Ken Reitz	3B81	R	30	82	260	10	56	9	1	2	28	15	56	0	.215	.281
Leon Durham	OF83, 1B3	L	23	87	328	42	95	14	6	10	35	27	53	25	.290	.460
Jerry Morales	OF72	R	32	84	245	27	70	6	2	1	25	22	29	1	.286	.339
Steve Henderson	OF77	R	28	82	287	32	84	9	5	5	35	42	61	5	.293	.411
Jody Davis	C56	R	24	56	180	14	46	5	1	4	21	21	28	0	.256	.361
Tim Blackwell	C56	B	28	58	158	21	37	10	2	1	11	23	23	2	.234	.342
Scot Thompson	OF30, 1B3	L	25	57	115	8	19	5	0	0	8	7	8	2	.165	.209
Steve Dillard	2B32, 3B7, SS2	R	30	53	119	18	26	7	1	2	11	8	20	0	.218	.345
Heity Cruz	3B1, OF16	R	28	53	109	15	25	5	0	7	15	17	24	2	.229	.468
Mike Tyson	2B36, SS1	B	31	50	92	6	17	2	0	2	8	7	15	1	.185	.272
Bobby Bonds	OF45	R	35	45	163	26	35	7	1	6	19	24	44	5	.215	.380
Jim Tracy	OF11	L	25	45	63	6	15	2	1	0	5	12	14	1	.238	.302
2 Mike Lum	OF14, 1B1	L	35	41	58	5	14	1	0	2	7	5	5	0	.241	.362
Ty Waller	3B22, 2B3, OF3	R	24	30	71	10	19	2	1	3	13	4	18	2	.268	.451
Joe Strain	2B20	R	27	25	74	7	14	1	0	0	1	5	7	0	.189	.203
Scott Fletcher	2B13, SS4, 3B1	R	22	19	46	6	10	4	0	0	1	2	4	0	.217	.304
Mel Hall	OF3	L	20	10	11	1	1	0	0	1	2	1	4	0	.091	.364
1 Barry Foote	C8	R	29	9	22	0	0	0	0	0	1	3	7	0	.000	.000
Carlos Lezcano	OF5	R	25	7	14	1	1	0	0	0	2	0	4	0	.071	.071
Gary Krug		L	26	7	5	0	2	0	0	0	0	1	1	0	.400	.400
Bill Hayes	C1	R	23	1	0	0	0	0	0	0	0	0	0	0	—	—
Steve Macko 26 (IL - cancer)																

NAME	T	AGE	W	L	PCT	SV	G	GS	CG	IP	H	BB	SO	SHO	ERA
		28	38	65	.369	20	106	106	6	957	983	388	532	2	4.01
Mike Krukow	R	29	9	9	.500	0	25	25	2	144	146	55	101	1	3.69
Randy Martz	R	25	5	7	.417	6	33	14	1	108	103	49	32	0	3.67
2 Doug Bird	R	31	5	4	.444	0	12	12	2	75	72	16	34	1	3.60
1 Rick Reuschel	R	32	4	7	.364	0	13	13	1	86	87	23	53	0	3.45
Lee Smith	R	23	3	6	.333	1	40	1	0	67	57	31	50	0	3.49
Dick Tidrow	R	34	3	10	.231	9	51	0	0	75	73	30	39	0	5.04
Dave Geisel	L	26	2	0	1.000	0	11	2	0	16	11	10	7	0	0.56
Jay Howell	R	25	2	0	1.000	0	10	2	0	22	23	10	10	0	4.91
2 Mike Griffin	R	24	3	5	.286	1	16	9	0	52	64	9	20	0	4.50
Doug Capilla	L	29	1	0	1.000	0	42	0	0	51	52	34	28	0	3.18
1 Lynn McGlothen	R	31	1	4	.200	0	20	6	0	55	71	28	26	0	4.75
Bill Caudill	R	24	1	5	.167	0	30	10	0	71	87	31	45	0	5.83
Ken Kravec	L	29	1	6	.143	0	7	7	0	78	80	39	50	0	5.08
Willie Hernandez	L	26	0	0	—	2	12	0	0	14	14	8	13	0	3.86
Rawly Eastwick (EJ)	R	30	0	1	.000	1	30	0	0	43	43	15	24	0	2.30

LINE SCORES

TEAM	1 2 3	4 5 6	7 8 9	10 11	R	H	E

EAST DIVISIONAL SERIES: MONTREAL 3   PHILADELPHIA 2

Game 1   October 7 at Montreal

PHI	010	000	000		1	10	1
MON	110	100	00X		3	8	0

Carlton, R. Reed (7)   **Rogers**, Reardon (9)

Game 2   October 8 at Montreal

PHI	000	000	010		1	6	2
MON	012	000	00X		3	7	0

Ruthven, Brusstar (5),   **Gullickson**, Reardon (8)
Lyle (7), McGraw (8)

Game 3   October 9 at Philadelphia

MON	010	000	010		2	8	4
PHI	020	002	20X		6	13	0

Burris, Lee (6)   **Christenson**, Lyle (7)
Sosa (7)   R. Reed (8)

Game 4   October 10 at Philadelphia

MON	000	112	100	0	5	10	1
PHI	202	001	000	1	6	9	0

Sanderson, Bahnsen (3),   Noles, Brusstar (5), Lyle (6)
Sosa (5), Fryman (6),   R. Reed (7), **McGraw** (8)
Reardon (7)

Game 5   October 11 at Philadelphia

MON	000	021	000		3	8	1
PHI	000	000	000		0	6	0

Rogers   Carlton, R. Reed (9)

COMPOSITE BATTING

NAME	POS	G	AB	R	H	2B	3B	HR	RBI	BA
Montreal										
TOTALS		5	161	16	41	10	1	2	16	.255
Cromartie	1B	5	22	1	5	2	0	0	1	.227
Dawson	CF	5	20	1	6	0	1	0	0	.300
Parrish	3B	5	20	3	3	1	0	0	1	.150
Carter	C	5	19	3	8	3	0	2	6	.421
White	LF-RF	5	18	3	3	1	0	0	1	.167
Speier	SS	5	15	4	6	2	0	0	3	.400
Manuel	2B	5	14	0	1	0	0	0	0	.071
Francona	LF	5	12	0	4	0	0	0	0	.333
Rogers	P	2	5	0	2	0	0	0	2	.400
Wallach	OF-PH	4	4	1	1	0	0	0	0	.250
Gullickson	P	1	3	0	0	0	0	0	0	.000
W. Johnson	PH	2	2	0	1	0	0	0	1	.500
Milner	PH	2	2	0	1	0	0	0	1	.500
Burris	P	1	2	0	0	0	0	0	0	.000
Phillips	2B-PR	2	1	0	0	0	0	0	0	.000
Reardon	P	3	1	0	0	0	0	0	0	.000
Sanderson	P	1	1	0	0	0	0	0	0	.000
Sosa	P	2	0	0	0	0	0	0	0	—
Bahnsen	P	1	0	0	0	0	0	0	0	—
Fryman	P	1	0	0	0	0	0	0	0	—
Lee	P	1	0	0	0	0	0	0	0	—
Mills	PH	1	0	0	0	0	0	0	0	—

NAME	POS	G	AB	R	H	2B	3B	HR	RBI	BA
Philadelphia										
TOTALS		5	166	14	44	6	1	4	12	.265
Matthews	LF	5	20	3	8	0	1	1	1	.400
Rose	1B	5	20	1	6	1	0	0	2	.300
Smith	CF	5	19	1	5	1	0	0	0	.263
Bowa	SS	5	17	0	3	1	0	0	1	.176
Schmidt	3B	5	16	3	4	1	0	1	2	.250
Trillo	2B	5	16	1	3	0	0	0	1	.188
McBride	RF	4	15	1	3	1	0	0	0	.200
Moreland	C	4	13	2	6	0	0	1	3	.462
G. Vukovich	LF-RF-PH	5	9	1	4	0	0	1	2	.444
Boone	C	3	5	0	0	0	0	0	0	.000
Carlton	P	2	4	0	1	0	0	0	0	.250
Gross	LF-RF-PH	4	4	0	0	0	0	0	0	.000
Maddox	CF	2	3	0	1	1	0	0	0	.333
Christenson	P	1	2	0	0	0	0	0	0	.000
D. Davis	RF-PH	1	2	0	0	0	0	0	0	.000
Ruthven	P	1	1	0	0	0	0	0	0	.000
Aguayo	PR	2	0	1	0	0	0	0	0	—
R. Reed	P	4	0	0	0	0	0	0	0	—
Lyle	P	3	0	0	0	0	0	0	0	—
Brusstar	P	2	0	0	0	0	0	0	0	—
McGraw	P	2	0	0	0	0	0	0	0	—
Aviles	PH	1	0	0	0	0	0	0	0	—
Noles	P	1	0	0	0	0	0	0	0	—

COMPOSITE PITCHING

NAME	G	IP	H	BB	SO	W	L	SV	ERA
Montreal									
TOTALS	5	44	44	13	19	3	2	2	2.05
Rogers	2	17.2	16	3	5	2	0	0	0.50
Gullickson	1	7.2	6	1	3	1	0	0	1.13
Burris	1	5.1	7	4	4	0	0	0	5.40
Reardon	3	4.1	1	1	2	0	1	2	2.25
Sosa	2	3	4	0	1	0	0	0	3.00
Sanderson	1	2.2	4	1	0	0	0	0	6.00
Bahnsen	1	1.1	1	1	1	0	0	0	0.00
Fryman	1	1.1	4	1	2	0	0	0	9.00
Lee	1	2	1	0	1	0	0	0	0.00

NAME	G	IP	H	BB	SO	W	L	SV	ERA
Philadelphia									
TOTALS	5	44	41	18	36	2	3	0	3.07
Carlton	2	14	14	8	13	0	2	0	3.86
Christenson	1	6	4	1	8	1	0	0	1.50
R. Reed	4	6	5	3	4	0	0	0	3.00
McGraw	2	4	2	0	2	1	0	0	0.00
Noles	1	4	4	2	5	0	0	0	4.50
Ruthven	1	4	3	1	0	0	1	0	4.50
Brusstar	2	3.2	5	1	3	0	0	0	4.50
Lyle	3	2.1	4	2	1	0	0	0	0.00

LOS ANGELES

		1st 36-21 .632														
		4th 27-26 .509 6														
		— 63-47 .573 —	TOMMY LASORDA													

Name	G by Pos	B	AGE	G	AB	R	H	2B	3B	HR	RBI	BB	SO	SB	BA	SA
			29	110	3751	450	984	133	20	82	427	331	550	73	.262	.374
Steve Garvey	1B110	R	32	110	431	63	122	23	1	10	64	25	49	3	.283	.411
Davey Lopes (NJ)	2B55	R	36	58	214	35	44	2	0	5	17	22	35	20	.206	.289
Bill Russell	SS80	R	32	82	262	20	61	9	2	0	22	19	20	2	.283	.282
Ron Cey	3B84	R	33	85	312	42	90	15	2	13	50	40	55	0	.288	.474
Pedro Guerrero	OF75, 3B21, 1B1	R	25	98	347	46	104	17	2	12	48	34	57	5	.300	.464
Ken Landreaux	OF95	L	26	99	390	48	98	16	4	7	41	25	42	18	.251	.367
Dusty Baker	OF101	R	32	103	400	48	128	17	3	9	49	29	43	10	.320	.445
Mike Scioscia	C91	L	22	93	290	27	80	10	0	2	29	36	18	0	.276	.331
Derrel Thomas	2B30, SS26, OF18, 3B10	B	30	80	218	25	54	4	0	4	24	25	23	7	.248	.321
Rick Monday	OF41	L	35	66	130	24	41	1	2	11	25	24	42	1	.315	.608
Jay Johnstone	OF16, 1B2	L	35	61	83	8	17	3	0	3	6	7	13	0	.205	.349
Steve Yeager	C40	R	32	42	86	5	18	2	0	3	7	6	14	0	.209	.337
Reggie Smith (SJ)	1B2	R	36	41	35	5	7	1	0	1	8	7	8	0	.200	.314
Steve Sax	2B29	R	21	31	119	15	33	2	0	2	9	7	14	5	.277	.345
Pep Frias	SS15, 2B6, 3B1	R	32	25	36	6	9	1	0	0	3	1	3	0	.250	.278
Ron Roenicke	OF20	B	24	22	47	6	11	0	0	0	0	6	8	1	.234	.234
1 Joe Ferguson	OF1	R	34	17	14	2	2	1	0	0	1	2	5	0	.143	.214
Mike Marshall	1B3, 3B3, OF2	R	21	14	25	2	5	3	0	0	1	1	4	0	.200	.320
Gary Weiss	SS13	R	25	14	19	2	2	0	0	0	1	1	4	0	.105	.105
Candy Maldonado	OF9	R	20	11	12	0	1	0	0	0	0	0	5	0	.083	.083
Bobby Mitchell	OF7	L	26	10	8	0	1	0	0	0	0	0	1	0	.125	.125
Mark Bradley	OF6	R	24	9	6	2	1	1	0	0	0	0	1	0	.167	.333
Jack Perconte	2B2	L	26	8	9	2	2	0	1	0	1	2	2	1	.222	.444
Jerry Grote	C1	R	38	2	1	0	0	0	0	0	0	0	1	0	.000	.000

NAME	T	AGE	W	L	PCT	SV	G	GS	CG	IP	H	BB	SO	SHO	ERA
		26	63	47	.573	24	110	110	26	997	904	302	603	19	3.01
Fernando Valenzuela	L	20	13	7	.650	0	25	25	11	192	140	61	180	8	2.48
Burt Hooton	R	31	11	6	.647	0	22	22	8	142	124	33	74	4	2.28
Jerry Reuss	L	32	10	4	.714	0	22	22	8	153	138	27	51	2	2.29
Bob Welch	R	24	9	5	.643	0	23	23	2	141	141	41	88	1	3.45
Steve Howe	L	23	5	3	.625	8	41	0	0	54	51	18	32	0	2.50
Dave Stewart	R	24	4	3	.571	6	32	0	0	43	40	14	29	0	2.51
Tom Niedenfuer	R	21	3	1	.750	2	17	0	0	26	25	6	12	0	3.81
Rick Sutcliffe	R	25	2	2	.500	0	14	6	0	47	41	20	16	0	4.02
Bobby Castillo	R	26	2	4	.333	5	34	1	0	51	50	24	35	0	5.29
Dave Goltz	R	32	2	7	.222	1	26	8	0	77	83	25	48	0	4.09
Alejandro Pena	R	22	1	1	.500	2	14	0	0	25	18	11	14	0	2.88
Ted Power	R	26	1	3	.250	0	5	2	0	14	16	7	7	0	3.21
Terry Forster	L	29	0	1	.000	0	21	0	0	31	37	15	17	0	4.06

Joe Beckwith 26 (Vision Problems)

HOUSTON

		3rd 28-29 .491 8														
		1st 33-20 .623														
		— 61-49 .555 —	BILL VIRDON													

Name	G by Pos	B	AGE	G	AB	R	H	2B	3B	HR	RBI	BB	SO	SB	BA	SA
			29	110	3693	394	948	160	35	45	369	340	488	81	.257	.356
Cesar Cedeno	1B46, OF34	R	30	82	306	42	83	19	0	5	34	24	31	12	.271	.382
2 Phil Garner	2B31	R	32	31	113	13	27	3	1	0	6	15	11	6	.239	.283
Craig Reynolds	SS85	L	28	87	232	43	84	10	12	4	31	12	31	3	.260	.402
Art Howe	3B98, 1B2	R	34	103	361	43	107	22	4	3	36	41	21	1	.296	.404
Terry Puhl	OF88	L	24	96	350	43	88	19	4	3	28	31	49	22	.251	.354
2 Tony Scott	OF55	B	29	55	225	28	66	13	2	2	22	15	32	8	.293	.396
Jose Cruz	OF105	L	33	107	409	53	109	16	5	13	55	35	49	5	.267	.425
Alan Ashby	C81	B	29	83	255	20	69	13	0	4	33	35	33	0	.271	.369
Denny Walling	1B27, OF27	L	27	65	158	23	37	6	0	5	23	28	17	2	.234	.367
Gary Woods	OF40	R	26	54	110	10	23	4	1	0	12	11	22	2	.209	.364
Joe Pittman	2B35, 3B4	R	27	52	135	11	38	4	2	0	7	11	16	4	.281	.341
Dickie Thon	2B28, SS13, 3B5	R	23	49	95	13	26	6	0	0	3	9	13	6	.274	.337
Kiko Garcia	SS28, 3B13, 2B9	R	27	48	136	9	37	6	1	0	15	10	10	2	.272	.331
Luis Pujols	C39	R	25	40	117	5	28	3	1	1	14	10	17	1	.239	.308
1 Rafael Landestoy	2B31	B	28	35	74	6	11	1	1	0	4	16	9	4	.149	.189
Danny Heep	1B22, OF1	L	23	33	96	6	24	3	0	0	11	10	11	0	.250	.281
2 Harry Spilman	1B13	L	26	28	34	5	10	0	0	1	2	3	0	.294	.294
Dave Roberts	1B10, 3B7, 2B3, C1	R	30	27	54	4	13	3	0	1	5	3	6	1	.241	.352
2 Mike Ivie (IL)	1B5	R	28	19	42	2	10	3	0	0	6	2	11	0	.238	.310
Scott Loucks	OF5	R	24	10	7	2	4	0	0	0	0	1	3	1	.571	.571
1 Jeff Leonard	1B2, OF2	R	25	7	18	1	3	1	1	0	3	0	4	1	.167	.333
1 Dave Bergman	1B1	L	28	6	6	1	1	0	0	1	1	0	0	0	.167	.667
Tim Tolman	OF3	R	25	4	8	0	1	0	0	0	0	0	0	0	.125	.125
Bert Pena	SS3	R	21	4	2	0	1	0	0	0	0	0	1	0	.500	.500
Alan Knicely	C2, OF1	R	26	3	7	2	4	0	0	2	2	0	1	0	.571	.429

NAME	T	AGE	W	L	PCT	SV	G	GS	CG	IP	H	BB	SO	SHO	ERA
		30	61	49	.555	25	110	110	23	990	842	300	610	19	2.66
Nolan Ryan	R	34	11	5	.688	0	21	21	5	149	99	68	140	3	1.69
Don Sutton	R	36	11	9	.550	0	23	23	6	159	132	29	104	3	2.60
Bob Knepper	L	27	9	5	.643	0	22	22	6	157	128	38	75	5	2.18
Joe Niekro	R	36	9	9	.500	0	24	24	5	166	150	47	77	2	2.82
Dave Smith	R	26	5	3	.625	8	42	0	0	75	54	23	52	0	2.76
Joe Sambito	L	29	5	5	.500	10	49	0	0	64	43	22	41	0	1.83
Frank LaCorte	R	29	4	2	.667	5	37	0	0	42	41	21	40	0	3.64
Vern Ruhle	R	30	4	6	.400	1	20	15	1	102	97	20	39	0	2.91
1 Joaquin Andujar	R	28	2	3	.400	0	9	3	0	24	29	12	18	0	4.88
Billy Smith	R	26	1	1	.500	1	10	1	0	21	20	3	3	0	3.00
Gordy Pladson	R	24	0	0	—	0	2	0	0	4	3	3	1	0	9.00
Bobby Sprowl	L	25	0	0	.000	0	15	1	0	29	40	14	18	0	5.90

Randy Niemann 25 (EJ)
J.R. Richard 31 (IL)

CINCINNATI

		2nd 35-21 .625 .5														
		2nd 31-21 .596 1.5														
		— 66-42 .611 —	JOHN McNAMARA													

Name	G by Pos	B	AGE	G	AB	R	H	2B	3B	HR	RBI	BB	SO	SB	BA	SA
			30	108	3637	464	972	190	24	64	429	375	553	58	.267	.385
Dan Driessen	1B74	L	29	82	233	35	55	14	0	7	33	40	31	2	.236	.386
Ron Oester	2B103, SS9	B	25	105	354	45	96	16	4	5	33	40	49	2	.271	.398
Dave Concepcion	SS106	R	33	106	421	57	129	28	0	5	67	37	61	4	.306	.409
Ray Knight	3B105	R	26	106	386	43	100	23	1	6	34	33	51	2	.259	.370
Dave Collins	OF94	B	28	95	360	63	98	18	6	3	23	41	41	26	.272	.381
Ken Griffey	OF99	L	31	101	396	65	123	21	6	2	34	39	42	12	.311	.409
George Foster	OF108	R	32	108	414	64	122	23	2	22	90	51	75	4	.295	.519
Joe Nolan	C81	R	30	81	236	25	73	18	1	1	26	24	19	1	.309	.407
Sammy Mejias	OF58	R	29	66	49	6	14	2	0	0	7	2	9	1	.286	.327
Mike O'Berry	C55	R	27	55	111	6	20	3	1	1	5	14	19	0	.180	.252
Johnny Bench (BN)	1B38, C7	R	33	52	178	14	55	8	0	8	25	17	21	0	.309	.489
Larry Biittner	1B8, OF3	L	35	42	61	1	13	4	0	0	8	4	4	0	.213	.279
Mike Vail	OF3	R	29	31	31	1	5	0	0	0	3	0	9	0	.161	.161
Junior Kennedy	2B16, 3B5	R	30	27	44	5	11	1	0	0	5	1	5	0	.250	.273
Paul Householder	OF19	R	22	23	69	12	19	4	0	2	9	10	16	3	.275	.420
1 Harry Spilman	3B3, 1B2	R	26	23	24	4	4	1	0	0	3	3	7	0	.167	.208
2 Rafael Landestoy	2B3	B	28	12	11	2	2	0	0	0	1	1	0	1	.182	.182
German Barranca		L	24	9	6	2	2	0	0	0	1	0	0	0	.333	.333
Eddie Milner	OF4	L	26	8	5	0	1	1	0	0	1	1	1	0	.200	.400
2 Neil Fiala		L	24	2	2	1	1	0	0	0	1	0	1	0	.500	.500

NAME	T	AGE	W	L	PCT	SV	G	GS	CG	IP	H	BB	SO	SHO	ERA
		27	66	42	.611	20	108	108	25	966	863	393	593	14	3.73
Tom Seaver	R	36	14	2	.875	0	23	23	6	166	120	66	87	1	2.55
Mario Soto	R	24	12	9	.571	0	25	25	10	175	142	61	151	3	3.29
Tom Hume	R	28	9	4	.692	13	51	0	0	68	63	31	27	0	3.44
Bruce Berenyi	R	26	9	6	.600	0	21	20	5	126	97	77	106	3	3.50
Joe Price	L	24	6	1	.857	4	41	0	0	54	42	18	41	0	2.50
Mike LaCross	R	25	4	7	.364	1	20	13	1	78	102	30	22	1	6.12
Frank Pastore	R	23	4	9	.308	0	22	22	2	132	125	35	81	1	4.02
Paul Moskau	R	27	2	1	.667	2	27	1	0	55	54	32	32	0	4.91
1 Doug Bair	R	31	2	2	.500	0	24	0	0	39	42	17	16	0	5.77
Geoff Combe	R	25	1	0	1.000	0	14	0	0	18	27	10	9	0	7.50
Scott Brown	R	24	1	0	1.000	0	10	0	0	13	16	1	7	0	2.77
2 Joe Edelen	R	25	1	0	1.000	0	5	0	0	13	13	5	5	0	0.69
Charlie Leibrandt	L	24	1	1	.500	0	7	4	1	30	28	15	9	1	3.60

Bill Bonham 32 (EJ)

SAN FRANCISCO

		5th 27-32 .458 10														
		3rd 29-23 .558 3.5														
		— 56-55 .505 —	FRANK ROBINSON													

Name	G by Pos	B	AGE	G	AB	R	H	2B	3B	HR	RBI	BB	SO	SB	BA	SA
			30	111	3766	427	941	161	26	63	399	386	543	89	.250	.357
Enos Cabell	1B69, 3B22	R	31	96	396	41	101	20	1	2	36	10	47	3	.255	.326
Joe Morgan	2B87	L	37	90	308	47	74	16	1	8	31	66	37	14	.240	.377
Johnnie LeMaster	SS103	R	27	104	324	27	82	9	1	0	28	24	46	3	.253	.287
Darrell Evans	3B87, 1B12	L	34	102	357	51	92	13	4	12	48	54	33	2	.258	.417
Jack Clark	OF98	R	25	99	385	60	103	19	2	17	53	45	45	1	.268	.460
Jerry Martin	OF64	R	32	72	241	23	58	5	3	4	25	21	52	6	.241	.336
Larry Herndon	OF93	R	27	96	364	48	105	15	8	5	41	20	55	15	.288	.415
Milt May	C93	L	30	97	316	20	98	17	0	2	33	34	29	1	.310	.383
2 Dave Bergman	1B33, OF15	L	28	63	145	16	37	9	0	3	13	19	18	2	.255	.379
Jim Wohlford	OF10	R	30	50	68	4	11	3	0	1	7	4	9	0	.162	.250
Billy North	OF37	B	33	46	131	22	29	7	0	1	12	26	28	26	.221	.298
Rennie Stennett	2B19	R	30	38	87	8	20	0	0	1	7	3	6	2	.230	.264
2 Jeff Leonard	OF28, 1B5	R	25	37	127	20	39	11	3	4	26	12	21	4	.307	.535
Billy Smith	SS21, 2B5, 3B3	B	27	36	61	6	11	0	0	1	5	9	16	0	.180	.230
Joe Pettini	2B12, SS12, 3B9	R	26	35	29	3	2	1	0	0	2	4	5	1	.069	.103
Bob Brenly	C14, 3B3, OF1	R	27	19	45	5	15	2	1	0	4	6	7	0	.333	.489
Mike Sadek	C19	R	35	19	36	5	6	3	0	0	3	8	7	0	.167	.250
Max Venable	OF5	L	24	18	32	2	6	.0	2	0	1	4	3	1	.188	.313
Guy Sularz	2B6, 3B1	R	25	20	20	0	4	0	0	0	0	2	2		.200	.200
Chili Davis	OF6	B	21	8	15	1	2	0	0	0	0	1	2	1	.133	.133
1 Mike Ivie	1B10	R	28	7	17	1	5	2	0	0	3	0	1	0	.294	.412
Jeff Ransom	C5	R	20	5	15	2	4	1	0	0	0	0	0	0	.267	.333

NAME	T	AGE	W	L	PCT	SV	G	GS	CG	IP	H	BB	SO	SHO	ERA
		29	56	55	.505	33	111	111	8	1009	970	393	561	9	3.28
Doyle Alexander	R	30	11	7	.611	0	24	24	1	152	156	44	77	1	2.90
Vida Blue	L	31	8	6	.571	0	18	18	1	125	97	54	63	0	2.45
Tom Griffin	R	33	8	8	.500	0	22	22	3	129	121	57	83	1	3.77
Al Holland	L	28	7	5	.583	7	47	3	0	101	87	44	78	0	2.41
Ed Whitson	R	26	6	9	.400	0	22	22	2	123	130	47	65	1	4.02
Fred Breining	R	25	4	2	.714	4	45	1	0	78	66	38	37	0	2.54
Allen Ripley	R	28	4	4	.500	0	19	14	1	91	103	27	47	0	4.05
Greg Minton	R	29	4	4	.444	21	55	0	0	84	84	36	29	0	2.89
Gary Lavelle	L	32	2	6	.250	4	34	3	0	66	58	23	45	0	3.82
Alan Hargesheimer	R	24	1	2	.333	0	6	3	0	19	20	9	6	0	4.26
Bob Tufts	L	25	0	0		0	11	0	0	13	6	6	12	0	3.60
Randy Moffitt (IL)	R	32	0	0	—	0	11	0	0	11	15	2	11	0	8.18
Mike Rowland	R	28	0	1	.000	0	9	1	0	16	13	6	8	0	3.38

Bill Bordley 23 (EJ)

Name	G by Pos	B	AGE	G	AB	R	H	2B	3B	HR	RBI	BB	SO	SB	BA	SA

ATLANTA   4th 25-29 .463 9.5   **BOBBY COX**
         5th 25-27 .481 7.5
         — 50-56 .472 —

Name	G by Pos	B	AGE	G	AB	R	H	2B	3B	HR	RBI	BB	SO	SB	BA	SA
			26	107	3642	395	886	148	22	64	366	321	540	98	.243	.349
Chris Chambliss	1B107	L	32	107	404	44	110	25	2	8	51	44	41	4	.272	.403
Glenn Hubbard	2B98	R	23	99	361	39	85	13	5	6	33	33	59	4	.235	.349
Rafael Ramirez	SS95	R	23	95	307	30	67	16	2	2	20	24	47	7	.218	.303
Bob Horner (WJ)	3B79	R	23	79	300	42	83	10	0	15	42	32	39	2	.277	.460
Claudell Washington	OF79	L	26	85	320	37	93	22	3	5	37	15	47	12	.291	.425
Dale Murphy	OF103, 1B3	R	25	104	369	43	91	12	1	13	50	44	72	14	.247	.390
Rufino Linares	OF60	R	30	78	253	27	67	9	2	5	25	9	28	8	.265	.375
Bruce Benedict	C90	R	25	90	295	26	78	12	1	5	35	33	21	1	.264	.363
Jerry Royster	3B24, 2B13	R	28	64	93	13	19	4	1	0	9	7	14	7	.204	.269
Biff Pocoroba	3B21, C9	B	27	57	122	4	22	4	0	0	8	12	15	0	.180	.213
Brian Asselstine	OF36	L	27	56	86	8	22	5	0	2	10	5	7	1	.256	.384
Eddie Milner	OF36	B	23	50	134	29	31	3	1	0	7	7	29	23	.231	.269
Brett Butler	OF37	L	24	40	126	17	32	2	3	0	4	19	17	9	.254	.317
Terry Harper	OF27	R	25	40	73	9	19	1	0	2	8	11	17	5	.260	.356
Luis Gomez	SS21, 3B9, 2B3, P1	R	29	35	35	4	7	0	0	0	1	6	4	0	.200	.200
Bob Porter		L	21	17	14	2	4	1	0	0	4	2	1	0	.286	.357
Bill Nahorodny	C3, 1B1	R	27	14	13	0	3	1	0	0	2	1	3	0	.231	.308
Larry Owen	C10	R	26	13	16	0	0	0	0	0	0	1	4	0	.000	.000
Matt Sinatro	C12	R	21	12	32	4	9	1	1	0	4	5	4	1	.281	.375
Brook Jacoby	3B3	R	21	11	10	0	2	0	0	0	1	0	3	0	.200	.200
Paul Runge	SS10	R	23	10	27	2	7	1	0	0	2	4	4	0	.259	.296
1 Mike Lum	OF1	L	35	10	11	1	1	0	0	0	0	2	2	0	.091	.091
Larry Whisenton	OF2	L	24	9	5	1	1	0	0	0	0	2	1	0	.200	.200
Albert Hall	OF2	B	23	6	2	1	0	0	0	0	0	1	1	0	.000	.000
Ken Smith	1B4	L	23	5	3	0	1	0	0	0	1	0	1	0	.333	.667

NAME	T	AGE	W	L	PCT	SV	G	GS	CG	IP	H	BB	SO	SHO	ERA
		31	50	56	.472	24	107	107	11	968	936	330	471	4	3.45
Rick Camp	R	28	9	3	.750	17	48	0	0	76	68	12	47	0	1.78
Rick Mahler	R	27	8	6	.571	2	34	14	1	112	109	43	54	0	2.81
Gaylord Perry	R	42	8	9	.471	0	23	23	3	151	182	24	60	0	3.93
Phil Niekro	R	42	7	7	.500	0	22	22	3	139	120	56	62	3	3.11
Gene Garber (BN)	R	33	4	6	.400	2	35	0	0	59	49	20	34	0	2.59
Tommy Boggs	R	25	3	13	.188	0	25	24	2	143	140	54	81	0	4.09
Larry Bradford	L	31	2	0	1.000	1	25	0	0	27	26	12	14	0	3.67
Preston Hanna	R	26	2	1	.667	0	20	1	0	35	45	23	22	0	6.43
Larry McWilliams	L	27	2	1	.667	0	6	5	2	38	31	8	23	1	3.08
John Montefusco	R	31	2	3	.400	1	26	9	0	77	75	27	34	0	3.51
Al Hrabosky (GJ)	L	31	1	1	.500	1	24	0	0	34	24	9	13	0	1.06
Steve Bedrosian	R	23	1	2	.333	0	15	1	0	24	15	15	9	0	4.50
Bob Walk (VJ)	R	24	1	4	.200	0	12	8	0	43	41	23	16	0	4.60
Rick Matula	R	27	0	0	—	0	5	0	0	7	8	2	0	0	6.43
Luis Gomez	R	29	0	0	—	0	1	0	0	1	3	2	0	0	27.00
Jose Alavarez	R	25	0	0	—	0	1	0	0	2	0	0	2	0	0.00

SAN DIEGO   6th 23-33 .411 12.5   **FRANK HOWARD**
         6th 18-36 .333 15.5
         — 41-69 .373 —

Name	G by Pos	B	AGE	G	AB	R	H	2B	3B	HR	RBI	BB	SO	SB	BA	SA
			26	110	3757	382	963	170	35	32	350	311	525	83	.256	.346
Broderick Perkins	1B80, OF3	L	26	92	254	27	71	18	3	2	40	14	16	0	.280	.398
Juan Bonilla	2B97	R	25	99	369	30	107	13	2	1	25	25	23	4	.290	.344
Ozzie Smith	S110	B	26	110	450	53	100	11	2	0	21	41	37	22	.222	.256
Luis Salazar	3B94, OF23	R	25	109	400	37	121	19	6	3	38	16	72	11	.303	.403
Joe Lefebvre	OF84	L	25	86	246	31	63	13	4	8	31	35	33	6	.256	.439
Ruppert Jones	OF104	L	26	104	397	53	99	34	1	4	39	43	66	7	.249	.370
Gene Richards	OF102	L	27	104	393	47	113	14	12	3	42	53	44	20	.288	.407
Terry Kennedy	C100	L	25	101	382	32	115	24	1	2	41	22	53	0	.301	.385
Randy Bass	1B50	L	27	69	176	13	67	4	1	4	20	20	28	0	.210	.313
Dave Edwards	OF49	R	27	58	112	13	24	4	1	2	13	11	24	3	.214	.321
Barry Evans	3B24, 1B10, 2B6, SS2	R	24	54	93	11	30	5	0	0	7	9	9	2	.323	.376
Tim Flannery	3B15, 2B7	L	23	37	67	4	17	4	1	0	6	2	4	1	.254	.343
Jose Moreno	OF9, 2B1	R	23	34	48	5	11	2	0	0	6	1	8	4	.229	.271
1 Jerry Turner	OF4	L	27	33	31	5	7	0	0	2	6	4	3	0	.226	.419
Steve Swisher	C10	R	29	16	28	2	4	0	0	0	2	11	0	4	.143	.143
Doug Gwosdz	C13	R	21	16	24	1	4	0	0	0	3	3	6	0	.167	.250
Alan Wiggins	OF4	B	23	15	14	4	5	0	0	0	0	1	0	2	.357	.357
1 Mike Phillips	2B9, SS1	L	30	14	29	1	6	0	1	0	0	3	1	1	.207	.276
Mario Ramirez	SS2, 3B2	R	23	13	.13	1	1	0	0	0	1	2	5	0	.077	.077
Craig Stimac		R	26	9	9	0	1	0	0	0	0	0	3	0	.111	.111

NAME	T	AGE	W	L	PCT	SV	G	GS	CG	IP	H	BB	SO	SHO	ERA
		28	41	69	.373	23	110	110	9	1002	1013	414	492	6	3.72
Juan Eichelberger	R	27	8	8	.500	0	25	24	3	141	136	74	61	1	3.51
Gary Lucas	L	26	7	7	.500	13	57	0	0	90	78	36	53	0	2.00
Chris Welsh	L	26	6	7	.462	0	22	19	4	124	122	41	51	2	3.77
Steve Mura	R	26	5	14	.263	0	23	22	2	139	156	50	70	0	4.27
Rick Wise	R	35	4	8	.333	0	18	18	0	98	116	19	27	0	3.77
John Urrea	R	26	2	2	.500	2	38	0	0	49	43	28	19	0	2.39
John Littlefield	R	27	2	3	.400	2	42	0	0	64	53	28	21	0	3.66
John Curtis	L	33	2	6	.250	0	28	8	0	67	70	30	31	0	5.10
Tim Lollar	L	25	2	8	.200	1	24	11	0	77	87	51	38	0	6.08
Dan Boone	L	27	1	0	1.000	2	37	0	0	63	63	21	43	0	2.86
Fred Kuhaulua	L	28	1	0	1.000	0	5	4	0	29	28	9	16	0	2.48
Eric Show	R	25	1	3	.250	3	15	0	0	23	17	9	22	0	3.13
Steve Fireovid	R	24	0	1	.000	0	3	3	0	26	30	7	11	0	2.77
Mike Armstrong	R	27	0	2	.000	0	10	0	0	12	14	11	9	0	6.00

LINE SCORES

TEAM	1 2 3	4 5 6	7 8 9	10 11	R	H	E

WEST DIVISIONAL SERIES: LOS ANGELES 3   HOUSTON 2

Game 1   October 6 at Houston
LA   0 0 0   0 0 0   1 0 0   1 2 0
HOU   0 0 0   0 0 1   0 0 2   3 8 0
   Valenzuela, Stewart(9)   **Ryan**

Game 2   October 7 at Houston
LA   0 0 0   0 0 0   0 0 0   0 0   0 9 1
HOU   0 0 0   0 0 0   0 0 0   0 1   1 9 0
   Reuss, Howe(10),   Niekro, D. Smith(9), **Sambito**(11)
   Stewart(11), Forster(11),
   Niedenfuer(11)

Game 3   October 9 at Los Angeles
HOU   0 0 1   0 0 0   0 0 0   1 3 2
LA   3 0 0   0 0 0   0 3 X   6 10 0
   Knepper, LaCorte(6)   Hooton, Howe(8), Welch(9)
   Sambito(8), B. Smith(8)

Game 4   October 10 at Los Angeles
HOU   0 0 0   0 0 0   0 0 1   1 4 0
LA   0 0 0   0 1 0   1 0 X   2 4 0
   Ruhle   Valenzuela

Game 5   October 11 at Los Angeles
HOU   0 0 0   0 0 0   0 0 0   0 5 3
LA   0 0 0   0 0 3   1 0 X   4 7 2
   Ryan, D. Smith (7),   Reuss
   LaCorte(7)

COMPOSITE BATTING

NAME	POS	G	AB	R	H	2B	3B	HR	RBI	BA
Los Angeles										
TOTALS		5	162	13	32	6	1	3	12	.198
Landreaux	CF	5	20	1	4	1	0	0	1	.200
Lopes	2B	5	20	1	4	0	0	0	0	.200
Garvey	1B	5	19	4	7	0	1	2	4	.368
Baker	LF	5	18	2	3	1	0	0	1	.167
Guerrero	3B	5	17	3	3	1	0	1	1	.176
Russell	SS	5	16	1	4	1	0	0	2	.250
Monday	RF	5	14	1	3	0	0	0	1	.214
Scioscia	C	4	13	0	2	0	0	0	1	.154
Reuss	P	2	8	0	0	0	0	0	0	.000
Yeager	C-PH	2	5	1	2	1	0	0	0	.400
Valenzuela	P	2	4	0	0	0	0	0	0	.000
Hooton	P	2	3	0	0	0	0	0	0	.000
Thomas	RF-PH-PR	4	2	1	0	0	0	0	0	.000
Smith	PH	2	1	0	0	0	0	0	1	.000
Johnstone	PH	1	1	0	0	0	0	0	0	.000
Marshall	PH	1	1	0	0	0	0	0	0	.000
Howe	P	2	0	0	0	0	0	0	0	—
Stewart	P	2	0	0	0	0	0	0	0	—
Forster	P	1	0	0	0	0	0	0	0	—
Niedenfuer	P	1	0	0	0	0	0	0	0	—
Sax	2B	1	0	0	0	0	0	0	0	—
Welch	P	1	0	0	0	0	0	0	0	—
Houston										
TOTALS		5	162	6	29	3	0	2	6	.179
Puhl	RF	5	21	2	4	1	0	0	0	.190
Cruz	LF	5	20	0	6	1	0	0	0	.300
Scott	CF	5	20	0	3	0	0	0	2	.150
Garner	2B	5	18	1	2	0	0	0	0	.111
Howe	3B	5	17	1	4	0	0	1	1	.235
Cedeno	1B	4	13	0	3	1	0	0	0	.231
Thon	SS-PH	4	11	0	2	0	0	0	0	.182
Ashby	C	3	9	1	1	0	0	1	2	.111
Walling	1B-RF-PH	3	6	0	2	0	0	0	1	.333
PujoLs	C	2	6	0	0	0	0	0	0	.000
Ryan	P	2	4	0	1	0	0	0	0	.250
Garcia	SS-PH	2	4	0	0	0	0	0	0	.000
Reynolds	SS-PH	3	3	1	1	0	0	0	0	.333
Pittman	PH	2	2	0	0	0	0	0	0	.000
Woods	PH	2	2	0	0	0	0	0	0	.000
Niekro	P	1	1	0	0	0	0	0	0	.000
Knepper	P	1	1	0	0	0	0	0	0	.000
Roberts	PH	1	1	0	0	0	0	0	0	.000
Ruhle	P	1	1	0	0	0	0	0	0	.000
Spilman	PH	1	1	0	0	0	0	0	0	.000
LaCorte	P	2	0	0	0	0	0	0	0	—
Sambito	P	2	0	0	0	0	0	0	0	—
D. Smith	P	2	0	0	0	0	0	0	0	—
B. Smith	P	1	0	0	0	0	0	0	0	—

COMPOSITE PITCHING

NAME	G	IP	H	BB	SO	W	L	SV	ERA
Los Angeles									
TOTALS	5	46.1	29	13	24	3	2	0	1.17
Reuss	2	18	10	5	7	1	0	0	0.00
Valenzuela	2	17	10	3	10	1	0	0	1.03
Hooton	1	7	3	3	2	1	0	0	1.29
Howe	2	2	1	0	2	0	0	0	0.00
Welch	1	1	0	1	1	0	0	0	0.00
Stewart	2	.2	4	0	1	0	2	0	27.00
Forster	1	.1	0	0	0	0	0	0	0.00
Niedenfuer	1	.1	1	1	1	0	0	0	0.00
Houston									
TOTALS	5	44	32	13	34	2	3	0	2.45
Ryan	2	15	6	3	14	1	1	0	1.80
Niekro	1	8	7	1	4	0	0	0	0.00
Ruhle	1	8	4	2	1	0	1	0	2.25
Knepper	1	5	6	2	4	0	1	0	5.40
LaCorte	2	3.2	2	1	5	0	0	0	0.00
D. Smith	2	2.1	2	0	4	0	0	0	4.50
Sambito	2	1.2	5	2	2	1	0	0	13.50
B.Smith	1	1	0	0	0	0	0	0	0.00

LINE SCORES

Team	1	2	3	4	5	6	7	8	9	10	11		R	H	E

AMERICAN LEAGUE CHAMPIONSHIPS: NEW YORK (EAST) 3   OAKLAND (WEST) 0

Game 1 October 13 at New York
```
OAK   0 0 0 0 0 1 0 0 0      1  6  1
NY    3 0 0 0 0 0 0 0 X      3  7  1
Norris, Underwood (8)        John, Davis (7), Gossage (8)
```

Game 2 October 14 at New York
```
OAK   0 0 1 2 0 0 0 0 0      3 11  1
NY    1 0 0 7 0 1 4 0 X     13 19  0
McCatty, Beard (4), Jones (5)      May, Frazier (4)
Kingman (7), Owchinko (7)
```

Game 3 October 15 at Oakland
```
NY    0 0 0 0 0 0 1 0 3      4 10  0
OAK   0 0 0 0 0 0 0 0 0      0  5  2
Righetti, Davis (7),         Keough, Underwood (9)
Gossage (9)
```

NATIONAL LEAGUE CHAMPIONSHIPS: LOS ANGELES (WEST) 3   MONTREAL (EAST) 2

Game 1 October 13 at Los Angeles
```
MON   0 0 0 0 0 0 0 0 1      1  9  1
LA    0 2 0 0 0 0 0 3 X      5  8  0
Gullickson, Reardon (8)      Hooton, Welch (8), Howe (9)
```

Game 2 October 14 at Los Angeles
```
MON   0 2 0 0 0 1 0 0 0      3 10  1
LA    0 0 0 0 0 0 0 0 0      0  5  1
Burris                       Valenzuela, Niedenfuer (7)
                             Foster (7), Pena (7), Castillo (9)
```

Game 3 October 16 at Montreal
```
LA    0 0 0 1 0 0 0 0 0      1  7  0
MON   0 0 0 0 0 4 0 0 X      4  7  1
Reuss, Pena (8)              Rogers
```

Game 4 October 17 at Montreal
```
LA    0 0 1 0 0 0 0 2 4      7 12  1
MON   0 0 0 1 0 0 0 0 0      1  5  1
Hooton, Welch (8),           Gullickson, Fryman (8)
Howe (9)                     Sosa (9), Lee (9)
```

Game 5 October 19 at Montreal
```
LA    0 0 0 0 1 0 0 0 1      2  6  0
MON   1 0 0 0 0 0 0 0 0      1  3  1
Valenzuela, Welch (9)        Burris, Rogers (9)
```

Game 1 October 20 at New York
```
LA    0 0 0 0 0 1 0 2 0      3  5  0
NY    3 0 1 1 0 0 0 0 X      5  6  0
Reuss, Castillo (3),         Guildry, Davis (8),
Goltz (4), Niedenfuer (5),   Gossage (8)
Stewart (8)
```

Game 2 October 21 at New York
```
LA    0 0 0 0 0 0 0 0 0      0  4  2
NY    0 0 0 0 0 1 0 2 X      3  6  1
Hooton, Forster (7),         John, Gossage (8)
Howe (8), Stewart (8)
```

Game 3 October 23 at Los Angeles
```
NY    0 2 2 0 0 0 0 0 0      4  9  0
LA    3 0 0 0 0 2 0 0 X      5 11  1
Righetti, Frazier (3),       Valenzuela
May (5), Davis (8)
```

Game 4 October 24 at Los Angeles
```
NY    2 1 1 0 0 2 0 1 0      7 13  1
LA    0 0 2 0 1 3 2 0 X      8 14  2
Reuschel, May (4),           Welch, Goltz (1),
Davis (5), Frazier (5),      Forster (4),
John (7)                     Niedenfuer (5), Howe (7)
```

Game 5 October 25 at Los Angeles
```
NY    0 1 0 0 0 0 0 0 0      1  5  0
LA    0 0 0 0 0 2 0 X        2  4  3
Guidry, Gossage (8)          Reuss
```

Game 6 October 28 at New York
```
LA    0 0 0 1 3 4 0 1 0      9 13  1
NY    0 0 1 0 0 1 0 0 0      2  7  2
Hooton, Howe (6)             John, Frazier (5), Davis (6)
Reuschel (6), May (7), LaRoche (9)
```

COMPOSITE BATTING

New York

NAME	POS	G	AB	R	H	2B	3B	HR	RBI	BA
TOTALS		3	107	20	36	4	0	3	20	.336
Milbourne	SS	3	13	4	6	0	0	0	0	.462
Winfield	LF	3	13	2	2	1	0	0	2	.154
Nettles	3B	3	12	2	6	2	0	1	9	.500
Mumphrey	CF	3	12	6	6	1	0	0	0	.500
Randolph	2B	3	12	2	4	0	0	1	2	.333
Watson	1B	3	12	0	3	0	0	0	0	.250
Cerone	C	3	10	1	1	0	0	0	0	.100
Gamble	RF-DH	3	6	2	1	0	0	0	0	.167
Piniella	RF-PH-DH	3	5	2	3	0	0	1	3	.600
Jackson	RF	2	4	1	0	0	0	0	1	.000
Murcer	DH	1	3	0	1	0	0	0	0	.333
Revering	1B	2	2	0	1	0	0	0	0	.500
Brown	RF-PR	2	1	2	1	0	0	0	0	1.000
Foote	C-PH	2	1	0	1	0	0	0	0	1.000
Robertson	SS-PH	1	1	0	0	0	0	0	0	.000
Rodriguez	3B	1	0	0	0	0	0	0	0	—

Oakland

NAME	POS	G	AB	R	H	2B	3B	HR	RBI	BA
TOTALS		3	99	4	22	4	1	0	4	.222
Armas	RF	3	12	0	2	0	0	0	0	.167
Henderson	LF	3	11	0	4	2	1	0	1	.364
McKay	2B	3	11	0	3	0	0	0	0	.273
Moore	1B	3	9	0	2	0	0	0	0	.222
Murphy	CF	3	8	0	2	1	0	0	1	.250
Klutts	3B	3	7	1	3	0	0	0	0	.429
Heath	LF-C	3	6	1	2	0	0	0	0	.333
Johnson	DH	2	6	0	0	0	0	0	0	.000
Picciolo	SS	2	5	1	1	0	0	0	0	.200
Gross	3B-PH	3	5	0	0	0	0	0	0	.000
Newman	C	2	5	0	0	0	0	0	0	.000
Bosetti	CF-PH-DH	2	4	1	1	1	0	0	0	.250
Drumright	PH-DH	1	4	0	0	0	0	0	0	.000
Stanley	SS	2	3	0	1	0	0	0	1	.333
Spencer	1B-PH	2	2	0	0	0	0	0	0	.000
Davis	PH	1	1	0	1	0	0	0	0	1.000

Los Angeles

NAME	POS	G	AB	R	H	2B	3B	HR	RBI	BA
TOTALS		5	163	15	38	3	1	4	15	.233
Garvey	1B	5	21	2	6	0	0	1	2	.286
Baker	LF	5	19	3	6	1	0	0	3	.316
Guerrero	CF-RF	5	19	1	2	0	0	1	2	.105
Cey	3B	5	18	1	5	1	0	0	3	.278
Lopes	2B	5	18	0	5	0	0	0	0	.278
Russell	SS	5	16	2	5	0	1	0	1	.313
Scioscia	C	5	15	1	2	0	0	1	1	.133
Landreaux	CF	5	10	0	1	1	0	0	0	.100
Monday	RF-PH	3	9	2	3	0	0	1	1	.333
Hooton	P	2	5	0	0	0	0	0	0	.000
Valenzuela	P	2	5	0	0	0	0	0	1	.000
Yeager	C-PH	1	2	1	1	1	0	0	0	.500
Smith	PH	1	1	0	1	0	0	0	1	1.000

Johnstone PH 0-2, Thomas 3B-RF-PR 1-1, Reuss P 0-2, Castillo P 0-0, Forster P 0-0, Howe P 0-0, Niedenfuer P 0-0, Sax 2B 0-0, Welch P 0-0

Montreal

NAME	POS	G	AB	R	H	2B	3B	HR	RBI	BA
TOTALS		5	158	10	34	7	0	1	8	.215
Raines	LF	5	21	1	5	2	0	0	1	.238
Dawson	CF	5	20	2	3	0	0	0	0	.150
Parrish	3B	5	19	2	5	2	0	0	2	.263
Cromartie	1B	5	18	0	3	1	0	0	2	.167
Scott	2B	5	18	0	3	0	0	0	0	.167
Carter	C	5	16	3	7	1	0	0	0	.438
White	RF	5	16	2	5	1	0	1	3	.313
Speier	SS	5	16	0	3	0	0	0	0	.188
Burris	P	2	6	0	0	0	0	0	0	.000
Gullickson	P	2	3	0	0	0	0	0	0	.000
Rogers	P	2	2	0	0	0	0	0	0	.000
Francona	1B-LF	2	1	0	0	0	0	0	0	.000

Milner PH 0-1, Wallach PH 0-1, Fryman P 0-0, Lee P 0-0, Manuel PR 0-0, Reardon P 0-0, Sosa P 0-0

Los Angeles

NAME	POS	G	AB	R	H	2B	3B	HR	RBI	BA
TOTALS		6	198	27	51	6	1	6	26	.258
Russell	SS	6	25	1	6	0	0	0	2	.240
Garvey	1B	6	24	3	10	1	0	0	4	.417
Baker	LF	6	24	3	4	0	0	0	0	.167
Lopes	2B	6	22	6	5	1	0	0	2	.227
Guerrero	CF-RF	6	21	2	7	1	1	2	7	.333
Cey	3B	6	20	3	7	0	0	1	6	.350
Yeager	C-PH	6	14	2	4	1	0	2	4	.286
Monday	RF-PH	6	13	1	3	1	0	0	1	.231
Thomas	3B-CF-PH	5	7	2	0	0	0	0	1	.000
Landreaux	CF-PR-PH	5	6	1	1	1	0	0	0	.167
Scioscia	C-PH	5	4	1	1	0	0	0	0	.250
Hooton	P	2	4	1	0	0	0	0	0	.000
Johnstone	PH	3	3	1	2	0	0	0	0	.667

Reuss, P 0-3, Valenzuela P 0-3, Smith PH 1-2, Howe P 0-2, Sax PR-PH 0-1, Castillo P 0-0, Foster P 0-0, Niedenfuer P 0-0, Stewart P 0-0, Welch P 0-0

New York

NAME	POS	G	AB	R	H	2B	3B	HR	RBI	BA
TOTALS		6	193	22	46	8	1	6	22	.238
Watson	1B	6	22	2	7	1	0	2	7	.318
Winfield	LF-CF	6	22	0	1	0	0	0	1	.045
Cerone	C	6	21	2	4	1	0	1	3	.190
Milbourne	SS	6	20	2	5	2	0	0	3	.250
Randolph	2B	6	18	5	4	1	1	2	3	.222
Piniella	LF-RF-PH	6	16	2	7	1	0	0	3	.438
Mumphrey	CF	5	15	2	3	0	0	0	0	.200
Rodriguez	3B-PR	4	12	1	5	0	0	0	0	.417
Jackson	RF	3	12	4	3	0	0	1	1	.333
Nettles	3B	3	10	1	4	1	0	0	0	.400
Gamble	LF-RF	3	6	1	2	0	0	0	0	.333
Guidry	P	2	3	0	0	0	0	0	0	.000

Murcer PH 0-3, Frazier P 0-2, John P 0-2, Brown CF-PR-PH 0-1, Foote PH 0-1, Gossage P 0-1, May P 0-1, Righetti P 0-1, Davis P 0-0, LaRoche P 0-0, Robertson PR 0-0

COMPOSITE PITCHING

New York

NAME	G	IP	H	BB	SO	W	L	SV	ERA
TOTALS	3	27	22	6	23	3	0	1	1.33
Righetti	1	6	4	2	4	1	0	0	0.00
John	1	6	6	1	3	1	0	0	1.50
Frazier	1	5.2	5	1	5	1	0	0	0.00
Davis	2	3.1	0	2	4	0	0	0	0.00
May	1	3.1	6	0	5	0	0	0	8.10
Gossage	2	2.2	1	0	2	0	0	1	0.00

Oakland

NAME	G	IP	H	BB	SO	W	L	SV	ERA
TOTALS	3	25	36	13	10	0	3	0	6.12
Keough	1	8.1	7	6	2	0	1	0	1.08
Norris	1	7.1	6	2	4	0	1	0	3.86
McCatty	1	3.1	6	2	2	0	1	0	13.50
Jones	1	2	2	1	0	0	0	0	4.50
Owchinko	1	1.2	3	0	0	0	0	0	5.40
Underwood	2	1.1	4	2	2	0	0	0	13.50
Beard	1	0.2	5	0	0	0	0	0	40.50
Kingman	1	0.1	3	0	0	0	0	0	81.00

Los Angeles

NAME	G	IP	H	BB	SO	W	L	SV	ERA
TOTALS	5	44	34	12	25	3	2	1	1.84
Hooton	2	14.2	11	6	7	2	0	0	0.00
Valenzuela	2	14.2	10	5	10	1	1	0	2.40
Reuss	1	7	7	1	2	0	1	0	5.14
Pena	2	2.1	1	0	0	0	0	0	0.00
Howe	2	2	1	0	2	0	0	0	0.00
Welch	3	1.2	2	0	2	0	0	1	4.50
Castillo	1	1	0	1	0	0	0	0	0.00
Forster	1	0.1	0	0	1	0	0	0	0.00
Niedenfuer	1	0.1	2	0	0	0	0	0	0.00

Montreal

NAME	G	IP	H	BB	SO	W	L	SV	ERA
TOTALS	5	44	38	12	23	2	3	0	2.86
Burris	2	17	10	3	4	1	0	0	0.53
Gullickson	2	14.1	12	6	12	0	2	0	2.57
Rogers	2	10	8	1	6	1	1	0	1.80
Reardon	1	1	3	0	0	0	0	0	27.00
Fryman	1	1	3	1	1	0	0	0	36.00
Lee	1	0.1	1	0	0	0	0	0	0.00
Sosa	1	0.1	1	0	0	0	0	0	0.00

Los Angeles

NAME	G	IP	H	BB	SO	W	L	SV	ERA
TOTALS	6	52	46	33	24	4	2	1	3.29
Reuss	2	11.2	10	3	8	1	1	0	3.86
Hooton	2	11.1	8	9	3	1	1	0	1.59
Valenzuela	1	9	9	7	6	1	0	0	4.00
Howe	3	7	7	1	4	1	0	1	3.86
Niedenfuer	2	5	3	1	0	0	0	0	0.00
Goltz	2	3.1	4	1	2	0	0	0	5.40
Forster	2	2	1	3	0	0	0	0	0.00
Stewart	2	1.2	1	2	1	0	0	0	0.00
Castillo	1	1	0	5	0	0	0	0	9.00
Welch	1	0	3	1	0	0	0	0	∞

New York

NAME	G	IP	H	BB	SO	W	L	SV	ERA
TOTALS	6	51	51	20	44	2	4	2	4.24
Guidry	2	14	8	4	15	1	1	0	1.93
John	3	13	11	0	8	1	0	0	0.69
May	3	6.1	5	1	5	0	0	0	2.84
Gossage	3	5	2	2	5	0	0	2	0.00
Reuschel	2	3.2	7	3	2	0	0	0	4.91
Frazier	3	3.2	9	3	2	0	3	0	17.18
Davis	4	2.1	4	5	4	0	0	0	23.14
Righetti	1	2	5	2	1	0	0	0	13.50
LaRoche	1	1	0	0	2	0	0	0	0.00

WORLD SERIES — LOS ANGELES (NL) 4 NEW YORK (AL) 2

1982 — Coming Back from a Strike

America hungered for a normal baseball season. An unusual April snowstorm, however, scratched 19 games, including six home openers. Once the weather hit its stride, baseball marched through a glorious post-strike campaign of record attendance and four close pennant races.

The earliest clinching came on September 27, when the Cardinals iced the National League East title. The Cards had traded over the winter for speedster Lonnie Smith and fielding whiz Ozzie Smith, blending their talents with the relief heroics of Bruce Sutter and strong late-season pitching by Joaquin Andujar. Although they had the fewest home runs in the major leagues, the Redbirds got strong RBI production from George Hendrick and Keith Hernandez. St. Louis moved into first place on September 13, passing the fading Phillies. Weak defense spoiled Montreal's chance to repeat as divisional champs.

Each of the other divisions was settled only on the final weekend. On Saturday morning, October 2, the Braves led the Dodgers by one game and the Giants by two. The Dodgers eliminated the Giants on Saturday 15-2 while the Braves beat San Diego 4-2. The Giants then beat the Dodgers 5-3 on Sunday, leaving the Braves as N.L. West champs. New manager Joe Torre led the Braves to a record 13-0 start and kept them in the running despite a wretched ten day stretch starting on July 30 in which they lost eight games to the Dodgers. Power hitter Dale Murphy won the MVP award, while old-timer Phil Niekro and relievers Steve Bedrosian and Gene Garber led a shallow mound staff. The Dodgers got terrific work from Pedro Guerrero, Fernando Valenzuela, and rookie-of-the-year Steve Sax, but an eight game losing streak in September did them in. Steady losers this year were the Reds, shorn of George Foster, Ken Griffey, and Dave Collins by a tight salary policy.

The New York Yankees paid top dollar for Griffey and Collins, but their new emphasis on speed fizzled into a fifth place finish. The Brewers and Orioles fought through the summer over the vacant American League East throne. The Brewers languished in fifth place on June 2 when Buck Rodgers

was replaced by coach Harvey Kuenn. Under the relaxed hand of Kuenn, the Brewers caught fire and built a 6 1/2 game lead by late August. Led by MVP Robin Yount and Cecil Cooper, the Brewer lineup shredded A.L. pitching and earned the nickname Harvey's Wallbangers. The Milwaukee hill staff was less impressive but hung together behind Cy Young winner Pete Vuckovich and reliever Rollie Fingers. After an elbow injury sidelined Fingers on September 2, the Orioles slowly closed the gap. Baltimore manager Earl Weaver had announced that he would retire at the end of the season, and he coaxed star performances from Eddie Murray, Jim Palmer, and rookie-of-the-year Cal Ripken. The Orioles swept a doubleheader on Friday and a Saturday afternoon game from the Brewers to deadlock the race with one game left. With veterans Palmer and Don Sutton on the mound, a sell-out Baltimore crowd sat through two Yount homers and a 10-2 Brewer victory which capped Weaver's 14 1/2 years on the job.

A new arrival to Anaheim pushed the Angels over the top in the A.L. West. Reggie Jackson joined the veteran California stars as a free-agent and furnished inspirational long-ball hitting. The Royals held first place into mid-September, but a streak of 10 losses in 11 games opened the way for the Angels to clinch the title on October 2. Never in the running were the Oakland A's, who collapsed into fifth place despite Rickey Henderson's record 130 stolen bases. A highlight in Seattle was Gaylord Perry's 300th career victory on May 6.

The A.L. Championship Series started out all California and ended all Milwaukee. The Angels won the first two games, then the Brewers swept the next three, prompting Angel manager Gene Mauch to resign. The Cardinals soothed manager Whitey Herzog's soul by dumping the Braves in three straight games.

In the World Series of midwestern teams, the Brewers took game one 10-0. The teams split the next four games, leaving the Brewers one victory from the championship. They never got that victory, as the Cards won games six and seven and grabbed the brass ring.

EAST DIVISION

1982 AMERICAN LEAGUE

Name	G by Pos	B	AGE	G	AB	R	H	2B	3B	HR	RBI	BB	SO	SB	BA	SA
MILWAUKEE 1st 95-67 .586	**BUCK RODGERS 23-24 .489 HARVEY KUENN 72-43 .626**															
TOTALS			30	163	5733	891	1599	277	41	216	843	484	714	84	.279	.455
Cecil Cooper	1B154, DH1	L	32	155	654	104	205	38	3	32	121	32	53	2	.313	.528
Jim Gantner (SJ)	2B131	L	29	132	447	48	132	17	2	4	43	26	36	6	.295	.360
Robin Yount	SS154, DH1	R	26	156	635	129	210	46	12	29	114	54	63	14	.331	.578
Paul Molitor	3B150, DH6, SS4	R	25	160	666	136	201	26	8	19	71	69	93	41	.302	.450
Charlie Moore	OF115, C20, 2B1	R	29	133	456	53	116	22	4	6	45	29	49	2	.254	.360
Gorman Thomas	OF157	R	31	158	567	96	139	29	1	39	112	84	143	3	.245	.506
Ben Oglivie	OF159	L	33	159	602	92	147	22	1	34	102	70	81	3	.244	.453
Ted Simmons	C121, DH15	B	32	137	539	73	145	29	0	23	97	32	40	0	.269	.451
Roy Howell	DH84, 1B4, OF2	L	28	98	300	31	78	11	2	4	38	21	39	0	.260	.350
Don Money	DH66, 3B16, 1B11, 2B1	R	35	96	275	40	78	14	3	16	55	32	38	0	.284	.531
Marshall Edwards	OF54, DH6	L	29	69	178	24	44	4	1	2	14	4	8	10	.247	.315
Ed Romero	2B39, SS10, 3B2, OF1	R	24	52	144	18	36	8	0	1	7	8	16	0	.250	.326
Mark Brouhard	OF30, DH7	R	26	40	108	16	29	4	1	4	10	9	17	0	.269	.435
Ned Yost	C39, DH1	R	27	40	98	13	27	6	3	1	8	7	20	3	.276	.429
Bob Picciolo	2B11, SS6, DH1	R	29	22	21	7	6	1	0	0	1	1	4	0	.286	.333
Kevin Bass	OF14, DH2	B	23	18	9	4	0	0	0	0	1	0	5	0	.000	.000
Larry Hisle (SJ)	DH8	R	35	9	31	7	4	0	0	2	5	5	13	0	.129	.323
Bob Skube	OF1, DH1	L	24	4	3	0	2	0	0	0	0	0	0	0	.667	.667

NAME	T	AGE	W	L	PCT	SV	G	GS	CG	IP	H	BB	SO	SHO	ERA
		30	95	67	.586	47	163	163	34	1467	1514	511	717	6	3.98
Pete Vuckovich	R	29	18	6	.750	0	30	30	9	224	234	102	105	1	3.34
Mike Caldwell	L	33	17	13	.567	0	35	34	12	258	269	58	75	3	3.91
Bob McClure	L	30	12	7	.632	0	34	26	5	173	160	74	99	0	4.22
Moose Haas	R	26	11	8	.579	1	32	27	3	193	232	39	104	0	4.47
Jim Slaton	R	32	10	6	.625	6	39	7	0	118	117	41	59	0	3.29
1 Randy Lerch	L	27	8	7	.533	0	21	20	1	109	123	51	33	1	4.97
2 Doc Medich	R	33	5	4	.556	0	10	10	1	63	57	32	36	0	5.00
Rollie Fingers (EJ)	R	35	5	6	.455	29	50	0	0	80	63	20	71	0	2.60
2 Don Sutton	R	37	4	1	.800	0	7	7	2	55	55	18	36	1	3.29
Dwight Bernard	R	30	3	1	.750	6	47	0	0	79	78	27	45	0	3.76
Jerry Augustine	L	29	1	3	.250	0	20	2	1	62	63	26	22	0	5.08
Pete Ladd	R	25	1	3	.250	3	16	0	0	18	16	6	12	0	4.00
Doug Jones	R	25	0	0	—	0	4	0	0	3	5	1	1	0	10.13
Chuck Porter	R	26	0	0	—	0	3	0	0	4	3	1	3	0	4.91
Jamie Easterly (KJ)	L	29	0	2	.000	2	28	0	0	31	39	15	16	0	4.70

NAME	G by Pos	B	AGE	G	AB	R	H	2B	3B	HR	RBI	BB	SO	SB	BA	SA
BALTIMORE 2nd 94-68 .580 1	**EARL WEAVER**															
TOTALS			30	163	5557	774	1478	259	27	179	735	634	796	49	.266	.419
Eddie Murray	1B149, DH2	B	26	151	550	87	174	30	1	32	110	70	82	7	.316	.549
Rich Dauer	2B123, 3B61	R	29	158	558	75	156	24	2	8	57	50	34	0	.280	.373
Cal Ripken	SS94, 3B71	R	21	160	598	90	158	32	5	28	93	46	95	3	.264	.475
Glenn Gulliver	3B50	L	27	50	145	24	29	7	0	1	5	37	18	0	.200	.269
Dan Ford	OF119, DH1	R	30	123	421	46	99	21	3	10	43	23	71	5	.235	.371
Al Bumbry	OF147, DH1	L	35	150	562	77	147	20	4	5	40	44	77	10	.262	.338
John Lowenstein	OF111	L	35	122	322	69	103	15	2	24	66	54	59	7	.320	.602
Rick Dempsey	C124, DH1	R	32	125	344	35	88	15	1	5	36	46	37	0	.256	.349
Ken Singleton	DH148, OF5	B	35	156	561	71	141	27	2	14	77	86	93	0	.251	.381
Gary Roenicke	OF125, 1B10	R	27	137	393	58	106	25	1	21	74	70	73	6	.270	.499
Lenn Sakata	2B83, SS56	R	28	136	343	40	89	18	1	6	31	30	39	7	.259	.370
Joe Nolan	C72	L	31	77	219	24	51	7	1	6	35	16	35	1	.233	.356
Jim Dwyer	OF49, 1B1, DH1	L	32	71	148	28	45	4	3	6	15	27	24	2	.304	.493
Terry Crowley	DH14, 1B10	L	35	65	93	8	22	2	0	3	17	21	9	0	.237	.355
Benny Ayala	OF25, DH17, 1B3	R	31	64	128	17	39	6	0	6	24	5	14	1	.305	.492
Bob Bonner	SS38, 2B3	R	25	41	77	8	13	3	1	0	5	3	12	0	.169	.234
Floyd Rayford	3B27, C2, DH2	R	24	34	53	7	7	0	0	3	5	6	14	0	.132	.302
John Shelby	OF24	B	24	26	35	8	11	3	0	1	2	0	5	0	.314	.486
Mike Young	DH2, OF1	B	22	6	2	2	0	0	0	0	0	0	1	0	.000	.000
Jose Morales		R	37	3	3	0	0	0	0	0	0	0	0	0	.000	.000
Leo Hernandez		R	22	3	2	0	0	0	0	0	0	0	2	0	.000	.000

NAME	T	AGE	W	L	PCT	SV	G	GS	CG	IP	H	BB	SO	SHO	ERA
		29	94	68	.580	34	163	163	38	1462	1436	488	719	8	3.99
Dennis Martinez	R	27	16	12	.571	0	40	39	10	252	262	87	111	2	4.21
Jim Palmer	R	36	15	5	.750	1	36	32	8	227	195	63	103	2	3.13
Mike Flanagan	L	30	15	11	.577	0	36	35	11	236	233	76	103	1	3.97
Scott McGregor	L	28	14	12	.538	0	37	37	7	226	238	52	84	1	4.61
Sammy Stewart	R	27	10	9	.526	5	38	12	1	139	140	62	69	1	4.14
Storm Davis	R	20	8	4	.667	0	29	8	1	101	96	28	67	0	3.49
Tippy Martinez	L	32	8	8	.500	16	76	0	0	95	81	37	78	0	3.41
Tim Stoddard (SJ-KJ)	R	29	3	4	.429	12	50	0	0	56	53	29	42	0	4.02
John Flinn	R	27	2	0	1.000	0	5	0	0	14	13	3	13	0	1.32
Mike Boddicker	R	24	1	0	1.000	0	7	0	0	26	25	12	20	0	3.51
Don Welchel	R	25	1	0	1.000	0	2	0	0	4	6	2	3	0	8.31
Ross Grimsley	L	32	1	2	.333	0	21	0	0	60	65	22	18	0	5.25
Don Stanhouse (SJ)	R	31	0	1	.000	0	17	0	0	27	29	15	8	0	5.40
Steve Stone 34 (EJ-VR)															

BOSTON — 3rd 89-73 .549 6 — RALPH HOUK

Name	G by Pos	B	AGE	G	AB	R	H	2B	3B	HR	RBI	BB	SO	SB	BA	SA
TOTALS			29	162	5596	753	1536	271	31	136	705	547	736	42	.274	.407
Dave Stapleton	1B106, SS27, 2B9, 3B5, DH4, OF1	R	28	150	538	66	142	28	1	14	65	31	40	2	.264	.398
Jerry Remy	2B154	L	29	155	636	89	178	22	3	0	47	55	77	16	.280	.324
Glenn Hoffman	SS150	R	23	150	469	53	98	23	2	7	49	30	69	0	.209	.311
Carney Lansford (NJ)	3B114, DH13	R	25	128	482	65	145	28	4	11	63	46	48	9	.301	.444
Dwight Evans	OF161, DH1	R	30	162	609	122	178	37	7	32	98	112	125	3	.292	.534
Rick Miller	OF127	L	34	135	409	50	104	13	2	4	38	40	41	5	.254	.325
Jim Rice	OF145	R	29	145	573	86	177	24	5	24	97	55	98	0	.309	.494
Gary Allenson	C91	R	27	92	264	25	54	11	0	6	33	38	39	0	.205	.314
Carl Yastrzemski	DH102, 1B14, OF2	L	42	131	459	53	126	22	1	16	72	59	50	0	.275	.431
Wade Boggs	1B49, 3B44, DH3, OF1	L	24	104	338	51	118	14	1	5	44	35	21	1	.349	.441
Rich Gedman	C86	L	22	92	289	30	72	17	2	4	26	10	37	0	.249	.363
Reid Nichols	OF82, DH4	R	23	92	245	35	74	16	1	7	33	14	28	5	.302	.461
Tony Perez	DH46, 1B2	R	40	69	196	18	51	14	2	6	31	19	48	0	.260	.444
Julio Valdez	SS22, DH1	B	26	28	20	3	5	1	0	0	1	0	7	1	.250	.300
Ed Jurak	3B11, OF1	R	24	12	21	3	7	0	0	0	7	2	4	0	.333	.333
Garry Hancock	OF7	L	28	11	14	3	0	0	0	0	0	1	1	0	.000	.000
Marty Barrett	2B7	R	24	8	18	0	1	0	0	0	0	0	1	0	.056	.056
Roger LaFrancois	C8	L	25	8	10	1	4	1	0	0	1	0	0	0	.400	.500
Marc Sullivan	C2	R	23	2	6	0	2	0	0	0	0	0	2	0	.333	.333

NAME	T	AGE	W	L	PCT	SV	G	GS	CG	IP	H	BB	SO	SHO	ERA
TOTALS		29	89	73	.549	33	162	162	23	1453	1557	478	816	11	4.03
Mark Clear	R	26	14	9	.609	14	55	0	0	105	92	61	109	0	3.00
John Tudor	L	28	13	10	.565	0	32	30	6	196	215	59	146	1	3.63
Dennis Eckersley	R	27	13	13	.500	0	33	33	11	224	228	43	127	3	3.73
Bob Stanley	R	27	12	7	.632	14	48	0	0	168	161	50	83	0	3.10
Mike Torrez	R	35	9	9	.500	0	31	31	1	176	196	74	84	0	5.23
Tom Burgmeier	L	38	7	0	1.000	7	40	0	0	102	98	22	44	0	2.29
Chuck Rainey	R	27	7	5	.583	0	27	25	3	129	146	63	57	3	5.02
Bob Ojeda (L)	L	24	4	6	.400	0	22	14	0	78	95	29	52	0	5.63
Brian Denman	R	26	3	4	.429	0	9	9	2	49	55	9	9	1	4.78
Bruce Hurst	L	24	3	7	.300	0	28	19	0	117	161	40	53	0	5.77
Luis Aponte	R	29	2	2	.500	3	40	0	0	85	78	25	44	0	3.18
Steve Crawford (EJ)	R	24	1	0	1.000	0	5	0	0	9	14	2	2	0	2.00
Mike Brown	R	23	1	0	1.000	0	3	1	0	6	7	1	4	0	0.00
Oil Can Boyd	R	22	0	1	.000	0	3	1	0	8	11	2	2	0	5.40

DETROIT — 4th 83-79 .512 12 — SPARKY ANDERSON

Name	G by Pos	B	AGE	G	AB	R	H	2B	3B	HR	RBI	BB	SO	SB	BA	SA
TOTALS			28	162	5590	729	1489	237	40	177	684	470	807	93	.266	.418
Enos Cabell	1B83, 3B59, OF3	R	32	125	464	45	121	17	3	2	37	15	48	15	.261	.323
Lou Whitaker	2B149, DH1	L	25	152	560	76	160	22	8	15	65	48	58	11	.286	.434
Alan Trammell	SS157	R	24	157	489	66	126	34	3	9	57	52	47	19	.258	.395
Tom Brookens	3B113, 2B26, SS9, OF1	R	28	140	398	40	92	15	3	9	58	27	63	5	.231	.352
Chet Lemon	OF121, DH1	R	27	125	436	75	116	20	1	19	52	56	69	1	.266	.447
Kirk Gibson (WJ)	OF64, DH4	L	25	69	266	34	74	16	2	8	35	25	41	9	.278	.444
Larry Herndon	OF155, DH4	R	28	157	614	92	179	21	13	23	88	38	92	12	.292	.480
Lance Parrish	C132, OF1	R	26	133	486	75	138	19	2	32	87	40	99	3	.284	.529
2 Mike Ivie	DH79	R	29	89	259	35	60	12	1	14	38	24	51	0	.232	.448
Jerry Turner	DH50, OF13	L	28	85	210	21	52	3	0	8	27	20	37	1	.248	.376
Glenn Wilson	OF80, DH1	R	23	84	322	39	94	15	1	12	34	15	51	2	.292	.457
Rick Leach (SJ)	1B56, OF14, DH1	L	25	82	218	23	52	7	2	3	12	21	29	4	.239	.330
John Wockenfuss	C24, 1B17, DH17, OF10, 3B1	R	33	70	193	28	58	9	0	8	32	29	21	0	.301	.472
1 Richie Hebner	1B40, DH20	L	34	68	179	25	49	6	0	8	18	25	21	1	.274	.441
Lynn Jones	OF56, DH1	R	28	59	139	15	31	3	1	0	14	7	14	0	.223	.259
Howard Johnson	3B33, DH10, OF9	B	21	54	155	23	49	5	0	4	14	16	30	7	.316	.426
Bill Fahey (KJ)	C28	L	32	28	67	7	10	2	0	0	4	0	5	1	.149	.179
Mike Laga	1B19, DH8	L	22	27	88	6	23	9	0	3	11	4	23	1	.261	.466
Mark DeJohn	SS20, 3B4, 2B1	B	24	21	24	1	4	2	0	0	1	4	4	0	.190	.286
Eddie Miller	OF8, DH1	B	25	14	25	1	1	0	0	0	0	4	4	1	.040	.040
1 Mick Kelleher	2B1, 3B1	R	34	2	1	0	0	0	0	0	0	0	0	0	.000	.000
Marty Castillo	C1	R	25	1	0	0	0	0	0	0	0	0	0	0	—	—
Rickey Peters 26 (EJ)																

NAME	T	AGE	W	L	PCT	SV	G	GS	CG	IP	H	BB	SO	SHO	ERA
TOTALS		27	83	79	.512	27	162	162	45	1451	1371	554	740	5	3.80
Jack Morris	R	27	17	16	.515	0	37	37	17	266	247	96	135	3	4.06
Dan Petry	R	23	15	9	.625	0	35	35	8	246	220	100	132	1	3.22
Milt Wilcox	R	32	12	10	.545	0	29	29	9	194	187	85	112	1	3.62
Jerry Ujdur	R	25	10	10	.500	0	25	25	7	178	150	69	86	0	3.69
Dave Rucker	L	24	5	6	.455	0	27	4	1	64	62	23	31	0	3.38
Larry Pashnick	R	26	4	4	.500	0	28	13	1	94	110	25	19	0	4.01
Pat Underwood	L	25	4	8	.333	3	33	12	2	99	108	22	43	0	4.73
Dave Tobik	R	29	4	9	.308	9	51	1	0	99	86	38	63	0	3.56
Dave Rozema (KJ)	R	25	3	0	1.000	1	8	2	0	28	17	7	15	0	1.63
Kevin Saucier	L	25	3	1	.750	5	31	1	0	40	35	29	23	0	3.12
Aurelio Lopez (SJ)	R	33	3	1	.750	3	19	0	0	41	41	19	26	0	5.27
Elias Sosa	R	32	3	3	.500	4	38	0	0	61	64	18	24	0	4.43
Howard Bailey	L	24	0	0	—	0				10	6	2	3	0	0.00
Dave Gumpert	R	24	0	1			5	1		7	2			0	27.00
Juan Berenguer	R	27	0	1			2	1		7	5	9	8		6.75
Larry Rothschild	R	28	0	0			2	0		3	4	2		0	13.50
2 Bob James	R	23	0	2	.000	0	12	0	0	20	22	8	20	0	5.03

NEW YORK — 5th 79-83 .488 16 — BOB LEMON 6-8 .429 GENE MICHAEL 44-42 .512 CLYDE KING 29-33 .468

Name	G by Pos	B	AGE	G	AB	R	H	2B	3B	HR	RBI	BB	SO	SB	BA	SA
TOTALS			29	162	5526	709	1417	225	37	161	666	590	719	69	.256	.398
2 John Mayberry	1B63, DH4	L	33	69	215	20	45	7	0	8	27	28	38	0	.209	.353
Willie Randolph	2B142, DH1	R	27	144	553	85	155	21	4	3	36	75	35	16	.280	.349
2 Roy Smalley	SS89, 3B53, DH4, 2B1	B	29	142	486	55	125	14	2	20	67	68	100	0	.257	.418
Graig Nettles	3B113, DH3	L	37	122	405	47	94	11	2	18	55	51	49	1	.232	.402
Ken Griffey	OF125	L	32	127	484	70	134	23	2	12	54	39	58	10	.277	.417
Jerry Mumphrey (BG)	OF123	B	29	123	477	76	143	24	10	9	68	50	66	11	.300	.449
Dave Winfield	OF135, DH4	R	30	140	539	84	151	24	8	37	106	45	64	5	.280	.560
Rick Cerone (BG)	C89	R	28	89	300	29	68	10	0	5	28	19	27	2	.227	.310
Oscar Gamble	DH74, OF29	L	32	108	316	49	86	21	2	18	57	58	47	2	.272	.522
Dave Collins	OF60, 1B52, DH1	B	29	111	348	41	88	12	3	3	25	28	49	13	.253	.330
Lou Piniella	DH55, OF40	R	38	102	261	33	80	17	1	6	37	18	18	0	.307	.448
Bobby Murcer	DH47	L	36	65	141	12	32	6	0	7	30	12	15	2	.227	.418
2 Butch Wynegar (IL)	C62	B	26	80	191	27	56	8	1	3	20	40	21	0	.293	.393
1 Bucky Dent	SS58	R	30	59	160	11	27	1	1	0	9	8	11	0	.169	.188
Andre Robertson	SS27, 2B15, 3B2	R	24	44	118	16	26	5	0	2	9	8	19	0	.220	.314
2 Lee Mazzilli	1B23, DH9, OF2	B	27	37	128	20	34	2	0	6	17	15	15	2	.266	.422
Steve Balboni	1B26, DH5	R	25	33	107	8	20	2	1	2	4	6	34	0	.187	.280
Butch Hobson	DH15, 1B11	R	30	30	52	3	10	2	0	0	3	1	14	0	.172	.207
Barry Foote (RJ)	C17	R	30	17	48	4	7	5	0	0	2	1	11	0	.146	.250
Barry Evans	2B8, 3B6, SS4	R	29	17	31	2	8	3	0	0	2	6	6	0	.258	.355
1 Dave Revering	1B13, DH1	L	29	14	40	4	6	1	0	1	5	3	9	0	.150	.200
1 Larry Milbourne	SS9, 2B3, 3B3	B	31	14	27	2	4	1	0	0	1	2	1	0	.148	.185
Mike Patterson	OF9, DH1	L	24	11	16	3	3	1	0	1	1	2	6	1	.188	.438
2 Rodney Scott	SS6, 2B4	B	29	10	26	5	5	0	0	0	2	4	6	2	.192	.192
1 Bob Watson	1B6, DH1	R	36	7	17	3	4	3	0	0	3	0	0	0	.235	.412
Don Mattingly	OF6, 1B1	L	21	7	12	0	2	0	0	0	1	0	1	0	.167	.167
Bobby Ramos	C4	R	26	4	11	1	1	0	0	0	0	1	2	0	.091	.364
Eddie Rodriguez	2B3	R	21	3	9	2	3	0	0	0	0	0	1	0	.333	.333
Juan Espino	C3	R	26	3	2	0	0	0	0	0	0	0	0	0	.000	.000
Dave Stegman	DH1	R	28	2	1	0	0	0	0	0	0	0	0	0	—	—

NAME	T	AGE	W	L	PCT	SV	G	GS	CG	IP	H	BB	SO	SHO	ERA
TOTALS		30	79	83	.488	39	162	162	24	1459	1471	491	939	8	3.99
Ron Guidry	L	31	14	8	.636	0	34	33	6	222	216	69	162	1	3.81
Shane Rawley	L	26	11	10	.524	3	47	17	3	164	165	54	111	0	4.06
Dave Righetti	L	23	11	10	.524	1	33	27	4	183	155	108	163	0	3.79
1 Tommy John	L	39	10	10	.500	0	30	26	9	187	190	34	54	2	3.66
Mike Morgan	R	22	7	11	.389	0	30	23	2	150	167	67	71	0	4.37
Rudy May	L	37	6	6	.500	3	41	6	0	106	109	14	85	0	2.89
Dave LaRoche	L	34	4	2	.667	0	25	0	0	50	54	11	31	0	3.42
George Frazier	R	27	4	4	.500	1	63	0	0	112	103	39	69	0	3.47
Goose Gossage (SJ)	R	30	4	5	.444	30	56	0	0	93	63	28	102	0	2.23
2 Roger Erickson (SJ)	R	25	4	5	.444	1	16	11	0	71	86	17	37	0	4.46
Jay Howell	R	26	2	3	.400	0	6			28	42	13	21	0	7.71
Curt Kaufman	R	24	1	0	1.000	0	9			9	6	1	5	0	5.19
Doyle Alexander (BG-SJ)	R	31	1	7	.125	0	16	11	0	67	81	14	26	0	6.08
Lynn McGlothen	R	32	0	0	—	0	4			9	9	3	2	0	10.80
Jim Lewis	R	26	0	0	—	0	1			3	3	0	0	0	54.00
1 John Pacella	R	25	0	0	.000	0	10			13		9	2		7.20
Stefan Wever	R	24	0	1	.000	0	3	1	0						27.00
Rick Reuschel 33 (SJ)															

CLEVELAND — 6th(tie) 78-84 .481 17 — DAVE GARCIA

Name	G by Pos	B	AGE	G	AB	R	H	2B	3B	HR	RBI	BB	SO	SB	BA	SA
TOTALS			28	162	5559	683	1458	225	32	109	639	651	625	151	.262	.373
Mike Hargrove	1B153, DH5	L	32	160	591	67	160	26	1	4	65	101	58	2	.271	.338
Jack Perconte	2B82, DH2	L	27	93	219	27	52	4	4	0	15	22	25	9	.237	.292
Mike Fischlin	SS101, 3B8, 2B6, C1	R	26	112	276	34	74	12	1	0	21	34	36	9	.268	.319
Toby Harrah	3B159, 2B3, SS2	R	33	162	602	100	183	29	4	25	78	84	52	17	.304	.490
Von Hayes	OF139, 3B5, 1B4	L	23	150	527	65	132	25	3	14	82	42	63	32	.250	.389
Rick Manning	OF152	L	27	152	562	71	152	18	2	8	44	54	60	12	.270	.352
Miguel Dilone	OF97, DH1	B	27	104	379	50	89	12	3	0	25	25	36	33	.235	.306
Ron Hassey	C105, 1B2, DH2	L	29	113	323	33	81	18	0	5	34	53	32	2	.251	.353
Andre Thornton	DH152, 1B8	R	32	161	589	90	161	26	1	32	116	109	81	6	.273	.484
Alan Bannister (LJ)	OF55, 2B48, SS2, 3B1, DH1	R	30	101	348	40	93	16	1	4	41	42	41	18	.267	.353
3 Larry Milbourne	2B63, SS21, 3B9, DH1	B	31	82	291	29	80	11	4	2	25	12	20	2	.275	.361
Jerry Dybzinski	SS77, 3B3	R	26	80	212	19	49	6	2	0	22	21	25	3	.231	.278
Chris Bando (BG)	C63, 3B2	B	26	66	184	13	39	6	1	3	16	24	30	0	.212	.304
Rodney Craig	OF22, DH4	B	24	49	65	7	15	2	0	0	1	4	9	3	.231	.262
Carmen Castillo	OF43, DH1	R	24	47	120	11	25	4	0	2	11	6	17	0	.208	.292
Bill Nahorodny	C35	R	28	39	94	6	21	5	1	4	18	2	9	0	.223	.426
Bake McBride (IJ)	OF22	L	33	27	85	8	31	3	3	0	13	2	12	2	.365	.471
Karl Pagel	1B10, DH1	L	27	23	18	3	3	0	0	0	2	2	7	0	.167	.167
Joe Charboneau	OF18, DH1	R	27	22	56	7	12	2	1	2	9	7	16	0	.214	.393
Kevin Rhomberg	OF7, DH4, 3B1	R	26	16	18	3	6	0	0	1	1	2	4	5	.333	.500

NAME	T	AGE	W	L	PCT	SV	G	GS	CG	IP	H	BB	SO	SHO	ERA
TOTALS		28	78	84	.481	30	162	162	31	1468	1433	589	882	9	4.11
Len Barker	R	26	15	11	.577	0	33	33	10	245	211	88	187	1	3.90
Rick Sutcliffe	R	26	14	8	.636	1	34	27	6	216	174	98	142	11	2.96
Dan Spillner	R	30	12	10	.545	21	65	0	0	134	117	45	90	0	2.49
Lary Sorensen	R	26	10	15	.400	0	32	30	6	189	251	55	62	1	5.61
1 John Denny (SJ)	R	29	6	11	.353	0	21	21	5	138	126	73	94	0	5.01
Ed Glynn	L	29	5	2	.714	4	47	0	0	50	43	30	54	0	4.17
Ed Whitson	R	27	4	2	.667	2	40	9	1	108	91	58	61	1	3.26
Tom Brennan	R	24	4	2	.667	2	30	4	0	93	112	10	46	0	4.27
Bud Anderson	R	26	3	4	.429	0	25	5	1	81	84	30	44	0	3.35
Bert Blyleven (EJ)	R	31	2	2	.500	0	4	4	1	20	16	11	19	0	4.87
Rick Waits (KJ)	L	30	2	13	.133	0	25	21	2	115	128	57	44	0	5.40
2 Jerry Reed	R	26	1	1	.500	0				16	15	3	10		3.45
Sandy Wihtol	R	27	1	1	.500	0	9	1		5	7	8			4.63
John Bohnet	L	21	0	0	—	0	12			11	7	4			6.94
Dennis Lewallyn	R	28	0	0	—	0	10			13	1	3			6.97
Neal Heaton	R	22	0	0	.000	0	4			31	32	16	14	0	5.23
Silvio Martinez 26 (AJ)															

TORONTO   6th(tie) 78-84 .481 17   BOBBY COX

Name	G by Pos	B	AGE	G	AB	R	H	2B	3B	HR	RBI	BB	SO	SB	BA	SA
TOTALS			27	162	5526	651	1447	262	45	106	605	415	749	118	.262	.383
Willie Upshaw	1B155, DH5	L	25	160	580	77	151	25	7	21	75	52	91	8	.287	.443
Damaso Garcia	2B141, DH4	R	27	147	597	89	185	32	3	5	42	21	44	54	.310	.399
Alfredo Griffin	SS162	B	24	162	539	57	130	20	8	1	48	22	48	10	.241	.314
Rance Mulliniks	3B102, SS16	L	26	112	311	32	76	25	0	4	35	37	49	3	.244	.363
Jesse Barfield	OF137, DH1	R	22	139	394	54	97	13	2	18	58	42	79	1	.246	.426
Lloyd Moseby	OF145	L	22	147	487	51	115	20	9	9	52	33	106	11	.236	.370
Barry Bonnell	OF125, 3B9, DH6	R	28	140	437	59	128	26	3	6	49	32	51	14	.293	.407
Ernie Whitt	C98, DH1	L	30	105	284	28	74	14	2	11	42	26	34	1	.261	.440
13 Wayne Nordhagen (XJ)	DH60, OF10	R	33	72	185	12	50	6	0	1	20	10	22	0	.270	.319
Garth Iorg	3B100, 2B30, DH1	R	27	129	417	45	119	20	5	1	36	12	38	1	.285	.365
Hosken Powell	OF75, DH19	L	27	112	265	43	73	13	4	3	26	12	23	4	.275	.389
Buck Martinez	C93	R	33	96	260	26	63	17	0	10	37	24	34	1	.242	.423
Al Woods	OF64, DH10	L	28	85	201	20	47	11	1	3	24	21	20	1	.234	.343
Tony Johnson	OF28, DH28	R	26	70	98	17	23	4	1	3	14	11	26	3	.235	.367
2 Dave Revering	DH49, 1B4	L	34	55	135	15	29	6	0	5	18	22	30	0	.215	.370
2 Leon Roberts	DH21, OF16	R	31	40	105	6	24	4	0	1	5	7	16	1	.229	.295
Glenn Adams	DH27	L	34	30	66	2	17	4	0	1	11	4	5	0	.258	.364
Otto Velez	DH24	R	31	28	52	4	10	1	0	1	5	13	15	1	.192	.269
1 John Mayberry	DH13, 1B4	R	33	17	33	7	9	0	0	2	3	7	5	0	.273	.455
Geno Petralli	C12, 3B3	B	22	16	44	3	16	2	0	0	1	4	6	0	.364	.409
Dave Baker	3B8	L	24	9	20	3	5	1	0	0	2	3	3	0	.250	.300
Pedro Hernandez	DH3, 3B2, OF1	R	23	8	9	1	0	0	0	0	0	0	3	0	.000	.000
2 Dick Davis	OF1, DH1	R	28	3	7	0	2	0	0	0	0	0	1	0	.286	.286

NAME	T	AGE	W	L	PCT	SV	G	GS	CG	IP	H	BB	SO	SHO	ERA
		26	78	84	.481	25	162	162	41	1444	1428	493	776	13	3.95
Dave Stieb	R	24	17	14	.548	0	38	38	19	288	271	75	141	5	3.25
Jim Clancy	R	26	16	14	.533	0	40	40	11	267	251	77	139	3	3.71
Luis Leal	R	25	12	15	.444	0	38	38	10	250	250	79	111	0	3.93
Joey McLaughlin (SJ)	R	25	8	6	.571	8	44	0	0	70	54	30	49	0	3.21
Dale Murray	R	32	8	7	.533	11	56	0	0	111	115	32	60	0	3.16
Roy Lee Jackson	R	28	8	8	.500	8	48	2	0	97	77	31	71	0	3.06
Jim Gott	R	22	5	10	.333	0	30	23	1	136	134	66	82	1	4.43
Ken Schrom	R	27	1	0	1.000	0	6	0	0	15	13	15	8	0	5.87
Jerry Garvin	L	26	1	1	.500	0	32	4	0	58	81	26	35	0	7.25
Dave Geisel	L	27	1	1	.500	0	16	2	0	32	32	17	22	0	3.98
Mark Bomback	R	29	1	5	.167	0	16	8	0	60	87	25	22	0	6.03
Steve Senteney	R	26	0	0	—	0	11	0	0	22	23	6	20	0	4.91
Mark Eichhorn	R	21	0	3	.000	0	7	7	0	38	40	14	16	0	5.45

WEST DIVISION

CALIFORNIA   1st 93-69 .574   GENE MAUCH

Name	G by Pos	B	AGE	G	AB	R	H	2B	3B	HR	RBI	BB	SO	SB	BA	SA
TOTALS			33	162	5532	814	1518	268	26	186	760	613	760	55	.274	.433
Rod Carew	1B134	L	36	138	523	88	167	25	5	3	44	67	49	10	.319	.403
Bobby Grich	2B142, DH1	R	33	145	506	74	132	28	5	19	65	82	109	3	.261	.449
Tim Foli	SS139, 2B8, 3B2	R	31	150	480	46	121	14	2	3	56	14	22	2	.252	.308
Doug DeCinces	3B153, SS2	R	31	153	575	94	173	42	5	30	97	66	80	7	.301	.548
Reggie Jackson	OF139, DH5	L	36	153	530	92	146	17	1	39	101	85	156	4	.275	.532
Fred Lynn	OF133	L	30	138	472	89	141	38	1	21	86	58	72	7	.299	.517
Brian Downing	OF158	R	31	158	623	109	175	37	2	28	84	86	58	2	.281	.482
Bob Boone	C143	R	34	143	472	42	121	17	0	7	58	39	34	0	.256	.337
Don Baylor	DH155	R	33	157	608	80	160	24	1	24	93	57	69	10	.263	.424
Juan Beniquez	OF107	R	32	112	196	25	52	11	2	3	24	15	21	3	.265	.388
Bobby Clark	OF102	R	27	102	90	11	19	2	0	1	9	6	29	1	.211	.289
2 Rob Wilfong	2B28, 3B5, OF3, SS2, DH1	L	28	55	102	17	25	4	2	1	11	7	17	4	.245	.353
Ron Jackson	1B37, 3B9	R	29	53	142	15	47	6	0	2	19	10	12	0	.331	.415
Joe Ferguson	C32, OF2	R	35	36	84	10	19	2	0	3	8	12	19	0	.226	.357
2 Mick Kelleher	SS28, 3B6	R	34	34	49	9	8	1	0	0	1	5	5	1	.163	.184
Daryl Sconiers	1B3, DH1	L	23	12	13	0	2	0	0	0	0	1	3	0	.154	.154
Rick Burleson (SJ)	SS11	R	31	11	45	4	7	1	0	0	2	6	3	0	.156	.178
Jose Moreno	2B2, DH1	B	24	11	3	3	0	0	0	0	0	0	0	0	.000	.000
Gary Pettis	OF8	R	24	10	5	5	1	0	0	1	0	2	0		.200	.800
Rick Adams	SS8	R	23	8	14	1	2	0	0	0	0	0	0	1	.143	.143
Ed Ott 30 (SJ)																

NAME	T	AGE	W	L	PCT	SV	G	GS	CG	IP	H	BB	SO	SHO	ERA
		31	93	69	.574	27	162	162	40	1464	1436	482	728	10	3.82
Geoff Zahn	L	36	18	8	.692	0	34	34	12	229	225	65	81	4	3.73
Ken Forsch	R	35	13	11	.542	0	37	35	12	228	225	57	73	4	3.87
Steve Renko	R	37	11	6	.647	0	31	23	4	156	163	51	81	0	4.44
Bruce Kison	R	32	10	5	.667	1	33	16	3	142	120	44	86	1	3.17
2 Dave Goltz (RJ)	R	33	8	5	.615	3	28	7	1	86	82	32	49	0	4.08
Mike Witt	R	21	8	6	.571	0	33	26	5	180	177	47	85	1	3.51
Luis Sanchez	R	28	7	4	.636	5	46	0	0	93	89	34	58	0	3.21
2 Tommy John	L	39	4	2	.667	0	7	7	1	35	49	5	14	0	3.86
Don Aase (EJ)	R	27	3	3	.500	4	24	0	0	52	45	23	40	0	3.46
Angel Moreno	L	27	3	7	.300	1	13	8	2	49	55	23	22	0	4.74
Mickey Mahler	L	29	2	0	1.000	0	6	0	0	9	6	5	0	0	1.13
Andy Hassler	L	30	2	1	.667	4	54	0	0	71	58	40	38	0	2.78
Luis Tiant	R	41	2	2	.500	0	6	5	0	30	39	8	30	0	5.76
Rick Steirer	R	25	1	0	1.000	0	10	1	0	26	25	11	14	0	3.76
2 Doug Corbett	R	29	1	1	.500	8	33	0	0	57	46	25	37	0	5.05
2 John Curtis	L	34	0	1	.000	0	12	2	0	12	16	3	10	0	6.00
1 Stan Bahnsen	R	37	0	1	.000	0	7	0	0	10	13	8	5	0	4.66
Bill Travers 29 (SJ)															

KANSAS CITY   2nd 90-72 .556 3   DICK HOWSER

Name	G by Pos	B	AGE	G	AB	R	H	2B	3B	HR	RBI	BB	SO	SB	BA	SA
TOTALS			30	162	5629	784	1603	295	58	132	746	442	758	133	.285	.428
Willie Aikens	1B128	L	34	134	466	50	131	29	1	17	74	45	70	0	.281	.457
Frank White	2B144	R	31	145	524	71	156	45	6	11	56	16	65	10	.298	.469
U.L. Washington (XJ)	SS117, DH1	B	28	119	437	64	125	19	3	10	60	38	48	23	.286	.412
George Brett	3B134, OF12	L	29	144	552	101	166	32	9	21	82	71	51	6	.301	.505
Jerry Martin	OF142, DH3	R	33	147	519	52	138	22	1	15	65	38	138	1	.266	.399
Amos Otis	OF125	R	35	125	475	73	136	25	3	11	88	37	65	9	.286	.421
Willie Wilson (KJ)	OF135	B	26	136	585	87	194	19	15	3	46	26	81	37	.332	.431
John Wathan (BN)	C120, 1B34	R	32	121	448	79	121	11	3	5	51	48	46	36	.270	.388
Hal McRae	DH158, OF1	R	36	159	613	91	189	46	8	27	133	55	61	4	.308	.542
Onix Concepcion	SS46, 2B24, DH1	R	24	74	205	17	48	9	1	0	15	5	18	2	.234	.288
Greg Pryor	3B40, 2B15, 1B14, SS7	R	32	73	152	23	41	10	1	2	12	10	20	2	.270	.388
Cesar Geronimo (VJ)	OF44, DH1	L	34	53	119	14	32	6	3	4	23	8	16	2	.269	.471
Steve Hammond	OF37, DH1	L	25	46	126	14	29	5	1	1	11	4	18	0	.230	.310
Don Slaught	C43	R	23	43	115	14	32	6	0	3	8	9	12	0	.278	.409
Lee May	1B32, DH2	R	39	42	91	12	28	5	2	3	12	14	18	0	.308	.505
Dennis Werth	1B35, C2	R	29	41	15	5	2	0	0	0	2	4	2	0	.133	.133
Jamie Quirk (XJ)	C29, 1B6, 3B1, OF1	L	27	36	78	8	18	3	0	1	5	3	15	0	.231	.308
Tom Poquette	OF23	L	30	24	62	4	9	1	0	0	3	4	5	1	.145	.161
Ron Johnson	1B7	R	26	8	14	2	4	2	0	0	0	4	3	0	.286	.429
Tim Ireland (BH)	2B4, OF2, 3B1	R	29	7	7	2	1	0	0	0	0	1	0	0	.143	.143
Mark Ryal	OF5	L	22	6	13	0	1	0	0	0	0	0	0	0	.077	.077
Bombo Rivera	OF3	R	29	5	10	1	1	0	0	0	0	0	3	0	.100	.100
Buddy Biancalana	SS3	B	22	3	2	1	1	0	0	0	0	0	1	0	.500	1.500
Kelly Heath	2B1	R	24	1	1	0	0	0	0	0	0	0	0	0	.000	.000

NAME	T	AGE	W	L	PCT	SV	G	GS	CG	IP	H	BB	SO	SHO	ERA
		31	90	72	.556	45	162	162	16	1431	1443	471	650	12	4.08
Larry Gura	L	34	18	12	.600	0	37	37	8	248	251	64	98	3	4.03
Vida Blue	L	32	13	12	.520	0	31	31	6	181	163	80	103	2	3.78
Dennis Leonard (BG)	R	31	10	6	.625	0	21	21	2	131	145	46	58	0	5.10
Paul Splittorff	L	35	10	10	.500	0	29	28	0	162	166	57	74	0	4.28
Dan Quisenberry	R	29	9	7	.563	35	72	0	0	137	126	12	46	0	2.57
Dave Frost (EJ-KJ)	R	29	6	6	.500	0	21	14	0	82	103	30	26	0	5.51
Mike Armstrong	R	28	5	5	.500	6	52	0	0	113	88	43	75	0	3.20
Don Hood	L	32	4	0	1.000	1	30	3	0	67	71	22	31	0	3.51
Bud Black	L	25	4	6	.400	0	22	14	0	88	92	34	40	0	4.58
1 Grant Jackson	L	39	3	1	.750	0	20	0	0	38	42	21	15	0	5.17
Bill Castro	R	28	3	2	.600	1	21	4	0	76	72	20	37	0	3.45
Bob Tufts	L	26	2	0	1.000	2	10	0	0	24	3	13		0	4.50
Derek Botelho	R	25	2	1	.667	0	8	4	0	24	25	8	12	0	4.13
Keith Creel	R	23	1	4	.200	0	9	6	0	45	43	25	13	0	5.40
Jim Wright	R	27	0	0	—	0	7	0	0	24	32	6	9	0	5.32
Scott Brown 25 (EJ)															
Mike Jones 22 (AA)															

CHICAGO   3rd 87-75 .537 6   TONY LARUSSA

Name	G by Pos	B	AGE	G	AB	R	H	2B	3B	HR	RBI	BB	SO	SB	BA	SA
TOTALS			29	162	5575	786	1523	266	52	136	747	533	866	136	.273	.413
Tom Paciorek	1B102, OF6	R	35	104	382	49	119	27	4	11	55	24	53	3	.312	.490
Tony Bernazard	2B137	B	25	137	540	90	138	25	9	11	56	67	88	11	.256	.396
Bill Almon	SS108, DH1	R	29	111	308	40	79	10	4	4	26	25	49	10	.256	.354
Aurelio Rodriguez	3B112, 2B3, SS2	R	34	118	257	24	62	15	1	3	31	11	35	0	.241	.342
Harold Baines	OF161	L	23	161	608	89	165	29	8	25	105	49	95	10	.271	.469
Ron LeFlore (ST)	OF83, DH2	L	34	91	334	58	96	15	4	4	25	22	91	28	.287	.392
Steve Kemp	OF154, DH2	L	27	160	580	91	166	23	1	19	98	89	83	7	.286	.428
Carlton Fisk	C133, 1B2	R	34	135	476	66	127	17	3	14	65	46	60	17	.267	.403
Greg Luzinski	DH156	R	31	159	583	87	170	37	1	18	102	89	120	1	.292	.451
Rudy Law	OF94, DH3	L	25	131	336	55	107	15	8	3	32	23	41	36	.318	.438
Mike Squires	1B109	L	30	116	195	33	52	9	3	1	21	14	13	3	.267	.359
Vance Law	SS85, 3B39, 2B10, OF1	R	25	114	359	40	101	20	1	5	54	26	46	4	.281	.384
Jerry Hairston	OF36, DH2	R	30	85	90	11	21	5	0	5	18	9	15	0	.233	.456
Marc Hill	C49, 1B1, 3B1	R	30	53	88	9	23	2	0	3	17	8	15	0	.261	.386
1 Jim Morrison	3B50, DH1	R	29	51	166	17	37	7	3	7	19	13	15	0	.223	.428
Chris Nyman	1B24, OF2	R	27	28	65	6	16	1	0	0	2	3	6	3	.246	.262
Marv Foley	C15, 3B2, 1B1, DH1	L	28	27	36	1	4	0	0	0	1	6	4	0	.111	.111
Rusty Kuntz	OF21	R	27	21	26	4	5	1	0	0	2	6	6	0	.192	.231
Ron Kittle	OF5, DH3	R	24	20	29	3	7	2	0	1	7	3	12	0	.241	.414
Lorenzo Gray	3B16	R	24	17	28	4	8	1	0	0	2	1	6	1	.286	.321
Steve Dillard	2B16	R	31	16	41	1	7	0	0	1	5	1	5	0	.171	.293
Jay Loviglio	2B13, DH2	B	26	15	31	5	6	0	0	0	2	1	4	2	.194	.194
Greg Walker	DH4	L	22	11	17	3	7	1	0	0	3	1	0	0	.412	1.000

NAME	T	AGE	W	L	PCT	SV	G	GS	CG	IP	H	BB	SO	SHO	ERA
		27	87	75	.537	41	162	162	30	1439	1502	460	753	10	3.87
LaMarr Hoyt	R	27	19	15	.559	0	39	32	14	240	248	48	124	2	3.53
Britt Burns	L	23	13	5	.722	0	28	28	5	169	168	67	116	1	4.04
Jerry Koosman	L	39	11	7	.611	3	42	19	3	173	194	38	88	1	3.84
Dennis Lamp	R	29	11	8	.579	5	44	27	3	190	206	59	78	2	3.99
Rich Dotson	R	23	11	15	.423	0	34	31	3	197	219	73	109	1	3.84
Salome Barojas	R	25	6	6	.500	21	61	0	0	107	96	46	56	0	3.54
Steve Trout	L	24	6	9	.400	0	25	19	2	120	130	50	62	0	4.26
Kevin Hickey	L	25	4	4	.500	0	60	0	0	78	73	30	38	0	3.00
2 Warren Brusstar	R	30	2	2	1.000	0	40	0	+0	18	19	3	8	0	3.44
2 Jim Kern	R	33	2	1	.667	3	13	1	0	28	20	12	23	0	5.14
2 Eddie Solomon	R	31	1	0	1.000	0	6	0	0	13	19	3	3	0	3.68
Chico Escarrega	R	32	1	3	.250	1	38	2	0	74	73	16	33	0	3.67
2 Sparky Lyle	L	37	0	0	—	1	11	0	0	12	11	7	6	0	3.00
Jim Siwy	R	23	0	1	.000	0	2	1	0	7	10	5	3	0	10.29
Juan Agosto	L	24	0	0	—	0	3	0	0	1	2	1	0	0	18.00
Rich Barnes	L	22	0	2	.000	0	7	1	0	17	21	4	6	0	4.76

SEATTLE 4th 76-86 .469 17 — RENE LACHEMANN

Name	G by Pos	B	AGE	G	AB	R	H	2B	3B	HR	RBI	BB	SO	SB	BA	SA
TOTALS			27	162	5626	651	1431	259	33	130	614	456	806	131	.254	.381
Gary Gray	1B60, DH14	R	29	80	269	26	69	14	2	7	29	24	59	1	.257	.401
Julio Cruz	2B151, SS2, DH2, 3B1	B	27	154	549	83	133	22	5	8	49	57	71	46	.242	.344
Todd Cruz	SS136	R	26	136	492	44	113	20	2	16	57	12	95	2	.230	.376
Manny Castillo	3B130, 2B9	R	25	138	506	49	130	29	1	3	49	22	35	2	.257	.336
Al Cowens	OF145, DH1	R	30	146	560	72	151	39	8	20	78	46	81	11	.270	.475
Dave Henderson	OF101	R	23	104	324	47	82	17	1	14	48	36	67	2	.253	.441
Bruce Bochte	OF99, 1B34, DH12	L	31	144	509	58	151	21	0	12	70	67	71	8	.297	.409
2 Rick Sweet	C83	B	29	88	258	29	66	6	1	4	24	20	24	3	.256	.333
Richie Zisk	DH130	R	33	131	503	61	147	28	1	21	62	49	89	2	.292	.477
Joe Simpson	OF97	L	30	105	296	39	76	14	4	2	23	22	48	8	.257	.351
Bobby Brown	OF68, DH3	B	28	79	245	29	59	7	1	4	17	17	32	28	.241	.327
Paul Serna	SS31, 2B18, 3B15, DH2	R	23	65	169	15	38	3	0	3	8	4	13	0	.225	.296
Jim Maler	1B57, DH5	R	23	64	221	18	50	8	3	4	26	12	35	0	.226	.344
Terry Bulling (JJ)	C56	R	29	56	154	17	34	7	0	1	8	19	16	2	.221	.286
Jim Essian (BN)	C48	R	31	48	153	14	42	8	0	3	20	11	7	2	.275	.386
Dave Edler	3B31, OF2, DH2	R	25	40	104	14	29	2	2	2	18	11	13	4	.279	.394
Lenny Randle	DH13, 3B9, 2B6	B	33	30	46	10	8	2	0	0	1	4	4	2	.174	.217
3 Dave Revering	1B27	L	29	29	82	8	17	3	1	3	12	9	17	0	.207	.378
Steve Stroughter	DH9, OF3	L	30	26	47	4	8	1	0	1	3	3	9	0	.170	.255
Thad Bosley	OF19	L	25	22	46	3	8	1	0	0	2	4	8	3	.174	.196
John Moses	OF19	B	24	22	44	7	14	5	1	1	3	4	5	5	.318	.545
Orlando Mercado	C8, DH1	R	20	9	17	1	2	0	0	1	6	0	5	0	.118	.294
Domingo Ramos	SS8	R	24	8	26	3	4	2	0	0	1	3	2	0	.154	.231
Dan Firova	C3	R	25	3	5	0	0	0	0	0	0	0	0	0	.000	.000
Vance McHenry	SS1, DH1	R	25	3	1	0	0	0	0	0	0	0	0	0	.000	.000

NAME	T	AGE	W	L	PCT	SV	G	GS	CG	IP	H	BB	SO	SHO	ERA
TOTALS		27	76	86	.469	39	162	162	23	1476	1431	547	1002	11	3.88
Bill Caudill	R	25	12	9	.571	26	70	0	0	96	65	35	111	0	2.35
Floyd Bannister	L	27	12	13	.480	0	35	35	5	247	225	77	209	3	3.43
Gaylord Perry	R	43	10	12	.455	0	32	32	6	217	245	54	116	0	4.40
Ed Vande Berg	L	23	9	4	.692	5	78	0	0	76	54	32	60	0	2.37
Jim Beattie	R	27	8	12	.400	0	28	27	5	172	149	65	140	1	3.34
Mike Moore	R	22	7	14	.333	0	28	27	1	144	159	79	73	1	5.36
Gene Nelson	R	21	6	9	.400	0	22	19	2	123	133	60	71	1	4.62
Bryan Clark	L	25	5	2	.714	0	37	5	1	115	104	58	70	1	2.75
Bob Stoddard	R	25	3	3	.500	0	9	9	2	67	48	18	24	1	2.41
Mike Stanton	R	29	2	4	.333	7	56	1	0	71	70	21	49	0	4.16
Ron Musselman	R	27	1	0	1.000	0	12	0	0	16	18	6	9	0	3.45
Edwin Nunez (BH)	R	19	1	2	.333	0	8	5	0	35	36	16	27	0	4.58
Larry Andersen	R	29	0	0	—	1	40	1	0	80	100	23	32	0	5.99
Jerry Don Gleaton	L	24	0	0	—	0	3	0	0	5	7	2	1	0	13.50
Rich Bordi	R	23	0	2	.000	0	7	2	0	13	18	1	10	0	8.31
Glenn Abbott 31 (EJ)															
Brian Allard 24 (SJ)															

OAKLAND 5th 68-94 .420 25 — BILLY MARTIN

Name	G by Pos	B	AGE	G	AB	R	H	2B	3B	HR	RBI	BB	SO	SB	BA	SA
TOTALS			31	162	5448	691	1286	211	27	149	659	582	948	232	.236	.367
Dan Meyer	1B58, DH38, OF11	L	29	120	383	28	92	17	3	8	59	18	33	1	.240	.363
Davey Lopes	2B125, OF6	R	37	128	450	58	109	19	3	11	42	40	51	28	.242	.371
Fred Stanley	SS98, 2B2	R	34	101	228	33	44	7	0	2	17	29	32	0	.193	.250
Wayne Gross	3B108, 1B16, DH1	L	30	129	386	43	97	14	0	9	41	53	50	0	.251	.358
Tony Armas	OF135, DH1	R	28	138	536	58	125	19	2	28	89	33	128	2	.233	.433
Dwayne Murphy	OF147, SS1, DH1	L	27	151	543	84	129	15	1	27	94	94	122	26	.238	.418
Rickey Henderson	OF144, DH4	R	23	149	536	119	143	24	4	10	51	116	94	130	.267	.382
Mike Heath	C90, OF14, DH1	R	27	101	318	43	77	18	4	3	39	27	36	8	.242	.352
Cliff Johnson (NJ)	DH48, 1B11	R	34	73	214	19	51	10	0	7	31	26	41	1	.238	.383
Jeff Burroughs	DH48, OF34	R	31	113	285	42	79	13	2	16	48	45	61	1	.277	.505
Dave McKay	2B59, 3B16, SS3	B	32	78	212	25	42	4	1	4	17	11	35	6	.198	.283
Jeff Newman	C67, 1B3, 3B1, DH1	R	33	72	251	19	50	11	0	6	30	14	49	0	.199	.315
Joe Rudi	1B49, OF14, DH3	R	35	71	193	21	41	6	1	5	18	24	35	0	.212	.332
Jimmy Sexton	SS47, 3B8, DH5	R	30	69	139	19	34	4	0	2	14	9	24	16	.245	.317
Mickey Klutts	3B49	R	27	55	157	10	28	8	0	1	14	9	18	0	.178	.229
Tony Phillips	SS39	B	23	40	81	11	17	2	2	0	8	12	26	2	.210	.284
Jim Spencer	1B32	L	34	33	101	6	17	3	1	2	5	3	20	0	.168	.277
Mitchell Page	DH24	L	30	31	78	14	20	5	0	4	7	7	24	3	.256	.474
Mike Davis	OF13, 1B7	L	23	23	75	12	30	4	0	1	10	2	9	3	.400	.493
Bob Kearney	C22	R	25	25	71	7	12	3	0	0	5	3	10	0	.169	.211
Kelvin Moore	1B20	L	24	21	67	6	15	1	1	2	6	3	23	0	.224	.358
1 Rob Picciolo	SS18	R	29	18	49	3	11	1	0	0	3	1	10	1	.224	.245
Danny Goodwin	DH15	L	28	17	52	6	11	2	1	2	8	2	13	0	.212	.404
Darrell Brown	OF7, DH1	B	26	8	18	2	6	0	1	0	3	1	2	1	.333	.444
Rick Bosetti	OF6	R	28	6	15	1	3	0	0	0	0	0	1	0	.200	.200
Kevin Bell	3B3, DH1	R	26	4	9	1	3	1	0	0	0	0	3	0	.333	.444

NAME	T	AGE	W	L	PCT	SV	G	GS	CG	IP	H	BB	SO	SHO	ERA
TOTALS		27	68	94	.420	22	162	162	42	1456	1506	648	697	6	4.54
Rick Langford	R	30	11	16	.407	0	32	31	15	237	265	49	79	2	4.21
Matt Keough	R	26	11	18	.379	0	34	34	10	209	233	101	75	2	5.72
Tom Underwood	L	28	10	6	.625	7	56	10	2	153	136	68	79	0	3.29
Dave Beard	R	22	10	9	.526	11	54	2	0	92	85	35	73	0	3.44
Mike Norris	R	27	7	11	.389	0	28	28	7	166	154	84	83	1	4.76
Steve McCatty	R	28	6	3	.667	0	21	20	2	129	124	70	66	0	3.99
Brian Kingman	R	27	4	12	.250	1	23	20	3	123	131	57	46	0	4.48
Jeff Jones (SJ)	R	25	3	1	.750	0	18	2	0	37	44	26	18	0	5.11
Tim Conroy	L	22	2	2	.500	0	5	5	1	25	20	18	17	0	3.55
Bob Owchinko	L	27	2	4	.333	3	54	0	0	102	111	52	67	0	5.21
Steve Baker	R	25	1	1	.500	0	5	3	0	26	30	4	14	0	4.56
Chris Codiroli	R	24	1	2	.333	0	3	1	0	17	16	4	5	0	4.32
2 Fernando Arroyo	R	30	0	0	—	0	10	0	0	22	23	7	9	0	5.24
Dennis Kinney	L	30	0	0	—	0	3	0	0	4	9	4	0	0	8.31
John D'Acquisto	R	30	0	1	.000	0	11	0	0	17	20	9	7	0	5.29
2 Preston Hanna	R	27	0	4	.000	0	23	2	1	48	54	33	32	0	5.59
Bo McLaughlin	R	28	0	0	.000	0	21	2	1	48	51	27	27	0	4.84

TEXAS 6th 64-98 .395 29 — DON ZIMMER 38-58 .396 / DARRELL JOHNSON 26-40 .394

Name	G by Pos	B	AGE	G	AB	R	H	2B	3B	HR	RBI	BB	SO	SB	BA	SA
TOTALS			29	162	5445	590	1354	204	26	115	558	447	750	63	.249	.359
Dave Hostetler	1B109, DH3	R	26	113	418	53	97	12	3	22	67	42	113	2	.232	.433
Mike Richardt	2B98, DH15, OF6	R	24	119	402	34	97	10	0	3	43	23	42	3	.241	.289
Mark Wagner (IL)	SS60	R	28	60	179	14	43	4	1	0	8	10	24	1	.240	.274
Buddy Bell	3B145, SS4	R	30	148	537	62	159	27	2	13	67	70	50	5	.296	.426
Larry Parrish	OF124, 3B3, DH2	R	28	128	440	59	116	15	0	17	62	30	84	5	.264	.414
George Wright	OF149	B	23	150	557	69	147	20	5	11	50	30	78	3	.264	.377
Billy Sample	OF91, DH1	R	27	97	360	56	94	14	2	10	27	27	35	10	.261	.394
Jim Sundberg	C132, OF1	R	31	139	470	57	118	22	5	10	47	49	57	2	.251	.383
Lamar Johnson	DH77, 1B12	R	31	105	324	37	84	11	0	7	38	31	40	3	.259	.358
Johnny Grubb	OF77, DH18	L	33	103	308	35	86	13	3	3	26	39	37	0	.279	.370
1 Doug Flynn	2B55, SS35	R	31	88	270	13	57	6	2	0	19	4	14	6	.211	.248
Bill Stein	2B34, 3B28, SS6, DH3, 1B2, OF1	R	35	85	184	14	44	8	0	1	16	12	23	0	.239	.299
1 Lee Mazzilli (WJ)	OF26, DH24	B	27	58	195	23	47	8	0	4	17	28	26	11	.241	.344
2 Bucky Dent	SS45	R	30	46	146	16	32	9	0	1	14	13	10	0	.219	.301
Pat Putnam	1B39, 3B1, OF1	L	28	43	122	14	28	9	0	2	9	10	18	0	.230	.344
Wayne Tolleson	SS26, 3B4, 2B1	B	26	38	70	6	8	1	0	0	2	5	14	1	.114	.129
1 Leon Roberts	OF28, DH1	R	31	31	73	7	17	3	0	1	6	4	14	0	.233	.315
Terry Bogener	OF16, DH4	R	26	24	60	6	13	2	1	1	4	4	8	2	.217	.333
Don Werner	C22	R	29	22	59	4	12	2	0	0	3	3	7	0	.203	.237
Pete O'Brien	OF11, DH4, 1B3	L	24	20	67	13	16	4	1	4	13	6	8	1	.239	.507
Bobby Johnson	OF14, 1B3	R	22	20	56	4	7	2	0	2	3	3	22	0	.125	.268
Mickey Rivers (KJ)	DH16	L	33	19	68	6	16	1	1	1	4	0	7	0	.235	.324
2 Randy Bass	DH7, 1B6	L	28	16	48	5	10	2	0	1	6	1	7	0	.208	.313
Nick Capra	OF9	R	24	13	15	2	4	0	0	0	1	3	4	2	.267	.467
Mario Mendoza	SS12	R	31	12	17	1	2	0	0	0	0	0	3	0	.118	.118

NAME	T	AGE	W	L	PCT	SV	G	GS	CG	IP	H	BB	SO	SHO	ERA
TOTALS		29	64	98	.395	24	162	162	32	1431	1554	483	690	5	4.28
Charlie Hough	R	34	16	13	.552	0	34	34	12	228	217	72	128	2	3.95
Danny Darwin	R	26	10	8	.556	7	56	1	0	89	95	37	61	0	3.44
Jon Matlack	L	32	7	7	.500	1	33	14	1	148	158	37	78	0	3.53
1 Doc Medich	R	33	7	11	.389	0	21	21	2	123	146	61	37	0	5.06
Frank Tanana	L	28	7	18	.280	0	30	30	7	194	199	55	87	0	4.21
Rick Honeycutt	L	28	5	17	.227	0	30	26	4	164	201	54	64	1	5.27
Dave Schmidt	R	25	4	6	.400	6	33	8	0	110	118	25	69	0	3.20
Mike Smithson	R	24	1	4	.429	0	8	8	3	47	51	13	24	0	5.01
Tom Henke	R	24	1	0	1.000	0	8	0	0	16	14	8	9	0	1.15
Paul Mirabella	L	28	1	1	.500	3	40	0	0	51	46	22	29	0	4.80
Mike Mason	R	23	1	2	.333	0	4	4	0	23	21	9	8	0	5.09
John Butcher	R	25	1	5	.167	1	18	13	2	94	102	34	39	0	4.87
Steve Comer (BF)	R	28	0	6	.143	6	37	3	1	97	133	36	23	0	5.10
Danny Boitano	R	29	0	0	—	0	19	0	0	30	33	13	28	0	5.34
Jim Farr	R	26	0	0	—	1	18	0	0	20	7	6	0	0	2.50

MINNESOTA 7th 60-102 .370 33 — BILLY GARDNER

Name	G by Pos	B	AGE	G	AB	R	H	2B	3B	HR	RBI	BB	SO	SB	BA	SA
TOTALS			25	162	5544	657	1427	234	44	148	624	474	887	38	.257	.396
Kent Hrbek	1B138, DH2	L	22	140	532	82	160	21	4	23	92	54	80	3	.301	.485
John Castino	2B96, 3B21, OF6, DH1	R	22	117	410	48	99	12	6	6	37	36	51	2	.241	.344
Lenny Faedo	SS88, DH1	R	22	90	255	16	62	9	3	1	22	16	22	1	.243	.310
Gary Gaetti	3B142, SS2, DH1	R	23	145	508	59	117	25	4	25	84	37	107	0	.230	.443
Tom Brunansky	OF127	R	21	127	463	77	126	30	1	20	46	71	101	1	.272	.471
Bobby Mitchell	OF121	L	27	124	454	48	113	11	6	2	28	58	34	8	.249	.313
Gary Ward	OF150, DH2	R	28	152	570	85	165	33	7	28	91	37	105	13	.289	.519
Tim Laudner	C93	R	24	93	306	37	78	19	1	7	33	34	74	0	.255	.392
Randy Johnson	DH67, OF2	R	23	89	234	26	58	10	0	10	33	30	46	0	.248	.419
Ron Washington	SS91, 2B37, 3B1	R	30	119	451	48	122	17	6	5	39	14	79	3	.271	.368
Mickey Hatcher	OF47, DH29, 3B5	R	27	84	277	23	69	13	2	3	26	8	27	0	.249	.343
Jesus Vega	DH39, 1B18, OF1	R	26	71	199	23	53	6	0	5	29	8	19	6	.266	.372
Dave Engle	OF34, DH20	R	25	58	186	20	42	7	2	4	16	10	22	0	.226	.349
Randy Bush	DH26, OF6	L	23	55	119	13	29	6	1	4	13	8	28	0	.244	.412
Sal Butera	C29	R	29	54	126	9	32	6	0	0	8	17	12	0	.254	.270
Jim Eisenreich (IL)	OF30	L	23	34	99	10	30	6	0	2	9	11	13	0	.303	.424
2 Larry Milbourne	2B26	B	31	29	98	9	23	1	1	0	5	7	8	1	.235	.265
1 Rob Wilfong	2B22	L	29	25	81	7	13	1	0	0	5	7	13	0	.160	.173
1 Butch Wynegar	C24	B	26	24	86	9	18	4	0	0	8	10	12	0	.209	.291
Greg Wells	1B10, DH5	L	28	15	54	5	11	1	2	0	3	1	4	0	.204	.315
Ray Smith	C9	B	26	9	23	1	5	1	0	0	1	1	3	0	.217	.304
1 Roy Smalley	SS4	B	29	4	13	1	2	1	0	0	3	4	0	0	.154	.231

NAME	T	AGE	W	L	PCT	SV	G	GS	CG	IP	H	BB	SO	SHO	ERA
TOTALS		25	60	102	.370	30	162	162	26	1433	1484	643	812	7	4.72
Bobby Castillo	R	27	13	11	.542	0	40	25	6	219	194	85	123	1	3.66
Brad Havens	L	22	10	14	.417	0	33	32	4	209	201	80	129	1	4.31
Al Williams	R	28	9	7	.563	0	26	26	3	154	166	55	61	0	4.22
Jack O'Connor	L	24	8	9	.471	0	23	19	6	126	122	57	56	1	4.29
Pete Redfern (EJ)	R	27	5	11	.313	0	27	13	2	94	122	51	40	0	6.58
1 Roger Erickson	R	25	4	3	.571	0	7	7	2	41	56	12	12	0	4.87
Frank Viola	L	22	4	10	.286	0	22	22	3	126	152	38	84	1	5.21
Ron Davis	R	26	3	9	.250	22	63	0	0	106	106	47	89	0	4.42
Jeff Little	L	27	2	0	1.000	0	33	0	0	36	33	27	26	0	4.21
Paul Boris	R	26	1	2	.333	0	23	0	0	50	46	19	30	0	3.99
2 John Pacella	R	25	1	2	.333	2	21	1	0	52	61	37	20	0	7.32
1 Fernando Arroyo	R	30	1	0	—	0	4	0	0	14	17	6	4	0	5.27
Don Cooper	R	26	0	1	.000	0	11	0	0	14	11	5	9	0	9.53
1 Doug Corbett	R	29	0	2	.000	9	22	0	0	37	10	15	0	5.32	
Pete Filson	L	23	0	0	—	0	7	0	0	12	17	8	10	0	8.76
Darrell Jackson (SA)	R	26	0	5	.000	0	13	7	1	45	51	24	16	0	6.25
Terry Felton	R	24	0	13	.000	3	48	6	0	117	99	76	92	0	4.99

LINE SCORES

Team	1	2	3	4	5	6	7	8	9	10	11		R	H	E

AMERICAN LEAGUE CHAMPIONSHIPS: MILWAUKEE (EAST) 3   CALIFORNIA (WEST) 2

Game 1 October 5 at California

														R	H	E
MIL	0	2	1	0	0	0	0	0	0					3	7	2
CAL	1	0	4	2	1	0	0	0	X					8	10	0

Caldwell, Slaton (4),   John
Ladd (7), Bernard (8)

Game 2 October 6 at California

											R	H	E
MIL	0	0	0	0	2	0	0	0	0		2	5	0
CAL	0	2	1	1	0	0	0	X			4	6	0

Vuckovich   Kison

Game 3 October 8 at Milwaukee

											R	H	E
CAL	0	0	0	0	0	0	0	3	0		3	8	0
MIL	0	0	0	3	0	0	2	0	X		5	6	0

Zahn, Witt (4),   Sutton, Ladd (8)
Hassler (7)

Game 4 October 9 at Milwaukee

											R	H	E
CAL	0	0	0	0	0	1	0	4	0		5	5	3
MIL	0	3	0	3	0	1	0	2	X		9	9	2

John, Goltz (4),   Haas, Slaton (8)
Sanchez (8)

Game 5 October 10 at Milwaukee

											R	H	E
CAL	1	0	1	1	0	0	0	0	0		3	11	1
MIL	1	0	0	1	0	0	2	0	X		4	6	4

Kison, Sanchez (6),   Vuckovich, McClure (7)
Hassler (7)   Ladd (9)

NATIONAL LEAGUE CHAMPIONSHIPS: ST. LOUIS (EAST) 3   ATLANTA (WEST) 0

Game 1 October 7 at St. Louis

											R	H	E
ATL	0	0	0	0	0	0	0	0	0		1	13	0
STL	0	0	1	0	0	5	0	1	X		7	13	1

Perez, Bedrosian (6),   Forsch
Moore (6), Walk (8)

Game 2 October 9 at St. Louis

											R	H	E
ATL	0	0	2	0	1	0	0	0	0		3	6	0
STL	1	0	0	0	0	1	0	1	1		4	9	1

Niekro, Garber (7)   Stuper, Bair (7)
    Sutter (8)

Game 3 October 10 at Atlanta

											R	H	E
STL	0	4	0	0	0	1	0	0	1		6	12	0
ATL	0	0	0	0	0	0	2	0	0		2	6	1

Andujar, Sutter (7)   Camp, Perez (2)
    Moore (5), Mahler (7)
    Bedrosian (8), Garber (9)

WORLD SERIES — ST. LOUIS (NL) 4   MILWAUKEE (AL) 3

Game 1 October 12 at St. Louis

											R	H	E
MIL	2	0	0	1	1	2	0	0	4		10	17	0
STL	0	0	0	0	0	0	0	0	0		0	3	1

Caldwell   Forsch, Kaat (6)
    LaPoint (8), Lahti (9)

Game 2 October 13 at St. Louis

											R	H	E
MIL	0	1	2	0	1	0	0	0	0		4	10	1
STL	0	0	2	0	0	0	0	1	X		5	8	0

Sutton, McClure (7),   Stuper, Kaat (5), Bair (5)
Ladd (8)   Sutter (7)

Game 3 October 15 at Milwaukee

											R	H	E
STL	0	0	0	0	3	0	2	0	1		6	6	1
MIL	0	0	0	0	0	0	0	2	0		2	5	3

Andujar, Kaat (7)   Vuckovich, McClure (9)
Bair (7), Sutter (7)

Game 4 October 16 at Milwaukee

											R	H	E
STL	1	3	0	0	0	1	0	0	0		5	8	1
MIL	0	0	0	0	0	1	0	6	X		7	10	0

LaPoint, Bair (7),   Haas, Slaton (6),
Kaat (7), Lahti (7)   McClure (8)

Game 5 October 17 at Milwaukee

											R	H	E
STL	0	0	1	0	0	0	1	0	2		4	15	2
MIL	1	0	1	0	0	0	1	2	X		6	11	1

Forsch, Sutter (8)   Caldwell, McClure (9)

Game 6 October 19 at St. Louis

											R	H	E
MIL	0	0	0	0	0	0	0	1	0		1	4	4
STL	0	2	0	3	0	2	6	0	0		13	12	1

Sutton, Slaton (5)   Stuper
Medich (6), Bernard (8)

Game 7 October 20 at St. Louis

											R	H	E
MIL	0	0	0	0	1	2	0	0	0		3	7	0
STL	0	0	0	1	0	3	0	2	X		6	15	1

Vuckovich, McClure (6),   Andujar, Sutter (8)
Haas (6), Caldwell (8)

COMPOSITE BATTING

Milwaukee

NAME	POS	G	AB	R	H	2B	3B	HR	RBI	BA
TOTALS		5	151	23	33	4	0	5	20	.219
Cooper	1B	5	20	1	3	2	0	0	4	.150
Molitor	3B	5	19	4	6	1	0	2	5	.316
Simmons	C	5	18	3	3	0	0	1	1	.167
Yount	SS	5	16	1	4	0	0	0	0	.250
Gantner	2B	5	16	1	3	0	0	0	0	.188
Oglivie	LF	4	15	1	2	0	0	1	1	.133
Thomas	CF	5	15	1	1	0	0	1	3	.067
Moore	RF	5	13	3	6	0	0	0	0	.462
Money	DH	4	11	2	2	0	0	0	0	.182
Brouhard	LF	1	4	4	3	1	0	1	3	.750
Howell	DH	1	3	0	0	0	0	0	0	.000
Edwards	CF-DH-PR	3	1	2	0	0	0	0	0	.000

California

NAME	POS	G	AB	R	H	2B	3B	HR	RBI	BA
TOTALS		5	157	23	40	8	1	4	23	.255
DeCinces	3B	5	19	5	6	2	0	0	0	.316
Downing	LF	5	19	4	3	1	0	0	0	.158
Lynn	CF	5	18	4	11	2	0	1	5	.611
Re. Jackson	RF	5	18	2	2	0	0	1	2	.111
Baylor	DH	5	17	2	5	1	1	1	10	.294
Carew	1B	5	17	2	3	1	0	0	0	.176
Boone	C	5	16	3	4	0	0	1	4	.250
Foli	SS	5	16	0	2	0	0	0	1	.125
Grich	2B	5	15	1	3	1	0	0	1	.200
Ro. Jackson	PH	1	1	0	1	0	0	0	0	1.000
Wilfong	DH-PR	2	1	0	0	0	0	0	0	.000
Beniquez	LF	2	0	0	0	0	0	0	0	—
Clark	RF	2	0	0	0	0	0	0	0	—

St. Louis

NAME	POS	G	AB	R	H	2B	3B	HR	RBI	BA
TOTALS		3	103	17	34	4	2	1	16	.330
Oberkfell	3B	3	15	1	3	0	0	0	2	.200
McGee	CF	3	13	4	4	0	2	1	5	.308
Hendrick	RF	3	13	2	4	0	0	0	2	.308
Herr	2B	3	13	1	3	1	0	0	1	.231
Hernandez	1B	3	12	3	4	0	0	0	1	.333
L. Smith	LF	3	11	1	3	0	0	0	1	.273
O. Smith	SS	3	9	5	5	0	0	0	3	.556
Porter	C	3	9	3	5	3	0	0	1	.556
Forsch	P	1	3	1	2	0	0	0	1	.667
Green	LF	2	1	1	1	0	0	0	0	1.000
Braun	PH	1	1	0	0	0	0	0	0	.000
Andujar	P	1	1	0	0	0	0	0	0	.000

Stuper P 0-1, Sutter P 0-1, Bair P 0-0

Atlanta

NAME	POS	G	AB	R	H	2B	3B	HR	RBI	BA
TOTALS		3	89	5	15	1	0	0	3	.169
Murphy	CF-LF	3	11	1	3	0	0	0	0	.273
Ramirez	SS	3	11	1	2	0	0	0	1	.182
Royster	LF-3B	3	11	0	2	0	0	0	0	.182
Horner	3B	3	11	0	1	0	0	0	0	.091
Chambliss	1B	3	10	0	0	0	0	0	0	.000
Washington	RF	3	9	0	3	0	0	0	0	.333
Hubbard	2B	3	9	1	2	0	0	0	1	.222
Benedict	C	3	8	1	2	1	0	0	1	.250
Perez	P	2	3	0	0	0	0	0	0	.000
Whisenton	PH	2	2	0	0	0	0	0	0	.000
Harper	RF-PR	1	1	1	0	0	0	0	0	.000
Butler	CF-PH	2	1	0	0	0	0	0	0	.000
Pocoroba	PH	1	1	0	0	0	0	0	0	.000
Garber	P	2	1	0	0	0	0	0	0	.000
Bedrosian	P	2	0	0	0	0	0	0	0	—
Moore	P	1	0	0	0	0	0	0	0	—

Camp P 0-0, Mahler P 0-0, Niekro P 0-0, Walk P 0-0

St. Louis

NAME	POS	G	AB	R	H	2B	3B	HR	RBI	BA
TOTALS		7	245	39	67	16	3	4	34	.273
Hendrick	RF	7	28	5	9	0	0	0	5	.321
L. Smith	LF-DH	7	28	6	9	4	1	0	1	.321
Porter	C	7	28	1	8	2	0	1	5	.286
Hernandez	1B	7	27	4	7	2	0	1	8	.259
McGee	CF	6	25	6	6	0	0	2	5	.240
Herr	2B	7	25	2	4	2	0	0	5	.160
Oberkfell	3B	7	24	4	7	1	0	0	1	.292
O. Smith	SS	7	24	3	5	0	0	0	1	.208
Iorg	DH	5	17	4	9	4	1	0	1	.529
Green	CF-LF-PH-PR	7	10	3	2	1	1	0	0	.200
Tenace	DH-PH	5	6	0	0	0	0	0	0	.000
Braun	DH-PH	2	2	0	1	0	0	0	2	.500
Ramsey	3B-PH	3	1	1	0	0	0	0	0	.000
Brummer	C	1	0	0	0	0	0	0	0	.000

Milwaukee

NAME	POS	G	AB	R	H	2B	3B	HR	RBI	BA
TOTALS		7	238	33	64	12	2	5	28	.269
Molitor	3B	7	31	5	11	0	0	0	2	.355
Yount	SS	7	29	6	12	3	0	1	6	.414
Cooper	1B	7	28	3	8	1	0	1	6	.286
Oglivie	LF	7	27	4	6	0	1	1	2	.222
Moore	RF	7	26	3	9	3	0	0	2	.346
Thomas	CF	7	26	3	0	0	0	0	3	.115
Gantner	2B	7	24	5	8	4	1	0	4	.333
Simmons	C	7	23	2	4	0	0	2	3	.174
Money	DH	5	13	4	3	1	0	0	1	.231
Howell	DH	4	11	0	0	0	0	0	0	.000
Edwards	CF	1	0	0	0	0	0	0	0	—
Yost	C	1	0	0	0	0	0	0	0	—

COMPOSITE PITCHING

Milwaukee

NAME	G	IP	H	BB	SO	W	L	SV	ERA
TOTALS	5	43	40	16	34	3	2	3	4.19
Vuckovich	2	14.1	15	7	8	0	1	0	4.40
Sutton	1	7.2	8	2	9	1	0	0	3.52
Haas	1	7.1	5	5	7	1	0	0	4.91
Slaton	2	4.2	3	1	3	0	0	0	1.93
Ladd	3	3.1	0	0	5	0	0	2	0.00
Caldwell	1	3	7	1	2	0	1	0	15.00
McClure	1	1.2	2	0	0	1	0	0	0.00
Bernard	1	1	0	0	0	0	0	0	0.00

California

NAME	G	IP	H	BB	SO	W	L	SV	ERA
TOTALS	5	42	33	15	28	2	3	0	4.29
Kison	2	14	8	3	12	1	0	0	1.93
John	2	12.1	11	6	6	1	1	0	5.11
Goltz	1	3.2	4	2	2	0	0	0	7.36
Zahn	1	3.2	4	1	2	0	1	0	7.36
Witt	1	3	2	3	3	0	0	0	6.00
Hassler	2	2.2	0	0	2	0	0	0	0.00
Sanchez	2	2.2	4	1	1	0	1	0	6.75

St. Louis

NAME	G	IP	H	BB	SO	W	L	SV	ERA
TOTALS	3	27	15	6	15	3	0	1	1.33
Forsch	1	9	3	0	6	1	0	0	0.00
Andujar	1	6.2	6	2	4	1	0	0	2.70
Stuper	1	6	4	1	4	0	0	0	3.00
Sutter	2	4.1	0	0	1	1	0	1	0.00
Bair	1	1	2	3	0	0	0	0	0.00

Atlanta

NAME	G	IP	H	BB	SO	W	L	SV	ERA
TOTALS	3	25.1	34	12	16	0	3	0	6.04
Perez	2	8.2	10	2	4	0	1	0	5.19
Niekro	1	6	6	4	5	0	0	0	3.00
Garber	2	3.1	4	1	3	0	1	0	8.10
Moore	2	2.2	2	0	1	0	0	0	0.00
Mahler	1	1.2	3	2	0	0	0	0	9.00
Walk	1	1	2	1	1	0	0	0	9.00
Bedrosian	2	1	3	1	2	0	0	0	18.00
Camp	1	1	4	1	0	0	1	0	36.00

St. Louis

NAME	G	IP	H	BB	SO	W	L	SV	ERA
TOTALS	7	61	64	19	28	4	3	2	3.39
Andujar	2	13.1	10	1	4	2	0	0	1.35
Stuper	2	13	10	5	5	1	0	0	3.46
Forsch	2	12.2	18	3	4	0	2	0	4.97
LaPoint	2	8.1	10	2	3	0	0	0	3.24
Sutter	4	7.2	6	3	6	1	0	2	4.70
Kaat	4	2.1	4	2	2	0	0	0	3.86
Bair	3	2	4	2	3	0	1	0	9.00
Lahti	2	1.2	4	1	1	0	0	0	10.80

Milwaukee

NAME	G	IP	H	BB	SO	W	L	SV	ERA
TOTALS	7	60	67	20	26	3	4	2	4.80
Caldwell	3	17.2	19	3	6	2	0	0	2.04
Vuckovich	2	14.1	16	5	4	0	1	0	4.50
Sutton	2	10.1	12	1	5	0	1	0	7.84
Haas	2	7.1	8	3	4	0	0	0	7.36
McClure	5	4.1	5	3	5	0	2	2	4.15
Slaton	2	2.2	1	2	1	1	0	0	0.00
Medich	1	2	4	0	1	0	0	0	18.00
Bernard	1	1	0	1	0	0	0	0	0.00
Ladd	1	1	2	1	0	0	0	0	0.00

ST. LOUIS   1st 92-70 .568   WHITEY HERZOG

Name	G by Pos	B	AGE	G	AB	R	H	2B	3B	HR	RBI	BB	SO	SB	BA	SA
TOTALS			27	162	5455	685	1439	239	52	67	632	569	805	200	.264	.364
Keith Hernandez	1B158, OF4	L	28	160	579	79	173	33	6	7	94	100	67	19	.299	.413
Tommy Herr	2B128	B	26	135	493	83	131	19	4	0	36	57	56	25	.266	.320
Ozzie Smith	SS139	B	27	140	488	58	121	24	1	2	43	68	32	25	.248	.314
Ken Oberkfell	3B135, 2B1	L	26	137	470	55	136	22	5	2	34	40	31	11	.289	.370
George Hendrick	OF134	R	32	136	515	65	145	20	5	19	104	37	80	3	.282	.450
Willie McGee	OF117	B	23	123	422	43	125	12	8	4	56	12	58	24	.296	.391
Lonnie Smith	OF149	R	26	156	592	120	182	35	8	8	69	64	74	68	.307	.434
Darrell Porter	C111	L	30	120	373	46	86	18	5	12	48	66	66	1	.231	.402
Mike Ramsey	2B43, 3B28, SS22, OF2	B	28	112	256	18	59	8	2	1	21	22	34	6	.230	.289
Dane Iorg	OF63, 1B10, 3B2	L	32	102	238	17	70	14	1	0	34	23	23	0	.294	.361
Tito Landrum	OF56	R	27	79	72	12	20	3	0	2	14	8	18	0	.278	.403
David Green	OF68	R	21	76	166	21	47	7	1	2	23	8	29	11	.283	.373
Gene Tenace (BH)	C37, 1B7	R	35	66	124	18	32	9	0	7	18	36	31	1	.258	.500
Steve Braun	OF8, 3B5	L	34	58	62	6	17	4	0	0	4	11	10	0	.274	.339
Julio Gonzalez	3B21, 2B9, SS1	R	29	42	87	9	21	3	2	1	7	1	24	1	.241	.356
Glenn Brummer	C32	R	27	35	64	4	15	4	0	0	8	0	12	2	.234	.297
Orlando Sanchez	C15	L	25	26	37	6	7	0	1	0	3	5	5	0	.189	.243
Kelly Paris	3B5, SS4	B	24	12	29	1	3	0	0	0	1	1	9	0	.103	.103
Gene Roof	OF5	B	24	11	15	3	4	0	0	0	2	1	4	2	.267	.267

NAME	T	AGE	W	L	PCT	SV	G	GS	CG	IP	H	BB	SO	SHO	ERA
		29	92	70	.568	47	162	162	25	1465	1420	502	689	10	3.37
Bob Forsch	R	32	15	9	.625	1	36	34	6	233	238	54	69	2	3.48
Joaquin Andujar	R	29	15	10	.600	0	38	37	9	266	237	50	137	5	2.47
Steve Mura	R	27	12	11	.522	0	35	30	7	184	196	80	84	1	4.05
Dave LaPoint	L	22	9	3	.750	0	42	21	0	153	170	52	81	0	3.42
John Stuper	R	25	9	7	.563	0	23	21	2	137	137	55	53	0	3.36
Bruce Sutter	R	29	9	8	.529	36	70	0	0	102	88	34	61	0	2.90
Doug Bair	R	32	5	3	.625	8	63	0	0	92	69	36	68	0	2.55
Jim Kaat	L	43	5	3	.625	2	62	2	0	75	79	23	35	0	4.08
Jeff Lahti	R	25	5	4	.556	0	33	1	0	57	53	21	22	0	3.81
John Martin	L	26	4	5	.444	0	24	7	0	66	56	30	21	0	4.23
Andy Rincon	R	23	2	3	.400	0	11	6	1	40	35	25	11	0	4.73
Jeff Keener	R	23	1	1	.500	1	9	0	0	22	19	19	25	0	1.61
Eric Rasmussen	R	30	1	2	.333	0	8	3	0	18	21	8	15	0	4.42
Mark Littell	R	29	0	0	.000	1	16	0	0	21	22	15	7	0	5.23

PHILADELPHIA   2nd 89-73 .549 3   PAT CORRALES

Name	G by Pos	B	AGE	G	AB	R	H	2B	3B	HR	RBI	BB	SO	SB	BA	SA
TOTALS			31	162	5454	664	1417	245	25	112	624	506	831	128	.260	.376
Pete Rose	1B162	B	41	162	634	80	172	25	4	3	54	66	32	8	.271	.338
Manny Trillo	2B149	R	31	149	549	52	149	24	1	0	39	33	53	8	.271	.319
Ivan DeJesus	SS154, 3B7	R	29	161	536	53	128	21	5	3	59	54	70	14	.239	.313
Mike Schmidt	3B148	R	32	148	514	108	144	26	3	35	87	107	131	14	.280	.547
George Vukovich	OF102	L	26	123	335	41	91	18	2	6	42	32	47	2	.272	.391
Garry Maddox	OF111	R	32	119	412	39	117	27	2	8	61	12	32	7	.284	.417
Gary Matthews	OF162	R	31	162	616	89	173	31	4	19	83	66	87	21	.281	.427
Bo Diaz	C144	R	29	144	525	69	151	29	1	18	85	36	87	3	.288	.450
Bob Dernier	OF119	R	25	122	370	56	92	10	2	4	21	36	69	42	.249	.319
Greg Gross	OF71	L	29	119	134	14	40	4	0	0	10	19	8	4	.299	.328
Luis Aguayo	2B21, SS15, 3B5	R	23	50	56	11	15	1	2	3	7	5	7	1	.268	.518
Ozzie Virgil	C35	R	25	49	101	11	24	6	0	3	8	10	26	0	.238	.386
2 Bill Robinson	OF19, 1B5	R	39	35	69	6	18	6	0	3	19	7	15	1	.261	.478
1 Dick Davis	OF16	R	28	28	68	5	19	3	1	2	9	2	9	1	.279	.441
Dave Roberts	3B11, CO, 2B7	R	31	28	33	2	6	1	0	0	2	2	8	0	.182	.212
Len Matuszek	3B8, 1B3	L	27	25	39	1	3	1	0	0	3	1	10	0	.077	.103
2 Bob Molinaro		L	32	19	14	4	4	0	0	0	2	3	1	1	.286	.286
Del Unser	1B5, OF2	L	37	19	14	0	0	0	0	0	0	3	2	0	.000	.000
2 Willie Montanez	1B6	L	34	18	16	0	1	0	0	0	1	1	3	0	.063	.063
Julio Franco	SS11, 3B2	R	23	16	29	3	8	1	0	0	3	2	4	0	.276	.310
Alex Sanchez	OF4	R	23	7	14	3	4	1	0	2	4	0	4	0	.286	.786

NAME	T	AGE	W	L	PCT	SV	G	GS	CG	IP	H	BB	SO	SHO	ERA
		32	89	73	.549	33	162	162	38	1456	1395	472	1002	13	3.61
Steve Carlton	L	37	23	11	.676	0	38	38	19	296	253	86	286	6	3.10
Mike Krukow	R	30	13	11	.542	0	33	33	7	208	211	82	138	2	3.12
Dick Ruthven	R	31	11	11	.500	0	33	31	8	204	189	59	115	2	3.79
Larry Christenson	R	28	9	10	.474	0	33	33	3	223	212	53	145	0	3.47
Sid Monge	L	31	7	1	.875	2	47	0	0	72	70	22	43	0	3.75
Porfi Altamirano	R	30	5	1	.833	2	29	0	0	39	41	14	26	0	4.15
Ron Reed	R	39	5	5	.500	14	57	2	0	98	85	24	57	0	2.66
Marty Bystrom (SJ)	R	23	5	6	.455	0	19	16	1	89	93	35	50	0	4.85
Tug McGraw (EJ)	L	37	3	3	.500	5	34	0	0	40	50	12	25	0	4.31
1 Sparky Lyle	L	37	3	3	.500	2	34	0	0	37	50	12	12	0	5.15
1 Warren Brusstar	R	30	2	3	.400	2	22	0	0	23	31	5	11	0	4.76
Ed Farmer	R	32	2	6	.250	6	47	4	0	76	66	50	58	0	4.86
1 Jerry Reed	R	26	1	0	1.000	0	9	1	1	9	11	3	1	0	5.19
2 Stan Bahnsen	R	37	0	0	—	0	8	0	0	13	8	3	9	0	1.35
Jay Baller	R	21	0	0	—	0	8	7	2	7	6	7	2	0	3.38
2 John Denny	R	29	0	2	.000	0	4	4	0	22	18	10	19	0	4.03

MONTREAL   3rd 86-76 .531 6   JIM FANNING

Name	G by Pos	B	AGE	G	AB	R	H	2B	3B	HR	RBI	BB	SO	SB	BA	SA
TOTALS			28	162	5557	697	1454	270	38	133	656	503	816	156	.262	.396
Al Oliver	1B159	L	35	160	617	90	204	43	2	22	109	61	59	5	.331	.514
2 Doug Flynn	2B58	R	31	58	193	14	47	6	2	0	20	4	23	0	.244	.295
Chris Speier	SS155	R	32	156	530	41	136	26	4	7	60	47	67	1	.257	.360
Tim Wallach	3B156, OF2, 1B1	R	24	158	596	89	160	31	3	28	97	36	81	6	.268	.471
Warren Cromartie	OF136, 1B9	L	28	144	497	59	126	24	4	14	62	69	60	3	.254	.398
Andre Dawson	OF147	R	27	148	608	107	183	37	7	23	83	34	96	39	.301	.498
Tim Raines	OF120, 2B14	B	22	156	647	90	179	32	8	4	43	75	83	78	.277	.369
Gary Carter	C153	R	28	154	557	91	163	32	1	29	97	78	64	2	.293	.510
Jerry White	OF30	R	29	69	115	13	28	6	1	2	13	8	26	3	.243	.365
Brad Mills	3B13	L	25	54	67	6	15	3	0	1	2	5	11	0	.224	.313
Dan Norman	OF31	R	27	53	66	6	14	3	0	2	7	2	20	0	.212	.348
Frank Taveras	SS26, 2B19	R	32	48	87	9	14	5	1	0	4	7	6	4	.161	.241
Terry Francona (KJ)	OF33, 1B16	L	23	46	131	14	42	3	0	0	9	8	11	2	.321	.344
2 Joel Youngblood	OF35	R	30	40	90	16	18	2	0	0	8	9	21	2	.200	.222
Mike Gates	2B36	B	22	35	121	16	28	2	3	0	9	9	19	0	.231	.298
Wallace Johnson	2B16, SS10	B	25	35	57	5	11	0	2	0	3	5	5	4	.193	.263
Bryan Little	1B5	B	22	29	42	6	9	0	0	0	3	4	6	2	.214	.214
1 John Milner	1B5	L	32	26	28	1	3	0	0	0	1	5	6	0	.107	.107
Tim Blackwell	C18	R	29	23	42	2	8	2	1	0	3	3	11	0	.190	.286
Roy Johnson	OF11	R	23	17	32	2	7	2	0	0	1	6	10	0	.219	.281
1 Rodney Scott	2B12	B	28	14	25	2	5	0	0	0	1	3	2	5	.200	.200
Mike Phillips	2B10, SS2	L	31	14	8	0	1	0	0	0	1	0	3	0	.125	.125
Ken Phelps		L	27	10	8	0	2	0	0	0	0	1	1	0	.250	.250
Brad Gulden	C2	L	26	5	6	1	0	0	0	0	0	0	1	1	.000	.000
Rowland Office	OF1	L	29	3	3	0	1	1	0	0	0	0	1	0	.333	.667
Chris Smith		B	24	3	2	0	0	0	0	0	0	0	0	0	.000	.000
Mike Stenhouse		L	24	1	1	0	0	0	0	0	0	0	1	0	.000	.000

NAME	T	AGE	W	L	PCT	SV	G	GS	CG	IP	H	BB	SO	SHO	ERA
		29	86	76	.531	43	162	162	34	1461	1371	448	936	10	3.31
Steve Rogers	R	32	19	8	.704	0	35	35	14	277	245	65	179	4	2.40
Charlie Lea	R	25	12	10	.545	0	27	27	4	178	145	56	115	2	3.24
Scott Sanderson	R	25	12	12	.500	0	32	32	7	224	212	58	158	0	3.46
Bill Gullickson	R	23	12	14	.462	0	34	34	6	237	231	61	155	0	3.57
Woody Fryman	L	42	9	4	.692	12	60	0	0	70	66	26	46	0	3.75
Jeff Reardon	R	26	7	4	.636	26	75	0	0	109	87	36	86	0	2.06
David Palmer (EJ)	R	24	6	4	.600	0	13	13	1	74	60	36	46	0	3.18
Ray Burris	R	31	4	14	.222	2	37	15	2	124	143	53	55	0	4.73
2 Randy Lerch	L	27	2	0	1.000	0	6	4	0	24	26	8	4	0	3.42
Bryn Smith	R	26	2	4	.333	1	47	1	0	79	81	23	50	0	4.20
1 Tom Gorman	L	24	1	0	1.000	0	5	0	0	7	8	4	5	0	5.14
Bill Lee	L	35	0	0	—	0	7	0	0	12	19	1	8	0	4.38
1 Bob James	R	23	0	0	—	0	7	0	0	9	11	8	11	0	6.00
Dave Tomlin	L	33	0	0	—	0	2	0	0	2	1	1	3	0	4.50
2 Dan Schatzeder	L	27	0	2	.000	0	26	1	0	36	37	12	15	0	3.50

PITTSBURGH   4th 84-78 .519 8   CHUCK TANNER

Name	G by Pos	B	AGE	G	AB	R	H	2B	3B	HR	RBI	BB	SO	SB	BA	SA
TOTALS			29	162	5614	724	1535	272	40	134	688	447	862	161	.273	.408
Jason Thompson	1B155	L	27	156	550	87	156	32	0	31	101	101	107	1	.284	.511
Johnny Ray	2B162	B	25	162	647	79	182	30	7	7	63	36	34	6	.281	.382
Dale Berra	SS153, 3B6	R	25	156	529	64	139	25	5	10	61	33	83	6	.263	.382
Bill Madlock	3B146, 1B3	R	31	154	568	92	181	33	3	19	95	48	39	18	.319	.488
Dave Parker (WJ-RJ)	OF63	L	31	73	244	41	66	19	3	6	29	22	45	7	.270	.447
Omar Moreno	OF157	L	29	158	645	82	158	18	9	3	44	44	121	60	.245	.315
Mike Easler	OF138	L	31	142	475	63	132	27	2	15	58	40	85	1	.276	.436
Tony Pena	C137	R	25	138	497	53	147	28	4	11	63	17	57	2	.296	.435
Lee Lacy	OF113, 3B2	R	34	121	359	66	112	18	3	5	31	32	57	40	.312	.415
Willie Stargell	1B8	L	42	74	73	6	17	4	0	3	17	10	24	0	.233	.411
2 Jim Morrison	3B26, OF2, 2B1, SS1	R	29	44	86	10	24	4	1	4	15	5	14	2	.279	.488
Jimmy Smith	SS29, 2B3, 3B1	R	27	42	42	5	10	2	1	0	4	5	7	2	.238	.333
Steve Nicosia	C35, OF3	R	26	39	100	6	28	3	0	1	7	11	13	0	.280	.340
3 Dick Davis	OF28	R	28	39	77	7	14	2	1	2	10	5	9	1	.182	.312
1 Willie Montanez	1B2, OF2	L	34	36	32	4	9	1	0	1	3	3	3	0	.281	.313
2 John Milner	1B1	L	32	33	25	5	6	2	0	2	8	6	9	0	.240	.560
1 Bill Robinson	OF22	R	39	31	71	8	17	3	0	4	12	5	19	0	.239	.451
2 Richie Hebner	OF21, 1B4, 3B1	L	34	25	70	6	21	2	0	2	12	5	3	4	.300	.414
Brian Harper	OF8	R	22	20	29	4	8	1	0	2	4	1	4	0	.276	.517
Doug Frobel	OF12	L	23	16	34	5	7	2	0	2	3	1	11	1	.206	.441
Reggie Walton	OF2	R	29	13	15	1	3	1	1	0	1	2	6	0	.200	.267
Rafael Belliard	SS4	R	20	9	2	3	1	0	0	0	1	1	0	1	.500	.500
Hedi Vargas	1B5	R	23	8	16	1	6	1	0	1	6	0	3	0	.375	.500
Junior Ortiz	C7	R	22	7	15	1	3	0	0	0	1	1	1	0	.200	.267
Ken Reitz	3B4	R	31	7	10	0	0	0	0	0	0	1	1	0	.000	.000
Nelson Norman	2B2, SS1	B	24	3	3	0	0	0	0	0	0	0	1	0	.000	.000
2 Wayne Nordhagen	OF1	R	33	1	4	0	2	1	0	0	0	0	0	0	.500	.500

NAME	T	AGE	W	L	PCT	SV	G	GS	CG	IP	H	BB	SO	SHO	ERA
		29	84	78	.519	39	162	162	19	1467	1434	521	933	7	3.81
Don Robinson	R	25	15	13	.536	0	38	30	6	227	213	103	165	0	4.28
John Candelaria	L	28	12	7	.632	0	31	30	1	175	166	37	133	1	2.94
Kent Tekulve	R	35	12	8	.600	20	85	0	0	129	113	46	66	0	2.87
Rick Rhoden	R	29	11	14	.440	0	35	35	6	230	239	70	128	1	4.14
Enrique Romo	R	34	9	3	.750	1	45	0	0	87	81	36	58	0	4.36
Manny Sarmiento	R	26	9	4	.692	1	35	17	4	165	153	46	81	0	3.11
2 Larry McWilliams	L	28	6	5	.545	1	19	18	2	122	106	24	94	2	3.11
Rod Scurry	L	26	4	5	.444	14	76	0	0	104	79	64	94	0	1.74
1 Eddie Solomon	R	31	2	6	.250	0	11	10	0	47	69	18	18	0	6.75
Randy Niemann	L	26	1	1	.500	1	20	0	0	35	34	17	26	0	5.09
Lee Tunnell	R	21	1	0	1.000	0	5	3	0	18	17	5	4	0	3.93
Paul Moskau (SJ)	R	28	1	0	1.000	0	13	5	0	35	43	8	15	0	4.37
Tom Griffin	R	34	1	3	.250	0	6	4	0	32	32	15	8	0	8.87
Cecilio Guante	R	22	0	0	—	0	10	0	0	27	28	5	26	0	3.33
2 Grant Jackson	L	39	0	0	—	0	7	0	0	1	0	0	1	0	13.50
Ross Baumgarten(BG-SJ)	L	27	0	5	.000	0	12	10	0	44	60	27	17	0	6.55
Jim Bibby 37 (SJ)															

CHICAGO — 5th 73-89 .451 19 — LEE ELIA

Name	G by Pos	B	AGE	G	AB	R	H	2B	3B	HR	RBI	BB	SO	SB	BA	SA
TOTALS			29	162	5531	676	1436	239	46	102	647	460	869	132	.260	.375
Bill Buckner	1B161	L	32	161	657	93	201	34	5	15	105	36	26	15	.306	.441
Bump Wills	2B103	B	29	128	419	64	114	18	4	6	38	46	76	35	.272	.377
Larry Bowa	SS140	B	36	142	499	50	123	15	7	0	29	39	38	8	.246	.305
Ryne Sandberg	3B133, 2B24	R	22	156	635	103	172	33	5	7	54	36	90	32	.271	.372
2 Jay Johnstone	OF86	L	36	98	269	39	67	13	1	10	43	40	41	0	.249	.416
Leon Durham	OF143, 1B1	L	24	148	539	84	168	33	7	22	90	66	77	28	.312	.512
Keith Moreland	OF86, C44, 3B24	R	28	138	476	50	124	17	2	15	68	46	71	0	.261	.399
Jody Davis	C129	R	25	130	418	41	109	20	2	12	52	36	92	0	.261	.404
Gary Woods	OF103	R	27	117	245	28	66	15	1	4	30	21	48	3	.269	.388
Junior Kennedy	2B71, SS28, 3B7	R	31	105	242	22	53	3	1	2	25	21	34	1	.219	.264
Steve Henderson	OF70	R	29	92	257	23	60	12	4	2	29	22	64	6	.233	.335
Jerry Morales (KJ)	OF41	R	33	65	116	14	33	2	2	4	30	9	7	1	.284	.440
1 Bob Molinaro	OF4	L	32	65	66	6	13	1	0	1	12	6	5	1	.197	.258
Scot Thompson (BC)	OF23, 1B4	L	26	49	74	11	27	5	1	0	7	5	4	0	.365	.459
Dan Briggs (JL)	OF10, 1B4	L	29	48	48	1	6	0	0	0	1	0	9	0	.125	.125
Pat Tabler	3B25	R	24	25	85	9	20	4	2	1	7	6	20	0	.235	.365
Mel Hall	OF22	L	21	24	80	6	21	3	2	0	4	1	17	0	.263	.350
Ty Waller	OF7, 3B1	R	25	17	21	4	5	0	0	0	1	2	5	0	.238	.238
Heity Cruz	OF4	R	29	17	19	1	4	1	0	0	0	2	4	0	.211	.263
Scott Fletcher	SS11	R	23	11	24	4	4	0	0	0	1	4	5	1	.167	.167
Butch Benton	C4	R	24	4	7	0	1	0	0	0	0	0	1	0	.143	.143
Larry Cox	C2	R	34	2	4	1	0	0	0	0	0	1	2	1	.000	.000

NAME	T	AGE	W	L	PCT	SV	G	GS	CG	IP	H	BB	SO	SHO	ERA
		30	73	89	.451	43	162	162	9	1447	1510	452	764	7	3.92
Ferguson Jenkins	R	38	14	15	.483	0	34	34	4	217	221	68	134	1	3.15
Randy Martz (SJ)	R	26	11	10	.524	1	28	24	1	148	157	36	40	0	4.21
Dickie Noles	R	25	10	13	.435	0	31	30	2	171	180	61	85	2	4.42
Doug Bird	R	32	9	14	.391	0	35	33	2	191	230	30	71	1	5.14
Dick Tidrow	R	35	8	3	.727	6	65	0	0	104	106	29	62	0	3.39
Mike Proly	R	31	5	3	.625	1	44	1	0	82	77	22	24	0	2.30
Allen Ripley	R	29	5	7	.417	0	28	19	0	123	130	38	57	0	4.26
Willie Hernandez	L	27	4	6	.400	10	75	0	0	75	74	24	54	0	3.00
Bill Campbell	R	33	3	6	.333	8	62	0	0	100	89	40	71	0	3.69
Lee Smith	R	24	2	5	.286	17	72	5	0	117	105	37	99	0	2.69
Ken Kravec	R	30	1	1	.500	0	13	2	0	25	27	18	20	0	6.12
Tom Filer	R	25	1	2	.333	0	8	8	0	41	50	18	15	0	5.53
Randy Stein	R	29	0	0	—	0	6	0	0	10	7	7	6	0	3.48
Herman Segelke	R	24	0	0	—	0	3	0	0	4	6	6	4	0	8.31
Dan Larson	R	27	0	4	.000	0	12	6	0	40	51	18	22	0	5.67

NEW YORK — 6th 65-97 .401 27 — GEORGE BAMBERGER

Name	G by Pos	B	AGE	G	AB	R	H	2B	3B	HR	RBI	BB	SO	SB	BA	SA
TOTALS			29	162	5510	609	1361	227	26	97	568	456	1005	137	.247	.350
Dave Kingman	1B143	R	33	149	535	80	109	9	1	37	99	59	156	4	.204	.432
Wally Backman (BL)	2B88, 3B6, SS1	B	22	96	261	37	71	13	2	3	22	49	47	8	.272	.372
Ron Gardenhire	SS135, 2B1, 3B1	R	24	141	384	29	92	17	1	3	33	23	55	5	.240	.313
Hubie Brooks	3B126	R	25	126	457	40	114	21	2	2	40	28	76	6	.249	.317
Ellis Valentine	OF98	R	27	111	337	33	97	14	1	8	48	5	38	1	.288	.407
Mookie Wilson	OF156	B	26	159	639	90	178	25	9	5	55	32	102	58	.279	.369
George Foster	OF138	R	33	151	550	64	136	23	2	13	70	50	123	1	.247	.367
John Stearns (EJ)	C81, 3B12	R	30	98	352	46	103	25	3	4	28	30	35	17	.293	.415
Mike Jorgensen	1B56, OF16	L	33	120	114	16	29	6	0	2	14	21	24	2	.254	.360
Rusty Staub	OF27, 1B18	L	38	112	219	11	53	9	0	3	27	24	10	0	.242	.324
Bob Bailor	SS60, 2B56, 3B21, OF4	R	31	110	376	44	104	14	1	0	31	20	17	20	.277	.319
Ron Hodges	C74	L	33	80	228	26	56	12	1	5	27	41	40	4	.246	.373
1 Joel Youngblood	OF63, 2B8, 3B1, SS1	R	30	80	202	21	52	12	0	3	21	8	37	1	.257	.361
Gary Rajsich	OF35, 1B2	L	27	80	162	17	42	8	3	2	12	17	40	1	.259	.383
Brian Giles	2B45, SS2	R	22	45	138	14	29	5	0	3	10	12	29	6	.210	.312
Tom Veryzer (LJ)	2B26, SS16	R	29	40	54	6	18	2	0	0	4	3	4	1	.333	.370
Mike Howard	OF22, 2B3	R	24	33	39	5	7	0	0	1	3	6	7	2	.179	.256
Bruce Bochy	C16, 1B1	R	27	17	49	4	15	4	0	2	8	4	6	0	.306	.510
Phil Mankowski	3B13	L	29	13	35	2	8	1	0	0	4	1	6	0	.229	.257
Rusty Tillman	OF3	R	21	12	13	4	2	1	0	0	0	0	4	1	.154	.231
1 Rick Sweet		B	29	3	3	0	1	0	0	0	0	0	1	0	.333	.333
Ronn Reynolds	C2	R	23	2	4	0	0	0	0	0	0	0	1	1	.000	.000

NAME	T	AGE	W	L	PCT	SV	G	GS	CG	IP	H	BB	SO	SHO	ERA
		28	65	97	.401	37	162	162	15	1447	1508	582	759	5	3.88
Craig Swan	R	31	11	7	.611	1	37	21	2	166	165	37	67	0	3.35
Charlie Puleo	R	27	9	9	.500	1	36	24	1	171	179	90	98	1	4.47
Pete Falcone	L	28	8	10	.444	2	40	23	3	171	159	71	101	0	3.84
Randy Jones	L	32	7	10	.412	0	28	20	2	108	130	51	44	1	4.60
Mike Scott	R	27	7	13	.350	3	37	22	1	147	185	60	63	0	5.14
Pat Zachry	R	30	6	9	.400	1	36	16	2	138	149	57	69	0	4.05
Ed Lynch	R	26	4	8	.333	2	43	12	0	139	145	40	51	0	3.55
Jesse Orosco	L	25	4	10	.286	4	54	2	0	109	92	40	89	0	2.72
Neil Allen (EJ)	R	24	3	7	.300	19	50	0	0	65	65	30	59	0	3.06
Terry Leach	R	28	2	1	.667	3	21	1	1	45	46	18	30	1	4.17
Scott Holman	R	23	1	1	.667	0	4	4	1	27	23	7	11	0	2.36
1 Tom Hausman(EJ-SJ)	R	29	1	2	.333	0	21	0	0	37	44	6	16	0	4.42
Rick Ownbey	R	24	1	2	.333	0	8	8	2	50	44	43	28	0	3.75
2 Carlos Diaz	L	24	0	0	—	0	4	0	0	4	6	4	9	0	1.04
Doug Sisk	R	24	0	0	.000	0	9	0	0	9	5	4	4	0	0.96
2 Tom Gorman	L	24	0	1	.000	0	3	0	0	5	3	1	2	0	0.96
Brent Gaff	R	23	0	0	.000	0	7	5	0	32	41	10	14	0	4.55
Walt Terrell	R	24	0	3	.000	0	3	3	0	21	22	14	8	0	3.43

WEST DIVISION

ATLANTA — 1st 89-73 .549 — JOE TORRE

Name	G by Pos	B	AGE	G	AB	R	H	2B	3B	HR	RBI	BB	SO	SB	BA	SA
TOTALS			27	162	5507	739	1411	215	22	146	687	554	869	151	.256	.383
Chris Chambliss	1B151	L	33	157	534	57	144	25	2	20	86	57	57	7	.270	.436
Glenn Hubbard	2B144	R	24	145	532	75	132	25	1	9	59	59	62	4	.248	.350
Rafael Ramirez	SS157	R	24	157	609	74	169	24	4	10	52	36	49	27	.278	.379
Bob Horner	3B137	R	24	140	499	85	130	24	0	32	97	66	75	3	.261	.501
Claudell Washington	OF139	L	27	150	563	94	150	24	6	16	80	50	107	33	.266	.416
Dale Murphy	OF162	R	26	162	598	113	168	23	2	36	109	93	134	23	.281	.507
Rufino Linares	OF53	R	31	77	191	28	57	7	1	2	17	7	29	5	.298	.372
Bruce Benedict	C118	R	26	118	386	34	95	11	1	3	44	37	40	4	.246	.303
Jerry Royster	3B62, OF25, 2B16, SS10	R	29	108	261	43	77	13	2	2	25	22	36	14	.295	.383
Brett Butler	OF77	L	25	89	240	35	52	2	0	0	7	25	35	21	.217	.225
Larry Whisenton	OF34	L	25	84	143	21	34	7	2	4	17	23	33	2	.238	.399
2 Bob Watson	1B27, OF2	R	36	57	114	16	28	3	1	5	22	14	20	1	.246	.421
Biff Pocoroba	C36, 3B2	R	26	58	120	5	33	7	0	2	22	13	12	0	.275	.383
Terry Harper (BJ)	OF41	R	26	48	150	16	43	3	2	2	16	14	26	7	.287	.347
Ken Smith	1B6, OF3	L	24	48	41	6	12	1	0	0	3	6	13	0	.293	.317
Matt Sinatro	C35	R	22	37	81	10	11	2	0	1	4	4	9	0	.136	.198
Randy Johnson	2B13, 3B4	R	26	27	46	5	11	5	0	0	6	6	4	0	.239	.348
Bob Porter	OF4, 1B1	L	22	24	27	1	3	0	0	0	0	1	9	0	.111	.111
Albert Hall		B	24	5	0	1	0	0	0	0	0	0	0	0	—	—
Paul Runge		R	24	4	2	0	0	0	0	0	0	0	0	0	.000	.000
Larry Owen	C2	R	27	3	3	1	1	1	0	0	0	1	0	0	.333	.667
Paul Zuvella	SS1	R	23	2	1	0	0	0	0	0	0	0	0	0	.000	.000

NAME	T	AGE	W	L	PCT	SV	G	GS	CG	IP	H	BB	SO	SHO	ERA
		28	89	73	.549	51	162	162	15	1463	1484	502	813	11	3.82
Phil Niekro	R	43	17	4	.810	0	35	35	4	234	225	73	144	2	3.61
Bob Walk	R	25	11	9	.550	0	32	27	3	164	179	59	84	1	4.87
Rick Camp	R	29	11	13	.458	5	51	21	3	177	199	52	68	0	3.65
Rick Mahler	R	28	9	10	.474	0	39	33	5	205	213	62	105	2	4.21
Steve Bedrosian	R	24	8	6	.571	11	64	3	0	138	102	57	123	0	2.42
Gene Garber	R	34	8	10	.444	30	69	0	0	119	100	32	68	0	2.34
Ken Dayley	L	23	5	6	.455	0	20	11	0	71	79	25	34	0	4.54
Pascual Perez	R	25	4	4	.500	0	16	11	0	79	85	17	29	0	3.06
1 Preston Hanna	R	27	3	0	1.000	0	20	1	0	36	36	28	17	0	3.75
Donnie Moore	R	28	3	1	.750	1	16	0	0	32	32	7	17	0	4.23
1 Carlos Diaz	L	24	3	2	.600	1	19	0	0	25	31	9	16	0	4.62
Al Hrabosky	L	32	2	1	.667	3	31	0	0	37	41	17	20	0	5.54
Tommy Boggs (SJ)	R	26	2	2	.500	0	10	10	0	46	43	22	29	0	3.30
1 Larry McWilliams (SJ)	L	28	2	3	.400	0	27	2	0	38	52	20	24	0	6.21
Joe Cowley (SJ)	R	23	1	2	.333	0	17	8	0	52	53	16	27	0	4.70
Jose Alvarez	R	26	0	0	—	0	8	2	0	8	8	2	6	0	4.70
2 Tom Hausman	R	29	0	0	—	0	3	0	0	4	6	4	2	0	4.91

LOS ANGELES — 2nd 88-74 .543 1 — TOMMY LASORDA

Name	G by Pos	B	AGE	G	AB	R	H	2B	3B	HR	RBI	BB	SO	SB	BA	SA
TOTALS			30	162	5642	691	1487	222	32	138	661	528	804	151	.264	.388
Steve Garvey	1B158	R	33	162	625	66	176	35	1	16	86	20	86	5	.282	.418
Steve Sax	2B149	R	22	150	638	88	180	23	7	4	47	49	53	49	.282	.359
Bill Russell	SS150	R	33	153	497	64	136	20	2	3	46	63	30	10	.274	.340
Ron Cey	3B149	R	34	150	556	62	141	23	1	24	79	57	99	3	.254	.428
Pedro Guerrero	OF137, 1B24	R	26	150	575	87	175	27	5	32	100	65	89	22	.304	.536
Ken Landreaux	OF117	L	27	129	461	71	131	20	7	7	50	39	54	31	.284	.410
Dusty Baker	OF144	R	33	147	570	80	171	19	1	23	88	56	62	17	.300	.458
Mike Scioscia	C123	L	23	129	365	31	80	11	1	5	38	44	31	2	.219	.296
Ron Roenicke	OF72	B	25	109	143	18	37	8	0	1	12	21	32	5	.259	.336
Rick Monday	OF57, 1B4	L	36	104	210	37	54	6	4	11	42	39	51	2	.257	.481
Jorge Orta	OF17	L	31	86	115	13	25	5	0	2	8	12	13	0	.217	.313
Steve Yeager (KJ)	C76	R	33	82	196	13	48	5	2	2	18	13	28	0	.245	.321
Derrel Thomas (BL)	OF28, 2B18, 3B14, SS8	B	31	66	98	13	26	2	1	0	10	12	22	5	.265	.306
Mark Belanger	SS44, 2B1	R	38	54	50	6	12	1	0	0	4	5	10	1	.240	.260
Mike Marshall	OF19, 1B13	R	22	49	95	10	23	3	0	5	9	13	23	2	.242	.432
2 Jose Morales		R	37	35	30	1	9	1	0	1	8	4	8	0	.300	.433
1 Jay Johnstone		L	36	17	13	2	1	0	0	0	0	1	5	0	.077	.154
Greg Brock	1B3	L	25	18	17	1	2	1	0	0	1	2	6	0	.118	.176
Alex Taveras	2B4, 3B4, SS2	R	26	11	3	1	1	0	0	0	0	0	1	0	.333	.333
Mark Bradley	OF3	R	25	8	3	2	1	0	0	0	0	0	3	1	.333	.333
Candy Maldonado	OF3	R	21	6	4	0	0	0	0	0	0	0	2	0	.000	.000
Don Crow	C4	R	23	4	4	0	0	0	0	0	0	2	0	0	.000	.000
Dave Sax	OF1	R	23	2	1	1	0	0	0	0	0	0	0	0	.000	.000
Manny Mota		R	44	2	1	0	0	0	0	0	0	0	0	0	.000	.000

NAME	T	AGE	W	L	PCT	SV	G	GS	CG	IP	H	BB	SO	SHO	ERA
		27	88	74	.543	28	162	162	37	1488	1356	468	932	16	3.26
Fernando Valenzuela	L	21	19	13	.594	0	37	37	18	285	247	83	199	4	2.87
Jerry Reuss	L	33	18	11	.621	0	39	37	8	255	232	50	138	4	3.11
Bob Welch	R	25	16	11	.593	0	36	36	9	236	199	81	176	3	3.36
Dave Stewart	R	25	9	8	.529	1	45	14	0	146	137	49	80	0	3.81
Steve Howe	L	24	7	5	.583	13	66	0	0	99	87	17	49	0	2.08
Terry Forster	L	30	5	4	.455	3	56	0	0	83	66	31	52	0	3.04
Burt Hooton (KJ)	R	32	4	7	.364	0	21	21	2	121	130	33	51	2	4.03
Tom Niedenfuer	R	22	3	4	.429	9	55	0	0	70	71	25	60	0	2.71
Joe Beckwith	R	27	2	1	.667	1	19	1	0	40	38	14	33	0	2.70
Ricky Wright	L	23	2	1	.667	0	14	5	0	33	28	20	24	0	3.03
Ted Power	R	27	1	1	.500	0	12	4	0	34	38	23	15	0	6.68
Steve Shirley	L	25	1	1	.500	0	13	1	0	13	15	7	8	0	4.26
Vincente Romo (JJ)	R	39	1	2	.333	1	15	6	0	36	25	14	24	0	3.03
1 Dave Goltz	R	33	0	1	.000	2	19	1	0	36	37	21	20	0	4.91
Alejandro Pena	R	23	0	0	—	0	29	0	0	36	37	21	20	0	4.79

SAN FRANCISCO 3rd 87-75 .537 2 — FRANK ROBINSON

Name	G by Pos	B	AGE	G	AB	R	H	2B	3B	HR	RBI	BB	SO	SB	BA	SA
TOTALS			30	162	5499	673	1393	213	30	133	631	607	915	130	.253	.376
Reggie Smith	1B99	B	37	106	349	51	99	11	0	18	56	46	46	7	.284	.470
Joe Morgan	2B120, 3B3	L	38	134	463	68	134	19	4	14	61	85	60	24	.289	.438
Johnnie LeMaster	SS130	R	28	130	436	34	94	14	1	2	30	31	78	13	.216	.266
Darrell Evans	3B84, 1B49, SS13	L	35	141	465	64	119	20	4	16	61	77	64	6	.256	.419
Jack Clark	OF155	R	26	157	563	90	154	30	3	27	103	90	91	6	.274	.481
Chili Davis	OF153	B	22	154	641	86	167	27	6	19	76	45	115	24	.261	.410
Jeff Leonard (WJ)	OF74, 1B1	R	26	80	278	32	72	16	1	9	49	19	65	18	.259	.421
Milt May	C110	L	31	114	395	29	104	19	0	9	39	28	38	0	.263	.380
Duane Kuiper	2B51	L	32	107	218	26	61	9	1	0	17	32	24	2	.280	.330
Dave Bergman	1B69, OF6	L	29	100	121	22	33	3	1	4	14	18	11	3	.273	.413
Jim Wohlford	OF72	R	31	97	250	37	64	12	1	2	25	30	36	8	.256	.336
Tom O'Malley	3B83, 2B1, SS1	L	21	92	291	26	80	12	4	2	27	33	39	0	.275	.364
Max Venable (IL)	OF53	L	25	71	125	17	28	2	1	1	7	7	16	9	.224	.280
Champ Summers	OF31, 1B3	L	36	70	125	15	31	5	0	4	19	16	17	0	.248	.384
Bob Brenly (SJ)	C61, 3B1	R	28	65	180	26	51	4	1	4	15	18	26	6	.283	.383
Guy Sularz	SS37, 3B14, 2B9	R	26	63	101	15	23	3	0	1	7	9	11	3	.228	.287
Joe Pettini	SS26, 3B1	R	27	29	39	5	8	1	0	0	2	3	4	0	.205	.231
Jeff Ransom	C14	R	21	15	44	5	7	0	0	0	3	6	7	0	.159	.159
Jose Barrios	1B7	R	25	10	19	2	3	0	0	0	0	1	4	0	.158	.158
Brad Wellman	2B2	R	22	6	4	1	1	0	0	0	0	0	1	0	.250	.250
Ron Pruitt	C1, OF1	R	30	5	4	1	2	1	0	0	2	1	1	0	.500	.750
John Rabb	OF1	R	22	2	2	0	1	0	1	0	0	0	1	0	.500	1.500

NAME	T	AGE	W	L	PCT	SV	G	GS	CG	IP	H	BB	SO	SHO	ERA
		28	87	75	.537	45	162	162	18	1465	1507	466	810	4	3.64
Bill Laskey	R	24	13	12	.520	0	34	34	4	189	186	43	88	1	3.14
Atlee Hammaker	L	24	12	8	.600	0	29	27	4	175	189	28	102	1	4.11
Fred Breining	R	26	11	6	.647	0	54	9	2	143	146	52	98	0	3.08
Greg Minton	R	30	10	4	.714	30	78	0	0	123	108	42	58	0	1.83
Gary Lavelle	L	33	10	7	.588	8	68	0	0	105	97	29	76	0	2.67
Al Holland	L	29	7	3	.700	5	58	7	0	130	115	40	97	0	3.33
Renie Martin	R	26	7	10	.412	0	29	25	1	141	148	64	63	0	4.65
Rich Gale	R	28	7	14	.333	0	33	29	2	170	193	81	102	0	4.23
Alan Fowlkes	R	23	4	2	.667	0	21	15	1	85	111	24	50	0	5.19
Jim Barr	R	34	4	3	.571	2	53	9	1	129	125	20	36	1	3.29
Andy McGaffigan	R	25	1	0	1.000	0	4	0	0	8	5	1	4	0	0.00
1 Dan Schatzeder	L	27	1	4	.200	0	13	3	0	33	47	12	18	0	7.29
Mark Dempsey	R	24	0	0	—	0	3	1	0	6	1	2	4	0	7.94
Scott Garrelts	R	20	0	0	—	0	1	0	0	2	3	2	4	0	13.50
Mike Chris	L	24	0	2	.000	0	9	6	0	26	23	26	10	0	4.85
Bill Bordley 24 (EJ)															

SAN DIEGO 4th 81-81 .500 8 — DICK WILLIAMS

Name	G by Pos	B	AGE	G	AB	R	H	2B	3B	HR	RBI	BB	SO	SB	BA	SA
TOTALS			26	162	5575	675	1435	217	52	81	611	429	877	165	.257	.359
Broderick Perkins	1B98, OF11	L	27	125	347	32	94	10	4	2	34	26	20	2	.271	.340
Tim Flannery	2B104, 3B5, SS2	L	24	122	379	40	100	11	7	0	30	30	32	1	.264	.330
Garry Templeton	SS136	B	26	141	563	76	139	25	8	6	64	26	87	27	.247	.352
Luis Salazar	3B129, SS18, OF1	R	26	145	524	55	127	15	5	8	62	23	80	32	.242	.336
Sixto Lezcano	OF134	R	28	138	470	73	136	26	6	16	84	78	69	2	.289	.472
Ruppert Jones	OF114	L	27	116	424	69	120	20	2	12	61	62	90	10	.283	.425
Gene Richards (KJ)	OF103, 1B25	L	28	132	521	63	149	13	8	3	28	36	52	30	.286	.359
Terry Kennedy	C139, 1B12	L	26	153	562	75	166	42	1	21	97	26	91	1	.295	.486
Joe Lefebvre	3B39, OF36, C3	L	26	102	239	25	57	9	0	4	21	18	50	0	.238	.326
Alan Wiggins (SD)	OF68, 2B1	B	24	72	254	40	65	3	3	1	15	13	19	33	.256	.303
Dave Edwards	OF45, 1B1	R	28	71	55	7	10	2	0	1	2	1	14	0	.182	.273
Kurt Bevacqua	1B30, OF3, 3B1	R	35	64	123	15	31	9	0	0	24	17	22	2	.252	.325
2 Joe Pittman	2B30, SS13	R	28	55	118	16	30	2	0	0	7	9	13	8	.254	.271
Tony Gwynn	OF52	L	22	54	190	33	55	12	2	1	17	14	16	8	.289	.389
Juan Bonilla (BW)	2B45	R	27	45	182	21	51	6	2	0	8	11	15	0	.280	.335
Steve Swisher (KJ)	C26	R	30	26	58	2	10	1	0	2	3	5	24	0	.172	.293
Rick Lancellotti	1B7, OF3	L	25	17	39	2	7	2	0	0	4	2	8	0	.179	.231
1 Randy Bass	1B9	L	28	13	30	1	6	0	0	1	8	2	4	0	.200	.300
Mario Ramirez	SS8, 2B1, 3B1	R	24	13	23	1	4	1	0	0	1	2	4	0	.174	.217
Jody Lansford	1B9	R	21	13	22	6	4	0	0	0	3	6	4	0	.182	.182
Ron Tingley	C8	R	23	8	20	0	2	0	0	0	0	0	7	0	.100	.100
Doug Gwosdz	C7	R	22	7	17	1	3	0	0	0	0	2	7	0	.176	.176
George Hinshaw	OF6	R	22	6	15	1	4	0	0	0	1	3	5	0	.267	.267
Jerry Manuel	2B1, SS1, 3B1	B	28	5	5	0	1	0	1	0	1	1	0	0	.200	.600

NAME	T	AGE	W	L	PCT	SV	G	GS	CG	IP	H	BB	SO	SHO	ERA
		27	81	81	.500	41	162	162	20	1476	1348	502	765	11	3.52
Tim Lollar	L	26	16	9	.640	0	34	34	4	233	192	87	150	2	3.13
Eric Show	R	26	10	6	.625	3	47	14	2	150	117	48	88	2	2.64
John Montefusco	R	32	10	11	.476	0	32	32	1	184	177	41	83	0	4.00
Luis DeLeon	R	23	9	5	.643	15	61	0	0	102	77	16	60	0	2.03
1 John Curtis	L	34	8	6	.571	0	26	18	1	116	121	46	54	1	4.10
Chris Welsh	L	27	8	8	.500	0	28	20	3	139	146	63	48	1	4.91
Juan Eichelberger	R	28	7	14	.333	0	31	24	8	178	171	72	74	0	4.20
Dave Dravecky	L	26	5	3	.625	2	31	10	0	105	86	33	59	0	2.57
Floyd Chiffer	R	26	4	3	.571	4	51	0	0	79	73	34	48	0	2.95
Andy Hawkins	R	22	2	5	.286	0	15	10	1	64	66	27	25	0	4.10
1 Dan Boone	L	28	1	0	1.000	1	10	0	0	16	21	3	8	0	5.63
Gary Lucas	L	27	1	10	.091	16	65	0	0	97	89	29	64	0	3.24
Rick Wise	R	36	0	0	—	0	1	0	0	2	3	0	0	0	9.00
Mike Griffin	R	25	0	0	.000	0	7	0	0	9	3	4	9	0	3.48

HOUSTON 5th 77-85 .475 12 — BILL VIRDON 49-62 .441 — BOB LILLIS 28-23 .549

Name	G by Pos	B	AGE	G	AB	R	H	2B	3B	HR	RBI	BB	SO	SB	BA	SA
TOTALS			31	162	5440	569	1342	236	48	74	533	435	830	140	.247	.349
Ray Knight	1B96, 3B67	R	29	158	609	72	179	36	6	6	70	48	58	2	.294	.402
Phil Garner	2B136, 3B18	R	33	155	588	65	161	33	8	13	83	40	92	24	.274	.423
Dickie Thon	SS119, 3B8, 2B1	R	24	136	496	73	137	31	10	3	36	37	48	37	.276	.397
Art Howe (LJ)	3B72, 1B35	R	35	110	365	29	87	15	1	5	38	41	45	2	.238	.326
Terry Puhl	OF138	L	32	145	507	64	133	17	9	8	50	51	49	17	.262	.379
Tony Scott	OF129	B	30	132	460	43	110	16	3	1	29	15	56	10	.239	.293
Jose Cruz	OF155	L	34	155	570	62	157	27	2	9	68	60	67	21	.275	.381
Alan Ashby	C95	B	30	100	339	40	87	14	2	12	49	27	53	2	.257	.416
Danny Heep	OF39, 1B16	L	24	85	198	16	47	14	1	4	22	21	31	0	.237	.379
Denny Walling	OF32, 1B20	L	28	85	146	22	30	4	1	1	14	23	19	4	.205	.267
Luis Pujols	C64	R	26	65	176	8	35	6	2	4	15	10	40	0	.199	.324
Alan Knicely	C23, OF16, 3B1	R	27	59	133	10	25	2	0	2	12	14	30	0	.188	.248
Craig Reynolds	SS35, 3B7	L	29	54	118	16	30	2	3	1	7	11	9	3	.254	.347
Scott Loucks	OF37	R	25	44	49	6	11	2	0	0	3	3	17	4	.224	.265
Harry Spilman	1B11	L	27	38	61	7	17	2	0	3	11	5	10	0	.279	.459
Kiko Garcia (XJ)	SS21, 3B2, 2B1	R	28	34	76	5	16	5	0	1	5	3	15	1	.211	.316
Bill Doran	2B26	B	24	26	97	11	27	3	0	0	6	4	11	5	.278	.309
Tim Tolman	OF5, 1B1	R	26	15	26	4	5	2	0	1	3	4	3	0	.192	.385
1 Joe Pittman	3B3, OF1	R	28	15	10	0	2	1	0	0	1	0	4	0	.200	.300
2 Kevin Bass	OF7	B	23	12	24	2	1	0	0	0	0	1	8	0	.042	.042
1 Mike Ivie		R	29	7	6	0	2	0	0	0	1	0	4	0	.333	.333
Larry Ray	OF1	L	24	5	6	0	1	0	0	0	1	0	4	0	.167	.167

NAME	T	AGE	W	L	PCT	SV	G	GS	CG	IP	H	BB	SO	SHO	ERA
		31	77	85	.475	31	162	162	37	1447	1338	479	899	16	3.42
Joe Niekro	R	37	17	12	.586	0	35	35	16	270	224	64	130	5	2.47
Nolan Ryan	R	35	16	12	.571	0	35	35	10	250	196	109	245	3	3.16
1 Don Sutton	R	37	13	8	.619	0	27	27	4	195	169	46	139	0	3.00
Vern Ruhle	R	31	9	13	.409	1	31	21	3	149	169	24	56	2	3.93
Mike LaCoss	R	26	6	6	.500	0	41	8	0	115	107	54	51	0	2.90
Dave Smith (XJ)	R	27	5	4	.556	11	49	1	0	63	69	31	28	0	3.84
Bob Knepper	L	28	5	15	.250	1	33	29	4	180	193	60	108	4	4.45
Frank DiPino	L	25	2	2	.500	0	6	6	0	28	32	11	25	0	6.04
Randy Moffitt	R	33	2	4	.333	3	30	0	0	42	36	13	20	0	3.02
Bert Roberge	R	27	1	2	.333	3	22	0	0	26	29	6	18	0	4.21
Frank LaCorte	R	30	1	5	.167	7	55	0	0	76	71	46	51	0	4.48
Joe Sambito (EJ)	L	30	0	0	—	4	9	0	0	13	7	2	7	0	0.71
Mark Ross	R	24	0	0	—	0	4	0	0	6	3	0	4	0	1.50
Gordy Pladson	R	25	0	0	—	0	2	0	0	1	10	2	0	0	54.00
2 Dan Boone	L	28	0	1	.000	0	10	0	0	13	19	7	4	0	3.55
George Cappuzzello	L	28	0	1	.000	0				19	16	7	13	0	2.79
J.R. Richard 32 (IL)															

CINCINNATI 6th 61-101 .377 28 — JOHN McNAMARA 34-58 .370 — RUSS NIXON 27-43 .386

Name	G by Pos	B	AGE	G	AB	R	H	2B	3B	HR	RBI	BB	SO	SB	BA	SA
TOTALS			29	162	5479	545	1375	228	34	82	496	470	817	131	.251	.350
Dan Driessen	1B144	L	30	149	516	64	139	25	1	17	57	82	62	11	.269	.421
Ron Oester	2B118, SS29, 3B13	B	26	151	549	63	143	19	4	9	47	35	82	5	.260	.359
Dave Concepcion	SS145, 1B1, 3B1	R	34	147	572	48	164	25	4	5	53	43	61	13	.287	.371
Johnny Bench	3B107, 1B8, C1	R	34	119	399	44	103	16	0	13	38	37	58	1	.258	.396
Paul Householder	OF131	B	23	138	417	40	88	11	5	9	34	30	77	17	.211	.326
Cesar Cedeno	OF131, 1B1	R	31	138	492	52	142	35	1	8	57	41	41	16	.289	.413
Eddie Milner (LJ)	OF107	L	27	113	407	61	109	23	5	4	31	41	40	18	.268	.378
Alex Trevino	C116, 3B2	R	24	120	355	24	89	10	3	1	33	34	34	3	.251	.304
Larry Biittner	OF31, 1B15	L	36	97	184	18	57	9	2	2	24	17	16	1	.310	.413
Wayne Krenchicki	3B70, 2B9	L	27	94	187	19	53	6	1	2	21	13	23	5	.283	.358
Duane Walker	OF69	L	25	86	239	26	52	10	0	5	22	27	58	9	.218	.322
Mike Vail	OF52	R	30	78	189	9	48	10	1	4	29	6	33	0	.254	.381
Rafael Landestoy	3B21, 2B16, OF3, SS2	B	29	73	111	11	21	3	0	1	9	8	14	2	.189	.243
Dave Van Gorder	C51	R	25	51	137	4	25	3	1	0	7	14	19	1	.182	.219
Tom Lawless	2B47	R	25	49	165	19	35	6	0	0	4	9	30	16	.212	.248
German Barranca	2B6	L	25	46	51	11	13	1	3	0	2	2	9	2	.255	.392
Mike O'Berry	C21	R	28	21	45	5	10	2	0	0	3	10	13	0	.222	.267
Gary Redus	OF20	R	25	20	83	12	18	3	2	1	7	5	21	11	.217	.337
Clint Hurdle	OF17	L	24	19	34	7	7	1	0	0	1	2	6	0	.206	.235

NAME	T	AGE	W	L	PCT	SV	G	GS	CG	IP	H	BB	SO	SHO	ERA
		27	61	101	.377	31	162	162	22	1460	1414	570	998	7	3.66
Mario Soto	R	25	14	13	.519	0	35	34	13	258	202	71	274	2	2.79
Bruce Berenyi	R	27	9	18	.333	0	34	34	4	222	208	96	157	1	3.36
Bob Shirley	L	28	8	13	.381	0	41	20	1	153	138	73	89	0	3.60
Frank Pastore	R	24	8	13	.381	0	31	29	3	188	210	57	94	2	3.97
Charlie Leibrandt	L	25	5	7	.417	2	36	11	0	108	130	48	34	0	5.10
Tom Seaver (SJ)	R	37	5	13	.278	0	21	21	0	111	136	44	62	0	5.50
Joe Price	L	25	3	4	.429	3	59	1	0	73	73	32	71	0	2.85
1 Jim Kern	R	33	3	3	.375	2	50	0	0	76	61	48	43	0	2.84
Ben Hayes	R	24	2	2	.500	1	28	0	0	46	37	22	38	0	1.97
Tom Hume (KJ)	R	29	2	6	.250	17	46	0	0	64	57	21	22	0	3.11
Greg Harris	R	26	2	6	.250	1	34	10	1	91	96	37	67	0	4.83
Joe Edelen	R	26	0	0	—	0	9	0	0	15	22	8	11	0	8.80
Bill Scherrer	L	24	0	1	.000	0	5	0	0	17	17	0	7	0	2.60
Brad Lesley	R	23	0	2	.000	4	28	0	0	38	27	13	29	0	2.58

1983 — Weaver's Replacement Does it All

It didn't much affect the pennant race, but the July 24 meeting of the Royals and Yankees captured the public's imagination as the Pine Tar Game. With two out in the top of the ninth, George Brett drove a two-run homer off Goose Gossage to put the Royals ahead 5-4. Out of the dugout charged Billy Martin, in his third hitch as Yankee manager, claiming that Brett had violated an obscure rule by having pine tar on his bat more than 18 inches up from the knob. The umpires agreed with Martin, declared Brett out, and gave a 4-3 victory to the Yanks. Amidst lively debate among fans over the sanctity of rules versus the injustice of hypertechnical enforcement, American League president Lee McPhail overruled the umpires and reinstated Brett's homer. On August 18, the teams reassembled at Yankee Stadium and played out the ninth inning, with the Royals holding out their 5-4 lead.

Neither the Yanks nor Royals made the playoffs this year. In the East, the Orioles combined a few stars with a sterling supporting cast in winning first place. The Birds had a new manager in Joe Altobelli, endured sub-par play from pitcher Dennis Martinez and all their third basemen, and survived serious injuries to pitchers Jim Palmer, Mike Flanagan, and Tippy Martinez. None of that stopped the Orioles. MVP Cal Ripken and Eddie Murray anchored a platoon-heavy lineup which led the majors in homers, while pitcher Mike Boddicker came up from the minors to baffle the A.L. with his foshball. The defending champion Brewers dropped from contention in September when they stopped hitting just as the Orioles caught fire.

In the A.L. Championship Series, the Birds met the White Sox, runaway winners in the West. The Sox' motto was winning ugly, and won often with strong offense and a talented starting staff that featured burly LaMarr Hoyt and Rich Dotson. Over the second half of the season, Hoyt went 13-0. Slugger Ron Kittle won the rookie of the year award, while catcher Carlton Fisk was the heart of the club with his timely hitting and flawless defense. The White Sox captured game one of the playoffs 2-1 behind Hoyt, but Boddicker's 14 strikeouts in game two turned the tide for the

Orioles to sweep the next three decisions.

In the World Series, the Orioles confronted the Phillies, so laden with ancient stars that they were called the Wheeze Kids. Pete Rose and Joe Morgan brought a winning habit to the lineup, but the real stars were slugger Mike Schmidt, starters Steve Carlton and John Denny, and reliever Al Holland. Manager Pat Corrales had been fired on July 18 despite his team's sharing first place. General Manager Paul Owens stepped into uniform and made his decision look good by leading the Phils through a torrid 22-7 September. Falling off the pace were the surprisingly strong Pirates, the Andre Dawson-led Expos, and the disappointing Cardinals. The Phils reached the Series by taking three of four games from the Dodgers in the playoffs. The Dodgers had sent Steve Garvey and Ron Cey packing, yet took the Western crown on strong pitching and a star season by Pedro Guerrero. Atlanta finished three games back despite Dale Murphy's second straight MVP performance.

The N.L. champion Phillies took the first game of the Series, but then Mike Boddicker spun a three-hitter for a 4-1 Oriole evener. The Birds came from behind in the next three contests behind Rick Dempsey's hot bat and capped a resourceful season with a World Championship.

Of the season's milestones, one must note that Steve Garvey injured his thumb on July 29, ending his consecutive game streak at a N.L. record 1,207. Also, the closing days of the regular season saw the final appearances of three outstanding baseball players, Gaylord Perry, Carl Yastrzemski, and Johnny Bench.

EAST DIVISION

1983 AMERICAN LEAGUE

BALTIMORE 1st 98-64 .605 — JOE ALTOBELLI

Name	G by Pos	B	AGE	G	AB	R	H	2B	3B	HR	RBI	BB	SO	SB	BA	SA
	TOTALS		30	162	5546	799	1492	283	27	168	761	601	800	61	.269	.421
Eddie Murray	1B153, DH2	B	27	156	582	115	178	30	3	33	111	86	90	5	.306	.538
Rich Dauer	2B131, 3B17	R	30	140	459	49	108	19	0	5	41	47	29	1	.235	.309
Cal Ripken	SS162	R	22	162	663	121	211	47	2	27	102	58	97	0	.318	.517
Todd Cruz	2B79, 3B2	R	27	81	221	16	46	9	1	3	27	15	52	3	.208	.299
Dan Ford (KJ)	OF103	R	31	103	407	63	114	30	4	9	55	29	55	9	.280	.440
Tom Brumby	OF104, DH11	L	36	124	378	63	104	14	4	3	31	31	33	12	.275	.357
John Lowenstein	OF107, 2B1, DH1	L	36	122	310	52	87	13	2	15	60	49	55	2	.281	.481
Rick Dempsey	C127	R	33	128	347	33	80	16	2	4	32	40	54	1	.231	.323
Ken Singleton	DH150	B	36	151	507	52	140	21	3	18	84	99	83	0	.276	.436
John Shelby	OF115, DH1	B	25	126	325	52	84	15	2	5	27	18	64	15	.258	.363
Gary Roenicke	OF100, 1B7, 3B2, DH2	R	28	115	323	45	84	13	0	19	64	30	35	2	.260	.477
Jim Dwyer	OF56, DH10, 1B4	L	33	100	196	37	56	17	1	8	38	31	29	1	.286	.505
Joe Nolan	C65	L	32	73	184	25	51	11	1	5	24	16	31	0	.277	.429
Lenn Sakata	2B60, C1, DH3	R	29	66	134	23	34	7	0	3	12	16	31	8	.254	.373
Leo Hernandez	3B64	R	23	64	203	21	50	6	1	6	26	12	19	1	.246	.374
Benny Ayala	OF24, DH11	R	32	47	104	12	23	7	0	4	13	9	18	0	.221	.404
Aurelio Rodriguez	3B45	R	35	45	67	0	8	0	0	0	4	1	13	0	.119	.119
Tito Landrum	OF26	R	28	26	42	8	13	2	0	1	4	1	11	0	.310	.429
Mike Young	OF22, DH3	B	23	24	36	5	6	2	1	0	2	2	8	1	.167	.278
Glenn Gulliver	3B21	L	25	23	47	5	10	3	0	0	2	9	5	0	.213	.277
John Stefero	C9	L	23	9	11	2	5	1	0	0	4	3	2	0	.455	.545
Bob Bonner	2B5, DH1	R	26	6	0	0	0	0	0	0	0	0	0	0	—	—
Dave Huppert	C2	R	26	2	0	0	0	0	0	0	0	0	0	0	—	—

NAME	T	AGE	W	L	PCT	SV	G	GS	CG	IP	H	BB	SO	SHO	ERA
		28	98	64	.605	38	162	162	36	1452	1451	452	774	15	3.63
Scott McGregor	L	29	18	7	.720	0	36	36	12	260	271	45	86	2	3.18
Mike Boddicker	R	25	16	8	.667	0	27	26	10	179	141	52	120	5	2.77
Storm Davis	R	21	13	7	.650	0	34	29	6	200	180	64	125	1	3.59
Mike Flanagan (KJ)	L	31	12	4	.750	0	20	20	3	125	135	31	50	1	3.30
Tippy Martinez (IL)	L	33	9	3	.750	21	65	0	0	103	76	37	81	0	2.35
Sammy Stewart	R	28	9	4	.692	7	58	1	0	144	138	67	95	0	3.62
Dennis Martinez	R	28	7	16	.304	0	32	25	4	153	209	45	71	0	5.53
Jim Palmer (SJ)	R	37	5	4	.556	0	14	11	0	77	86	19	34	0	4.23
Tim Stoddard	R	30	4	3	.571	9	47	0	0	58	65	29	50	0	6.09
Allan Ramirez	R	26	4	4	.500	0	11	10	1	57	46	30	20	0	3.47
Bill Swaggerty	R	26	1	1	.500	0	7	2	0	22	23	6	7	0	2.91
Paul Mirabella	L	29	0	0	—	0	3	2	0	10	9	7	4	0	5.59
Dan Morogiello	L	28	0	1	.000	1	22	0	0	38	39	10	15	0	2.39
Don Welchel	R	26	0	2	.000	0	11	0	0	27	33	10	16	0	5.40

DETROIT 2nd 92-70 .568 6 — SPARKY ANDERSON

Name	G by Pos	B	AGE	G	AB	R	H	2B	3B	HR	RBI	BB	SO	SB	BA	SA
	TOTALS		28	162	5592	789	1530	283	53	156	749	508	831	93	.274	.427
Enos Cabell	1B106, DH8, 3B4, SS1	R	33	121	392	62	122	23	5	5	46	16	41	4	.311	.434
Lou Whitaker	2B160	L	26	161	643	94	206	40	6	12	72	67	70	17	.320	.457
Alan Trammell	SS140	R	25	142	505	83	161	31	2	14	66	57	64	30	.319	.471
Tom Brookens	3B103, SS30, 2B10, DH1	R	29	138	332	50	71	13	3	6	32	29	46	10	.214	.325
Glenn Wilson	OF143	R	24	144	503	55	135	25	6	11	65	25	79	1	.268	.408
Chet Lemon	OF145	R	28	145	491	78	125	21	5	24	69	54	70	0	.255	.464
Larry Herndon	OF133, DH19	R	29	153	603	88	182	28	9	20	92	46	95	9	.302	.478
Lance Parrish	C131, DH27	R	27	155	605	80	163	42	3	27	114	44	106	1	.269	.483
Kirk Gibson	DH66, OF54	L	26	128	401	60	91	12	9	15	51	53	96	14	.227	.414
Rick Leach	1B73, OF13, DH3	L	26	99	242	22	60	17	0	3	26	19	21	2	.248	.355
John Wockenfuss	DH39, C29, 1B13, 3B1, OF1	R	34	92	245	32	66	8	1	9	44	31	37	1	.269	.420
Marty Castillo	3B58, C10	R	26	67	119	10	23	4	0	2	10	7	22	2	.193	.277
Wayne Krenchicki	3B48, 2B6, SS6, 1B3	L	28	59	133	18	37	7	0	1	16	11	27	0	.278	.353
Johnny Grubb (BG)	OF26, DH18	L	34	57	134	20	34	5	2	4	22	28	17	0	.254	.410
Lynn Jones	OF31, DH6	R	29	46	64	9	17	1	2	0	6	3	6	1	.266	.344
Howard Johnson	3B21, DH2	B	22	27	66	11	14	0	0	3	5	7	10	0	.212	.348
Bill Fahey (BG)	C18	L	33	19	22	4	6	1	0	0	2	5	3	0	.273	.318
Mike Ivie	1B12	R	30	12	42	4	9	4	0	0	7	2	4	0	.214	.310
Mike Laga	DH6, 1B5	L	23	12	21	2	4	0	0	2	1	9	0	.190	.190
Julio Gonzalez	SS6, 2B5, 3B1	R	30	12	21	0	3	1	0	0	2	1	7	9	.143	.190
Bob Molinari	DH1	L	30	5	3	2	3	0	0	0	0	1	1	0	1.000	1.000
Sal Butera	C4	R	30	4	5	1	1	0	0	0	0	0	0	0	.200	.200
Bill Nahorodny		R	29	2	1	0	0	0	0	0	0	1	0	0	.000	.000

NAME	T	AGE	W	L	PCT	SV	G	GS	CG	IP	H	BB	SO	SHO	ERA
		28	92	70	.568	28	162	162	42	1451	1318	522	875	9	3.80
Jack Morris	R	28	20	13	.606	0	37	37	20	294	257	83	232	1	3.34
Dan Petry	R	24	19	11	.633	0	38	38	9	266	256	99	122	2	3.92
Milt Wilcox (SJ)	R	33	11	10	.524	0	26	26	9	186	164	74	101	2	3.97
Juan Berenguer	R	28	9	5	.643	1	37	19	2	158	110	71	129	1	3.14
Aurelio Lopez	R	34	9	8	.529	18	57	0	0	115	87	49	90	0	2.81
Dave Rozema	R	26	8	3	.727	2	29	16	1	105	100	29	63	0	3.43
Doug Bair	R	33	7	3	.700	4	27	1	0	56	51	19	39	0	3.88
Howard Bailey	L	25	5	5	.500	0	33	3	0	72	69	25	21	0	4.88
Glenn Abbott	R	32	2	1	.667	0	7	7	1	47	43	7	11	1	1.93
Dave Rucker	L	25	1	2	.333	1	4	3	0	9	18	8	6	0	17.00
Larry Pashnick	R	27	1	3	.250	0	12	6	0	38	48	18	17	0	5.26
John Martin	L	27	0	0	—	1	15	0	0	13	15	4	11	0	7.43
Pat Underwood	L	26	0	0	—	0	4	0	0	10	11	6	2	0	8.71
Bob James	R	24	0	0	—	2	26	0	0	4	5	3	4	0	11.25
Dave Gumpert	R	25	0	2	.000	2	26	0	0	44	43	7	14	0	2.64
Jerry Ujdur	R	26	0	4	.000	0	11	6	0	34	41	20	13	0	7.15

NEW YORK   3rd 91-71 .562 7   BILLY MARTIN

Name	G by Pos	B	AGE	G	AB	R	H	2B	3B	HR	RBI	BB	SO	SB	BA	SA
TOTALS			30	162	5631	770	1535	269	40	153	728	533	686	84	.273	.416
Ken Griffey (LJ)	1B101, OF14, DH2	L	33	118	458	60	140	21	3	11	46	34	45	6	.306	.437
Willie Randolph (LJ)	2B104	L	28	104	420	73	117	21	1	2	38	53	32	12	.279	.348
Roy Smalley	SS91, 3B26, 1B22	B	30	130	451	70	124	24	1	18	62	58	58	3	.275	.452
Graig Nettles	3B126, DH1	L	38	129	462	56	123	17	3	20	75	51	65	0	.266	.446
Steve Kemp	OF101, DH2	L	28	109	373	53	90	17	3	12	49	41	37	1	.241	.399
1 Jerry Mumphrey	OF83	B	30	83	267	41	70	11	4	7	36	28	33	2	.262	.412
Dave Winfield	OF151	R	31	152	598	99	169	26	8	32	116	58	77	15	.283	.513
Butch Wynegar	C93	B	27	94	301	40	89	18	2	6	42	52	29	1	.296	.429
Don Baylor	DH136, OF5, 1B1	R	34	144	534	82	162	33	3	21	85	40	53	17	.303	.494
Andre Robertson (AA)	SS78, 2B29	R	25	98	322	37	80	16	3	1	22	8	54	2	.248	.326
Don Mattingly	OF48, 1B41, 2B1	L	22	91	279	34	79	15	4	4	32	21	31	0	.283	.409
Rick Cerone	C78, 3B1	R	29	80	246	18	54	7	0	2	22	15	29	0	.220	.272
Oscar Gamble	OF32, DH21	L	33	74	180	26	47	10	2	7	26	25	23	0	.261	.456
Bert Campaneris	2B32, 3B24	R	41	60	143	19	46	5	0	0	11	8	9	6	.322	.357
Lou Piniella	OF43, DH1	R	39	53	148	19	43	9	1	2	16	11	12	1	.291	.405
2 Omar Moreno	OF48	L	30	48	152	17	38	9	1	1	17	8	31	7	.250	.342
Steve Balboni	1B23, DH4	R	26	32	86	8	20	2	0	5	17	8	23	0	.233	.430
2 Larry Milbourne	2B19, SS6, 3B4	B	32	31	70	5	14	4	0	0	2	5	10	1	.200	.257
Bobby Meacham	SS18, 3B4	B	22	22	51	5	12	2	0	0	4	4	10	8	.235	.275
Otis Nixon	OF9	B	24	13	14	2	2	0	0	0	0	1	5	2	.143	.143
Brian Dayett	OF9	R	26	11	29	3	6	0	1	0	5	2	4	0	.207	.276
Juan Espino	C10	R	27	10	23	1	6	0	0	1	3	1	5	0	.261	.391
Bobby Murcer	DH5	L	37	9	22	2	4	2	0	1	1	1	1	0	.182	.409
Rowland Office	OF2	L	30	2	2	0	0	0	0	0	1	0	0	0	.000	.000

NAME	T	AGE	W	L	PCT	SV	G	GS	CG	IP	H	BB	SO	SHO	ERA
		29	91	71	.562	32	162	162	47	1457	1449	455	892	12	3.86
Ron Guidry	L	32	21	9	.700	0	31	31	21	250	232	60	156	3	3.42
Dave Righetti	L	24	14	8	.636	0	31	31	7	217	194	67	169	2	3.44
Shane Rawley	L	27	14	14	.500	1	34	33	13	238	246	79	124	2	3.78
Goose Gossage	R	31	13	5	.722	22	57	0	0	87	82	25	90	0	2.27
Ray Fontenot	L	25	8	2	.800	0	15	15	3	97	101	25	27	1	3.33
2 John Montefusco	R	33	5	0	1.000	0	6	6	0	38	39	10	15	0	3.32
Bob Shirley	L	29	5	8	.385	0	25	17	1	108	122	36	53	1	3.59
George Frazier	R	28	4	4	.500	8	61	0	0	115	94	45	78	0	3.43
2 Matt Keough	R	27	3	4	.429	0	12	12	0	56	59	20	26	0	5.17
Dale Murray	R	33	2	4	.333	1	40	0	0	94	113	22	45	0	4.48
Jay Howell (KJ)	R	27	1	5	.167	0	19	12	2	82	89	35	61	0	5.38
Rudy May (XJ)	R	38	1	5	.167	0	15	0	0	18	22	12	16	0	6.87
Curt Kaufman	R	25	0	0	—	0	4	0	0	9	10	4	8	0	3.12
Dave LaRoche	L	35	0	0	—	0	1	0	0	1	2	0	0	0	18.00
Roger Erickson	R	26	0	1	.000	0	5	0	0	17	13	8	7	0	4.32
1 Doyle Alexander	R	32	0	2	.000	0	8	5	0	28	31	7	17	0	6.35
1 Rick Reuschel 34 (SJ)															

TORONTO   4th 89-73 .549 9   BOBBY COX

Name	G by Pos	B	AGE	G	AB	R	H	2B	3B	HR	RBI	BB	SO	SB	BA	SA
TOTALS			29	162	5581	795	1546	268	58	167	748	510	810	131	.277	.436
Willie Upshaw	1B159, DH1	L	26	160	579	99	177	33	7	27	104	61	98	10	.306	.515
Damaso Garcia	2B130	R	28	131	525	84	161	23	6	3	38	24	34	31	.307	.390
Alfredo Griffin	SS157, 2B5, DH1	B	26	162	528	62	132	22	9	4	47	27	44	8	.250	.348
Rance Mulliniks	3B116, SS15, 2B2	L	27	129	364	54	100	34	3	10	49	57	43	0	.275	.467
Jesse Barfield	OF120, DH5	R	23	128	388	58	98	13	3	27	68	22	110	2	.253	.510
Lloyd Moseby	OF147	L	23	151	539	104	170	31	7	18	81	51	85	27	.315	.499
Dave Collins	OF112, 1B5, DH1	B	30	118	402	55	109	12	4	1	34	43	67	31	.271	.328
Ernie Whitt	C119	L	31	123	344	53	88	15	2	17	56	50	55	1	.256	.459
Cliff Johnson	DH130, 1B6	R	35	142	407	59	108	23	1	22	76	67	69	0	.265	.489
Garth Iorg	3B82, 2B39, SS1	R	28	122	375	40	103	22	5	2	39	13	45	7	.275	.376
Barry Bonnell	OF117, 3B4, DH1	R	29	121	377	49	120	21	3	10	54	33	52	10	.318	.469
Jorge Orta	DH69, OF17	L	32	103	245	30	58	6	3	10	38	19	29	1	.237	.408
Buck Martinez	C85	R	34	88	221	27	56	14	0	10	33	29	39	0	.253	.452
Hosken Powell	OF33, 1B1, DH1	L	28	40	83	6	14	0	0	1	7	5	8	2	.169	.205
George Bell	OF34, DH2	R	23	39	112	5	30	5	4	2	17	4	17	1	.268	.438
Mickey Klutts	3B17, DH2	R	28	22	43	3	11	0	0	3	5	1	11	0	.256	.465
Tony Fernandez	SS13, DH1	B	21	15	34	5	9	1	1	0	2	2	2	0	.265	.353
Mitch Webster	OF7, DH2	B	24	11	11	2	2	0	0	0	0	1	1	0	.182	.182
Geno Petralli	C5, DH1	B	23	6	4	0	0	0	0	0	0	1	1	0	.000	.000

NAME	T	AGE	W	L	PCT	SV	G	GS	CG	IP	H	BB	SO	SHO	ERA
		27	89	73	.549	32	162	162	43	1445	1434	517	835	8	4.12
Dave Stieb	R	25	17	12	.588	0	36	36	14	278	223	93	187	4	3.04
Jim Clancy	R	27	15	11	.577	0	34	34	11	223	238	61	99	1	3.91
Luis Leal	R	26	13	12	.520	0	35	35	7	217	216	65	116	1	4.31
Jim Gott	R	23	9	14	.391	0	34	30	6	177	195	68	121	1	4.74
Roy Lee Jackson	R	29	8	3	.727	7	49	0	0	92	92	41	48	0	4.50
Joey McLaughlin	R	26	7	6	.636	9	50	0	0	65	63	37	47	0	4.45
2 Doyle Alexander	R	32	7	6	.538	0	17	15	5	117	126	26	46	0	3.93
Randy Moffitt	R	34	6	2	.750	10	45	0	0	57	52	24	38	0	3.77
Jim Acker	R	24	5	1	.833	1	38	5	0	98	103	38	44	0	4.33
Stan Clarke	L	22	1	1	.500	0	10	0	0	11	10	5	7	0	3.27
Matt Williams	R	23	1	1	.500	0	4	3	0	8	13	7	5	0	14.63
Don Cooper	R	27	1	1	.500	—	4	0	0	5	8	0	5	0	6.75
Dave Geisel	L	28	0	0	.000	5	47	0	0	52	47	31	50	0	4.64
Mike Morgan (SJ)	R	23	0	3	.000	0	16	4	0	45	48	21	22	0	5.16

MILWAUKEE   5th 87-75 .537 11   HARVEY KUENN

Name	G by Pos	B	AGE	G	AB	R	H	2B	3B	HR	RBI	BB	SO	SB	BA	SA
TOTALS			30	162	5620	764	1556	281	57	132	732	475	665	101	.277	.418
Cecil Cooper	1B158, DH2	L	33	160	661	106	203	37	3	30	126	37	63	2	.307	.508
Jim Gantner	2B158	L	30	161	603	85	170	23	8	11	74	38	46	5	.282	.401
Robin Yount	SS139, DH8	R	27	149	578	102	178	42	10	17	80	72	58	12	.308	.503
Paul Molitor	3B148, DH2	R	26	152	608	95	164	28	6	15	47	59	74	41	.270	.410
Charlie Moore	OF150, C7, DH7	R	30	151	529	65	150	27	6	2	49	55	42	11	.284	.369
2 Rick Manning	OF108	L	28	108	375	40	86	14	4	3	32	26	40	11	.229	.312
Ben Oglivie	OF113, DH8	L	34	125	411	49	115	19	3	13	66	60	64	4	.280	.436
Ted Simmons	C86, DH66	B	33	153	600	76	185	39	3	13	108	41	51	4	.308	.448
Roy Howell	DH54, 1B2	L	29	69	194	23	54	9	6	4	25	15	29	1	.278	.448
Ned Yost (PJ)	C61	R	28	61	196	21	44	5	1	6	28	5	36	1	.224	.352
Ed Romero	SS22, OF15, 3B5, DH5, 2B3	R	25	59	145	17	46	7	0	1	18	8	8	1	.317	.386
Mark Brouhard (FJ)	OF42, DH11	R	27	56	185	25	51	10	1	7	23	9	39	0	.276	.454
Marshall Edwards	OF35, DH4	L	30	51	74	14	22	1	0	0	5	1	9	5	.297	.338
1 Gorman Thomas	OF46	R	32	46	164	21	30	6	1	5	18	23	50	2	.183	.323
Don Money (EJ)	DH28, 3B11, 1B2	R	36	43	114	5	17	5	0	1	8	11	17	0	.149	.219
Bill Schroeder	C23	R	24	23	73	7	13	2	1	3	7	3	23	0	.178	.356
Rob Picciolo	SS7, 2B2, 3B2, 1B1, DH1	R	30	14	27	2	6	3	0	0	1	0	4	0	.222	.333
Randy Ready	DH6, 3B4	R	23	12	37	8	15	3	2	1	6	4	3	0	.405	.676
Bob Skube	OF8, DH2, 1B1	L	25	12	25	2	5	1	1	0	9	4	7	0	.200	.320
Dion James	OF9, DH2	L	20	11	20	1	2	0	0	0	1	2	2	1	.100	.100

NAME	T	AGE	W	L	PCT	SV	G	GS	CG	IP	H	BB	SO	SHO	ERA
		30	87	75	.537	43	162	162	35	1454	1513	491	689	10	4.02
Jim Slaton	R	33	14	6	.700	5	46	0	0	112	112	56	38	0	4.33
Moose Haas	R	27	13	3	.813	0	25	25	7	179	170	42	75	3	3.27
Mike Caldwell	L	34	12	11	.522	0	32	32	10	228	269	51	58	2	4.53
Tom Tellmann	R	29	9	4	.692	8	44	0	0	100	95	35	48	0	2.80
Bob McClure	L	31	9	9	.500	0	24	23	4	142	152	68	68	0	4.50
Don Sutton	R	38	8	13	.381	0	31	31	4	220	209	54	134	0	4.08
Chuck Porter	R	27	7	9	.438	0	25	21	6	134	162	38	76	1	4.50
Tom Candiotti	R	25	4	4	.500	0	10	8	2	56	62	16	21	1	3.23
Jerry Augustine (AJ)	L	30	3	3	.500	2	34	7	1	64	89	25	40	0	5.74
Pete Ladd	R	26	3	4	.429	25	44	0	0	49	30	16	41	0	2.55
Bob Gibson	R	26	3	4	.429	2	27	7	0	81	71	46	46	0	3.90
Jaime Cocanower	R	26	2	0	1.000	0	5	3	1	30	21	12	8	0	1.80
Andy Beene	R	26	0	0	—	0	1	0	0	4	3	1	0	0	4.50
1 Jamie Easterly	L	30	0	1	.000	0	12	0	0	12	14	10	6	0	3.86
2 Rick Waits (SJ)	R	31	0	2	.000	0	10	2	0	30	39	11	20	0	5.10
Pete Vuckovich (SJ)	R	30	0	2	.000	0	3	3	0	15	15	10	10	0	4.91
Rollie Fingers 36 (EJ)															

BOSTON   6th 78-84 .481 20   RALPH HOUK

Name	G by Pos	B	AGE	G	AB	R	H	2B	3B	HR	RBI	BB	SO	SB	BA	SA
TOTALS			27	162	5590	724	1512	287	32	142	691	536	758	30	.270	.409
Dave Stapleton	1B145, 2B5	R	29	151	542	54	134	31	1	10	66	40	44	1	.247	.363
Jerry Remy	2B144	L	30	146	592	73	163	16	5	0	43	40	35	11	.275	.319
Glenn Hoffman	SS143	R	24	143	473	56	123	24	1	4	41	30	76	1	.260	.340
Wade Boggs	3B153	L	25	153	582	100	210	44	7	5	74	92	36	3	.361	.486
Dwight Evans (GJ)	OF99, DH21	R	31	126	470	74	112	19	4	22	58	70	97	3	.238	.436
Tony Armas	OF116, DH27	R	29	145	574	77	125	23	2	36	107	29	131	0	.218	.453
Jim Rice	OF151, DH1	R	30	155	626	90	191	34	1	39	126	52	102	0	.305	.550
Gary Allenson	C84	R	28	84	230	19	53	11	0	3	30	27	43	0	.230	.317
Carl Yastrzemski	DH107, 1B2, OF1	L	43	119	380	38	101	24	0	10	56	54	29	0	.266	.408
Rick Miller	OF66, 1B2, DH2	L	35	104	262	41	75	10	2	2	21	28	30	3	.286	.363
Reid Nichols	OF72, DH18, SS1	R	24	100	274	35	78	22	1	6	22	26	36	7	.285	.438
Rich Gedman	C69	L	23	81	204	21	60	16	1	2	18	15	37	0	.294	.412
Ed Jurak	SS38, 1B19, 3B12, DH5, 2B1	R	25	75	159	19	44	8	4	0	18	18	25	1	.277	.377
Jeff Newman	C51, DH6	R	34	59	132	11	25	4	0	3	7	10	31	0	.189	.288
Marty Barrett	2B23, DH5	R	25	33	44	7	10	1	1	0	2	3	1	0	.227	.295
Julio Valdez (ST)	2B9, SS2, DH1	B	27	12	25	3	3	0	0	0	1	0	4	0	.120	.120
Jackie Gutierrez	SS4	R	23	5	10	2	3	0	0	0	0	1	1	0	.300	.300
Lee Graham	OF3	L	23	6	2	0	0	0	0	0	1	0	0	1	.000	.000
Chico Walker	OF3	B	25	4	5	2	2	0	0	0	1	0	0	0	.400	.200

NAME	T	AGE	W	L	PCT	SV	G	GS	CG	IP	H	BB	SO	SHO	ERA
		27	78	84	.481	42	162	162	29	1446	1572	493	767	7	4.34
John Tudor	L	29	13	12	.520	0	34	34	7	242	236	81	136	2	4.09
Bob Ojeda	L	25	12	7	.632	0	29	28	5	174	173	73	94	0	4.04
Bruce Hurst	L	25	12	12	.500	0	33	32	6	211	241	62	115	2	4.09
Dennis Eckersley	R	28	9	13	.409	0	28	28	2	176	223	39	77	0	5.61
Bob Stanley	R	28	8	10	.444	33	64	0	0	145	145	38	65	0	2.85
Mike Brown (SJ)	R	24	6	6	.500	0	19	18	3	104	110	43	35	1	4.67
Luis Aponte	R	30	5	4	.556	3	34	0	0	62	74	23	32	0	3.63
Mark Clear	R	27	4	5	.444	4	48	0	0	96	101	68	81	0	6.28
Oil Can Boyd	R	23	4	8	.333	0	15	13	5	99	103	23	43	0	3.28
John Henry Johnson	L	26	3	2	.600	1	34	1	0	53	58	20	51	0	3.71
Al Nipper	R	24	1	1	.500	0	3	2	1	16	17	7	5	0	2.25
Doug Bird	R	33	1	4	.200	1	22	6	0	68	91	16	33	0	6.65

CLEVELAND — 7th 70-92 .432 28 — MIKE FERRARO 40-60 .400 — PAT CORRALES 30-32 .484

Name	G by Pos	B	AGE	G	AB	R	H	2B	3B	HR	RBI	BB	SO	SB	BA	SA
TOTALS			30	162	5476	704	1451	249	31	86	659	605	691	109	.265	.369
Mike Hargrove	1B131, DH1	L	33	134	469	57	134	21	4	3	57	78	40	0	.286	.367
1 Manny Trillo	2B88	R	32	89	320	33	87	13	1	1	29	21	46	1	.272	.328
Julio Franco	SS149	R	24	149	560	68	153	24	8	8	80	27	50	32	.273	.388
Toby Harrah (BH)	3B137, 2B1, DH1	R	34	138	526	81	140	23	1	9	53	75	49	16	.266	.365
George Vukovich	OF122	L	27	124	312	31	77	13	2	3	44	24	37	3	.247	.330
2 Gorman Thomas	OF106	R	32	106	371	51	82	17	0	17	51	57	98	2	.221	.404
Pat Tabler	OF88, 3B25, DH6, 2B2	R	25	124	430	56	125	23	5	6	65	56	63	2	.291	.409
Ron Hassey	C113, DH1	L	30	117	341	48	92	21	0	6	42	38	35	2	.270	.384
Andre Thornton	DH114, 1B27	R	33	141	508	78	143	27	1	17	77	87	72	4	.281	.439
Alan Bannister	OF91, 2B27, 1B3, DH3	R	31	117	377	51	100	25	4	5	45	31	43	6	.265	.393
Mike Fischlin	2B71, SS15, 3B4, DH1	R	27	95	225	31	47	5	2	2	23	26	32	9	.209	.276
Broderick Perkins	1B19, OF17, DH16	L	27	79	184	23	50	10	0	0	24	9	19	1	.272	.326
Bake McBride (SJ)	OF46, DH15	L	34	70	230	21	67	8	1	1	18	9	26	8	.291	.348
1 Rick Manning	OF50	L	28	50	194	20	54	6	0	1	10	12	22	7	.278	.325
Chris Bando	C43	B	27	48	121	15	31	3	0	4	15	15	19	0	.256	.380
Jim Essian	C47, 3B1	R	32	48	93	11	19	4	0	2	11	16	8	0	.204	.312
1 Miguel Dilone	OF19	B	28	32	68	15	13	3	1	0	7	10	5	5	.191	.265
Carmen Castillo	OF19, DH1	R	25	23	36	9	10	2	1	1	3	4	6	1	.278	.472
Jack Perconte	2B13	L	28	14	26	1	7	1	0	0	0	5	2	3	.269	.308
Kevin Rhomberg	OF9, DH1	R	27	12	21	2	10	0	0	0	2	2	4	1	.476	.476
Otto Velez	DH8	R	32	10	25	1	2	0	0	0	1	3	6	0	.080	.080
Karl Pagel	DH5, OF1	L	28	8	20	1	6	0	0	1	1	0	5	0	.300	.300
Wil Culmer	OF4, DH2	R	25	7	19	0	2	0	0	0	1	0	4	0	.105	.105

NAME	T	AGE	W	L	PCT	SV	G	GS	CG	IP	H	BB	SO	SHO	ERA
		28	70	92	.432	25	162	162	34	1441	1531	529	794	8	4.43
Rick Sutcliffe	R	27	17	11	.607	0	36	35	10	243	251	102	160	2	4.29
Lary Sorensen	R	27	12	11	.522	0	36	35	10	223	238	65	76	1	4.24
Neal Heaton	L	23	11	7	.611	7	39	16	4	149	157	44	75	1	4.16
1 Len Barker	R	27	8	13	.381	0	24	24	4	150	150	52	105	1	5.11
Bert Blyleven	R	32	7	10	.412	0	24	24	5	156	160	44	123	0	3.91
2 Jamie Easterly	L	30	4	2	.667	3	41	0	0	57	69	22	39	0	3.63
Juan Eichelberger	R	29	4	11	.267	0	28	15	2	134	132	59	56	0	4.90
Tom Brennan	R	30	2	2	.500	0	11	5	1	40	45	8	21	1	3.86
Dan Spillner	R	31	2	9	.182	8	60	0	0	92	117	38	48	0	5.07
Rich Barnes		23	1	1	.500	0	4	2	0	12	18	10	2	0	6.94
Mike Jeffcoat	L	23	1	3	.250	0	11	2	0	33	32	13	9	0	3.31
Bud Anderson	R	27	1	6	.143	0	39	1	0	68	64	32	32	0	4.08
Jerry Reed	R	27	0	0	—	0	7	0	0	21	26	9	11	0	7.17
1 Rick Waits	L	31	0	0	.000	0	8	0	0	20	23	9	13	0	4.58
Ernie Camacho	R	28	0	1	.000	0	4	0	0	5	5	2	2	0	5.06
Ed Glynn	L	30	0	2	.000	0	11	0	0	12	22	6	13	0	5.84
2 Rick Behenna	R	23	0	2	.000	0	5	4	0	26	22	14	9	0	4.15

WEST DIVISION

CHICAGO — 1st 99-63 .611 — TONY LARUSSA

Name	G by Pos	B	AGE	G	AB	R	H	2B	3B	HR	RBI	BB	SO	SB	BA	SA
TOTALS			28	162	5484	800	1439	270	42	157	762	527	888	165	.262	.413
Tom Paciorek	1B67, OF55, DH2	R	36	115	420	65	129	32	3	9	63	25	58	6	.307	.462
2 Julio Cruz	2B97	B	29	99	334	47	84	9	4	1	40	29	44	24	.251	.311
Jerry Dybzinski	SS118, 3B9	R	27	127	256	30	59	10	1	1	32	18	29	11	.230	.289
Vance Law	3B139, 2B3, SS2, OF1, DH1	R	26	145	408	55	99	21	5	4	51	51	56	3	.243	.348
Harold Baines	OF155	L	24	156	596	76	167	33	2	20	99	49	85	7	.280	.443
Rudy Law	OF132, DH3	L	25	145	501	95	142	20	7	3	34	42	36	77	.283	.369
Ron Kittle	OF139, DH4	R	25	145	520	75	132	19	3	35	100	39	150	8	.254	.504
Carlton Fisk	C133, DH2	R	35	138	488	85	141	26	4	26	86	46	88	9	.289	.518
Greg Luzinski	DH139, 1B2	R	32	144	502	73	128	26	1	32	95	70	117	2	.255	.502
Mike Squires	1B124, DH5, 3B1	L	31	143	153	21	34	4	1	1	11	22	11	3	.222	.281
Greg Walker	1B59, DH21	L	23	118	307	32	83	16	3	10	55	28	57	2	.270	.440
Scott Fletcher	SS100, 2B12, 3B7, DH1	R	24	114	262	42	62	16	5	3	31	29	22	5	.237	.370
Jerry Hairston	OF32, DH4	B	31	101	126	17	37	9	1	5	22	23	16	0	.294	.500
1 Tony Bernazard	2B59	B	26	59	233	30	61	16	2	2	26	17	45	2	.262	.373
Marc Hill	C55, DH2, 1B1	R	31	58	133	11	30	6	0	1	11	9	24	0	.226	.293
Lorenzo Gray	3B31, DH7	R	25	41	78	18	14	3	0	1	4	8	16	1	.179	.256
Dave Stegman	OF28	R	29	29	53	5	9	2	0	0	4	10	9	0	.170	.208
1 Rusty Kuntz	OF27, DH1	R	28	28	42	6	11	1	0	0	6	13	13	1	.262	.286
2 Aurelio Rodriguez	3B22	R	35	22	20	1	4	1	0	1	1	0	3	0	.200	.400
Chris Nyman	1B10, DH10	L	28	21	28	12	8	0	0	0	4	4	7	2	.286	.500
Casey Parsons	OF3, DH2	L	29	8	5	1	1	0	0	0	0	2	1	0	.200	.200
Joel Skinner	C6	R	22	6	11	2	3	0	0	0	1	0	1	0	.273	.273
Tim Hulett	2B6	R	23	6	5	0	1	0	0	0	0	0	1	0	.200	.200
2 Miguel Dilone	OF2, DH2	B	28	4	3	0	0	0	0	0	0	0	0	0	.000	.000

NAME	T	AGE	W	L	PCT	SV	G	GS	CG	IP	H	BB	SO	SHO	ERA
		29	99	63	.611	48	162	162	35	1445	1355	447	877	12	3.67
LaMarr Hoyt	R	28	24	10	.706	0	36	36	11	261	236	31	148	1	3.66
Rich Dotson	R	24	22	7	.759	0	35	35	8	240	209	106	137	1	3.23
Floyd Bannister	L	28	16	10	.615	0	34	34	5	217	191	71	193	2	3.35
Jerry Koosman	L	40	11	7	.611	2	37	24	2	170	176	53	90	1	4.77
Britt Burns (SJ)	L	24	10	11	.476	0	29	26	8	174	165	55	115	4	3.58
Dennis Lamp	R	30	7	7	.500	15	49	5	1	116	123	29	44	0	3.71
Salome Barojas	R	26	3	5	.500	12	52	0	0	87	70	32	38	0	2.47
Juan Agosto	L	25	2	2	.500	7	39	0	0	42	41	11	29	0	4.10
Dick Tidrow	R	36	2	4	.333	7	50	1	0	92	86	34	66	0	4.22
Guy Hoffman	L	26	1	0	1.000	0	11	0	0	6	14	2	2	0	7.50
Kevin Hickey (SJ)	L	26	1	2	.333	5	23	0	0	21	23	11	8	0	5.23
Steve Mura	R	28	0	0	—	0	6	0	0	13	16	6	4	0	4.38
Al Jones	R	24	0	0	—	0	2	0	0	2	3	2	2	0	3.86
Randy Martz	R	27	0	0	—	0	1	0	0	5	4	1	1	0	3.60
Jim Kern (EJ)	R	34	0	0	—	0	1	0	0	1	1	0	0	0	0.00

KANSAS CITY — 2nd 79-83 .488 20 — DICK HOWSER

Name	G by Pos	B	AGE	G	AB	R	H	2B	3B	HR	RBI	BB	SO	SB	BA	SA
TOTALS			30	163	5598	696	1515	273	54	109	653	397	722	182	.271	.397
Willie Aikens	1B112, DH6	L	28	125	410	49	124	26	1	23	72	45	75	0	.302	.539
Frank White	2B145	R	32	146	549	52	143	35	6	11	77	20	51	13	.260	.406
U. L. Washington	SS140, DH1	B	29	147	547	76	129	19	6	5	41	48	78	40	.236	.320
George Brett	3B102, 1B14, OF13, DH1	L	30	123	464	90	144	38	2	25	93	57	39	0	.310	.563
Amos Otis	OF96, DH1	R	36	98	356	35	93	16	3	4	41	27	63	5	.261	.357
Willie Wilson	OF136	B	27	137	576	90	159	22	8	2	33	33	75	59	.276	.352
Pat Sheridan	OF100	L	25	109	333	43	90	12	2	7	36	20	64	12	.270	.381
John Wathan	C92, 1B37, OF9	R	33	128	437	49	107	18	3	2	32	27	56	28	.245	.314
Hal McRae	DH156	R	37	157	589	84	183	41	6	12	82	50	68	2	.311	.462
Joe Simpson	1B54, OF38, P2, DH1	L	31	91	119	16	20	2	2	0	8	11	21	1	.168	.218
Leon Roberts	OF76, DH1	R	32	84	213	24	55	7	0	8	24	17	27	1	.258	.404
Don Slaught	C79, DH1	R	24	83	276	21	86	13	4	0	28	11	27	3	.312	.388
Onix Concepcion	3B31, 2B28, SS21, DH1	R	25	80	219	22	53	11	3	0	20	12	12	10	.242	.320
Greg Pryor	3B60, 1B6, 2B3, SS2	R	33	68	115	9	25	4	0	1	14	7	8	0	.217	.278
Cesar Geronimo (XJ)	OF35	L	35	38	87	2	18	4	0	0	4	2	13	0	.207	.253
Butch Davis	OF33	R	25	33	122	13	42	2	6	2	18	4	18	4	.344	.508
Darryl Motley	OF18, DH1	R	23	19	68	9	16	1	2	3	11	2	8	2	.235	.441
Jerry Martin (BW-BH)	OF13	R	34	13	44	4	14	2	0	2	13	1	7	1	.318	.500
Cliff Pastornicky	3B9	R	24	9	32	4	4	0	0	0	5	0	3	0	.125	.313
Ron Johnson	1B7, C2	R	27	9	27	2	7	0	0	0	3	0	1	0	.259	.259
Buddy Biancalana	SS6	B	23	6	15	2	3	0	0	0	0	0	7	1	.200	.200

NAME	T	AGE	W	L	PCT	SV	G	GS	CG	IP	H	BB	SO	SHO	ERA
		31	79	83	.488	49	163	163	19	1438	1535	471	593	8	4.25
Paul Splittorff	L	36	13	8	.619	0	27	27	4	256	259	52	61	0	3.63
Larry Gura	L	35	11	18	.379	0	34	31	5	200	220	76	57	0	4.90
Mike Armstrong	R	29	10	7	.588	3	58	0	0	103	86	45	52	0	3.86
Bud Black	L	26	10	7	.588	0	24	24	3	161	159	43	58	0	3.79
Dennis Leonard (KJ)	R	32	6	3	.667	0	10	10	1	63	69	19	31	0	3.71
Steve Renko	R	38	6	11	.353	1	25	17	1	121	144	36	54	0	4.30
Dan Quisenberry	R	30	5	3	.625	45	69	0	0	139	118	11	48	0	1.94
2 Gaylord Perry	R	44	4	4	.500	0	14	14	1	84	98	26	40	1	4.27
2 Eric Rasmussen	R	31	3	6	.333	0	11	9	2	53	61	22	18	1	4.78
Bill Castro	R	29	2	0	1.000	0	18	0	0	41	51	12	17	0	6.64
Mark Huismann	R	25	2	1	.667	0	13	0	0	31	29	17	20	0	5.58
Frank Wills	R	24	2	1	.667	0	4	3	0	35	35	15	23	0	4.15
Don Hood	L	33	2	3	.400	0	27	0	0	48	48	14	17	0	2.27
Keith Creel	R	24	2	5	.286	0	25	10	1	89	116	35	31	0	6.35
Danny Jackson	L	21	1	1	.500	0	4	3	0	19	26	6	9	0	5.21
Joe Simpson	L	31	0	0	—	0	2	0	0	3	4	2	1	0	3.00
Bob Tufts	L	27	0	0	—	0	7	0	0	7	16	5	3	0	8.10
Vida Blue	L	33	0	5	.000	0	19	14	1	85	96	35	53	0	6.01
Mike Jones 23 (ZJ)															

TEXAS — 3rd 77-85 .475 22 — DOUG RADER

Name	G by Pos	B	AGE	G	AB	R	H	2B	3B	HR	RBI	BB	SO	SB	BA	SA
TOTALS			29	163	5610	639	1429	242	33	106	587	442	767	119	.255	.366
Pete O'Brien	1B133, F27, DH1	L	25	154	524	53	124	24	5	8	53	58	62	5	.237	.347
Wayne Tolleson	2B112, SS26, DH1	B	27	134	470	64	122	13	2	3	20	40	68	33	.260	.315
Bucky Dent	SS129, DH1	R	31	131	417	36	99	15	2	2	34	23	31	3	.237	.297
Buddy Bell	3B154	R	31	156	618	75	171	35	3	14	66	50	48	3	.277	.411
Larry Parrish	OF132, DH13	R	29	145	555	76	151	26	4	26	88	46	91	0	.272	.474
George Wright	OF161	B	23	162	634	79	175	28	6	18	60	41	82	8	.276	.424
Billy Sample	OF146	R	28	147	554	80	152	28	3	12	57	44	46	44	.274	.401
Jim Sundberg	C131	R	32	131	378	30	76	14	0	2	36	35	64	0	.201	.254
Dave Hostetler	DH88, 1B2	R	27	94	304	31	67	9	2	11	46	42	103	0	.220	.372
Mickey Rivers	DH53, OF23	L	34	96	309	37	88	17	0	1	20	11	21	9	.285	.350
Bill Stein	2B32, 1B23, 3B10, DH6	R	36	78	232	21	72	15	1	2	33	8	31	2	.310	.409
Bobby Johnson	C62, 1B10	R	23	72	175	18	37	6	1	5	16	16	55	3	.211	.343
Larry Biittner	1B22, DH9, OF2	L	37	66	116	5	32	5	0	1	18	9	16	0	.276	.336
Jim Anderson	SS27, 2B17, 3B3, DH2, C1	R	26	50	102	8	22	1	1	0	5	5	22	1	.216	.245
Bobby Jones	OF11, DH11, 1B1	L	33	41	72	5	16	4	0	1	11	5	17	0	.222	.319
Mike Richardt (KJ)	2B20	R	25	22	83	9	13	2	1	1	7	2	11	0	.157	.241
Curt Wilkerson	SS9, 2B3, 3B2	B	22	16	35	7	6	0	1	0	2	3	5	3	.171	.229
Tommy Dunbar	OF9, DH1	L	23	12	24	3	6	0	0	0	3	3	3	0	.250	.250
Nick Capra	OF4	R	25	8	2	2	0	0	0	0	0	0	0	0	.000	.000
Donnie Scott	C2	B	21	4	0	0	0	0	0	0	0	0	0	0	.000	.000
Mark Wagner	SS2	R	29	2	2	0	0	0	0	0	0	0	1	0	.000	.000

NAME	T	AGE	W	L	PCT	SV	G	GS	CG	IP	H	BB	SO	SHO	ERA
		29	77	85	.475	32	163	163	43	1367	1392	471	826	11	3.31
Charlie Hough	R	35	15	13	.536	0	34	33	11	252	219	95	152	3	3.18
1 Rick Honeycutt	L	29	14	8	.636	0	25	25	5	175	168	37	56	2	2.42
Mike Smithson	R	28	10	14	.417	0	33	33	10	223	233	71	135	0	3.91
Danny Darwin	R	27	8	13	.381	0	28	26	9	183	175	62	92	2	3.49
Frank Tanana	L	29	7	9	.438	0	29	22	3	159	144	49	108	0	3.16
John Butcher	R	26	6	6	.500	5	38	6	1	123	128	41	58	1	3.51
2 Dave Stewart	R	26	5	2	.714	0	8	1	0	59	50	17	24	0	2.14
Dave Schmidt (EJ)	R	26	3	3	.500	2	31	0	0	46	42	14	29	0	3.88
Odell Jones (EJ)	R	30	3	6	.333	10	42	0	0	67	56	22	50	0	3.09
Dave Tobik	R	30	2	1	.667	9	27	0	0	44	36	13	30	0	3.68
Jon Matlack	L	33	2	4	.333	0	25	9	2	73	90	27	38	0	4.66
Tom Henke	R	25	1	0	1.000	1	8	0	0	16	16	4	17	0	3.38
Victor Cruz	R	25	1	3	.250	5	17	0	0	25	16	10	18	0	1.44
2 Ricky Wright	L	24	0	0	—	0	8	0	0	4	4	2	2	0	2.25
Al Lachowicz	R	22	0	0	—	0	1	0	0	4	8	4	4	0	2.25
Mike Mason	L	24	0	2	.000	0	7	2	0	11	10	6	9	0	5.91

OAKLAND — 4th 74-88 .457 25 — STEVE BOROS

Name	G by Pos	B	AGE	G	AB	R	H	2B	3B	HR	RBI	BB	SO	SB	BA	SA
TOTALS			28	162	5516	708	1447	237	28	121	662	524	872	236	.262	.381
Wayne Gross	1B74, 3B67, DH1, P1	L	31	137	339	34	79	18	0	12	44	36	52	3	.233	.392
Davey Lopes	2B123, DH12, OF7, 3B5	R	38	147	494	64	137	13	4	17	67	51	61	22	.277	.423
Tony Phillips	SS101, 2B63, 3B4, DH1	B	24	148	412	54	102	12	3	4	35	48	70	16	.248	.320
Carney Lansford (WJ)	3B78, SS1	R	26	80	299	43	92	16	2	10	45	22	33	3	.308	.475
Mike Davis (FJ)	OF121, DH3	L	24	128	443	61	122	24	4	8	62	27	74	33	.275	.402
Dwayne Murphy	OF124, DH7	L	28	130	471	55	107	17	2	17	75	62	105	7	.227	.380
Rickey Henderson	OF142, DH1	R	24	145	513	105	150	25	7	9	48	103	80	108	.292	.421
Mike Heath (XJ)	C80, OF24, 3B2, DH2	R	28	96	345	45	97	17	0	6	33	18	59	3	.281	.383
Jeff Burroughs	DH114	R	32	121	401	43	108	15	1	10	56	47	79	0	.269	.387
Bill Almon	SS52, 3B40, OF23, 2B5, DH4	R	30	143	451	45	120	29	1	4	63	26	67	26	.266	.361
Bob Kearney	C101, DH3	R	26	108	298	33	76	11	0	8	32	21	50	1	.255	.372
Garry Hancock	OF67, 1B27, DH9	L	29	101	256	29	70	7	3	8	30	5	13	2	.273	.418
Dan Meyer (SJ)	1B41, DH12, OF11, 3B1	L	30	69	169	15	32	9	0	1	19	19	11	0	.189	.260
Mitchell Page	DH34, OF10	L	31	57	79	16	19	3	0	0	1	10	22	3	.241	.278
Rickey Peters	OF47, DH8	B	27	55	178	20	51	7	0	0	20	12	21	4	.287	.278
Donnie Hill	SS53	B	22	53	158	20	42	7	0	2	15	4	21	1	.266	.348
Kelvin Moore	1B40	R	25	42	124	12	26	4	0	5	16	10	39	2	.210	.363
Darryl Cias	C19	R	26	20	18	1	6	1	0	0	1	2	4	1	.333	.389
Luis Quinones	2B6, 3B4, DH4, SS3	B	21	19	42	5	8	2	1	0	4	1	4	1	.190	.286
Rusty McNealy	DH7, OF5	L	24	15	4	5	0	0	0	0	0	0	0	0	.000	.000
Dave Hudgens	1B3, DH1	R	26	6	7	0	1	0	0	0	0	0	3	0	.143	.143
Marshall Brant	1B3, DH1	R	27	5	14	2	2	0	0	0	0	0	5	0	.143	.143
Joe Rudi 36 (LJ)																

NAME	T	AGE	W	L	PCT	SV	G	GS	CG	IP	H	BB	SO	SHO	ERA
		27	74	88	.457	33	162	162	22	1454	1462	626	719	12	4.34
Chris Codiroli	R	25	12	12	.500	1	37	31	7	206	208	72	85	2	4.46
Tom Underwood	L	29	9	7	.563	4	51	15	0	145	156	50	62	0	4.04
Bill Krueger (AJ)	L	25	7	6	.538	0	17	16	2	110	104	53	58	0	3.61
Tim Conroy	L	23	7	10	.412	0	39	18	3	162	141	98	112	1	3.94
Tom Burgmeier (SJ)	L	39	6	7	.462	4	49	0	0	96	89	32	39	0	2.81
Steve McCatty	R	29	6	9	.400	5	38	24	3	167	156	82	65	2	3.99
Mike Warren	R	22	5	3	.625	0	12	9	3	66	51	18	30	1	4.11
Dave Beard	R	23	5	5	.500	10	43	0	0	61	55	36	40	0	5.61
Mike Norris (SJ)	R	28	4	5	.444	0	16	16	2	89	68	36	63	0	3.76
1 Steve Baker	R	26	3	3	.500	1	35	1	0	54	59	26	23	0	4.33
Gorman Heimueller	L	27	3	5	.375	0	16	14	2	84	93	39	31	1	4.41
1 Matt Keough	R	27	2	3	.400	0	14	4	0	44	50	31	28	0	5.52
Keith Atherton	R	24	2	5	.286	4	29	0	0	68	53	23	40	0	2.77
Mark Smith	R	27	1	0	1.000	0	8	1	0	15	24	6	10	0	6.75
Jeff Jones (SJ)	R	26	1	1	.500	0	13	1	0	30	43	8	14	0	5.76
Ben Callahan	R	26	1	2	.330	0	4	2	0	9	18	5	2	0	12.54
Bert Bradley	R	26	0	0	—	0	6	0	0	8	14	4	3	0	6.48
2 Ed Farmer	R	33	0	0	—	0	5	1	0	10	15	0	7	0	3.48
Wayne Gross	L	31	0	0	—	0	1	0	0	2	2	1	0	0	0.00
Rich Wortham	L	29	0	0	—	0	1	0	0	3	1	3	0	0	∞
Curt Young	L	23	0	1	.000	0	8	2	0	9	17	5	5	0	16.00
Rick Langford (SJ-EJ)	R	31	0	4	.000	0	7	7	0	20	43	10	2	0	12.15

CALIFORNIA — (Tie)5th 70-92 .432 29 — JOHN McNAMARA

Name	G by Pos	B	AGE	G	AB	R	H	2B	3B	HR	RBI	BB	SO	SB	BA	SA
TOTALS			32	162	5640	722	1467	241	22	154	682	509	835	41	.260	.393
Rod Carew	1B89, DH24, 2B2	L	37	129	472	66	160	24	2	2	44	57	48	6	.339	.411
Bobby Grich (BH)	2B118, SS1	R	34	120	387	65	113	17	0	16	62	76	62	2	.292	.460
Tim Foli (SJ)	SS74, 3B13	R	32	88	330	29	83	10	0	2	29	5	18	2	.252	.300
Doug DeCinces (XJ)	3B85, DH10	R	32	95	370	49	104	19	3	18	65	32	56	2	.281	.495
Ellis Valentine (LJ)	OF85	R	28	86	271	30	65	10	2	13	43	18	48	2	.240	.435
Fred Lynn	OF113, DH2	L	31	117	437	56	119	20	3	22	74	55	83	2	.272	.483
Brian Downing (BW)	OF84, DH26	R	32	113	403	68	99	15	1	19	53	62	59	1	.246	.429
Bob Boone	C142	R	35	142	468	46	120	18	0	9	52	24	42	4	.256	.353
Reggie Jackson	DH62, OF47	L	37	116	397	43	77	14	1	14	49	52	140	0	.194	.340
Daryl Sconiers	1B57, DH27, OF1	L	24	106	314	49	86	19	3	8	46	17	41	4	.274	.430
Ron Jackson	3B38, 1B35, DH16, OF15	R	30	102	348	41	80	16	1	8	39	27	33	2	.230	.351
Juan Beniquez (BH)	OF84, DH20	R	33	92	315	44	96	15	0	3	34	15	29	4	.305	.381
Bobby Clark (SJ)	OF72, DH6, 3B1	R	28	76	212	17	49	9	1	5	21	9	45	0	.231	.354
Rob Wilfong	2B39, 3B13, SS6, DH1	L	19	65	177	17	45	7	1	2	17	10	25	0	.254	.339
Rick Adams	SS38, 3B16, 2B4	R	24	58	112	22	28	2	0	2	6	5	12	1	.250	.321
Steve Lubratich	SS23, 3B22, 2B14	R	25	57	156	12	34	9	0	0	7	4	17	0	.218	.276
Rick Burleson (SJ)	SS31	R	32	33	119	22	34	7	0	0	11	12	12	0	.286	.345
Mike Brown	OF31	R	23	31	104	12	24	5	1	3	9	7	20	1	.231	.385
Mike O'Berry	C26	R	29	26	60	7	10	1	0	1	5	3	11	0	.167	.233
Gary Pettis	OF21	B	25	22	85	19	25	2	3	3	6	7	15	8	.294	.494
Dick Schofield	SS21	R	20	21	54	4	11	2	0	3	4	6	8	0	.204	.407
Joe Ferguson	C9, OF3	R	36	12	27	3	2	0	0	0	2	5	8	0	.074	.074
Jerry Narron	C6, DH1	L	27	10	22	1	3	0	0	1	4	1	3	0	.136	.273
Ed Ott 31 (SJ)																

NAME	T	AGE	W	L	PCT	SV	G	GS	CG	IP	H	BB	SO	SHO	ERA
		32	70	92	.432	23	162	162	39	1474	1636	496	668	7	4.31
Bruce Kison (XJ)	R	33	11	5	.688	2	26	17	4	127	128	43	83	1	4.05
Ken Forsch	R	36	11	12	.478	0	31	31	11	219	226	61	81	1	4.06
Tommy John	L	40	11	13	.458	0	34	34	9	235	287	49	65	0	4.33
Luis Sanchez (SJ)	R	29	10	8	.556	7	56	1	0	98	92	40	49	0	3.66
Geoff Zahn (SA)	L	37	9	11	.450	0	29	28	11	203	212	51	81	3	3.33
Mike Witt	R	22	7	14	.333	5	43	19	2	154	173	75	77	0	4.91
Rick Steirer	R	26	3	2	.600	0	19	5	0	62	77	18	25	0	4.82
Steve Brown	R	26	2	3	.400	0	12	4	2	46	45	16	23	1	3.52
Byron McLaughlin(EJ)	R	27	2	4	.333	0	16	7	0	56	63	22	45	0	5.17
Doug Corbett	R	30	1	1	.500	0	11	0	0	17	26	4	18	0	3.63
Curt Brown	R	23	1	1	.500	0	10	0	0	16	25	4	7	0	7.31
John Curtis	L	35	1	2	.333	5	37	3	0	90	89	40	36	0	3.49
Bob Lacey	L	29	1	2	.333	0	8	0	0	9	12	0	7	0	5.19
Bill Travers	L	30	0	3	.000	0	10	7	0	43	58	19	24	0	5.91
Andy Hassler	L	31	0	5	.000	4	42	0	0	36	42	17	20	0	5.45
Dave Goltz	R	34	0	6	.000	0	15	6	0	64	81	37	27	0	6.22
Don Aase 28 (EJ)															

MINNESOTA — (Tie)5th 70-92 .432 29 — BILLY GARDNER

Name	G by Pos	B	AGE	G	AB	R	H	2B	3B	HR	RBI	BB	SO	SB	BA	SA
TOTALS			26	162	5601	709	1463	280	41	141	671	467	802	44	.261	.401
Kent Hrbek	1137, DH2	L	23	141	515	75	153	41	5	16	84	57	71	4	.297	.489
John Castino	2B132, 3B8, DH1	R	28	142	563	83	156	30	4	11	57	62	54	4	.277	.403
Ron Washington	SS81, 2B14, 3B1, DH1	R	31	99	317	28	78	7	3	4	26	20	50	10	.246	.325
Gary Gaetti	3B154, SS3, DH1	R	24	157	584	81	143	30	3	21	78	54	121	7	.245	.414
Tom Brunansky	OF146, DH4	R	22	151	542	70	123	24	5	28	82	61	95	2	.227	.445
Darrell Brown	OF81, DH3	B	27	91	309	40	84	6	2	0	22	10	28	3	.272	.304
Gary Ward	OF152, DH2	R	29	157	623	76	173	34	5	19	88	44	98	8	.278	.440
Dave Engle	C73, DH29, OF4	R	26	120	374	46	114	24	3	8	43	28	39	2	.305	.449
Randy Bush	DH103, 1B3	L	24	124	373	43	93	24	3	11	56	34	51	0	.249	.418
Mickey Hatcher	OF56, DH39, 1B7, 3B1	R	28	106	375	50	119	15	3	9	47	14	19	2	.317	.445
Tim Laudner	C57, DH4	R	25	62	168	20	31	9	0	6	18	15	49	0	.185	.345
Bobby Mitchell	OF44	L	28	59	152	26	35	4	2	1	15	28	21	1	.230	.303
Ray Smith	C59	R	27	59	152	11	34	5	0	0	8	10	12	1	.224	.257
Lenny Faedo (LJ)	SS51	R	23	51	173	16	48	7	0	1	18	4	19	0	.277	.335
Houston Jimenez	SS36	R	25	35	86	5	15	5	1	0	9	4	11	0	.174	.256
Scott Ullger	1B30, 3B3, DH1	L	27	35	79	8	15	4	0	0	5	5	21	0	.190	.241
2 Rusty Kuntz	OF30	R	28	31	100	13	19	3	0	3	5	12	28	0	.190	.310
Tim Teufel	2B18, SS1, DH1	R	24	21	78	11	24	7	1	3	6	2	8	0	.308	.538
Gerg Gagne	SS10	R	21	10	27	2	3	1	0	0	3	0	6	0	.111	.148
Tack Wilson	DH2, OF1	R	27	5	4	4	1	1	0	0	1	0	0	0	.250	.500
Jim Eisenreich (IL)	OF2	L	24	2	7	1	2	1	0	0	0	1	1	0	.286	.429

NAME	T	AGE	W	L	PCT	SV	G	GS	CG	IP	H	BB	SO	SHO	ERA
		26	70	92	.432	39	162	162	20	1437	1559	580	748	5	4.66
Ken Schrom	R	28	15	8	.652	0	33	28	6	196	196	80	80	1	3.71
Al Williams	R	29	11	14	.440	1	36	29	4	193	196	68	68	1	4.14
Bobby Castillo (SJ)	R	28	8	12	.400	0	27	25	3	158	170	65	90	0	4.77
Len Whitehouse	L	25	7	1	.875	2	60	0	0	74	70	44	44	0	4.15
Frank Viola	L	23	7	15	.318	0	35	34	4	210	242	92	127	0	5.49
Ron Davis	R	27	6	3	.385	30	66	0	0	89	89	33	84	0	3.34
Brad Havens	L	23	5	8	.385	0	16	14	1	80	110	38	40	0	8.18
Rick Lysander	R	30	5	12	.294	3	61	4	1	125	132	43	58	1	3.38
Pete Filson (SJ)	L	24	4	1	.800	1	26	8	0	90	87	29	49	0	3.43
Jack O'Connor	L	25	2	3	.400	0	27	0	0	83	107	36	56	0	5.86
Mike Walters	R	25	1	1	.500	2	23	0	0	59	52	20	21	0	4.12
Jim Lewis	R	27	0	0	—	0	6	0	0	18	24	7	8	0	6.50
Jay Pettibone	R	26	0	4	.000	0	7	7	0	27	28	8	10	0	5.33
Bryan Oelkers	L	22	0	5	.000	0	10	8	0	34	56	17	13	0	8.65

SEATTLE — 7th 60-102 .370 39 — RENE LACHEMANN 26-47 .356 DEL CRANDALL 34-55 .382

Name	G by Pos	B	AGE	G	AB	R	H	2B	3B	HR	RBI	BB	SO	SB	BA	SA
TOTALS			27	162	5336	558	1280	247	31	111	536	460	840	144	.240	.360
Pat Putnam	1B125, DH11	R	29	144	469	58	126	23	2	19	67	39	57	2	.269	.448
2 Tony Bernazard	2B79	B	26	80	300	35	80	18	1	6	30	38	52	21	.267	.393
Spike Owen	SS80	B	22	80	306	36	60	11	3	2	21	24	44	10	.196	.271
Jamie Allen	3B82, DH2	R	25	86	273	23	61	10	0	4	21	33	52	6	.223	.304
Al Cowens (SJ)	OF70, DH34	R	31	110	356	39	73	19	2	7	35	23	38	10	.205	.329
Dave Henderson	OF133, DH3	R	24	137	484	50	130	24	5	17	55	28	93	9	.269	.444
Steve Henderson	OF112, DH6	R	30	121	436	50	128	32	3	10	54	44	82	10	.294	.450
Rick Sweet	C85	B	30	93	249	18	55	9	0	1	22	13	26	2	.221	.269
Richie Zisk	DH84	R	34	90	285	30	69	12	0	12	36	30	61	0	.242	.411
Ricky Nelson	OF91, DH1	L	24	98	291	32	74	13	3	6	36	17	50	7	.254	.371
John Moses	OF71, DH6	B	25	93	130	19	27	4	1	0	6	12	20	11	.208	.254
Manny Castillo	3B55, 1B11, DH6, 2B5, P1	R	26	91	203	13	42	6	3	0	24	7	20	1	.207	.266
Orlando Mercado	C65	R	21	66	178	10	35	11	2	1	16	14	27	2	.197	.298
1 Todd Cruz	SS83	R	27	65	216	21	41	4	2	7	21	7	56	1	.190	.324
1 Julio Cruz	2B60, DH1	B	28	61	181	24	46	10	1	2	12	20	22	33	.254	.354
2 Ron Roenicke	OF54, 1B8, DH1	B	26	59	198	23	50	12	0	4	23	33	22	6	.253	.374
Domingo Ramos	SS28, 2B8, 3B8, DH2	R	25	53	127	14	36	4	0	2	10	7	12	3	.283	.362
Ken Phelps	1B22, DH19	L	28	50	127	10	30	4	1	7	16	13	25	0	.236	.449
Jamie Nelson	C39	R	23	40	96	9	21	3	0	1	5	13	12	4	.219	.281
Al Chambers	DH2, OF3	L	22	32	67	11	14	3	0	1	7	18	20	0	.209	.299
Dave Edler	3B13, DH6, 1B5, OF1	R	26	29	63	2	12	1	1	1	8	5	11	3	.190	.286
Darnell Coles	3B26	R	21	27	92	9	25	7	0	1	6	2	12	0	.283	.391
Jim Maler	1B19, DH5	R	24	26	66	5	12	1	0	1	3	5	11	0	.182	.242
Phil Bradley	OF27, DH1	R	24	23	67	8	18	2	0	0	1	5	5	1	.269	.299
Harold Reynolds	2B18	B	22	20	59	8	12	4	1	0	1	2	6	5	.203	.305
Rod Allen	DH3, OF2	R	23	11	12	1	2	0	0	0	0	1	3	0	.167	.167

NAME	T	AGE	W	L	PCT	SV	G	GS	CG	IP	H	BB	SO	SHO	ERA
		28	60	102	.370	39	162	162	25	1418	1455	544	910	9	4.12
Matt Young	L	24	11	15	.423	0	33	32	5	204	178	79	130	2	3.27
Jim Beattie (SJ)	R	28	10	15	.400	0	30	29	8	197	197	66	132	2	3.84
Bob Stoddard	R	26	9	17	.346	0	35	23	2	176	182	58	87	1	4.41
Bryan Clark	L	26	7	10	.412	0	41	17	2	162	160	72	76	0	3.94
Mike Moore	R	23	6	8	.429	0	22	21	3	128	130	60	108	2	4.71
1 Glenn Abbott (EJ)	R	32	5	3	.625	0	14	14	2	82	103	15	38	0	4.59
Roy Thomas	R	30	3	1	.750	1	43	0	0	89	95	32	77	0	3.45
1 Gaylord Perry	R	44	3	10	.231	0	16	16	2	102	116	23	42	0	4.94
Mike Stanton	R	30	2	3	.400	7	50	0	0	65	65	28	47	0	3.32
Ed Vande Berg	L	24	2	4	.333	0	68	0	0	94	59	22	49	0	3.36
Bill Caudill	R	26	2	4	.200	26	63	0	0	73	70	38	73	0	4.71
Bobby Castillo	R	28	0	0	—	0	4	0	0	3	3	2	5	0	23.63
Karl Best	R	24	0	1	.000	0	4	0	0	5	8	5	3	0	13.50
Gene Nelson	R	22	0	0	—	0	10	5	1	32	38	21	11	0	7.88
Edwin Nunez	R	20	0	4	.000	0	5	5	0	37	40	22	35	0	4.38

LINE SCORES

Team	1	2	3	4	5	6	7	8	9	10	11		R	H	E

AMERICAN LEAGUE CHAMPIONSHIPS: BALTIMORE (EAST) 3 CHICAGO (WEST) 1

Game 1 October 5 at Baltimore

| CHI | 0 0 1 | 0 0 1 | 0 0 0 | | 2 | 7 | 0 |
| BAL | 0 0 0 | 0 0 0 | 0 0 1 | | 1 | 5 | 0 |

Hoyt   McGregor,Stewart (7)
                                  T. Martinez (8)

Game 2 October 6 at Baltimore

| CHI | 0 0 0 | 0 0 0 | 0 0 0 | | 0 | 5 | 2 |
| BAL | 0 1 0 | 1 0 2 | 0 0 X | | 4 | 6 | 0 |

Bannister, Barojas (7),   Boddicker
Lamp (8)

Game 3 October 7 at Chicago

| BAL | 3 1 0 | 0 2 0 | 0 1 4 | | 11 | 8 | 1 |
| CHI | 0 1 0 | 0 0 0 | 0 0 0 | | 1 | 6 | 1 |

Flanagan, Stewart (6)   Dotson, Tidrow (6),
                                  Koosman (9), Lamp (9)

Game 4 October 8 at Chicago

| BAL | 0 0 0 | 0 0 0 | 0 0 3 | | 3 | 9 | 0 |
| CHI | 0 0 0 | 0 0 0 | 0 0 0 | | 0 | 10 | 0 |

Davis, T. Martinez (7)   Burns, Barojas (10),
                                  Agosto (10), Lamp (10)

NATIONAL LEAGUE CHAMPIONSHIPS: PHILADELPHIA (EAST) 3 LOS ANGELES (WEST) 1

Game 1 October 4 at Los Angeles

| PHI | 1 0 0 | 0 0 0 | 0 0 0 | | 1 | 5 | 1 |
| LA | 0 0 0 | 0 0 0 | 0 0 0 | | 0 | 7 | 0 |

Carlton, Holland (8)   Reuss, Niedenfuer (9)

Game 2 October 5 at Los Angeles

| PHI | 0 1 0 | 0 0 0 | 0 0 0 | | 1 | 7 | 2 |
| LA | 1 0 0 | 0 2 0 | 0 1 X | | 4 | 6 | 1 |

Denny, Reed (7)   Valenzuela, Niedenfuer (9)

Game 3 October 7 at Philadelphia

| LA | 0 0 0 | 2 0 0 | 0 0 0 | | 2 | 4 | 0 |
| PHI | 0 2 1 | 1 2 0 | 1 0 X | | 7 | 9 | 1 |

Welch, Pena (2)   Hudson
Honeycutt (5), Beckwith (5),
Zachry (7)

Game 4 October 8 at Philadelphia

| LA | 0 0 0 | 1 0 0 | 0 1 0 | | 2 | 10 | 0 |
| PHI | 3 0 0 | 0 2 2 | 0 0 X | | 7 | 13 | 1 |

Reuss, Beckwith (5),   Carlton, Reed (7),
Honeycutt (5), Zachry (7)   Holland (8)

WORLD SERIES — BALTIMORE (AL) 4 PHILADELPHIA (NL) 1

Game 1 October 11 at Baltimore

| PHI | 0 0 0 | 0 0 1 | 0 1 0 | | 2 | 5 | 0 |
| BAL | 1 0 0 | 0 0 0 | 0 0 0 | | 1 | 5 | 1 |

Denny, Holland (8)   McGregor, Stewart (9),
                                  T. Martinez (9)

Game 2 October 12 at Baltimore

| PHI | 0 0 0 | 1 0 0 | 0 0 0 | | 1 | 3 | 0 |
| BAL | 0 0 0 | 0 3 0 | 1 0 X | | 4 | 9 | 1 |

Hudson, Hernandez (5),   Boddicker
Andersen (6), Reed (8)

Game 3 October 14 at Philadelphia

| BAL | 0 0 0 | 0 0 1 | 2 0 0 | | 3 | 6 | 1 |
| PHI | 0 1 1 | 0 0 0 | 0 0 0 | | 2 | 8 | 2 |

Flanagan, Palmer (5),   Carlton
Stewart (7), T. Martinez (9)

Game 4 October 15 at Philadelphia

| BAL | 0 0 0 | 2 0 2 | 1 0 0 | | 5 | 10 | 1 |
| PHI | 0 0 0 | 1 2 0 | 0 0 0 | | 4 | 10 | 0 |

Davis, Stewart (6),   Denny, Hernandez (6),
T. Martinez (8)   Reed (6), Andersen (8)

Game 5 October 16 at Philadelphia

| BAL | 0 1 1 | 2 1 0 | 0 0 0 | | 5 | 5 | 0 |
| PHI | 0 0 0 | 0 0 0 | 0 0 0 | | 0 | 5 | 1 |

McGregor   Hudson, Bystrom (5),
                                  Hernandez (6), Reed (9)

COMPOSITE BATTING

NAME	POS	G	AB	R	H	2B	3B	HR	RBI	BA
Baltimore										
TOTALS		4	129	19	28	9	0	3	17	.217
Ripken	SS	4	15	5	6	2	0	0	1	.400
Murray	1B	4	15	5	4	0	0	1	0	.267
T. Cruz	3B	4	15	0	2	0	0	0	1	.133
Dauer	2B	4	14	0	0	0	0	0	0	.000
Singleton	DH	4	12	0	3	2	0	0	1	.250
Dempsey	C	4	12	1	2	0	0	0	0	.167
Landrum	RF-PH-PR	4	10	2	2	0	0	1	1	.200
Shelby	CF-PH	3	9	1	2	0	0	0	0	.222
Bumbry	CF-PR	3	8	0	1	1	0	0	1	.125
Lowenstein	LF-PH	2	6	0	1	1	0	0	2	.167
Ford	RF-PH	2	5	0	1	1	0	0	0	.200
Roenicke	LF-PH	3	4	4	3	1	0	1	4	.750
Dwyer	RF-PH	2	4	1	1	1	0	0	0	.250
Ayala	PH	1	1	0	0	0	0	0	1	—
Nolan	PH	1	0	0	0	0	0	0	1	—
Chicago										
TOTALS		4	133	3	28	4	0	0	2	.211
R. Law	CF	4	18	1	7	1	0	0	0	.389
Fisk	C	4	17	0	3	1	0	0	0	.176
Paciorek	1B-LF	4	16	1	4	0	0	0	0	.250
Baines	RF	4	16	0	2	0	0	0	0	.125
Luzinski	DH	4	15	0	2	0	0	0	0	.133
J. Cruz	2B	4	12	0	4	0	0	0	0	.333
V. Law	3B	4	11	0	2	0	0	0	1	.182
Kittle	LF	3	7	1	2	1	0	0	0	.286
Fletcher	SS	3	7	0	0	0	0	0	0	.000
Dybzinski	SS	2	4	0	1	0	0	0	0	.250
Squires	1B-PH-PR	4	4	0	0	0	0	0	0	.000
Walker	1B-PH	2	3	0	1	0	0	0	0	.333
Hairston	RF-LF-PH	2	3	0	0	0	0	0	0	.000
Rodriguez	3B	2	0	0	0	0	0	0	0	—
Philadelphia										
TOTALS		4	130	16	34	4	0	5	15	.262
Rose	1B	4	16	3	6	0	0	0	0	.375
Schmidt	3B	4	15	1	7	2	0	1	2	.467
Morgan	2B	4	15	1	1	0	0	0	0	.067
Matthews	LF	4	14	4	6	0	0	3	8	.429
Lezcano	RF-LF-PH	4	13	2	4	0	0	1	1	.308
Diaz	C	4	13	0	2	1	0	0	0	.154
DeJesus	SS	4	12	0	3	0	0	0	1	.250
Maddox	CF	3	11	0	3	1	0	0	0	.273
Carlton	P	2	5	0	1	0	0	0	0	.200
G. Gross	CF-LF-DH	4	5	1	0	0	0	0	0	.000
Hudson	P	1	2	0	0	0	0	0	0	.000
Lefebrve	RF-PH	2	2	0	0	0	0	0	0	.000
Hayes	RF-PH	2	2	0	0	0	0	0	0	.000
Perez	PH	1	1	0	1	0	0	0	0	1.000

Virgil PH 0-1, Denny P 0-1, Dernier CF 0-0, Samuel PR 0-0.
Holland P 0-0, Reed P 0-0

NAME	POS	G	AB	R	H	2B	3B	HR	RBI	BA
Los Angeles										
TOTALS		4	129	8	27	5	1	2	7	.209
S. Sax	2B	4	16	1	4	0	0	0	0	.250
Marshall	1B-RF	4	15	1	2	1	0	1	2	.133
Baker	LF	4	14	4	5	1	0	1	1	.357
Russell	SS	4	14	1	4	0	0	0	0	.286
Landreaux	CF	4	14	0	2	0	0	0	1	.143
Guerrero	3B	4	12	1	3	1	1	0	2	.250
Thomas	RF-PH	4	9	0	4	1	0	0	0	.444
Brock	1B	3	8	0	0	0	0	0	0	.000
Fimple	C	3	7	0	1	0	0	0	1	.143
Yeager	C	2	6	0	1	1	0	0	0	.167
Reuss	P	2	3	0	0	0	0	0	0	.000
Valenzuela	P	1	3	0	0	0	0	0	0	.000
Landestoy	PH	2	2	0	0	0	0	0	0	.000
Maldonado	PH	2	2	0	0	0	0	0	0	.000
Morales	PH	2	2	0	0	0	0	0	0	.000
Pena	P	1	1	0	1	0	0	0	0	1.000

Monday PH 0-0, Beckwith P 0-0, Honeycutt P 0-0,
Niedenfuer P 0-0, Welch P 0-0, Zachry P 0-0

NAME	POS	G	AB	R	H	2B	3B	HR	RBI	BA
Baltimore										
TOTALS		5	164	18	35	8	0	6	17	.213
Murray	1B	5	20	2	5	0	0	2	3	.250
Dauer	2B-3B	5	19	2	4	1	0	0	3	.211
Ripken	SS	5	18	2	3	0	0	0	0	.167
Cruz	3B	5	16	1	2	0	0	0	0	.125
Dempsey	C	5	13	3	5	4	0	1	2	.385
Lowenstein	LF	4	13	2	5	1	0	1	1	.385
Ford	RF-PH	5	12	1	2	0	0	1	1	.167
Bumbry	CF	4	11	0	1	1	0	0	1	.091
Shelby	CF-PH-PR	5	9	1	4	0	0	0	0	.444
Dwyer	RF-PH	2	8	3	3	1	0	1	1	.375
Roenicke	LF-PH	3	7	0	0	0	0	0	0	.000
McGregor	P	2	5	0	0	0	0	0	0	.000
Boddicker	P	1	3	0	0	0	0	0	0	.000
Nolan	C-PH	2	2	0	0	0	0	0	0	.000
Ayala	PH	1	1	1	1	0	0	0	1	1.000

Davis P 0-2, Stewart P 0-2, Sakata 2B-PR 0-1, Singleton PH 0-1,
Flanagan P 0-1, Landrum RF-LF-PR 0-0, T. Martinez P 0-0, Palmer P 0-0

NAME	POS	G	AB	R	H	2B	3B	HR	RBI	BA
Philadelphia										
TOTALS		5	159	9	31	4	1	4	9	.195
Schmidt	3B	5	20	1	1	0	0	0	0	.050
Morgan	2B	5	19	3	5	0	1	2	2	.263
Rose	1B-RF-PH	5	16	1	5	1	0	0	1	.313
Matthews	LF	5	16	1	4	0	0	1	1	.250
DeJesus	SS	5	16	0	2	0	0	0	0	.125
Diaz	C	5	15	1	5	1	0	0	0	.333
Maddox	CF-PH	4	12	1	3	1	0	1	0	.250
Perez	1B-PH	4	10	0	2	0	0	0	2	.200
Lezcano	RF-PH	4	8	0	1	0	0	0	0	.125
G. Gross	CF	2	2	0	0	0	0	0	0	.000
Lefebvre	RF-PH	3	5	0	1	1	0	0	0	.200
Denny	P	2	5	0	1	0	0	0	1	.200
Hayes	RF-PH	4	4	0	0	0	0	0	0	.000
Carlton	P	1	3	0	0	0	0	0	0	.000
Virgil	C-PH	3	2	0	1	0	0	0	0	.500

Hudson, P 0-2, Samuel PH-PR 0-1, Dernier PR 0-0, Andersen P 0-0,
Bystrom, P 0-0, Hernandez P 0-0, Holland P 0-0, Reed P 0-0

COMPOSITE PITCHING

NAME	G	IP	H	BB	SO	W	L	SV	ERA
Baltimore									
TOTALS	4	37	28	12	26	3	1	1	0.49
Boddicker	1	9	5	3	14	1	0	0	0.00
McGregor	1	6.2	6	3	2	0	1	0	1.35
Davis	1	6	5	2	6	0	0	0	0.00
T. Martinez	2	6	5	3	5	1	0	0	0.00
Flanagan	1	5	5	0	1	1	0	0	1.80
Stewart	2	4.1	2	1	2	0	0	1	0.00
Chicago									
TOTALS	4	36	28	16	24	1	3	0	4.00
Burns	0	9.1	6	5	8	0	1	0	0.96
Hoyt	1	9	5	0	4	1	0	0	1.00
Bannister	0	6	5	1	5	0	1	0	4.50
Dotson	0	5	6	3	3	0	1	0	10.80
Tidrow	0	3	1	3	3	0	0	0	3.00
Lamp	3	2	0	2	1	0	0	0	0.00
Barojas	2	1	4	0	0	0	0	0	18.00
Agosto	1	0.1	0	1	0	0	0	0	0.00
Koosman	1	0.1	1	2	0	0	0	0	54.00
Philadelphia									
TOTALS	4	35	27	11	31	3	1	1	1.03
Carlton	2	13.2	13	5	13	2	0	0	0.66
Hudson	1	9	4	2	9	1	0	0	2.00
Denny	1	6	3	2	6	0	1	0	0.00
Reed	2	3.1	4	1	3	0	0	1	2.70
Holland	2	3	1	0	3	0	0	1	0.00
Los Angeles									
TOTALS	4	34	34	15	22	1	3	1	3.97
Reuss	2	12	14	3	4	0	2	0	4.50
Valenzuela	1	8	7	4	5	1	0	0	1.13
Zachry	2	4	4	2	2	0	0	0	2.25
Pena	1	2.2	4	1	3	0	0	0	6.75
Beckwith	2	2.1	1	2	3	0	0	0	0.00
Niedenfuer	2	2	0	1	3	0	0	1	0.00
Honeycutt	2	1.2	4	0	2	0	0	0	21.60
Welch	1	1.1	0	2	0	0	1	0	6.75
Baltimore									
TOTALS	5	45	31	7	29	4	1	2	1.60
McGregor	2	17	9	2	12	1	1	0	1.06
Boddicker	1	9	3	0	6	1	0	0	0.00
Stewart	3	5	2	2	6	0	0	0	0.00
Davis	1	5	6	1	3	0	0	0	5.40
Flanagan	1	4	6	1	1	0	0	0	4.50
T. Martinez	3	3	3	0	0	0	0	2	3.00
Palmer	1	2	2	1	1	1	0	0	0.00
Philadelphia									
TOTALS	5	44	35	10	37	1	4	1	3.48
Denny	2	13	12	3	9	1	1	0	3.46
Hudson	1	8.1	9	1	6	0	2	0	8.64
Carlton	1	6.2	5	3	7	0	1	0	2.70
Hernandez	3	4	1	1	3	0	0	0	0.00
Andersen	2	4	4	0	1	0	0	0	2.25
Holland	3	3.2	1	0	5	0	0	1	0.00
Reed	3	3.1	4	2	4	0	0	0	2.70
Bystrom	1	1	0	0	1	0	0	0	0.00

PHILADELPHIA 1st 90-72 .556   PAT CORRALES 43-42 .506   PAUL OWENS 47-30 .610

Name	G by Pos	B	AGE	G	AB	R	H	2B	3B	HR	RBI	BB	SO	SB	BA	SA
TOTALS			32	163	5426	696	1352	209	45	125	649	640	906	143	.249	.373
Pete Rose	1B112, OF35	B	42	151	493	52	121	14	3	0	45	52	28	7	.245	.286
Joe Morgan	2B117	L	39	123	404	72	93	20	1	16	59	89	54	18	.230	.403
Ivan DeJesus	SS158	R	30	158	497	60	126	15	7	4	45	53	77	11	.254	.336
Mike Schmidt	3B153, SS2	R	33	154	534	104	136	16	4	40	109	128	148	7	.255	.524
Von Hayes	OF103	L	24	124	351	45	93	9	5	6	32	36	55	20	.265	.370
Garry Maddox	OF95	R	33	97	324	27	89	14	2	4	32	11	31	8	.275	.367
Gary Matthews	OF122	R	32	132	446	66	115	18	2	10	50	69	81	13	.258	.374
Bo Diaz	C134	R	30	136	471	49	111	17	0	15	64	38	57	1	.236	.367
Greg Gross	OF110, 1B1	L	30	136	245	25	74	12	3	0	29	34	16	3	.302	.376
Bob Dernier	OF107	R	26	122	221	41	51	10	0	1	15	18	21	35	.231	.290
2 Joe Lefebvre	OF74, 3B9, C3	L	27	101	258	34	80	20	8	8	38	31	46	5	.310	.543
Tony Perez	1B69	R	41	91	253	18	61	11	2	6	43	28	57	1	.241	.372
Kiko Garcia	2B52, SS22, 3B10	R	29	84	118	22	34	7	1	2	9	9	20	1	.288	.415
Ozzie Virgil	C51	R	26	55	140	11	30	7	0	6	23	8	34	0	.214	.393
1 Larry Milbourne	2B27, SS8, 3B3	B	32	41	66	3	16	0	1	0	4	4	7	2	.242	.273
Len Matuszek	1B21	L	28	28	80	12	22	6	1	4	16	4	14	0	.275	.525
1 Bob Molinaro		L	33	19	18	1	2	1	0	1	3	0	2	0	.111	.333
Juan Samuel	2B18	R	22	18	65	14	18	1	2	2	5	4	16	3	.277	.446
2 Sixto Lezcano	OF15	R	29	18	39	8	11	1	0	0	7	5	9	1	.282	.308
Steve Jeltz	2B4, SS2, 3B2	R	24	13	8	0	1	0	1	0	1	1	2	0	.125	.375
Bill Robinson	1B3, 3B2, OF1	R	40	10	7	0	1	0	0	0	2	1	4	0	.143	.143
Jeff Stone	OF1	L	22	9	4	2	3	0	2	0	3	0	1	4	.750	1.750
Alex Sanchez	OF2	R	24	8	7	2	2	0	0	0	2	0	2	0	.286	.286
Tim Corcoran	1B3	L	30	3	0	0	0	0	0	0	0	0	0	0	—	—
Luis Aguayo (BH)	SS2	R	24	2	4	1	1	0	0	0	0	1	2	0	.250	.250
Darren Daulton	C2	L	21	2	3	1	1	0	0	0	0	0	1	0	.333	.333
Dave Roberts 32 (KJ)																

NAME	T	AGE	W	L	PCT	SV	G	GS	CG	IP	H	BB	SO	SHO	ERA
TOTALS		30	90	72	.556	41	163	163	20	1462	1429	464	1092	10	3.34
John Denny	R	30	19	6	.760	0	36	36	7	243	229	53	139	1	2.37
Steve Carlton	L	38	15	16	.484	0	37	37	8	284	277	84	275	3	3.11
Ron Reed	R	40	9	1	.900	8	61	0	0	96	89	34	73	0	3.48
Al Holland	L	30	8	4	.667	25	68	0	0	93	63	30	100	0	2.26
2 Willie Hernandez	L	28	8	4	.667	7	63	0	0	96	93	26	75	0	3.29
Charlie Hudson	R	24	8	8	.500	0	26	26	3	169	158	53	101	0	3.35
Marty Bystrom(XJ-EJ)	R	24	6	9	.400	0	24	23	1	119	136	44	87	0	4.60
Kevin Gross	R	22	4	6	.400	0	17	17	1	96	100	35	66	1	3.56
1 Sid Monge	L	32	3	0	1.000	1	14	0	0	12	20	6	7	0	6.94
Tug McGraw	L	38	2	1	.667	0	34	1	0	56	58	19	30	0	3.56
Porfi Altamirano	R	31	2	3	.400	0	31	0	0	41	38	15	24	0	3.70
Larry Christenson(EJ)	R	29	2	4	.333	0	9	9	0	48	42	17	14	0	3.91
Larry Andersen	R	30	1	0	1.000	0	17	0	0	26	19	9	14	0	2.39
Steve Comer	R	29	1	0	1.000	0	3	1	0	9	11	3	1	0	5.19
Tony Ghelfi	R	21	1	1	.500	0	3	3	0	14	15	6	14	0	3.14
1 Dick Ruthven	R	32	1	3	.250	0	7	7	0	34	46	10	26	0	5.61
Don Carman	L	23	0	0	—	0	1	0	0	1	0	0	0	0	0.00
1 Ed Farmer (VJ)	R	33	0	6	.000	0	12	3	0	27	35	20	16	0	6.08

PITTSBURGH 2nd 84-78 .519 6   CHUCK TANNER

Name	G by Pos	B	AGE	G	AB	R	H	2B	3B	HR	RBI	BB	SO	SB	BA	SA
TOTALS			29	162	5531	659	1460	238	29	121	612	497	873	124	.264	.383
Jason Thompson	1B151	L	28	152	517	70	134	20	1	18	76	99	128	1	.259	.406
Johnny Ray	2B151	B	26	151	576	68	163	38	7	5	53	35	26	18	.283	.399
Dale Berra	SS161	R	26	161	537	51	135	25	1	10	52	61	84	8	.251	.358
Bill Madlock	3B126	R	32	130	473	68	153	21	0	12	68	49	24	3	.323	.444
Dave Parker	OF142	L	32	144	552	68	154	29	4	12	69	28	89	12	.279	.411
Marvell Wynne	OF102	L	23	103	366	66	89	16	2	7	26	38	52	12	.243	.355
Mike Easler	OF105	L	32	115	381	44	117	17	2	10	54	22	64	4	.307	.441
Tony Pena	C149	R	26	151	542	51	163	22	3	15	70	31	73	6	.301	.435
Lee Mazzilli	OF57, 1B7	B	28	109	246	37	59	9	0	5	24	49	43	15	.240	.337
Lee Lacy	OF98	R	35	108	288	40	87	12	3	4	13	22	36	31	.302	.406
Richie Hebner	3B40, 1B7, OF7	L	35	78	162	23	43	4	1	5	26	17	28	8	.265	.395
Jim Morrison	2B28, 3B26, SS7	R	30	66	158	16	48	7	2	6	25	9	25	2	.304	.487
Brian Harper	OF35, 1B1	R	23	61	131	16	29	4	1	7	20	2	15	0	.221	.427
Gene Tenace	1B19, C3, OF1	R	36	53	62	7	11	5	0	0	6	12	17	0	.177	.258
Doug Frobel	OF24	L	24	32	60	10	17	4	1	3	11	4	17	1	.283	.533
1 Steve Nicosia (SJ)	C15	R	27	21	46	4	6	2	0	1	5	3	3	0	.130	.239
2 Milt May	C4	L	32	7	12	0	3	0	0	0	1	0	1	0	.250	.250
Joe Orsulak	OF4	L	21	7	11	0	2	0	0	0	1	0	2	0	.182	.182
2 Miguel Dilone		B	27	7	0	1	0	0	0	0	0	0	2	0	—	—
1 Junior Ortiz	C4	R	23	5	8	1	1	0	0	0	0	0	0	0	.125	.125
Ron Wotus	SS2, 2B1	R	22	5	3	0	0	0	0	0	0	0	1	0	.000	.000
Rafael Belliard	SS3	R	21	4	1	1	0	0	0	0	0	0	1	0	.000	.000

NAME	T	AGE	W	L	PCT	SV	G	GS	CG	IP	H	BB	SO	SHO	ERA
TOTALS		28	84	78	.519	41	162	162	25	1462	1378	563	1061	14	3.55
Larry McWilliams	L	29	15	8	.652	0	35	35	8	238	205	87	199	4	3.25
John Candelaria	L	29	15	8	.652	0	33	32	2	198	191	45	157	0	3.23
Rick Rhoden	R	30	13	13	.500	1	36	35	7	244	256	68	153	2	3.09
Lee Tunnell	R	22	11	6	.647	0	35	25	5	178	167	58	95	3	3.65
Jose DeLeon	R	22	7	3	.700	0	15	15	3	108	75	47	118	2	2.83
Kent Tekulve	R	36	7	5	.583	18	76	0	0	99	78	36	52	0	1.64
Jim Bibby	R	38	5	12	.294	2	29	12	0	78	92	51	44	0	6.69
Rod Scurry	L	27	3	9	.308	7	61	0	0	68	63	53	67	0	5.56
Manny Sarmiento	R	27	3	5	.375	4	52	0	0	84	74	36	49	0	2.99
Don Robinson (SJ)	R	26	2	2	.500	0	9	6	0	36	43	21	28	0	4.46
Cecilio Guante	R	23	2	6	.250	9	49	0	0	100	90	46	82	0	3.32
Jim Winn	R	23	0	0	—	0	7	0	0	11	12	6	3	0	7.36
Dave Tomlin	L	34	0	0	—	0	5	0	0	4	4	1	1	0	6.75
Alfonso Pulido	L	26	0	0	—	0	1	0	0	2	4	1	0	0	9.00
Bob Owchinko	L	28	0	0	—	0	1	0	0	1	0	0	1	0	0.00
Randy Niemann	L	27	0	1	.000	0	8	1	0	14	20	7	8	0	9.22

MONTREAL 3rd 82-80 .506 8   BILL VIRDON

Name	G by Pos	B	AGE	G	AB	R	H	2B	3B	HR	RBI	BB	SO	SB	BA	SA
TOTALS			28	163	5611	677	1482	297	41	102	632	509	733	138	.264	.386
Al Oliver	1B153, OF1	L	36	157	614	70	184	38	3	8	84	44	44	1	.300	.410
Doug Flynn	2B107, SS37	R	32	143	452	44	107	18	4	0	26	19	38	2	.237	.294
Chris Speier	SS74, 3B12, 2B1	R	33	88	261	31	67	12	2	2	22	29	37	2	.257	.341
Tim Wallach	3B156	R	26	156	581	54	156	33	3	19	70	55	97	0	.269	.434
Warren Cromartie	OF101, 1B1	L	29	120	360	37	100	26	2	3	43	43	48	8	.278	.386
Andre Dawson	OF157	R	28	159	644	104	189	36	10	32	113	38	81	25	.299	.539
Tim Raines	OF154, 2B7	B	23	156	615	133	183	32	8	11	71	97	70	90	.298	.429
Gary Carter	C144, 1B1	R	29	145	541	63	146	37	3	17	79	51	57	1	.270	.444
Terry Francona	OF51, 1B47	L	24	120	230	21	59	11	1	3	22	6	20	0	.257	.352
Bryan Little	SS66, 2B51	B	23	106	350	48	91	15	3	1	36	50	22	4	.260	.329
Jim Wohlford	OF61	R	32	83	141	7	39	8	0	1	14	3	14	0	.277	.355
Terry Crowley	1B4	L	36	50	44	2	8	0	0	0	3	9	4	0	.182	.182
Jerry White	OF13	R	30	40	34	4	5	1	0	0	0	12	8	4	.147	.176
Angel Salazar	SS34	R	21	36	37	5	8	1	1	0	1	1	8	1	.216	.297
2 Mike Vail	OF15, 1B1, 3B1	R	31	34	53	5	15	2	0	2	4	8	10	0	.283	.434
2 Manny Trillo	2B31	R	32	32	121	16	32	8	0	2	16	10	18	0	.264	.380
Bobby Ramos	C25	R	27	27	61	2	14	3	1	0	5	8	11	0	.230	.311
Mike Stenhouse	OF9, 1B5	L	25	24	40	2	5	1	0	0	2	4	10	0	.125	.150
Brad Mills	3B3, 1B1	L	26	14	20	1	5	0	0	0	1	2	3	0	.250	.250
2 Gene Roof	OF5	B	25	8	12	2	2	0	0	0	2	0	3	0	.167	.333
Tim Blackwell	C5	B	30	6	15	0	3	1	0	0	2	1	3	0	.200	.267
Mike Fuentes		R	24	6	4	1	1	0	0	0	0	0	2	0	.250	.250
Mike Phillips	SS3, 3B2	L	32	5	2	0	0	0	0	0	0	0	0	0	.000	.000
Wallace Johnson		B	26	3	2	1	1	0	0	0	0	1	0	1	.500	.500
Razor Shines	OF1	R	26	3	2	0	1	0	0	0	0	0	0	0	.500	.500
Tom Wieghaus	C1	R	26	2												

NAME	T	AGE	W	L	PCT	SV	G	GS	CG	IP	H	BB	SO	SHO	ERA
TOTALS		28	82	80	.506	34	163	163	38	1471	1406	479	899	15	3.58
Steve Rogers	R	33	17	12	.586	0	36	36	13	273	258	78	146	5	3.23
Bill Gullickson	R	24	17	12	.586	0	34	34	10	242	230	59	120	1	3.75
Charlie Lea	R	26	16	11	.593	0	33	33	8	222	195	84	137	4	3.12
Jeff Reardon	R	27	7	9	.438	21	66	0	0	92	87	44	78	0	3.03
Scott Sanderson (RJ)	R	26	6	7	.462	1	18	16	0	81	98	20	55	0	4.65
Bryn Smith	R	27	6	11	.353	3	49	12	5	155	142	43	101	3	2.49
Dan Schatzeder	L	28	3	2	.600	2	58	2	0	87	88	25	48	0	3.21
Ray Burris	R	32	4	7	.364	0	40	17	2	154	139	56	100	1	3.68
Greg Bargar	R	24	2	0	1.000	0	3	3	0	20	23	9	8	0	6.75
2 Bob James	R	24	1	0	1.000	1	27	0	0	50	37	23	56	0	2.88
1 Randy Lerch	L	28	1	3	.250	0	19	5	0	39	45	18	24	0	6.75
2 Chris Welsh	L	28	0	0	—	0	16	5	0	45	46	18	17	0	5.04
Tom Dixon	R	28	0	1	.000	0	4	0	0	6	4	1	4	0	9.82
Dick Grapenthin	R	25	0	0	—	0	4	0	0	4	1	3	1	0	9.00
Woody Fryman (EJ)	L	43	0	3	.000	0	6	0	0	8	8	1	1	0	1.00
David Palmer 25 (EJ)															

ST. LOUIS 4th 79-83 .488 11   WHITEY HERZOG

Name	G by Pos	B	AGE	G	AB	R	H	2B	3B	HR	RBI	BB	SO	SB	BA	SA
TOTALS			27	162	5550	679	1496	262	63	83	636	543	879	207	.270	.384
George Hendrick	1B92, OF51	R	33	144	529	73	168	33	3	18	97	51	76	3	.318	.494
Tommy Herr (KJ)	2B86	B	27	89	313	43	101	14	4	2	31	43	27	6	.323	.412
Ozzie Smith	SS158	B	28	159	552	69	134	30	6	3	50	64	36	34	.243	.335
Ken Oberkfell	3B127, 3B32, SS11	L	27	151	488	62	143	26	5	3	38	61	27	12	.293	.385
David Green	OF136	R	22	146	422	52	120	14	10	8	69	26	76	34	.284	.422
Willie McGee	OF145	R	24	147	601	75	172	22	8	5	75	26	98	39	.286	.374
Lonnie Smith (DR)	OF126	R	27	130	492	83	158	31	5	8	45	41	55	43	.321	.453
Darrell Porter	C133	L	31	145	443	57	116	24	3	15	66	68	94	1	.262	.431
Andy Van Slyke	OF69, 3B30, 1B9	L	22	101	309	51	81	15	5	8	38	46	64	21	.262	.421
Mike Ramsey	2B66, SS20, 3B8, OF1	B	22	97	175	25	46	4	3	1	16	12	23	4	.263	.337
Steve Braun	SS	L	35	78	92	8	25	2	1	0	11	22	10	0	.272	.413
Dane Iorg (WJ)	OF22, 1B11	L	33	58	116	6	31	9	1	0	11	10	11	1	.267	.362
Floyd Rayford	3B33	R	25	56	104	5	22	4	0	3	14	1	10	1	.212	.337
1 Keith Hernandez	1B54	L	29	55	218	34	62	15	4	3	26	24	30	1	.284	.431
Jamie Quirk	C22, 3B7, SS1	L	28	48	86	3	18	2	1	2	4	2	21	0	.209	.326
Glenn Brummer	C41	R	28	45	87	7	24	7	0	0	9	10	11	1	.276	.356
Billy Lyons	2B23, 3B8, SS2	R	25	42	60	3	10	1	1	0	5	3	10	3	.167	.217
Rafael Santana	2B9, SS6, 3B4	R	25	30	14	1	3	0	0	0	2	0	6	0	.214	.214
Jeff Doyle	2B12	B	26	13	37	4	11	2	0	0	2	2	3	0	.297	.432
Jim Adduci	1B6, OF1	L	23	9	20	1	1	0	0	0	3	1	4	0	.050	.050
Jimmy Sexton	SS4, 3B2	R	31	9	9	1	1	0	0	0	1	1	4	1	.111	.222
Orlando Sanchez	C1	L	25	5	5	0	0	0	0	0	0	0	2	0	.000	.000
1 Tito Landrum	OF5	R	28	5	5	0	1	0	0	0	0	2	1	0	.200	.600
1 Gene Roof	OF1	B	25	3	5	0	0	0	0	0	0	0	0	0	.000	.000

NAME	T	AGE	W	L	PCT	SV	G	GS	CG	IP	H	BB	SO	SHO	ERA
TOTALS		29	79	83	.488	27	162	162	22	1461	1479	525	709	10	3.79
Dave LaPoint	L	23	12	9	.571	0	37	29	1	191	191	84	113	0	3.95
John Stuper	R	26	12	11	.522	1	40	30	6	198	202	71	81	1	3.68
2 Neil Allen	R	25	10	6	.625	0	25	18	4	122	122	48	74	2	3.70
Bob Forsch	R	33	10	12	.455	0	34	30	6	187	190	54	56	2	4.28
Bruce Sutter	R	30	9	10	.474	21	60	0	0	89	90	30	64	0	4.23
Joaquin Andujar	R	30	6	16	.273	1	39	34	5	225	215	75	125	2	4.16
2 Dave Rucker	L	25	3	5	.625	0	34	0	0	37	36	18	22	0	2.43
1 John Martin	L	27	3	1	.750	0	26	5	0	66	60	26	29	0	3.53
Dave Von Ohlen	L	24	3	2	.600	2	46	0	0	68	71	25	21	0	3.29
Jeff Lahti	R	26	3	4	.429	3	53	0	0	74	64	29	26	0	3.16
Danny Cox	R	23	3	6	.333	0	12	12	0	83	92	23	36	0	3.25
Kevin Hagen	R	23	2	3	.400	0	9	4	0	34		7	7	0	4.84
1 Doug Bair	R	33	1	1	.500	1	26	0	0	30	24	13	21	0	3.03
Jim Kaat	L	44	0	0	—	0	24	0	0	35	48	10	19	0	3.89
Ralph Citarella	R	25	0	0	—	0	6	0	0	11	3	4	1	0	1.64
1 Eric Rasmussen	R	31	0	1	.000	0	2	1	0	4	6	1	4	0	1.74
Jeff Keener	R	24	0	0	—	0	6	0	0	4	4	1	5	0	8.31
2 Steve Baker	R	26	0	0	—	0	2	0	0	10	14	1	5	0	1.80

CHICAGO — 5th 71-91 .438 19   LEE ELIA 54-69 .439   CHARLIE FOX 17-22 .436

Name	G by Pos	B	AGE	G	AB	R	H	2B	3B	HR	RBI	BB	SO	SB	BA	SA
TOTALS			29	162	5512	701	1436	272	42	140	649	470	868	84	.261	.401
Bill Buckner	1B144, OF15	L	33	153	626	79	175	38	6	16	66	25	30	12	.280	.438
Ryne Sandberg	2B157, SS11	R	23	158	633	94	165	25	4	8	48	51	79	37	.261	.351
Larry Bowa	SS145	B	37	147	499	73	133	20	5	2	43	35	30	7	.267	.339
Ron Cey	3B157	R	35	159	581	73	160	33	1	24	90	62	85	0	.275	.460
Keith Moreland	OF151, C3	R	29	154	533	76	161	30	3	16	70	68	73	0	.302	.460
Mel Hall (BG)	OF112	L	22	112	410	60	116	23	5	17	56	42	101	6	.283	.488
Leon Durham (BG)	OF95, 1B6	L	25	100	337	58	87	18	8	12	55	66	83	12	.258	.466
Jody Davis	C150	R	26	151	510	56	138	31	2	24	84	33	93	0	.271	.480
Gary Woods	OF73, 2B1	R	28	93	190	25	46	9	0	4	22	15	27	5	.242	.353
Jay Johnstone	OF44	L	37	86	140	16	36	7	0	6	22	20	24	1	.257	.436
Jerry Morales	OF29	R	34	63	87	11	17	9	0	0	11	7	19	0	.195	.299
Tom Veryzer	SS28, 3B17	R	30	59	88	5	18	3	0	1	3	3	13	0	.205	.273
Scot Thompson	OF29, 1B1	L	27	53	88	4	17	3	1	0	10	3	14	0	.193	.250
Thad Bosley	OF20	L	26	43	72	12	21	4	1	2	12	10	12	1	.292	.458
Steve Lake	C32	R	26	38	85	9	22	4	1	1	7	2	6	0	.259	.365
Carmelo Martinez	1B26, 3B1, OF1	R	22	29	89	8	23	3	0	6	16	4	19	0	.258	.494
Joe Carter	OF16	R	23	23	51	6	9	1	1	0	1	0	21	1	.176	.235
Dan Rohn	2B6, SS1	L	27	23	31	3	12	3	2	0	6	2	2	1	.287	.613
Wayne Nordhagen	OF7	R	34	21	35	1	5	1	0	1	4	0	5	0	.143	.257
Junior Kennedy	2B7, 3B4, SS1	R	32	17	22	3	3	0	0	0	3	1	6	0	.136	.136
Dave Owen	SS14, 3B3	B	25	16	22	1	2	0	1	0	2	2	7	1	.091	.182
Tom Grant	OF10	R	26	16	20	2	3	1	0	0	2	3	4	0	.150	.200
Fritz Connally	3B3	R	25	8	10	0	1	0	0	0	0	0	5	0	.100	.100
Mike Diaz	C3	R	23	6	7	2	2	1	0	0	1	0	0	0	.286	.429
Jay Loviglio		R	27	1	1	0	0	0	0	0	0	0	0	0	.000	.000

NAME	T	AGE	W	L	PCT	SV	G	GS	CG	IP	H	BB	SO	SHO	ERA
TOTALS		30	71	91	.438	42	162	162	9	1429	1496	498	807	10	4.08
Chuck Rainey	R	28	14	13	.519	0	34	34	1	191	219	74	84	1	4.48
2 Dick Ruthven	R	32	12	9	.571	0	25	25	5	149	156	28	73	2	4.10
Steve Trout	L	25	10	14	.417	0	34	32	1	180	217	59	80	0	4.65
Bill Campbell	R	34	6	8	.429	8	82	0	0	122	128	49	97	0	4.49
Ferguson Jenkins	R	39	6	9	.400	0	33	29	1	167	176	46	96	1	4.30
Dickie Noles (AL)	R	26	5	10	.333	0	24	18	1	116	133	37	59	1	4.72
Lee Smith	R	25	4	10	.286	29	66	0	0	103	70	41	91	0	1.65
Warren Brusstar	R	31	3	1	.750	1	59	0	0	80	67	37	46	0	2.35
Paul Moskau	R	29	3	2	.600	0	8	8	0	32	44	14	16	0	6.75
Craig Lefferts	L	25	3	4	.429	1	56	5	0	89	80	29	60	0	3.13
1 Willie Hernandez	L	28	1	0	1.000	1	11	1	0	20	16	6	18	0	3.20
Bill Johnson	R	22	1	0	1.000	0	10	0	0	12	17	3	4	0	4.38
2 Rick Reuschel	R	34	1	1	.500	0	4	4	0	21	18	10	9	0	3.92
Reggie Patterson	R	24	1	2	.333	0	5	2	0	19	17	6	10	0	4.82
Mike Proly	R	32	1	5	.167	1	60	0	0	83	79	38	31	0	3.58
Alan Hargesheimer	R	26	0	0	—	0	5	0	0	4	4	5	1	0	9.00
Don Schulze	R	20	0	1	.000	0	4	3	0	14	19	7	8	0	7.07
Rich Bordi	R	24	0	2	.000	1	11	1	0	25	34	12	20	0	4.97

NEW YORK — 6th 68-94 .420 22   GEORGE BAMBERGER 16-30 .348   FRANK HOWARD 52-64 .448

Name	G by Pos	B	AGE	G	AB	R	H	2B	3B	HR	RBI	BB	SO	SB	BA	SA
TOTALS			27	162	5444	575	1314	172	26	112	542	436	1031	141	.241	.344
2 Keith Hernandez	1B90	L	29	95	320	43	98	8	3	9	37	64	42	8	.306	.434
Brian Giles	2B140, SS12	R	23	145	400	49	98	15	0	2	27	36	77	7	.245	.298
Jose Oquendo	SS116	R	19	120	328	29	70	7	0	1	17	19	60	8	.213	.244
Hubie Brooks	3B145, OF2	R	26	150	586	53	147	18	4	5	58	24	96	6	.251	.321
Darryl Strawberry	OF117	L	21	122	420	63	108	15	7	26	74	47	128	19	.257	.512
Mookie Wilson	OF148	B	27	152	638	91	176	25	6	7	51	18	103	54	.276	.387
George Foster	OF153	R	34	157	601	74	145	19	2	28	90	38	111	1	.241	.419
2 Junior Ortiz	C67	R	23	68	185	10	47	5	0	0	12	3	34	1	.254	.281
Bob Bailor	SS75, 2B50, 3B11, OF3	R	31	118	340	35	85	8	0	1	30	20	23	18	.250	.282
Danny Heep	OF61, 1B14	L	25	115	253	30	64	12	0	8	21	29	40	1	.253	.395
Ron Hodges	C96	L	34	110	250	20	65	12	0	0	21	49	42	0	.260	.308
Rusty Staub	1B5, OF5	R	39	104	115	5	34	6	0	3	28	14	10	0	.296	.426
Dave Kingman	1B50, OF5	R	34	100	248	25	49	7	0	13	29	22	57	2	.198	.383
Mark Bradley	OF35	R	26	73	104	10	21	4	0	3	5	11	35	4	.202	.327
1 Mike Jorgensen	1B19	L	34	38	24	5	6	3	0	1	3	2	4	0	.250	.500
Tucker Ashford	3B15, 2B13, C1	R	28	35	56	3	10	0	1	0	2	7	4	0	.179	.214
Wally Backman	2B14, 3B2	B	23	26	42	6	7	0	1	0	3	2	8	0	.167	.214
Ronn Reynolds	C24	R	24	24	66	4	13	1	0	0	2	8	12	0	.197	.212
Ron Gardenhire	SS15	R	25	17	32	1	2	0	0	0	1	1	4	0	.063	.063
Clint Hurdle	3B9, OF1	L	25	15	13	3	3	0	2	0	2	2	10	0	.182	.242
Gary Rajsich	1B10	L	28	11	36	5	12	3	0	1	3	3	1	0	.333	.500
Mike Fitzgerald	C8	R	22	8	20	1	2	0	0	1	2	3	6	0	.100	.250
John Stearns (EJ)		R	31	4	4	0	2	0	0	0	0	0	0	0	.250	.500
Mike Bishop	C3	R	24	3	8	2	1	1	0	0	0	3	4	0	.125	.250
Mike Howard	OF1	B	25	1	3	0	1	0	0	0	1	0	0	0	.333	.333

NAME	T	AGE	W	L	PCT	SV	G	GS	CG	IP	H	BB	SO	SHO	ERA
TOTALS		28	68	94	.420	33	162	162	18	1451	1384	615	717	17	3.68
Jesse Orosco	L	26	13	7	.650	17	62	0	0	110	76	38	84	0	1.47
Ed Lynch	R	27	10	10	.500	0	30	27	1	175	208	41	44	0	4.28
Mike Torrez	R	36	10	17	.370	0	39	34	5	222	227	113	94	0	4.37
Tom Seaver	R	38	9	14	.391	0	34	34	5	231	201	86	135	2	3.55
Walt Terrell	R	25	8	8	.500	0	21	20	4	134	123	55	59	2	3.57
Doug Sisk	R	25	5	4	.556	11	67	0	0	104	88	59	33	0	2.24
Carlos Diaz	L	25	3	1	.750	2	54	0	0	83	62	35	64	0	2.05
1 Neil Allen	R	25	2	7	.222	2	21	4	1	54	57	36	32	1	4.50
Craig Swan	R	32	2	8	.200	1	27	18	0	96	112	42	43	0	5.51
Brent Gaff	R	24	1	0	1.000	0	4	0	0	10	18	1	4	0	6.10
Tim Leary	R	24	1	1	.500	0	2	2	0	12	15	4	9	0	3.39
Rick Ownbey	R	24	1	3	.250	0	10	4	0	35	31	21	19	0	4.67
Ron Darling	R	22	1	3	.250	0	5	5	1	35	31	17	23	0	2.80
Tom Gorman	L	25	1	4	.200	1	8	2	0	49	45	15	30	0	4.93
Scott Holman	R	24	1	7	.125	0	35	10	0	101	90	52	44	0	3.74

WEST DIVISION

LOS ANGELES — 1st 91-71 .562   TOMMY LASORDA

Name	G by Pos	B	AGE	G	AB	R	H	2B	3B	HR	RBI	BB	SO	SB	BA	SA
TOTALS			30	163	5440	654	1358	197	34	146	613	541	925	166	.250	.379
Greg Brock	1B140	L	26	145	455	64	102	14	2	20	66	83	81	5	.224	.396
Steve Sax	2B152	R	23	155	623	94	175	18	5	5	41	58	73	56	.281	.350
Bill Russell	SS127	R	34	131	451	47	111	13	1	0	30	33	31	13	.246	.286
Pedro Guerrero	3B157, 1B1	R	27	160	584	87	174	28	6	32	103	72	110	23	.298	.531
Mike Marshall	OF109, 1B33	R	23	140	465	47	132	17	1	17	65	43	127	7	.284	.434
Ken Landreaux	OF137	L	28	141	481	63	135	25	3	17	66	34	52	30	.281	.451
Dusty Baker	OF143	R	34	149	531	71	138	25	1	15	73	72	59	7	.260	.395
Steve Yeager	C112	R	34	113	335	31	68	8	3	15	41	23	57	1	.203	.379
Derrell Thomas (RJ)	OF82, SS13, 2B9, 3B7	B	32	118	192	38	48	6	6	2	8	27	36	9	.250	.375
Rick Monday	OF44, 1B4	L	37	99	178	21	44	7	1	6	20	29	42	0	.247	.399
1 Ron Roenicke	OF62	R	26	81	145	12	32	4	0	2	12	14	26	3	.221	.290
2 Rafael Landestoy	2B14, 3B10, OF10, SS1	B	30	64	64	6	11	1	1	1	3	3	8	0	.172	.266
Dave Anderson	SS53, 3B1	R	22	61	115	12	19	4	2	1	2	12	15	6	.165	.261
Jack Fimple	C54	R	24	54	148	16	37	8	1	2	22	11	39	1	.250	.358
Jose Morales	1B4	R	38	47	53	4	15	3	0	3	8	1	11	0	.283	.509
Candy Maldonado	OF33	R	22	42	62	5	12	1	1	1	6	5	14	0	.194	.290
R.J. Reynolds	OF18	B	24	24	55	5	13	0	0	2	11	3	11	5	.236	.345
Cecil Espy	OF15	B	20	20	11	4	3	1	0	0	1	1	2	0	.273	.364
Gil Reyes	C19	R	19	19	31	1	5	2	0	0	0	0	5	0	.161	.226
Sid Bream	1B4	L	22	15	11	0	2	0	0	0	2	2	2	0	.182	.182
German Rivera	3B8	R	23	13	17	1	6	1	0	0	3	0	4	0	.353	.412
Mike Scioscia (SJ)	C11	R	24	12	35	3	11	3	0	1	7	5	2	0	.314	.486
Alex Taveras	S3, 2B2, 3B1	R	27	10	4	0	0	0	0	0	0	1	0	0	.000	.000
Dave Sax	C4	R	24	7	4	0	0	0	0	0	0	0	1	0	.000	.000

NAME	T	AGE	W	L	PCT	SV	G	GS	CG	IP	H	BB	SO	SHO	ERA
TOTALS		27	91	71	.562	40	163	163	27	1464	1336	495	1000	12	3.10
Fernando Valenzuela	L	22	15	10	.600	0	35	35	9	257	245	99	189	4	3.75
Bob Welch	R	26	15	12	.556	0	31	31	4	204	164	72	156	3	2.65
Alejandro Pena	R	24	12	9	.571	1	34	26	4	177	152	51	120	3	2.75
Jerry Reuss	L	34	12	11	.522	0	32	31	7	223	233	50	143	0	2.94
Burt Hooton	R	33	8	8	.529	0	33	27	2	160	156	59	87	0	4.22
Tom Niedenfuer	R	23	8	3	.727	11	66	0	0	95	55	29	66	0	1.90
Pat Zachry	R	31	6	1	.857	0	40	1	0	61	63	21	36	0	2.49
1 Dave Stewart	R	26	5	2	.714	8	46	0	0	76	67	33	54	0	2.96
Steve Howe (DR)	L	25	4	7	.364	18	46	0	0	69	55	12	52	0	1.44
Joe Beckwith	R	28	3	4	.429	1	42	3	0	71	73	35	50	0	3.55
2 Rick Honeycutt	L	29	2	3	.400	0	9	7	1	39	46	13	18	0	5.77
Orel Hershiser	R	24	0	0	—	1	8	0	0	8	7	6	5	0	3.38
Rich Rodas	L	23	0	0	—	0	6	0	0	6	3	5	5	0	1.93
1 Ricky Wright	L	24	0	0	—	0	6	0	0	6	6	3	2	0	2.84
Larry White	R	24	0	0	—	0	4	0	0	4	7	3	5	0	1.29
Sid Fernandez	L	20	0	1	.000	0	2	2	0	6	7	7	9	0	6.00

ATLANTA — 2nd 88-74 .543 3   JOE TORRE

Name	G by Pos	B	AGE	G	AB	R	H	2B	3B	HR	RBI	BB	SO	SB	BA	SA
TOTALS			27	162	5472	746	1489	218	45	130	691	582	847	146	.272	.400
Chris Chambliss	1B126	L	34	131	447	59	125	24	3	20	78	63	68	2	.280	.481
Glenn Hubbard	2B148	R	25	148	517	65	136	24	6	12	70	55	71	3	.263	.402
Rafael Ramirez	SS152	R	25	152	622	82	185	13	5	7	58	36	48	16	.297	.368
Bob Horner (BW)	3B104, 1B1	R	25	104	386	75	117	25	1	20	68	50	63	4	.303	.528
Claudell Washington	OF128	L	28	134	496	75	138	24	8	9	44	40	103	31	.278	.413
Dale Murphy	OF160	R	27	162	589	131	178	24	4	36	121	90	110	30	.302	.540
Brett Butler	OF143	L	26	151	549	84	154	21	13	5	37	54	56	39	.281	.393
Bruce Benedict	C134	R	27	134	423	43	126	19	1	3	43	61	24	1	.298	.348
Jerry Royster	3B47, 2B26, OF18, SS13	R	30	91	268	32	63	10	3	3	30	28	35	11	.235	.328
Randy Johnson	3B53, 2B4	R	27	86	144	22	36	3	0	1	17	20	27	1	.250	.292
Terry Harper	OF60	R	27	80	201	19	53	13	1	3	26	20	43	6	.264	.383
Bob Watson	1B34	R	37	65	149	14	46	9	0	6	37	18	23	0	.309	.490
2 Mike Jorgensen	1B19, OF6	L	34	47	48	5	12	1	0	1	8	8	8	0	.250	.333
Biff Pocoroba	C34	B	29	55	120	11	32	6	0	2	16	12	7	0	.267	.367
Ken Smith	1B13	L	25	30	12	2	2	0	0	1	5	1	5	0	.167	.417
Gerald Perry	1B7, OF1	L	22	27	39	5	14	2	0	0	6	5	4	1	.359	.487
Brad Komminsk	OF13	R	22	19	26	4	7	2	0	0	1	0	7	0	.222	.278
Larry Owen	C16	R	28	17	17	0	2	2	0	0	1	0	4	0	.118	.118
Albert Hall	OF25	B	25	10	8	2	2	0	0	0	1	0	0	0	1.000	1.000
Matt Sinatro	C7	R	23	7	12	0	2	0	0	0	1	0	4	0	.167	.167
Paul Runge	2B2	R	25	5	4	2	1	0	0	0	0	2	0	0	.250	.250
Brook Jacoby	3B2	R	23	4	5	1	0	0	0	0	0	1	0	0	.000	.000
Paul Zuvella	SS2	R	24	3	5	0	0	0	0	0	0	2	1	0	.000	.000

NAME	T	AGE	W	L	PCT	SV	G	GS	CG	IP	H	BB	SO	SHO	ERA
TOTALS		30	88	74	.543	48	162	162	18	1441	1412	540	895	4	3.67
Pascual Perez	R	26	15	8	.652	0	33	33	7	215	213	51	144	1	3.43
Craig McMurtry	R	23	15	9	.625	0	36	35	6	224	204	88	105	3	3.08
Phil Niekro	R	44	11	10	.524	0	34	33	2	202	212	105	128	0	3.97
Rick Camp (HJ)	R	30	10	9	.526	0	40	16	1	140	146	38	61	0	3.79
Pete Falcone	L	29	9	4	.692	0	33	15	2	107	102	60	59	0	3.63
Steve Bedrosian	R	25	9	10	.474	19	70	1	0	120	100	51	114	0	3.60
Ken Dayley	L	24	5	8	.385	0	24	16	0	100	100	39	70	0	4.30
Gene Garber (EJ)	R	35	4	5	.444	9	43	0	0	61	72	23	45	0	4.60
Terry Forster	L	31	3	2	.600	13	56	0	0	79	60	31	54	0	2.16
1 Rick Behenna	R	23	3	3	.500	0	14	6	0	37	37	12	17	0	4.58
Donnie Moore	R	29	2	3	.400	0	43	0	0	69	72	10	41	0	3.67
Tony Brizzolara	R	26	1	0	1.000	1	14	0	0	20	22	6	9	0	3.54
2 Len Barker	R	27	1	3	.250	0	8	8	0	33	31	14	21	0	3.82
Rick Mahler	R	29	0	0	—	0	5	0	0	6	6	1	5	0	5.02
Tommy Boggs (SJ)	R	27	0	0	—	0	4	2	0	8	9	1	6	0	5.68
Jeff Dedmon	R	22	0	0	—	0	4	0	0	10	0	3	6	0	3.50
Bob Walk	R	26	0	0	—	0	3	3	0	14	15	8	6	0	7.36

HOUSTON 3rd 85-77 .525 6   BOB LILLIS

Name	G by Pos	B	AGE	G	AB	R	H	2B	3B	HR	RBI	BB	SO	SB	BA	SA
	TOTALS		29	162	5502	643	1412	239	60	97	615	517	869	164	.257	.375
Ray Knight	1B143	R	30	145	507	43	154	36	4	9	70	42	62	0	.304	.444
Bill Doran	2B153	B	25	154	535	70	145	12	7	8	39	86	67	12	.271	.364
Dickie Thon	SS154	R	25	154	619	81	177	28	9	20	79	54	73	34	.286	.457
Phil Garner	3B154	R	34	154	567	76	135	24	2	14	79	63	84	18	.238	.362
Terry Puhl	OF124	L	26	137	465	66	136	25	7	8	44	36	48	24	.292	.428
1 Omar Moreno	OF97	L	30	97	405	48	98	12	11	0	25	22	72	30	.242	.326
Jose Cruz	OF160	L	35	160	594	85	189	28	8	14	92	65	86	30	.318	.463
Alan Ashby (IL)	C85	B	31	87	275	31	63	18	1	8	34	31	38	0	.229	.389
Denny Walling	1B42, 3B13, OF13	L	29	100	135	24	40	5	3	3	19	15	16	2	.296	.444
Kevin Bass	OF52	B	24	88	195	25	46	7	3	2	18	6	27	2	.236	.333
Tony Scott	OF61	B	31	80	186	20	42	6	1	2	17	11	39	5	.226	.301
Craig Reynolds	2B26, 3B15, SS8, OF1	L	30	65	98	10	21	3	0	1	6	6	10	0	.214	.276
2 Jerry Mumphrey	OF43	B	30	44	143	17	48	10	2	1	17	22	23	5	.336	.455
Tim Tolman	1B7, OF3	R	27	43	56	4	11	4	0	2	10	6	9	0	.196	.375
Harry Spilman	1B19, C6	L	28	42	78	7	13	3	0	1	9	5	12	0	.167	.244
Luis Pujols	C39	R	27	40	87	4	17	2	0	0	12	5	14	0	.195	.218
John Mizerock (SJ)	C33	L	22	33	85	8	13	4	1	1	10	12	15	0	.153	.259
George Bjorkman	C29	R	26	29	75	8	17	4	0	2	14	16	29	0	.227	.360
Scott Loucks	OF6	R	26	7	14	2	3	0	0	0	0	1	4	2	.214	.214
Bert Pena	SS4	R	23	4	8	0	1	0	0	0	0	2	2	0	.125	.125
Art Howe 36 (EJ-NJ)																

NAME	T	AGE	W	L	PCT	SV	G	GS	CG	IP	H	BB	SO	SHO	ERA
		30	85	77	.525	48	162	162	22	1466	1276	570	904	14	3.45
Joe Niekro	R	38	15	14	.517	0	38	38	9	264	238	101	152	2	3.48
Nolan Ryan (LJ)	R	36	14	9	.609	0	29	29	5	196	134	101	183	2	2.98
Mike Scott (SJ)	R	28	10	6	.625	0	24	24	2	145	143	46	73	2	3.72
Mike Madden (EJ)	L	25	9	5	.643	0	28	13	0	95	76	45	44	0	3.14
Vern Ruhle	R	32	8	5	.615	3	41	9	0	115	107	36	43	0	3.69
Bill Dawley	R	25	6	6	.500	14	48	0	0	80	57	22	60	0	2.90
Bob Knepper	L	29	6	13	.316	0	35	29	4	203	202	71	125	3	3.19
Mike LaCoss (RJ)	R	27	5	7	.417	1	38	17	2	138	142	56	53	0	4.43
Frank LaCorte (SJ)	R	31	4	4	.500	3	37	0	0	53	35	28	48	0	5.06
Dave Smith	R	28	3	1	.750	6	42	0	0	73	72	36	41	0	3.10
Frank DiPino	L	26	3	4	.429	20	53	0	0	71	52	20	67	0	2.65
Jeff Heathcock	R	23	2	1	.667	1	6	3	0	28	19	4	12	0	3.21
Julio Solano	R	23	0	0	.000	0	4	0	0	6	5	4	3	0	6.00
Joe Sambito 31 (IL)															
J.R. Richard 33 (IL)															

SAN DIEGO 4th 81-81 .500 10   DICK WILLIAMS

Name	G by Pos	B	AGE	G	AB	R	H	2B	3B	HR	RBI	BB	SO	SB	BA	SA
	TOTALS		28	163	5527	653	1384	207	34	93	592	482	822	179	.250	.351
Steve Garvey (RJ)	1B100	R	34	100	388	76	114	22	0	14	59	29	39	4	.294	.459
Juan Bonilla	3B149	R	28	152	556	55	132	17	4	4	45	50	40	3	.237	.304
Garry Templeton	SS123	B	27	126	460	39	121	20	2	3	40	21	57	16	.263	.335
Luis Salazar	3B118, SS19	R	27	134	481	52	124	16	2	14	45	17	80	24	.258	.387
1 Sixto Lezcano	OF91	R	29	97	317	41	74	11	2	8	40	47	68	0	.233	.356
Ruppert Jones	OF111, 1B5	L	28	133	335	42	78	12	3	12	49	35	58	11	.233	.394
Alan Wiggins	OF105, 1B45	B	25	144	503	83	139	20	2	0	22	65	43	66	.276	.324
Terry Kennedy	C143, 1B4	L	27	149	549	47	156	27	2	17	98	51	89	1	.284	.434
Gene Richrds	OF54	L	29	95	233	37	64	11	3	3	22	17	17	14	.275	.386
Tim Flannery	3B52, 2B21, SS7	L	25	92	214	24	50	7	3	3	19	20	23	2	.234	.336
Tony Gwynn (BW)	OF81	L	23	86	304	34	94	12	2	1	37	23	21	7	.309	.372
Kurt Bevacqua	1B27, 3B12, OF12	R	36	74	156	17	38	7	0	2	24	18	33	0	.244	.327
Bobby Brown	OF54	B	29	57	225	40	60	5	3	5	22	23	38	27	.267	.382
Mario Ramirez	SS38, 3B1	R	25	55	107	11	21	6	3	0	12	20	23	0	.196	.308
Kevin McReynolds	OF38	R	23	39	140	15	31	3	1	4	14	12	29	2	.221	.343
Doug Gwosdz	C32	R	23	39	55	7	6	1	0	1	4	7	19	0	.109	.182
Jerry Turner	OF1	L	29	25	23	1	3	0	0	0	1	8	0	0	.130	.130
Bruce Bochy	C11	R	28	23	42	2	9	1	0	0	3	0	9	0	.214	.286
1 Joe Lefebvre	OF6, 3B4, C2	L	27	18	20	1	5	0	0	0	1	2	3	0	.250	.250
Jody Lansford	1B8	R	22	12	8	1	2	0	0	1	2	0	3	0	.250	.625
George Hinshaw	3B5, 2B1	R	23	7	16	1	7	1	0	0	4	0	1	1	.438	.500
Eddie Rodriguez	2B5, SS2, 3B1	R	22	7	12	1	2	1	0	0	0	0	4	0	.167	.250
Jerry Davis	OF5	R	24	5	15	3	5	2	0	0	1	3	4	1	.333	.467

NAME	T	AGE	W	L	PCT	SV	G	GS	CG	IP	H	BB	SO	SHO	ERA
		28	81	81	.500	44	163	163	23	1468	1389	528	850	5	3.62
Eric Show	R	27	15	12	.556	0	35	33	4	201	201	74	120	2	4.17
Dave Dravecky	L	27	14	10	.583	0	28	28	9	184	181	44	74	1	3.58
1 John Montefusco	R	33	9	4	.692	4	31	10	1	95	94	32	52	0	3.30
2 Sid Monge	L	32	7	3	.700	7	47	0	0	69	65	31	32	0	3.15
Mark Thurmond	L	26	7	3	.700	0	21	18	2	115	104	33	49	0	2.65
Tim Lollar	L	27	7	12	.368	0	30	30	1	176	170	85	135	0	4.61
Luis DeLeon	R	24	6	6	.500	13	63	0	0	111	89	27	90	0	2.68
Ed Whitson (KJ)	R	28	5	7	.417	1	31	21	2	144	143	50	81	0	4.30
Andy Hawkins	R	23	5	7	.417	0	21	19	4	120	106	48	59	1	2.93
Gary Lucas	L	28	5	8	.385	17	62	0	0	91	85	34	60	0	2.87
Elias Sosa	R	33	1	4	.200	1	41	1	0	72	72	30	45	0	4.35
Dennis Rasmussen	L	24	0	0	—	0	4	1	0	14	10	8	13	0	1.98
Marty Decker	R	26	0	0	—	0	4	0	0	9	5	3	9	0	2.08
Steve Fireovid	R	26	0	0	—	0	3	0	0	5	4	2	1	0	1.80
Mike Couchee (BR)	R	25	0	1	.000	0	3	3	0	14	12	6	5	0	5.14
1 Chris Welsh	L	28	0	1	.000	0	7	1	0	14	13	2	5	0	2.51
Greg Booker	R	23	0	1	.000	0	6	1	0	12	18	9	5	0	7.71
Floyd Chiffer	R	27	0	1	.000	1	15	0	0	23	17	10	15	0	3.18

SAN FRANCISCO 5th 79-83 .488 12   FRANK ROBINSON

Name	G by Pos	B	AGE	G	AB	R	H	2B	3B	HR	RBI	BB	SO	SB	BA	SA
	TOTALS		28	162	5369	687	1324	206	30	142	638	619	990	140	.247	.375
Darrell Evans	1B113, 3B32, SS9	L	36	142	523	94	145	29	3	30	82	84	81	6	.277	.516
Brad Wellman	2B74, SS2	R	23	82	182	15	39	3	0	1	16	22	39	5	.214	.247
Johnnie LeMaster	SS139	R	29	141	534	81	128	16	1	6	30	60	96	39	.240	.307
Tom O'Malley	3B117	L	22	135	410	40	106	16	1	5	45	52	47	2	.259	.339
Jack Clark	OF133, 1B2	R	27	135	492	82	132	25	0	20	66	74	79	5	.268	.441
Chili Davis	OF133	B	23	137	486	54	113	21	2	11	59	55	108	10	.233	.352
Jeff Leonard	OF136	R	27	139	516	74	144	17	7	21	87	35	116	26	.279	.461
Bob Brenly	C90, 1B10, OF2	R	29	104	281	36	63	12	2	7	34	37	48	10	.244	.356
Joel Youngblood	2B63, 3B28, OF22	R	31	124	373	59	109	20	3	17	53	33	59	7	.292	.499
Max Venable	OF66	L	26	94	228	28	50	7	4	6	27	22	34	15	.219	.364
Dave Bergman	1B50, OF6	L	30	90	140	16	40	4	1	6	24	24	21	2	.286	.457
Duane Kuiper (BC)	2B64	L	33	72	176	14	44	2	2	0	14	27	13	0	.250	.284
1 Milt May	C56	L	32	66	186	18	46	6	0	6	20	21	23	2	.247	.376
Joe Pettini	SS26, 2B14, 3B12	R	28	61	86	11	16	0	1	0	7	9	11	4	.186	.209
John Rabb	C31, OF2	R	23	40	104	10	24	9	0	1	14	9	17	1	.231	.346
Champ Summers (SJ)	OF1	L	37	29	22	3	3	0	0	3	7	8	0	0	.136	.136
Chris Smith	1B15, OF4, 3B1	R	25	22	67	13	22	6	1	1	11	7	12	0	.238	.493
Dan Gladden	OF18	R	25	18	63	6	14	2	0	1	9	5	11	4	.222	.302
1 Mike Vail	1B4, OF2	R	31	18	26	1	4	1	0	0	3	0	7	0	.154	.192
2 Steve Nicosia	C9	R	27	15	33	4	11	0	0	0	6	3	2	0	.333	.333
Guy Sularz	SS6, 3B4	R	27	10	20	3	2	0	0	0	0	0	6	0	.100	.100
2 Wallace Johnson	2B1	B	26	9	8	0	1	0	0	0	1	0	0	0	.125	.125
Jeff Ransom	C6	R	22	6	20	3	4	0	0	1	3	4	7	0	.200	.350
Rich Murray	1B3	R	25	4	10	0	2	0	0	0	1	0	3	0	.200	.200
Ron Pruitt		R	31	1	1	0	0	0	0	0	0	0	0	0	.000	.000

NAME	T	AGE	W	L	PCT	SV	G	GS	CG	IP	H	BB	SO	SHO	ERA
		28	79	83	.488	47	162	162	20	1446	1431	520	881	9	3.70
Bill Laskey (XJ)	R	25	13	10	.565	0	25	25	1	148	151	45	81	0	4.19
Mike Krukow (EJ)	R	31	11	11	.500	0	31	31	2	184	189	76	136	1	3.95
Fred Breining	R	27	11	12	.478	0	32	32	6	203	202	60	117	0	3.82
Atlee Hammaker (SJ)	L	25	10	9	.526	0	23	23	8	172	147	32	127	3	2.25
Gary Lavelle	L	34	7	4	.636	20	56	0	0	87	73	19	68	0	2.59
Greg Minton	R	31	7	11	.389	22	73	0	0	107	117	47	38	0	3.54
Mark Davis	L	22	6	4	.600	0	20	20	2	111	93	50	83	2	3.49
Jim Barr	R	35	3	6	.333	2	53	0	0	93	106	20	47	0	3.98
Andy McGaffigan	R	26	3	9	.250	2	43	16	0	134	131	39	93	0	4.29
Scott Garrelts	R	21	2	2	.500	0	5	5	1	36	33	19	16	1	2.52
Renie Martin	R	27	2	4	.333	1	37	6	0	94	95	51	43	0	4.20
2 Randy Lerch	L	28	1	0	1.000	0	7	0	0	11	9	8	6	0	3.38
Mark Calvert	R	26	1	4	.200	0	18	4	0	37	46	34	14	0	6.27
Mike Chris	L	25	0	0	—	0	7	0	0	13	16	16	5	0	8.10
Pat Larkin	L	23	0	0	—	0	5	0	0	10	13	3	6	0	4.35
Brian Kingman	R	28	0	0	—	0	5	0	0	5	10	1	1	0	7.71

CINCINNATI 6th 74-88 .457 17   RUSS NIXON

Name	G by Pos	B	AGE	G	AB	R	H	2B	3B	HR	RBI	BB	SO	SB	BA	SA
	TOTALS		28	162	5333	623	1274	236	35	107	577	588	1006	154	.239	.356
Dan Driessen (LJ)	1B112	L	31	122	386	57	107	17	1	12	57	75	51	6	.277	.420
Ron Oester	2B154	B	27	157	549	63	145	23	5	11	58	49	106	2	.264	.384
Dave Concepcion	SS139, 3B6, 1B1	R	35	143	528	54	123	22	0	1	47	56	81	14	.233	.280
Nick Esasky	3B84	R	23	85	302	41	80	10	5	12	46	27	99	6	.265	.450
Paul Householder	OF112	B	24	123	380	40	97	24	4	6	43	44	60	12	.255	.387
Eddie Milner	OF139	L	28	146	502	77	131	23	6	9	33	68	60	41	.261	.384
Gary Redus	OF120	R	26	125	453	90	112	20	9	17	51	71	111	39	.247	.444
Dann Bilardello	C105	R	24	109	298	27	71	18	0	9	38	15	49	2	.238	.389
Johnny Bench	3B42, 1B32, C5, OF1	R	35	110	310	32	79	15	2	12	54	24	38	0	.255	.432
Duane Walker	OF60	L	26	109	225	14	53	12	1	2	29	20	43	6	.236	.324
Cesar Cedeno	OF73, 1B17	R	32	98	332	40	77	16	0	9	39	33	53	13	.232	.361
Alex Trevino	C63, 3B4	R	25	74	167	14	36	8	1	1	13	17	20	0	.216	.293
Tom Foley	SS37, 2B5	L	23	68	98	7	20	4	1	0	9	13	17	1	.204	.265
Alan Knicely	C31, OF8, 1B2	R	28	59	98	11	22	3	0	2	10	16	28	0	.224	.316
Kelly Paris	3B16, 2B10, SS7, 1B3	B	25	56	120	13	30	6	0	0	7	1	22	8	.250	.300
1 Wayne Krenchicki	3B39, 2B1	L	28	51	77	6	21	2	0	0	11	8	4	0	.273	.299
Dallas Williams	OF12	L	25	18	36	2	2	0	0	0	1	0	6	0	.056	.056
Jeff Jones	OF13, 1B1	R	25	16	44	6	10	3	0	0	5	11	13	2	.227	.295
Skeeter Barnes	1B7, 3B7	R	26	15	34	5	7	0	0	1	4	1	3	2	.206	.294
Steve Christmas	C7	L	25	9	17	0	1	0	0	0	1	1	3	0	.059	.059
1 Rafael Landestoy	1B2, 3B1, OF1	B	30	7	5	0	0	0	0	0	0	0	0	0	.000	.000

NAME	T	AGE	W	L	PCT	SV	G	GS	CG	IP	H	BB	SO	SHO	ERA
		27	74	88	.457	29	162	162	34	1441	1365	627	934	5	3.98
Mario Soto	R	26	17	13	.567	0	34	34	18	274	207	95	242	3	2.70
Joe Price (SJ)	L	26	10	6	.625	0	21	21	5	144	118	46	83	0	2.88
Frank Pastore	R	25	9	12	.429	0	36	29	4	184	207	64	93	1	4.68
Bruce Berenyi	R	28	9	14	.391	0	32	31	4	186	173	102	151	1	3.86
Charlie Puleo (KJ)	R	28	6	12	.333	0	27	14	0	144	145	91	71	0	4.89
Ted Power	R	28	6	6	.455	2	49	6	1	111	120	49	57	0	4.54
Jeff Russell	R	21	4	5	.444	0	10	10	2	68	58	22	40	0	3.03
Ben Hayes	R	25	4	6	.400	7	60	0	0	69	82	37	44	0	6.49
Rich Gale	R	29	4	6	.400	1	33	7	0	90	103	43	53	0	5.82
Tom Hume (EJ)	R	30	3	5	.375	9	48	0	0	66	66	41	34	0	4.77
Bill Scherrer	L	25	3	3	.400	10	73	0	0	92	73	33	57	0	2.74
Keefe Cato	R	25	1	0	1.000	0	4	0	0	4	2	1	5	0	2.45
Brad Lesley	R	24	0	0	—	1	5	0	0	8	8	0	5	0	2.16
Greg Harris	R	27	0	0	—	0	2	1	0	3	1	4	3	0	7.00

1984 — And The Lights Did Not Go On

The first pounce of the Detroit Tigers stunned the baseball world. They won 10 of their first 11 games, including a no-hitter by Jack Morris. By late May, they cruised far in front of the American League East with a 35-5 record. The other teams in the division issued a lot of brave talk, but the race was over before the summer really began. Sparky Anderson orchestrated a slew of talented players into a championship unit. Lance Parrish, Alan Trammell, Lou Whitaker, and Chet Lemon anchored the Tigers up the middle, while Kirk Gibson paid an immediate dividend on his vast potential. Anderson had three solid starters in Jack Morris, Dan Petry, and Milt Wilcox, but the spring trade for reliever Willie Hernandez gave the Tigers their last missing piece. Coupled in the bullpen with Aurelio Lopez, Hernandez used the screwball in such flawless fashion that he won both the MVP and Cy Young awards.

But while the Tigers owned the spring, all eyes focused on the Chicago Cubs in the summer. Never champions of anything since 1945, the Cubs started the season strong and delighted their fans by staying in contention. New manager Jim Frey guided a veteran club assembled in a series of crafty trades. Shining brightest amidst the veterans was Ryne Sandberg, a scintillating second baseman who blossomed into the National League MVP. The pitching staff lacked depth but found a leader in tall Rick Sutcliffe, a June pick-up from Cleveland who was practically unbeatable in a Chicago uniform.

The Cubs trailed the New York Mets by 4 1/2 games on July 28. The Mets had a spectacular rookie in hard-throwing Dwight Gooden and had fans dreaming about a miracle pennant for New York. Over the next two weeks, however, the Cubs beat the Mets seven out of eight times in head-on meetings. With the Mets dispatched, the Cubs drove home to their first N.L. East title.

In the league playoffs, the Cubs and Tigers were favored to win. The Kansas City Royals had survived Willie Wilson's suspension until May 15, George Brett's knee injury, and the aging of several key players to inch onto the A.L. West throne. Wilson sparked the offense after his return, while starter Bud Black and reliever Dan Quisenberry starred on the mound. Late season collapses by the Angels and the upstart Twins paved the way for the Royals. Once in the playoffs, however, the Royals were blown away by the Tigers in three straight games.

In the N.L., the Cubs started out with two straight victories over the San Diego Padres. A hot June and July gave the Padres an unbeatable lead in the surprisingly weak N.L. West. Newly acquired Graig Nettles and Rich Gossage combined their winning touch with Steve Garvey's, while young Padre outfielders Tony Gwynn and Kevin McReynolds grew into productive starters. With Garvey's clutch hitting in the lead, the Padres beat back the Cubs and took the last three games of the Championship Series, ending the debate over whether lights should be installed in Wrigley Field for the World Series.

The Series looked like a mismatch and was played like one. The Tigers won the title five games, with Trammell winning the Series MVP award. Kings of the early season, the Tigers held first place from the first day to the last.

Elsewhere this season, Pete Rose got his 4,000th career hit while in a Montreal uniform on April 13, then returned to Cincinnati in August as a player-manager. A new commissioner took office on October 1, as Peter Ueberroth succeeded Bowie Kuhn after serving as president of the Los Angeles Olympic Organizing Committee. Two owners left the stage, as Calvin Griffith sold the Twins to a group of local bankers and Ray Kroc died in January, nine months before his Padres would make their first World Series appearance.

EAST DIVISION

1984 AMERICAN LEAGUE

Name	G by Pos	B	AGE	G	AB	R	H	2B	3B	HR	RBI	BB	SO	SB	BA	SA
DETROIT 1st 104-58 .642 SPARKY ANDERSON																
TOTALS			29	162	5644	829	1529	254	46	187	788	602	941	106	.271	.432
Dave Bergman	1B114, OF2	L	31	120	271	42	74	8	5	7	44	33	40	3	.273	.417
Lou Whitaker	2B142	L	27	143	558	90	161	25	1	13	56	62	63	6	.289	.407
Alan Trammell	SS114, DH23	R	26	139	555	85	174	34	5	14	69	90	63	19	.314	.468
Howard Johnson	3B108, SS9, DH4, 1B1, OF1	B	23	116	355	43	88	14	1	12	50	40	67	10	.248	.394
Kirk Gibson	OF139, DH6	L	27	149	531	92	150	23	10	27	91	63	103	29	.282	.516
Chet Lemon	OF140, DH1	R	29	141	509	77	146	34	6	20	76	51	83	5	.287	.495
Larry Herndon	OF117, DH4	R	30	125	407	52	114	18	5	7	43	32	63	6	.280	.400
Lance Parrish	C127, DH22	R	28	147	578	75	137	16	2	33	98	41	120	2	.237	.443
Darrell Evans	DH62, 1B47, 3B19	L	37	131	401	60	93	11	1	16	63	77	70	2	.232	.384
Tom Brookens	3B68, SS28, 2B26, DH1	R	30	113	224	32	55	11	4	5	26	19	33	6	.246	.397
Barbaro Garbey	1B65, 3B20, DH17, OF10, 2B3	R	27	110	327	45	94	17	1	5	52	17	35	6	.287	.391
Johnny Grubb	OF36, DH33	L	35	86	176	25	47	5	0	8	17	36	36	1	.267	.432
Rusty Kuntz	OF67, DH10	R	29	84	140	32	40	12	0	2	22	25	28	2	.286	.414
Ruppert Jones	OF73, DH2	L	29	79	215	26	61	12	1	12	37	21	47	2	.284	.516
Marty Castillo	3B33, C36, DH1	R	27	70	141	16	33	5	2	4	17	10	33	1	.234	.383
Doug Baker	SS39, 2B5, DH1	B	23	43	108	15	20	4	1	0	12	7	22	3	.185	.241
Dwight Lowry	C31	L	26	32	45	8	11	2	0	2	7	3	11	0	.244	.422
Rod Allen	DH11, OF2	R	24	15	27	6	8	1	0	0	3	2	8	1	.296	.333
Scott Earl	2B14	R	23	14	35	3	4	0	1	0	1	0	9	1	.114	.171
Nelson Simmons	OF5, DH4	B	20	9	30	4	13	2	0	0	3	2	5	1	.433	.500
Mike Laga	1B4, DH4	L	24	9	11	1	6	0	0	0	1	1	2	0	.545	.545

NAME	T	AGE	W	L	PCT	SV	G	GS	CG	IP	H	BB	SO	SHO	ERA
		30	104	58	.642	51	162	162	19	1464	1358	489	914	8	3.49
Jack Morris	R	29	19	11	.633	0	35	35	9	240	221	87	148	1	3.60
Dan Petry	R	25	18	8	.692	0	35	35	7	233	231	66	144	2	3.24
Milt Wilcox	R	34	17	8	.680	0	33	33	0	194	183	66	119	0	4.00
Juan Berenguer	R	29	11	10	.524	0	31	27	2	168	146	79	118	1	3.48
Aurelio Lopez	R	35	10	1	.909	14	71	0	0	138	109	52	94	0	2.94
Willie Hernandez	L	29	9	3	.750	32	80	0	0	140	96	36	112	0	1.92
Dave Rozema	R	27	7	6	.538	0	29	16	0	101	110	18	48	0	3.74
Doug Bair	R	34	5	3	.625	4	47	1	0	94	82	36	57	0	3.75
Glenn Abbott	R	33	3	4	.429	0	13	8	1	44	62	8	8	0	5.93
Randy O'Neal	R	23	2	1	.667	0	4	3	0	19	16	6	12	0	3.38
2 Sid Monge	L	33	1	0	1.000	0	19	0	0	36	40	12	19	0	4.25
2 Bill Scherrer	L	26	1	0	1.000	0	18	0	0	19	14	8	16	0	1.89
Roger Mason	R	25	1	1	.500	0	5	2	0	22	23	10	15	0	4.50
1 Carl Willis	R	23	0	2	.000	0	10	2	0	16	25	5	4	0	7.31

Name	G by Pos	B	AGE	G	AB	R	H	2B	3B	HR	RBI	BB	SO	SB	BA	SA
TORONTO 2nd 89-73 .549 15 BOBBY COX																
TOTALS			28	163	5687	750	1555	275	68	143	702	460	816	193	.273	.421
Willie Upshaw	1B151, DH1	L	27	152	569	79	158	31	9	19	84	55	86	10	.278	.464
Damaso Garcia	2B149, DH1	R	29	152	633	79	180	32	5	5	46	16	46	46	.284	.374
Alfredo Griffin	SS115, 2B21, DH5	B	26	140	419	53	101	8	2	4	30	4	33	11	.241	.298
Rance Mulliniks	3B119, SS3, 2B1	L	28	125	343	41	111	21	5	3	42	33	44	2	.324	.440
George Bell	OF147, DH7, 3B3, 2B1	R	24	159	606	85	177	39	4	26	87	24	86	11	.292	.498
Lloyd Moseby	OF156	L	24	158	592	97	166	28	15	18	92	78	122	39	.280	.470
Dave Collins	OF108, 1B6, DH6, 3B1	B	31	128	441	59	136	24	15	2	44	43	41	60	.308	.444
Ernie Whitt	C118	L	32	124	315	35	75	12	1	15	46	43	49	0	.238	.425
Cliff Johnson	DH109, 1B2	R	36	127	359	51	109	23	1	16	61	50	62	0	.304	.507
Garth Iorg	3B112, 2B7, SS2, DH1	R	29	121	247	24	56	10	3	1	25	5	16	1	.227	.304
Jesse Barfield	OF88, DH9	R	24	110	320	51	91	14	1	14	49	35	81	8	.284	.466
Buck Martinez	C98, DH1	R	35	102	232	24	51	13	1	5	37	29	49	0	.220	.349
Willie Aikens (SD)	DH81, 1B2	L	29	93	234	21	48	7	0	11	26	29	56	0	.205	.376
Tony Fernandez (BH)	SS73, 3B10, DH1	B	22	88	233	29	63	5	3	3	19	17	15	5	.270	.356
Rick Leach	OF23, 1B15, DH6, P1	L	27	65	88	11	23	6	2	0	7	8	14	0	.261	.375
Mitch Webster	OF10, DH9, 1B1	B	25	26	22	9	5	2	1	0	4	1	7	0	.227	.409
Kelly Gruber	3B12, OF2, DH1	R	22	15	16	1	1	0	0	1	0	2	0	5	.063	.250
Ron Shepherd	OF5, DH4	R	23	12	4	0	0	0	0	0	0	0	3	0	.000	.000
Fred Manrique	2B9, DH1	R	23	10	9	0	3	0	0	0	0	1	0	1	.333	.333
Geno Petralli	C1, DH1	B	24	3	3	0	0	0	0	0	0	0	0	0	.000	.000
Toby Hernandez	C3	R	25	3	2	1	1	0	0	0	0	0	0	0	.500	.500

NAME	T	AGE	W	L	PCT	SV	G	GS	CG	IP	H	BB	SO	SHO	ERA
		27	89	73	.549	33	163	163	34	1464	1433	528	875	10	3.86
Doyle Alexander	R	33	17	6	.739	0	36	35	11	262	238	59	139	2	3.13
Dave Stieb	R	26	16	8	.667	0	35	35	11	267	215	88	198	2	2.83
Luis Leal	R	27	13	8	.619	0	35	35	6	222	221	77	134	2	3.89
Jim Clancy	R	28	13	15	.464	0	36	36	5	220	249	88	118	0	5.12
Dennis Lamp	R	31	8	8	.500	9	56	4	0	85	97	38	45	0	4.55
Jim Gott	R	24	7	6	.538	2	35	12	1	110	93	49	73	1	4.02
Roy Lee Jackson	R	30	7	8	.467	10	54	0	0	86	73	31	58	0	3.56
Jimmy Key	L	23	4	5	.444	10	63	0	0	62	70	32	44	0	4.65
Jim Acker	R	25	3	5	.375	1	32	3	0	72	79	25	33	0	4.38
Bryan Clark	L	27	1	2	.333	0	20	3	0	46	66	22	21	0	5.91
1 Joey McLaughlin	R	27	0	0	—	0	6	0	0	11	12	7	3	0	2.53
Rick Leach	L	27	0	0		0	1	0	0	1	2	2	0		27.00
Ron Musselman	R	29	0	2	.000	1	11	0	0	21	18	10	9	0	2.11

NEW YORK — 3rd 87-75 .537 17 — YOGI BERRA

Name	G by Pos	B	AGE	G	AB	R	H	2B	3B	HR	RBI	BB	SO	SB	BA	SA
TOTALS			30	162	5661	758	1560	275	32	130	725	534	673	62	.276	.404
Don Mattingly	1B133, OF19	L	23	153	603	91	207	44	2	23	110	41	33	1	.343	.537
Willie Randolph	2B142	B	29	142	564	86	162	24	2	2	31	86	42	10	.287	.348
Bobby Meacham	SS96, 2B2	B	23	99	360	62	91	13	4	2	25	32	70	9	.253	.328
Toby Harrah	3B74, 2B4, DH2, OF1	R	35	88	253	40	55	9	4	1	26	42	28	3	.217	.296
Dave Winfield	OF140	R	32	141	567	106	193	34	4	19	100	53	71	6	.340	.515
Omar Moreno	OF108, DH1	L	31	117	355	37	92	12	6	4	38	18	48	20	.259	.361
Steve Kemp	OF75, DH12	L	29	94	313	37	91	12	1	7	41	40	54	4	.291	.403
Butch Wynegar	C126	B	28	129	442	48	118	3	1	6	45	65	35	1	.267	.342
Don Baylor	DH127, OF5	R	35	134	493	84	129	29	1	27	89	38	68	1	.262	.489
Ken Griffey	OF82, 1B27, DH2	L	34	120	399	44	109	20	1	7	56	29	32	2	.273	.381
1 Roy Smalley	3B35, SS13, 1B5, DH5	B	31	67	209	17	50	8	1	7	26	15	35	2	.239	.388
Mike Pagliarulo	3B67	R	24	67	201	24	48	15	3	7	34	15	46	0	.239	.448
Brian Dayett	OF62, DH1	R	27	64	127	14	31	8	0	4	23	9	14	0	.244	.402
Tim Foli	SS28, 2B21, 3B10, 1B2	R	33	61	163	8	41	11	0	0	16	2	16	0	.252	.319
Oscar Gamble (LJ)	DH28, OF12	L	34		125	17	23	2	0	10	27	25	18	1	.184	.440
Andre Robertson	SS49, 2B6	R	26	52	140	10	30	5	1	0	6	4	20	0	.214	.264
Rick Cerone (EJ)	C38	R	30	38	120	8	25	3	0	2	13	9	15	1	.208	.283
Vic Mata	OF28	R	23	30	70	8	23	5	0	1	6	0	12	1	.329	.443
Lou Piniella	OF24, DH2	R	40	29	86	8	26	4	1	1	6	7	5	0	.302	.407
Mike O'Berry	C12, 3B1	R	30	13	32	3	8	2	0	0	5	2	2	0	.250	.313
Scott Bradley	OF5, C3	L	24	9	21	3	6	1	0	0	2	1	1	0	.286	.333
Rex Hudler	2B9	R	23	9	7	2	1	1	0	0	0	1	5	0	.143	.286
Stan Javier	OF5	B	20	7	7	1	1	0	0	0	0	0	1	0	.143	.143
Keith Smith	SS2	R	22	4	0	0	0	0	0	0	0	0	2	0	.000	.000

NAME	T	AGE	W	L	PCT	SV	G	GS	CG	IP	H	BB	SO	SHO	ERA
TOTALS		29	87	75	.537	43	162	162	15	1465	1485	518	992	12	3.78
Phil Niekro	R	45	16	8	.667	0	32	31	5	216	219	76	136	1	3.09
Ron Guidry (VJ)	L	33	10	11	.476	0	29	28	5	196	223	44	127	1	4.51
Joe Cowley	R	25	9	2	.818	0	16	11	3	83	75	31	71	1	3.56
Jay Howell	R	28	9	4	.692	7	61	1	0	104	86	34	109	0	2.69
Dennis Rasmussen	L	25	9	6	.600	0	24	24	1	148	127	60	110	0	4.57
Ray Fontenot	L	26	8	9	.471	0	35	24	0	169	189	58	85	0	3.61
John Montefusco (ZJ)	R	34	5	3	.625	0	11	11	0	55	55	13	23	0	3.58
Dave Righetti	L	25	5	6	.455	31	64	0	0	96	79	37	90	0	2.34
Mike Armstrong (EJ)	R	30	3	2	.600	1	36	0	0	54	47	26	43	0	3.48
Bob Shirley	L	30	3	3	.500	0	41	7	1	114	119	38	48	0	3.38
2 Marty Bystrom (EJ)	R	25	2	2	.500	0	7	7	0	39	34	13	24	0	2.97
1 Shane Rawley	L	28	2	3	.400	0	11	10	0	42	46	27	24	0	6.21
Clay Christiansen	R	26	2	4	.333	2	24	1	0	39	50	12	27	0	6.05
Jose Rijo	R	19	2	8	.200	2	24	5	0	62	74	33	47	0	4.76
Curt Brown	R	24	1	1	.500	0	13	0	0	17	18	4	10	0	2.70
Dale Murray (LJ)	R	34	1	3	.250	0	19	0	0	24	30	5	13	0	4.94
Jim Deshaies	L	24	0	1	.000	0	2	2	0	7	14	7	5	0	11.57
Rudy May 39 (XJ)															

BOSTON — 4th 86-76 .531 18 — RALPH HOUK

Name	G by Pos	B	AGE	G	AB	R	H	2B	3B	HR	RBI	BB	SO	SB	BA	SA
TOTALS			29	162	5648	810	1598	259	45	181	767	500	842	38	.283	.441
2 Bill Buckner	1B113	L	34	114	439	51	122	21	2	11	67	24	38	2	.278	.410
Marty Barrett	2B136	R	26	139	475	56	144	23	3	3	45	42	25	5	.303	.383
Jackie Gutierrez	SS150	R	24	151	449	55	118	12	3	2	29	15	49	12	.263	.316
Wade Boggs	3B156, DH2	L	26	158	625	109	203	31	4	6	55	89	44	3	.325	.416
Dwight Evans	OF161, DH1	R	32	162	630	121	186	37	8	32	104	96	115	3	.295	.532
Tony Armas	OF126, DH31	R	30	157	639	107	171	29	5	43	123	32	156	1	.268	.531
Jim Rice	OF157, DH1	R	31	159	657	98	184	25	7	28	122	44	102	4	.280	.467
Rich Gedman	C125	R	24	133	449	54	121	26	4	24	72	29	72	0	.269	.506
Mike Easler	DH126, 1B29	L	33	156	601	87	188	31	5	27	91	58	134	1	.313	.516
Rick Miller	OF31, 1B8	L	36	95	123	17	32	5	1	0	12	17	22	1	.260	.317
Reid Nichols	OF48, DH1	R	25	74	124	14	28	5	1	1	14	12	18	2	.226	.306
Glenn Hoffman	SS56, 3B4, 2B2	R	25	64	74	8	14	4	0	0	4	5	10	0	.189	.243
Ed Jurak	1B19, 2B14, 3B9, SS1	R	26	47	66	6	16	3	1	1	7	12	12	0	.242	.364
Gary Allenson	C35	R	29	35	83	9	19	2	0	2	8	9	14	0	.229	.325
Jerry Remy	2B24	L	31	30	104	8	26	1	1	0	8	7	11	4	.250	.279
Jeff Newman	C24	R	35	24	63	5	14	2	0	1	3	5	16	0	.222	.302
Dave Stapleton (KJ)	1B10, DH1	R	30	13	39	4	9	2	0	0	1	3	3	0	.231	.333
Chico Walker	2B1	B	26	3	2	0	0	0	0	0	0	0	1	0	.000	.000
Marc Sullivan	C2	R	25	2	6	1	3	0	0	0	1	0	1	0	.500	.500

NAME	T	AGE	W	L	PCT	SV	G	GS	CG	IP	H	BB	SO	SHO	ERA
TOTALS		26	86	76	.531	32	162	162	40	1442	1524	517	927	12	4.18
Bruce Hurst	L	26	12	12	.500	0	33	33	0	218	232	88	136	2	3.92
Bob Ojeda	L	26	12	12	.500	0	33	32	8	217	211	96	137	5	3.99
Oil Can Boyd	R	24	12	12	.500	0	29	26	10	198	207	53	134	3	4.37
Al Nipper	R	25	11	6	.647	0	29	24	6	183	183	52	84	0	3.89
Roger Clemens	R	21	9	4	.692	0	21	20	5	133	146	29	126	1	4.32
Bob Stanley	R	29	9	10	.474	22	57	0	0	107	113	23	52	0	3.54
Mark Clear	R	28	8	3	.727	8	47	0	0	67	47	70	76	0	4.03
Steve Crawford	R	26	5	0	1.000	1	35	0	0	62	69	21	21	0	3.34
1 Dennis Eckersley	R	29	4	4	.500	0	9	9	2	65	71	13	33	0	5.01
Rich Gale	R	30	2	3	.400	0	13	4	0	44	57	18	28	0	5.56
John Henry Johnson	L	27	1	2	.333	1	30	3	0	64	64	27	57	0	3.53
Mike Brown	R	25	1	8	.111	0	15	11	0	67	104	19	32	0	6.85
Charlie Mitchell	R	22	0	0	—	0	10	0	0	16	14	6	7	0	2.76
Jim Dorsey	R	28	0	0	—	0	2	0	0	3	2	4		0	10.13

BALTIMORE — 5th 85-77 .525 19 — JOE ALTOBELLI

Name	G by Pos	B	AGE	G	AB	R	H	2B	3B	HR	RBI	BB	SO	SB	BA	SA
TOTALS			30	162	5456	681	1374	234	23	160	647	620	884	51	.252	.391
Eddie Murray	1B159, DH3	B	28	162	588	97	180	26	3	29	110	107	87	10	.306	.509
Rich Dauer	2B123, 3B3	R	31	127	397	29	101	26	0	2	24	24	23	1	.254	.335
Cal Ripken	SS162	R	23	162	641	103	195	37	7	27	86	71	89	2	.304	.510
Wayne Gross	3B117, 1B3, DH1	L	32	127	342	53	74	9	1	22	64	68	69	1	.216	.442
Mike Young	OF115, DH1	B	24	123	401	59	101	17	2	17	52	58	110	6	.252	.431
John Shelby	OF124	B	26	128	383	44	80	12	5	6	30	20	71	12	.209	.313
Gary Roenicke	OF117	R	29	121	326	36	73	19	1	10	44	58	43	1	.224	.380
Rick Dempsey	C108	R	34	109	330	37	76	11	0	11	34	40	58	1	.230	.364
Ken Singleton	DH103	B	37	111	363	28	78	7	1	6	36	37	60	0	.215	.289
Al Bumbry	OF99, DH9	L	37	119	344	47	93	12	1	3	24	25	35	9	.270	.337
John Lowenstein	OF67, DH22, 1B2	L	37	105	270	34	64	13	0	8	28	33	54	1	.237	.374
Todd Cruz	3B89, DH1, P1	R	28	96	142	15	31	4	0	3	9	8	33	1	.218	.310
Floyd Rayford	C86, 3B22, 1B1	R	26	86	250	24	64	14	0	4	27	12	51	0	.256	.350
Lenn Sakata	2B76, OF1	R	30	81	157	23	30	1	0	3	11	6	15	4	.191	.255
Jim Dwyer (KJ)	OF52, DH3	L	34	76	161	22	41	9	1	2	21	23	24	0	.255	.360
Benny Ayala	DH34, OF13	R	33	60	118	9	25	6	0	4	24	8	24	1	.212	.364
Joe Nolan (KJ)	DH11, C6	L	33	35	62	2	18	1	1	1	9	12	10	0	.290	.387
Dan Ford (KJ-WJ)	OF15, DH8	R	32	25	91	7	21	4	0	1	5	7	13	0	.231	.308
2 Ron Jackson	3B10	R	31	12	28	0	8	2	0	0	2	0	4	0	.286	.357
Vic Rodriguez	2B7, DH1	R	22	11	17	4	7	3	0	0	2	0	1	0	.412	.588
Jim Traber	DH9	L	22	10	21	3	5	0	0	1	2	3	2	0	.238	.238
Larry Sheets	OF7	L	24	8	16	3	7	1	0	1	2	0	3	0	.438	.688
2 Orlando Sanchez	C4	L	27	5	8	0	2	0	0	0	1	0	2	0	.250	.250

NAME	T	AGE	W	L	PCT	SV	G	GS	CG	IP	H	BB	SO	SHO	ERA
TOTALS		29	85	77	.525	32	162	162	48	1439	1393	512	714	13	3.71
Mike Boddicker	R	26	20	11	.645	0	34	34	16	261	218	81	128	4	2.79
Scott McGregor (BG)	L	30	15	12	.556	0	30	30	10	196	216	54	67	3	3.94
Storm Davis	R	22	14	9	.609	1	35	31	10	225	205	71	105	2	3.12
Mike Flanagan	L	32	13	13	.500	0	34	34	10	227	213	81	115	2	3.53
Sammy Stewart	R	29	7	4	.636	13	60	0	0	93	81	47	56	0	3.29
Dennis Martinez	R	29	6	9	.400	0	34	20	2	142	145	37	77	0	5.02
Tippy Martinez	L	34	4	9	.308	17	55	0	0	90	88	51	72	0	3.91
Bill Swaggerty	R	27	3	2	.600	0	23	6	0	57	68	21	18	0	5.21
Tom Underwood	L	30	2	0	1.000	1	37	1	0	72	78	31	39	0	3.52
Nate Snell	R	31	1	0	.500	0	5	0	0	8	1	7		0	2.35
Mark Brown	R	24	1	2	.333	0	9	0	0	23	22	7	10	0	3.91
Todd Cruz	R	28	0	0		0	1	0	0	1	0	0	0	0	0.00
John Pacella	R	27	0	0	.000	0	6	1	0	15	15	9	8	0	6.75
Ken Dixon	R	23	0	1	.000	0	2	0	0	13	14	4	8	0	4.15
Jim Palmer	R	38	0	3	.000	0	5	3	0	18	22	17	4	0	9.17

CLEVELAND — 6th 75-87 .463 29 — PAT CORRALES

Name	G by Pos	B	AGE	G	AB	R	H	2B	3B	HR	RBI	BB	SO	SB	BA	SA
TOTALS			27	163	5643	761	1498	222	39	123	704	600	815	126	.265	.384
Mike Hargrove	1B124	L	34	133	352	44	94	14	2	2	44	53	38	0	.267	.335
Tony Bernazard	2B136, DH1	B	27	140	439	44	97	15	4	2	38	43	70	20	.221	.287
Julio Franco	SS159, DH1	R	25	160	658	82	188	22	5	3	79	43	68	19	.286	.348
Brook Jacoby (BH)	3B123, SS1	R	24	126	439	64	116	19	3	7	40	32	73	3	.264	.369
George Vukovich	OF130	L	28	134	437	38	133	22	5	9	60	34	61	1	.304	.439
Brett Butler	OF156	L	27	159	602	108	162	25	9	3	49	86	62	52	.269	.355
2 Mel Hall	OF69, DH9	L	23	83	257	43	66	13	1	7	30	35	55	1	.257	.397
Jerry Willard	C76, DH11	L	24	87	246	21	55	8	1	10	37	26	55	1	.224	.386
Andre Thornton	DH144, 1B11	R	34	155	587	91	159	26	0	33	99	91	79	6	.271	.484
Pat Tabler	1B67, OF43, 3B36, 2B1, DH1	R	26	144	473	66	137	21	3	10	68	47	62	3	.290	.410
Carmen Castillo	OF70, DH2	R	26	87	211	36	55	9	2	10	36	21	52	1	.261	.464
Mike Fischlin	2B55, 3B22, SS15	R	28	85	133	17	30	4	2	1	14	12	18	3	.226	.308
Chris Bando	C63, 1B1, 3B1, DH1	B	28	75	220	38	64	11	0	12	41	33	35	1	.291	.505
Joe Carter	OF59, 1B7	R	24	66	244	32	67	6	1	13	41	11	48	2	.275	.467
Broderick Perkins	DH10, 1B2	L	29	58	66	5	13	1	0	0	7	8	6	0	.197	.212
Otis Nixon	OF46	B	25	49	91	16	14	0	0	0	8	8	12	12	.154	.154
1 Ron Hassey	C44, 1B1, DH1	L	31	48	149	11	38	5	1	0	19	15	26	1	.255	.302
Junior Noboa	2B19, DH1	R	19	23	11	3	4	0	0	0	0	2	1	0	.364	.364
Kevin Rhomberg	OF7, 1B1, 2B1, DH1	R	24	13	8	0	2	0	0	0	3	0	0	0	.250	.250
Jeff Moronko	3B6, DH1	R	24	7	19	1	3	1	0	0	3	0	5	0	.158	.211
2 Jamie Quirk	C1	L	29	1	1	1	0	0	0	0	0	0	0	0	1.000	4.000

NAME	T	AGE	W	L	PCT	SV	G	GS	CG	IP	H	BB	SO	SHO	ERA
TOTALS		27	75	87	.463	35	163	163	21	1468	1523	545	803	7	4.26
Bert Blyleven	R	33	19	7	.731	0	33	32	12	245	204	74	170	4	2.87
Neal Heaton	L	24	12	15	.444	0	38	34	4	199	231	75	75	1	5.21
Tom Waddell	R	25	7	4	.636	6	58	0	0	97	66	37	59	0	3.06
Mike Jeffcoat	L	24	5	2	.714	1	63	1	0	75	82	24	41	0	2.99
Roy Smith	R	22	5	5	.500	0	22	14	0	86	91	40	55	0	4.59
Ernie Camacho	R	29	5	9	.357	23	69	0	0	100	83	37	48	0	2.43
1 Rick Sutcliffe	R	28	4	5	.444	0	15	15	2	94	111	46	58	0	5.15
Steve Comer	R	30	4	3	.333	0	22	20	1	117	146	39	39	0	5.68
Jamie Easterly (XJ)	L	31	3	2	.750	2	26	1	0	69	74	23	42	0	3.38
1 George Frazier	R	29	3	1	.600	1	22	0	0	44	45	14	24	0	3.65
2 Don Schulze	R	21	3	6	.333	0	19	14	2	86	105	27	39	0	4.83
Steve Farr	R	27	3	11	.214	1	31	16	0	116	106	46	83	0	4.58
Luis Aponte	R	31	1	0	1.000	0	25	0	0	50	53	15	25	0	4.11
Jery Ujdur	R	27	1	2	.333	0	4	3	0	14	22	14	6	0	6.91
Jeff Barkley	R	24	0	0	—	0	7	0	0	12	13	6	6	0	6.75
Ramon Romero	L	25	0	0	—	0	3	0	0	3	4	0	0	0	0.00
Jose Roman	R	21	0	1	.000	0	6	1	0	9	11	3	0	0	18.00
Rick Behenna (SJ)	R	24	0	3	.000	0	10	5	0	51	70	22	23	0	13.97
1 Dan Spillner	R	32	0	5	.000	1	14	8	0	51	70	22	23	0	5.65

MILWAUKEE — 7th 67-94 .416 36.5 — RENE LACHEMANN

Name	G by Pos	B	AGE	G	AB	R	H	2B	3B	HR	RBI	BB	SO	SB	BA	SA
TOTALS			30	161	5511	641	1446	232	36	96	598	432	673	52	.262	.370
Cecil Cooper	1B122, DH26	L	34	148	603	63	166	28	3	11	67	27	59	8	.275	.386
Jim Gantner	2B153	L	31	153	613	61	173	27	1	3	56	30	51	6	.282	.344
Robin Yount	SS120, DH39	R	28	160	624	105	186	27	7	16	80	67	67	14	.298	.441
Ed Romero	3B59, SS39, 2B11, 1B4, DH2, OF1	R	26	116	357	36	90	12	0	1	31	29	25	3	.252	.294
Dion James	OF118	L	21	128	387	52	114	19	5	1	30	32	41	10	.295	.377
Rick Manning	OF114, DH1	L	29	119	341	53	85	10	5	7	31	34	32	5	.249	.370
Ben Oglivie	OF125, DH1	L	35	131	461	49	121	16	2	12	60	44	56	0	.262	.384
Jim Sundberg (XJ)	C109	R	33	110	348	43	91	19	4	7	43	38	63	1	.261	.399
Ted Simmons	DH77, 1B37, 3B14	B	34	132	497	44	110	23	2	4	52	30	40	3	.221	.300
Charlie Moore	OF61, C7	R	31	70	188	13	44	7	1	2	17	10	26	0	.234	.314
Roy Howell	346, DH8, 1B4	L	30	68	164	12	38	5	1	4	17	8	32	0	.232	.348
Mark Brouhard	OF52, DH8	R	28	66	197	20	47	7	0	6	22	16	36	1	.239	.365
Bill Schroeder	C58, DH3, 1B1	R	25	61	210	29	54	6	0	14	25	8	54	0	.257	.486
Bobby Clark (LJ)	OF56	R	29	58	169	17	44	7	2	2	16	16	35	1	.260	.361
Willie Lozado	3B36, SS6, 2B1, DH1	R	25	43	128	17	35	9	2	1	20	12	23	0	.271	.411
Randy Ready	3B36	R	24	37	123	13	23	6	1	3	13	14	18	0	.187	.325
Doug Loman	OF23	L	26	23	76	13	21	4	0	2	12	15	7	0	.276	.408
Paul Molitor (EJ)	3B7, DH4	R	27	13	46	3	10	1	0	0	6	2	8	1	.217	.239

NAME	T	AGE	W	L	PCT	SV	G	GS	CG	IP	H	BB	SO	SHO	ERA
TOTALS		31	67	94	.416	41	161	161	13	1433	1532	480	785	7	4.06
Don Sutton	R	39	14	12	.538	0	33	33	7	213	224	51	143	0	3.77
Moose Haas	R	28	9	11	.450	0	31	30	4	189	205	43	84	0	3.99
Jaime Cocanower	R	27	8	16	.333	0	33	27	1	175	188	78	65	0	4.02
Tom Tellmann	R	30	6	3	.667	4	50	0	0	81	82	31	28	0	2.78
Chuck Porter (EJ)	R	28	6	4	.600	0	17	12	1	81	92	12	48	0	3.87
Mike Caldwell (XJ)	L	35	6	13	.316	0	26	19	4	126	160	21	34	1	4.64
Bob McClure	L	32	4	8	.333	1	39	18	1	140	154	52	68	0	4.38
Pete Ladd	R	27	4	9	.308	3	54	1	0	91	94	38	75	0	5.24
Ray Searage	L	29	2	1	.667	6	21	0	0	38	20	16	29	0	0.70
Tom Candiotti (SJ)	R	26	2	2	.500	0	8	6	0	32	38	10	23	0	5.29
Rick Waits	L	32	2	4	.333	3	47	1	0	73	84	24	49	0	3.58
Bob Gibson	R	27	2	5	.286	0	18	9	1	69	61	47	54	1	4.96
2 Jim Kern	R	35	1	0	1.000	0	6	0	0	9	5	4	4	0	0.00
Rollie Fingers (XJ)	R	37	1	2	.333	23	33	0	0	46	38	13	40	0	1.96
Jerry Augustine	L	31	0	0	—	0	3	0	0	4	5	4	0	0	0.00
Jack Lazorko	R	28	0	1	.000	1	15	1	0	40	37	22	24	0	4.31
Paul Hartzell	R	30	0	1	.000	0	4	1	0	10	17	6	3	0	7.84
Andy Beene	R	27	0	2	.000	0	5	3	0	19	28	9	11	0	11.09
Pete Vuckovich (SJ) 31															

WEST DIVISION

KANSAS CITY — 1st 84-78 .519 — DICK HOWSER

Name	G by Pos	B	AGE	G	AB	R	H	2B	3B	HR	RBI	BB	SO	SB	BA	SA
TOTALS			30	162	5543	673	1487	269	52	117	639	400	832	106	.268	.399
Steve Balboni	1B125, DH1	R	27	126	438	58	107	23	2	28	77	45	139	0	.244	.498
Frank White	2B129	R	33	129	479	58	130	22	5	17	56	27	72	5	.271	.445
Onix Concepcion (SJ-BH)	SS85, 2B6, 3B1	R	26	90	287	36	81	9	2	1	23	14	33	9	.282	.338
George Brett (KJ)	3B101	L	31	104	377	42	107	21	3	13	69	38	37	0	.284	.459
Pat Sheridan	OF134	L	26	138	481	64	136	24	4	8	53	41	91	19	.283	.399
Willie Wilson (SD)	OF128	B	28	128	541	81	163	24	9	2	44	39	56	47	.301	.390
Darryl Motley	OF138	R	24	146	522	64	146	25	6	15	70	28	73	10	.284	.441
Don Slaught	C123, DH1	R	25	124	409	48	108	27	4	4	42	20	55	0	.264	.379
Jorge Orta	DH83, OF24, DH1	L	33	122	447	50	120	23	7	9	50	28	39	0	.298	.457
Greg Pryor	3B105, 2B22, SS2, 1B1, DH1	R	34	123	270	32	71	11	1	4	25	12	28	0	.263	.356
Hal McRae	DH94	R	38	106	317	30	96	13	4	3	42	34	47	0	.303	.397
John Wathan	C59, 1B33, DH4, OF1	R	34	97	171	17	31	7	1	2	10	21	34	6	.181	.269
2 Dan Iorg	1B43, OF22, DH5, 3B1	L	34	78	235	27	60	16	2	5	30	13	15	0	.255	.404
Buddy Biancalana	SS33, 2B29	B	24	66	134	18	26	6	1	2	9	6	44	1	.194	.299
U.L. Washington (AJ)	SS61	B	30	63	170	18	38	6	0	1	10	14	31	4	.224	.276
Lynn Jones (BH-BG)	OF45	R	31	47	103	11	31	8	0	1	10	4	9	1	.301	.388
Butch Davis	OF35, DH2	R	26	41	116	11	17	3	0	2	1	10	19	4	.147	.224
Leon Roberts (XJ)	OF16, DH3, P1	R	33	29	45	4	10	1	1	0	3	4	3	0	.222	.289
Bucky Dent	SS9, 3B2	R	32	11	9	2	3	0	0	0	1	1	2	0	.333	.333
1 Orlando Sanchez	C1	L	27	10	10	0	1	1	0	0	2	0	2	0	.100	.200
Tucker Ashford	3B9	R	29	9	13	1	2	1	0	0	0	1	2	0	.154	.231
Dave Leeper	OF2, DH1	L	24	6	6	1	0	0	0	0	0	0	3	0	.000	.000
Luis Pujols	C4	R	28	4	5	0	1	0	0	0	1	0	1	0	.200	.200
Jim Scranton	SS1, 3B1	R	24	2	2	0	0	0	0	0	0	0	0	0	.000	.000

NAME	T	AGE	W	L	PCT	SV	G	GS	CG	IP	H	BB	SO	SHO	ERA
TOTALS		26	84	78	.519	50	162	162	18	1444	1426	433	724	9	3.92
Bud Black	L	27	17	12	.586	0	35	35	8	257	226	64	140	1	3.12
Larry Gura	L	36	12	9	.571	0	31	25	3	169	175	67	68	0	5.18
Charlie Leibrandt	L	27	11	7	.611	0	23	23	0	144	158	38	53	0	3.63
Bret Saberhagen	R	20	10	11	.476	1	38	18	2	158	138	36	73	1	3.48
Mark Gubicza	R	21	10	14	.417	0	29	29	4	189	172	75	111	2	4.05
Joe Beckwith	R	29	8	4	.667	2	49	1	0	101	92	25	75	0	3.40
Dan Quisenberry	R	31	6	3	.667	44	72	0	0	129	121	12	41	0	2.64
Mark Huismann	R	26	3	3	.500	3	38	0	0	75	84	21	54	0	4.20
Mike Jones	L	24	2	3	.400	0	23	12	0	81	86	36	43	0	4.89
Frank Wills	R	25	2	3	.400	0	10	5	0	37	39	13	21	0	5.11
Danny Jackson	L	22	2	6	.250	0	15	11	1	76	84	35	40	0	4.26
Paul Splittorff	L	27	1	3	.250	0	12	3	0	28	47	10	4	0	7.71
Leon Roberts (KJ)	R	33	0	0	—	0	1	0	0	1	4	1	1	1*	27.00
Dennis Leonard 33 (KJ)															

CALIFORNIA (TIE) — 2nd 81-81 .500 3 — JOHN McNAMARA

Name	G by Pos	B	AGE	G	AB	R	H	2B	3B	HR	RBI	BB	SO	SB	BA	SA
TOTALS			32	162	5470	696	1363	211	30	150	649	556	928	80	.249	.381
Rod Carew	1B83, DH1	L	38	93	329	42	97	8	1	3	31	40	39	4	.295	.352
Rob Wilfong	2B97, SS4, DH1	L	30	108	307	31	76	13	2	6	33	20	53	3	.248	.362
Dick Schofield	SS140	R	21	140	400	39	77	10	3	4	21	33	79	5	.193	.263
Doug DeCinces	3B140, DH5	R	33	146	547	77	147	23	3	20	82	53	79	4	.269	.431
Fred Lynn	OF140	L	32	142	517	84	140	28	4	23	79	77	97	2	.271	.474
Gary Pettis	OF134	B	26	140	397	63	90	11	6	2	29	60	115	48	.227	.300
Brian Downing	OF131, DH1	R	33	156	539	65	148	28	2	23	91	70	66	0	.275	.462
Bob Boone	C137	R	36	139	450	33	91	16	1	3	32	25	45	3	.202	.262
Reggie Jackson	DH134, OF3	L	38	143	525	67	117	17	2	25	81	55	141	8	.223	.406
Bobby Grich	2B91, 1B25, 3B21	R	35	116	363	60	93	15	1	18	58	57	70	2	.256	.452
Juan Beniquez	OF98	R	34	110	354	60	119	17	0	8	39	18	43	3	.336	.452
Rob Picciolo	SS66, 3B13, 2B9, OF1	R	31	87	119	18	24	6	0	1	9	0	21	0	.202	.277
Jerry Narron	C46, 1B7	L	28	69	150	9	37	5	0	3	17	8	12	0	.247	.340
Mike Brown	OF44, DH3	R	24	62	148	19	42	8	3	7	22	13	23	0	.284	.520
Daryl Sconiers (XJ)	1B41, DH1	L	25	57	160	14	39	4	0	4	17	13	17	1	.244	.344
1 Ron Jackson	1B21, 3B9, OF1	R	31	33	91	5	15	2	1	0	5	7	13	0	.165	.209
Darrell Miller	1B16, OF1	R	26	17	41	5	7	0	0	0	4	4	9	0	.171	.171
2 Derrel Thomas	OF7, SS4, 3B3	B	33	14	29	3	4	0	1	0	3	4	4	0	.138	.207
Rick Burleson (SJ)		R	33	7	4	2	0	0	0	0	0	0	2	0	.000	.000
Ellis Valentine 29 (FJ)																

NAME	T	AGE	W	L	PCT	SV	G	GS	CG	IP	H	BB	SO	SHO	ERA
TOTALS		31	81	81	.500	26	162	162	36	1458	1526	474	754	12	3.96
Mike Witt	R	23	15	11	.577	0	34	34	9	247	227	84	196	2	3.47
Geoff Zahn	L	38	13	10	.565	0	28	27	9	199	200	48	61	5	3.12
Ron Romanick	R	23	12	12	.500	0	33	33	8	230	240	61	87	2	3.76
Luis Sanchez	R	30	9	7	.563	11	49	0	0	84	84	33	62	0	3.33
Jim Slaton	R	34	7	10	.412	0	32	22	5	163	192	56	67	1	4.97
Tommy John	L	41	7	13	.350	0	32	29	4	181	223	56	47	1	4.52
Doug Corbett	R	31	5	1	.833	4	45	1	0	85	76	30	48	0	2.12
Don Aase (EJ)	R	29	4	1	.800	8	23	0	0	39	30	19	28	0	1.62
Bruce Kison (XJ)	R	34	4	5	.444	2	20	7	0	65	72	28	66	0	5.37
Curt Kaufman	R	26	2	3	.400	1	29	1	0	69	68	20	41	0	4.57
Ken Forsch (SJ)	R	37	1	1	.500	0	2	2	1	16	14	3	10	0	2.20
John Curtis (HJ)	L	36	1	2	.333	0	17	0	0	29	30	11	18	0	4.40
Frank LaCorte (AJ)	R	32	1	2	.333	0	13	1	0	29	33	13	13	0	7.06
Stew Cliburn	R	27	0	0	—	0	1	0	0	3	1	1	1	0	13.50
D.W. Smith	R	26	0	0	—	0	1	0	0	1	3	1	1	0	18.00
Steve Brown	R	24	0	0	—	0	3	0	0	11	16	9	5	0	10.80
2 Craig Swan (AJ)	R	33	0	1	.000	0	3	1	0	5	8	0	2	0	10.80
Rick Steirer	R	27	0	1	.000	0	1	0	0	5	8	2	0	0	16.88

MINNESOTA (TIE) — 2nd 81-81 .500 3 — BILLY GARDNER

Name	G by Pos	B	AGE	G	AB	R	H	2B	3B	HR	RBI	BB	SO	SB	BA	SA
TOTALS			26	162	5562	673	1473	259	33	114	636	437	735	39	.265	.385
Kent Hrbek	1B148, DH1	L	24	149	559	80	174	31	3	27	107	65	87	1	.311	.522
Tim Teufel	2B157	R	25	157	568	76	149	30	3	14	61	76	73	1	.262	.400
Houston Jimenez	SS107	R	26	108	298	28	60	11	1	0	19	15	34	0	.201	.245
Gary Gaetti	3B154, OF8, SS2	R	25	162	588	55	154	29	4	5	65	44	81	11	.262	.350
Tom Brunansky	OF153, DH1	R	23	155	567	75	144	21	0	32	85	57	94	4	.254	.460
Kirby Puckett	OF128	R	24	128	557	63	165	12	5	0	31	16	69	14	.296	.336
Mickey Hatcher	OF100, DH37, 1B17, 3B1	R	29	152	576	61	174	35	5	5	69	37	34	0	.302	.404
Dave Engle	C86, DH22	R	26	131	441	56	104	20	1	4	42	30	53	0	.266	.353
Randy Bush	DH89, 1B2	L	25	113	311	46	69	17	1	11	43	31	60	1	.222	.389
Darrell Brown	OF55, DH13	B	28	95	260	36	71	9	3	1	19	14	16	4	.273	.342
Ron Washington	SS71, 2B9, DH4, 3B2	R	32	88	197	25	58	11	5	3	23	4	31	1	.294	.447
Tim Laudner	C81, DH2	R	26	87	262	31	54	16	1	10	35	18	78	0	.206	.389
Dave Meier	OF50, DH4, 3B1	R	24	59	147	18	35	8	1	0	13	6	9	0	.238	.306
Andre David	OF14, DH2	L	24	33	48	5	12	2	0	1	5	7	11	0	.250	.354
Jeff Reed	C18	L	21	18	21	3	3	3	0	0	1	2	6	0	.143	.286
Lenny Faedo	SS15, 1B1	R	24	16	52	6	13	1	0	1	1	6	4	0	.250	.327
2 Pat Putnam	DH11	L	30	14	38	1	3	1	0	0	4	4	12	0	.079	.105
Mike Hart	OF11	L	26	13	29	0	5	0	0	0	3	1	7	0	.172	.172
3 Chris Speier	SS12	R	34	12	33	2	7	0	0	0	3	7	7	0	.212	.212
Jim Eisenreich (VR)	DH6, OF3	L	25	12	32	1	7	1	0	0	3	2	4	2	.219	.250
John Castino (XJ)	3B8	R	29	8	27	5	12	1	0	0	5	5	2	0	.444	.481
Greg Gagne	SS1	R	22	2	1	0	0	0	0	0	0	0	0	0	.000	.000
Alvaro Espinoza	SS1	R	22	2												

NAME	T	AGE	W	L	PCT	SV	G	GS	CG	IP	H	BB	SO	SHO	ERA
TOTALS		27	81	81	.500	38	162	162	32	1438	1429	463	713	9	3.85
Frank Viola	L	24	18	12	.600	0	35	35	10	258	225	73	149	4	3.21
Mike Smithson	R	29	15	13	.536	0	36	36	10	252	246	54	144	1	3.68
John Butcher	R	27	13	11	.542	0	34	34	8	225	242	53	83	1	3.44
Ron Davis	R	28	7	11	.389	29	64	0	0	83	79	41	74	0	4.55
Pete Filson	L	25	6	5	.545	1	55	7	0	119	106	54	59	0	4.10
Ken Schrom (SJ)	R	29	5	11	.313	0	25	21	3	137	156	44	47	0	4.47
Rick Lysander	R	31	4	3	.571	5	36	0	0	57	62	27	22	0	3.49
Ed Hodge	L	26	4	3	.571	0	25	15	0	100	116	29	59	0	4.77
Al Williams (EJ)	R	30	3	5	.375	0	17	11	1	69	75	22	22	0	5.77
Larry Pashnick	R	28	2	1	.667	0	13	1	0	38	38	11	10	0	3.52
Bobby Castillo (EJ)	R	29	2	1	.667	0	10	2	0	25	14	19	7	0	1.78
Len Whitehouse	L	26	2	2	.500	1	30	0	0	31	29	17	18	0	3.16
Keith Comstock	L	28	0	0	—	0	2	0	0	1	4	0	1	0	8.53
Jack O'Connor	L	23	0	0	—	0	2	0	0	5	4	0	0	0	1.93
Curt Wardle	L	23	0	0	—	0	2	0	0	4	4	4	0	0	4.50
Mike Walters	R	26	0	3	.000	2	23	0	0	29	31	14	10	0	3.72

OAKLAND — 4th 77-85 .475 7 — STEVE BOROS 20-24 .455 — JACKIE MOORE 57-61 .483

Name	G by Pos	B	AGE	G	AB	R	H	2B	3B	HR	RBI	BB	SO	SB	BA	SA
TOTALS			30	162	5457	738	1415	257	29	158	697	568	871	145	.259	.404
Bruce Bochte	1B144, DH2	L	33	148	469	58	124	23	0	5	52	52	59	2	.264	.345
Joe Morgan	2B100, DH5	L	40	116	365	50	89	21	0	6	43	66	39	8	.244	.351
Tony Phillips	SS91, 2B90, OF1	B	25	154	451	62	120	24	3	4	37	42	86	10	.266	.359
Carney Lansford	3B151	R	27	151	597	70	179	31	5	14	74	40	62	9	.300	.424
Mike Davis	OF127, DH4	L	25	134	382	47	88	18	3	9	46	31	66	14	.230	.364
Dwayne Murphy	OF153	L	29	153	559	93	143	18	2	33	88	74	111	4	.256	.472
Rickey Henderson	OF140	R	25	142	502	113	147	27	4	16	58	86	81	66	.293	.458
Mike Heath	C108, OF45, 3B2, SS1	R	28	140	475	49	118	21	5	13	64	26	72	7	.248	.346
Dave Kingman	DH139, 1B9	R	35	147	549	68	147	23	1	35	118	44	119	2	.268	.505
Bill Almon	OF48, 1B44, DH12, 3B4, SS1, C1	R	31	106	211	24	47	11	0	7	16	10	42	5	.223	.374
Mark Wagner	SS58, 3B15, 2B8, DH3, P1	R	30	87	87	8	20	5	1	0	12	7	11	2	.230	.310
Donnie Hill (IL)	SS66, 2B4, 3B2, DH2	B	23	73	174	21	40	6	0	2	16	5	12	1	.230	.299
1 Davey Lopes (IJ)	OF42, 2B17, DH9, 3B5	R	39	72	230	32	59	11	1	9	36	31	36	12	.257	.430
Jim Essian (BH)	C59, 3B1, DH1	R	33	63	136	17	32	9	0	2	10	23	17	1	.235	.346
Jeff Burroughs (BH)	DH33	R	33	58	71	5	15	1	0	2	8	18	23	0	.211	.310
Garry Hancock (EJ)	OF18, DH5, 1B4, P1	L	30	51	60	2	13	2	0	0	8	0	1	0	.217	.250
Mickey Tettleton	C32	R	23	33	76	10	20	2	1	1	5	11	21	0	.263	.355
Steve Kiefer	SS17, DH3, 3B2	R	23	23	40	7	7	1	2	0	2	2	10	2	.175	.300
Dan Meyer	1B3, DH2	L	31	20	22	1	7	3	1	0	4	0	2	0	.318	.545

NAME	T	AGE	W	L	PCT	SV	G	GS	CG	IP	H	BB	SO	SHO	ERA
		28	77	85	.475	44	162	162	15	1430	1554	592	695	6	4.48
Ray Burris	R	33	13	10	.565	0	34	28	5	212	193	90	93	1	3.15
Bill Krueger	L	26	10	10	.500	0	26	24	1	142	156	85	61	0	4.75
Curt Young	L	24	9	4	.692	0	20	17	2	109	118	31	41	1	4.06
Steve McCatty	R	30	8	14	.364	0	33	30	4	180	206	71	63	0	4.76
Keith Atherton	R	25	7	6	.538	2	57	0	0	104	110	39	58	0	4.33
Chris Codiroli	R	26	6	4	.600	1	28	14	1	89	111	34	44	0	5.84
Lary Sorensen	R	28	6	13	.316	1	46	21	2	183	240	44	63	0	4.91
Tom Burgmeier (SJ)	L	40	3	1	1.000	2	17	0	0	23	15	8	8	0	2.35
Mike Warren	R	23	3	6	.333	0	24	12	0	90	104	44	61	0	4.90
Dave Leiper	L	22	1	0	1.000	0	8	0	0	7	12	5	3	0	9.00
2 Chuck Rainey	R	29	1	1	.500	1	16	0	0	31	43	17	10	0	6.75
Tim Conroy	L	24	1	6	.143	0	38	14	0	93	82	63	69	0	5.23
Jeff Bettendorf	R	23	0	0	—	0	3	0	0	10	9	5	5	0	4.66
Rick Langford (EJ)	R	32	0	0	—	0	3	2	0	9	15	2	2	0	8.31
2 Mike Torrez	R	37	0	0	—	0	2	0	0	2	2	3	2	0	27.00
Mark Wagner	R	30	0	0	—	0	1	0	0	2	2	1	0	0	0.00
Garry Hancock	L	30	0	0	—	0	1	0	0	1	0	0	0	0	0.00
Gorman Heimueller	L	28	0	1	.000	0	6	0	0	15	21	7	3	0	6.14
Jeff Jones (EJ)	R	27	0	3	.000	0	13	0	0	33	31	12	19	0	3.55
Mike Norris 29 (SJ)															

CHICAGO — 5th 74-88 .457 10 — TONY LaRUSSA

Name	G by Pos	B	AGE	G	AB	R	H	2B	3B	HR	RBI	BB	SO	SB	BA	SA
TOTALS			29	162	5513	679	1360	225	38	172	640	523	883	109	.247	.395
Greg Walker	1B101, DH21	L	24	136	442	62	130	29	2	24	75	35	66	8	.294	.532
Julio Cruz	2B141	B	29	143	415	42	92	14	4	5	43	45	58	14	.222	.311
Scott Fletcher	SS134, 2B28, 3B3	R	25	149	456	46	114	13	3	3	35	46	46	10	.250	.311
Vance Law	3B137, 2B22, OF5, SS4	R	27	151	481	60	121	18	2	17	59	41	75	4	.252	.403
Harold Baines	OF147	L	25	147	569	72	173	28	10	29	94	54	75	1	.304	.541
Rudy Law	OF130	L	26	136	487	68	122	14	7	6	37	39	42	29	.251	.345
Ron Kittle	OF124, DH7	R	26	139	466	67	100	15	0	32	74	49	137	3	.215	.453
Carlton Fisk	C90, DH5	R	36	102	359	54	83	20	1	21	43	26	60	6	.231	.468
Greg Luzinski	OF114	R	33	125	412	47	98	13	0	13	58	56	80	5	.238	.364
Jerry Hairston	OF37, DH20	B	32	115	227	41	59	13	2	5	19	41	29	2	.260	.401
Tom Paciorek (BH)	OF67, OF41	R	37	111	363	35	93	21	2	4	29	25	69	6	.296	.358
Mike Squires	1B77, 3B13, OF3, P1	L	32	104	82	9	15	1	0	0	6	6	7	2	.183	.195
Jerry Dybzinski	SS76, 3B14, 2B1, DH1	R	28	94	132	17	31	5	1	1	10	13	12	7	.235	.311
Marc Hill	C72, 1B2	R	32	77	193	15	45	10	1	5	20	9	26	0	.233	.373
Dave Stegman	OF46, DH3	R	30	55	92	13	24	1	2	2	11	4	18	3	.261	.380
2 Roy Smalley	3B38, SS3, DH2, 1B1	B	31	47	135	15	23	4	0	4	13	22	30	1	.170	.289
Joel Skinner	C43	R	23	43	80	4	17	2	0	3	7	19	1	.213	.238	
Daryl Boston	OF34, DH1	L	21	35	83	8	14	3	1	0	3	4	20	6	.169	.229
2 Tom O'Malley	3B6	L	23	12	16	0	2	0	0	3	0	5	0	.125	.125	
Steve Christmas	C1	R	26	12	11	1	4	1	0	1	4	0	2	0	.364	.727
Tim Hulett	3B4, 2B3	R	24	8	7	1	0	0	0	0	0	1	1	0	.000	.000
1 Jamie Quirk	3B1	L	29	3	2	0	0	0	0	0	0	0	2	0	.000	.000
Casey Parsons		L	30	1	1	0	0	0	0	0	0	0	1	0	.000	.000

NAME	T	AGE	W	L	PCT	SV	G	GS	CG	IP	H	BB	SO	SHO	ERA
		29	74	88	.457	32	162	162	43	1454	1416	483	840	9	4.13
Tom Seaver	R	39	15	11	.577	0	34	33	10	237	216	61	131	4	3.95
Floyd Bannister	L	29	14	11	.560	0	34	33	4	218	211	80	152	0	4.83
Rich Dotson	R	25	14	15	.483	0	32	32	14	246	216	103	120	1	3.59
LaMarr Hoyt	R	29	13	18	.419	0	34	34	11	236	244	43	126	1	4.47
Britt Burns (IL)	L	25	4	12	.250	0	34	16	2	117	130	45	85	0	5.00
1 Salome Barojas	R	27	3	2	.600	1	24	0	0	39	48	19	18	0	4.58
Bert Roberge (EJ)	R	29	3	3	.500	0	21	0	0	41	36	15	25	0	3.76
Gene Nelson	R	23	3	5	.375	1	20	9	2	75	72	17	36	0	4.46
Juan Agosto	L	26	2	1	.667	7	49	0	0	55	54	34	26	0	3.09
2 Dan Spillner	R	32	1	0	1.000	1	22	0	0	48	51	14	26	0	4.10
Al Jones	R	25	1	1	.500	5	20	0	0	20	23	11	15	0	4.43
Jerry Don Gleaton	L	26	1	2	.333	2	11	1	0	18	20	6	4	0	3.44
Randy Niemann	L	28	0	0	—	0	5	0	0	5	5	5	5	0	1.69
Bob Fallon	L	24	0	0	—	0	3	0	0	5	12	11	10	0	3.68
Jim Siwy	R	25	0	0	—	0	1	0	0	4	3	2	1	0	2.08
Mike Squires	L	32	0	0	—	0	1	0	0	1	0	0	0	0	0.00
Tom Brennan	R	31	0	1	.000	0	4	1	0	7	8	3	3	0	4.05
Ron Reed	R	41	0	6	.000	12	51	0	0	73	67	14	57	0	3.08

SEATTLE — 5th 74-88 .457 10 — DEL CRANDALL 59-76 .437 — CHUCK COTTIER 15-12 .556

Name	G by Pos	B	AGE	G	AB	R	H	2B	3B	HR	RBI	BB	SO	SB	BA	SA
TOTALS			28	162	5546	682	1429	244	34	129	635	519	871	116	.258	.497
Alvin Davis	1B147, DH7	L	23	152	567	80	161	34	3	27	116	97	78	5	.284	.497
Jack Perconte	2B150	L	29	155	612	93	180	24	4	0	31	57	47	29	.294	.346
Spike Owen	SS151	B	23	152	530	67	130	18	8	3	43	46	63	16	.245	.326
Jim Presley	3B69, DH1	R	22	70	251	27	57	12	1	10	36	6	63	1	.227	.402
Al Cowens	OF130, DH7	R	32	139	524	60	145	34	2	15	78	27	83	9	.277	.435
Dave Henderson	OF97, DH10	R	25	112	350	42	98	23	0	14	43	19	56	5	.280	.466
Barry Bonnell	OF94, 3B10, DH8, 1B5	R	30	110	363	42	96	15	4	8	48	25	51	5	.264	.394
Bob Kearney	C133	R	28	133	431	39	97	24	1	7	43	18	72	7	.225	.334
Ken Phelps (BG)	DH84, 1B9	L	29	101	290	52	70	9	0	24	51	61	73	3	.241	.521
Phil Bradley	OF117, DH3	R	25	124	322	49	97	12	4	0	24	34	61	21	.301	.363
Steve Henderson	OF53, DH51	R	31	109	325	42	85	12	3	10	35	38	62	2	.262	.409
Larry Milbourne	3B40, 2B14, DH6, SS5	B	33	79	211	22	56	5	1	1	22	12	16	0	.265	.313
1 Pat Putnam	DH30, OF13, 1B6	L	30	64	155	11	31	6	0	2	16	12	27	3	.200	.277
Domingo Ramos	3B38, SS13, 1B5, 2B3	R	26	59	81	6	15	2	0	0	2	5	12	2	.185	.210
Darnell Coles	3B42, OF3, DH3	R	22	48	143	15	23	1	0	6	17	26	2	.161	.196	
Gorman Thomas (SJ)	OF34, DH1	R	33	35	108	6	17	3	1	0	13	28	27	0	.157	.213
Orlando Mercado	C29	R	22	30	78	5	17	3	1	0	5	4	12	1	.218	.282
Al Chambers	OF13, DH1	L	23	22	49	4	11	1	0	1	4	3	12	2	.224	.306
John Moses	OF19, DH1	B	26	19	35	3	12	1	1	0	2	2	5	1	.343	.429
Dave Valle	C13	R	23	13	27	4	8	1	0	1	4	1	5	0	.296	.444
Bill Nahorodny	C10, 1B1	R	30	12	25	2	6	0	0	1	3	1	7	0	.240	.360
Ivan Calderon (HJ)	OF11	R	22	11	24	2	5	1	0	1	2	5	1	0	.208	.375
Danny Tartabull	SS8, 2B1	R	21	10	20	3	6	1	0	2	7	2	3	0	.300	.650
Harold Reynolds	2B6	R	23	10	10	3	3	1	0	0	0	1	1	0	.300	.300
Ricky Nelson	DH3, OF2	L	25	9	15	2	3	0	0	1	2	2	4	0	.200	.400
Richie Zisk 34 (KJ)																

NAME	T	AGE	W	L	PCT	SV	G	GS	CG	IP	H	BB	SO	SHO	ERA
		27	74	88	.457	35	162	162	26	1442	1497	619	972	14	4.31
Mark Langston	L	23	17	10	.630	0	35	33	5	225	188	118	204	2	3.40
Jim Beattie	R	29	12	16	.429	0	32	32	12	211	206	75	119	2	3.41
Ed Vande Berg	L	25	8	12	.400	7	50	17	2	130	165	50	71	0	4.76
Mike Moore	R	24	7	17	.292	0	34	33	6	212	236	85	158	0	4.97
2 Salome Barojas	R	27	6	5	.545	1	19	14	0	95	88	41	37	0	3.97
Matt Young	L	25	6	8	.429	0	22	22	1	113	141	57	73	0	5.72
Mike Stanton	R	31	4	4	.500	8	54	0	0	61	55	22	55	0	3.54
Dave Beard (EJ)	R	24	3	2	.600	5	43	0	0	76	88	33	40	0	5.80
Roy Thomas	R	31	3	2	.600	1	21	1	0	50	52	37	42	0	5.26
Edwin Nunez	R	21	2	2	.500	7	37	0	0	68	55	21	57	0	3.19
Bob Stoddard	R	27	2	3	.400	0	27	6	0	79	86	37	39	0	5.13
Paul Mirabella	L	30	2	5	.286	3	52	1	0	68	74	32	41	0	4.37
Dave Geisel	L	29	1	1	.500	3	20	3	0	43	47	9	28	0	4.15
Karl Best	R	25	1	1	.500	0	5	0	0	6	7	0	6	0	3.00
Lee Guetterman	L	25	0	2	.000	0	4	2	0	4	9	2	2	0	4.15

TEXAS — 7th 69-92 .429 14.5 — DOUG RADER

Name	G by Pos	B	AGE	G	AB	R	H	2B	3B	HR	RBI	BB	SO	SB	BA	SA
TOTALS			28	161	5569	656	1452	227	29	120	618	420	807	81	.261	.377
Pete O'Brien	1B141, OF1	L	26	142	520	57	149	26	2	18	80	53	50	3	.287	.448
Wayne Tolleson	2B109, SS7, 3B5, OF1, DH1	B	28	118	338	35	72	9	2	0	9	27	47	22	.213	.251
Curt Wilkerson	SS116, 2B47	B	23	153	484	47	120	12	0	1	26	33	72	12	.248	.279
Buddy Bell	3B147	R	32	148	553	88	174	36	5	11	83	63	54	2	.315	.458
George Wright (KJ)	OF80, DH18	B	25	101	383	40	93	19	4	9	48	15	54	0	.243	.384
Gary Ward	OF148, DH5	R	30	155	602	97	171	21	7	21	79	55	95	7	.284	.447
Billy Sample	OF122, DH2	R	29	130	489	67	121	20	2	5	33	29	46	18	.247	.327
Donnie Scott	C80	B	21	81	235	16	52	9	0	3	20	20	44	0	.221	.298
Larry Parrish	DH63, OF81, 3B12	R	30	156	613	72	175	42	1	22	101	42	116	2	.285	.465
Mickey Rivers	DH48, OF30	L	35	102	313	40	94	13	1	4	33	9	23	5	.300	.387
Ned Yost	C78	R	29	80	242	15	44	4	0	6	25	6	47	1	.182	.273
Bobby Jones	OF22, 1B15, DH4	L	34	64	143	14	37	4	0	4	22	10	19	1	.259	.371
Marv Foley	C36, DH4, 1B1, 3B1	L	30	63	115	13	25	2	0	6	19	15	24	1	.217	.391
Jeff Kunkel	SS48, DH1	R	22	50	142	13	29	2	3	2	7	2	35	4	.204	.324
2 Alan Bannister (VJ)	2B25, DH9, OF3, 1B1, 3B1	R	32	47	112	20	33	2	1	2	9	21	17	3	.295	.384
Jim Anderson	SS31, 3B6, 2B1	R	28	39	47	2	5	0	1	0	2	2	13	0	.106	.106
Dave Hostetler	1B14, DH13	R	28	37	82	7	18	2	1	3	10	13	27	0	.220	.378
Tommy Dunbar	OF20, DH6	L	24	34	97	9	25	2	0	0	10	6	16	1	.258	.340
Bill Stein (WJ-XJ)	2B11, DH4, 1B3, 3B3	R	37	27	43	3	12	1	0	0	3	6	5	0	.279	.302
1 Mike Richardt	2B4	R	26	9	7	1	1	1	0	0	2	1	0	0	.111	.111
Kevin Buckley	DH3	R	25	5	7	1	2	1	0	0	2	0	4	0	.286	.429

NAME	T	AGE	W	L	PCT	SV	G	GS	CG	IP	H	BB	SO	SHO	ERA
		29	69	92	.429	21	161	161	38	1438	1443	518	863	6	3.91
Charlie Hough	R	36	16	14	.533	0	36	36	17	266	260	94	164	1	3.76
Frank Tanana	L	30	15	15	.500	0	35	35	9	246	234	81	141	1	3.25
Mike Mason	L	25	9	13	.409	0	36	24	4	184	159	51	113	0	3.61
Danny Darwin	R	28	8	12	.400	0	35	32	5	223	249	54	123	1	3.94
Dave Stewart	R	27	7	14	.333	0	32	27	3	192	193	87	119	0	4.73
Dave Schmidt	R	27	6	6	.500	12	43	0	0	70	69	20	46	0	2.56
2 Joey McLaughlin	R	27	2	1	.667	0	15	0	0	33	33	13	21	0	4.41
2 Dickie Noles	R	27	2	3	.400	0	18	6	0	58	60	30	39	0	5.15
Odell Jones	R	31	2	4	.333	2	33	0	0	59	62	23	28	0	3.64
Tom Henke	R	26	1	1	.500	2	25	0	0	28	36	20	25	0	6.35
Dave Tobik	R	31	1	6	.143	5	24	0	0	42	44	17	30	0	3.61
Jim Bibby	R	39	0	0	—	0	8	0	0	16	19	10	6	0	4.41
Dwayne Henry	R	22	0	0	—	0	4	0	0	8	8	7	2	0	8.31
Ricky Wright	L	25	0	2	.000	0	8	1	0	14	20	11	6	0	6.14

LINE SCORES

AMERICAN LEAGUE CHAMPIONSHIPS: DETROIT (EAST) 3 KANSAS CITY (WEST) 0

Game 1 October 2 at Kansas City

Team	1	2	3	4	5	6	7	8	9	R	H	E
DET	2	0	0	1	1	0	1	2	1	8	14	0
KC	0	0	0	0	0	0	0	1	0	1	5	1

Morris, Hernandez (8) | Black, Huismann (6), Jones (8)

Game 2 October 3 at Kansas City

Team	1	2	3	4	5	6	7	8	9	R	H	E
DET	2	0	1	0	0	0	0	0	2	5	8	1
KC	0	0	0	1	0	0	1	1	0	3	10	3

Petry, Hernandez (8), Lopez (9) | Saberhagen, Quisenberry (9)

Game 3 October 5 at Detroit

Team	1	2	3	4	5	6	7	8	9	R	H	E
KC	0	0	0	0	0	0	0	0	0	0	3	0
DET	0	1	0	0	0	0	0	0	x	1	3	0

Leibrandt | **Wilcox**, Hernandez (9)

NATIONAL LEAGUE CHAMPIONSHIPS: SAN DIEGO (WEST) 3 CHICAGO (EAST) 2

Game 1 October 2 at Chicago

Team	1	2	3	4	5	6	7	8	9	R	H	E
SD	0	0	0	0	0	0	0	0	0	0	6	1
CHI	2	0	3	0	6	2	0	0	x	13	16	0

Show, Harris (5), Booker (7) | **Sutcliffe**, Brusstar (8)

Game 2 October 3 at Chicago

Team	1	2	3	4	5	6	7	8	9	R	H	E
SD	0	0	0	1	0	1	0	0	0	2	5	0
CHI	1	0	2	1	0	0	0	0	x	4	8	1

Thurmond, Hawkins (4), Dravecky (6), Lefferts (8) | **Trout**, Smith (9)

Game 3 October 4 at San Diego

Team	1	2	3	4	5	6	7	8	9	R	H	E
CHI	0	1	0	0	0	0	0	0	0	1	5	0
SD	0	0	0	0	3	4	0	0	x	7	11	0

Eckersley, Frazier (6), Stoddard (8) | **Whitson**, Gossage (9)

Game 4 October 6 at San Diego

Team	1	2	3	4	5	6	7	8	9	R	H	E
CHI	0	0	0	2	0	3	0	0	0	5	8	1
SD	0	0	2	0	1	0	2	0	2	7	11	0

Sanderson, Brusstar (5), Stoddard (7), **Smith** (8) | Lollar, Hawkins (5), Dravecky (6), Gossage (8), **Lefferts** (9)

Game 5 October 7 at San Diego

Team	1	2	3	4	5	6	7	8	9	R	H	E
CHI	2	1	0	0	0	0	0	0	0	3	5	1
SD	0	0	0	0	0	2	4	0	x	6	8	0

Sutcliffe, Trout (7), Brusstar (8) | Show, Hawkins (2), Dravecky (4), **Lefferts** (6), Gossage (8)

WORLD SERIES —DETROIT (AL) 4 SAN DIEGO (NL) 1

Game 1 October 9 at San Diego

Team	1	2	3	4	5	6	7	8	9	R	H	E
DET	1	0	0	0	2	0	0	0	0	3	8	0
SD	2	0	0	0	0	0	0	0	0	2	8	1

Morris | Thurmond, Hawkins (6), Dravecky

Game 2 October 10 at San Diego

Team	1	2	3	4	5	6	7	8	9	R	H	E
DET	3	0	0	0	0	0	0	0	0	3	7	2
SD	1	0	0	1	3	0	0	0	x	5	11	0

Petry, Lopez (5), Scherrer (6), Bair (7), Hernandez (8) | Whitson, **Hawkins** (1), Lefferts (8)

Game 3 October 12 at Detroit

Team	1	2	3	4	5	6	7	8	9	R	H	E
SD	0	0	1	0	0	0	1	0	0	2	10	0
DET	0	4	1	0	0	0	0	0	x	5	7	0

Lollar, Booker (2), Harris (3) | **Wilcox**, Scherrer (7), Hernandez (7)

Game 4 October 13 at Detroit

Team	1	2	3	4	5	6	7	8	9	R	H	E
SD	0	1	0	0	0	0	0	0	1	2	10	2
DET	2	0	2	0	0	0	0	0	x	4	7	0

Show, Dravecky (3), Lefferts (7), Gossage (8) | **Morris**

Game 5 October 14 at Detroit

Team	1	2	3	4	5	6	7	8	9	R	H	E
SD	0	0	1	2	0	0	0	1	0	4	10	1
DET	3	0	0	1	0	0	0	4	x	8	11	1

Thurmond, **Hawkins** (1), Lefferts (5), Gossage (7) | Petry, Scherrer (4), **Lopez** (5), Hernandez (8)

COMPOSITE BATTING

Detroit

NAME	POS	G	AB	R	H	2B	3B	HR	RBI	BA
TOTALS		3	107	14	25	4	1	4	14	.234
Whitaker	2B	3	14	3	2	0	0	0	0	.143
Lemon	CF	3	13	1	0	0	0	0	0	.000
Gibson	RF	3	12	2	5	1	0	1	2	.417
Parrish	C	3	12	1	3	1	0	0	1	.250
Trammell	SS	3	11	2	4	0	1	1	3	.364
Evans	1B-3B	3	10	1	3	1	0	0	1	.300
Garbey	DH-PH	3	9	1	3	0	0	0	0	.333
Castillo	3B	3	8	0	2	0	0	0	2	.250
Herndon	LF	2	5	1	1	0	0	1	1	.200
Jones	LF-PH	2	5	1	0	0	0	0	0	.000
Grubb	DH	1	4	0	1	1	0	0	0	.250
Brookens	3B	2	2	0	0	0	0	0	0	.000
Bergman	1B-PR	2	1	1	1	0	0	0	0	1.000
Kuntz	LF-PH	1	1	0	0	0	0	0	0	.000
Baker	SS	1	0	0	0	0	0	0	0	—

Kansas City

NAME	POS	G	AB	R	H	2B	3B	HR	RBI	BA
TOTALS		3	106	4	18	1	1	0	4	.170
Brett	3B	3	13	0	3	0	0	0	0	.231
Wilson	CF	3	13	0	2	0	0	0	0	.154
Motley	LF	3	12	0	2	0	0	0	0	.167
White	2B	3	12	1	1	0	0	0	0	.083
Slaught	C	3	11	0	4	0	0	0	0	.364
Orta	DH	3	10	1	1	0	1	0	1	.100
Balboni	1B	3	10	0	1	0	0	0	1	.100
Concepcion	SS	3	7	0	0	0	0	0	0	.000
Sheridan	RF	3	6	1	0	0	0	0	0	.000
Jones	RF-PH	3	5	1	1	0	0	0	0	.200
McRae	PH	2	2	0	2	1	0	0	1	1.000
Iorg	PH	2	2	0	1	0	0	0	0	.500
Biancalana	SS-PR	2	1	0	0	0	0	0	0	.000
Washington	PH	2	1	0	0	0	0	0	0	.000
Wathan	DH-PR	1	1	0	0	0	0	0	0	.000
Pryor	3B-PR	1	0	0	0	0	0	0	0	—

San Diego

NAME	POS	G	AB	R	H	2B	3B	HR	RBI	BA
TOTALS		5	155	22	41	5	1	2	20	.265
Garvey	1B	5	20	1	8	1	0	1	7	.400
Gwynn	RF	5	19	6	7	3	0	0	3	.368
Wiggins	2B	5	19	4	6	0	0	0	3	.316
Kennedy	C	5	18	2	4	0	0	1	2	.222
Martinez	LF	5	17	1	3	0	0	0	1	.176
Templeton	SS	5	15	2	5	1	0	0	2	.333
Nettles	3B	5	14	1	2	0	0	0	2	.143
McReynolds	CF	4	10	2	3	0	0	0	4	.300
Salazar	3B-CF-PH	3	5	0	1	0	1	0	0	.200
Brown	CF-PH	3	4	1	0	0	0	0	0	.000
Flannery	PH	3	2	2	1	0	0	0	0	.500
Bevacqua	PH	2	2	0	0	0	0	0	0	.000
Ramirez	PH	2	2	0	0	0	0	0	0	.000
Summers	PH	2	2	0	0	0	0	0	0	.000

Whitson P 0-3, Thurmond 1-1, Show P 0-1, Lollar P 0-1, Booker P 0-0, Dravecky P 0-0, Gossage P 0-0, Harris P 0-0, Hawkins P 0-0, Lefferts P 0-0

Chicago

NAME	POS	G	AB	R	H	2B	3B	HR	RBI	BA
TOTALS		5	162	26	42	11	0	9	25	.259
Durham	1B	5	20	2	3	0	0	2	4	.150
Sandberg	2B	5	19	3	7	2	0	0	3	.368
Cey	3B	5	19	3	3	1	0	1	3	.158
Davis	C	5	18	3	7	2	0	2	6	.389
Moreland	RF	5	18	3	6	2	0	0	2	.333
Dernier	CF	5	17	5	4	0	0	1	1	.235
Matthews	LF	5	15	4	3	0	0	2	5	.200
Bowa	SS	5	15	1	3	1	0	0	1	.200
Sutcliffe	P	2	6	1	3	0	0	1	1	.500
Bosley	PH	2	2	0	0	0	0	0	0	.000
Lake	C	1	1	0	1	1	0	0	0	1.000
Cotto	LF-PR	3	1	1	1	0	0	0	0	1.000
Veryzer	SS-3B	3	1	0	0	0	0	0	0	.000
Lopes	RF-PH	2	1	0	0	0	0	0	0	.000
Hebner	PH	2	1	0	0	0	0	0	0	.000

Eckersley P 0-2, Sanderson P 0-2, Trout 1-2, Brusstar P 0-1, Woods RF-PH 0-1, Frazier P 0-0, Smith P 0-0, Stoddard P 0-0

World Series — Detroit

NAME	POS	G	AB	R	H	2B	3B	HR	RBI	BA
TOTALS		5	158	23	40	4	0	7	22	.253
Trammell	SS	5	20	5	9	1	0	2	6	.450
Gibson	RF	5	18	4	6	0	0	2	7	.333
Parrish	C	5	18	3	5	1	0	1	1	.278
Whitaker	2B	5	18	6	5	2	0	0	0	.278
Lemon	CF	5	17	1	5	0	0	0	1	.294
Herndon	LF-PH	5	15	1	5	0	0	1	3	.333
Evans	1B-3B	5	15	1	1	0	0	0	3	.067
Garbey	DH-PH	4	12	0	0	0	0	0	0	.000
Castillo	3B	3	9	2	3	0	0	1	2	.333
Bergman	1B-PR	5	5	0	0	0	0	0	0	.000
Grubb	DH-PH	4	3	0	1	0	0	0	0	.333
Brookens	3B-PH	3	3	0	0	0	0	0	0	.000
Jones	LF-PH	2	3	0	0	0	0	0	0	.000
Kuntz	DH-PH	3	1	0	0	0	0	0	0	.000
Johnson	DH-PH	1	1	0	0	0	0	0	0	.000

World Series — San Diego

NAME	POS	G	AB	R	H	2B	3B	HR	RBI	BA
TOTALS		5	166	15	44	7	0	3	14	.265
Wiggins	2B	5	22	2	8	1	0	0	1	.364
Garvey	1B	5	20	2	4	2	0	0	2	.200
Templeton	SS	5	19	1	6	1	0	0	0	.316
Gwynn	RF	5	19	1	5	0	0	0	0	.263
Kennedy	C	5	19	2	4	1	0	1	3	.211
Bevacqua	DH	5	17	4	7	2	0	2	4	.412
Martinez	LF	5	17	0	3	0	0	0	0	.176
Brown	CF	5	15	1	1	0	0	0	0	.067
Nettles	3B	5	12	2	3	0	0	0	2	.250
Salazar	3B-CF-LF-PH-PR	4	3	0	1	0	0	0	0	.333
Bochy	PH	1	1	0	1	0	0	0	0	1.000
Flannery	2B-PH	1	1	0	1	0	0	0	0	1.000
Summers	PH	1	1	0	0	0	0	0	0	.000
Roenicke	LF-PR	2	0	0	0	0	0	0	0	—

COMPOSITE PITCHING

Detroit

NAME	G	IP	H	BB	SO	W	L	SV	ERA
TOTALS	3	29	18	6	21	3	0	1	1.24
Wilcox	1	8	2	2	8	1	0	0	0.00
Morris	1	7	5	1	4	1	0	0	1.29
Petry	1	7	4	1	4	0	0	0	2.57
Hernandez	3	4	3	1	3	0	0	1	2.25
Lopez	1	3	4	1	2	1	0	0	0.00

Kansas City

NAME	G	IP	H	BB	SO	W	L	SV	ERA
TOTALS	3	28	25	8	17	0	3	0	3.86
Leibrandt	1	8	3	4	6	0	1	0	1.13
Saberhagen	1	8	6	1	5	0	0	0	2.25
Black	1	5	7	1	3	0	1	0	7.20
Quisenberry	1	3	2	1	1	0	1	0	3.00
Huismann	1	2.2	6	1	2	0	0	0	10.13
Jones	1	1.1	1	0	0	0	0	0	6.75

San Diego

NAME	G	IP	H	BB	SO	W	L	SV	ERA
TOTALS	5	43	42	20	28	3	2	1	5.23
Whitson	1	8	5	2	6	1	0	0	1.13
Dravecky	3	6	2	0	5	0	0	0	0.00
Show	2	5.1	8	4	2	0	1	0	13.50
Lollar	1	4.1	3	4	3	0	0	0	6.23
Lefferts	3	4	1	1	2	2	0	0	0.00
Gossage	3	4	5	1	5	0	0	1	4.50
Hawkins	3	3.2	0	2	1	0	0	0	0.00
Thurmond	1	3.2	7	2	1	0	1	0	9.82
Booker	1	2	2	1	2	0	0	0	0.00
Harris	1	2	9	3	2	0	0	0	31.50

Chicago

NAME	G	IP	H	BB	SO	W	L	SV	ERA
TOTALS	5	42.1	41	14	22	2	3	1	4.25
Suitcliffe	2	13.1	9	8	10	1	1	0	3.38
Trout	2	9	5	3	3	1	0	0	2.00
Eckersley	1	5.1	9	0	0	0	1	0	8.44
Sanderson	1	4.2	6	1	2	0	0	0	5.79
Brusstar	3	4.1	6	0	1	0	0	0	0.00
Stoddard	2	2	1	2	0	0	0	0	4.50
Smith	2	2	3	0	1	0	0	1	9.00
Frazier	1	1.2	2	0	1	0	0	0	10.80

World Series — Detroit

NAME	G	IP	H	BB	SO	W	L	SV	ERA
TOTALS	5	44	44	11	26	4	1	2	3.07
Morris	2	18	13	3	13	2	0	0	2.00
Petry	2	8	14	5	4	0	1	0	9.00
Wilcox	1	6	7	2	4	1	0	0	1.50
Hernandez	3	5.1	4	0	0	0	0	2	1.69
Scherrer	3	3	5	0	0	0	0	0	3.00
Lopez	2	3	1	1	4	1	0	0	0.00
Bair	1	0.2	0	0	1	0	0	0	0.00

World Series — San Diego

NAME	G	IP	H	BB	SO	W	L	SV	ERA
TOTALS	5	42	40	24	27	1	4	1	4.71
Hawkins	3	12	4	6	4	1	1	0	0.75
Lefferts	3	6	2	1	7	0	0	1	0.00
Thurmond	2	5.1	12	3	2	0	1	0	10.13
Harris	1	5.1	3	3	5	0	0	0	0.00
Dravecky	2	4.2	3	1	5	0	0	0	0.00
Gossage	2	2.2	3	1	2	0	1	0	13.50
Show	1	2.2	4	1	2	0	0	0	10.13
Lollar	1	1.2	4	4	0	0	0	0	21.60
Booker	1	1	4	0	1	0	0	0	9.00
Whitson	1	0.2	5	0	0	0	0	0	40.50

Name	G by Pos	B	AGE	G	AB	R	H	2B	3B	HR	RBI	BB	SO	SB	BA	SA

CHICAGO 1st 96-65 .596 **JIM FREY**

	TOTALS		30	161	5437	762	1415	240	47	136	703	567	967	154	.260	.397
Leon Durham	1B130	L	26	137	473	86	132	30	4	23	96	69	86	16	.279	.505
Ryne Sandberg	2B156	R	24	156	636	114	200	36	19	19	84	52	101	32	.314	.520
Larry Bowa	SS132	B	38	133	391	33	87	14	2	0	17	28	24	10	.233	.269
Ron Cey	3B144	R	36	146	505	71	121	27	0	25	97	61	108	3	.240	.442
Keith Moreland	OF103, 1B29, 3B8, C3	R	30	140	495	59	138	17	3	16	80	34	71	1	.279	.422
Bob Dernier	OF140	R	27	143	536	94	149	26	5	3	32	63	60	45	.278	.362
Gary Matthews	OF145	R	33	147	491	101	143	21	2	14	82	103	47	17	.291	.429
Jody Davis	C146	R	27	150	523	55	134	25	2	19	94	47	99	5	.256	.421
Henry Cotto	OF88	R	23	105	146	24	40	5	0	0	9	10	23	9	.274	.308
Gary Woods	OF62, 2B3	R	29	87	98	13	23	4	1	3	10	15	21	2	.235	.388
Thad Bosley	OF33	L	27	55	98	17	29	2	2	2	14	13	22	5	.296	.418
Jay Johnstone	OF15	L	38	52	73	8	21	2	0	3	7	18	0	.288	.370
1 Mel Hall	OF46	L	23	48	150	25	42	11	3	4	22	12	23	2	.280	.473
Dave Owen	SS35, 3B6, 2B4	B	26	47	93	8	18	2	1	0	10	8	15	1	.194	.290
Richie Hebner (SJ)	3B14, 1B3, OF3	L	36	44	81	12	27	3	0	2	8	10	15	1	.333	.444
Tom Veryzer (BG)	SS36, 3B5, 2B4	R	31	44	74	5	14	1	0	0	4	3	11	0	.189	.203
Steve Lake (IL)	C24	R	27	25	54	4	12	4	0	2	7	0	7	0	.222	.407
Dan Rohn	3B7, 2B5, SS3	L	28	25	31	1	4	0	0	1	3	1	6	0	.129	.226
1 Bill Buckner	1B7, OF2	L	34	21	43	4	9	0	0	0	2	1	1	0	.209	.209
2 Ron Hassey (KJ)	C6, 1B4	L	31	19	33	5	11	0	0	2	5	4	6	0	.333	.515
2 Davey Lopes	OF9, 2B2	R	39	16	17	5	4	1	0	0	0	6	5	3	.235	.294
Billy Hatcher	OF4	R	23	8	9	1	1	0	0	0	1	0	1	0	.111	.111

NAME	T	AGE	W	L	PCT	SV	G	GS	CG	IP	H	BB	SO	SHO	ERA
		29	96	65	.596	50	161	161	19	1434	1458	442	879	8	3.75
2 Rick Sutcliffe	R	28	16	1	.914	0	20	20	7	150	123	39	155	3	2.69
Steve Trout	L	26	13	7	.650	0	32	31	6	190	205	59	81	2	3.41
Tm Stoddard	R	31	10	6	.625	7	58	0	0	92	77	57	87	0	3.82
2 Dennis Eckersley	R	29	10	8	.556	0	24	24	2	160	152	36	81	0	3.03
Lee Smith	R	26	9	7	.563	33	69	0	0	101	98	35	86	0	3.65
Scott Sanderson (XJ)	R	27	8	5	.615	0	24	24	3	141	140	24	76	0	3.14
2 George Frazier	R	29	6	3	.667	3	37	0	0	64	53	26	58	0	4.10
Dick Ruthven (SJ)	R	33	6	10	.375	0	23	22	0	127	154	41	55	0	5.04
Rich Bordi	R	25	5	2	.714	4	31	7	0	83	78	20	41	0	3.46
Rick Reuschel (XJ)	R	35	5	5	.500	0	19	14	1	92	123	23	43	0	5.17
1 Chuck Rainey	R	29	5	7	.417	0	17	16	0	88	102	38	45	0	4.28
1 Dickie Noles	R	27	2	2	.500	0	21	1	0	51	60	16	14	0	5.15
Warren Brusstar	R	32	1	1	.500	3	41	0	0	64	57	21	36	0	3.11
Porfi Altamirano	R	32	0	0	—	0	5	0	0	11	8	1	7	0	4.76
Bill Johnson	R	23	0	0	—	0	4	0	0	5	4	1	3	0	1.69
Ron Meridith	L	27	0	0	—	0	3	0	0	5	6	2	4	0	3.38
1 Don Schulze	R	21	0	0	—	0	1	1	0	3	8	1	2	0	12.00
Reggie Patterson	R	25	0	1	.000	0	3	1	0	6	10	2	5	0	10.50

NEW YORK 2nd 90-72 .556 6.5 **DAVEY JOHNSON**

	TOTALS		26	162	5438	652	1400	235	25	107	607	500	1001	149	.257	.369
Keith Hernandez	1B153	L	30	154	550	83	171	31	0	15	94	97	89	2	.311	.449
Wally Backman	2B115, SS8	B	24	128	436	68	122	19	2	1	26	56	63	32	.280	.339
Ron Gardenhire	SS49, 2B18, 3B7	R	26	74	207	20	51	7	1	1	10	9	43	6	.246	.304
Hubie Brooks	3B129, SS26	R	27	153	561	61	159	23	2	16	73	48	79	6	.283	.417
Darryl Strawberry	OF146	L	22	147	522	75	131	27	4	26	97	75	131	27	.251	.467
Mookie Wilson	OF146	B	28	154	587	88	162	28	10	10	54	26	90	46	.276	.409
George Foster	OF141	R	35	146	553	67	149	22	1	24	86	30	122	2	.269	.443
Mike Fitzgerald	C107	R	23	112	360	20	87	15	1	2	33	24	71	1	.242	.306
Danny Heep	OF48, 1B10	L	26	99	199	36	46	9	2	1	12	27	22	3	.231	.312
Jose Oquendo	SS67	R	20	81	189	23	42	5	0	0	10	15	26	10	.222	.249
Rusty Staub	1B3	L	40	78	72	2	19	4	0	1	18	4	9	0	.264	.361
Kelvin Chapman	2B57, 3B3	R	27	75	197	27	57	13	0	3	23	19	30	8	.289	.401
Ron Hodges	C35	L	35	64	106	5	22	1	0	1	11	23	18	1	.208	.264
Rafael Santana	SS50	R	26	51	152	14	42	11	1	1	12	9	17	0	.276	.382
Jerry Martin (SD)	OF30, 1B3	R	35	51	91	6	14	1	0	3	5	6	29	0	.154	.264
Junior Ortiz	C32	R	24	40	91	6	18	3	0	0	11	5	15	1	.198	.231
2 Ray Knight	3B27, 1B3	R	31	27	93	13	26	4	0	1	6	7	13	0	.280	.355
Ross Jones	SS6, 3B1	R	24	17	10	2	1	1	0	0	1	3	4	0	.100	.200
Herm Winningham	OF10	L	22	14	27	5	11	1	0	0	5	1	7	2	.407	.519
John Gibbons (EJ)	C9	R	22	11	31	1	2	0	0	0	1	3	11	0	.065	.065
John Stearns (EJ)	C4, 1B2	R	32	8	17	6	3	1	0	0	1	4	1	1	.176	.235
Kevin Mitchell	3B5	R	22	7	14	0	3	0	0	0	1	0	3	0	.214	.214
John Christensen	OF5	R	23	5	11	2	3	2	0	0	3	1	2	0	.273	.455
Billy Beane	OF5	R	22	5	10	0	1	0	0	0	0	2	1	0	.100	.100

		25	90	72	.556	50	162	162	12	1443	1371	573	1028	15	3.60
Dwight Gooden	R	19	17	9	.654	0	31	31	7	218	161	73	276	3	2.60
Ron Darling	R	23	12	9	.571	0	33	33	2	206	179	104	136	2	3.81
Walt Terrell	R	26	11	12	.478	0	33	33	3	215	232	80	114	1	3.52
Jesse Orosco	L	27	10	6	.625	31	60	0	0	87	58	34	85	0	2.59
2 Bruce Berenyi	R	29	9	6	.600	0	19	19	0	115	100	53	81	0	3.76
Ed Lynch	R	28	9	8	.529	2	40	13	0	124	169	24	62	0	4.50
Tom Gorman	L	26	6	0	1.000	0	36	0	0	58	51	13	40	0	2.97
Sid Fernandez	L	21	6	6	.500	0	15	15	0	90	74	34	62	0	3.50
Brent Gaff	R	25	3	2	.600	1	47	0	0	84	77	36	42	0	3.63
Tim Leary	R	25	3	3	.500	0	20	7	0	54	61	18	29	0	4.02
1 Craig Swan	R	33	1	0	1.000	0	10	0	0	19	18	7	10	0	8.20
Wes Gardner	R	23	1	1	.500	1	21	0	0	25	34	8	19	0	6.39
Doug Sisk	R	26	1	3	.250	15	50	0	0	78	57	54	32	0	2.09
1 Mike Torrez	R	37	1	5	.167	0	9	8	0	38	55	18	16	0	5.02
Dick Tidrow	R	37	0	0	—	0	11	0	0	16	25	7	8	0	9.19
Calvin Schiraldi	R	22	0	2	.000	0	5	3	0	17	20	10	16	0	5.71

ST. LOUIS 3rd 84-78 .519 12.5 **WHITEY HERZOG**

	TOTALS		27	162	5433	652	1369	225	44	75	610	516	924	220	.252	.351
David Green	1B117, OF14	R	23	126	452	29	121	14	4	15	65	20	105	17	.268	.416
Tommy Herr	2B144	B	28	145	558	67	154	23	2	4	49	49	56	13	.276	.346
Ozzie Smith (BW)	SS124	B	29	124	412	53	106	20	5	1	44	56	17	35	.257	.337
Terry Pendleton	3B66	B	23	67	262	37	85	16	3	1	33	16	32	20	.324	.420
George Hendrick (IL)	OF116, 1B1	R	34	120	441	57	122	28	1	9	69	25	52	0	.277	.406
Willie McGee	OF141	B	25	145	571	82	166	19	11	6	50	29	80	43	.291	.394
Lonnie Smith	OF10	R	28	145	504	77	126	20	4	6	49	70	90	50	.250	.341
Darrell Porter	C122	L	32	127	422	56	98	16	3	11	68	60	79	5	.232	.363
Andy Van Slyke	OF81, 3B32, 1B30	L	23	137	361	45	88	16	4	7	50	63	71	28	.244	.368
Tito Landrum	OF88	R	29	105	173	21	47	9	1	3	26	10	27	3	.272	.387
Art Howe	3B45, 1B11, 2B8, SS5	R	37	89	139	17	30	5	0	2	12	18	18	0	.216	.295
Steve Braun	OF19, 3B1	L	36	86	98	6	27	3	1	0	16	17	17	0	.276	.327
2 Mike Jorgensen	1B39	L	35	59	98	5	24	4	1	2	12	10	17	0	.245	.395
1 Ken Oberkfell	3B46, 2B2, SS1	L	28	50	152	17	47	11	1	0	11	16	10	1	.309	.395
Billy Lyons	2B25, SS11, 3B3	R	26	46	73	13	16	3	0	0	3	9	13	3	.219	.260
2 Chris Speier	SS34, 3B2	R	34	38	118	9	21	7	1	3	8	9	19	0	.178	.331
Tom Nieto	C32	R	23	33	86	7	24	4	0	3	12	5	18	0	.279	.430
Glenn Brummer (NJ)	C26	R	29	28	58	3	12	0	0	1	3	3	7	0	.207	.259
1 Mike Ramsey	2B7, SS7, 3B1	B	30	21	15	1	1	1	0	0	1	6	3	0	.067	.133
1 Dane Iorg	1B6, OF5	L	34	15	28	3	4	2	0	0	3	2	3	0	.143	.214
Mark Salas	OF3, C4	L	23	14	20	1	2	0	0	0	1	0	3	0	.100	.150
2 Paul Householder	OF8	B	25	13	14	1	2	0	0	0	0	0	3	0	.143	.143
Jose Gonzalez	SS5, 2B1	B	25	8	19	4	4	0	0	0	2	1	11	0	.211	.211
Gary Rajsich	1B3	L	29	7	7	1	1	0	0	0	2	2	1	0	.143	.143

		27	84	78	.519	51	162	162	19	1449	1427	494	808	12	3.58
Joaquin Andujar	R	31	20	14	.588	0	36	36	12	261	218	70	147	4	3.34
Dave La Point	L	24	12	10	.545	0	33	33	2	193	205	77	130	1	3.96
Ricky Horton	L	24	9	4	.692	1	37	18	1	126	140	39	76	1	3.44
Neil Allen	R	26	9	6	.600	3	57	1	0	119	105	49	66	0	3.55
Danny Cox	R	24	9	11	.450	0	29	27	1	156	171	54	70	1	4.03
Kurt Kepshire	R	24	6	5	.545	0	17	16	2	109	100	44	71	2	3.30
Bruce Sutter	R	31	5	7	.417	45	71	0	0	123	109	23	77	0	1.54
Jeff Lahti	R	27	4	2	.667	1	63	0	0	85	69	34	45	0	3.72
John Stuper	R	27	3	5	.375	0	15	12	0	61	73	20	19	0	5.28
Dave Rucker	L	26	2	3	.400	0	50	0	0	73	62	34	38	0	2.10
Bob Forsch (XJ)	R	34	2	5	.286	0	16	11	1	52	64	19	21	0	6.02
Dave Von Ohlen	L	25	1	0	1.000	1	27	0	0	35	39	8	19	0	3.12
Kevin Hagen	R	24	1	0	1.000	0	4	0	0	7	1	2	1	0	2.45
Andy Hassler	L	32	1	1	.500	0	4	0	0	2	4	2	1	0	11.57
Ralph Citarella	R	26	0	1	.000	0	10	2	0	22	20	7	15	0	3.63
2 Ken Dayley	L	25	0	2	.000	0	5	1	0	5	16	5	0	0	18.00
Rick Ownbey	R	26	0	0	—	0	3	0	0	19	23	8	11	0	4.74

PHILADELPHIA 4th 81-81 .500 15.5 **PAUL OWENS**

	TOTALS		32	162	5614	720	1494	248	51	147	673	555	1084	186	.266	.407
Len Matuszek (BG)	1B81, OF1	L	29	101	262	40	65	17	1	12	43	39	54	4	.248	.458
Juan Samuel	2B160	R	23	160	701	105	191	36	19	15	69	28	168	72	.272	.442
Ivan DeJesus	SS141	R	31	144	435	40	112	15	3	0	35	43	76	12	.257	.306
Mike Schmidt	3B145, 1B2, SS1	R	34	151	528	93	146	23	3	36	106	92	116	5	.277	.536
Von Hayes	OF148	L	25	152	561	85	164	27	6	16	67	59	84	48	.292	.447
Garry Maddox (XJ)	OF69	R	34	77	241	29	68	11	0	5	19	13	29	3	.282	.390
Glenn Wilson	OF109, 3B4	R	25	132	341	28	82	21	3	6	31	17	56	7	.240	.372
Ozzie Virgil	C137	R	27	141	456	61	119	21	2	18	68	45	91	1	.261	.434
Greg Gross	OF48, 1B28	L	31	112	202	19	65	9	1	0	16	24	11	1	.322	.376
Sixto Lezcano	OF87	R	30	109	256	36	71	6	2	14	40	38	43	0	.277	.480
Tim Corcoran	1B51, OF17	L	31	102	208	30	71	13	1	5	36	37	27	0	.341	.486
John Wockenfuss	1B39, 3B2	R	35	86	180	20	52	3	1	6	24	30	24	1	.289	.417
Luis Aguayo	3B14, 2B12, SS10	R	25	58	72	15	20	4	0	3	11	8	16	0	.278	.458
Kiko Garcia	SS30, 3B23, 2B1	R	30	57	60	6	14	2	0	0	6	6	14	0	.233	.267
Joe LeFebvre (KJ)	OF47, 3B1	L	28	52	160	22	40	9	0	3	18	23	37	0	.250	.363
Jeff Stone (GJ)	OF46	L	23	51	185	27	67	4	6	1	15	9	26	27	.362	.465
John Russell	OF29, C2	R	23	39	99	11	28	3	1	2	11	12	33	0	.283	.444
2 Al Oliver	1B19, OF5	L	37	28	93	9	29	7	0	0	14	7	8	0	.312	.387
Steve Jeltz	SS27, 3B1	B	25	28	68	7	14	0	1	0	7	7	11	2	.206	.279
Bo Diaz (KJ)	C23	R	31	27	75	5	16	4	0	1	6	4	5	13	0	.213	.307
Francisco Melendez	1B10	L	20	21	23	0	3	0	0	0	2	1	2	0	.130	.130
Rick Schu	3B15	R	22	17	29	12	8	2	1	2	5	6	6	1	.276	.621
Mike LaValliere	C6	L	23	6	1	0	0	0	0	0	0	1	0	0	.000	.000

		29	81	81	.500	35	162	162	11	1458	1416	448	904	6	3.62
Jerry Koosman	L	41	14	15	.483	0	36	34	3	224	232	60	137	1	3.25
Steve Carlton	L	39	13	7	.650	0	33	33	1	229	214	79	163	0	3.58
2 Shane Rawley	R	28	10	6	.625	0	18	18	3	120	117	27	58	0	3.81
Charlie Hudson	R	25	9	11	.450	0	30	30	1	174	181	52	94	1	4.04
Kevin Gross	R	23	8	5	.615	1	44	14	1	129	140	44	84	0	4.12
John Denny (EJ)	R	31	7	7	.500	0	22	22	2	154	122	29	94	0	2.45
Bill Campbell	R	35	5	4	.545	1	57	0	0	81	68	35	52	0	3.43
Al Holland	L	31	5	10	.333	29	68	0	0	98	82	30	61	0	3.39
1 Marty Bystrom	R	25	4	4	.500	0	11	11	0	57	66	22	36	0	5.08
Larry Andersen	R	31	3	7	.300	4	64	0	0	91	85	25	54	0	2.38
Tug McGraw (SJ)	L	39	2	0	1.000	0	25	0	0	38	36	10	26	0	3.79
Dave Wehrmeister	R	31	0	0	—	0	7	0	0	15	18	7	13	0	7.20
Stee Fireovid	R	27	0	0	—	0	1	0	0	3	5	1	1	0	1.59
Don Carman	L	24	0	1	.000	0	11	0	0	13	14	6	16	0	5.40
1 Jim Kern	R	35	0	1	.000	0	4	0	0	9	9	5	4	0	10.13
2 Renie Martin	R	28	0	2	.000	0	9	0	0	16	17	12	5	0	4.60

Tony Ghelfi 22 (EJ)
Larry Christensen 30 (EJ)

MONTREAL 5th 78-83 .484 18 — BILL VIRDON 64-67 .489 — JIM FANNING 14-16 .467

Name	G by Pos	B	AGE	G	AB	R	H	2B	3B	HR	RBI	BB	SO	SB	BA	SA
TOTALS			29	161	5439	593	1367	242	36	96	553	470	782	131	.251	.362
Terry Francona (KJ)	1B50, OF6	L	25	58	214	18	74	19	2	1	18	5	12	0	.346	.467
Doug Flynn	2B88, SS34	R	33	124	366	23	89	12	1	0	17	12	41	0	.243	.281
Angel Salazar	SS80	R	22	80	174	12	27	4	2	0	12	4	38	1	.155	.201
Tim Wallach	3B160, SS1	R	26	160	582	55	143	25	4	18	72	50	101	3	.246	.395
Andre Dawson	OF134	R	29	138	533	73	132	23	6	17	86	41	80	13	.246	.409
Tim Raines	OF160, 2B2	B	24	160	622	106	192	38	9	8	60	87	69	75	.309	.437
Jim Wohlford	OF59, 3B2	R	33	95	213	20	64	13	2	5	29	14	19	3	.300	.451
Gary Carter	C143, 1B25	R	30	159	596	75	175	32	1	27	106	64	57	2	.294	.487
1 Derrel Thomas	SS62, OF48, 2B15, 3B4, 1B1	B	33	108	243	26	62	12	2	0	20	20	33	0	.255	.321
1 Pete Rose	1B40, OF28	B	43	95	278	34	72	6	2	0	23	31	20	1	.259	.295
Miguel Dilone	OF41	B	29	88	169	28	47	8	2	1	10	17	18	27	.278	.367
Bryan Little	2B77, SS2	B	24	85	266	31	65	11	1	0	9	34	19	2	.244	.293
Mike Stenhouse	OF48, 1B14	L	26	80	175	14	32	8	0	4	16	26	32	0	.183	.297
2 Tony Scott	OF17	B	32	45	71	8	18	4	0	0	5	7	21	1	.254	.310
2 Dan Driessen	1B45	L	32	51	169	20	43	11	0	9	32	17	15	0	.254	.479
Max Venable	OF27	L	27	38	71	7	17	2	0	2	7	3	7	1	.239	.352
2 Mike Ramsey	SS26, 2B12	B	30	37	70	2	15	1	0	0	3	0	13	0	.214	.229
Bobby Ramos	C31	R	28	31	83	8	16	1	0	2	5	6	13	0	.193	.277
Rene Gonzales	SS27	R	23	29	30	5	7	1	0	0	2	2	5	0	.233	.267
1 Chris Speier	SS13, 3B4	R	34	25	40	1	6	0	0	0	1	1	8	1	.150	.150
Wallace Johnson	1B4	B	27	17	24	3	5	0	0	0	4	5	4	0	.208	.208
Roy Johnson	OF10	L	25	16	33	2	5	2	0	1	2	7	10	1	.152	.303
Razor Shines	1B3, 3B1	B	27	12	20	0	6	1	0	0	2	0	3	0	.300	.350
2 Tom Lawless	2B9	R	27	11	17	1	3	1	0	0	0	0	4	1	.176	.235
Ron Johnson	1B2, OF1	R	28	5	5	0	1	0	0	0	1	0	0	0	.200	.200
Mike Fuentes	OF1	R	25	3	4	0	1	0	0	0	0	1	2	0	.250	.250
Sal Butera	C2	R	31	3	3	0	0	0	0	0	0	0	0	0	.000	.000

NAME	T	AGE	W	L	PCT	SV	G	GS	CG	IP	H	BB	SO	SHO	ERA
		28	78	83	.484	48	161	161	19	1431	1333	474	861	10	3.31
Charlie Lea	R	28	15	10	.600	0	30	30	8	224	198	68	123	0	2.89
Bill Gullickson	R	25	12	9	.571	0	32	32	3	227	230	37	100	0	3.61
Bryn Smith	R	28	12	13	.480	0	28	28	4	179	178	51	101	2	3.32
David Palmer (SJ)	R	26	7	3	.700	0	20	19	1	105	101	44	66	1	3.84
Jeff Reardon	R	28	7	7	.500	23	68	0	0	87	70	37	79	0	2.90
Dan Schatzeder	L	29	7	7	.500	1	36	14	1	136	132	36	89	1	2.71
Bob James	R	25	6	6	.500	10	62	0	0	96	92	45	91	0	3.66
Steve Rogers	R	34	6	15	.286	0	31	28	1	169	171	78	64	0	4.31
1 Andy McGaffigan	R	27	3	4	.429	1	21	3	0	46	37	15	39	0	2.54
Joe Hesketh	L	25	2	2	.500	1	11	5	1	45	38	15	32	1	1.80
Dick Grapenthin	R	26	1	2	.333	2	13	1	0	23	19	7	9	0	3.52
Randy St Claire	R	23	0	0	—	0	4	0	0	8	11	2	4	0	4.50
Fred Breining (SJ)	R	28	0	0	—	0	4	0	0	7	4	5	5	0	1.35
1 Greg Harris	R	28	0	1	.000	2	15	0	0	18	10	7	15	0	2.04
Greg Barger	R	25	0	1	.000	0	3	1	0	8	8	7	2	0	7.88
Gary Lucas	L	29	0	3	.000	8	55	0	0	53	54	20	42	0	2.72

PITTSBURGH 6th 75-87 .463 21.5 — CHUCK TANNER

Name	G by Pos	B	AGE	G	AB	R	H	2B	3B	HR	RBI	BB	SO	SB	BA	SA
TOTALS			29	162	5537	615	1412	237	33	98	586	438	841	96	.255	.363
Jason Thompson	1B152	L	29	154	543	61	138	22	0	17	74	87	73	0	.254	.389
Johnny Ray	2B149	B	27	155	555	75	173	38	6	6	67	37	31	11	.312	.434
Dale Berra	SS135, 3B1	R	27	136	450	31	100	16	0	9	52	34	78	1	.222	.318
Bill Madlock (EJ)	3B98, 1B1	R	33	103	403	38	102	16	4	4	44	26	29	3	.253	.323
Doug Frobel	OF112	L	25	126	276	33	56	9	3	12	28	24	84	7	.203	.388
Marvell Wynne	OF154	L	24	154	653	77	174	24	11	0	39	42	81	24	.266	.337
Lee Lacy	OF127, 2B2	R	36	138	474	66	152	26	3	12	70	32	61	21	.321	.464
Tony Pena	C146	R	27	147	546	77	156	27	2	15	78	36	79	12	.286	.425
Lee Mazzilli	OF74, 1B5	B	29	111	268	37	64	11	1	4	21	40	42	8	.237	.331
Jim Morrison	3B61, 2B26, SS2, 1B1	R	31	100	304	38	87	14	2	11	45	20	52	0	.286	.454
Milt May	C26	L	33	50	96	4	17	3	0	1	8	10	15	0	.177	.240
Brian Harper (BT)	OF37, C2	R	24	46	112	4	29	4	0	2	11	5	11	0	.259	.348
Benny Distefano	OF20, 1B17	L	22	45	78	10	13	1	2	3	9	5	13	0	.167	.364
Amos Otis (VJ)	OF32	R	37	40	97	6	16	4	0	0	10	7	15	0	.165	.346
Joe Orsulak	OF25	L	22	32	67	12	17	1	2	0	3	1	7	3	.254	.328
Ron Wotus	SS17, 2B7	R	23	27	55	4	12	6	0	0	2	6	8	0	.218	.327
Denny Gonzalez	3B11, SS10, OF3	R	22	26	82	9	15	3	1	0	4	7	21	1	.183	.244
Rafael Belliard (BL)	SS12, 2B1	R	22	20	22	3	5	0	0	0	0	0	1	4	.227	.227
Hedi Vargas	1B13	R	25	18	31	3	7	2	0	0	2	3	5	0	.226	.290
Mitchell Page		L	32	16	12	2	4	1	0	0	0	3	4	0	.333	.417

NAME	T	AGE	W	L	PCT	SV	G	GS	CG	IP	H	BB	SO	SHO	ERA
		28	75	87	.463	34	162	162	27	1470	1344	502	995	13	3.11
Rick Rhoden	R	31	14	9	.609	0	33	33	6	238	216	62	136	3	2.72
Larry McWilliams	L	30	12	11	.522	1	34	32	7	227	226	78	149	2	2.93
John Candelaria	L	30	12	11	.522	2	33	28	3	185	179	34	133	1	2.72
John Tudor	L	30	12	11	.522	0	32	32	6	212	200	56	117	1	3.27
Jose DeLeon	R	23	7	13	.350	0	30	28	5	192	147	92	153	1	3.74
Don Robinson	R	27	5	6	.455	10	51	1	0	122	99	49	110	0	3.02
Rod Scurry (DR)	L	28	5	6	.455	4	43	0	0	46	28	22	48	0	2.53
Kent Tekulve	R	37	3	9	.250	13	72	0	0	88	86	33	36	0	2.66
Cecilio Guante	R	24	2	3	.400	2	27	0	0	41	32	16	30	0	2.61
Jim Winn	R	24	1	0	1.000	1	9	0	0	19	19	9	11	0	3.88
Bob Walk (EJ)	R	27	1	1	.500	0	2	2	0	10	8	4	10	0	2.61
Lee Tunnell	R	23	1	7	.125	1	26	6	0	68	81	40	51	0	5.27
Ray Krawczyk	R	24	0	0	—	0	4	0	0	5	7	4	3	0	3.38
Mike Bielecki	R	24	0	0	—	0	4	0	0	3	5	3	1	0	0.00
Chris Green	L	23	0	0	—	0	4	0	0	3	5	1	3	0	6.00
Jeff Zaske	R	23	0	0	—	0	2	0	0	3	3	4	2	0	0.00
Alfonso Pulido	L	27	0	0	—	0	1	0	0	2	3	1	2	0	9.00

WEST DIVISION

SAN DIEGO 1st 92-70 .568 — DICK WILLIAMS

Name	G by Pos	B	AGE	G	AB	R	H	2B	3B	HR	RBI	BB	SO	SB	BA	SA
TOTALS			29	162	5504	686	1425	207	42	109	629	472	810	152	.259	.371
Steve Garvey	1B160	R	35	161	617	72	175	27	2	8	86	24	64	1	.284	.373
Alan Wiggins	2B157	B	26	158	596	106	154	19	7	3	34	75	57	70	.258	.329
Garry Templeton	SS146	B	28	148	493	40	127	19	3	2	35	39	81	8	.258	.320
Graig Nettles	3B119	L	39	124	395	56	90	11	1	20	65	58	55	0	.228	.320
Tony Gwynn	OF156	L	24	158	606	88	213	21	10	5	71	59	23	33	.351	.444
Kevin McReynolds	OF143	R	24	147	525	68	146	26	6	20	75	34	69	3	.278	.465
Carmelo Martinez	OF142, 1B2	R	23	149	488	64	122	28	2	13	66	68	82	1	.250	.005
Terry Kennedy	C147	L	28	148	530	54	127	16	1	14	57	33	99	1	.240	.353
Luis Salazar	3B58, OF24, SS4	R	28	93	228	20	55	7	2	3	17	6	38	11	.241	.329
Tim Flannery	2B22, SS14, 3B14	L	26	86	128	24	35	3	3	2	10	12	17	4	.273	.391
Bobby Brown	OF53	B	29	85	171	28	43	7	2	3	29	11	33	16	.251	.368
Kurt Bevacqua	1B20, 3B10, OF3	R	37	59	80	7	16	3	0	1	9	14	19	0	.200	.275
Mario Ramirez	SS33, 3B6, 2B2	R	26	48	59	12	7	1	0	2	9	13	14	0	.119	.237
Champ Summers	1B8	L	38	47	54	5	10	3	0	1	12	4	15	0	.185	.296
Bruce Bochy	C36	R	29	37	92	10	21	5	1	4	15	3	21	0	.228	.435
Eddie Miller	OF8	R	27	13	14	4	4	0	1	1	2	0	4	4	.286	.643
Ron Roenicke	OF10	B	27	12	20	4	6	1	0	1	2	2	5	0	.300	.500
Doug Gwosdz	C6	R	24	7	8	0	2	0	0	0	1	2	5	0	.250	.250

NAME	T	AGE	W	L	PCT	SV	G	GS	CG	IP	H	BB	SO	SHO	ERA
		27	92	70	.568	44	162	162	13	1460	1327	563	812	17	3.48
Eric Show	R	28	15	9	.625	0	32	32	3	207	175	88	104	1	3.48
Mark Thurmond	L	27	14	8	.636	0	32	29	1	179	174	55	57	1	2.97
Ed Whitson	R	29	14	8	.636	0	31	31	1	189	181	42	103	0	3.24
Tim Lollar	L	28	11	13	.458	0	31	31	3	196	168	105	131	2	3.91
Goose Gossage	R	32	10	6	.625	25	62	0	0	102	75	36	84	0	2.90
Dave Dravecky	L	28	9	8	.529	8	50	14	3	157	125	51	71	2	2.93
Andy Hawkins	R	24	8	9	.471	0	36	22	2	146	143	72	77	1	4.68
Craig Lefferts	L	26	3	4	.429	10	62	0	0	106	88	24	56	0	2.13
2 Greg Harris	R	28	2	1	.667	1	19	1	0	37	28	18	30	0	2.70
1 Sid Monge	L	33	2	1	.667	0	13	0	0	15	17	17	7	0	4.80
Luis DeLeon (EJ-AJ)	R	25	2	2	.500	0	43	0	0	43	44	12	44	0	5.48
Floyd Chiffer	R	28	1	0	1.000	0	15	1	0	28	42	16	20	0	7.71
Greg Booker	R	24	1	1	.500	0	32	1	0	57	68	27	28	0	3.30

ATLANTA 2nd 80-82 .494 12 — JOE TORRE

Name	G by Pos	B	AGE	G	AB	R	H	2B	3B	HR	RBI	BB	SO	SB	BA	SA
TOTALS			28	162	5422	632	1388	234	27	111	578	555	896	140	.247	.361
Chris Chambliss	1B109	L	35	135	389	47	100	14	0	9	44	58	54	1	.257	.362
Glenn Hubbard	2B117	R	26	120	397	53	93	27	2	9	43	55	61	4	.234	.380
Rafael Ramirez	SS145	R	26	145	591	51	157	22	4	2	48	26	70	14	.266	.327
Randy Johnson	3B81	R	26	91	294	28	82	13	0	5	30	21	30	1	.279	.374
Claudell Washington	OF107	L	29	120	416	62	119	21	2	17	61	59	77	21	.286	.469
Dale Murphy	OF160	R	28	162	607	94	176	32	8	36	100	79	134	19	.290	.547
Brad Komminsk	OF80	R	23	90	301	37	61	10	0	8	36	29	77	18	.203	.316
Bruce Benedict	C95	R	28	95	300	26	67	8	1	4	25	34	35	1	.223	.297
Gerald Perry	1B64, OF53	L	23	122	347	52	92	12	2	7	47	61	38	15	.265	.372
Albert Hall	OF66	B	26	87	142	25	37	6	1	1	7	18	18	6	.261	.338
Jerry Royster	2B29, 3B17, SS16, OF11	R	31	81	227	22	47	13	2	1	21	15	41	6	.207	.295
2 Alex Trevino	C79	R	26	79	266	36	65	16	0	3	28	16	27	5	.244	.338
2 Ken Oberkfell (BG)	3B45, 2B6	L	28	50	172	21	40	8	1	1	10	15	17	1	.233	.308
Bob Watson	1B19	R	38	49	85	4	18	4	0	2	12	9	12	0	.212	.329
Terry Harper	OF29	R	28	40	102	4	16	3	1	0	8	4	21	4	.157	.206
Rufino Linares	OF13	R	33	34	58	4	12	3	0	1	10	6	12	0	.207	.310
Bob Horner (BW)	3B32	R	26	32	113	15	31	8	0	3	19	14	17	0	.274	.425
1 Mike Jorgensen	1B8, OF4	L	35	31	26	4	7	1	0	0	3	6	3	0	.269	.308
Paul Runge	2B22, SS7, 3B3	R	26	28	90	5	24	3	1	0	3	10	14	5	.267	.322
Milt Thompson	OF25	L	25	25	99	16	30	1	0	0	2	4	11	14	.303	.374
Paul Zuvella	2B6, SS6	R	25	11	25	2	5	1	0	0	1	2	3	0	.200	.240
Biff Pocoroba		L	30	4	2	1	2	0	0	0	0	0	1	0	.500	.500
Matt Sinatro	C2	R	24	2	4	0	0	0	0	0	0	0	0	0	.000	.000

NAME	T	AGE	W	L	PCT	SV	G	GS	CG	IP	H	BB	SO	SHO	ERA
		29	80	82	.494	49	162	162	17	1447	1401	525	859	7	3.57
Pascual Perez (SD)	R	27	14	8	.636	0	30	30	4	212	208	51	145	1	3.74
Rick Mahler	R	30	13	10	.565	0	38	29	9	222	209	62	106	1	3.12
Steve Bedrosian (AJ)	R	26	9	6	.600	11	40	4	0	84	65	33	81	0	2.37
Craig McMurty	R	24	9	17	.346	0	37	30	0	183	184	102	99	0	4.32
Rick Camp	R	31	8	6	.571	0	31	21	1	149	134	63	69	0	3.27
Len Barker (EJ)	R	28	7	8	.467	0	21	20	1	126	120	38	95	0	3.85
Pete Falcone	L	30	5	7	.417	2	35	16	2	120	115	57	55	1	4.13
Jeff Dedmon	R	24	4	3	.571	4	54	0	0	81	86	35	51	0	3.78
Donnie Moore (KJ)	R	30	4	5	.444	16	47	0	0	64	63	18	47	0	2.94
Gene Garber	R	36	3	6	.333	11	62	0	0	106	103	24	55	0	3.06
Terry Forster (LJ)	L	32	2	0	1.000	5	25	0	0	27	30	7	10	0	2.70
Zane Smith	L	23	1	0	1.000	0	3	3	0	20	16	13	16	0	2.25
Tony Brizzolara	R	27	1	2	.333	0	10	4	0	29	33	13	17	0	5.28
Mike Payne	R	22	0	1	.000	0	3	2	0	6	7	3	3	0	6.35
1 Ken Dayley	L	25	0	0	—	0	4	0	0	19	28	6	10	0	5.30

HOUSTON 2nd 80-82 .494 12 — BOB LILLIS

Name	G by Pos	B	AGE	G	AB	R	H	2B	3B	HR	RBI	BB	SO	SB	BA	SA
TOTALS			30	162	5548	693	1465	222	67	79	630	494	837	105	.264	.371
Enos Cabell	1B112	R	34	127	436	52	135	17	3	8	44	21	47	8	.310	.417
Bill Doran	2B139, SS13	L	26	147	548	92	143	18	11	4	41	66	69	21	.261	.356
Craig Reynolds	SS143, 3B1	L	31	146	527	61	137	15	11	6	60	22	53	7	.260	.364
Phil Garner	3B82, 2B35	R	35	128	374	60	104	17	6	4	45	43	63	3	.278	.388
Terry Puhl (EJ)	OF128	L	27	132	449	66	135	19	7	9	55	59	45	13	.301	.434
Jerry Mumphrey	OF137	B	31	151	524	66	152	20	3	9	83	56	79	15	.290	.391
Jose Cruz	OF160	L	36	160	600	96	187	28	13	12	95	73	68	22	.312	.462
Mark Bailey	C108	B	22	108	344	38	73	16	1	9	34	53	71	0	.212	.343
Kevin Bass	OF81	R	25	121	331	33	86	17	5	2	29	6	57	5	.260	.360
1 Ray Knight	3B54, 1B24	R	31	88	278	15	62	10	0	2	29	14	30	1	.223	.281
Denny Walling	3aB52, 1B16, OF6	L	30	87	249	37	70	11	5	3	31	16	28	7	.281	.402
Alan Ashby (BT)	C63	B	32	66	191	16	50	7	0	4	27	20	22	0	.262	.361
Jim Pankovits	2B15, SS4, OF3	R	28	53	81	6	23	7	0	1	14	2	20	2	.284	.407
Harry Spilman	1B18, C8	L	29	32	72	14	19	2	0	2	15	12	10	0	.264	.375
1 Tony Scott	OF6	B	32	25	21	2	4	1	0	0	0	4	3	0	.190	.238
Bert Pena	SS21	R	24	24	39	3	8	1	0	1	4	3	8	0	.205	.308
Glenn Davis	1B61	R	23	18	61	6	13	5	0	2	8	4	12	0	.213	.393
2 Mike Richardt	OF3, 1B1	R	26	16	15	1	4	1	0	0	2	0	1	0	.267	.333
Tim Tolman	OF3, OF1	L	28	14	17	2	3	1	0	0	0	0	3	0	.176	.235
1 Alan Bannister	SS4, OF1	R	32	9	20	2	4	0	0	0	2	1	2	0	.200	.300
Tom Wieghaus	C6	R	27	6	10	0	0	0	0	0	1	1	3	0	.000	.000
Dickie Thon (IJ)	SS5	R	26	5	17	3	6	0	1	0	1	0	3	0	.353	.471
Scott Loucks 27 (SJ)																
John Mizerock 23 (EJ)																

NAME	T	AGE	W	L	PCT	SV	G	GS	CG	IP	H	BB	SO	SHO	ERA
		30	80	82	.494	29	162	162	24	1449	1350	502	950	13	3.32
Joe Niekro	R	39	16	12	.571	0	38	38	6	248	223	89	127	1	3.04
Bob Knepper	L	30	15	10	.600	0	35	34	11	234	223	55	140	3	3.20
Nolan Ryan	R	37	12	11	.522	0	30	30	5	184	143	69	197	2	3.04
Bill Dawley	R	26	11	4	.733	5	60	0	0	98	82	35	47	0	1.93
Mike LaCoss	R	28	7	5	.583	3	39	18	2	132	132	55	86	1	4.02
Dave Smith	R	29	5	4	.556	5	53	0	0	77	60	20	45	0	2.21
Mike Scott	R	29	5	11	.313	0	31	29	0	154	179	43	83	0	4.68
Frank DiPino	L	27	4	9	.308	14	57	0	0	75	74	36	65	0	3.35
Mike Madden	L	26	2	3	.400	0	17	7	0	41	46	35	29	0	5.53
Mark Ross	R	26	1	0	1.000	0	2	0	0	2	1	0	1	0	0.00
Julio Solano	R	24	1	3	.250	0	31	0	0	51	31	18	33	0	1.95
Vern Ruhle	R	33	1	9	.100	2	40	6	0	90	112	29	60	0	4.58
Joe Sambito (EJ)	L	32	0	0	.000	0	32	0	0	48	39	16	26	0	3.02
Jeff Calhoun	L	26	0	1	.000	0	9	0	0	15	5	2	11	0	1.17

LOS ANGELES 4th 79-83 .488 13 — TOMMY LASORDA

Name	G by Pos	B	AGE	G	AB	R	H	2B	3B	HR	RBI	BB	SO	SB	BA	SA
TOTALS			27	162	5399	580	1316	213	23	102	530	488	829	109	.244	.348
Greg Brock (WJ)	1B83	L	27	88	271	33	61	6	0	14	34	39	77	0	.225	.402
Steve Sax	2B141	R	24	145	569	70	138	24	4	1	35	47	53	34	.243	.304
Dave Anderson	SS111, 3B11	R	23	121	374	51	94	16	2	3	34	45	55	15	.251	.329
German Rivera	3B90	R	24	94	227	20	59	12	2	2	17	20	30	1	.260	.357
Pedro Guerrero	OF58, 3B76, 1B16	R	28	144	535	85	162	29	4	16	72	49	105	9	.303	.462
Ken Landreaux	OF129	L	29	134	438	39	110	11	5	11	47	29	35	10	.251	.374
Mike Marshall	OF118, 1B15	R	24	134	495	68	127	27	0	21	65	40	93	4	.257	.438
Mike Scioscia	C112	L	25	114	341	29	93	18	0	5	38	52	26	2	.273	.370
Candy Maldonado	OF102, 3B4	R	23	116	254	25	68	14	0	5	28	19	29	0	.268	.382
Bill Russell	SS65, OF18, 2B5	R	35	89	262	25	70	12	1	0	19	25	24	4	.267	.321
Franklin Stubbs	1B51, OF20	L	23	87	217	22	42	2	3	8	17	24	63	2	.194	.341
Terry Whitfield (BG)	OF58	L	31	87	180	15	44	8	0	4	18	17	35	1	.244	.356
Steve Yeager	C65	R	35	74	197	16	45	4	0	4	29	20	38	1	.228	.310
R.J. Reynolds	OF63	B	25	73	240	24	62	12	2	2	24	14	38	7	.258	.350
Bob Bailor (SJ-KJ)	2B23, 3B17, SS16	R	32	65	131	11	36	4	0	0	8	8	1	3	.275	.305
Rafael Landestoy	2B14, 3B11, OF5	R	31	53	54	10	10	0	0	1	2	1	6	2	.185	.241
Ed Amelung	OF23	L	23	34	46	7	10	0	0	0	4	2	4	3	.217	.217
Rick Monday	1B10, OF2	L	38	31	47	4	9	2	0	1	7	8	16	0	.191	.298
Sid Bream	1B14	L	23	27	49	2	9	3	0	0	6	6	9	1	.184	.245
Tony Brewer	OF10	L	26	24	37	3	4	1	0	1	4	4	9	1	.108	.216
Jose Morales		R	39	22	19	0	3	0	0	0	0	1	2	0	.158	.158
Mike Vail	OF1	R	32	16	16	1	1	0	0	0	2	1	7	0	.063	.063
Jack Fimple	C12	R	25	12	26	2	5	1	0	0	3	1	6	0	.192	.231
Lemmie Miller	OF5	R	24	8	12	1	2	0	0	0	1	2	0		.167	.167
Gil Reyes	C2	R	20	4	5	0	0	0	0	0	0	0	3	0	.000	.000

NAME	T	AGE	W	L	PCT	SV	G	GS	CG	IP	H	BB	SO	SHO	ERA
		29	79	83	.488	27	162	162	39	1461	1381	499	1033	16	3.17
Bob Welch	R	29	13	13	.500	0	31	29	3	179	191	58	126	1	3.78
Alejandro Pena	R	25	12	6	.667	0	28	28	8	199	186	46	135	4	2.48
Fernando Valenzuela	L	23	12	17	.414	0	34	34	12	261	218	106	240	2	3.03
Orel Hershiser	R	25	11	8	.579	2	45	20	8	190	160	50	150	4	2.66
Rick Honeycutt	L	30	10	9	.526	0	29	28	6	184	180	51	75	2	2.84
Ken Howell	R	23	5	5	.500	6	32	1	0	51	51	9	54	0	3.33
Pat Zachry	R	32	5	6	.455	2	58	0	0	83	84	51	55	0	3.81
Jerry Reuss (EJ)	L	35	5	7	.417	1	30	15	2	99	102	31	44	0	3.82
Burt Hooton	R	34	3	6	.333	4	54	6	0	110	109	43	62	0	3.44
Tom Niedenfuer (EJ)	R	24	2	5	.286	11	33	0	0	47	39	23	45	0	2.47
Carlos Diaz	L	26	1	0	1.000	1	37	0	0	41	47	24	36	0	5.49
Rich Rodas (EJ)	L	24	0	0	.---	0	5			5	5	1	1	0	5.40
Larry White	R	25	0	1	.000	0	7	1	0	12	9	6	10	0	3.00
Steve Howe 26 (SD)															

CINCINNATI 5th 70-92 .432 22 — VERN RAPP 51-70 .421   PETE ROSE 19-22 .463

Name	G by Pos	B	AGE	G	AB	R	H	2B	3B	HR	RBI	BB	SO	SB	BA	SA
TOTALS			28	162	5498	627	1342	238	30	106	578	566	978	160	.244	.356
1 Dan Driessen	1B70	L	32	81	218	27	61	13	0	7	28	37	25	2	.280	.436
Ron Oester	2B147, SS1	B	28	150	553	54	134	26	3	3	38	41	97	7	.242	.316
Dave Concepcion	SS104, 3B54, 1B6	R	36	154	531	46	130	26	1	4	58	52	72	22	.245	.320
Nick Esasky	3B82, 1B25	R	24	113	322	30	62	10	5	10	45	52	103	1	.193	.348
Dave Parker	OF151	R	33	156	607	73	173	28	0	16	94	41	89	11	.285	.410
Eddie Milner (IL)	OF108	L	27	117	336	44	78	17	2	4	29	51	50	21	.232	.342
Gary Redus	OF114	R	27	123	394	69	100	21	3	7	22	52	71	48	.254	.376
Brad Gulden	C100	L	28	107	292	31	66	8	2	4	33	33	35	2	.226	.308
Cesar Cedeno	OF77, 1B4	R	33	110	380	59	105	24	2	10	47	25	54	19	.276	.429
Tom Foley	SS83, 2B10, 3B1	L	24	106	277	26	70	8	3	5	27	24	36	3	.253	.357
Wayne Krenchicki	3B62, 1B3, 2B3, 1B	R	29	97	181	18	54	9	2	6	22	19	23	0	.298	.470
Duane Walker (LJ)	OF68	L	27	83	195	35	57	10	3	10	28	33	35	7	.292	.528
Tony Perez	1B31	R	42	71	137	9	33	6	1	2	15	11	21	0	.241	.343
Dann Bilardello	C68	R	25	68	182	16	38	7	0	2	10	19	34	0	.209	.280
Eric Davis	OF51	R	22	57	174	33	39	10	1	10	30	24	48	10	.224	.466
1 Tom Lawless	2B23, 3B6	R	27	43	80	10	20	2	0	2	8	12	6	2	.250	.313
Dave Van Gorder	C36, 1B1	R	27	38	101	10	23	2	0	0	6	12	17	0	.228	.248
Skeeter Barnes	3B11, OF3	R	27	32	42	5	5	0	1	0	3	4	6	0	.119	.190
2 Pete Rose	1B23	B	43	26	96	9	35	9	0	0	11	9	7	0	.365	.458
1 Paul Householder	OF10	B	25	14	12	3	1	1	0	0	0	3	3	1	.083	.167
Alan Knicely	1B8, C1	R	29	10	29	0	4	0	0	0	5	3	9	0	.136	.138
1 Alex Trevino	C4	R	26	6	6	0	1	0	0	0	0	0	1	0	.167	.167
Wade Rowden	SS1, 3B1	R	24	4	7	0	2	0	0	0	0	0	1	0	.286	.286

NAME	T	AGE	W	L	PCT	SV	G	GS	CG	IP	H	BB	SO	SHO	ERA
		27	70	92	.432	25	162	162	25	1461	1445	578	946	6	4.16
Mario Soto	R	27	18	7	.720	0	33	33	13	237	181	87	185	0	3.53
Ted Power	R	29	9	7	.563	11	78	0	0	109	93	46	81	0	2.82
Joe Price	L	27	7	13	.350	0	30	30	3	172	176	61	129	1	4.19
John Franco	L	23	6	2	.750	4	54	0	0	79	74	36	55	0	2.61
Jay Tibbs	R	22	6	2	.750	0	14	14	3	101	87	33	40	1	2.86
Jeff Russell	R	22	6	18	.250	0	33	30	4	182	186	65	101	2	4.26
Tom Hume	R	31	4	13	.235	3	54	8	0	113	142	41	59	0	5.64
Bob Owchinko	L	29	3	5	.375	2	49	4	0	94	91	39	60	0	4.12
1 Bruce Berenyi	R	29	3	7	.300	0	13	11	0	51	63	42	53	0	6.00
Frank Pastore	R	26	3	8	.273	0	24	16	1	98	110	40	53	0	6.50
Mike Smith	R	23	1	0	1.000	0	8	0	0	10	12	5	7	0	5.23
Tom Browning	R	24	1	0	1.000	0	3	3	2	23	27	5	14	1	1.54
1 Bill Scherrer	L	26	1	1	.500	1	36	0	0	52	64	15	35	0	4.99
Ron Robinson	R	22	1	2	.333	0	12	5	1	40	35	13	24	0	2.72
Charlie Puleo	R	29	1	2	.333	0	5	4	0	22	27	15	6	0	5.73
Freddie Toliver	R	23	0	0	.---	0	3	1	0	10	7	7	4	0	0.90
Brad Lesley	R	25	0	1	.000	2	16	0	0	19	14	7	6	0	5.12
Keefe Cato	R	26	0	1	.000	0	16			22	4		12	0	8.04
2 Carl Willis	R	23	0	1	.000	1	7	0	0	19	28	2	3	0	3.72
1 Andy McGaffigan	R	27	0	2	.000	0	5	0	0	23	23	8	18	0	5.48
Ben Hayes 26 (EJ)															

SAN FRANCISCO 6th 66-96 .407 26 — FRANK ROBINSON 42-64 .396   DANNY OZARK 24-32 .429

Name	G by Pos	B	AGE	G	AB	R	H	2B	3B	HR	RBI	BB	SO	SB	BA	SA
TOTALS			30	162	5650	682	1499	229	26	112	646	528	980	126	.265	.375
1 Al Oliver	1B82	L	37	91	339	27	101	19	2	0	34	20	27	2	.298	.368
Manny Trillo (BH)	2B96, 3B4	R	33	98	401	45	102	21	4	4	36	25	55	0	.254	.342
Johnnie LeMaster	SS129	R	30	132	451	46	98	13	2	4	32	31	97	17	.217	.282
Joel Youngblood	3B117, OF11, 2B5	R	33	134	469	50	119	17	1	10	51	48	86	5	.254	.358
Chili Davis	OF123	B	24	137	499	87	157	21	6	21	81	42	74	12	.315	.507
Dan Gladden	OF85	R	26	86	342	71	120	17	2	4	31	33	41	31	.351	.447
Jeff Leonard	OF131	R	28	136	514	76	155	27	2	21	86	47	123	17	.302	.484
Bob Brenly	C127, 1B22, OF3	R	30	145	506	74	147	28	0	20	80	48	52	6	.291	.464
Scot Thompson	1B87, OF6	L	28	120	245	30	75	7	1	1	31	30	26	5	.306	.355
Dusty Baker	OF62	R	35	100	243	31	71	7	2	3	32	40	27	4	.292	.374
Brad Wellman	2B54, SS33, 3B10	R	24	93	265	23	60	9	1	2	25	19	41	10	.226	.291
Gene Richards	OF26	L	30	87	135	18	34	4	0	0	4	18	28	5	.252	.281
Duane Kuiper	2B31, 1B1	L	34	83	115	8	23	1	0	0	11	12	10	0	.200	.209
Jack Clark (KJ)	OF54, 1B4	R	28	57	203	33	65	9	1	11	44	43	29	1	.320	.537
Fran Mullins (SJ)	SS28, 3B28, 2B4	R	27	57	110	8	24	6	0	0	9	3	28	3	.218	.345
John Rabb	1B13, OF8, C6	R	24	54	82	10	16	1	0	3	9	10	33	1	.195	.317
Steve Nicosia (NJ)	C41	R	28	48	132	9	40	11	2	2	19	8	14	1	.303	.462
Chris Brown	3B23	R	22	23	84	6	24	7	0	1	11	9	19	2	.286	.405
Joe Pittman	SS6, 2B5, 3B2	R	30	17	22	2	5	0	0	0	2	0	5	1	.227	.227
Randy Gomez	C14	R	26	14	30	0	5	0	0	0	0	0	1	0	.167	.200
Alex Sanchez	OF11	R	23	13	41	3	8	2	0	0	5	0	12	0	.195	.244
1 Tom O'Malley	3B7	L	23	13	25	2	3	0	0	0	3	1	6	0	.120	.120
Rob Deer	OF9	R	23	13	24	5	4	0	0	3	7	10	1		.167	.542

NAME	T	AGE	W	L	PCT	SV	G	GS	CG	IP	H	BB	SO	SHO	ERA
		27	66	96	.407	38	162	162	9	1461	1589	549	854	7	4.39
Mike Krukow	R	32	11	12	.478	0	35	33	3	199	234	78	141	1	4.56
Frank Williams	R	26	9	4	.692	0	3	61	1	106	98	51	91	1	3.55
Bill Laskey	R	26	9	14	.391	0	35	34	2	208	222	50	71	0	4.33
Jeff Robinson	R	23	7	15	.318	0	34	33	1	172	195	52	102	1	4.56
Randy Lerch (GJ)	L	29	5	3	.625	2	37	4	0	72	80	36	48	0	4.23
Gary Lavelle	L	35	5	4	.556	12	77	0	0	101	92	42	71	0	2.76
Mark Davis	L	23	5	17	.227	0	46	27	1	175	201	54	124	0	5.36
Greg Minton	R	29	4	9	.308	19	74	0	0	124	130	57	48	0	3.76
Atlee Hammaker(SJ-EJ)	L	26	2	0	1.0000	0	6	6	0	33	32	9	24	0	2.18
Scott Garrelts	R	22	2	3	.400	0	21	3	0	43	45	34	32	0	5.65
Mark Calvert	R	27	2	4	.333	0	15	1	0	32	40	9	5	0	5.06
George Riley	L	27	1	0	1.000	0	5	4	0	29	39	7	12	0	3.99
1 Renie Martin	R	28	1	1	.500	0	28	0	0	35	29	16	8	0	3.86
Bob Lacey	L	30	1	0	.250	0	34	0	0	51	55	13	26	0	3.88
Jeff Cornell	R	27	1	3	.250	0	23	0	0	58	51	22	19	0	6.10
Mark Grant	R	20	1	4	.200	1	11	10	0	54	56	19	32	0	6.37

1985 — A Good Year Nevertheless

Baseball soared to new heights despite two black eyes. The first was a mid-season players strike that threatened to abort the schedule. The usual financial issues sparked hardball rhetoric between Donald Fehr, the executive director of the players union, and Lee McPhail, the representative of the team owners. With no new contract in hand, the players walked off the job on August 6. While public opinion turned ugly, a compromise solution ended the strike after only two days. The new labor contract settled matters for the next five years without any radical changes.

One month later, a criminal trial in Pittsburgh further soiled baseball's good name. A former caterer in the Phillies' clubhouse, Curtis Strong, was charged with selling cocaine to various baseball players. A parade of players testified about their purchase and use of the illegal drug. After two weeks of unsavory testimony, the jury found Strong guilty. He wound up with a sentence of four to twelve years, while baseball wound up with a public relations disaster.

Despite these body blows, major league attendance climbed to a new record. A flood of individual heroics washed away some of the bad taste. At center stage, 44 year old Pete Rose set a new career record for hits, passing Ty Cobb with number 4,192 on September 11. Nolan Ryan struck out his 4,000th batter, Rod Carew swatted his 3,000th hit, and both Tom Seaver and Phil Niekro won their 300th games, paving the way for Hall of Fame inductions in a few years.

While these oldsters basked in the limelight, three pennant races sizzled into late September. The Los Angeles Dodgers had the easiest path to the play-offs, holding first place in the N.L.West comfortably from mid-July to the end. Fernando Valenzuela and Orel Hershiser led the typically strong Dodger pitching, while Pedro Guerrero's bat caught fire after he moved from third base to left field on June 1. The Padres led the West by five games on July 4 but faded.

Over in the N.L.East, the Cardinals edged the Mets after a summer-long battle. Picked by some experts for last place, the Cards featured speed, defense, and pitching. Center fielder Willie McGee won the MVP award with his .353 batting, 56 stolen bases, and superb fielding for the Cardinals. Starring around him were rookie speedster Vince Coleman (110 stolen bases), newly-acquired Jack Clark (22 homers, 87 rbi's), veteran Tommy Herr (110 rbi's), and defensive whiz Ozzie Smith. Joaquin Andujar and John Tudor each won 21 games, with Tudor winning 20 of his last 21 decisions with impeccable control. Dwight Gooden's 24-4 season won the Cy Young award and led the Met challenge.

In A.L.East, the Blue Jays cashed in their potential for a divisional title.

With youngsters George Bell, Jesse Barfield, and Damaso Garcia playing championship ball, the Jays led most of the way under the calm hand of manager Bobby Cox. When the chips were on the table, the Jays came through with three victories in a four-game series in New York on September 12-15. The Yankees had charged to within 1 1/2 games after winning the first game of that series, but they then lost eight straight games. The slump wasted an MVP season by Don Mattingly.

The A.L. West race came down to the Kansas City Royals and the California Angels nose to nose. On September 30, they began a four-game series in Kansas City with the Angels ahead by one game. Losers of their three previous games, the Royals won three of the four games to take the lead. When both clubs won two of their remaining three games, the Royals had repeated as divisional champs. George Brett anchored the K.C. lineup, while 21 year old Bret Saberhagen blossomed with a 20-6 Cy Young season.

For the first time, the League Championship Series were best-of-seven affairs, and each showcased a fevered comeback. In the A.L., the Blue Jays won the first two games in Toronto and three of the first four. Owners of the best record in the league, the young Blue Jays plummeted into a hitting slump and dropped the final three games to the Royals.

After dropping the first two contests of the N.L. series, the Cards swept four straight. They won the final two games on dramatic ninth inning homers by Ozzie Smith and Jack Clark, both off relief ace Tom Niedenfuer. The Cards staged their comeback despite a bizarre injury which ended Vince Coleman's season. Before the start of game four, an automatic tarp rolled over his left leg and benched a key part of the jackrabbit Cardinal offense.

The series matched Missouri's two teams in what was called the I-70 Series. The Cards swept the first two games in Kansas City in a pair of pitching duels. After the Royals took game three behind Saberhagen, the Cards closed in with a masterful Tudor shutout in game four. Danny Jackson's five-hitter sent the Series back across the state for a conclusion. In game six, the Cards took a 2-1 lead into the bottom of the ninth, only to lose on a questionable call in a two-run uprising which sent the Series to a seventh game. The Royals decided it early, rushing out to a 11-0 lead after five innings. The Cardinals took out their frustrations in a couple of rhubarbs in that fifth inning, but nothing could turn back the fate that had smiled upon the lightly-regarded Royals of Dick Howser.

EAST DIVISION

Name	G by Pos	B	AGE	G	AB	R	H	2B	3B	HR	RBI	BB	SO	SB	BA	SA
TORONTO	**1st 99-62 .615**				**BOBBY COX**											
	TOTALS		29	161	5508	759	1482	281	53	158	714	503	807	144	.269	.425
Willie Upshaw	1B147, DH1	L	28	148	501	79	138	31	5	15	65	48	71	8	.275	.447
Damaso Garcia	2B143	R	30	146	600	70	169	25	4	8	65	15	41	28	.282	.377
Tony Fernandez	SS160	B	23	161	564	71	163	31	10	2	51	43	41	13	.289	.390
Rance Mulliniks	3B119	L	29	129	366	55	108	26	1	10	57	55	54	2	.295	.454
Jesse Barfield	OF154	R	25	155	539	94	156	34	9	27	84	66	143	22	.289	.536
Lloyd Moseby	OF152	L	25	152	584	92	151	30	7	18	70	76	91	37	.259	.426
George Bell	OF157, 3B2	R	25	157	607	87	167	28	6	28	95	43	90	21	.275	.479
Ernie Whitt	C134	L	33	139	412	55	101	21	2	19	64	47	59	3	.245	.444
Cliff Burroughs	DH75	R	34	86	191	19	49	9	3	6	28	34	36	0	.257	.429
Garth Iorg	3B104, 2B23	R	30	131	288	33	90	22	1	7	37	21	26	3	.313	.469
Manny Lee	2B38, SS8, 3B5	B	20	64	40	9	8	0	0	0	0	2	9	1	.200	.200
Len Matuszek	DH54, 1B5	L	30	62	151	23	32	6	2	4	15	11	24	2	.212	.318
Al Oliver	DH59, 1B1	L	38	61	187	20	47	6	1	5	23	7	13	0	.251	.374
Lou Thornton	OF35, DH16	L	22	56	72	18	17	1	1	1	8	2	24	1	.236	.319
Buck Martinez (BN)	C42	R	36	42	99	11	16	3	0	4	14	10	12	0	.162	.313
Ron Shepherd	OF16, DH15	R	24	38	35	7	4	2	0	0	1	2	12	3	.114	.171
Cecil Fielder	1B25	R	21	30	74	6	23	4	0	4	16	6	16	0	.311	.527
Cliff Johnson	DH21, 1B3	R	37	24	73	4	20	0	0	1	10	9	15	0	.274	.315
Rick Leach	1B10, OF4	L	28	16	35	2	7	0	1	0	1	3	9	0	.200	.257
Gary Allenson	C14	R	30	14	34	2	4	1	0	0	3	0	10	0	.118	.147
Willie Aikens	DH11	L	30	12	20	2	4	1	0	1	5	3	6	0	.200	.400
Steve Nicosia	C6	R	29	6	15	0	4	0	0	0	1	0	0	0	.267	.267
Kelly Gruber	3B5, 2B1	R	23	5	13	0	3	0	0	0	1	0	3	0	.231	.231
Jeff Hearron	C4	R	23	4	7	0	1	0	0	0	0	0	2	0	.143	.143
Mitch Webster	OF2, DH2	B	26	4	1	0	0	0	0	0	0	0	1	0	.000	.000

Name	G by Pos	B	AGE	G	AB	R	H	2B	3B	HR	RBI	BB	SO	SB	BA	SA
NEW YORK	**2nd 97-64 .602 2**				**YOGI BERRA 6-10 .375 BILLY MARTIN 91-54 .628**											
	TOTALS		29	161	5458	839	1458	272	31	176	793	620	771	155	.267	.425
Don Mattingly	1B159	L	24	159	652	107	211	48	3	35	145	56	41	2	.324	.567
Willie Randolph	2B143	R	30	143	497	75	137	21	2	5	40	85	39	16	.276	.356
Bobby Meacham	SS155	B	24	156	481	70	105	16	2	1	47	54	102	25	.218	.266
Mike Pagliarulo	3B134	L	25	138	380	55	91	16	2	19	62	45	86	0	.239	.442
Dave Winfield	OF152, DH2	R	33	155	633	105	174	34	6	26	114	52	96	19	.275	.471
Rickey Henderson	OF141, DH1	R	26	143	547	146	172	28	5	24	72	99	65	80	.314	.516
Ken Griffey	OF110, DH7, 1B1	L	35	127	438	68	120	28	4	10	69	41	51	7	.274	.425
Butch Wynegar	C96	B	29	102	309	27	69	15	0	5	32	64	43	0	.233	.320
Don Baylor	DH140	R	36	142	477	70	110	24	1	23	91	52	90	0	.231	.430
Ron Hassey	C69, 1B2, DH2	L	32	92	167	31	79	16	1	13	42	28	21	0	.296	.509
Andre Pasqua	OF37, DH14	L	23	60	148	17	31	3	1	9	25	16	38	0	.209	.426
Billy Sample	OF55	R	30	59	139	18	40	5	0	1	15	9	10	2	.288	.345
Andre Robertson (KJ)	3B33, SS14, 2B2	R	27	50	125	16	41	5	0	2	17	6	24	1	.328	.416
Dale Berra	3B41, SS6	R	28	48	109	8	25	5	1	4	8	7	20	1	.229	.321
Omar Moreno	OF26, DH1	L	32	34	66	12	13	4	1	0	1	6	13	1	.197	.333
Henry Cotto (EarJ)	OF30	R	24	34	56	4	17	1	1	0	6	3	12	1	.304	.375
Rex Hudler	2b16, 1B1, SS1	R	24	20	51	4	8	0	1	0	1	1	5	0	.157	.196
Scott Bradley (BG)	DH9, C3	L	25	19	49	4	8	2	1	0	1	1	5	0	.163	.245
Juan Espino	C9	R	29	9	11	0	4	0	0	0	1	0	3	0	.364	.364
Juan Bonilla	2B7	R	29	8	16	0	2	1	0	0	2	0	3	0	.125	.188
Vic Mata	OF3	R	24	6	7	1	1	0	0	0	0	0	0	0	.143	.143
Keith Smith	SS3	R	23	4	1	0	0	0	0	0	0	0	0	0	.000	.000

1985 AMERICAN LEAGUE

NAME	T	AGE	W	L	PCT	SV	G	GS	CG	IP	H	BB	SO	SHO	ERA
		29	99	62	.615	47	161	161	18	1448	1312	484	823	9	3.29
Doyle Alexander	R	34	17	10	.630	0	36	36	6	261	268	67	142	1	3.45
Jimmy Key	L	24	14	6	.700	0	35	32	3	213	188	50	85	0	3.00
Dave Stieb	R	27	14	13	.519	0	36	36	8	265	206	96	167	2	2.48
Dennis Lamp	R	32	11	0	1.000	2	53	1	0	106	96	27	68	0	3.32
Jim Clancy (SJ)	R	29	9	6	.600	0	23	23	1	129	117	37	66	0	3.78
Tom Filer	R	28	7	0	1.000	0	11	9	0	49	38	18	24	0	3.88
Jim Acker	R	26	7	2	.778	10	61	0	0	86	86	43	42	0	3.23
Gary Lavelle	L	36	5	7	.417	8	69	0	0	73	54	36	50	0	3.10
Bill Caudill	R	28	4	6	.400	14	67	0	0	69	53	35	46	0	2.99
Ron Musselman	R	30	3	0	1.000	0	25	4	0	52	59	24	29	0	4.47
Tom Henke	R	27	3	3	.500	13	28	0	0	40	29	8	42	0	2.03
Luis Leal	R	28	3	6	.333	0	15	14	0	67	82	24	33	0	5.75
Steve Davis	L	24	2	1	.667	0	10	5	0	28	23	13	22	0	3.54
Stan Clarke	L	24	0	0	—	0	4	0	0	4	3	2	2	0	4.50
John Cerutti	L	25	0	2	.000	0	4	1	0	7	10	4	5	0	5.40

NAME	T	AGE	W	L	PCT	SV	G	GS	CG	IP	H	BB	SO	SHO	ERA
		30	97	64	.602	49	161	161	25	1440	1373	518	907	9	3.69
Ron Guidry	L	34	22	6	.786	0	34	33	11	259	243	42	143	2	3.27
Phil Niekro	R	46	16	12	.571	0	33	33	7	220	203	120	149	1	4.09
Joe Cowley	R	26	12	6	.667	0	30	26	1	160	132	85	97	0	3.95
Dave Righetti	R	26	12	7	.632	29	74	0	0	107	96	45	92	0	2.78
Ed Whitson	R	30	10	8	.556	0	30	30	2	159	201	43	89	2	4.88
Rich Bordi	R	26	6	8	.429	2	51	3	0	98	95	29	64	0	3.21
Bob Shirley	L	31	5	5	.500	2	48	8	2	109	103	26	55	0	2.64
Brian Fisher	R	23	4	4	.500	14	55	0	0	98	77	29	85	0	2.38
Marty Bystrom (EJ)	R	26	3	2	.600	0	8	8	0	41	44	19	16	0	5.71
Dennis Rasmussen	L	26	3	5	.375	0	22	16	2	102	97	42	63	0	3.98
2 Joe Niekro	R	40	2	1	.667	0	3	3	0	12	14	8	4	0	5.84
2 Neil Allen	R	27	1	0	1.000	1	17	0	0	29	26	13	16	0	2.76
2 Rod Scurry	L	29	0	0	1.000	1	5	0	0	13	5	10	17	0	2.84
Mike Armstrong	R	31	0	0	—	0	9	0	0	15	9	2	11	0	3.07
Don Cooper	R	29	0	0	—	0	7	0	0	10	12	3	4	0	5.40
John Montefusco (PJ)	R	35	0	0	—	0	7	7	0	12	12	2	0	0	10.29
1 Dale Murray	R	35	0	0	—	0	4	0	0	6	12	4	0	0	13.50

DETROIT 3rd 84-77 .522 15 — SPARKY ANDERSON

Name	G by Pos	B	AGE	G	AB	R	H	2B	3B	HR	RBI	BB	SO	SB	BA	SA
	TOTALS		29	161	5575	729	1413	254	45	202	703	526	926	75	.253	.424
Darrell Evans	1B113, DH33, 3B7	L	38	151	505	81	125	17	0	40	94	85	85	0	.248	.519
Lou Whitaker	2B105	L	28	152	609	102	170	29	8	21	73	80	56	6	.279	.456
Alan Trammell	SS149	R	27	149	605	79	156	21	7	13	57	50	71	14	.258	.380
Tom Brookens	3B151, 2B3, C1, DH1	R	31	156	485	54	115	34	6	7	47	27	78	14	.237	.375
Kirk Gibson	OF144, DH8	L	28	154	581	96	167	37	5	29	97	71	137	30	.287	.518
Chet Lemon	OF144	R	30	145	517	69	137	28	4	18	68	45	93	0	.265	.439
Larry Herndon	OF136	R	31	137	442	45	106	12	7	12	37	33	79	2	.244	.385
Lance Parrish	C120, DH22	R	29	140	549	64	150	27	1	28	98	41	90	2	.273	.479
Barbaro Garbey	1B37, OF24, DH21, 3B1	R	28	86	237	27	61	9	1	6	29	15	37	3	.257	.380
Johnny Grubb	DH33, OF18	L	36	78	155	19	38	7	1	5	25	24	25	0	.245	.400
Alex Sanchez	OF31, DH28	R	26	71	133	19	33	6	2	6	12	0	39	2	.248	.459
Dave Bergman (EJ)	1B44, DH5, OF1	L	32	69	140	8	25	2	0	3	7	14	15	0	.179	.257
Marty Castillo	C32, 3B25	R	28	57	84	4	10	2	0	2	5	2	19	0	.119	.214
Bob Melvin	C41	R	23	41	82	10	18	4	1	0	4	3	21	0	.220	.293
2 Doug Flynn	2B20, SS8, 3B4	R	34	32	51	2	13	2	1	0	2	0	3	0	.255	.333
Chris Pittaro	3B22, 2B4, DH1	R	23	28	62	10	15	3	1	0	7	5	13	1	.242	.323
Doug Baker	SS12, 2B1	B	24	15	27	4	5	1	0	0	1	0	9	0	.185	.222
Jim Weaver	DH4, OF4	L	25	12	7	2	1	1	0	0	0	1	4	0	.143	.286
Mike Laga	DH5, 1B4	L	25	9	36	3	6	1	0	2	6	0	9	0	.167	.361
Scotti Madison	DH3, C1	B	25	6	11	0	0	0	0	0	0	1	2	0	.000	.000
Rusty Kuntz	DH3, 1B1	R	30	5	5	0	0	0	0	0	0	2	2	0	.000	.000

NAME	T	AGE	W	L	PCT	SV	G	GS	CG	IP	H	BB	SO	SHO	ERA
	R	29	84	77	.522	40	161	161	31	1456	1313	556	943	11	3.78
Jack Morris	R	30	16	11	.593	0	35	35	13	257	212	110	191	4	3.33
Walt Terrell	R	27	15	10	.600	0	34	34	5	229	221	95	130	1	3.85
Dan Petry	R	26	15	13	.536	0	34	34	8	239	190	81	109	0	3.36
2 Frank Tanana	L	31	10	7	.558	0	20	20	4	137	131	34	107	0	3.34
Willie Hernandez	L	30	8	10	.444	31	74	0	0	107	82	14	76	0	2.70
Randy O'Neal	R	24	5	5	.500	2	28	12	1	94	82	36	52	1	3.24
Juan Berenguer	R	30	5	6	.445	0	31	13	0	95	96	48	82	0	5.59
Bill Scherrer	L	27	3	2	.600	0	48	0	0	66	62	41	46	0	4.36
Aurelio Lopez	R	36	3	7	.300	5	51	0	0	86	82	41	53	0	4.80
1 Doug Bair	R	35	2	0	1.000	0	21	3	0	49	54	25	30	0	6.24
2 Mickey Mahler	L	32	1	2	.333	0	3	2	0	21	19	4	14	0	1.74
Milt Wilcox (SJ)	R	35	1	3	.250	0	8	8	0	39	51	14	20	0	4.85
Bob Stoddard	R	28	0	0	—	1	8	0	0	13	15	5	11	0	6.75
Chuck Cary	L	25	0	1	.000	2	16	0	0	24	16	8	22	0	3.42

BALTIMORE 4th 83-78 .516 16 — JOE ALTOBELLI 29-26 .527 CAL RIPKEN SR. 1-0 1.000 EARL WEAVER 53-52 .505

Name	G by Pos	B	AGE	G	AB	R	H	2B	3B	HR	RBI	BB	SO	SB	BA	SA
	TOTALS		30	161	5517	818	1451	234	22	214	773	604	908	69	.263	.430
Eddie Murray	1B54, DH2	B	29	156	583	111	173	37	1	31	124	84	68	5	.297	.523
2 Alan Wiggins	2B76	B	27	76	298	43	85	11	4	0	21	29	16	30	.285	.349
Cal Ripken	SS161	R	24	161	642	116	181	32	5	26	110	67	68	2	.282	.469
Floyd Rayford	3B78, DH2, DH1	R	27	105	359	55	110	21	1	18	48	10	68	3	.306	.521
Lee Lacy (RJ)	OF115, DH5	R	37	121	492	69	144	22	4	9	48	39	95	10	.293	.409
Fred Lynn	OF123	L	33	124	448	59	118	12	1	23	68	53	100	7	.263	.449
Mike Young	OF90, DH37	B	25	139	450	72	123	22	1	28	81	48	104	1	.273	.513
Rick Dempsey	C131	R	35	132	362	54	92	19	0	12	52	50	87	0	.254	.406
Larry Sheets	DH39, OF9, 1B1	L	25	113	328	43	86	8	0	17	50	28	52	0	.262	.442
Gary Roenicke	OF89, DH17	R	30	114	225	36	49	9	0	15	43	44	36	2	.218	.458
Wayne Gross	3B67, DH10, 1B9	L	33	103	217	31	51	8	0	11	18	46	48	1	.235	.424
Jim Dwyer	OF78, DH3	L	35	101	233	35	58	8	1	7	36	37	31	0	.249	.399
Rich Dauer	2B73, 3B17, 1B1	R	32	85	206	25	42	7	0	2	14	20	7	0	.204	.262
John Shelby	OF59, DH3, 2B1	B	27	69	205	28	58	6	2	7	27	7	44	5	.283	.434
Lenn Sakata	2B50, DH4	R	31	55	97	15	22	3	0	3	6	6	15	3	.227	.351
Fritz Connally	3B46, 1B2, DH1	R	27	50	112	16	26	4	0	3	15	19	21	0	.232	.348
Al Pardo	C29	B	22	34	75	3	10	1	0	0	1	3	15	0	.133	.147
Joe Nolan (KJ)	C5, DH4	L	34	31	38	1	5	2	0	0	6	5	6	0	.132	.184
Dan Ford (KJ)	DH28	R	33	28	75	4	14	2	0	1	6	7	17	0	.187	.253
John Lowenstein	DH6, OF4	L	38	12	26	0	2	0	0	0	2	2	3	0	.077	.077
Leo Hernandez	DH8, OF1, 1B1	R	25	12	21	0	1	0	0	0	0	0	4	0	.048	.048
Tom O'Malley	3B3	L	24	8	14	1	1	0	0	1	0	0	1	0	.071	.286
Kelly Paris	2B2, DH2	R	27	5	9	0	0	0	0	0	0	0	1	0	.000	.000

NAME	T	AGE	W	L	PCT	SV	G	GS	CG	IP	H	BB	SO	SHO	ERA
		29	83	78	.516	33	161	161	32	1427	1480	568	793	6	4.38
Scott McGregor	L	31	14	14	.500	0	35	34	8	204	228	65	86	1	4.81
Dennis Martinez	R	30	13	11	.542	0	33	31	3	180	203	63	68	1	5.15
Mike Boddicker	R	27	12	17	.414	0	32	32	9	203	227	89	135	2	4.07
Don Aase	R	30	10	6	.625	14	54	0	0	88	83	35	67	0	3.78
Storm Davis	R	23	10	8	.556	0	31	28	8	175	172	70	93	1	4.53
Ken Dixon	R	24	8	4	.667	1	34	18	3	162	144	64	108	1	3.67
Sammy Stewart	R	30	5	7	.417	9	56	1	0	130	117	66	77	0	3.61
Mike Flanagan (FJ)	L	33	4	5	.444	0	15	15	1	86	101	28	42	0	5.13
Nate Snell (BR)	R	32	3	2	.600	5	43	0	0	100	100	30	41	0	2.69
Tippy Martinez	L	35	3	3	.500	4	49	0	0	70	70	37	47	0	5.40
John Habyan	R	21	1	0	1.000	0	2	2	0	3	3	2	2	0	0.00
Eric Bell	L	21	0	0	—	0	4	0	0	6	4	4	4	0	4.76
Phil Huffman	R	27	0	0	—	0	2	1	0	5	7	5	2	0	15.43
Bill Swaggerty	R	28	0	1	.000	0	8	1	0	14	14	7	6	0	5.40
Brad Havens	L	25	0	1	.000	0	8	1	0	14	20	10	19	0	8.79

BOSTON 5th 81-81 .500 18.5 — JOHN McNAMARA

Name	G by Pos	B	AGE	G	AB	R	H	2B	3B	HR	RBI	BB	SO	SB	BA	SA
	TOTALS		29	163	5720	800	1615	292	31	162	760	562	816	66	.282	.429
Bill Buckner	1B162	L	35	162	673	89	201	46	3	16	110	30	36	18	.299	.447
Marty Barrett	2B155	R	27	156	534	59	142	26	0	5	56	56	50	7	.266	.343
Glenn Hoffman (SJ)	SS93, 3B3	R	26	96	279	40	77	17	2	6	34	25	40	2	.276	.416
Wade Boggs	3B161	L	27	161	653	107	240	42	3	8	78	96	61	2	.368	.478
Dwight Evans	OF152, DH7	R	33	159	617	110	162	29	1	29	78	114	105	1	.263	.454
Tony Armas (LJ)	OF79, DH19	R	32	103	385	50	102	17	5	23	64	18	90	0	.265	.514
Jim Rice	OF130, DH7	R	32	140	546	85	159	20	3	27	103	51	75	2	.291	.487
Rich Gedman	C139	L	25	144	498	66	147	30	5	18	80	50	79	2	.295	.484
Mike Easler	DH130, OF20	L	34	155	568	71	149	29	4	16	74	53	129	0	.262	.412
Steve Lyons	OF114, DH5, 3B1, SS1	L	25	133	371	52	98	14	3	5	30	32	64	12	.264	.358
Jackie Gutierrez	SS99	R	25	103	275	33	60	5	2	2	21	12	37	10	.218	.273
Rick Miller (PJ)	OF8, DH4	L	37	41	45	5	15	2	0	0	9	5	6	1	.333	.378
Marc Sullivan (BW)	C32	R	26	32	69	10	12	2	0	2	3	6	15	0	.174	.290
Dave Stapleton (KJ)	2B14, 1B8, DH5	R	31	30	66	4	15	6	0	0	4	2	11	0	.227	.318
Ed Jurak	3B7, SS3, DH2, 1B1, OF1	R	27	26	13	4	3	0	0	0	1	3	0	0	.231	.231
Kevin Romine	OF23, DH1	R	24	24	28	3	6	2	0	0	1	4	9	1	.214	.286
Dave Sax	C16, OF1	R	26	22	36	2	11	3	0	0	6	3	3	0	.306	.389
1 Reid Nichols	OF10, DH4, 2B3	R	26	21	32	3	6	1	0	1	3	2	4	1	.188	.313
Mike Greenwell	OF17	L	21	17	31	7	10	1	0	4	8	1	4	0	.323	.742
Jerry Remy 32 (KJ)																

NAME	T	AGE	W	L	PCT	SV	G	GS	CG	IP	H	BB	SO	SHO	ERA
		27	81	81	.500	29	163	163	35	1461	1487	540	913	8	4.06
Oil Can Boyd	R	25	15	13	.536	0	35	35	13	272	273	61	154	3	3.70
Bruce Hurst	L	27	11	13	.458	0	35	31	6	229	243	70	189	1	4.51
Bob Ojeda	L	27	9	11	.450	1	39	22	5	158	166	48	102	0	4.00
Al Nipper	R	26	9	12	.429	0	25	25	5	162	157	82	85	0	4.06
Roger Clemens (SJ)	R	22	7	5	.583	0	15	15	3	96	83	37	74	1	3.29
Steve Crawford	R	27	6	5	.545	12	44	1	0	91	103	28	58	0	3.76
Bob Stanley (RJ)	R	30	6	6	.500	10	48	0	0	88	76	30	46	0	2.87
Bruce Kison (LJ)	R	35	5	3	.625	1	22	9	0	92	98	32	56	0	4.11
2 Tim Lollar	L	29	5	5	.500	1	16	10	1	67	57	40	44	0	4.57
Mike Trujillo	R	25	4	4	.500	1	27	7	1	84	112	23	19	0	4.82
Jeff Sellers	R	21	2	0	1.000	0	4	4	1	22	24	7	6	0	3.63
Rob Woodward	R	22	1	0	1.000	0	3	2	0	27	17	9	16	0	1.69
Mark Clear	R	29	1	3	.250	3	41	0	0	56	45	50	55	0	3.72
Tom McCarthy	R	24	0	0	—	0	2	0	0	5	6	0	4	0	10.80
Mike Brown	R	26	0	0	—	0	2	2	0	5	8	3	2	0	21.60
Charlie Mitchell	R	23	0	0	—	0	5	0	0	5	6	5	2	0	16.20
Jim Dorsey	R	29	0	1	.000	0	5	1	0	12	12	10	2	0	20.25

MILWAUKEE 6th 71-90 .441 28 — GEORGE BAMBERGER

Name	G by Pos	B	AGE	G	AB	R	H	2B	3B	HR	RBI	BB	SO	SB	BA	SA
	TOTALS		30	161	5568	690	1467	250	44	101	636	462	746	69	.263	.379
Cecil Cooper	1B123, DH30	L	35	154	631	82	185	39	8	16	99	30	77	10	.293	.456
Jim Gantner	2B124, 3B24, SS1	L	32	143	523	63	133	15	4	5	44	33	42	11	.254	.327
Ernest Riles	SS115, DH1	L	24	116	448	54	128	12	7	5	45	36	54	2	.286	.377
Paul Molitor	3B135, DH4	R	28	140	576	93	171	28	3	10	48	54	80	21	.297	.408
Paul Householder	OF79, DH1	B	26	95	299	41	77	15	0	11	34	27	46	1	.258	.418
Robin Yount	OF108, DH12, 1B2	R	29	122	466	76	129	26	3	15	68	49	56	10	.277	.442
Ben Oglivie	OF91, DH4	L	36	101	341	40	99	17	2	10	41	37	51	0	.290	.440
Charlie Moore	C102, OF3	R	32	105	349	35	81	13	4	0	31	27	53	4	.232	.292
Ted Simmons	DH99, 1B28, C15, 3B2	B	35	143	528	60	144	28	2	12	76	57	32	1	.273	.402
Ed Romero	SS43, 2B31, OF14, 3B1	R	27	88	251	24	63	11	1	0	21	26	20	1	.176	.303
Rick Manning	OF74, DH2	L	30	79	216	19	47	9	1	2	18	14	19	1	.218	.296
Bill Schroeder (EJ)	C48, DH4, 1B1	R	26	53	194	18	47	8	0	8	25	12	61	0	.242	.407
Randy Ready (FJ)	OF37, 3B7, 2B3, DH1	R	25	48	181	29	48	9	5	1	21	14	23	0	.265	.387
Mark Brouhard	OF29, DH1	R	29	37	108	11	28	7	1	2	13	5	26	0	.259	.389
Brian Giles	SS20, 2B13, DH2	R	25	34	58	6	10	1	0	1	7	16	7	2	.172	.241
Bobby Clark	OF27	R	30	29	93	6	21	3	0	0	9	7	19	1	.226	.258
Doug Loman	OF20	L	27	24	66	10	14	2	0	1	7	1	12	0	.212	.318
Carlos Ponce	1B10, OF6, DH3	R	26	21	62	4	10	2	0	1	5	1	9	0	.161	.242
Billy Jo Robidoux	OF11, 1B6, DH3	L	21	18	51	5	9	2	0	1	6	12	16	0	.176	.392
Dion James (SJ)	OF11, DH3	L	22	18	49	5	11	1	0	0	3	6	6	0	.224	.245
Mike Felder	OF14	B	23	15	56	8	11	1	0	0	0	5	6	4	.196	.214
Dave Huppert	C15	R	28	15	21	0	1	0	0	0	2	0	7	0	.048	.048

NAME	T	AGE	W	L	PCT	SV	G	GS	CG	IP	H	BB	SO	SHO	ERA
		31	71	90	.441	37	161	161	34	1437	1510	499	777	5	4.39
Teddy Higuera	L	26	15	8	.652	0	32	30	7	212	186	63	127	2	3.90
Ray Burris	R	34	9	13	.409	0	29	28	6	170	182	53	81	0	4.81
Moose Haas	R	29	8	8	.500	0	27	26	6	162	165	25	78	1	3.84
Danny Darwin	R	29	8	18	.308	2	39	29	11	218	212	65	125	1	3.80
Bob Gibson	R	28	6	7	.462	11	41	1	0	92	86	49	53	0	3.90
Jaime Cocanower	R	28	6	8	.429	0	24	15	3	116	122	73	44	1	4.33
Pete Vuckovich (SJ)	R	32	6	10	.375	0	22	22	1	113	134	48	55	0	5.51
Bob McClure	L	33	4	1	.800	3	38	1	0	86	91	30	57	0	4.31
Rick Waits	L	33	3	2	.600	1	24	0	0	47	67	20	24	0	6.51
Bill Wegman	R	22	2	0	1.000	0	3	3	0	18	17	3	6	0	3.57
Brad Lesley	R	26	1	0	1.000	0	5	0	0	5	8	2	5	0	9.95
Ray Searage	L	30	1	1	.500	3	38	0	0	54	54	24	36	0	5.92
Tim Leary	R	26	1	4	.200	0	5	5	0	33	40	8	29	0	4.05
Rollie Fingers	R	38	1	6	.143	17	47	0	0	55	59	19	24	0	5.04
Pete Ladd	R	28	0	0	—	2	29	0	0	46	58	16	22	0	4.53
Chuck Porter (EJ)	R	29	0	0	—	0	6	1	0	14	15	2	8	0	1.96
Jim Kern	R	36	0	0	—	0	15	0	0	11	14	5	3	0	6.55

CLEVELAND 7th 60-102 .370 39.5   PAT CORRALES

Name	G by Pos	B	AGE	G	AB	R	H	2B	3B	HR	RBI	BB	SO	SB	BA	SA
TOTALS			28	162	5527	729	1465	254	31	116	689	492	817	132	.265	.385
Pat Tabler (KJ)	1B92, DH16, 3B4, 2B1	R	27	117	404	47	111	18	3	5	59	27	55	0	.275	.371
Tony Bernazard	2B147, SS1	B	28	153	500	73	137	26	3	11	59	69	72	17	.274	.404
Julio Franco	SS151, 2B8, DH1	R	26	160	636	97	183	33	4	6	90	54	74	13	.288	.381
Brook Jacoby	3B161, 2B1	R	25	161	606	72	166	26	3	20	87	48	120	2	.274	.426
George Vuckovich	OF137	L	29	149	434	43	106	22	0	8	45	30	75	2	.244	.350
Brett Butler	OF150, DH1	L	28	152	591	106	184	28	14	5	50	63	42	47	.311	.431
Joe Carter	OF135, 1B11, DH7, 3B1, 2B1	R	25	143	489	64	128	27	0	15	59	25	74	24	.262	.409
Jerry Willard	C96, DH1	L	25	104	300	39	81	13	0	7	36	28	59	0	.270	.383
Andre Thornton	DH122	R	35	124	461	49	109	13	0	22	68	47	75	2	.236	.408
Mike Hargrove	1B84, DH2, OF1	L	35	107	284	31	81	14	1	1	27	39	29	1	.285	.352
Otis Nixon	OF80, DH11	B	26	104	162	34	38	4	0	3	9	8	27	20	.235	.315
Chris Bando	C67	R	29	75	173	11	24	4	1	0	13	22	21	0	.139	.173
Mike Fischlin	2B31, SS22, 1B6, DH5, 3B3	R	29	73	60	12	12	4	1	0	2	5	7	0	.200	.300
Carmen Castillo	OF51, DH9	R	27	67	184	27	45	5	1	11	25	11	40	3	.245	.462
Benny Ayala	DH3	R	34	46	76	10	19	7	0	2	15	4	17	0	.250	.421
Butch Benton	C26	R	27	31	67	5	12	4	0	0	7	3	9	0	.179	.239
Mel Hall (BC)	OF15, DH5	L	24	23	66	7	21	6	0	0	12	8	12	0	.318	.409
2 Johnnie LeMaster	SS10	R	31	11	20	0	3	0	0	0	2	0	6	0	.150	.150
Jim Wilson	1B2, DH2	R	24	4	14	2	5	0	0	0	4	1	3	0	.357	.357

NAME	T	AGE	W	L	PCT	SV	G	GS	CG	IP	H	BB	SO	SHO	ERA
TOTALS		27	60	102	.370	28	162	162	24	1421	1556	547	702	7	4.91
1 Bert Blyleven	R	34	9	11	.450	0	23	23	15	180	163	49	129	4	3.26
Neal Heaton	L	25	9	17	.346	0	36	33	5	208	244	80	82	1	4.90
Tom Waddell	R	26	8	6	.571	9	49	9	1	113	104	39	53	0	4.87
2 Curt Wardle	L	24	7	5	.538	0	15	12	0	66	78	34	37	0	6.68
Jamie Easterly	L	32	4	1	.800	0	50	7	0	99	96	53	58	0	3.92
Don Schulze	R	22	4	10	.286	0	19	18	1	94	128	19	37	0	6.01
Dave Von Ohlen (AJ)	L	26	3	2	.600	0	26	0	0	43	47	20	12	0	2.91
Bryan Clark	L	28	3	4	.429	2	31	3	0	53	78	34	24	0	6.32
Jerry Reed	R	29	3	5	.375	8	33	5	0	72	67	19	37	0	4.11
Rich Thompson	R	26	3	8	.273	5	57	0	0	80	95	48	30	0	6.30
Ramon Romero	L	26	2	3	.400	0	19	10	0	64	69	38	38	0	6.58
Keith Creel	R	26	2	5	.286	0	15	8	0	62	73	23	31	0	4.79
Vern Ruhle (ZJ)	R	34	2	10	.143	3	42	16	1	125	139	30	54	0	4.32
Roy Smith (CN)	R	23	1	4	.200	0	12	11	1	62	84	17	28	0	5.34
1 Mike Jeffcoat	L	25	0	0	.000	0	9	0	0	10	8	6	4	0	2.79
Ernie Camacho (EJ)	R	30	0	1	.000	2	9	0	0	3	4	1	2	0	8.10
Rick Behenna (SJ)	R	25	0	2	.000	0	4	4	0	20	29	8	4	0	7.78
Jeff Barkley	R	25	0	3	.000	1	21	0	0	41	37	15	30	0	5.27
Jose Roman	R	22	0	0	.000	0	5	3	0	16	13	14	12	0	6.61

Blyleven, also with Minnesota, league leader in GS with 37, CG with 24, IP with 294, SO with 206 and ShO with 5

WEST DIVISION

KANSAS CITY 1st 91-71 .562   DICK HOWSER

Name	G by Pos	B	AGE	G	AB	R	H	2B	3B	HR	RBI	BB	SO	SB	BA	SA
TOTALS			31	162	5500	687	1384	261	49	154	657	473	840	128	.252	.401
Steve Balboni	1B160	R	28	160	600	74	146	28	2	36	88	52	166	1	.243	.477
Frank White	2B149	R	34	149	563	62	140	25	4	22	69	28	86	10	.249	.414
Onix Concepcion	SS128, 2B2	R	27	131	314	32	64	5	1	2	20	16	29	4	.204	.245
George Brett	3B152, DH1	L	32	155	550	108	184	38	5	30	112	103	49	9	.335	.585
Darryl Motley	OF114, DH7	R	25	123	383	45	85	20	1	17	49	18	57	6	.222	.413
Willie Wilson	OF140	B	29	141	605	87	168	25	21	4	43	29	94	43	.278	.408
2 Lonnie Smith	OF119	R	29	120	448	77	115	23	4	6	41	41	69	40	.257	.366
Jim Sundberg	C112	R	34	115	367	38	90	12	4	10	35	33	57	1	.245	.381
Hal McRae	DH106	R	39	112	320	41	83	19	0	14	70	44	45	0	.259	.450
Jorge Orta	DH85	L	34	110	300	32	80	21	1	4	45	22	28	2	.267	.383
Lynn Jones	OF100, DH2	R	32	110	152	32	32	7	0	0	9	8	15	0	.211	.257
Buddy Biancalana	SS74, 2B4, DH2	B	25	81	138	21	26	5	1	1	6	17	34	1	.188	.261
Pat Sheridan (LJ)	OF69, DH1	L	27	78	206	18	47	9	2	3	17	23	38	11	.228	.335
Dane Iorg (LJ)	OF32, 1B2, DH2, 31	L	35	64	130	7	29	9	1	1	21	8	16	0	.223	.331
Greg Pryor	3B26, 2B20, SS13, DH1, 1B1	R	35	63	114	8	25	3	0	1	9	5	9	1	.219	.272
John Wathan	C49, 1B6, DH2	R	35	60	145	11	34	8	1	1	9	17	15	1	.234	.324
2 Omar Moreno	OF21	L	32	24	70	9	17	1	3	2	12	3	8	0	.243	.429
Jamie Quirk	C17, 1B1	R	30	19	57	3	16	3	1	0	4	1	3	0	.281	.368
Dave Leeper	OF8	L	25	15	34	1	3	0	0	0	4	1	3	0	.068	.068
Jim Scanlon	SS5	R	25	6	4	1	0	0	0	0	0	0	0	0	.000	.000
Bob Hegman	2B1	R	27	1	0	0	0	0	0	0	0	0	1	0	—	—

NAME	T	AGE	W	L	PCT	SV	G	GS	CG	IP	H	BB	SO	SHO	ERA
TOTALS		27	91	71	.562	41	162	162	27	1461	1433	463	846	11	3.49
Bret Saberhagen	R	21	20	6	.769	0	32	32	10	235	211	38	158	1	2.87
Charlie Leibrandt	L	28	17	9	.654	0	33	33	8	238	223	68	108	3	2.69
Mark Gubicza	R	22	14	10	.583	0	29	28	0	177	160	77	99	0	4.06
Danny Jackson	L	23	14	12	.538	0	32	32	4	208	209	76	114	3	3.42
Bud Black	L	28	10	15	.400	0	33	33	5	206	216	59	122	2	4.33
Dan Quisenberry	R	32	8	9	.471	37	84	0	0	129	142	16	54	0	2.37
Mike Jones	L	25	3	3	.500	0	33	1	0	64	62	39	32	0	4.78
Steve Farr	R	28	2	1	.667	1	16	3	0	38	34	20	36	0	3.11
Mark Huismann	R	27	1	0	1.000	0	9	0	0	19	14	3	9	0	1.93
Mike LaCoss	R	29	1	1	.500	1	21	0	0	41	49	29	26	0	5.09
Joe Beckwith	R	30	1	5	.167	1	49	0	0	95	99	32	80	0	4.07
1 Larry Gura	L	37	0	0	—	0	3	0	0	4	7	4	2	0	12.46
Tony Ferreira (KJ)	L	22	0	0	—	0	2	0	0	6	6	2	5	0	7.94
Dennis Leonard (KJ)	R	34	0	0	—	0	2	0	0	1	0	1	0	0	0.00

CALIFORNIA 2nd 90-72 .556 1   GENE MAUCH

Name	G by Pos	B	AGE	G	AB	R	H	2B	3B	HR	RBI	BB	SO	SB	BA	SA
TOTALS			33	162	5442	732	1364	215	31	153	685	648	902	106	.251	.386
Rod Carew	1B116, DH6	L	39	127	443	69	124	17	3	2	39	64	47	5	.280	.345
Bobby Grich	2B116, 1B16, 3B15	R	36	144	479	74	116	13	3	13	53	81	77	3	.242	.372
Dick Schofield	SS147	R	22	147	438	50	96	19	3	8	41	35	70	11	.219	.331
Doug DeCinces	3B111, DH3	R	34	120	427	50	104	22	1	20	78	47	71	1	.244	.440
Reggie Jackson	OF81, DH52	L	39	143	460	64	116	27	0	27	85	78	138	1	.252	.487
Gary Pettis (WJ)	OF122	B	25	125	443	67	114	10	8	1	32	62	125	56	.257	.323
Brian Downing	OF121, DH25	R	34	150	520	80	137	23	1	20	85	78	61	1	.263	.427
Bob Boone	C147	R	37	150	460	37	114	17	0	5	55	37	35	1	.248	.317
Ruppert Jones	OF73, DH43	L	30	125	389	66	90	17	2	21	67	57	82	7	.231	.447
Juan Beniquez	OF71, 1B46, DH14, SS1, 3B1	R	35	132	411	54	125	13	5	8	42	34	46	4	.304	.418
Rob Wilfong	2B69, DH1	L	31	83	217	16	41	3	0	4	13	16	32	4	.189	.258
Jerry Narron	C45, DH7, 1B1	R	29	67	132	12	29	4	0	5	14	11	17	0	.220	.364
Craig Gerber	SS53, 3B9, 2B1, DH1	L	25	65	91	8	24	1	2	0	6	2	9	1	.264	.319
1 Mike Brown	OF48, DH7	R	25	60	153	23	41	9	1	4	20	7	21	0	.268	.418
Darrell Miller (KJ)	OF45, DH4, C1, 3B1	R	27	51	48	8	18	2	1	2	7	1	10	0	.375	.583
Daryl Sconiers (DR, WJ)	DH20, 1B6	L	26	44	98	14	28	6	1	2	12	15	18	2	.286	.429
Jack Howell	3B42	L	23	43	137	19	27	4	0	5	18	16	33	1	.197	.336
Devon White	OF16	R	22	21	7	7	1	0	0	0	0	1	3	3	.143	.143
Rufino Linares	DH14, OF2	R	34	18	43	7	11	2	0	3	11	2	5	2	.256	.512
2 George Hendrick	OF12, DH1	R	35	16	41	5	5	1	0	2	6	4	8	0	.122	.293
Pat Keedy	3B2, OF1	R	27	3	4	1	2	1	0	1	1	0	0	0	.500	1.500
Gus Polidor	SS1, OF1	R	23	2	1	1	1	0	0	0	0	0	1	0	1.000	1.000
Rick Burleson 34 (SJ)																

NAME	T	AGE	W	L	PCT	SV	G	GS	CG	IP	H	BB	SO	SHO	ERA
TOTALS		28	90	72	.556	41	162	162	22	1457	1453	514	767	8	3.91
Mike Witt	R	24	15	9	.625	0	25	25	6	250	228	98	180	1	3.56
Ron Romanick	R	24	14	9	.609	0	31	31	6	195	210	62	64	1	4.11
Kirk McCaskill	R	24	12	12	.500	0	30	29	6	190	189	64	102	1	4.70
Stew Cliburn	R	28	9	3	.750	6	44	0	0	99	87	26	58	0	2.09
Donnie Moore	R	31	8	8	.500	31	65	0	0	103	91	21	72	0	1.92
2 John Candelaria	L	31	7	3	.700	0	13	13	1	71	70	24	53	1	3.80
Jim Slaton	R	35	6	10	.375	1	29	24	1	148	162	63	60	0	4.37
1 Pat Clements	L	23	5	0	1.000	1	41	0	0	62	47	25	19	0	3.34
Doug Corbett (KJ)	R	32	5	3	.500	0	30	0	0	46	49	20	24	0	3.69
Urbano Lugo	R	23	4	4	.429	0	20	10	1	83	86	29	42	0	3.69
Luis Sanchez (ZJ)	R	31	2	0	1.000	2	28	0	0	61	67	27	34	0	5.72
Geoff Zahn (SJ)	L	39	2	2	.500	0	7	7	1	37	44	14	14	1	4.38
2 Don Sutton	R	40	2	2	.500	0	5	5	0	32	27	8	16	0	3.69
1 Tommy John	L	42	2	4	.333	0	12	6	0	38	51	15	17	0	4.70
D.W. Smith	R	27	0	0	—	0	4	0	0	5	5	1	3	0	7.20
Alan Fowlkes (EJ)	R	26	0	0	—	0	2	0	0	7	4	5	0	0	9.00
3 Al Holland	L	32	0	0	.000	0	15	0	0	24	17	10	14	0	1.48
1 Bob Kipper	L	20	0	1	.000	0	4	1	0	3	7	3	0	0	21.60
Tony Mack	R	24	0	0	—	0	1	1	0	7	7	2	3	0	15.43
Ken Forsch 38 (EJ)																
Frank LaCorte 33 (SJ)																

CHICAGO 2nd 85-77 .525 6   TONY LaRUSSA

Name	G by Pos	B	AGE	G	AB	R	H	2B	3B	HR	RBI	BB	SO	SB	BA	SA
TOTALS			27	163	5470	736	1386	247	37	146	695	471	843	106	.253	.392
Greg Walker	1B151, DH7	L	25	163	601	77	155	38	4	24	92	44	100	5	.258	.454
Julio Cruz	2B87, DH2	B	30	91	234	28	46	2	3	0	15	32	40	8	.197	.231
Ozzie Guillen	SS150	L	21	150	491	71	134	21	9	1	33	12	36	7	.273	.358
Tim Hulett	3B115, 2B28, OF1	R	25	141	395	52	106	19	4	5	37	30	81	6	.268	.375
Harold Baines	OF159, DH1	L	26	160	640	86	196	29	3	22	113	42	89	1	.309	.467
Daryl Boston	OF93, DH2	L	22	95	232	20	53	13	1	3	15	14	44	8	.228	.332
Rudy Law	OF120, DH3	L	28	123	390	62	101	21	6	4	36	27	40	29	.259	.374
Carlton Fisk	C130, DH28	R	37	153	543	85	129	23	1	37	107	52	81	17	.238	.488
Ron Kittle	DH57, OF57	R	27	116	379	51	87	12	0	26	58	31	92	1	.230	.467
Luis Salazar	OF84, 3B39, DH8, 1B6	R	29	122	327	39	80	18	2	10	45	12	60	14	.245	.404
Scott Fletcher	3B55, SS44, 2B37, DH2	R	26	119	301	38	77	8	1	2	31	35	47	5	.256	.309
Jerry Hairston	OF35, DH29	B	33	95	140	9	34	8	0	2	20	29	18	0	.243	.343
Bryan Little	2B68, 3B2, SS1	B	25	73	188	35	47	9	1	2	27	26	21	0	.250	.340
Oscar Gamble	DH48	L	35	70	148	20	30	5	0	4	24	34	22	0	.203	.318
2 Reid Nichols	OF48, DH1	R	26	51	118	20	35	7	1	1	15	15	13	2	.297	.398
1 Tom Paciorek	OF23, DH12, 1B6	R	38	46	122	14	30	2	0	0	9	8	22	2	.246	.262
Marc Hill	C37, 3B1	R	33	40	75	5	10	2	0	0	4	12	9	0	.133	.160
Joe DeSa	1B9, DH4, OF1	L	25	28	44	5	8	2	0	2	7	3	6	0	.182	.364
Joel Skinner	C21	R	24	22	44	9	15	4	1	1	5	5	13	0	.341	.545
Mark Ryal	OF12	L	25	12	33	4	5	3	0	0	3	3	5	0	.152	.242
Mark Gilbert	OF7	B	28	7	22	1	6	0	0	0	2	4	3	1	.273	.318
John Cangelosi	OF3, DH2	B	22	5	2	1	0	0	0	0	0	1	0	0	.000	.000
Mike Squires		L	33	2	0	0	0	0	0	0	0	0	0	0	—	—

NAME	T	AGE	W	L	PCT	SV	G	GS	CG	IP	H	BB	SO	SHO	ERA
TOTALS		29	85	77	.525	39	163	163	20	1452	1411	569	1023	8	4.07
Britt Burns	L	26	18	11	.621	0	36	34	8	227	206	79	172	4	3.96
Tom Seaver	R	40	16	11	.593	0	35	33	6	239	223	69	134	1	3.17
Gene Nelson	R	24	10	10	.500	2	48	18	1	146	144	67	101	0	4.26
Floyd Bannister	L	30	10	14	.417	0	34	34	4	211	211	100	198	1	4.87
Bob James	R	26	8	7	.533	32	69	0	0	110	90	23	88	0	2.13
Juan Agosto	L	27	4	1	.571	1	54	0	0	60	45	23	39	0	3.58
Dan Spillner	R	33	4	3	.571	1	52	3	0	92	83	33	41	0	3.44
Joel Davis	R	20	3	3	.500	0	12	11	1	71	71	26	37	0	4.16
Rich Dotson (SJ)	R	26	3	4	.429	0	9	9	0	52	53	17	33	0	4.47
1 Tim Lollar	L	29	3	5	.375	0	18	13	0	83	83	58	61	0	4.66
Dave Wehrmeister	R	32	2	2	.500	2	23	0	0	39	35	10	32	0	3.43
Jerry Don Gleaton	L	27	1	0	1.000	1	31	0	0	30	37	13	22	0	5.76
Ed Correa	R	19	1	0	1.000	0	5	1	0	11	11	10	10	0	6.97
Al Jones (EJ)	R	28	1	1	.500	0	6	0	0	6	3	3	2	0	1.50
Bruce Tanner	R	23	1	2	.333	0	10	4	0	27	34	13	9	0	5.33
Bob Fallon	R	28	0	0	—	0	10	0	0	7	11	2	5	0	6.19
Steve Fireovid	R	28	0	0	—	0	5	1	0	7	17	2	2	0	5.14
2 Mike Stanton	R	32	0	1	.000	11	41	0	0	13	18	12	10	0	9.26
Bill Long	R	25	0	0	—	0	3	1	0	14	25	5	13	0	10.29

MINNESOTA (TIE) 4th 77-85 .475 14   BILLY GARDNER 27-35 .435   RAY MILLER 50-50 .500

Name	G by Pos	B	AGE	G	AB	R	H	2B	3B	HR	RBI	BB	SO	SB	BA	SA
TOTALS			26	162	5509	705	1453	282	41	141	678	502	779	68	.264	.407
Kent Hrbek	1B156, DH2	L	25	158	593	78	165	31	2	21	93	67	87	1	.278	.444
Tim Teufel	2B137, DH1	R	26	138	434	58	113	24	3	10	50	48	70	4	.260	.399
Greg Gagne	SS106, DH5	R	23	114	293	37	66	15	3	2	23	20	57	10	.225	.317
Gary Gaetti	3B156, OF4, DH1, 1B1	R	26	160	560	71	138	31	0	20	63	37	89	13	.246	.409
Tom Brunansky	OF155	R	24	157	567	71	137	28	4	27	90	71	86	5	.242	.448
Kirby Puckett	OF161	R	25	161	691	80	199	29	13	4	74	41	87	21	.288	.385
Mickey Hatcher	OF97, DH11, 1B4	R	30	116	444	46	125	28	0	3	49	16	23	0	.282	.365
Mark Salas	C115, DH3	L	24	120	360	51	108	20	5	9	41	18	37	0	.300	.458
Roy Smalley	DH56, SS49, 3B14, 1B1	B	32	129	388	57	100	20	0	12	45	60	65	0	.258	.402
Randy Bush	OF41, DH28, 1B1	L	26	97	234	26	56	13	3	10	35	24	30	3	.239	.449
Mike Stenhouse	DH27, OF16, 1B8	L	27	81	179	23	40	5	0	5	21	29	18	1	.223	.335
Tim Laudner	C68, 1B1	R	27	72	164	16	39	5	0	7	19	12	45	0	.238	.396
Dave Meier	OF63, DH3	R	25	71	104	15	27	6	0	1	8	18	12	0	.260	.346
Dave Engle	DH38, C17, OF3	R	28	70	172	28	44	8	2	7	25	21	28	2	.256	.448
Ron Washington	SS31, 2B24, 3B7, DH7, 1B1	R	33	70	135	24	37	6	4	1	14	8	15	5	.274	.400
Alvaro Espinoza	SS31	R	23	32	57	5	15	2	0	0	6	1	9	0	.263	.298
Steve Lombardozzi	2B26	R	25	28	54	10	20	4	1	0	6	6	6	3	.370	.481
Mark Funderburk	DH15, OF5, 1B1	R	28	23	70	7	22	7	1	2	13	5	12	0	.313	.529
Jeff Reed	C7	L	22	7	10	2	2	0	0	0	0	0	3	0	.200	.200
John Castino 30 (XJ)																

NAME	T	AGE	W	L	PCT	SV	G	GS	CG	IP	H	BB	SO	SHO	ERA
		28	77	85	.475	34	162	162	41	1426	1468	462	767	7	4.48
Frank Viola	L	25	18	14	.563	0	36	36	9	251	262	68	135	0	4.09
Mike Smithson	R	30	15	14	.517	0	37	37	8	257	264	78	127	0	4.34
John Butcher	R	28	11	14	.440	0	34	33	8	208	239	43	92	2	4.98
Ken Schrom	R	30	9	12	.429	0	29	26	6	161	164	59	74	0	4.99
2 Bert Blyleven	R	34	8	5	.615	0	14	14	9	114	101	26	77	1	3.00
Frank Eufemia	R	25	4	2	.667	2	39	0	0	62	56	21	30	0	3.79
Pete Filson	L	26	4	5	.444	2	40	6	1	96	93	30	42	0	3.67
Dennis Burtt	R	27	2	2	.500	0	5	2	0	28	20	7	9	0	3.81
2 Steve Howe	L	27	2	3	.400	0	13	0	0	19	28	7	10	0	6.16
Ron Davis	R	29	2	6	.250	25	57	0	0	65	55	35	72	0	3.48
1 Curt Wardle	L	24	1	3	.250	0	35	0	0	49	49	28	47	0	5.51
Mark Portugal	R	22	1	3	.250	0	6	4	0	24	24	14	12	0	5.55
Tom Klawitter (EJ)	L	27	0	0	—	0	7	0	0	9	7	13	5	0	6.75
Mark Brown	R	25	0	0	—	0	6	0	0	16	21	7	5	0	6.89
Len Whitehouse	L	27	0	0	—	1	5	0	0	7	12	2	4	0	11.05
Rich Yett	R	22	0	0	—	0	1	1	0	1	1	2	0	0	27.00
Rick Lysander	R	32	0	2	.000	3	35	1	0	61	72	22	26	0	6.05

Blyleven, also with Minnesota, league leader in GS with 37, CG with 24, IP with 294, SO with 206 and ShO with 5

OAKLAND (TIE) 4th 77-85 .475 14   JACKIE MOORE

Name	G by Pos	B	AGE	G	AB	R	H	2B	3B	HR	RBI	BB	SO	SB	BA	SA
TOTALS			28	162	5581	757	1475	230	34	155	690	508	861	117	.264	.401
Bruce Bochte	1B128	L	34	137	424	48	125	17	1	14	60	49	58	3	.295	.439
Donnie Hill (BH)	2B122	B	24	123	393	45	112	13	2	3	48	23	33	9	.285	.351
Alfredo Griffin	SS162	B	27	162	614	75	166	18	7	3	64	20	50	24	.270	.332
Carney Lansford (BW)	3B97	R	28	98	401	51	111	18	2	13	46	18	27	2	.277	.429
Mike Davis	OF151	L	26	154	547	92	157	34	4	24	82	50	99	24	.287	.484
Dwayne Murphy	OF150	R	30	152	523	77	122	21	3	20	59	84	123	4	.233	.400
Dave Collins	OF91	R	32	112	379	52	95	16	4	4	29	29	37	29	.251	.346
Mike Heath	C112, OF35, 3B13	R	30	138	436	71	109	18	6	13	55	41	63	7	.250	.408
Dave Kingman	DH149, 1B9	R	36	158	592	66	141	16	0	30	91	62	114	3	.238	.417
Dusty Baker	1B58, OF35, DH13	R	36	111	343	48	92	15	1	14	52	50	47	2	.268	.440
Steve Henderson	OF58, DH1	R	32	85	193	25	58	8	3	3	31	18	34	0	.301	.420
Mickey Tettleton	C24	R	24	78	211	23	53	12	0	3	15	28	59	2	.251	.351
Mike Gallego	2B42, SS21, 3B12	R	24	76	77	13	16	5	1	1	9	12	14	1	.208	.338
Rob Picciolo (IL)	3B19, 2B17, 1B13, DH10, SS9, OF2	R	32	71	102	19	28	2	0	1	8	2	17	3	.275	.324
Tony Philips (BF)	3B31, 2B24	B	26	42	161	23	45	12	2	4	17	13	34	3	.280	.453
Steve Kiefer	3B34, DH2	R	24	40	66	8	13	1	1	1	10	1	18	0	.197	.288
Jose Canseco	OF26	R	20	29	96	16	29	3	0	5	13	4	31	1	.302	.490
Charlie O'Brien	C16	R	25	16	11	3	3	1	0	0	1	3	3	0	.273	.364
Dan Meyer	OF1, DH1, 3B1	L	32	14	12	2	0	0	0	0	0	1	0	0	.000	.000

NAME	T	AGE	W	L	PCT	SV	G	GS	CG	IP	H	BB	SO	SHO	ERA
		28	77	85	.475	41	162	162	4	1453	1451	607	785	6	4.39
Chris Codiroli	R	27	14	14	.500	0	37	37	4	226	228	78	111	0	4.46
1 Don Sutton	R	40	13	8	.619	0	29	29	1	194	194	51	91	1	3.89
Tim Birtsas	L	24	10	6	.625	0	29	25	2	141	124	91	94	0	4.01
Jay Howell	R	29	9	8	.529	29	63	0	0	98	98	31	68	0	2.85
Bill Krueger	L	27	9	10	.474	0	32	23	2	151	165	69	56	0	4.52
Jose Rijo	R	20	6	4	.600	0	12	9	0	64	57	28	65	0	3.53
Steve McCatty	R	31	4	4	.500	0	30	9	1	86	95	41	36	0	5.57
Keith Atherton	R	26	4	7	.364	3	56	0	0	105	89	42	77	0	4.30
Rick Lanford (EJ)	R	33	5	3	.375	0	23	3	0	59	60	15	21	0	3.51
2 Tommy John	R	42	2	6	.250	0	11	11	0	48	66	13	8	0	6.19
Steve Mura	R	30	1	1	.500	0	23	1	0	48	41	25	29	0	4.13
Steve Ontiveros	R	24	1	3	.250	8	39	0	0	75	45	19	36	0	1.93
Mike Warren	R	24	1	4	.200	0	16	6	0	49	52	38	48	0	6.61
Jeff Kaiser	L	24	0	0	—	0	15	0	0	17	25	20	10	0	14.58
Tom Tellmann (XJ)	R	31	0	0	—	0	11	0	0	21	33	9	8	0	5.06
Tim Conroy	L	25	0	1	.000	0	16	2	0	25	22	15	8	0	4.26
Curt Young (SJ)	L	25	0	1	.000	0	19	7	0	46	57	22	19	0	7.24
Mike Norris 30 (SJ, DR)															

SEATTLE 5th 74-88 .457 17   CHUCK COTTIER

Name	G by Pos	B	AGE	G	AB	R	H	2B	3B	HR	RBI	BB	SO	SB	BA	SA
TOTALS			27	162	5521	719	1410	277	38	171	686	564	942	94	.255	.412
Alvin Davis	1B154	L	24	155	578	78	166	33	1	18	78	90	71	1	.287	.441
Jack Perconte	2B125	L	30	125	485	60	128	17	7	2	23	50	35	31	.264	.340
Spike Owen	SS117	B	24	118	352	41	91	10	6	6	37	34	27	11	.259	.372
Jim Presley	3B154	R	23	155	570	71	157	33	1	28	84	44	100	2	.275	.484
Al Cowens	OF110, DH5	R	33	122	452	59	120	32	5	14	69	30	56	0	.265	.451
Dave Henderson	OF138	R	26	139	502	70	121	28	2	14	68	48	104	6	.241	.388
Phil Bradley	OF159	R	26	159	641	100	192	33	8	26	88	55	129	22	.300	.498
Bob Kearney (BW)	C108	R	29	108	305	24	74	14	1	6	27	11	59	1	.243	.354
Gorman Thomas	DH133	R	34	135	484	76	104	16	1	32	87	84	126	3	.210	.450
Donnie Scott	C74	B	23	80	185	18	41	13	0	4	23	15	41	1	.222	.357
Domingo Ramos	SS36, 2B20, 1B14, 3B7	R	27	75	168	19	33	6	0	1	15	17	23	0	.196	.250
Ivan Calderon (BW)	OF53, DH3, 1B2	R	23	67	210	37	60	16	4	8	28	19	45	4	.286	.514
Harold Reynolds	2B61	B	24	67	104	15	15	3	1	0	6	17	14	3	.144	.192
Ken Phelps	DH25, 1B8	L	30	61	116	18	24	3	0	9	24	24	33	2	.207	.466
Barry Bonnell (LJ)	OF22, 1B5, DH2	R	31	48	111	9	27	8	0	1	10	6	19	1	.243	.342
John Moses	OF29	B	27	33	62	4	12	0	0	0	3	2	8	5	.194	.194
Dave Valle	C31	R	24	31	70	2	11	1	0	0	4	1	17	0	.157	.171
Darnell Coles	SS15, 3B7, OF2, DH2	R	23	27	59	8	14	4	0	1	5	4	6	0	.237	.356
Danny Tartabull	SS16, 3B4	R	22	19	61	8	20	7	1	1	7	4	14	1	.328	.525
Ricky Nelson	OF3	L	26	6	2	2	0	0	0	0	0	0	0	0	.000	.000
Al Chambers		L	24	1	4	0	0	0	0	0	0	0	1	0	.000	.000
Larry Milbourne 34 (WJ)																

NAME	T	AGE	W	L	PCT	SV	G	GS	CG	IP	H	BB	SO	SHO	ERA
		27	74	88	.457	30	162	162	23	1432	1456	637	868	8	4.68
Mike Moore	R	25	17	10	.630	0	35	34	14	247	230	70	155	2	3.46
Matt Young	L	26	12	19	.387	1	37	35	5	218	242	76	136	2	4.91
Roy Thomas	R	32	7	3	.700	0	40	0	0	94	66	48	70	0	3.36
Edwin Nunez	R	22	9	3	.700	16	70	0	0	90	79	34	58	0	3.09
Mark Langston (EJ)	L	24	7	14	.333	0	24	24	2	127	122	91	72	0	5.47
Bill Swift	R	23	6	10	.375	0	23	21	0	121	131	48	35	0	4.77
Jim Beattie (SJ)	R	30	5	6	.455	0	18	15	1	70	93	33	45	1	7.29
Frank Wills	R	26	5	11	.313	1	24	18	1	123	122	68	67	0	6.00
Ed Vande Berg	L	26	5	2	.714	3	76	0	0	68	71	31	34	0	3.72
Karl Best (SJ)	R	26	2	1	.667	4	15	0	0	32	25	6	32	0	1.95
Dave Tobik	R	32	1	0	1.000	3	9	0	0	9	10	3	8	0	6.00
Mike Morgan (LJ)	R	25	1	1	.500	0	2	2	0	6	9	2	1	0	12.00
1 Mike Stanton	R	32	1	2	.333	1	24	0	0	29	32	21	17	0	5.28
Brian Snyder	L	27	1	2	.333	1	15	6	0	35	44	19	23	0	6.37
Bob Long	R	30	1	0	1.000	0	8	0	0	38	30	17	29	0	3.76
Jack Lazorko	R	29	0	0	—	1	3	0	0	5	8	4	1	0	3.54
Dave Geisel	L	30	0	0	—	0	27	0	0	27	35	15	17	0	6.33
Paul Mirabella	L	31	0	0	—	0	10	0	0	14	18	4	5	0	1.32
Jim Lewis	R	29	0	1	.000	0	5	1	0	5	8	1	1	0	7.71
Bill Wilkinson	L	20	0	2	.000	0	2	0	0	7	7	6	4	0	13.50
Salome Barojas	R	28	0	5	.000	17	29	0	0	53	66	33	27	0	5.98
(left team when son died)																

TEXAS 7th 62-99 .385 28.5   DOUG RADER 9-23 .281   BOBBY VALENTINE 53-76 .411

Name	G by Pos	B	AGE	G	AB	R	H	2B	3B	HR	RBI	BB	SO	SB	BA	SA
TOTALS			29	161	5361	617	1359	213	41	129	578	530	819	130	.253	.381
Pete O'Brien	1B159	L	27	159	573	69	153	34	3	22	92	69	53	5	.267	.542
Toby Harrah	2B122, SS2, DH1	R	36	126	401	65	107	18	1	9	44	113	60	11	.270	.389
Curt Wilkerson	SS110, 2B19, DH2	B	24	129	360	35	88	11	6	0	22	22	46	14	.244	.308
1 Buddy Bell	3B83	R	33	84	313	33	74	13	3	4	32	33	21	3	.236	.335
Larry Parrish	OF69, DH22, 3B2	R	31	94	346	44	86	11	1	17	51	33	77	0	.259	.434
Oddibe McDowell	OF103, DH4	L	22	111	406	63	97	14	5	18	42	36	85	25	.239	.434
Gary Ward	OF153, DH1	R	31	154	593	79	170	28	7	15	70	39	97	26	.287	.433
Don Slaught (LJ)	C102, DH1	R	26	102	343	34	96	17	4	8	35	20	41	5	.280	.423
1 Cliff Johnson (KJ)	DH82	R	37	82	296	31	76	17	1	12	56	31	44	0	.257	.443
Wayne Tolleson	SS81, 2B29, 3B12, DH6	B	29	123	323	45	101	9	5	1	18	21	46	21	.313	.381
George Wright	OF102, DH4	B	26	109	363	21	69	13	0	2	18	25	49	4	.190	.242
Bobby Jones	OF30, DH10, 1B4	L	35	83	134	14	30	2	0	5	23	19	31	1	.224	.351
Steve Buechele	3B69, 2B1	R	23	69	219	22	48	6	3	6	21	14	38	3	.219	.356
Alan Bannister	DH21, OF14, 2B10, 3B5, 1B4	R	33	57	122	17	32	4	1	1	6	14	17	4	.262	.336
2 Duane Walker	OF7, DH4	L	28	53	132	14	23	7	0	5	11	15	29	2	.174	.303
Glenn Brummer	C47, OF1, DH1	R	30	49	108	7	30	4	0	2	5	11	22	1	.278	.315
Tommy Dunbar	DH18, OF14	L	25	45	104	7	21	4	0	1	12	9	15	0	.202	.269
Bill Stein	3B11, 1B8, DH6, 2B3, OF3	R	38	44	79	5	20	3	1	1	12	1	15	0	.253	.354
Geno Petralli	C41	B	25	42	100	7	27	2	0	0	11	8	12	1	.270	.290
Ellis Valentine	OF7, DH4	R	30	11	38	5	8	1	0	0	2	1	6	0	.211	.395
Nick Capra	OF8	R	27	8	8	1	1	0	0	0	0	1	2	1	.125	.125
Jeff Kunkel	SS2	R	23	4	4	1	1	0	0	0	0	0	4	0	.250	.250
Luis Pujols (SJ)	C1	R	29	1	1	0	1	0	0	0	0	0	0	0	1.000	1.000

NAME	T	AGE	W	L	PCT	SV	G	GS	CG	IP	H	BB	SO	SHO	ERA
		29	62	99	.385	33	161	161	18	1412	1479	501	863	5	4.56
Charlie Hough	R	37	14	16	.467	0	34	34	14	250	198	83	141	1	3.31
Mike Mason	L	26	8	15	.348	0	38	30	1	179	212	73	92	1	4.83
Dave Schmidt	R	28	7	6	.538	5	51	4	1	86	81	22	46	1	3.15
Greg Harris	R	29	5	4	.556	11	58	0	0	113	74	43	111	0	2.47
Burt Hooton	R	35	5	8	.385	0	29	20	2	124	149	40	62	0	5.23
Dickie Noles (SJ)	R	28	4	8	.333	1	28	13	0	110	129	33	59	0	5.06
Jose Guzman	R	22	3	2	.600	0	5	5	0	33	27	14	24	0	2.76
Jeff Russell	R	23	3	6	.333	0	13	13	0	62	85	27	44	0	7.55
Dave Rozema (KJ)	R	28	3	3	.500	7	34	4	0	88	100	22	42	0	4.19
Matt Williams	R	25	2	1	.667	0	6	3	0	26	20	10	22	0	2.42
Dwayne Henry	R	23	2	1	.667	3	16	0	0	21	16	7	20	0	2.57
Glen Cook	R	25	2	3	.400	0	7	5	0	40	53	18	19	0	9.45
Chris Welsh	L	30	2	5	.286	0	5	5	0	76	101	25	31	0	4.13
1 Frank Tanana	L	31	2	7	.222	0	13	13	0	78	89	23	52	0	5.91
Ricky Wright	L	26	0	0	—	0	8	5	0	8	5	7	0	0	4.70
Tommy Boggs	R	29	0	0	—	0	1	1	0	7	13	2	6	0	11.57
2 Dale Murray	R	35	0	0	—	0	5	0	0	7	11	4	1	0	18.00
2 Rick Surhoff	R	22	0	0	—	0	5	0	0	8	5	7	4	0	7.56
Bob Sebra	R	23	0	2	.000	0	6	3	0	20	26	14	13	0	7.52
1 Dave Stewart	R	28	0	6	.000	4	42	6	0	81	86	37	64	0	5.42

ST. LOUIS   1st 101-61 .623   WHITEY HERZOG

Name	G by Pos	B	AGE	G	AB	R	H	2B	3B	HR	RBI	BB	SO	SB	BA	SA
TOTALS			27	162	5467	747	1446	245	59	87	687	586	853	314	.264	.390
Jack Clark (VJ)	1B121, OF12	R	29	126	442	71	124	26	3	22	87	83	88	1	.281	.502
Tommy Herr	2B158	B	29	159	596	97	180	38	3	8	110	80	55	31	.302	.416
Ozzie Smith	SS158	B	30	158	537	70	148	22	3	6	54	66	27	31	.276	.361
Terry Pendleton	3B149	B	24	149	559	56	134	16	3	5	69	37	75	17	.240	.306
Andy Van Slyke	OF142, 1B2	L	24	146	424	61	110	25	6	13	55	47	54	34	.259	.439
Willie McGee	OF149	B	26	152	612	114	216	26	18	10	82	34	86	56	.353	.439
Vince Coleman	OF150	B	24	151	636	107	170	20	10	1	40	50	115	110	.267	.335
Darrell Porter (BG)	C82	L	33	84	240	30	53	12	2	10	36	41	48	6	.221	.413
Tom Nieto	C95	R	24	95	253	15	57	10	2	0	34	26	37	0	.225	.218
Tito Landrum	OF73	R	30	85	161	21	45	8	2	4	21	19	30	1	.280	.429
Mike Jorgensen	1B49, OF2	L	36	72	112	14	22	6	0	0	11	31	27	2	.196	.250
Steve Braun	OF14	L	37	64	67	7	16	4	0	1	6	10	9	0	.239	.343
Ivan DeJesus	3B20, SS13	R	32	59	72	11	16	5	0	0	7	4	16	2	.222	.292
Tom Lawless	3B13, 2B11	R	28	47	58	8	12	3	1	0	8	5	4	2	.207	.293
Brian Harper	OF13, 3B6, C2, 1B1	R	25	43	52	5	13	4	0	0	8	2	3	0	.250	.327
1 Lonnie Smith	OF28	R	29	28	96	15	25	2	2	0	7	15	20	12	.260	.323
2 Cesar Cedeno	1B23, OF2	R	34	28	76	14	33	4	1	6	19	5	7	5	.434	.750
Randy Hunt	C13	R	25	14	19	1	3	0	0	0	1	0	5	0	.158	.158
Mike LaValliere	C12	L	24	12	34	2	5	1	0	0	6	7	3	0	.147	.176
Curt Ford	OF4	L	24	11	12	2	6	2	0	0	3	4	1	1	.500	.667
Art Howe	3B1, 1B1	R	38	4	3	0	0	0	0	0	0	0	0	0	.000	.000

NAME	T	AGE	W	L	PCT	SV	G	GS	CG	IP	H	BB	SO	SHO	ERA
		29	101	61	.623	44	162	162	37	1464	1343	453	798	20	3.10
John Tudor	L	31	21	8	.724	0	36	36	14	275	209	49	169	10	1.93
Joaquin Andujar	R	32	21	12	.636	0	38	38	10	270	265	82	112	2	3.40
Danny Cox	R	25	18	9	.667	0	35	35	10	241	226	64	131	4	2.88
Kurt Kepshire	R	25	10	9	.526	0	32	29	0	153	155	71	67	0	4.75
Bob Forsch	R	35	9	6	.600	0	34	19	3	136	132	47	48	1	3.90
Jeff Lahti	R	28	5	2	.714	19	52	0	0	68	63	26	41	0	1.84
Bill Campbell	R	40	5	3	.625	4	50	0	0	64	55	21	41	0	3.50
Ken Dayley	L	26	4	4	.500	11	57	0	0	65	65	18	62	0	2.76
Todd Worrell	R	25	3	0	1.000	5	17	0	0	22	17	7	17	0	2.91
Ricky Horton	L	25	3	2	.600	1	49	3	0	90	84	34	59	0	2.91
Pat Perry	L	26	1	0	1.000	0	6	0	0	12	3	3	6	0	0.00
1 Neil Allen	R	27	1	4	.200	2	23	1	0	29	32	17	10	0	5.59
Joe Boever	R	25	0	0	—	0	13	0	0	16	17	4	20	0	4.41
2 Doug Bair	R	35	0	0	—	0	2	0	0	2	1	2	0	0	0.00
Andy Hassler	L	33	0	1	.000	0	10	0	0	10	9	4	5	0	1.80
Matt Keough	R	29	0	1	.000	0	4	1	0	10	10	4	4	0	4.50

NEW YORK   2nd 98-64 .605   3   DAVEY JOHNSON

Name	G by Pos	B	AGE	G	AB	R	H	2B	3B	HR	RBI	BB	SO	SB	BA	SA
TOTALS			28	162	5549	695	1425	239	35	134	651	546	872	117	.257	.385
Keith Hernandez	1B157	L	31	158	593	87	183	34	4	10	91	77	59	3	.309	.430
Wally Backman	2B140, SS1	B	25	145	520	77	142	24	5	1	38	36	72	30	.273	.344
Rafael Santana	SS153	R	27	154	529	41	136	19	1	1	29	29	54	1	.257	.302
Howard Johnson	3B113, SS7, OF1	B	24	126	389	38	94	18	4	11	46	34	78	6	.242	.393
Darryl Strawberry (RJ)	OF110	L	23	111	393	78	109	15	4	29	79	73	96	26	.277	.557
Mookie Wilson (SJ)	OF83	B	29	93	337	56	93	16	8	6	26	28	52	24	.276	.424
George Foster	OF123	R	36	129	452	57	119	24	1	21	77	46	87	0	.263	.460
Gary Carter	C143, 1B6, OF1	R	31	149	555	83	156	17	1	32	100	69	46	1	.281	.488
Danny Heep	OF78, 1B4	L	27	95	271	26	76	17	0	7	42	27	27	2	.280	.421
Ray Knight	3B73, 2B2, 1B1	R	32	90	271	22	59	12	0	6	36	13	32	1	.218	.328
Lenny Dykstra	OF74	L	22	83	236	40	60	9	3	1	19	30	24	15	.254	.331
Kelvin Chapman	2B48, 3B1	R	29	62	144	16	25	3	0	0	7	9	15	5	.174	.194
Rusty Staub	OF1	L	41	54	45	2	12	3	0	1	8	10	4	0	.267	.400
John Christensen	OF38	R	24	51	113	10	21	4	1	3	13	19	23	1	.186	.319
2 Tom Paciorek	OF29, 1B8	R	38	46	116	14	33	3	1	1	11	6	14	1	.284	.353
Clint Hurdle	C17, OF10	L	28	43	82	7	16	4	0	3	7	13	20	0	.195	.354
Ronn Reynolds	C25	R	27	28	43	4	9	2	0	0	1	0	18	0	.209	.256
Ron Gardenhire (LJ)	SS13, 2B5, 3B2	R	27	26	39	5	7	2	1	0	2	8	11	0	.179	.282
Terry Blocker	OF5	L	25	18	15	1	1	0	0	0	0	1	2	0	.067	.067
2 Larry Bowa	SS9, 2B4	B	39	14	19	2	2	1	0	0	2	2	2	0	.105	.158
Billy Beane	OF2	R	23	8	4	0	1	1	0	0	0	0	3	0	.250	.375

NAME	T	AGE	W	L	PCT	SV	G	GS	CG	IP	H	BB	SO	SHO	ERA
		26	98	64	.605	37	162	162	32	1488	1306	515	1039	19	3.11
Dwight Gooden	R	20	24	4	.857	0	35	35	16	277	198	69	268	8	1.53
Ron Darling	R	24	16	6	.727	0	36	35	4	248	214	114	167	2	2.90
Rick Aguilera	R	23	10	7	.588	0	21	19	2	122	118	37	74	0	3.24
Ed Lynch	R	29	10	8	.556	0	31	29	6	191	188	27	65	1	3.44
Sid Fernandez	L	22	9	9	.500	0	26	26	3	170	108	80	180	0	2.80
Jesse Orosco	R	28	8	6	.571	17	54	0	0	79	66	34	68	0	2.73
Roger McDowell	R	24	6	5	.545	17	62	2	0	127	108	37	70	0	2.83
Tom Gorman	R	27	4	4	.500	0	34	2	0	53	56	18	32	0	5.13
Doug Sisk	R	27	4	5	.444	2	42	0	0	73	86	40	26	0	5.30
Terry Leach	R	31	3	4	.429	1	22	4	1	56	48	14	30	1	2.91
Calvin Schiraldi	R	23	2	1	.667	0	10	4	0	26	43	11	21	0	8.89
Bruce Berenyi (SJ)	R	30	1	0	1.000	0	3	3	0	14	8	10	10	0	2.63
Bill Latham	L	24	1	3	.250	0	7	3	0	23	21	7	10	0	3.97
Joe Sambito	L	33	0	0	—	0	8	0	0	11	21	8	3	0	12.66
Randy Niemann	L	29	0	0	—	0	4	0	0	5	2	1	2	0	0.00
Randy Meyers	R	22	0	0	—	0	1	0	0	1	3	2	1	0	0.00
Wes Gardner	R	24	0	2	.000	0	12	18	8	11				0	5.25
Brent Gaff 26 (SJ)	R														

MONTREAL   3rd 84-77 .522   16.5   BUCK RODGERS

Name	G by Pos	B	AGE	G	AB	R	H	2B	3B	HR	RBI	BB	SO	SB	BA	SA
TOTALS			27	161	5429	633	1342	242	49	118	593	492	880	77	.247	.375
1 Dan Driessen	1B88	L	33	91	312	31	78	18	0	6	25	33	29	2	.250	.365
Vance Law	2B126, 1B20, 3B11, OF1	R	28	147	519	75	138	30	6	10	52	86	96	6	.266	.405
Hubie Brooks	SS155	R	28	156	605	67	163	34	7	13	100	34	79	6	.269	.413
Tim Wallach	3B154	R	27	155	569	70	148	36	3	22	81	38	79	9	.260	.450
Andre Dawson	OF131	R	30	139	529	65	135	27	2	23	91	29	92	13	.255	.444
Herm Winningham	OF116	L	23	125	312	30	74	6	5	3	21	28	72	20	.237	.317
Tim Raines	OF146	B	25	150	575	115	184	30	13	11	41	81	60	70	.320	.475
Mike Fitzgerald	C108	R	24	108	295	25	61	7	1	5	34	38	55	5	.207	.288
Terry Francona	1B57, OF28, 3B1	L	26	107	281	19	75	15	1	2	31	12	12	5	.267	.349
2 Mitch Webster	OF64	B	26	74	212	32	58	7	2	11	30	20	33	15	.274	.486
Jim Wohlford	OF43	R	34	70	125	7	24	5	1	1	15	16	18	0	.192	.272
U.L. Washington (LJ)	2B43, SS9, 3B3	B	31	68	193	24	48	9	4	1	17	15	33	6	.249	.352
Sal Butera	C66	R	32	67	120	11	24	1	0	3	12	13	12	0	.200	.283
1 Miguel Dilone	OF22	B	30	51	84	10	16	0	2	0	6	6	11	7	.190	.238
Razor Shines	1B5	B	28	47	50	6	6	0	0	0	4	3	9	0	.120	.120
1 Steve Nicosia (SJ)	C23, 1B2	R	29	42	71	4	12	2	0	0	1	7	11	1	.169	.197
2 Scot Thompson	OF3, 1B3	L	29	34	32	2	9	1	0	0	4	3	4	0	.281	.313
Al Newman	2B15, SS2	B	25	29	7	5	1	1	0	0	1	3	4	2	.172	.207
Andres Galarraga	1B23	R	24	24	75	9	14	1	0	2	4	3	18	1	.187	.280
Mike O'Berry	C20	R	31	20	21	2	4	0	0	0	4	3	6	0	.190	.190
Skeeter Barnes	3B4, OF3, 1B1	R	28	19	26	0	4	1	0	0	0	0	4	0	.154	.192
2 Doug Frobel	OF6	L	26	12	23	3	3	1	0	1	1	2	6	0	.130	.304
Fred Manrique	2B2, SS2, 3B1	R	24	9	13	5	4	1	1	1	1	1	3	0	.308	.769
1 Doug Flynn	2B6, SS1	R	34	9	6	0	1	0	0	0	0	0	0	0	.167	.167
Ned Yost	C5	R	30	5	11	1	2	0	0	0	0	0	0	0	.182	.182
Roy Johnson	OF3	L	26	3	5	0	0	0	0	0	0	0	3	0	.000	.000

NAME	T	AGE	W	L	PCT	SV	G	GS	CG	IP	H	BB	SO	SHO	ERA
		28	84	77	.522	53	161	161	13	1457	1346	509	870	13	3.55
Bryn Smith	R	29	18	5	.783	0	32	32	4	222	193	41	127	2	2.91
Bill Gullickson	R	26	14	12	.538	0	29	29	4	181	187	47	68	1	3.52
Joe Hesketh (BL)	L	26	10	5	.667	0	25	25	2	155	125	45	113	1	2.49
Tim Burke	R	26	9	4	.692	8	78	0	0	120	86	44	87	0	2.39
David Palmer (EJ)	R	27	7	10	.412	0	24	23	0	136	128	67	106	0	3.71
Gary Lucas (XJ)	L	30	6	2	.750	1	49	0	0	68	63	24	31	0	3.19
Randy St. Claire	R	24	5	3	.625	4	42	0	0	69	69	26	25	0	3.93
Floyd Youmans	R	22	4	3	.571	0	14	12	0	77	57	49	54	0	2.45
Bert Roberge (SJ)	R	30	3	3	.500	2	42	0	0	68	58	22	34	0	3.44
Dan Schatzeder (SJ)	L	30	3	5	.375	0	24	15	1	104	101	31	64	0	3.80
Steve Rogers	R	35	2	4	.333	0	8	7	1	38	51	20	18	0	5.68
Jeff Reardon	R	29	2	8	.200	41	63	0	0	88	68	26	67	0	3.18
1 Mickey Mahler	L	32	1	4	.200	1	14	0	0	48	40	24	32	1	3.54
Dick Grapenthin	R	27	0	0	—	0	7	0	0	7	13	8	4	0	14.14
Ed Glynn	L	32	0	0	—	0	3	0	0	1	1	0	1	0	19.29
Sal Butera	R	32	0	0	—	0	1	0	0	1	2	0	0	0	0.00
Razor Shines	R	28	0	0	—	0	1	0	0	2	1	0	0	0	
Jack O'Connor	L	27	0	0	—	0	4	3	0	24	13	16	0		4.94
John Dopson	R	21	0	0	—	0	4	3	0	13	55	14	18	0	11.08
2 Bill Laskey	R	27	0	5	.000	0	11	9	0	34	55	14	18	0	9.44
Charlie Lea 28 (SJ)															

CHICAGO   4th 77-84 .478   23.5   JIM FREY

Name	G by Pos	B	AGE	G	AB	R	H	2B	3B	HR	RBI	BB	SO	SB	BA	SA
TOTALS			31	162	5492	686	1397	239	28	150	640	562	937	182	.254	.390
Leon Durham	1B151	L	27	153	542	58	153	32	2	21	75	64	99	7	.282	.465
Ryne Sandberg	2B153, SS1	R	25	153	609	113	186	31	6	26	83	57	97	51	.305	.504
Shawon Dunston	SS73	R	22	74	250	40	65	12	4	4	18	19	42	11	.260	.388
Ron Cey	3B140	R	37	145	500	64	116	18	2	22	63	58	106	1	.232	.408
Keith Moreland	OF148, 1B12, 3B11, C2	R	31	161	587	74	180	30	3	14	106	68	58	12	.307	.440
Bob Dernier (FJ)	OF116	R	28	121	469	63	119	20	3	1	21	40	44	31	.254	.316
Gary Matthews (KJ)	OF85	R	34	97	298	45	70	12	0	13	40	59	64	2	.235	.406
Jody Davis	C138	R	28	142	482	47	112	30	0	17	58	48	83	1	.232	.440
Thad Bosley	OF55	L	28	108	180	25	59	6	3	7	27	20	29	5	.328	.511
Chris Speier	SS58, 3B31, 2B13	R	35	106	218	16	53	11	0	4	24	17	34	1	.243	.349
Davey Lopes	OF79, 3B4, 2B1	R	40	99	275	52	78	11	0	11	44	46	37	47	.284	.444
Richie Hebner	1B12, 3B7, OF1	L	37	83	120	10	26	3	0	3	22	7	15	0	.217	.308
Gary Woods	OF56	R	30	81	82	11	20	3	0	0	4	14	18	0	.244	.280
1 Larry Bowa	SS66	B	39	72	195	13	48	6	0	1	13	11	20	5	.246	.318
Steve Lake	C55	R	28	58	119	5	18	2	0	1	11	3	21	1	.151	.193
Billy Hatcher	OF44	R	24	53	163	24	40	12	1	2	10	8	12	2	.245	.368
Brian Dayett (NJ)	OF10	R	28	22	26	1	6	0	0	0	4	2	4	0	.231	.346
Dave Owen	SS7, 3B7, 2B4	B	27	22	19	6	7	0	0	0	4	0	1	0	.368	.368
Chico Walker	OF6, 2B2	B	27	21	12	3	1	0	0	0	0	5	0		.083	.083
Darrin Jackson	OF4	R	22	5	11	0	1	0	0	0	0	0	3	0	.091	.091

NAME	T	AGE	W	L	PCT	SV	G	GS	CG	IP	H	BB	SO	SHO	ERA
		29	77	84	.478	42	162	162	20	1442	1492	519	820	8	4.16
Dennis Eckersley (SJ)	R	30	11	7	.611	0	25	25	6	169	145	19	117	2	3.08
Steve Trout (EJ)	L	27	9	7	.563	0	24	24	3	141	142	63	44	1	3.39
Rick Sutcliffe (SJ)	R	29	8	8	.500	0	20	20	6	130	119	44	102	3	3.18
Lee Smith	R	27	7	4	.636	33	65	0	0	98	87	32	112	0	3.04
George Frazier	R	30	7	7	.467	2	51	0	0	76	88	52	46	0	6.39
Ray Fontenot	R	27	6	10	.375	0	38	23	0	155	177	45	70	0	4.36
Scott Sanderson (KJ)	R	28	5	6	.455	0	19	19	2	121	100	27	80	0	3.12
Warren Brusstar	R	33	4	3	.571	4	51	0	0	74	87	36	34	0	6.05
Dick Ruthven (BT)	R	34	4	7	.364	0	20	15	0	87	103	37	26	0	4.53
Reggie Patterson	R	27	3	0	1.000	0	8	5	1	39	36	10	17	0	3.00
Ron Meridith	L	28	3	2	.600	1	32	0	0	46	53	24	23	0	4.47
Lary Sorensen	R	29	3	7	.300	0	45	3	0	82	86	24	34	0	4.26
Jay Baller	R	27	1	0	1.000	1	20	4	0	52	52	17	31	0	3.46
Dave Gumpert (GJ)	R	27	1	0	1.000	0	10	0	0	10	12	7	4	0	3.48
Jon Perlman	R	22	1	0	1.000	0	8	0	0	11	12	8	8	0	11.42
Johnny Abrego	R	28	1	1	.500	0	5	5	0	24	32	12	13	0	6.38
Derek Botelho	R	28	1	3	.250	0	5	1	0	29	23	23	0		5.32
Steve Engel	L	23	1	5	.167	0	11	8	1	52	61	26	29	0	5.57
Dave Beard	R	26	0	2	.000	0	13	0	0	16	17	7	4	0	6.39
2 Larry Gura	L	37	0	3	.000	0	8	5	0	20	34	6	7	0	8.41

PHILADELPHIA 5th 75-87 .463 26 — JOHN FELSKE

Name	G by Pos	B	AGE	G	AB	R	H	2B	3B	HR	RBI	BB	SO	SB	BA	SA
TOTALS			28	162	5477	667	1343	238	47	141	628	527	1095	122	.245	.383
Mike Schmidt	1B106, 3B54, SS1	R	35	158	549	89	152	31	5	33	93	87	117	1	.277	.532
Juan Samuel	2B159	R	24	161	663	101	175	31	13	19	74	33	141	53	.264	.436
Steve Jeltz	SS86	R	26	89	196	17	37	4	1	0	12	26	55	1	.189	.219
Rick Schu	3B111	R	23	112	416	54	105	21	4	7	24	38	78	8	.252	.373
Glenn Wilson	OF158	R	26	161	608	73	167	39	5	14	102	35	117	7	.275	.424
Von Hayes	OF146	L	26	152	570	76	150	30	4	13	70	61	99	21	.263	.398
Jeff Stone	OF69	L	24	88	264	36	70	4	3	3	11	15	50	15	.265	.337
Ozzie Virgil	C120	R	28	131	426	47	105	16	3	19	55	49	85	0	.246	.432
Garry Maddox	OF94	R	35	105	218	22	52	8	1	4	23	13	26	4	.239	.339
Tim Corcoran	1B59, OF3	L	32	103	182	11	39	6	1	0	22	29	20	0	.214	.258
Greg Gross (BG)	OF52, 1B8	L	32	93	169	21	44	5	2	0	14	32	9	1	.260	.314
Luis Aguayo	SS60, 2B17, 3B7	R	26	91	165	27	46	7	3	6	21	22	26	1	.279	.467
John Russell	OF49, 1B18	R	24	81	216	22	47	12	0	9	23	18	72	2	.218	.398
Derrel Thomas	SS21, OF7, 3B1,2B, C1	B	34	63	92	16	19	2	0	4	12	11	14	2	.207	.359
2 Tom Foley	SS45	L	25	46	158	17	42	8	0	3	17	13	18	1	.266	.373
Darren Daulton (SJ)	C28	L	23	36	103	14	21	3	1	4	11	16	37	3	.204	.369
John Wockenfuss	1B7, C2	R	36	32	37	1	6	0	0	0	2	8	7	0	.162	.162
1 Bo Diaz (BW)	C24	R	32	26	76	9	16	5	1	2	16	6	7	0	.211	.382
2 Alan Knicely	1B1	R	30	7	7	0	0	0	0	0	0	0	4	0	.000	.000
Kiko Garcia	SS3, 3B1	R	31	4	3	0	0	0	0	0	0	0	1	0	.000	.000
Joe Lefebvre 29 (KJ)																

NAME	T	AGE	W	L	PCT	SV	G	GS	CG	IP	H	BB	SO	SHO	ERA
		30	75	87	.463	30	162	162	24	1447	1424	596	899	9	3.68
Kevin Gross	R	24	15	13	.536	0	38	31	6	206	194	81	151	2	3.41
Shane Rawley	L	29	13	8	.619	0	36	31	6	199	188	81	106	2	3.31
John Denny	R	32	11	14	.440	0	33	33	6	231	252	83	123	2	3.82
Don Carman	L	25	9	4	.692	7	71	0	0	86	52	38	87	0	2.08
Charlie Hudson	R	26	8	13	.381	0	38	26	3	193	188	74	122	0	3.78
Jerry Koosman (KJ)	L	42	6	4	.600	0	19	18	3	99	107	34	60	1	4.62
2 Kent Telkuve	R	38	4	10	.286	14	58	0	0	72	67	25	36	0	2.99
Dave Rucker	L	27	3	2	.600	1	39	3	0	79	83	40	41	0	4.31
Larry Andersen	R	32	3	3	.500	3	57	0	0	73	78	26	50	0	4.32
1 Rick Surhoff	R	22	1	0	1.000	0	2	0	0	1	2	0	1	0	0.00
Dave Shipanoff	R	25	1	2	.333	3	26	0	0	36	33	16	26	0	3.22
Steve Carlton (SJ)	L	40	1	8	.111	0	16	16	0	92	84	53	48	0	3.33
Pat Zachry	R	33	0	0	—	0	10	0	0	13	14	11	8	0	4.26
2 Dave Stewart	R	28	0	0	—	0	4	0	0	4	5	4	2	0	6.23
Rocky Childress	R	23	0	1	.000	0	16	1	0	33	45	9	1	0	6.21
1 Al Holland	L	32	0	1	.000	1	3	0	0	4	5	4	1	0	4.50
Freddie Toliver	R	24	0	4	.000	0	11	3	0	25	27	17	23	0	4.68

PITTSBURGH 6th 57-104 .354 43.5 — CHUCK TANNER

Name	G by Pos	B	AGE	G	AB	R	H	2B	3B	HR	RBI	BB	SO	SB	BA	SA
TOTALS			29	161	5436		1340	251	28	80	535	514	842	110	.247	.347
Jason Thompson	1B114	L	30	123	402	42	97	17	1	12	61	84	58	0	.241	.378
Johnny Ray	2B151	B	28	154	594	67	163	33	3	7	70	46	24	13	.274	.375
Sammy Khalifa	SS95	R	21	95	320	30	76	14	3	2	31	34	56	5	.238	.319
1 Bill Madlock	3B98, 1B12	R	34	110	399	49	100	23	1	10	41	39	42	3	.251	.388
1 George Hendrick	OF65	R	35	69	256	23	59	15	0	2	25	18	42	1	.230	.313
Marvell Wynne	OF99	L	25	103	337	21	69	6	3	2	18	18	48	10	.205	.258
Joe Orsulak	OF115	L	23	121	397	54	119	14	6	0	21	26	27	24	.300	.365
Tony Pena	C146, 1B1	R	28	147	546	53	136	27	2	10	59	29	67	12	.249	.361
Jim Morrison	3B59, 2B15, OF1	R	32	92	244	17	62	10	0	4	22	8	44	3	.254	.344
Steve Kemp	OF63	L	30	92	236	19	59	13	2	2	21	25	54	1	.250	.347
Lee Mazzilli	1B19, OF5	B	30	92	117	20	33	8	0	1	9	29	17	4	.282	.376
Bill Almon	SS43, OF32, 3B7, 1B7	R	32	88	244	33	66	17	0	6	29	22	61	10	.270	.414
Sixto Lezcano	OF40	R	31	72	116	16	24	2	0	3	9	35	17	0	.207	.302
2 Mike Brown	OF56	R	25	57	205	29	68	18	2	5	33	22	27	2	.332	.512
1 Doug Frobel	OF36	L	26	53	109	14	22	5	0	0	7	19	24	4	.202	.248
Denny Gonzalez	3B21, OF13, 2B6	R	21	35	124	11	28	4	0	4	12	13	27	2	.226	.355
2 R.J. Reynolds	OF31	B	25	31	130	22	40	5	3	3	17	9	18	12	.308	.462
2 Sid Bream	1B25	L	24	26	95	14	27	7	0	3	15	11	14	0	.284	.453
Junior Ortiz	C23	R	25	23	72	4	21	2	0	1	5	3	17	1	.292	.361
3 Johnnie LeMaster (NJ)	SS21	R	31	22	58	4	9	0	0	1	6	5	12	1	.155	.207
Tim Foli	SS13	R	34	19	37	1	7	0	0	0	2	4	2	0	.189	.189
Rafael Belliard	SS12	R	23	17	20	1	4	0	0	0	1	0	5	0	.200	.200
Jerry Dybzinski	SS5	R	29	5	4	0	0	0	0	0	0	0	0	0	.000	.000
Scott Loucks	OF4	R	28	4	7	1	2	2	0	0	1	2	0	0	.286	.571
Trench Davis	OF2	L	24	2	7	1	1	0	0	0	0	0	1	0	.143	.143
Ron Wotus 24 (SJ)																

NAME	T	AGE	W	L	PCT	SV	G	GS	CG	IP	H	BB	SO	SHO	ERA
		28	57	104	.354	29	161	161	15	1445	1406	584	962	6	3.97
Rick Reuschel	R	46	14	8	.636	1	31	26	9	194	153	52	138	1	2.27
Rick Rhoden	R	32	10	15	.400	0	35	35	2	213	254	69	128	0	4.47
Larry McWilliams (SJ)	L	31	7	9	.438	0	30	19	2	126	139	62	52	0	4.70
Don Robinson	R	28	5	11	.313	3	44	6	0	95	95	42	65	0	3.87
Cecilio Guante	R	24	4	6	.400	5	63	0	0	109	84	40	92	0	2.70
Lee Tunnell	R	24	4	10	.286	0	24	23	0	132	126	57	74	0	4.01
Jim Winn	R	25	3	6	.333	0	30	7	0	76	77	31	22	0	5.23
Mike Bielecki	R	25	2	3	.400	0	12	7	0	46	45	31	22	0	4.53
Bob Walk	R	28	2	3	.400	0	9	9	1	59	60	18	40	1	3.68
1 John Candelaria	L	31	2	4	.333	9	37	0	0	54	57	14	47	0	3.64
Jose DeLeon	R	24	2	19	.095	3	31	25	1	163	138	89	149	0	4.70
2 Bob Kipper	L	20	1	2	.333	0	5	4	0	25	21	7	13	0	5.11
1 Al Holland	L	32	1	3	.250	4	38	0	0	59	48	17	47	0	3.38
2 Kent Tekulve	R	38	1	0	1.000	0	3	0	0	3	7	5	4	0	16.20
Dave Tomlin	L	36	0	0	—	0	1	0	0	1	1	1	0	0	0.00
1 Rod Scurry (DR)	L	29	0	1	.000	2	30	0	0	48	42	28	43	0	3.21
2 Pat Clements	L	23	0	2	.000	2	27	0	0	34	39	15	17	0	3.67
Ray Krawczyk	R	25	0	2	.000	0	6	0	0	6	9	6	9	0	14.04

WEST DIVISION

LOS ANGELES 1st 95-67 .586 — TOMMY LASORDA

Name	G by Pos	B	AGE	G	AB	R	H	2B	3B	HR	RBI	BB	SO	SB	BA	SA
TOTALS			28	162	5502	682	1434	226	28	129	632	539	846	136	.261	.382
Greg Brock	1B122	L	28	129	438	64	110	19	0	21	66	54	72	4	.251	.438
Steve Sax	2B135, 3B1	R	25	136	488	62	136	8	4	1	42	54	43	27	.279	.318
Mariano Duncan	SS123, 2B19	B	22	142	562	74	137	24	6	6	39	38	113	38	.244	.340
Dave Anderson (XJ)	3B51, SS25, 2B2	R	24	77	221	24	44	6	0	4	18	35	42	5	.199	.281
Mike Marshall (IL)	OF125, 1B7	R	25	135	518	72	152	27	2	28	95	37	137	3	.293	.515
Ken Landreaux	OF140	L	30	147	482	70	129	26	2	12	50	33	37	15	.268	.405
Pedro Guerrero	OF81, 3B44, 1B12	R	29	137	487	99	156	22	2	33	87	83	68	12	.320	.577
Mike Scioscia	C139	L	26	141	429	47	127	26	3	7	53	77	21	3	.296	.420
Candy Maldonado	OF113	R	24	121	213	20	48	7	1	5	19	19	40	1	.225	.338
Terry Whitfield	OF28	L	32	79	104	8	27	7	0	3	16	6	27	0	.260	.413
Bill Russell (IJ)	SS23, OF21, 2B8, 3B5	R	36	76	169	19	44	6	1	0	13	18	9	4	.260	.308
Bob Bailor	3B45, 2B16, SS5, OF1	R	33	74	118	8	29	3	1	0	7	5	13	1	.246	.288
2 Enos Cabell	3B32, 1B21, OF4	R	36	73	207	22	55	10	4	0	25	13	31	6	.266	.353
1 R.J. Reynolds	OF54	B	25	57	192	20	56	11	0	0	22	14	21	6	.292	.349
Steve Yeager	C48	R	36	53	121	4	25	4	1	0	9	7	24	0	.207	.256
2 Len Matuszek	OF17, 1B10, 3B1	L	30	43	63	10	14	2	1	3	13	8	14	0	.222	.429
1 Al Oliver	OF17	L	38	35	79	1	20	5	0	0	8	5	11	1	.253	.316
2 Bill Matlock	3B32	R	34	34	114	20	41	4	0	2	15	10	11	7	.360	.447
1 Sid Bream	1B16	L	24	24	53	4	7	0	0	3	6	7	10	0	.132	.302
Jose Gonzalez	OF18	R	20	23	11	6	3	2	0	0	0	1	3	1	.273	.455
Reggie Williams	OF15	R	24	22	9	4	3	0	0	0	0	0	4	1	.333	.333
Jay Johnstone (PJ-XJ)		L	39	17	15	0	2	1	0	0	2	1	3	0	.133	.200
Franklin Stubbs	1B4	L	24	10	9	0	2	0	0	0	2	0	3	0	.222	.222
Mike Ramsey	SS4, 2B2	B	30	9	15	1	2	1	0	0	2	4	0	.133	.200
Stu Pederson	OF5	L	25	8	4	1	0	0	0	0	1	0	0	.000	.000
Ralph Bryant	OF3	L	21	6	6	0	2	0	0	0	0	0	3	0	.333	.333
Gil Reyes	C6	R	21	6	1	0	0	0	0	0	0	1	1	0	.000	.000

NAME	T	AGE	W	L	PCT	SV	G	GS	CG	IP	H	BB	SO	SHO	ERA
		27	95	67	.586	36	162	162	37	1465	1280	462	979	21	2.96
Orel Hershiser	R	26	19	3	.864	0	36	34	9	240	179	68	157	5	2.03
Fernando Valenzuela	L	24	17	10	.630	0	35	35	14	272	211	101	208	5	2.45
Bob Welch (EJ)	R	28	14	4	.778	0	23	23	8	167	141	35	96	3	2.31
Jerry Reuss	L	36	14	10	.583	0	34	44	5	213	210	58	84	3	2.92
Rick Honeycutt	L	31	8	12	.400	1	31	25	1	142	141	49	67	0	3.42
Tom Niedenfuer	R	25	7	9	.438	19	64	0	0	106	86	24	102	0	2.71
Carlos Diaz	L	27	6	3	.667	0	46	0	0	79	70	18	73	0	2.61
Ken Howell	R	24	4	7	.364	12	56	0	0	86	66	35	85	0	3.77
Bobby Castillo	R	30	2	2	.500	0	35	5	0	68	59	41	57	0	5.43
1 Steve Howe	L	27	1	1	.500	3	19	0	0	22	30	5	11	0	4.91
Dennis Powell	L	21	1	1	.500	1	16	2	0	29	30	13	19	0	5.22
Brian Holton	R	25	1	1	.500	0	3	0	0	4	9	1	1	0	9.00
Tom Brennan	R	32	1	3	.250	0	12	4	0	32	41	11	17	0	7.39
Alejandro Pena (SJ)	R	26	0	1	.000	0	2	0	0	4	7	3	2	0	8.31

CINCINNATI 2nd 89-72 .553 5.5 — PETE ROSE

Name	G by Pos	B	AGE	G	AB	R	H	2B	3B	HR	RBI	BB	SO	SB	BA	SA
TOTALS			33	162	5431	677	1385	249	34	114	634	576	865	159	.255	.376
Pete Rose	1B110	B	44	119	405	60	107	12	2	2	46	86	35	8	.264	.319
Ron Oester	2B149	B	29	152	526	59	155	26	3	1	34	51	65	5	.295	.361
Dave Concepcion	SS151, 3B5	R	37	155	560	59	141	19	2	7	48	50	67	16	.252	.330
2 Buddy Bell	3B67	R	33	67	247	28	54	15	2	6	36	34	27	0	.219	.368
Dave Parker	OF159	L	34	160	635	88	198	42	4	34	125	52	80	5	.312	.551
Eddie Milner	OF135	L	30	145	453	82	115	19	7	3	33	61	31	35	.254	.347
Gary Redus	OF85	R	28	101	246	51	62	14	4	6	28	44	52	48	.252	.415
2 Bo Diaz	C51	R	32	51	161	12	42	8	0	3	15	15	18	0	.261	.366
Nick Esasky	3B62, OF54, 1B12	R	25	125	413	61	108	21	0	21	66	41	102	3	.262	.465
Wayne Krenchicki	3B52, 2B3	L	30	90	173	16	47	9	0	4	25	28	20	0	.272	.393
1 Cesar Cedeno	OF53, 1B34	R	34	83	220	24	53	12	0	3	30	19	35	9	.241	.355
Max Venable	OF39	L	28	77	135	21	39	12	3	0	10	6	17	11	.289	.422
Dave Van Gorder	C70	R	28	73	151	12	36	7	0	2	24	9	19	0	.238	.325
Tony Perez	1B50	R	43	72	183	25	60	8	0	6	33	22	22	0	.328	.470
Eric Davis	OF47	R	23	56	122	26	30	3	3	8	18	7	39	16	.246	.516
1 Alan Knicely	C46	R	30	48	158	17	40	9	0	5	26	16	34	0	.253	.405
1 Tom Foley	2B18, SS15, 3B1	L	25	43	92	7	18	5	1	0	6	4	16	0	.196	.272
Dann Bilardello	C42	R	26	42	102	6	17	6	0	4	15			0	.167	.196
1 Duane Walker	OF10	L	28	37	48	5	9	1	0	3	7	6	18	1	.167	.375
Tom Runnells	SS11, 2B1	B	30	28	35	3	7	1	0	0	3	4	0	.200	.229
Paul O'Neill	OF2	L	22	5	12	1	4	1	0	0	1	0	0	.333	.417
Wade Rowdon	3B4	R	24	5	9	1	2	0	0	0	0	0	2	0	.222	.222

NAME	T	AGE	W	L	PCT	SV	G	GS	CG	IP	H	BB	SO	SHO	ERA
		27	89	72	.553	45	162	162	24	1451	1347	535	910	11	3.71
Tom Browning	L	25	20	9	.690	0	38	38	6	261	242	73	155	4	3.55
John Franco	L	24	12	3	.800	12	67	0	0	99	83	40	61	0	2.18
Mario Soto	R	28	12	15	.444	0	36	36	9	257	196	104	214	1	3.58
Jay Tibbs	R	23	10	16	.385	0	35	34	5	218	216	83	98	2	3.92
John Stuper	R	28	8	5	.615	0	33	13	1	99	116	37	38	0	4.55
Ted Power	R	30	8	6	.571	27	64	0	0	80	65	45	42	0	2.70
Ron Robinson	R	23	7	7	.500	3	33	12	0	108	107	32	76	0	3.99
Andy McGaffigan	R	28	3	3	.500	0	15	15	2	94	88	30	83	0	3.72
Tom Hume	R	32	3	5	.375	3	56	0	0	80	65	35	50	0	3.26
Frank Pastore (EJ)	R	27	1	1	.667	0	17	6	1	54	60	16	29	0	3.83
Joe Price (EJ)	L	28	2	1	.500	1	26	8	0	65	59	23	52	0	3.90
Bob Buchanan (EJ)	L	24	1	0	1.000	0	1	0	0	3	5	9	3	0	8.44
Carl Willis	R	24	1	0	1.000	1	11	0	0	14	21	5	6	0	9.00
Mike Smith	R	24	0	0	—	0	2	0	0	3	2	1	2	0	5.40
Rob Murphy	L	25	0	0	—	0	2	0	0	3	4	1	1	0	6.00

HOUSTON (TIE) 3rd 83-79 .512 12   BOB LILLIS

Name	G by Pos	B	AGE	G	AB	R	H	2B	3B	HR	RBI	BB	SO	SB	BA	SA
TOTALS			30	162	5582	706	1457	261	42	121	666	477	873	96	.261	.388
Glenn Davis	1B89, OF9	R	24	100	350	51	95	11	0	20	64	27	68	0	.271	.474
Bill Doran	2B147	B	27	148	578	84	166	31	6	14	59	71	69	23	.287	.434
Craig Reynolds	SS102, 2B1	L	32	107	379	43	103	18	8	4	32	12	30	4	.272	.393
Phil Garner	3B123, 2B15	R	36	135	463	65	124	23	10	6	51	34	72	4	.268	.400
Jerry Mumphrey	OF126	B	32	130	444	52	123	25	2	8	61	37	57	6	.277	.396
Kevin Bass	OF141	B	26	150	539	72	145	27	5	16	68	31	63	19	.268	.427
Jose Cruz	OF137	L	37	141	544	69	163	34	4	9	79	43	74	16	.300	.426
Mark Bailey	C110, 1B2	B	23	114	332	47	88	14	0	10	45	67	70	0	.265	.398
Denny Walling	3B51, 1B46, OF13	L	31	119	345	44	93	20	1	7	45	25	26	5	.270	.394
Dickie Thon (IJ)	SS79	R	27	84	251	26	63	6	1	6	29	18	50	2	.251	.355
Jim Pankovits (LJ)	OF33, 2B21, 3B1, SS1	R	29	75	172	24	42	3	0	4	14	17	29	1	.244	.331
Alan Ashby (BG)	C60	B	33	65	189	20	53	8	0	8	25	24	27	0	.280	.450
1 Enos Cabell	1B49	R	35	60	143	20	35	8	1	2	14	16	15	3	.245	.357
Terry Puhl (LJ)	OF53	L	28	57	194	34	55	14	3	2	23	18	23	6	.284	.418
Harry Spilman	1B19, C2	L	30	44	66	3	9	1	0	1	4	3	7	0	.136	.197
Tim Tolman	OF9, 1B6	R	29	31	43	4	6	1	0	2	8	1	10	0	.140	.302
Chris Jones	OF15	L	27	31	25	0	5	0	0	0	2	4	7	0	.200	.200
Bert Pena (IJ-WJ)	3B7, SS6, 2B2	R	25	20	29	7	8	2	0	0	4	1	6	0	.276	.345
Eric Bullock	OF7	L	25	18	25	3	7	2	0	0	2	1	3	0	.280	.360
John Mizerock	C15	R	25	15	38	6	9	4	0	0	6	2	8	0	.237	.342
Ty Gainey	OF9	L	24	13	37	5	6	0	0	0	2	0	9	0	.162	.162
Grerman Rivera	3B11	R	25	13	36	3	7	2	1	0	2	4	8	0	.194	.306
Mike Richardt 27 (SJ)																

NAME	T	AGE	W	L	PCT	SV	G	GS	CG	IP	H	BB	SO	SHO	ERA
TOTALS		30	83	79	.512	42	162	162	17	1458	1393	543	909	9	3.66
Mike Scott	R	30	18	8	.692	0	36	35	4	222	194	80	137	2	3.29
Bob Knepper	L	31	15	13	.536	0	37	37	4	241	253	54	131	0	3.50
Nolan Ryan	R	38	10	12	.455	0	35	35	4	232	205	95	209	0	3.80
Dave Smith	R	30	9	5	.643	27	64	0	0	79	69	17	40	0	2.27
1 Joe Niekro	R	40	9	12	.429	0	32	32	4	213	197	99	117	1	3.72
Bill Dawley	R	27	5	3	.625	2	49	0	0	81	76	37	48	0	3.56
Charley Kerfeld	R	21	4	2	.667	0	11	6	0	44	44	25	30	0	4.06
Jeff Heathcock	R	25	3	1	.750	1	14	7	1	56	50	13	25	0	3.36
Ron Mathis	R	26	3	5	.375	1	23	8	0	70	83	27	34	0	6.04
Frank DiPino	L	28	3	7	.300	6	54	0	0	76	69	43	49	0	4.03
Julio Solano	R	25	2	2	.500	0	20	0	0	34	34	3	17	0	3.48
Jeff Calhoun	L	27	2	5	.286	4	44	0	0	64	56	24	47	0	2.54
Mike Madden (BG)	L	27	1	0	—	0	13	0	0	19	29	11	16	0	4.26
Jim Deshaies	L	25	0	0	—	0	2	0	0	3	1	0	2	0	0.00
Mark Ross	R	27	0	2	.000	1	8	0	0	13	12	2	3	0	4.85
Mark Knudson	R	24	0	2	.000	0	7	1	0	11	21	3	4	0	9.00

SAN DIEGO (TIE) 3rd 83-79 .512 12   DICK WILLIAMS

Name	G by Pos	B	AGE	G	AB	R	H	2B	3B	HR	RBI	BB	SO	SB	BA	SA
TOTALS			30	162	5507	650	1405	241	28	109	611	513	809	60	.255	.368
Steve Garvey	1B162	R	36	162	654	80	184	34	6	17	81	35	67	0	.281	.430
Tim Flannery	2B121, 3B1	L	27	126	384	50	108	14	3	1	40	58	39	2	.281	.341
Garry Templeton	SS148	B	29	148	546	63	154	30	2	6	55	41	88	16	.282	.377
Graig Nettles	3B130	L	40	137	440	66	115	23	1	15	61	72	59	0	.261	.420
Tony Gwynn	OF152	L	25	154	622	90	197	29	5	6	46	45	33	14	.317	.408
Kevin McReynolds	OF150	R	25	152	564	61	132	24	4	15	75	43	81	4	.234	.371
Carmelo Martinez	OF150, 1B3	R	24	150	514	64	130	28	1	21	72	87	82	0	.253	.434
Terry Kennedy	C140, 1B5	L	29	143	532	54	139	27	1	10	74	31	102	0	.261	.372
Jerry Royster	2B58, 3B29, SS7, OF2	R	32	90	249	31	70	13	2	5	31	32	31	6	.281	.410
Bobby Brown	OF28	B	31	79	84	8	13	3	0	0	6	5	20	6	.155	.190
Kurt Bevacqua	3B33, 1B9, OF1	R	38	71	138	17	33	6	0	3	25	25	17	0	.239	.349
Al Brumbry	OF17	L	38	68	95	6	19	3	0	1	10	7	9	2	.200	.263
Bruce Bochy	C46	R	30	48	112	16	30	2	0	6	13	6	30	0	.268	.446
Jerry Davis	OF23	R	26	44	58	10	17	3	1	0	2	5	7	0	.293	.379
Mario Ramirez	SS27, 2B7	R	27	37	60	6	17	0	0	2	5	3	11	0	.283	.383
2 Miguel Dilone	OF14	B	30	27	46	8	10	0	1	0	1	4	8	10	.217	.261
1 Alan Wiggins (DR)	2B9	B	27	10	37	3	2	1	0	0	0	2	4	0	.054	.081
Eddie Rodriguez		R	24	1	1	0	0	0	0	0	0	0	0	0	.000	.000

NAME	T	AGE	W	L	PCT	SV	G	GS	CG	IP	H	BB	SO	SHO	ERA
TOTALS		28	83	79	.512	44	162	162	19	1451	1399	443	727	19	3.40
Andy Hawkins	R	25	18	8	.692	0	33	33	5	229	229	65	69	2	3.15
LaMarr Hoyt	R	30	16	8	.667	0	31	31	8	210	210	20	83	3	3.47
Dave Dravecky	L	29	13	11	.542	0	34	31	7	215	205	57	105	2	2.93
Eric Show	R	29	12	11	.522	0	35	35	5	233	212	87	141	2	3.09
Craig Lefferts	L	27	7	6	.538	2	60	0	0	83	75	30	48	0	3.35
Mark Thurmond	L	29	7	11	.389	2	36	23	1	138	154	44	57	1	3.97
Goose Gossage (KJ)	R	33	5	3	.625	26	50	0	0	79	64	17	52	0	1.82
Roy Lee Jackson	R	31	2	3	.400	2	22	2	0	40	32	13	28	0	2.70
Ed Wojna	R	24	2	4	.333	0	15	7	0	42	53	19	18	0	5.79
Tim Stoddard	R	32	1	6	.143	1	44	0	0	60	63	37	42	0	4.65
Bob Patterson	R	26	0	0	—	0	4	0	0	13	3	1	7	0	24.75
Greg Booker	R	25	0	1	.000	0	17	0	0	22	20	17	7	0	6.85
Lance McCullers	R	22	0	2	.000	5	21	0	0	35	23	16	27	0	2.31
Gene Walter	L	24	0	2	.000	3	15	0	0	22	12	8	18	0	2.05
Luis DeLeon	R	26	0	3	.000	1	39	0	0	39	39	16	31	0	4.19

ATLANTA 5th 66-96 .407 29   EDDIE HAAS 50-71 .413   BOBBY WINE 16-25 .390

Name	G by Pos	B	AGE	G	AB	R	H	2B	3B	HR	RBI	BB	SO	SB	BA	SA
TOTALS			28	162	5526	632	1359	213	28	126	598	553	849	72	.246	.363
Bob Horner	1B87, 3B40	R	27	130	483	61	129	25	3	27	89	50	57	1	.267	.499
Glenn Hubbard	2B140	R	27	142	439	51	102	21	0	5	39	56	54	4	.232	.314
Rafael Ramirez	SS133	R	27	138	568	54	141	25	4	5	58	20	63	2	.248	.333
Ken Oberkfell	3B117, 2B16	L	29	134	412	30	112	19	4	3	35	51	38	1	.272	.359
Claudell Washington	OF99	L	30	122	398	62	110	14	6	15	43	40	66	14	.276	.455
Dale Murphy	OF161	R	29	162	616	118	185	32	3	37	111	90	141	10	.300	.539
Terry Harper	OF131	R	29	138	492	58	130	15	2	17	72	44	76	9	.264	.407
Rick Cerone	C91	R	31	96	282	15	61	9	0	3	25	29	25	0	.216	.280
Gerald Perry	1B55, OF1	L	24	110	238	22	51	5	0	3	13	23	28	9	.214	.273
Brad Komminsk	OF92	R	24	106	300	52	68	12	3	4	21	38	71	10	.227	.327
Chris Chambliss	1B36	L	36	101	170	16	40	7	0	3	21	18	22	0	.235	.329
Paul Zuvella	2B42, SS33, 3B5	R	26	81	190	16	48	8	1	0	4	16	14	2	.253	.305
Milt Thompson	OF49	L	26	73	182	17	55	7	2	0	6	7	36	9	.302	.363
Bruce Benedict	C70	R	29	70	208	12	42	6	0	0	20	22	12	0	.202	.231
Albert Hall	OF13	R	27	54	47	5	7	0	1	0	3	9	12	1	.149	.191
Paul Runge	3B28, SS5, 2B2	R	27	50	87	15	19	3	0	1	5	18	18	0	.218	.287
Larry Owen	C25	R	30	26	71	7	17	3	0	2	12	8	17	0	.239	.366
Andres Thomas	SS10	R	21	15	18	6	5	0	0	0	2	0	2	0	.278	.278
John Rabb	OF1	R	25	3	3	0	0	0	0	0	0	0	1	0	.000	.000

NAME	T	AGE	W	L	PCT	SV	G	GS	CG	IP	H	BB	SO	SHO	ERA
TOTALS		29	66	96	.407	29	162	162	9	1457	1512	642	776	9	4.19
Rick Mahler	R	31	17	15	.531	0	39	39	6	267	272	79	107	1	3.48
Zane Smith (XJ)	L	24	9	10	.474	0	42	18	2	147	135	80	85	2	3.80
Bruce Sutter	R	32	7	7	.500	23	58	0	0	88	91	29	52	0	4.48
Steve Bedrosian	R	27	7	15	.318	0	37	37	0	207	198	111	134	0	3.83
Jeff Dedmon	R	25	6	6	.667	0	60	0	0	86	84	49	41	0	4.08
Gene Garber	R	37	6	6	.500	1	59	0	0	97	98	25	66	0	3.61
Joe Johnson	R	23	4	4	.500	0	15	14	1	86	95	24	34	0	4.10
Rick Camp	R	32	4	6	.400	3	66	2	0	128	130	61	49	0	3.95
Terry Forster	L	33	2	3	.400	1	46	0	0	59	49	28	37	0	2.28
Len Barker (EJ)	R	29	2	9	.182	0	20	18	0	74	84	37	47	0	6.35
Steve Shields	R	26	1	2	.333	0	23	6	0	68	86	32	29	0	5.16
Pascual Perez (SJ)	R	28	1	13	.071	0	22	22	0	95	115	57	57	0	6.14
Dave Schuler	R	31	0	0	—	0	11	0	0	11	13	3	10	0	6.75
Craig McMurtry	R	25	0	3	.000	1	17	6	0	45	56	27	28	0	6.60

SAN FRANCISCO 6th 62-100 .383 33   JIM DAVENPORT 56-88 .389   ROGER CRAIG 6-12 .333

Name	G by Pos	B	AGE	G	AB	R	H	2B	3B	HR	RBI	BB	SO	SB	BA	SA
TOTALS			28	162	5420	556	1263	217	31	115	517	488	962	99	.233	.348
David Green	1B78, OF12	R	24	106	294	36	73	10	2	5	20	22	58	6	.248	.347
Manny Trillo	2B120, 3B1	R	34	125	451	36	101	16	2	3	25	40	44	2	.224	.288
Jose Uribe	SS145, 2B1	B	26	147	476	46	113	20	4	3	26	30	57	8	.237	.315
Chris Brown	3B120	R	23	131	432	50	117	20	3	16	61	38	78	2	.271	.412
Chili Davis	OF126	B	25	136	481	53	130	25	2	13	56	62	74	15	.270	.412
Dan Gladden	OF124	R	27	142	502	64	122	15	8	7	41	40	78	32	.243	.359
Jeff Leonard	OF126	R	29	133	507	49	122	20	3	17	62	21	107	11	.241	.393
Bob Brenly	C110, 3B17, 1B10	R	31	123	440	41	97	16	1	19	56	57	62	1	.220	.391
Joel Youngblood	OF56, 3B1	R	33	95	230	24	62	6	0	4	24	30	37	3	.270	.348
Rob Deer	OF37, 1B10	R	24	78	162	22	30	5	1	8	20	23	71	0	.185	.377
Brad Wellman (KJ)	2B36, 3B25, SS3	R	25	71	174	16	41	11	1	0	16	4	33	5	.236	.310
Ron Roenicke	OF35	B	28	65	133	23	34	9	1	3	13	35	27	6	.256	.406
1 Scot Thompson	1B24	L	29	64	111	8	23	5	0	0	2	2	10	0	.207	.252
Alex Trevino	C55, 3B1	R	27	57	157	17	34	10	1	6	19	20	24	0	.217	.408
2 Dan Driessen	1B49	L	33	54	181	22	42	8	0	3	22	17	22	0	.232	.326
Rick Adams	SS25, 3B16, 2B6	R	26	54	121	12	23	3	1	2	10	5	23	1	.190	.281
Gary Rajsich	1B23	L	30	51	91	5	15	6	0	0	10	17	2	0	.165	.231
Mike Woodward	2B23	L	25	24	82	12	20	1	0	0	9	5	3	6	.244	.256
Matt Nokes	C14	L	21	19	53	3	11	2	0	2	5	1	9	0	.208	.358
1 Johnnie LeMaster	SS10	R	31	12	16	1	0	0	0	0	0	0	6	0	.000	.000
Duane Kuiper (NJ)		L	35	9	5	0	3	0	0	0	0	1	0	0	.600	.600

NAME	T	AGE	W	L	PCT	SV	G	GS	CG	IP	H	BB	SO	SHO	ERA
TOTALS		28	62	100	.383	24	162	162	13	1448	1348	572	985	5	3.61
Scott Garrelts	R	23	9	6	.600	13	74	0	0	106	78	58	106	0	2.30
Vida Blue	L	35	8	8	.500	0	33	20	1	131	115	80	103	0	4.47
Mike Krukow (RJ)	R	33	8	11	.421	0	28	28	6	195	176	49	150	1	3.38
Jim Gott	R	25	7	10	.412	0	26	26	2	148	144	51	78	0	3.88
Dave LaPoint	L	25	7	17	.292	0	31	31	2	207	215	74	122	1	3.57
Greg Minton	R	33	5	4	.556	4	68	0	0	97	98	54	37	0	3.54
1 Bill Laskey	R	27	5	11	.313	0	19	19	0	114	110	39	42	0	3.55
Mark Davis	L	24	5	12	.294	7	77	1	0	114	89	41	131	0	3.54
Atlee Hammaker	L	27	5	12	.294	0	29	29	1	171	161	47	100	1	3.74
Frank Williams	R	27	2	4	.333	0	49	0	0	73	56	35	54	0	4.19
Roger Mason	R	26	1	3	.250	0	5	5	1	30	28	11	26	1	2.12
Bobby Moore	R	26	0	0	—	0	11	0	0	17	18	10	10	0	3.24
Jeff Robinson	R	24	0	0	—	0	8	0	0	12	16	10	8	0	5.11
Colin Ward	L	24	0	0	—	0	6	2	0	12	10	7	8	0	4.38
2 Mike Jeffcoat	L	25	0	2	.000	0	19	1	0	22	27	6	10	0	5.32

LINE SCORES

Team	1	2	3	4	5	6	7	8	9	10	11		R	H	E

AMERICAN LEAGUE CHAMPIONSHIPS: KANSAS CITY (WEST) 4   TORONTO (EAST) 3

Game 1 October 8 at Toronto

												R	H	E
KC	0	0	0	0	0	0	0	0	1	1	5	1
TOR	0	2	3	1	0	0	0	0	X	6	11	0

Leibrandt, Farr (3)   Stieb, Henke (9)
Gubicza (5), Jackson (8)

Game 2 October 9 at Toronto

												R	H	E
KC	0	0	2	1	0	0	0	0	1	1	5	10	3
TOR	0	0	0	1	0	2	0	1	0	2	6	10	0

Black, **Quisenberry** (8)   Key, Lamp (4), Lavelle (8)
                                     Henke (8)

Game 3 October 11 at Kansas City

											R	H	E
TOR	0	0	0	0	5	0	0	0	0	5	13	1
KC	1	0	0	1	1	2	0	1	X	6	10	1

Alexander, Lamp (6),   Saberhagen, Black (5),
Clancy (8)   Farr (5)

Game 4 October 12 at Kansas City

											R	H	E
TOR	0	0	0	0	0	0	0	0	3	3	7	0
KC	0	0	0	0	0	1	0	0	0	1	2	0

Stieb, **Henke** (7)   Leibrandt, Quisenberry (9)

Game 5 October 13 at Kansas City

											R	H	E
TOR	0	0	0	0	0	0	0	0	0	0	8	0
KC	1	1	0	0	0	0	0	0	X	2	8	0

Key, Acker (6)   Jackson

Game 6 October 15 at Toronto

											R	H	E
KC	1	0	1	0	1	2	0	0	0	5	8	1
TOR	1	0	1	0	0	1	0	0	0	3	8	2

Gubicza, Black (6),   Alexander, Lamp (6)
Quisenberry

Game 7 October 16 at Toronto

											R	H	E
KC	0	1	0	1	0	4	0	0	0	6	8	0
TOR	0	0	0	1	0	0	0	0	1	2	8	1

Saberhagen, Leibrandt (4),   Stieb, Acker (6)
Quisenberry

NATIONAL LEAGUE CHAMPIONSHIPS: ST. LOUIS (EAST) 4   LOS ANGELES (WEST) 2

Game 1 October 9 at Los Angeles

											R	H	E
STL	0	0	0	0	0	0	1	0	0	1	8	1
LA	0	0	0	1	0	3	0	0	X	4	8	0

Tudor, Dayley (6),   Valenzuela, Niedenfuer (7)
Campbell (7), Worrell (8)

Game 2 October 10 at Los Angeles

											R	H	E
STL	0	0	1	0	0	0	0	0	1	2	8	1
LA	0	0	3	2	1	2	0	0	X	8	13	1

Andujar, Horton (5)   Hershiser
Campbell (6), Dayley (7),
Lahti (8)

Game 3 October 12 at St. Louis

											R	H	E
LA	0	0	0	1	0	0	1	0	0	2	7	2
STL	2	2	0	0	0	0	0	0	X	4	8	0

Welch, Honeycutt (3),   Cox, Horton (7), Worrell (7),
Diaz (5), Howell (7)   Dayley (9)

Game 4 October 13 at St. Louis

											R	H	E
LA	0	0	0	0	0	0	1	1	0	2	5	2
STL	0	9	0	1	1	0	0	1	X	12	15	0

Reuss, Honeycutt (2),   Tudor, Horton (8).
Castillo (2), Diaz (8)   Campbell (9)

Game 5 October 14 at St. Louis

											R	H	E
LA	0	0	0	2	0	0	0	0	0	2	5	1
STL	2	0	0	0	0	0	0	0	1	3	5	0

Valenzuela, **Niedenfuer** (9)   Forsch, Dayley (4), Worrell (7),
                                    Lahti (9)

Game 6 October 16 at Los Angeles

											R	H	E
STL	0	0	1	0	0	0	3	0	3	7	12	1
LA	1	1	0	0	2	0	0	1	0	5	8	0

Andujar, **Worrell** (7),   Hershiser, **Niedenfuer** (7)
Dayley

COMPOSITE BATTING

Kansas City

NAME	POS	G	AB	R	H	2B	3B	HR	RBI	BA
	TOTALS	7	227	26	51	9	1	7	26	.225
Wilson	CF	7	29	5	9	0	0	1	2	.310
Smith	LF	7	28	2	7	2	0	0	1	.250
White	2B	7	25	1	5	0	0	0	3	.200
Balboni	1B	7	25	1	3	0	0	0	1	.120
Sundberg	C	7	24	3	4	1	1	1	6	.167
Brett	3B	7	23	6	8	2	0	3	5	.348
McRae	DH	6	23	1	6	2	0	0	3	.261
Sheridan	RF-PH	7	20	4	3	0	0	2	3	.150
Biancalana	SS	7	18	2	4	1	0	0	1	.222
Orta	DH-PH	2	5	0	0	0	0	0	0	.000
Motley	RF	3	3	1	1	0	0	0	1	.333
D. Iorg	PH	4	2	0	1	1	0	0	0	.500
Concepcion	SS-PR	4	1	0	0	0	0	0	0	.000
Quirk	PH	1	1	0	0	0	0	0	0	.000
Jones	LF	5	0	0	0	0	0	0	0	—

Toronto

NAME	POS	G	AB	R	H	2B	3B	HR	RBI	BA
	TOTALS	7	242	25	65	19	0	2	23	.269
Moseby	CF	7	31	5	7	1	0	0	4	.226
Garcia	2B	7	30	4	7	4	0	0	1	.233
Bell	LF	7	28	4	9	3	0	0	1	.321
Upshaw	1B	7	26	2	6	2	0	0	1	.231
Barfield	RF	7	25	3	7	1	0	1	4	.280
Fernandez	SS	7	24	2	8	2	0	0	3	.333
Whitt	C	7	21	1	4	1	0	0	2	.190
Johnson	DH-PH	7	19	1	7	2	0	0	2	.368
G. Iorg	3B-PH	6	15	1	2	0	0	0	0	.133
Mulliniks	PH-3B	5	11	4	4	1	0	1	3	.364
Oliver	PH-DH	4	8	0	3	1	0	0	3	.375
Fielder	PH	3	3	0	1	0	0	0	0	.333
Burroughs	PH	1	1	0	0	0	0	0	0	.000
Thornton	PR	2	0	1	0	0	0	0	0	—
Hearron	C	2	0	0	0	0	0	0	0	—
Lee	PR-2B	1	0	0	0	0	0	0	0	—

St. Louis

NAME	POS	G	AB	R	H	2B	3B	HR	RBI	BA
	TOTALS	6	201	29	56	10	1	3	26	.279
McGee	CF	6	26	6	7	1	0	0	3	.269
Pendleton	3B	6	24	2	5	1	0	0	4	.208
Smith	SS	6	23	4	10	1	1	1	3	.435
Clark	1B	6	21	4	8	0	0	1	4	.381
Herr	2B	6	21	2	7	4	0	1	6	.333
Porter	C	5	15	1	4	1	0	0	0	.267
Landrum	LF-RF-PH	5	14	2	6	0	0	0	4	.429
Coleman	LF	3	14	2	4	0	0	0	1	.286
Cedeno	RF-PH	5	12	2	2	1	0	0	0	.167
Van Slyke	RF-PR	5	11	1	1	0	0	0	0	.091
Andujar	P	2	4	1	1	1	0	0	0	.250
Tudor	P	2	4	1	0	0	0	0	0	.000
Nieto	C	1	3	1	0	0	0	0	0	.000
Dayley	P	5	2	0	1	0	0	0	0	.500
Braun	PH	2	2	0	0	0	0	0	0	.000
Jorgensen	PH	2	2	0	0	0	0	0	0	.000
Cox	P	1	2	0	0	0	0	0	0	.000
Harper	PH	1	1	0	0	0	0	0	0	.000
Worrell	P	4	0	0	0	0	0	0	0	—
Campbell	P	3	0	0	0	0	0	0	0	—
Horton	P	3	0	0	0	0	0	0	0	—
Lahti	P	2	0	0	0	0	0	0	0	—
Forsch	P	1	0	0	0	0	0	0	0	—

Los Angeles

NAME	POS	G	AB	R	H	2B	3B	HR	RBI	BA
	TOTALS	6	197	23	46	12	1	5	23	.234
Madlock	3B	6	24	5	8	1	0	3	7	.333
Marshall	RF	6	23	1	5	2	0	1	3	.217
Sax	2B	6	20	1	6	3	0	0	1	.300
Guerrero	LF	6	20	2	5	1	0	0	4	.250
Landreaux	CF-PH	6	18	4	7	3	0	0	2	.389
Duncan	SS	5	18	4	4	2	1	0	1	.222
Scioscia	C	6	16	2	4	0	0	0	1	.250
Cabell	1B-PH	5	13	1	1	0	0	0	0	.077
Brock	1B-PH	5	12	2	1	0	0	1	2	.083
Hershiser	P	2	7	1	2	0	0	0	1	.286
Maldonado	CF-LF-PH	4	7	0	1	0	0	0	1	.143
Valenzuela	P	2	5	1	1	0	0	0	0	.200
Anderson	SS-3B-PR	4	5	1	0	0	0	0	0	.000
Yeager	C-PH	2	2	0	0	0	0	0	0	.000
Castillo	P	1	2	0	0	0	0	0	0	.000
Matuszek	PH-LF-1B	3	1	1	1	0	0	0	0	1.000
Niedenfuer	P	3	1	0	0	0	0	0	0	.000
Bailor	3B-PR	2	1	0	0	0	0	0	0	.000
Johnstone	PH	1	1	0	0	0	0	0	0	.000
Welch	P	1	1	0	0	0	0	0	0	.000
Diaz	P	2	0	0	0	0	0	0	0	—
Honeycutt	P	2	0	0	0	0	0	0	0	—
Howell	P	1	0	0	0	0	0	0	0	—
Reuss	P	1	0	0	0	0	0	0	0	—
Whitfield	PH	1	0	0	0	0	0	0	0	—

COMPOSITE PITCHING

Kansas City

NAME	G	IP	H	BB	SO	W	L	SV	ERA
TOTALS	7	62.2	65	16	37	4	3	1	3.16
Leibrandt	3	15.1	17	4	6	1	2	0	5.28
Black	3	10.2	11	4	8	0	0	0	1.69
Jackson	2	10	10	1	7	1	0	0	0.00
Gubicza	2	8.1	4	4	4	1	0	0	3.24
Saberhagen	2	7.1	12	2	6	0	0	0	6.14
Farr	2	6.1	4	1	3	1	0	0	1.42
Quisenberry	4	4.2	7	0	3	0	1	1	3.86

Toronto

NAME	G	IP	H	BB	SO	W	L	SV	ERA
TOTALS	7	62	51	22	51	3	4	0	3.77
Stieb	3	20.1	11	10	18	1	1	0	3.10
Alexander	2	10.1	14	3	9	0	1	0	8.71
Lamp	3	9.1	1	1	10	0	0	0	0.00
Key	2	8.2	15	2	5	0	1	0	5.19
Henke	3	6.1	5	4	4	2	0	0	4.26
Acker	2	6	2	0	5	0	0	0	0.00
Clancy	1	1	2	1	0	0	1	0	9.00
Lavelle	1	1	0	1	0	0	0	0	0.00

St. Louis

NAME	G	IP	H	BB	SO	W	L	SV	ERA
TOTALS	6	52	46	19	31	4	2	2	3.46
Tudor	2	12.2	10	3	8	1	1	0	2.84
Andujar	2	10.1	14	4	9	0	1	0	6.97
Worrell	4	6.1	4	2	3	1	0	0	1.42
Dayley	5	6	2	1	3	0	0	2	0.00
Cox	1	6	4	5	4	1	0	0	1.50
Forsch	1	3.1	3	2	0	0	0	0	5.40
Horton	3	3	4	2	1	0	0	0	12.00
Campbell	3	2.1	3	0	2	0	0	0	0.00
Lahti	2	2	2	0	1	1	0	0	0.00

Los Angeles

NAME	G	IP	H	BB	SO	W	L	SV	ERA
TOTALS	6	51.1	56	30	34	2	4	1	3.61
Hershiser	2	15.1	17	6	5	1	0	0	3.52
Valenzuela	2	14.1	11	10	13	1	0	0	1.88
Niedenfuer	3	5.2	5	2	5	0	2	1	6.35
Castillo	1	5.1	4	2	4	0	0	0	3.38
Diaz	2	3	5	1	2	0	0	0	3.00
Welch	1	2.2	5	6	2	0	1	0	6.75
Howell	1	2	0	0	2	0	0	0	0.00
Reuss	1	1.2	5	1	0	0	1	0	10.80
Honeycutt	2	1.1	4	2	1	0	0	0	13.50

LINE SCORES

Team	1	2	3	4	5	6	7	8	9	10		R	H	E

WORLD SERIES: KANSAS CITY (AL) 4 : ST. LOUIS (NL) 3

Game 1 October 19 at Kansas City

	1	2	3	4	5	6	7	8	9	10	R	H	E
STL	0	0	1	0	0	1	0	0	0	1	3	7	1
KC	0	1	0	0	0	0	0	0	0		1	8	0

Tudor, Worrell (7)   Jackson, Quisenberry (8)
                            Black (9)

Game 2 October 20 at Kansas City

	1	2	3	4	5	6	7	8	9	R	H	E
STL	0	0	0	0	0	0	0	0	4	4	6	0
KC	0	0	0	2	0	0	0	0	0	2	9	0

Cox, Dayley (8), Lahti   Liebrandt, Quisenberry (9)

Game 3 October 22 at St. Louis

	1	2	3	4	5	6	7	8	9	R	H	E
KC	0	0	0	2	2	0	2	0	0	6	11	0
STL	0	0	0	0	0	1	0	0	0	1	6	0

Saberhagen   Andujar, Campbell (5),
                    Horton (6), Dayley (8)

Game 4 October 23 at St. Louis

	1	2	3	4	5	6	7	8	9	R	H	E
KC	0	0	0	0	0	0	0	0	0	0	5	1
STL	0	1	1	0	1	0	0	0	X	3	6	0

Black, Beckwith (6),   Tudor
Quisenberry

Game 5 October 24 at St. Louis

	1	2	3	4	5	6	7	8	9	R	H	E
KC	1	3	0	0	0	0	0	1	1	6	11	2
STL	1	0	0	0	0	0	0	0	0	1	5	1

Jackson   Forsch, Horton (2), Campbell (4),
                 Worrell (6), Lahti (8)

Game 6 October 26 at Kansas City

	1	2	3	4	5	6	7	8	9	R	H	E
STL	0	0	0	0	0	0	1	0		1	5	0
KC	0	0	0	0	0	0	0	2		2	10	0

Cox, Dayley (8), Worrell (9)   Liebrandt, Quisenberry (8)

Game 7 October 27 at Kansas City

	1	2	3	4	5	6	7	8	9	R	H	E
STL	0	0	0	0	0	0	0	0	0	0	5	0
KC	0	2	3	0	6	0	0	0	X	11	14	0

Tudor, Campbell (3),   Saberhagen
Lahti (5), Horton (5),
Andujar (5), Forsch (5),
Dayley (7)

COMPOSITE BATTING

KANSAS CITY

NAME	POS	G	AB	R	H	2B	3B	HR	RBI	BA
TOTALS		7	236	28	68	12	2	2	26	.288
Wilson	CF	7	30	2	11	0	1	0	3	.367
White	2B	7	28	4	7	3	0	1	6	.250
Brett	3B	7	27	5	10	1	0	0	1	.370
L. Smith	LF	7	27	4	9	3	0	0	4	.333
Balboni	1B	7	25	2	8	0	0	0	3	.320
Sundberg	C	7	24	6	6	2	0	0	1	.250
Biancalana	SS	7	18	2	5	0	0	0	1	.278
Sheridan	RF-PH	5	18	0	4	2	0	0	1	.222
Motley	RF-PH	5	11	1	4	0	0	1	3	.364
Saberhagen	P	2	7	1	0	0	0	0	0	.000
Jackson	P	2	6	0	0	0	0	0	0	.000
Leibrandt	P	2	4	0	0	0	0	0	0	.000
Jones	LF-PH	6	3	0	2	1	1	0	0	.667
Iorg	PH	3	3	0	1	0	0	0	0	.333
Orta	PH	2	2	0	1	0	0	0	2	.500
McRae	PH	2	1	0	0	0	0	0	0	.000
Wathan	PH-PR	2	1	0	0	0	0	0	0	.000
Black	P	2	1	0	0	0	0	0	0	.000
Quisenberry	P	4	0	0	0	0	0	0	0	—
Concepcion	SS-PR	3	0	0	0	0	0	0	0	0
Pryor	3B	1	0	0	0	0	0	0	0	0
Beckwith	P	1	0	0	0	0	0	0	0	—

ST. LOUIS

NAME	POS	G	AB	R	H	2B	3B	HR	RBI	BA
TOTALS		7	216	13	40	10	1	2	13	.185
McGee	CF	7	27	2	7	2	0	1	2	.259
Herr	2B	7	26	4	7	3	0	1	6	.154
Landrum	LF	7	25	3	9	2	0	1	1	.360
Clark	1B	7	25	1	6	2	0	0	4	.240
Pendleton	3B	7	23	3	6	1	1	0	3	.261
O. Smith	SS	7	23	1	2	0	0	0	0	.087
Cedeno	RF	5	15	2	1	0	0	0	0	.133
Porter	C	5	15	0	2	0	0	0	0	.133
Van Slyke	RF-PH-PR	6	11	0	1	0	0	0	0	.091
Tudor	P	3	5	0	0	0	0	0	0	.000
Nieto	C	2	5	0	0	0	0	0	1	.000
Harper	PH	4	4	0	1	0	0	0	0	.250
Cox	P	2	4	0	0	0	0	0	0	.000
Jorgensen	LF-PH	2	3	0	0	0	0	0	0	.000
Horton	P	3	1	0	0	0	0	0	0	.000
Worrell	P	3	1	0	0	0	0	0	0	.000
Andujar	P	2	1	0	0	0	0	0	0	.000
Braun	PH	1	1	0	0	0	0	0	0	.000
DeJesus	PH	1	1	0	0	0	0	0	0	.000
Dayley	P	4	0	0	0	0	0	0	0	—
Campbell	P	3	0	0	0	0	0	0	0	—
Lahti	P	3	0	0	0	0	0	0	0	—
Forsch	P	2	0	0	0	0	0	0	0	—
Lawless	PR	1	0	0	0	0	0	0	0	—

COMPOSITE PITCHING

KANSAS CITY

NAME	G	IP	H	BB	SO	W	L	SV	ERA
TOTALS	7	62	40	18	42	4	3	0	1.89
Saberhagen	2	18	11	1	10	2	0	0	0.50
Leibrandt	2	16.1	10	4	10	0	1	0	2.76
Jackson	2	16	9	5	12	1	1	0	1.69
Black	2	5.1	4	5	4	0	1	0	5.06
Quisenberry	4	4.1	5	3	3	1	0	0	2.08
Beckwith	1	2	1	0	3	0	0	0	0.00

ST. LOUIS

NAME	G	IP	H	BB	SO	W	L	SV	ERA
TOTALS	7	61.1	68	28	56	3	4	2	3.96
Tudor	3	18	15	7	14	2	1	0	3.00
Cox	2	14	14	4	13	0	0	0	1.29
Dayley	4	6	1	3	5	1	0	0	0.00
Worrell	3	4.2	4	2	6	0	1	1	3.86
Campbell	3	4	4	2	5	0	0	0	2.25
Horton	3	4	4	5	5	0	0	0	6.75
Andujar	2	4	10	4	3	0	1	0	9.00
Lahti	3	3.2	10	0	4	0	0	1	12.27
Forsch	2	3	6	1	3	0	1	0	12.00

MISCELLANEOUS 1985 INDIVIDUAL LEADERS

BATTING

On Base Average

American League			National League	
1	Boggs, Bos.	.450	1 Guerrero, L.A.	.422
2	Brett, K.C.	.436	2 Scioscia, L.A.	.407
3	Harrah, Tex.	.432	3 Raines, Mon.	.405
4	Henderson, N.Y.	.419	4 Clark, St. L.	.393
5	Murray, Bal.	.383	5 Murphy, Atl.	.388

Caught Stealing

American League			National League	
1	Butler, Cle.	20	1 Coleman, St. L.	25
2	Garcia, Tor.	15	2 Samuel, Phi.	19
2	Moseby, Tor.	15	3 McGee, St. L.	16
4	Wiggins, Bal.	13	4 Doran, Hou.	15
5	Puckett, Min.	12	4 Gladden, S.F.	15
	Tolleson, Tex.	12		

Hit by Pitcher

American League			National League	
1	Baylor, N.Y.	24	1 Brown, S.F.	11
2	Fisk, Chi.	17	2 Flannery, S.D.	9
3	Downing, Cal.	13	3 Madlock, Pit.-L.A.	8
4	Bradley, Sea.	12	4 Davis, Hou.	7
5	Lemon, Det.	10	5 Gladden, S.F.	7

Sacrifice Hits

American League			National League	
1	Meacham, N.Y.	23	1 Backman, N.Y.	14
2	Boone, Cal.	16	1 Ryan, Hou.	14
	Hill, Oak.	16	3 Darling, N.Y.	13
4	Barrett, Bos.	12		Duncan, L.A.	13
	Concepcion, K.C.	12		Hawkins, S.D.	13
	Schofield, Cal.	12		

Game Winning RBI's

American League			National League	
1	Mattingly, N.Y.	21	1 Hernandez, N.Y.	24
2	Winfield, N.Y.	19	2 Carter, N.Y.	18
	Brett, K.C.	16		Parker, Cin.	18
	Parrish, Det.	16	4 McGee, St. L.	16
5	Murray, Bal.	15		Guerrero, L.A.	16
	Ripkin, Bal.	15		

Grounded Into Double Play

American League			National League	
1	Rice, Bos.	35	1 Parker, Cin.	26
2	Ripkin, Bal.	32	2 Garvey, S.D.	25
3	Presley, Sea.	29	3 Wilson, Phi.	24
	Franco, Cle.	26		Concepcion, Cin.	23
5	Cooper, Mil.	24	5 Ramirez, Atl.	21
	Randolph, N.Y.	24		

Total Bases

American League			National League	
1	Mattingly, N.Y.	370	1 Parker, Cin.	350
2	Brett, K.C.	322	2 Murphy, Atl.	332
3	Bradley, Sea.	319	3 McGee, St. L.	308
4	Boggs, Bos.	312	4 Sandberg, Chi.	307
5	Murray, Bal.	305	5 Schmidt, Phi.	292

Sacrifice Flies

American League			National League	
1	Mattingly, N.Y.	15	1 Herr, St. L.	13
2	Brunansky, Min.	13	2 Hemandez, N.Y.	10
3	Buckner, Bos.	11	3 Moreland, Chi.	9
4	Baines, Chi.	10	4 Brooks, Mon.	8
	Baylor, N.Y.	10		Landreaux, L.A.	8
	Cooper, Mil.	10		
	Gibson, Det.	10		
	Oglivie, Mil.	10		

FIELDING

American League

	PO	A	E	DP	Pct.
1B Mattingly, N.Y.	1318	87	7	154	.995
2B Grich, Cal.	224	380	2	99	.997
SS Guillen, Chi.	220	382	12	80	.980
3B Mulliniks, Tor.	75	162	7	16	.971
OF Butler, Cle.	437	19	1	5	.998
OF Wilson, K.C.	378	4	2	1	.995
OF Baines, Chi.	318	8	2	2	.994
C Kearney, Sea.	529	50	3	7	.993
P Petry, Det.	36	26	0	3	1.000

National League

	PO	A	E	DP	Pct.
1B Hemandez, N.Y.	1310	139	4	113	.997
2B Backman, N.Y.	272	370	7	76	.989
SS O. Smith, St. L.	264	549	14	111	.983
3B Brown, S.F.	94	243	10	15	.971
OF Bass, Hou.	328	10	1	1	.997
OF Van Slyke, St. L.	234	13	1	4	.996
OF Raines, Mon.	284	8	2	4	.993
C Virgil, Phi.	667	52	4	11	.994
P Reuschel, Pit.	24	40	0	2	1.000

PITCHING

Wild Pitches

American League			National League	
1	Morris, Det.	15	1 Niekro, Hou.	21
2	Cocanower, Mil.	13	2 Tibbs, Cin.	12
3	Gubicza, K.C.	12	3 LaPointe, S.F.	10
4	Bannister, Chi.	11		Valenzuela, L.A.	10
	Hough, Tex.	11		Krukow, S.F.	10
	Nelson, Chi.	11		
	Witt, Cal.	11		

Hit Batters

American League			National League	
1	Smithson, Min.	15	1 Andujar, St. L.	11
2	Blyleven, Cle.-Min.	9	2 Ryan, Hou.	9
3	D. Martinez, Bal.	9	3 Burke, Mon.	7
	Nipper, Bos.	9	4 Gross, Phi.	7
	Stieb, Tor.	9	5 McWilliams, Phi.	7

Home Runs Allowed

American League			National League	
1	Darwin, Min.	34	1 Soto, Cin.	30
	McGregor, Bal.	34	2 Browning, Cin.	29
3	Hurst, Bos.	31	3 Shaw, S.D.	27
	Bannister, Chi.	30	4 Mahler, Atl.	24
5	Cowley, N.Y.	29	5 Fontenot, Chi.	23
	D. Martinez, Bal.	29		Hudson, Phi.	23
	P. Niekro, N.Y.	29		
	Romanick, Cal.	29		

Balks

American League		
1	Hurst, Bos.	4
2	11 tied with	3

National League		
1	Roberge, Mon.	5
2	Hammaker, S.F.	4
	Hoyt, S.D.	4
	Welch, L.A.	4
5	8 tied with	3

1986 — Heroics upon Heroics

The playoffs treated a national audience to gourmet baseball. The Mets, Astros, Red Sox, and Angels stacked comeback on comeback in a frenzy of one-upmanship. Each team charged into October with clear dominance in its division.

The Mets built last year's near-miss into a passionate rout in the N.L. East. They blew their rivals away with a torrid start and had first place practically locked up by the All-Star break. Gary Carter, Keith Hernandez, and Darryl Strawberry were the backbone of the lineup, with outstanding supporting performances by Len Dykstra, Wally Backman, and Ray Knight. Although he fell off from his 1985 peak, Dwight Gooden still starred on a pitching-deep staff made richer by the arrival of lefty Bob Ojeda from Boston. Philadelphia captured a distant second-place behind Mike Schmidt's MVP year. Even with Ozzie Smith's excellence, the Cards suffered from a team-wide slump and the trading of Joaquin Andujar to Oakland. The Expos mad an early run at the Mets and featured Tim Raines' league-leading .334 hitting.

In the N.L. West, Pedro Guerrero's springtime knee injury crippled the Dodgers and created a vacuum at the top. The Astros seized the moment with good pitching and sound fundamentals. Glenn Davis and Kevin Bass blossomed into offensive leaders, while Mike Scott won the Cy Young award with his split-fingered fastball. The Reds charged down the stretch behind Dave Parker's bat but could not dent Houston's lead. The Giants jumped up to third place, and the Dodgers fell to fifth despite Fernando Valenzuela's first twenty-win season and Steve Sax's hot hitting.

Each of the A.L. divisional champs slumped at the end and still finished comfortably ahead. The Red Sox took an early lead in the East and hung on despite a summer-long watch for an expected swoon. The Sox got the usual good work from Jim Rice, Wade Boggs, and Rich Gedman, but two new elements brought the championship to Boston. Don Baylor came from the Yankees with long-ball power and boosted morale in the clubhouse. Free of his past arm worries, Roger Clemens had an overpowering 24-4 season crowned with both MVP and Cy Young awards. The Keynote of his season was a record twenty-strikeout masterpiece against Seattle on April 29. The Yankees stayed within earshot of Don Mattingly's consistent brilliance. Toronto failed to defend the crown despite star turns by Tony Fernandez, George Bell, and Jesse Barfield, hurt by Dave Stieb's flop.

The Angels won the West by coaxing good season out of a crew of oldsters and a few youngsters. Gene Mauch piloted his team to the playoffs behind the hitting of rookie Wally Joyner and veteran Doug DeCinces. Mike Witt and Kirk McCaskill led a pitching staff which profited from Don Sutton's endless savvy. The Texas Rangers launched a surprise challenge and finished second. The Royals were cursed with ill fortune and never got un tracked. Bret Saberhagen became a ordinary pitcher, and manager Dick Howser left the team after the All-Star break for treatment for a brain tumor. The Royals did make a splash by signin Bo Jackson, winner of football's Heisman Trophy at Auburn, to a $7 millio contract.

The playoffs unfolded into high drama. One thunderbolt struck in the fifth game of the A.L. series. The Angels won three of the first four games and took a 5-2 lead into the top of the ninth. With two out, the Sox had only the faintes heartbeat. Don Baylor narrowed the margin to 5-4 with a two-run homer off Mike Witt. Gary Lucas came on in relief and hit Gedman in the ribs. Mauch next called on Donnie Moore. Dave Henderson, a late-season Boston pick-up, swatted a 2-2 pitch over the left field fence for a stunning 6-5 Red Sox lead. Although the Angeles recovered enough to tie the score in the bottom of the ninth, the Sox won in 11 innings. Risen from their deathbed the Red Sox then blew the Angels away in games six and seven. The collapse perpetuated the curse of Gene Mauch, never a pennant winner in 25 years of managing.

The N.L. series careened from one highlight to another. Mike Scott struck out 14 Mets in a 1-0 opening game victory over Dwight Gooden. The Mets won the next two games, with Dykstra capping game three with a two-run homer in the bottom of the ninth. Scott got the Astros even in game four.. The Next two games were overtime classics. Gary Carter won the fifth game 2-1 on an RBI single in the twelfth inning. The next day, Houston led 3-0 after eight innings in the Astrodome. The Mets woke up with three runs in the ninth. The game stretched on into excruciatingly tense extra innings. Each team scored once in the 14th inning. In the 16th inning, the Mets broke through for three runs and hung on through a final two-run Astro rally.

In the World Series, the Red Sox shocked the Mets by sweeping the first two game in Shea Stadium. The Mets took the next two games in Fenway Park, but Bruce Hurst shut them own in game five. The score in game six stood at 3-3 after nine innings. The Red Sox scored in the top of the tenth on a home run by Henderson, then added an insurance run. The first two Mets went down to start the bottom of the tenth. Suddenly, Carter, Kevin Mitchell, and Knight all singled off Calvin Schiraldi. Bob Stanley came in and promptly wild-pitched the tying run home. Mookie Wilson then poked a slow roller through the legs of first baseman Bill Buckner for an improbable 6-5 victory. With fate smiling on the Mets, they came from behind in game seven to cap a season custom made for highlight films.

EAST DIVISION

1986 AMERICAN LEAGUE

Name	G by Pos	B	AGE	G	AB	R	H	2B	3B	HR	RBI	BB	SO	SB	BA	SA
BOSTON 1st 95-66 .590	JOHN McNAMARA															
TOTALS			30	161	5498	794	1488	320	21	144	752	595	707	41	.271	.415
Bill Buckner	1B138, DH15	L	36	153	629	73	168	39	2	18	102	40	25	6	.267	.421
Marty Barrett	2B158	R	28	158	625	94	179	39	4	4	60	65	31	15	.286	.381
1 Rey Quinones	SS62	R	22	62	190	26	45	12	1	2	15	19	26	3	.237	.342
Wade Boggs	3B149	L	28	149	580	107	207	47	2	8	71	105	44	0	.357	.486
Dwight Evans	OF149, DH1	R	34	152	529	86	137	33	2	26	97	97	117	3	.259	.467
Tony Armas	OF117, DH1	R	33	121	425	40	112	21	4	11	58	24	77	0	.264	.409
Jim Rice	OF156, DH1	R	33	157	618	98	200	39	2	20	110	62	78	0	.324	.490
Rich Gedman	C134	L	26	135	462	49	119	29	0	16	65	37	61	1	.258	.424
Don Baylor	DH143, 1B13, OF3	R	37	160	585	93	139	23	1	31	94	62	111	3	.238	.439
Ed Romero	SS75, 3B18, 2B4, OF1	R	28	100	233	41	49	11	0	2	23	18	16	2	.212	.283
1 Steve Lyons	OF55	L	26	59	124	20	31	7	2	1	14	12	23	2	.250	.363
2 Spike Owen	SS42	B	25	42	126	21	23	2	1	1	10	17	9	3	.183	.238
Marc Sullivan	C41	R	27	41	119	15	23	4	0	1	14	7	32	0	.193	.252
Dave Stapleton	1B29, 2B6, 3B2	R	32	39	29	4	5	1	0	0	3	2	10	0	.128	.154
2 Dave Henderson	OF32	R	27	36	51	8	10	3	0	1	3	2	15	1	.196	.314
Kevin Romine	OF33	R	25	35	35	6	9	2	0	0	2	3	9	2	.257	.314
Mike Greenwell	OF15, DH3	L	22	31	35	4	11	2	0	4	5	7	1	0	.314	.371
Mike Stenhouse	OF4, 1B3	L	28	21	21	1	2	1	0	0	1	12	5	0	.095	.143
LaSchelle Tarver	OF9	L	27	13	25	3	3	0	0	0	1	1	4	0	.120	.120
Glenn Hoffman (NJ-IL)	SS11, 3B1	R	27	12	23	1	5	2	0	1	2	3	3	0	.217	.304
Pat Dodson	1B7	L	26	9	12	3	5	2	0	1	4	3	3	0	.417	.838
Dave Sax	C2, 1B1	R	27	4	11	1	5	1	0	1	1	0	1	0	.455	.818

NAME	T	AGE	W	L	PCT	SV	G	GS	CG	IP	H	BB	SO	SHO	ERA
		29	95	66	.590	41	161	161	36	1430	1469	474	1033	6	3.93
Roger Clemens	R	23	24	4	.857	0	33	33	10	254	179	67	238	1	2.48
Oil Can Boyd	R	26	16	10	.615	0	30	30	10	214	222	45	129	0	3.78
Bruce Hurst (GJ)	L	28	13	8	.619	0	25	25	1	174	169	50	167	4	2.99
Al Nipper (KJ)	R	27	10	12	.455	0	26	26	3	159	186	47	79	0	5.38
Bob Stanley	R	31	6	6	.500	16	66	1	0	82	109	22	54	0	4.37
2 Tom Seaver	R	41	5	7	.417	0	16	16	1	104	114	29	72	0	3.80
Sammy Stewart (AJ)	R	31	4	1	.800	0	17	0	0	64	64	48	47	0	4.38
Calvin Schiraldi	R	24	4	2	.667	9	25	0	0	51	36	15	55	0	1.41
1 Mike Brown	R	27	4	4	.500	0	15	10	0	57	72	25	32	0	5.34
Jeff Sellers	R	22	3	7	.300	0	14	13	1	82	90	40	51	0	4.94
Joe Sambito	L	34	2	0	1.000	12	53	0	0	45	54	16	30	0	4.84
Tim Lollar	L	30	2	1	1.000	0	32	1	0	43	51	34	28	0	6.91
Rob Woodward	R	23	2	3	.400	0	9	6	0	36	46	11	14	0	5.30
1 Mike Trujillo	R	26	0	0		0	3	0	0	6	7	6	4	0	9.53
Wes Gardner (SJ)	R	25	0	0		0	1	1	0	1	1	0	1	0	9.00
Steve Crawford (SJ)	R	28	0	2	.000	4	40	0	0	57	69	19	32	0	3.92

Name	G by Pos	B	AGE	G	AB	R	H	2B	3B	HR	RBI	BB	SO	SB	BA	SA
NEW YORK 2nd 90-72 .556 5.5	LOU PINIELLA															
TOTALS			29	162	5570	797	1512	275	23	188	745	645	911	139	.271	.430
Don Mattingly	1B160, 3B3, DH1	L	25	162	677	117	238	53	2	31	113	53	35	0	.352	.573
Willie Randolph	2B139, DH1	R	31	141	492	76	136	15	2	5	50	94	49	15	.276	.346
2 Wayne Tolleson	SS56, 3B7, 2B3	B	30	60	215	22	61	9	2	0	14	14	33	4	.284	.344
Mike Pagliarulo	3B143, SS2	L	26	149	504	71	120	24	3	28	71	54	120	4	.238	.464
Dave Winfield	OF145, DH6, 3B2	R	34	154	565	90	148	31	5	24	104	77	106	6	.262	.462
Rickey Henderson	OF146, DH5	R	27	153	608	130	160	31	5	28	74	89	81	87	.263	.469
Dan Pasqua	OF81, 1B5, DH1	L	24	102	280	44	82	17	0	16	45	47	78	2	.293	.525
2 Joel Skinner	C54	R	25	54	166	6	43	4	0	1	17	7	40	0	.259	.301
Mike Easler	DH129, OF1	L	35	146	490	64	148	26	2	14	78	49	87	3	.302	.449
Mike Fischlin	SS42, 2B27	R	30	71	102	9	21	2	0	0	3	8	29	0	.206	.225
Gary Roenicke	OF37, DH15, 3B3, 1B2	R	31	69	136	11	36	5	0	3	18	27	30	1	.265	.368
1 Ron Hassey	C51, DH3	L	33	64	191	23	57	14	0	6	29	24	16	1	.298	.466
Butch Wynegar (IL)	C57	B	30	61	194	19	40	4	1	7	29	30	21	0	.206	.345
1 Ken Griffey	OF51, DH2	L	36	59	198	33	60	7	0	9	26	15	24	2	.303	.475
Bobby Meacham	SS56	B	25	56	161	19	36	7	1	0	10	17	39	3	.224	.280
2 Claudell Washington	OF39	L	31	54	135	19	32	5	0	6	16	7	33	6	.237	.407
Dale Berra	SS19, 3B18, DH4	R	29	42	108	10	25	7	0	2	13	9	14	0	.231	.352
Henry Cotto	OF29, DH1	R	25	35	80	11	17	3	0	1	6	4	17	3	.213	.288
2 Ron Kittle	DH24, OF1	R	28	30	80	8	19	2	0	4	12	7	23	2	.238	.413
Juan Espino	C27	R	30	27	37	1	6	2	0	0	5	2	9	0	.162	.216
Paul Zuvella	SS21	R	27	21	48	2	4	1	0	0	2	5	4	0	.083	.104
Phil Lombardi	OF8, C3	R	23	20	36	6	10	3	0	2	4	4	7	0	.278	.528
2 Bryan Little	2B14	B	28	14	41	3	8	1	0	0	3	6	3	0	.195	.220
Leo Hernnadez	3B7, 2B1	R	26	7	22	2	5	2	0	1	4	1	8	0	.227	.455
Ivan DeJesus	SS7	R	33	7	4	1	0	0	0	0	1	1	1	0	.000	.000

NAME	T	AGE	W	L	PCT	SV	G	GS	CG	IP	H	BB	SO	SHO	ERA
		30	90	72	.556	58	162	162	13	1443	1461	492	878	8	4.11
Dennis Rasmussen	L	27	18	6	.750	0	31	31	3	202	160	74	131	1	3.88
Brian Fisher	R	24	9	5	.643	6	62	0	0	97	105	37	67	0	4.93
Bob Tewksbury	R	25	9	5	.643	0	23	20	2	130	144	31	49	0	3.31
Joe Niekro	R	41	9	10	.474	0	25	25	0	126	139	63	59	0	4.87
Ron Guidry	L	35	9	12	.429	0	30	30	5	192	202	38	140	0	3.98
Dave Righetti	R	27	8	8	.500	46	74	0	0	107	88	35	83	0	2.45
Doug Drabek	R	23	7	8	.467	0	27	21	0	132	126	50	76	0	4.10
1 Ed Whitson	R	31	5	2	.714	0	14	4	0	37	54	23	27	0	7.54
Tommy John (LJ-BG)	L	43	5	3	.625	0	13	10	1	71	73	15	28	0	2.93
2 Tim Stoddard	R	33	4	1	.800	0	24	0	0	49	41	23	34	0	3.83
Scott Nielson	R	27	4	4	.500	0	10	9	2	56	66	12	20	2	4.02
Al Holland	L	33	1	0	1.000	0	25	1	0	41	44	9	37	0	5.09
Alfonso Pulido	L	30	1	1	.500	1	10	3	0	31	38	9	13	0	4.70
John Montefusco (PJ)	R	36	0	0		0	4	0	0	12	6	9	5	0	2.19
Brad Arnsberg	R	22	0	0		0	2	0	0	6	6	6	4	0	3.38
Mike Armstong	R	32	0	1	.000	0	3	0	0	8	13	6	8	0	9.35
Bob Shirley	L	32	0	4		3	39	6	0	105	108	40	64	0	5.04
Britt Burns (PJ) 27															

DETROIT — 3rd 87-75 .537 8.5 — SPARKY ANDERSON

Name	G by Pos	B	AGE	G	AB	R	H	2B	3B	HR	RBI	BB	SO	SB	BA	SA
TOTALS			31	162	5512	798	1447	234	30	198	751	613	885	138	.263	.424
Darrell Evans	1B105, DH42, 3B2	L	39	151	507	78	122	15	0	29	85	91	105	3	.241	.442
Lou Whitaker	2B141	L	29	144	584	95	157	26	6	20	73	63	70	13	.269	.437
Alan Trammell	SS149, DH2	R	28	151	574	107	159	33	7	21	75	59	57	25	.277	.469
Darnell Coles	3B133, DH7, OF2, SS2	R	24	142	521	67	142	30	2	20	86	45	84	6	.273	.453
Kirk Gibson (NJ)	OF114, DH4	L	29	119	441	84	118	11	2	28	86	68	107	34	.268	.492
Chet Lemon	OF124	R	31	126	403	45	101	21	3	12	53	39	53	2	.251	.407
Dave Collins	OF94, DH24	B	33	124	419	44	113	18	2	1	27	44	49	27	.270	.329
Lance Parrish (XJ)	C85, DH6	R	30	91	327	53	84	6	1	22	62	38	83	0	.257	.483
Johnny Grubb (SJ)	DH52, OF19	L	37	81	210	32	70	13	1	13	51	28	70	0	.333	.590
Larry Herndon	OF83, DH18	R	32	106	283	33	70	13	1	8	37	27	40	2	.247	.385
Tom Brookens	3B35, 2B31, DH14, SS14, OF3	R	32	98	281	42	76	11	2	3	25	20	42	11	.270	.356
Pat Sheridan	OF90, DH5	L	28	98	236	41	56	9	1	6	19	21	57	9	.237	.360
Dave Bergman	1B41, DH6, OF2	L	33	65	130	14	30	6	1	1	9	21	16	0	.231	.315
Dwight Lowry	C55, 1B1, OF1	L	28	56	150	21	46	4	0	3	18	17	19	0	.307	.393
Dave Engle (WJ)	1B23, DH5, OF4, C3	R	29	35	86	6	22	7	0	0	4	7	13	0	.256	.337
2 Mike Heath	C29, 3B1	R	31	30	98	11	26	3	0	4	11	4	17	4	.265	.418
1 Harry Spilman	OF11, DH6, 1B2, C1	L	31	24	49	6	12	2	0	3	8	3	8	0	.245	.469
Brian Harper	OF11, DH6, 1B2, C2	R	26	19	36	2	5	1	0	0	3	3	3	0	.139	.167
Bruce Fields	OF14, DH1	L	25	16	43	4	12	1	1	0	6	1	6	1	.279	.349
Tim Tolman	DH9, OF4, 1B3	R	30	16	34	4	6	1	0	0	2	6	4	1	.176	.206
1 Mike Laga (BW)	1B12, DH2	L	26	15	45	6	9	1	0	3	8	5	13	0	.200	.422
Doug Baker	SS10, 2B2, DH1	B	25	13	24	1	3	1	0	0	0	2	7	1	.125	.167
Matt Nokes	C7	B	22	7	24	2	8	1	0	1	2	1	1	0	.333	.500
Scotti Madison	3B1, DH1	B	26	2	7	0	0	0	0	0	1	0	1	0	.000	.000

NAME	T	AGE	W	L	PCT	SV	G	GS	CG	IP	H	BB	SO	SHO	ERA
		29	87	75	.537	38	162	162	33	1444	1374	571	880	12	4.02
Jack Morris	R	31	21	8	.724	0	35	35	15	267	229	82	223	6	3.27
Walt Terrell	R	28	15	12	.556	0	34	33	9	217	199	98	93	2	4.56
Frank Tanana	L	32	12	9	.571	0	32	31	3	188	196	65	119	1	4.16
Eric King	R	22	11	4	.733	3	33	16	3	138	148	63	79	1	3.51
Willie Hemandez	L	31	8	7	.533	24	64	0	0	89	87	21	77	0	3.55
Dan Petry (EJ)	R	27	5	10	.333	0	20	20	2	116	122	53	56	0	4.66
2 Mark Thurmond	L	29	4	1	.800	1	25	5	0	52	44	17	17	0	1.92
Bill Campbell (EJ)	R	41	3	6	.333	3	34	0	0	56	46	21	37	0	3.88
1 Dave LaPoint	L	28	3	6	.333	0	16	8	0	68	85	32	36	0	5.72
Randy O'Neal	R	25	3	7	.300	2	37	11	1	123	121	44	68	0	4.33
Chuck Cary	L	26	1	2	.333	0	22	0	0	32	33	15	21	0	3.41
Bryan Kelly	R	27	1	2	.333	0	6	4	0	20	21	10	18	0	4.50
2 Jim Slaton	R	36	0	0	—	2	22	0	0	40	46	11	12	0	4.05
John Pacella	R	29	0	0	—	1	5	0	0	11	10	13	5	0	4.09
Jack Lazorko	R	30	0	0	—	3	3	0	0	7	8	4	3	0	4.05
Bill Scherrer	L	28	0	0	.000	0	13	0	0	21	19	22	16	0	7.29

TORONTO — 4th 86-76 .531 9.5 — JIMY WILLIAMS

Name	G by Pos	B	AGE	G	AB	R	H	2B	3B	HR	RBI	BB	SO	SB	BA	SA
TOTALS			29	163	5716	809	1540	285	35	181	767	496	848	110	.269	.427
Willie Upshaw	1B154, DH1	L	29	163	573	85	144	28	6	9	60	78	87	23	.251	.368
Damaso Garcia	2B106, DH11, 1B1	R	31	122	424	57	119	22	0	6	46	13	32	9	.281	.375
Tony Fernandez	SS163	R	24	163	687	91	213	33	9	10	65	27	52	25	.310	.428
Rance Mulliniks	3B110, DH5, 2B1	L	30	117	348	50	90	22	0	11	45	43	60	1	.259	.417
Jesse Barfield	OF157	R	26	158	589	107	170	35	2	40	108	69	146	8	.289	.559
Lloyd Moseby	OF147, DH3	L	26	152	589	89	149	24	5	21	86	64	122	32	.253	.418
George Bell	OF147, DH11, 3B2	R	26	159	641	101	198	38	6	31	108	41	62	7	.309	.532
Ernie Whitt	C127	L	34	131	395	48	106	19	2	16	56	35	39	0	.268	.448
Cliff Johnson	DH95, 1B1	R	38	107	336	48	84	12	1	15	55	52	57	0	.250	.426
Garth Iorg	3B90, 2B52, SS2	R	31	137	327	30	85	19	1	3	44	20	47	3	.260	.352
Rick Leach	DH42, OF39, 1B7	L	29	103	246	35	76	14	1	5	39	13	24	0	.309	.435
Kelly Gruber	3B42, 2B14, DH14, OF9, SS5	R	24	87	143	20	28	4	1	5	15	5	27	2	.196	.343
Buck Martinez	C78, DH3	R	37	81	160	13	29	8	0	2	12	20	25	0	.181	.269
Ron Shepherd	OF32, DH16	R	25	65	69	16	14	4	0	2	4	3	22	0	.203	.348
Manny Lee	2B29, SS5, 3B2	B	21	35	78	8	16	0	1	1	7	4	10	0	.205	.269
Cecil Fielder	DH22, 1B7, 3B2, OF1	R	22	34	83	7	13	2	0	4	13	6	27	0	.157	.325
Jeff Hearron	C12	R	24	12	23	2	5	1	0	0	4	3	7	0	.217	.261
Fred McGriff	DH2, 1B1	L	22	3	5	1	1	0	0	0	0	0	2	0	.200	.200

NAME	T	AGE	W	L	PCT	SV	G	GS	CG	IP	H	BB	SO	SHO	ERA
		28	86	76	.531	44	163	163	16	1476	1467	847	1002	12	4.08
Mark Eichhorn	R	25	14	6	.700	10	69	0	0	157	105	45	166	0	1.72
Jimmy Key	L	25	14	11	.560	0	36	35	4	232	222	74	141	2	3.57
Jim Clancy	R	30	14	14	.500	0	34	34	6	219	202	63	126	3	3.94
John Cerutti	L	26	9	4	.692	1	34	20	2	145	150	47	89	1	4.15
Tom Henke	R	28	9	5	.643	27	63	0	0	91	63	32	118	0	3.35
2 Joe Johnson	R	24	7	2	.778	0	16	15	0	88	94	22	39	0	3.89
Dave Stieb	R	28	7	12	.368	1	37	34	1	205	239	87	127	1	4.74
1 Doyle Alexander	R	35	5	4	.556	0	17	17	3	111	120	20	65	0	4.46
Bill Caudill	R	29	2	4	.333	2	40	0	0	36	36	17	32	0	6.19
1 Jim Acker	R	27	2	4	.333	0	23	5	0	60	63	22	32	0	4.35
Dennis Lamp	R	33	2	6	.250	2	40	2	0	73	93	23	30	0	5.05
Luis Aquino	R	22	1	1	.500	0	7	0	0	11	14	3	5	0	6.35
Jeff Musselman	L	23	0	0	—	0	6	0	0	4	8	5	5	0	10.13
Steve Davis	L	23	0	0	—	0	2	0	0	4	8	4	1	0	17.18
2 Mickey Mahler	L	33	0	0	—	1	4	0	0	1	1	0	0	0	0.00
Don Gordon	R	26	0	1	.000	1	14	0	0	22	28	8	13	0	7.06
Stan Clarke	L	25	0	0	.000	0	10	0	0	13	12	10	9	0	9.24
2 Duane Ward	R	22	0	1	.000	0	2	1	0	3	4	4	5	0	13.50
Gary Lavelle (EJ) 37															
Tom Filer (EJ) 29															

CLEVELAND — 5th 84-78 .519 11.5 — PAT CORRALES

Name	G by Pos	B	AGE	G	AB	R	H	2B	3B	HR	RBI	BB	SO	SB	BA	SA
TOTALS			28	163	5702	831	1620	270	45	157	775	456	944	141	.284	.430
Pat Tabler	1B107, DH18	R	28	130	473	61	154	29	2	6	48	29	75	3	.326	.433
Tony Bernazard	2B146	B	29	146	562	88	169	28	4	17	73	53	77	17	.301	.456
Julio Franco	SS134, 2B13, DH3	R	27	149	599	80	183	30	5	10	74	32	66	10	.306	.422
Brook Jacoby	3B158	R	26	158	583	83	168	30	4	17	80	56	137	2	.288	.441
Joe Carter	OF104, 1B70	R	26	162	663	108	200	36	9	29	121	32	95	29	.302	.514
Brett Butler	OF159	L	29	161	587	92	163	17	14	4	51	70	65	32	.278	.375
Mel Hall	OF126, DH7	L	25	140	442	68	131	29	2	18	77	33	65	6	.296	.493
Andy Allanson	C99	R	24	101	293	30	66	7	3	1	29	14	36	10	.225	.280
Andre Thornton (KJ)	DH110	R	36	120	401	49	92	14	0	17	66	65	67	4	.229	.392
Otis Nixon	OF95, DH5	B	27	105	95	33	25	4	1	0	8	13	12	23	.263	.326
Cory Snyder	OF74, SS34, 3B11, DH1	R	23	103	416	58	113	21	1	24	69	16	123	2	.272	.500
Chris Bando	C86	B	30	92	254	28	68	9	0	2	26	22	49	0	.268	.327
Carmen Castillo	OF37, DH35	R	28	85	205	34	57	9	0	8	32	9	48	2	.276	.439
Fran Mullins (SJ)	2B13, SS11, DH1, 1B1	R	29	28	40	3	7	4	0	0	5	2	11	0	.175	.275
Dave Clark	OF10, DH7	L	23	18	58	10	16	1	0	3	9	7	11	0	.276	.448
Dan Rohn	2B2, 3B2, SS1	L	30	6	10	1	2	0	0	0	1	0	3	0	.200	.200
Jay Bell	2B2, DH2	R	20	5	14	3	5	2	0	1	4	3	7	0	.357	.714
Eddie Williams	OF4	R	21	5	7	2	1	0	0	0	1	0	3	0	.143	.143

NAME	T	AGE	W	L	PCT	SV	G	GS	CG	IP	H	BB	SO	SHO	ERA
		30	84	78	.519	34	163	163	31	1448	1548	605	744	7	4.58
Tom Candiotti	R	28	16	12	.571	0	36	34	17	252	234	106	167	3	3.57
Ken Schrom	R	31	14	7	.667	0	34	33	3	206	217	49	97	0	4.54
Phil Niekro	R	47	11	11	.500	0	34	32	5	210	241	95	81	0	4.32
Scott Bailes	L	24	10	10	.500	7	62	10	0	113	123	43	60	0	4.95
Greg Swindell	R	21	5	2	.714	0	9	9	1	62	57	15	46	0	4.23
Rich Yett	R	23	5	3	.625	1	39	3	1	79	84	37	50	1	5.15
Frank Wills	R	27	4	4	.500	0	26	0	0	40	43	16	32	0	4.91
Don Schulze (SJ)	R	23	4	4	.500	0	19	13	1	85	88	34	33	0	5.00
Dickie Noles (BF)	R	29	3	2	.600	0	32	0	0	55	56	30	32	0	5.10
Bryan Oelkers	L	26	3	3	.500	1	35	4	0	69	70	40	33	0	4.70
1 Neal Heaton	L	26	3	6	.333	0	12	12	2	74	73	34	24	0	4.24
Ernie Camacho	R	31	2	4	.333	20	51	0	0	57	60	31	36	0	4.08
Doug Jones	R	29	1	0	1.000	1	11	0	0	18	18	6	12	0	2.50
Jim Kern	R	37	1	1	.500	0	16	0	0	27	34	23	11	0	7.90
Jose Roman	R	23	1	2	.333	0	5	0	0	22	23	17	9	0	6.55
2 John Butcher (ZJ)	R	29	1	5	.167	0	9	5	0	51	86	13	16	1	6.93
Reggie Ritter	R	26	0	0	—	0	5	0	0	10	14	4	6	0	6.30
Jamie Easterly (SJ)	L	33	0	2	.000	0	13	0	0	18	27	12	9	0	7.64
Tom Waddell (EJ) 27															

MILWAUKEE — 6th 77-84 .478 18 — GEORGE BAMBERGER 71-81 .467 TOM TREBELHORN 6-3 .667

Name	G by Pos	B	AGE	G	AB	R	H	2B	3B	HR	RBI	BB	SO	SB	BA	SA
TOTALS			29	161	5461	667	1393	255	38	127	625	530	986	100	.255	.385
Cecil Cooper	1B90, DH44	L	36	134	542	46	140	24	1	12	75	41	87	1	.258	.373
Jim Gantner	2B135, 3B3, DH1, SS1	L	33	139	497	58	136	25	1	7	28	26	50	13	.274	.370
Ernest Riles	SS142	L	25	145	524	69	132	24	2	9	47	54	80	7	.252	.357
Paul Molitor (LJ)	3B91, DH10, OF4	R	29	105	437	62	123	24	6	9	55	40	81	20	.281	.426
Rob Deer	OF131, 1B4	R	25	134	466	75	108	17	3	33	86	72	179	5	.232	.494
Robin Yount	OF131, DH6, 1B3	R	30	140	522	82	163	31	7	9	46	62	73	14	.312	.450
Glenn Braggs	OF19, DH2	R	23	58	215	19	51	8	2	4	18	11	47	1	.237	.349
Charlie Moore	C72, OF4, DH2, 2B1	R	33	80	235	24	61	12	3	3	39	21	38	5	.260	.374
Ben Oglivie	OF50, DH42	L	37	103	346	31	98	20	1	5	53	30	33	1	.283	.390
Dale Sveum	3B65, SS13, 2B13	B	22	91	317	35	78	13	2	7	35	32	63	4	.246	.366
Rick Manning	OF83, DH5	L	31	89	205	31	52	7	3	8	27	17	20	5	.254	.434
Rick Cerone	C68	R	32	68	216	22	56	14	0	4	18	15	28	1	.259	.380
Bill Schroeder	C35, 1B19, DH10	R	27	64	217	32	46	14	0	7	19	9	59	1	.212	.373
Billy Jo Robidoux (KJ)	1B43, DH10	L	22	58	181	15	41	8	0	1	21	33	36	0	.227	.287
Mike Felder (LJ)	OF42, DH1	B	24	44	155	24	37	2	4	1	13	13	16	16	.239	.323
2 Gorman Thomas	DH36, 1B6	R	35	44	145	21	26	4	1	6	10	31	50	2	.179	.345
Paul Householder	OF22, DH3	B	27	26	78	4	17	3	1	1	16	7	16	1	.218	.321
Juan Castillo	2B17, SS4, 3B2, DH2, OF1	B	24	26	54	6	9	0	1	0	5	5	12	1	.167	.204
1 Randy Ready	OF11, 2B7, 3B3, DH1	R	26	23	79	8	15	4	0	1	4	0	3	0	.190	.278
Eddie Diaz	SS5	R	22	5	13	0	3	0	0	0	0	2	4	0	.231	.231
Jim Adduci	1B3	L	26	3	11	2	1	1	0	0	1	0	2	0	.091	.182
Steve Kiefer	SS2	R	25	2	7	0	0	0	0	0	0	0	4	0	.000	.000

NAME	T	AGE	W	L	PCT	SV	G	GS	CG	IP	H	BB	SO	SHO	ERA
		27	77	84	.478	32	161	161	29	1432	1478	494	952	12	4.01
Teddy Higuera	L	27	20	11	.645	0	34	34	15	248	226	74	207	4	2.79
Tim Leary	R	27	12	12	.500	0	33	30	3	188	216	53	110	2	4.21
Juan Nieves	L	21	11	12	.478	0	35	33	4	185	224	77	116	3	4.92
Dan Plesac	L	24	10	7	.588	14	51	0	0	91	81	29	75	0	2.97
1 Danny Darwin	R	30	8	8	.429	0	27	14	5	130	120	35	80	1	3.52
Mark Clear	R	30	5	5	.500	16	59	0	0	74	53	36	85	0	2.20
Bill Wegman	R	23	5	12	.294	0	35	32	2	198	217	43	82	0	5.13
John Henry Johnson	L	29	2	1	.667	1	19	0	0	44	43	10	42	0	2.66
1 Bob McClure	L	34	2	1	.667	0	16	18	1	10	11	12	0	3.86	
Pete Vuckovich (VR)	R	33	2	4	.333	0	6	6	0	32	33	11	12	0	3.06
Mike Birkbeck	R	25	1	1	.500	0	7	4	0	33	43	11	33	0	4.50
Bob Gibson	R	29	1	1	.333	0	11	1	0	22	23	11	11	0	4.73
Bryan Clutterbuck	R	26	1	0	1.000	0	17	0	0	57	68	16	18	0	4.29
Jaime Cocanower	R	29	0	1	.000	0	17	0	0	45	40	38	22	0	4.43
1 Ray Searage	L	31	0	1	.000	0	4	0	0	9	9	10	0	6.95	
2 Mark Knudson	R	25	0	1	.000	0	4	4	1	18	22	5	9	0	7.64
Chris Bosio	R	23	0	4	.000	0	10	4	0	35	41	13	29	0	7.01

1986 AMERICAN LEAGUE — EAST DIVISION

BALTIMORE 7th 73-89 .451 22.5 EARL WEAVER

Name	G by Pos	B	AGE	G	AB	R	H	2B	3B	HR	RBI	BB	SO	SB	BA	SA
TOTALS			30	162	5524	708	1425	223	13	169	669	563	862	64	.258	.395
Eddie Murray (LJ)	1B119, DH16	B	30	137	495	61	151	25	1	17	84	78	59	3	.305	.463
Juan Bonilla	2B70, 3B33, DH2	R	31	102	284	33	69	10	1	1	18	25	21	0	.243	.296
Cal Ripken	SS162	R	25	162	627	98	177	35	1	25	81	70	60	4	.282	.461
Floyd Rayford	3B72, C10, DH1	R	28	81	210	15	37	4	0	8	19	15	50	0	.176	.310
Lee Lacy	OF120, DH3	R	38	130	491	77	141	18	0	11	47	37	71	4	.287	.391
Fred Lynn	OF107, DH1	L	34	112	397	67	114	13	1	23	67	53	59	2	.287	.499
Mike Young	OF69, DH38	B	26	117	369	43	93	15	1	9	42	49	90	3	.252	.371
Rick Dempsey	C121	R	36	122	327	42	68	15	1	13	29	45	78	1	.208	.379
Larry Sheets	DH58, OF32, C6, 1B4, 3B2	L	26	112	338	42	92	17	1	18	60	21	56	2	.272	.488
John Shelby	OF121, DH2	B	28	135	404	54	92	14	4	11	49	18	75	18	.228	.364
Juan Beniquez	OF54, 3B25, DH16, 1B14	R	36	113	343	48	103	15	0	6	36	40	49	2	.300	.397
Jim Dwyer	OF24, DH24, 1B1	L	36	94	160	18	39	13	1	8	31	23	31	0	.244	.488
Alan Wiggins	2B66, DH1	B	28	71	239	30	60	3	1	0	11	22	20	21	.251	.272
Jim Traber	1B29, DH21, OF8	L	24	65	212	28	54	7	0	13	44	18	31	0	.255	.472
Jackie Gutierrez (IL)	2B53, 3B6, DH1	R	26	61	145	8	27	3	0	0	4	3	27	3	.186	.207
Tom O'Malley	3B55	L	25	56	181	19	46	9	0	1	18	17	21	0	.254	.320
John Stefero	C50, 2B1	L	25	52	120	14	28	2	0	2	13	16	25	0	.233	.300
Ken Gerhart	OF20	R	25	20	69	4	16	2	0	1	7	4	18	0	.232	.304
Al Pardo	C14, DH1	B	23	16	51	3	7	1	0	1	3	0	14	0	.137	.216
Ricky Jones	2B11, 3B6	R	28	16	33	2	6	2	0	0	4	6	8	0	.182	.242
Rex Hudler	2B13, 3B1	R	25	14	1	1	0	0	0	0	0	0	1	0	1.000	.000
Tom Dodd	DH6, 3B1	R	27	8	13	1	3	0	0	0	1	2	2	0	.231	.462
Kelly Paris	3B3, SH2	R	28	5	10	0	2	0	0	0	0	0	3	0	.200	.200
Carl Nichols	C5	R	23	5	5	0	0	0	0	0	0	1	4	0	.000	.000

NAME	T	AGE	W	L	PCT	SV	G	GS	CG	IP	H	BB	SO	SHO	ERA
		29	73	89	.451	39	162	162	17	1437	1451	535	954	6	4.30
Mike Boddicker	R	28	14	12	.538	0	33	33	7	218	214	74	175	0	4.70
Ken Dixon	R	25	11	13	.458	0	33	33	2	202	194	83	170	0	4.58
Scott McGregor	L	32	11	15	.423	0	34	33	4	203	216	57	95	2	4.52
Storm Davis (NJ)	R	24	9	12	.429	0	25	25	2	154	166	49	96	0	3.62
Mike Flanagan	L	34	7	11	.389	0	29	28	2	172	179	66	96	0	4.24
Rich Bordi	R	27	6	4	.600	1	32	11	0	107	105	41	83	0	4.46
Don Aase	R	31	6	7	.462	34	66	0	0	82	71	28	67	0	2.98
Brad Havens	L	26	3	3	.500	1	46	0	0	71	64	29	57	0	4.56
Nate Snell	R	33	2	1	.667	0	34	0	0	72	69	22	29	0	3.86
Odell Jones	R	33	2	2	.500	0	21	0	0	49	58	23	32	0	3.83
Eric Bell	L	22	2	2	.500	0	4	4	0	23	23	14	18	0	5.01
John Habyan	R	22	1	3	.250	0	6	5	0	26	24	18	14	0	4.44
Mike Kinnunen	L	28	0	0	—	0	9	0	0	7	8	5	1	0	6.43
1 Dennis Martinez (SJ)	R	31	0	0	—	0	4	0	0	7	11	2	2	0	6.75
Bill Swaggerty	R	29	0	0	—	0	1	0	0	1	6	1	1	0	18.00
Tippy Martinez (IL-SJ)	L	36	0	2	.000	0	14	0	0	16	18	12	11	0	5.63
Tony Arnold	R	27	0	2	.000	0	11	0	0	25	25	11	7	0	3.55

WEST DIVISION

CALIFORNIA 1st 92-70 .568 GENE MAUCH

Name	G by Pos	B	AGE	G	AB	R	H	2B	3B	HR	RBI	BB	SO	SB	BA	SA
TOTALS			33	162	5433	786	1387	236	26	167	743	671	860	109	.255	.404
Wally Joyner	1B152	L	24	154	593	82	172	27	3	22	100	57	58	5	.290	.457
Rob Wilfong	2B90	L	32	92	288	25	63	11	3	3	33	30	28	1	.219	.309
Dick Schofield	SS137	R	23	139	458	67	114	17	6	13	57	48	55	23	.249	.397
Doug DeCinces	3B132, DH3, SS1	R	35	140	512	69	131	20	3	26	96	52	74	2	.256	.459
Ruppert Jones	OF121	L	31	126	393	73	90	21	3	17	49	64	87	10	.229	.427
Gary Pettis	OF153, DH1	B	28	154	539	93	139	23	4	5	58	69	132	50	.258	.343
Brian Downing	OF138, DH10	R	35	152	513	90	137	27	4	20	95	90	84	4	.267	.452
Bob Boone	C144	R	38	144	442	48	98	12	2	7	49	43	30	1	.222	.305
Reggie Jackson	DH121, OF4	L	40	132	419	65	101	12	2	18	58	92	115	1	.241	.408
George Hendrick	OF93, 1B7, DH4	R	36	102	283	45	77	13	1	14	47	26	41	1	.272	.473
Bobby Grich	2B87, 1B11, 3B2	R	37	98	313	42	84	18	0	9	30	39	54	1	.268	.412
Rick Burleson	DH38, SS37, 2B6, 3B4	R	25	93	271	35	77	14	0	5	29	33	32	1	.284	.391
Jack Howell	3B39, OF8, DH2	L	24	63	151	26	41	14	2	4	21	19	28	2	.272	.470
Jerry Narron	C51, DH2	L	30	57	95	5	21	3	1	1	8	9	14	0	.221	.305
Darrell Miller	OF23, C10, DH2	R	28	33	57	6	13	2	1	0	4	3	7	0	.228	.298
Devon White	OF28	R	23	29	51	8	12	1	1	1	3	6	8	6	.235	.353
Mark Ryal	OF6, 1B4, DH2	L	26	13	32	6	12	0	0	2	5	2	4	1	.375	.563
Gus Polidor	2B4, 3B1, SS1	R	24	6	19	1	5	1	0	0	1	0	2	0	.263	.316
Mark McLemore	2B2	B	21	5	4	0	0	0	0	0	0	0	1	0	.000	.000

NAME	T	AGE	W	L	PCT	SV	G	GS	CG	IP	H	BB	SO	SHO	ERA
		30	92	70	.568	40	62	162	29	1456	1356	478	955	12	3.84
Mike Witt	R	25	18	10	.643	0	34	34	14	269	218	73	208	3	2.84
Kirk McCaskill	R	25	17	10	.630	0	34	33	10	246	207	92	202	2	3.36
Don Sutton	R	41	15	11	.577	0	34	34	3	207	192	49	116	1	3.74
John Candelaria (EJ)	L	32	10	2	.833	0	16	16	1	92	68	26	81	1	2.55
Ron Romanick	R	25	5	8	.385	0	18	18	1	106	124	44	38	1	5.50
Terry Forster (NJ)	L	34	4	1	.800	2	41	0	0	41	47	17	28	0	3.51
Gary Lucas (XJ)	L	31	4	1	.800	5	41	0	0	46	45	6	31	0	3.15
Doug Corbett	R	33	4	2	.667	10	46	0	0	79	66	22	36	0	3.66
Donnie Moore (SJ)	R	32	4	5	.444	21	49	0	0	73	60	22	53	0	2.97
1 Jim Slaton	R	36	4	6	.400	0	14	12	0	73	84	29	31	0	5.65
Chuck Finley	L	23	3	1	.750	0	25	0	0	46	40	23	37	0	3.30
T.R. Bryden	R	27	1	2	.667	0	16	0	0	34	38	21	25	0	6.55
Urbano Lugo (EJ)	R	23	1	1	.500	0	5	3	0	21	21	6	9	0	3.80
Vern Ruhle	R	35	1	3	.250	1	16	3	0	54	46	7	23	0	4.15
Todd Fischer	R	22	0	0	—	0	9	0	0	17	18	7	6	0	4.24
Willie Fraser	R	22	0	0	—	0	1	1	0	6	8	1	2	0	8.31
Ken Forsch	R	39	0	1	.000	1	10	0	0	17	24	10	13	0	9.53
Mike Cook	R	22	0	0	—	0	5	1	0	6	4	7	4	0	9.00
Ray Chadwick	R	23	0	5	.000	0	7	7	0	27	39	15	9	0	7.24

TEXAS 2nd 87-75 .537 5 BOBBY VALENTINE

Name	G by Pos	B	AGE	G	AB	R	H	2B	3B	HR	RBI	BB	SO	SB	BA	SA
TOTALS			28	162	5529	771	1479	248	43	184	725	511	1088	103	.267	.428
Pete O'Brien	1B155	L	28	156	551	86	160	23	3	23	90	87	66	4	.290	.468
Toby Harrah	2B93	R	37	95	289	36	63	18	2	7	41	44	53	2	.218	.367
Scott Fletcher	SS136, 3B12, 2B11, DH1	R	27	147	530	82	159	34	5	3	50	47	59	12	.300	.406
Steve Buechele	3B137, 2B33, OF2	R	24	153	461	54	112	19	2	18	54	35	98	5	.243	.410
Pete Incaviglia	OF114, DH36	R	22	153	540	82	135	21	2	30	88	55	185	3	.250	.463
Oddibe McDowell	OF148, DH1	L	23	154	572	105	152	24	7	18	49	65	112	33	.266	.427
Gary Ward (IL)	OF104, DH1	R	32	105	380	54	120	15	2	5	51	31	72	12	.316	.405
Don Slaught	C91, DH2	R	27	95	314	39	83	17	1	13	46	16	59	3	.264	.449
Larry Parrish	DH99, 3B30	R	32	129	464	67	128	22	1	28	94	52	114	3	.276	.509
Ruben Sierra	OF107, DH3	B	20	113	382	50	101	13	10	16	55	22	65	7	.264	.476
Curt Wilkerson	2B60, SS56, DH2	B	25	110	236	27	56	10	3	0	15	11	42	9	.237	.305
To Paciorek	OF25, 1B23, 3B21, DH9, SS1	R	39	88	213	17	61	7	0	4	22	3	41	1	.286	.376
Geno Petralli	C41, 3B15, DH2, 2B2	B	27	69	137	17	35	9	3	2	18	5	14	3	.255	.409
Darrell Porter	C25, DH19	L	34	68	155	21	41	6	0	12	29	22	51	1	.265	.535
1 George Wright	OF42, DH16	B	27	49	106	10	23	3	1	2	7	4	23	2	.217	.321
Orlando Mercado	C45	R	24	46	102	7	24	1	1	1	7	6	13	0	.235	.294
Bob Brower	OF17, DH1	R	26	21	9	3	1	1	0	0	0	3	1	1	.111	.222
Mike Stanley	3B7, DH3, OF1	R	23	15	30	4	10	3	0	1	1	3	7	1	.333	.533
Bobby Jones	OF9, 1B2	L	36	13	21	1	2	0	0	0	3	2	6	0	.095	.095
Jerry Browne	2B8	B	20	12	24	6	10	2	0	0	3	4	1	1	.417	.500
Jeff Kunkel	SS5, DH1	R	24	8	13	3	3	1	0	0	2	0	3	0	.231	.462

NAME	T	AGE	W	L	PCT	SV	G	GS	CG	IP	H	BB	SO	SHO	ERA
		27	87	75	.537	41	162	162	15	1450	1356	736	1059	8	4.11
Charlie Hough (BG)	R	38	17	10	.630	0	33	33	7	230	188	89	146	2	3.79
Ed Correa	R	20	12	14	.462	0	32	32	4	202	167	126	189	2	4.23
Bobby Witt	R	22	11	9	.550	0	31	31	0	158	130	143	174	0	5.48
Greg Harris	R	30	10	8	.556	20	73	0	0	111	103	42	95	0	2.83
Jose Guzman	R	23	9	15	.375	0	29	29	2	172	199	60	87	0	4.54
Mitch Williams	L	21	8	6	.571	8	80	0	0	98	69	79	90	0	3.58
Mike Mason	L	27	7	3	.700	0	27	22	2	135	135	56	85	1	4.33
Jeff Russell	R	24	5	2	.714	2	37	3	1	82	74	31	54	0	3.40
Mike Loynd	R	22	2	2	.500	0	9	8	0	42	49	19	33	0	5.36
Dale Mohorcic	R	30	2	4	.333	7	58	0	0	79	86	15	29	0	2.51
Ricky Wright (GJ)	L	27	1	0	1.000	0	21	1	0	39	44	21	23	0	5.03
Dwayne Henry (EJ)	R	24	1	0	1.000	0	19	0	0	14	14	22	17	0	4.66
Ron Meridith	R	29	1	0	1.000	0	5	0	0	11	9	3	3	0	3.00
Kevin Brown	R	21	1	0	1.000	0	1	1	0	5	6	0	4	0	3.60
Dave Rozema	R	28	0	1	.000	3	29	0	0	11	19	3	3	0	5.91
1 Mickey Mahler	L	33	0	2	.000	3	29	5	0	63	71	29	28	0	4.14

OAKLAND (TIE) 3rd 76-86 .469 16 JACKIE MOORE 29-44 .397 JEFF NEWMAN 2-8 .200 TONY LaRUSSA 45-34 .570

Name	G by Pos	B	AGE	G	AB	R	H	2B	3B	HR	RBI	BB	SO	SB	BA	SA
TOTALS			29	162	5435	731	1370	213	25	163	683	553	983	139	.252	.390
Bruce Bochte	1B115, DH1	L	35	125	407	57	104	13	1	6	43	65	68	3	.256	.337
Tony Phillips (KJ)	2B88, 3B30, OF4, DH2, SS1	B	27	118	441	76	113	14	5	5	52	76	82	15	.256	.345
Alfredo Griffin	SS162	B	28	162	594	74	169	23	6	4	51	35	52	33	.285	.364
Carney Lansford	3B100, 1B60, DH3, 2B1	R	29	151	591	80	168	16	4	19	72	39	51	16	.284	.421
Mike Davis	OF139	L	27	142	489	77	131	28	3	19	55	34	91	27	.268	.454
Dwayne Murphy (XJ)	OF97, DH1	L	31	98	329	50	83	11	3	9	39	56	80	3	.252	.386
Jose Canseco	OF155, DH1	R	21	157	600	85	144	29	1	33	117	65	175	15	.240	.457
Mickey Tettleton (FJ)	C89	B	25	90	211	26	43	9	0	10	35	39	51	7	.204	.389
Dave Kingman	DH140, 1B2	R	37	144	561	70	118	19	0	35	94	33	126	3	.210	.431
Donnie Hill	2B68, 3B33, DH3, SS2	B	25	108	339	37	96	16	2	4	29	23	38	5	.283	.378
Dusty Baker	OF55, DH15, 1B3	R	37	83	242	25	58	9	0	4	19	27	37	0	.240	.322
Jerry Willard	C71, DH1	L	26	75	161	17	43	7	0	4	26	22	28	0	.267	.385
Stan Javier	OF51, DH2	B	22	59	114	13	23	8	0	0	8	16	27	8	.202	.272
Rickey Peters (AJ)	OF27, DH1, 2B1	B	29	44	38	7	7	1	0	0	1	7	7	2	.184	.211
Bill Bathe	C39	R	25	39	103	9	19	3	0	3	11	2	20	0	.184	.359
Rusty Tillman	OF17	R	25	22	39	6	10	1	0	1	3	6	11	2	.256	.359
Mike Gallego	2B19, 3B2, SS1	R	25	20	37	2	10	2	0	0	4	1	9	0	.270	.324
Mark McGwire	3B16	R	23	18	53	10	10	1	0	3	9	4	18	0	.189	.377
Lenn Sakata	2B16, DH1	R	32	17	34	4	12	2	0	0	3	2	6	0	.353	.412
Steve Henderson	OF7, DH1	R	33	11	26	2	2	0	0	0	1	3	7	0	.077	.115
Terry Steinbach	C5	R	24	6	15	3	5	0	0	2	4	1	0	0	.333	.733
Rob Nelson	1B2, DH1	L	22	9	9	4	2	0	0	0	3	4	0	0	.222	.333
Wayne Gross	3B1	L	34	3	2	0	0	0	0	0	0	0	0	0	.000	.000

NAME	T	AGE	W	L	PCT	SV	G	GS	CG	IP	H	BB	SO	SHO	ERA
		28	76	86	.469	37	162	162	22	1433	1334	667	937	8	4.31
Curt Young	L	26	13	9	.591	0	29	27	5	198	176	57	116	2	3.45
Joaquin Andujar (LJ)	R	33	12	7	.632	1	28	26	7	155	139	56	72	1	3.82
2 Dave Stewart	R	29	9	5	.643	0	29	17	4	149	137	65	102	1	3.74
Jose Rijo	R	21	9	11	.450	0	39	26	4	194	172	108	176	0	4.65
Moose Haas (SJ)	R	30	7	2	.778	0	12	12	1	72	58	19	40	0	2.74
Chris Codiroli (EJ)	R	25	5	8	.385	0	16	16	1	92	91	38	43	0	4.03
Bill Mooneyham	R	24	4	5	.444	2	45	0	0	80	103	67	75	0	4.52
Eric Plunk	R	22	4	7	.364	0	26	15	0	120	91	102	98	0	5.31
Jay Howell (EJ)	R	30	3	6	.333	16	38	0	0	53	53	23	42	0	3.38
Steve Ontiveros (EJ)	R	25	2	2	.500	10	46	0	0	73	72	25	54	0	4.71
Dave Leiper	L	24	2	2	.500	1	33	0	0	32	28	18	15	0	4.83
Doug Bair	R	36	2	4	.400	4	31	0	0	45	37	18	40	0	3.00
1 Keith Atherton	R	27	1	2	.333	1	13	0	0	15	18	11	9	0	5.87
Bill Krueger (AJ)	L	28	1	1	.500	0	11	3	0	34	40	13	11	0	8.03
Rick Rodriguez	R	25	1	1	.500	0	8	1	0	16	17	7	2	0	6.61
Rick Langford	R	34	1	10	.091	0	16	11	0	55	69	18	30	0	7.36
Tom Dozier	R	25	0	0	—	0	11	0	0	18	18	12	5	0	5.88
Darrel Akerfelds	R	24	0	0	—	0	1	1	0	6	5	4	6	0	6.75
Tim Birtsas	L	25	0	0	—	0	2	1	0	7	8	5	4	0	22.50
Fernando Arroyo	R	34	0	0	—	0	1	0	0	3	7	0	1	0	
Dave Von Ohlen	L	27	0	3	.000	1	24	0	0	15	18	7	4	0	3.52

Name	G by Pos	B	AGE	G	AB	R	H	2B	3B	HR	RBI	BB	SO	SB	BA	SA

KANSAS CITY(TIE)3rd 76-86 .469 16 DICK HOWSER (IL) 40-48 .455 MIKE FERRARO 36-38 .486

Name	G by Pos	B	AGE	G	AB	R	H	2B	3B	HR	RBI	BB	SO	SB	BA	SA
TOTALS			31	162	5561	654	1403	264	45	137	618	474	919	97	.252	.390
Steve Balboni (XJ)	1B137	R	29	138	512	54	117	25	1	29	88	43	146	0	.229	.451
Frank White	2B151, SS1, 3B1	R	35	151	566	76	154	37	3	22	84	43	88	4	.272	.465
Angel Salazar (KJ)	SS115, 2B1	R	24	117	298	24	73	20	2	0	24	7	47	1	.245	.326
George Brett	3B115, DH7, SS2	L	33	124	441	70	128	28	4	16	73	80	45	1	.290	.481
Rudy Law	OF77, DH2	L	29	87	307	42	80	28	5	1	36	29	22	14	.261	.388
Willie Wilson	OF155	B	30	156	631	77	170	20	7	9	44	31	97	34	.269	.366
Lonnie Smith	OF118, DH10	R	30	134	508	80	146	25	7	8	44	46	78	26	.287	.411
Jim Sundberg	C134	R	35	140	429	41	91	9	1	12	42	57	91	1	.212	.322
Jorge Orta	DH87	L	35	106	336	35	93	14	2	9	46	23	34	0	.277	.411
Hal McRae	DH75	R	40	112	278	22	70	14	0	7	37	18	39	0	.252	.378
Buddy Biancalana	SS89, 2B12	B	26	100	190	24	46	4	4	2	8	15	50	5	.242	.337
Jamie Quirk	C41, 3B24, 1B6, OF1	L	31	80	219	24	47	10	0	8	26	17	41	0	.215	.370
1 Darryl Motley	OF66, DH2	R	26	72	217	22	44	9	1	7	20	11	31	0	.203	.350
Lynn Jones	OF62, DH3, 2B1	R	33	67	47	1	6	2	0	0	1	6	5	0	.128	.170
Greg Pryor	3B35, SS17, 2B12, 1B1	R	36	63	112	7	19	4	0	0	7	3	14	1	.170	.205
Mike Kingery	OF59	L	25	62	209	25	54	8	5	3	14	12	30	7	.258	.388
Kevin Seitzer	1B22, OF5, 3B3	R	24	28	96	16	31	4	1	2	11	19	14	0	.323	.448
Bo Jackson	OF23, DH1	R	23	25	82	9	17	2	1	2	9	7	34	3	.207	.329
Bill Pecota	3B12, SS2	R	26	12	29	3	6	2	0	0	2	3	3	0	.207	.276
Mike Brewer	OF9, DH1	R	26	12	18	0	3	1	0	0	0	2	6	0	.167	.222
Ron Johnson	2B11	R	27	11	31	1	8	0	1	0	2	0	3	0	.258	.323
Terry Bell	C8	R	23	8	3	0	0	0	0	0	0	0	0	0	.000	.000
Dwight Taylor	DH2, OF1	L	26	4	1	0	0	0	0	0	0	0	0	0	.000	.000

CHICAGO 5th 72-90 .444 20 TONY LaRUSSA 26-38 .406 DOUG RADER 1-1 .500 JIM FREGOSI 45-51 .469

Name	G by Pos	B	AGE	G	AB	R	H	2B	3B	HR	RBI	BB	SO	SB	BA	SA
TOTALS			28	162	5406	644	1335	197	34	121	605	487	940	115	.247	.363
Greg Walker (BW-BH)	1B77, DH1	L	26	78	282	37	78	10	6	13	51	29	44	1	.277	.493
Julio Cruz	2B78, SS3	B	31	81	209	38	45	2	0	0	19	42	28	7	.215	.225
Ozzie Guillen	SS157, DH1	L	22	159	547	58	137	19	4	2	47	12	52	8	.250	.311
Tim Hulett	3B89, 2B66	R	26	150	520	53	120	16	5	17	44	21	91	4	.231	.379
Harold Baines	OF141, DH3	L	27	145	570	72	169	29	2	21	88	38	89	2	.296	.465
Daryl Boston	OF53, DH1	L	23	56	199	29	53	11	3	5	22	21	33	9	.266	.427
John Cangelosi	OF129, DH3	B	23	137	438	65	103	16	3	2	32	71	61	50	.235	.299
Carlton Fisk	C71, OF20	R	38	125	457	42	101	11	0	14	63	22	92	2	.221	.337
1 Ron Kittle	DH62, OF20	R	28	86	296	34	63	11	0	17	48	28	87	2	.213	.422
Jerry Hairston	DH29, 1B19, OF11	B	34	101	225	32	61	15	0	5	26	26	26	0	.271	.404
1 Wayne Tolleson	3B65, SS18, DH2, OF2	B	30	81	260	39	65	7	3	3	29	38	43	13	.250	.335
1 Bobby Bonilla	OF43, 1B30	B	23	75	234	27	63	10	2	2	26	33	49	4	.269	.355
Reid Nichols (KJ)	OF53, DH3, 2B2	R	27	74	136	9	31	4	0	2	18	11	23	5	.201	.329
1 Joel Skinner	C60	R	25	60	149	17	30	5	1	4	20	9	43	1	.201	.329
2 Ron Hassey	DH34, C11	L	33	49	150	22	53	11	1	3	20	22	11	0	.353	.500
Russ Morman	1B47	R	24	49	159	18	40	5	0	4	17	16	36	1	.252	.358
2 Steve Lyons	OF35, 3B3, DH1, 1B1	L	26	42	123	10	25	2	1	0	6	7	24	2	.203	.236
Ron Karkovice	C37	R	22	37	97	13	24	7	0	4	13	9	37	1	.247	.443
Jack Perconte	2B24	L	31	24	73	6	16	1	0	0	4	11	10	2	.219	.233
Marc Hill	C22	R	34	22	19	2	3	0	0	0	2	4	3	0	.158	.158
1 Bryan Little	2B12, SS7, 3B1	B	26	20	35	3	6	1	0	0	2	4	4	0	.171	.200
Dave Cochrane	3B18, SS1	B	23	19	62	4	12	2	0	1	2	5	22	0	.194	.274
2 George Foster	OF11, DH3	R	37	15	51	2	11	0	0	2	5	8	10	0	.216	.353
Kenny Williams	OF10, DH1	R	22	15	31	2	4	0	0	1	1	1	11	1	.129	.226
2 Ivan Calderon	DH6, OF5	R	24	13	33	3	10	2	1	0	5	3	6	0	.303	.424
Rodney Craig	OF1	B	28	10	10	3	2	0	0	0	0	0	2	0	.200	.200
1 Scott Bradley	DH6, OF1	L	26	9	21	3	6	0	0	0	1	0	0	0	.286	.286
Brian Giles (NJ)	2B7, SS1	R	26	9	11	0	3	1	0	0	0	0	2	0	.273	.364

MINNESOTA 6th 71-91 .438 21 RAY MILLER 59-80 .424 TOM KELLY 12-11 .522

Name	G by Pos	B	AGE	G	AB	R	H	2B	3B	HR	RBI	BB	SO	SB	BA	SA
TOTALS			27	162	5531	741	1446	257	39	196	700	501	977	81	.261	.428
Kent Hrbek	1B147, DH1	L	26	149	550	85	147	27	1	29	91	71	81	2	.267	.418
Steve Lombardozzi	2B155	R	26	156	453	53	103	20	5	8	33	52	76	3	.227	.347
Greg Gagne	SS155, 2B4	R	24	156	472	63	118	22	6	12	54	30	108	12	.250	.398
Gary Gaetti	3B156, SS2, OF1, 2B1	R	27	157	596	91	171	34	1	34	108	52	108	14	.287	.518
Tom Brunansky	OF152, DH2	R	25	157	593	69	152	28	1	23	75	53	98	12	.256	.423
Kirby Puckett	OF160	R	26	161	680	119	223	37	6	31	96	34	99	20	.328	.537
Randy Bush	OF102, DH6, 1B3	L	27	130	357	50	96	16	7	7	45	39	63	5	.269	.460
Mark Salas	C69, DH8	L	25	91	258	28	60	7	4	8	33	18	34	0	.233	.384
Roy Smalley	DH114, SS19, 3B8	B	33	143	459	59	113	20	4	20	57	68	80	1	.246	.438
Mickey Hatcher	OF46, DH28, 1B22, 3B3	R	31	115	317	40	88	13	3	3	32	19	26	2	.278	.366
Billy Beane	OF67, DH5	R	24	80	183	20	39	6	0	3	15	11	54	2	.213	.295
Tim Laudner	C68	R	28	76	193	21	47	10	0	10	29	24	56	1	.244	.451
Jeff Reed	C64	L	23	68	165	13	39	6	1	2	9	16	19	1	.236	.321
Ron Washington	2B16, DH15, SS7, 3B3	R	34	48	74	15	19	3	0	4	11	3	21	1	.257	.459
Alvaro Espinoza	2B19, SS18	R	24	37	42	4	9	1	0	0	2	0	12	0	.214	.238
Mark Davidson	OF31, DH3	R	25	36	66	5	8	1	0	2	6	6	22	2	.121	.303
Al Woods	DH7	L	32	23	28	5	9	1	0	2	8	3	5	0	.321	.571
Chris Pittaro	2B8, SS4	R	24	11	21	0	2	0	0	0	0	0	3	0	.095	.095
Alex Sanchez	DH3, OF1	R	27	8	16	1	2	0	0	0	2	0	6	0	.125	.125
Andre David	DH1	L	28	5	5	0	1	0	0	0	0	0	0	0	.200	.200

SEATTLE 7th 67-95 .414 25 CHUCK COTTIER 9-19 .321 MARTY MARTINEZ 0-1 .000 DICK WILLIAMS 58-75 .436

Name	G by Pos	B	AGE	G	AB	R	H	2B	3B	HR	RBI	BB	SO	SB	BA	SA
TOTALS			27	162	5498	718	1392	243	41	158	681	572	1148	93	.253	.399
Alvin Davis	1B101, DH32	L	25	135	479	66	130	18	1	18	72	76	68	0	.271	.426
Harold Reynolds	2B126	B	25	126	445	46	99	19	4	1	24	29	42	30	.222	.290
1 Spike Owen	SS112	B	25	112	402	46	99	22	6	0	35	34	42	1	.246	.331
Jim Presley	3B155	R	24	155	616	83	163	33	4	27	107	32	172	0	.265	.463
Danny Tartabull	OF101, 2B321, DH3, 3B1	R	23	137	511	76	138	25	6	25	96	61	157	4	.270	.489
John Moses	OF93, 1B7, DH4	B	28	103	399	56	102	16	3	3	34	34	65	26	.256	.333
Phil Bradley	OF140	R	27	143	526	88	163	27	4	12	50	77	134	21	.310	.445
Bob Kearney	C79	R	30	81	204	23	49	10	0	6	25	12	33	0	.240	.377
Ken Phelps	1B55, DH52	L	31	125	344	69	85	16	4	24	64	88	96	2	.247	.526
1 Dave Henderson	OF80, DH22	R	27	103	337	51	93	19	4	14	44	37	95	1	.276	.481
2 Scott Bradley	C59, DH2	L	26	68	199	17	60	8	3	5	28	12	7	1	.302	.447
1 Gorman Thomas	DH52, 1B6	R	35	57	170	24	33	4	0	10	26	27	55	1	.194	.394
Steve Yeager	C49	R	37	50	130	10	27	2	0	2	12	12	23	0	.208	.269
Domingo Ramos	SS21, 2B16, 3B8, DH1	R	28	49	99	8	13	2	0	0	5	6	13	0	.131	.162
1 Ivan Calderon	OF32	R	24	37	131	13	31	5	0	2	13	6	33	3	.237	.321
2 Rey Quinones	SS36	R	22	30	122	6	23	4	0	0	4	5	31	1	.189	.221
Al Cowens	OF19, DH1	R	34	28	82	5	15	4	0	0	9	7	10	1	.183	.232
Mickey Brantley	OF25	R	25	27	102	12	20	3	2	3	7	7	7	0	.196	.353
Dave Valle	C12, 1B4	R	25	22	53	10	18	5	0	5	15	7	7	0	.340	.679
Dave Hengel	DH11, OF8	R	24	21	63	3	12	1	0	1	6	5	13	0	.190	.254
Barry Bonnell	OF9, 1B8, DH2	R	33	17	51	4	10	2	0	0	4	4	5	0	.196	.235
Ross Jones	SS4, 2B3, 3B2, DH1	R	26	15	21	0	2	0	0	0	0	4	4	0	.095	.095
Ricky Nelson	DH4, OF1	L	27	10	12	1	2	0	0	0	0	0	2	0	.167	.167

NAME	T	AGE	W	L	PCT	SV	G	GS	CG	IP	H	BB	SO	SHO	ERA
		27	76	86	.469	31	162	162	24	1441	1413	479	888	13	3.82
Charlie Leibrandt	L	29	14	11	.560	0	35	34	8	231	238	63	108	1	4.09
Mark Gubicza	R	23	12	6	.667	0	35	24	3	181	155	84	118	2	3.64
Danny Jackson	L	24	11	12	.478	1	32	27	4	186	177	79	115	1	3.20
Steve Farr	R	29	8	4	.667	8	56	0	0	109	90	39	83	0	3.13
Scott Bankhead	R	22	8	9	.471	0	24	17	0	121	121	37	94	0	4.61
Dennis Leonard	R	35	8	13	.381	0	33	30	5	193	207	51	114	2	4.44
Bret Saberhagen	R	22	7	12	.368	0	30	25	4	156	165	29	112	2	4.15
Bud Black	L	29	5	10	.333	9	56	4	0	121	100	43	68	0	3.20
Dan Quisenberry	R	33	3	7	.300	12	62	0	0	81	92	24	36	0	2.77
David Cone	R	23	0	0	—	0	11	0	0	23	29	13	21	0	5.56
2 Steve Shields	R	27	0	0	—	3	0	0	9	3	4	2	2	0	2.08
1 Mark Huismann	R	28	0	1	.000	1	10	0	0	17	18	6	13	0	4.15
Alan Hargesheimer(SJ)	R	29	0	1	.000	0	5	0	0	13	18	7	4	0	6.23

NAME	T	AGE	W	L	PCT	SV	G	GS	CG	IP	H	BB	SO	SHO	ERA
		27	72	90	.444	38	162	162	18	1442	1361	561	895	8	3.93
Joe Cowley	R	27	11	11	.500	0	27	27	4	162	133	83	132	0	3.88
Floyd Bannister (KJ)	L	31	10	14	.417	0	28	27	6	165	162	48	92	1	3.54
Rich Dotson	R	27	10	17	.370	0	34	34	3	197	226	69	110	1	5.48
Neil Allen (AJ)	R	28	7	2	.778	0	22	17	2	113	101	38	57	2	3.82
Gene Nelson	R	25	6	6	.500	6	54	1	0	115	118	41	70	0	3.85
Bob James (AJ)	R	27	5	4	.556	14	49	0	0	58	61	23	40	0	5.25
3 Steve Carlton	L	41	4	3	.571	0	10	10	0	63	58	25	40	0	3.69
Joel Davis	R	21	4	5	.444	0	19	19	1	105	115	51	54	0	4.70
2 Jose DeLeon	R	25	4	5	.444	0	13	13	1	79	49	42	68	0	2.96
Joel McKeon (IL)	L	23	3	1	.750	1	30	0	0	33	18	17	18	0	2.45
Dave Schmidt	R	29	3	6	.333	8	49	1	0	92	94	27	67	0	3.31
Bobby Thigpen	R	22	2	0	1.000	7	20	0	0	36	26	12	20	0	1.77
1 Tom Seaver	R	41	2	6	.250	0	12	12	1	72	66	27	31	0	4.38
2 Ray Searage	L	31	1	0	1.000	0	29	0	0	29	15	19	26	0	0.62
Bryan Clark	L	29	0	0	—	0	4	0	0	5	5	3	4	0	4.50
2 Pete Filson	L	27	0	1	.000	0	9	0	0	12	14	5	4	0	6.17
1 Juan Agosto	L	27	0	1	.000	0	9	0	0	5	6	4	3	0	7.71
Bill Dawley	R	28	0	7	.000	2	46	0	0	98	91	28	66	0	3.32

NAME	T	AGE	W	L	PCT	SV	G	GS	CG	IP	H	BB	SO	SHO	ERA
		28	71	91	.438	24	162	162	39	1433	1579	503	937	6	4.77
Bert Blyleven	R	35	17	14	.548	0	36	36	16	272	262	58	215	3	4.01
Frank Viola	L	26	16	13	.552	0	37	37	7	246	257	83	191	1	4.51
Mike Smithson	R	31	13	14	.481	0	34	33	8	198	234	57	114	1	4.77
Mark Portugal	R	23	6	1	.375	1	27	15	3	113	112	50	67	0	4.31
1 Keith Atherton	R	27	5	8	.385	10	47	0	0	82	82	35	59	0	3.75
2 Neal Heaton	L	26	4	9	.308	1	21	17	3	124	128	47	66	0	3.98
Frank Pastore (SJ)	R	28	3	1	.750	0	2	33	1	49	54	24	18	0	4.01
Allan Anderson	L	22	3	6	.333	0	21	11	0	84	106	30	51	0	5.55
1 Ron Davis	R	30	2	6	.250	7	2	36	0	99	55	29	30	0	9.08
2 George Frazier	R	31	1	1	.500	6	15	0	0	27	23	16	25	0	4.39
2 Juan Agosto	L	28	1	2	.333	1	17	1	0	20	43	14	9	0	8.85
2 Ray Fontenot	L	27	0	0	—	0	15	0	0	16	24	4	10	0	9.92
1 Pete Filson	L	27	0	0	—	0	6	0	0	6	13	2	4	0	5.68
Dennis Burtt	R	28	0	0	—	0	4	0	0	8	13	4	1	0	31.50
Roy Lee Jackson	R	32	0	1	.000	1	28	0	0	58	57	16	32	0	3.86
Bill Latham	L	25	0	1	.000	0	7	2	0	14	18	8	6	0	7.31
Roy Smith	R	24	0	3	.000	0	16	10	1	70	82	24	29	0	6.30
1 John Butcher	R	29	0	3	.000	0	16	10	1	70	82	24	29	0	6.30

NAME	T	AGE	W	L	PCT	SV	G	GS	CG	IP	H	BB	SO	SHO	ERA
		27	67	95	.414	27	162	162	33	1440	1590	585	944	5	4.65
Mark Langston	L	25	12	14	.462	0	37	36	9	239	234	123	245	0	4.85
Mike Moore	R	26	11	13	.458	1	38	37	11	266	279	94	146	1	4.30
Mike Morgan	R	26	11	17	.393	1	37	33	9	216	243	86	116	1	4.53
Matt Young	L	27	8	6	.571	13	65	5	1	104	108	46	82	0	3.82
Pete Ladd	R	29	8	6	.571	6	52	0	0	71	69	18	53	0	3.82
Jerry Reed (BW)	R	30	4	1	1.000	0	4	0	0	35	38	13	16	0	3.12
2 Mike Trujillo	R	26	3	3	.500	4	36	1	0	80	80	19	59	0	3.71
2 Mark Huismann	R	28	3	5	.500	4	36	1	0	80	80	19	59	0	3.71
Steve Fireovid	R	29	2	0	1.000	0	26	0	0	36	35	21	23	0	4.04
Karl Best	R	27	2	3	.400	1	26	0	0	29	17	11	15	5	5.46
Bill Swift	R	24	2	9	.182	0	29	17	1	115	148	55	55	0	5.82
Edwin Nunez (SJ)	R	23	0	6	.000	0	14	1	0	22	25	5	17	0	5.82
Paul Mirabella	L	32	0	0	—	0	5	0	0	16	19	11	9	0	8.53
2 Mike Brown	R	27	0	0	—	0	41	4	1	76	100	30	38	0	7.47
Lee Guetterman	L	27	0	4	.000	0	41	4	1	76	100	30	38	0	7.34
Jim Beattie (SJ)	R	31	0	3	.000	0	10	10	0	40	57	14	24	0	6.02
Milt Wilcox	R	36	0	0	—	0	13	10	0	56	74	28	26	0	5.50
Roy Thomas (EJ) 33															

NEW YORK — 1st 108-54 .667 — DAVEY JOHNSON

Name	G by Pos	B	AGE	G	AB	R	H	2B	3B	HR	RBI	BB	SO	SB	BA	SA
TOTALS		28		162	5558	783	1462	261	31	148	730	631	968	118	.263	.401
Keith Hernandez	1B149	L	32	149	551	94	171	34	1	13	83	94	69	2	.310	.446
Wally Backman	2B113	R	26	124	387	67	124	18	2	1	27	36	32	13	.320	.385
Rafael Santana	SS137, 2B1	R	28	139	394	38	86	11	0	1	28	36	43	0	.218	.254
Ray Knight	3B132, 1B1	R	33	137	486	51	145	24	2	11	76	40	63	2	.298	.424
Darryl Strawberry	OF131	L	24	136	475	76	123	27	5	27	93	72	141	28	.259	.507
Lenny Dykstra	OF139	L	23	147	431	77	127	27	7	8	45	58	55	31	.295	.445
Mookie Wilson (SJ-IJ)	OF114	B	30	123	381	61	110	17	5	9	45	32	72	25	.289	.430
Gary Carter	C122, 1B9, OF4, 3B1	R	32	132	490	81	125	24	2	24	105	62	63	1	.255	.439
Kevin Mitchell	OF68, SS24, 3B7, 1B2	R	24	108	328	51	91	22	2	12	43	33	61	3	.277	.466
Tim Teufel	2B84, 1B3, 3B1	R	27	93	279	35	69	20	1	4	31	32	42	1	.247	.369
Howard Johnson	3B45, SS34, OF1	R	25	88	220	30	54	14	0	10	39	31	64	8	.245	.445
Danny Heep	OF56	L	28	86	195	24	55	8	2	5	33	30	31	1	.282	.421
1 George Foster	OF62	R	37	72	233	28	53	6	1	13	38	21	53	1	.227	.429
Ed Hearn	C45	R	25	49	136	16	36	5	0	4	10	12	19	0	.265	.390
2 Lee Mazzilli	OF10, 1B8	L	31	39	58	10	16	3	0	2	7	12	11	1	.276	.431
Kevin Elster	SS19	R	21	19	30	3	5	1	0	0	0	3	8	0	.167	.200
Stan Jefferson	OF7	B	23	14	24	6	5	1	0	1	3	2	8	0	.208	.375
Dave Magadan	1B9	L	23	10	18	3	8	0	0	0	3	3	1	0	.444	.444
John Gibbons	C8	R	24	8	19	4	9	4	0	1	1	3	6	0	.474	.842
Barry Lyons	C3	R	26	6	9	1	0	0	0	0	0	2	1	0	.000	.000
Tim Corcoran	1B1	L	33	6	7	1	0	0	0	0	0	0	1	0	.000	.000

NAME	T	AGE	W	L	PCT	SV	G	GS	CG	IP	H	BB	SO	SHO	ERA
		26	108	54	.667	46	162	162	27	1484	1304	509	1083	11	3.11
Bob Ojeda	L	28	18	5	.783	0	32	30	7	217	185	52	148	2	2.57
Dwight Gooden	R	21	17	6	.739	0	33	33	12	250	197	80	200	2	2.84
Sid Fernandez	L	23	16	6	.727	1	32	31	2	204	161	91	200	1	3.52
Ron Darling	R	25	15	6	.714	0	34	34	4	237	203	81	184	2	2.81
Roger McDowell	R	25	14	9	.609	22	75	0	0	128	107	42	65	0	3.02
Rick Aguilera	R	24	10	7	.588	0	28	20	2	142	145	36	104	0	3.88
Jesse Orosco	L	29	8	6	.571	21	58	0	0	81	64	35	62	0	2.33
Doug Sisk	R	28	4	2	.667	1	41	0	0	71	77	31	31	0	3.06
Rick Anderson	R	29	2	1	.667	1	15	5	0	50	45	11	21	0	2.72
Bruce Berenyi	R	31	2	2	.500	0	14	7	0	40	47	22	30	0	6.35
Randy Niemann	L	30	2	3	.400	0	31	0	0	36	44	12	18	0	3.79
Randy Myers	L	23	0	0	—	0	10	0	0	11	11	9	13	0	4.22
1 Ed Lynch (KJ)	R	30	0	0	—	0	1	0	0	2	2	1	0	0	0.00
Terry Leach	R	32	0	0	—	0	6	0	0	7	6	3	4	0	2.70
John Mitchell	R	20	0	1	.000	0	4	1	0	10	10	4	2	0	3.60

PHILADELPHIA — 2nd 86-75 .534 21.5 — JOHN FELSKE

Name	G by Pos	B	AGE	G	AB	R	H	2B	3B	HR	RBI	BB	SO	SB	BA	SA
TOTALS		27		161	5739	739	1386	266	39	154	696	589	1154	153	.253	.400
Von Hayes	1B134, OF31	L	27	158	610	107	186	46	2	19	98	74	77	24	.305	.480
Juan Samuel	2B143	R	25	145	591	90	157	36	12	16	78	26	142	42	.266	.448
Steve Jeltz	SS141	B	27	145	439	44	96	11	4	0	36	65	97	6	.219	.262
Mike Schmidt	3B124, 1B35	R	36	160	552	97	160	29	1	37	119	89	84	1	.290	.547
Glenn Wilson	OF154	R	27	155	584	70	158	30	4	15	84	42	91	5	.271	.413
Milt Thompson	OF89	L	27	96	299	38	75	7	1	6	23	26	62	19	.251	.341
Gary Redus (EJ)	OF89	R	29	90	340	62	84	22	4	11	33	47	78	25	.247	.432
John Russell	C89	R	25	93	315	35	76	21	2	13	60	25	103	0	.241	.444
Ron Roenicke	OF83	B	29	102	275	42	68	13	1	5	42	61	52	2	.247	.356
Rick Schu	3B58	R	24	93	208	32	57	10	1	8	25	18	44	2	.274	.447
Greg Gross	OF27, 1B5	L	33	87	101	11	25	5	0	0	8	21	11	1	.248	.297
Jeff Stone	OF58	L	25	82	249	32	69	6	4	6	19	20	52	19	.277	.406
Luis Aguayo	2B31, SS20, 3B1	R	27	62	133	17	28	6	1	4	13	8	26	1	.211	.361
Darren Daulton (KJ)	C48	L	24	49	138	18	31	4	0	8	21	38	41	2	.225	.428
Ronn Reynolds	C42	R	27	43	126	8	27	4	0	3	10	5	30	0	.214	.317
1 Tom Foley	SS24, 2B1, 3B1	R	26	39	61	8	18	2	1	0	5	10	11	2	.295	.361
Chris James (BN)	OF11	R	23	16	46	5	13	3	0	1	5	1	13	0	.283	.413
Joe Lefebvre	OF3	L	30	14	18	0	2	0	0	0	0	3	5	0	.111	.111
Greg Legg	2B4, SS1	R	26	11	20	2	9	1	0	0	1	0	3	0	.450	.500
Francisco Melendez	1B2	L	22	9	8	0	2	0	0	0	0	1	2	0	.250	.250
Garry Maddox (XJ)	OF3	R	36	6	7	1	3	0	0	0	1	2	1	0	.429	.429

NAME	T	AGE	W	L	PCT	SV	G	GS	CG	IP	H	BB	SO	SHO	ERA
		29	86	75	.534	39	161	161	22	1452	1473	553	874	11	3.85
Kevin Gross	R	25	12	12	.500	0	37	36	7	242	240	94	154	2	4.02
Kent Tekulve	R	39	11	5	.688	4	73	0	0	110	99	25	57	0	2.54
Shane Rawley (BS)	L	30	11	7	.611	0	23	23	7	158	166	50	73	1	3.54
Don Carman	L	26	10	5	.667	1	50	14	2	134	113	52	98	1	3.22
Bruce Ruffin	L	22	9	4	.692	0	21	21	6	146	138	44	70	0	2.46
Steve Bedrosian	R	28	8	6	.571	29	68	0	0	90	79	34	82	0	3.39
Charlie Hudson	R	27	7	10	.412	0	33	23	0	144	165	58	82	0	4.94
Tom Hume (KJ)	R	33	4	1	.800	4	48	1	0	94	89	34	51	0	2.77
1 Steve Carlton	L	41	4	8	.333	0	16	16	0	83	102	45	62	0	6.18
2 Dan Schatzeder	L	31	3	3	.500	1	29	5	0	29	28	16	14	0	3.38
Mike Maddux	R	24	3	7	.300	0	16	16	0	78	88	34	44	0	5.42
Marvin Freeman	R	23	2	0	1.000	0	3	3	0	16	6	10	8	0	2.25
Randy Lerch	L	31	1	1	.500	0	4	0	0	8	10	7	5	0	7.88
Jeff Bittiger	R	24	1	1	.500	0	4	0	0	9	14	7	6	0	5.52
1 Larry Andersen	R	33	0	0	—	0	10	0	0	13	19	3	9	0	4.26
Mike Jackson	R	21	0	0	—	0	9	0	0	13	12	4	9	0	3.38
1 Dave Stewart	R	29	0	0	—	0	8	0	0	12	15	4	9	0	6.57
Rocky Childress	R	24	0	0	—	0	8	0	0	12	14	4	9	0	6.75
Greg Gross	L	33	0	0	—	0	1	0	0	1	1	1	2	0	0.00
Tom Gorman	R	29	0	1	.000	0	8	0	0	12	21	5	8	0	7.71
Dave Rucker	L	28	0	2	.000	0	19	0	0	25	34	14	14	0	5.76
Freddie Toliver (BA)	R	25	0	2	.000	0	5	5	0	26	28	11	20	0	3.51

ST. LOUIS — 3rd 79-82 .491 28.5 — WHITEY HERZOG

Name	G by Pos	B	AGE	G	AB	R	H	2B	3B	HR	RBI	BB	SO	SB	BA	SA
TOTALS		28		161	5478	601	1270	216	48	58	550	568	905	262	.236	.327
Jack Clark (RJ)	1B64	R	30	65	232	34	58	12	2	9	23	45	61	1	.237	.422
Tommy Herr	2B152	B	30	152	559	48	141	30	4	2	61	73	75	22	.252	.331
Ozzie Smith	SS144	B	31	153	514	67	144	19	4	0	54	79	27	31	.280	.333
Terry Pendleton	3B156 OF1	B	25	159	578	56	138	26	5	1	59	34	59	24	.239	.306
Andy Van Slyke	OF110 1B38	L	25	137	418	48	113	23	7	13	61	47	85	21	.270	.452
Willie McGee (LJ)	OF121	R	27	124	497	65	127	22	7	7	48	37	82	19	.256	.370
Vince Coleman	OF149	B	25	154	600	94	139	13	8	0	29	60	98	107	.232	.280
Mike LaValliere	C108	L	25	110	303	18	71	10	2	3	30	36	37	0	.234	.310
Tito Landrum	OF78	R	31	96	205	24	43	7	1	2	17	20	41	3	.210	.283
Curt Ford	OF64	R	25	85	214	30	53	15	2	2	29	23	29	13	.248	.364
Clint Hurdle	1B39 OF10 C5 3B4	L	28	78	154	18	30	5	1	3	15	26	38	0	.195	.299
Jose Oquendo	SS29 2B21 3B1 OF1	B	22	76	138	20	41	4	1	0	13	15	20	2	.297	.341
1 Mike Heath	C63 OF2	R	31	65	190	19	39	8	1	4	25	23	36	2	.205	.321
Tom Lawless	3B12 2B7 OF1	R	29	46	39	5	11	1	0	0	3	2	8	8	.282	.308
John Morris	0F31	R	25	39	100	8	24	0	1	1	14	7	15	6	.240	.290
Alan Knicely	1B29 C2	R	31	34	82	8	16	3	0	1	6	17	21	1	.195	.268
2 Steve Lake	C26	R	29	28	49	4	12	1	0	2	10	2	5	0	.294	.368
Jerry White	OF6	B	33	25	24	1	3	0	0	1	3	2	3	0	.125	.250
Jim Lindeman	1B17 3B1 OF1	R	24	19	55	7	14	1	0	1	6	2	10	1	.255	.327
2 Mike Laga	1B16	L	26	18	46	7	10	4	0	3	8	5	18	0	.217	.500
Fred Manrique	3B4 2B1	R	25	18	17	2	3	0	0	1	1	1	5	0	.176	.353

NAME	T	AGE	W	L	PCT	SV	G	GS	CG	IP	H	BB	SO	SHO	ERA
		28	79	82	.491	46	161	161	17	1466	1364	485	761	4	3.37
Bob Forsch	R	36	14	10	.583	0	33	33	3	230	211	68	104	0	3.25
John Tudor	L	32	13	7	.650	0	30	30	3	219	197	53	107	0	2.92
Danny Cox	R	26	12	13	.480	0	32	32	8	220	189	60	108	0	2.90
Greg Matthews	L	24	11	8	.579	0	23	22	1	145	139	44	67	0	3.65
Todd Worrell	R	26	9	10	.474	36	74	0	0	104	86	41	73	0	2.08
Tim Conroy (SJ)	L	26	5	11	.313	0	25	21	1	115	122	56	79	0	5.23
Ray Soff	R	27	4	2	.667	0	30	0	0	38	37	13	22	0	3.29
Ricky Horton (EJ)	L	26	4	3	.571	3	42	9	1	100	77	26	49	0	2.24
Ray Burris	R	35	4	4	.444	0	23	10	0	82	92	32	34	0	5.60
Pat Perry	R	27	2	3	.400	2	46	0	0	69	59	34	29	0	3.80
Rick Ownbey	R	28	1	3	.250	0	17	3	0	43	47	19	25	0	3.80
Jeff Lahti (SJ)	R	29	0	0	—	0	4	0	0	4	2	1	0	0	1.66
Bill Earley	R	30	0	0	—	0	1	0	0	1	1	1	0	0	1.66
Joe Boever	R	25	0	1	.000	0	11	0	0	8	8	4	4	0	4.50
Kurt Kepshire	R	26	0	1	.000	0	2	1	0	8	9	11	8	0	5.60
Greg Bargar	R	27	0	2	.000	0	22	0	0	27	36	10	12	0	5.60
Ken Dayley (EJ)	L	27	0	3	.000	1	31	0	0	39	42	11	33	0	3.26

MONTREAL — 4th 78-83 .484 29.5 — BUCK RODGERS

Name	G by Pos	B	AGE	G	AB	R	H	2B	3B	HR	RBI	BB	SO	SB	BA	SA
TOTALS		27		161	5508	637	1401	255	50	110	602	537	1016	193	.254	.379
Andres Galarraga	1B102	R	25	105	321	39	87	13	0	10	42	30	79	6	.271	.405
Vance Law (IF)	2B94, 1B20, 3B13, P3, OF1	R	29	112	360	37	81	17	2	5	44	37	66	3	.225	.325
Hubie Brooks (RJ)	SS80	R	29	80	306	50	104	18	5	14	58	25	60	4	.340	.569
Tim Wallach	3B132	R	28	134	480	50	112	22	1	18	71	44	72	8	.233	.396
Andre Dawson	OF127	R	31	130	496	65	141	32	2	20	78	37	79	18	.284	.478
Mitch Webster	OF146	B	27	151	576	89	167	31	13	8	49	57	78	36	.290	.431
Tim Raines	OF147	B	26	151	580	91	194	35	10	9	62	78	60	70	.334	.476
Mike Fitzgerald (BG)	C71	R	25	73	209	20	59	13	1	6	37	27	34	3	.282	.440
Wayne Krenchicki	1B41, 3B24, 2B1, OF1	L	31	101	221	21	53	6	2	2	23	22	32	2	.240	.312
Al Newman	2B59, SS22	B	26	95	185	23	37	3	0	1	8	21	20	11	.200	.232
Herm Winningham	OF66, SS1	L	24	90	185	23	40	6	3	1	11	18	51	12	.216	.346
Dann Bilardello	C77	R	27	79	191	12	37	5	0	4	17	14	32	1	.194	.283
Jim Wohlford	OF22, 3B6	R	35	70	120	12	32	4	2	1	11	9	17	0	.266	.383
2 Tom Foley	SS29, 2B25, 3B16	L	26	64	202	18	52	13	2	1	18	20	26	8	.257	.356
Wallace Johnson	1B27	R	29	61	127	13	36	3	1	1	10	7	9	6	.283	.346
2 George Wright	OF32	B	27	56	117	12	22	5	2	0	5	11	28	1	.188	.265
Luis Rivera	SS55	R	22	55	166	20	34	11	1	0	13	17	33	1	.205	.283
Casey Candaele	2B24, 3B4	B	25	30	104	9	24	4	1	0	6	5	15	3	.231	.288
Tom Nieto	C30	R	25	30	65	5	13	3	1	1	7	2	16	0	.200	.323
Jason Thompson	1B15	L	31	30	51	6	10	4	0	0	4	18	12	0	.196	.275
Randy Hunt	C21	R	26	26	61	4	10	1	0	2	5	5	16	0	.208	.333
Rene Gonzales	SS6, 3B5	R	25	11	26	1	3	0	0	0	0	1	5	0	.115	.115
Wil Tejada	C10	R	23	10	25	1	6	1	0	0	2	1	6	0	.240	.280
Billy Moore	1B3, OF1	R	25	6	12	2	2	1	0	0	2	0	4	0	.167	.167

NAME	T	AGE	W	L	PCT	SV	G	GS	CG	IP	H	BB	SO	SHO	ERA
		28	78	83	.484	50	161	161	15	1466	1350	566	1051	9	3.78
Floyd Youmans	R	22	13	12	.520	0	33	32	6	219	145	118	202	2	3.53
Andy McGaffigan	R	29	10	5	.667	2	48	14	1	143	114	55	104	1	2.65
Bryn Smith (BE)	R	30	10	8	.556	0	30	30	1	187	182	63	105	0	3.94
Tim Burke	R	27	9	7	.563	4	68	2	0	101	103	46	82	0	2.93
Jeff Reardon	R	30	7	9	.438	35	62	0	0	89	83	26	67	0	3.94
Jay Tibbs	R	27	7	9	.438	0	35	31	3	190	181	70	117	2	3.97
Joe Hesketh (XJ)	L	27	6	5	.545	0	15	15	0	83	92	31	67	0	5.01
Bob Sebra	R	24	5	5	.500	0	17	13	3	91	82	25	66	1	3.55
1 Dan Schatzeder	L	31	5	2	.600	1	30	1	0	59	53	19	33	0	3.20
2 Dennis Martinez	R	31	3	6	.333	0	19	15	1	98	103	28	63	1	4.59
Randy St. Claire	R	25	2	0	1.000	1	11	0	0	19	13	6	21	0	2.37
2 Bob McClure	L	34	2	5	.286	6	52	0	0	63	53	23	42	0	3.02
Bob Owchinko	L	31	0	0	1.000	0	3	3	0	15	17	3	6	0	3.60
George Riley	L	29	0	0	—	0	10	0	0	13	17	7	6	0	4.15
Dave Tomlin (FJ)	L	37	0	0	—	0	13	0	0	13	17	7	6	0	5.23
Vance Law	R	29	0	0	—	0	2	0	0	2	2	1	0	0	2.25
Jeff Parrett	R	24	0	1	.000	0	12	0	0	20	19	13	21	0	4.87
Curt Brown	R	26	0	1	.000	0	12	1	0	14	21	6	9	0	3.00
Bert Roberge	R	31	0	4	.000	1	21	0	0	29	33	10	20	0	6.28
Sergio Valdez	R	21	0	4	.000	0	5	5	0	25	39	11	20	0	6.84
Charlie Lea (SJ)		29													

EAST DIVISION

CHICAGO — 5th 70-90 .438 37 — JIM FREY 23-33 .411 · JOHN VUKOVICH 1-1 .500 · GENE MICHAEL 46-56 .451

Name	G by Pos	B	AGE	G	AB	R	H	2B	3B	HR	RBI	BB	SO	SB	BA	SA
TOTALS			30	160	5499	680	1409	258	27	155	638	508	966	132	.256	.398
Leon Durham	1B141	L	28	141	484	66	127	18	7	20	65	67	98	8	.262	.452
Ryne Sandberg	2B153	R	26	154	627	68	178	28	5	14	76	46	79	34	.284	.411
Shawon Dunston	SS149	R	23	150	581	66	145	37	3	17	68	21	114	13	.250	.411
Ron Cey	3B77	R	38	97	256	42	70	21	0	13	36	55	66	0	.273	.508
Keith Moreland	OF121, 3B24, C13, 1B12	R	32	156	586	72	159	30	0	12	79	53	48	3	.271	.384
Bob Dernier (SJ)	OF105	R	29	108	324	32	73	14	1	4	18	22	41	27	.225	.312
Gary Matthews	OF105	R	35	123	370	49	96	16	1	21	46	60	59	3	.259	.428
Jody Davis	C145, 1B1	R	29	148	528	61	132	27	2	21	74	41	110	0	.250	.428
Jerry Mumphrey	OF92	B	33	111	309	37	94	11	2	5	32	26	45	2	.304	.401
Chris Speier	3B53, SS23, 2B7	R	36	95	155	21	44	8	0	6	23	15	32	2	.284	.452
Thad Bosley	OF41	L	29	87	120	15	33	4	1	9	18	24	3		.275	.350
Terry Francona	OF30, 1B23	L	27	86	124	13	31	3	0	2	8	6	8	0	.250	.323
Manny Trillo (RJ)	3B53, 1B11, 2B6	R	35	81	152	22	45	10	0	1	19	16	21	0	.296	.382
1 Davey Lopes	3B32, OF22	R	41	59	157	38	47	8	2	6	22	31	16	17	.299	.490
Dave Martinez	OF46	L	21	53	108	13	15	1	1	1	7	6	22	4	.139	.194
Chico Walker	OF26	B	28	28	101	21	28	5	2	1	7	10	20	15	.277	.376
Brian Dayett	OF24	R	24	67	7	18	4	0	4	11	6	10	0		.269	.507
Rafael Palmeiro	OF20	L	21	22	73	9	18	4	0	3	12	4	6	1	.247	.425
1 Steve Lake	C10	R	29	10	19	4	8	1	0	0	4	1	2	0	.421	.474
Mike Martin	C8	R	27	8	13	1	1	1	0	0	0	2	4	0	.077	.154
Steve Christmas (EJ)	C1, 1B1	L	28	3	9	0	1	1	0	0	2	0	1	0	.111	.222

NAME	T	AGE	W	L	PCT	SV	G	GS	CG	IP	H	BB	SO	SHO	ERA
		29	70	90	.438	42	160	160	11	1445	1546	557	962	6	4.49
Lee Smith	R	28	9	9	.500	31	66	0	0	90	69	42	93	0	3.09
Scott Sanderson	R	29	9	11	.450	0	37	28	1	170	165	37	124	1	4.19
Jamie Moyer	L	23	7	4	.636	0	16	16	1	87	107	42	45	1	5.05
2 Ed Lynch	R	30	7	5	.583	0	23	13	1	100	105	23	57	1	3.79
Guy Hoffman	L	29	6	2	.750	0	32	8	1	84	92	29	47	0	3.86
Dennis Eckersley	R	31	6	11	.353	0	33	32	1	201	226	43	137	0	4.57
Steve Trout	L	28	5	7	.417	0	37	25	0	161	184	78	69	0	4.75
Rick Sutcliffe	R	30	5	14	.263	0	28	27	4	177	166	96	122	1	4.64
1 Ray Fontenot	R	28	3		.375	2	42	0	0	56	57	21	24	0	3.86
Dave Gumpert	R	28	2	0	1.000	2	38	0	0	60	60	28	45	0	4.37
1 Matt Keough	R	30	2	2	.500	0	19	2	0	29	36	12	19	0	4.97
Jay Baller	R	25	2	2	.330	5	36	0	0	54	58	28	42	0	5.37
1 George Frazier	R	31	2	4	.333	0	35	0	0	52	63	34	41	0	5.40
1 Frank DiPino	L	29	2	4	.333	0	30	0	0	40	47	14	43	0	5.18
Greg Maddux	R	20	2	4	.333	0	6	5	1	31	44	11	20	0	5.52
Drew Hall	L	23	1	2	.333	1	5	4	1	24	24	10	21	0	4.56
Dick Ruthven	R	35	0	0	—	0	6	0	0	11	12	6	3	0	5.06
2 Ron Davis	R	30	0	2	.000	0	17	0	0	20	31	3	10	0	7.65

PITTSBURGH — 6th 64-98 .395 44 — JIM LEYLAND

Name	G by Pos	B	AGE	G	AB	R	H	2B	3B	HR	RBI	BB	SO	SB	BA	SA
TOTALS			27	162	5456	663	1366	273	33	111	618	569	929	152	.250	.374
Sid Bream	1B153, OF2	L	25	154	522	73	140	37	5	16	77	60	73	13	.268	.450
Johnny Ray	2B151	B	29	155	579	67	174	33	0	7	78	58	47	6	.301	.394
Rafael Belliard	SS96, 2B23	R	24	117	309	33	72	5	2	0	31	26	54	12	.233	.262
Jim Morrison	3B151, 2B1, SS1	R	33	154	537	58	147	35	4	23	88	47	88	9	.274	.482
Joe Orsulak	OF120	L	24	138	401	60	100	19	6	2	19	28	38	24	.249	.342
Barry Bonds	OF110	L	21	113	413	72	92	26	3	16	48	65	102	36	.223	.416
R.J. Reynolds	OF112	B	27	118	402	63	108	30	2	9	48	40	73	16	.269	.420
Tony Pena	C139, 1B4	R	29	144	510	56	147	26	2	10	52	53	69	9	.288	.406
Bill Almon	OF54, 3B28, SS19, 1B4	R	33	102	196	29	43	7	2	7	27	30	38	11	.219	.383
Mike Diaz	OF38, 1B20, 3B5, C1	R	26	97	209	22	56	9	0	12	36	19	43	0	.268	.483
Mike Brown	OF71	R	26	87	243	18	53	7	0	4	26	28	32	2	.218	.296
U.L. Washington	SS51, 2B3	B	32	72	135	14	27	0	4	0	10	15	27	6	.200	.259
Sammy Khalifa	SS60, 2B6	R	22	64	151	8	28	6	0	0	4	19	28	0	.185	.225
2 Bobby Bonilla	OF52, 3B4, 1B4	R	23	63	192	28	46	6	2	1	17	29	39	4	.240	.307
1 Lee Mazzilli	OF18, 1B7	B	31	61	93	1	21	2	1	1	8	26	25	3	.226	.301
Junior Ortiz	C36	R	25	49	110	11	37	6	0	0	14	9	13	0	.336	.391
Benny Distefano	OF9, 1B1	L	24	31	39	3	7	1	0	1	5	1	5	0	.179	.282
Trench Davis	OF7	L	25	15	23	2	3	0	0	0	1	0	4	0	.130	.130
Steve Kemp	OF4	L	31	13	16	1	3	0	0	0	1	4	6	1	.188	.375
Rich Renteria	2B1	R	24	10	12	2	3	1	0	0	1	0	4	0	.250	.333

NAME	T	AGE	W	L	PCT	SV	G	GS	CG	IP	H	BB	SO	SHO	ERA
		28	64	98	.395	30	162	162	17	1451	1397	570	924	9	3.90
Rick Rhoden	R	33	15	12	.556	0	34	34	12	254	211	76	159	1	2.85
Rick Reuschel	R	37	9	16	.360	0	35	34	4	216	232	57	125	2	3.96
Bob Walk	R	29	7	8	.467	2	44	15	1	142	129	64	78	1	3.75
Bob Kipper (SJ)	L	21	6	8	.429	0	20	19	0	114	123	34	81	0	4.03
Mike Bielecki	R	26	6	11	.353	0	31	27	0	149	149	83	83	0	4.66
Cecilio Guante (WJ)	R	26	5	2	.714	4	52	0	0	78	65	29	63	0	3.35
Don Robinson (KJ)	R	29	3	4	.429	14	50	0	0	69	61	27	53	0	3.38
Barry Jones	R	23	3	4	.429	3	26	0	0	37	29	21	29	0	2.89
Jim Winn	R	26	3	5	.375	3	50	3	0	88	85	38	70	0	3.58
Larry McWilliams	R	32	3	11	.214	0	49	15	0	122	129	49	80	0	5.15
Bob Patterson	L	27	1	3	.400	0	11	5	0	36	49	5	20	0	4.95
John Smiley	L	21	1	0	1.000	0	12	0	0	12	4	4	9	0	3.86
1 Jose DeLeon	R	25	1	3	.250	1	9	3	0	16	17	11	11	0	8.27
Rich Sauveur	L	22	0	0	—	0	3	0	0	12	17	6	6	0	6.00
Ray Krawczyk (KJ)	R	26	0	1	.000	0	12	0	0	12	17	10	7	0	7.30
Hipolito Pena	L	22	0	0	—	1	10	1	0	8	7	3	6	0	8.64
Stan Fansler	R	22	0	3	.000	0	5	5	0	20	15	13	10	0	3.75
Pat Clements	L	24	0	4	.000	2	65	0	0	61	53	32	31	0	2.80

WEST DIVISION

HOUSTON — 1st 96-66 .593 — HAL LANIER

Name	G by Pos	B	AGE	G	AB	R	H	2B	3B	HR	RBI	BB	SO	SB	BA	SA
TOTALS			31	162	5441	654	1388	244	32	125	613	536	916	163	.255	.381
Glenn Davis	1B156	R	25	158	574	91	152	32	3	31	101	64	72	3	.265	.493
Bill Doran	2B144	B	28	145	550	92	152	29	3	6	37	81	57	42	.276	.373
Dickie Thon	SS104	R	28	106	278	24	69	13	1	3	21	29	49	6	.248	.335
Denny Walling	3B102, OF11, 1B4	L	32	130	382	54	119	23	1	13	58	36	31	1	.312	.479
Kevin Bass	OF155	R	27	157	591	83	184	33	5	20	79	38	72	22	.311	.486
Billy Hatcher	OF121	R	25	127	419	55	108	15	4	6	36	22	52	38	.258	.356
Jose Cruz	OF134	L	38	141	479	48	133	22	4	10	72	55	86	3	.278	.403
Alan Ashby	C103	B	34	120	315	24	81	15	0	7	38	39	56	1	.257	.371
Phil Garner	3B84, 2B7	R	37	107	313	43	83	14	3	9	41	30	45	12	.265	.415
Craig Reynolds	SS98, 1B5, 3B4, OF2, P1	L	33	114	313	32	78	7	3	6	41	12	31	3	.249	.348
Tony Walker	OF68	R	27	84	90	19	20	7	0	2	10	11	15	11	.222	.367
Terry Puhl	OF47	L	29	81	172	17	42	10	0	3	14	15	24	3	.244	.355
Jim Pankovits	2B28, OF5, C1	R	30	70	113	12	32	6	1	1	7	11	25	1	.283	.381
Mark Bailey	C53, 1B5	B	24	57	153	9	27	5	0	4	15	28	45	1	.176	.288
John Mizerock	C42	R	25	44	81	9	15	1	1	1	4	26	16	0	.185	.259
2 Davey Lopes	OF19, 3B5	R	41	37	98	11	23	2	1	1	13	12	9	8	.235	.306
Ty Gainey	OF19	L	25	26	50	6	15	3	1	1	6	6	19	3	.300	.460
2 Dan Driessen	1B12	L	34	17	24	5	7	1	0	1	3	5	2	0	.292	.458
Bert Pena	SS10, 3B2, 2B1	R	26	15	29	3	6	1	0	0	2	5	5	1	.207	.241
Robbie Wine	C8	R	23	9	12	2	3	1	0	0	0	1	4	0	.250	.333
Eric Bullock	OF6	L	25	9	21	0	1	0	0	0	0	0	1	0	.048	.048
Louie Meadows	OF1	L	25	6	3	1	2	0	0	0	0	0	0	0	.333	.333

NAME	T	AGE	W	L	PCT	SV	G	GS	CG	IP	H	BB	SO	SHO	ERA
		30	96	66	.593	51	162	162	18	1456	1203	523	1160	19	3.15
Mike Scott	R	31	18	10	.643	0	37	37	7	275	182	72	306	5	2.22
Bob Knepper	L	32	17	12	.586	0	40	38	8	258	232	62	143	5	3.14
Jim Deshaies	L	26	12	5	.706	0	26	26	1	144	124	59	128	1	3.25
Nolan Ryan (EJ)	R	39	12	8	.600	0	30	30	1	178	119	82	194	0	3.34
Charley Kerfeld	R	22	11	2	.846	7	61	0	0	94	71	42	77	0	2.59
2 Danny Darwin	R	30	5	2	.714	0	12	8	1	54	50	9	40	0	2.32
Dave Smith	R	31	4	7	.364	33	54	0	0	56	39	22	46	0	2.73
Julio Solano	R	26	3	1	.750	0	16	1	0	32	39	22	21	0	3.09
2 Matt Keough	R	30	3	2	.600	0	10	5	0	35	22	18	25	0	3.09
Aurelio Lopez	R	37	3	3	.500	7	45	0	0	78	64	25	44	0	3.46
2 Larry Andersen	R	33	2	1	.667	1	38	0	0	65	64	23	33	0	2.78
Manny Hernandez	R	25	2	3	.400	0	9	4	0	28	32	12	9	0	3.90
Jeff Calhoun	L	28	1	0	1.000	0	20	0	0	27	28	12	14	0	3.71
Mike Madden	L	28	1	2	.333	0	13	6	0	40	47	22	30	0	4.08
1 Frank DiPino	L	29	1	3	.250	3	31	0	0	40	47	16	27	0	3.57
1 Mark Knudson	R	25	1	5	.167	0	10	5	0	43	48	15	20	0	4.32
Tom Funk	R	24	0	0	—	0	8	0	0	10	6	2	6	0	6.48
Rafael Montalvo	R	21	0	0	—	0	1	0	0	1	1	1	0	0	9.00
Craig Reynolds	R	33	0	0	—	0	1	0	0	1	2	1	1	0	27.00

CINCINNATI — 2nd 86-76 .531 10 — PETE ROSE

Name	G by Pos	B	AGE	G	AB	R	H	2B	3B	HR	RBI	BB	SO	SB	BA	SA
TOTALS			32	162	5536	732	1404	237	35	144	670	586	920	177	.254	.387
Nick Esasky (LJ)	1B70, OF42, 3B1	R	26	102	330	35	76	17	2	12	41	47	97	0	.230	.403
Ron Oester	2B151	B	30	153	523	52	135	23	2	8	44	52	84	9	.258	.356
Kurt Stillwell	SS80	B	21	104	279	31	64	6	1	0	26	30	47	6	.229	.258
Buddy Bell	3B151, 2B1	R	34	155	568	89	158	29	3	20	75	73	49	2	.278	.445
Dave Parker	OF159	R	35	162	637	89	174	31	3	31	116	56	126	1	.273	.477
Eddie Milner	OF127	L	31	145	424	70	110	22	6	15	47	36	56	18	.259	.446
Eric Davis	OF121	R	24	132	415	97	115	15	3	27	71	68	100	80	.277	.523
Bo Diaz	C134	R	33	134	474	50	129	21	0	10	56	40	52	1	.272	.380
Max Venable	OF57	L	29	108	147	17	31	7	1	2	15	17	24	7	.211	.313
Dave Concepcion (BH)	SS60, 1B12, 2B10, 3B10	R	38	90	311	42	81	13	2	3	30	26	43	13	.260	.344
Tony Perez	1B55	R	44	77	200	14	51	12	1	2	29	25	25	0	.255	.395
Kal Daniels	OF47	L	22	74	181	34	58	10	4	6	23	22	30	15	.320	.519
Pete Rose	1B61	B	45	72	237	15	52	8	2	0	25	30	31	3	.219	.270
Sal Butera	C53, P1	R	33	56	113	14	27	6	1	2	16	21	10	0	.239	.363
Tracy Jones (WJ)	OF24, 1B2	R	22	46	86	16	30	3	0	2	10	9	16	7	.349	.453
Barry Larkin	SS36, 2B3	R	22	41	159	27	45	4	3	3	19	9	21	8	.283	.403
Wade Rowdon	3B7, SS6, OF5, 2B3	R	25	38	80	9	20	5	1	0	10	9	17	2	.250	.338
Tom Runnells	2B4, 3B3	R	31	12	11	1	1	0	0	0	0	1	2	0	.091	.182
Dave Van Gorder (BW)	C7	R	29	9	10	0	0	0	0	0	0	0	0	0	.000	.000
Paul O'Neill		L	23	3	2	0	1	0	0	0	0	0	1	0	.000	.000

NAME	T	AGE	W	L	PCT	SV	G	GS	CG	IP	H	BB	SO	SHO	ERA
		27	86	76	.531	45	162	162	14	1468	1465	524	924	8	3.91
Bill Gullickson	R	28	15	12	.556	0	37	37	6	245	245	60	121	2	3.38
Tom Browning	L	26	14	13	.519	0	39	39	4	243	225	70	147	2	3.81
John Denny (WJ)	R	33	11	10	.524	0	27	27	2	171	179	56	115	1	4.20
Ron Robinson	R	24	10	3	.769	14	70	0	0	117	110	43	117	0	3.24
Ted Power	R	31	10	6	.625	1	56	10	0	129	115	52	95	0	3.70
Rob Murphy	L	26	6	0	1.000	1	34	0	0	50	26	21	36	0	0.72
John Franco	L	25	6	6	.500	29	74	0	0	101	90	44	84	0	2.94
Chris Welsh	L	31	6	9	.400	0	24	24	1	139	163	40	40	0	4.78
Mario Soto (SJ)	R	29	5	10	.333	0	19	19	1	105	113	46	67	1	4.71
Scott Terry	R	26	1	2	.333	0	28	3	0	56	66	32	32	0	6.14
Joe Price (EJ)	L	29	1	2	.333	0	25	2	0	42	49	22	30	0	5.40
Carl Willis	R	25	1	3	.250	0	29	0	0	52	54	23	14	0	4.47
Bill Landrum	R	28	0	0	—	0	10	0	0	13	23	4	14	0	6.75
Mike Smith	R	33	0	0	—	0	1	1	0	3	9	1	2	0	13.50
Sal Butera	R	33	0	0	—	0	1	0	0	2	1	0	0	0	0.00

SAN FRANCISCO 3rd 83-79 .512 13 — ROGER CRAIG

Name	G by Pos	B	AGE	G	AB	R	H	2B	3B	HR	RBI	BB	SO	SB	BA	SA
TOTALS			27	162	5501	698	1394	269	29	114	637	536	1087	148	.253	.375
Will Clark (WJ)	1B102	L	22	111	408	66	117	27	2	11	41	34	76	4	.287	.444
Robby Thompson	2B149, SS1	R	24	149	549	73	149	27	3	7	47	42	112	12	.271	.370
Jose Uribe	SS156	B	27	157	453	46	101	15	1	3	43	61	76	22	.223	.280
Chris Brown (SJ)	3B111, SS2	R	24	116	416	57	132	16	3	7	49	33	43	13	.317	.421
Chili Davis	OF148	B	26	153	526	71	146	28	3	13	70	84	96	16	.278	.416
Dan Gladden (RJ)	OF89	R	28	102	351	55	97	16	1	4	29	39	59	27	.276	.362
Jeff Leonard (WJ)	OF87	R	30	89	341	48	95	11	3	6	42	20	62	16	.279	.381
Bob Brenly	C101, 3B45, 1B19	R	32	149	472	60	116	26	0	16	62	74	97	10	.246	.403
Candy Maldonado	OF101, 3B1	R	25	133	405	49	102	31	3	18	85	20	77	4	.252	.477
Joel Youngblood	OF45, 1B7, 3B5, 2B4, SS1	R	34	97	184	20	47	12	0	5	28	18	34	1	.255	.402
Bob Melvin	C84, 3B1	R	24	89	268	24	60	14	2	5	25	15	69	3	.224	.347
Mike Aldrete	1B37, OF31	L	25	84	216	27	54	18	3	2	25	33	34	1	.250	.389
Randy Kutcher	OF51, 3B4, 2B3	R	26	71	186	28	44	9	1	7	16	11	41	6	.237	.409
Luis Quinones	SS33, 3B31, 2B8	B	24	71	106	13	19	1	3	0	11	3	17	3	.179	.245
2 Harry Spilman	1B19, 3B5, 2B1, OF1, C1	L	31	58	94	12	27	7	0	2	22	12	13	0	.287	.426
Mike Woodard	2B23, SS2, 3B2	L	26	48	79	14	20	2	1	1	5	10	9	7	.253	.342
Brad Gulden	C10	L	30	17	22	2	2	0	0	0	1	2	5	0	.091	.091
1 Dan Driessen	1B4	L	34	15	16	2	3	2	0	0	0	4	4	0	.188	.313
Rick Lancellotti	1B1, OF1	L	29	15	18	2	4	0	0	2	6	0	7	0	.222	.556
Brad Wellman	SS8, 2B1, 3B1	R	26	12	13	0	2	0	0	0	1	1	2	0	.154	.154
Phil Duellette	C9	B	24	10	23	1	4	0	0	0	0	3	3	0	.174	.174
Chris Jones		L	28	3	1	0	0	0	0	0	0	0	0	1	.000	.000

NAME	T	AGE	W	L	PCT	SV	G	GS	CG	IP	H	BB	SO	SHO	ERA
		29	83	79	.512	35	162	162	18	1460	1264	591	992	10	3.33
Mike Krukow	R	34	20	9	.690	0	34	34	10	245	204	55	178	2	3.05
Scott Garrelts	R	24	13	9	.591	10	53	18	2	174	144	74	125	0	3.11
Vita Blue (LJ)	L	36	10	10	.500	0	28	28	0	157	137	77	100	0	3.27
Mike LaCoss	R	30	10	13	.435	0	37	31	4	204	179	70	86	1	3.57
Jeff Robinson	R	25	6	3	.667	8	64	1	0	104	92	52	90	0	3.36
Mark Davis	L	25	5	7	.417	4	67	2	0	84	63	34	90	0	2.99
Greg Minton (VJ)	R	34	4	4	.500	5	48	0	0	69	63	34	34	0	3.93
Kelly Downs	R	25	4	4	.500	0	14	14	1	88	78	30	64	0	2.75
Frank Williams	R	28	3	1	.750	1	36	0	0	52	35	21	33	0	1.20
Roger Mason (EJ)	R	27	3	4	.429	0	11	11	1	60	56	30	43	0	4.80
Juan Berenguer	R	31	2	3	.400	1	46	4	0	73	64	44	72	0	2.70
Bill Laskey	R	28	1	1	.500	1	20	0	0	27	28	13	8	0	4.28
2 Steve Carlton	L	41	1	3	.250	0	6	6	0	30	36	16	18	0	5.10
Terry Mulholland	L	23	1	7	.125	0	15	10	0	55	51	35	27	0	4.94
Chuck Hensley	L	27	0	0	—	1	11	0	0	7	5	2	6	0	2.45
Jim Gott (AJ)	R	26	0	0	—	1	9	2	0	13	16	13	9	0	7.62
Randy Bockus	L	25	0	0	—	0	5	0	0	7	7	6	4	0	2.57
Mark Grant	R	22	0	1	.000	0	4	1	0	10	6	5	5	0	3.60
Atlee Hammaker (SJ)		28													

SAN DIEGO 4th 74-88 .457 22 — STEVE BOROS

Name	G by Pos	B	AGE	G	AB	R	H	2B	3B	HR	RBI	BB	SO	SB	BA	SA
TOTALS			29	162	5515	656	1442	239	25	136	629	484	917	96	.261	.388
Steve Garvey	1B148	R	37	155	557	58	142	22	0	21	81	23	72	1	.255	.408
Tim Flannery	2B108, 3B23, SS8	L	28	134	368	48	103	11	2	3	28	54	61	3	.280	.345
Garry Templeton	SS144	B	30	147	510	42	162	21	2	2	44	35	86	10	.247	.308
Graig Nettles	3B114	L	41	126	354	36	77	9	0	16	55	41	62	0	.218	.379
Tony Gwynn	OF160	L	26	160	642	107	211	33	7	14	59	52	35	37	.329	.467
Kevin McReynolds	OF154	R	26	158	560	89	161	31	6	26	96	66	83	8	.288	.504
John Kruk	OF74, 1B9	L	25	122	278	33	86	16	2	4	38	45	58	2	.309	.424
Terry Kennedy	C123	L	30	141	432	46	114	22	1	12	57	37	74	0	.264	.403
Marvell Wynne	OF125	L	26	137	288	34	76	19	2	7	37	15	45	11	.264	.417
Jerry Royster	3B59, SS24, 2B21, OF7	R	33	118	257	31	66	12	0	5	26	32	45	5	.257	.362
Carmelo Martinez	OF60, 1B26, 3B1	R	25	113	244	28	58	10	0	9	25	35	46	1	.238	.389
Bip Roberts	2B87	B	22	101	241	34	61	5	2	1	12	14	29	14	.253	.303
Dane Iorg	1B10, 3B6, OF3	L	36	90	106	10	24	2	1	2	11	2	21	0	.226	.321
Bruce Bochy	C48	R	31	63	127	16	32	9	0	8	22	14	23	1	.252	.512
Benito Santiago	C17	R	20	17	62	10	18	2	0	3	6	2	12	0	.290	.468
Randy Asadoor	3B15, 2B2	R	23	15	55	9	20	5	0	0	7	3	13	1	.364	.455
Tim Pyznarski	1B13	R	26	15	42	3	10	1	0	0	4	11	12	2	.238	.262
Gary Green	SS13	R	24	13	33	2	7	1	0	0	2	1	11	0	.212	.242
Mark Parent	C3	R	24	8	14	1	2	0	0	0	0	1	3	0	.143	.143
Mark Wasinger	3B3, 2B1	R	24	7	8	0	0	0	0	0	1	0	2	0	.000	.000
2 Randy Ready	3B1	R	26	1	3	0	0	0	0	0	0	0	1	0	.000	.000

NAME	T	AGE	W	L	PCT	SV	G	GS	CG	IP	H	BB	SO	SHO	ERA
		29	74	88	.457	32	162	162	13	1443	1406	607	934	7	3.99
Andy Hawkins	R	26	10	8	.556	0	37	35	3	209	218	75	117	1	4.30
Lance McCullers	R	22	10	10	.500	5	70	7	0	136	103	58	92	0	2.78
Eric Show (EJ)	R	30	9	5	.643	0	24	22	2	136	109	69	94	0	2.97
Craig Lefferts	L	28	9	8	.529	4	83	0	0	108	98	44	72	0	3.09
Dave Dravecky (EJ)	L	30	9	11	.450	0	26	26	3	161	149	54	87	1	3.07
LaMarr Hoyt	R	31	8	11	.421	0	35	25	1	159	170	68	85	0	5.15
Goose Gossage	R	34	5	7	.417	21	45	0	0	65	69	20	63	0	4.45
1 Mark Thurmond	L	29	3	3	.350	0	17	15	2	71	96	27	32	1	6.50
Jimmy Jones	R	22	2	0	1.000	0	3	3	1	18	10	3	15	1	2.50
Gene Walter	L	25	2	2	.500	1	57	0	0	98	89	49	84	0	3.86
Ed Wojna	R	25	2	2	.500	0	7	7	1	39	42	16	19	0	3.23
Bob Stoddard	R	29	1	0	1.000	1	18	0	0	23	20	11	17	0	2.31
Greg Booker	R	26	1	0	1.000	0	9	0	0	11	10	4	7	0	1.64
1 Tim Stoddard	R	33	1	1	.250	0	30	0	0	45	33	34	37	0	3.77
2 Dave LaPoint	L	26	1	4	.200	0	24	4	0	61	67	24	41	0	4.26
2 Ed Whitson	R	31	1	7	.125	0	17	12	0	76	85	37	46	0	5.59
Dane Iorg	R	36	0	0	—	0	2	0	0	3	5	1	2	0	12.00
Ed Vosberg	L	24	0	1	.000	0	5	3	0	14	17	9	8	0	6.59
Ray Hayward	L	25	0	0	.000	0	1	0	0	16	14	6	5	0	9.00

LOS ANGELES 5th 73-89 .451 23 — TOMMY LASORDA

Name	G by Pos	B	AGE	G	AB	R	H	2B	3B	HR	RBI	BB	SO	SB	BA	SA
TOTALS			29	162	5471	638	1373	232	14	130	599	478	966	155	.251	.370
Greg Brock (KJ)	1B99	L	29	115	325	33	76	13	0	16	52	37	60	2	.234	.422
Steve Sax	2B154	R	26	157	633	91	210	43	4	6	56	59	58	40	.332	.441
Mariano Duncan (BF)	SS106	B	23	109	407	47	93	7	0	8	30	30	58	48	.229	.305
Bill Madlock	3B101, 1B2	R	35	111	379	38	106	17	0	10	60	30	43	3	.280	.404
Mike Marshall	OF97	R	26	103	330	47	77	11	0	19	53	27	90	4	.233	.439
Ken Landreaux	OF85	L	31	103	283	34	74	13	2	4	29	22	39	10	.261	.364
Franklin Stubbs	OF124, 1B13	L	25	132	420	55	95	11	1	23	58	37	107	7	.226	.421
Mike Scioscia (NJ)	C119	L	27	122	374	36	94	18	1	5	26	62	23	3	.251	.345
Reggie Williams	OF124	R	25	128	303	35	84	14	2	4	32	23	57	9	.277	.376
Enos Cabell	1B61, OF16, 3B7	R	38	107	277	27	71	13	0	2	29	14	26	10	.256	.318
Bill Russell	OF48, SS32, 2B8, 3B1	R	37	105	216	21	54	11	0	0	18	15	23	1	.250	.301
Dave Anderson (BG)	3B51, SS34, 2B5	R	25	92	216	31	53	9	0	1	15	22	39	5	.245	.301
Len Matuszek (SJ)	OF37, 1B31	L	31	91	199	26	52	7	0	9	28	21	47	2	.261	.432
Alex Trevino	C63, 1B1	R	28	89	202	31	53	13	0	4	26	27	35	0	.262	.386
Jeff Hamilton	3B66, SS2	R	22	71	147	22	33	5	0	5	19	2	43	0	.224	.361
Jose Gonzalez	OF57	R	21	57	93	15	20	5	1	2	6	7	29	4	.215	.355
Cesar Cedeno	OF31	R	35	37	78	5	18	2	0	6	6	7	13	1	.231	.282
Pedro Guerrero (KJ)	OF10, 1B4	R	30	31	61	7	15	3	0	5	10	2	19	0	.246	.541
Ralph Bryant	OF26	L	25	27	75	15	19	4	2	6	13	5	25	0	.253	.600
Terry Whitfield	OF1	L	33	19	14	0	1	0	0	0	0	5	2	0	.071	.071
Larry See	1B9	R	26	13	20	1	5	2	0	0	2	2	5	0	.250	.350
Jack Fimple	C7, 1B1, 2B1	R	27	13	13	2	1	0	0	0	2	6	6	0	.077	.077
Craig Shipley	SS10, 3B1, 2B1	R	23	12	27	3	3	1	0	0	4	2	5	0	.111	.148
Ed Amelung	OF4	L	27	8	11	0	1	0	0	0	0	0	4	0	.091	.091

NAME	T	AGE	W	L	PCT	SV	G	GS	CG	IP	H	BB	SO	SHO	ERA
		28	73	89	.451	25	162	162	35	1454	1428	499	1051	14	3.76
Fernando Valenzuela	L	25	21	11	.656	0	34	34	20	269	226	85	242	3	3.14
Orel Hershiser	R	27	14	14	.500	0	35	35	8	231	213	86	153	1	3.85
Rick Honeycutt	L	32	11	9	.550	0	32	28	0	171	164	45	100	0	3.32
Bob Welch	R	29	7	13	.350	0	33	33	7	236	227	55	183	3	3.28
Tom Niedenfuer	R	26	6	6	.500	11	60	0	0	80	86	29	55	0	3.71
Ken Howell	R	25	6	12	.333	12	62	0	0	98	86	63	104	0	3.87
Brian Holton	R	25	2	3	.400	0	12	3	0	24	28	6	24	0	4.44
Jerry Reuss (EJ)	L	37	2	6	.250	1	19	13	0	74	96	17	29	0	5.84
Dennis Powell (EJ)	L	22	2	7	.222	0	27	6	0	65	65	25	31	0	4.27
Alejandro Pena (SJ)	R	27	1	2	.333	1	24	10	0	70	74	30	46	0	4.89
Ed Vande Berg	L	27	1	5	.167	0	60	0	0	71	83	33	42	0	3.41
Carlos Diaz	L	28	0	0	—	0	19	0	0	25	33	7	18	0	4.26
Joe Beckwith	R	31	0	0	—	0	15	0	0	18	28	6	13	0	6.87
Balvino Galvez	R	22	0	0	.000	0	10	0	0	21	19	12	11	0	3.92

ATLANTA 6th 72-89 .447 23.5 — CHUCK TANNER

Name	G by Pos	B	AGE	G	AB	R	H	2B	3B	HR	RBI	BB	SO	SB	BA	SA
TOTALS			30	161	5384	615	1348	241	24	138	575	538	904	93	.250	.381
Bob Horner	1B139	R	28	141	517	70	141	22	0	27	87	52	72	1	.273	.472
Glenn Hubbard	2B142	R	28	143	408	42	94	16	1	4	36	66	74	3	.230	.304
Andres Thomas	SS97	R	22	102	323	26	81	17	2	6	32	8	49	4	.251	.372
Ken Oberkfell	3B130 2B41	L	30	151	503	62	136	24	3	5	48	83	40	7	.270	.360
Omar Moreno	OF97	L	33	118	359	46	84	18	6	4	27	21	77	17	.234	.351
Dale Murphy	OF159	R	30	160	614	89	163	29	7	29	83	75	141	7	.265	.477
Ozzie Virgil	C111	R	29	114	359	45	80	9	0	15	48	63	73	1	.223	.373
Rafael Ramirez	SS86 3B57 OF3	R	28	134	496	57	119	21	1	8	33	21	60	19	.240	.335
Terry Harper	OF83	R	30	106	265	26	68	12	0	8	30	29	39	3	.257	.392
Chris Chambliss	1B20	L	37	97	122	13	38	8	0	2	14	15	24	0	.311	.426
Billy Sample	OF56 2B1	R	31	92	200	23	57	11	0	6	14	14	26	4	.285	.386
Ted Simmons	1B14 C10 3B9	B	36	76	127	14	32	5	4	4	25	12	14	1	.252	.386
Bruce Benedict	C57	R	30	64	160	11	36	10	1	0	13	16	10	1	.225	.300
1 Claudell Washington (ZJ)	OF38	L	31	40	137	17	37	11	0	5	14	14	26	4	.270	.460
Gerald Perry	OF21 1B1	R	25	29	70	6	19	2	0	0	7	4	8	0	.271	.386
Albert Hall	OF14	B	28	16	50	6	12	2	0	0	1	5	6	8	.240	.280
Paul Runge	2B5	R	27	8	7	8	1	2	0	1	0	0	2	6	0	.250	.250
2 Darryl Motley	OF3	R	26	5	10	1	2	1	0	0	0	1	1	0	.200	.300
Brad Komminsk	3B2 OF2	R	25	5	5	1	2	1	0	0	1	0	2	0	.400	.400

NAME	T	AGE	W	L	PCT	SV	G	GS	CG	IP	H	BB	SO	SHO	ERA
		29	72	89	.447	39	161	161	17	1425	1443	576	932	5	3.97
Rick Mahler	R	32	14	18	.438	0	39	39	7	238	283	95	137	1	4.88
David Palmer	R	28	11	10	.524	0	35	35	2	210	181	102	170	0	3.65
Zane Smith	L	25	8	16	.333	1	38	32	3	205	209	105	139	1	4.05
Paul Assenmacher	L	25	7	3	.700	7	61	0	0	68	61	26	56	0	2.50
Jeff Dedmon	R	26	6	6	.500	3	57	0	0	100	90	39	58	0	2.98
2 Doyle Alexander	R	35	6	6	.500	0	17	17	2	117	135	17	74	0	3.84
1 Joe Johnson	R	24	6	7	.462	0	17	15	2	87	101	35	49	0	4.97
Gene Garber	R	38	5	5	.500	24	61	0	0	78	76	20	56	0	2.54
2 Jim Acker	R	27	3	8	.273	0	21	14	0	95	100	26	37	0	3.79
Bruce Sutter (SJ)	R	33	2	0	1.000	3	16	0	0	19	17	9	16	0	4.34
Cliff Speck	R	29	2	1	.667	0	13	1	0	28	25	15	21	0	4.13
Charlie Puleo	R	31	1	3	.333	0	13	5	1	24	13	12	18	0	2.96
Craig McMurtry (RJ)	R	26	1	6	.143	0	37	5	0	80	82	43	50	0	4.74
Ed Olwine	L	28	0	0	—	0	49	0	0	48	35	17	37	0	3.40
Steve Shields	R	27	0	0	—	0	13			13	7	7	6	0	7.11
1 Duane Ward	R	22	0	0	.000	0	10	0	0	16	22	8	9	0	7.31

LINE SCORES

Team	1	2	3	4	5	6	7	8	9	10	11	12	R	H	E

AMERICAN LEAGUE CHAMPIONSHIPS: BOSTON (EAST) 4   CALIFORNIA (WEST) 3

Game 1 October 7 at Boston

| CAL | 0 | 4 | 1 | 0 | 0 | 0 | | 0 | 3 | 0 | | | 8 | 11 | 0 |
| BOS | 0 | 0 | 0 | 0 | 0 | 1 | | 0 | 0 | 0 | | | 1 | 5 | 1 |

Witt — Clemens, Sambito (8), Stanley (8)

Game 2 October 8 at Boston

| CAL | 0 | 0 | 0 | 1 | 1 | 0 | | 0 | 0 | 0 | | | 2 | 11 | 3 |
| BOS | 1 | 1 | 0 | 0 | 3 | 3 | | 3 | X | | | | 9 | 13 | 2 |

McCaskill, Lucas (8), Corbett (8) — Hurst

Game 3 October 10 at California

| BOS | 0 | 1 | 0 | 0 | 0 | 0 | | 2 | 0 | | | | 3 | 9 | 1 |
| CAL | 0 | 0 | 0 | 0 | 0 | 1 | | 3 | 1 | X | | | 5 | 8 | 0 |

Boyd, Sambito (7), Schiraldi (8) — Candelaria, Moore (8)

Game 4 October 11 at California

| BOS | 0 | 0 | 0 | 0 | 0 | 1 | | 0 | 2 | 0 | 0 | 0 | 3 | 6 | 1 |
| CAL | 0 | 0 | 0 | 0 | 0 | 0 | | 0 | 0 | 3 | 0 | 1 | 4 | 11 | 2 |

Clemens, **Schiraldi** (9) — Sutton, Lucas (7), Ruhle (7), Finley (8), **Corbett** (8)

Game 5 October 12 at California

| BOS | 0 | 2 | 0 | 0 | 0 | 0 | | 0 | 0 | 4 | 0 | 1 | 7 | 12 | 0 |
| CAL | 0 | 0 | 1 | 0 | 0 | 2 | | 2 | 0 | 1 | 0 | 0 | 6 | 13 | 0 |

Hurst, Stanley (7), Sambito (9), **Crawford** (9), Schiraldi (11) — Witt, Lucas (9), **Moore** (9), Finley (11)

Game 6 October 14 at Boston

| CAL | 2 | 0 | 0 | 0 | 0 | 0 | | 1 | 1 | 0 | | | 4 | 11 | 1 |
| BOS | 2 | 0 | 5 | 0 | 1 | 0 | | 2 | 0 | X | | | 10 | 16 | 1 |

McCaskill, Lucas (3), Corbett (4), Finley (7) — Boyd, Stanley (8)

Game 7 October 15 at Boston

| CAL | 0 | 0 | 0 | 0 | 0 | 0 | | 0 | 1 | 0 | | | 1 | 6 | 2 |
| BOS | 0 | 3 | 0 | 4 | 0 | 0 | | 1 | 0 | X | | | 8 | 8 | 1 |

Candeleria, Sutton (4), Moore (8) — Clemens, Schiraldi (8)

NATIONAL LEAGUE CHAMPIONSHIPS: NEW YORK (EAST) 4   HOUSTON (WEST) 2

Game 1 October 8 at Houston

| NY | 0 | 0 | 0 | 0 | 0 | 0 | | 0 | 0 | 0 | | | 0 | 5 | 0 |
| HOU | 0 | 1 | 0 | 0 | 0 | 0 | | 0 | 0 | X | | | 1 | 7 | 1 |

Gooden, Orosco (8) — Scott

Game 2 October 9 at Houston

| NY | 0 | 0 | 0 | 2 | 3 | 0 | | 0 | 0 | 0 | | | 5 | 10 | 0 |
| HOU | 0 | 0 | 0 | 0 | 0 | 1 | | 0 | 0 | | | | 1 | 10 | 2 |

Ojeda — Ryan, Anderson (6), Lopez (8), Kerfeld (9)

Game 3 October 11 at New York

| HOU | 2 | 2 | 0 | 0 | 0 | 0 | | 1 | 0 | 0 | | | 5 | 8 | 1 |
| NY | 0 | 0 | 0 | 0 | 0 | 4 | | 0 | 0 | 2 | | | 6 | 10 | 1 |

Knepper, Kerfeld (8), **Smith** (9) — Darling, Aquilera (6), **Orosco** (8)

Game 4 October 12 at New York

| HOU | 0 | 2 | 0 | 0 | 0 | 1 | | 0 | 0 | 0 | | | 3 | 4 | 1 |
| NY | 0 | 0 | 1 | 0 | 0 | 0 | | 0 | 1 | 0 | | | 1 | 3 | 0 |

Scott — Fernandez, McDowell (7), Sisk (9)

Game 5 October 14 at New York

| HOU | 0 | 0 | 0 | 0 | 1 | 0 | | 0 | 0 | 0 | 0 | 0 | 1 | 9 | 1 |
| NY | 0 | 0 | 0 | 0 | 1 | 0 | | 0 | 0 | 0 | 0 | 1 | 2 | 4 | 0 |

Ryan, Kerfeld (10) — Gooden, Orosco (11)

Game 6 October 15 at Houston (16 innings)

NY	0	0	0	0	0	0	0	0	3	0	0	0	7	11	0
			0	1	0	3									
HOU	3	0	0	0	0	0	0	0	0	0	0	0	6	11	1
			0	1	0	2									

Ojeda, Aquilera (6), McDowell (9), **Orosco** (14) — Knepper, Smith (9), Anderson (11), **Lopez** (14), Calhoun (16)

COMPOSITE BATTING

NAME	POS	G	AB	R	H	2B	3B	HR	RBI	BA
Boston										
TOTALS		7	254	41	69	11	2	6	35	.272
Rice	LF	7	31	8	5	1	0	2	6	.161
Barrett	2B	7	30	4	11	2	0	0	5	.367
Boggs	3B	7	30	3	7	1	1	0	2	.233
Gedman	C	7	28	4	10	1	0	1	6	.357
Buckner	1B	7	28	3	6	1	0	0	3	.214
Evans	RF	7	28	6	6	1	0	1	4	.214
Baylor	DH	7	26	6	9	3	0	1	2	.346
Owen	SS	7	21	5	9	0	1	0	3	.429
Armas	CF	5	16	1	2	1	0	0	0	.125
Henderson	CF	5	9	3	1	0	0	1	4	.111
Stapleton	1B-PR	4	3	2	2	0	0	0	0	.667
Greenwell	PH	2	2	0	1	0	0	0	0	.500
Romero	PR-SS	1	2	0	0	0	0	0	0	.000
California										
TOTALS		7	256	30	71	11	0	7	29	.277
DeCinces	3B	7	32	2	9	3	0	1	3	.281
Schofield	SS	7	30	4	9	1	0	1	2	.300
Downing	LF	7	27	2	6	0	0	1	7	.222
Pettis	CF	7	26	4	9	1	0	1	4	.346
Jackson	DH	6	26	2	5	2	0	0	2	.192
Grich	1B-2B	6	24	1	5	0	0	1	3	.208
Boone	C	7	22	4	10	0	0	0	1	.455
Jones	RF-PR	6	17	4	3	1	0	0	2	.176
Wilfong	2B-PH	4	13	1	4	1	0	0	2	.194
Hendrick	RF-1B	3	12	0	1	0	0	0	0	.083
Joyner	1B	3	11	3	5	2	0	1	2	.455
Burleson	2B-DH-PH	4	11	0	3	0	0	0	0	.273
Narron	C-PH	4	2	1	1	0	0	0	0	.500
White	RF-PR	4	2	2	1	0	0	0	0	.500
Howell	PH	2	1	0	0	0	0	0	0	.000
New York										
TOTALS		6	227	21	43	4	2	3	19	.189
Carter	C	6	27	1	4	1	0	0	2	.148
Hernandez	1B	6	26	3	7	1	1	0	3	.269
Wilson	LF-CF	6	26	2	3	0	0	0	1	.115
Knight	3B	6	24	1	4	0	0	0	2	.167
Dykstra	CF-PH	6	23	3	7	1	1	1	3	.304
Strawberry	RF	6	22	4	5	1	0	2	5	.227
Backman	2B	6	21	5	5	0	0	0	2	.238
Santana	SS	6	17	0	3	0	0	0	0	.176
Mitchell	LF	2	8	1	2	0	0	0	0	.250
Teufel	2B	2	6	0	1	0	0	0	0	.167
Mazzilli	PH	5	5	0	1	0	0	0	0	.200
Gooden	P	2	5	0	0	0	0	0	0	.000
Ojeda	P	2	5	1	0	0	0	0	0	.000
Heep	PH-LF	5	4	0	1	0	0	0	1	.250
Elster	PR-SS	4	3	0	0	0	0	0	0	.000
Johnson	PH	2	2	0	0	0	0	0	0	.000
McDowell	P	2	1	0	0	0	0	0	0	.000
Darling	P	1	1	0	0	0	0	0	0	.000
Fernandez	P	1	1	0	0	0	0	0	0	.000
Orosco	P	4	0	0	0	0	0	0	0	—
Aguilera	P	2	0	0	0	0	0	0	0	—
Sisk	P	1	0	0	0	0	0	0	0	—
Houston										
TOTALS		6	225	17	49	6	0	5	17	.218
Doran	2B	6	27	3	6	0	0	1	3	.220
Davis	1B	6	26	3	7	1	0	1	3	.269
Cruz	LF	6	26	0	5	0	0	0	2	.192
Hatcher	CF	6	25	4	7	0	0	1	2	.280
Bass	RF	6	24	0	7	2	0	0	0	.292
Ashby	C	6	23	2	3	1	0	1	2	.130
Walling	3B-PH	5	19	1	3	1	0	0	2	.158
Thon	SS-PH	6	12	1	3	0	0	1	1	.250
Reynolds	SS	4	12	1	4	0	0	0	0	.333
Garner	3B	3	9	1	2	1	0	0	2	.222
Scott	P	2	6	0	0	0	0	0	0	.000
Knepper	P	2	5	0	0	0	0	0	0	.000
Ryan	P	2	4	0	0	0	0	0	0	.000
Puhl	PH	3	3	0	2	0	0	0	0	.667
Lopes	PH	3	2	1	0	0	0	0	0	.000
Pankovits	PH	2	2	0	0	0	0	0	0	.000
Kerfeld	P	3	0	0	0	0	0	0	0	—
Andersen	P	2	0	0	0	0	0	0	0	—
Lopez	P	2	0	0	0	0	0	0	0	—
Smith	P	2	0	0	0	0	0	0	0	—
Calhoun	P	1	0	0	0	0	0	0	0	—

COMPOSITE PITCHING

NAME	G	IP	H	BB	SO	W	L	SV	ERA
Boston									
TOTALS	7	65.1	71	20	44	4	3	1	3.58
Clemens	3	22.2	22	7	17	1	0	0	4.37
Hurst	2	15	18	1	8	1	0	0	2.40
Boyd	2	13.2	17	3	8	1	1	0	4.61
Schiraldi	4	6	5	3	9	0	1	1	1.50
Stanley	3	5.2	7	3	1	0	0	0	3.18
Crawford	1	1.2	1	1	1	0	0	0	0.00
Sambito	3	0.2	1	1	0	0	0	0	13.50
California									
TOTALS	7	64	69	19	31	3	4	1	3.94
Witt	2	17.2	13	2	8	1	0	0	2.55
Candelaria	2	10.2	11	6	7	1	1	0	0.84
Sutton	2	9.2	6	1	4	0	0	0	1.86
McCaskill	2	9.1	16	5	7	0	2	0	7.71
Corbett	3	6.2	9	2	2	1	0	0	5.40
Moore	3	5	8	2	0	0	1	1	7.20
Lucas	4	2.1	3	1	2	0	0	0	11.57
Finley	3	2	1	0	1	0	0	0	0.00
Ruhle	1	0.2	2	0	0	0	0	0	13.50
New York									
TOTALS	6	63	49	17	40	4	2	0	2.29
Gooden	2	17	16	5	9	0	1	0	1.06
Ojeda	2	14	15	4	6	1	0	0	2.57
Orosco	4	8	5	2	10	3	0	0	3.38
McDowell	2	7	1	0	3	0	0	0	0.00
Fernandez	1	6	3	1	5	0	1	0	4.50
Aguilera	2	5	2	2	2	0	0	0	0.00
Darling	1	5	6	2	5	0	0	0	7.20
Sisk	1	1	1	1	0	0	0	0	0.00
Houston									
TOTALS	6	62.2	43	14	57	2	4	0	2.87
Scott	2	18	8	1	19	2	0	0	0.50
Knepper	2	15.1	13	1	9	0	0	0	3.52
Ryan	2	14	9	1	17	0	1	0	3.86
Andersen	2	5	1	2	3	0	0	0	0.00
Kerfeld	3	4	2	1	4	0	1	0	2.25
Lopez	2	3.1	7	4	3	0	1	0	8.10
Smith	2	2	2	3	2	0	1	0	9.00
Calhoun	1	1	1	1	0	0	0	0	9.00

LINE SCORES

Team	1	2	3	4	5	6	7	8	9	10			R	H	E

WORLD SERIES: NEW YORK (NL) 4 : BOSTON (AL) 3

Game 1 October 18 at New York

													R	H	E
BOS	0	0	0	0	0	0	1	0	0				1	5	0
NY	0	0	0	0	0	0	0	0	0				0	4	1

Hurst, Schiraldi (9)   Darling, McDowell (9)

Game 2 October 19 at New York

													R	H	E
BOS	0	0	3	1	2	0	2	0	1				9	18	0
NY	0	0	2	0	1	0	0	0	0				3	8	1

Clemens, Crawford (5),   Gooden, Aguilera (6),
Stanley (7)   Orosco (7), Fernandez (9), Sisk (9)

Game 3 October 21 at Boston

													R	H	E
NY	4	0	0	0	0	0	2	1	0				7	13	0
BOS	0	0	1	0	0	0	0	0	0				1	5	0

Ojeda, McDowell (8)   Boyd, Sambito (8), Stanley (9)

Game 4 October 22 at Boston

													R	H	E
NY	0	0	0	3	0	0	2	1	0				6	12	0
BOS	0	0	0	0	0	0	0	2	0				2	7	1

Darling, McDowell (7), Orosco (7)   Nipper, Crawford (7), Stanley (9)

Game 5 October 23 at Boston

													R	H	E
NY	0	0	0	0	0	0	0	1	1				2	10	1
BOS	0	1	1	0	2	0	0	0	X				4	12	0

Gooden, Fernandez (5)   Hurst

Game 6 October 25 at New York

													R	H	E
BOS	1	1	0	0	0	0	1	0	0	2			5	13	3
NY	0	0	0	2	0	0	1	0	3				6	8	2

Clemens, Schiraldi (8),   Ojeda, McDowell (7), Orosco (8),
Stanley (10)   Aguilera (9)

Game 7 October 27 at New York

													R	H	E
BOS	0	3	0	0	0	0	0	2	0				5	9	0
NY	0	0	0	0	0	3	3	2	X				8	10	0

Hurst, Schiraldi (7),   Darling, Fernandez (4),
Sambito (7), Stanley (7),   McDowell (8), Orosco (9)
Nipper (8), Crawford (8)

COMPOSITE BATTING

New York

NAME	POS	G	AB	R	H	2B	3B	HR	RBI	BA
TOTALS		7	240	32	65	6	0	7	29	.271
Carter	C	7	29	4	8	2	0	2	9	.276
Dykstra	CF	7	27	4	8	0	0	2	3	.296
Wilson	LF	7	26	3	7	1	0	0	0	.269
Hernandez	1B	7	26	1	6	0	0	0	4	.231
Strawberry	RF	7	24	4	5	1	0	1	1	.208
Knight	3B	6	23	4	9	1	0	1	5	.391
Santana	SS	7	20	3	5	0	0	0	2	.250
Backman	2B-PR	6	18	4	6	0	0	0	1	.333
Heep	PH-LF-DH	5	11	0	1	0	0	0	2	.091
Teufel	2B	3	9	1	4	1	0	1	2	.444
Mitchell	PH-LF-DH	5	8	1	2	0	0	0	0	.250
Mazzilli	PH-RF	4	5	2	2	0	0	0	0	.400
Johnson	3B-PH-SS	2	5	0	0	0	0	0	0	.000
Darling	P	3	3	0	0	0	0	0	0	.000
Gooden	P	2	2	1	1	0	0	0	0	.500
Ojeda	P	2	2	0	0	0	0	0	0	.000
Orosco	P	4	1	0	1	0	0	0	1	1.000
Elster	SS	2	1	0	0	0	0	0	0	.000
McDowell	P	5	1	0	0	0	0	0	0	—
Fernandez	P	3	0	0	0	0	0	0	0	—
Aguilera	P	2	0	0	0	0	0	0	0	—
Sisk	P	1	0	0	0	0	0	0	0	—

Boston

NAME	POS	G	AB	R	H	2B	3B	HR	RBI	BA
TOTALS		7	248	27	69	11	2	5	26	.278
Buckner	1B	7	32	2	6	0	0	0	1	.188
Boggs	3B	7	31	3	9	3	0	0	3	.290
Barrett	2B	7	30	1	13	2	0	0	4	.433
Gedman	C	7	30	1	6	1	0	1	1	.200
Rice	LF	7	27	6	9	1	1	0	0	.333
Evans	RF	7	26	4	8	2	0	2	9	.308
Henderson	CF	7	25	6	10	1	1	2	5	.400
Owen	SS	7	20	2	6	0	0	0	2	.300
Baylor	DH-PH	4	11	1	2	1	0	1	1	.182
Clemens	P	2	4	1	1	0	0	0	1	.000
Greenwall	PH	4	3	0	1	0	0	0	0	.000
Hurst	P	3	3	0	0	0	0	0	0	.000
Stanley	P	5	1	0	0	0	0	0	0	.000
Romero	PR-SS	3	1	0	0	0	0	0	0	.000
Stapleton	1B-PR	3	1	0	0	0	0	0	0	.000
Crawford	P	3	1	0	0	0	0	0	0	.000
Schiraldi	P	3	1	0	0	0	0	0	0	.000
Armas	PH	1	1	0	0	0	0	0	0	.000
Nipper	P	2	0	0	0	0	0	0	0	—
Sambito	P	2	0	0	0	0	0	0	0	—
Boyd	P	1	0	0	0	0	0	0	0	—

COMPOSITE PITCHING

New York

NAME	G	IP	H	BB	SO	W	L	SV	ERA
TOTALS	7	63	69	28	53	4	3	2	3.29
Darling	3	17.2	13	10	12	1	1	0	1.53
Ojeda	2	13	3	5	9	1	0	0	2.08
Gooden	2	9	17	4	9	0	2	0	8.00
McDowell	5	7.1	10	6	2	1	0	0	4.91
Fernandez	3	6.2	6	1	10	0	0	0	1.35
Orosco	4	5.2	2	0	6	0	0	2	0.00
Aguilera	2	3	8	1	4	1	0	0	12.00
Sisk	1	0.2	0	1	1	0	0	0	0.00

Boston

NAME	G	IP	H	BB	SO	W	L	SV	ERA
TOTALS	7	62.2	65	21	43	3	4	2	4.31
Hurst	3	23	18	6	17	2	0	0	1.96
Clemens	2	11.1	9	6	11	0	0	0	3.18
Boyd	1	7	9	1	3	0	1	0	7.71
Stanley	5	6.1	5	1	4	0	0	1	0.00
Nipper	2	6.1	10	2	2	0	1	0	7.11
Crawford	3	4.1	5	0	4	1	0	0	6.23
Schiraldi	3	4	7	3	2	0	2	1	13.50
Sambito	2	0.1	2	2	0	0	0	0	27.00

MISCELLANEOUS 1986 INDIVIDUAL LEADERS

BATTING

On Base Average

American League		National League	
1 Boggs, Bos.	.453	1 Raines, Mon.	.415
2 P. Bradley, Sea.	.405	2 Hernandez, N.Y.	.413
3 Brett, K.C.	.401	3 Sax, L.A.	.390
4 Murray, Bal.	.396	4 Schmidt, Phi.	.390
5 Mattingly, N.Y.	.394	5 Gwynn, S.D.	.381

Caught Stealing

American League		National League	
1 Henderson, N.Y.	18	1 Doran, Hou.	19
Moses, Sea.	18	2 Sax, L.A.	17
3 Cangelosi, Chi.	17	3 Morena, Atl.	16
4 Griffin, Oak.	16	4 Thompson, S.F.	15
5 Butler, Cle.	15	5 Webster, Mon.	15
Gaetti, Min.	15		
McDowell, Tex.	15		

Hit by Pitcher

American League		National League	
1 Baylor, Bos.	35	1 Wallach, Mon.	10
2 Downing, Cal.	17	2 Brown, S.F.	9
3 L. Smith, K.C.	10	3 Davis, Hou.	9
4 Wilson, K.C.	9	4 Samuel, Phi.	8
5 4 tied	8	5 Schmidt, Phi.	7

Sacrifice Hits

American League		National League	
1 Barrett, Bos.	18	1 Thompson, S.F.	18
2 Butler, Cle.	17	2 Cox, St. L.	16
3 Pettis, Cal.	15	3 Bachman, N.Y.	14
4 Gagne, Min.	13	4 Gooden, N.Y.	13
Tolleson, Chi.+N.Y.	13	5 Tudor, St. L.	13

Game Winning RBI's

American League		National League	
1 Bell, Tor.	15	1 Carter, N.Y.	16
Mattingly, N.Y.	15	Davis, Hou.	16
Ripken, Bal.	15	3 Strawberry, N.Y.	15
4 Canseco, Oak.	14	4 Hayes, Phi.	14
Joyner, Cal.	14	Maldonado, S.F.	14
O'Brien, Tex.	14	McReynolds, S.D.	14

Grounded Into Double Play

American League		National League	
1 Franco, Cle.	28	1 Carter, N.Y.	21
2 Buckner, Bos.	25	Pena, Pit.	21
3 Lynn, Bal.	20	Ray, Pit.	21
Whitaker, Det.	20	4 Gwynn, S.D.	20
Winfield, N.Y.	20	5 Knight, N.Y.	19

Total Bases

American League		National League	
1 Mattingly, N.Y.	388	1 Parker, Cin.	304
2 Puckett, Min.	365	2 Schmidt, Phi.	302
3 Bell, Tor.	341	3 Gwynn, S.D.	300
4 Carter, Cle.	329	4 Hayes, Phi.	293
5 Barfield, Tor.	309	Murphy, Atl.	293

Sacrifice Flies

American League		National League	
1 Joyner, Cal.	12	1 Carter, N.Y.	15
2 Mattingly, N.Y.	10	2 Moreland, Chi.	11
3 Canseco, Oak.	9	3 Horner, Atl.	10
Rice, Bos.	9	4 McReynolds, S.D.	9
Schofield, Cal.	9	Schmidt, Phi.	9
		Strawberry, N.Y.	9
		Wilson, Phi	9

FIELDING

American League	PO	A	E	DP	Pct.
1B Mattingly, N.Y.	1377	100	6	132	.996
2B Lombardozzi, Min.	289	407	6	102	.991
SS Fernandez, Tor.	294	445	13	103	.983
3B Mulliniks, Tor.	60	176	6	13	.975
OF Yount, Mil.	352	9	1	4	.997
OF P. Bradley, Sea.	250	11	1	0	.996
OF Butler, Cle.	434	9	3	3	.993
C Sundberg, K.C.	686	46	4	11	.995
P Key, Tor.	18	42	0	4	1.000

National League	PO	A	E	DP	Pct.
1B Hernandez, N.Y.	1199	149	5	115	.996
2B Sandberg, Chi.	309	492	5	86	.994
SS Smith, St. L.	229	453	15	96	.978
3B Schmidt, Phi.	78	220	6	27	.980
OF McGee, St. L.	325	9	3	0	.991
OF Milner, Cin.	292	6	3	0	.990
OF Dykstra, N.Y.	283	8	3	2	.990
C Brenly, S.F.	518	55	3	4	.995
P Rhoden, Pit.	32	34	0	4	1.000

PITCHING

Wild Pitches

American League		National League	
1 Witt, Tex.	22	1 Ryan, Hou.	15
2 Correa, Tex.	19	2 Sutcliffe, Chi.	13
3 Hough, Tex.	16	3 Valenzuela, L.A.	13
4 Gubicza, K.C.	15	4 Walk, Pit.	12
Smithson, Min.	15	Hershiser, L.A.	12

Hit Batters

American League		National League	
1 Stieb, Tor.	15	1 K. Gross, Phi.	8
2 Smithson, Min.	14	Reuschel, Pit.	8
3 Moore, Sea.	12	3 Aguilera, N.Y.	7
Schrom, Cle.	12	McWilliams, Pit.	7
5 Boddicker, Bal.	11	Welch, L.A.	7
Williams, Tex.	11		

Home Runs Allowed

National League		American League	
1 Blyleven, Min.	50	1 K. Gross, Phi.	28
2 Morris, Det.	40	2 Hoyt, S.D.	27
3 Viola, Min.	37	3 Browning, Cin.	26
4 McGregor, Bal.	35	4 Mahler, Atl.	25
5 Schrom, Cle.	34	5 Gullickson, Cin.	24
		Hawkins, S.D.	24
		Krukow, S.F.	24

Balks

American League	
1 Plunk, Oak.	6
2 Williams, Tex.	5
3 Andujar, Oak.	4
Candiotti, Cle.	4
Rijo, Oak.	4

National League	
1 Deshaies, Hou.	7
2 Matthews, St. L.	6
3 Bielecki, Pit.	5
Eckersley, Chi.	5
LaCross, S.F.	5

1987 A Year of Homers and Heroics

Home runs flew out of ballparks in record numbers this year. Some people credited batting skill, others blamed pitching weakness, and others thought the ball had been juiced up. Regardless of the reason, the offense was dominant throughout the summer. In this new mood, the defending champions fell on hard times. Despite an impressive batting order and a pitching ace in Roger Clemens, the American League Cy Young Award winner for the second straight year, the Red Sox fell to a fifth-place finish in the A.L. East. The aging Angels fell even harder, winding up in last place in the A.L. West. In the N.L. West, the Astros stayed in the pennant race for most of the summer. Beginning on August 25, however, they lost 19 of 26 games to disappear from sight.

The Mets kept their hopes of another championship in sight alive into the last week of the season. Before spring training had ended, the Mets had lost Dwight Gooden to a cocaine abuse problem and Roger McDowell to a hernia operation, both of them to be gone for about two months. Their worst fears were realized, however, when the Cardinals regained their championship form of 1985. The Cards had speed in abundance, the league's best shortstop in Ozzie Smith, and a consistent heavy hitter in Jack Clark. A deep bullpen held the St. Louis pitching staff together. Even early injuries to John Tudor and newly acquired Tony Pena did not keep the Cardinals from soaring to a large midseason lead. During July and August, however, the Mets and Expos inched back into the race. With Jack Clark shelved with an ankle injury, the Cards limped into a key three-game series in New York only 1 1/2 games ahead of the Mets. On Friday night, September 11, the Mets held a 4-1 lead with two outs in the top of the ninth. Terry Pendleton resuscitated the Cards with a three-run homer to center field. St. Louis then beat the stunned Mets 6-4 in 10 innings. On Saturday, the Cardinals blasted Gooden for another victory. Although the Mets salvaged the third game, the Cards had beaten their strongest challenge and won their third divisional crown in six years.

The San Francisco Giants had finished last in the N.L. West two years ago. Under manager Roger Craig, the quick learning Giants captured first place in the division. The Giants started out fast, slumped in early summer, then broke away from the field late in the season. The San Francisco offense was centered around Will Clark and Candy Maldonado, with Kevin Mitchell contributing after a midseason trade with San Diego. Key pitchers Rick Reuschel, Dave Dravecky and Don Robinson arrived in midsummer swaps. Cincinnati fell short despite strong offensive seasons by Eric Davis and Kal Daniels. Houston's September swoon could not detract from the achievements of oldster Nolan Ryan, who led the league in both E.R.A. and strikeouts, despite an 8-16 record.

No one in the A.L. West took charge of the divisional race until late in the season. The Twins finally grabbed first-place, primarily because their home record of 56-25 was the best in the major leagues. Manager Tom Kelly, in his first full season, had a solid lineup built around Kelly Puckett, Kent Hrbek, Gary Gaetti and Tom Brunansky. Frank Viola spearheaded a thin starting staff, while newly acquired Jeff Reardon gave the Twins unaccustomed relief help. The second place Royals endured manager Dick Howser's resignation in spring training and midseason death from cancer. The third-place Athletics showcased Mark McGwire, whose 49 homers set a rookie record.

The Milwaukee Brewers rocked the A.L East by winning their first 13 games. Although they soon fell back into the pack, Paul Molitor brightened the Milwaukee summer with a 39-game hitting streak in July and August. Don Mattingly of the Yankees reached similar heights by homering in eight straight games in July and swatting a season record of six grand slam homers. The divisional title race came down to the Tigers and Blue Jays, both rich in hitting and pitching. The Detroit stars were Alan Trammell, Darrell Evans, Matt Nokes, Jack Morris and August acquisition Doyle Alexander. Toronto's top performers were MVP George Bell, Tony Fernandez and Jimmy Key. The last 11 days settled the issue. On September 24, the Tigers went to Toronto for a four-game set, trailing the Blue Jays by half a game. The Jays came from behind to win each of the first three games, pushing the Tigers to the brink. Toronto, however, lost star shortstop Tony Fernandez with a broken elbow in the first game. The Tigers won the final game of the series. During the next week, the Tigers split four games with the Orioles, while the Jays alarmingly dropped three straight to the Brewers in Toronto. The two contenders then convened in Detroit for an October 2-4 finale. The Tigers tied the race with a victory on Friday night, clinched a tie for first place with a victory on Saturday, then kicked the Blue Jays into bitter oblivion on Sunday.

In the League Championship Series, the Cardinals won the N.L. pennant by shutting down the Giants without a run in games six and seven. The Twins upset the Tigers in five games, eliminating the team with baseball's best record. As fate would have it, the World Series began in the park of the A.L. champion this year. The lightly regarded Twins did what they did best, win at home. They won the first two games with offensive fireworks under the Dome at home, lost three straight in St. Louis, then came from behind twice in win games six and seven back home. For the Twins, it was their first World Series championship ever. For the Cards, it was a reversal of their LCS comeback success and a replay of their 1985 Series frustration.

EAST DIVISION

Name	G by Pos	B	AGE	G	AB	R	H	2B	3B	HR	RBI	BB	SO	SB	BA	SA
DETROIT	1st 98-64 .605		**SPARKY ANDERSON**													
TOTALS			32	162	5649	896	1535	274	32	225	840	653	913	106	.272	.451
Darrell Evans	1B105, DH44, 3B7	R	40	150	499	90	128	20	0	34	99	100	84	6	.257	.501
Lou Whitaker	2B148	L	30	149	604	110	160	38	6	16	59	71	108	13	.265	.427
Alan Trammell	SS149	R	29	151	597	109	205	34	3	28	105	60	47	21	.343	.551
Tom Brookens	3B122, SS16, 2B1	R	33	143	444	55	107	15	3	13	59	33	63	7	.241	.376
Pat Sheridan	OF137	L	29	141	421	57	109	19	3	6	49	44	90	18	.259	.361
Chet Lemon	OF145	R	32	146	470	75	130	30	3	20	75	70	82	0	.277	.481
Matt Nokes	C109, DH19, OF3, 3B2	L	23	135	461	69	133	14	2	32	87	35	70	2	.289	.536
Kirk Gibson (UJ)	OF121, DH4	L	30	128	487	95	135	25	3	24	79	71	117	26	.277	.489
Bill Madlock	DH64, 1B22, 3B5	R	36	87	326	56	91	17	0	14	50	28	45	4	.279	.460
Mike Heath	C67, OF24, 1B4, 3B4, SS2, 2B1, DH1	R	32	93	270	34	76	16	0	8	33	21	42	1	.281	.430
Dave Bergman	1B65, OF7, DH7	L	34	91	172	25	47	7	3	6	22	30	23	0	.273	.453
Larry Herndon	OF57, DH23	R	33	89	225	32	73	13	2	9	47	23	35	1	.324	.520
Johnny Grubb	OF31, DH16, 3B1	L	38	59	114	9	23	6	0	2	13	15	16	0	.202	.307
Darnell Coles (VJ)	3B36, 1B9, OF8, DH3, SS1	R	25	53	149	14	27	5	1	4	15	15	23	0	.181	.309
Jim Walewander	2B24, 3B17, DH8, SS3	B	25	53	54	24	13	3	1	1	4	7	6	2	.241	.389
Jim Morrison	3B16, DH8, OF3, SS3, 2B3, 1B1	R	34	34	117	15	24	1	1	4	19	2	26	2	.205	.333
Terry Harper	DH15, OF14	R	31	31	64	4	13	3	0	3	10	9	8	1	.203	.391
Billy Bean	OF24	L	23	26	66	6	17	2	0	0	4	5	11	1	.258	.288
Scott Lusader	OF22, DH1	L	22	23	47	8	15	3	1	1	8	5	7	1	.319	.489
Dwight Lowry	C12, 1B1	L	29	13	25	0	5	2	0	0	1	0	6	0	.200	.280
Orlando Mercado	C10	R	25	10	22	2	3	0	0	0	1	2	0	0	.136	.136
Tim Tolman	OF7, DH2	R	31	9	12	3	1	1	0	0	1	1	7	2	.083	.167
Doug Baker	SS6, 2B1, 3B1	B	26	8	1	0	0	0	0	0	0	0	1	0	.000	.000
TORONTO	2nd 96-66 .593 2		**JIMY WILLIAMS**													
TOTALS			26	162	5635	845	1514	277	38	215	790	555	970	126	.269	.446
Willie Upshaw	1B146	L	30	150	512	68	125	22	4	15	58	58	78	10	.244	.391
Garth Iorg	2B91, 3B28, DH5	R	32	122	310	35	65	11	0	4	30	21	52	2	.210	.284
Tony Fernandez	SS146	B	25	146	578	90	186	29	8	5	67	51	48	32	.322	.426
Kelly Gruber	3B119, SS21, 2B7, OF2, DH1	R	25	138	341	50	80	14	3	12	36	17	70	12	.235	.399
Jesse Barfield	OF158	R	27	159	590	89	155	25	3	28	84	58	141	3	.263	.458
Lloyd Moseby	OF158, DH2	L	27	155	592	106	167	27	4	26	96	70	124	39	.282	.473
George Bell	OF148, DH7, 3B1, 2B1	R	27	156	610	111	188	32	4	47	134	39	75	5	.308	.605
Ernie Whitt	C131	L	35	135	446	57	120	24	1	19	75	44	50	0	.269	.455
Fred McGriff	DH90, 1B14	L	23	107	295	58	73	16	0	20	43	60	104	3	.247	.505
Rance Mulliniks	3B96, DH22, SS1	L	31	124	332	37	103	28	1	11	44	34	55	1	.310	.500
Rick Leach	OF43, DH30, 1B5	L	30	98	195	26	55	13	1	3	25	25	25	0	.282	.405
Cecil Fielder	DH55, 1B16, 3B2	R	23	82	175	30	47	7	1	14	32	20	48	0	.269	.426
Manny Lee	2B27, SS26, DH1	B	22	56	121	14	31	2	3	1	11	6	13	2	.256	.347
Charlie Moore	C44, OF5	R	34	51	107	15	23	10	1	1	7	13	12	0	.215	.355
Juan Beniquez	DH15, OF7, 1B2	R	37	39	81	6	23	5	1	5	21	5	13	0	.284	.556
Nelson Liriano	2B37	B	23	37	158	29	38	6	2	2	10	16	22	13	.241	.342
Rob Ducey	OF28, DH1	L	22	34	48	12	9	1	1	0	6	5	10	2	.188	.271
Mike Sharperson	2B32	R	25	32	96	4	20	7	0	0	9	7	15	2	.208	.271
Jeff DeWillis	C13	R	23	13	25	2	3	1	0	0	0	2	12	0	.120	.280
Lou Thornton	DH6, OF4	L	24	12	12	5	6	1	0	0	0	0	1	0	.500	.500
Greg Myers	C7	L	21	7	9	1	1	0	0	0	0	0	3	0	.111	.111
Matt Stark (SJ)	C5	R	22	5	12	0	1	0	0	0	0	1	1	0	.083	.083
Alex Infante		R	25	1	0	0	0	0	0	0	0	0	0	0		

1987 AMERICAN LEAGUE

NAME	T	AGE	W	L	PCT	SV	G	GS	CG	IP	H	BB	SO	SHO	ERA
		29	98	64	.605	31	162	162	33	1456	1430	563	976	10	4.02
Jack Morris	R	32	18	11	.621	0	34	34	13	266	227	93	208	0	3.38
Walt Terrell	R	29	17	10	.630	0	35	35	10	245	254	94	143	1	4.05
Frank Tanana	L	33	15	10	.600	0	34	34	5	219	216	56	146	3	3.91
Mike Henneman	R	25	11	3	.786	7	55	0	0	97	86	30	75	0	2.98
2 Doyle Alexander	R	36	9	0	1.000	0	11	11	3	88	63	26	44	3	1.53
Jeff Robinson	R	25	9	6	.600	0	29	21	2	127	132	54	98	1	5.37
Dan Petry	R	28	9	7	.563	0	30	21	0	135	148	76	93	0	5.61
Eric King	R	23	6	9	.400	9	55	4	0	116	111	60	89	0	4.89
Guillermo Hernandez (AJ)	L	32	3	4	.429	8	45	0	0	49	53	20	30	0	3.67
Nate Snell	R	34	1	2	.333	0	22	0	0	39	39	19	19	0	3.96
2 Dickie Noles	R	30	1	0	—	2	4	0	0	2	2	1	0	0	4.50
Morris Madden	L	26	0	0	—	0	2	0	0	2	4	3	0	0	16.20
Mark Thurmond	L	30	0	1	.000	5	48	0	0	62	83	24	21	0	4.23
Bryan Kelly	R	28	0	1	.000	0	5	0	0	11	12	7	10	0	5.06
		28	96	66	.593	43	162	162	18	1454	1323	567	1064	8	3.74
Jimmy Key	L	26	17	8	.680	0	36	36	8	261	210	66	161	1	2.76
Jim Clancy	R	31	15	11	.577	0	37	37	5	241	234	80	180	1	3.54
Dave Stieb	R	29	13	9	.591	0	33	31	3	185	164	87	115	1	4.09
Jeff Musselman	L	24	12	5	.706	3	68	1	0	89	75	54	54	0	4.15
John Cerutti	L	27	11	4	.733	0	44	21	2	151	144	59	92	0	4.40
Mark Eichhorn	R	26	10	6	.625	4	89	0	0	128	110	52	96	0	3.17
Jose Nunez	R	23	5	2	.714	0	37	9	0	97	91	58	99	0	5.01
David Wells	L	24	4	3	.571	1	18	2	0	29	37	12	32	0	3.99
2 Mike Flanagan	L	35	3	2	.600	0	7	7	0	49	46	15	43	0	2.37
Joe Johnson	R	25	3	5	.375	0	14	14	0	67	77	18	27	0	5.13
1 Gary Lavelle (EJ)	L	38	2	3	.400	1	23	0	0	28	36	19	17	0	5.53
Duane Ward	R	23	1	0	1.000	0	12	1	0	12	14	12	10	0	6.94
1 Don Gordon	R	27	0	0	—	0	5	0	0	11	8	3	3	0	4.09
2 Phil Niekro	R	48	0	2	.000	0	3	0	0	12	15	7	7	0	8.25
Tom Henke	R	29	0	6	.000	34	72	0	0	94	62	25	128	0	2.49

MILWAUKEE 3rd 91-71 .562 7 — TOM TREBELHORN

Name	G by Pos	B	AGE	G	AB	R	H	2B	3B	HR	RBI	BB	SO	SB	BA	SA
TOTALS			28	162	5625	862	1552	272	46	163	832	598	1040	176	.276	.428
Greg Brock	1B141	L	30	141	532	81	159	29	3	13	85	57	63	5	.299	.438
Juan Castillo	2B97, SS13, 3B7	B	25	116	321	44	72	11	4	3	28	33	76	15	.224	.312
Dale Sveum	SS142, 2B13	B	23	153	535	86	135	27	3	25	95	40	133	2	.252	.454
Ernest Riles (RJ)	3B65, SS21	L	26	83	276	38	72	11	1	4	38	30	47	3	.261	.351
Glenn Braggs	OF123, DH8	R	24	132	505	67	136	28	7	13	77	47	96	12	.269	.430
Robin Yount	OF150, DH8	R	31	158	635	99	198	25	9	21	103	76	94	19	.312	.479
Rob Deer	OF123, 1B12, DH4	R	26	134	474	71	113	15	2	28	80	86	186	12	.238	.456
B.J. Surhoff	C98, 3B10, DH7, 1B1	L	22	115	395	50	118	22	3	7	68	36	30	11	.299	.423
Paul Molitor (LJ)	DH58, 3B41, 2B19	R	30	118	465	114	164	41	5	16	75	69	67	45	.353	.566
Mike Felder	OF99, DH3, 2B1	B	25	108	289	48	77	5	7	2	31	28	23	34	.266	.353
Rick Manning	OF78, DH2	L	32	97	114	21	26	7	1	0	13	12	18	4	.228	.307
Jim Gantner (LJ)	2B57, 3B38, DH1	L	33	81	265	37	72	14	0	4	30	19	22	6	.272	.370
Bill Schroeder	C67, 1B4, DH2	R	26	75	250	35	83	12	0	14	42	16	56	5	.332	.548
Cecil Cooper	DH62	L	37	63	250	25	62	13	0	6	36	17	51	1	.248	.372
Jim Paciorek	1B21, 3B15, C05, DH2	R	27	48	101	16	23	5	0	2	10	12	20	1	.228	.337
Steve Kiefer	3B26, 2B4	R	26	28	99	17	20	4	0	5	17	7	28	0	.202	.394
Billy Jo Robidoux	1B10, DH10	L	23	23	62	9	12	0	0	0	4	8	17	0	.194	.194
Charlie O'Brien	C10	R	27	10	35	2	7	3	1	0	0	4	0	.200	.343
Brad Komminsk	OF5, DH1	R	26	7	15	0	1	0	0	0	0	1	7	1	.067	.067
Stan Stanicek	DH1	R	26	4	7	2	2	0	0	0	0	0	2	0	.286	.286

NAME	T	AGE	W	L	PCT	SV	G	GS	CG	IP	H	BB	SO	SHO	ERA
TOTALS		26	91	71	.562	45	162	162	28	1464	1548	529	1039	6	4.62
Teddy Higuera	L	28	18	10	.643	0	35	35	14	262	236	87	240	3	3.85
Juan Nieves	L	22	14	8	.636	0	34	33	3	196	199	100	163	1	4.88
Bill Wegman	R	24	12	11	.522	0	34	33	7	225	229	53	102	0	4.24
Chris Bosio	R	24	11	8	.579	2	46	19	2	170	187	50	150	1	5.24
Mark Clear	R	31	8	5	.615	6	58	1	0	78	75	55	81	0	4.48
Chuck Crim	R	25	6	8	.429	12	53	5	0	130	133	39	56	0	3.67
Dan Plesac	L	25	5	6	.455	23	57	0	0	79	63	23	89	0	2.61
Mark Knudson	R	26	4	4	.500	0	15	8	1	62	88	14	26	0	5.37
Jay Aldrich	R	26	3	1	.750	0	31	0	0	58	71	13	22	0	4.94
Dave Stapleton	L	25	2	0	1.000	0	4	0	0	15	13	3	14	0	1.84
Paul Mirabella	L	33	2	1	.667	2	29	0	0	29	30	16	14	0	4.91
Len Barker (EJ)	R	31	2	1	.667	0	11	11	0	44	54	17	22	0	5.36
Ray Burris (RF)	R	36	2	2	.500	0	10	2	0	23	33	12	8	0	5.87
Mark Ciardi	R	25	1	1	.500	0	4	3	0	16	26	9	8	0	9.37
Mike Birkbeck (SJ)	R	26	1	4	.200	0	10	10	1	45	63	19	25	0	6.20
Alex Madrid	R	24	0	0	—	0	3	0	0	5	11	1	1	0	15.19
John Henry Johnson	L	30	0	1	.000	0	10	2	0	26	42	18	18	0	9.57

NEW YORK 4th 89-73 .549 9 — LOU PINIELLA

Name	G by Pos	B	AGE	G	AB	R	H	2B	3B	HR	RBI	BB	SO	SB	BA	SA
TOTALS			30	162	5611	788	1445	239	16	196	749	604	949	105	.262	.418
Don Mattingly	1B140, DH1	L	26	141	569	93	186	38	2	30	115	51	38	1	.327	.559
Willie Randolph (KJ)	2B119, DH1	R	32	120	449	96	137	24	2	7	67	82	25	11	.305	.414
Wayne Tolleson	SS119, 3B3	B	31	121	349	48	77	4	0	1	22	43	56	5	.221	.241
Mike Pagliarulo	3B147, 1B1	L	27	150	522	76	122	26	3	32	87	53	111	1	.234	.479
Dave Winfield	OF145, DH8	R	35	156	575	83	158	22	1	27	97	76	96	5	.275	.457
Rickey Henderson (LJ)	OF69, DH24	R	28	95	358	78	104	17	3	17	37	80	52	41	.291	.497
Gary Ward	OF94, DH36, 1B15	R	33	146	529	65	131	22	1	16	78	33	101	9	.248	.384
Rick Cerone	C111, 1B2, P2	R	33	113	284	28	69	12	1	4	23	30	46	0	.243	.335
Ron Kittle (ZJ)	DH49, OF2	R	29	59	159	21	44	5	0	12	28	10	36	0	.277	.535
Dan Pasqua	OF74, DH20, 1B12	L	25	113	318	42	74	7	1	17	42	40	99	0	.233	.421
Claudell Washington	OF72, DH13	L	32	102	312	42	87	17	0	9	44	27	54	10	.279	.429
Bobby Meacham	SS56, 2B25, DH1	B	26	77	203	28	55	11	1	5	21	19	33	6	.271	.409
Henry Cotto	OF57	R	26	68	149	21	35	10	0	5	20	6	35	4	.235	.403
2 Mike Easler	DH32, OF15	L	36	65	167	13	47	9	0	4	21	14	32	1	.281	.389
Joel Skinner	C64	R	26	64	139	9	19	4	0	3	14	8	46	0	.137	.237
2 Mark Salas	C41, DH4, OF1	L	26	50	115	13	23	4	0	3	12	10	17	0	.200	.313
Juan Bonilla	2B22, DH1, 3B1	R	32	23	55	6	14	3	0	1	3	5	6	0	.255	.364
Roberto Kelly	OF17, DH2	R	22	23	52	12	14	3	0	1	7	5	15	9	.269	.385
Lenn Sakata (NJ)	3B12, 2B6	R	33	19	45	5	12	0	1	2	4	2	4	0	.267	.444
2 Jerry Royster	3B13, 2B1, SS1, OF1	R	34	18	42	1	15	2	0	0	4	4	4	2	.357	.405
Paul Zuvella	2B7, SS6, 3B1	R	28	14	34	2	6	0	0	0	0	4	4	0	.176	.176
Orestes Destrade	1B3, DH2	B	25	9	19	5	5	0	0	0	1	5	5	0	.263	.263
Randy Velarde	SS8	R	24	8	22	1	4	0	0	0	1	1	6	0	.182	.182
Jay Buhner	OF7	R	22	7	22	0	5	2	0	0	1	1	6	0	.227	.318
Jeff Moronko	3B3, SS2, DH1	R	27	7	11	0	1	0	0	0	0	0	2	0	.125	.125
Phil Lombardi	C3	R	24	5	8	0	1	0	0	0	0	0	2	0	.091	.091
1 Keith Hughes		L	23	1	0	0	0	0	0	0	0	0	0	0	.000	.000

NAME	T	AGE	W	L	PCT	SV	G	GS	CG	IP	H	BB	SO	SHO	ERA
TOTALS		31	89	73	.549	47	162	162	19	1446	1475	542	900	10	4.36
Rick Rhoden	R	34	16	10	.615	0	30	29	4	182	184	61	107	0	3.86
Tommy John	L	44	13	6	.684	0	33	33	3	188	212	47	63	1	4.03
Charlie Hudson	R	28	11	7	.611	0	35	16	6	155	137	57	100	3	3.61
1 Dennis Rasmussen	L	28	9	7	.563	0	26	25	2	146	145	55	89	0	4.75
Dave Righetti	L	28	8	6	.571	31	60	0	0	95	95	44	77	0	3.51
Ron Guidry (FH-EJ)	L	36	5	8	.385	0	22	17	2	118	111	38	96	0	3.67
2 Bill Gullickson	R	28	4	2	.667	0	8	8	1	48	41	11	28	0	4.88
Tim Stoddard	R	34	4	3	.571	8	57	0	0	93	83	30	78	0	3.50
Rich Bordi	R	28	3	1	.750	0	16	1	0	33	42	12	23	0	7.64
Cecilio Guante (EJ)	R	27	3	2	.600	1	23	0	0	44	42	20	46	0	5.73
1 Pat Clements	L	25	3	3	.500	7	55	0	0	80	91	30	36	0	4.95
1 Joe Niekro	R	42	3	4	.429	0	8	8	1	51	40	19	30	0	3.55
Al Leiter	L	21	2	2	.500	0	4	4	0	23	24	15	28	0	6.35
1 Bob Shirley	L	33	1	0	1.000	0	12	1	0	34	36	16	12	0	4.50
Pete Filson	L	28	1	0	1.000	0	7	2	0	22	26	9	10	0	3.27
Bill Fulton	R	23	1	0	1.000	0	3	0	0	5	9	1	2	0	11.57
Brad Arnsberg (EJ)	R	23	1	1	.500	0	6	2	0	19	22	13	14	0	5.59
1 Bob Tewksbury	R	26	1	4	.250	0	8	6	0	33	47	7	12	0	6.75
Al Holland	L	34	0	0	—	0	3	0	0	6	9	9	5	0	14.21
Rick Cerone	R	33	0	0	—	0	2	0	0	1	1	1	0	0	0.00
2 Neil Allen	R	29	0	1	.000	0	7	1	0	25	23	10	16	0	3.65
2 Steve Trout	L	29	0	4	.000	0	14	9	0	46	51	37	27	0	6.60

BOSTON 5th 78-84 .481 20 — JOHN McNAMARA

Name	G by Pos	B	AGE	G	AB	R	H	2B	3B	HR	RBI	BB	SO	SB	BA	SA
TOTALS			29	162	5586	842	1554	273	26	174	802	606	825	77	.278	.430
Dwight Evans	1B79, OF77, DH4	R	35	154	541	109	165	37	2	34	123	106	98	4	.305	.569
Marty Barrett	2B137	R	29	137	559	72	164	23	0	3	43	51	38	15	.293	.351
Spike Owen	SS130	B	26	132	437	50	113	17	7	2	48	53	43	11	.259	.343
Wade Boggs	3B145, 1B1, DH1	L	29	147	551	108	200	40	6	24	89	105	48	1	.363	.588
Mike Greenwell	OF91, DH15, C1	L	23	125	412	71	135	31	6	19	89	35	45	5	.328	.570
Ellis Burks	OF132, DH1	R	22	133	558	94	152	30	2	20	59	41	98	27	.272	.441
Jim Rice (KJ)	OF94, DH12	R	34	108	404	66	112	14	0	13	62	45	77	1	.277	.408
Rich Gedman (FH-RJ)	C51	L	27	52	151	11	31	8	1	0	13	10	24	0	.205	.278
1 Don Baylor	DH97	R	38	108	339	64	81	8	0	16	57	40	41	5	.239	.404
Ed Romero	2B29, SS24, 3B24, 1B8	R	29	88	235	23	64	5	0	0	14	18	22	0	.272	.294
1 Bill Buckner	1B74	L	37	75	286	23	78	6	1	2	42	13	19	1	.273	.322
1 Dave Henderson	OF64, DH1	R	28	75	184	30	43	10	0	8	25	22	48	1	.234	.418
Todd Benzinger	OF61, 1B2	B	24	73	223	36	62	11	1	8	43	22	41	2	.278	.444
Marc Sullivan	C60	R	28	60	160	11	27	5	2	2	10	4	43	0	.169	.237
John Marzano	C52	R	24	52	168	20	41	11	0	5	24	7	41	0	.244	.399
Sam Horn	DH40	L	23	46	158	31	44	7	0	14	34	17	55	0	.278	.589
Pat Dodson	1B21, DH1	L	27	26	42	4	7	3	0	2	6	3	16	0	.167	.381
Danny Sheaffer	C25	R	25	25	66	5	8	1	0	1	5	0	14	0	.121	.182
1 Glenn Hoffman	SS16, 3B3, 2B2	R	28	21	55	5	11	3	0	0	6	3	9	0	.200	.255
Jody Reed	SS4, 2B2, 3B1	R	24	9	30	4	9	1	1	0	8	4	0	1	.300	.400
Kevin Romine	OF7, DH2	R	26	9	24	5	7	2	0	0	2	2	6	1	.292	.375
Dave Sax	C2	R	28	2	3	0	0	0	0	0	0	0	1	0	.000	.000

NAME	T	AGE	W	L	PCT	SV	G	GS	CG	IP	H	BB	SO	SHO	ERA
TOTALS		28	78	84	.481	16	162	162	47	1436	1584	517	1034	13	4.77
Roger Clemens	R	24	20	9	.690	0	36	36	18	282	248	83	256	7	2.97
Bruce Hurst	L	29	15	13	.536	0	33	33	15	239	239	76	190	3	4.41
Al Nipper	R	28	11	12	.478	0	30	30	6	174	196	62	89	0	5.43
Calvin Schiraldi	R	25	8	5	.615	6	62	1	0	84	75	40	93	0	4.41
Jeff Sellers	R	23	7	8	.467	0	25	22	4	140	161	61	99	2	5.28
Steve Crawford	R	29	5	4	.556	0	29	0	0	73	91	32	43	0	5.33
Bob Stanley	R	32	4	15	.211	0	34	20	4	153	198	42	67	1	5.01
Wes Gardner	R	26	3	6	.333	10	49	1	0	90	98	42	70	0	5.42
Joe Sambito	L	35	2	6	.250	0	47	0	0	38	46	16	35	0	6.93
Tom Bolton	L	25	1	0	1.000	0	9	0	0	62	83	27	49	0	4.38
Rob Woodward	R	24	1	1	.500	0	7	6	0	37	53	15	15	0	7.05
Oil Can Boyd (SJ)	R	27	1	3	.250	0	7	7	0	37	47	9	12	0	5.89
John Leister	R	23	0	2	.000	0	8	4	0	30	49	12	16	0	9.20

BALTIMORE 6th 67-95 .414 31 — CAL RIPKEN SR.

Name	G by Pos	B	AGE	G	AB	R	H	2B	3B	HR	RBI	BB	SO	SB	BA	SA
TOTALS			31	162	5576	729	1437	219	20	211	701	524	939	69	.258	.418
Eddie Murray	1B156, DH4	B	31	160	618	89	171	38	3	30	91	73	80	1	.277	.477
Billy Ripken	2B58	R	22	58	234	27	72	9	0	2	20	21	23	4	.308	.372
Cal Ripken	SS162	R	26	162	624	97	157	28	3	27	98	81	77	3	.252	.436
Ray Knight	3B130, DH14, 1B6	R	34	150	563	46	144	24	0	14	65	39	90	0	.256	.373
Larry Sheets	OF124, DH7, 1B3	L	27	135	469	74	148	23	0	31	94	31	67	1	.316	.563
Fred Lynn	OF101, DH8	L	35	111	396	49	100	24	0	23	60	39	72	3	.253	.487
Ken Gerhart (BW)	OF91	R	26	92	284	41	69	10	2	14	34	17	53	9	.243	.440
Terry Kennedy	C142	R	30	143	512	51	128	13	1	18	62	35	100	1	.250	.385
Mike Young (RJ)	OF60, DH47	B	27	110	363	46	87	10	1	16	39	46	91	10	.240	.405
Jim Dwyer	DH41, OF30	L	37	92	241	54	66	7	1	15	33	37	57	4	.274	.498
Lee Lacy	OF80, DH4	R	39	87	258	35	63	13	3	7	28	32	49	3	.244	.399
Alan Wiggins (SC)	DH44, 2B33, OF5	B	29	85	306	37	71	4	2	1	15	28	34	20	.232	.298
Rick Burleson	2B55, DH7	R	36	62	206	26	43	14	1	2	14	17	30	0	.209	.316
Rene Gonzales	3B29, 2B6, SS1	R	26	37	60	14	16	2	1	1	7	3	11	1	.267	.383
Mike Hart	OF32	L	29	34	76	7	12	2	0	4	12	6	19	1	.158	.342
Pate Stanicek	2B19, DH10, 3B2	B	24	30	113	9	31	3	0	0	9	6	19	8	.274	.301
Ron Washington	3B20, 2B3, OF2, DH2, SS1	R	35	26	79	7	16	3	1	1	6	1	15	0	.203	.304
1 John Shelby	OF19, DH1	B	29	21	32	4	6	0	0	0	1	1	13	0	.188	.281
Floyd Rayford	C17, 3B1, DH1	R	29	20	50	5	11	0	0	2	3	2	9	0	.220	.340
Nelson Simmons	OF13, DH1	B	24	16	49	3	13	1	1	1	4	3	11	0	.265	.388
Carl Nichols	C13	R	24	13	21	4	8	1	0	0	3	1	4	0	.381	.429
Dave Van Gorder	C12	R	30	12	21	4	5	0	0	0	1	3	6	0	.238	.381
Jackie Gutierrez	2B1, 3B1	R	27	3	2	1	0	0	0	0	0	0	0	0	.000	.000

NAME	T	AGE	W	L	PCT	SV	G	GS	CG	IP	H	BB	SO	SHO	ERA
TOTALS		28	67	95	.414	30	162	162	17	1440	1555	547	870	6	5.01
Dave Schmidt	R	30	10	5	.667	1	35	14	2	124	128	26	70	2	3.77
Mike Boddicker	R	29	10	12	.455	0	33	33	7	226	212	78	152	2	4.18
Eric Bell	L	23	10	13	.435	0	33	29	2	165	174	78	111	0	5.45
Mark Williamson	R	26	8	9	.471	3	61	2	0	125	122	41	73	0	4.03
Ken Dixon	R	26	7	10	.412	5	34	15	0	105	128	27	91	0	6.43
John Habyan	R	23	6	7	.462	1	27	13	0	116	110	40	64	0	4.80
2 Tom Niedenfuer	R	27	3	5	.375	13	45	0	0	52	55	22	37	0	4.99
Mike Griffin	R	30	3	5	.375	1	23	6	1	74	78	33	42	0	4.36
1 Mike Flanagan (EJ)	L	35	3	6	.333	0	16	16	4	95	102	36	50	0	4.94
Scott McGregor (SJ)	L	33	2	7	.222	0	26	15	1	85	112	35	39	1	6.64
Jeff Ballard	L	23	2	8	.200	0	14	14	0	70	100	35	27	0	6.59
Don Aase	R	32	1	1	.500	2	7	0	0	8	8	4	3	0	2.25
Jack O'Connor (SJ)	L	29	1	1	.500	2	29	0	0	46	46	23	33	0	4.30
Jose Mesa	R	21	1	3	.250	0	6	5	0	31	38	15	17	0	6.03
Tony Arnold (XJ)	R	28	0	0	—	0	27	0	0	53	71	17	18	0	5.77
Mike Kinnunen	R	28	0	0	—	0	18	0	0	20	27	16	14	0	4.95
Doug Corbett	R	34	0	0	—	0	11	0	0	23	25	13	16	0	7.83
Luis DeLeon	R	28	0	2	.000	0	11	0	0	21	19	8	13	0	4.79
Tippy Martinez (SJ) 37															

CLEVELAND — 7th 61-101 .377 37 — PAT CORRALES 31-56 .356 — DOC EDWARDS 30-45 .400

Name	G by Pos	B	AGE	G	AB	R	H	2B	3B	HR	RBI	BB	SO	SB	BA	SA
TOTALS			28	162	5606	742	1476	267	30	187	691	489	977	140	.263	.422
Joe Carter	1B84, OF62, DH5	R	27	149	588	83	155	27	2	32	106	27	105	31	.264	.480
1 Tony Bernazard	2B78	B	30	149	293	39	70	12	1	11	30	25	49	7	.239	.399
Julio Franco (EJ)	SS111, 2B9, DH8	R	28	128	495	86	158	24	3	8	52	57	56	32	.319	.428
Brook Jacoby	3B144, 1B7, DH4	R	27	155	540	73	162	26	4	32	69	75	73	2	.300	.541
Cory Snyder	OF139, SS18	R	24	157	577	74	136	24	2	33	82	31	166	5	.236	.456
Brett Butler	OF136	L	30	137	522	91	154	25	8	9	41	91	55	33	.295	.425
Mel Hall	OF122, DH14	L	26	142	485	57	136	21	1	18	76	20	68	5	.280	.439
Chris Bando	C86	B	31	89	211	20	46	9	0	5	16	12	28	0	.218	.332
Pat Tabler	1B82, DH66	R	29	151	553	66	170	34	3	11	86	51	84	5	.307	.439
Carmen Castillo	DH43, OF23	R	29	89	220	27	55	17	0	11	31	16	52	1	.250	.477
Tommy Hinzo	2B67	B	23	67	257	31	68	9	3	3	21	10	47	9	.265	.358
Rick Dempsey (RJ)	C59	R	37	60	141	16	25	10	0	1	9	23	29	0	.177	.270
Andy Allanson	C50	R	25	50	154	17	41	6	0	3	16	9	30	1	.266	.364
Junior Noboa	2B21, SS8, 3B5, DH1	R	22	39	80	7	18	2	1	0	7	3	6	1	.225	.275
Jay Bell	SS38	R	21	38	125	14	27	9	1	2	13	8	31	2	.216	.352
Andre Thornton	DH21	R	37	36	85	8	10	2	0	0	5	10	25	1	.118	.141
Dave Clark	OF13, DH12	L	24	29	87	11	18	5	0	3	12	2	24	1	.207	.368
Doug Frobel	OF12, DH5	L	28	29	40	5	4	0	0	2	5	5	13	0	.100	.250
Eddie Williams	3B22	R	22	22	64	9	11	4	0	1	4	9	19	0	.172	.281
Otis Nixon	OF17, DH1	B	28	19	17	2	1	0	0	0	1	3	4	2	.059	.059
Casey Parsons	DH5, OF2, 1B1	L	33	18	25	2	4	0	0	1	5	0	5	0	.160	.280
Dave Gallagher	OF14	R	26	15	36	2	4	1	1	0	1	2	5	2	.111	.194
Brian Dorsett	C4	R	26	5	11	2	3	0	0	1	3	0	3	0	.273	.545

NAME	T	AGE	W	L	PCT	SV	G	GS	CG	IP	H	BB	SO	SHO	ERA
		30	61	101	.377	25	162	162	24	1423	1566	606	849	8	5.28
Scott Bailes	L	25	7	8	.467	6	39	17	0	120	145	47	65	0	4.64
1 Phil Niekro	R	48	7	11	.389	0	22	22	2	124	142	53	57	0	5.89
Tom Candiotti	R	29	7	18	.280	0	32	32	7	202	193	93	111	2	4.78
Doug Jones	R	30	6	5	.545	8	49	0	0	91	101	24	87	0	3.15
Ken Schrom	R	32	6	13	.316	0	32	29	4	154	185	57	61	1	6.50
John Farrell	R	24	5	1	.833	0	10	9	1	69	68	22	28	0	3.39
1 Steve Carlton	L	42	5	9	.357	1	23	14	3	109	111	63	71	0	5.37
Sammy Stewart (VJ)	R	22	4	2	.667	3	25	0	0	27	25	21	25	0	5.67
Greg Swindell (EJ)	R	22	3	8	.273	0	16	15	4	102	112	37	97	1	5.10
Rick Yett	R	24	3	9	.250	1	37	11	2	98	96	49	59	0	5.25
2 Mark Huismann	R	29	2	3	.400	2	20	0	0	35	38	8	23	0	5.09
Darrel Akerfelds	R	25	2	6	.250	0	16	13	1	75	84	38	42	0	6.75
Ed Vande Berg	L	28	1	0	1.000	0	55	0	0	72	96	21	40	0	5.10
Mike Armstrong	R	33	1	0	1.000	0	14	0	0	19	27	10	9	0	8.68
Jamie Easterly (SJ)	L	34	1	1	.500	0	16	0	0	32	26	13	22	0	4.55
Reggie Ritter (BJ)	R	27	1	1	.500	0	14	0	0	27	33	16	11	0	6.08
Jeff Kaiser (TJ)	R	26	0	0	—	0	2	0	0	3	4	3	2	0	16.20
Ernie Camacho	R	32	0	1	.000	1	15	0	0	14	21	5	9	0	9.22
Tom Waddell	R	28	0	1	.000	0	6	0	0	6	7	7	6	0	14.29
Frank Wills	R	28	0	1	.000	1	6	0	0	5	3	7	4	0	5.06
2 Don Gordon	R	27	0	3	.000	1	21	0	0	40	49	12	20	0	4.08

WEST DIVISION

MINNESOTA — 1st 85-77 .525 — TOM KELLY

Name	G by Pos	B	AGE	G	AB	R	H	2B	3B	HR	RBI	BB	SO	SB	BA	SA
TOTALS			28	162	5441	786	1422	258	35	196	733	523	898	113	.261	.430
Kent Hrbek	1B137, DH1	L	27	143	477	85	136	20	1	34	90	84	60	5	.285	.545
Steve Lombardozzi	2B133	R	27	136	432	51	103	19	3	8	38	33	66	5	.238	.352
Greg Gagne	SS136, OF4, 2B1, DH1	R	25	137	437	68	116	28	7	10	40	25	84	6	.265	.430
Gary Gaetti	3B150, DH2	R	28	154	584	95	150	36	2	31	109	37	92	10	.257	.485
Tom Brunansky	OF138, DH17	R	26	155	532	83	138	22	2	32	85	74	104	11	.259	.489
Kirby Puckett	OF147, DH8	R	27	157	624	96	207	32	5	28	99	32	91	12	.332	.534
Dan Gladden	OF111, DH4	R	29	121	438	69	109	21	2	8	38	38	72	25	.249	.361
Tim Laudner	C101, 1B7, DH2	R	29	113	288	30	55	7	1	16	43	23	80	1	.191	.389
Roy Smalley	DH73, 3B14, SS4	B	34	110	309	32	85	16	1	8	34	36	52	2	.275	.411
Randy Bush	OF75, 1B9, DH9	L	28	122	293	46	74	10	2	11	46	43	43	10	.253	.413
Al Newman	SS55, 2B47, 3B12, DH5, OF2	B	27	110	307	44	68	15	5	0	29	34	27	15	.221	.303
Mark Davidson	OF86, DH9	R	26	102	150	32	40	4	1	1	14	13	26	9	.267	.327
Gene Larkin	DH40, 1B26	B	24	85	233	23	62	11	2	4	28	25	31	1	.266	.382
2 Sal Butera	C51	R	34	51	111	7	19	5	0	1	12	7	16	0	.171	.243
Tom Nieto (BH)	C40, DH1	R	26	41	105	7	21	7	1	1	12	8	24	0	.200	.314
1 Mark Salas	C14	L	26	22	45	8	17	2	0	3	9	5	6	0	.378	.622
1 Don Baylor	DH14	R	38	20	49	3	14	1	0	0	6	5	12	0	.286	.306
Chris Pittaro	2B8, DH2	B	25	14	12	6	4	0	0	0	0	1	0	1	.333	.333
Billy Beane	OF7	R	25	12	15	1	4	2	0	0	1	0	6	0	.267	.400

NAME	T	AGE	W	L	PCT	SV	G	GS	CG	IP	H	BB	SO	SHO	ERA
		32	85	77	.525	39	162	162	16	1427	1465	564	990	4	4.63
Frank Viola	L	27	17	10	.630	0	36	36	7	252	230	66	197	1	2.90
Bert Blyleven	R	36	15	12	.556	0	37	37	8	267	249	101	196	1	4.01
Juan Berenguer	R	32	8	1	.889	4	47	6	0	112	100	47	110	0	3.94
Jeff Reardon	R	31	8	8	.500	31	63	0	0	80	70	28	83	0	4.48
Les Straker	R	27	8	10	.444	0	31	26	1	154	150	59	76	0	4.37
Keith Atherton	R	28	7	5	.583	2	59	0	0	79	81	30	51	0	4.54
George Frazier	R	32	5	5	.500	2	54	0	0	81	77	51	58	0	4.98
Mike Smithson	R	32	4	7	.364	0	21	20	0	109	126	38	53	0	5.94
2 Joe Niekro	R	42	4	9	.308	0	19	18	0	96	115	45	54	0	6.26
2 Dan Schatzeder	L	32	3	1	.750	0	30	1	0	44	64	18	30	0	6.39
Roy Smith	R	25	1	0	1.000	0	7	1	0	16	20	6	8	0	4.96
Randy Niemann	L	31	1	0	1.000	0	6	0	0	5	3	7	1	0	8.44
Allan Anderson	L	23	1	0	1.000	0	2	2	0	10	20	3	3	0	10.95
Jeff Bittiger	R	25	1	0	1.000	0	8	1	0	8	11	0	5	0	5.40
Mark Portugal	R	24	1	3	.250	0	13	7	0	44	58	24	28	0	7.77
2 Steve Carlton	L	42	1	5	.167	0	12	0	0	43	54	23	20	0	6.70
Joe Klink	L	25	0	1	.000	0	12	0	0	23	37	11	17	0	6.65

KANSAS CITY — 2nd 83-77 .512 2 — BILLY GARDNER 62-64 .492 — JOHN WATHAN 21-15 .583

Name	G by Pos	B	AGE	G	AB	R	H	2B	3B	HR	RBI	BB	SO	SB	BA	SA
TOTALS			28	162	5499	715	1443	239	40	168	677	523	1034	125	.262	.412
George Brett (KJ)	1B83, DH21, 3B11	L	34	115	427	71	124	18	2	22	78	72	47	6	.290	.496
Frank White	2B152, DH1	R	36	154	563	67	138	32	2	17	78	51	86	1	.245	.400
Angel Salazar	SS116	R	25	116	317	24	65	7	0	2	21	6	46	4	.205	.262
Kevin Seitzer	3B141, 1B25, OF3, DH1	R	25	161	641	105	207	33	8	15	83	80	85	12	.323	.470
Danny Tartabull	OF149, DH6	R	24	158	582	95	180	27	3	34	101	79	136	9	.309	.541
Willie Wilson	OF143, DH2	B	31	146	610	97	170	18	15	4	30	32	88	59	.279	.377
Bo Jackson	OF113, DH1	R	24	116	396	46	93	17	2	22	53	30	158	10	.235	.455
Jamie Quirk	C108, SS1	L	32	109	296	24	70	17	0	5	33	28	56	1	.236	.345
Steve Balboni	1B55, DH53	R	30	121	386	44	80	11	1	24	60	34	97	0	.207	.442
Thad Bosley	OF28, DH13	L	30	80	140	13	39	6	1	1	16	9	26	0	.279	.357
Larry Owen	C75	R	32	76	164	17	31	6	0	5	14	16	51	0	.189	.317
Bill Pecota	SS36, 3B17, 2B15, DH1	R	27	66	156	22	43	5	1	3	14	15	25	5	.276	.378
1 Juan Beniquez	OF22, DH15, 1B6, 3B6	R	37	57	174	14	41	7	0	3	26	11	26	0	.236	.328
Lonnie Smith (FJ)	OF32, DH15	R	31	48	167	26	42	7	1	3	8	24	31	9	.251	.359
Jim Eisenreich	DH26	L	28	44	105	10	25	8	2	4	21	7	13	1	.238	.467
Ross Jones	SS36, 2B3	R	27	39	114	10	29	4	2	0	10	5	15	1	.254	.325
1 Buddy Biancalana	SS22, 2B12, DH1	B	27	37	47	4	10	1	0	1	7	1	10	0	.213	.298
Gary Thurman	OF27	R	22	27	81	12	24	2	0	0	5	8	20	7	.296	.321
Jorge Orta	DH12	L	36	21	50	3	9	4	0	2	4	3	8	0	.180	.380
Hal McRae (RC)	DH7	R	41	18	32	5	10	3	0	1	9	5	1	0	.313	.500
Mike Macfarlane	C8	R	23	8	19	0	4	1	0	0	3	2	2	0	.211	.263
Scotti Madison	1B4, C3	B	27	7	15	4	4	3	0	0	1	1	5	0	.267	.467
Ed Hearn (SJ)	C5	R	26	6	17	2	5	2	0	0	3	4	2	0	.294	.412

NAME	T	AGE	W	L	PCT	SV	G	GS	CG	IP	H	BB	SO	SHO	ERA
		28	83	79	.512	26	162	162	44	1424	1424	548	923	11	3.86
Bret Saberhagen	R	23	18	10	.643	0	33	33	15	257	246	53	163	4	3.36
Charlie Leibrandt	L	30	16	11	.593	0	35	35	8	240	235	74	151	3	3.41
Mark Gubicza	R	24	13	18	.419	0	35	35	10	242	231	120	166	2	3.98
Danny Jackson	R	25	9	18	.333	0	36	34	11	224	219	109	152	2	4.02
Bud Black	R	30	8	6	.571	1	29	18	0	122	126	35	61	0	3.60
John Davis	R	24	5	2	.714	2	27	0	0	44	29	26	24	0	2.27
Dan Quisenberry	R	34	4	1	.800	8	47	0	0	49	58	10	17	0	2.76
Steve Farr	R	30	4	3	.571	1	47	0	0	91	97	44	88	0	4.15
Jerry Don Gleaton	L	29	4	4	.500	5	48	0	0	51	38	28	44	0	4.26
Melido Perez	R	21	1	1	.500	0	3	3	0	10	18	5	5	0	7.84
Bob Stoddard	R	30	1	3	.250	1	17	2	0	40	51	22	23	0	4.28
2 Gene Garber	R	39	0	0	—	0	13	0	0	14	13	1	3	0	2.51
Dave Gumpert	R	29	0	0	—	0	13	0	0	19	27	6	13	0	6.05
2 Bob Shirley	L	33	0	0	—	0	7	0	0	10	6	1	6	0	14.73
Rick Anderson	R	30	0	2	.000	0	13	0	0	13	26	9	12	0	13.85

OAKLAND — 3rd 81-81 .500 4 — TONY LaRUSSA

Name	G by Pos	B	AGE	G	AB	R	H	2B	3B	HR	RBI	BB	SO	SB	BA	SA
TOTALS			28	162	5511	806	1432	263	33	199	761	593	1056	140	.260	.428
Mark McGwire	1B145, 3B8, OF3	R	24	151	557	97	161	28	4	49	118	71	131	1	.289	.618
Tony Phillips (BA)	2B87, 3B11, SS9, OF2, DH1	B	28	111	379	48	91	20	0	10	46	57	76	7	.240	.372
Alfredo Griffin	SS137, 2B1	B	29	144	494	69	130	23	5	3	60	28	41	26	.263	.348
Carney Lansford	3B142, 1B17, DH4	R	30	151	554	89	160	27	4	19	76	60	44	27	.289	.455
Mike Davis	OF124, DH14	L	28	139	494	69	131	32	1	22	72	42	94	19	.265	.468
Luis Polonia	OF104, DH18	B	22	125	435	78	125	16	10	4	49	32	64	29	.287	.398
Jose Canseco	OF159, DH2	R	22	159	630	81	162	35	3	31	113	50	157	15	.257	.470
Terry Steinbach	C107, 3B10, DH8, 1B1	R	25	122	391	66	111	16	3	16	56	32	66	1	.284	.463
Reggie Jackson	DH79, OF20	L	41	115	336	42	74	14	1	15	43	33	97	2	.220	.402
Dwayne Murphy (KJ)	OF79, 1B1, 2B1	L	32	82	219	39	51	7	0	8	35	58	61	4	.233	.374
Mickey Tettleton	C80, DH1, 1B1	B	26	82	211	19	41	3	0	8	26	30	65	1	.194	.322
Stan Javier (VJ)	OF71, 1B6, DH1	B	23	81	151	22	28	3	1	2	9	19	33	3	.185	.265
Mike Gallego (WJ)	2B31, 3B24, SS17	R	26	72	124	18	31	6	0	2	14	12	21	0	.250	.347
2 Tony Bernazard	2B59, DH3	B	30	61	214	34	57	14	1	3	19	30	34	4	.266	.383
Steve Henderson	OF31, DH9	R	34	46	114	14	33	7	0	3	19	12	19	0	.289	.430
Ron Cey	DH30, 1B7, 3B3	R	39	45	104	12	23	6	0	4	11	22	32	0	.221	.394
Johnnie LeMaster	3B8, SS7, 2B5, DH1	R	33	32	42	2	2	0	0	1	4	9	6	0	.083	.083
Walt Weiss	SS11, DH2	B	23	16	26	3	12	4	0	0	1	2	2	1	.462	.615
Brian Harper	DH7, OF1, 1B1	R	27	11	17	1	4	1	0	0	3	0	4	0	.235	.294
1 Rob Nelson	1B7	L	23	7	24	1	4	1	0	0	0	6	12	0	.167	.208
Jerry Willard (XJ)	DH3, 1B1, 3B1	L	27	6	6	1	1	0	0	0	0	1	0	0	.167	.167
Matt Sinatro	C6	R	27	6	8	0	0	0	0	0	0	0	1	0	.000	.000
Alex Sanchez	OF1, DH1	R	28	2	3	0	0	0	0	0	0	0	0	0	.000	.000

NAME	T	AGE	W	L	PCT	SV	G	GS	CG	IP	H	BB	SO	SHO	ERA
		27	81	81	.500	40	162	162	18	1446	1442	531	1042	6	4.32
Dave Stewart	R	30	20	13	.606	0	37	37	8	261	224	105	205	1	3.68
Curt Young	L	27	13	7	.650	0	31	31	6	203	194	44	124	0	4.08
Steve Ontiveros	R	26	10	8	.556	1	35	22	2	151	141	50	97	1	4.00
Greg Cadaret	L	25	6	2	.750	0	29	0	0	40	37	24	30	0	4.54
Gene Nelson	R	26	6	5	.545	3	54	6	0	124	120	35	94	0	3.93
Dennis Eckersley	R	32	6	8	.429	16	54	2	0	116	99	17	113	0	3.03
Eric Plunk	R	23	4	6	.400	2	32	11	0	95	91	62	90	0	4.74
Jay Howell (EJ)	R	31	3	4	.429	16	36	0	0	44	48	21	55	0	5.89
Joaquin Andujar (EJ)	R	34	3	5	.375	0	13	13	1	61	63	26	32	0	6.08
1 Moose Haas (EJ)	R	31	2	2	.500	0	9	9	0	41	57	9	13	0	5.75
Jose Rijo	R	22	2	7	.222	0	21	14	1	82	106	41	67	0	5.90
Rick Rodriguez	R	26	1	0	1.000	0	15	0	0	24	32	15	9	0	2.96
2 Storm Davis	R	25	1	1	.500	0	5	3	0	31	43	10	23	0	3.26
Dennis Lamp	R	34	1	3	.250	0	36	5	0	57	76	22	36	0	5.08
2 Rick Honeycutt	L	33	1	4	.200	0	7	6	0	24	25	9	10	0	5.32
Bill Caudill (BH)	R	30	0	0	—	0	8	0	0	8	10	1	8	0	9.00
2 Gary Lavelle	L	38	0	0	—	0	6	0	0	6	6	6	3	0	8.31
Dave Von Ohlen	L	28	0	0	—	0	7	0	0	7	13	5	1	0	7.50
Dave Otto	L	22	0	0	—	0	3	0	0	9	9	4	0	0	9.00
Chris Codiroli	R	29	0	0	.000	0	3	0	0	11	9	8	4	0	8.74
1 Bill Krueger	L	29	0	3	.000	0	11	6	0	41	50	27	23	0	9.53

SEATTLE 4th 78-84 .481 7 DICK WILLIAMS

Name	G by Pos	B	AGE	G	AB	R	H	2B	3B	HR	RBI	BB	SO	SB	BA	SA
TOTALS			27	162	5508	760	1499	282	48	161	717	500	863	174	.272	.428
Alvin Davis	1B157	L	26	157	580	86	171	37	2	29	100	72	84	0	.295	.516
Harold Reynolds	2B160	B	26	160	530	73	146	31	8	1	35	39	34	60	.275	.370
Rey Quinones	SS135	R	23	135	478	55	132	18	2	12	56	26	71	1	.276	.397
Jim Presley	3B148, SS4, DH1	R	25	152	575	78	142	23	6	24	88	38	157	2	.247	.433
Mike Kingery	OF114, DH4	L	26	120	354	38	99	25	4	9	52	27	43	7	.280	.449
John Moses	OF100, 1B16, DH5	B	29	116	390	58	96	16	4	3	38	29	49	23	.246	.331
Phil Bradley	OF158	R	28	158	603	101	179	38	10	14	67	84	119	40	.297	.463
Scott Bradley	C82, 3B8, DH6, OF2	L	27	102	342	34	95	15	1	5	43	15	18	0	.278	.371
Ken Phelps	DH114, 1B1	L	32	120	332	68	86	13	1	27	68	80	75	1	.259	.548
Dave Valle	C75, DH14, 1B2, OF1	R	26	95	324	40	83	16	3	12	53	15	46	2	.256	.435
Mickey Brantley (VJ)	OF82, DH8	R	26	92	351	52	106	23	2	14	54	24	44	13	.302	.499
John Christensen (KJ)	OF43, DH8	R	26	53	132	19	32	6	1	2	12	12	28	2	.242	.348
Donell Nixon	OF32, DH6	R	25	46	132	17	33	4	0	3	12	13	28	21	.250	.348
2 Gary Matthews	DH39	R	36	45	119	10	28	1	0	3	15	15	22	0	.235	.319
Domingo Ramos	SS25, 3B7, 2B6, DH2	R	29	42	103	9	32	6	0	2	11	3	12	0	.311	.427
Bob Kearney	C24	R	31	24	47	5	8	4	0	1	1	1	9	0	.170	.298
Edgar Martinez	3B12, DH1	R	24	13	43	6	16	5	2	0	5	2	5	0	.372	.581
Rich Renteria	2B4, DH4, SS1	R	25	12	10	2	1	1	0	0	0	1	2	1	.100	.200
Mario Diaz	SS10	R	25	11	23	4	7	0	1	0	3	0	1	0	.304	.391
Dave Hengel	OF7, DH1	R	25	10	19	2	6	0	0	1	4	0	4	0	.316	.474
Jim Weaver	OF4	L	27	7	4	2	0	0	0	0	0	2	3	1	.000	.000
Brick Smith	1B3, DH1	L	28	5	8	1	1	0	0	0	0	2	4	0	.125	.125
Jerry Narron	C3	L	31	4	8	0	0	0	0	0	0	0	2	0	.000	.000

NAME	T	AGE	W	L	PCT	SV	G	GS	CG	IP	H	BB	SO	SHO	ERA
		26	78	84	.481	33	162	162	39	1431	1503	497	919	10	4.49
Mark Langston	L	26	19	13	.594	0	35	35	14	272	242	114	262	3	3.84
Mike Morgan	R	27	12	17	.414	0	34	31	8	207	245	53	85	2	4.65
Lee Guetterman	L	28	11	4	.733	0	25	17	2	113	117	35	42	1	3.81
Scott Bankhead	R	23	9	8	.529	0	27	25	2	149	168	37	95	0	5.42
Mike Moore	R	27	9	19	.321	0	33	33	12	231	268	84	115	0	4.71
Mike Trujillo	R	27	4	4	.500	1	28	7	0	66	70	26	36	0	6.17
Bill Wilkinson	L	22	3	4	.429	10	56	0	0	76	61	21	73	0	3.66
Edwin Nunez	R	24	3	4	.429	12	48	0	0	47	45	18	34	0	3.80
Steve Shields (BY)	R	28	2	0	1.000	3	20	0	0	30	43	12	22	0	6.60
Stan Clarke	L	26	2	2	.500	0	22	0	0	23	31	10	13	0	5.48
Roy Thomas	R	34	1	0	1.000	0	8	0	0	21	23	11	14	0	5.23
Jerry Reed	R	31	1	2	.333	7	39	1	0	82	79	24	51	0	3.42
Dennis Powell	L	23	1	3	.250	0	16	3	0	34	32	15	17	0	3.15
Mike Campbell	R	23	1	4	.200	0	9	9	1	49	41	25	35	0	4.74
1 Mike Huismann	R	29	0	0	—	0	6	0	0	15	10	4	15	0	4.91
Clay Parker	R	24	0	0	—	0	3	1	0	8	5	4	8	0	10.57
Rich Monteleone	R	24	0	0	—	0	3	0	0	7	10	4	2	0	6.43
Mike Brown	R	28	0	0	—	0	1	0	0	1	3	0	0	0	54.00

CHICAGO 5th 77-85 .475 8 JIM FREGOSI

Name	G by Pos	B	AGE	G	AB	R	H	2B	3B	HR	RBI	BB	SO	SB	BA	SA
TOTALS			28	162	5538	748	1427	283	36	173	706	487	971	138	.258	.415
Greg Walker	1B154, DH3	L	27	157	566	85	145	33	2	27	94	75	112	2	.256	.465
Donnie Hill	2B84, 3B32, DH6	B	26	111	410	57	98	16	4	9	46	30	35	1	.239	.368
Ozzie Guillen	SS149	L	23	149	560	64	156	22	7	2	51	22	52	25	.279	.354
Tim Hulett	3B61, 2B8	R	27	68	240	20	52	10	0	7	28	10	41	0	.217	.346
Ivan Calderon	OF139, DH3	R	25	144	542	93	159	38	2	28	83	60	109	10	.293	.526
Kenny Williams	OF115	R	23	116	391	48	110	13	5	11	50	10	83	21	.281	.422
Gary Redus	OF123, DH3	R	30	130	475	78	112	26	6	12	48	69	90	52	.236	.392
Carlton Fisk	C122, 1B9, DH7, OF2	R	39	135	454	68	116	22	1	23	71	39	72	1	.256	.460
Harold Baines (KJ)	DH117, OF8	L	28	132	505	59	148	26	4	20	93	46	82	0	.293	.479
Fred Manrique	2B92, SS23, DH5	R	26	115	298	30	77	13	3	4	29	19	69	5	.258	.362
Daryl Boston	OF92, DH5	L	24	103	337	51	87	21	2	10	29	25	68	12	.258	.421
Steve Lyons	3B51, OF15, DH6, 1B7	L	27	76	193	26	54	11	1	1	19	12	37	3	.280	.363
Jerry Hairston	DH13, OF13, 1B7	B	35	66	126	14	29	8	0	5	20	25	25	0	.230	.413
1 Jerry Royster	3B30, OF13, 2B5, DH1	R	34	55	154	25	37	11	0	7	23	19	28	2	.240	.448
Ron Hassey (AJ)	C24, DH18	L	34	49	145	15	31	9	0	3	12	17	11	0	.214	.338
Ron Karkovice	C37, DH1	R	23	39	85	7	6	0	0	2	7	7	40	3	.071	.141
Pat Keedy	3B11, 1B2, 2B1, SS1, OF1, DH1	R	29	17	41	6	7	1	0	2	2	2	14	1	.171	.341
Bill Lindsey	C9	R	27	9	16	2	3	0	0	0	1	0	3	0	.188	.188

NAME	T	AGE	W	L	PCT	SV	G	GS	CG	IP	H	BB	SO	SHO	ERA
		28	77	85	.475	37	162	162	29	1448	1436	537	792	12	4.30
Floyd Bannister	L	32	16	11	.593	0	34	34	11	229	216	49	124	2	3.58
Jose DeLeon	R	26	11	12	.478	0	33	31	2	206	177	97	153	0	4.02
Rich Dotson	R	28	11	12	.478	0	31	31	7	211	201	86	114	2	4.17
Bill Long	R	27	8	8	.500	1	29	23	5	169	179	28	72	2	4.37
Bobby Thigpen	R	23	7	5	.583	16	51	0	0	89	86	24	52	0	2.73
2 Dave LaPoint	L	27	6	3	.667	0	14	12	2	83	69	31	43	1	2.94
Jim Winn	R	27	4	6	.400	6	56	0	0	94	95	62	44	0	4.79
Bob James (SJ)	R	28	4	6	.400	10	56	0	0	54	54	17	34	0	4.67
Jack McDowell	R	21	3	0	1.000	0	4	4	0	28	16	6	15	0	1.93
Scott Nielson	R	28	3	5	.375	2	19	7	1	66	83	25	23	1	6.24
Ray Searage	L	32	2	3	.400	2	58	0	0	56	56	24	33	0	4.20
Joel McKeon	L	24	1	2	.333	0	13	0	0	21	27	15	14	0	9.43
Joel Davis	R	22	1	5	.167	0	13	9	1	55	56	29	25	0	5.73
Bryan Clark	L	30	0	0	—	0	11	0	0	19	19	8	8	0	2.41
Ralph Citarella	R	29	0	0	—	0	5	0	0	11	13	4	9	0	7.36
John Pawlowski	R	23	0	0	—	0	4	3	2	9	4	3	1	0	4.91
Adam Peterson	R	21	0	0	—	0	1	1	0	4	8	3	1	0	13.50
1 Neil Allen (AJ-LJ)	R	29	0	7	.000	0	15	10	0	50	74	26	26	0	7.07

CALIFORNIA 6th(tie) 75-87 .463 10 GENE MAUCH

Name	G by Pos	B	AGE	G	AB	R	H	2B	3B	HR	RBI	BB	SO	SB	BA	SA
TOTALS			31	162	5570	770	1406	257	26	172	709	590	926	125	.252	.401
Wally Joyner	1B149	L	25	149	564	100	161	33	1	34	117	72	64	8	.285	.528
Mark McLemore	2B132, SS6, DH3	B	22	138	433	61	102	13	3	3	41	48	72	25	.236	.300
Dick Schofield (SJ)	SS131, 2B2, DH1	R	24	134	479	52	120	17	3	9	46	37	63	19	.251	.355
1 Doug DeCinces	3B128, 1B4, SS1, DH1	R	36	133	453	65	106	23	0	16	63	70	87	3	.234	.391
Devon White	OF159	B	24	159	639	103	168	33	5	24	87	39	135	32	.263	.443
Gary Pettis	OF131	B	29	133	394	49	82	13	2	1	17	52	124	24	.208	.259
Jack Howell	OF89, 3B48, 2B13	L	25	138	449	64	110	18	5	23	64	57	118	4	.245	.461
Bob Boone (FH)	C127, DH1	R	39	128	389	42	94	18	0	3	33	35	36	0	.242	.311
Brian Downing	DH118, OF34	R	36	155	567	110	154	29	3	29	77	106	85	5	.272	.487
Ruppert Jones	OF66, DH3	L	32	85	192	25	47	8	2	8	28	20	38	2	.245	.432
George Hendrick (BG)	OF45, 1B9, DH6	R	37	65	162	14	39	10	0	5	25	14	18	0	.241	.395
Gus Polidor	SS46, 3B11, 2B3	R	25	63	137	12	36	3	0	2	15	2	15	0	.263	.328
Mark Ryal	OF21, DH5, 1B4	L	27	58	100	7	20	6	0	5	18	3	15	0	.200	.410
2 Bill Buckner (BG)	DH39, 1B5	L	37	57	183	16	56	12	1	3	32	9	7	1	.306	.432
Darrell Miller (BG)	C33, OF18, 3B1, DH1	R	29	53	108	14	26	5	0	4	16	9	13	1	.241	.398
Butch Wynegar (FJ)	C28, DH1	B	31	31	92	4	19	2	0	1	6	9	13	0	.207	.228
2 Johnny Ray	2B29, DH1	B	30	30	127	16	44	11	0	0	15	3	10	0	.346	.433
Tony Armas	OF27	R	34	28	81	8	16	3	1	3	9	1	11	1	.198	.370
Jack Fimple	C13	R	28	13	10	1	2	0	0	0	1	1	2	0	.200	.200
Jim Eppard	OF1	L	27	8	9	2	3	0	0	0	0	1	0	0	.333	.333
Tack Wilson	OF4, DH2	R	31	7	2	5	1	0	0	0	0	1	0	0	.500	.500

NAME	T	AGE	W	L	PCT	SV	G	GS	CG	IP	H	BB	SO	SHO	ERA
		31	75	87	.463	36	162	162	20	1457	1481	504	941	7	4.38
Mike Witt	R	26	16	14	.533	0	36	36	10	247	252	84	192	0	4.01
Don Sutton	R	42	11	11	.500	0	35	34	1	192	199	41	99	0	4.70
Willie Fraser	R	23	10	10	.500	1	26	23	5	177	160	63	106	1	3.92
1 John Candelaria (AL)	L	33	8	6	.571	0	20	20	0	117	127	20	74	0	4.71
DeWayne Buice	R	29	6	7	.462	17	57	0	0	114	87	40	109	0	3.39
2 Greg Minton	R	35	5	4	.556	10	41	0	0	76	71	29	35	0	3.08
Jack Lazorko	R	31	5	4	.455	0	26	11	2	118	108	44	55	0	4.59
3 Jerry Reuss	L	38	4	5	.444	0	17	16	1	82	112	17	37	1	5.25
Kirk McCaskill (EJ)	R	26	4	6	.400	0	14	13	1	75	84	34	56	1	5.67
Donnie Moore (VJ)	R	33	2	2	.500	5	14	0	0	27	28	13	17	0	2.70
Chuck Finley	L	24	2	7	.222	0	35	3	0	91	102	43	63	0	4.67
Mike Cook	R	23	1	2	.333	0	16	1	0	34	34	18	27	0	5.50
Gary Lucas	L	32	1	5	.167	3	48	0	0	74	66	35	44	0	3.63
Bryan Harvey	R	24	0	0	—	0	3	0	0	6	6	2	3	0	0.00
1 Miguel Garcia	L	20	0	0	—	0	2	0	0	2	3	0	1	0	16.20
Urbano Lugo	R	24	0	2	.000	0	7	5	0	28	42	18	24	0	9.32

TEXAS 6th(tie) 75-87 .463 10 BOBBY VALENTINE

Name	G by Pos	B	AGE	G	AB	R	H	2B	3B	HR	RBI	BB	SO	SB	BA	SA
TOTALS			26	162	5564	823	1478	264	35	194	772	567	1081	120	.266	.430
Pete O'Brien	1B158, OF2, DH1	L	29	159	569	84	163	26	1	23	88	59	61	0	.286	.457
Jerry Browne	2B130, DH1	B	21	132	454	63	123	16	6	1	38	61	50	27	.271	.339
Scott Fletcher	SS155	R	28	156	588	82	169	28	4	5	63	61	66	13	.287	.374
Steve Buechele	3B123, 2B18, OF2	R	25	136	363	45	86	20	0	13	50	28	66	2	.237	.399
Ruben Sierra	OF157	B	21	158	643	97	169	35	4	30	109	39	114	16	.263	.470
Oddibe McDowell	OF125	L	24	128	407	65	98	28	4	14	52	51	99	24	.241	.428
Pete Incaviglia	OF132, DH6	R	23	139	509	85	138	26	4	27	80	48	168	9	.271	.497
Don Slaught	C85, DH5	R	28	95	237	25	53	15	2	8	16	24	41	0	.224	.405
Larry Parrish	DH122, 3B28, OF1	R	33	152	557	79	149	22	1	32	100	49	154	3	.268	.483
Bob Brower	OF106, DH7	R	27	127	303	63	79	10	3	14	46	36	66	15	.261	.452
Geno Petralli	C63, 3B17, 1B5, 2B4, OF3, DH2	B	27	101	202	28	61	11	2	7	31	27	29	0	.302	.480
Curt Wilkerson	SS33, 2B28, 3B18, DH4	B	26	85	138	28	37	5	3	2	14	6	16	6	.268	.391
Darrell Porter	DH35, C7, 1B5	L	35	85	130	19	31	3	0	7	21	30	43	0	.238	.423
Mike Stanley	C61, 1B12, DH5, OF1	R	24	78	216	34	59	8	1	6	37	30	48	3	.273	.403
Tom O'Malley	3B40, DH1	L	26	45	117	10	32	8	0	1	12	15	9	0	.274	.368
Tom Paciorek (LJ)	1B12, OF12, DH3	R	40	27	60	6	17	3	0	3	12	1	19	0	.283	.483
Jeff Kunkel (SJ)	2B10, 3B3, OF3, SS1, 1B1, DH1	R	25	15	32	1	7	0	0	1	2	0	10	0	.219	.313
Cecil Espy	OF8	B	24	14	8	1	0	0	0	0	0	1	3	2	.000	.000
Dave Meier	OF8	R	27	13	21	4	6	1	0	0	0	4	4	0	.286	.333
Greg Tabor	2B4, DH1	R	26	9	9	1	2	1	0	0	0	0	4	0	.111	.222

NAME	T	AGE	W	L	PCT	SV	G	GS	CG	IP	H	BB	SO	SHO	ERA
		27	75	87	.463	27	162	162	20	1444	1388	760	1103	3	4.63
Charlie Hough	R	39	18	13	.581	0	40	40	13	285	238	124	223	0	3.79
Jose Guzman	R	24	14	14	.500	0	37	36	6	208	196	82	143	0	4.67
Mitch Williams	L	22	8	6	.571	6	85	1	0	109	63	94	129	0	3.23
Bobby Witt (SJ)	R	23	8	10	.444	0	26	25	1	143	114	140	160	0	4.91
Dale Mohorcic	R	31	7	6	.538	16	74	0	0	99	88	19	48	0	2.99
Jeff Russell (EJ)	R	25	5	4	.556	3	52	2	0	97	109	52	56	0	4.44
Greg Harris	R	31	5	10	.333	0	42	19	0	141	157	56	106	0	4.86
Steve Howe (SD)	L	29	3	3	.500	1	24	0	0	31	33	8	19	0	4.31
Ed Correa (BS)	R	21	3	5	.375	0	15	15	0	70	83	52	61	0	7.59
Paul Kilgus	L	25	2	7	.222	0	25	12	0	89	95	31	42	0	4.13
Ron Meredith	L	30	1	0	1.000	0	11	0	0	21	25	12	17	0	6.10
Mike Loynd	R	23	1	5	.167	1	26	8	0	69	82	38	48	0	6.10
Keith Creel	R	25	0	0	—	0	4	0	0	10	12	5	5	0	4.66
Dwayne Henry	R	25	0	0	—	0	3	0	0	10	12	9	7	0	9.00
Gary Mielke	R	24	0	0	—	0	3	0	0	11	13	3	6	0	6.00
Bob Malloy	R	22	0	0	—	0	2	1	0	11	13	3	8	0	6.55
Scott Anderson	R	24	0	1	.000	0	3	0	0	8	15	6	6	0	9.53
Mike Jeffcoat	L	28	0	0	—	0	8	0	0	7	11	4	1	0	12.86
1 Mike Mason	L	28	0	2	.000	0	8	6	0	28	37	22	21	0	5.59

ST. LOUIS 1st 95-67 .586 — WHITEY HERZOG

Name	G by Pos	B	AGE	G	AB	R	H	2B	3B	HR	RBI	BB	SO	SB	BA	SA
TOTALS			28	162	5500	798	1449	252	49	94	746	644	933	248	.263	.378
Jack Clark (NJ)	1B126, OF1	R	31	131	419	93	120	23	1	35	106	136	139	1	.286	.597
Tommy Herr	2B137	R	31	141	510	73	134	29	0	2	83	68	62	19	.263	.331
Ozzie Smith	SS158	B	32	158	600	104	182	40	4	0	75	89	36	43	.303	.383
Terry Pendleton	3B158	B	26	159	583	82	167	29	4	12	96	70	74	19	.286	.412
Curt Ford (BH)	OF75	L	26	89	228	32	65	9	5	3	26	14	32	11	.285	.434
Willie McGee	OF152, SS1	B	28	153	620	76	177	37	11	11	105	24	90	16	.285	.434
Vince Coleman	OF150	B	26	151	623	121	180	14	10	3	43	70	126	109	.289	.358
Tony Pena (BG)	C112, 1B4, OF2	R	30	116	384	40	82	13	4	5	44	36	54	6	.214	.307
Jose Oquendo	OF46, 2B32, SS23, 1B3, P1	B	23	116	248	43	71	9	0	1	24	54	29	4	.286	.335
John Morris	OF74	L	26	101	157	22	41	6	4	3	23	11	22	5	.261	.408
Jim Lindeman (LJ)	OF49, 1B20	R	25	75	207	20	43	13	0	8	28	11	56	3	.208	.386
Steve Lake	C59	R	30	74	179	19	45	7	2	2	19	10	18	0	.251	.346
Rod Booker	2B18, 3B4, SS1	L	28	44	47	9	13	1	1	0	8	7	7	2	.277	.340
Lance Johnson	OF25	L	23	33	59	4	13	2	1	0	7	4	6	6	.220	.288
1 Tito Landrum (FJ)	OF23, 1B1	R	32	30	50	2	10	1	0	0	6	7	14	1	.200	.220
Tom Pagnozzi	C25, 1B1	R	24	27	48	8	9	1	1	0	9	4	13	1	.188	.333
Dan Driessen	1B21	L	35	24	60	5	14	2	0	1	11	7	8	0	.233	.317
Tom Lawless	2B7, 3B3, OF1	R	30	19	25	5	2	1	0	0	0	3	5	2	.080	.120
Mike Laga	1B12	L	27	17	29	4	4	1	0	1	4	2	7	0	.138	.276
David Green	OF10, 1B3	R	26	14	30	4	8	2	1	1	4	2	5	0	.267	.500
2 Doug DeCinces	3B3	R	36	4	9	1	2	2	0	0	1	0	2	0	.222	.444
Skeeter Barnes	3B1	R	30	4	4	1	1	0	0	1	0	0	0		.250	1.000

NAME	T	AGE	W	L	PCT	SV	G	GS	CG	IP	H	BB	SO	SHO	ERA
		28	95	67	.586	48	162	162	10	1466	1484	533	873	7	3.91
Bob Forsch	R	37	11	7	.611	0	33	30	2	179	189	45	89	1	4.32
Danny Cox (BF)	R	27	11	9	.550	0	31	31	2	199	224	71	101	0	3.88
Greg Mathews	L	25	11	11	.500	0	32	32	2	198	184	71	108	1	3.73
John Tudor (KJ)	L	33	10	2	.833	0	16	16	0	96	100	32	54	0	3.84
Ken Dayley (EJ)	L	28	9	5	.643	4	53	0	0	61	52	33	63	0	2.66
Joe Magrane	L	22	9	7	.563	0	27	26	4	170	157	60	101	2	3.54
Ricky Horton	L	27	8	3	.727	7	67	6	0	125	127	42	55	0	3.82
Todd Worrell	R	27	8	6	.571	33	75	0	0	95	86	34	92	0	2.66
Bill Dawley	R	29	5	8	.385	2	60	0	0	97	93	38	65	0	4.47
1 Pat Perry	L	28	4	2	.667	1	45	0	0	66	54	21	33	0	4.39
Lee Tunnell (SJ)	R	26	4	4	.500	0	32	9	0	74	90	34	49	0	4.84
Tim Conroy (SJ)	L	27	3	2	.600	0	10	9	0	41	48	25	22	0	5.53
Ray Soff	R	28	1	0	1.000	0	12	0	0	15	18	5	9	0	6.46
1 Dave LaPoint	L	27	1	1	.500	0	6	2	0	16	26	5	8	0	6.75
Steve Peters	L	24	0	0	—	1	12	0	0	15	17	6	11	0	1.80
Scott Terry	R	27	0	0	—	0	11	0	0	13	13	8	9	0	3.38
2 Randy O'Neal	R	26	0	0	—	0	1	1	0	5	2	2	4	0	1.80
Jose Oquendo	R	23	0	0	—	0	1	0	0	1	4	1	0	0	27.00
Jeff Lahti (SJ) 30															

NEW YORK 2nd 92-70 .568 3 — DAVEY JOHNSON

Name	G by Pos	B	AGE	G	AB	R	H	2B	3B	HR	RBI	BB	SO	SB	BA	SA
TOTALS			28	162	5601	823	1499	287	34	192	771	592	1012	159	.268	.434
Keith Hernandez	1B154	L	33	154	587	87	170	28	2	18	89	81	104	0	.290	.436
Tim Teufel	2B92, 1B1	R	28	97	299	55	92	29	0	14	61	44	53	3	.308	.545
Rafael Santana	SS138	R	29	139	439	41	112	29	1	5	44	29	57	1	.255	.346
Howard Johnson	3B140, SS38, OF2	B	26	157	554	93	147	22	1	36	99	83	113	32	.265	.504
Darryl Strawberry	OF151	L	25	154	532	108	151	32	5	39	104	97	122	36	.284	.583
Lenny Dykstra	OF118	L	24	132	431	86	123	37	3	10	43	40	67	27	.285	.455
Kevin McReynolds	OF150	R	27	151	590	86	163	32	5	29	95	39	70	14	.276	.495
Gary Carter	C135, 1B4, OF1	R	33	139	523	55	123	18	2	20	83	42	73	0	.235	.392
Mookie Wilson	OF109	B	31	124	385	58	115	19	7	9	34	35	85	21	.299	.455
Wally Backman	2B87	B	27	94	300	43	75	6	1	1	23	25	43	11	.250	.287
Lee Mazzilli	OF25, 1B13	B	32	88	124	26	38	8	1	3	24	21	14	5	.306	.460
Dave Magadan	3B50, 1B13	L	24	85	192	21	61	13	1	3	24	22	22	0	.318	.443
Barry Lyons	C49	R	27	53	130	15	33	4	1	4	24	8	24	0	.254	.392
2 Bill Almon	SS22, 2B10, 1B2, OF1	R	34	49	54	8	13	3	0	0	4	8	16	1	.241	.296
Keith Miller (RJ)	2B16	R	24	25	51	14	19	2	2	0	1	2	6	8	.373	.490
Mark Carreon	OF5	R	23	9	12	0	3	0	0	0	1	1	1	0	.250	.250
Gregg Jefferies		B	19	6	6	0	3	1	0	0	2	0	0	0	.500	.667
Kevin Elster	SS3	R	22	5	10	1	4	2	0	0	1	0	1	0	.400	.600
1 Al Pedrique	SS4, 2B1	R	26	5	6	1	0	0	0	0	0	1	2	0	.000	.000
Clint Hurdle	1B1	L	29	3	3	1	1	0	0	0	0	0	1	0	.333	.333
Randy Milligan		R	25	3	1	0	0	0	0	0	0	0	0	0	.000	.000

NAME	T	AGE	W	L	PCT	SV	G	GS	CG	IP	H	BB	SO	SHO	ERA
		26	92	70	.568	51	162	162	16	1454	1407	510	1032	7	3.84
Dwight Gooden (DR)	R	22	15	7	.682	0	25	25	7	180	162	53	148	3	3.21
Ron Darling	R	26	12	8	.600	0	32	32	2	208	183	96	167	0	4.29
Sid Fernandez	L	24	12	8	.600	0	28	27	3	156	130	67	134	1	3.81
Terry Leach	R	33	11	1	.917	0	44	12	1	131	132	29	61	1	3.22
Rick Aguilera (EJ)	R	25	11	3	.786	0	18	17	1	115	124	33	77	0	3.60
Roger McDowell (GJ)	R	26	7	5	.583	25	56	0	0	89	95	28	32	0	4.16
David Cone (BG)	R	24	5	6	.455	1	21	13	1	99	87	44	68	0	3.71
Doug Sisk	R	29	3	1	.750	3	55	0	0	78	83	22	37	0	3.46
Bob Ojeda (EJ)	L	29	3	5	.375	0	10	7	0	46	45	10	21	0	3.88
Randy Myers	L	24	3	6	.333	6	54	0	0	75	61	30	92	0	3.96
John Mitchell	R	21	3	6	.333	0	20	19	1	112	124	36	57	0	4.11
Jesse Orosco	L	30	3	9	.250	16	58	0	0	77	78	31	78	0	4.44
2 John Candelaria	L	33	2	0	1.000	0	3	3	0	12	17	3	10	0	5.84
Gene Walter	L	26	1	2	.333	0	21	0	0	20	18	13	11	0	3.20
Don Schulze	R	24	1	2	.333	0	5	4	0	22	24	6	6	0	6.23
Tom Edens	R	26	0	0	—	0	2	2	0	8	15	4	4	0	6.75
Jeff Innis	R	24	0	0	—	0	17	1	0	26	29	4	28	0	3.16
Bob Gibson	R	30	0	1	.000	0	1	0	0	1	2	0	0	0	0.00

MONTREAL 3rd 91-71 .562 4 — BUCK RODGERS

Name	G by Pos	B	AGE	G	AB	R	H	2B	3B	HR	RBI	BB	SO	SB	BA	SA
TOTALS			27	162	5527	741	1467	310	39	120	695	501	918	166	.265	.401
Andres Galarraga	1B146	R	26	147	551	72	168	40	3	13	90	41	127	7	.305	.459
Vance Law	2B106, 3B22, 1B17, P3	R	30	133	436	52	119	27	1	12	56	51	62	8	.273	.422
Hubie Brooks (BW)	SS109	R	30	112	430	57	113	22	3	14	72	24	72	4	.263	.426
Tim Wallach	3B150, P1	R	29	153	593	89	177	42	4	26	123	37	98	9	.298	.514
Mitch Webster	OF153	B	28	156	588	101	165	30	8	15	63	70	95	33	.281	.435
Herm Winningham	OF131	L	25	137	347	34	83	20	3	4	41	34	68	29	.239	.349
Tim Raines (FJ)	OF139	B	27	139	530	123	175	34	8	18	68	90	52	50	.330	.526
Mike Fitzgerald	C104, 1B1, 2B1	R	26	107	287	32	69	11	0	3	36	42	54	3	.240	.310
Casey Candaele	2B68, OF67, SS25, 1B1	B	26	138	449	62	122	23	4	1	23	38	28	7	.272	.347
Tom Foley	SS49, 2B39, 3B9	L	27	106	280	35	82	18	3	5	28	11	40	6	.293	.432
Reid Nichols	OF59, 3B3	R	28	77	147	22	39	8	2	4	20	14	13	2	.265	.429
Jeff Reed (SJ)	C74	L	24	75	207	15	44	11	0	1	21	12	20	0	.213	.280
Wallace Johnson	1B9	B	30	75	85	7	21	5	0	1	14	7	6	5	.247	.341
Dave Engle	OF11, C6, 1B2, 3B1	R	30	59	84	7	19	4	0	1	14	6	11	1	.226	.310
John Stefero	C17	L	27	18	56	4	11	0	0	1	3	3	17	0	.196	.250
Luis Rivera	SS15	R	23	18	32	0	5	2	0	0	4	1	8	0	.156	.219
Alonzo Powell	OF11	R	22	14	41	3	8	3	0	0	4	5	17	0	.195	.268
Jack Daugherty	1B1	R	26	11	10	1	1	1	0	0	1	0	2	0	.100	.200
Tom Romano	OF3	R	28	7	3	1	0	0	0	0	0	0	3	0	.000	.000
Razor Shines	1B2	B	30	6	9	0	2	0	0	0	0	1	0	1	.222	.222
Nelson Santovenia	C1	R	25	2	1	0	0	0	0	0	0	0	0	0	.000	.000
Nelson Norman	SS1	B	29	1	0	0	0	0	0	0	0	0	0	0	.000	.000

NAME	T	AGE	W	L	PCT	SV	G	GS	CG	IP	H	BB	SO	SHO	ERA
		28	91	71	.562	50	162	162	16	1450	1428	446	1012	8	3.92
Neal Heaton	L	27	13	10	.565	0	32	32	3	193	207	37	105	1	4.52
Dennis Martinez	R	32	11	4	.733	0	22	22	2	145	133	40	84	1	3.30
Bryn Smith	R	31	10	9	.526	0	26	26	2	150	164	31	94	0	4.37
Floyd Youmans (EJ)	R	23	9	8	.529	0	23	23	3	116	112	47	94	3	4.64
Tim Burke	R	28	7	0	1.000	18	55	0	0	91	64	17	58	0	1.19
Pasqual Perez (SD)	R	30	7	0	1.000	0	10	10	2	70	52	16	58	0	2.30
Jeff Parrett	R	25	7	6	.538	6	45	0	0	62	63	30	56	0	4.21
Bob McClure	L	35	6	1	.857	5	52	0	0	52	47	20	33	0	3.44
Bob Sebra	R	25	6	15	.286	0	36	27	4	177	184	67	156	1	4.42
Andy McGaffigan	R	30	5	2	.714	12	69	0	0	120	105	42	100	0	2.39
Jay Tibbs	R	25	4	5	.444	0	19	12	0	83	95	34	54	0	4.99
Randy St. Claire	R	26	3	3	.500	7	44	0	0	67	64	20	43	0	4.03
Lary Sorensen	R	31	3	4	.429	1	23	5	0	48	56	12	21	0	4.72
Joe Hesketh (SJ)	L	28	0	0	—	0	18	0	0	29	23	15	31	0	3.14
Bill Campbell	R	42	0	0	—	0	7	0	0	10	18	4	4	0	8.10
Vance Law	R	30	0	0	—	0	3	0	0	1	0	0	2	0	5.40
Tim Wallach	R	29	0	0	—	0	1	0	0	1	0	1	1	0	0.00
Curt Brown	R	27	0	1	.000	0	5	0	0	7	10	4	6	0	7.71
Jeff Fischer	R	23	0	1	.000	0	2	2	0	14	21	5	6	0	8.56
Ubaldo Heredia	R	31	0	1	.000	0	2	1	0	11	10	3	6	0	5.40
Charlie Lea (SJ)	R	30	0	0	—	0	1	1	0	1	0	1	1	0	36.00

PHILADELPHIA 4th(tie) 80-82 .494 15 — JOHN FELSKE 29-32 .475 LEE ELIA 51-51 .505

Name	G by Pos	B	AGE	G	AB	R	H	2B	3B	HR	RBI	BB	SO	SB	BA	SA
TOTALS			29	162	5475	702	1390	248	51	169	662	587	1109	111	.254	.410
Von Hayes	1B144, OF32	L	28	158	556	84	154	36	5	21	84	121	77	16	.277	.473
Juan Samuel	2B160	R	26	160	655	113	178	37	15	28	100	60	162	35	.272	.502
Steve Jeltz	SS114, OF1	B	28	114	293	37	68	9	6	0	12	39	54	1	.232	.304
Mike Schmidt	3B138, 1B9, SS3	R	37	147	522	88	153	28	0	35	113	83	80	2	.293	.548
Glenn Wilson	OF154, P1	R	28	154	569	55	150	21	2	14	54	38	82	3	.264	.381
Milt Thompson	OF146	L	28	150	527	86	159	26	9	7	43	42	87	46	.302	.425
Chris James	OF108	R	24	115	358	48	105	20	6	17	54	27	67	3	.293	.525
Lance Parrish	C127	R	31	130	466	42	114	21	0	17	67	47	104	0	.245	.399
Greg Gross	OF50, 1B11	L	34	114	133	14	38	4	1	1	12	25	12	0	.286	.353
Luis Aguayo	SS78, 2B6, 3B2	R	28	94	209	25	43	9	1	12	21	15	56	0	.206	.431
Rick Schu	3B45, 1B28	R	25	92	196	24	46	6	3	7	23	20	36	0	.235	.403
Jeff Stone (HJ)	OF25	L	26	66	125	19	32	7	1	1	16	9	38	3	.256	.352
Ron Roenicke	OF26	B	30	63	78	9	13	3	1	1	4	14	15	1	.167	.269
2 Darren Daulton (KJ)	C40, 1B1	L	25	53	129	10	25	6	0	3	13	16	37	0	.194	.310
1 Keith Hughes	OF19	L	23	37	76	8	20	2	0	0	10	7	11	0	.263	.289
Mike Easler	OF15	L	36	33	110	7	31	4	0	1	10	6	20	0	.282	.345
John Russell	OF10, C7	R	26	24	62	5	9	1	0	3	8	3	17	0	.145	.306
Ken Dowell	SS15	R	26	15	39	4	5	1	0	0	1	3	5	0	.128	.128
Greg Jelks	3B4, 1B2, OF1	R	25	10	11	2	1	1	0	0	0	0	4	0	.091	.182
Ken Jackson	SS8	R	23	8	16	1	4	2	0	0	1	4	0		.250	.375
Greg Legg	2B1, 3B1, SS1	R	27	3	2	1	0	0	0	0	0	0	0	0	.000	.000

NAME	T	AGE	W	L	PCT	SV	G	GS	CG	IP	H	BB	SO	SHO	ERA
		29	80	82	.494	48	162	162	13	1448	1453	587	877	7	4.18
Shane Rawley	L	31	17	11	.607	0	36	36	4	230	250	86	123	1	4.39
Don Carman	L	27	13	11	.542	0	35	35	3	211	194	69	125	2	4.22
Bruce Ruffin	L	23	11	14	.440	0	35	35	3	205	236	73	93	1	4.35
Kevin Gross	R	26	9	16	.360	0	34	33	3	201	205	87	110	1	4.35
Kent Tekulve	R	40	6	4	.600	0	90	0	0	105	96	29	60	0	3.09
Steve Bedrosian	R	29	5	3	.625	40	65	0	0	89	79	28	74	0	2.83
Jeff Calhoun (SJ)	L	29	3	1	.750	0	42	0	0	43	25	26	31	0	1.48
1 Dan Schatzeder	L	32	3	1	.750	0	26	0	0	38	40	14	28	0	4.06
Wally Ritchie	L	21	3	2	.600	3	49	0	0	62	60	29	45	0	3.75
Mike Jackson	R	22	3	10	.231	1	55	7	0	109	88	56	93	0	4.20
Doug Bair	R	37	2	0	1.000	0	11	0	0	14	17	5	10	0	5.93
Mike Maddux	R	25	2	0	1.000	0	7	6	0	17	17	5	15	0	2.65
Todd Frohwirth	R	24	1	0	1.000	0	10	0	0	11	12	2	4	0	0.00
Freddie Toliver	R	26	1	1	.500	0	10	4	0	30	34	17	25	0	5.64
1 Tom Hume	R	34	1	4	.200	0	38	6	0	71	75	41	29	0	5.60
Tom Newell	R	24	0	0	—	0	2	0	0	2	4	3	1	0	36.00
Glenn Wilson	R	28	0	0	—	0	1	0	0	1	1	0	0	0	0.00
Joe Cowley	R	28	0	4	.000	0	5	4	0	12	21	17	5	0	15.43

PITTSBURGH 4th(tie) 80-82 .494 15 — JIM LEYLAND

Name	G by Pos	B	AGE	G	AB	R	H	2B	3B	HR	RBI	BB	SO	SB	BA	SA
TOTALS			27	162	5536	723	1464	282	45	131	684	535	914	140	.264	.403
Sid Bream	1B144	L	26	149	516	64	142	25	3	13	65	49	69	9	.275	.411
Johnny Ray	2B119	B	30	123	472	48	129	19	3	5	54	41	36	4	.273	.358
2 Al Pedrique	SS76,3B3,2B2	R	26	88	246	23	74	10	1	1	27	18	27	5	.301	.362
Bobby Bonilla	3B89,OF46,1B6	R	24	141	466	58	140	33	3	15	77	39	64	3	.300	.481
R.J. Reynolds	OF99	B	28	117	335	47	87	24	1	7	51	34	80	14	.260	.400
Andy Van Slyke	OF150,1B1	L	26	157	564	93	165	36	11	21	82	56	122	34	.293	.507
Barry Bonds	OF145	L	22	150	551	99	144	34	9	25	59	54	88	32	.261	.492
Mike LaValliere	C112	L	26	121	340	33	102	19	0	1	36	43	32	0	.300	.365
John Cangelosi	OF47	B	24	104	182	44	50	8	3	4	18	46	33	21	.275	.418
Mike Diaz	OF37,1B32,C8	R	27	103	241	28	58	8	2	16	48	31	42	1	.241	.490
1 Jim Morrison	3B82,SS17,2B9	R	34	96	348	41	92	22	1	9	46	27	57	8	.264	.411
Rafael Belliard (BL)	SS7,2B7	R	25	81	203	26	42	4	3	1	15	20	25	5	.207	.271
Junior Ortiz	C72	R	27	75	192	16	52	8	1	1	22	15	23	0	.271	.339
Darnell Coles	OF26,3B10,1B1	R	25	40	119	20	27	8	0	6	24	19	20	1	.227	.445
2 Terry Harper	OF20	R	31	36	66	8	19	3	0	1	7	7	11	0	.288	.379
Jose Lind	2B35	R	23	35	143	21	46	8	4	0	11	8	12	2	.322	.434
Felix Fermin (BG)	SS23	R	23	23	68	6	17	0	0	0	4	4	9	0	.250	.250
1 Bill Almon	SS4,OF2,3B1	R	34	19	20	5	4	1	0	0	1	1	5	0	.200	.250
2 Mackey Sasser	C5	L	24	12	23	2	5	0	0	0	2	0	2	0	.217	.217
U.L. Washington	SS1,3B1	B	33	10	10	1	3	0	0	0	0	0	3	0	.300	.300
Tommy Gregg	OF4	R	23	10	8	3	2	1	0	0	0	0	0	0	.250	.375
Butch Davis	OF1	R	29	7	7	3	1	1	0	0	0	0	1	3	.143	.286
Sammy Khalifa	SS5	R	23	5	17	1	3	0	0	0	2	0	2	1	.176	.176
Denny Gonzalez	SS1	R	23	5	7	1	0	0	0	0	0	1	2	0	.000	.000
Houston Jimenez	SS2,2B2	R	29	5	6	0	0	0	0	0	0	0	1	2	.000	.000
Tom Prince	C4	R	22	4	9	1	2	1	0	1	2	0	2	0	.222	.667
Onix Concepcion (LJ)		R	29	1	1	0	1	0	0	0	0	0	0	0	1.000	1.000

NAME	T	AGE	W	L	PCT	SV	G	GS	CG	IP	H	BB	SO	SHO	ERA
		26	80	82	.494	39	162	162	25	1445	1377	562	914	13	4.20
Mike Dunne	R	24	13	6	.684	0	23	23	5	163	143	68	72	1	3.03
Brian Fisher	R	25	11	9	.550	0	37	26	6	185	185	72	117	3	4.52
Doug Drabek (LJ)	R	24	11	12	.478	0	29	28	1	176	165	46	120	1	3.88
Bob Walk	R	30	8	2	.800	0	39	12	1	117	107	51	78	1	3.31
1 Rick Reuschel	R	38	8	5	.571	0	25	25	*9	177	163	35	80	*3	2.75
1 Don Robinson	R	30	6	6	.500	12	42	0	0	65	66	22	53	0	3.86
John Smiley	L	22	5	5	.500	4	63	0	0	75	69	50	58	0	5.76
Bob Kipper	L	22	5	9	.357	0	24	20	1	111	117	52	83	1	5.94
2 Jeff Robinson	R	26	2	1	.667	4	18	0	0	27	20	6	19	0	3.04
Vicente Palacios	R	23	2	1	.667	0	6	4	0	29	27	9	13	0	4.30
Dorn Taylor	R	28	2	3	.400	0	14	8	0	53	48	28	37	0	5.74
Mike Bielecki	R	27	2	3	.400	0	8	8	2	46	43	12	25	0	4.73
Barry Jones	R	24	2	4	.333	1	32	0	0	43	55	23	28	0	5.61
Logan Easley	L	25	1	1	.500	1	17	0	0	26	23	17	21	0	5.47
Bob Patterson	L	27	1	2	.333	0	15	7	0	43	49	22	27	0	6.70
Brett Gideon	R	23	1	5	.167	3	29	0	0	37	34	10	31	0	4.66
Tim Drummond	R	22	0	0	—	0	6	0	0	6	5	3	5	0	4.50
Dave Johnson	R	27	0	0	—	0	5	0	0	6	13	2	4	0	9.95
Mark Ross	R	29	0	0	—	0	1	0	0	1	4	1	0	0	9.00
2 Miguel Garcia	L	20	0	0	—	0	1	0	0	1	0	0	0	0	0.00
2 Jim Gott	R	27	0	2	.000	13	25	0	0	31	28	8	27	0	1.45
Hipolito Pena	L	23	0	3	.000	1	16	1	0	26	16	26	16	0	4.56

*Reuschel, also with San Francisco, league leader in CG with 12 and ShO with 4.

CHICAGO 6th 76-85 .472 18.5 — GENE MICHAEL 68-68 .500 FRANK LUCCHESI 8-17 .320

Name	G by Pos	B	AGE	G	AB	R	H	2B	3B	HR	RBI	BB	SO	SB	BA	SA
TOTALS			29	161	5583	720	1475	244	33	209	683	504	1064	109	.264	.432
Leon Durham	1B123	L	29	131	439	70	120	22	1	27	63	51	92	2	.273	.513
Ryne Sandberg (NJ)	2B131	R	27	132	523	81	154	25	2	16	59	59	79	21	.294	.442
Shawon Dunston (BG)	SS94	R	24	95	346	40	85	18	3	5	22	10	68	12	.246	.358
Keith Moreland	3B150,1B1	R	33	153	563	63	150	29	1	27	88	39	66	3	.266	.465
Andre Dawson	OF152	R	32	153	621	90	178	24	2	49	137	32	103	11	.287	.568
Dave Martinez	OF139	L	22	142	459	70	134	18	8	8	36	57	96	16	.292	.418
Jerry Mumphery	OF85	B	34	118	309	41	103	19	2	13	44	35	47	1	.333	.534
Jody Davis	C123	R	30	125	428	57	106	12	2	19	51	52	91	1	.248	.418
Manny Trillo	1B47,3B35,2B10,SS6	R	36	108	214	27	63	8	0	8	26	25	37	0	.294	.444
Brian Dayett	OF78	R	30	97	177	20	49	14	1	5	25	20	37	0	.277	.452
Bob Dernier	OF71	R	30	93	199	38	63	4	4	8	21	19	19	16	.317	.497
Rafael Palmeiro	OF45,1B18	L	22	84	221	32	61	15	1	14	30	20	26	2	.276	.544
Paul Noce	2B36,SS35,3B2	R	27	70	180	17	41	9	2	3	14	6	49	5	.228	.350
Jim Sundberg	C57	R	36	61	139	9	28	2	0	4	15	19	40	0	.201	.302
Luis Quinones	SS28,2B4,3B1	B	25	49	101	12	22	6	0	0	8	10	16	0	.218	.277
Chico Walker	OF33,3B2	B	29	47	105	15	21	4	0	0	7	12	23	11	.200	.238
1 Gary Matthews	OF2	R	36	44	42	3	11	3	0	0	8	4	11	0	.262	.333
Mike Brumley	SS34,2B1	B	24	39	104	8	21	2	2	1	9	10	30	7	.202	.288
Damon Berryhill	C11	R	23	12	28	2	5	1	0	0	1	3	5	0	.179	.214
Wade Rowdon	3B9	R	26	11	31	2	7	1	1	1	3	3	10	0	.226	.419
Darrin Jackson	OF5	R	24	7	5	2	4	1	0	0	0	0	2	0	.800	1.000

NAME	T	AGE	W	L	PCT	SV	G	GS	CG	IP	H	BB	SO	SHO	ERA
		28	76	85	.472	48	161	161	11	1435	1524	628	1024	5	4.55
Rick Sutcliffe	R	31	18	10	.643	0	34	34	6	237	223	106	174	1	3.68
Jamie Moyer	L	24	12	15	.444	0	35	33	1	201	210	97	147	0	5.10
Les Lancaster	R	25	8	3	.727	0	27	18	0	132	138	51	78	0	4.90
Scott Sanderson	R	30	8	9	.471	2	32	22	0	145	156	50	106	0	4.29
1 Steve Trout (LJ)	L	29	6	3	.667	0	11	11	3	75	72	27	32	2	3.00
Greg Maddux	R	21	6	14	.300	0	30	27	1	156	181	74	101	1	5.61
2 Mike Mason	L	28	4	1	.800	0	17	4	0	38	43	23	28	0	5.68
Dickie Noles (WJ)	R	30	4	2	.667	2	41	1	0	64	59	27	33	0	3.50
Frank DiPino	L	30	3	3	.500	4	69	0	0	80	75	34	61	0	3.15
Ed Lynch	R	31	2	3	.400	0	9	6	0	43	58	9	23	0	5.38
Drew Hall	L	24	1	1	.500	0	21	0	0	33	40	14	20	0	6.89
1 Ron Davis	R	31	0	0	—	0	21	0	0	32	43	12	31	0	5.85
Jay Baller	R	26	0	0	.000	0	23	0	0	29	38	20	27	0	6.75
2 Bob Tewksbury (SJ)	R	26	0	4	.000	0	3	3	0	18	32	13	10	0	6.50

WEST DIVISION

SAN FRANCISCO 1st 90-72 .556 — ROGER CRAIG

Name	G by Pos	B	AGE	G	AB	R	H	2B	3B	HR	RBI	BB	SO	SB	BA	SA
TOTALS			28	162	5608	783	1458	274	32	205	731	511	1094	126	.260	.430
Will Clark	1B139	L	23	150	529	89	163	29	5	35	91	49	98	5	.308	.580
Robby Thompson	2B126	R	25	132	420	62	110	26	5	10	44	40	91	16	.262	.419
Jose Uribe (LJ)	SS95	B	28	95	309	44	90	16	5	5	30	24	35	12	.291	.424
2 Kevin Mitchell	3B68,OF3,SS1	R	25	69	268	49	82	13	1	15	44	28	50	9	.306	.530
Candy Maldonado (BG)	OF116	R	26	118	442	69	129	28	4	20	85	34	78	8	.292	.509
Chili Davis	OF135	B	27	149	500	80	125	22	1	24	76	72	109	16	.250	.442
Jeff Leonard (LJ)	OF127	R	31	131	503	70	141	29	4	19	63	21	68	16	.280	.467
Bob Brenly	C108,1B6,3B2	R	33	123	375	55	100	19	1	18	51	47	85	10	.267	.467
Mike Aldrete	OF79,1B33	L	26	126	357	50	116	18	2	9	51	43	50	6	.325	.462
Chris Speier	2B55,3B44,SS22	R	37	111	317	39	79	13	0	11	39	42	51	4	.249	.394
Eddie Milner (DR)	OF84	L	32	101	214	38	54	14	0	4	19	24	33	10	.252	.374
Bob Melvin	C78,1B1	R	25	84	246	31	49	8	0	11	31	17	44	0	.199	.366
Matt Williams	SS70,3B17	R	21	84	245	28	46	9	2	8	21	16	68	4	.188	.339
Harry Spilman	3B10,1B9,C1	L	32	83	90	5	24	5	0	2	14	9	20	1	.267	.356
Joel Youngblood	OF22,3B2	R	35	69	91	9	23	3	0	3	11	5	13	1	.253	.385
Mark Wasinger	3B21,2B10,SS2	R	25	44	80	16	22	3	0	1	3	8	14	2	.275	.350
1 Chris Brown (BY)	3B37,SS1	R	25	38	132	17	32	6	0	6	17	9	16	1	.242	.424
2 Dave Henderson	OF9	R	28	15	21	2	5	2	0	0	1	8	5	2	.238	.333
Randy Kutcher	OF6,2B2,3B2,SS1	R	27	14	16	7	3	1	1	0	1	1	5	1	.188	.375
Francisco Melendez	1B5	L	23	12	16	2	5	0	0	1	5	0	3	0	.313	.500
Mike Woodard	2B8	L	27	10	19	0	4	1	0	0	1	0	2	0	.211	.263
Ivan DeJesus	SS9	R	34	9	10	0	2	0	0	0	1	0	3	0	.200	.200
Jessie Reid	OF3	L	25	6	8	1	1	0	0	0	1	1	5	0	.125	.500
Kirt Manwaring	C6	R	21	6	7	0	1	0	0	0	0	0	1	0	.143	.143
Rob Wilfong	2B2	L	33	2	8	1	1	0	0	1	2	1	2	0	.125	.500
1 Mackey Sasser	C1	L	24	2	0	0	0	0	0	0	0	0	0	0	.000	.000

NAME	T	AGE	W	L	PCT	SV	G	GS	CG	IP	H	BB	SO	SHO	ERA
		29	90	72	.556	38	162	162	19	1471	1407	547	1038	10	3.68
Mike LaCoss	R	31	13	10	.565	0	39	26	2	171	184	63	79	1	3.68
Kelly Downs	R	26	12	9	.571	1	41	28	4	186	185	67	137	3	3.63
Scott Garrelts	R	25	11	7	.611	12	64	0	0	106	70	55	127	0	3.22
Atlee Hammaker (EJ)	L	29	10	10	.500	0	31	27	2	168	159	57	107	1	3.58
2 Dave Dravecky	L	31	7	5	.583	0	18	18	4	112	115	33	78	3	3.20
1 Jeff Robinson	R	26	6	8	.429	10	63	0	0	97	69	48	82	0	2.79
2 Don Robinson	R	30	5	1	.833	7	25	0	0	42	39	18	26	0	2.74
1 Rick Reuschel	R	38	5	3	.625	0	9	9	*3	50	44	7	27	*1	4.32
Mike Krukow	R	35	5	6	.455	0	30	28	3	163	182	46	104	0	4.80
1 Mark Davis	L	26	4	5	.444	0	20	11	1	71	72	28	51	0	4.71
1 Craig Lefferts	L	29	3	3	.500	4	44	0	0	47	36	18	18	0	3.23
1 Keith Comstock	L	31	1	2	.333	0	25	0	0	21	19	10	21	0	3.05
Joe Price	L	30	2	2	.500	1	20	0	0	35	19	13	42	0	2.57
1 Jim Gott	R	27	1	1	.500	0	30	0	0	56	53	32	63	0	4.50
1 Greg Minton	R	35	1	1	.500	0	15	0	0	23	30	10	9	0	3.47
Randy Bockus	R	26	1	0	1.000	0	12	0	0	17	14	9	9	0	3.63
Roger Mason	R	28	1	1	.500	0	5	1	0	26	30	10	18	0	4.50
1 Mark Grant	R	23	1	1	.333	1	16	8	0	61	66	21	32	0	3.54
Jon Perlman	R	30	0	0	—	0	10	0	0	11	11	4	3	0	3.97
John Burkett	R	22	0	0	—	0	3	0	0	6	7	3	3	0	4.50

*Reuschel, also with Pittsburgh, league leader in CG with 12 and ShO with 4.

CINCINNATI 2nd 84-78 .519 6 — PETE ROSE

Name	G by Pos	B	AGE	G	AB	R	H	2B	3B	HR	RBI	BB	SO	SB	BA	SA
TOTALS			29	162	5560	783	1478	262	29	192	747	514	928	169	.266	.427
Nick Esasky (BW)	1B93,OF1,3B1	R	27	100	346	48	94	19	2	22	59	29	76	0	.272	.529
Ron Oester (KJ)	2B69	B	31	84	237	28	60	9	6	2	23	22	51	2	.253	.350
Barry Larkin	SS119	R	23	125	439	64	107	16	2	12	43	36	52	21	.244	.371
Buddy Bell	3B142	R	35	153	522	77	142	19	2	17	70	71	39	4	.284	.425
Dave Parker	OF142,1B9	L	36	153	589	77	149	28	0	26	97	44	104	7	.253	.433
Eric Davis	OF128	R	25	129	474	120	139	23	4	37	100	84	134	50	.293	.593
Kal Daniels	OF94	L	23	108	368	73	123	24	1	26	64	60	62	26	.334	.617
Bo Diaz	C137	R	34	140	496	49	134	28	1	15	82	19	73	1	.270	.421
Kurt Stillwell	SS51,2B37,3B20	B	22	131	395	54	102	20	7	4	33	32	50	4	.258	.375
Tracy Jones	OF95	R	26	117	359	53	104	17	3	10	44	23	40	31	.290	.437
Dave Concepcion	2B59,1B26,3B13,SS2	R	39	104	279	32	89	15	0	1	33	28	24	4	.319	.384
Terry Francona	1B57,OF8	L	28	102	207	16	47	5	3	3	12	10	12	2	.227	.295
Paul O'Neill	OF42,1B2,P1	L	24	84	160	24	41	14	1	7	28	18	29	2	.256	.488
Dave Collins	OF21	L	34	57	85	19	25	5	0	0	5	11	12	6	.294	.353
Lloyd McClendon	C12,1B5,OF1,3B1	R	28	45	72	8	15	5	0	2	13	4	15	1	.208	.361
Terry McGriff	C33	R	23	34	89	6	20	2	0	3	8	8	17	0	.225	.326
Leo Garcia	OF14	L	24	31	30	6	6	0	0	0	3	2	3	0	.200	.300
Jeff Treadway	2B21	L	24	23	84	9	28	4	0	2	4	4	1	0	.333	.452
Max Venable	OF4	L	30	7	7	2	1	0	0	0	0	1	2	0	.143	.143
1 Sal Butera	C5	R	34	5	11	1	2	0	0	0	2	0	1	0	.182	.455

NAME	T	AGE	W	L	PCT	SV	G	GS	CG	IP	H	BB	SO	SHO	ERA
		28	84	78	.519	44	162	162	7	1452	1486	485	919	6	4.24
1 Bill Gullickson	R	28	10	11	.476	0	27	27	3	165	172	39	89	1	4.85
Ted Power	R	32	10	13	.435	0	34	34	2	204	213	71	133	1	4.50
Tom Browning	L	27	10	13	.435	0	32	31	2	183	201	61	117	0	5.02
Guy Hoffman	L	30	9	10	.474	0	36	22	0	159	160	49	87	0	4.37
Rob Murphy	L	27	8	5	.615	3	87	0	0	101	91	32	99	0	3.04
John Franco	L	26	8	5	.615	32	68	0	0	82	76	27	61	0	2.52
Ron Robinson	R	25	7	5	.583	4	48	18	0	154	148	43	99	0	3.68
Frank Williams	R	29	4	0	1.000	2	85	0	0	106	101	39	60	0	2.30
2 Dennis Rasmussen	L	28	4	1	.800	0	7	7	0	45	39	12	39	0	3.97
Bill Landrum	R	29	3	2	.600	2	44	0	0	65	68	34	42	0	4.71
Mario Soto (SJ)	R	30	3	2	.600	0	6	6	0	32	34	12	11	0	5.12
Pat Pacillo	R	23	3	3	.500	0	12	7	1	40	41	19	23	0	6.13
Jeff Montgomery	R	25	2	2	.500	0	14	1	0	19	25	9	13	0	6.52
2 Pat Perry	L	28	1	0	1.000	1	7	0	0	8	8	4	5	0	0.00
2 Tom Hume	R	34	1	0	1.000	0	11	0	0	13	14	2	4	0	4.05
Bill Scherrer	L	29	1	1	.500	0	23	0	0	33	43	16	24	0	4.36
Paul O'Neill	L	24	0	0	—	0	1	0	0	1	4	1	0	0	13.50
2 Jerry Reuss	L	38	0	5	.000	0	7	7	0	35	52	12	10	0	7.79

Name	G by Pos	B	AGE	G	AB	R	H	2B	3B	HR	RBI	BB	SO	SB	BA	SA
HOUSTON 3rd 76-86 .469 14	**HAL LANIER**		29	162	5485	648	1386	238	28	122	603	526	936	162	.253	.373
TOTALS																
Glenn Davis	1B151	R	26	151	578	70	145	35	2	27	93	47	84	4	.251	.458
Bill Doran	2B162, SS3	B	29	162	625	82	177	23	3	16	79	82	64	31	.283	.406
Craig Reynolds	SS129, 3B2	L	34	135	374	35	95	17	3	4	28	30	44	5	.254	.348
Denny Walling	3B79, 1B16, OF7	L	33	110	325	45	92	21	4	5	33	39	37	5	.283	.418
Kevin Bass	OF155	B	28	157	592	83	168	31	5	19	85	53	77	21	.284	.449
Billy Hatcher	OF140	R	26	141	564	96	167	28	3	11	63	42	70	53	.296	.415
Jose Cruz	OF97	L	39	126	365	47	88	17	4	11	38	36	65	4	.241	.400
Alan Ashby	C110	B	35	125	386	53	111	16	0	14	63	50	52	0	.288	.438
Terry Puhl	OF40	L	30	90	122	9	28	5	0	2	15	11	16	1	.230	.320
Gerald Young	OF67	B	22	71	274	44	88	9	2	1	15	26	27	26	.321	.380
Ken Caminiti	3B61	B	24	63	203	10	50	7	1	3	23	12	44	0	.246	.335
Jim Pankovits	2B9, OF6, 3B4	R	31	50	61	7	14	2	0	1	8	6	13	2	.230	.311
Davey Lopes (EJ)	OF5	R	42	47	43	4	10	2	0	1	6	13	8	2	.233	.349
1 Phil Garner	3B36, 2B2	R	38	43	112	15	25	5	0	3	15	8	20	1	.223	.348
Ronn Reynolds	C38	R	28	38	102	5	17	4	0	1	7	3	29	0	.167	.235
Chuck Jackson	3B16, OF13, SS1	R	24	35	71	3	15	3	0	1	6	7	19	1	.211	.296
Mark Bailey	C27	B	25	35	64	5	13	1	0	0	3	10	21	1	.203	.219
Dickie Thon (IJ)	SS31	R	29	32	66	6	14	1	0	1	3	16	13	3	.212	.273
Bert Pena	SS19, 3B1	R	27	21	46	5	7	0	0	0	2	7	8	0	.152	.152
Dale Berra	SS18, 2B3	R	30	19	45	3	8	3	0	0	2	8	12	0	.178	.244
Ty Gainey	OF6	L	26	18	24	1	3	0	0	1	2	9	9	1	.125	.125
2 Buddy Biancalana	SS16, 2B3	B	27	18	24	1	1	0	0	0	0	1	12	0	.042	.042
Robbie Wine (IL)	C12	R	24	14	29	1	3	1	0	0	1	0	10	0	.103	.138
Paul Householder	OF7	B	28	14	12	2	1	1	0	0	1	4	2	0	.083	.167
Ty Waller	OF3	R	30	14	12	2	1	0	0	0	0	0	3	0	.167	.333
Troy Afenir	C10	R	23	10	20	1	6	1	0	0	1	0	12	0	.300	.350

Name	T	AGE	W	L	PCT	SV	G	GS	CG	IP	H	BB	SO	SHO	ERA
		30	76	86	.469	33	162	162	13	1441	1363	525	**1137**	13	3.84
Mike Scott	R	32	16	13	.552	0	36	36	8	248	199	79	233	3	3.23
Jim Deshaies	L	27	11	6	.647	0	26	25	1	152	149	57	104	0	4.62
Larry Andersen	R	34	9	5	.643	5	67	0	0	102	95	41	94	0	3.45
Danny Darwin	R	31	9	10	.474	0	33	30	3	196	184	69	134	1	3.59
Nolan Ryan	R	40	8	16	.333	0	34	34	0	212	154	87	**270**	0	**2.76**
Bob Knepper	L	33	8	17	.320	0	33	31	1	178	226	54	76	0	5.27
Dave Meads	L	23	5	3	.625	0	45	0	0	49	60	16	32	0	5.55
Jeff Heathcock	R	27	4	2	.667	1	19	2	0	43	44	9	15	0	3.16
Aurelio Lopez	R	38	2	1	.667	1	26	0	0	38	39	12	21	0	4.50
Dave Smith	R	32	2	3	.400	24	50	0	0	60	39	21	73	0	1.65
Juan Agosto	L	29	1	1	.500	2	27	0	0	27	26	10	6	0	2.63
Rocky Childress	R	25	1	2	.333	0	32	0	0	48	46	18	26	0	2.98
Julio Solano	R	27	0	0	—	0	11	0	0	20	25	9	12	0	7.65
Rob Mallicoat	L	22	0	0	—	0	4	1	0	7	8	6	4	0	6.75
Ron Mathis	R	28	0	1	.000	0	8	1	0	12	10	11	8	0	5.25
Charley Kerfeld (EJ)	R	23	0	2	.000	0	21	0	0	30	34	21	17	0	6.67
Manny Hernandez	R	26	0	4	.000	0	6	3	0	22	25	5	12	0	5.40

Name	G by Pos	B	AGE	G	AB	R	H	2B	3B	HR	RBI	BB	SO	SB	BA	SA
LOS ANGELES 4th 73-89 .451 17	**TOMMY LASORDA**		28	162	5517	635	1389	236	23	125	594	445	923	128	.252	.371
TOTALS																
Franklin Stubbs	1B111, OF18	L	26	129	386	48	90	16	3	16	52	31	85	8	.233	.415
Steve Sax	2B152, 3B1, OF1	R	27	157	610	84	171	22	7	6	46	44	61	37	.280	.369
Mariano Duncan (KJ)	SS67, 2B7, OF2	B	24	76	261	31	56	8	1	6	18	17	62	11	.215	.322
Mickey Hatcher	3B49, 1B37, OF7	R	32	101	282	27	81	19	1	7	42	20	19	2	.282	.429
Mike Marshall	OF102	R	27	104	402	45	118	19	0	16	72	18	79	0	.294	.460
2 John Shelby	OF117	B	29	120	476	61	132	26	0	21	69	31	97	16	.277	.464
Pedro Guerrero	OF109, 1B40	R	31	152	545	89	184	25	2	27	89	74	85	9	.338	.539
Mike Scioscia	C138	L	28	142	461	44	122	26	1	6	38	55	23	7	.265	.364
Ken Landreaux	OF63	L	32	115	182	17	37	4	0	6	23	16	28	5	.203	.324
Dave Anderson	SS65, 3B35, 2B5	R	26	108	265	32	62	12	3	1	13	24	43	5	.234	.313
Alex Trevino	C45, OF2, 3B1	R	29	72	144	16	32	7	1	3	16	6	28	1	.222	.347
2 Phil Garner	3B46, 2B12, SS2	R	38	70	126	14	24	4	0	2	8	20	24	5	.190	.270
Danny Heep	OF22, 1B6	L	29	60	98	7	16	4	0	0	9	8	10	1	.163	.204
Tracy Woodson (WJ)	3B45, 1B7	R	24	53	136	14	31	8	1	1	11	9	21	1	.228	.324
2 Tito Landrum	OF31	R	32	51	67	8	16	3	0	1	6	11	16	1	.239	.328
Mike Ramsey	OF43	R	26	48	125	18	29	4	2	0	12	10	32	2	.232	.296
Ralph Bryant	OF19	L	26	46	69	7	17	2	1	2	10	10	24	2	.246	.391
2 Glenn Hoffman	SS40	R	28	40	132	10	29	5	0	0	10	7	23	0	.220	.258
Reggie Williams	OF30	R	26	39	36	6	4	0	0	0	1	9	13	1	.111	.111
Jeff Hamilton (NJ)	3B31, SS1	R	23	35	83	5	18	3	0	1	7	2	22	0	.217	.253
Craig Shipley	SS18, 3B6	R	24	26	35	3	9	1	0	0	2	0	6	0	.257	.286
1 Bill Madlock	3B16, 1B1	R	36	21	61	5	11	1	0	3	7	6	5	0	.180	.344
Mike Devereaux	OF18	R	24	19	54	7	12	3	0	0	1	3	10	3	.222	.278
Jose Gonzalez	OF16	R	22	19	16	2	3	2	0	0	1	2	5	1	.188	.313
Chris Gwynn	OF10	L	22	17	32	2	7	1	0	0	2	1	7	0	.219	.250
Len Matuszek (FJ)	1B3	L	32	16	15	0	1	0	0	0	0	1	6	0	.067	.067
2 Mike Sharperson	3B7, 2B6	R	25	10	33	7	9	2	0	0	1	4	5	0	.273	.333
2 Orlando Mercado	C7	R	25	7	5	1	3	1	0	1	1	0	1	0	.600	.800
Brad Wellman (IJ)	3B1, SS1, 2B1	R	27	3	4	1	1	0	0	0	1	1	1	0	.250	.250
Gil Reyes	C1	R	23	1	0	0	0	0	0	0	0	0	0	0	—	—

Name	T	AGE	W	L	PCT	SV	G	GS	CG	IP	H	BB	SO	SHO	ERA
		28	73	89	.451	32	162	162	**29**	1455	1415	565	1097	8	3.72
Orel Hershiser	R	28	16	16	.500	1	37	35	10	**265**	247	74	190	1	3.06
Bob Welch	R	30	15	9	.625	0	35	35	6	252	204	86	196	4	3.22
Fernando Valenzuela	L	26	14	14	.500	0	34	34	**12**	251	**254**	124	190	1	3.98
Matt Young	L	28	5	8	.385	11	47	0	0	54	67	17	42	0	4.47
Tim Belcher	R	25	4	2	.667	0	6	5	0	34	30	7	23	0	2.38
Shawn Hillegas	R	22	4	3	.571	0	12	10	0	58	52	31	51	0	3.57
Brian Holton	R	26	3	2	.600	2	53	1	0	83	87	32	58	0	3.89
Ken Howell	R	26	3	4	.429	1	40	2	0	55	54	29	60	0	4.91
Tim Leary	R	28	3	11	.214	1	39	12	0	108	121	36	61	0	4.76
Alejandro Pena	R	28	2	7	.222	11	37	7	0	87	82	37	76	0	3.50
1 Rick Honeycutt	L	33	2	12	.167	0	27	20	1	116	133	45	92	1	4.59
1 Tom Niedenfuer	R	27	1	0	1.000	1	15	0	0	16	13	9	10	0	2.76
Tim Crews	R	26	1	1	.500	3	20	0	0	29	30	8	20	0	2.48
Brad Havens (VJ)	L	27	0	0	—	1	31	1	0	35	30	23	23	0	4.33
2 Ron Davis	R	31	0	0	—	0	4	0	0	7	6	1	6	0	6.75
Jack Savage	R	23	0	0	—	0	2	0	0	3	4	1	0	0	2.70
2 Bill Krueger	L	29	0	0	—	0	2	0	0	3	1	2	0	0	0.00
1 Jerry Reuss	L	38	0	0	—	0	2	0	0	4	3	1	2	0	4.50

Name	G by Pos	B	AGE	G	AB	R	H	2B	3B	HR	RBI	BB	SO	SB	BA	SA
ATLANTA 5th 69-92 .429 20.5	**CHUCK TANNER**		30	161	5428	747	1401	284	24	152	696	641	834	135	.258	.403
TOTALS																
Gerald Perry	1B136, OF7	L	26	142	533	77	144	35	2	12	74	48	63	42	.270	.411
Glenn Hubbard	2B139	R	29	141	443	69	117	33	2	5	38	77	57	1	.264	.381
Andre Thomas (KJ)	SS81	R	23	82	324	29	75	11	0	5	39	14	50	6	.231	.312
Ken Oberkfell	3B126, 2B11	L	31	135	508	62	142	29	2	3	48	48	29	3	.280	.362
Dale Murphy	OF159	R	31	159	566	115	167	27	1	44	105	115	136	16	.295	.580
Dion James	OF126	L	24	134	494	80	154	37	6	10	61	70	63	10	.312	.472
Ken Griffey	OF107, 1B3	L	37	122	399	65	114	24	1	14	64	46	54	4	.286	.516
Ozzie Virgil	C122	R	30	123	429	57	106	13	1	27	72	47	81	0	.247	.471
Graig Nettles	3B40, 1B6	L	42	112	177	16	37	8	1	5	33	22	25	1	.209	.350
Albert Hall	OF69	B	29	92	292	54	83	20	4	3	24	38	36	33	.284	.411
Ted Simmons	1B28, C15, 3B2	B	37	73	177	20	49	8	0	4	30	21	23	1	.277	.390
Gary Roenicke	OF44, 1B9	R	32	67	151	25	33	8	0	9	28	32	23	0	.219	.450
Rafael Ramirez (KJ)	SS38, 3B12	R	29	56	179	22	47	12	0	1	21	8	13	6	.263	.346
Jeff Blauser	SS50	R	21	51	165	11	40	6	3	2	15	18	34	7	.242	.352
Bruce Benedict	C35	R	31	37	95	4	14	1	0	1	5	17	15	0	.147	.189
Paul Runge	3B10, SS9, 2B2	R	29	27	47	9	10	1	0	3	8	5	10	0	.213	.426
Ron Gant	2B20	R	22	21	83	9	22	4	0	2	9	1	11	4	.265	.386
Darryl Motley	OF2	R	26	8	8	0	0	0	0	0	0	1	0	1	.000	.000
Trench Davis		L	26	6	3	0	0	0	0	0	0	0	1	0	.000	.000
Terry Bell		R	24	1	1	0	0	0	0	0	0	0	1	0	.000	.000
Mike Fischlin		R	31	1	0	0	0	0	0	0	0	0	0	0	—	—
Bob Horner (JL) 29																
Damaso Garcia (KJ) 32																

Name	T	AGE	W	L	PCT	SV	G	GS	CG	IP	H	BB	SO	SHO	ERA
		30	69	92	.429	32	161	161	16	1428	**1529**	587	837	4	4.63
Zane Smith	L	26	15	10	.600	0	36	**36**	9	242	245	91	130	3	4.09
1 Gene Garber	R	39	8	10	.444	10	49	0	0	69	87	28	48	0	4.41
David Palmer (EJ)	R	29	8	11	.421	0	28	28	0	152	169	64	111	0	4.90
Rick Mahler	R	33	8	13	.381	0	39	28	3	197	212	85	95	1	4.98
Charlie Puleo	R	32	8	8	.429	0	35	16	1	123	122	40	99	0	4.23
1 Doyle Alexander (FJ)	R	36	5	10	.333	0	16	16	3	118	115	27	64	0	4.13
1 Randy O'Neal	R	26	4	2	.667	0	16	10	0	61	79	24	33	0	5.61
Jim Acker	R	28	4	9	.308	14	68	0	0	115	109	51	68	0	4.16
Jeff Dedmon	R	27	3	4	.429	4	53	0	0	90	82	42	40	0	3.91
Kevin Coffman	R	22	2	3	.400	0	5	5	0	25	31	22	14	0	4.62
Tom Glavine	L	21	2	4	.333	0	9	9	0	50	55	33	20	0	5.54
Joe Boever	R	26	1	0	1.000	1	14	0	0	18	19	12	18	0	7.36
Paul Assenmacher	L	26	1	1	.500	2	52	0	0	55	58	24	39	0	5.10
Chuck Cary	L	27	1	1	.500	1	13	0	0	17	17	4	15	0	3.78
Pete Smith	R	21	1	2	.333	0	6	6	0	32	39	14	11	0	4.83
3 Phil Niekro	R	48	0	0	—	0	1	1	0	6	8	6	0	0	15.00
Ed Olwine	L	28	0	0	.000	1	27	0	0	23	25	8	12	0	5.01
Larry McWilliams	L	33	0	0	.000	0	2	0	0	20	25	7	13	0	5.75
Marty Clary	R	24	0	0	.000	0	7	1	0	15	23	7	4	0	6.14
Steve Ziem	R	25	0	1	.000	0	2	1	0	2	4	1	0	0	7.71
Bruce Sutter (SJ) 34																

Name	G by Pos	B	AGE	G	AB	R	H	2B	3B	HR	RBI	BB	SO	SB	BA	SA
SAN DIEGO 6th 65-97 .401 25	**LARRY BOWA**		26	162	5456	668	1419	209	48	113	621	577	992	198	.260	.378
TOTALS																
John Kruk	1B101, OF29	L	26	138	447	72	140	14	2	20	91	73	93	18	.313	.488
Tim Flannery	2B84, 3B8, SS2	L	30	148	276	23	63	5	1	0	20	42	30	2	.228	.254
Garry Templeton	SS146	B	31	148	510	42	113	13	5	5	48	42	92	14	.222	.296
Randy Ready	3B52, 2B51, OF16	R	27	124	350	69	108	26	6	12	54	67	44	7	.309	.520
Tony Gwynn	OF156	L	27	157	589	119	218	36	13	7	54	82	35	56	.370	.511
Stan Jefferson	OF107	B	24	116	422	59	97	8	7	8	29	39	82	34	.230	.339
Carmelo Martinez	OF78, 1B65	R	26	139	447	59	122	21	2	15	70	70	82	5	.273	.430
Benito Santiago	C146	R	21	146	546	64	164	33	2	18	79	16	112	21	.300	.467
Shane Mack	OF91	R	23	105	238	28	57	11	3	4	25	18	47	4	.239	.361
Marvell Wynne	OF71	L	27	98	188	17	47	8	2	4	20	20	37	11	.250	.346
Luis Salazar	3B38, SS22, OF10, P2, 1B1	R	31	84	189	13	48	5	0	3	17	14	30	3	.254	.328
Joey Cora	2B66, SS6	B	22	77	241	23	57	7	2	0	13	28	26	15	.237	.282
2 Kevin Mitchell	3B51, OF3	R	25	62	196	19	48	7	1	7	26	20	38	0	.245	.396
James Steels	OF28	L	26	62	68	9	13	1	1	0	6	3	14	3	.191	.235
2 Chris Brown	3B43	R	25	44	155	17	36	9	0	6	23	11	30	1	.232	.368
Bruce Bochy	C23	R	32	38	75	8	12	3	0	2	11	5	12	0	.160	.280
Steve Garvey (AJ)	1B20	R	38	27	76	5	16	2	0	1	9	1	10	0	.211	.276
Shawn Abner	OF14	R	21	16	47	5	13	3	1	2	7	2	17	1	.277	.511
Mark Parent	C10	R	25	12	25	0	2	1	0	0	1	0	8	0	.080	.080
Randy Byers	OF5	L	22	10	16	1	5	1	0	0	1	0	5	1	.313	.375
2 Rob Nelson	1B2	L	23	10	11	0	1	0	0	0	0	3	6	0	.091	.091

Name	T	AGE	W	L	PCT	SV	G	GS	CG	IP	H	BB	SO	SHO	ERA
		28	65	97	.401	33	162	162	14	1433	1402	602	897	10	4.27
Ed Whitson	R	32	10	13	.435	0	36	34	3	206	197	64	135	1	4.73
Jimmy Jones	R	23	9	7	.563	0	30	22	2	146	154	54	51	1	4.14
Lance McCullers	R	23	8	10	.444	16	78	0	0	123	115	59	126	0	3.72
Eric Show	R	31	8	16	.333	0	34	34	5	206	188	85	117	3	3.84
2 Mark Grant	R	23	7	4	.462	0	17	17	2	102	104	52	58	1	4.66
2 Mark Davis	L	26	5	3	.625	2	43	0	0	62	54	31	47	0	3.18
Goose Gossage (VJ)	R	35	5	4	.556	11	40	0	0	52	47	19	44	0	3.12
1 Dave Dravecky	L	31	3	7	.300	0	30	13	1	79	71	31	60	0	3.76
Andy Hawkins (SJ)	R	27	3	10	.231	0	24	20	0	118	131	49	51	0	5.05
1 Craig Lefferts	L	29	3	2	.500	2	33	0	0	51	56	15	39	0	4.38
Eric Nolte	L	23	2	6	.250	0	12	12	1	67	57	36	44	0	3.21
1 Storm Davis (VJ)	R	25	2	7	.222	0	21	10	0	63	70	36	37	0	6.18
2 Dave Leiper	L	25	2	0	1.000	1	12	0	0	16	16	5	10	0	4.50
Greg Booker	R	27	1	4	.200	0	11	11	5	8	11	1	5	0	4.09
Tom Gorman (EJ)	L	29	1	1	.500	1	44	0	0	68	62	30	17	0	3.96
Ray Hayward	L	26	0	1	.000	0	6	2	1	9	11	5	8	0	16.50
Luis Salazar	R	31	0	0	—	0	2	0	0	5	6	4	3	0	4.50
2 Keith Comstock	L	31	0	0	.000	0	26	0	0	36	33	21	38	0	5.50
Ed Wojna	R	26	0	3	.000	0	10	1	0	21	26	6	11	0	5.89

LINE SCORES

Team	1	2	3	4	5	6	7	8	9	10	11	12	R	H	E

AMERICAN LEAGUE CHAMPIONSHIPS: MINNESOTA (WEST) 4   DETROIT (EAST) 1

Game 1   October 7 at Minnesota

	1	2	3	4	5	6	7	8	9	R	H	E
DET	0	0	1	0	0	1	0	1	2	5	10	0
MIN	0	1	0	0	3	0	0	4	X	8	10	0

Alexander, Henneman (8), Hernandez (8), King (8), **Viola**, Reardon (8)

Game 2   October 8 at Minnesota

	1	2	3	4	5	6	7	8	9	R	H	E
DET	0	2	0	0	0	0	0	1	0	3	7	1
MIN	0	3	0	2	1	0	0	0	X	6	6	0

Morris, **Blyleven**, Berenguer (8)

Game 3   October 10 at Detroit

	1	2	3	4	5	6	7	8	9	R	H	E
MIN	0	0	0	2	0	2	0	2	0	6	8	1
DET	0	0	5	0	0	0	0	2	X	7	7	0

Straker, Schatzeder (3), Berenguer (7), **Reardon** (8), Terrell, **Henneman** (7)

Game 4   October 11 at Detroit

	1	2	3	4	5	6	7	8	9	R	H	E
MIN	0	0	1	1	1	1	0	1	0	5	7	1
DET	1	0	0	0	1	1	0	0	0	3	7	1

Viola, Atherton (6), Berenguer (6), Reardon (9), **Tanana**, Petry (6), Thurmond (9)

Game 5   October 12 at Detroit

	1	2	3	4	5	6	7	8	9	R	H	E
MIN	0	4	0	0	0	0	0	1	3	9	15	1
DET	0	0	0	3	0	0	0	1	1	5	9	1

Blyleven, Schatzeder (7), Berenguer (8), Reardon (8), **Alexander**, King (2), Henneman (7), Robinson (9)

NATIONAL LEAGUE CHAMPIONSHIPS: ST. LOUIS (EAST) 4 SAN FRANCISCO (WEST) 3

Game 1   October 6 at St. Louis

	1	2	3	4	5	6	7	8	9	R	H	E
SF	1	0	0	1	0	0	0	1	0	3	7	1
STL	0	0	1	1	0	3	0	0	X	5	10	1

Reuschel, Lefferts (7), Garrelts (8), **Mathews**, Worrell (8), Dayley (8)

Game 2   October 7 at St. Louis

	1	2	3	4	5	6	7	8	9	R	H	E
SF	0	2	0	1	0	0	0	2	0	5	10	0
STL	0	0	0	0	0	0	0	0	0	0	2	1

Dravecky, **Tudor**, Forsch (9)

Game 3   October 9 at San Francisco

	1	2	3	4	5	6	7	8	9	R	H	E
STL	0	0	0	0	0	2	4	0	0	6	11	1
SF	0	3	1	0	0	0	0	0	1	5	7	1

Magrane, **Forsch** (5), Worrell (7), Hammaker, **Robinson** (7), Lefferts (7), LaCoss (8)

Game 4   October 10 at San Francisco

	1	2	3	4	5	6	7	8	9	R	H	E
STL	0	2	0	0	0	0	0	0	0	2	9	0
SF	0	0	0	1	2	0	0	1	X	4	9	2

Cox, **Krukow**

Game 5   October 11 at San Francisco

	1	2	3	4	5	6	7	8	9	R	H	E
STL	1	0	1	1	0	0	0	0	0	3	7	0
SF	1	0	1	4	0	0	0	0	X	6	7	1

Mathews, **Forsch** (4), Horton (4), Dayley (7), **Reuschel**, Price (5)

Game 6   October 13 at St. Louis

	1	2	3	4	5	6	7	8	9	R	H	E
SF	0	0	0	0	0	0	0	0	0	0	6	0
STL	0	1	0	0	0	0	0	0	0	1	5	0

Dravecky, Robinson (7), **Tudor**, Worrell (8), Dayley (9)

Game 7   October 14 at St. Louis

	1	2	3	4	5	6	7	8	9	R	H	E
SF	0	0	0	0	0	0	0	0	0	0	8	1
STL	0	4	0	0	0	2	0	0	X	6	12	0

Hammaker, Price (3), Downs (3), Garrelts (5), Lefferts (6), LaCoss (6), Robinson (8), **Cox**

COMPOSITE BATTING

MINNESOTA

NAME	POS	G	AB	R	H	2B	3B	HR	RBI	BA
		5	171	34	46	13	1	8	33	.269
Puckett	OF	5	24	3	5	1	0	1	3	.208
Gladden	LF	5	20	5	7	2	0	0	5	.350
Gaetti	3B	5	20	5	6	1	0	2	5	.300
Hrbek	1B	5	20	4	3	0	0	1	1	.150
Gagne	SS	5	18	5	5	3	0	2	3	.278
Brunansky	RF	5	17	5	7	4	0	2	9	.412
Lombardozzi	2B	5	15	2	4	0	0	0	2	.267
Laudner	C	5	14	1	1	1	0	0	2	.071
Bush	DH	4	12	4	3	0	1	0	0	.250
Baylor	DH	2	5	0	2	0	0	0	1	.400
Butera	C	1	3	0	2	0	0	0	0	.667
Newman	2B	1	2	0	0	0	0	0	0	.000
Larkin	DH-PH	1	1	0	1	1	0	0	1	1.000
Davidson	PH	1	0	0	0	0	0	0	0	—

DETROIT

NAME	POS	G	AB	R	H	2B	3B	HR	RBI	BA
		5	167	23	40	4	0	7	21	.240
Gibson	RF	5	21	4	6	1	0	1	4	.286
Trammell	SS	5	20	3	4	1	0	0	4	.200
Lemon	CF	5	18	4	5	0	0	2	4	.278
Evans	1B	5	17	0	5	0	0	0	2	.294
Whitaker	2B	5	17	4	3	0	0	1	1	.176
Nokes	C	5	14	2	2	0	0	1	2	.143
Brookens	3B	5	13	0	0	0	0	0	0	.000
Sheridan	PH-DH	5	10	2	3	1	0	1	2	.300
Herndon	LF	3	9	1	3	1	0	0	2	.333
Grubb	DH-PH	4	7	0	4	0	0	0	0	.571
Heath	C	3	7	1	2	0	0	1	2	.286
Morrison	3B	2	5	1	2	0	0	0	0	.400
Madlock	3B	1	5	0	0	0	0	0	0	.000
Bergman	1B	4	4	0	1	0	0	0	2	.250
Morris	P	2	0	1	0	0	0	0	0	—

ST. LOUIS

NAME	POS	G	AB	R	H	2B	3B	HR	RBI	BA
		7	215	23	56	4	4	2	22	.260
Herr	2B	7	27	0	6	0	0	0	3	.222
McGee	CF	7	26	3	8	1	1	0	2	.308
Coleman	LF	7	26	3	7	1	0	0	4	.269
Smith	SS	7	25	2	5	0	1	0	1	.200
Pena	C	7	21	5	8	0	1	0	0	.361
Pendleton	3B	6	19	3	4	0	0	1	0	.211
Lindeman	1B	5	13	1	4	0	0	1	3	.308
Driessen	1B-PH	5	12	1	3	2	0	0	1	.250
Oquendo	RF-3B	5	12	3	2	0	0	1	4	.167
Ford	RF	4	9	2	3	0	0	0	0	.333
Lawless	3B	3	6	0	2	0	0	0	0	.333
Cox	P	2	6	0	2	0	0	0	1	.333
Tudor	P	2	4	0	0	0	0	0	0	.000
Morris	RF	2	3	0	0	0	0	0	0	.000
Mathews	P	2	2	0	2	0	0	0	0	.000
Worrell	P	3	1	0	0	0	0	0	0	.000
Clark	PH	1	1	0	0	0	0	0	0	.000
Pagnozzi	C	1	1	0	0	0	0	0	0	.000
Magrane	P	1	1	0	0	0	0	0	2	.000
Dayley	P	3	0	0	0	0	0	0	0	—
Forsch	P	3	0	0	0	0	0	0	0	—
Johnson	PR	1	0	1	0	0	0	0	0	—
Horton	P	1	0	0	0	0	0	0	0	—

SAN FRANCISCO

NAME	POS	G	AB	R	H	2B	3B	HR	RBI	BA
		7	226	23	54	7	1	9	20	.239
Mitchell	3B	7	30	2	8	1	0	1	2	.267
Uribe	SS	7	26	1	7	1	0	0	2	.269
Clark	1B	7	25	3	9	2	0	1	3	.360
Leonard	LF	7	24	5	10	0	0	4	5	.417
Thompson	2B	7	20	4	2	0	1	1	2	.100
Davis	CF	6	20	2	3	1	0	0	0	.150
Maldonado	RF	5	19	2	4	1	0	0	2	.211
Brenly	C	6	17	3	4	1	0	1	2	.235
Aldrete	RF	5	10	0	1	0	0	0	1	.100
Melvin	PH-C	3	7	0	3	0	0	0	0	.429
Milner	CF-PR	6	7	0	1	0	0	0	0	.143
Dravecky	P	2	6	0	1	0	0	0	0	.167
Speier	SS	3	5	0	0	0	0	0	0	.000
Hammaker	P	2	3	0	0	0	0	0	0	.000
Spilman	PH	3	2	1	1	0	0	1	1	.500
Reuschel	P	2	2	0	0	0	0	0	0	.000
Krukow	P	1	2	0	0	0	0	0	0	.000
Price	P	2	1	0	0	0	0	0	0	.000
Lefferts	P	3	0	0	0	0	0	0	0	—
Robinson	P	3	0	0	0	0	0	0	0	—
Garrelts	P	2	0	0	0	0	0	0	0	—
LaCoss	P	2	0	0	0	0	0	0	0	—
Downs	P	1	0	0	0	0	0	0	0	—

COMPOSITE PITCHING

MINNESOTA

NAME	G	IP	H	BB	SO	W	L	SV	ERA
	5	44	40	18	35	4	1	3	4.50
Blyleven	2	13.1	12	3	9	2	0	0	4.05
Viola	2	12	14	5	9	1	0	0	5.25
Berenguer	4	6	1	3	6	0	0	1	1.50
Reardon	4	5.1	7	3	5	1	1	2	5.06
Schatzeder	2	4.1	2	0	5	0	0	0	0.00
Straker	1	2.2	3	4	1	0	0	0	16.88
Atherton	1	0.1	1	0	0	0	0	0	0.00

DETROIT

NAME	G	IP	H	BB	SO	W	L	SV	ERA
	5	43	46	20	25	1	4	0	6.70
Alexander	2	9	14	1	5	0	2	0	10.00
Morris	1	8	6	3	7	0	1	0	6.75
Terrell	1	6	7	4	4	0	0	0	9.00
King	2	5.1	3	2	4	0	0	0	1.69
Tanana	1	5.1	6	4	1	0	1	0	5.06
Henneman	3	5	6	6	3	1	0	0	10.80
Petry	1	3.1	0	1	0	0	0	0	0.00
Robinson	1	0.1	1	0	0	0	0	0	0.00
Thurmond	1	0.1	0	0	0	0	0	0	0.00
Hernandez	1	0.1	2	0	0	0	0	0	0.00

ST. LOUIS

NAME	G	IP	H	BB	SO	W	L	SV	ERA
	7	61	54	17	51	4	3	3	2.95
Cox	2	17	17	3	11	1	1	0	2.12
Tudor	2	15.1	16	5	12	1	1	0	1.76
Mathews	2	10.1	6	3	10	1	0	0	3.48
Worrell	3	4.1	4	1	6	0	0	1	2.08
Dayley	3	4	1	2	4	0	0	2	0.00
Magrane	1	4	4	2	3	0	0	0	9.00
Horton	3	3	2	0	2	0	0	0	0.00
Forsch	3	3	4	1	3	1	1	0	12.00

SAN FRANCISCO

NAME	G	IP	H	BB	SO	W	L	SV	ERA
	7	60	56	16	42	3	4	0	3.30
Dravecky	2	15	7	4	14	1	1	0	0.60
Reuschel	2	10	15	2	2	0	1	0	6.30
Krukow	1	9	9	1	3	1	0	0	2.00
Hammaker	2	8	12	0	7	0	1	0	7.88
Price	2	5.2	3	1	7	1	0	0	0.00
LaCoss	2	3.1	1	3	2	0	0	0	0.00
Robinson	3	3	3	0	3	0	1	0	9.00
Garrelts	2	2.2	2	4	4	0	0	0	6.75
Lefferts	3	2	3	1	0	0	0	0	0.00
Downs	1	1.1	1	0	0	0	0	0	0.00

LINE SCORES

Team	1	2	3	4	5	6	7	8	9	10	R	H	E

WORLD SERIES: MINNESOTA (AL) 4 : ST. LOUIS (NL) 3

Game 1 October 17 at Minnesota

| STL | 0 | 1 | 0 | 0 | 0 | 0 | 0 | 0 | 0 | | 1 | 5 | 1 |
| MIN | 0 | 0 | 0 | 7 | 2 | 0 | 1 | 0 | X | | 10 | 11 | 0 |

Magrane, Forsch (4),   Viola, Atherton (9)
Horton (7)

Game 2 October 18 at Minnesota

| STL | 0 | 0 | 0 | 0 | 1 | 0 | 1 | 2 | 0 | | 4 | 9 | 0 |
| MIN | 0 | 1 | 0 | 6 | 0 | 1 | 0 | 0 | X | | 8 | 10 | 0 |

Cox, Tunnell (4),   Blyleven, Berenguer (8),
Dayley (7), Worrell (8)   Reardon (9)

Game 3 October 20 at St. Louis

| MIN | 0 | 0 | 0 | 0 | 0 | 1 | 0 | 0 | 0 | | 1 | 5 | 1 |
| STL | 0 | 0 | 0 | 0 | 0 | 0 | 3 | 0 | X | | 3 | 9 | 1 |

Straker, Berenguer (7),   Tudor, Worrell (8)
Schatzeder (7)

Game 4 October 21 at St. Louis

| MIN | 0 | 0 | 1 | 0 | 1 | 0 | 0 | 0 | 0 | | 2 | 7 | 1 |
| STL | 0 | 0 | 1 | 6 | 0 | 0 | 0 | 0 | X | | 7 | 10 | 1 |

Viola, Schatzeder (4),   Matthews, Forsch (4),
Niekro (5), Frazier (7)   Dayley (7)

Game 5 October 22 at St. Louis

| MIN | 0 | 0 | 0 | 0 | 0 | 0 | 2 | 0 | 0 | | 2 | 6 | 1 |
| STL | 0 | 0 | 0 | 0 | 3 | 0 | 1 | 0 | X | | 4 | 10 | 0 |

Blyleven, Atherton (7),   Cox, Dayley (8),
Reardon (7)   Worrell (8)

Game 6 October 24 at Minnesota

| STL | 1 | 1 | 0 | 2 | 1 | 0 | 0 | 0 | 0 | | 5 | 11 | 2 |
| MIN | 2 | 0 | 0 | 0 | 4 | 4 | 0 | 1 | X | | 11 | 15 | 0 |

Tudor, Horton (5), Forsch (6),   Straker, Schatzeder (4),
Dayley (6), Tunnel (7)   Berenguer (6), Reardon (9)

Game 7 October 25 at Minnesota

| STL | 0 | 2 | 0 | 0 | 0 | 0 | 0 | 0 | 0 | | 2 | 6 | 1 |
| MIN | 0 | 1 | 0 | 0 | 1 | 1 | 0 | 1 | X | | 4 | 10 | 1 |

Magrane, Cox (5),   Viola, Reardon (9)
Worrell (6)

COMPOSITE BATTING

NAME	POS	G	AB	R	H	2B	3B	HR	RBI	BA
MINNESOTA										
TOTALS		7	238	38	64	10	3	7	38	.269
Gladden	LF	7	31	3	9	2	1	1	7	.290
Gagne	SS	7	30	5	6	1	0	1	3	.200
Puckett	CF	7	28	5	10	1	1	0	3	.357
Gaetti	3B	7	27	4	7	2	1	1	4	.259
Brunansky	RF	7	25	5	5	0	0	0	2	.200
Hrbek	1B	7	24	4	5	0	0	1	6	.208
Laudner	C	7	22	4	7	1	0	1	4	.318
Lombardozzi	2B	6	17	3	7	1	0	1	4	.412
Baylor	DH-PH	5	13	3	5	0	0	1	3	.385
Bush	DH	4	6	1	1	1	0	0	2	.167
Newman	2B	4	5	0	1	0	0	0	0	.200
Larkin	PH	5	3	1	0	0	0	0	0	.000
Smalley	PH	4	2	0	1	1	0	0	0	.500
Straker	P	2	2	0	0	0	0	0	0	.000
Viola	P	3	1	0	0	0	0	0	0	.000
Blyleven	P	2	1	0	0	0	0	0	0	.000
Davidson	PH	2	1	0	0	0	0	0	0	.000
Reardon	P	4	0	0	0	0	0	0	0	—
Berenguer	P	3	0	0	0	0	0	0	0	—
Schatzeder	P	3	0	0	0	0	0	0	0	—
Atherton	P	2	0	0	0	0	0	0	0	—
Butera	C	1	0	0	0	0	0	0	0	—
Frazier	P	1	0	0	0	0	0	0	0	—
Niekro	P	1	0	0	0	0	0	0	0	—
ST. LOUIS										
TOTALS		7	232	26	60	8	0	2	25	.259
Herr	2B	7	28	2	7	0	0	1	1	.250
Smith	SS	7	28	3	6	0	0	2	2	.214
Coleman	LF	7	28	5	4	2	0	0	2	.143
McGee	CF	7	27	2	10	2	0	0	4	.370
Oquendo	RF-3B	7	24	2	6	0	0	0	4	.250
Pena	C	7	22	2	9	1	0	0	4	.409
Lindeman	1B	6	15	3	5	1	0	0	2	.308
Ford	RF-PH-DH	5	13	1	4	0	0	0	2	.308
Driessen	DH-1B	4	13	3	3	2	0	0	1	.231
Lawless	3B	3	10	1	1	0	0	1	3	.100
Pendleton	3B	7	2	3	0	0	0	0	1	.429
Pagnozzi	C	2	4	0	1	0	0	0	1	.250
Lake	C	3	3	0	1	0	0	0	1	.333
Morris	RF	1	2	0	0	0	0	0	0	.000
Cox	P	3	2	0	0	0	0	0	0	.000
Forsch	P	3	2	0	0	0	0	0	0	.000
Tudor	P	2	2	0	0	0	0	0	0	.000
Dayley	P	4	1	0	0	0	0	0	0	.000
Matthews	P	1	1	0	0	0	0	0	0	.000
Worrell	P	4	0	0	0	0	0	0	0	—
Horton	P	2	0	0	0	0	0	0	0	—
Magrane	P	2	0	0	0	0	0	0	0	—
Tunnell	P	2	0	0	0	0	0	0	0	—
Johnson	RF	1	0	0	0	0	0	0	0	—

COMPOSITE PITCHING

NAME	G	IP	H	BB	SO	W	L	SV	ERA
MINNESOTA									
TOTALS	7	60	60	13	44	4	3	1	3.75
Viola	3	19.1	17	3	16	2	1	0	3.72
Blyleven	2	13	13	2	12	1	1	0	2.77
Straker	2	9	9	3	6	0	0	0	4.00
Reardon	4	4.2	5	0	3	0	0	1	0.00
Schatzeder	3	4.1	4	3	3	1	0	0	6.23
Berenguer	3	4.1	10	0	1	0	1	0	10.38
Frazier	1	2	1	0	2	0	0	0	0.00
Niekro	1	2	1	1	1	0	0	0	0.00
Atherton	2	1.1	0	1	0	0	0	0	6.75
ST. LOUIS									
TOTALS	7	59	64	29	36	3	4	3	5.64
Cox	3	11.2	13	8	9	1	2	0	7.71
Tudor	2	11	15	3	8	1	1	0	5.73
Magrane	2	7.1	9	5	5	0	1	0	8.59
Worrell	4	7	6	4	3	0	0	2	1.29
Forsch	3	6.1	8	5	3	1	0	0	9.95
Dayley	4	4.2	2	0	3	0	0	1	1.93
Tunnell	2	4.1	4	2	1	0	0	0	2.08
Matthews	1	3.2	2	2	3	0	0	0	2.45
Horton	2	3	5	0	1	0	0	0	6.00

MISCELLANEOUS 1987 INDIVIDUAL LEADERS

BATTING

On Base Average

	American League				National League	
1	Boggs, Bos.	.461	1	Clark, St. L.		.459
2	Molitor, Mil.	.438	2	Gwynn, S.D.		.447
3	Evans, Bos.	.417	3	Raines, Mon.		.429
4	Randolph, N.Y.	.411	4	Murphy, Atl.		.417
5	Trammel, Det.	.402	5	Guerrero, L.A.		.416

Caught Stealing

	American League				National League	
1	Reynolds, Sea.	20	1	Coleman, St. L.		22
2	Browne, Tex.	17	2	Clark, S.F.		17
3	Butler, Cle.	16	3	Perry, Atl.		16
4	Moses, Sea.	15	4	Samuel, Phi.		15
5	Griffin, Oak.	13	5	5 tied with		12
	Sheridan, Det.	13				

Hit by Pitcher

	American League				National League	
1	Baylor, Bos.-Min.	28	1	Galarraga, Mon.		10
2	Downing, Cal.	17	2	Hatcher, Hou.		9
3	Madlock, Det.	10	3	Parker, Cin.		8
4	Carter, Cle.	9	4	Thompson, S.F.		8
	Lansford, Oak.	9	5	5 tied with		7

Sacrifice Hits

	American League				National League	
1	Barrett, Bos.	22	1	Smith, Atl.		14
2	McLemore, Cal.	15	2	Rawley, Phi.		12
3	Boone, Cal.	14	3	Smith, St. L.		12
	Castillo, Mil.	14	4	Forsch, St. L.		11
	White, Cal.	14		Sutcliffe, Chi.		11

Game Winning RBI's

	American League				National League	
1	Tartabull, K.C.	25	1	Dawson, Chi.		16
2	Canseco, Oak.	17	2	Johnson, N.Y.		16
	Fisk, Chi.	17		Parker, Cin.		16
	Young, Mil.	17		Wallach, Mon.		16
	Bell, Tor.	16	5	Clark, St. L.		15
5	Trammell, Det.	16				

Grounded Into Double Play

	American League				National League	
1	Gaetti, Min.	25	1	McGee, St. L.		24
2	Franco, Cle.	23	2	Parrish, Phi.		23
3	Rice, Bos.	22	3	Bream, Pit.		19
4	Braggs, Mil.	20	4	Pena, St. L.		19
	Ward, N.Y.	20	5	5 tied with		18
	Winfield, N.Y.	20				

Total Bases

	American League				National League	
1	Bell, Tor.	369	1	Dawson, Chi.		353
2	McGwire, Oak.	344	2	Samuel, Phi.		329
3	Puckett, Min.	333	3	Murphy, Atl.		328
4	Trammell, Det.	329	4	Strawberry, N.Y.		310
5	Boggs, Bos.	324	5	Clark, St. L.		307

Sacrifice Flies

	American League				National League	
1	Sierra, Tex.	12	1	Herr, St. L.		12
2	C. Ripken, Bal.	11	2	Moreland, Chi.		9
3	Joyner, Cal.	10	3	Pendleton, St. L.		9
	O'Brien, Tex.	10		Shelby, L.A.		9
5	Bell, Tor.	9	5	Bonilla, Pit.		8
	Canseco, Oak.	9		McReynolds, N.Y.		8
	Surhoff, Mil.	9		Reynolds, Hou.		8

PITCHING

Wild Pitches

	American League				National League	
1	Morris, Det.	24	1	Valenzuela, L.A.		14
2	Bosio, Mil.	14	2	Downs, S.F.		12
3	Gubicza, K.C.	14	3	Hershiser, L.A.		11
4	Blyleven, Min.	13	4	Moyer, Chi.		11
	Candiotti, Cle.	13	5	O'Neal, Atl.-St. L.		10
	Niekro, N.Y.-Cle.	13		Ryan, Hou.		10
				Scott, Hou.		10

Hit Batters

	American League				National League	
1	Hough, Tex.	19	1	Gross, Phi.		10
2	DeLeon, Chi.	10		Magrane, St. L.		10
	Niekro, N.Y.-Min.	10	3	Hershiser, L.A.		9
	Petry, Det.	10		Show, S.D.		9
	Blyleven, Min.	9	5	Fernandez, N.Y.		8
	Clemens, Bos.	9		Rueschel, Pit.-S.F.		8
	Smithson, Min.	9				

Home Runs Allowed

	American League				National League	
1	Blyleven, Min.	46	1	Whitson, S.D.		36
2	Morris, Det.	39	2	Carmen, Phi.		34
3	Bannister, Chi.	38	3	Gullickson, Cin.		33
	Sutton, Cal.	38	4	Moyer, Chi.		28
	Young, Oak.	38		Power, Cin.		28

FIELDING

	American League	PO	A	E	DP	Pct.
1B	Mattingly, N.Y.	1239	91	5	122	.996
2B	Barrett, Bos.	320	438	8	108	.988
SS	Schofield, Cal.	204	348	9	76	.984
3B	Lansford, Oak.	98	249	7	15	.908
OF	Wilson, K.C.	342	3	1	1	.997
C	Cerone, N.Y.	538	38	1	6	.998
P	Tanana, Det.	14	35	0	2	1.000

	National League	PO	A	E	DP	Pct.
1B	Stubbs, L.A.	802	78	5	65	.994
2B	Doran, Hou.	300	431	6	70	.992
SS	Smith, St. L.	245	516	10	111	.987
3B	Bell, Cin.	93	241	7	17	.979
OF	James, Atl.	262	4	1	1	.996
C	Ashby, Hou.	778	46	6	6	.993
P	Welch, L.A.	25	38	0	3	1.000

Balks

American League

1	Hough, Tex.	9
2	Carlton, Cle.-Min.	5
	Guzman, Tex.	5
	Key, Tor.	5
	Straker, Min.	5

National League

1	Jackson, Phi.	8
	Lancaster, Chi.	8
3	Gross, Phi.	7
	Hammaker, S.F.	7
	Maddox, Chi.	7
	Magrane, St. L.	7

1988 The Unexpected Dodgers

In the early spring, there was an omen. The Dodgers had signed Kirk Gibson to a lucrative contract as a free agent. Gibson took the field on March 3 for the opening spring training game. Before the game began, he discovered that a prankster had coated the inside of his cap with shoe polish. Gibson stormed off the field and out of the park, enraged at the embarrassing behavior and cavalier attitude of a teammate. After his one-day walkout, Gibson's intensity and big-bat transformed the rebuilt Dodgers into a winning team. The Dodgers took first place in early May and kept it all the way in the N.L. West despite various injuries and a late-season hitting slump. While Gibson bolstered the offense, Orel Hershiser pitched in unbeatable fashion down the stretch. Starting on August 30, Hershiser threw a record 59 straight scoreless innings, ending the season with six straight shutouts. With MVP Gibson and Cy Young Award winner Hershiser leading the way, the Dodgers beat back challenges by Cincinnati, Houston, and San Francisco. The Padres stumbled to a 16-30 start under Larry Bowa, but surged to a 67-48 record under new manager Jack McKeon.

As the season started, the floor opened up beneath the Atlanta Braves and the Baltimore Orioles. The Braves lost their first ten games. The Orioles, however, obliterated the previous record of thirteen losses at the start of a season by losing an amazing 21 games in a row before winning their first. The Indians, on the other hand, led the A.L. East in April, then faded as the Tigers and the Yankees rose to the top. The Tigers stayed in contention despite the loss of Kirk Gibson, relying heavily on veteran Alan Trammell and young pitcher Jeff Robinson. The Yankees had an array of heavy hitters and a shortage of pitching. Dave Winfield, Don Mattingly, and free-agent signee Jack Clark led the New York attack. Billy Martin returned to the Yankees as manager for the fifth time, only to be fired for the fifth time on June 23. Another manager to get the axe was John McNamara, who led Boston to a 43-42 mark at the All Star break. With coach Joe Morgan elevated to manager, the Red Sox won their first twelve games after the break to charge back into contention. The Sox prospered at Fenway Park, winning a record 24 straight home games between June 24 and August 14. Wade Boggs, Mike Greenwell, and Dwight Evans were the backbone of the Boston lineup, while Roger Clemens and Bruce Hurst were twin mound aces. In September, New York's pitching collapsed and Detroit's hitting wilted. The Sox, meanwhile, hung on to capture the A.L. East title despite losing their last three games and seven of their last ten.

In the heat of the summer, the Oakland Athletics and New York Mets coasted through relaxed pennant races. The Athletics had an abundance of hitting, with MVP Jose Canseco swinging the heaviest lumber. The Oakland pitching staff did the job, led by starter Dave Stewart and reliever Dennis Eckersley. The defending champion Twins finished a strong but distant second in the A. L. West. Kirby Puckett, Kent Hrbek, and Gary Gaetti battered opposing pitchers, while Allan Anderson unexpectedly joined Cy Young Award winner Frank Viola as

a star pitcher. The Mets sprinted out to a comfortable lead in the N.L. East, then fell int[o] a batting lethargy for most of the summer. The superb New York pitching staff, howeve[r] kept the Mets in first place from early May onwards despite hot streaks by Pittsburgh an[d] Montreal. Dwight Gooden was the recognized ace of the New York staff, while David Con[e] and Randy Myers blossomed into stoppers. Darryl Strawberry and Kevin McReynolds wer[e] the top Met run producers. The Cardinals were never in the race, crippled by Jack Clark'[s] defection to the Yankees.

The spring and summer brought a variety of noteworthy events and trends. Umpire[s] strictly enforced the rules regarding the stretch delivery used by pitchers with men on base[s.] The result was a spate of balk calls in April and May, with the season's record total balk[s] being broken a mere 41 days into the campaign. On April 30, Reds manager Pete Ros[e] shoved an umpire during a dispute. N.L. president Bart Giamatti suspended Rose for thirt[y] days. In Chicago, the Cubs installed lights at Wrigley Field and played at night at home fo[r] the first time on August 8 against the Phillies. Rain ended that contest before it becam[e] official, so the Mets played the first Wrigley night game that counted on August 9. The floo[d] of home runs abated from last year's level, and a rash of near-no-hitters were broken up i[n] ninth innings.

Autumn brought the playoffs and mixed results. The Oakland juggernaut had won nin[e] of twelve games from the Red Sox during the season. The A's turned the heat up in the LCS and swept the Sox in four straight. Canseco's three homers led the Oakland blitz. In th[e] National League LCS, the Mets came into the series with eleven regular-season victorie[s] over the Dodgers in twelve games. The lightly-regarded Dodgers battled the Met[s] heroically, but still lost two of the first three games. Trailing 4-2 in the ninth inning of gam[e] four, the Dodgers shocked Dwight Gooden with a two-run homer by Mike Scioscia. Wit[h] that blow, the momentum swung almost palpably. The Dodgers went on to win game fou[r] and took game five the next day. The Mets captured game six to force a showdown. Wit[h] Orel Hershiser taming the New York batters, the Dodgers took advantage of shoddy Me[t] fielding to win game seven and an unexpected pennant.

The surprises did not stop there. The Dodgers were behind 4-3 in the bottom of the ninth inning of game one of the World Series. Oakland ace Dennis Eckersley retired the first tw[o] batters, then walked Mike Davis. Kirk Gibson hobbled into action as a pinch-hitter, unabl[e] to run because of hamstring and knee injuries. Gibson lined a game-winning homerun int[o] the right field grandstand of Dodger Stadium. Even with Gibson disabled, the over[-] achieving Dodgers knocked off the A's in five games. The transformation that began i[n] spring training was complete.

EAST DIVISION — 1988 AMERICAN LEAGUE

Name	G by Pos	B	AGE	G	AB	R	H	2B	3B	HR	RBI	BB	SO	SB	BA	SA
BOSTON 1st 89-73 .549	JOHN McNAMARA 43-42 .506		JOE MORGAN 46-31 .597													
TOTALS			29	162	5545	813	1569	310	39	124	760	623	728	65	.283	.420
Todd Benzinger	1B85 OF48 DH1	B	25	120	405	47	103	28	1	13	70	22	80	2	.254	.425
Marty Barrett	2B150	R	30	150	612	83	173	28	1	1	65	40	35	7	.283	.337
Jody Reed	SS94 2B11 3B4	R	25	109	338	60	99	23	1	1	28	45	21	1	.293	.376
Wade Boggs	3B151 DH3	L	30	155	584	128	214	45	6	5	58	125	34	2	.366	.490
Dwight Evans	OF85 1B64 DH6	R	36	149	559	96	164	31	7	21	111	76	99	5	.293	.487
Ellis Burks	OF142 DH2	R	23	144	540	93	159	37	5	18	92	62	89	25	.294	.481
Mike Greenwell	OF147 DH11	L	24	158	590	86	192	39	8	22	119	87	38	16	.325	.531
Rich Gedman (BT)	C93 DH1	L	28	95	299	33	69	14	0	9	39	18	49	0	.231	.368
Jim Rice	DH112 OF19	R	35	135	485	57	128	18	3	15	72	48	89	1	.264	.406
Spike Owen	SS76 DH7	B	27	89	257	40	64	14	1	5	18	27	27	0	.249	.370
Rick Cerone	C83 DH1	R	34	84	264	31	71	13	1	3	27	20	32	0	.269	.360
Kevin Romine	OF45 DH5	R	27	57	78	17	15	2	1	1	6	7	15	2	.192	.282
2 Larry Parrish	1B36 DH14	R	34	52	158	10	41	5	0	7	26	8	32	1	.259	.424
1 Brady Anderson	OF41	L	24	41	148	14	34	5	3	0	12	15	35	4	.230	.304
Ed Romero (KJ)	3B15 SS8 2B5 1B1 DH1	R	30	31	75	3	18	3	0	0	5	3	8	0	.240	.280
Sam Horn	DH16	L	24	24	61	4	9	0	0	2	8	11	20	0	.148	.246
Randy Kutcher	DH 7 OF7 3B2	R	28	19	12	2	2	1	0	0	0	0	2	0	.167	.250
Pat Dodson	1B17	L	27	17	45	5	8	3	1	1	6	17	0	.178	.356	
John Marzano	C10	R	25	10	29	3	4	1	0	0	1	1	3	0	.138	.172
Carlos Quintana	OF3 DH1	R	22	5	6	1	2	0	0	0	2	3	1	0	.333	.333
DETROIT 2nd 88-74 .543 1	SPARKY ANDERSON															
TOTALS			32	162	5433	703	1358	213	28	143	650	588	841	87	.250	.378
Dave Bergman	1B64 DH30 OF13 3B1	L	35	116	289	37	85	14	0	5	35	38	34	0	.294	.394
Lou Whitaker (KJ)	2B110	L	31	115	403	54	111	18	2	12	55	66	61	2	.275	.419
Alan Trammell	SS125	R	30	128	466	73	145	24	1	15	69	46	46	7	.311	.464
Tom Brookens	3B136 SS3 2B1	R	34	136	441	62	107	23	5	5	38	44	74	4	.243	.351
Chet Lemon	OF144	R	33	144	512	67	135	29	4	17	64	59	65	1	.264	.436
Gary Pettis	OF126 DH2	B	30	129	458	65	96	14	4	3	36	47	85	44	.210	.277
Pat Sheridan	OF111 DH3	L	30	127	347	47	88	9	5	11	47	44	64	8	.254	.403
Mat Nokes	C110 DH4	L	24	122	382	53	96	18	0	16	53	34	58	0	.251	.424
Darrell Evans	DH72 1B65	L	41	144	437	48	91	9	0	22	64	84	89	1	.208	.380
Luis Salazar	OF68 SS37 3B31 2B5 1B4	R	32	130	452	61	122	14	1	12	62	21	70	6	.270	.385
Ray Knight	1B64 DH25 3B11 OF2	R	35	105	299	34	65	12	2	3	33	20	30	1	.217	.301
Jim Walewander	2B61 DH9 SS8 3B3	B	26	88	175	23	37	5	0	0	6	12	26	11	.211	.240
Mike Heath	C75 OF9	R	33	86	219	24	54	7	2	5	18	18	32	1	.247	.365
Larry Herndon	DH53 OF15	R	34	76	174	16	39	5	0	4	20	23	37	0	.224	.322
Dwayne Murphy	OF43 DH3	L	32	49	144	14	36	5	0	4	19	24	26	1	.250	.368
2 Fred Lynn	OF22 DH3	L	36	27	90	9	20	1	0	7	19	5	16	0	.222	.467
1 Jim Morrison	DH14 3B4 1B4 OF2 SS1	R	35	74	7	16	5	0	0	6	3	16	0	.216	.284	
Scott Lusader	DH6 OF4	L	23	16	16	3	1	0	0	0	1	3	4	0	.063	.250
Torri Lovullo	2B93B3	B	22	12	21	2	8	1	1	0	2	3	0	.381	.667	
Billy Bean	OF4 1B2 DH1	L	24	10	11	2	2	0	0	0	0	0	2	0	.182	.364
Ivan DeJesus	SS7	R	35	7	17	1	3	0	0	0	0	1	4	0	.176	.176
Billy Beane	OF6	R	26	6	6	1	1	0	0	0	1	0	2	0	.167	.167

NAME	T	AGE	W	L	PCT	SV	G	GS	CG	IP	H	BB	SO	SHO	ERA
		29	89	73	.549	37	162	162	26	1427	1415	493	1085	14	3.97
Bruce Hurst	L	30	18	6	.750	0	33	32	7	217	222	65	166	1	3.66
Roger Clemens	R	25	18	12	.600	0	35	35	14	264	217	62	291	8	2.93
Mike Smithson	R	33	9	6	.600	0	31	18	1	127	149	37	73	0	5.97
Oil Can Boyd (SJ)	R	28	9	7	.562	0	23	23	1	130	147	41	71	0	5.34
Wes Gardner	R	27	8	6	.571	2	36	18	1	149	119	64	106	0	3.50
2 Mike Boddicker	R	30	7	3	.700	0	15	14	1	89	85	26	56	1	2.63
Dennis Lamp	R	35	7	6	.538	0	46	0	0	83	92	19	49	0	3.19
Bob Stanley (HJ)	R	33	6	4	.600	5	57	0	0	102	90	29	57	0	3.19
Lee Smith	R	30	4	5	.444	29	64	0	0	84	72	37	96	0	2.67
Tom Bolton	L	26	1	3	.250	1	28	0	0	30	35	14	21	0	4.75
Steve Ellsworth	R	27	1	6	.143	0	8	7	0	36	47	16	16	0	6.75
Jeff Sellers (BG-FJ)	R	24	1	7	.125	0	18	12	1	86	89	56	70	0	4.83
Mike Rochford	L	25	0	0	—	0	2	0	0	2	4	1	1	0	0.00
Zach Crouch	L	22	0	0	—	0	3	0	0	1	4	2	0	0	6.75
Rob Woodward	R	25	0	0	—	0	1	0	0	2	1	0	0	0	13.50
John Trautwein	R	25	0	1	.000	0	9	0	0	16	26	9	8	0	9.00
Steve Curry	R	22	0	1	.000	0	3	0	1	11	15	14	4	0	8.18
		30	88	74	.543	36	162	162	34	1445	1361	497	890	8	3.71
Jack Morris	R	33	15	13	.536	0	34	34	10	235	225	83	168	2	3.94
Doyle Alexander	R	37	14	11	.560	0	34	34	5	229	260	46	126	1	4.32
Frank Tanana	L	34	14	11	.560	0	32	32	2	203	213	64	127	0	4.21
Jeff Robinson (RJ)	R	26	13	6	.684	0	24	23	6	172	121	72	114	2	2.98
Mike Henneman	R	26	9	6	.600	22	65	0	0	91	72	24	58	0	1.87
Walt Terrell	R	30	7	16	.304	0	29	29	11	206	199	78	84	1	3.97
Guillermo Hernandez	L	33	6	5	.545	10	63	0	0	68	50	31	59	0	3.06
Eric King	R	24	4	1	.800	3	23	5	0	69	60	34	45	0	3.41
Paul Gibson	L	28	4	2	.667	0	40	1	0	92	83	34	50	0	2.93
Mark Huismann	R	30	1	0	1.000	0	5	0	0	6	2	6	6	0	
2 Ted Power	R	33	1	1	.500	0	4	2	0	19	23	8	13	0	5.79
Don Heinkel (XJ)	R	28	0	0	—	0	21	0	0	36	30	12	30	0	3.96
Mike Trujillo	R	28	0	0	—	0	6	0	0	12	11	5	5	0	5.11
Steve Sercy	L	24	0	0	.000	0	2	0	0	8	8	4	5	0	5.63

MILWAUKEE — 3rd (tie) 87-75 .537 2 TOM TREBLEHORN

Name	G by Pos	B	AGE	G	AB	R	H	2B	3B	HR	RBI	BB	SO	SB	BA	SA
TOTALS			29	162	5488	682	1409	258	26	113	632	439	911	159	.257	.375
Greg Brock (VJ)	1B114 DH1	L	31	115	364	53	77	16	1	6	50	63	48	6	.212	.310
Jim Gantner	2B154 DH1	L	35	155	539	67	149	28	2	0	47	34	50	20	.276	.336
Dale Sveum (BL)	SS127 2B1 DH1	B	24	129	467	41	113	14	4	9	51	21	122	1	.242	.347
Paul Molitor	3B105 DH49 2B1	R	31	154	609	115	190	34	6	13	60	71	54	41	.312	.452
Rob Deer	OF133 DH1	R	27	135	492	71	124	24	0	23	85	51	153	9	.252	.441
Robin Yount	OF158 DH4	R	32	162	621	92	190	38	11	13	91	63	63	22	.306	.465
2 Jeff Leonard	OF91 DH2	R	32	94	374	45	88	19	0	8	44	16	68	10	.235	.350
B. J. Surhoff	C106 3B27 1B2 SS1 OF1	L	23	139	493	47	121	21	0	5	38	31	49	21	.245	.318
Joey Meyer	DH66 1B33	R	26	103	327	22	86	18	0	11	45	23	88	0	.263	.419
Glenn Braggs (SJ)	OF54 DH18	R	25	72	272	30	71	14	0	10	42	14	60	6	.261	.423
Juan Castillo (BH)	2B18 3B17 SS13 DH3 OF1	B	26	54	90	10	20	0	0	0	3	14	22	2	.222	.222
Mike Felder (LJ)	OF28 DH16 2B1	B	26	56	81	14	14	1	0	0	5	0	11	8	.173	.185
Darryl Hamilton	OF37 DH3	L	23	44	103	14	19	4	0	1	11	12	9	7	.184	.252
Jim Adduci	OF24 DH12 1B3	L	28	44	94	8	25	6	1	1	15	0	15	0	.266	.383
1 Ernest Riles	3B28 SS9 DH5	L	27	41	127	7	32	6	1	1	9	7	26	2	.252	.339
Bill Schroeder (KJ)	C30 1B10 DH1	R	29	41	122	9	19	2	0	5	10	6	36	0	.156	.295
Charlie O'Brien	C40	R	28	40	118	12	26	6	0	2	9	5	16	0	.220	.322
Billy Jo Robidoux	1B30 DH1	L	24	33	91	9	23	5	0	0	5	8	14	1	.253	.308
Gary Sheffield	SS24	R	19	24	80	12	19	1	0	4	12	7	7	3	.238	.400
2 Mike Young	DH5 OF2	B	28	8	14	2	0	0	0	0	0	2	5	0	.000	.000
Steve Kiefer	2B4 3B4	R	27	7	10	2	3	1	0	1	2	3	0		.300	.700
Steve Stanicek (KJ) 27																

NAME	T	AGE	W	L	PCT	SV	G	GS	CG	IP	H	BB	SO	SHO	ERA
Teddy Higuera	L	29	16	9	.640	0	31	31	8	227	168	59	192	1	2.45
Don August	R	24	13	7	.650	0	24	22	6	148	137	48	66	1	3.09
Bill Wegman	R	25	13	13	.500	0	32	31	4	199	207	50	84	1	4.12
Mike Birkbeck	R	27	10	8	.556	0	23	23	0	124	141	37	64	0	4.72
Juan Nieves (SJ)	R	23	7	5	.583	1	25	15	1	110	84	50	73	1	4.08
Chuck Crim	R	26	7	6	.538	9	70	0	0	105	95	28	58	0	2.91
Chris Bosio	R	25	7	15	.318	6	38	22	9	182	190	38	84	1	3.36
Odell Jones	R	35	5	0	1.000	1	28	2	0	81	75	29	48	0	4.35
Tom Filer (SJ)	R	31	5	8	.385	0	19	16	2	102	108	33	39	1	4.43
Paul Mirabella	L	34	2	2	.500	4	38	0	0	60	44	21	33	0	1.65
Mark Clear (EJ)	R	32	1	0	1.000	0	25	0	0	29	23	21	26	0	2.79
Dan Plesac	R	26	1	2	.333	30	50	0	0	52	46	12	52	0	2.41
Mark Knudson	R	27	0	0	—	0	5	0	0	16	17	2	7	0	1.13
Dave Stapleton (SJ)	L	26	0	0	—	0	6	0	0	14	20	9	6	0	5.93

TORONTO — 3rd (tie) 87-75 .537 2 JIMY WILLIAMS

Name	G by Pos	B	AGE	G	AB	R	H	2B	3B	HR	RBI	BB	SO	SB	BA	SA
TOTALS			27	162	5557	763	1491	271	47	158	706	521	935	107	.268	.419
Fred McGriff	1B153	L	24	154	536	100	151	35	4	34	82	79	149	6	.282	.552
Manny Lee	2B98 SS19 3B8 DH2	B	23	116	381	38	111	16	3	2	38	26	64	3	.291	.365
Tony Fernandez	SS154	L	24	154	648	76	186	41	4	5	70	45	65	15	.287	.386
Kelly Gruber	3B156 2B7 OF2 SS1 DH1	R	26	158	569	75	158	33	5	16	81	38	92	23	.278	.438
Jesse Barfield	OF138 DH1	R	28	137	468	62	114	21	5	18	56	41	108	7	.244	.425
Lloyd Moseby	OF125 DH1	L	28	128	472	77	113	17	7	10	42	70	93	31	.239	.369
George Bell	OF149 DH7	R	28	156	614	78	165	27	5	24	97	34	66	4	.269	.446
Ernie Whitt	C123	L	36	127	398	63	100	11	2	16	70	61	38	4	.251	.410
Rance Mulliniks	DH108 3B7	L	32	119	337	49	101	21	1	12	48	56	57	1	.300	.475
Nelson Liriano	2B80 DH11 3B1	B	24	99	276	36	73	6	2	3	23	11	40	12	.264	.333
Rick Leach	OF49 DH25 1B4	L	31	87	199	21	55	13	1	0	23	18	27	0	.276	.352
Cecil Fielder	DH50 1B17 3B3 DH2	R	24	74	174	24	40	6	1	9	23	14	53	0	.230	.431
Sil Campusano (NJ)	O69 DH2	R	21	73	142	14	31	10	2	2	12	9	33	0	.218	.359
Pat Borders (VJ)	C43 DH7 3B1 2B1	R	25	56	154	15	42	6	3	5	21	3	24	0	.273	.448
Juan Beniquez	DH1 OF1	R	38	27	58	9	17	2	0	1	6	8	6	0	.293	.379
Rob Ducey	OF26	L	23	27	54	15	17	4	1	0	6	5	7	1	.315	.426
Sal Butera	C23	R	35	23	60	3	14	2	1	1	6	1	9	0	.233	.350
Alex Infante	3B9 DH7 SS2	R	26	19	15	7	3	0	0	0	0	2	4	0	.200	.200
Lou Thornton	OF10 DH1	L	25	11	2	1	0	0	0	0	0	0	1	0	.000	.000
Matt Stark (SJ) 23																

NAME	T	AGE	W	L	PCT	SV	G	GS	CG	IP	H	BB	SO	SHO	ERA
		29	87	75	.537	47	162	162	16	1449	1404	528	904	17	3.80
Dave Stieb	R	30	16	8	.667	0	32	31	8	207	157	79	147	4	3.04
Mike Flanagan	L	36	13	13	.500	0	34	34	2	211	220	80	99	1	4.18
Jimmy Key (EJ)	L	27	12	5	.706	0	21	21	2	131	127	30	65	2	3.29
Jim Clancy	R	32	11	13	.458	1	36	31	4	196	207	47	118	0	4.49
Duane Ward	R	24	9	3	.750	15	64	0	0	112	101	60	91	0	3.30
Jeff Musselman (SJ)	R	25	8	5	.615	0	15	15	0	85	80	30	39	0	3.18
John Cerutti	L	28	6	7	.462	1	46	12	0	124	120	42	65	0	3.13
Tom Henke	R	30	4	4	.500	25	52	0	0	68	60	24	66	0	2.91
Todd Stottlemyre	R	23	4	8	.333	0	28	16	0	98	109	46	67	0	5.69
David Wells	L	25	3	5	.375	4	41	0	0	64	65	31	56	0	4.62
Tony Castillo	L	25	1		1.000	0	14	0	0	15	10	2	14	0	3.00
Frank Wills	R	29	0	0	—	0	14	0	0	21	22	6	19	0	5.23
Doug Bair	R	38	0	0	—	0	10	0	0	13	14	3	8	0	4.05
Mark Ross	R	30	0	0	—	0	3	0	0	7	5	4	4	0	4.91
Jose Nunez	R	24	0	1	.000	0	13	2	0	29	28	17	18	0	3.07
Mark Eichhorn	R	27	0	3	.000	1	37	0	0	67	79	27	28	0	4.19

NEW YORK — 5th 85-76 .530 5 BILLY MARTIN 40-28 .588 LOU PINIELLA 45-48 .484

Name	G by Pos	B	AGE	G	AB	R	H	2B	3B	HR	RBI	BB	SO	SB	BA	SA
TOTALS			31	161	5592	772	1469	272	12	148	713	588	935	146	.263	.395
Don Mattingly	1B143 DH1	L	27	144	599	94	186	37	0	18	88	41	29	1	.311	.462
Willie Randolph (VJ)	2B110	R	33	110	404	43	93	20	1	2	34	55	39	8	.230	.300
Rafael Santana	SS148	R	30	148	480	50	115	12	1	4	38	33	61	1	.240	.294
Mike Pagliarulo	3B124	L	28	125	444	46	96	20	1	15	67	37	104	1	.216	.367
Dave Winfield	OF141 DH4	R	36	149	559	96	180	37	2	25	107	69	88	9	.322	.530
Claudell Washington	OF117 DH1	L	33	126	455	62	140	22	3	11	64	24	74	15	.308	.442
Rickey Henderson	OF138 DH3	R	29	140	554	118	169	30	2	6	50	82	54	93	.305	.399
Don Slaught (GJ)	C94 DH1	R	29	97	322	33	91	25	1	9	43	24	54	1	.283	.450
Jack Clark	DH112 OF19 1B11	R	32	150	496	81	120	14	0	27	93	113	141	3	.242	.433
Gary Ward	OF54 1B11 DH9 3B2	R	34	91	231	26	52	8	0	4	24	24	41	0	.225	.312
Joel Skinner	C85 OF2 1B1	R	27	88	251	23	57	15	0	4	23	14	72	0	.227	.335
2 Luis Aguayo	3B33 2B13 SS6	R	29	50	140	12	35	4	0	3	8	7	33	0	.250	.343
Randy Velarde	2B24 SS14 3B10	R	25	48	115	18	20	6	0	5	12	8	24	1	.174	.357
Bobby Meacham (ZJ)	SS24 2B21 3B5	R	27	47	115	18	25	9	0	0	7	14	22	7	.217	.296
2 Ken Phelps	DH28 1B1	L	33	45	107	17	24	5	0	10	22	19	26	0	.224	.551
Jose Cruz	DH12 OF8	L	40	38	80	9	16	2	0	1	7	8	8	0	.200	.263
Roberto Kelly (WJ)	OF30 DH3	R	23	38	77	9	19	4	1	1	7	3	15	5	.247	.364
1 Jay Buhner	OF22	R	23	25	69	8	13	0	0	3	13	3	25	0	.188	.319
Wayne Tolleson (SJ-LJ)	2B12 3B11 SS1	B	32	21	59	8	15	2	0	0	5	8	12	1	.254	.288
Hal Morris	OF4 DH1	L	23	15	20	1	2	0	0	0	0	0	9	0	.100	.100
Bob Geren	C10	R	26	10	10	0	1	0	0	0	0	1	3	0	.100	.100
Alvaro Espinoza	2B2 SS1	R	26	3	3	0	0	0	0	0	0	0	1	0	.000	.000
Chris Chambliss (RC)		L	39	1	1	0	0	0	0	0	0	0	0	0	.000	.000

NAME	T	AGE	W	L	PCT	SV	G	GS	CG	IP	H	BB	SO	SHO	ERA
		32	85	76	.528	43	161	161	16	1456	1512	487	861	5	4.26
John Candelaria (KJ)	L	34	13	7	.650	1	25	24	6	157	150	23	121	2	3.38
Rich Dotson	R	29	12	9	.571	0	32	29	4	171	178	72	77	0	5.00
Rick Rhoden	R	35	12	12	.500	0	30	30	5	197	206	56	94	1	4.29
Tommy John	L	45	9	8	.529	0	35	32	0	176	221	46	81	0	4.49
Charlie Hudson (SJ)	R	29	6	6	.500	2	28	12	1	106	93	36	58	0	4.49
Neil Allen (UJ)	R	30	5	3	.625	0	41	2	0	117	121	37	61	1	3.84
Dave Righetti	R	29	5	4	.556	25	60	0	0	87	86	37	70	0	3.52
Steve Shields	R	29	5	4	.500	0	39	0	0	82	96	30	55	0	4.37
1 Cecelio Guante	R	28	5	6	.455	11	56	0	0	75	59	22	61	0	2.88
Al Leiter (RJ)	R	22	4	4	.500	0	14	14	0	57	49	33	60	0	3.92
Tim Stoddard	R	35	2	2	.500	3	28	0	0	55	62	27	33	0	6.38
2 Dale Mohorcic	R	32	2	2	.500	1	13	0	0	23	21	9	13	0	2.78
Ron Guidry (SJ-LJ)	L	37	2	3	.400	0	12	10	0	56	57	15	32	0	4.18
Hipolito Pena	L	24	1	1	.500	0	16	0	0	14	10	9	10	0	3.14
Lee Guetterman	R	29	1	2	.333	0	20	2	0	41	49	14	15	0	4.65
Scott Nielsen	R	29	1	2	.333	0	7	3	0	27	27	13	4	0	6.86
Dave Eiland	R	21	0	0	—	0	3	0	0	13	15	4	7	0	6.39
Pat Clements	L	26	0	0	—	0	6	0	0	5	3	6	1	0	6.48

CLEVELAND — 6th 78-84 .481 11 DOC EDWARDS

Name	G by Pos	B	AGE	G	AB	R	H	2B	3B	HR	RBI	BB	SO	SB	BA	SA
TOTALS			28	162	5505	666	1435	235	28	134	629	416	866	97	.261	.387
Willie Upshaw	1B144	L	31	149	493	58	121	22	3	11	50	62	66	12	.245	.369
Julio Franco	2B151 DH1	R	29	152	613	88	186	23	6	10	54	56	72	25	.303	.409
Jay Bell	SS72 DH1	R	22	73	211	23	46	5	1	2	21	21	53	4	.218	.280
Brook Jacoby	3B151	R	28	152	552	59	133	25	0	9	49	48	101	2	.241	.335
Cory Snyder	OF141 DH1	R	25	142	511	71	139	24	3	26	75	42	101	5	.272	.483
Joe Carter	OF156	R	28	157	621	85	168	36	6	27	98	35	82	27	.271	.478
Mel Hall	OF141 DH6	L	27	150	515	69	144	32	4	6	71	28	50	7	.280	.392
Andy Allanson	C133	R	26	133	434	44	111	10	5	5	50	25	63	5	.256	.323
Ron Kittle	DH63	R	30	75	225	31	58	8	0	18	43	16	65	0	.258	.533
Ron Washington	SS54 3B8 2B7	R	36	69	223	30	57	14	2	2	21	9	35	3	.256	.363
Carmen Castillo	OF45 OF2 1B1	R	30	66	176	12	48	8	0	4	14	5	31	6	.273	.386
Dave Clark	DH27 OF23	L	25	63	156	11	41	4	1	3	18	17	28	0	.263	.359
Terry Francona	DH38 1B5 OF5	L	29	62	212	24	66	8	0	1	12	5	18	0	.311	.363
Paul Zuvella	SS49	R	29	51	130	9	30	5	1	0	7	8	13	0	.231	.285
1 Pat Tabler	DH29 1B10	R	30	41	143	16	32	5	1	1	17	23	27	1	.224	.294
1 Chris Bando	C32	B	32	32	72	6	9	1	0	1	8	8	12	0	.125	.181
1 Domingo Ramos	3B2	R	30	22	46	7	12	1	0	0	5	3	7	0	.261	.283
Luis Medina	1B16	R	25	16	51	10	13	0	0	6	8	2	18	0	.255	.608
Reggie Williams	OF11	R	27	11	31	7	7	2	0	0	3	0	6	0	.226	.387
Eddie Williams	3B10	R	23	10	21	3	4	0	0	0	1	0	3	0	.190	.190
Ron Tingley	C9	R	29	9	24	1	4	0	0	1	2	2	4	0	.167	.292
Houston Jimenez	2B7 SS2	R	30	9	21	1	1	0	0	0	1	0	2	0	.048	.048
Scott Jordan	OF6	R	25	7	9	0	1	0	0	0	1	0	1	1	.111	.111
Rod Allen	DH4	R	29	7	11	0	1	0	0	0	1	0	0	0	.091	.182
Tom Lampkin	C3	L	24	4	4	0	0	0	0	0	0	0	0	0	.000	.000
Dan Firova	C1	R	31	4	1	0	0	0	0	0	0	0	0	0	.000	.000

NAME	T	AGE	W	L	PCT	SV	G	GS	CG	IP	H	BB	SO	SHO	ERA
		28	78	84	.481	46	162	162	35	1434	1501	442	812	10	4.16
Greg Swindell	L	23	18	14	.562	0	33	33	12	242	234	45	180	4	3.20
Tom Candiotti	R	30	14	8	.636	0	31	31	11	217	225	53	137	1	3.28
John Farrell	R	25	14	10	.583	0	31	30	4	210	216	67	92	0	4.24
Rich Yett (XJ)	R	25	9	6	.600	0	23	22	0	134	146	55	71	0	4.62
Scott Bailes	L	26	9	14	.391	0	37	21	5	145	149	46	53	2	4.90
Doug Jones	R	31	3	4	.429	37	51	0	0	83	69	16	72	0	2.27
Don Gordon	R	28	3	4	.429	1	38	0	0	59	65	19	20	0	4.40
2 Bud Black (EJ)	L	31	2	3	.400	1	16	7	0	59	59	23	44	0	5.03
2 Brad Havens	L	28	2	3	.400	1	28	0	0	57	62	17	30	0	3.14
Jeff Dedmon	R	28	1	0	1.000	1	21	0	0	34	35	21	17	0	4.54
Bill Laskey	R	30	1	0	1.000	0	17	0	0	24	32	6	17	0	5.18
Rick Rodriguez (EJ)	R	28	1	2	.333	0	10	5	0	33	43	17	9	0	7.09
Rod Nichols	R	23	1	7	.125	0	11	10	3	69	73	23	31	0	5.06
Jeff Kaiser	L	27	0	0	—	0	9	1	0	9	16	7	7	0	7.27
Mike Walker	R	21	0	1	.000	0	3	1	0	9	8	10	7	0	7.27
Jon Perlman (EJ)	R	30	0	1	.000	0	15	0	0	25	11	10	6	0	5.49
1 Dan Schatzeder (EJ)	L	33	0	0	—	0	16	0	0	16	26	2	10	0	9.56
Chris Codiroli	R	30	0	4	.000	2	19	0	0	19	32	10	12	0	9.31

Name	G by Pos	B	AGE	G	AB	R	H	2B	3B	HR	RBI	BB	SO	SB	BA	SA

BALTIMORE 7th 54-107 .335 34.5   CAL RIPKEN SR. 0-6 .000   FRANK ROBINSON 54-101 .348

Name	G by Pos	B	AGE	G	AB	R	H	2B	3B	HR	RBI	BB	SO	SB	BA	SA
TOTALS		28	161	5358	550	1275	199	20	137	517	504	869	69	.238	.359	
Eddie Murray	1B103 DH58	B	32	161	603	75	171	27	2	28	84	75	78	5	.284	.474
Billy Ripken	2B149 3B2 DH1	R	23	150	512	52	106	18	1	2	34	33	63	8	.207	.258
Cal Ripken	SS161	R	27	161	575	87	152	25	1	23	81	102	69	2	.264	.431
Rick Schu (EJ)	3B72 DH9 1B4	R	26	89	270	22	69	9	4	4	20	21	49	6	.256	.363
Joe Orsulak	OF117	L	26	125	379	48	109	21	3	8	27	23	30	9	.288	.422
1 Fred Lynn (NJ)	OF83 DH2	L	36	87	301	37	76	13	1	18	37	28	66	2	.252	.482
Pete Stanicek	OF65 2B16 DH1	B	25	83	261	29	60	7	1	4	17	28	45	12	.230	.310
Mickey Tettleton	C80	B	27	86	283	31	74	11	1	11	37	28	70	0	.261	.424
Larry Sheets	OF76 DH50 1B3	L	28	136	452	38	104	19	1	10	47	42	72	1	.230	.343
Jim Traber	1B57 DH30 OF11	L	26	103	352	25	78	6	0	10	45	19	42	1	.222	.324
Ken Gerhart	OF93 DH3	R	27	103	262	27	51	10	1	9	23	21	57	7	.195	.344
Rene Gonzales	3B80 2B14 SS2 OF1 1B1	R	27	92	237	13	51	6	0	2	15	13	32	2	.215	.266
Terry Kennedy	C79	L	32	85	265	20	60	10	0	3	16	15	53	0	.226	.298
2 Brady Anderson	OF49	L	24	53	177	17	35	8	1	1	9	8	40	6	.198	.271
Keith Hughes	OF31 DH1	L	24	41	108	10	21	4	2	2	14	16	27	1	.194	.324
1 Jim Dwyer (EJ)	DH17 OF2	L	38	53	53	3	12	0	0	3	12	11		0	.226	.226
Craig Worthington	3B26	R	23	26	81	5	15	2	0	2	4	9	24	1	.185	.284
Jeff Stone (RJ)	OF21 DH1	L	27	26	61	4	10	1	0	0	1	4	11	4	.164	.180
Wade Rowdon	3B8 OF5 DH5	R	27	20	30	1	3	0	0	0	0	6		1	.100	.100
Carl Nichols	C13 OF3	R	25	18	47	2	9	1	0	0	1	3	10	0	.191	.213
Butch Davis	OF10 DH1	R	30	13	25	2	6	1	0	0	0	0	8	1	.240	.280
Tito Landrum	OF12 DH1	R	33	13	24	2	3	0	1	0	2	4	5	1	.125	.208

NAME	T	AGE	W	L	PCT	SV	G	GS	CG	IP	H	BB	SO	SHO	ERA
		28	54	107	.335	26	161	161	20	1416	1506	523	709	7	4.54
Dave Schmidt	R	31	8	5	.615	2	41	9	0	130	129	38	67	0	3.40
Jeff Ballard	R	24	8	12	.400	0	25	25	6	153	167	42	41	1	4.40
1 Mike Boddicker	R	30	6	12	.333	0	21	21	4	147	149	51	100	0	3.86
Jose Bautista	R	23	6	15	.286	0	33	25	3	172	171	45	76	0	4.30
Oswald Peraza	R	25	5	7	.417	0	19	15	1	86	98	37	61	0	5.55
Mark Williamson	R	28	5	8	.385	2	37	10	2	118	125	40	69	0	4.90
Jay Tibbs	R	26	4	15	.211	0	30	24	1	159	184	63	82	0	5.39
Doug Sisk (FJ)	R	30	3	3	.500	0	52	0	0	94	109	45	26	0	3.72
Tom Niedenfuer	R	28	3	4	.429	18	52	0	0	59	59	19	40	0	3.51
Bob Milacki	R	23	2	0	1.000	0	3	3	1	25	9	9	18	1	0.72
John Habyan	R	24	1	0	1.000	0	7	0	0	15	22	4	4	0	4.30
Gregg Olson	R	21	1	1	.500	0	10	0	0	11	10	10	9	0	3.27
Mike Morgan (FJ)	R	28	1	6	.143	1	22	10	2	71	70	23	29	0	5.43
Mark Thurmond	L	31	1	8	.111	3	43	6	0	75	80	27	29	0	4.68
Don Aase (SJ)	R	33	0	0	—	0	35	0	0	47	40	37	28	0	4.05
Gordon Dillard	R	24	0	0	—	0	2	1	0	3	3	4	2	0	6.00
1 Bill Scherrer	L	30	0	1	.000	0	4	0	0	4	8	3	3	0	13.50
Pete Harnisch	R	21	0	2	.000	0	2	2	0	13	13	9	10	0	5.54
Dickie Noles	R	31	0	2	.000	0	3	2	0	3	11	0	1	0	24.30
Scott McGregor	L	34	0	3	.000	0	4	4	0	17	27	7	10	0	8.83
Curt Schilling	R	21	0	3	.000	0	4	4	0	15	22	10	4	0	9.82

WEST DIVISION

OAKLAND 1st 104-58 .642   TONY LARUSSA

Name	G by Pos	B	AGE	G	AB	R	H	2B	3B	HR	RBI	BB	SO	SB	BA	SA
TOTALS		28	162	5602	800	1474	251	22	156	752	580	926	129	.263	.399	
Mark McGwire	1B154 OF1	R	24	155	550	87	143	22	1	32	99	76	117	0	.260	.478
Glenn Hubbard	2B104 DH1	R	30	105	294	35	75	12	2	3	33	33	50	1	.255	.340
Walt Weiss	SS147	B	24	147	452	44	113	17	3	3	39	35	56	4	.250	.321
Carney Lansford	3B143 1B9 2B1 DH1	R	31	150	556	80	155	20	2	7	57	35	35	29	.279	.360
Jose Canseco	OF144 DH13	R	23	158	610	120	187	34	0	42	124	78	128	40	.307	.569
Dave Henderson	OF143	R	29	146	507	100	154	38	1	24	94	47	92	2	.304	.525
Luis Polonia	OF76 DH2	L	23	84	288	51	84	11	4	2	27	21	40	24	.292	.378
Terry Steinbach (IJ)	C84 3B9 1B8 DH7 OF1	R	26	104	351	42	93	19	1	9	51	33	47	3	.265	.402
Don Baylor	DH80	R	39	92	264	28	58	7	0	7	34	34	44	0	.220	.326
Mike Gallego	2B83 SS42 3B16	R	29	129	277	38	58	8	0	2	20	34	53	2	.209	.260
Stan Javier	OF115 1B4 DH2	B	24	125	397	49	102	13	3	2	35	32	63	20	.257	.320
Ron Hassey	C91 DH9	L	35	107	323	32	83	15	0	7	45	30	42	2	.257	.368
Dave Parker (RJ)	DH61 OF34 1B1	L	37	101	377	43	97	18	1	12	55	32	70	0	.257	.406
Tony Phillips (LJ)	3B32 OF31 2B27 SS10 1B3	B	29	79	212	32	43	8	4	2	17	36	50	0	.203	.307
Doug Jennings (XJ)	OF23 1B14 DH2	L	23	71	101	9	21	6	0	1	15	21	28	0	.208	.297
Orlando Mercado	C16	R	26	16	24	3	3	0	0	1	1	3	8	0	.125	.250
Matt Sinatro	C9	R	28	10	9	1	3	2	0	0	5	0	1	0	.333	.556
Lance Blankenship	2B4 DH4	R	24	10	3	1	0	0	0	0	0	2	2	0	.000	.000
Felix Jose	OF6	B	23	8	6	2	2	1	0	0	1	0	1	1	.333	.500
Ed Jurak	3B1	R	30	3	1	1	0	0	0	0	0	0	0	0	.000	.000

NAME	T	AGE	W	L	PCT	SV	G	GS	CG	IP	H	BB	SO	SHO	ERA
		29	104	58	.642	64	162	162	22	1489	1376	553	983	9	3.44
Dave Stewart	R	31	21	12	.636	0	37	37	14	276	240	110	192	2	3.23
Bob Welch	R	31	17	9	.654	0	36	36	4	245	237	81	158	2	3.64
Storm Davis	R	26	16	7	.696	0	33	33	1	202	211	91	127	0	3.70
Curt Young	L	28	11	8	.579	0	26	26	1	156	162	50	69	0	4.14
Gene Nelson	R	27	9	6	.600	3	54	1	0	112	93	36	67	0	3.06
Todd Burns	R	24	8	2	.800	1	17	14	2	103	93	34	57	0	3.16
Eric Plunk	R	24	7	2	.777	5	49	0	0	78	62	39	79	0	3.00
Greg Cadaret	L	26	5	2	.714	3	58	0	0	72	60	36	64	0	2.89
Dennis Eckersley	R	33	4	2	.667	45	60	0	0	73	52	11	70	0	2.35
Rick Honeycutt	L	34	3	2	.600	7	55	0	0	80	74	25	47	0	3.50
Steve Ontiveros (EJ)	R	27	3	4	.429	0	10	10	0	55	57	21	30	0	4.61
Dave Otto	L	23	0	0	—	0	3	2	0	10	9	6	7	0	1.80
Jeff Shaver	R	24	0	0	—	0	1	0	0	4	0	0	0	0	0.00
Jim Corsi	R	26	0	1	.000	0	11	1	0	21	20	6	10	0	3.80
Rich Bordi	R	29	0	1	.000	0	2	2	0	8	6	5	6	0	4.70
Matt Young (SJ) 29															

MINNESOTA 2nd 91-71 .582 13   TOM KELLY

Name	G by Pos	B	AGE	G	AB	R	H	2B	3B	HR	RBI	BB	SO	SB	BA	SA
TOTALS		29	162	5510	759	1508	294	31	151	710	528	832	107	.274	.421	
Kent Hrbek	1B105 DH37	L	28	143	510	75	159	31	0	25	76	67	54	0	.312	.520
2 Tommy Herr (LJ)	2B73 DH3 SS2	B	32		304	42	80	16	0	1	21	40	47	10	.263	.326
Greg Gagne	SS146 OF2 2B1 3B1	R	26	149	461	70	109	20	6	14	48	27	110	15	.236	.397
Gary Gaetti	3B115 DH5 SS2	R	29	133	468	66	141	29	2	28	88	36	85	7	.301	.561
Randy Bush	OF109 DH17 1B6	L	29	136	394	51	103	20	3	14	51	58	49	8	.261	.434
Kirby Puckett	OF158	R	28	158	657	109	234	42	5	24	121	23	83	6	.356	.545
Dan Gladden	OF140 2B1 3B1 P1	R	30	141	576	91	155	32	6	11	62	46	74	28	.269	.403
Tim Laudner	C108 DH4 1B3	R	30	117	375	38	94	18	1	13	54	36	89	0	.251	.408
Gene Larkin	DH86 1B60	B	25	149	505	56	135	30	2	8	70	68	55	3	.267	.382
Al Newman	3B60 2B23 SS21 DH2	B	28	105	260	35	58	7	0	0	19	29	34	12	.223	.250
John Moses	OF82 DH2	B	30	105	206	33	65	10	3	2	12	15	21	11	.316	.422
Steve Lombardozzi	2B90 SS12 3B5	R	27	103	287	34	60	15	2	3	27	35	48	2	.209	.307
Mark Davidson	OF91 DH3 3B1	R	27	100	106	22	23	7	0	1	10	10	20	3	.217	.311
Brian Harper	C48 DH5 3B2	R	28	60	166	15	49	11	1	3	20	10	12	0	.295	.428
Tom Nieto	C24	R	27	24	60	1	4	0	0	0	3	5	17	0	.067	.067
John Christensen	OF17 DH1	R	27	23	38	5	10	4	0	0	5	3	5	0	.263	.368
2 Jim Dwyer	DH13 OF2	L	38	20	41	6	12	1	0	2	15	13	8	0	.293	.463
Eric Bullock	OF4 DH2	L	28	16	17	3	5	0	0	0	3	3	1	1	.294	.294
1 Tom Brunansky	OF13 DH1	R	27	14	49	5	9	1	0	1	6	7	11	1	.184	.265
Kelvin Torve	1B4 DH1	L	28	12	16	1	3	0	0	0	2	1	2	0	.188	.375
Doug Baker	SS9 3B1 2B1	B	27	11	7	1	0	0	0	0	0	0	5	0	.000	.000
Dwight Lowry	C5	L	30	7	7	0	0	0	0	0	0	0	0	0	.000	.000

NAME	T	AGE	W	L	PCT	SV	G	GS	CG	IP	H	BB	SO	SHO	ERA
		29	91	71	.562	52	162	162	18	1431	1457	453	897	9	3.93
Frank Viola	L	28	24	7	.774	0	35	35	7	255	236	54	193	2	2.64
Allan Anderson	L	24	16	9	.640	0	30	30	3	202	199	37	83	1	2.45
Bert Blyleven	R	37	10	17	.370	0	33	33	7	207	240	51	145	0	5.43
Juan Berenguer	R	33	8	4	.667	2	57	1	0	100	74	61	99	0	3.96
Keith Atherton	R	29	7	5	.583	3	49	0	0	74	65	22	43	0	3.41
Freddie Toliver	R	27	7	6	.538	0	21	19	0	115	116	52	69	0	4.24
Charlie Lea (AJ)	R	31	7	7	.500	0	24	23	0	130	156	50	72	0	4.85
Roy Smith	R	26	3	0	1.000	0	9	4	0	37	29	12	17	0	2.68
Mark Portugal	R	25	3	3	.500	3	26	0	0	58	60	17	31	0	4.53
Jeff Reardon	R	32	2	4	.333	42	63	0	0	73	68	15	56	0	2.47
Les Straker (EJ)	R	28	2	5	.286	1	16	14	1	83	86	25	23	1	3.92
Jim Winn (EJ)	R	28	1	0	1.000	9	9	0	0	21	33	10	9	0	6.00
Joe Niekro	R	43	1	1	.500	0	5	1	0	17	16	9	7	0	10.03
German Gonzalez	R	26	0	0	—	1	16	0	0	21	20	8	19	0	3.38
Karl Best	R	29	0	0	—	0	11	0	0	12	15	7	9	0	6.00
Tippy Martinez	L	38	0	0	—	0	3	0	0	4	4	3	4	0	18.00
Dan Gladden	R	30	0	0	—	0	1	0	0	1	1	0	0	0	0.00
Steve Carlton	L	43	0	1	.000	0	4	1	0	10	20	5	5	0	16.76
2 Dan Schatzeder	L	33	0	1	.000	0	10	0	0	10	8	5	1	0	1.74
Mike Mason	L	29	0	1	.000	0	5	0	0	6	9	6	4	0	10.80

KANSAS CITY 3rd 84-77 .522 19.5   JOHN WATHAN

Name	G by Pos	B	AGE	G	AB	R	H	2B	3B	HR	RBI	BB	SO	SB	BA	SA
TOTALS		30	161	5469	704	1419	275	40	121	671	486	944	137	.259	.391	
George Brett	1B124 DH33 SS1	L	35	157	589	90	180	42	3	24	103	82	51	14	.306	.509
Frank White	2B148 DH3	R	37	150	537	48	126	25	1	8	58	21	67	7	.235	.330
Kurt Stillwell	SS124	B	23	128	459	63	115	28	5	10	53	47	76	6	.251	.399
Kevin Seitzer	3B147 OF1 DH1	R	26	149	559	90	170	32	5	5	60	72	64	10	.304	.406
Danny Tartabull	OF130 DH13	R	25	146	507	80	139	38	3	26	102	76	119	8	.274	.515
Willie Wilson	OF142	B	32	147	591	81	155	17	11	1	37	22	106	35	.262	.333
Bo Jackson (LJ)	OF121 DH2	R	25	124	439	63	108	16	4	25	68	25	146	27	.246	.472
Jamie Quirk	C79 3B1 1B1	L	33	84	196	22	47	7	1	8	25	28	41	1	.240	.408
2 Pat Tabler	DH40 1B7	R	30	89	301	37	93	17	2	1	49	23	41	2	.309	.389
Bill Pecota	3B21 1B11 OF9 DH4 2B3 C1	R	28	90	178	25	37	3	3	1	15	18	34	7	.208	.275
2 Bill Buckner	DH42 1B21	L	38	89	242	18	62	14	0	3	34	13	19	3	.256	.351
Jim Eisenreich	OF64 DH13	L	29	82	202	26	44	8	1	1	19	6	31	9	.218	.282
Brad Wellman	2B46 SS15 3B4 DH3	R	28	71	107	11	29	3	0	1	6	6	23	1	.271	.327
Mike Macfarlane	C68	R	24	70	211	25	56	15	0	4	26	21	37	0	.265	.393
Larry Owen	C37	R	33	37	81	5	17	1	0	1	9	6	20	0	.210	.259
Gary Thurman	OF32 DH1	R	23	35	66	6	11	1	0	0	2	5	20	5	.167	.182
1 Steve Balboni	1B13 DH6	R	31	21	63	2	9	2	0	0	5	1	20	0	.143	.270
Scotti Madison	DH4 C4 OF3 1B2	B	28	16	35	4	6	2	0	0	2	4	5	1	.171	.229
1 Thad Bosley	OF6 DH4	L	31	15	21	1	4	1	0	0	1	0	5	0	.190	.190
Nick Capra	OF11 DH1	R	30	14	29	3	4	1	0	0	4	3	4	1	.138	.172
Luis de los Santos	1B5 DH3	R	21	11	22	1	5	1	0	0	2	2	2	0	.091	.227
Ed Hearn (SJ)	C4 DH2	R	27	7	18	1	4	1	0	0	4	1	0	0	.222	.333
Dave Owen	SS7	B	30	7	5	0	0	0	0	0	0	0	0	0	.000	.000
Rey Palacios	C3 3B1 DH1	R	25	5	11	2	1	0	0	0	0	0	4	0	.091	.091

NAME	T	AGE	W	L	PCT	SV	G	GS	CG	IP	H	BB	SO	SHO	ERA
		30	84	77	.522	32	161	161	29	1428	1415	465	886	12	3.65
Mark Gubicza	R	25	20	8	.714	0	35	35	8	270	237	83	183	4	2.70
Bret Saberhagen	R	24	14	16	.467	0	35	35	9	261	271	59	171	0	3.80
Charlie Liebrandt	L	31	13	12	.520	0	35	35	7	243	244	62	125	2	3.19
Floyd Bannister	L	33	12	13	.480	0	31	31	2	189	182	68	113	0	4.33
Jeff Montgomery	R	26	7	2	.778	1	45	0	0	63	54	30	47	0	3.45
Steve Farr	R	31	5	4	.556	20	62	1	0	83	74	30	72	0	2.50
1 Ted Power	R	33	5	6	.455	0	22	12	2	80	98	30	44	2	5.94
Israel Sanchez	L	24	3	2	.600	1	19	1	0	36	36	18	14	0	4.54
Rick Anderson	R	31	2	1	.667	0	17	3	0	34	41	9	9	0	4.24
1 Bud Black	L	31	2	3	.667	0	17			22	23	11	19	0	4.91
Luis Aquino	R	24	1	0	1.000	0	7	5	1	29	33	17	11	1	2.79
Mark Lee		23	0	0	—	0	5			5	6	1	3	0	3.60
1 Dan Quisenberry	R	35	0	1	.000	1	20	0	0	25	32	5	9	0	3.55
Jose DeJesus	R	23	0	1	.000	0	3	1	0	3	6	5	2	0	27.00
Tom Gordon	R	20	0	2	.000	0	5	1	0	16	7	18		0	5.17
Jerry Don Gleaton	L	30	0	4	.000	0	42	0	0	38	33	17	29	0	3.55
Gene Garber	R	40	0	4	.000	6	26	0	0	33	29	13	20	0	3.58

CALIFORNIA — 4th 75-87 .463 29 COOKIE ROJAS 75-79 .487 MOOSE STUBING 0-8 .000

Name	G by Pos	B	AGE	G	AB	R	H	2B	3B	HR	RBI	BB	SO	SB	BA	SA
TOTALS			30	162	5582	714	1458	258	31	124	660	469	819	86	.261	.385
Wally Joyner	1B156	L	26	158	597	81	176	31	2	13	85	55	51	8	.295	.419
Johnny Ray	2B 104 OF 40 DH6	B	31	153	602	75	184	42	7	6	83	36	38	4	.306	.429
Dick Schofield	SS155	R	25	155	527	61	126	11	6	6	34	40	57	20	.239	.317
Jack Howell	3B152 OF2	L	26	154	500	59	127	32	2	16	63	46	130	2	.254	.422
Chili Davis	OF153 DH3	B	28	158	600	81	161	29	3	21	93	56	118	9	.268	.432
Devon White (KJ)	OF116	B	25	122	455	76	118	22	2	11	51	23	84	17	.259	.389
Tony Armas	OF113 DH1	R	34	120	368	42	100	20	2	13	49	22	87	1	.272	.443
Bob Boone	C121	R	40	122	352	38	104	17	0	5	39	29	26	2	.295	.386
Brian Downing	DH132	R	37	135	484	80	117	18	2	25	64	81	63	3	.242	.442
Mark McLemore (EJ)	2B63 3B3 DH1	B	23	77	233	38	56	11	2	2	16	25	28	13	.240	.330
Darrell Miller	C53 OF8 DH1	R	30	70	140	21	31	4	1	2	7	9	29	2	.221	.307
George Hendrick	OF24 1B12 DH3	R	38	69	127	12	31	1	0	3	19	7	20	0	.244	.323
Jim Eppard	OF 17 DH10 1B6	L	28	56	113	7	32	3	1	0	14	11	15	0	.283	.327
Gus Polidor	SS25 3B22 2B3 DH1	R	26	54	81	4	12	3	0	0	4	3	11	0	.148	.185
2 Thad Bosley	OF26 DH2	L	31	35	75	9	21	5	0	0	7	6	12	1	.280	.347
Chico Walker	OF17 2B7 3B2	B	30	33	78	8	12	1	0	0	2	6	15	2	.154	.167
Butch Wynagar (FJ)	C26	B	32	27	55	8	14	1	1	1	8	8	7	0	.255	.418
Dante Bichette	OF21	R	24	21	46	1	12	2	0	0	8	0	7	0	.261	.304
Junior Noboa	2B9 SS3 3B2	R	23	21	16	4	1	0	0	0	0	0	1	0	.063	.063
1 Bill Buckner	DH11 1B1	L	38	19	43	1	9	0	0	0	9	4	0	2	.209	.209
Mike Brown	OF18	R	28	18	50	4	11	2	0	0	3	1	6	0	.220	.260
2 Domingo Ramos	3B8	R	30	10	15	3	2	0	0	0	0	0	1	0	.133	.133
Brian Dorsett (EJ)	C7	R	27	7	11	0	1	0	0	0	2	1	5	0	.091	.091
Doug Davis	C3 3B3	R	25	6	12	1	0	0	0	0	0	0	3	0	.000	.000
Joe Redfield	3B1	R	27	1	0	0	0	0	0	0	0	0	0	0	.000	.000

NAME	T	AGE	W	L	PCT	SV	G	GS	CG	IP	H	BB	SO	SHO	ERA
		28	75	87	.463	33	162	162	26	1455	1503	568	817	9	4.32
Mike Witt	R	27	13	16	.448	0	34	34	12	250	263	87	133	2	4.15
Willie Fraser	R	24	12	13	.480	0	34	32	2	195	203	80	86	0	5.41
Chuck Finley	L	25	9	15	.375	0	31	31	2	194	191	82	111	0	4.17
Kirk McCaskill (AJ)	R	27	8	6	.571	0	23	23	4	146	155	61	98	2	4.31
Bryan Harvey	R	25	7	5	.583	17	50	0	0	76	59	20	67	0	2.13
Terry Clark	R	27	6	6	.500	0	15	15	2	94	120	31	39	1	5.07
Donnie Moore (KJ)	R	34	5	2	.714	4	27	0	0	33	48	8	22	0	4.91
Stew Clburn	R	31	4	2	.667	0	40	1	0	84	83	32	42	0	4.07
Greg Minton (EJ)	R	36	4	5	.444	7	44	0	0	79	67	34	46	0	2.85
Dan Petry (NJ)	R	29	3	9	.250	0	22	22	4	140	139	59	64	1	4.38
Sherman Corbett	L	25	2	1	.667	1	34	0	0	46	47	23	28	0	4.14
DeWayne Buice (LJ)	R	30	2	4	.333	3	32	0	0	41	45	19	38	0	5.88
Frank DiMichele	L	23	0	0	—	0	4	0	0	5	5	2	1	0	9.64
Rich Monteleone	R	25	0	0	—	0	3	0	0	4	4	1	3	0	0.00
Urbano Lugo	R	25	0	0	—	0	1	0	0	2	2	1	1	0	9.00
Vance Lovelace	L	24	0	0	—	0	3	0	1	2	3	0	0	0	13.50
Jack Lazorko	R	32	0	1	.000	0	10	3	0	38	37	16	19	0	3.35
Ray Krawczyk	R	28	0	1	.000	1	14	1	0	24	29	8	17	0	4.81
Mike Cook	R	24	0	1	.000	0	4	4	1	2	4	1	2	0	4.91

CHICAGO — 5th 71-90 .441 32.5 JIM FREGOSI

Name	G by Pos	B	AGE	G	AB	R	H	2B	3B	HR	RBI	BB	SO	SB	BA	SA
TOTALS			28	161	5449	631	1327	224	35	132	573	446	908	98	.244	.370
Greg Walker (IL)	1B98	L	28	99	377	45	93	22	1	8	42	29	77	0	.247	.374
Fred Manrique	2B 129 SS12 DH1	R	27	140	345	43	81	10	6	5	37	21	54	6	.235	.342
Ozzie Guillen	SS156	R	24	156	566	58	148	16	7	0	39	25	40	25	.261	.314
Steve Lyons	3B128 OF14 2B4 C2 1B1	L	28	146	472	59	127	28	3	5	45	32	59	1	.269	.373
Ivan Calderon (SJ)	OF67 DH3	R	26	73	264	40	56	14	0	14	35	34	66	4	.212	.424
Dave Gallagher	OF95 DH2	R	27	101	347	59	105	15	3	5	31	29	40	5	.303	.406
Dan Pasqua	OF112 1B7 DH2	L	26	129	422	48	96	16	2	20	50	46	100	1	.227	.417
Carlton Fisk (BH)	C74	R	40	76	253	37	70	8	1	19	50	37	40	0	.277	.542
Harold Baines	DH147 OF9	L	29	158	599	55	166	39	1	13	81	67	109	0	.277	.411
Daryl Boston	OF85 DH5	L	25	105	281	37	61	12	2	15	31	21	44	9	.217	.434
Donnie Hill	2B59 3B12 DH5	R	27	83	221	17	48	6	1	2	20	26	32	3	.217	.281
1 Gary Redus	OF68 DH2	R	31	77	262	42	69	10	4	6	34	33	52	26	.263	.401
Mark Sales	OF69 DH1	R	27	75	196	17	49	7	0	3	9	12	17	0	.250	.332
Kenny Williams (NJ)	OF38 3B32 DH3	R	24	73	220	18	35	4	2	8	28	10	64	6	.159	.305
Ron Karkovice	C46	R	24	46	115	10	20	4	0	3	9	7	30	4	.174	.287
2 Mike Diaz	SS21 2B4 DH1 1B1 3B1	R	28	40	152	12	36	6	0	3	12	5	30	0	.237	.336
Russ Morman	1B22 OF10 DH3	R	26	40	75	8	18	2	0	0	3	3	17	0	.240	.267
Lance Johnson	OF31	L	24	33	124	11	23	4	1	0	6	6	11	6	.185	.234
Mike Woodard	2B14 DH2	L	28	18	45	3	6	0	1	0	4	1	5	1	.133	.178
Carlos Martinez	3B15 DH2	R	22	17	55	5	9	1	0	0	0	0	12	1	.164	.182
Kelly Paris (EJ)	1B9 3B4 DH1	R	30	14	44	6	11	0	0	3	6	0	6	0	.250	.455
Sap Randall	1B2 OF1 DH1	R	27	4	12	1	0	0	0	0	1	2	3	0	.000	.000
Jerry Hairston		B	36	2	2	0	0	0	0	0	0	0	0	0	.000	.000

NAME	T	AGE	W	L	PCT	SV	G	GS	CG	IP	H	BB	SO	SHO	ERA
		26	71	90	.441	43	161	161	11	1439	1467	533	754	9	4.12
Jerry Reuss	L	39	13	9	.591	0	32	29	2	183	183	43	73	0	3.44
Melido Perez	R	22	12	10	.545	0	32	32	3	197	186	72	138	1	3.79
1 Dave LaPoint	L	28	10	11	.476	0	25	25	1	161	151	47	79	1	3.40
Bill Long	R	28	8	11	.421	2	47	18	3	174	187	43	77	0	4.03
1 Ricky Horton	L	28	6	10	.375	2	52	9	1	109	120	36	28	0	4.80
Bobby Thigpen	R	24	5	8	.385	34	68	0	0	90	96	33	62	0	3.30
Jack McDowell (EJ)	R	22	5	10	.333	0	26	26	1	159	147	68	84	0	3.97
2 Shawn Hillegas	R	23	3	2	.600	0	6	6	0	40	30	18	26	0	3.15
Tom McCarthy	R	27	2	0	1.000	0	9	0	0	13	9	2	5	0	1.38
2 Barry Jones	R	24	2	2	.500	1	17	0	0	26	15	17	17	0	2.42
Jeff Bittiger	R	26	2	4	.333	0	25	7	0	62	59	29	33	0	4.23
John Davis	R	25	2	5	.286	1	34	1	0	64	77	50	37	0	6.64
John Pawlowski	R	24	1	0	1.000	0	6	0	0	14	20	3	10	0	8.36
Carl Willis	R	27	1	0	—	0	12	0	0	12	17	7	6	0	8.25
Jose Segura	R	25	0	0	—	0	4	0	0	9	19	8	2	0	13.50
Steve Rosenberg	L	23	0	1	—	1	33	0	0	46	53	19	28	0	4.30
Joel Davis	R	23	0	1	—	0	5	2	0	16	21	5	10	0	6.75
Ravelo Manzanillo	L	24	0	1	—	0	2	0	0	2	7	12	10	0	5.79
Adam Peterson	R	22	0	1	—	0	2	2	0	6	5	1	6	0	3.00
Donn Pall	R	26	0	2	—	0	17	0	0	29	39	8	16	0	3.45
Ken Patterson	L	23	0	2	.000	0	2	1	0	21	25	7	8	0	4.79

TEXAS — 6th 70-91 .435 33.5 BOBBY VALENTINE

Name	G by Pos	B	AGE	G	AB	R	H	2B	3B	HR	RBI	BB	SO	SB	BA	SA
TOTALS			26	161	5479	637	1378	227	39	112	589	542	1022	130	.252	.368
Pete O'Brien	1B155 DH1	L	30	156	547	57	149	24	1	16	71	72	73	1	.272	.408
Curt Wilkerson	2B87 SS24 3B11 DH1	B	27	117	338	41	99	12	5	0	28	26	43	9	.293	.358
Scott Fletcher	SS138	R	29	140	515	59	142	19	4	0	47	62	34	8	.276	.328
Steve Buechele	3B153 2B2	R	26	155	503	68	126	21	4	16	58	65	79	2	.250	.424
Ruben Sierra	OF153 DH1	B	22	156	615	77	156	32	2	23	91	44	91	18	.254	.424
Oddibe McDowell	OF153 DH1	L	25	120	437	55	108	19	5	6	37	41	89	33	.247	.355
Pete Incaviglia (HJ)	OF93 DH21	R	24	116	418	59	104	19	3	22	54	39	153	6	.249	.467
Geno Petralli	C85 DH23 3B9 1B2 2B2	L	28	129	351	35	99	14	2	7	36	41	52	0	.282	.393
1 Larry Parrish	DH67	R	34	68	248	22	47	9	1	7	26	20	79	0	.190	.319
Cecil Espy	OF98 DH12 SS3 C2 2B1 1B1	B	25	123	347	46	86	17	6	2	39	20	83	33	.248	.349
Mike Stanley	C64 DH18 1B7 3B2	R	21	94	249	21	57	8	0	3	27	37	62	0	.229	.297
Bob Brower	OF59 DH1	R	28	82	201	29	45	7	0	1	11	27	38	10	.224	.274
Jerry Browne	2B70	B	22	73	214	26	49	9	2	1	17	25	32	7	.229	.304
Jeff Kunkel	2B28 SS12 3B10 OF6 DH3 P1	R	26	55	154	14	35	8	3	2	15	4	35	0	.227	.357
2 Jim Sundberg	C36	R	37	38	91	13	26	4	0	4	13	5	17	0	.286	.462
James Steels	OF17 DH1	R	26	36	53	4	10	1	0	0	5	0	15	2	.189	.208
Barbaro Garbey (VJ)	OF8 1B7 DH7 3B3	R	31	30	62	4	12	2	0	0	5	3	7	0	.194	.226
Chad Kreuter	C16	B	23	16	51	3	14	2	1	1	5	7	13	0	.275	.412
Steve Kemp	DH7 OF5 1B1	L	33	16	36	2	8	0	0	0	2	6	9	1	.222	.222
Larry See	DH7 1B2 C2 3B1	R	28	13	23	0	3	0	0	1	3	0	3	0	.130	.130
Kevin Reimer	DH7	R	24	12	25	2	3	0	0	0	0	1	8	0	.120	.240

NAME	T	AGE	W	L	PCT	SV	G	GS	CG	IP	H	BB	SO	SHO	ERA
		28	70	91	.435	31	161	161	41	1438	1310	654	912	11	4.05
Charlie Hough	R	40	15	16	.484	0	34	34	10	252	202	126	174	0	3.32
Paul Kilgus	L	26	12	15	.444	0	32	32	5	203	190	71	88	3	4.16
Jose Guzman	R	25	11	13	.458	0	30	30	6	207	180	82	157	2	3.70
Jeff Russell	R	26	10	9	.526	0	34	24	5	189	183	66	88	0	3.82
Bobby Witt	R	24	8	10	.444	0	22	22	13	174	134	101	148	2	3.92
Ray Hayward (SJ)	L	27	4	6	.400	0	12	12	1	63	63	35	37	1	5.46
Craig McMurty	R	28	3	4	.500	3	32	0	0	60	37	24	35	0	2.25
Ed Vande Berg	L	29	2	2	.500	2	26	0	0	37	44	11	18	0	4.14
1 Dale Mohorcic	R	32	2	6	.250	5	43	0	0	52	62	20	25	0	4.85
Mitch Williams	L	23	2	7	.222	18	67	0	0	68	48	47	61	0	4.63
Kevin Brown	R	23	1	1	.500	0	4	4	1	23	33	8	12	0	4.24
Jose Cecena (EJ)	R	24	0	0	—	1	22	0	0	20	20	23	27	0	4.78
Guy Hoffman	L	31	0	0	—	0	11	0	0	22	22	8	9	0	5.24
DeWayne Vaughn	R	28	0	0	—	0	8	0	0	15	24	4	8	0	7.63
Steve Wilson	L	23	0	0	—	0	2	2	0	8	8	4	4	0	5.87
Scott May	R	26	0	0	—	0	3	0	0	4	4	1	4	0	8.59
Tony Fossas	L	30	0	0	—	0	5	0	0	4	4	4	4	0	4.76
2 Cecelio Guante	R	28	0	0	—	0	7	0	0	5	8	1	6	0	1.93
Jeff Kunkel	R	26	0	0	.000	0	1	0	0	1	0	1	0	0	0.00
Dwayne Henry	R	26	0	0	.000	0	11	0	0	11	9	15	10	0	8.71
Mike Jeffcoat	L	28	0	1	.000	0	11	0	0	5	4	5	1	0	11.70
Brad Arnsberg (EJ) 24															
Ed Correa (SJ) 22															

SEATTLE — 7th 68-93 .420 35.5 DICK WILLIAMS 23-33 .411 JIMMY SNYDER 45-60 .429

Name	G by Pos	B	AGE	G	AB	R	H	2B	3B	HR	RBI	BB	SO	SB	BA	SA
TOTALS			27	161	5436	664	1397	271	24	148	617	461	787	95	.257	.398
Alvin Davis	1B115 DH25	L	27	140	478	67	141	24	1	18	69	95	53	1	.295	.462
Harold Reynolds	2B158	B	27	158	598	61	169	26	11	4	41	51	51	35	.283	.383
Rey Quinones	SS135 DH4	R	24	140	499	63	124	30	3	12	52	23	71	0	.248	.393
Jim Presley	3B146 DH4	R	26	150	544	50	125	26	0	14	62	36	114	3	.230	.355
1 Glenn Wilson	OF75 DH2	R	29	98	284	29	71	10	1	3	17	15	52	1	.250	.324
Henry Cotto	OF120 DH2	R	27	133	386	50	100	18	1	8	33	23	52	27	.259	.373
Mickey Brantley	OF147 DH2	R	27	149	577	76	152	26	4	15	56	26	64	18	.263	.399
Dave Valle (WJ)	C84 DH13 DH2	R	27	93	290	29	67	15	2	10	50	18	30	0	.231	.400
2 Steve Balboni	DH56 1B40	R	31	97	350	44	88	15	1	21	61	23	67	0	.251	.480
Scott Bradley	C85 DH4 OF4 3B1 1B2	L	28	103	335	45	86	17	1	4	33	17	16	1	.257	.349
1 Ken Phelps	DH64 1B3	L	33	72	190	37	54	8	0	14	32	51	35	1	.284	.547
2 Jay Buhner	OF59	R	23	60	192	28	43	13	1	10	25	25	68	1	.224	.458
Mike Kingery	OF44 1B10	L	27	57	123	21	25	6	0	1	9	19	23	3	.203	.276
2 Darnell Coles	OF47 DH7 1B1	R	26	55	195	32	57	10	1	10	34	17	26	3	.292	.508
Bruce Fields	OF23 DH6	L	27	39	67	8	18	5	0	1	5	4	11	0	.269	.388
Rich Renteria	DH12 SS11 3B5 1B2	R	26	31	88	6	18	9	0	0	5	6	13	1	.205	.307
Mario Diaz	SS21 2B4 1B1 3B1	R	30	28	72	6	22	5	0	0	2	3	6	0	.306	.375
Dave Hengal	OF12 DH12	R	26	26	60	3	10	1	0	2	7	1	15	0	.167	.283
Edgar Martinez	3B13	R	25	14	32	0	9	4	0	0	5	4	7	0	.281	.406
Greg Briley	OF11	L	23	13	36	6	9	2	0	1	4	5	9	0	.250	.389
Bill McGuire	C9	R	24	9	16	1	3	0	0	0	2	3	6	0	.188	.188
John Rabb	DH5 OF2 1B4	R	29	8	14	2	5	2	0	0	2	0	4	0	.357	.500
Brick Smith	1B4	R	29	4	10	1	1	0	0	0	1	0	3	0	.100	.100

NAME	T	AGE	W	L	PCT	SV	G	GS	CG	IP	H	BB	SO	SHO	ERA
		27	68	93	.422	28	161	161	28	1428	1385	558	981	11	4.15
Mark Langston	L	27	15	11	.577	0	35	35	9	261	222	110	235	3	3.34
Mike Moore	R	28	9	15	.375	0	37	32	9	229	196	63	182	3	3.78
Bill Swift	R	26	8	12	.400	0	38	24	6	175	199	65	47	1	4.59
Scott Bankhead (SJ-VJ)	R	24	7	9	.438	0	21	21	2	135	115	38	102	1	3.07
Mike Jackson	R	23	6	5	.545	4	62	0	0	99	74	43	76	0	2.63
Mike Campbell	R	24	6	10	.375	0	20	20	2	115	128	43	63	0	5.89
Mike Schooler	R	25	5	8	.385	15	40	0	0	48	45	24	54	0	3.54
Steve Trout (BG-AJ)	L	30	4	7	.364	0	15	13	0	56	86	31	14	0	7.83
Bill Wilkinson (SJ)	L	23	2	3	.400	3	30	0	0	31	35	15	25	0	3.88
Erik Hanson	R	23	2	3	.400	0	6	6	0	42	35	12	36	0	3.24
2 Gene Walter	L	27	1	0	—	0	16	0	0	26	21	15	13	0	5.13
Jerry Reed	R	33	1	1	.500	1	46	0	0	86	82	33	48	0	3.96
Dennis Powell	L	24	1	3	.250	0	12	9	0	19	29	11	15	0	8.68
1 Edwin Nunez	R	25	1	4	.200	0	14	3	0	29	45	14	19	0	7.98
Julio Solano	R	28	0	0	—	3	17	0	0	22	22	12	10	0	4.09
Terry Taylor	R	23	0	1	.000	0	5	5	0	23	26	11	9	0	6.26
Rod Scurry	L	32	0	0	.000	2	39	0	0	37	32	18	33	0	4.02

NEW YORK 1st 100-60 .625 DAVEY JOHNSON

Name	G by Pos	B	AGE	G	AB	R	H	2B	3B	HR	RBI	BB	SO	SB	BA	SA
TOTALS			26	160	5408	703	1387	251	24	152	659	544	842	140	.256	.395
Keith Hernandez (LJ)	1B93	L	34	95	348	43	96	16	0	11	55	31	57	2	.276	.417
Wally Backman	2B92	B	28	99	294	44	89	12	0	0	17	41	49	9	.303	.344
Kevin Elster	SS148	R	23	149	406	41	87	11	1	9	37	35	47	2	.214	.313
Howard Johnson	3B 131 SS52	B	27	148	495	85	114	21	1	24	68	86	104	23	.230	.422
Darryl Strawberry	OF150	L	26	153	543	101	146	27	3	39	101	85	127	29	.269	.545
Lenny Dykstra	OF112	L	25	126	429	57	116	19	3	8	33	30	43	30	.270	.385
Kevin McReynolds	OF147	R	28	147	552	82	159	30	2	27	99	38	56	21	.288	.496
Gary Carter	C119 3B1 1B10	R	34	130	455	39	110	16	2	11	46	34	52	0	.242	.358
Mookie Wilson	OF104	B	32	112	378	61	112	17	5	8	41	27	63	15	.296	.431
Dave Magadan	3B48 1B71	L	25	112	314	39	87	15	0	1	35	60	39	0	.277	.334
Tim Teufel	2B84 1B3	R	29	90	273	35	64	20	0	4	31	29	41	0	.234	.352
Lee Mazzilli	OF18 1B16	B	33	68	116	9	17	2	0	0	12	12	16	4	.147	.164
Mackey Sasser	OF1 C42 3B1	L	25	60	123	9	35	10	1	1	17	6	9	0	.285	.407
Barry Lyons	C32 1B1	R	28	50	91	5	21	7	1	0	11	3	12	0	.231	.330
Keith Miller	2B16 SS8 3B6 OF1	R	25	40	70	9	15	1	1	1	5	6	10	0	.214	.300
Gregg Jefferies	3B20 2B10	B	20	29	109	19	35	8	2	6	17	8	10	5	.321	.596
Mark Carreon	OF4	R	24	7	9	5	5	2	0	1	1	2	1	0	.556	1.111

NAME	T	AGE	W	L	PCT	SV	G	GS	CG	IP	H	BB	SO	SHO	ERA
		27	100	60	.625	46	160	160	31	1439	1253	404	1100	22	2.91
David Cone	R	25	20	3	.870	0	35	28	8	231	178	80	213	4	2.22
Dwight Gooden	R	23	18	9	.667	0	34	34	10	248	242	57	175	3	3.19
Ron Darling	R	27	17	9	.654	0	34	34	7	241	218	60	161	4	3.25
Sid Fernandez	L	25	12	10	.545	0	31	31	1	187	127	70	189	1	3.03
Bob Ojeda	L	30	10	13	.435	0	29	29	5	190	158	33	133	5	2.88
Terry Leach	R	34	7	2	.778	3	52	0	0	92	95	24	51	0	2.54
Randy Meyers	L	25	7	3	.700	26	55	0	0	68	45	17	69	0	1.72
Roger McDowell	R	27	5	5	.500	16	62	0	0	89	80	31	46	0	2.63
2 Edwin Nunez	R	25	1	0	1.000	0	10	0	0	14	21	3	8	0	4.50
2 Bob McClure	L	36	1	0	1.000	1	14	0	0	11	12	2	7	0	4.09
David West	L	23	1	0	1.000	0	2	1	0	6	6	3	3	0	3.00
Jeff Innis	R	25	1	1	.500	0	12	0	0	19	19	2	14	0	1.89
John Mitchell	R	22	0	0	—	0	1	0	0	1	1	1	0	0	0.00
1 Gene Walter	L	27	0	1	.000	0	17	0	0	17	21	11	14	0	3.78
Rick Aguilera (EJ)	R	26	0	4	.000	0	11	3	0	25	29	16	15	0	6.93

PITTSBURGH 2nd 85-75 .531 15 JIM LEYLAND

Name	G by Pos	B	AGE	G	AB	R	H	2B	3B	HR	RBI	BB	SO	SB	BA	SA
TOTALS			26	160	5379	651	1327	240	45	110	619	553	947	119	.247	.369
Sid Bream	1B138	L	27	148	462	50	122	37	0	10	65	47	64	9	.264	.409
Jose Lind	2B153	R	24	154	611	82	160	24	4	2	49	42	75	15	.262	.324
Rafael Belliard	SS117 2B3	R	26	122	286	28	61	0	4	0	11	26	47	7	.213	.241
Bobby Bonilla	3B159	B	25	159	584	87	160	32	7	24	100	85	82	3	.274	.476
R.J. Reynolds	OF95	B	29	130	323	35	80	14	2	6	51	20	62	15	.248	.359
Andy Van Slyke	OF152	L	27	154	587	101	169	23	15	25	100	57	126	30	.288	.506
Barry Bonds	OF136	L	23	144	538	97	152	30	5	24	58	72	82	17	.283	.491
Mike La Valliere	C114	L	27	120	352	24	92	18	0	2	47	50	34	3	.261	.330
John Cangelosi	OF24 P1	B	25	75	118	18	30	4	1	0	8	17	16	9	.254	.305
1 Darnell Coles	OF55 3B1 1B1	R	26	68	211	20	49	13	1	5	36	20	41	1	.232	.374
Al Pedrique	SS44 3B5	R	27	50	128	7	23	5	0	0	4	8	17	0	.180	.219
Junior Ortiz (BC)	C40	R	28	49	118	8	33	6	0	2	18	9	9	1	.280	.381
1 Mike Diaz (RJ)	OF19 1B6 C1	R	28	47	74	6	17	3	0	0	5	16	13	0	.230	.270
Felix Fermin	SS43	R	24	43	87	9	24	0	2	0	2	8	3	0	.276	.322
Randy Milligan	1B25 OF1	R	26	40	82	10	18	5	0	3	8	20	24	1	.220	.390
2 Glenn Wilson	OF35	R	29	37	126	11	34	8	0	2	15	3	18	0	.270	.381
Orestes Destrade	1B8	B	26	36	47	2	7	1	0	1	3	5	17	0	.149	.234
2 Gary Redus	OF19	R	31	30	71	12	14	2	0	2	4	15	19	5	.197	.310
Tom Prince	C28	R	23	29	74	3	13	2	0	0	6	4	15	0	.176	.203
Denny Gonzalez	SS14 2B4 3B2	R	24	24	32	5	6	1	0	0	1	6	10	0	.188	.219
1 Ken Oberkfell	2B11 3B2	L	32	20	54	7	12	2	0	0	2	5	6	0	.222	.259
Benny Distefano	1B5 OF2	L	26	16	29	6	10	3	1	1	6	3	4	0	.345	.621
1 Tommy Gregg	OF6	L	24	14	15	4	3	1	0	1	3	1	4	0	.200	.467
Dave Hostetler	1B4 C1	R	32	6	8	0	2	0	0	0	0	1	4	0	.250	.250
Ruben Rodriguez	C2	R	23	5	5	1	1	0	1	0	1	0	2	0	.200	.600

NAME	T	AGE	W	L	PCT	SV	G	GS	CG	IP	H	BB	SO	SHO	ERA
		26	85	75	.531	46	160	160	12	1440	1349	469	790	11	3.47
Doug Drabek	R	25	15	7	.682	0	33	32	3	219	194	50	127	1	3.08
John Smiley	L	23	13	11	.542	0	34	32	5	205	185	46	129	1	3.25
Bob Walk	R	31	12	10	.545	0	32	32	1	213	183	65	81	1	2.71
Jeff Robinson	R	27	11	5	.688	9	75	0	0	125	113	39	87	0	3.03
Brian Fisher	R	26	8	10	.444	1	33	22	1	146	157	57	66	1	4.61
Mike Dunne	R	25	7	11	.389	0	30	28	1	170	163	88	70	0	3.92
Jim Gott	R	28	6	6	.500	34	67	0	0	77	68	22	76	0	3.49
2 Dave LaPoint	L	28	4	2	.667	0	8	8	1	52	54	10	19	0	2.77
Scott Medvin	R	26	3	0	1.000	0	17	0	0	28	23	9	16	0	4.88
Bob Kipper	L	23	2	6	.250	0	50	0	0	65	54	26	39	0	3.74
Rick Reed	R	23	1	0	1.000	0	2	2	0	12	10	2	6	0	3.00
1 Barry Jones	R	25	1	1	.500	2	42	0	0	56	57	21	31	0	3.04
Vicente Palacios	R	24	1	2	.333	0	7	3	0	24	28	15	15	0	6.66
Randy Kramer	R	27	1	2	.333	0	5	1	0	10	12	1	7	0	5.40
Morris Madden	L	27	0	0	—	0	6	0	0	6	5	7	3	0	0.00
John Cangelosi	L	25	0	0	—	0	1	0	0	2	3	2	0	0	4.50
Miguel Garcia	L	21	0	0	—	0	1	0	0	2	1	2	2	0	4.50
Dave Rucker	L	30	0	2	.000	0	31	0	0	28	39	9	16	0	4.76

MONTREAL 3rd 81-81 .500 19 BUCK RODGERS

Name	G by Pos	B	AGE	G	AB	R	H	2B	3B	HR	RBI	BB	SO	SB	BA	SA
TOTALS			22	163	5573	628	1400	260	48	107	575	454	1053	189	.251	.373
Andres Galarraga	1B156	R	27	157	609	99	184	42	8	29	92	39	153	13	.302	.540
Tom Foley	2B89 SS32 3B9	L	28	127	377	33	100	21	3	5	43	30	49	2	.265	.377
Luis Rivera	SS116	R	24	123	371	35	83	17	3	4	30	24	69	3	.224	.318
Tim Wallach	3B153 2B1	R	30	159	592	52	152	32	5	12	69	38	88	2	.257	.389
Hubie Brooks	OF149	R	31	151	588	61	164	35	2	20	90	35	108	7	.279	.447
Otis Nixon	OF82	B	29	90	271	47	66	8	2	0	15	28	42	46	.244	.288
Tim Raines (SJ)	OF108	B	28	109	429	66	116	19	7	12	48	53	44	33	.270	.431
Nelson Santovenia	C86 1B1	R	26	92	309	26	73	20	2	8	41	24	77	2	.236	.392
Wallace Johnson	1B13 2B1	B	31	86	94	7	29	5	1	0	3	12	15	0	.309	.383
1 Mitch Webster	OF71	B	29	81	259	33	66	5	2	2	13	36	37	12	.255	.313
Graig Nettles	3B12 1B5	L	43	80	93	5	16	4	0	1	14	9	19	0	.172	.247
Rex Hudler	2B41 SS27 OF4	R	27	77	216	38	59	14	2	4	14	10	34	29	.273	.412
2 Dave Martinez	OF60	L	23	63	191	24	49	3	5	2	12	17	48	16	.257	.356
Mike Fitzgerald	C47 OF4	R	27	63	155	17	42	5	2	1	23	19	22	2	.271	.419
2 Tracy Jones	OF43	R	27	53	141	20	47	5	1	2	15	12	12	9	.333	.426
1 Herm Winningham	OF30	L	26	47	90	10	21	2	1	0	6	12	18	4	.233	.278
1 Jeff Reed	C39	L	25	43	123	10	27	3	2	0	9	13	22	1	.220	.275
1 Casey Candaele	2B35	B	27	36	116	9	20	5	1	0	4	10	11	1	.172	.233
Johnny Paredes	2B28 OF1	R	25	35	91	6	17	2	0	1	10	9	17	5	.187	.242
Dave Engle	C9 OF4 3B1	R	31	34	37	4	8	3	0	1	5	5	5	0	.216	.297
Jeff Huson	SS15 2B2 OF1 3B1	L	23	20	42	7	13	2	0	0	3	4	3	2	.310	.357
Tom O'Malley	3B7	L	27	14	27	3	7	0	0	0	2	3	4	0	.259	.259
Wil Tejada	C7	R	25	8	15	1	4	2	0	0	1	0	3	0	.267	.400

NAME	T	AGE	W	L	PCT	SV	G	GS	CG	IP	H	BB	SO	SHO	ERA
		30	81	81	.500	43	163	163	18	1482	1310	476	923	12	3.08
Dennis Martinez	R	33	15	13	.536	0	34	34	9	235	215	55	120	2	2.72
Jeff Parrett (RJ)	R	26	12	4	.750	6	61	0	0	92	66	45	62	0	2.65
Pascual Perez (BG)	R	31	12	8	.600	0	27	27	4	188	133	44	131	2	2.44
Bryn Smith	R	32	12	10	.545	0	32	32	1	198	179	32	122	0	3.00
Andy McGaffigan	R	31	6	0	1.000	4	63	0	0	91	81	37	71	0	2.76
Joe Hesketh	L	29	4	3	.571	9	60	0	0	73	63	35	64	0	2.85
Brian Holman	R	23	4	8	.333	0	18	16	1	100	101	34	58	1	3.23
Randy Johnson	L	24	3	0	1.000	0	4	4	1	26	23	7	25	0	2.42
Tim Burke	R	29	3	5	.375	18	61	0	0	82	84	25	42	0	3.40
Floyd Youmans (SD)	R	24	3	6	.333	0	14	13	1	84	64	41	54	1	3.21
Neal Heaton	L	28	3	10	.231	2	32	11	0	97	98	43	43	0	4.99
John Dopson	R	24	3	11	.214	0	26	26	1	169	150	58	101	0	3.04
1 Bob McClure	L	36	1	3	.250	2	19	0	0	19	23	6	12	0	6.16
Tim Barrett	R	27	0	0	—	1	4	0	0	9	10	2	5	0	5.79
Mike Smith	R	27	0	0	—	0	1	0	0	5	6	4	3	0	3.12
1 Randy St. Claire	R	27	0	0	—	0	6	0	0	7	11	5	6	0	6.14
Rick Sauverur	L	24	0	0	—	0	4	0	0	3	2	3	0	0	6.00

CHICAGO 4th 77-85 .475 24 DON ZIMMER

Name	G by Pos	B	AGE	G	AB	R	H	2B	3B	HR	RBI	BB	SO	SB	BA	SA
TOTALS			28	163	5675	660	1481	262	46	113	612	403	910	120	.261	.383
Mark Grace	1B133	L	24	134	486	65	144	23	4	7	57	60	43	3	.296	.403
Ryne Sandberg	2B153	R	28	155	618	77	163	23	8	19	69	54	91	25	.264	.419
Shawon Dunston	SS151	R	25	155	575	69	143	23	6	9	56	16	108	30	.249	.357
Vance Law	3B150 OF1	R	31	151	556	73	163	29	2	11	78	55	79	1	.293	.412
Andre Dawson	OF147	R	33	157	591	78	179	31	8	24	79	37	73	12	.303	.504
2 Dave Martinez	OF72	L	23	75	256	27	65	10	1	4	34	21	46	7	.254	.348
Rafael Palmeiro	OF147 1B5	L	23	152	580	75	178	41	5	8	53	38	34	12	.307	.436
Damon Berryhill	C90	B	24	95	309	19	80	19	1	7	38	17	56	1	.259	.395
Darrin Jackson	OF74	R	25	100	188	29	50	11	3	6	20	5	28	4	.266	.452
1 Jody Davis	C74	R	31	88	249	19	57	9	0	6	33	29	51	0	.229	.337
Manny Trillo	1B24 3B17 2B13 SS7	R	37	76	164	15	41	5	0	1	14	8	32	2	.250	.299
2 Mitch Webster	OF65	B	29	70	264	36	70	11	6	4	26	19	50	10	.265	.398
Jerry Mumphrey	OF4	B	35	63	66	3	9	2	0	0	9	7	16	0	.136	.167
Gary Varsho	OF18	L	27	46	73	6	20	3	0	0	5	1	6	5	.274	.315
Angel Salazar	SS29 2B2 3B1	R	26	34	60	4	15	1	1	0	4	1	11	0	.250	.300
Doug Dascenzo	OF20	B	24	26	75	9	16	3	0	0	4	9	4	6	.213	.253
1 Leon Durham	1B20	L	30	24	73	10	16	6	1	3	6	9	20	0	.219	.452
1 Jim Sundberg	C20	R	37	24	54	8	13	1	0	2	8	8	15	0	.241	.370
Rolando Roomes	OF5	R	26	17	16	3	3	0	0	0	0	0	6	0	.188	.188
Rick Wrona	C2	R	24	4	6	0	0	0	0	0	0	0	1	0	.000	.000
Dave Meier	3B1	R	28	2	5	0	2	0	0	0	1	0	1	0	.400	.400

NAME	T	AGE	W	L	PCT	SV	G	GS	CG	IP	H	BB	SO	SHO	ERA
		28	77	85	.475	29	163	163	30	1464	1494	490	897	10	3.84
Greg Maddux	R	22	18	8	.692	0	34	34	9	249	230	81	140	3	3.18
Rick Sutcliffe	R	32	13	14	.481	0	32	32	12	226	232	70	144	2	3.86
Calvin Schiraldi	R	26	9	13	.409	1	29	27	2	166	166	63	140	1	4.38
Jamie Moyer	L	25	9	15	.375	0	34	30	3	202	212	55	121	1	3.48
Jeff Pico	R	22	6	7	.462	1	29	13	3	113	108	37	57	2	4.15
Goose Gossage	R	36	4	4	.500	13	46	0	0	44	50	15	30	0	4.33
Les Lancaster (BF)	R	26	4	6	.400	5	44	3	1	86	89	34	36	0	3.78
Mike Capel	R	26	2	1	.667	0	22	0	0	29	34	13	19	0	4.91
Mike Bielecki	R	28	2	2	.500	0	19	5	0	48	55	16	33	0	3.35
2 Pat Perry	L	29	2	2	.500	1	35	0	0	48	47	24	24	0	3.32
Frank DiPino	L	31	2	3	.400	6	63	0	0	90	102	32	69	0	4.98
Al Nipper (EJ)	R	29	2	4	.333	1	22	12	0	80	72	34	27	0	3.04
Bill Landrum	R	30	1	0	1.000	0	7	0	0	12	19	3	6	0	5.84
2 Kevin Blankenship	R	25	1	0	1.000	0	1	1	1	7	4	1	4	0	7.20
Drew Hall	L	25	1	1	.500	1	19	0	0	22	26	9	22	0	7.66
Scott Sanderson (XJ)	R	31	1	2	.333	0	11	0	0	15	13	3	6	0	5.28
Bob Tewksbury	R	27	0	0	—	0	1	0	0	3	6	1	1	0	8.10
Mike Harkey	R	21	0	0	—	0	5	5	0	35	33	15	18	0	2.60

ST. LOUIS 5th 76-86 .469 25 WHITEY HERZOG

Name	G by Pos	B	AGE	G	AB	R	H	2B	3B	HR	RBI	BB	SO	SB	BA	SA
TOTALS			28	162	5518	578	1373	207	33	71	536	484	827	234	.249	.337
Bob Horner (SJ)	1B57	R	30	60	206	15	53	9	1	3	33	32	23	0	.257	.354
Hose Oquendo	2B69 3B47 SS17 1B16 OF15 C1 P1	B	24	148	451	36	125	10	1	7	46	52	40	4	.277	.350
Ozzie Smith	SS150	B	33	153	575	80	155	27	1	3	51	74	43	57	.270	.336
Terry Pendleton (LJ)	3B101	B	27	110	391	44	99	20	2	6	53	21	51	3	.253	.361
2 Tom Brunansky	OF143	R	27	143	523	69	128	22	4	22	79	79	82	16	.245	.428
Willie McGee	OF135	R	29	137	562	73	164	24	6	3	50	32	84	41	.292	.372
Vince Coleman	OF150	B	27	153	616	77	160	20	10	3	38	49	111	81	.260	.339
Tony Pena	C142 1B3	R	31	149	505	55	133	23	1	10	51	33	60	6	.263	.372
Luis Alicea	2B91	B	22	93	297	20	63	10	4	1	24	25	32	1	.212	.283
Curt Ford	OF40 1B7	L	27	91	128	11	25	6	0	1	18	8	26	6	.195	.266
Tom Pagnozzi	C28 1B28 3B5	R	25	81	195	17	55	9	0	0	15	11	32	0	.282	.328
Tom Lawless	3B24 OF6 2B5 1B1	R	31	54	65	9	10	2	1	1	3	7	9	6	.154	.262
2 Pedro Guerrero	1B37 OF7	R	32	44	149	16	40	7	1	5	30	21	26	2	.268	.430
Mike Laga (SJ)	1B37	L	28	41	100	5	13	0	0	1	4	2	21	0	.130	.160
Steve Lake	C19	R	31	36	54	5	15	3	0	1	4	3	15	0	.278	.389
Tim Jones	SS9 2B8 3B1	L	25	31	52	2	14	0	0	0	3	4	10	4	.269	.269
Duane Walker	OF4 1B1	L	31	24	22	1	4	1	0	0	3	2	7	0	.182	.227
John Morris (XJ)	OF16	L	27	20	38	3	11	2	1	0	3	1	7	0	.289	.395
2 Denny Walling	3B5 1B1	L	34	19	58	3	13	3	0	0	1	2	7	1	.224	.276
Rod Booker	3B13 2B1	L	29	18	35	6	12	3	0	0	3	4	3	2	.343	.429
Jim Lindeman (XJ)	OF12 1B3	R	26	17	43	3	9	1	0	2	7	2	9	0	.209	.372
1 Tommy Herr	2B15 1B	R	32	15	50	4	13	0	1	0	3	11	4	3	.260	.320
Mike Fitzgerald	1B12	R	24	13	46	4	9	1	0	0	1	0	9	0	.196	.217

NAME	T	AGE	W	L	PCT	SV	G	GS	CG	IP	H	BB	SO	SHO	ERA
		30	76	86	.469	42	162	162	17	1470	1387	486	881	14	3.47
Jose DeLeon	R	27	13	10	.565	0	34	34	3	225	198	86	208	1	3.67
Bob Forsch	R	38	9	4	.692	0	30	12	1	109	111	38	40	1	3.73
1 Scott Terry	R	28	9	6	.600	3	51	11	1	129	119	34	65	0	2.92
1 John Tudor	L	34	6	5	.545	0	21	21	4	145	131	31	55	1	2.29
Larry McWilliams	L	38	6	9	.400	1	42	17	2	136	130	45	70	1	3.90
John Costello	R	27	5	2	.714	5	34	0	0	50	44	25	38	0	1.81
Joe Magrane (UJ)	L	23	5	9	.357	0	24	24	4	165	133	51	100	3	2.18
Todd Worrell	R	28	5	9	.357	32	68	0	0	90	69	34	78	0	3.00
Greg Mathews (SJ)	L	26	4	6	.400	0	13	13	1	68	61	33	31	0	4.24
Steve Peters	L	25	3	3	.500	0	44	0	0	45	57	22	30	0	6.40
Danny Cox (EJ-SJ)	R	28	3	8	.273	0	13	13	0	86	89	25	47	0	3.98
2 Dan Quisenberry	R	35	2	0	1.000	0	33	0	0	38	54	6	19	0	6.16
Randy O'Neal (XJ)	R	27	2	3	.400	0	10	8	0	53	57	10	20	0	4.58
Chris Carpenter	R	23	2	3	.400	0	8	8	1	48	56	9	24	0	4.72
Ken Dayley (XJ)	L	29	2	7	.220	5	54	0	0	55	48	19	38	0	2.77
Scott Arnold	R	25	0	0	—	0	6	0	0	7	9	4	8	0	5.40
Gibson Alba	L	28	0	0	—	0	3	0	0	3	1	2	3	0	2.70
Ken Hill	R	22	0	1	.000	0	4	1	0	14	16	6	6	0	5.14
Jose Oquendo	R	24	0	1	.000	0	4	0	0	4	4	6	1	0	4.50

PHILADELPHIA 6th 65-96 .404 35.5 LEE ELIA 60-92 .395 JOHN VUKOVICH 5-4 .556

Name	G by Pos	B	AGE	G	AB	R	H	2B	3B	HR	RBI	BB	SO	SB	BA	SA
TOTALS			29	162	5403	597	1294	246	31	106	567	489	981	112	.240	.355
Von Hayes (EJ)	1B85 OF16 3B3	L	29	104	367	43	100	28	2	6	45	49	59	20	.272	.409
Juan Samuel	2B152 OF3 3B1	R	27	157	629	68	153	32	9	12	67	39	151	33	.243	.380
Steve Jeltz	SS148	B	29	148	379	39	71	11	4	0	27	59	58	3	.187	.237
Mike Schmidt (SJ)	3B104 1B3	R	38	108	390	52	97	21	2	12	62	49	42	3	.249	.405
Chris James	OF116 3B31	R	25	150	566	57	137	24	1	19	66	31	73	7	.242	.389
Milt Thompson	OF112	L	29	122	378	53	109	16	2	2	33	39	59	17	.288	.357
Phil Bradley	OF153	R	29	154	569	77	160	20	5	11	56	54	106	11	.264	.392
1 Lance Parrish	C117 1B1	R	32	123	424	44	91	17	2	15	60	47	93	0	.215	.370
Greg Gross	OF37 1B14	L	35	98	133	10	27	1	0	0	5	16	3	0	.203	.211
1 Mike Young	OF42	B	28	75	146	13	33	14	0	1	14	26	43	0	.226	.342
Ricky Jordan	1B69	R	23	69	273	41	84	15	1	11	43	7	39	1	.308	.491
Bob Dernier	OF54	R	31	68	166	19	48	3	1	1	10	9	19	13	.289	.337
Darren Daulton (BH)	C44 1B1	L	26	58	144	13	30	6	0	1	12	17	26	2	.208	.271
1 Luis Aguayo	SS27 3B13 2B2	R	29	49	97	9	24	3	0	3	5	13	17	2	.247	.371
Keith Miller	OF4 3B3 SS1	R	25	47	48	4	8	3	0	0	6	5	13	0	.167	.229
Tommy Barrett	2B10	R	24	36	54	5	11	1	0	0	3	7	8	0	.204	.222
Ron Jones	OF32	L	24	33	124	15	36	6	1	8	26	2	14	0	.290	.548
Jackie Gutierrez	SS20 3B13	R	28	33	77	8	19	4	0	0	9	2	9	0	.247	.299
John Russell	C15	R	27	22	49	5	12	1	0	2	4	3	15	0	.245	.388
Bill Almon	3B9 SS5 1B1	R	35	20	26	1	3	2	0	0	1	3	11	0	.115	.192
Shane Turner	3B8 SS5	L	25	18	35	1	6	0	0	0	1	5	9	0	.171	.171
Al Pardo	C2	B	25	2	2	0	0	0	0	0	0	0	2	0	.000	.000

NAME	T	AGE	W	L	PCT	SV	G	GS	CG	IP	H	BB	SO	SHO	ERA
		29	65	96	.404	36	162	162	16	1433	1447	628	859	6	4.14
Kevin Gross	R	27	12	14	.462	0	33	33	5	232	209	89	162	1	3.69
Don Carman	L	28	10	14	.417	0	36	32	2	201	211	70	116	0	4.29
Shane Rawley	L	32	8	16	.333	0	32	32	4	198	220	78	87	1	4.18
David Palmer (SJ)	R	30	7	9	.438	0	22	22	1	129	129	48	85	1	4.47
Steve Bedrosian (IL)	R	30	6	6	.500	28	57	0	0	74	75	27	61	0	3.75
Bruce Ruffin	L	24	6	10	.375	3	55	15	3	144	151	80	82	0	4.43
Mike Maddux	R	26	4	3	.571	0	25	11	0	89	91	34	59	0	3.76
Greg Harris	R	32	4	6	.400	1	66	1	0	107	80	52	71	0	2.36
Kent Tekulve	R	41	3	7	.300	4	70	0	0	80	87	22	43	0	3.60
Marvin Freeman	R	25	2	3	.400	0	11	11	0	52	55	43	37	0	6.10
Alex Madrid	R	25	1	1	.500	0	5	2	1	15	16	5	2	0	2.76
Todd Frohwirth	R	25	1	2	.333	1	12	0	0	12	16	11	11	0	8.25
Bob Sebra	R	26	1	2	.333	0	3	3	0	11	15	10	7	0	7.94
Wally Ritchie	R	22	0	0	—	0	19	0	0	26	19	17	8	0	3.12
2 Bill Scherrer	L	30	0	0	—	0	6	0	0	9	7	7	3	0	5.40
Brad Moore	R	24	0	0	—	0	5	0	0	8	7	2	3	0	0.00
Scott Service	R	21	0	0	—	0	3	0	0	5	7	1	6	0	1.69
Jeff Calhoun (SJ)	L	30	0	0	—	0	3	0	0	4	2	1	1	0	15.43
Danny Clay	R	26	0	1	.000	0	17	0	0	24	27	21	12	0	6.00
Bill Dawley (EJ)	R	30	0	2	.000	0	8	0	0	9	16	4	3	0	13.50

WEST DIVISION

LOS ANGELES 1st 94-67 .584 TOMMY LASORDA

Name	G by Pos	B	AGE	G	AB	R	H	2B	3B	HR	RBI	BB	SO	SB	BA	SA
TOTALS			29	162	5431	628	1346	217	25	99	587	437	947	131	.248	.352
Franklin Stubbs	1B84 OF13	L	27	115	242	30	54	13	0	8	34	23	61	11	.223	.376
Steve Sax	2B158	R	28	160	632	70	175	19	4	5	57	45	51	42	.277	.343
Alfredo Griffin (BW)	SS93	B	30	95	316	39	63	8	3	1	27	24	30	7	.199	.253
Jeff Hamilton (VJ)	3B105 SS2 1B1	R	24	111	309	34	73	14	2	6	33	10	51	0	.236	.353
Mike Marshall	OF90 1B53	R	28	144	542	63	150	27	2	20	82	24	93	4	.277	.445
John Shelby	OF140	B	30	140	494	65	130	23	6	10	64	44	128	16	.263	.395
Kirk Gibson	OF148	L	31	150	542	106	157	28	1	25	76	73	120	31	.290	.483
Mike Scioscia	C123	L	29	130	408	29	105	18	0	3	35	38	31	0	.257	.324
Dave Anderson	SS82 3B12 2B11	R	27	116	285	31	71	10	2	2	20	32	45	4	.249	.319
Mike Davis	aOF76	L	29	108	281	29	55	11	2	2	17	25	59	7	.196	.270
Danny Heep	OF32 1B12 P1	L	30	95	149	14	36	2	0	0	11	22	13	2	.242	.255
Mickey Hatcher	OF29 1B25 3B3	R	33	88	191	22	56	8	0	1	25	7	7	0	.293	.351
Rick Dempsey	C74	R	38	77	167	25	42	13	0	7	30	25	44	1	.251	.455
Tracy Woodson	3B41 1B25	R	25	65	173	15	43	4	1	3	15	7	32	1	.249	.335
1 Pedro Guerrero (ZJ)	3B455 1B15 OF2	R	32	59	215	24	64	7	1	5	35	25	33	2	.298	.409
Mike Sharperson	2B20 3B6 SS4	R	26	46	59	8	16	1	0	0	4	1	12	0	.271	.288
Jose Gonzalez	OF24	R	23	37	24	7	2	1	0	0	4	2	10	3	.083	.125
Mike Devereaux	OF26	R	25	30	43	4	5	1	0	0	4	2	10	0	.116	.140
Chris Gwynn	OF4	L	23	12	11	1	2	1	0	0	0	1	2	0	.182	.182
Gil Reyes	C5	R	24	5	9	1	1	0	0	0	0	0	3	0	.111	.111

NAME	T	AGE	W	L	PCT	SV	G	GS	CG	IP	H	BB	SO	SHO	ERA
		30	94	67	.584	49	162	162	32	1463	1291	473	1029	24	2.96
Orel Hershiser	R	29	23	8	.742	1	35	34	15	267	208	73	178	8	2.26
Tim Leary	R	29	17	11	.607	0	35	34	9	229	201	56	180	6	2.91
Tim Belcher	R	26	12	6	.667	4	36	27	4	180	143	51	152	1	2.91
Brian Holton	R	28	7	3	.700	1	45	0	0	85	69	26	49	0	1.70
Alejandro Pena	R	29	6	7	.462	12	60	0	0	94	75	27	83	0	1.91
Jay Howell	R	32	5	3	.625	21	50	0	0	65	44	21	70	0	2.08
Fernando Valenzuela(SJ)	L	27	5	8	.385	1	23	22	3	142	142	76	64	0	4.24
Tim Crews	R	27	4	0	1.000	0	42	0	0	72	77	16	45	0	3.14
2 John Tudor	L	34	4	3	.571	0	9	9	1	52	58	10	32	0	2.41
Jesse Orosco	L	31	3	2	.600	9	55	0	0	53	51	30	43	0	2.72
1 Shawn Hillegas	R	23	3	4	.429	0	11	10	0	57	54	17	30	0	4.13
Don Sutton (EJ)	R	43	3	6	.333	0	16	16	0	87	91	30	44	0	3.92
1 Ricky Horton	L	28	1	1	.500	0	12	0	0	9	11	2	8	0	5.00
Ramon Martinez	R	20	1	3	.250	0	9	6	0	36	27	22	23	0	3.79
1 Brad Havens	L	28	0	0	—	0	10	0	0	10	15	4	8	0	4.66
Danny Heep	L	30	0	0	—	0	1	0	0	2	2	0	0	0	9.00
Bill Krueger	R	30	0	0	—	0	1	1	0	3	4	2	1	0	11.57
Ken Howell (SJ-KJ)	R	27	0	0	.000	0	13	16	4	12	6	39	0	6.39	
Bill Brennan	R	25	0	1	.000	0	9	0	0	13	6	7	6	0	6.75
2 Mano Soto (SJ) 31															

CINCINNATI 2nd 87-74 .540 7 PETE ROSE

Name	G by Pos	B	AGE	G	AB	R	H	2B	3B	HR	RBI	BB	SO	SB	BA	SA
TOTALS			29	162	5426	641	1334	246	25	122	588	479	922	207	.246	.368
Nick Esasky	1B116	R	28	122	391	40	95	17	2	15	62	48	104	7	.243	.412
Jeff Treadway (SJ)	2B97 3B2	L	25	103	301	30	76	19	4	2	23	27	30	2	.252	.362
Barry Larkin	SS148	R	24	151	588	91	174	32	5	12	56	41	24	40	.296	.429
Chris Sabo	3B135 SS2	R	26	137	538	74	146	40	2	11	44	29	52	46	.271	.414
Paul O'Neill	OF118 1B21	L	25	145	485	58	122	25	3	16	73	38	65	8	.252	.414
Eric Davis	OF130	R	26	135	472	81	129	18	3	26	93	65	124	35	.273	.489
Kal Daniels	OF137	L	24	140	495	95	144	29	1	18	64	87	94	27	.291	.463
Bo Diaz (KJ)	C88	R	35	92	315	26	69	9	0	10	35	7	41	0	.219	.343
Dave Collins	OF35 1B3	B	35	99	174	12	41	6	2	0	14	11	27	7	.236	.293
Dave Concepcion	2B46 1B16 SS13 3B9 P1	R	40	84	197	11	39	9	0	0	8	13	23	3	.198	.244
Lloyd McClendon	C23 OF17 1B12 3B2	R	29	72	137	9	30	4	0	3	14	15	22	4	.219	.314
Ron Oester	SS5 2B49	B	32	54	150	20	42	7	0	0	10	9	24	0	.280	.327
1 Herm Winningham	OF42	L	26	53	113	6	26	1	3	0	15	5	27	8	.230	.292
2 Jeff Reed	C49	L	25	49	142	10	33	6	1	1	7	15	19	0	.232	.296
1 Tracy Jones	OF25	R	27	37	83	9	19	1	0	1	9	8	6	9	.229	.277
Terry McGriff	C32	R	24	35	96	9	19	3	0	1	4	12	31	1	.198	.260
2 Ken Griffey	1B11	L	38	25	50	5	14	1	0	2	4	5	8	0	.280	.420
Luis Quinones	SS10 3B4 2B4	B	26	23	52	4	12	3	0	1	11	2	11	1	.231	.346
Eddie Milner (SD)	OF15	L	33	23	51	3	9	1	0	0	4	5	10	0	.176	.196
Leo Garcia	OF9	L	25	23	28	2	4	1	0	0	2	0	5	0	.143	.179
1 Buddy Bell (KJ)	3B13 1B2	R	36	21	54	3	10	0	0	1	5	5	5	0	.185	.185
1 Leon Durham (DR)	1B17	L	30	21	51	4	11	3	0	1	2	5	12	0	.216	.333
Lenny Harris	3B10 2B6	L	23	16	43	7	16	1	0	0	8	5	4	4	.372	.395
Ron Roenicke	OF14	B	31	14	37	4	5	1	0	0	6	10	3	0	.135	.162
Van Snider	OF8	L	24	11	28	4	6	0	0	1	6	0	13	0	.214	.357
Marty Brown	3B8	R	25	10	16	1	3	0	0	0	2	1	5	0	.188	.250

NAME	T	AGE	W	L	PCT	SV	G	GS	CG	IP	H	BB	SO	SHO	ERA
		27	87	74	.540	43	161	161	19	1455	1271	504	934	13	3.35
Danny Jackson	L	26	23	8	.742	0	35	35	15	261	206	71	161	6	2.73
Tom Browning	L	28	18	5	.783	0	36	36	5	251	205	64	124	2	3.41
Jose Rijo	R	23	13	8	.619	0	49	19	0	162	120	63	160	0	2.39
John Franco	R	27	6	6	.500	39	70	0	0	86	60	27	46	0	1.57
Norm Charlton	L	25	4	5	.444	0	10	10	0	61	60	20	39	0	3.96
Jack Armstrong	R	23	4	7	.364	0	14	13	0	65	63	38	45	0	5.79
Frank Williams	R	30	3	2	.600	1	60	0	0	63	59	35	43	0	2.59
1 Mario Soto	R	31	3	7	.300	0	14	14	3	87	88	34	31	1	4.66
1 Ron Robinson (EJ)	R	26	3	7	.300	0	10	10	0	79	88	26	38	0	4.12
Keith Brown	R	24	2	1	.667	0	4	3	0	16	14	4	6	0	2.76
1 Pat Perry	R	29	2	2	.500	0	23	0	0	21	21	9	11	0	5.66
1 Dennis Rasmussen	L	29	2	6	.250	0	11	11	1	56	68	22	27	1	5.75
2 Randy St. Claire	R	27	1	0	1.000	0	10	0	0	14	13	5	8	0	2.63
Pat Pacillo	R	24	1	0	1.000	0	6	0	0	11	14	4	11	0	5.06
Rob Dibble	R	24	1	1	.500	0	37	0	0	59	43	21	59	0	1.82
Tim Birtsas	L	27	1	3	.250	0	36	4	0	64	61	24	38	0	4.20
Jeff Gray	R	25	0	0	—	0	9	0	0	12	4	5	3	0	3.86
2 Candy Sierra	R	21	0	0	—	0	4	0	0	4	5	1	4	0	4.50
Dave Concepcion	R	40	0	0	—	0	1	0	0	1	0	0	0	0	0.00
Rob Murphy	L	28	0	0	.000	3	76	0	0	85	69	38	74	0	3.08

SAN DIEGO   3rd 83-78 .516 11   LARRY BOWA 16-30 .348   JACK McKEON 67-48 .583

Name	G by Pos	B	AGE	G	AB	R	H	2B	3B	HR	RBI	BB	SO	SB	BA	SA
TOTALS			28	161	5366	594	1325	205	35	94	566	494	892	123	.247	.351
Keith Moreland	1B73 OF64 3B2	R	34	143	511	40	131	23	0	5	64	40	51	2	.256	.331
Roberto Alomar	2B143	B	20	143	545	84	145	24	6	9	41	47	83	24	.266	.382
Garry Templeton	SS105 3B2	R	32	110	362	35	90	15	7	3	36	20	50	8	.249	.354
Chris Brown	3B72	R	26	80	247	14	58	6	0	2	19	19	49	0	.235	.283
Tony Gwynn	OF133	L	28	133	521	64	163	22	5	7	70	51	40	26	.313	.415
Marvell Wynne	OG113	L	28	128	333	37	88	13	4	11	42	31	62	3	.264	.426
Carmelo Martinez	OF64 1B41	R	27	121	365	48	86	12	0	18	65	35	57	1	.236	.416
Benito Santiago	C136	R	23	139	492	49	122	22	2	10	46	24	82	15	.248	.362
John Kruk	1B63 OF55	L	27	120	378	54	91	17	1	9	44	80	68	5	.241	.362
Randy Ready	3B55 2B26 OF16	R	28	114	331	43	88	16	2	7	39	39	38	6	.266	.390
Dickie Thon	SS70 2B2 3B1	R	30	95	258	36	68	12	2	1	18	33	49	19	.264	.337
Tim Flannery	3B51 2B2 SS1	L	30	79	170	16	45	5	4	0	19	24	32	3	.265	.341
Shane Mack	OF55	R	24	56	119	13	29	3	0	0	12	14	21	5	.244	.269
Stan Jefferson	OF38	B	25	49	111	16	16	1	2	1	4	9	22	5	.144	.216
Mark Parent	C36	R	26	41	118	9	23	3	0	6	15	6	23	0	.195	.373
Shawn Abner	OF35	R	22	37	83	6	15	3	0	2	5	4	19	0	.181	.289
Randy Byers	OF2	L	23	11	10	0	2	1	0	0	0	0	5	0	.200	.300
Rob Nelson	1B5	L	24	7	21	4	4	0	0	1	3	2	9	0	.190	.333
Jerald Clark	OF4	R	24	6	15	0	3	1	0	0	3	0	4	0	.200	.267
Bib Roberts	3B2 2B1	B	24	5	9	1	3	0	0	0	1	1	2	0	.333	.333
Sandy Alomar		R	22	1	1	0	0	0	0	0	0	0	1	0	.000	.000

NAME	T	AGE	W	L	PCT	SV	G	GS	CG	IP	H	BB	SO	SHO	ERA
TOTALS		27	83	78	.516	39	161	161	30	1449	1332	439	885	9	3.28
Eric Show	R	32	16	11	.593	0	32	32	13	235	201	53	144	1	3.26
Dennis Rasmussen	L	29	14	4	.778	0	20	20	6	148	131	36	85	0	2.55
Andy Hawkins	R	28	14	11	.560	0	33	33	4	218	196	76	91	2	3.35
Ed Whitson	R	33	13	11	.542	0	34	33	3	205	202	45	118	1	3.77
Jimmy Jones	R	24	9	14	.391	0	29	29	3	179	192	44	82	0	4.12
Mark Davis	L	27	5	10	.333	28	62	0	0	98	70	42	102	0	2.01
Dave Leiper	L	26	3	0	1.000	1	35	0	0	54	45	14	33	0	2.17
Lance McCullers	R	24	3	6	.333	10	60	0	0	98	70	55	81	0	2.49
Greg Harris	R	24	2	0	1.000	0	3	1	1	18	13	3	15	0	1.50
Greg Booker	R	28	2	2	.500	0	34	2	0	64	68	19	43	0	3.39
Mark Grant	R	24	2	8	.200	0	33	11	0	98	97	36	61	0	3.69
Keith Comstock	L	32	0	0	—	0	7	0	0	8	8	3	9	0	6.75
Eric Nolte	L	24	0	0	—	0	2	0	0	3	3	2	1	0	6.00
1 Candy Sierra	R	21	0	1	.000	0	15	0	0	24	36	11	20	0	5.70

SAN FRANCISCO   4th 83-79 .512 11.5   ROGER CRAIG

Name	G by Pos	B	AGE	G	AB	R	H	2B	3B	HR	RBI	BB	SO	SB	BA	SA
TOTALS			29	162	5450	670	1353	227	44	113	629	550	1023	121	.248	.368
Will Clark	1B158	L	24	162	575	102	162	31	6	29	109	100	129	9	.282	.508
Robby Thompson	2B134	R	26	138	477	66	126	24	6	7	48	40	111	14	.264	.384
Jose Uribe	SS140	R	29	141	493	47	124	10	7	3	35	36	69	14	.252	.318
Kevin Mitchell	3B102 OF40	R	26	148	505	60	127	25	7	19	80	48	85	5	.251	.442
Candy Maldonado	OF139	R	27	142	499	53	127	23	1	12	68	37	89	6	.255	.377
Brett Butler	OF155	L	31	157	568	109	163	27	9	6	43	97	64	43	.287	.398
Mike Aldrete	OF115 1B10	L	27	139	389	44	104	15	0	3	50	56	65	6	.267	.329
Bob Melvin	C89 1B1	R	26	92	273	23	64	13	1	8	27	13	46	0	.234	.377
Joel Youngblood	OF45	R	36	83	123	12	31	4	0	0	16	10	17	1	.252	.285
Chris Speier	2B45 3B22 SS12	R	38	82	171	26	37	9	1	3	18	23	39	1	.216	.333
2 Ernest Riles	3B30 2B17 SS16	L	27	79	187	26	55	7	2	3	28	10	33	1	.294	.401
Bob Brenly	C69	R	34	73	206	13	39	7	0	5	22	20	40	1	.189	.296
Donell Nixon	OF46	R	26	59	78	15	27	3	0	0	6	10	12	11	.346	.436
Matt Williams	SS14 3B43	R	22	52	156	17	32	6	1	8	19	8	41	0	.205	.410
1 Jeff Leonard	OF43	R	32	44	160	12	41	8	1	2	20	9	24	7	.256	.356
Kirt Manwaring	C40	R	22	40	116	12	29	7	0	1	15	2	21	0	.250	.336
1 Harry Spilman	1B33	L	33	40	40	4	7	1	1	1	3	4	6	0	.175	.325
Francisco Melendez (LJ)	1B6 OF1	L	24	23	26	1	5	0	0	0	3	2	2	0	.192	.192
Phil Garner (XJ)	3B2	R	39	15	13	0	2	0	0	0	1	0	3	0	.154	.154
Charlie Hayes	OF4 3B3	R	23	7	11	0	1	0	0	0	0	0	2	0	.091	.091
Tony Perezchica	2B6	R	22	7	8	1	1	0	0	0	1	2	1	0	.125	.125
Rusty Tillman	OF1	R	27	4	4	1	1	0	0	0	0	3	1	0	.250	1.000
Angel Escobar	SS1 3B1	B	23	3	3	1	1	0	0	0	0	2	1	0	.333	.333
Mark Wasinger	3B1	R	26	3	2	1	0	0	0	0	0	0	0	0	.000	.000
Jessie Reid		L	26	2	2	0	0	0	0	0	0	0	1	0	.000	.000

NAME	T	AGE	W	L	PCT	SV	G	GS	CG	IP	H	BB	SO	SHO	ERA
TOTALS		31	83	79	.512	42	162	162	25	1462	1323	422	875	13	3.39
Rick Reuschel	R	39	19	11	.633	0	36	36	7	245	242	42	92	2	3.12
Kelly Downs (SJ)	R	27	13	9	.591	0	27	26	6	168	140	47	118	3	3.32
Don Robinson	R	31	10	5	.667	6	51	19	3	177	152	49	122	2	2.45
Atlee Hammaker	L	30	9	9	.500	5	43	17	3	145	136	41	65	1	3.73
Mike Krukow (SJ)	R	36	7	4	.636	0	20	20	1	125	111	31	75	0	3.54
Mike LaCoss (EJ)	R	32	7	7	.500	0	19	19	1	114	99	47	70	1	3.62
Scott Garrelts	R	26	5	9	.357	13	65	0	0	98	80	46	86	0	3.58
Craig Lefferts	L	30	3	8	.273	11	64	0	0	92	74	23	58	0	2.92
Terry Mulholland (BA)	L	25	3	1	.667	0	9	6	2	46	50	7	18	1	3.72
Dennis Cook	L	25	2	1	.667	0	4	4	1	22	9	11	13	1	2.86
Dave Dravecky (SJ-IL)	L	32	2	2	.500	0	7	7	1	37	33	8	19	0	3.16
Randy Bockus	L	28	2	2	.500	0	9	0	0	32	35	13	18	0	4.78
Ron Davis	R	32	1	1	.500	0	9	0	0	17	15	6	15	0	4.67
Roger Samuels	L	27	1	2	.333	0	15	0	0	23	17	7	22	0	3.47
Joe Price (SJ)	L	31	1	6	.143	4	38	3	0	62	59	27	49	0	3.94
Lary Sorensen	R	33	0	0	—	2	12	0	0	17	24	3	9	0	4.86
Jeff Brantley	R	24	0	1	.000	0	9	1	0	21	22	6	11	0	5.66
Trevor Wilson	L	22	0	2	.000	0	4	4	0	22	25	8	15	0	4.09

HOUSTON   5th 82-80 .506 12.5   HAL LANIER

Name	G by Pos	B	AGE	G	AB	R	H	2B	3B	HR	RBI	BB	SO	SB	BA	SA
TOTALS			30	152	5494	617	1338	239	31	96	575	474	840	198	.244	.351
Glenn Davis	1B151	R	27	152	561	78	152	26	0	30	99	53	77	4	.271	.478
Bill Doran	2B130	B	30	132	480	66	119	18	1	7	53	65	60	17	.248	.333
Rafael Ramirez	SS154	R	30	155	566	51	156	30	5	6	59	18	61	3	.276	.378
2 Buddy Bell	3B64 1B7	R	36	74	269	24	68	10	1	7	37	19	29	1	.253	.375
Kevin Bass	OF147	B	29	157	541	57	138	27	2	14	72	42	65	31	.255	.390
Gerald Young	OF145	B	23	149	576	79	148	21	9	0	37	66	66	65	.257	.325
Billy Hatcher	OF142	R	27	145	530	79	142	25	4	7	52	37	56	32	.268	.370
Alan Ashby (XJ)	C66	B	36	73	227	19	54	10	0	7	33	29	36	0	.238	.374
Terry Puhl	OF78	L	31	113	234	42	71	7	2	3	19	35	30	22	.303	.389
Alex Trevino	C74 OF1	R	30	78	193	19	48	17	0	2	13	24	29	5	.249	.368
Craig Reynolds	SS22 3B19 2B11 1B10	L	35	78	161	20	41	7	0	1	14	8	23	3	.255	.317
Jim Pankovits	2B31 3B11 1B2	R	32	68	140	13	31	7	1	2	12	8	28	2	.221	.329
1 Denny Walling (XJ)	3B51 1B3 OF1	L	34	65	176	19	43	10	2	1	20	15	18	1	.244	.341
Craig Biggio	C50	R	22	50	123	14	26	6	1	3	5	7	29	6	.211	.350
Chuck Jackson	3B32 SS3 OF3	R	25	46	83	7	19	5	1	1	8	7	16	1	.229	.349
Steve Henderson	OF8 1B1	R	35	42	46	4	10	2	0	0	5	7	14	1	.217	.261
Louie Meadows	OF10	L	27	35	42	5	8	0	1	2	3	6	8	4	.190	.381
Ken Caminiti	3B28	B	25	30	83	5	15	2	0	1	7	5	18	0	.181	.241
2 Casey Candaele	2B10	B	27	21	31	2	5	3	0	0	1	1	6	0	.161	.258
John Fishel	OF6	R	25	19	26	1	6	0	1	0	1	2	3	6	.231	.346
Mark Bailey	C8	B	26	8	23	1	3	0	0	0	0	5	6	0	.130	.130
Craig Smajstrla	2B2	B	26	8	3	2	0	0	0	0	0	1	0	0	.000	.000
Cameron Drew	OF5	L	24	7	16	1	3	0	1	0	1	0	4	0	.188	.313
2 Harry Spilman	1B1	L	33	5	0	0	0	0	0	0	0	0	0	0	.000	.000
Ty Gainey (WJ) 27																

NAME	T	AGE	W	L	PCT	SV	G	GS	CG	IP	H	BB	SO	SHO	ERA
TOTALS		32	82	80	.506	40	162	162	21	1474	1339	478	1049	15	3.41
Bob Knepper	L	32	14	5	.737	0	27	27	3	175	156	67	103	2	3.14
Mike Scott	R	33	14	8	.636	0	32	32	8	219	162	53	190	5	2.92
Nolan Ryan	R	41	12	11	.522	0	33	33	4	220	186	87	228	1	3.52
Jim Deshaies	L	28	11	14	.440	0	31	31	3	207	164	72	127	2	3.00
Juan Agosto	L	30	10	2	.833	4	75	0	0	92	74	30	33	0	2.26
Danny Darwin	R	32	8	13	.381	3	44	20	3	192	189	48	129	0	3.84
Dave Smith	R	33	4	5	.444	27	51	0	0	58	60	19	38	0	2.67
Dave Meads	L	24	3	1	.750	0	22	0	0	40	37	14	27	0	3.18
Larry Andersen	R	35	2	4	.333	5	53	0	0	83	82	20	66	0	2.94
Joaquin Andujar (VJ-KJ)	R	35	2	5	.286	0	23	10	0	79	94	21	35	0	4.00
Rocky Childress	R	26	1	0	1.000	0	11	0	0	23	26	9	24	0	6.17
2 Bob Forsch	R	38	1	4	.200	0	6	6	0	28	42	6	14	0	6.51
Brian Meyer	R	25	1	0	—	0	8	0	0	12	9	4	10	0	1.46
Ernie Camacho	R	33	0	0	.000	1	13	0	0	18	25	12	13	0	7.64
Jeff Heathcock	R	28	0	5	.000	0	17	1	0	37	36	12	12	0	5.81
Charlie Kerfeld (SJ) 24																

ATLANTA   6th 54-106 .338 39.5   CHUCK TANNER 12-27 .308   RUSS NIXON 42-79 .347

Name	G by Pos	B	AGE	G	AB	R	H	2B	3B	HR	RBI	BB	SO	SB	BA	SA
TOTALS			29	160	5440	555	1319	228	28	96	527	432	848	95	.242	.348
Gerald Perry	1B141	L	27	141	547	61	164	29	1	8	74	36	49	29	.300	.400
Ron Gant	2B122 3B22	R	23	146	563	85	146	28	8	19	60	46	118	19	.259	.439
Andres Thomas	SS154	R	24	153	606	54	153	22	2	13	68	14	95	7	.252	.360
1 Ken Oberkfell	3B113 2B1	L	32	120	422	42	117	20	4	3	40	32	28	1	.277	.365
Dale Murphy	OF156	R	32	156	592	77	134	35	4	24	77	74	125	3	.226	.421
Albert Hall (LJ)	OF63	B	29	85	231	27	57	7	1	1	15	21	35	15	.247	.299
Dion James	OF120	L	25	132	386	46	99	17	5	3	30	58	59	9	.256	.350
Ozzie Virgil	C96	R	31	107	320	23	82	10	0	9	31	22	54	2	.256	.372
Bruce Benedict	C89	R	32	90	236	11	57	7	0	0	19	19	26	0	.242	.271
Ted Simmons	1B19 C10	B	38	78	107	6	21	6	0	2	11	15	9	0	.196	.308
1 Ken Griffey	OF42 1B10	L	38	69	193	21	48	5	0	2	19	17	26	1	.249	.306
Jerry Royster	OF26 3B10 2B2 SS2	R	35	68	102	8	18	3	0	1	6	16	16	0	.176	.206
Terry Blocker	OF61	L	28	66	198	13	42	4	2	2	10	10	20	1	.212	.283
Paul Runge	3B19 SS6 2B7	R	30	52	76	11	16	5	0	0	7	14	21	0	.211	.276
2 Jim Morrison	3B20 OF4 P3	R	35	51	92	6	14	2	0	2	13	10	13	0	.152	.239
Gary Roenicke	OF35 1B1	R	33	49	114	11	26	5	0	1	7	8	15	0	.228	.298
Lonnie Smith	OF35	R	32	43	114	14	27	3	0	3	9	25	20	4	.237	.342
Damaso Garcia	2B13	R	33	21	60	3	7	1	0	1	4	3	10	1	.117	.183
Jeff Blauser	SS8 2B9	R	22	18	67	7	16	3	1	2	7	6	13	0	.239	.403
Mark Lemke	2B16	B	22	16	58	8	13	4	0	0	2	4	5	0	.224	.293
2 Tommy Gregg	OF7	L	24	11	29	1	10	3	0	0	0	1	0	0	.345	.448
Jody Davis	C2	R	31	2	8	2	2	0	0	0	0	0	1	0	.250	.625

NAME	T	AGE	W	L	PCT	SV	G	GS	CG	IP	H	BB	SO	SHO	ERA
TOTALS		29	54	106	.338	25	160	160	14	1446	1481	524	810	4	4.09
Rick Mahler	R	34	9	16	.360	0	39	34	5	249	279	42	131	0	3.69
Paul Assenmacher	L	27	8	7	.533	5	64	0	0	79	72	32	71	0	3.06
Pete Smith	R	22	7	15	.318	0	32	32	5	195	183	88	124	3	3.69
Tom Glavine	L	22	7	17	.292	0	34	34	1	195	201	63	84	0	4.56
Charlie Puleo	R	33	5	5	.500	1	53	3	0	106	101	47	70	0	3.47
Jose Alvarez	R	32	5	6	.455	2	60	0	0	102	88	53	81	0	2.99
Zane Smith (EJ)	L	27	5	10	.333	0	23	22	3	140	159	44	59	0	4.30
Juan Eichelberger	R	34	2	0	1.000	0	20	0	0	37	44	10	13	0	3.86
Kevin Coffman	R	23	2	6	.250	0	18	11	0	67	62	54	24	0	5.78
John Smoltz	R	21	2	7	.222	0	12	12	0	64	74	33	37	0	5.48
Bruce Sutter	R	35	1	4	.200	14	38	0	0	45	49	11	40	0	4.76
German Jimenez	L	25	1	6	.143	0	15	9	0	56	65	12	26	0	5.01
Ed Olwine (EJ)	L	30	0	0	—	1	16	0	0	19	22	4	5	0	6.75
Chuck Cary (KJ)	L	28	0	0	—	0	7	0	0	8	8	3	6	0	6.48
Gary Eave	R	24	0	0	—	0	5	0	0	5	7	3	0	0	9.00
2 Jim Morrison	R	35	0	0	—	0	5	0	0	5	7	3	0	0	0.00
1 Kevin Blankenship	R	25	0	1	.000	1	2	1	1	11	7	1	5	0	3.00
Joe Boever	R	28	0	2	.000	1	16	0	0	20	12	1	7	0	1.77
Jim Acker (EJ)	R	29	0	4	.000	0	21	1	0	42	45	14	25	0	4.71

LINE SCORES

Team	1	2	3	4	5	6	7	8	9	10	11		R	H	E

AMERICAN LEAGUE CHAMPIONSHIPS: OAKLAND (WEST) 4 BOSTON (EAST) 0

Game 1 October 5 at Boston

													R	H	E
OAK	0	0	0	1	0	0	0	1	0				2	6	0
BOS	0	0	0	0	0	1	0	0					1	6	0

Stewart, Honeycutt (7), Eckersley (8) Hurst

Game 2 October 6 at Boston

													R	H	E
OAK	0	0	0	0	0	0	3	0	1				4	10	1
BOS	1	0	0	0	0	2	1	0	0				3	4	1

Davis, Cadaret (7), **Nelson** (7), Eckersley (9) Clemens, Stanley (8), **Smith** (8)

Game 3 October 8 at Oakland

													R	H	E
BOS	3	2	0	0	0	0	0	1	0				6	12	0
OAK	0	4	2	0	1	0	1	2	X				10	15	1

Boddicker, Gardner (3), Stanley (8) Welch, **Nelson** (2), Young (6), Plunk (7), Honeycutt (7), Eckersley (8)

Game 4 October 9 at Oakland

													R	H	E
BOS	0	0	0	0	0	1	0	0	0				1	4	0
OAK	1	0	1	0	0	0	0	2	X				4	10	1

Hurst, Smithson (5), Smith (7) **Stewart**, Honeycutt (8), Eckersley (9)

NATIONAL LEAGUE CHAMPIONSHIPS: LOS ANGELES (WEST) 4 NEW YORK (EAST) 3

Game 1 October 4 at Los Angeles

													R	H	E
NY	0	0	0	0	0	0	0	0	3				3	8	1
LA	1	0	0	0	0	0	1	0	0				2	4	0

Gooden, **Myers** (8) Hershiser, **Howell** (9)

Game 2 October 5 at Los Angeles

													R	H	E
NY	0	0	0	2	0	0	0	0	1				3	6	0
LA	1	4	0	0	1	0	0	0	X				6	7	0

Cone, Aguilera (3), Leach (6), McDowell (8) **Belcher**, Orosco (9), Pena (9)

Game 3 October 8 at New York

													R	H	E
LA	0	2	1	0	0	0	1	0					4	7	1
NY	0	0	1	0	0	2	0	5	X				8	9	2

Hershiser, Howell (8), **Pena** (8), Orosco (8), Horton (8) Darling, McDowell (7), **Myers** (8), Cone (9)

Game 4 October 9 at New York

													R	H	E
LA	2	0	0	0	0	0	2	0	0	1			5	7	1
NY	0	0	0	3	0	1	0	0	0	0			4	10	2

Tudor, Holton (6), Horton (7), **Pena** (9), Leary (12), Orosco (12), Hershiser (12) Gooden, Myers (9), **McDowell** (11)

Game 5 October 10 at New York

													R	H	E
LA	0	0	0	3	3	0	0	0	1				7	12	0
NY	0	0	0	0	3	0	0	1	0				4	9	1

Belcher, Horton (8), Holton (8) Fernandez, Leach (5), Aguilera (6), McDowell (8)

Game 6 October 11 at Los Angeles

													R	H	E
NY	1	0	1	0	2	1	0	0	0				5	11	0
LA	0	0	0	0	1	0	0	0	0				1	5	2

Cone Leary, Holton (5), Horton (6), Orosco (8)

Game 7 October 12 at Los Angeles

													R	H	E
NY	0	0	0	0	0	0	0	0	0				0	5	2
LA	1	5	0	0	0	0	0	0	X				6	10	0

Darling, Gooden (4), Leach (5), Aguilera (7) **Hershiser**

COMPOSITE BATTING

NAME	POS	G	AB	R	H	2B	3B	HR	RBI	BA
OAKLAND										
TOTALS		4	137	20	41	8	0	7	20	.299
Lansford	3B	4	17	4	5	1	0	1	2	.294
Henderson	CF	4	16	2	5	1	0	1	3	.375
Canseco	RF	4	16	4	5	1	0	3	4	.313
McGwire	1B	4	15	2	5	0	0	1	3	.333
Weiss	SS	4	15	2	5	2	0	0	2	.333
Parker	DH-LF	3	12	1	3	1	0	0	0	.250
Gallego	2B	4	12	1	1	0	0	0	0	.083
Hassey	C	4	8	2	4	0	0	1	3	.500
Phillips	LF-2B	2	7	0	2	1	0	0	0	.286
Baylor	DH	2	6	0	0	0	0	0	1	.000
Polonia	PR-LF-PH	3	5	0	2	0	0	0	0	.400
Javier	LF-PR	2	4	0	2	0	0	0	1	.500
Steinbach	C	2	4	0	1	0	0	0	0	.250
BOSTON										
TOTALS		4	126	11	26	4	0	2	10	.203
Burks	CF	4	17	2	4	1	0	0	1	.235
Barrett	2B	4	15	2	1	0	0	0	0	.067
Gedman	C	4	14	1	5	0	0	1	1	.357
Greenwell	LF	4	14	3	3	1	0	1	3	.214
Boggs	3B	4	13	2	5	0	0	0	3	.385
Rice	DH	4	13	0	2	0	0	0	1	.154
Evans	RF	4	12	1	2	1	0	0	1	.167
Reed	SS	4	11	0	3	1	0	0	0	.273
Benzinger	1B-PH	4	11	0	1	0	0	0	0	.091
Parrish	PH-1B	4	6	0	0	0	0	0	0	.000
Owen	PH	1	0	0	0	0	0	0	0	—
Romine	PR	2	0	1	0	0	0	0	0	—
Romero	PR	1	0	0	0	0	0	0	0	—
LOS ANGELES										
TOTALS		7	243	31	52	7	1	3	30	.210
Sax	2B	7	30	7	8	0	0	0	3	.267
Marshall	RF	7	30	3	7	1	1	0	5	.233
Gibson	LF	7	26	2	4	0	0	2	6	.154
Griffin	SS	7	25	1	4	1	0	0	3	.160
Shelby	CF	7	24	3	4	0	0	0	3	.167
Hamilton	3B	7	23	2	5	0	0	0	1	.217
Scioscia	C	7	22	3	8	1	0	1	2	.364
Hatcher	1B-LF	6	21	4	5	2	0	0	3	.268
Hershiser	P	4	9	1	0	0	0	0	1	.000
Stubbs	1B-PH	4	8	0	2	0	0	0	0	.250
Belcher	P	2	8	1	1	0	0	0	0	.125
Dempsey	PH-C	4	5	1	2	2	0	0	2	.400
Woodson	PH-1B	3	4	0	1	0	0	0	0	.250
Davis	PH	4	2	0	0	0	0	0	0	.000
Tudor	P	1	2	0	0	0	0	0	0	.000
Holton	P	3	1	1	1	0	0	0	0	1.000
Heep	PH	3	1	0	0	0	0	0	0	.000
Sharperson	PH-SS-3B	3	1	0	0	0	0	0	1	.000
Leary	P	2	1	0	0	0	0	0	0	.000
Gonzalez	LF-PH-PR	5	0	2	0	0	0	0	0	—
NEW YORK										
TOTALS		7	240	27	58	12	1	5	27	.242
Strawberry	RF	7	30	5	9	2	0	1	6	.300
McReynolds	LF	7	28	4	7	2	0	2	4	.250
Jefferies	3B	7	27	2	9	2	0	0	1	.333
Carter	C	7	27	0	6	1	1	0	4	.222
Hernandez	1B	7	26	2	7	0	0	1	5	.269
Backman	2B	7	22	2	6	1	0	0	2	.273
Johnson	SS-PH-3B	6	18	3	1	0	0	0	0	.056
Dykstra	PH-CF	7	14	6	6	3	0	1	3	.429
Wilson	CF-PH	4	13	2	2	0	0	0	1	.154
Elster	SS-PR	5	8	1	2	1	0	0	1	.250
Sasser	PH-C	4	5	0	1	0	0	0	0	.200
Gooden	PH-CF	3	5	0	1	0	0	0	0	.200
Cone	PH-CF	3	4	0	0	0	0	0	0	.000
Magaden	PH	3	3	0	0	0	0	0	0	.000
Teufel	2B	1	3	0	0	0	0	0	0	.000
Darling	P-PR	3	3	0	0	0	0	0	0	.000
Mazzilli	PH	3	2	0	1	0	0	0	0	.500
Aguilera	P	3	1	0	0	0	0	0	0	.000
Fernandez	P	1	1	0	0	0	0	0	0	.000

COMPOSITE PITCHING

NAME	G	IP	H	BB	SO	W	L	SV	ERA
OAKLAND									
TOTALS	4	36	26	18	23	4	0	4	2.00
Stewart	2	13.1	9	6	11	1	0	0	1.35
Davis	1	6.1	2	5	4	0	0	0	0.00
Eckersley	4	6	1	2	5	0	0	4	0.00
Nelson	2	4.2	5	1	4	2	0	0	0.00
Honeycutt	3	2	0	2	0	1	0	0	0.00
Welch	1	1.2	6	2	0	0	0	0	27.00
Young	1	1.1	1	0	2	0	0	0	0.00
Plunk	1	0.1	0	1	0	0	0	0	0.00
Caderet	1	0.1	1	0	0	0	0	0	27.00
BOSTON									
TOTALS	4	34	41	10	35	0	4	0	5.29
Hurst	2	13	10	5	12	0	2	0	2.77
Clemens	1	7	6	0	8	0	0	0	3.86
Gardner	1	4.2	6	2	8	0	0	0	5.79
Smith	2	3.1	6	1	4	0	1	0	8.10
Boddicker	1	2.2	8	1	2	0	1	0	20.25
Smithson	1	2.1	3	0	1	0	0	0	0.00
Stanley	2	1	2	1	0	0	0	0	9.00
LOS ANGELES									
TOTALS	7	65	58	28	42	4	3	3	3.32
Hershiser	4	24.2	18	7	15	1	0	1	1.09
Belcher	2	15.1	12	4	16	2	0	0	4.11
Tudor	1	5	8	1	1	0	0	0	7.20
Horton	4	4.1	4	2	3	0	0	0	0.00
Pena	3	4.1	1	5	1	1	1	1	4.15
Leary	2	4.1	8	3	3	0	1	0	6.23
Holton	3	4	2	1	2	0	0	0	2.25
Orosco	4	2.1	4	3	0	0	0	0	7.71
Howell	2	0.2	1	2	1	0	1	0	27.00
NEW YORK									
TOTALS	7	64	52	25	54	3	4	0	3.94
Gooden	3	18.1	10	8	20	0	0	0	2.95
Cone	3	12	10	5	9	1	1	0	4.50
Aguilera	3	7	3	2	4	0	0	0	1.29
Darling	2	7	11	4	7	0	1	0	7.71
McDowell	4	6	6	2	5	0	1	0	4.50
Leach	3	5	4	1	4	0	0	0	0.00
Myers	3	4.2	1	2	2	0	0	0	0.00
Fernandez	1	4	7	1	5	0	1	0	13.50

LINE SCORES

Team	1	2	3	4	5	6	7	8	9	10			R	H	E

WORLD SERIES: LOS ANGELES (NL) 4 : OAKLAND (AL) 1

Game 1 October 15 at Los Angeles

												R	H	E
OAK	0	4	0	0	0	0	0	0	0			4	7	0
LA	2	0	0	0	0	1	0	0	2			5	7	0

Stewart, Ekersley (9) Belcher, Leary (3)
Holton (6), Pena (8)

Game 2 October 16 at Los Angeles

												R	H	E
OAK	0	0	0	0	0	0	0	0	0			0	3	0
LA	0	0	5	1	0	0	0	0	X			6	10	1

Davis, Nelson (4), Hershiser
Young (6), Plunk (7),
Honeycutt (8)

Game 3 October 18 at Oakland

												R	H	E
LA	0	0	0	0	1	0	0	0	0			1	8	1
OAK	0	0	1	0	0	0	0	0	1			2	5	0

Tudor, Leary (2), Welch, Cadaret (6),
Pena (6), **Howell** (9) Nelson (6), **Honeycutt** (8)

Game 4 October 19 at Oakland

												R	H	E
LA	2	0	1	0	0	0	1	0	0			4	8	1
OAK	1	0	0	0	0	1	1	0	0			3	9	2

Belcher, Howell (7) **Stewart**, Cadaret (7),
Eckersley (9)

Game 5 October 20 at Oakland

												R	H	E
LA	2	0	0	2	0	1	0	0	0			5	8	0
OAK	0	0	1	0	0	0	0	1	0			2	4	0

Hershiser Davis, Cadaret (5),
Nelson (5), Honeycutt (8)
Plunk (9), Burns (9)

COMPOSITE BATTING

LOS ANGELES

NAME	POS	G	AB	R	H	2B	3B	HR	RBI	BA
TOTALS		5	167	21	41	8	1	5	19	.246
Sax	2B	5	20	3	6	0	0	0	1	.300
Hatcher	LF-RF	5	19	5	7	1	0	2	5	.368
Hamilton	3B	5	19	1	2	0	0	0	0	.105
Shelby	CF	5	18	0	4	1	0	0	1	.222
Stubbs	1B	5	17	3	5	2	0	0	2	.294
Griffin	SS	5	16	2	3	0	0	0	0	.188
Scioscia	C	4	14	0	3	0	0	0	1	.214
Marshall	RF	5	13	2	3	0	1	1	3	.231
Heep	PH-LF-DH	3	8	0	2	1	0	0	0	.250
Davis	PH-DH-RF	4	7	3	1	0	0	1	2	.143
Dempsey	C	2	5	0	1	0	0	0	1	.200
Woodson	PH-1B	4	4	0	0	0	0	0	1	.000
Hershiser	P	2	3	1	3	2	0	0	1	1.000
Gonzalez	PH-RF-LF	4	2	0	0	0	0	0	0	.000
Gibson	PH	1	1	1	1	0	0	1	2	1.000
Anderson	DH-PH	1	1	0	0	0	0	0	0	—

OAKLAND

NAME	POS	G	AB	R	H	2B	3B	HR	RBI	BA
TOTALS		5	158	11	28	3	0	2	11	.177
Henderson	CF	5	20	1	6	2	0	0	1	.300
Canseco	RF	5	19	1	1	0	0	1	5	.053
Lansford	3B	5	18	2	3	0	0	0	1	.167
McGwire	1B	5	17	1	1	0	0	1	1	.059
Weiss	SS	5	16	1	1	0	0	0	0	.063
Parker	LF-DH	4	15	0	3	0	0	0	0	.200
Hubbard	2B	4	12	2	3	0	0	0	0	.250
Steinbach	C-DH	3	11	0	4	1	0	0	1	.364
Polonia	PH-LF	3	9	1	1	0	0	0	0	.111
Hassey	C-PH	5	8	0	2	0	0	0	1	.250
Javier	PR-LF	3	4	0	2	0	0	0	2	.500
Phillips	LF-2B	2	4	1	1	0	0	0	0	.250
Stewart	P	2	3	1	0	0	0	0	0	.000
Davis	P	2	1	0	0	0	0	0	0	.000
Baylor	PH	1	1	0	0	0	0	0	0	.000
Gallego	PR-2B	1	0	0	0	0	0	0	0	—

COMPOSITE PITCHING

LOS ANGELES

NAME	G	IP	H	BB	SO	W	L	SV	ERA
TOTALS	5	44.1	28	17	41	4	1	1	2.03
Hershiser	2	18	7	6	17	2	0	0	1.00
Belcher	2	8.2	10	6	10	1	0	0	6.23
Leary	2	6.2	6	2	4	0	0	0	1.35
Pena	2	5	2	1	7	1	0	0	0.00
Howell	2	2.2	3	1	2	0	1	1	3.38
Holton	1	2	0	1	0	0	0	0	0.00
Tudor	1	1.1	0	0	1	0	0	0	0.00

OAKLAND

NAME	G	IP	H	BB	SO	W	L	SV	ERA
TOTALS	5	43.2	41	13	36	1	4	0	3.92
Stewart	2	14.1	12	5	5	0	1	0	3.14
Davis	2	8	14	1	7	0	2	0	11.25
Nelson	3	6.1	4	3	3	0	0	0	1.42
Welch	1	5	6	3	8	0	0	0	1.80
Honeycutt	3	3.1	0	0	5	1	0	0	0.00
Cadaret	3	2	2	0	3	0	0	0	0.00
Plunk	2	1.2	0	0	3	0	0	0	0.00
Eckersley	2	1.2	1	2	1	0	1	0	10.80
Young	1	1	1	0	0	0	0	0	0.00
Burns	1	0.1	0	0	0	0	0	0	0.00

MISCELLANEOUS 1988 INDIVIDUAL LEADERS

BATTING

On Base Average

American League
1 Boggs, Bos. .476
2 Greenwell, Bos. .416
3 Davis, Sea. .412
4 Winfield, N.Y. .398
5 Henderson, N.Y. .394

National League
1 Daniels, Cin. .397
2 Butler, S.F. .393
3 Clark, S.F. .386
4 Gibson, L.A. .377
5 Gwynn, S.D. .373

Caught Stealing

American League
1 Reynolds, Sea. 29
2 Canseco, Oak. 16
3 Guillen, Chi. 13
   Henderson, N.Y. 13
5 Franco, Cle. 11

National League
1 Coleman, St. L. 27
   Young, Hou. 27
3 Butler, S.F. 20
   Perry, Atl. 14
5 Sabo, Cin. 14
   Strawberry, N.Y. 14
   Webster, Mon.-Chi. 14

Hit by Pitcher

American League
1 Larkin, Min. 15
2 Downing, Cal. 14
3 Baylor, Oak. 12
   Fletcher, Tex. 12
5 Canseco, Oak. 10

National League
1 Bradley, Phi. 16
2 Samuel, Phi. 12
3 Davis, Hou. 11
4 Galarraga, Mon. 10
5 Hatcher, Hou. 8
   Larkin, Cin. 8
   Webster, Mon.-Chi. 8

Sacrifice Hits

American League
1 Barrett, Bos. 20
2 Gantner, Mil. 18
3 Manrique, Chi. 16
4 Fletcher, Tex. 15
   Lyons, Chi. 15

National League
1 Hershiser, L.A. 19
2 Reuschel, S.F. 19
3 R. Alomar, S.D. 16
4 Knepper, Hou. 14
   Thompson, S.F. 14

Game Winning RBI's

American League
1 Greenwell, Bos. 23
2 McGwire, Oak. 20
3 Bell, Tor. 17
4 Canseco, Oak. 16
   Clark, N.Y. 16

National League
1 Davis, Cin. 21
2 McReynolds, N.Y. 19
3 Galarraga, Mon. 16
   Van Slyke, Pit. 16
5 Strawberry, N.Y. 15

Grounded Into Double Play

American League
1 Boggs, Bos. 23
2 Baines, Chi. 21
   Bell, Tor. 21
   Yount, Mil. 21
5 Gruber, Tor. 20
   Murray, Bal. 20

National League
1 Murphy, Atl. 24
2 Brooks, Mon. 21
3 Wallach, Mon. 19
4 Perry, Atl. 18
   Santiago, S.D. 18

Total Bases

American League
1 Puckett, Min. 358
2 Canseco, Oak. 347
3 Greenwell, Bos. 313
4 Brett, K.C. 300
5 Carter, Cle. 297

National League
1 Galarraga, Mon. 329
2 Dawson, Chi. 298
3 Van Slyke, Pit. 297
4 Strawberry, N.Y. 296
5 Clark, S.F. 292

Sacrifice Flies

American League
1 C. Davis, Cal. 10
   C. Ripken, Bal. 10
3 Puckett, Min. 9
4 Seven tied with 8

National League
1 Van Slyke, Pit. 13
2 Clark, S.F. 10
3 Perry, Atl. 10
4 Davis, Hou. 9
   Moreland, S.D. 9
   Strawberry, N.Y. 9

FIELDING

American League

	PO	A	E	DP	Pct.
1B McGriff, Tor.	1344	93	5	143	.997
2B White, K.C.	293	426	4	88	.994
SS Schofield, Cal.	278	492	13	125	.983
3B Lansford, Oak.	113	220	7	16	.979
OF Pasqua, Chi.	258	6	1	2	.996
C Cerone, Bos.	471	28	0	4	1.000
P August, Mil.	22	24	0	2	1.000

National League

	PO	A	E	DP	Pct.
1B Davis, Hou.	1355	103	6	104	.996
2B Doran, Hou.	260	371	8	73	.987
SS Belliard, Pit.	131	258	9	50	.977
3B Sabo, Cin.	75	318	14	31	.966
OF Brunansky, St. L.	267	10	1	0	.996
C Pena, St. L.	777	70	5	8	.994
P Perez, Mon.	13	38	0	2	1.000

Balks

American League
1 Stewart, Oak. 16
2 Welch, Oak. 13
3 Candelaria, N.Y. 12
   Guzman, Tex. 12
5 Birbeck, Mil. 11
   Morris, Det. 11
   Scurry, N.Y. 11

National League

PITCHING

Wild Pitches

American League
1 Davis, Oak. 16
   Witt, Tex. 16
3 Stewart, Oak. 14
4 McCaskill, Cal. 13
   Perez, Chi. 13

National League
1 Walk, Pit. 13
2 Dunne, Pit. 12
   Ruffin, Phi. 12
4 Coffman, Atl. 11
   Robinson, Pit. 11
   Sutcliffe, Chi. 11

Hit Batters

American League
1 Blyleven, Min. 16
2 Boddicker, Bal.-Bos. 14
3 Stieb, Tor. 13
4 Hough, Tex. 12
5 Kilgus, Tex. 10
   Wegman, Mil. 10

National League
1 Gross, Phi. 11
2 Smith, Mon. 10
3 Maddux, Chi. 9
4 Glavine, Atl. 8
   Mahler, Atl. 8
   Scott, Hou. 8

Home Runs Allowed

American League
1 Fraser, Cal. 33
2 Langston, Sea. 32
3 Alexander, Det. 30
4 Dotson, N.Y. 27
   Clancy, Tor. 26
   Perez, Chi. 26

National League
1 Browning, Cin. 36
2 Rawley, Phi. 27
3 Darling, N.Y. 24
4 Show, S.D. 22
5 Drabek, Pit. 21
   Martinez, Mon. 21

1 Cone, N.Y. 10
   Martinez, Mon. 10
   Perez, Mon. 10
   Fernandez, N.Y. 9
4 Walk, Pit. 9

1989 Giamatti/Rose And The Quake

Bart Giamatti became Commissioner of Baseball on April 1, 1989. He was a Renaissance literature scholar, had been president of Yale University, and had served for two years as president of the National League. His obvious love of baseball endeared him to the fans. Bill White, a former player and broadcaster, became the new N.L. president, the first black man to hold such a high administrative post in sports history.

From its start, Giamatti's regime was absorbed almost totally with the investigation of Pete Rose. The media reported as early as spring training that Reds manager Rose had bet on numerous sporting events, including baseball and, probably, Reds games. Although no one accused Rose of betting on the Reds to lose, the allegations were nevertheless grounds for a lifetime suspension under baseball's internal rules. Rose brought a lawsuit aimed at preventing Giamatti from passing judgment on him. After the legal proceedings played on through most of the summer, Rose gave up the battle. On August 23, he and Giamatti signed an agreement in which Rose did not admit guilt on the gambling charges. He did, however, accept a lifetime suspension from baseball. Although he could apply for reinstatement after one year, no one expected to see Rose back in uniform anytime soon.

Nine days after the suspension, Giamatti died. He suffered a fatal heart attack on September 1 at the age of 51 years. The deputy commissioner, Fay Vincent, became the new commissioner and dedicated the World Series to the popular Giamatti.

The World Series capped a quirky regular season in which teams rose and fell precipitously. In the A.L. East, the Tigers tumbled off the edge completely into the cellar, with worst record in the major leagues. Swapping roles with the Tigers were the Orioles. Forelorn losers last year, the Birds combined improved pitching and tightened defense to lead the East for most of the summer. They finally were overtaken in September, however, by the Blue Jays, who engineered a comeback story of their own. Their 12-24 start cost manager Jimy Williams his job in May. Under Cito Gaston, the Jays regrouped and began a successful drive for first place. The new Toronto Skydome opened on June 5 and inspired a major league attendance record of 3,375,573 fans. George Bell, Kelly Gruber, and Fred McGriff powered the offense with late-season help from Mookie Wilson. Although Milwaukee never made a strong challenge for the top, Robin Yount's overall excellence won him the MVP award.

In the A.L. West, Oakland slugger Jose Canseco missed the first half of the season with a broken wrist. The Athletics pulled away from the pack in late August to repeat as divisional champs. Canseco came back strongly to join Carney Lansford, Mark McGwire, Rickey Henderson, and Dave Parker in a feared lineup. The Athletics had a talented pitching staff, with Dave Stewart and Mike Moore the top starters and Dennis Eckersley the ace reliever. The Royals contended behind Bo Jackson's 32 homers and 105 runs batted in and Bret Saberhagen's Cy Young Award pitching. One part of the Angels' resurgence was rookie pitcher Jim Abbott, born with only one hand.

In the N.L. East, age, injuries, and slumps sank the Mets. The Expos made a strong run during the summer, fueled in part by the acquisition of star pitcher Mark Langston. When the Expos faded, however, the surprising Cubs stepped forward to take the title. The Cubs had two rookie stars in Jerome Walton and Dwight Smith and infield excellence in Mark Grace, Tyne Sandberg, and Shawon Dunston. The Chicago pitching lacked depth but profited from the arrival of reliever Mitch Williams. The Phillies came in last and lost Mike Schmidt to retirement on May 29.

In the N.L. West, the Dodgers and Reds fell off the pace. The Giants filled the vacuum and held first place from June 13 onward. Kevin Mitchell and Will Clark both punished pitchers all season long, with Mitchell edging Clark for the MVP award. Scott Garrelts and Rich Reuschel led a pitching staff that was cursed with injuries. The Padres challenged in the late summer, led by Tony Gwynn's third straight batting title and reliever Mark Davis' Cy Young Award season.

Both league championship series lasted only five games. The Athletics beat the Blue Jays in large part because of Rickey Henderson's hitting and running. The Giants beat the Cubs in a lively series full of offensive heroics. The two young first basemen, Clark and Grace, spewed base hits with extraordinary regularity.

The World Series was the first metropolitan series since the Yankees and Dodgers met in 1956. The Athletics won the first two games in Oakland, living up to their billing as favorites. On October 17, the teams convened in Candlestick Park for game three. At 5:04 p.m., just minutes before the scheduled start, a catastrophic earthquake hit the Bay Area. The ballpark shook without appreciable damage, but dozens of people died in the Bay Area amid great destruction of property. Commissioner Vincent immediately postponed the game. After ten days of mourning and regrouping, the Series resumed. The Athletics blew the Giants out twice more to complete a four-game sweep. Dave Stewart won the MVP award with his victories in games one and three, but his heroics would be shadowed in memory by the quake.

EAST DIVISION — 1989 AMERICAN LEAGUE

TORONTO — 1st 89-73 .549 — JIMY WILLIAMS 12-24 .333 — CITO GASTON 77-49 .611

Name	G by Pos	B	AGE	G	AB	R	H	2B	3B	HR	RBI	BB	SO	SB	BA	SA
TOTALS			28	162	5581	731	1449	265	40	142	685	521	923	144	.260	.398
Fred McGriff	1B159 DH2	L	25	161	551	98	148	27	3	36	92	119	132	7	.269	.525
Nelson Liriano	2B122 DH5	B	25	132	418	51	110	26	3	5	53	43	51	16	.263	.376
Tony Fernandez	SS140	B	27	140	573	64	147	25	9	11	64	29	51	22	.257	.389
Kelly Gruber	3B119 OF16 DH1 SS1	R	27	135	545	83	158	24	4	18	73	30	60	10	.290	.448
Junior Felix	OF 107 DH2	B	21	110	415	62	107	14	8	9	46	33	101	18	.258	.395
Lloyd Moseby	OF 120 DH14	L	29	135	502	72	111	25	3	11	43	56	101	24	.221	.349
George Bell	OF 134 DH19	R	29	153	613	88	182	41	2	18	104	33	60	4	.297	.458
Ernie Whitt	C115 DH8	L	37	129	385	42	101	24	1	11	53	52	53	5	.262	.416
Rance Mulliniks	DH73 3B29	L	33	103	273	25	65	11	2	3	29	34	40	1	.238	.326
Manny Lee (NJ)	2B40 SS28 3B17 DH13 OF1	B	24	99	300	27	78	9	2	3	34	20	60	4	.260	.333
Pat Borders	C68 DH19	R	26	94	241	22	62	11	1	3	29	11	45	2	.257	.349
Tom Lawless	OF16 3B12 DH12 2B7 C1	R	32	59	70	20	16	1	0	0	3	7	12	12	.229	.243
Mookie Wilson	OF54	B	33	54	238	32	71	9	1	2	17	3	37	12	.298	.370
Bob Brenly	DH28 C13 1B5	R	35	48	88	9	15	3	1	1	6	10	17	1	.170	.261
Rob Ducey (KJ)	OF35 DH1	L	24	41	76	5	16	4	0	0	7	9	25	2	.211	.263
Lee Mazzilli	DH19 OF2 1B2	B	34	28	66	12	15	3	0	4	11	17	16	2	.227	.455
Jesse Barfield	OF21	R	29	21	80	8	16	4	0	5	11	5	28	0	.200	.438
Alex Infante	SS9 3B4 DH3 2B1	R	27	20	12	1	2	0	0	0	0	1	1	0	.167	.167
Glenallen Hill	OF16 DH3	R	24	19	52	4	15	0	0	1	7	3	12	2	.288	.346
Greg Myers (SJ)	C11 DH6	L	23	17	44	0	5	2	0	0	1	2	9	0	.114	.159
Ozzie Virgil	DH6 C1	R	32	9	11	2	2	1	0	1	2	4	3	0	.182	.545
John Olerud	1B5 DH1	L	20	6	8	2	3	0	0	0	0	1	3	0	.375	.375
Kevin Batiste	OF5	R	22	6	8	1	2	0	0	0	0	0	5	1	.250	.250
Francisco Hill	DH3	R	22	3	12	1	2	1	0	0	0	1	3	0	.167	.250

NAME	T	AGE	W	L	PCT	SV	G	GS	CG	IP	H	BB	SO	SHO	ERA
		29	89	73	.549	38	162	162	12	1467	1408	478	849	12	3.58
Dave Stieb	R	31	17	8	.680	0	33	33	3	207	164	76	101	2	3.35
Jimmy Key	L	28	13	14	.481	0	33	33	5	216	226	27	118	1	3.88
John Cerutti	L	29	11	11	.500	0	33	31	3	205	214	53	69	1	3.07
Tom Henke	R	31	8	3	.727	20	64	0	0	89	66	25	116	0	1.92
Mike Flanagan	L	37	8	10	.444	0	30	30	1	172	186	47	47	1	3.93
David Wells	R	26	7	4	.636	2	54	0	0	86	66	28	78	0	2.40
Todd Stottlemyre	R	24	7	7	.500	0	27	18	0	128	137	44	63	0	3.88
Mauro Gozzo	R	23	4	1	.800	0	9	3	0	32	35	9	10	0	4.83
Duane Ward	R	26	4	10	.286	15	66	0	0	115	94	58	122	0	3.77
Frank Wills	R	30	3	1	.750	0	24	4	0	71	65	30	41	0	3.66
Steve Cummings	R	24	2	0	1.000	0	5	2	0	21	18	11	8	0	3.00
Jim Acker	R	30	2	1	.667	0	14	0	0	28	24	12	24	0	1.59
Xavier Hernandez	R	23	1	0	1.000	0	7	0	0	23	25	8	7	0	4.76
DeWayne Buice	R	31	1	0	1.000	1	7	0	0	17	13	13	10	0	5.82
Tony Castillo	L	26	1	1	.500	1	17	0	0	18	23	10	10	0	6.11
Jose Nunez	R	25	0	0	—	0	6	1	0	11	8	2	14	0	2.53
Al Leiter (SJ)	L	23	0	0	—	0	1	1	0	7	9	2	4	0	4.05
Jeff Musselman (AL)	L	26	0	1	.000	0	5	3	0	11	19	9	3	0	10.64
Alex Sanchez	R	23	0	0	.000	0	4	3	0	12	16	14	4	0	10.03

BALTIMORE — 2nd 87-75 .537 2 — FRANK ROBINSON

Name	G by Pos	B	AGE	G	AB	R	H	2B	3B	HR	RBI	BB	SO	SB	BA	SA
TOTALS			27	162	5440	708	1369	238	33	129	659	593	957	118	.252	.379
Randy Milligan	1B 117 DH1	R	27	124	365	56	98	23	5	12	45	74	75	9	.268	.458
Billy Ripken	2B 114 DH1	R	24	115	318	31	76	11	2	2	26	22	53	1	.239	.305
Cal Ripken	SS162	R	28	162	646	80	166	30	0	21	93	57	72	3	.257	.401
Craig Worthington	3B145	R	24	145	497	57	123	23	0	15	70	61	114	1	.247	.384
Joe Orsulak	OF109 DH5	L	27	123	390	59	111	22	5	7	55	41	35	5	.285	.421
Mike Devereaux	OF112 DH5	R	26	122	391	55	104	14	3	8	46	36	60	22	.266	.379
Phil Bradley	OF140 DH2	R	30	144	545	83	151	23	10	11	55	70	103	20	.277	.417
Mickey Tettleton (KJ)	C75 DH43	B	28	117	411	72	106	21	2	26	65	73	117	3	.258	.509
Larry Sheets	DH88	L	29	102	304	33	74	12	1	7	33	26	58	1	.243	.359
Brady Anderson	OF79 DH8	L	25	94	266	44	55	12	2	4	16	43	45	16	.207	.312
Jim Traber	1B69 DH5	L	27	86	234	14	49	8	0	4	26	19	41	4	.209	.295
Bob Melvin	C75 DH9	R	27	85	278	22	67	10	1	1	32	15	53	1	.241	.295
Steve Finley	OF76 DH3	L	24	81	217	35	54	5	2	2	25	15	30	17	.249	.318
Rene Gonzales	2B54 3B17 SS1	R	28	71	166	16	36	4	0	1	11	12	30	5	.217	.259
Stan Jefferson	OF32 DH2	B	26	35	127	19	33	7	0	4	20	4	22	9	.260	.409
Keith Moreland	DH29	R	35	33	107	11	23	4	0	1	10	4	12	0	.215	.280
Tim Hulett	2B23 3B11	R	29	33	57	7	5	2	0	0	4	3	16	0	.088	.123
Jamie Quirk	C24 OF1	L	34	25	51	5	11	2	0	0	9	9	11	0	.216	.255
Francisco Melendez	1B5	L	25	9	5	0	0	0	0	0	0	0	0	0	.273	.273
Juan Bell	DH4 2B2 SS2	R	21	8	4	2	0	0	0	0	0	0	1	0	1.000	.000
Chris Hoiles	C3 DH3	R	24	6	9	0	1	0	0	0	1	1	3	0	.111	.222
Butch Davis	OF3 DH1	R	31	5	6	1	1	1	0	0	0	0	3	0	.167	.333
Rich Schu	2B1	R	27	1	0	0	0	0	0	0	0	0	0	0	—	—

NAME	T	AGE	W	L	PCT	SV	G	GS	CG	IP	H	BB	SO	SHO	ERA
		27	87	75	.537	44	162	162	16	1448	1518	486	676	7	4.00
Jeff Ballard	L	25	18	8	.692	0	35	35	4	215	240	57	62	1	3.43
Bob Milacki	R	24	14	12	.538	0	37	36	3	243	233	88	113	2	3.74
Mark Williamson	R	29	10	5	.667	9	65	0	0	107	105	30	55	0	2.93
Dave Schmidt	R	32	10	13	.435	0	38	26	2	157	196	36	46	0	5.69
Jay Tibbs (SJ)	R	27	5	0	1.000	0	10	8	1	54	62	20	30	0	3.48
Gregg Olson	R	22	5	2	.714	27	64	0	0	85	57	46	90	0	1.69
Brian Holton	R	29	5	7	.417	0	39	12	0	116	140	39	51	0	4.02
Pete Harnisch	R	22	5	9	.357	0	18	17	2	103	97	64	70	0	4.62
Dave Johnson	R	29	4	7	.364	0	14	14	4	89	90	28	26	0	4.23
Jose Bautista	R	24	3	4	.429	0	15	10	0	78	84	15	30	0	5.31
Mike Smith	R	25	2	0	1.000	0	13	1	0	20	25	14	12	0	7.65
Kevin Hickey	L	32	2	3	.400	2	51	0	0	49	38	23	28	0	2.92
Mark Thurmond	L	32	2	4	.333	4	49	2	0	90	102	17	34	0	3.90
Mickey Weston (SJ)	R	28	1	0	1.000	0	7	0	0	13	18	2	7	0	5.54
Ben McDonald	R	21	1	0	1.000	0	6	0	0	7	8	4	3	0	8.59
Mark Huismann (SJ)	R	31	0	0	—	0	6	0	0	11	11	0	13	0	6.35
Curt Schilling	R	22	0	1	.000	0	5	0	0	9	10	3	6	0	6.23
Oswald Peraza (SJ) 26															

BOSTON — 3rd 83-79 .512 6 — JOE MORGAN

Name	G by Pos	B	AGE	G	AB	R	H	2B	3B	HR	RBI	BB	SO	SB	BA	SA
TOTALS			30	162	5666	774	1571	326	30	108	716	643	755	56	.277	.403
Nick Esasky	1B153 OF1	R	29	154	564	79	156	26	5	30	108	66	117	1	.277	.500
Marty Barrett (KJ)	2B80 DH4	R	31	86	336	31	86	18	0	1	27	32	12	4	.256	.318
Jody Reed	SS77 2B70 3B4 DH1 OF1	R	26	146	524	76	151	42	2	3	40	73	44	4	.288	.393
Wade Boggs	3B152 DH3	L	31	156	621	113	205	51	7	3	54	107	51	2	.330	.449
Dwight Evans	OF77 DH69	R	37	146	520	82	148	27	3	20	100	99	84	3	.285	.463
Ellis Burks (SJ)	OF95 DH1	R	24	97	399	73	121	19	6	12	61	36	52	21	.303	.471
Mike Greenwell	OF139 DH5	L	25	145	578	87	178	36	0	14	95	56	44	13	.308	.443
Rick Cerone	C97 DH1 OF1	R	35	102	296	28	72	16	1	4	48	34	40	0	.243	.345
Jim Rice (EJ)	DH55	R	36	56	209	22	49	10	2	3	28	13	39	1	.234	.344
Danny Heep	OF75 1B19 DH9	L	31	113	320	36	96	17	0	5	49	29	26	0	.300	.400
Luis Rivera	SS90 2B1 DH1	R	25	93	323	35	83	17	1	5	29	20	60	2	.257	.362
Rich Gedman	C91	L	29	93	260	24	55	9	0	4	16	23	47	0	.212	.292
Kevin Romine	OF89 DH1	R	28	92	274	30	75	13	0	1	23	21	53	1	.274	.332
Randy Kutcher	OF57 3B6 DH6 C1	R	29	77	160	28	36	10	3	2	18	11	46	3	.225	.363
1 Ed Romero	2B22 3B14 SS10 DH1	R	31	46	113	14	24	4	0	0	6	7	7	1	.212	.248
Carlos Quintana (NJ)	OF21 DH7 1B1	R	23	34	77	6	16	5	0	0	6	7	12	0	.208	.273
Sam Horn (VJ)	DH14 1B2	L	25	33	54	1	8	2	0	0	4	8	16	1	.148	.185
2 Jeff Stone	OF11 DH3	L	28	18	15	3	3	0	0	0	1	1	2	1	.200	.200
Dana Williams	DH2 OF1	R	26	8	5	1	1	1	0	0	0	0	1	0	.200	.400
John Marzano	C7	R	26	7	18	5	8	1	0	0	3	0	4	0	.444	.778

NAME	T	AGE	W	L	PCT	SV	G	GS	CG	IP	H	BB	SO	SHO	ERA
TOTALS		31	83	79	.512	42	162	162	14	1460	1448	548	1054	9	4.01
Roger Clemens	R	26	17	11	.607	0	35	35	8	253	215	93	230	3	3.13
Mike Boddicker	R	31	15	11	.577	0	34	34	3	212	217	71	145	2	4.00
John Dopson (AJ)	R	25	12	8	.600	0	29	28	2	169	166	69	95	0	3.99
Mike Smithson	R	34	7	14	.333	2	40	19	1	144	170	35	61	1	4.95
Lee Smith	R	31	6	1	.857	25	64	0	0	71	53	33	96	0	3.57
Bob Stanley	R	34	5	2	.714	4	43	0	0	79	102	26	32	0	4.88
Rob Murphy	L	29	5	7	.417	9	74	0	0	105	97	41	107	0	2.74
Dennis Lamp	R	36	4	2	.667	2	42	0	0	112	96	27	61	0	2.32
Oil Can Boyd (SJ)	R	29	3	2	.600	0	10	10	0	59	57	19	26	0	4.42
Wes Gardner (BY)	R	28	3	7	.300	0	22	16	0	86	97	47	81	0	5.97
2 Greg Harris	R	33	2	2	.500	0	15	0	0	28	21	15	25	0	2.57
Eric Hetzel	R	25	2	3	.400	0	12	11	0	50	61	28	33	0	6.26
2 Joe Price	L	32	2	5	.286	0	31	5	0	70	71	30	52	0	4.35
Mike Rochford	L	26	0	0	—	0	4	0	0	4	4	4	1	0	6.75
Tom Bolton	L	27	0	4	.000	0	4	0	0	17	21	10	9	0	8.31

MILWAUKEE — 4th 81-81 .500 8 — TOM TRERELHORN

Name	G by Pos	B	AGE	G	AB	R	H	2B	3B	HR	RBI	BB	SO	SB	BA	SA
TOTALS			28	162	5473	707	1415	235	32	126	660	455	791	165	.259	.382
Greg Brock (SJ)	1B100 DH7	L	32	107	373	40	99	16	0	12	52	43	49	6	.265	.405
Jim Gantner (KJ)	2B114 DH2	L	36	116	409	51	112	18	3	0	34	21	33	20	.274	.333
Bill Spiers	SS89 3B12 2B4 DH4 1B2	L	23	114	345	44	88	9	3	4	33	21	63	10	.255	.333
Paul Molitor	3B112 DH28 2B16	R	32	155	615	84	194	35	4	11	56	64	67	27	.315	.439
Rob Deer	OF125 DH5	R	28	130	466	72	98	18	2	26	65	60	158	4	.210	.425
Robin Yount	OF143 DH17	R	33	160	614	101	195	38	9	21	103	63	71	19	.318	.511
Glenn Braggs	OF132 DH13	R	26	144	514	77	127	12	3	15	66	42	111	17	.247	.370
B.J. Surhoff	C106 DH2 3B6	L	24	126	436	42	108	17	4	5	55	25	29	14	.248	.339
Joey Meyer	DH31 1B18	R	27	53	147	13	33	6	0	7	29	12	36	1	.224	.408
Mike Felder	OF93 DH11 2B10	B	27	117	315	50	76	11	3	3	23	23	38	26	.241	.324
Gary Sheffield (BF)	SS70 3B21 DH4	R	20	95	368	34	91	18	0	5	32	27	33	10	.247	.337
Terry Francona	1B46 DH23 OF16 P1	L	30	90	233	26	54	10	1	3	23	8	20	2	.232	.322
Gus Polidor	3B30 2B29 SS21 DH2	R	27	79	175	15	34	7	0	0	14	6	18	0	.194	.234
Charlie O'Brien	C62	R	29	62	188	22	44	10	0	6	35	21	11	0	.234	.383
Greg Vaughn (SJ)	OF24 DH13	R	23	38	113	18	30	3	0	5	23	13	23	4	.265	.425
Dave Engle	1B18 C3 DH3	R	32	27	65	5	14	3	0	2	8	4	13	0	.215	.354
3 Ed Romero	2B11 3B4 SS1	R	31	15	50	3	10	3	0	0	3	0	10	0	.200	.260
George Canale	1B11	L	23	13	26	5	5	1	0	1	4	2	9	1	.192	.346
Billy Bates (SJ)	2B7	L	25	7	14	3	3	0	0	0	0	0	1	2	.214	.214
Juan Castillo	2B3	R	27	3	4	0	0	0	0	0	0	3	0	2	.000	.000
LaVel Freeman		L	26	2	1	0	0	0	0	0	0	0	2	0	.000	.000
Dale Sveum (BL) 25																

NAME	T	AGE	W	L	PCT	SV	G	GS	CG	IP	H	BB	SO	SHO	ERA
TOTALS		27	81	81	.500	45	162	162	16	1432	1463	457	812	8	3.80
Chris Bosio	R	26	15	10	.600	0	33	33	8	235	225	48	173	2	2.95
Don August	R	25	12	12	.500	0	31	25	2	142	175	58	51	1	5.31
Teddy Higuera (XJ-SJ)	L	30	9	6	.600	0	22	22	2	135	125	48	91	1	3.46
Chuck Crim	R	27	9	7	.563	7	76	0	0	118	114	36	59	0	2.83
Mark Knudson	R	28	8	5	.615	0	40	7	1	124	110	29	47	0	3.35
Tom Filer (SJ)	R	32	7	3	.700	0	13	13	0	72	74	23	20	0	3.61
Jaime Navarro	R	22	7	8	.467	0	19	17	1	110	119	32	56	0	3.12
Bill Krueger	L	31	3	2	.600	3	34	5	0	94	96	33	72	0	3.84
Dan Plesac	R	27	3	4	.429	33	52	0	0	61	47	17	52	0	2.35
Tony Fossas	L	31	2	2	.500	1	51	0	0	61	57	22	42	0	3.54
Bryan Clutterbuck (SJ)	R	28	2	5	.286	0	14	11	1	67	73	16	29	0	4.14
Bill Wegman (SJ)	R	26	2	6	.250	0	11	8	0	51	69	21	27	0	6.71
1 Jay Aldrich	R	28	1	0	1.000	1	16	0	0	26	24	13	12	0	3.81
2 Jerry Reuss	L	40	1	4	.200	0	7	7	0	34	36	13	13	0	5.35
Paul Mirabella (SJ)	L	35	0	0	—	0	13	0	0	15	18	7	6	0	7.63
Ray Krawczyk	R	30	0	0	—	0	1	0	0	1	0	1	1	0	0.00
Terry Francona	L	30	0	0	—	0	1	0	0	1	0	1	1	0	13.50
Randy Veres	R	23	0	1	.000	0	3	1	0	9	8	4	6	0	4.32
Jeff Peterek	R	25	0	2	.000	0	7	4	0	31	14	16	0		4.02
Mike Birkbeck (SJ)	R	28	0	4	.000	0	9	9	1	45	57	22	31	0	5.44
Juan Nieves (SJ) 24															

NEW YORK — 5th 74-87 .460 14.5 — DALLAS GREEN 56-65 .463 — BUCKY DENT 18-22 .450

Name	G by Pos	B	AGE	G	AB	R	H	2B	3B	HR	RBI	BB	SO	SB	BA	SA
TOTALS			29	161	5458	698	1470	229	23	130	657	502	831	137	.269	.391
Don Mattingly	1B145 DH17 OF1	L	28	158	631	79	191	37	2	23	113	51	30	3	.303	.477
Steve Sax	2B158	R	29	158	651	88	205	26	3	5	63	52	44	43	.315	.387
Alvaro Espinoza	SS146	R	27	146	503	51	142	23	1	0	41	14	60	3	.282	.332
1 Mike Pagliarulo	3B69 DH1	L	29	74	223	19	44	10	0	4	16	19	43	1	.197	.296
2 Jesse Barfield	OF129	R	29	129	441	71	106	19	1	18	56	82	122	5	.240	.410
Roberto Kelly	OF137	R	24	137	441	65	133	18	3	9	48	41	89	35	.302	.417
Mel Hall (LJ)	OF75 DH34	L	28	113	361	54	94	9	0	17	58	21	37	0	.260	.427
Don Slaught	C105 DH3	R	30	117	350	34	88	21	3	5	38	30	57	1	.251	.371
Steve Balboni	DH82 1B20	R	32	110	300	33	71	12	2	17	59	25	67	0	.237	.460
1 Ken Phelps	DH55 1B8	L	34	86	185	26	46	3	0	7	29	47	47	0	.249	.378
Wayne Tolleson	3B28 SS28 2B13 DH10	B	29	80	140	16	23	5	2	1	9	16	23	5	.164	.250
1 Luis Polonia	OF53 DH9	L	24	66	227	39	71	11	2	2	29	16	29	9	.313	.405
Tom Brookens (MJ)	3B51 SS7 2B5 1B3 OF3 DH3	R	35	66	168	14	38	6	0	4	14	11	27	1	.226	.333
1 Rickey Henderson	OF65	R	30	65	235	*41	58	13	1	3	22	*56	29	*25	.247	.349
Bob Geren	C60 DH2	R	27	65	205	26	59	5	1	9	27	12	44	0	.288	.454
Randy Velarde	3B27 SS9	R	26	33	100	12	34	4	2	2	11	7	14	0	.340	.480
Bob Brower	OF25	R	28	26	69	6	16	3	0	2	3	6	11	3	.232	.362
Hal Morris	OF5 1B2 DH1	L	24	15	18	2	5	0	0	0	4	1	4	0	.278	.278
Deion Sanders (LF)	OF14	L	21	14	47	7	11	2	0	2	7	3	9	1	.234	.404
Mike Blowers	3B13	R	24	13	38	2	10	0	0	0	3	3	13	0	.263	.263
1 Jamie Quirk	C6 DH1 SS1	L	34	13	24	0	2	0	0	0	0	3	5	0	.083	.083
Marcus Lawton	OF8 DH1	B	23	10	14	1	3	0	0	0	0	1	2	1	.214	.214
1 Stan Jefferson	OF7 DH1	B	26	12	12	1	1	0	0	0	1	0	4	1	.083	.083
Hensley Meulens	3B8	R	22	8	28	2	5	0	0	0	0	4	14	0	.179	.179
Brian Dorsett	C8	R	28	8	22	1	8	1	0	0	3	0	6	0	.364	.409
1 Gary Ward	OF6 DH1	R	35	8	17	1	5	1	0	0	3	0	4	0	.294	.353
Steve Kiefer (NJ)	3B5	R	28	5	0	0	0	0	0	0	0	0	2	0	.125	.125
Dave Winfield (XJ) 37																
Rafael Santana (EJ) 31																

* Henderson, also with Oakland, league leader in R(113), BB(126), SB(77).

NAME	T	AGE	W	L	PCT	SV	G	GS	CG	IP	H	BB	SO	SHO	ERA
TOTALS		29	74	87	.460	44	161	161	15	1415	1550	521	787	9	4.50
Andy Hawkins	R	29	15	15	.500	0	34	34	5	208	238	76	98	2	4.80
Eric Plunk	R	25	7	5	.583	0	27	7	0	76	65	52	61	0	3.69
2 Walt Terrell	L	31	6	5	.545	0	13	13	1	83	102	24	30	1	5.20
Dave LaPoint (J)	L	29	6	9	.400	0	20	20	0	114	146	45	51	0	5.62
Lee Guetterman	L	30	5	5	.500	13	70	0	0	103	98	26	51	0	2.45
2 Greg Cadaret	R	27	5	5	.500	0	20	13	3	92	109	38	66	1	4.58
Lance McCullers	R	25	4	3	.571	3	52	1	0	85	83	37	82	0	4.57
Chuck Cary (XJ)	L	29	4	4	.500	0	22	11	2	99	78	29	79	0	3.26
Clay Parker	R	26	4	5	.444	0	22	17	2	120	123	31	53	0	3.68
1 John Candelaria (KJ)	L	35	3	3	.500	0	10	6	1	49	49	12	37	0	5.14
Dale Mohorcic	R	33	2	1	.667	2	32	0	0	58	65	18	24	0	4.99
Jimmy Jones	R	25	2	1	.667	0	11	6	0	48	56	16	25	0	5.25
1 Rich Dotson	R	30	2	5	.286	0	11	9	1	52	69	17	14	0	5.57
Dave Righetti	L	30	2	6	.250	25	55	0	0	69	73	26	51	0	3.00
Tommy John	L	46	2	7	.222	0	10	10	0	64	87	22	18	0	5.80
2 Goose Gossage	R	37	1	1	1.000	1	11	0	0	14	14	3	6	0	3.77
Scott Nielsen	R	30	1	0	1.000	0	1	0	0	2	1	0	2	0	13.50
1 Don Schulze	R	26	1	1	.500	0	2	0	0	11	12	5	4	0	4.09
1 Al Leiter	L	23	1	2	.333	0	4	4	0	21	23	22	26	0	6.08
Dave Eiland	R	22	1	0	.250	0	6	4	0	34	44	13	11	0	5.77
Bobby Davidson	R	26	0	0	—	0	4	0	0	2	1	8	1	0	18.00
Kevin Mmahat	L	24	0	2	.000	0	4	2	0	8	13	8	3	0	12.91

CLEVELAND — 6th 73-89 .461 16 — DOC EDWARDS 65-78 .455 — JOHN HART 8-11 .421

Name	G by Pos	B	AGE	G	AB	R	H	2B	3B	HR	RBI	BB	SO	SB	BA	SA
TOTALS			27	162	5463	604	1340	221	26	127	567	499	934	74	.245	.365
Pete O'Brien	1B154 DH1	L	31	155	554	75	144	24	1	12	55	83	48	3	.260	.372
Jerry Browne	2B151 DH2	B	23	153	598	83	179	31	4	5	45	68	64	14	.299	.390
Felix Fermin	SS153 2B2	R	25	156	484	50	115	9	1	0	21	41	27	6	.238	.260
Brook Jacoby	3B144 DH3	R	29	147	519	49	141	26	5	13	64	62	90	2	.272	.416
Cory Snyder	OF125 SS7 DH2	R	26	132	489	49	105	17	0	18	59	23	134	6	.215	.360
Joe Carter	OF146 1B15 DH1	R	29	162	651	84	158	32	4	35	105	39	112	13	.243	.460
1 Oddibe McDowell	OF64 DH2	L	26	69	239	30	53	5	2	3	22	25	36	12	.222	.297
Andy Allanson	C111	R	27	111	323	30	96	9	2	3	17	23	54	3	.237	.279
Dave Clark	DH55 OF21	L	26	102	253	21	60	12	0	8	29	30	63	0	.237	.379
Joel Skinner	C79	R	28	79	178	10	41	10	0	1	13	9	42	1	.230	.303
2 Dion James	OF37 DH22 1B1	L	26	71	245	26	75	11	0	4	29	24	26	1	.306	.400
Brad Komminsk (IL)	OF68	R	28	71	198	27	47	8	2	8	33	24	55	8	.237	.419
Joey Belle	OF44 DH17	R	22	62	218	22	49	8	4	7	37	12	55	2	.225	.394
Luis Aguayo	3B19 SS15 2B10 DH2	R	30	47	97	7	17	4	1	1	8	7	19	0	.175	.268
Mike Young	DH15 OF1	R	29	32	59	2	11	0	0	1	5	6	13	1	.186	.237
Luis Medina	DH25 OF3 1B1	R	26	30	83	8	17	1	0	4	9	6	35	0	.205	.361
Mark Salas	DH20 C5	L	28	30	77	4	17	4	1	2	7	0	11	0	.221	.377
Paul Zuvella	SS15 3B5 DH3	R	30	24	58	10	16	2	0	0	1	11	0	4	.276	.414
Tommy Hinzo	2B6 SS1 DH1	B	25	18	17	4	0	0	0	0	0	1	5	1	.000	.000
Beau Allred	OF5 DH2	L	24	13	24	0	6	3	0	0	2	2	10	0	.250	.391
Dave Hengel (EJ)	OF9 DH3	R	27	12	25	0	3	1	0	0	0	0	9	0	.120	.160
Pat Keedy	OF3 3B2 SS1 1B1 DH1	R	31	9	14	3	3	2	0	0	1	0	5	0	.214	.357
Tom Magrann	C9	R	25	9	10	1	2	0	0	0	1	0	0	0	.200	.200
Denny Gonzalez	DH6 3B1	R	25	7	17	1	6	0	0	0	3	0	5	0	.353	.353
Danny Sheaffer	DH3 3B2 OF1	R	28	7	16	1	1	0	0	0	0	0	4	0	.063	.063
Mark Higgins	1B5	L	25	5	7	0	1	0	0	0	0	0	0	0	.100	.100
Pete Dalena	DH1	L	29	5	7	0	1	0	0	0	0	0	0	0	.143	.286

NAME	T	AGE	W	L	PCT	SV	G	GS	CG	IP	H	BB	SO	SHO	ERA
TOTALS		28	73	89	.451	38	162	162	23	1453	1423	452	844	13	3.65
Greg Swindell (EJ)	L	24	13	6	.684	0	28	28	5	184	170	51	129	2	3.37
Tom Candiotti	R	31	13	10	.565	0	31	31	4	206	188	55	124	0	3.10
Bud Black	R	32	12	11	.522	0	33	33	6	222	213	52	88	3	3.36
John Farrell	R	26	9	14	.391	0	31	31	7	208	196	71	132	2	3.63
Doug Jones	R	32	7	10	.412	32	59	0	0	81	76	13	65	0	2.34
Rich Yett	R	26	5	6	.455	0	32	12	1	99	111	47	47	0	5.00
Scott Bailes	L	27	5	9	.357	0	34	11	0	114	116	29	47	0	4.28
Rod Nichols (SJ)	R	24	4	6	.400	0	15	11	0	72	81	24	42	0	4.40
Jesse Orosco	L	32	3	4	.429	3	69	0	0	78	54	26	79	0	2.08
Steve Davis	L	28	1	1	.500	0	12	2	0	24	14	12	8	0	8.06
Steve Olin	R	23	1	4	.200	1	25	0	0	36	35	14	24	0	3.75
Tim Stoddard (AJ)	R	36	0	0	—	0	14	0	0	14	18	7	12	0	2.95
Brad Havens	L	29	0	0	—	0	13	0	0	13	18	7	6	0	3.38
Rudy Seanez	R	20	0	0	—	0	5	0	0	5	1	5	4	0	3.60
Kevin Wicklander	L	24	0	0	—	0	3	0	0	5	5	3	3	0	3.38
Ed Wojna	R	28	0	1	.000	0	33			31	14	10		0	4.09
Jeff Kaiser	R	27	0	0	—	0	6	0	0	4	5	4	7	0	7.36
Neil Allen (BG)	R	31	0	0	—	0	3	0	0	5	6	4	0		15.00
Joe Skalski	R	24	0	2	.000	0	5	0	0	9	6	6	0		6.75
Keith Atherton	R	30	0	3	.000	0	32	0	0	39	48	13	13	0	4.15

Name	G by Pos	B	AGE	G	AB	R	H	2B	3B	HR	RBI	BB	SO	SB	BA	SA
DETROIT	**7th 59-103 .364 30**									SPARKY ANDERSON					
TOTALS			31	162	5432	617	1315	198	24	116	564	585	899	103	.242	.351
Dave Bergman	1B123 DH7 OF1	L	36	137	385	38	103	13	1	7	37	44	44	1	.268	.361
Lou Whitaker	2B146 DH2	L	32	148	509	77	128	21	1	28	85	89	59	6	.251	.462
Alan Trammell	SS117 DH2	R	31	121	449	54	109	20	3	5	43	45	45	10	.243	.334
2 Rick Schu	3B83 DH9 2B5 SS3 1B3	R	27	98	266	25	57	11	0	7	21	24	37	1	.214	.335
Chet Lemon	OF111 DH6	R	34	127	414	45	98	19	2	7	47	46	71	1	.237	.343
Gary Pettis (RJ)	OF119	B	31	119	444	77	114	8	6	1	18	84	106	43	.257	.309
Fred Lynn	OF68 DH46	L	37	117	353	44	85	11	1	11	46	47	71	1	.241	.371
Mike Heath	C117 3B4 OF3 DH1	R	34	122	396	38	104	16	2	10	43	24	71	7	.263	.389
1 Keith Moreland	DH51 1B31 3B12 C1	R	35	90	318	34	95	16	0	5	35	27	33	3	.299	.396
2 Gary Ward	OF51 1B26 DH26	R	35	105	275	24	69	10	2	9	29	21	54	1	.251	.400
Kenny Williams (VJ)	OF87 1B1 DH1	R	25	94	258	29	53	5	1	6	23	18	63	9	.205	.302
Mike Brumley	SS42 2B24 3B11 DH8 OF4	B	26	92	212	33	42	5	2	1	11	14	45	8	.198	.255
Matt Nokes (KJ)	C51 DH33	L	25	87	268	15	67	10	0	9	39	17	37	1	.250	.388
Doug Strange	3B54 SS9 2B9 DH1	B	25	64	196	16	42	4	1	1	14	17	36	3	.214	.260
2 Pat Sheridan	OF35 DH8	L	31	50	120	16	29	3	0	3	15	17	21	4	.242	.342
2 Tracy Jones	OF36 DH8	R	28	46	158	17	41	10	0	3	26	16	16	1	.259	.380
Scott Lusader (SJ)	OF33 DH1	L	25	40	103	15	26	4	0	1	8	9	21	3	.252	.320
Al Pedrique	SS12 3B12 2B8	R	28	31	69	1	14	3	0	0	5	2	15	0	.203	.246
Torey Lovullo	1B18 3B11 DH1	B	23	29	87	8	10	2	0	1	4	14	20	0	.115	.172
Rob Ritchie	OF13 DH4	L	23	19	49	6	13	4	2	1	10	5	10	0	.265	.490
Chris Brown	3B17	R	27	17	57	3	11	3	0	0	4	1	17	0	.193	.246
Matt Sinatro	C13	R	29	13	25	2	3	0	0	0	1	3	1	0	.120	.120
1 Billy Bean	OF6 1B2	L	25	9	11	0	0	0	0	0	0	1	2	0	.000	.000
Jeff Datz	C6 DH1	R	29	7	10	1	2	0	0	0	0	1	1	0	.200	.200

NAME	T	AGE	W	L	PCT	SV	G	GS	CG	IP	H	BB	SO	SHO	ERA
		31	59	103	.364	26	162	162	24	1427	1514	652	831	4	4.53
Mike Henneman	R	27	11	4	.733	8	60	0	0	90	84	51	69	0	3.70
Frank Tanana	L	35	10	14	.417	0	33	33	6	224	227	74	147	1	3.58
Jack Morris (EJ)	R	34	6	14	.300	0	24	24	10	170	189	59	115	0	4.86
Doyle Alexander	R	38	6	18	.250	0	33	33	5	223	245	76	95	1	4.44
Jeff Robinson (UJ)	R	27	4	5	.444	0	16	16	1	78	76	46	40	1	4.73
Kevin Ritz	R	24	4	6	.400	0	12	12	1	74	75	44	56	0	4.38
Paul Gibson	L	29	4	8	.333	0	45	13	0	132	129	57	77	0	4.64
Frank Williams (EJ)	R	31	3	3	.500	1	42	0	0	72	70	46	33	0	3.64
Edwin Nunez	R	26	3	4	.429	1	27	0	0	54	49	36	41	0	4.17
Guillermo Hernandez (EJ)	L		2	2	.500	15	32	0	0	31	36	16	30	0	5.74
Mike Schwabe	R	24	2	4	.333	0	13	4	0	45	58	16	13	0	6.04
2 Steve Searcy (SJ)	L	25	1	1	.500	0	8	2	0	22	27	12	11	0	6.04
2 Brad Havens	L	29	1	2	.333	0	13	1	0	23	28	14	15	0	5.96
Mike Trujillo	R	29	1	2	.333	0	8	4	1	26	35	13	13	0	5.96
Charlie Hudson (LJ-BL)	R	30	1	5	.167	0	18	7	0	67	75	31	23	0	6.35
Ramon Pena (LJ)	R	27	0	0	—	0	8	0	0	18	26	8	12	0	6.00
Shawn Holman	R	24	0	0	—	0	5	0	0	10	8	11	9	0	1.80
Randy Bockus	R	28	0	0	—	0	5	0	0	5	7	2	2	0	5.06
Dave Beard	R	29	0	2	.000	0	5	0	0	5	9	2	1	0	5.06
Randy Nosek	R	22	0	2	.000	0	2	2	0	5	5	7	2	0	13.50
David Palmer	R	31	0	3	.000	0	5	5	0	17	25	11	12	0	7.79
Brian DuBois	L	24	0	4	.000	0	6	5	0	36	29	11	13	0	1.75

WEST DIVISION

OAKLAND	**1st 99-63 .611**									TONY LaRUSSA					
TOTALS			29	162	5416	712	1414	220	25	127	659	562	855	157	.261	.381
Mark McGwire	1B141 DH2	R	25	143	490	74	113	17	0	33	95	83	94	1	.231	.467
Tony Phillips	2B84 3B49 SS17 OF16 1B1	B	30	143	451	48	118	15	6	4	47	58	66	3	.262	.348
Mike Gallego	SS94 2B41 3B3 DH1	R	28	133	357	45	90	14	2	3	30	35	43	7	.252	.328
Carney Lansford	3B136 1B15 DH3	R	32	148	551	81	185	28	2	2	52	51	25	37	.336	.405
Jose Canseco (BW)	OF56 DH5	R	24	65	227	40	61	9	1	17	57	23	69	6	.269	.542
Dave Henderson	OF149 DH2	R	30	152	579	77	145	24	3	15	80	54	131	8	.250	.380
2 Rickey Henderson	OF82 DH3	R	30	85	306	*72	90	13	2	9	35	*70	39	*52	.294	.438
Terry Steinbach	C103 OF14 1B10 DH4 3B8	R	27	130	454	37	124	13	1	7	42	30	66	1	.273	.352
Dave Parker	DH140 OF1	L	38	144	553	56	146	27	0	22	97	38	91	0	.264	.432
Stan Javier	OF107 2B1 1B1	B	25	112	310	42	77	12	3	1	28	31	45	12	.248	.316
Ron Hassey	C78 DH2 1B1	L	36	97	268	29	61	12	0	5	23	24	45	1	.228	.328
Walt Weiss (KJ)	SS84	B	25	84	236	30	55	11	0	3	21	21	39	6	.233	.318
1 Luis Polonia	OF55	L	24	59	206	31	59	6	4	1	17	9	15	13	.286	.369
Lance Blankenship	OF25 2B24 DH10	R	25	58	125	22	29	5	1	1	4	8	31	5	.232	.312
Glenn Hubbard	2B48 DH3	R	31	53	131	12	26	6	0	3	12	19	20	2	.198	.313
Billy Beane	OF25 1B4 DH4 3B1 C1	R	27	37	79	8	19	5	0	0	11	0	13	3	.241	.304
Felix Jose	OF19	B	24	20	57	3	11	2	0	0	5	4	13	0	.193	.228
2 Ken Phelps	1B1 DH1	L	34	11	9	0	1	1	0	0	4	2	4	0	.111	.222
2 Jamie Quirk	3B3 C2 1B1	L	34	9	10	1	2	0	0	0	1	0	4	0	.200	.500
Doug Jennings	OF3	L	24	4	4	0	0	0	0	0	0	0	2	0	.000	.000
Scott Hemond	DH3	R	23	4	0	2	0	0	0	0	0	0	0	0		
Dean Howitt	OF1 1B1	L	25	3	3	0	0	0	0	0	0	0	1	0	.000	.000
Dick Scott	SS3	R	26	3	2	0	0	0	0	0	0	0	1	0	.000	.000
Larry Arndt	1B1 3B1	R	26	2	6	1	1	0	0	0	0	0	1	0	.167	.167
Chris Bando	C1	B	32	2	2	1	1	0	0	0	0	1	0	0	.500	.500

	T	AGE	W	L	PCT	SV	G	GS	CG	IP	H	BB	SO	SHO	ERA
		29	99	63	.611	57	162	162	17	1448	1271	510	931	20	3.09
Dave Stewart	R	32	21	9	.700	0	36	36	8	258	260	69	155	0	3.32
Storm Davis	R	27	19	7	.731	0	31	31	1	169	187	68	91	0	4.36
Mike Moore	R	29	19	11	.633	0	35	35	6	242	193	83	172	3	2.61
Bob Welch	R	32	17	8	.680	0	33	33	1	210	191	78	137	0	3.00
Todd Burns	R	25	6	5	.545	8	50	2	0	96	66	28	49	0	2.24
Curt Young	L	29	5	9	.357	0	25	20	1	111	117	47	55	0	3.73
Dennis Eckersley (SJ)	R	34	4	0	1.000	33	51	0	0	58	32	3	55	0	1.56
Gene Nelson	R	28	3	5	.375	3	50	0	0	80	60	30	70	0	3.26
Rick Honeycutt	L	35	2	2	.500	12	64	0	0	77	56	26	52	0	2.35
1 Eric Plunk	R	25	1	1	.500	1	23	0	0	29	17	12	24	0	2.20
Jim Corsi	R	27	1	2	.333	0	22	0	0	38	26	10	21	0	1.88
Matt Young (EJ)	R	30	1	4	.200	0	37	7	0	37	42	31	27	0	6.75
1 Greg Cadaret	L	27	0	0	—	0	26	0	0	28	21	19	14	0	2.28
Bill Dawley	R	31	0	0	—	0	4	0	0	9	11	2	3	0	4.00
Brian Snyder	L	31	0	0	—	0	3	0	0	3	3	3	1	0	27.00
Dave Otto	L	24	0	1	—	0	1	0	0	7	6	2	4	0	2.70

*Rickey Henderson, also with New York, League leader in R(113),BB (126), SB (77).

KANSAS CITY	**2nd 92-70 .568 7**									JOHN WATHAN					
TOTALS			32	162	5475	690	1428	227	41	101	653	554	897	154	.261	.373
George Brett (KJ)	1B104 DH17 OF2	L	36	124	457	67	129	26	3	12	80	59	47	14	.282	.431
Frank White	2B132	R	38	135	418	34	107	22	1	2	36	30	52	3	.256	.328
Kurt Stillwell	SS130	B	24	130	463	52	121	20	7	7	54	42	64	9	.261	.380
Kevin Seitzer	3B159 SS6 OF3 DH1	R	27	160	597	78	168	17	2	4	48	102	76	17	.281	.337
Jim Eisenreich	OF123 DH10	L	30	134	475	64	139	33	7	9	59	37	44	27	.293	.448
Willie Wilson	OF108 DH1	B	33	112	383	58	97	17	7	3	43	27	78	24	.253	.358
Bo Jackson	OF110 DH24	R	26	135	515	86	132	15	6	32	105	39	172	26	.256	.495
Bob Boone	C129	R	41	131	405	33	111	13	2	1	43	49	37	3	.274	.323
Danny Tartabull	OF71 DH55	R	26	133	441	54	118	22	0	18	62	69	123	4	.268	.440
Pat Tabler	OF55 DH39 1B20 2B3 3B1	R	31	123	390	36	101	11	1	2	42	37	42	0	.259	.308
Brad Wellman	2B64 SS34 3B3 OF1 DH1	R	29	103	178	30	41	4	0	2	12	7	36	5	.230	.287
Bill Buckner	1B24 DH19	L	39	79	176	7	38	4	1	1	16	6	11	1	.216	.267
Gary Thurman (WJ)	OF60 DH4	R	24	72	87	24	17	2	1	0	5	15	26	16	.195	.241
Mike Macfarlane	C59 DH4	R	25	69	157	13	35	6	0	2	19	7	27	0	.223	.299
Bill Pecota	SS29 OF15 2B12 3B7 1B4	R	29	65	83	21	17	4	2	3	5	9	14	5	.205	.410
Rex Palacios	3B21 1B18 C13 OF1	R	26	55	47	12	8	2	0	1	8	2	14	0	.170	.277
Matt Winters	OF31 DH3	L	29	42	107	14	25	6	0	2	9	14	23	0	.234	.346
Luis de los Santos	1B27	R	22	28	87	6	22	3	1	0	6	5	14	0	.253	.310
Jeff Schulz	OF5	L	28	7	9	0	2	0	0	0	1	0	2	0	.222	.222
Buddy Biancalana (XJ) 29																

	T	AGE	W	L	PCT	SV	G	GS	CG	IP	H	BB	SO	SHO	ERA
		28	92	70	.568	38	162	162	27	1452	1415	455	978	13	3.55
Bret Saberhagen	R	25	23	6	.793	0	36	35	12	262	209	43	193	4	2.16
Tom Gordon	R	21	17	9	.654	1	49	16	1	163	122	86	153	1	3.64
Mark Gubicza	R	26	15	11	.577	0	36	36	8	255	252	63	173	2	3.04
Jeff Montgomery	R	27	7	3	.700	18	63	0	0	92	66	25	94	0	1.37
Luis Aquino	R	25	6	8	.429	0	34	16	2	141	148	35	68	1	3.50
2 Terry Leach	R	35	5	6	.455	0	30	3	0	74	78	36	34	0	4.15
Charlie Leibrandt	L	32	5	11	.313	0	33	27	3	161	196	54	73	1	5.14
Floyd Bannister (SJ)	L	34	4	1	.800	0	14	14	0	75	87	18	35	0	4.66
Steve Crawford	R	31	3	1	.750	0	25	0	0	54	48	19	33	0	2.83
Rick Luecken	R	28	2	1	.667	1	19	0	0	24	23	13	16	0	3.42
2 Larry McWilliams	L	35	2	2	.500	0	8	5	1	33	31	8	24	0	4.13
Steve Farr (KJ)	R	32	2	5	.286	18	51	0	0	63	75	22	56	0	4.12
Kevin Appier	R	21	1	4	.200	0	6	5	0	22	34	12	10	0	9.14
Jerry Don Gleaton	L	31	0	0	—	0	14	0	0	20	6	9	5	0	5.65
Jose DeJesus	R	24	0	0	—	0	3	1	0	5	4	3	4	0	1.80
Bob Buchanan	L	28	0	1	—	0	3	0	0	5	3	1	5	0	16.20
Stan Clarke	L	28	0	1	.000	0	7	0	0	14	14	4	2	0	15.43
Israel Sanchez (EJ) 25																

CALIFORNIA	**3rd 91-71 .552 8**									DOUG RADER					
TOTALS			30	162	5545	669	1422	208	37	145	624	429	1011	89	.256	.386
Wally Joyner	1B159	L	27	159	593	78	167	30	2	16	79	46	58	3	.282	.420
Johnny Ray	2B130	B	32	134	530	52	153	16	3	5	62	36	30	6	.289	.358
Dick Schofield (BH)	SS90	R	26	91	302	42	69	11	2	4	26	28	47	9	.228	.318
Jack Howell	3B142 OF4	L	27	144	474	56	108	19	4	20	52	52	125	0	.228	.411
Claudell Washington	OF100 DH7	L	34	110	418	54	114	18	4	13	42	27	84	13	.273	.445
Devon White	OF154 DH1	B	26	156	636	86	156	18	13	12	56	31	129	44	.245	.371
Chili Davis	OF147 DH7	B	29	154	560	81	152	24	1	22	90	61	109	3	.271	.436
Lance Parrish	C122 DH2	R	33	124	433	48	103	12	1	17	50	42	104	1	.238	.388
Brian Downing	DH141	R	38	142	544	59	154	25	2	14	59	56	87	0	.283	.414
Kent Anderson	SS70 2B7 3B5 OF2 DH1	R	25	86	223	27	51	6	1	0	17	17	42	1	.229	.265
Tony Armas (LJ)	OF47 DH6 1B2	R	35	60	202	22	52	7	1	11	30	7	48	0	.257	.465
Dante Bichette	OF40 DH1	R	25	48	138	13	29	7	0	3	15	6	24	3	.210	.326
Glenn Hoffman	SS23 3B18 2B4 1B1 DH1	R	30	48	104	9	22	3	0	1	3	13	22	0	.212	.269
Bill Schroeder (EJ)	C33 1B8	R	30	41	138	16	28	2	0	6	15	3	44	0	.203	.348
Mark McLemore	2B27 DH1	B	24	32	103	12	25	3	1	0	14	7	19	6	.243	.291
Max Venable	OF13	L	32	20	53	7	19	4	0	0	4	1	16	0	.358	.434
John Orton	C16	R	23	16	39	4	7	1	0	0	4	2	17	0	.179	.205
Bobby Rose	3B10 2B3	R	22	14	38	4	8	1	2	1	3	2	10	0	.211	.421
Jim Eppard	1B4	L	29	12	12	0	3	0	0	0	2	1	4	0	.250	.250
Ron Tingley	C4	R	30	4	3	0	1	0	0	0	0	1	1	0	.333	.333
Brian Brady	OF1	L	26	2	2	0	1	0	0	1	0	1	0	1	.500	1.000
Gary DiSarcina	SS1	R	21	2	0	0	0	0	0	0	0	0	0	0	.000	.000

	T	AGE	W	L	PCT	SV	G	GS	CG	IP	H	BB	SO	SHO	ERA
		29	91	71	.562	38	162	162	32	1454	1384	465	897	20	3.28
Bert Blyleven	R	38	17	5	.773	0	33	33	8	241	225	44	131	5	2.73
Chuck Finley	L	26	16	9	.640	0	29	29	9	200	171	82	156	1	2.57
Kirk McCaskill	R	28	15	10	.600	0	32	32	6	212	202	59	107	4	2.93
Jim Abbott	L	21	12	12	.500	0	29	29	4	181	190	74	115	2	3.92
Mike Witt	R	28	9	15	.375	0	33	33	5	220	252	48	123	0	4.54
Bob McClure	L	37	6	1	.857	3	48	0	0	52	39	15	36	0	1.55
Greg Minton	R	37	4	3	.571	8	62	0	0	90	76	37	42	0	2.20
Willie Fraser	R	25	4	7	.364	2	44	0	0	92	80	23	46	0	3.24
Dan Petry	R	30	3	2	.600	0	19	4	0	51	53	23	21	0	5.47
Bryan Harvey	R	26	3	3	.500	25	51	0	0	55	36	41	78	0	3.44
Rich Monteleone	R	26	2	2	.500	0	24	0	0	40	39	13	27	0	3.18
Sherman Corbett	L	26	0	0	—	0	9	0	0	8	8	3	3	0	3.38
Mike Fetters	R	24	0	0	—	0	1	0	0	3	5	1	4	0	8.10
Vance Lovelace	L	26	0	0	—	0	2	0	0	1	1	1	0	0	0.00
Terry Clark (SJ)	R	28	0	2	.000	0	4	2	0	11	13	3	7	0	4.91

TEXAS 4th 83-79 .512 16 BOBBY VALENTINE

Name	G by Pos	B	AGE	G	AB	R	H	2B	3B	HR	RBI	BB	SO	SB	BA	SA
TOTALS			27	162	5458	695	1433	260	46	122	654	503	989	101	.263	.394
Rafael Palmeiro	1B147 DH6	L	24	156	559	76	154	23	4	8	64	63	48	4	.275	.374
Julio Franco	2B140 DH10	R	30	150	548	80	173	31	5	13	92	66	69	21	.316	.462
1 Scott Fletcher	SS81 DH1	R	30	83	314	47	75	14	1	0	22	38	41	1	.239	.290
Steve Buechele	3B145 2B18 SS1 DH1	R	27	155	486	60	114	22	2	16	59	36	107	1	.235	.387
Ruben Sierra	OF162	B	23	162	634	101	194	35	14	29	119	43	82	8	.306	.543
Cecil Espy	OF133 DH3	B	26	142	475	65	122	12	7	3	31	38	99	45	.257	.331
Pete Incaviglia	OF125 DH5	R	25	133	453	48	107	27	4	21	81	32	136	5	.236	.453
Chad Kreuter	C85	B	24	87	158	16	24	3	0	5	9	27	40	0	.152	.266
2 Harold Baines	DH46 OF1	L	30	50	172	18	49	9	0	3	16	30	27	0	.285	.390
Rick Leach	DH44 OF41 1B4	L	32	110	239	32	65	14	1	1	23	32	33	2	.272	.351
Jeff Kunkel	SS59 OF30 2B8 DH5 3B4 P1	R	27	108	293	39	79	21	2	8	29	20	75	3	.270	.437
Jim Sundberg	C73 DH1	R	38	76	117	13	29	7	1	2	8	23	37	0	.197	.299
Geno Petralli	C49 DH16	L	29	70	184	18	56	7	0	4	23	17	24	0	.304	.408
Mike Stanley	C25 DH21 1B7 3B3	R	26	67	122	9	30	3	1	1	11	12	29	1	.246	.311
2 Fred Manrique	SS37 2B17 3B6	R	28	59	191	23	55	12	0	2	22	9	33	4	.288	.382
Jack Daugherty	1B23 DH8 OF5	B	28	52	106	15	32	4	2	1	10	11	21	2	.302	.406
Thad Bosley	OF8 DH5	L	32	37	40	5	9	2	0	1	9	3	11	2	.225	.350
Buddy Bell	DH22 3B9 1B1	L	37	34	82	4	15	4	0	0	3	7	10	0	.183	.232
1 Sammy Sosa	OF19 DH6	R	20	25	84	8	20	3	0	1	3	0	20	0	.238	.310
Scott Coolbaugh	3B23 DH2	R	23	25	51	7	14	1	0	2	7	4	12	0	.275	.412
Juan Gonzalez	OF24	R	19	24	60	6	9	3	0	1	7	6	17	0	.150	.250
1 Jeff Stone	DH15 OF3	L	28	22	36	5	6	1	2	0	5	3	5	2	.167	.306
Dean Palmer	3B6 DH6 OF1 SS1	R	20	16	19	0	2	2	0	0	1	0	12	0	.105	.211
Kevin Reimer	DH1	L	25	3	5	0	0	0	0	0	0	0	1	0	.000	.000

NAME	T	AGE	W	L	PCT	SV	G	GS	CG	IP	H	BB	SO	SHO	ERA
TOTALS		29	83	79	.512	44	162	162	26	1434	1279	654	1112	7	3.91
Nolan Ryan	R	42	16	10	.615	0	32	32	6	239	162	98	301	2	3.20
Kevin Brown	R	24	12	9	.571	0	28	28	7	191	167	70	104	0	3.35
Bobby Witt	R	25	12	13	.480	0	31	31	5	194	182	114	166	1	5.14
Charlie Hough	R	41	10	13	.435	0	30	30	5	182	168	95	94	1	4.35
Mike Jeffcoat	L	29	9	6	.600	0	22	22	2	131	139	33	64	2	3.58
Jeff Russell	R	27	6	4	.600	38	71	0	0	73	45	24	77	0	1.98
Cecilio Guante	R	29	6	6	.500	2	50	0	0	69	66	36	69	0	3.91
Jamie Moyer (SJ)	L	26	4	9	.308	0	15	15	1	76	84	33	44	0	4.86
Kenny Rogers	L	24	3	4	.429	2	73	0	0	74	60	42	63	0	2.93
Drew Hall	L	26	2	1	.667	0	38	0	0	58	42	33	45	0	3.70
Brad Arnsberg	R	25	2	1	.667	1	16	1	0	48	45	22	26	0	4.13
Gary Mielke	R	26	1	0	.000	0	43	0	0	50	52	25	26	0	3.26
Craig McMurtry (SJ)	R	29	0	0	—	0	19	0	0	23	29	13	14	0	7.43
Paul Wilmet	R	30	0	0	—	0	3	0	0	2	5	2	1	0	15.43
Jeff Kunkel	R	27	0	0	—	0	1	0	0	2	4	3	0	0	21.60
Darrel Akerfelds	R	27	0	1	.000	0	6	0	0	11	11	5	9	0	3.27
John Barfield	L	24	0	1	.000	0	4	2	0	12	15	4	9	0	6.17
Wilson Alvarez	L	19	0	1	.000	0	1	1	0	0	3	2	0	0	∞
Ed Correa (SJ) 23															
Jose Guzman (SJ) 26															

MINNESOTA 5th 80-82 .494 19 TOM KELLY

Name	G by Pos	B	AGE	G	AB	R	H	2B	3B	HR	RBI	BB	SO	SB	BA	SA
TOTALS			30	162	5581	740	1542	278	35	117	691	478	743	111	.276	.402
Kent Hrbek (SJ)	1B89 DH18	L	29	109	375	59	102	17	0	25	84	53	35	3	.272	.517
Wally Backman (SJ)	2B84 DH1	B	29	87	299	33	69	9	2	1	26	32	45	1	.231	.284
Greg Gagne	SS146 OF1	R	27	149	460	69	125	29	7	9	48	17	80	11	.272	.424
Gary Gaetti	OF125 DH3 1B2	R	30	130	498	63	125	11	4	19	75	25	87	6	.251	.404
Randy Bush	OF109 1B25 DH5	L	30	141	391	60	103	17	4	14	54	48	73	5	.263	.435
Kirby Puckett	OF157 DH2	R	29	159	635	75	215	45	4	9	85	41	59	11	.339	.465
Dan Gladden (LJ)	OF117 DH2 P1	R	31	121	461	69	136	23	3	8	46	23	53	23	.295	.410
Brian Harper	C101 DH19 OF3 1B2 3B2	R	29	126	385	43	125	24	0	8	57	13	16	2	.325	.449
1 Jim Dwyer	DH74 OF1	L	37	88	225	34	71	11	0	3	23	28	23	1	.316	.404
Al Newman	2B84 3B37 SS31 OF4 DH2	B	29	141	446	62	113	18	2	0	38	59	46	25	.253	.303
Gene Larkin	1B67 DH41 OF32	B	26	136	446	61	119	25	1	6	46	54	57	5	.267	.368
John Moses	OF108 1B2 DH3 P1	B	31	129	242	33	68	12	3	1	31	19	23	14	.281	.368
Tim Laudner	C68 DH19 1B11	R	31	100	239	24	53	11	1	6	27	25	65	1	.222	.351
Carmen Castillo	OF67 DH16	R	31	94	218	23	56	13	3	8	33	15	40	1	.257	.454
Doug Baker	2B25 SS19 DH1	B	28	44	96	13	17	3	1	0	9	9	18	0	.295	.385
Chip Hale	2B16 3B9 DH2	L	24	28	67	6	14	3	0	0	4	1	6	0	.209	.254
Orlando Mercado	C19	R	27	19	38	1	4	0	0	0	4	1	4	0	.105	.105
Paul Sorrento	1B5 DH5	L	23	14	21	2	5	0	0	0	5	4	4	0	.238	.238
Lenny Webster	C14	R	24	14	20	3	6	2	0	1	3	2	0	0	.300	.400
Terry Jorgensen	3B9	R	22	10	23	1	4	1	0	0	2	4	5	0	.174	.217
Vic Rodriguez	3B5 DH1	R	27	6	11	2	5	2	0	0	0	0	0	0	.455	.636
Greg Olson	C3	R	28	3	2	0	1	0	0	0	0	0	1	0	.500	.500

NAME	T	AGE	W	L	PCT	SV	G	GS	CG	IP	H	BB	SO	SHO	ERA
TOTALS		28	80	82	.494	38	162	162	19	1429	1495	500	851	8	4.28
Allan Anderson	L	25	17	10	.630	0	33	33	4	197	214	53	69	1	3.80
Roy Smith	R	27	10	6	.625	1	32	26	2	172	180	51	92	0	3.92
Juan Berenguer	R	34	9	3	.750	3	56	0	0	106	96	47	93	0	3.48
1 Frank Viola	L	29	8	12	.400	0	24	24	7	176	171	47	138	1	3.79
Jeff Reardon	R	33	5	4	.556	31	65	0	0	73	68	12	46	0	4.07
Shane Rawley	L	33	5	12	.294	0	27	25	1	145	167	60	68	0	5.21
Mike Dyer	R	22	4	7	.364	0	16	12	1	71	74	37	37	0	4.82
2 David West	L	24	3	2	.600	0	10	5	0	39	48	19	31	0	6.41
Gary Wayne	L	26	3	4	.429	1	60	0	0	71	55	36	41	0	3.30
Francisco Oliveras	R	26	3	4	.429	0	12	8	1	56	64	15	24	0	4.53
2 Rick Aguilera	R	27	3	5	.375	0	11	11	3	76	71	17	57	0	3.21
2 Kevin Tapani	R	25	2	2	.500	0	5	5	0	33	34	8	21	0	3.86
Mark Guthrie	L	23	2	4	.333	0	13	8	0	57	66	21	38	0	4.55
Randy St. Claire	R	28	1	0	1.000	1	14	0	0	22	19	10	14	0	5.24
Lee Tunnell	R	28	1	0	1.000	0	10	0	0	12	18	6	7	0	6.00
1 Freddie Toliver	R	28	1	3	.250	0	5	5	0	29	39	15	11	0	7.76
Tim Drummond	R	24	0	0	—	0	10	0	0	16	16	8	9	0	3.86
2 Greg Booker	R	29	0	0	—	0	9	0	0	9	11	2	3	0	4.15
John Moses	L	31	0	0	—	0	1	0	0	1	0	0	1	0	0.00
Dan Gladden	R	31	0	0	—	0	1	0	0	1	2	1	0	0	9.00
Mike Cook	R	25	0	1	.000	0	15	0	0	21	22	17	15	0	5.06
Steve Shields (NJ)	R	30	0	1	.000	0				17	28	6	12	0	7.79

SEATTLE 6th 73-89 .451 26 JIM LEFEBVRE

Name	G by Pos	B	AGE	G	AB	R	H	2B	3B	HR	RBI	BB	SO	SB	BA	SA
TOTALS			26	162	5512	694	1417	237	29	134	653	489	838	81	.257	.384
Alvin Davis	1B125 DH14	L	28	142	498	84	152	30	1	21	95	101	49	0	.305	.496
Harold Reynolds	2B151 DH1	B	28	153	613	87	184	24	9	0	43	55	45	25	.300	.369
Omar Vizquel	SS143	B	22	143	387	45	85	7	3	1	20	28	40	1	.220	.261
Jim Presley	3B90 1B30 DH1	R	27	117	390	42	92	20	1	12	41	21	107	0	.236	.385
Darnell Coles	OF89 3B26 1B18 DH1	R	27	146	535	54	135	21	3	10	59	27	61	5	.252	.359
Ken Griffey Jr. (BG)	OF127	L	19	127	455	61	120	23	0	16	61	44	83	16	.264	.420
Greg Briley	OF105 2B10 DH2	L	24	115	394	52	105	22	4	13	52	39	82	11	.266	.442
Dave Valle (KJ)	C93	R	28	94	316	32	75	10	3	7	34	29	32	0	.237	.354
Jeff Leonard	DH123 OF24 DH1	R	33	150	566	69	144	20	1	24	93	38	125	6	.254	.420
Scott Bradley	C70 DH6 1B2 OF1	L	29	103	270	21	74	16	0	3	37	21	23	1	.274	.367
Henry Cotto	OF90 DH2	R	28	100	295	44	78	11	2	9	33	12	44	10	.264	.407
Edgar Martinez	3B61	R	26	65	171	20	41	5	0	2	20	17	26	2	.240	.304
Jay Buhner (WJ)	OF57	R	24	58	204	27	56	15	1	9	33	19	55	1	.275	.490
Dave Cochrane	SS30 1B9 3B9 2B4 OF3 C2	B	26	54	102	13	24	4	1	3	14	27	27	0	.235	.382
Mario Diaz	SS37 2B14 3B3	R	27	52	74	9	10	0	1	0	7	7	7	0	.135	.176
Mickey Brantley	OF23 DH7	R	28	34	108	14	17	5	0	0	3	7	15	1	.157	.204
Mike Kingery	OF23	L	28	31	76	14	17	3	0	2	6	7	14	1	.224	.342
Bill McGuire	C14	R	25	14	28	2	5	0	0	1	4	2	6	0	.179	.286
1 Rey Quinones	SS7	R	25	7	19	2	2	0	0	0	1	1	6	0	.105	.105
Jim Wilson	DH5	R	28	5	8	0	0	0	0	0	0	0	3	0	.000	.000
Bruce Fields	OF1	L	28	3	3	1	1	0	0	0	0	0	1	0	.333	.667

NAME	T	AGE	W	L	PCT	SV	G	GS	CG	IP	H	BB	SO	SHO	ERA
TOTALS		27	73	89	.451	44	162	162	15	1438	1422	560	897	10	4.00
Scott Bankhead	R	25	14	6	.700	0	33	33	3	210	187	63	140	2	3.34
Erik Hanson (SJ)	R	24	9	5	.643	0	17	17	1	113	103	32	75	0	3.18
2 Brian Holman	R	24	8	10	.444	0	23	22	6	160	160	62	82	2	3.44
Bill Swift	R	27	7	3	.700	1	37	16	0	130	140	38	45	0	4.43
Jerry Reed	R	33	7	7	.500	0	52	1	0	102	89	43	50	0	3.19
2 Randy Johnson	L	25	7	9	.438	0	22	22	2	131	118	70	104	0	4.40
Steve Trout	L	31	4	3	.571	0	19	3	0	30	43	17	7	0	6.60
1 Mark Langston	L	28	4	5	.444	0	10	10	2	73	60	19	60	1	3.56
Mike Jackson	R	24	4	6	.400	7	65	0	0	99	81	54	94	0	3.17
Dennis Powell	L	25	2	2	.500	2	43	1	0	45	49	21	27	0	5.00
2 Mike Dunne	R	26	2	9	.182	0	15	15	1	85	104	37	38	0	5.27
Keith Comstock	L	33	1	2	.333	0	31	0	0	26	26	10	22	0	7.29
Mike Campbell	R	25	1	2	.333	0	5	5	0	28	28	16	10	0	5.89
2 Gene Harris (UJ)	R	24	1	4	.200	0	10	6	0	33	47	15	14	0	6.48
Clint Zavaras	R	22	1	6	.143	0	10	10	0	52	49	30	21	0	5.19
Mike Schooler	R	26	1	7	.125	33	67	0	0	77	81	19	69	0	2.81
Julio Solano	R	29	0	0	—	0	1	0	0	4	6	1	4	0	5.59
Luis DeLeon	R	30	0	0	—	0	1	0	0	1	3	1	2	0	5.06
Tom Niedenfuer (BW)	R	29	0	3	.000	0	25	0	0	38	46	15	15	0	6.69
Gene Walter (AJ) 28															

CHICAGO 7th 69-92 .429 29.5 JEFF TORBORG

Name	G by Pos	B	AGE	G	AB	R	H	2B	3B	HR	RBI	BB	SO	SB	BA	SA
TOTALS			28	161	5504	693	1493	262	36	94	661	464	873	97	.271	.383
Greg Walker	1B48 DH23	L	29	77	233	25	49	14	0	5	26	23	50	0	.210	.335
Steve Lyons	2B70 1B40 3B28 OF20 C1 SS3 2B1 DH1	L	29	140	443	51	117	21	3	2	50	35	68	9	.264	.339
Ozzie Guillen	SS155	L	25	155	597	63	151	20	8	1	54	15	48	36	.253	.318
Carlos Martinez	3B68 1B34 OF10 DH1	R	23	109	350	44	105	22	0	5	32	21	57	4	.300	.406
Ivan Calderon	OF103 DH36 1B26	R	27	157	622	83	178	34	9	14	87	43	94	7	.286	.437
Dave Gallagher	OF160 DH1	R	28	161	601	74	160	22	2	1	46	46	79	5	.266	.314
Dan Pasqua (BW-KJ)	OF66 DH5	L	27	73	246	26	61	9	1	11	47	25	58	1	.248	.427
Carlton Fisk (BH)	C90 DH13	R	41	103	375	47	110	25	2	13	68	36	60	1	.293	.475
1 Harold Baines	DH70 OF25	L	30	96	333	55	107	20	1	13	56	60	52	0	.321	.505
Daryl Boston	OF75 DH9	L	26	101	218	34	55	3	4	5	23	24	31	7	.252	.372
Ron Karkovice	C68 DH2	R	25	71	182	21	48	9	2	3	24	10	56	0	.264	.385
Eddie Williams	3B65	R	24	66	201	25	55	8	0	3	10	18	31	1	.274	.358
1 Fred Manrique	2B57 SS2 3B2	R	28	65	187	23	56	13	1	2	30	8	30	0	.299	.412
2 Scott Fletcher	2B53 SS8	R	30	59	232	30	63	11	1	1	21	26	19	1	.272	.341
Ron Kittle (XJ)	1B27 DH17 OF5	R	31	51	169	26	51	10	0	11	37	22	42	0	.302	.556
Lance Johnson	OF45 DH1	L	25	50	180	28	54	8	2	0	16	17	24	16	.300	.367
Russ Morman	1B35	R	27	37	58	5	13	2	0	0	8	6	16	1	.224	.259
2 Sammy Sosa	OF33	R	20	33	99	19	27	5	0	3	10	11	27	7	.273	.414
Matt Merullo	C27	L	23	31	81	5	18	1	0	1	8	6	14	0	.222	.272
Robin Ventura	3B16	R	21	16	45	5	8	3	0	0	7	8	6	0	.178	.244
Billy Jo Robidoux	1B15 OF1	R	25	16	39	2	5	2	0	0	4	9	6	0	.128	.179
Jeff Schaefer	SS5 2B4 3B4 DH1	R	29	15	10	2	1	0	0	0	1	1	5	1	.100	.100
Jerry Hairston	DH2	B	37	8	3	0	1	0	0	0	0	0	1	0	.333	.333

NAME	T	AGE	W	L	PCT	SV	G	GS	CG	IP	H	BB	SO	SHO	ERA
TOTALS		27	69	92	.429	46	161	161	9	1422	1472	539	778	5	4.23
Melido Perez	R	23	11	14	.440	0	31	31	2	183	187	90	141	0	5.01
Eric King (SJ)	R	25	9	10	.474	0	25	25	1	159	144	64	72	1	3.39
1 Jerry Reuss	L	40	8	5	.615	0	23	19	1	107	135	21	27	1	5.06
Shawn Hillegas	R	24	7	11	.389	0	50	13	0	120	132	51	76	0	4.74
Ken Patterson	L	24	6	1	.857	0	50	1	0	66	64	28	43	0	4.52
Greg Hibbard	R	24	6	7	.462	0	23	23	2	137	142	41	55	0	3.21
Bill Long	R	29	5	5	.500	1	30	8	0	99	101	37	51	0	3.92
Donn Pall	R	27	4	5	.444	6	53	0	0	87	90	19	58	0	3.31
Steve Rosenberg	L	24	4	13	.235	0	38	21	2	142	148	58	77	0	4.94
Barry Jones (EJ)	R	26	3	2	.600	1	22	0	0	30	22	8	17	0	2.37
2 Rich Dotson	R	30	3	7	.300	0	17	17	1	100	112	41	55	0	3.88
Bobby Thigpen	R	25	2	6	.250	34	61	0	0	79	62	40	47	0	3.76
Tom McCarthy	R	28	1	2	.333	0	31	0	0	67	72	20	27	0	3.51
Wayne Edwards	L	25	0	0	—	0	5	0	0	7	3	6	3	0	3.68
Jack Hardy	R	29	0	0	—	0	2	0	0	12	14	5	4	0	6.57
Jose Segura	R	26	0	1	.000	0	5	0	0	13	23	4	6	0	15.00
John Davis	R	26	0	1	.000	0	4	0	0	5	5	6	3	0	4.50
Adam Peterson	R	24	0	1	.000	0	1	1	0	4	5	1	3	0	15.19
Jeff Bittiger (GJ)	R	27	0	1	.000	0	2	1	0	2	1	9	6	1	6.52

CHICAGO — 1st 93-69 .571 — DON ZIMMER

Name	G by Pos	B	AGE	G	AB	R	H	2B	3B	HR	RBI	BB	SO	SB	BA	SA
TOTALS			28	162	5513	702	1438	235	45	124	663	472	921	136	.261	.387
Mark Grace	1B142	L	25	142	510	74	160	28	3	13	79	80	42	14	.314	.457
Ryne Sandberg	2B155	R	29	157	606	104	176	25	5	30	76	59	85	15	.290	.497
Shawon Dunston	SS138	R	26	138	471	52	131	20	6	9	60	30	86	19	.278	.403
Vance Law	3B119 OF1	R	32	130	408	38	96	22	3	7	42	38	73	2	.235	.355
Andre Dawson (KJ)	OF112	R	34	118	416	62	105	18	6	21	77	35	62	8	.252	.476
Jerome Walton (LJ)	OF115	R	23	116	475	64	139	23	3	5	46	27	77	24	.293	.385
Dwight Smith	OF102	L	25	109	343	52	111	19	6	9	52	31	51	9	.324	.493
Damon Berryhill (SJ)	C89	B	25	91	334	37	86	13	0	5	41	16	54	1	.257	.341
Mitch Webster	OF74	B	30	98	272	40	70	12	4	3	19	30	55	14	.257	.364
Lloyd McClendon	OF45 1B28 3B6 C5	R	30	92	259	47	74	12	1	12	40	37	31	6	.286	.479
Domingo Ramos	SS42 3B30	R	31	85	179	18	47	6	2	1	19	17	23	1	.263	.335
Curt Wilkerson	3B26 2B15 SS7 OF1	B	28	77	160	18	39	4	2	1	10	8	33	4	.244	.313
Gary Varsho	OF21	L	26	61	87	10	16	4	2	0	6	4	13	3	.184	.276
Joe Girardi	C59	R	24	59	157	15	39	10	0	1	14	11	26	2	.248	.331
Doug Dascenzo	OF45	B	25	47	139	20	23	1	0	1	12	13	13	6	.165	.194
1 Darrin Jackson	OF39	R	26	45	83	7	19	4	0	1	8	6	17	1	.229	.313
2 Rick Wrona	C37	R	25	38	92	11	26	2	1	2	14	2	21	0	.283	.391
2 Luis Salazar	3B25 OF2	R	33	26	80	7	26	5	0	1	12	4	13	0	.325	.425
1 Marvell Wynne	OF13	L	29	20	48	8	9	2	1	1	4	1	7	2	.188	.333
Phil Stephenson	OF3	L	28	17	21	0	3	0	0	0	0	2	3	1	.142	.143
Greg Smith	2B2 OF1	B	22	4	5	1	2	0	0	0	2	0	0	0	.400	.400

NAME	T	AGE	W	L	PCT	SV	G	GS	CG	IP	H	BB	SO	SHO	ERA
		27	93	67	.571	55	162	162	18	1460	1369	532	918	10	3.43
Greg Maddux	R	23	19	12	.613	0	35	35	7	238	222	82	135	1	2.95
Mike Bielecki	R	29	18	7	.720	0	33	33	4	212	187	81	147	3	3.14
Rick Sutcliffe	R	33	16	11	.593	0	35	34	5	229	202	69	153	1	3.66
Scott Sanderson	R	32	11	9	.550	0	37	23	2	146	155	31	86	0	3.94
Steve Wilson	L	24	6	4	.600	2	53	8	0	86	83	31	65	0	4.20
Paul Kilgus	R	27	6	10	.375	2	33	23	0	146	164	49	61	0	4.39
Les Lancaster	R	27	4	2	.667	8	42	0	0	73	60	15	56	0	1.36
Mitch Williams	L	24	4	4	.500	36	76	0	0	82	71	52	67	0	2.76
Jeff Pico	R	23	3	1	.750	2	53	5	0	91	99	31	38	0	3.77
1 Calvin Schiraldi	R	27	3	6	.333	4	54	0	0	79	60	50	54	0	3.78
2 Paul Assenmacher	L	28	2	1	.667	0	14	0	0	18	19	12	15	0	5.21
Dean Wilkins	R	22	1	0	1.000	0	11	0	0	16	13	9	14	0	4.60
Kevin Blankenship	R	26	0	0	—	0	2	0	0	5	4	2	2	0	1.69
Pat Perry (SJ)	L	30	0	1	.000	1	19	0	0	36	23	16	20	0	1.77
Joe Kraemer	L	24	0	1	.000	0	11	0	0	4	7	2	5	0	4.91

NEW YORK — 2nd 87-75 .537 6 — DAVEY JOHNSON

Name	G by Pos	B	AGE	G	AB	R	H	2B	3B	HR	RBI	BB	SO	SB	BA	SA
TOTALS			28	162	5489	683	1351	280	21	147	633	504	934	158	.246	.385
Dave Magadan	1B87 3B28	L	26	127	374	47	107	22	3	4	41	49	37	1	.286	.393
Gregg Jefferies	2B123 3B20	B	21	141	508	72	137	28	2	12	56	39	46	21	.258	.392
Kevin Elster	SS150	R	24	151	458	52	106	25	2	10	55	34	77	4	.231	.360
Howard Johnson	3B143 SS31	B	28	153	571	104	164	41	3	36	101	77	126	41	.287	.559
Darryl Strawberry	OF131	L	27	134	476	69	107	26	1	29	77	61	105	11	.225	.446
2 Juan Samuel	OF84	R	28	86	333	37	76	13	1	3	28	24	75	31	.228	.300
Kevin McReynolds	OF145	R	29	148	545	74	148	25	3	22	85	46	74	15	.272	.450
Barry Lyons	C76	R	29	79	235	15	58	13	0	3	27	11	28	0	.247	.340
Tim Teufel	2B40 1B33	R	30	83	219	27	56	7	2	2	15	32	40	1	.256	.333
1 Mookie Wilson	OF71	B	33	80	249	22	51	10	1	3	18	10	47	7	.205	.289
Keith Hernandez (KJ)	1B58	L	35	75	215	18	50	8	0	4	19	27	30	0	.233	.326
Mackey Sasser	C62 3B1	R	26	72	182	17	53	14	2	1	22	7	15	0	.291	.407
Mark Carreon	OF39	R	26	68	133	20	41	6	0	6	16	12	17	2	.308	.489
Keith Miller	2B23 OF14 SS8 3B2	R	26	57	143	15	33	7	0	1	7	5	27	6	.231	.301
1 Lenny Dykstra	OF51	L	26	56	159	27	43	12	1	3	13	23	15	13	.270	.415
Gary Carter (KJ)	C47 1B1	R	35	50	153	14	28	8	0	2	15	12	15	0	.183	.275
1 Lee Mazzilli	OF10 1B8	B	34	48	60	10	11	2	0	2	7	17	19	3	.183	.317
Phil Lombardi	C16 1B1	R	26	18	48	4	11	1	0	1	3	5	8	0	.229	.313
Lou Thornton	OF6	L	25	13	13	5	4	1	0	0	1	0	1	2	.308	.385
Tom O'Malley	3B3	L	28	9	11	2	6	2	0	0	8	0	2	0	.545	.727
Jeff McKnight	2B4 3B1 SS1 1B1	B	26	6	12	2	3	0	0	0	0	2	1	0	.250	.250
Craig Shipley	SS3 3B2	R	26	4	7	3	1	0	0	0	0	0	1	0	.143	.143

NAME	T	AGE	W	L	PCT	SV	G	GS	CG	IP	H	BB	SO	SHO	ERA
		27	87	75	.537	38	162	162	24	1454	1260	532	1108	12	3.29
Sid Fernandez	L	26	14	5	.737	0	35	32	6	219	157	75	198	2	2.83
David Cone	R	26	14	8	.636	0	34	33	7	220	183	74	190	2	3.52
Ron Darling	R	28	14	14	.500	0	33	33	4	217	214	70	153	0	3.52
Bob Ojeda	L	31	13	11	.542	0	31	31	5	192	179	78	95	2	3.47
Dwight Gooden (SJ)	R	24	9	4	.692	1	19	17	0	118	93	47	101	0	2.89
Randy Myers	L	26	7	4	.636	24	65	0	0	84	62	40	88	0	2.35
1 Rick Aguilera	R	27	6	6	.500	7	36	0	0	69	59	21	80	0	2.34
2 Jeff Musselman	L	26	3	2	.600	0	20	0	0	26	27	14	11	0	3.08
Don Aase	R	34	1	5	.167	2	49	0	0	59	56	26	34	0	3.94
1 Roger McDowell	R	28	1	5	.167	4	25	0	0	35	34	16	15	0	3.31
2 Terry Leach	R	35	0	0	—	0	10	0	0	21	19	4	2	0	4.22
1 Kevin Tapani	R	25	0	0	—	0	3	0	0	7	5	4	2	0	3.68
Blaine Beatty	L	25	0	0	—	0	2	1	0	6	1	2	1	0	1.50
Manny Hernandez	R	28	0	0	—	0	1	0	0	1	0	0	1	0	0.00
Jeff Innis	R	26	0	1	.000	0	29	0	0	40	38	8	16	0	3.18
Julio Machado	R	23	0	0	—	0	10	0	0	11	9	3	14	0	3.27
Wally Whitehurst	R	25	0	1	.000	0	9	1	0	14	17	5	9	0	4.50
John Mitchell	R	23	0	1	.000	0	2	0	0	3	3	4	4	0	6.00
1 David West	L	24	0	2	.000	0	11	2	0	24	25	14	19	0	7.40

ST. LOUIS — 3rd 86-76 .531 7 — WHITEY HERZOG

Name	G by Pos	B	AGE	G	AB	R	H	2B	3B	HR	RBI	BB	SO	SB	BA	SA
TOTALS			30	164	5492	632	1418	263	47	73	587	507	848	155	.258	.363
Pedro Guerrero	1B160	R	33	162	570	60	177	42	1	17	117	79	84	2	.311	.477
Jose Oquendo	2B156 SS7 1B1	B	25	163	556	59	162	28	7	1	48	79	59	3	.291	.372
Ozzie Smith	SS153	B	34	155	593	82	162	30	8	2	50	55	37	29	.273	.361
Terry Pendleton	3B161	B	28	162	613	83	162	28	5	13	74	44	81	9	.264	.390
Tom Brunansky	OF155 1B1	R	28	158	556	67	133	29	3	20	85	59	107	5	.239	.410
Milt Thompson	OF147	L	30	155	545	60	158	28	8	4	68	39	91	27	.290	.393
Vince Coleman	OF142	B	28	145	563	94	143	21	9	2	28	50	90	65	.254	.332
Tony Pena	C134 OF1	R	32	141	424	36	110	17	2	4	37	35	33	5	.259	.337
John Morris	OF51	L	28	96	117	8	28	4	1	2	14	4	22	1	.239	.342
Jim Lindeman (XJ)	3B7 OF5	R	27	73	45	8	5	1	0	0	2	3	18	0	.111	.133
Denny Walling	1B20 3B9 OF6	L	35	69	79	9	24	7	0	1	11	14	12	0	.304	.430
Willie McGee (VJ-WJ)	OF47	B	30	58	199	23	47	10	2	3	17	10	34	8	.236	.352
Tom Pagnozzi	C38 1B2 3B1	R	26	52	80	3	12	2	0	0	3	6	19	0	.150	.175
Tim Jones	SS12 2B12 3B5 OF1 C1	L	26	42	75	11	22	6	0	0	7	7	8	1	.293	.373
Leon Durham	1B18	L	31	29	18	2	1	1	0	0	2	4	6	0	.056	.111
Todd Zeile	C23	R	23	28	82	7	21	3	1	1	8	9	14	0	.256	.354
Rod Booker	2B5 3B1	L	30	10	8	1	2	0	0	0	0	0	1	0	.250	.250
Craig Wilson	3B2	R	24	6	4	1	1	0	0	0	1	1	2	0	.250	.250

NAME	T	AGE	W	L	PCT	SV	G	GS	CG	IP	H	BB	SO	SHO	ERA
		29	86	76	.531	43	164	164	18	1461	1330	482	844	18	3.36
Joe Magrane	L	24	18	9	.667	0	34	33	9	235	219	72	127	3	2.91
Jose DeLeon	R	28	16	12	.571	0	36	36	5	245	173	80	201	3	3.05
Frank DiPino	L	32	9	0	1.000	0	67	0	0	88	73	20	44	0	2.45
Scott Terry (SJ)	R	29	8	10	.444	2	31	24	1	149	142	43	69	0	3.57
Ted Power (VJ)	R	34	7	7	.500	0	23	15	0	97	96	21	43	0	3.71
Ken Hill	R	23	7	15	.318	0	33	33	2	197	186	99	112	1	3.80
John Costello	R	28	5	4	.556	3	48	0	0	62	48	20	40	0	3.32
Ken Dayley	L	30	4	3	.571	12	71	0	0	75	63	30	40	0	2.87
Cris Carpenter	R	24	4	4	.500	0	36	5	0	68	70	26	35	0	3.18
Dan Quisenberry	R	36	3	1	.750	6	63	0	0	78	78	14	37	0	2.64
1 Todd Worrell (EJ)	R	29	3	5	.375	20	47	0	0	52	42	24	41	0	2.96
Bob Tewksbury	R	28	1	0	1.000	0	7	4	1	30	25	10	17	1	3.30
Don Heinkel	R	29	1	1	.500	0	5	0	0	26	40	7	16	0	5.81
Matt Kinzer	R	25	0	1	.000	0	8	1	0	13	25	4	8	0	12.83
1 Ricky Horton	L	29	0	3	.000	0	11	8	0	46	50	10	14	0	4.73

Danny Cox (EJ) 29
Greg Matthews (EJ) 27

MONTREAL — 4th 81-81 .500 12 — BUCK ROGERS

Name	G by Pos	B	AGE	G	AB	R	H	2B	3B	HR	RBI	BB	SO	SB	BA	SA
TOTALS			29	162	5482	632	1353	267	30	100	587	572	958	160	.247	.361
Andres Galarraga	1B147	R	28	152	572	76	147	30	1	23	85	48	158	12	.257	.434
Tom Foley	2B108 3B16 SS14	L	28	122	375	34	86	19	2	7	39	45	53	2	.229	.347
Spike Owen	SS142	B	28	142	437	52	102	17	4	6	41	76	44	3	.233	.332
Tim Wallach	3B153 P1	R	31	154	573	76	159	42	0	13	77	58	81	3	.277	.419
Hubie Brooks	OF140	R	32	148	542	56	145	30	1	14	70	39	108	6	.268	.404
Dave Martinez	OF118	L	24	126	361	41	99	16	7	3	27	27	57	23	.274	.382
Tim Raines	OF139	B	29	145	517	76	148	29	6	9	60	93	48	41	.286	.418
Nelson Santovenia (BG)	C89 1B1	R	27	97	304	30	76	14	1	5	31	24	37	2	.250	.352
Otis Nixon	OF98	B	30	126	258	41	56	7	2	0	21	33	36	37	.217	.260
Mike Fitzgerald	C77 3B8 OF6	R	28	100	290	33	69	18	2	7	42	35	61	3	.238	.386
Rex Hudler	2B38 OF23 SS18	R	28	92	155	21	38	7	0	6	13	6	23	15	.245	.406
Wallace Johnson	1B18	B	32	85	114	9	31	3	1	2	17	7	12	1	.272	.368
Damaso Garcia	2B62 3B1	R	34	80	203	26	55	9	1	3	18	15	20	5	.271	.369
Mike Aldrete	OF37 1B10	L	28	76	136	12	30	8	1	1	12	19	30	1	.221	.316
Jeff Huson	SS20 2B9 3B1	L	24	32	74	1	12	5	0	0	2	6	3	3	.162	.230
Marquis Grissom	OF23	R	22	26	74	16	19	2	0	1	2	12	21	1	.257	.324
Junior Noboa	2B13 SS4 3B1	R	24	21	44	3	10	0	0	0	1	3	1	0	.227	.227
Larry Walker	OF15	L	22	20	47	4	8	0	0	0	4	5	13	1	.170	.170
Marty Pevey	C11 OF1	L	27	13	41	2	9	1	1	0	3	0	8	0	.220	.293
2 Jim Dwyer		L	37	13	10	1	3	1	0	0	2	1	1	0	.300	.400
Gil Reyes	C4	R	25	4	5	0	1	0	0	0	0	1	1	0	.200	.200

Johnny Paredes (EJ) 26

NAME	T	AGE	W	L	PCT	SV	G	GS	CG	IP	H	BB	SO	SHO	ERA
		30	81	81	.500	35	162	162	20	1468	1344	519	1059	13	3.48
Dennis Martinez	R	34	16	7	.696	0	34	33	5	232	227	49	142	2	3.18
2 Mark Langston	L	28	12	9	.571	0	24	24	6	177	138	93	175	4	2.39
Kevin Gross	R	28	11	12	.478	0	31	31	4	201	188	88	158	3	4.38
Bryn Smith	R	33	10	11	.476	0	33	32	3	216	177	54	129	1	2.84
Tim Burke	R	30	9	3	.750	28	68	0	0	85	68	22	54	0	2.55
Pascual Perez	R	32	9	13	.409	0	33	28	2	198	178	45	152	0	3.31
Joe Hesketh	L	30	6	4	.600	3	43	0	0	48	54	26	44	0	5.77
Steve Frey	L	25	3	2	.600	0	20	0	0	21	29	11	15	0	5.48
Andy McGaffigan	R	32	3	5	.375	2	57	0	0	75	85	30	40	0	4.68
1 Gene Harris	R	24	1	1	.500	0	11	0	0	26	10	10	11	0	4.95
1 Brian Holman	R	24	1	2	.333	0	10	3	0	32	34	15	23	0	4.83
Brett Gideon	R	25	0	0	—	0	4	0	0	5	5	5	2	0	1.93
Urbano Lugo	R	26	0	0	—	0	3	0	0	4	2	0	3	0	6.75
Tim Wallach	R	31	0	0	—	0	1	0	0	0.1	0	0	0	0	9.00
Tom Foley	R	29	0	0	—	0	1	0	0	0.1	1	0	0	0	27.00
1 Zane Smith	L	28	0	0	.000	2	31	0	0	48	39	19	35	0	1.50
Rich Thompson	R	30	0	2	.000	0	19	1	0	33	27	11	15	0	2.18
2 John Candelaria	L	35	0	0	—	0	16	17	4	14	0	3.31			
Mark Gardner	R	27	0	3	.000	0	7	4	0	26	21	11	11	0	5.13
1 Randy Johnson	L	25	0	4	.000	0	7	6	0	30	29	26	26	0	6.67

PITTSBURGH 5th 74-88 .457 19 JIM LEYLAND

Name	G by Pos	B	AGE	G	AB	R	H	2B	3B	HR	RBI	BB	SO	SB	BA	SA
	TOTALS		27	164	5539	637	1334	263	53	95	584	563	914	155	.241	.359
Gary Redus	1B72 OF16	R	32	98	279	42	79	18	7	6	33	40	51	25	.283	.462
Jose Lind	2B151	R	25	153	578	52	134	21	3	2	48	39	64	15	.232	.289
Jay Bell	SS78	B	23	78	271	33	70	13	3	2	27	19	47	5	.258	.351
Bobby Bonilla	3B156 1B8 OF1	B	26	163	616	96	173	37	10	24	86	76	93	8	.281	.490
1 Glenn Wilson	OF85 1B10	R	30	100	330	42	93	20	4	9	49	32	39	1	.282	.403
Andy Van Slyke (VJ)	OF123 1B2	L	28	130	476	64	113	18	9	9	53	47	100	16	.237	.370
Barry Bonds	OF156	L	24	159	580	96	144	34	6	19	58	93	93	32	.248	.426
Mike LaValliere (KJ)	C65	L	28	68	190	15	60	10	0	2	23	29	24	0	.316	.400
R.J. Reynolds	OF98	B	30	125	363	45	98	16	2	6	48	34	66	22	.270	.375
John Cangelosi	0F46	B	26	112	160	18	35	4	2	0	9	35	20	11	.219	.269
Benny Distefano	1B48 C3 OF1	L	27	96	154	12	38	8	0	2	15	17	30	1	.247	.338
Junior Ortiz	C84	R	29	91	230	16	50	6	1	1	22	20	22	2	.217	.265
Jeff King	1B46 3B13 2B7 SS1	R	24	75	215	31	42	13	3	5	19	20	34	4	.195	.353
2 Rey Quinones	SS69	R	25	71	225	21	47	11	0	3	29	15	40	0	.209	.298
Rafael Belliard	SS40 2B20 3B6	R	27	67	154	10	33	4	0	0	8	8	22	5	.214	.240
Dann Bilardello	C33	R	30	33	80	11	18	6	0	2	8	2	18	1	.225	.375
1 Billy Hatcher	OF20	R	28	27	86	10	21	4	0	1	7	0	9	2	.244	.326
Tom Prince	C21	R	24	21	52	1	7	4	0	1	5	6	12	1	.135	.212
Albert Hall	OF12	B	30	20	33	4	6	2	1	0	1	3	5	3	.182	.303
Sid Bream (KJ)	1B13	L	28	19	36	3	8	3	0	0	4	12	10	0	.222	.306
1 Ken Oberkfell	1B9 2B3	L	33	14	40	2	5	1	0	0	2	2	2	0	.125	.150
Steve Carter	OF5	L	24	9	16	2	2	1	0	0	1	0	3	0	.125	.375
Scott Little	OF1	R	26	3	4	0	1	0	0	0	0	0	1	0	.250	.250

NAME	T	AGE	W	L	PCT	SV	G	GS	CG	IP	H	BB	SO	SHO	ERA
		28	74	88	.457	40	164	164	20	1488	1394	539	827	9	3.64
Doug Drabek	R	26	14	12	.538	0	35	34	8	244	215	69	123	5	2.80
Bob Walk	R	32	13	10	.565	0	33	31	2	196	208	65	83	0	4.41
John Smiley	L	24	12	8	.600	0	28	28	8	205	174	49	123	1	2.81
Jeff Robinson	R	28	7	13	.350	4	50	19	0	141	161	59	95	0	4.58
Neal Heaton	L	29	6	7	.462	0	42	11	1	147	127	55	67	0	3.05
Randy Kramer	R	28	5	9	.357	2	35	15	1	111	90	61	52	1	3.96
Bob Patterson	L	30	4	3	.571	1	12	3	0	27	23	8	20	0	4.05
Bob Kipper (EJ)	L	24	3	4	.429	4	52	0	0	83	55	33	58	0	2.93
Morris Madden	L	28	2	2	.500	0	9	3	0	14	17	13	6	0	7.07
Bill Landrum	R	31	2	3	.400	26	56	0	0	81	60	28	51	0	1.67
Doug Bair	R	39	2	3	.400	1	44	0	0	67	52	28	56	0	2.27
Logan Easley	R	27	1	0	1.000	1	10	0	0	12	8	7	6	0	4.38
Dom Taylor	R	30	1	1	.500	0	9	0	0	11	14	5	3	0	5.06
1 Mike Dunne	R	26	1	1	.500	0	3	3	0	14	21	9	4	0	7.53
Rick Reed	R	24	1	4	.200	0	15	7	0	55	62	11	34	0	5.60
Roger Samuels	L	28	0	0	—	0	5	0	0	4	4	1	2	0	9.82
Jim Gott (EJ)	R	29	0	0	—	0	1	0	0	1	1	1	1	0	0.00
Mike Smith	R	28	0	1	.000	0	16	0	0	24	28	10	12	0	3.75
Stan Belinda	R	22	0	1	.000	0	8	0	0	10	13	2	10	0	6.10
Scott Medvin	R	27	0	1	.000	0	6	0	0	6	6	5	4	0	5.68
Miguel Garcia	L	22	0	2	.000	0	11	0	0	16	25	7	9	0	8.44
Brian Fisher (KJ)	R	27	0	3	.000	1	9	3	0	17	25	10	8	0	7.94

PHILADELPHIA 6th 67-95 .414 26 NICK LEYVA

Name	G by Pos	B	AGE	G	AB	R	H	2B	3B	HR	RBI	BB	SO	SB	BA	SA
	TOTALS		28	163	5447	629	1324	215	36	123	594	558	926	106	.243	.364
Ricky Jordan	1B140	R	24	144	523	63	149	22	3	12	75	23	62	4	.285	.407
Tommy Herr	2B144	B	33	151	561	55	161	25	6	2	37	54	63	10	.287	.364
Dicky Thon	SS129	R	31	136	435	45	118	18	4	15	60	33	81	6	.271	.434
2 Charlie Hayes	3B82	R	24	84	299	26	77	15	1	8	43	11	49	3	.258	.401
Von Hayes	OF128 1B30 3B10	L	30	154	540	93	140	27	2	26	78	101	103	28	.259	.461
2 Lenny Dykstra	OF88	L	26	90	352	39	78	20	3	4	19	37	38	17	.222	.330
John Kruk	OF72187	L	28	81	281	46	93	13	6	5	38	27	39	3	.331	.473
Darren Daulton	C126	L	27	131	368	29	74	12	2	8	44	52	58	2	.201	.310
Steve Jeltz	SS63 3B30 2B23 OF1	B	30	116	263	28	64	7	3	4	25	45	44	4	.243	.338
Curt Ford	OF52 1B1 2B1	L	28	108	142	13	31	5	1	1	13	16	33	5	.218	.289
Bob Dernier	OF74	R	32	107	187	26	32	5	0	1	13	14	28	11	.171	.214
Dwayne Murphy	OF52	L	33	98	156	20	34	5	0	9	27	29	44	0	.218	.423
2 Randy Ready	OF36 3B14 2B7	R	29	72	187	33	50	11	1	8	21	31	31	4	.267	.465
Steve Lake (KJ)	C55	R	32	58	155	9	39	5	1	2	14	12	20	0	.252	.335
1 Juan Samuel	OF50	R	28	51	199	32	49	3	1	8	20	18	45	11	.246	.392
1 Chris James	OF37 3B11	R	26	45	179	14	37	4	0	2	19	4	23	3	.207	.263
Mike Schmidt	3B42	R	39	42	148	19	30	7	0	6	28	21	17	0	.203	.372
Mark Ryal	OF4 184	L	29	29	33	2	8	2	0	0	5	1	6	0	.242	.303
Tommy Barrett	2B9	R	24	14	27	3	6	0	0	0	1	1	7	0	.222	.222
Jim Adduci	1B4 OF1	L	29	13	19	1	7	1	0	0	4	0	4	1	.368	.421
Ron Jones (KJ)	OF12	L	25	12	31	7	9	0	0	2	4	9	1	1	.290	.484
Tom Nieto (HJ)	C11	R	28	11	20	1	3	0	0	0	0	6	7	0	.150	.150
Steve Stanicek		R	28	9	9	0	1	0	0	0	0	1	0	0	.111	.111
Keith Miller	OF2	R	28	8	10	3	1	0	0	0	0	0	3	0	.300	.400
Eric Bullock	OF3	L	29	6	4	1	0	0	0	0	0	0	1	0	.000	.000
Al Pardo	C1	R	26	1	1	0	0	0	0	0	0	0	1	0	.000	.000

NAME	T	AGE	W	L	PCT	SV	G	GS	CG	IP	H	BB	SO	SHO	ERA
		28	67	95	.414	33	163	163	10	1433	1408	613	899	10	4.04
Jeff Parrett	R	27	12	6	.667	6	72	0	0	106	90	44	98	0	2.98
Ken Howell	R	28	12	12	.500	0	33	32	1	204	155	86	164	1	3.44
2 Dennis Cook	L	26	6	8	.429	0	21	16	1	106	97	33	58	1	3.99
Bruce Ruffin	L	25	6	10	.375	0	24	23	1	126	152	62	70	0	4.44
Don Carman	L	29	5	15	.250	0	49	20	0	149	152	86	81	0	5.24
Pat Combs	L	22	4	0	1.000	0	6	6	1	39	36	6	30	1	2.09
2 Terry Mulholland	R	26	4	7	.364	0	20	17	2	104	122	32	60	1	5.00
2 Roger McDowell	R	28	3	3	.500	19	44	0	0	57	45	22	32	0	1.11
Steve Ontiveros (EJ)	R	28	2	1	.667	0	5	0	0	31	34	15	12	0	3.82
1 Greg Harris	R	33	2	1	.667	1	44	0	0	75	64	43	51	0	3.58
1 Steve Bedrosian	R	31	2	3	.400	6	28	0	0	34	21	17	24	0	3.21
Bob Sebra	R	27	2	3	.400	0	6	5	0	35	31	10	21	0	4.46
Larry McWilliams	L	35	2	11	.154	0	40	16	2	121	123	49	54	1	4.10
Todd Frohwirth	R	26	1	0	1.000	0	45	0	0	63	56	18	39	0	3.59
Alex Madrid	R	26	1	1	.333	0	4	3	0	25	32	14	13	0	5.47
Mike Maddux	R	27	1	3	.250	1	16	4	2	44	52	14	26	1	5.15
Jason Grimsley	R	21	1	3	.250	0	4	4	0	14	17	20	17	0	5.89
Floyd Youmans (SJ)	R	25	1	5	.167	0	10	10	0	43	50	25	20	0	5.70
Chuck McElroy	L	21	0	0	—	0	11	0	0	10	12	4	8	0	1.74
Gordon Dillard	L	25	0	0	—	0	5	0	0	4	7	0	2	0	6.75
Marvin Freeman (AJ)	R	26	0	0	—	0	3	1	0	3	2	5	0	0	6.00
Randy O'Neal	R	28	0	1	.000	0	20	1	0	39	46	9	29	0	6.23

WEST DIVISION

SAN FRANCISCO 1st 92-70 .568 ROGER CRAIG

Name	G by Pos	B	AGE	G	AB	R	H	2B	3B	HR	RBI	BB	SO	SB	BA	SA
	TOTALS		28	162	5469	699	1365	241	52	141	647	508	1071	87	.250	.390
Will Clark	1B158	L	25	159	588	104	196	38	9	23	111	74	103	8	.333	.546
Robby Thompson	2B148	R	27	148	547	91	132	26	11	13	50	51	133	12	.241	.400
Jose Uribe	SS150	B	30	151	453	34	100	12	6	1	30	34	74	6	.221	.280
Matt Williams	3B73 SS30	R	23	84	292	31	59	18	1	18	50	14	72	1	.202	.455
Candy Maldonado	OF116	R	28	129	345	39	75	23	0	9	41	37	69	4	.217	.362
Brett Butler	OF152	L	32	154	594	100	168	22	4	4	36	59	69	31	.283	.354
Kevin Mitchell	OF147 3B2	R	27	154	543	100	158	34	6	47	125	87	115	3	.291	.635
Terry Kennedy	C121 1B2	L	33	125	355	19	85	15	0	5	34	35	56	1	.239	.324
Ernest Riles	3B83 2B18 SS7 OF5	L	28	122	302	43	84	13	2	7	40	28	50	0	.278	.404
Donell Nixon	OF64	R	27	95	166	23	44	2	0	1	15	11	30	10	.265	.295
Dirt Manwaring	C81	R	23	85	200	14	42	4	2	0	18	11	28	2	.210	.250
2 Ken Oberkfell	3B38 2B7 1B7	L	33	83	116	17	37	5	1	2	15	8	8	0	.319	.431
Greg Litton	3B34 2B15 SS9 OF6 C2	R	24	71	143	12	36	5	3	4	17	7	29	0	.252	.413
2 Pat Sheridan	OF66	L	31	70	161	20	33	3	4	3	14	13	45	4	.205	.329
1 Tracy Jones	OF30	R	28	40	97	5	18	4	0	0	12	5	14	2	.186	.227
Ed Jurak	SS6 3B5 2B4 OF2 1B1	R	31	30	42	2	10	0	0	0	5	5	5	0	.238	.238
Bill Bathe	C7	R	28	30	32	3	9	4	0	2	6	0	5	0	.281	.313
Chris Sperer (XJ)	SS9 3B9 2B4 1B1	R	39	28	37	7	9	4	0	2	3	1	6	1	.243	.351
Mike Laga	1B4	L	29	17	20	1	4	1	0	1	1	1	6	0	.200	.400
Mike Benjamin	SS8	R	23	14	6	6	1	0	0	0	0	2	4	0	.167	.167
James Steels	1B3 OF1	R	28	13	12	0	1	0	0	0	0	2	4	0	.083	.083
2 Bob Brenly	C12	R	35	12	22	2	4	2	0	0	2	1	7	0	.182	.273
Jim Weaver	OF8	L	29	12	20	2	4	3	0	0	2	1	7	0	.200	.350
1 Charlie Hayes	3B3	R	24	3	5	0	1	0	0	0	0	0	1	0	.200	.200

NAME	T	AGE	W	L	PCT	SV	G	GS	CG	IP	H	BB	SO	SHO	ERA
		31	92	70	.568	47	162	162	12	1457	1320	471	802	16	3.30
Rick Reuschel	R	40	17	8	.680	0	32	32	2	208	195	54	111	0	2.94
Scott Garrelts	R	27	14	5	.737	0	30	29	2	193	149	46	119	1	2.28
Don Robinson	R	32	12	11	.522	0	34	32	5	197	184	37	96	1	3.43
Mike LaCoss	R	33	10	10	.500	6	45	18	1	150	143	65	78	0	3.17
Jeff Brantley	R	25	7	1	.875	0	59	1	0	97	101	37	69	0	4.07
Atlee Hammaker (AJ-KJ)	L	31	6	6	.500	0	28	9	0	77	78	23	30	0	3.76
Mike Krukow (SJ)	R	37	4	3	.571	0	8	8	0	43	37	18	18	0	3.98
Kelly Downs (SJ)	R	28	4	8	.333	0	18	15	0	83	82	26	49	0	4.79
Ernie Camacho	R	34	3	0	1.000	0	13	0	0	16	10	11	14	0	2.76
2 Bob Knepper	L	35	3	2	.600	0	13	6	1	52	55	15	19	1	3.46
Dave Dravecky (IL-BA)	L	33	2	0	1.000	0	3	2	0	13	8	4	5	0	3.46
1 Goose Gossage	R	37	2	1	.667	4	31	0	0	44	32	27	24	0	2.68
Trevor Wilson	L	23	2	3	.400	0	14	4	0	39	28	24	22	0	4.35
Craig Lefferts	L	31	2	4	.333	20	70	0	0	107	93	22	71	0	2.69
1 Dennis Cook	R	26	1	0	1.000	0	2	1	0	8	3	3	6	0	1.80
Randy McCament	R	26	1	1	.500	0	25	0	0	37	32	23	12	0	3.93
1 Joe Price	L	32	1	1	.500	0	14	0	0	16	14	10	15	0	3.45
2 Steve Bedrosian	R	31	1	2	.333	17	40	0	0	51	35	22	34	0	2.65
Terry Mulholland	L	26	0	0	—	0	1	0	0	11	15	4	6	0	4.09
Stu Tate	R	27	0	0	—	0	5	0	0	7	11	2	2	0	
Russ Swan	L	25	0	2	.000	0	2	0	0	7	11	0	2	0	10.80
Karl Best (EJ)	30														

SAN DIEGO 2nd 89-73 .549 3 JACK McKEON

Name	G by Pos	B	AGE	G	AB	R	H	2B	3B	HR	RBI	BB	SO	SB	BA	SA
	TOTALS		28	162	5422	642	1360	215	32	120	598	552	1013	136	.251	.369
Jack Clark	1B131 OF12	R	33	142	455	76	110	19	1	26	94	132	145	6	.242	.459
Roberto Alomar	2B157	B	21	158	623	82	184	27	1	7	56	53	76	42	.295	.376
Garry Templeton	SS140	B	33	142	506	43	129	26	3	6	40	23	80	1	.255	.354
Luis Salazar	3B72 OF14 SS9 1B2	R	33	95	246	27	66	7	2	8	22	11	44	1	.268	.411
Tony Gwynn	OF157	R	29	158	604	82	203	27	7	4	62	56	30	40	.336	.424
Marvell Wynne	OF96	R	29	105	294	19	74	11	1	6	35	12	41	4	.252	.357
2 Chris James	OF79 3B6	R	26	87	303	41	80	13	2	11	46	22	45	2	.264	.429
Benito Santiago	C127	R	24	129	462	50	109	16	3	16	62	26	89	11	.236	.387
Bip Roberts	OF54 3B37 SS14 2B9	B	25	117	329	81	99	15	8	3	25	49	45	21	.301	.422
Carmelo Martinez	OF65 1B32	R	28	111	267	23	59	12	2	6	39	32	54	0	.221	.348
Tim Flannery	3B33 2B1	L	31	73	130	9	30	5	0	0	8	13	20	2	.231	.269
Shawn Abner	OF51	R	23	57	102	13	18	4	0	2	14	5	20	1	.176	.275
Mark Parent	C41 1B1	R	27	52	141	12	27	3	0	7	21	8	41	0	.191	.369
2 Mike Pagliarulo	3B49	L	29	50	148	12	29	7	0	3	14	18	39	2	.196	.304
Rob Nelson	1B31	L	25	42	82	6	16	2	0	1	5	17	29	1	.195	.329
John Kruk	OF27	L	28	31	76	7	14	0	0	1	6	17	10	0	.184	.303
1 Randy Ready	3B18 2B2 OF2	R	29	28	47	2	12	3	0	1	9	5	6	0	.254	.313
Darrin Jackson	OF14	R	25	25	87	10	18	3	1	3	12	7	17	0	.207	.345
Jerald Clark	OF14	R	25	17	41	3	10	2	0	0	3	0	9	0	.195	.317
Gary Green	SS11 3B1	R	27	15	27	1	7	3	0	0	1	3	5	0	.259	.370
Joey Cora	SS7 3B2 2B1	B	24	12	19	5	6	1	0	0	1	1	3	2	.316	.368
2 Phil Stephenson	1B8	L	28	10	17	4	6	1	0	1	6	3	4	0	.353	.706
Sandy Alomar	C6	R	23	7	19	1	4	1	0	1	6	3	1	0	.211	.421

NAME	T	AGE	W	L	PCT	SV	G	GS	CG	IP	H	BB	SO	SHO	ERA
		29	89	73	.549	52	162	162	21	1457	1359	481	933	11	3.38
Ed Whitson	R	34	16	11	.593	0	33	33	5	227	198	48	117	1	2.66
Bruce Hurst	L	31	15	11	.577	0	33	33	10	245	214	66	179	2	2.69
Dennis Rasmussen	L	30	10	10	.500	0	33	33	1	184	190	72	87	0	4.26
Mark Grant	R	25	8	2	.800	2	50	0	0	116	105	32	69	0	3.33
Eric Show (XJ)	R	33	8	6	.571	0	16	16	1	106	113	39	66	0	4.23
Greg Harris	R	25	8	9	.471	6	56	8	0	135	106	52	106	0	2.60
Andy Benes	R	21	6	3	.667	0	10	10	0	67	51	31	66	0	3.51
1 Walt Terrell	R	31	5	13	.278	0	19	19	4	123	134	26	63	1	4.01
Pat Clements	L	27	4	1	.800	0	23	0	0	39	39	15	18	0	3.92
Mark Davis	L	28	4	3	.571	44	70	0	0	93	66	31	92	0	1.85
2 Calvin Schiraldi	R	27	3	1	.750	0	21	12	1	13	17	0	2.53		
2 Don Schulze	R	28	2	1	.667	0	7	1	0	34	38	6	15	0	5.55
Freddie Toliver	R	28	0	1		0	8	1	0	14	17	9	14	0	7.07
Dan Murphy	R														
Eric Nolte	L	25	0	0	—	0	3	1	0	7	15	4	8	0	11.00
Dave Leiper (EJ)	L	25	0	0	—	0	9	0	0	29	40	20	7	0	5.02
1 Greg Booker	R	29	0	1	.000	0	11	0	0	15	15	10	8	0	4.26

HOUSTON   3rd 86-76 .531 6   ART HOWE

Name	G by Pos	B	AGE	G	AB	R	H	2B	3B	HR	RBI	BB	SO	SB	BA	SA
TOTALS			29	162	5516	647	1316	239	28	97	598	530	860	144	.239	.345
Glenn Davis	1B156	R	28	158	581	87	156	26	1	34	89	69	123	4	.269	.492
Bill Doran	2B138	B	31	142	507	65	111	25	2	8	58	59	63	22	.219	.323
Rafael Ramirez	SS149	R	31	151	537	46	132	20	2	6	54	29	64	3	.246	.324
Ken Caminiti	3B160	B	26	161	585	71	149	31	3	10	72	51	93	4	.255	.369
Kevin Bass (BL)	OF84	R	30	87	313	42	94	19	4	5	44	29	44	11	.300	.435
Gerald Young	OF143	B	24	146	533	71	124	17	3	0	38	74	60	34	.233	.270
1 Billy Hatcher	OF104	R	28	108	395	49	90	15	3	3	44	30	53	22	.228	.304
Craig Biggio	C125 OF5	R	23	134	443	64	114	21	2	13	60	49	64	21	.257	.402
Terry Puhl	OF103 1B3	L	32	121	354	41	96	25	4	0	27	45	39	9	.271	.364
Craig Reynolds	2B29 SS26 3B10 1B5 OF1 P1	L	36	101	189	16	38	4	0	2	14	19	18	1	.201	.254
Eric Yelding	SS15 2B13 OF8	R	24	70	90	19	21	2	0	0	9	7	19	11	.233	.256
Greg Gross	OF12 1B6 P1	L	36	60	75	2	15	0	0	0	4	11	6	0	.200	.200
Alex Trevino	C32 3B2 1B2	R	31	59	131	15	38	7	1	2	16	7	18	0	.290	.405
Mark Davidson	OF23	R	28	33	65	7	13	2	1	1	5	7	14	1	.200	.308
Harry Spilman	1B9 C1	L	34	32	36	7	10	3	0	0	3	7	2	0	.278	.361
Louie Meadows	OF14 1B1	L	28	31	51	5	9	0	0	3	10	1	14	1	.176	.353
2 Glenn Wilson	OF25	R	30	28	102	8	22	6	0	2	15	5	14	0	.216	.333
Eric Anthony	OF21	L	21	25	61	7	11	2	0	4	7	9	16	0	.180	.410
Alan Ashby	C19	B	37	22	61	4	10	1	1	0	3	7	8	0	.164	.213
Steve Lombardozzi	2B18 3B1	R	29	21	37	5	8	3	1	1	3	4	9	0	.216	.432
Carl Nichols	C6	R	26	8	13	0	1	0	0	0	2	0	3	0	.077	.077
Ron Washington	2B1 3B1	R	37	7	7	1	1	1	0	0	0	0	1	0	.143	.286

NAME	T	AGE	W	L	PCT	SV	G	GS	CG	IP	H	BB	SO	SHO	ERA
TOTALS		33	86	76	.531	38	162	162	19	1479	1379	551	965	12	3.64
Mike Scott	R	34	20	10	.667	0	33	32	9	229	180	62	172	2	3.10
Jim Deshaies	L	29	15	10	.600	0	34	34	6	226	180	79	153	3	2.91
Danny Darwin	R	33	11	4	.733	7	68	0	0	122	92	33	104	0	2.36
Mark Portugal	R	26	7	1	.875	0	20	15	2	108	91	37	86	1	2.75
Jim Clancy	R	33	7	14	.333	2	33	26	1	147	155	66	91	0	5.08
Dan Schatzeder (SJ)	L	34	4	1	.800	1	36	0	0	57	64	28	46	0	4.45
Larry Andersen	R	36	4	4	.500	3	60	0	0	88	63	24	85	0	1.54
Juan Agosto	L	31	4	5	.444	1	71	0	0	83	81	32	46	0	2.93
Bob Forsch	R	37	4	5	.444	0	37	15	0	108	133	46	40	0	5.32
1 Bob Knepper	L	35	4	10	.286	0	22	20	0	113	135	60	45	0	5.89
Dave Smith	R	34	3	4	.429	25	52	0	0	58	49	19	31	0	2.64
Rick Rhoden (VJ)	R	36	2	6	.250	0	20	17	0	97	108	41	41	0	4.28
Jose Cano	R	27	1	1	.500	0	6	3	1	23	24	7	8	0	5.09
Roger Mason	R	30	0	0	—	0	2	0	0	1	2	2	3	0	20.25
Greg Gross	L	36	0	0	—	0	1	0	0	1	3	1	1	0	18.00
Craig Reynolds	R	36	0	0	—	0	1	0	0	1	3	1	0	0	27.00
Brian Meyer	R	26	0	1	.000	1	12	0	0	18	16	13	13	0	4.50
Dave Meads (EJ) 25															

LOS ANGELES   4th 77-83 .481 14   TOM LASORDA

Name	G by Pos	B	AGE	G	AB	R	H	2B	3B	HR	RBI	BB	SO	SB	BA	SA
TOTALS			30	160	5465	554	1313	241	17	89	513	507	885	81	.240	.339
Eddie Murray	1B159 3B2	B	33	160	594	66	147	29	1	20	88	87	85	7	.247	.401
Willie Randolph	2B140	R	34	145	549	62	155	18	0	2	36	71	51	7	.282	.326
Alfredo Griffin	SS131	B	31	136	506	49	125	27	2	0	29	29	57	10	.247	.308
Jeff Hamilton	3B147 2B1 SS1 P1	R	25	151	548	45	134	35	1	12	56	20	71	0	.245	.378
Mike Marshall (XJ)	OF102	R	29	105	377	41	98	21	1	11	42	33	78	2	.260	.408
John Shelby	OF98	B	31	108	345	28	63	11	1	1	12	25	92	10	.183	.229
Kirk Gibson (LJ)	OF70	L	32	71	253	35	54	8	2	9	28	35	55	12	.213	.368
Mike Scioscia	C130	L	30	133	408	40	102	16	0	10	44	52	29	0	.250	.363
Jose Gonzalez	OF87	R	24	95	261	31	70	11	2	3	18	23	53	9	.268	.360
Mickey Hatcher	OF48 3B16 1B5 P1	R	34	94	224	18	66	9	2	2	25	13	16	1	.295	.379
Dave Anderson	SS33 3B18 2B7	R	28	87	140	15	32	2	0	1	14	17	26	2	.229	.264
Rick Dempsey	C62	R	39	79	151	16	27	7	0	4	16	30	37	1	.179	.305
Franklin Stubbs (KJ)	OF28 1B7	L	28	69	103	11	30	6	0	4	15	16	27	3	.291	.466
Mike Davis (KJ)	OF48	L	30	67	173	21	43	7	1	5	19	16	28	4	.249	.387
2 Lenny Harris	OF21 2B14 3B8 SS1	L	24	54	147	19	37	6	1	1	15	11	13	4	.252	.327
2 Billy Bean	OF44	L	25	51	71	7	14	4	0	0	3	4	10	0	.197	.254
1 Mariano Duncan	SS16 2B8 OF6	R	26	49	84	9	21	5	1	0	8	0	15	3	.250	.333
Chris Gwynn (BF)	OF19	L	24	32	68	8	16	4	1	0	7	2	9	1	.235	.324
Mike Sharperson	2B4 3B2 1B2 SS1	R	27	27	28	2	7	3	0	0	5	4	7	0	.250	.357
Mike Huff	OF9	R	25	12	25	4	5	1	0	1	2	3	6	0	.200	.360
2 Kal Daniels (KJ)	OF11	L	25	11	38	7	13	2	0	2	8	7	5	3	.342	.553
Jose Vizcaino	SS5	B	21	7	10	2	2	0	0	0	0	1	1	0	.200	.200
Darrin Fletcher	C5	L	22	5	8	1	4	1	0	0	2	1	0	0	.500	.875
Tracy Woodson	3B1	R	26	4	7	0	0	0	0	0	0	0	1	0	.000	.000

NAME	T	AGE	W	L	PCT	SV	G	GS	CG	IP	H	BB	SO	SHO	ERA
TOTALS		28	77	83	.481	36	160	160	25	1463	1278	504	1052	19	2.95
Tim Belcher	R	27	15	12	.556	1	39	30	10	230	182	80	200	8	2.82
Orel Hershiser	R	30	15	15	.500	0	35	33	8	257	226	77	178	4	2.31
Fernando Valenzuela	L	28	10	13	.435	0	31	31	3	197	185	98	116	0	3.43
Mike Morgan	R	29	8	11	.421	0	40	19	0	153	130	33	72	0	2.53
Ramon Martinez	R	21	6	4	.600	0	15	15	2	99	79	41	89	2	3.19
1 Tim Leary	R	30	6	7	.462	0	19	17	2	117	107	37	59	0	3.38
Jay Howell	R	33	5	3	.625	28	56	0	0	80	60	22	55	0	1.58
John Wetteland	R	22	5	8	.385	1	31	12	0	103	81	34	96	0	3.77
Alejandro Pena	R	30	4	3	.571	5	53	0	0	76	62	18	75	0	2.13
Ray Searage	L	34	3	4	.429	0	41	0	0	36	29	18	24	0	3.53
1 Ricky Horton	L	29	0	0	—	0	23	0	0	27	35	11	12	0	5.06
John Tudor (EJ)	L	35	0	0	—	0	6	3	0	14	17	6	9	0	3.14
Mike Munoz	L	23	0	0	—	0	3	0	0	3	5	2	3	0	16.88
Jeff Fischer	R	25	0	0	—	0	3	0	0	4	8	1	3	0	13.50
Mickey Hatcher	R	34	0	0	—	0	1	0	0	1	3	0	0	0	9.00
Tim Crews	R	28	0	1	.000	1	44	0	0	62	69	23	56	0	3.21
Mike Hartley	R	27	0	0	—	0	5	0	0	6	2	4	1	0	1.50
Jeff Hamilton	R	25	0	1	.000	0	1	0	0	2	1	2	0	0	5.40

CINCINNATI   5th 75-87 .463 17   PETE ROSE(DL) 61-66 .480   TOMMY HELMS 14-21 .400

Name	G by Pos	B	AGE	G	AB	R	H	2B	3B	HR	RBI	BB	SO	SB	BA	SA
TOTALS			28	162	5520	632	1362	243	28	128	588	493	1028	128	.247	.370
Todd Benzinger	1B158	B	26	161	628	79	154	28	3	17	76	44	120	3	.245	.381
Ron Oester (LJ)	2B102 SS2	R	33	109	305	23	75	15	0	1	14	32	47	1	.246	.305
Barry Larkin (KJ)	SS82	R	25	97	325	47	111	14	4	4	36	20	23	10	.342	.446
Chris Sabo (KJ)	3B76	R	27	82	304	40	79	21	1	6	29	25	33	14	.260	.395
Paul O'Neill (BG)	OF115	L	26	117	428	49	118	24	2	15	74	46	64	20	.276	.446
Eric Davis	OF125	R	27	131	462	74	130	14	2	34	101	68	116	21	.281	.541
Rolando Roomes	OF100	R	27	107	315	36	83	18	5	7	34	13	100	12	.263	.419
Jeff Reed	C99	L	26	102	287	16	64	11	0	3	23	34	46	0	.223	.293
Herm Winningham	OF85	L	27	115	251	40	63	11	3	3	13	24	50	14	.251	.355
Ken Griffey	OF58 1B9	L	39	106	236	26	62	8	3	8	30	29	43	4	.263	.424
Luis Quinones	2B53 3B50 SS5	B	27	97	340	43	83	13	4	12	34	25	46	2	.244	.412
Dave Collins	OF16	B	36	78	106	12	25	4	0	0	7	10	17	3	.236	.274
Joel Youngblood	OF45	R	37	76	118	13	25	5	0	3	13	13	21	0	.212	.331
1 Lenny Harris	2B32 SS17 3B16	L	24	61	188	17	42	4	2	1	9	20	10	0	.223	.277
Jeff Richardson	SS39 3B8	R	23	53	125	10	21	4	0	2	11	10	23	1	.168	.248
Joe Oliver	C47	R	23	49	151	13	41	8	0	3	23	6	28	0	.272	.384
2 Mariano Duncan	SS44 OF7 2B5	R	26	45	174	23	43	10	1	3	13	8	36	6	.247	.368
1 Kal Daniels (KJ)	OF38	L	25	44	133	26	29	11	0	2	9	36	28	6	.218	.346
Bo Diaz (KJ)	C43	R	36	43	132	6	27	5	0	1	8	6	7	0	.205	.265
Scotti Madison	3B26	R	29	40	98	13	17	7	0	1	7	8	9	0	.173	.276
Manny Trillo	2B10 1B3 SS1	R	38	17	39	3	8	0	0	0	2	4	9	0	.205	.205
Marty Brown	3B11	R	26	16	30	2	5	1	0	0	4	4	9	0	.167	.200
Van Snider	OF6	L	25	8	7	1	1	0	0	0	0	0	5	0	.143	.143
Terry McGriff	C6	R	25	6	11	1	3	0	0	0	2	2	3	0	.273	.273
Skeeter Barnes		R	32	5	3	1	0	0	0	0	0	0	0	0	.000	.000

NAME	T	AGE	W	L	PCT	SV	G	GS	CG	IP	H	BB	SO	SHO	ERA
TOTALS		29	75	87	.463	37	162	162	16	1464	1404	559	981	9	3.73
Tom Browning	L	29	15	12	.556	0	37	37	9	250	241	64	118	2	3.39
Rob Dibble	R	25	10	5	.667	2	74	0	0	99	62	39	141	0	2.09
Rick Mahler	R	35	9	13	.409	0	40	31	5	221	242	51	102	2	3.83
Norm Charlton	L	26	8	3	.727	0	69	0	0	95	67	40	98	0	2.93
Jose Rijo (XJ)	R	24	7	6	.538	0	19	19	1	111	101	48	86	1	2.84
Danny Jackson (SJ)	L	27	6	11	.353	0	20	20	1	116	122	57	70	0	5.60
Ron Robinson (EJ)	R	27	5	3	.625	0	15	15	0	83	80	28	36	0	3.35
John Franco	L	28	4	8	.333	32	60	0	0	81	77	36	60	0	3.12
Scott Scudder	R	21	4	9	.308	0	23	17	0	100	91	61	66	0	4.49
Tim Birtsas	R	28	2	2	.500	1	42	1	0	70	68	27	57	0	3.75
Jack Armstrong	R	24	2	3	.400	0	9	8	0	43	40	21	23	0	4.64
2 Tim Leary	R	30	2	7	.222	0	14	14	0	90	88	31	64	0	3.71
Rosario Rodriguez	L	19	1	1	.500	0	7	0	0	4	3	3	0	0	6.48
2 Bob Sebra	R	27	0	0	—	0	15	0	0	21	14	14	0	0	6.48
Mike Griffin	R	32	0	0	—	0	3	0	0	4	3	1	2	0	12.46
Mike Roesler	R	25	0	1	.000	0	17	0	0	25	22	9	14	0	3.96
Kent Tekulve	R	42	0	3	.000	0	37	0	0	52	56	23	31	0	5.02
Jeff Sellers (SJ) 25															

ATLANTA   6th 63-97 .394 28   RUSS NIXON

Name	G by Pos	B	AGE	G	AB	R	H	2B	3B	HR	RBI	BB	SO	SB	BA	SA
TOTALS			29	161	5463	584	1281	201	22	128	544	485	996	83	.234	.350
Gerald Perry (SJ)	1B72	L	28	72	266	24	67	11	0	4	21	32	28	10	.252	.338
Jeff Treadway	2B123 3B6	L	26	134	473	58	131	18	3	8	40	30	38	3	.277	.378
Andres Thomas	SS138	R	25	141	554	41	118	18	0	13	57	12	62	3	.213	.316
Jeff Blauser	3B78 2B39 SS30 OF2	R	23	142	456	63	123	24	2	12	46	38	101	5	.270	.410
Dale Murphy	OF151	R	33	154	574	60	131	16	0	20	84	65	142	3	.228	.361
2 Oddibe McDowell	OF68	L	26	76	280	56	85	18	4	7	24	27	37	15	.304	.461
Lonnie Smith	OF132	R	33	134	482	89	152	34	4	21	79	76	95	25	.315	.533
Jody Davis	C72 1B2	R	32	78	231	12	39	5	0	4	19	23	61	0	.169	.242
Darrell Evans	1B50 3B28	L	42	107	276	31	57	6	1	11	39	41	46	0	.207	.355
Tommy Gregg (BF)	OF48 1B37	L	25	102	276	24	67	8	0	6	23	18	45	3	.243	.337
Geronimo Berroa	OF34	R	24	81	136	7	36	4	0	2	9	7	32	0	.265	.338
Ron Gant	3B53 OF14	R	24	75	260	26	46	8	3	9	25	20	63	9	.177	.335
John Russell	C45 OF14 1B2 3B2 P1	R	28	74	159	14	29	2	0	2	8	9	46	0	.182	.233
Bruce Benedict	C65	R	33	66	160	12	31	3	0	1	6	23	18	0	.194	.231
1 Dion James	OF46 1B8	L	26	63	170	15	44	7	0	1	11	25	23	1	.259	.318
Jeff Wetherby	OF9	L	25	52	48	5	10	2	1	1	7	4	6	1	.208	.354
Ed Whited	3B29 1B3	R	25	36	74	5	13	3	0	1	4	6	15	1	.162	.243
Terry Blocker	OF8 P1	L	29	26	31	1	7	1	0	0	1	5	1	1	.226	.258
David Justice	OF16	L	23	16	51	7	12	3	0	1	8	7	9	2	.235	.353
Mark Lemke	2B14	R	23	14	55	4	10	2	1	2	10	5	7	0	.182	.364
Drew Denson	1B12	R	23	12	36	1	9	1	0	0	1	1	9	0	.250	.278
John Mizerock	C11	L	28	11	27	1	6	0	0	0	2	2	2	0	.222	.222
Kelly Mann	C7	R	21	7	24	1	6	1	0	0	2	0	8	0	.208	.292
2 Ed Romero	2B4 SS2 3B1	R	31	7	19	1	5	1	0	0	3	0	1	0	.263	.474
2 Francisco Cabrera	1B2 C1	R	22	4	14	0	3	0	0	0	0	3	1	0	.214	.357

NAME	T	AGE	W	L	PCT	SV	G	GS	CG	IP	H	BB	SO	SHO	ERA
TOTALS		27	63	97	.394	33	161	161	15	1448	1370	468	966	8	3.70
Tom Glavine	L	23	14	8	.636	0	29	29	6	186	172	40	90	4	3.68
John Smoltz	R	22	12	11	.522	0	29	29	5	208	160	72	168	0	2.94
Derek Lilliquist	L	23	8	10	.444	0	32	30	0	166	202	34	79	0	3.97
Mark Eichhorn	R	28	5	5	.500	0	45	0	0	68	70	19	49	0	4.35
Pete Smith	R	23	5	14	.263	0	28	27	1	142	144	57	115	0	4.75
Marty Clary	R	27	4	3	.571	0	18	17	2	109	103	31	30	1	3.15
Joe Boever	R	28	4	11	.267	21	66	0	0	82	78	34	68	0	3.94
Jose Alvarez (KJ)	R	33	3	3	.500	2	30	5	0	50	44	24	45	0	2.86
Gary Eave	R	25	2	0	1.000	0	3	3	0	21	15	12	9	0	1.31
Charlie Puleo	R	34	1	1	.500	0	19	0	0	29	26	16	17	0	4.66
Sergio Valdez	R	24	1	2	.333	0	19	1	0	33	31	17	26	0	6.06
2 Jay Aldrich	R	28	1	1	.500	0	8	0	0	12	12	6	7	0	2.19
Tommy Greene	R	22	1	2	.333	0	4	4	1	26	22	6	17	1	4.10
1 Paul Assenmacher	L	28	1	3	.250	0	49	0	0	58	56	16	64	0	3.59
1 Zane Smith	L	28	1	12	.077	0	17	17	0	99	102	33	58	0	4.45
Rusty Richards	R	24	0	1	.000	0	2	2	0	9	10	6	4	0	4.82
Kent Mercker	L	21	0	0	—	0	2	0	0	0	0	2	4	0	12.46
Terry Blocker	L	29	0	0	—	0	1	0	0	1	0	1	0	0	0.00
John Russell	R	28	0	0	—	0	1	0	0	2	1	1	0	0	4.50
Mike Stanton	L	22	0	1	.000	0	20	0	0	24	17	8	27	0	1.50
2 Tony Castillo	L	26	0	1	.000	0	17	0	0	24	27	8	26	0	4.82
Dwayne Henry	R	27	0	2	.000	0	12	0	0	12	10	15	16	0	4.26
1 Jim Acker	R	30	0	6	.000	0	59	0	0	98	84	20	68	0	2.67
Bruce Sutter (SJ) 36															

LINE SCORES

Team	1	2	3	4	5	6	7	8	9	10	11	12	R	H	E

AMERICAN LEAGUE CHAMPIONSHIPS: OAKLAND (WEST) 4 TORONTO (EAST) 1

Game 1   October 3 at Oakland
TOR 0 2 0 1 0 0 0 0 0   3 5 1
OAK 0 1 0 0 1 3 0 2 X   7 11 0
Stieb, Acker (6), Ward (8)
Stewart, Eckersley (9)

Game 2   October 4 at Oakland
TOR 0 0 1 0 0 0 0 2 0   3 5 1
OAK 0 0 0 2 0 3 1 0 X   6 9 1
Stottleymyre, Acker (6), Wells (6), Henke (7), Cerutti (8)
Moore, Honeycutt (8), Eckersley (9)

Game 3   October 6 at Toronto
OAK 1 0 1 1 0 0 0 0 0   3 8 1
TOR 0 0 0 4 0 0 3 0 X   7 8 0
Davis, Honeycutt (7), Nelson (7), M. Young (8)
Key, Acker (7), Henke (9)

Game 4   October 7 at Toronto
OAK 0 0 3 0 2 0 1 0 0   6 11 1
TOR 0 0 0 1 0 1 1 2 0   5 13 0
Welch, Honeycutt (6), Eckersley (8)
Flanagan, Ward (5), Cerutti (8), Acker (9)

Game 5   October 8 at Toronto
OAK 1 0 1 0 0 0 2 0 0   4 4 0
TOR 0 0 0 0 0 0 0 1 2   3 9 0
Stewart, Eckersley (9)
Stieb, Acker (7), Henke (9)

NATIONAL LEAGUE CHAMPIONSHIPS: SAN FRANCISCO (WEST) 4   CHICAGO (EAST) 1

Game 1   October 4 at Chicago
S.F. 3 0 1 4 0 0 0 3 0   11 13 0
CHI   2 0 1 0 0 0 0 0 0   3 10 1
Garrelts, Brantley (8), Hammaker (9)
Maddux, Kilgus (5), Wilson (8)

Game 2   October 5 at Chicago
S.F. 0 0 0 2 0 0 0 2 1   5 10 0
CHI   6 0 0 0 3 0 0 0 X   9 11 0
Reuschel, Downs (1), Lefferts (6), Brantley (7), Bedrosian (8)
Bielecki (5), Assenmacher (5), Lancaster (6)

Game 3   October 7 at San Francisco
CHI   2 0 0 1 0 0 1 0 0   4 10 0
S.F. 3 0 0 0 0 0 2 0 X   5 8 3
Sutcliffe, Assenmacher (7), Lancaster (7)
LaCoss, Brantley (4), Robinson (7), Lefferts (8), Bedrosian (9)

Game 4   October 8 at San Francisco
CHI   1 1 0 0 2 0 0 0 0   4 12 1
S.F. 1 0 2 1 2 0 0 0 X   6 9 1
Maddux, Wilson (4), Sanderson (6), Mi. Williams (8)
Garrelts, Downs (5), Bedrosian (9)

Game 5   October 9 at San Francisco
CHI   0 0 1 0 0 0 0 0 1   2 10 1
S.F. 0 0 0 0 0 0 1 2 X   3 4 1
Bielecki, McWilliams (8), Lancaster (8)
Reuschel, Bedrosian (9)

COMPOSITE BATTING

OAKLAND

NAME	POS	G	AB	R	H	2B	3B	HR	RBI	BA
Totals		5	158	26	43	9	1	7	23	.272
D. Henderson	CF	5	19	4	5	3	0	1	1	.263
McGwire	1B	5	18	3	7	1	0	1	3	.294
Phillips	2B-3B	5	18	1	3	1	0	0	1	.167
Canseco	RF	5	17	2	5	1	0	1	2	.294
Parker	DH	4	16	2	3	0	0	2	3	.188
R. Henderson	LF	5	15	8	6	1	1	2	5	.400
Steinbach	C-DH	5	15	0	3	0	0	0	1	.200
Gallego	SS	4	11	3	3	1	0	0	1	.273
Lansford	3B	5	11	2	5	0	0	0	4	.455
Weiss	SS	4	9	1	1	0	0	0	1	.111
Hassey	C	2	6	0	1	0	0	0	1	.167
Javier	RF	1	2	0	0	0	0	0	0	.000
Phelps	PH	1	1	0	1	1	0	0	0	1.000
Blankenship	2B	1	0	0	0	0	0	0	0	—

TORONTO

NAME	POS	G	AB	R	H	2B	3B	HR	RBI	BA
Totals		5	165	21	40	5	0	3	19	.242
McGriff	1B	5	21	1	3	0	0	0	3	.143
Fernandez	SS	5	20	6	7	3	0	0	1	.350
Bell	LF-DH	5	20	2	4	0	0	1	2	.200
Wilson	RF-LF	5	19	2	5	0	0	0	2	.263
Gruber	3B	5	17	2	5	1	0	0	0	.294
Moseby	CF	5	16	4	5	0	0	1	2	.313
Whitt	C	5	16	1	2	0	0	0	0	.125
Felix	RF	3	11	0	3	1	0	0	3	.273
Mazzilli	DH-PH	3	8	0	0	0	0	0	0	.000
Lee	2B	2	8	2	2	0	0	0	0	.250
Lirano	2B	3	7	1	3	0	0	0	1	.429
Borders	C	3	1	0	1	0	0	0	0	1.000
Mulliniks	PH	1	1	0	0	0	0	0	0	.000

SAN FRANCISCO

NAME	POS	G	AB	R	H	2B	3B	HR	RBI	BA
Totals		5	165	30	44	6	2	8	29	.267
Clark	1B	5	20	8	13	3	1	2	8	.650
Ma. Williams	3B	5	20	2	6	1	0	2	9	.300
Butler	CF	5	19	6	4	0	0	0	0	.211
Thompson	2B	5	18	5	5	0	0	2	3	.278
Uribe	SS	5	17	2	4	1	0	0	0	.235
Mitchell	LF	5	17	5	6	0	0	2	7	.353
Kennedy	C	5	16	0	3	1	0	0	0	.188
Sheridan	RF	5	13	1	2	0	1	0	0	.154
Oberkfell	3B-PH	3	4	0	0	0	0	0	0	.000
Garrelts	P	2	4	0	0	0	0	0	0	.000
Maldonado	RF	3	3	1	0	0	0	0	1	.000
Nixon	RF	3	3	0	0	0	0	0	0	.000
Downs	P	2	3	0	0	0	0	0	0	.000
Manwaring	C	3	2	0	0	0	0	0	0	.000
Reuschel	P	2	2	0	0	0	0	0	0	.000
Litton	3B	1	1	0	1	0	0	0	0	1.000
Bathe	PH	1	1	0	0	0	0	0	0	.000
Riles	PH	1	1	0	0	0	0	0	0	.000
LaCoss	P	1	1	0	0	0	0	0	0	.000
Bedrosian	P	4	0	0	0	0	0	0	0	—
Brantley	P	3	0	0	0	0	0	0	0	—
Lefferts	P	2	0	0	0	0	0	0	0	—
Hammaker	P	1	0	0	0	0	0	0	0	—
Robinson	P	1	0	0	0	0	0	0	0	—

CHICAGO

NAME	POS	G	AB	R	H	2B	3B	HR	RBI	BA
Totals		5	175	22	53	9	3	3	21	.303
Walton	CF	5	22	4	8	0	0	0	2	.364
Sandberg	2B	5	20	6	8	3	1	1	4	.400
Dunston	SS	5	19	2	6	0	0	0	0	.316
Dawson	RF	5	19	0	2	1	0	0	3	.105
Salazar	3B	5	19	2	7	0	1	1	2	.368
Grace	1B	5	17	3	11	3	1	1	8	.647
Smith	LF	4	15	2	3	1	0	0	0	.200
Girardi	C	4	10	1	1	0	0	0	0	.100
Wynne	CF-LF	4	6	0	1	0	0	0	0	.167
Bielicki	P	2	5	0	1	0	0	0	2	.200
Wrona	C	2	5	0	0	0	0	0	0	.000
McClendon	LF-C	3	3	0	2	0	0	0	0	.667
Webster	LF-RF	3	3	0	1	0	0	0	0	.333
Madddux	P	3	3	1	0	0	0	0	0	.000
Law	3B	2	3	0	0	0	0	0	0	.000
Wilkerson	3B	3	2	1	1	0	0	0	0	.500
Sutcliffe	P	3	2	0	1	0	0	0	0	.500
Lancaster	P	3	1	0	0	0	0	0	0	.000
Ramos	PH	1	1	0	0	0	0	0	0	.000
Assenmacher	P	2	0	0	0	0	0	0	0	—
Mi. Williams	P	2	0	0	0	0	0	0	0	—
Wilson	P	2	0	0	0	0	0	0	0	—
Kilgus	P	1	0	0	0	0	0	0	0	—
Sanderson	P	1	0	0	0	0	0	0	0	—

COMPOSITE PITCHING

OAKLAND

NAME	G	IP	H	BB	SO	W	L	SV	ERA
Totals	5	44	40	15	24	4	1	3	3.89
Stewart	2	16	13	3	9	2	0	0	2.81
Moore	1	7	3	2	3	1	0	0	0.00
Davis	1	6.1	5	2	3	0	1	0	7.11
Eckersley	4	5.2	4	0	2	0	0	3	1.59
Welch	1	5.2	8	1	4	1	0	0	2.81
Honeycutt	3	1.2	6	5	1	0	0	0	32.40
Nelson	1	1.1	1	0	2	0	0	0	0.00
Young	1	0.1	0	2	0	0	0	0	0.00

TORONTO

NAME	G	IP	H	BB	SO	W	L	SV	ERA
Totals	5	43	43	20	32	1	4	0	5.02
Stieb	2	11.1	12	6	10	0	2	0	6.35
Acker	5	6.1	4	1	4	0	0	0	1.42
Key	1	6	7	2	2	1	0	0	4.50
Stottlemyre	1	5	7	2	2	0	1	0	7.20
Flanagan	1	4.1	7	1	3	0	1	0	10.39
Ward	2	3.2	6	3	5	0	0	0	7.36
Henke	3	2.2	0	0	3	0	0	0	0.00
Cerutti	2	2.2	0	3	1	0	0	0	0.00
Wells	1	1	0	2	1	0	0	0	0.00

SAN FRANCISCO

NAME	G	IP	H	BB	SO	W	L	SV	ERA
Totals	5	44	53	16	27	4	1	3	4.09
Garrelts	2	11.2	16	2	8	1	0	0	5.40
Downs	2	8.2	8	6	6	1	0	0	3.12
Reuschel	2	8.2	12	2	5	1	1	0	5.19
Brantley	3	5	1	2	3	0	0	0	0.00
Bedrosian	4	3.1	4	2	2	0	0	3	2.70
LaCoss	1	3	5	1	2	0	0	0	9.00
Robinson	1	1.2	3	0	1	0	1	0	0.00
Hammaker	1	1	0	1	0	0	0	0	0.00
Lefferts	2	1	1	2	1	0	0	0	9.00

CHICAGO

NAME	G	IP	H	BB	SO	W	L	SV	ERA
Totals	5	42	44	17	29	1	4	0	5.57
Bielecki	2	12	7	6	11	0	1	0	3.65
Maddux	2	7.1	13	4	5	0	1	0	13.50
Lancaster	2	6	6	1	3	1	1	0	6.35
Sutcliffe	1	6	5	4	2	0	0	0	4.50
Wilson	2	3.2	3	1	4	0	1	0	4.91
Kilgus	1	3	4	1	1	0	0	0	0.00
Sanderson	1	2	2	0	1	0	0	0	0.00
Mi. Williams	2	1	1	0	2	0	0	0	13.50
Assenmacher	2	0.2	3	0	0	0	0	0	13.50

LINE SCORES

Team	1	2	3	4	5	6	7	8	9	10	11	12	R	H	E

WORLD SERIES: OAKLAND (AL) 4 SAN FRANCISCO (NL) 0

Game 1   October 14 at Oakland

SF	0	0	0	0	0	0	0	0	0				0	5	1
OAK	0	3	1	1	0	0	0	0	X				5	11	1

Garrelts, Hammaker (5),   **Stewart**
Brantley (6), LaCoss (8)

Game 2   October 15 at Oakland

SF	0	0	1	0	0	0	0	0	0				1	4	0
OAK	1	0	0	4	0	0	0	0	X				5	7	0

Reuschel, Downs (5),   **Moore**, Honeycutt (8),
Lefferts (7), Bedrosian (8)   Eckersley (9)

Game 3   October 27 at San Francisco

OAK	2	0	0	2	4	1	0	4	0				13	14	0
SF	0	1	0	2	0	0	0	0	4				7	10	3

Stewart, Honeycutt (8),   **Garrelts**, Downs (4),
Nelson (9), Burns (9)   Brantley (5), Hammaker (8),
                        Lefferts (8)

Game 4   October 28 at San Francisco

OAK	1	3	0	0	3	1	0	1	0				9	12	0
SF	0	0	0	0	0	2	4	0	0				6	9	0

Moore, Nelson (7),   **Robinson**, LaCoss (2),
Honeycutt (7), Burns (7),   Brantley (6), Downs (6),
Eckersley (9)   Lefferts (8), Bedrosian (8)

COMPOSITE BATTING

NAME	POS	G	AB	R	H	2B	3B	HR	RBI	BA
OAKLAND		4	136	32	44	8	3	9	30	.301
R. Henderson	LF	4	19	4	9	1	2	1	3	.474
McGwire	1B	4	17	0	5	1	0	1		.294
Phillips	2B-3B-LF	4	17	2	4	1	0	1	3	.235
Lansford	3B	4	16	5	7	1	0	1	4	.438
Steinbach	C	4	16	4	4	0	0	1	7	.250
Weiss	SS	4	15	3	2	0	0	1	1	.133
Canseco	RF	4	14	5	5	0	0	1	3	.357
D. Henderson	CF	4	13	6	4	2	0	2	4	.308
Parker	DH-PH	3	9	2	2	1	0	1	2	.222
Moore	P	2	3	1	1	1	0	0	2	.333
Stewart	P	2	3	0	0	0	0	0	0	.000
Blankenship	PH-2B	1	2	1	1	0	0	0	0	.000
Gallego	2B-PH-3B	1	1	0	0	0	0	0	0	.000
Phelps	PH	1	1	0	0	0	0	0	0	.000
Javier	RF	1	0	0	0	0	0	0	0	—

NAME	POS	G	AB	R	H	2B	3B	HR	RBI	BA
SAN FRANCISCO		4	134	14	28	4	1	4	14	.209
Mitchell	LF	4	17	2	5	0	0	1	2	.294
Clark	1B	4	16	2	4	1	0	0	0	.250
Williams	3B-SS	4	16	1	2	0	0	1	1	.125
Butler	CF	4	14	1	4	1	0	0	1	.286
Kennedy	C	4	12	1	2	0	0	0	2	.167
Maldonado	RF-PH	4	11	1	1	0	1	0	0	.091
Thompson	2B-PH	4	11	0	1	0	0	0	0	.091
Riles	DH-PH	4	8	0	0	0	0	0	0	.000
Litton	2B-3B-PH	2	6	1	3	1	0	1	3	.500
Oberkfell	PH-3B	4	6	1	2	0	0	0	3	.333
Uribe	SS	3	5	1	0	0	0	0	0	.000
Nixon	PH-CF-RF	3	5	1	1	0	0	0	0	.200
Bathe	PH	2	2	1	1	0	0	1	3	.500
Sheridan	RF	1	2	0	0	0	0	0	0	.000
Marwaring	C	1	1	1	1	1	0	0	0	1.000
LaCoss	P	2	1	0	0	0	0	0	0	.000
Garrelts	P	1	1	0	0	0	0	0	0	.000

COMPOSITE PITCHING

NAME	G	IP	H	BB	SO	W	L	SV	ERA
OAKLAND	4	36	28	8	27	4	0	1	3.50
Stewart	2	16	10	2	14	2	0	0	1.69
Moore	2	13	9	3	10	2	0	0	2.08
Honeycutt	3	2.2	4	0	2	0	0	0	6.75
Burns	2	1.2	1	1	0	0	0	0	0.00
Eckersley	2	1.2	0	0	0	0	0	1	0.00
Nelson	2	1	4	2	1	0	0	0	54.00

NAME	G	IP	H	BB	SO	W	L	SV	ERA
SAN FRANCISCO	4	34	44	18	22	0	4	0	8.21
Garrelts	2	7.1	13	1	8	0	2	0	9.82
Downs	4	4.2	3	2	4	0	0	0	7.71
Brantley	3	4.1	5	3	1	0	0	0	4.15
LaCoss	2	4.1	4	3	2	0	0	0	6.23
Reuschel	1	4	5	4	2	0	1	0	11.25
Lefferts	3	2.2	2	1	2	0	0	0	3.38
Bedrosian	2	2.2	0	2	2	0	0	0	0.00
Hammaker	2	2.1	8	0	2	0	0	0	15.43
Robinson	1	1.2	4	1	0	0	1	0	21.60

MISCELLANEOUS 1989 INDIVIDUAL LEADERS

BATTING

On Base Percentage

American League		National League	
Boggs, Bos.	.430	1 L. Smith, Atl.	.415
A. Davis, Sea.	.424	2 Ja. Clark, S.D.	.410
Henderson, N.Y.+Oak.	.411	3 W. Clark, S.F.	.407
McGwire, Tor.	.399	4 Grace, Chi.	.405
Lansford, Oak.	.398	5 Raines, Mon.	.395

Caught Stealing

American League		National League	
Espy, Tex.	20	1 Young, Hou.	25
Reynolds, Sea.	18	2 R. Alomar, S.D.	17
Guillen, Chi.	17	3 Butler, S.F.	16
Sax, N.Y.	17	T. Gwynn, S.D.	16
White, Cal.	16	5 Dykstra, N.Y. + Phi.	12
		Nixon, Mon.	12
		Samuel, Phi. + N.Y.	12
		L. Smith, Atl.	12

Hit By Pitch

American League		National League	
Gantner, Mil.	10	1 Galarraga, Mon.	13
Lansford, Oak.	9	Thompson, S.F.	13
Larkin, Min.	9	3 Samuel, Phi. + N.Y.	11
C. O'Brien, Mil.	9	L. Smith, Atl.	11
Carter, Cle.	8	5 G. Davis, Hou.	7
Lemon, Det.	8		

Sacrifice Hits

American League		National League	
Fermin, Cle.	32	1 R. Alomar, S.D.	17
Espinoza, N.Y.	23	2 Reuschel, S.F.	16
B. Ripken, Bal.	19	3 Browning, Cin.	14
Gallagher, Chi.	16	4 Butler, S.F.	13
Barrett, Bos.	15	Lind, Pit.	13

Wild Pitches

American League		National League	
Ryan, Tex.	19	1 K. Howell, Phi.	21
Moore, Oak.	17	2 Wetteland, L.A.	16
Black, Cle.	13	3 Cone, N.Y.	14
Stewart, Oak.	13	Magrane, St. L.	14
Ward, Tor.	13	J. Robinson, Pit.	14

Extra Base Hits

American League		National League	
Sierra, Tex.	78	1 Mitchell, S.F.	87
Carter, Cle.	71	2 H. Johnson, N.Y.	80
Yount, Mil.	68	3 Bonilla, Pit.	71
McGriff, Tor.	66	4 W. Clark, S.F.	70
Mattingly, N.Y.	62	5 G. Davis, Hou.	61

Ground into Double Play

American League		National League	
Franco, Tex.	27	1 Wallach, Mon.	21
McGwire, Oak.	23	2 C. James, Phi. + S.D.	20
C. Ripken, Bal.	22	3 Jordan, Phi.	19
Buechele, Tex.	21	Pena, St. L.	19
C. Davis, Cal.	21	5 Guerrero, St. L.	17
Greenwell, Bos.	21	Thomas, Atl.	17
Lansford, Oak.	21		
Moreland, Det. + Bal.	21		
Parker, Oak.	21		
Puckett, Min.	21		

Total Bases

American League		National League	
Sierra, Tex.	344	1 Mitchell, S.F.	345
Yount, Mil.	314	2 Clark, S.F.	321
Carter, Cle.	303	3 Johnson, N.Y.	319
Mattingly, N.Y.	301	4 Bonilla, Pit.	302
Puckett, Min.	295	5 Sandberg, Chi.	301

Sacrifice Flies

American League		National League	
Bell, Tor.	14	1 Guerrero, St. L.	12
Leonard, Sea.	12	2 E. Davis, Cin.	11
Ray, Cal.	12	3 R. Alomar, S.D.	8
McGwire, Oak.	11	Benzinger, Cin.	8
Fernandez, Tor.	10	5 Brooks, Mon.	8
Mattingly, N.Y.	10	W. Clark, S.F.	8
Sierra, Tex.	10	Elster, N.Y.	8
Surhoff, Mil.	10	Jordan, Phi.	8
		Larkin, Cin.	8
		Oquendo, St. L.	8
		Quinones, Pit.	8

PITCHING
Hit Batters

American League		National League	
Stieb, Tor.	13	1 Mahler, Cin.	10
Boddicker, Bos.	10	2 Williams, Chi.	8
Smithson, Bos.	10	3 Belcher, L.A.	7
Ryan, Tex.	9	Kramer, Pit.	7
Blyleven, Cal.	8	5 LaCoss, S.F.	7
Clemens, Bos.	8	D. Martinez, Mon.	7
Pall, Chi.	8	Sebra, Phi. + Cin.	7
Tanana, Det.	8		

Home Runs Allowed

American League		National League	
Alexander, Det.	28	1 Browning, Cin.	31	1 P. Smith, Atl.	7
Hough, Tex.	28	2 Scott, Hou.	23	2 Sutcliffe, Chi.	6
M. Witt, Cal.	26	3 D. Robinson, S.F.	22	3 Forsch, Hou.	5
Schmidt, Bal.	24	Smiley, Pit.	22	Gooden, N.Y.	5
Hawkins, N.Y.	23	Whitson, S.D.	22	K. Gross, Mon.	5
Morris, Det.	23			Heaton, Pit."	5
Perez, Chi.	23			LaCoss, S.F.	5
Stewart, Oak.	23			Magrane, St. L.	5

FIELDING AVERAGE

American League	PO	A	E	DP	Pct.
1B Brett, K.C.	896	80	2	71	.998
2B Sax, N.Y.	312	460	10	117	.987
3B Howell, Phi.	95	322	11	27	.974
SS Fernandez, Tor.	260	475	6	93	.992
OF Snyder, Cle.	291	18	1	5	.997
C Macfarlane, K.C.	249	17	1	4	.996
P Tanana, Det.	16	41	0	2	1.000

National League	PO	A	E	DP	Pct.
1B Murray, L.A.	1316	137	6	122	.996
2B Oquendo, St. L.	346	500	5	106	.994
3B Pendleton, St. L.	113	392	15	25	.971
SS S. Owen, Mon.	232	388	13	65	.979
OF Young, Hou.	412	15	1	5	.998
C Pena, St. L.	674	70	2	13	.997
P Hurst, S.D.	8	42	0	2	1.000

Balks

American League		National League	
Dopson, Bos.	15	1 P. Smith, Atl.	7
Candiotti, Cle.	8	2 Sutcliffe, Chi.	6
Black, Cle.	5	3 Forsch, Hou.	5
Hough, Tex.	5	Gooden, N.Y.	5
R. Johnson, Sea.	5	K. Gross, Mon.	5
Perez, Chi.	5	Heaton, Pit."	5
		LaCoss, S.F.	5
		Magrane, St. L.	5

1990 Reds Rise and The Year of the No-Hitter

The Reds under Lou Piniella led from start to finsih in a season highlighted by a lock-out, 9 no hitters, the jailing of Pete Rose, the barring of "Boss" George Steinbrenner plus many on the field achievements.

The spring-training season was delayed by an owner's lock-out which stayed in effect until both sides could reach an agreement. After 32 days, on March 18, an agreement was reached for four years. Spring training finally began and the first week's games were delayed until later in the season. Opening day was April 9. The major concern was that pitchers would need longer than the three week training period. On the third day of the season, the Angel's Mark Langston and Mike Witt combined for a no-hitter. This was the first of nine during the season including Nolan Ryan's sixth on June 11 over Oakland. He became the oldest ever to pitch a no-hitter at the age of 43. On June 29, two no-hitters were pitched on the same day. Two days later, Andy Hawkins pitched a no-hitter only to lose 0-4 at Chicago on errors.

Pete Rose was sentenced to five months in federal prison and fined $50,000 for tax evasion. He began serving his sentence on August 8 at Marion (Ill.) Federal Prison Camp. Meanwhile, the "Boss" George Steinbrenner was faring no better. Commissioner Vincent ordered an investigation into Steinbrenner's relationship with gambler Howard Spira (who was allegedly working for Steinbrenner trying to hunt out material on Dave Winfield). After many long meetings, it was announced on July 30 that Steinbrenner agreed to resign as general managing partner of the Yankees (permanently) for his violation of "the best interest of baseball rule". The Yankees finished their season 67-95, their worst record in over 70 years.

On the field the big hitter was Cecil Fielder of the Tigers. Fielder, who played the 1989 season in Japan, became the first Major Leaguer since 1977 and the first American Leaguer since 1961 to hit over 50 home runs. He hit numbers 50 and 51 on the final night of the season at Yankee Stadium. In the National League, Ryne Sandberg became the first second baseman since Rogers Hornsby to lead the league in homers. The ageless Ryan won his 300th game on July 31 in Milwaukee. He also again led the league in strikeouts (now nine times) continuing to add to his lifetime lead. Rickey Henderson got to within two stolen bases of Lou Brock's record. George Brett at age 37 became the only player in baseball history to win a batting crown in three different decades. Bob Welch won 27 games, the most in the AL since 1968. History was also made in Seattle where a father and son played for the same team: Ken Griffey Jr. & Sr..

The Reds with new skipper Piniella at the helm, were never out of first place with nine straight wins to start the season. The closest anyone got after April was in late September when the Dodgers trailed by only three games. Piniella had basically the same team inherited from Pete Rose and Tommy Helms, that had finished in fifth place and 17 games out.

The N.L. East was a surprise when the Pirates upstaged the heavily favored Mets. The Pirates were led by MVP winner Barry Bonds and Bobby Bonilla who combined for 65 homers and 234 RBI's. Late in the season the Pirates traded for Zane Smith who went 6-1 in the last seven weeks. The biggest series of the season was a three game set at Three Rivers Stadium on Sept. 5-6. The Pirates were only leading by 1/2 game but swept the Mets in three.

The A's were a new dynasty (or so they thought). The White Sox did make a couple of spurts but were never able to close ground. Rickey Henderson won the MVP, Dave Stewart won 20 games for the fourth consecutive year, Bob Welch won 27. The A's were helped further with late season additions in Harold Baines and the winner of the N.L. batting title, Willie McGee. The Red Sox just nosed out the Blue Jays in the A.L. East. Not picked by anyone to be close to the top, the Sox got good seasons from a suspect pitching staff. On Sept. 4 they led by 6 1/2 games when Roger Clemens was sidelined with a shoulder injury. By Sept 23 the Blue Jays were leading by one but lost six of their last eight to hand Boston the title. The Blue Jays played to almost 4,000,000 home fans.

The Championship Series in the American League was no contest with the A's sweeping the Sox in four. The Red Sox only scored one run in each game. In game four Clemens faced Stewart trying to avert the sweep. Clemens was ejected from the game (for verbal abuse) in the second inning, which led to a subsequent suspension to begin in 1991.

The Reds were having a tougher time with the Pirates who won game one 4-3 at Cincinnati. The Reds came back to beat Doug Drabek 2-1. The Reds won game three on homers by Duncan and Hatcher. They took a three games to one lead in the fourth game 5-3. But game five saw the Pirates come back 3-2. Back to Cincinnati for game six where Red's pitchers combined for a one-hitter and won 2-1.

The World Series began in Cincinnati with Oakland a heavy favorite. Eric Davis hit a 2-run homer in the first leading the Reds to an easy 7-0 win. Billy Hatcher went 3 for 3. The big winner Bob Welch started game two. The Reds took a lead in the bottom of the first 2-1. Oakland scored three in the top of the third to go up 4-2. The Reds scored one in the fourth to trail by one. In the eighth Hatcher tripled off of Canseco's glove and later scored. Ace reliever Dennis Eckersly came in to pitch in the tenth, but he gave up three successive singles to lose 4-5. Game three moved to Oakland and with the A's leading 2-1 in the third, the Reds scored seven runs on seven hits and that essentially was the game as the Reds won 8-3. In game four, Tony LaRussa benched Canseco due to a back injury. The A's scored in the first. Eric Davis suffered a rib and kidney injury diving for a ball in the first. Hatcher suffered an injured left hand when hit by a Stewart pitch in the first. The A's nursed this 1-0 lead into the eighth when Larkin singled, Winningham bunt singled on a 0-2 pitch, O'Neill was safe on a bunt when Stewart made an error on the play. With the bases loaded Braggs grounded out, scoring one. Morris hit a sacrifice fly and the Reds went on to win 2-1 and a four-game sweep of the series. Jose Riho was MVP, Billy Hatcher went 9 for 12 and Chris Sabo went 9-16. A fitting finish for Piniella who left New York on a murky cloud and woundup in Cincinnati with a team of destiny.

EAST DIVISION

Name	G by Pos	B	AGE	G	AB	R	H	2B	3B	HR	RBI	BB	SO	SB	BA	SA
BOSTON 1st 88-74 .543 JOE MORGAN																
TOTALS			29	162	5516	699	1502	298	31	106	660	598	795	53	.272	.395
Carlos Quintana	1B148 OF3	R	24	149	512	56	147	28	0	7	67	52	74	1	.287	.383
Jody Reed	2B119 SS50 DH1	R	27	155	598	70	173	45	0	5	51	75	65	4	.289	.390
Luis Rivera	SS112 2B3 3B1	R	26	118	346	38	78	20	0	7	45	25	58	4	.225	.344
Wade Boggs	3B152 DH3	L	32	155	619	89	187	44	5	6	63	87	68	0	.302	.386
2 Tom Brunansky	OF121 DH7	R	29	129	461	61	123	24	5	15	71	54	105	5	.267	.438
Ellis Burks	OF143 DH6	R	25	152	588	89	174	33	8	21	89	48	82	9	.296	.486
Mike Greenwell	OF159	L	26	159	610	71	181	30	6	14	73	65	43	8	.297	.434
Tony Pena	C142 1B1	R	33	143	491	62	129	19	1	7	56	43	71	8	.263	.348
Dwight Evans	DH122	R	38	123	445	66	111	18	3	13	63	67	73	3	.249	.391
Kevin Romine	OF64 DH1	R	29	70	136	21	37	7	0	2	14	12	27	4	.272	.368
Randy Kutcher	OF34 3B11 2B5 DH5	R	30	63	74	18	17	4	1	1	5	13	18	3	.230	.351
Marty Barrett	2B60 3B1 DH1	R	32	62	159	15	36	4	0	0	13	15	13	1	.226	.252
Danny Heep (XJ)	OF14 DH6 1B5 P1	L	32	41	69	3	12	1	1	0	8	7	14	0	.174	.217
John Marzano	C32	R	27	32	83	8	20	4	0	0	6	5	10	0	.241	.289
2 Mike Marshall (IL)	DH14 1B8 OF4	R	30	30	112	10	32	6	1	4	12	4	26	0	.286	.464
Billy Jo Robidoux (SJ)	1B11 DH4	L	26	27	44	3	8	4	0	1	4	6	14	0	.182	.341
Tim Naehring (XJ)	SS19 3B5 2B1	R	23	24	85	10	23	6	0	2	12	8	15	0	.271	.412
Bill Buckner	1B15	L	40	22	43	4	8	0	0	1	3	3	2	0	.186	.256
Phil Plantier	DH4 OF1	L	21	14	15	1	2	1	0	0	3	4	6	0	.133	.200
1 Rich Gedman	C9	L	30	10	15	3	3	0	0	0	0	5	6	0	.200	.200
Jeff Stone	DH2	L	29	10	2	1	1	0	0	0	1	0	1	0	.500	.500
Rick Lancellotti	1B2	L	33	4	8	0	0	0	0	0	1	0	3	0	.000	.000
Scott Cooper	2B1	L	22	2	1	0	0	0	0	0	0	0	1	0	.000	.000
Jim Panovits	2B2	R	34	2	0	0	0	0	0	0	0	0	0	0	—	—
TORONTO 2nd 86-76 .531 2 CITO GASTON																
TOTALS			26	162	5589	767	1479	263	50	167	729	526	970	111	.265	.419
Fred McGriff	1B147 DH6	L	26	153	557	91	167	21	1	35	88	94	108	5	.300	.530
Manny Lee	2B112 SS9	B	25	117	391	45	95	12	4	6	41	26	90	3	.243	.340
Tony Fernandez	SS161	B	28	161	635	84	175	27	17	4	66	71	70	26	.276	.371
Kelly Gruber	3B145 OF6 DH1	R	28	150	592	92	162	36	6	31	118	48	94	14	.274	.512
Junior Felix	OF125 DH1	B	22	127	463	73	122	23	7	15	65	45	99	13	.263	.441
Mookie Wilson	OF141 DH6	B	34	147	588	81	156	36	4	3	51	31	102	23	.265	.355
George Bell	OF108 DH36	R	30	142	562	67	149	25	0	21	86	32	80	3	.265	.422
Pat Borders	C115 DH1	R	27	125	346	36	99	24	2	15	49	18	57	0	.286	.497
John Olerud	DH90 1B18	L	21	111	358	43	95	15	1	14	48	57	75	0	.265	.430
Greg Myers	C87	L	24	87	250	33	56	7	3	5	22	22	33	0	.236	.332
Glenallen Hill	OF60 DH20	R	25	84	260	47	60	11	3	12	32	18	62	8	.231	.435
Rance Mulliniks	3B22 DH10 1B3	L	34	57	97	11	28	4	0	2	16	22	19	2	.289	.392
1 Nelson Liriano	2B49	B	26	50	170	16	36	7	2	1	15	16	20	3	.212	.294
2 Kenny Williams	OF29 DH12	R	26	49	72	13	14	6	1	0	7	7	18	7	.194	.306
Mark Whiten	OF30 DH1	B	23	33	88	12	24	1	1	2	7	7	14	2	.273	.375
Luis Sojo	2B15 OF5 SS5 3B4 DH3	R	24	33	80	14	18	3	0	1	9	5	5	1	.225	.300
Rob Ducey	OF19	L	25	53	7	16	0	5	0	0	7	7	15	1	.302	.396
Tom Lawless	DH5 3B4 OF2 2B1	R	33	15	12	1	1	0	0	0	0	0	1	0	.083	.083
Carlos Diaz	C9	R	24	10	6	0	2	0	0	0	0	0	5	0	.333	.333
Jim Eppard	1B30	L	30	5	0										.200	.200
Ozzie Virgil	C2 DH1	R	33	4	8	0	0	0	0	0	0	0	1	0	.000	.000
Tom Quinlan	3B1	R	22	1	2	0	0	0	0	0	0	0	0	0	.500	.500

1990 AMERICAN LEAGUE

NAME	T	AGE	W	L	PCT	SV	G	GS	CG	IP	H	BB	SO	SHO	ERA
		31	88	74	.543	44	162	162	15	1442	1439	519	997	13	3.72
Roger Clemens	R	27	21	6	.778	0	31	31	7	228	193	54	209	4	1.93
Mike Boddicker	R	32	17	8	.680	0	34	34	2	228	225	69	143	0	3.36
Greg Harris	R	34	13	9	.591	0	34	30	1	184	186	77	117	0	4.00
Tom Bolton	L	28	10	5	.667	0	21	16	3	120	111	47	65	0	3.38
Dana Kiecker	R	29	8	9	.471	0	32	25	0	152	145	54	93	0	3.97
Jeff Reardon (XJ)	R	34	5	3	.625	21	47	0	0	51	39	19	33	0	3.16
Dennis Lamp	R	37	3	5	.375	0	47	1	0	106	114	30	49	0	4.68
Wes Gardner	R	29	3	7	.300	0	34	9	0	77	77	35	58	0	4.89
2 Jerry Reed	R	34	2	1	.667	2	29	0	0	45	55	16	17	0	4.80
1 Lee Smith	R	32	2	1	.667	4	11	0	0	14	13	9	17	0	1.88
Jeff Gray	R	27	2	4	.333	9	41	0	0	51	53	15	50	0	4.44
Daryl Irvine	R	25	1	1	.500	0	11	0	0	17	15	10	9	0	4.67
Eric Hetzel	R	26	1	4	.200	0	9	8	0	35	39	21	20	0	5.91
1 Larry Andersen	R	37	0	0	—	1	15	0	0	22	18	3	25	0	1.23
John Dopson (EJ)	R	26	0	0	—	0	4	4	0	18	13	9	9	0	2.04
John Leister	R	29	0	0	—	0	2	1	0	6	7	4	3	0	4.76
Danny Heep	L	32	0	0		0	1	0	0	1	0	4	0	0	9.00
Mike Rochford	L	27	0	1	.000	0	2	1	0	4	10	4	0	0	18.00
3 Joe Hesketh	L	31	0	4	.000	0	12	2	0	26	37	11	26	0	3.51
Rob Murphy	L	30	0	6	.000	7	68	0	0	57	85	32	54	0	6.32
		29	86	76	.531	48	162	162	6	1454	1434	445	892	9	3.84
Dave Stieb	R	32	18	6	.750	0	33	33	2	209	179	64	125	2	2.93
Jimmy Key (LJ)	L	29	13	7	.650	0	27	27	0	155	169	22	88	0	4.25
Todd Stottlemyre	R	25	13	17	.433	0	33	33	4	203	214	69	115	0	4.34
David Wells	L	27	11	6	.647	3	43	25	0	189	165	45	115	0	3.14
John Cerutti	L	30	9	9	.500	0	30	23	0	140	162	49	49	0	4.76
Frank Wills	R	31	6	4	.600	0	44	4	0	99	101	38	72	0	4.73
Jim Acker	R	31	4	4	.500	1	59	0	0	92	103	30	54	0	3.83
Willie Blair	R	24	3	5	.375	0	27	6	0	69	66	28	43	0	4.06
2 Bud Black	L	33	2	1	.667	0	6	6	0	21	16	10	3	3	4.02
Mike Flanagan	L	38	2	2	.500	0	5	5	0	20	28	8	5	0	5.31
Tom Henke	R	32	2	4	.333	32	61	0	0	75	58	19	75	0	2.17
Duane Ward	R	26	2	8	.200	11	73	0	0	128	101	42	112	0	3.45
Tom Gilles	R	27	1	0	1.000	0	2	0	0	1	2	0	1	0	6.75
Paul Kilgus	L	28	0	0		0	11	0	0	16	19	7	7	0	6.06
Steve Cummings	R	25	0	0	—	0	5	5	0	12	12	5	4	0	5.11
Al Leiter	L	24	0	0	—	0	4	1	0	6	9	2	5	0	6.00
Rob MacDonald	L	25	0	0		0	3	0	0	2	1	0	0	0	0.00
2 Rick Luecken	R	28	0	0	—	0	5	0	0	1	3	2	0	0	9.00
2 John Candelaria	L	36	0	3	.000	1	13	2	0	21	32	11	19	0	5.48

DETROIT — 3rd 79-83 .488 9 — SPARKY ANDERSON

Name	G by Pos	B	AGE	G	AB	R	H	2B	3B	HR	RBI	BB	SO	SB	BA	SA
TOTALS		R	31	162	5479	750	1418	241	32	172	714	634	952	82	.259	.409
Cecil Fielder	1B143 DH15	R	26	159	573	104	159	25	1	51	132	90	182	0	.277	.592
Lou Whitaker	2B130 DH1	L	33	132	472	75	112	22	2	18	60	74	71	4	.237	.407
Alan Trammell	SS142 DH3	R	32	146	559	71	170	37	1	14	89	68	55	12	.304	.449
Tony Phillips	3B104 2B47 SS11 OF8 DH4	B	31	152	573	97	144	23	5	8	55	99	85	19	.251	.351
Chet Lemon	OF96 DH6	R	35	104	322	39	83	16	4	5	32	48	61	3	.258	.379
Lloyd Moseby	OF116 DH4	L	30	122	431	64	107	16	5	14	51	48	77	17	.248	.406
Gary Ward	OF85 DH13 1B2	R	36	106	309	32	79	11	2	9	46	30	50	2	.256	.392
Mike Heath	C117 OF3 DH2 SS1	R	35	122	370	46	100	18	2	7	38	19	71	7	.270	.386
Dave Bergman	DH51 1B27 OF5	L	37	100	205	21	57	10	1	2	26	33	17	3	.278	.366
Larry Sheets	OF79 DH44	L	30	131	360	40	94	17	2	10	52	24	42	1	.261	.403
2 John Shelby	OF68 DH5	B	32	78	222	22	55	9	3	4	20	10	51	3	.248	.369
Mark Salas	C57 DH3 3B1	L	29	74	164	18	38	3	0	9	24	21	28	0	.232	.415
Travis Fryman	3B48 SS17 DH1	R	21	66	232	32	69	11	1	9	27	17	51	3	.297	.470
1 Kenny Williams	OF48 DH3	R	26	57	83	10	11	2	0	0	5	3	24	2	.133	.157
2 Darnell Coles	DH30 OF11 3B8	R	28	52	108	13	22	2	0	1	4	12	21	0	.204	.250
1 Tracy Jones	OF27 DH20	R	29	50	118	15	27	4	1	4	9	6	13	1	.229	.381
Scott Lusader	OF42 DH2	L	25	45	87	13	21	2	0	2	16	12	8	0	.241	.333
1 Matt Nokes	DH24 C19	L	26	44	111	12	30	5	1	3	8	4	14	0	.270	.414
Ed Romero	3B27 DH3	R	32	32	70	8	16	3	0	0	4	6	4	0	.229	.271
Milt Cuyler	OF17	B	21	19	51	8	13	3	1	0	8	5	10	1	.255	.353
Jim Lindeman	DH10 1B1	R	28	12	32	5	7	1	0	2	8	2	13	0	.219	.438
Rich Rowland	C5 DH2	R	26	7	19	3	3	1	0	0	0	2	4	0	.158	.211
1 Johnny Paredes	2B4	R	27	6	8	2	1	0	0	0	0	1	0	0	.125	.125

NAME	T	AGE	W	L	PCT	SV	G	GS	CG	IP	H	BB	SO	SHO	ERA
		30	79	83	.488	45	162	162	15	1430	1401	661	856	12	4.39
Jack Morris	R	35	15	18	.455	0	36	36	11	250	231	97	162	3	4.51
Dan Petry (SJ)	R	31	10	9	.526	0	32	23	1	150	148	77	73	0	4.45
Jeff Robinson (EJ)	R	28	10	9	.526	0	32	27	1	145	141	88	76	1	5.96
Frank Tanana	L	36	9	8	.529	1	34	29	1	176	190	66	114	0	5.31
Mike Henneman	R	28	8	6	.571	22	69	0	0	94	90	33	50	0	3.05
2 Walt Terrell	L	32	6	4	.600	0	13	12	0	75	86	24	30	0	4.54
Paul Gibson	L	30	5	4	.556	3	61	0	0	97	99	44	56	0	3.05
Edwin Nunez (HJ)	R	27	3	1	.750	6	42	0	0	80	65	37	66	0	2.24
1 Brian DuBois	L	25	3	5	.375	0	12	11	0	58	70	22	34	0	5.09
Urbano Lugo	R	27	2	0	1.000	3	1	0		24	30	13	12	0	7.03
Clay Parker	R	27	2	2	.500	0	24	1	0	51	45	25	20	0	3.18
Steve Searcy	L	22	2	7	.222	0	16	12	1	75	76	51	66	0	4.66
Lance McCullers (SJ)	R	26	1	0	1.000	9	1	0		30	18	13	20	0	2.73
Randy Nosek	R	23	1	1	.500	0	3	2	0	7	7	9	3	0	7.71
Scott Aldred	L	22	1	2	.333	0	4	3	0	14	13	10	7	0	3.77
Jerry Don Gleaton	L	32	1	3	.250	13	57	0	0	83	62	25	56	0	2.94
Steve Wapnick	R	24	0	0	—	0	4	0	0	7	8	10	6	0	6.43
Mike Schwabe	R	25	0	0	—	1	0	0		4	5	0	1	0	2.45
Matt Kinzer (EJ)	R	27	0	0	—	0	2	0	0	2	3	3	1	0	16.20
Kevin Ritz	R	25	0	4	.000	0	4	4	0	14	14	14	3	0	11.05

CLEVELAND — 4th 77-85 .475 11 — JOHN McNAMARA

Name	G by Pos	B	AGE	G	AB	R	H	2B	3B	HR	RBI	BB	SO	SB	BA	SA
TOTALS		B	26	162	5485	732	1465	266	41	110	675	458	836	107	.267	.391
Keith Hernandez (LJ)	1B42	L	36	43	130	7	26	2	0	1	8	14	17	0	.200	.238
Jerry Browne	2B139	B	26	140	513	92	137	26	5	6	50	72	46	12	.267	.372
Felix Fermin	SS147 2B1	R	26	148	414	47	106	13	2	1	40	26	22	3	.256	.304
Brook Jacoby	3B99 1B78	R	30	155	553	77	162	24	4	14	75	63	58	1	.293	.427
Cory Snyder	OF120 SS5	R	27	123	438	46	102	27	3	14	55	21	118	1	.233	.404
Mitch Webster	OF118 1B3 DH3	B	31	128	437	58	110	20	6	12	55	20	61	22	.252	.407
Candy Maldonado	OF134 DH20	R	29	155	590	76	161	32	2	22	95	49	134	3	.273	.446
Sandy Alomar	C129	R	24	132	445	60	129	26	2	9	66	25	46	4	.290	.418
Chris James	DH124 OF14	R	27	140	528	62	158	32	4	12	70	31	71	4	.299	.443
Carlos Baerga	3B50 SS48 2B8	B	21	108	312	46	81	17	2	7	47	16	57	0	.260	.394
Dion James	1B35 OF33 DH10	L	27	87	248	28	68	15	2	1	22	27	23	5	.274	.363
Tom Brookens	3B35 2B21 SS3 1B2 DH1	R	36	64	154	18	41	7	2	1	20	14	25	0	.266	.357
Alex Cole	OF59 DH1	L	24	63	227	43	68	5	4	0	13	28	38	40	.300	.357
Joel Skinner	C49	R	29	49	139	16	35	4	1	2	16	7	44	0	.252	.338
2 Stan Jefferson	OF34 DH5	B	27	49	98	21	27	8	0	2	10	8	18	8	.276	.418
Jeff Manto	1B25 3B5	R	25	30	76	12	17	5	1	2	14	21	18	0	.224	.395
2 Ken Phelps	1B14 DH6	L	35	24	61	4	7	0	0	0	0	10	11	1	.115	.115
Turner Ward	OF13 DH1	R	25	14	46	10	16	2	1	1	10	3	8	3	.348	.500
Joey Belle	DH6 OF1	R	23	9	23	1	4	0	0	1	3	1	6	0	.174	.304
2 Mark McLemore	3B4 2B3 DH1	B	25	8	12	2	2	0	0	0	0	0	6	0	.167	.167
Rafael Santana	SS7	R	32	7	13	3	3	0	0	1	3	0	3	0	.231	.462
Beau Allred	OF4	L	25	4	16	2	3	1	0	1	2	2	3	0	.188	.438
Steve Springer	3B3 DH1	R	29	4	12	1	2	0	0	0	1	0	6	0	.167	.167

NAME	T	AGE	W	L	PCT	SV	G	GS	CG	IP	H	BB	SO	SHO	ERA
		28	77	85	.475	47	162	162	12	1427	1491	518	860	10	4.26
Tom Candiotti	R	32	15	11	.577	0	31	29	3	202	207	55	128	1	3.65
Greg Swindell	L	25	12	9	.571	0	34	34	3	215	245	47	135	0	4.40
1 Bud Black	L	33	11	10	.524	0	29	29	5	191	171	58	103	2	3.53
2 Sergio Valdez	R	25	6	6	.500	0	24	13	0	102	109	35	63	0	4.75
Jesse Orosco	L	33	5	4	.556	2	55	0	0	65	58	38	55	0	3.90
Doug Jones	R	33	5	5	.500	43	66	0	0	84	66	22	55	0	2.56
Steve Olin	R	24	4	4	.500	1	50	1	0	92	96	26	64	0	3.41
John Farrell (EJ)	R	27	4	5	.444	0	17	17	1	97	108	33	44	0	4.28
Jeff Shaw	R	23	3	4	.429	0	12	9	0	49	73	20	25	0	6.66
Rudy Seanez	R	21	2	1	.667	0	24	0	0	27	22	25	24	0	5.60
Cecilio Guante	R	30	2	3	.400	0	26	1	0	47	38	18	30	0	5.01
Al Nipper	R	31	2	3	.400	0	9	8	0	45	53	19	12	0	6.75
Charles Nagy	R	23	2	4	.333	0	9	8	0	46	58	21	26	0	5.91
Mike Walker	R	23	2	6	.250	0	18	11	0	76	82	42	34	0	4.88
Efrain Valdez	L	23	1	1	.500	0	13	0	0	24	20	14	13	0	3.04
Colby Ward	R	26	1	3	.250	1	22	0	0	36	31	21	23	0	4.25
Jeff Kaiser (XJ)	L	29	0	0	—	0	5	0	0	13	16	7	9	0	3.55
Mauro Gozzo	R	24	0	1	.000	0	3	2	0	6	9	4	1	0	0.00
Kevin Wickander (BE)	L	25	0	1	.000	0	10	0	0	12	14	4	10	0	3.65
Kevin Bearse	R	24	0	2	.000	0	3	3	0	8	15	5	2	0	12.91
Rod Nichols	R	24	0	2	.000	0	4	2	0	16	24	6	3	0	7.88

BALTIMORE — 5th 76-85 .472 11.5 — FRANK ROBINSON

Name	G by Pos	B	AGE	G	AB	R	H	2B	3B	HR	RBI	BB	SO	SB	BA	SA
TOTALS			27	161	5410	669	1328	234	22	132	623	660	962	94	.245	.370
Randy Milligan (SJ)	1B98 DH9	R	28	109	362	64	96	20	1	20	60	88	68	6	.265	.492
Billy Ripken	2B127	R	25	129	406	48	108	28	1	3	38	28	43	5	.291	.387
Cal Ripken	SS161	R	29	161	600	78	150	28	4	21	84	82	66	3	.250	.415
Craig Worthington	3B131 DH2	R	25	133	425	46	96	17	0	8	44	63	96	1	.226	.322
Steve Finley	OF133 DH2	L	25	142	464	46	119	16	4	3	37	32	53	22	.256	.328
Mike Devereaux (LJ)	OF104 DH3	R	27	108	367	48	88	18	1	12	49	28	48	13	.240	.392
1 Phil Bradley	OF70 DH2	R	31	72	289	39	78	9	1	4	26	30	35	10	.270	.349
Mickey Tettleton	C90 DH40 1B5 OF1	B	29	135	444	68	99	21	2	15	51	106	160	2	.223	.381
Sam Horn	DH63 1B10	L	26	79	246	30	61	13	0	14	45	32	62	0	.248	.472
Joe Orsulak	OF109 DH4	L	28	124	413	49	111	14	3	11	57	46	48	6	.269	.397
Bob Melvin	C76 DH10 1B1	R	28	93	301	30	73	14	1	5	37	11	54	0	.243	.346
Brady Anderson (NJ)	OF63 DH11	L	26	89	234	24	54	5	2	3	24	31	46	15	.231	.308
Rene Gonzales	2B43 3B16 SS9 OF1	R	29	67	103	13	22	3	1	1	12	12	14	1	.214	.291
Tim Hulett	3B24 2B16 DH8	R	30	53	153	16	39	7	1	3	16	15	41	1	.255	.373
2 Brad Komminsk	OF40 DH2	R	29	46	101	18	24	4	0	3	8	14	29	1	.238	.366
David Segui	1B40 DH3	B	24	40	123	14	30	7	0	2	15	11	15	0	.244	.350
Jeff McKnight	1B15 OF8 2B5 SS1 DH1	B	27	29	75	11	15	2	0	1	4	5	17	0	.200	.267
Chris Hoiles	C7 DH7 1B6	R	25	23	63	7	12	3	0	1	6	5	12	0	.190	.286
3 Dave Gallagher	OF20 DH2	R	29	23	51	7	11	1	0	0	4	3	1	0	.216	.235
2 Ron Kittle	DH14 1B5	R	32	22	61	4	10	2	0	2	3	2	14	0	.164	.295
2 Greg Walker	3B12	L	30	14	34	2	5	0	0	0	3	3	9	1	.147	.147
Leo Gomez	3B12	R	23	12	39	3	9	0	0	0	1	8	7	0	.231	.231
1 Stan Jefferson	OF5 DH1	R	27	10	19	1	0	0	0	0	0	2	8	1	.000	.000
Marty Brown	DH4 2B3 3B2	R	27	9	15	1	3	0	0	0	1	0	7	0	.200	.200
Donell Nixon	OF4 DH3	R	28	8	20	1	5	2	0	0	2	1	9	0	.250	.350
Juan Bell	SS1 DH1	B	22	5	2	1	0	0	0	0	0	0	2	0	.000	.000

NAME	T	AGE	W	L	PCT	SV	G	GS	CG	IP	H	BB	SO	SHO	ERA
		27	76	85	.472	43	161	161	10	1435	1445	537	776	5	4.04
Dave Johnson	R	30	13	9	.591	0	30	29	3	180	196	43	68	0	4.10
Pete Harnisch	R	23	11	11	.500	0	31	31	3	189	189	86	122	0	4.34
Mark Williamson (BG)	R	30	8	2	.800	1	49	0	0	85	65	28	60	0	2.21
Ben McDonald (PJ)	R	22	8	5	.615	0	21	15	3	119	88	35	65	2	2.43
Gregg Olson	R	23	6	5	.545	37	64	0	0	74	57	31	74	0	2.42
John Mitchell	R	24	6	6	.500	0	24	17	0	114	133	48	43	0	4.64
Bob Milacki (SJ)	R	25	5	8	.385	0	27	24	1	135	143	61	60	1	4.46
Jose Mesa	R	24	3	2	.600	0	7	7	0	47	37	27	24	0	3.86
Anthony Telford	R	24	3	3	.500	0	8	8	0	36	43	19	20	0	4.95
Joe Price	L	33	3	4	.429	0	50	0	0	65	62	24	54	0	3.58
Brian Holton	R	30	2	3	.400	0	33	0	0	58	68	21	27	0	4.50
2 Jay Tibbs	R	28	2	2	.222	0	10	10	0	51	55	14	23	0	5.68
Jeff Ballard	L	26	2	11	.154	0	44	17	0	133	152	42	50	0	4.93
Jose Bautista	R	25	1	0	1.000	0	22	0	0	27	28	7	15	0	4.05
Curt Schilling	R	23	1	2	.333	3	35	0	0	46	38	19	32	0	2.54
Jay Aldrich	R	29	1	2	.333	1	7	0	0	12	17	7	5	0	8.25
Kevin Hickey	L	33	1	3	.250	1	37	0	0	26	13	17	12	0	5.13
Dan Boone	L	36	0	0	—	1	4	0	0	10	4	3	5	0	2.79
Mike Smith	R	26	0	0	—	0	1	0	0	6	10	6	4	0	12.00
Mickey Weston	R	29	0	0	—	0	9	0	0	21	28	6	9	0	7.71
Dorn Taylor	R	31	0	0	—	0	1	0	0	2	1	4	2	0	2.45
2 Brian DuBois (EJ) 25															

MILWAUKEE — 6th 74-88 .457 14 — TOM TREBELHORN

Name	G by Pos	B	AGE	G	AB	R	H	2B	3B	HR	RBI	BB	SO	SB	BA	SA
TOTALS			29	162	5503	732	1408	247	36	128	680	519	821	164	.256	.384
Greg Brock	1B115	L	33	123	367	42	91	23	0	7	50	43	45	4	.248	.368
Jim Gantner (KJ)	2B80 3B9	L	37	88	323	36	85	8	5	0	25	29	19	18	.263	.319
Bill Spiers (SJ)	SS111	L	24	112	363	44	88	15	3	2	36	16	45	11	.242	.317
Gary Sheffield	3B125	R	21	125	487	67	143	30	1	10	67	44	41	25	.294	.421
Rob Deer	OF117 1B21 DH1	R	29	134	440	57	92	15	1	27	69	64	147	2	.209	.432
Robin Yount	OF107 DH1	R	34	158	587	98	145	17	5	17	77	78	89	15	.247	.380
Greg Vaughn	OF106 DH8	R	24	120	382	51	84	26	2	17	61	33	91	7	.220	.432
B.J. Surhoff	C125 3B11	L	25	135	474	55	131	21	4	6	59	41	37	18	.276	.376
Dave Parker	DH153 1B3	L	39	157	610	71	176	30	3	21	92	41	102	4	.289	.451
Mike Felder	OF109 3B1 2B1 DH1	B	28	121	237	38	65	7	2	3	27	22	17	20	.274	.359
Paul Molitor (BG)	2B60 1B37 DH4 3B2	R	33	103	418	64	119	27	6	12	45	37	51	18	.285	.464
Darryl Hamilton	OF72 DH9	L	25	89	156	27	46	5	0	1	18	9	12	10	.295	.346
Eddie Diaz	SS65 2B15 3B7 DH1	R	26	86	218	27	59	2	2	0	14	21	32	3	.271	.298
Dale Sveum	3B22 2B16 SS5 1B5	B	26	48	117	15	23	7	0	1	12	12	30	0	.197	.282
1 Charlie O'Brien	C46	R	30	46	145	11	27	7	2	0	11	11	26	0	.186	.262
1 Glenn Braggs	OF32 DH2	R	27	37	113	17	28	5	0	3	13	12	21	5	.248	.372
Gus Polidor	3B14 2B2 SS2	R	29	27	30	2	2	1	0	0	1	0	9	0	.067	.067
1 Billy Bates	2B14	L	26	14	29	6	3	1	0	0	1	4	7	3	.103	.138
George Canale	1B6 DH3	L	24	10	13	4	1	1	0	0	2	5	6	0	.077	.154
Tim McIntosh	C4	R	25	5	4	1	1	0	0	0	2	0	4	0	.250	.500
Terry Francona	1B2 DH1	L	31	3	4	0	0	0	0	0	0	0	0	0	.000	.000

NAME	T	AGE	W	L	PCT	SV	G	GS	CG	IP	H	BB	SO	SHO	ERA
		29	74	88	.457	42	162	162	23	1445	1558	469	771	13	4.08
2 Ron Robinson	R	28	12	5	.706	0	22	22	7	148	158	37	57	2	2.91
Teddy Higuera	L	31	11	10	.524	0	27	27	4	170	167	50	129	1	3.76
Mark Knudson	R	29	10	9	.526	0	30	27	4	168	187	40	56	2	4.12
Jaime Navarro	R	23	8	7	.533	1	32	22	3	149	176	41	75	0	4.46
Bill Krueger	L	32	6	8	.429	0	30	17	0	129	137	54	64	0	3.98
Paul Mirabella	L	36	4	2	.667	0	44	2	0	59	66	27	28	0	3.97
Tom Edens	R	29	4	5	.444	2	35	6	0	89	89	33	40	0	4.45
Chris Bosio (KJ)	R	27	4	9	.308	0	20	20	4	133	131	38	76	1	4.00
Chuck Crim	R	28	3	5	.375	11	67	0	0	91	114	23	39	0	3.47
Dan Plesac	L	28	3	7	.300	24	66	0	0	69	67	31	65	0	4.43
Bill Wegman (EJ)	R	27	2	2	.500	0	8	5	1	30	37	6	20	0	1.85
Tony Fossas	L	32	2	3	.400	0	32	0	0	29	44	10	24	0	6.44
Tom Filer (SJ)	R	33	2	3	.400	0	7	7	0	32	36	9	8	0	6.14
Mark Lee	L	26	1	1	1.000	0	11	0	0	24	14	12	11	0	2.11
2 Kevin Brown	R	24	1	1	.500	0	5	3	0	21	14	7	12	0	2.57
Bob Sebra	R	28	1	2	.333	0	10	0	0	13	9	8	12	0	8.18
2 Julio Machado	R	24	0	0	—	0	10	0	0	13	9	8	12	0	0.69
Narciso Elvira	L	23	0	0	—	0	1	0	0	0.1	6	1	1	0	135.00
Mike Capel	R	28	0	0	—	0	6	0	0	5	6	6	3	0	5.40
Randy Veres	R	23	0	0	1.000	0	4	0	0	13	9	8	12	0	3.67
Don August	R	26	0	3	.000	0	5	0	0	11	13	5	1	0	6.55
2 Dennis Powell	L	26	0	4	.000	0	9	7	0	39	59	19	23	0	6.86
Juan Nieves (SJ) 25															

NEW YORK　7th 67-95 .414 21　BUCKY DENT 18-31 .367　STUMP MERRILL 49-64 .434

Name	G by Pos	B	AGE	G	AB	R	H	2B	3B	HR	RBI	BB	SO	SB	BA	SA
TOTALS			28	162	5483	603	1322	208	19	147	561	427	1027	119	.241	.366
Don Mattingly (XJ)	1B89 DH13 OF1	L	29	102	394	40	101	16	0	5	42	28	20	1	.256	.335
Steve Sax	2B154	R	30	155	615	70	160	24	2	4	42	49	46	43	.260	.325
Alvaro Espinoza	SS150	R	28	150	438	31	98	12	2	2	20	16	54	1	.224	.274
Jim Leyritz	3B69 OF14 C11	R	26	92	303	28	78	13	1	5	25	27	51	2	.257	.356
Jesse Barfield	OF151	R	30	153	476	69	117	21	2	25	78	82	150	4	.246	.456
Roberto Kelly	OF160 DH1	R	25	162	641	85	183	32	4	15	61	33	148	42	.285	.418
Oscar Azocar	OF57 DH1	L	25	65	214	18	53	8	0	5	19	2	15	7	.248	.355
Bob Geren	C107 DH1	R	28	110	277	21	59	7	0	8	31	13	73	0	.213	.325
Steve Balboni	DH72 1B28	R	33	116	266	24	51	6	0	17	34	35	91	0	.192	.406
Mel Hall	DH54 OF50	L	29	113	360	41	93	23	2	12	46	6	46	0	.258	.433
Randy Velarde	3B74 SS15 OF5 2B3 DH3	R	27	95	229	21	48	6	2	5	19	20	53	0	.210	.319
2 Matt Nokes	C46 DH30 OF2	L	26	92	240	21	57	4	0	8	32	20	33	2	.238	.354
Kevin Maas	1B57 DH18	L	25	79	254	42	64	9	0	21	41	43	76	1	.252	.535
Wayne Tolleson	SS45 2B13 DH5 3B3	B	34	73	74	12	11	1	1	0	4	6	21	1	.149	.189
Deion Sanders (LF)	OF42 DH4	L	22	57	133	24	21	2	2	3	9	13	27	8	.158	.271
Rick Cerone (KJ)	C35 DH6 2B1	R	36	49	139	12	42	6	0	2	11	5	13	0	.302	.388
Mike Blowers	3B45 DH2	R	25	48	144	16	27	4	0	5	21	12	50	1	.188	.319
2 Claudell Washington (RJ)	OF21 DH2	L	35	33	80	4	13	1	1	0	6	2	17	3	.163	.200
Hensley Meulens	OF23	R	23	23	83	12	20	7	0	3	10	9	25	1	.241	.434
1 Dave Winfield	OF12 DH7	R	38	20	61	7	13	3	0	2	6	4	13	0	.213	.361
Brian Dorsett	C9 DH5	R	29	14	35	2	5	2	0	0	2	4	1	0	.143	.200
1 Luis Polonia	DH4	L	25	11	22	2	7	0	0	0	3	0	1	1	.318	.318
Jim Walewander	2B2 3B2 DH2 SS1	B	28	9	5	1	1	1	0	0	1	0	1	0	.200	.400

NAME	T	AGE	W	L	PCT	SV	G	GS	CG	IP	H	BB	SO	SHO	ERA
		29	67	95	.414	41	162	162	15	1445	1430	618	909	6	4.21
Lee Guetterman	L	31	11	7	.611	2	64	0	0	93	80	26	48	0	3.39
Tim Leary	R	31	9	19	.321	0	31	31	6	208	202	78	138	1	4.11
Dave LaPoint	L	30	7	10	.412	0	28	27	2	158	180	57	67	0	4.11
Eric Plunk	R	26	6	3	.667	0	47	0	0	73	58	43	67	0	2.72
Chuck Cary (EJ)	L	30	6	12	.333	0	28	27	2	157	155	55	134	0	4.19
Greg Cadaret	L	28	5	4	.556	3	54	6	0	121	120	64	80	0	4.15
2 Mike Witt (EJ)	R	29	5	6	.455	0	16	16	2	97	87	34	60	1	4.47
Andy Hawkins	R	30	5	12	.294	0	28	26	2	158	156	82	74	1	5.37
Jeff Robinson	R	29	3	6	.333	0	54	4	1	89	82	34	43	0	3.45
Dave Eiland	R	23	2	1	.667	0	5	5	0	30	31	5	16	0	3.56
1 Lance McCullers	R	26	1	0	1.000	0	11	0	0	15	14	6	11	0	3.60
Dave Righetti	R	31	1	1	.500	36	53	0	0	53	48	26	43	0	3.57
Mark Leiter	R	27	1	1	.500	0	8	3	0	26	33	9	21	0	6.84
1 Clay Parker	R	27	1	1	.500	0	5	2	0	22	19	7	20	0	4.50
Jimmy Jones	R	26	1	2	.333	0	17	7	0	50	72	23	25	0	6.30
Steve Adkins	L	25	1	2	.333	0	5	5	0	24	19	29	14	0	6.38
Pasual Perez (SJ)	R	33	1	2	.333	0	3	3	0	14	8	3	12	0	1.29
Alan Mills	R	23	1	5	.167	0	36	0	0	42	48	33	24	0	4.10
John Habyan	R	26	0	0	—	0	6	0	0	9	10	2	4	0	2.08
Rich Monteleone	R	27	0	0	.000	0	7	0	0	7	8	1	8	0	6.14

WEST DIVISION

OAKLAND　1st 103-59 .636　TONY LARUSSA

Name	G by Pos	B	AGE	G	AB	R	H	2B	3B	HR	RBI	BB	SO	SB	BA	SA
TOTALS			30	162	5433	733	1379	209	22	164	693	651	992	141	.254	.391
Mark McGwire	1B154 DH2	R	26	156	523	87	123	16	0	39	108	110	116	2	.235	.489
2 Willie Randolph	2B84 DH6	R	35	93	292	37	75	9	3	1	21	32	25	6	.257	.318
Walt Weiss	SS137	B	26	138	445	50	118	17	1	2	35	46	53	9	.265	.321
Carney Lansford	3B126 1B5 DH5	R	33	134	507	58	136	15	1	3	50	45	50	16	.268	.320
Jose Canseco	OF88 DH43	R	25	131	481	83	132	14	2	37	101	72	158	19	.274	.543
Dave Henderson (KJ)	OF116 DH6	R	31	127	450	65	122	28	0	20	63	40	105	3	.271	.467
Rickey Henderson	OF118 DH15	R	31	136	489	119	159	33	3	28	61	97	60	65	.325	.577
Terry Steinbach	C83 DH25 1B3	R	28	114	379	32	95	15	2	9	57	19	66	0	.251	.372
2 Harold Baines	DH30	L	31	32	94	11	25	5	0	3	21	20	17	0	.266	.415
Mike Gallego	2B83 SS38 3B27 OF1 DH1	R	29	140	389	36	80	13	2	3	34	35	50	5	.206	.272
1 Felix Jose	OF92 DH7	B	25	101	341	42	90	12	0	8	39	16	65	8	.264	.370
Ron Hassey	C59 DH15 1B3	L	37	94	254	18	54	7	0	5	22	27	29	0	.213	.299
Lance Blankenship	3B28 OF28 2B20 DH6 1B1	R	26	86	136	18	26	3	0	0	10	20	23	3	.191	.213
Doug Jennings	OF45 DH8 1B4	L	25	64	156	19	30	7	2	2	14	17	48	0	.192	.301
Jamie Quirk	C37 3B8 1B8 OF1 DH1	L	35	56	121	12	34	5	1	3	26	14	34	0	.281	.413
1 Ken Phelps	DH15 1B5	L	35	32	59	6	11	2	0	1	6	12	10	0	.186	.271
2 Willie McGee	OF28 DH1	B	31	29	113	23	31	3	2	0	15	10	18	3	.274	.336
Darren Lewis	OF23 DH2	R	22	25	35	4	8	0	0	0	1	7	4	2	.229	.229
Mike Bordick	3B10 SS9 2B7	R	24	25	14	0	1	0	0	0	0	1	4	0	.071	.071
Steve Howard	OF14 DH7	R	26	21	52	5	12	4	0	0	1	4	17	0	.231	.308
1 Stan Javier	OF13 DH2	B	26	19	33	4	8	0	2	0	3	6	6	0	.242	.364
Dann Howitt	OF11 1B5 3B1	L	26	14	22	3	3	0	1	0	1	3	12	0	.136	.227
Troy Afenir	C14 DH1	R	26	14	14	0	2	0	0	0	2	0	6	0	.143	.143
Ozzie Canseco	DH4 OF2	R	25	9	19	1	2	1	0	0	1	1	10	0	.105	.158
Scott Hemond	3B7 2B1	R	24	7	13	0	2	0	0	0	1	0	5	0	.154	.154

NAME	T	AGE	W	L	PCT	SV	G	GS	CG	IP	H	BB	SO	SHO	ERA
		30	103	59	.636	64	162	162	18	1456	1287	494	831	16	3.18
Bob Welch	R	33	27	6	.818	0	35	35	2	238	214	77	127	2	2.95
Dave Stewart	R	33	22	11	.667	0	36	36	11	267	226	83	166	4	2.56
Scott Sanderson	R	33	17	11	.607	0	34	34	2	206	205	66	128	1	3.88
Mike Moore	R	30	13	15	.464	0	33	33	3	199	204	84	73	0	4.65
Curt Young	L	30	9	6	.600	0	26	21	0	124	124	53	56	0	4.85
Dennis Eckersley	R	35	4	2	.667	48	63	0	0	73	41	4	73	0	0.61
Gene Nelson	R	29	3	3	.500	5	51	0	0	75	55	17	38	0	1.57
Todd Burns	R	26	3	3	.500	3	43	2	0	79	78	32	43	0	2.97
Rick Honeycutt	L	36	2	2	.500	7	63	0	0	63	46	22	38	0	2.70
Reggie Harris (IL)	R	21	1	0	1.000	0	16	1	0	41	25	21	31	0	3.48
Mike Norris	R	35	1	1	.500	0	14	0	0	27	24	9	16	0	3.00
Steve Chitren	R	23	1	0	1.000	0	8	0	0	18	7	4	19	0	1.02
Joe Klink	L	28	0	0	—	2	40	0	0	40	34	18	19	0	2.04
Dave Otto (KJ)	L	25	0	0	—	0	2	0	0	2	3	2	0	0	7.71
1 Joe Bitker	R	26	0	0	—	0	1	0	0	1	1	1	2	0	0.00
Dave Leiper (IL) 28															
Jim Corsi (EJ) 28															

CHICAGO　2nd 94-68 .580 9　JEFF TORBORG

Name	G by Pos	B	AGE	G	AB	R	H	2B	3B	HR	RBI	BB	SO	SB	BA	SA
TOTALS			27	162	5402	682	1393	251	44	106	637	478	903	140	.258	.379
Carlos Martinez	1B82 DH3 OF1	R	24	92	272	18	61	6	5	4	24	10	40	0	.224	.327
Scott Fletcher	2B151	R	31	151	509	54	123	18	3	4	56	45	63	1	.242	.312
Ozzie Guillen	SS159	L	26	160	516	61	144	21	4	1	58	26	37	13	.279	.341
Robin Ventura	3B147 1B1	L	22	150	493	48	123	17	1	5	54	55	53	1	.249	.318
Sammy Sosa	OF152	R	21	153	532	72	124	26	10	15	70	33	150	32	.233	.404
Lance Johnson	OF148 DH1	L	26	151	541	76	154	18	9	1	51	33	45	36	.285	.357
Ivan Calderon	OF130 DH27 1B2	R	28	158	607	85	166	44	2	14	74	51	79	32	.273	.422
Carlton Fisk	C116 DH14	R	42	137	452	65	129	21	0	18	65	61	73	7	.285	.451
Dan Pasqua	DH57 OF43	L	28	112	325	43	89	27	3	13	58	37	66	1	.274	.495
Steve Lyons	1B61 2B15 OF7 3B5 DH3 SS1 P1	L	30	94	146	22	28	6	1	1	11	10	41	1	.192	.267
1 Ron Kittle	DH53 1B25	R	32	83	277	29	68	14	0	16	43	24	77	0	.245	.469
Ron Karkovice	C64 DH1	R	26	68	183	30	45	10	0	6	20	16	52	2	.246	.399
Frank Thomas	1B51 DH8	R	22	60	191	39	63	11	3	7	31	44	54	0	.330	.529
Craig Grebeck	3B35 SS16 2B6 DH1	R	25	59	119	7	20	3	1	1	9	8	24	0	.168	.235
2 Phil Bradley	OF38 DH7	R	31	45	133	20	30	5	1	0	5	20	26	7	.226	.278
1 Dave Gallagher (LJ)	OF37 DH4	R	29	45	75	5	21	3	1	0	5	4	9	0	.280	.347
Rodney McCray	OF13 DH7	R	26	32	6	8	0	0	0	0	1	6	0	.000	.000
Matt Stark	DH6	R	25	8	16	0	4	1	0	0	5	0	3	0	.250	.313
1 Daryl Boston	DH3 OF1	L	27	5	1	0	0	0	0	0	0	0	1	0	.000	.000
Jerry Willard	C1	L	30	3	3	0	0	0	0	0	0	0	2	0	.000	.000
1 Greg Walker	1B1 DH1	L	30	2	5	0	1	0	0	0	0	0	1	0	.200	.200

NAME	T	AGE	W	L	PCT	SV	G	GS	CG	IP	H	BB	SO	SHO	ERA
		25	94	68	.580	68	162	162	17	1449	1313	548	914	10	3.61
Greg Hibbard	L	25	14	9	.609	0	33	33	3	211	202	55	92	1	3.16
Jack McDowell	R	24	14	9	.609	0	33	33	4	205	189	77	165	0	3.82
Melido Perez	R	24	13	14	.481	0	35	35	3	197	177	86	161	3	4.61
Eric King (SJ)	R	26	12	4	.750	0	25	25	2	151	135	40	70	2	3.28
Barry Jones	R	27	11	4	.733	1	65	0	0	74	62	33	45	0	2.31
Scott Radinsky	L	22	6	1	.857	4	62	0	0	52	47	36	46	0	4.82
Wayne Edwards	L	26	5	3	.625	2	42	5	0	95	81	41	63	0	3.22
Alex Fernandez	R	20	5	5	.500	0	13	13	3	88	89	34	61	0	3.80
Bobby Thigpen	R	26	4	6	.400	57	77	0	0	89	60	32	70	0	1.83
Donn Pall	R	28	3	5	.375	2	56	0	0	76	63	24	39	0	3.32
Ken Patterson	L	25	2	1	.667	2	43	0	0	66	58	34	40	0	3.39
Jerry Kutzler	R	25	2	3	.400	0	7	7	0	31	38	14	21	0	6.03
Adam Peterson	R	24	2	5	.286	0	20	11	2	85	90	26	29	0	4.55
Steve Rosenberg	L	25	1	0	1.000	0	6	0	0	10	10	5	4	0	5.40
Shawn Hillegas	R	25	1	2	.333	0	6	0	0	11	4	5	1	0	0.79
Steve Lyons	R	30	0	0	—	0	1	0	0	2	4	1	0	0	4.50
1 Bill Long	R	30	0	1	.000	0	8	0	0	17	21	6	2	0	6.35

TEXAS　3rd 83-79 .512 20　BOBBY VALENTINE

Name	G by Pos	B	AGE	G	AB	R	H	2B	3B	HR	RBI	BB	SO	SB	BA	SA
TOTALS			28	162	5469	676	1416	257	27	110	641	575	1054	115	.259	.376
Rafael Palmeiro	1B146 DH6	L	25	154	598	72	191	35	6	14	89	40	59	3	.319	.468
Julio Franco	2B152 DH3	R	31	157	582	96	172	27	1	11	69	82	83	31	.296	.402
Jeff Huson	SS119 3B36 2B12	L	25	145	396	57	95	12	2	0	28	46	54	12	.240	.280
Steve Buechele (BW)	3B88 2B4	R	28	91	251	30	54	10	0	7	30	27	63	1	.215	.339
Ruben Sierra	OF151 DH7	B	24	159	608	70	170	37	2	16	96	49	86	9	.280	.426
Gary Pettis	OF128 DH2	B	32	136	423	66	101	16	8	3	31	57	118	38	.239	.336
Pete Incaviglia	OF145 DH2	R	26	153	529	59	123	27	0	24	85	45	146	3	.233	.420
Geno Petralli	C118 3B7 2B3	L	30	133	325	28	83	13	1	0	21	50	49	0	.255	.302
1 Harold Baines	DH95 OF2	L	31	103	321	41	93	10	1	13	44	47	63	0	.290	.449
Jack Daugherty	OF42 1B30 DH21	B	29	125	310	36	93	20	2	6	47	22	49	0	.300	.435
Mike Stanley	C63 DH14 3B8 1B6	R	27	103	189	21	47	8	1	2	19	30	25	1	.249	.333
Jeff Kunkel (ZJ)	SS67 3B15 2B13 OF5 DH1	R	28	99	200	17	34	11	1	3	17	11	66	2	.170	.280
John Russell	C31 DH19 OF6 1B3 3B1	R	29	68	128	16	35	4	0	2	8	11	41	1	.273	.352
Scott Coolbaugh	3B66	R	24	67	180	21	36	6	0	2	13	15	47	1	.200	.267
Kevin Reimer	DH21 OF9	L	26	64	100	5	26	9	1	2	15	10	22	0	.260	.430
Gary Green	SS58	R	28	62	88	10	19	3	0	0	6	1	10	0	.216	.250
Cecil Espy	OF39 DH4 2B1	B	27	52	115	15	9	0	0	1	10	20	11	7	.127	.127
Thad Bosley	OF9 DH4	L	33	30	29	3	4	0	0	1	3	3	6	1	.138	.241
Juan Gonzalez	OF16 DH9	R	20	25	90	11	26	7	1	4	12	2	18	0	.289	.522
Chad Kreuter	C20 DH1	B	25	22	22	2	1	0	0	2	8	0	6	0	.045	.091
Kevin Belcher	OF9	R	22	16	15	4	2	1	0	0	3	0	3	0	.133	.200
Bill Haselman	DH3 C1	R	24	7	13	0	2	0	0	0	3	1	4	0	.154	.154

NAME	T	AGE	W	L	PCT	SV	G	GS	CG	IP	H	BB	SO	SHO	ERA
		30	83	79	.512	36	162	162	25	1445	1343	623	997	9	3.83
Bobby Witt	R	26	17	10	.630	0	33	32	7	222	197	110	221	1	3.36
Nolan Ryan	R	43	13	9	.591	0	30	30	5	204	137	74	232	2	3.44
Kevin Brown (EJ)	R	25	12	10	.545	0	26	26	6	180	175	60	88	3	3.60
Charlie Hough	R	42	12	12	.500	0	32	32	5	219	190	119	114	0	4.07
Kenny Rogers	L	25	10	6	.625	15	69	3	0	98	93	42	74	0	3.13
Brad Arnsberg	R	26	6	1	.857	5	53	0	0	63	56	33	44	0	2.15
Mike Jeffcoat (XJ)	L	30	5	6	.455	5	44	12	1	111	122	28	58	0	4.47
John Barfield	L	25	4	3	.571	1	33	0	0	44	42	13	17	0	4.67
Jamie Moyer	L	27	2	6	.250	0	33	10	1	102	115	39	58	0	4.66
Scott Chiamparino	R	23	1	2	.333	0	6	6	0	38	36	12	19	0	2.63
Jeff Russell (EJ)	R	28	1	5	.167	10	27	0	0	25	23	16	16	0	4.26
2 Joe Bitker	R	26	0	0	—	0	3	0	0	6	6	3	6	0	3.00
Gerald Alexander	R	22	0	1	.000	0	2	0	0	7	14	5	8	0	7.71
John Hoover	R	27	0	1	.000	0	3	0	0	5	8	1	2	0	5.40
Ramon Manon	R	22	0	0	—	0	2	0	0	2	9	1	4	0	13.50
Gary Mielke (RJ)	R	30	0	0	.000	0	23	0	0	42	43	30	14	0	3.73
Craig McMurtry	R	30	0	0	.000	0	23	0	0	42	43	30	14	0	4.32
Brian Bohanon	R	21	0	0	—	0	11	0	0	34	40	18	15	0	6.62
Jose Guzman (SJ) 27															

CALIFORNIA 4th 80-82 .494 23 DOUG RADER

Name	G by Pos	B	AGE	G	AB	R	H	2B	3B	HR	RBI	BB	SO	SB	BA	SA
TOTALS			30	162	5570	690	1448	237	27	147	646	566	1000	69	.260	.391
Wally Joyner (KJ)	1B83	L	28	83	310	35	83	15	0	8	41	41	34	2	.268	.394
Johnny Ray	2B100 DH1	B	33	105	404	47	112	23	0	5	43	19	44	2	.277	.371
Dick Schofield (LJ)	SS99	R	27	99	310	41	79	8	1	1	18	52	61	3	.255	.297
Jack Howell	3B102 SS1 1B1	R	28	105	316	35	72	19	1	8	33	46	61	3	.228	.370
2 Dave Winfield	OF108 DH3	R	38	112	414	63	114	18	2	19	72	48	68	0	.275	.466
Devon White	OF122	B	27	125	443	57	96	17	3	11	44	44	116	21	.217	.343
2 Luis Polonia	OF85 DH11	L	25	109	381	50	128	7	9	2	32	25	42	20	.336	.417
Lance Parrish	C131 1B4 DH1	R	34	133	470	54	126	14	0	24	70	46	107	2	.268	.451
Brian Downing	DH87	R	39	96	330	47	90	18	2	14	51	50	45	0	.273	.467
Chili Davis	DH60 OF52	B	30	113	412	58	109	17	1	12	58	61	89	1	.265	.398
Dante Bichette	OF105	R	26	109	349	40	89	15	1	15	53	16	79	5	.255	.433
Donnie Hill	2B60 SS24 3B21 1B3 DH1 P1	B	29	103	352	36	93	18	2	3	32	29	27	1	.264	.352
Max Venable	OF77 DH1	L	33	93	189	26	49	9	3	4	21	24	31	5	.259	.402
Lee Stevens	1B67	L	22	67	248	28	53	10	0	7	32	22	75	1	.214	.339
Rick Schu	3B38 1B15 OF4 2B1	R	28	61	157	19	42	8	0	6	14	11	25	0	.268	.433
Kent Anderson	SS28 3B16 2B5	R	26	49	143	16	44	6	1	1	5	13	19	0	.308	.385
John Orton	C31	R	24	31	84	8	16	5	0	1	6	5	31	0	.190	.286
1 Mark McLemore (WJ)	2B8 SS8 DH1	B	25	20	48	4	7	2	0	0	2	4	9	1	.146	.188
Bill Schroeder (EJ)	C15 1B3	R	31	18	58	7	13	3	0	4	9	1	10	0	.224	.483
Gary DiSarcina	SS14 2B3	R	22	18	57	8	8	1	1	0	3	1	4	0	.140	.193
Pete Coachman	3B9 2B2 DH2	R	28	16	45	3	14	3	0	0	5	1	7	0	.311	.378
1 Claudell Washington	OF9	L	35	12	34	3	6	1	0	1	3	2	8	1	.176	.294
Bobby Rose	2B4 3B3	R	23	7	13	5	5	0	0	1	2	2	1	0	.385	.615
Ron Tingley (HJ)	C5	R	31	5	3	0	0	0	0	0	0	1	1	0	.000	.000

NAME	T	AGE	W	L	PCT	SV	G	GS	CG	IP	H	BB	SO	SHO	ERA
		28	80	82	.494	42	162	162	21	1454	1482	544	944	13	3.79
Chuck Finley	L	27	18	9	.667	0	32	32	7	236	210	81	177	2	2.40
Kirk McCaskill	R	29	12	11	.522	0	29	29	2	174	161	72	78	1	3.25
Jim Abbott	L	22	10	14	.417	0	33	33	4	212	246	72	105	1	4.51
Mark Langston	R	29	10	17	.370	0	33	33	5	223	215	104	195	1	4.40
Bert Blyleven (SJ)	R	39	8	7	.533	0	23	23	2	134	163	25	69	0	5.24
Willie Fraser	R	26	5	4	.556	2	45	0	0	76	69	24	32	0	3.08
Bryan Harvey	R	27	4	4	.500	25	54	0	0	64	45	35	82	0	3.22
Joe Grahe	R	22	3	4	.429	0	8	8	0	43	51	23	25	0	4.98
Scott Bailes	L	28	2	0	1.000	0	27	0	0	35	46	20	16	0	6.37
Bob McClure (EJ)	L	38	2	0	1.000	0	11	0	0	7	7	3	6	0	6.43
Mark Eichhorn	R	29	2	5	.286	13	60	0	0	85	98	23	69	0	3.08
Mike Fetters	R	25	1	1	.500	1	26	2	0	68	77	20	35	0	4.12
Cliff Young	R	25	1	1	.500	0	17	0	0	31	40	7	19	0	3.52
Greg Minton (EJ)	R	38	1	1	.500	0	11	0	0	15	11	7	4	0	2.35
Scott Lewis	R	24	1	1	.500	0	2	2	1	16	10	2	9	0	2.20
Mark Clear	R	34	0	0	—	0	4	0	0	8	5	9	6	0	5.87
Sherman Corbett	L	27	0	0	—	0	4	0	0	5	8	3	2	0	9.00
Donnie Hill	R	29	0	0	—	0	1	0	0	1	1	0	1	0	0.00
Jeff Richardson	R	26	0	0	—	0	1	0	0	0.1	0	1	0	0	0.00
1 Mike Witt	R	29	0	3	.000	1	10	0	0	20	19	13	14	0	1.77

SEATTLE 5th 77-85 .475 26 JIM LEFEBVRE

Name	G by Pos	B	AGE	G	AB	R	H	2B	3B	HR	RBI	BB	SO	SB	BA	SA
TOTALS			28	162	5474	640	1419	251	26	107	610	596	749	105	.259	.373
Pete O'Brien (BG)	1B97 OF6 DH6	L	32	108	366	32	82	18	0	5	27	44	33	0	.244	.314
Harold Reynolds	2B160	B	29	160	642	100	162	36	5	5	55	81	52	31	.252	.347
Omar Vizquel (KJ)	SS81	B	23	81	255	19	63	3	2	2	18	18	22	4	.247	.298
Edgar Martinez	3B143 DH2	R	27	144	487	71	147	27	2	11	49	74	62	1	.302	.433
Jay Buhner (NJ-BA)	OF40 DH10	R	25	51	163	16	45	12	0	7	33	17	50	2	.276	.479
Ken Griffey Jr.	OF151 DH2	L	20	155	597	91	179	28	7	22	80	63	81	16	.300	.481
Jeff Leonard	OF79 DH48	R	34	134	478	39	120	20	0	10	75	37	97	4	.251	.356
Dave Valle (VJ)	C104 1B1	R	29	107	308	37	66	15	0	7	33	45	48	1	.214	.331
Alvin Davis	DH87 1B52	L	29	140	494	63	140	21	0	17	68	85	48	0	.283	.429
Henry Cotto	OF118 DH3	R	29	127	355	40	92	14	3	4	33	22	52	21	.259	.349
Greg Briley	OF107 DH4	L	25	125	337	40	83	18	2	5	29	37	48	16	.246	.356
Scott Bradley	C36 DH6 3B5 1B1	L	30	101	233	11	52	9	0	1	28	15	20	0	.223	.275
Mike Brumley (MJ)	SS47 2B6 3B5 OF2 DH1	B	27	62	147	19	33	5	4	0	7	10	22	2	.224	.313
Jeff Schaefer	3B26 SS24 2B3	R	30	55	107	11	22	3	0	0	6	3	11	4	.206	.234
Brian Giles	SS37 2B6 3B1	R	30	45	95	15	22	6	0	4	11	15	24	2	.232	.421
1 Darnell Coles	OF20 2B6 1B4 DH1	R	28	37	107	9	23	5	1	2	16	4	17	0	.215	.336
Matt Sinatro	C28	R	30	30	50	2	15	1	0	0	4	4	10	1	.300	.320
2 Tracy Jones (KJ)	OF18 DH5	R	29	25	86	8	26	4	0	2	15	3	12	0	.302	.419
Tino Martinez	1B23	L	22	24	68	4	15	4	0	0	5	9	9	0	.221	.279
2 Ken Griffey Sr.	OF20	L	40	21	77	13	29	2	0	3	18	10	3	0	.377	.519
Dave Cochrane	SS5 3B3 1B3 C1	B	26	15	20	0	3	0	0	0	0	0	8	0	.150	.150

NAME	T	AGE	W	L	PCT	SV	G	GS	CG	IP	H	BB	SO	SHO	ERA
		27	77	85	.475	41	162	162	21	1443	1319	606	1064	7	3.69
Erik Hanson	R	25	18	9	.667	0	33	33	5	236	205	68	211	1	3.24
Randy Johnson	R	26	14	11	.560	0	33	33	5	220	174	120	194	2	3.65
Brian Holman (EJ)	R	25	11	11	.500	0	28	28	3	190	188	66	121	0	4.03
Matt Young	L	31	8	18	.308	0	34	33	7	225	198	107	176	1	3.51
Keith Comstock	L	34	4	3	.636	2	60	0	0	56	40	26	50	0	2.89
Bill Swift	R	28	6	4	.600	6	55	8	0	128	135	21	42	0	2.39
Mike Jackson	R	25	5	7	.417	3	63	0	0	77	64	44	69	0	4.54
Bryan Clark	L	33	2	0	1.000	0	12	0	0	11	9	10	3	0	3.27
2 Russ Swan (AJ)	L	26	2	3	.400	0	11	8	0	47	42	18	15	0	3.64
Brent Knackert	R	20	1	1	.500	0	24	2	0	37	50	21	28	0	6.51
Gene Harris (BL)	R	25	1	2	.333	1	25	0	0	38	31	30	43	0	4.74
Rich DeLucia	R	25	1	2	.333	0	5	5	1	36	30	9	20	0	2.00
Mike Schooler (SJ)	R	27	1	4	.200	30	49	0	0	56	47	16	45	0	2.25
Dave Burba	R	23	0	0	—	0	6	0	0	8	8	2	4	0	4.50
Vance Lovelace	L	27	0	0	—	0	5	0	0	2	1	4	2	0	3.86
Jose Melendez	R	24	0	0	—	0	3	0	0	5	8	3	7	0	11.81
1 Dennis Powell	L	26	0	0	—	0	4	0	0	6	9	6	6	0	9.00
Scott Medvin	R	28	0	1	.000	0	4	0	0	7	2	1	6	0	6.23
1 Jerry Reed	R	34	0	1	.000	0	4	0	0	4	8	4	3	0	4.91
Mike Gardiner	R	24	0	1	.000	0	5	0	0	13	22	5	6	0	10.66
Scott Bankhead (SJ)	R	26	0	2	.000	0	4	4	0	14	18	7	10	0	11.08
Gary Eave	R	26	0	3	.000	0	8	4	0	30	27	20	16	0	4.20
Clint Zavaras (SJ) 23															

KANSAS CITY 6th 75-86 .466 27.5 JOHN WATHAN

Name	G by Pos	B	AGE	G	AB	R	H	2B	3B	HR	RBI	BB	SO	SB	BA	SA
TOTALS			30	161	5488	707	1465	316	44	100	660	498	879	107	.267	.395
George Brett	1B102 DH32 OF9 3B1	L	37	142	544	82	179	45	7	14	87	56	63	9	.329	.515
Frank White	2B79 OF1	R	39	82	241	20	52	14	1	2	21	10	32	1	.216	.307
Kurt Stillwell	SS141	B	25	144	506	60	126	35	4	3	51	39	60	0	.249	.322
Kevin Seitzer	3B152 2B10	R	28	158	622	91	171	31	5	6	38	67	66	7	.275	.370
Danny Tartabull (LJ)	OF52 DH32	R	27	88	313	41	84	19	0	15	60	36	93	1	.268	.473
Bo Jackson (SJ)	OF97 DH10	R	27	111	405	74	110	16	1	28	78	44	128	15	.272	.523
Jim Eisenreich	OF138 DH2	L	31	142	496	61	139	29	7	5	51	42	51	12	.280	.397
Mike Macfarlane	C112 DH5	R	26	124	400	37	102	24	4	6	58	25	69	1	.255	.380
Gerald Perry	DH68 1B51	L	29	133	465	57	118	22	2	8	57	39	56	17	.254	.361
Willie Wilson	OF105 DH1	B	34	115	307	49	89	13	3	2	42	30	57	24	.290	.371
Bill Pecota	2B50 SS21 3B11 OF6 1B4 DH2	R	30	87	240	43	58	15	2	5	20	33	39	8	.242	.383
1 Pat Tabler	OF42 DH15 3B6 1B5	R	32	75	195	12	53	14	0	1	19	20	21	0	.272	.359
Steve Jeltz	2B34 SS23 OF13 3B3 DH3	B	31	74	103	11	16	4	0	0	10	6	21	1	.155	.194
Brian McRae	OF45	B	22	46	168	21	48	8	3	2	23	9	29	4	.286	.405
Rey Palacios (SJ)	C27 1B7 3B3 OF1	R	27	41	56	8	13	3	0	2	9	5	24	2	.232	.393
Bob Boone (BG)	C40	R	42	40	117	11	28	3	0	0	9	17	12	1	.239	.265
Terry Shumpert (RJ)	2B27 DH3	R	23	32	91	7	25	6	1	0	8	2	17	3	.275	.363
Jeff Schulz (VJ)	OF22 DH1	L	23	30	66	5	17	5	1	0	6	6	13	0	.258	.364
Gary Thurman	OF21	R	25	23	60	5	14	3	0	0	3	2	12	1	.233	.283
Russ Morman	OF8 1B3 DH1	R	28	12	37	5	10	4	2	1	3	3	3	0	.270	.568
Jeff Conine	1B9	R	24	9	20	3	5	2	0	0	2	2	5	0	.250	.350
Sean Berry	3B8	R	24	8	23	2	5	1	1	0	4	2	5	0	.217	.348
Brent Mayne	C5	L	22	5	13	2	3	0	0	0	1	3	3	0	.231	.231

NAME	T	AGE	W	L	PCT	SV	G	GS	CG	IP	H	BB	SO	SHO	ERA
		28	75	86	.466	33	161	161	18	1421	1449	560	1006	8	3.93
Steve Farr	R	33	13	7	.650	1	57	6	1	127	99	48	94	1	1.98
Kevin Appier	R	22	12	8	.600	0	32	24	3	186	179	54	127	3	2.76
Tom Gordon	R	22	12	11	.522	0	32	32	6	195	192	99	175	1	3.73
Storm Davis	R	28	7	10	.412	0	21	20	0	112	129	35	62	0	4.74
Jeff Montgomery	R	28	6	5	.545	24	73	0	0	94	81	34	94	0	2.39
Steve Crawford (EJ)	R	32	5	4	.556	1	46	0	0	80	79	23	54	0	4.16
Bret Saberhagen (EJ)	R	26	5	9	.357	0	20	20	5	135	146	28	87	0	3.27
2 Andy McGaffigan	R	33	4	3	.571	1	24	11	0	79	75	28	49	0	3.09
Mark Gubicza (SJ)	R	27	4	7	.364	0	16	16	2	94	101	38	71	0	4.50
Mark Davis (EJ)	L	29	2	7	.222	6	53	0	0	69	71	52	73	0	5.11
Jim Campbell (SJ)	L	24	1	0	1.000	0	2	0	0	10	5	1	5	0	8.38
Larry McWilliams	L	36	0	0	—	0	13	0	0	8	10	9	7	0	9.72
Israel Sanchez	L	26	0	0	—	0	11	0	0	10	16	4	5	0	8.38
Luis Encarnacion	R	26	0	0	—	0	4	0	0	11	14	4	8	0	7.84
Carlos Maldonado	R	23	0	0	—	0	4	0	0	9	14	4	8	0	9.00
Mel Stottlemyre	R	26	0	1	.000	0	13	0	0	13	12	14	0	0	4.88
Chris Codiroli	R	32	0	1	.000	0	4	0	0	10	13	17	8	0	9.58
Jay Baller	R	29	0	1	.000	0	4	0	0	7	4	6	6	0	4.05
Daryl Smith	R	23	0	2	.000	0	5	5	0	23	32	11	14	0	8.10
Hector Wagner	R	21	0	2	.000	0	4	4	0	19	26	5	10	0	8.53
Pete Filson (SJ)	L	31	0	4	.000	0	8	7	0	35	42	13	14	0	5.91
Rich Dotson	R	31	0	4	.000	0	9	7	0	29	43	14	9	0	8.48

MINNESOTA 7th 74-88 .457 29 TOM KELLY

Name	G by Pos	B	AGE	G	AB	R	H	2B	3B	HR	RBI	BB	SO	SB	BA	SA
TOTALS			29	162	5499	666	1458	281	39	100	625	445	749	96	.265	.385
Kent Hrbek	1B120 DH20 3B1	L	30	143	492	61	141	26	0	22	79	69	45	5	.287	.474
Al Newman	2B89 SS48 3B28 OF3	B	30	144	388	43	94	14	0	0	30	33	34	13	.242	.278
Greg Gagne	SS135 DH2 OF1	R	28	138	388	38	91	22	3	7	38	24	76	8	.235	.361
Gary Gaetti	3B151 OF2 1B2 SS2	R	31	154	577	61	132	27	5	16	85	36	101	6	.229	.376
Shane Mack	OF109 DH4	R	26	125	313	50	102	10	4	8	44	29	69	13	.326	.460
Kirby Puckett	OF141 DH4 3B1 2B1 SS1	R	30	146	551	82	164	40	3	12	80	57	73	5	.298	.416
Dan Gladden	OF133 DH2	R	32	136	534	64	147	27	6	5	40	26	67	25	.275	.376
Brian Harper	C120 DH11 3B3 1B2	R	30	134	479	61	141	42	3	6	54	19	27	3	.294	.432
Gene Larkin	OF47 DH43 1B28	B	27	119	401	46	108	26	4	5	42	42	55	5	.269	.392
John Moses	OF85 DH10 P1	B	32	115	172	26	38	3	1	1	14	19	19	2	.221	.267
Randy Bush (LJ)	OF32 DH29 1B6	L	31	73	181	17	44	8	0	6	18	21	27	0	.243	.387
Junior Ortiz	C68 DH3	R	30	71	170	18	57	7	1	0	18	12	16	0	.335	.384
Fred Manrique	2B67 DH1	R	28	69	228	22	54	10	0	5	29	4	35	2	.237	.346
Carmen Castillo	DH35 OF21	R	32	64	137	11	30	4	0	12	3	23	24	0	.219	.248
2 Nelson Liriano	2B50 DH24 SS1	B	25	53	185	30	47	5	7	1	13	12	31	1	.254	.357
Paul Sorrento	DH23 1B15	L	24	41	121	11	25	4	1	5	13	12	31	0	.207	.380
Jim Dwyer	DH23	L	38	37	67	7	12	0	0	1	5	12	7	0	.190	.238
Pedro Munoz	OF21 DH1	R	21	22	85	13	23	4	1	0	5	2	16	3	.271	.341
Scott Leius	SS12 3B1	R	24	14	25	6	6	1	0	1	4	2	5	0	.240	.400
Doug Baker	2B3	B	29	3	1	0	0	0	0	0	0	0	1	0	.000	.000
Lenny Webster	C2	R	25	2	6	1	2	0	0	0	2	1	0	0	.333	.500
Chip Hale	2B1	L	25	1	2	0	1	0	0	0	1	0	0	0	.500	.500

NAME	T	AGE	W	L	PCT	SV	G	GS	CG	IP	H	BB	SO	SHO	ERA
		28	74	88	.457	43	162	162	13	1436	1509	489	872	13	4.12
Kevin Tapani	R	26	12	8	.600	0	28	28	1	159	164	29	101	1	4.07
Scott Erickson	R	22	8	4	.667	0	19	17	1	113	108	51	53	0	2.87
Juan Berenguer	R	35	8	5	.615	0	51	0	0	100	85	58	77	0	3.41
1 Juan Candelaria	L	36	7	3	.700	4	34	1	0	58	55	9	44	0	3.39
David West (LJ)	L	25	7	9	.438	0	29	27	2	146	142	78	92	0	5.10
Mark Guthrie	L	24	7	9	.438	0	24	21	3	145	154	39	101	1	3.79
Allan Anderson	L	26	7	18	.280	0	31	31	5	189	214	39	82	1	4.53
Rick Aguilera	R	28	5	3	.625	32	56	0	0	65	55	19	61	0	2.76
Roy Smith	R	28	5	10	.333	0	32	23	1	153	191	47	87	1	4.81
Tim Drummond	R	26	3	3	.500	1	35	4	0	91	104	36	49	0	4.35
Larry Casian	L	24	2	1	.667	0	5	3	0	22	26	4	11	0	3.22
Terry Leach	R	36	2	5	.286	2	55	2	0	82	84	21	46	0	3.20
Gary Wayne	L	27	1	1	.500	1	38	0	0	39	38	13	28	0	4.19
Rich Garces	R	19	0	0	—	0	5	0	0	6	4	4	1	0	1.59
Rich Yett	R	27	0	0	—	0	4	0	0	4	6	1	2	0	2.08
John Moses	L	32	0	0	—	0	1	0	0	2	6	1	1	0	13.50
Jack Savage	R	26	0	0	—	0	17	0	0	26	37	11	12	0	8.31
Paul Abbott	R	22	0	5	.000	0	7	7	0	35	37	28	25	0	5.97

PITTSBURGH 1st 95-67 .586 — JIM LEYLAND

Name	G by Pos	B	AGE	G	AB	R	H	2B	3B	HR	RBI	BB	SO	SB	BA	SA
TOTALS			28	162	5388	733	1395	288	42	138	693	582	914	137	.259	.405
Sid Bream	1B142	L	29	147	389	39	105	23	2	15	67	48	65	8	.270	.455
Jose Lind	2B152	R	26	152	514	46	134	28	5	1	48	35	52	8	.261	.340
Jay Bell	SS159	R	24	159	583	93	148	28	7	7	52	65	109	10	.254	.362
Jeff King	3B115 1B1	R	25	127	371	46	91	17	1	14	53	21	50	3	.245	.410
Bobby Bonilla	OF149 3B14 1B3	B	27	160	625	112	175	39	7	32	120	45	103	4	.280	.518
Andy Van Slyke	OF133	L	29	136	493	67	140	26	6	17	77	66	89	14	.284	.465
Barry Bonds	OF150	L	25	151	519	104	156	32	3	33	114	93	83	52	.301	.565
Mike LaValliere	C95	L	29	96	279	27	72	15	0	3	31	44	20	0	.258	.344
Wally Backman	3B71 2B15	B	30	104	315	62	92	21	3	2	28	42	53	6	.292	.397
Gary Redus	1B72 OF7	R	33	96	227	32	56	15	3	6	23	33	38	11	.247	.419
R.J. Reynolds	OF59	R	31	95	215	25	62	10	1	0	19	23	35	12	.288	.344
Don Slaught	C78	R	31	84	230	27	69	18	3	4	29	27	27	0	.300	.457
John Cangelosi	OF12	B	27	58	76	13	15	2	0	0	1	11	12	7	.197	.224
Rafael Belliard	2B21 SS10 3B5	R	28	47	54	10	11	3	0	0	6	5	13	1	.204	.259
Orlando Merced	OF1 C1	B	23	25	24	3	5	1	0	0	0	1	9	0	.208	.250
Dann Bilardello	C19	R	31	19	37	1	2	0	0	0	3	4	10	0	.054	.054
2 Carmelo Martinez	1B4 OF2	R	29	12	19	3	4	1	0	2	4	1	5	0	.211	.579
Mark Ryal	OF4	R	30	9	12	0	1	0	0	0	0	0	3	0	.083	.083
Steve Carter	OF3	L	25	5	5	0	1	0	0	0	0	0	1	0	.200	.200
Tom Prince	C3	R	25	4	10	1	1	0	0	0	0	0	1	2	.100	.100
Carlos Garcia	SS3	R	22	4	4	1	2	0	0	0	0	0	2	0	.500	.500
2 Lloyd McClendon	OF1	R	31	4	3	1	1	0	0	0	1	2	0	1	.333	.333
1 Moises Alou	OF2	R	23	2	2	0	0	0	0	0	0	0	0	0	.200	.200

NAME	T	AGE	W	L	PCT	SV	G	GS	CG	IP	H	BB	SO	SHO	ERA
	R	30	95	67	.586	43	162	162	18	1447	1367	413	848	8	3.40
Doug Drabek	R	27	22	6	.786	0	33	33	9	231	190	56	131	3	2.76
Neal Heaton	L	30	12	9	.571	0	30	24	0	146	143	38	68	0	3.45
John Smiley (BH)	L	25	9	10	.474	0	26	25	2	149	161	36	86	0	4.64
Bob Patterson	L	31	8	5	.615	5	55	5	0	95	88	21	70	0	2.95
Bill Landrum	R	32	7	3	.700	13	54	0	0	72	69	21	39	0	2.13
Bob Walk	R	33	7	5	.583	1	26	24	1	130	136	36	73	1	3.75
2 Zane Smith	L	29	6	2	.750	0	11	10	3	76	55	9	50	2	1.30
Bob Kipper (EJ)	L	25	5	2	.714	3	41	1	0	63	44	26	35	0	3.02
Randy Tomlin	L	24	4	4	.500	0	12	12	2	78	62	12	42	0	2.55
Stan Belinda	R	23	3	4	.429	8	55	0	0	58	48	29	55	0	3.55
1 Scott Ruskin	L	27	2	2	.500	2	44	0	0	48	50	28	34	0	3.02
Rick Reed	R	25	2	3	.400	1	13	8	1	54	62	12	27	1	4.36
1 Walt Terrell	R	32	2	7	.222	0	16	16	0	83	98	33	34	0	5.88
Mark Ross	R	32	1	0	1.000	0	9	0	0	13	11	4	5	0	3.55
2 Jay Tibbs	R	28	1	0	1.000	0	5	0	0	7	7	2	4	0	2.57
Mike Roesler	R	26	1	0	1.000	0	5	0	0	6	6	1	2	0	3.00
Mark Huismann	R	32	1	0	1.000	0	2	0	0	3	6	1	2	0	9.00
Mike York	R	25	1	1	.500	0	4	1	0	13	13	5	4	0	2.84
Ted Power (AJ)	R	35	1	3	.250	7	40	0	0	52	50	17	42	0	3.66
Doug Bair	R	40	0	0	—	0	22	0	0	24	30	11	19	0	4.81
Vicente Palacios	R	26	0	0	—	3	7	0	0	15	4	2	8	0	0.00
Jerry Reuss	L	41	0	1	.000	0	4	1	0	8	8	3	1	0	3.52
1 Randy Kramer	R	29	0	1	.000	0	12	0	0	26	27	9	15	0	4.91

NEW YORK 2nd 91-71 .562 4 — DAVEY JOHNSON 20-22 .476 BUD HARRELSON 71-49 .592

Name	G by Pos	B	AGE	G	AB	R	H	2B	3B	HR	RBI	BB	SO	SB	BA	SA
TOTALS			27	162	5504	775	1410	278	21	172	734	536	851	110	.256	.408
Dave Magadan	1B113 3B19	L	27	144	451	74	148	28	6	6	72	74	55	2	.328	.457
Gregg Jefferies	2B118 3B34	B	22	153	604	96	171	40	3	15	68	46	40	11	.283	.434
Kevin Elster (SJ)	SS92	R	25	92	314	36	65	20	1	9	45	30	54	2	.207	.363
Howard Johnson	3B92 SS73	B	29	154	590	89	144	37	3	23	90	69	100	34	.244	.434
Darryl Strawberry	OF149	L	28	152	542	92	150	18	1	37	108	70	110	15	.277	.518
4 Daryl Boston	OF109	L	27	115	366	65	100	21	2	12	45	28	50	18	.273	.440
Kevin McReynolds	OF144	R	30	147	521	75	140	23	1	24	82	71	61	9	.269	.455
Mackey Sasser	C87 1B1	R	27	100	270	31	83	14	0	6	41	15	19	0	.307	.426
Keith Miller	OF61 2B11 SS4	R	27	88	233	42	60	8	0	1	12	23	46	16	.258	.305
Mark Carreon (KJ)	OF60	R	26	82	188	30	47	12	0	10	26	15	29	1	.250	.473
Tom O'Malley	3B38 1B3	L	29	82	121	14	27	7	0	3	14	11	20	0	.223	.355
Tim Teufel	2B24 1B24 3B10	R	31	80	175	28	43	11	0	10	24	15	33	0	.246	.480
1 Mike Marshall	1B42 OF1	R	30	53	163	24	39	8	1	6	27	7	40	0	.239	.411
4 Orlando Mercado	C40	R	28	42	90	10	19	1	0	3	7	8	11	0	.211	.322
Todd Hundley	C36	B	21	36	67	8	14	6	0	0	2	6	18	0	.209	.299
2 Charlie O'Brien	C28	R	30	28	68	6	11	3	0	0	9	10	8	2	.162	.206
2 Tommy Herr	2B26	B	34	27	100	9	25	5	0	1	10	14	11	0	.250	.330
Darren Reed	OF14	R	24	26	39	5	8	4	1	1	2	3	11	1	.205	.436
1 Barry Lyons (XJ)	C23	R	30	24	80	8	19	0	0	2	7	2	9	0	.238	.313
Kelvin Torve	1B9 OF1	L	30	20	38	0	11	4	0	0	2	4	9	0	.289	.395
2 Pat Tabler	OF10	R	32	17	43	6	12	1	1	0	10	3	6	0	.279	.419
Mario Diaz	SS10 2B1	R	28	16	22	0	3	1	0	0	1	0	2	0	.136	.182
2 Alex Trevino	C7	R	32	9	10	0	3	1	0	0	2	1	0	0	.300	.400
Keith Hughes	OF5	L	26	8	9	0	0	0	0	0	0	0	4	0	.000	.000
Kevin Baez	SS4	R	23	5	12	0	2	1	0	0	0	0	5	0	.167	.250
Chris Jelic	OF4	R	24	4	11	2	1	0	0	1	1	0	3	0	.091	.364
Chuck Carr	OF1	B	22	4	2	0	0	0	0	0	0	0	1	1	.000	.000
Lou Thornton	OF2	L	26	3	0	0	0	0	0	0	0	0	0	0	.000	.000
Dave Liddell	C1	R	24	1	1	1	1	0	0	0	0	0	0	0	1.000	1.000

NAME	T	AGE	W	L	PCT	SV	G	GS	CG	IP	H	BB	SO	SHO	ERA
		28	91	71	.562	41	162	162	18	1440	1339	444	1217	14	3.43
Frank Viola	L	30	20	12	.625	0	35	35	7	250	227	60	182	3	2.67
Dwight Gooden	R	25	19	7	.731	0	34	34	2	233	229	70	223	1	3.83
David Cone	R	27	14	10	.583	0	31	30	6	212	177	65	233	2	3.23
Sid Fernandez	L	27	9	14	.391	0	30	30	2	179	130	67	181	1	3.46
Bob Ojeda	L	32	7	6	.538	0	38	12	0	118	123	40	62	0	3.66
Ron Darling	R	29	7	9	.438	0	33	18	1	126	135	44	99	0	4.50
John Franco	L	29	5	3	.625	33	55	0	0	68	66	21	56	0	2.53
1 Julio Machado	R	24	4	1	.800	0	27	0	0	34	32	17	27	0	3.15
Alejandro Pena	R	31	3	3	.500	5	52	0	0	76	71	22	76	0	3.20
Wally Whitehurst	R	26	1	0	1.000	2	38	0	0	66	63	9	46	0	3.29
Julio Valera	R	21	1	1	.500	0	3	3	0	13	20	7	4	0	6.92
Jeff Innis	R	27	1	3	.250	1	18	0	0	26	19	10	12	0	2.39
1 Kevin Brown	L	35	0	0	—	0	6	0	0	6	5	0	2	0	0.00
Jeff Musselman	L	24	0	0	—	0	6	0	0	2	1	0	0	0	0.00
Blaine Beatty (EJ) 26	L	27	0	2	.000	0	28	0	0	40	41	11	14	0	5.63

MONTREAL 3rd 85-77 .525 10 — BUCK RODGERS

Name	G by Pos	B	AGE	G	AB	R	H	2B	3B	HR	RBI	BB	SO	SB	BA	SA
TOTALS			28	162	5453	662	1363	227	43	114	607	576	1024	235	.250	.370
Andres Galarraga	1B154	R	27	155	579	65	148	29	0	20	87	40	169	10	.256	.409
Delino DeShields	2B128	R	21	129	499	69	144	28	6	4	45	66	96	42	.289	.393
Spike Owen	SS148	B	29	149	453	55	106	24	5	5	35	70	60	8	.234	.342
Tim Wallach	3B161	R	32	161	626	69	185	37	5	21	98	42	80	6	.296	.471
Larry Walker	OF124	L	23	133	419	59	101	18	3	19	51	49	112	21	.241	.434
Dave Martinez	OF108 P1	L	25	118	391	60	109	13	5	11	39	24	48	13	.279	.422
Tim Raines	OF123	B	30	130	457	65	131	11	5	9	62	70	43	49	.287	.392
Mike Fitzgerald	C98 OF6	R	29	111	313	36	76	18	1	9	41	60	60	8	.243	.393
Otis Nixon	OF88 SS1	B	31	119	231	46	58	6	2	1	20	28	33	50	.251	.307
Marquis Grissom (BH)	OF87	R	23	98	288	42	74	14	2	3	29	27	40	22	.257	.351
Mike Aldrete	OF38 1B18	R	29	96	161	22	39	7	1	1	18	37	31	1	.242	.317
Junior Noboa	2B31 OF9 3B8 SS7 P1	R	25	81	158	15	42	7	2	0	14	7	14	4	.266	.335
Tom Foley	SS45 2B20 3B7 1B1	L	30	73	164	11	35	2	1	0	12	12	22	0	.213	.238
Nelson Santovenia (KJ)	C51	R	28	59	163	13	31	3	1	6	28	8	31	0	.190	.331
Jerry Goff	C38 1B3 3B3	L	26	52	119	14	27	1	0	3	7	21	36	0	.227	.311
Wallace Johnson	1B7	B	33	47	49	6	8	1	0	1	5	7	6	1	.163	.245
2 Rolando Roomes	OF6	R	28	16	14	1	4	0	0	0	1	1	6	0	.286	.429
2 Moises Alou	OF5	R	23	14	15	4	3	0	1	0	0	0	3	0	.200	.233
2 Orlando Mercado	C8	R	28	8	8	0	2	0	0	0	0	0	2	0	.250	.250
1 Rex Hudler		R	29	8	3	1	1	0	0	0	0	0	1	0	.333	.333
Eric Bullock		L	29	4	2	0	1	0	0	0	0	0	0	0	.500	.500
2 Johnny Paredes	2B2	R	27	3	6	0	2	1	0	0	1	1	0	0	.333	.500

NAME	T	AGE	W	L	PCT	SV	G	GS	CG	IP	H	BB	SO	SHO	ERA
		29	85	77	.525	50	162	162	18	1473	1349	510	991	11	3.37
Bill Sampen	R	27	12	7	.632	2	59	4	0	90	94	33	69	0	2.99
Oil Can Boyd	R	30	10	6	.625	0	31	31	3	191	164	52	113	3	2.93
Dennis Martinez	R	35	10	11	.476	0	32	32	7	226	191	49	156	2	2.95
Kevin Gross	R	29	9	12	.429	0	31	26	2	163	171	65	111	1	4.57
Steve Frey	L	26	8	2	.800	9	51	0	0	56	44	29	29	0	2.10
Mark Gardner	R	28	7	9	.438	0	27	26	3	153	129	61	135	3	3.42
Chris Nabholz	L	23	6	2	.750	0	11	11	1	70	43	32	53	1	2.83
2 Zane Smith (SJ)	L	29	6	7	.462	0	22	21	1	139	141	41	80	0	3.23
Drew Hall (SJ)	L	27	4	7	.364	3	42	0	0	58	52	29	40	0	5.09
Mel Rojas	R	23	3	1	.750	1	23	0	0	40	34	24	26	0	3.60
Tim Burke (BL)	R	31	3	3	.500	20	58	0	0	75	71	21	47	0	2.52
Dave Schmidt (SJ)	R	33	3	3	.500	13	34	0	0	48	58	13	22	0	4.31
2 Scott Ruskin	L	27	1	0	1.000	0	23	0	0	28	25	10	23	0	2.28
1 Joe Hesketh	L	31	1	0	1.000	0	2	2	0	3	2	3	1	0	0.00
Brian Barnes	L	23	1	1	.500	0	4	4	1	28	25	7	23	0	2.89
Dale Mohorcic	R	34	1	2	.333	2	34	0	0	53	56	18	29	0	3.23
2 John Costello (GJ)	R	29	0	0	—	0	4	0	0	6	5	1	1	0	5.68
Bob Malloy	R	25	0	0	—	0	1	0	0	1	0	0	0	0	0.00
Rich Thompson	R	31	0	0	—	0	1	0	0	1	1	0	1	0	9.00
Brett Gideon (EJ)	R	26	0	0	—	0	1	0	0	1	0	0	0	0	0.00
Junior Noboa	R	25	0	0	—	0	1	0	0	1	0	1	0	0	9.00
Dave Martinez	L	25	0	0	—	0	1	0	0	0.1	2	1	0	0	54.00
Scott Anderson	R	27	0	1	.000	0	4	3	0	18	12	5	16	0	3.00
Howard Farmer	R	23	0	3	.000	0	6	5	0	23	26	10	14	0	7.04

CHICAGO 4th(Tie) 77-85 .475 18 — DON ZIMMER

Name	G by Pos	B	AGE	G	AB	R	H	2B	3B	HR	RBI	BB	SO	SB	BA	SA
TOTALS			29	162	5600	690	1474	240	36	136	649	406	869	151	.263	.392
Mark Grace	1B153	L	26	157	589	72	182	32	1	9	82	59	54	15	.309	.413
Ryne Sandberg	2B154	R	30	155	615	116	188	30	3	40	100	50	84	25	.306	.559
Shawon Dunston	SS144	R	27	146	545	73	143	22	8	17	66	15	87	25	.262	.426
Luis Salazar	3B91 OF28	R	34	115	410	44	104	13	3	12	47	19	59	3	.254	.388
Andre Dawson	OF139	R	35	147	529	72	164	28	5	27	100	42	65	16	.310	.535
Jerome Walton (BH)	OF98	R	24	101	392	63	103	16	2	2	21	50	70	14	.263	.329
Dwight Smith	OF81	L	26	117	290	34	76	15	0	6	27	28	46	11	.262	.376
Joe Girardi	C133	R	25	133	419	36	113	24	2	1	38	17	50	8	.270	.344
Doug Dascenzo	OF107 P1	B	26	113	241	27	61	9	5	1	26	21	18	15	.253	.344
Domingo Ramos	3B66 SS21 2B1	R	32	98	226	22	60	5	0	2	17	27	29	0	.265	.314
Marvell Wynne	OF66	L	30	92	186	21	38	8	2	4	19	14	25	3	.204	.333
Dave Clark	OF39	L	27	84	171	22	47	4	2	5	20	8	40	7	.275	.409
Curt Wilkerson	3B52 2B14 SS1 OF1	B	29	77	186	21	41	5	1	0	16	7	36	2	.220	.258
Hector Villanueva	C23 1B14	R	25	52	114	14	31	4	1	7	18	4	27	1	.272	.509
1 Lloyd McClendon	OF23 1B8 C8	R	31	49	107	5	17	3	0	1	10	14	21	1	.159	.215
Gary Varsho	OF3	L	29	46	48	10	12	4	0	0	1	1	6	2	.250	.333
Greg Smith	SS7 2B7	B	23	18	44	4	9	2	1	0	2	5	1	5	.205	.295
Derrick May	OF17	L	21	17	61	8	15	3	0	1	11	2	7	1	.246	.344
Damon Berryhill (SJ)	C15	R	26	17	53	6	10	1	0	0	2	5	14	0	.189	.321
Rick Wrona		R	26	16	29	3	5	0	0	0	0	2	11	1	.172	.172

NAME	T	AGE	W	L	PCT	SV	G	GS	CG	IP	H	BB	SO	SHO	ERA
		26	77	85	.475	42	162	162	13	1443	1510	572	877	7	4.34
Mike Harkey (SJ)	R	23	12	6	.667	0	27	27	2	174	153	59	94	1	3.26
Greg Maddux	R	24	15	15	.500	0	35	35	8	237	242	71	144	2	3.46
Les Lancaster	R	28	9	5	.643	6	55	6	0	109	121	40	65	1	4.62
Mike Bielecki	R	30	8	11	.421	1	36	29	0	168	188	70	103	0	4.93
Paul Assenmacher	L	29	7	2	.778	10	74	0	0	103	90	36	95	0	2.80
2 Bill Long	R	30	6	1	.857	5	42	0	0	56	66	21	32	0	4.37
Shawn Boskie (EJ)	R	23	5	6	.455	0	15	15	1	98	99	31	49	0	3.69
Jeff Pico	R	24	4	4	.500	2	31	8	0	92	120	37	37	0	4.79
Jose Nunez	R	26	4	9	.364	0	21	10	0	61	61	34	40	0	6.53
Steve Wilson	L	25	4	9	.308	1	45	15	1	139	140	43	95	0	4.79
1 Dave Pavlas	R	27	2	1	1.000	0	13	0	0	21	23	6	12	0	2.11
Mitch Williams (KJ)	L	25	1	8	.111	16	59	2	0	66	60	50	55	0	3.93
Joe Kraemer	L	25	0	0	—	0	18	0	0	25	31	14	16	0	7.20
Dean Wilkins	R	23	0	0	—	0	1	0	0	7	11	7	3	0	9.82
Doug Dascenzo	R	26	0	0	—	0	1	0	0	0	1	0	0	0	0.00
2 Randy Kramer	R	29	0	0	—	0	10	2	0	20	20	12	12	0	3.98
Kevin Coffman	R	25	0	0	—	0	2	0	0	3	3	4	1	0	11.29
Rick Sutcliffe (SJ)	R	34	0	2	.000	0	5	5	0	21	25	12	7	0	5.91
Kevin Blankenship	R	27	0	0	—	0	3	3	0	14	13	6	5	0	5.84
Lance Dickson	L	20	0	3	.000	0	3	3	0	14	20	4	4	0	7.24

PHILADELPHIA   4th(Tie)   77-85   .475   18   NICK LEYVA

Name	G by Pos	B	AGE	G	AB	R	H	2B	3B	HR	RBI	BB	SO	SB	BA	SA
TOTALS			30	162	5535	646	1410	237	27	103	619	582	915	108	.255	.363
Ricky Jordan	1B84	R	25	92	324	32	78	21	0	5	44	13	39	2	.241	.352
1 Tommy Herr	2B114	B	34	119	447	39	118	21	3	4	50	36	47	1	.264	.351
Dickie Thon	SS148	R	32	149	552	54	141	20	4	8	48	37	77	12	.255	.350
Charlie Hayes	3B146 1B4 2B1	R	25	152	561	56	145	20	0	10	57	28	91	4	.258	.348
Von Hayes	OF127	L	31	129	467	70	122	14	3	17	73	87	81	16	.261	.413
Lenny Dykstra	OF149	L	27	149	590	106	192	35	3	9	60	89	48	33	.325	.441
John Kruk	OF87 1B61	L	29	142	443	52	129	25	8	7	67	69	70	10	.291	.431
Darren Daulton	C139	L	28	143	459	62	123	30	1	12	57	72	72	7	.268	.416
Randy Ready	OF30 2B28	R	30	101	217	26	53	9	1	1	26	29	35	3	.244	.309
Rod Booker	SS27 2B23 3B10	L	31	73	131	19	29	5	2	0	10	15	26	3	.221	.290
Dave Hollins	3B30 1B1	B	24	72	114	14	21	0	0	5	15	10	28	0	.184	.316
1 Carmelo Martinez	1B44 OF20	R	29	71	198	23	48	8	0	8	31	29	37	2	.242	.404
Sil Campusano	OF47	R	24	66	85	10	18	1	1	2	9	6	16	1	.212	.318
2 Dale Murphy	OF55	R	34	57	214	22	57	9	1	7	28	20	46	0	.266	.416
1 Jim Vatcher	OF24	R	25	36	46	5	12	1	0	1	4	4	6	0	.261	.348
Steve Lake (HJ)	C28	R	33	29	80	4	20	2	0	0	6	3	12	0	.250	.275
Mickey Morandini	2B25	L	24	25	79	9	19	4	0	1	3	6	19	3	.241	.329
Ron Jones (KJ)	OF16	L	26	24	58	5	16	2	0	3	7	9	9	0	.276	.466
Curt Ford	OF3	L	29	22	18	0	2	0	0	0	0	1	5	0	.111	.111
Wes Chamberlain	OF10	R	24	18	46	9	13	3	0	2	4	1	9	4	.283	.478
Tom Nieto	C17	R	29	17	30	1	5	0	0	0	4	3	11	0	.167	.167
2 Louie Meadows	OF7	L	29	15	14	1	1	0	0	0	0	1	2	0	.071	.071
2 Darrin Fletcher	C6	L	23	9	22	3	3	1	0	0	1	1	5	0	.136	.182
Tommy Barrett (KJ) 30																

NAME	T	AGE	W	L	PCT	SV	G	GS	CG	IP	H	BB	SO	SHO	ERA
		27	77	85	.475	35	162	162	18	1449	1381	651	840	7	4.07
Pat Combs	L	23	10	10	.500	0	32	31	3	183	179	86	108	2	4.07
1 Terry Mulholland	L	27	9	10	.474	0	33	26	6	181	172	42	75	1	3.34
Dennis Cook	L	27	8	3	.727	1	42	13	2	142	132	54	58	1	3.56
Ken Howell	R	29	8	7	.533	0	18	18	2	107	106	49	70	0	4.64
Jose DeJesus	R	25	7	8	.467	0	22	22	3	130	97	73	87	1	3.74
Don Carman	L	30	6	2	.750	1	59	0	0	87	69	38	58	0	4.15
Roger McDowell	R	29	6	8	.429	22	72	0	0	86	92	35	39	0	3.86
Bruce Ruffin	L	26	6	13	.316	0	32	25	2	149	178	62	79	1	5.38
Darrel Akerfelds	R	28	5	2	.714	3	71	0	0	93	65	54	42	0	3.77
1 Jeff Parrett	R	28	4	9	.308	1	47	5	0	82	92	36	69	0	5.18
Jason Grimsley	R	22	3	2	.600	0	11	11	0	57	47	43	41	0	3.30
2 Joe Boever	R	29	2	3	.400	6	34	0	0	46	37	16	40	0	2.15
2 Tommy Greene	R	23	2	3	.400	0	10	7	0	39	36	17	17	0	4.15
Chuck Malone	R	24	1	0	1.000	0	7	0	0	7	3	11	7	0	3.68
Steve Ontiveros (EJ)	R	29	0	0	—	0	5	0	0	10	9	3	6	0	2.70
Brad Moore	R	26	0	0	—	0	3	0	0	3	4	2	1	0	3.38
Chuck McElroy	L	22	0	1	.000	0	16	0	0	14	24	10	16	0	7.71
Todd Frohwirth	R	27	0	1	.000	0	5	0	0	1	3	6	1	0	18.00
Dickie Noles (SJ)	R	33	0	1	.000	1	1	0	0	0.1	2	0	0	0	27.00
1 Marvin Freeman	R	27	0	0	.000	1	16	3	0	32	34	14	26	0	5.57
Floyd Youmans (SJ) 26															

ST. LOUIS   6th   70-92   .432   25   WHITEY HERZOG 33-47 .413   RED SCHOENDIENST 13-11 .542   JOE TORRE 24-34 .414

Name	G by Pos	B	AGE	G	AB	R	H	2B	3B	HR	RBI	BB	SO	SB	BA	SA
TOTALS			30	162	5462	599	1398	255	41	73	554	517	844	221	.256	.358
Pedro Guerrero	1B132	R	34	136	498	42	140	31	1	13	80	44	70	1	.281	.426
Jose Oquendo	2B150 SS4	B	26	156	469	38	118	17	5	1	37	74	46	1	.252	.316
Ozzie Smith	SS140	B	35	143	512	61	130	21	1	1	50	61	33	32	.254	.305
Terry Pendleton	3B117	B	29	121	447	46	103	20	2	6	58	30	58	7	.230	.324
Milt Thompson	OF116	L	31	135	418	42	91	14	7	6	30	39	60	25	.218	.328
1 Willie McGee	OF124	B	31	125	501	76	168	32	5	3	62	38	86	28	.335	.437
Vince Coleman	OF120	B	29	124	497	73	145	18	9	6	39	35	88	77	.292	.400
Todd Zeile	C105 3B24 1B11 OF1	R	24	144	495	62	121	25	3	15	57	67	77	2	.244	.398
Dave Collins	1B49 OF12	B	37	99	58	12	13	1	0	0	3	13	10	7	.224	.241
2 Rex Hudler	OF45 2B10 3B6 1B6 SS1	R	29	89	217	30	61	11	2	7	22	12	31	18	.281	.447
Denny Walling	1B15 3B11 OF8	L	36	78	127	7	28	5	0	1	19	8	15	0	.220	.283
Tom Pagnozzi	C63 1B2	R	27	69	220	20	61	15	0	2	23	14	37	1	.277	.373
Tim Jones	SS29 2B19 3B6 P1	L	27	67	128	9	28	7	1	1	12	12	20	3	.219	.313
Craig Wilson	3B13 OF13 2B9 1B1	R	24	55	121	13	30	2	0	0	7	8	14	0	.248	.264
Ray Lankford	OF35	L	23	39	126	12	36	10	1	3	12	13	27	8	.286	.452
2 Felix Jose	OF23	B	25	25	85	12	23	4	1	3	13	8	16	4	.271	.447
1 Tom Brunansky	OF17	R	29	19	57	5	9	3	0	2	12	10	0		.158	.263
2 Bernard Gilkey	OF18	R	23	18	64	11	19	5	2	1	3	8	5	6	.297	.484
Geronimo Pena	2B11	B	23	18	45	5	11	2	0	0	2	4	14	1	.244	.289
John Morris (XJ)	OF6	R	29	18	18	0	2	0	0	0	3	0	6	0	.111	.111
Rod Brewer	1B9	L	24	14	25	4	6	1	0	0	2	0	4	0	.240	.280
Ray Stephens	C5	R	27	5	15	2	2	1	0	1	1	0	3	0	.133	.400

NAME	T	AGE	W	L	PCT	SV	G	GS	CG	IP	H	BB	SO	SHO	ERA
		30	70	92	.432	39	162	162	8	1443	1432	475	833	13	3.87
John Tudor	L	36	12	4	.750	0	25	22	1	146	120	30	63	1	2.40
Bob Tewksbury	R	29	10	9	.526	1	28	20	3	145	151	15	50	2	3.47
Joe Magrane	L	25	10	7	.370	0	31	31	3	203	204	59	100	2	3.59
Bryn Smith (SJ)	R	34	9	8	.529	0	26	25	0	141	160	30	78	0	4.27
Jose DeLeon	R	29	7	19	.269	0	32	32	0	183	168	86	164	0	4.43
Frank DiPino	L	33	5	2	.714	3	62	0	0	81	92	31	49	0	4.56
Ken Hill	R	24	5	6	.455	0	17	14	1	79	79	33	58	0	5.49
Ken Dayley	L	31	4	4	.500	2	58	0	0	73	63	30	51	0	3.56
2 Lee Smith	R	32	3	4	.429	27	53	0	0	69	58	20	70	0	2.10
Scott Terry	R	30	2	6	.250	2	50	2	0	72	75	27	35	0	4.75
Mike Perez	R	25	1	0	1.000	1	13	0	0	14	12	3	5	0	3.95
Ricky Horton	L	30	1	1	.500	1	32	0	0	42	52	22	18	0	4.93
Omar Olivares	R	22	1	1	.500	0	9	6	0	49	45	17	20	0	2.92
Tim Sherrill	L	24	0	0	—	0	4	0	0	4	10	3	3	0	6.23
2 Ernie Camacho	R	35	0	0	—	0	6	0	0	6	7	6	7	0	7.94
Chris Carpenter	R	25	0	0	—	0	4	0	0	4	5	2	6	0	4.50
1 John Costello	R	29	0	0	—	0	2	0	0	3	2	1	1	0	6.23
Stan Clarke	L	29	0	0	—	0	2	0	0	3	2	1	3	0	2.70
Howard Hilton	R	26	0	0	—	0	2	0	0	2	3	1	3	0	0.00
Tim Jones	R	27	0	0	—	0	1	0	0	1	0	0	0	0	6.75
Greg Mathews	L	28	0	5	.000	0	11	10	0	51	53	30	18	0	5.33
Tom Niedenfuer	R	30	0	0	.000	2	52	0	0	65	66	25	32	0	3.46
Danny Cox (EJ) 30															
Todd Worrell (EJ) 30															

WEST DIVISION

CINCINNATI   1st   91-71   .562   LOU PINIELLA

Name	G by Pos	B	AGE	G	AB	R	H	2B	3B	HR	RBI	BB	SO	SB	BA	SA
TOTALS			27	162	5525	693	1466	284	40	125	644	466	913	166	.265	.399
Todd Benzinger	1B95 OF10	B	27	118	376	35	95	14	2	5	46	19	69	3	.253	.340
Mariano Duncan	2B115 SS12 OF1	R	27	125	435	67	133	22	11	10	55	24	67	13	.306	.476
Barry Larkin	SS156	R	26	158	614	85	185	25	6	7	67	49	49	30	.301	.396
Chris Sabo	3B146	R	28	148	567	95	153	38	2	25	71	61	58	25	.270	.476
Paul O'Neill	OF141	L	27	145	503	59	136	28	0	16	78	53	103	13	.270	.421
Eric Davis	OF122	R	28	127	453	84	118	26	2	24	86	60	100	21	.260	.486
Billy Hatcher	OF131	R	29	139	504	68	139	28	5	5	33	42	30		.276	.381
Joe Oliver	C118	R	24	121	364	34	84	23	0	8	52	37	75	1	.231	.360
Hal Morris	1B80 OF6	L	25	107	309	50	105	22	3	7	36	21	32	9	.340	.498
Herm Winningham	OF64	L	28	84	160	20	41	8	5	3	17	14	31	6	.256	.425
Luis Quinones	3B22 2B13 SS9 LB1	B	28	83	145	10	35	7	0	2	17	13	29	0	.241	.331
2 Glenn Braggs	OF60	R	27	72	201	22	60	9	1	6	28	26	43	3	.299	.443
Jeff Reed	C70	L	27	72	175	12	44	8	1	3	16	24	26	0	.251	.360
Ron Oester	2B50 3B4	R	34	64	154	10	46	10	1	0	13	10	29	1	.299	.377
1 Ken Griffey	1B9 OF6	L	40	46	63	6	13	2	0	1	8	2	5	2	.206	.286
1 Rolando Roomes	OF19	R	28	30	61	5	13	0	0	2	7	0	20	0	.213	.311
2 Bill Doran	2B12 3B4	B	32	17	59	10	22	8	0	1	5	8	5	5	.373	.559
Terry Lee	1B6	R	28	12	19	1	4	1	0	0	3	2	2	0	.211	.263
1 Billy Bates	2B1	L	26	8	5	2	0	0	0	0	0	2	0	0	.000	.000
3 Alex Trevino	C2	R	32	7	7	0	3	1	0	0	1	0	0	0	.429	.571
1 Terry McGriff	C1	R	26	4	2	0	0	0	0	0	0	0	1	0	.000	.000
Paul Noce		R	29	1	1	0	1	0	0	0	0	0	0	0	1.000	1.000
Glenn Sutko	C1	R	22	1	1	0	0	0	0	0	0	0	1	0	.000	.000

NAME	T	AGE	W	L	PCT	SV	G	GS	CG	IP	H	BB	SO	SHO	ERA
		27	91	71	.562	50	162	162	14	1456	1338	543	1029	12	3.39
Tom Browning	L	30	15	9	.625	0	35	35	2	228	235	52	99	1	3.80
Jose Rijo	R	25	14	8	.636	0	29	29	7	197	151	78	152	1	2.70
Norm Charlton	L	27	12	9	.571	2	56	16	1	154	131	70	117	1	2.74
Jack Armstrong	R	25	12	9	.571	0	29	27	2	166	151	59	110	1	3.42
Rob Dibble	R	26	8	3	.727	11	68	0	0	98	62	34	136	0	1.74
Rick Mahler	R	36	7	6	.538	4	35	16	2	135	134	39	68	1	4.28
Danny Jackson (SJ)	L	28	6	6	.500	0	22	21	0	117	119	40	76	0	3.61
Tim Layana	R	26	5	3	.625	2	55	0	0	80	71	44	53	0	3.49
Scott Scudder	R	22	5	5	.500	0	21	10	0	72	74	30	42	0	4.90
Randy Myers	L	27	4	6	.400	31	66	0	0	87	59	38	98	0	2.08
1 Ron Robinson	R	28	2	2	.500	0	6	6	0	31	36	14	14	0	4.88
Tim Birtsas	L	29	1	3	.250	0	29	0	0	51	69	24	41	0	3.86
Rosario Rodriguez	L	20	0	0	—	0	9	0	0	10	15	2	8	0	6.10
Keith Brown	R	26	0	1	.000	0	1	0	0	11	12	3	6	0	4.76
Kip Gross	R	25	0	0	—	0	1	0	0	6	2	3	4	0	4.26
Gino Minutelli	L	26	0	0	—	0	1	0	0	2	1	1	0	0	9.00
Chris Hammond	L	24	0	2	.000	0	3	1	0	11	13	12	4	0	6.35

LOS ANGELES   2nd   86-76   .531   5   TOMMY LASORDA

Name	G by Pos	B	AGE	G	AB	R	H	2B	3B	HR	RBI	BB	SO	SB	BA	SA
TOTALS			30	162	5491	728	1436	222	27	129	669	538	952	141	.262	.382
Eddie Murray	1B150	B	34	155	558	96	184	22	3	26	95	82	64	8	.330	.520
Juan Samuel	2B108 OF31	R	29	143	492	62	119	24	3	13	52	51	126	38	.242	.382
Alfredo Griffin	SS139	B	32	141	461	38	97	11	3	1	35	29	65	6	.210	.254
Mike Sharperson	3B106 SS15 2B9 1B6	R	29	129	357	42	106	14	2	3	36	46	39	15	.297	.373
Hubie Brooks	OF150	R	33	153	568	74	151	28	1	20	91	33	108	2	.266	.424
Kirk Gibson	OF81	L	33	89	315	59	82	20	0	8	38	39	65	26	.260	.400
Kal Daniels	OF127	L	26	130	450	81	133	23	1	27	94	68	104	4	.296	.531
Mike Scioscia	C132	L	31	135	435	46	115	25	0	12	66	55	31	4	.264	.405
Lenny Harris	3B94 2B44 OF2 SS1	B	25	137	431	61	131	16	4	2	29	29	31	15	.304	.374
Jose Gonzales	OF81	B	25	106	99	15	23	5	3	2	8	9	23	1	.232	.404
2 Stan Javier	OF87	B	26	104	276	56	84	9	4	3	24	37	44	15	.304	.399
Chris Gwynn	OF44	L	25	101	141	19	40	7	1	5	22	7	28	0	.284	.418
Mickey Hatcher	1B25 3B10 OF10	R	35	85	132	12	28	3	1	0	13	6	22	0	.212	.250
Rick Dempsey	C53	R	40	62	128	13	25	5	0	4	15	23	29	1	.195	.281
Jose Vizcaino	SS11 2B6	B	22	37	51	3	14	1	0	0	2	4	7	1	.275	.333
Jose Offerman	SS27	B	21	29	58	7	9	0	0	1	7	4	14	1	.155	.207
1 Willie Randolph	2B26	R	35	26	96	15	26	4	0	1	9	13	9	1	.271	.344
1 John Shelby	OF12	B	32	32	25	2	6	1	0	0	2	3	6	0	.250	.292
Carlos Hernandez	C10	R	23	10	20	2	4	1	0	0	1	0	5	0	.200	.250
Brian Traxler	1B3	L	22	9	11	0	1	1	0	0	0	1	5	0	.091	.182
Jeff Hamilton (SJ)	3B7	R	26	7	24	1	3	0	0	0	1	0	5	0	.125	.125
Luis Lopez	1B1	R	25	6	7	0	1	0	0	0	0	0	0	0	.000	.000
Dave Hansen	3B2	L	21	5	7	0	1	0	0	0	0	0	2	0	.143	.143
2 Barry Lyons	C2	R	27	3	5	1	1	0	0	0	1	0	0	0	.200	.800
1 Darrin Fletcher	C1	L	23	2	1	0	0	0	0	0	0	0	0	0	.000	.000

NAME	T	AGE	W	L	PCT	SV	G	GS	CG	IP	H	BB	SO	SHO	ERA
		29	86	76	.531	29	162	162	29	1442	1364	478	1021	12	3.72
Ramon Martinez	R	22	20	6	.769	0	33	33	12	234	191	67	223	3	2.92
Fernando Valenzuela	L	29	13	13	.500	0	33	33	5	204	223	77	115	2	4.59
Mike Morgan	R	30	11	15	.423	0	33	33	6	211	216	60	106	4	3.75
Tim Belcher (SJ)	R	28	9	9	.500	0	24	24	5	153	136	48	102	2	4.00
Mike Hartley	R	28	6	3	.667	1	32	6	1	79	58	30	76	1	2.95
Jim Neidlinger	R	25	5	3	.625	0	12	12	0	74	67	15	46	0	3.28
Jay Howell (KJ)	R	34	5	5	.500	16	45	0	0	66	59	20	59	0	2.18
Tim Crews	R	29	4	5	.444	5	66	2	0	107	98	24	76	0	2.77
Don Aase (SJ)	R	35	1	1	.750	3	32	0	0	38	33	19	24	0	4.97
Jim Gott (EJ)	R	30	3	5	.375	3	50	0	0	62	59	34	44	0	2.90
John Wetteland	R	23	2	4	.333	0	22	5	0	43	44	17	36	0	4.81
Ray Searage (EJ)	L	35	1	0	1.000	0	29	0	0	32	30	10	19	0	2.78
Dave Walsh	L	29	1	0	1.000	1	20	0	0	16	15	6	15	0	3.86
2 Dennis Cook	L	27	1	1	.500	0	5	3	0	14	23	2	6	0	7.53
Orel Hershiser (SJ)	R	31	1	1	.500	0	4	4	0	25	26	4	16	0	4.26
Terry Wells	L	26	1	2	.333	0	5	5	0	21	25	14	18	0	7.84
Jim Poole	L	24	1	0	1.000	0	16	0	0	11	15	6	13	0	4.22
Pat Perry (SJ)	L	31	0	0	—	0	17	0	0	7	7	5	2	0	8.10
Darren Holmes	R	24	0	1	.000	0	14	0	0	15	11	11	19	0	5.19
Mike Maddux	R	28	0	1	.000	0	11	2	0	21	24	11	11	0	6.53
Mike Munoz	L	24	0	0	—	0	8	0	0	4	6	2	4	0	3.18

Name	G by Pos	B	AGE	G	AB	R	H	2B	3B	HR	RBI	BB	SO	SB	BA	SA

SAN FRANCISCO 3rd 85-77 .525 6   ROGER CRAIG

Name	G by Pos	B	AGE	G	AB	R	H	2B	3B	HR	RBI	BB	SO	SB	BA	SA
TOTALS			30	162	5573	719	1459	221	35	152	681	488	973	109	.262	.396
Will Clark	1B153	L	26	154	600	91	177	25	5	19	95	62	97	8	.295	.448
Robby Thompson	2B142	R	28	144	498	67	122	22	3	15	56	34	96	14	.245	.392
Jose Uribe	SS134	B	31	138	415	35	103	8	6	1	24	29	49	5	.248	.304
Matt Williams	3B159	R	24	159	617	87	171	27	2	33	122	33	138	7	.277	.488
Kevin Bass (KJ)	OF55	B	31	61	214	25	54	9	1	7	32	14	26	2	.252	.402
Brett Butler	OF159	L	33	160	622	108	192	20	9	3	44	90	62	51	.309	.384
Kevin Mitchell	OF138	R	28	140	524	90	152	24	2	35	93	58	87	4	.290	.544
Terry Kennedy	C103	L	34	107	303	25	84	22	0	2	26	31	38	1	.277	.370
Mike Kingery	OF95	L	29	105	207	24	61	7	1	0	24	12	19	6	.295	.338
Greg Litton	OF56 2B18 SS7 3B5	R	25	93	204	17	50	9	1	1	24	11	45	1	.245	.314
Gary Carter	C80 1B3	R	36	92	244	24	62	10	0	9	27	25	31	1	.254	.406
Ernest Riles	SS26 2B24 3B10	L	29	92	155	22	31	2	1	8	21	26	26	0	.200	.381
Rick Leach (SD)	OF52 1B7	L	32	78	174	24	51	13	0	2	16	21	20	0	.293	.402
Dave Anderson	SS29 2B13 1B3 3B2	R	29	60	100	14	35	5	1	1	6	3	20	1	.350	.450
Rick Parker	OF35 2B2 3B1 SS1	R	27	54	107	19	26	5	0	2	14	10	15	6	.243	.346
Bill Bathe (KJ)	C	R	29	52	48	3	11	0	1	3	12	7	12	0	.229	.458
Mike Benjamin	SS21	R	24	22	56	7	12	3	1	2	3	3	10	1	.214	.411
Steve Decker	C15	R	24	15	54	5	16	2	0	3	8	1	10	0	.296	.500
Mark Leonard	OF7	L	25	11	17	3	3	1	0	1	2	3	8	0	.176	.412
Kirt Manwaring	C8	R	24	8	13	0	2	0	1	0	1	3	0	0	.154	.308
1 Brad Komminsk	OF7	R	29	8	5	2	1	0	0	0	0	1	2	0	.200	.200
Andres Santana	SS3	R	22	6	2	0	0	0	0	0	0	1	0	0	.000	.000
Mark Bailey	C1	B	28	5	7	1	1	0	0	1	0	3	0	2	.143	.571
Tony Perezchica	2B2 SS2	R	24	4	3	1	1	0	0	0	0	1	2	0	.333	.333

NAME	T	AGE	W	L	PCT	SV	G	GS	CG	IP	H	BB	SO	SHO	ERA
		30	85	77	.525	45	162	162	14	1446	1477	553	788	6	4.08
John Burkett	R	25	14	7	.667	1	33	32	2	204	201	61	118	0	3.79
Scott Garrelts	R	28	12	11	.522	0	31	31	4	182	190	70	80	2	4.15
Don Robinson (KJ)	R	33	10	7	.528	0	26	25	4	158	173	41	78	0	4.57
Steve Bedrosian	R	32	9	9	.500	17	68	0	0	79	72	44	43	0	4.20
Trevor Wilson	L	24	8	7	.533	0	27	17	3	110	87	49	66	2	4.00
Mike LaCoss (KJ)	R	34	6	4	.600	0	13	12	1	78	75	39	39	0	3.94
Jeff Brantley	R	26	5	3	.625	19	55	0	0	87	77	33	61	0	1.56
Atlee Hammaker (AJ)	L	32	4	5	.444	0	25	6	0	67	69	21	28	0	4.28
Kelly Downs (SJ)	R	29	3	2	.600	0	13	9	0	63	56	20	31	0	3.43
Bob Knepper	L	36	3	3	.500	0	12	7	0	44	56	19	24	0	5.68
Rick Reuschel (KJ)	R	41	3	6	.333	1	15	13	0	87	102	31	49	0	3.93
Francisco Oliveras	R	27	2	2	.500	2	33	2	0	55	47	21	41	0	2.77
Mark Thurmond (SJ)	L	33	2	3	.400	4	43	0	0	57	53	18	24	0	3.34
Randy O'Neal	R	29	1	0	1.000	0	26	0	0	47	58	18	30	0	3.83
Ed Vosburg	L	28	1	1	.500	0	18	0	0	24	21	12	12	0	5.55
Mark Dewey	R	25	1	1	.500	0	14	0	0	23	22	5	11	0	2.78
Eric Gunderson	L	24	1	2	.333	0	7	4	0	20	24	11	14	0	5.49
Ernie Camacho	R	35	0	0	—	0	8	0	0	10	10	3	8	0	3.60
Andy McGaffigan	R	33	0	0	—	0	4	0	0	5	10	4	4	0	17.36
Randy McCament	R	27	0	0	—	0	3	0	0	6	8	5	5	0	3.00
Rick Rodriguez	R	29	0	0	—	0	3	0	0	3	5	2	2	0	8.10
Greg Booker	R	30	0	0	—	0	2	0	0	2	7	0	1	0	13.50
Rafael Novoa	L	22	0	1	.000	0	2	0	0	19	21	13	14	0	6.75
Dan Quisenberry	R	37	0	1	.000	0	7	0	0	7	13	3	2	0	13.50
Paul McClellan	R	24	0	1	.000	0	1	0	0	8	14	6	2	0	11.74
Russ Swan	L	26	0	1	.000	0	4	2	0	6	4	1	0	0	3.86
Jose Alvarez (AJ) 34															

HOUSTON 4th(Tie) 75-87 .463 16   ART HOWE

Name	G by Pos	B	AGE	G	AB	R	H	2B	3B	HR	RBI	BB	SO	SB	BA	SA
TOTALS			28	162	5379	573	1301	209	32	94	536	548	997	179	.242	.345
Glenn Davis (VJ)	1B91	R	29	93	327	44	82	15	4	22	64	46	54	0	.251	.523
1 Bill Doran	2B99	B	32	109	344	49	99	21	2	6	32	71	53	18	.288	.413
Rafael Ramirez	SS129	R	32	132	445	44	116	19	3	2	37	24	46	10	.261	.330
Ken Caminiti	3B149	B	27	153	541	52	131	20	2	4	51	48	97	9	.242	.309
Glenn Wilson	OF108 1B1	R	31	118	368	42	90	14	0	10	55	26	64	0	.245	.364
Eric Yelding	OF94 SS40 2B10 3B3	R	25	142	511	69	130	9	5	1	28	39	87	64	.254	.297
Franklin Stubbs	1B72 OF71	L	29	146	448	59	117	23	2	23	71	48	114	19	.261	.475
Craig Biggio	C113 OF50	R	24	150	555	53	153	24	2	4	42	53	79	25	.276	.348
Casey Candaele	OF58 2B49 SS13 3B1	B	29	130	262	30	77	8	6	3	22	31	42	7	.286	.397
Eric Anthony	OF71	L	22	84	239	26	46	8	0	10	29	29	78	5	.192	.351
Ken Oberkfell	3B24 2B11 1B11	L	34	77	150	10	31	6	1	1	12	15	17	1	.207	.280
Dave Rohde	2B32 3B4 SS2	B	25	59	98	8	18	4	0	0	5	20	20	0	.184	.224
Gerald Young	OF50	B	25	57	154	15	27	4	1	1	4	20	23	6	.175	.234
Mark Davidson (XJ)	OF51	R	29	57	130	12	38	5	1	1	11	10	18	0	.292	.369
1 Alex Trevino	C30 1B1	R	32	42	69	3	13	3	0	1	10	6	11	0	.188	.275
2 Rich Gedman	C39	L	30	40	104	4	21	7	0	1	10	15	24	0	.202	.298
Tuffy Rhodes	OF30	L	21	38	86	12	21	6	1	1	3	13	12	4	.244	.372
Terry Puhl (BS)	OF8 1B1	L	33	37	41	5	12	1	0	0	8	5	7	1	.293	.317
Carl Nichols	C15 1B3 OF1	R	27	32	49	7	10	3	0	0	11	8	11	0	.204	.265
Javier Ortiz (KJ)	OF25	R	27	30	77	7	21	5	1	1	10	12	11	1	.273	.403
1 Louie Meadows	OF9	L	29	15	14	3	2	0	0	0	2	1	4	0	.143	.143
Luis Gonzalez	3B4 1B2	L	22	12	21	1	4	2	0	0	0	2	5	0	.190	.286
Mike Simms	1B6	R	23	12	13	3	4	1	0	1	2	0	4	0	.308	.615
Jeff Baldwin	OF3	L	24	7	8	1	0	0	0	0	0	1	2	0	.000	.000
Andujar Cedeno	SS3	R	20	7	8	0	0	0	0	0	0	0	4	0	.000	.000
2 Terry McGriff	C4	R	26	4	5	0	0	0	0	0	0	0	1	0	.000	.000
Steve Lombardozzi (BT)		R	30	2	1	0	0	0	0	0	0	0	1	1	.000	.000

NAME	T	AGE	W	L	PCT	SV	G	GS	CG	IP	H	BB	SO	SHO	ERA
		32	75	87	.463	37	162	162	12	1450	1396	496	854	6	3.61
Danny Darwin	R	34	11	4	.733	2	48	17	3	163	136	31	109	0	2.21
Mark Portugal	R	27	11	10	.524	0	32	32	1	197	187	67	136	0	3.62
Bill Gullickson	R	31	10	14	.417	0	32	32	2	193	221	61	73	1	3.82
Juan Agosto	L	32	9	8	.529	4	82	0	0	92	91	39	50	0	4.29
Mike Scott	R	35	9	13	.409	0	32	32	4	206	194	66	121	2	3.81
Jim Deshaies	L	30	7	12	.368	0	34	34	2	209	186	84	119	0	3.78
Dave Smith	R	35	6	6	.500	23	49	0	0	60	45	20	50	0	2.39
1 Larry Andersen	R	37	5	2	.714	6	50	0	0	74	61	24	68	0	1.95
Al Osuna	L	24	2	0	1.000	0	12	0	0	11	10	6	6	0	4.76
Xavier Hernandez	R	24	2	1	.667	0	34	1	0	62	60	24	24	0	4.62
Jim Clancy	R	34	2	8	.200	1	33	10	0	76	100	33	44	0	6.51
1 Dan Schatzeder	L	35	1	3	.250	0	45	2	0	64	61	23	37	0	2.39
Brian Fisher	R	28	0	0	—	0	4	0	0	9	3	0	1	0	7.20
Randy Hennis	R	24	0	0	—	0	3	1	0	10	1	3	4	0	0.00
Terry Clark	R	29	0	0	—	0	3	0	0	9	6	1	0	0	13.50
1 Charley Kerfeld	R	26	0	2	.000	0	9	0	0	20	16	6	6	0	16.20
Brian Meyer	R	27	0	4	.000	1	14	0	0	20	16	6	6	0	2.21

SAN DIEGO 4th(Tie) 75-87 .463 16   JACK McKEON 37-43 .463   GREG RIDDOCH 38-44 .463

Name	G by Pos	B	AGE	G	AB	R	H	2B	3B	HR	RBI	BB	SO	SB	BA	SA
TOTALS			29	162	5554	673	1429	243	35	123	628	590	902	138	.257	.380
Jack Clark (XJ)	1B109	L	34	115	334	59	89	12	1	25	62	104	91	4	.266	.533
Roberto Alomar	2B137 SS5	B	22	147	586	80	168	27	5	6	60	48	72	24	.287	.381
Garry Templeton	SS135	B	34	144	505	45	125	25	3	9	59	24	59	1	.248	.362
Mike Pagliarulo	3B116	R	30	128	398	29	101	23	2	7	38	39	66	1	.254	.374
Tony Gwynn	OF141	L	30	141	573	79	177	29	10	4	72	44	23	17	.309	.415
Joe Carter	OF150 1B14	R	30	162	634	79	147	27	1	24	115	48	93	22	.232	.391
Bip Roberts	OF75 3B56 SS18 2B8	B	26	149	556	104	172	36	3	9	44	55	65	46	.309	.433
Benito Santiago (BA)	C98	R	25	100	344	42	93	8	5	11	53	27	55	5	.270	.419
Phil Stephenson	1B60	L	29	103	182	26	38	9	1	4	19	30	43	2	.209	.335
Shawn Abner	OF62	R	24	91	184	17	45	9	0	1	15	9	28	2	.245	.310
Fred Lynn	OF55	L	38	90	196	18	47	3	1	6	23	22	44	2	.240	.357
Mark Parent	C60	R	28	65	189	13	42	11	0	3	16	16	29	1	.222	.328
Darrin Jackson	OF39	R	27	58	113	10	29	3	0	3	9	5	24	3	.257	.363
Jerald Clark	1B15 OF13	R	26	52	101	12	27	4	1	5	11	5	24	0	.267	.475
Joey Cora	SS21 2B15 C1	B	25	51	100	12	27	3	0	0	2	6	9	8	.270	.300
Tom Lampkin	C20	L	26	26	63	4	14	0	1	1	4	4	9	0	.222	.302
Thomas Howard	OF13	B	25	20	44	4	12	2	0	0	0	0	11	0	.273	.318
Eddie Williams	3B13	R	25	14	42	5	12	3	0	3	4	5	6	0	.286	.571
Paul Faries	2B7 SS4 3B1	R	25	14	37	4	7	1	0	0	2	4	7	0	.189	.216
Ronn Reynolds	C8	R	31	8	15	1	1	0	0	0	1	1	6	0	.067	.133
Rob Nelson		L	25	5	5	0	0	0	0	0	0	0	4	0	.000	.000

NAME	T	AGE	W	L	PCT	SV	G	GS	CG	IP	H	BB	SO	SHO	ERA
		29	75	87	.463	35	162	162	21	1462	1437	507	928	12	3.68
Ed Whitson	R	35	14	9	.609	0	32	32	6	229	215	47	127	3	2.60
Bruce Hurst	L	32	11	9	.550	0	33	33	9	224	188	63	162	4	3.14
Dennis Rasmussen	L	31	11	15	.423	0	32	32	3	188	217	62	86	1	4.51
Andy Benes	R	22	10	11	.476	0	32	31	2	192	177	69	140	0	3.60
Greg Harris	R	26	8	8	.500	9	73	0	0	117	92	49	97	0	2.30
Craig Lefferts	L	32	7	5	.583	23	56	0	0	79	68	22	60	0	2.52
Eric Show	R	34	6	8	.429	1	39	12	0	106	131	41	55	0	5.76
2 Derek Lilliquist	L	24	3	3	.500	0	16	7	1	60	61	23	29	1	4.33
Calvin Schiraldi	R	28	3	8	.273	1	42	8	0	104	105	60	74	0	4.41
Rich Rodriguez	L	27	1	1	.500	0	32	0	0	48	52	16	22	0	2.83
1 Mark Grant	R	26	1	1	.500	0	26	0	0	39	47	19	29	0	4.85
Pat Clements	L	28	0	0	—	0	4	0	0	13	20	7	6	0	4.15
John Davis	R	27	0	1	.000	0	3	0	0	6	11	2	3	0	11.12
Rafael Valdez	R	22	0	1	.000	0	3	0	0	6	11	2	3	0	11.12
Mike Dunne (SJ)	R	27	0	3	.000	0	10	6	0	29	28	17	15	0	5.65
2 Atlee Hammaker	L	32	0	4	.000	0	14	0	0	19	16	6	16	0	4.66

ATLANTA 6th 65-97 .401 26   RUSS NIXON 25-40 .385   BOBBY COX 40-57 .412

Name	G by Pos	B	AGE	G	AB	R	H	2B	3B	HR	RBI	BB	SO	SB	BA	SA
TOTALS			28	162	5504	682	1376	263	26	162	636	473	1010	92	.250	.396
David Justice	1B69 OF61	L	24	127	439	76	124	23	2	28	78	64	92	11	.282	.535
Jeff Treadway	2B122	R	27	128	474	56	134	20	2	11	59	25	42	3	.283	.403
Jeff Blauser	SS93 3B14 3B9 OF1	R	24	115	386	46	104	24	3	8	39	35	70	3	.269	.409
Jim Presley	3B133 1B7	R	28	140	541	59	131	34	1	19	72	29	130	1	.242	.414
1 Dale Murphy	OF97	R	34	97	349	38	81	14	0	17	55	41	84	9	.232	.418
Ron Gant	OF146	R	25	152	575	107	174	34	3	32	84	50	86	33	.303	.539
Lonnie Smith	OF122	R	34	135	466	72	142	27	9	9	42	58	69	10	.305	.459
Greg Olson	C97 3B1	R	29	100	298	36	78	12	1	7	36	30	51	1	.262	.379
Tommy Gregg	1B50 OF20	L	26	124	239	18	63	13	1	5	32	20	39	4	.264	.389
Oddibe McDowell	OF72	L	27	113	305	47	74	14	0	7	25	21	53	13	.243	.357
Mark Lemke (NJ)	2B44 3B35 SS1	B	24	102	239	22	54	13	0	0	21	21	22	0	.226	.280
Andres Thomas	SS72 3B5	R	26	84	278	26	61	8	0	5	30	11	43	2	.219	.302
Ernie Whitt (RJ)	C59	L	38	67	180	14	37	6	2	10	23	27	17	0	.206	.400
Francisco Cabrera	1B48 C3	R	23	63	137	14	38	5	1	7	25	5	21	1	.277	.482
Mike Bell	1B24	L	22	36	45	8	11	5	1	1	9	2	8	0	.244	.467
Jimmy Kremers	C27	L	24	29	73	7	8	1	1	0	8	6	27	0	.110	.192
2 Jim Vatcher	OF6	R	23	21	27	1	7	1	0	0	1	6	9	0	.259	.370
Alex Infante	2B10 3B4 SS3	R	27	20	28	1	1	0	0	0	0	3	8	0	.036	.071
Jody Davis	1B6 C4	R	33	12	28	0	2	0	0	0	0	2	9	0	.071	.071
Kelly Mann	C10	R	22	11	14	2	2	0	0	0	1	0	6	0	.143	.143
Nick Esasky (IL)	1B9	R	30	9	35	1	3	1	0	0	1	0	14	0	.171	.171
Victor Rosario	SS3 2B1	B	23	9	7	1	1	0	0	0	0	1	2	0	.143	.143
Geronimo Berroa	OF3	R	25	7	4	0	0	0	0	0	0	0	3	0	.000	.000

NAME	T	AGE	W	L	PCT	SV	G	GS	CG	IP	H	BB	SO	SHO	ERA
		27	65	97	.401	30	162	162	17	1430	1527	579	938	8	4.58
John Smoltz	R	23	14	11	.560	0	34	34	6	231	206	90	170	2	3.85
Tom Glavine	L	24	10	12	.455	0	33	33	1	214	232	78	129	2	4.28
Charlie Leibrandt (SJ)	L	33	9	11	.450	0	24	24	5	162	164	35	76	2	3.16
Tony Castillo	L	27	5	1	.833	1	52	0	0	77	93	20	64	1	4.23
Pete Smith (SJ)	R	24	5	6	.455	0	13	13	3	77	77	24	56	0	4.79
Kent Mercker	L	22	4	7	.364	7	36	0	0	48	43	24	39	0	3.17
2 Charley Kerfeld	R	26	3	1	.750	2	25	0	0	31	31	23	27	0	5.58
Steve Avery	L	20	3	11	.214	0	21	20	1	99	121	45	75	1	5.64
Dwayne Henry	R	28	2	2	.500	0	34	0	0	38	41	25	34	0	5.63
1 Derek Lilliquist	L	24	2	8	.200	0	12	6	0	62	75	19	34	0	6.28
Marvin Freeman	R	27	1	0	1.000	0	9	0	0	12	6	3	9	0	1.72
1 Tommy Greene	R	23	1	1	.500	1	20	0	0	27	27	19	17	0	3.00
Jeff Parrett	R	28	5	10	.333	1	27	27	19	17						
Mark Grant	R	26	1	2	.333	3	33	1	0	52	61	18	40	0	4.64
Paul Marak	R	24	1	2	.333	0	7	7	1	39	39	19	15	0	3.69
Joe Boever	R	29	1	3	.250	8	34	0	0	45	45	35	35	0	4.68
Rick Luecken	R	29	1	4	.200	1	36	0	0	53	73	30	35	0	5.77
Marty Clary	R	28	1	10	.091	0	34	14	0	102	128	39	44	0	5.67
Sergio Valdez (EJ)	R	26	0	0	—	0	3	0	0	2	8	2	2	0	6.75
Doug Sisk (EJ)	R	33	0	0	—	0	14	0	0	31	30	12	21	0	5.81
Rusty Richards	R	25	0	0	—	0	2	1	0	9	8	3	2	0	27.00
2 Joe Hesketh	L	31	0	2	.000	0	31	0	0	31	30	12	21	0	5.81
Mike Stanton (SJ)	L	23	0	3	.000	2	7	0	0	7	16	4	7	0	18.00

LINE SCORES

Team	1	2	3	4	5	6	7	8	9	10	11		R	H	E

AMERICAN LEAGUE CHAMPIONSHIPS: OAKLAND (WEST) 4   BOSTON (EAST) 0

Game 1 October 6 at Boston

	1	2	3	4	5	6	7	8	9		R	H	E
OAK	0	0	0	0	0	0	1	1	7		9	13	0
BOS	0	0	0	1	0	0	0	0	0		1	5	1

Stewart, Eckersley (9)   Clemens, **Andersen** (7), Bolton (8), Gray (8), Lamp (9), Murphy (9)

Game 2 October 7 at Boston

	1	2	3	4	5	6	7	8	9		R	H	E
OAK	0	0	0	1	0	0	1	0	2		4	13	1
BOS	0	0	1	0	0	0	1	0	0		1	6	0

Welch, Honeycutt (8), Eckersley (8)   Kiecker, **Harris** (6), Andersen (7), Reardon (8)

Game 3 October 9 at Oakland

	1	2	3	4	5	6	7	8	9		R	H	E
BOS	0	1	0	0	0	0	0	0	0		1	8	3
OAK	0	0	0	2	0	2	0	0	X		4	6	0

Boddicker   Moore, Nelson (7), Honeycutt (8), Eckersley (9)

Game 4 October 10 at Oakland

	1	2	3	4	5	6	7	8	9		R	H	E
BOS	0	0	0	0	0	0	0	0	1		1	4	1
OAK	0	3	0	0	0	0	0	0	X		3	6	0

Clemens, Bolton (2), Gray (5), Andersen (8)   **Stewart**, Honeycutt (9)

NATIONAL LEAGUE CHAMPIONSHIPS: CINCINNATI (WEST) 4   PITTSBURGH (EAST) 2

Game 1 October 4 at Cincinnati

	1	2	3	4	5	6	7	8	9		R	H	E
PIT	0	0	1	2	0	0	1	0	0		4	7	1
CIN	3	0	0	0	0	0	0	0	0		3	5	0

Walk, Belinda (7), Patterson (8), Power (9)   Rijo, **Charlton** (6), Dibble (9)

Game 2 October 5 at Cincinnati

	1	2	3	4	5	6	7	8	9		R	H	E
PIT	0	0	0	0	1	0	0	0	0		1	6	0
CIN	1	0	0	0	1	0	0	0	X		2	5	0

Drabek   Browning, Dibble (7), Myers (8)

Game 3 October 8 at Pittsburgh

	1	2	3	4	5	6	7	8	9		R	H	E
CIN	0	2	0	0	3	0	0	0	1		6	13	0
PIT	0	0	0	2	0	0	1	0	0		3	8	0

Jackson, Dibble (6), Charlton (8), Myers (9)   **Smith**, Landrum (6), Smiley (7), Belinda (9)

Game 4 October 9 at Pittsburgh

	1	2	3	4	5	6	7	8	9		R	H	E
CIN	0	0	0	2	0	0	2	0	1		5	10	1
PIT	1	0	0	1	0	0	0	1	0		3	8	0

Rijo, Myers (8), Dibble (9)   **Walk**, Power (8)

Game 5 October 10 at Pittsburgh

	1	2	3	4	5	6	7	8	9		R	H	E
CIN	1	0	0	0	0	0	0	1	0		2	7	0
PIT	2	0	0	1	0	0	0	0	X		3	6	1

Browning, Mahler (4), Charlton (7), Scudder (8)   **Drabek**, Patterson (9)

Game 6 October 12 at Cincinnati

	1	2	3	4	5	6	7	8	9		R	H	E
PIT	0	0	0	0	1	0	0	0	0		1	1	3
CIN	1	0	0	0	0	0	1	0	X		2	9	0

Power, **Smith** (3), Belinda (7), Landrum (8)   Jackson, **Charlton** (7), Myers (8)

COMPOSITE BATTING

OAKLAND

NAME	POS	G	AB	R	H	2B	3B	HR	RBI	BA
TOTALS		4	127	20	38	4	0	0	18	.299
R. Henderson	LF	4	17	1	5	0	0	0	3	.294
Lansford	3B	4	16	2	7	1	0	0	2	.438
Baines	DH	4	14	2	5	1	0	0	3	.357
McGwire	1B	4	13	2	2	0	0	0	1	.154
Canseco	RF	4	11	3	2	0	0	0	1	.182
Steinbach	C	3	11	2	5	0	0	0	1	.455
Gallego	2B-SS	4	10	1	4	1	0	0	2	.400
McGee	CF-PR	3	9	3	2	1	0	0	0	.222
Randolph	2B-SS	4	8	1	3	0	0	0	3	.375
Weiss	SS	2	7	2	0	0	0	0	0	.000
D. Henderson	CF	2	6	0	1	0	0	0	1	.167
Hassey	C-PH	2	3	0	1	0	0	0	0	.333
Quirk	PH	1	1	0	1	0	0	0	0	1.000
Jennings	RF	1	1	0	0	0	0	0	0	.000
Blankenship	PR	3	0	1	0	0	0	0	0	—

BOSTON

NAME	POS	G	AB	R	H	2B	3B	HR	RBI	BA
TOTALS		4	126	1	23	5	0	1	4	.183
Boggs	3B	4	16	1	7	1	0	1	1	.438
Burks	CF	4	15	0	4	2	0	0	0	.267
Reed	2B	4	15	0	2	0	0	0	1	.133
Pena	C	4	14	1	3	0	0	0	0	.214
Greenwell	LF	4	14	0	0	0	0	0	0	.000
Evans	DH	4	13	0	3	1	0	0	0	.231
Quintana	1B	4	13	0	0	0	0	0	0	.000
Brunansky	RF	4	12	1	1	0	0	0	1	.083
Rivera	SS	4	9	0	2	1	0	0	0	.222
Marshall	PH	3	3	0	1	0	0	0	0	.333
Heep	PH	2	2	0	0	0	0	0	0	.000
Barrett	2B	3	0	0	0	0	0	0	0	—
Kutcher	PR	2	0	0	0	0	0	0	0	—

CINCINNATI

NAME	POS	G	AB	R	H	2B	3B	HR	RBI	BA
TOTALS		6	192	20	49	9	0	4	20	.255
Davis	LF	6	23	2	4	1	0	0	2	.174
Larkin	SS	6	23	5	6	2	0	0	1	.261
Sabo	3B	6	22	1	5	0	0	1	3	.227
Duncan	2B	6	20	1	6	0	0	1	4	.300
O'Neill	RF	5	17	1	8	3	0	1	4	.471
Hatcher	CF	4	15	2	5	1	0	1	2	.333
Oliver	C	5	14	1	2	1	0	0	0	.143
Morris	1B	5	12	3	5	0	0	0	1	.417
Benzinger	PH-1B	5	9	0	3	0	0	0	0	.333
Reed	C	4	7	0	0	0	0	0	0	.000
Winningham	CF-PH	3	7	1	2	1	0	0	1	.286
Braggs	RF	2	5	0	1	0	0	0	0	.200
Rijo	PH-1B	2	5	0	0	0	0	0	0	.000
Oester	2B-PH	3	3	1	1	0	0	0	0	.333
Browning	P	2	3	0	0	0	0	0	0	.000
Jackson	P	2	3	0	0	0	0	0	0	.000
Quinones	PH	3	2	1	1	0	0	0	2	.000
Dibble	P	4	2	0	0	0	0	0	0	.000
Bates	PR	2	0	1	0	0	0	0	0	—

PITTSBURGH

NAME	POS	G	AB	R	H	2B	3B	HR	RBI	BA
TOTALS		6	186	15	36	9	2	3	14	.194
Van Slyke	CF	6	24	3	5	1	1	0	3	.208
Lind	2B	6	21	1	5	1	1	1	2	.238
Bonilla	RF-3B	6	21	0	4	1	0	0	1	.190
Bell	SS	6	20	3	5	1	0	1	1	.250
Bonds	LF	6	18	4	3	0	0	0	1	.167
Slaught	C	4	11	0	1	1	0	0	1	.091
Reynolds	PH-RF	4	10	0	2	0	0	0	0	.200
King	3B-PH	4	10	0	1	0	0	0	0	.100
Bream	1B	3	8	1	4	1	0	1	3	.500
Martinez	1B	2	8	0	2	2	0	0	2	.250
Redus	PH-1B	6	8	1	2	0	0	0	0	.250
Backman	PH-3B	3	7	1	1	1	0	0	0	.143
Drabek	P	2	6	0	1	0	0	0	0	.167
LaValliere	C	2	6	1	0	0	0	0	0	.000
Walk	P	2	4	0	0	0	0	0	0	.000
Smith	P	2	3	0	0	0	0	0	0	.000
Power	P	2	1	0	0	0	0	0	0	.000

COMPOSITE PITCHING

OAKLAND

NAME	G	IP	H	BB	SO	W	L	SV	ERA
TOTALS	4	36	23	6	16	4	0	3	1.00
Stewart	2	16	8	2	4	2	0	0	1.13
Welch	1	7.1	6	3	4	1	0	0	1.23
Moore	1	6	4	1	5	1	0	0	1.50
Eckersley	3	3.1	2	0	3	0	0	2	0.00
Honeycutt	3	1.2	0	0	0	0	0	1	0.00
Nelson	1	1.2	3	0	0	0	0	0	0.00

BOSTON

NAME	G	IP	H	BB	SO	W	L	SV	ERA
TOTALS	4	34	38	19	21	0	4	0	4.50
Boddicker	1	8	6	3	7	0	1	0	2.25
Clemens	2	7.2	7	5	4	0	1	0	3.52
Kiecker	1	5.2	6	1	2	0	0	0	1.59
Gray	2	3.1	4	1	2	0	0	0	2.70
Bolton	2	3	2	2	3	0	0	0	0.00
Andersen	3	3	3	3	3	0	1	0	6.00
Reardon	1	2	3	1	0	0	0	0	9.00
Murphy	1	0.2	2	1	0	0	0	0	13.50
Harris	1	0.1	3	0	0	0	1	0	27.00
Lamp	1	0.1	2	2	0	0	0	0	108.00

CINCINNATI

NAME	G	IP	H	BB	SO	W	L	SV	ERA
TOTALS	6	53	36	27	49	4	2	4	2.38
Rijo	2	12.1	10	7	15	1	0	0	4.38
Jackson	2	11.1	8	7	8	1	0	0	2.38
Browning	2	11	9	6	5	1	1	0	3.27
Myers	4	5.2	2	3	7	0	0	3	0.00
Charlton	4	5	4	3	4	1	1	0	1.80
Dibble	4	5	0	1	10	0	0	1	0.00
Mahler	1	1.2	2	0	0	0	0	0	0.00
Scudder	1	1	1	0	1	0	0	0	0.00

PITTSBURGH

NAME	G	IP	H	BB	SO	W	L	SV	ERA
TOTALS	6	52.1	49	10	37	2	4	2	3.29
Drabek	2	16.2	12	3	13	1	1	0	1.65
Walk	2	12	11	2	8	1	1	0	4.85
Smith	2	9	14	1	8	0	2	0	6.00
Power	3	5	6	2	3	0	0	1	3.60
Belinda	3	3.2	3	0	4	0	0	0	2.45
Landrum	2	2	0	1	0	0	0	0	0.00
Smiley	1	2	2	0	0	0	0	0	0.00
Patterson	2	1	1	2	0	0	0	1	0.00

LINE SCORES

Team	1	2	3	4	5	6	7	8	9	10			R	H	E

WORLD SERIES: CINCINNATI (NL) 4 : OAKLAND (AL) 0

Game 1 October 16 at Cincinnati

	1	2	3	4	5	6	7	8	9	10			R	H	E
OAK	0	0	0	0	0	0	0	0	0				0	9	1
CIN	2	0	2	0	3	0	0	0	X				7	10	0

Stewart, Burns (5),   **Rijo**, Dibble (8),
Nelson (5), Sanderson (7),   Myers (9)
Eckersley (8)

Game 2 October 17 at Cincinnati

	1	2	3	4	5	6	7	8	9	10			R	H	E
OAK	1	0	3	0	0	0	0	0	0	0			4	10	2
CIN	2	0	0	1	0	0	0	1	0	1			5	14	2

Welch, Honeycutt (8),   Jackson, Scudder (3),
Eckersley (10)   Armstrong (5), Charlton (8),
     Dibble (9)

Game 3 October 19 at Oakland

	1	2	3	4	5	6	7	8	9	10			R	H	E
CIN	0	1	7	0	0	0	0	0	0				8	14	1
OAK	0	2	1	0	0	0	0	0	0				3	7	1

Browning, Dibble (7),   **Moore**, Sanderson (3),
Myers (8)   Klink (4), Nelson (4),
     Burns (8), Young (9)

Game 4 October 20 at Oakland

	1	2	3	4	5	6	7	8	9	10			R	H	E
CIN	0	0	0	0	0	0	0	2	0				2	7	1
OAK	1	0	0	0	0	0	0	0	0				1	2	1

Rijo, Myers (9)   **Stewart**

COMPOSITE BATTING

NAME	POS	G	AB	R	H	2B	3B	HR	RBI	BA
CINCINNATI										
TOTALS		4	142	22	45	9	2	3	22	.317
Oliver	C	4	18	2	6	3	0	0	2	.333
Larkin	SS	4	17	3	6	1	1	0	1	.353
Sabo	3B	4	16	2	9	1	0	2	5	.563
Davis	LF	4	14	3	4	0	0	1	5	.286
Duncan	2B	4	14	1	2	0	0	0	1	.143
Morris	DH-1B	4	14	0	1	0	0	0	2	.071
Hatcher	CF	4	12	6	9	4	1	0	2	.750
O'Neill	RF	4	12	2	1	0	0	0	1	.083
Benzinger	1B-PH	4	11	1	2	0	0	0	0	.182
Winningham	PH-CF	2	4	1	2	0	0	0	0	.500
Braggs	PH-LF	2	4	0	0	0	0	0	2	.000
Rijo	P	2	3	0	1	0	0	0	0	.333
Bates	PH	1	1	1	1	0	0	0	0	1.000
Oester	PH	1	1	0	1	0	0	0	1	1.000
Jackson	P	1	1	0	0	0	0	0	0	.000
Dibble	P	3	0	0	0	0	0	0	0	—
Myers	P	3	0	0	0	0	0	0	0	—
Armstrong	P	1	0	0	0	0	0	0	0	—
Browning	P	1	0	0	0	0	0	0	0	—
Charlton	P	1	0	0	0	0	0	0	0	—
Scudder	P	1	0	0	0	0	0	0	0	—
OAKLAND										
TOTALS		4	135	8	28	4	0	3	8	.207
R. Henderson	LF	4	15	2	5	2	0	1	1	.333
Lansford	3B	4	15	0	4	0	0	0	1	.267
Randolph	2B	4	15	0	4	0	0	0	1	.267
McGwire	1B	4	14	1	3	0	0	0	0	.214
D. Henderson	CF-PH	4	13	2	3	1	0	0	0	.231
Canseco	RF-PH	4	12	1	1	0	0	1	2	.083
Gallego	SS	4	11	0	1	0	0	0	1	.091
McGee	CF-RF-PH	4	10	1	2	1	0	0	0	.200
Steinbach	C	3	8	0	1	0	0	0	0	.125
Baines	DH-PH	3	7	1	1	0	0	1	2	.143
Hassey	C-PH	3	6	0	2	0	0	0	1	.333
Quirk	C	1	3	0	0	0	0	0	0	.000
Welch	P	3	3	0	0	0	0	0	0	.000
Stewart	P	2	1	0	0	0	0	0	0	.000
Blankenship	PH	1	1	0	0	0	0	0	0	.000
Jennings	PH	1	1	0	1	0	0	0	0	1.000
Bordick	SS-PR	3	0	0	0	0	0	0	0	—
Burns	P	2	0	0	0	0	0	0	0	—
Eckersley	P	2	0	0	0	0	0	0	0	—
Nelson	P	2	0	0	0	0	0	0	0	—
Sanderson	P	2	0	0	0	0	0	0	0	—
Honeycutt	P	1	0	0	0	0	0	0	0	—
Klink	P	1	0	0	0	0	0	0	0	—
Moore	P	1	0	0	0	0	0	0	0	—
Young	P	1	0	0	0	0	0	0	0	—

COMPOSITE PITCHING

NAME	G	IP	H	BB	SO	W	L	SV	ERA
CINCINNATI									
TOTALS	4	37	28	12	28	4	0	0	1.70
Rijo	2	15.1	9	5	14	2	0	0	0.59
Browning	1	6	6	2	2	1	0	0	4.50
Dibble	3	4.2	3	1	4	1	0	0	0.00
Myers	3	3	2	0	3	0	0	0	0.00
Armstrong	1	3	1	0	3	0	0	0	0.00
Jackson	1	2.2	6	2	0	0	0	0	10.13
Scudder	1	1.1	0	2	2	0	0	0	0.00
Charlton	1	1	1	0	0	0	0	0	0.00
OAKLAND									
TOTALS	4	35.1	45	15	9	0	4	0	4.33
Stewart	2	13	10	6	5	0	2	0	3.46
Welch	2	7.1	9	2	2	0	0	0	4.91
Nelson	2	5	3	2	0	0	0	0	0.00
Moore	1	2.2	8	0	1	0	1	0	6.75
Honeycutt	1	1.2	1	0	0	0	0	0	0.00
Sanderson	2	1.2	4	1	0	0	0	0	10.80
Burns	2	1.2	5	2	0	0	0	0	16.20
Eckersley	2	1.1	3	0	1	0	0	0	6.75
Young	1	1	1	0	0	0	0	0	0.00
Klink	1	0	0	1	0	0	0	0	0.00

MISCELLANEOUS 1990 INDIVIDUAL LEADERS

BATTING

On Base Average

American League			National League		
1	R. Henderson, Oak.	.439	1	Dykstra, Phi.	.418
2	McGriff, Tor.	.400	2	Magadan, N.Y.	.417
3	Martinez, Sea.	.397	3	Murray, L.A.	.414
4	Brett, K.C.	.387	4	Bonds, Pit.	.406
5	A. Davis, Sea.	.387	5	Butler, S.F.	.397

Caught Stealing

American League			National League		
1	Johnson, Chi.	22	1	Yelding, Hou.	25
2	Guillen, Chi.	17	2	DeShields, Mon.	22
	Kelly, N.Y.	17	3	Samuel, L.A.	20
4	Calderon, Chi.	16	4	Butler, S.F.	19
	Reynolds, Sea.	16	5	Coleman, St. L.	17
	Sosa, Chi.	16			

Hit by Pitcher

American League			National League		
1	Bradley, Chi.	11	1	G. Davis, Hou.	8
2	Incaviglia, Tex.	9	2	Carter, S.D.	7
3	Gruber, Tor.	8	3	Dykstra, Phi.	7
4	8 players with	7		Larkin, Cin.	7
				Williams, S.F.	7

Sacrifice Hits

American League			National League		
1	Gallego, Oak.	17	1	Bell, Pit.	39
	B. Ripken, Bal.	17	2	Gooden, N.Y.	14
3	Guillen, Chi.	15	3	Armstrong, Cin.	13
4	Fermin, Cle.	13		Whitson, S.D.	13
	Schoefield, Sea.	13	5	Boyd, Mon.	12
	Ventura, Chi.	13		De. Martinez, Mon.	12

Extra Base Hits

American League			National League		
1	Fielder, Det.	77	1	Bonilla, Pit.	78
2	Gruber, Tor.	73	2	Sandberg, Chi.	73
3	Brett, K.C.	66	3	Gant, Atl.	69
4	R. Henderson, Oak.	64	4	Bonds, Pit.	68
5	Burks, Bos.	62	5	Sabo, Cin.	65

Grounded Into Double Play

American League			National League		
1	Calderon, Chi.	26	1	Murphy, Atl. + Phi.	22
2	Palmeiro, Tex.	24	2	Lind, Pit.	20
3	Pena, Bos.	23	3	Murray, L.A.	19
4	Gaetti, Min.	22	4	Templeton, S.D.	17
5	Harper, Min.	20	5	Alomar, S.D.	16
	Jacoby, Cle.	20		Raines, Mon.	16
	Leonard, Sea.	20			

Total Bases

American League			National League		
1	Fielder, Det.	339	1	Sandberg, Chi.	344
2	Gruber, Tor.	303	2	Bonilla, Pit.	324
3	McGriff, Tor.	295	3	Gant, Atl.	310
4	K. Griffey, Jr., Sea.	287	4	Williams, S.F.	301
5	Burks, Bos.	286	5	Wallach, Mon.	295

Sacrifice Flies

American League			National League		
1	Parker, Mil.	14	1	Bonilla, Pit.	15
2	Gruber, Tor.	13	2	Clark, S.F.	13
3	Bell, Tor.	11	3	Brooks, L.A.	11
	Browne, Cle.	11		Guerrero, St. L.	11
5	Davis, Sea.	9	5	Hayes, Phi.	10
	McGwire, Oak.	9		Magadan, N.Y.	10
	Sheffield, Mil.	9		O. Smith, St. L.	10

FIELDING

American League	PO	A	E	DP	Pct.
1B	Hrbek, Min.	1057	81	3	100	.997
2B	Lee, Tor.	259	286	4	65	.993
3B	Lansford, Oak.	100	194	9	22	.970
SS	C. Ripken, Bal.	242	435	3	94	.996
OF	Wilson, K.C.	187	2	0	1	1.000
OF	Eisenreich, K.C.	261	6	1	3	.996
OF	Burks, Bos.	324	7	2	0	.994
C	Valle, Sea.	631	44	2	9	.997
P	Welch, Oak. (51 TC)	20	31	0	2	1.000

National League	PO	A	E	DP	Pct.
1B	Magadan, N.Y.	830	71	2	52	.998
2B	Oquendo, St. L.	285	393	3	65	.996
3B	Sabo, Cin.	70	273	12	17	.966
SS	S. Owen, Mon.	216	340	6	52	.989
OF	Hatcher, Cin.	308	10	1	2	.997
OF	O'Neill, Cin.	271	12	2	0	.993
OF	Strawberry, N.Y.	268	10	3	4	.989
C	Oliver, Cin.	686	59	6	8	.992
P	Maddux, Chi. (94 TC)	39	55	0	6	1.000

PITCHING

Wild Pitches

American League			National League		
1	Leary, N.Y.	23	1	Smoltz, Atl.	14
2	Morris, Det.	16	2	Valenzuela, L.A.	13
	Robinson, Det.	16	3	Magrane, St.L.	11
	Young, Sea.	16		Viola, N.Y.	11
5	Perez, Chi.	14		Bielecki, Chi.	11

Hit Batters

American League			National League		
1	Hough, Tex.	11	1	Gardner, Mon.	9
2	Boddicker, Bos.	10	2	Deshaies, Hou.	8
3	Stieb, Tor.	10	3	Magrane, St. L.	8
4	Kiecker, Bos.	9	4	Agosto, Hou.	7
	Tanana, Det.	9		Gooden, N.Y.	7
				Harkey, Chi.	7

Home Runs Allowed

American League			National League		
1	Johnson, Bal.	30	1	Rasmussen, S.D.	28
2	Sanderson, Oak.	27	2	Scott, Hou.	27
3	Swindell, Cle.	27	3	Browning, Cin.	24
4	Johnson, Sea.	26	4	Martinez, L.A.	22
	Morris, Det.	26	5	5 players with	21
	Welch, Oak.	26			

Balks

American League		
1	Navarro, Mil.	5
2	Perez, Chi.	4
3	Abbott, Cal.	3
	Anderson, Min.	3
	Candiotti, Cle.	3

National League		
1	Armstrong, Chi.	5
	Benes, S.D.	5
	Kipper, Pit.	5
	Rijo, Cin.	5
	Smith, Hou.	5

1991 And The Last Shall Be First

In a year of individual landmarks, Rickey Henderson broke the all-time career stolen base mark, Cecil Fielder became the first American Leaguer since Jimmie Foxx to lead in home runs and RBI in two consecutive years, Nolan Ryan pitched his seventh no-hitter, Dennis Martinez threw a perfect game, Lee Smith set a new National League save record, and David Cone tied the N.L. single game strike out record on the last day of the season. Other players completed hitting and pitching masterpieces, but individual achievements paled beside a pair of monumental team accomplishments. Two clubs - Minnesota and Atlanta - that finished last in their divisions in 1990 jumped all the way to division championships in '91, a leap that had never before been executed even once in the 20th Century. Furthermore, St. Louis made an only slightly lesser vault from last to second in its division. Then, both the Braves and Twins added to their unprecedented seasons by winning their league's pennants.

In the A.L. East, Toronto was buoyed by outfielder Joe Carter and second baseman Roberto Alomar, both acquired in a blockbuster off-season trade with San Diego. The Blue Jays took the lead early and held it amid predictions of an expected collapse. Pitching ace Dave Stieb was lost for most of the season with back pains, but rookie Juan Guzman stepped forward to become unbeatable down the stretch. Toronto became the first pro sports team to draw four million. Detroit, with a lineup of home run hitters, challenged until sinking under a sea of its own strikeouts and weak pitching. Boston, treated to a mock funeral by disappointed Red Sox fans in August, battled back to make it close in September. But, with only Roger Clemens and retread Joe Hesketh as reliable starters the BoSox slipped at the end.

The A.L. West was baseball's strongest division, with all seven teams finishing at .500 or better. Three-time champ Oakland was favored at the start. Dave Henderson's hot early hitting carried them for a while, but shortstop Walt Weiss and third baseman Carney Lansford missed virtually the whole season with injuries, first baseman Mark McGwire slumped badly, and Rickey Henderson never caught fire. Most damaging was the collapse of the pitching, long the team's greatest strength. 1990 Cy Young winner Bob Welch and perennial 20-game winner Dave Stewart were ineffective most of the year, as was the once-proud middle relief corps.

Into the breech left by the A's stepped the Twins. The solid pitching provided by youngsters Scott Erickson and Kevin Tapani, free agent pickup Jack Morris, and reliever Rick Aguilera and the hitting of Kirby Puckett, Brian Harper, Kent Hrbek, Shane Mack and Chili Davis kept Minnesota narrowly in front through the summer. In summer, they widened their lead and coasted home. The White Sox, enjoying their first season in new Comiskey Park, and the heavy-hitting Rangers challenged briefly. Seattle had the first winning season in its history.

The Chicago Cubs were pre-season favorites in the N.L. East, but free agent pitchers Danny Jackson and Dave Smith were hurt and others disappointed. Despite a lineup that featured Mark Grace, Ryne Sandberg, Andre Dawson, and George Bell, the Cubbies spent the year trying to avoid last place. The Mets were done in by their own shoddy defense, spotty hitting, and surprisingly unreliable pitching. Only Howard Johnson, the N.L.'s homer and RBI leader, had a strong season.

That cleared the road for the "Killer B's", Barry Bonds, Bobby Bonilla, and Jay Bell. Pittsburgh took over first place in April and was never headed. The surprising Cardinals dogged them all the way, largely due to the efforts of the Smiths, Ozzie, Lee, and Bryn.

The Dodgers got off to an early lead in the N.L. West on the strength of their superior starting pitching and threatened to make a runaway of their race. They never actually faltered, as Darryl Strawberry and Eddie Murray began hitting in the second half after slow starts. Instead, they were simply swept aside by red-hot Atlanta. The young Braves, last place finishers in four of the last five years, were nine-and-a-half games out at the All-Star break. But Terry Pendleton, the season's best free agent addition, gave them timely hitting and inspirational leadership. Ron Gant and David Justice provided power. And Tom Glavine, Steve Avery, and John Smoltz were the finest trio of young starters in baseball. As the Braves closed with a rush, they became through Superstation TBS somewhat "America's Team," and their fans' trademark tomahawk chop was seen in every league park. On the next-to last day of the regular season, Smoltz won over Houston while Los Angeles lost at San Francisco to make the Braves division champions.

The Twins took the ALCS in five games, thanks to timely and frequent hitting, particularly by Puckett and rookie second baseman Chuck Knoblauch.

The NLCS was a nail-biter with three 1-0 games. The Braves won in seven on the remarkable pitching of Avery, Smoltz and reliever Alejandro Pena. For the second year in a row, the Pirates' big bats - Van Slyke, Bonilla and Bonds - were silent in the playoffs.

The World Series was one of the closest of all time. Three games went into extra innings, four games were decided on the final pitch, and five games were decided by a run. Both the Twins and Braves won all their home games. In the finale, Series MVP Jack Morris shutout the Braves inning after inning to keep Minnesota alive until Gene Larkin's one-out, pinch-hit single in the last of the tenth drove in the only run to make the Twins world champions.

EAST DIVISION

1991 AMERICAN LEAGUE

Name	G by Pos	B	AGE	G	AB	R	H	2B	3B	HR	RBI	BB	SO	SB	BA	SA
TORONTO 1st 91-71 .562					**CITO GASTON**											
TOTALS			29	162	5489	684	1412	295	45	133	649	499	1043	148	.257	.400
John Olerud	1B135 DH1	L	22	139	454	64	116	30	1	17	68	68	84	0	.256	.438
Roberto Alomar	2B160	B	23	161	637	88	188	41	11	9	69	57	86	53	.295	.436
Manny Lee	SS138	B	26	138	445	41	104	18	3	0	29	24	107	7	.234	.288
Kelly Gruber (RJ)	3B111 DH2	R	29	113	429	58	108	18	2	20	65	31	70	12	.252	.443
Joe Carter	OF151 DH11	R	31	162	638	89	174	42	3	33	108	49	112	20	.273	.503
Devon White	OF156	B	28	156	642	110	181	40	10	17	60	55	135	33	.282	.455
Candy Maldonado	OF52 DH9	R	30	52	177	26	49	9	0	7	28	23	53	4	.277	.446
Greg Myers	C104	L	25	107	309	25	81	22	0	8	36	21	45	0	.262	.411
Rance Mulliniks (FJ)	DH81 3B5	L	35	97	240	27	60	12	1	2	24	44	44	0	.250	.333
Pat Borders	C102	R	28	105	291	22	71	17	0	5	36	11	45	0	.244	.354
Mookie Wilson	OF41 DH34	B	35	86	241	26	58	12	4	2	28	8	35	11	.241	.349
Pat Tabler	DH57 1B20 OF1	R	33	82	185	20	40	5	1	1	21	29	21	0	.216	.270
Rene Gonzales	SS36 3B26 2B11 1B2	R	30	71	118	16	23	3	0	1	6	12	22	0	.195	.246
Ed Sprague	3B35 1B22 C2 DH2	R	23	61	160	17	44	7	0	4	20	19	43	0	.275	.394
1 Mark Whiten	OF42	B	24	46	149	12	33	4	3	2	19	11	35	0	.221	.329
Rob Ducey	OF24 DH2	L	26	39	68	8	16	2	2	1	4	6	26	2	.235	.368
4 Glenallen Hill	DH16 OF13	R	26	35	99	14	25	5	2	3	11	7	24	2	.253	.434
2 Cory Snyder	OF14 1B4 3B3	R	28	21	49	4	7	0	1	0	6	3	19	0	.143	.184
Derek Bell	OF13	R	22	18	28	5	4	0	0	0	1	6	5	3	.143	.143
Eddie Zosky	SS18	R	23	18	27	2	4	1	1	0	2	0	8	0	.148	.259
2 Dave Parker	DH11	L	40	13	36	2	12	4	0	0	3	4	7	0	.333	.444
1 Kenny Williams	OF9 DH2	R	27	13	29	5	6	2	0	1	3	4	5	1	.207	.379
Ray Giannelli	3B9	L	25	9	24	2	4	1	0	0	0	5	9	1	.167	.208
2 Turner Ward	OF6	R	26	8	13	1	4	0	0	0	2	1	2	0	.308	.308
Randy Knorr	C3	R	22	3	1	0	0	0	0	0	0	0	1	0	.000	.000
BOSTON (TIE) 2nd 84-78 .519 7					**JOE MORGAN**											
TOTALS			29	162	5530	731	1486	305	25	126	691	593	820	59	.269	.401
Carlos Quintana	1B138 OF13 DH1	R	25	149	478	69	141	21	1	11	71	61	66	1	.295	.412
Jody Reed	2B152 SS6	R	28	153	618	87	175	42	2	5	60	60	53	6	.283	.382
Luis Rivera	SS129	R	27	129	414	64	107	22	3	8	40	35	86	4	.258	.384
Wade Boggs	3B140	L	33	144	546	93	181	42	2	8	51	89	32	1	.332	.460
Tom Brunansky	OF137 DH1	R	30	142	459	54	105	24	1	16	70	49	72	1	.229	.390
Ellis Burks	OF126 DH2	R	26	130	474	56	119	33	3	14	56	39	81	6	.251	.422
Mike Greenwell	OF143 DH1	L	27	147	544	76	163	26	6	9	83	43	35	15	.300	.419
Tony Pena	C140	R	34	141	464	45	107	23	2	5	48	37	53	8	.231	.321
Jack Clark	DH135	R	35	140	481	75	120	18	1	28	87	96	133	0	.249	.466
Steve Lyons	OF45 2B16 3B12 1B2 DH2 SS1 P1	L	31	87	212	15	51	10	1	4	17	11	35	10	.241	.354
Mo Vaughn	1B49 DH16	L	23	74	219	21	57	12	0	4	32	26	43	2	.260	.370
Mike Brumley	SS31 3B17 2B7 OF4 DH2	B	28	63	118	16	25	5	0	0	7	5	22	4	.212	.254
Phil Plantier	OF40 DH5	L	22	53	148	27	49	7	1	11	35	23	38	1	.331	.615
John Marzano	C48	R	28	49	114	10	30	8	0	0	9	1	16	0	.263	.333
Kevin Romine	OF23 DH14	R	30	44	55	7	9	2	0	0	3	3	10	1	.164	.255
1 Mike Marshall	DH7 1B5 OF4	R	31	22	62	4	18	4	0	1	5	3	15	0	.290	.403
Tim Naehring (XJ)	SS17 3B2 2B1	R	24	20	55	1	6	1	0	0	3	6	15	0	.109	.127
Bob Zupcic	OF16	R	25	18	25	3	4	0	0	0	3	1	6	0	.160	.280
Scott Cooper	3B13	L	23	14	35	6	16	4	2	0	7	2	2	0	.457	.686
Wayne Housie	OF4 DH2	B	26	11	8	2	2	1	0	0	1	0	3	1	.250	.375
Eric Wedge	DH1	R	23	1	1	0	1	0	0	0	1	0	0	0	1.000	1.000

NAME	T	AGE	W	L	PCT	SV	G	GS	CG	IP	H	BB	SO	SHO	ERA
		28	91	71	.562	60	162	162	10	1463	1301	523	971	16	3.50
Jimmy Key	L	30	16	12	.571	0	33	33	2	209	207	44	125	2	3.05
Todd Stottlemyre	R	26	15	8	.652	0	34	34	1	219	194	75	116	0	3.78
David Wells	L	28	15	10	.600	1	40	28	2	198	188	49	106	0	3.72
Mike Timlin	R	25	11	6	.647	3	63	3	0	108	94	50	85	0	3.16
Juan Guzman	R	24	10	3	.769	0	23	23	1	139	98	66	123	0	2.99
2 Tom Candiotti	R	33	6	7	.462	0	19	19	3	130	114	45	81	0	2.98
Dave Stieb (SJ-XJ)	R	33	4	3	.571	0	9	9	1	60	52	23	29	0	3.17
Bob MacDonald	L	26	3	3	.500	0	45	0	0	54	51	25	24	0	2.85
Jim Acker	R	32	3	5	.375	1	54	4	0	88	77	36	44	0	5.20
David Weathers	R	21	1	0	1.000	0	15	0	0	15	15	17	13	0	4.91
Ken Dayley (IL)	L	32	0	0	—	0	8	0	0	4	7	5	3	0	6.23
Vince Horsman	L	24	0	0	—	0	4	0	0	4	2	3	2	0	0.00
Pat Hentgen	R	22	0	0	—	0	3	1	0	7	5	3	3	0	2.45
Al Leiter (EJ)	L	25	0	0	—	0	3	0	0	2	3	5	1	0	27.00
Mickey Weston	R	30	0	0	—	0	2	0	0	2	1	1	1	0	0.00
Frank Wills	R	32	0	1	.000	0	4	0	0	4	8	5	2	0	16.62
Tom Henke (GJ)	R	33	0	2	.000	32	49	0	0	50	33	11	53	0	2.32
1 Willie Fraser	R	27	0	2	.000	0	13	1	0	26	33	11	12	0	6.15
1 Denis Boucher	L	23	0	3	.000	0	7	7	0	35	39	16	16	0	4.58
		31	84	78	.519	45	162	162	15	1440	1405	530	999	13	4.01
Roger Clemens	R	28	18	10	.643	0	35	35	13	271	219	65	241	4	2.62
Joe Hesketh	L	32	12	4	.750	0	39	17	0	153	142	53	104	0	3.29
Greg Harris	R	35	11	12	.478	2	53	21	1	173	157	69	127	0	3.85
Mike Gardiner	R	25	9	10	.474	0	22	22	0	130	140	47	91	0	4.85
Tom Bolton (XJ)	L	29	8	9	.471	0	25	19	0	110	136	51	64	0	5.24
Dennis Lamp	R	38	6	3	.667	0	51	0	0	92	100	31	57	0	4.70
Kevin Morton	L	22	6	5	.545	0	16	15	1	86	93	40	45	0	4.59
Tony Fossas	L	33	3	2	.600	1	64	0	0	57	49	28	29	0	3.47
Danny Darwin (SJ)	R	35	3	6	.333	0	12	12	0	68	71	15	42	0	5.16
Matt Young (SJ)	L	32	3	7	.300	0	19	16	0	89	92	53	69	0	5.18
Jeff Gray (IL)	R	28	2	3	.400	1	50	0	0	62	39	10	41	0	2.34
Dana Kiecker (EJ)	R	30	2	3	.400	0	18	5	0	40	56	23	21	0	7.36
Jeff Reardon	R	35	1	4	.200	40	57	0	0	59	54	16	44	0	3.03
3 Dan Petry	R	32	0	0	—	0	13	0	0	22	21	12	12	0	4.43
Daryl Irvine (SJ)	R	26	0	0	—	0	9	0	0	18	25	9	8	0	6.00
Jeff Plympton	R	25	0	0	—	0	4	0	0	5	4	2	0	0	0.00
John Dopson (EJ)	R	27	0	0	—	0	1	1	0	4	4	1	1	0	18.00
Josias Manzanillo	R	23	0	1	.000	0	1	0	0	2	2	1	3	0	18.00
Steve Lyons	R	31	0	0	—	0	1	0	0	1	0	0	1	0	0.00

DETROIT (TIE) 2nd 84-78 .519 7 SPARKY ANDERSON

Name	G by Pos	B	AGE	G	AB	R	H	2B	3B	HR	RBI	BB	SO	SB	BA	SA
TOTALS			30	162	5547	817	1372	259	26	209	778	699	1185	109	.247	.416
Cecil Fielder	1B122 DH42	R	27	162	624	102	163	25	0	44	133	78	151	0	.261	.513
Lou Whitaker	2B135 DH3	L	34	138	470	94	131	26	2	23	78	90	45	4	.279	.489
Alan Trammell (NJ)	SS92 DH6	R	33	101	375	57	93	20	0	9	55	37	39	11	.248	.373
Travis Fryman	3B86 SS71	R	22	149	557	65	144	36	3	21	91	40	149	12	.259	.447
Rob Deer	OF132 DH2	R	30	134	448	64	80	14	2	25	64	89	175	1	.179	.386
Milt Cuyler	OF151	B	22	154	475	77	122	15	7	3	33	52	92	41	.257	.337
Lloyd Moseby	OF64 DH7	L	31	74	260	37	68	15	1	6	35	21	43	8	.262	.396
Mickey Tettleton	C125 DH24 OF3 1B1	B	30	154	501	85	132	17	2	31	89	101	131	3	.263	.491
Pete Incaviglia	OF54 DH41	R	27	97	337	38	72	12	1	11	38	36	92	1	.214	.353
Tony Phillips	OF56 3B46 2B36 DH18 SS13	B	32	146	564	87	160	28	4	17	72	79	95	10	.284	.438
Dave Bergman	1B49 DH13 OF4	L	38	86	194	23	46	10	1	7	29	35	40	1	.237	.407
Skeeter Barnes	OF33 3B17 1B9 2B7 DH3	R	34	75	159	28	46	13	2	5	17	9	24	10	.289	.491
Andy Allanson	C56 1B2 DH1	R	29	60	151	10	35	10	0	1	16	7	31	0	.232	.318
John Shelby	OF47 DH4	B	33	53	143	19	22	8	1	3	8	8	23	0	.154	.287
Scott Livingstone	3B43	L	25	44	127	19	37	5	0	2	11	10	25	2	.291	.378
Mark Salas	C11 DH8 1B5	L	30	33	57	2	5	1	0	1	7	0	10	0	.088	.158
Luis de los Santos	DH9 OF3 1B2 3B2	R	24	16	30	1	5	2	0	0	2	4	0	0	.167	.233
Johnny Paredes	2B7 DH2 3B1 SS1	R	28	16	18	4	6	0	0	0	0	1	1	1	.333	.333
John Moses	OF12	B	33	13	21	5	1	1	0	0	1	2	7	4	.048	.095
Shawn Hare	OF6 DH2	L	24	9	19	0	1	1	0	0	0	2	1	0	.053	.105
Tony Bernazard	2B2 DH2	B	34	6	12	0	2	0	0	0	0	0	4	0	.167	.167
Rich Rowland	C2 DH1	R	27	4	4	0	1	0	0	0	1	1	2	0	.250	.250

NAME	T	AGE	W	L	PCT	SV	G	GS	CG	IP	H	BB	SO	SHO	ERA
		31	84	78	.519	38	162	162	18	1450	1570	593	739	8	4.51
Bill Gullickson	R	32	20	9	.690	0	35	35	4	226	256	44	91	0	3.90
Frank Tanana	L	37	13	12	.520	0	33	33	3	217	217	78	107	2	3.77
Walt Terrell	R	33	12	14	.462	0	35	33	8	219	257	79	80	2	4.24
Mike Henneman (SJ)	R	29	10	2	.833	21	60	0	0	84	81	34	61	0	2.88
Mark Leiter	R	28	9	7	.563	1	38	15	1	135	125	50	103	0	4.21
Paul Gibson	L	31	5	7	.417	8	68	0	0	96	112	48	52	0	4.59
Jerry Don Gleaton(SJ)	L	33	3	2	.600	2	47	0	0	75	74	39	47	0	4.06
John Cerutti	L	31	3	6	.333	2	38	8	1	89	94	37	29	0	4.57
Rusty Meacham	R	23	2	1	.667	0	10	4	0	28	35	11	14	0	5.20
1 Dan Petry	R	32	2	3	.400	0	17	6	0	55	66	19	18	0	4.94
Scott Aldred	L	23	2	4	.333	0	11	11	1	57	58	30	35	0	5.18
Dave Haas	R	25	1	0	1.000	0	11	0	0	11	8	12	6	0	6.75
1 Steve Searcy	L	27	1	2	.333	0	16	5	0	41	52	30	32	0	8.41
Dan Gakeler	R	27	1	4	.200	2	31	7	0	74	73	39	43	0	5.74
Mike Munoz	L	25	0	0	—	0	6	0	0	9	14	5	3	0	9.64
Mike Dalton	L	28	0	0	—	0	4	0	0	8	12	2	4	0	3.38
Jeff Kaiser	L	30	0	1	.000	2	10	0	0	5	6	5	4	0	9.00
John Kiely	R	26	0	1	.000	0	7	0	0	7	13	9	1	0	14.85
Kevin Ritz	R	26	0	3	.000	0	11	5	0	15	17	22	9	0	11.74

MILWAUKEE 4th 83-79 .512 8 TOM TREBELHORN

Name	G by Pos	B	AGE	G	AB	R	H	2B	3B	HR	RBI	BB	SO	SB	BA	SA
TOTALS			29	162	5611	799	1523	247	53	116	750	556	802	106	.271	.396
Franklin Stubbs	1B92 OF4 DH4	L	30	103	362	48	77	16	2	11	38	35	71	13	.213	.359
Willie Randolph	2B149 DH2	R	36	124	431	60	141	14	3	0	54	75	38	4	.327	.414
Bill Spiers	SS128 DH2 OF1	L	25	133	414	71	117	13	6	8	54	34	55	14	.283	.401
Jim Gantner	3B90 2B59	L	38	140	526	63	149	27	4	2	47	27	34	4	.283	.361
Dante Bichette	OF127 3B1	R	27	134	445	53	106	18	3	15	59	22	107	14	.238	.393
Robin Yount	OF117 DH13	R	35	130	503	66	131	20	4	10	77	54	79	6	.260	.376
Greg Vaughn	OF135 DH10	R	25	145	542	81	132	24	5	27	98	62	125	2	.244	.456
B. J. Surhoff	C127 DH6 3B5 OF2 2B1	L	26	143	505	57	146	19	4	5	68	26	33	5	.289	.372
Paul Molitor	DH112 1B46	R	34	158	665	133	216	32	13	17	75	77	62	19	.325	.489
Darryl Hamilton	OF117	L	26	122	405	64	126	15	6	1	57	33	38	16	.311	.385
Dale Sveum	SS51 3B38 DH3 2B2	B	27	90	266	33	64	19	1	4	43	32	78	2	.241	.365
Rick Dempsey	C56 1B1 P1	R	41	61	147	15	34	5	0	4	21	23	20	0	.231	.347
Gary Sheffield (WJ)	3B43 DH5	R	22	50	175	25	34	12	2	2	22	19	15	5	.194	.320
1 Candy Maldonado (BF)	OF24 DH9	R	30	34	111	11	23	6	0	5	20	13	23	1	.207	.396
Greg Brock	1B25	L	34	31	60	9	17	4	0	1	6	14	9	1	.283	.400
George Canale	1B19	L	25	21	34	6	6	2	0	3	10	8	6	0	.176	.500
Jim Olander	OF9 DH3	R	28	12	9	2	0	0	0	0	0	0	3	0	.000	.000
Tim McIntosh	OF4 DH2 1B1	R	26	7	11	2	4	1	0	1	1	0	4	0	.364	.727
Matias Carrillo	OF3	L	28	3	0	0	0	0	0	0	0	0	0	0		

NAME	T	AGE	W	L	PCT	SV	G	GS	CG	IP	H	BB	SO	SHO	ERA
		27	83	79	.512	41	162	162	23	1464	1498	527	859	11	4.14
Bill Wegman	R	28	15	7	.682	0	28	28	7	193	176	40	89	2	2.84
Jaime Navarro	R	24	15	12	.556	0	34	34	10	234	237	73	114	2	3.92
Chris Bosio	R	28	14	10	.583	0	32	32	5	205	187	58	117	1	3.25
Don August	R	27	9	8	.529	0	28	23	1	138	166	47	62	1	5.47
Chuck Crim	R	29	8	5	.615	3	66	0	0	91	115	25	39	0	4.63
Teddy Higuera (SJ)	L	32	3	2	.600	0	7	6	0	36	37	10	33	0	4.46
Julio Machado	R	25	3	3	.500	3	54	0	0	89	65	55	98	0	3.45
Cal Eldred	R	23	2	0	1.000	0	3	3	0	16	20	6	10	0	4.50
Doug Henry	R	27	2	1	.667	15	32	0	0	36	16	14	28	0	1.00
Edwin Nunez (XJ)	R	28	2	1	.667	8	23	0	0	25	28	13	24	0	6.04
Mike Ignasiak (LJ)	R	25	2	1	.667	0	4	1	0	13	7	8	10	0	5.68
Kevin Brown	L	26	2	4	.333	0	15	10	0	64	66	34	30	0	5.51
Mark Lee	L	26	2	5	.286	1	62	0	0	68	72	31	43	0	3.86
Dan Plesac	L	29	2	7	.222	8	45	10	0	92	92	39	61	0	4.29
Mark Knudson (SJ)	R	30	1	3	.250	0	12	7	0	35	54	15	23	0	7.97
Darren Holmes	R	25	1	4	.200	3	40	0	0	76	90	27	59	0	4.72
Jim Austin (EJ)	R	27	0	0	—	0	9	0	0	9	8	11	3	0	8.31
Chris George	R	24	0	0	—	0	2	0	0	3	3	1	0	0	3.00
Rick Dempsey	R	41	0	0	—	0	1	0	0	2	3	2	0	0	4.50
Ron Robinson (EJ)	R	29	0	1	.000	0	1	1	0	4	6	3	0	0	6.23
Jim Hunter	R	27	0	5	.000	0	8	6	0	31	45	17	14	0	7.26

NEW YORK 5th 71-91 .438 20 STUMP MERRILL

Name	G by Pos	B	AGE	G	AB	R	H	2B	3B	HR	RBI	BB	SO	SB	BA	SA
TOTALS			27	162	5541	674	1418	249	19	147	630	473	861	109	.256	.387
Don Mattingly	1B127 DH22	L	30	152	587	64	169	35	0	9	68	46	42	2	.288	.394
Steve Sax	2B149 3B54 DH4	R	31	158	652	85	198	38	2	10	56	41	38	31	.304	.414
Alvaro Espinoza	SS147 3B2 P1	R	29	148	480	51	123	23	2	5	33	16	57	4	.256	.344
Pat Kelly	3B80 2B19	R	23	96	298	35	72	12	4	3	23	15	52	12	.242	.339
Jesse Barfield (NJ)	OF81	R	31	84	284	37	64	12	0	17	48	36	80	1	.225	.447
Roberto Kelly (WJ)	OF125	R	26	126	486	68	130	22	2	20	69	45	77	32	.267	.444
Mel Hall	OF120 DH10	L	30	141	492	67	140	23	2	19	80	26	40	0	.285	.455
Matt Nokes	C130 DH3	L	27	135	456	52	122	20	0	24	77	25	49	3	.268	.469
Kevin Maas	DH109 1B36	L	26	148	500	69	110	14	1	23	63	83	128	5	.220	.390
Hensley Meulens	OF73 DH13 1B7	R	24	96	288	37	64	8	1	6	29	18	97	3	.222	.319
Bernie Williams	OF85	B	22	85	320	43	76	19	4	3	34	48	57	10	.238	.350
Randy Velarde	3B50 SS31 OF2	R	28	80	184	19	45	11	1	1	15	18	43	3	.245	.332
Bob Geren	C63	R	29	64	128	7	28	3	0	2	12	9	31	0	.219	.289
Pat Sheridan	OF34 DH2	L	33	62	113	13	23	3	0	4	7	13	30	1	.204	.336
Jim Leyritz	3B18 C5 1B3 DH1	R	27	32	77	8	14	3	0	0	4	13	15	0	.182	.221
Mike Humphreys	OF9 DH7 3B6	R	24	25	40	9	8	0	0	3	9	7	2	2	.200	.300
Torey Lovullo	3B22	B	25	22	51	0	9	2	0	0	2	5	7	0	.176	.216
Carlos Rodriguez	SS11 3B3	B	23	15	37	1	7	0	0	0	1	4	3	0	.189	.189
Mike Blowers	3B14	R	26	15	35	3	7	0	0	1	1	4	5	0	.200	.286
Scott Lusader (MJ)	OF4 DH1	L	26	11	7	2	1	0	0	0	0	1	3	0	.143	.143
John Ramos	C5 DH4	R	25	10	26	4	8	1	0	0	3	1	3	0	.308	.346

NAME	T	AGE	W	L	PCT	SV	G	GS	CG	IP	H	BB	SO	SHO	ERA
		29	71	91	.438	37	162	162	3	1444	1510	506	936	11	4.42
Scott Sanderson	R	34	16	10	.615	0	34	34	2	208	200	29	130	2	3.81
Greg Cadaret	L	29	8	6	.571	3	68	5	0	122	110	59	105	0	3.62
Wade Taylor	R	25	7	12	.368	0	23	22	0	116	144	53	72	0	6.27
Jeff Johnson	L	24	6	11	.353	0	23	23	0	127	156	33	62	0	5.95
Steve Farr	R	34	5	5	.500	23	60	0	0	70	57	20	60	0	2.19
John Habyan	R	27	4	2	.667	2	66	0	0	90	73	20	70	0	2.30
Scott Kamieniecki (XJ)	R	27	4	4	.500	0	9	9	0	55	54	22	34	0	3.90
Tim Leary	R	32	4	10	.286	0	28	18	1	121	150	57	83	0	6.49
Steve Howe (EJ)	L	33	3	1	.750	3	37	0	0	48	39	7	34	0	1.68
Rich Monteleone	R	28	3	1	.750	0	26	0	0	47	42	19	34	0	3.64
Lee Guetterman	L	32	3	4	.429	6	64	0	0	88	91	25	35	0	3.68
Pascual Perez (SJ)	R	34	2	4	.333	0	14	14	0	74	68	24	41	0	3.18
Eric Plunk	R	27	2	5	.286	0	43	8	0	112	128	62	103	0	4.76
Dave Eiland (FJ)	R	24	2	5	.286	0	18	13	0	73	87	23	18	0	5.33
Alan Mills	R	24	1	1	.500	0	6	2	0	16	16	8	11	0	4.41
Chuck Cary	L	31	1	6	.143	0	10	9	0	53	61	32	34	0	5.91
Alvaro Espinoza	R	29	0	0	—	0	1	0	0	1	0	0	0	0	0.00
Darrin Chapin	R	25	0	1	.000	0	3	0	0	5	3	6	5	0	5.06
Mike Witt (EJ)	R	31	0	1	.000	2	2	1	0	5	8	1	0	0	10.13
1 Andy Hawkins	R	31	0	2	.000	0	4	3	0	13	23	6	5	0	9.95

BALTIMORE 6th 67-95 .414 24 FRANK ROBINSON 13-24 .351 JOHNNY OATES 54-71 .432

Name	G by Pos	B	AGE	G	AB	R	H	2B	3B	HR	RBI	BB	SO	SB	BA	SA
TOTALS			28	162	5604	686	1421	256	29	170	660	528	974	50	.254	.401
Glenn Davis (ZJ)	1B36 DH12	R	30	49	176	29	40	9	1	10	28	16	29	4	.227	.460
Billy Ripken (VJ)	2B103	R	26	104	287	24	62	11	1	0	14	15	31	0	.216	.261
Cal Ripken	SS162	R	30	162	650	99	210	46	5	34	114	53	46	6	.323	.566
Leo Gomez	3B105 DH10 1B3	R	24	118	391	40	91	17	2	16	45	40	82	1	.233	.409
Dwight Evans (LJ)	OF67 DH21	R	39	101	270	35	73	9	1	6	38	54	54	2	.270	.376
Mike Devereaux	OF149	R	28	149	608	82	158	27	10	19	59	47	115	16	.260	.431
Joe Orsulak	OF132 DH2	L	29	143	486	57	135	22	1	5	43	28	45	6	.278	.358
Chris Hoiles	C89 DH13 1B8	R	26	107	341	36	83	15	0	11	31	29	61	0	.243	.384
Sam Horn	DH102	L	27	121	317	45	74	16	0	23	61	41	99	0	.233	.502
Randy Milligan	1B106 DH25 OF9	R	29	141	483	57	127	17	2	16	70	84	108	0	.263	.406
Brady Anderson	OF101 DH3	L	27	113	256	40	59	12	3	2	27	38	44	12	.230	.324
Juan Bell	2B77 SS15 DH4 OF1	B	23	100	209	26	36	9	2	1	15	8	51	0	.172	.249
David Segui	1B42 OF33 DH4	B	24	86	212	15	59	7	0	2	22	12	19	1	.278	.340
Bob Melvin	C72 DH4	R	29	79	228	11	57	10	0	1	23	11	46	0	.250	.307
Tim Hulett	3B39 2B26 DH15 SS1	R	31	79	206	29	42	9	0	7	18	13	49	0	.204	.350
Chito Martinez	OF54 DH4 1B1	L	25	67	216	32	58	12	1	13	33	11	51	1	.269	.514
Ernie Whitt	C20 DH2	L	39	35	62	5	15	2	0	3	8	12	22	0	.242	.274
Craig Worthington (LJ)	3B30	R	26	31	102	11	23	7	0	4	12	12	14	0	.225	.373
Luis Mercedes	OF15 DH1	R	23	19	54	10	11	2	0	0	4	4	6	2	.204	.241
Jeff McKnight (WJ)	OF7 DH4 1B2	L	28	16	41	2	7	1	0	1	5	2	7	1	.171	.195
Jeff Tackett	C6	R	25	6	8	1	1	0	0	0	0	0	6	0	.125	.125
Shane Turner	2B1 DH1	L	28	4	1	0	0	0	0	0	0	0	0	0	.000	.000

NAME	T	AGE	W	L	PCT	SV	G	GS	CG	IP	H	BB	SO	SHO	ERA
		29	67	95	.414	42	162	162	8	1458	1534	504	868	8	4.59
Bob Milacki	R	26	10	9	.526	0	31	26	3	184	175	53	108	1	4.01
Todd Frohwirth	R	28	7	3	.700	3	51	0	0	96	64	29	77	0	1.87
Ben McDonald (EJ)	R	23	6	8	.429	0	21	21	1	126	126	43	85	0	4.84
Jose Mesa	R	25	6	11	.353	0	23	23	2	124	151	62	64	1	5.97
Jeff Ballard	L	27	6	12	.333	0	26	22	0	124	153	28	37	0	5.60
Roy Smith	R	29	4	5	.556	0	17	14	0	80	99	24	25	0	5.60
Mark Williamson	R	31	5	5	.500	4	65	0	0	80	87	35	53	0	4.48
Mike Mussina	R	22	4	5	.444	0	12	12	2	88	77	21	52	0	2.87
Gregg Olson	R	24	4	6	.400	31	72	0	0	74	74	29	72	0	3.18
Dave Johnson (GJ)	R	31	4	8	.333	0	22	14	0	84	127	24	38	0	7.07
Jeff Robinson	R	29	4	9	.308	0	21	19	0	104	119	51	65	0	5.18
2 Jim Poole	L	25	3	2	.600	0	24	0	0	36	19	9	34	0	2.00
Mike Flanagan	L	39	2	7	.222	3	64	1	0	98	84	25	55	0	2.38
Kevin Hickey	L	34	1	0	1.000	0	9	0	0	14	15	6	10	0	9.00
Anthony Telford	R	25	0	0	—	0	9	1	0	27	27	6	24	0	4.05
Stacy Jones	R	24	0	0	—	0	2	0	0	4	6	2	1	0	4.50
Francisco de la Rosa	B	25	0	0	—	0	4	0	0	6	2	1	0	0	1.50
Jose Bautista	R	25	0	0	—	0	1	0	0	1	0	0	0	0	0.00
Jose Bautista	R	27	0	0	—	0	1	0	0	1	3	0	0	0	16.88
Paul Kilgus	L	29	0	0	—	1	38	0	0	62	60	24	32	0	5.08
Arthur Rhodes	L	21	0	3	.000	0	8	8	0	36	47	23	23	0	8.00
Brian DuBois (SJ) 24															

CLEVELAND   7th 57-105 .352 34   JOHN McNAMARA 25-52 .325   MIKE HARGROVE 32-53 .376

#	Name	G by Pos	B	AGE	G	AB	R	H	2B	3B	HR	RBI	BB	SO	SB	BA	SA
	TOTALS			26	162	5470	576	1390	236	26	79	546	449	888	84	.254	.350
1	Brook Jacoby	1B55 3B15	R	31	66	231	14	54	9	1	4	24	16	32	0	.234	.333
	Mark Lewis	2B50 SS36	R	21	84	314	29	83	15	1	5	30	15	45	2	.264	.318
	Felix Fermin	SS129	R	27	129	424	30	111	13	2	0	31	26	27	5	.262	.302
	Carlos Baerga	3B89 2B75 SS2	B	22	158	593	80	171	28	2	11	69	48	74	3	.288	.398
2	Mark Whiten (XJ)	OF67 DH3	B	24	70	258	34	66	14	4	7	26	19	50	4	.256	.388
	Alex Cole	OF107 DH6	L	25	122	387	58	114	17	3	0	21	58	47	27	.295	.354
	Albert Belle	OF89 DH32	R	24	123	461	60	130	31	2	28	95	25	99	3	.282	.540
	Sandy Alomar (SJ-PJ)	C46 DH4	R	25	51	184	10	40	9	0	0	7	8	24	0	.217	.266
	Chris James (SJ)	DH60 OF39 1B15	R	28	115	437	31	104	16	2	5	41	18	61	3	.238	.318
	Jerry Browne	2B47 OF17 3B15 DH7	B	25	107	290	28	66	5	2	1	29	27	29	2	.228	.269
	Joel Skinner	C99	R	30	99	284	23	69	14	0	1	24	14	67	0	.243	.303
2	Mike Aldrete	1B47 OF16 DH7	L	30	85	183	22	48	6	1	1	19	36	37	1	.262	.322
	Carlos Martinez	DH41 1B31	R	25	72	257	22	73	14	0	5	30	10	43	3	.284	.397
1	Mike Huff	OF48 2B2	R	27	51	146	28	35	6	1	2	10	25	30	11	.240	.336
	Beau Allred	OF42 DH1	L	26	48	125	17	29	3	0	3	12	25	35	2	.232	.328
	Jeff Manto	3B32 1B14 C5 OF1	R	26	47	128	15	27	7	0	2	13	14	22	1	.211	.313
1	Turner Ward	OF42 DH1	L	26	40	100	11	23	7	0	0	5	10	16	0	.230	.300
2	Glenallen Hill	OF33 DH1	R	26	37	122	15	32	3	0	5	14	16	30	1	.262	.410
	Luis Lopez	C12 1B10 DH6 OF1 3B1	R	26	35	82	7	18	4	1	0	7	4	7	0	.220	.293
2	Jose Gonzalez	OF32	R	26	33	69	10	11	2	1	1	4	11	27	5	.159	.261
	Jim Thome	3B27	L	20	27	98	7	25	4	2	1	9	5	16	1	.255	.367
2	Reggie Jefferson	1B26	B	22	26	101	10	20	3	0	2	12	3	22	0	.198	.287
	Eddie Taubensee	C25	L	22	26	66	5	16	2	1	0	8	5	16	0	.242	.303
	Wayne Kirby	OF21	L	27	21	43	4	9	2	0	0	5	2	6	1	.209	.256
2	Tony Perezchica	SS6 3B3 2B2 DH1	R	25	17	22	4	8	2	0	0	3	3	9	2	.364	.455
1	Mitch Webster	OF10	B	32	13	32	4	4	0	0	0	0	3	9	2	.125	.125
	Jose Escobar	SS5 2B4 3B1	R	30	10	15	0	3	0	0	0	1	0	4	0	.200	.200
	Luis Medina	DH5	R	28	5	16	0	1	0	0	0	0	1	3	0	.063	.063
	Ever Magallanes	SS2	B	25	3	2	0	0	0	0	0	0	1	1	0	.000	.000
	Keith Hernandez (XJ) 37																

#	NAME	T	AGE	W	L	PCT	SV	G	GS	CG	IP	H	BB	SO	SHO	ERA
			28	57	105	.352	33	162	162	22	1441	1551	441	862	8	4.23
	Charles Nagy	R	24	10	15	.400	0	33	33	6	211	228	66	109	1	4.13
	Greg Swindell	L	26	9	16	.360	0	33	33	7	238	241	31	169	0	3.48
1	Tom Candiotti	R	33	7	6	.538	0	15	15	3	108	88	28	86	0	2.24
	Eric King (SJ)	R	27	6	11	.353	0	25	24	2	151	166	44	59	1	4.60
	Eric Bell	L	27	4	0	1.000	0	10	0	0	18	5	5	7	0	0.50
	Doug Jones	R	34	4	8	.333	7	36	4	0	63	87	17	48	0	5.54
	Shawn Hillegas	R	26	3	4	.429	7	51	3	0	83	67	46	66	0	4.34
	Steve Olin	R	25	3	6	.333	17	48	0	0	56	61	23	38	0	3.36
	Jesse Orosco	L	34	2	0	1.000	0	47	0	0	46	52	15	36	0	3.74
	Willie Blair	R	25	2	3	.400	0	11	5	0	36	58	10	13	0	6.75
	Dave Otto	L	26	2	8	.200	0	18	14	1	100	108	27	47	0	4.23
	Rod Nichols	R	26	2	11	.154	1	31	16	3	137	145	30	76	1	3.54
	Sergio Valdez	R	26	1	1	.500	0	6	0	0	16	15	5	11	0	5.51
	Mike York (EJ)	R	26	1	4	.200	0	14	4	0	35	45	19	19	0	6.75
2	Denis Boucher	L	23	1	4	.200	0	5	5	0	23	35	8	13	0	8.34
	Efrain Valdez	L	24	0	0	—	0	7	0	0	5	3	1	1	0	1.50
	Garland Kiser	L	22	0	0	—	0	7	0	0	5	7	4	3	0	9.64
	Bruce Egloff	R	26	0	0	—	0	6	0	0	6	8	4	4	0	4.76
	Rudy Seanez	R	22	0	0	—	0	5	0	0	5	10	7	7	0	16.20
	Tommy Kramer	R	23	0	0	—	0	4	0	0	5	8	5	3	0	17.36
	Mauro Gozzo	R	25	0	0	—	0	3	0	0	6	9	3	0	0	19.29
	Mike Walker	R	24	0	1	.000	0	3	0	0	7	11	6	2	0	2.08
	Jeff Mutis	L	24	0	3	.000	0	3	3	0	12	23	7	6	0	11.68
	Jeff Shaw	R	24	0	5	.000	1	29	1	0	72	72	27	31	0	3.36
	John Farrell (EJ) 28																

WEST DIVISION

MINNESOTA   1st 95-67 .586   TOM KELLY

#	Name	G by Pos	B	AGE	G	AB	R	H	2B	3B	HR	RBI	BB	SO	SB	BA	SA
	TOTALS			29	162	5556	776	1557	270	42	140	733	526	747	107	.280	.420
	Kent Hrbek	1B128	L	31	132	462	72	131	20	1	20	89	67	48	4	.284	.461
	Chuck Knoblauch	2B148 SS2	R	22	151	565	78	159	24	6	1	50	59	40	25	.281	.350
	Greg Gagne	SS137 DH1	R	29	139	408	52	108	23	3	8	42	26	72	11	.265	.395
	Mike Pagliarulo	3B118 2B1	L	31	121	365	38	102	20	0	6	36	21	55	1	.279	.384
	Shane Mack	OF140 DH1	R	27	143	442	79	137	27	8	18	74	34	79	13	.310	.529
	Kirby Puckett	OF152	R	31	152	611	92	195	29	6	15	89	31	78	11	.319	.460
	Dan Gladden	OF126	R	33	126	461	65	114	14	9	6	52	36	60	15	.247	.356
	Brian Harper	C119 DH2 1B1 OF1	R	31	123	441	54	137	28	1	10	69	14	22	1	.311	.447
	Chili Davis	DH150 OF2	B	31	153	534	84	148	34	1	29	93	95	117	5	.277	.507
	Al Newman	SS55 2B35 3B35 DH3 OF1 1B1	B	31	118	246	25	47	5	0	0	19	23	21	4	.191	.211
	Scott Leius	3B79 SS19 OF2	R	25	109	199	35	57	7	2	5	20	30	35	5	.286	.417
	Gene Larkin	OF47 1B39 DH4 3B1	B	28	98	255	34	73	14	1	2	19	30	21	2	.286	.373
	Randy Bush	OF38 1B12 DH10	L	32	93	165	21	50	10	1	6	23	24	25	0	.303	.485
	Junior Ortiz	C60	R	31	61	134	19	28	5	1	0	11	15	12	0	.209	.261
	Pedro Munoz	OF44 DH2	R	22	51	138	15	39	7	1	7	26	9	31	3	.283	.500
	Jarvis Brown	OF32 DH4	R	24	38	37	10	8	0	0	0	4	5	12	7	.216	.216
	Paul Sorrento	1B13 DH2	L	25	26	47	6	12	2	0	4	13	4	11	0	.255	.553
	Lenny Webster	C17	R	26	18	34	7	10	1	0	3	8	4	6	0	.294	.588
	Carmen Castillo	OF4 DH2	R	33	9	12	0	2	1	0	0	1	0	3	0	.167	.333

#	NAME	T	AGE	W	L	PCT	SV	G	GS	CG	IP	H	BB	SO	SHO	ERA
			28	95	67	.586	53	162	162	21	1449	1402	488	876	12	3.69
	Scott Erickson	R	23	20	8	.714	0	32	32	5	204	189	71	108	3	3.18
	Jack Morris	R	36	18	12	.600	0	35	35	10	247	226	92	163	2	3.43
	Kevin Tapani	R	27	16	9	.640	0	34	34	4	244	225	40	135	1	2.99
	Carl Willis	R	30	8	3	.727	2	40	0	0	89	76	19	53	0	2.63
	Mark Guthrie	L	25	7	5	.583	2	41	12	0	98	116	41	72	0	4.32
	Steve Bedrosian	R	33	5	3	.625	6	56	0	0	77	70	35	44	0	4.42
	Allan Anderson	L	26	5	11	.313	0	29	22	2	134	148	42	51	0	4.96
	David West (EJ)	L	26	4	4	.500	0	15	12	0	71	66	28	52	0	4.54
	Rick Aguilera	R	29	4	5	.444	42	63	0	0	69	44	30	61	0	2.35
	Paul Abbott	R	23	3	1	.750	0	15	3	0	47	38	36	43	0	4.75
	Tom Edens	R	30	2	2	.500	0	8	6	0	33	34	10	19	0	4.09
	Gary Wayne	L	28	1	0	1.000	0	8	0	0	12	11	4	7	0	5.11
	Willie Banks	R	22	1	1	.500	0	5	3	0	17	21	12	16	0	5.71
	Terry Leach	R	37	1	2	.333	0	50	0	0	67	82	14	32	0	3.61
	Larry Casian	L	25	0	0	—	0	15	0	0	18	28	7	6	0	7.36
	Denny Neagle	L	22	0	0	—	0	7	3	0	20	28	7	14	0	4.05

CHICAGO   2nd 87-75 .537 8   JEFF TORBORG

#	Name	G by Pos	B	AGE	G	AB	R	H	2B	3B	HR	RBI	BB	SO	SB	BA	SA
	TOTALS			28	162	5594	758	1464	226	39	139	722	610	896	134	.262	.391
	Dan Pasqua	1B83 OF59 DH8	L	29	134	417	71	108	22	5	18	66	62	86	0	.259	.465
	Scott Fletcher	2B86 3B4	R	32	90	248	14	51	10	1	1	28	17	26	0	.206	.266
	Ozzie Guillen	SS149	L	27	154	524	52	143	20	3	4	49	11	38	21	.273	.340
	Robin Ventura	3B151 1B31	L	23	157	606	92	172	25	1	23	100	80	67	2	.284	.442
	Sammy Sosa	OF111 DH2	R	22	116	316	39	64	10	1	10	33	14	98	13	.203	.335
	Lance Johnson	OF157	L	27	159	588	72	161	14	**13**	0	49	26	58	26	.274	.342
	Tim Raines	OF133 DH19	B	31	155	609	102	163	20	6	5	50	83	68	51	.268	.345
	Carlton Fisk	C106 DH13 1B12	R	43	134	460	42	111	25	0	18	74	32	86	1	.241	.413
	Frank Thomas	DH101 1B56	R	23	158	559	104	178	31	2	32	109	**138**	112	1	.318	.553
	Craig Grebeck	3B49 2B36 SS26	R	26	107	224	37	63	16	3	6	31	38	40	1	.281	.460
	Joey Cora	2B80 SS5 DH2 3B2	B	26	100	228	37	55	2	3	0	18	20	21	11	.241	.276
	Matt Merullo	C27 1B16 DH6	L	25	80	140	8	32	1	0	5	21	9	18	0	.229	.343
	Ron Karkovice	C69 OF1	R	27	75	167	25	41	13	0	5	22	15	42	0	.246	.413
	Warren Newson	OF50 DH3	L	26	71	132	20	39	5	0	4	25	28	34	2	.295	.424
2	Mike Huff	OF48 2B2 DH2	R	27	51	97	14	26	4	1	1	15	12	18	3	.268	.361
1	Cory Snyder (PJ)	OF29 1B18 DH3	R	28	50	117	10	22	4	0	3	11	6	41	0	.188	.299
	Bo Jackson (PJ)	DH21	R	28	23	71	8	16	4	0	3	14	12	25	0	.225	.408
	Don Wakamatsu	C18	R	28	18	31	2	7	0	0	0	6	0	6	0	.226	.226
	Ron Kittle	1B15	R	33	17	47	7	9	2	0	4	7	5	9	0	.191	.319
	Rodney McCray	OF8 DH6	R	27	17	7	2	2	0	0	0	0	1	3	1	.286	.286
	Esteban Beltre	SS8	R	23	9	6	0	1	0	0	0	1	1	1	0	.167	.167

#	NAME	T	AGE	W	L	PCT	SV	G	GS	CG	IP	H	BB	SO	SHO	ERA
			26	87	75	.537	40	162	162	28	1478	1302	601	923	8	3.79
	Jack McDowell	R	25	17	10	.630	0	35	35	15	254	212	82	191	3	3.41
	Greg Hibbard	L	26	11	11	.500	0	32	29	5	194	196	57	71	0	4.31
	Charlie Hough	R	43	9	10	.474	0	31	29	4	199	167	94	107	1	4.02
	Alex Fernandez	R	21	9	13	.391	0	34	32	2	192	186	88	145	0	4.51
	Melido Perez	R	25	8	7	.533	1	49	8	0	136	111	52	128	0	3.12
	Donn Pall	R	29	7	2	.778	0	51	0	0	71	59	20	40	0	2.41
	Bobby Thigpen	R	27	7	5	.583	30	67	0	0	70	63	38	47	0	3.49
	Scott Radinsky	L	23	5	5	.500	8	67	0	0	71	53	23	49	0	2.02
	Ramon Garcia	R	21	4	4	.500	0	16	15	0	78	79	31	40	0	5.40
	Ken Patterson	L	26	3	0	1.000	1	43	0	0	64	48	35	32	0	2.83
	Brian Drahman	R	24	3	2	.600	0	28	0	0	31	21	13	18	0	3.23
	Wilson Alvarez	L	21	3	2	.600	0	10	9	2	56	47	29	32	1	3.51
	Roberto Hernandez	R	26	1	0	1.000	0	9	3	0	15	18	7	6	0	7.80
	Tom Drees	L	28	0	0	—	0	7	0	0	10	6	2	2	0	12.27
	Steve Wapnick	R	25	0	0	—	0	5	0	0	6	7	6	3	0	1.80
	Jeff Carter	R	25	0	0	—	0	13	0	0	23	22	17	12	0	5.25
	Wayne Edwards	L	27	0	0	—	0	13	0	0	23	22	17	12	0	3.86

TEXAS   3rd 85-77 .525 10   BOBBY VALENTINE

#	Name	G by Pos	B	AGE	G	AB	R	H	2B	3B	HR	RBI	BB	SO	SB	BA	SA
	TOTALS			28	162	5703	829	1539	288	31	177	774	596	1039	102	.270	.424
	Rafael Palmeiro	1B157 DH2	L	26	159	631	115	203	49	3	26	88	68	72	4	.322	.532
	Julio Franco	2B146	R	32	146	589	108	201	27	3	15	78	65	78	36	.341	.474
	Jeff Huson	SS116 2B2 3B1	L	26	119	268	36	57	8	3	2	26	39	32	8	.213	.287
1	Steve Buechele	3B111 2B13 SS4	R	29	121	416	58	111	17	2	18	66	39	69	0	.267	.447
	Ruben Sierra	OF161	R	25	161	661	110	203	44	5	25	116	56	91	16	.307	.502
	Juan Gonzalez	OF136 DH4	R	21	142	545	78	144	34	1	27	102	42	118	4	.264	.479
	Kevin Reimer	OF66 DH56	L	27	136	394	46	106	22	0	20	69	33	93	0	.269	.477
	Ivan Rodriguez	C88	R	19	88	280	24	74	16	0	3	27	5	42	0	.264	.354
	Brian Downing	DH109	R	40	123	407	76	113	17	2	17	49	58	70	1	.278	.455
	Gary Pettis	OF126 DH3	B	33	137	282	37	61	7	5	0	19	54	91	29	.216	.277
	Mario Diaz	SS65 2B20 3B8 DH1	R	29	96	182	24	48	7	0	1	22	15	18	0	.264	.319
	Mike Stanley	C58 1B12 3B6 DH6 OF1	R	31	95	181	25	45	13	1	3	25	34	44	0	.249	.381
	Geno Petralli (XJ)	C66 3B7 DH5	B	31	99	199	21	54	8	1	2	20	25	23	0	.271	.352
	Dean Palmer	3B50 OF29 DH5	R	22	81	268	38	50	9	2	15	37	32	98	0	.187	.403
	Jack Daugherty (IL)	OF37 1B11 DH1	B	30	58	144	8	28	3	2	1	11	16	23	1	.194	.264
	Jose Hernandez	SS44 3B1	R	21	45	98	8	18	2	1	0	4	3	31	0	.184	.224
	Denny Walling	3B14 OF5	L	37	24	44	1	4	1	0	0	3	6	8	0	.091	.114
	John Russell (EJ)	OF8 C15 DH5	R	30	22	71	8	16	4	0	3	10	6	27	0	.111	.111
	Monty Fariss	OF8 2B4 DH4	R	23	19	31	6	8	1	1	0	7	11	16	0	.258	.387
	Donald Harris	OF12 DH3	R	23	18	20	4	3	0	0	1	4	3	11	0	.375	.750
	Rob Maurer	1B4 DH2	L	24	13	16	0	1	0	0	0	4	6	6	0	.063	.063
	Gary Green (LJ)	SS8	R	29	12	20	4	3	0	0	0	3	0	4	0	.150	.200
	Tony Scruggs	OF5	R	25	5	5	1	1	0	0	0	0	0	3	0	.200	.200
	Chad Kreuter	C1	R	26	5	4	0	0	0	0	0	0	4	0	0	.000	.000
	Mike Parent (KJ)	C3	R	29	3	1	0	0	0	0	0	0	0	1	0	.000	.000
	Nick Capra	OF2	R	33	3	1	0	0	0	0	0	0	0	0	0	.000	.000
	Jeff Kunkel (KJ) 29																

#	NAME	T	AGE	W	L	PCT	SV	G	GS	CG	IP	H	BB	SO	SHO	ERA
			29	85	77	.525	41	162	162	9	1479	1486	662	1022	10	4.47
	Jose Guzman	R	28	13	7	.650	0	25	25	5	170	152	84	125	1	3.08
	Nolan Ryan	R	44	12	6	.667	0	27	27	2	173	102	72	203	2	2.91
	Kenny Rogers	L	26	10	10	.500	5	63	9	0	110	121	61	73	0	5.42
	Kevin Brown	R	26	9	12	.429	0	33	33	0	211	233	90	96	0	4.40
	Jeff Russell	R	29	6	4	.600	30	68	0	0	79	71	26	52	0	3.29
	Mike Jeffcoat	L	31	5	3	.625	1	70	0	0	80	104	25	43	0	4.63
	Gerald Alexander	R	23	5	3	.625	0	30	9	0	89	93	48	50	0	5.24
	Terry Mathews	R	26	4	0	1.000	1	34	0	0	54	18	11	51	0	3.61
	Goose Gossage (SJ)	R	39	4	2	.667	1	44	0	0	40	33	16	28	0	3.57
	Brian Bohanon (SJ)	L	22	4	3	.571	0	11	11	1	61	66	23	34	0	4.84
	John Barfield	R	26	4	4	.500	1	28	0	0	83	96	22	27	0	4.54
	Bobby Witt (SJ)	R	27	3	7	.300	0	17	16	1	89	84	74	82	1	6.09
2	Oil Can Boyd	R	31	2	7	.222	0	12	12	0	62	81	17	33	0	6.68
	Joe Bitker	R	27	1	0	1.000	0	9	0	0	16	7	6	5	0	1.13
	Barry Manuel	R	25	1	1	.500	0	8	0	0	16	7	6	5	0	5.25
	Scott Chiamparino (EJ)	R	24	1	0	1.000	0	3	3	0	22	25	7	8	0	4.03
	Wayne Rosenthal	R	26	1	4	.200	1	36	0	0	70	72	36	61	0	5.25
1	Jim Poole	L	25	0	0	—	0	5	0	0	6	6	6	6	0	4.50
2	Eric Nolte	L	27	0	0	—	0	5	0	0	12	9	7	8	0	3.38
	Brad Arnsberg (EJ)	R	27	0	1	.000	0	9	0	0	5	6	6	3	0	8.38
	Mark Petkovsek	R	25	0	1	.000	0	4	1	0	12	18	8	2	0	14.46
	Calvin Schiraldi	R	29	0	1	.000	0	19	0	0	25	34	15	15	0	11.57
2	Hector Fajardo	R	20	0	2	.000	0	4	1	0	15	15	4	6	0	5.68

OAKLAND 4th 84-78 .519 11 TONY LaRUSSA

Name	G by Pos	B	AGE	G	AB	R	H	2B	3B	HR	RBI	BB	SO	SB	BA	SA
TOTALS			30	162	5410	760	1342	246	19	159	716	642	981	151	.248	.389
Mark McGwire	1B152	R	27	154	483	62	97	22	0	22	75	93	116	2	.201	.383
Mike Gallego	2B135 SS55	R	30	159	482	67	119	15	4	12	49	67	84	6	.247	.369
Walt Weiss (NJ)	SS40	R	27	40	133	15	30	6	1	0	13	12	14	6	.226	.286
Ernest Riles	3B69 SS20 2B7 1B5	L	30	108	281	30	60	8	4	5	32	31	42	3	.214	.324
Jose Canseco	OF131 DH24	R	26	154	572	115	152	32	1	44	122	78	152	26	.266	.556
Dave Henderson	OF140 DH7 2B1	R	32	150	572	86	158	33	0	25	85	58	113	6	.276	.465
Rickey Henderson	OF119 DH10	R	32	134	470	105	126	17	1	18	57	98	73	58	.268	.423
Terry Steinbach	C117 1B9 DH2	R	29	129	456	50	125	31	1	6	67	22	70	2	.274	.386
Harold Baines	DH125 OF12	L	32	141	488	76	144	25	1	20	90	72	67	0	.295	.473
Willie Wilson	OF87 DH9	B	35	113	294	38	70	14	4	0	28	18	43	20	.238	.313
Mike Bordick	SS84 2B5 3B1	R	25	90	235	21	56	5	1	0	21	14	37	3	.238	.268
Lance Blankenship	2B45 OF28 3B14 DH6	R	27	90	185	33	46	8	0	3	21	23	42	12	.249	.341
Jamie Quirk	C54 1B8 3B1 DH1	L	36	76	203	16	53	4	0	1	17	16	28	0	.261	.296
Vance Law	3B67 SS3 OF3 1B1 DH1	R	34	74	134	11	28	7	1	0	9	18	27	0	.209	.276
2 Brook Jacoby	3B52 1B3	R	31	56	188	14	40	12	0	0	20	11	22	2	.213	.277
Scott Brosius	2B18 OF13 3B7 DH1	R	24	36	68	9	16	5	0	2	4	3	11	3	.235	.397
Brad Komminsk	OF22	R	30	24	25	1	3	1	0	0	2	2	9	1	.120	.160
Scott Hemond	C8 2B7 DH4 3B2 SS1	R	25	23	23	4	5	0	0	0	0	1	7	1	.217	.217
Dann Howitt	OF20 1B1	L	27	21	42	5	7	1	0	1	3	1	12	0	.167	.262
Ron Witmeyer	1B8	L	24	11	19	0	1	0	0	0	0	0	5	0	.053	.053
Fred Manrique	SS7 2B2	R	30	9	21	2	3	0	0	0	0	2	1	0	.143	.143
Doug Jennings	OF6	L	26	8	9	0	1	0	0	0	0	0	3	0	.111	.111
Carney Lansford (KJ)	3B4 DH1	R	34	5	16	0	1	0	0	0	1	0	2	0	.063	.063
Troy Afenir	C4 DH1	R	27	5	11	0	1	0	0	0	0	0	2	0	.091	.091

NAME	T	AGE	W	L	PCT	SV	G	GS	CG	IP	H	BB	SO	SHO	ERA
TOTALS		31	84	78	.519	49	162	162	11	1444	1425	655	892	10	4.57
Mike Moore	R	31	17	8	.680	0	33	33	3	210	176	105	153	1	2.96
Bob Welch	R	34	12	13	.480	0	35	35	7	220	220	91	101	1	4.58
Dave Stewart	R	34	11	11	.500	0	35	35	2	226	245	105	144	1	5.18
Joe Klink (BF)	L	29	10	3	.769	2	62	0	0	62	60	21	34	0	4.35
Dennis Eckersley	R	36	5	4	.556	43	67	0	0	76	60	9	87	0	2.96
Joe Slusarski	R	24	5	7	.417	0	20	19	1	109	121	52	60	0	5.27
Curt Young	L	31	4	2	.667	0	41	1	0	68	74	34	27	0	5.00
2 Andy Hawkins	R	31	4	4	.500	0	15	14	1	77	68	36	40	0	4.79
Kirk Dressendorfer (IL)	R	22	3	3	.500	0	7	7	0	35	33	21	17	0	5.45
3 Ron Darling	R	30	3	7	.300	0	12	12	0	75	64	38	60	0	4.08
Rick Honeycutt (SJ)	L	37	2	4	.333	0	43	0	0	38	37	20	26	0	3.58
Kevin Campbell	R	26	1	0	1.000	0	14	0	0	23	13	14	16	0	2.74
Bruce Walton	R	28	1	0	1.000	0	12	0	0	13	11	6	10	0	6.23
Todd Burns (SJ)	R	27	1	0	1.000	0	9	0	0	13	10	8	3	0	3.38
Johnny Guzman	L	20	1	0	1.000	0	5	0	0	5	1	4	1	0	9.00
Dana Allison	L	24	1	1	.500	0	11	0	0	11	16	5	4	0	7.36
Eric Show	R	35	1	2	.333	0	23	5	0	52	62	17	20	0	5.92
Steve Chitren	R	24	1	2	.200	4	56	0	0	60	59	32	47	0	4.33
Gene Nelson (BG)	R	30	1	5	.167	0	44	0	0	49	60	23	23	0	6.84
John Briscoe	R	23	0	0	—	0	11	0	0	14	12	10	9	0	7.07
Reggie Harris	R	22	0	0	—	0	2	0	0	3	3	4	1	0	12.00
Todd Van Poppel	R	19	0	0	—	0	1	1	0	5	7	2	6	0	9.64
Vance Law	R	34	0	0	—	0	1	0	0	1	1	1	0	0	0.00

SEATTLE 5th 83-79 .512 12 JIM LEFEBVRE

Name	G by Pos	B	AGE	G	AB	R	H	2B	3B	HR	RBI	BB	SO	SB	BA	SA
TOTALS			30	162	5494	702	1400	268	29	126	665	588	811	97	.255	.383
Pete O'Brien	1B132 DH18 OF13	L	33	152	560	58	139	29	3	17	88	44	61	0	.248	.402
Harold Reynolds	2B159 DH1	B	30	161	631	95	160	34	6	3	57	72	63	28	.254	.341
Omar Vizquel	SS138 2B1	B	24	142	426	42	98	16	4	1	41	45	37	7	.230	.293
Edgar Martinez	3B144 DH2	R	28	150	544	98	167	35	1	14	52	84	72	0	.307	.452
Jay Buhner	OF131	R	26	137	406	64	99	14	4	27	77	53	117	0	.244	.498
Ken Griffey Jr.	OF152 DH1	L	21	154	548	76	179	42	1	22	100	71	82	18	.327	.527
Greg Briley	OF125 DH2 2B3 3B1	L	26	139	381	39	99	17	3	2	26	27	51	23	.260	.336
Dave Valle	C129 1B2	R	30	132	324	38	63	8	1	8	32	34	49	0	.194	.299
Alvin Davis	DH126 1B14	L	30	145	462	39	102	15	1	12	69	56	78	0	.221	.335
Jeff Schaefer	SS46 3B30 2B11 DH1	R	31	84	164	19	41	7	1	1	15	5	25	3	.250	.323
Scott Bradley	C65 3B4 DH2 1B1	L	31	83	172	10	35	7	0	0	11	19	19	0	.203	.244
Tracy Jones (LJ)	DH37 OF34	R	30	79	175	30	44	8	1	3	24	18	22	2	.251	.360
Henry Cotto (SJ)	OF56 DH6	R	30	66	177	35	54	6	2	6	23	10	27	16	.305	.463
Dave Cochrane	OF26 C19 3B13 1B4 DH1	B	27	65	178	16	44	13	0	2	22	9	38	0	.247	.354
Alonzo Powell	OF40 1B7 DH7	R	26	57	111	16	24	6	1	3	12	11	24	0	.216	.369
Tino Martinez	1B29 DH15	L	23	36	112	11	23	2	0	4	9	11	24	0	.205	.330
Ken Griffey Sr. (ZJ)	OF26 DH1	L	41	30	85	10	24	7	0	1	9	13	13	0	.282	.400
Rich Amaral (EJ)	2B5 SS2 3B2 DH2 1B1	R	29	14	16	2	1	0	0	0	1	3	5	0	.063	.063
Patrick Lennon	DH5 OF1	R	23	9	8	2	1	1	0	0	0	1	3	1	.125	.250
Chris Howard	C9	R	25	9	6	1	1	1	0	0	1	0	1	0	.167	.333
Matt Sinatro	C5	R	31	5	8	1	2	1	0	0	1	0	2	0	.250	.250

NAME	T	AGE	W	L	PCT	SV	G	GS	CG	IP	H	BB	SO	SHO	ERA
TOTALS		27	83	79	.512	48	162	162	10	1464	1387	628	1003	13	3.79
Randy Johnson	L	27	13	10	.565	0	33	33	2	201	151	152	228	1	3.98
Brian Holman	R	26	13	14	.481	0	30	30	5	195	199	77	108	3	3.69
Rich DeLucia	R	26	12	13	.480	0	32	31	0	182	176	78	98	0	5.09
Bill Krueger	L	33	11	8	.579	0	35	25	1	175	194	60	91	0	3.60
Erik Hanson (EJ)	R	26	8	8	.500	0	27	27	2	175	182	56	143	1	3.81
Mike Jackson	R	26	7	7	.500	14	72	0	0	89	64	34	74	0	3.25
Russ Swan	L	27	6	2	.750	2	63	0	0	79	81	28	33	0	3.43
Mike Schooler (AJ)	R	28	3	3	.500	7	34	0	0	34	25	10	31	0	4.90
Scott Bankhead (SJ)	R	27	3	6	.333	0	17	9	0	61	73	21	28	0	4.90
Calvin Jones	R	27	2	2	.500	2	27	0	0	46	33	29	42	0	2.53
Dave Burba	L	24	2	2	.500	1	22	2	0	37	34	14	16	0	3.68
Dave Fleming	L	21	1	0	1.000	0	9	3	0	18	19	3	11	0	6.62
Pat Rice	R	27	1	1	.500	0	7	2	0	21	18	10	12	0	3.00
Bill Swift	R	29	1	2	.333	17	71	0	0	90	74	26	48	0	1.99
Gene Harris	R	26	0	0	—	1	3	0	0	5	13	15	10	0	4.05
Keith Comstock	L	35	0	0	—	0	1	0	0	0.1	2	1	0	0	54.00
Rob Murphy (NJ)	L	31	0	1	.000	4	57	0	0	48	47	19	34	0	3.00

KANSAS CITY 6th 82-80 .506 13 JOHN WATHAN 15-22 .405 BOB SCHAEFER 1-0 1.000 HAL McRAE 66-58 .532

Name	G by Pos	B	AGE	G	AB	R	H	2B	3B	HR	RBI	BB	SO	SB	BA	SA
TOTALS			28	162	5584	727	1475	290	41	117	689	523	969	119	.264	.394
2 Todd Benzinger	1B75 DH1	B	28	121	293	29	86	15	3	2	40	17	46	2	.294	.386
Terry Shumpert	2B144	R	24	144	369	45	80	16	4	5	34	30	75	17	.217	.322
Kurt Stillwell	SS118	R	26	122	385	44	102	17	1	6	51	33	56	3	.265	.361
Bill Pecota	3B102 2B34 SS9 1B8 DH2 OF1 P1	R	31	125	398	53	114	23	2	6	45	41	45	16	.286	.399
Danny Tartabull	OF124 DH6	R	28	132	484	78	153	35	3	31	100	65	121	6	.316	.593
Brian McRae	OF150	B	23	152	629	86	164	28	9	8	64	24	99	20	.261	.372
Kirk Gibson	OF94 DH30	L	34	132	462	81	109	17	6	16	55	69	103	18	.236	.403
Mike Macfarlane	C69 DH4	R	27	84	267	34	74	18	2	13	41	25	52	1	.277	.506
George Brett (KJ)	DH118 1B10	L	38	131	505	77	129	40	2	10	61	58	75	2	.255	.402
Jim Eisenreich	OF105 1B15 DH1	L	32	135	375	47	113	22	3	2	47	20	35	5	.301	.392
David Howard	SS63 2B26 3B1 OF1 DH1	B	24	94	236	20	51	7	0	1	17	16	45	3	.216	.258
Kevin Seitzer	3B68 DH3	R	29	85	234	28	62	11	3	1	25	29	21	4	.265	.350
Brent Mayne	C80 DH1	L	23	85	231	22	58	8	0	3	31	23	42	2	.251	.325
Gary Thurman (KJ)	OF72	R	26	80	184	24	51	9	0	2	13	11	42	15	.277	.359
Warren Cromartie	1B29 OF96 P1	L	37	69	131	13	41	7	2	1	20	15	18	1	.313	.420
2 Carmelo Martinez	1B43 DH1	R	30	44	121	17	25	6	0	4	17	27	25	0	.207	.355
Tim Spehr	C37	R	24	37	74	7	14	5	0	3	14	9	18	1	.189	.378
Sean Berry	3B30	R	25	31	60	5	8	3	0	0	1	6	13	0	.133	.183
Harvey Pulliam	OF15	R	23	18	33	4	9	1	0	3	4	3	9	0	.273	.576
Bobby Moore	OF13	R	25	18	14	3	5	1	0	0	0	1	2	3	.357	.429
Terry Puhl	DH2 OF1	L	34	15	18	0	4	0	0	0	0	0	5	0	.222	.222
Russ Morman	1B8 OF2 DH1	R	29	12	23	1	6	0	0	0	1	0	5	0	.261	.261
Dave Clark	OF1 DH1	L	28	11	10	1	2	0	0	0	1	0	0	0	.200	.200
Nelson Liriano	2B10	B	27	10	22	5	9	0	0	0	1	0	4	0	.409	.409
George Pedre	C9 1B1	R	24	10	19	2	5	1	1	0	3	3	5	0	.263	.421
Stu Cole	2B5 DH2 SS1	R	25	9	7	1	1	0	0	0	0	1	3	0	.143	.143
Paul Zuvella	3B2	R	32	2	1	0	0	0	0	0	0	0	0	0	.000	.000

NAME	T	AGE	W	L	PCT	SV	G	GS	CG	IP	H	BB	SO	SHO	ERA
TOTALS		28	82	80	.506	41	162	162	17	1466	1473	529	1004	12	3.92
Bret Saberhagen (SJ)	R	27	13	8	.619	0	28	28	7	196	165	45	136	2	3.07
Kevin Appier	R	23	13	10	.565	0	34	31	6	208	205	61	158	3	3.42
Mike Boddicker	R	33	12	12	.500	0	30	29	1	181	188	59	79	0	4.08
Mark Gubicza (SJ)	R	28	9	12	.429	0	26	26	0	133	168	42	89	0	5.68
Tom Gordon	R	23	9	14	.391	1	45	14	1	158	129	87	167	0	3.87
Luis Aquino	R	27	8	4	.667	3	38	18	1	157	152	47	80	1	3.44
Mark Davis (RJ)	L	30	6	3	.667	1	29	5	0	63	55	39	47	0	4.45
Jeff Montgomery	R	29	4	4	.500	33	67	0	0	90	83	28	77	0	2.90
Steve Crawford (KJ)	R	33	3	2	.600	1	33	0	0	47	60	18	38	0	5.98
Storm Davis	R	29	3	9	.250	2	51	9	1	114	140	46	53	1	4.96
Joel Johnston	R	24	1	0	1.000	0	13	0	0	22	9	9	21	0	0.40
Hector Wagner	R	22	1	1	.500	0	4			10	16	3	5	0	7.20
Dan Schatzeder	L	36	0	0	—	0	7	0	0	7	11	7	4	0	9.45
Carlos Maldonado	R	24	0	0	—	0	11	0	0	8	11	9	1	0	8.22
Andy McGaffigan	R	34	0	0	—	0	8	0	0	8	14	2	3	0	4.50
2 Wes Gardner	R	30	0	0	—	0	2	0	0	2	4	5	1	0	1.59
Archie Corbin	R	23	0	0	—	0	2	0	0	1	1	4	0	0	3.86
Bill Pecota	R	31	0	0	—	0	1	0	0	0	0	0	0	0	4.50
Mike Magnante	L	26	0	1	.000	0	38	0	0	55	55	23	42	0	2.45

CALIFORNIA 7th 81-81 .500 14 DOUG RADER 61-63 .492 BUCK RODGERS 20-18 .526

Name	G by Pos	B	AGE	G	AB	R	H	2B	3B	HR	RBI	BB	SO	SB	BA	SA
TOTALS			31	162	5470	653	1396	245	29	115	607	448	928	94	.255	.374
Wally Joyner	1B141	L	29	143	551	79	166	34	3	21	96	52	66	2	.301	.488
Luis Sojo	2B107 SS2 3B1 OF1 DH1	R	26	113	364	38	94	14	1	3	20	14	26	4	.258	.327
Dick Schofield	SS133	R	28	134	427	44	96	9	3	0	31	50	69	8	.225	.260
Gary Gaetti	3B152	R	32	152	586	58	144	22	1	18	66	33	104	5	.246	.379
Dave Winfield	OF115 DH34	R	39	150	568	75	149	27	4	28	86	56	109	7	.262	.472
Junior Felix (LJ)	OF65	R	23	66	230	32	65	10	2	2	26	11	55	7	.283	.370
Luis Polonia	OF143 DH4	L	26	150	604	92	179	28	8	2	50	52	74	48	.296	.379
Lance Parrish	C111 DH5 1B3	R	35	119	402	38	87	12	0	19	51	35	117	0	.216	.388
1 Dave Parker	DH119	L	40	119	466	45	108	22	2	11	56	29	91	2	.232	.358
Dave Gallagher	OF87 DH2	R	30	90	270	32	79	17	0	1	30	24	43	2	.293	.367
Max Venable	OF65 DH3	L	34	82	187	24	46	8	2	3	21	11	30	2	.246	.358
Donnie Hill	2B39 SS29 3B1	B	30	77	209	36	50	8	1	1	20	30	21	1	.239	.301
Ron Tingley	C45	R	32	45	115	11	23	7	0	1	13	8	34	1	.200	.287
2 Shawn Abner	OF38 DH3	R	25	41	101	12	23	6	1	2	9	4	16	1	.228	.366
Jack Howell	2B12 3B8 OF5 1B3 DH1	L	29	32	81	11	17	2	0	2	7	11	11	1	.210	.309
John Orton	C25	R	29	29	69	7	14	4	0	0	3	10	17	0	.203	.261
Bobby Rose (SJ)	2B8 OF7 3B4 1B3	R	24	22	65	5	18	5	1	1	8	3	13	0	.277	.431
Lee Stevens	1B11 OF9	L	23	18	58	8	17	7	0	0	6	5	12	1	.293	.414
Gary DiSarcina	SS10 2B7 3B2	R	23	18	57	5	12	2	0	0	3	4	9	0	.211	.246
Ruben Amaro	OF5 2B4 DH1	B	26	10	23	0	5	1	0	0	2	4	3	1	.217	.261
Chris Cron	1B5 DH1	R	27	6	15	0	2	0	0	0	1	0	3	0	.133	.133
Kevin Flora	2B3	R	23	3	8	1	1	0	0	0	1	1	2	1	.125	.125
Mark Davis	OF3	R	26	3	2	0	0	0	0	0	0	0	1	0	.000	.000
2 Mike Marshall	1B1 DH1	R	31	4	5	0	0	0	0	0	0	0	2	0	.000	.000
2 Barry Lyons	1B2	R	31	3	5	0	1	0	0	0	0	0	1	0	.200	.200

NAME	T	AGE	W	L	PCT	SV	G	GS	CG	IP	H	BB	SO	SHO	ERA
TOTALS		28	81	81	.500	50	162	162	18	1442	1351	543	990	10	3.69
Mark Langston	L	30	19	8	.704	0	34	34	7	246	190	96	183	0	3.00
Chuck Finley	L	28	18	9	.667	0	34	34	4	227	205	101	171	2	3.80
Jim Abbott	L	23	18	11	.621	0	34	34	5	243	222	73	158	1	2.89
Kirk McCaskill	R	30	10	19	.345	0	30	30	1	178	193	66	71	0	4.26
Mark Eichhorn	R	30	3	3	.500	1	70	0	0	82	63	13	49	0	1.98
Scott Lewis	R	25	3	5	.375	0	16	11	0	60	81	21	37	0	6.27
Joe Grahe	R	23	3	7	.300	0	18	10	1	73	84	33	40	0	4.81
Bryan Harvey	R	28	2	4	.333	46	67	0	0	79	51	17	101	0	1.60
Mike Fetters	R	26	2	5	.286	0	19	4	0	45	53	28	24	0	4.84
Cliff Young	L	27	2	1	.667	0	11	0	0	13	12	3	6	0	4.26
Scott Bailes	L	29	1	2	.333	0	42	0	0	52	41	22	41	0	4.18
Kyle Abbott	L	23	1	2	.333	0	5	3	0	20	22	13	12	0	4.58
Floyd Bannister (SJ)	L	36	1	1	.500	0	16	0	0	15	25	10	16	0	3.96
Bob McClure	L	39	0	0	—	0	14	0	0	10	13	5	5	0	9.25
Chris Beasley	R	29	0	1	.000	0	22	0	0	27	26	10	14	0	3.38
Fernando Valenzuela	L	30	0	2	.000	0	2	2	0	6	14	3	5	0	12.15
Jeff Robinson	R	30	0	3	.000	2	39	0	0	57	56	29	57	0	5.37
Bert Blyleven (SJ) 40															

PITTSBURGH — 1st 98-64 .605 — JIM LEYLAND

Name	G by Pos	B	AGE	G	AB	R	H	2B	3B	HR	RBI	BB	SO	SB	BA	SA
TOTALS			29	162	5449	768	1433	259	50	126	725	620	901	124	.263	.398
Orlando Merced	1B105 OF7	B	24	120	411	83	113	17	2	10	50	64	81	8	.275	.399
Jose Lind	2B149	R	27	150	502	53	133	16	6	3	54	30	56	2	.265	.339
Jay Bell	SS156	R	25	157	608	96	164	32	8	16	67	52	99	10	.270	.428
Jeff King (XJ)	3B33	R	26	33	109	16	26	1	1	4	18	14	15	3	.239	.376
Bobby Bonilla	OF104 3B67 1B4	B	28	157	577	102	174	44	6	18	100	90	67	2	.302	.492
Andy Van Slyke	OF135	L	30	138	491	87	130	24	7	17	83	71	85	10	.265	.446
Barry Bonds	OF150	L	26	153	510	95	149	28	5	25	116	107	73	43	.292	.514
Mike LaValliere	C105	L	30	108	336	25	97	11	2	3	41	33	27	2	.289	.360
Gary Varsho	OF54 1B3	L	30	99	187	23	51	11	2	4	23	19	34	9	.273	.417
Gary Redus	1B47 OF33	R	34	98	252	45	62	12	2	7	24	28	39	17	.246	.393
Curt Wilkerson	2B30 SS15 3B14	B	30	85	191	20	36	9	1	2	18	15	40	2	.188	.277
Lloyd McClendon	OF32 1B22 C2	R	32	85	163	24	47	7	0	7	24	18	23	2	.288	.460
Don Slaught	C69 3B1	R	32	77	220	19	65	17	1	1	29	21	32	1	.295	.395
Cecil Espy	OF35	B	28	43	82	7	20	4	0	1	11	5	17	4	.244	.329
John Wehner (XJ)	3B36	R	24	37	106	15	36	7	0	0	7	7	17	3	.340	.406
2 Mitch Webster	OF29	B	32	36	97	9	17	3	4	1	9	9	31	0	.175	.320
2 Steve Buechele	3B31	R	29	31	114	16	28	5	1	4	19	10	28	0	.246	.412
Tom Prince	C19 1B1	R	26	26	34	4	9	3	0	1	2	7	3	0	.265	.441
2 Jose Gonzalez	OF14	R	26	16	20	2	2	0	0	1	3	0	6	0	.100	.250
Carlos Garcia	SS9 3B2 2B1	R	23	12	24	2	6	0	2	0	1	1	8	0	.250	.417
Joe Redfield	3B9	R	30	11	18	1	2	0	0	0	4	1	7	0	.111	.111
1 Carmelo Martinez	1B8	R	30	11	16	1	4	0	0	0	0	5	2	0	.250	.250
Scott Bullett	OF3	L	22	11	4	2	1	0	0	0	0	0	1	1	.250	.250
Jeff Richardson	3B3 SS2	R	25	6	4	0	1	0	0	0	0	0	3	0	.250	.250
Jeff Schulz		L	30	3	3	0	0	0	0	0	0	0	1	0	.000	.000
Jeff Banister		R	26	1	1	0	1	0	0	0	0	0	0	0	1.000	1.000

NAME	T	AGE	W	L	PCT	SV	G	GS	CG	IP	H	BB	SO	SHO	ERA
		28	98	64	.605	51	162	162	18	1457	1411	401	919	11	3.44
John Smiley	L	26	20	8	.714	0	33	32	2	208	194	44	129	1	3.08
Zane Smith	L	30	16	10	.615	0	35	35	6	228	234	29	120	3	3.20
Doug Drabek	R	28	15	14	.517	0	35	35	5	235	245	62	142	2	3.07
Bob Walk (GJ-LJ)	R	34	9	2	.818	0	25	20	0	115	104	35	67	0	3.60
Randy Tomlin	L	25	8	7	.533	0	31	27	4	175	170	54	104	2	2.98
Stan Belinda	R	24	7	5	.583	16	60	0	0	78	50	35	71	0	3.45
Vicente Palacios (SJ)	R	27	6	3	.667	3	36	7	1	82	69	38	64	1	3.75
Bob Patterson	L	32	4	3	.571	2	54	1	0	66	67	15	57	0	4.11
Bill Landrum	R	33	4	4	.500	17	61	0	0	76	76	19	45	0	3.18
Roger Mason	R	32	3	2	.600	3	24	0	0	30	21	6	21	0	3.03
Neal Heaton	L	31	3	3	.500	0	42	1	0	69	72	21	34	0	4.33
Bob Kipper	R	26	2	2	.500	4	52	0	0	60	66	22	38	0	4.65
Rosario Rodriguez	L	21	1	1	.500	6	18	0	0	15	14	8	10	0	4.11
Mark Huismann	R	33	0	0	—	0	5	0	0	5	7	2	5	0	7.20
1 Hector Fajardo	R	20	0	0	—	0	2	2	0	6	10	7	8	0	9.95
Paul Miller	R	26	0	0	—	0	1	0	0	5	4	3	2	0	5.40
Rick Reed	R	26	0	0	—	0	1	1	0	4	8	1	2	0	10.38

ST. LOUIS — 2nd 84-78 .519 14 — JOE TORRE

Name	G by Pos	B	AGE	G	AB	R	H	2B	3B	HR	RBI	BB	SO	SB	BA	SA
TOTALS			28	162	5362	651	1366	239	53	68	599	532	857	202	.255	.357
Pedro Guerrero (BL)	1B112	R	35	115	427	41	116	12	1	8	70	37	46	4	.272	.361
Jose Oquendo	2B118 SS22 1B3	B	27	127	366	37	88	11	4	1	26	67	48	1	.240	.301
Ozzie Smith	SS150	B	36	150	550	96	157	30	3	3	50	83	36	35	.285	.367
Todd Zeile	3B154	R	25	155	565	76	158	36	3	11	81	62	94	17	.280	.412
Felix Jose	OF153	B	26	154	568	69	173	40	6	8	77	50	113	20	.305	.438
Ray Lankford	OF149	L	24	151	566	83	142	23	15	9	69	41	114	44	.251	.400
Bernard Gilkey (BG)	OF74	R	24	81	268	28	58	7	2	5	20	39	33	14	.216	.313
Tom Pagnozzi	C139 1B3	R	28	140	459	38	121	24	5	2	57	36	63	9	.264	.351
Milt Thompson	OF91	L	32	115	326	55	100	16	5	6	34	32	53	16	.307	.442
Gerald Perry	1B61 OF5	L	30	109	242	29	58	8	4	6	36	32	34	15	.240	.380
Geronimo Pena	2B83 OF4	R	24	104	185	38	45	8	3	5	17	18	45	15	.243	.400
Rex Hudler	OF58 1B12 2B5	R	30	101	207	21	47	10	2	1	15	10	29	12	.227	.309
Craig Wilson	3B12 OF5 1B4 2B3	R	25	60	82	5	14	2	0	0	13	6	10	0	.171	.195
Luis Alicea	2B11 3B2 SS1	B	25	56	68	5	13	3	0	0	0	8	19	0	.191	.235
Rich Gedman	C43	L	31	46	94	7	10	1	0	3	8	4	15	0	.106	.213
Rod Brewer	1B15 OF3	L	25	19	13	0	1	0	0	0	1	0	5	0	.077	.077
Tim Jones	SS14 2B4	L	28	16	24	1	4	2	0	0	2	1	6	0	.167	.250
Stan Royer	3B5	R	23	9	21	1	6	1	0	0	1	1	2	0	.286	.333
Ray Stephens	C6	R	28	6	7	0	2	0	0	0	1	1	3	0	.286	.286

NAME	T	AGE	W	L	PCT	SV	G	GS	CG	IP	H	BB	SO	SHO	ERA
		30	84	78	.519	51	162	162	9	1435	1367	454	822	5	3.69
Bryn Smith	R	35	12	9	.571	0	31	31	3	199	188	45	94	0	3.85
Omar Olivares	R	23	11	7	.611	1	28	24	0	167	148	61	91	0	3.71
Ken Hill	R	25	11	10	.524	0	30	30	0	181	147	67	121	0	3.57
Bob Tewksbury	R	30	11	12	.478	0	30	30	3	191	206	38	75	0	3.25
Cris Carpenter (RJ)	R	26	10	4	.714	0	59	0	0	66	53	20	47	0	4.23
Lee Smith	R	33	6	3	.667	47	67	0	0	73	70	13	67	0	2.34
Juan Agosto	L	33	5	3	.625	2	72	0	0	86	92	39	34	0	4.81
Jose DeLeon	R	30	5	9	.357	0	28	28	1	163	144	61	118	0	2.71
Scott Terry	R	31	4	4	.500	1	65	0	0	80	76	32	52	0	2.80
Rheal Cormier	L	24	4	5	.444	0	11	10	2	68	74	8	38	0	4.12
2 Willie Fraser	R	27	3	3	.500	0	35	0	0	49	44	21	25	0	4.93
2 Bob McClure	L	39	1	1	.500	0	32	0	0	23	24	8	15	0	3.13
Mark Clark	R	23	1	1	.500	0	7	2	0	22	17	11	13	0	4.03
Tim Sherrill	L	25	0	0	—	0	10	0	0	14	20	3	4	0	8.16
Mark Grater	R	27	0	0	—	0	3	0	0	3	5	2	0	0	0.00
Jose Oquendo	R	27	0	0	—	0	1	0	0	2	1	2	1	0	27.00
Mike Perez	R	26	0	0	—	0	14	0	0	17	19	7	7	0	5.82
Jamie Moyer	L	28	0	5	.000	0	8	7	0	31	38	16	20	0	5.74
Joe Magrane (EJ) 26															
Todd Worrell (EJ) 31															
Frank DiPino (EJ) 34															

PHILADELPHIA — 3rd 78-84 .481 20 — NICK LEYVA 4-9 .308 — JIM FREGOSI 74-75 .497

Name	G by Pos	B	AGE	G	AB	R	H	2B	3B	HR	RBI	BB	SO	SB	BA	SA
TOTALS			29	162	5521	629	1332	248	33	111	590	490	1026	92	.241	.358
John Kruk	1B102 OF52	L	30	152	538	84	158	27	6	21	92	67	100	7	.294	.483
Mickey Morandini	2B97	L	25	98	325	38	81	11	4	1	20	29	45	13	.249	.317
Dickie Thon	SS146	R	33	146	539	44	136	18	4	9	44	25	84	11	.252	.351
Charlie Hayes	3B138 SS2	R	26	142	460	34	106	23	1	12	53	16	75	3	.230	.363
Dale Murphy	OF147	R	35	153	544	66	137	33	1	18	81	48	93	1	.252	.415
Lenny Dykstra (AA-BC)	OF63	L	28	63	246	48	73	13	5	3	12	37	20	24	.297	.427
Von Hayes (BW)	OF72	L	32	77	284	43	64	15	1	0	21	31	42	9	.225	.285
Darren Daulton (AA-KJ)	C88	L	29	89	285	36	56	12	0	12	42	41	66	5	.196	.365
Wes Chamberlain	OF98	R	25	101	383	51	92	16	2	13	50	31	73	9	.240	.399
Ricky Jordan	1B72	R	26	101	301	38	82	21	3	9	49	14	49	0	.272	.452
Wally Backman	2B36 3B20	B	31	94	185	20	45	12	0	0	15	30	30	3	.243	.308
John Morris	OF57	L	30	85	127	15	28	2	1	1	6	12	25	2	.220	.276
Randy Ready (XJ)	2B66	R	31	76	205	32	51	10	1	1	20	47	25	2	.249	.322
Jim Lindeman	OF30 1B1	R	29	65	95	13	32	5	0	3	12	13	14	0	.337	.389
Steve Lake	C58	R	34	58	158	12	36	4	1	1	11	2	26	0	.228	.285
Dave Hollins	3B36 1B6	B	25	56	151	18	45	10	2	6	21	17	26	1	.298	.510
Darrin Fletcher	C45	L	24	46	136	5	31	8	0	1	12	5	15	0	.228	.309
Rod Booker	SS20 3B3	L	32	28	53	3	12	1	0	0	7	1	7	0	.226	.245
Braulio Castillo	OF26	R	23	28	52	3	9	3	0	0	2	1	15	1	.173	.231
Ron Jones (KJ)		L	27	28	26	0	4	2	0	0	1	0	5	0	.154	.231
Rick Schu	3B3 1B1	R	29	17	22	1	2	0	0	0	2	1	7	0	.091	.091
Sil Campusano	OF15	R	25	15	35	2	4	0	0	1	2	1	10	0	.114	.200
Kim Batiste	SS7	R	23	10	27	2	6	0	0	0	3	0	8	0	.222	.222
Doug Lindsey	C1	R	23	1	3	0	0	0	0	0	0	0	0	0	.000	.000

NAME	T	AGE	W	L	PCT	SV	G	GS	CG	IP	H	BB	SO	SHO	ERA
		28	78	84	.481	35	162	162	16	1463	1346	670	988	11	3.86
Terry Mulholland	L	28	16	13	.552	0	34	34	8	232	231	49	142	3	3.61
Tommy Greene	R	24	13	7	.650	0	36	27	3	208	177	66	154	2	3.38
Mitch Williams	L	26	12	5	.706	30	69	0	0	88	56	62	84	0	2.34
Jose DeJesus	R	26	10	9	.526	1	31	29	3	182	147	128	118	0	3.42
Danny Cox	R	31	4	6	.400	0	23	17	0	102	98	39	46	0	4.57
Bruce Ruffin	R	27	4	7	.364	0	31	15	1	119	125	38	85	1	3.78
Joe Boever	R	30	3	5	.375	0	68	0	0	98	90	54	89	0	3.84
1 Roger McDowell	R	30	3	6	.333	3	38	0	0	59	61	32	28	0	3.20
Darrel Akerfelds	R	29	2	1	.667	0	30	0	0	50	49	27	31	0	5.26
2 Steve Searcy	L	27	2	1	.667	0	18	0	0	30	29	14	21	0	4.15
2 Mike Hartley	R	29	2	1	.667	1	18	0	0	26	21	10	19	0	3.76
Cliff Brantley	R	23	2	2	.500	0	6	5	0	32	26	19	25	0	3.41
Pat Combs	L	24	2	6	.250	0	14	13	1	64	64	43	41	0	4.90
Wally Ritchie	L	25	1	2	.333	0	39	0	0	50	44	17	26	0	2.50
Andy Ashby	R	23	1	5	.167	0	8	8	0	42	41	19	26	0	6.00
Jason Grimsley	R	23	1	7	.125	0	12	12	0	61	54	41	42	0	4.87
Tim Mauser	R	24	0	0	—	0	3	0	0	11	18	3	6	0	7.59
Amalio Carreno	R	27	0	0	—	0	3	0	0	3	6	3	2	0	16.20
Dave LaPoint	L	31	0	1	.000	0	2	2	0	5	10	6	3	0	16.20
Ken Howell (SJ) 30															
Steve Ontiveros (SJ) 30															

CHICAGO — 4th 77-83 .481 20 — DON ZIMMER 18-19 .486 — JOE ALTOBELLI 0-1 .000 — JIM ESSIAN 59-63 .484

Name	G by Pos	B	AGE	G	AB	R	H	2B	3B	HR	RBI	BB	SO	SB	BA	SA
TOTALS			28	162	5522	695	1395	232	26	159	654	442	879	123	.253	.390
Mark Grace	1B160	L	27	160	619	87	169	28	5	8	58	70	53	3	.273	.373
Ryne Sandberg	2B157	R	31	158	585	104	170	32	2	26	100	87	89	22	.291	.485
Shawon Dunston	SS142	R	28	142	492	59	128	22	7	12	50	23	64	21	.260	.407
Luis Salazar	3B86 1B7 OF7	R	35	139	333	34	86	14	1	14	38	15	45	0	.258	.432
Andre Dawson	OF137	R	36	149	563	69	153	21	4	31	104	22	80	4	.272	.488
Jerome Walton	OF101	R	25	123	270	42	59	13	1	5	17	19	55	7	.219	.330
George Bell	OF146	R	31	149	558	63	159	27	0	25	86	32	62	2	.285	.468
Rick Wilkins	C82	L	24	86	203	21	45	9	0	6	22	19	56	3	.222	.355
Chico Walker	3B57 OF53 2B6	B	33	124	374	51	96	10	1	5	34	33	57	15	.257	.337
Doug Dascenzo	OF86 P3	B	27	118	239	40	61	11	0	1	18	24	26	14	.255	.314
Jose Vizcaino	3B57 SS33 2B9	B	23	93	145	7	38	5	0	0	10	5	18	2	.262	.297
Dwight Smith	OF42	L	27	90	167	16	38	7	2	3	21	11	32	2	.228	.347
Hector Villanueva	C55 1B6	R	26	71	192	23	53	10	1	13	32	21	30	0	.276	.542
1 Damon Berryhill	C48	B	27	62	159	13	30	7	0	5	14	11	41	1	.189	.277
Ced Landrum	OF44	L	27	56	86	28	20	2	1	0	6	10	18	27	.233	.279
Gary Scott	3B31	R	22	31	79	8	13	5	0	1	5	6	14	0	.165	.241
Joe Girardi (XJ)	C21	R	26	21	47	3	9	2	0	0	6	6	6	0	.191	.234
Derrick May	OF7	L	22	15	22	1	5	2	0	0	2	1	4	0	.227	.455
Rey Sanchez	SS10 2B2	R	23	13	23	1	6	0	0	0	2	4	3	0	.261	.261
Erik Pappas	C6	R	25	7	17	1	3	1	0	0	1	1	5	0	.176	.176
Doug Strange	3B3	B	27	3	9	0	4	0	0	0	1	0	1	0	.444	.556

NAME	T	AGE	W	L	PCT	SV	G	GS	CG	IP	H	BB	SO	SHO	ERA
		28	77	83	.481	40	160	160	12	1457	1415	542	927	4	4.03
Greg Maddux	R	25	15	11	.577	0	37	37	7	263	232	66	198	2	3.35
1 Mike Bielecki	R	31	13	11	.542	0	39	25	0	172	169	54	72	0	4.50
Les Lancaster	R	29	9	7	.563	0	64	11	1	156	150	49	102	0	3.52
Paul Assenmacher	L	30	7	8	.467	15	75	0	0	103	85	31	117	0	3.24
Bob Scanlan	R	24	7	8	.467	1	40	13	0	111	114	40	44	0	3.89
Chuck McElroy	L	23	6	2	.750	3	71	0	0	101	73	57	92	0	1.95
Rick Sutcliffe (SJ)	R	35	6	5	.545	0	19	18	0	97	96	45	52	0	4.10
Frank Castillo	R	22	6	7	.462	0	18	18	4	112	107	33	73	0	4.35
Shawn Boskie	R	24	4	9	.308	0	28	20	0	129	150	52	62	0	5.23
Heathcliff Slocumb	R	25	2	1	.667	1	52	0	0	63	53	30	34	0	3.45
Yorkis Perez	L	23	1	0	1.000	0	3	0	0	4	2	3	2	0	2.08
Danny Jackson (MJ)	L	29	1	5	.667	0	17	14	0	71	89	48	31	0	6.75
1 Steve Wilson	L	26	0	0	—	0	9	0	0	12	13	5	9	0	4.38
Doug Dascenzo	L	27	0	0	—	0	3	0	0	5	2	1	1	0	0.00
Scott May	R	28	0	0	—	0	2	0	0	2	6	1	1	0	18.00
Dave Pavlas	R	28	0	0	—	0	4	0	0	3	9	0	2	0	18.00
Laddie Renfroe	R	29	0	2	.000	0	4	0	0	4	11	2	1	0	13.50
Mike Harkey (SJ)	R	24	0	2	.000	0	4	4	0	21	6	15	0	5.30	
Dave Smith (KJ)	R	36	0	6	.000	17	35	0	0	33	39	19	16	0	6.00

NEW YORK 5th 77-84 .478 20.5　　BUD HARRELSON 74-80 .481　　MIKE CUBBAGE 3-4 .429

Name	G by Pos	B	AGE	G	AB	R	H	2B	3B	HR	RBI	BB	SO	SB	BA	SA
TOTALS			30	161	5359	640	1305	250	24	117	605	578	789	153	.244	.365
Dave Magadan (SJ)	1B122	L	28	124	418	58	108	23	0	4	51	83	50	1	.258	.342
Gregg Jefferies	2B77 3B51	B	28	136	486	59	132	19	2	9	62	47	58	26	.272	.374
Kevin Elster	SS107	R	26	115	348	33	84	16	2	6	36	40	53	2	.241	.351
Howard Johnson	3B104 OF30 SS28	B	30	156	564	108	146	34	4	38	117	78	120	30	.259	.535
Hubie Brooks (XL)	OF100	R	34	103	357	48	85	11	1	16	50	44	62	3	.238	.409
Vince Coleman (LJ)	OF70	B	30	72	278	45	71	7	5	1	17	39	47	37	.255	.327
Kevin McReynolds	OF141	R	31	143	522	65	135	32	1	16	74	49	46	6	.259	.416
Rick Cerone	C81	R	37	90	227	18	62	13	0	2	16	30	24	1	.273	.357
Daryl Boston	OF115	L	28	137	255	40	70	16	4	4	21	30	42	15	.275	.416
Mark Carreon	OF77	R	27	106	254	18	66	6	0	4	21	12	26	2	.260	.331
Keith Miller	2B60 OF28 3B2 SS2	R	28	98	275	41	77	22	1	4	23	23	44	14	.280	.411
Mackey Sasser	C43 OF21 1B10	L	28	96	228	18	62	14	2	5	35	9	15	0	.272	.417
2 Garry Templeton	SS40 1B25 3B2 OF2	B	35	80	219	20	50	9	1	2	20	9	29	3	.228	.306
1 Tommy Herr	2B57 OF1	B	35	70	155	17	30	7	0	1	14	32	21	7	.194	.258
Charlie O'Brien	C67	R	31	69	168	16	31	6	0	2	14	17	25	0	.185	.256
Chris Donnels	1B15 3B11	L	25	37	89	7	20	2	0	0	5	14	19	1	.225	.247
Terry McDaniel	OF16	R	24	23	29	3	6	1	0	0	2	1	11	2	.207	.241
Todd Hundley	C20	B	22	21	60	5	8	0	1	1	7	6	14	0	.133	.217
1 Tim Teufel	1B6 3B5 2B1	R	32	20	34	2	4	0	0	1	2	2	8	1	.118	.206
Jeff Gardner	SS8 2B3	L	27	13	37	3	6	0	0	0	1	4	6	0	.162	.162
Chuck Carr (LJ)	OF9	B	23	12	11	1	2	0	0	0	1	0	2	1	.182	.182
Kelvin Torve	1B1	L	31	10	8	0	0	0	0	0	0	1	0	0	.000	.000

NAME	T	AGE	W	L	PCT	SV	G	GS	CG	IP	H	BB	SO	SHO	ERA
		28	77	84	.478	39	161	161	12	1437	1403	410	1028	11	3.56
David Cone	R	28	14	14	.500	0	34	34	5	233	204	73	241	2	3.29
Dwight Gooden (SJ)	R	26	13	7	.650	0	27	27	3	190	185	56	150	1	3.60
Frank Viola	L	31	13	15	.464	0	35	35	3	231	259	54	132	0	3.97
Wally Whitehurst	R	27	7	12	.368	1	36	20	0	133	142	25	87	0	4.19
1 Alejandro Pena	R	32	6	1	.857	4	44	0	0	63	63	19	49	0	2.71
Pete Schourek	L	22	5	4	.556	2	35	8	1	86	82	43	67	1	4.27
1 Ron Darling	R	30	5	6	.455	0	17	17	0	102	96	28	58	0	3.87
John Franco	L	30	5	9	.357	30	52	0	0	55	61	18	45	0	2.93
2 Tim Burke	R	32	3	3	.500	1	35	0	0	56	55	12	34	0	2.75
Doug Simons	L	24	2	3	.400	1	42	1	0	61	55	19	38	0	5.19
Anthony Young	R	25	2	5	.286	0	10	8	0	49	48	12	20	0	3.10
2 Tony Castillo	L	28	1	0	1.000	0	10	3	0	24	27	6	10	0	1.90
Sid Fernandez(BW-KJ)	L	28	1	3	.250	0	8	8	0	44	36	9	31	0	2.86
Terry Bross	R	25	0	0	—	0	8	0	0	10	7	3	5	0	1.80
Rich Sauveur	L	27	0	0	—	0	6	0	0	3	7	2	4	0	10.80
Blaine Beatty	L	27	0	0	—	0	5	0	0	10	9	4	7	0	2.79
Julio Valera	R	22	0	0	.000	0	2	0	0	2	1	4	3	0	0.00
Jeff Innis	R	28	0	2	.000	0	69	0	0	85	66	23	47	0	2.66

MONTREAL 6th 71-90 .441 26.5　　BUCK RODGERS 20-29 .408　　TOM RUNNELLS 51-61 .455

Name	G by Pos	B	AGE	G	AB	R	H	2B	3B	HR	RBI	BB	SO	SB	BA	SA
TOTALS			28	161	5412	579	1329	236	42	95	536	484	1056	221	.246	.357
Andres Galarraga (KJ)	1B105	R	30	107	375	34	82	13	2	9	33	23	86	5	.219	.336
Delino DeShields	2B148	L	22	151	563	83	134	15	4	10	51	95	151	56	.238	.332
Spike Owen	SS133	B	30	139	424	39	108	22	8	3	26	42	61	2	.255	.366
Tim Wallach	3B149	R	33	151	577	60	130	22	1	13	73	50	100	2	.225	.334
Larry Walker	OF102 1B39	L	24	137	487	59	141	30	2	16	64	42	102	14	.290	.458
Marquis Grissom	OF138	R	24	148	558	73	149	23	9	6	39	34	89	76	.267	.373
Ivan Calderon	OF122 1B4	R	29	134	470	69	141	22	3	19	75	53	64	31	.300	.481
Gil Reyes	C80	R	27	83	207	11	45	9	0	0	13	19	51	2	.217	.261
Dave Martinez	OF112	L	26	124	396	47	117	18	5	7	42	20	54	16	.295	.419
Tom Foley	SS43 1B31 3B6 2B2	L	31	86	168	12	35	11	1	0	15	14	30	2	.208	.286
Eric Bullock	OF9 1B3	L	30	73	72	6	16	4	0	1	6	9	13	6	.222	.319
Mike Fitzgerald (BW)	C54 1B3 OF3	R	30	71	198	17	40	5	2	4	28	22	35	4	.202	.308
Junior Noboa	OF7 2B6 3B2 SS2 1B1	R	26	67	95	5	23	3	0	1	2	1	8	2	.242	.305
Bret Barberie	SS19 2B10 3B10 1B1	B	23	57	136	16	48	12	2	2	18	20	22	0	.353	.515
Ron Hassey (KJ)	C34	L	38	52	119	5	27	8	0	1	14	13	16	1	.227	.319
Nelson Santovenia	C30 1B7	R	29	41	96	7	24	5	0	2	14	2	18	0	.250	.365
2 Kenny Williams	OF24	R	27	34	70	11	19	5	2	0	1	3	22	2	.271	.400
John Vander Wal	OF17	L	25	21	61	4	13	4	1	1	8	1	18	0	.213	.361
Nikco Riesgo	OF2	R	24	7	1	1	0	0	0	0	3	1	5	0	.143	.143
Darren Reed (BA) 25																
Moises Alou (SJ) 24																

NAME	T	AGE	W	L	PCT	SV	G	GS	CG	IP	H	BB	SO	SHO	ERA
		28	71	90	.441	39	161	161	12	1440	1304	584	909	14	3.64
Dennis Martinez	R	36	14	11	.560	0	31	31	9	222	187	62	123	5	2.39
Bill Sampen	R	28	9	5	.643	0	43	8	0	92	96	46	52	0	4.00
Mark Gardner (SJ)	R	29	9	11	.450	0	27	27	0	168	139	75	107	0	3.85
Chris Nabholz (SJ)	L	24	8	7	.533	0	24	24	1	154	134	57	99	0	3.63
1 Oil Can Boyd	R	31	6	8	.429	0	19	19	1	120	115	40	82	1	3.52
Brian Barnes	L	24	5	8	.385	0	28	27	1	160	135	84	117	0	4.22
Scott Ruskin	L	28	4	4	.500	6	64	0	0	64	57	30	46	0	4.24
Barry Jones	R	28	4	9	.308	13	77	0	0	89	76	33	46	0	3.35
Mel Rojas	R	24	3	3	.500	6	37	0	0	48	42	13	37	0	3.75
1 Tim Burke	R	32	3	4	.429	5	37	0	0	46	41	14	25	0	4.11
Chris Haney	L	22	3	7	.300	0	16	16	0	85	94	43	51	0	4.04
Jeff Fassero	L	28	2	5	.286	8	51	0	0	55	39	17	42	0	2.44
1 Rick Mahler	R	37	1	3	.250	0	10	6	0	37	37	15	17	0	3.62
Doug Piatt	R	25	0	0	—	0	21	0	0	35	29	17	29	0	2.60
Bill Long	R	31	0	0	—	0	3	2	0	2	4	4	0	0	10.80
Steve Frey	L	27	0	1	.000	1	31	0	0	40	43	23	21	0	4.99
Dave Schmidt	R	34	0	0	.000	0	4	0	0	4	2	3	2	0	10.38
Dave Wainhouse	R	23	0	1	.000	0	2	0	0	3	2	4	1	0	6.75
2 Ron Darling	R	30	0	2	.000	0	3	0	0	17	25	5	11	0	7.41

WEST DIVISION

ATLANTA 1st 94-68 .580　　BOBBY COX

Name	G by Pos	B	AGE	G	AB	R	H	2B	3B	HR	RBI	BB	SO	SB	BA	SA
TOTALS			28	162	5456	749	1407	255	30	141	704	563	906	165	.258	.393
Sid Bream (KJ)	1B85	L	30	91	265	32	67	12	0	11	45	25	31	0	.253	.423
Jeff Treadway	2B93	L	28	106	306	41	98	17	2	3	32	23	19	2	.320	.418
Rafael Belliard	SS145	R	29	149	353	36	88	9	2	0	27	22	63	3	.249	.286
Terry Pendleton	3B148	B	30	153	586	94	187	34	8	22	86	43	70	10	.319	.517
David Justice (XJ)	OF106	L	25	109	396	67	109	25	1	21	87	65	81	8	.275	.503
Ron Gant	OF148	R	26	154	561	101	141	35	3	32	105	71	104	34	.251	.496
Otis Nixon	OF115	B	32	124	401	81	119	10	1	0	26	47	40	72	.297	.327
Greg Olson	C127	R	30	133	411	46	99	25	0	6	44	44	48	1	.241	.345
Mark Lemke	2B110 3B15	B	25	136	269	36	63	11	2	2	23	29	27	1	.234	.312
Jeff Blauser	SS85 2B32 3B18	R	25	129	352	49	91	14	3	11	54	54	59	5	.259	.409
Lonnie Smith	OF99	R	35	122	353	58	97	19	1	7	44	50	64	9	.275	.394
Brian Hunter	1B85 OF6	R	23	97	271	32	68	16	1	12	50	17	48	0	.251	.450
Tommy Gregg (BH)	OF14 1B13	L	27	72	107	13	20	8	1	1	4	12	24	2	.187	.308
Deion Sanders (LF)	OF44	L	23	54	110	16	21	1	2	4	13	12	23	11	.191	.345
Mike Heath (EJ)	C45	R	36	49	139	4	29	3	1	1	12	7	26	0	.209	.266
Keith Mitchell	OF34	R	21	48	66	11	21	0	0	2	5	8	12	3	.318	.409
Francisco Cabrera	C17 1B14	R	24	44	95	7	23	6	0	4	23	6	20	1	.242	.432
Mike Bell	1B14	R	23	17	30	4	4	0	0	1	2	1	6	0	.133	.233
Jerry Willard	C1	L	31	17	14	1	3	0	0	1	4	2	5	0	.214	.429
Danny Heep	OF1 1B1	L	34	12	12	4	5	1	0	0	3	1	4	0	.417	.500
Vinny Castilla	SS12	R	23	12	5	1	1	0	0	0	1	0	2	0	.200	.200
Rico Rossy	SS1	R	27	5	1	0	0	0	0	0	0	0	1	0	.000	.000
2 Damon Berryhill	C1	B	27	1	1	0	0	0	0	0	0	0	0	0	.000	.000
Nick Esasky (IL) 31																

NAME	T	AGE	W	L	PCT	SV	G	GS	CG	IP	H	BB	SO	SHO	ERA
		28	94	68	.580	48	162	162	18	1453	1304	481	969	7	3.49
Tom Glavine	L	25	20	11	.645	0	34	34	9	247	201	69	192	1	2.55
Steve Avery	L	21	18	8	.692	0	35	35	3	210	189	65	137	1	3.38
Charlie Leibrandt	L	34	15	13	.536	0	36	36	1	230	212	56	128	1	3.49
John Smoltz	R	24	14	13	.519	0	36	36	5	230	206	77	148	0	3.80
Kent Mercker	L	23	5	3	.625	6	50	4	0	73	56	35	62	0	2.58
Mike Stanton	L	24	5	5	.500	7	74	0	0	78	62	21	54	0	2.88
Mark Wohlers	R	21	3	1	.750	2	17	0	0	20	17	13	13	0	3.20
2 Jim Clancy	R	35	3	2	.600	3	24	0	0	35	36	14	17	0	5.71
2 Alejandro Pena	R	32	2	0	1.000	11	15	0	0	19	11	3	13	0	1.40
Doug Sisk (SJ)	R	33	2	1	.667	0	14	0	0	14	21	8	5	0	5.02
Armando Reynoso	R	25	2	1	.667	0	6	5	0	23	26	10	10	0	6.17
Marvin Freeman (XJ)	R	28	1	0	1.000	1	34	0	0	48	37	13	34	0	3.00
1 Rick Mahler	R	37	1	1	.500	0	13	2	0	29	33	13	10	0	5.65
1 Tony Castillo	L	28	1	0	1.000	0	7	0	0	9	13	5	8	0	7.27
Jeff Parrett	R	29	1	2	.333	1	18	0	0	21	31	12	14	0	6.33
Pete Smith (SJ)	R	24	1	3	.250	0	14	10	0	48	48	22	29	0	5.06
Randy St. Claire	R	30	0	0	—	0	19	0	0	29	31	9	30	0	4.08
2 Dan Petry	R	32	0	0	—	0	10	0	0	24	29	14	9	0	5.55
2 Mike Bielecki	R	31	0	0	—	0	2	0	0	4	2	1	3	0	0.00
Juan Berenguer (SJ)	R	36	0	3	.000	17	49	0	0	64	43	20	53	0	2.24
Mark Grant (SJ) 27																

LOS ANGELES 2nd 93-69 .574 1　　TOMMY LASORDA

Name	G by Pos	B	AGE	G	AB	R	H	2B	3B	HR	RBI	BB	SO	SB	BA	SA
TOTALS			31	162	5408	665	1366	191	29	108	605	583	957	126	.253	.359
Eddie Murray	1B149 3B1	B	35	153	576	69	150	23	1	19	96	55	74	10	.260	.403
Juan Samuel	2B152	R	30	153	594	74	161	22	6	12	58	49	133	23	.271	.389
Alfredo Griffin	SS109	B	33	109	350	27	85	6	2	0	27	22	49	5	.243	.271
Lenny Harris	3B113 2B27 SS20 OF1	L	26	145	429	59	121	16	1	3	38	37	32	12	.287	.350
Darryl Strawberry	OF136	L	29	139	505	86	134	22	4	28	99	75	125	10	.265	.491
Brett Butler	OF161	L	34	161	615	112	182	13	5	2	38	108	79	38	.296	.343
Kal Daniels	OF132	L	27	137	461	54	115	15	1	17	73	63	116	6	.249	.397
Mike Scioscia	C115	L	32	119	345	39	91	16	2	8	40	47	32	4	.264	.391
Stan Javier	OF69 1B2	B	27	121	176	21	36	5	3	1	11	16	36	7	.205	.284
Mike Sharperson	3B68 SS16 1B10 2B5	R	29	105	216	24	60	11	2	2	20	25	24	1	.278	.375
Gary Carter	C68 1B10	R	37	101	248	22	61	14	0	6	26	22	26	2	.246	.375
Chris Gwynn	OF41	L	26	94	139	18	35	5	1	5	22	10	23	1	.252	.410
2 Mitch Webster	OF36 1B3	B	32	58	74	12	21	5	1	1	10	9	21	0	.284	.419
Dave Hansen	3B21 SS1	L	22	53	56	3	15	4	0	1	5	2	12	1	.268	.393
Jose Offerman	SS50	B	22	52	113	10	22	3	0	3	25	32	5	.195	.212	
1 Jose Gonzalez	OF27	R	26	42	28	3	0	0	0	0	0	0	9	0	.000	.000
Jeff Hamilton	3B33 SS1	R	27	41	94	4	21	1	0	1	14	4	21	0	.223	.298
Tom Goodwin	OF5	R	22	16	7	3	1	0	0	0	0	0	1	1	.143	.143
Carlos Hernandez	C13 3B1	R	24	15	14	1	3	1	0	0	1	1	3	0	.214	.286
Eric Karros	1B10	R	23	14	14	0	1	0	0	0	1	0	6	0	.071	.143
1 Barry Lyons	C6	R	31	9	14	0	0	0	0	0	0	0	0	0	.000	.000
Greg Smith	2B1	B	24	8	3	0	0	0	0	0	0	0	2	0	.000	.000
Butch Davis		R	33	4	1	0	0	0	0	0	0	0	1	0	.000	.000

NAME	T	AGE	W	L	PCT	SV	G	GS	CG	IP	H	BB	SO	SHO	ERA
		31	93	69	.574	40	162	162	15	1458	1312	500	1028	14	3.06
Ramon Martinez	R	23	17	13	.567	0	33	33	6	220	190	69	150	4	3.27
Mike Morgan	R	31	14	10	.583	1	34	33	5	236	197	61	140	1	2.78
Bob Ojeda	L	33	12	9	.571	0	31	31	2	189	181	70	120	1	3.18
Tim Belcher	R	29	10	9	.526	0	33	33	2	209	189	75	156	1	2.62
Kevin Gross	R	30	10	11	.476	3	46	10	0	116	123	50	95	0	3.58
Orel Hershiser	R	32	7	2	.778	0	21	21	0	112	112	32	73	0	3.46
2 Roger McDowell (SJ)	R	30	6	3	.667	7	33	0	0	42	39	16	22	0	2.55
Jay Howell (EJ)	R	35	6	5	.545	16	44	0	0	51	39	11	40	0	3.18
Jim Gott	R	31	4	3	.571	2	55	0	0	76	63	32	73	0	2.96
1 Mike Hartley	R	29	2	0	1.000	1	40	0	0	57	53	37	44	0	4.42
Tim Crews	R	30	2	3	.400	0	40	0	0	76	75	19	53	0	3.43
Dennis Cook	L	28	1	0	1.000	0	20	1	0	18	12	7	8	0	0.51
John Wetteland	R	24	1	0	1.000	0	6	0	0	9	5	3	9	0	0.00
John Candelaria	L	37	1	1	.500	2	59	0	0	34	31	11	38	0	3.74
2 Steve Wilson	L	26	0	0	—	0	11	0	0	8	1	4	5	0	0.00
Mike Christopher	R	28	0	0	—	0	3	0	0	4	2	1	2	0	0.00

SAN DIEGO 3rd 84-78 .519 10 GREG RIDDOCH

Name	G by Pos	B	AGE	G	AB	R	H	2B	3B	HR	RBI	BB	SO	SB	BA	SA
TOTALS			28	162	5408	636	1321	204	36	121	591	501	1069	101	.244	.362
Fred McGriff	1B153	L	27	153	528	84	147	19	1	31	106	105	135	4	.278	.494
Bip Roberts	2B68 OF46	B	27	117	424	66	119	13	3	3	32	37	71	26	.281	.347
Tony Fernandez	SS145	R	29	145	558	81	152	27	5	4	38	55	74	23	.272	.360
Scott Coolbaugh	3B54	R	25	60	180	12	39	8	1	2	15	19	45	0	.217	.306
Tony Gwynn	OF134	L	31	134	530	69	168	27	11	4	62	34	19	8	.317	.432
Darrin Jackson	OF98 P1	R	28	122	359	51	94	12	1	21	49	27	66	5	.262	.476
Jerald Clark	OF96 1B16	R	26	118	369	26	84	16	0	10	47	31	90	2	.228	.352
Benito Santiago	C151 OF1	R	26	152	580	60	155	22	3	17	87	23	114	8	.267	.403
Thomas Howard	OF86	B	26	106	281	30	70	12	3	4	22	24	57	10	.249	.356
2 Tim Teufel	2B65 3B48	R	32	97	307	39	70	16	0	11	42	49	69	8	.228	.388
2 Jack Howell	3B54	L	29	58	160	24	33	3	1	6	16	18	33	0	.206	.350
Paul Faries	2B36 3B12 SS8	R	26	57	130	13	23	3	1	0	7	14	21	3	.177	.215
1 Shawn Abner	OF39	R	25	53	115	15	19	4	1	1	5	7	25	0	.165	.243
Kevin Ward	OF33	R	29	44	107	13	26	7	2	2	8	9	27	1	.243	.402
Tom Lampkin	C11	R	27	38	58	4	11	3	1	0	3	3	9	0	.190	.276
Oscar Azocar	OF13 1B1	L	26	38	57	5	14	2	0	0	9	1	9	2	.246	.281
Craig Shipley	SS19 3B14	R	28	37	91	6	25	3	0	1	6	2	14	0	.275	.341
1 Garry Templeton	3B15 SS1	B	35	32	57	5	11	1	1	1	6	1	9	0	.193	.298
Jim Presley	3B16	R	29	20	59	3	8	0	0	1	5	4	16	0	.136	.186
Jose Mota	2B13 SS3	B	26	17	36	4	8	0	0	0	2	2	7	0	.222	.222
Jim Vatcher	OF11	R	26	17	20	3	4	0	0	0	2	4	6	1	.200	.200
Dann Bilardello	C13	R	32	15	26	4	7	2	1	0	5	3	4	0	.269	.423
Marty Barrett (KJ)	2B2 3B2	R	33	12	16	1	3	1	0	1	3	0	3	0	.188	.438
1 Mike Aldrete	OF5	L	30	12	15	2	0	0	0	0	1	3	4	0	.000	.000
Brian Dorsett	1B2	R	30	11	12	0	1	0	0	0	0	2	3	0	.083	.083
Phil Stephenson (KJ)		L	30	11	7	0	2	0	0	0	0	2	5	0	.286	.286

NAME	T	AGE	W	L	PCT	SV	G	GS	CG	IP	H	BB	SO	SHO	ERA
		30	84	78	.519	47	162	162	14	1453	1385	457	921	11	3.57
Bruce Hurst	L	33	15	8	.562	0	31	31	4	222	201	59	141	4	3.29
Andy Benes	R	27	15	11	.577	0	33	33	4	223	194	59	167	1	3.03
Greg Harris (EJ)	R	25	9	5	.643	0	20	20	3	133	116	27	95	2	2.23
Jose Melendez	R	25	8	5	.615	3	31	9	0	94	77	24	60	0	3.27
Mike Maddux	R	29	7	2	.778	5	64	1	0	99	78	27	57	0	2.46
Dennis Rasmussen(SJ)	L	32	6	13	.316	0	24	24	1	147	155	49	75	1	3.74
Ed Whitson (EJ)	R	36	4	6	.400	0	13	12	2	79	93	17	40	0	5.03
Ricky Bones	R	22	4	6	.400	0	11	11	0	54	57	18	31	0	4.83
Rich Rodriguez	L	28	3	1	.750	0	64	1	0	80	66	44	40	0	3.26
1 Eric Nolte	L	27	3	2	.600	0	6	6	0	22	37	10	15	0	11.05
Larry Andersen	R	38	3	4	.429	13	38	0	0	47	39	13	40	0	2.30
Adam Peterson	R	25	3	4	.429	0	11	11	0	55	50	28	37	0	4.45
John Costello	R	30	1	0	1.000	0	27	0	0	35	37	17	24	0	3.09
Pat Clements (SJ)	L	29	1	0	1.000	0	12	0	0	14	13	9	8	0	3.77
Steve Rosenberg	L	26	1	1	.500	0	10	0	0	12	11	5	6	0	6.94
Craig Lefferts	L	33	1	6	.143	23	54	0	0	69	74	14	48	0	3.91
Jim Lewis	R	24	0	0	—	0	12	0	0	13	14	11	10	0	4.15
Jeremy Hernandez	R	24	0	0	—	2	9	0	0	14	8	5	9	0	0.00
Tim Scott	R	24	0	0	—	0	2	0	0	1	2	0	1	0	9.00
Darrin Jackson	R	28	0	0	—	0	1	0	0	2	3	2	0	0	9.00
1 Wes Gardner	R	30	0	1	.000	1	14	0	0	20	27	12	9	0	7.08
Atlee Hammaker(SJ)	L	33	0	1	.000	0	1	1	0	5	8	3	1	0	5.79
Derek Lilliquist	L	25	0	2	.000	0	6	2	0	14	25	4	7	0	8.79

SAN FRANCISCO 4th 75-87 .463 19 ROGER CRAIG

Name	G by Pos	B	AGE	G	AB	R	H	2B	3B	HR	RBI	BB	SO	SB	BA	SA
TOTALS			29	162		649	1345	215	48	141	605	471	973	95	.246	.381
Will Clark	1B144	L	27	148	565	84	170	32	7	29	116	51	91	4	.301	.536
Robby Thompson	2B144	R	29	144	492	74	129	24	5	19	48	63	95	14	.262	.447
Jose Uribe	SS87	B	32	90	231	23	51	8	4	1	12	20	33	3	.221	.303
Matt Williams	3B155 SS4	R	25	157	589	72	158	24	5	34	98	33	128	5	.268	.499
Kevin Bass (KJ)	OF101	R	32	124	361	43	84	10	4	10	40	36	56	7	.233	.366
Willie McGee (VJ)	OF128	B	32	131	497	67	155	30	3	4	43	34	74	17	.312	.408
Kevin Mitchell	OF100 1B1	R	29	113	371	52	95	13	1	27	69	43	57	2	.256	.515
Kirt Manwaring	C67	R	25	67	178	16	40	9	0	0	19	9	22	1	.225	.275
Mike Felder	OF107 3B3 2B1	B	29	132	348	51	92	10	6	0	18	30	31	21	.264	.328
Dave Anderson	SS63 1B16 3B11 2B6	R	30	100	226	24	56	5	2	2	13	12	35	2	.248	.314
Mike Kingery	OF38 1B6	L	30	91	110	13	20	2	2	0	8	15	21	1	.182	.236
Steve Decker	C78	R	25	79	233	11	48	7	1	5	24	16	44	0	.206	.309
Darren Lewis	OF68	R	23	72	222	41	55	5	3	1	15	36	30	13	.248	.311
Terry Kennedy	C58 1B2	L	35	69	171	12	40	7	1	3	13	11	31	0	.234	.339
Mark Leonard	OF34	L	26	64	129	14	31	7	1	2	14	12	25	0	.240	.357
Greg Litton	2B15 1B15 3B11 SS9 OF6 C1 P1	R	26	59	127	13	23	7	1	1	15	11	25	0	.181	.276
Mike Benjamin	SS51 3B1	R	25	54	106	12	13	3	0	2	8	7	26	3	.123	.208
2 Tommy Herr	2B15 3B3	B	35	32	60	6	15	1	1	0	7	13	7	2	.250	.300
1 Tony Perezchica	SS13 2B6	R	25	23	48	2	11	4	1	0	3	2	12	0	.229	.354
Rick Parker (LJ)	OF4	R	28	13	14	0	1	0	0	0	1	1	5	0	.071	.071
Darnell Coles	OF3 1B1	R	29	11	14	1	3	0	0	0	0	2	1	0	.214	.214
Ted Wood	OF8	L	24	10	25	0	3	1	0	0	1	2	11	0	.120	.120
Royce Clayton	SS8	R	21	9	26	0	3	0	0	0	2	1	2	0	.115	.154

NAME	T	AGE	W	L	PCT	SV	G	GS	CG	IP	H	BB	SO	SHO	ERA
		29	75	87	.463	45	162	162	10	1442	1397	544	905	10	4.03
Trevor Wilson	L	25	13	11	.542	0	44	29	2	202	173	77	139	1	3.56
John Burkett	R	26	12	11	.522	0	36	34	3	207	223	60	131	1	4.18
Bud Black	L	34	12	16	.429	0	34	34	3	214	201	71	104	3	3.99
Kelly Downs	R	30	10	4	.714	0	45	11	0	112	99	53	62	0	4.19
Francisco Oliveras	R	28	6	6	.500	3	55	1	0	79	69	22	48	0	3.86
Jeff Brantley	R	27	5	2	.714	15	67	0	0	95	78	52	81	0	2.45
Don Robinson	R	34	5	9	.357	1	34	16	0	121	123	50	78	0	4.38
Paul McClellan	R	25	3	6	.333	0	13	12	1	71	68	25	44	0	4.56
Mike Remlinger	L	25	2	1	.663	0	8	6	1	35	36	20	19	1	4.37
Bryan Hickerson	L	27	2	2	.500	0	17	6	0	50	53	17	43	0	3.60
Dave Righetti	L	32	2	7	.222	24	61	0	0	72	64	28	51	0	3.39
Rod Beck	R	22	1	1	.500	1	31	0	0	52	53	13	38	0	3.78
Scott Garrelts (EJ)	R	29	1	1	.500	0	8	5	0	20	25	9	8	0	6.41
Mike LaCoss	R	35	1	5	.167	0	18	5	0	47	61	24	30	0	7.23
Eric Gunderson	L	25	0	0	—	1	2	0	0	4	3	2	2	0	5.40
Greg Litton	R	26	0	0	—	0	1	0	0	1	1	3	0	0	9.00
Jose Segura	R	28	0	1	.000	0	11	0	0	26	30	10	10	0	4.41
Gil Heredia	R	25	0	2	.000	0	7	4	0	33	27	7	13	0	3.82
Rick Reuschel (KJ)	R	42	0	2	.000	0	4	1	0	11	17	7	4	0	4.22

CINCINNATI 4th 74-88 .457 20 LOU PINIELLA

Name	G by Pos	B	AGE	G	AB	R	H	2B	3B	HR	RBI	BB	SO	SB	BA	SA
TOTALS			28	162	5463	689	1419	250	27	164	654	488	1006	124	.258	.403
Hal Morris	1B128 OF1	L	26	136	478	72	152	33	1	14	59	46	61	10	.318	.479
Bill Doran	2B88 OF6 1B4	B	33	111	361	51	101	12	2	6	35	46	39	5	.280	.374
Barry Larkin	SS119	R	27	123	464	88	140	27	4	20	69	55	64	24	.302	.506
Chris Sabo	3B151	R	28	153	582	91	175	35	3	26	88	44	79	19	.301	.505
Paul O'Neill	OF150	L	28	152	532	71	136	36	0	28	91	73	107	12	.256	.481
Eric Davis (IL)	OF81	R	29	89	285	39	67	10	0	11	33	48	92	14	.235	.386
Billy Hatcher	OF121	R	30	138	442	45	116	25	3	4	41	26	55	11	.262	.360
Jeff Reed	C89	L	28	91	270	20	72	15	2	3	31	23	38	0	.267	.370
Mariano Duncan	2B62 SS32 OF7	R	28	100	333	46	86	7	4	12	40	12	57	5	.258	.411
Herm Winningham	OF66	L	29	98	169	17	38	6	1	1	4	11	40	4	.225	.290
Luis Quinones	2B33 3B19 SS5	B	29	97	212	15	47	4	3	2	20	21	31	1	.222	.325
Joe Oliver	C90	R	25	94	269	21	58	11	0	11	41	18	53	0	.216	.379
Glenn Braggs (LJ)	OF74	R	28	85	250	36	65	10	0	11	39	23	46	11	.260	.432
Carmelo Martinez	1B25 OF16	R	30	53	138	12	32	5	0	6	19	15	37	0	.232	.399
Chris Jones	OF26	R	25	52	89	14	26	1	2	2	6	2	31	2	.292	.416
1 Todd Benzinger	1B21 OF15	B	28	51	123	7	23	3	2	1	11	10	22	1	.187	.268
Freddie Benavides	SS20 2B3	R	25	24	63	11	18	1	0	0	3	1	15	1	.286	.302
Stan Jefferson	OF5	B	28	13	19	2	1	0	0	0	0	0	3	0	.053	.053
Donnie Scott	C8	B	29	10	19	0	3	0	0	0	0	2	6	0	.158	.158
Glenn Sutko	C9	R	23	10	10	0	1	0	0	0	1	0	9	0	.100	.100
Reggie Sanders (SJ)	OF9	R	23	9	40	6	8	0	1	1	2	6	9	1	.200	.275
1 Reggie Jefferson	1B2	B	22	5	9	1	1	0	0	0	1	2	5	0	.143	.571
Terry Lee	1B2	R	29	6	6	0	0	0	0	0	0	0	0	0	.000	.000

NAME	T	AGE	W	L	PCT	SV	G	GS	CG	IP	H	BB	SO	SHO	ERA
		28	74	88	.457	43	162	162	7	1440	1372	560	997	11	3.83
Jose Rijo (BN)	R	26	15	6	.714	0	30	30	3	204	165	55	172	1	2.51
Tom Browning	L	31	14	14	.500	0	36	36	1	230	241	56	115	0	4.18
Chris Hammond (EJ)	L	25	7	7	.500	0	20	18	0	100	92	48	50	0	4.06
Jack Armstrong	R	26	7	13	.350	0	27	24	1	140	158	54	93	0	5.48
Kip Gross	R	26	6	4	.600	0	29	9	1	86	93	40	40	0	3.47
Scott Scudder (AJ)	R	23	6	9	.400	1	27	14	0	101	91	56	51	0	4.35
Randy Myers	L	28	6	13	.316	6	58	12	1	132	116	80	108	0	3.55
Ted Power	R	36	5	3	.625	3	68	0	0	87	87	31	51	0	3.62
Rob Dibble	R	27	3	5	.375	31	67	0	0	82	67	25	124	0	3.17
Norm Charlton (SJ)	L	28	3	5	.375	1	39	11	0	108	92	34	77	0	2.91
Milt Hill	R	25	1	1	.500	0	22	0	0	33	36	8	20	0	3.78
Mo Sanford	R	24	1	2	.333	0	5	5	0	28	19	15	31	0	3.86
Steve Foster	R	24	0	0	—	1	11	0	0	14	7	4	11	0	1.93
Keith Brown	R	27	0	0	—	0	2	0	0	12	15	6	4	0	2.25
Don Carman	L	31	0	0	—	0	2	0	0	36	40	19	15	0	5.25
Tim Layana	R	27	0	2	.000	0	22	0	0	21	23	11	14	0	6.97
Gino Minutelli	L	27	0	0	—	0	16	3	0	38	18	21	21	0	6.04

HOUSTON 6th 65-97 .401 29 ART HOWE

Name	G by Pos	B	AGE	G	AB	R	H	2B	3B	HR	RBI	BB	SO	SB	BA	SA
TOTALS			26	162	5504	605	1345	240	43	79	570	502	1027	125	.244	.347
Jeff Bagwell	1B155	R	23	156	554	79	163	26	4	15	82	75	116	7	.294	.437
Casey Candaele	2B109 OF26 3B11	B	30	151	461	44	121	20	7	4	50	40	49	9	.262	.362
Eric Yelding	SS72 OF4	R	26	78	276	19	67	11	1	2	20	13	46	11	.243	.301
Ken Caminiti	3B152	B	28	152	574	65	145	30	3	13	80	46	85	4	.253	.383
Karl Rhodes	OF44	L	22	44	136	7	29	3	1	1	12	14	26	2	.213	.272
Steve Finley	OF153	L	26	159	596	84	170	28	10	8	54	42	65	34	.285	.406
Luis Gonzalez	OF133	L	23	137	473	51	120	28	9	13	69	40	101	10	.254	.433
Craig Biggio	C139 2B3 OF2	R	25	149	546	79	161	23	4	4	46	53	71	19	.295	.374
Gerald Young	OF84	B	26	108	142	26	31	3	1	1	11	24	17	16	.218	.275
Rafael Ramirez	SS45 2B27 3B2	R	33	101	233	17	55	10	1	1	20	13	40	3	.236	.292
Mark Davidson	OF63	R	30	85	161	17	26	7	0	2	15	12	28	0	.190	.275
Andujar Cedeno	SS66	R	21	67	251	27	61	13	2	9	36	9	74	4	.243	.418
Ken Oberkfell (IL)	1B13 3B4	L	35	53	77	7	16	4	0	0	14	14	8	0	.229	.286
Mike Simms	OF41	R	24	49	123	18	25	5	0	3	16	18	38	1	.203	.317
Javier Ortiz	OF24	R	28	43	87	7	23	4	1	1	6	14	14	0	.277	.386
Jose Tolentino	1B10 OF1	L	30	44	54	6	14	4	0	0	6	4	10	0	.259	.389
Eric Anthony	OF37	L	23	39	118	11	18	6	0	5	11	12	41	1	.153	.229
Dave Rohde	2B4 3B3 SS3 1B1	B	27	29	41	3	5	0	0	0	5	8	11	0	.122	.122
Andy Mota	2B27	R	25	27	90	4	17	2	0	1	6	2	13	0	.189	.244
Mark McLemore (LJ)	2B19	B	26	21	61	6	9	1	0	0	2	6	13	0	.148	.164
Kenny Lofton	OF20	L	24	20	74	9	15	1	0	0	0	5	19	2	.203	.216
Carl Nichols	C17	R	24	17	55	3	10	1	0	0	2	1	9	0	.196	.255
Scott Servais (BH)	C14	R	24	16	37	0	6	1	0	0	6	5	8	0	.162	.243
Tony Eusebio	C9	R	24	10	14	0	2	0	0	0	1	0	5	0	.105	.158
Gary Cooper	3B4	R	26	9	16	1	4	1	0	0	1	3	1	0	.250	.313

NAME	T	AGE	W	L	PCT	SV	G	GS	CG	IP	H	BB	SO	SHO	ERA
		27	65	97	.401	36	162	162	7	1453	1347	651	1033	13	4.00
Pete Harnisch	R	24	12	9	.571	0	33	33	4	217	169	83	172	2	2.70
Mark Portugal	R	28	10	12	.455	1	32	27	1	168	163	59	120	0	4.49
Al Osuna	L	25	7	6	.538	12	71	0	0	82	59	46	68	0	3.42
Darryl Kile	R	22	7	11	.389	0	37	22	0	154	144	84	100	0	3.69
Ryan Bowen	R	23	6	4	.600	0	14	13	0	72	73	36	49	0	5.15
Jimmy Jones (EJ)	R	27	6	8	.429	0	26	22	1	135	143	51	88	1	4.39
Jim Deshaies	L	31	5	12	.294	0	28	28	1	161	156	72	98	0	4.98
Dwayne Henry	R	29	3	2	.600	2	52	0	0	68	51	39	71	0	3.19
Curt Schilling	R	24	3	5	.375	8	56	0	0	76	79	39	71	0	3.81
Dean Wilkins	R	24	2	1	.667	1	9	0	0	8	16	10	4	0	11.25
Xavier Hernandez (SJ)	R	25	2	7	.222	3	32	6	0	63	66	32	55	0	4.71
Chris Gardner	R	22	1	3	.333	0	5	4	0	25	19	14	12	0	4.01
Mike Capel	R	29	1	3	.250	3	25	0	0	33	33	15	23	0	3.03
Brian Williams	R	22	0	1	.000	0	2	1	0	12	11	4	4	0	3.75
Rob Mallicoat	L	26	0	3	.000	0	24	0	0	23	22	13	18	0	3.86
Jeff Juden	R	20	0	2	.000	0	4	4	0	18	19	7	11	0	6.00
Mike Scott (SJ)	R	36	0	2	.000	0	2	2	0	7	11	4	1	0	12.86
1 Jim Clancy	R	35	0	3	.000	0	30	0	0	55	57	20	33	0	2.78
Jim Corsi	R	29	0	5	.000	0	47	0	0	78	76	23	53	0	3.71

LINE SCORES

Team	1	2	3	4	5	6	7	8	9	10	11	12	R	H	E

AMERICAN LEAGUE CHAMPIONSHIPS: MINNESOTA (WEST) 4 TORONTO (EAST) 1

Game 1 October 8 at Minnesota

| TOR | 0 | 0 | 0 | 1 | 0 | 3 | 0 | 0 | 0 | | | | 4 | 9 | 3 |
| MIN | 2 | 2 | 1 | 0 | 0 | 0 | 0 | 0 | X | | | | 5 | 11 | 0 |

Candiotti, Wells (3), Timlin (6) **Morris**, Willis (8), Aguilera (8)

Game 2 October 9 at Minnesota

| TOR | 1 | 0 | 2 | 0 | 0 | 0 | 2 | 0 | 0 | | | | 5 | 9 | 0 |
| MIN | 0 | 0 | 1 | 0 | 0 | 1 | 0 | 0 | 0 | | | | 2 | 5 | 1 |

Guzman, Henke (6), D. Ward (8) **Tapani**, Bedrosian (7), Guthrie (7)

Game 3 October 11 at Toronto

| MIN | 0 | 0 | 0 | 0 | 1 | 1 | 0 | 0 | 1 | | | | 3 | 7 | 0 |
| TOR | 2 | 0 | 0 | 0 | 0 | 0 | 0 | 0 | 0 | 0 | | | 2 | 5 | 1 |

Erickson, **West** (5), Willis (7) Key, Wells (7), Henke (8), **Timlin** (10)
Guthrie, (9), Aguilera (10)

Game 4 October 12 at Toronto

| MIN | 0 | 0 | 4 | 0 | 2 | 1 | 1 | | | | | | 9 | 13 | 1 |
| TOR | 0 | 1 | 0 | 0 | 0 | 1 | 0 | 0 | 1 | | | | 3 | 11 | 2 |

Morris, Bedrosian (9) **Stottlemyre**, Wells (4), Acker (6)
Timlin (7), MacDonald (9)

Game 5 October 13 at Toronto

| MIN | 1 | 1 | 0 | 0 | 0 | 3 | 0 | 3 | 0 | | | | 8 | 14 | 2 |
| TOR | 0 | 0 | 3 | 2 | 0 | 0 | 0 | 0 | 0 | | | | 5 | 9 | 1 |

Tapani, **West** (5), Willis (8), Candiotti, Timlin (6), **D. Ward** (6),
Aguilera (9) Wells (8)

NATIONAL LEAGUE CHAMPIONSHIPS: ATLANTA (WEST) 4   PITTSBURGH (EAST) 3

Game 1 October 9 at Pittsburgh

| ATL | 0 | 0 | 0 | 0 | 0 | 0 | 0 | 1 | | | | | 1 | 5 | 1 |
| PIT | 1 | 0 | 2 | 0 | 0 | 1 | 0 | 1 | X | | | | 5 | 8 | 1 |

Glavine, Wohlers(7), Stanton(8) **Drabek**, Walk (7)

Game 2 October 10 at Pittsburgh

| ATL | 0 | 0 | 0 | 0 | 0 | 1 | 0 | 0 | 0 | | | | 1 | 8 | 0 |
| PIT | 0 | 0 | 0 | 0 | 0 | 0 | 0 | 0 | 0 | | | | 0 | 6 | 0 |

Avery, Pena(9) **Smith**, Mason(8), Belinda(9)

Game 3 October 12 at Atlanta

| PIT | 1 | 0 | 0 | 1 | 0 | 0 | 1 | 0 | 0 | | | | 3 | 10 | 2 |
| ATL | 4 | 1 | 1 | 0 | 0 | 0 | 1 | 3 | X | | | | 10 | 11 | 0 |

Smiley, Landrum(3), Patterson(4) **Smoltz**, Stanton(7), Wohlers(8),
Kipper(6), Rodriguez(8) Pena(8)

Game 4 October 13 at Atlanta

| PIT | 0 | 1 | 0 | 0 | 1 | 0 | 0 | 0 | 1 | | | | 3 | 11 | 1 |
| ATL | 2 | 0 | 0 | 0 | 0 | 0 | 0 | 0 | 0 | | | | 2 | 7 | 1 |

Tomlin, Walk(7), **Belinda**(9) Leibrandt, Clancey(7), Stanton(8),
Mercker(10), Wohlers(10)

Game 5 October 14 at Atlanta

| PIT | 0 | 0 | 0 | 0 | 1 | 0 | 0 | 0 | 0 | | | | 1 | 6 | 2 |
| ATL | 0 | 0 | 0 | 0 | 0 | 0 | 0 | 0 | 0 | | | | 0 | 9 | 1 |

Smith, Mason (8) **Glavine**, Pena (9)

Game 6 October 16 at Pittsburgh

| ATL | 0 | 0 | 0 | 0 | 0 | 0 | 0 | 0 | 1 | | | | 1 | 7 | 0 |
| PIT | 0 | 0 | 0 | 0 | 0 | 0 | 0 | 0 | 0 | | | | 0 | 4 | 0 |

Avery, Pena (9) **Drabek**

Game 7 October 17 at Pittsburgh

| ATL | 3 | 0 | 0 | 0 | 1 | 0 | 0 | 0 | 0 | | | | 4 | 6 | 1 |
| PIT | 0 | 0 | 0 | 0 | 0 | 0 | 0 | 0 | 0 | | | | 0 | 6 | 0 |

Smoltz **Smiley**, Walk (1), Mason (6),
Belinda (8)

COMPOSITE BATTING

NAME	POS	G	AB	R	H	2B	3B	HR	RBI	BA
MINNESOTA										
Totals		5	181	27	50	9	1	3	25	.276
Gladden	LF	5	23	4	6	0	0	0	3	.261
Puckett	CF	5	21	4	9	1	0	2	6	.429
Hrbek	1B	5	21	0	3	0	0	0	3	.143
Knoblauch	2B	5	20	5	7	2	0	0	3	.350
Mack	RF	5	18	4	6	1	1	0	3	.333
Harper	C	5	18	1	5	2	0	1	2	.278
Davis	DH	5	17	3	5	2	0	0	3	.294
Gagne	SS	5	17	2	4	0	0	0	1	.235
Pagliarulo	3B-PH	5	15	3	5	1	0	1	3	.333
Leius	PH-3B	3	4	0	0	0	0	0	0	.000
Larkin	PH	3	3	0	0	0	0	0	0	.000
Ortiz	C	3	3	0	0	0	0	0	0	.000
Sorrento	PH	1	1	0	0	0	0	0	0	.000
Newman	3B-SS	2	0	0	0	0	0	0	0	—
Brown	PR	1	0	1	0	0	0	0	0	—
TORONTO										
Totals		5	173	19	43	6	0	1	18	.249
White	CF	5	22	6	8	1	0	0	0	.364
Gruber	3B	5	21	1	5	0	0	0	4	.238
Maldonado	LF-RF	5	20	1	2	1	0	0	1	.100
Alomar	2B	5	19	3	9	0	0	0	1	.474
Borders	C	5	19	0	5	1	0	0	2	.263
Carter	RF-DH	5	19	3	5	2	0	1	4	.263
Olerud	1B	5	19	1	4	1	0	0	3	.211
Lee	SS	5	16	3	2	0	0	0	0	.125
Mulliniks	DH-PH	5	8	1	1	0	0	0	0	.125
Wilson	PR-DH-LF	3	8	1	2	0	0	0	0	.250
Ducey	PR-RF	1	1	0	0	0	0	0	0	.000
Tabler	PH	1	1	0	0	0	0	0	0	.000
Gonzales	PR-1B-SS	2	0	0	0	0	0	0	0	—
ATLANTA										
Totals		7	229	19	53	10	1	5	19	.231
Pendleton	3B	7	30	1	5	1	1	0	1	.167
Gant	CF	7	27	4	7	1	0	1	3	.259
Justice	RF	7	25	4	5	1	0	1	2	.200
Olson	C	7	24	3	8	1	0	1	4	.333
L. Smith	LF	7	24	3	6	3	0	0	0	.225
Lemke	2B	7	20	1	4	1	0	0	1	.200
Belliard	SS	7	19	0	4	0	0	0	1	.211
Hunter	1B	5	18	2	6	2	0	1	4	.333
Bream	1B-PH	4	10	1	3	0	0	1	3	.300
Avery	P	2	7	0	1	0	0	0	0	.143
Smoltz	P	2	5	0	1	0	0	0	0	.200
Mitchell	PR-LF-PH	5	4	0	0	0	0	0	0	.000
Gregg	PH	4	4	0	1	0	0	0	0	.250
Glavine	P	2	4	0	1	0	0	0	0	.250
Treadway	2B	1	3	0	1	0	0	0	0	.333
Blauser	SS-PH	2	2	0	0	0	0	0	0	.000
Willard	PH	2	2	0	0	0	0	0	0	.000
Leibrandt	P	2	1	0	0	0	0	0	0	.000
PITTSBURGH										
Totals		7	228	12	51	10	0	3	11	.224
Bell	SS	7	29	2	12	2	0	1	1	.414
Bonds	LF	7	27	1	4	1	0	0	0	.148
Lind	2B	7	25	0	4	0	0	0	3	.160
Van Slyke	CF	7	25	3	4	2	0	1	2	.160
Bonilla	RF	7	23	2	7	2	0	0	1	.304
Buechele	3B	7	23	2	7	0	0	0	0	.304
Redus	1B	5	19	1	3	0	0	0	0	.158
Slaught	C-PH	6	17	0	4	0	0	0	1	.235
Merced	1B-PH	7	9	1	2	0	0	1	1	.222
LaValliere	C-PH	3	6	0	2	0	0	0	1	.333
Drabek	P	2	5	0	1	1	0	0	1	.200
Z. Smith	P	2	5	0	0	0	0	0	0	.000
Wilkerson	PH	4	4	0	0	0	0	0	0	.000
McClendon	PH-1B	3	2	0	0	0	0	0	0	.000
Walk	P	3	2	0	0	0	0	0	0	.000
Varsho	PH	2	2	0	1	0	0	0	0	.500
Espy	PH	2	2	0	0	0	0	0	0	.000
Tomlin	P	1	2	0	0	0	0	0	0	.000
Mason	P	3	1	0	0	0	0	0	0	.000

COMPOSITE PITCHING

NAME	G	IP	H	BB	SO	W	L	SV	ERA
MINNESOTA									
Totals	5	46	43	15	30	4	1	3	3.33
Morris	2	13.1	17	1	7	2	0	0	4.05
Tapani	2	10.1	16	3	9	0	1	0	7.84
West	3	5.2	1	4	4	1	0	0	0.00
Willis	3	5.1	2	0	3	0	0	0	0.00
Erickson	1	4	3	5	2	0	0	0	4.50
Aguilera	3	3.1	1	0	3	0	0	3	0.00
Guthrie	2	2.2	0	0	1	0	0	0	0.00
Bedrosian	2	1.1	3	2	2	1	0	0	0.00
TORONTO									
Totals	5	45	50	15	37	1	4	1	4.60
Wells	4	7.2	6	2	9	0	0	0	2.35
Candiotti	2	7.2	17	2	5	0	1	0	8.22
Key	1	6	5	1	1	0	0	0	3.00
Timlin	4	5.2	5	2	5	1	0	1	3.18
Guzman	1	5.2	4	4	2	1	0	0	3.18
Ward	2	4.1	4	1	6	0	1	1	6.23
Stottlemyre	1	3.2	7	1	3	0	1	0	9.81
Henke	2	2.2	0	1	5	0	0	0	0.00
MacDonald	1	1	1	0	0	0	0	0	9.00
Acker	1	0.2	1	0	1	0	0	0	0.00
ATLANTA									
Totals	7	63	51	22	57	4	3	3	1.57
Avery	2	16.1	9	4	17	2	0	0	0.00
Smoltz	2	15.1	14	3	15	2	0	0	1.76
Glavine	2	14	12	6	11	0	2	0	3.21
Leibrandt	1	6.2	8	1	6	0	0	0	1.35
Pena	4	4.1	1	0	4	0	0	3	0.00
Stanton	3	3.2	4	3	3	0	0	0	2.45
Wohlers	3	1.2	3	1	1	0	0	0	0.00
Mercker	1	0.2	0	1	0	0	0	0	13.50
Clancy	1	0.1	0	0	0	0	0	0	0.00
PITTSBURGH									
Totals	7	63	53	22	42	3	4	2	2.57
Drabek	2	15	10	5	10	1	1	0	0.60
Z. Smith	2	14.2	15	3	10	1	1	0	0.61
Walk	3	9.1	5	3	5	0	0	1	1.43
Tomlin	1	6	6	2	1	0	0	0	3.00
Belinda	3	5	0	3	4	1	0	0	0.00
Mason	3	4.1	3	1	2	0	0	1	0.00
Smiley	2	2.2	8	1	3	0	2	0	23.63
Kipper	1	2	2	0	1	0	0	0	4.50
Patterson	1	2	1	0	3	0	0	0	0.00
Landrum	1	1	2	2	2	0	0	0	9.00
Rodriguez	1	1	1	2	1	0	0	0	27.00

LINE SCORES

WORLD SERIES MINNESOTA (AL) 4: ATLANTA (NL) 3

Team	1	2	3	4	5	6	7	8	9	10	11	12	R	H	E

Game 1 October 19 at Minnesota

Team	1	2	3	4	5	6	7	8	9	R	H	E
ATL	0	0	0	0	0	0	1	0	1	2	6	1
MIN	0	0	1	0	3	1	0	0	X	5	9	1

Leibrandt Clancy (5), **Morris**, Guthrie (8), Aguilera (8)
Wohlers (7), Stanton (8),

Game 2 October 20 at Minnesota

Team	1	2	3	4	5	6	7	8	9	R	H	E
ATL	0	1	0	0	1	0	0	0		2	8	1
MIN	2	0	0	0	0	0	0	1	X	3	4	1

Glavine   **Tapani**, Aguilera (9),

Game 3 October 22 at Atlanta

Team	1	2	3	4	5	6	7	8	9	10	11	12	R	H	E
MIN	1	0	0	0	0	0	1	2	0	0	0	0	4	10	1
ATL	0	1	0	1	2	0	0	0	0	0	1		5	8	2

Erickson, West (5), Leach (5)   Avery, Pena (8), Stanton (10)
Bedrosian (6), Willis (8),   Wohlers (12), Mercker (12),
Guthrie (10), **Aguilera (12)**   Clancy (12)

Game 4 October 23 at Atlanta

Team	1	2	3	4	5	6	7	8	9	R	H	E
MIN	0	1	0	0	0	0	1	0	0	2	7	0
ATL	0	0	1	0	0	0	1	0	1	3	8	0

Morris, Willis (9), Guthrie (8),   Smoltz, Wohlers (8), **Stanton (8)**
Bedrosian (9)

Game 5 October 24 at Atlanta

Team	1	2	3	4	5	6	7	8	9	R	H	E
MIN	0	0	0	0	0	3	0	1	1	5	7	1
ATL	0	0	4	1	0	6	3	X		14	17	1

Tapani, Leach (5), West (7),   **Glavine**, Mercker (6), Clancy (7),
Bedrosian (7), Willis (8)   St. Claire (9)

Game 6 October 26 at Minnesota

Team	1	2	3	4	5	6	7	8	9	10	11	R	H	E
ATL	0	0	0	0	2	0	1	0	0	0	0	3	9	1
MIN	2	0	0	1	0	0	0	0	0	0	1	4	9	0

Avery, Stanton (7), Pena (9),   Erickson, Guthrie (7), Willis (7),
Leibrandt (11)   **Aguilera (10)**

Game 7 October 27 at Minnesota

Team	1	2	3	4	5	6	7	8	9	10	R	H	E
ATL	0	0	0	0	0	0	0	0	0	0	0	7	0
MIN	0	0	0	0	0	0	0	0	1		1	10	0

Smoltz, Stanton (8), **Pena (9)**   **Morris**

COMPOSITE BATTING

NAME	POS	G	AB	R	H	2B	3B	HR	RBI	BA
MINNESOTA										
Totals		7	241	24	56	8	4	8	24	.232
Gladden	LF	7	30	5	7	2	2	0	0	.233
Knoblauch	2B	7	26	3	8	1	0	0	2	.308
Hrbek	1B	7	26	2	3	1	0	1	2	.115
Puckett	CF	7	24	4	6	0	1	2	4	.250
Gagne	SS	7	24	1	4	1	0	1	3	.167
Mack	RF	6	23	0	3	1	0	0	1	.130
Harper	C-PH	7	21	2	8	2	0	0	1	.381
Davis	DH-RF-PH	6	18	4	4	0	0	2	4	.222
Leius	3B-SS-PH	7	14	2	5	0	0	1	2	.357
Pagliarulo	3B-PH	6	11	1	3	0	0	1	2	.273
Ortiz	C	3	5	0	1	0	0	0	1	.200
Larkin	PH	4	4	0	2	0	0	0	1	.500
Bush	RF-PH	3	4	0	1	0	0	0	0	.250
Newman	3B-2B-SS-PH	3	2	0	1	0	1	0	1	.500
Brown	RF-CF-PH-PR	4	2	0	0	0	0	0	0	.000
Sorrento	1B-PH	3	2	0	0	0	0	0	0	.000
Morris	P	3	2	0	0	0	0	0	0	.000
Aguilera	P-PH	4	1	0	0	0	0	0	0	.000
Erickson	P	2	1	0	0	0	0	0	0	.000
Tapani	P	1	1	0	0	0	0	0	0	.000
Willis	P	4	0	0	0	0	0	0	0	—
Guthrie	P	4	0	0	0	0	0	0	0	—
Bedrosian	P	3	0	0	0	0	0	0	0	—
Leach	P	2	0	0	0	0	0	0	0	—
West	P	2	0	0	0	0	0	0	0	—
ATLANTA										
Totals		7	249	29	63	10	4	8	29	.253
Pendleton	3B	7	30	6	11	3	0	2	3	.367
Gant	CF	7	30	3	8	0	1	0	4	.267
Justice	RF	7	27	5	7	0	0	2	6	.259
Olson	C	7	27	3	6	2	0	0	1	.222
Smith	DH-LF	7	26	5	6	0	0	3	3	.231
Lemke	2B	6	24	4	10	1	3	0	4	.417
Bream	1B	7	24	0	3	2	0	0	0	.125
Hunter	LF-1B-PH	7	21	2	4	1	0	1	3	.190
Belliard	SS	7	16	0	6	1	0	0	4	.375
Blauser	SS-PH	5	6	0	1	0	0	0	0	.167
Treadway	2B-PH	3	4	1	1	0	0	0	0	.250
Gregg	PH	4	3	0	0	0	0	0	0	.000
Avery	P	2	3	0	0	0	0	0	0	.000
Mitchell	LF-PR	3	2	0	0	0	0	0	0	.000
Smoltz	P	2	2	0	0	0	0	0	0	.000
Glavine	P	2	2	0	0	0	0	0	0	.000
Cabrera	C-PH	2	1	0	0	0	0	0	0	.000
Clancy	P	2	1	0	0	0	0	0	0	.000
Willard	PH	1	0	0	0	0	0	0	1	—
Stanton	P	5	0	0	0	0	0	0	0	—
Pena	P	3	0	0	0	0	0	0	0	—
Wohlers	P	3	0	0	0	0	0	0	0	—
Leibrandt	P	2	0	0	0	0	0	0	0	—
Mercker	P	2	0	0	0	0	0	0	0	—
St. Claire	P	1	0	0	0	0	0	0	0	—

COMPOSITE PITCHING

NAME	G	IP	H	BB	SO	W	L	SV	ERA
MINNESOTA									
Totals	7	67.1	63	26	39	4	3	2	3.74
Morris	3	23	18	9	15	2	0		1.17
Tapani	2	12	13	2	7	1	1	0	4.50
Aguilera	4	5	6	1	3	1	1	2	1.80
Erickson	2	10.2	10	4	5	0	0		5.06
Willis	4	7	6	2	2	0	0		5.14
Bedrosian	3	3.1	3	0	2	0	0		5.40
Leach	2	2.1	2	0	2	0	0		3.86
West	2	0	2	4	0	1	0		∞
Guthrie	4	4	3	4	3	0	1		2.25
ATLANTA									
Totals	7	65.1	56	21	48	3	4	0	2.89
Stanton	5	7.1	5	2	7	1	0	0	0.00
Clancy	3	4.1	3	4	2	1	0	0	4.15
Glavine	2	13.1	8	7	8	1	1	0	2.70
Smoltz	2	14.1	13	1	11	0	0	0	1.26
Avery	2	13	10	1	8	0	0	0	3.46
Wohlers	3	1.2	2	1	0	0	0	0	0.00
Mercker	2	1	0	1	0	0	0	0	0.00
St. Claire	1	1	1	0	0	0	0	0	9.00
Pena	3	5.1	6	3	7	0	1	0	3.38
Leibrandt	2	4	8	1	3	0	2	0	11.25

MISCELLANEOUS 1991 INDIVIDUAL LEADERS

BATTING

On Base Average

	American League			National League	
1	Thomas, Chi.	.453	1	Bonds, Pit.	.410
2	Randolph, Mil.	.424	2	Butler, L.A.	.401
3	Boggs, Bos.	.421	3	McGriff, S.D.	.396
4	Franco, Tex.	.408	4	Bonilla, Pit.	.391
5	E. Martinez, Sea.	.405	5	Bagwell, Hou.	.387

Caught Stealing

	American League			National League	
1	Polonia, Cal.	23	1	Butler, L.A.	28
2	R. Henderson, Oak.	18	2	DeShields, Mon.	23
3	Cole, Cle.	17	3	Nixon, Atl.	21
4	Raines, Chi.	15	4	Lankford, St.L.	20
	Guillen, Chi.	15	5	Finley, Hou.	18

Hit By Pitcher

	American League			National League	
1	Carter, Tor.	10	1	Bagwell, Hou.	13
2	Valle, Sea.	9	2	Smith, Atl.	9
	Canseco, Oak.	9	3	Gonzalez, Hou.	8
4	Downing, Tex.	8	4	Carter, L.A.	7
	Gaetti, Cal.	8		Hatcher, Cin.	7
	E. Martinez, Sea.	8			

Sacrifice Hits

	American League			National League	
1	Sojo, Cal.	19	1	Bell, Pit.	30
2	Alomar, Tor.	16	2	Glavine, Atl.	15
3	Reynolds, Sea.	14	3	Tomlin, Pit.	13
4	Fermin, Cle.	13		Smith, Pit.	13
	Surhoff, Mil.	13	5	Leibrandt, Atl.	12
	Guillen, Chi.	13		Hurst, S.D..	12
				Harris, L.A.	12

Extra Base Hits

	American League			National League	
1	C. Ripken, Bal.	85	1	Johnson, N.Y.	76
2	Carter, Tor.	78	2	Gant, Atl.	70
	Palmeiro, Tex.	78	3	Clark, S.F.	68
4	Canseco, Oak.	77		Bonilla, Pit.	68
5	Sierra, Tex.	74	5	O'Neill, Cin.	64
				Sabo, Cin.	64
				Pendleton, Atl.	64

Ground into Double Play

	American League			National League	
1	Puckett, Min.	27	1	Santiago, S.D.	21
2	Belle, Cle.	24	2	Lind, Pit.	20
3	Milligan, Bal.	23		Murphy, Phi.	20
	Pena, Bos.	23	4	Caminiti, Hou.	18
5	Ventura, Chi.	22	5	Murray, L.A.	17

Total Bases

	American League			National League	
1	C. Ripken, Bal.	368	1	Clark, S.F.	303
2	Palmeiro, Tex.	336		Pendleton, Atl.	303
3	Sierra, Tex.	332	3	Johnson, N.Y.	302
4	Molitor, Mil.	325	4	Sabo, Cin.	294
5	Carter, Tor.	321		Wiliams, S.F.	294

Sacrifice Flies

	American League			National League	
1	Davis, Sea.	10	1	Johnson, N.Y.	15
2	Olerud, Tor.	10	2	Bonds, Pit.	13
			3	Bonilla, Pit.	11
				Dunston, Chi.	11
				Van Slyke, Pit.	11

FIELDING AVERAGE

		PO	A	E	DP	Pct.
American League						
1B	O'Brien, Sea.	1047	86	3	124	.997
2B	Whitaker, Det.	255	362	4	91	.994
3B	Pecota, K.C.	69	158	4	14	.983
SS	C. Ripken, Bal.	267	529	11	114	.986
OF	White, Tor.	439	8	1	2	.998
C	Parrish, Cal.	658	57	2	11	.997
National League						
1B	Kruk, Phi.	736	49	2	54	.997
2B	Sandberg, Chi.	267	515	4	66	.995
3B	Wallach, Mon.	107	310	14	27	.968
SS	Smith, St.L.	244	387	8	79	.987
OF	Butler, L.A.	372	8	0	3	1.000
C	LaValliere, Pit.	565	46	1	4	.998

PITCHING

Wild Pitches

	American League			National League	
1	Morris, Min..	15	1	Smoltz, Atl.	20
2	Hanson, Sea.	14	2	Cone, N.Y.	17
	Moore, Oak.	14	3	Grimsley, Phi.	14
4	Stewart, Oak.	13	4	Charlton, Cin.	11
5	Brown, Tex.	12		Walk, Pit.	11
	Johnson, Sea.	12			

Home Runs Allowed

	American League			National League	
1	DeLucia, Sea.	31	1	Browning, Cin.	32
2	Langston, Cal.	30	2	Armstrong, Cin.	25
3	Tanana, Det.	26		Black, S.F.	25
4	Welch, Oak..	25		Viola, N.Y.	25
	Anderson, Min.	24	5	Benes, S.D.	23
	Wells, Tor.	24			
	Stewart, Oak.	24			

Home Runs Allowed per 9 IP
(Minimum 10 Home Runs Allowed)

	American League			National League	
1	Nelson, Oak.	2.22	1	Peterson, S.D.	1.65
2	Darwin, Bos.	1.98	2	McClellan, S.F.	1.52
3	Johnson, Bal.	1.93	3	Oliveras, S.F.	1.36
4	Boucher, Tor.-Cle.	1.86	4	Palacios, Pit.	1.32
5	Boyd, Tex.	1.74			

1992 OH, CANADA !

Like too many recent seasons, 1992 was memorable as much for what happened off the field as on it. The year's biggest story was the forced resignation of Commissioner Fay Vincent in August. Vincent had incurred the owners' wrath with his attempt to realign the National League by shifting St. Louis and Chicago to the West Division, by his handling of the suspensions of Yankees owner George Steinbrenner and pitcher Steve Howe, and by his refusal to deal himself out of upcoming negotiations with the Players' Association. In the wake of Vincent's departure, baseball owners proposed a complete restructuring of the commissioner's office and duties.

Other news-making events included the sale of the Seattle Mariners to interests with part of their base in Japan, the passing of the Detroit Tigers from the hands of one pizza king to another, and a proposed sale and migration of the San Francisco Giants to interests in St. Petersburg, Florida. Ever-increasing salaries paid to players sometimes produced contract numbers that were better-known than their batting averages. Bobby Bonilla's $5.9 million deal with the New York Mets was eclipsed by Ryne Sandberg's long-term contract with the Cubs that will eventually be worth more than $7 million per year. Meanwhile, much of the daily sports page was given over to speculation as to how high the next crop of free agents would go for.

The pennant races themselves were somewhat mundane. In the National League East, Pittsburgh, led by Barry Bonds and Andy Van Slyke, went in front early, held off a challenge by the young and talented Montreal Expos, and took their third straight division title. The pre-season favored Mets were hamstrung by decimating injuries and disappointing performances.

Injuries to key players shaped the final standings in both leagues. After a strong start, the Cincinnati Reds bogged down at mid-year in the N.L. West under a growing hospital list. Atlanta, led by Terry Pendleton and the league's strongest starting rotation, moved to the front and won in a walk. The proud Dodgers could blame injuries, a punchless lineup, and baseball's most inept fielding for finishing last for the first time since 1905.

In the American League West, defending champ Minnesota could look to injuries and undependable pitching as the reasons for a disastrous mid-season slump. Ironically, Oakland, which suffered as heavy an injury outbreak as anyone, was able to overcome and triumph as Manager Tony LaRussa squeezed strong performances out of journeyman reserves. In August, the A's pulled off the deal of the season when they sent superstar Jose Canseco to Texas for Ruben Sierra, Bobby Witt and Jeff Russell. The one constant in the Athletics' division win was reliever Dennis Eckersley, who saved 51 games and was all but unbeatable.

Amid predictions that they would once more fold in the clutch, Toronto's Blue Jays shook off good efforts by Baltimore and Milwaukee to win the A.L. East. Joe Carter, Dave Winfield, and Roberto Alomar provided the punch, and the sometimes shaky pitching was buoyed by the late-season acquisition of David Cone from the Mets.

In the landmark category, both Robin Yount of Milwaukee and George Brett of Kansas City passed the 3,000 hit mark, Winfield became the oldest player ever to drive in 100 runs, and Detroit's Cecil Fielder became the first since Babe Ruth to lead in RBI'S three consecutive years. Among pitchers, Kevin Gross of Los Angeles pitched the season's only no-hitter. In the same year Rollie Fingers was enshrined in the Hall of Fame, his all-time saves record was surpassed by Jeff Reardon of Boston and Lee Smith of St. Louis. The Cardinals' Bob Tewksbury dazzled by allowing only 20 bases on balls in 233 innings. The season's most unusual fielding was turned in by Philadelphia's Mickey Morandini with an unassisted triple play.

The Blue Jays took the American League took the American League Championship Series from the Athletics in six games. The key moment came when Toronto rallied from a 6-1 deficit in Game Four to tie on Alomar's ninth-inning homer off Eckersley. They then went on to win in the tenth.

The Braves took a 3-1 advantage in the National League Championship Series with Pittsburgh's only win coming from knuckleballing rookie Tim Wakefield in the third game. With the Pirates' backs to the wall, journeyman Bob Walk pitched the best game of his career to win Game Five, and when Wakefield won again the series was tied. Pirate ace Doug Drabek held a 2-0 lead into the ninth inning of the final game only to see the Braves load the bases with no outs. Reliever Stan Belinda allowed a sacrifice fly and a walk but had two outs when Francisco Cabrera, the last man named to the Braves' post-season roster, pinch-hit a single to left. Sid Bream, the slowest man on the field, pounded around third carrying the winning run. When he slid home under the flag, the Braves had the pennant.

Toronto was not to be denied in the World Series. Although Jack Morris, the 1991 Series MVP while with the Twins, lost both his starts, the Blue Jays won four other games, each by one run. In the final game, Winfield's double down the left field line plated two runs to put Toronto in front in the top of the 11th. The Braves rallied furiously in the bottom of the frame but fell a run short. For the first time in history, the major league baseball championship resided outside the United States.

EAST DIVISION   1992 AMERICAN LEAGUE

Name	G by Pos	B	AGE	G	AB	R	H	2B	3B	HR	RBI	BB	SO	SB	BA	SA
TORONTO 1st 96-66 .593	**CITO GASTON**		29	162	5536	780	1458	265	40	163	737	561	933	129	.263	.414
John Olerud	1B133 DH1	L	23	138	458	68	130	28	0	16	66	70	61	1	.284	.450
Roberto Alomar	2B150 DH1	B	24	152	571	105	177	27	8	8	76	87	52	49	.310	.427
Manuel Lee	SS128	B	27	128	396	49	104	10	1	3	39	50	73	6	.263	.316
Kelly Gruber	3B120	R	30	120	446	42	102	16	3	11	43	26	72	7	.229	.352
Joe Carter	OF129 DH24 1B4	R	32	158	622	97	164	30	7	34	119	36	109	12	.264	.498
Devon White	OF152 DH1	B	29	153	641	98	159	26	7	17	60	47	133	37	.248	.390
Candy Maldonado	OF132 DH4	R	31	137	489	64	133	25	4	20	66	59	112	2	.272	.462
Pat Borders	C137	R	29	138	480	47	116	26	2	13	53	33	75	1	.242	.385
Dave Winfield	DH130 OF26	R	40	156	583	92	169	33	3	26	108	82	89	2	.290	.491
1 Jeff Kent	3B49 2B17 1B3	R	24	65	192	36	46	13	1	8	35	20	47	2	.240	.443
Alfredo Griffin	SS48 2B16	B	34	63	150	21	35	7	0	0	10	9	19	3	.233	.280
Derek Bell (BW)	OF56 DH1	R	23	61	161	23	39	6	3	2	15	15	34	7	.242	.354
Pat Tabler	1B34 OF8 DH2 3B1	R	34	49	135	11	34	5	0	0	16	11	14	0	.252	.289
1 Rob Ducey	OF13 DH4	L	27	23	21	3	1	1	0	0	0	0	10	0	.048	.095
1 Greg Myers	C18	L	26	22	61	4	14	6	0	1	13	5	5	0	.230	.377
Ed Sprague	C15 1B4 DH2 3B1	R	24	22	47	6	11	2	0	1	7	3	7	0	.234	.340
Turner Ward	B	27	18	29	7	10	3	0	1	3	4	4	0	.345	.552
Tom Quinlan	3B13	R	24	13	15	2	1	1	0	0	2	2	9	0	.067	.133
Randy Knorr (RJ)	C8	R	23	8	19	1	5	0	0	1	2	1	5	0	.263	.421
Eddie Zosky	SS8	R	24	8	7	1	2	0	1	0	1	0	2	0	.286	.571
Domingo Martinez	1B7	R	24	7	8	2	5	0	0	1	3	0	1	0	.625	1.000
Mike Maksudian	1B1	L	26	3	3	0	0	0	0	0	0	0	1	0	.000	.000
Rance Mulliniks (XJ)	DH2	L	36	3	2	1	1	0	0	0	0	1	0	0	.500	.500
MILWAUKEE 2nd 92-70 .568 4	**PHIL GARNER**		30	162	5504	740	1477	272	35	82	683	511	779	256	.268	.375
Franklin Stubbs	1B68 DH16 OF1	L	31	92	288	37	66	11	1	9	42	27	68	11	.229	.368
Scott Fletcher	2B106 SS22 3B1	R	33	123	386	53	106	18	3	3	51	30	33	17	.275	.360
Pat Listach	SS148 2B1 OF1	B	24	149	579	93	168	19	6	1	47	55	124	54	.290	.349
Kevin Seitzer	3B146 2B2 1B1	R	30	148	540	74	146	35	1	5	71	57	44	13	.270	.367
Darryl Hamilton	OF124	L	27	128	470	67	140	19	7	5	62	45	42	41	.298	.400
Robin Yount	OF139 DH11	R	36	150	557	71	147	40	3	8	77	53	81	15	.264	.390
Greg Vaughn	OF131 DH7	R	26	141	501	77	114	18	2	23	78	60	123	15	.228	.409
B.J. Surhoff	C109 1B17 DH9 OF7 3B3	L	27	139	480	63	121	19	1	4	62	46	41	14	.252	.321
Paul Molitor	DH108 1B48	R	35	158	609	89	195	36	7	12	89	73	66	31	.320	.461
Dante Bichette	OF101 DH4	R	28	112	387	37	111	27	2	5	41	16	74	18	.287	.406
Jim Gantner	2B68 3B31 1B2 DH2	L	39	101	256	22	63	12	1	1	18	12	17	6	.246	.313
Dave Nilsson (WJ)	C46 1B3 DH2	R	22	51	164	15	38	8	0	4	25	17	18	2	.232	.354
John Jaha	1B38 DH8 OF1	R	26	47	133	17	30	3	1	2	10	12	30	10	.226	.308
Tim McIntosh (RJ)	C14 OF10 1B7 DH3	R	26	35	77	7	14	3	0	0	6	3	9	1	.182	.221
Alex Diaz	OF11 DH2	B	23	22	9	5	1	0	0	0	1	0	0	3	.111	.111
William Suero	2B15 DH2 SS1	R	25	18	16	4	3	1	0	0	1	2	6	1	.188	.250
Bill Spiers (XJ)	SS5 2B4 3B1 DH1	L	26	12	16	2	5	2	0	0	2	1	4	1	.313	.438
Andy Allanson (LJ)	C9	R	30	9	25	6	8	1	0	0	0	1	2	0	.320	.360
Jim Tatum	3B5	R	24	5	8	0	1	0	0	0	0	1	2	0	.125	.125
Jose Valentin	2B1 SS1	B	22	4	3	1	0	0	0	0	1	0	0	0	.000	.000

NAME	T	AGE	W	L	PCT	SV	G	GS	CG	IP	H	BB	SO	SHO	ERA
		30	96	66	.593	49	162	162	18	1441	1346	541	954	14	3.91
Jack Morris	R	37	21	6	.778	0	34	34	6	241	222	80	132	1	4.04
Juan Guzman (BJ)	R	25	16	5	.762	0	28	28	1	181	135	72	165	0	2.64
Jimmy Key	L	31	13	13	.500	0	33	33	4	217	205	59	117	2	3.53
Todd Stottlemyre (KJ)	R	27	12	11	.522	0	28	27	6	174	175	63	98	2	4.50
Duane Ward	R	28	7	4	.636	12	79	0	0	101	76	39	103	0	1.95
David Wells	L	29	7	9	.438	2	41	14	0	120	138	36	62	0	5.40
Pat Hentgen(EJ)	R	23	5	2	.714	0	28	2	0	50	49	32	39	0	5.36
2 David Cone	R	29	4	3	.571	0	8	7	0	53	39	29	47	0	2.55
Dave Stieb (EJ)	R	34	4	6	.400	0	21	14	1	96	98	43	45	0	5.04
Tom Henke	R	34	3	2	.600	34	57	0	0	56	40	22	46	0	2.28
2 Mark Eichhorn	R	31	2	0	1.000	2	23	0	0	31	35	7	19	0	4.35
Bob MacDonald	L	27	1	0	1.000	0	27	0	0	47	50	16	26	0	4.37
Doug Linton	R	27	1	3	.250	0	8	3	0	24	31	17	16	0	8.63
David Weathers	R	22	0	0	—	0	2	0	0	3	5	2	3	0	8.10
Ricky Trlicek	R	23	0	0	—	0	2	0	0	2	2	2	1	0	10.80
Al Leiter	L	26	0	0	—	0	1	0	0	1	1	2	0	0	9.00
Mike Timlin (EJ)	R	26	0	2	.000	1	26	0	0	44	45	20	35	0	4.12
Ken Dayley (EJ) 33															
		28	92	70	.568	39	162	162	19	1457	1344	435	793	14	3.43
Jaime Navarro	R	25	17	11	.607	0	34	34	5	246	224	64	100	3	3.33
Chris Bosio	R	29	16	6	.727	0	33	33	4	231	223	44	120	2	3.62
Bill Wegman	R	29	13	14	.481	0	35	35	7	262	251	55	127	0	3.20
Cal Eldred	R	24	11	2	.846	0	14	14	2	100	76	23	62	1	1.79
Ricky Bones	R	23	9	10	.474	0	31	28	0	163	169	48	65	0	4.57
Mike Fetters	R	27	5	1	.833	2	50	0	0	63	38	24	43	0	1.87
Jim Austin	R	28	5	2	.714	0	47	0	0	58	38	32	30	0	1.85
Dan Plesac	L	30	5	4	.556	1	44	4	0	79	64	35	54	0	2.96
Darren Holmes	R	26	4	4	.500	6	41	0	0	42	35	11	31	0	2.55
Jesse Orosco	L	35	3	1	.750	1	59	0	0	39	33	13	40	0	3.23
1 Edwin Nunez	R	29	3	1	.500	0	10	0	0	14	12	6	10	0	2.63
Doug Henry	R	28	1	4	.200	29	68	0	0	65	64	24	52	0	4.02
Ron Robinson (BR)	R	30	1	4	.200	0	8	0	0	35	51	14	12	0	5.86
Bruce Ruffin	L	28	1	6	.143	0	25	6	1	58	66	41	45	0	6.67
2 Neal Heaton	L	32	0	1	.000	0	4	0	0	7	7	1	2	0	0.00
Teddy Higuera (SJ) 33															
Julio Machado (AV) 26															

BALTIMORE   3rd 89-73 .549   7   JOHNNY OATES

Name	G by Pos	B	AGE	G	AB	R	H	2B	3B	HR	RBI	BB	SO	SB	BA	SA
TOTALS			28	162	5485	705	1423	243	36	148	680	647	827	89	.259	.398
Randy Milligan	1B129 DH6	R	30	137	462	71	111	21	1	11	53	106	81	0	.240	.361
Billy Ripken	2B108	R	27	111	330	35	76	15	0	4	36	18	26	2	.230	.312
Cal Ripken	SS162	R	31	162	637	73	160	29	1	14	72	64	50	4	.251	.366
Leo Gomez	3B137	R	25	118	468	62	124	24	0	17	64	63	78	2	.265	.425
Joe Orsulak	OF110 DH1	L	30	117	391	45	113	18	3	4	39	28	34	5	.289	.381
Mike Devereaux	OF155	R	29	156	653	76	180	29	11	24	107	44	94	10	.276	.464
Brady Anderson	OF158	L	28	159	623	100	169	28	10	21	80	98	98	53	.271	.449
Chris Hoiles (BW)	C95 DH1	R	27	96	310	49	85	10	1	20	40	55	60	0	.274	.506
Glenn Davis (VJ)	DH103 1B2	R	31	106	398	46	110	15	2	13	48	37	65	1	.276	.422
David Segui	1B95 OF18	B	25	115	189	21	44	9	0	1	17	20	23	1	.233	.296
Mark McLemore	2B70 DH17	B	27	101	228	40	56	7	2	0	27	21	26	11	.246	.294
Chito Martinez	OF52 DH4	L	26	83	198	26	53	10	1	5	25	31	47	0	.268	.404
Jeff Tackett	C64 3B1	R	26	65	179	21	43	8	1	5	24	17	28	0	.240	.380
Sam Horn	DH46	R	28	73	162	13	38	10	1	5	19	21	60	0	.235	.401
Tim Hulett	3B27 DH13 2B10 SS5	R	32	57	142	11	41	7	2	2	21	10	31	0	.289	.408
Luis Mercedes	OF16 DH7	R	24	23	50	7	7	2	0	0	4	8	9	0	.140	.180
Mark Parent	C16	R	30	17	34	4	8	1	0	2	4	3	7	0	.235	.441
2 Steve Scarsone	2B5 3B2 SS1	R	26	11	17	2	3	0	0	0	0	1	6	0	.176	.176
Rick Dempsey (RC)	C8	R	42	8	9	2	1	0	0	0	0	2	1	0	.111	.111
Manny Alexander	SS3	R	21	4	5	1	1	0	0	0	0	1	0	0	.200	.200
Tommy Shields		R	27	2	0	0	0	0	0	0	0	0	0	0	—	—
Jack Voight		R	26	1	0	0	0	0	0	0	0	0	0	0	—	—

NAME	T	AGE	W	L	PCT	SV	G	GS	CG	IP	H	BB	SO	SHO	ERA
		28	89	73	.549	48	162	162	20	1464	1419	518	846	16	3.79
Mike Mussina	R	23	18	5	.783	0	32	32	8	241	212	48	130	4	2.54
Rick Sutcliffe	R	36	16	15	.516	0	36	36	5	237	251	74	109	2	4.47
Ben McDonald	R	24	13	13	.500	0	35	35	4	227	213	74	158	2	4.24
Alan Mills	R	25	10	4	.714	2	35	3	0	103	78	54	60	0	2.61
Storm Davis	R	30	7	3	.700	4	48	2	0	89	79	36	53	0	3.43
Arthur Rhodes	L	22	7	5	.583	0	15	15	2	94	87	38	77	1	3.63
Bob Milacki	R	27	6	8	.429	1	23	20	0	116	140	44	51	0	5.84
Todd Frohwirth	R	29	4	3	.571	4	65	0	0	106	97	41	58	0	2.46
1 Jose Mesa	R	26	3	8	.273	0	13	12	0	68	77	27	22	0	5.19
2 Pat Clements	L	30	2	0	1.000	0	23	0	0	25	23	11	9	0	3.28
Richie Lewis	R	26	1	1	.500	0	2	2	0	7	13	7	4	0	10.80
2 Craig Lefferts	L	34	1	3	.250	0	5	5	1	33	34	6	23	0	4.09
Gregg Olson	R	25	1	5	.167	36	60	0	0	61	46	24	58	0	2.05
Mike Flanagan	L	40	0	0	—	0	42	0	0	35	50	23	17	0	8.05
Mark Williamson (EJ)	R	32	0	0	—	1	12	0	0	19	16	10	14	0	0.96
Jim Poole (SJ)	L	26	0	0	—	0	3	3	1	3	3	1	3	0	0.00

CLEVELAND   4th(tie) 76-86 .469   20   MIKE HARGROVE

Name	G by Pos	B	AGE	G	AB	R	H	2B	3B	HR	RBI	BB	SO	SB	BA	SA
TOTALS			27	162	5620	674	1495	227	24	127	637	448	885	144	.266	.383
Paul Sorrento	1B121 DH 11	L	26	140	458	52	123	24	1	18	60	51	89	0	.269	.443
Carlos Baerga	2B160 DH1	B	23	161	657	92	205	32	1	20	105	35	76	10	.312	.455
Mark Lewis	SS121 3B1	R	22	122	413	44	109	21	0	5	30	25	69	4	.264	.351
Brook Jacoby	3B111 1B10	R	32	120	291	30	76	7	0	4	36	28	54	0	.261	.326
Mark Whiten	OF144 DH2	R	25	148	508	73	129	19	4	9	43	72	102	16	.254	.360
Kenny Lofton	OF143	L	25	148	576	96	164	15	8	5	42	68	54	66	.285	.365
Glenallen Hill (GJ)	OF59 DH34	R	27	102	369	38	89	16	1	18	49	20	73	9	.241	.436
Sandy Alomar (KJ)	C88 DH1	R	26	89	299	22	75	16	0	2	26	13	32	3	.251	.324
Albert Belle	DH100 OF52	R	25	153	585	81	152	23	1	34	112	52	128	8	.260	.477
2 Thomas Howard	OF97 DH2	R	27	117	358	36	99	15	2	2	32	17	60	15	.277	.346
Junior Ortiz	C86	R	32	86	244	20	61	7	0	0	24	12	23	1	.250	.279
Felix Fermin	SS55 3B17 2B7 1B2	R	28	79	215	27	58	7	2	0	13	18	10	0	.270	.321
Carlos Martinez (XJ)	1B37 3B28 DH4	R	26	69	228	23	60	9	1	5	35	7	21	1	.263	.377
1 Alex Cole	OF24 DH4	L	26	41	97	11	20	1	0	0	5	10	21	9	.206	.216
Jim Thome (WJ-SJ)	3B40	L	21	40	117	8	24	3	1	2	12	10	34	2	.205	.299
Jesse Levis	C21 DH1	L	24	28	43	2	12	4	0	1	3	0	5	0	.279	.442
Reggie Jefferson (EJ)	1B15 DH7	R	23	24	89	8	30	6	2	1	6	1	17	0	.337	.483
Wayne Kirby	DH4 OF2	L	28	21	18	9	3	1	0	1	3	2	2	0	.167	.389
Tony Perezchica	3B9 2B4 SS4 DH1	R	26	18	20	2	2	1	0	0	2	1	6	0	.100	.150
Craig Worthington	3B9	R	27	9	24	0	4	0	0	0	2	2	4	0	.167	.167
Dave Rohde	3B5	B	28	5	7	0	0	0	0	0	0	0	3	0	.000	.000
Jose Hernandez	SS3	R	22	3	4	0	0	0	0	0	0	0	2	0	.000	.000
Joel Skinner (SJ) 31																

NAME	T	AGE	W	L	PCT	SV	G	GS	CG	IP	H	BB	SO	SHO	ERA
		27	76	86	.531	46	162	162	13	1470	1507	566	890	7	4.11
Charles Nagy	R	25	17	10	.630	0	33	33	10	252	245	57	169	3	2.96
Eric Plunk	R	28	9	6	.600	4	58	0	0	72	61	38	50	0	3.64
Steve Olin	R	26	8	5	.615	29	72	0	0	88	80	27	47	0	2.34
Scott Scudder (SJ)	R	24	6	10	.375	0	23	22	0	109	134	55	66	0	5.28
Jack Armstrong	R	27	6	15	.286	0	35	23	1	167	176	67	114	0	4.64
Derek Lilliquist	L	26	5	3	.625	6	71	0	0	62	39	18	47	0	1.75
Dennis Cook	L	29	5	7	.417	0	32	25	1	158	156	50	96	0	3.82
Dave Otto	L	27	5	9	.357	0	18	16	0	80	110	33	32	0	7.06
Rod Nichols	R	27	4	3	.571	0	30	9	0	105	114	31	56	0	4.53
2 Jose Mesa	R	26	4	4	.500	0	15	15	1	93	92	43	40	1	4.16
Ted Power	R	37	3	3	.500	6	64	0	0	99	88	35	51	0	2.54
Kevin Wickander	L	27	2	0	1.000	1	44	0	0	41	39	28	38	0	3.07
Denis Boucher	L	24	2	2	.500	0	8	7	0	41	48	17	20	0	6.37
Mike Christopher	R	28	0	0	—	0	10	0	0	18	17	10	13	0	3.00
Brad Arnsberg	R	28	0	1	.000	0	4	0	0	11	13	11	5	0	11.81
Jeff Shaw	R	25	0	1	.000	0	2	1	0	8	7	4	3	0	8.22
Eric Bell	L	28	0	1	.000	0	4	1	0	15	22	9	10	0	7.63
Dave Mlicki	R	24	0	2	.000	0	4	4	0	22	23	16	16	0	4.98
Alan Embree	L	22	0	2	.000	0	4	4	0	18	19	8	12	0	7.00
Jeff Mutis	L	25	0	2	.000	0	3	2	0	11	24	6	8	0	9.53
Bruce Egloff (EJ) 27																

NEW YORK   4th(tie) 76-86 .469   20   BUCK SHOWALTER

Name	G by Pos	B	AGE	G	AB	R	H	2B	3B	HR	RBI	BB	SO	SB	BA	SA
TOTALS			28	162	5593	733	1462	281	18	163	703	536	903	78	.261	.406
Don Mattingly	1B143 DH15	L	31	157	640	89	184	40	0	14	86	39	43	3	.288	.416
Pat Kelly	2B101 DH1	R	24	106	318	38	72	22	2	7	27	25	72	8	.226	.374
Andy Stankiewicz	SS81 2B34 DH1	R	27	116	400	52	107	22	2	2	25	38	42	9	.268	.348
Charlie Hayes	3B139 1B4	R	27	142	509	52	131	19	2	18	66	28	100	3	.257	.409
Danny Tartabull	OF69 DH53	R	29	123	421	72	112	19	0	25	85	103	115	2	.266	.489
Roberto Kelly	OF146	R	27	152	580	81	158	31	2	10	66	41	96	28	.272	.384
Mel Hall	OF136 DH11	L	31	152	583	67	163	36	3	15	81	29	53	4	.280	.429
Matt Nokes	C111	R	28	121	384	42	86	9	1	22	59	37	62	0	.224	.424
Kevin Maas	DH62 1B22	L	27	98	286	35	71	12	0	11	35	25	63	3	.248	.406
Randy Velarde	SS75 3B26 OF23 2B3	R	29	121	412	57	112	24	1	7	46	38	78	7	.272	.386
Mike Stanley	C55 1B4 DH6	R	29	68	173	24	43	7	0	8	27	33	45	0	.249	.428
Dion James	OF46 DH1	L	29	67	145	24	38	8	0	3	17	22	15	1	.262	.379
Jim Leyritz	DH31 C18 3B2 OF2 1B2 2B1	R	28	63	144	17	37	6	0	7	26	14	22	0	.257	.444
Bernie Williams	OF62	B	23	62	261	39	73	14	2	5	26	29	36	7	.280	.406
Mike Gallego (FJ-WJ)	2B40 SS14	R	31	53	173	24	44	7	3	3	14	20	22	0	.254	.358
Jessie Barfield (WJ)	OF30	R	32	30	95	8	13	2	0	2	7	9	27	1	.137	.221
Gerald Williams	OF12	R	25	15	27	7	8	2	0	3	6	0	3	2	.296	.704
J.T. Snow	1B6 DH1	B	24	7	14	1	2	1	0	0	2	5	5	0	.143	.214
Dave Silvestri	SS6	R	24	7	13	3	4	0	2	0	1	4	3	0	.308	.615
Mike Humphreys	OF2 DH1	R	25	4	10	0	1	0	0	0	0	0	1	0	.100	.100
Hensley Meulens	3B2	R	25	2	5	1	3	0	0	1	1	1	0	0	.600	1.200
John Ramos (EJ) 26																

NAME	T	AGE	W	L	PCT	SV	G	GS	CG	IP	H	BB	SO	SHO	ERA
		30	76	86	.469	44	162	162	20	1453	1453	612	851	9	4.21
Melido Perez	R	26	13	16	.448	0	33	33	10	248	212	93	218	1	2.87
Scott Sanderson	R	35	12	11	.522	0	33	33	2	193	220	64	104	1	4.93
Rich Monteleone	R	29	7	3	.700	0	47	0	0	93	82	27	62	0	3.30
Bob Wickman	R	23	6	1	.857	0	8	8	0	50	51	20	21	0	4.11
Scott Kamieniecki	R	28	6	14	.300	0	28	28	4	188	193	74	88	0	4.36
John Habyan	R	28	5	6	.455	7	56	0	0	73	84	21	44	0	3.84
1 Tim Leary	R	33	5	6	.455	0	18	15	2	97	84	57	34	0	5.57
Greg Cadaret	L	30	4	8	.333	1	46	11	1	104	104	74	73	1	4.25
Steve Howe (SD)	L	34	3	0	1.000	6	20	0	0	22	9	3	12	0	2.45
2 Curt Young (LJ)	L	32	3	0	1.000	0	13	5	0	43	51	10	13	0	3.32
Sam Militello	R	22	3	3	.500	0	9	9	0	60	43	32	42	0	3.45
Steve Farr	R	35	2	2	.500	30	50	0	0	52	34	19	37	0	1.56
2 Tim Burke (EJ)	R	33	2	2	.500	0	23	0	0	28	30	11	8	0	3.25
Jeff Johnson	L	25	2	3	.400	0	13	8	0	53	71	23	14	0	6.66
Jerry Nielsen	L	23	1	0	1.000	0	20	0	0	20	17	18	12	0	4.58
1 Lee Guetterman	L	33	1	1	.500	0	15	0	0	23	35	13	5	0	9.53
1 Shawn Hillegas	R	27	1	8	.111	0	21	8	1	78	96	33	46	1	5.51
Russ Springer	R	23	0	0	—	0	14	0	0	16	18	10	12	0	6.19
Sterling Hitchcock	L	21	0	2	.000	0	3	3	0	13	23	6	6	0	8.31
Mike Witt (EJ) 31																
Pascual Perez (SD) 35																

DETROIT   6th 75-87 .463   21   SPARKY ANDERSON

Name	G by Pos	B	AGE	G	AB	R	H	2B	3B	HR	RBI	BB	SO	SB	BA	SA
TOTALS			30	162	5515	791	1411	256	16	182	746	675	1055	66	.256	.407
Cecil Fielder	1B114 DH43	R	28	155	594	80	145	22	0	35	124	73	151	0	.244	.458
Lou Whitaker	2B160 DH10	L	35	130	453	77	126	26	0	19	71	81	46	6	.278	.461
Travis Fryman	SS137 3B26	R	23	161	659	87	175	31	4	20	96	45	144	8	.266	.416
Scott Livingstone	3B112	L	26	117	354	43	100	21	0	4	46	21	36	1	.282	.376
Rob Deer (NJ)	OF106 DH2	R	31	110	393	66	97	20	1	32	64	51	131	4	.247	.547
Milt Cuyler (KJ)	OF89	B	23	89	291	39	70	11	1	3	28	10	62	8	.241	.316
Dan Gladden (RJ)	OF108 DH2	L	34	113	417	57	106	20	1	7	42	30	64	4	.254	.357
Mickey Tettleton	C113 DH40 1B3 OF2	B	31	157	525	82	125	25	0	32	83	122	137	0	.238	.469
Tony Phillips	OF73 2B57 DH34 3B20 SS1	B	33	159	606	114	167	32	3	10	64	114	93	12	.276	.388
Mark Carreon	OF83 DH13	R	28	101	336	34	78	11	1	10	41	22	57	3	.232	.360
Skeeter Barnes	3B39 1B17 OF15 2B7 DH7	R	35	95	165	27	45	8	1	3	25	10	18	3	.273	.388
Dave Bergman	1B55 DH12 OF1	L	39	87	181	17	42	3	0	1	10	20	19	1	.232	.265
Chad Kreuter	C62 DH1	R	27	67	190	22	48	9	0	2	16	20	38	0	.253	.332
2 Gary Pettis	OF46	B	34	48	129	27	26	4	3	1	12	27	34	13	.202	.302
Alan Trammell (BN)	SS27	R	34	29	102	11	28	7	1	1	11	15	4	2	.275	.392
Phil Clark	OF13 DH7	R	24	23	54	3	22	4	0	1	5	6	9	1	.407	.537
Shawn Hare (KJ)	OF9 1B4	L	25	15	26	0	3	1	0	0	5	2	4	0	.115	.154
Rico Brogna	1B8 DH2	L	22	9	26	3	5	1	0	0	3	1	10	0	.192	.346
Rich Rowland	C3 DH2 1B1 3B1	R	28	6	14	2	3	0	0	0	3	0	3	0	.214	.214

NAME	T	AGE	W	L	PCT	SV	G	GS	CG	IP	H	BB	SO	SHO	ERA
		29	75	87	.463	36	162	162	10	1436	1534	564	693	4	4.60
Bill Gullickson	R	33	14	13	.519	0	34	34	4	222	228	50	64	1	4.34
Frank Tanana	L	38	13	11	.542	0	32	31	3	187	188	90	91	0	4.39
Mark Leiter (GJ)	R	29	8	5	.615	0	35	14	1	112	116	43	75	0	4.18
John Doherty	R	25	7	4	.636	3	47	11	0	116	131	25	37	0	3.88
Walt Terrell	R	34	7	10	.412	0	36	14	1	137	163	48	61	0	5.20
Dave Haas	R	26	5	3	.625	0	12	11	1	62	68	16	29	1	3.94
John Kiely (SJ)	R	27	4	2	.667	0	39	0	0	55	44	28	18	0	2.13
Eric King (SJ)	R	28	4	4	.400	1	17	14	0	79	90	28	45	0	5.22
Les Lancaster	R	30	3	4	.429	0	41	1	0	87	101	51	35	0	6.33
Scott Aldred	L	24	3	8	.273	0	16	13	0	65	80	33	34	0	6.78
Kurt Knudsen	R	25	2	3	.400	5	48	1	0	71	70	41	51	0	4.58
Kevin Ritz (EJ)	R	27	2	5	.286	0	23	11	0	80	88	44	57	0	5.60
Mike Henneman	R	30	2	6	.250	24	60	0	0	77	75	20	58	0	3.96
Mike Munoz	L	27	1	2	.333	2	65	0	0	48	44	25	23	0	3.00
Buddy Groom	L	27	0	5	.000	0	12	7	0	39	48	22	15	0	5.82
Dan Gakeler (SJ) 28																

BOSTON 7th 73-89 .451 23 BUTCH HOBSON

Name	G by Pos	B	AGE	G	AB	R	H	2B	3B	HR	RBI	BB	SO	SB	BA	SA
TOTALS			28	162	5461	599	1343	259	21	84	567	591	865	44	.246	.347
Mo Vaughn	1B85 DH20	R	24	113	355	42	83	16	2	13	57	47	67	3	.234	.400
Jody Reed	2B142 DH1	R	29	143	550	64	136	27	1	3	40	62	44	7	.247	.316
Luis Rivera	SS93 2B1 DH2	R	28	102	288	17	62	11	1	0	29	26	56	4	.215	.260
Wade Boggs	3B117 DH21	L	34	143	514	62	133	22	4	7	50	74	31	1	.259	.358
Tom Brunansky	OF92 1B28 DH17	R	31	138	458	47	122	31	3	15	74	66	96	2	.266	.445
Ellis Burks (WJ)	OF63 DH1	R	27	66	235	35	60	8	3	8	30	25	48	5	.255	.417
Mike Greenwell (KJ)	OF41 DH6	L	28	49	180	16	42	2	0	2	18	18	19	2	.233	.278
Tony Pena	C132	R	35	133	410	39	99	21	1	1	38	24	61	3	.241	.305
Jack Clark (SJ)	DH64 1B13	R	36	81	257	32	54	11	0	5	33	56	87	1	.210	.311
Bob Zupcic	OF114 DH5	R	25	124	392	46	108	19	1	3	43	25	60	2	.276	.352
Scott Cooper	1B62 3B47 DH2 2B1 SS1	L	24	123	337	34	93	21	0	5	33	37	33	1	.276	.383
Phil Plantier	OF69 DH23	L	23	108	349	46	86	19	0	7	30	44	83	2	.246	.361
Herm Winningham	OF67 DH6	L	30	105	234	27	55	8	1	1	14	10	53	6	.235	.291
2 Billy Hatcher	OF75	R	31	75	315	37	75	16	2	1	23	17	41	4	.238	.311
Tim Naehring (WJ)	SS30 2B23 3B10 DH4 OF1	R	25	72	186	12	43	8	0	3	14	18	31	0	.231	.323
John Valentin	SS58	R	25	58	185	21	51	13	0	5	25	20	17	1	.276	.427
John Flaherty	C34	R	24	35	66	3	13	2	0	0	2	3	7	0	.197	.227
Eric Wedge	DH20 C5	R	24	27	68	11	17	2	0	5	11	13	18	0	.250	.500
3 Steve Lyons	1B8 OF5 2B1	L	32	21	28	3	7	0	1	0	2	0	5	0	.250	.321
John Marzano (SJ)	C18 DH1	R	29	19	50	4	4	2	1	0	1	2	12	0	.080	.160
Tommy Barrett	2B2	B	32	4	3	1	0	0	0	0	0	0	2	0	.000	.000
Mike Brumley		B	29	2	1	0	0	0	0	0	0	0	0	0	.000	.000
Carlos Quintana (AA)26																

NAME	T	AGE	W	L	PCT	SV	G	GS	CG	IP	H	BB	SO	SHO	ERA
		31	73	89	.451	39	162	162	22	1449	1403	535	943	13	3.58
Roger Clemens	R	29	18	11	.621	0	32	32	11	247	203	62	208	5	2.41
Frank Viola	L	32	13	12	.520	0	35	35	6	238	214	89	121	1	3.44
Danny Darwin	R	36	9	9	.500	3	51	15	2	161	159	53	124	0	3.96
Joe Hesketh	L	33	8	9	.471	1	30	25	1	149	162	58	104	0	4.36
John Dopson (EJ)	R	28	7	11	.389	0	25	25	0	141	159	38	55	0	4.08
Greg Harris	R	36	4	9	.308	4	70	2	1	108	82	60	73	0	2.51
Mike Gardiner	R	26	4	10	.286	0	28	18	0	131	126	58	79	0	4.75
Daryl Irvine	R	27	3	4	.429	0	21	0	0	28	31	14	10	0	6.11
1 Jeff Reardon	R	36	2	2	.500	27	46	0	0	42	53	7	32	0	4.25
Paul Quantrill	R	23	2	3	.400	1	27	0	0	49	55	15	24	0	2.19
Scott Taylor	L	24	1	1	.500	0	4	1	0	15	13	4	7	0	4.91
Tony Fossas	L	34	1	2	.333	2	60	0	0	30	31	14	19	0	2.43
1 Tom Bolton	L	30	1	2	.333	0	21	1	0	29	34	14	23	0	3.41
Ken Ryan	R	23	0	0	—	1	7	0	0	7	4	5	5	0	6.43
Peter Hoy	R	25	0	0	—	0	5	0	0	4	8	2	2	0	7.36
Matt Young	L	33	0	4	.000	0	28	8	1	71	69	42	57	0	4.58
Jeff Gray (IL) 29															

WEST DIVISION

OAKLAND 1st 96-66 .593 TONY LaRUSSA

Name	G by Pos	B	AGE	G	AB	R	H	2B	3B	HR	RBI	BB	SO	SB	BA	SA
TOTALS			28	162	5387	745	1389	219	24	142	693	707	831	143	.258	.386
Mark McGwire	1B139	R	28	139	467	87	125	22	0	42	104	90	105	0	.268	.585
Mike Bordick	2B95 SS70	R	26	154	504	62	151	19	4	3	48	40	59	12	.300	.371
Walt Weiss (VJ)	SS103	B	28	103	316	36	67	5	2	0	21	43	39	6	.212	.241
Carney Lansford	3B119 1B18 DH2 SS1	R	35	135	496	65	130	30	1	7	75	43	39	7	.262	.369
1 Jose Canseco	OF77 DH20	R	27	97	366	66	90	11	0	22	72	48	104	5	.246	.456
Willie Wilson	OF120 DH5	B	36	132	396	38	107	15	5	0	37	35	65	28	.270	.333
Rickey Henderson	OF108 DH6	R	33	117	396	77	112	18	3	15	46	95	56	48	.283	.457
Terry Steinbach	C124 1B5 DH2	R	30	128	438	48	122	20	1	12	53	45	58	2	.279	.411
Harold Baines	DH116 OF23	L	33	140	478	58	121	18	0	16	76	59	61	1	.253	.391
Lance Blankenship(BG)	2B78 OF51 1B7 DH3	R	28	123	349	59	84	24	1	3	34	82	57	21	.241	.341
Jerry Browne	3B58 OF43 2B19 SS1 DH1	B	26	111	324	43	93	12	2	3	40	40	40	3	.287	.364
Jamie Quirk	C59 1B9 3B2 DH1	L	37	78	177	13	39	7	1	2	11	16	28	0	.220	.305
Randy Ready	OF24 DH24 3B7 2B4 1B4	R	32	61	125	17	25	2	0	3	17	25	23	1	.200	.288
Eric Fox	OF43 DH4	B	28	51	143	24	34	5	2	3	13	13	29	3	.238	.364
Scott Brosius (IL)	OF20 3B12 1B3 SS1 DH1	R	25	38	87	13	19	2	0	4	13	3	13	3	.218	.379
2 Ruben Sierra	OF25 DH2	B	26	27	101	17	28	4	1	3	17	14	9	2	.277	.426
Troy Neel	OF9 DH9 1B2	L	26	24	53	8	14	3	0	3	9	5	15	0	.264	.491
1 Dann Howitt	OF19	L	27	22	48	1	6	0	0	2	5	4	12	0	.125	.188
Dave Henderson (LJ)	OF12 DH4	R	33	20	63	1	9	1	0	0	2	2	16	0	.143	.159
1 Scott Hemond	C8 3B2 OF2 DH1	R	26	17	27	7	6	1	0	1	1	3	7	1	.222	.259
Mike Kingery	OF10	L	31	12	28	3	3	0	0	0	1	1	3	0	.107	.107
Henry Mercedes	C9	R	22	9	5	1	4	0	0	0	1	0	1	0	.800	1.200

NAME	T	AGE	W	L	PCT	SV	G	GS	CG	IP	H	BB	SO	SHO	ERA
		32	96	66	.593	58	162	162	8	1447	1396	601	843	9	3.73
Mike Moore	R	32	17	12	.586	0	36	36	2	223	229	103	117	0	4.12
Ron Darling	R	31	15	10	.600	0	33	33	4	206	198	72	99	3	3.66
Dave Stewart	R	35	12	10	.545	0	31	31	2	199	175	79	130	0	3.66
Bob Welch (EJ)	R	35	11	7	.611	0	20	20	0	124	114	43	47	0	3.27
Jeff Parrett	R	30	9	1	.900	0	66	0	0	98	81	42	78	0	3.02
Dennis Eckersley	R	37	7	1	.875	51	69	0	0	80	62	11	93	0	1.91
2 Kelly Downs	R	31	5	5	.500	0	18	13	0	82	72	46	38	0	3.29
Joe Slusarski	R	25	5	5	.500	0	15	14	0	76	85	27	38	0	5.45
Gene Nelson	R	31	3	1	.750	0	28	2	0	52	68	22	23	0	6.45
2 Jeff Russell	R	30	2	0	1.000	2	8	0	0	10	4	3	5	0	0.00
Vince Horsman	L	25	2	1	.667	1	58	0	0	43	39	21	18	0	2.49
Kevin Campbell	R	27	2	3	.400	1	32	5	0	65	66	45	38	0	5.12
2 Bobby Witt	R	28	1	1	.500	0	6	6	0	32	31	19	25	0	3.41
Rick Honeycutt	L	38	1	4	.200	3	54	0	0	39	41	10	32	0	3.69
Mike Raczka	L	29	0	0	—	0	8	0	0	6	10	3	6	0	8.53
Bruce Walton	R	29	0	0	—	0	5	0	0	10	17	3	7	0	9.90
2 Shawn Hillegas	R	27	0	0	—	0	5	0	0	8	4	3	0	0	2.35
Johnny Guzman	L	21	0	0	—	0	2	0	0	3	1	3	0	0	12.00
Todd Revenig	R	23	0	0	—	0	2	0	0	2	2	1	0	0	0.00
John Briscoe	R	24	0	1	.000	0	2	0	0	7	12	9	4	0	6.43
Goose Gossage (AJ)	R	40	0	0	—	0	30	0	0	38	32	19	26	0	2.84
Joe Klink (EJ) 30															
Kirk Dressendorfer (SJ) 23															

MINNESOTA 2nd 90-72 .556 6 TOM KELLY

Name	G by Pos	B	AGE	G	AB	R	H	2B	3B	HR	RBI	BB	SO	SB	BA	SA
TOTALS			29	162	5582	747	1544	275	27	104	701	527	834	123	.277	.391
Kent Hrbek (SJ)	1B104 DH8	L	32	112	394	52	96	20	0	15	58	71	56	5	.244	.409
Chuck Knoblauch	2B154 SS1 DH1	R	23	155	600	104	178	19	6	2	56	88	60	34	.297	.358
Greg Gagne	SS141	R	30	146	439	53	108	23	0	7	39	19	83	6	.246	.346
Scott Leius	3B125 SS10	R	26	129	409	50	102	18	2	2	35	34	61	6	.249	.318
Pedro Munoz	OF122 DH3	R	23	127	418	44	113	16	3	12	71	17	90	4	.270	.409
Kirby Puckett	OF149 DH9 2B2 3B2 SS1	R	32	160	639	104	210	38	4	19	110	44	97	17	.329	.490
Shane Mack	OF155	R	28	156	600	101	189	31	6	16	75	64	106	26	.315	.467
Brian Harper	C133 DH2	R	32	140	502	58	154	25	0	9	73	26	22	0	.307	.410
Chili Davis	DH125 OF14 1B1	B	32	138	444	63	128	27	2	12	66	73	76	4	.288	.439
Gene Larkin	1B55 OF43 DH4	B	29	115	337	38	83	18	1	6	42	28	43	7	.246	.359
Randy Bush	OF24 DH24 1B8	L	33	100	182	14	39	8	1	2	22	11	37	1	.214	.302
Jeff Reboulet	SS36 3B22 2B13 OF7 DH1	R	28	73	137	15	26	7	1	1	16	23	26	3	.190	.277
J.T. Bruett	OF45 DH3	L	24	56	76	7	19	4	0	0	2	6	12	6	.250	.303
Lenny Webster	C49 DH1	R	27	53	118	10	33	10	1	1	13	9	11	0	.280	.407
Mike Pagliarulo (BW)	3B37 DH1	L	32	42	105	10	21	4	0	0	9	1	17	1	.200	.238
Jarvis Brown	OF31 DH2	R	25	35	15	8	1	0	0	0	0	2	6	2	.067	.067
Donnie Hill (XJ)	SS10 2B7 3B5 OF1	B	31	25	51	7	15	3	0	0	2	5	6	0	.294	.353
Terry Jorgensen	1B13 3B9 SS2	R	25	22	58	5	18	1	0	0	5	3	11	1	.310	.328
2 Darren Reed	OF13 DH1	R	26	14	33	2	6	2	0	0	4	2	11	0	.182	.242
Bernardo Brito	OF3 DH1	R	28	8	14	1	2	1	0	0	2	0	4	0	.143	.214
Derek Parks	C7	R	23	7	6	1	2	0	0	0	0	1	0	0	.333	.333
Luis Quinones	3B1 SS1 DH1	B	30	3	5	1	1	0	0	0	0	0	0	0	.200	.200

NAME	T	AGE	W	L	PCT	SV	G	GS	CG	IP	H	BB	SO	SHO	ERA
		28	90	72	.556	50	162	162	16	1453	1391	479	923	13	3.70
John Smiley	L	27	16	9	.640	0	34	34	5	241	205	65	163	2	3.21
Kevin Tapani	R	28	16	11	.593	0	34	34	4	220	226	48	138	1	3.97
Scott Erickson	R	24	13	12	.520	0	32	32	5	212	197	83	101	3	3.40
1 Bill Krueger	L	34	10	6	.625	0	27	27	2	161	166	46	86	2	4.30
Carl Willis	R	31	7	3	.700	1	59	0	0	79	73	11	45	0	2.72
Tom Edens	R	31	6	3	.667	3	52	0	0	76	65	36	57	0	2.83
Willie Banks	R	23	4	4	.500	0	16	12	0	71	80	37	37	0	5.70
Mike Trombley	R	25	3	2	.600	0	10	7	0	46	43	17	38	0	3.30
Gary Wayne	L	27	3	3	.500	0	41	0	0	48	46	19	29	0	2.63
Bob Kipper	L	27	3	3	.500	0	25	0	0	39	40	14	22	0	4.42
Pat Mahomes	R	21	3	4	.429	0	14	13	0	70	73	37	44	0	5.04
Mark Guthrie	L	26	2	3	.400	5	54	0	0	75	59	23	76	0	2.88
Rick Aguilera	R	30	2	6	.250	41	64	0	0	67	60	17	52	0	2.84
Larry Casian	L	26	1	0	1.000	0	5	0	0	2	2	1	2	0	2.70
David West	L	27	1	3	.250	0	9	0	0	28	32	20	19	0	6.99
Paul Abbott (SJ)	R	24	0	0	—	0	6	0	0	11	12	5	13	0	3.27
Mauro Gozzo	R	26	0	0	—	0	2	0	0	2	7	0	1	0	27.00

CHICAGO 3rd 86-76 .531 10 GENE LAMONT

Name	G by Pos	B	AGE	G	AB	R	H	2B	3B	HR	RBI	BB	SO	SB	BA	SA
TOTALS			30	162	5498	738	1434	269	36	110	686	622	784	160	.261	.383
Frank Thomas	1B158 DH2	R	24	160	573	108	185	46	2	24	115	122	88	6	.323	.536
Steve Sax	2B141	R	32	143	567	74	134	26	4	4	47	43	42	30	.236	.317
Ozzie Guillen (KJ)	SS12	L	28	12	40	5	8	4	1	0	7	1	5	1	.200	.300
Robin Ventura	3B157 1B2	L	24	157	592	85	167	38	1	16	93	93	71	2	.282	.431
Dan Pasqua	OF81 1B5 DH1	L	30	93	265	26	56	16	1	6	33	36	57	0	.211	.347
Lance Johnson	OF157	L	28	157	567	67	158	15	12	3	47	34	33	41	.279	.363
Tim Raines	OF129 DH14	B	32	144	551	102	162	22	9	7	54	81	48	45	.294	.405
Ron Karkovice	C119 OF1	R	28	123	342	39	81	12	1	13	50	30	89	10	.237	.392
George Bell	DH140 OF15	R	32	155	627	74	160	27	0	25	112	31	97	5	.255	.418
Shawn Abner	OF94 DH1	R	26	97	208	21	58	10	1	1	16	12	35	1	.279	.351
Craig Grebeck (BF)	SS85 3B7 OF2	R	27	88	287	24	77	21	2	3	35	30	34	0	.268	.387
Joey Cora	2B28 DH18 SS6 3B5	B	27	68	122	27	30	7	1	0	9	22	13	10	.246	.320
Warren Newson	OF50 DH4	L	27	63	136	19	30	3	0	1	11	37	38	3	.221	.265
Carlton Fisk (FJ)	C54 DH2	R	44	62	188	12	43	4	1	3	21	23	38	3	.229	.309
Mike Huff (SJ)	OF56 DH1	R	28	60	115	13	24	5	0	0	8	10	24	1	.209	.252
Esteban Beltre	SS43 DH4	R	25	49	110	21	21	4	0	0	10	3	18	1	.191	.236
2 Dale Sveum	SS37 3B2 1B2	B	28	40	114	15	25	9	0	2	12	12	29	1	.219	.351
Matt Merullo	C16 DH1	L	26	24	50	3	9	1	0	1	8	1	8	0	.180	.240
Shawn Jeter	OF8 DH3	L	26	13	18	1	2	0	0	0	1	0	7	0	.111	.111
2 Scott Hemond	DH4 SS3 OF2 3B1 C1	R	26	8	13	1	3	1	0	0	1	4	5	1	.231	.308
Chris Cron	1B5 OF1	R	28	6	10	0	0	0	0	0	0	0	4	0	.000	.000
Nelson Santovenia	C2	R	30	3	1	1	0	0	0	0	0	0	1	0	.333	1.333
Bo Jackson (PJ) 29																

NAME	T	AGE	W	L	PCT	SV	G	GS	CG	IP	H	BB	SO	SHO	ERA
		29	86	76	.531	52	162	162	21	1462	1400	550	810	5	3.82
Jack McDowell	R	26	20	10	.667	0	34	34	13	261	247	75	178	1	3.18
Kirk McCaskill	R	31	12	13	.480	0	34	34	0	209	193	95	109	0	4.18
Greg Hibbard	L	27	10	7	.588	1	31	28	0	176	187	57	69	0	4.40
Alex Fernandez	R	22	8	11	.421	0	29	29	4	188	199	50	95	2	4.27
Roberto Hernandez	R	27	7	3	.700	12	43	0	0	71	45	20	68	0	1.65
Charlie Hough	R	44	7	12	.368	0	27	27	4	176	160	66	76	0	3.93
Terry Leach	R	38	6	5	.545	0	51	0	0	74	57	20	22	0	1.95
Donn Pall	R	30	5	2	.714	1	39	0	0	73	79	27	27	0	4.93
Wilson Alvarez	L	22	5	3	.625	1	34	9	0	100	103	65	66	0	5.20
Scott Radinsky	L	24	3	7	.300	15	68	0	0	59	54	34	48	0	2.73
Mike Dunne	R	29	2	0	1.000	0	13	1	0	13	12	6	2	0	4.26
Bobby Thigpen	R	28	1	6	.250	22	55	0	0	55	58	33	45	0	4.75
Brian Drahman	R	28	0	0	—	0	5	0	0	7	6	2	1	0	2.57

TEXAS — 4th 77-85 .475 19 — BOBBY VALENTINE 45-41 .523 — TOBY HARRAH 32-44 .421

Name	G by Pos	B	AGE	G	AB	R	H	2B	3B	HR	RBI	BB	SO	SB	BA	SA
TOTALS			28	162	5537	682	1387	266	23	159	646	550	1036	81	.250	.393
Rafael Palmeiro	1B156 DH2	L	27	159	608	84	163	27	4	22	85	72	83	2	.268	.434
Jeff Frye	2B67	R	25	67	199	24	51	9	1	1	12	16	27	1	.256	.327
Dickie Thon (SJ)	SS87	R	34	95	275	30	68	15	3	4	37	20	40	12	.247	.367
Dean Palmer	3B150	R	23	152	541	74	124	25	0	26	72	62	154	10	.229	.420
1 Ruben Sierra	OF119 DH4	B	26	124	500	66	139	30	6	14	70	31	59	12	.278	.446
Juan Gonzalez	OF148 DH4	R	22	155	584	77	152	24	2	43	109	35	143	0	.260	.529
Kevin Reimer	OF110 DH32	L	28	148	494	56	132	32	2	16	58	42	103	1	.267	.437
Ivan Rodriguez	C116 DH2	R	20	123	420	39	109	16	1	8	37	24	73	0	.260	.360
Brian Downing	DH93	R	41	107	320	53	89	18	0	10	39	62	58	1	.278	.428
Jeff Huson	SS82 2B47 OF2	L	27	123	318	49	83	14	3	4	24	41	43	18	.261	.362
Al Newman	2B72 3B28 SS20 OF1	B	32	116	246	25	54	5	0	0	12	34	26	9	.220	.240
Geno Petralli	C54 DH14 3B4 2B2		32	94	192	11	38	12	0	1	18	20	34	1	.198	.276
John Cangelosi	OF65 DH6	B	29	73	85	12	16	2	0	1	6	18	16	6	.188	.247
Monty Fariss	OF49 2B17 DH4 1B1		24	67	166	13	36	7	1	3	21	17	51	0	.217	.325
Jack Daugherty (RJ)	OF26 DH13 1B8	L	31	59	127	13	26	9	0	0	9	16	21	2	.205	.325
Julio Franco (KJ)	DH15 2B9 OF4	R	33	35	107	19	25	7	0	2	8	15	17	1	.234	.355
David Hulse	OF31	L	24	32	92	14	28	4	0	0	2	3	18	3	.304	.348
Donald Harris	OF24		24	24	33	3	6	1	0	0	1	0	15	1	.182	.212
2 Jose Canseco	OF13 DH8	R	27	22	73	8	17	4	0	1	15	15	24	1	.233	.452
Mario Diaz	SS16 2B3 3B2	R	30	19	31	2	7	1	0	0	1	1	2	0	.226	.258
Cris Colon	SS14	B	23	14	36	5	6	0	0	0	1	1	8	0	.167	.167
Russ Mc Ginnis	C10 1B2 3B2	R	29	14	33	2	8	4	0	0	4	3	7	0	.242	.364
Dan Peltier	OF10	L	24	12	24	1	4	0	0	0	2	0	3	0	.167	.167
Ray Stephens	C8 DH1	R	29	8	13	0	2	0	0	0	0	0	5	0	.154	.154
Rob Maurer	1B3 DH1	L	25	8	9	1	2	0	0	0	1	1	2	0	.100	.100
John Russell (RJ)	C4 OF2 1B1	R	31	7	10	1	1	0	0	0	2	1	4	0	.222	.222
Doug Davis	C1	R	29	1	1	0	1	0	0	0	0	0	0	0	1.000	1.000

NAME	T	AGE	W	L	PCT	SV	G	GS	CG	IP	H	BB	SO	SHO	ERA
TOTALS		29	77	85	.475	42	162	162	19	1460	1471	598	1034	3	4.09
Kevin Brown	R	27	21	11	.656	0	35	35	11	266	262	76	173	1	3.32
Jose Guzman	R	29	16	11	.593	0	33	33	5	224	229	73	179	0	3.66
1 Bobby Witt	R	28	9	13	.409	0	25	25	0	161	152	95	100	0	4.46
Nolan Ryan	R	45	5	9	.357	0	27	27	2	157	138	69	157	0	3.72
1 Jeff Robinson	R	30	4	4	.500	0	16	4	0	46	50	21	18	0	5.72
Roger Pavlik	R	24	4	4	.500	0	13	12	1	62	66	34	45	0	4.21
Todd Burns	R	28	3	5	.375	1	35	10	0	103	97	32	55	0	3.84
Kenny Rogers	L	27	3	6	.333	6	81	0	0	79	80	26	70	0	3.09
1 Jeff Russell	R	30	2	3	.400	28	51	0	0	57	51	22	43	0	1.91
Terry Mathews (EJ)	R	27	2	4	.333	0	40	0	0	42	48	31	26	0	5.95
Lance McCullers	R	28	1	0	1.000	0	5	1	0	8	3			0	5.40
Steve Fireovid	R	35	1	0	1.000	0	3	0	0	7	10	4	0	0	4.05
Barry Manuel	R	26	1	0	1.000	3	0	0	0	6	1	9	0		4.76
Gerald Alexander	R	24	1	0	1.000	0	3	0	0	2	5	1		0	27.00
Floyd Bannister	L	37	1	1	.500	0	36	0	0	37	39	21	30	0	8.32
Matt Whiteside	R	24	1	1	.500	4	20	0	0	28	26	11	13	0	1.93
Brian Bohanon	L	23	1	1	.500	0	18	7	0	46	57	25	29	0	6.31
Danny Leon (EJ)	R	23	1	1	.500	0	15	0	0	18	18	10	15	0	5.89
Wayne Rosenthal	R	27	0	0	---	0	6	0	0	5	7	1	7	0	7.71
Dan Carman	L	32	0	0	---	0	5	0	0	2	5	1	0	0	7.71
Mike Jeffcoat	L	32	0	1	.000	0	6	3	0	20	28	5	6	0	7.32
Mike Campbell	R	28	0	1	.000	0	1	0	0	4	3	4	0		9.82
2 Edwin Nunez	R	29	0	2	.000	3	39	0	0	46	51	16	39	0	5.52
Dan Smith	L	23	0	3	.000	0	4	2	0	14	18	5	5	0	5.02
Scott Chiamparino (EJ)	R	25	0	4	.000	0	6	5	0	21	25	5	13	0	3.55

CALIFORNIA — 5th(tie) 72-90 .444 24 — BUCK RODGERS

Name	G by Pos	B	AGE	G	AB	R	H	2B	3B	HR	RBI	BB	SO	SB	BA	SA
TOTALS			28	162	5364	579	1306	202	20	88	537	416	882	160	.243	.338
Lee Stevens	1B91 DH2	L	24	106	312	25	69	19	0	7	37	29	64	1	.221	.349
Luis Sojo	2B96 3B9 SS5	R	27	106	368	37	100	12	3	7	43	14	24	7	.272	.378
Gary DiSarcina	SS157	R	24	157	518	48	128	19	0	3	42	20	50	9	.247	.301
Rene Gonzales (BA)	3B53 2B42 1B13 SS8	R	31	104	329	47	91	17	1	7	38	41	46	7	.277	.398
Chad Curtis	OF135 DH1	R	23	139	441	59	114	16	2	10	46	51	71	43	.259	.372
Junior Felix	OF128 DH8	B	24	139	509	63	125	22	5	9	72	33	128	8	.246	.361
Luis Polonia	OF99 DH47	L	27	149	577	83	165	17	4	0	35	45	64	51	.286	.329
Mike Fitzgerald	C74 OF11 3B3 1B2 2B1 DH1	R	31	95	189	19	40	2	0	6	17	22	34	2	.212	.317
Hubie Brooks (ZJ)	DH70 1B6	R	35	82	306	28	66	13	0	8	36	12	46	3	.216	.337
Gary Gaetti	3B67 1B44 DH17	R	33	130	456	41	103	13	2	12	48	21	79	3	.226	.342
Von Hayes	OF85 DH5 1B4	L	33	94	307	35	69	17	1	4	29	37	54	11	.225	.326
Ron Tingley	C69	R	33	71	127	15	25	2	1	3	8	13	35	0	.197	.299
Damion Easley	3B45 SS3	R	22	47	151	14	39	5	0	1	12	8	26	9	.258	.311
John Orton (SJ)	C43	R	26	43	114	11	25	3	0	2	12	7	32	1	.219	.298
John Morris	OF14 DH6	L	31	43	57	4	11	1	0	1	3	4	11	1	.193	.263
Ken Oberkfell	2B21 DH5 1B2	L	36	41	91	6	24	1	0	0	10	8	5	0	.264	.275
Alvin Davis	1B22 DH9	L	31	40	104	5	26	8	0	0	16	13	9	0	.250	.327
Jose Gonzalez	OF22	R	27	33	55	4	10	2	0	0	2	7	20	0	.182	.218
2 Rob Ducey	OF20 DH1	L	27	31	59	4	14	3	0	0	2	5	12	2	.237	.288
Bobby Rose (NJ)	2B28 1B2	R	25	30	84	10	18	5	0	2	10	8	9	1	.214	.345
1 Lance Parrish	C22 DH2	R	36	24	83	7	19	2	0	4	11	5	22	0	.229	.398
Tim Salmon	OF21	R	23	23	79	8	14	1	0	2	6	11	23	1	.177	.266
Reggie Williams	OF12 DH2	B	25	14	26	5	6	1	1	0	2	1	10	0	.231	.346
2 Greg Myers (WJ)	C9	L	26	8	17	0	4	1	0	0	0	0	6	0	.235	.294
1 Dick Schofield	SS1	R	29	1	3	0	1	0	0	0	0	0	0	0	.333	.333

NAME	T	AGE	W	L	PCT	SV	G	GS	CG	IP	H	BB	SO	SHO	ERA
TOTALS		29	72	90	.444	42	162	162	26	1446	1449	532	888	13	3.84
Mark Langston	L	31	13	14	.481	0	32	32	9	229	206	74	174	2	3.66
Julio Valera	R	23	8	11	.421	0	30	28	4	188	188	64	113	2	3.73
Bert Blyleven (SJ)	R	41	8	12	.400	0	25	24	1	133	150	29	70	0	4.74
Chuck Crim	R	30	7	6	.538	1	57	0	0	87	100	29	30	0	5.17
Chuck Finley	L	29	7	12	.368	0	31	31	4	204	212	98	124	1	3.96
Jim Abbott	L	24	7	15	.318	0	29	29	7	211	208	68	130	0	2.77
Joe Grahe	R	24	5	6	.455	21	46	7	0	95	85	39	39	0	3.52
Scott Lewis	R	26	1	0	1.000	0	21	2	0	38	36	14	18	0	3.99
Steve Frey	L	28	4	2	.667	4	51	0	0	45	39	22	24	0	3.57
Scott Bailes	L	30	3	1	.750	0	32	0	0	39	59	28	25	0	7.45
Mike Butcher	R	27	2	2	.500	0	19	0	0	28	23	13	24	0	3.25
1 Mark Eichhorn	R	31	2	4	.333	2	42	0	0	57	51	18	42	0	2.38
1 Don Robinson (XJ)	R	35	1	0	1.000	0	3	3	0	16	19	3	9	0	2.20
Tim Fortugno	L	30	1	1	.500	1	14	5	1	42	37	19	31	1	5.18
Hilly Hathaway	L	22	0	0	---	0	2	1	0	6	8	4	1	0	7.94
Bryan Harvey (EJ)	R	29	0	4	---	13	25	0	0	29	22	11	34	0	2.83
John Farrell (EJ) 29															

KANSAS CITY — 6th(tie) 72-90 .444 24 — HAL McRAE

Name	G by Pos	B	AGE	G	AB	R	H	2B	3B	HR	RBI	BB	SO	SB	BA	SA
TOTALS			29	162	5610	610	1411	284	42	75	568	439	741	131	.256	.364
Wally Joyner	1B145 DH4	R	30	149	572	66	154	36	2	9	66	55	50	11	.269	.386
Keith Miller (LJ)	2B93 OF16 DH1	R	29	106	416	57	118	24	4	4	38	31	46	16	.284	.389
David Howard (XJ)	SS74 OF2	B	25	74	219	19	49	6	2	1	18	15	43	3	.224	.283
Gregg Jefferies	3B146 2B1 DH1	B	24	152	604	66	172	36	3	10	75	43	29	19	.285	.404
Jim Eisenreich (VJ)	OF88 DH6	L	33	113	353	31	95	13	3	2	28	24	36	11	.269	.340
Brian McRae	OF148	B	24	149	533	63	119	23	5	4	52	42	88	18	.223	.308
Kevin McReynolds (SJ)	OF106 DH1	R	32	109	373	45	92	25	0	13	49	67	48	7	.247	.416
Mike Macfarlane	C104 DH13	R	28	129	402	51	94	28	3	17	48	30	89	1	.234	.445
George Brett	DH132 1B15 3B3	L	39	152	592	55	169	35	5	7	61	35	69	8	.285	.397
Curt Wilkerson	SS69 2B39 3B5 DH1	B	31	111	296	27	74	10	1	2	29	18	47	18	.250	.314
Gary Thurman	OF67 DH9	R	27	88	200	25	49	6	3	0	20	9	34	9	.245	.305
Brent Mayne	C62 3B8	L	24	82	213	16	48	10	0	0	18	11	26	0	.225	.272
Rico Rossy	SS51 3B9 2B3	R	28	59	149	21	32	8	1	1	12	20	20	1	.215	.302
Kevin Koslofski	OF52	L	25	55	133	20	33	3	2	3	13	12	23	2	.248	.346
Terry Shumpert (FJ)	2B33 SS1 DH1	R	25	36	94	6	14	5	1	1	11	3	17	2	.149	.255
Chris Gwynn (LJ-SJ)	OF23 1B4	L	27	34	84	10	24	3	2	1	7	3	10	0	.286	.405
Bob Melvin	C21 1B3	R	30	32	70	5	22	5	0	0	6	5	13	0	.314	.386
2 Juan Samuel	OF18 2B10 DH1	R	31	29	102	15	29	3	0	0	8	7	27	6	.284	.392
Jeff Conine	OF23 1B4	R	26	28	91	10	23	5	0	0	9	8	23	0	.253	.352
Harvey Pulliam	DH2 OF1	R	24	8	4	5	2	1	0	0					.200	.400

NAME	T	AGE	W	L	PCT	SV	G	GS	CG	IP	H	BB	SO	SHO	ERA
TOTALS		28	72	90	.444	44	162	162	9	1447	1426	512	834	12	3.81
Kevin Appier	R	24	15	8	.652	0	30	30	3	208	167	68	150	0	2.46
Rusty Meacham	R	24	10	4	.714	2	64	0	0	102	88	21	64	0	2.74
Hipolito Pichardo	R	22	9	6	.600	0	31	24	1	144	148	49	59	1	3.95
Mark Gubicza (SJ)	R	29	7	6	.538	0	18	18	2	111	110	36	81	1	3.72
Tom Gordon	R	24	6	10	.375	0	40	11	0	118	116	55	98	0	4.59
2 Dennis Rasmussen	L	33	4	1	.800	0	5	5	1	38	25	8	12	1	1.43
Mike Magnante	L	27	4	9	.308	0	44	12	0	89	115	35	31	0	4.94
1 Neal Heaton	L	32	3	1	.750	0	31	0	0	41	43	22	29	0	4.17
Luis Aquino (SJ)	R	28	3	6	.333	0	15	13	0	68	81	20	11	0	4.52
Rick Reed	R	27	3	7	.300	0	19	18	1	100	105	20	49	1	3.68
2 Chris Haney	L	23	2	3	.400	0	7	7	1	42	35	16	27	1	3.86
1 Curt Young	L	32	1	3	.333	0	10	2	0	24	29	7	5	0	5.18
1 Mark Davis	L	31	1	3	.250	0	13	6	0	36	42	36	19	0	7.18
Steve Shifflett	R	26	1	0	1.000	0	34	0	0	52	55	17	25	0	2.60
Mike Boddicker (XJ-LJ)	R	34	1	4	.200	0	29	12	0	87	92	37	47	0	4.98
2 Juan Berenguer	R	37	1	4	.200	1	12	0	0	20	22	20	26	0	5.64
Jeff Montgomery	R	30	1	6	.143	39	65	0	0	83	61	27	69	0	2.18
Joel Johnston	R	25	0	0	---	0	4	0	0	4	9	1	1	0	13.50
Ed Pierce	R	28	0	0	---	0	2	0	0	3	6	3	2	0	3.38
Rich Sauveur	L	28	0	0	---	0	6	0	0	14	15	4	7	0	4.40
2 Bill Sampen	R	29	0	2	.000	0	13	0	0	20	21	14	10	0	3.63
Dennis Moeller	L	24	0	3	.000	0	6	3	0	18	14	11	6	0	7.00

SEATTLE — 7th 64-98 .395 32 — BILL PLUMMER

Name	G by Pos	B	AGE	G	AB	R	H	2B	3B	HR	RBI	BB	SO	SB	BA	SA
TOTALS			29	162	5564	679	1466	278	24	149	638	474	841	100	.263	.402
Pete O'Brien	1B81 DH35	L	34	134	396	40	88	15	1	14	52	40	27	2	.222	.371
Harold Reynolds	2B134 OF1 DH1	B	31	140	458	55	113	23	3	3	33	45	41	15	.247	.330
Omar Vizquel (KJ)	SS136	B	25	136	483	49	142	20	4	0	21	32	38	15	.294	.352
Edgar Martinez	3B103 DH28 1B2	R	29	135	528	100	181	46	3	18	73	54	61	14	.343	.544
Jay Buhner	OF150	R	27	152	543	69	132	16	3	25	79	71	146	0	.243	.422
Ken Griffey Jr.	OF137 DH3	L	22	142	565	83	174	39	4	27	103	44	67	10	.308	.535
Kevin Mitchell (BF)	OF69 DH26	R	30	99	360	48	103	24	0	9	67	35	46	0	.286	.428
Dave Valle	C31	R	31	124	367	39	88	16	1	9	30	27	58	0	.240	.362
Tino Martinez	1B78 DH48	L	24	136	460	53	118	19	2	16	66	42	77	2	.257	.411
Henry Cotto	OF92 DH3	R	31	108	294	42	76	11	1	5	27	14	49	23	.259	.354
Greg Briley	OF42 DH12 2B4 3B1	L	27	86	200	18	55	10	0	5	12	4	31	9	.275	.400
2 Lance Parrish	C34 1B16 DH14	R	36	69	192	19	45	11	1	8	21	19	48	1	.234	.427
Dave Cochrane (FJ)	OF25 C21 3B10 1B3 SS3 DH2 2B1	B	28	65	152	10	38	12	0	2	12	12	34	1	.250	.322
Jeff Schaefer	SS33 3B21 2B7	R	32	65	70	5	8	2	0	1	3	2	9	1	.114	.186
Rich Amaral	3B17 SS17 OF3 1B2 2B1	R	30	35	100	9	24	3	0	0	7	5	16	4	.240	.300
Shane Turner	3B18 OF15	L	29	34	74	8	20	5	0	0	6	4	9	2	.270	.338
Bret Boone	2B32 3B1	R	23	33	129	15	25	4	0	4	15	4	34	1	.194	.318
Mike Blowers	3B29 1B3	R	27	31	73	7	14	3	0	1	7	6	25	0	.192	.274
John Moses	OF18	B	34	21	22	3	4	0	0	0	3	3	2	0	.136	.182
Matt Sinatro	C18	R	32	18	28	0	3	0	0	0	1	4	5	0	.107	.107
2 Dann Howitt	OF11 1B4 DH1	L	27	13	37	4	10	3	0	1	5	5	11	0	.270	.514
Bill Haselman	C5 OF2	R	26	8	19	1	5	0	0	0	2	0	7	0	.263	.263
Bert Heffernan	C5	L	27	8	11	0	1	1	0	0	0	1	2	0	.091	.182
1 Scott Bradley	C1	L	32	2	1	0	0	0	0	0	0	0	0	0	.000	.000
Patrick Lennon	1B1	R	24	1	2	0	0	0	0	0	0	0	0	0	.000	.000

NAME	T	AGE	W	L	PCT	SV	G	GS	CG	IP	H	BB	SO	SHO	ERA
TOTALS		28	64	98	.395	30	162	162	21	1445	1467	661	894	9	4.55
Dave Fleming	L	22	17	10	.630	0	33	33	7	228	225	60	112	4	3.39
Randy Johnson	L	28	12	14	.462	0	31	31	6	210	154	144	241	2	3.77
Erik Hanson	R	27	8	17	.320	0	31	30	6	187	209	57	112	1	4.82
Dennis Powell	L	28	4	2	.667	0	49	0	0	57	49	29	35	0	4.58
Brian Fisher	R	30	4	3	.571	1	22	14	0	91	80	47	26	0	4.53
2 Tim Leary	R	33	3	4	.429	0	8	8	0	44	47	30	12	0	4.91
Calvin Jones	R	28	3	5	.375	0	38	1	0	62	50	47	49	0	5.69
Rich DeLucia (EJ)	R	28	3	6	.333	1	30	11	0	84	100	35	66	0	5.49
Russ Swan	L	28	3	10	.231	9	55	0	0	104	104	45	45	0	4.74
Eric Gunderson	L	26	2	1	.667	0	9	1	0	13	14	4	3	0	8.68
Mark Grant	R	28	2	4	.333	0	23	0	0	81	100	22	42	0	3.89
Mike Schooler (SA)	R	27	2	7	.222	13	53	0	0	52	55	24	33	0	4.70
Jeff Nelson	R	25	1	7	.125	6	66	0	0	81	71	44	46	0	3.44
Jim Acker (BW)	R	33	1	1	.500	0	31	0	0	45	51	11	15	0	5.28
2 Juan Agosto	L	34	1	0	1.000	0	18	0	0	18	27	12	3	0	5.89
1 Gene Harris	R	27	0	0	---	0	4	0	0	5	5	5	3	0	7.00
Dave Schmidt	R	35	0	0	---	0	1	0	0	2	8	0	1	0	18.90
Kevin Brown	R	26	0	0	---	0	1	0	0	2	5	2	1	0	9.00
Shawn Barton	L	29	0	0	---	0	14	0	0	14	14	5	6	0	2.92
Kerry Woodson (EJ)	R	23	0	0	---	0	6	0	0	14	16	11	6	0	3.29
Randy Kramer	R	31	0	1	.000	0	16	0	0	30	17	6	9	0	7.71
Clay Parker (EJ)	R	29	0	2	.000	0	11	2	0	33	47	11	20	0	7.56
Mike Walker	R	27	0	3	.000	0	15	0	0	21	19	5	5	0	7.36
Brian Holman (SJ) 27															

PITTSBURGH 1st 96-66 .593 — JIM LEYLAND

Name	G by Pos	B	AGE	G	AB	R	H	2B	3B	HR	RBI	BB	SO	SB	BA	SA
TOTALS			29	162	5527	693	1409	272	54	106	656	569	872	110	.255	.381
Orlando Merced	1B114 OF17	B	25	134	405	50	100	28	5	6	60	52	63	5	.247	.385
Jose Lind	2B134	R	28	135	468	38	110	14	1	0	39	26	29	3	.235	.269
Jay Bell	SS159	R	26	159	632	87	167	36	6	9	55	55	103	7	.264	.383
Jeff King	3B73 2B32 1B32 SS6 OF1	R	27	130	480	56	111	21	2	14	65	27	56	4	.231	.371
2 Alex Cole	OF53	L	26	64	205	33	57	3	7	0	10	18	46	7	.278	.361
Andy Van Slyke	OF154	L	31	154	614	103	199	45	12	14	89	58	99	12	.324	.505
Barry Bonds	OF139	L	27	140	473	109	147	36	5	34	103	127	69	39	.311	.624
Mike LaValliere	C92 3B1	L	31	95	293	22	75	13	1	2	29	44	21	0	.256	.328
Cecil Espy	OF82	B	29	112	194	21	50	7	3	1	20	15	40	6	.258	.340
Gary Varsho	OF44	L	31	103	162	22	36	6	3	4	22	10	32	5	.222	.370
Don Slaught	C79	R	33	87	255	26	88	17	3	4	37	17	23	2	.345	.482
Lloyd McClendon	OF60 1B18	R	33	84	190	26	48	8	1	3	20	28	24	1	.253	.353
1 Steve Buechele	3B80	R	30	80	285	27	71	14	1	8	43	34	61	0	.249	.389
Gary Redus (LJ)	1B36 OF15	R	35	76	176	26	45	7	3	3	12	17	25	11	.256	.381
John Wehner	3B34 1B13 2B5	R	25	55	123	11	22	6	0	0	4	12	22	3	.179	.228
Tom Prince	C19 3B1	R	27	27	44	1	4	2	0	0	5	6	9	1	.091	.136
Dave Clark	OF8	L	29	23	33	3	7	0	0	2	7	6	8	0	.212	.394
Carlos Garcia	2B14 SS8	R	24	22	39	4	8	1	0	0	4	0	9	0	.205	.231
Kirk Gibson	OF13	L	35	16	56	6	11	0	0	2	5	3	12	1	.196	.304
Will Pennyfeather	OF10	R	24	15	9	2	2	0	0	0	0	0	5	0	.222	.222
Al Martin	OF7	L	24	12	12	1	2	0	1	0	2	0	5	0	.167	.333
Kevin Young	3B7 1B1	R	23	10	7	2	4	0	0	0	4	2	0	1	.571	.571

NAME	T	AGE	W	L	PCT	SV	G	GS	CG	IP	H	BB	SO	SHO	ERA
		30	96	66	.593	43	162	162	20	1480	1410	455	844	20	3.35
Doug Drabek	R	29	15	11	.577	0	34	34	10	257	218	54	177	4	2.77
Randy Tomlin	L	26	14	9	.609	0	35	33	1	209	226	42	90	1	3.41
Bob Walk	R	35	10	6	.625	2	36	19	1	135	132	43	60	0	3.20
Tim Wakefield (SJ)	R	25	8	1	.889	0	13	13	4	92	76	35	51	1	2.15
Zane Smith (SJ)	L	31	8	8	.500	0	23	22	4	141	138	19	56	3	3.06
Bob Patterson	L	33	6	3	.667	9	60	0	0	65	59	23	43	0	2.92
Stan Belinda	R	25	6	4	.600	18	59	0	0	71	58	29	57	0	3.15
Roger Mason	R	33	5	7	.417	8	65	0	0	88	80	33	56	0	4.09
2 Danny Jackson	L	30	4	4	.500	0	15	15	0	88	94	29	46	0	3.36
Denny Neagle	L	23	4	6	.400	2	55	6	0	86	81	43	77	0	4.48
2 Danny Cox	R	32	3	1	.750	3	16	0	0	24	20	8	18	0	3.33
2 Jeff Robinson	R	30	3	1	.750	0	8	7	0	36	33	15	14	0	4.46
Vincente Palacios (AJ)	R	28	3	2	.600	0	20	8	0	53	56	27	33	0	4.25
Steve Cooke	L	22	2	0	1.000	1	11	0	0	23	22	4	10	0	3.52
Paul Wagner	R	24	2	0	1.000	0	6	1	0	13	9	5	5	0	0.69
Jerry Don Gleaton	L	34	2	0	1.000	0	23	0	0	32	34	19	18	0	4.26
Paul Miller	R	27	1	0	1.000	0	6	0	0	11	11	1	5	0	2.38
Dennis Lamp	R	39	1	1	.500	0	21	0	0	28	33	9	15	0	5.14
Blas Minor	R	26	0	0	—	0	1	0	0	2	3	0	4	0	4.50
Miguel Batista	R	21	0	0	—	0	1	0	0	2	4	3	1	0	9.00
Victor Cole	R	24	0	2	.000	0	8	4	0	23	23	14	12	0	5.48

MONTREAL 2nd 87-75 .537 9 — TOM RUNNELLS 17-20 .459   FELIPE ALOU 70-55 .560

Name	G by Pos	B	AGE	G	AB	R	H	2B	3B	HR	RBI	BB	SO	SB	BA	SA
TOTALS			27	162	5477	648	1381	263	37	102	601	463	976	196	.252	.370
Tim Wallach	3B85 1B71	R	34	150	537	53	120	29	1	9	59	50	90	2	.223	.331
Delino DeShields	2B134	L	23	135	530	82	155	19	4	7	56	54	108	46	.292	.398
Spike Owen	SS116	B	31	122	386	52	104	16	3	7	40	50	30	9	.269	.381
Bret Barberie	3B63 2B26 SS1	B	24	111	285	26	66	11	0	1	24	47	62	3	.232	.281
Larry Walker	OF139	L	25	143	528	85	159	31	4	23	93	41	97	18	.301	.506
Marquis Grissom	OF157	R	25	159	653	99	180	39	6	14	66	42	81	78	.276	.418
Ivan Calderon (SJ)	OF46	R	30	48	170	19	45	14	2	3	24	14	22	1	.265	.424
Gary Carter	C85 1B5	R	38	95	285	24	62	18	1	5	29	33	37	0	.218	.340
Moises Alou	OF100	R	25	115	341	53	96	28	2	9	56	25	46	16	.282	.455
John Vander Wal	OF57 1B7	L	26	105	213	21	51	8	2	4	20	24	36	3	.239	.352
Archi Cianfrocco	1B56 3B19 OF5	R	25	86	232	25	56	5	2	6	30	11	66	3	.241	.358
Darrin Fletcher (IL)	C69	R	25	83	222	13	54	10	2	2	26	14	28	0	.243	.333
Tom Foley	SS33 2B13 1B12 3B4 OF1	L	32	72	115	7	20	3	1	0	5	8	21	3	.174	.217
Greg Colbrunn	1B47	R	22	52	168	12	45	8	2	2	18	6	34	3	.268	.351
Wil Cordero	SS35 2B9	R	20	45	126	17	38	4	1	2	8	9	31	0	.302	.397
1 Darren Reed (AJ)	OF29	R	26	42	81	10	14	2	0	5	10	6	23	0	.173	.383
Rick Cerone	C28	R	38	33	63	10	17	4	0	1	7	3	5	1	.270	.381
Tim Laker	C28	R	22	28	46	8	10	3	0	0	4	2	14	1	.217	.283
Sean Berry	3B20	R	26	24	57	5	19	1	0	1	4	1	11	2	.333	.404
2 Jerry Willard	1B5	R	32	21	25	0	3	0	0	1	1	1	7	0	.120	.120
2 Steve Lyons	OF8 1B1	L	32	18	13	2	3	0	0	0	1	1	3	0	.231	.231
Matt Stairs	OF10	L	24	13	30	2	5	2	0	0	5	7	7	0	.167	.233
Eric Bullock		L	31	8	5	0	0	0	0	0	0	0	0	0	.000	.000
Todd Haney	2B5	R	26	7	10	0	3	1	0	0	1	0	0	0	.300	.400
Rob Natal	C4	R	26	5	6	0	0	0	0	0	0	1	1	0	.000	.000
Jerry Goff		L	28	3	3	0	0	0	0	0	0	0	0	0	.000	.000

NAME	T	AGE	W	L	PCT	SV	G	GS	CG	IP	H	BB	SO	SHO	ERA
		28	87	75	.537	49	162	162	11	1468	1296	525	1014	14	3.25
Ken Hill	R	26	16	9	.640	0	33	33	3	218	187	75	150	3	2.68
Dennis Martinez	R	37	16	11	.593	0	32	32	6	226	172	60	147	0	2.47
Mark Gardner	R	30	12	10	.545	0	33	30	0	180	179	60	132	0	4.36
Chris Nabholz	L	25	11	12	.478	0	32	32	1	195	176	74	130	1	3.32
Jeff Fassero	L	29	8	7	.533	1	70	0	0	86	81	34	63	0	2.84
Mel Rojas	R	25	7	1	.875	10	68	0	0	101	71	34	70	0	1.43
Brian Barnes	L	25	6	6	.500	0	21	17	0	100	77	46	65	0	2.97
John Wetteland	R	25	4	4	.500	37	67	0	0	83	64	36	99	0	2.92
1 Chris Haney	L	23	2	3	.400	0	9	6	1	38	40	10	27	1	5.45
Bill Risley	R	25	1	0	1.000	0	1	1	0	5	4	1	2	0	1.80
Bill Landrum (SJ)	R	34	1	1	.500	0	18	0	0	20	27	9	7	0	7.20
Jonathan Hurst	R	25	1	1	.500	0	3	3	0	16	18	7	4	0	5.51
Kent Bottenfield	R	23	1	2	.330	1	10	4	0	32	26	11	14	0	2.23
1 Bill Sampen	R	29	1	4	.200	0	44	1	0	63	62	29	23	0	3.13
Pete Young	R	24	0	0	—	0	13	0	0	20	18	9	11	0	3.98
2 Gil Heredia	R	26	0	0	—	0	7	1	0	15	12	4	7	0	1.84
Doug Simons	L	25	0	0	—	0	5	1	0	15	15	2	6	0	23.63
Scott Service	R	25	0	0	—	0	5	0	0	7	4	5	11	0	14.14
Matt Maysey	R	25	0	0	—	0	7	0	0	7	4	5	11	0	3.86
Sergio Valdez	R	27	0	0	—	0	27	0	0	37	25	12	32	0	2.41
2 Bill Krueger	L	34	0	0	—	0	9	2	0	17	23	7	13	0	6.75

ST LOUIS 3rd 83-79 .512 13 — JOE TORRE

Name	G by Pos	B	AGE	G	AB	R	H	2B	3B	HR	RBI	BB	SO	SB	BA	SA
TOTALS			28	162	5594	631	1464	262	44	94	599	495	996	208	.262	.375
Andres Galarraga (BW)	1B90	R	31	95	325	38	79	14	2	10	39	11	69	5	.243	.391
Geronimo Pena (BC-SJ)	2B57	B	25	62	203	31	62	12	1	7	31	24	37	13	.305	.478
Ozzie Smith	SS132	B	37	132	518	73	153	20	2	0	31	59	34	43	.295	.342
Todd Zeile	3B121	R	26	126	439	51	113	18	4	7	48	68	70	7	.257	.364
Felix Jose	OF127	B	27	131	509	62	150	22	3	14	75	40	100	28	.295	.432
Ray Lankford	OF153	L	25	153	598	87	175	40	6	20	86	72	147	42	.293	.480
Bernard Gilkey	OF111	R	25	131	384	56	116	19	4	7	43	39	52	18	.302	.427
Tom Pagnozzi	C138	R	29	139	485	33	121	26	3	7	44	28	64	2	.249	.359
Milt Thompson	OF45	L	33	109	208	31	61	9	1	4	17	16	39	18	.293	.404
Gerald Perry	1B29	L	31	87	143	14	34	6	0	1	18	15	23	3	.238	.315
Luis Alicea (VJ)	2B75 SS4	B	26	85	265	26	65	9	11	2	32	27	40	2	.245	.385
Tim Jones (VJ)	SS34 2B28 3B2 OF1	L	29	67	145	9	29	4	0	0	3	11	29	5	.200	.228
Craig Wilson	3B18 2B11 OF3	R	26	61	106	6	33	6	0	0	13	10	18	1	.311	.368
Rex Hudler (KJ)	2B16 OF12 1B8	R	31	61	98	17	24	4	0	3	5	2	23	2	.245	.378
Brian Jordan (LJ)	OF53	R	25	55	193	17	40	9	4	5	22	10	48	7	.207	.373
Pedro Guerrero (SJ)	1B28 OF10	R	36	43	146	10	32	6	1	1	16	11	25	2	.219	.295
Rich Gedman	C40	L	32	41	105	5	23	4	0	1	8	11	22	0	.219	.286
Tracy Woodson	3B26 1B3	R	29	31	114	9	35	8	1	2	22	3	10	0	.307	.404
Rod Brewer	1B27 OF4	L	26	29	103	11	31	6	0	0	10	8	12	0	.301	.359
Chuck Carr	OF19	B	24	22	64	8	14	3	0	0	3	9	6	10	.219	.266
Jose Oquendo (SJ-FJ)	2B9 SS5	B	28	14	35	3	9	3	0	0	3	5	3	0	.257	.400
Stan Royer	3B5 1B4	R	24	13	31	6	10	2	0	2	9	1	4	0	.323	.581
Bien Figueroa	SS9 2B3	R	28	12	11	1	2	1	0	0	4	1	2	0	.182	.273
Ozzie Canseco	OF8	R	27	9	29	7	8	5	0	1	3	7	4	0	.276	.448

NAME	T	AGE	W	L	PCT	SV	G	GS	CG	IP	H	BB	SO	SHO	ERA
		29	83	79	.512	47	162	162	10	1480	1405	400	842	9	3.38
Bob Tewksbury	R	31	16	5	.762	0	33	32	5	233	217	20	91	0	2.16
Donovan Osborne	L	23	11	9	.550	0	34	29	0	179	193	38	104	0	3.77
Rheal Cormier	L	25	10	10	.500	0	31	30	3	186	194	33	117	0	3.68
Mike Perez	R	27	9	3	.750	0	77	0	0	93	70	32	46	0	1.84
Omar Olivares	R	24	9	9	.500	0	32	30	1	197	189	63	124	0	3.84
Todd Worrell	R	32	5	3	.625	3	67	0	0	64	45	25	64	0	2.11
Cris Carpenter	R	27	5	4	.556	1	73	0	0	88	69	27	46	0	2.97
Bryn Smith (EJ)	R	36	4	2	.667	0	13	1	0	29	37	5	9	0	4.64
Lee Smith	R	34	4	9	.308	43	70	0	0	75	62	26	60	0	3.12
Mark Clark	R	24	3	10	.231	0	20	20	1	113	117	36	44	1	4.45
Bob McClure	L	40	2	2	.500	0	71	0	0	54	52	25	24	0	3.17
1 Juan Agosto	L	34	2	4	.333	0	22	0	0	32	39	9	13	0	6.25
1 Jose Deleon	R	31	2	7	.222	0	29	15	0	102	95	43	72	0	4.57
Joe Magrane (EJ)	L	27	1	2	.333	0	5	5	0	31	34	15	20	0	4.02
Frank DiPino (EJ)	L	35	0	0	—	0	0	0	0	11	9	3	8	0	1.64
Scott Terry (SJ) 32															

CHICAGO 4th 78-84 .481 18 — JIM LEFEBVRE

Name	G by Pos	B	AGE	G	AB	R	H	2B	3B	HR	RBI	BB	SO	SB	BA	SA
TOTALS			28	162	5590	593	1420	221	41	104	566	417	816	77	.254	.364
Mark Grace	1B157	L	28	158	603	72	185	37	5	9	79	72	36	6	.307	.430
Ryne Sandberg	2B157	R	32	158	612	100	186	32	8	26	87	68	73	17	.304	.510
Shawon Dunston (XJ)	SS18	R	29	18	73	8	23	3	1	0	2	3	13	2	.315	.384
2 Steve Buechele	3B63 2B2	R	30	65	239	25	66	9	3	1	21	18	44	1	.276	.351
Andre Dawson	OF143	R	37	143	542	60	150	27	2	22	90	30	70	6	.277	.456
Sammy Sosa (BH-BN)	OF67	R	23	67	262	41	68	7	2	8	25	19	63	15	.260	.393
Derrick May	OF108	L	23	124	351	33	96	11	0	8	45	14	40	5	.274	.373
Joe Girardi	C86	R	27	91	270	19	73	3	1	1	12	19	38	0	.270	.300
Doug Dascenzo	OF122	B	28	139	376	37	96	13	4	0	20	27	32	6	.255	.311
Dwight Smith	OF63	L	28	109	217	28	60	10	3	3	24	13	40	9	.276	.392
Luis Salazar	3B40 OF34 SS12 1B5	R	36	98	255	20	53	7	2	5	25	11	34	1	.208	.310
Jose Vizcaino (HJ)	SS50 3B29 2B5	B	24	86	285	25	64	10	4	1	17	14	35	3	.225	.298
Rick Wilkins	C73	L	25	83	244	20	66	9	1	8	22	28	53	0	.270	.414
Rey Sanchez (XJ)	SS68 2B4	R	24	74	255	24	64	14	3	1	19	10	17	2	.251	.341
Doug Strange	3B33 2B12	B	28	52	94	7	15	1	0	1	5	5	20	1	.160	.202
Hector Villanueva	C28 1B6	R	27	51	112	9	17	6	0	2	13	11	24	0	.152	.259
2 Kal Daniels	OF28	L	28	48	108	12	27	6	0	4	17	12	24	0	.250	.417
Gary Scott	3B30 SS2	R	23	36	96	8	15	2	0	2	11	5	14	0	.156	.240
Alex Arias	SS30	R	24	32	99	14	29	6	0	0	7	11	13	0	.293	.354
Jerome Walton	OF24	R	26	30	55	7	7	1	0	0	1	0	9	3	.127	.164
Jeff Kunkel	SS6 2B3 OF3	R	30	20	29	0	4	2	0	0	4	0	8	0	.138	.207
1 Chico Walker	OF6 2B2 3B2	B	34	19	26	3	3	0	0	0	4	1	5	0	.115	.115
Fernando Ramsey	OF15	R	26	18	25	0	3	0	0	0	0	0	6	0	.120	.120
George Pedre	C4	R	25	4	4	0	0	0	0	0	0	0	1	0	.000	.000

NAME	T	AGE	W	L	PCT	SV	G	GS	CG	IP	H	BB	SO	SHO	ERA
		27	78	84	.481	37	162	162	16	1469	1337	575	901	11	3.39
Greg Maddux	R	26	20	11	.645	0	35	35	9	268	201	70	199	4	2.18
Mike Morgan	R	32	16	8	.667	0	34	34	6	240	203	79	123	1	2.55
Frank Castillo	R	23	10	11	.476	0	33	33	0	205	179	63	135	0	3.46
Shawn Boskie (ZJ)	R	25	5	11	.313	0	23	18	0	92	96	36	39	0	5.01
Mike Harkey (SJ-KJ)	R	25	4	0	1.000	0	7	7	0	38	34	15	21	0	1.89
Jeff Robinson	L	31	4	3	.571	1	49	5	0	78	76	40	46	0	3.00
Paul Assenmacher	L	31	4	4	.500	0	70	0	0	68	72	26	67	0	4.10
Chuck McElroy	L	24	4	7	.364	6	72	0	0	84	73	51	83	0	3.55
1 Danny Jackson	L	30	4	9	.308	0	19	19	0	113	117	48	51	0	4.22
Bob Scanlan	R	25	3	6	.333	14	69	0	0	87	76	30	42	0	2.89
Ken Patterson (SJ)	L	27	2	3	.400	0	32	1	0	42	41	27	23	0	3.89
Jim Bullinger	R	26	2	8	.200	7	39	9	1	85	72	54	36	0	4.66
Dave Smith (EJ)	R	37	0	3	.000	0	11	0	0	14	15	4	3	0	2.51
Jeff Hartsock	R	25	0	0	—	0	4	0	0	9	15	4	6	0	6.75
Jessie Hollins	R	25	0	0	—	0	5	0	0	5	7	2	0	0	13.50
1 Dennis Rasmussen	L	33	0	0	—	0	5	1	0	7	2	0	0	0	10.80
Heathcliff Slocumb	R	26	0	0	.000	0	30	0	0	36	52	21	27	0	6.50

NEW YORK — 5th 72-90 .444 24 — JEFF TORBORG

Name	G by Pos	B	AGE	G	AB	R	H	2B	3B	HR	RBI	BB	SO	SB	BA	SA
TOTALS		B	30	162	5340	599	1254	259	17	93	564	572	956	129	.235	.342
Eddie Murray	1B154	B	36	156	551	64	144	37	2	16	93	66	74	4	.261	.423
Willie Randolph (BW)	2B79	R	27	90	286	29	72	15	1	2	15	40	34	1	.252	.318
2 Dick Schofield	SS141	R	29	142	420	52	86	18	2	4	36	60	82	1	.205	.286
Dave Magadan (BW)	3B93 1B2	L	29	99	321	33	91	9	1	3	28	56	44	1	.283	.346
Bobby Bonilla	OF121 1B6	B	29	128	438	62	109	23	0	19	70	66	73	4	.249	.432
Howard Johnson (SJ)	OF98	B	31	100	350	48	78	19	0	7	43	55	79	22	.223	.337
Vince Coleman	OF61	B	31	71	229	37	63	11	1	2	21	27	41	24	.275	.358
Todd Hundley	C121	B	23	123	358	32	75	17	0	7	32	19	76	3	.209	.316
Daryl Boston	OF95	L	29	130	289	37	72	14	2	11	35	38	60	12	.249	.426
Bill Pecota	3B48 SS39 2B38 1B1	R	32	117	269	28	61	13	0	2	26	25	40	9	.227	.297
2 Chico Walker	3B36 2B16 OF15	B	34	107	227	24	70	12	1	4	36	24	46	14	.308	.423
Dave Gallagher (BH)	OF76	R	31	98	175	20	42	11	1	1	21	19	16	4	.240	.331
Mackey Sasser	C27 1B12 OF9	L	29	92	141	7	34	6	0	2	18	3	10	0	.241	.326
Charlie O'Brien	C64	R	32	68	156	15	33	12	0	2	13	16	18	0	.212	.327
2 Kevin Bass	OF39	B	33	46	137	15	37	12	2	2	9	7	17	7	.270	.431
Junior Noboa	2B16 3B3 SS2	R	27	46	47	7	7	0	0	0	3	3	8	1	.149	.149
Chris Donnels	3B29 2B12	L	26	45	121	8	21	4	0	0	6	17	25	1	.174	.207
Jeff Kent	2B34 3B1 SS1	R	24	37	113	16	27	8	1	3	15	7	29	0	.239	.407
2 Jeff McKnight	2B14 1B9 3B3 SS3 OF1	B	24	28	31	85	10	23	3	1	2	13	2	8	0	.271	.400
Pat Howell	OF28	B	23	31	75	9	14	1	0	0	1	2	15	4	.187	.200
Ryan Thompson	OF29	R	24	30	108	15	24	7	1	3	10	8	24	2	.222	.389
D.J. Dozier	OF13	B	26	25	47	4	9	2	0	0	2	4	19	4	.191	.234
Rodney McCray	OF13	R	28	18	1	3	1	0	0	0	1	0	0	2	1.000	1.000
Kevin Elster (SJ)	SS5	R	27	6	18	0	4	0	0	0	0	0	0	0	.222	.222
Kevin Baez (BG)	SS5	R	24	6	13	0	2	0	0	0	0	0	2	0	.154	.154
Steve Springer	2B1 3B1	R	31	4	5	0	2	1	0	0	0	0	2	0	.400	.600

NAME	T	AGE	W	L	PCT	SV	G	GS	CG	IP	H	BB	SO	SHO	ERA
		29	72	90	.444	34	162	162	17	1447	1404	482	1025	13	3.66
Sid Fernandez	L	29	5	6	.560	0	32	32	5	215	162	67	193	2	2.73
1 David Cone	R	29	13	7	.650	0	27	27	7	197	162	82	214	5	2.88
Dwight Gooden	R	27	10	13	.435	0	31	31	3	206	197	70	145	0	3.67
John Franco (EJ)	L	31	6	2	.750	15	31	0	0	33	24	11	20	0	1.64
Pete Schourek	L	23	6	8	.429	0	22	21	0	136	137	44	60	0	3.64
Jeff Innis	R	29	6	9	.400	1	76	0	0	88	85	36	39	0	2.86
2 Lee Guetterman	L	33	3	4	.429	2	43	0	0	43	57	14	15	0	5.82
Bret Saberhagen (RJ)	R	28	3	5	.375	0	17	15	1	98	84	27	81	1	3.50
Wally Whitehurst	R	28	3	9	.250	0	44	11	0	97	99	33	70	0	3.62
2 Barry Jones	R	29	2	0	1.000	1	17	0	0	15	20	11	11	0	9.39
Eric Hillman	L	26	2	2	.500	0	11	8	0	52	67	10	16	0	5.33
Anthony Young	R	26	2	14	.125	15	52	13	1	121	134	31	64	0	4.17
Mark Dewey	R	27	1	0	1.000	2	20	0	0	33	37	10	24	0	4.32
1 Tim Burke	R	33	1	2	.000	0	15	0	0	16	26	3	7	0	5.74
Bill Pecota	R	32	0	0	—	0	1	0	0	1	0	0	0	0	9.00
Paul Gibson	L	32	0	1	.000	0	43	1	0	62	70	25	49	0	5.23
Tom Filer	R	35	0	1	.000	0	9	1	0	22	18	6	9	0	2.05
Joe Vitko	R	22	0	1	.000	0	3	1	0	5	12	1	6	0	13.50
Mike Birkbeck	R	31	0	1	.000	0	1	0	0	7	12	1	2	0	9.00
Steve Rosenberg (SJ) 27															

PHILADELPHIA — 6th 70-92 .432 26 — JIM FREGOSI

Name	G by Pos	B	AGE	G	AB	R	H	2B	3B	HR	RBI	BB	SO	SB	BA	SA
TOTALS			28	162	5500	686	1392	255	36	118	638	509	1059	127	.253	.377
John Kruk	1B108 OF35	L	31	144	507	86	164	30	4	10	70	92	88	3	.323	.458
Mickey Morandini	2B124 SS3	L	26	127	422	47	112	8	8	3	30	25	64	8	.265	.344
Juan Bell	SS46	B	24	46	147	12	30	3	1	1	8	18	29	5	.204	.259
Dave Hollins	3B156 1B1	B	26	156	586	104	158	28	4	27	93	76	110	9	.270	.469
Wes Chamberlin (NJ)	OF73	R	26	76	275	26	71	18	0	9	41	10	55	4	.258	.422
Lenny Dykstra (J)	OF85	L	29	85	345	53	104	18	0	6	39	40	32	30	.301	.406
Mariano Duncan	OF65 2B52 SS42 3B4	R	29	142	574	71	153	40	3	8	50	17	108	23	.267	.389
Darren Daulton	C141	R	30	145	485	80	131	32	5	27	109	88	103	11	.270	.524
Ruben Amaro	OF113	B	26	126	374	43	82	15	6	7	34	37	54	11	.219	.348
Ricky Jordan (BJ)	1B54 OF11	R	27	94	276	33	84	19	0	4	34	5	44	1	.304	.417
2 Stan Javier	OF84	B	28	74	276	36	72	14	1	0	24	31	43	18	.261	.319
Jeff Grotewald	OF2 C2 1B1	L	26	72	65	7	13	2	0	3	5	9	20	0	.200	.369
1 Dale Sveum	SS34 3B5 1B4	B	28	54	135	13	24	4	0	2	16	16	39	0	.178	.252
Kim Batiste	SS41	R	24	44	136	9	28	4	0	1	10	4	18	0	.206	.257
Tom Marsh (VJ)	OF35	R	26	42	125	7	25	3	2	2	16	2	23	0	.200	.304
Wally Backman (BG)	2B10 3B2	B	32	42	48	6	13	1	0	0	6	8	19	1	.271	.292
Joe Millette	SS26 3B32 B1	R	25	33	78	5	16	0	0	0	2	5	10	1	.205	.205
Jim Lindeman (XJ)	OF9	R	30	29	39	6	10	1	0	1	3	3	11	0	.256	.359
Braulio Castillo	OF24	R	23	28	76	12	15	3	1	2	7	4	15	1	.197	.342
Steve Lake (KJ)	C17	R	35	20	53	3	13	2	0	1	2	1	9	0	.245	.340
Dale Murphy (KJ)	OF16	R	36	18	62	5	10	1	0	2	7	1	13	0	.161	.274
Todd Pratt	C11	R	25	16	46	6	13	1	0	2	10	4	12	0	.283	.435
Julio Peguero	OF14	B	23	14	9	3	2	0	0	0	1	1	5	0	.222	.222
1 Steve Scarsone	2B3	R	26	7	13	1	2	0	0	0	0	1	5	0	.154	.154

NAME	T	AGE	W	L	PCT	SV	G	GS	CG	IP	H	BB	SO	SHO	ERA
		26	70	92	.432	34	162	162	27	1428	1387	549	851	7	4.11
Curt Schilling	R	25	14	11	.560	2	42	26	10	226	165	59	147	4	2.35
Terry Mulholland	L	29	13	11	.542	0	32	32	12	229	227	46	125	2	3.81
1 Ben Rivera	R	24	7	3	.700	0	20	14	4	102	78	32	66	1	2.82
Mike Hartley (LJ)	R	30	7	6	.538	0	46	0	0	55	54	23	53	0	3.44
1 Barry Jones	R	29	5	6	.455	0	44	0	0	54	65	24	19	0	4.64
Mitch Williams	L	27	5	8	.385	29	66	0	0	81	69	64	74	0	3.78
Tommy Greene (SJ)	R	25	3	3	.500	0	13	12	0	64	75	34	39	0	5.32
Wally Ritchie	L	26	2	1	.667	1	40	0	0	39	44	17	19	0	3.00
Bob Ayrault	R	26	2	2	.500	0	30	0	0	43	32	17	27	0	3.12
1 Danny Cox	R	32	2	2	.500	0	9	7	0	38	46	19	30	0	5.40
Greg Mathews	L	30	2	3	.400	0	14	7	0	52	54	24	27	0	5.16
Cliff Brantley	R	24	2	6	.250	0	28	9	0	76	71	58	32	0	4.60
Keith Shepherd	R	23	1	1	.500	2	12	0	0	22	19	6	10	0	3.27
Mike Williams	R	23	1	1	.500	0	5	4	0	19	20	12	11	0	7.71
Pat Combs	L	25	1	1	.500	0	4	4	0	19	21	12	7	0	7.54
Andy Ashby (BG)	R	24	1	3	.250	0	10	8	0	37	42	21	24	0	7.54
2 Don Robinson	R	35	1	4	.200	0	8	8	0	44	49	4	17	0	6.13
Kyle Abbott	L	24	1	14	.067	0	31	19	0	133	147	45	88	0	5.13
Steve Searcy	L	28	0	0	—	0	10	0	0	13	13	6	9	0	8.18
Jay Baller	R	31	0	0	—	0	2	0	0	1	10	10	9	0	8.18
Darrin Chapin	R	26	0	0	—	0	1	0	0	2	1	1	2	0	9.00
2 Jose DeLeon	R	31	0	1	.000	0	3	0	0	15	16	5	7	0	3.00
Mickey Weston	R	31	0	1	.000	0	1	0	0	1	4	1	0	0	12.27
Brad Brink	R	27	0	1	.000	0	7	7	0	41	53	13	16	0	4.14
Ken Howell (SJ) 31, Jose DeJesus (SJ) 27															

WEST DIVISION

ATLANTA — 1st 98-64 .605 — BOBBY COX

Name	G by Pos	B	AGE	G	AB	R	H	2B	3B	HR	RBI	BB	SO	SB	BA	SA
TOTALS			28	162	5480	682	1391	223	48	138	641	493	924	126	.254	.388
Sid Bream	1B120	L	28	125	372	30	97	25	1	10	61	46	51	6	.261	.414
Mark Lemke	2B145 3B13	B	26	155	427	38	97	7	4	6	26	50	39	0	.227	.304
Rafael Belliard	SS139 2B1	R	30	144	285	20	60	6	1	0	14	14	43	0	.211	.239
Terry Pendleton	3B158	B	31	160	640	98	199	39	1	21	105	37	67	5	.311	.473
David Justice	OF140	L	26	144	484	78	124	19	5	21	72	79	85	2	.256	.473
Otis Nixon	OF111	B	33	120	456	79	134	14	2	2	22	39	54	41	.294	.346
Ron Gant	OF147	R	27	153	544	74	141	22	6	17	80	45	101	32	.259	.415
Greg Olson (BN)	C94	R	31	95	302	27	72	14	2	3	27	34	31	2	.238	.328
Jeff Blauser	SS106 2B21 3B1	R	26	123	343	61	90	19	3	14	46	46	82	5	.262	.458
Brian Hunter	1B92 OF8	R	24	102	238	34	57	13	2	14	41	21	50	1	.239	.487
Damon Berryhill	C84	B	28	101	307	21	70	16	1	10	43	17	67	0	.228	.384
Deion Sanders	OF75	L	24	97	303	54	92	6	14	8	28	18	52	26	.304	.495
Lonnie Smith	OF35	R	36	84	158	23	39	8	2	6	33	17	37	4	.247	.437
Jeff Treadway (HJ)	2B45 3B1	L	29	61	126	5	28	6	1	0	5	9	16	1	.222	.286
1 Jerry Willard	C1	L	32	26	23	2	8	1	0	2	7	1	3	0	.348	.652
Tommy Gregg (BH)	OF9	L	28	18	19	1	5	0	0	1	2	1	3	0	.263	.421
Ryan Klesko	1B5	L	21	13	14	0	0	0	0	0	0	2	5	0	.000	.000
Melvin Nieves	OF6	B	20	12	19	0	4	1	0	0	1	2	7	0	.211	.263
Francisco Cabrera	C1	R	25	12	10	2	3	0	0	2	3	1	1	0	.300	.900
1 Steve Lyons	OF6 2B2	L	32	11	14	0	1	0	0	0	1	0	4	0	.071	.214
Javy Lopez	C9	R	21	9	16	3	6	2	0	0	0	0	1	0	.375	.500
Vinny Castilla	3B4 SS4	R	24	9	16	1	4	1	0	0	0	0	4	0	.250	.313
Nick Esasky (IL)32																

NAME	T	AGE	W	L	PCT	SV	G	GS	CG	IP	H	BB	SO	SHO	ERA
		28	98	64	.605	41	162	162	26	1460	1321	489	948	24	3.14
Tom Glavine	L	26	20	8	.714	0	33	33	7	225	197	70	129	5	2.76
Charlie Leibrandt	L	35	15	7	.682	0	32	31	5	193	191	42	104	2	3.36
John Smoltz	R	25	15	12	.556	0	35	35	9	247	206	80	215	3	2.85
Steve Avery	L	22	11	11	.500	0	35	35	2	234	216	71	129	2	3.20
Pete Smith	R	26	7	0	1.000	0	12	11	2	79	63	28	43	1	2.05
Marvin Freeman	R	29	7	5	.583	3	58	0	0	64	61	29	41	0	3.22
Mike Stanton	L	25	5	4	.556	8	65	0	0	64	59	20	44	0	4.10
2 Jeff Reardon	R	36	3	0	1.000	3	14	0	0	23	10	5	19	0	1.15
David Nied	R	23	3	0	1.000	0	6	2	0	23	10	5	19	1	1.17
1 Juan Berenguer	R	37	1	3	.750	1	29	0	0	33	35	16	19	0	5.13
Kent Mercker	L	24	3	2	.600	6	53	0	0	68	51	35	49	0	3.42
Mike Bielecki (EJ)	R	32	2	4	.333	0	19	14	1	81	77	27	62	1	2.57
2 Mark Davis	L	31	1	0	1.000	0	14	0	0	17	22	13	15	0	7.02
Armando Reynoso	R	26	1	0	1.000	1	3	0	0	8	10	3	1	0	4.70
Mark Wohlers	R	22	1	2	.333	4	32	0	0	35	28	14	17	0	2.55
Alejandro Pena (EJ)	R	33	1	6	.143	15	41	0	0	42	40	13	34	0	4.07
Randy St. Claire	R	31	0	0	—	0	10	0	0	15	15	7	9	0	5.87
1 Ben Rivera	R		0	0	.000	0	8	0	0	15	13	11	10	0	4.70
Pedro Borbon	L	24	0	0	.000	0	0	0	0	0	0	0	0	0	6.75

CINCINNATI — 2nd 90-72 .556 8 — LOU PINIELLA

Name	G by Pos	B	AGE	G	AB	R	H	2B	3B	HR	RBI	BB	SO	SB	BA	SA
TOTALS			28	162	5460	660	1418	281	44	99	606	563	888	125	.260	.382
Hal Morris (BH)	1B109	L	27	115	395	41	107	21	3	6	53	45	53	6	.271	.385
Bill Doran	2B104 1B25	B	34	132	387	48	91	16	2	8	47	64	40	7	.235	.349
Barry Larkin	SS140	R	28	140	533	76	162	32	6	12	78	63	58	15	.304	.454
Chris Sabo	3B93	R	30	96	344	42	84	19	3	12	43	30	54	4	.244	.422
Paul O'Neill	OF143	L	29	148	496	59	122	19	1	14	66	77	85	6	.246	.373
Reggie Sanders	OF116	R	24	116	385	62	104	26	6	12	36	48	98	16	.270	.480
Bip Roberts	OF79 2B42 3B36	B	28	147	532	92	172	34	6	4	45	62	54	44	.323	.432
Joe Oliver	C141 1B1	R	26	143	485	42	131	25	1	10	57	35	75	2	.270	.388
Dave Martinez	OF111 1B21	L	27	135	393	47	100	20	5	3	31	42	54	12	.254	.354
Glenn Braggs (BH)	OF79	R	29	92	266	40	63	16	3	8	39	36	48	3	.237	.410
Freddie Benavides	2B37 SS34 3B1	R	26	74	173	14	40	10	1	1	17	10	34	1	.231	.318
Jeff Branson	2B33 3B8 SS1	L	25	72	115	12	34	7	1	0	15	5	16	0	.296	.374
Darnell Coles (NJ)	3B23 1B20 OF5	R	30	55	141	16	44	11	2	3	18	3	15	1	.312	.482
1 Billy Hatcher	OF93	R	31	43	94	10	27	3	2	2	10	5	11	0	.287	.383
Cesar Hernandez	OF18	R	25	34	51	6	14	4	0	0	4	6	10	4	.275	.353
Willie Greene	3B25	L	20	29	93	10	25	5	2	2	13	10	23	0	.269	.430
Jacob Brumfield	OF16	R	27	24	30	6	4	0	0	0	1	3	6	3	.133	.133
Troy Afenir	C15	R	29	15	34	3	6	3	0	0	5	4	12	0	.176	.324
Jeff Reed (EJ)	C6	L	29	15	25	2	4	0	0	0	0	1	1	0	.160	.160
Geronimo Berroa	OF3	R	27	13	25	4	4	0	0	1	2	0	6	0	.267	.333
Tim Costo	1B12	R	23	12	36	3	8	2	0	0	5	3	6	0	.222	.278
Dan Wilson	C9	R	23	12	25	0	5	1	0	0	3	0	4	0	.200	.400
Rick Wrona	C10 1B1	R	28	11	23	0	4	0	0	0	0	0	5	0	.174	.174
Gary Green	SS6 3B1	R	30	8	12	3	4	1	0	0	0	0	3	0	.333	.417
2 Scott Bradley	C2	L	32	5	5	1	2	0	0	0	0	0	0	0	.400	.400

NAME	T	AGE	W	L	PCT	SV	G	GS	CG	IP	H	BB	SO	SHO	ERA
		28	90	72	.556	55	162	162	9	1450	1362	470	1060	11	3.46
Jose Rijo	R	27	15	10	.600	0	33	33	2	211	185	44	171	0	2.56
Tim Belcher	R	30	15	14	.517	0	35	34	2	228	201	80	149	3	3.91
Greg Swindell	L	27	12	8	.600	0	31	30	5	214	210	41	138	2	2.70
Scott Bankhead	R	28	10	4	.714	1	54	0	0	71	57	29	53	0	2.93
Chris Hammond	L	26	7	10	.412	0	28	26	0	147	149	55	79	0	4.21
Tom Browning (KJ)	L	32	6	5	.545	0	16	16	0	87	108	28	33	0	5.07
Norm Charlton	L	29	4	2	.667	26	64	0	0	81	79	26	90	0	2.99
Tim Pugh	R	25	4	2	.667	0	7	7	0	45	47	13	18	0	2.58
Scott Ruskin	L	29	4	3	.571	0	57	0	0	54	56	29	43	0	5.03
Dwayne Henry	R	30	3	3	.500	0	16	0	0	46	59	44	72	0	3.33
2 Tom Bolton	L	30	3	4	.429	0	18	16	0	68	64	36	39	0	5.24
Rob Dibble	R	28	3	5	.375	25	63	0	0	70	48	31	110	0	3.07
Bobby Ayala	R	22	2	1	.667	0	5	3	0	29	33	13	23	0	4.34
Tony Menendez	R	27	1	0	1.000	0	3	0	0	5	5	1	6	0	1.93
Steve Foster	R	26	1	1	.500	2	31	0	0	50	52	12	34	0	2.88
Milt Hill	R	26	1	1	.500	0	14	0	0	20	15	5	10	0	3.15
Keith Brown	R	28	0	0	.000	0	2	0	0	5	5	1	5	0	4.50

SAN DIEGO — 3rd 82-80 .506 16 GREG RIDDOCH 78-72 .520 JIM RIGGLEMAN 4-8 .333

Name	G by Pos	B	AGE	G	AB	R	H	2B	3B	HR	RBI	BB	SO	SB	BA	SA
TOTALS			28	162	5476	617	1396	255	30	135	576	453	864	69	.255	.386
Fred McGriff	1B151	L	28	152	531	79	152	30	4	35	104	96	108	8	.286	.556
Kurt Stillwell	2B111	B	27	114	379	35	86	15	3	2	24	26	58	4	.227	.298
Tony Fernandez	SS154	B	30	155	622	84	171	32	4	4	37	56	62	20	.275	.359
Gary Sheffield	3B144	R	23	146	557	87	184	34	3	33	100	48	40	5	.330	.580
Tony Gwynn	OF127	L	32	128	520	77	165	27	3	6	41	46	16	3	.317	.415
Darrin Jackson	OF153	R	29	155	587	72	146	23	5	17	70	26	106	14	.249	.392
Jerald Clark	OF134 1B11	R	27	146	496	45	120	22	6	12	58	22	97	3	.242	.383
Benito Santiago (BG)	C103	R	27	106	386	37	97	21	0	10	42	21	52	2	.251	.383
Tim Teufel	2B52 3B26 1B5	R	33	101	246	23	55	10	0	6	25	31	45	2	.224	.337
Oscar Azocar	OF37	L	27	99	168	15	32	6	0	0	8	9	12	1	.190	.226
Kevin Ward	OF51	R	30	81	147	12	29	5	0	3	12	14	38	2	.197	.293
Dan Walters	C55	R	25	57	179	14	45	11	1	4	22	10	28	1	.251	.391
Phil Stephenson	OF15 1B7	L	31	53	71	5	11	2	1	0	8	10	11	0	.155	.211
Craig Shipley	SS23 2B11 3B8	R	29	52	105	7	26	6	0	0	7	2	21	1	.248	.305
Gary Pettis	OF14	L	34	30	30	0	6	1	0	0	0	2	11	1	.200	.233
1 Dann Bilardello (XJ)	C14	R	33	17	33	2	4	1	0	0	1	4	8	0	.121	.152
Guillermo Velasquez	1B3 OF2	L	24	15	23	1	7	0	0	1	5	1	7	0	.304	.435
Jeff Gardner	2B11	L	28	15	19	0	2	0	0	0	0	1	8	0	.105	.105
Jim Vatcher	OF13	R	27	13	16	1	4	1	0	0	2	3	6	0	.250	.313
Paul Faries	2B4 3B2 SS1	R	27	10	11	3	5	1	0	0	1	1	2	0	.455	.545
Tom Lampkin	C7 OF1	L	28	9	17	3	4	0	0	0	0	6	1	2	.235	.235
1 Thomas Howard		B	27	5	3	1	1	0	0	0	0	0	0	0	.333	.333

NAME	T	AGE	W	L	PCT	SV	G	GS	CG	IP	H	BB	SO	SHO	ERA
		29	82	80	.506	46	162	162	9	1461	1444	439	971	11	3.56
Bruce Hurst	L	34	14	9	.609	0	32	32	6	217	223	51	131	4	3.85
1 Craig Lefferts	L	34	13	9	.591	0	27	27	0	163	180	35	81	0	3.69
Andy Benes	R	24	13	14	.481	0	34	34	2	231	230	61	169	2	3.35
Frank Seminara	R	25	9	4	.692	0	19	18	0	100	98	46	61	0	3.68
Rich Rodriguez	R	29	6	3	.667	0	61	1	0	91	77	29	64	0	2.37
Jose Melendez	R	26	6	7	.462	0	56	3	0	89	82	20	82	0	2.92
Tim Scott	R	25	4	1	.800	0	34	0	0	38	39	21	30	0	5.26
Jim Deshaies	L	32	4	7	.364	0	15	15	0	96	92	33	46	0	3.28
Greg Harris (BG)	R	28	4	8	.333	0	20	20	1	118	113	35	66	0	4.12
Randy Myers	L	29	3	6	.333	38	66	0	0	80	84	34	66	0	4.29
1 Pat Clements	R	30	2	1	.667	0	27	0	0	24	25	12	11	0	2.66
Mike Maddux	R	30	2	2	.500	5	50	1	0	80	71	24	60	0	2.37
Larry Andersen (EJ)	R	39	1	1	.500	2	34	0	0	35	26	8	35	0	3.34
Jeremy Hernandez	R	25	1	4	.200	1	26	0	0	37	39	11	25	0	4.17
Doug Brocail	R	25	0	0	—	0	3	3	0	14	17	5	15	0	6.43
2 Gene Harris	R	27	0	0	.000	0	14	1	0	21	15	9	19	0	2.95
Dave Eiland (BJ-NJ)	R	25	0	2	.000	0	7	7	0	27	33	5	10	0	5.67
Ed Whitson (SJ) 37															

HOUSTON — 4th 81-81 .500 17 ART HOWE

Name	G by Pos	B	AGE	G	AB	R	H	2B	3B	HR	RBI	BB	SO	SB	BA	SA
TOTALS			26	162	5480	608	1350	255	38	96	582	506	1025	139	.246	.359
Jeff Bagwell	1B159	R	24	162	586	87	160	34	6	18	96	84	97	10	.273	.444
Craig Biggio	2B161	R	26	162	613	96	170	32	3	6	39	94	95	38	.277	.369
Andujar Cedeno	SS70	R	22	71	220	15	38	13	2	2	13	14	71	2	.173	.277
Ken Caminiti	3B129	B	29	135	506	68	149	31	2	13	62	44	68	10	.294	.441
Eric Anthony	OF115	L	24	137	440	45	105	15	1	19	80	38	98	5	.239	.407
Steve Finley	OF160	L	27	162	607	84	177	29	13	5	55	58	63	44	.292	.407
Luis Gonzalez	OF111	L	24	122	387	40	94	19	3	10	55	24	52	7	.243	.385
Eddie Taubensee	C103	L	23	104	297	23	66	15	0	5	28	31	78	2	.222	.323
Casey Candaele	SS65 3B29 OF21 2B9	B	31	135	320	19	68	12	1	1	18	24	36	7	.213	.266
Pete Incaviglia	OF98	R	28	113	349	31	93	22	1	11	44	25	99	2	.266	.430
Juan Guerrero	SS19 3B12 OF3 2B2	R	25	79	125	8	25	4	2	1	14	10	32	1	.200	.288
Scott Servais	C73	R	25	77	205	12	49	9	0	0	15	11	25	0	.239	.283
Gerald Young (BW)	OF57	B	27	74	76	14	14	1	0	0	4	10	11	6	.184	.224
Rafael Ramirez (SJ)	SS57 3B1	R	34	73	176	17	44	6	0	1	13	7	24	0	.250	.301
Chris Jones	OF43	R	26	54	63	7	12	2	1	1	4	7	21	1	.190	.302
Benny Distefano	OF12 1B6	L	30	52	60	4	14	0	2	0	7	5	14	0	.233	.300
Ernest Riles	SS6 3B5 1B4 2B2	L	31	39	61	5	16	1	0	1	4	2	11	1	.262	.328
Scooter Tucker	C19	R	25	20	50	5	6	1	0	0	3	3	13	1	.120	.140
Mike Simms	OF9 1B1	R	25	15	24	1	6	1	0	1	3	2	9	0	.250	.417
Eric Yelding	SS2 OF2	R	27	9	8	1	2	0	0	0	3	0	3	2	.250	.250
Karl Rhodes	OF1	L	23	5	4	0	0	0	0	0	0	0	2	0	.000	.000
Denny Walling (XJ)		L	38	3	3	1	1	0	0	0	0	0	0	0	.333	.333

NAME	T	AGE	W	L	PCT	SV	G	GS	CG	IP	H	BB	SO	SHO	ERA
		27	81	81	.500	45	162	162	5	1459	1386	539	978	12	3.72
Doug Jones	R	35	11	8	.579	36	80	0	0	112	96	17	93	0	1.85
Jimmy Jones (EJ)	R	28	10	6	.625	0	25	23	0	139	135	39	69	0	4.07
Xavier Hernandez	R	26	9	1	.900	7	77	0	0	111	81	42	96	0	2.11
Pete Harnisch	R	25	9	10	.474	0	34	34	0	207	182	64	164	0	3.70
Brian Williams	R	23	7	6	.538	0	16	16	0	96	92	42	54	0	3.92
Al Osuna	L	26	6	3	.667	0	66	0	0	62	52	38	37	0	4.23
Mark Portugal (EJ)	R	29	6	3	.667	0	18	16	1	101	76	41	62	1	2.66
Butch Henry (SJ)	L	23	6	9	.400	0	28	28	2	166	185	41	96	1	4.02
Willie Blair	R	26	5	7	.417	0	29	8	0	79	74	25	48	0	4.00
Darryl Kile	R	23	5	10	.333	0	22	22	2	125	124	63	90	0	3.95
Rob Murphy	L	32	3	1	.750	0	56	0	0	56	56	21	42	0	4.04
Joe Boever	R	31	3	6	.333	2	81	0	0	111	103	45	67	0	2.51
Shane Reynolds	R	24	1	3	.250	0	8	5	0	25	42	6	10	0	7.11
Rob Mallicoat	L	27	0	0	—	0	23	0	0	24	26	19	20	0	7.23
Rich Scheid	L	27	0	1	.000	0	1	1	0	12	14	6	4	0	6.00
Ryan Bowen	R	24	0	7	.000	0	11	9	0	34	48	30	22	0	10.96

SAN FRANCISCO — 5th 72-90 .444 26 ROGER CRAIG

Name	G by Pos	B	AGE	G	AB	R	H	2B	3B	HR	RBI	BB	SO	SB	BA	SA
TOTALS			29	162	5456	574	1330	220	36	105	532	435	1067	112	.244	.355
Will Clark	1B141	L	28	144	513	69	154	40	1	16	73	73	82	12	.300	.476
Robby Thompson	2B120	R	30	128	443	54	115	25	1	14	49	43	75	5	.260	.415
Royce Clayton	SS94 3B1	R	22	98	321	31	72	7	4	4	24	26	63	8	.224	.308
Matt Williams	3B144	R	26	146	529	58	120	13	5	20	66	39	109	7	.227	.384
Willie McGee	OF119	B	33	138	474	56	141	20	2	1	36	29	88	13	.297	.356
Darren Lewis	OF94	R	24	100	320	38	74	8	1	1	18	29	46	28	.231	.272
Mike Felder	OF105 2B3	B	30	145	322	44	92	13	3	4	23	21	29	14	.286	.382
Kirt Manwaring	C108	R	26	109	349	24	85	10	5	4	26	29	42	2	.244	.335
Cory Snyder	OF70 1B27 3B14 2B4 SS3	R	29	124	390	48	105	22	2	14	57	23	96	4	.269	.444
Chris James	OF62	R	29	111	248	25	60	10	4	5	32	14	45	2	.242	.375
1 Kevin Bass	OF72	B	33	89	265	25	71	11	3	7	30	16	53	7	.268	.411
Greg Litton	2B31 3B10 1B8 SS3 OF1	R	27	68	140	9	32	5	0	4	15	11	33	0	.229	.350
Jose Uribe (VJ)	SS62	B	33	66	162	24	39	9	1	2	13	14	25	2	.241	.346
Mark Leonard (LJ)	OF37	L	27	55	128	13	30	7	0	4	16	16	31	0	.234	.383
Craig Colbert	C35 3B9 2B2	R	27	49	126	10	29	5	2	1	16	9	22	1	.230	.325
Mike Benjamin (KJ)	SS33 3B2	R	26	40	75	4	13	2	1	1	3	4	15	1	.173	.267
John Patterson	2B22 OF5	B	25	32	103	10	19	1	1	0	4	5	24	5	.184	.214
Jim McNamara	C30	L	27	30	74	6	16	1	0	1	9	6	25	0	.216	.270
Ted Wood (BG)	OF16	L	25	24	58	5	12	2	0	1	3	6	15	0	.207	.293
Steve Hosey	OF18	R	23	21	56	6	14	1	0	1	6	0	15	1	.250	.321
Steve Decker	C15	R	26	15	43	3	7	1	0	0	1	3	7	0	.163	.186
Mark Bailey (XJ)	C7	B	30	13	26	0	4	1	0	0	1	3	9	0	.154	.192
Andres Santana (SJ) 24																

NAME	T	AGE	W	L	PCT	SV	G	GS	CG	IP	H	BB	SO	SHO	ERA
		28	72	90	.444	30	162	162	9	1461	1385	502	927	12	3.61
John Burkett	R	28	13	9	.591	0	32	32	3	190	194	45	107	1	3.84
Bill Swift (SJ)	R	30	10	4	.714	1	30	22	3	165	144	43	77	2	2.08
Bud Black (XJ)	L	35	10	12	.455	0	28	28	2	177	178	59	82	1	3.97
Trevor Wilson	L	26	8	14	.364	0	26	26	1	154	152	64	88	1	4.21
Jeff Brantley	R	28	7	7	.500	7	56	4	0	92	67	45	86	0	2.95
Mike Jackson	R	27	6	6	.500	2	67	0	0	82	76	33	80	0	3.73
Bryan Hickerson	L	28	5	3	.625	0	61	1	0	87	74	21	68	0	3.09
Rod Beck	R	23	3	3	.500	17	65	0	0	92	62	15	87	0	1.76
1 Gil Heredia	R	26	2	3	.400	0	13	4	0	30	32	16	15	0	5.40
Dave Righetti	L	33	2	7	.222	0	54	0	0	78	79	36	47	0	5.06
Dave Burba	R	25	2	7	.222	0	23	11	0	71	80	31	47	0	4.97
Steve Reed	R	27	1	0	1.000	0	18	0	0	16	13	3	11	0	2.30
Jim Pena	L	27	1	1	.500	0	25	2	0	44	49	20	32	0	3.48
1 Kelly Downs	R	31	1	3	.333	0	19	7	0	62	65	24	33	0	3.47
Larry Carter	R	27	1	5	.167	0	6	6	0	33	34	18	21	0	4.64
Kevin Rogers	L	23	0	2	.000	0	6	6	0	34	37	13	26	0	4.24
Pat Rapp	R	24	0	2	.000	0	3	2	0	10	8	6	3	0	7.20
Francisco Oliveras	R	29	0	3	.000	0	16	7	0	45	41	10	17	0	3.63
Scott Garrelts (EJ) 30															

LOS ANGELES — 6th 63-99 .389 35 TOMMY LASORDA

Name	G by Pos	B	AGE	G	AB	R	H	2B	3B	HR	RBI	BB	SO	SB	BA	SA
TOTALS			28	162	5368	548	1333	201	34	72	499	503	899	142	.248	.339
Eric Karros	1B143	R	24	149	545	63	140	30	1	20	88	37	103	2	.257	.426
Lenny Harris	2B81 3B33 OF15 SS10	L	27	135	347	28	94	11	0	0	30	24	29	19	.271	.303
Jose Offerman	SS149	B	23	149	534	67	139	20	8	1	30	57	98	23	.260	.333
Dave Hansen	3B108	L	23	132	341	30	73	11	0	6	22	34	49	0	.214	.299
Darryl Strawberry (XJ)	OF42	L	30	43	156	20	37	8	0	5	25	19	34	3	.237	.410
Brett Butler	OF155	L	35	157	553	86	171	14	11	3	39	95	67	41	.309	.391
Eric Davis (SJ)	OF74	R	30	76	267	21	61	8	1	5	32	36	71	19	.228	.382
Mike Scioscia	C108	L	33	117	348	19	77	6	3	3	24	32	31	3	.221	.282
Mitch Webster	OF90	B	33	135	262	33	70	12	5	6	35	27	49	11	.267	.420
Mike Sharperson	2B63 3B60 SS2	R	30	128	317	48	95	21	0	3	36	47	33	2	.300	.394
Todd Benzinger	OF51 1B42	R	29	121	293	24	70	16	2	4	31	15	54	2	.239	.348
Carlos Hernandez	C63	R	25	69	173	11	45	4	0	3	17	11	21	0	.260	.335
Tom Goodwin	OF45	L	23	73	15	17	1	1	0	3	6	10	7	.233	.274	
1 Stan Javier	OF27	B	28	56	58	6	11	3	0	1	5	6	11	1	.190	.329
Henry Rodriguez	OF48 1B1	L	24	53	146	11	32	7	0	3	14	8	30	0	.219	.329
Dave Anderson	3B26 SS7	R	31	51	84	10	24	4	0	3	8	4	11	0	.286	.440
Eric Young	2B43	R	25	49	132	9	34	1	0	1	11	8	9	6	.258	.288
1 Juan Samuel (BG)	2B38 OF1	R	31	47	122	7	32	3	1	0	15	7	22	2	.262	.303
1 Kal Daniels	OF21 1B8	L	28	35	104	9	24	5	0	2	8	10	30	0	.231	.337
Billy Ashley	OF27	R	21	29	95	6	21	5	0	2	6	5	34	0	.221	.337
Mike Piazza	C16	R	23	21	69	5	16	3	0	1	7	4	12	0	.232	.319
Rafael Bournigal	SS9	R	26	10	20	1	3	1	0	0	1	0	2	0	.150	.200

NAME	T	AGE	W	L	PCT	SV	G	GS	CG	IP	H	BB	SO	SHO	ERA
		32	63	99	.389	29	162	162	18	1438	1401	553	981	13	3.41
Tom Candiotti	R	34	11	15	.423	0	32	30	6	204	177	63	152	2	3.00
Orel Hershiser	R	33	10	15	.400	0	33	33	1	211	209	69	130	0	3.67
Ramon Martinez (EJ)	R	24	8	11	.421	0	25	25	1	151	141	69	101	1	4.00
Kevin Gross	R	31	8	13	.381	0	34	30	4	205	182	77	158	3	3.17
Bob Ojeda	L	34	6	9	.400	0	29	29	2	166	169	81	94	1	3.63
Roger McDowell	R	31	6	10	.375	14	65	0	0	84	103	42	50	0	4.09
Pedro Astacio	R	22	5	5	.500	0	11	11	4	82	80	20	43	4	1.98
Jim Gott	R	32	3	3	.500	6	68	0	0	88	72	41	75	0	2.45
Steve Wilson	L	27	2	5	.286	0	60	0	0	67	74	29	54	0	4.19
John Candelaria	L	38	2	5	.286	5	50	0	0	25	20	13	23	0	2.84
Kip Gross	R	27	1	1	.500	0	16	1	0	24	32	10	14	0	4.18
Jay Howell (SJ)	R	36	1	3	.250	4	41	0	0	47	41	18	36	0	1.54
Perdo Martinez	R	20	0	1	.000	0	2	1	0	8	6	1	8	0	2.25
Tim Crews	R	31	0	3	.000	0	49	2	0	78	95	20	43	0	5.19
Rudy Seanez (XJ) 23															

LINE SCORES

Team	1	2	3	4	5	6	7	8	9	10	11	12	R	H	E

AMERICAN LEAGUE CHAMPIONSHIPS: TORONTO (EAST) 4 OAKLAND (WEST) 2

Game 1 October 7 at Toronto

OAK	0	3	0	0	0	0	0	0	1				4	6	1
TOR	0	0	0	0	1	1	0	1	0				3	9	0

Stewart, **Russell** (8), Eckersley (9) **Morris**

Game 2 October 8 at Toronto

OAK	0	0	0	0	0	0	0	0	1				1	6	0
TOR	0	0	0	0	2	0	1	0	X				3	4	0

Moore, Corsi (8), Parrett (8) **Cone**, Henke (9)

Game 3 October 10 at Oakland

TOR	0	1	0	1	1	0	2	1	1				7	9	1
OAK	0	0	0	2	0	0	2	1	0				5	13	3

Guzman, Ward (7), Timlin (8), Henke (8) **Darling**, Downs (7), Corsi (8), Russell (8), Honeycutt (9), Eckersley (9)

Game 4 October 11 at Oakland

TOR	0	1	0	0	0	0	3	2	0	1			7	17	4
OAK	0	0	5	0	0	1	0	0	0	0			6	12	2

Morris, Stottlemyre (4), Timlin (8), **Ward** (9), Henke (11) Welch, Parrett (8), Eckersley (8), Corsi (9), **Downs** (10)

Game 5 October 12 at Oakland

TOR	0	0	0	1	0	0	1	0	0				2	7	3
OAK	2	0	1	0	3	0	0	0	X				6	8	0

Stewart Cone, Key (5), Eichorn (8)

Game 6 October 14 at Toronto

OAK	0	0	0	0	0	1	0	1	0				2	7	1
TOR	2	0	4	0	1	0	0	2	X				9	13	0

Moore, Parrett (3), Honeycutt (5), Russell (7), Witt (8) **Guzman**, Ward (8), Henke (9)

NATIONAL LEAGUE CHAMPIONSHIPS: ATLANTA (WEST) 4 PITTSBURGH (EAST) 3

Game 1 October 6 at Atlanta

PIT	0	0	0	0	0	0	0	1	0				1	5	1
ATL	0	1	0	2	1	0	1	0	X				5	8	0

Drabek, Patterson (5), Neagle (7), Cox (8) **Smoltz**, Stanton (9)

Game 2 October 7 at Atlanta

PIT	0	0	0	0	0	0	4	1	0				5	7	0
ATL	0	4	0	0	4	0	5	0	X				13	14	0

Jackson, Mason (2) Walk (3), Tomlin (5), Neagle (7), Patterson (7), Belinda (9) **Avery**, Freeman (7), Stanton (7), Wohlers (8), Reardon (9)

Game 3 October 9 at Pittsburgh

ATL	0	0	0	1	0	0	1	0	0				2	5	0
PIT	0	0	0	0	1	1	1	0	X				3	8	1

Glavine, Stanton (7), Wohlers (8) **Wakefield**

Game 4 October 10 at Pittsburgh

ATL	0	2	0	0	0	2	2	0	0				6	11	1
PIT	0	2	1	0	0	0	1	0	0				4	6	1

Smoltz, Stanton (7), Reardon (9) **Drabek**, Tomlin (5), Cox (6), Mason (7)

Game 5 October 11 at Pittsburgh

ATL	0	0	0	0	0	0	0	1	0				1	3	0
PIT	4	0	1	0	0	1	0	1	X				7	13	0

Avery, Smith (1), Leibrandt (5), Freeman (6), Mercker (8) **Walk**

Game 6 October 13 at Atlanta

PIT	0	8	0	0	4	1	0	0	0				13	13	1
ATL	0	0	0	1	0	0	1	0	2				4	9	1

Wakefield **Glavine**, Leibrandt (2), Freeman (5), Mercker (7), Wohlers (9)

Game 7 October 14 at Atlanta

PIT	1	0	0	0	0	1	0	0	0				2	7	1
ATL	0	0	0	0	0	0	0	0	3				3	7	0

Drabek, Belinda (9) Smoltz, Stanton (7), Smith (7), Avery (7), **Reardon** (9)

COMPOSITE BATTING

TORONTO

NAME	POS	G	AB	R	H	2B	3B	HR	RBI	BA
	Totals	6	210	31	59	8	1	10	30	.281
Alomar	2B	6	26	4	11	1	0	2	4	.423
Carter	RF-1B	6	26	2	5	0	0	1	3	.192
Winfield	DH	6	24	7	6	1	0	2	3	.250
Olerud	1B	6	23	4	8	2	0	1	4	.348
White	CF	6	23	2	8	2	0	0	2	.348
Borders	C	6	22	3	7	0	0	1	3	.318
Maldonado	LF	6	22	3	6	0	0	2	6	.273
Gruber	3B	6	22	3	2	1	0	1	2	.091
Lee	SS	6	18	2	5	1	1	0	3	.278
Sprague	PH	2	2	0	1	0	0	0	0	.500
Griffin	SS	2	2	0	0	0	0	0	0	.000
Bell	RF	2	0	1	0	0	0	0	0	—

OAKLAND

NAME	POS	G	AB	R	H	2B	3B	HR	RBI	BA
	Totals	6	207	24	52	5	1	4	23	.251
Baines	DH	6	25	6	11	2	0	1	4	.440
Sierra	RF	6	24	4	8	2	1	1	7	.333
Steinbach	C	6	24	1	7	0	0	1	5	.292
R. Henderson	LF	6	23	5	6	0	0	1	0	.261
Wilson	CF	5	22	0	5	1	0	0	0	.227
McGwire	1B	6	20	1	3	0	0	1	3	.150
Bordick	SS-2B	6	19	1	1	0	0	0	0	.053
Lansford	3B	4	18	0	3	0	0	0	1	.167
Blankenship	2B	5	13	2	3	0	0	0	0	.231
Browne	CF-3B	4	10	3	4	0	0	0	2	.400
Weiss	SS	3	6	1	1	0	0	0	0	.167
Fox	LF-DH	4	1	0	0	0	0	0	0	.000
Quirk	PH	1	1	0	0	0	0	0	0	.000
Ready	PH	1	1	0	0	0	0	0	0	.000

ATLANTA

NAME	POS	G	AB	R	H	2B	3B	HR	RBI	BA
	Totals	7	234	34	57	11	2	6	32	.244
Pendleton	3B	7	30	2	7	2	0	0	3	.233
Nixon	CF	7	28	5	8	2	0	0	2	.286
Justice	RF	7	25	5	7	1	0	2	6	.280
Blauser	SS	7	24	3	5	0	1	1	4	.208
Berryhill	C	7	24	1	4	1	0	0	1	.167
Bream	1B	7	22	5	6	3	0	1	2	.273
Gant	LF	7	22	5	4	0	0	2	6	.182
Lemke	2B-3B	7	21	2	7	1	0	0	2	.333
Smoltz	P	3	7	1	2	0	0	0	1	.286
L. Smith	PH	4	6	1	2	0	1	0	1	.333
Hunter	1B	3	5	1	1	0	0	0	0	.200
Sanders	LF-CF	4	5	0	0	0	0	0	0	.000
Treadway	2B	3	3	1	2	0	0	0	0	.667
Belliard	SS-2B	3	2	1	0	0	0	0	0	.000
Avery	P	3	2	0	0	0	0	0	1	.000
Cabrera	PH	2	2	0	1	0	0	0	2	.500
Glavine	P	2	2	0	0	0	0	0	0	.000
Stanton	P	3	1	1	1	1	0	0	1	1.000
Leibrandt	P	2	1	0	0	0	0	0	0	.000
P. Smith	P	2	1	0	0	0	0	0	0	.000
Lopez	C	1	1	0	0	0	0	0	0	.000

PITTSBURGH

NAME	POS	G	AB	R	H	2B	3B	HR	RBI	BA
	Totals	7	231	35	59	20	3	5	32	.255
Van Slyke	CF	7	29	1	8	3	1	0	4	.276
King	3B	7	29	4	7	4	0	0	2	.241
Bell	SS	7	29	3	5	2	0	1	4	.172
Lind	2B	7	27	5	6	2	1	1	5	.222
Bonds	LF	7	23	5	6	1	0	1	2	.261
Redus	1B	5	16	4	7	4	1	0	3	.438
Slaught	C	5	12	5	4	1	0	1	5	.333
McClendon	RF	5	11	4	8	2	0	1	4	.727
Cole	RF	4	10	2	2	0	0	0	0	.200
LaValliere	C	3	10	1	2	0	0	0	0	.200
Merced	1B	3	10	0	1	1	0	0	2	.100
Drabek	P	3	6	0	0	0	0	0	0	.000
Wakefield	P	2	6	1	0	0	0	0	0	.000
Walk	P	2	5	0	0	0	0	0	0	.000
Espy	RF	2	3	0	2	0	0	0	0	.667
Varsho	RF	2	2	0	1	0	0	0	0	.500
Wehner	PH	2	2	0	0	0	0	0	0	.000
Garcia	2B	1	1	0	0	0	0	0	0	.000

COMPOSITE PITCHING

TORONTO

NAME	G	IP	H	BB	SO	W	L	SV	ERA
Totals	6	55	52	24	33	4	2	3	3.44
Guzman	2	13	12	5	11	2	0	0	2.08
Morris	2	12.1	11	9	6	0	1	0	6.57
Cone	2	12	11	5	9	1	1	0	3.00
Henke	4	4.2	4	2	2	0	0	3	0.00
Ward	3	4	5	1	2	1	0	0	6.75
Stottlemyre	1	3.2	3	0	1	0	0	0	2.46
Key	1	3	2	2	1	0	0	0	0.00
Timlin	3	1.1	4	0	1	0	0	0	6.75
Eichhorn	1	1	1	0	0	0	0	0	0.00

OAKLAND

NAME	G	IP	H	BB	SO	W	L	SV	ERA
Totals	6	54	59	23	29	2	4	1	4.50
Stewart	2	16.2	14	6	7	1	0	0	2.70
Moore	2	9.2	11	5	7	0	2	0	7.45
Welch	1	7	7	1	7	0	0	0	2.57
Darling	1	6	4	2	3	0	1	0	3.00
Eckersley	3	3	8	0	2	0	0	1	6.00
Parrett	3	2.1	6	0	1	0	0	0	11.57
Downs	2	2.1	3	1	0	0	1	0	3.86
Russell	3	2	4	0	1	0	0	0	9.00
Corsi	3	2	2	3	0	0	0	0	0.00
Honeycutt	2	2	0	1	0	0	0	0	0.00
Witt	1	1	1	1	1	0	0	0	18.00

ATLANTA

NAME	G	IP	H	BB	SO	W	L	SV	ERA
Totals	7	61	59	29	42	4	3	1	4.72
Smoltz	3	20.1	14	10	19	2	0	0	2.66
Avery	3	8	13	2	3	1	1	0	9.00
Glavine	2	7.1	13	3	2	0	2	0	12.27
Leibrandt	2	4.2	4	3	3	0	0	0	1.93
Stanton	5	4.1	2	2	5	0	0	0	0.00
Freeman	3	3.2	8	2	1	0	0	0	14.73
P. Smith	2	3.2	2	3	3	0	0	0	2.45
Reardon	3	3	0	2	3	1	0	1	0.00
Wohlers	3	3	1	1	2	0	0	0	0.00
Mercker	2	3	1	1	1	0	0	0	0.00

PITTSBURGH

NAME	G	IP	H	BB	SO	W	L	SV	ERA
Totals	7	60.2	57	29	28	3	4	0	4.45
Wakefield	2	18	14	5	7	2	0	0	3.00
Drabek	3	17	18	7	10	0	3	0	3.71
Walk	2	11.2	6	7	6	1	0	0	3.86
Mason	2	3.1	0	2	1	0	0	0	6.75
Tomlin	2	2.2	5	1	0	0	0	0	6.75
Belinda	2	1.2	2	0	2	0	0	0	0.00
Patterson	2	1.2	3	1	1	0	0	0	5.40
Neagle	2	1.2	4	3	0	0	0	0	27.00
Jackson	1	1.2	4	2	0	0	0	1	21.60
Cox	2	1.1	1	1	1	0	0	0	0.00

LINE SCORES

Team	1	2	3	4	5	6	7	8	9	10	11	12	R	H	E

WORLD SERIES TORONTO (AL) 4: ATLANTA (NL) 2

Game 1 October 17 at Atlanta

| TOR | 0 | 0 | 0 | 1 | 0 | 0 | 0 | 0 | 0 | | | | 1 | 4 | 0 |
| ATL | 0 | 0 | 0 | 0 | 0 | 3 | 0 | 0 | X | | | | 3 | 4 | 0 |

Morris, Stottlemyre (7), Wells (8)   **Glavine**

Game 2 October 18 at Atlanta

| TOR | 0 | 0 | 0 | 0 | 2 | 0 | 0 | 1 | 2 | | | | 5 | 9 | 2 |
| ATL | 0 | 1 | 0 | 2 | 0 | 0 | 0 | 0 | 0 | | | | 4 | 5 | 1 |

Cone, Wells (5), Stottlemyre (7),   Smoltz, Stanton (8), **Reardon** (8)
Ward (8), Henke (9)

Game 3 October 20 at Toronto

| ATL | 0 | 0 | 0 | 0 | 0 | 1 | 0 | 1 | 0 | | | | 2 | 9 | 0 |
| TOR | 0 | 0 | 1 | 0 | 0 | 0 | 0 | 1 | 1 | | | | 3 | 6 | 1 |

Avery, Wohlers (9), Stanton (9),   Guzman, **Ward** (9)
Reardon (9)

Game 4 October 21 at Toronto

| ATL | 0 | 0 | 0 | 0 | 0 | 0 | 0 | 1 | 0 | | | | 1 | 5 | 0 |
| TOR | 0 | 1 | 0 | 0 | 0 | 1 | 0 | X | | | | | 2 | 6 | 0 |

Glavine   **Key**, Ward (8), Henke (9)

Game 5 October 22 at Toronto

| ATL | 1 | 0 | 0 | 1 | 5 | 0 | 0 | 0 | 0 | | | | 7 | 13 | 0 |
| TOR | 0 | 1 | 0 | 1 | 0 | 0 | 0 | 0 | 0 | | | | 2 | 6 | 0 |

Smoltz, Stanton (7)   **Morris**, Wells (5), Timlin (7),
Eichhorn (8), Stottlemyre (9)

Game 6 October 24 at Atlanta

| TOR | 1 | 0 | 0 | 1 | 0 | 0 | 0 | 0 | 2 | | | | 4 | 14 | 1 |
| ATL | 0 | 0 | 1 | 0 | 0 | 0 | 0 | 0 | 1 | 0 | 1 | | 3 | 8 | 1 |

Cone, Stottlemyre (7),   Avery, Smith (5), Stanton (8),
Wells (7), Ward (8),   Wohlers (9), **Leibrandt** (10)
Henke (9), **Key** (9), Timlin (11)

COMPOSITE BATTING

TORONTO

NAME	POS	G	AB	R	H	2B	3B	HR	RBI	BA
	Totals	6	196	17	45	8	0	6	17	.230
White	CF	6	26	2	6	1	0	0	2	.231
Alomar	2B	6	24	3	5	1	0	0	0	.208
Carter	1B-RF-LF	6	22	2	6	2	0	2	3	.273
Winfield	RF-DH	6	22	0	5	1	0	0	3	.227
Borders	C	6	20	2	9	3	0	1	3	.450
Maldonado	LF-PH	6	19	1	3	0	0	1	2	.158
Gruber	3B	6	19	2	2	0	0	1	1	.105
Lee	SS	6	19	1	2	0	0	0	0	.105
Olerud	1B	4	13	2	4	0	0	0	0	.308
Cone	P	2	4	0	2	0	0	0	1	.500
Sprague	1B-PH	3	2	1	1	0	0	1	2	.500
Tabler	PH	2	2	0	0	0	0	0	0	.000
Morris	P	2	2	0	0	0	0	0	0	.000
Bell	PH	2	1	1	0	0	0	0	0	.000
Key	P	2	1	0	0	0	0	0	0	.000
Wells	P	4	0	0	0	0	0	0	0	—
Stottlemyre	P	4	0	0	0	0	0	0	0	—
Ward	P	4	0	0	0	0	0	0	0	—
Henke	P	3	0	0	0	0	0	0	0	—
Griffin	SS	2	0	0	0	0	0	0	0	—
Timlin	P	2	0	0	0	0	0	0	0	—
Guzman	P	1	0	0	0	0	0	0	0	—
Eichhorn	P	1	0	0	0	0	0	0	0	—

ATLANTA

NAME	POS	G	AB	R	H	2B	3B	HR	RBI	BA
	Totals	6	200	20	44	6	0	3	19	.220
Nixon	CF	6	27	3	8	1	0	0	1	.296
Pendleton	3B	6	25	2	6	2	0	0	2	.240
Blauser	SS	6	24	2	6	0	0	0	0	.250
Berryhill	C	6	22	1	2	0	0	1	3	.091
Lemke	2B	6	19	0	4	0	0	0	2	.211
Justice	RF	6	19	4	3	0	0	1	3	.158
Bream	1B	5	15	1	3	0	0	0	0	.200
Sanders	LF	4	15	4	8	2	0	0	1	.533
L. Smith	DH-PH	5	12	1	2	0	0	1	5	.167
Gant	LF-PH-PR	4	8	2	1	1	0	0	0	.125
Hunter	1B-PH-PR	4	5	1	1	0	0	0	2	.200
Smoltz	P-PR	3	3	0	0	0	0	0	0	.000
Glavine	P	2	2	0	0	0	0	0	0	.000
Avery	P	2	1	0	0	0	0	0	0	.000
Cabrera	PH	1	1	0	0	0	0	0	0	.000
Treadway	PH	1	1	0	0	0	0	0	0	.000
P. Smith	P	1	1	0	0	0	0	0	0	.000
Belliard	SS-2B	4	0	0	0	0	0	0	0	—
Stanton	P	4	0	0	0	0	0	0	0	—
Reardon	P	2	0	0	0	0	0	0	0	—
Wohlers	P	2	0	0	0	0	0	0	0	—
Leibrandt	P	1	0	0	0	0	0	0	0	—

COMPOSITE PITCHING

TORONTO

NAME	G	IP	H	BB	SO	W	L	SV	ERA
	Totals	6	55	44	20	48	4	2	3	2.78
Morris	2	10.2	13	6	12	0	2	0	8.44
Cone	2	10.1	9	8	8	0	0	0	3.48
Key	2	9	6	0	6	2	0	0	1.00
Guzman	1	8	8	1	7	0	0	0	1.13
Wells	4	4.1	1	2	3	0	0	0	0.00
Stottlemyre	4	3.2	4	0	4	0	0	0	0.00
Ward	4	3.1	1	1	6	2	0	0	0.00
Henke	3	3.1	2	1	1	0	0	2	2.70
Timlin	2	1.1	0	0	0	0	0	0	0.00
Eichhorn	1	1	0	1	0	0	0	0	0.00

ATLANTA

NAME	G	IP	H	BB	SO	W	L	SV	ERA
	Totals	6	54.1	45	18	33	2	4	1	2.65
Glavine	2	17	10	4	8	1	1	0	1.59
Smoltz	2	13.1	13	7	12	1	0	0	2.70
Avery	2	12	11	3	11	0	1	0	3.75
Stanton	4	5	3	2	1	0	0	0	0.00
P. Smith	1	3	3	0	0	0	0	0	0.00
Leibrandt	1	2	3	0	0	0	1	0	9.00
Reardon	2	1.1	2	1	1	0	1	0	13.50
Wohlers	2	0.2	0	1	0	0	0	0	0.00

MISCELLANEOUS 1992 INDIVIDUAL LEADERS

BATTING

On Base Average

	American League			National League	
1	Thomas, Chi.	.439	1	Bonds, Pit.	.456
2	Tartabull, N.Y.	.409	2	Kruk, Phi.	.423
3	Alomar, Tor.	.405	3	Butler, L.A.	.413
4	E. Martinez, Sea.	.404	4	McGriff, S.D.	.394
5	Mack, Min.	.394	5	Roberts, Cin.	.393
6	Molitor, Mil.	.389	6	Sheffield, S.D.	.385
7	Phillips, Det.	.387	7	Daulton, Phi.	.385
8	Whitaker, Det.	.386	8	Clark, S.F.	.384
9	Davis, Min.	.386	9	Van Slyke, Pit.	.381
10	McGwire, Oak.	.385	10	Grace, Chi.	.380

Caught Stealing

	American League			National League	
1	Polonia, Cal.	21	1	Lankford, St.L	24
2	Curtis, Cal.	18	2	Butler, L.A.	21
	Listach, Mil.	18	3	Fernandez, S.D.	20
4	Anderson, Bal.	16	4	Nixon, Atl.	18
5	Vaughn, Mil.	15	5	Offerman, L.A.	16
				Roberts, Cin.	16

Stolen Base Percentage
(Minimum 20 Attempts)

	American League			National League	
1	Cotto, Sea.	92	1	Davis, L.A.	95
2	White, Tor.	90	2	Duncan, Phi.	88
3	Raines, Chi.	88	3	Dykstra, Phi.	86
4	R. Kelly, N.Y.	85	4	Javier, L.A.-Phi.	86
5	Lofton, Cle.	85	5	Finley, Hou.	83

On Base Average plus Slugging Average

	American League			National League	
1	Thomas, Chi.	.975	1	Bonds, Pit.	1.080
2	McGwire, Oak.	.970	2	Sheffield, S.D.	.965
3	E. Martinez, Sea.	.948	3	McGriff, S.D.	.950
4	Tartabull, N.Y.	.898	4	Daulton, Phi.	.909
5	Griffey, Sea.	.896	5	Van Slyke, Pit.	.886
6	Winfield, Tor.	.868	6	Sandberg, Chi.	.881
7	Puckett, Min.	.864	7	Kruk, Phi.	.881
8	Mack, Min.	.861	8	Walker, Mon.	.859
9	Molitor, Mil.	.850	9	Hollins, Phi.	.858
10	Whitaker, Det.	.847	10	Lankford, St. L.	.851

Extra Base Hits

	American League			National League	
1	Thomas, Chi.	72	1	Bonds, Pit.	75
2	Carter, Tor.	71	2	Van Slyke, Pit.	71
3	Griffey, Sea.	70	3	Sheffield, S.D.	70
4	Gonzalez, Tex.	69	4	McGriff, S.D.	69
5	E. Martinez, Sea.	67	5	Sandberg, Chi.	66
				Lankford, St. L.	66

Total Bases

	American League			National League	
1	Puckett, Min.	313	1	Sheffield, S.D.	323
2	Carter, Tor.	310	2	Sandberg, Chi.	312
3	Gonzalez, Tex.	309	3	Van Slyke, Pit.	310
4	Thomes, Chi.	307	4	Pendleton, Atl.	303
5	Devereaux, Bal.	303	5	Bonds, Pit.	295
				McGriff, S.D.	295

FIELDING

Fielding Average
(Minimum 90 Games)

American League			National League	
B. Ripken, Bal.	.993	2B-best	Lind, Pit.	.992
Alomar, Tor.	.993	2nd	Morandini, Phi.	.991
Miller, K.C.	.971	worst	Stillwell, S.D.	.970
Vizquel, Sea.	.989	SS-best	Schofield, N.Y.	.988
Lee, Tor.	.987	2nd	Smith, St. L.	.985
Lewis, Cle.	.954	worst	Offerman, L.A.	.935
Seitzer, Mil.	.969	3B-best	Hansen, L.A.	.968
Lansford, Oak.	.965	2nd	Caminiti, Hou.	.966
Jefferies, K.C.	.939	worst	Williams, S.F.	.944

Putouts plus Assists per 9 Innings Played
(Minimum 90 Games)

American League			National League	
Bordick, Oak.	5.75	2B-best	Thompson, S.F.	5.81
Reed, Bos.	5.55	2nd	Lind, Pit.	5.56
Alomar, Tor.	4.68	worst	DeShields, Mon.	4.66
Gagne, Min.	5.06	SS-best	Bell, Pit.	5.07
Rivera, Bos.	4.95	2nd	Smith, St. L.	5.05
Lee, Tor.	4.30	worst	Offerman, L.A.	4.23
Ventura, Chi.	3.30	3B-best	Pendleton, Atl.	2.95
E. Martinez, Sea.	2.90	2nd	Sheffield, S.D.	2.87
Lansford, Oak.	2.29	worst	Magadan, N.Y.	2.10

PITCHING

Wild Pitches

	American League			National League	
1	Moore, Oak.	21	1	Smoltz, Atl.	17
2	Guzman, Tor.	14	2	Henry, Cin.	12
3	Darling, Oak.	13	3	Castillo, Chi.	11
	Johnson, Sea.	13		Hill, Mon.	11
	M. Perez, N.Y.	13		Morgan, Chi.	11
				Drabek, Pit.	11

Home Runs Allowed

	American League			National League	
1	Gullickson, Det.	35	1	Black, S.F.	23
2	McDonald, Bal.	32	2	Hurst, S.D.	22
3	Cook, Cle.	29	3	Abbott, Phi.	20
4	Sanderson, N.Y.	28		Olivares, St. L.	20
	Wegman, Mil.	28	5	Castillo, Chi.	19

Home Runs Allowed per 9 IP
(Minimum 10 Home Runs Allowed)

	American League			National League	
1	Slusarski, Oak.	1.78	1	Oliveras, S.F.	2.22
2	Aldred, Det.	1.66	2	Boskie, Chi.	1.37
3	Cook, Cle.	1.65	3	Abbott, Phi.	1.35
4	Bones, Mil.	1.49	4	Black, S.F.	1.17
5	Gullickson, Det.	1.42	5	Mason, Pit.	1.12

1993 Carter's Blast Makes Jays' Reign Last

Joe Carter's last-of-the-ninth home run wrote an appropriate and sudden end to an exciting and improbable 1993 baseball season. While baseball went without a commissioner, fussed over realignment, and worried that TV money was drying up, fans enjoyed a bang-up year.

Among the continuing stories in the National League were the utter collapse of the New York Mets and the not-quite-so-utter fall in Cincinnati, San Diego's determination to reduce its payroll by selling most of its movable players, and the moderate success on the field and enormous success at the turnstiles by expansion teams in Miami and Denver. In the American League, no-hitters by Jim Abbott and Chris Bosio, Dave Winfield's 3,000th hit, Nolan Ryan's injury-filled final season, the retirement of George Brett, and the refreshing silence of reinstated owner George Steinbrenner all made headlines, but the big news was a pair of hot pennant races.

The National League pennant races appeared to be settled by mid-season. After finishing last the year before, Jim Fregosi's Philadelphia Phillies took a commanding lead in the East. With their scruffy, tobacco-chewing, belly-over-the-belt style, the Phillies seemed a throwback to an earlier age but they won with a lot more than personality. Len Dykstra played inspired ball all season and had one of the best years of any leadoff man in history. John Kruk, Dave Hollins, and Darren Daulton gave the middle of the lineup solid power. Role-players filled in the gaps. In 1992, the Phillies' pitching collapsed with injuries; in 1993, the starters were healthy, and, though the middle relief was often shaky, Mitch "The Wild Thing" Williams provided a usually effective, though nail-bitingly scary, closer. In September, Montreal challenged with a long winning streak, causing nightmare memories of 1964 to resurface in Philadelphia, but Fregosi's men fought off the charge and cruised home.

Although Houston's Darryl Kile pitched the National League's only 1993 no-hitter, the league's pitching center was in Georgia. The Atlanta Braves had been conceded the Western Division title in many quarters when they added free agent Greg Maddox to their already glittering starting staff. Maddox, Tom Glavine, John Smoltz, and Steve Avery pitched well enough during the early season, but the offense was unreliable. In the meantime, the San Francisco Giants' led by their free agent acquisition Barry Bonds, who put up Ruthian numbers most of the way, ran far out in front. Rookie Giants' manager Dusty Baker also received superior work from Matt Williams, Robby Thompson, John Burkett, and Bill Swift. At mid-season, the Giants had a seemingly insurmountable ten-game lead. Then Atlanta received a home run transfusion with the addition of Fred McGriff from the Great San Diego Fire Sale, and the Braves began to climb. Although the Giants suffered one six-game losing streak, they refused to collapse as Atlanta closed in. The Braves were simply too hot. On the final day of the season, Atlanta won its 104th game, while San Francisco, with 103 wins, lost to the Dodgers.

Not only did the N.L. West have the league's best player in Bonds, best pitcher in Maddux, and top rookie in the Dodgers' Mike Piazza, it also produced the top comeback story in Denver's Andre Galarraga. "The Big Cat" had been on a downward spiral for several years, in part because of injuries. First Montreal and then St. Louis gave up on him. When he hit only .243 with 39 RBI for the Cardinals in 1992, many assumed he'd reached the end of the line. Signed as a free agent by the Colorado Rockies, he became the first Venezuelan ever to lead a major league in hitting when he batted a resounding .370 and drove in 98 runs. He received plenty of encouragement from Rockies fans who averaged a record 56,750 per game at Mile High Stadium.

The American League's season began and ended in tragedy. During spring training, two Cleveland Indians pitchers, Steve Olin and Tim Crews, were killed in a boating accident. A third pitcher, Bob Ojeda, was seriously injured. Cleveland players dealt with their grief throughout the season. Then, in early November, an auto accident claimed the life of still another Cleveland hurler, Cliff Young.

The American League East was a donnybrook for most of the season with Detroit, Boston, Baltimore, and the Yankees all taking shots at 1992 champ Toronto. Cito Gaston's Blue Jays had undergone a near 50 percent roster turnover from the previous season. The pitching was under siege with the loss of Jimmy Key and Tom Henke and ineffective work from Jack Morris and free agent Dave Stewart. On the other hand, John Olerud flirted with .400 for much of the season, Paul Molitor had a sensational year, and Roberto Alomar continued to be the best second baseman in the league. Toronto was tied for league leadership several times but never headed.

In the West, Chicago had to overcome some serious side issues; Bo Jackson's comeback with an artificial hip, Carlton Fisk's breaking of the record for most games by a catcher folowed immediately by his involuntary retirement, and George Bell's grumping. But Gene Lamont won the division and Manager of the Year honors by parlaying a monster season by slugger Frank Thomas and fine pitching by Jack McDowell and his other young starters. Texas, despite the distracting hooplah of Ryan's final season, made a game try before falling short.

Dave Stewart won his second AL Championship Series MVP Award by tossing two of Toronto's victories in the Blue Jays' win over Chicago. Stewart, who ran his ALCS career mark to 8-0, won the sixth and final game 6-3 with a strong 7 2/3 inning outing at Chicago to make the Blue Jays American League champions for the second consecutive year.

The Phillies also won the LCS in six games, spoiling Atlanta's bid for three straight pennants. Tommy Greene, routed in the Braves' 14-3 Game Two win, came back to pitch seven strong innings in the Phils' final-game 6-3 win. Phillies' righthander Curt Schilling was named MVP even though he didn't win a game. He did, however turn in strong starts in Game One and Five to make victories in extra innings possible. The key to the World Series was Game Four. Trailing two games to one, the Phillies held a 14-9 lead into the eighth inning of a see-saw game, only to see the Blue Jays rally for six runs to win 15-14. The game set World Series records for runs, hits, and length, as well as several records for individuals. Schilling held off the Blue Jays in Game Five 2-0, with his best start of the postseason to force the Series back to Toronto. The Blue Jays led 5-1 in Game Six when Philadelphia kayoed Stewart and Danny Cox with a five-run outburst to go up 6-5. That held to the bottom of the ninth, when, with Rickey Henderson and Paul Molitor aboard and one out, Joe Carter made the Blue Jays champs for the second year in a row with a drive off Mitch Williams into the left field seats.

TORONTO   1st 95-67 .586   CITO GASTON

Name	G by Pos	B	AGE	G	AB	R	H	2B	3B	HR	RBI	BB	SO	SB	BA	SA
TOTALS			30	162	5579	847	1556	317	42	159	796	588	861	170	.279	.436
John Olerud	1B137 DH20	L	24	158	551	109	200	54	2	24	107	114	65	0	.363	.599
Roberto Alomar	2B150	B	25	153	589	109	192	35	6	17	93	80	67	55	.326	.492
2 Tony Fernandez	SS94	B	31	94	353	45	108	18	9	4	50	31	26	15	.306	.442
Ed Sprague	3B150	R	25	150	546	50	142	31	1	12	73	32	85	1	.260	.386
Joe Carter	OF151 DH3	R	33	155	603	92	153	33	5	33	121	47	113	8	.254	.489
Devon White	OF145	B	30	146	598	116	163	42	6	15	52	57	127	34	.273	.438
2 Rickey Henderson	OF44	R	34	44	163	37	35	3	1	4	12	35	19	22	.215	.319
Pat Borders	C138	R	30	138	488	38	124	30	4	9	55	20	66	2	.254	.371
Paul Molitor	DH137 1B23	R	36	160	636	121	211	37	5	22	111	77	71	22	.332	.509
Turner Ward (SJ)		B	28	72	167	20	32	4	2	4	28	23	26	3	.192	.311
Darnell Coles	OF44 3B16 1B1 DH1	R	31	64	194	26	49	9	1	4	26	16	29	1	.253	.371
1 Darrin Jackson	OF46	R	30	46	176	15	38	8	0	5	19	8	53	0	.216	.347
Alfredo Griffin (SJ)	SS20 2B11 3B6	R	35	46	95	15	20	3	0	1	3	3	13	0	.211	.242
Randy Knorr	C39	R	24	39	101	11	25	3	2	4	20	9	29	0	.248	.436
Willie Canate (IL)	OF31 DH1	R	21	38	47	12	10	0	0	1	3	6	15	1	.213	.277
Dick Schofield (BA)	SS36	R	30	36	110	11	21	1	2	0	5	16	25	3	.191	.236
Luis Sojo	2B8 SS8 3B3	R	28	19	47	5	8	2	0	0	6	4	2	1	.170	.213
Rob Butler (RJ)	OF16	L	23	17	48	8	13	4	0	0	2	7	12	2	.271	.354
Domingo Cedeno	SS10 2B5	B	24	15	46	5	8	0	0	0	7	1	10	1	.174	.174
Domingo Martinez	1B7 3B1	R	27	8	14	2	4	0	0	1	3	1	7	0	.286	.500
Shawn Green	OF2 DH1	L	20	3	6	0	0	0	0	0	0	0	1	0	.000	.000
Carlos Delgado	C1 DH1	L	21	2	1	0	0	0	0	0	0	0	1	0	.000	.000
Eddie Zosky 25 (EJ)																

NAME	T	AGE	W	L	PCT	SV	G	GS	CG	IP	H	BB	SO	SHO	ERA
		30	95	67	.586	50	162	162	11	1441	1441	620	1023	11	4.21
Pat Hentgen	R	24	19	9	.679	0	34	32	3	218	215	74	122	0	3.87
Juan Guzman	R	26	14	3	.824	0	33	33	2	221	211	110	194	1	3.99
Dave Stewart (EJ)	R	36	12	8	.600	0	26	26	0	162	146	72	96	0	4.44
Todd Stottlemyre	L	28	11	12	.479	0	30	28	1	177	204	69	98	1	4.84
Al Leiter	L	27	9	6	.600	2	34	12	1	105	93	56	66	1	4.11
Danny Cox	R	33	7	6	.538	2	44	0	0	84	73	29	84	0	3.12
Jack Morris (EJ)	R	38	7	12	.368	0	27	27	4	153	189	65	103	1	6.19
Mike Timlin	R	27	4	2	.667	1	54	0	0	56	63	27	49	0	4.69
Mark Eichhorn	R	32	3	1	.750	0	54	0	0	73	76	22	47	0	2.72
Woody Williams	R	26	3	1	.750	0	37	0	0	37	40	22	24	0	4.38
Tony Castillo	L	30	3	2	.600	0	51	0	0	51	44	22	28	0	3.38
Duane Ward	R	29	2	3	.400	45	71	0	0	72	49	25	97	0	2.13
Scott Brow	R	24	1	1	.500	0	6	3	0	18	19	10	7	0	6.00
Huck Flener	L	24	0	0	—	0	6	0	0	7	4	2	0	0	4.05
Ken Dayley	L	34	0	0	—	0	2	0	0	1	1	4	2	0	0.00
1 Doug Linton	R	27	0	1	.000	0	4	1	0	11	11	9	4	0	6.55

NEW YORK   2nd 88-74 .543 7   BUCK SHOWALTER

Name	G by Pos	B	AGE	G	AB	R	H	2B	3B	HR	RBI	BB	SO	SB	BA	SA
TOTALS			30	162	5615	821	1568	294	24	178	793	629	910	39	.279	.435
Don Mattingly (VJ)	1B130 DH5	L	32	134	530	78	154	27	2	17	86	61	42	0	.291	.445
Pat Kelly	2B125	R	25	127	406	49	111	24	1	7	51	24	68	14	.273	.389
Spike Owen	SS96 DH2	B	32	103	334	41	78	16	2	2	20	29	30	3	.234	.311
Wade Boggs	3B134 DH8	L	35	143	560	83	169	26	1	2	59	74	49	0	.302	.363
Paul O'Neill	OF138 DH2	L	30	141	498	71	155	34	1	20	75	44	69	2	.311	.504
Bernie Williams	OF139	B	24	139	567	67	152	31	4	12	68	53	106	9	.268	.400
Dion James	OF103 1B1 DH1	L	30	115	343	62	114	21	2	7	36	31	31	0	.332	.466
Mike Stanley	C122 DH2	R	30	130	423	70	129	17	1	26	84	57	85	1	.305	.534
Danny Tartabull	DH88 OF50	R	30	138	513	87	128	33	2	31	102	92	156	0	.250	.503
Mike Gallego	SS55 2B52 3B27	R	32	119	403	63	114	20	1	10	54	50	65	3	.283	.412
Jim Leyritz	1B29 OF28 DH21 C12	R	29	95	259	43	80	14	0	14	53	37	59	0	.309	.525
Randy Velarde (FP)	OF50 SS26 3B16 DH1	R	30	85	226	28	68	13	2	7	24	18	39	2	.301	.469
Matt Nokes	C56 DH11	L	29	76	217	25	54	8	0	10	35	16	31	0	.249	.424
Kevin Maas	DH31 1B17	L	28	59	151	20	31	4	0	9	25	24	32	1	.205	.411
Gerald Williams	OF37	R	26	42	67	11	10	2	3	0	6	1	14	2	.149	.269
Hensley Meulens	OF23 1B3 3B1	R	26	30	53	8	9	1	1	2	5	8	19	0	.170	.340
Mike Humphreys	OF21 DH3	R	26	25	35	6	6	2	1	1	6	4	13	0	.171	.371
Andy Stankiewicz	2B6 3B4 SS1 DH1	R	28	16	9	5	0	0	0	0	0	1	1	0	.000	.000
Dave Silvestri	SS4 3B3	R	25	7	21	4	6	1	0	1	4	5	3	0	.286	.476

NAME	T	AGE	W	L	PCT	SV	G	GS	CG	IP	H	BB	SO	SHO	ERA
		30	88	74	.543	38	162	162	11	1438	1467	552	899	13	4.35
Jimmy Key	L	32	18	6	.750	0	34	34	4	237	219	43	173	2	3.00
Bob Wickman	R	24	14	4	.778	0	41	19	1	140	156	69	70	1	4.63
Jim Abbott	L	25	11	14	.440	0	32	32	4	214	221	73	95	1	4.37
Scott Kamieniecki	R	29	10	7	.588	1	30	20	2	154	163	59	72	0	4.08
Rich Monteleone	R	30	7	4	.636	0	42	0	0	86	85	35	50	0	4.94
Melido Perez	R	27	6	14	.300	0	25	25	0	163	173	64	148	0	5.19
Mike Witt (SJ)	R	32	3	2	.600	0	9	9	0	41	39	22	30	0	5.27
Bobby Munoz	R	25	3	3	.500	0	38	0	0	46	48	26	33	0	5.32
Steve Howe (NJ)	L	35	3	5	.375	4	51	0	0	51	58	10	19	0	4.97
2 Paul Gibson	L	33	2	0	1.000	0	20	0	0	35	31	9	25	0	3.06
1 John Habyan	R	29	2	1	.667	1	36	0	0	42	45	16	29	0	4.04
Steve Farr	R	36	2	2	.500	25	49	0	0	47	44	28	39	0	4.21
2 Paul Assenmacher	L	32	2	2	.500	0	26	0	0	17	10	9	11	0	3.12
Neal Heaton	R	33	1	0	1.000	0	8	0	0	27	34	11	15	0	6.00
Domingo Jean	R	24	1	1	.500	0	10	6	0	40	37	19	20	0	4.46
Mark Hutton	R	23	1	1	.500	0	7	4	0	22	24	17	12	0	5.73
Sam Militello	R	23	1	1	.500	0	9	9	0	9	10	7	5	0	6.75
Sterling Hitchcock	L	22	1	2	.333	0	6	6	0	31	32	14	26	0	4.65
2 Lee Smith	R	35	0	0	—	3	8	0	0	8	4	5	11	0	0.00
Andy Cook	R	25	0	1	.000	0	4	0	0	5	7	4	5	0	5.06
2 Frank Tanana	L	39	0	0	—	0	3	3	0	20	18	7	12	0	3.20
Jeff Johnson	L	26	0	0	—	0	2	0	0	3	12	2	0	0	30.38

BALTIMORE   3rd(tie) 85-77 .525 10   JOHNNY OATES

Name	G by Pos	B	AGE	G	AB	R	H	2B	3B	HR	RBI	BB	SO	SB	BA	SA
TOTALS			30	162	5508	786	1470	287	24	157	744	655	930	73	.267	.713
David Segui	1B144 DH1	B	26	146	450	54	123	27	0	10	60	58	53	2	.273	.400
Harold Reynolds	2B141	B	32	145	485	64	122	20	4	4	47	66	47	12	.252	.334
Cal Ripken	SS162	R	32	162	641	87	165	26	3	24	90	65	58	1	.257	.420
Leo Gomez (WJ)	3B70 DH1	R	26	71	244	30	48	7	0	10	25	32	60	0	.197	.348
Mark McLemore	OF124 2B25 3B4 DH1	B	28	148	581	81	165	27	5	4	72	64	92	21	.284	.368
Mike Devereaux	OF130	R	30	131	527	72	132	31	3	14	75	43	99	3	.250	.425
Brady Anderson	OF140 DH2	L	29	142	560	87	147	36	8	13	66	82	99	24	.263	.425
Chris Hoiles	C124 DH1	R	28	126	419	80	130	28	0	29	82	69	94	1	.310	.585
Harold Baines	DH116	L	34	118	416	64	130	22	0	20	78	57	52	0	.313	.510
Tim Hulett	3B75 SS8 2B4 DH2	R	33	85	260	40	78	15	0	2	23	23	56	1	.300	.381
Jack Voigt	OF43 DH4	R	27	64	152	32	45	11	1	6	23	25	33	1	.296	.500
Damon Buford	OF30 DH17	R	23	53	79	18	18	5	2	0	9	9	19	2	.228	.367
Jeff Tackett	C38 P1	R	27	39	87	8	15	3	0	0	9	13	28	0	.172	.207
2 Mike Pagliarulo	3B28 1B4	L	33	38	117	24	38	9	0	6	21	8	15	0	.325	.556
Jeffrey Hammonds (ZJ)	OF23 DH8	R	22	33	105	10	32	8	0	3	19	2	16	4	.305	.467
Sherman Obando (LJ)	DH21 OF8	R	23	31	92	8	25	2	0	3	15	4	26	0	.272	.391
Glenn Davis	1B22 DH7	R	32	30	113	8	20	3	0	1	9	7	29	0	.177	.230
Mark Parent	C21 DH1	R	31	22	54	7	14	2	0	4	12	3	14	0	.259	.519
Paul Carey	1B9 DH1	L	25	18	47	1	10	1	0	0	3	5	14	0	.213	.234
1 Luis Mercedes	OF8 DH2	R	25	10	24	1	7	2	0	0	4	5	4	1	.292	.375
Mark Leonard	OF4 DH3	L	28	10	15	1	1	1	0	0	3	2	3	0	.067	.133
2 Lonnie Smith	DH5 OF4	R	37	9	24	8	5	1	0	2	4	8	10	0	.208	.500
Chito Martinez	OF5 DH2	L	27	8	15	0	0	0	0	0	0	4	4	0	.000	.000
Manny Alexander		R	22	3	0	0	0	0	0	0	0	0	0	0	—	—

NAME	T	AGE	W	L	PCT	SV	G	GS	CG	IP	H	BB	SO	SHO	ERA
		28	85	77	.525	42	162	162	21	1443	1427	579	900	10	4.31
Mike Mussina (SJ)	R	24	14	6	.700	0	25	25	3	168	163	44	117	2	4.46
Ben McDonald	R	25	13	14	.481	0	34	34	7	220	185	86	171	1	3.39
Jamie Moyer	L	30	12	9	.571	0	25	25	3	152	154	38	90	1	3.43
Rick Sutcliffe (KJ)	R	37	10	10	.500	0	29	28	2	166	212	74	80	0	5.75
Fernando Valenzuela	L	32	8	10	.444	0	32	31	5	179	179	79	78	2	4.94
Mark Williamson	R	33	7	5	.583	0	48	1	0	88	106	25	45	0	4.91
Todd Frohwirth	R	30	6	7	.462	3	70	0	0	96	91	44	50	0	3.83
Alan Mills	R	26	5	4	.556	4	45	0	0	100	80	51	68	0	3.23
Arthur Rhodes (KJ)	R	23	5	6	.455	0	17	17	0	86	91	49	49	0	6.51
Brad Pennington	L	24	3	2	.600	4	34	0	0	33	34	25	39	0	6.55
Jim Poole	L	27	2	1	.667	2	55	0	0	50	30	21	29	0	2.15
Kevin McGehee	R	24	0	0	—	0	5	0	0	17	18	7	7	0	5.94
Mike Oquist	R	25	0	0	—	0	12	12	4						3.86
Anthony Telford	R	27	0	0	—	0	2	0	0	7	11	1	3	0	9.82
Mike Cook	R	29	0	0	—	0	2	0	0	1	1	3	0	0	0.00
Jeff Tackett															
John O'Donoghue	L	24	0	1	.000	0	11	1	0	20	22	10	16	0	4.58
Gregg Olson (EJ)	R	26	0	2	.000	29	50	0	0	45	37	18	44	1	1.60

DETROIT   3rd(tie) 85-77 .525 10   SPARKY ANDERSON

Name	G by Pos	B	AGE	G	AB	R	H	2B	3B	HR	RBI	BB	SO	SB	BA	SA
TOTALS			31	162	5620	899	1546	282	38	178	853	765	1122	104	.275	.434
Cecil Fielder	1B119 DH36	R	29	154	573	80	153	23	0	30	117	90	125	0	.267	.464
Lou Whitaker	2B110	L	36	119	383	72	111	32	1	9	67	78	46	3	.290	.449
Travis Fryman	SS81 3B69 DH1	R	24	151	607	98	182	37	5	22	97	77	128	9	.300	.486
Scott Livingstone	3B62 DH32	L	27	98	304	39	89	10	2	2	39	19	32	1	.293	.359
1 Rob Deer	OF86 DH4	R	32	90	323	48	70	11	0	14	39	38	120*	3	.217	.381
Milt Cuyler (KJ)	OF80	B	24	82	249	46	53	11	7	0	19	19	53	13	.213	.313
Tony Phillips	OF108 2B51 DH4 3B3	B	34	151	566	113	177	27	0	7	57	132	102	16	.313	.398
Chad Kreuter	C112 DH2 1B1	B	28	119	374	59	107	23	3	15	51	49	92	2	.286	.484
Kirk Gibson	DH76 OF32	L	36	116	403	62	105	16	6	13	62	44	87	15	.261	.432
Mickey Tettleton	1B59 C56 OF55 DH4	B	32	152	522	79	128	25	4	32	110	109	139	3	.245	.492
Alan Trammell	SS63 3B35 OF8 DH6	R	35	112	401	72	132	25	3	12	60	38	38	12	.329	.496
Dan Gladden (LJ)	OF35 DH5	R	35	91	356	52	95	16	2	13	56	21	50	8	.267	.433
Skeeter Barnes	1B27 OF18 DH13 3B13 2B10 SS2	R	36	84	160	24	45	8	1	2	27	11	19	5	.281	.381
Gary Thurman	OF53 DH8	R	28	75	89	22	19	2	2	0	13	11	30	7	.213	.281
Chris Gomez	SS29 2B17 DH1	R	22	46	128	11	32	7	1	0	11	9	17	2	.250	.320
2 Eric Davis	OF18 DH5	R	31	23	75	14	19	1	1	6	15	14	18	2	.253	.533
Rich Rowland	C17 DH3	R	29	21	46	2	10	0	0	4	5	4	16	0	.217	.283
Danny Bautista	OF16	R	21	17	61	6	19	1	1	3	11	4	16	3	.311	.410

NAME	T	AGE	W	L	PCT	SV	G	GS	CG	IP	H	BB	SO	SHO	ERA
		30	85	77	.525	36	162	162	11	1437	1547	542	828	7	4.65
John Doherty	R	26	14	11	.560	0	32	31	3	185	205	48	63	2	4.44
Mike Moore	R	33	13	9	.591	0	36	36	4	214	227	89	89	3	5.22
Bill Gullickson (KJ)	R	34	13	9	.591	0	28	28	2	159	186	44	70	0	5.37
David Wells	L	30	11	9	.550	0	32	30	0	187	183	42	139	0	4.19
Bill Krueger (EJ)	L	35	8	6	.600	0	32	7	0	82	90	30	60	0	3.40
Tom Bolton	L	31	6	6	.500	0	43	8	0	103	113	45	66	0	4.47
Mark Leiter (SJ)	R	30	6	6	.500	0	27	13	1	107	111	44	70	0	4.73
Mike Henneman	R	31	5	3	.625	24	63	0	0	72	69	32	58	0	2.64
Kurt Knudsen (EJ)	R	27	3	2	.600	2	30	0	0	38	41	16	29	0	4.78
Bob MacDonald	L	28	3	3	.500	3	68	0	0	66	67	33	39	0	5.35
2 Joe Boever	R	32	2	1	.667	3	19	0	0	23	14	11	14	0	2.74
Dave Johnson (SJ)	R	33	1	1	.500	0	8				13			0	12.96
Dave Haas (LJ)	R	27	1	1	.333	0	20	0	0	28	45	8	17	0	6.11
Sean Bergman	R	23	1	4	.200	0	10	10	0	40	47	23	19	0	5.67
Greg Gohr	R	25	0	0	—	0	10	0	0	11	12	7	4	0	5.96
2 Mike Gardiner	R	27	0	0	—	0	10	0	0	11	12	7	4	0	3.97
Mark Grater	R		0	0	—	0	2	0	0	1	2			0	5.40
John DeSilva	R	25	0	0	—	0	2	0	0	1	2	0		0	6.00
1 Mike Munoz	L	27	0	1	.000	0	24	0	0	35	25	15	36	0	3.00
2 Storm Davis	R	31	0	2	.000	4	18	0	0	35	40	15	15	0	3.06
Buddy Groom	L	28	0	2	.000	0	19	3	0	37	48	13	15	0	6.14
John Kiely	R	28	0	0	—	0	12	0	0	13	13	5	5	0	7.71

* Deer, also with Boston, league leader in SO with 169

BOSTON — 5th 80-82 .494 15 — BUTCH HOBSON

Name	G by Pos	B	AGE	G	AB	R	H	2B	3B	HR	RBI	BB	SO	SB	BA	SA
TOTALS			30	162	5496	686	1451	319	29	114	644	508	871	73	.264	.395
Mo Vaughn	1B131 DH19	R	25	152	539	86	160	34	1	29	101	79	130	4	.297	.525
Scott Fletcher	2B116 SS2 3B1 DH1	R	34	121	480	81	137	31	5	5	45	37	35	16	.285	.402
John Valentin	SS144	R	26	144	468	50	130	40	3	11	66	49	77	3	.278	.447
Scott Cooper	3B154 1B2 SS1	L	25	156	526	67	147	29	3	9	63	58	81	5	.279	.397
Bob Zupcic	OF122 DH5	R	26	141	286	40	69	24	2	2	26	27	54	1	.241	.360
Billy Hatcher	OF130 2B2	R	32	136	508	71	146	24	4	9	57	28	46	14	.287	.402
Mike Greenwell	OF134 DH10	L	29	146	540	77	170	38	6	13	72	54	46	5	.315	.480
Tony Pena	C125 DH1	R	36	126	304	20	55	11	0	4	19	25	46	1	.181	.257
Andre Dawson	DH97 OF20	R	38	121	461	44	126	29	1	13	67	17	49	2	.273	.425
Carlos Quintana	1B53 OF51	R	27	101	303	31	74	5	0	1	19	31	52	1	.244	.271
Ernest Riles	2B20 DH15 3B11 1B1	L	32	94	143	15	27	8	0	5	20	20	40	1	.189	.350
Bob Melvin	C76 1B1	R	31	77	176	13	39	7	0	3	23	7	44	0	.222	.313
1 Ivan Calderon	OF47 DH19	R	31	73	213	25	47	8	2	1	19	21	28	4	.221	.291
Luis Rivera (VJ)	2B27 SS27 DH7 3B2	R	29	62	130	13	27	8	1	1	7	11	36	1	.208	.308
Tim Naehring (SJ)	2B15 DH10 3B9 SS4	R	26	39	127	14	42	10	0	1	17	10	26	1	.331	.433
2 Rob Deer	OF36 DH2	R	32	38	143	18	28	6	1	7	16	20	49*	2	.196	.399
Steve Lyons	OF10 2B9 3B1 1B1 C1 DH1	L	33	28	23	4	3	1	0	0	0	2	5	1	.130	.174
Jeff McNeely	OF13 DH3	R	22	21	37	10	11	1	1	0	1	7	9	6	.297	.378
Greg Blosser	OF9 DH1	L	22	17	28	1	2	1	0	0	1	2	7	1	.071	.107
Jeff Richardson (XJ)	2B8 SS5 3B1	R	27	15	24	3	5	2	0	0	2	1	3	0	.208	.292
John Flaherty	C13	R	25	13	25	3	3	2	0	0	2	2	6	0	.120	.200
Luis Ortiz	3B5 DH3	R	23	9	12	0	3	0	0	0	1	0	2	0	.250	.250
Jim Byrd		R	24	2	0	0	0	0	0	0	0	0	0	0	—	—

* Deer, also with Detroit, league leader in SO with 169

NAME	T	AGE	W	L	PCT	SV	G	GS	CG	IP	H	BB	SO	SHO	ERA
		30	80	82	.494	44	162	162	9	1452	1379	552	997	11	3.77
Danny Darwin	R	37	15	11	.577	0	34	34	2	229	196	49	130	1	3.26
Frank Viola	L	33	11	8	.579	0	29	29	2	184	180	72	91	1	3.14
Roger Clemens (GJ)	R	30	11	14	.440	0	29	29	2	192	175	67	160	1	4.46
Ken Ryan	R	24	7	2	.778	1	47	0	0	50	43	29	49	0	3.60
Aaron Sele	R	23	7	2	.778	0	18	18	0	112	100	48	93	0	2.74
John Dopson	R	29	7	11	.389	0	34	28	1	156	170	59	89	1	4.97
Greg Harris	R	37	6	7	.462	8	80	0	0	112	95	60	103	0	3.77
Paul Quantrill	R	24	6	12	.333	1	49	14	1	138	151	44	66	1	3.91
Joe Hesketh (EJ)	L	34	3	4	.429	1	28	5	0	53	62	29	34	0	5.06
Scott Bankhead	R	29	2	1	.667	0	40	0	0	64	59	29	47	0	3.50
Jose Melendez (RJ,ZJ)	R	27	2	1	.667	0	9	0	0	16	10	5	14	0	2.25
Tony Fossas	L	35	1	1	.500	0	71	0	0	40	38	15	39	0	5.18
Nate Minchey	R	23	1	2	.333	0	5	5	1	33	35	8	18	0	3.55
Jeff Russell (NJ)	R	31	1	4	.200	33	51	0	0	47	39	14	45	0	2.70
Scott Taylor	L	25	0	1	.000	0	16	0	0	11	14	12	8	0	8.18
Cory Bailey	R	22	0	1	.000	0	11	0	0	16	12	12	11	0	3.45

CLEVELAND — 6th 76-86 .469 19 — MIKE HARGROVE

Name	G by Pos	B	AGE	G	AB	R	H	2B	3B	HR	RBI	BB	SO	SB	BA	SA
TOTALS			28	162	5619	790	1547	264	31	141	747	488	843	159	.275	.409
Paul Sorrento	1B144 OF3 DH1	L	27	148	463	75	119	26	1	18	65	58	121	3	.257	.434
Carlos Baerga	2B150 DH4	B	24	154	624	105	200	28	6	21	114	34	68	15	.321	.486
Felix Fermin	SS140	R	29	140	480	48	126	16	2	2	45	24	14	4	.263	.317
Alvaro Espinoza	3B99 SS35 2B2	R	31	129	263	34	73	15	0	4	27	8	36	2	.278	.380
Wayne Kirby	OF123 DH6	L	29	131	458	71	123	19	5	6	60	37	58	17	.269	.385
Kenny Lofton	OF146	L	26	148	569	116	185	28	8	1	42	81	83	70	.325	.408
Albert Belle	OF150 DH6	R	26	159	594	93	172	36	3	38	129	76	96	23	.290	.552
Sandy Alomar (XJ)	C64	R	27	64	215	24	58	7	1	6	32	11	20	3	.270	.395
Reggie Jefferson	DH88 1B15	B	24	113	366	35	91	11	2	10	34	28	78	1	.249	.372
Jeff Treadway	3B42 2B19 DH4	L	30	97	221	25	67	14	1	2	27	14	21	1	.303	.403
Junior Ortiz	C95	R	33	95	249	19	55	13	0	0	20	14	26	1	.221	.273
Carlos Martinez	3B35 1B22 DH19	R	27	80	262	26	64	10	0	5	31	20	29	1	.244	.340
1 Thomas Howard	OF47 DH7	B	28	74	178	26	42	7	0	3	23	12	42	5	.236	.326
1 Glenallen Hill	OF39 DH18	R	28	66	174	19	39	7	2	5	25	11	50	7	.224	.374
Jim Thome	3B47	L	22	47	154	28	41	11	0	7	22	29	36	2	.266	.474
Jesse Levis	C29	L	25	31	63	7	11	2	0	0	4	2	10	0	.175	.206
2 Candy Maldonado	OF26 DH2	R	32	28	81	11	20	2	0	5	20	11	18	0	.247	.457
Manny Ramirez	DH21 OF1	R	21	22	53	5	9	1	0	2	5	2	8	0	.170	.302
2 Randy Milligan	1B18 DH1	R	31	19	47	7	20	7	0	0	7	14	4	0	.426	.574
Mark Lewis	SS13	R	23	14	52	6	13	2	0	1	5	0	7	3	.250	.346
Sam Horn	DH11	L	29	12	33	8	15	1	0	4	8	1	5	0	.455	.848
Lance Parrish	C10	R	37	10	20	2	4	1	0	1	2	4	5	1	.200	.400
Joel Skinner 32 (SJ)																

NAME	T	AGE	W	L	PCT	SV	G	GS	CG	IP	H	BB	SO	SHO	ERA
		27	76	86	.469	45	162	162	7	1446	1591	591	888	8	4.58
Jose Mesa	R	27	10	12	.455	0	34	33	3	209	232	62	118	0	4.92
Tommy Kramer	R	25	7	3	.700	0	39	16	1	121	126	59	71	0	4.02
Mark Clark (XJ)	R	25	7	5	.583	0	26	15	1	109	119	25	57	0	4.28
2 Jeremy Hernandez	R	26	6	5	.545	8	49	0	0	77	75	27	44	0	3.14
Dennis Cook	L	30	5	5	.500	0	25	6	0	54	62	16	34	0	5.67
Derek Lilliquist	L	27	4	4	.500	10	56	2	0	64	64	19	40	0	2.25
Jerry Dipoto	R	25	4	4	.500	11	46	0	0	56	57	30	41	0	2.79
Eric Plunk	R	29	4	5	.444	15	70	0	0	71	61	30	77	0	2.79
Mike Bielecki	R	33	4	5	.444	0	13	13	0	69	90	23	38	0	5.90
2 Heathcliff Slocumb	R	27	3	1	.750	0	20	0	0	27	28	16	18	0	4.28
Albie Lopez	R	21	3	1	.750	0	9	9	1	50	49	32	25	0	5.98
Cliff Young	L	28	3	3	.500	1	21	7	0	60	74	18	31	0	4.62
Jason Grimsley	R	25	3	4	.429	0	10	6	0	42	52	20	27	0	5.31
Jeff Mutis	L	26	3	6	.333	0	17	13	1	81	93	33	29	1	5.78
Bob Ojeda (YJ)	L	35	2	1	.667	0	9	7	0	43	48	21	27	0	4.40
Julian Tavarez	R	20	2	2	.500	0	8	7	0	37	53	13	19	0	6.57
Bill Wertz	R	26	2	3	.400	0	34	0	0	60	54	32	53	0	3.62
Charles Nagy (SJ)	R	26	2	6	.250	0	9	9	1	49	48	13	30	0	6.29
Bob Milacki	R	28	1	1	.500	0	9	1	0	16	19	11	7	0	3.38
Matt Young	L	34	1	6	.143	0	22	8	0	74	75	57	65	0	5.21
1 Kevin Wickander	L	28	0	0	—	0	11	0	0	9	15	3	3	0	4.15
Mike Christopher	R	29	0	0	—	0	6	0	0	12	14	2	8	0	3.86
Dave Mlicki (SJ)	R	25	0	0	—	0	3	3	0	13	11	6	7	0	3.38
Paul Abbott	R	25	0	1	.000	0	5	0	0	18	19	11	7	0	6.38
Scott Scudder (XJ)	R	25	0	1	.000	0	2	1	0	4	5	1	4	0	9.00
1 Ted Power (AJ)	R	38	0	2	.000	0	20	0	0	20	30	8	11	0	7.20

Steve Olin 27 killed in boating accident March 22
Tim Crews 32 died from injuries in boating accident March 23

MILWAUKEE — 7th 69-93 .426 26 — PHIL GARNER

Name	G by Pos	B	AGE	G	AB	R	H	2B	3B	HR	RBI	BB	SO	SB	BA	SA
TOTALS			29	162	5525	733	1426	240	25	125	688	555	932	138	.258	.378
John Jaha	1B150 3B1 2B1	R	27	153	515	78	136	21	0	19	70	51	109	13	.264	.416
Bill Spiers	2B104 OF7 SS4	L	27	113	340	43	81	8	4	2	36	29	51	9	.238	.300
Pat Listach (LJ)	SS95 OF6	B	25	98	356	50	87	15	1	3	30	37	70	18	.244	.317
B.J. Surhoff	3B121 OF24 1B8 C3 DH1	L	28	148	552	66	151	38	3	7	79	36	47	12	.274	.391
Darryl Hamilton	OF129 DH1	L	28	135	520	74	161	21	1	9	48	45	62	21	.310	.406
Robin Yount	OF114 1B7 DH6	R	37	127	454	62	117	25	3	8	51	44	93	9	.258	.379
Greg Vaughn	OF94 DH58	R	27	154	569	97	152	28	2	30	97	89	118	10	.267	.482
Dave Nilsson (KJ)	C91 1B4 DH4	L	23	100	296	35	76	10	2	7	40	37	36	3	.257	.375
Kevin Reimer	DH83 OF37	L	29	125	437	53	109	22	1	13	60	30	72	5	.249	.394
2 Juan Bell	2B47 SS40 OF3 DH2	B	25	91	286	42	67	6	2	5	29	36	64	6	.234	.322
Dickie Thon	SS28 3B25 2B22 DH14	R	35	85	245	23	66	10	1	1	33	22	39	6	.269	.331
Tom Brunansky (XJ)	OF71 DH6	R	32	80	224	20	41	7	3	6	29	25	59	3	.183	.321
Tom Lampkin	C60 OF3 DH1	L	28	73	162	22	32	8	0	4	25	20	26	7	.198	.321
Joe Kmak	C50	R	30	51	110	9	24	5	0	0	7	14	13	6	.218	.264
Alex Diaz (BN)	OF28 DH1	B	24	32	69	9	22	2	0	1	0	12	5	5	.319	.348
2 Kevin Seitzer	3B33 1B7 DH3 2B1 OF1	R	31	47	162	21	47	6	0	5	30	17	15	3	.290	.457
Bill Doran (SJ)	2B17 1B4	B	35	28	60	7	13	4	0	0	6	6	3	1	.217	.283
Matt Mieske	OF22	R	25	23	58	9	14	0	0	3	7	4	14	0	.241	.397
Jose Valentin	SS19	B	23	19	53	10	13	1	2	1	7	7	16	1	.245	.396
Troy O'Leary	OF19	L	23	19	41	3	12	3	0	0	3	5	9	0	.293	.366
William Suero	2B8 3B1	R	26	15	14	0	4	0	0	0	0	1	3	0	.286	.286
1 Tim McIntosh	C1	R	27	1	0	0	0	0	0	0	0	0	0	0	—	—

NAME	T	AGE	W	L	PCT	SV	G	GS	CG	IP	H	BB	SO	SHO	ERA
		27	69	93	.426	29	162	162	26	1447	1511	522	810	6	4.45
Cal Eldred	R	25	16	16	.500	0	36	36	8	258	232	91	180	1	4.01
Ricky Bones	R	24	11	11	.500	0	32	31	3	204	222	63	63	0	4.86
Jaime Navarro	R	26	11	12	.478	0	35	34	5	214	254	73	114	1	5.33
Doug Henry	R	29	4	4	.500	17	54	0	0	55	67	25	38	0	5.56
Angel Miranda (SJ)	L	23	4	5	.444	0	22	17	2	120	100	52	88	0	3.30
Bill Wegman (EJ)	R	30	4	14	.222	0	20	18	5	121	135	34	50	0	4.48
Mike Fetters	R	28	3	3	.500	0	45	0	0	59	59	22	23	0	3.34
Graeme Lloyd	L	26	3	4	.429	0	55	0	0	64	64	13	31	0	2.83
Jesse Orosco	L	36	3	5	.375	8	57	0	0	57	47	17	67	0	3.18
2 Mike Boddicker (KJ)	R	35	3	5	.375	0	10	10	1	54	77	15	24	0	5.67
Carlos Maldonado	R	26	2	2	.500	1	29	0	0	37	40	17	18	0	4.58
Mike Ignasiak	R	27	2	2	.500	0	27	0	0	37	36	11	28	0	3.65
1 Josias Manzanillo	R	25	1	1	.500	1	10	1	0	17	12	10	15	0	9.53
Jim Austin	R	29	1	2	.333	0	11	0	0	33	28	13	15	0	3.82
Matt Maysey	R	26	1	2	.333	1	23	0	0	22	28	13	10	0	5.73
Teddy Higuera (SJ)	L	34	1	3	.250	0	8	8	0	30	43	16	27	0	7.20
Mark Kiefer	R	24	0	0	—	1	6	0	0	9	5	1	7	0	0.00
Rafael Novoa	L	25	0	3	.000	0	15	7	2	56	58	22	17	0	4.50

WEST DIVISION

CHICAGO — 1st 94-68 .580 — GENE LAMONT

Name	G by Pos	B	AGE	G	AB	R	H	2B	3B	HR	RBI	BB	SO	SB	BA	SA
TOTALS			29	162	5483	776	1454	228	44	162	731	604	834	106	.265	.411
Frank Thomas	1B150 DH4	R	25	153	549	106	174	36	0	41	128	112	54	4	.317	.607
Joey Cora	2B151 3B3	B	28	153	579	95	155	15	13	2	51	67	63	20	.268	.349
Ozzie Guillen	SS133	L	29	134	457	44	128	23	4	4	50	10	41	5	.280	.374
Robin Ventura	3B155 1B4	L	25	157	554	85	145	27	1	22	94	105	82	1	.262	.433
Ellis Burks	OF146 DH4	R	28	146	499	75	137	24	4	17	74	60	97	6	.275	.441
Lance Johnson	OF146	L	29	147	540	75	168	18	14	0	47	36	33	35	.311	.396
Tim Raines (RJ)	OF112	B	33	115	415	75	127	16	4	16	54	64	35	21	.306	.480
Ron Karkovice	C127	R	29	128	403	60	92	17	1	20	54	29	126	2	.228	.424
George Bell (KJ)	DH102	R	33	102	410	36	89	17	2	13	64	13	49	1	.217	.363
Bo Jackson	OF47 DH36	R	30	85	284	32	66	9	0	16	45	23	106	0	.232	.433
Dan Pasqua	OF37 1B32 DH6	L	31	78	176	22	36	10	1	5	20	26	51	2	.205	.358
Craig Grebeck	SS46 2B16 3B14	R	28	72	190	25	43	5	0	1	12	26	26	1	.226	.268
Steve Sax	OF32 DH21 2B1	R	33	57	119	20	28	5	0	1	8	8	20	7	.235	.303
Mike Huff	OF43	R	29	43	44	4	8	1	0	0	9	6	15	1	.182	.295
2 Mike LaValliere	C37	L	32	37	97	6	25	2	0	0	8	14	6	0	.258	.278
Warren Newson	DH10 OF5	L	28	26	40	9	12	0	0	2	6	12	10	0	.300	.450
Carlton Fisk	C25	R	45	25	53	2	10	0	0	1	4	3	11	1	.189	.245
2 Ivan Calderon	DH6	R	31	9	26	1	3	2	0	0	0	2	6	0	.115	.192
Matt Merullo	DH6	L	27	8	20	0	1	0	0	0	0	1	5	0	.050	.050
Norberto Martin	2B5 DH1	R	26	8	14	3	5	0	0	0	1	0	2	0	.357	.357
Rick Wrona	C4	R	30	8	8	1	1	0	0	0	0	1	2	0	.125	.125
Drew Denson	1B3	R	28	4	5	0	1	0	0	0	1	0	1	0	.200	.200
2 Doug Lindsey	C2	R	25	2	1	0	0	0	0	0	0	0	0	0	.000	.000

NAME	T	AGE	W	L	PCT	SV	G	GS	CG	IP	H	BB	SO	SHO	ERA
		27	94	68	.580	48	162	162	16	1454	1398	566	974	11	3.70
Jack McDowell	R	27	22	10	.688	0	34	34	10	257	261	69	158	4	3.37
Alex Fernandez	R	23	18	9	.667	0	34	34	3	247	221	67	169	1	3.13
Wilson Alvarez	L	23	15	8	.652	0	31	31	1	208	168	122	155	1	2.95
Jason Bere	R	22	12	5	.706	0	24	24	1	143	109	81	129	0	3.47
Scott Radinsky	L	25	8	2	.800	4	73	0	0	55	61	19	44	0	4.28
Kirk McCaskill	R	32	4	8	.333	2	30	14	0	114	144	36	65	0	5.23
Roberto Hernandez	R	28	3	4	.429	38	70	0	0	79	66	20	71	0	2.29
2 Tim Belcher	R	31	3	5	.375	0	12	11	1	72	64	27	34	1	4.40
Jeff Schwarz	R	29	2	2	.500	0	41	0	0	51	35	38	41	0	3.71
1 Donn Pall	R	31	2	3	.400	1	39	0	0	59	62	11	29	0	3.22
Rodney Bolton	R	24	2	6	.250	0	9	8	0	43	55	16	17	0	7.44
Chuck Cary (EJ,XJ)	L	33	1	0	1.000	0	16	0	0	21	22	11	10	0	5.23
Chris Howard	R	27	1	0	1.000	0	4	0	0	8	6	4	3	0	4.05
Dave Stieb	R	35	1	3	.250	0	4	4	0	22	27	14	11	0	6.04
1 Bobby Thigpen	R	29	0	0	—	1	25	0	0	40	51	12	19	0	5.71
Terry Leach (EJ)	R	39	0	1	.000	0	14	0	0	16	15	2	3	0	2.81
2 Jose DeLeon	R	32	0	0	—	0	11	0	0	10	5	3	6	0	1.74
Brian Drahman	R	26	0	0	—	0	5	0	0	7	4	5	3	0	6.39
Barry Jones	R	30	0	1	.000	0	2	0	0	3	5	3	7	0	8.59
Scott Ruffcorn	R	23	0	2	.000	0	2	2	0	10	9	10	2	0	8.10
Mike Dunne 30 (EJ)															

TEXAS 2nd 86-76 .531 8 KEVIN KENNEDY

Name	G by Pos	B	AGE	G	AB	R	H	2B	3B	HR	RBI	BB	SO	SB	BA	SA
TOTALS			28	162	5510	835	1472	284	39	181	780	483	984	113	.267	.431
Rafael Palmeiro	1B160	L	28	160	597	124	176	40	2	37	105	73	85	22	.295	.554
Doug Strange	2B135 3B9 SS1	L	29	145	484	58	124	29	4	7	60	43	69	6	.256	.360
Manuel Lee (RJ)	SS72 DH1	B	28	73	205	31	45	3	1	1	12	22	39	2	.220	.259
Dean Palmer	3B148 SS1	R	24	148	519	88	127	31	2	33	96	53	154	11	.245	.503
Jose Canseco (EJ)	OF49 DH9 P1	R	28	60	231	30	59	14	1	10	46	16	62	6	.255	.455
David Hulse	OF112 DH2	L	25	114	407	71	118	9	10	1	29	26	57	29	.290	.369
Juan Gonzalez	OF129 DH10	R	23	140	536	105	166	33	1	46	118	37	99	4	.310	.632
Ivan Rodriguez	C134 DH1	R	21	137	473	56	129	28	4	10	66	29	70	8	.273	.412
Julio Franco	DH140	R	34	144	532	85	154	31	3	14	84	62	95	9	.289	.438
Gary Redus	OF61 1B5 2B1 DH1	R	36	77	222	28	64	12	4	6	31	23	35	4	.288	.459
Doug Dascenzo	OF68 DH2	B	29	76	146	20	29	5	1	2	10	8	22	2	.199	.288
Mario Diaz	SS57 3B12 1B1	R	31	71	205	24	56	10	1	2	24	8	13	1	.273	.361
Dan Peltier	OF55 1B5	L	25	65	160	23	43	7	1	1	17	20	27	0	.269	.344
Butch Davis	OF44 DH11	R	35	62	159	24	39	10	4	3	20	5	28	3	.245	.415
Geno Petralli (EJ)	C39 DH2 3B1	L	33	59	133	16	32	5	0	1	13	22	17	2	.241	.301
Billy Ripken (LJ)	2B34 SS18 3B1	R	28	50	132	12	25	4	0	0	11	11	19	0	.189	.220
Donald Harris	OF38 DH3	R	25	40	76	10	15	2	0	1	8	5	18	0	.197	.263
Rob Ducey	OF26	L	28	27	85	15	24	6	3	2	9	10	17	2	.282	.494
Jeff Huson (SJ,BT)	SS12 2B5 3B2	L	28	23	45	3	6	1	1	0	2	0	10	0	.133	.200
Benji Gil	SS22	R	20	22	57	3	7	0	0	0	2	5	22	1	.123	.123
John Russell (RC)	C11 1B1 OF1 3B1	R	32	18	22	1	5	1	0	1	3	2	10	0	.227	.409
Jon Shave	SS9 2B8	R	25	17	47	3	15	2	0	0	7	0	8	1	.319	.362
2 Chris James	OF7	R	30	8	31	5	11	1	0	3	7	3	6	0	.355	.677
Steve Balboni	DH2	R	36	5	5	0	3	0	0	0	0	0	2	0	.600	.600

Rob Maurer 26 (KJ), Jeff Fyre 26 (KJ)

NAME	T	AGE	W	L	PCT	SV	G	GS	CG	IP	H	BB	SO	SHO	ERA
		30	86	76	.531	45	162	162	20	1438	1476	562	957	6	4.28
Kenny Rogers	L	28	16	10	.615	0	35	33	5	208	210	71	140	0	4.10
Kevin Brown	R	28	15	12	.556	0	34	34	12	233	228	74	142	3	3.59
Roger Pavlik	R	25	12	6	.667	0	26	26	2	166	151	80	131	0	3.41
Charlie Leibrandt (SJ)	L	36	9	10	.474	0	26	26	1	150	169	45	89	0	4.55
Tom Henke	R	35	5	5	.500	40	66	0	0	74	55	27	79	0	2.91
Nolan Ryan (PJ)	R	46	5	5	.500	0	13	13	0	66	54	40	46	0	4.88
2 Cris Carpenter	R	28	4	1	.800	1	27	0	0	32	35	12	27	0	4.22
Brian Bohanon	L	24	4	4	.500	0	36	8	0	93	107	46	45	0	4.76
Mike Schooler	R	30	3	3	.500	0	17	0	0	24	30	10	16	0	5.55
Steve Dreyer	R	23	3	3	.500	0	10	6	0	41	48	20	23	0	5.71
Craig Lefferts	L	35	3	9	.250	0	52	8	0	83	102	28	58	0	6.05
Matt Whiteside	R	25	2	1	.667	1	60	0	0	73	78	23	39	0	4.32
Bob Patterson	L	34	2	4	.333	1	52	0	0	53	59	11	46	0	4.78
2 Rick Reed	R	28	1	0	1.000	0	2	0	0	4	6	1	2	0	2.25
Jeff Bronkey	R	27	1	1	.500	1	21	0	0	36	39	11	18	0	4.00
1 Robb Nen (GJ)	R	23	1	1	.500	0	9	3	0	23	28	26	12	0	6.35
2 Gene Nelson	R	32	0	0	—	1	6	0	0	8	10	1	4	0	3.38
Darren Oliver	L	22	0	0	—	0	2	0	0	3	4	3	0	0	2.70
Jose Canseco	R	28	0	0	—	0	1	0	0	1	2	3	0	0	27.00
Hector Fajardo (EJ)	R	22	0	0	—	0	1	1	0	1	0	1	1	0	0.00
1 Todd Burns	R	29	0	4	.000	0	25	6	0	65	63	32	35	0	4.57

KANSAS CITY 3rd 84-78 .519 10 HAL McRAE

Name	G by Pos	B	AGE	G	AB	R	H	2B	3B	HR	RBI	BB	SO	SB	BA	SA
TOTALS			30	162	5522	675	1455	294	35	125	641	428	936	100	.263	.397
Wally Joyner	1B140	L	31	141	497	83	145	36	3	15	65	66	67	5	.292	.467
Jose Lind	2B136	R	29	136	431	33	107	13	2	0	37	13	36	3	.248	.288
Greg Gagne	SS159	R	31	159	540	66	151	32	3	10	57	33	93	10	.280	.406
2 Gary Gaetti	3B72 1B18 DH1	R	34	82	281	37	72	18	1	14	46	16	75	0	.256	.477
Felix Jose	OF144 DH1	B	28	149	499	64	126	24	3	6	43	36	95	31	.253	.349
Brian McRae	OF153	B	25	153	627	78	177	28	9	12	69	37	105	23	.282	.413
Kevin McReynolds	OF104 DH1	R	33	110	351	44	86	22	4	11	42	37	56	2	.245	.425
Mike Macfarlane	C114	R	29	117	388	55	106	27	0	20	67	40	83	2	.273	.497
George Brett	DH140	L	40	145	560	69	149	31	3	19	75	39	67	7	.266	.434
Chris Gwynn	OF83 DH5 1B1	L	28	103	287	36	86	14	4	1	25	24	34	0	.300	.387
Phil Hiatt	3B70 DH9	R	24	81	238	30	52	12	1	7	36	16	82	6	.218	.366
Hubie Brooks	OF40 DH9 1B3	R	36	75	168	14	48	12	0	1	24	11	27	0	.286	.375
Brent Mayne	C68 DH1	L	25	71	205	22	52	9	1	2	22	18	31	3	.254	.337
Rico Rossy	2B24 3B16 SS11	R	29	46	86	10	19	4	0	2	12	9	11	0	.221	.337
Keith Miller (RJ)	3B21 DH6 OF4 2B3	R	30	37	108	9	18	3	0	1	8	4	18	3	.167	.194
Harvey Pulliam	OF26	R	25	27	62	7	16	5	0	1	6	2	14	0	.258	.387
Craig Wilson (PP)	3B15 2B1 OF1	R	27	21	49	6	13	1	0	1	3	7	6	1	.265	.347
Bob Hamelin	1B15	L	25	16	49	2	11	3	0	2	5	6	15	0	.224	.408
Kevin Koslofski	OF13	L	26	15	26	4	7	0	0	1	4	2	5	0	.269	.385
David Howard (LJ)	2B7 SS3 3B2 OF1	B	26	15	24	5	8	0	1	0	2	1	6	2	.333	.417
Curt Wilkerson (BN)	2B10 SS4	B	32	12	28	1	4	0	0	0	1	0	6	1	.143	.143
Terry Shumpert	2B8	R	26	8	10	0	1	0	0	0	0	2	0	1	.100	.100
Nelson Santovenia	C4	R	31	4	8	1	1	0	0	0	0	1	2	0	.125	.125

NAME	T	AGE	W	L	PCT	SV	G	GS	CG	IP	H	BB	SO	SHO	ERA
		27	84	78	.519	48	162	162	16	1445	1379	571	985	6	4.04
Kevin Appier	R	25	18	8	.692	0	34	34	5	239	183	81	186	1	2.56
Tom Gordon	R	25	12	6	.667	1	48	14	2	156	125	77	143	0	3.58
David Cone	R	30	11	14	.440	0	34	34	6	254	205	114	191	1	3.33
Chris Haney	L	24	9	9	.500	0	23	23	1	124	141	53	65	1	6.02
Jeff Montgomery	R	31	7	5	.583	45	69	0	0	87	65	23	66	0	2.27
Hipolito Pichardo	R	23	7	8	.467	0	30	25	2	165	183	53	70	0	4.04
Mark Gubicza	R	30	5	8	.385	2	49	6	0	104	128	43	80	0	4.66
Mark Gardner (SJ)	R	31	4	6	.400	0	17	16	0	92	92	36	54	0	6.19
Billy Brewer	L	25	2	2	.500	0	46	0	0	39	31	20	28	0	3.46
Bill Sampen	R	30	2	1	.667	1	18	0	0	18	25	9	5	0	5.89
Rusty Meacham (EJ)	R	25	2	2	.500	0	15	0	0	21	31	5	13	0	5.57
2 Stan Belinda	R	26	1	1	.500	0	23	0	0	27	30	6	25	0	4.28
2 Greg Cadaret	L	31	1	1	.500	0	13	0	0	15	14	7	2	0	2.93
Frank DiPino (ZJ)	L	36	1	1	.500	0	11	0	0	16	21	6	5	0	6.89
Dennis Rasmussen (NJ)	L	34	1	2	.333	0	4	0	0	29	40	14	12	0	7.45
Mike Magnante	L	28	1	2	.333	0	7	0	0	35	37	11	16	0	4.08
2 John Habyan	R	29	0	0	—	0	12	0	0	14	14	4	10	0	4.50
1 Rick Reed	R	28	0	0	—	0	1	0	0	2	2	0	2	0	9.82
Jeff Granger	L	21	0	0	—	0	1	1	0	4	2	1	5	0	27.00
Enrique Burgos	L	27	0	1	.000	0	5	0	0	5	5	6	6	0	9.00

1 Mike Boddicker 35 (KJ)

SEATTLE 4th 82-80 .506 12 LOU PINIELLA

Name	G by Pos	B	AGE	G	AB	R	H	2B	3B	HR	RBI	BB	SO	SB	BA	SA
TOTALS			29	162	5494	734	1429	272	24	161	681	624	901	91	.260	.406
Tino Martinez (KJ)	1B103 DH6	L	25	109	408	48	108	25	1	17	60	45	56	0	.265	.456
Rich Amaral	2B77 3B19 SS14 DH9 1B3	R	31	110	373	53	108	24	1	1	44	33	54	19	.290	.367
Omar Vizquel	SS155 DH2	B	26	158	560	68	143	14	2	2	31	50	71	12	.255	.298
Mike Blowers	3B117 DH3 OF2 1B1 C1	R	28	127	379	55	106	23	3	15	57	44	98	1	.280	.475
Jay Buhner	OF148 DH10	R	28	158	563	91	153	28	3	27	98	100	144	2	.272	.476
Ken Griffey Jr.	OF139 DH19 1B1	L	23	156	582	113	180	38	3	45	109	96	91	17	.309	.617
Mike Felder	OF95 DH6 3B2	B	31	109	342	31	72	7	5	1	20	22	35	15	.211	.269
Dave Valle	C135	R	32	135	423	48	109	19	0	13	63	48	56	1	.258	.395
Edgar Martinez (LJ)	DH24 3B16	R	30	42	135	20	32	7	0	4	13	28	19	0	.237	.378
Mackey Sasser	OF37 DH19 C4 1B1	L	30	83	188	18	41	10	2	1	21	15	30	1	.218	.309
Bret Boone	2B74 DH1	R	24	76	271	31	68	12	2	12	38	17	52	2	.251	.443
Pete O'Brien	DH52 1B9 OF1	L	35	72	210	30	54	7	0	7	27	26	21	0	.257	.390
Greg Litton	OF22 2B17 1B13 DH12 3B7 SS6	R	28	72	174	25	52	17	0	3	25	18	30	0	.299	.448
2 Dave Magadan	1B41 3B27 DH2	L	30	71	228	27	59	11	0	1	21	36	33	2	.259	.320
Bill Haselman	C49 DH4 OF2	R	27	58	137	21	35	8	0	5	16	12	19	2	.255	.423
1 Henry Cotto	OF34 DH15	R	32	54	105	10	20	1	0	2	7	2	22	5	.190	.257
Brian Turang	OF38 3B2 2B1 DH1	R	26	40	140	22	35	11	1	0	7	17	20	6	.250	.343
Dann Howitt	OF29 DH2	L	28	32	76	6	16	3	1	2	4	4	18	0	.211	.355
Fernando Vina	2B16 SS4 DH2	R	24	24	45	5	10	2	0	0	2	6	4	0	.222	.267
Marc Newfield	DH15 OF5	R	20	22	66	5	15	3	0	1	7	2	8	0	.227	.318
Lee Tinsley	OF6 DH2	B	24	11	19	2	3	1	0	1	2	4	6	2	.158	.368
Larry Sheets	DH5 OF1	L	33	11	17	0	2	2	0	0	1	0	3	0	.118	.176
Wally Backman	3B9 2B1	B	33	10	29	2	4	0	0	0	1	6	5	0	.138	.138
Greg Pirkl	1B5 DH2	R	22	7	23	1	4	0	0	1	2	0	8	0	.174	.304
Chris Howard	C4	R	27	1	0	0	0	0	0	0	0	0	0	0	.000	.000

NAME	T	AGE	W	L	PCT	SV	G	GS	CG	IP	H	BB	SO	SHO	ERA
		29	82	80	.506	41	162	162	22	1454	1421	605	1083	10	4.20
Randy Johnson	L	29	19	8	.704	1	35	34	10	255	185	99	308	3	3.24
Dave Fleming (EJ)	L	23	12	5	.706	0	26	26	1	167	189	67	75	1	4.36
Tim Leary	R	34	11	9	.550	0	33	27	0	169	202	58	68	0	5.05
Erik Hanson	R	28	11	12	.478	0	31	30	7	215	215	60	163	0	3.47
Chris Bosio (BC)	R	30	9	9	.500	1	29	24	3	164	138	59	119	1	3.45
Jeff Nelson	R	26	5	3	.625	1	71	0	0	60	57	34	61	0	4.35
Russ Swan	L	29	3	3	.500	0	23	0	0	25	18	10	9	0	9.15
Rich DeLucia	R	28	3	6	.333	0	30	1	0	43	46	23	48	0	4.64
2 Dwayne Henry (EJ)	R	31	2	1	.667	2	31	0	0	54	56	35	35	0	6.67
2 Ted Power	R	38	2	2	.500	13	25	0	0	25	27	9	16	0	3.91
2 Bob Ayrault	R	27	1	1	.500	0	14	0	0	20	17	8	10	0	3.90
Norm Charlton (EJ)	L	30	1	3	.250	18	34	0	0	35	22	17	48	0	2.34
Brad Holman	R	25	1	3	.250	0	19	0	0	36	27	16	17	0	3.72
Mike Hampton	R	21	1	3	.250	1	13	3	0	17	17	17	8	0	9.53
Jim Converse	R	21	1	3	.250	0	4	4	0	20	23	14	10	0	5.31
Dennis Powell	L	24	0	0	—	0	33	2	0	48	42	24	32	0	4.15
Erik Plantenberg	L	22	0	0	—	0	10	0	0	10	11	12	3	0	6.52
Roger Salkeld	R	22	0	0	—	0	3	3	0	14	13	4	13	0	2.51
Dave Wainhouse	R	25	0	0	—	0	2	0	0	4	9	7	1	0	27.00
Zak Shinall	R	24	0	0	—	0	3	0	0	3	3	0	1	0	3.38
Kevin King	L	24	0	0	—	0	13	0	0	12	14	10	4	0	6.17
Steve Ontiveros	R	32	0	0	—	0	1	0	0	18	18	6	13	0	1.00
John Cummings	L	24	0	0	—	0	10	8	1	46	59	16	19	0	6.02

Kerry Woodson 24 (EJ)
Brian Holman 28 (SJ)

CALIFORNIA 5th(tie) 71-91 .438 23 BUCK RODGERS

Name	G by Pos	B	AGE	G	AB	R	H	2B	3B	HR	RBI	BB	SO	SB	BA	SA
TOTALS			27	162	5391	684	1399	259	24	114	644	564	930	169	.260	.380
J. T. Snow	1B129	B	25	129	419	60	101	18	2	16	57	55	88	3	.241	.408
Torey Lovullo	2B91 3B14 SS9 OF2 1B1	B	27	116	367	42	92	20	0	6	30	36	49	7	.251	.354
Gary DiSarcina (BG)	SS126	R	25	126	416	44	99	20	1	3	45	15	38	5	.238	.313
Rene Gonzales	3B79 1B31 SS5 2B4 P1	R	32	118	335	34	84	17	0	2	31	49	45	5	.251	.313
Tim Salmon	OF140 DH1	R	24	142	515	93	146	35	1	31	95	82	135	5	.283	.536
Chad Curtis	OF151 2B3	R	24	152	583	94	166	25	3	6	59	70	89	48	.285	.393
Luis Polonia	OF141 DH4	L	28	152	576	75	156	17	6	1	32	48	59	55	.271	.326
Greg Myers	C97 DH2	L	27	108	290	27	74	10	0	7	40	17	47	3	.255	.362
Chili Davis	DH150 P1	B	33	153	573	74	139	32	0	27	112	71	135	4	.243	.440
Stan Javier	OF64 1B12 2B2 DH1	B	29	92	237	33	69	10	4	3	28	27	33	12	.291	.405
Damion Easley (LJ)	2B54 3B14 DH1	R	23	73	230	33	72	13	2	2	22	28	35	6	.313	.413
Rod Correia	SS40 2B11 DH6 3B3	R	25	64	128	12	34	5	0	0	12	5	22	2	.266	.305
Ron Tingley	C58	R	34	58	90	7	18	7	0	0	12	6	22	1	.200	.278
Eduardo Perez	3B45 DH3	R	23	52	180	16	45	6	2	4	30	9	39	5	.250	.372
John Orton (EJ)	C35 OF1	R	27	37	95	5	18	5	0	1	9	7	24	1	.189	.274
Chris Turner	C25	R	24	25	75	9	21	5	0	1	13	8	12	1	.280	.387
2 Kurt Stillwell	2B18 SS7	L	28	22	61	2	16	2	0	2	4	4	11	2	.262	.361
1 Gary Gaetti	3B7 1B6 DH5	R	34	20	50	3	9	2	0	2	4	1	10	0	.180	.220
Kelly Gruber (SJ-ZJ)	3B17 OF1 DH1	R	31	18	65	10	18	4	0	1	9	2	11	0	.277	.462
Jim Edmonds	OF17	L	23	18	61	5	15	4	0	0	4	2	16	0	.246	.344
Ty Van Burkleo	1B12	L	29	12	28	1	4	0	0	0	2	4	10	0	.143	.143
Jim Walewander	SS6 DH3 2B3	R	27	11	21	3	5	1	0	0	1	1	5	1	.238	.286
Jerome Walton	DH4 OF1	R	27	5	5	0	5	0	0	0	0	0	1	0	1.000	1.000
Larry Gonzales	C2	R	26	3	2	0	1	0	0	0	0	0	0	0	.500	.500

NAME	T	AGE	W	L	PCT	SV	G	GS	CG	IP	H	BB	SO	SHO	ERA
		29	71	91	.438	41	162	162	26	1430	1482	550	843	6	4.34
Mark Langston	L	32	16	11	.593	0	35	35	7	256	220	85	196	0	3.20
Chuck Finley	L	30	16	14	.533	0	35	35	13	251	243	82	187	2	3.15
1 Scott Sanderson	R	36	7	11	.389	0	21	21	4	135	163	27	66	1	4.46
Joe Grahe (SJ)	R	25	4	1	.800	11	45	0	0	57	54	25	31	0	2.86
Hilly Hathaway	L	23	4	3	.571	0	11	11	0	57	71	26	11	0	5.02
Phil Leftwich	R	24	4	6	.400	0	12	12	1	81	81	27	31	0	3.79
2 Joe Magrane	L	28	3	2	.600	0	8	8	0	48	48	21	24	0	3.90
Julio Valera (EJ)	R	25	3	6	.333	4	19	5	0	53	57	15	28	0	6.62
John Farrell	R	30	3	12	.200	0	21	17	0	91	110	44	45	0	7.35
2 Doug Linton	R	27	2	0	1.000	0	19	0	0	26	35	14	19	0	7.71
Chuck Crim	R	31	2	2	.500	0	11	0	0	15	17	5	10	0	5.87
Steve Frey	L	29	2	3	.400	13	55	0	0	48	41	26	22	0	2.98
Mike Butcher (SJ,EJ)	R	28	2	1	1.000	0	23	0	0	21	15	24	15	0	2.86
Ken Patterson	L	28	1	1	.500	1	46	0	0	59	54	35	36	0	4.58
Darryl Scott	R	24	1	2	.333	0	16	0	0	19	11	9	13	0	5.85
Scott Lewis	R	27	1	1	.333	0	4	0	0	32	37	12	10	0	4.22
Russ Springer (XJ)	R	24	1	6	.143	0	14	9	0	60	73	32	31	0	7.20
Jerry Nielsen	L	27	0	0	—	0	10	0	0	12	18	4	8	0	8.03
Brian Anderson	L	21	0	0	—	0	4	4	0	11	11	2	4	0	3.97
Chili Davis	R	33	0	0	—	0	1	0	0	1	0	0	0	0	0.00
Rene Gonzales	R	31	0	0	—	0	1	0	0	1	1	0	0	0	0.00
Paul Swingle	R	26	0	0	—	0	10	0	0	15	15	10	8	0	8.38
Mark Holzemer	L	24	0	3	.000	0	13	5	0	24	31	13	10	0	8.87
1 Gene Nelson	R	32	0	5	.000	0	46	0	0	53	50	23	31	0	3.08

MINNESOTA 5th(tie) 71-91 .438 23   TOM KELLY

Name	G by Pos	B	AGE	G	AB	R	H	2B	3B	HR	RBI	BB	SO	SB	BA	SA
TOTALS			29	162	5601	693	1480	261	27	121	642	493	850	83	.264	.385
Kent Hrbek	1B115 DH2	L	33	123	392	60	95	11	1	25	83	71	57	4	.242	.467
Chuck Knoblauch	2B148 SS6 OF1	R	24	153	602	82	167	27	4	2	41	65	44	29	.277	.346
Pat Meares	SS111	R	24	111	346	33	87	14	3	0	33	7	52	4	.251	.309
1 Mike Pagliarulo	3B79	L	33	83	253	31	74	16	4	3	23	18	34	6	.292	.423
Pedro Munoz	OF102	R	24	104	326	34	76	11	1	13	38	25	97	1	.233	.393
Kirby Puckett	OF139 DH17	R	33	156	622	89	184	39	2	22	89	47	93	8	.296	.474
Shane Mack	OF128	R	29	128	503	66	139	30	4	10	61	41	76	15	.276	.412
Brian Harper	C134 DH7	R	33	147	530	52	161	26	1	12	73	29	29	1	.304	.425
Dave Winfield	DH105 OF31 1B5	R	41	143	547	72	148	27	2	21	76	45	106	2	.271	.442
Jeff Reboulet	SS62 3B35 2B11 OF3 DH1	R	29	109	240	33	62	8	0	1	15	35	37	5	.258	.304
Dave McCarty	OF67 1B36 DH2	L	23	98	350	36	75	15	2	2	21	19	80	2	.214	.286
Chip Hale	2B21 3B19 DH19 1B1 SS1	L	28	69	186	25	62	6	1	3	27	18	17	2	.333	.425
Terry Jorgensen	3B45 1B9 SS6	R	26	59	152	15	34	7	0	1	12	10	21	1	.224	.289
Gene Larkin (LJ)	OF28 1B18 DH3 3B2	B	30	56	144	17	38	7	1	1	19	21	16	0	.264	.347
Leeny Webster	C45 DH1	R	28	49	106	14	21	2	0	1	8	11	8	1	.198	.245
Randy Bush	DH5 1B4 OF1	L	34	35	45	1	7	2	0	0	3	7	13	0	.156	.200
Bernardo Brito	OF10 DH7	R	29	27	54	8	13	2	0	4	9	1	20	0	.241	.500
Scott Stahoviak	3B19	L	23	20	57	1	11	4	0	0	1	3	22	0	.193	.263
J. T. Bruett	OF13	L	26	15	20	2	5	2	0	0	1	1	4	0	.250	.350
Denny Hocking	SS12 2B1	B	23	15	36	7	5	1	0	0	0	6	8	1	.139	.167
Derek Lee	OF13	L	26	15	33	3	5	1	0	0	4	1	4	0	.152	.182
Scott Leius (SJ)	SS9	R	27	10	18	4	3	0	0	0	2	2	4	1	.167	.167
Derek Parks	C7	R	24	7	20	3	4	0	0	0	1	1	2	0	.200	.200
Mike Maksudian (EJ)	1B4 3B1	L	27	5	12	2	2	1	0	0	2	4	2	0	.167	.250
Rich Becker	OF3	B	21	3	7	3	2	2	0	0	0	5	4	1	.286	.571

NAME	T	AGE	W	L	PCT	SV	G	GS	CG	IP	H	BB	SO	SHO	ERA
		28	71	91	.438	44	162	162	5	1444	1591	514	901	3	4.71
Kenin Tapani	R	29	12	15	.444	0	36	35	3	226	243	57	150	1	4.43
Willie Banks	R	24	11	12	.478	0	31	30	0	171	186	78	138	0	4.04
1 Jim Deshaies	L	33	11	13	.458	0	27	27	1	167	159	51	80	0	4.41
Scott Erickson	R	25	8	19	.296	0	34	34	1	219	266	71	116	0	5.19
Mike Trombley	R	26	6	6	.500	2	44	10	0	114	131	41	85	0	4.88
Larry Casian (EJ)	L	27	5	3	.625	1	54	0	0	57	59	14	31	0	3.02
Rick Aguilera	R	31	4	3	.571	34	65	0	0	72	60	14	59	0	3.11
Carl Willis (SJ)	R	32	3	0	1.000	0	53	0	0	58	56	17	44	0	3.10
Eddie Guardado	L	22	3	8	.273	0	19	16	0	95	123	36	46	0	6.18
Mark Guthrie (SJ)	L	27	2	1	.667	0	22	0	0	21	20	16	15	0	4.71
2 Greg Brummett	R	26	2	1	.667	0	5	5	0	27	29	15	10	0	5.74
Brett Merriman	R	26	1	1	.500	0	19	0	0	27	36	23	14	0	9.67
Mike Hartley	R	31	1	2	.333	1	53	0	0	81	86	36	57	0	4.00
George Tsamis	L	26	1	3	.333	0	41	0	0	68	86	27	30	0	6.19
Pat Mahomes	R	22	1	5	.167	0	12	5	0	37	47	16	23	0	7.71
Rich Garces	R	22	0	0	—	0	3	0	0	4	4	2	3	0	0.00

OAKLAND 7th 68-94 .420 26   TONY LaRUSSA

Name	G by Pos	B	AGE	G	AB	R	H	2B	3B	HR	RBI	BB	SO	SB	BA	SA
TOTALS			28	162	5543	715	1408	260	21	158	679	622	1048	131	.254	.394
Mark McGwire (FJ)	1B25	R	29	27	84	16	28	6	0	9	24	21	19	0	.333	.726
Brent Gates	2B139	R	23	139	535	64	155	29	2	7	69	56	75	7	.290	.391
Mike Bordick	SS159 2B1	R	27	159	546	60	136	21	2	3	48	60	58	0	.249	.311
Craig Paquette	3B104 OF1 DH1	R	24	105	393	35	86	20	4	12	46	14	108	4	.219	.382
Ruben Sierra	OF133 DH25	B	27	158	630	77	147	23	5	22	101	52	97	25	.233	.390
Dave Henderson	OF76 DH28	R	34	107	382	37	84	19	0	20	53	32	113	0	.220	.427
1 Rickey Henderson	OF74 DH16	R	34	90	318	77	104	19	1	17	47	85	46	31	.327	.553
Terry Steinbach (BW)	C86 1B15 DH6	R	31	104	389	47	111	19	1	10	43	25	65	3	.285	.416
Troy Neel	DH85 1B34	L	27	123	427	59	124	21	0	19	63	49	101	3	.290	.473
Mike Aldrete	1B59 OF20 DH6	L	32	95	255	40	68	13	1	10	33	34	45	1	.267	.443
Lance Blankenship	OF66 2B19 1B6 DH5 SS2	R	29	94	252	43	48	8	1	2	23	67	64	13	.190	.254
Scott Hemond	C75 OF6 DH3 1B2 2B1	R	27	91	215	31	55	16	0	6	26	32	55	14	.256	.414
Jerry Browne (BH)	OF56 3B13 2B3 1B2	B	27	76	260	27	65	13	0	2	19	22	17	4	.250	.323
1 Kevin Seitzer	3B46 1B24 OF3 DH3 2B2 SS1 P1	R	31	73	255	24	65	10	2	4	27	27	33	4	.255	.357
Scott Brosius	OF46 1B11 3B10 SS6 DH2	R	26	70	213	26	53	10	1	6	25	14	37	6	.249	.390
Scott Lydy	OF38 DH2	R	24	41	102	11	23	5	0	2	7	8	39	2	.225	.333
Dale Sveum	1B14 3B7 2B4 DH2 SS1 OF1	R	29	30	79	12	14	2	1	2	6	16	21	0	.177	.304
Eric Fox	OF26 DH2	B	29	28	56	5	8	1	0	1	5	2	7	0	.143	.214
Kurt Abbott	OF13 SS6 2B2	R	24	20	61	11	15	1	0	3	9	3	20	2	.246	.410
Henry Mercedes	C18 DH1	R	23	20	47	5	10	2	0	0	3	2	15	1	.213	.255
Marcos Armas	1B12 DH2 OF1	R	23	15	31	7	6	2	0	1	1	1	12	1	.194	.355
Eric Helfand	C5	L	24	8	13	1	3	0	0	0	1	0	1	0	.231	.231

NAME	T	AGE	W	L	PCT	SV	G	GS	CG	IP	H	BB	SO	SHO	ERA
		31	68	94	.420	42	162	162	8	1452	1551	680	864	2	4.90
Bobby Witt	R	29	14	13	.519	0	35	33	5	220	226	91	131	4	4.21
Bob Welch	R	36	9	11	.450	0	30	28	0	167	208	56	63	0	5.29
Todd Van Poppel	R	21	6	6	.500	0	16	16	0	84	76	62	47	0	5.04
Ron Darling	R	32	5	9	.357	0	31	29	3	178	198	72	95	0	5.16
Kelly Downs	R	32	5	10	.333	0	42	12	0	120	135	60	66	0	5.64
1 Joe Boever	R	32	4	2	.667	0	42	0	0	79	87	33	49	0	3.86
Goose Gossage	R	41	4	5	.444	1	39	0	0	48	49	26	40	0	4.53
Steve Karsay	R	21	3	3	.500	0	8	8	0	49	49	16	33	0	4.04
Edwin Nunez	R	30	3	6	.333	1	56	0	0	76	89	29	58	0	3.81
Shawn Hillegas	R	28	3	0	.333	0	18	11	0	61	78	33	29	0	6.97
Vince Horsman	L	26	2	1	1.000	0	40	0	0	25	25	15	17	0	5.40
Dennis Eckersley	R	38	2	4	.333	36	64	0	0	67	67	13	80	0	4.16
1 Storm Davis	R	31	2	6	.250	0	19	8	0	62	68	33	37	0	6.18
John Briscoe	R	25	1	0	1.000	0	17	0	0	25	26	26	24	0	8.03
Miguel Jimenez	R	23	1	0	1.000	0	5	4	0	27	27	16	13	0	4.00
Curt Young (SJ)	L	33	1	1	.500	0	3	3	0	15	14	6	4	0	4.30
Roger Smithberg	R	27	1	2	.333	1	13	0	0	20	13	7	4	0	2.75
Rick Honeycutt (BW)	L	39	1	4	.200	1	52	0	0	42	30	20	21	0	2.81
Mike Mohler	L	24	1	6	.143	0	42	9	0	64	57	44	42	0	5.60
Kevin Campbell	R	28	0	0	—	0	11	0	0	16	20	11	9	0	5.19
Joe Slusarski	R	26	0	0	—	0	2	1	0	9	9	11	1	0	5.19
1 Kevin Seitzer	R	31	0	0	—	0	1	0	0	0.1	0	1	0	0	0.00
Todd Revenig 24 (EJ)															

1993 CHAMPIONSHIPS

LINE SCORES

Team	1	2	3	4	5	6	7	8	9	10	11	12	R	H	E

AMERICAN LEAGUE CHAMPIONSHIPS: TORONTO (EAST) 4 CHICAGO (WEST) 2

Game 1 October 5 at Chicago

TOR	0	0	0	2	3	0	2	0	0				7	17	1
CHI	0	0	0	3	0	0	0	0	0				3	6	1

Guzman, Cox(7), Ward(9)   McDowell, DeLeon(7), Radinsky(8), McCaskill(9)

Game 2 October 6 at Chicago

TOR	1	0	0	2	0	0	0	0	0				3	8	0
CHI	1	0	0	0	0	0	0	0	0				1	7	2

Stewart, Leiter(7), Ward(9)   Fernandez, Hernandez(9)

Game 3 October 8 at Toronto

CHI	0	0	5	1	0	0	0	0	0				6	12	0
TOR	0	0	1	0	0	0	0	0	0				1	7	1

Alvarez   Hentgen, Cox(4), Eichhorn(7), Castillo(9)

Game 4 October 9 at Toronto

CHI	0	2	0	0	0	3	1	0	1				7	11	0
TOR	0	0	3	0	0	0	1	0	0				4	9	0

Bere, **Belcher**(3), McCaskill(7), Radinsky(8), Hernandez(9)   Stottlemyre, Leiter(7), Timlin(7)

Game 5 October 10 at Toronto

CHI	0	0	0	0	1	0	0	2	0				3	5	1
TOR	1	1	1	1	0	0	1	0	X				5	14	0

McDowell, DeLeon(3), Radinsky(7), Hernandez(7)   Guzman, Castillo(9), Ward(9)

Game 6 October 12 at Chicago

TOR	0	2	0	1	0	0	0	0	3				6	10	0
CHI	0	0	2	0	0	0	0	0	1				3	5	3

Stewart, Ward(8)   Fernandez, McCaskill(8), Radinsky(9), Hernandez(9)

COMPOSITE BATTING

NAME	POS	G	AB	R	H	2B	3B	HR	RBI	BA
TORONTO										
Totals		6	216	26	65	8	3	2	24	.301
White	CF	6	27	3	12	1	1	1	2	.444
Carter	RF	6	27	2	7	0	0	0	2	.259
Henderson	LF	6	25	4	3	2	0	0	0	.120
Alomar	2B	6	24	3	7	1	0	0	4	.292
Borders	C	6	24	1	6	1	0	0	3	.250
Molitor	DH	6	23	7	9	2	1	1	5	.391
Olerud	1B	6	23	5	8	1	1	0	3	.348
Fernandez	SS	6	22	1	7	0	0	0	1	.318
Sprague	3B	6	21	0	6	0	1	0	4	.286
CHICAGO										
Totals		6	194	23	46	6	1	5	22	.237
Raines	LF	6	27	5	12	3	0	0	1	.444
Burks	RF	6	23	4	7	1	0	1	3	.304
Johnson	CF	6	23	2	5	1	1	1	6	.217
Guillen	SS	6	22	4	6	1	0	0	2	.273
Cora	2B	6	22	1	3	0	0	0	1	.136
Ventura	3B-1B	6	20	2	4	0	0	1	5	.200
Thomas	1B-DH	6	17	2	6	0	0	1	3	.353
Karkovice	C	6	15	0	0	0	0	0	0	.000
Jackson	DH	5	10	1	0	0	0	0	0	.000
Pasqua	1B	2	6	1	0	0	0	0	0	.000
Newson	DH	2	5	1	1	0	0	0	1	.200
LaValliere	C	2	3	0	1	0	0	0	0	.333
Grebeck	3B	1	1	0	0	0	0	0	0	.100

COMPOSITE PITCHING

NAME	G	IP	H	BB	SO	W	L	SV	ERA
TORONTO									
Totals	6	54	46	32	43	4	2	2	3.67
Stewart	2	13.1	8	8	8	2	0	0	2.03
Guzman	2	13	8	9	9	2	0	0	2.08
Stottlemyre	1	6	6	4	4	0	1	0	7.50
Cox	2	5	3	2	5	0	0	0	0.00
Ward	4	4.2	4	3	8	0	0	2	5.79
Hentgen	1	3	9	2	3	0	1	0	18.00
Leiter	2	2.2	4	2	2	0	0	0	3.86
Timlin	1	2.1	3	0	2	0	0	0	3.86
Castillo	2	2	1	1	1	0	0	0	0.00
Eichhorn	1	2	1	1	0	0	0	0	0.00
CHICAGO									
Totals	6	53	65	21	36	2	4	1	3.57
Fernandez	2	15	15	6	10	0	2	0	1.80
McDowell	2	9	18	5	6	0	2	0	10.00
Alvarez	1	9	7	2	6	1	0	0	1.00
DeLeon	2	4.2	7	1	6	0	0	0	1.93
Hernandez	4	4	4	0	1	0	0	0	0.00
McCaskill	3	3.2	3	1	0	0	0	0	0.00
Belcher	1	3.2	3	3	1	0	0	0	2.45
Bere	1	2.1	5	2	3	0	0	0	11.57
Radinsky	4	1.2	3	1	1	0	0	0	10.80

PHILADELPHIA   1st 97-65 .599   JIM FREGOSI

Name	G by Pos	B	AGE	G	AB	R	H	2B	3B	HR	RBI	BB	SO	SB	BA	SA
TOTALS			29	162	5685	877	1555	297	51	156	811	665	1049	91	.274	.426
John Kruk	1B144	L	32	150	535	100	169	33	5	14	85	111	87	6	.316	.475
Mickey Morandini	2B111	L	27	120	425	57	105	19	9	3	33	34	73	13	.247	.355
Kevin Stocker	SS70	B	23	70	259	46	84	12	3	2	31	30	43	5	.324	.417
Dave Hollins	3B143	B	27	143	543	104	148	30	4	18	93	85	109	2	.273	.442
Jim Eisenreich	OF137 1B1	L	34	153	362	51	115	17	4	7	54	26	36	5	.318	.445
Lenny Dykstra	OF160	L	30	161	637	143	194	44	6	19	66	129	64	37	.305	.482
Milt Thompson	OF106	L	34	129	340	42	89	14	2	4	44	40	57	9	.262	.350
Darren Daulton	C146	L	31	147	510	90	131	35	4	24	105	117	111	5	.257	.482
Mariano Duncan	2B65 SS59	R	30	124	496	68	140	26	4	11	73	12	88	6	.282	.417
Pete Incaviglia	OF97	R	29	116	368	60	101	16	3	24	89	21	82	1	.274	.530
Wes Chamberlain	OF76	R	27	96	284	34	80	20	2	12	45	17	51	2	.282	.493
Ricky Jordan	1B33	R	28	90	159	21	46	4	1	5	18	8	32	0	.289	.421
Kim Batiste	3B58 SS24	R	25	79	156	14	44	7	1	5	29	3	29	0	.282	.436
Todd Pratt (NJ)	C26	R	26	33	87	8	25	6	0	5	13	5	19	0	.287	.529
Ruben Amaro	OF16	B	28	25	48	7	16	2	2	1	6	6	5	0	.333	.521
1 Juan Bell	SS22	B	25	24	65	5	13	6	1	0	7	5	12	0	.200	.323
Tony Longmire	OF2	L	24	11	13	1	3	0	0	0	1	0	1	0	.231	.231
Joe Millette	SS7 3B3	R	26	10	10	3	2	0	0	0	2	1	2	0	.200	.200
Jeff Manto	3B6 SS1	R	28	8	18	0	1	0	0	0	0	0	3	0	.056	.056
1 Doug Lindsey	C2	R	25	2	2	0	1	0	0	0	0	0	1	0	.500	.500

NAME	T	AGE	W	L	PCT	SV	G	GS	CG	IP	H	BB	SO	SHO	ERA
		30	97	65	.599	46	162	162	24	1473	1419	573	1117	11	3.95
Tommy Greene	R	26	16	4	.800	0	31	30	7	200	175	62	167	2	3.42
Curt Schilling	R	26	16	7	.696	0	34	34	7	235	234	57	186	2	4.02
Ben Rivera	R	25	13	9	.591	0	30	28	1	163	175	85	123	1	5.02
Terry Mulholland (PJ)	L	30	12	9	.571	0	29	28	7	191	177	40	116	2	3.25
Danny Jackson	L	31	12	11	.522	0	32	32	2	210	214	80	120	1	3.77
David West	L	28	6	4	.600	2	76	0	0	86	60	51	87	0	2.92
2 Roger Mason	R	34	5	5	.500	0	34	0	0	50	47	16	32	0	4.89
1 Jose DeLeon	R	32	3	0	1.000	0	24	3	0	47	39	27	34	0	3.26
Bobby Thigpen	R	29	3	1	.750	0	17	0	0	19	23	9	10	0	6.05
Larry Andersen	R	40	3	2	.600	0	64	0	0	62	54	21	67	0	2.92
Mitch Williams	L	28	3	7	.300	43	65	0	0	62	56	44	60	0	3.34
1 Bob Ayrault	R	27	1	0	1.000	0	10	0	0	10	18	10	8	0	9.58
1 Donn Pall	R	31	1	0	1.000	0	8	0	0	18	15	3	11	0	2.55
1 Mark Davis	L	32	1	2	.333	0	25	0	0	31	35	24	28	0	5.17
Mike Williams	R	24	1	3	.250	0	17	4	0	51	50	22	33	0	5.29
1 Tim Mauser	R	26	0	0	—	0	8	0	0	16	15	7	14	0	4.96
Tyler Green	R	23	0	0	—	0	3	2	0	7	16	5	7	0	7.36
Brad Brink	R	28	0	0	—	0	2	0	0	6	3	3	8	0	3.00
Paul Fletcher	R	26	0	0	—	0	1	0	0	0.1	0	1	0	0	0.00
Kevin Foster	R	24	0	1	.000	0	1	1	0	7	13	7	6	0	14.85
Jose DeJesus 28 (SJ)															

MONTREAL   2nd 94-68 .580 3   FELIPE ALOU

Name	G by Pos	B	AGE	G	AB	R	H	2B	3B	HR	RBI	BB	SO	SB	BA	SA
TOTALS			26	163	5493	732	1410	270	36	122	682	542	860	228	.257	.386
Greg Colbrunn (EJ)	1B61	R	23	70	153	15	39	9	0	4	23	4	33	4	.255	.392
Delino DeShields (RJ)	2B123	L	24	123	481	75	142	17	7	2	29	72	64	43	.295	.372
Wil Cordero	SS134 3B2	R	21	138	475	56	118	32	2	10	58	34	60	12	.248	.387
Sean Berry	3B96	R	27	122	299	50	78	15	2	14	49	41	70	12	.261	.465
Larry Walker	OF132 1B4	R	26	138	490	85	130	24	5	22	86	80	76	29	.265	.469
Marquis Grissom	OF157	R	26	157	630	104	188	27	2	19	95	52	76	53	.298	.438
Moises Alou	OF136	R	26	136	482	70	138	29	6	18	85	38	53	17	.286	.493
Darrin Fletcher	C127	L	26	133	396	33	101	20	1	9	60	34	40	0	.255	.379
Mike Lansing	3B81 SS51 2B25	R	25	141	491	64	141	29	1	3	45	46	56	23	.287	.369
Lou Frazier	OF60 1B8 2B1	R	28	112	189	27	54	7	1	1	16	16	24	17	.286	.349
John Vander Wal	1B42 OF38	L	27	106	215	34	50	7	4	5	30	27	30	6	.233	.372
Frank Bolick	1B51 3B24	B	27	95	213	25	45	13	0	4	24	23	37	1	.211	.329
Tim Spehr	C49	R	26	53	87	14	20	6	0	2	10	6	20	2	.230	.368
Tim Laker	C43	R	23	43	86	3	17	2	1	0	7	2	16	2	.198	.244
Randy Ready	2B28 1B13 3B3	R	33	40	134	22	34	8	1	1	10	23	8	2	.254	.351
Oreste Marrero	1B32	R	23	32	81	10	17	5	1	0	4	14	16	1	.210	.333
Rondell White	OF21	R	21	23	73	9	19	3	1	2	15	7	16	1	.260	.411
2 Tim McIntosh	OF7 C5	R	27	20	21	2	2	0	0	0	2	0	7	0	.095	.143
Joe Siddall	C15 1B1 OF1	L	25	19	20	0	2	1	0	0	1	1	5	0	.100	.150
Derrick White	1B17	R	23	17	49	6	11	3	0	2	4	2	12	2	.224	.408
Ted Wood	OF8	L	26	13	26	4	5	1	0	0	3	3	3	0	.192	.231
1 Archi Cianfrocco	1B11	R	26	12	17	3	4	1	0	1	1	0	5	0	.235	.471
Cliff Floyd	1B10	L	20	10	31	3	7	0	0	1	2	0	9	0	.226	.323
Curtis Pride	OF2	L	24	10	9	3	4	1	1	1	5	0	3	1	.444	1.111
Matt Stairs	OF1	L	25	6	8	1	3	1	0	0	2	0	1	0	.375	.500
Charlie Montoyo	2B3	R	27	4	5	1	2	1	0	0	3	0	1	0	.400	.600

NAME	T	AGE	W	L	PCT	SV	G	GS	CG	IP	H	BB	SO	SHO	ERA
		27	94	68	.580	61	163	163	8	1457	1369	521	934	7	3.55
Dennis Martinez	R	38	15	9	.625	1	35	34	2	225	211	64	138	0	3.85
Jeff Fassero	R	30	12	5	.706	1	56	15	1	150	119	54	140	0	2.29
John Wetteland	R	26	9	3	.750	43	70	0	0	85	58	28	113	0	1.37
Ken Hill	R	27	9	7	.563	0	28	28	2	184	163	74	90	0	3.23
Chris Nabholz (AJ)	L	26	9	8	.529	0	26	21	1	117	100	63	74	0	4.09
Kirk Rueter	L	22	8	0	1.000	0	14	14	1	86	85	18	31	0	2.73
2 Tim Scott	R	26	5	2	.714	1	32	0	0	34	31	19	35	0	3.71
Mel Rojas	R	26	5	8	.385	10	66	0	0	88	80	30	48	0	2.95
Jimmy Jones (EJ)	R	29	4	1	.800	0	12	6	0	40	47	9	21	0	6.35
Gil Heredia	R	26	4	2	.667	2	20	9	1	57	66	14	40	0	3.92
Denis Boucher	L	25	3	1	.750	0	5	5	0	28	24	3	14	0	1.91
1 Mike Gardiner	R	27	2	3	.400	0	24	2	0	38	40	19	21	0	5.21
1 Kent Bottenfield	R	24	2	5	.286	0	23	11	0	83	93	33	33	0	4.12
Brian Barnes	L	26	2	6	.250	3	52	8	0	100	105	48	60	0	4.41
Jeff Shaw	R	26	2	7	.222	0	55	8	0	96	91	32	50	0	4.14
Pete Young	R	25	1	0	1.000	0	9	0	0	9	5	1	4	0	3.38
2 Scott Aldred (EJ)	L	25	1	0	1.000	0	5	0	0	9	4	6	0	0	6.75
1 Butch Henry	R	24	1	1	.500	0	10	1	0	18	18	4	6	0	3.93
Bruce Walton	R	30	0	0	—	0	6	0	0	11	3	0	9	0	9.53
Sergio Valdez	R	28	0	0	—	0	2	0	0	6	1	3	0	0	9.00
Brian Looney	L	23	0	0	—	0	3	0	0	2	4	6	0	0	3.00
Bill Risley	R	26	0	0	—	0	2	0	0	3	2	2	2	0	6.00

ST LOUIS   3rd 87-75 .537 10   JOE TORRE

Name	G by Pos	B	AGE	G	AB	R	H	2B	3B	HR	RBI	BB	SO	SB	BA	SA
TOTALS			28	162	5551	758	1508	262	34	118	724	588	882	153	.272	.395
Gregg Jefferies	1B140 2B1	B	25	142	544	89	186	24	3	16	83	62	32	46	.342	.485
Luis Alicea	2B96 OF4 3B1	B	27	115	362	50	101	19	3	3	46	47	54	11	.279	.373
Ozzie Smith	SS134	B	38	141	545	75	157	22	6	1	53	43	18	21	.288	.356
Todd Zeile	3B153	R	27	157	571	82	158	36	1	17	103	70	76	5	.277	.433
Mark Whiten	OF148	B	26	152	562	81	142	13	4	25	99	58	110	15	.253	.423
Ray Lankford	OF121	L	26	127	407	64	97	17	3	7	45	81	111	14	.238	.346
Bernard Gilkey	OF134 1B3	R	26	137	557	99	170	40	5	16	70	56	66	15	.305	.481
Tom Pagnozzi (KJ)	C92	R	30	92	330	31	85	15	1	7	41	19	30	1	.258	.373
Rod Brewer	OF33 1B32 P1	L	27	110	147	15	42	8	0	2	20	17	26	1	.286	.381
Gerald Perry	1B15 OF1	L	32	96	98	21	33	5	0	4	16	18	23	1	.337	.510
Erik Pappas	C63 OF16 1B2	R	27	82	228	25	63	12	0	1	28	35	35	1	.276	.342
Geronimo Pena	2B64	B	26	74	254	34	65	19	2	5	30	25	71	13	.256	.406
Brian Jordan (SJ)	OF65	R	26	67	223	33	69	10	6	10	44	12	35	6	.309	.543
Tracy Woodson	3B28 1B11	R	30	62	77	4	16	2	0	2	14	1	14	0	.208	.234
Jose Oquendo (EJ)	SS22 2B16	R	29	46	73	7	15	0	0	0	4	12	8	0	.205	.205
Tim Jones	SS21 2B7	L	30	29	61	13	16	6	0	0	1	9	8	2	.262	.361
Stan Royer	3B10 1B2	R	25	24	46	4	14	2	0	1	8	2	14	0	.304	.413
Hector Villanueva	C17	R	28	17	55	7	8	1	0	3	9	4	17	0	.145	.327
Lonnie Maclin	OF5	L	26	12	13	2	1	0	0	0	1	0	5	1	.077	.077
Tripp Cromer	SS9	R	25	10	23	1	2	0	0	0	0	1	6	0	.087	.087
Ozzie Canseco	OF5	R	28	8	17	0	3	0	0	0	0	0	5	0	.176	.176
Marc Ronan	C6	L	23	6	12	0	1	0	0	0	1	0	5	0	.083	.083

NAME	T	AGE	W	L	PCT	SV	G	GS	CG	IP	H	BB	SO	SHO	ERA
		29	87	75	.537	54	162	162	5	1453	1553	383	775	7	4.09
Bob Tewksbury	R	32	17	10	.630	0	32	32	2	214	258	20	97	0	3.83
Rene Arocha	R	27	11	8	.579	0	32	29	1	188	197	31	96	0	3.78
Donovan Osborne (SJ)	L	24	10	7	.588	0	26	26	1	156	153	47	83	0	3.76
1 Joe Magrane	L	28	8	10	.444	0	22	20	0	116	127	37	38	0	4.97
Mike Perez (SJ)	R	26	7	2	.778	7	65	0	0	73	65	20	58	0	2.48
Rheal Cormier	L	26	7	6	.538	0	38	21	1	145	163	27	75	0	4.33
Allen Watson	L	22	6	7	.462	0	16	15	0	86	90	28	49	0	4.60
Omar Olivares	R	25	5	3	.625	1	58	9	0	119	134	54	63	0	4.17
Rob Murphy	L	33	5	7	.417	1	73	0	0	65	73	20	41	0	4.87
Les Lancaster (EJ)	R	31	4	1	.800	0	50	0	0	61	56	21	36	0	2.93
Lee Guetterman	L	34	3	3	.500	1	40	0	0	46	41	16	19	0	2.93
1 Lee Smith	R	35	2	4	.333	43	55	0	0	50	49	9	49	0	4.50
Paul Kilgus (BF)	L	31	1	0	1.000	1	18	0	0	18	21	8	21	0	0.63
1 Tom Urbani	L	25	1	3	.250	0	18	9	0	62	73	26	33	0	4.65
Rich Batchelor	R	26	0	0	—	0	10	0	0	14	3	4	8	0	2.10
Steve Dixon	L	23	0	0	—	0	3	0	0	3	7	5	2	0	33.75
Rod Brewer	L	27	0	0	—	0	1	0	0	3	3	0	0	0	45.00
2 Todd Burns	R	29	0	4	.000	0	24	0	0	31	32	9	10	0	6.16

CHICAGO   4th 84-78 .519 13   JIM LEFEBVRE

Name	G by Pos	B	AGE	G	AB	R	H	2B	3B	HR	RBI	BB	SO	SB	BA	SA
TOTALS			28	163	5627	738	1521	259	32	161	706	446	923	100	.270	.414
Mark Grace	1B154	L	29	155	594	86	193	39	4	14	98	71	32	8	.325	.475
Ryne Sandberg	2B115	R	33	117	456	67	141	20	9	9	45	37	62	9	.309	.412
Rey Sanchez	SS98	R	25	105	344	35	97	11	2	0	28	15	22	1	.282	.326
Steve Buechele	3B129 1B6	R	31	133	460	53	125	27	2	15	65	48	87	1	.272	.437
Sammy Sosa	OF158	R	24	159	598	92	156	25	5	33	93	38	135	36	.261	.485
Dwight Smith (BG)	OF89	L	29	111	310	51	93	17	5	11	35	25	51	8	.300	.494
Derrick May	OF122	L	24	128	465	62	137	25	2	10	77	31	41	10	.295	.422
Rick Wilkins	C133	L	26	136	446	78	135	23	1	30	73	50	99	2	.303	.561
Jose Vizcaino	SS81 3B44 2B34	B	25	151	551	74	158	19	4	4	54	46	71	12	.287	.358
Willie Wilson	OF82	B	37	105	221	29	57	11	3	1	11	11	40	7	.258	.348
1 Candy Maldonado	OF41	R	32	70	140	8	26	5	0	3	15	13	40	0	.186	.286
Eric Yelding	2B32 3B7 SS1 OF1	R	28	69	108	14	22	5	1	1	10	11	22	3	.204	.296
Kevin Roberson	OF51	B	25	62	180	23	34	6	3	9	27	12	48	0	.189	.372
Steve Lake	C41	R	36	44	120	11	27	6	0	5	13	4	19	0	.225	.400
Doug Jennings	1B10	L	28	42	52	8	13	3	1	2	8	9	20	0	.250	.462
2 Glenallen Hill	OF21	R	28	31	87	14	30	7	0	10	22	6	21	1	.345	.770
Tommy Shields	2B7 3B7 1B1 OF1	R	29	30	34	4	6	1	0	0	1	2	10	0	.176	.206
2 Karl Rhodes	OF14	L	24	15	52	12	15	2	1	1	7	11	9	2	.288	.538
Matt Walbeck	C11	B	23	11	30	2	6	2	0	0	6	1	6	0	.200	.367
Eddie Zambrano	OF4 1B2	R	27	8	17	1	5	0	0	0	2	0	6	0	.294	.294
Shawon Dunston (XJ)	SS2	R	30	7	10	3	4	2	0	0	2	0	2	0	.400	.600

NAME	T	AGE	W	L	PCT	SV	G	GS	CG	IP	H	BB	SO	SHO	ERA
		28	84	78	.519	56	163	163	8	1450	1514	470	905	5	4.18
Greg Hibbard	L	28	15	11	.577	0	31	31	1	191	209	47	82	0	3.96
Jose Guzman	R	30	12	10	.545	0	30	30	2	191	188	74	163	1	4.34
Jose Bautista	R	28	10	3	.769	2	58	7	1	112	105	27	63	0	2.82
Mike Harkey	R	26	10	10	.500	0	28	28	1	157	187	43	67	0	5.26
Mike Morgan	R	33	10	15	.400	0	32	32	1	208	206	74	111	1	4.03
Shawn Boskie	R	26	5	3	.625	0	39	2	0	66	63	21	39	0	3.43
Frank Castillo	R	24	5	8	.385	0	29	25	2	141	162	39	84	0	4.84
Bob Scanlan	R	26	4	5	.444	0	70	0	0	75	79	28	44	0	4.54
Dan Plesac	L	31	2	1	.667	0	57	0	0	63	74	21	47	0	4.74
1 Paul Assenmacher	L	32	2	1	.667	0	46	0	0	39	44	13	34	0	3.49
Bill Brennan	R	30	2	1	.667	0	4	0	0	15	16	8	11	0	4.20
Chuck McElroy	L	25	2	2	.500	0	49	0	0	47	51	25	31	0	4.56
Randy Myers	L	30	2	4	.333	53	73	0	0	75	65	26	86	0	3.11
Jim Bullinger	R	27	1	0	1.000	0	15	0	0	17	18	9	10	0	4.32
1 Heathcliff Slocumb	R	27	1	0	1.000	0	10	0	0	11	7	4	4	0	3.38
Turk Wendell	R	26	1	2	.333	0	7	4	0	23	24	8	15	0	4.37
Steve Trachsel	R	22	0	2	.000	0	3	3	0	20	16	3	14	0	4.58
Jessie Hollins 23 (AJ)															

PITTSBURGH 5th 75-87 .463 — JIM LEYLAND

Name	G by Pos	B	AGE	G	AB	R	H	2B	3B	HR	RBI	BB	SO	SB	BA	SA
TOTALS			29	162	5549	707	1482	287	50	110	664	536	972	92	.267	.393
Kevin Young	1B135 3B6	R	24	141	449	38	106	24	3	6	47	36	82	2	.236	.343
Carlos Garcia	2B140 SS3	R	25	141	546	77	147	25	5	12	47	31	67	18	.269	.399
Jay Bell	SS154	R	27	154	604	102	187	32	9	9	51	77	122	16	.310	.437
Jeff King	3B156 2B2 SS2	R	28	158	611	82	180	35	3	9	98	59	54	8	.295	.406
Orlando Merced	OF109 1B42	R	26	137	447	68	140	26	4	8	70	77	64	3	.313	.437
Andy Van Slyke (BC)	OF78	L	32	83	323	42	100	13	4	8	50	24	40	11	.310	.449
Al Martin	OF136	L	25	143	480	85	135	26	8	18	64	42	122	16	.281	.481
Don Slaught	C105	R	34	116	377	34	113	19	2	10	55	29	56	2	.300	.440
Dave Clark	OF91	L	30	110	277	43	75	11	2	11	46	38	58	1	.271	.444
1 Lonnie Smith	OF60	R	37	94	199	35	57	5	4	6	24	43	42	9	.286	.442
Lloyd McClendon	OF61 1B6	R	34	88	181	21	40	11	1	2	19	23	17	0	.221	.326
Tom Foley	2B35 1B12 3B7 SS6	L	33	86	194	18	49	11	1	3	22	11	26	0	.253	.366
Tom Prince	C59	R	28	66	179	14	35	14	0	2	24	13	38	1	.196	.307
John Wehner	OF13 3B3 2B3	R	26	29	35	3	5	0	0	0	0	6	10	0	.143	.143
Andy Tomberlin	OF7	L	26	27	42	4	12	0	1	1	5	2	14	0	.286	.405
Scott Bullett	OF19	L	24	23	55	2	11	0	2	0	4	3	15	3	.200	.273
Will Pennyfeather	OF17	R	25	21	34	4	7	1	0	0	2	0	6	0	.206	.235
Ben Shelton	OF6 1B2	R	23	15	24	3	6	1	0	2	7	3	3	0	.250	.542
Tony Womack	SS6	L	23	15	24	5	2	0	0	0	0	3	3	2	.083	.083
Jerry Goff	C14	R	29	14	37	5	11	2	0	2	6	8	9	0	.297	.514
Midre Cummings	OF11	L	21	13	36	5	4	1	0	0	3	4	9	0	.111	.139
Rich Aude	1B7 OF1	R	21	13	26	1	3	1	0	0	4	1	7	0	.115	.154
Glenn Wilson	OF5	R	34	10	14	0	2	0	0	0	0	0	5	0	.143	.143
1 Mike LaValliere	C1	L	32	1	5	0	1	0	0	0	0	0	0	0	.200	.200

NAME	T	AGE	W	L	PCT	SV	G	GS	CG	IP	H	BB	SO	SHO	ERA
		28	75	87	.463	34	162	162	12	1446	1557	485	832	5	4.77
Bob Walk	R	36	13	14	.481	0	32	32	3	187	214	70	80	0	5.68
Steve Cooke	L	23	10	10	.500	0	32	32	3	211	207	59	132	1	3.89
Blas Minor	R	27	8	6	.571	2	65	0	0	94	94	26	84	0	4.10
Paul Wagner	R	25	8	8	.500	2	44	17	1	141	143	42	114	1	4.27
Tim Wakefield	R	26	6	11	.353	0	24	20	3	128	145	75	59	2	5.61
Jeff Ballard	L	29	4	1	.800	0	25	5	0	54	70	15	16	0	4.86
Randy Tomlin (EJ)	R	27	4	8	.333	0	18	18	1	98	109	15	44	0	4.85
Mark Petkovsek	R	27	3	0	1.000	0	26	0	0	32	43	9	14	0	6.96
1 Stan Belinda	R	27	3	1	.750	19	40	0	0	42	35	11	30	0	3.61
Dave Otto	L	28	3	4	.429	0	28	8	0	68	85	28	30	0	5.03
Denny Neagle	L	24	3	5	.375	1	50	7	0	81	82	37	73	0	5.31
Zane Smith (SJ)	L	32	3	7	.300	0	14	14	1	83	97	22	32	0	4.55
Tony Menendez	R	28	2	0	1.000	0	14	0	0	21	20	4	13	0	3.00
Joel Johnston	R	26	2	4	.333	2	33	0	0	53	38	19	31	0	3.38
Freddie Toliver	R	32	1	0	1.000	0	12	0	0	22	20	8	14	0	3.74
Dennis Moeller	L	25	1	0	1.000	0	10	0	0	16	26	7	13	0	9.92
Mark Dewey	R	28	1	2	.333	7	21	0	0	27	14	10	14	0	2.36
Dan Miceli	R	22	0	0	—	0	9	0	0	5	6	3	4	0	5.08
Brian Shouse	L	24	0	0	—	0	6	0	0	4	7	2	3	0	9.00
Paul Miller	R	28	0	0	—	3	2	0	0	10	15	2	2	0	5.40
Rich Robertson	L	24	0	1	.000	0	9	0	0	9	15	4	5	0	6.00
John Hope	R	22	0	2	.000	0	7	7	0	38	47	8	8	0	4.03
John Candelaria	L	39	0	3	.000	1	24	0	0	20	25	9	17	0	8.24
Alejandro Pena 34 (EJ)															

FLORIDA 6th 64-98 .395 33 — RENE LACHEMANN

Name	G by Pos	B	AGE	G	AB	R	H	2B	3B	HR	RBI	BB	SO	SB	BA	SA
TOTALS			27	162	5475	581	1356	197	31	94	542	498	1054	117	.248	.346
Orestes Destrade	1B152	B	31	153	569	61	145	20	3	20	87	58	130	0	.255	.406
Bret Barberie (EJ-KJ)	2B97	B	25	99	375	45	104	16	2	5	33	33	58	2	.277	.371
Walt Weiss	SS153	B	29	158	500	50	133	14	2	1	39	79	73	7	.266	.308
2 Gary Sheffield	3B65	R	24	72	236	33	69	8	3	10	37	29	34	12	.292	.479
Darrell Whitmore	OF69	L	24	76	250	24	51	8	2	4	19	10	72	4	.204	.300
Chuck Carr	OF139	B	25	142	551	75	147	19	2	4	41	49	74	58	.267	.330
Jeff Conine	OF147 1B43	R	27	162	595	75	174	24	3	12	79	52	135	2	.292	.403
Benito Santiago	C136 OF1	R	28	139	469	49	108	19	6	13	50	37	88	10	.230	.380
Greg Briley	OF67	L	28	120	177	17	33	6	0	3	12	12	42	6	.194	.282
Rich Renteria	2B45 3B25 OF1	R	31	103	263	27	67	9	2	2	30	21	31	0	.255	.327
Alex Arias	2B30 3B22 SS18	R	25	96	249	27	67	5	1	2	20	27	18	1	.269	.321
1 Dave Magadan	3B63 1B2	L	30	66	227	22	65	12	0	4	29	44	30	0	.286	.392
Junior Felix	OF52	B	25	57	214	25	51	11	1	7	22	10	50	2	.238	.397
2 Henry Cotto	OF46	R	32	54	135	15	40	7	0	3	14	3	18	11	.296	.415
Bob Natal	C38	R	27	41	117	3	25	4	1	1	6	6	22	1	.214	.291
Matias Carrillo	OF16	L	30	24	55	4	14	6	0	3	1	7	9	0	.255	.364
Monty Fariss	OF8	R	25	18	29	3	5	2	1	0	2	5	13	0	.172	.310
Scott Pose	OF10	L	26	15	41	0	8	2	0	0	3	4	9	1	.195	.244
Geronimo Berroa	OF9	R	28	14	34	3	4	1	0	0	0	2	7	0	.118	.147
Carl Everett	OF8	B	22	11	19	0	2	0	0	0	0	1	5	1	.105	.105
Steve Decker (XJ)	C5	R	27	8	15	0	0	0	0	0	1	3	3	0	.000	.000
Nigel Wilson	OF3	L	23	7	16	0	0	0	0	0	0	0	11	0	.000	.000
Gus Polidor	2B1 3B1	R	31	7	6	0	1	0	0	0	1	0	2	0	.167	.333
Mitch Lyden	C2	R	28	6	10	2	3	0	0	1	1	0	3	0	.300	.600
Terry McGriff	C3	R	29	3	7	0	0	0	0	0	0	0	1	2	.000	.000

NAME	T	AGE	W	L	PCT	SV	G	GS	CG	IP	H	BB	SO	SHO	ERA
		29	64	98	.395	48	162	162	4	1440	1437	598	945	5	4.13
Chris Hammond	L	27	11	12	.478	0	32	32	1	191	207	66	108	0	4.66
Charlie Hough	R	45	9	16	.360	0	34	34	0	204	202	71	126	0	4.27
Jack Armstrong	R	28	9	17	.346	0	36	33	0	196	210	78	118	0	4.49
Ryan Bowen (KJ)	R	25	8	12	.400	0	27	27	2	157	156	87	98	1	4.42
Richie Lewis	R	27	6	3	.667	0	57	0	0	77	68	43	65	0	3.26
Luis Aquino (SJ)	R	28	6	8	.429	0	38	13	0	111	115	40	67	0	3.42
Matt Turner	R	26	4	5	.444	0	55	0	0	68	55	26	59	0	2.91
Pat Rapp	R	25	4	6	.400	0	16	16	1	94	101	39	57	0	4.02
1 Trevor Hoffman	R	25	2	4	.333	3	28	0	0	36	24	19	26	0	3.28
David Weathers	R	23	2	3	.400	0	14	6	0	46	57	13	34	0	5.12
2 Robb Nen	R	23	1	0	1.000	0	15	1	0	33	35	20	27	0	7.02
Bob McClure	L	41	1	1	.500	0	14	0	0	6	13	5	6	0	7.11
Bryan Harvey	R	30	1	5	.167	45	59	0	0	69	45	13	73	0	1.70
2 Rich Rodriguez	L	30	0	1	.000	1	36	0	0	46	39	24	21	0	4.11
1 Cris Carpenter	R	28	0	1	.000	0	29	0	0	37	29	13	26	0	3.28
Joe Klink	L	31	0	2	.000	0	59	0	0	38	37	24	22	0	5.02
Jim Corsi (SJ)	R	31	0	2	.000	0	15	0	0	20	28	10	7	0	6.64
John Johnstone	R	24	0	2	.000	0	7	0	0	11	16	7	5	0	5.91
Scott Chiamparino 26 (EJ)															

NEW YORK 7th 59-103 .364 38 — JEFF TORBORG 13-25 .342 DALLAS GREEN 46-78 .371

Name	G by Pos	B	AGE	G	AB	R	H	2B	3B	HR	RBI	BB	SO	SB	BA	SA
TOTALS			30	162	5448	672	1350	228	37	158	632	448	870	79	.248	.390
Eddie Murray	1B154	B	37	154	610	77	174	28	1	27	100	40	61	2	.285	.467
Jeff Kent	2B127 3B12 SS2	R	25	140	496	65	134	24	0	21	80	30	88	4	.270	.446
Tim Bogar (WJ)	SS66 3B7 2B6	R	26	78	205	19	50	13	0	3	25	14	29	0	.244	.351
Howard Johnson (BG)	3B67	B	32	72	235	32	56	8	2	7	26	43	43	6	.238	.379
Bobby Bonilla (SJ)	OF85 3B52 1B6	B	30	139	502	81	133	21	3	34	87	72	96	3	.265	.522
Ryan Thompson	OF76	R	25	80	288	34	72	19	2	11	26	19	81	2	.250	.479
Vince Coleman (ST)	OF90	B	32	92	373	64	104	14	8	2	25	21	58	38	.279	.375
Todd Hundley	C123	B	24	130	417	40	95	17	2	11	53	23	62	1	.228	.357
Joe Orsulak	OF114 1B4	L	31	134	409	59	116	15	4	8	35	28	25	5	.284	.399
Chico Walker	2B24 3B23 OF15	B	35	115	213	18	48	7	1	5	19	14	29	7	.225	.338
Jeff McKnight	SS29 2B15 1B10 3B9 C1	B	29	105	164	19	42	3	1	2	13	13	31	0	.256	.323
Dave Gallagher	OF72 1B9	R	32	99	201	34	55	12	2	6	28	20	18	1	.274	.443
Jeromy Burnitz	OF79	L	24	86	263	49	64	10	6	13	38	38	66	3	.243	.475
Charlie O'Brien	C85	R	33	67	188	15	48	11	0	4	23	14	14	1	.255	.378
Kevin Baez	SS52	R	26	52	126	10	23	6	0	0	7	13	17	0	.183	.254
1 Tony Fernandez	SS48	B	31	48	173	20	39	5	2	1	14	25	19	6	.225	.295
2 Darrin Jackson (IL)	OF26	R	30	31	87	4	17	1	0	1	7	2	22	0	.195	.241
Doug Saunders	2B22 3B4 SS1	R	23	28	67	8	14	2	0	0	3	4	9	0	.209	.239
Ced Landrum	OF3	R	29	22	19	2	5	1	0	0	1	0	5	0	.263	.316
Wayne Housie	OF2	B	28	18	16	2	3	1	0	0	1	1	1	0	.188	.250
Butch Huskey	3B13	R	21	13	41	2	6	1	0	0	3	1	13	0	.146	.171
Tito Navarro	SS2	B	22	12	17	1	1	0	0	0	1	0	4	0	.059	.059

NAME	T	AGE	W	L	PCT	SV	G	GS	CG	IP	H	BB	SO	SHO	ERA
		29	59	103	.364	22	162	162	16	1438	1483	434	867	8	4.05
Dwight Gooden (SJ)	R	28	12	15	.444	0	29	29	7	209	188	61	149	2	3.45
Bret Saberhagen (EJ)	R	29	7	7	.500	0	19	19	4	139	131	17	93	1	3.29
1 Frank Tanana	L	39	7	15	.318	0	29	29	0	183	198	48	104	0	4.48
Dave Telgheder	R	26	6	2	.750	0	24	7	0	76	82	21	35	0	4.76
Sid Fernandez (KJ)	L	30	5	6	.455	0	18	18	1	120	82	36	81	1	2.93
Pete Schourek	L	24	5	12	.294	0	41	18	0	128	168	45	72	0	5.96
John Franco (EJ)	L	32	4	3	.571	10	35	0	0	36	46	19	29	0	5.20
Mike Maddux	R	31	3	8	.273	5	58	0	0	75	67	27	57	0	3.60
Jeff Innis	R	30	2	3	.400	3	67	0	0	77	81	38	36	0	4.11
Bobby Jones	R	23	2	4	.333	0	9	9	2	62	61	22	35	0	3.65
Eric Hillman	L	27	2	9	.182	0	27	22	3	145	173	24	60	1	3.97
Kenny Greer	R	26	1	0	1.000	0	1	0	0	3	3	1	3	0	0.00
Mike Draper (EJ)	R	26	1	1	.500	0	29	1	0	42	53	14	16	0	4.25
1 Paul Gibson	L	33	1	1	.500	8	0	9	0	14	2	12	5	0	5.19
Anthony Young	R	27	1	16	.059	3	39	10	1	100	103	42	62	0	3.77
2 Josias Manzanillo	R	25	0	0	—	0	12	8	0	12	8	9	11	0	3.00
2 Jeff Kaiser	L	32	0	0	—	0	6	0	0	5	11	5	2	0	11.57
Mickey Weston	R	32	0	0	—	0	6	0	0	6	11	1	2	0	7.94
Mauro Gozzo	R	27	0	1	.000	1	10	0	0	14	11	5	6	0	2.57

WEST DIVISION

ATLANTA 1st 104-58 .642 — BOBBY COX

Name	G by Pos	B	AGE	G	AB	R	H	2B	3B	HR	RBI	BB	SO	SB	BA	SA
TOTALS			28	162	5515	767	1444	239	29	169	712	560	946	125	.262	.408
2 Fred McGriff	1B66	L	29	68	255	59	79	18	1	19	55	34	51	1	.310	.612
Mark Lemke	2B150	B	27	151	493	52	124	19	2	7	49	65	50	1	.252	.341
Jeff Blauser	SS161	R	27	161	597	110	182	29	2	15	73	85	109	16	.305	.436
Terry Pendleton	3B161	B	32	161	633	81	172	33	1	17	84	36	97	5	.272	.408
David Justice	OF157	L	27	157	585	90	158	15	4	40	120	78	90	3	.270	.515
Otis Nixon	OF116	B	34	134	461	77	124	12	3	1	24	61	63	47	.269	.315
Ron Gant	OF155	R	28	157	606	113	166	27	4	36	117	67	117	26	.274	.510
Damon Berryhill	C105	B	29	115	335	24	82	18	2	8	43	21	64	0	.245	.382
Sid Bream	1B90	L	32	117	277	33	72	14	1	9	35	31	43	0	.260	.415
Deion Sanders	OF60	L	25	95	272	42	75	18	6	6	28	16	42	19	.276	.452
Rafael Belliard	SS58 2B24	R	31	91	79	6	18	5	0	0	6	4	13	0	.228	.291
Greg Olson (AJ)	C81	R	32	83	262	23	59	10	0	4	24	29	27	1	.225	.309
Bill Pecota	3B23 2B4 OF1	R	33	72	62	17	20	2	1	0	5	2	5	1	.323	.387
Francisco Cabrera	1B12 C2	R	26	70	83	8	20	3	0	4	11	8	21	0	.241	.422
Brian Hunter (WJ)	1B29 OF2	R	25	37	80	4	11	3	1	2	8	2	15	0	.138	.200
Tony Tarasco	OF12	L	22	24	35	6	8	2	0	0	2	0	5	0	.229	.286
Ryan Klesko	1B3 OF2	L	22	22	17	3	6	1	0	2	5	3	4	0	.353	.765
Javy Lopez	C7	R	22	8	16	1	6	1	1	1	2	0	2	0	.375	.750
Chipper Jones	SS3	B	21	8	3	2	2	1	0	0	1	0	1	0	.667	1.000
Ramon Caraballo	2B5	B	24	6	0	0	0	0	0	0	0	0	0	0	—	—

NAME	T	AGE	W	L	PCT	SV	G	GS	CG	IP	H	BB	SO	SHO	ERA
		28	104	58	.642	46	162	162	18	1455	1297	480	1036	16	3.14
Tom Glavine	L	27	22	6	.786	0	36	36	4	239	236	90	120	2	3.20
Greg Maddux	R	27	20	10	.667	0	36	36	8	267	228	52	197	1	2.36
Steve Avery	L	23	18	6	.750	0	35	35	3	223	216	43	125	1	2.94
John Smoltz	R	26	15	11	.577	0	35	35	3	244	208	100	208	1	3.62
Mark Wohlers	R	23	6	2	.750	0	46	0	0	48	37	22	45	0	4.50
Steve Bedrosian	R	35	5	2	.714	0	49	0	0	50	34	14	33	0	1.63
Mike Stanton	L	26	4	6	.400	27	63	0	0	52	51	29	43	0	4.67
Pete Smith (SJ)	R	27	4	8	.333	0	20	14	0	91	92	36	53	0	4.37
Kent Mercker	L	25	3	1	.750	0	43	6	0	66	52	36	59	0	2.86
Jay Howell	R	37	3	3	.500	0	54	0	0	58	48	16	37	0	2.31
Marvin Freeman (AJ)	R	30	2	0	1.000	0	21	0	0	24	24	10	25	0	6.08
Greg McMichael	R	26	2	3	.400	19	74	0	0	92	68	29	89	0	2.06
Pedro Borbon	L	25	0	0	—	0	3	0	0	3	3	2	0	0	21.60

SAN FRANCISCO 2nd 103-59 .636 1 — DUSTY BAKER

Name	G by Pos	B	AGE	G	AB	R	H	2B	3B	HR	RBI	BB	SO	SB	BA	SA
TOTALS			28	162	5557	808	1534	269	33	168	759	516	930	120	.276	.427
Will Clark	1B129	L	29	132	491	82	139	27	2	14	73	63	68	2	.283	.432
Robby Thompson	2B128	R	31	128	494	85	154	30	2	19	65	45	97	10	.312	.496
Royce Clayton	SS153	R	23	153	549	54	155	21	5	6	70	38	91	11	.282	.372
Matt Williams	3B144	R	27	145	579	105	170	33	4	38	110	27	80	1	.294	.561
Willie McGee	OF126	B	34	130	475	53	143	28	4	4	46	38	67	10	.301	.389
Darren Lewis	OF131	R	26	136	522	84	132	17	7	2	48	30	40	46	.253	.324
Barry Bonds	OF157	L	28	159	539	129	181	38	4	46	123	126	79	29	.336	.677
Kirt Manwaring	C130	R	27	130	432	48	119	15	1	5	49	41	76	1	.275	.350
Dave Martinez (LJ)	OF73	L	28	91	241	28	58	12	1	5	27	27	39	6	.241	.361
Todd Benzinger	1B40 OF7 3B1	B	30	86	177	25	51	7	2	6	26	13	35	0	.288	.452
Mark Carreon	OF41 1B3	R	29	78	150	22	49	9	1	7	33	13	16	1	.327	.540
Jeff Reed (LJ)	C37	L	30	66	119	10	31	3	0	6	12	16	22	0	.261	.437
Mike Benjamin (FJ)	2B23 SS23 3B16	R	27	63	146	22	29	7	0	4	16	9	23	1	.199	.329
Steve Scarsone (BG)	2B20 3B8 1B6	R	27	44	103	16	26	9	0	2	15	4	32	0	.252	.398
Craig Colbert (BR)	C10 2B2 3B1	R	28	23	37	2	6	2	0	1	5	3	13	0	.162	.297
2 Luis Mercedes	OF5	R	25	18	25	1	4	0	1	0	3	1	3	0	.160	.240
John Patterson (KJ)		B	26	16	16	1	3	0	0	1	2	0	5	0	.188	.375
Paul Faries	2B7 SS4 3B1	R	28	15	36	6	8	2	1	0	4	1	4	2	.222	.333
Andy Allanson	C8 1B2	R	31	13	24	3	4	1	0	0	2	1	2	0	.167	.208
J. R. Phillips	1B5	L	23	11	16	1	5	1	1	1	4	0	5	0	.313	.688
Rikkert Faneyte	OF6	R	24	7	15	2	2	0	0	0	2	4	0	0	.133	.133
Jim McNamara	C4	L	28	4	7	0	1	0	0	0	1	0	1	0	.143	.143
Erik Johnson	2B2 3B1 SS1	R	27	4	5	1	2	2	0	0	0	0	1	0	.400	.800
Steve Hosey	OF1	R	24	3	2	0	1	1	0	0	1	0	0	0	.500	1.000

NAME	T	AGE	W	L	PCT	SV	G	GS	CG	IP	H	BB	SO	SHO	ERA
		29	103	59	.636	50	162	162	4	1457	1385	442	982	9	3.61
John Burkett	R	28	22	7	.759	0	34	34	2	232	224	40	145	1	3.65
Bill Swift	R	31	21	8	.724	0	34	34	1	233	195	55	157	1	2.82
Dave Burba	R	26	10	3	.769	0	54	5	0	95	95	37	88	0	4.25
Bud Black (EJ)	L	36	8	2	.800	0	16	16	0	94	89	33	45	0	3.56
Bryan Hickerson	L	29	7	5	.583	0	47	15	0	120	137	39	69	0	4.26
Trevor Wilson (SJ)	L	27	7	5	.583	0	22	18	1	110	110	40	57	0	3.60
Mike Jackson	R	28	6	6	.500	1	81	0	0	77	58	24	70	0	3.03
Jeff Brantley	R	29	5	6	.455	0	53	12	0	114	112	46	76	0	4.28
2 Scott Sanderson	R	36	4	2	.667	0	11	8	0	49	48	7	36	0	3.51
Rod Beck	R	24	3	1	.750	48	76	0	0	79	57	13	86	0	2.16
Salomon Torres	R	21	3	5	.375	0	8	8	0	45	37	27	23	0	4.03
Kevin Rogers	L	24	2	2	.500	0	64	0	0	81	71	28	62	0	2.68
2 Jim Deshaies	L	33	2	2	.500	0	5	4	0	17	24	6	5	0	4.24
2 Greg Brummett	R	26	2	3	.400	0	8	8	0	46	53	13	20	0	4.70
Dave Righetti	L	34	1	1	.500	1	51	0	0	47	58	17	31	0	5.70
Terry Bross	R	27	0	0	—	0	2	0	0	2	3	1	1	0	9.00
Tim Layana	R	29	0	0	—	0	1	0	0	2	7	1	1	0	22.50
Gino Minutelli	L	29	0	1	.000	0	9	0	0	14	7	15	10	0	3.77

HOUSTON 3rd 85-77 .525 19 — ART HOWE

Name	G by Pos	B	AGE	G	AB	R	H	2B	3B	HR	RBI	BB	SO	SB	BA	SA
TOTALS			27	162	5464	716	1459	288	37	138	656	497	911	103	.267	.409
Jeff Bagwell	1B140	R	25	142	535	76	171	37	4	20	88	62	73	13	.320	.516
Craig Biggio	2B155	R	27	155	610	98	175	41	5	21	64	77	93	15	.287	.474
Andujar Cedeno	SS149 3B1	R	23	149	505	69	143	24	4	11	56	49	97	9	.283	.412
Ken Caminiti	3B143	B	30	143	543	75	142	31	0	13	75	49	88	8	.262	.390
Eric Anthony	OF131	L	25	145	486	70	121	19	4	15	66	49	88	3	.249	.397
Steve Finley	OF140	L	28	142	545	69	145	15	13	8	44	28	65	19	.266	.385
Luis Gonzalez	OF149	L	25	154	540	82	162	34	3	15	72	47	83	20	.300	.457
Eddie Taubensee	C90	L	24	94	288	26	72	11	1	9	42	21	44	1	.250	.389
Kevin Bass	OF64	B	34	111	229	31	65	18	0	3	37	26	31	7	.284	.402
Chris Donnels	3B31 1B23 2B1	L	27	88	179	18	46	14	2	2	24	19	33	2	.257	.391
Scott Servais	C82	R	26	85	258	24	63	11	0	11	32	22	45	0	.244	.415
Casey Candaele	2B19 OF17 SS14 3B4	B	32	75	121	18	29	8	0	1	7	10	14	2	.240	.331
1 Chris James	OF34	R	30	65	129	19	33	10	1	6	19	15	34	2	.256	.488
Jose Uribe	SS41	B	34	45	53	4	13	1	0	0	3	8	5	1	.245	.264
Rick Parker	OF16 2B1 SS1	R	30	45	45	11	15	3	0	0	4	3	8	1	.333	.400
Scooter Tucker	C8	R	26	9	26	1	5	1	0	0	3	2	3	0	.192	.231
Jim Lindeman	1B9	R	31	9	23	2	8	3	0	0	0	0	7	0	.348	.478
Mike Brumley	3B1 SS1 OF1	B	30	8	10	1	3	0	0	0	2	1	3	0	.300	.300
1 Karl Rhodes	OF4	L	24	5	2	0	0	0	0	0	0	0	0	0	.000	.000
1 Jack Daugherty	1B1 OF1	B	32	4	3	0	1	0	0	0	0	0	1	0	.333	.333

NAME	T	AGE	W	L	PCT	SV	G	GS	CG	IP	H	BB	SO	SHO	ERA
		28	85	77	.525	42	162	162	18	1441	1363	476	1056	14	3.49
Mark Portugal	R	30	18	4	.818	0	33	33	1	208	194	77	131	1	2.77
Pete Harnisch	R	26	16	9	.640	0	33	33	5	218	171	79	185	4	2.98
Darryl Kile	R	24	15	8	.652	0	32	26	4	172	152	69	141	2	3.51
Greg Swindell	L	28	12	13	.480	0	31	30	1	190	215	40	124	1	4.16
Doug Drabek	R	30	9	18	.333	0	34	34	7	238	242	60	157	2	3.79
Brian Williams	R	24	4	4	.500	3	42	5	0	82	76	38	56	0	4.83
Xavier Hernandez	R	27	4	5	.444	9	72	0	0	97	75	28	101	0	2.61
Doug Jones	R	36	4	10	.286	26	71	0	0	85	102	21	66	0	4.54
Al Osuna	L	27	1	1	.500	2	44	0	0	25	17	13	21	0	3.20
Tom Edens (SJ)	R	32	1	1	.500	0	38	0	0	49	47	19	21	0	3.12
Todd Jones	R	25	1	2	.333	2	27	0	0	37	28	15	25	0	3.13
1 Mark Grant	R	29	0	0	—	0	6	0	0	11	11	5	6	0	0.82
Juan Agosto	L	35	0	0	—	0	6	0	0	6	8	0	3	0	6.00
Shane Reynolds	R	25	0	0	—	0	5	1	0	11	11	6	10	0	0.82
Eric Bell	L	29	0	1	.000	0	10	0	0	7	10	2	2	0	6.14
Jeff Juden	R	22	0	1	.000	0	2	0	0	5	4	4	7	0	5.40
Rob Mallicoat 28 (SJ)															

LOS ANGELES 4th 81-81 .500 23 — TOMMY LASORDA

Name	G by Pos	B	AGE	G	AB	R	H	2B	3B	HR	RBI	BB	SO	SB	BA	SA
TOTALS			29	162	5588	675	1458	234	28	130	639	492	937	126	.261	.383
Eric Karros	1B157	R	27	158	619	74	158	27	2	23	80	34	82	0	.247	.409
Jody Reed (EJ)	2B132	R	30	132	445	48	123	21	2	2	31	38	40	1	.276	.346
Jose Offerman	SS158	B	24	158	590	77	159	21	6	1	62	71	75	30	.269	.331
Tim Wallach	3B130 1B1	R	35	133	477	42	106	19	1	12	62	32	70	0	.222	.342
Darryl Strawberry (XJ)	OF29	L	31	32	100	12	14	2	0	5	12	16	19	1	.140	.310
Brett Butler	OF155	L	36	156	607	80	181	21	10	1	42	86	69	39	.298	.371
1 Eric Davis	OF103	R	31	108	376	57	88	17	0	14	53	41	88	33	.234	.391
Mike Piazza	C146 1B1	R	24	149	547	81	174	24	2	35	112	46	86	3	.318	.561
Cory Snyder	OF115 3B23 1B12 SS2	R	30	143	516	61	137	33	1	11	56	47	147	4	.286	.397
Lenny Harris	2B35 3B17 SS3 OF2	L	28	107	160	20	38	6	1	2	11	15	15	3	.238	.325
Mitch Webster	OF56	B	34	88	172	26	42	6	2	2	14	11	24	4	.244	.337
Dave Hansen	3B18	L	24	84	105	13	38	3	0	4	30	21	13	0	.362	.505
Henry Rodriguez	OF48 1B13	L	25	76	176	20	39	9	0	8	23	11	39	1	.222	.415
Mike Sharperson	2B17 3B6 SS3 1B1 OF1	R	31	73	90	13	23	4	0	2	10	5	17	2	.256	.367
Carlos Hernandez	C43	R	26	50	99	6	25	5	0	2	7	2	11	0	.253	.364
Raul Mondesi	OF40	R	22	42	86	13	25	3	1	4	10	4	16	4	.291	.488
Orel Hershiser	P33 3B1	R	34	33	73	11	26	4	0	0	6	2	5	0	.356	.411
Tom Goodwin	OF12	L	24	30	17	6	5	1	0	0	1	1	4	1	.294	.353
Billy Ashley	OF11	R	22	14	37	0	9	0	0	0	0	2	11	0	.243	.243
Jerry Brooks	OF2	R	26	9	9	2	2	1	0	0	1	0	2	0	.222	.667
Rafael Bournigal	SS4 2B4	R	27	8	18	0	9	1	0	0	3	0	2	0	.500	.556

NAME	T	AGE	W	L	PCT	SV	G	GS	CG	IP	H	BB	SO	SHO	ERA
		28	81	81	.500	36	162	162	17	1473	1406	567	1043	9	3.50
Pedro Astacio	R	23	14	9	.609	0	31	31	3	186	165	68	122	2	3.57
Kevin Gross	R	32	13	13	.500	0	33	32	3	202	224	74	150	0	4.14
Orel Hershiser	R	34	12	14	.462	0	33	33	5	216	201	72	141	1	3.59
Pedro Martinez	R	21	10	5	.667	2	65	2	0	107	76	57	119	0	2.61
Ramon Martinez	R	25	10	12	.455	0	32	32	4	212	202	104	127	3	3.44
Tom Candiotti	R	35	8	10	.444	0	33	32	2	214	192	71	155	0	3.12
Roger McDowell	R	32	5	3	.625	2	54	0	0	68	76	30	27	0	2.25
Jim Gott	R	33	4	8	.333	25	62	0	0	78	71	17	67	0	2.32
Omar Daal	L	21	2	3	.400	0	47	0	0	35	36	21	19	0	5.09
Steve Wilson	L	28	1	0	1.000	1	25	0	0	26	30	14	23	0	4.56
Todd Worrell (AJ,EJ)	R	33	1	1	.500	5	35	0	0	39	46	11	31	0	6.05
Ricky Trlicek	R	24	1	2	.333	1	41	0	0	64	59	21	41	0	4.08
Kip Gross	R	28	0	0	—	0	10	0	0	15	13	4	12	0	0.60
2 John DeSilva	R	25	0	0	—	0	3	0	0	5	6	1	6	0	6.75
Rod Nichols	R	28	0	1	.000	0	4	0	0	6	9	2	3	0	5.68

CINCINNATI 5th 73-89 .451 31 — TONY PEREZ 20-24 .455 / DAVEY JOHNSON 53-65 .449

Name	G by Pos	B	AGE	G	AB	R	H	2B	3B	HR	RBI	BB	SO	SB	BA	SA
TOTALS			29	162	5517	722	1457	261	28	137	669	485	1025	142	.264	.396
Hal Morris (SJ)	1B98	L	28	101	379	48	120	18	0	7	49	34	51	2	.317	.420
Bip Roberts (RJ)	2B64 OF11 3B3 SS1	B	29	83	292	46	70	13	0	1	18	38	46	26	.240	.295
Barry Larkin (RJ)	SS99	R	29	100	384	57	121	20	3	8	51	51	33	14	.315	.445
Chris Sabo	3B148	R	31	148	552	86	143	33	2	21	82	43	105	6	.259	.440
Reggie Sanders	OF137	R	25	138	496	90	136	16	4	20	83	51	118	27	.274	.444
Bobby Kelly (SJ)	OF77	R	28	78	320	44	102	17	3	9	35	17	43	21	.319	.475
Kevin Mitchell (SJ)	OF87	R	31	93	323	56	110	21	3	19	64	25	48	1	.341	.601
Joe Oliver	C133 1B12 OF1	R	28	139	482	40	115	28	0	14	75	27	91	0	.239	.384
Jeff Branson	SS59 2B45 3B14 1B1	L	26	125	381	40	92	15	1	3	22	19	73	4	.241	.310
Jacob Brumfield	OF96 2B4	R	28	103	272	40	73	17	3	6	23	21	47	20	.268	.419
Juan Samuel	2B70 1B6 3B4 OF3	R	32	103	261	31	60	10	4	4	26	23	53	9	.230	.345
1 Randy Milligan	1B61 OF9	R	31	83	234	30	64	11	1	6	29	46	49	0	.274	.406
Gary Varsho	OF22	L	32	77	95	8	22	6	0	2	11	9	19	1	.232	.358
2 Jack Daugherty	OF16 1B2	B	32	46	59	7	13	2	0	2	9	11	15	0	.220	.356
Cecil Espy	OF18	B	30	40	60	6	14	2	0	0	8	4	14	2	.233	.267
2 Thomas Howard	OF37	B	28	38	141	22	39	8	3	4	13	12	21	5	.277	.461
Dan Wilson	C35	R	24	36	76	6	17	3	0	0	8	4	16	0	.224	.303
Greg Tubbs	OF21	R	30	35	59	10	11	0	0	0	2	14	10	3	.186	.237
Tim Costo	OF26 1B2 3B2	R	24	31	98	13	22	5	1	3	17	4	26	1	.224	.387
Cesar Hernandez	OF23	R	26	27	24	3	2	0	0	0	1	1	8	1	.083	.083
Brian Dorsett	C18 1B3	R	32	25	63	7	16	6	0	2	11	5	14	0	.254	.413
Willie Greene (RJ)	SS10 3B5	R	21	15	50	7	14	2	1	5	13	6	17	0	.160	.340
Keith Kessinger	SS11	B	26	11	24	3	7	1	0	0	2	4	4	0	.259	.407
Tommy Gregg	OF1	L	29	10	12	1	2	0	0	0	1	2	3	0	.167	.167
Brian Koelling	2B3 SS2	R	24	7	15	2	1	0	0	0	0	0	5	0	.067	.067
Keith Gordon	OF2	R	24	3	6	0	1	0	0	0	0	0	1	0	.167	.167
Keith Hughes	OF1	R	29	3	4	0	0	0	0	0	0	0	0	0	.000	.000

NAME	T	AGE	W	L	PCT	SV	G	GS	CG	IP	H	BB	SO	SHO	ERA
		28	73	89	.451	37	162	162	11	1434	1510	508	996	8	4.51
Jose Rijo	R	28	14	9	.609	0	36	36	2	257	218	62	227	1	2.48
Tim Pugh	R	26	10	15	.400	0	31	27	3	164	200	59	94	1	5.26
1 Tim Belcher	R	31	9	6	.600	0	22	22	4	137	134	47	101	2	4.47
Tom Browning (BG)	L	33	7	7	.500	0	21	20	0	114	159	20	53	0	4.74
Bobby Ayala	R	23	7	10	.412	3	43	9	0	98	106	45	65	0	5.60
Jeff Reardon	R	37	4	8	.400	8	58	0	0	62	66	10	35	0	4.09
1 Milt Hill	R	27	3	0	1.000	0	19	0	0	29	34	9	23	0	5.65
John Smiley (EJ)	L	28	3	9	.250	0	18	18	2	106	117	31	60	0	5.62
Jerry Spradlin	R	26	2	1	.667	2	37	0	0	49	44	9	24	0	3.49
1 Greg Cadaret	L	31	2	1	.667	1	34	0	0	33	40	23	23	0	4.96
Johnny Ruffin	R	21	2	1	.667	2	21	0	0	38	36	11	30	0	3.58
2 Scott Service	R	26	2	2	.500	2	26	0	0	41	36	15	40	0	3.70
Steve Foster (SJ)	R	26	1	2	.500	0	5	0	0	26	23	5	16	0	1.75
John Roper (UJ)	R	21	2	5	.286	0	16	15	0	80	92	36	54	0	5.63
Larry Luebbers	R	23	2	5	.286	0	14	14	0	77	74	38	38	0	4.54
2 Kevin Wickander	L	28	1	0	1.000	0	33	0	0	22	20	10	20	0	6.75
Rob Dibble (BA)	R	29	1	4	.200	19	45	0	0	42	34	42	49	0	6.48
Chris Bushing	R	25	0	0	—	0	7	0	0	4	1	4	1	0	12.46
Scott Ruskin	L	30	0	0	—	0	1	0	0	1	3	2	1	0	18.00
Mike Anderson	R	26	0	0	—	0	4	0	0	2	4	4	2	0	18.56
1 Jeff Kaiser	L	29	0	0	—	0	9	0	0	7	7	4	4	0	2.70
1 Dwayne Henry	R	31	0	0	—	0	5	0	0	3	3	3	1	0	3.86
Bill Landrum (EJ)	R	35	0	0	—	0	18	0	0	22	18	6	14	0	3.74
Ross Powell	L	25	0	3	.000	0	9	1	0	16	13	6	17	0	4.41

COLORADO — 6th 67-95 .414 37 — DON BAYLOR

Name	G by Pos	B	AGE	G	AB	R	H	2B	3B	HR	RBI	BB	SO	SB	BA	SA
TOTALS		28		162	5517	758	1507	278	59	142	704	388	944	146	.273	.422
Andres Galarraga (KJ)	1B119	R	32	120	470	71	174	35	4	22	98	24	73	2	.370	.602
Eric Young	2B79 OF52	R	26	144	490	82	132	16	4	3	42	63	41	42	.269	.353
Vinny Castilla	SS104	R	25	105	337	36	86	9	7	9	30	13	45	2	.255	.404
Charlie Hayes	3B154 SS1	R	28	157	573	89	175	45	2	25	98	43	82	11	.305	.522
Dante Bichette	OF137	R	29	141	538	93	167	43	5	21	89	28	99	14	.310	.526
Alex Cole	OF93	L	27	126	348	50	89	9	4	0	24	43	58	30	.256	.305
Jerald Clark	OF96 1B37	R	28	140	478	65	135	26	6	13	67	20	60	9	.282	.444
Joe Girardi (WJ)	C84	R	28	86	310	35	90	14	5	3	31	24	41	6	.290	.397
Daryl Boston	OF79	L	30	124	291	46	76	15	1	14	40	26	57	1	.261	.464
Jim Tatum	1B12 3B6 OF3	R	25	92	98	7	20	5	0	1	12	5	27	0	.204	.286
Chris Jones	OF70	R	27	86	209	29	57	11	4	6	31	10	48	9	.273	.450
Danny Sheaffer	C65 1B7 OF2 3B1	R	32	82	216	26	60	9	1	4	32	8	15	2	.278	.384
Freddie Benavides (KJ)	SS48 2B19 3B5 1B1	R	27	74	213	20	61	10	3	3	26	6	27	3	.286	.404
Roberto Mejia	2B65	R	21	65	229	31	53	14	5	5	20	13	63	4	.231	.402
Nelson Liriano	SS35 2B16 3B1	B	29	48	151	28	46	6	3	2	15	18	22	6	.305	.424
Pedro Castellano	3B13 1B10 SS2 2B4	R	23	34	71	12	13	2	0	3	7	8	16	1	.183	.338
Jayhawk Owens	C32	R	24	33	86	12	18	5	0	3	6	6	30	1	.209	.372
Dale Murphy	OF13	R	37	26	42	1	6	1	0	0	7	5	15	0	.143	.167
Jay Gainer	1B7	L	26	23	41	4	7	0	0	3	6	4	12	1	.171	.390
Gerald Young	OF11	B	28	19	19	5	1	0	0	0	1	4	4	0	.053	.053
Eric Wedge (EJ)	C1	R	25	9	11	2	2	0	0	0	1	0	4	0	.182	.182

SAN DIEGO — 7th 61-101 .377 43 — JIM RIGGLEMAN

Name	G by Pos	B	AGE	G	AB	R	H	2B	3B	HR	RBI	BB	SO	SB	BA	SA
TOTALS		27		162	5503	679	1386	239	28	153	633	443	1046	92	.252	.389
1 Fred McGriff	1B83	L	29	83	302	52	83	11	1	18	46	42	55	4	.275	.497
Jeff Gardner	2B133 SS1 3B1	L	29	140	404	53	106	21	7	1	24	45	69	2	.262	.356
Ricky Gutierrez	SS117 2B6 OF5 3B4	R	23	133	438	76	110	10	5	5	26	50	97	4	.251	.331
1 Gary Sheffield	3B67	R	24	68	258	34	76	12	2	10	36	13	46	5	.295	.473
Tony Gwynn (KJ)	OF121	R	33	122	489	70	175	41	3	7	59	36	19	14	.358	.497
Derek Bell	OF125 3B19	R	24	150	542	73	142	19	1	21	72	23	122	26	.262	.417
Phil Plantier	OF134	L	24	138	462	67	111	20	1	34	100	61	124	4	.240	.509
Kevin Higgins	C59 3B4 1B3 OF3 2B1	L	25	71	181	17	40	4	1	0	13	16	17	0	.221	.254
Craig Shipley	SS38 3B37 2B12 OF5	R	30	105	230	25	54	9	0	4	22	10	31	12	.235	.326
Phil Clark	OF36 1B24 C11 3B5	R	25	102	240	33	75	17	0	9	33	8	31	2	.313	.496
Tim Teufel	2B52 3B9 1B8	R	34	96	200	26	50	11	2	7	31	27	39	2	.250	.430
Billy Bean	OF54 1B12	L	29	88	177	19	46	9	0	5	32	6	29	2	.260	.395
2 Archi Cianfrocco	3B64 1B31	R	26	84	279	27	68	10	2	11	47	17	64	2	.244	.412
Guillermo Velasquez	1B38 OF6	L	25	79	143	7	30	2	0	3	20	13	35	0	.210	.287
Bob Geren	C49 1B3	R	31	58	145	8	31	6	0	3	6	13	28	0	.214	.317
Kurt Stillwell	SS30 3B3	B	28	57	121	9	26	4	0	1	11	11	22	2	.215	.273
Brad Ausmus	C49	R	24	49	160	18	41	9	5	1	12	6	28	2	.256	.413
Jarvis Brown	OF43	R	26	47	133	21	31	9	2	0	8	15	26	3	.233	.331
Darrell Sherman	OF26	L	25	37	63	8	14	1	0	0	2	6	8	2	.222	.238
Dan Walters	C26	R	26	27	94	6	19	3	0	1	10	7	13	0	.202	.266
Melvin Nieves	OF15	B	21	19	47	4	9	0	0	2	3	3	21	0	.191	.319
Luis Lopez	2B15	R	22	17	43	1	5	1	0	0	1	0	8	0	.116	.140
Dave Staton	1B12	R	23	17	42	7	11	3	0	5	9	3	12	0	.262	.690
Mike Scioscia 34 (SJ)																

Colorado Pitching

NAME	T	AGE	W	L	PCT	SV	G	GS	CG	IP	H	BB	SO	SHO	ERA
		27	67	95	.414	35	162	162	9	1431	1664	609	913	0	5.41
Armando Reynoso	R	27	12	11	.522	0	30	30	4	189	206	63	117	0	4.00
Steve Reed	L	28	9	5	.643	3	64	0	0	84	80	30	51	0	4.48
Bruce Ruffin	L	29	6	5	.545	2	59	12	0	140	145	69	126	0	3.87
Willie Blair	R	27	6	10	.375	0	46	18	1	146	184	42	84	0	4.75
Gary Wayne	R	30	5	3	.625	1	65	0	0	62	68	26	49	0	5.05
David Nied (EJ)	R	24	5	9	.357	0	16	16	1	87	99	42	46	0	5.17
Marcus Moore	R	23	3	1	.750	0	27	0	0	26	30	20	13	0	6.84
Darren Holmes	R	27	3	3	.500	25	62	0	0	67	56	20	60	0	4.05
Jeff Parrett (EJ)	R	31	3	3	.500	1	40	6	0	74	78	45	66	0	5.38
1 Kent Bottenfield	R	24	3	5	.375	0	14	14	1	77	86	38	30	0	6.10
2 Mike Munoz	L	27	2	1	.667	0	21	0	0	18	21	9	16	0	4.50
Lance Painter	L	25	2	2	.500	0	10	6	1	39	52	9	16	0	6.00
Bryn Smith	R	37	2	4	.333	0	11	5	0	30	47	11	9	0	8.49
1 Butch Henry	R	24	2	8	.200	0	20	15	1	85	117	24	39	0	6.59
Mo Sanford	R	26	1	2	.333	0	11	6	0	36	37	27	36	0	5.30
Keith Shepherd	R	25	1	1	.500	0	11	6	0	19	26	4	7	0	6.98
Curtis Leskanic	R	25	1	5	.167	0	18	8	0	57	59	27	30	0	5.37
1 Greg Harris	R	29	1	8*	.111	0	13	13	0	73	88	30	40	0	6.50
1 Scott Aldred	L	25	0	0	—	0	5	0	0	7	10	9	5	0	10.80
Mark Knudson	R	32	0	0	—	0	6	0	0	16	16	3	4	0	22.24
1 Scott Service	R	26	0	0	—	0	5	0	0	5	6	1	3	0	9.64
Scott Fredrickson	R	25	0	1	.000	0	25	0	0	39	33	17	20	0	6.21
2 Mark Grant	R	29	0	1	.000	0	14	0	0	14	23	6	8	0	12.56
2 Bruce Hurst (SJ)	L	35	0	1	.000	0	3	3	0	9	6	3	6	0	5.19
1 Andy Ashby	R	25	0	4	.000	1	20	9	0	54	89	32	33	0	8.50
Kevin Ritz 28 (AJ)															

* Harris, also with San Diego, league leader in L with 17

San Diego Pitching

NAME	T	AGE	W	L	PCT	SV	G	GS	CG	IP	H	BB	SO	SHO	ERA
		27	61	101	.377	32	162	162	8	1438	1470	558	957	6	4.23
Andy Benes	R	25	15	15	.500	0	34	34	4	231	200	86	179	2	3.78
1 Greg Harris	R	29	10	9*	.526	0	22	22	4	152	151	39	83	0	3.67
Gene Harris	R	28	6	6	.500	23	59	0	0	59	57	37	39	0	3.03
Wally Whitehurst (EJ,SJ)	R	29	4	7	.364	0	21	19	0	106	109	30	57	0	3.83
Doug Brocail	R	26	4	13	.235	0	24	24	0	128	143	42	70	0	4.56
Pedro Martinez	L	24	3	1	.750	0	32	0	0	37	23	13	32	0	2.43
Frank Seminara	R	26	3	3	.500	0	18	7	0	46	53	21	22	0	4.47
Scott Sanders	R	24	3	3	.500	0	9	9	0	52	54	23	37	0	4.13
2 Andy Ashby	R	25	3	6	.333	1	12	12	0	69	79	24	44	0	5.48
1 Tim Scott	R	26	2	0	1.000	0	24	0	0	38	38	15	30	0	2.29
1 Rich Rodriguez	L	30	2	3	.400	2	34	0	0	30	34	19	22	0	3.30
1 Trevor Hoffman	R	25	2	4	.333	3	39	0	0	54	56	20	53	0	4.31
Tim Worrell	R	26	2	7	.222	0	21	16	0	101	104	43	52	0	4.92
Mark Ettles	R	26	1	0	1.000	0	14	0	0	18	23	4	9	0	6.50
Pat Gomez (EJ)	L	25	1	2	.333	0	27	1	0	32	35	19	26	0	5.12
Rudy Seanez	R	24	0	0	—	0	3	0	0	3	8	2	1	0	13.50
2 Tim Mauser	R	26	0	0	—	0	28	0	0	38	36	17	32	0	3.58
1 Bruce Hurst (SJ)	L	35	0	1	.000	0	2	2	0	4	9	3	3	0	12.46
1 Jeremy Hernandez	R	26	0	2	.000	0	21	0	0	34	41	7	26	0	4.72
2 Mark Davis	L	32	0	3	.000	4	35	0	0	38	44	20	42	0	3.52
Dave Eiland	R	26	0	3	.000	0	10	9	0	48	58	17	14	0	5.21
Kerry Taylor	R	22	0	5	.000	0	36	7	0	68	72	49	45	0	6.45
1 Roger Mason	R	34	0	7	.000	0	34	0	0	50	43	18	39	0	3.24

* Harris, also with Colorado, league leader in L with 17

1993 CHAMPIONSHIPS

LINE SCORES

NATIONAL LEAGUE CHAMPIONSHIPS: PHILADELPHIA (EAST) 4 ATLANTA (WEST) 2

Game 1 October 6 at Philadelphia

Team	1	2	3	4	5	6	7	8	9	10	R	H	E
ATL	0	0	1	1	0	0	0	0	1	0	3	9	0
PHI	1	0	0	1	0	1	0	0	0	1	4	9	1

Avery, Mercker(7), **McMichael**(9) — Schilling, **Williams**(9)

Game 2 October 7 at Philadelphia

Team	1	2	3	4	5	6	7	8	9	R	H	E
ATL	2	0	6	0	1	0	0	4	1	14	16	0
PHI	0	0	0	2	0	0	0	0	1	3	7	2

Maddux, Stanton(8), Wohlers(9) — **Greene**, Thigpen(3), Rivera(4), Mason(6), West(8), Anderson(9)

Game 3 October 9 at Atlanta

Team	1	2	3	4	5	6	7	8	9	R	H	E
PHI	0	0	0	1	0	0	0	1	1	4	10	1
ATL	0	0	0	0	5	4	0	X		9	12	0

Mulholland, Mason(6), Andersen(7), West(7), Thigpen(8) — **Glavine**, Mercker(8), McMichael(9)

Game 4 October 10 at Atlanta

Team	1	2	3	4	5	6	7	8	9	R	H	E
PHI	0	0	0	2	0	0	0	0	0	2	8	1
ATL	0	1	0	0	0	0	0	0	0	1	10	1

Jackson, Williams(8) — Smoltz, **Mercker**(7), Wohlers(8)

Game 5 October 11 at Atlanta

Team	1	2	3	4	5	6	7	8	9	10	R	H	E
PHI	1	0	0	1	0	0	0	0	1	1	4	6	1
ATL	0	0	0	0	0	0	3	0			3	7	1

Schilling, **Williams**(9), Andersen(10) — Avery, Mercker(8), McMichael(9), **Wohlers**(10)

Game 6 October 13 at Philadelphia

Team	1	2	3	4	5	6	7	8	9	R	H	E
ATL	0	0	0	0	1	0	2	0	0	3	5	3
PHI	0	0	2	0	2	2	0	0	X	6	7	1

Maddux, Mercker(6), McMichael(7), Wohlers(7) — **Greene**, West(8), Williams(9)

COMPOSITE BATTING

PHILADELPHIA

NAME	POS	G	AB	R	H	2B	3B	HR	RBI	BA
Totals		6	207	23	47	11	4	7	22	.227
Dykstra	CF	6	25	5	7	1	0	2	2	.280
Kruk	1B	6	24	4	6	2	1	1	5	.250
Stocker	SS	6	22	0	4	1	0	0	0	.182
Hollins	3B	6	20	2	4	1	0	2	4	.200
Daulton	C	6	19	2	5	1	0	1	3	.263
Morandini	2B	4	16	1	4	0	1	0	2	.250
Duncan		3	15	3	4	0	2	0	0	.267
Eisenreich	RF	6	15	0	2	1	0	0	0	.133
Thompson	LF	6	13	2	3	1	0	0	1	.231
Incaviglia	LF	3	12	2	2	0	0	0	1	.167
Chamberlain	RF	4	11	1	4	3	0	0	1	.364
Schilling	P	2	5	0	0	0	0	0	0	.000
Jackson	P	1	4	0	1	0	0	0	1	.250
Mulholland	P	1	2	0	0	0	0	0	0	.000
Batiste	3B	4	2	0	1	0	0	0	1	1.000
Jordan	PH	1	2	0	0	0	0	0	0	.000
Longmire	PH	1	1	0	0	0	0	0	0	.000
Pratt	C	1	1	0	0	0	0	0	0	.000
Greene	P	2	1	0	1	0	0	0	0	—

ATLANTA

NAME	POS	G	AB	R	H	2B	3B	HR	RBI	BA
Totals		6	215	33	59	14	0	5	32	.274
Gant	LF	6	27	4	5	3	0	0	3	.185
Pendleton	3B	6	26	4	9	1	0	1	5	.346
Blauser	SS	6	25	5	7	1	0	2	4	.280
Lemke	2B	6	24	2	5	2	0	0	4	.208
McGriff	1B	6	23	6	10	2	0	1	4	.435
Nixon	CF	6	23	3	8	2	0	0	4	.348
Justice	RF	6	21	2	3	1	0	0	4	.143
Berryhill	C	6	19	2	4	1	0	1	3	.211
Avery	P	2	4	1	2	1	0	0	0	.500
Maddux	P	2	4	1	1	0	0	0	0	.250
Sanders	CF	5	3	0	0	0	0	0	0	.000
Pecota	PH	4	3	1	1	0	0	0	0	.333
Cabrera	C	2	3	0	2	0	0	0	1	.667
Olson	C	2	3	1	1	0	0	0	0	.333
Glavine	P	1	3	0	0	0	0	0	0	.000
Belliard	2B-SS	2	1	0	0	0	0	0	0	.000
Tarasco	LF-RF	2	1	0	1	0	0	0	0	1.000
Bream	1B	2	1	1	1	0	0	0	0	1.000
Smoltz	P	1	1	0	0	0	0	0	0	.000

COMPOSITE PITCHING

PHILADELPHIA

NAME	G	IP	H	BB	SO	W	L	SV	ERA
Totals	6	55	59	22	54	4	2	3	4.75
Schilling	2	16	11	5	19	0	0	0	1.67
Greene	2	9.1	12	7	7	1	1	0	9.64
Jackson	1	7.2	9	2	6	1	0	0	1.17
Williams	4	5.1	6	2	5	2	0	2	1.69
Mulholland	1	5	4	1	3	0	1	0	7.20
Mason	2	3	1	0	2	0	0	0	0.00
West	3	2.2	5	2	5	0	0	0	13.50
Andersen	3	2.1	4	1	3	0	0	1	15.43
Rivera	1	2	1	1	2	0	0	0	4.50
Thigpen	2	1.2	1	1	0	0	0	0	5.40

ATLANTA

NAME	G	IP	H	BB	SO	W	L	SV	ERA
Totals	6	54.1	47	26	51	2	4	0	3.15
Avery	2	13	9	6	10	0	0	0	2.77
Maddux	2	12.2	11	7	11	1	1	0	4.97
Glavine	1	7	6	5	1	0	0	0	2.57
Smoltz	1	6.1	8	5	10	1	0	0	0.00
Wohlers	4	5.1	2	3	10	0	0	1	3.38
Mercker	5	5	4	2	4	0	0	0	1.80
McMichael	4	4	7	2	1	0	1	0	6.75
Stanton	1	1	1	1	0	0	1	0	0.00

LINE SCORES

Team	1	2	3	4	5	6	7	8	9	10	11	12	R	H	E

WORLD SERIES TORONTO (AL) 4: PHILADELPHIA (NL) 2

Game 1 October 16 at Toronto

	1	2	3	4	5	6	7	8	9	R	H	E
PHI	2	0	1	0	1	0	0	0	1	5	11	1
TOR	0	2	1	0	1	1	3	0	X	8	10	2

Schilling, West(7), Andersen(7), Guzman, **Leiter**(6), Ward(8)
Mason(8)

Game 2 October 17 at Toronto

	1	2	3	4	5	6	7	8	9	R	H	E
PHI	0	0	5	0	0	0	1	0	0	6	12	0
TOR	0	0	0	2	0	1	0	1	0	4	8	0

Mulholland, Mason(6), **Stewart**, Castillo(7), Eichhorn(8),
Williams(8) Timlin(8)

Game 3 October 19 at Philadelphia

	1	2	3	4	5	6	7	8	9	R	H	E
TOR	3	0	1	0	0	1	3	0	2	10	13	1
PHI	0	0	0	0	0	1	1	0	1	3	9	0

Hentgen, Cox(7), Ward(9) **Jackson**, Rivera(6), Thigpen(7),
Andersen(9)

Game 4 October 20 at Philadelphia

	1	2	3	4	5	6	7	8	9	R	H	E
TOR	3	0	4	0	0	2	0	6	0	15	18	1
PHI	4	2	0	1	5	1	0	0	1	14	14	0

Stottlemyre, Leiter(3), Greene, Mason(3), West(6),
Castillo(5), Timlin(8), Ward(8) Andersen(7), **Williams**(8), Thigpen(9)

Game 5 October 21 at Philadelphia

	1	2	3	4	5	6	7	8	9	R	H	E
TOR	0	0	0	0	0	0	0	0	0	0	5	1
PHI	1	1	0	0	0	0	0	0	0	2	5	1

Guzman, Cox(8) **Schilling**

Game 6 October 23 at Toronto

	1	2	3	4	5	6	7	8	9	R	H	E
PHI	0	0	0	1	0	0	5	0	0	6	7	0
TOR	3	0	1	1	0	0	0	0	3	8	10	2

Mulholland, Mason(6), West(8), Stewart, Cox(7), Leiter(7),
Andersen(8), **Williams**(9) **Ward**(9)

COMPOSITE BATTING

NAME	POS	G	AB	R	H	2B	3B	HR	RBI	BA
TORONTO										
Totals		6	206	45	64	13	5	6	45	.311
Alomar	2B	6	25	5	12	2	1	0	6	.480
Carter	RF	6	25	6	7	1	0	2	8	.280
Molitor	DH-1B-3B	6	24	10	12	2	2	2	8	.500
White	CF	6	24	8	7	3	2	1	7	.292
Borders	C	6	23	2	7	0	0	0	1	.304
Henderson	LF	6	22	6	5	2	0	0	2	.227
Fernandez	SS	6	21	2	7	1	0	0	9	.333
Olerud	1B	5	17	5	4	1	0	1	2	.235
Sprague	3B-1B-PH	5	15	0	1	0	0	0	2	.067
Hentgen	P	1	3	0	0	0	0	0	0	.000
Butler	PH	2	2	1	1	0	0	0	0	.500
Guzman	P	2	2	0	0	0	0	0	0	.000
Leiter	P	3	1	0	1	1	0	0	1	1.000
Cox	P	3	1	0	0	0	0	0	0	.000
Castillo	P	2	1	0	0	0	0	0	0	.000
Ward	P	4	0	0	0	0	0	0	0	—
Griffin	3B-PR	3	0	0	0	0	0	0	0	—
Stewart	P	2	0	0	0	0	0	0	0	—
Timlin	P	2	0	0	0	0	0	0	0	—
Knorr	C	1	0	0	0	0	0	0	0	—
Canate	PR	1	0	0	0	0	0	0	0	—
Stottlemyre	P	1	0	0	0	0	0	0	0	—
Eichhorn	P	1	0	0	0	0	0	0	0	—
PHILADELPHIA										
Totals		6	212	36	58	7	2	7	35	.274
Duncan	2B-DH	6	29	5	10	0	1	0	2	.345
Eisenreich	RF	6	26	3	6	0	0	1	7	.231
Dykstra	CF	6	23	9	8	1	0	4	8	.348
Kruk	1B	6	23	4	8	1	0	0	4	.348
Hollins	3B	6	23	5	6	1	0	0	2	.261
Daulton	C	6	23	4	5	2	0	1	4	.217
Stocker	SS	6	19	1	4	1	0	0	1	.211
Thompson	LF-PR	5	16	3	5	1	1	1	6	.313
Jordan	DH-PH	3	10	0	2	0	0	0	0	.200
Incaviglia	LF-PH	4	8	0	1	0	0	0	1	.125
Morandini	2B-PH	3	5	1	1	0	0	0	0	.200
Schilling	P	2	2	0	1	0	0	0	0	.500
Chamberlain	PH	2	2	0	0	0	0	0	0	.000
Mason	P	4	1	0	0	0	0	0	0	.000
Greene	P	1	1	1	1	0	0	0	0	1.000
Jackson	P	1	1	0	0	0	0	0	0	.000
Andersen	P	4	0	0	0	0	0	0	0	—
Williams	P	3	0	0	0	0	0	0	0	—
West	P	3	0	0	0	0	0	0	0	—
Batiste	3B	2	0	0	0	0	0	0	0	—
Mulholland	P	2	0	0	0	0	0	0	0	—
Thigpen	P	2	0	0	0	0	0	0	0	—
Rivera	P	1	0	0	0	0	0	0	0	—

COMPOSITE PITCHING

NAME	G	IP	H	BB	SO	W	L	SV	ERA
TORONTO									
Totals	6	53	58	34	50	4	2	2	5.77
Guzman	2	12	10	8	12	0	1	0	3.75
Stewart	2	12	10	8	8	1	0	0	6.75
Leiter	3	7	12	5	5	1	0	0	7.71
Hentgen	1	6	5	3	6	1	0	0	1.50
Ward	4	4.2	3	0	7	1	0	2	1.93
Cox	3	3.1	6	5	6	0	0	0	8.10
Castillo	2	3.1	6	3	1	1	0	0	8.10
Timlin	2	2.1	2	0	4	0	0	0	0.00
Stottlemyre	1	2	3	4	1	0	0	0	27.00
Eichhorn	1	0.1	1	1	0	0	0	0	0.00
PHILADELPHIA									
Totals	6	52.1	64	25	30	2	4	1	7.57
Schilling	2	15.1	13	5	9	1	1	0	3.52
Mulholland	2	10.2	14	3	5	1	0	0	6.75
Mason	4	7.2	4	1	7	0	0	0	1.17
Jackson	1	5	6	1	1	0	1	0	6.75
Andersen	4	3.2	5	3	3	0	0	0	12.27
Williams	3	2.2	5	4	1	0	2	1	20.25
Thigpen	2	2.2	1	1	0	0	0	0	0.00
Greene	1	2.1	7	4	1	0	0	0	27.00
Rivera	1	1.1	4	2	3	0	0	0	27.00
West	3	1	5	1	0	0	0	0	27.00

MISCELLANEOUS 1993 INDIVIDUAL LEADERS

BATTING

On Base Average

	American League			National League	
1	Olerud, Tor.	.473	1	Bonds, S.F.	.458
2	Phillips, Det.	.443	2	Kruk, Phi.	.430
3	Henderson, Oak+Tor.	.432	3	Dystra, Phi.	.420
4	Thomas, Chi.	.426	4	Merced, Pit.	.414
5	Hoiles, Bal.	.416	5	Jefferies, St.L.	.408
6	Griffey, Sea.	.408	6	Galarraga, Col.	.403
7	Alomar, Tor.	.408	7	Blauser, Atl.	.401
8	Lofton, Cle.	.408	8	Gwynn, S.D.	.398
9	Molitor, Tor.	.402	9	Grace, Chi.	.393
10	Vaughn, Bos.	.390	10	Daulton, Phi.	.392

Caught Stealing

	American League			National League	
1	Polonia, Cal.	24	1	Carr, Fla.	22
	Curtis, Cal.	24	2	Young, Col.	19
3	Alomar, Tor.	15		Butler, L.A.	19
	McLemore, Bal.	15	4	Biggio, Hou.	17
5	Lofton, Cle.	14	5	Lewis, S.F.	15
	McRae, K.C.	14			
	Vizquel, Sea.	14			

Stolen Base Percentage
(Minimum 20 Attempts)

	American League			National League	
1	White, Tor.	89	1	Davis, L.A.	87
2	Palmeiro, Tex.	88	2	Grissom, Mon.	84
3	Henderson, Oak.	87	3	Bell, S.D.	84
4	Molitor, Tor.	85		Jefferies, St.L.	84
5	Lofton, Cle.	83	5	Roberts, Cin.	81
	Johnson, Chi.	83			
	Sierra, Oak.	83			

On Base Average plus Slugging Average

	American League			National League	
1	Olerud, Tor.	1.072	1	Bonds, S.F.	1.135
2	Thomas, Chi.	1.033	2	Galarraga, Col.	1.005
3	Griffey, Sea.	1.025	3	Piazza, L.A.	.931
4	Hoiles, Bal.	1.001	4	McGriff, S.D.-Atl.	.924
5	Gonzalez, Tex.	1.000	5	Kruk, Phi.	.905
6	Palmeiro, Tex.	.925	6	Bagwell, Hou.	.904
7	Belle, Cle.	.922	7	Dykstra, Phi.	.902
8	Salmon, Cal.	.918	8	Gwynn, S.D.	.895
9	Vaughn, Bos.	.915	9	Jefferies, St.L.	.893
10	Molitor, Tor.	.911	10	Williams, S.F.	.886

Extra Base Hits

	American League			National League	
1	Griffey, Sea.	86	1	Bonds, S.F.	88
2	Gonzalez, Tex.	80	2	Williams, S.F.	75
	Olerud, Tor.	80	3	Hayes, Col.	72
4	Palmeiro, Tex.	79	4	Bichette, Col.	69
5	Belle, Cle.	77	5	Dykstra, Phi.	69
	Thomas, Chi.	77			

Total Bases

	American League			National League	
1	Griffey, Sea.	359	1	Bonds, S.F.	365
2	Gonzalez, Tex.	339	2	Williams, S.F.	325
3	Thomas, Chi.	333	3	Gant, Atl.	309
4	Palmeiro, Tex.	331	4	Dykstra, Phi.	307
5	Olerud, Tor.	330	5	Piazza, L.A.	307

FIELDING

Fielding Average
(Minimum 90 Games)

American League			National League	
Lind, K.C.	.994	2B-best	Reed, L.A.	.993
Knoblauch, Min.	.988	2nd	Morandini, Phi.	.990
Spiers, Mil.	.971	worst	Kent, N.Y.	.969
Gagne, K.C.	.986	SS-best	Bell, Pit.	.986
Fernandez, Tor.	.985	2nd	Weiss, Fla.	.977
Fermin, Cle.	.960	worst	Cordero, Mon.	.941
Boggs, N.Y.	.970	3B-best	Buechele, Chi.	.975
Pagliarulo, Min.-Bal.	.969	2nd	Williams, S.F.	.970
Palmer, Tex.	.922	worst	Sheffield, S.D.-Fla.	.899

Putouts plus Assists per 9 Innings Played
(Minimum 90 Games)

American League			National League	
Whitaker, Det.	5.80	2B-best	Alicea, St.L.	5.57
Baerga, Cle.	5.47	2nd	Reed, L.A.	5.50
Alomar, Tor.	4.79	worst	Kent, N.Y.	4.71
Fernandez, Tor.	4.98	SS-best	Sanchez, Chi.	5.60
Valentin, Bos.	4.93	2nd	Smith, St. L.	5.56
Fermin, Cle.	4.23	worst	Cedeno, Hou.	3.88
Boggs, N.Y.	3.09	3B-best	King, Pit.	3.02
Blowers, Sea.	2.82	2nd	Pendleton, Atl.	2.89
Cooper, Bos.	2.45	worst	Hollins, Phi.	2.13

PITCHING

Wild Pitches

	American League			National League	
1	Guzman, Tor.	26	1	Greene, Phi.	15
2	Gordon, K.C.	17	2	Benes, S.D.	14
3	Morris, Tor.	14	3	Rivera, Phi.	13
	Cone, K.C.	14		Smoltz, Atl.	13
5	Wells, Det.	13	5	Wagner, Pit.	12
				Drabek, Hou.	12

Home Runs Allowed

	American League			National League	
1	Moore, Det.	35	1	Harris, S.D.-Col.	33
2	Eldred, Mil.	32	2	Armstrong, Fla.	29
3	Darwin, Bos.	31	3	Martinez, Mon.	27
4	Gullickson, Det.	28	4	Tanana, N.Y.	26
	Bones, Mil.	28	5	Guzman, Chi.	25

Home Runs Allowed per 9 IP
(Minimum 10 Home Runs Allowed)

	American League			National League	
1	Farrell, Cal.	2.18	1	Sanderson, S.F.	2.22
2	Lefferts, Tex.	1.84	2	Righetti, S.F.	2.09
3	Rhodes, Bal.	1.68	3	Smith, St.L.	1.98
4	Gardner, K.C.	1.67	4	Brantley, S.F.	1.50
5	Springer, Col.	1.65	5	Smith, Atl.	1.49

1994 The Fans Are Struck Out

If Charles Dickens were alive today, he'd call the 1994 baseball season "the best of times" and "the worst of times." It was a season that some called the best in fifty years right up until it was assassinated.

Before the 1994 season opened, purists fretted about the realignment of each league into three divisions and the additional round of playoffs that would ensue. They predicted the end of traditional pennant races. No longer could two teams be locked in a death struggle for a division championship; with the inclusion of a wild card team in the playoffs, coming in second would be as good as finishing first. A team with a losing record might actually win a weak division. Mediocrity would rule.

Sure enough, when the last game was played on August 11, the Texas Rangers led the American League West with a 52-62 mark. The Oakland Athletics were one game behind in second place. In the National League West, the Los Angeles Dodgers just managed to creep two games over .500 to hold first place there.

Did fans gnash their teeth in frustration? Far from it. With sixteen of the 28 teams still holding a legitimate shot at the playoffs, more fans than ever before looked forward to an exciting September. As it turned out, they were to be profoundly disappointed.

World champion Toronto was betrayed by its pitching, but the New York Yankees, with Paul O'Neill winning the batting championship and Jimmy Key the winningest pitcher, put up the A.L.'s best record. Yankee rooters dreamed of seeing longtime pinstripe hero Don Mattingly in a World Series at last.

In the A.L. Central, Chicago had Frank Thomas trying for a Triple Crown while Cleveland's Albert Belle nearly matched his numbers. The White Sox were in first place by a game when play ceased in August, but the Indians were hanging tough and the Royals looked to make it a three-way race.

All four teams in the American League West had losing records. Nevertheless, Seattle's Ken Griffey, Jr. created plenty of excitement with an early flurry of home runs. When the games stopped, he had cashed 40 and was only a few games off Roger Maris' pace for 61.

In the National League West, Matt Williams of the San Francisco Giants was dead-on Maris' pace with 43 homers and Barry Bonds was putting up MVP numbers as usual. Yet the Giants, with major pitching problems, couldn't overtake the surprising Dodgers, whose Raul Mondesi seemed poised to give L.A. its third consecutive N.L. Rookie of the Year. Though San Diego was far out of the race, interest centered on Tony Gwynn's chances of becoming the first .400 hitter since Ted Williams in 1941.

The Central Division saw a race between a well-balanced Cincinnati Reds team and the Houston Astros led by Jeff Bagwell's incredible season that included 116 RBI's in 110 games, a .368 batting average and a .750 slugging average. When play stopped, the Reds held a half-game lead thanks to one less loss than the Astros.

The Atlanta Braves, boasting the strongest starting pitching in baseball, were favored to take the N.L. East when the season opened, with 1993 N.L. champion Philadelphia getting some votes. However, the Phillies were kayoed early by a crippling rash of injuries, and the Braves, except for Greg Maddux, who nailed down a record third Cy Young Award in a row, never really caught fire. In the meantime, the speedy Montreal Expos raced to baseball's best record. Moises Alou (son of the Expo's manager), Larry Walker, Marquis Grissom, and Ken Hill were among the young stars who brought the Expos to the fore.

With new teams fighting for championships and more teams in the races than ever, and with batting records apparently ready to fall while numerous new stars were on the rise, baseball was enjoying perhaps the greatest season in its history. But, from the start, that joy was tempered by the possibility of a strike.

Team owners insisted that 19 of the 28 teams were losing money. While many observers suggested that such a figure was obtained through creative bookkeeping, no one doubted that small-market teams such as Milwaukee, Pittsburgh, San Diego and Seattle were in deep financial trouble.

After much hand-wringing and some arm-twisting, the large-market owners agreed to a revenue-sharing plan that would include giving the small-markets a part of the much bigger TV revenues enjoyed in large-markets. This appeared likely to save the small-market teams, but the agreement was predicated on the players accepting a salary cap. That, argued the owners, would allow the small-market clubs to spend as much on player salaries as the large-market clubs and therefore ensure a competitive balance. The owners also insisted on a change in the arbitration rules which they said led to runaway salaries.

The players refused to consider any kind of salary cap, maintaining it was only a plot to reduce salaries and break the union. After a series of meetings between the two sides found neither willing to budge, the players went out on strike at midnight on August 11. At that point, the players had received about 75 percent of their pay for the season whereas the owners were depending on post-season play for much of their income. The players, solidly behind union leader Donald Fehr, confidently expected the owners to blink.

They didn't. Even after a federal mediator was brought in, the owners refused to soften their demands and the union remained intransigent. On September 14, the baseball season, including the World Series, was officially called off.

And so America saw a season end without an ending while a set of millionaires walked the golf course instead of picket lines in protest against the fiscal policies of another group of millionaires. Many fans wondered if there would be a 1995 season. Many others answered, "Who cares?"

EAST DIVISION   1994 AMERICAN LEAGUE

Name	G by Pos	B	AGE	G	AB	R	H	2B	3B	HR	RBI	BB	SO	SB	BA	SA
NEW YORK 1st 70-43 .619			**BUCK SHOWALTER**													
TOTALS			30	113	3986	670	1155	238	16	139	632	530	660	55	.290	.462
Don Mattingly	1B97	L	33	97	372	62	113	20	1	6	51	60	24	0	.304	.411
Pat Kelly	2B93	R	26	93	286	35	80	21	2	3	41	19	51	6	.280	.399
Mike Gallego	SS72, 2B26	R	33	89	306	39	73	17	1	6	41	38	46	0	.239	.359
Wade Boggs	3B93, 1B4	L	36	97	366	61	125	19	1	11	55	61	29	2	.342	.489
Paul O'Neill	OF99, DH4	L	31	103	368	68	132	25	1	21	83	72	56	5	.359	.603
Bernie Williams	OF107	B	25	108	408	80	118	29	1	12	57	61	54	16	.289	.453
Luis Polonia	OF84, DH2	L	29	95	350	62	109	21	6	1	36	37	38	20	.311	.414
Mike Stanley	C72, 1B7, DH4	R	31	82	290	54	87	20	0	17	57	39	56	0	.300	.545
Danny Tartabull	DH78, OF26	R	31	104	399	68	102	24	1	19	67	66	111	1	.256	.464
Randy Velarde	SS49, 3B27, OF7, 2B5	R	31	77	280	47	78	16	1	9	34	22	61	4	.279	.439
Jim Leyritz	C37, DH25, 1B10	R	30	75	249	47	66	12	0	17	58	35	61	0	.265	.518
Gerald Williams	OF43	R	27	57	86	19	25	8	0	4	13	4	17	1	.291	.523
Daryl Boston	OF16, DH9	L	32	52	77	11	14	2	0	4	14	6	20	0	.182	.364
Matt Nokes (BH)	C17, DH5, 1B4	L	30	28	79	11	23	3	0	7	19	5	16	0	.291	.595
Dave Silvestri	2B9, 3B2, SS1	R	26	12	18	3	2	0	1	1	2	4	9	0	.111	.389
Bob Melvin	1B4, C4, DH1	R	32	9	14	2	4	0	0	1	3	0	3	0	.286	.500
Kevin Elster (SJ)	SS7	R	29	7	20	0	0	0	0	0	1	0	6	0	.000	.000
Russ Davis	3B4	R	24	4	14	0	2	0	0	0	1	0	4	0	.143	.143
Robert Eenhoorn	SS3	R	26	3	4	1	2	1	0	0	0	0	0	0	.500	.750
BALTIMORE 2nd 63-49 .563 6.5			**JOHNNY OATES**													
TOTALS			30	112	3856	589	1047	185	20	139	557	438	655	69	.272	.438
Rafael Palmeiro	1B111	L	29	111	436	82	139	32	0	23	76	54	63	7	.319	.550
Mark McLemore	2B96, OF7	B	29	104	343	44	88	11	1	3	29	51	50	20	.257	.321
Cal Ripken	SS112	R	33	112	444	71	140	19	3	13	75	32	41	1	.315	.459
Leo Gomez	3B78, DH5, 1B1	R	27	84	285	46	78	20	0	15	56	41	55	0	.274	.502
Jeffrey Hammonds (KJ)	OF66	R	23	68	250	45	74	18	2	8	31	17	39	5	.296	.480
Mike Devereaux	OF84	R	31	85	301	35	61	8	2	9	33	22	72	1	.203	.332
Brady Anderson	OF109	L	30	111	453	78	119	25	5	12	48	57	75	31	.263	.419
Chris Hoiles	C98	R	29	99	332	45	82	10	0	19	53	63	73	2	.247	.449
Harold Baines	DH91	L	35	94	326	44	96	12	1	16	54	30	49	0	.294	.485
Chris Sabo	3B37, OF22, DH10	R	32	68	258	41	66	15	3	11	42	20	38	1	.256	.465
Jack Voigt	OF54, 1B6, DH2	R	28	59	141	15	34	5	0	3	20	28	25	0	.241	.340
Tim Hulett	2B23, 3B9, SS6	R	34	36	92	11	21	2	1	2	15	12	24	1	.228	.337
Lonnie Smith	DH30, OF2	R	38	35	59	13	12	3	0	2	11	18	1	.203	.254
Dwight Smith	OF22, DH3	L	28	29	74	12	23	2	1	3	12	5	17	0	.311	.486
Jeff Tackett	C26	R	28	26	53	5	12	1	1	2	9	5	13	0	.226	.434
Damon Buford	OF1	R	24	4	2	2	1	0	0	0	0	0	1	0	.500	.500
Mark Smith	OF3	R	24	3	7	0	1	0	0	0	2	0	1	0	.143	.143
Paul Carey 26 (BA)																

NAME	T	AGE	W	L	PCT	SV	G	GS	CG	IP	H	BB	SO	SHO	ERA
		30	70	43	.619	31	113	113	8	1020	1045	398	656	2	4.34
Jimmy Key	L	33	17	4	.810	0	25	25	1	168	177	52	97	0	3.27
Melido Perez	R	28	9	4	.692	0	22	22	1	151	134	58	109	0	4.10
Jim Abbott	L	26	9	8	.529	0	24	24	2	160	167	64	90	0	4.55
Scott Kamienicki	R	30	8	6	.571	0	22	16	1	117	115	59	71	0	3.76
Terry Mulholland	L	31	6	7	.462	0	24	19	2	121	150	37	72	0	6.49
Bob Wickman	R	25	5	4	.556	6	53	0	0	70	54	27	56	0	3.09
Sterling Hitchcock	L	23	4	1	.800	2	23	5	1	49	48	29	37	0	4.20
Xavier Hernandez	R	28	4	4	.500	6	31	0	0	40	48	21	37	0	5.85
Steve Howe	L	36	3	0	1.000	15	40	0	0	40	28	7	18	0	1.80
Joe Ausanio	R	28	2	1	.667	0	13	0	0	16	16	6	15	0	5.17
Jeff Reardon	R	38	1	0	1.000	2	11	0	0	10	17	3	4	0	8.38
Paul Gibson	L	34	1	1	.500	0	30	0	0	29	26	17	21	0	4.97
1 Donn Pall	R	32	1	2	.333	0	26	0	0	35	43	9	21	0	3.60
2 Rob Murphy	L	34	0	0	—	0	3	0	0	2	3	0	0	0	16.20
Mark Hutton	R	24	0	0	—	0	2	0	0	4	4	0	1	0	4.91
Bob Ojeda	L	36	0	0	—	0	2	2	0	3	11	6	3	0	24.00
2 Greg Harris	R	38	0	1	.000	0	3	0	0	5	4	3	4	0	5.40
		30	63	49	.563	37	112	112	13	998	1005	351	666	4	4.31
Mike Mussina	R	25	16	5	.762	0	24	24	3	176	163	42	99	0	3.06
Ben McDonald	R	26	14	7	.667	0	24	24	5	157	151	54	94	1	4.06
Mark Eichhorn	R	33	6	5	.545	1	43	0	0	71	62	19	35	0	2.15
Sid Fernandez	L	31	6	6	.500	0	19	19	2	115	109	46	95	0	5.15
Jamie Moyer	L	31	5	7	.417	0	23	23	0	149	158	38	87	0	4.77
Mark Williamson	R	34	3	1	.750	1	28	2	0	67	75	17	28	0	4.01
Alan Mills	R	27	3	3	.500	2	47	0	0	45	43	24	44	0	5.16
Mike Oquist	R	26	3	3	.500	0	15	9	0	58	70	33	39	0	6.17
Arthur Rhodes	L	24	3	5	.375	0	10	10	3	53	51	30	47	2	5.81
Jim Poole	L	28	1	0	1.000	0	38	0	0	20	32	11	18	0	6.64
Scott Klingenbeck	R	23	1	0	1.000	0	1	1	0	7	6	4	5	0	3.86
Tom Bolton	L	32	1	2	.333	0	22	0	0	29	37	13	12	0	5.40
Lee Smith	R	36	1	4	.200	33	41	0	0	38	34	11	42	0	3.29
Armando Benitez	R	21	0	0	—	0	3	0	0	10	4	4	14	0	0.90
Brad Pennington	L	25	0	0	—	0	8	0	0	6	4	5	3	0	12.00

TORONTO — 3rd 55-60 .478 16 — CITO GASTON

Name	G by Pos	B	AGE	G	AB	R	H	2B	3B	HR	RBI	BB	SO	SB	BA	SA
TOTALS			29	115	3962	566	1064	210	30	115	534	387	691	79	.269	.424
John Olerud	1B104, DH3	L	25	108	384	47	114	29	2	12	67	61	53	1	.297	.477
Roberto Alomar	2B106	B	26	107	392	78	120	25	4	8	38	51	41	19	.306	.452
Dick Schofield	SS95	R	31	95	325	38	83	14	1	4	32	34	62	7	.255	.342
Ed Sprague	3B107, 1B3	R	26	109	405	38	97	19	1	11	44	23	95	1	.240	.373
Joe Carter	OF110, DH1	R	34	111	435	70	118	25	2	27	103	33	64	11	.271	.524
Devon White	OF98	B	31	100	403	67	109	24	6	13	49	21	80	11	.270	.457
Mike Huff	OF76	R	30	80	207	31	63	15	3	3	25	27	27	2	.304	.449
Pat Borders	C85	R	31	85	295	24	73	13	1	3	26	15	50	1	.247	.329
Paul Molitor	DH110, 1B5	R	37	115	454	86	155	30	4	14	75	55	48	20	.341	.518
Darnell Coles	OF29, 1B10, 3B7, DH1	R	32	48	143	15	30	6	1	4	15	10	25	0	.210	.350
Domingo Cedeno	2B28, SS8, 3B6, OF1	B	25	47	97	14	19	2	3	0	10	10	31	1	.196	.278
Carlos Delgado	OF41, C1	L	22	43	130	17	28	2	0	9	24	25	46	1	.215	.438
Rob Butler	OF31, DH1	L	24	41	74	13	13	0	1	0	5	7	8	0	.176	.203
Randy Knorr	C40	R	25	40	124	20	30	2	0	7	19	10	35	0	.242	.427
Alex Gonzalez (LJ)	SS15	R	21	15	53	7	8	3	1	0	1	4	17	3	.151	.245
Shawn Green	OF14	L	21	14	33	1	3	1	0	0	1	1	8	1	.091	.121
Robert Perez	OF4	R	25	4	8	0	1	0	0	0	0	0	1	0	.125	.125

NAME	T	AGE	W	L	PCT	SV	G	GS	CG	IP	H	BB	SO	SHO	ERA
		29	55	60	.478	26	115	115	13	1025	1053	482	832	4	4.70
Pat Hentgen	R	25	13	8	.619	0	24	24	6	175	158	59	147	3	3.40
Juan Guzman	R	27	12	11	.522	0	25	25	2	147	165	76	124	0	5.68
Todd Stottlemyre	R	29	7	7	.500	1	26	19	3	141	149	48	105	1	4.22
Dave Stewart	R	37	7	8	.467	0	22	22	1	133	151	62	111	0	5.87
Al Leiter	L	28	6	7	.462	0	20	20	1	112	125	65	100	0	5.08
Tony Castillo	L	31	5	2	.714	1	41	0	0	68	66	28	43	0	2.51
Darren Hall	R	29	2	3	.400	17	30	0	0	32	26	14	28	0	3.41
Danny Cox (SJ)	R	34	1	1	.500	3	10	0	0	19	7	7	14	0	1.45
Woody Williams	R	27	1	3	.250	0	38	0	0	59	44	33	56	0	3.64
Brad Cornett	R	25	1	3	.250	0	9	4	0	31	40	11	22	0	6.68
Randy St.Claire	R	33	0	0	—	0	2	0	0	2	4	2	2	0	9.00
Aaron Small	R	22	0	0	—	0	1	0	0	2	5	2	0	0	9.00
Mike Timlin	R	28	0	1	.000	2	34	0	0	40	41	20	38	0	5.18
1 Greg Cadaret	L	32	0	1	.000	0	21	0	0	20	24	17	15	0	5.85
2 Paul Righetti	L	35	0	1	.000	0	13	0	0	13	9	10	10	0	6.75
Paul Spoljaric	L	23	0	1	.000	0	2	1	0	2	5	9	2	0	38.57
Scott Brow	R	25	0	3	.000	0	18	0	0	29	34	19	15	0	5.90
Duane Ward 30 (SJ)															

BOSTON — 4th 54-61 .470 17 — BUTCH HOBSON

Name	G by Pos	B	AGE	G	AB	R	H	2B	3B	HR	RBI	BB	SO	SB	BA	SA
TOTALS			30	115	3940	552	1038	222	19	120	523	404	723	81	.263	.421
Mo Vaughn	1B106, DH1	L	26	111	394	65	122	25	1	26	82	57	112	4	.310	.576
Scott Fletcher (LJ)	2B53, DH4	R	35	63	185	31	42	9	1	3	11	16	14	8	.227	.335
John Valentin (KJ)	SS83, DH1	R	27	84	301	53	95	26	2	9	49	42	38	3	.316	.505
Scott Cooper	3B104	L	26	104	369	49	104	16	4	13	53	30	65	0	.282	.453
2 Tom Brunansky	OF42, 1B5, DH3	R	33	48	177	22	42	10	1	0	34	23	48	0	.237	.475
Otis Nixon	OF103	B	35	103	398	60	109	15	1	0	25	55	65	42	.274	.317
Mike Greenwell	OF84, DH6	L	30	95	327	60	88	25	1	11	45	38	26	2	.269	.453
Damon Berryhill	C67, DH6	B	30	82	255	30	67	17	2	6	34	19	59	0	.263	.416
Andre Dawson	DH74	R	39	75	292	34	70	18	0	16	48	7	53	2	.240	.466
Tim Naehring (NJ)	2B49, 3B11, SS8, 1B8, DH7	R	27	80	297	41	82	18	1	7	42	30	56	1	.276	.414
Lee Tinsley	OF60, DH10	B	25	78	144	27	32	4	0	2	14	19	36	13	.222	.292
Carlos Rodriguez	SS32, 2B20, 3B4	B	26	57	174	15	50	14	1	1	13	11	13	1	.287	.397
2 Wes Chamberlain	OF34, DH12	R	28	51	164	13	42	9	1	4	20	12	38	0	.256	.396
Rich Rowland	C39, DH4, 1B1	R	30	46	118	14	27	3	0	9	20	11	35	0	.229	.483
1 Billy Hatcher	OF43, DH1	R	33	44	164	24	40	9	1	1	18	11	14	4	.244	.329
1 Dave Valle	C28, 1B2	R	33	30	76	6	12	2	1	1	5	9	18	0	.158	.250
Andy Tomberlin (YJ)	OF11, DH5	L	27	18	36	1	7	0	1	1	6	1	12	1	.194	.333
Greg Litton	2B4, 1B3, 3B2, DH1	R	28	11	21	2	2	0	0	0	1	0	5	0	.095	.095
Luis Ortiz	DH2	R	24	7	18	3	3	2	0	0	1	1	4	0	.167	.278
Greg Blosser	OF3, DH1	L	23	5	11	2	1	0	0	0	0	1	4	0	.091	.091
2 Stan Royer	3B3, 1B1	R	26	4	9	0	1	0	0	0	1	0	4	0	.111	.111
1 Bob Zupcic	OF2	R	27	4	4	0	0	0	0	0	0	0	1	0	.000	.000
Eric Wedge	DH2	R	26	2	6	0	0	0	0	0	0	1	3	0	.000	.000

NAME	T	AGE	W	L	PCT	SV	G	GS	CG	IP	H	BB	SO	SHO	ERA
		30	54	61	.470	30	115	115	6	1029	1104	450	729	3	4.93
Roger Clemens	R	31	9	7	.563	0	24	24	3	171	124	71	168	1	2.85
Joe Hesketh	L	35	8	5	.615	0	25	20	0	114	117	46	83	0	4.26
Aaron Sele	R	24	8	7	.533	0	22	22	2	143	140	60	105	0	3.83
Danny Darwin (XJ)	R	38	7	5	.583	0	13	13	0	76	101	24	54	0	6.30
Scott Bankhead (GJ)	R	30	3	2	.600	0	27	0	0	38	34	12	25	0	4.54
1 Greg Harris	R	38	3	4	.429	2	35	0	0	46	60	23	44	0	8.28
2 Chris Nabholz	L	27	3	4	.429	0	8	8	0	42	44	29	23	0	6.64
Tony Fossas	L	36	2	0	1.000	1	44	0	0	34	35	15	31	0	4.76
Ken Ryan	R	25	2	3	.400	13	42	0	0	48	46	17	32	0	2.44
Tim VanEgmond	R	24	2	3	.400	0	7	7	1	38	38	21	22	0	6.34
Nate Minchey	R	24	2	3	.400	0	6	5	0	23	44	14	15	0	8.61
Chris Howard	L	28	1	0	1.000	1	37	0	0	40	35	12	22	0	3.63
2 Steve Farr	R	37	1	0	1.000	1	11	0	0	13	24	3	8	0	6.23
1 Paul Quantrill	R	25	1	1	.500	0	17	0	0	23	25	5	15	0	3.52
Ricky Trlicek	R	25	1	1	.500	1	12	0	0	22	32	16	7	0	8.06
Frank Viola (EJ)	L	34	1	1	.500	0	6	6	0	31	34	17	9	0	4.65
Andy Tomberlin	L	27	0	0	—	0	1	0	0	1	1	1	0	0	0.00
Sergio Valdez	R	29	0	1	.000	0	12	1	0	14	25	8	4	0	8.16
Jose Melendez	R	28	0	1	.000	0	10	0	0	16	20	8	9	0	5.06
Cory Bailey	R	23	0	1	.000	0	4	0	0	4	10	3	4	0	12.46
Todd Frohwirth	R	31	0	3	.000	1	22	0	0	27	40	17	13	0	10.80
Gar Finnvold (VJ)	R	26	0	4	.000	0	8	8	0	36	45	15	17	0	5.94
1 Jeff Russell	R	32	0	5	.000	12	29	0	0	28	30	13	18	0	5.14

DETROIT — 5th 53-62 .461 18 — SPARKY ANDERSON

Name	G by Pos	B	AGE	G	AB	R	H	2B	3B	HR	RBI	BB	SO	SB	BA	SA
TOTALS			31	115	3955	652	1048	216	25	161	622	520	897	46	.265	.454
Cecil Fielder	1B102, DH7	R	30	109	425	67	110	16	2	28	90	50	110	0	.259	.504
Lou Whitaker	2B83, DH5	L	37	92	322	67	97	21	2	12	43	41	47	2	.301	.491
Alan Trammell	SS63, DH11	R	36	76	292	38	78	17	1	8	28	16	35	3	.267	.414
Travis Fryman	3B114	R	25	114	464	66	122	34	5	18	85	45	126	2	.263	.474
Junior Felix	OF81, DH2	B	26	86	301	54	92	25	1	13	49	26	76	1	.306	.525
Eric Davis (ZJ)	OF35	R	32	37	120	19	22	4	0	3	13	18	45	5	.183	.292
Tony Phillips	OF104, 2B12, DH6	B	35	114	438	91	123	19	3	19	61	95	105	13	.281	.468
Chad Kreuter	C64, OF1, 1B1	B	29	65	170	17	38	8	0	1	19	28	36	0	.224	.288
Kirk Gibson	DH56, OF38	L	37	98	330	71	91	17	2	23	72	42	69	4	.276	.548
Mickey Tettleton	C53, 1B24, DH22, OF18	B	33	107	339	57	84	18	2	17	51	97	98	0	.248	.463
Chris Gomez	SS57, 2B30	R	23	84	296	32	76	19	0	8	53	33	64	5	.257	.402
Juan Samuel	OF27, DH10, 2B8, 1B2	R	33	59	136	32	42	9	5	5	21	10	26	5	.309	.559
Milt Cuyler (RJ)	OF45	B	25	48	116	20	28	3	1	1	11	13	21	5	.241	.310
John Flaherty	C33, DH1	R	26	34	40	2	6	1	0	0	4	1	11	0	.150	.175
Danny Bautista (BG)	OF30, DH1	R	22	31	99	12	23	4	1	4	15	3	18	1	.232	.414
Skeeter Barnes	1B15, OF4, DH1	R	37	24	21	4	6	0	0	1	4	0	2	0	.286	.429
1 Scott Livingstone	DH5, 1B5, 3B1	L	28	15	23	0	5	1	0	0	1	4	0	0	.217	.261
Riccardo Ingram	OF8, DH1	R	27	12	23	3	5	0	0	0	2	1	2	0	.217	.217

NAME	T	AGE	W	L	PCT	SV	G	GS	CG	IP	H	BB	SO	SHO	ERA
		31	53	62	.461	20	115	115	15	1018	1139	449	560	1	5.38
Mike Moore	R	34	11	10	.524	0	25	25	4	154	152	89	62	0	5.42
Joe Boever	R	33	9	2	.818	3	46	0	0	81	80	37	49	0	3.98
Tim Belcher	R	32	7	15	.318	0	25	25	3	162	192	78	76	0	5.89
John Doherty (XJ)	R	27	6	7	.462	0	18	17	2	101	139	26	28	0	6.48
David Wells (EJ)	L	31	5	7	.417	0	16	16	5	111	113	24	71	1	3.96
Bill Gullickson	R	35	4	5	.444	0	21	19	1	115	156	25	65	0	5.93
Sean Bergman	R	24	2	1	.667	0	3	3	0	18	22	7	12	0	5.60
Mike Gardiner	R	28	2	2	.500	5	38	1	0	59	53	23	31	0	4.14
Greg Gohr	R	26	2	2	.500	0	8	6	0	34	36	21	21	0	4.50
Storm Davis	R	32	2	4	.333	0	35	0	0	48	36	34	38	0	3.56
2 Greg Cadaret	L	32	1	0	1.000	2	17	0	0	20	17	16	14	0	3.60
Kurt Knudsen	R	29	1	0	1.000	0	4	0	0	5	7	11	1	0	13.50
Mike Henneman	R	32	1	3	.250	8	30	0	0	35	43	17	27	0	5.19
2 Gene Harris (EJ)	R	29	0	0	—	1	11	0	0	11	13	4	10	0	7.15
Phil Stidham	R	26	0	0	—	0	3	0	0	3	8	4	2	0	24.92
Buddy Groom	L	28	0	1	.000	1	40	0	0	32	31	13	27	0	3.94
Jose Lima	R	21	0	1	.000	0	3	1	0	7	11	3	7	0	13.50
1 Bill Krueger	L	36	0	2	.000	0	16	2	0	20	26	17	17	0	9.61

CENTRAL DIVISION

CHICAGO — 1st 67-46 .593 — GENE LAMONT

Name	G by Pos	B	AGE	G	AB	R	H	2B	3B	HR	RBI	BB	SO	SB	BA	SA
TOTALS			30	113	3942	633	1133	175	39	121	602	497	568	77	.287	.444
Frank Thomas	1B99, DH13	R	26	113	399	106	141	34	1	38	101	109	61	2	.353	.729
Joey Cora	2B84	B	29	90	312	55	86	13	4	2	30	38	32	8	.276	.362
Ozzie Guillen	SS99	L	30	100	365	46	105	9	5	1	39	14	35	5	.288	.348
Robin Ventura	3B108, 1B3, SS1	L	26	109	401	57	113	15	1	18	78	61	69	3	.282	.459
Darrin Jackson	OF102	R	31	104	369	43	115	17	3	10	51	27	56	7	.312	.455
Lance Johnson	OF103	L	30	106	412	56	114	11	14	3	54	26	23	26	.277	.393
Tim Raines	OF96	B	34	101	384	80	102	15	5	10	52	61	43	13	.266	.409
Ron Karkovice	C76	R	30	77	207	33	44	9	1	11	29	36	68	0	.213	.425
Julio Franco	DH99, 1B14	R	35	112	433	72	138	19	2	20	98	62	75	8	.319	.510
Warren Newson	OF34, DH3	L	29	63	102	16	26	5	0	2	7	14	23	1	.255	.363
Mike LaValliere	C57	L	33	59	139	6	39	4	0	1	24	20	15	0	.281	.331
Norberto Martin	2B28, SS6, 3B5, OF2, DH1	R	27	45	131	19	36	7	1	1	16	9	16	4	.275	.366
Craig Grebeck (NJ)	2B14, SS14, 3B7	R	29	35	97	17	30	5	0	0	5	12	5	0	.309	.361
2 Bob Zupcic	OF28, 3B2, 1B1	R	27	32	88	10	18	4	1	1	8	4	16	0	.205	.307
Joe Hall (LJ)	OF9, DH2	L	28	17	28	6	11	3	0	1	5	2	4	0	.393	.607
Dan Pasqua (KJ)	OF5, 1B3	L	32	11	23	2	5	2	0	0	4	0	9	0	.217	.565
2 Bob Melvin	C11	R	32	11	19	3	3	0	0	0	1	1	4	0	.158	.158
Dann Howitt	OF7, 1B4	L	29	10	14	4	5	3	0	0	1	0	7	0	.357	.571
Olmedo Saenz	3B5	R	23	9	14	2	2	0	1	0	1	3	3	0	.143	.286
2 Ron Tingley	C5	R	35	5	5	0	0	0	0	0	0	0	1	0	.000	.000

NAME	T	AGE	W	L	PCT	SV	G	GS	CG	IP	H	BB	SO	SHO	ERA
		30	67	46	.593	20	113	113	13	1011	964	377	754	9	3.96
Jason Bere	R	23	12	2	.857	0	24	24	0	142	119	80	127	0	3.81
Wilson Alvarez	L	24	12	8	.600	0	24	24	2	162	147	62	108	1	3.45
Alex Fernandez	R	24	11	7	.611	0	24	24	4	170	163	50	122	3	3.86
Jack McDowell	R	28	10	9	.526	0	25	25	6	181	186	42	127	2	3.73
Scott Sanderson	R	37	8	4	.667	0	18	14	1	92	110	12	36	0	5.09
Roberto Hernandez	R	29	4	4	.500	14	45	0	0	48	44	19	50	0	4.91
Dennis Cook	L	31	3	1	.750	0	38	0	0	33	29	14	26	0	3.55
Jose DeLeon	R	33	3	2	.600	2	42	0	0	67	48	31	67	0	3.36
Dane Johnson	R	31	2	1	.667	0	15	0	0	12	16	11	7	0	6.57
Paul Assenmacher	L	33	1	2	.333	1	44	0	0	33	26	13	29	0	3.55
Kirk McCaskill	R	33	1	4	.200	3	40	0	0	53	51	22	37	0	3.42
1 Jeff Schwarz	R	30	0	0	—	0	11	9	16	14	6	0	6.35
Atlee Hammaker	L	36	0	0	—	0	2	0	0	1	1	1	0	0.00
Scott Ruffcorn	R	24	0	2	.000	0	2	2	0	6	15	5	3	0	12.79
Scott Radinsky 26 (IL)															

CLEVELAND 2nd 66-47 .584 1 MIKE HARGROVE

Name	G by Pos	B	AGE	G	AB	R	H	2B	3B	HR	RBI	BB	SO	SB	BA	SA
TOTALS			28	113	4022	679	1165	240	20	167	647	382	629	131	.290	.484
Paul Sorrento	1B86, DH8	L	28	95	322	43	90	14	0	14	62	34	68	0	.280	.453
Carlos Baerga	2B102, DH1	B	25	103	442	81	139	32	2	19	80	10	45	1	.314	.525
Omar Vizquel (KJ)	SS69	B	27	69	286	39	78	10	1	1	33	23	23	13	.273	.325
Jim Thome	3B94	B	23	98	321	58	86	20	1	20	52	46	84	3	.268	.523
Manny Ramirez	OF84, DH5	R	22	91	290	51	78	22	0	17	60	42	72	4	.269	.521
Kenny Lofton	0F112	L	27	112	459	105	160	32	9	12	57	52	56	60	.349	.536
Albert Belle	OF104, DH2	R	27	106	412	90	147	35	2	36	101	58	71	9	.357	.714
Sandy Alomar	C78	R	28	80	292	44	84	15	1	14	43	25	31	8	.288	.490
Eddie Murray	DH82, 1B26	B	38	108	433	57	110	21	1	17	76	31	53	8	.254	.425
Alvaro Espinoza	3B37, SS36, 2B20, 1B3	R	32	90	231	27	55	13	0	1	19	6	33	1	.238	.307
Wayne Kirby	OF68, DH2	L	30	78	191	33	56	6	0	5	23	13	30	11	.293	.403
Candy Maldonado	DH25, OF5	R	33	42	92	14	18	5	1	5	12	19	31	1	.196	.435
Tony Pena	C40	R	37	40	112	18	33	8	1	2	10	9	11	0	.295	.438
Ruben Amaro	OF12, DH3	R	29	26	23	5	5	1	0	2	5	2	3	2	.217	.522
Rene Gonzales	3B13, SS4, 1B4, 2B1	R	33	22	23	6	8	1	1	1	5	5	3	2	.348	.609
Mark Lewis	SS13, 3B6, 2B1	R	24	20	73	6	15	5	0	1	8	2	13	1	.205	.315
Herbert Perry	1B2, 3B2	R	24	4	9	1	1	0	0	0	1	3	1	0	.111	.111
Matt Merullo	C4	L	28	4	10	1	1	0	0	0	0	2	1	0	.100	.100
Jesse Levis		L	26	1	1	0	0	0	0	0	0	0	0	0	1.000	1.000

NAME	T	AGE	W	L	PCT	SV	G	GS	CG	IP	H	BB	SO	SHO	ERA
		32	66	47	.584	21	113	113	17	1019	1097	404	666	5	4.36
Mark Clark	R	26	11	3	.786	0	20	20	4	127	133	40	60	1	3.82
Dennis Martinez	R	39	11	6	.647	0	24	24	7	177	166	44	92	3	3.52
Jack Morris	R	39	10	6	.625	0	23	23	1	141	163	67	100	0	5.60
Charles Nagy	R	27	10	8	.556	0	23	23	3	169	175	48	108	0	3.45
Eric Plunk	R	30	7	2	.778	3	41	0	0	71	61	37	73	0	2.54
Jose Mesa	R	28	7	5	.583	2	51	0	0	73	71	26	63	0	3.82
Jason Grimsley	R	26	5	2	.714	0	14	13	1	83	91	34	59	0	4.57
Matt Turner (IL)	R	27	1	0	1.000	1	9	0	0	13	13	7	5	0	2.13
1 Steve Farr	R	37	1	1	.500	4	19	0	0	15	17	15	12	0	5.28
2 Jeff Russell	R	32	1	1	.500	5	13	0	0	13	13	3	10	0	4.97
Albie Lopez	R	22	1	2	.333	0	4	4	1	17	20	6	18	1	4.24
Derek Lilliquist	L	28	1	3	.250	1	36	0	0	29	34	8	15	0	4.91
Jerry Dipoto (IL)	R	26	0	0	—	0	7	0	0	16	26	10	9	0	8.04
Bill Wertz	R	27	0	0	—	0	1	0	0	4	9	1	1	0	10.38
Paul Shuey	R	23	0	1	.000	5	14	0	0	12	14	12	16	0	8.49
Russ Swan	L	30	0	0	—	0	12	0	0	8	13	7	2	0	11.25
1 Chris Nabholz (SJ)	L	27	0	1	.000	0	6	4	0	11	23	9	5	0	11.45
1 Brian Barnes	L	27	0	1	.000	0	4	0	0	13	12	15	5	0	5.40
Chad Ogea	R	23	0	0	.000	0	6	0	0	16	21	10	11	0	6.06
Julian Tavarez	R	21	0	0	.000	0	1	1	0	2	6	1	0	0	21.60
2 Larry Casian	L	28	0	2	.000	0	7	0	0	8	16	4	2	0	8.64

KANSAS CITY 3rd 64-51 .557 4 HAL McRAE

Name	G by Pos	B	AGE	G	AB	R	H	2B	3B	HR	RBI	BB	SO	SB	BA	SA
TOTALS			30	115	3911	574	1051	211	38	100	538	376	698	140	.269	.419
Wally Joyner	1B86, DH11	L	32	97	363	52	113	20	3	8	57	47	43	3	.311	.449
Jose Lind	2B84, DH1	R	30	85	290	34	78	16	2	1	31	16	34	0	.269	.348
Greg Gagne	SS106	R	32	107	375	39	97	23	3	7	51	27	79	10	.259	.392
Gary Gaetti	3B85, 1B9	R	35	90	327	53	94	15	3	12	57	19	63	0	.287	.462
Felix Jose	OF98	B	29	99	366	56	111	28	1	11	55	35	75	10	.303	.475
Brian McRae	OF110, DH4	B	26	114	436	71	119	22	6	4	40	54	67	28	.273	.378
Vince Coleman	OF99, DH5	B	33	104	438	61	105	14	12	2	33	29	72	50	.240	.340
Mike Macfarlane	C81, DH8	R	30	92	314	53	80	17	3	14	47	35	71	1	.255	.462
Bob Hamelin	DH70, 1B24	L	26	101	312	64	88	25	1	24	65	56	62	4	.282	.599
Terry Shumpert	2B38, 3B24, DH2, SS1	R	27	64	183	28	44	6	2	8	24	13	39	18	.240	.426
Dave Henderson	OF40, DH16	R	35	56	198	27	49	14	1	5	31	16	28	2	.247	.404
Brent Mayne	C42, DH3	L	26	46	144	19	37	5	1	2	20	14	27	1	.257	.347
David Howard	3B25, SS15, 2B3, DH2, OF1, P1	R	27	46	83	9	19	4	0	1	13	11	23	3	.229	.313
Hubie Brooks	DH19, 1B4	R	37	34	61	5	14	2	0	1	14	2	10	1	.230	.311
Keith Miller (XJ)	OF4, 3B2	R	31	5	15	1	2	0	0	0	0	0	3	1	.133	.133
Kevin Koslofski	OF2	L	27	2	4	0	1	0	0	0	0	1	2	0	.250	.250
Tom Goodwin	OF1	L	25	2	2	0	0	0	0	0	0	0	1	0	.000	.000

NAME	T	AGE	W	L	PCT	SV	G	GS	CG	IP	H	BB	SO	SHO	ERA
		28	64	51	.557	38	115	115	0	1032	1018	392	717	6	4.23
David Cone	R	31	16	5	.762	0	23	23	4	172	130	54	132	3	2.94
Tom Gordon	R	26	11	7	.611	0	24	24	0	155	136	87	126	0	4.35
Kevin Appier	R	26	7	6	.538	0	23	23	1	155	137	63	145	0	3.83
Mark Gubicza	R	31	7	9	.438	0	22	22	0	130	158	23	59	0	4.50
Hipolito Pichardo	R	24	5	3	.625	3	45	0	0	68	82	24	36	0	4.92
Billy Brewer	L	26	4	1	.800	3	50	0	0	39	28	16	25	0	2.56
Jose DeJesus	R	29	3	1	.750	5	4	0	0	27	27	13	12	0	4.73
Rusty Meacham	R	26	3	3	.500	4	36	0	0	51	51	12	36	0	3.73
Stan Belinda	R	27	2	2	.500	1	37	0	0	49	47	24	37	0	5.14
Chris Haney	L	25	2	2	.500	0	8	0	0	28	36	11	18	0	7.31
Jeff Montgomery	R	32	2	3	.400	27	42	0	0	45	48	15	50	0	4.03
Mike Magnante	L	29	2	3	.400	0	36	1	0	47	55	16	21	0	4.60
David Howard	R	26	0	0	.000	0	1	0	0	2	5	0	0	0	4.50
Jeff Granger	L	22	0	1	.000	0	2	2	0	9	13	6	3	0	6.75
Bob Milacki	R	28	0	5	.000	0	10	10	0	56	68	20	17	0	6.14

MINNESOTA 4th 53-60 .469 14 TOM KELLY

Name	G by Pos	B	AGE	G	AB	R	H	2B	3B	HR	RBI	BB	SO	SB	BA	SA
TOTALS			30	113	3952	594	1092	239	23	103	556	359	635	94	.276	.427
Kent Hrbek (LJ)	1B72, DH4	L	34	81	274	34	74	11	0	10	53	37	28	0	.270	.420
Chuck Knoblauch	2B109, SS1	R	25	109	445	85	139	45	3	5	51	41	56	35	.312	.461
Pat Meares	SS79	R	25	80	229	29	61	12	1	2	24	14	50	5	.266	.354
Scott Leius	3B95, SS2	R	28	97	350	57	86	16	1	14	49	37	58	2	.246	.417
Kirby Puckett	OF95, DH13	R	34	108	439	79	139	32	3	20	112	28	47	6	.317	.540
Alex Cole	OF100	L	28	105	345	68	102	15	5	4	23	44	60	29	.296	.403
Shane Mack (SJ)	OF75, DH4	R	30	81	303	55	101	21	2	15	61	32	51	4	.333	.564
Matt Walbeck	C95, DH1	B	24	97	338	31	69	12	0	5	35	17	37	1	.204	.284
Dave Winfield	DH76, OF1	R	42	77	294	35	74	15	3	10	43	31	51	2	.252	.425
Pedro Munoz	OF58, DH12	R	25	75	244	35	72	15	2	11	36	19	67	0	.295	.508
Jeff Reboulet	SS42, 2B14, 1B10, 3B6, OF4, DH1	R	30	74	189	28	49	11	1	3	23	18	23	0	.259	.376
Chip Hale	3B21, DH10, 1B7, 2B5, OF1	L	29	67	118	13	31	9	0	1	11	16	14	0	.263	.364
Dave McCarty	1B32, DH4	R	24	44	131	21	34	8	2	1	12	7	32	2	.260	.374
Derek Parks	C31	R	25	31	89	6	17	6	0	1	9	4	20	0	.191	.292
Rich Becker	OF26, DH1	B	22	28	68	12	26	3	0	1	8	13	25	6	.265	.327
Steve Dunn	1B12	L	24	14	35	2	8	5	0	0	4	1	12	0	.229	.371
Denny Hocking	SS10	B	24	11	31	3	10	3	0	0	2	0	4	1	.323	.419

NAME	T	AGE	W	L	PCT	SV	G	GS	CG	IP	H	BB	SO	SHO	ERA
		28	53	60	.469	29	113	113	6	1005	1197	388	602	4	5.68
Kevin Tapani	R	30	11	7	.611	0	24	24	4	156	181	39	91	1	4.62
Pat Mahomes	R	23	9	5	.643	0	21	21	0	120	121	62	53	0	4.73
Scott Erickson	R	26	8	11	.421	0	23	23	2	144	173	59	104	1	5.44
Jim Deshaies	L	34	6	12	.333	0	25	25	0	130	170	54	78	0	7.39
Dave Stevens	R	24	5	2	.714	0	24	0	0	45	55	23	24	0	6.80
Mark Guthrie	L	28	4	2	.667	1	50	2	0	51	65	18	38	0	6.14
Carlos Pulido	L	22	3	7	.300	0	19	14	0	84	87	40	32	0	5.98
Mike Trombley	R	27	2	0	1.000	0	24	0	0	48	56	18	32	0	6.33
Carl Willis	R	33	4	4	.333	0	59	0	0	59	89	12	37	0	5.92
Kevin Campbell	R	29	1	0	1.000	0	14	0	0	25	20	5	15	0	2.92
1 Larry Casian	L	28	1	3	.250	1	33	0	0	41	57	12	18	0	7.08
Rick Aguilera	R	32	1	4	.200	23	44	0	0	45	57	10	46	0	3.63
Erik Schullstrom	R	25	0	0	—	1	9	0	0	13	13	5	13	0	2.77
Keith Garagozzo	L	24	0	0	—	0	2	1	0	9	13	3	3	0	9.64
Brett Merriman	R	27	0	1	.000	0	15	0	0	17	18	14	10	0	6.35
Eddie Guardado	L	23	0	2	.000	0	4	4	0	17	26	4	8	0	8.47

MILWAUKEE 5th 53-62 .461 15 PHIL GARNER

Name	G by Pos	B	AGE	G	AB	R	H	2B	3B	HR	RBI	BB	SO	SB	BA	SA
TOTALS			28	115	3978	547	1045	238	21	99	510	417	680	59	.263	.408
John Jaha	1B73, DH11	R	28	84	291	45	70	14	0	12	39	32	75	3	.241	.412
Jody Reed	2B106	R	31	108	399	48	108	22	0	2	37	57	34	5	.271	.341
Pat Listach (KJ)	SS16	R	26	16	54	6	16	3	0	0	2	3	8	2	.296	.352
Kevin Seitzer (LJ)	3B43, 1B35, DH4	R	32	80	309	44	97	24	2	5	49	30	38	2	.314	.453
Matt Mieske	OF80	R	26	84	259	39	67	13	1	10	38	21	62	3	.259	.432
Darryl Hamilton (EJ)	OF32, DH4	L	29	36	141	23	37	10	1	1	13	15	17	3	.262	.369
Greg Vaughn	OF81, DH14	R	28	95	370	59	94	24	1	19	55	51	93	9	.254	.478
Dave Nilsson	C60, DH43, 1B5	L	24	109	397	51	109	28	3	12	69	34	61	1	.275	.451
Brain Harper (BA)	DH36, C25, OF3	R	34	64	251	23	73	15	0	4	32	9	18	0	.291	.398
Turner Ward	OF99, 3B1	B	29	102	367	55	85	15	2	9	45	52	68	6	.232	.357
Jose Valentin	SS83, 2B18, 3B1, DH1	B	24	97	285	47	68	19	0	11	46	38	75	12	.239	.421
Alex Diaz	OF73, 2B2	R	25	79	187	17	47	5	7	1	17	10	19	5	.251	.369
Bill Spiers	3B35, SS35, DH2, OF1	L	28	73	214	27	54	10	1	0	17	19	42	7	.252	.308
B.J. Surhoff (MJ)	3B18, C12, 1B8, OF3, DH1	L	29	40	134	20	35	11	2	5	22	16	14	0	.261	.485
Jeff Cirillo	3B37, 2B1	R	24	39	126	17	30	9	0	3	12	11	16	0	.238	.381
Mike Matheny	C27	R	23	28	53	3	12	3	0	1	2	3	13	0	.226	.340
Troy O'Leary (MJ)	OF21, DH1	L	24	27	66	9	18	1	1	2	7	5	12	1	.273	.409
2 Dave Valle	C12, DH2	R	33	16	36	8	14	6	0	1	5	9	4	0	.389	.639
1 Tom Brunansky	OF6, 1B2, DH2	R	33	16	28	2	6	2	0	0	0	1	9	0	.214	.286
Rick Wrona	C5, 1B1	R	30	6	10	2	5	4	0	1	5	1	0	0	.500	1.200
Duane Singleton	OF2	L	21	2	0	0	0	0	0	0	0	0	0	0		

NAME	T	AGE	W	L	PCT	SV	G	GS	CG	IP	H	BB	SO	SHO	ERA
		29	53	62	.461	23	115	115	11	1036	1071	421	577	3	4.62
Cal Eldred	R	26	11	11	.500	0	25	25	4	179	158	84	98	0	4.68
Ricky Bones	R	25	10	9	.526	0	24	24	4	171	166	45	57	1	3.43
Bill Wegman (MJ)	R	31	8	4	.667	0	19	19	0	116	140	26	59	0	4.51
Jaime Navarro	R	27	4	9	.308	0	29	10	0	90	115	35	65	0	6.62
Jesse Orosco	L	37	3	1	.750	0	40	0	0	39	32	26	36	0	5.08
Mike Ignasiak	R	28	3	1	.750	0	23	5	0	48	51	13	24	0	4.53
Jose Mercedes (PJ)	R	23	2	1	1.000	0	19	14	0	31	22	16	11	0	2.32
Graeme Lloyd	L	27	2	3	.400	3	43	0	0	47	49	15	31	0	5.17
Doug Henry	R	30	2	3	.400	0	31	0	0	31	32	23	20	0	4.60
Angel Miranda (KJ)	L	24	2	5	.286	0	8	8	1	46	39	27	24	0	5.28
Bob Scanlan	R	27	2	6	.250	2	30	12	0	103	117	28	65	0	4.11
Mark Kiefer	R	25	1	0	1.000	0	7	0	0	11	15	8	8	0	8.44
Jeff Bronkey (EJ)	R	28	1	1	.500	1	16	0	0	21	20	12	13	0	4.35
Mike Fetters	R	29	1	4	.200	17	42	0	0	46	41	27	31	0	2.54
Teddy Higuera	L	35	1	5	.167	17	12	0	0	59	74	36	35	0	7.06

TEXAS — 1st 52-62 .456 — KEVIN KENNEDY

Name	G by Pos	B	AGE	G	AB	R	H	2B	3B	HR	RBI	BB	SO	SB	BA	SA
TOTALS			27	114	3983	613	1114	198	27	124	582	437	730	82	.280	.436
Will Clark	1B107, DH1	L	30	110	389	73	128	24	2	13	80	71	59	5	.329	.501
Jeff Frye	2B54, 3B1, DH1	R	27	57	205	37	67	20	3	0	18	29	23	6	.327	.454
Manuel Lee	SS85, 2B13	R	29	95	335	41	93	18	2	2	38	21	66	3	.278	.361
Dean Palmer	3B91	R	25	93	342	50	84	14	2	19	59	26	89	3	.246	.465
Rusty Greer	OF73, 1B9	L	25	80	277	36	87	16	1	10	46	46	46	0	.314	.487
David Hulse	OF76	L	26	77	310	58	79	8	4	1	19	21	53	18	.255	.316
Juan Gonzalez	OF107	R	24	107	422	57	116	18	4	19	85	30	66	6	.275	.472
Ivan Rodriguez	C99	R	22	99	363	56	108	19	1	16	57	31	42	6	.298	.488
Jose Canseco	DH111	R	29	111	429	88	121	19	2	31	90	69	114	15	.282	.552
Doug Strange	2B53, 3B13, OF3	B	30	73	226	26	48	12	1	5	26	15	38	1	.212	.341
Oddibe McDowell	OF53, DH2	L	31	59	183	34	48	5	1	1	15	28	39	14	.262	.317
Chris James	OF48	R	31	52	133	28	34	8	4	7	19	20	38	0	.256	.534
Esteban Beltre	SS41, 1B5, 2B4	R	29	48	131	12	37	5	0	0	12	16	25	2	.282	.321
Billy Ripken (PJ)	3B18, 2B12, SS2, 1B1	R	29	32	81	9	25	5	0	0	6	3	11	2	.309	.370
Junior Ortiz	C28	R	34	29	76	3	21	2	0	0	9	5	11	0	.276	.303
Gary Redus (LJ)	OF7, 1B5	R	37	18	33	2	9	1	0	0	2	4	6	2	.273	.303
Rob Ducey	OF10	L	29	11	29	1	5	1	0	0	1	2	1	0	.172	.207
Butch Davis	OF4	R	26	4	17	2	4	3	0	0	0	0	3	1	.235	.412
Chuck Jackson	3B1	R	31	1	2	0	0	0	0	0	0	0	0	0	.000	.000
Jeff Huson 29 (KJ)																

NAME	T	AGE	W	L	PCT	SV	G	GS	CG	IP	H	BB	SO	SHO	ERA
		30	52	62	.456	26	114	114	10	1023	1176	394	683	4	5.45
Kenny Rogers	L	29	11	8	.579	0	24	24	6	187	169	52	120	2	4.46
Kevin Brown	R	29	7	9	.438	0	26	25	3	170	218	50	123	0	4.82
Hector Fajardo	R	23	5	7	.417	0	18	12	0	83	95	26	45	0	6.91
Darren Oliver	L	23	4	0	1.000	2	43	0	0	50	40	35	50	0	3.42
Jay Howell	R	38	4	1	.800	2	40	0	0	43	44	16	22	0	5.44
Rick Helling	R	23	3	2	.600	0	9	9	1	52	62	18	25	1	5.88
Tom Henke (XJ)	R	36	3	6	.333	15	37	0	0	38	33	12	39	0	3.79
Bruce Hurst (SJ)	L	36	2	1	.667	0	8	8	0	38	53	16	24	0	7.11
Matt Whiteside	R	26	2	2	.500	1	47	0	0	61	68	28	37	0	5.02
Brian Bohanon	L	25	2	2	.500	0	11	5	0	37	51	8	26	0	7.23
Chris Carpenter	R	29	2	5	.286	5	47	0	0	59	69	20	39	0	5.03
Roger Pavlik (SJ)	R	26	2	5	.286	0	11	11	0	50	61	30	31	0	7.69
Tim Leary	R	35	1	1	.500	0	6	3	0	21	26	11	9	0	8.14
Steve Dreyer	R	24	1	1	.500	0	5	3	0	17	19	8	11	0	5.71
Rick Reed	R	29	1	1	.500	0	4	3	0	17	17	7	12	0	5.94
Rick Honeycutt	L	40	1	2	.333	1	42	0	0	25	37	9	18	0	7.20
Dan Smith (BE)	L	25	1	2	.333	0	13	0	0	15	18	12	9	0	4.30
James Hurst	L	25	0	0	—	0	8	0	0	11	17	8	5	0	10.13
Duff Brumley	R	23	0	0	—	0	2	0	0	3	6	5	4	0	16.20
Terry Burrows	L	25	0	0	—	0	1	1	0	1	1	0	0	0	9.00
Jack Armstrong (SJ)	R	29	0	1	.000	0	2	2	0	10	9	2	7	0	3.60
John Dettmer	R	24	0	6	.000	0	11	9	0	54	63	20	27	0	4.33

OAKLAND — 2nd 51-63 .447 1 — TONY LaRUSSA

Name	G by Pos	B	AGE	G	AB	R	H	2B	3B	HR	RBI	BB	SO	SB	BA	SA
TOTALS			29	114	3885	549	1009	178	13	113	515	417	686	91	.260	.399
Mark McGwire (FJ)	1B40, DH5	R	30	47	135	26	34	3	0	9	25	37	40	0	.252	.474
Brent Gates	2B63, 1B1	B	24	64	233	29	66	11	1	2	24	21	32	3	.283	.365
Mike Bordick	SS112, 2B4	R	28	114	391	38	99	18	4	2	37	38	44	7	.253	.335
Scott Brosius	3B93, OF7, 1B1	R	27	96	324	31	77	14	1	14	49	24	57	2	.238	.417
Ruben Sierra	OF98, DH10	B	28	110	426	71	114	21	1	23	92	23	64	8	.268	.484
Stan Javier	OF108, 3B1, 1B4	B	30	109	419	75	114	23	0	10	44	49	76	24	.272	.399
Rickey Henderson	OF71, DH13	R	35	87	296	66	77	13	0	6	20	72	45	22	.260	.365
Terry Steinbach	C93, 1B6, DH6	R	32	103	369	51	105	21	2	11	57	26	62	2	.285	.442
Geronimo Berroa	DH44, OF42, 1B9	R	29	96	340	55	104	18	2	13	65	41	62	7	.306	.485
Scott Hemond	C39, 2B25, 3B12, 1B7, OF2	R	28	91	198	23	44	11	0	3	20	16	51	7	.222	.323
Troy Neel	1B45, DH35	L	28	83	278	43	74	13	0	15	48	38	61	2	.266	.475
Mike Aldrete	OF35, 1B27, DH1	L	33	76	178	23	43	5	0	4	18	20	35	2	.242	.337
Eric Fox	OF24	R	30	46	44	7	9	2	0	1	3	8	2	.205	.318	
1 Junior Noboa	2B14, SS1	R	29	17	40	3	13	1	1	0	6	2	5	1	.325	.400
Fausto Cruz	SS10, 3B4, 2B1	R	22	17	28	2	3	0	0	0	0	4	6	0	.107	.107
Craig Paquette	3B14	R	25	14	49	0	7	2	0	0	0	0	14	1	.143	.184
Francisco Matos	2B12	R	24	14	28	1	7	1	0	0	2	1	2	1	.250	.286
Ernie Young	OF10, DH1	R	24	11	30	2	2	1	0	0	3	1	8	0	.067	.100
Mike Brumley (FJ)	2B4, 3B4, OF3, SS1	B	31	11	25	0	6	0	0	0	2	1	8	0	.240	.240
Steve Sax (FJ)	2B6	R	34	7	24	2	6	0	1	0	1	0	2	0	.250	.333
Eric Helfand	C6	R	25	7	6	1	1	0	0	0	1	2	3	0	.167	.167
Jim Bowie	1B6	L	29	6	14	0	3	0	0	0	0	1	2	0	.214	.214
Jeff Schaefer	3B3, SS2, 1B1	R	33	6	8	0	1	0	0	0	0	0	1	0	.125	.125
Lance Blankenship 30 (SJ)																

NAME	T	AGE	W	L	PCT	SV	G	GS	CG	IP	H	BB	SO	SHO	ERA
		30	51	63	.447	23	114	114	12	1003	979	510	732	9	4.80
Ron Darling	R	33	10	11	.476	0	25	25	4	160	162	59	108	0	4.50
Bobby Witt	R	30	8	10	.444	0	24	24	5	136	151	70	111	3	5.04
Todd Van Poppel	R	22	7	10	.412	0	23	23	0	117	108	89	83	0	6.09
Steve Ontiveros	R	33	6	4	.600	0	27	13	2	115	93	26	56	0	2.65
Mark Acre	R	25	5	1	.833	0	34	0	0	34	24	23	21	0	3.41
Dennis Eckersley	R	39	5	4	.556	19	45	0	0	44	49	13	47	0	4.26
John Briscoe (SJ)	R	26	4	2	.667	1	37	0	0	49	31	39	45	0	4.01
Bob Welch	R	37	3	6	.333	0	25	8	0	69	79	43	44	0	7.08
Steve Karsay (EJ)	R	22	1	1	.500	0	4	4	1	28	28	8	15	0	2.57
Billy Taylor	R	32	1	3	.250	1	41	0	0	46	38	18	48	0	3.50
Miquel Jimenez	R	24	1	4	.200	0	8	7	0	34	38	32	22	0	7.41
Dave Leiper	L	32	0	0	—	1	26	0	0	19	13	6	14	0	1.93
Edwin Nunez	R	31	0	0	—	0	15	0	0	15	26	10	15	0	12.00
1 Dave Righetti	L	35	0	0	—	0	7	0	0	4	13	9	4	0	16.71
Steve Phoenix	R	26	0	0	—	0	2	0	0	4	4	3	2	0	6.23
Roger Smithberg	R	27	0	0	—	0	3	0	0	5	9	1	3	0	15.43
Vince Horsman	L	27	0	0	.000	0	33	0	0	29	29	11	20	0	4.91
Mike Mohler	L	25	0	1	.000	1	10	2	0	2	2	2	4	0	7.71
Ed Vosberg	L	32	0	0	.000	0	16	0	0	14	16	5	12	0	3.95
Carlos Reyes	R	25	0	3	.000	1	27	9	0	78	71	44	57	0	4.15

SEATTLE — 3rd 49-63 .438 2 — LOU PINIELLA

Name	G by Pos	B	AGE	G	AB	R	H	2B	3B	HR	RBI	BB	SO	SB	BA	SA
TOTALS			28	112	3883	569	1045	211	18	153	549	372	652	48	.269	.451
Tino Martinez	1B82, DH8	L	26	97	329	42	86	21	0	20	61	29	52	1	.261	.508
Rich Amaral	2B42, OF16, SS7, DH6, 1B2	R	32	77	228	37	60	10	2	4	18	24	28	5	.263	.377
Felix Fermin	SS77, 2B25	R	30	101	379	52	120	21	0	1	35	11	22	4	.317	.380
Edgar Martinez	3B64, DH23	R	31	89	326	47	93	23	1	13	51	53	42	6	.285	.482
Jay Buhner	OF96, DH4	R	29	101	358	74	100	23	4	21	68	66	63	0	.279	.542
Ken Griffey Jr.	OF103, DH9	L	24	111	433	94	140	24	4	40	90	56	73	11	.323	.674
Eric Anthony	OF71, DH4	L	26	79	262	31	62	14	1	10	30	23	66	6	.237	.412
Dan Wilson	C91	R	25	91	282	24	61	14	2	3	27	10	57	1	.216	.312
Reggie Jefferson	DH32, 1B13, OF2	B	25	63	162	24	53	11	0	8	32	17	32	0	.327	.543
Mike Blowers	3B48, 1B20, OF9, DH9	R	29	85	270	37	78	13	0	9	49	25	60	2	.289	.437
Luis Sojo	2B40, SS24, 3B1	R	29	63	213	32	59	9	2	6	22	8	25	2	.277	.423
Keith Mitchell (FJ)	OF38, DH6	R	24	46	128	21	29	2	0	5	15	18	22	0	.227	.359
Brian Turang	OF30, 2B5, DH4	R	27	38	112	9	21	5	1	1	7	7	25	3	.188	.277
Bill Haselman	C33, DH3, OF2	R	28	38	83	11	16	7	1	1	8	3	11	1	.193	.337
Torey Lovullo	2B20, 3B5, DH2	B	28	36	72	9	16	5	0	2	7	9	13	1	.222	.375
Greg Pirkl	DH10, 1B7	R	23	19	53	7	14	3	0	6	11	1	12	0	.264	.660
Alex Rodriguez	SS17	R	18	17	54	4	11	0	0	0	2	3	20	3	.204	.204
Marc Newfield	DH9, OF3	R	21	12	38	3	7	1	0	1	4	2	4	0	.184	.289
Dale Sveum	DH4, 3B3	R	30	10	27	3	5	0	0	1	2	2	10	0	.185	.296
Chris Howard	C9	R	28	9	25	2	5	1	0	0	2	1	6	0	.200	.240
Darren Bragg	OF3, DH3	L	24	8	19	4	3	1	0	0	2	3	2	0	.158	.211
Jerry Willard	C1, DH1	L	34	6	5	1	1	0	0	0	1	1	0	0	.200	.800
Quinn Mack	OF4, DH1	L	28	5	21	1	5	3	0	0	2	1	3	2	.238	.381
Mackey Sasser (KJ)	C1, OF1	L	31	3	4	1	0	0	0	0	0	0	0	0	.000	.000

NAME	T	AGE	W	L	PCT	SV	G	GS	CG	IP	H	BB	SO	SHO	ERA
		28	49	63	.438	21	112	112	13	984	1051	486	763	7	4.99
Randy Johnson	L	30	13	6	.684	0	23	23	9	172	132	72	204	4	3.19
Bill Risley	R	27	9	6	.600	0	37	0	0	52	31	19	61	0	3.44
Dave Fleming	L	24	7	11	.389	0	23	23	0	117	152	65	65	0	6.46
Bobby Ayala	R	24	4	3	.571	18	46	0	0	57	42	26	76	0	2.86
Chris Bosio (KJ)	R	31	4	10	.286	0	19	19	4	125	137	40	67	0	4.32
Goose Gossage	R	42	0	0	1.000	1	36	0	0	47	44	15	29	0	4.18
Tim Davis	L	23	2	2	.500	2	42	1	0	49	57	25	28	0	4.01
John Cummings	L	25	2	4	.333	0	13	13	0	64	66	37	33	0	5.63
Roger Salkeld	R	23	2	5	.286	0	13	13	0	59	76	45	46	0	7.17
2 Mik Hill	R	28	2	0	1.000	0	0	0	0	24	30	11	16	0	6.46
2 Bob Wells	R	27	1	0	1.000	1	0	0	0	9	9	2	3	0	2.25
Greg Hibbard (SJ)	L	29	1	5	.167	0	15	14	0	81	115	31	39	0	6.69
Jeff Nelson	R	27	0	0	—	0	28	0	0	42	35	20	44	0	2.76
Erik Plantenberg	L	25	0	0	—	0	6	0	0	7	4	7	1	0	13.50
Jeff Darwin	R	24	0	0	—	0	2	0	0	4	3	1	6	0	13.50
George Glinatsis	R	25	0	0	—	0	2	0	0	5	9	6	1	0	13.50
3 Shawn Boskie	R	27	0	0	.000	0	2	2	0	24	30	11	18	0	6.75
Kevin King	L	25	0	2	.000	0	19	0	0	15	21	17	6	0	7.04
Bobby Thigpen	R	30	0	2	.000	0	8	0	0	12	8	5	4	0	9.39
Jim Converse	R	22	0	5	.000	0	13	8	0	49	73	40	39	0	8.00
Ted Power 39 (SJ)																

CALIFORNIA — 4th 47-68 .395 5.5 — BUCK RODGERS 16-23 .410 — MARCEL LACHEMANN 31-45 .408

Name	G by Pos	B	AGE	G	AB	R	H	2B	3B	HR	RBI	BB	SO	SB	BA	SA
TOTALS			28	115	3943	543	1042	178	16	120	518	402	715	65	.264	.409
J.T. Snow	1B61	B	26	61	223	22	49	4	0	8	30	19	48	0	.220	.345
Harold Reynolds	2B65	B	33	74	207	33	48	10	1	0	11	23	18	10	.232	.290
Gary DiSarcina	SS110	R	26	112	389	53	101	14	2	3	33	18	28	3	.260	.329
Spike Owen	3B70, SS5, 1B4, DH2, 2B1	B	33	82	268	30	83	17	2	3	37	49	17	2	.310	.422
Tim Salmon	OF99	R	25	100	373	67	107	18	2	23	70	54	102	1	.287	.531
Chad Curtis	OF114	R	25	114	453	67	116	23	4	11	50	37	69	25	.256	.397
Jim Edmonds	OF77, 1B22	R	24	94	289	35	79	13	1	5	37	30	72	4	.273	.377
Chris Turner	C57	R	25	58	149	23	36	7	1	1	12	10	29	3	.242	.322
Chili Davis	DH106, OF2	B	34	108	392	72	122	18	1	26	84	69	84	3	.311	.561
Damon Easley	3B47, 2B40	R	24	88	316	41	68	16	1	6	30	29	48	4	.215	.329
Bo Jackson	DH49, OF46, DH9	R	31	75	201	23	56	7	0	13	43	20	72	1	.279	.507
Rex Hudler	2B22, OF18, 3B4, DH4, 1B1	R	33	56	124	17	37	8	0	8	20	6	28	2	.298	.556
Greg Myers (KJ)	C41, DH1	L	28	45	126	10	31	6	0	2	8	10	27	0	.246	.341
1 Dwight Smith	OF31, DH2	L	30	45	122	19	32	5	1	5	18	7	20	2	.262	.443
Jorge Fabregas	C41	L	24	43	127	12	36	4	0	0	16	7	18	1	.283	.307
Eduardo Perez	1B38	R	24	38	129	10	27	7	0	1	15	12	29	3	.209	.380
Mark Dalesandro	C11, 3B5, OF2	R	26	19	25	5	5	1	0	0	2	2	1	0	.200	.360
Rod Correia	2B5, SS11	R	26	6	17	4	4	1	0	0	0	0	4	0	.235	.294
Garret Anderson	OF4	L	22	5	13	0	5	1	0	0	4	0	3	0	.385	.385
Andy Allanson 32 (BG)																

NAME	T	AGE	W	L	PCT	SV	G	GS	CG	IP	H	BB	SO	SHO	ERA
		29	47	68	.409	21	115	115	11	1027	1149	436	682	4	5.42
Chuck Finley	L	31	10	10	.500	0	25	25	7	183	178	71	148	2	4.32
Brian Anderson (BJ)	L	22	7	5	.583	0	18	18	0	102	120	27	47	0	5.22
Mark Langston (EJ)	L	33	7	8	.467	0	18	18	2	119	121	54	109	1	4.68
Phil Leftwich	R	25	5	10	.333	0	20	20	1	114	127	42	67	0	5.68
Mark Leiter	R	31	4	7	.364	2	40	7	0	95	99	35	71	0	4.72
Mike Butcher	R	29	2	1	.667	1	33	0	0	30	31	23	19	0	6.67
Russ Springer	R	25	2	2	.500	2	18	5	0	46	53	14	28	0	5.52
Bob Patterson	L	35	2	3	.400	1	47	0	0	42	35	15	30	0	4.07
Joe Grahe	R	26	2	5	.286	13	40	0	0	43	68	18	26	0	6.65
Joe Magrane (EJ)	L	29	2	6	.250	0	20	11	1	74	89	51	33	0	7.30
Craig Lefferts	L	36	1	1	.500	1	30	0	0	35	50	12	27	0	4.67
Bill Sampen	R	31	1	1	.500	0	10	3	0	16	18	13	9	0	6.46
John Farrell	R	31	1	1	.333	0	3	3	0	13	16	8	10	0	9.00
John Dopson (SJ)	R	31	1	4	.200	1	5	5	0	59	67	26	33	0	6.14
2 Jeff Schwarz	R	30	0	0	—	0	4	0	0	7	5	4	4	0	4.05
Ken Patterson (EJ)	R	29	0	0	—	0	4	0	0	3	3	5	1	0	6.75
Scott Lewis (ZJ)	R	28	0	0	.000	0	20	0	0	31	46	10	10	0	6.10
Andrew Lorraine	L	21	0	2	.000	0	4	3	0	19	30	11	10	0	10.61
Julio Valera 25 (SJ)																
Paul Swingle 27 (SJ)																

MONTREAL — 1st 74-40 .649 — FELIPE ALOU

Name	G by Pos	B	AGE	G	AB	R	H	2B	3B	HR	RBI	BB	SO	SB	BA	SA
TOTALS			26	114	4000	585	1111	246	30	108	542	379	669	137	.278	.435
Cliff Floyd	1B77, OF26	L	21	100	334	43	94	19	4	4	41	24	63	10	.281	.398
Mike Lansing	2B82, 3B27, SS12	R	26	106	394	44	105	21	2	5	35	20	37	12	.266	.368
Wil Cordero	SS109	R	22	110	415	65	122	30	3	15	63	41	62	16	.294	.489
Sean Berry	3B100	R	28	103	320	43	89	19	2	11	41	32	50	14	.278	.453
Larry Walker	OF68, 1B35	L	27	103	395	76	127	44	2	19	86	47	74	15	.322	.587
Marquis Grissom	OF109	R	27	110	475	96	137	25	4	11	45	41	66	36	.288	.427
Moises Alou	OF106	R	27	107	422	81	143	31	5	22	78	42	63	7	.339	.592
Darrin Fletcher	C81	L	27	94	285	28	74	18	1	10	57	25	23	0	.260	.435
Lou Frazier	OF36, 2B6, 1B1	B	29	76	140	25	38	3	1	0	14	18	23	20	.271	.307
Lenny Webster	C46	R	29	57	143	13	39	10	0	5	23	16	24	0	.273	.448
Tim Spehr	C46, OF2	R	27	52	36	8	9	3	1	0	5	4	11	2	.250	.389
Freddie Benavides	2B36, 3B5, SS3, 1B3	R	28	47	85	8	16	5	1	0	6	3	15	0	.188	.271
Randy Milligan	1B33	R	32	47	82	10	19	2	0	2	12	14	21	0	.232	.329
Rondell White	OF29	R	22	40	97	16	27	10	1	2	13	9	18	1	.278	.464
Juan Bell	2B25, 3B3, SS1	B	26	38	97	12	27	4	0	2	10	15	21	4	.278	.381
Jeff Gardner	3B9, 2B4	L	30	18	32	4	7	0	1	0	1	3	5	0	.219	.281

NAME	T	AGE	W	L	PCT	SV	G	GS	CG	IP	H	BB	SO	SHO	ERA
		27	74	40	.649	46	114	114	4	1037	970	288	805	8	3.56
Ken Hill	R	28	16	5	.762	0	23	23	2	155	145	44	85	1	3.32
Pedro Martinez	R	22	11	5	.688	0	24	23	1	145	115	45	142	1	3.42
Butch Henry	L	25	8	3	.727	1	24	15	0	107	97	20	70	0	2.43
Jeff Fassero	L	31	8	6	.571	0	21	21	1	139	119	40	119	0	2.99
Kirk Rueter	R	23	7	3	.700	0	20	20	0	92	106	23	50	0	5.17
Gil Heredia	R	28	6	3	.667	0	39	3	0	75	85	13	62	0	3.46
Tim Scott	R	27	5	2	.714	1	40	0	0	53	51	18	37	0	2.70
John Wetteland	R	27	4	6	.400	25	52	0	0	64	46	21	68	0	2.83
Mel Rojas	R	27	3	2	.600	16	58	0	0	84	71	21	84	0	3.32
Gabe White	L	22	1	1	.500	1	7	5	0	24	24	11	17	0	6.08
Heath Haynes	R	25	0	0	—	0	4	0	0	4	3	1	1	0	0.00
Brian Looney	L	24	0	0	—	0	1	0	0	3	4	2	2	0	22.50
Joey Eischen	L	24	0	0	—	0	1	0	0	1	4	0	1	0	54.00
Denis Boucher	L	26	0	1	.000	0	10	2	0	19	24	7	17	0	6.75
Rod Henderson	R	23	0	1	.000	0	3	2	0	7	9	7	3	0	9.45

ATLANTA — 2nd 68-46 .596 6 — BOBBY COX

Name	G by Pos	B	AGE	G	AB	R	H	2B	3B	HR	RBI	BB	SO	SB	BA	SA
TOTALS			28	114	3861	542	1031	198	18	137	510	377	668	48	.267	.434
Fred McGriff	1B112	L	30	113	424	81	135	25	1	34	94	50	76	7	.318	.623
Mark Lemke	2B103	B	28	104	350	40	103	15	0	3	31	38	37	0	.294	.363
Jeff Blauser	SS96	R	28	96	380	56	98	21	4	6	45	38	64	1	.258	.382
Terry Pendleton (XJ)	3B77	R	33	77	309	25	78	18	3	7	30	12	57	2	.252	.398
David Justice	OF102	L	28	104	352	61	110	16	2	19	59	69	45	2	.313	.531
2 Roberto Kelly	OF63	R	29	63	255	44	73	15	3	6	24	24	36	10	.286	.439
Ryan Klesko	OF74, 1B6	L	23	92	245	42	68	13	3	17	47	26	48	1	.278	.563
Javy Lopez	C75	R	23	80	277	27	68	9	0	13	35	17	61	0	.245	.419
Dave Gallagher	OF77, 1B1	R	33	89	152	27	34	5	0	2	14	22	17	0	.224	.296
Tony Tarasco	OF45	L	23	87	132	16	36	6	0	5	19	9	17	5	.273	.432
Bill Pecota	3B31, 2B1, OF1	R	34	64	112	11	24	5	0	2	16	16	16	1	.214	.313
Charlie O'Brien	C48	R	34	51	152	24	37	11	0	8	28	15	24	0	.243	.474
1 Deion Sanders	OF46	L	26	46	191	32	55	10	0	4	21	16	28	19	.288	.403
Rafael Belliard	SS26, 2B18	R	32	46	120	9	29	7	1	0	9	2	29	0	.242	.317
Mike Kelly	OF25	R	24	30	77	14	21	10	1	2	9	2	18	0	.273	.506
Jose Oliva	3B16	R	23	19	59	9	17	5	0	6	11	7	10	0	.288	.678
Jarvis Brown	OF9	R	27	17	15	3	2	1	0	1	1	0	2	0	.133	.400
Mike Mordecai	SS4	R	26	4	4	1	1	0	0	0	0	0	0	0	.250	1.000
Chipper Jones 22 (KJ)																

NAME	T	AGE	W	L	PCT	SV	G	GS	CG	IP	H	BB	SO	SHO	ERA
		28	68	46	.596	26	114	114	16	1026	929	378	865	8	3.57
Greg Maddux	R	28	16	6	.727	0	25	25	10	202	150	31	156	3	1.56
Tom Glavine	L	28	13	9	.591	0	25	25	2	165	173	70	140	0	3.97
Kent Mercker	L	26	9	4	.692	0	20	17	2	112	90	45	111	1	3.45
Steve Avery	L	24	8	3	.727	0	24	24	1	152	127	55	122	0	4.04
Mark Wohlers	R	24	7	2	.778	1	51	0	0	51	51	33	58	0	4.59
John Smoltz	R	27	6	10	.375	0	21	21	1	135	120	48	113	0	4.14
Greg McMichael	R	27	4	6	.400	21	51	0	0	59	66	19	47	0	3.84
Mike Stanton	R	27	3	1	.750	3	49	0	0	46	41	26	35	0	3.55
Mike Bielecki	R	34	2	0	1.000	0	19	1	0	27	28	12	18	0	4.00
1 Milt Hill	R	28	0	0	—	0	10	0	0	11	18	6	10	0	7.94
Brad Woodall	L	25	0	1	.000	0	6	5	2	6	5	2	2	0	4.50
Steve Bedrosian	R	36	0	0	.000	0	46	0	0	46	41	18	43	0	3.33
Gregg Olson (EJ)	R	27	0	2	.000	1	16	0	0	15	19	13	10	0	9.20

NEW YORK — 3rd 55-58 .487 18.5 — DALLAS GREEN

Name	G by Pos	B	AGE	G	AB	R	H	2B	3B	HR	RBI	BB	SO	SB	BA	SA
TOTALS			27	113	3869	506	966	164	21	117	477	336	807	25	.250	.394
David Segui	1B78, OF21	B	27	92	336	46	81	17	1	10	43	33	43	0	.241	.387
Jeff Kent	2B107	R	26	107	415	53	121	24	5	14	68	23	84	1	.292	.475
Jose Vizcaino	SS102	B	26	103	410	47	105	13	3	3	33	33	62	1	.256	.324
Bobby Bonilla	3B107	B	31	108	403	60	117	24	1	20	67	55	101	1	.290	.504
Joe Orsulak	OF90, 1B6	L	32	96	292	39	76	14	3	8	42	16	21	4	.260	.353
Ryan Thompson	OF98	R	26	98	334	39	75	14	1	18	59	28	94	1	.225	.434
Kevin McReynolds	OF47	R	34	51	180	23	46	11	2	4	21	20	34	2	.256	.406
Todd Hundley	C82	B	25	91	291	45	69	10	1	16	42	25	73	2	.237	.443
Fernando Vina	2B13, 3B12, SS9, OF6	L	25	79	124	20	31	6	0	0	6	12	11	3	.250	.298
John Cangelosi	OF50	B	31	62	111	14	28	4	1	0	4	19	20	5	.252	.288
Jim Lindeman	OF33, 1B4	R	32	52	137	18	37	8	1	7	20	6	35	0	.270	.496
Tim Bogar (WJ)	3B22, 1B14, SS7, 2B1, OF	R	27	50	52	5	8	0	0	2	5	4	11	1	.154	.269
Kelly Stinnett	C44	R	24	47	150	20	38	4	2	2	14	11	28	2	.253	.360
Jeremy Burnitz	OF42	L	25	45	143	26	34	4	0	3	15	23	45	1	.238	.329
Rico Brogna	1B35	L	24	39	131	16	46	11	2	7	20	6	29	1	.351	.626
Luis Rivera	SS11, 2B5	R	30	32	43	11	12	2	1	3	5	4	14	0	.279	.581
Jeff McKnight (VJ)	1B2	B	30	31	27	1	4	1	0	0	2	4	12	0	.148	.185
Shawn Hare	OF14	L	27	22	40	7	9	1	0	1	2	4	11	0	.225	.300
Rick Parker	OF6	R	31	8	16	1	1	0	0	0	0	0	2	0	.063	.063

NAME	T	AGE	W	L	PCT	SV	G	GS	CG	IP	H	BB	SO	SHO	ERA
		29	55	58	.487	35	113	113	7	1023	1069	332	640	3	4.13
Bret Saberhagen	R	30	14	4	.778	0	24	24	4	177	169	13	143	0	2.74
Bobby Jones	R	24	12	7	.632	0	24	24	1	160	157	56	80	1	3.15
Doug Linton	R	29	6	2	.750	0	32	3	0	50	74	20	29	0	4.47
Jason Jacome	L	23	4	3	.571	0	8	8	1	54	54	17	30	1	2.67
Pete Smith	R	28	4	10	.286	0	21	21	1	131	145	42	62	0	5.55
Josias Manzanillo	R	26	3	2	.600	2	37	0	0	47	34	13	48	0	2.66
Dwight Gooden (TJ-DR)	R	29	3	4	.429	0	7	7	0	41	46	15	40	0	6.31
Mauro Gozzo	R	28	3	5	.375	0	23	6	0	69	86	28	33	0	4.83
Mike Maddux	R	32	2	1	.667	2	27	0	0	44	45	13	32	0	5.11
2 Roger Mason	R	35	2	4	.333	1	41	0	0	51	44	20	26	0	3.51
John Franco	L	33	1	4	.200	30	47	0	0	50	47	19	42	0	2.70
Mike Remlinger	L	28	1	5	.167	0	10	9	0	55	55	35	33	0	4.61
Eric Gunderson	L	28	0	0	—	0	14	0	0	9	5	4	4	0	0.00
Juan Castillo	R	24	0	0	—	2	9	0	0	12	17	5	1	0	6.94
Jonathan Hurst	R	27	0	1	.000	0	6	0	0	10	15	5	6	0	12.60
Dave Telgheder	R	27	0	1	.000	0	7	0	0	10	11	8	4	0	7.20
Frank Seminara	R	27	0	1	.000	0	10	1	0	17	20	8	7	0	5.82
Eric Hillman	L	28	0	0	—	0	11	6	0	35	45	11	20	0	7.79

PHILADELPHIA — 4th 54-61 .470 20.5 — JIM FREGOSI

Name	G by Pos	B	AGE	G	AB	R	H	2B	3B	HR	RBI	BB	SO	SB	BA	SA
TOTALS			30	115	3927	521	1028	208	28	80	484	396	711	67	.262	.390
John Kruk	1B69	L	33	75	255	35	77	17	0	5	38	42	51	4	.302	.427
Mickey Morandini	2B79	L	28	87	274	40	80	16	5	2	26	34	33	10	.292	.409
Kevin Stocker (WJ)	SS82	B	24	82	271	38	74	11	2	2	28	44	41	2	.273	.351
Dave Hollins (BH)	3B43, OF1	B	28	44	162	28	36	7	1	4	26	23	32	1	.222	.352
Jim Eisenreich	OF93	L	35	104	290	42	87	15	4	4	43	33	31	6	.300	.421
Lenny Dykstra (IL)	OF82	L	31	84	315	68	86	26	5	5	24	68	48	15	.273	.435
1 Milt Thompson	OF79	L	35	87	220	29	60	7	3	1	30	23	28	7	.273	.345
Darren Daulton (BC)	C68	L	32	69	257	43	77	17	1	15	56	33	43	4	.300	.549
Mariano Duncan	2B37, 3B28, SS19, 1B6	R	31	88	347	49	93	22	1	8	48	17	72	10	.268	.406
Pete Incaviglia	OF63	R	30	80	244	28	56	10	1	13	32	16	71	1	.230	.439
Ricky Jordan	1B49	R	29	72	220	29	62	14	2	8	37	6	32	0	.282	.473
Tony Longmire	OF32	L	25	69	139	10	33	6	1	0	17	10	27	2	.237	.317
Kim Batiste	3B42, SS17	R	26	64	209	17	49	6	0	1	13	1	32	1	.234	.278
2 Billy Hatcher	OF40	R	33	43	134	15	33	5	1	2	13	6	14	4	.246	.343
Todd Pratt	C28	R	27	28	102	10	20	6	1	2	9	12	29	1	.196	.333
Mike Lieberthal	C22	R	22	24	79	6	21	5	1	1	5	3	5	0	.266	.367
1 Wes Chamberlain	OF18	R	28	24	69	7	19	5	0	2	6	3	12	0	.275	.435
Tom Quinlan	3B20	R	26	24	35	6	7	2	0	1	3	3	13	0	.200	.343
Randy Ready	2B11, 3B1	R	34	17	42	5	16	1	0	0	3	8	6	0	.381	.476
Tom Marsh	OF7	R	28	8	18	3	5	1	1	0	3	1	1	0	.278	.444

NAME	T	AGE	W	L	PCT	SV	G	GS	CG	IP	H	BB	SO	SHO	ERA
		30	54	61	.470	30	115	115	7	1024	1028	377	699	6	3.85
Danny Jackson	L	32	14	6	.700	0	25	25	4	179	183	46	129	1	3.26
Bobby Munoz	R	26	7	5	.583	1	21	14	1	104	101	35	59	0	2.67
Heathcliff Slocumb	R	28	5	1	.833	0	52	0	0	72	75	28	58	0	2.86
2 Shawn Boskie	R	27	4	6	.400	0	18	14	1	84	85	29	59	0	5.23
David West	L	29	4	10	.286	0	31	14	0	99	74	61	83	0	3.55
Ben Rivera (SJ)	R	25	3	4	.429	0	9	7	0	38	40	22	19	0	6.87
Tommy Greene (SJ)	R	27	2	0	1.000	0	7	7	0	36	37	22	28	0	4.54
2 Paul Quantrill	R	25	2	2	.500	1	18	1	0	30	39	10	13	0	6.00
Doug Jones	R	37	2	4	.330	27	47	0	0	54	55	6	38	0	2.17
Mike Williams	R	25	2	4	.333	0	12	8	0	50	61	20	29	0	5.01
Curt Schilling (EJ)	R	27	2	8	.200	0	13	13	1	82	87	28	58	0	4.48
Toby Borland	R	25	1	0	1.000	0	24	0	0	34	31	14	26	0	2.36
1 Bob Wells	R	27	1	0	1.000	0	4	1	0	4	1	1	2	0	1.80
2 Tom Edens	R	33	1	0	.500	0	8	0	0	4	4	1	1	0	2.25
2 Roger Mason	R	35	1	2	.333	1	9	0	0	17	18	4	10	0	5.19
Larry Andersen	R	41	1	2	.333	0	29	0	0	33	33	15	27	0	4.41
Fernando Valenzuela	L	33	1	2	.333	0	7	7	0	45	42	7	19	0	3.00
Jeff Juden	R	23	1	0	.200	0	6	6	0	28	29	12	22	0	6.18
Ricky Bottalico	R	24	0	0	—	0	1	0	0	3	1	3	0	0.00	
Andy Carter	L	25	0	0	.000	0	20	0	0	34	31	12	18	0	4.46
Norm Charlton 31 (EJ)															

FLORIDA 5th 51-64 .443 23.5   RENE LACHEMANN

Name	G by Pos	B	AGE	G	AB	R	H	2B	3B	HR	RBI	BB	SO	SB	BA	SA
TOTALS			28	115	3926	468	1043	180	24	94	451	349	746	65	.266	.396
Greg Colbrunn (KJ)	1B41	R	24	47	155	17	47	10	0	6	31	9	27	1	.303	.484
Bret Barberie	2B106	B	26	107	372	40	112	20	2	5	31	23	65	2	.301	.406
Kurt Abbott	SS110	R	25	101	345	41	86	17	3	9	33	16	98	3	.249	.394
Jerry Browne	3B62, OF/30, 2B15	B	28	101	329	42	97	17	4	3	30	52	23	1	.295	.398
Gary Sheffield (SJ)	OF87	R	25	87	322	61	89	16	1	27	78	51	50	12	.276	.584
Chuck Carr	OF104	B	26	106	433	61	114	19	2	2	30	22	71	32	.263	.330
Jeff Conine	OF97, 1B46	R	28	115	451	60	144	27	6	18	82	40	92	1	.319	.525
Benito Santiago	C97	R	29	101	337	35	92	14	2	11	41	25	57	1	.273	.424
Matias Carrillo	OF49	L	31	80	136	13	34	7	0	0	9	9	31	3	.250	.301
Dave Magadan	3B48, 1B16	L	31	74	211	30	58	7	0	1	17	39	25	0	.275	.322
Alex Arias	SS20, 3B15	R	26	59	113	4	27	5	0	0	15	9	19	0	.239	.283
Orestes Destrade	1B37	B	32	39	130	12	27	4	0	5	15	19	32	1	.208	.354
Mario Diaz	3B11, SS7, 2B7	R	32	32	77	10	25	4	2	0	11	6	6	0	.325	.429
Rich Renteria (LJ)	3B14, 2B6, OF2	R	32	28	49	5	11	0	0	2	4	1	4	0	.224	.347
1 Ron Tingley	C18	R	25	19	52	4	9	3	1	1	2	5	18	0	.173	.327
Jesus Tavarez	OF11	B	23	17	39	4	7	0	0	0	4	1	5	1	.179	.179
Carl Everett	OF16	B	23	16	51	7	11	1	0	2	6	3	15	4	.216	.353
Russ Morman	1B8	R	32	13	33	2	7	0	1	1	2	2	9	0	.212	.364
Greg O'Halloran	C1	L	26	12	11	1	2	0	0	0	1	0	1	0	.182	.182
Bob Natal	C8	R	28	10	29	2	8	2	0	0	2	5	5	1	.276	.345
Darrell Whitmore	OF6	L	25	9	22	1	5	1	0	0	0	3	5	0	.227	.273
Charles Johnson	C4	R	22	4	11	5	5	1	0	1	4	1	4	0	.455	.818

NAME	T	AGE	W	L	PCT	SV	G	GS	CG	IP	H	BB	SO	SHO	ERA
		29	51	64	.443	30	115	115	5	1015	1069	428	649	7	4.50
David Weathers	R	24	8	12	.400	0	24	24	0	135	166	59	72	0	5.27
Pat Rapp	R	26	7	8	.467	0	24	23	2	133	132	69	75	1	3.85
Robb Nen	R	24	5	5	.500	15	44	0	0	58	46	17	60	0	2.95
Charlie Hough	R	46	5	9	.357	0	21	21	1	114	118	52	65	1	5.15
Mark Gardner	R	32	4	4	.500	0	20	14	0	92	97	30	57	0	4.87
Chris Hammond (XJ)	L	28	4	4	.500	0	13	13	1	73	79	23	40	1	3.07
Yorkis Perez	L	26	3	0	1.000	0	44	0	0	41	33	14	41	0	3.54
Jeremy Hernandez (ZJ)	R	27	3	3	.500	9	21	0	0	23	16	14	13	0	2.70
Willie Fraser	R	30	2	0	1.000	0	9	0	0	12	20	6	7	0	5.84
Luis Aquino (BT)	R	30	2	1	.667	0	29	1	0	51	39	22	22	0	3.73
Terry Mathews	R	29	2	1	.667	0	24	2	0	43	45	9	21	0	3.35
Jeff Mutis	L	27	1	0	1.000	0	35	0	0	38	51	15	30	0	5.40
John Johnstone	R	25	1	2	.333	0	17	0	0	21	23	16	23	0	5.91
Rich Scheid	L	29	1	3	.250	0	8	5	0	32	35	8	17	0	3.34
Kurt Miller	R	21	1	3	.250	0	4	4	0	20	26	7	11	0	8.10
Richie Lewis	R	28	1	4	.200	0	45	0	0	54	62	38	45	0	5.67
Ryan Bowen (VJ)	R	26	1	5	.167	0	8	8	1	47	50	19	32	0	4.94
Bryan Harvey (EJ-GJ)	R	31	0	0	—	6	12	0	0	10	12	4	10	0	5.23
Brian Drahman	R	27	0	0	—	0	9	0	0	13	15	6	7	0	6.23
Mike Jeffcoat	L	34	0	0	—	0	4	0	0	3	4	0	1	0	10.13

CENTRAL DIVISION

CINCINNATI 1st 66-48 .579   DAVEY JOHNSON

Name	G by Pos	B	AGE	G	AB	R	H	2B	3B	HR	RBI	BB	SO	SB	BA	SA
TOTALS			29	115	3999	609	1142	211	36	124	569	388	738	119	.286	.449
Hal Morris	1B112	L	29	112	436	60	146	30	4	10	78	34	62	6	.335	.491
Bret Boone	2B106, 3B2	R	25	108	381	59	122	25	2	12	68	24	74	3	.320	.491
Barry Larkin	SS110	R	30	110	427	78	119	23	5	9	52	64	58	26	.279	.419
Tony Fernandez	3B93, SS9, 2B5	B	32	104	366	50	102	18	6	8	50	44	40	12	.279	.426
Reggie Sanders	OF104	R	26	107	400	66	105	20	8	17	62	41	114	21	.263	.480
2 Deion Sanders	OF45	L	26	46	184	26	51	7	4	0	7	16	35	19	.277	.359
Kevin Mitchell	OF89, 1B1	R	32	95	310	57	101	18	1	30	77	59	62	2	.326	.681
Brian Dorsett	C73, 1B1	R	33	76	216	21	53	8	0	5	26	21	33	0	.245	.352
Thomas Howard	OF57	B	29	83	178	24	47	11	0	5	24	10	30	4	.264	.410
Jacob Brumfield	OF43	R	29	68	122	36	38	10	2	4	11	15	18	6	.311	.525
Lenny Harris	3B15, 1B4, OF3, 2B2	L	29	66	100	13	31	3	1	0	14	5	13	7	.310	.360
2 Eddie Taubensee	C61	L	25	61	177	29	52	8	2	8	21	15	28	2	.294	.497
Jeff Branson	2B19, 3B18, SS8, 1B2	L	27	58	109	18	31	4	1	6	16	5	16	0	.284	.505
1 Roberto Kelly (FJ)	OF47	R	29	47	179	29	54	8	0	3	21	11	35	9	.302	.397
Jerome Walton (FJ)	OF26, 1B7	R	28	46	68	10	21	4	0	1	9	4	12	1	.309	.412
Willie Greene	3B13, OF1	L	22	16	37	5	8	2	0	0	3	6	14	0	.216	.270
1 Steve Peques	OF4	R	26	11	10	1	3	0	0	0	1	3	0	.300	.300	
2 Brian Hunter	OF5, 1B1	R	26	9	23	6	7	1	0	4	10	2	1	.304	.870	
Joe Oliver (NJ)	C6	R	28	6	19	1	4	0	0	1	5	2	3	0	.211	.368
Ron Gant 29 (BL)																

NAME	T	AGE	W	L	PCT	SV	G	GS	CG	IP	H	BB	SO	SHO	ERA
		27	66	48	.579	27	115	115	6	1038	1037	339	799	6	3.78
John Smiley		29	11	10	.524	0	24	24	1	159	169	37	112	1	3.86
Jose Rijo	R	29	9	6	.600	0	26	26	2	172	177	52	171	0	3.08
Johnny Ruffin	R	22	7	2	.778	1	51	0	0	70	57	27	44	0	3.09
Pete Schourek	L	25	7	2	.778	0	22	10	0	81	90	29	69	0	4.09
John Roper	R	22	6	2	.750	0	16	15	0	92	90	30	51	0	4.50
Jeff Brantley	R	30	6	6	.500	15	50	0	0	65	46	28	63	0	2.48
Erik Hanson	R	29	5	5	.500	0	22	21	0	123	137	23	101	0	4.11
Hector Carrasco	R	24	5	6	.455	6	45	0	0	56	42	30	41	0	2.24
Tom Browning (BA)	L	34	3	1	.750	0	7	7	2	41	34	13	22	1	4.20
Tim Pugh (XJ)	R	27	3	3	.500	0	11	8	0	48	60	26	24	0	6.04
Tim Fortugno	L	32	1	0	1.000	0	25	0	0	30	32	14	29	0	4.20
Kevin Jarvis	R	24	1	1	.500	0	6	3	0	18	22	5	10	0	7.13
Chuck McElroy	L	26	1	2	.333	5	52	0	0	58	52	15	38	0	2.34
Scott Service	R	27	1	2	.333	0	8	3	0	32	35	8	17	0	7.36
Rich DeLucia	R	29	0	0	—	0	11	0	0	9	5	5	15	0	4.22
Jerry Spradlin	R	26	0	0	—	0	8	0	0	8	12	2	4	0	10.13
Rob Dibble 30 (SJ)																
Steve Foster 27 (SJ)																

HOUSTON 2nd 66-49 .574 0.5   TERRY COLLINS

Name	G by Pos	B	AGE	G	AB	R	H	2B	3B	HR	RBI	BB	SO	SB	BA	SA
TOTALS			28	115	3955	602	1099	252	25	120	573	394	718	124	.278	.445
Jeff Bagwell	1B109, OF1	R	26	110	400	104	147	32	2	39	116	65	65	15	.368	.750
Craig Biggio	2B113	R	28	114	437	88	139	44	5	6	56	62	58	39	.318	.483
Andujar Cedeno	SS95	R	24	98	342	38	90	26	0	9	49	29	79	1	.263	.418
Ken Caminiti	3B108	R	31	111	406	63	115	28	2	18	75	43	71	4	.283	.495
James Mouton	OF96	R	25	99	310	43	76	11	0	2	16	27	69	24	.245	.300
Steve Finley	OF92	L	29	94	373	64	103	16	5	11	33	28	52	13	.276	.434
Luis Gonzalez	OF111	L	26	112	392	57	107	29	4	8	67	49	57	15	.273	.429
Scott Servais	C78	R	27	78	251	27	49	15	1	9	41	10	44	0	.195	.371
Kevin Bass	OF57	B	35	82	203	37	63	15	1	6	35	28	24	2	.310	.483
Mike Felder	OF32	B	32	58	117	10	28	2	2	0	13	4	12	3	.239	.291
Tony Eusebio	C52	R	27	55	159	18	47	9	1	5	30	8	33	0	.296	.459
Chris Donnels	3B14, 2B4, 1B4	L	28	54	86	12	23	5	0	3	5	13	18	1	.267	.430
Sid Bream	1B10	L	33	46	61	7	21	5	0	0	7	9	9	0	.344	.426
Andy Stankiewicz	SS17, 2B6, 3B1	R	29	37	54	10	14	3	0	1	5	12	12	1	.259	.370
Orlando Miller	SS11, 2B3	R	25	16	40	3	13	0	1	2	9	2	12	1	.325	.525
2 Milt Thompson	OF6	L	35	9	21	5	6	0	0	1	3	1	3	0	.286	.429
Roberto Petagine	1B2	B	23	8	7	0	0	0	0	0	0	1	3	0	.000	.000
Brian Hunter	OF6	R	23	8	24	2	6	1	0	0	1	2	6	0	.250	.292
Mike Simms	OF3	R	27	6	12	1	1	0	0	0	1	0	5	0	.083	.167
1 Eddie Taubensee	C5	L	25	5	10	0	1	0	0	0	0	0	3	0	.100	.100

NAME	T	AGE	W	L	PCT	SV	G	GS	CG	IP	H	BB	SO	SHO	ERA
		27	66	49	.574	29	115	115	9	1030	1043	367	739	6	3.97
Doug Drabek	R	31	12	6	.667	0	23	23	6	165	132	45	121	2	2.84
Darryl Kile	R	25	9	6	.600	0	24	24	0	148	153	82	105	0	4.57
Shane Reynolds	R	26	8	5	.615	0	33	14	1	124	128	21	110	1	3.05
Pete Harnisch (SJ)	R	27	8	5	.615	0	17	17	1	95	100	39	62	0	5.40
Greg Swindell	L	29	8	9	.471	0	24	24	1	148	175	26	74	0	4.37
Brian Williams	R	25	6	5	.545	0	20	13	0	78	112	41	49	0	5.74
Todd Jones	R	26	5	2	.714	5	48	0	0	73	52	26	63	0	2.72
1 Tom Edens	R	33	4	1	.800	1	39	0	0	50	55	17	38	0	4.50
Dave Veres	R	27	3	3	.500	1	32	0	0	41	39	7	28	0	2.41
Mike Hampton	L	21	2	1	.667	0	44	0	0	41	46	16	24	0	3.70
Mitch Williams	L	29	1	4	.200	6	25	0	0	20	21	24	21	0	7.65
Ross Powell	L	26	0	0	—	0	7	6	5	5	1	0	1.23		
John Hudek	R	27	0	2	.000	16	42	0	0	39	24	18	39	0	2.97

PITTSBURGH 3rd(tie) 53-61 .465 13   JIM LEYLAND

Name	G by Pos	B	AGE	G	AB	R	H	2B	3B	HR	RBI	BB	SO	SB	BA	SA
TOTALS			30	114	3864	466	1001	198	23	80	435	349	725	53	.259	.384
1 Brian Hunter	1B59, OF5	R	26	78	233	28	53	15	1	11	47	15	55	0	.227	.442
Carlos Garcia	2B98	R	26	98	412	49	114	15	2	6	28	16	67	18	.277	.367
Jay Bell	SS110	R	28	110	424	68	117	35	4	9	45	49	82	2	.276	.441
Jeff King	3B91, 2B1	R	29	94	339	36	89	23	0	5	42	30	38	3	.263	.375
Orlando Merced	OF68, 1B55	L	27	108	386	48	105	21	3	9	51	42	58	4	.272	.412
Andy Van Slyke	OF99	L	33	105	374	41	92	18	3	6	30	52	72	7	.246	.358
Al Martin (WJ)	OF77	L	26	82	276	48	79	12	4	9	33	34	56	15	.286	.457
Don Slaught	C74	R	35	76	240	21	69	7	0	2	21	34	31	0	.288	.342
Dave Clark	OF57	L	31	86	223	37	66	11	1	10	46	22	48	2	.296	.489
Gary Varsho	OF36, 1B1	L	33	67	82	15	21	6	3	0	5	4	19	0	.256	.402
Tom Foley	2B17, 3B14, SS8, 1B3	L	34	59	123	13	29	7	0	3	15	13	18	0	.236	.366
Kevin Young	1B37, 3B17, OF1	R	25	59	122	15	25	7	2	1	11	8	34	1	.205	.320
Lloyd McClendon	OF20, 1B2	R	35	51	92	9	22	4	0	4	12	4	11	0	.239	.413
Lance Parrish	C38, 1B1	R	38	40	126	10	34	5	0	3	16	18	28	1	.270	.381
Midre Cummings	OF24	L	22	24	86	11	21	4	0	0	12	4	18	0	.244	.326
Jerry Goff	C7	L	30	8	25	0	2	0	0	0	0	4	11	0	.080	.080
2 Steve Pegues	OF7	R	26	7	26	1	10	2	0	0	2	0	5	1	.385	.462
Tony Womack	2B3, SS2	L	24	5	12	4	4	0	0	0	0	1	1	3	.333	.333
Will Pennyfeather	OF1	R	26	4	3	0	0	0	0	0	0	0	2	0	.000	.000
John Wehner	3B1	R	27	2	4	1	1	0	0	0	1	0	1	0	.250	.500
2 Junior Noboa	SS1	R	29	2	2	0	0	0	0	0	0	0	0	0	.000	.000

NAME	T	AGE	W	L	PCT	SV	G	GS	CG	IP	H	BB	SO	SHO	ERA
		28	53	61	.465	24	114	114	8	1006	1094	370	650	2	4.64
Zane Smith	L	33	10	8	.556	0	25	24	2	157	162	34	57	1	3.27
Denny Neagle	L	25	9	10	.474	0	24	24	2	137	135	49	122	0	5.12
Paul Wagner	R	26	8	8	.467	0	29	17	1	120	136	50	86	0	4.59
Jon Lieber	R	24	6	7	.462	0	17	17	1	109	116	25	71	0	3.73
Ravelo Manzanillo	L	30	4	4	.667	1	46	0	0	50	45	42	39	0	4.14
Rick White	R	25	4	5	.444	8	43	5	0	75	79	17	38	0	3.82
Steve Cooke	L	24	4	11	.267	0	25	23	2	134	157	46	74	0	5.02
Alejandro Pena (IL)	R	35	3	2	.600	7	22	0	0	29	22	10	27	0	5.02
Mark Dewey	R	29	2	1	.667	1	45	0	0	51	61	19	30	0	3.68
Dan Miceli	R	23	2	1	.667	2	28	0	0	27	28	11	27	0	5.93
Jeff Ballard	L	30	1	1	.500	2	28	0	0	24	32	10	11	0	6.66
Mike Dyer	R	27	1	1	.500	4	14	0	0	15	15	12	13	0	5.87
John Hope	R	23	0	0	—	0	4	4	0	14	18	4	6	0	5.79
Rich Robertson	L	25	0	0	—	0	16	0	0	16	20	10	9	0	6.89
1 Jeff Tabaka	L	30	0	0	—	0	4	0	0	4	4	8	2	0	18.00
Joel Johnston	R	27	0	0	—	0	4	0	0	3	4	5	2	0	29.70
Blas Minor	R	28	0	0	.000	0	17	0	0	19	27	9	17	0	8.05
Randy Tomlin	L	28	0	3	.000	0	4	4	0	21	23	10	17	0	3.92

ST. LOUIS — 3rd(tie) 53-61 .465 13 — JOE TORRE

Name	G by Pos	B	AGE	G	AB	R	H	2B	3B	HR	RBI	BB	SO	SB	BA	SA
TOTALS			29	115	3902	535	1026	213	27	108	506	434	686	76	.263	.414
Gregg Jefferies	1B102	B	26	103	397	52	129	27	1	12	55	45	26	12	.325	.489
Geronimo Pena	2B59, 3B1	B	27	83	213	33	54	13	1	11	34	24	54	9	.254	.479
Ozzie Smith	SS96	B	39	98	381	51	100	18	3	3	30	38	26	6	.262	.349
Todd Zeile	3B112	B	27	113	415	62	111	25	1	19	75	52	56	1	.267	.470
Mark Whiten	OF90	B	27	92	334	57	98	18	2	14	53	37	75	10	.293	.485
Ray Lankford	OF104	L	27	109	416	89	111	25	5	19	57	58	113	11	.267	.488
Bernard Gilkey	OF102	R	27	105	380	52	96	22	1	6	45	39	65	15	.253	.363
Tom Pagnozzi (KJ)	C70, 1B1	R	31	70	243	21	66	12	1	7	40	21	39	0	.272	.416
Luis Alicea	2B53, OF2	B	28	88	205	32	57	12	5	5	29	30	38	4	.278	.459
Gerald Perry	1B13	L	33	60	77	12	25	7	0	3	18	15	12	-1	.325	.532
Jose Oquendo	SS28, 2B16	B	30	55	129	13	34	7	2	0	9	21	16	1	.264	.310
Brian Jordan (BR)	OF46, 1B1	R	27	53	178	14	46	8	2	5	15	16	40	4	.258	.410
Terry McGriff	C39	R	30	42	114	10	25	6	0	0	13	13	11	0	.219	.272
1 Stan Royer	1B11, 3B5	R	26	39	57	3	10	5	0	1	2	0	18	0	.175	.316
Gerald Young	OF11	B	29	16	41	5	13	3	2	0	3	3	8	2	.317	.488
Erik Pappas	C15	R	28	15	44	8	4	1	0	0	5	10	13	0	.091	.114
Scott Coolbaugh	1B4, 3B4	R	28	15	21	4	4	0	0	2	6	1	4	0	.190	.476
John Mabry	OF6	L	23	6	23	2	7	3	0	0	3	2	4	0	.304	.435
Tripp Cromer	SS2	R	26	2	0	1	0	0	0	0	0	0	0	0	—	—

NAME	T	AGE	W	L	PCT	SV	G	GS	CG	IP	H	BB	SO	SHO	ERA
		30	53	61	.465	29	115	115	7	1018	1154	355	632	7	5.14
Bob Tewksbury	R	33	12	10	.545	0	24	24	4	156	190	22	79	1	5.32
Rick Sutcliffe (LJ)	R	38	6	4	.600	0	16	14	0	68	93	32	26	0	6.52
Allen Watson	L	23	6	5	.545	0	22	22	0	116	130	53	74	0	5.52
1 Rob Murphy	L	34	4	3	.571	2	50	0	0	40	35	13	25	0	3.79
Rene Arocha	R	28	4	4	.500	11	45	7	1	83	94	21	62	1	4.01
Rheal Cormier (XJ)	L	27	3	2	.600	0	7	7	0	40	40	7	26	0	5.45
Omar Olivares	R	26	3	4	.429	1	14	12	1	74	84	37	26	0	5.74
Rich Rodriguez	L	31	3	5	.375	0	56	0	0	60	62	26	43	0	4.03
Tom Urbani	L	26	3	7	.300	0	20	10	0	80	98	21	43	0	5.15
Vicente Palacios	R	30	3	8	.273	1	31	17	1	118	104	43	95	1	4.44
Bryan Eversgerd	L	25	2	3	.400	0	40	1	0	68	75	20	47	0	4.52
Mike Perez	R	29	2	3	.400	12	36	0	0	31	52	10	20	0	8.71
John Habyan	R	30	1	0	1.000	1	52	0	0	47	50	20	46	0	3.23
Willie Smith	R	26	1	1	.500	0	8	0	0	7	9	3	7	0	9.00
Frank Cimorelli	R	25	0	0	—	1	11	0	0	13	20	10	1	0	8.78
Steve Dixon	L	24	0	0	—	0	2	0	0	2	3	6	1	0	23.14
Gary Buckels	R	28	0	1	.000	0	10	0	0	12	8	7	9	0	2.25
John Frascatore	R	24	0	1	.000	0	1	1	0	7	7	2	2	0	16.20
Donovan Osborne 25 (SJ)															
Paul Kilgus 32 (SJ)															

CHICAGO — 5th 49-64 .434 16.5 — TOM TREBELHORN

Name	G by Pos	B	AGE	G	AB	R	H	2B	3B	HR	RBI	BB	SO	SB	BA	SA
TOTALS			28	113	3918	500	1015	189	26	109	464	364	750	69	.259	.404
Mark Grace	1B103	L	30	106	403	55	120	23	3	6	44	48	41	0	.298	.414
Rey Sanchez	2B50, SS30, 3B17	R	26	96	291	26	83	13	1	0	24	20	29	2	.285	.337
Shawon Dunston	SS84	R	31	88	331	38	92	19	0	11	35	16	48	3	.278	.435
Steve Buechele	3B99, 1B6, 2B1	R	32	104	339	33	82	11	1	14	52	39	80	1	.242	.404
Sammy Sosa	OF105	R	25	105	426	59	128	17	6	25	70	25	92	22	.300	.545
Karl Rhodes	OF76	L	25	95	269	39	63	17	0	8	19	33	64	6	.234	.387
Derrick May	OF92	L	25	100	345	43	98	19	2	8	51	30	34	3	.284	.420
Rick Wilkins	C95, 1B2	L	27	100	313	44	71	25	2	7	39	40	86	4	.227	.387
Glenallen Hill	OF78	R	29	89	269	48	80	12	1	10	38	29	57	19	.297	.461
Eddie Zambrano	OF27, 1B9, 3B4	R	28	67	116	17	30	7	0	6	18	16	29	2	.259	.474
Ryne Sandberg (VR)	2B57	R	34	57	223	36	53	9	5	5	24	23	40	2	.238	.390
Jose Hernandez	3B28, SS21, 2B8, OF1	R	24	56	132	18	32	2	3	1	9	8	29	2	.242	.326
Mark Parent	C37	R	32	44	99	8	26	4	0	3	16	13	24	0	.263	.394
Kevin Roberson (BH)	OF9	R	26	44	55	8	12	4	0	4	9	2	14	0	.218	.509
Mike Maksudian	1B3, C2, 3B2	L	28	26	26	6	7	2	0	0	4	10	4	0	.269	.346
Todd Haney	2B11, 3B3	R	28	17	37	6	6	0	1	2	3	3	2	.162	.243	
Willie Wilson	OF10	B	38	17	21	4	5	0	2	0	1	6	1	.238	.429	

NAME	T	AGE	W	L	PCT	SV	G	GS	CG	IP	H	BB	SO	SHO	ERA
		29	49	64	.434	27	113	113	5	1024	1054	392	717	5	4.47
Steve Trachsel	R	29	9	7	.563	0	22	22	1	146	133	54	108	0	3.21
Willie Banks	R	25	8	12	.400	0	23	23	1	138	139	56	91	1	5.40
Jim Bullinger	R	28	8	2	.750	2	33	10	1	100	87	34	72	0	3.60
Chuck Crim	R	33	5	4	.556	2	49	1	0	64	69	24	43	0	4.48
Jose Bautista	R	29	4	5	.444	1	58	0	0	69	75	17	45	0	3.89
Anthony Young (EJ)	R	28	4	6	.400	0	20	19	0	115	103	46	65	0	3.92
Kevin Foster	R	25	3	4	.429	0	13	13	0	81	70	35	75	0	2.89
Frank Castillo (RJ)	R	25	2	1	.667	0	4	4	1	23	25	5	19	0	4.30
Jose Guzman (SJ)	R	31	2	2	.500	0	4	4	0	20	22	13	11	0	9.15
Dan Plesac	L	32	2	3	.400	1	54	0	0	55	61	13	53	0	4.61
Mike Morgan	R	34	2	10	.167	0	15	15	1	81	111	35	57	0	6.69
Randy Veres	R	28	1	1	.500	0	10	0	0	10	12	2	5	0	5.59
Randy Myers	L	31	1	5	.167	21	38	0	0	40	40	16	32	0	3.79
Blaise Ilsey	L	30	0	0	—	0	10	0	0	15	25	9	9	0	7.80
2 Donn Pall	R	32	0	0	—	0	2	0	0	4	8	1	2	0	4.50
1 Shawn Boskie	R	27	0	0	—	0	2	0	0	4	5	1	0	0	0.00
Dave Otto	L	29	0	1	.000	0	36	0	0	45	49	22	19	0	3.80
Turk Wendell	R	27	0	1	.000	0	6	2	0	14	22	10	9	0	11.93
Jessie Hollins 24 (SJ)															

WEST DIVISION

LOS ANGELES — 1st 58-56 .509 — TOMMY LASORDA

Name	G by Pos	B	AGE	G	AB	R	H	2B	3B	HR	RBI	BB	SO	SB	BA	SA
TOTALS			28	114	3904	532	1055	160	29	115	505	366	687	74	.270	.414
Eric Karros	1B109	R	26	114	406	51	108	21	1	14	46	29	112	2	.266	.426
Delino DeShields	2B88, SS10	L	25	89	320	51	80	11	3	2	33	54	53	27	.250	.322
Jose Offerman	SS72	B	25	72	243	27	51	8	4	1	25	38	38	2	.210	.288
Tim Wallach	3B113	R	36	113	414	68	116	21	1	23	78	46	80	0	.280	.502
Raul Mondesi	OF112	R	23	112	434	63	133	27	8	16	56	16	78	11	.306	.516
Brett Butler	OF111	L	37	111	417	79	131	13	9	8	33	68	52	27	.314	.446
Henry Rodriguez	OF86, 1B17	L	26	104	306	33	82	14	2	8	49	17	58	0	.268	.405
Mike Piazza	C104	R	26	107	405	64	129	18	0	24	92	33	65	1	.319	.541
Mitch Webster	OF48	B	35	82	84	16	23	4	0	4	12	8	13	1	.274	.464
Cory Snyder	OF50, 1B9, 3B6, SS4, 2B3	R	31	73	153	18	36	6	0	6	18	14	47	1	.235	.392
Chris Gwynn	OF20	L	29	58	71	9	19	0	0	3	13	7	7	0	.268	.394
Jeff Treadway	2B24, 3B3	L	31	52	67	14	20	3	0	0	5	5	8	1	.299	.343
Rafael Bournigal	SS40	R	28	40	116	2	26	3	1	0	11	9	5	0	.224	.267
Dave Hansen	3B7	L	25	40	44	3	15	3	0	0	5	5	5	0	.341	.409
Carlos Hernandez	C27	R	27	32	64	6	14	2	0	2	6	1	14	0	.219	.344
Garey Ingram	2B23	R	23	26	78	10	22	1	0	3	8	7	22	0	.282	.410
Eddie Pye	SS3, 2B3	R	27	7	10	2	1	1	0	0	0	1	4	0	.100	.100
Tom Prince	C3	R	29	3	6	2	2	1	0	0	1	1	3	0	.333	.333
Billy Ashley	OF2	R	23	2	6	0	2	1	0	0	0	0	2	0	.333	.500
1 Darryl Strawberry 32 (DR)																

NAME	T	AGE	W	L	PCT	SV	G	GS	CG	IP	H	BB	SO	SHO	ERA
		29	58	56	.509	20	114	114	14	1014	1041	354	732	5	4.17
Ramon Martinez	R	26	12	7	.632	0	24	24	4	170	160	56	119	3	3.97
Kevin Gross	R	33	7	7	.500	0	25	23	1	157	162	43	124	0	3.60
Tom Candiotti	R	36	7	7	.500	0	23	22	5	153	149	54	102	0	4.12
Todd Worrell	R	34	5	5	.545	11	38	0	0	42	37	12	44	0	4.29
Orel Hershiser	R	35	6	6	.500	0	21	21	1	135	146	42	72	0	3.79
Pedro Astacio	R	24	6	8	.429	0	23	23	3	149	142	47	108	1	4.29
Jim Gott (IL)	R	34	5	3	.625	2	37	0	0	36	46	20	29	0	5.94
Ismael Valdes	R	20	3	1	.750	0	21	1	0	28	21	10	28	0	3.18
Al Osuna	L	28	2	0	1.000	0	15	0	0	9	13	4	7	0	6.23
Rudy Seanez	R	25	1	1	.500	0	17	0	0	24	24	9	18	0	2.66
Gary Wayne	L	31	1	3	.250	0	19	0	0	17	19	6	10	0	4.67
Omar Daal	L	22	0	0	—	0	24	0	0	14	12	5	9	0	3.29
2 Brian Barnes	L	27	0	0	—	0	5	0	0	5	10	4	5	0	7.20
Chan Ho Park	R	21	0	0	—	0	2	0	0	4	5	5	6	0	11.25
Roger McDowell	R	33	0	3	.000	0	32	0	0	41	50	22	29	0	5.23
Darren Dreifort	R	22	0	5	.000	6	27	0	0	29	45	15	22	0	6.21

SAN FRANCISCO — 2nd 55-60 .478 3.5 — DUSTY BAKER

Name	G by Pos	B	AGE	G	AB	R	H	2B	3B	HR	RBI	BB	SO	SB	BA	SA
TOTALS			29	115	3869	504	963	159	32	123	472	364	719	114	.249	.402
Todd Benzinger	1B99	B	31	107	328	32	87	13	2	9	31	17	84	2	.265	.399
Robby Thompson (SJ)	2B35	R	32	35	129	13	27	8	2	2	7	15	32	3	.209	.349
Royce Clayton	SS108	R	24	108	385	38	91	14	6	3	30	30	74	23	.236	.327
Matt Williams	3B110	R	28	112	445	74	119	16	3	43	96	33	87	1	.267	.607
Willie McGee (LJ)	OF42	B	35	45	156	19	44	3	0	5	23	15	24	3	.282	.397
Darren Lewis	OF113	R	26	114	451	70	116	15	9	4	29	53	50	30	.257	.357
Barry Bonds	OF112	L	29	115	391	89	122	18	1	37	81	74	43	29	.312	.647
Kirt Manwaring	C97	R	28	97	316	30	79	17	1	1	29	25	50	1	.250	.320
Dave Martinez	OF58, 1B25	L	29	97	235	23	58	9	3	4	27	21	22	3	.247	.362
John Patterson	2B63	B	27	85	240	36	57	10	1	3	32	16	43	13	.238	.325
Steve Scarsone	2B22, 3B8, 1B6, SS1	R	28	52	103	21	28	8	0	2	13	10	20	0	.272	.408
Mark Carreon	OF33	R	30	51	100	8	27	4	0	3	20	7	20	0	.270	.400
Jeff Reed	C33	L	31	50	103	11	18	3	0	1	7	11	21	0	.175	.233
Mike Benjamin	SS18, 2B10, 3B5	R	28	38	62	9	16	5	1	1	9	5	16	5	.258	.419
2 Darryl Strawberry	OF27	L	32	29	92	13	22	3	1	4	27	21	22	3	.239	.424
Rikkert Faneyte	OF6	R	25	19	26	1	3	3	0	0	4	3	11	0	.115	.231
J.R. Phillips	1B10	L	24	15	38	1	5	0	0	1	3	1	13	1	.132	.211
Mark Leonard	OF2	L	29	14	11	2	4	1	0	2	3	2	3	0	.364	.636
Erik Johnson	2B2, SS1	R	28	5	13	0	2	0	0	0	4	0	4	0	.154	.154

NAME	T	AGE	W	L	PCT	SV	G	GS	CG	IP	H	BB	SO	SHO	ERA
		28	55	60	.478	33	115	115	2	1025	1014	372	655	4	3.99
Mark Portugal	R	31	10	8	.556	0	21	21	1	137	135	45	87	0	3.93
William VanLandingham	R	23	8	2	.800	0	16	14	0	84	70	43	56	0	3.54
Bill Swift (SJ)	R	32	8	7	.533	0	17	17	0	109	109	31	62	0	3.38
John Burkett	R	29	6	8	.429	0	25	25	0	159	176	36	85	0	3.62
Bud Black (KJ-EJ)	L	37	4	2	.667	0	10	10	0	54	50	16	28	0	4.47
Rich Monteleone (FJ)	R	31	4	3	.571	0	25	4	0	45	43	13	16	0	3.18
Bryan Hickerson	L	30	4	8	.333	1	28	14	0	98	118	38	59	0	5.40
Mike Jackson (SJ)	R	29	3	2	.600	4	36	0	0	42	23	11	51	0	1.49
Dave Burba	R	27	3	6	.333	0	57	0	0	74	59	45	84	0	4.38
Rod Beck	R	25	2	4	.333	28	48	0	0	49	49	13	39	0	2.77
Salomon Torres	R	22	2	8	.200	0	16	14	1	84	95	34	42	0	5.44
Steve Frey	L	30	1	0	1.000	0	44	0	0	31	37	15	20	0	4.94
Kevin Rogers (SJ)	L	25	0	0	—	0	10	0	0	10	6	7	3	0	3.48
Brad Brink	R	29	0	0	—	0	4	0	0	5	0	0	6	0	10.80
2 Kent Bottenfield	R	25	0	0	—	0	2	0	0	2	5	0	0	0	0.00
Pat Gomez	L	26	0	1	.000	0	26	0	0	33	23	20	14	0	3.78
Tony Menendez	R	29	0	1	.000	0	6	0	0	3	8	2	2	0	21.60
Trevor Wilson 28 (SJ)															

Name	G by Pos	B	AGE	G	AB	R	H	2B	3B	HR	RBI	BB	SO	SB	BA	SA
COLORADO 3rd 53-64 .453 6.5 DON BAYLOR																
TOTALS			30	117	4006	573	1098	206	39	125	540	378	761	91	.274	.439
Andres Galarraga	1B103	R	33	103	417	77	133	21	0	31	85	19	93	8	.319	.592
Nelson Liriano	2B79, SS3, 3B2	B	30	87	255	39	65	17	5	3	31	42	44	0	.255	.396
Walt Weiss	SS110	B	30	110	423	58	106	11	4	1	32	56	58	12	.251	.303
Charlie Hayes	3B110	R	29	113	423	46	122	23	4	10	50	36	71	3	.288	.433
Dante Bichette	OF116	R	30	116	484	74	147	33	2	27	95	19	70	21	.304	.548
Ellis Burks (WJ)	OF39	R	29	42	149	33	48	8	3	13	24	16	39	3	.322	.678
Eric Young	OF60, 2B1	R	27	90	228	37	62	13	1	7	30	38	17	18	.272	.430
Joe Girardi	C93	R	29	93	330	47	91	9	4	4	34	21	48	3	.276	.364
Mike Kingery	OF98, 1B1	L	33	105	301	56	105	27	8	4	41	30	26	5	.349	.532
Howard Johnson	OF62, 1B1	B	33	93	227	30	48	10	2	10	40	39	73	11	.211	.405
John Vander Wal	1B14, OF7	L	28	91	110	12	27	3	1	5	15	16	31	2	.245	.427
Vinny Castilla	SS18, 2B14, 3B9, 1B2	R	26	52	130	16	43	11	1	3	18	7	23	2	.331	.500
Danny Sheaffer	C30, 1B2, OF1	R	33	44	110	11	24	4	0	1	12	10	11	0	.218	.282
Roberto Mejia	2B34	R	22	38	116	11	28	8	1	4	14	15	33	3	.241	.431
Chris Jones	OF14	R	21	21	40	6	12	2	1	0	2	2	14	0	.300	.400
Trenidad Hubbard	OF5	R	30	18	25	3	7	1	1	1	3	3	4	0	.280	.520
Jayhawk Owens	C6	R	25	6	12	4	3	0	1	0	1	3	3	0	.250	.417
Ty Van Burkleo	1B2	L	30	2	5	0	0	0	0	0	0	0	0	1	.000	.000

NAME	T	AGE	W	L	PCT	SV	G	GS	CG	IP	H	BB	SO	SHO	ERA
		28	53	64	.453	28	117	117	4	1031	1185	448	703	5	5.15
Marvin Freeman	R	31	10	2	.833	0	19	18	0	113	113	23	67	0	2.80
David Nied	R	25	9	7	.563	0	22	22	2	122	137	47	74	1	4.80
Kevin Ritz	R	29	5	6	.455	0	15	15	0	74	88	35	53	0	5.62
Mike Munoz	L	28	4	2	.667	1	57	0	0	46	37	31	32	0	3.74
Bruce Ruffin	L	30	4	5	.444	16	56	0	0	56	55	30	65	0	4.04
Lance Painter	L	26	4	6	.400	0	15	14	0	74	91	26	41	0	6.11
Kent Bottenfield (BH)	R	25	3	1	.750	1	15	1	0	25	28	10	15	0	5.84
Steve Reed	R	29	3	2	.600	3	61	0	0	64	79	26	51	0	3.94
Armando Reynoso (EJ)	R	28	3	4	.429	0	9	9	1	52	54	22	25	0	4.82
Greg Harris	R	30	3	12	.200	1	29	19	1	130	154	52	82	0	6.65
Bruce Walton	R	31	1	0	1.000	0	4	0	0	5	6	1	2	0	8.44
Marcus Moore	R	24	1	1	.500	0	29	0	0	34	33	21	33	0	6.15
Curtis Leskanic	R	26	1	1	.500	0	8	3	0	22	27	10	17	0	5.64
Mark Thompson	R	23	1	1	.500	0	2	2	0	9	16	8	5	0	9.00
Mike Harkey	R	27	1	6	.143	0	24	13	0	92	125	35	39	0	5.79
Jim Czajkowski	R	30	0	0	.—	0	5	0	0	9	9	6	2	0	4.15
Darren Holmes	R	28	0	3	.000	3	29	0	0	28	35	24	33	0	6.35
Willie Blair	R	28	0	5	.000	3	47	1	0	78	98	39	68	0	5.79
Scott Fredrickson 26 (BK)															

Name	G by Pos	B	AGE	G	AB	R	H	2B	3B	HR	RBI	BB	SO	SB	BA	SA
SAN DIEGO 4th 47-70 .402 12.5 JIM RIGGLEMAN																
TOTALS			27	117	4068	479	1117	200	19	92	445	319	762	79	.275	.401
Eddie Williams	1B46, 3B1	R	29	49	175	32	58	11	1	11	42	15	26	0	.331	.594
Bip Roberts	2B90, OF2	B	30	105	403	52	129	15	5	2	31	39	57	21	.320	.397
Ricky Gutierrez	SS78, 2B7	R	24	90	275	27	66	11	2	1	28	32	54	2	.240	.305
? Scott Livingstone	3B50	L	28	57	180	11	49	12	1	2	10	6	22	2	.272	.383
Tony Gwynn	OF106	L	34	110	419	79	**165**	35	1	12	64	48	19	5	**.394**	.568
Derek Bell	OF108	R	25	108	434	54	135	20	0	14	54	29	88	24	.311	.454
Phil Plantier	OF91	L	25	96	341	44	75	21	0	18	41	36	91	3	.220	.440
Brad Ausmus	C99, 1B1	R	25	101	327	45	82	12	1	7	24	30	63	5	.251	.358
Billy Bean	OF39, 1B16	L	30	84	135	7	29	5	1	0	14	7	25	0	.215	.267
Craig Shipley	3B53, SS14, 2B13, OF2, 1B1	R	31	81	240	32	80	14	4	4	30	9	28	6	.333	.475
Luis Lopez	SS43, 2B29, 3B5	R	23	77	235	29	65	16	1	2	20	15	39	3	.277	.379
Phil Clark	1B24, OF17, C5, 3B1	R	26	61	149	14	32	6	0	5	20	5	17	1	.215	.356
Archi Cianfrocco	3B37, 1B16, SS1	R	27	59	146	9	32	8	0	4	13	3	39	2	.219	.356
Tim Hyers (SJ)		L	22	52	113	10	30	3	0	0	7	9	15	3	.254	.280
Brian Johnson	C24, 1B5	R	26	36	93	7	23	4	1	3	16	5	21	0	.247	.409
Dave Staton	1B19	R	24	28	66	6	12	2	0	4	6	10	18	0	.182	.394
Keith Lockhart	3B13, 2B5, SS1, OF1	L	29	27	43	4	9	2	0	2	6	4	10	1	.209	.349
Melvin Nieves	OF6	B	22	10	19	2	5	1	0	1	4	3	10	0	.263	.474
Ray McDavid	OF7	L	22	9	28	2	7	1	0	0	2	1	8	1	.250	.286
Ray Holbert	SS1	R	23	5	5	1	1	0	0	0	0	1	3	0	.200	.200

NAME	T	AGE	W	L	PCT	SV	G	GS	CG	IP	H	BB	SO	SHO	ERA
		28	47	70	.402	27	117	117	8	1046	1008	393	862	6	4.08
Joey Hamilton	R	23	9	6	.600	0	16	16	1	109	98	29	61	1	2.98
Andy Ashby	R	26	6	11	.353	0	24	24	4	164	145	43	121	0	3.40
Andy Benes	R	26	6	14	.300	0	25	25	2	172	155	51	**189**	2	3.86
Trevor Hoffman	R	26	4	4	.500	20	47	0	0	56	39	20	68	0	2.57
Wally Whitehurst (EJ)	R	30	4	7	.364	0	13	13	0	64	84	26	43	0	4.92
Scott Sanders	R	25	4	8	.333	1	23	20	0	111	103	48	109	0	4.78
Jeff Tabaka	L	30	3	1	.750	1	34	0	0	37	28	19	30	0	3.89
Pedro Martinez	L	25	2	2	.600	3	48	1	0	68	52	49	52	0	2.90
Bill Krueger	L	36	3	2	.600	8	7	1	0	41	42	7	30	0	4.83
Tim Mauser	R	27	2	4	.333	2	35	0	0	49	50	19	32	0	3.49
Gene Harris	R	29	1	1	.500	0	13	0	0	12	21	9	8	0	8.03
Mike Campbell	R	30	1	1	.500	0	3	2	0	8	13	5	10	0	12.96
A.J. Sager	R	29	1	4	.200	0	22	3	0	47	62	16	26	0	5.98
Doug Brocail (EJ)	R	27	0	0	.—	0	12	0	0	17	21	5	11	0	5.82
Bryce Florie	R	24	0	0	.—	0	9	0	0	9	3	8	0	0	0.96
Kerry Taylor	R	23	0	0	.—	0	1	1	0	4	9	1	3	0	8.31
Donnie Elliott (SJ)	R	25	0	1	.000	0	30	1	0	33	31	21	24	0	3.27
Mark Davis	L	33	0	1	.000	0	20	0	0	16	20	13	15	0	8.82
Tim Worrell (EJ)	R	26	0	2	.000	0	3	0	0	15	9	5	14	0	3.68
Jose Martinez	R	23	0	2	.000	0	4	1	0	12	18	5	7	0	6.75

MISCELLANEOUS 1994 INDIVIDUAL LEADERS

BATTING

On Base Average

#	American League		#	National League	
1	Thomas, Chi.	.487	1	Gwynn, S.D.	.454
2	O'Neill, N.Y.	.460	2	Bagwell, Hou.	.451
3	Belle, Cle.	.438	3	Mitchell, Cin.	.429
4	Boggs, N.Y.	.433	4	Justice, Atl.	.427
5	Clark, Tex.	.431	5	Bonds, S.F.	.426
6	Tettleton, Tex.	.419	6	Biggio, Hou.	.411
7	Lofton, Cle.	.412	7	Butler, L.A.	.411
8	Henderson, Oak.	.411	8	Alou, Mon.	.397
9	Molitor, Tor.	.410	9	Walker, Mon.	.394
	Davis, Cal.	.410	10	Browne, Fla.	.392

Caught Stealing

#	American League		#	National League	
1	Gagne, K.C.	17	1	D. Sanders, Atl.+Cin.	16
2	Jose, K.C.	12	2	Gonzalez, Hou.	13
	Polonia, Cal.	12		Sosa, Chi.	13
	Lofton, Cle.	12		Lewis, Chi.	13
5	Curtis, Cal.	11	5	Vizcaino, N.Y.	11
				Kelly, Cin.+Atl.	11

Stolen Base Percentage
(Minimum 20 Attempts)

#	American League		#	National League	
1	Molitor, Tor.	100	1	Larkin, Cin.	93
2	Anderson, Bal.	97	2	Biggio, Hou.	91
3	Coleman, K.C.	86	3	Clayton, S.F.	88
	Shumpert, K.C.	86	4	Grissom, Mon.	86
5	Knoblauch, Min.	85	5	Frazier, Mon.	83

On Base Average plus Slugging Average

#	American League		#	National League	
1	Thomas, Chi.	1.216	1	Bagwell, Hou.	1.201
2	Belle, Cle.	1.152	2	Mitchell, Cin.	1.110
3	Griffey, Sea.	1.076	3	Bonds, S.F.	1.073
4	O'Neill, N.Y.	1.063	4	Gwynn, S.D.	1.022
5	Hamelin, K.C.	.987	5	McGriff, Atl.	1.012
6	Vaughn, Bos.	.984	6	Alou, Mon.	.989
7	Davis, Cal.	.971	7	Walker, Mon.	.981
8	Lofton, Cle.	.948	8	Sheffield, Fla.	.964
9	Palmeiro, Bal.	.942	9	Justice, Atl.	.958
10	Canseco, Tex.	.938	10	Galarraga, Col.	.948

Extra Base Hits

#	American League		#	National League	
1	Thomas, Chi.	73	1	Bagwell, Hou.	73
	Belle, Cle.	73	2	Walker, Mon.	65
3	Griffey, Sea.	68	3	Williams, S.F.	62
4	Fryman, Det.	57		Bichette, Col.	62
5	Palmeiro, Bal.	55	5	McGriff, Atl.	60
	Puckett, Min.	55			

Total Bases

#	American League		#	National League	
1	Belle, Cle.	294	1	Bagwell, Hou.	300
2	Griffey, Sea.	292	2	Williams, S.F.	270
3	Thomas, Chi.	291	3	Bichette, Col.	265
4	Lofton, Cle.	246	4	McGriff, Atl.	264
5	Palmeiro, Bal.	240		Bonds, S.F.	253

FIELDING

Fielding Average
(Minimum 70 Games)

American League			National League	
Reed, Mil.	.995	2B-best	Lemke, Atl.	.994
Knoblauch, Min.	.994	2nd	Biggio, Hou.	.98
Whitaker, Det.	.970	worst	Liriano, Col.	.97
Ripken, Bal.	.985	SS-best	Smith, St. L.	.982
DiSarcina, Cal.	.983	2nd	Larkin, Cin.	.98
Valentin, Mil.	.954	worst	Gutierrez, S.D.	.92
Gaetti, K.C.	.982	3B-best	Fernandez, Cin.	.98
Gomez, Bal.	.975	2nd	Buechele, Chi.	.97
Palmer, Tex.	.912	worst	Berry, Mon.	.9

Putouts plus Assists per 9 Innings Played
(Minimum 70 Games)

American League			National League	
Reed, Mil.	5.65	2B-best	Barberie, Fla.	5.69
Baerga, Cle.	5.45	2nd	Garcia, Pit.	5.68
Knoblauch, Min.	4.61	worst	Boone, Cin.	4.61
Valentin, Mil.	5.36	SS-best	Bell, Pit.	5.08
Gallego, N.Y.	5.21	2nd	Clayton, S.F.	4.91
Guillen, Chi.	3.93	worst	Gutierrez, S.D.	3.94
Boggs, N.Y.	2.92	3B-best	King, Pit.	2.94
Gaetti, K.C.	2.83	2nd	Williams, S.F.	2.93
Sprague, Tor.	2.34	worst	Buechele, Chi.	2.18

PITCHING

Wild Pitches

#	American League		#	National League	
1	Guzman, Tor.	13	1	Lewis, Fla.	10
2	Gordon, K.C.	12		Sanders, S.D.	10
3	Appier, K.C.	11		Kile, Hou.	10
4	Davis, Det.	10	4	Slocumb, Phi.	9
	Erickson, Min.	10		West, Phi.	9
	Moore, Det.	10		Hough, Fla.	9
	Finley, Cal.	10		Candiotti, L.A.	9

Home Runs Allowed

#	American League		#	National League	
1	Deshaies, Min.	30	1	Smith, N.Y.	25
2	Fernandez, Bal.	27	2	Harris, Col.	22
	Moore, Det.	27	3	Cooke, Pit.	21
4	Stewart, Tor.	26	4	Henderson, S.F.	20
5	Fernandez, Chi.	25		Swindell, Hou.	20
				Benes, S.D.	20

Home Runs Allowed per 9 IP
(Minimum 10 Home Runs Allowed)

#	American League		#	National League	
1	Casian, Min.+Cle.	2.20	1	Beck, S.F.	1.85
2	Magrane, Cal.	2.19	2	Hickerson, S.F.	1.83
3	Fernandez, Bal.	2.11	3	Smith, N.Y..	1.71
4	Deshaies, Min.	2.07	4	Roper, Cin.	1.57
5	Higuera, Mil.	1.99	5	Harris, Col.	1.52

1995 A Season For Healing

The high point of the 1995 season came on the night of September 6 when Baltimore's Cal Ripken, Jr. broke Lou Gehrig's long-standing consecutive-game record. Before a packed house at Camden Yards and before a huge television audience, Ripken played his 2,131st consecutive game and even cracked a home run to boot. When the game became official in the middle of the fifth inning, the Orioles' shortstop received a twenty-two minute standing ovation. To baseball fans, Ripken represented all the good things they wanted to see in their game—a modest, hard-working star who cared about the game's integrity and the fans than he did about a paycheck. Too much of the season was given over to economic talk, but Ripken was a nice guy who finished first—at least in the hearts of the fans.

The strike that ended the 1994 season was not settled as Opening Day approached. But faced with the prospect of seeing "replacement players"—mostly marginally talented amateurs—take the field, the major leaguers returned to work on the eve of the scheduled opening of the season. To allow them to get into playing shape, the start was pushed back three weeks and the season shortened to 144 games for each club.

When the season finally began, many fans showed the depth of their anger by staying home from the ballparks. Attendance plunged in almost every city, dangerously so in several. The situation wasn't helped by the absence of pennant races. Baseball had restructured itself into three divisions in each league in 1994, but only two of the divisions produced any down-to-the-wire excitement in '95. The saving grace was the wild card addition to the playoffs. Much maligned by purists before the season began, the possibility of earning the fourth-spot in the league playoffs kept the fans hopeful into September in more than half of the major league cities as interest in the National Pastime slowly returned.

In the National League East, Philadelphia got off to a fast start, but a horrendous rash of injuries soon derailed their hopes. That left the way open for Atlanta with the league's best pitching to cakewalk to the division championship. Greg Maddux, Tom Glavine, Mark Wohlers, and the rest could nearly always be counted on. Maddux, on his way to a fourth Cy Young Award, set a record for consecutive road victories.

The story was much the same in the Central Division where Houston was also kayoed by injuries, particularly a broken hand that put 1994 MVP Jeff Bagwell out of action for an extended period. Cincinnati, perhaps the league's best balanced team, coasted to victory.

Only in the West was there a real race. The Dodgers found a drawing card and a fine pitcher in Japanese import Hideo Nomo, the N.L. Rookie of the Year, but surprising Colorado stayed neck and neck with L.A. until the end. The Rockies blended terrific home run power, an aggressive style, and truly awful pitching into a contender in only their third season of existence.

The Red Sox, led by a super season by slugger Mo Vaughn, ran away with the American League East. A storybook comeback by knuckle-baller Tim Wakefield added the necessary pitching when staff ace Roger Clemens made a slow recovery from arm surgery.

In the A.L. Central, the long-suffering Cleveland Indians with 100 wins were undoubtedly baseball's best team during the season. The Tribe's lineup brimmed with power from top to bottom and their pitching was the best in the league. Albert Belle posted a remarkable year, reaching a lofty 50 home runs and 103 extra base hits in the shortened season. The Indians made a habit of come-from-behind victories, and their route to the playoffs was, in the words of one observer, "not a race but a coronation."

For much of the season, the California Angels seemed to be on their way to an easy victory in the West. Combining young sluggers and veteran pitching, the Angels zoomed to a commanding lead. But after an injury to shortstop Gary DiSarcina, the team began to slide. Meanwhile, the Seattle Mariners survived a mid-summer wrist injury to Ken Griffey, Jr. to stay a viable wild card contender. Edgar Martinez's hitting and Randy Johnson's overpowering pitching kept them afloat until Griffey returned to action. Then, as California stumbled, Seattle suddenly found itself vying for the division lead. The two teams tied at the end of the regular season, and the Mariners won a one-game playoff.

The playoffs produced one exciting series, as Seattle narrowly bested the wild card Yankees, but in the long run Cleveland and Atlanta came out on top as expected.

In an enjoyable six-game World Series, the Braves' pitching—particularly that of Glavine—shut down the Indians vaunted bats. For Atlanta, the third time proved the charm when, after Series losses in 1991 and 1992, they finally claimed a World Championship.

Although the 1995 season ended with still no end in sight to the divisions between owners and players that led to the strike in '94, the play of Vaughn, Belle, Johnson, Maddux, Nomo, and others, the revitalization of Cleveland and the surprising improvement in Colorado, the close wild car races, the satisfactory World Series, and, perhaps most of all, the example of Cal Ripken, Jr. went a long way toward healing the fans' wounds.

EAST DIVISION — 1995 AMERICAN LEAGUE

BOSTON — 1st 86-58 .597 — KEVIN KENNEDY (Batting)

Name	G by Pos	B	AGE	G	AB	R	H	2B	3B	HR	RBI	BB	SO	SB	BA	SA
TOTALS			29	144	4997	791	1399	286	31	175	754	560	923	99	.280	.455
Mo Vaughn	1B138 DH2	L	27	140	550	98	165	28	3	39	126	68	150	11	.300	.575
Luis Alicea	2B132	B	29	132	419	64	113	20	3	6	44	63	61	13	.270	.375
John Valentin	SS135	R	28	135	520	108	155	37	2	27	102	81	67	20	.298	.533
Tim Naehring	3B124 DH1	R	28	126	433	61	133	27	2	10	57	77	66	0	.307	.448
Troy O'Leary	OF105 DH3	L	25	112	399	60	123	31	6	10	49	29	64	5	.308	.491
Lee Tinsley	OF97	B	26	100	341	61	97	17	1	7	41	39	74	18	.284	.402
Mike Greenwell	OF118 DH2	L	31	120	481	67	143	25	4	15	76	38	35	9	.297	.459
Mike Macfarlane	C111 DH3	R	31	115	364	45	82	18	1	15	51	38	78	2	.225	.404
Jose Canseco (VJ)	DH101 OF1	R	30	102	396	64	121	25	1	24	81	42	93	4	.306	.556
Willie McGee	OF64	B	36	67	200	32	57	11	3	2	15	9	41	5	.285	.400
Bill Haselman	C48 DH11 1B1 3B1	R	29	64	152	22	37	6	1	5	23	17	30	0	.243	.395
Reggie Jefferson (XJ)	DH32 1B7 OF2	L	26	46	121	21	35	8	0	5	26	9	24	0	.289	.479
Chris Donnels	3B27 1B8 2B1	L	26	40	91	13	23	2	2	2	11	9	18	0	.253	.385
Matt Stairs	OF23 DH2	L	27	39	88	8	23	7	1	1	17	4	14	0	.261	.398
Mark Whiten	OF31 DH1	B	28	32	108	13	20	3	0	1	10	8	23	1	.185	.241
Dwayne Hosey	OF21 DH1	B	28	24	68	20	23	8	1	3	7	8	16	6	.338	.618
Terry Shumpert	2B8 3B5 SS3 DH2	R	28	21	47	6	11	3	0	0	3	4	13	3	.234	.298
Wes Chamberlain	OF12 DH5 1B1	R	29	19	42	4	5	1	0	1	1	3	11	1	.119	.214
Juan Bell	SS6 2B5 3B1	B	27	17	26	7	4	2	0	1	2	2	10	0	.154	.346
Chris James	OF8 DH5 3B2	R	32	16	24	2	4	1	0	0	1	1	4	0	.167	.208
Rich Rowland	C11 DH3	R	31	14	29	1	5	1	0	0	1	0	11	0	.172	.207
Carlos Rodriguez	2B7 SS8 3B1	B	27	13	30	5	10	2	0	0	5	2	2	0	.333	.400
Karl Rhodes	OF9	L	26	10	25	2	2	1	0	1	1	3	4	0	.080	.120
Steve Rodriguez	SS4 2B1 DH1	R	24	8	8	1	1	0	0	0	0	1	1	1	.125	.125
Ron Mahay	OF5	L	24	5	20	3	4	2	0	1	3	1	6	0	.200	.450
Dave Hollins (WJ)	DH3 OF2	B	29	5	13	2	2	0	0	0	1	4	7	0	.154	.154
Scott Hatteberg	C2	L	25	2	2	1	1	0	0	0	0	0	0	0	.500	.500

BOSTON (Pitching)

NAME	T	AGE	W	L	PCT	SV	G	GS	CG	IP	H	BB	SO	SHO	ERA
		30	86	58	.597	39	144	144	7	1293	1338	476	888	9	4.39
Tim Wakefield	R	28	16	8	.667	0	27	27	6	195	163	68	119	1	2.95
Erik Hanson	R	30	15	5	.750	0	29	29	1	187	187	59	139	1	4.24
Roger Clemens (SJ)	R	32	10	5	.667	0	23	23	0	140	141	60	132	0	4.18
Stan Belinda	R	28	8	1	.889	10	63	0	0	70	51	28	57	0	5.10
Zane Smith	L	34	8	8	.500	0	24	21	0	111	144	23	47	0	5.61
Rheal Cormier	L	28	7	5	.583	0	48	12	0	115	131	31	69	0	4.07
Vaughn Eshelman	L	26	6	3	.667	0	23	14	0	82	86	36	41	0	4.85
2 Mike Maddux	R	33	4	1	.800	1	36	4	0	90	86	15	65	0	3.61
Aaron Sele (SJ)	R	25	3	1	.750	0	6	6	0	32	32	14	21	0	3.06
Derek Lilliquist	L	29	2	1	.667	0	28	.0	0	23	27	9	9	0	6.26
2 Eric Gunderson	L	29	2	1	.667	0	19	.0	0	12	13	9	9	0	5.11
2 Rick Aguilera	R	33	2	2	.500	20	30	0	0	30	26	7	23	0	2.67
2 Mike Stanton	L	28	1	0	1.000	0	22	0	0	21	17	8	10	0	3.00
1 Alejandro Pena	R	36	1	1	.500	0	17	0	0	24	33	12	25	0	7.40
Jeff Suppan	R	20	1	2	.333	0	8	3	0	23	29	5	19	0	5.96
1 Mike Hartley	R	33	0	0	—	0	5	0	0	7	8	2	2	0	9.00
Brian Bark	L	26	0	0	—	0	3	0	0	2	2	1	0	0	0.00
Keith Shepherd (SJ)	R	27	0	0	—	0	2	0	0	1	4	2	0	0	36.00
Joe Hudson	R	24	0	1	.000	0	39	0	0	46	53	23	29	0	4.11
Tim VanEgmond	R	26	0	1	.000	0	4	1	0	7	9	6	5	0	9.45
Joel Johnston	R	28	0	1	.000	0	4	0	0	5	12	4	3	0	11.25
Brian Looney	L	25	0	0	—	0	3	1	0	5	12	4	2	0	17.36
2 Matt Murray	R	24	0	1	.000	0	2	1	0	3	11	3	1	0	18.90
1 Frankie Rodriguez	R	22	0	2	.000	0	2	0	0	15	21	10	14	0	10.57
Jeff Pierce	R	26	0	3	.000	0	12	0	0	15	16	14	12	0	6.60
Ken Ryan	R	26	0	4	.000	1	28	0	0	33	34	24	34	0	4.96

NEW YORK — 2nd 79-65 .549 7 (Wild Card) — BUCK SHOWALTER (Batting)

Name	G by Pos	B	AGE	G	AB	R	H	2B	3B	HR	RBI	BB	SO	SB	BA	SA
TOTALS			31	145	4947	749	1365	280	34	122	709	625	851	50	.276	.420
Don Mattingly	1B125 DH1	L	34	128	458	59	132	32	2	7	49	40	35	0	.288	.413
Pat Kelly (WJ)	2B87 DH1	R	27	89	270	32	64	12	1	4	29	23	65	8	.237	.333
Tony Fernandez	SS103 2B4	B	33	108	384	57	94	20	2	5	45	42	40	6	.245	.346
Wade Boggs	3B117 1B9	L	37	126	460	76	149	22	4	5	63	74	50	1	.324	.422
Paul O'Neill	OF121 DH4	L	32	127	460	82	138	30	4	22	96	71	76	1	.300	.526
Bernie Williams	OF144	B	26	144	563	93	173	29	9	18	82	75	98	8	.307	.487
Luis Polonia	OF64	L	30	67	238	37	62	9	3	2	15	25	29	10	.261	.349
Mike Stanley	C107 DH10	R	32	118	399	63	107	29	1	18	83	57	106	1	.268	.481
Ruben Sierra	DH46 OF10	B	29	56	215	33	56	15	0	7	44	22	34	1	.260	.428
Randy Velarde	2B62 SS28 OF20 3B19	R	32	111	367	60	102	19	1	7	46	55	64	5	.278	.392
Gerald Williams	OF92 DH1	R	28	100	182	33	45	18	2	6	28	22	34	4	.247	.467
Dion James	OF29 DH27 1B6	L	32	85	209	22	60	6	1	2	26	20	16	2	.287	.354
Jim Leyritz	C46 1B18 DH15	R	31	77	264	37	71	12	0	7	37	37	73	1	.269	.394
Danny Tartabull	DH39 OF18	R	32	59	192	25	43	12	0	6	28	33	54	0	.224	.380
Russ Davis	3B34 DH4 1B2	R	25	40	98	14	27	5	2	2	12	10	26	0	.276	.429
Darryl Strawberry (SD)	DH15 OF11	L	33	32	87	15	24	4	1	3	13	10	22	0	.276	.448
Dave Silvestri	2B7 1B4 DH4 SS1	R	27	17	21	4	2	0	0	1	4	4	9	0	.095	.238
Derek Jeter	SS15	R	21	15	48	5	12	4	1	0	7	3	11	0	.250	.375
Kevin Elster	SS10 2B1	R	30	10	17	1	2	1	0	0	0	1	5	0	.118	.176
Robert Eenhoorn	2B3 SS2	R	27	5	14	1	2	1	0	0	2	1	3	0	.143	.214
Ruben Rivera	OF4	R	21	5	1	0	0	0	0	0	0	0	2	0	.000	.000
Jorge Posada	C1	B	23	1	0	0	0	0	0	0	0	0	0	0		

NEW YORK (Pitching)

NAME	T	AGE	W	L	PCT	SV	G	GS	CG	IP	H	BB	SO	SHO	ERA
		28	79	65	.549	35	144	144	18	1285	1286	535	908	5	4.56
Jack McDowell	R	29	15	10	.600	0	30	30	8	218	211	78	157	2	3.93
Andy Pettitte	L	23	12	9	.571	0	30	26	3	175	183	63	114	0	4.17
Sterling Hitchcock	L	24	11	10	.524	0	27	27	4	168	155	68	121	1	4.70
2 David Cone	R	32	9	2	.818	0	13	13	1	99*	82	47	89	0	3.82
Scott Kamieniecki (EJ)	R	31	7	6	.538	0	17	16	1	90	83	49	43	0	4.01
Steve Howe	R	37	3	3	.667	2	56	0	0	49	66	17	28	0	4.96
Mariano Rivera	R	25	5	3	.625	0	19	10	0	67	71	30	51	0	5.51
Melido Perez (SJ)	R	29	5	5	.500	0	13	12	1	69	70	31	44	0	5.58
Joe Ausanio	R	29	2	0	1.000	1	28	0	0	38	42	23	36	0	5.73
Bob Wickman	R	26	2	4	.333	1	63	1	0	80	77	33	51	0	4.05
Bob MacDonald	L	30	3	0	1.000	0	33	0	0	46	50	22	41	0	4.86
Scott Bankhead	R	31	1	1	.500	0	20	1	0	39	44	16	20	0	6.00
Dave Eiland	R	28	0	1	.000	0	4	1	0	10	18	3	6	0	6.30
Jimmy Key (SJ)	L	34	1	2	.333	0	5	5	0	30	40	6	14	0	5.64
John Wetteland	R	28	1	5	.167	31	60	0	0	61	40	14	66	0	2.93
2 Josias Manzanillo (EJ)	R	27	0	0	—	0	17			19	9	11	0		2.08
Dave Pavlas	R	32	0	0	—	0	3	0	0	18	17	6	9	0	3.18
Jeff Patterson	R	26	0	0	—	0	2	0	0	3	3	2	3	0	2.70
2 Rick Honeycutt	L	41	0	0	—	0	2	0	0	2	9	1	2	0	27.00
Brian Boehringer	R	26	0	3	.000	0	7	2	0	18	24	12	10	0	13.75

*Cone, also with Toronto, league leader in Innings Pitched with 229

BALTIMORE — 3rd 71-73 .493 15 — PHIL REGAN

Name	G by Pos	B	AGE	G	AB	R	H	2B	3B	HR	RBI	BB	SO	SB	BA	SA
TOTALS			30	144	4837	704	1267	229	27	173	668	574	803	92	.262	.428
Rafael Palmeiro	1B142	L	30	143	554	89	172	30	2	39	104	62	65	3	.310	.583
Manny Alexander	2B81 SS7 3B2 DH1	R	24	94	242	35	57	9	1	3	23	20	30	11	.236	.318
Cal Ripken	SS144	R	34	144	550	71	144	33	2	17	88	52	59	0	.262	.422
Jeff Manto	3B69 DH13 1B4	R	30	89	254	31	65	9	0	17	38	24	69	0	.256	.492
Jeffrey Hammonds (SJ)	OF46 DH5	R	24	57	178	18	43	9	1	4	23	9	30	4	.242	.371
Curtis Goodwin	OF84 DH2	L	22	87	289	40	76	11	3	1	24	15	53	22	.263	.332
Brady Anderson	OF142	L	31	143	554	108	145	33	10	16	64	87	111	26	.262	.444
Chris Hoiles	C107 DH6	R	30	114	352	53	88	15	1	19	58	67	80	1	.250	.460
Harold Baines	DH122	L	36	127	385	60	115	19	1	24	63	70	45	0	.299	.540
Kevin Bass	OF77 DH19	R	36	111	295	32	72	12	0	5	32	24	47	8	.244	.336
Bret Barberie	2B74 DH5 3B3	R	27	90	237	32	57	14	0	2	25	36	50	3	.241	.325
Jeff Huson	3B33 2B21 DH2 SS1	L	30	66	161	24	40	4	2	1	19	15	20	5	.248	.317
2 Bobby Bonilla (NJ)	OF39 3B24	B	32	61	237	47	79	12	4	10	46	23	31	0	.333	.544
Leo Gomez (NJ)	3B44 DH5 1B3	R	28	53	127	16	30	5	0	4	12	18	23	0	.236	.370
Gregg Zaun	C39	B	24	40	104	18	27	5	0	3	14	16	14	1	.260	.394
Mark Smith	OF32 DH6	R	25	37	104	11	24	5	0	3	15	12	22	3	.231	.365
1 Matt Nokes	C16 DH2	L	31	26	49	4	6	1	0	2	6	4	11	0	.122	.265
1 Damon Buford	OF24	R	25	24	32	6	2	0	0	0	2	6	7	3	.063	.063
Jarvis Brown	OF17	R	28	18	27	2	4	1	0	0	1	7	9	1	.148	.185
1 Andy Van Slyke	OF17	L	34	17	63	6	10	1	0	3	8	5	15	0	.159	.317
Sherman Obando	OF7 DH7	R	25	16	38	0	10	1	0	3	2	2	12	1	.263	.289
Cesar Devarez	C6	R	25	6	4	0	0	0	0	0	0	0	0	0	.000	.000
1 Jack Voigt	1B1 DH1	R	29	3	1	1	1	0	0	0	0	0	0	0	1.000	1.000

NAME	T	AGE	W	L	PCT	SV	G	GS	CG	IP	H	BB	SO	SHO	ERA
		30	71	73	.493	29	144	144	19	1267	1165	523	930	10	4.31
Mike Mussina	R	26	19	9	.679	0	32	32	7	222	187	50	158	4	3.29
Kevin Brown	R	30	10	9	.526	0	26	26	3	172	155	48	117	1	3.60
2 Scott Erickson	R	27	9	4	.692	0	17	16	7	109	111	35	61	2	3.89
Jamie Moyer	L	32	8	6	.571	0	27	18	0	116	117	30	65	0	5.21
Alan Mills	R	28	3	0	1.000	0	21	0	0	23	30	18	16	0	7.43
Ben McDonald (SJ)	R	27	3	6	.333	0	14	13	1	80	67	38	62	0	4.16
Mark Lee	L	29	2	0	1.000	0	39	0	0	33	31	18	27	0	4.86
Mike Oquist	R	27	2	1	.667	0	27	0	0	54	51	41	27	0	4.17
Jimmy Haynes	R	22	2	1	.667	0	4	3	0	24	11	12	22	0	2.25
1 Scott Klingenbeck	R	24	2	2	.500	0	6	5	0	31	32	18	15	0	4.89
Jesse Orosco	L	38	2	4	.333	3	65	0	0	50	28	27	58	0	3.26
2 Terry Clark	R	34	2	5	.286	1	38	0	0	39	40	15	18	0	3.46
Arthur Rhodes (SJ)	L	25	2	5	.286	0	19	9	0	75	68	48	77	0	6.21
Rick Krivda	L	25	2	7	.222	0	13	13	1	75	76	25	53	0	4.54
2 Mike Hartley	R	33	1	0	1.000	0	3	0	0	7	5	1	4	0	1.29
John DeSilva	R	27	1	0	1.000	0	2	2	0	9	8	7	1	0	7.27
Armando Benitez	R	22	1	5	.167	2	44	0	0	48	37	37	56	0	5.66
Jim Dedrick	R	27	0	0	—	0	6	0	0	8	8	6	3	0	2.35
Joe Borowski	R	24	0	0	—	0	6	0	0	7	5	4	3	0	1.23
2 Gene Harris (EJ)	R	30	0	0	—	0	3	0	0	4	4	1	4	0	4.50
1 Brad Pennington	L	26	0	1	.000	0	8	0	0	7	3	11	10	0	8.10
Doug Jones	R	38	0	4	.000	22	52	0	0	47	55	16	42	0	5.01
1 Sid Fernandez	L	32	0	4	.000	0	8	7	0	28	36	17	31	0	7.39
Mark Eichhorn (SJ) 34															

DETROIT — 4th 60-84 .417 26 — SPARKY ANDERSON

Name	G by Pos	B	AGE	G	AB	R	H	2B	3B	HR	RBI	BB	SO	SB	BA	SA
TOTALS			30	144	4865	604	1204	228	29	159	619	551	987	73	.247	.404
Cecil Fielder	1B77 DH58	R	31	136	494	70	120	18	1	31	82	75	116	0	.243	.472
Lou Whitaker	2B63 DH8	L	38	84	249	36	73	14	0	14	44	31	41	4	.293	.518
Chris Gomez	SS97 2B31 DH1	R	24	123	431	49	96	20	2	11	50	41	96	4	.223	.355
Travis Fryman	3B144	R	26	144	567	79	156	21	5	15	81	63	100	4	.275	.409
Danny Bautista	OF86	R	23	89	271	28	55	9	0	7	27	12	68	4	.203	.314
Chad Curtis	OF144	R	26	144	586	96	157	29	3	21	67	70	93	27	.268	.435
Bobby Higginson	OF123 DH2	L	24	131	410	61	92	17	5	14	43	62	107	6	.224	.393
John Flaherty	C112	R	27	112	354	39	86	22	1	11	40	18	47	0	.243	.404
Kirk Gibson	DH63 OF1	L	38	70	227	37	59	12	2	9	35	33	61	9	.260	.449
1 Juan Samuel	1B37 DH16 OF9 2B6	R	34	76	171	28	48	10	1	10	34	24	38	5	.281	.526
Alan Trammell	SS60 DH6	R	37	74	223	28	60	12	0	2	23	27	19	3	.269	.350
Scott Fletcher	2B63 SS3 1B1	R	36	67	182	19	42	10	1	1	17	19	27	1	.231	.313
Franklin Stubbs	OF20 1B20 DH3	L	34	62	116	13	29	11	0	2	19	19	27	0	.250	.397
Ron Tingley	C53 1B1	R	36	54	124	14	28	8	1	4	18	15	38	0	.226	.403
Milt Cuyler	OF36 DH2	B	26	41	88	15	18	1	4	0	5	8	16	2	.205	.307
Derrick White	1B16 OF9 DH8	R	25	39	48	3	9	2	0	0	2	0	7	1	.188	.229
Todd Steverson (WJ)	OF27 DH1	R	23	30	42	11	11	0	0	2	6	6	10	2	.262	.405
2 Phil Nevin	OF27 DH4	R	24	29	96	9	21	3	1	2	12	11	27	0	.219	.333
Tony Clark	1B27	B	23	27	101	10	24	5	1	3	11	8	30	0	.238	.396
2 Steve Rodriguez	2B12 SS1	R	24	12	31	4	6	1	0	0	3	0	5	0	.194	.226
Rudy Pemberton	OF8 DH3	R	25	12	30	3	9	3	1	0	3	1	5	0	.300	.467
Joe Hall	OF5 DH1	R	29	7	15	2	2	0	0	0	2	3	4	0	.133	.133
Shannon Penn	2B3	B	25	3	9	0	3	0	0	0	0	1	2	0	.333	.333

NAME	T	AGE	W	L	PCT	SV	G	GS	CG	IP	H	BB	SO	SHO	ERA
		29	60	84	.417	38	144	144	5	1275	1509	536	729	3	5.49
1 David Wells	L	32	10	3	.769	0	18	18	3	130	120	37	83	0	3.04
Felipe Lira	R	23	9	13	.409	1	37	22	0	146	151	56	89	0	4.31
Sean Bergman	R	25	7	10	.412	0	28	28	1	135	169	67	86	1	5.12
Joe Boever	R	34	5	7	.417	3	60	0	0	99	128	44	71	0	6.39
John Doherty	R	28	5	9	.357	6	48	2	0	113	130	37	46	0	5.10
Mike Moore	R	35	5	15	.250	0	25	25	1	133	179	68	64	0	7.53
Mike Christopher	R	31	4	0	1.000	1	36	0	0	61	71	14	34	0	3.82
Brian Maxcy	R	24	4	5	.444	0	41	0	0	52	61	31	20	0	6.88
Jose Lima	R	22	3	9	.250	0	15	15	0	74	85	18	37	0	6.11
Clint Sodowsky	R	22	2	2	.500	0	6	6	0	23	24	18	14	0	5.01
2 Mike Myers	L	26	1	0	1.000	0	11	0	0	6	10	4	4	0	9.95
Greg Gohr (AJ)	R	27	1	0	1.000	0	3	0	0	9	3	12	0	0	0.87
Dwayne Henry	R	33	1	0	1.000	5	10	0	0	9	11	10	9	0	8.23
Brian Bohanon	L	26	1	1	.500	1	52	10	0	106	121	41	63	0	5.54
1 Buddy Groom	L	29	1	3	.250	1	23	4	0	41	55	26	23	0	7.52
2 C.J. Nitkowski	L	22	1	4	.250	0	11	11	0	39	53	20	13	0	7.09
1 Kevin Wickander	R	30	0	0	—	0	21	0	0	17	18	9	9	0	2.60
Ben Blomdahl	R	24	0	0	—	0	14	0	0	24	36	13	15	0	7.77
Mike Gardiner (IL)	R	29	0	0	—	0	9	0	0	12	27	2	7	0	14.59
Sean Whiteside	L	24	0	0	—	0	9	0	0	4	7	4	2	0	14.73
1 Mike Henneman	R	33	0	1	.000	18	29	0	0	29	24	9	24	0	1.53
Pat Aheame	R	24	0	2	.000	0	10	2	0	10	20	5	4	0	11.70

TORONTO — 5th 56-88 .389 30 — CITO GASTON

Name	G by Pos	B	AGE	G	AB	R	H	2B	3B	HR	RBI	BB	SO	SB	BA	SA
TOTALS			29	144	5036	642	1309	275	27	140	613	492	906	75	.260	.409
John Olerud	1B133	L	26	135	492	72	143	32	0	8	54	84	54	0	.291	.404
Roberto Alomar	2B128 DH3	B	27	130	517	71	155	24	7	13	66	47	45	30	.300	.449
Alex Gonzalez	SS97 3B9 DH3	R	22	111	367	51	89	19	4	10	42	44	114	4	.243	.398
Ed Sprague	3B139 1B7 DH2	R	27	144	521	77	127	27	2	18	74	58	96	0	.244	.407
Shawn Green	OF109	L	22	121	379	52	109	31	4	15	54	20	68	1	.288	.509
Devon White (BF)	OF99	B	32	101	427	61	121	23	5	10	53	29	97	11	.283	.431
Joe Carter	OF128 1B7 DH4	R	35	139	558	70	141	23	0	25	76	37	87	12	.253	.428
Sandy Martinez	C61	L	24	62	191	12	46	12	0	2	25	7	45	0	.241	.335
Paul Molitor	DH129	R	38	130	525	63	142	31	2	15	60	61	57	12	.270	.423
Lance Parrish	C67 DH1	R	39	70	178	15	36	9	0	4	22	15	52	0	.202	.320
Mike Huff	OF55	R	31	61	138	14	32	9	1	1	9	22	21	1	.232	.333
1 Candy Maldonado	OF58 DH1	R	34	61	160	22	43	13	0	7	25	25	45	1	.269	.481
Domingo Cedeno	SS30 2B20 3B1	B	26	51	161	18	38	6	4	1	14	10	35	0	.236	.360
Randy Knorr (BG)	C45	R	26	45	132	18	28	8	0	3	16	11	28	0	.212	.341
Tomas Perez	SS31 2B7 3B1	B	21	41	98	12	24	3	1	1	8	7	18	0	.245	.327
Carlos Delgado	OF17 DH7 1B4	L	23	37	91	7	15	3	0	3	11	6	26	0	.165	.297
Robert Perez	OF15	R	26	17	48	2	9	1	0	0	3	0	5	0	.188	.292
Shannon Stewart	OF12	R	21	12	38	2	8	1	0	0	1	5	5	2	.211	.211
Howard Battle	3B6 DH1	R	23	9	15	3	3	0	0	0	1	0	3	1	.200	.200

NAME	T	AGE	W	L	PCT	SV	G	GS	CG	IP	H	BB	SO	SHO	ERA
		28	56	88	.389	22	144	144	16	1293	1336	654	894	8	4.88
Al Leiter	L	29	11	11	.500	0	28	28	2	183	162	108	153	1	3.64
Pat Hentgen	R	26	10	14	.417	0	30	30	2	201	236	90	135	0	5.11
1 David Cone	R	32	9	6	.600	0	17	17	5	130*	113	41	102	2	3.38
Edwin Hurtado	R	25	5	2	.714	0	14	10	1	78	81	40	33	0	5.45
Mike Timlin	R	29	4	3	.571	5	31	0	0	42	38	17	36	0	2.14
Juan Guzman	R	28	4	14	.222	0	24	24	3	135	151	73	94	0	6.32
Jeff Ware	R	24	2	1	.667	0	5	0	0	24	28	21	18	0	5.47
Jimmy Rogers	R	28	2	3	.333	0	17	0	0	24	21	18	13	0	5.70
Giovanni Carrara	R	27	2	4	.333	0	12	7	1	49	64	25	27	0	7.21
Ricardo Jordan	L	25	1	0	1.000	0	15	0	0	15	18	13	10	0	6.60
Woody Williams	R	28	1	2	.333	0	23	3	0	54	44	28	41	0	3.69
Ken Robinson	R	25	1	2	.333	0	21	0	0	39	25	22	31	0	3.69
Danny Cox	R	35	1	3	.250	0	24	0	0	45	57	33	38	0	7.40
Paul Menhart	R	26	1	4	.200	0	21	9	1	79	72	47	50	0	4.92
Tony Castillo	L	32	1	5	.167	13	55	0	0	73	64	24	38	0	3.22
1 Danny Darwin	R	39	1	8	.111	0	13	11	1	65	91	24	36	0	7.62
Brad Cornett	R	26	0	0	—	0	5	0	0	5	9	3	4	0	9.00
Duane Ward (SJ)	R	31	0	1	.000	0	4	0	0	3	11	5	3	0	27.00
Darren Hall	R	30	0	2	.000	3	17	0	0	16	21	9	11	0	4.41
Tim Crabtree	R	25	0	2	.000	0	31	0	0	32	30	13	21	0	3.09

*Cone, also with New York, league leader in Innings Pitched with 229

CENTRAL DIVISION

CLEVELAND — 1st 100-44 .694 — MIKE HARGROVE

Name	G by Pos	B	AGE	G	AB	R	H	2B	3B	HR	RBI	BB	SO	SB	BA	SA
TOTALS			29	144	5028	840	1461	279	23	207	803	542	766	132	.291	.479
Paul Sorrento	1B91 DH1	L	29	104	323	50	76	14	0	25	79	51	71	1	.235	.511
Carlos Baerga	2B134 DH1	B	26	135	557	87	175	28	2	15	90	35	31	11	.314	.452
Omar Vizquel	SS136	B	28	136	542	87	144	28	0	6	56	59	59	29	.266	.351
Jim Thome	3B134 DH1	L	24	137	452	92	142	29	3	25	73	97	113	4	.314	.558
Manny Ramirez	OF131 DH5	R	23	137	484	85	149	26	1	31	107	75	112	6	.308	.558
Kenny Lofton	OF114 DH2	L	28	118	481	93	149	22	13	7	53	40	49	54	.310	.453
Albert Belle	OF142 DH1	R	28	143	546	121	173	52	1	50	126	73	80	5	.317	.690
Sandy Alomar (KJ)	C61	R	29	66	203	32	61	6	0	10	35	7	26	3	.300	.478
Eddie Murray (BR)	DH95 1B18	B	39	113	436	68	141	21	0	21	82	39	65	5	.323	.516
Wayne Kirby	OF68 DH7	L	31	101	188	29	39	10	2	1	14	13	32	10	.207	.298
Tony Pena	C91	R	38	91	263	25	69	15	0	5	28	14	44	1	.262	.376
Alvaro Espinoza	3B22 2B22 SS19 1B2 DH1	R	33	66	143	15	36	4	0	2	17	2	16	0	.252	.322
Herbert Perry	1B45 DH5 3B1	R	25	52	162	23	51	13	1	3	23	13	28	1	.315	.463
Dave Winfield (SJ)	DH39	R	43	46	115	11	22	5	0	2	4	14	26	1	.191	.287
Ruben Amaro (LJ)	OF22 DH3	B	30	28	60	5	12	3	0	1	5	4	6	1	.200	.300
2 Scooter Tucker	C17	R	28	17	20	2	0	0	0	0	0	5	4	0	.000	.000
Jesse Levis	C12	L	27	12	18	1	6	2	0	0	3	3	1	0	.333	.444
Jeromy Burnitz	OF6 DH2	L	26	9	7	4	4	1	0	2	8	0	1	0	.571	.714
Billy Ripken	2B7 3B1	R	30	8	17	4	7	1	0	0	4	2	3	0	.412	.765
Brian Giles	OF3 DH1	L	24	6	9	6	5	0	0	1	3	4	1	0	.556	.889
1 David Bell	3B2	R	22	2	1	0	0	0	0	0	0	0	1	0	.000	.000

NAME	T	AGE	W	L	PCT	SV	G	GS	CG	IP	H	BB	SO	SHO	ERA
		29	100	44	.694	50	144	144	10	1301	1261	445	926	10	3.83
Charles Nagy	R	28	16	6	.727	0	29	29	2	178	194	61	139	1	4.55
Orel Hershiser	R	36	16	6	.727	0	26	26	1	167	151	51	111	1	3.87
Dennis Martinez	R	40	12	5	.706	0	28	28	3	187	174	46	99	2	3.08
Julian Tavarez	R	22	10	2	.833	0	57	0	0	85	76	21	68	0	2.44
Mark Clark	R	27	9	7	.563	0	22	21	2	125	143	42	68	0	5.27
Chad Ogea	R	24	8	3	.727	0	20	14	1	106	95	29	57	0	3.05
Eric Plunk	R	31	6	2	.750	2	56	0	0	64	48	27	71	0	2.67
2 Paul Assenmacher	L	34	6	2	.750	0	47	0	0	38	32	12	40	0	2.82
2 Ken Hill	R	29	4	1	.800	0	12	11	1	75	77	32	48	0	3.98
Bud Black	L	38	4	2	.667	0	11	10	0	47	63	16	34	0	6.85
Jose Mesa	R	29	3	0	1.000	46	62	0	0	64	49	17	58	0	1.13
Alan Embree	L	25	3	2	.600	1	23	0	0	25	23	16	23	0	5.11
Jim Poole	L	29	3	3	.500	0	42	0	0	50	40	17	41	0	3.75
Jason Grimsley	R	27	0	0	—	0	15	2	0	34	37	32	25	0	6.09
1 Dennis Cook	L	32	0	0	—	0	11	0	0	13	16	10	13	0	6.39
Albie Lopez	R	23	0	0	—	0	6	2	0	23	17	7	22	0	3.13
1 Gregg Olson	R	28	0	0	—	3	5	0	0	3	5	6	0	0	13.50
John Farrell	R	28	0	1	.000	0	6	0	0	3	3	8	3	0	3.86
Joe Roa	R	23	0	0	—	0	5	0	0	5	8	5	5	0	4.26
Paul Shuey	R	24	0	2	.000	0	7	0	0	11	14	9	5	0	4.26

KANSAS CITY 2nd 70-74 .486 30 BOB BOONE

Name	G by Pos	B	AGE	G	AB	R	H	2B	3B	HR	RBI	BB	SO	SB	BA	SA
TOTALS			28	144	4903	629	1275	240	35	119	578	475	849	120	.260	.396
Wally Joyner	1B126 DH2	L	33	131	465	69	144	28	0	12	83	69	65	3	.310	.447
Keith Lockhart	2B61 3B17 DH14	L	30	94	274	41	88	19	3	6	33	14	21	8	.321	.478
Greg Gagne	SS118	R	33	120	430	58	110	25	4	6	49	38	60	3	.256	.374
Gary Gaetti	3B123 1B11 DH6	R	36	137	514	76	134	27	0	35	96	47	91	3	.261	.518
Jon Nunnally	OF107 DH4	L	23	119	303	51	74	15	6	14	42	51	86	6	.244	.472
Tom Goodwin	OF130 DH2	L	26	133	480	72	138	16	3	4	28	38	72	50	.288	.358
Vince Coleman	OF69 DH4	B	34	75	293	39	84	13	4	4	20	27	48	26	.287	.399
Brent Mayne	C103	L	27	110	307	23	77	18	1	1	27	25	41	0	.251	.326
Bob Hamelin	DH56 1B8	L	27	72	208	20	35	7	1	7	25	24	56	0	.168	.313
David Howard	2B41 SS33 OF30 1B1 DH1	B	28	95	255	23	62	13	4	0	19	24	41	6	.243	.325
Michael Tucker	OF36 DH22	L	24	62	177	23	46	10	4	4	17	18	51	2	.260	.384
Edgar Caceres	2B36 SS8 1B6 3B3 DH3	B	31	55	117	13	28	6	2	1	17	8	15	2	.239	.350
Joe Vitiello	DH38 1B8	R	26	53	130	13	33	4	0	7	21	8	25	0	.254	.446
Pat Borders	C45 DH3	R	32	52	143	14	33	8	1	4	13	7	22	0	.231	.385
Phil Hiatt	OF47 DH2	R	26	52	113	11	23	6	0	4	12	9	37	1	.204	.363
Johnny Damon	OF47	L	21	47	188	32	53	11	5	3	23	12	22	7	.282	.441
Joe Randa	3B22 2B9 DH2	R	25	34	70	6	12	2	0	1	5	6	17	0	.171	.243
Jose Lind (JT)	2B29	R	31	29	97	4	26	3	0	0	6	3	8	0	.268	.299
Chris James (SJ)	DH14 OF5	R	32	26	58	6	18	3	0	2	7	6	10	1	.310	.466
Les Norman	OF17 DH5	R	26	24	40	6	9	0	1	0	4	6	6	2	.225	.275
Henry Mercedes	C22	R	25	23	43	7	11	2	0	0	9	8	13	0	.256	.302
Chris Stynes	2B17 DH1	R	22	22	35	7	6	1	0	0	2	4	3	1	.171	.200
Brent Cookson	OF12 DH2	R	25	21	35	2	5	1	0	0	5	2	7	1	.143	.171
Jeff Grotewald	DH11 1B1	L	29	15	36	4	10	1	0	1	6	9	7	0	.278	.389
Juan Samuel	DH7 OF5 1B1	R	34	15	34	3	6	0	0	2	5	5	11	1	.176	.353
Felix Jose	OF7	B	30	9	30	2	4	1	0	0	1	2	9	0	.133	.167
Keith Miller	OF4 DH4	R	32	9	15	2	5	0	0	1	3	2	4	0	.333	.533
Mike Sweeney	C4	R	21	4	4	1	1	0	0	0	0	0	0	0	.250	.250
Russ McGinnis	OF1 1B1 3B1	R	32	3	5	1	0	0	0	0	0	0	1	0	.000	.000
Jose Mota (GJ)	2B2	R	30	2	2	0	0	0	0	0	0	0	0	0	.000	.000

NAME	T	AGE	W	L	PCT	SV	G	GS	CG	IP	H	BB	SO	SHO	ERA
TOTALS		28	70	74	.486	37	144	144	11	1288	1323	503	763	10	4.49
Kevin Appier	R	27	15	10	.600	0	31	31	4	201	163	80	185	1	3.89
Tom Gordon	R	27	12	12	.500	0	31	31	2	189	204	89	119	0	4.43
Mark Gubicza	R	32	12	14	.462	0	33	33	3	213	222	62	81	2	3.75
Hipolito Pichardo	R	25	8	4	.667	1	44	0	0	64	66	30	43	0	4.36
Rusty Meacham	R	27	4	3	.571	2	49	0	0	60	72	19	30	0	4.98
2 Jason Jacome	L	24	4	6	.400	0	15	14	1	84	101	21	39	0	5.36
2 Gregg Olson	R	28	3	3	.500	3	20	0	0	30	23	17	21	0	3.26
Chris Haney (XJ)	L	26	3	4	.429	0	16	13	1	81	78	33	31	0	3.65
Jeff Montgomery	R	33	2	3	.400	31	54	0	0	66	60	25	49	0	3.43
Billy Brewer	L	27	2	4	.333	0	48	0	0	45	54	20	31	0	5.56
2 Jim Converse	R	23	1	0	1.000	0	9	0	0	12	12	8	5	0	5.84
Scott Anderson	R	32	1	0	1.000	0	6	4	0	25	29	8	6	0	5.33
Mike Magnante	L	30	1	1	.500	0	28	0	0	45	45	16	28	0	4.23
Dilson Torres	R	25	1	2	.333	0	24	2	0	44	56	17	28	0	6.09
Melvin Bunch	R	23	1	3	.250	0	13	5	0	40	42	14	19	0	5.63
Rick Huisman	R	26	0	0	—	0	7	0	0	10	14	1	12	0	7.45
Jim Pittsley (EJ)	R	23	0	0	—	0	1	1	0	3	7	1	0	0	13.50
2 Dave Fleming	L	25	0	1	.000	0	9	5	0	32	27	19	14	0	3.66
Doug Linton	R	30	0	1	.000	0	7	2	0	22	22	10	13	0	7.25
Dennis Rasmussen	L	36	0	1	.000	0	5	1	0	10	13	8	6	0	9.00
Tom Browning (SJ)	R	35	0	2	.000	0	2	2	0	10	15	3	5	0	8.10

CHICAGO 3rd 68-76 .472 32 GENE LAMONT 11-20 .355   TERRY BEVINGTON 57-56 .504

Name	G by Pos	B	AGE	G	AB	R	H	2B	3B	HR	RBI	BB	SO	SB	BA	SA
TOTALS			30	145	5060	755	1417	252	37	146	712	576	767	110	.280	.431
Frank Thomas	1B90 DH53	R	27	145	493	102	152	27	0	40	111	136	74	3	.308	.606
Ray Durham	2B122 DH1	B	23	125	471	68	121	27	6	7	51	31	83	18	.257	.384
Ozzie Guillen	SS120 DH1	L	31	122	415	50	103	20	3	1	41	13	25	6	.248	.318
Robin Ventura	3B121 1B18 DH1	L	27	135	492	79	145	22	0	26	93	75	98	4	.295	.498
Mike Devereaux	OF90	R	32	92	333	48	102	21	1	10	55	25	51	6	.306	.465
Lance Johnson	OF140 DH1	L	31	142	607	98	186	18	12	10	57	32	31	40	.306	.425
Tim Raines	OF107 DH22	B	35	133	502	81	143	25	4	12	67	70	52	13	.285	.422
Ron Karkovice	C113	R	32	113	323	44	70	14	1	13	51	39	84	2	.217	.387
John Kruk	DH42 1B1	L	34	45	159	13	49	7	0	2	23	26	33	0	.308	.390
Dave Martinez	OF59 1B47 DH4 P1	L	30	119	303	49	93	16	4	5	37	32	41	8	.307	.436
Norberto Martin	2B17 OF12 DH10 3B9 SS7	R	28	72	160	17	43	7	4	2	17	3	25	5	.269	.400
Lyle Mouton	OF53 DH2	R	26	58	179	23	54	16	0	5	27	19	46	1	.302	.475
Craig Grebeck	SS31 3B18 2B8	R	30	53	154	19	40	12	0	1	18	21	23	0	.260	.357
1 Warren Newson	OF24 DH71	L	30	51	85	19	20	0	2	3	9	23	27	1	.235	.388
Mike LaValliere	C46	L	34	46	98	7	24	6	0	1	19	9	15	0	.245	.337
Mike Cameron	OF22	R	22	28	38	4	7	2	0	1	2	3	15	0	.184	.316
Barry Lyons	C16 DH7 1B4	R	35	27	64	8	17	2	0	5	16	4	14	0	.266	.531
Chris Snopek	3B17 SS6	R	24	22	68	12	22	4	0	1	7	9	12	1	.324	.426
Chris Sabo	DH15 3B1 1B1	R	33	20	71	10	18	5	0	1	8	3	12	2	.254	.366
Doug Brady	2B6 DH2	B	25	12	21	4	4	1	0	0	3	2	4	0	.190	.238
Chris Tremie	C9 DH1	R	25	10	24	0	4	0	0	0	0	1	2	0	.167	.167

NAME	T	AGE	W	L	PCT	SV	G	GS	CG	IP	H	BB	SO	SHO	ERA
TOTALS		29	68	76	.472	36	145	145	3	1285	1374	617	892	4	4.85
Alex Fernandez	R	25	12	8	.600	0	30	30	5	204	200	65	159	2	3.80
Wilson Alvarez	L	25	8	11	.421	0	29	29	3	175	171	93	118	0	4.32
Jason Bere	R	24	8	15	.348	0	27	27	1	138	151	106	110	0	7.19
Kirk McCaskill	R	34	6	4	.600	2	55	1	0	81	97	33	50	0	4.89
1 Jim Abbott	L	27	6	4	.600	0	17	17	3	112	116	35	45	0	3.36
1 Jose DeLeon	R	34	5	3	.625	0	38	0	0	68	60	28	53	0	5.19
Brian Keyser	R	28	5	6	.455	0	23	10	0	92	114	27	48	0	4.97
Matt Karchner	R	28	4	2	.667	0	31	0	0	32	33	12	24	0	1.69
Dave Righetti	L	36	3	2	.600	0	10	9	0	49	65	18	29	0	4.20
Roberto Hernandez	R	30	3	7	.300	32	60	0	0	60	63	28	84	0	3.92
Scott Radinsky (GJ)	R	27	2	1	.667	1	46	0	0	38	46	17	14	0	5.45
Luis Andujar	R	22	2	1	.667	0	5	5	0	30	26	14	9	0	3.26
Bill Simas	R	23	1	1	.500	1	14	0	0	14	15	10	16	0	2.57
Mike Bertotti	L	25	1	1	.500	0	4	4	0	14	23	11	15	0	12.56
Mike Sirotka	L	24	1	2	.333	0	6	6	0	34	39	17	19	0	4.19
Tim Fortugno	L	33	1	3	.250	0	37	0	0	39	30	19	24	0	5.59
Larry Thomas	L	25	0	0	—	0	17	0	0	14	6	6	12	0	1.32
Atlee Hammaker	L	37	0	0	—	0	13	0	0	6	11	8	3	0	12.79
2 Jeff Shaw	R	28	0	0	—	0	9	0	0	10	12	1	6	0	6.52
Andrew Lorraine	L	22	0	0	—	0	3	0	0	8	13	2	5	0	3.38
Scott Ruffcorn	R	25	0	0	—	0	2	0	0	7	10	13	5	0	7.88
Dave Martinez	L	30	0	0	—	0	1	1	0	1	0	2	0	0	0.00
1 Rob Dibble	R	31	0	1	.000	1	16	0	0	14	7	27	16	0	6.28
Isidro Marquez	R	30	0	1	.000	0	7	0	0	7	9	2	6	0	6.75
James Baldwin	R	23	0	1	.000	0	1	1	0	5	12	9	10	0	12.89
Rodney Bolton	R	27	0	2	.000	0	8	3	0	22	33	14	10	0	8.18

MILWAUKEE 4th 65-79 .451 35 PHIL GARNER

Name	G by Pos	B	AGE	G	AB	R	H	2B	3B	HR	RBI	BB	SO	SB	BA	SA
TOTALS			28	144	5000	740	1329	249	42	128	700	502	800	105	.266	.409
John Jaha (GJ)	1B81 DH6	R	29	88	316	59	99	20	2	20	65	36	66	2	.313	.579
Fernando Vina	2B99 SS6 3B2	L	26	113	288	46	74	7	7	3	29	22	28	6	.257	.361
Jose Valentin (BG)	SS104 DH3 3B1	B	25	112	338	62	74	23	3	11	49	37	83	16	.219	.402
Kevin Seitzer	3B88 1B18 DH14	R	33	132	492	56	153	33	3	5	69	64	57	2	.311	.421
Matt Mieske	OF108 DH2	R	27	117	267	42	67	13	1	12	48	27	45	2	.251	.442
Darryl Hamilton	OF109 DH2	L	30	112	398	54	108	20	6	5	44	47	35	11	.271	.389
B.J. Surhoff	OF60 1B55 C18 DH3	L	30	117	415	72	133	26	3	13	73	37	43	7	.320	.442
Joe Oliver (BW)	C91 DH6 1B2	R	29	97	337	43	92	20	0	12	51	27	48	2	.273	.439
Greg Vaughn	DH104	R	29	108	392	67	88	19	1	17	59	55	89	10	.224	.408
Jeff Cirillo	3B108 2B25 1B3 SS2	R	25	125	328	57	91	19	4	9	39	47	42	7	.277	.442
David Hulse	OF115	L	26	119	339	46	85	11	6	3	47	18	60	15	.251	.345
Pat Listach	2B59 SS36 OF11 3B2	B	27	101	334	35	73	8	2	0	25	26	61	13	.219	.254
Dave Nilsson (IL)	OF58 DH14 1B7 C2	L	25	81	263	41	73	12	1	12	53	24	41	2	.278	.468
Mike Matheny	C80	R	24	80	166	13	41	9	1	0	21	12	28	2	.247	.313
Turner Ward (LJ)	OF40 DH1	B	30	44	129	19	34	3	1	4	16	14	21	6	.264	.395
1 Derrick May	OF32	L	26	32	113	15	28	4	0	1	9	5	18	0	.248	.319
Mark Loretta	SS13 2B4 DH1	R	23	19	50	13	13	3	0	1	3	4	7	1	.260	.380
Duane Singleton	OF11	L	22	13	31	0	2	0	0	0	1	0	10	1	.065	.065
Tim Unroe	1B2	R	24	2	4	0	1	0	0	0	0	1	1	0	.250	.250

NAME	T	AGE	W	L	PCT	SV	G	GS	CG	IP	H	BB	SO	SHO	ERA
TOTALS		28	65	79	.451	31	144	144	7	1286	1391	603	699	4	4.82
Ricky Bones	R	26	10	12	.455	0	32	31	3	200	218	83	77	0	4.63
Steve Sparks	R	29	9	11	.450	0	33	27	3	202	210	86	96	0	4.63
Sid Roberson	L	23	6	4	.600	0	26	13	0	84	102	37	40	0	5.76
Scott Karl	L	23	6	7	.462	0	25	18	1	124	141	50	59	0	4.14
Bill Wegman	R	32	5	7	.417	2	37	4	0	71	89	21	50	0	5.35
Brian Givens	L	29	5	7	.417	0	19	19	0	107	116	54	73	0	4.95
Mike Ignasiak (XJ)	R	29	4	1	.800	0	25	0	0	40	51	23	26	0	5.90
Mark Kiefer	R	26	4	1	.800	0	24	0	0	50	57	27	41	0	3.44
Angel Miranda (KJ)	L	25	4	5	.444	1	30	10	0	74	83	49	45	0	5.23
Bob Scanlan (EJ)	R	28	4	7	.364	0	17	14	0	83	101	44	29	0	6.59
Ron Rightnowar	L	30	2	1	.667	1	34	0	0	37	35	18	22	0	5.40
Jamie McAndrew (KJ)	R	27	2	3	.400	0	10	4	0	36	37	12	19	0	4.71
Alberto Reyes (EJ)	R	24	1	1	.500	1	27	0	0	33	19	18	29	0	2.43
2 Rob Dibble	R	31	1	1	.500	0	15	0	0	12	9	19	10	0	8.25
Joe Slusarski	R	28	1	1	.500	0	12	0	0	15	16	5	9	0	5.40
Cal Eldred (EJ)	R	27	1	1	.500	0	4	4	0	24	24	10	18	0	3.42
Jeff Bronkey (SJ)	R	29	0	0	—	0	12	0	0	12	15	6	5	0	3.65
2 Kevin Wickander	L	30	0	0	—	0	4	0	0	3	3	6	1	0	0.00
Mike Thomas	L	25	0	0	—	0	5	0	0	6	14	6	6	0	9.82
Jose Mercedes (EJ)	R	24	0	1	.000	0	7	0	0	12	8	6	5	0	5.79
Mike Fetters	R	30	0	3	.000	22	40	0	0	35	40	20	33	0	3.38
Graeme Lloyd (RJ)	L	28	0	5	.000	4	33	0	0	32	28	8	13	0	4.50

MINNESOTA 5th 56-88 .389 44 TOM KELLY

Name	G by Pos	B	AGE	G	AB	R	H	2B	3B	HR	RBI	BB	SO	SB	BA	SA
TOTALS			27	144	5005	703	1398	270	34	120	662	471	916	105	.279	.419
Scott Stahoviak	1B69 3B22 DH1	L	25	94	263	28	70	19	0	3	23	30	61	5	.266	.373
Chuck Knoblauch	2B136 SS2	R	26	136	538	107	179	34	8	11	63	78	95	46	.333	.487
Pat Meares	SS114 OF3	R	26	116	390	57	105	19	4	12	49	15	68	10	.269	.431
Scott Leius	3B112 SS7 DH3	R	29	117	372	51	92	16	5	4	45	49	54	2	.247	.349
Kirby Puckett	OF109 DH28 2B1 3B1 SS1	R	35	137	538	83	169	39	0	23	99	56	89	3	.314	.515
Rich Becker	OF105	B	23	106	392	45	93	15	1	2	33	34	95	8	.237	.296
Marty Cordova	OF137	R	25	137	512	81	142	27	4	24	84	52	111	20	.277	.486
Matt Walbeck	C113	B	25	115	393	40	101	18	1	1	44	25	71	3	.257	.316
Pedro Munoz	DH77 OF26 1B1	R	26	104	376	45	113	17	0	18	58	19	86	0	.301	.489
Jeff Reboulet	SS39 3B22 1B17 2B15 C1	R	31	87	216	39	63	11	0	4	23	27	34	1	.292	.398
Matt Merullo	C46 DH13 1B2	L	29	76	195	19	55	14	1	1	27	14	27	0	.282	.379
Dan Masteller	1B48 OF2 DH1	L	27	91	198	21	47	12	0	3	21	18	19	1	.237	.343
Chip Hale	DH27 2B7 3B5 1B3	L	30	69	103	10	27	4	0	2	18	11	20	0	.262	.359
Ron Coomer	1B22 3B13 DH4 OF1	R	28	37	101	15	26	3	1	5	19	9	11	0	.257	.455
Jerald Clark (KJ)	OF23 1B11 DH3	R	31	36	109	17	37	8	3	3	15	2	11	0	.339	.550
Alex Cole (BL)	OF23	L	29	28	79	10	27	3	1	1	14	8	15	5	.342	.468
1 Dave McCarty	1B18 OF5	R	25	25	55	10	12	3	1	0	4	4	18	0	.218	.309
Kevin Maas	DH12 1B8	L	30	22	57	5	11	1	0	1	9	7	11	0	.193	.316
Matt Lawton	OF19 DH1	L	23	21	60	11	19	4	1	1	12	7	11	1	.317	.467
Denny Hocking	SS6	B	25	9	25	4	9	0	0	0	1	2	10	0	.360	.360
Brian Raabe	2B4 3B2	R	27	6	14	4	3	0	0	0	2	0	1	0	.214	.214
Steve Dunn	1B3	L	25	5	6	0	0	0	0	0	0	1	3	0	.000	.000
Bernardo Brito	DH3	R	31	5	5	1	1	0	0	0	1	0	4	0	.200	.800
Riccardo Ingram	DH3	R	28	4	8	0	1	0	0	0	2	1	0	0	.125	.125

NAME	T	AGE	W	L	PCT	SV	G	GS	CG	IP	H	BB	SO	SHO	ERA
TOTALS		26	56	88	.389	27	144	144	7	1273	1450	533	790	2	5.76
Brad Radke	R	22	11	14	.440	0	29	28	2	181	195	47	75	1	5.32
1 Kevin Tapani	R	31	6	11	.353	0	20	20	3	134	155	34	88	1	4.92
1 Mark Guthrie	L	29	5	3	.625	0	36	0	0	42	47	16	48	0	4.46
Dave Stevens	R	25	5	4	.556	10	56	0	0	66	74	32	47	0	5.07
2 Frankie Rodriguez	R	22	5	5	.455	0	16	16	0	90	93	47	45	0	5.38
1 Scott Erickson	R	27	4	6	.400	0	15	15	0	88	102	32	45	0	5.95
Mike Trombley	R	28	4	8	.333	0	20	18	0	98	107	42	68	0	5.62
Eddie Guardado	L	24	4	9	.308	2	51	5	0	91	99	45	71	0	5.12
Pat Mahomes	R	24	4	10	.286	3	47	7	0	95	100	47	67	0	6.37
Rich Robertson	L	26	2	0	1.000	0	25	4	1	52	48	31	38	0	3.83
Oscar Munoz	R	25	2	1	.667	0	10	3	0	35	40	17	25	0	5.60
LaTroy Hawkins	R	22	2	3	.400	0	6	6	1	27	39	12	19	0	8.67
1 Rick Aguilera	R	33	1	1	.500	12	22	0	0	30	42	6	29	0	2.52
2 Jose Parra	R	22	1	5	.167	0	12	12	0	62	83	29	29	0	7.59
Erik Schullstrom	R	25	0	0	—	0	37	0	0	44	66	22	30	0	6.89
Scott Watkins	L	25	0	0	—	0	27	0	0	22	22	11	11	0	5.40
Mo Sanford	R	29	0	0	—	0	1	0	0	16	16	17	17	0	5.30
Vince Horsman	L	28	0	0	—	0	4	0	0	3	6	4	2	0	7.00
Kevin Campbell	R	30	0	0	—	0	10	0	0	9	6	10	5	0	4.66
Carl Willis	R	34	0	0	—	0	2	0	0	1	5	0	2	0	94.50
2 Scott Klingenbeck	R	24	0	2	.000	0	8	6	0	48	69	24	27	0	8.57
Greg Harris (BW)	R	31	0	5	.000	0	7	6	0	33	50	16	21	0	8.82

SEATTLE — 1st 79-66 .545 — LOU PINIELLA (defeated California in a 1 game playoff)

Name	G by Pos	B	AGE	G	AB	R	H	2B	3B	HR	RBI	BB	SO	SB	BA	SA
TOTALS			29	145	4996	796	1377	276	20	182	767	549	871	110	.276	.448
Tino Martinez	1B139 DH1	L	27	141	519	92	152	35	3	31	111	62	91	0	.293	.551
Joey Cora	2B112 SS1	B	30	120	427	64	127	19	2	3	39	37	31	18	.297	.372
Luis Sojo	SS80 2B19 OF6	R	30	102	339	50	98	18	2	7	39	23	19	4	.289	.416
Mike Blowers	3B126 1B7 OF5	R	30	134	439	59	113	24	1	23	96	53	128	2	.257	.474
Jay Buhner	OF120 DH4	R	30	126	470	86	123	23	0	40	121	60	120	0	.262	.566
Ken Griffey Jr. (BW)	OF70 DH2	L	25	72	260	52	67	7	0	17	42	52	53	4	.258	.481
2 Vince Coleman	OF38	B	34	40	162	27	47	10	2	1	9	10	32	16	.290	.395
Dan Wilson	C119	R	26	119	399	40	111	22	3	9	51	33	63	2	.278	.416
Edgar Martinez	DH138 3B4 1B3	R	32	145	511	121	182	52	0	29	113	116	87	4	.356	.628
Alex Diaz	OF88	B	26	103	270	44	67	14	0	3	27	13	27	18	.248	.333
Rich Amaral	OF78 DH1	R	33	90	238	45	67	14	2	2	19	21	33	21	.282	.382
Doug Strange	3B41 2B5 OF4 DH1	B	31	74	155	19	42	9	2	2	21	10	25	0	.271	.394
Felix Fermin	SS46 2B29	R	31	73	200	21	39	6	0	0	15	6	6	2	.195	.225
Darren Bragg	OF47 DH1	L	25	52	145	20	34	5	1	3	12	18	37	9	.234	.345
Alex Rodriguez	SS46 DH1	R	19	48	142	15	33	6	2	5	19	6	42	4	.232	.408
2 Warren Newson	OF23	L	30	33	72	15	21	2	0	2	6	16	18	1	.292	.403
Chad Kreuter	C23	B	30	26	75	12	17	5	0	1	8	5	22	0	.227	.333
1 Marc Newfield	OF24	R	22	24	85	7	16	3	0	3	14	3	16	0	.188	.329
Chris Widger	C19 OF3 DH1	R	24	23	45	2	9	0	0	1	2	3	11	0	.200	.267
Gary Thurman	OF9	R	30	13	25	3	8	2	0	0	3	1	3	5	.320	.400
Greg Pirkl (LJ)	1B6 DH1	R	24	10	17	2	4	0	0	0	0	1	7	0	.235	.235
Arquimedez Pozo	2B1	R	21	1	1	0	0	0	0	0	0	0	1	0	.000	.000

NAME	T	AGE	W	L	PCT	SV	G	GS	CG	IP	H	BB	SO	SHO	ERA
TOTALS		28	79	66	.545	39	145	145	9	1289	1343	591	1068	8	4.50
Randy Johnson	L	31	18	2	.900	0	30	30	6	214	159	65	294	3	2.48
Chris Bosio	R	32	10	8	.556	0	31	31	0	170	211	69	85	0	4.92
Tim Belcher	R	33	10	12	.455	0	28	28	1	179	188	88	96	0	4.52
2 Andy Benes	R	27	7	2	.778	0	12	12	0	63	72	33	45	0	5.86
Jeff Nelson	R	28	7	3	.700	2	62	0	0	79	58	27	96	0	2.17
Bobby Ayala	R	25	6	5	.545	19	63	0	0	71	73	30	77	0	4.44
Bob Wells	R	28	4	3	.571	0	30	4	0	77	88	39	38	0	5.75
Bob Wolcott	R	21	3	2	.600	0	7	6	0	37	43	14	19	0	4.42
2 Salomon Torres	R	23	3	8	.273	0	16	13	1	72	87	42	45	0	6.00
Bill Risley	R	28	2	1	.667	1	45	0	0	60	55	18	65	0	3.13
2 Norm Charlton	L	32	2	1	.667	14	30	0	0	48	23	16	58	0	1.51
2 Bill Krueger	L	37	2	1	.667	0	6	5	0	20	37	4	10	0	5.85
Tim Davis	L	24	2	1	.667	0	5	5	0	24	30	18	19	0	6.38
Rafael Carmona	R	22	2	4	.333	1	15	3	0	48	55	34	28	0	5.66
1 Dave Fleming	L	25	1	5	.167	0	16	7	1	48	57	34	26	0	7.50
Lee Guetterman	L	36	0	0	—	1	23	0	0	17	21	11	11	0	6.48
1 John Cummings	L	23	0	0	—	0	4	0	0	5	8	7	4	0	11.81
Scott Davison	R	24	0	0	—	0	3	0	0	4	7	1	3	0	6.23
Jim Mecir	R	25	0	0	—	0	2	0	0	5	5	2	3	0	0.00
Kevin King	L	26	0	0	—	0	2	0	0	1	3	4	1	0	12.27
Tim Harikkala	R	23	0	0	—	0	1	0	0	3	7	1	1	0	16.20
1 Ron Villone	L	25	0	2	.000	0	19	0	0	19	20	23	26	0	7.91
2 Steve Frey	L	31	0	3	.000	0	13	0	0	11	16	6	7	0	4.76
1 Jim Converse	R	23	0	3	.000	1	6	1	0	11	16	8	9	0	7.36
Greg Hibbard (SJ) 30															

CALIFORNIA — 2nd 78-67 .538 1 — MARCEL LACHEMANN (defeated by Seattle in a 1 game playoff)

Name	G by Pos	B	AGE	G	AB	R	H	2B	3B	HR	RBI	BB	SO	SB	BA	SA
TOTALS			29	145	5019	801	1390	252	25	186	761	564	889	57	.277	.448
J.T. Snow	1B143	B	27	143	544	80	157	22	1	24	102	52	91	2	.289	.465
Damion Easley	2B88 SS25	R	25	114	357	35	77	14	2	4	35	32	47	5	.216	.300
Gary DiSarcina (RJ)	SS98	R	27	99	362	61	111	28	6	5	41	20	25	7	.307	.459
Tony Phillips	3B88 OF48 DH2	B	36	139	525	119	137	21	1	27	61	113	135	13	.261	.459
Tim Salmon	OF142 DH1	R	26	143	537	111	177	34	3	34	105	91	111	5	.330	.594
Jim Edmonds	OF139	L	25	141	558	120	162	30	4	33	107	51	130	1	.290	.536
Garret Anderson	OF100 DH1	L	23	106	374	50	120	19	1	16	69	19	65	6	.321	.505
Jorge Fabregas	C73	L	25	73	227	24	56	10	0	1	22	17	28	0	.247	.304
Chili Davis (LJ)	DH119	B	35	119	424	81	135	23	0	20	86	89	79	3	.318	.514
Greg Myers	C61 DH16	L	29	85	273	35	71	12	2	9	38	17	49	0	.260	.418
Rex Hudler	2B52 2B22 DH3 1B2	R	34	84	223	30	59	16	0	6	27	10	48	13	.265	.417
Spike Owen (SJ)	3B29 SS25 2B16	B	34	82	218	17	50	9	3	1	28	18	22	1	.229	.312
Andy Allanson	C35	R	33	35	82	5	14	3	0	3	10	7	12	0	.171	.317
Rene Gonzales	3B18 2B6 SS1	R	34	30	18	1	6	1	0	0	3	0	4	0	.333	.556
Eduardo Perez	3B23 DH1	R	25	29	71	9	12	4	1	1	7	12	9	0	.169	.296
Carlos Martinez	3B16 1B4 DH2	R	29	26	61	7	11	1	0	1	9	6	7	0	.180	.246
2 Mike Aldrete	DH2 OF2 1B1	L	34	18	24	1	6	0	0	0	3	0	8	0	.250	.250
2 Jose Lind	2B15	R	31	15	43	5	7	2	0	0	1	3	4	0	.163	.209
Orlando Palmeiro	DH1	L	26	15	20	3	7	0	0	0	1	1	1	0	.350	.350
Rod Correia	SS7 2B3 3B2 DH1	R	27	14	21	3	5	1	1	0	3	0	5	0	.238	.381
2 Dick Schofield	SS12	R	32	12	20	1	5	0	0	0	2	5	2	0	.250	.250
2 Dave Gallagher	OF6 DH1	R	34	11	16	1	3	1	0	0	1	0	2	0	.188	.250
Mark Dalesandro	C8 OF1 DH1	R	27	11	10	1	1	1	0	0	0	0	0	0	.100	.200
Chris Turner	C4	R	26	5	10	0	1	0	0	0	0	0	1	0	.100	.100
1 Kevin Flora	DH1	R	26	2	1	1	0	0	0	0	0	0	1	0	.000	.000

NAME	T	AGE	W	L	PCT	SV	G	GS	CG	IP	H	BB	SO	SHO	ERA
TOTALS		30	78	67	.538	42	145	145	8	1284	1310	486	901	9	4.52
Mark Langston	L	34	15	7	.682	0	31	31	2	200	212	64	142	1	4.63
Chuck Finley	L	32	15	12	.556	0	32	32	2	203	192	93	195	1	4.21
Shawn Boskie (EJ)	R	28	7	7	.500	0	20	20	1	112	127	25	51	0	5.64
Mike Butcher	R	30	6	1	.857	0	40	0	0	51	49	31	29	0	4.73
Brian Anderson (AJ)	L	23	6	8	.429	0	18	17	1	100	110	30	45	0	5.87
Bob Patterson	L	36	5	2	.714	0	62	0	0	53	48	13	41	0	3.04
2 Jim Abbott	L	27	5	4	.556	0	13	13	1	85	93	29	41	1	4.15
2 Mike Harkey	R	28	4	3	.571	0	12	8	1	61	80	16	28	0	4.55
2 Mike Bielecki (SJ)	R	35	4	6	.400	0	22	11	0	75	80	31	45	0	5.97
Mike James	R	27	3	0	1.000	1	46	0	0	56	49	26	36	0	3.88
Troy Percival	R	25	3	2	.600	3	62	0	0	74	37	26	94	0	1.95
Rich Monteleone	R	32	1	0	1.000	0	24	0	0	59	60	16	22	0	2.00
2 John Habyan	R	31	1	2	.333	0	28	0	0	33	36	12	25	0	4.13
Mitch Williams	L	30	1	2	.333	0	20	0	0	11	13	21	9	0	6.75
1 Russ Springer	R	26	1	2	.333	1	19	6	0	52	60	25	38	0	6.10
Scott Sanderson (XJ)	R	38	1	3	.250	0	7	7	0	39	48	4	23	0	4.12
Ken Edenfield	R	28	0	0	—	0	7	0	0	13	15	5	6	0	4.26
Erik Bennett	R	25	0	0	—	0	3	0	0	0.1	0	0	0	0	0.00
Mark Holzemer	L	25	0	1	.000	0	12	0	0	8	11	7	5	0	5.40
Lee Smith	R	37	0	5	.000	37	52	0	0	49	42	25	43	0	3.47
Phil Leftwich (SJ) 26															

TEXAS — 3rd 74-70 .514 4.5 — JOHNNY OATES

Name	G by Pos	B	AGE	G	AB	R	H	2B	3B	HR	RBI	BB	SO	SB	BA	SA
TOTALS			29	144	4921	691	1304	247	24	138	651	526	877	90	.265	.410
Will Clark	1B122 DH1	L	31	123	454	85	137	27	3	16	92	68	50	0	.302	.480
Jeff Frye	2B83	R	28	90	313	38	87	15	2	4	29	24	45	3	.278	.377
Benji Gil	SS130	R	22	130	415	36	91	20	3	9	46	26	147	2	.219	.347
Dean Palmer (AJ)	3B36	R	26	36	119	30	40	6	0	9	24	21	21	1	.336	.613
Rusty Greer	OF125 1B3	L	26	131	417	58	113	21	2	13	61	55	66	3	.271	.424
Otis Nixon	OF138	B	36	139	589	87	174	21	2	0	45	58	85	50	.295	.338
Mark McLemore	OF73 2B66 DH1	B	30	129	467	73	122	20	5	5	41	59	71	21	.261	.358
Ivan Rodriguez	C127 DH1	R	23	130	492	56	149	32	2	12	67	16	48	0	.303	.449
Juan Gonzalez (XJ)	DH83 OF5	R	25	90	352	57	104	20	2	27	82	17	66	0	.295	.594
Mickey Tettleton	OF63 DH58 1B9 C3	B	34	134	429	76	102	19	1	32	78	107	110	0	.238	.510
Mike Pagliarulo	3B68 1B11	L	35	86	241	27	56	16	0	4	27	15	49	0	.232	.349
Esteban Beltre	SS36 2B15 3B1	R	27	54	92	7	20	8	0	0	7	4	15	0	.217	.304
2 Lou Frazier	OF47 DH2	B	30	49	99	19	21	2	0	0	8	7	20	9	.212	.232
Luis Ortiz	3B35 DH3	R	25	41	108	10	25	5	2	1	18	6	18	0	.231	.343
Dave Valle (SJ)	C29 1B7	R	34	36	75	7	18	3	0	0	5	6	18	1	.240	.280
2 Jack Voigt	OF25 1B5 DH1	R	29	33	62	8	10	3	0	2	8	10	14	0	.161	.306
2 Craig Worthington	3B26	R	30	26	68	4	15	4	0	2	6	5	9	0	.221	.368
Shawn Hare	OF9 DH2 1B1	L	28	18	24	2	6	1	0	0	2	4	6	0	.250	.292
2 Candy Maldonado	OF11	R	34	13	30	6	7	1	0	2	5	7	5	0	.233	.533
Sam Horn	DH1	L	31	11	9	0	1	0	0	0	0	3	6	0	.111	.111
Eric Fox	OF8 DH1	B	31	10	15	2	0	0	0	0	0	3	4	0	.000	.000
2 Steve Buechele	3B9	R	33	9	24	0	3	0	0	0	0	4	3	0	.125	.125
Billy Hatcher	OF5 DH1	R	34	6	12	2	1	1	0	0	0	0	2	0	.083	.167
John Marzano	C2	R	32	2	6	1	2	0	0	0	0	0	1	0	.333	.333

NAME	T	AGE	W	L	PCT	SV	G	GS	CG	IP	H	BB	SO	SHO	ERA
TOTALS		29	74	70	.514	34	144	144	14	1285	1385	514	838	4	4.66
Kenny Rogers	L	30	17	7	.708	0	31	31	3	208	192	76	140	1	3.38
Roger Pavlik	R	27	10	10	.500	0	31	31	2	192	174	90	149	1	4.37
Kevin Gross	R	34	9	15	.375	0	31	30	4	184	200	89	106	0	5.54
Bob Tewksbury (BR)	R	34	8	7	.533	0	21	21	4	130	169	20	53	1	4.58
Roger McDowell	R	34	7	4	.636	4	64	0	0	85	86	34	49	0	4.02
Matt Whiteside	R	27	5	4	.556	3	40	0	0	53	48	19	46	0	4.08
Ed Vosberg	L	33	5	5	.500	4	44	0	0	36	32	16	36	0	3.00
Darren Oliver (SJ)	L	24	4	2	.667	0	17	7	0	49	47	32	39	0	4.22
2 Bobby Witt	R	31	3	4	.429	0	10	10	1	61	81	21	46	0	4.55
Terry Burrows	L	26	2	2	.500	1	28	3	0	45	60	19	22	0	6.45
2 Danny Darwin	R	39	2	2	.500	0	7	4	0	34	40	7	22	0	7.15
Jeff Russell	R	33	1	0	1.000	20	37	0	0	33	36	9	21	0	3.03
Scott Taylor	R	28	1	2	.333	0	3	1	0	15	25	5	10	0	9.39
Chris Nichting	R	29	0	0	—	0	13	0	0	24	36	13	6	0	7.03
Jose Alberro	R	26	0	0	—	0	12	0	0	12	12	6	10	0	7.40
Hector Fajardo	R	24	0	0	—	0	5	5	0	15	19	5	9	0	7.80
Chris Howard	L	29	0	0	—	0	1	0	0	2	0	0	0	0	27.00
John Dettmer	R	25	0	0	—	0	3	0	0	0.1	2	0	0	0	27.00
Mark Brandenburg	R	24	0	1	.000	0	11	0	0	27	36	7	21	0	5.93
Wilson Heredia	R	23	0	1	.000	0	3	0	0	3	9	15	6	0	3.75
2 Dennis Cook	L	32	0	2	.000	2	35	1	0	45	47	16	40	0	4.00
Rick Helling	R	24	0	3	.000	0	3	0	0	6	12	1	8	0	6.57
Dan Smith (EJ) 26															

OAKLAND — 4th 67-77 .465 11.5 — TONY LaRUSSA

Name	G by Pos	B	AGE	G	AB	R	H	2B	3B	HR	RBI	BB	SO	SB	BA	SA
TOTALS			29	144	4915	730	1296	228	18	169	694	565	911	112	.264	.421
Mark McGwire	1B91 DH10	R	31	104	317	75	87	13	0	39	90	88	77	1	.274	.685
Brent Gates	2B132 DH3 1B1	B	25	136	524	60	133	24	4	5	56	46	84	3	.254	.344
Mike Bordick	SS126 DH3	R	29	126	428	46	113	13	0	8	44	35	48	11	.264	.350
Craig Paquette	3B75 OF20 SS8 1B3	R	26	105	283	42	64	13	1	13	49	12	88	5	.226	.417
1 Ruben Sierra	OF62 DH7	B	29	70	264	40	70	17	0	12	42	24	42	4	.265	.466
Stan Javier	OF124 3B1	B	31	130	442	81	123	20	2	8	56	49	63	36	.278	.387
Rickey Henderson	OF90 DH19	R	36	112	407	67	122	31	1	9	54	72	66	32	.300	.447
Terry Steinbach	C111 1B2	R	33	114	406	43	113	26	1	15	65	25	74	1	.278	.458
Geronimo Berroa	DH72 OF71	R	30	141	546	87	152	22	3	22	88	63	98	7	.278	.451
Scott Brosius	3B60 OF49 1B18 2B3 SS3 DH2	R	28	123	389	69	102	19	2	17	46	41	67	4	.262	.452
1 Mike Aldrete	1B35 OF16	L	34	60	125	18	34	7	1	2	21	19	23	0	.272	.432
Jason Giambi	3B30 1B26 DH2	L	24	54	176	27	45	7	0	6	25	28	31	2	.256	.398
Andy Tomberlin	OF42 DH1	L	28	46	85	15	18	4	0	5	10	5	22	4	.212	.353
Mike Gallego (FJ)	2B18 SS14 3B12	R	34	43	120	11	28	0	0	0	8	9	24	0	.233	.233
Eric Helfand	C36	L	26	38	86	9	14	2	1	0	7	11	25	0	.163	.209
Jose Herrera	OF25 DH5	L	23	33	70	9	17	1	2	0	2	6	11	1	.243	.314
George Williams	C13 DH10	B	26	29	79	13	23	5	1	3	14	11	21	0	.291	.494
Ernie Young	OF24	R	25	26	50	9	10	3	0	2	5	8	12	0	.200	.380
2 Danny Tartabull (VJ)	DH22 OF1	R	32	24	88	9	23	9	0	1	7	10	28	0	.261	.375
Fausto Cruz	SS8	R	23	8	23	0	5	1	0	0	1	1	4	0	.217	.217
Brian Harper	C2	R	35	2	6	1	2	0	0	0	0	0	0	0	.333	.333

NAME	T	AGE	W	L	PCT	SV	G	GS	CG	IP	H	BB	SO	SHO	ERA
TOTALS		31	67	77	.465	34	144	144	8	1273	1320	556	890	4	4.93
Todd Stottlemyre	R	30	14	7	.667	0	31	31	2	210	228	80	205	0	4.55
Steve Ontiveros (AJ)	R	34	9	6	.600	0	22	22	2	130	144	38	77	1	4.37
1 Rick Honeycutt	L	41	5	1	.833	2	49	0	0	45	37	9	21	0	2.42
Doug Johns	L	27	5	3	.625	0	11	9	1	55	44	26	25	1	4.61
Dennis Eckersley	R	40	4	6	.400	29	52	0	0	50	53	11	40	0	4.83
Carlos Reyes	R	26	4	6	.400	0	40	14	0	69	71	28	48	0	5.09
1 Mike Harkey	R	34	4	7	.364	0	21	21	1	104	124	46	69	0	6.23
Ron Darling	R	34	4	7	.364	0	25	25	1	122	124	46	69	0	6.23
Todd Van Poppel	R	23	4	8	.333	0	36	14	1	138	125	56	122	0	4.88
Dave Stewart	R	38	3	7	.300	0	16	16	0	81	101	39	58	0	6.89
Steve Wojciechowski	L	24	2	3	.400	0	14	7	0	49	51	28	13	0	5.18
Jim Corsi	R	33	2	4	.333	2	38	0	0	45	31	26	26	0	2.20
Ariel Prieto	R	25	2	6	.250	0	14	9	1	58	57	32	37	0	4.97
Mike Mohler	L	27	1	1	.500	1	28	0	0	23	23	13	10	0	3.04
1 Dave Leiper	L	33	1	1	.500	0	24	0	0	23	23	13	10	0	3.57
Don Wengert	R	24	1	1	.500	0	19	0	0	17	14	3	6	0	3.34
John Wasdin	R	22	1	1	.500	0	5	5	0	17	14	3	6	0	4.67
Mark Acre	R	27	1	3	.250	0	43	0	0	52	52	28	47	0	5.71
Chris Eddy	L	25	0	1	.000	0	3	1	0	4	5	5	3	0	7.36
Scott Baker	L	25	0	1	.000	0	3	0	0	3	4	5	1	0	9.82
Steve Phoenix	R	27	0	1	.000	0	2	0	0	3	3	1	0	0	32.40
Ramon Fermin	R	22	0	1	.000	0	4	1	0	4	11	0	0	0	13.50
John Briscoe (SJ)	R	27	0	1	.000	0	16	0	0	18	25	21	19	0	8.35
Steve Karsay (EJ) 23															

1995 AMERICAN LEAGUE

DIVISION SERIES

LINE SCORES

CLEVELAND 3 : BOSTON 0

```
Game 1        October 3 at Cleveland
BOS  0 0 2 0 0 0 0 1 0 0 1 0 0   4 11 2
CLE  0 0 0 0 3 0 0 0 0 0 1 0 1   5 10 2
Clemens, Cormier (8),          Martinez, Tavarez (7)
Belinda (8), Stanton (8),      Assenmacher (8), Plunk (8)
Aquilera (11), Maddux (11),    Mesa (10), Poole (11), Hill (13)
Smith (12)

Game 2        October 4 at Cleveland
BOS  0 0 0 0 0 0 0 0 0           0 3 1
CLE  0 0 0 0 0 2 0 0 2 X         4 4 2
Hanson                          Hershiser, Tavarez (8),
                                Assenmacher (8), Mesa (9)

Game 3        October 6 at Boston
CLE  0 2 1 0 0 5 0 0 0           8 11 2
BOS  0 0 0 1 0 0 0 1 0           2 7 1
Nagy, Tavarez (8),              Wakefield, Cormier (6),
Assenmacher (9)                 Maddux (6), Hudson (9)
```

SEATTLE 3 : NEW YORK 2

```
Game 1        October 3 at New York
SEA  0 0 0 1 0 1 0 2 0 2         6 9 0
NY   0 0 2 0 0 2 4 1 X           9 13 0
Bosio, Nelson (6), Ayala (7),   Cone, Wetteland (9)
Risley (7), Wells (8)

Game 2        October 4 at New York
SEA  0 0 1 0 0 1 2 0 0 0 0 0 1
NY   0 0 0 0 1 2 0 0 0 0 0 0 1

SEA  (14th and 15th innings)    0 0  5 16 2
NY                              0 2  7 11 0
Benes, Risley (6), Charlton (7), Pettitte, Wickman (8)
Nelson (11), Belcher (12)       Wetteland (9), Rivera (12)

Game 3        October 6 at Seattle
NY   0 0 0 1 0 0 1 2 0           4 6 2
SEA  0 0 0 0 2 4 1 0 X           7 7 0
McDowell, Howe (6), Wickman (6), Johnson, Risley (8), Charlton (8)
Hitchcock (7), Rivera (7)

Game 4        October 7 at Seattle
NY   3 0 2 0 0 0 0 1 2           8 14 1
SEA  0 0 4 0 1 1 0 5 X          11 16 0
Kamieniecki, Hitchcock (6),     Bosio, Nelson (3), Belcher (7),
Wickman (7), Wetteland (8),     Charlton (8), Ayala (9), Risley (9)
Howe (8)

Game 5        October 8 at Seattle
NY   0 0 0 2 0 2 0 0 0 1         5 6 0
SEA  0 0 1 1 0 0 0 2 0 2         6 15 0
Cone, Rivera (8),               Benes, Charlton (7),
McDowell (9)                    Johnson (9)
```

AMERICAN LEAGUE CHAMPIONSHIPS: CLEVELAND 4 : SEATTLE 2

```
Game 1        October 10 at Seattle
CLE  0 0 1 0 0 0 1 0 0           2 10 1
SEA  0 2 0 0 0 0 0 1 X           3 7 0
Martinez, Tavarez (7)           Wolcott, Nelson (8), Charlton (8)
Assenmacher (8), Plunk (8)

Game 2        October 11 at Seattle
CLE  0 0 0 0 2 2 0 1 0           5 12 0
SEA  0 0 0 0 1 0 0 1             2 6 1
Hershiser, Mesa (9)             Belcher, Ayala (6), Risley (9)

Game 3        October 13 at Cleveland
SEA  0 1 1 0 0 0 0 0 3           5 9 1
CLE  0 0 0 1 0 0 0 1 0           2 4 2
Johnson, Charlton (9)           Nagy, Mesa (9), Tavarez (10),
                                Assenmacher (11), Plunk (11)

Game 4        October 14 at Cleveland
SEA  0 0 0 0 0 0 0 0 0           0 6 1
CLE  3 1 2 0 0 1 0 X             7 9 0
Benes, Wells (3), Ayala (6),    Hill, Poole (8), Ogea (9), Embree (9)
Nelson (7), Risley (8)

Game 5        October 15 at Cleveland
SEA  0 0 1 0 0 1 0 0 0           2 5 2
CLE  1 0 0 0 0 0 2 0 X           3 10 4
Bosio, Nelson (6), Risley (7)   Hershiser, Tavarez (7)
                                Assenmacher (7), Plunk (8), Mesa (9)

Game 6        October 17 at Seattle
CLE  0 0 0 0 1 0 0 3 0           4 8 0
SEA  0 0 0 0 0 0 0 0 0           0 4 1
Martinez, Tavarez (8),          Johnson, Charlton (8)
Mesa (9)
```

COMPOSITE BATTING — DIVISION SERIES

CLEVELAND

NAME	POS	G	AB	R	H	2B	3B	HR	RBI	BA
TOTALS		3	114	17	25	4	1	4	17	.219
Baerga	2B	3	14	2	4	1	0	0	1	.286
Murray	DH	3	13	3	5	0	1	1	3	.385
Lofton	CF	3	13	1	2	0	0	0	0	.154
Thome	3B	3	13	1	2	0	0	1	3	.154
Vizquel	SS	3	12	2	2	1	0	0	4	.167
Ramirez	RF	3	12	1	0	0	0	0	0	.000
Belle	LF	3	11	3	3	1	0	1	3	.273
Alomar	C	3	11	1	2	1	0	0	1	.182
Sorrento	1B	3	10	2	3	0	0	0	1	.300
Pena	C	2	2	1	1	0	0	1	1	.500
Kirby	RF	2	1	0	1	0	0	0	0	1.000
Perry	1B	1	1	0	0	0	0	0	0	.000
Espinoza	3B	1	1	0	0	0	0	0	0	.000

BOSTON

NAME	POS	G	AB	R	H	2B	3B	HR	RBI	BA
TOTALS		3	114	6	21	2	0	3	6	.184
Greenwell	LF	3	15	0	3	0	0	0	0	.200
Vaughn	1B	3	14	0	0	0	0	0	0	.000
Naehring	3B	3	13	2	4	0	0	1	1	.308
Canseco	DH-RF	3	13	0	0	0	0	0	0	.000
Valentin	SS	3	12	1	3	1	0	1	2	.250
Hosey	CF-RF	3	12	1	0	0	0	0	0	.000
Alicea	2B	3	10	1	6	1	0	1	1	.600
Macfarlane	C	3	9	0	3	0	0	0	1	.333
Tinsley	CF	1	5	0	0	0	0	0	0	.000
McGee	RF-CF	2	4	0	1	0	0	0	1	.250
Jefferson	DH	1	4	1	1	0	0	0	0	.250
Haselman	C	1	2	0	0	0	0	0	0	.000
Stairs	PH	1	1	0	0	0	0	0	0	.000

SEATTLE

NAME	POS	G	AB	R	H	2B	3B	HR	RBI	BA
TOTALS		5	200	35	63	6	1	11	33	.315
Buhner	RF	5	24	2	11	1	0	1	3	.458
Griffey	CF	5	23	9	9	0	0	5	7	.391
Coleman	LF	5	23	6	5	0	1	1	1	.217
T. Martinez	1B	5	22	4	9	1	0	1	5	.409
E. Martinez	DH	5	21	6	12	3	0	2	10	.571
Sojo	SS	5	20	0	5	0	0	0	3	.250
Cora	2B	5	19	7	6	1	0	1	1	.316
Blowers	3B-1B	5	18	0	3	0	0	0	1	.167
Wilson	C	5	17	0	2	0	0	0	1	.118
Strange	3B	2	4	0	0	0	0	0	1	.000
Diaz	LF	2	3	0	1	0	0	0	0	.333
Widger	C	2	3	0	0	0	0	0	0	.000
Fermin	2B-SS	3	1	0	0	0	0	0	0	.000
Rodriguez	SS	1	1	1	0	0	0	0	0	.000
Newson	PH	1	1	0	0	0	0	0	0	.000

NEW YORK

NAME	POS	G	AB	R	H	2B	3B	HR	RBI	BA
TOTALS		5	193	33	50	12	0	11	32	.259
Mattingly	1B	5	24	3	10	4	0	1	6	.417
Sierra	DH	5	23	2	4	2	0	2	5	.174
B. Williams	CF	5	21	8	9	2	0	2	5	.429
Fernandez	SS	5	21	0	5	2	0	0	0	.238
Boggs	3B	4	19	4	5	2	0	1	3	.263
O'Neill	RF	5	18	5	6	0	0	3	6	.333
Velarde	2B-LF-3B	5	17	3	3	0	0	0	1	.176
Stanley	C	5	16	2	5	0	0	1	3	.313
James	LF	4	12	1	1	0	0	0	0	.083
Leyritz	C	2	7	1	1	0	0	1	2	.143
G. Williams	LF-RF	5	5	1	0	0	0	0	0	.000
Davis	3B	2	5	0	1	0	0	0	0	.200
Kelly	2B	4	3	3	0	0	0	0	1	.000
Strawberry	PH	2	2	0	0	0	0	0	0	.000
Posada	PR	1	0	1	0	0	0	0	0	—

COMPOSITE PITCHING — DIVISION SERIES

CLEVELAND

NAME	G	IP	H	BB	SO	W	L	SV	ERA
TOTALS	3	31	21	11	26	3	0	1	1.74
Hershiser	1	7.1	3	2	7	1	0	0	0.00
Nagy	1	7	4	5	6	1	0	0	0.78
Martinez	1	6	5	0	2	0	0	0	3.00
Tavarez	3	2.2	5	0	3	0	0	0	6.75
Mesa	2	2	0	2	0	0	0	1	0.00
Assenmacher	3	1.2	0	0	3	0	0	0	0.00
Poole	1	1.2	2	1	2	0	0	0	5.40
Hill	1	1.1	1	0	2	1	0	0	0.00
Plunk	1	1.1	1	1	1	0	0	0	0.00

BOSTON

NAME	G	IP	H	BB	SO	W	L	SV	ERA
TOTALS	3	29.2	25	13	22	0	3	0	5.16
Hanson	1	8	4	4	5	0	1	0	4.50
Clemens	1	7	5	1	5	0	0	0	3.86
Wakefield	1	5.1	5	5	4	0	1	0	11.81
Maddux	2	3	2	1	1	0	0	0	0.00
Stanton	1	2.1	1	0	4	0	0	0	0.00
Smith	1	1.1	1	0	0	0	1	0	6.75
Hudson	1	1	2	1	0	0	0	0	0.00
Cormier	2	0.2	1	2	0	0	0	0	13.49
Aguilera	1	0.2	3	0	1	0	0	0	13.50
Belinda	1	0.1	0	0	0	0	0	0	0.00

SEATTLE

NAME	G	IP	H	BB	SO	W	L	SV	ERA
TOTALS	5	51.1	50	32	43	3	2	2	5.79
Benes	2	11.2	10	9	8	0	0	0	5.40
Johnson	2	10	5	6	16	2	0	0	2.70
Bosio	2	7.2	10	4	2	0	0	0	10.57
Charlton	4	7.1	4	3	9	1	0	1	2.45
Nelson	3	5.2	7	3	7	0	1	0	3.18
Belcher	2	4.1	4	5	0	0	1	0	6.23
Risley	4	3	2	0	1	0	1	0	6.00
Wells	1	1	2	1	0	0	0	0	9.00
Ayala	2	0.2	6	1	0	0	0	0	54.00

NEW YORK

NAME	G	IP	H	BB	SO	W	L	SV	ERA
TOTALS	5	50	63	25	41	2	3	0	5.94
Cone	2	15.2	15	9	14	1	0	0	4.60
McDowell	2	7	8	4	6	0	2	0	9.00
Pettitte	1	7	9	3	0	0	0	0	5.14
Rivera	3	5.1	3	1	8	1	0	0	0.00
Kamieniecki	1	5	9	4	4	0	0	0	7.20
Wetteland	3	4.1	8	2	5	0	1	0	14.55
Wickman	3	3	5	0	3	0	0	0	0.00
Hitchcock	2	1.2	2	2	1	0	0	0	5.40
Howe	2	1	4	0	0	0	0	0	18.00

AMERICAN LEAGUE CHAMPIONSHIP

COMPOSITE BATTING

CLEVELAND

NAME	POS	G	AB	R	H	2B	3B	HR	RBI	BA
TOTALS		6	206	23	53	6	3	7	21	.257
Baerga	2B	6	25	3	10	0	0	1	4	.400
Lofton	CF	6	24	4	11	0	2	0	3	.458
Murray	DH	6	24	2	6	1	0	1	3	.250
Vizquel	SS	6	23	2	2	1	0	0	2	.087
Ramirez	RF	6	21	2	6	0	0	2	2	.286
Belle	LF	5	18	1	4	1	0	1	1	.222
Thome	3B	5	15	2	4	0	0	2	5	.267
Alomar	C	5	15	0	4	1	1	0	1	.267
Sorrento	1B	4	13	2	2	1	0	0	0	.154
Espinoza	3B	4	8	1	1	0	0	0	0	.125
Perry	1B	3	8	0	0	0	0	0	0	.000
Pena	C	4	6	1	2	1	0	0	0	.333
Kirby	LF-RF	5	5	2	1	0	0	0	0	.200
Amaro	PR-DH	3	1	0	0	0	0	0	0	.000

SEATTLE

NAME	POS	G	AB	R	H	2B	3B	HR	RBI	BA
TOTALS		6	201	12	37	8	0	5	10	.184
Buhner	RF	6	23	5	7	2	0	3	5	.304
Cora	2B	6	23	2	4	1	0	0	0	.174
E. Martinez	DH	6	23	0	2	0	0	0	0	.087
T. Martinez	1B	6	22	0	3	0	0	0	0	.136
Griffey	CF	6	21	2	7	2	0	1	2	.333
Sojo	SS	6	20	2	5	2	0	0	1	.250
Coleman	LF	6	20	0	2	0	0	0	0	.100
Blowers	3B	6	18	1	4	0	0	1	2	.222
Wilson	C	6	16	0	0	0	0	0	0	.000
Diaz	LF	4	7	0	3	1	0	0	0	.429
Strange	3B	4	4	0	0	0	0	0	0	.000
Amaral	PH	2	2	0	0	0	0	0	0	.000
Widger	C	3	1	0	0	0	0	0	0	.000
Rodriguez	PH	1	1	0	0	0	0	0	0	.000
Fermin	2B	1	1	0	0	0	0	0	0	—

COMPOSITE PITCHING

CLEVELAND

NAME	G	IP	H	BB	SO	W	L	SV	ERA
TOTALS	6	55	37	15	46	4	2	1	1.64
Hershiser	2	14	9	3	15	2	0	0	1.29
Martinez	2	13.1	10	3	7	1	1	0	2.03
Nagy	1	8	5	0	6	0	0	0	1.12
Hill	1	7	5	3	6	1	0	0	0.00
Mesa	4	4	1	1	4	0	0	2	2.25
Tavarez	4	3.1	3	1	2	0	1	0	2.70
Plunk	2	2	1	2	2	0	0	0	9.00
Assenmacher	3	1.1	0	1	2	0	0	0	0.00
Poole	1	1	0	0	2	0	0	0	0.00
Ogea	1	0.2	1	0	2	0	0	0	0.00
Embree	1	0.1	0	1	0	0	0	0	0.00

SEATTLE

NAME	G	IP	H	BB	SO	W	L	SV	ERA
TOTALS	6	54	53	25	37	2	4	1	3.33
Johnson	2	15.1	12	2	13	1	1	0	2.35
Wolcott	1	7	8	5	2	1	0	0	2.57
Charlton	3	6	1	1	5	1	0	1	0.00
Belcher	1	5.2	9	2	1	0	1	0	6.35
Bosio	1	5.1	7	2	3	0	1	0	3.38
Ayala	3	3.2	3	3	3	0	0	0	2.45
Nelson	3	3	3	5	3	0	0	0	0.00
Wells	1	3	3	1	2	0	0	0	3.00
Risley	3	2.2	1	1	2	0	0	0	0.00
Benes	1	2.1	6	2	3	0	1	0	3.14

ATLANTA — 1st 90-54 .625 — BOBBY COX

Name	G by Pos	B	AGE	G	AB	R	H	2B	3B	HR	RBI	BB	SO	SB	BA	SA
TOTALS			29	144	4814	645	1202	210	27	168	618	520	933	73	.250	.409
Fred McGriff	1B144	R	31	144	528	85	148	27	1	27	93	65	99	3	.280	.489
Mark Lemke	2B115	B	29	116	399	42	101	9	1	5	38	44	40	1	.253	.356
Jeff Blauser	SS115	R	29	115	431	60	91	16	2	12	31	57	107	8	.211	.341
Chipper Jones	3B123 OF20	B	23	140	524	87	139	22	3	23	86	73	99	8	.265	.450
David Justice	OF120	L	29	120	411	73	104	17	2	24	78	73	68	4	.253	.479
Marquis Grissom	OF136	R	28	139	551	80	142	23	3	12	42	47	61	29	.258	.376
Ryan Klesko	OF102 1B4	L	24	107	329	48	102	25	2	23	70	47	72	5	.310	.608
Javy Lopez	C93	R	24	100	333	37	105	11	4	14	51	14	57	0	.315	.498
Dwight Smith	OF25	L	31	103	131	16	33	8	2	3	21	13	35	0	.252	.412
Mike Kelly	OF83	R	25	97	137	26	26	6	1	3	17	11	49	7	.190	.314
Rafael Belliard	SS40 2B32	R	33	75	180	12	40	2	1	0	7	6	28	2	.222	.244
Mike Mordecai	2B21 1B9 SS6 3B6 OF1	R	27	69	75	10	21	6	0	3	11	9	16	0	.280	.480
Charlie O'Brien	C64	R	35	67	198	18	45	7	0	9	23	29	40	0	.227	.399
1 Jose Oliva	3B25 1B1	R	24	48	109	7	17	4	0	5	12	7	22	0	.156	.330
2 Mike Devereaux	OF27	R	32	29	55	7	14	3	0	1	8	2	11	2	.255	.364
2 Luis Polonia	OF15	L	30	28	53	6	14	7	0	0	2	3	9	3	.264	.396
Ed Giovanola	2B7 3B3 SS1	L	26	13	14	2	1	0	0	0	0	3	5	0	.071	.071
Brian Kowitz	OF8	L	25	10	24	3	4	1	0	0	3	2	5	0	.167	.208
Eddie Perez	C5 1B1	R	27	7	13	1	4	1	0	1	4	0	2	0	.308	.615
Mike Sharperson	3B1	R	33	7	7	1	1	1	0	0	2	0	1	0	.143	.286

NAME	T	AGE	W	L	PCT	SV	G	GS	CG	IP	H	BB	SO	SHO	ERA
TOTALS		28	90	54	.625	34	144	144	18	1292	1184	436	1087	11	3.44
Greg Maddux	R	29	19	2	.905	0	28	28	10	210	147	23	181	3	1.63
Tom Glavine	L	29	16	7	.696	0	29	29	3	199	182	66	127	1	3.08
John Smoltz	R	28	12	7	.632	0	29	29	2	193	166	72	193	1	3.18
Brad Clontz	R	24	8	1	.889	4	59	0	0	69	71	22	55	0	3.65
Greg McMichael	R	28	7	2	.778	2	67	0	0	81	64	32	74	0	2.79
Mark Wohlers	R	25	7	3	.700	25	65	0	0	65	51	24	90	0	2.09
Kent Mercker	L	27	7	8	.467	0	29	26	0	143	140	61	102	0	4.15
Steve Avery	L	25	7	13	.350	0	29	29	3	173	165	52	141	1	4.67
Pedro Borbon	L	27	2	2	.500	2	41	0	0	32	29	17	33	0	3.09
Jason Schmidt	R	22	2	2	.500	0	9	2	0	25	27	18	19	0	5.76
1 Mike Stanton	L	28	1	1	.500	1	26	0	0	19	31	6	13	0	5.59
Brad Woodall	L	26	1	1	.500	0	9	0	0	10	13	5	6	0	6.10
Steve Bedrosian	R	37	1	2	.333	0	29	0	0	28	40	12	22	0	6.11
3 Alejandro Pena	R	36	0	0	—	0	14	0	0	13	11	4	18	0	4.15
Rod Nichols	R	30	0	0	—	0	5	0	0	7	14	5	3	0	5.40
1 Terry Clark	R	34	0	0	—	0	3	0	0	4	3	5	2	0	4.91
Tom Thobe	L	25	0	0	—	0	3	0	0	3	7	0	2	0	10.80
Darrell May	L	23	0	0	—	0	2	0	0	4	4	0	1	0	11.25
Terrell Wade	L	22	0	1	.000	0	2	0	0	4	3	4	3	0	4.50
1 Matt Murray	R	24	0	2	.000	0	4	1	0	11	16	5	3	0	6.75

NEW YORK — 2nd(tie) 69-75 .479 21 — DALLAS GREEN

Name	G by Pos	B	AGE	G	AB	R	H	2B	3B	HR	RBI	BB	SO	SB	BA	SA
TOTALS			28	144	4958	657	1323	218	34	125	617	446	994	58	.267	.400
Rico Brogna	1B131	L	25	134	495	72	143	27	2	22	76	39	111	0	.289	.485
Jeff Kent	2B122	R	27	125	472	65	131	22	3	20	65	29	89	3	.278	.464
Jose Vizcaino	SS134 2B7	B	27	135	509	66	146	21	5	3	56	35	76	8	.287	.365
Edgardo Alfonzo (XJ)	3B58 2B29 SS6	R	21	101	335	26	93	13	5	4	41	12	37	1	.278	.382
Carl Everett	OF77	R	24	79	289	48	75	13	1	12	54	39	67	2	.260	.436
1 Brett Butler	OF90	L	38	90	367	54	114	13	7*	1	25	43	42	21	.311	.392
Joe Orsulak	OF86 1B1	L	33	108	290	41	82	19	2	1	37	19	35	1	.283	.372
Todd Hundley (WJ)	C89	R	26	90	275	39	77	11	0	15	51	42	64	1	.280	.484
1 Bobby Bonilla	3B46 OF31 1B10	B	32	80	317	49	103	25	4	18	53	31	48	0	.325	.599
Chris Jones	OF52 1B5	R	29	79	182	33	51	6	2	8	31	13	45	2	.280	.467
Tim Bogar	SS27 3B25 1B10 2B7 OF1	R	28	78	145	17	42	7	0	1	21	9	25	1	.290	.359
Kelly Stinnett	C67	R	25	77	196	23	43	8	1	4	18	29	65	2	.219	.332
Ryan Thompson (EJ-LJ)	OF74	R	27	75	267	39	67	13	0	7	31	19	77	3	.251	.378
Bill Spiers	3B11 2B6	L	29	63	72	5	15	2	1	0	11	12	15	0	.208	.264
2 Damon Buford	OF39	R	25	44	136	24	32	5	0	4	12	19	28	7	.235	.360
Ricky Otero	OF23	B	23	35	51	5	7	2	0	0	1	3	10	2	.137	.176
1 David Segui	OF18 1B10	B	28	33	73	9	24	3	1	2	11	12	9	1	.329	.479
Butch Huskey	3B27 OF1	R	23	28	90	8	17	1	0	3	11	10	16	1	.189	.300
Aaron Ledesma	3B10 1B2 SS2	R	24	21	33	4	8	0	0	0	3	6	7	0	.242	.242
Jeff Barry	OF2	R	26	15	15	2	2	1	0	0	0	1	8	0	.133	.200
Alberto Castillo	C12	R	25	13	29	2	3	1	0	0	2	2	4	0	.103	.103
Alex Ochoa	OF10	R	23	11	37	7	11	1	0	0	0	2	10	1	.297	.324
Brook Fordyce	C5	R	25	4	2	1	1	1	0	0	0	1	0	0	.500	1.000

NAME	T	AGE	W	L	PCT	SV	G	GS	CG	IP	H	BB	SO	SHO	ERA
TOTALS		28	69	75	.479	36	144	144	9	1291	1296	401	901	9	3.88
Bobby Jones	R	25	10	10	.500	0	30	30	3	196	209	53	127	1	4.19
Jason Isringhausen	R	22	9	2	.818	0	14	14	1	93	88	31	55	0	2.81
Dave Mlicki	R	27	9	7	.563	0	29	25	0	161	160	54	123	0	4.26
John Franco	L	34	5	3	.625	29	48	0	0	52	48	17	41	0	2.44
1 Bret Saberhagen	R	31	5	5	.500	0	16	16	3	110	105	20	71	0	3.35
Bill Pulsipher	L	21	5	7	.417	0	17	17	2	127	122	45	81	0	3.98
Blas Minor (BR)	R	29	4	2	.667	1	35	0	0	47	44	13	43	0	3.66
Jerry Dipoto	R	27	4	6	.400	2	58	0	0	79	77	29	49	0	3.78
Don Florence	L	28	3	0	1.000	0	14	0	0	12	17	6	5	0	1.50
2 Reid Cornelius	R	25	3	7	.300	0	10	10	0	58	64	25	35	0	5.15
Paul Byrd	R	24	2	1	.667	0	17	0	0	22	18	7	26	0	2.05
Pete Harnisch (SJ)	R	28	2	8	.200	0	18	18	0	110	111	24	82	0	3.68
Pete Walker	R	26	1	0	1.000	0	13	0	0	18	24	5	5	0	4.58
Robert Person	R	25	1	1	.500	2	13	0	0	12	5	2	10	0	0.75
Eric Gunderson	L	29	1	1	.500	0	30	0	0	24	25	8	19	0	3.70
1 Josias Manzanillo	R	27	1	2	.333	0	12	0	0	16	18	6	14	0	7.88
Dave Telgheder	R	28	1	2	.333	0	7	3	0	34	7	16	0	5.61	
Kevin Lomon	R	23	0	1	.000	0	6	0	0	9	17	5	6	0	6.75
1 Mike Remlinger	L	29	0	1	.500	0	3	2	0	8	11	6	5	0	6.35
Mike Birkbeck	R	33	0	1	.000	0	2	1	0	28	22	2	14	0	1.63
1 Jason Jacome	L	24	0	4	.000	0	5	5	0	21	33	15	11	0	10.29

*Butler, also with Los Angeles, tied for league lead in triples with 9

PHILADELPHIA — 2nd(tie) 69-75 .479 21 — JIM FREGOSI

Name	G by Pos	B	AGE	G	AB	R	H	2B	3B	HR	RBI	BB	SO	SB	BA	SA
TOTALS			31	144	4950	615	1296	263	30	94	576	497	884	72	.262	.384
Gregg Jefferies	1B59 OF55	B	27	114	480	69	147	31	2	11	56	35	26	9	.306	.448
Mickey Morandini	2B122	L	29	127	494	65	140	34	7	6	49	42	80	9	.283	.417
Kevin Stocker	SS125	B	25	125	412	42	90	14	3	1	32	43	75	6	.218	.274
Charlie Hayes	3B141	R	30	141	529	58	146	30	3	11	85	50	88	5	.276	.406
2 Mark Whiten	OF55	B	28	60	212	38	57	10	1	11	37	31	63	7	.269	.481
Lenny Dykstra	OF61	L	32	62	254	37	67	15	1	2	18	33	28	10	.264	.354
Jim Eisenreich	OF111	L	36	129	377	46	119	22	2	10	55	38	44	10	.316	.464
Darren Daulton (KJ)	C95	L	33	98	342	44	85	19	3	9	55	55	52	3	.249	.401
Gary Varsho	OF25	L	34	72	103	7	26	1	1	0	11	7	17	2	.252	.282
1 Dave Hollins	1B61	B	29	65	205	46	47	12	2	7	25	53	38	1	.229	.410
1 Andy Van Slyke (VJ)	OF56	L	34	63	214	26	52	10	2	3	16	28	41	7	.243	.350
1 Dave Gallagher	OF55	R	34	62	157	12	50	12	0	1	12	16	20	0	.318	.414
Tony Longmire (BW)	OF23	L	26	59	104	21	37	7	3	0	19	11	19	1	.356	.510
1 Mariano Duncan	2B24 SS14 1B12	R	32	52	196	20	56	12	1	3	23	0	43	1	.286	.403
Lenny Webster	C43	R	30	49	150	18	40	9	0	4	14	16	27	0	.267	.407
Tom Marsh	OF29	R	29	43	109	13	32	3	1	3	15	4	25	0	.294	.422
2 Kevin Elster	SS19 1B4 3B2	R	30	26	53	10	11	4	1	1	9	7	14	0	.208	.377
2 Kevin Flora	OF20	R	26	24	75	12	16	3	0	2	7	4	22	1	.213	.333
Gene Schall	1B14 OF4	R	25	24	65	2	15	2	0	0	5	6	16	0	.231	.262
Kevin Jordan	2B9 3B1	R	25	24	54	6	10	1	0	2	6	2	9	0	.185	.315
Randy Ready	1B3 2B1	R	35	23	29	3	4	0	0	0	3	8	5	0	.138	.138
Mike Lieberthal	C14	R	23	16	47	1	12	2	0	0	4	5	8	0	.255	.298
Kevin Sefcik	3B2	R	24	5	4	1	0	0	0	0	0	0	1	0	.000	.000
Gary Bennett		R	23	1	1	0	0	0	0	0	0	0	0	0	.000	.000

NAME	T	AGE	W	L	PCT	SV	G	GS	CG	IP	H	BB	SO	SHO	ERA
TOTALS		27	69	75	.479	41	144	144	8	1290	1241	538	980	8	4.21
Paul Quantrill	R	26	11	12	.478	0	33	29	0	179	212	44	103	0	4.67
Michael Mimbs	L	26	9	7	.563	1	35	19	2	137	127	75	93	1	4.15
Tyler Green	R	25	8	9	.471	0	26	25	4	141	157	66	85	2	5.31
Curt Schilling	R	28	7	5	.583	0	17	17	1	116	96	26	114	0	3.57
2 Sid Fernandez	L	32	6	1	.857	0	11	11	0	65	48	21	79	0	3.34
Ricky Bottalico	R	25	5	3	.625	1	62	0	0	88	50	42	87	0	2.46
Heathcliff Slocumb	R	29	5	6	.455	32	61	0	0	65	64	35	63	0	2.89
David West (SJ)	L	30	3	2	.600	0	8			38	34	19	25	0	3.79
Mike Williams	R	26	3	3	.500	0	33	8	0	88	78	29	57	0	3.29
Kyle Abbott (SJ)	L	27	2	0	1.000	0	18	0	0	28	28	16	21	0	3.81
1 Gene Harris	R	30	2	2	.500	0	21	0	0	19	19	8	9	0	4.26
Jeff Juden	R	24	2	4	.333	0	13	10	1	63	53	31	47	0	4.02
1 Norm Charlton	L	32	2	5	.286	0	25	0	0	22	23	15	12	0	7.36
Paul Fletcher	R	27	1	0	1.000	0	10	0	0	3	5	5	3	0	5.40
Chuck Ricci	R	26	1	0	1.000	0	9	0	0	9	9	3	9	0	1.80
Mike Grace	R	26	1	0	1.000	0	2	0	0	11	10	4	7	0	3.18
Toby Borland (VJ)	R	26	1	3	.250	6	50	0	0	74	81	37	59	0	3.77
2 Russ Springer	R	26	0	0	—	0	14	0	0	27	22	10	32	0	3.71
Steve Frey	L	31	0	0	—	0	9	0	0	11	3	2	7	0	0.84
Andy Carter	L	26	0	0	—	0	4	0	0	1	1	1	4	0	6.14
Ryan Karp	L	25	0	0	—	0	4	0	0	4	4	1	4	0	4.50
2 Omar Olivares	R	27	0	1	.000	0	3	0	0	10	11	2	7	0	5.40
Jim Deshaies	L	35	0	1	.000	0	4	0	0	5	15	1	6	0	20.25
Bobby Munoz (EJ)	R	27	0	1	.000	0	4	3	0	16	15	9	6	0	5.74
Dennis Springer	R	30	0	1	.000	0	4	0	0	22	21	9	15	0	4.84
Tommy Greene (SJ)	R	28	0	5	.000	0	11	6	0	34	45	20	24	0	8.29

FLORIDA — 4th 67-76 .469 22.5 — RENE LACHEMANN

Name	G by Pos	B	AGE	G	AB	R	H	2B	3B	HR	RBI	BB	SO	SB	BA	SA
TOTALS			28	144	4886	673	1278	214	29	144	636	517	916	131	.262	.406
Greg Colbrunn	1B134	R	25	138	528	70	146	22	1	23	89	22	69	11	.277	.453
Quilvio Veras	2B122 OF2	B	24	124	440	86	115	20	7	5	32	80	66	56	.261	.373
Kurt Abbott	SS115	R	26	120	420	60	107	18	7	17	60	36	110	4	.255	.452
Terry Pendleton	3B129	B	34	133	513	70	149	32	1	14	78	38	84	1	.290	.439
Gary Sheffield (RJ)	OF61	R	26	63	213	46	69	8	0	16	46	55	45	19	.324	.587
Chuck Carr	OF103	B	27	105	308	54	70	20	0	2	20	46	49	25	.227	.312
Jeff Conine	OF118 1B14	R	29	133	483	72	146	26	2	25	105	66	94	2	.302	.520
Charles Johnson	C97	R	23	97	315	40	79	15	1	11	39	46	71	0	.251	.410
Alex Arias	SS36 3B21 2B6	R	27	94	216	22	58	9	2	3	26	22	20	1	.269	.370
Andre Dawson	OF59	R	40	79	226	30	58	10	3	8	37	9	45	0	.257	.434
Jerry Browne (LJ)	OF30 2B29 3B7	B	29	77	184	21	47	4	0	1	17	25	20	1	.255	.293
Tommy Gregg	OF38 1B2	L	31	72	156	20	37	5	0	6	20	16	33	3	.237	.385
Jesus Tavarez	OF61	B	24	63	190	31	55	6	2	3	16	16	27	1	.289	.374
Steve Decker	C46 1B2	R	29	51	133	12	30	2	1	3	13	19	22	1	.226	.323
Mario Diaz	2B49 SS3 5B3	R	33	49	87	5	20	3	0	1	9	3	12	0	.230	.299
Russ Morman	OF18 1B3	R	33	34	72	9	20	2	1	3	7	3	12	0	.278	.458
Darrell Whitmore (SJ)	OF16	L	26	27	58	6	11	2	0	2	6	1	15	0	.190	.276
Bob Natal	C13	R	29	16	43	2	10	2	1	2	6	1	9	0	.233	.465
Eddie Zosky	SS4 2B1	R	27	8	5	0	1	0	0	0	0	0	0	1	.200	.200

NAME	T	AGE	W	L	PCT	SV	G	GS	CG	IP	H	BB	SO	SHO	ERA
TOTALS		29	67	76	.469	29	143	143	12	1286	1299	562	994	7	4.27
Pat Rapp	R	29	14	7	.667	0	28	28	3	167	158	76	102	2	3.44
John Burkett	R	30	14	14	.500	0	30	30	4	188	208	57	126	0	4.30
Chris Hammond	L	29	9	6	.600	0	25	24	3	161	157	47	126	2	3.80
Mark Gardner	R	33	5	5	.500	1	39	11	1	102	109	43	87	1	4.49
Terry Mathews	R	30	4	4	.500	3	57	0	0	83	70	27	72	0	3.38
Randy Veres	R	29	4	4	.500	1	47	0	0	49	46	22	31	0	3.88
David Weathers	R	25	4	5	.444	0	28	15	0	90	104	52	60	0	5.98
2 Alejandro Pena	R	36	2	0	1.000	0	13	0	0	18	11	3	21	0	1.50
Ryan Bowen (KJ)	R	27	2	0	1.000	0	3	3	0	17	23	12	15	0	3.78
3 Willie Banks	R	26	2	3	.400	0	9	9	0	50	43	30	30	0	4.32
Yorkis Perez	L	27	2	6	.250	1	69	0	0	47	35	28	47	0	5.21
1 Bobby Witt	R	31	2	7	.222	0	19	19	1	111	104	47	95	0	3.90
Aaron Small	R	23	1	0	1.000	0	7	0	0	7	6	7	5	0	1.42
2 Rob Murphy	L	35	1	1	.500	0	7	0	0	7	7	5	3	0	9.82
2 Buddy Groom	L	29	1	2	.333	0	14	0	0	15	26	6	12	0	7.20
Jay Powell	R	23	0	0	—	0	7	0	0	7	12	3	6	0	1.08
Jeremy Hernandez (ZJ)	R	28	0	0	—	0	7	0	0	7	12	5	4	0	11.57
Rick Scheid	L	30	0	0	—	0	10			14	7	10	0	6.10	
John Johnstone (EJ)	R	26	0	0	—	0	4	0	0	7	14	2	10	0	3.86
Marc Valdes	R	23	0	0	—	0	2	2	0	7	4	7	2	0	14.14
1 Mike Myers	L	26	0	0	—	0	2	0	0	1	2	3	0	0	0.00
Bryan Harvey (EJ)	R	32	0	0	—	0	1	0	0	1	0	1	0	0	∞
Richie Lewis	R	29	0	1	.000	0	21	0	0	36	30	15	32	0	3.75
Matt Mantei (XJ)	R	22	0	1	.000	0	6	0	0	13	12	13	15	0	4.73
Matt Dunbar	L	26	0	1	.000	0	3	0	0	7	12	11	5	0	11.57
2 Rich Garces	R	24	0	2	.000	0	11	0	0	14	14	8	16	0	5.40
Robb Nen	R	25	0	7	.000	23	62	0	0	66	62	23	68	0	3.29

MONTREAL   5th 66-78 .458 24   FELIPE ALOU

Name	G by Pos	B	AGE	G	AB	R	H	2B	3B	HR	RBI	BB	SO	SB	BA	SA
TOTALS			26	144	4905	621	1268	265	24	118	572	400	901	120	.259	.394
2 David Segui	1B97 OF2	B	28	97	383	59	117	22	3	10	57	28	38	1	.305	.457
Mike Lansing	2B127 SS2	R	27	127	467	47	119	30	2	10	62	28	65	27	.255	.392
Wil Cordero	SS105 OF26	R	23	131	514	64	147	35	2	10	49	36	88	9	.286	.420
Sean Berry	3B83 1B3	R	29	103	314	38	100	22	1	14	55	25	53	3	.318	.529
Tony Tarasco	OF116	L	24	126	438	64	109	18	4	14	40	51	78	24	.249	.404
Rondell White	OF119	R	23	130	474	87	140	33	4	13	57	41	87	25	.295	.464
Moises Alou (SJ)	OF92	R	28	93	344	48	94	22	0	14	58	29	56	4	.273	.459
Darrin Fletcher	C98	L	28	110	350	42	100	21	1	11	45	32	23	0	.286	.446
Shane Andrews	3B51 1B29	R	23	84	220	27	47	10	1	8	31	17	68	1	.214	.377
Mark Grudzielanek	SS34 3B31 2B13	R	25	78	269	27	66	12	2	1	20	14	47	0	.245	.316
Tim Laker	C61	R	25	64	141	17	33	8	1	3	20	14	38	0	.234	.369
Curtis Pride	OF24	L	26	48	63	10	11	1	0	0	2	5	16	3	.175	.190
2 Jeff Treadway	2B11 3B1	L	32	41	50	4	12	2	0	0	10	5	2	0	.240	.280
Tim Spehr (IL)	C38	R	28	41	35	4	9	5	0	1	3	6	7	0	.257	.486
2 Dave Silvestri	SS9 3B8 1B4 2B3 OF3	R	27	39	72	12	19	6	0	2	7	9	27	2	.264	.431
F.P. Santangelo	OF25 2B5	B	27	35	98	11	29	5	1	1	9	12	9	1	.296	.398
1 Lou Frazier	OF25 2B1	B	30	35	63	6	12	2	0	0	3	8	12	4	.190	.222
Cliff Floyd (BW)	1B18 OF4	L	22	29	69	6	9	1	0	1	8	7	22	3	.130	.188
Roberto Kelly	OF24	R	30	24	95	11	26	4	0	1	9	7	14	4	.274	.347
1 Henry Rodriguez (BL)	1B10 OF8	L	27	24	58	7	12	0	0	1	5	6	11	0	.207	.259
Yamil Benitez	OF14	R	22	14	39	8	15	2	1	2	7	1	7	0	.385	.641
1 Chad Fonville	2B2	B	24	14	12	2	4	0	0	0	0	0	3	0	.333	.333
Tom Foley	1B4 2B3	L	35	11	24	2	5	2	0	0	2	2	4	1	.208	.292
Joe Siddall	C7	L	27	7	10	4	3	0	0	0	1	3	1	0	.300	.300

NAME	T	AGE	W	L	PCT	SV	G	GS	CG	IP	H	BB	SO	SHO	ERA
		29	66	78	.458	42	144	144	7	1284	1286	416	950	9	4.11
Pedro Martinez	R	23	14	10	.583	0	30	30	2	195	158	66	174	2	3.51
Jeff Fassero	L	32	13	14	.481	0	30	30	1	189	207	74	164	0	4.33
Carlos Perez	L	24	10	8	.556	0	28	23	2	141	142	28	106	1	3.69
Butch Henry (EJ)	L	26	7	9	.438	0	21	21	1	127	133	28	60	1	2.84
Kirk Rueter	L	24	5	3	.625	0	9	9	1	47	38	9	28	1	3.23
Gil Heredia	R	29	5	6	.455	1	40	18	0	119	137	21	74	0	4.31
Tim Scott	R	28	2	0	1.000	2	62	0	0	63	52	23	57	0	3.98
Willie Fraser	R	31	2	2	.500	2	22	0	0	26	25	9	12	0	5.61
Ugueth Urbina	R	21	2	2	.500	0	7	4	0	23	26	14	15	0	6.17
Greg Harris	R	39	2	3	.400	0	45	0	0	48	45	16	47	0	2.61
Gabe White	L	23	1	2	.333	0	19	1	0	26	26	9	25	0	7.01
Mel Rojas	R	28	1	4	.200	30	59	0	0	68	69	29	61	0	4.12
Tavo Alvarez	R	23	1	5	.167	0	8	8	0	37	46	14	17	0	6.75
1 Jeff Shaw	R	28	1	6	.143	3	50	0	0	62	58	26	45	0	4.62
Bryan Eversgerd	L	26	0	0	—	0	25	0	0	21	22	9	8	0	5.14
Curt Schmidt	R	25	0	0	—	0	11	0	0	10	15	9	7	0	6.97
Reid Cornelius	R	25	0	0	—	0	8	0	0	9	11	5	4	0	8.00
J.J. Thobe	R	24	0	0	—	0	4	0	0	4	6	3	0	0	7.56
2 Jose DeLeon	R	34	0	1	.000	0	7	0	0	8	7	7	12	0	7.56
1 Luis Aquino	R	31	0	2	.000	2	29	0	0	37	47	11	22	0	3.86
2 Dave Leiper	L	33	0	2	.000	2	26	0	0	22	16	6	12	0	2.86

CENTRAL DIVISION

CINCINNATI   1st 85-59 .590   DAVEY JOHNSON

Name	G by Pos	B	AGE	G	AB	R	H	2B	3B	HR	RBI	BB	SO	SB	BA	SA
TOTALS			28	144	4903	747	1326	277	35	161	694	519	946	190	.270	.440
Hal Morris	1B99	L	30	101	359	53	100	25	2	11	51	29	58	1	.279	.451
Bret Boone	2B138	R	26	138	513	63	137	34	2	15	68	41	84	5	.267	.429
Barry Larkin	SS130	R	31	131	496	98	158	29	6	15	66	61	49	51	.319	.492
Jeff Branson	3B98 SS32 2B6 1B1	L	28	122	331	43	86	18	2	12	45	44	60	2	.260	.435
Reggie Sanders	OF130	R	27	133	484	91	148	36	6	28	99	69	122	36	.306	.579
2 Darren Lewis	OF57	R	27	58	163	19	40	3	0	0	17	20	11	6	.245	.264
Ron Gant	OF117	R	30	119	410	79	113	19	4	29	88	74	108	23	.276	.554
Benito Santiago	C75 1B8	R	30	81	266	40	76	20	0	11	44	24	48	2	.286	.485
Thomas Howard		B	30	113	281	42	85	15	2	3	26	20	37	17	.302	.402
Jerome Walton	OF82	R	29	102	162	32	47	12	1	8	22	17	25	10	.290	.525
Lenny Harris	3B24 1B23 OF8 2B1	L	30	101	197	32	41	8	3	2	16	14	20	10	.208	.310
Mark Lewis	3B72 2B2 SS2	R	25	81	171	25	58	13	1	3	30	21	33	0	.339	.480
Eddie Taubensee	C65 1B3	L	26	80	218	32	62	14	2	9	44	22	52	2	.284	.491
Eric Anthony (EJ-KJ)	OF24 1B17	L	27	47	134	19	36	6	0	5	23	13	30	2	.269	.425
Brian Hunter (LJ)	1B23 OF4	R	27	40	79	9	17	6	0	1	9	9	21	2	.215	.329
Damon Berryhill (EJ)	C29 1B1	B	31	34	82	6	15	3	0	2	11	10	19	0	.183	.293
1 Deion Sanders (NJ)	OF33	L	27	33	129	19	31	2	3	1	10	9	18	16	.240	.326
2 Mariano Duncan	2B7 SS6 1B6 OF3 3B1	R	32	29	69	16	20	2	1	3	13	5	19	0	.290	.478
1 Craig Worthington	1B4 3B2	R	30	10	18	1	5	1	0	1	2	2	1	0	.278	.500
Willie Greene	3B7	L	23	8	19	1	2	0	0	0	0	3	7	0	.105	.105
Nigel Wilson	OF2	L	25	5	7	0	0	0	0	0	0	0	4	0	.000	.000
Steve Gibralter	OF2	R	23	4	3	0	1	0	0	0	0	0	0	0	.333	.333
Eric Owens	3B2	R	24	2	0	2	0	0	0	0	0	1	0	0	01.000	1.000

NAME	T	AGE	W	L	PCT	SV	G	GS	CG	IP	H	BB	SO	SHO	ERA
		28	85	59	.590	38	144	144	8	1289	1270	424	903	10	4.03
Pete Schourek	L	26	18	7	.720	0	29	29	2	190	158	45	160	0	3.22
John Smiley	L	30	12	5	.706	0	28	27	1	177	173	39	124	0	3.46
Xavier Hernandez	R	29	7	2	.778	3	59	0	0	90	95	31	84	0	4.60
Mike Jackson (SJ)	R	30	6	1	.857	2	40	0	0	49	38	19	41	0	2.39
2 Dave Burba	R	28	6	2	.750	0	15	9	1	63	52	26	50	1	3.27
Tim Pugh	R	28	6	5	.545	0	28	12	0	98	100	32	38	0	3.84
2 Mark Portugal	R	32	6	5	.545	0	14	14*	0	78	79	22	33	0	3.82
2 David Wells	L	32	6	5	.545	0	11	11	3	73	74	16	50	0	3.59
Jose Rijo (EJ)	R	30	5	4	.556	0	14	14*	0	69	76	22	62	0	4.17
Jeff Brantley	R	31	3	2	.600	28	56	0	0	70	53	20	62	0	2.82
Chuck McElroy	L	27	3	4	.429	0	44	0	0	40	46	15	27	0	6.02
Kevin Jarvis	R	25	3	4	.429	0	19	11	1	79	91	32	33	1	5.70
Hector Carrasco	R	25	2	7	.222	5	64	0	0	87	86	46	64	0	4.12
Pete Smith	R	29	1	2	.333	0	11	2	0	24	30	7	14	0	6.66
1 C.J. Nitkowski	L	22	1	3	.250	0	9	7	0	32	41	15	18	0	6.12
Johnny Ruffin (KJ)	R	23	0	0	—	0	10	0	0	13	4	11	11	0	1.35
2 Brad Pennington	L	26	0	0	—	0	6	0	0	9	11	9	11	0	5.59
Rick Reed	R	30	0	0	—	0	3	0	0	17	18	3	10	0	5.82
Scott Sullivan	R	24	0	0	—	0	2	0	0	3	4	1	4	0	9.00
1 John Roper (SJ)	R	23	0	1	.000	0	7	1	0	13	4	6	6	0	10.29
Matt Grott	R	28	0	0	—	0	1	0	0	1	2	1	1	0	21.60
2 Mike Remlinger	L	29	0	0	—	0	1	0	0	1	2	2	1	0	9.00
John Courtright	L	25	0	0	—	0	0	0	0	1	1	0	0	0	9.00
Frank Viola	L	26	0	1	.000	0	3	3	0	14	20	3	4	0	6.28

*Porgugal, also with San Francisco, tied for league lead in Games Started with 31

HOUSTON   2nd 76-49 .528 9   TERRY COLLINS

Name	G by Pos	B	AGE	G	AB	R	H	2B	3B	HR	RBI	BB	SO	SB	BA	SA
TOTALS			28	144	5097	747	1403	260	22	109	694	566	992	176	.275	.399
Jeff Bagwell (BH)	1B114	R	27	114	448	88	130	29	0	21	87	79	102	12	.290	.496
Craig Biggio	2B141	R	29	141	553	123	167	30	2	22	77	80	85	33	.302	.483
Orlando Miller (KJ)	SS89	R	26	92	324	36	85	20	1	5	36	22	71	3	.262	.377
Dave Magadan	3B100 1B11	L	32	127	348	44	109	24	0	2	51	71	56	2	.313	.399
Derek Bell (LJ)	OF110	R	26	112	452	63	151	21	2	8	86	33	71	27	.334	.442
Brian Hunter	OF74	R	24	78	321	52	97	14	5	2	28	21	52	24	.302	.396
James Mouton	OF94	R	26	104	298	42	78	18	2	4	27	25	59	25	.262	.376
Tony Eusebio	C103	R	28	113	368	46	110	21	1	6	58	31	59	0	.299	.410
Craig Shipley	3B65 SS11 2B4 1B1	R	32	92	232	23	61	8	1	3	24	8	28	6	.263	.345
Milt Thompson	OF34	L	36	92	132	14	29	9	0	2	19	14	37	4	.220	.333
John Cangelosi	OF59 P1	B	32	90	201	46	64	5	2	2	18	48	42	21	.318	.393
2 Derrick May	OF55 1B1	L	26	78	206	29	62	15	1	8	41	19	24	5	.301	.500
1 Luis Gonzalez	OF55	R	27	56	209	35	54	10	4	6	35	18	30	1	.258	.431
Ricky Gutierrez	SS44 3B2	R	25	52	156	22	43	6	0	0	12	10	33	5	.276	.314
Mike Simms	1B25 OF12	R	28	50	121	14	31	4	0	9	24	13	28	1	.256	.512
Andy Stankiewicz (KJ)	SS14 2B6 3B3	R	30	43	52	6	6	1	0	0	7	12	19	4	.115	.135
2 Scott Servais	C28	R	28	28	89	7	20	10	0	1	12	9	15	0	.225	.371
Phil Plantier (BH-LJ)	OF20	R	26	22	68	12	17	2	0	4	15	11	19	0	.250	.456
1 Chris Donnels	3B9 2B1	L	29	19	30	4	9	0	0	2	3	6	4	0	.300	.300
1 Phil Nevin	3B16	R	24	18	60	4	7	1	0	0	1	7	13	1	.117	.133
Mike Brumley	SS3 OF3 3B1 1B1	B	32	18	18	1	1	0	0	1	0	1	7	0	.056	.222
2 Rick Wilkins (ZJ)	C13	R	28	15	40	6	10	1	0	1	5	10	10	0	.250	.350
Jerry Goff	C11	L	31	12	26	2	4	2	0	1	3	4	13	0	.154	.423
2 Pat Borders	C11	R	32	11	35	1	4	0	0	0	1	0	5	0	.114	.114
1 Scooter Tucker	C3	R	28	5	7	1	2	0	0	1	1	0	0	0	.286	.714
Dave Hajek		R	27	5	2	0	0	0	0	0	0	1	1	0	.000	.000

NAME	T	AGE	W	L	PCT	SV	G	GS	CG	IP	H	BB	SO	SHO	ERA
		28	76	68	.528	32	144	144	6	1320	1357	460	1056	8	4.06
Greg Swindell	L	30	10	9	.526	0	33	26	1	153	180	39	96	1	4.47
Doug Drabek	R	32	10	9	.526	0	31	31	2	185	205	54	143	1	4.77
Shane Reynolds	R	27	10	11	.476	0	30	30	3	189	196	37	175	2	3.47
Mike Hampton	L	22	9	8	.529	0	24	24	0	151	141	49	115	0	3.35
Jim Dougherty	R	27	8	4	.667	0	56	0	0	68	76	25	49	0	4.92
Doug Brocail	R	28	6	4	.600	1	36	7	0	77	87	22	39	0	4.19
Todd Jones	R	27	6	5	.545	15	68	0	0	100	89	52	96	0	3.07
Dave Veres	R	28	5	1	.833	1	72	0	0	103	89	30	94	0	2.26
Darryl Kile	R	26	4	12	.250	0	25	21	0	127	114	73	113	0	4.96
Donne Wall	R	27	3	1	.750	0	6	5	0	24	33	5	16	0	5.55
Dean Hartgraves	L	28	2	0	1.000	1	40	0	0	36	30	16	24	0	3.22
1 John Hudek (AJ)	R	28	2	2	.500	7	19	0	0	19	5	29	0		5.40
2 Jeff Tabaka	L	31	1	0	1.000	0	24	0	0	24	17	12	19	0	7.40
Pedro Martinez	R	26	0	0	—	0	25	0	0	21	29	16	17	0	11.00
1 Ross Powell	L	27	0	0	—	0	15	0	0	9	16	11	4	0	0.00
John Cangelosi	B	32	0	0	—	0	1	0	0	1	0	1	0	0	0.00
Billy Wagner	L	23	0	0	—	0	1	0	0	0.1	0	1	0	0	0.00
2 Mike Henneman	R	33	0	1	.000	8	21	0	0	21	21	4	19	0	3.00
Craig McMurtry	R	35	0	0	—	0	11	0	0	10	15	9	4	0	7.84

CHICAGO   3rd 73-71 .507 12   JIM RIGGLEMAN

Name	G by Pos	B	AGE	G	AB	R	H	2B	3B	HR	RBI	BB	SO	SB	BA	SA
TOTALS			28	144	4963	693	1315	267	39	158	648	440	953	105	.265	.430
Mark Grace	1B143	L	31	143	552	97	180	51	3	16	92	65	46	6	.326	.516
Rey Sanchez	2B111 SS4	R	27	114	428	57	119	22	2	3	27	14	46	6	.278	.360
Shawon Dunston	SS125	R	32	127	477	58	141	30	6	14	69	10	75	10	.296	.472
2 Todd Zeile	3B70 OF2 1B1	R	29	79	299	34	68	16	0	9	30	16	53	0	.227	.371
Sammy Sosa	OF143	R	26	144	564	89	151	17	3	36	119	58	134	34	.268	.500
Brian McRae	OF137	B	27	137	580	92	167	38	7	12	48	47	92	27	.288	.440
2 Luis Gonzalez	OF76	L	27	77	262	34	76	19	4	7	34	39	33	5	.290	.473
2 Scott Servais	C52	R	28	52	175	31	50	12	0	12	35	23	37	2	.286	.560
Scott Bullett	OF64	L	26	104	150	19	41	5	3	3	22	12	30	8	.273	.460
Jose Hernandez	SS43 2B29 3B20	R	25	93	245	37	60	11	4	13	40	13	69	1	.245	.482
Howard Johnson	3B34 OF13 2B8 1B3 SS1	B	34	87	169	26	33	4	1	7	22	34	46	1	.195	.355
Ozzie Timmons	OF55	R	24	77	171	30	45	10	1	8	28	13	32	3	.263	.474
1 Rick Wilkins	C49 1B2	L	28	50	162	24	31	2	0	6	14	36	51	0	.191	.315
1 Steve Buechele	3B32	R	33	32	106	10	20	2	0	1	9	11	19	0	.189	.236
Kevin Roberson		B	27	32	38	5	7	1	0	4	6	4	16	0	.184	.526
Todd Haney	2B17 3B4	R	29	25	73	11	30	8	0	0	7	7	11	0	.411	.603
Todd Pratt	C25	R	28	25	60	3	8	2	0	2	6	6	12	0	.133	.167
Joe Kmak (KJ)	C18 3B1	R	32	19	53	7	13	0	0	0	2	5	8	6	.245	.358
Matt Franco	2B3 3B1 1B1	L	26	16	17	3	5	1	0	0	3	0	4	0	.294	.353
Mike Hubbard	C9	R	24	15	23	2	4	0	0	0	1	0	7	0	.174	.174
1 Karl Rhodes	OF11	L	26	13	16	2	2	0	0	0	3	4	4	0	.125	.125
1 Mark Parent	C10	R	33	12	32	1	8	2	0	2	5	1	6	0	.250	.594

NAME	T	AGE	W	L	PCT	SV	G	GS	CG	IP	H	BB	SO	SHO	ERA
		28	73	71	.507	45	144	144	6	1301	1313	518	926	12	4.13
Jaime Navarro	R	28	14	6	.700	0	29	29	1	200	194	56	128	1	3.28
Jim Bullinger (EJ)	R	29	12	8	.600	0	24	24	1	150	152	65	93	1	4.14
Kevin Foster	R	26	12	11	.522	0	30	28	0	168	149	65	146	0	4.51
Frank Castillo	R	26	11	10	.524	0	29	29	2	188	179	52	135	2	3.21
Steve Trachsel	R	24	7	13	.350	0	30	29	2	161	174	76	117	0	5.15
Turk Wendell (SJ)	R	28	3	1	.750	0	43	0	0	60	71	24	50	0	4.92
Anthony Young (EJ-LJ)	R	29	3	4	.429	2	32	1	0	41	47	14	15	0	3.70
1 Mike Morgan (VJ)	R	35	2	1	.667	0	4	4	0	25	19	9	15	0	2.19
1 Bryan Hickerson	L	31	2	3	.400	1	38	0	0	32	36	15	28	0	6.82
Mike Perez	R	30	2	6	.250	0	68	0	0	71	72	27	49	0	3.66
Larry Casian (SJ)	L	28	1	0	1.000	0	42	0	0	23	23	15	11	0	1.93
Tom Edens	R	34	1	0	1.000	0	5	0	0	6	8	4	6	0	6.50
Terry Adams	R	28	1	1	.500	1	18	0	0	18	22	18	15	0	6.50
Randy Myers	L	32	1	2	.333	38	57	0	0	56	49	28	59	0	3.88
Mike Walker	R	28	1	3	.250	1	42	0	0	45	45	24	20	0	3.22
1 Rich Garces	R	24	0	0	—	0	1	0	0	2	2	1	2	0	0.00
Dave Swartzbaugh	R	27	0	0	—	0	2	0	0	8	6	5	6	0	9.00
Roberto Rivera	L	27	0	0	—	0	1	0	0	1	1	0	0	0	9.00
Tanyon Sturtze	R	24	0	0	—	0	2	0	0	3	5	4	1	0	5.40
Chris Nabholz (XJ)	R	28	0	1	.000	1	14	0	0	14	21	10	5	0	5.40
1 Willie Banks (SJ) 32	R	26	0	0	—	0	11	0	0	12	17	12	6	0	15.43

ST. LOUIS — 4th 62-81 .434 22.5   JOE TORRE 20-27 .426   MIKE JORGENSEN 42-54 .438

Name	G by Pos	B	AGE	G	AB	R	H	2B	3B	HR	RBI	BB	SO	SB	BA	SA
TOTALS			29	144	4779	563	1182	238	24	107	533	247	920	79	.247	.374
John Mabry	1B73 OF39	L	24	129	388	35	119	21	1	5	41	24	45	0	.307	.405
Geronimo Pena (BL-KJ)	2B25	B	28	32	101	20	27	6	1	1	8	16	30	3	.267	.376
Ozzie Smith (SJ)	SS41	B	40	44	156	16	31	5	0	0	11	17	12	4	.199	.244
Scott Cooper	3B110	L	29	118	374	29	86	18	2	3	40	49	85	0	.230	.313
Brian Jordan	OF126	R	28	131	490	83	145	20	4	22	81	22	79	24	.296	.488
Ray Lankford	OF129	L	28	132	483	81	134	35	2	25	82	63	110	24	.277	.513
Bernard Gilkey	OF118	R	28	121	480	73	143	33	4	17	69	42	70	12	.298	.490
Tom Pagnozzi (KJ-BW)	C61	R	32	62	219	17	47	14	1	2	15	11	31	0	.215	.315
Tripp Cromer	SS95 2B11	R	27	105	345	36	78	19	0	5	18	14	66	0	.226	.325
Jose Oquendo	2B62 SS24 3B2 OF1	B	31	88	220	31	46	8	3	2	17	35	21	1	.209	.300
Danny Sheaffer	C67 1B3 3B1	R	34	76	208	24	48	10	1	5	30	23	38	0	.231	.361
Gerald Perry		L	34	65	79	4	13	4	0	0	5	6	12	0	.165	.215
Darnell Coles	3B22 1B18 OF1	R	33	63	138	13	31	7	0	3	16	16	20	0	.225	.341
Allen Battle	OF32	R	26	61	118	13	32	5	0	2	5	15	26	3	.271	.314
Scott Hemond	C38 2B6	R	29	57	118	11	17	1	0	3	9	12	31	0	.144	.229
David Bell	2B37 3B3	R	22	39	144	13	36	7	2	1	19	4	25	1	.250	.368
Mark Sweeney	1B19 OF1	L	25	37	77	5	21	2	0	1	13	10	15	1	.273	.377
Todd Zeile	1B34	R	29	34	127	16	37	6	0	5	22	18	23	1	.291	.457
Ramon Caraballo	2B24	B	26	34	99	10	20	4	1	2	6	8	33	3	.202	.323
Jose Oliva	3B18 1B2	R	24	22	74	8	9	1	0	2	8	5	24	0	.122	.216
Terry Bradshaw	OF10	L	26	19	44	6	10	1	1	0	2	2	10	1	.227	.295
Ray Giannelli	1B2 OF2	L	29	9	11	0	1	0	0	0	0	3	4	0	.091	.091
Chris Sabo (XJ)	1B2 3B1	R	33	5	13	0	2	1	0	0	3	1	2	1	.154	.231
Tim Hulett	2B2 SS1	R	35	4	11	0	2	0	0	0	0	0	3	0	.182	.182
Manuel Lee (NJ)	2B1	B	30	4	1	1	1	0	0	0	0	0	0	0	1.000	1.000

NAME	T	AGE	W	L	PCT	SV	G	GS	CG	IP	H	BB	SO	SHO	ERA
TOTALS		30	62	81	.434	38	143	143	4	1266	1290	445	842	6	4.09
Rich DeLucia	R	30	8	7	.533	0	56	0	0	82	63	36	76	0	3.39
Allen Watson (AJ)	L	24	7	9	.438	0	21	19	0	114	126	41	49	0	4.96
Mark Petkovsek	R	29	6	6	.500	0	26	21	1	137	136	35	71	1	4.00
Ken Hill	R	29	6	7	.462	0	18	18	0	110	125	45	50	0	5.06
Mike Morgan	R	35	5	6	.455	0	17	17	1	107	114	25	46	0	3.88
Donovan Osborne (EJ)	L	26	4	6	.400	0	19	19	0	113	112	34	82	0	3.81
Jeff Parrett	R	33	4	7	.364	0	59	0	0	77	71	28	71	0	3.64
Tony Fossas	L	37	3	0	1.000	0	58	0	0	37	28	10	40	0	1.47
John Habyan	R	31	3	2	.600	0	31	0	0	41	32	15	35	0	2.88
Rene Arocha (EJ)	R	29	3	5	.375	0	41	0	0	50	55	18	25	0	3.99
Tom Urbani	L	27	3	5	.375	0	24	13	0	83	99	21	52	0	3.70
Brian Barber	R	22	2	1	.667	0	9	4	0	29	31	16	27	0	5.22
Vincente Palacios (SJ)	R	31	2	3	.400	0	20	5	0	40	48	19	34	0	5.80
Danny Jackson (NJ)	L	33	2	12	.143	0	19	19	2	101	120	48	52	1	5.90
Tom Henke	R	37	1	1	.500	36	52	0	0	54	42	18	48	0	1.82
T.J. Mathews	R	25	1	1	.500	2	23	0	0	30	21	11	28	0	1.52
John Frascatore	R	25	1	1	.500	0	14	4	0	33	39	16	21	0	4.41
Alan Benes	R	23	1	2	.333	0	3	3	0	16	24	4	20	0	8.44
Doug Creek	R	26	0	0	—	0	6	0	0	7	2	3	10	0	0.00
Cory Bailey	R	24	0	0	—	0	9	0	0	4	2	2	5	0	7.36
Rich Rodriguez (SJ)	L	32	0	0	—	0	1	0	0	2	0	1	0	0	0.00

PITTSBURGH — 5th 58-86 .403 27   JIM LEYLAND

Name	G by Pos	B	AGE	G	AB	R	H	2B	3B	HR	RBI	BB	SO	SB	BA	SA
TOTALS			28	144	4937	629	1281	245	27	125	587	456	972	84	.259	.396
Mark Johnson	1B70	L	28	79	221	32	46	6	1	13	28	37	66	5	.208	.421
Carlos Garcia	2B92 SS15	R	27	104	367	41	108	24	2	6	50	25	55	8	.294	.420
Jay Bell	SS136 3B3	R	29	138	530	79	139	28	4	13	55	55	110	2	.262	.404
Jeff King	3B84 1B35 2B8 SS22	R	30	122	445	61	118	27	2	18	87	55	63	7	.265	.456
Orlando Merced	OF107 1B35	L	28	132	487	75	146	29	4	15	83	52	74	7	.300	.488
Jacob Brumfield	OF104	R	30	116	402	64	109	23	2	4	26	37	71	22	.271	.368
Al Martin	OF122	L	27	124	439	70	124	25	3	13	41	44	92	20	.282	.442
Mark Parent	C67	R	33	69	233	25	54	9	0	15	33	23	62	0	.232	.464
Nelson Liriano	2B67 3B5 SS1	B	31	107	259	29	74	12	1	5	38	24	34	2	.286	.398
Steve Pegues	OF53	R	27	82	171	17	42	8	0	6	16	4	36	1	.246	.398
Dave Clark (BC)	OF61	L	32	77	196	30	55	6	0	4	24	24	38	3	.281	.372
Midre Cummings	OF41	B	23	59	152	13	37	7	1	2	15	13	30	1	.243	.342
Angelo Encarnacion	C55	R	26	58	159	18	36	7	2	2	10	13	28	1	.226	.333
Kevin Young	3B48 1B6	R	26	56	181	13	42	9	0	6	22	8	53	1	.232	.381
John Wehner	OF23 3B19 SS1 C1	R	28	52	107	13	33	3	0	5	10	10	17	3	.308	.364
Rich Aude	1B32	R	23	42	109	10	27	8	0	2	19	6	20	1	.248	.376
Freddy Garcia	OF10 3B8	R	22	42	57	5	8	1	1	0	1	8	17	0	.140	.193
Don Slaught (LJ)	C33	R	36	35	112	13	34	6	0	0	13	9	8	0	.304	.357
Mackey Sasser	C11	L	32	14	26	1	4	1	0	0	0	0	5	0	.154	.192

NAME	T	AGE	W	L	PCT	SV	G	GS	CG	IP	H	BB	SO	SHO	ERA
TOTALS		27	58	86	.403	29	144	144	11	1275	1407	477	871	7	4.70
Denny Neagle	L	26	13	8	.619	0	31	31	5	210	221	45	150	1	3.43
Esteban Loaiza	R	23	8	9	.471	0	32	31	1	173	205	55	85	0	5.16
Steve Parris	R	27	6	6	.500	0	15	15	1	82	89	33	61	1	5.38
Paul Wagner	R	27	5	16	.238	1	33	25	3	165	174	72	120	1	4.80
Dan Plesac	L	33	4	4	.500	3	58	0	0	60	53	27	57	0	3.58
Dan Miceli	R	24	4	4	.500	21	58	0	0	58	61	28	56	0	4.66
Mike Dyer	R	28	4	5	.444	0	55	0	0	75	81	30	53	0	4.34
Jon Lieber	R	25	4	7	.364	0	21	12	0	73	103	14	45	0	6.32
Jon Ericks	R	28	3	9	.250	0	19	18	1	106	108	50	80	0	4.58
Rick White (EJ)	R	26	2	3	.400	0	19	5	0	55	66	18	29	0	4.75
Jim Gott (EJ)	R	35	2	4	.333	3	25	0	0	31	38	12	19	0	6.03
Mike Maddux	R	33	1	0	1.000	0	9	0	0	9	14	3	4	0	9.00
Jason Christiansen	L	25	1	3	.250	0	63	0	0	56	49	34	53	0	4.15
Jeff McCurry	R	25	1	4	.200	1	55	0	0	61	82	30	27	0	5.02
Lee Hancock	L	29	0	0	—	0	11	0	0	14	10	2	6	0	1.93
Ravelo Manzanillo	L	31	0	0	—	0	5	0	0	4	3	2	1	0	4.91
John Hope	R	24	0	0	—	0	3	2	0	8	4	2	2	0	30.86
Dennis Konuszewski	R	24	0	0	—	0	1	0	0	0.1	3	1	0	0	54.00
Gary Wilson	R	25	0	0	—	0	10	0	0	14	13	5	8	0	5.02
Ramon Morel	R	20	0	1	.000	0	10	0	0	11	16	2	3	0	2.84
Ross Powell	L	27	0	2	.000	0	12	3	0	21	20	10	12	0	5.20
Steve Cooke (SJ) 25															

WEST DIVISION

LOS ANGELES — 1st 78-66 .544   TOMMY LASORDA

Name	G by Pos	B	AGE	G	AB	R	H	2B	3B	HR	RBI	BB	SO	SB	BA	SA
TOTALS			28	144	4942	634	1303	191	31	140	593	468	1023	127	.264	.400
Eric Karros	1B143	R	27	143	551	83	164	29	3	32	105	61	115	4	.298	.535
Delino DeShields	2B113	L	26	127	425	66	109	18	3	8	37	63	83	39	.256	.369
Jose Offerman	SS115	B	26	119	429	69	123	14	6	4	33	69	67	2	.287	.375
Tim Wallach	3B96 1B1	R	37	97	327	24	87	22	2	9	38	27	69	0	.266	.428
Raul Mondesi	OF138	R	24	139	536	91	153	23	6	26	88	33	96	27	.285	.496
Roberto Kelly	OF110	R	30	112	409	47	114	19	2	6	48	15	65	15	.279	.379
Billy Ashley	OF69	R	24	81	215	17	51	5	0	8	27	25	88	0	.237	.372
Mike Piazza	C112	R	26	112	434	82	150	17	0	32	93	39	80	1	.346	.606
Dave Hansen	3B58	L	26	100	181	19	52	10	0	1	14	28	28	0	.287	.359
Chad Fonville	SS38 2B36 OF11	B	24	88	308	41	85	6	1	0	16	23	39	20	.276	.302
Chris Gwynn	OF17 1B2	L	30	67	84	8	18	3	2	1	10	6	23	0	.214	.333
Mitch Webster	OF25	B	36	54	56	6	10	1	1	1	3	4	14	0	.179	.286
Carlos Hernandez	C115	R	28	45	94	3	14	1	0	2	7	4	25	0	.149	.223
Garey Ingram	3B12 2B7 OF4	R	24	44	55	5	11	2	0	3	9	8	3	3	.200	.236
Todd Hollandsworth (BW-BG)	OF37	L	22	41	103	16	24	2	0	5	13	10	29	2	.233	.398
Roger Cedeno	OF36	B	20	40	42	4	10	2	0	0	3	3	10	1	.238	.286
Brett Butler	OF21 3B2 SS2	L	38	39	146	24	40	5	2*	0	13	24	9	11	.274	.336
Rick Parker	OF20 1B1	R	32	27	29	3	8	0	0	0	4	2	4	1	.276	.276
Henry Rodriguez	OF20 1B1	L	27	21	80	6	21	4	1	1	10	5	17	0	.263	.375
Tom Prince	C17	R	30	18	40	3	8	2	1	1	4	4	10	0	.200	.375
Jeff Treadway	3B2 2B1	L	32	17	17	2	2	0	1	0	3	0	2	0	.118	.235
Reggie Williams	OF14	R	29	15	11	2	1	0	0	0	1	2	4	0	.091	.091
Karim Garcia	OF5	L	19	13	20	1	4	0	0	0	0	0	4	0	.200	.200
Mike Busch	3B10 1B2	R	26	13	17	3	4	0	0	1	6	0	7	0	.235	.765
Juan Castro	3B7 SS4	R	23	11	4	0	1	0	0	0	0	0	1	0	.250	.250
Dick Schofield	SS3 3B1	R	32	9	10	0	1	0	0	0	1	3	1	0	.100	.100
Eddie Pye	3B2	R	28	7	8	0	0	0	0	0	0	0	2	0	.000	.000
Noe Munoz	C1	R	27	2	1	0	0	0	0	0	0	0	0	0	.000	.000

NAME	T	AGE	W	L	PCT	SV	G	GS	CG	IP	H	BB	SO	SHO	ERA
TOTALS		26	78	66	.542	37	144	144	16	1295	1188	462	1060	11	3.66
Ramon Martinez	R	27	17	7	.708	0	30	30	4	206	176	81	138	2	3.66
Hideo Nomo	R	26	13	6	.684	0	28	28	4	191	124	78	236	3	2.54
Ismael Valdes	R	21	13	11	.542	1	33	27	6	198	168	51	150	2	3.05
Pedro Astacio	R	25	7	8	.467	0	48	11	1	104	103	29	80	1	4.24
Tom Candiotti	R	37	7	14	.333	0	30	30	1	190	187	58	141	1	3.50
Omar Daal	L	23	4	0	1.000	0	28	0	0	20	29	15	11	0	7.20
Todd Worrell	R	35	4	1	.800	32	59	0	0	62	50	19	61	0	2.02
Kevin Tapani	R	31	4	2	.667	0	13	11	0	57	72	14	43	0	5.05
John Cummings	L	26	3	1	.750	0	35	0	0	39	38	10	21	0	3.00
Todd Williams	R	24	3	2	.500	0	16	0	0	19	19	7	8	0	5.12
Antonio Osuna (GJ)	R	22	2	4	.333	0	39	0	0	45	39	20	46	0	4.43
Felix Rodriguez	R	22	1	1	.500	0	11	0	0	11	11	5	5	0	2.53
Rudy Seanez	R	26	1	3	.250	3	37	0	0	35	39	18	29	0	6.75
Joey Eischen	L	25	0	0	—	0	17	0	0	20	19	11	15	0	3.10
Jim Bruske	R	30	0	0	—	0	9	0	0	10	12	4	5	0	4.50
Jose Parra	R	22	0	0	—	0	1	0	0	4	2	2	7	0	4.50
Chan Ho Park	R	22	0	0	—	0	2	0	0	4	6	7	7	0	7.45
Greg Hansell	R	24	0	1	.000	0	20	0	0	19	29	6	13	0	7.45
Rob Murphy	L	35	0	1	.000	0	6	0	0	5	6	3	2	0	12.60
Mark Guthrie	L	29	0	2	.000	0	24	0	0	19	19	9	19	0	3.66
Willie Banks	R	26	0	0	—	0	6	0	0	29	36	16	23	0	4.50
Darren Dreifort (EJ) 23															

*Butler, also with New York, tied for league lead in triples with 9

COLORADO — 2nd 77-67 .535 1 (Wild Card)   DON BAYLOR

Name	G by Pos	B	AGE	G	AB	R	H	2B	3B	HR	RBI	BB	SO	SB	BA	SA
TOTALS			30	144	4994	785	1406	259	43	200	749	484	943	125	.282	.471
Andres Galarraga	1B142	R	34	143	554	89	155	29	3	31	106	32	146	12	.280	.511
Eric Young	2B77 OF79	R	28	120	366	68	116	21	9	6	36	49	29	35	.317	.473
Walt Weiss	SS136	B	31	137	427	65	111	17	3	1	25	98	57	15	.260	.321
Vinny Castilla	3B137 SS5	R	27	139	527	82	163	34	2	32	90	30	87	2	.309	.564
Larry Walker	OF129	L	28	131	494	96	151	31	5	36	101	49	72	16	.306	.607
Mike Kingery	OF108 1B5	L	34	119	350	66	94	18	4	8	37	45	40	13	.269	.411
Dante Bichette	OF136	R	31	139	579	102	197	38	2	40	128	22	96	13	.340	.620
Joe Girardi	C122	R	30	125	462	63	121	17	2	8	55	29	76	3	.262	.359
Jason Bates	2B82 SS20 3B15	B	24	116	322	42	86	17	4	8	46	42	70	3	.267	.419
John Vander Wal	OF10 1B10	L	29	105	101	15	35	8	1	5	21	16	23	1	.347	.594
Ellis Burks	OF80	R	30	103	278	41	74	10	6	14	49	39	72	7	.266	.496
Jim Tatum	OF2 C1	R	27	34	34	4	8	1	1	0	4	1	7	0	.235	.324
Trenidad Hubbard	OF16	R	31	24	58	13	18	4	0	3	8	6	9	4	.310	.534
Roberto Mejia	2B16	R	26	23	52	5	8	1	0	2	4	2	17	1	.154	.231
Jorge Brito	C18	R	29	18	51	11	9	2	1	2	17	11	20	1	.216	.275
Jayhawk Owens	C16	R	26	18	45	7	11	2	0	2	9	2	15	0	.244	.556
Matt Nokes (RJ)	C3	L	31	10	11	1	2	1	0	0	2	3	1	0	.182	.273
Harvey Pulliam	OF1	R	27	5	5	1	2	1	0	0	1	0	1	0	.400	1.200
Pedro Castellano	3B3	R	25	4	5	0	0	0	0	0	0	2	3	0	.000	.000
Craig Counsell	SS3	L	24	3	1	0	0	0	0	0	0	1	0	0	.000	.000
Quinton McCracken	OF1	B	25	3	1	0	0	0	0	0	0	0	1	0	.000	.000

NAME	T	AGE	W	L	PCT	SV	G	GS	CG	IP	H	BB	SO	SHO	ERA
TOTALS		28	77	67	.535	43	144	144	1	1288	1443	512	891	1	4.97
Kevin Ritz	R	30	11	11	.500	2	31	28	0	173	171	65	120	0	4.21
Bill Swift (SJ)	R	33	9	3	.750	0	19	19	0	106	122	43	68	0	4.94
Roger Bailey	R	24	7	6	.538	0	39	6	0	81	88	39	33	0	4.98
Armando Reynoso (EJ)	R	29	7	7	.500	0	20	18	0	93	116	36	40	0	5.32
Darren Holmes	R	29	6	1	.857	14	68	0	0	67	59	28	61	0	3.24
Curtis Leskanic	R	27	6	3	.667	10	76	0	0	98	83	33	107	0	3.40
Steve Reed	R	30	5	2	.714	3	71	0	0	84	61	21	79	0	2.14
Joe Grahe (SJ)	R	27	4	3	.571	0	17	7	0	59	69	27	27	0	5.08
Juan Acevedo	R	25	4	6	.400	0	17	11	0	66	82	20	40	0	6.44
Bryan Rekar	R	23	4	6	.400	0	15	14	1	85	95	24	60	0	4.98
Lance Painter	L	26	3	0	1.000	0	17	3	0	45	55	10	36	0	4.37
Marvin Freeman	R	32	3	7	.300	0	22	18	0	94	122	41	61	0	5.89
Bret Saberhagen	R	24	2	1	.667	0	9	9	0	43	60	13	29	0	6.28
Mark Thompson	R	24	2	3	.400	0	21	5	0	51	73	22	30	0	6.53
Mike Munoz	L	29	2	4	.333	2	64	0	0	44	54	27	37	0	7.42
Bryan Hickerson	L	31	1	0	1.000	0	37	0	0	33	13	12	0	11.88
Omar Olivares	R	30	0	0	—	0	11	0	0	7	9	7	0	7.39
A.J. Sager	R	30	0	0	—	0	10	0	0	16	32	44	21	15	0	7.36
David Nied (EJ)	R	26	0	0	—	0	4	4	1	11	3	0	20.77
Bruce Ruffin (EJ)	L	31	0	1	.000	11	37	0	0	34	26	19	23	0	2.12

Name	G by Pos	B	AGE	G	AB	R	H	2B	3B	HR	RBI	BB	SO	SB	BA	SA
SAN DIEGO 3rd 70-74 .486 8				**BRUCE BOCHY**												
TOTALS			29	144	4950	668	1345	231	20	116	618	447	872	124	.272	.397
Eddie Williams	1B81	R	30	97	296	35	77	11	1	12	47	23	47	0	.260	.426
Jody Reed	2B130 SS5	R	32	131	445	58	114	18	1	4	40	59	38	6	.256	.328
Adujar Cedeno	SS116 3B1	R	25	120	390	42	82	16	2	6	31	28	92	5	.210	.308
Ken Caminiti	3B143	B	32	143	526	74	159	33	0	26	94	69	94	12	.302	.513
Tony Gwynn	OF133	L	35	135	535	82	197	33	1	9	90	35	15	17	.368	.484
Steve Finley	OF138	L	30	139	562	104	167	23	8	10	44	59	62	36	.297	.420
Bip Roberts (LJ)	OF50 OF79 1B22	B	31	73	296	40	90	14	0	2	25	17	36	20	.304	.372
Brad Ausmus	C100 1B1	R	26	103	328	44	96	16	4	5	34	31	56	16	.293	.412
Scott Livingstone	1B43 3B13 2B4	L	29	99	196	26	66	15	0	5	32	15	22	2	.337	.490
Melvin Nieves	OF79 1B29	B	23	98	234	32	48	6	1	14	38	19	88	2	.205	.419
Roberto Petagine	1B51 OF2	L	24	89	124	15	29	8	0	3	17	26	41	0	.234	.371
Phil Clark	OF34 1B2	R	27	75	97	12	21	3	0	2	7	8	18	0	.216	.309
Brian Johnson	C55 1B2	R	27	68	207	20	52	9	0	3	29	11	39	0	.251	.338
Ray Holbert (NJ)	SS30 2B7 OF1	R	24	63	73	11	13	2	1	2	5	8	20	4	.178	.315
Phil Plantier	OF39	L	26	54	148	21	38	4	0	5	19	17	29	1	.257	.385
Archi Cianfrocco	1B30 SS15 OF7 3B3 2B3	R	28	51	118	22	31	7	0	5	31	11	28	0	.263	.449
Marc Newfield	OF19	R	22	21	55	6	17	5	1	1	7	2	8	0	.309	.491
Ray McDavid	OF7	L	23	11	17	2	3	0	0	0	0	0	6	1	.176	.176
Tim Hyers	1B1	L	23	6	5	0	0	0	0	0	0	0	0	0	.000	.000
Billy Bean	OF4	L	31	4	7	1	0	0	0	0	0	0	1	0	.000	.000
Luis Lopez (EJ) 24																
SAN FRANCISCO 4th 67-77 .465 11				**DUSTY BAKER**												
TOTALS			28	144	4971	652	1256	229	33	152	610	472	1060	138	.253	.404
Mark Carreon	1B81 OF22	R	31	117	396	53	119	24	0	17	65	23	37	0	.301	.490
Robby Thompson	2B91	R	33	95	336	51	75	15	0	8	23	42	76	1	.223	.339
Royce Clayton	SS116	R	25	138	509	56	124	29	3	5	58	38	109	24	.244	.342
Matt Williams (BF)	3B74	R	29	76	283	53	95	17	1	23	65	30	58	2	.336	.647
Glenallen Hill	OF125	R	30	132	497	71	131	29	4	24	86	39	98	25	.264	.483
Darren Lewis	OF73	R	27	74	309	47	78	10	3	1	16	17	37	21	.252	.314
Barry Bonds	OF143	L	30	144	506	109	149	30	7	33	104	120	83	31	.294	.577
Kirt Manwaring	C118	R	29	118	379	21	95	15	2	4	36	27	72	1	.251	.332
John Patterson	2B53	B	28	95	205	27	42	5	3	1	14	14	41	4	.205	.273
J.R. Phillips	1B79 OF1	L	25	92	231	27	45	9	0	9	28	19	69	1	.195	.351
Steve Scarsone	3B50 2B13 1B11	R	29	80	233	33	62	10	3	11	29	18	82	3	.266	.476
Mike Benjamin	3B43 SS16 2B8	R	29	68	186	19	41	6	0	3	12	8	51	11	.220	.301
Jeff Reed	C42	L	32	66	113	12	30	2	0	0	9	20	17	0	.265	.283
Tom Lampkin	C17 OF6	L	31	65	76	8	21	2	0	1	9	9	8	2	.276	.342
Deion Sanders	OF52	L	27	52	214	29	61	9	5	5	18	18	42	8	.285	.444
Rikkert Faneyte	OF34	R	26	46	86	7	17	4	1	0	4	11	27	1	.198	.267
Mark Leonard	OF6	L	30	14	21	4	4	1	0	1	4	5	2	0	.190	.381
Marvin Benard	OF7	L	25	13	34	5	13	2	0	1	4	1	7	1	.382	.529
Dave McCarty	OF4 1B2	L	25	12	20	1	5	1	0	0	2	2	4	1	.250	.300
Rich Aurilia	SS6	R	23	9	19	4	9	3	0	2	4	1	2	1	.474	.947
Todd Benzinger	1B5	B	32	9	10	2	2	0	0	1	2	2	3	0	.200	.500

NAME	T	AGE	W	L	PCT	SV	G	GS	CG	IP	H	BB	SO	SHO	ERA
		26	70	74	.486	35	144	144	6	1285	1242	512	1047	10	4.13
Andy Ashby	R	27	12	10	.545	0	31	31	2	193	180	62	150	2	2.94
Fernando Valenzuela	L	34	8	3	.727	0	29	15	0	90	101	34	57	0	4.98
Trevor Hoffman	R	27	7	4	.636	31	55	0	0	53	48	14	52	0	3.88
Willie Blair	R	29	7	5	.583	0	40	12	0	114	112	45	83	0	4.34
Joey Hamilton	R	24	6	9	.400	0	31	30	2	204	189	56	123	2	3.08
Scott Sanders (EJ)	R	26	5	5	.500	0	17	15	1	90	79	31	88	0	4.30
Doug Bochtler	R	24	4	4	.500	1	34	0	0	45	38	19	45	0	3.57
1 Andy Benes	R	27	4	7	.364	0	19	19	1	119	121	45	126	1	4.17
Glenn Dishman	L	24	4	8	.333	0	19	16	0	97	104	34	43	0	5.01
Dustin Hermanson	R	22	3	1	.750	0	26	0	0	32	35	22	19	0	6.82
Brian Williams	R	26	3	10	.231	0	44	6	0	72	79	38	75	0	6.00
2 Ron Villone	L	25	2	1	.667	1	19	0	0	26	24	11	37	0	4.21
Bryce Florie	R	25	2	2	.500	1	47	0	0	69	49	38	68	0	3.01
Andres Berumen	R	23	2	3	.400	1	37	0	0	44	37	36	42	0	5.68
Tim Worrell (EJ)	R	27	1	0	1.000	0	9	0	0	13	16	6	13	0	4.73
1 Jeff Tabaka	L	31	0	0	—	0	10	0	0	6	10	5	6	0	7.11
1 Bill Krueger	L	37	0	0	—	0	6	0	0	8	13	4	6	0	7.04
Donnie Elliott (SJ)	R	26	0	0	—	0	1	0	0	2	2	1	3	0	0.00
Tim Mauser	R	28	0	1	.000	0	5	0	0	6	4	9	9	0	9.53
Marc Kroon	R	22	0	1	.000	0	2	0	0	2	1	2	2	0	10.80
		29	67	77	.465	34	144	144	12	1294	1368	505	801	5	4.86
Mark Leiter	R	32	10	12	.455	0	30	29	7	196	185	55	129	1	3.82
William VanLandingham (VJ)	R	24	6	3	.667	0	18	18	1	123	124	40	95	0	3.67
Jamie Brewington	R	23	6	4	.600	0	13	13	0	75	68	45	45	0	4.54
Chris Hook	R	26	5	1	.833	0	45	0	0	52	55	29	40	0	5.50
1 Mark Portugal	R	32	5	5	.500	0	17	17*	1	104	106	34	63	0	4.15
Rod Beck	R	26	5	6	.455	33	60	0	0	59	60	21	42	0	4.45
Terry Mulholland (EJ)	L	32	5	13	.278	0	29	24	2	149	190	38	65	0	5.80
Shawn Barton	L	32	4	1	.800	1	52	0	0	44	37	19	22	0	4.26
1 Dave Burba	R	28	4	2	.667	0	37	0	0	43	38	25	46	0	4.98
Sergio Valdez	R	30	4	5	.444	0	13	11	1	66	78	17	29	0	4.75
Scott Service	R	28	3	1	.750	0	28	0	0	31	18	20	30	0	3.19
Trevor Wilson (SJ)	L	29	3	4	.429	0	17	17	0	83	82	38	38	0	3.92
Jose Bautista	R	30	3	8	.273	0	52	6	0	101	120	26	45	0	6.44
Joe Rosselli (SJ)	L	22	2	1	.667	0	9	5	0	30	39	20	7	0	8.70
Mark Dewey (VJ)	R	30	1	0	1.000	0	27	0	0	32	30	17	32	0	3.13
Steve Mintz	R	26	1	2	.333	0	14	0	0	19	12	7	7	0	7.45
Pat Gomez (VJ)	L	27	0	0	—	0	18	0	0	14	16	12	15	0	5.14
Enrique Burgos	R	29	0	0	—	1	8	0	0	8	14	6	12	0	8.64
2 John Roper	R	23	0	0	—	0	1	0	0	1	2	0	0	0	27.00
Carlos Valdez	R	23	0	1	.000	0	11	0	0	15	19	8	7	0	6.14
1 Steve Frey	L	31	0	0	—	0	9	0	0	6	7	2	5	0	4.26
2 Luis Aquino (TJ)	R	31	0	1	.000	0	5	0	0	5	10	2	4	0	14.40
1 Salomon Torres	R	23	0	1	.000	0	4	1	0	8	13	7	2	0	9.00
Kenny Greer	R	28	0	2	.000	0	5	0	0	12	15	5	7	0	5.25
Shawn Estes	L	22	0	3	.000	0	3	3	0	17	16	5	14	0	6.75
Kevin Rogers (SJ) 26															

*Portugal, also with Cincinnati, tied for league lead in Games Started with 31

DIVISION SERIES

LINE SCORES

Team	1	2	3	4	5	6	7	8	9		R	H	E
DIVISION SERIES: ATLANTA 3 COLORADO 1													

Game 1   October 3 at Colorado

| ATL | 0 | 0 | 1 | 0 | 0 | 2 | 0 | 1 | 1 | | 5 | 12 | 1 |
| COL | 0 | 0 | 3 | 0 | 0 | 1 | 0 | | | | 4 | 13 | 4 |

Maddux, McMichael (8), **Pena** (8), Wohlers (9)   Ritz, Reed (6), Ruffin (7), Munoz (8), Holmes (8), **Leskanic** (9)

Game 2   October 4 at Colorado

| ATL | 1 | 0 | 1 | 1 | 0 | 0 | 0 | 0 | 4 | | 7 | 13 | 1 |
| COL | 0 | 0 | 0 | 0 | 3 | 0 | 1 | 0 | | | 4 | 8 | 2 |

Glavine, Avery (8), **Pena** (8), Wohlers (9)   Painter, Reed (6), Ruffin (7), Leskanic (8), **Munoz** (9), Holmes (9)

Game 3   October 6 at Atlanta

| COL | 1 | 0 | 2 | 0 | 0 | 2 | 0 | 0 | 2 | | 7 | 9 | 0 |
| ATL | 0 | 0 | 0 | 3 | 0 | 0 | 1 | 0 | 1 | | 5 | 11 | 0 |

Swift, Reed (7), Munoz (7), Leskanic (7), Ruffin (8), **Holmes** (9), Thompson (10)   Smoltz, Clontz (6), Borbon (8), McMichael (9), **Wohlers** (10), Mercker (10)

Game 4   October 7 at Atlanta

| COL | 0 | 0 | 3 | 0 | 0 | 1 | 0 | 0 | 0 | | 4 | 11 | 1 |
| ATL | 0 | 0 | 4 | 2 | 1 | 3 | 0 | X | | | 10 | 15 | 0 |

Saberhagen, Ritz (5), Munoz (6), Reynoso (7), Ruffin (8)   **Maddux**, Pena (8)

COMPOSITE BATTING

NAME	POS	G	AB	R	H	2B	3B	HR	RBI	BA
ATLANTA										
TOTALS		4	154	27	51	8	0	7	24	.331
Grissom	CF	4	21	5	11	2	0	3	4	.524
Lemke	2B	4	19	3	4	1	0	0	1	.211
Jones	3B	4	18	4	7	0	0	2	4	.389
McGriff	1B	4	18	4	6	0	0	2	4	.333
Klesko	LF	4	15	5	7	1	0	0	1	.467
Justice	RF	4	13	2	3	1	0	0	2	.231
Lopez	C	3	9	0	4	0	0	0	3	.444
Blauser	SS	3	6	0	0	0	0	0	0	.000
Maddux	P	2	6	1	1	0	0	0	0	.167
Belliard	SS	4	5	1	0	0	0	0	0	.000
Devereaux	LF	4	5	1	1	0	0	0	0	.200
O'Brien	C	2	5	0	1	0	0	0	0	.200
Smith	PH	4	3	0	2	1	0	0	1	.667
Polonia	PH	3	3	0	1	0	0	0	2	.333
Mordecai	SS	2	3	1	2	1	0	0	2	.667
Glavine	P	1	3	0	1	0	0	0	0	.333
Smoltz	P	1	2	0	0	0	0	0	0	.000
Pena	P	3								—
Wohlers	P	4								—
McMichael	P	2								—
Clontz	P	1								—
Borbon	P	1								—
Avery	P	1								—
Mercker	P	1								—
COLORADO										
TOTALS		4	143	19	41	7	0	6	18	.287
Galarraga	1B	4	18	1	5	1	0	0	2	.278
Bichette	LF	4	17	6	10	3	0	1	2	.588
Young	2B	4	16	3	7	1	0	1	2	.438
Girardi	C	4	16	0	2	0	0	0	0	.125
Castilla	3B	4	15	3	7	1	0	3	6	.467
Walker	RF	4	14	3	3	0	0	1	2	.214
Weiss	SS	4	12	1	2	0	0	0	0	.167
Kingery	CF	4	10	1	2	0	0	0	0	.200
Burks	CF	4	6	1	2	1	0	0	0	.333
Bates	3B	4	4	0	1	0	0	0	0	.250
Vander Wal	PH	4	3	0	0	0	0	0	0	.000
Swift	P	1	3	0	0	0	0	0	0	.000
Hubbard	PH-PR	2	2	0	0	0	0	0	0	.000
Painter	P-PH	2	2	0	0	0	0	0	0	.000
Ritz	P	2	2	0	0	0	0	0	0	.000
Owens	C	1	1	0	0	0	0	0	0	.000
Saberhagen	P	1	1	0	0	0	0	0	0	.000
Ruffin	P	4								—
Munoz	P	3								—
Leskanic	P	3								—
Reed	P	3								—
Holmes	P	3								—
Thompson	P	1								—
Reynoso	P	1								—

COMPOSITE PITCHING

NAME	G	IP	H	BB	SO	W	L	SV	ERA
ATLANTA									
TOTALS	4	37	41	9	29	3	1	2	4.38
Maddux	2	14	19	2	7	1	0	0	4.50
Glavine	1	7	5	1	3	0	0	0	2.57
Smoltz	1	5.2	5	1	6	0	0	0	7.94
Pena	3	3	3	1	2	2	0	0	0.00
Wohlers	4	2.2	6	2	4	0	1	2	6.75
McMichael	2	1.1	1	1	0	0	0	0	6.75
Clontz	1	1.1	0	0	2	0	0	0	0.00
Borbon	1	1.1	0	1	3	0	0	0	0.00
Avery	1	0.2	1	0	1	0	0	0	13.50
Mercker	1	0.1	0	0	0	0	0	0	0.00
COLORADO									
TOTALS	4	36	51	12	27	1	3	1	5.75
Ritz	2	7	12	3	5	0	0	0	7.71
Swift	1	6	7	2	3	0	0	0	6.00
Painter	1	5	5	2	4	0	0	0	5.40
Saberhagen	1	4	7	3	3	0	1	0	11.25
Ruffin	4	3.1	3	2	2	0	0	0	2.70
Leskanic	3	3	3	0	4	0	1	0	6.00
Reed	3	2.2	1	3	0	0	0	0	0.00
Holmes	3	1.2	6	0	2	1	0	0	13.50
Munoz	4	1.1	4	1	1	0	1	0	13.50
Thompson	1	1	1	0	0	0	0	0	0.00
Reynoso	1	1	2	0	1	0	0	0	0.00

LINE SCORES

Team	1	2	3	4	5	6	7	8	9	10	11			R	H	E

DIVISION SERIES: CINCINNATI 3 : LOS ANGELES 0

Game 1   October 3 at Los Angeles

	1	2	3	4	5	6	7	8	9			R	H	E
CIN	4	0	0	0	3	0	0	0	0			7	12	0
LA	0	0	0	0	1	1	0	0	0			2	8	0

Schourek, Jackson (8)   **Martinez**, Cummings (5)
Brantley (9)   Astacio (6), Guthrie (8), Osuna (9)

Game 1   October 4 at Los Angeles

	1	2	3	4	5	6	7	8	9			R	H	E
CIN	0	0	0	2	0	0	0	1	2			5	6	0
LA	1	0	0	1	0	0	0	0	2			4	14	2

Smiley, **Burba** (7), Jackson (8),   Valdes, **Osuna** (8), Tapani (9)
Brantley (9)   Guthrie (9), Astacio (9)

Game 3   October 6 at Cincinnati

	1	2	3	4	5	6	7	8	9			R	H	E
LA	0	0	0	1	0	0	0	0	0			1	9	1
CIN	0	0	2	1	0	4	3	0	X			10	11	2

Nomo, Tapani (6), Guthrie (6),   **Wells**, Jackson (7), Brantley (9)
Astacio (6), Cummings (7)
Osuna (7)

NATIONAL LEAGUE CHAMPIONSHIP: ATLANTA 4 : CINCINNATI 0

Game 1   October 10 at Cincinnati

	1	2	3	4	5	6	7	8	9	10	11		R	H	E
ATL	0	0	0	0	0	0	0	0	1	0	1		2	7	0
CIN	0	0	0	0	0	0	0	0	1	0	0		1	8	0

Glavine, Pena (8), **Wohlers** (9),   Schourek, Brantley (9),
Clontz (11), Avery (11),   **Jackson** (11)
McMichaels (11)

Game 2   October 11 at Cincinnati

	1	2	3	4	5	6	7	8	9	10			R	H	E
ATL	1	0	0	1	0	0	0	0	0	4			6	11	1
CIN	0	0	0	2	0	0	0	0	0	0			2	9	1

Smoltz, Pena (8)   Smiley, Burba (6), Jackson (8),
McMichael (9), Wohlers (9)   Brantley (9), Portugal (10)

Game 3   October 13 at Atlanta

	1	2	3	4	5	6	7	8	9			R	H	E
CIN	0	0	0	0	0	0	1	1				2	8	0
ATL	0	0	0	0	0	3	2	0	X			5	12	1

Wells, Hernandez (7),   **Maddux**, Wohlers (9)
Carrasco (7)

Game 4   October 14 at Atlanta

	1	2	3	4	5	6	7	8	9			R	H	E
CIN	0	0	0	0	0	0	0	0				0	3	1
ATL	0	0	1	0	0	0	5	0	X			6	12	1

Schourek, Jackson (7),   **Avery**, McMichael (7),
Burba (7)   Pena (8), Wohlers (9)

DIVISION SERIES

COMPOSITE BATTING

NAME	POS	G	AB	R	H	2B	3B	HR	RBI	BA
CINCINNATI										
TOTALS		3	104	22	29	6	0	5	22	.279
Larkin	SS	3	13	2	5	0	0	0	1	.385
Gant	LF	3	13	3	3	0	0	1	2	.231
Sanders	RF	3	13	3	2	1	0	1		.154
Morris	1B	3	10	5	5	1	0	0	2	.500
Boone	2B	3	10	4	3	1	0	1	1	.300
Howard	CF	3	10	0	1	1	0	0	0	.100
Santiago	C	3	9	2	3	0	0	1	3	.333
Branson	3B	3	7	0	2	1	0	0	2	.286
D. Lewis	CF	3	3	0	0	0	0	0	0	.000
Walton	LF-CF	3	3	0	0	0	0	0	0	.000
Duncan	2B	2	3	1	2	0	0	0	1	.667
Wells	P	1	3	0	1	0	0	0	0	.333
M. Lewis	3B	3	2	2	1	0	0	1	5	.500
Schourek	P	1	2	0	0	0	0	0	0	.000
Smiley	P	1	2	0	0	0	0	0	0	.000
Jackson	P	3	1	0	1	1	0	0	3	1.000
Brantley	P	3	0	0	0	0	0	0	0	—
Burba	P	1	0	0	0	0	0	0	0	—

NAME	POS	G	AB	R	H	2B	3B	HR	RBI	BA
LOS ANGELES										
TOTALS		3	111	7	31	2	0	3	7	.279
Butler	CF	3	15	1	4	0	0	0	1	.267
Piazza	C	3	14	1	3	1	0	1	1	.214
Karros	1B	3	12	3	6	1	0	2	4	.500
Fonville	SS	3	12	1	6	0	0	0	0	.500
DeShields	2B	3	12	1	3	0	0	0	0	.250
Wallach	3B	3	12	0	1	0	0	0	0	.083
Kelly	LF	3	11	0	4	0	0	0	0	.364
Mondesi	RF	3	9	0	2	0	0	0	1	.222
Hansen	PH	3	3	0	2	0	0	0	0	.667
Valdes	P	1	3	0	0	0	0	0	0	.000
Hollandsworth	RF	2	2	0	0	0	0	0	0	.000
Webster	PH	2	2	0	0	0	0	0	0	.000
Nomo	P	1	2	0	0	0	0	0	0	.000
Gwynn	PH	1	1	0	0	0	0	0	0	.000
Martinez	P	1	1	0	0	0	0	0	0	.000
Astacio	P	3	0	0	0	0	0	0	0	—
Osuna	P	3	0	0	0	0	0	0	0	—
Guthrie	P	3	0	0	0	0	0	0	0	—
Cummings	P	2	0	0	0	0	0	0	0	—
Tapani	P	2	0	0	0	0	0	0	0	—
Offerman	PR	1	0	0	0	0	0	0	0	—

COMPOSITE PITCHING

NAME	G	IP	H	BB	SO	W	L	SV	ERA
CINCINNATI									
TOTALS	3	27	31	5	17	3	0	1	2.00
Schourek	1	7	5	3	5	1	0	0	2.57
Wells	1	6.1	6	1	8	1	0	0	0.00
Smiley	1	6	9	0	1	0	0	0	3.00
Jackson	3	3.2	4	0	1	0	0	0	0.00
Brantley	3	3	5	0	2	0	0	1	6.00
Burba	1	1	2	1	0	1	0	0	0.00

NAME	G	IP	H	BB	SO	W	L	SV	ERA
LOS ANGELES									
TOTALS	3	26	29	13	28	0	3	0	6.92
Valdes	1	7	3	1	6	0	0	0	0.00
Nomo	1	5	7	2	6	0	1	0	9.00
Martinez	1	4.1	10	2	3	0	1	0	14.54
Astacio	3	3.1	1	0	5	0	0	0	.000
Osuna	3	3.1	3	1	3	0	1	0	2.70
Guthrie	3	1.1	2	1	1	0	0	0	6.75
Cummings	2	1.1	3	2	3	0	0	0	20.25
Tapani	2	0.1	0	4	1	0	0	0	81.00

NATIONAL LEAGUE CHAMPIONSHIP

COMPOSITE BATTING

NAME	POS	G	AB	R	H	2B	3B	HR	RBI	BA
ATLANTA										
TOTALS		4	149	19	42	6	1	4	17	.282
Grissom	OF	4	19	2	5	0	1	0	0	.263
Lemke	2B	4	18	2	3	0	0	0	1	.167
Jones	3B	4	16	3	7	0	0	1	3	.438
McGriff	1B	4	16	5	7	4	0	0	0	.438
Lopez	C	4	14	2	5	1	0	1	3	.357
Devereaux	LF-RF	4	13	2	4	1	0	1	5	.308
Belliard	SS	4	11	1	3	0	0	0	0	.273
Justice	RF	3	11	1	3	0	0	0	0	.273
Klesko	LF	4	7	0	0	0	0	1	0	.000
O'Brien	C	2	5	1	2	0	0	0	0	.400
Blauser	SS	1	4	0	0	0	0	0	0	.000
Smoltz	P	1	3	0	1	0	0	0	0	.333
Maddux	P	1	3	0	0	0	0	0	0	.000
Polonia	LF	3	2	0	1	0	0	0	1	.500
Avery	P	2	2	0	1	0	0	0	0	.500
Mordecai	SS	2	2	0	0	0	0	0	0	.000
Smith	PH	2	2	0	0	0	0	0	0	.000
Glavine	P	1	1	0	0	0	0	0	0	.000
Wohlers	P	4	0	0	0	0	0	0	0	—
Pena	P	3	0	0	0	0	0	0	0	—
McMichael	P	3	0	0	0	0	0	0	0	—
Clontz	P	1	0	0	0	0	0	0	0	—

NAME	POS	G	AB	R	H	2B	3B	HR	RBI	BA
CINCINNATI										
TOTALS		4	134	5	28	5	1	0	4	.209
Larkin	SS	4	18	1	7	2	1	0	0	.389
Gant	LF	4	16	1	3	0	0	0	0	.188
Sanders	RF	4	16	0	2	0	0	0	0	.125
Boone	2B	4	14	1	3	0	0	0	0	.214
Santiago	C	4	13	0	3	0	0	0	0	.231
Morris	1B	4	12	0	2	1	0	0	1	.167
Branson	3B	4	9	2	1	1	0	0	0	.111
Howard	CF	4	8	0	2	1	0	0	1	.250
Walton	CF-LF	2	7	0	0	0	0	0	0	.000
Schourek	Pos	2	5	0	0	0	0	0	0	.000
M. Lewis	3B	2	4	0	1	0	0	0	0	.250
Duncan	1B	3	3	0	0	0	0	0	0	.000
Harris	PH	3	2	0	2	0	0	0	1	1.000
Taubensee	C	2	2	0	1	0	0	0	0	.500
Wells	P	1	2	0	1	0	0	0	0	.500
D. Lewis	CF	2	1	0	0	0	0	0	0	.000
Anthony	PH	2	1	0	0	0	0	0	0	.000
Smiley	P	1	1	0	0	0	0	0	0	.000
Jackson	P	3	0	0	0	0	0	0	0	—
Burba	P	2	0	0	0	0	0	0	0	—
Brantley	P	2	0	0	0	0	0	0	0	—
Carrasco	P	1	0	0	0	0	0	0	0	—
Portugal	P	1	0	0	0	0	0	0	0	—
Hernandez	P	1	0	0	0	0	0	0	0	—

COMPOSITE PITCHING

NAME	G	IP	H	BB	SO	W	L	SV	ERA
ATLANTA									
TOTALS	4	39	28	12	31	4	0	1	1.15
Maddux	1	8	7	2	4	1	0	0	1.12
Glavine	1	7	7	2	5	0	0	0	1.29
Smoltz	1	7	7	2	2	0	0	0	2.57
Avery	2	6	2	4	6	1	0	0	0.00
Wohlers	4	5	2	0	8	1	0	0	1.80
Pena	3	3	2	1	4	0	0	0	0.00
McMichael	3	2.2	0	1	2	1	0	1	0.00
Clontz	1	0.1	1	0	0	0	0	0	0.00

NAME	G	IP	H	BB	SO	W	L	SV	ERA
CINCINNATI									
TOTALS	4	37	42	16	22	0	4	0	4.62
Schourek	2	14.1	14	3	13	0	1	0	1.26
Wells	1	6	8	2	3	0	1	0	4.50
Smiley	1	5	5	0	1	0	0	0	3.60
Burba	2	3.2	3	4	0	0	0	0	0.00
Brantley	2	2.2	0	2	1	0	0	0	0.00
Jackson	3	2.1	5	4	1	0	1	0	23.14
Carrasco	1	1.1	1	0	3	0	0	0	0.00
Portugal	1	1	3	1	0	0	1	0	36.00
Hernandez	1	0.2	3	0	0	0	0	0	27.00

LINE SCORES

Team	1	2	3	4	5	6	7	8	9	10	11		R	H	E

WORLD SERIES: ATLANTA (NL) 4 : CLEVELAND (AL) 2

Game 1   October 21 at Atlanta

CLE	1	0	0	0	0	0	0	0	1				2	2	0
ATL	0	1	0	0	0	3	0	X					3	3	2

Hershiser, Assenmacher (7),   Maddux
Tavarez (7), Embree (8)

Game 2   October 22 at Atlanta

CLE	0	2	0	0	0	0	1	0	0				3	6	2
ATL	0	0	2	0	0	2	0	0	X				4	8	2

Martinez, Embree (6), Poole (7),   Glavine, McMichael (7),
Tavarez (8)   Pena (7), Wohlers (8)

Game 3   October 24 at Cleveland

ATL	1	0	0	0	0	1	1	3	0	0	0		6	12	1
CLE	2	0	2	0	0	1	0	0	1	0	1		7	12	2

Smoltz, Clontz (3), Mercher (5),   Nagy, Assenmacher (8),
McMichael (7), Wohlers (8),   Tavarez (8), Mesa (9)
Pena (11)

Game 4   October 25 at Cleveland

ATL	0	0	0	0	0	1	3	0	1				5	11	1
CLE	0	0	0	0	0	1	0	0	1				2	6	0

Avery, McMichael (7), Wohlers (9)   Hill, Assenmacher (7),
Borbon (9)   Tavarez (8), Embree (8)

Game 5   October 26 at Cleveland

ATL	0	0	0	1	1	0	0	0	2				4	7	0
CLE	2	0	0	0	0	2	0	1	X				5	8	1

Maddux, Clontz (8)   Hershiser, Mesa (9)

Game 6   October 28 at Atlanta

CLE	0	0	0	0	0	0	0	0	0				0	1	1
ATL	0	0	0	0	0	1	0	0	X				1	6	0

Martinez, Poole (5), Hill (7),   Glavine, Wohlers (9)
Embree (7), Tavarez (8),
Assenmacher (8)

COMPOSITE BATTING

NAME	POS	G	AB	R	H	2B	3B	HR	RBI	BA
ATLANTA										
TOTALS		6	193	23	47	10	0	8	23	.244
Grissom	CF	6	25	3	9	1	0	0	1	.360
McGriff	1B	6	23	5	6	2	0	2	3	.261
Lemke	2B	6	22	1	6	0	0	0	0	.273
Jones	3B	6	21	3	6	3	0	0	1	.286
Justice	RF	6	20	3	5	1	0	1	5	.250
Lopez	C	6	17	1	3	2	0	1	3	.176
Klesko	LF-DH	6	16	4	5	0	0	3	4	.313
Belliard	SS	6	16	0	0	0	0	0	0	.000
Polonia	LF	6	14	3	4	1	0	1	4	.286
Devereaux	LF-RF	5	4	0	1	0	0	0	1	.250
Glavine	P	2	4	0	0	0	0	0	0	.000
Mordecai	SS	2	3	0	1	0	0	0	0	.333
O'Brien	C	2	3	0	0	0	0	0	0	.000
Maddux	P	2	3	0	0	0	0	0	0	.000
Smith	PH	3	2	0	1	0	0	0	0	.500
Wohlers	P	4	0	0	0	0	0	0	0	—
McMichael	P	3	0	0	0	0	0	0	0	—
Clontz	P	2	0	0	0	0	0	0	0	—
Pena	P	2	0	0	0	0	0	0	0	—
Avery	P	1	0	0	0	0	0	0	0	—
Smoltz	P	1	0	0	0	0	0	0	0	—
Mercker	P	1	0	0	0	0	0	0	0	—
Borbon	P	1	0	0	0	0	0	0	0	—
CLEVELAND										
TOTALS		6	195	19	35	7	1	5	17	.179
Baerga	2B	6	26	1	5	2	0	0	4	.192
Lofton	CF	6	25	6	5	1	0	0	0	.200
Vizquel	SS	6	23	3	4	0	1	0	1	.174
Thome	3B	6	19	1	4	1	0	1	2	.211
Murray	1B-DH	6	19	1	2	0	0	1	3	.105
Ramirez	RF	6	18	2	4	0	0	1	2	.222
Belle	LF	6	17	4	4	0	0	2	4	.235
Alomar	C	5	15	0	3	2	0	0	1	.200
Sorrento	1B	5	11	0	2	1	0	0	0	.182
Pena	C	2	6	0	1	0	0	0	0	.167
Perry	1B	3	5	0	0	0	0	0	0	.000
Martinez	P	2	3	0	0	0	0	0	0	.000
Espinoza	3B	2	2	1	1	0	0	0	0	.500
Amaro	RF	2	2	0	0	0	0	0	0	.000
Hershiser	P	2	2	0	0	0	0	0	0	.000
Kirby	RF	2	1	0	0	0	0	0	0	.000
Poole	P	2	1	0	0	0	0	0	0	.000
Tavarez	P	5	0	0	0	0	0	0	0	—
Assenmacher	P	4	0	0	0	0	0	0	0	—
Embree	P	4	0	0	0	0	0	0	0	—
Hill	P	2	0	0	0	0	0	0	0	—
Mesa	P	2	0	0	0	0	0	0	0	—
Nagy	P	1	0	0	0	0	0	0	0	—

COMPOSITE PITCHING

NAME	G	IP	H	BB	SO	W	L	SV	ERA
ATLANTA									
TOTALS	6	54	35	25	37	4	2	3	2.67
Maddux	2	16	9	3	8	1	1	0	2.25
Glavine	2	14	4	6	11	2	0	0	1.29
Avery	1	6	3	5	3	1	0	0	1.50
Wohlers	4	5	4	3	3	0	0	2	1.80
McMichael	3	3.1	3	2	2	0	0	0	2.70
Clontz	2	3.1	2	0	2	0	0	0	2.70
Smoltz	1	2.1	6	2	4	0	0	0	15.43
Mercker	1	2	1	2	2	0	0	0	4.50
Pena	2	1	3	2	0	0	1	0	9.00
Borbon	1	1	0	2	0	0	0	0	0.00
CLEVELAND									
TOTALS	6	53	47	25	34	2	4	1	3.57
Hershiser	2	14	8	4	13	1	1	0	2.57
Martinez	2	10.1	12	8	5	0	1	0	3.48
Nagy	1	7	8	1	4	0	0	0	6.43
Hill	2	6.1	7	4	1	0	1	0	4.26
Tavarez	5	4.1	3	2	1	0	0	0	0.00
Mesa	2	4	5	1	4	1	0	1	4.50
Embree	4	3.1	2	2	2	0	0	0	2.70
Poole	2	2.1	1	0	1	0	1	0	3.86
Assenmacher	4	1.1	1	3	3	0	0	0	6.75

MISCELLANEOUS 1995 INDIVIDUAL LEADERS

BATTING

On Base Average

American League		National League	
1 E. Martinez, Sea.	.479	1 Bonds, S.F.	.431
2 Thomas, Chi.	.454	2 Biggio, Hou.	.406
3 Thome, Cle.	.438	3 Gwynn, S.D.	.404
4 Salmon, Cal.	.429	4 Weiss, Col.	.403
5 Davis, Cal.	.429	5 Piazza, L.A.	.400
6 Knoblauch, Min.	.424	6 Bagwell, Hou.	.399
7 Naehring, Bos.	.415	7 Sanders, Cin.	.397
8 Boggs, N.Y.	.412	8 Grace, Chi	.395
9 Henderson, Oak.	.407	9 Larkin, Cin.	.394
10 Baines, Bal.	.403	10 Offerman, L.A.	.389

Caught Stealing

American League		National League	
1 Nixon, Tex.	21	1 Veras, Fla.	21
2 Knoblauch, Min.	20	2 D. Lewis, S.F. + Cin.	18
3 Goodwin, K.C.	20	3 DeShields, L.A.	14
4 Coleman, K.C.-Sea.	16	4 Brumfield, Pit.	12
5 Curtis, Det.	15	5 Young, Col.	12
Lofton, Cle.	15	Sanders, Cin.	12
		Finley, S.D.	12

Stolen Base Percentage
(Minimum 20 Attempts)

American League		National League	
1 Amaral, Sea.	91	1 Larkin, Cin.	91
2 Alomar, Tor.	91	2 Roberts, S.D.	91
3 Javier, Oak.	88	3 Tarasco, Mon.	89
4 Johnson, Chi.	87	4 Lansing, Mon.	87
5 Goodwin, Bal.	85	5 Mondesi, L.A.	87

On Base Average plus Slugging Average

American League		National League	
1 E. Martinez, Sea.	1.107	1 Bonds, S.F.	1.008
2 Belle, Cle.	1.091	2 Piazza, L.A.	1.006
3 Thomas, Chi.	1.060	3 Walker, Col.	.988
4 Salmon, Cal.	1.023	4 Bichette, Col.	.984
5 Thome, Cle.	.996	5 Sanders, Cin.	.976
6 Vaughn, Bos.	.963	6 Gant, Cin.	.940
7 Palmeiro, Bal.	.963	7 Castilla, Col.	.911
8 Ramirez, Cle.	.960	8 Karros, L.A.	.904
9 Davis, Cal.	.943	9 Conine, Fla.	.899
Baines, Bal.	.943	10 Bagwell, Hou.	.895

Extra Base Hits

American League		National League	
1 Belle, Cle.	103	1 Bichette, Col.	80
2 E. Martinez, Sea.	81	2 Walker, Col.	72
3 Palmeiro, Bal.	71	3 Sanders, Cin.	70
4 Salmon, Cal.	71	Bonds, S.F.	70
5 Vaughn, Bos.	70	Grace, Chi.	70

Total Bases

American League		National League	
1 Belle, Cle.	377	1 Bichette, Col.	359
2 Palmeiro, Bal.	323	2 Walker, Col.	300
3 E. Martinez, Sea.	321	3 Castilla, Col.	297
4 Salmon, Cal.	319	4 Karros, L.A.	295
5 Vaughn, Bos.	316	5 Bonds, S.F.	292

FIELDING

Fielding Average
(Minimum 80 Games)

American League			National League	
Alomar, Tor.	.994	2B-best	Boone, Cin.	.994
Alexander, Bal.	.986	2nd	Reed, S.D.	.994
Cora, Sea.	.953	worst	Garcia, Pit.	.970
Ripken, Bal.	.989	SS-best	Vizcaino, N.Y.	.984
DeSarcina, Cal.	.986	2nd	Larkin, Cin.	.980
Gonzalez, Tor.	.952	worst	Offerman, L.A.	.932
Boggs, N.Y.	.981	3B-best	Wallach, L.A.	.976
Fryman, Det.	.969	2nd	Hayes, Phi.	.963
Phillips, Cal.	.920	worst	Magadan, Hou.	.922

Putouts plus Assists per 9 Innings Played
(Minimum 80 Games)

American League			National League	
Vina, Mil.	5.86	2B-best	Garcia, Pit.	5.66
Frye, Tex.	5.50	2nd	Reed, S.D.	5.61
Easley, Cal.	4.54	worst	Lemke, Atl.	4.75
Gil, Tex.	5.19	SS-best	Clayton, S.F.	4.88
Valentin, Mil.	5.06	2nd	Vizcaino, N.Y.	4.82
Gonzalez, Tor.	4.00	worst	Cordero, Mon.	3.91
Fryman, Det.	3.13	3B-best	Cooper, St. L.	3.05
Cirillo, Mil.	2.90	2nd	Branson, Cin.	3.05
Blowers	2.22	worst	Wallach, L.A.	2.34

PITCHING

Wild Pitches

American League		National League	
1 Leiter, Tor.	14	1 Nomo, L.A.	19
2 Bergman, Det.	13	2 Carrasco, Cin.	15
3 Finley, Cal.	13	3 Smoltz, Atl.	13
4 Hurtado, Tor.	11	4 Borland, Phi.	12
Wakefield, Bos.	11	5 Ericks, Pit.	11
Stottlemyre, Oak.	11	Kile, Hou.	11
Cone, Tor. + N.Y.	11		

Home Runs Allowed

American League		National League	
1 Radke, Min.	32	1 Foster, Chi.	32
2 Gross, Tex.	27	2 Mulholland, S.F.	25
3 Bones, Mil.	26	3 Trachsel, Chi.	25
Rogers, Tex.	26	4 Bautista, S.F.	24
Stottlemyre, Oak.	26	5 Micki, N.Y.	23

Home Runs Allowed per 9 IP
(Minimum 10 Home Runs Allowed)

American League		National League	
1 Klingenbeck, Bal.+Min.	2.49	1 Bautista, S.F.	2.15
2 Darwin, Tor. + Tex.	2.27	2 Acevedo, Col.	2.06
3 Burrows, Tex.	2.22	3 Foster, Chi.	1.72
4 Anderson, Cal.	2.17	4 Hoffman, S.D.	1.69
5 Fleming, Sea. + K.C.	2.14	5 Wendell, Chi.	1.64

1996: THE YEAR OF THE HOMER

Offense, particularly home runs, boomed in 1996. No doubt it was the merest coincidence that just when baseball was struggling to regain the attendance lost during its disastrous 1994 strike and had not completely recouped in 1995, its traditional gate stimulus arrived to captivate fans in 1996. A number of explanations circulated for the deluge of long balls: juicier baseballs, springier bats, smaller ballparks, bigger players, a shrinking strike zone, and a growing use of second-line pitchers.

With three weeks to go in the season, the old record for total major league homers set in 1987 tumbled as Florida's Gary Sheffield hit the 4,459th of the year. When the season closed, the new mark was 4,962. Baltimore set a new team record with 257 home runs; Seattle and Oakland also cruised past the old mark of 240 by the 1961 Yankees. For the fourth time ever, two players reached 50 homers – one of them a lead-off man! Seventeen players had 40 or more, forty-three players had at least 30 homers; and fifty players had at least 100 RBI.

Although early season predictions held that a half dozen players might surpass Roger Maris' 61 home runs, Oakland's Mark McGwire earned the individual leadership with "only" 52. Significantly, because of injuries, he played in only 130 games – setting a pace that, if maintained, would have produced 64 homers.

Injury-plagued Tony Gwynn was able to win his seventh National League batting title by the rule that allows the addition of hitless at-bats to a player's record. Although he came up four shy of the minimum required plate appearances, Gwynn still had the N.L.'s highest batting mark when four "ophers" were added.

With all the hitting going on, pitchers still had a few bright spots. Boston's Roger Clemens tied his own single game strike out mark. Florida's Al Leiter, the Dodgers' Hideo Nomo, and the Yankees' Dwight Gooden tossed no-hitters. Gooden's feat was part of a popular comeback for the onetime Met, while Nomo's no-no was doubly amazing in that it was performed at Coors Field, A.K.A. "Hitter's Paradise."

All the individual feats helped disguise the fact that there were no really scintillating pennant races. In the American League, Baltimore's pitching woes let the Yankee's get far in front early and a late Oriole spurt brought them no closer than two games behind. Cleveland, generally regarded as the *creme de la creme* of the American League, cruised past the White Sox on the Central. In the West, Texas took the lead early. Seattle never quite recovered from the loss of Randy Johnson despite exceptional work by Ken Griffey, Jr., Edgar Martinez, and prodigy shortstop Alex Rodriguez.

The defending champs, Atlanta, as expected, easily took the National League East over young Montreal. Houston started well but eventually faded and lost to a resurgent

St. Louis, buoyed by an expensive transfusion of talent. The one race that might hav produced real sparks – San Diego and Los Angeles, which came down to the last da – was somewhat dampened by fan's knowledge that the loser would still go to into th playoffs as a wild card.

Neither the Padres nor the Dodgers lasted past the minimum in the opening of th playoff round. In the A.L., the Orioles shocked the suddenly punchless Indians i quick fashion. Only the Yankees and Rangers produced a close opening series, b relief work by set-up man Mariano Rivera and closer John Wetteland, plus a pencha for comeback rallies, gave New York the brass ring.

In the closing days of the regular season, a controversy erupted when Oriole second baseman Robby Alomar spit in the face of umpire John Hirschbeck. Tha Alomar would not have to serve his five-day suspension until 1997 brought com plaints that his punishment was too little and much too late. When Alomar helpe defeat Cleveland in the playoffs, criticism became intense. Then a 12-year-old Ne York fan replaced Alomar as storm center. In the opening ALCS game at Yanke Stadium, he reached into the playing field to pull what should have been only a dee fly out into the stands for a New York home run. The umpire missed seeing his gra and the home run helped the Yankees win the game over the Orioles. New Yor quickly closed out the series and then sat back to await the outcome of the Braves Cardinals NLCS.

Atlanta had great starting pitching, but the Braves appeared to have burned the bats through the first four games, as St. Louis went up three games to one. Then, ju in the nick of time, Atlanta remembered how to hit – and hit. They scored 32 runs the Cardinals' one over the final three games to earn their annual trip to the Worl Series.

The Series opened in New York with Atlanta still in a hitting mode, as they too the first two games. The teams moved on to Atlanta amid predictions that the Brave would sweep, liberally mixed with proclamations that Atlanta ranked among th greatest teams of all time. However, the '96 Yankees rescued the pride of the ol Yankees by zapping the Braves thrice on Atlanta's home field. The third victory wa a brilliant 1-0 win by Andy Pettitte over John Smoltz.

During the travel day, Yankees manager Joe Torre's brother Frank, the erstwhi Milwaukee first baseman, received a heart transplant. Then, the Yankees gladdene Joe's heart by winning the sixth and final game, 3-2. Wetteland, who saved all fou New York victories, was named Series MVP.

1996 AMERICAN LEAGUE — EAST DIVISION

NEW YORK 1st 92-70 .568 JOE TORRE

Name	G by Pos	B	AGE	G	AB	R	H	2B	3B	HR	RBI	BB	SO	SB	BA	SA
TOTALS			31	162	5628	871	1621	293	28	162	830	632	909	96	.288	.436
Tino Martinez	1B151 DH3	L	28	155	595	82	174	28	0	25	117	68	85	2	.292	.466
Mariano Duncan	2B104 3B3 OF3 DH2	R	33	109	400	62	136	34	3	8	56	9	77	4	.340	.500
Derek Jeter	SS157	R	22	157	582	104	183	25	6	10	78	48	102	14	.314	.430
Wade Boggs	3B123 DH4	L	38	132	501	80	156	29	2	2	41	67	32	1	.311	.389
Paul O'Neill	OF146 DH3 1B1	L	33	150	546	89	165	35	1	19	91	102	76	0	.302	.474
Bernie Williams	OF140 DH2	B	27	143	551	108	168	26	7	29	102	82	72	17	.305	.535
Tim Raines (LJ)	OF50 DH2	B	36	59	201	45	57	10	0	9	33	34	29	10	.284	.468
Joe Girardi	C120 DH2	R	31	124	422	55	124	22	3	2	45	30	55	13	.294	.374
1 Ruben Sierra	DH61 OF33	B	30	96	360	39	93	17	1	11	52	40	58	1	.258	.403
Andy Fox	2B72 3B31 SS9 DH3 OF1	L	25	113	189	26	37	4	0	3	13	20	28	11	.196	.265
1 Gerald Williams	OF92 DH2	R	29	99	233	37	63	15	4	5	30	15	39	7	.270	.433
Jim Leyritz	C55 3B13 1B5 OF3 2B2	R	32	88	265	23	70	10	0	7	40	30	68	2	.264	.381
Darryl Strawberry	OF34 DH26	L	34	63	202	35	53	13	0	11	36	31	55	6	.262	.490
2 Cecil Fielder	DH43 1B9	R	32	53	200	30	52	8	0	13	37	24	48	0	.260	.495
Ruben Rivera	OF45	R	22	46	88	17	25	6	1	2	16	13	26	6	.284	.443
Matt Howard	2B30 3B6	R	28	35	54	9	11	1	0	1	9	2	8	1	.204	.278
2 Mike Aldrete	OF9 DH9 1B8 P1	L	35	32	68	11	17	5	0	3	12	9	15	0	.250	.456
2 Charlie Hayes	3B19	R	31	20	67	7	19	3	0	2	13	1	12	0	.284	.418
2 Luis Sojo	2B14 SS4 3B1	R	31	18	40	3	11	2	0	0	5	1	4	0	.275	.325
Pat Kelly (SJ)	2B10 DH3	R	28	13	21	4	3	0	0	0	2	2	9	0	.143	.143
1 Robert Eenhoorn	2B10 3B2	R	28	12	14	2	1	0	0	0	2	2	3	0	.071	.071
Jorge Posada	C4 DH3	B	24	8	14	1	1	0	0	0	0	1	6	0	.071	.071
Dion James	OF4 DH1	L	33	6	12	1	2	0	0	0	0	1	2	1	.167	.167
Tim McIntosh	C1 1B1 3B1	R	31	3	3	0	0	0	0	0	0	0	1	0	.000	.000
Matt Luke	DH1	L	25	1	0	0	0	0	0	0	0	0	0	0	.─	.─

2 Pat Listach (BF) 28, Tony Fernandez (BE) 34

NAME	T	AGE	W	L	PCT	SV	G	GS	CG	IP	H	BB	SO	SHO	ERA
		30	92	70	.568	52	162	162	6	1440	1469	610	1139	9	4.6
Andy Pettitte	L	24	21	8	.724	0	35	34	2	221	229	72	162	0	3.8
Kenny Rogers	L	31	12	8	.600	0	30	30	2	179	179	83	92	1	4.6
Jimmy Key	L	35	12	11	.522	0	30	30	0	169	171	58	116	0	4.6
Dwight Gooden	R	31	11	7	.611	0	29	29	1	171	169	88	126	1	5.0
Mariano Rivera	R	26	8	3	.727	5	61	0	0	108	73	34	130	0	2.8
David Cone (SJ)	R	33	7	2	.778	0	11	11	1	72	50	34	71	0	2.8
1 Bob Wickman	R	27	4	1	.800	0	58	0	0	79	94	34	61	0	4.6
Jeff Nelson	R	29	4	4	.500	2	73	0	0	74	75	36	91	0	4.3
Ramiro Mendoza	R	24	4	5	.444	0	12	11	0	53	80	10	34	0	6.7
John Wetteland	R	29	2	3	.400	43	62	0	0	64	54	21	69	0	2.8
Brian Boehringer	R	27	2	4	.333	0	15	3	0	46	46	21	37	0	5.4
Billy Brewer	L	28	1	0	1.000	0	4	0	0	6	7	8	8	0	9.5
Jim Mecir	R	26	1	1	.500	0	26	0	0	40	42	23	38	0	5.1
Wally Whitehurst	R	32	1	1	.500	0	2	2	0	8	11	2	1	0	5.1
Scott Kamieniecki	R	32	1	2	.333	0	7	5	0	23	36	19	15	0	11.1
Dale Polley	L	30	1	3	.250	0	32	0	0	22	23	11	14	0	7.8
Dave Pavlas	R	33	0	0	.─	1	16	0	0	23	23	7	18	0	2.3
2 Ricky Bones	R	27	0	0	.─	0	4	1	0	7	14	6	4	0	14.1
Paul Gibson	L	36	0	0	.─	0	4	0	0	6	3	0	6	0	6.2
Mike Aldrete	L	35	0	0	.─	0	1	0	0	1	1	0	0	0	0.0
Steve Howe	L	38	0	1	.000	1	25	0	0	17	19	6	5	0	6.3
2 Graeme Lloyd	L	29	0	2	.000	0	13	0	0	6	12	5	6	0	17.4
1 Mark Hutton (GJ)	R	26	0	2	.000	0	12	4	0	30	32	18	25	0	5.0
2 David Weathers	R	26	0	2	.000	0	11	4	0	17	23	14	13	0	9.3
Melido Perez (EJ) 30															

BALTIMORE 2nd 88-74 .543 4 (Wild Card) DAVEY JOHNSON

Name	G by Pos	B	AGE	G	AB	R	H	2B	3B	HR	RBI	BB	SO	SB	BA	SA
TOTALS			32	163	5689	949	1557	299	29	257	914	645	915	76	.274	.472
Rafael Palmeiro	1B159 DH3	L	31	162	626	110	181	40	2	39	142	95	96	8	.289	.543
Roberto Alomar	2B141 DH10	B	28	153	588	132	193	43	4	22	94	90	65	17	.328	.527
Cal Ripken	SS158 3B8	R	35	163	640	94	178	40	1	26	102	59	78	1	.278	.466
B.J. Surhoff	3B106 OF27 DH10 1B2	L	31	143	537	74	157	27	6	21	82	47	79	0	.292	.482
Bobby Bonilla	OF108 DH44 1B9 3B4	B	33	159	595	107	171	27	5	28	116	75	85	1	.287	.491
Brady Anderson	OF143 DH2	L	32	149	579	117	172	37	5	50	110	76	106	21	.297	.637
Jeffrey Hammonds (KJ)	OF70 DH1	R	25	71	248	38	56	10	1	9	27	23	53	3	.226	.383
Chris Hoiles	C126 1B1	R	31	127	407	64	105	13	0	25	73	57	97	0	.258	.474
2 Eddie Murray	DH62	B	40	64	230	36	59	12	0	10	34	27	42	1	.257	.439
Mike Devereaux	OF112 DH10	R	33	127	323	49	74	11	2	8	34	34	53	8	.229	.350
1 Luis Polonia	OF34 DH18	L	31	58	175	25	42	4	1	2	14	10	20	4	.240	.309
Billy Ripken	2B30 3B25 1B1	R	31	57	135	19	31	8	0	2	12	9	18	0	.230	.333
Manny Alexander	SS21 2B7 3B7 OF3 DH1 P1	R	25	54	68	6	7	0	0	0	4	3	27	1	.103	.103
1 Gregg Zaun	C49	B	25	50	108	16	25	1	1	1	13	11	15	0	.231	.352
Tony Tarasco	OF23 DH6	L	25	31	84	14	20	3	0	1	9	7	15	5	.238	.310
2 Todd Zeile	3B29	R	30	29	117	17	28	6	0	5	19	15	16	0	.239	.436
Mark Smith (LJ)	OF20 DH6	R	26	27	78	9	19	2	0	4	10	3	20	0	.244	.423
Brent Bowers	OF21	L	25	21	39	6	12	2	0	0	3	0	6	2	.308	.359
2 Mark Parent	C18	R	34	18	33	4	6	1	0	1	6	2	10	0	.182	.394
Jeff Huson (KJ)	2B12 3B3 OF1	L	31	17	25	3	5	9	1	0	2	1	3	0	.321	.357
2 Pete Incaviglia	OF7 DH4	R	32	12	33	4	10	2	0	2	6	1	7	0	.303	.545
Cesar Devarez	C10	R	26	10	18	3	2	1	0	0	1	0	5	0	.111	.222
Eugene Kingsale	OF2	B	19	3	7	0	0	0	0	0	0	0	0	0	.─	.─

NAME	T	AGE	W	L	PCT	SV	G	GS	CG	IP	H	BB	SO	SHO	ERA
		29	88	74	.543	44	163	163	13	1469	1604	597	1047	1	5.14
Mike Mussina	R	27	19	11	.633	0	36	36	4	243	264	69	204	1	4.81
Scott Erickson	R	28	13	12	.520	0	34	34	6	222	262	66	100	0	5.02
David Wells	L	33	11	14	.440	0	34	34	3	224	247	51	130	0	5.14
Rocky Coppinger	R	22	10	6	.625	0	23	22	0	125	126	60	104	0	5.18
Arthur Rhodes (SJ)	L	26	9	1	.900	1	28	2	0	53	48	23	62	0	4.08
Randy Myers	L	33	4	4	.500	31	62	0	0	59	60	29	74	0	3.53
Jesse Orosco	L	39	3	1	.750	0	66	0	0	56	42	28	52	0	3.40
Alan Mills (SJ)	R	29	3	6	.333	3	49	0	0	55	40	35	50	0	4.28
Rick Krivda	L	26	3	5	.375	0	22	11	0	82	89	39	54	0	4.96
Jimmy Haynes	R	23	3	6	.333	0	26	11	0	89	122	58	65	0	8.29
1 Kent Mercker	L	28	3	6	.333	0	14	12	0	58	73	35	22	0	7.76
Archie Corbin	R	28	3	0	1.000	0	18	0	0	27	20	22	20	0	2.30
2 Terry Mathews	R	31	2	1	.667	0	18	0	0	18	14	6	20	0	3.77
Armando Benitez (EJ)	R	23	1	0	1.000	4	14	0	0	14	7	6	20	0	3.77
2 Mike Milchin	L	28	1	0	1.000	0	13	0	0	13	14	9	6	0	5.73
Roger McDowell (SJ)	R	35	1	1	.500	4	41	0	0	59	69	23	20	0	4.25
Jimmy Myers	R	27	0	0	.─	0	14	0	0	14	18	3	6	0	7.07
Esteban Yan	R	22	0	0	.─	0	3	0	0	4	5	2	2	0	9.00
Brian Sackinsky	R	25	0	0	.─	0	2	0	0	2	6	2	0	0	3.86
Manny Alexander	R	25	0	0	.─	0	1	0	0	1	2	0	0	0	67.50
Keith Shepherd	R	28	0	0	.─	0	13	0	0	21	31	18	17	0	8.71
Nerio Rodriguez	R	25	0	1	.000	0	6	1	0	18	17	3	12	0	4.32
Garrett Stephenson	R	24	0	0	.─	0	4	0	0	6	13	3	3	0	12.79

BOSTON 3rd 85-77 .525 7 — KEVIN KENNEDY

Name	G by Pos	B	AGE	G	AB	R	H	2B	3B	HR	RBI	BB	SO	SB	BA	SA
TOTALS			29	162	5756	928	1631	308	31	209	882	642	1020	91	.283	.457
Mo Vaughn	1B146 DH15	L	28	161	635	118	207	29	1	44	143	95	154	2	.326	.583
Jeff Frye	2B100 OF5 SS3 DH1	R	29	105	419	74	120	27	2	4	41	54	57	18	.286	.389
John Valentin	SS118 3B12 DH1	R	29	131	527	84	156	29	3	13	59	63	59	9	.296	.436
Tim Naehring	3B116 2B1	R	29	116	430	77	124	16	0	17	65	49	63	2	.288	.444
Troy O'Leary	OF146	L	26	149	497	68	129	28	5	15	81	47	80	3	.260	.427
Darren Bragg	OF58	L	26	58	222	38	56	14	1	3	22	36	39	6	.252	.365
Mike Greenwell (BG)	OF83	L	32	77	295	35	87	20	1	7	44	18	27	4	.295	.441
Mike Stanley	C105 DH10	R	33	121	397	73	107	20	1	24	69	69	62	0	.270	.506
Jose Canseco (XJ)	DH84 OF11	R	31	96	360	68	104	22	1	28	82	63	82	3	.289	.589
Reggie Jefferson	DH49 OF45 1B16	L	27	122	386	67	134	30	4	19	74	25	89	0	.347	.593
Lee Tinsley	OF83	B	27	92	192	28	47	6	1	3	14	13	56	6	.245	.333
Bill Haselman	C69 1B2 DH2	R	30	77	237	33	65	13	1	8	34	19	52	1	.274	.439
Wil Cordero (KJ)	2B37 DH13 1B1	R	24	59	198	29	57	14	0	3	37	11	31	2	.288	.404
Milt Cuyler (XJ)	OF45 DH2	B	27	50	110	19	22	1	2	2	12	13	19	7	.200	.300
Jose Malave	OF38	R	25	41	102	12	24	3	0	4	17	2	25	0	.235	.382
Bill Selby	2B14 3B14 OF6	L	26	40	95	12	26	4	0	3	6	9	11	1	.274	.411
Dwayne Hosey	OF26 DH2	B	29	28	78	13	17	2	2	1	3	7	17	6	.218	.333
Kevin Mitchell (LJ)	OF21 DH4	R	34	27	92	9	28	4	0	2	13	11	14	0	.304	.413
Tony Rodriguez	SS21 3B5	R	25	27	67	7	16	1	0	1	9	4	8	0	.239	.299
Esteban Beltre	3B13 2B8 SS6 DH1	R	28	27	64	6	16	2	0	0	6	4	14	1	.258	.290
Alex Delgado	C14 OF6 3B4 2B1 1B1	R	25	26	20	5	5	0	0	0	1	3	3	0	.250	.250
Nomar Garciaparra	SS22 2B1 DH1	R	22	24	87	11	21	2	3	4	16	4	14	5	.241	.471
Alex Cole	OF24	L	30	24	72	13	16	5	1	0	7	8	11	5	.222	.319
Jeff Manto (KJ)	3B10 2B4 SS4 1B1	R	31	22	48	8	10	3	1	2	6	8	12	0	.208	.438
Arquimedez Pozo	2B10 3B10	R	22	21	58	4	10	3	1	1	11	2	10	1	.172	.310
Rudy Pemberton	OF13	R	26	13	41	11	21	4	0	1	10	2	4	3	.512	.780
Scott Hatteberg	C10	L	26	10	11	3	2	1	0	0	0	3	2	0	.182	.273
Phil Clark	1B1 3B1 DH1	R	28	3	3	0	0	0	0	0	0	0	0	0	.000	.000
Jim Tatum	3B2	R	28	2	8	1	1	0	0	0	0	0	1	0	.125	.125
Trot Nixon	OF2	L	22	2	4	2	2	1	0	0	0	0	1	0	.500	.700
Greg Pirkl	C1	R	25	2	2	0	0	0	0	0	0	0	0	1	.000	.000
Walt McKeel	C1	R	24	1												

NAME	T	AGE	W	L	PCT	SV	G	GS	CG	IP	H	BB	SO	SHO	ERA
TOTALS		29	85	77	.525	37	162	162	17	1458	1606	722	1165	5	4.98
Tim Wakefield	R	29	14	13	.519	0	32	32	6	212	238	90	140	0	5.14
Tom Gordon	R	28	12	9	.571	0	34	34	4	216	249	105	171	1	5.59
Roger Clemens	R	33	10	13	.435	0	34	34	6	243	216	106	257	2	3.63
Jamie Moyer	L	33	7	1	.875	0	23	10	0	90	111	27	50	0	4.50
Aaron Sele	R	26	7	11	.389	0	29	29	1	157	192	67	137	0	5.32
Vaughn Eshelman (HJ)	L	27	3	3	.667	0	39	10	0	88	112	58	59	0	7.08
Heathcliff Slocumb	R	30	5	5	.500	31	75	0	0	83	68	55	88	0	3.02
Mark Brandenburg	R	25	4	2	.667	0	29	0	0	28	28	8	29	0	3.81
Mike Stanton	L	29	4	3	.571	1	59	0	0	56	58	23	46	0	3.83
Rich Garces (TJ)	R	25	3	2	.600	0	37	0	0	44	42	33	55	0	4.91
Mike Maddux (EJ)	R	34	3	2	.600	0	23	7	0	64	76	27	32	0	4.48
Joe Hudson	R	25	3	5	.375	1	36	0	0	45	57	32	19	0	5.40
Pat Mahomes	R	25	2	1	1.000	2	11	0	0	12	9	6	6	0	5.84
Kerry Lacy	R	23	2	0	1.000	0	11	0	0	11	15	8	9	0	3.38
Stan Belinda (EJ-GJ)	R	29	2	1	.667	2	31	0	0	29	31	20	18	0	6.59
Jeff Suppan (EJ)	R	21	1	1	.500	0	8	3	0	23	29	13	13	0	7.54
Reggie Harris	R	27	0	0	—	0	4	0	0	4	7	5	4	0	12.46
John Doherty	R	29	0	0	—	0	3	0	0	6	8	4	3	0	5.68
Ken Grundt	L	26	0	0	—	0	1	0	0	0.1	0	1	0	0	27.00
Eric Gunderson	L	30	0	1	.000	0	28	0	0	17	21	8	7	0	8.31
Brent Knackert	R	26	0	1	.000	0	8	0	0	10	16	7	5	0	9.00
Brad Pennington	L	27	0	0	—	0	6	0	0	13	6	15	13	0	2.77
Nate Minchey (EJ)	R	26	0	2	.000	0	2	2	0	16	6	8	4	0	15.00
Butch Henry (SJ) 27															

TORONTO 4th 74-88 .457 18 — CITO GASTON

Name	G by Pos	B	AGE	G	AB	R	H	2B	3B	HR	RBI	BB	SO	SB	BA	SA
TOTALS			29	162	5599	766	1451	302	35	177	712	529	1105	116	.259	.420
John Olerud	1B101 DH15	L	27	125	398	59	109	25	0	18	61	60	37	1	.274	.472
Tomas Perez	2B75 3B11 SS5	B	22	91	295	24	74	13	4	1	19	25	29	1	.251	.332
Alex Gonzalez	SS147	R	23	147	527	64	124	30	5	14	64	45	127	16	.235	.391
Ed Sprague	3B148 DH10	R	28	159	591	88	146	35	2	36	101	60	146	0	.247	.496
Shawn Green	OF127 DH1	L	23	132	422	52	118	32	3	11	45	33	75	5	.280	.448
Otis Nixon	OF125	B	37	125	496	87	142	15	1	1	29	71	68	54	.286	.327
Joe Carter	OF115 1B41 DH15	R	36	157	625	84	158	35	7	30	107	44	106	7	.253	.475
Charlie O'Brien	C105	R	36	109	324	33	77	17	0	13	44	29	68	0	.238	.410
Carlos Delgado	DH108 1B27	L	24	138	488	68	132	28	2	25	92	58	139	0	.270	.490
Jacob Brumfield	OF83 DH5	R	31	90	308	52	79	19	2	12	52	24	58	12	.256	.448
Robert Perez	OF79 DH2	R	26	86	202	30	66	10	2	2	21	8	17	3	.327	.406
Domingo Cedeno	2B62 3B6 SS5	B	27	77	282	44	79	10	2	2	17	15	60	5	.280	.351
Sandy Martinez	C75	L	25	76	229	17	52	9	3	3	18	16	58	0	.227	.332
Juan Samuel	OF24 DH24 1B17	R	35	69	188	34	48	7	3	8	26	15	65	9	.255	.457
Tilson Brito	2B18 SS5 DH2	R	24	26	80	10	19	7	0	1	7	10	18	1	.238	.363
Felipe Crespo	2B10 3B6 1B2	B	23	22	49	6	9	4	0	0	4	12	13	1	.184	.265
Mike Huff	OF9 3B3	R	31	11	29	5	5	0	1	0	1	6	5	0	.172	.241
Miguel Cairo	2B9	R	22	9	27	5	6	2	0	0	1	2	9	0	.222	.296
Julio Mosquera	C8	R	24	8	22	2	5	2	0	0	2	0	3	0	.227	.318
Shannon Stewart	OF6	R	22	7	17	2	3	1	0	0	2	1	4	1	.176	.235

NAME	T	AGE	W	L	PCT	SV	G	GS	CG	IP	H	BB	SO	SHO	ERA
TOTALS		28	74	88	.457	35	162	162	19	1446	1476	610	1033	7	4.57
Pat Hentgen	R	27	20	10	.667	0	35	35	10	266	238	94	177	3	3.22
Erik Hanson	R	31	13	17	.433	0	35	35	4	215	243	102	156	1	5.41
Juan Guzman (IL)	R	29	11	8	.579	0	27	27	4	188	158	53	165	1	2.93
Tim Crabtree	R	26	5	3	.625	1	53	0	0	67	59	22	57	0	2.54
Paul Quantrill	R	27	5	14	.263	0	38	20	0	134	172	51	86	0	5.43
Woody Williams (SJ)	R	29	5	4	.444	0	12	10	1	59	64	21	43	0	4.73
Marty Janzen	R	23	4	6	.400	0	15	11	0	74	95	38	47	0	7.33
Huck Flener	L	27	3	2	.600	0	15	11	0	71	68	33	44	0	4.58
Paul Spoljaric	L	25	2	2	.500	1	28	0	0	38	30	19	38	0	3.08
Tony Castillo	L	33	2	4	.333	1	40	0	0	72	72	20	48	0	4.23
Scott Brow	R	27	1	0	1.000	0	18	1	0	39	45	25	23	0	5.59
Luis Andujar	R	23	1	1	.500	0	3	2	0	14	14	1	5	0	5.02
Frank Viola	L	36	1	3	.250	0	6	6	0	30	43	21	18	0	7.71
Jeff Ware	R	25	1	5	.167	0	13	4	0	33	35	31	11	0	9.09
Mike Timlin	R	30	1	6	.143	31	59	0	0	57	47	18	52	0	3.65
Dane Johnson	R	33	0	0	—	0	9	0	0	2	5	5	7	0	13.50
Jose Silva	R	22	0	0	—	0	2	0	0	2	0	0	0	0	
Bill Risley (SJ)	R	29	0	1	.000	0	25	0	0	42	33	25	29	0	3.89
Brian Bohanon	L	27	0	1	.000	0	20	0	0	22	27	19	17	0	7.77
Giovanni Carrara	R	28	0	1	.000	0	11	0	0	15	23	12	10	0	11.40

DETROIT 5th 53-109 .327 39 — BUDDY BELL

Name	G by Pos	B	AGE	G	AB	R	H	2B	3B	HR	RBI	BB	SO	SB	BA	SA
TOTALS			27	162	5530	783	1413	257	21	204	741	546	1268	87	.256	.420
Tony Clark	1B86 DH12	B	24	100	376	56	94	14	0	27	72	29	127	0	.250	.503
Mark Lewis	2B144 DH1	R	26	145	545	69	147	30	3	11	55	42	109	6	.270	.396
Alan Trammell (NJ)	SS43 2B11 3B8 OF1	R	38	66	193	16	45	2	0	1	16	10	21	6	.233	.259
Travis Fryman	3B128 SS29	R	27	157	616	90	165	32	3	22	100	57	118	4	.268	.437
Melvin Nieves	OF105 DH11	B	24	120	431	71	106	23	4	24	60	44	158	1	.246	.485
Chad Curtis	OF104	R	27	104	400	65	105	20	1	10	37	53	73	16	.263	.393
Bobby Higginson (FJ)	OF123 DH4	L	25	130	440	75	141	35	6	26	81	65	66	6	.320	.577
Brad Ausmus	C73	R	27	75	226	30	54	12	0	4	22	26	45	3	.248	.354
Eddie Williams	DH52 1B7 3B3 OF2	R	31	77	215	22	43	6	0	6	26	18	50	0	.200	.307
Kimera Bartee	OF99 DH2	R	23	110	217	32	55	6	1	1	14	17	77	20	.253	.304
Cecil Fielder	1B71 DH36	R	32	107	391	55	97	12	0	26	80	63	91	2	.248	.478
Curtis Pride	OF48 DH31	L	27	95	267	52	80	17	5	10	31	31	63	11	.300	.513
Andujar Cedeno	SS51 3B1	R	26	52	179	19	35	4	2	7	20	4	37	2	.196	.358
Chris Gomez	SS47	R	25	48	128	21	31	5	0	1	16	18	20	1	.242	.305
John Flaherty	C46	R	28	47	152	18	38	12	0	4	23	8	25	1	.250	.408
Ruben Sierra	OF23 DH20	B	30	46	158	22	35	9	1	1	20	20	25	2	.222	.310
Phil Nevin	3B24 OF9 C4 DH1	R	25	38	120	15	35	5	0	8	19	8	39	1	.292	.533
Mark Parent	C33 1B1	R	34	38	104	13	25	6	0	7	17	3	27	0	.240	.500
Raul Casanova (BW)	C22 DH3	B	23	25	85	6	16	1	0	4	9	6	18	1	.188	.341
Danny Bautista	OF22 DH1	R	24	25	64	12	16	2	0	3	8	9	15	1	.250	.375
Damion Easley	2B8 SS8 3B2 DH1	R	26	21	67	10	23	1	0	2	10	4	13	3	.343	.448
Duane Singleton	OF15	L	23	18	56	5	9	1	0	0	3	4	15	0	.161	.179
Tim Hyers	1B9 DH2 OF1	L	24	17	26	1	2	1	0	0	1	1	6	0	.077	.115
Fausto Cruz	2B8 SS4 DH1	R	24	14	38	5	9	2	0	0	1	1	11	0	.237	.289
Phil Hiatt	3B3 OF2 DH1	R	27	7	21	3	4	1	0	0	1	2	11	0	.190	.286
Shannon Penn	DH4 OF1	B	26	6	14	0	1	0	0	0	0	1	4	0	.071	.071

NAME	T	AGE	W	L	PCT	SV	G	GS	CG	IP	H	BB	SO	SHO	ERA
TOTALS		27	53	109	.327	22	162	162	10	1433	1699	784	957	4	6.38
Omar Olivares (LJ)	R	28	7	11	.389	0	25	25	4	160	169	75	81	0	4.89
Felipe Lira	R	24	6	14	.300	0	32	32	3	195	204	66	113	2	5.22
Jose Lima	R	23	5	6	.455	3	39	4	0	73	87	22	59	0	5.70
A.J. Sager	R	30	4	5	.444	0	22	9	0	79	91	29	52	0	5.01
Richie Lewis	R	30	4	6	.400	0	72	0	0	90	78	65	78	0	4.18
Greg Gohr (KJ)	R	28	4	8	.333	0	17	16	0	92	129	34	60	0	7.17
Gregg Olson	R	29	3	0	1.000	8	43	0	0	43	43	28	29	0	5.02
John Cummings	L	27	3	3	.500	0	21	0	0	32	36	20	24	0	5.12
Greg Keagle (XJ)	R	25	3	6	.333	0	26	8	0	88	104	68	70	0	7.39
Brian Williams	R	28	3	10	.231	2	40	17	2	121	145	85	72	1	6.77
Tom Urbani	L	28	2	2	.500	0	16	2	0	24	31	14	20	0	8.37
C.J. Nitkowski (XJ)	L	23	2	3	.400	0	11	8	0	46	62	38	36	0	8.08
Todd Van Poppel	R	24	2	4	.333	0	9	9	1	36	53	29	16	1	11.39
Joey Eischen	L	26	1	1	.500	0	24	0	0	25	27	14	15	0	3.24
Mike Christopher	R	32	1	1	.500	0	13	0	0	30	47	11	19	0	9.30
Clint Sodowsky	R	23	1	3	.250	0	7	7	0	24	40	20	9	0	11.84
Mike Myers	L	27	1	5	.167	0	83	0	0	65	70	34	69	0	5.01
Justin Thompson (SJ)	L	23	1	6	.143	0	11	11	0	59	62	31	44	0	4.58
Mike Walker	R	29	0	0	—	0	20	0	0	28	40	17	13	0	8.46
Bob Scanlan	R	29	0	0	—	0	1	1	0	11	16	9	3	0	10.64
Brian Maxcy	R	25	0	0	—	0	7	0	0	8	12	10	1	0	13.50
Jeff McCurry	R	26	0	0	—	0	11	0	0	12	11	6	2	0	24.30
Brian Moehler	R	24	0	1	.000	0	2	2	0	10	11	3	6	0	4.35
John Farrell	R	33	0	1	.000	0	11	0	0	11	11	8	2	0	14.21
Randy Veres	R	29	0	1	.000	0	7	0	0	11	16	9	3	0	8.31
Scott Aldred	L	28	0	1	.000	0	11	8	0	43	64	28	36	0	9.35
Trever Miller	L	23	0	4	.000	0	5	5	0	25	39	20	19	0	9.18

CENTRAL DIVISION

CLEVELAND 1st 99-62 .615 — MIKE HARGROVE

Name	G by Pos	B	AGE	G	AB	R	H	2B	3B	HR	RBI	BB	SO	SB	BA	SA
TOTALS			31	161	5681	952	1665	335	23	218	904	671	844	160	.293	.475
Julio Franco	1B97 DH13	R	37	112	432	72	139	20	1	14	76	61	82	8	.322	.470
Carlos Baerga	2B100	R	27	100	424	54	113	20	0	10	55	16	25	1	.267	.396
Omar Vizquel	SS150	B	29	151	542	98	161	36	1	9	64	56	42	35	.297	.417
Jim Thome	3B150 DH1	L	25	151	505	122	157	28	5	38	116	123	141	2	.311	.612
Manny Ramirez	OF149 DH3	R	24	152	550	94	170	45	3	33	112	85	104	8	.309	.582
Kenny Lofton	OF152	L	29	154	662	132	210	35	4	14	67	61	82	75	.317	.446
Albert Belle	OF152 DH6	R	29	158	602	124	187	38	3	48	148	99	87	11	.311	.623
Sandy Alomar	C124 1B1	R	30	127	418	53	110	23	0	11	50	19	42	1	.263	.397
Eddie Murray	DH87 1B1	B	40	88	336	33	88	9	1	12	45	34	45	3	.262	.402
Jeromy Burnitz	OF30 DH15	L	27	71	128	30	36	10	0	7	26	25	31	2	.281	.523
Tony Pena	C67	R	39	67	174	14	34	4	0	1	27	15	25	0	.195	.236
Alvaro Espinoza	3B20 1B18 SS16 2B5 DH1	R	34	59	112	12	25	4	2	4	11	6	18	1	.223	.402
Brian Giles	DH21 OF16	L	25	51	121	26	43	14	1	5	27	19	13	3	.355	.612
Jose Vizcaino	2B45 SS4 DH1	B	28	48	179	23	51	5	2	0	13	7	24	6	.285	.335
Jeff Kent	1B20 2B9 3B6 DH1	R	28	39	102	16	27	7	0	3	16	10	22	2	.265	.422
Mark Carreon (LJ)	1B34 OF5 DH2	R	32	38	142	16	46	12	0	2	14	11	9	1	.324	.451
Scott Leius	3B8 1B7 2B6 DH1	R	30	27	43	3	6	4	1	0	0	8	9	0	.140	.302
Wayne Kirby	OF18	L	32	27	16	3	4	1	0	0	0	2	5	0	.250	.313
Casey Candaele	2B11 3B3 SS1	B	35	24	44	8	11	2	0	0	5	2	6	0	.250	.364
Kevin Seitzer	DH17 1B5	R	34	22	83	11	32	10	0	1	16	14	11	0	.386	.542
Nigel Wilson	DH3 OF1	L	26	10	12	2	3	0	1	0	2	1	5	0	.250	.750
Ryan Thompson	OF8	R	28	8	22	2	7	2	0	0	5	1	6	0	.318	.455
Herbert Perry (KJ)	1B5 3B1 DH1	R	26	7	12	1	1	0	0	0	0	1	2	0	.083	.167
Damian Jackson	SS5	R	22	5	10	2	3	0	0	0	0	1	3	0	.300	.500
Geronimo Pena	3B3 2B1	B	29	5	9	1	1	0	0	0	0	0	4	0	.111	.444
Einar Diaz	C4	R	23	4											.000	.000

NAME	T	AGE	W	L	PCT	SV	G	GS	CG	IP	H	BB	SO	SHO	ERA
TOTALS		30	99	62	.615	46	161	161	13	1452	1530	484	1033	9	4.34
Charlie Nagy	R	29	17	5	.773	0	32	32	5	222	217	61	167	0	3.41
Orel Hershiser	R	37	15	9	.625	0	33	33	1	206	238	58	125	0	4.24
Jack McDowell	R	30	13	9	.591	0	30	30	5	192	214	67	141	1	5.11
Chad Ogea (SJ)	R	25	10	6	.625	0	29	21	1	147	151	42	101	1	4.79
Dennis Martinez (EJ)	R	41	9	6	.600	0	20	20	1	112	122	37	48	1	4.50
Paul Shuey	R	25	5	2	.714	4	42	0	0	54	45	26	44	0	2.85
Albie Lopez	R	24	5	4	.556	0	13	10	0	62	80	22	45	0	6.39
Jim Poole	L	30	4	0	1.000	0	32	0	0	27	29	14	19	0	3.04
Paul Assenmacher	L	35	4	2	.667	1	63	0	0	47	46	14	44	0	3.09
Julian Tavarez	R	23	4	7	.364	0	51	4	0	81	101	22	46	0	5.36
Brian Anderson	L	24	3	1	.750	0	53	15	0	51	58	14	21	0	4.91
Eric Plunk	R	32	3	2	.600	2	56	0	0	78	56	34	85	0	2.43
Danny Graves	R	30	2	0	1.000	1	15	0	0	30	44	9	22	0	4.55
Jose Mesa	R	30	2	7	.222	39	69	0	0	72	69	28	64	0	3.73
Kent Mercker	L	28	1	0	1.000	0	24	0	0	13	10	7	3	0	3.09
Alan Embree (PJ)	L	26	1	1	.500	0	24	0	0	31	30	21	33	0	6.39
Greg Swindell	L	31	0	1	.500	0	13	0	0	7	8	3	21	0	6.59
Joe Roa	R	24	0	0	—	0	1	1	0	7	10			0	10.80

CHICAGO — 2nd 85-77 .525 14.5 — TERRY BEVINGTON

Name	G by Pos	B	AGE	G	AB	R	H	2B	3B	HR	RBI	BB	SO	SB	BA	SA
TOTALS			31	162	5644	898	1586	284	33	195	860	701	927	105	.281	.447
Frank Thomas	1B139	R	28	141	527	110	184	26	0	40	134	109	70	1	.349	.626
Ray Durham	2B150 DH3	B	24	156	557	79	153	33	5	10	65	58	95	30	.275	.406
Ozzie Guillen	SS146 OF2	L	32	150	499	62	131	24	8	4	45	10	27	6	.263	.367
Robin Ventura	3B150 1B14	L	28	158	586	96	168	31	2	34	105	78	81	1	.287	.520
Danny Tartabull	OF122 DH10	R	33	132	472	58	120	23	3	27	101	64	128	1	.254	.487
Darren Lewis	OF138	R	28	141	337	55	77	12	2	4	53	45	40	21	.228	.312
Tony Phillips	OF150 2B2 1B3	B	37	153	581	119	161	29	3	12	63	125	132	13	.277	.399
Ron Karkovice	C111	R	33	111	355	44	78	22	0	10	38	24	93	0	.220	.366
Harold Baines	DH141	L	37	143	495	80	154	29	0	22	95	73	62	3	.311	.503
Dave Martinez	OF121 1B23	L	31	146	440	85	140	20	8	10	53	52	52	15	.318	.468
Lyle Mouton	OF47 DH28	R	27	87	214	25	63	8	1	7	39	22	50	4	.294	.439
Norberto Martin (IJ)	SS24 DH22 2B10 3B3	R	29	70	140	30	49	7	0	1	14	6	17	10	.350	.421
Chad Kreuter (BS)	C38 1B2	R	31	46	114	14	25	8	0	3	18	13	29	0	.219	.368
Chris Snopek	3B27 SS12 DH3	R	25	46	104	18	27	6	1	6	18	6	16	0	.260	.510
Pat Borders	C30 DH1	R	33	31	94	6	26	1	0	3	6	5	18	0	.277	.383
Jose Munoz	2B7 SS2 DH2 3B1 OF1	B	28	17	27	7	7	0	0	0	1	4	1	0	.259	.259
Don Slaught	C12 DH1	R	37	14	36	2	9	1	0	0	4	2	2	0	.250	.278
Domingo Cedeno	SS2 2B2 DH1	B	27	12	19	2	3	2	0	0	3	0	4	1	.158	.263
Greg Norton	SS6 3B2 DH1	R	23	11	23	4	5	0	0	2	3	4	6	0	.217	.478
Mike Cameron	OF8 DH2	R	23	11	11	1	1	0	0	0	1	3	0	.091	.091
Mike Robertson	1B2 DH1	L	25	6	7	0	1	1	0	0	0	0	1	0	.143	.286
Robert Machado	C4	R	23	4	6	1	4	1	0	0	2	0	0	.667	.833

NAME	T	AGE	W	L	PCT	SV	G	GS	CG	IP	H	BB	SO	SHO	ERA
TOTALS		28	85	77	.525	43	162	162	7	1461	1529	616	1039	4	4.52
Alex Fernandez	R	26	16	10	.615	0	35	35	6	258	248	72	200	1	3.45
Wilson Alvarez	L	26	15	10	.600	0	35	35	0	217	216	97	181	0	4.22
Kevin Tapani	R	32	13	10	.565	0	34	34	1	225	236	76	150	0	4.59
James Baldwin	R	34	11	6	.647	0	28	28	0	169	168	57	127	0	4.42
Matt Karchner (LJ)	R	29	7	4	.636	0	50	0	0	59	61	41	46	0	5.76
Roberto Hernandez	R	31	6	5	.545	38	72	0	0	85	65	38	85	0	1.91
Kirk McCaskill	R	35	5	5	.500	0	29	4	0	52	72	31	28	0	6.97
Tony Castillo	L	33	3	1	.750	1	15	0	0	23	23	4	9	0	1.59
Mike Bertotti	L	26	2	0	1.000	0	15	2	0	28	28	20	19	0	5.14
Larry Thomas (EJ)	R	26	2	3	.400	0	57	0	0	31	32	14	20	0	3.23
Bill Simas	R	24	2	8	.200	2	64	0	0	73	75	39	65	0	4.58
Brian Keyser	R	29	1	2	.333	1	28	0	0	60	78	28	19	0	4.98
Mike Sirotka	L	25	1	2	.333	0	15	4	0	26	34	12	11	0	7.18
Joe Magrane	L	31	1	5	.167	0	19	8	0	54	70	25	21	0	6.88
Rich Sauveur	L	32	0	0	—	0	3	0	0	2	0	1	1	0	15.00
Stacy Jones	R	29	0	0	—	0	2	0	0	2	0	1	1	0	4.50
Marvin Freeman	R	33	0	1	.000	0	2	1	0	2	4	1	1	0	13.50
Jeff Darwin	R	26	0	1	.000	0	22	0	0	31	26	9	15	0	2.93
Al Levine	R	28	0	1	.000	0	16	0	0	18	22	7	12	0	5.40
Jason Bere (EJ)	R	25	0	1	.000	0	5	5	0	17	26	18	19	0	10.26
Scott Ruffcorn	R	26	0	1	.000	0	2	2	0	7	10	6	6	0	11.37
Luis Andujar	R	23	0	2	.000	0	5	5	0	23	32	15	6	0	8.22

MILWAUKEE — 3rd 80-82 .494 19.5 — PHIL GARNER

Name	G by Pos	B	AGE	G	AB	R	H	2B	3B	HR	RBI	BB	SO	SB	BA	SA
TOTALS			28	162	5662	894	1578	304	40	178	845	624	986	101	.279	.441
John Jaha	1B85 DH63	R	30	148	543	108	163	28	1	34	118	85	118	3	.300	.543
Fernando Vina	2B137	R	27	140	554	94	157	19	10	7	46	38	35	16	.283	.392
Jose Valentin	SS151	B	26	154	552	90	143	33	7	24	95	66	145	17	.259	.475
Jeff Cirillo	3B154 DH3 1B2 2B1	R	26	158	566	101	184	46	5	15	83	58	69	4	.325	.504
Matt Mieske	OF122	R	28	127	374	46	104	24	3	14	64	26	76	1	.278	.471
Chuck Carr (KJ)	OF27	B	28	27	106	18	29	6	1	1	11	6	21	5	.274	.377
Greg Vaughn	OF100 DH1	R	30	102	375	78	105	16	0	31	95	58	99	5	.280	.571
Mike Matheny	C104 DH1	R	25	106	313	31	64	15	2	8	46	14	80	3	.204	.342
Kevin Seitzer	1B65 DH56 3B12	R	34	132	490	74	155	25	3	12	62	73	68	6	.316	.453
Dave Nilsson (FJ)	OF61 DH40 1B24 C2	L	26	123	453	81	150	33	2	17	84	57	68	2	.331	.525
Jesse Levis	C90 DH6	L	28	104	233	27	55	6	1	1	21	38	15	0	.236	.283
Pat Listach	OF68 2B12 SS7	B	28	87	317	51	76	16	2	1	33	36	51	25	.240	.312
David Hulse (SJ)	OF68 DH4	L	28	81	117	18	26	3	0	0	6	8	16	4	.222	.248
Mark Loretta	2B28 3B23 SS21	R	24	73	154	20	43	3	0	1	13	14	15	2	.279	.318
Marc Newfield	OF49	R	23	49	179	21	55	15	0	7	31	11	26	0	.307	.508
Turner Ward (SJ)	OF32 DH1	B	31	43	67	7	12	2	1	2	10	13	17	3	.179	.328
Gerald Williams	OF26	R	29	26	92	6	19	4	0	0	4	4	18	3	.207	.250
Kevin Koslofski	OF22 DH1	L	29	25	42	5	9	3	2	0	6	4	12	0	.214	.381
Jeromy Burnitz	OF22	L	27	23	72	8	17	4	0	2	14	8	16	2	.236	.375
Kelly Stinnett	C14 DH1	R	26	14	26	1	2	0	0	0	0	2	11	0	.077	.077
Tim Unroe	1B11 3B3 OF1 DH1	R	25	14	16	5	3	0	0	0	0	4	5	0	.188	.188
Todd Dunn	OF6	R	25	6	10	2	3	1	0	0	1	0	3	0	.300	.400
Brian Banks	OF3 1B1	B	25	4	7	2	4	2	0	1	2	1	2	0	.571	1.286
Danny Perez	OF3	R	25	4	4	0	0	0	0	0	0	0	0	0	.000	.000

NAME	T	AGE	W	L	PCT	SV	G	GS	CG	IP	H	BB	SO	SHO	ERA
TOTALS		28	80	82	.494	42	162	162	6	1447	1570	635	846	4	5.14
Scott Karl	L	24	13	9	.591	0	32	32	3	207	220	72	121	1	4.86
Ben McDonald	R	28	12	10	.545	0	35	35	2	221	228	67	146	0	3.90
Angel Miranda	R	26	7	6	.538	1	46	12	0	109	116	69	78	0	4.94
Ricky Bones	R	27	7	14	.333	0	32	23	0	145	170	62	59	0	5.83
Jeff D'Amico	R	20	6	6	.500	0	17	17	0	86	88	31	53	0	5.44
Doug Jones	R	39	5	0	1.000	2	24	0	0	32	31	13	34	0	3.41
Ramon Garcia	R	26	4	4	.500	0	37	2	0	76	84	21	40	0	6.66
Cal Eldred (EJ)	R	28	4	4	.500	0	15	15	0	85	82	38	50	0	4.46
Steve Sparks	R	30	4	7	.364	0	20	13	1	89	103	52	21	0	6.60
Bob Wickman	R	27	3	3	.500	0	17	0	0	16	12	10	14	0	3.24
Mike Fetters	R	31	3	3	.500	32	61	0	0	61	65	26	53	0	3.38
Tim VanEgmond	R	27	3	5	.375	0	12	9	0	55	58	23	33	0	5.27
Kevin Wickander (SJ)	L	31	2	0	1.000	0	21	0	0	25	26	17	19	0	4.97
Terry Burrows	L	27	2	0	1.000	0	13	0	0	12	10	5	5	0	2.84
Graeme Lloyd	L	29	2	4	.333	0	52	0	0	51	49	17	24	0	2.82
Alberto Reyes	R	25	1	0	1.000	0	6	0	0	8	8	2	2	0	7.94
Mike Potts	L	25	1	2	.333	1	24	0	0	45	58	30	21	0	7.15
Brian Givens (XJ)	L	30	1	3	.250	1	14	12	0	63	75	37	43	0	12.86
Ron Villone	L	26	0	0	—	0	23	0	0	25	14	18	19	0	3.28
Cris Carpenter	R	31	0	0	—	0	2	0	0	5	5	2	5	0	7.56
Mark Kiefer	R	27	0	0	—	0	3	0	0	10	15	5	9	0	9.00
Bryce Florie	R	26	0	1	.000	0	15	0	0	19	20	13	12	0	6.63
Marshall Boze	R	25	0	1	.000	1	25	0	0	32	47	25	19	0	7.53
Jose Mercedes	R	25	0	0	—	0	11	0	0	17	20	5	6	0	9.18

Jamie McAndrew (KJ) 28

MINNESOTA — 4th 78-84 .481 21.5 — TOM KELLY

Name	G by Pos	B	AGE	G	AB	R	H	2B	3B	HR	RBI	BB	SO	SB	BA	SA
TOTALS			29	162	5673	877	1633	332	47	118	812	576	958	143	.288	.425
Scott Stahoviak	1B114 DH9	L	26	130	405	72	115	30	3	13	61	59	114	3	.284	.469
Chuck Knoblauch	2B151 DH2	R	27	153	578	140	197	35	14	13	72	98	74	45	.341	.517
Pat Meares	SS150 OF1	R	27	152	517	66	138	26	7	8	67	17	90	9	.267	.391
Dave Hollins	3B116 DH3 SS1	B	30	121	422	71	102	26	0	13	53	71	102	6	.242	.396
Roberto Kelly	OF93 DH2	R	31	98	322	41	104	17	4	6	47	23	53	10	.323	.457
Rich Becker	OF146	L	24	148	525	92	153	31	4	12	71	68	118	19	.291	.434
Marty Cordova	OF145	R	26	145	569	97	176	46	1	16	111	53	96	11	.309	.478
Greg Myers	C90	L	30	97	329	37	94	22	3	6	47	19	52	0	.286	.426
Paul Molitor	DH143 1B17	R	39	161	660	99	225	41	8	9	113	56	72	18	.341	.468
Jeff Reboulet	SS37 3B36 2B22 1B13 OF7 DH3	R	32	107	234	20	52	9	0	0	23	25	34	4	.222	.261
Ron Coomer	1B57 OF23 3B9 DH3	R	29	95	233	34	69	12	1	12	41	17	24	3	.296	.511
Chip Hale	2B14 DH10 1B6 3B3 OF3	L	31	85	87	8	24	5	0	1	16	10	6	0	.276	.368
Matt Lawton	OF75 DH1	L	24	79	252	34	65	7	1	6	42	28	28	4	.258	.365
Matt Walbeck (BH)	C61	R	26	63	215	25	48	10	0	2	24	9	34	3	.223	.298
Denny Hocking (BJ-KJ-VJ)	OF33 SS6 2B2 1B1 DH1	B	26	49	127	16	25	6	0	1	10	8	24	3	.197	.268
Mike Durant	C37	R	26	40	81	15	17	3	0	0	5	10	15	3	.210	.247
Todd Walker	3B20 2B4 DH1	L	23	25	82	8	21	6	0	0	6	4	13	2	.256	.329
Brent Brede	OF7	L	24	10	20	2	6	0	1	0	2	1	5	0	.300	.400
Brian Raabe	3B6 2B1	R	28	7	9	0	2	0	0	0	1	0	1	0	.222	.222
Tom Quinlan	3B4	R	28	4	6	0	0	0	0	0	0	0	3	0	.000	.000
Kirby Puckett (IJ) 36																

NAME	T	AGE	W	L	PCT	SV	G	GS	CG	IP	H	BB	SO	SHO	ERA
TOTALS		26	78	84	.481	31	162	162	13	1440	1561	581	959	5	5.28
Frankie Rodriguez	R	23	13	14	.481	2	38	33	2	207	218	78	110	0	5.05
Brad Radke	R	23	11	16	.407	0	35	35	3	232	231	57	148	0	4.46
Rick Aguilera (WJ)	R	34	8	6	.571	0	19	19	2	111	124	27	83	0	5.42
Rich Robertson	L	27	7	17	.292	0	36	31	5	186	197	116	114	3	5.12
Eddie Guardado	L	25	6	5	.545	4	83	0	0	74	61	33	74	0	5.25
Scott Aldred	L	28	6	5	.545	0	25	17	0	122	134	42	75	0	5.09
Mike Trombley	R	29	5	1	.833	6	43	0	0	69	61	25	57	0	3.01
Jose Parra	R	23	5	5	.500	0	27	5	0	70	88	27	50	0	6.04
Greg Hansell	R	25	3	0	1.000	0	50	0	0	74	83	31	46	0	5.69
Dan Naulty (AJ)	R	26	3	2	.600	4	49	0	0	57	43	35	56	0	3.79
Dave Stevens	R	26	3	3	.500	11	49	0	0	58	58	25	29	0	4.66
Erik Bennett	R	27	2	0	1.000	1	24	0	0	27	33	16	13	0	7.90
Mike Milchin	L	28	2	1	.667	0	26	0	0	22	31	12	19	0	8.31
Scott Klingenbeck	R	25	1	1	.500	0	10	3	0	29	42	10	15	0	7.85
LaTroy Hawkins	R	23	1	1	.500	0	7	6	0	26	42	9	24	0	8.20
Travis Miller	L	24	1	2	.333	0	7	7	0	26	42	19	24	0	8.20
Pat Mahomes	R	25	1	4	.200	0	20	5	0	45	63	27	30	0	7.20
Dan Serafini	L	22	0	1	.000	0	4	4	0	4	7	2	1	0	10.38

KANSAS CITY — 5th 75-86 .469 24 — BOB BOONE

Name	G by Pos	B	AGE	G	AB	R	H	2B	3B	HR	RBI	BB	SO	SB	BA	SA
TOTALS			27	161	5542	746	1477	286	38	123	689	529	943	195	.267	.398
Jose Offerman	1B96 2B38 SS36 OF1	B	27	151	561	85	170	33	8	5	47	74	98	24	.303	.417
Bip Roberts (LJ)	2B63 DH16 OF11	B	32	90	339	39	96	21	2	0	52	25	38	12	.283	.357
David Howard	SS135 2B3 1B2 OF1	B	29	143	420	51	92	14	5	4	48	40	74	5	.219	.305
Joe Randa	3B92 2B15 1B7 DH1	R	26	110	337	36	102	24	1	6	47	26	47	13	.303	.433
Michael Tucker (RJ)	OF98 1B9 DH5	L	25	108	339	55	88	18	4	12	53	40	69	10	.260	.442
Johnny Damon	OF144 DH1	L	22	145	517	61	140	22	5	6	50	31	64	25	.271	.368
Tom Goodwin	OF136 DH5	L	27	143	524	80	148	14	5	3	35	39	79	66	.282	.330
Mike Macfarlane	C99 DH9	R	32	112	379	58	104	24	2	19	54	31	57	3	.274	.499
Joe Vitiello	DH70 1B9 OF1	R	27	85	257	29	62	15	1	8	40	38	69	2	.241	.401
Keith Lockhart	2B84 3B55 DH1	L	31	138	433	49	118	33	3	7	55	30	40	11	.273	.414
Craig Paquette	3B51 OF47 1B19 SS11 DH6	R	27	118	429	61	111	15	1	22	67	23	101	5	.259	.452
Bob Hamelin (UJ)	DH47 1B33	L	28	89	239	31	61	14	1	9	40	54	58	5	.255	.435
Kevin Young	1B27 OF17 3B7 DH3	R	27	55	132	20	32	6	0	8	23	11	32	3	.242	.470
Les Norman (SJ)	OF38 DH7	R	27	54	49	9	6	1	0	1	1	12	0	.122	.122
Sal Fasano	C51	R	24	51	143	20	29	2	0	6	19	14	25	1	.203	.343
Mike Sweeney	C26 DH22	R	22	50	165	23	46	10	0	4	24	18	21	1	.279	.412
Chris Stynes	OF19 2B5 DH3 3B2	R	23	36	92	6	27	6	2	0	6	2	5	5	.293	.359
Jon Nunnally	OF29 DH4	L	24	35	90	16	19	3	0	3	11	21	26	3	.211	.456
Rod Myers	OF19	L	23	22	63	9	18	7	1	1	11	7	16	3	.286	.444
Patrick Lennon	OF11 DH1	R	28	14	30	1	7	1	0	0	7	7	10	0	.233	.333
Henry Mercedes	C4	R	26	4	4	1	1	0	0	0	0	2	0	.250	.250

NAME	T	AGE	W	L	PCT	SV	G	GS	CG	IP	H	BB	SO	SHO	ERA
TOTALS		28	75	86	.469	35	161	161	17	1450	1563	460	926	8	4.55
Tim Belcher	R	34	15	11	.577	0	35	35	4	239	262	68	113	0	3.92
Kevin Appier	R	28	14	11	.560	0	32	32	5	211	192	75	207	1	3.62
Chris Haney	L	27	10	14	.417	0	35	35	4	228	267	51	115	1	4.70
Jose Rosado	L	21	8	6	.571	0	16	16	2	107	101	26	64	1	3.21
Doug Linton	R	31	7	9	.438	0	21	18	0	104	111	26	87	0	5.02
Jeff Montgomery (SJ)	R	34	4	6	.400	24	48	0	0	63	59	19	45	0	4.26
Mark Gubicza (BL)	R	33	4	12	.250	0	19	19	2	119	132	34	55	1	5.13
Julio Valera	R	27	3	3	.500	1	31	2	0	61	75	27	31	0	6.46
Hipolito Pichardo	R	27	3	5	.375	3	57	0	0	68	74	26	43	0	5.43
Rick Huisman	R	27	2	1	.667	1	22	0	0	29	25	18	23	0	4.60
Mike Magnante	L	31	2	2	.500	0	38	0	0	54	58	24	32	0	5.67
Ken Robinson	R	26	1	0	1.000	0	5	0	0	8	6	7	5	0	5.73
Brian Bevil	R	24	1	0	1.000	0	3	0	0	8	7	1	6	0	5.73
Terry Clark	R	35	1	0	.500	0	12	0	0	17	28	7	12	0	7.07
Jaime Bluma	L	24	0	0	—	0	17	0	0	16	21	10	11	0	3.60
Jeff Granger	L	24	0	0	—	0	1	0	0	5	6	3	2	0	6.61
Tim Pugh	R	27	0	1	.000	0	19	1	0	36	42	12	27	0	5.45
Bob Scanlan	R	29	0	1	.000	0	11	0	0	17	20	5	6	0	3.18
Jason Jacome	L	25	0	4	.000	1	49	0	0	48	67	22	32	0	4.72

Jim Pittsley (EJ) 24, Jim Converse (SJ) 24

TEXAS — 1st 90-72 .556 — JOHNNY OATES

Name	G by Pos	B	AGE	G	AB	R	H	2B	3B	HR	RBI	BB	SO	SB	BA	SA
TOTALS		B	30	163	5702	928	1622	323	32	221	890	660	1041	83	.284	.469
Will Clark (VJ)	1B117	L	32	117	436	69	124	25	1	13	72	64	67	2	.284	.436
Mark McLemore	2B147 OF1	B	31	147	517	84	150	23	4	5	46	87	69	27	.290	.379
Kevin Elster	SS157	R	31	157	515	79	130	32	2	24	99	52	138	4	.252	.462
Dean Palmer	3B154 DH1	R	27	154	582	98	163	26	2	38	107	59	145	2	.280	.527
Juan Gonzalez	OF102 DH32	R	26	134	541	89	170	33	2	47	144	45	82	2	.314	.643
Darryl Hamilton	OF147	L	31	148	627	94	184	29	6	6	51	54	66	15	.293	.381
Rusty Greer	OF137 1B1 DH1	L	27	139	542	96	180	41	6	18	100	62	86	9	.332	.530
Ivan Rodriguez	C146 DH6	R	24	153	639	116	192	47	3	19	86	38	55	5	.300	.473
Mickey Tettleton	DH115 1B23	B	35	143	491	78	121	26	1	24	83	95	137	2	.246	.450
Warren Newson	OF66 DH9	L	31	91	235	34	60	14	1	10	31	37	82	3	.255	.451
Damon Buford	OF80	R	26	90	145	30	41	9	0	6	20	15	34	8	.283	.469
Rene Gonzales	1B23 3B15 SS10 2B5 OF1	R	35	51	92	19	20	4	0	2	5	10	11	2	.217	.326
Kurt Stillwell	2B21 SS9 3B6 1B1 DH1	R	31	46	77	12	21	4	0	1	4	10	11	1	.273	.364
Dave Valle	C35 1B5 DH1	R	35	42	86	14	26	6	1	3	17	9	17	0	.302	.500
Lou Frazier	OF15 DH13 2B1	L	31	50	50	5	13	2	1	0	5	8	10	4	.260	.340
Lee Stevens (GJ)	1B18 OF5	L	28	27	78	6	18	2	3	3	12	6	22	0	.231	.449
Craig Worthington	3B7 1B6	R	31	13	19	2	3	0	0	1	4	6	0	0	.158	.316
Rikkert Faneyte	OF6 DH2	R	27	8	5	0	1	0	0	0	1	0	3	0	.200	.200
Jack Voigt	OF3 3B1	R	30	5	9	1	1	0	0	0	0	1	1	0	.111	.111
Benji Gil (XJ)	SS5	R	23	5	5	0	2	0	0	0	1	1	1	0	.400	.400
Luis Ortiz	DH1	R	26	3	7	1	2	0	1	0	1	0	0	0	.286	1.000
Kevin Brown	C2 DH1	R	23	3	4	1	0	0	0	0	0	1	2	0	.000	.000

NAME	T	AGE	W	L	PCT	SV	G	GS	CG	IP	H	BB	SO	SHO	ERA
		31	90	72	.556	43	163	163	19	1449	1569	582	976	6	4.65
Ken Hill	R	30	16	10	.615	0	35	35	7	251	250	95	170	1	3.63
Bobby Witt	R	32	16	12	.571	0	33	33	2	200	235	96	157	0	5.41
Roger Pavlik	R	28	15	8	.652	0	34	34	7	201	216	81	127	0	5.19
Darren Oliver	L	25	14	6	.700	0	30	30	1	174	190	76	112	1	4.66
Kevin Gross	R	35	11	8	.579	0	28	19	1	129	151	50	78	0	5.22
Dennis Cook	L	33	5	2	.714	0	70	0	0	70	53	35	64	0	4.09
2 John Burkett	R	31	5	2	.714	0	10	10	1	69	75	16	47	1	4.06
Jeff Russell	R	34	3	3	.500	2	55	0	0	56	58	22	23	0	3.38
Gil Heredia	R	30	2	5	.286	1	44	0	0	73	91	14	43	0	5.89
Ed Vosberg	L	34	1	1	.500	8	52	0	0	44	51	21	32	0	3.27
1 Rick Helling	R	25	1	2	.333	0	6	2	0	20	23	9	16	0	7.52
1 Mark Brandenburg	R	25	1	3	.250	0	26	0	0	48	48	25	37	0	3.21
Danny Patterson	R	25	0	0	—	0	7	0	0	9	10	3	5	0	0.00
2 Mike Stanton	L	29	0	1	.000	0	22	0	0	22	20	4	14	0	3.22
Matt Whiteside	R	28	0	1	.000	0	14	0	0	32	43	11	15	0	6.68
Jose Alberro	R	27	0	1	.000	0	5	1	0	9	14	7	2	0	5.79
Mike Henneman	R	34	0	7	.000	31	49	0	0	42	41	17	34	0	5.79

Chris Nichting (ZJ) 30, Chris Howard (SJ) 30

SEATTLE — 2nd 85-76 .525 4.5 — LOU PINIELLA

Name	G by Pos	B	AGE	G	AB	R	H	2B	3B	HR	RBI	BB	SO	SB	BA	SA
TOTALS			29	161	5668	993	1625	343	19	245	954	670	1052	90	.287	.484
Paul Sorrento	1B138	L	30	143	471	67	136	32	1	23	93	57	103	0	.289	.507
Joey Cora	2B140 3B1	R	31	144	530	90	154	37	6	6	45	35	32	5	.291	.417
Alex Rodriguez	SS146	R	20	146	601	141	215	54	1	36	123	59	104	15	.358	.631
Russ Davis (BL)	3B51	R	26	51	167	24	39	9	0	5	18	17	50	2	.234	.377
Jay Buhner	OF142 DH8	R	31	150	564	107	153	29	0	44	138	84	159	0	.271	.557
Ken Griffey Jr.	OF137 DH5	L	26	140	545	125	165	26	2	49	140	78	104	16	.303	.628
Rich Amaral	OF91 2B15 1B10 DH6 3B1	R	34	118	312	69	91	11	3	1	29	47	55	25	.292	.356
Dan Wilson	C135	R	27	138	491	51	140	24	0	18	83	32	88	1	.285	.444
Edgar Martinez	DH134 1B4 3B2	R	33	139	499	121	163	52	2	26	103	123	84	3	.327	.595
Doug Strange	3B39 OF11 DH10 2B3 1B3	B	32	88	183	19	43	7	1	3	23	14	31	1	.235	.333
1 Luis Sojo	3B33 2B27 SS19	R	30	77	247	20	52	8	1	1	16	10	13	2	.211	.263
Brian Hunter	1B41 OF29 DH2	L	26	69	198	21	53	10	0	7	28	15	43	0	.268	.424
1 Darren Bragg	OF63	L	26	69	195	36	53	12	1	7	25	33	35	8	.272	.451
Andy Sheets	3B25 2B18 SS7	R	24	47	110	18	21	8	0	0	9	10	41	2	.191	.264
John Marzano	C39	R	33	41	106	8	26	6	0	0	6	7	15	0	.245	.302
3 Mark Whiten	OF39	B	29	40	140	31	42	7	0	12	33	21	40	2	.300	.607
Alex Diaz (LJ)	OF28 DH1	B	27	38	79	11	19	2	0	1	5	2	8	6	.241	.304
2 Dave Hollins	3B28 1B1	R	30	28	94	17	33	3	0	3	25	13	15	0	.351	.479
2 Jeff Manto	3B16 DH2 OF1	R	31	21	54	7	10	3	0	1	4	9	12	0	.185	.296
Ricky Jordan	1B9 DH2	R	31	15	28	4	7	0	0	1	4	1	6	0	.250	.357
1 Manny Martinez	OF8	R	25	9	17	3	4	2	1	0	3	3	5	2	.235	.471
Chris Widger	C7	R	25	8	11	1	2	0	0	0	0	0	3	0	.182	.182
1 Greg Pirkl	DH3 1B2	R	25	7	21	2	4	1	0	0	1	0	9	0	.190	.381
Raul Ibanez	DH2	L	24	4	5	0	0	0	0	0	0	0	1	0	.000	.000

NAME	T	AGE	W	L	PCT	SV	G	GS	CG	IP	H	BB	SO	SHO	ERA
		29	85	76	.525	34	161	161	4	1432	1562	605	1000	4	5.21
Sterling Hitchcock	L	35	13	9	.591	0	35	35	0	197	245	73	132	0	5.35
Bob Wells	R	29	12	7	.632	0	36	16	1	131	141	46	94	1	5.30
Rafael Carmona	R	23	8	3	.727	1	53	1	0	90	95	55	62	0	4.28
Bob Wolcott	R	22	7	10	.412	0	30	28	1	149	179	54	78	0	5.73
2 Jamie Moyer	L	33	6	2	.750	0	11	11	0	71	66	19	29	0	3.31
Bobby Ayala (HJ)	R	26	6	3	.667	3	50	0	0	67	65	25	61	0	5.88
Randy Johnson (XJ)	L	32	5	0	1.000	1	14	8	0	61	48	25	85	0	3.67
2 Terry Mulholland	L	33	5	4	.556	0	12	12	0	69	75	28	34	0	4.67
Chris Bosio (KJ)	R	33	4	4	.500	0	18	0	0	61	72	24	39	0	5.93
Norm Charlton	R	33	4	7	.364	20	70	0	0	76	68	38	73	0	4.04
Salomon Torres	R	24	3	3	.500	0	10	7	1	49	44	23	36	1	4.59
Matt Wagner	R	24	3	5	.375	0	15	14	1	80	91	38	41	0	6.86
Tim Davis (BL)	L	25	2	2	.500	0	40	0	0	43	45	17	34	0	4.01
Paul Menhart	R	27	2	2	.500	0	11	6	0	42	55	25	18	0	7.29
Edwin Hurtado	R	25	2	2	.500	0	16	4	0	48	61	30	36	0	7.74
Mike Jackson	R	31	1	5	.500	0	73	0	0	72	61	24	70	0	3.63
Rusty Meacham	R	28	1	1	.500	1	15	5	0	42	57	13	25	0	5.74
Bob Milacki	R	31	1	4	.200	0	7	4	0	21	30	15	13	0	6.86
Greg McCarthy	L	27	0	0	—	0	10	0	0	9	4	4	9	0	1.86
Scott Davison	R	25	0	0	.000	0	9	0	0	9	11	4	9	0	9.00
Joe Klink	L	34	0	0	—	0	7	0	0	3	2	2	1	0	3.86
Mac Suzuki	R	21	0	0	—	0	2	1	0	2	5	1	0	0	20.25
2 Blas Minor	R	30	0	1	.000	0	25	0	0	25	27	11	14	0	4.97
Tim Harikkala	R	24	0	3	.000	0	11	6	0	25	33	11	12	0	12.46
Lee Guetterman	L	37	0	0	.000	0	11	0	0	11	11	10	6	0	4.09

Greg Hibbard (SJ) 31

OAKLAND — 3rd 78-84 .481 12 — ART HOWE

Name	G by Pos	B	AGE	G	AB	R	H	2B	3B	HR	RBI	BB	SO	SB	BA	SA
TOTALS			28	162	5630	861	1492	283	21	243	823	640	1114	58	.265	.452
Mark McGwire	1B109 DH18	R	32	130	423	104	132	21	0	52	113	116	112	0	.312	.730
Brent Gates (BL)	2B63	R	26	64	247	28	65	19	2	2	30	18	35	1	.263	.381
Mike Bordick	SS155	R	30	155	525	46	126	18	4	5	54	52	59	5	.240	.318
Scott Brosius (BH)	3B109 1B10 OF4	R	29	114	428	73	130	25	0	22	71	59	85	7	.304	.516
Jose Herrera	OF100 DH1	L	23	108	320	44	86	15	1	6	30	20	58	9	.269	.378
Ernie Young	OF140	R	26	141	462	72	112	19	4	19	64	52	118	7	.242	.424
Jason Giambi	OF45 1B45 3B39 DH12	L	25	140	536	84	156	40	1	20	79	51	95	0	.291	.481
Terry Steinbach	C137 DH4 1B1	R	34	145	514	79	140	25	1	35	100	49	115	0	.272	.529
Geronimo Berroa	DH91 OF61	R	31	153	586	101	170	32	1	36	106	47	122	0	.290	.532
Rafael Bournigal	2B64 SS23	R	30	88	252	33	61	14	2	0	18	16	19	4	.242	.313
Tony Batista	2B52 3B18 SS4 DH4	R	22	74	238	38	71	10	2	6	25	19	49	7	.298	.433
Phil Plantier	OF68 DH1	L	27	73	231	29	49	8	1	7	31	28	56	2	.212	.346
Torey Lovullo	1B42 3B11 DH4 2B2 SS1 OF1	B	30	65	82	15	18	4	0	3	9	11	17	1	.220	.378
Matt Stairs	OF44 DH5 1B1	L	28	61	137	21	38	5	1	10	23	19	23	1	.277	.547
George Williams	C43 DH1	B	27	56	132	17	20	5	3	0	10	28	32	0	.152	.258
Allen Battle	OF47	R	27	50	105	20	28	7	1	3	12	16	31	4	.267	.438
Damon Mashore (SJ)	OF48	R	26	47	130	20	35	3	0	1	5	17	26	10	.192	.238
Pedro Munoz (KJ)	DH18 OF14	R	27	34	121	17	31	5	0	8	18	9	31	0	.256	.446
Brian Lesher	OF25 1B1	R	25	26	82	11	19	5	0	5	16	5	17	0	.232	.451
Kerwin Moore	OF18 DH2	B	25	22	16	4	1	1	0	0	2	3	6	1	.063	.125
Izzy Molina	C12 DH1	R	24	25	14	2	5	2	0	0	1	1	3	0	.200	.280
Scott Spiezio	3B5 DH4	B	23	9	29	6	9	2	2	0	8	4	4	0	.310	.586
Webster Garrison	2B3 1B1	R	30	5											.000	.000

NAME	T	AGE	W	L	PCT	SV	G	GS	CG	IP	H	BB	SO	SHO	ERA
		28	78	84	.481	34	162	162	7	1456	1638	644	884	5	5.20
John Wasdin	R	23	8	7	.533	0	25	21	1	131	145	50	75	0	5.96
Carlos Reyes	R	27	7	10	.412	0	46	10	0	122	154	50	78	0	4.78
Don Wengert	R	26	7	11	.389	0	36	25	1	161	200	60	75	1	5.58
Jim Corsi	R	34	6	0	1.000	3	56	0	0	74	71	34	43	0	4.03
Mike Mohler	L	27	6	3	.667	7	72	0	0	81	79	41	64	0	3.67
Billy Taylor (GJ)	R	34	6	3	.667	17	55	0	0	60	52	25	67	0	4.33
Ariel Prieto (EJ)	R	26	6	7	.462	0	21	21	2	126	130	54	75	0	4.15
Doug Johns	L	28	6	12	.333	1	40	23	1	158	187	69	71	0	5.98
Buddy Groom	L	30	5	0	1.000	2	72	1	0	77	85	34	57	0	3.84
Steve Wojciechowski	L	25	5	5	.500	0	16	15	0	80	97	28	30	0	5.65
Bobby Chouinard	R	24	4	2	.667	0	13	11	0	59	75	32	32	0	6.10
Dave Telgheder	R	23	4	3	.364	0	16	14	1	79	92	26	43	1	4.65
Willie Adams	R	23	3	4	.429	0	12	12	1	76	76	23	68	1	4.01
Steve Montgomery	R	25	1	0	1.000	0	8	0	0	13	12	5	12	0	9.22
Jay Witasick	R	23	1	1	.500	0	2	2	0	13	13	12	6	0	6.23
Mark Acre	R	27	1	2	.333	0	25	0	0	38	38	9	16	0	6.12
Aaron Small	R	24	1	3	.250	0	12	3	0	29	37	17	10	0	8.16
1 Todd Van Poppel	R	24	1	5	.167	0	14	0	0	63	86	33	37	0	7.71
Paul Fletcher	R	29	0	0	—	0	1	0	0	6	6	1	0	0	20.25
John Briscoe	R	28	0	0	.000	0	26	0	0	18	24	14	0	0	3.76

Steve Karsay (EJ) 24

CALIFORNIA — 4th 70-91 .435 19.5 — MARCEL LACHEMANN 52-59 .468 / JOHN McNAMARA 18-32 .360

Name	G by Pos	B	AGE	G	AB	R	H	2B	3B	HR	RBI	BB	SO	SB	BA	SA
TOTALS			30	161	5686	762	1571	256	24	192	727	527	974	53	.276	.431
J.T. Snow	1B154	B	28	155	575	69	148	20	1	17	67	56	96	1	.257	.384
Randy Velarde	2B114 3B28 SS7	R	33	136	530	82	151	27	3	14	54	70	118	7	.285	.426
Gary DiSarcina	SS155	R	28	150	536	62	137	26	4	5	48	21	36	2	.256	.347
George Arias	3B83 DH1	R	24	84	252	19	60	8	1	6	28	16	50	2	.238	.349
Tim Salmon	OF153 DH1	R	26	155	581	90	166	27	4	30	98	93	125	4	.286	.501
Jim Edmonds (RJ)	OF111 DH1	R	26	114	431	73	131	28	3	27	66	46	101	4	.304	.571
Garret Anderson	OF146 DH1	L	24	150	607	79	173	33	2	12	72	27	84	7	.285	.405
Jorge Fabregas	C89 DH1	L	26	90	254	18	73	6	0	2	26	17	22	0	.287	.335
Chili Davis	DH143	B	36	145	530	73	155	24	0	28	95	86	99	5	.292	.496
Rex Hudler	2B53 OF21 DH8 1B7	R	35	92	302	60	94	20	3	16	40	9	54	14	.311	.556
Jack Howell (LJ)	3B43 DH4 1B2 C1	R	34	66	126	20	34	4	1	8	21	10	30	1	.270	.508
1 Don Slaught	C59 DH1	R	37	62	207	23	67	9	0	6	32	13	20	0	.324	.454
Darin Erstad	OF48	R	22	57	208	34	59	5	1	4	20	17	29	3	.284	.375
1 Tim Wallach	3B46 DH8 1B3	R	38	55	190	23	45	7	0	8	20	18	47	1	.237	.400
Orlando Palmeiro	OF31 DH4	L	27	50	87	6	25	6	1	0	8	6	13	0	.287	.379
1 Mike Aldrete	OF6 DH1 1B1	L	35	31	40	5	6	1	3	0	5	6	9	0	.150	.400
Todd Greene	C26	R	25	29	79	9	15	1	0	2	6	4	11	0	.190	.278
1 Damion Easley (SJ)	SS13 2B9 3B3 OF2 DH2	R	26	28	73	8	11	2	0	2	5	9	11	4	.151	.311
2 Pat Borders	C19	R	33	19	57	6	13	0	0	2	5	1	5	0	.228	.386
Dick Schofield (RP)	SS7 2B2 3B1 DH1	R	33	13	16	3	4	0	0	1	2	3	5	0	.250	.250
2 Robert Eenhoorn	SS4 2B2	R	28	11	15	1	4	1	0	0	3	0	3	0	.267	.267
Chris Pritchett	1B5	L	26	5	13	1	2	0	0	0	1	1	6	0	.154	.154
Chris Turner	C3 OF1	R	27	4	3	1	1	0	0	0	0	0	1	0	.333	.333

NAME	T	AGE	W	L	PCT	SV	G	GS	CG	IP	H	BB	SO	SHO	ERA
		29	70	91	.435	38	161	161	12	1439	1546	662	1052	8	5.30
Chuck Finley	L	33	15	16	.484	0	35	35	4	238	241	94	215	1	4.16
Shawn Boskie	R	29	12	11	.522	0	37	28	1	189	226	67	133	0	5.32
Mark Langston (KJ)	L	35	6	5	.545	0	18	18	2	123	116	45	83	0	4.82
2 Chuck McElroy	L	28	5	1	.833	0	40	0	0	37	32	13	32	2	2.95
Mike James	R	28	5	5	.500	1	69	0	0	81	62	42	65	0	2.67
Dennis Springer	R	31	5	6	.455	0	20	15	3	90	150	74	92	1	5.51
Jason Grimsley	R	28	5	7	.417	0	35	20	2	130	150	74	82	1	6.84
Ryan Hancock	R	24	4	1	.800	0	11	4	0	28	29	21	19	0	7.48
Mike Holtz	L	23	3	3	.500	0	30	0	0	32	31	17	31	0	3.90
Pep Harris	R	23	2	0	1.000	0	9	0	0	13	18	7	8	0	7.88
Jeff Schmidt	R	25	2	0	1.000	0	9	0	0	8	13	8	2	0	7.48
Jim Abbott	L	28	2	18	.100	0	27	23	1	142	171	78	58	0	7.48
Mark Holzemer (SJ)	L	26	1	1	.500	0	25	0	0	25	35	8	20	0	8.76
2 Greg Gohr	R	28	1	4	.200	0	15	0	0	24	34	15	10	0	7.50
Mark Eichhorn (SJ)	R	35	1	2	.333	0	24	0	0	30	36	11	24	0	5.04
Jason Dickson	R	23	1	4	.200	0	7	7	0	43	52	18	20	0	4.57
1 Lee Smith	R	38	0	0	.000	0	11	0	0	9	13	8	11	0	7.00
2 Brad Pennington	L	27	0	0	—	0	7	0	0	7	9	12	7	0	12.27
2 Darrell May	L	24	0	0	.000	0	7	0	0	7	13	4	5	0	10.13
Todd Frohwirth	R	33	0	0	—	0	8	0	0	6	13	4	2	0	11.12
Robert Ellis	R	25	0	0	.000	0	3	0	0	6	8	6	3	0	5.54
Ken Edenfield	R	29	0	0	—	0	11	0	0	9	14	7	4	0	10.38
Ben VanRyn	L	28	0	0	—	0	4	0	0	6	11	1	0	0	7.50
Kyle Abbott	L	28	0	0	—	0	5	0	0	4	4	5	5	0	20.25
Phil Leftwich	R	26	0	0	—	0	3	0	0	7	8	2	2	0	7.36
Troy Percival	R	26	0	2	.000	36	62	0	0	74	38	31	100	0	2.31
Shad Williams	R	26	0	3	.000	0	18	0	0	28	42	21	26	0	8.89
Scott Sanderson	R	39	0	0	.000	0	7	0	0	18	39	4	7	0	5.04
Rich Monteleone (XJ)	R	33	0	0	.000	0	15	0	0	15	23	2	6	0	5.87

Bryan Harvey (EJ) 33, Steve Ontiveros (EJ) 35

LINE SCORES

Team	1	2	3	4	5	6	7	8	9	10	11	12	R	H	E

DIVISION SERIES: NEW YORK 3 : TEXAS 1

Game 1   October 1 at New York

TEX	0 0 0 5 0 1 0 0 0	6 8 0
NY	1 0 0 1 0 0 0 0 0	2 10 0

Burkett   **Cone**, Lloyd (7)
Weathers (9)

Game 2   October 2 at New York

TEX	0 1 3 0 0 0 0 0 0 0 0 0	4 8 1
NY	0 1 0 1 0 0 1 1 0 0 0 1	5 8 0

Hill, Cook (7), Russell (8),   Pettitte, Rivera (7), Wetteland (10),
Stanton (11), Henneman (12)   Lloyd (12), Nelson (12), Rogers (12),
   Boehringer (12)

Game 3   October 4 at Texas

NY	1 0 0 0 0 0 0 0 2	3 7 1
TEX	0 0 0 1 1 0 0 0 0	2 6 1

Key, **Nelson** (6),   **Oliver**, Henneman (9),
Wetteland (9)   Stanton (9)

Game 4   October 5 at Texas

NY	0 0 0 3 1 0 1 0 1	6 12 1
TEX	0 2 2 0 0 0 0 0 0	4 9 0

Rogers, Boehringer (3),   Witt, Patterson (4), Cook (4)
Weathers (4), Rivera (7),   **Pavlik** (5), Vosberg (7), Russell (7),
Wetteland (9)   Stanton (8), Henneman (8)

DIVISION SERIES: BALTIMORE 3 : CLEVELAND 1

Game 1   October 1 at Baltimore

CLE	0 1 0 2 0 0 1 0 0	4 10 0
BAL	1 1 2 0 0 5 1 0 X	10 12 1

Nagy, Embree (6),   **Wells**, Orosco (7), Mathew (7),
Shuey (6), Tavarez (8)   Rhodes (8), Myers (9)

Game 2   October 2 at Baltimore

CLE	0 0 0 0 0 3 0 1 0	4 8 2
BAL	1 0 0 0 3 0 0 3 X	7 9 0

Hershiser, **Plunk** (6),   Erickson, Orosco (7),
Assenmacher (8), Tavarez (8)   **Benitez** (8), Myers (9)

Game 3   October 4 at Cleveland

BAL	0 1 0 3 0 0 0 0 0	4 8 2
CLE	1 2 0 1 0 0 4 1 X	9 10 0

Mussina, **Ososco** (7), Benitez (7)   McDowell, Embree (6), Shuey (7),
Rhodes (8), Mathews (8)   **Assenmacher** (7), Plunk (8), Mesa (9)

Game 4   October 5 at Cleveland

BAL	0 2 0 0 0 0 0 1 0 0 1	4 14 1
CLE	0 0 0 2 1 0 0 0 0 0 0	3 7 1

Wells, Mathews (9), Orosco (9),   Nagy, Embree (7), Shuey (7),
Benitez (10), Myers (12)   Assenmacher (7), Plunk (8),
   Mesa (9), Ogea (12)

AMERICAN LEAGUE CHAMPIONSHIPS: NEW YORK 4 : BALTIMORE 1

Game 1   October 9 at New York

BAL	0 1 1 1 0 1 0 0 0	4 11 1
NY	1 1 0 0 0 0 1 0 0 1	5 11 0

Erickson, Orosco (7), Benitez (7),   Pettitte, Nelson (8), Wetteland (9),
Rhodes (8), Mathews (9), **Myers** (9)   **Rivera** (10)

Game 2   October 10 at New York

BAL	0 0 2 0 0 0 0 2 1 0	5 10 0
NY	2 0 0 0 0 0 1 0 0	3 11 1

Wells, Mills (7), Orosco (7),   Cone, **Nelson** (7), Lloyd (9),
Myers (9), Benitez (9)   Weathers (9)

Game 3   October 11 at Baltimore

NY	0 0 0 1 0 0 0 4 0	5 8 0
BAL	2 0 0 0 0 0 0 0 0	2 3 2

Key, Wetteland (9)   **Mussina**, Orosco (8), Mathews (9)

Game 4   October 12 at Baltimore

NY	2 1 0 2 0 0 0 3 0	8 9 0
BAL	1 0 1 2 0 0 0 0 0	4 11 0

Rogers, **Weathers** (4), Lloyd (6),   Coppinger, Rhodes (6), Mills (7)
Rivera (7), Wetteland (9)   Orosco (8), Benitez (8), Mathews (9)

Game 5   October 13 at Baltimore

NY	0 0 6 0 0 0 0 0 0	6 11 0
BAL	0 0 0 0 0 1 0 1 2	4 4 1

Pettitte, Wetteland (9)   **Erickson**, Rhodes (6), Mills (7),
   Myers (8)

DIVISION SERIES

COMPOSITE BATTING

NEW YORK

NAME	POS	G	AB	R	H	2B	3B	HR	RBI	BA
TOTALS		4	140	16	37	4	0	4	15	.264
Jeter	SS	4	17	2	7	1	0	0	1	.412
Duncan	2B	4	16	0	5	0	0	0	1	.313
Raines	LF	4	16	3	4	0	0	0	0	.250
Williams	CF	4	15	5	7	0	0	3	5	.467
Martinez	1B	4	15	3	4	2	0	0	0	.267
O'Neill	RF	4	15	0	2	0	0	0	0	.133
Boggs	3B	3	12	0	1	1	0	0	0	.083
Fielder	DH	3	11	2	4	0	0	1	4	.364
Girardi	C	4	9	1	2	0	0	0	0	.222
Hayes	3B	3	5	0	1	0	0	0	1	.200
Strawberry	DH	2	5	0	0	0	0	0	0	.000
Leyritz	C	2	3	0	0	0	0	0	0	.000
R. Rivera	RF	2	1	0	0	0	0	0	0	.000
Sojo	2B	2	0	0	0	0	0	0	0	—
Fox	DH	2	0	0	0	0	0	0	0	—

TEXAS

NAME	POS	G	AB	R	H	2B	3B	HR	RBI	BA
TOTALS		4	142	16	31	4	0	6	16	.218
Palmer	3B	4	19	3	4	1	0	1	2	.211
Hamilton	CF	4	19	0	3	0	0	0	0	.158
Gonzalez	RF	4	16	5	7	0	0	5	9	.438
Rodriguez	C	4	16	1	6	1	0	0	2	.375
Clark	1B	4	16	1	2	0	0	0	0	.125
Greer	LF	4	16	2	2	1	0	0	0	.125
McLemore	2B	4	15	1	2	0	0	0	2	.133
Elster	SS	4	12	2	4	2	0	0	0	.333
Tettleton	DH	4	12	1	1	0	0	0	1	.083
Newson	PH	3	1	0	0	0	0	0	0	.000
Buford	PR	3	0	0	0	0	0	0	0	—

BALTIMORE

NAME	POS	G	AB	R	H	2B	3B	HR	RBI	BA
TOTALS		4	150	25	43	6	0	9	23	.289
Zeile	3B	4	19	2	5	1	0	0	0	.263
C. Ripken	SS	4	18	2	8	3	0	0	0	.444
Anderson	CF	4	17	3	5	0	0	2	4	.294
Alomar	2B	4	17	2	5	0	0	1	4	.294
Palmeiro	1B	4	17	4	3	1	0	1	2	.176
Murray	DH	4	15	1	6	1	0	1	1	.400
Bonilla	RF	4	15	4	3	0	0	2	5	.200
Surhoff	LF	4	13	5	5	0	0	3	5	.385
Hoiles	C	4	8	1	1	0	0	0	0	.125
Parent	C	4	5	0	1	0	0	0	0	.200
Incaviglia	LF	2	5	1	1	0	0	0	0	.200
Devereaux	RF-LF	4	1	0	0	0	0	0	0	.000
Alexander	DH	3	0	2	0	0	0	0	0	—

CLEVELAND

NAME	POS	G	AB	R	H	2B	3B	HR	RBI	BA
TOTALS		4	143	20	35	7	0	4	20	.245
Lofton	CF	4	18	3	3	0	0	0	0	.167
Seitzer	DH-1B	4	17	1	5	1	0	0	4	.294
Ramirez	RF	4	16	4	6	2	0	2	2	.375
Alomar	C	4	16	0	2	0	0	0	3	.125
Belle	LF	4	15	2	3	0	0	2	6	.200
Franco	1B-DH	4	15	1	2	0	0	0	2	.133
Vizquiel	SS	4	14	4	6	1	0	0	4	.429
Vizcaino	2B	3	12	1	4	2	0	0	2	.333
Thome	3B	4	10	1	3	0	0	0	0	.300
Kent	2B-1B-3B	4	8	2	1	1	0	0	0	.125
Giles	PH	1	1	0	0	0	0	0	0	.000
Wilson	PH	1	1	0	0	0	0	0	0	.000
Candaele	DH	2	0	1	0	0	0	0	0	—
Pena	C	1	0	0	0	0	0	0	0	—

COMPOSITE PITCHING

NEW YORK

NAME	G	IP	H	BB	SO	W	L	SV	ERA
TOTALS	4	39	31	20	30	3	1	2	3.46
Pettitte	1	6	4	6	3	0	0	0	5.68
Cone	1	6	8	2	8	0	1	0	9.00
Weathers	2	5	1	0	5	1	0	0	0.00
Key	1	5	5	1	3	0	0	0	3.60
M. Rivera	2	4.2	0	1	1	0	0	0	0.00
Wetteland	3	4	2	4	4	0	0	2	0.00
Nelson	2	3.2	2	2	5	1	0	0	0.00
Rogers	2	2	5	2	1	0	0	0	9.00
Boehringer	2	1.1	3	2	0	1	0	0	6.75
Lloyd	2	1	1	0	0	0	0	0	0.00

TEXAS

NAME	G	IP	H	BB	SO	W	L	SV	ERA
TOTALS	4	38	37	13	20	1	3	0	3.55
Burkett	1	9	10	1	7	1	0	0	2.00
Oliver	1	8	6	2	3	0	1	0	3.38
Hill	1	6	0.5	3	1	0	0	0	4.50
Witt	1	3.1	4	2	3	0	0	0	8.10
Stanton	3	3.1	2	3	3	0	1	0	2.70
Russell	2	3	3	0	1	0	0	0	0.00
Pavlik	1	2.2	4	0	1	0	1	0	6.75
Cook	2	1.1	0	1	0	0	0	0	0.00
Henneman	3	1	1	1	1	0	0	0	0.00
Patterson	1	.1	1	0	0	0	0	0	0.00
Vosberg	1	0	1	0	0	0	0	0	—

BALTIMORE

NAME	G	IP	H	BB	SO	W	L	SV	ERA
TOTALS	4	38	35	15	32	3	1	2	4.50
Wells	2	13.2	15	4	6	1	0	0	4.61
Erickson	1	6.2	6	2	6	0	0	0	4.05
Mussina	1	6.0	7	2	6	0	0	0	4.50
Benitez	3	4.0	1	2	6	2	0	0	2.25
Myers	3	3	0	0	3	0	0	2	0.00
Mathews	3	2.2	3	1	2	0	0	0	0.00
Orosco	4	1	2	3	2	0	1	0	36.00
Rhodes	2	1	1	1	1	0	0	0	9.00

CLEVELAND

NAME	G	IP	H	BB	SO	W	L	SV	ERA
TOTALS	4	37	43	17	40	1	3	0	5.84
Nagy	2	11.1	15	5	13	0	1	0	7.15
McDowell	1	5.2	6	1	5	0	0	0	6.35
Hershiser	1	5	7	3	3	0	0	0	5.40
Mesa	2	4.2	8	0	7	0	1	0	3.86
Plunk	3	4	1	2	6	0	1	0	6.75
Shuey	3	2	5	2	2	0	0	0	9.00
Assenmacher	3	1.2	0	1	2	1	0	0	0.00
Tavarez	2	1.1	1	2	1	0	0	0	0.00
Embree	3	1	0	1	0	0	0	0	9.00
Ogea	1	.1	0	1	1	0	0	0	0.00

AMERICAN LEAGUE CHAMPIONSHIP

COMPOSITE BATTING

NEW YORK

NAME	POS	G	AB	R	H	2B	3B	HR	RBI	BA
TOTALS		5	183	27	50	9	1	10	24	.273
Jeter	SS	5	24	5	10	2	0	1	1	.417
Martinez	1B	5	22	3	4	1	0	0	0	.182
Williams	CF	5	19	6	9	3	0	2	6	.474
Fielder	DH	5	18	3	3	0	0	2	8	.167
Raines	LF	5	15	2	4	1	0	0	0	.267
Duncan	2B	4	15	4	3	2	0	0	0	.200
Boggs	3B	3	15	1	2	0	0	0	0	.133
Strawberry	RF-LF	4	12	4	5	0	0	3	5	.417
Girardi	C	4	12	1	3	0	1	0	0	.250
O'Neill	RF	4	11	1	3	0	0	1	2	.273
Leyritz	C-RF	3	8	1	2	0	0	1	2	.250
Hayes	3B	4	7	0	1	0	0	0	0	.143
Sojo	2B	3	5	0	1	0	0	0	0	.200

BALTIMORE

NAME	POS	G	AB	R	H	2B	3B	HR	RBI	BA
TOTALS		5	176	19	39	4	0	9	19	.222
Alomar	2B	5	23	2	5	2	0	0	1	.217
Zeile	3B	5	22	3	8	0	0	3	5	.364
Anderson	CF	5	21	5	4	1	0	1	1	.190
C. Ripken	SS	5	20	1	5	1	0	0	0	.250
Bonilla	RF	5	20	1	1	0	0	1	2	.050
Palmeiro	1B	5	17	4	4	0	0	2	4	.235
Murray	DH	5	15	1	4	0	0	1	2	.267
Surhoff	LF	5	15	0	4	0	0	1	2	.267
Hoiles	C	4	12	1	2	0	0	1	2	.167
Parent	C	3	6	0	1	0	0	0	0	.167
Devereaux	LF	3	2	0	0	0	0	0	0	.000
Incaviglia	DH	1	2	1	1	0	0	0	0	.500
Tarasco	RF	2	1	0	0	0	0	0	0	.000

COMPOSITE PITCHING

NEW YORK

NAME	G	IP	H	BB	SO	W	L	SV	ERA
TOTALS	5	47	39	15	33	4	1	1	3.64
Pettitte	2	15	10	5	7	1	0	0	3.60
Key	1	8	3	1	5	1	0	0	2.25
Cone	1	6.0	5	1	5	0	0	0	3.00
Wetteland	4	4.0	2	1	5	0	0	1	4.50
Rivera	2	4	6	1	5	1	0	0	0.00
Weathers	2	3.0	3	0	1	0	0	0	12.00
Rogers	1	3.0	5	2	3	0	0	0	12.00
Nelson	2	2.1	5	0	2	0	1	0	11.57
Lloyd	2	1.2	0	1	0	0	0	0	0.00

BALTIMORE

NAME	G	IP	H	BB	SO	W	L	SV	ERA
TOTALS	5	46	50	20	37	1	4	1	4.11
Erickson	2	11.1	14	4	8	0	1	0	2.38
Mussina	1	7.2	8	2	6	0	1	0	5.87
Wells	1	6.2	8	3	6	1	0	0	4.05
Coppinger	1	5.1	6	1	3	0	0	0	8.44
Myers	3	4	4	3	2	0	1	0	2.25
Benitez	3	2.1	3	3	2	0	1	1	7.71
Mathews	3	2.1	0	2	3	0	0	0	3.86
Mills	3	2.1	1	3	2	0	0	0	3.86
Orosco	4	2	1	2	4	0	0	0	4.50
Rhodes	3	2	1	2	1	0	0	0	0.00

ATLANTA 1st 96-66 .593 — BOBBY COX

Name	G by Pos	B	AGE	G	AB	R	H	2B	3B	HR	RBI	BB	SO	SB	BA	SA
TOTALS			28	162	5614	773	1514	264	28	197	735	530	1032	83	.270	.432
Fred McGriff	1B158	L	32	159	617	81	182	37	1	28	107	68	116	7	.295	.494
Mark Lemke	2B133	B	30	135	498	64	127	17	0	5	37	53	48	5	.255	.319
Jeff Blauser (BH)	SS79	R	30	83	265	48	65	14	1	10	35	40	54	6	.245	.419
Chipper Jones	3B118 SS38 OF1	B	24	157	598	114	185	32	5	30	110	87	88	14	.309	.530
David Justice (SJ)	OF40	L	30	40	140	23	45	9	0	6	25	21	22	1	.321	.514
Marquis Grissom	OF158	R	29	158	671	106	207	32	10	23	74	41	73	28	.308	.489
Ryan Klesko	OF144 1B2	L	25	153	528	90	149	21	4	34	93	68	129	6	.282	.530
Javy Lopez	C135	R	25	138	489	56	138	19	1	23	69	28	84	1	.282	.466
Dwight Smith	OF29	L	32	101	153	16	31	5	0	3	16	17	42	1	.203	.294
Jermaine Dye	OF92	R	22	98	292	32	82	16	0	12	37	8	67	1	.281	.459
Rafael Belliard	SS63 2B15	R	34	87	142	9	24	7	0	0	3	2	22	3	.169	.218
Eddie Perez	C54 1B7	R	28	68	156	19	40	9	1	4	17	8	19	0	.256	.404
Mike Mordecai	2B20 3B10 SS6 1B1	R	28	66	108	12	26	5	0	2	8	9	24	1	.241	.343
Ed Giovanola	SS25 3B6 2B5	L	27	43	82	10	19	2	0	0	7	8	13	1	.232	.256
2 Terry Pendleton	3B41	R	35	42	162	21	33	6	0	4	17	15	36	2	.204	.315
Jerome Walton (PJ)	OF28	R	30	37	47	9	16	5	0	1	4	5	10	0	.340	.511
Mark Whiten	OF29	B	29	36	90	12	23	5	1	3	17	16	25	2	.256	.433
1 Tyler Houston	1B11 OF1	L	25	33	27	3	6	2	1	1	8	1	9	0	.222	.481
Andruw Jones	OF29	R	19	31	106	11	23	7	1	5	13	7	29	3	.217	.443
Tony Graffanino	2B18	R	24	22	46	7	8	1	1	0	2	4	13	0	.174	.239
2 Luis Polonia	OF7	L	31	22	31	3	13	0	0	0	1	2	3	1	.419	.419
2 Danny Bautista (BZ)	OF14	R	24	17	20	1	3	0	0	0	1	2	5	0	.150	.150
Joe Ayrault	C7	R	24	7	5	0	1	0	0	0	0	0	1	0	.200	.200
Pablo Martinez	SS1	B	27	4	2	1	1	0	0	0	0	0	0	0	.500	.500

NAME	T	AGE	W	L	PCT	SV	G	GS	CG	IP	H	BB	SO	SHO	ERA
TOTALS		28	96	66	.593	46	162	162	14	1469	1372	451	1245	9	3.52
John Smoltz	R	29	24	8	.750	0	35	35	6	254	199	55	276	2	2.94
Tom Glavine	L	30	15	10	.600	0	36	36	1	235	222	85	181	0	2.98
Greg Maddux	R	30	15	11	.577	0	35	35	5	245	225	28	172	1	2.72
Steve Avery (UJ)	L	26	7	10	.412	0	24	23	1	131	146	40	86	0	4.47
Brad Clontz	R	25	6	3	.667	1	81	0	0	81	78	33	49	0	5.69
Terrell Wade	L	23	5	0	1.000	1	44	8	0	70	57	47	79	0	2.97
Greg McMichael	R	29	5	3	.625	2	73	0	0	87	84	27	78	0	3.22
Mike Bielecki	R	36	4	3	.571	2	40	5	0	75	63	33	71	0	2.63
Pedro Borbon (EJ)	L	28	3	0	1.000	1	43	0	0	36	26	7	31	0	2.75
1 Jason Schmidt (BR)	R	23	3	4	.429	0	13	11	0	59	69	32	48	0	6.75
Brad Woodall	L	27	2	2	.500	0	8	3	0	21	27	9	7	0	7.32
2 Denny Neagle	L	27	2	3	.400	0	6	6	1	39	40	14	18	0	5.59
Mark Wohlers	R	26	2	4	.333	39	77	0	0	77	71	21	100	0	3.03
Joe Borowski	R	25	2	4	.333	0	22	0	0	26	33	13	15	0	4.85
2 Dean Hartgraves	L	29	1	0	1.000	0	20	0	0	19	16	7	14	0	4.34
Kevin Lomon	R	24	0	0	—	0	6	0	0	7	7	3	1	0	4.91
Carl Schutz	L	24	0	0	—	0	3	0	0	3	3	2	5	0	2.70
Tom Thobe	L	26	0	0	.000	0	3	0	0	1	1	0	1	0	1.50

MONTREAL 2nd 88-74 .543 8 — FELIPE ALOU

Name	G by Pos	B	AGE	G	AB	R	H	2B	3B	HR	RBI	BB	SO	SB	BA	SA
TOTALS			27	162	5505	741	1441	297	27	148	696	492	1077	108	.262	.406
David Segui (BG)	1B113	B	29	115	416	69	119	30	1	11	58	60	54	4	.286	.442
Mike Lansing	2B159 SS2	R	28	159	641	99	183	40	2	11	53	44	85	23	.285	.406
Mark Grudzielanek	SS153	R	26	153	657	99	201	34	4	6	49	26	83	33	.306	.397
Shane Andrews	3B123	R	24	127	375	43	85	15	2	19	64	35	119	3	.227	.429
Moises Alou	OF142	R	29	143	540	87	152	28	2	21	96	49	83	9	.281	.457
Rondell White (SJ)	OF86	R	24	88	334	35	98	19	4	6	41	22	53	14	.293	.428
Henry Rodriguez	OF89 1B51	L	28	145	532	81	147	42	1	36	103	37	160	2	.276	.562
Darrin Fletcher	C112	L	29	127	394	41	105	22	0	12	57	27	42	0	.266	.414
F.P. Santangelo	OF124 3B23 2B5 SS1	B	28	152	393	54	109	20	5	7	56	49	61	5	.277	.407
Cliff Floyd	OF85 1B2	L	23	117	227	29	55	15	4	6	26	30	52	7	.242	.423
Sherman Obando	OF47	R	26	89	178	30	44	9	0	8	22	22	48	2	.247	.433
Dave Silvestri	3B47 SS10 OF2 2B1 1B1	R	26	86	162	16	33	4	0	1	17	34	41	2	.204	.247
Lenny Webster	C63	R	31	78	174	18	40	10	0	2	17	25	21	0	.230	.322
Andy Stankiewicz	2B19 SS13 3B1	R	31	64	77	12	22	5	1	0	9	6	12	1	.286	.377
Tim Spehr	C58 OF1	R	29	63	44	4	4	1	0	1	3	3	15	1	.091	.182
Yamil Benitez	OF4	R	23	11	12	0	2	0	0	2	0	1	4	0	.167	.167
Vladimir Guerrero	OF8	R	20	9	27	2	5	0	0	1	1	0	3	0	.185	.296
Raul Chavez	C3	R	23	4	5	1	1	0	0	0	0	0	1	0	.200	.200
Rob Lukachyk		L	27	2	2	0	0	0	0	0	0	0	1	0	.000	.000
Rick Schu	3B1	R	34	1	4	0	0	0	0	0	0	0	0	0	.000	.000
Tony Barron		R	29	1	1	0	0	0	0	0	0	0	0	0	.000	.000
Tim Laker (EJ) 26																

NAME	T	AGE	W	L	PCT	SV	G	GS	CG	IP	H	BB	SO	SHO	ERA
TOTALS		27	88	74	.543	43	162	162	11	1441	1353	462	1206	7	3.78
Jeff Fassero	L	33	15	11	.577	0	34	34	5	232	217	55	222	1	3.30
Pedro Martinez	R	24	13	10	.565	0	33	33	4	217	189	70	222	1	3.70
Ugueth Urbina	R	22	10	5	.667	0	33	17	0	114	102	44	108	0	3.71
Mel Rojas	R	29	7	4	.636	36	74	0	0	81	56	28	92	0	3.22
Rheal Cormier	L	29	7	10	.412	0	33	27	1	160	165	41	100	1	4.17
Dave Veres	R	29	6	3	.667	4	68	0	0	78	85	32	81	0	4.17
Mike Dyer	R	29	5	5	.500	2	70	1	0	76	79	34	51	0	4.40
1 Kirk Rueter	L	25	5	6	.455	0	16	16	0	79	91	22	30	0	4.58
Barry Manuel	R	30	4	1	.800	0	53	0	0	86	70	26	62	0	3.24
2 Mark Leiter	R	33	4	2	.667	0	12	12	1	70	68	19	46	0	4.39
Omar Daal	L	24	4	5	.444	0	64	6	0	87	74	37	82	0	4.02
1 Tim Scott	R	29	3	5	.375	1	45	0	0	46	41	21	37	0	3.11
Tavo Alvarez	R	24	2	1	.667	0	11	5	0	21	19	12	9	0	3.00
Jose Paniagua	R	22	2	4	.333	0	13	11	0	51	55	23	27	0	3.53
2 Jeff Juden	R	25	1	0	1.000	0	22	0	0	33	22	14	26	0	2.20
Alex Pacheco	R	22	0	0	—	0	5	0	0	6	8	1	7	0	11.12
2 Dave Leiper	L	34	0	1	.000	0	7	0	0	4	9	2	3	0	11.25
Derek Aucoin	R	26	0	1	.000	0	3	0	0	1	1	1	0		3.38
Carlos Perez (SJ) 25															

FLORIDA 3rd 80-82 .494 16 — RENE LACHEMANN 39-47 .453   COOKIE ROJAS 1-0 1.000   JOHN BOLES 40-35 .533

Name	G by Pos	B	AGE	G	AB	R	H	2B	3B	HR	RBI	BB	SO	SB	BA	SA
TOTALS			27	162	5498	688	1413	240	30	150	650	553	1122	99	.257	.393
Greg Colbrunn	1B134	R	26	141	511	60	146	26	2	16	69	25	76	4	.286	.438
Quilvio Veras (LJ)	2B67	B	25	73	253	40	64	8	1	4	14	51	42	8	.253	.340
Edgar Renteria	SS106	R	20	106	431	68	133	18	3	5	31	33	68	16	.309	.399
1 Terry Pendleton	3B108	B	35	111	406	30	102	20	1	7	58	26	75	0	.251	.357
Gary Sheffield	OF161	R	27	161	519	118	163	33	1	42	120	142	66	16	.314	.624
Devon White	OF139	B	33	146	552	77	151	37	6	17	84	38	99	22	.274	.455
Jeff Conine	0F128 1B48	R	30	157	597	84	175	32	2	26	95	62	121	1	.293	.484
Charles Johnson (RJ)	C120	R	24	120	386	34	84	13	1	13	37	40	91	1	.218	.358
Joe Orsulak	OF59 1B2	L	34	120	217	23	48	6	1	2	19	16	38	1	.221	.286
Kurt Abbott	SS44 3B33 2B20	R	27	109	320	37	81	18	7	8	33	22	99	3	.253	.428
Alex Arias	3B59 SS20 2B1 1B1	R	28	100	224	27	62	11	2	3	26	17	28	2	.277	.384
Jesus Tavarez	OF65	B	25	98	114	14	25	3	0	0	6	7	18	5	.219	.246
Craig Grebeck (EJ)	2B29 SS2 3B1	R	31	50	95	8	20	1	0	1	9	4	14	0	.211	.253
Bob Natal	C43	R	30	44	90	4	12	1	1	0	2	15	31	0	.133	.167
Andre Dawson (KJ)	OF6	R	41	42	58	6	16	2	0	2	14	2	13	0	.276	.414
Luis Castillo	2B41	B	20	41	164	26	43	2	1	1	8	14	40	17	.262	.305
Billy McMillon	OF15	L	24	28	51	4	11	0	0	0	4	5	14	0	.216	.216
Ralph Milliard	2B24	R	22	24	62	7	10	2	0	1	1	14	16	2	.161	.194
Joe Siddall	C18	L	28	18	47	0	7	1	0	0	3	2	5	1	.149	.170
2 Gregg Zaun	C10	B	25	10	31	4	9	1	0	1	2	3	5	1	.290	.419
Jerry Brooks	OF2 1B1	R	29	8	5	2	2	0	0	0	1	1	1	0	.400	.800
Russ Morman	1B2	R	30	6	6	0	1	0	0	0	0	0	1	0	.167	.333
Josh Booty	3B1	R	21	2	2	1	1	0	0	0	0	0	1	0	.500	.500

NAME	T	AGE	W	L	PCT	SV	G	GS	CG	IP	H	BB	SO	SHO	ERA
TOTALS		27	80	82	.494	41	162	162	8	1443	1386	598	1050	13	3.95
Kevin Brown	R	31	17	11	.607	0	32	32	5	233	187	33	159	3	1.89
Al Leiter	L	30	16	12	.571	0	33	33	2	215	153	119	200	1	2.93
Pat Rapp	R	28	8	16	.333	0	30	29	0	162	184	91	86	0	5.10
1 John Burkett	R	31	6	10	.375	0	24	24	1	154	154	42	108	0	4.32
Robb Nen	R	26	5	1	.833	35	75	0	0	83	67	21	92	0	1.95
2 Mark Hutton	R	26	5	1	.833	0	13	9	0	56	47	18	31	0	3.67
Chris Hammond (IL)	L	30	5	8	.385	0	38	9	0	81	104	27	50	0	6.56
Jay Powell	R	24	3	4	.571	2	67	0	0	71	71	36	52	0	4.54
Yorkis Perez	L	28	3	4	.429	0	64	0	0	48	51	31	47	0	5.29
2 Rick Helling	R	25	2	1	.667	0	5	4	0	28	14	7	26	0	1.95
2 David Weathers	R	26	2	2	.500	0	31	8	0	71	85	28	40	0	4.54
1 Terry Mathews	R	31	2	4	.333	4	57	0	0	55	59	27	49	0	4.91
Matt Mantei (SJ)	R	23	1	0	1.000	0	14	0	0	18	13	21	25	0	6.38
Felix Heredia	L	20	1	1	.500	0	21	0	0	17	21	10	10	0	4.32
Donn Pall	R	34	1	1	.500	0	12	0	0	19	16	9	9	0	5.79
Kurt Miller	R	23	1	1	.500	0	26	4	0	46	57	33	30	0	6.80
Marc Valdes	R	24	1	3	.250	0	11	8	0	49	63	23	13	0	4.81
Miguel Batista	R	24	0	0	—	0	9	0	0	11	9	7	6	0	5.56
Joel Adamson	L	24	0	0	—	0	9	0	0	11	18	7	7	0	7.36
Bill Hurst	R	26	0	0	—	0	1	0	0	1	1	3	1	0	0.00
Andy Larkin	R	22	0	0	—	0	1	1	0	3	5	4	2	0	1.80
Livan Hernandez	R	21	0	0	—	0	2	0	0	5	3	4	2	0	0.00
Alejandro Pena (SJ)	R	37	0	1	.000	0	4	0	0	4	5	1	5	0	4.50
Wilson Heredia (EJ) 24															

NEW YORK 4th 71-91 .438 25 — DALLAS GREEN 59-72 .450   BOBBY VALENTINE 12-19 .387

Name	G by Pos	B	AGE	G	AB	R	H	2B	3B	HR	RBI	BB	SO	SB	BA	SA
TOTALS			26	162	5618	746	1515	267	47	147	697	445	1069	97	.270	.412
Rico Brogna	1B52	L	26	55	188	18	48	10	1	7	30	19	50	0	.255	.431
1 Jose Vizcaino	2B93	B	28	96	363	47	110	12	6	1	32	28	58	9	.303	.377
Rey Ordonez	SS150	R	25	151	502	51	129	12	4	1	30	22	53	1	.257	.303
1 Jeff Kent	3B89	R	28	89	335	45	97	20	1	9	39	21	56	4	.290	.436
Alex Ochoa	OF76	R	24	82	282	37	83	19	3	4	33	17	30	4	.294	.426
Lance Johnson	OF157	L	32	160	682	117	227	31	21	9	69	33	40	50	.333	.479
Bernard Gilkey	OF151	R	29	153	571	108	181	44	3	30	117	73	125	17	.317	.562
Todd Hundley	C150	B	27	153	540	85	140	32	1	41	112	79	146	1	.259	.550
Edgardo Alfonzo	2B66 3B36 SS15	R	22	123	368	36	96	15	2	4	40	25	56	2	.261	.345
Butch Huskey	1B75 OF40 3B6	R	24	118	414	43	115	16	2	15	60	27	77	1	.278	.435
Carl Everett	OF55	B	25	101	192	29	46	8	1	1	16	21	53	6	.240	.307
Tim Bogar	1B32 3B25 SS19 2B8	R	29	91	89	17	19	4	0	0	18	12	42	1	.213	.258
Chris Jones	OF66 1B5	R	30	89	149	22	36	7	0	4	18	12	42	1	.242	.369
Brent Mayne	C21	L	28	70	99	9	26	6	0	1	6	12	12	0	.263	.354
Andy Tomberlin	OF17 1B1	L	29	63	66	12	17	3	0	4	19	9	27	0	.258	.455
Roberto Petagine	1B40	L	25	50	99	10	23	4	0	3	17	12	31	0	.232	.384
2 Alvaro Espinoza	3B38 SS7 2B2 1B1	R	34	48	134	19	41	7	2	4	16	4	19	0	.306	.478
Kevin Roberson	OF10	B	28	27	36	8	8	1	0	2	8	4	17	0	.222	.500
2 Carlos Baerga	1B16 3B6 2B1	B	27	26	83	5	16	5	0	1	5	2	12	0	.193	.301
Jason Hardtke	2B18	B	24	18	31	3	11	5	0	0	3	6	6	0	.194	.323
Matt Franco	3B8 1B2	L	26	14	31	4	6	1	0	0	4	3	5	0	.194	.323
Alberto Castillo	C6	R	26	6	11	1	4	0	0	0	3	1	4	0	.364	.364
Charlie Greene	C1	R	25	2	1	0	0	0	0	0	0	0	1	0	.000	.000

NAME	T	AGE	W	L	PCT	SV	G	GS	CG	IP	H	BB	SO	SHO	ERA
TOTALS		28	71	91	.438	41	162	162	10	1440	1517	532	999	10	4.22
Mark Clark	R	28	14	11	.560	0	32	32	2	212	217	48	142	0	3.43
Bobby Jones	R	26	12	8	.600	0	31	31	3	196	219	46	116	1	4.42
Pete Harnisch	R	29	8	12	.400	0	31	31	2	195	195	61	114	1	4.21
Jerry Dipoto	R	28	7	2	.778	0	57	0	0	77	91	45	52	0	4.19
Dave Mlicki	R	28	6	7	.462	1	51	2	0	90	95	33	83	0	3.30
Jason Isringhausen	R	23	6	14	.300	0	27	27	2	172	190	73	114	1	4.77
Paul Wilson (SJ)	R	23	5	12	.294	0	26	26	1	149	157	71	109	0	5.38
John Franco	L	35	4	3	.571	28	51	0	0	54	54	21	48	0	1.83
Robert Person	R	26	4	5	.444	0	27	13	0	90	86	35	76	0	4.52
Derek Wallace	R	24	2	3	.400	3	19	0	0	25	29	14	15	0	4.01
Doug Henry	R	32	2	3	.200	9	58	0	0	75	82	36	58	0	4.68
Paul Byrd (XJ)	R	25	1	2	.333	0	38	0	0	47	48	21	31	0	4.24
1 Blas Minor	R	30	0	0	—	0	17	0	0	26	23	6	20	0	3.51
1 Pedro Martinez	L	27	0	1	.000	0	5	0	0	8	7	3	6	0	6.43
Ricky Trlicek	R	27	0	0	—	0	5	0	0	7	8	3	3	0	3.38
Mike Fyhrie	R	26	0	0	—	0	1	1	0	7	11	2	4	0	15.43
Bob MacDonald	L	31	0	2	.000	0	20	0	0	19	16	9	12	0	4.26
Bill Pulsipher (EJ) 22															

PHILADELPHIA — 5th 67-95 .414 29 — JIM FREGOSI

Name	G by Pos	B	AGE	G	AB	R	H	2B	3B	HR	RBI	BB	SO	SB	BA	SA
TOTALS			29	162	5499	650	1405	249	39	132	604	536	1092	117	.256	.387
Gregg Jefferies (BG)	1B53 OF51	B	28	104	404	59	118	17	3	7	51	36	21	20	.292	.401
Mickey Morandini	2B137	L	30	140	539	64	135	24	6	3	32	49	87	26	.250	.334
Kevin Stocker	SS119	B	26	119	394	46	100	22	6	5	41	43	89	6	.254	.378
1 Todd Zeile	3B106 1B28	R	30	134	500	61	134	24	0	20	80	67	88	1	.268	.436
Jim Eisenreich (BF)	OF91	L	37	113	338	45	122	24	3	3	41	31	32	11	.361	.476
Lenny Dykstra (XJ)	OF39	L	33	40	134	21	35	6	3	3	13	26	25	3	.261	.418
1 Pete Incaviglia (XJ)		R	32	99	269	33	63	7	2	16	42	30	82	2	.234	.454
Benito Santiago	C114 1B14	R	31	136	481	71	127	21	2	30	85	49	104	2	.264	.503
Ricky Otero	OF100	B	24	104	411	54	112	11	7	2	32	34	30	16	.273	.348
Ruben Amaro	OF35 1B1	B	31	61	117	14	37	10	0	2	15	9	18	0	.316	.453
1 Mark Whiten	OF51	R	29	60	182	33	43	8	0	7	21	33	62	13	.236	.396
Mike Lieberthal	C43	R	24	50	166	21	42	8	0	7	23	10	30	0	.253	.428
Kevin Sefcik	SS21 3B20 2B1	R	25	44	116	10	33	5	3	0	9	9	16	3	.284	.379
Kevin Jordan (KJ)	1B30 2B7 3B1	R	26	43	131	15	37	10	0	3	12	5	20	2	.282	.427
David Doster	2B24 3B1	R	25	39	105	14	28	8	0	1	8	7	21	0	.267	.371
Wendell Magee	OF37	R	23	38	142	9	29	7	0	2	14	9	33	0	.204	.296
Glenn Murray (WJ)	OF27	R	25	38	97	8	19	3	0	2	6	7	36	1	.196	.289
Scott Rolen	3B37	R	21	37	130	10	33	7	0	4	18	13	27	0	.254	.400
Mike Benjamin (WJ-ZJ)	SS31 2B1	R	30	35	103	13	23	5	1	4	13	12	21	3	.223	.408
2 J.R. Phillips	OF15 1B11	L	26	35	79	9	12	5	0	5	10	10	38	0	.152	.405
1 Lee Tinsley	OF22	B	27	31	52	1	7	0	0	0	2	4	22	2	.135	.135
Jon Zuber	1B22	L	26	30	91	7	23	4	0	1	10	6	11	1	.253	.330
Gene Schall	1B19	R	26	28	66	7	18	5	1	2	10	12	15	0	.273	.470
Desi Relaford	SS9 2B4	B	22	15	40	2	7	2	0	0	1	3	9	1	.175	.225
2 Manny Martinez	OF11	R	25	13	36	2	8	0	2	0	0	1	11	2	.222	.333
Bobby Estalella	C4	R	21	7	17	5	6	0	0	0	4	1	6	1	.353	.706
Gary Bennett	C5	R	24	6	16	0	4	0	0	0	1	0	5	0	.250	.250
Darren Daulton (KJ)	OF5	L	34	5	12	3	2	0	0	0	0	0	7	0	.167	.167
Howard Battle	3B1	R	24	5	5	0	0	0	0	0	0	0	2	0	.000	.000
Tony Longmire (BW) 27																

NAME	T	AGE	W	L	PCT	SV	G	GS	CG	IP	H	BB	SO	SHO	ERA
		29	67	95	.415	42	162	162	12	1423	1463	510	1044	6	4.48
Curt Schilling (SJ)	R	29	9	10	.474	0	26	26	8	183	149	50	182	2	3.19
1 Terry Mulholland	L	33	8	7	.533	0	21	21	3	133	157	21	52	0	4.66
Mike Grace (SJ)	R	26	7	2	.778	0	12	12	1	80	72	16	49	1	3.49
Toby Borland	R	27	7	3	.700	0	69	0	0	91	83	43	76	0	4.07
Mike Williams	R	27	6	14	.300	0	32	29	0	167	188	67	103	0	5.44
Ricky Bottalico	R	26	4	5	.444	34	61	0	0	68	47	23	74	0	3.19
Ron Blazier	R	24	3	1	.750	0	27	0	0	38	49	10	25	0	5.87
Ken Ryan	R	27	3	5	.375	8	62	0	0	89	71	45	70	0	2.43
Sid Fernandez (EJ)	L	33	3	6	.333	0	11	11	0	63	50	26	77	0	3.43
Rich Hunter	R	21	3	7	.300	0	14	14	0	69	84	33	32	0	6.49
Michael Mimbs	L	27	3	9	.250	0	21	17	0	99	116	41	56	0	5.53
Russ Springer	R	27	3	10	.231	0	51	7	0	97	106	38	94	0	4.66
1 Dave Leiper	L	34	2	1	1.000	0	26	0	0	21	31	7	10	0	6.43
Ricardo Jordan	L	26	2	2	.500	0	26	0	0	25	18	12	17	0	1.80
David West (SJ)	L	31	2	2	.500	0	7	6	0	28	31	11	22	0	4.76
2 Jeff Parrett	R	34	1	1	.500	0	18	0	0	24	24	11	33	0	1.88
Matt Beech	L	24	1	4	.200	0	8	8	0	41	49	11	33	0	6.97
Larry Mitchell	R	24	0	0	—	0	7	0	0	12	14	5	7	0	4.50
2 Glenn Dishman	L	25	0	0	—	0	4	1	0	7	9	2	3	0	7.71
Bronson Heflin	R	24	0	0	—	0	3	0	0	7	11	3	4	0	6.75
Steve Frey	L	32	0	0	.000	0	31	0	0	34	38	18	12	0	4.72
Calvin Maduro	R	21	0	1	.000	0	2	2	0	15	13	3	11	0	3.52
Carlos Crawford	R	24	0	1	.000	0	4	1	0	4	7	2	4	0	4.91
Rafael Quirico	R	26	0	1	.000	0	1	1	0	2	4	5	1	0	37.80
Bobby Munoz (EJ-SJ)	R	28	0	2	.000	0	8	2	0	25	42	7	22	0	7.82
Tyler Green (SJ) 26															

CENTRAL DIVISION

ST. LOUIS — 1st 88-74 .543 — TONY LaRUSSA

Name	G by Pos	B	AGE	G	AB	R	H	2B	3B	HR	RBI	BB	SO	SB	BA	SA
TOTALS			32	162	5502	759	1468	281	31	142	711	495	1089	149	.267	.407
John Mabry	1B146 OF14	L	25	151	543	63	161	30	2	13	74	37	84	3	.297	.431
Luis Alicea	2B125	L	30	129	380	54	98	26	3	5	42	52	78	11	.258	.382
Royce Clayton	SS113	R	26	129	491	64	136	20	4	6	35	33	89	33	.277	.371
Gary Gaetti	3B133 1B14	R	37	141	522	71	143	27	4	23	80	35	97	2	.274	.473
Brian Jordan	OF136 1B1	R	29	140	513	82	159	36	1	17	104	29	84	22	.310	.483
Ray Lankford	OF144	L	29	149	545	100	150	36	8	21	86	79	133	35	.275	.486
Ron Gant (LJ)	OF116	R	31	122	419	74	103	14	2	30	82	73	98	13	.246	.504
Tom Pagnozzi	C116 1B1	R	33	119	407	48	110	23	0	13	55	24	78	4	.270	.423
Willie McGee	OF83 1B6	B	37	123	309	52	95	15	2	5	41	18	60	5	.307	.417
Mark Sweeney	OF43 1B15	L	26	98	170	32	45	9	0	3	22	33	29	3	.265	.371
Ozzie Smith	SS52	R	41	82	227	36	64	10	2	2	18	25	9	7	.282	.370
Danny Sheaffer	C47 3B17 1B6 OF3	R	35	79	198	10	45	9	3	2	20	9	25	3	.227	.333
David Bell	3B45 2B20 SS1	R	23	62	145	12	31	6	0	1	9	10	22	1	.214	.276
Mike Gallego (LJ)	2B43 3B7 SS1	R	35	51	129	12	30	2	0	0	4	12	31	0	.210	.224
Miguel Mejia (LJ)	OF21	R	21	45	23	10	2	0	0	0	0	0	10	6	.087	.087
1 Pat Borders	C17 1B1	R	33	26	69	3	22	3	0	0	4	1	14	0	.319	.362
Dmitri Young	1B10	R	22	16	29	3	7	0	0	0	2	4	5	0	.241	.241
Terry Bradshaw	OF7	L	27	15	21	4	7	1	0	0	3	3	2	0	.333	.381
Mike DiFelice	C4	R	27	4	7	0	2	1	0	0	2	0	1	0	.286	.429
Aaron Holbert	2B1	R	23	1	3	0	0	0	0	0	0	0	0	0	.000	.000

NAME	T	AGE	W	L	PCT	SV	G	GS	CG	IP	H	BB	SO	SHO	ERA
		32	88	74	.543	43	162	162	0	1452	1380	539	1050	11	3.97
Andy Benes	R	28	18	10	.643	1	36	34	3	230	215	77	160	1	3.83
Todd Stottlemyre	R	31	14	11	.560	0	34	33	5	223	191	93	194	2	3.87
Donovan Osborne	L	27	13	9	.591	0	30	30	2	199	191	57	134	1	3.53
Alan Benes	R	24	13	10	.565	0	34	32	3	191	192	87	131	1	4.90
Mark Petkovsek	R	30	11	2	.846	0	48	6	0	89	83	35	45	0	3.55
Cory Bailey	R	25	5	2	.714	0	51	0	0	57	57	30	38	0	3.00
1 Mike Morgan	R	36	4	8	.333	0	18	18	0	103	118	40	55	0	5.24
Rich Batchelor	R	29	2	0	1.000	0	11	0	0	15	9	1	11	0	1.20
Rick Honeycutt	L	42	2	1	.667	4	61	0	0	47	42	7	30	0	2.85
1 Jeff Parrett	R	34	2	2	.500	0	43	0	0	42	40	20	42	0	4.25
T.J. Mathews	R	26	2	6	.250	6	67	0	0	84	62	32	80	0	3.01
1 Tom Urbani	L	28	1	0	1.000	0	3	2	0	12	15	4	1	0	7.71
Danny Jackson	L	34	1	1	.500	0	13	4	0	36	33	16	27	0	4.46
Brian Barber	R	23	0	1	.000	0	1	1	0	3	4	6	1	0	15.00
Eric Ludwick	R	24	0	1	.000	0	6	1	0	9	11	3	12	0	9.00
Mike Busby	R	23	0	1	.000	0	1	1	0	4	9	4	4	0	18.00
Tony Fossas	L	38	0	2	.000	0	65	0	0	47	43	21	36	0	2.68
Dennis Eckersley	R	41	0	6	.000	30	63	0	0	60	65	6	49	0	3.30

HOUSTON — 2nd 82-80 .506 6 — TERRY COLLINS

Name	G by Pos	B	AGE	G	AB	R	H	2B	3B	HR	RBI	BB	SO	SB	BA	SA
TOTALS			28	162	5508	753	1445	297	29	129	703	554	1057	180	.262	.397
Jeff Bagwell	1B162	R	28	162	568	111	179	48	2	31	120	135	114	21	.315	.570
Craig Biggio	2B162	R	30	162	605	113	174	24	4	15	75	75	72	25	.288	.415
Orlando Miller	SS117 3B29	R	27	139	468	43	120	26	2	15	58	14	116	3	.256	.417
Sean Berry	3B110	R	30	132	431	55	121	38	1	17	95	23	58	12	.281	.492
Derek Bell	OF157	R	27	158	627	84	165	40	3	17	113	40	123	29	.263	.418
Brian Hunter (VJ)	OF127	R	25	132	526	74	145	27	2	5	35	17	92	35	.276	.363
James Mouton	OF108	R	27	122	300	40	79	15	1	3	34	34	55	21	.263	.350
1 Rick Wilkins	C82	L	29	84	254	34	54	8	2	6	23	46	81	0	.213	.331
Bill Spiers	3B77 2B7 SS4 1B4 OF2	L	30	122	218	27	55	10	1	6	26	20	34	7	.252	.390
Derrick May	OF71	L	27	109	259	24	65	12	3	5	33	30	33	2	.251	.378
John Cangelosi	OF78	B	33	108	262	49	69	11	4	1	16	44	41	17	.263	.347
Ricky Gutierrez	SS74 3B6 2B5	R	26	89	218	28	62	8	1	1	15	23	42	6	.284	.344
Tony Eusebio (WJ-BH)	C29	R	29	58	152	15	41	7	2	1	19	18	20	0	.270	.362
Mike Simms	OF12 1B5	R	29	49	68	6	12	2	1	1	8	4	16	1	.176	.279
2 Kirt Manwaring	C37	R	30	37	82	5	18	3	0	0	6	3	15	0	.220	.256
Randy Knorr	C33	R	27	37	87	7	17	5	0	1	7	5	18	0	.195	.287
Bobby Abreu	OF7	L	22	15	22	1	5	1	0	0	1	2	3	0	.227	.273
Ray Montgomery	OF6	R	26	14	14	3	3	1	0	1	4	1	5	0	.214	.500
Dave Hajek	3B3 2B2	R	28	8	10	3	3	1	0	0	0	2	1	0	.300	.400
3 Andujar Cedeno	SS2 3B1	R	26	3	2	1	0	0	0	0	0	1	2	0	.000	.000
Jerry Goff	C1	L	32	4	4	1	2	1	0	0	2	0	1	0	.500	1.250

NAME	T	AGE	W	L	PCT	SV	G	GS	CG	IP	H	BB	SO	SHO	ERA
		29	82	80	.506	35	162	162	13	1447	1541	539	1163	4	4.37
Shane Reynolds	R	28	16	10	.615	0	35	35	4	239	227	44	204	1	3.65
Darryl Kile	R	27	12	11	.522	0	35	33	4	219	233	97	219	0	4.19
Mike Hampton	R	23	10	10	.500	0	27	27	2	160	175	49	101	1	3.59
Donne Wall	R	28	9	8	.529	0	26	23	2	150	170	34	99	1	4.56
Doug Drabek	R	33	7	9	.438	0	30	30	1	175	208	60	137	0	4.57
Todd Jones	R	28	6	3	.667	17	51	0	0	57	61	32	44	0	4.40
2 Xavier Hernandez	R	30	5	5	.500	6	58	0	0	75	69	26	78	0	4.22
Alvin Morman	L	27	4	1	.800	0	53	0	0	42	43	24	31	0	4.93
2 Danny Darwin	R	40	3	2	.600	0	15	6	0	42	43	11	27	0	5.95
Anthony Young	R	30	3	3	.500	0	28	0	0	33	38	22	19	0	4.59
John Hudek (VJ)	R	29	2	2	.500	2	15	0	0	16	12	5	14	0	2.81
Billy Wagner	L	24	2	2	.500	9	37	0	0	52	28	30	67	0	2.44
John Johnstone	R	27	1	1	.500	0	13	0	0	17	5	5	5	0	5.54
2 Gregg Olson	R	29	1	0	1.000	0	9	0	0	13	17	8	12	0	4.82
1 Dean Hartgraves	L	29	0	0	—	0	19	0	0	19	16	16	16	0	5.21
Mark Small	R	28	0	1	.000	0	10	0	0	24	33	13	16	0	5.92
Chris Holt	R	24	0	1	.000	0	3	3	0	16	19	5	7	0	5.79
Jeff Tabaka	L	32	0	1	.000	0	18	0	0	20	14	11	18	0	8.64
Jim Dougherty	R	28	0	2	.000	0	12	0	0	13	14	11	6	0	9.00
2 Terry Clark (LJ)	R	35	0	2	.000	0	8	0	0	16	16	2	5	0	11.37
1 Greg Swindell (GJ)	L	31	0	3	.000	0	8	0	0	23	35	11	15	0	7.83

CINCINNATI — 3rd 81-81 .500 7 — RAY KNIGHT

Name	G by Pos	B	AGE	G	AB	R	H	2B	3B	HR	RBI	BB	SO	SB	BA	SA
TOTALS			29	162	5455	778	1398	259	36	191	733	604	1134	171	.256	.422
Hal Morris	1B140	L	31	142	528	82	165	32	4	16	80	50	76	7	.313	.479
Bret Boone	2B141	R	27	142	520	56	121	21	3	12	69	31	100	3	.233	.354
Barry Larkin	SS151	R	32	152	517	117	154	32	4	33	89	96	52	36	.298	.567
Jeff Branson	3B64 SS38 2B31	L	29	129	311	34	76	16	4	9	37	31	67	2	.244	.408
Reggie Sanders (XJ)	OF80	R	28	81	287	49	72	17	1	14	33	44	86	24	.251	.463
Eric Davis	OF126 1B1	R	34	129	415	81	119	20	0	26	83	70	121	23	.287	.523
Thomas Howard	OF103	L	31	121	360	50	98	19	10	6	42	17	91	6	.272	.431
Joe Oliver	C97 1B3 OF3	R	30	106	289	31	70	12	1	11	46	28	54	2	.242	.405
Lenny Harris	OF37 3B24 1B16 2B8	L	31	125	302	33	86	17	2	5	32	21	31	14	.285	.404
Willie Greene	3B74 OF10 1B2 SS1	L	24	115	287	48	70	5	5	19	63	36	88	0	.244	.495
Eddie Taubensee	C94	L	27	108	327	46	95	20	0	12	48	26	64	3	.291	.462
Eric Owens	OF52 2B6 3B5	R	25	88	205	26	41	6	0	0	9	23	38	16	.200	.229
Chris Sabo	3B43	R	34	54	125	15	32	7	1	3	16	18	27	2	.256	.400
Curtis Goodwin	OF42	L	23	49	136	20	31	3	0	1	5	19	34	15	.228	.250
1 Eric Anthony (LJ)	OF37	L	28	47	123	22	30	6	0	8	13	22	36	0	.244	.488
2 Kevin Mitchell	OF31 1B3	R	34	37	114	18	37	11	0	6	26	26	16	0	.325	.579
Chad Mottola	OF31	R	24	35	79	10	13	2	0	3	6	4	21	0	.215	.367
Vince Coleman	OF20	B	35	33	84	10	13	1	0	1	4	9	31	12	.155	.226
Mike Kelly	OF17	R	26	19	49	5	9	4	0	1	3	4	16	3	.184	.327
Eduardo Perez	1B8 3B3	R	26	18	36	4	7	1	0	0	3	5	13	0	.222	.472
Keith Mitchell	OF5	R	26	11	15	2	4	0	0	0	1	6	3	0	.267	.333
Tim Belk	1B6	R	26	7	15	2	3	0	0	0	0	0	2	0	.200	.200
Brook Fordyce	C4	R	26	4	7	0	2	0	0	0	0	0	1	0	.286	.429
Steve Gibralter	OF2	R	26	2	1	0	0	0	0	0	0	0	0	0	.000	.000

NAME	T	AGE	W	L	PCT	SV	G	GS	CG	IP	H	BB	SO	SHO	ERA
		29	81	81	.500	52	162	162	6	1443	1447	591	1089	8	4.32
John Smiley	L	31	13	14	.481	0	35	34	2	217	207	54	171	2	3.64
Dave Burba	R	29	11	13	.458	0	34	33	0	195	179	97	148	0	3.83
Roger Salkeld	R	25	8	5	.615	0	29	19	1	116	114	54	82	1	5.20
Jeff Shaw	R	29	8	6	.571	4	78	0	0	105	99	29	69	0	2.49
Mark Portugal	R	33	8	9	.471	0	27	26	1	156	146	42	93	1	3.98
Kevin Jarvis	R	26	8	9	.471	0	24	20	2	120	152	43	63	1	5.98
Hector Carrasco	R	26	4	3	.571	0	56	0	0	74	58	45	59	0	3.75
Pete Schourek (EJ)	L	27	4	5	.444	0	12	12	0	67	79	24	54	0	6.01
Marcus Moore	R	25	3	3	.500	2	23	0	0	31	22	22	27	0	5.81
2 Lee Smith	R	38	3	4	.429	2	43	0	0	44	49	23	35	0	4.06
1 Chuck McElroy	L	28	2	1	.667	0	40	0	0	49	49	23	35	0	6.57
Curt Lyons	R	21	2	2	.500	0	7	7	0	35	31	16	32	0	5.20
2 Mike Morgan	R	36	2	3	.400	0	28	7	0	53	53	19	29	0	2.30
Scott Service	R	29	1	0	1.000	0	34	1	0	48	50	18	46	0	3.94
2 Giovanni Carrara	R	28	1	0	1.000	0	23	1	0	33	31	13	13	0	5.87
1,3 Tim Pugh	R	29	1	0	.500	0	10	1	0	15	15	5	11	0	11.49
Jeff Brantley	R	32	1	2	.333	44	66	0	0	71	54	28	76	0	2.41
Johnny Ruffin	R	26	1	3	.250	0	21	0	0	71	37	69	50	0	5.49
Scott Sullivan	R	25	0	0	—	0	5	0	0	8	9	3	4	0	2.25
Derek Lilliquist	L	30	0	0	.000	0	14	0	0	11	18	4	9	0	7.36
2 Pedro Martinez	L	27	0	0	—	0	6	0	0	12	14	6	9	0	6.00
1 Xavier Hernandez	R	28	0	0	—	0	2	0	0	2	5	1	3	0	13.50
Jerry Spradlin	R	28	0	0	—	0	1	0	0	1	0	0	1	0	.00
Mike Remlinger	L	30	0	0	.000	0	19	4	0	27	24	19	19	0	5.60
Jose Rijo (EJ) 31															

CHICAGO — 4th 76-86 .469 12 — JIM RIGGLEMAN

Name	G by Pos	B	AGE	G	AB	R	H	2B	3B	HR	RBI	BB	SO	SB	BA	SA
TOTALS			29	162	5531	772	1388	267	19	175	725	523	1090	108	.251	.401
Mark Grace	1B141	L	32	142	547	88	181	39	1	9	75	62	41	2	.331	.455
Ryne Sandberg	2B146	R	36	150	554	85	135	28	4	25	92	54	116	12	.244	.444
Rey Sanchez (BH)	SS92	R	28	95	289	28	61	9	0	1	12	22	42	7	.211	.253
Leo Gomez	3B124 1B8 SS1	R	29	136	362	44	86	19	0	17	56	53	94	1	.238	.431
Sammy Sosa (BH)	OF124	R	27	124	498	84	136	21	2	40	100	34	134	18	.273	.564
Brian McRae	OF155	B	28	157	624	111	172	32	5	17	66	73	84	37	.276	.425
Luis Gonzalez	0F139 1B2	L	28	146	483	70	131	30	4	15	79	61	49	9	.271	.443
Scott Servais	C128 1B1	R	29	129	445	42	118	20	0	11	63	30	75	0	.265	.384
Jose Hernandez	SS87 3B43 2B1 OF1	R	26	131	331	52	80	14	1	10	41	24	97	4	.242	.381
Scott Bullett	OF58	L	27	109	165	26	35	5	0	3	16	10	54	7	.212	.297
Dave Magadan (HJ)	3B51 1B10	L	33	78	169	23	43	10	0	3	17	29	23	0	.254	.367
Ozzie Timmons	OF35	R	25	65	140	18	28	4	0	7	16	15	30	1	.200	.379
Doug Glanville	OF49	R	25	49	83	10	20	5	1	1	10	3	11	2	.241	.361
Todd Haney	2B23 3B4 SS3	R	30	49	82	11	11	1	0	0	3	7	15	1	.134	.146
2 Tyler Houston	C27 3B9 2B2 1B1	L	25	46	115	18	39	7	0	2	19	8	18	3	.339	.452
Robin Jennings	OF11	L	24	31	58	7	13	5	0	0	4	3	9	1	.224	.310
Brant Brown	1B18	L	25	29	69	11	21	1	0	5	9	2	17	3	.304	.536
Terry Shumpert	3B10 2B4 SS1	R	29	27	31	5	7	1	0	2	6	2	11	0	.226	.452
Brooks Kieschnick	OF8	L	24	25	29	6	10	2	0	1	6	3	6	0	.345	.517
Mike Hubbard	C14	R	25	21	38	1	4	0	0	1	4	0	15	0	.105	.184
Brian Dorsett	C15	R	35	17	41	3	5	0	0	1	3	4	8	0	.122	.195
Bret Barberie	2B6 3B2 SS1	B	28	15	29	4	1	0	0	1	2	5	11	0	.034	.138
Felix Fermin	2B6 SS2	R	32	11	16	4	2	1	0	0	1	2	0	0	.125	.188
Pedro Valdes	OF2	L	23	9	8	2	1	1	0	0	1	1	5	0	.125	.250

NAME	T	AGE	W	L	PCT	SV	G	GS	CG	IP	H	BB	SO	SHO	ERA
		29	76	86	.469	34	162	162	10	1456	1447	546	1027	10	4.36
Jaime Navarro	R	29	15	12	.556	0	35	35	4	237	244	72	158	1	3.92
Steve Trachsel	R	25	13	9	.591	0	31	31	3	205	181	62	132	2	3.03
Kevin Foster	R	27	7	8	.538	0	17	16	1	87	98	35	53	0	6.21
Frank Castillo	R	27	7	16	.304	0	33	33	1	182	209	46	139	1	5.28
Jim Bullinger	R	30	6	10	.375	1	37	20	1	129	144	68	90	1	6.54
Amaury Telemaco	R	22	5	7	.417	0	25	17	0	97	108	31	64	0	5.46
Turk Wendell	R	29	4	5	.444	18	70	0	0	79	58	44	75	0	2.84
Mike Campbell (EJ)	R	32	3	1	.750	0	13	5	0	36	29	10	19	0	4.46
Bob Patterson	L	33	3	3	.500	8	79	0	0	55	46	22	53	0	3.13
Kent Bottenfield	R	27	3	5	.375	1	48	0	0	62	59	19	33	0	2.63
Terry Adams	R	23	3	6	.333	4	69	0	0	101	84	49	78	0	2.94
Rodney Myers	R	27	2	1	.667	0	45	0	0	67	61	38	50	0	4.68
1 Doug Jones	R	39	2	2	.500	2	28	0	0	32	41	7	26	0	5.01
Mike Perez	R	31	1	0	1.000	0	24	0	0	27	29	13	22	0	4.67
Tanyon Sturtze	R	25	1	0	1.000	0	6	0	0	11	16	5	7	0	9.00
Larry Casian	L	30	1	1	.500	0	35	0	0	24	14	11	15	0	1.88
Dave Swartzbaugh	R	28	0	2	.000	0	6	5	0	24	26	14	13	0	6.38

PITTSBURGH — 5th 73-89 .451 15 — JIM LEYLAND

Name	G by Pos	B	AGE	G	AB	R	H	2B	3B	HR	RBI	BB	SO	SB	BA	SA
TOTALS			29	162	5665	776	1509	319	33	138	738	510	989	126	.266	.407
Jeff King	1B92 2B71 3B17	R	31	155	591	91	160	36	4	30	111	70	95	15	.271	.497
Carlos Garcia (LJ)	2B77 SS19 3B14	R	28	101	390	66	111	18	4	6	44	23	58	16	.285	.397
Jay Bell	SS151	R	30	151	527	65	132	29	3	13	71	54	108	6	.250	.391
1 Charlie Hayes	3B124	R	31	128	459	51	114	21	2	10	62	36	78	6	.248	.368
Orlando Merced	OF115 1B1	L	29	120	453	69	130	24	1	17	80	51	74	8	.287	.457
Mike Kingery	OF83	L	35	117	276	32	68	12	2	3	27	23	29	2	.246	.337
Al Martin	OF152	L	28	155	630	101	189	40	1	18	72	54	116	38	.300	.452
Jason Kendall	C129	R	22	130	414	54	124	23	5	3	42	35	30	5	.300	.401
Mark Johnson	1B100 OF1	R	28	127	343	55	94	24	0	13	47	44	64	6	.274	.458
Nelson Liriano	2B36 3B9 SS5	B	32	112	217	23	58	14	2	3	30	14	22	2	.267	.392
1 Dave Clark		L	33	92	211	28	58	12	2	8	35	31	51	2	.275	.464
John Wehner	OF29 3B24 2B12 C1	R	29	86	139	19	36	9	1	2	13	8	22	1	.259	.381
Jermaine Allensworth	OF61	R	24	61	229	32	60	9	3	4	31	23	50	11	.262	.380
Keith Osik (BH)	C41 3B2 OF2	R	27	48	140	18	41	14	1	1	14	14	21	1	.293	.429
1 Jacob Brumfield	OF22	R	31	29	80	11	20	9	0	2	8	5	17	3	.250	.438
Midre Cummings	OF21	L	24	24	85	11	19	3	1	3	7	0	16	0	.224	.388
Troy Beamon	OF14	L	22	24	51	7	11	2	0	0	6	4	5	1	.216	.255
Tony Womack	OF6 2B4	L	26	17	30	11	10	3	1	0	7	6	1	2	.333	.500
2 Dale Sveum	3B10	B	32	12	34	9	12	5	0	1	5	6	6	0	.353	.588
Angelo Encarnacion	C7	R	24	7	22	3	7	2	0	0	1	0	8	0	.318	.409
Rich Aude	1B4	R	24	7	16	0	4	0	0	0	0	0	6	0	.250	.250

NAME	T	AGE	W	L	PCT	SV	G	GS	CG	IP	H	BB	SO	SHO	ERA
		28	73	89	.451	37	162	162	5	1453	1602	479	1044	7	4.61
1 Denny Neagle	L	27	14	6	.700	0	27	27	1	183	186	34	131	0	3.05
Jon Lieber	R	26	9	5	.643	1	51	15	0	142	156	28	94	0	3.99
1 Danny Darwin	R	40	7	9	.438	0	19	19	0	122	117	16	69	0	3.02
Dan Plesac	L	34	6	5	.545	11	73	0	0	70	67	24	76	0	4.09
Marc Wilkins	R	25	4	5	.571	1	47	2	0	75	75	36	62	0	3.84
John Ericks	R	29	4	5	.444	8	28	4	0	47	56	19	46	0	5.79
Zane Smith	L	35	4	6	.400	0	16	16	1	83	104	21	47	1	5.08
Francisco Cordova	R	24	4	7	.364	12	59	6	0	99	103	20	95	0	4.09
Paul Wagner (EJ)	R	28	4	8	.333	0	16	15	1	82	86	39	81	0	5.40
Jason Christiansen	L	26	3	3	.500	0	33	0	0	44	56	19	38	0	6.70
Ramon Morel	R	21	2	1	.667	0	29	0	0	42	57	19	22	0	5.36
2 Jason Schmidt	R	23	2	2	.500	0	6	6	1	38	39	21	26	0	4.06
Esteban Loaiza	R	24	2	3	.400	0	10	10	1	53	65	19	32	1	4.96
Chris Peters	L	24	2	4	.333	0	16	10	0	64	72	25	28	0	5.63
Dan Miceli	R	25	2	10	.167	1	44	0	0	86	99	45	66	0	5.78
Dave Wainhouse	R	28	1	0	1.000	0	17	0	0	24	22	10	16	0	5.70
Rich Loiselle	R	24	1	1	.500	1	26	7	0	59	64	25	22	0	4.60
Matt Ruebel	L	26	1	1	.500	0	26	7	0	59	64	25	22	0	4.60
John Hope	R	25	1	3	.250	0	9	4	0	19	17	11	13	0	6.98
Lee Hancock	L	29	0	0	—	0	13	0	0	18	21	10	13	0	6.38
Steve Cooke (SJ)	L	26	0	0	—	0	8	0	0	11	15	7	7	0	7.56
1 Darrell May	L	24	0	1	.000	0	5	2	0	9	15	4	5	0	9.35
Elmer Dessens (UJ)	R	25	0	2	.000	0	15	3	0	25	40	4	13	0	8.28
Joe Boever	R	35	0	2	.000	0	13	0	0	15	17	6	6	0	5.40
Steve Parris (SJ-UJ)	R	28	0	3	.000	0	8	4	0	26	35	11	22	0	7.18

WEST DIVISION

SAN DIEGO — 1st 91-71 .562 — BRUCE BOCHY

Name	G by Pos	B	AGE	G	AB	R	H	2B	3B	HR	RBI	BB	SO	SB	BA	SA
TOTALS			31	162	5665	771	1499	285	24	147	718	601	1015	109	.265	.402
Wally Joyner (BG)	1B119	L	34	121	433	59	120	29	1	8	65	69	71	5	.277	.404
Jody Reed	2B145	R	33	146	495	45	121	20	0	2	49	59	53	2	.244	.297
2 Chris Gomez	SS89	R	25	89	328	32	86	16	1	3	29	39	64	2	.262	.345
Ken Caminiti	3B145	B	33	146	546	109	178	37	2	40	130	78	99	11	.326	.621
Tony Gwynn (LJ)	OF111	L	36	116	451	67	159	27	2	3	50	39	17	11	.353	.441
Steve Finley	OF160	L	31	161	655	126	195	45	9	30	95	56	87	22	.298	.531
Ricky Henderson	OF134	R	37	148	465	110	112	17	2	9	29	125	90	37	.241	.344
2 John Flaherty	C72	R	28	72	264	22	80	12	0	9	41	9	36	2	.303	.451
Scott Livingstone	1B22 3B16	L	30	102	172	20	51	4	1	2	20	9	22	0	.297	.366
1 Marc Newfield	OF51 1B2	R	23	84	191	27	48	11	0	5	26	16	44	1	.251	.387
Brian Johnson	C66 1B1 3B1	R	28	82	243	18	66	13	1	8	35	4	36	0	.272	.432
Chris Gwynn	OF29 1B1	L	31	81	90	8	16	4	0	1	10	10	28	0	.178	.256
Archi Cianfrocco	1B33 3B11 SS10 OF8 2B6 C1	R	29	79	192	21	54	13	3	2	32	8	56	1	.281	.411
Luis Lopez (SJ)	SS35 2B22 3B2	B	25	63	139	10	25	3	0	2	11	6	27	0	.180	.245
1 Brad Ausmus	C46	R	27	50	149	16	27	4	0	1	13	13	27	1	.181	.228
Andujar Cedeno	SS47 3B2	R	26	49	154	10	36	2	1	3	18	9	36	1	.234	.318
Greg Vaughn	OF39	R	30	43	141	20	29	3	1	10	22	24	31	4	.206	.454
Craig Shipley (LJ)	2B17 SS7 3B4 OF3	R	33	33	92	13	29	5	0	1	7	2	15	7	.315	.402
Rob Deer	OF18	R	35	25	50	9	9	3	0	4	9	14	30	0	.180	.480
Doug Dascenzo	OF10	B	32	21	9	3	1	0	0	0	0	1	2	0	.111	.111
Jason Thompson	1B13	L	25	13	49	4	11	4	0	2	6	1	14	0	.224	.429
2 Jim Tatum	3B1	R	28	5	3	0	0	0	0	0	0	0	1	0	.000	.000
Sean Mulligan		R	26	2	1	0	0	0	0	0	0	0	1	0	.000	.000
Todd Steverson		R	24	1	1	0	0	0	0	0	0	0	0	0	.000	.000

NAME	T	AGE	W	L	PCT	SV	G	GS	CG	IP	H	BB	SO	SHO	ERA
		28	91	71	.562	47	162	162	5	1489	1395	506	1194	11	3.72
Joey Hamilton	R	25	15	9	.625	0	34	33	3	212	206	83	184	1	4.17
Fernando Valenzuela	L	35	13	8	.619	0	33	31	0	172	177	67	95	0	3.62
Bob Tewksbury	R	35	10	10	.500	0	36	33	1	207	224	43	126	0	4.31
Trevor Hoffman	R	28	9	5	.643	42	70	0	0	88	50	31	111	0	2.25
Scott Sanders	R	27	9	5	.643	0	46	16	0	144	117	48	157	0	3.38
Andy Ashby (SJ)	R	28	9	5	.643	0	24	24	1	151	147	34	85	0	3.23
Tim Worrell	R	28	9	7	.563	1	50	11	0	121	109	39	99	0	3.05
Sean Bergman	R	26	6	8	.429	0	41	14	0	113	119	33	85	0	4.37
Dario Veras	R	23	3	1	.750	0	23	0	0	29	24	10	23	0	2.79
1 Bryce Florie	R	26	2	2	.500	0	39	0	0	49	45	27	51	0	4.01
Doug Bochtler	R	25	2	4	.333	3	63	0	0	66	45	39	68	0	3.02
Willie Blair	R	30	2	6	.250	1	60	0	0	88	80	29	67	0	4.60
Dustin Hermanson	R	23	1	0	1.000	0	14	0	0	18	4	11	11	0	8.56
1 Ron Villone	L	26	1	1	.500	0	21	0	0	18	17	7	19	0	2.95
Al Osuna	L	30	0	0	—	0	10	0	0	4	5	2	4	0	2.25
Mike Oquist	R	28	0	0	—	0	8	0	0	13	19	5	6	0	2.35
Andres Berumen	R	25	0	0	—	0	3	0	0	3	3	1	5	0	5.40
1 Glenn Dishman	L	25	0	1	.000	0	2	2	0	9	14	2	3	0	7.71
Pete Walker	R	27	0	0	—	0	3	0	0	6	8	1	1	0	0.00

LOS ANGELES — 2nd 90-72 .556 1 (Wild Card) — TOMMY LASORDA 41-35 .539 BILL RUSSELL 49-37 .570

Name	G by Pos	B	AGE	G	AB	R	H	2B	3B	HR	RBI	BB	SO	SB	BA	SA
TOTALS			28	162	5568	703	1396	215	33	150	661	516	1190	124	.252	.384
Eric Karros	1B154	R	28	154	608	84	158	29	1	34	111	53	121	8	.260	.479
Delino DeShields	2B145	L	27	154	581	75	130	12	8	5	41	53	124	48	.224	.298
Greg Gagne (NJ)	SS127	R	34	128	428	48	109	13	2	10	55	50	93	4	.255	.364
Mike Blowers (KJ)	3B90 1B6 SS1	R	31	92	317	31	84	19	2	6	38	37	77	0	.265	.394
Raul Mondesi	OF157	R	25	157	634	98	188	40	7	24	88	32	122	14	.297	.495
Brett Butler (IL)	OF34	L	39	34	131	22	35	1	1	0	8	9	22	8	.267	.290
Todd Hollandsworth	OF142	L	23	149	478	64	139	26	4	12	59	41	93	21	.291	.437
Mike Piazza	C146	R	27	148	547	87	184	16	0	36	105	81	93	0	.336	.563
Chad Fonville	OF35 2B23 SS20 3B2	B	25	103	201	34	41	4	1	0	13	17	31	7	.204	.234
Roger Cedeno	OF71	B	21	86	211	26	52	11	1	2	18	24	47	5	.246	.336
Dave Hansen	3B19 1B8	L	27	80	104	7	23	1	0	0	6	19	21	0	.221	.231
Billy Ashley (LJ)	OF38	R	25	71	110	18	22	1	2	9	25	21	44	0	.200	.482
Juan Castro	SS30 3B23 2B9 OF1	R	24	70	132	16	26	5	3	0	5	10	27	1	.197	.280
2 Wayne Kirby	OF53	L	32	65	188	23	51	10	1	1	17	11	17	4	.271	.351
Milt Thompson	OF17	L	37	48	51	2	6	1	0	0	1	6	10	1	.118	.137
2 Tim Wallach	3B45	R	38	45	162	14	37	3	1	4	22	12	32	0	.228	.333
2 Chad Curtis	OF40	R	27	43	104	20	22	6	0	1	9	17	15	2	.212	.317
Tom Prince	C35	R	31	40	64	6	19	4	0	1	6	4	15	0	.297	.438
Mike Busch	3B23 1B1	R	27	38	83	8	18	4	0	7	17	5	33	0	.217	.410
Rick Parker	OF4	R	33	16	14	2	4	1	0	0	1	0	4	1	.286	.357
2 Dave Clark	OF1	L	33	15	15	0	3	0	0	0	0	0	3	0	.200	.200
Carlos Hernandez (XJ)	C9	R	29	13	14	1	4	0	0	0	0	0	4	0	.286	.286
Oreste Marrero	1B1	L	26	10	8	1	3	0	0	0	1	1	3	0	.375	.500
Wilton Guerrero		R	21	5	2	0	0	0	0	0	0	0	0	0	.000	.000
Karim Garcia		L	20	1	1	0	0	0	0	0	0	0	1	0	.000	.000

NAME	T	AGE	W	L	PCT	SV	G	GS	CG	IP	H	BB	SO	SHO	ERA
		28	90	72	.556	50	162	162	6	1466	1378	534	1212	9	3.46
Hideo Nomo	R	27	16	11	.593	0	33	33	3	228	180	85	234	2	3.19
Ramon Martinez (GJ)	R	28	15	6	.714	0	28	27	2	169	153	86	133	2	3.42
Ismael Valdes	R	22	15	7	.682	0	33	33	0	225	219	54	173	0	3.32
Antonio Osuna	R	26	9	6	.600	4	73	0	0	84	65	32	85	0	3.00
Pedro Astacio	R	26	9	8	.529	0	35	32	0	212	207	67	130	0	3.44
Tom Candiotti	R	38	9	11	.450	0	28	27	1	152	172	43	79	0	4.49
Scott Radinsky	L	28	5	1	.833	1	58	0	0	52	52	17	48	0	2.41
Chan Ho Park	R	23	5	5	.500	0	48	10	0	109	82	71	119	0	3.64
Todd Worrell	R	36	4	6	.400	44	72	0	0	65	70	15	66	0	3.03
Mark Guthrie	L	30	2	3	.400	1	66	0	0	73	65	22	56	0	2.22
Darren Dreifort (EJ)	R	24	1	4	.200	0	19	0	0	24	23	12	24	0	4.94
Jim Bruske	R	31	0	0	—	0	13	0	0	13	13	3	12	0	5.68
1 Joey Eischen	L	26	0	0	.000	0	28	0	0	43	48	20	36	0	4.78
1 John Cummings	L	27	0	0	.000	0	4	0	0	5	12	2	5	0	6.75
Darren Hall (EJ)	R	31	0	2	.000	0	9	0	0	13	13	5	12	0	6.00

Name	G by Pos	B	AGE	G	AB	R	H	2B	3B	HR	RBI	BB	SO	SB	BA	SA
COLORADO 3rd 83-79 .512 8	**DON BAYLOR**															
TOTALS			30	162	5590	961	1607	297	37	221	909	527	1108	201	.287	.472
Andres Galarraga	1B159 3B1	R	35	159	626	119	190	39	3	47	150	40	157	18	.304	.601
Eric Young	2B139	R	29	141	568	113	184	23	4	8	74	47	31	53	.324	.421
Walt Weiss	SS155	B	32	155	517	89	146	20	2	8	48	80	78	10	.282	.375
Vinny Castilla	3B160	R	28	160	629	97	191	34	0	40	113	35	88	7	.304	.548
Dante Bichette	OF156	R	32	159	633	114	198	39	3	31	141	45	105	31	.313	.531
Larry Walker (BC)	OF83	L	29	83	272	58	75	18	4	18	58	20	58	18	.276	.570
Ellis Burks	OF152	R	31	156	613	142	211	45	8	40	128	61	114	32	.344	.639
Jeff Reed	C111	L	33	116	341	34	97	20	1	8	37	43	65	2	.284	.419
Quinton McCracken	OF93	B	26	124	283	50	82	13	6	3	40	32	62	17	.290	.410
John Vander Wal	OF26 1B10	L	30	104	151	20	38	6	2	5	31	19	38	2	.252	.417
Jason Bates	2B37 SS18 3B12	B	25	88	160	19	33	8	1	1	9	23	34	2	.206	.288
Jayhawk Owens	C68	R	27	73	180	31	43	9	1	4	17	27	56	4	.239	.367
1 Trenidad Hubbard	OF19	R	32	45	60	12	13	5	1	1	12	9	22	2	.217	.383
2 Eric Anthony	OF19	L	28	32	62	10	15	2	0	4	9	10	20	0	.242	.468
Angel Echevarria	OF11	R	25	26	21	2	6	0	0	0	6	2	5	0	.286	.286
Neifi Perez	SS14 2B4	B	21	17	45	4	7	2	0	0	3	0	8	2	.156	.200
2 Milt Thompson	OF1	L	37	14	15	1	1	0	0	0	2	1	3	0	.067	.133
Pedro Castellano	2B3 3B1 OF1	R	26	13	17	1	2	0	0	0	2	3	6	0	.118	.118
Terry Jones	OF4	B	25	12	10	6	3	0	0	0	1	0	3	0	.300	.300
2 Steve Decker	C10	R	30	10	25	8	8	2	0	1	8	3	1	0	.320	.520
Harvey Pulliam (KJ)	OF3	R	28	10	15	2	2	0	0	0	0	2	6	0	.133	.133
Alan Cockrell	OF1	R	33	9	8	0	2	1	0	0	2	1	4	0	.250	.375
Jorge Brito	C8	R	30	8	14	1	1	0	0	0	0	0	6	0	.071	.071

NAME		T	AGE	W	L	PCT	SV	G	GS	CG	IP	H	BB	SO	SHO	ERA
			29	83	79	.512	34	162	162	5	1423	1597	624	932	4	5.59
Kevin Ritz		R	31	17	11	.607	0	35	35	2	213	236	105	105	0	5.28
Mark Thompson		R	25	9	11	.450	0	34	28	3	170	189	74	99	1	5.30
Armando Reynoso		R	30	8	9	.471	0	30	30	0	169	195	49	88	0	4.96
Bruce Ruffin		L	32	7	5	.583	24	71	0	0	70	55	29	74	0	4.00
Curtis Leskanic		R	28	7	5	.583	6	70	0	0	74	82	38	76	0	6.23
1 Marvin Freeman		R	33	7	9	.438	0	26	23	0	130	151	57	71	0	6.04
Darren Holmes		R	30	5	4	.556	1	62	0	0	77	78	28	73	0	3.97
Lance Painter (SJ)		L	28	4	2	.667	0	34	1	0	51	56	25	48	0	5.86
Steve Reed		R	31	4	3	.571	0	70	0	0	75	66	19	51	0	3.96
Jamey Wright		R	21	4	4	.500	0	16	15	0	91	105	41	45	0	4.93
John Burke		R	26	3	1	.667	0	11	0	0	16	21	7	19	0	7.47
Mike Munoz		L	30	2	2	.500	0	54	0	0	45	55	16	45	0	6.65
Roger Bailey		R	25	2	3	.400	1	24	11	0	84	94	52	45	0	6.24
Bryan Rekar		R	24	2	4	.333	0	14	11	0	58	87	26	25	0	8.95
Garvin Alston		R	24	1	0	1.000	0	6	0	0	9	3	5	9	0	9.00
John Habyan		R	32	1	1	.500	0	19	0	0	24	34	14	25	0	7.13
Bill Swift (SJ)		R	34	1	1	.500	2	7	3	0	18	23	5	5	0	5.40
Robbie Beckett		R	23	1	0	1.000	0	5	0	0	5	6	9	6	0	13.50
Ryan Hawblitzel		R	25	0	1	.000	0	5	0	0	15	18	6	7	0	6.00
Mike Farmer		L	27	0	1	.000	0	7	4	0	28	32	13	16	0	7.71
David Nied		R	27	0	2	.000	0	6	1	0	5	5	4	4	0	13.50
Bret Saberhagen (SJ) 32																

Name	G by Pos	B	AGE	G	AB	R	H	2B	3B	HR	RBI	BB	SO	SB	BA	SA
SAN FRANCISCO 4th 68-94 .420 23	**DUSTY BAKER**															
TOTALS			29	162	5533	752	1400	245	21	153	707	615	1189	113	.253	.388
1 Mark Carreon	1B73 OF5	R	32	132	476	22	3	9	51	22	33	2	.260	.449		
Robby Thompson (PJ)	2B62	R	24	63	227	35	48	11	1	5	21	24	69	1	.211	.335
Shawon Dunston (IJ)	SS78	R	33	82	287	27	86	12	2	5	25	13	40	8	.300	.408
Matt Williams (SJ)	3B92 SS1 1B13	R	30	105	404	69	122	16	1	22	85	39	91	1	.302	.510
Glenallen Hill (BW)	OF98	R	31	98	379	56	106	26	0	19	67	33	95	6	.280	.499
Stan Javier (LJ)	OF71	B	32	71	274	44	74	25	0	2	22	25	51	14	.270	.383
Barry Bonds	OF152	L	31	158	517	122	159	27	3	42	129	151	76	40	.308	.615
1 Kirt Manwaring (BH)	C49	R	30	49	145	9	34	6	0	1	14	16	24	0	.234	.297
Marvin Benard	OF132	L	26	135	488	89	121	17	4	5	27	59	84	25	.248	.330
Rich Aurilia	SS93 2B11	R	24	105	318	27	76	7	1	3	26	25	52	4	.239	.296
Steve Scarsone	2B74 3B14 SS1 1B1	R	30	105	283	28	62	12	1	5	23	25	91	2	.219	.322
Dave Martinez	1B51 OF20	R	26	91	175	16	38	3	0	6	24	18	43	2	.217	.337
Tom Lampkin (BG)	C53	L	32	66	177	26	41	8	0	6	29	20	22	1	.232	.379
1 Steve Decker	C30 1B3 3B2	R	30	57	122	16	28	1	0	1	12	15	26	0	.230	.262
Bill Mueller	3B45 2B8	B	25	55	200	31	66	15	1	0	19	24	26	0	.330	.415
Kim Batiste	3B25 SS7	R	28	54	130	17	27	6	0	3	11	5	33	3	.208	.323
2 Rick Wilkins	C42 1B7	L	29	52	157	19	46	10	0	8	36	21	40	0	.293	.510
Jay Canizaro	2B35 SS7	R	22	43	120	11	24	4	1	2	8	9	38	0	.200	.300
Desi Wilson	1B33	L	28	41	118	10	32	2	0	2	12	12	27	0	.271	.339
Dax Jones	OF33	R	26	34	59	7	10	0	2	1	7	8	12	2	.172	.293
Jacob Cruz	OF23	L	23	33	77	10	18	3	0	3	10	12	24	0	.234	.390
Dan Peltier	1B13 OF1	L	28	31	59	3	15	2	0	0	9	7	9	0	.254	.288
Mel Hall	OF4	L	35	25	25	3	3	0	0	0	5	1	4	0	.120	.120
1 J.R. Phillips	1B10	L	26	15	25	5	5	0	0	2	5	1	13	0	.200	.440
2 Trenidad Hubbard	OF9	R	32	10	29	3	6	0	1	1	2	2	5	0	.207	.379
Keith Williams	OF4	R	24	9	20	0	5	0	0	0	0	0	6	0	.250	.250
Marcus Jensen	C7	B	23	9	19	4	4	1	0	0	4	8	7	0	.211	.263
Doug Mirabelli	C8	R	25	9	18	2	4	1	0	0	1	3	4	0	.222	.278
Wilson Delgado	SS6	B	23	6	22	3	8	0	0	0	2	1	5	1	.364	.364

NAME		T	AGE	W	L	PCT	SV	G	GS	CG	IP	H	BB	SO	SHO	ERA
			28	68	94	.420	35	162	162	9	1442	1520	570	997	8	4.71
Mark Gardner		R	34	12	7	.632	0	30	28	4	179	200	57	145	1	4.42
William VanLandingham	R	25	9	14	.391	0	32	32	0	182	196	78	97	0	5.40
Allen Watson		L	25	8	12	.400	0	29	29	2	186	189	69	128	0	4.61
Osvaldo Fernandez		R	27	7	13	.350	0	30	28	2	172	193	57	106	0	4.61
Mark Dewey		R	31	6	3	.667	0	78	0	0	83	79	41	57	0	4.21
1 Jeff Juden		R	24	0	1.000	0	36	0	0	42	39	20	35	0	4.10	
1 Mark Leiter		R	33	4	10	.286	0	23	22	1	135	151	50	118	0	5.19
Jose Bautista		R	31	3	4	.429	0	37	1	0	70	66	15	28	0	3.36
Shawn Estes		L	23	3	5	.375	0	11	11	0	70	63	39	60	0	3.60
Rich DeLucia (SJ)		R	31	3	6	.333	1	56	0	0	62	62	31	55	0	5.84
Steve Soderstrom		R	24	2	0	1.000	0	3	3	0	14	16	6	9	0	5.27
2 Jim Poole		L	30	2	1	.667	0	35	0	0	24	15	13	19	0	2.66
2 Tim Scott		R	29	2	2	.500	0	20	0	0	20	24	9	10	0	8.24
Dan Carlson		R	26	1	0	1.000	0	5	0	0	10	13	2	4	0	2.70
2 Kirk Rueter		L	25	1	2	.333	0	4	3	0	22	18	5	16	0	1.93
Steve Bourgeois		R	23	1	3	.250	0	15	5	0	40	60	21	17	0	6.30
Shawn Barton		L	33	0	0	—	0	7	0	0	8	19	1	3	0	9.72
Chris Hook		R	27	0	0	—	0	13	16	14	4	7	0	7.43		
Doug Creek		L	27	0	2	.000	0	63	0	0	48	45	32	38	0	6.52
Rod Beck		R	27	0	9	.000	35	63	0	0	62	56	10	48	0	3.34
Sergio Valdez (SJ) 31																

LINE SCORES

Team	1	2	3	4	5	6	7	8	9	10			R	H	E

DIVISION SERIES: ATLANTA 3 : LOS ANGELES 0

Game 1   October 2 at Los Angeles

	1	2	3	4	5	6	7	8	9	10		R	H	E
ATL	0	0	0	1	0	0	0	0	0	1		2	4	1
LA	0	0	0	0	0	0	0	0	0	0		1	5	0

Smoltz, Wohlers (10)   Martinez, Radinsky (9), Osuna (9)

Game 2   October 3 at Los Angeles

	1	2	3	4	5	6	7	8	9		R	H	E
ATL	0	1	0	0	0	0	2	0	0		3	5	2
LA	1	0	0	1	0	0	0	0	0		2	3	0

Maddux, McMichael (8), Wohlers (9)   **Valdes**, Astacio (7), Worrell (9)

Game 3   October 5 at Atlanta

	1	2	3	4	5	6	7	8	9		R	H	E
LA	0	0	0	0	0	0	1	1	0		2	6	1
ATL	1	0	0	4	0	0	0	0	X		5	7	0

Nomo, Guthrie (4), Candiotti (5), Radinsky (7), Osuna (8), Dreifort (8)   **Glavine**, McMichael (7), Bielecki (8), Wohlers (8)

DIVISION SERIES

COMPOSITE BATTING

NAME	POS	G	AB	R	H	2B	3B	HR	RBI	BA
ATLANTA										
TOTALS		3	89	10	16	3	0	5	10	.180
Lemke	2B	3	12	1	2	1	0	0	2	.167
Grissom	CF	3	12	2	1	0	0	0	0	.083
Dye	RF	3	11	1	2	0	0	1	1	.182
McGriff	1B	3	9	1	3	1	0	1	3	.333
Jones	3B	3	9	2	2	0	0	1	2	.222
Blauser	SS	3	9	0	1	0	0	0	0	.111
Klesko	LF	3	8	1	1	0	0	1	1	.125
Lopez	C	2	7	1	2	0	0	1	1	.286
Perez	C	1	3	0	1	0	0	0	0	.333
Polonia	PH	2	2	0	0	0	0	0	0	.000
Glavine	P	1	2	1	1	1	0	0	0	.500
Smoltz	P	1	2	0	0	0	0	0	0	.000
Maddux	P	1	2	0	0	0	0	0	0	.000
Pendleton	PH	1	1	0	0	0	0	0	0	.000
Wohlers	P	3	0	0	0	0	0	0	0	—
McMichael	P	2	0	0	0	0	0	0	0	—
Bielecki	P	1	0	0	0	0	0	0	0	—
LOS ANGELES										
TOTALS		3	95	5	14	7	0	0	5	.147
Hollandsworth	LF	3	12	1	4	3	0	0	1	.333
Gagne	SS	3	11	2	3	1	0	0	0	.273
Mondesi	RF	3	11	0	2	2	0	0	1	.182
Wallach	3B	3	11	0	0	0	0	0	0	.000
Piazza	C	3	10	1	3	0	0	0	2	.300
Karros	1B	3	9	0	0	0	0	0	0	.000
Kirby	CF	3	8	1	1	0	0	0	0	.125
Castro	2B	2	5	0	1	1	0	0	1	.200
DeShields	2B	2	4	0	0	0	0	0	0	.000
Martinez	P	1	3	0	0	0	0	0	0	.000
Ashley	PH	2	2	0	0	0	0	0	0	.000
Clark	PH	2	2	0	0	0	0	0	0	.000
Hansen	PH	2	2	0	0	0	0	0	0	.000
Curtis	CF	1	2	0	0	0	0	0	0	.000
Valdes	P	1	1	0	0	0	0	0	0	.000
Nomo	P	1	1	0	0	0	0	0	0	.000
Osuna	P	2	0	0	0	0	0	0	0	—
Radinsky	P	2	0	0	0	0	0	0	0	—
Candiotti	P	1	0	0	0	0	0	0	0	—
Astacio	P	1	0	0	0	0	0	0	0	—
Worrell	P	1	0	0	0	0	0	0	0	—
Dreifort	P	1	0	0	0	0	0	0	0	—
Guthrie	P	1	0	0	0	0	0	0	0	—

COMPOSITE PITCHING

NAME	G	IP	H	BB	SO	W	L	SV	ERA
ATLANTA									
TOTALS	3	28	14	7	29	3	0	2	0.96
Smoltz	1	9	4	2	7	1	0	0	1.00
Maddux	1	7	3	0	7	1	0	0	0.00
Glavine	1	6.2	5	3	7	1	0	0	1.35
Wohlers	3	3.1	1	0	4	0	0	2	0.00
McMichael	2	1.1	1	1	3	0	0	0	6.75
Bielecki	1	.2	0	1	1	0	0	0	0.00
LOS ANGELES									
TOTALS	3	27	16	12	24	0	3	0	3.33
Martinez	1	8	3	3	6	0	0	0	1.12
Valdes	1	6.1	5	0	5	0	1	0	4.26
Nomo	1	3.2	5	5	3	0	1	0	12.27
Osuna	2	2	3	1	4	0	1	0	4.50
Candiotti	1	2	0	1	0	0	0	0	0.00
Astacio	1	1.2	0	1	0	0	0	0	0.00
Radinsky	2	1.1	0	1	2	0	0	0	0.00
Worrell	1	1	0	1	1	0	0	0	0.00
Dreifort	1	.2	0	0	1	0	0	0	0.00
Guthrie	1	.1	0	1	1	0	0	0	0.00

LINE SCORES

Team	1	2	3	4	5	6	7	8	9	10	11	R	H	E

DIVISION SERIES: ST. LOUIS 3 : SAN DIEGO 0

Game 1 — October 1 at St. Louis

	1	2	3	4	5	6	7	8	9		R	H	E
SD	0	0	0	0	0	1	0	0	0		1	8	1
StL	3	0	0	0	0	0	0	0	X		3	6	0

Hamilton, Blair (7)
Stottlemyre, Honeycutt (7), Eckersley (8)

Game 2 — October 3 at St. Louis

	1	2	3	4	5	6	7	8	9	10	R	H	E
SD	0	0	0	0	0	1	2	0	1	0	4	6	0
StL	0	0	1	0	3	0	0	1	X		5	5	1

Sanders, Veras (5), Worrell (6), Bochtler (8), Hoffman (8)
Andy Benes, Honeycutt (8), Eckersley (9)

Game 3 — October 5 at San Diego

	1	2	3	4	5	6	7	8	9	R	H	E
StL	1	0	0	0	0	3	1	0	2	7	13	1
SD	0	2	1	1	0	0	0	1	0	5	11	2

Osborne, Petkovsek (5), Honeycutt (7), Mathews (8), Eckersley (9)
Ashby, Worrell (6), Valenzuela (8), Veras (8), Hoffman (9)

NATIONAL LEAGUE CHAMPIONSHIP: ATLANTA 4 : ST. LOUIS 3

Game 1 — October 9 at Atlanta

	1	2	3	4	5	6	7	8	9	10	R	H	E
StL	0	1	0	0	0	0	0	1	0	0	2	5	1
ATL	0	0	0	0	0	2	0	0	2	X	4	9	0

Andy Benes, Petkovsek (7), Fossas (8), Mathews (8)
Smoltz, Wohlers (9)

Game 2 — October 10 at Atlanta

	1	2	3	4	5	6	7	8	9	R	H	E
StL	1	0	2	0	0	0	5	0	0	8	11	2
ATL	0	0	2	0	1	0	0	0	0	3	5	2

Stottlemyre, Petkovsek (7), Honeycutt (8), Eckersley (8)
Maddux, McMichael (7), Neagle (8), Avery (9)

Game 3 — October 12 at St. Louis

	1	2	3	4	5	6	7	8	9	R	H	E
ATL	1	0	0	0	0	0	1	0	0	2	8	1
StL	2	0	0	0	0	1	0	0	X	3	7	0

Glavine, Bielecki (7), McMichael (8)
Osborne, Petkovsek (8) Honeycutt (9), Eckersley (9)

Game 4 — October 13 at St. Louis

	1	2	3	4	5	6	7	8	9	R	H	E
ATL	0	1	0	0	0	2	0	0	0	3	9	1
StL	0	0	0	0	0	0	3	1	X	4	5	0

Neagle, McMichael (7), Wohlers (9)
Andy Benes, Fossas (6), Mathews (6), Alan Benes (6), Honeycutt (8), Eckersley (8)

Game 5 — October 14 at St. Louis

	1	2	3	4	5	6	7	8	9	R	H	E
ATL	5	2	0	3	1	0	0	1	2	14	22	0
StL										0	7	0

Smoltz, Bielecki (8), Wade (9), Clontz (9)
Stottlemyre, Jackson (2), Fossas (5), Petkovsek (7), Honeycutt (9)

Game 6 — October 16 at Atlanta

	1	2	3	4	5	6	7	8	9	R	H	E
StL	0	0	0	0	0	0	0	1	0	1	6	1
ATL	0	1	0	0	1	0	0	1	X	3	7	0

Alan Benes, Fossas (6), Petkovsek (6), Stottlemyre (8)
Maddux, Wohlers (8)

Game 7 — October 17 at Atlanta

	1	2	3	4	5	6	7	8	9	R	H	E
StL	0	0	0	0	0	0	0	0	0	0	4	2
ATL	6	0	0	4	0	3	2	0	X	15	17	0

Osborne, Andy Benes (1), Petkovsek (6), Honeycutt (6), Fossas (8)
Glavine, Bielecki (8), Avery (9)

COMPOSITE BATTING

DIVISION SERIES

ST. LOUIS

NAME	POS	G	AB	R	H	2B	3B	HR	RBI	BA
TOTALS		3	94	15	24	3	1	3	14	.255
Jordan	RF	3	12	4	4	0	0	1	3	.333
Pagnozzi	C	3	11	0	3	0	0	0	2	.273
Alicea	2B	3	11	1	2	2	0	0	0	.182
Gaetti	3B	3	11	1	1	0	0	1	3	.091
Gant	LF	3	10	3	4	1	0	1	4	.400
Mabry	1B	3	10	1	3	0	1	0	1	.300
McGee	CF	3	10	1	1	0	0	0	1	.100
Clayton	SS	2	6	1	2	0	0	0	0	.333
Smith	SS	2	3	1	1	0	0	0	0	.333
Lankford	CF	1	2	1	1	0	0	0	0	.500
Andy Benes	P	1	2	1	1	0	0	0	0	.500
Stottlemyre	P	1	2	0	0	0	0	0	0	.000
Honeycutt	P	3	1	0	0	0	0	0	0	.000
Gallego	2B	2	1	0	0	0	0	0	0	.000
Sweeney	PH	1	1	0	1	0	0	0	0	1.000
Osborne	P	1	1	0	0	0	0	0	0	.000
Eckersley	P	3	0	0	0	0	0	0	0	—
Petkovsek	P	1	0	0	0	0	0	0	0	—
Mathews	P	1	0	0	0	0	0	0	0	—

SAN DIEGO

NAME	POS	G	AB	R	H	2B	3B	HR	RBI	BA
TOTALS		3	105	10	25	3	0	3	9	.238
T. Gwynn	RF	3	13	0	4	1	0	0	1	.308
Henderson	LF	3	12	2	4	0	0	0	1	.333
Gomez	SS	3	12	0	2	0	0	0	1	.167
Finley	CF	3	12	0	1	0	0	0	1	.083
Reed	2B	3	11	0	3	1	0	0	2	.273
Caminiti	3B	3	10	3	3	0	0	3	3	.300
Joyner	1B	3	9	0	1	0	0	0	0	.111
Johnson	C	2	8	2	3	1	0	0	0	.375
Flaherty	C	2	4	0	0	0	0	0	0	.000
Cianfrocco	1B	3	3	1	1	0	0	0	0	.333
Vaughn	LF	3	3	0	0	0	0	0	0	.000
C. Gwynn	PH	2	2	1	2	0	0	0	0	1.000
Livingstone	PH	2	2	1	1	0	0	0	0	.500
Hamilton	P	1	2	0	0	0	0	0	0	.000
Ashby	P	1	1	0	0	0	0	0	0	.000
Sanders	P	1	1	0	0	0	0	0	0	.000
Worrell	P	2	0	0	0	0	0	0	0	—
Hoffman	P	2	0	0	0	0	0	0	0	—
Veras	P	2	0	0	0	0	0	0	0	—
Blair	P	1	0	0	0	0	0	0	0	—
Valenzuela	P	1	0	0	0	0	0	0	0	—
Bochtler	P	1	0	0	0	0	0	0	0	—

COMPOSITE PITCHING

DIVISION SERIES

ST. LOUIS

NAME	G	IP	H	BB	SO	W	L	SV	ERA
TOTALS	3	27	25	4	28	3	0	3	3.33
Andy Benes	1	7	6	1	9	0	0	0	5.14
Stottlemyre	1	6.2	5	2	7	1	0	0	1.35
Osborne	1	4	7	0	5	0	0	0	9.00
Eckersley	3	3.2	3	0	2	0	0	3	0.00
Honeycutt	3	2.2	3	1	2	1	0	0	3.38
Petkovsek	1	2	0	0	1	0	0	0	0.00
Mathews	1	1	1	0	2	1	0	0	0.00

SAN DIEGO

NAME	G	IP	H	BB	SO	W	L	SV	ERA
TOTALS	3	25	24	13	23	0	3	0	5.40
Hamilton	1	6	5	0	6	0	1	0	4.50
Ashby	1	5.1	7	1	5	0	0	0	6.75
Sanders	1	4.1	3	4	4	0	0	0	8.31
Worrell	2	3.2	4	1	2	0	0	0	2.45
Blair	1	2	1	2	3	0	0	0	0.00
Hoffman	2	1.2	3	1	2	0	1	0	10.00
Veras	2	1	1	0	1	0	0	0	0.00
Valenzuela	1	.2	0	2	0	0	0	0	0.00
Bochtler	1	.1	0	2	0	0	0	1	27.00

NATIONAL LEAGUE CHAMPIONSHIP

COMPOSITE BATTING

ATLANTA

NAME	POS	G	AB	R	H	2B	3B	HR	RBI	BA
TOTALS		7	249	44	77	11	3	8	43	.309
Grissom	CF	7	35	7	10	1	0	1	3	.286
McGriff	1B	7	28	6	7	0	1	2	7	.250
Dye	RF	7	28	2	6	1	0	0	4	.214
Lemke	2B	7	27	4	12	2	0	1	5	.444
C. Jones	3B	7	25	6	11	2	0	0	4	.440
Lopez	C	7	24	8	13	5	0	2	6	.542
Blauser	SS	7	17	5	3	0	1	0	2	.176
Klesko	LF	6	16	1	4	0	0	1	3	.250
A. Jones	LF	5	9	3	2	0	0	1	3	.222
Smoltz	P	2	7	1	2	0	0	0	1	.286
Pendleton	PH	6	6	0	0	0	0	0	0	.000
Belliard	SS	4	6	0	4	0	0	0	2	.667
Glavine	P	2	6	0	1	0	1	0	3	.167
Mordecai	3B	4	4	1	1	0	0	0	0	.250
Maddux	P	2	4	0	0	0	0	0	0	.000
Polonia	PH	3	3	0	0	0	0	0	0	.000
Neagle	P	2	2	0	1	0	0	0	0	.500
Perez	C	4	1	0	0	0	0	0	0	.000
Wohlers	P	3	1	0	0	0	0	0	0	.000
Bielecki	P	3	0	0	0	0	0	0	0	—
McMichael	P	3	0	0	0	0	0	0	0	—
Avery	P	2	0	0	0	0	0	0	0	—
Clontz	P	1	0	0	0	0	0	0	0	—
Wade	P	1	0	0	0	0	0	0	0	—

ST. LOUIS

NAME	POS	G	AB	R	H	2B	3B	HR	RBI	BA
TOTALS		7	221	18	45	4	2	4	15	.204
Gant	LF	7	25	3	6	1	0	2	4	.240
Jordan	RF-CF	7	25	3	6	1	1	1	2	.240
Gaetti	3B	7	24	1	7	0	0	1	4	.292
Mabry	1B	7	23	1	6	0	0	0	0	.261
Clayton	SS	5	20	4	7	0	0	0	1	.350
Pagnozzi	C	7	19	1	3	1	0	0	1	.158
McGee	CF-RF	6	15	0	5	0	0	0	0	.333
Gallego	2B	7	14	1	2	0	0	0	0	.143
Lankford	CF	5	13	1	0	0	0	0	0	.000
Smith	SS	3	9	0	0	0	0	0	0	.000
Alicea	2B	5	8	0	0	0	0	0	0	.000
Young	1B	4	7	1	2	0	1	0	2	.286
Sweeney	RF	5	5	0	0	0	0	0	0	.000
Andy Benes	P	3	4	0	1	1	0	0	0	.250
Sheaffer	C	2	3	0	0	0	0	0	0	.000
Osborne	P	2	3	0	0	0	0	0	0	.000
Stottlemyre	P	2	2	0	0	0	0	0	0	.000
Mejia	CF	3	1	0	1	0	0	0	0	.000
Alan Benes	P	2	1	0	0	0	0	0	0	.000
Jackson	P	1	1	0	0	0	0	0	0	.000
Petkovsek	P	6	0	0	0	0	0	0	0	—
Fossas	P	5	0	0	0	0	0	0	0	—
Honeycutt	P	5	0	0	0	0	0	0	0	—
Eckersley	P	3	0	0	0	0	0	0	0	—
Mathews	P	2	0	0	0	0	0	0	0	—

COMPOSITE PITCHING

ATLANTA

NAME	G	IP	H	BB	SO	W	L	SV	ERA
TOTALS	7	61	45	11	53	4	3	2	1.92
Smoltz	2	15	12	3	12	2	0	0	1.20
Maddux	2	14.1	15	2	10	1	1	0	2.51
Glavine	2	13	10	0	9	1	1	0	2.08
Neagle	2	7.2	2	3	8	0	0	0	2.35
Wohlers	3	3	0	0	4	0	0	2	0.00
Bielecki	3	3	0	1	5	0	0	0	0.00
McMichael	3	2	4	1	3	0	1	0	9.00
Avery	2	2	2	1	1	0	0	0	0.00
Clontz	1	0.2	0	0	1	0	0	0	0.00
Wade	1	0.1	0	0	1	0	0	0	0.00

ST. LOUIS

NAME	G	IP	H	BB	SO	W	L	SV	ERA
TOTALS	7	60	77	25	51	3	4	1	6.60
Andy Benes	3	15.1	19	3	9	0	0	0	5.28
Stottlemyre	3	8	15	3	11	1	1	0	12.38
Osborne	2	7.2	12	4	6	1	1	0	9.39
Petkovsek	6	7.1	11	3	7	0	1	0	7.36
Alan Benes	2	6.1	3	2	5	0	1	0	2.84
Fossas	5	4.1	1	3	1	0	0	0	2.08
Honeycutt	5	4	5	3	3	0	0	0	9.00
Eckersley	3	3.1	2	0	4	1	0	1	0.00
Jackson	1	3	7	3	3	0	0	0	9.00
Mathews	2	.2	2	1	2	0	0	0	0.00

LINE SCORES

Team	1	2	3	4	5	6	7	8	9	10		R	H	E

WORLD SERIES: NEW YORK (AL) 4 : ATLANTA (NL) 2

Game 1   October 20 at New York
ATL	0	2	6	0	1	3	0	0	0		12	13	0
NY	0	0	0	0	1	0	0	0	0		1	4	1

Smoltz, McMichael (7), Neagle (8)   Pettitte, Boehringer (3)
Wade (9), Clontz (9)   Weathers (6), Nelson (8)
Wetteland (9)

Game 2   October 21 at New York
ATL	1	0	1	0	1	0	1	1	0	0		4	10	0
NY	0	0	0	0	0	0	0	0	0	0		0	7	1

Maddux, Wohlers (9)   Key, Lloyd (7), Nelson (7),
Rivera (9)

Game 3   October 22 at Atlanta
NY	1	0	0	1	0	0	0	3	0		5	8	1
ATL	0	0	0	0	0	1	0	1	0		2	6	1

Cone, Rivera (7), Lloyd (8),   Glavine, McMichael (8),
Wetteland (9)   Clontz (8), Bielecki (9)

Game 4   October 23 at Atlanta
NY	0	0	0	0	0	0	3	0	3	2		8	12	0
ATL	0	4	1	0	1	0	0	0	0		6	9	2

Rogers, Boehringer (3),   Neagle, Wade (6), Bielecki (6),
Weathers (5), Nelson (6), Rivera (8),   Wohlers (8), **Avery** (10), Clontz (10)
Lloyd (9), Wetteland (10)

Game 5   October 24 at Atlanta
NY	0	0	0	1	0	0	0	0	0		1	4	1
ATL	0	0	0	0	0	0	0	0	0		0	5	1

Pettitte, Wetteland (9)   **Smoltz**, Wohlers (9)

Game 6   October 26 at New York
ATL	0	0	0	1	0	0	0	0	1		2	8	0
NY	0	0	3	0	0	0	0	0	X		3	8	1

Maddux, Wohlers (8)   **Key**, Weathers (6), Lloyd (6),
Rivera (8), Wetteland (9)

COMPOSITE BATTING

NEW YORK

NAME	POS	G	AB	R	H	2B	3B	HR	RBI	BA
TOTALS		6	199	18	43	6	1	2	16	.216
Williams	CF	6	24	3	4	0	0	1	4	.167
Fielder	DH-1B	6	23	1	9	2	0	0	2	.391
Jeter	SS	6	20	5	5	0	0	1		.250
Duncan	2B	6	19	1	1	0	0	0	1	.053
Strawberry	LF-RF	5	16	0	3	0	0	0	1	.188
Hayes	3B-1B	5	16	2	3	0	0	0	1	.188
Raines	LF	5	14	2	3	0	0	0		.214
O'Neill	RF	5	12	1	2	2	0	0	1	.167
Martinez	1B	6	11	0	1	0	0	0		.091
Boggs	3B	5	11	0	3	1	0	0	2	.273
Girardi	C	4	10	1	2	1	0	1		.200
Leyritz	C	4	8	1	3	0	0	1	3	.375
Sojo	2B	5	5	0	3	1	0	0	1	.600
Pettitte	P	2	4	0	0	0	0	0		.000
Cone	P	1	2	0	0	0	0	0		.000
Rivera	P	4	1	0	0	0	0	0		.000
Lloyd	P	4	1	0	0	0	0	0		.000
Aldrete	RF	2	1	0	0	0	0	0		.000
Rogers	P	1	1	0	1	0	0	0		1.000
Wetteland	P	5	0	0	0	0	0	0		—
Fox	2B-3B	4	0	1	0	0	0	0		—
Nelson	P	3	0	0	0	0	0	0		—
Weathers	P	3	0	0	0	0	0	0		—
Key	P	2	0	0	0	0	0	0		—
Boehringer	P	2	0	0	0	0	0	0		—

ATLANTA

NAME	POS	G	AB	R	H	2B	3B	HR	RBI	BA
TOTALS		6	201	26	51	9	1	4	26	.254
Grissom	CF	6	27	4	12	2	1	0	5	.444
Lemke	2B	6	26	2	6	1	0	0	2	.231
C. Jones	3B-SS	6	21	3	6	3	0	0	3	.286
Lopez	C	6	21	3	4	0	0	1		.190
A. Jones	LF-RF	6	20	4	8	1	0	2	6	.400
McGriff	1B	6	20	4	6	0	0	2	6	.300
Blauser	SS	6	18	2	3	1	0	0	1	.167
Dye	RF	5	17	0	2	0	0	1	1	.118
Klesko	DH-LF-1B	5	10	0	1	0	0	0		.100
Pendleton	DH-3B	4	9	1	2	0	0	0		.222
Polonia	PH	6	5	0	0	0	0	0		.000
Smoltz	P	2	2	0	1	0	0	0		.500
Perez	C	2	1	0	0	0	0	0		.000
Neagle	P	2	1	0	0	0	0	0		.000
Bielecki	P	2	1	0	0	0	0	0		.000
Glavine	P	1	1	0	0	0	0	0		.000
Mordecai	PH	1	1	0	0	0	0	0		.000
Belliard	SS	4	0	0	0	0	0	0		—
Wohlers	P	4	0	0	0	0	0	0		—
Clontz	P	3	0	0	0	0	0	0		—
Maddux	P	2	0	0	0	0	0	0		—
McMichael	P	2	0	0	0	0	0	0		—
Wade	P	2	0	0	0	0	0	0		—
Avery	P	1	0	0	0	0	0	0		—

COMPOSITE PITCHING

NEW YORK

NAME	G	IP	H	BB	SO	W	L	SV	ERA
TOTALS	6	55	51	23	36	4	2	4	3.93
Key	2	11.1	15	5	1	1	1	0	3.97
Pettitte	2	10.2	11	4	5	1	1	0	5.90
Cone	1	6	4	4	3	1	0	0	1.50
Rivera	4	5.2	4	3	4	0	0	0	1.59
Boehringer	2	5	5	0	5	0	0	0	5.40
Wetteland	5	4.1	4	1	6	0	0	4	2.08
Nelson	3	4.1	1	1	5	0	0	0	0.00
Weathers	3	3	2	3	3	0	0	0	3.00
Lloyd	4	2.2	0	4	1	0	0	0	0.00
Rogers	1	2	5	2	0	0	0	0	22.50

ATLANTA

NAME	G	IP	H	BB	SO	W	L	SV	ERA
TOTALS	6	54	43	26	43	2	4	0	2.33
Maddux	2	15.2	14	1	5	1	1	0	1.72
Smoltz	2	14	6	8	14	1	1	0	0.64
Glavine	1	7	4	3	8	0	1	0	1.29
Neagle	2	6	5	4	3	0	0	0	3.00
Wohlers	4	4.1	7	2	4	0	0	0	6.23
Bielecki	2	3	0	3	6	0	0	0	0.00
Clontz	3	1.2	1	1	2	0	0	0	0.00
McMichael	2	1	5	0	1	0	0	0	27.00
Wade	2	.2	0	1	0	0	0	0	0.00
Avery	1	.2	1	3	1	0	0	1	13.50

MISCELLANEOUS 1996 INDIVIDUAL LEADERS

BATTING

On Base Average

	American League			National League	
1	McGwire, Oak.	.467	1	Sheffield, Fla.	.465
2	Martinez, Sea.	.464	2	Bonds, S.F.	.461
3	Thomas, Chi.	.459	3	Bagwell, Hou.	.451
4	Thome, Cle.	.450	4	Piazza, L.A.	.422
5	Knoblauch, Min.	.448	5	Henderson, S.D.	.410
6	Vaughn, Bos.	.420		Larkin, Cin.	.410
7	Seitzer, Mil. + Cle.	.416	7	Burks, Col.	.408
8	Rodriguez, Sea.	.414		Caminiti, S.D.	.408
9	Alomar, Bal.	.411	9	Gwynn, S.D.	.400
6	O'Neill, N.Y.	.411	10	Grace, Chi.	.396

On Base Average plus Slugging Average

	American League			National League	
1	McGwire, Oak.	1.197	1	Sheffield, Fla.	1.089
2	Thomas, Chi.	1.085	2	Bonds, S.F.	1.076
3	Thome, Cle.	1.062	3	Burks, Col.	1.047
4	Martinez, Sea.	1.059	4	Caminiti, S.D.	1.029
5	Rodriguez, Sea.	1.045	5	Bagwell, Hou.	1.021
6	Anderson, Bal.	1.033	6	Piazza, L.A.	.985
	Belle, Cle.	1.033	7	Larkin, Cin.	.977
8	Griffey, Sea.	1.020	8	Galarraga, Col.	.958
9	Gonzalez, Tex.	1.011	9	Gilkey, N.Y.	.955
10	Vaughn, Bos.	1.003	10	C. Jones, Atl.	.923

Total Bases

	American League			National League	
1	Rodriguez, Sea.	379	1	Burks, Col.	392
2	Belle, Cle.	375	2	Galarraga, Col.	376
3	Vaughn, Bos.	370	3	Finley, S.D.	348
4	Anderson, Bal.	369	4	Castilla, Col.	345
5	Gonzalez, Tex.	348	5	Caminiti, S.D.	339
6	Griffey, Sea.	342	6	Bichette, Col.	336
	Palmeiro, Bal.	342	7	Grissom, Atl.	328
8	Thomas, Chi.	330	8	Johnson, N.Y.	327
9	Ramirez, Cle.	320	9	Sheffield, Fla.	324
10	Buhner, Sea.	314	10	Bagwell, Hou.	324

Caught Stealing

	American League			National League	
1	Goodwin, K.C.	22	1	Young, Col.	19
2	Lofton, Cle.	17	2	Clayton, St. L.	15
3	Knoblauch, Min.	14		Henderson, S.D.	15
4	Nixon, Tor.	13	4	Bichette, Col.	12
5	5 tied with	10		Martin, Pit.	12
				Johnson, N.Y.	12

Stolen Base Percentage
(Minimum 20 Attempts)

	American League			National League	
1	Durham, Chi.	88	1	Bell, Hou.	91
2	Frye, Bos.	82	2	Walker, Col.	90
3	Lofton, Cle.	82	3	Bonds, S.F.	85
4	Burnitz, Cle. + Mil.	81	4	Burks, Col.	84
	Williams, N.Y.	81		Morandini, Phi.	84

Extra Base Hits

	American League			National League	
1	Anderson, Bal.	92	1	Burks, Col.	93
2	Rodriguez, Sea.	91	2	Galarraga, Col.	89
3	Belle, Cle.	89	3	Finley, S.D.	84
4	Gonzalez, Tex.	82	4	Bagwell, Hou.	81
5	Ramirez, Cle.	81	5	Caminiti, S.D.	79
	Palmeiro, Bal.	81		Rodriguez, Mon.	79

PITCHING

Fewest Hits Per 9 Innings Pitched

	American League			National League	
1	Guzman, Tor.	7.58	1	Leiter, Fla.	6.39
2	Clemens, Bos.	8.01	2	Smoltz, Atl.	7.06
3	Hentgen, Tor.	8.06	3	Nomo, L.A.	7.09
4	Appier, K.C.	8.18	4	Brown, Fla.	7.22
5	Fernandez, Chi.	8.65	5	Schilling, Phi.	7.31
6	Nagy, Cle.	8.80	6	Stottlemyre, StL.	7.70
7	Gooden, NY	8.91	7	Matinez, Mon.	7.85
8	Alvarez, Chi.	8.94	8	Trachsel, Chi.	7.95
9	Baldwin, Chi.	8.95	9	Martinez, L.A.	8.16
10	Radke, Min.	8.96	10	Burba, Cin.	8.26

Fewest Bases on Balls Per 9 Innings Pitched

	American League			National League	
1	Haney, K.C.	2.01	1	Maddux, Atl.	1.03
2	Clemens, Bos.	2.05	2	Brown, Fla.	1.27
3	Radke, Min.	2.21	3	Darwin, Pit. + Hou.	1.48
4	Nagy, Cle.	2.47	4	Reynolds, Hou.	1.66
5	Fernandez, Chi.	2.51	5	Tewksbury, S.D.	1.87
6	Hershiser, Cle.	2.53	6	Smoltz, Atl.	1.95
7	Guzman, Tor.	2.54	7	Neagle, Pit. + Atl.	1.95
8	Mussina, Bal.	2.55	8	Clark, NY	2.03
9	Belcher, K.C.	2.56	9	B. Jones, NY	2.12
10	Erickson, Bal.	2.67	10	Fassero, Mon.	2.14

Strikeouts Per 9 Innings Pitched

	American League			National League	
1	Clemens, Bos.	9.53	1	Smoltz, Atl.	9.79
2	Appier, K.C.	8.82	2	Nomo, L.A.	9.22
3	Finley, Cal.	8.13	3	Martinez, Mon.	9.22
4	Guzman, Tor.	7.91	4	Kile, Hou.	9.00
5	Mussina, Bal.	7.55	5	Schilling, Phi.	8.93
6	Alvarez, Chi.	7.50	6	Fassero, Mon.	8.62
7	Gordon, Bos.	7.14	7	Leiter, Fla.	8.36
8	Witt, Tex.	7.08	8	Hamilton, S.D.	7.82
9	Fernandez, Chi.	6.98	9	Stottlemyre, St.L.	7.82
10	Nagy, Cle.	6.77	10	Reynolds, Hou.	7.68

Lowest Batting Average Allowed

	American League			National League	
1	Guzman, Tor.	.228	1	Leiter, Fla.	.202
2	Clemens, Bos.	.237	2	Smoltz, Atl.	.216
3	Hentgen, Tor.	.241	3	Nomo, L.A.	.218
4	Appier, K.C.	.245	4	Brown, Fla.	.220
5	Fernandez, Chi.	.253	5	Schilling, Phi.	.223

Home Runs Allowed

	American League			National League	
1	Boskie, Cal.	40	1	Leiter, S.F. + Mon.	37
2	Radke, Min.	40	2	Hamisch, NY	30
3	Wakefield, Bos.	38		Stottlemyre, St.L	30
4	Tapani, Chi.	34		Trachsel, Chi.	30
	Fernandez, Chi.	34	5	Andy Benes, StL	28
				Castillo, Chi.	28
				Gardner, S.F.	28
				Watson, S.F.	28

Home Runs Allowed per 9 IP
(Minimum 10 Home Runs Allowed)

	American League			National League	
1	Christopher, Det.	3.60	1	Painter, Col.	2.13
2	Walker, Det.	3.25	2	Ericks, Pit.	2.12
3	Embree, Cle.	2.90	3	Creek, S.F.	2.05
4	Gohr, Det. + Cal.	2.41	4	Loaiza, Pit.	1.88
5	D'Amico, Mil.	2.20	5	Telemaco, Chi.	1.85

1997: PURISTS GO HOME

While purists groused, baseball inaugurated interleague play in 1997. Under special rules, the designated hitter was used in American League parks only. Although neither league had a clear advantage in the win-loss column, the innovation produced a turnstile boost and was pronounced a success by the baseball establishment. Meanwhile, those who remembered baseball's history nervously awaited the Lords of Baseball's decision on re-alignment proposals that threatened to switch as many as fifteen teams to their opposite leagues. The anticlimatic outcome saw the Milwaukee Brewers move to the N.L.

Money in gobs continued to speak loudly in '97, as the five teams with the highest payrolls reached the playoffs. The Pittsburgh Pirates achieved nationwide fan support by finishing slightly sub-500 with a $9 million payroll or less than Albert Belle received himself. But wealth did not necessarily buy happiness. Marlins owner Wayne Hulzinga spent $89 million on free agents before the season, then at mid-season threatened to sell the club because he was losing millions despite a 30% rise in Florida's attendance.

American League divisional races produced the nail-biting

In the East, the Baltimore Orioles, with perhaps the best balance of hitting, pitching, and fielding, moved out in front of the 1996-champion New York Yankees early and stayed there to the end. Cal Ripken Jr. turned his shortstop franchise over to Mike Bordick and continued his consecutive-game streak at third base. New York had sensational seasons from Tino Martinez and closer Mario Rivera but couldn't overtake the Orioles. Heralded rookie pitcher Hideki Irabu was a major disappointment.

The Cleveland Indians combined a plethora of home runs with an often chaotic pitching situation to hold off the White Sox in the Central. Cleveland's pitchers seemed jinxed. After ace Jack McDowell went out with an injury, they traded for John Smiley who promptly broke his pitching arm while warming up in the bullpen! The White Sox signed Albert Belle to an $11 million contract before the season and seemed poised to take the Central crown. Belle put up good, but hardly superstar numbers. Worse, Robin Ventura was lost for most of the year with a broken leg. In August, owner Jerry Reinsdorf pulled the plug and began dismantling his pitching staff.

In the West, the Seattle Mariners hit home runs in record numbers, led by Ken Grifey's 56. Lefty Randy Johnson was nearly unbeatable, but the same could not be said for the Mariner's bullpen. Seattle's arsonists masquerading as relievers made for high-scoring games, but the rest of the division couldn't take advantage.

The A.L. season saw a volatile brew of home runs and weak pitching. One exception to the latter was Toronto's Roger Clemens who put together his most impressive work since his last Cy Young Award.

In the National League east, Atlanta's dominance continued. Greg Maddux, Tom Glavine, John Smoltz, and Denny Neagle gave the Braves perhaps the most reliable starting pitching in modern baseball history. Although they won more games than any other team in the majors, a shaky bullpen and uneven attack kept the Braves from running away from the determined Marlins. Newcomers Moises Alou, Bobby Bonilla, and Darren Daulton made up for Gary Sheffield's off-year.

The Houston Astros, led by Craig Biggio and Jeff Bagwell, struggled to the Central Division title over the bargain basement Pirates. In a division that seemed no one was capable of winning, St. Louis and Cincinnati were disappointing and the Cubs were——well—the Cubs. The most interesting race may have been Mark McGwire's pursuit of Roger Maris's home run record. The big slugger hit 34 for Oakland and 24 for the Cardinals, setting split-league records but leading neither.

Baseball's top title chase was in the west. The surprising San Francisco Giants jumped out in front early thanks to revitalized pitching and Jeff Kent's hitting. Barry Bonds came on strong in the second half, but Los Angeles still caught the Giants and entered September with a two-and-a-half game lead. Using the usual suspects—strong pitching, Eric Karros, Raul Mondesi, and terrific Mike Piazza—the Dodgers appeared on their way until they ran into a 4-11 slump. They rallied, but so did the Giants who finally won by two. The Colorado Rockies produced MVP candidates in Larry Walker and Andres Gelarraga and the San Diego Padres' Tony Gwynn won yet another batting title, but neither team challenged for the crown.

In the playoffs, Atlanta swept Houston and Florida applied a broom to San Francisco. Baltimore had only slightly less trouble in polishing off Seattle. However, New York and Cleveland produced a slambang playoff that saw the Indians outlast the Yankees, largely on the efforts of rookie pitcher Jaret Wright who won two games.

The AICS pitted the team with the most season wins against the team with the least. Yet David outdueled Goliath in six games when Tony Ferandez delivered a run-scoring, eleventh-inning hit and Jose Mesa earned a save in the bottom half. The five-year-old Marlins also needed only six games to upset the Braves and become the "youngest" franchise to get to a World Series in modern baseball history.

Tony Fernandez and the eleventh inning came together again in the seventh of the World Series. Only this time Fernandez wore the goat horns when he bobbled a potential double-play grounder. Edgar Renteria's smash up the middle a few minutes later plated the final winning run of 1997. Until the thrilling final game, the series was underwhelming as it suffered through low television ratings, sloppy play, snow for one game, and seemingly interminable throws to first by lollygagging pitchers. It didn't help that the country's perception was that, because of baseball's playoff system, the two best teams—the Orioles and Braves—were home watching their own TVs.

EAST DIVISION — 1997 AMERICAN LEAGUE

Batting

Name	G by Pos	B	AGE	G	AB	R	H	2B	3B	HR	RBI	BB	SO	SB	BA	SA
BALTIMORE 1st 98-64 .605	DAVEY JOHNSON															
TOTALS		31		162	5584	812	1498	264	22	196	780	586	952	63	.268	.429
Rafael Palmeiro	1B155 DH3	L	32	158	614	95	156	24	2	38	110	67	109	5	.254	.485
Roberto Alomar	2B109 DH2	B	29	112	412	64	137	23	2	14	60	40	43	9	.333	.500
Mike Bordick	SS153	R	31	153	509	55	120	19	1	7	48	33	66	0	.236	.318
Cal Ripken	3B162 SS3	R	36	162	615	79	166	30	0	17	84	56	73	1	.270	.402
Eric Davis (IL)	OF30 DH12	R	35	42	158	29	48	11	0	8	25	14	47	5	.304	.525
Brady Anderson	OF124 DH25	L	33	151	590	97	170	39	7	18	73	84	105	18	.288	.469
B.J. Surhoff	OF133 DH9 1B3 3B3	L	32	147	528	80	150	30	4	18	88	49	60	1	.284	.458
Chris Hoiles (KJ)	C87 DH8 1B4 3B1	R	32	99	320	45	83	15	0	12	49	51	86	1	.259	.419
Geronimo Berroa	DH42 OF40	R	32	83	300	48	78	13	0	10	48	40	62	1	.260	.403
Jeffrey Hammonds	OF114 DH4	R	26	118	397	71	105	19	3	21	55	32	73	15	.264	.486
Tony Tarasco	OF81 DH2	L	26	100	166	26	34	8	1	7	26	25	33	2	.205	.392
Jeff Reboulet	2B63 SS22 3B12 OF1 DH1	R	33	99	228	26	54	9	0	4	27	23	44	3	.237	.329
Lenny Webster	C97 DH1	R	32	98	259	29	66	8	1	7	37	22	46	0	.255	.375
Pete Incaviglia	DH26 OF18	R	33	48	138	18	34	4	0	5	12	11	43	0	.246	.384
Harold Baines	DH35	L	38	44	134	15	39	5	0	4	15	14	15	0	.291	.418
Aaron Ledesma	2B22 3B11 1B5 SS4	R	26	43	88	24	31	5	1	2	11	13	9	1	.352	.500
Jerome Walton (LJ)	OF19 1B5 DH2	R	31	26	68	8	20	1	0	3	9	4	10	0	.294	.441
Dave Dellucci	OF9 DH5	L	23	17	27	3	6	1	0	1	3	4	7	0	.222	.370
Tim Laker	C7	R	27	7	14	0	0	0	0	0	0	0	6	0	.000	.000
Charlie Greene	C4	R	26	5	2	0	0	0	0	0	1	0	1	0	.000	.000
Mel Rosario	C4	R	24	4	3	0	0	0	0	0	0	0	1	0	.000	.000
Danny Clyburn	OF1	R	23	2	1	0	0	0	0	0	0	0	2	0	.000	.000
NEW YORK 2nd 96-66 .593 2 (Wild Card)	JOE TORRE															
TOTALS		31		162	5710	891	1636	325	23	161	846	676	954	99	.287	.436
Tino Martinez	1B150 DH7	L	29	158	594	96	176	31	2	44	141	75	75	3	.296	.577
Luis Sojo (BW)	2B72 SS4 3B3 1B2	R	32	77	215	27	66	6	1	2	25	16	14	3	.307	.372
Derek Jeter	SS159	R	23	159	654	116	190	31	7	10	70	74	125	23	.291	.405
Charlie Hayes	3B98 2B5	R	32	100	353	39	91	16	0	11	53	30	66	3	.258	.397
Paul O'Neill	OF146 1B2 DH2	L	34	149	553	89	179	42	0	21	117	75	92	10	.324	.514
Bernie Williams	OF128	B	28	129	509	107	167	35	6	21	100	73	80	15	.328	.544
Tim Raines (LJ)	OF57 DH13	B	37	74	271	56	87	20	2	4	38	41	34	8	.321	.454
Joe Girardi	C111 DH1	R	32	112	398	38	105	23	1	1	50	26	53	2	.264	.334
Cecil Fielder (RJ)	DH89 1B8	R	33	98	361	40	94	15	0	13	61	51	87	0	.260	.410
Wade Boggs	3B76 DH19 P1	L	39	104	353	55	103	23	1	4	28	48	38	0	.292	.397
Chad Curtis	OF92	R	28	93	320	51	93	21	1	12	50	36	49	12	.291	.475
Mark Whiten	OF57 DH7	B	30	69	215	34	57	11	0	5	24	30	47	4	.265	.386
Pat Kelly	2B48 DH6	R	29	67	122	19	29	8	1	2	10	14	37	8	.242	.358
Jorge Posada	C60	B	25	60	188	29	47	12	0	6	25	30	33	1	.250	.410
Scott Pose	OF45 DH5	L	30	54	87	19	19	2	1	0	5	9	11	3	.218	.264
Mariano Duncan	2B41 OF6 DH2	R	34	50	172	16	42	8	0	1	13	6	39	2	.244	.308
Rey Sanchez	2B37 SS6 DH2	R	29	38	134	21	43	12	0	1	15	5	21	0	.312	.420
Mike Stanley	DH16 1B12	R	34	28	87	16	25	8	0	3	12	15	22	0	.287	.483
Andy Fox	3B11 2B5 SS2 OF2 DH2	L	26	22	31	13	7	1	0	0	1	7	9	2	.226	.258
Darryl Strawberry (KJ)	OF4 DH1	L	35	11	29	1	3	1	0	0	1	5	10	0	.103	.138
Ivan Cruz	DH4 1B3 OF1	L	29	11	20	0	5	1	0	0	3	0	5	0	.250	.300
Homer Bush	2B8	R	24	10	11	2	4	0	0	0	0	0	1	0	.364	.364
Pete Incaviglia	DH5	R	33	5	16	1	4	1	0	0	2	0	5	0	.250	.250
Mike Figga	C1 DH1	R	26	2	4	0	0	0	0	0	0	0	3	0	.000	.000
Ruben Rivera (SJ) 23																

Pitching

NAME	T	AGE	W	L	PCT	SV	G	GS	CG	IP	H	BB	SO	SHO	ERA
(Baltimore totals)		31	98	64	.605	59	162	162	8	1461	1404	563	1139	10	3.91
Scott Erickson	R	29	16	7	.696	0	34	33	3	222	218	61	131	2	3.69
Jimmy Key	L	36	16	10	.615	0	34	34	1	212	210	82	141	1	3.43
Mike Mussina	R	28	15	8	.652	0	33	33	4	225	197	54	218	1	3.20
Arthur Rhodes	L	27	10	3	.769	1	53	0	0	95	75	26	102	0	3.02
Scott Kamieniecki	R	33	10	6	.625	0	30	30	0	179	179	67	109	0	4.01
Jesse Orosco	L	40	6	3	.667	0	71	0	0	50	29	30	46	0	2.32
Shawn Boskie	R	30	6	6	.500	1	28	9	0	77	95	26	50	0	6.43
Rick Krivda	L	27	4	2	.667	0	10	10	0	50	67	18	29	0	6.30
Terry Mathews	R	32	4	4	.500	1	57	0	0	63	63	36	39	0	4.41
Armando Benitez	R	24	4	5	.444	9	71	0	0	73	49	43	106	0	2.45
Nerio Rodriguez	R	26	2	1	.667	0	6	2	0	22	21	8	11	0	4.91
Randy Myers	L	34	2	3	.400	45	61	0	0	60	47	22	56	0	1.51
Alan Mills (SJ)	R	30	2	3	.400	0	39	0	0	39	41	33	32	0	4.89
Rocky Coppinger (EJ)	R	23	1	1	.500	0	5	4	0	20	21	16	22	0	6.30
Brian Williams	R	28	0	0	—	0	13	0	0	24	20	18	14	0	3.00
1 Mike Johnson	R	21	0	1	.000	2	14	5	0	40	52	16	29	0	7.94
Esteban Yan	R	22	0	1	.000	0	3	2	0	10	20	7	4	0	15.83
(New York totals)		30	96	66	.593	51	162	162	11	1468	1463	532	1165	10	3.84
Andy Pettitte	L	25	18	7	.720	0	35	35	4	240	233	65	166	1	2.88
David Wells	L	34	16	10	.615	0	32	32	5	218	239	45	156	2	4.21
David Cone	R	34	12	6	.667	0	29	29	1	195	155	86	222	0	2.82
Dwight Gooden (MJ)	R	32	9	5	.643	0	20	19	0	106	116	53	66	0	4.91
Ramiro Mendoza	R	25	8	6	.571	2	39	15	0	134	157	28	82	0	4.24
Mike Stanton	L	30	6	1	.857	3	64	0	0	67	50	34	70	0	2.57
Mariano Rivera	R	27	6	4	.600	43	66	0	0	72	65	20	68	0	1.88
Kenny Rogers	L	32	6	7	.462	0	31	22	1	145	161	62	78	0	5.65
Hideki Irabu	R	28	5	4	.556	0	13	9	0	53	69	20	56	0	7.09
Willie Banks	R	28	3	0	1.000	0	5	1	0	14	9	6	8	0	1.93
Brian Boehringer (EJ)	R	28	3	2	.600	0	34	0	0	48	39	32	53	0	2.63
Jeff Nelson	R	30	3	7	.300	2	77	0	0	79	53	37	81	0	2.86
Graeme Lloyd	L	30	1	1	.500	1	46	0	0	49	55	20	28	0	3.31
Danny Rios	R	24	0	0	—	0	2	0	0	2	9	2	1	0	19.29
Wade Boggs	R	39	0	0	—	0	1	0	0	1	1	1	0	0	0.00
1 David Weathers	R	27	0	0	.000	0	10	0	0	9	15	7	4	0	10.00
2 Joe Borowski	R	26	0	0	.000	0	1	0	0	2	4	2	0	0	9.00
Jim Mecir	R	27	0	4	.000	0	25	0	0	34	36	10	25	0	5.88

DETROIT — 3rd 79-83 .488 19 — BUDDY BELL

Name	G by Pos	B	AGE	G	AB	R	H	2B	3B	HR	RBI	BB	SO	SB	BA	SA
TOTALS			26	162	5481	784	1415	268	32	176	743	578	1164	161	.258	.415
Tony Clark	1B158 DH1	B	25	159	580	105	160	28	3	32	117	93	144	1	.276	.500
Damion Easley	2B137 SS21 DH4	R	27	151	527	97	139	37	3	22	72	68	102	28	.264	.471
Delvi Cruz	SS147	R	24	147	436	35	105	26	0	2	40	14	55	3	.241	.314
Travis Fryman	3B153	R	28	154	595	90	163	27	3	22	102	46	113	16	.274	.440
Melvin Nieves	OF99 DH12	B	25	116	359	46	82	18	1	20	64	39	157	1	.228	.451
Brian Hunter	OF162	R	26	162	658	112	177	29	7	4	45	66	121	74	.269	.353
Bobby Higginson	OF143 DH1	L	26	146	546	94	163	30	5	27	101	70	85	12	.299	.520
Raul Casanova	C92 DH1	B	24	101	304	27	74	10	1	5	24	26	48	1	.243	.332
Bob Hamelin	DH95 1B7	L	29	110	318	47	86	15	0	18	52	48	72	2	.270	.487
Phil Nevin	OF40 DH30 3B17 1B7 C1	R	26	93	251	32	59	16	1	9	35	25	68	0	.235	.414
1 Curtis Pride	OF35 DH23	L	28	79	162	21	34	4	2	10	19	24	45	6	.210	.321
Jody Reed	2B41 SS7	R	34	52	112	6	22	2	0	0	8	10	15	3	.196	.214
Orlando Miller (XJ)	SS31 DH11 3B4 1B3	R	28	50	111	13	26	7	1	2	10	5	24	1	.234	.369
Matt Walbeck (BW)	C44	R	27	47	137	18	38	3	0	3	10	12	19	3	.277	.365
1 Brian Johnson	C43 DH1	R	29	45	139	13	33	6	1	2	18	5	19	1	.237	.338
Bubba Trammell	OF28 DH14	R	25	44	123	14	28	5	0	4	13	15	35	3	.228	.366
Frank Catalanotto	2B6 DH3	L	23	13	26	2	8	2	0	0	3	3	7	0	.308	.385
Jimmy Hurst	OF12 DH1	R	25	13	17	1	3	1	0	1	2	6	6	0	.176	.412
Kimera Bartee	OF6 DH3	R	24	12	5	4	1	0	0	0	0	2	2	3	.200	.200
Juan Encarnacion	OF10	R	21	11	33	3	7	1	1	1	5	3	12	1	.212	.394
2 Marcus Jensen	C8	B	24	8	11	1	2	0	0	0	1	1	5	0	.182	.182
Vince Coleman	OF3 DH1	B	36	6	14	0	1	0	0	0	0	1	3	0	.071	.071
Joe Hall	OF1	R	31	2	4	1	2	1	0	0	3	0	0	0	.500	.750

NAME	T	AGE	W	L	PCT	SV	G	GS	CG	IP	H	BB	SO	SHO	ERA
TOTALS		28	79	83	.488	42	162	162	13	1446	1476	552	982	8	4.56
Willie Blair	R	28	16	8	.667	0	29	27	2	175	186	46	90	0	4.17
Justin Thompson	L	24	15	11	.577	0	32	32	4	223	188	66	151	0	3.02
Brian Moehler	R	25	11	12	.478	0	31	31	2	175	198	61	97	1	4.67
Todd Jones	R	29	5	4	.556	31	68	0	0	70	60	35	70	0	3.09
1 Omar Olivares	R	29	5	6	.455	0	19	19	3	115	110	53	74	2	4.70
1 Felipe Lira	R	25	5	7	.417	0	20	15	1	92	101	45	64	1	5.77
Dan Miceli	R	26	3	2	.600	3	71	0	0	82	77	38	79	0	5.01
A.J. Sager	R	32	3	4	.429	1	38	1	0	84	81	24	53	0	4.18
Doug Brocail	R	30	3	4	.429	2	61	4	0	78	74	36	60	0	3.23
Greg Keagle	R	26	3	5	.375	0	11	10	0	45	58	18	33	0	6.55
2 Scott Sanders	R	28	3	8	.273	0	14	14	1	74	79	24	58	1	5.33
John Cummings	L	28	2	0	1.000	0	19	0	0	25	32	14	8	0	5.47
1 Jose Bautista	R	32	2	2	.500	0	21	0	0	40	55	12	19	0	6.69
Eddie Gaillard	R	26	1	0	1.000	1	16	0	0	20	16	10	12	0	5.31
Tim Pugh	R	30	1	1	.500	0	2	0	0	9	6	5	4	0	5.00
Glenn Dishman	L	26	1	2	.333	0	7	4	0	29	30	8	20	0	5.28
Roberto Duran	L	24	0	0	—	0	13	0	0	11	7	15	11	0	7.59
Fernando Hernandez	R	26	0	0	—	0	2	0	0	1	5	3	2	0	40.50
3 Kevin Jarvis	R	27	0	3	.000	0	17	3	0	42	55	14	27	0	5.40
Mike Myers	L	28	0	4	.000	2	88	0	0	54	58	25	50	0	5.70

BOSTON — 4th 78-84 .481 20 — JIMY WILLIAMS

Name	G by Pos	B	AGE	G	AB	R	H	2B	3B	HR	RBI	BB	SO	SB	BA	SA
TOTALS			28	162	5781	851	1684	373	32	185	810	514	1044	68	.291	.463
Mo Vaughn	1B131 DH9	L	29	141	527	91	166	24	0	35	96	86	154	2	.315	.560
John Valentin	2B79 3B64	R	30	143	575	95	176	47	5	18	77	58	66	7	.306	.499
Nomar Garciaparra	SS153	R	23	153	684	122	209	44	11	30	98	35	92	22	.306	.534
Tim Naehring (EJ)	3B68 DH1	R	30	70	259	38	74	18	1	9	40	38	40	1	.286	.467
Troy O'Leary	OF142 DH1	L	27	146	499	65	154	32	4	15	80	39	70	0	.309	.479
Darren Bragg	OF150 3B1	R	27	153	513	65	132	35	4	9	57	61	102	10	.257	.386
Wil Cordero	OF137 DH2 2B1	R	25	140	570	82	160	26	3	18	72	31	122	1	.281	.432
Scott Hatteberg	C106 DH1	L	27	114	350	46	97	23	1	10	44	40	70	0	.277	.434
Reggie Jefferson	DH119 1B12	L	28	136	489	74	156	31	3	13	67	24	93	1	.319	.470
Jeff Frye	2B80 3B18 OF13 DH11 SS3 1B1	R	30	127	404	56	126	36	2	3	51	27	44	19	.312	.433
1 Mike Stanley	DH53 1B31 C15	R	34	97	260	45	78	17	0	13	53	39	50	0	.300	.515
Bill Haselman (BG)	C66	R	31	67	212	22	50	15	0	6	26	15	44	0	.236	.392
Shane Mack	OF45 DH5	R	33	60	130	13	41	7	0	3	17	9	24	2	.315	.438
Mike Benjamin	3B19 SS16 2B5 1B4 DH1 P	R	31	49	116	12	27	9	1	0	7	4	27	2	.233	.328
Jesus Tavarez	OF35 DH2	B	26	42	69	12	12	3	1	0	9	4	9	1	.174	.246
Rudy Pemberton	OF23	R	27	27	63	8	15	2	0	2	10	4	13	0	.238	.365
Michael Coleman	OF7	R	21	8	24	2	4	1	0	0	2	0	11	1	.167	.208
Walt McKeel	C4 1B1	R	25	5	3	0	0	0	0	0	0	0	1	0	.000	.000
Arquimedez Pozo	3B4	R	23	4	15	0	4	1	0	0	3	0	5	0	.267	.333
Jose Malave	OF4	R	26	4	4	0	0	0	0	0	0	0	2	0	.000	.000
2 Curtis Pride		L	28	2	2	1	1	0	0	1	1	1	0	1	.500	2.000
Jason Varitek	C1	B	25	1	1	0	1	0	0	0	1	0	0	0	1.000	1.000

NAME	T	AGE	W	L	PCT	SV	G	GS	CG	IP	H	BB	SO	SHO	ERA
TOTALS		28	78	84	.481	40	162	162	7	1452	1569	611	987	4	4.85
Aaron Sele	R	27	13	12	.520	0	33	33	1	177	198	80	122	0	5.38
Tim Wakefield	R	30	12	15	.444	0	35	29	4	201	193	87	151	2	4.25
Jeff Suppan	R	22	7	3	.700	0	23	22	0	112	140	36	67	0	5.69
Butch Henry (SJ)	L	28	7	3	.700	0	36	5	0	84	89	19	51	0	3.52
Steve Avery (GJ)	L	27	6	7	.462	0	22	18	0	97	127	49	51	0	6.42
Tom Gordon	R	29	6	10	.375	11	42	25	2	183	155	78	159	1	3.74
Jim Corsi	R	35	5	3	.625	2	52	0	0	58	56	21	40	0	3.43
John Wasdin	R	24	4	6	.400	0	53	7	0	125	121	38	84	0	4.40
Ron Mahay	R	26	3	1	.750	0	28	0	0	25	19	11	22	0	2.52
Joe Hudson	R	26	3	1	.750	0	39	0	0	36	39	14	14	0	3.53
Vaughn Eshelman	L	28	3	3	.500	0	21	6	0	43	58	17	18	0	6.33
Chris Hammond (EJ)	R	31	3	4	.429	1	29	8	0	65	81	27	48	0	5.92
1 Rick Trlicek	R	28	3	4	.429	0	18	0	0	23	26	18	10	0	4.63
Pat Mahomes (IL)	R	26	1	0	1.000	0	10	0	0	15	10	5	0	0	8.10
Kerry Lacy	R	24	1	1	.500	3	33	0	0	46	60	22	18	0	6.11
Robinson Checo (EJ)	R	25	1	1	.500	0	5	2	0	13	12	3	14	0	3.38
2 Toby Borland	R	28	0	0	—	0	2	0	0	5	7	1	1	0	13.50
Ken Grundt	L	27	0	0	—	0	3	0	0	3	5	0	0	0	9.00
Brian Rose	R	21	0	0	—	0	1	1	0	6	13	3	2	0	12.00
Mike Benjamin	R	31	0	0	—	0	1	0	0	1	1	1	0	0	0.00
Bret Saberhagen (SJ)	R	33	0	1	.000	0	6	6	0	26	30	10	14	0	6.58
Rich Garces (XJ)	R	26	0	1	.000	0	12	0	0	14	14	9	12	0	4.61
Mark Brandenburg (SJ)	R	26	0	2	.000	0	31	0	0	41	49	16	34	0	5.49
2 Derek Lowe	R	24	0	2	.000	0	8	0	0	16	15	3	13	0	3.38
1 Heathcliff Slocumb	R	31	0	5	.000	17	49	0	0	47	58	34	36	0	5.79

TORONTO — 5th 76-86 .469 22 — CITO GASTON 72-85 .459 MEL QUEEN 4-1 .800

Name	G by Pos	B	AGE	G	AB	R	H	2B	3B	HR	RBI	BB	SO	SB	BA	SA
TOTALS			30	162	5473	654	1333	275	41	147	627	487	1138	134	.244	.389
Carlos Delgado	1B119 DH33	L	25	153	519	79	136	42	3	30	91	64	133	0	.262	.528
Carlos Garcia	2B96 SS5 3B4	R	24	126	350	29	77	18	2	3	15	15	60	11	.220	.309
Alex Gonzalez (BG)	SS125	R	24	126	426	46	102	23	2	3	35	34	94	15	.239	.387
Ed Sprague	3B129 DH8	R	29	138	565	89	158	23	4	14	48	51	102	0	.228	.385
Orlando Merced (SJ)	OF96 1B1 DH1	L	30	98	368	45	98	23	2	9	40	47	62	7	.266	.413
1 Otis Nixon	OF102 DH1	B	38	103	401	54	105	12	1	1	26	52	54	47	.262	.304
Jose Cruz	OF55	R	23	55	212	31	49	7	0	14	34	28	72	6	.231	.462
Benito Santiago	C95 DH1	R	32	97	341	31	83	10	0	13	42	17	80	1	.243	.387
Joe Carter	DH64 OF51 1B42	R	37	157	612	76	143	30	4	21	102	40	105	8	.234	.399
Shawn Green	OF91 DH35	L	24	135	429	57	123	22	4	16	53	36	99	14	.287	.469
Charlie O'Brien	C69	R	37	69	225	22	49	15	1	4	27	22	45	0	.218	.347
Jacob Brumfield	OF47 DH4	R	32	58	174	22	36	5	1	2	20	14	31	4	.207	.282
1 Tilson Brito	2B25 3B17 SS8	R	25	49	126	9	28	3	0	0	8	9	28	1	.222	.246
Juan Samuel	DH15 3B9 1B7 2B4 OF2	R	36	45	95	13	27	3	1	3	15	10	28	5	.284	.516
Shannon Stewart	OF23	R	23	44	168	25	48	13	7	0	22	19	24	10	.286	.444
Tomas Perez	SS32 2B8	R	23	40	123	9	24	3	0	2	9	11	28	1	.195	.252
2 Mariano Duncan	2B39	R	34	39	167	20	38	6	0	2	12	6	39	4	.228	.263
Robert Perez	OF25 DH7	R	28	37	78	4	15	4	1	2	6	0	16	0	.192	.346
2 Ruben Sierra	OF7 DH6	B	31	14	48	4	10	4	0	2	5	2	13	0	.208	.354
Tom Evans	3B12	R	22	12	38	7	11	2	0	1	2	4	9	0	.289	.421
Felipe Crespo	3B7 DH2 2B1	B	24	12	28	3	8	0	1	1	5	2	6	0	.286	.464
Rich Butler	OF3 DH1	L	24	7	14	3	4	1	0	0	2	1	3	0	.286	.357
Julio Mosquera	C3	R	25	4	8	0	2	1	0	0	1	1	0	0	.250	.375
Sandy Martinez	C3	L	26	3	1	0	0	0	0	0	0	0	1	0	.000	.000

NAME	T	AGE	W	L	PCT	SV	G	GS	CG	IP	H	BB	SO	SHO	ERA
TOTALS		28	76	86	.469	34	162	162	19	1443	1453	497	1150	16	3.92
Roger Clemens	R	34	21	7	.750	0	34	34	9	264	204	68	292	3	2.05
Pat Hentgen	R	28	15	10	.600	0	35	35	9	264	253	71	160	3	3.68
Woody Williams	R	30	9	14	.391	0	31	31	0	195	201	66	124	0	4.35
Paul Quantrill	R	28	6	7	.462	5	77	0	0	88	103	17	56	0	1.94
Robert Person	R	27	5	10	.333	0	23	22	0	128	125	60	99	0	5.61
1 Mike Timlin	R	31	3	2	.600	9	38	0	0	47	41	15	36	0	2.87
Kelvim Escobar (EJ)	R	21	3	2	.600	14	27	0	0	31	28	19	36	0	2.90
Tim Crabtree (EJ)	R	27	3	3	.500	2	37	0	0	41	65	17	26	0	7.08
Juan Guzman (BG-SJ)	R	30	3	6	.333	0	13	13	0	60	48	31	52	0	4.95
Chris Carpenter	R	22	3	7	.300	0	14	13	1	81	108	37	55	1	5.09
Marty Janzen	R	24	2	1	.667	0	12	0	0	25	23	13	17	0	3.60
Dan Plesac	L	35	2	4	.333	1	73	0	0	50	47	19	61	0	3.58
2 Omar Daal	L	25	1	1	.500	0	3	0	0	27	34	6	18	0	2.70
Erik Hanson (SJ)	R	32	0	0	—	0	1	0	0	3	6	1	2	0	18.00
Ken Robinson	R	27	0	0	—	0	1	0	0	3	6	1	2	0	2.70
Huck Flener	L	28	0	1	.000	0	3	0	0	4	8	2	2	0	9.87
Bill Risley (AJ)	R	30	0	0	—	0	7	0	0	9	6	4	6	0	2.70
Carlos Almanzar	R	23	0	1	.000	0	4	0	0	8	13	3	8	0	2.70
1 Paul Spoljaric	L	26	0	2	.000	0	37	0	0	48	37	21	43	0	3.19
Luis Andujar	R	24	0	0	.000	0	17	8	0	50	76	21	28	0	6.48

CENTRAL DIVISION

CLEVELAND — 1st 86-75 .534 — MIKE HARGROVE

Name	G by Pos	B	AGE	G	AB	R	H	2B	3B	HR	RBI	BB	SO	SB	BA	SA
TOTALS			31	161	5556	868	1589	301	22	220	810	617	955	118	.286	.467
Jim Thome	1B145	L	26	147	496	104	142	25	0	40	102	120	146	1	.286	.579
Tony Fernandez	2B109 SS10 DH1	R	35	120	409	55	117	21	1	11	44	22	40	6	.286	.423
Omar Vizquel	SS152	B	30	153	565	89	158	23	6	5	49	57	58	43	.280	.368
Matt Williams	3B151	R	31	151	596	86	157	32	3	32	105	34	108	12	.263	.488
Manny Ramirez	OF146 DH4	R	25	150	561	99	184	40	0	26	88	79	115	2	.328	.538
Marquis Grissom	OF144	R	30	144	558	74	146	27	6	12	66	43	99	22	.262	.396
Brian Giles	OF115 DH9	L	26	130	377	62	101	15	3	17	61	63	50	13	.268	.459
Sandy Alomar	C119 DH1	R	31	125	451	63	146	37	0	21	83	19	48	0	.324	.545
David Justice	OF78 DH61	L	31	139	495	84	163	31	1	33	101	80	79	3	.329	.596
1 Julio Franco	DH42 2B35 1B1	R	38	78	289	46	82	13	1	3	25	38	75	8	.284	.367
Kevin Seitzer	DH24 1B19 3B13	R	35	64	198	27	53	14	0	2	24	18	25	1	.268	.369
Pat Borders	C53	R	34	55	159	17	47	7	1	4	15	9	27	0	.296	.428
2 Jeff Branson	2B19 3B6 SS2 DH1	L	30	29	72	5	19	4	0	2	7	7	17	0	.264	.403
2 Bip Roberts	2B13 OF10	B	33	23	85	19	23	3	0	3	8	7	14	3	.271	.412
1 Chad Curtis	OF19	R	28	22	29	8	6	1	0	0	2	2	5	3	.207	.552
Kevin Mitchell	DH18 OF1	R	35	20	59	7	9	1	0	4	11	9	11	1	.153	.373
Jeff Manto	3B7 1B6 OF1	R	32	16	30	3	8	2	0	2	7	1	10	0	.267	.567
Casey Candaele	2B9 3B1 DH1	B	36	14	26	5	8	1	0	0	3	4	3	0	.308	.346
Bruce Aven	OF13	R	25	9	19	1	4	0	0	1	2	1	6	0	.211	.263
1 Damian Jackson	SS5 2B1	R	23	9	9	2	1	0	0	0	0	1	2	0	.111	.111
Trenidad Hubbard	OF6	R	23	8	4	3	2	0	0	0	1	0	2	0	.250	.333
Sean Casey	DH3 1B1	L	22	6	10	1	2	0	0	0	1	0	2	0	.200	.200
Enrique Wilson	SS4 2B1	B	21	5	9	1	3	0	0	0	0	0	0	0	.333	.333
Richie Sexson	1B2 DH1	R	22	5	11	1	3	0	0	0	1	0	2	0	.273	.273
Einar Diaz	C5	R	24	5	7	1	1	0	0	0	0	1	0	0	.143	.286
Herbert Perry (KJ) 27																

NAME	T	AGE	W	L	PCT	SV	G	GS	CG	IP	H	BB	SO	SHO	ERA
TOTALS		28	86	75	.534	39	161	161	4	1426	1528	575	1036	3	4.73
Charles Nagy	R	30	15	11	.577	0	34	34	1	227	253	77	149	1	4.28
Orel Hershiser	R	38	14	6	.700	0	32	32	1	195	199	69	107	0	4.47
Jaret Wright	R	21	8	3	.727	0	16	16	0	90	81	35	63	0	4.38
Chad Ogea (EJ)	R	26	8	9	.471	0	21	21	1	126	139	47	80	0	4.99
Paul Assenmacher	L	36	5	0	1.000	4	75	0	0	49	43	15	53	0	2.94
Brian Anderson (EJ)	L	25	4	2	.667	0	8	6	0	48	55	11	22	0	4.69
Paul Shuey	R	26	4	2	.667	2	40	0	0	45	52	28	46	0	6.20
Jose Mesa	R	31	4	4	.500	16	66	0	0	82	83	28	69	0	2.40
Eric Plunk	R	33	4	5	.444	0	55	0	0	66	62	36	66	0	4.66
Bartolo Colon	R	24	4	7	.364	0	19	17	1	94	107	45	66	0	5.65
1 Steve Kline	L	24	1	1	.750	0	20	1	0	24	42	13	17	0	5.81
1 Jack McDowell (EJ)	R	31	3	5	.500	0	6	5	0	41	44	18	38	0	5.09
Albie Lopez	R	25	3	7	.300	0	37	6	0	77	101	40	63	0	6.93
2 Jason Jacome	L	26	2	0	1.000	0	21	4	0	43	45	15	24	0	5.27
2 John Smiley	L	32	2	4	.333	0	6	6	0	45	52	10	26	0	5.54
Mike Jackson	R	32	2	3	.286	15	71	0	0	75	59	29	74	0	3.24
3 David Weathers	R	27	1	2	.333	0	9	0	0	17	23	8	14	0	7.56
Alvin Morman (EJ)	L	28	0	0	—	0	34	0	0	18	19	14	13	0	5.89
1 Danny Graves	R	24	0	0	—	0	5	0	0	11	15	9	4	0	4.76
2 Jeff Juden	R	26	0	2	.000	0	8	6	0	32	36	15	26	0	5.46
1 Terry Clark	R	36	0	3	.000	0	4	0	0	13	13	10	6	0	6.15

CHICAGO — 2nd 80-81 .497 6 — TERRY BEVINGTON

Name	G by Pos	B	AGE	G	AB	R	H	2B	3B	HR	RBI	BB	SO	SB	BA	SA
TOTALS			29	161	5491	779	1498	260	28	158	740	569	901	106	.273	.417
Frank Thomas	1B97 DH49	R	29	146	530	110	184	35	0	35	125	109	69	1	.347	.611
Ray Durham	2B153 DH1	R	25	155	634	106	172	27	5	11	53	61	96	33	.271	.382
Ozzie Guillen	SS139	L	33	142	490	59	120	21	6	4	52	22	24	5	.245	.337
Robin Ventura (BL)	3B54	L	29	54	183	27	48	10	1	6	26	34	21	0	.262	.410
Dave Martinez	OF105 1B52 DH1	L	32	146	504	78	144	16	6	12	55	55	69	12	.286	.413
Mike Cameron	OF112 DH4	R	24	116	379	63	98	18	3	14	55	55	105	23	.259	.410
Albert Belle	OF154 DH7	R	30	161	634	90	174	45	1	30	116	53	105	4	.274	.491
2 Jorge Fabregas	C92 1B1	L	27	100	322	31	90	10	1	7	48	11	43	1	.280	.382
Harold Baines	DH86 OF1	L	38	93	318	40	97	18	0	12	52	41	47	0	.305	.475
Lyle Mouton	OF67 DH11	R	28	88	242	26	65	9	0	5	23	14	66	4	.269	.368
Chris Snopek	3B82 SS4	R	26	86	298	27	65	15	0	5	35	18	51	3	.218	.319
Darren Lewis	OF64 DH6	R	29	81	77	15	18	1	0	0	5	11	14	11	.234	.247
Norberto Martin	SS28 3B17 2B9 DH6	R	30	71	213	24	64	7	1	2	27	6	31	1	.300	.371
Mario Valdez	1B47 DH2 3B1	L	22	54	115	11	28	7	0	1	13	17	39	1	.243	.330
Ron Karkovice	C51	R	34	51	138	10	25	3	0	6	18	11	32	0	.181	.333
Tony Phillips	OF28 3B9	B	38	36	129	23	40	6	0	2	9	29	29	4	.310	.403
1 Tony Pena	C30 3B1	R	40	31	67	4	11	1	0	0	8	8	13	0	.164	.179
Magglio Ordonez	OF19	R	23	21	69	12	22	6	0	4	11	2	8	1	.319	.580
Jeff Abbott	OF10 DH3	R	23	19	38	8	10	1	0	1	2	0	6	0	.263	.368
Chad Kreuter	C13 1B2	B	32	19	37	6	8	2	1	1	3	8	9	0	.216	.405
Greg Norton	3B11 DH2	B	24	19	34	5	9	2	2	0	1	3	9	1	.265	.441
Robert Machado	C10	R	24	10	15	1	3	0	1	0	2	1	6	0	.200	.333
2 Chad Fonville	OF3 2B2 SS2 DH1	B	26	9	9	1	1	0	0	0	1	0	2	1	.111	.111

NAME	T	AGE	W	L	PCT	SV	G	GS	CG	IP	H	BB	SO	SHO	ERA
		29	80	81	.497	52	161	161	6	1422	1505	575	961	7	4.73
Doug Drabek	R	34	12	11	.522	0	31	31	0	169	170	69	85	0	5.74
James Baldwin	R	25	12	15	.444	0	32	32	1	200	205	83	140	0	5.27
1 Wilson Alvarez	L	27	9	8	.529	0	22	22	2	146	126	55	110	1	3.03
Jaime Navarro	R	30	9	14	.391	0	33	33	2	210	267	73	142	0	5.79
1 Roberto Hernandez	R	32	5	1	.833	27	46	0	0	48	38	24	47	0	2.44
Jason Bere (EJ)	R	26	4	4	.667	0	6	6	0	29	20	17	21	0	4.71
Tony Castillo	L	34	4	4	.500	0	64	0	0	62	74	23	42	0	4.91
Scott Eyre	L	25	4	4	.500	0	11	11	0	61	62	31	36	0	5.04
1 Danny Darwin	R	41	4	8	.333	0	21	17	1	113	130	31	62	0	4.13
Mike Sirotka	L	26	3	0	1.000	0	7	4	0	32	36	5	24	0	2.25
2 Keith Foulke	R	24	3	0	1.000	3	16	0	0	29	28	5	21	0	3.45
Matt Karchner	R	30	3	1	.750	15	52	0	0	53	50	26	30	0	2.91
Bill Simas (SJ)	R	25	3	1	.750	1	40	0	0	41	46	24	38	0	4.14
Carlos Castillo	R	22	2	1	.667	1	37	2	0	66	68	33	43	0	4.48
Al Levine	R	29	2	2	.500	0	25	0	0	27	35	16	22	0	6.91
2 Chuck McElroy	L	29	1	3	.250	1	48	0	0	59	56	19	44	0	3.94
Mike Bertotti	L	27	0	0	—	0	9	0	0	4	9	2	4	0	7.36
Larry Thomas	L	27	0	0	—	0	5	0	0	3	3	2	0	0	8.10
Tom Fordham	L	23	0	1	.000	0	7	1	0	17	17	10	10	0	6.23
Jeff Darwin	R	27	0	1	.000	0	14	0	0	14	17	7	9	0	5.27
Nelson Cruz	R	24	0	2	.000	0	19	0	0	26	29	9	23	0	6.49
Chris Clemons	R	24	0	2	.000	0	13	0	0	23	19	11	8	0	8.53
Roger McDowell (SJ) 36															

MILWAUKEE — 3rd 78-83 .484 8 — PHIL GARNER

Name	G by Pos	B	AGE	G	AB	R	H	2B	3B	HR	RBI	BB	SO	SB	BA	SA
TOTALS			28	162	5444	681	1415	294	27	135	643	494	967	103	.260	.398
John Jaha (SJ)	1B27 DH20	R	31	46	162	25	40	7	0	11	26	25	40	1	.247	.494
Fernando Vina (BN)	2B77 DH1	L	28	79	324	37	89	12	2	4	28	12	23	5	.275	.361
Jose Valentin	SS134 DH1	B	27	136	494	58	125	23	1	17	58	39	109	19	.253	.407
Jeff Cirillo	3B150 DH2	R	27	154	580	74	167	46	2	10	82	60	74	4	.288	.426
Jeromy Burnitz	OF149	L	28	153	494	85	139	37	8	27	85	75	111	20	.281	.553
Gerald Williams	OF154	R	30	155	566	73	143	32	2	10	41	19	90	23	.253	.369
Marc Newfield (SJ)	OF28 DH18	R	24	50	157	14	36	8	0	1	18	14	27	0	.229	.299
Mike Matheny	C121 1B2	R	26	123	320	29	78	16	1	4	32	17	68	0	.244	.338
Dave Nilsson	1B74 DH59 OF22	L	27	156	554	71	154	33	0	20	81	65	88	2	.278	.446
Mark Loretta	2B63 SS44 1B19 3B15 DH1	R	25	132	418	56	120	17	5	5	47	47	60	5	.287	.388
Jessie Levis	C78 DH8	L	29	99	200	19	57	7	0	1	19	24	17	1	.285	.335
Matt Mieske (LJ)	OF59 DH2	R	29	84	253	39	63	15	3	5	21	19	50	1	.249	.391
2 Jeff Huson	2B32 1B21 OF9 DH4 3B2	L	32	84	143	12	29	3	0	0	11	5	15	3	.203	.224
Jack Voigt	OF40 1B19 3B6 DH1	R	31	72	151	20	37	9	2	8	22	19	36	1	.245	.490
Todd Dunn	OF27 DH14	R	26	44	118	17	27	5	0	3	9	2	39	1	.229	.347
2 Julio Franco	DH28 1B13	R	38	42	141	22	34	3	0	4	19	31	41	7	.241	.348
Tim Unroe	1B23 3B2 OF2 2B1	R	26	32	16	3	4	1	0	2	5	2	9	2	.250	.688
Kelly Stinnett (VJ)	C25 DH1	R	27	30	36	2	9	4	0	0	3	3	9	0	.250	.361
Brian Banks	OF15 1B5 3B1 DH1	B	26	28	68	9	14	1	0	1	8	6	17	0	.206	.265
2 Darrin Jackson	OF26	R	34	26	81	7	22	7	0	2	15	2	10	2	.272	.432
1 Chuck Carr	OF23 DH1	B	29	26	46	3	6	3	0	0	2	0	11	1	.130	.196
Antone Williamson	1B14 DH4	L	23	24	54	2	11	0	0	1	6	4	8	0	.204	.259
Eddy Diaz	2B14 3B1 SS1	R	25	16	50	4	11	3	0	0	7	1	5	0	.220	.300

NAME	T	AGE	W	L	PCT	SV	G	GS	CG	IP	H	BB	SO	SHO	ERA
		29	78	83	.484	44	161	161	6	1427	1419	542	1016	8	4.22
Cal Eldred	R	29	13	15	.464	0	34	34	3	202	207	89	122	1	4.99
Scott Karl	L	25	10	13	.435	0	32	32	1	193	212	67	119	0	4.47
Jeff D'Amico (AJ)	R	21	9	7	.563	0	23	23	1	136	139	43	94	1	4.71
Ben McDonald (SJ)	R	29	8	7	.533	0	21	21	1	133	120	36	110	0	4.06
Bob Wickman	R	28	7	6	.538	1	74	0	0	96	89	41	78	0	2.73
Jose Mercedes	R	26	7	10	.412	0	29	23	2	159	146	53	80	1	3.79
Doug Jones	R	40	6	6	.500	36	75	0	0	80	62	9	82	0	2.02
Joel Adamson	L	25	5	3	.625	0	30	6	0	76	78	19	56	0	3.54
Bryce Florie (SJ)	R	27	4	4	.500	0	32	8	0	75	74	42	53	0	4.32
Steve Woodard (UJ)	R	22	3	3	.500	0	7	7	0	37	39	6	32	0	5.15
Ron Villone	L	27	3	1	.750	0	50	0	0	53	54	36	40	0	3.42
2 Paul Wagner	R	29	1	1	1.000	0	2	2	0	9	2	0	0	0	9.00
Jamie McAndrew	R	29	1	1	1.000	0	5	4	0	24	23	8	8	0	8.38
Pete Harnisch	R	30	1	1	.500	0	4	4	0	14	13	12	10	0	5.14
Alberto Reyes	R	26	1	2	.333	1	19	0	0	30	32	9	28	0	5.46
Mike Fetters (LJ)	R	32	1	5	.167	8	51	0	0	70	62	33	62	0	3.45
Mark Davis	L	36	0	0	—	0	19	0	0	14	11	9	5	0	5.51
Angel Miranda	L	27	0	0	—	0	4	1	0	14	17	9	14	0	3.86
Mike Misuraca	R	28	0	1	.000	0	10	1	0	15	17	10	10	0	11.32
Sean Maloney	R	26	0	0	—	0	7	0	0	7	2	5	5	0	5.14
Greg Hansell	R	26	0	3	.000	0	10	0	0	7	11	9	6	0	9.64
Steve Sparks (EJ) 31															

MINNESOTA — 4th 68-94 .420 18.5 — TOM KELLY

Name	G by Pos	B	AGE	G	AB	R	H	2B	3B	HR	RBI	BB	SO	SB	BA	SA
TOTALS			29	162	5634	772	1522	305	40	132	730	495	1121	151	.270	.409
Scott Stahoviak (BG)	1B81 DH5	L	27	91	275	33	63	17	0	10	33	24	73	5	.229	.400
Chuck Knoblauch	2B153 SS1 DH1	R	28	156	611	117	178	26	10	9	58	84	84	62	.291	.411
Pat Meares	SS134	R	28	134	439	63	121	23	3	10	60	18	86	7	.276	.410
Ron Coomer	3B119 1B9 OF7 DH7	R	30	140	523	63	156	30	2	13	85	22	91	4	.298	.438
Matt Lawton	OF138	L	25	142	460	74	114	29	3	14	60	76	81	7	.248	.415
Rich Becker	OF128	L	25	132	443	61	117	22	3	10	45	62	130	17	.264	.395
Marty Cordova (FJ)	OF101 DH2	R	27	103	378	44	93	18	4	9	51	30	92	5	.246	.434
Terry Steinbach	C116 1B2 DH1	R	35	122	447	60	111	27	1	12	54	35	106	0	.248	.394
Paul Molitor	DH122 1B12	R	40	135	538	63	164	32	4	10	89	45	73	11	.305	.435
Denny Hocking	SS44 3B39 OF20 2B15 1B1 DH1	B	27	115	253	28	65	12	4	2	25	18	51	3	.257	.360
1 Roberto Kelly	OF59 DH12	R	32	75	247	39	71	19	2	5	37	17	50	7	.287	.441
1 Greg Colbrunn	1B64 DH2	R	27	70	217	24	61	14	0	5	26	8	38	1	.281	.415
1 Greg Myers	C38 DH10	L	31	62	165	24	44	11	1	5	28	16	26	0	.267	.436
Brent Brede	OF42 1B15 DH1	L	25	61	190	25	52	11	3	3	21	18	38	1	.274	.389
Todd Walker	3B40 2B8 DH2	L	24	52	156	15	37	7	1	3	16	11	30	2	.237	.353
1 Darrin Jackson	OF44	R	34	49	130	19	33	2	1	3	21	4	21	2	.254	.354
Damian Miller	C20 DH3	R	27	25	66	5	18	1	0	2	13	2	12	0	.273	.379
David Ortiz	1B11 DH1	L	21	15	49	10	16	3	0	1	6	2	19	0	.327	.449
Chris Latham	OF10	B	24	15	22	4	4	1	0	0	2	1	8	0	.182	.227
Javier Valentin	C4	B	21	4	7	1	2	0	0	0	0	0	3	0	.286	.286
Torii Hunter	OF	R	21	1	0	0	0	0	0	0	0	0	0	0	—	—
Kirby Puckett (IJ) 37																

NAME	T	AGE	W	L	PCT	SV	G	GS	CG	IP	H	BB	SO	SHO	ERA
		28	68	94	.420	30	162	162	10	1434	1596	495	908	4	5.00
Brad Radke	R	24	20	10	.667	0	35	35	4	240	238	48	174	1	3.87
Rich Robertson	L	28	8	12	.400	0	31	26	0	147	169	70	69	0	5.69
Bob Tewksbury	R	36	8	13	.381	0	26	26	5	169	200	31	92	2	4.22
Greg Swindell	L	32	7	4	.636	1	65	1	0	116	102	25	75	0	3.58
LaTroy Hawkins	R	24	7	12	.368	0	20	20	0	103	134	47	58	0	5.84
Rick Aguilera	R	35	5	4	.556	26	61	0	0	68	65	22	68	0	3.82
Frankie Rodriguez	R	24	5	4	.333	0	43	15	0	142	147	60	65	0	4.62
Dan Serafini	L	23	2	1	.667	0	6	4	0	26	21	11	15	0	3.42
Mike Trombley	R	30	2	3	.400	0	67	0	0	82	77	31	74	0	4.37
Todd Ritchie	R	25	2	3	.400	0	42	0	0	75	87	28	44	0	4.58
Scott Aldred	L	29	2	10	.167	0	17	15	0	77	102	28	33	0	7.68
Dan Naulty (VJ)	R	27	1	1	.500	1	29	0	0	31	29	10	23	0	5.87
1 Dave Stevens	R	27	1	3	.250	0	6	6	0	23	41	17	16	0	9.00
Travis Miller	L	24	1	5	.167	0	6	6	0	13	23	8	9	0	7.63
2 Kevin Jarvis	R	27	0	0	—	0	6	2	0	13	23	8	9	0	12.46
1 Gregg Olson	R	30	0	0	—	0	11	0	0	8	19	11	6	0	18.36
Shane Bowers	R	25	0	3	.000	0	5	5	0	19	27	8	7	0	8.05
Eddie Guardado	L	26	0	4	.000	0	69	0	0	46	45	17	54	0	3.91

KANSAS CITY — 5th 67-94 .416 19 — BOB BOONE 36-46 .439 TONY MUSER 31-48 .392

Name	G by Pos	B	AGE	G	AB	R	H	2B	3B	HR	RBI	BB	SO	SB	BA	SA
TOTALS			29	161	5599	747	1478	256	35	158	711	561	1061	130	.264	.407
Jeff King	1B150 DH2	R	32	155	543	84	129	30	1	28	112	89	96	16	.238	.451
Jose Offerman	2B101 DH1	B	28	106	424	59	126	23	6	2	39	41	64	9	.297	.394
Jay Bell	SS149 3B4	R	31	153	573	89	167	28	3	21	92	79	101	10	.291	.461
Craig Paquette	3B72 OF4	R	28	77	252	26	58	15	1	8	30	10	51	2	.230	.393
Jermaine Dye (LJ)	OF75	R	23	75	263	26	62	14	0	7	22	10	52	2	.236	.369
1 Tom Goodwin	OF96	L	28	97	367	51	100	13	4	2	22	19	51	34	.272	.346
Bip Roberts	OF84 3B10	B	33	97	346	44	107	17	2	1	36	21	53	15	.309	.379
Mike Macfarlane	C81	R	33	97	257	34	61	14	2	8	31	24	60	1	.237	.401
Chili Davis	DH133	B	37	140	477	71	133	20	0	30	90	85	96	6	.279	.509
Johnny Damon	OF136 DH5	L	23	146	472	70	130	12	8	8	48	42	70	16	.275	.386
Mike Sweeney	C76 DH3	R	23	84	240	30	58	8	0	7	31	17	33	3	.242	.363
David Howard	2B34 OF23 SS9 3B7 DH5	B	30	80	162	24	39	8	1	0	13	10	31	2	.241	.321
Scott Cooper (LJ)	3B39 1B8 DH5	L	29	75	159	12	32	5	0	3	15	17	32	1	.201	.308
Shane Halter	OF32 2B18 3B12 SS5 DH4	R	27	74	123	16	34	5	1	2	10	10	28	4	.276	.382
Yamil Benitez	OF52	R	24	53	191	22	51	7	0	6	23	10	52	2	.267	.440
Joe Vitiello (KJ-KJ)	OF28 DH12 1B1	R	28	51	130	11	31	6	0	5	18	14	37	0	.238	.400
2 Dean Palmer	3B48 DH1	R	28	42	187	23	52	9	1	9	31	15	50	1	.278	.487
Jed Hansen	2B31	R	24	34	94	11	29	6	1	1	14	13	29	1	.309	.426
Rod Myers (BW)	OF26	L	27	34	101	14	26	7	0	2	9	17	22	5	.257	.386
Larry Sutton	1B12 DH3 OF1	L	27	27	69	9	20	2	0	2	6	5	12	0	.290	.406
1 Tim Spehr	C17	R	30	17	35	6	6	1	0	2	6	2	12	0	.171	.257
Felix Martinez	SS12 DH2	B	24	17	31	5	7	0	1	0	3	2	7	1	.226	.323
Sal Fasano	C12 DH1	R	25	13	38	4	7	2	0	1	3	2	10	0	.184	.342
1 Jon Nunnally	OF9	L	25	13	29	8	7	1	0	2	3	5	9	1	.241	.414
Ryan Long	OF5 DH1	R	24	9	17	3	2	0	0	0	2	0	5	0	.222	.222
Andy Stewart	C4 DH1	R	26	4	8	1	2	0	0	0	0	1	4	0	.250	.375

NAME	T	AGE	W	L	PCT	SV	G	GS	CG	IP	H	BB	SO	SHO	ERA
		28	67	94	.416	29	161	161	11	1443	1530	531	961	5	4.70
Tim Belcher	R	35	13	12	.520	0	32	32	3	213	242	70	113	1	5.02
Jose Rosado	L	22	9	12	.429	0	33	33	2	203	208	73	129	0	4.69
Kevin Appier	R	29	9	13	.409	0	34	34	4	236	215	74	196	1	3.40
Glendon Rusch	L	22	6	9	.400	0	30	27	1	170	206	52	116	0	5.50
Jim Pittsley	R	25	5	8	.385	0	21	21	0	112	120	54	52	0	5.46
Randy Veres (SJ)	R	31	4	0	1.000	1	24	0	0	35	36	7	28	0	3.31
2 Gregg Olson	R	30	4	0	.571	1	34	0	0	42	39	17	28	0	3.02
1 Ricky Bones	R	28	4	7	.364	0	21	11	1	78	102	25	36	0	5.97
Jamie Walker	L	26	3	1	.500	0	50	0	0	43	46	20	24	0	5.44
Hipolito Pichardo (SJ)	R	27	3	5	.375	11	47	0	0	49	51	24	34	0	4.22
Mike Perez	R	32	2	0	1.000	0	16	0	0	20	15	8	17	0	3.54
2 Matt Whisenant	L	26	1	0	1.000	0	16	0	0	16	11	13	9	0	2.84
Chris Haney (BN-EJ)	L	28	1	2	.333	0	5	3	0	25	29	5	16	0	4.38
Brian Bevil	R	25	1	2	.333	1	18	0	0	16	9	13	6	0	6.61
Jeff Montgomery	R	35	1	4	.200	14	55	0	0	59	53	18	48	0	3.49
2 Hector Carrasco	R	27	1	6	.143	1	29	16	0	56	53	30	54	0	5.45
1 Jason Jacome	L	26	0	1	.000	0	7	0	0	5	7	13	5	0	9.45
Jim Converse	R	22	0	1	.000	0	4	0	0	5	5	2	4	0	3.60
Jose Santiago	R	22	0	1	.000	0	12	3	0	24	21	11	16	0	1.93
Allen McDill	L	26	0	1	.000	0	9	0	0	7	13	5	3	0	13.50
Roland De La Maza	R	25	0	1	.000	0	7	0	0	9	13	6	4	0	4.50
Mitch Williams	L	32	0	0	—	0	7	0	0	11	10	10	6	0	10.80
2 Larry Casian	L	31	0	0	—	0	32	0	0	27	32	6	16	0	5.06
Mike Williams	R	28	0	0	—	0	14	0	0	20	8	10	0	6.43	
2 Scott Service	R	30	0	3	.000	0	17	0	0	17	5	19	0	4.76	
Jamie Bluma (SJ) 25																

SEATTLE — 1st 90-72 .556 — LOU PINIELLA

Name	G by Pos	B	AGE	G	AB	R	H	2B	3B	HR	RBI	BB	SO	SB	BA	SA
TOTALS			29	162	5614	925	1574	312	21	264	890	626	1110	89	.280	.485
Paul Sorrento	1B139 DH1	L	31	146	457	68	123	19	0	31	80	51	112	0	.269	.514
Joey Cora	2B142	B	32	149	574	105	172	40	4	11	54	53	49	6	.300	.441
Alex Rodriguez	SS140 DH1	R	21	141	587	100	176	40	3	23	84	41	99	29	.300	.496
Russ Davis (NJ)	3B117 DH1	R	27	119	420	57	114	29	1	20	63	27	100	6	.271	.488
Jay Buhner	OF154 DH2	R	32	157	540	104	131	18	2	40	109	119	175	0	.243	.506
Ken Griffey Jr.	OF153 DH4	L	27	157	608	125	185	34	3	56	147	76	121	15	.304	.646
1 Jose Cruz	OF49	R	23	49	183	28	49	12	1	12	34	13	45	1	.268	.541
Dan Wilson	C144	R	28	146	508	66	137	31	1	15	74	39	72	7	.270	.423
Edgar Martinez	DH144 1B7 3B1	R	34	155	542	104	179	35	1	28	108	119	86	2	.330	.554
Rich Amaral	OF52 1B14 2B11 DH3 3B1 SS1	R	35	89	190	34	54	5	0	1	21	10	34	12	.284	.326
Rob Ducey	OF69	L	32	76	143	25	41	15	2	5	10	6	31	3	.287	.524
Mike Blowers	1B49 3B10 OF6 DH1	R	32	68	150	22	44	5	0	5	20	21	33	0	.293	.427
Brent Gates	3B32 2B1 SS5 1B1 OF1 DH	B		27	65	151	18	36	8	0	3	20	14	20		.238
Lee Tinsley (EJ)	OF41 DH5	B	29	49	122	12	24	6	2	0	6	11	34	2	.197	.279
John Marzano	C37 DH1	R	34	39	87	7	25	3	0	1	10	7	15	0	.287	.356
Alvaro Espinoza	SS17 2B1 3B1	R	35	33	72	3	13	1	0	0	7	2	12	1	.181	.194
Andy Sheets	3B21 SS9 2B2	R	25	32	89	18	22	3	0	4	9	7	34	2	.247	.416
2 Roberto Kelly	OF29 DH1	R	32	30	121	19	36	7	0	7	22	5	17	2	.298	.529
Raul Ibanez	OF8 DH1	L	25	11	26	3	4	0	1	1	4	0	6	0	.154	.346
Dan Rohrmeier	DH4 1B3	R	31	7	9	4	3	0	0	0	2	2	4	0	.333	.333
2 Rick Wilkins	C3 DH2	L	30	5	12	2	3	1	0	1	4	1	2	0	.250	.583
Giomar Guevara	2B2 DH2 SS1	R	24	5	4	0	0	0	0	0	0	0	2	1	.000	.000
1 Brian Raabe	3B2 2B1	R	29	3	0	0	0	0	0	0	0	0	1	0	.000	.000

NAME	T	AGE	W	L	PCT	SV	G	GS	CG	IP	H	BB	SO	SHO	ERA
TOTALS		30	90	72	.556	38	162	162	9	1448	1500	598	1207	8	4.78
Randy Johnson	L	33	20	4	.833	0	30	29	5	213	147	77	1207	2	2.28
Jamie Moyer	L	34	17	5	.773	0	30	30	2	189	187	43	113	0	3.86
Jeff Fassero	L	34	16	9	.640	0	35	35	2	234	226	84	189	1	3.61
Bobby Ayala	R	27	10	5	.667	8	71	0	0	97	91	41	92	0	3.82
Bob Wolcott	R	23	5	6	.455	0	19	18	0	100	129	29	58	0	6.03
Ken Cloude	R	22	4	2	.667	0	10	9	0	51	41	26	46	0	5.12
2 Mike Timlin	R	31	3	2	.600	1	26	0	0	26	28	5	9	0	3.86
Scott Sanders	R	28	3	6	.333	2	33	6	0	65	73	38	62	0	6.47
Norm Charlton	L	34	3	8	.273	14	71	0	0	69	89	47	55	0	7.27
Bob Wells	R	30	2	0	1.000	2	46	1	0	67	88	18	51	0	5.75
1 Derek Lowe	R	24	2	4	.333	0	12	9	0	53	59	20	39	0	6.96
Mike Maddux	R	35	1	0	1.000	0	6	0	0	11	20	8	7	0	10.13
Greg McCarthy	L	28	1	1	.500	0	37	0	0	30	26	16	34	0	5.46
Edwin Hurtado	R	27	1	2	.333	0	13	1	0	19	25	15	10	0	9.00
Omar Olivares	R	29	1	4	.200	0	13	12	0	62	81	28	29	0	5.49
Dennis Martinez	R	42	1	5	.167	0	9	9	0	49	65	29	17	0	7.71
Paul Spoljaric	L	26	0	0	—	2	20	0	0	23	24	15	27	0	4.76
Mark Holzemer	L	27	0	0	—	1	14	0	0	9	9	8	7	0	6.00
Tim Davis (EJ)	L	26	0	0	—	0	7	0	0	6	4	10		0	6.75
Rafael Carmona	R	24	0	0	—	0	4	0	0	6	3	4	3	0	3.18
1 Salomon Torres	R	25	0	0	—	0	2	0	0	3	7	3	0	0	27.00
1 Josias Manzanillo (GJ-GJ)	R	29	0	1	.000	0	16	0	0	18	19	17	18	0	5.40
2 Heathcliff Slocumb	R	31	0	4	.000	10	27	0	0	28	26	15	28	0	4.13
2 Felipe Lira	R	24	0	1	.000	0	8	3	0	19	31	10	9	0	9.16

3 Tim Scott (EJ) 30 Greg Hibbard (SJ) 32

ANAHEIM — 2nd 84-78 .519 6 — TERRY COLLINS

Name	G by Pos	B	AGE	G	AB	R	H	2B	3B	HR	RBI	BB	SO	SB	BA	SA
TOTALS			30	162	5628	829	1531	279	25	161	775	617	953	126	.272	.416
Darin Erstad	1B126 DH9 OF1	L	23	139	539	99	161	34	4	16	77	51	86	23	.299	.466
Luis Alicea	2B105 3B12 DH6	B	31	128	388	59	98	16	7	5	37	69	65	22	.253	.369
Gary DiSarcina	SS153	R	29	154	549	52	135	28	2	4	47	17	29	7	.246	.326
Dave Hollins	3B135 1B14	R	31	149	572	101	165	29	2	16	85	62	124	16	.288	.430
Tim Salmon	OF153 DH4	R	28	157	582	95	172	28	1	33	129	95	142	4	.296	.517
Jim Edmonds	OF115 1B11 DH8	L	27	133	502	82	146	27	0	26	80	60	80	5	.291	.500
Garret Anderson	OF148 DH4	L	25	154	624	76	189	36	3	8	92	30	70	10	.303	.409
2 Chad Kreuter	C67 DH2	B	32	70	218	19	51	7	1	4	18	21	57	0	.234	.330
1 Eddie Murray (EJ)	DH45	R	41	46	160	13	35	7	0	3	15	13	24	1	.219	.319
2 Tony Phillips	2B43 OF35 DH26 3B1	B	38	105	405	73	107	28	2	6	48	73	89	9	.264	.388
1 Jim Leyritz	C58 1B15 DH13	R	33	84	294	47	81	7	0	11	50	37	56	1	.276	.412
Jack Howell	3B24 DH22 1B12	L	35	77	174	25	45	7	0	14	34	13	36	1	.259	.540
Orlando Palmeiro	OF52 DH11	L	28	74	134	19	29	2	2	0	8	17	11	2	.216	.261
Craig Grebeck	2B26 SS20 3B15 OF3 DH2	R	32	63	126	12	34	9	0	1	6	18	11	0	.270	.365
Todd Greene (BW)	C26 DH8	R	26	34	124	24	36	6	0	9	24	7	25	2	.290	.556
2 Rickey Henderson	DH19 OF13	R	38	32	115	21	21	3	0	2	7	26	23	16	.183	.261
1 Jorge Fabregas	C21	L	27	21	38	2	3	1	0	0	3	2	5	0	.079	.105
Chris Turner (WJ)	C8 1B2 OF1 DH1	R	28	18	23	4	6	1	1	1	2	5	8	0	.261	.522
Robert Eenhoorn	3B5 2B3 SS2	R	29	11	20	2	7	1	1	0	6	0	2	0	.350	.550
Angelo Encarnacion	C11	R	24	11	17	2	7	1	0	1	4	0	1	0	.412	.647
1 George Arias	3B1 DH1	R	25	3	6	1	2	0	0	0	1	0	0	0	.333	.333
Randy Velarde (EJ-EJ)		R	34	1	0	0	0	0	0	0	0	0	0	0	—	—

NAME	T	AGE	W	L	PCT	SV	G	GS	CG	IP	H	BB	SO	SHO	ERA
TOTALS		28	84	78	.519	39	162	162	9	1455	1506	605	1050	5	4.52
Chuck Finley (BW)	L	34	13	6	.684	0	25	25	3	164	152	65	155	1	4.23
Jason Dickson	R	24	13	9	.591	0	33	32	2	204	236	56	115	1	4.29
Allen Watson	L	26	12	12	.500	0	35	34	0	199	220	73	141	0	4.93
Dennis Springer	R	32	9	9	.500	0	32	28	3	195	199	73	75	1	5.18
2 Rich DeLucia (SJ)	R	32	6	4	.600	3	33	0	0	42	29	27	42	0	3.61
Pep Harris	R	24	5	4	.556	0	61	0	0	80	82	38	56	0	3.62
Mike James	R	29	5	5	.500	1	58	0	0	63	69	28	57	0	4.31
Troy Percival (EJ)	R	27	5	5	.500	27	55	0	0	52	40	22	72	0	3.46
2 Ken Hill	R	31	4		.500	0	12	12	1	79	65	39	38	0	3.65
Mike Holtz	L	24	3	4	.429	2	66	0	0	43	38	15	40	0	3.32
Shigetoshi Hasegawa	R	28	3	7	.300	0	50	7	0	117	118	46	83	0	3.93
Darrell May	L	25	2	1	.667	0	29	2	0	52	56	25	42	0	5.23
Kevin Gross	R	36	2	1	.667	0	13	0	0	25	30	20	20	0	6.75
Mark Langston (EJ-EJ)	L	36	2	4	.333	0	9	9	0	48	61	29	30	0	5.85
1 Chuck McElroy	L	29	0	0	—	0	13	0	0	16	17	3	18	0	3.45
Greg Cadaret	L	35	0	0	—	0	15	0	0	14	11	8	11	0	3.29
Tony Chavez	R	26	0	0	—	0	7	0	0	10	7	5	10	0	0.93
Mike Bovee	R	23	0	0	—	0	2	0	0	5	3	1	5	0	5.40
Shad Williams	R	24	0	0	—	0	1	0	0	3	1	2			
Mark Gubicza (SJ)	R	34	0	1	.000	0	2	1	0	6	13	3	5	0	25.07
Matt Perisho	R	22	0	2	.000	0	11	8	0	45	59	28	35	0	6.00

Steve Ontiveros (EJ) 36

TEXAS — 3rd 77-85 .475 13 — JOHNNY OATES

Name	G by Pos	B	AGE	G	AB	R	H	2B	3B	HR	RBI	BB	SO	SB	BA	SA
TOTALS			28	162	5651	807	1547	311	27	187	773	500	1116	72	.274	.438
Will Clark (FJ)	1B100 DH7	L	33	110	393	56	128	29	1	12	51	49	62	0	.326	.496
Mark McLemore (KJ)	2B89 OF1	B	32	89	349	47	91	17	2	1	25	40	54	7	.261	.330
Benji Gil	SS106 DH4	R	24	110	317	35	71	13	2	5	31	17	96	1	.224	.325
1 Dean Palmer	3B93	R	28	94	355	47	87	21	0	14	55	26	84	1	.245	.423
Juan Gonzalez (BG)	DH69 OF64	R	27	133	533	87	158	24	3	42	131	33	107	0	.296	.589
Damon Buford	OF117 DH3	R	27	122	366	49	82	18	0	8	39	30	83	18	.224	.339
Rusty Greer	OF153 DH2	L	28	157	601	112	193	42	3	26	87	83	87	9	.321	.531
Ivan Rodriguez	C143 DH5	R	25	150	597	98	187	34	4	20	77	38	89	7	.313	.484
Lee Stevens	1B62 DH38 OF22	L	29	137	426	58	128	24	2	21	74	23	83	1	.300	.514
Domingo Cedeno (VJ)	2B65 SS43 3B3 DH2	B	28	113	365	49	103	19	6	4	36	27	77	3	.282	.400
Warren Newson (FJ)	OF58 DH1	L	32	81	169	23	36	10	1	10	23	31	53	3	.213	.462
Billy Ripken	SS31 2B25 3B13 1B9	R	32	71	203	18	56	9	1	3	24	9	32	0	.276	.374
Fernando Tatis	3B60	R	22	60	223	29	57	9	0	8	29	14	42	3	.256	.404
Mike Simms	DH28 OF19 1B2	R	30	59	111	13	28	8	0	5	22	8	27	0	.252	.459
2 Tom Goodwin	OF51	L	28	53	207	39	49	13	2	0	17	15	22	16	.237	.319
2 Jim Leyritz	C11 1B9 OF4	R	33	37	85	11	24	4	0	0	14	23	22	1	.282	.329
Mike Devereaux	OF28	R	34	29	72	8	15	3	0	0	7	10	1	2	.208	.250
Alex Diaz	OF23 1B1 2B1	B	28	28	90	8	20	4	0	2	12	5	13	1	.222	.333
Henry Mercedes	C23	R	27	23	47	4	10	4	0	0	4	6	16	0	.213	.298
Marc Sagmoen	OF17 1B1 DH1	L	26	21	43	2	6	2	0	1	4	2	13	0	.140	.256
Mickey Tettleton	DH13	B	36	17	44	5	4	1	0	3	4	13	12	0	.091	.318
Hanley Frias	SS12 2B1	R	23	14	26	4	5	1	0	0	1	4	6	0	.192	.231
Kevin Brown	C4	R	24	4	15	2	6	0	0	0	1	0	1	0	.400	1.000
Dave Silvestri	3B1 SS1	R	29	3	0	0	0	0	0	0	0	0	1	0	.000	.000

NAME	T	AGE	W	L	PCT	SV	G	GS	CG	IP	H	BB	SO	SHO	ERA
TOTALS		30	77	85	.475	33	162	162	8	1430	1598	541	925	9	4.69
Darren Oliver	L	26	13	12	.520	0	32	32	3	201	213	82	104	1	4.20
Bobby Witt	R	33	12	12	.500	0	34	32	3	209	245	74	121	0	4.82
Danny Patterson	R	26	10	6	.625	1	54	0	0	71	70	23	69	0	3.42
John Burkett	R	32	9	12	.429	0	30	30	2	189	240	30	139	0	4.56
John Wetteland	R	30	7	2	.778	31	61	0	0	65	43	21	63	0	1.94
1 Ken Hill	R	31	5	8	.385	0	19	19	0	111	129	56	68	0	5.19
Matt Whiteside	R	29	4	1	.800	0	42	1	0	73	85	26	44	0	5.08
Julio Santana	R	24	4	0	.400	0	30	14	0	104	141	49	64	0	6.75
2 Rick Helling	R	26	4	3	.500	0	10	8	0	55	47	21	46	0	4.58
Roger Pavlik (EJ)	R	29	3	5	.375	0	11	11	0	58	59	31	35	0	4.37
Eric Gunderson	L	31	2	1	.667	1	60	0	0	50	45	15	31	0	3.26
Scott Bailes	L	35	1	0	1.000	0	24	0	0	22	18	10	14	0	2.86
Wilson Heredia	R	25	1	0	1.000	0	20	0	0	20	14	16	8	0	3.20
Tanyon Sturtze	L	26	1	1	.500	0	9	5	0	33	45	18	18	0	8.27
1 Ed Vosberg	L	35	1	2	.333	4	42	0	0	41	44	15	29	0	4.61
2 Terry Clark	R	36	1	4	.200	0	19	5	0	31	41	10	11	0	5.87
Eric Moody	R	26	1	1	.500	0	10	1	0	19	26	2	12	0	4.26
Bryan Eversgerd	L	28	0	1	.000	0	10	0	0	5	3	2		0	20.25
Jose Alberro	R	28	0	3	.000	0	10	4	0	28	37	17	11	0	7.94
Xavier Hernandez (SJ)	R	31	0	4	.000	0	44	0	0	49	51	22	36	0	4.56

OAKLAND — 4th 65-97 .401 25 — ART HOWE

Name	G by Pos	B	AGE	G	AB	R	H	2B	3B	HR	RBI	BB	SO	SB	BA	SA
TOTALS			28	162	5589	764	1451	274	23	197	714	642	1181	71	.260	.423
1 Mark McGwire	1B101	R	33	105	366	48	104	24	0	*34	81	58	98	1	.284	.628
Scott Spiezio	2B146 3B1	B	24	147	538	58	131	28	4	14	65	44	75	9	.243	.388
Rafael Bournigal	SS74 2B7	R	31	79	222	29	62	9	0	1	20	16	19	2	.279	.333
Scott Brosius	3B107 SS30 OF22	R	30	129	479	59	97	20	1	11	41	34	102	9	.203	.317
Matt Stairs	OF89 DH17 1B7	L	29	133	352	62	105	19	0	27	73	50	60	3	.298	.582
Damon Mashore (SJ)	OF89	R	27	92	279	55	69	10	2	3	16	50	82	5	.247	.330
Jason Giambi	OF68 1B51 DH25	L	26	142	519	66	152	41	2	20	81	55	89	0	.293	.495
Brent Mayne	C83	L	29	85	256	29	74	12	0	6	22	18	33	1	.289	.406
Jose Canseco (XJ)	DH60 OF44	R	32	108	388	56	91	19	0	23	74	51	122	8	.235	.461
Dave Magadan	3B49 1B30 DH25	L	34	128	271	38	82	10	1	4	30	50	40	1	.303	.391
Jason McDonald	OF74	B	25	78	236	47	62	11	4	4	14	36	49	13	.263	.394
George Williams (AJ)	C67 DH1	B	28	76	201	30	58	9	1	7	33	32	35	0	.289	.388
1 Geronimo Berroa	OF43 DH27	R	32	73	261	40	81	12	0	16	42	36	58	3	.310	.540
Ernie Young	OF66 DH1	R	27	71	175	22	39	7	0	5	15	19	57	1	.223	.349
Mark Bellhorn	3B40 2B17 DH3 SS3	B	22	68	224	33	51	9	1	6	19	32	70	7	.228	.357
Tony Batista	SS61 3B4 2B1 DH1	R	23	68	188	22	38	10	1	4	18	6	35	0	.202	.330
Patrick Lennon	OF36 DH17	R	29	56	116	14	34	6	1	1	14	15	35	0	.293	.388
Izzy Molina	C48	R	26	48	111	6	22	3	0	1	16	4	18	0	.198	.324
Brian Lesher	OF32 1B3 DH3	R	26	46	131	17	30	4	1	4	16	9	30	4	.229	.366
Miguel Tejada	SS26	R	21	26	99	10	20	3	0	2	10	2	22	2	.202	.333
Ben Grieve	OF24	L	21	24	93	12	29	6	0	3	24	13	25	0	.312	.473
2 Tilson Brito	3B10 SS6 2B2	R	28	17	46	4	13	2	1	1	10	1	6	0	.283	.500
Scott Sheldon	SS12 OF6 3B1	R	28	11	20	3	3	1	0	0	2	2	7	0	.150	.200

* McGwire, also with St. Louis, major league leader in HR with 58

NAME	T	AGE	W	L	PCT	SV	G	GS	CG	IP	H	BB	SO	SHO	ERA
TOTALS		29	65	97	.401	38	162	162	2	1445	1734	642	953	1	5.48
Aaron Small	R	25	9	5	.643	4	71	0	0	97	109	40	57	0	4.28
T.J. Mathews	R	27	6	2	.750	3	34	0	0	29	34	12	24	0	4.40
Ariel Prieto (SJ-SJ)	R	27	6	8	.429	0	22	22	0	125	155	70	90	0	5.04
Don Wengert	R	27	5	11	.313	2	49	12	1	134	177	41	68	0	6.04
Dane Johnson	R	34	4	1	.800	2	38	0	0	46	49	31	43	0	4.53
Mike Oquist (SJ)	R	29	4	6	.400	0	19	17	1	108	111	43	72	0	5.02
Dave Telgheder (RJ)	R	30	4	8	.400	0	20	19	0	101	134	35	55	0	6.06
Andrew Lorraine	L	24	1		.750	0	12	6	0	30	45	15	18	0	6.37
Carlos Reyes (KJ)	R	27	1	4	.429	0	37	6	0	77	101	25	43	0	5.82
Billy Taylor	R	35	3	4	.429	23	72	0	0	73	70	36	66	0	3.82
Willie Adams	R	24	3	5	.375	0	13	13	0	58	73	32	37	0	8.18
Jimmy Haynes	R	24	3	6	.333	0	13	13	0	73	74	40	65	0	4.42
Steve Karsay (AJ)	R	25	3	12	.200	0	24	24	0	133	166	47	92	0	5.77
1 Richie Lewis	R	31	1	0	1.000	0	14	0	0	19	14	15	12	0	9.64
Mark Acre	R	28	1	0	1.000	1	31	0	0	65	75	24	45	0	5.15
Buddy Groom	L	31	0	2	.000	0	78	0	0	56	64	18	45	0	4.87
2 Eric Ludwick	R	25	1	4	.200	0	5	3	0	32	36	14	14	0	8.25
Brad Rigby	R	24	1	7	.125	0	14	14	0	78	92	22	34	0	4.87
Mike Mohler	L	28	1	10	.091	1	62	0	0	102	116	54	66	0	5.13
Tim Kubinski	L	25	0	0	—	0	11	0	0	13	12	6	10	0	5.68
Gary Haught	R	26	0	0	—	0	4	0	0	5	11	4	6	0	7.15
Jay Witasick (EJ)	R	24	0	1	.000	0	5	1	0	11	14	6	5	0	5.73
1 John Johnstone	R	28	0	0	—	0	5	0	0	7	4	2	7	0	7.04
1 Billy Brewer	L	29	0	0	—	0	4	0	0	5	5	2	1	0	13.50
Steve Montgomery	R	26	0	0	—	0	4	0	0	8	11	8	1	0	9.95
Steve Wojciechowski (EJ)	L	26	0	2	.000	0	2	2	0	10	17	1	5	0	7.84

		LINE SCORES																
Team	1	2	3	4	5	6	7	8	9	10	11	12			R	H	E

	COMPOSITE BATTING									
NAME	POS	G	AB	R	H	2B	3B	HR	RBI	BA

	COMPOSITE PITCHING								
NAME	G	IP	H	BB	SO	W	L	SV	ERA

DIVISION SERIES

DIVISION SERIES: CLEVELAND 3 : NEW YORK 2

Game 1   September 30 at New York

	1	2	3	4	5	6	7	8	9		R	H	E
CLE	5	0	0	1	0	0	0	0	0		6	11	0
NYY	0	1	0	1	1	5	0	0	x		8	11	0

Hershiser, Morman (5), **Plunk** (5),   Cone, **Mendoza** (4), Stanton (7),
Assenmacher (7), Jackson (8)   Nelson (7), Rivera (8)

Game 2   October 2 at New York

	1	2	3	4	5	6	7	8	9		R	H	E
CLE	0	0	0	5	2	0	0	0	0		7	11	1
NYY	3	0	0	0	0	0	1	1			5	7	2

Wright, Jackson (7),   **Pettitte**, Boehringer (6),
Assenmacher (7), Mesa (8)   Lloyd (7), Nelson (9)

Game 3   October 4 at Cleveland

	1	2	3	4	5	6	7	8	9		R	H	E
NYY	1	0	1	4	0	0	0	0	0		6	4	1
CLE	0	1	0	0	0	0	0	0	0		1	5	1

Nagy, Ogea (4)   **Wells**

Game 4   October 5 at Cleveland

	1	2	3	4	5	6	7	8	9		R	H	E
NYY	2	0	0	0	0	0	0	0	0		2	9	1
CLE	0	0	0	0	0	0	1	1			3	9	0

Hershiser, Assenmacher (8),   Gooden, Lloyd (6), Nelson (6),
Jackson (8)   Stanton (7), Rivera (8), **Mendoza** (9)

Game 5   October 6 at Cleveland

	1	2	3	4	5	6	7	8	9		R	H	E
NYY	0	0	0	2	1	0	0	0			3	12	0
CLE	0	0	3	1	0	0	0	x			4	7	2

Wright, Jackson (6), Assenmacher (7), **Pettitte**, Nelson (7), Stanton (8)
Mesa (8)

DIVISION SERIES: BALTIMORE 3 : SEATTLE 1

Game 1   October 1 at Seattle

	1	2	3	4	5	6	7	8	9		R	H	E
BAL	0	0	1	0	4	0	4	0	0		9	13	0
SEA	0	0	0	1	0	0	1	0	1		3	7	1

Mussina, Orosco (8), Benitez (9)   **Johnson**, Timlin (6), Spoljaric (6), Wells (7),
Charlton (8)

Game 2   October 2 at Seattle

	1	2	3	4	5	6	7	8	9		R	H	E
BAL	0	1	0	0	2	0	2	4	0		9	14	0
SEA	2	0	0	0	0	1	0	0			3	9	0

Erickson, Benitez (7), Orosco (8),   **Moyer**, Spoljaric (5), Ayala (7), Charlton (8),
Myers (9)   Slocumb (9)

Game 3   October 4 at Baltimore

	1	2	3	4	5	6	7	8	9		R	H	E
SEA	0	0	1	0	1	0	0	0	2		4	11	0
BAL	0	0	0	0	0	0	0	0	2		2	5	0

Fassero, Slocumb (9)   **Key**, Mills (5), Rhodes (6), Mathews (9)

Game 4   October 5 at Baltimore

	1	2	3	4	5	6	7	8	9		R	H	E
SEA	0	1	0	0	0	0	0	0	0		1	2	0
BAL	2	0	0	0	1	0	0	0	x		3	7	0

Johnson   **Mussina**, Benitez (8), Myers (9)

CHAMPIONSHIP: CLEVELAND 4 : BALTIMORE 2

Game 1   October 8 at Baltimore

	1	2	3	4	5	6	7	8	9	10	11		R	H	E
CLE	0	0	0	0	0	0	0	0	0	0	0		0	4	1
BAL	1	0	2	0	0	0	0	0	x				3	6	1

Ogea, Anderson (7)   **Erickson**, Myers (9)

Game 2   October 9 at Baltimore

	1	2	3	4	5	6	7	8	9		R	H	E
CLE	2	0	0	0	0	0	0	3	0		5	6	3
BAL	0	2	0	0	2	0	0	0			4	8	1

Nagy, Morman (6), Juden (7),   Key, Kamieniecki (5), **Benitez** (8), Mills (9)
Assenmacher (7), Jackson (8), Mesa (9)

Game 3   October 11 at Cleveland

	1	2	3	4	5	6	7	8	9	10	11	12		R	H	E
BAL	0	0	0	0	0	0	0	1	0	0	0	1		8	1
CLE	0	0	0	0	0	0	1	0	0	0	0	2		6	0

Mussina, Benitez (8), Orosco (8),   Hershiser, Assenmacher (8), Jackson (8),
Mills (9), Rhodes (10), **Myers** (11)   Mesa (9), Juden (11), Morman (11), **Plunk** (12)

Game 4   October 12 at Cleveland

	1	2	3	4	5	6	7	8	9		R	H	E
BAL	0	1	4	0	0	0	1	0	1		7	12	2
CLE	0	2	0	1	4	0	0	0	1		8	13	0

Erickson, Rhodes (5), **Mills** (7),   Wright, Anderson (4), Juden (7),
Orosco (9), Benitez (9)   Assenmacher (7), Jackson (7), **Mesa** (8)

Game 5   October 13 at Cleveland

	1	2	3	4	5	6	7	8	9		R	H	E
BAL	0	0	2	0	0	0	0	0	2		4	10	0
CLE	0	0	0	0	0	0	0	0	2		2	8	1

Kamieniecki, Key (6), Myers (9)   Ogea, Assenmacher (8), Jackson (9)

Game 6   October 15 at Baltimore

	1	2	3	4	5	6	7	8	9	10	11		R	H	E
CLE	0	0	0	0	0	0	0	0	0	0	1		3	0
BAL	0	0	0	0	0	0	0	0	0	0	0		10	0

Nagy, Assenmacher (8), Jackson (8),   Mussina, Myers (9), **Benitez** (11)
Anderson (10), Mesa (11)

DIVISION SERIES — COMPOSITE BATTING

CLEVELAND

NAME	POS	G	AB	R	H	2B	3B	HR	RBI	BA
TOTALS		5	167	21	43	6	1	4	20	.257
Ramirez	RF	5	21	2	3	1	0	0	3	.143
Alomar	C	5	19	4	6	1	0	2	5	.316
Roberts	2B-LF	5	19	1	6	0	0	0	1	.316
Justice	DH	5	19	3	5	2	0	1	2	.263
Vizquel	SS	5	18	3	9	0	0	0	1	.500
Williams	3B	5	17	4	4	1	0	1	3	.235
Grissom	CF	5	17	3	4	0	1	0	0	.235
Thome	1B	4	15	1	3	0	0	0	1	.200
Fernandez	2B	4	11	0	2	1	0	0	4	.182
Giles	LF	3	7	0	1	0	0	0	0	.143
Seitzer	1B	1	4	0	0	0	0	0	0	.000

NEW YORK

NAME	POS	G	AB	R	H	2B	3B	HR	RBI	BA
TOTALS		5	166	24	43	7	0	6	23	.259
Jeter	SS	5	21	6	7	1	0	2	2	.333
O'Neill	RF	5	19	5	8	2	0	2	7	.421
Raines	DH-LF	5	19	4	4	0	0	1	3	.211
Martinez	1B	5	18	1	4	1	0	1	4	.222
Williams	CF	5	17	3	2	1	0	0	1	.118
Hayes	3B-2B	5	15	0	5	0	0	0	1	.333
Sanchez	2B	5	15	1	3	1	0	0	0	.200
Girardi	C	5	15	2	2	0	0	0	0	.133
Fielder	DH	2	8	0	1	0	0	0	1	.125
Boggs	3B-2B	3	7	1	3	0	0	0	2	.429
Curtis	LF	4	6	0	1	0	0	0	0	.167
Stanley	DH	2	4	1	3	1	0	0	1	.750
Posada	C	2	2	0	0	0	0	0	0	.000
Fox	2B	2	0	0	0	0	0	0	0	—
Pose	PR	1	0	0	0	0	0	0	0	—

BALTIMORE

NAME	POS	G	AB	R	H	2B	3B	HR	RBI	BA
TOTALS		4	135	23	39	11	0	6	23	.289
Anderson	CF	4	17	3	6	1	0	1	4	.353
Ripken	3B	4	16	1	7	2	0	1	5	.438
Berroa	DH-RF	4	13	4	5	1	0	2	2	.385
Palmeiro	1B	4	12	2	3	2	0	0	2	.250
Surhoff	LF	3	11	0	3	1	0	0	2	.273
Bordick	SS	4	10	4	4	1	0	0	4	.400
Alomar	2B	4	10	1	3	2	0	0	3	.300
Hammonds	LF-RF	4	10	3	1	0	0	0	2	.100
Davis	RF	3	9	0	2	0	0	0	0	.222
Hoiles	C	3	7	1	1	0	0	1	1	.143
Webster	C	2	6	1	1	0	0	0	1	.167
Baines	DH	2	5	2	2	0	0	1	1	.400
Reboulet	2B	2	5	1	1	0	0	1	1	.200
Walton	1B	2	4	0	0	0	0	0	0	—

SEATTLE

NAME	POS	G	AB	R	H	2B	3B	HR	RBI	BA
TOTALS		4	133	11	29	5	0	6	11	.218
Cora	2B	4	17	1	3	0	0	0	0	.176
Rodriguez	SS	4	16	1	5	1	0	1	1	.313
Martinez	DH	4	16	2	3	0	0	2	3	.188
Griffey	CF	4	15	0	2	0	0	0	2	.133
Kelly	LF	4	13	1	4	3	0	0	1	.308
Buhner	RF	4	13	2	3	0	0	2	2	.231
Wilson	C	4	13	0	0	0	0	0	0	.000
Sorrento	1B	4	10	2	3	1	0	1	1	.300
Blowers	3B	3	5	0	1	0	0	0	0	.200
Amaral	1B	2	4	2	2	0	0	0	0	.500
Ducey	LF	2	4	0	2	0	0	0	0	.500
Gates	3B	2	4	0	0	0	0	0	0	.000
Sheets	3B	2	3	0	1	0	0	0	0	.333
Wilkins	C	1	1	0	0	0	0	0	0	—

DIVISION SERIES — COMPOSITE PITCHING

CLEVELAND

NAME	G	IP	H	BB	SO	W	L	SV	ERA
TOTALS	5	44	43	20	26	3	2	1	4.50
Hershiser	2	11.1	14	2	4	0	0	0	3.97
Wright	2	11.1	11	7	10	2	0	0	3.97
Ogea	1	5.1	2	0	1	0	0	0	1.69
Jackson	4	4.1	3	1	5	1	0	0	0.00
Nagy	1	3.2	6	1	0	1	0	9.82
Mesa	2	3.1	5	1	2	0	0	1	2.70
Assenmacher	4	3.1	2	2	2	0	0	0	5.40
Plunk	2	1.1	4	0	1	0	1	0	27.00
Morman	1	0	0	1	0	0	0	0	—

NEW YORK

NAME	G	IP	H	BB	SO	W	L	SV	ERA
TOTALS	5	43.1	43	10	22	2	3	1	4.36
Pettitte	2	11.2	15	1	5	0	2	0	8.49
Wells	1	9	5	0	1	0	0	0	1.00
Gooden	1	5,2	5	3	5	0	0	0	1.59
Nelson	4	4	4	2	0	0	0	0	0.00
Mendoza	2	3.2	3	0	2	1	1	0	2.45
Cone	1	3.1	7	2	2	0	0	0	16.20
Rivera	2	2	2	0	1	0	0	1	4.50
Boehringer	1	1.2	1	1	2	0	0	0	0.00
Lloyd	2	1.1	0	1	0	0	0	0	0.00
Stanton	3	1	1	1	3	0	0	0	0.00

BALTIMORE

NAME	G	IP	H	BB	SO	W	L	SV	ERA
TOTALS	4	36	29	7	42	3	1	1	2.75
Mussina	2	14	7	3	16	2	0	0	1.93
Erickson	1	6.2	7	2	6	1	0	0	4.05
Key	1	4.2	8	0	4	0	1	0	3.86
Benitez	3	3	3	2	4	0	0	0	3.00
Rhodes	1	2.1	0	0	4	0	0	0	0.00
Myers	2	2	0	0	5	0	0	1	0.00
Orosco	2	1.1	1	0	1	0	0	0	0.00
Mills	1	1	1	0	1	0	0	0	0.00
Mathews	1	1	2	0	1	0	0	0	18.00

SEATTLE

NAME	G	IP	H	BB	SO	W	L	SV	ERA
TOTALS	4	35	39	16	27	1	3	0	5.91
Johnson	2	13	14	6	16	0	2	0	5.54
Fassero	1	8	3	4	3	1	0	0	1.13
Moyer	1	4.2	5	1	2	0	1	0	5.79
Charlton	2	2.1	2	0	1	0	0	0	0.00
Slocumb	2	2	3	1	0	0	0	0	4.50
Spoljaric	2	1.2	4	0	1	0	0	0	0.00
Wells	1	1.1	1	0	1	0	0	0	0.00
Ayala	1	1.1	4	3	2	0	0	0	40.50
Timlin	1	0.2	3	1	1	0	0	0	54.00

AMERICAN LEAGUE CHAMPIONSHIP

CLEVELAND

NAME	POS	G	AB	R	H	2B	3B	HR	RBI	BA
TOTALS		6	207	18	40	8	0	5	15	.193
Vizquel	SS	6	25	1	1	0	0	0	0	.040
Alomar	C	6	24	3	3	0	0	1	4	.125
Grissom	CF	6	23	2	6	0	0	1	4	.261
Williams	3B	6	23	1	5	1	0	0	2	.217
Justice	DH	6	21	3	7	1	0	0	0	.333
Ramirez	RF	6	21	3	6	1	0	2	3	.286
Roberts	2B-LF	5	20	0	3	1	0	0	0	.150
Giles	LF	6	16	1	3	3	0	0	4	.188
Fernandez	2B	6	14	1	5	1	0	1	2	.357
Thome	1B	6	14	3	1	0	0	0	0	.071
Seitzer	1B	4	4	0	0	0	0	0	0	.000
Branson	DH	1	2	0	0	0	0	0	0	.000

BALTIMORE

NAME	POS	G	AB	R	H	2B	3B	HR	RBI	BA
TOTALS		6	218	19	54	11	0	7	19	.248
Anderson	CF	6	25	5	9	2	0	2	3	.360
Palmeiro	1B	6	25	3	7	2	0	1	2	.280
Surhoff	LF-1B	6	25	4	5	2	0	0	1	.200
Ripken	3B	6	23	3	8	2	0	1	3	.348
Alomar	2B	6	22	2	4	0	0	1	2	.182
Berroa	RF-DH	6	21	1	6	2	0	0	0	.286
Bordick	SS	6	19	1	3	1	0	0	0	.158
Baines	DH	6	17	1	6	0	0	1	3	.353
Hoiles	C	4	14	1	2	0	0	1	1	.143
Davis	RF-DH	6	13	1	2	0	0	1	1	.154
Webster	C	4	9	0	2	0	0	0	0	.222
Hammonds	RF-LF	5	3	0	0	0	0	0	0	.000
Reboulet	SS	1	2	1	0	0	0	0	0	.000
Walton	RF	1	0	0	0	0	0	0	0	—

CLEVELAND

NAME	G	IP	H	BB	SO	W	L	SV	ERA
TOTALS	6	58	54	23	47	4	2	2	2.95
Ogea	2	14	12	5	7	0	2	0	3.21
Nagy	2	13	17	5	5	0	0	0	2.77
Hershiser	1	7	4	1	7	0	0	0	0.00
Anderson	3	6.1	3	3	7	1	0	0	1.42
Mesa	4	5.1	5	3	5	1	0	2	3.38
Jackson	5	4.1	1	1	7	0	0	0	0.00
Wright	2	3	6	2	3	0	0	0	15.00
Assenmacher	5	2	5	1	3	1	0	0	9.00
Morman	2	1.1	0	1	2	0	0	0	0.00
Juden	3	1	2	2	0	0	0	0	0.00
Plunk	1	0.2	1	0	1	1	0	0	0.00

BALTIMORE

NAME	G	IP	H	BB	SO	W	L	SV	ERA
TOTALS	6	58	40	23	62	2	4	1	2.64
Mussina	2	15	4	4	25	0	0	0	0.60
Erickson	2	12.2	15	1	6	1	0	0	4.26
Kamieniecki	2	8	4	2	5	1	0	0	0.00
Key	2	7	5	3	7	0	1	0	2.57
Myers	4	5.1	6	3	7	0	1	1	5.06
Mills	3	3.1	1	2	3	0	0	0	2.70
Benitez	4	3	3	4	6	0	2	0	12.00
Rhodes	2	2.1	2	3	2	0	0	0	0.00
Orosco	2	1.1	0	1	1	0	0	0	0.00

Name	G by Pos	B	AGE	G	AB	R	H	2B	3B	HR	RBI	BB	SO	SB	BA	SA

ATLANTA   1st 101-61 .623   **BOBBY COX**

Name	G by Pos	B	AGE	G	AB	R	H	2B	3B	HR	RBI	BB	SO	SB	BA	SA
	TOTALS		27	162	5528	791	1490	268	37	174	755	597	1160	108	.270	.426
Fred McGriff	1B149	L	33	152	564	77	156	25	1	22	97	68	112	5	.277	.441
Mark Lemke (NJ)	2B104	B	31	109	351	33	86	17	1	2	26	33	51	2	.245	.316
Jeff Blauser	SS149	R	31	151	519	90	160	31	4	17	70	70	101	5	.308	.482
Chipper Jones	3B152 OF5	B	25	157	597	100	176	41	3	21	111	76	88	20	.295	.479
Michael Tucker	OF129	L	26	138	499	80	141	25	7	14	56	44	116	12	.283	.445
Kenny Lofton	OF122	L	30	122	493	90	164	20	6	5	48	64	83	27	.333	.428
Ryan Klesko	OF130 1B22	L	26	143	467	67	122	23	6	24	84	48	130	4	.261	.490
Javy Lopez	C117	R	26	123	414	52	122	28	1	23	68	40	82	1	.295	.534
Andruw Jones	OF147	R	20	153	399	60	92	18	1	18	70	56	107	20	.231	.416
Tony Graffanino	2B75 3B2 SS2 1B1	R	25	104	186	33	48	9	1	8	20	26	46	6	.258	.446
Keith Lockhart	2B20 3B11	L	32	96	147	25	41	5	3	6	32	14	17	0	.279	.476
Eddie Perez	C64 1B6	R	29	73	191	20	41	5	0	6	18	10	35	1	.215	.335
Rafael Belliard	SS53 2B7	R	35	72	71	9	15	3	0	1	3	1	17	0	.211	.296
Danny Bautista	OF57	R	25	64	103	14	25	3	2	3	9	5	24	2	.243	.398
Mike Mordecai	3B19 2B4 SS4 1B3 OF1	R	29	61	81	8	14	2	1	0	3	6	16	0	.173	.222
2 Greg Colbrunn	1B14	R	27	28	54	3	15	3	0	2	9	2	11	0	.278	.444
Ed Giovanola	3B8 2B1 SS1	L	28	14	8	0	2	0	0	0	2	1	1	0	.250	.250
Tommy Gregg	OF6 1B1	L	33	13	19	1	5	2	0	0	1	1	2	1	.263	.368
Randall Simon	1B6	L	22	13	14	2	6	1	0	0	1	1	2	0	.429	.500
2 Greg Myers	C2	L	31	9	9	0	1	0	0	0	1	1	3	0	.111	.111
2 Tim Spehr	C7	R	30	8	14	2	3	1	0	1	4	0	4	1	.214	.500

NAME	T	AGE	W	L	PCT	SV	G	GS	CG	IP	H	BB	SO	SHO	ERA
		26	101	61	.623	37	162	162	21	1466	1319	450	1196	17	3.18
Denny Neagle	L	28	20	5	.800	0	34	34	4	233	204	49	172	4	2.97
Greg Maddux	R	31	19	4	.826	0	33	33	5	233	200	20	177	2	2.20
John Smoltz	R	30	15	12	.556	0	35	35	7	256	234	63	241	3	3.02
Tom Glavine	L	31	14	7	.667	0	33	33	5	240	197	79	152	2	2.96
Brad Clontz	R	26	5	1	.833	1	51	0	0	48	52	18	42	0	3.75
Kevin Millwood	R	22	5	3	.625	0	12	8	0	51	55	21	42	0	4.03
Mark Wohlers	R	27	5	7	.417	33	71	0	0	69	57	38	92	0	3.50
Paul Byrd	R	26	4	4	.500	0	31	4	0	53	47	28	37	0	5.26
Alan Embree	L	27	3	1	.750	0	66	0	0	46	36	20	45	0	2.54
Mike Bielecki (SJ)	R	37	3	7	.300	2	50	0	0	57	56	21	60	0	4.08
1 Joe Borowski	R	26	2	2	.500	0	20	0	0	24	27	16	6	0	3.75
Terrell Wade (PJ)	L	24	2	3	.400	0	12	9	0	42	60	16	35	0	5.36
Mike Cather	R	26	2	4	.333	0	35	0	0	38	23	19	29	0	2.39
Kerry Ligtenberg	R	26	1	0	1.000	1	15	0	0	15	12	4	19	0	3.00
John LeRoy	R	26	1	0	1.000	0	1	0	0	2	1	3	3	0	0.00
Chris Brock	R	27	0	0	—	0	7	6	0	31	34	19	16	0	5.58
Chad Fox	R	26	0	1	.000	0	30	0	0	27	24	16	28	0	3.29
Pedro Borbon (EJ-KJ)															

FLORIDA   2nd 92-70 .568 9 (Wild Card)   **JIM LEYLAND**

Name	G by Pos	B	AGE	G	AB	R	H	2B	3B	HR	RBI	BB	SO	SB	BA	SA
	TOTALS		29	162	5439	740	1410	272	28	136	703	686	1074	115	.259	.395
Jeff Conine	1B145 OF1	R	31	151	405	46	98	13	1	17	61	57	89	2	.242	.405
Luis Castillo	2B70	B	21	75	263	27	63	8	0	0	8	27	53	16	.240	.270
Edgar Renteria	SS153	R	21	154	617	90	171	21	3	4	52	45	108	32	.277	.340
Bobby Bonilla	3B149 1B2	B	34	153	562	77	167	39	3	17	96	73	94	6	.297	.468
Gary Sheffield	OF132	R	28	135	444	86	111	22	1	21	71	121	79	11	.250	.424
Devon White (KJ-LJ)	OF71	B	34	74	265	37	65	13	1	6	34	32	65	13	.245	.370
Moises Alou	OF150	R	30	150	538	88	157	29	5	23	115	70	85	9	.292	.493
Charles Johnson	C123	R	25	124	416	43	104	26	1	19	63	60	109	0	.250	.454
Jim Eisenreich	OF55 1B29	L	38	120	293	36	82	19	1	2	34	30	28	0	.280	.372
John Cangelosi	OF58 P1	B	34	103	192	28	47	8	0	1	12	19	33	5	.245	.302
Kurt Abbott	2B54 OF10 SS7 3B4	R	28	94	252	35	69	18	2	6	30	14	68	3	.274	.433
Alex Arias	3B37 SS11	R	29	74	93	13	23	2	0	1	11	12	12	0	.247	.301
Cliff Floyd (LJ)	OF38 1B9	L	24	61	137	23	32	9	1	6	19	24	33	6	.234	.445
Gregg Zaun	C50 1B1	R	26	58	143	21	43	10	2	2	20	26	8	1	.301	.441
2 Darren Daulton	1B39 OF3	L	35	52	126	22	33	8	2	3	21	22	17	2	.262	.429
2 Craig Counsell	2B51	L	26	51	164	20	49	9	2	1	16	18	17	1	.299	.396
John Wehner (SJ)	OF27 3B6	R	30	44	36	8	10	2	0	0	2	2	5	1	.278	.333
Todd Dunwoody	OF14	L	22	19	50	7	13	2	2	2	7	7	21	2	.260	.500
Mark Kotsay	OF14	L	21	14	52	5	10	1	1	0	4	4	7	3	.192	.250
1 Billy McMillon	OF2	L	25	13	18	0	2	1	0	0	1	0	7	0	.111	.167
Ralph Milliard	2B8	R	23	8	30	2	6	0	0	0	2	3	3	1	.200	.200
Russ Morman	OF2 1B1	R	35	7	3	2	1	0	1	0	2	0	2	1	.286	.857
Josh Booty	3B4	R	22	4	5	2	3	0	0	0	1	1	1	0	.600	.600
Bob Natal	C4	R	31	4	4	2	2	1	0	1	3	2	0	0	.500	1.500

NAME	T	AGE	W	L	PCT	SV	G	GS	CG	IP	H	BB	SO	SHO	ERA
		27	92	70	.568	39	162	162	12	1447	1353	639	1188	10	3.83
Alex Fernandez	R	27	17	12	.586	0	32	32	5	221	193	69	183	1	3.59
Kevin Brown	R	32	16	8	.667	0	33	33	6	237	214	66	205	2	2.69
Al Leiter	L	31	11	9	.550	0	27	27	0	151	133	91	132	0	4.34
Livan Hernandez	R	22	9	3	.750	0	17	17	0	96	81	38	72	0	3.18
Robb Nen	R	27	9	3	.750	35	73	0	0	74	72	40	81	0	3.89
Jay Powell	R	25	7	2	.778	2	74	0	0	80	71	30	65	0	3.28
Felix Heredia	L	22	5	3	.625	0	56	0	0	57	53	30	54	0	4.29
Tony Saunders (KJ)	L	23	4	6	.400	0	22	21	0	111	99	64	102	0	4.61
1 Pat Rapp	R	29	4	6	.400	0	19	19	1	109	121	51	64	1	4.47
1 Mark Hutton	R	27	3	1	.750	0	32	0	0	48	50	19	29	0	3.78
1 Rick Helling	R	26	2	6	.250	0	31	8	0	76	61	48	53	0	4.38
2 Ed Vosberg	L	35	1	1	.500	1	17	0	0	12	15	6	8	0	3.75
Dennis Cook	L	34	1	2	.333	0	59	0	0	62	64	28	63	0	3.90
Rob Stanifer	R	25	1	2	.333	1	36	0	0	45	43	16	28	0	4.60
Kirt Ojala	L	28	1	2	.333	0	7	5	0	29	28	18	19	0	3.14
Antonio Alfonseca	R	25	1	3	.250	0	17	0	0	26	36	10	19	0	4.91
1 Matt Whisenant (VJ)	L	26	0	1	.000	0	4	0	0	3	4	4	3	0	16.88
Donn Pall	R	35	0	0	—	0	2	0	0	2	3	1	0	0	3.86
John Cangelosi	L	34	0	0	—	0	1	0	0	1	0	1	0	0	0.00
Kurt Miller (EJ)	R	24	0	1	.000	0	7	0	1	7	12	7	7	0	9.82

NEW YORK   3rd 88-74 .543 13   **BOBBY VALENTINE**

Name	G by Pos	B	AGE	G	AB	R	H	2B	3B	HR	RBI	BB	SO	SB	BA	SA
	TOTALS		27	162	5524	777	1448	274	28	153	741	550	1029	97	.262	.405
John Olerud	1B146	L	28	154	524	90	154	34	1	22	102	85	67	0	.294	.489
Carlos Baerga	2B131	B	28	133	467	53	131	25	1	9	52	20	54	2	.281	.396
Rey Ordonez (BH)	SS118	R	26	120	356	35	77	5	3	1	33	18	36	11	.216	.256
Edgardo Alfonzo	3B143 SS12 2B3	R	23	151	518	84	163	27	2	10	72	63	56	11	.315	.432
Butch Huskey	OF92 1B22 3B15	R	25	142	471	61	135	26	2	24	81	25	84	8	.287	.503
1 Lance Johnson (LJ)	OF66	L	33	72	265	43	82	10	6	1	24	33	21	15	.309	.404
Bernard Gilkey	OF136	R	30	145	518	85	129	31	1	18	78	70	111	9	.249	.417
Todd Hundley	C122	B	28	132	417	78	114	21	2	30	86	83	116	2	.273	.549
Carl Everett	OF128	B	26	142	443	58	110	28	3	14	57	32	102	17	.248	.420
Alex Ochoa	OF88	R	25	113	238	31	58	14	1	3	22	18	32	3	.244	.349
Matt Franco	OF128 1B13 OF1	L	27	112	163	21	45	5	0	5	21	13	23	1	.276	.399
Luis Lopez	SS45 2B20 3B4	B	26	78	178	19	48	12	1	1	19	12	42	0	.270	.365
1 Manny Alexander	2B31 SS26 3B1	R	26	54	149	26	37	9	3	2	15	9	38	11	.248	.389
Steve Bieser	OF21 C2	L	29	47	69	16	17	3	0	0	4	7	20	2	.246	.290
2 Brian McRae	OF41	B	29	45	145	23	36	5	2	5	15	13	22	2	.248	.414
Todd Pratt	C36	R	30	39	106	12	30	6	0	2	19	13	32	0	.283	.396
Alberto Castillo	C34	R	27	35	59	3	12	1	0	0	7	9	16	0	.203	.220
Jason Hardtke	2B21 3B1	L	25	30	56	9	15	2	0	2	8	4	6	1	.268	.411
Shawn Gilbert	2B8 SS6 3B3 OF1	R	32	19	22	3	3	0	0	1	1	3	6	1	.136	.273
Carlos Mendoza	OF3	L	22	15	12	6	3	0	0	0	1	4	2	0	.250	.250
Roberto Petagine	1B6 OF1	L	26	12	15	2	1	0	0	0	0	3	6	0	.067	.067
Gary Thurman	OF7	R	32	11	6	0	1	0	0	0	0	0	2	0	.167	.167
Andy Tomberlin (ZJ)	OF2	L	30	6	7	0	2	0	0	0	0	1	2	0	.286	.286
Kevin Morgan	3B1	R	27	1	1	0	0	0	0	0	0	0	1	0	.000	.000

NAME	T	AGE	W	L	PCT	SV	G	GS	CG	IP	H	BB	SO	SHO	ERA
		29	88	74	.543	49	162	162	7	1459	1452	504	982	8	3.95
Bobby Jones	R	27	15	9	.625	0	30	30	2	193	177	63	125	1	3.63
Rick Reed	R	32	13	9	.591	0	33	31	2	208	186	31	113	0	2.89
1 Mark Clark	R	29	8	7	.533	0	23	22	1	142	158	47	72	0	4.25
Dave Mlicki	R	29	8	12	.400	0	32	32	1	194	194	76	157	1	4.00
Cory Lidle	R	25	7	2	.778	2	54	2	0	82	86	20	54	0	3.53
Greg McMichael	R	30	7	10	.412	7	73	0	0	88	73	27	81	0	2.98
Armando Reynoso (SJ)	R	31	6	3	.667	0	16	16	1	91	95	29	47	1	4.53
Brian Bohanon	L	28	6	4	.600	0	19	14	0	94	95	34	66	0	3.82
John Franco	L	36	5	3	.625	36	59	0	0	60	49	20	53	0	2.55
Joe Crawford	L	27	4	3	.571	0	19	2	0	46	36	13	25	0	3.30
Juan Acevedo	R	27	3	1	.750	0	25	2	0	48	52	22	33	0	3.59
Takashi Kashiwada	L	25	3	1	.750	0	35	0	0	31	38	18	19	0	4.31
Jason Isringhausen (SJ)	R	24	2	2	.500	0	6	6	0	30	40	22	25	0	7.58
Ricardo Jordan	L	27	1	2	.333	2	27	0	0	27	31	19	19	0	5.33
2 Turk Wendell	R	30	0	0	—	1	13	0	0	16	15	14	10	0	4.96
2 Rick Trlicek (RJ)	R	28	0	0	—	0	9	0	0	9	10	3	6	0	8.00
Barry Manuel	R	31	0	0	—	0	19	0	0	26	35	13	21	0	5.26
1 Pete Harnisch (IL)	R	30	0	1	.000	0	3	3	0	13	11	14	7	0	8.06
1 Toby Borland	R	28	0	1	.000	0	13	0	0	13	11	14	7	0	6.08
Yorkis Perez (SJ)	L	29	0	1	.000	0	9	0	0	9	15	4	7	0	8.31
2 Mel Rojas	R	30	0	1	.000	2	26	0	0	26	24	16	32	0	5.13
Bill Pulsipher (EJ) 23 Derek Wallace (SJ) 25 Paul Wilson (SJ) 24															

MONTREAL   4th 78-84 .481 23   **FELIPE ALOU**

Name	G by Pos	B	AGE	G	AB	R	H	2B	3B	HR	RBI	BB	SO	SB	BA	SA
	TOTALS		27	162	5526	691	1423	339	34	172	659	420	1084	75	.258	.425
David Segui	1B125	B	30	125	459	75	141	22	3	21	68	57	66	1	.307	.505
Mike Lansing	2B144	R	29	144	572	86	161	45	2	20	70	45	92	11	.281	.472
Mark Grudzielanek	SS156	R	27	156	649	76	177	54	3	4	51	23	76	25	.273	.384
Doug Strange	3B105 2B3 OF2 1B1	B	33	118	327	40	84	16	2	12	47	36	76	0	.257	.428
Vladimir Guerrero (BF)	OF85	R	21	90	325	44	98	22	2	11	40	19	39	3	.302	.483
Rondell White	OF151	R	25	151	592	84	160	29	5	28	82	31	111	16	.270	.478
Henry Rodriguez	OF126 1B3	L	29	132	476	55	116	28	3	26	83	42	149	3	.244	.479
Darrin Fletcher	C83	L	30	96	310	39	86	20	1	17	55	17	35	1	.277	.513
F.P. Santangelo	OF99 3B32 2B7 SS1	B	29	130	350	56	87	19	5	5	31	50	73	8	.249	.374
Joe Orsulak	OF63 1B15	L	35	106	150	13	34	12	1	1	7	18	17	0	.227	.340
Chris Widger	C85	R	26	91	278	30	65	20	3	7	37	22	59	2	.234	.403
Ryan McGuire	OF44 1B30	L	25	84	199	22	51	15	2	3	17	19	34	1	.256	.397
Andy Stankiewicz	2B25 SS14 3B3	R	32	76	101	12	24	9	0	1	5	4	22	1	.224	.336
Jose Vidro	3B36 2B5	B	22	67	169	19	42	12	1	2	17	11	20	1	.249	.367
Sherman Obando (EJ)	OF15	R	27	41	47	3	6	1	0	1	8	2	12	1	.128	.277
Brad Fullmer	1B8 OF2	L	22	19	40	4	12	2	0	3	8	4	9	0	.300	.575
Shane Andrews (SJ)	3B18	R	25	18	64	10	13	3	0	4	13	6	20	0	.203	.438
Hensley Meulens	OF8 1B3	R	30	16	24	6	7	2	0	2	4	6	10	0	.292	.583
Orlando Cabrera	SS6 2B4	R	22	16	18	4	4	0	1	0	1	1	2	2	.222	.222
Raul Chavez	C13	R	24	13	26	0	7	1	0	0	1	1	5	0	.269	.269

NAME	T	AGE	W	L	PCT	SV	G	GS	CG	IP	H	BB	SO	SHO	ERA
		27	78	84	.481	37	162	162	27	1447	1365	557	1138	14	4.14
Pedro Martinez	R	25	17	8	.680	0	31	31	13	241	158	67	305	4	1.90
Carlos Perez	L	26	12	13	.480	0	33	32	8	207	206	48	110	5	3.88
1 Jeff Juden	R	26	11	5	.688	0	22	22	3	130	125	57	107	0	4.22
Dustin Hermanson	R	24	8	8	.500	0	32	28	1	158	134	66	136	1	3.69
Jim Bullinger	R	31	7	12	.368	0	36	25	2	155	165	74	87	2	5.56
Ugueth Urbina	R	23	5	8	.385	27	63	0	0	64	52	29	84	0	3.78
Marc Valdes	R	25	4	4	.500	0	2	48	7	95	84	39	54	0	3.13
Anthony Telford	R	31	4	4	.500	1	65	0	0	89	77	33	61	0	3.24
Dave Veres	R	30	2	3	.400	1	53	0	0	62	68	27	47	0	3.48
2 Mike Johnson	R	21	2	5	.286	0	11	11	0	50	54	21	28	0	5.94
Mike Thurman	R	23	1	0	1.000	0	9	0	0	15	16	4	5	0	5.40
1 Omar Daal	L	25	1	3	.333	1	33	0	0	30	48	15	16	0	9.79
Jose Paniagua	R	23	1	3	.333	1	3	0	0	18	19	16	9	0	12.00
2 Steve Kline	L	24	1	1	.250	0	26	0	0	26	31	10	20	0	6.15
2 Salomon Torres	R	25	0	0	—	0	8	8	0	35	37	12	11	0	7.25
Steve Falteisek	R	25	0	0	—	0	3	0	0	8	3	2	2	0	3.38
Shayne Bennett	R	25	0	0	—	0	23	0	0	23	28	8	15	0	3.18
Lee Smith	R	39	0	1	.000	5	25	0	0	25	28	8	15	0	5.82
Everett Stull	R	25	0	0	—	0	1	1	0	7	4	1	0	0	16.20
Rheal Cormier (EJ)	L	30	0	0	—	0	1	1	0	1	1	1	0	0	33.75
Matt Wagner (SJ) 25															

PHILADELPHIA — 5th 68-94 .420 33 — TERRY FRANCONA

Name	G by Pos	B	AGE	G	AB	R	H	2B	3B	HR	RBI	BB	SO	SB	BA	SA
TOTALS			28	162	5443	668	1390	290	35	116	622	519	1032	92	.255	.385
Rico Brogna	1B145	L	27	148	543	68	137	36	1	20	81	33	116	12	.252	.433
Mickey Morandini	2B146 SS1	L	31	150	553	83	163	40	2	1	39	62	91	11	.295	.380
Kevin Stocker	SS147	B	27	149	504	51	134	23	5	4	40	51	91	11	.266	.355
Scott Rolen	3B155	R	22	156	561	93	159	35	3	21	92	76	138	16	.283	.469
1 Darren Daulton	OF70 1B3	L	35	84	269	46	71	13	6	11	42	54	57	4	.264	.480
2 Midre Cummings	OF54	L	25	63	208	24	63	16	4	1	23	23	30	2	.303	.433
Gregg Jefferies	OF124	B	29	130	476	68	122	25	3	11	48	53	27	12	.256	.391
Mike Lieberthal	C129	R	29	134	455	59	112	27	1	20	77	44	76	3	.246	.442
Ruben Amaro	OF72 1B1	B	32	117	175	18	41	6	1	2	21	21	24	1	.234	.314
Kevin Jordan	1B25 3B12 2B6	R	27	84	177	19	47	8	0	6	30	3	26	0	.266	.412
Derrick May	OF56	L	28	83	149	8	34	5	1	1	13	8	26	4	.228	.295
Kevin Sefcik	2B22 SS10 3B4	R	26	61	119	11	32	3	0	2	6	4	9	1	.269	.345
Tony Barron	OF53	R	30	57	189	22	54	12	1	4	24	12	38	0	.286	.423
Ricky Otero	OF42	B	25	50	151	20	38	6	2	0	3	19	15	0	.252	.318
Rex Hudler (KJ)	OF35 2B6	R	36	50	122	17	27	4	0	5	10	6	28	1	.221	.377
Rob Butler	OF25	L	27	43	89	10	26	9	1	0	13	5	8	1	.292	.416
Mark Parent	C38	R	35	39	113	4	17	3	0	8	7	39	0	.150	.177
Wendell Magee	OF38	L	24	38	115	7	23	4	0	1	9	9	20	1	.200	.261
2 Billy McMillon	OF21	L	25	24	72	10	21	4	1	2	13	6	17	2	.292	.458
Mike Robertson	1B5 OF5	L	26	22	38	3	8	2	1	0	4	6	11	1	.211	.316
Desi Relaford	SS12	B	23	15	38	3	7	1	2	0	6	5	6	3	.184	.316
Bobby Estalella	C11	R	22	13	29	9	10	1	0	4	9	7	7	0	.345	.793
Danny Tartabull (BF)	OF3	R	34	3	7	2	0	0	0	0	4	4	5	0	.000	.000
Lenny Dykstra (XJ) 34																

NAME	T	AGE	W	L	PCT	SV	G	GS	CG	IP	H	BB	SO	SHO	ERA
TOTALS		27	68	94	.420	35	162	162	13	1420	1441	616	1209	7	4.85
Curt Schilling	R	30	17	11	.607	0	35	35	7	254	208	58	319	2	2.97
Mark Leiter	R	34	10	17	.370	0	31	31	3	183	216	64	148	0	5.67
Garrett Stephenson	R	25	8	6	.571	0	20	18	2	117	104	38	81	0	3.15
Wayne Gomes	R	24	5	1	.833	0	37	0	0	43	45	24	24	0	5.27
Tyler Green (EJ-SJ)	R	27	4	4	.500	0	14	14	0	77	72	45	58	0	4.93
Jerry Spradlin	R	29	4	8	.333	1	70	0	0	82	86	27	67	0	4.74
Matt Beech	L	25	4	9	.308	0	24	24	0	137	147	57	120	0	5.07
Mike Grace (AJ)	R	27	3	2	.600	0	6	6	1	39	32	10	26	1	3.46
Calvin Maduro	R	22	3	7	.300	0	15	13	0	71	83	41	31	0	7.23
Darrin Winston	L	30	2	0	1.000	0	7	1	0	12	8	8	8	0	5.25
Ricky Bottalico	R	27	2	5	.286	34	69	0	0	74	68	42	89	0	3.65
Ken Ryan (EJ)	R	28	1	0	1.000	0	22	0	0	21	31	13	10	0	9.58
Ron Blazier	R	25	1	1	.500	0	36	0	0	54	62	21	42	0	5.03
Ryan Karp	L	27	1	1	.500	0	15	1	0	15	12	9	18	0	5.40
2 Billy Brewer (EJ)	L	29	1	2	.333	0	25	0	0	22	15	11	16	0	3.27
Reggie Harris	R	28	1	3	.250	0	50	0	0	54	55	43	45	0	5.30
Bobby Munoz	R	29	1	5	.167	0	8	7	0	33	47	15	20	0	8.91
Erik Plantenberg	L	28	0	0	—	0	35	0	0	26	25	12	12	0	4.91
Edgar Ramos (HJ)	R	22	0	2	.000	0	4	2	0	14	15	6	4	0	5.14
Mark Portugal (EJ)	R	34	0	2	.000	0	3	3	0	14	17	5	2	0	4.61
Ryan Nye	R	24	0	2	.000	0	4	2	0	12	20	9	7	0	8.25
Scott Ruffcorn (HJ)	R	27	0	3	.000	0	18	4	0	40	42	36	33	0	7.71
Michael Mimbs	L	28	0	3	.000	0	17	1	0	29	31	27	29	0	7.53

CENTRAL DIVISION

HOUSTON — 1st 84-78 .516 — LARRY DIERKER

Name	G by Pos	B	AGE	G	AB	R	H	2B	3B	HR	RBI	BB	SO	SB	BA	SA
TOTALS			29	162	5502	777	1427	314	40	133	720	633	1085	171	.259	.403
Jeff Bagwell	1B159	R	29	162	566	109	162	40	2	43	135	127	122	31	.286	.592
Craig Biggio	2B160	R	31	162	619	146	191	37	8	22	81	84	107	47	.309	.501
Tim Bogar	SS80 3B14 1B1	R	30	97	241	30	60	14	4	3	30	24	42	4	.249	.390
Sean Berry	3B85	R	31	96	301	37	77	16	2	8	43	25	53	1	.256	.422
Derek Bell	OF125	R	28	129	493	67	136	29	3	15	71	40	94	15	.276	.438
2 Chuck Carr	OF59	R	29	63	192	34	53	11	2	4	17	15	37	11	.276	.417
Luis Gonzalez	OF146 1B1	L	29	152	550	78	142	31	2	10	68	71	67	10	.258	.376
Brad Ausmus	C129	R	28	130	425	45	113	25	1	4	44	38	78	14	.266	.358
Bill Spiers	3B84 SS28 1B8 2B4	L	31	132	291	51	93	27	4	4	48	61	42	10	.320	.481
Thomas Howard	OF62	L	32	107	255	24	63	16	1	3	22	26	48	1	.247	.353
Ricky Gutierrez (BG)	SS64 3B22 2B9	R	27	102	303	33	79	14	4	3	34	21	50	5	.261	.363
James Mouton	OF61	R	28	86	180	24	38	9	1	3	23	18	30	9	.211	.322
Tony Eusebio	C43	R	30	60	164	12	45	2	0	1	18	19	27	0	.274	.305
Bobby Abreu (WJ)	OF53	L	23	59	188	22	47	10	2	3	26	21	48	7	.250	.372
Pat Listach	SS31 OF6	B	29	52	132	13	24	2	2	0	6	11	24	4	.182	.227
Ray Montgomery (SJ)	OF18	R	27	29	68	8	16	4	1	0	4	5	14	0	.235	.324
Russ Johnson	3B14 2B3	R	24	21	60	7	18	1	0	2	9	6	14	1	.300	.417
Richard Hidalgo	OF19	R	22	19	62	8	19	5	0	2	6	4	18	1	.306	.484
Ken Ramos	OF2	L	30	14	12	0	0	0	0	0	1	2	0	0	.000	.000
J.R. Phillips	1B3 OF3	L	27	13	15	2	2	0	0	1	4	0	7	0	.133	.333
2 Tony Pena	C8	R	40	9	19	2	4	3	0	0	2	2	3	0	.211	.368
Luis Rivera	SS6 2B1	R	33	7	13	2	3	0	1	0	3	1	6	0	.231	.385
Randy Knorr	C3 1B2	R	28	4	8	1	3	0	0	1	0	2	0		.375	.750

NAME	T	AGE	W	L	PCT	SV	G	GS	CG	IP	H	BB	SO	SHO	ERA
TOTALS		27	84	78	.519	37	162	162	16	1459	1379	511	1138	12	3.66
Darryl Kile	R	28	19	7	.731	0	34	34	6	256	208	94	205	4	2.57
Mike Hampton	L	24	15	10	.600	0	34	34	7	223	217	77	139	2	3.83
Ramon Garcia	R	27	8	8	.529	1	42	20	1	159	155	52	120	1	3.69
Shane Reynolds (KJ)	R	29	9	10	.474	0	30	30	2	181	189	47	152	0	4.23
Chris Holt	R	25	8	12	.400	0	33	32	0	210	211	61	95	0	3.52
Billy Wagner	L	25	7	8	.467	23	62	0	0	66	49	30	106	0	2.85
Tom Martin	L	27	5	3	.625	2	55	0	0	56	52	23	36	0	2.09
Mike Magnante	L	32	3	1	.750	1	40	0	0	48	39	11	43	0	2.27
Russ Springer	R	28	3	3	.500	3	54	0	0	55	48	27	74	0	4.23
Donne Wall	R	29	2	5	.286	0	8	8	0	42	53	16	25	0	6.26
Blas Minor	R	31	1	0	1.000	1	11	0	0	12	13	5	6	0	4.50
Sid Fernandez (AJ)	L	34	1	0	1.000	0	4	5	0	15	4	2	3	0	3.60
John Hudek	R	30	1	3	.250	4	40	0	0	41	36	33	36	0	5.98
Jose Lima	R	24	1	6	.143	2	52	1	0	75	79	16	63	0	5.28
Jose Cabrera	R	25	0	0	—	0	12	0	0	15	6	6	18	0	1.17
Manuel Barrios	R	22	0	0	—	0	2	0	0	3	6	3	3	0	12.00
Tommy Greene (SJ)	R	30	0	1	.000	0	2	0	0	4	2	3	1	0	7.00
Oscar Henriquez	R	23	0	1	.000	0	4	0	0	3	2	3	0		4.50

PITTSBURGH — 2nd 79-83 .488 5 — GENE LAMONT

Name	G by Pos	B	AGE	G	AB	R	H	2B	3B	HR	RBI	BB	SO	SB	BA	SA
TOTALS			27	162	5503	725	1440	291	52	129	686	481	1161	160	.262	.404
Kevin Young (BG)	1B77 3B12 OF11	R	28	97	333	59	100	18	3	18	74	16	89	11	.300	.535
Tony Womack	2B152 SS4	L	27	155	641	85	178	26	9	6	50	43	109	60	.278	.374
Kevin Polcovich	SS80 2B2 3B1	R	28	84	245	37	67	16	1	4	21	21	45	2	.273	.396
Joe Randa	3B120 2B13	R	27	126	443	58	134	27	9	7	60	41	64	4	.302	.451
Jose Guillen	OF136	R	21	143	498	58	133	20	5	14	70	17	88	1	.267	.412
Jermaine Allensworth (BH)	OF104	R	25	108	369	55	94	18	2	3	43	44	79	14	.255	.339
Al Martin (HJ)	OF110	L	29	113	423	64	123	24	7	13	59	45	83	23	.291	.473
Jason Kendall	C142	R	23	144	486	71	143	36	4	8	49	49	53	18	.294	.434
Dale Sveum	3B47 SS28 1B21 2B2	B	33	126	306	30	80	20	1	12	47	27	81	0	.261	.451
Mark Johnson	1B63	L	29	78	219	30	47	10	0	4	29	43	78	1	.215	.315
Mark Smith	OF42 1B9	R	27	93	193	29	55	13	1	9	35	28	36	3	.285	.503
Turner Ward	OF54	B	32	71	167	33	59	16	1	7	33	18	17	4	.353	.587
Emil Brown	OF42	R	22	66	95	16	17	2	1	2	6	10	32	5	.179	.284
1 Midre Cummings	OF25	L	25	52	106	11	20	6	2	3	8	8	26	0	.189	.368
Keith Osik	C32 2B4 1B1 3B1	R	28	49	105	10	27	9	1	0	10	13	18	8	.257	.362
Adrian Brown	OF38	B	23	48	147	17	28	6	0	2	7	13	18	8	.190	.252
Kevin Elster (BW)	SS39	R	32	39	138	14	31	6	2	7	25	21	39	0	.225	.449
2 Eddie Williams	1B26	R	32	30	89	12	22	5	0	3	11	10	24	1	.247	.404
Freddy Garcia	3B10 1B2	R	24	20	40	4	6	1	0	3	5	2	13	0	.150	.400
Abraham Nunez	SS12 2B9	B	21	19	40	3	9	2	2	0	6	3	8	1	.225	.375
2 Shawon Dunston	SS18	R	34	18	71	14	28	4	1	5	16	0	11	3	.394	.690
Lou Collier	SS18	R	24	18	37	3	5	0	0	0	3	1	11	1	.135	.135

NAME	T	AGE	W	L	PCT	SV	G	GS	CG	IP	H	BB	SO	SHO	ERA
TOTALS		26	79	83	.488	41	162	162	6	1436	1503	560	1080	8	4.28
Francisco Cordova	R	25	11	8	.579	0	29	29	2	179	175	49	121	2	3.63
Esteban Loaiza	R	25	11	11	.500	0	33	32	1	196	214	56	122	0	4.13
Jon Lieber	R	27	11	14	.440	0	33	32	1	188	193	51	160	0	4.49
Jason Schmidt	R	24	10	9	.526	0	32	32	2	188	193	76	136	0	4.60
Marc Wilkins	R	26	9	5	.643	2	70	0	0	76	65	33	47	0	3.69
Steve Cooke	L	27	9	15	.375	0	32	32	0	167	184	77	109	0	4.30
Ricardo Rincon	L	27	8	4	.333	4	62	0	0	60	51	24	71	0	3.45
Jason Christiansen (SJ)	L	27	3	0	1.000	0	39	0	0	34	37	17	37	0	2.94
Matt Ruebel	L	27	3	2	.600	0	44	0	0	63	77	27	50	0	6.32
Jose Silva	R	23	2	1	.667	0	11	4	0	36	52	16	30	0	5.94
Clint Sodowsky	R	24	2	2	.500	0	45	0	0	52	49	34	51	0	3.63
Chris Peters	L	25	2	2	.500	0	31	0	0	37	38	21	17	0	4.58
John Ericks (ZJ)	R	30	1	0	1.000	0	10	0	0	9	7	4	6	0	1.93
Rich Loiselle	R	25	1	5	.167	29	72	0	0	73	76	24	66	0	3.10
1 Paul Wagner (EJ)	R	27	1	1	.500	0	3	3	0	16	17	13	9	0	3.94
Jeff Wallace	L	21	0	0	—	0	11	0	0	12	8	14	0		0.75
1 Ramon Morel	R	22	0	0	—	0	3	0	0	8	11	4	4	0	4.70
Jason Johnson	R	23	0	0	—	0	3	0	0	6	10	1	3	0	6.00
Jeff Granger	L	25	0	0	—	0	3	0	0	10	18	4	2	0	18.00
Elmer Dessens	R	25	0	0	—	0	3	0	0	9	7	4	6	0	6.00
Dave Wainhouse	R	29	0	1	.000	0	25	0	0	28	34	17	21	0	8.04

CINCINNATI — 3rd 76-86 .469 8 — RAY KNIGHT 43-56 .434 — JACK McKEON 33-30 .524

Name	G by Pos	B	AGE	G	AB	R	H	2B	3B	HR	RBI	BB	SO	SB	BA	SA
TOTALS			28	162	5484	651	1386	269	27	142	612	518	1151	190	.253	.389
Hal Morris (SJ)	1B89	L	32	96	333	42	92	20	1	1	33	23	43	3	.276	.351
Bret Boone	2B136	R	28	139	443	40	99	25	1	7	46	45	101	5	.223	.332
Barry Larkin (LJ)	SS63	R	33	73	224	34	71	17	3	4	20	47	24	14	.317	.473
Willie Greene	3B103 OF39 1B7 SS3	L	25	151	495	62	125	22	1	26	91	78	111	6	.253	.459
Reggie Sanders (NJ)	OF85	R	29	86	312	52	79	19	2	19	56	42	93	13	.253	.510
Deion Sanders	OF113	L	29	115	465	53	127	13	7	5	23	34	67	56	.273	.363
Curtis Goodwin	OF71	L	24	85	265	27	67	11	0	1	12	24	55	22	.253	.306
Joe Oliver	C106 1B4	R	31	111	349	28	90	13	0	14	43	25	58	1	.258	.415
Pokey Reese	SS110 2B8 3B8	R	24	128	397	48	87	15	4	4	26	31	82	25	.219	.287
Lenny Harris	OF42 2B20 3B13 1B11	L	32	120	238	32	65	13	1	3	28	18	18	4	.273	.374
Eddie Taubensee	C64 OF11 1B7	L	28	108	254	28	68	18	0	10	34	22	66	0	.268	.457
Eduardo Perez	1B67 OF12 3B8	R	27	106	297	44	75	18	0	16	52	29	76	5	.253	.475
Mike Kelly	OF59	R	27	73	140	27	41	13	2	6	19	10	30	6	.293	.543
2 Jon Nunnally	OF60	L	25	65	201	38	64	19	2	13	35	26	51	7	.318	.602
1 Jeff Branson	3B27 2B14 SS11	L	30	65	98	9	15	3	1	1	11	7	22	0	.153	.235
Terry Pendleton	3B32	B	36	50	113	11	28	7	0	3	14	12	24	0	.248	.354
Chris Stynes	OF38 2B8 3B3	R	24	49	198	31	69	7	1	6	28	11	13	11	.348	.485
Brook Fordyce	C30	R	27	47	96	7	20	3	0	1	9	5	14	0	.208	.292
Eric Owens	OF18 2B2	R	26	27	57	8	15	0	0	0	3	3	13	3	.263	.263
1 Ruben Sierra	OF24	B	31	25	90	6	22	4	0	0	4	1	20	0	.244	.389
Pat Watkins	OF15	R	24	16	49	5	12	1	0	1	6	1	11	0	.207	.276
Aaron Boone	3B13 2B1	R	23	16	49	5	12	4	0	0	2	1	8	0	.222	.481
2 Damian Jackson	SS6 2B3	R	23	12	27	3	6	0	0	0	3	2	7	0	.143	.143
Pete Rose	3B2 1B1	R	27	11	14	2	2	0	0	0	0	0	4	0	.143	.143
Ozzie Timmons	OF1	R	26	9	9	1	3	0	0	0	0	1	5	0	.333	.444

NAME	T	AGE	W	L	PCT	SV	G	GS	CG	IP	H	BB	SO	SHO	ERA
TOTALS		29	76	86	.469	49	162	162	6	1449	1408	558	1159	8	4.41
Brett Tomko	R	24	11	7	.611	0	22	19	0	126	106	47	95	0	3.43
Dave Burba	R	30	11	10	.524	0	30	27	2	160	157	73	131	0	4.73
1 John Smiley	L	32	9	10	.474	0	20	20	3	117	139	31	94	0	5.23
Mike Morgan	R	37	9	12	.429	0	31	30	1	162	165	49	103	0	4.78
Mike Remlinger	L	29	8	8	.500	2	69	12	2	124	100	60	145	0	4.14
Kent Mercker	L	29	8	11	.421	0	28	25	0	145	135	62	75	0	3.92
Scott Sullivan	R	26	5	3	.625	1	59	0	0	97	79	30	96	0	3.24
Pete Schourek (AJ-EJ)	L	28	5	8	.385	0	18	17	0	85	78	38	59	0	5.42
Jeff Shaw	R	30	4	2	.667	42	78	0	0	95	79	12	74	0	2.38
Gabe White	L	25	2	2	.500	1	12	6	0	41	39	8	25	0	4.39
Jeff Brantley	R	33	1	1	.500	1	13	0	0	7	9	4	7	0	3.86
Pedro Martinez	L	28	1	1	.500	0	4	0	0	7	7	8	16	0	9.45
1 Hector Carrasco	R	27	1	1	.333	0	38	0	0	51	51	25	46	0	3.68
Stan Belinda	R	30	1	5	.167	1	84	0	0	99	84	33	114	0	3.71
Felix Rodriguez	R	24	0	0	—	0	26	0	0	46	48	28	34	0	4.30
2 Danny Graves	R	24	0	0	—	0	10	0	0	15	26	11	7	0	6.14
Scott Winchester	R	24	0	0	—	0	10	0	0	15	26	4	12	0	6.00
1 Richie Lewis	R	31	0	0	—	0	14	0	0	14	14	11	9	0	6.35
1 Scott Service	R	31	0	0	—	0	1	0	0	2	4	3	2	0	11.81
Jeff Tabaka	L	33	0	0	—	0	4	0	0	2	3	2	4	0	4.50
Joey Eischen (SJ)	L	27	0	0	—	0	3	0	0	4	6	3	3	0	6.75
1 Ricky Bones	R	28	0	1	.000	0	18	0	0	31	38	11	8	0	10.19
1 Kevin Jarvis	R	28	0	1	.000	0	14	6	0	41	66	17	12	0	10.13
Giovanni Carrara	R	29	0	0	—	0	9	0	0	14	6	12	5	0	7.84
Jim Crowell	L	23	0	0	—	0	4	0	0	6	12	5	3	0	9.95
Jose Rijo (EJ) 32															

ST. LOUIS 4th 73-89 .451 11 — TONY LaRUSSA

Name	G by Pos	B	AGE	G	AB	R	H	2B	3B	HR	RBI	BB	SO	SB	BA	SA
TOTALS			31	162	5524	689	1409	269	39	144	654	543	1191	164	.255	.396
Dmitri Young	1B74 OF17	B	23	110	333	38	86	14	3	5	34	38	63		.258	.363
Delino DeShields	2B147	L	28	150	572	92	169	26	14	11	58	55	72	55	.295	.448
Royce Clayton	SS153	R	27	154	576	75	153	39	5	9	61	33	109	30	.266	.398
Gary Gaetti	3B132 1B20 P1	R	38	148	502	63	126	24	1	17	69	36	88	7	.251	.404
Brian Jordan (XJ)	OF44	R	30	47	145	17	34	5	0	0	10	10	21	6	.234	.269
Ray Lankford	OF131	L	30	133	465	94	137	36	3	31	98	95	125	21	.295	.585
Ron Gant	OF128	R	32	139	502	68	115	21	4	17	62	58	162	14	.229	.388
Tom Pagnozzi (GJ)	C13 1B2 3B1	R	34	25	50	4	11	3	0	1	8	1	7	0	.220	.340
Willie McGee	OF81	B	38	122	300	29	90	19	4	3	38	22	59	8	.300	.420
John Mabry (CJ)	OF78 1B49 3B1	L	26	116	388	40	110	19	0	5	36	39	77	0	.284	.371
Tom Lampkin	C86	L	33	108	229	28	56	8	1	7	22	28	30	2	.245	.380
Mike DiFelice	C91 1B1	R	28	93	260	16	62	10	1	4	30	19	61	1	.238	.331
Danny Sheaffer	3B30 OF22 C9 2B3	R	36	76	132	10	33	5	0	0	11	8	17	1	.250	.288
David Bell (BH)	3B35 2B23 SS13 1B1	R	24	66	142	9	30	7	2	1	12	10	28	1	.211	.310
2 Mark McGwire	1B50	R	33	51	174	38	44	3	0	*24	42	43	61	2	.253	.684
1 Mark Sweeney	OF25 1B1	L	27	44	61	5	13	3	0	0	4	9	14	0	.213	.262
2 Phil Plantier	OF32	L	28	42	113	13	29	8	0	5	18	11	27	0	.257	.460
2 Scott Livingstone	3B2 OF1	L	31	42	41	3	7	1	0	0	3	1	10	1	.171	.195
Mike Gallego	2B11 SS10 3B7	R	36	27	43	6	7	2	0	0	1	1	6	0	.163	.209
Scarborough Green	OF19	B	23	20	31	5	3	0	0	0	2	2	13	4	.097	.097
Eli Marrero	C17	R	23	17	45	4	11	0	0	2	7	2	13	4	.244	.422
Micah Franklin	OF13	B	25	17	34	6	11	0	0	2	3	3	10	0	.324	.500
Luis Ordaz	SS11	R	21	12	22	3	6	1	0	0	1	1	2	3	.273	.318
Roberto Mejia (GJ)	2B3 OF1	R	25	7	14	0	1	1	0	0	2	0	5	0	.071	.143
Jeff Berblinger	2B4	R	26	7	5	1	0	0	0	0	0	0	1	0	.000	.000
Steve Scarsone	2B2 OF2 3B1	R	31	5	10	0	1	0	0	0	0	0	2	5	.100	.100
Mike Gulan	3B3	R	26	5	9	2	0	0	0	0	1	1	5	0	.000	.000

*McGwire, also with Oakland, major league leader in HR with 58

NAME	T	AGE	W	L	PCT	SV	G	GS	CG	IP	H	BB	SO	SHO	ERA
TOTALS		29	73	89	.451	39	162	162	5	1456	1422	536	1130	3	3.88
Matt Morris	R	22	12	9	.571	0	33	33	0	217	208	69	149	0	3.19
Todd Stottlemyre	R	32	12	9	.571	0	28	28	0	181	155	65	160	0	3.88
Andy Benes	R	29	10	7	.588	0	26	26	0	177	149	61	175	0	3.10
Alan Benes (SJ)	R	25	9	9	.500	0	23	23	0	162	128	68	160	0	2.89
John Frascatore	R	27	5	2	.714	0	59	0	0	80	74	33	58	0	2.48
Curtis King	R	26	4	2	.667	0	30	0	0	29	38	11	13	0	2.76
T.J. Mathews	R	27	4	4	.500	0	40	0	0	46	41	18	46	0	2.15
Mark Petkovsek	R	31	4	7	.364	2	55	2	0	96	109	31	51	0	5.06
Donovan Osborne (GJ)	L	28	3	7	.300	0	14	14	0	80	84	23	51	0	4.93
Manny Aybar	R	25	2	4	.333	0	12	12	0	68	66	29	41	0	4.24
Tony Fossas	L	39	2	7	.222	0	71	0	0	52	62	26	41	0	3.83
Lance Painter (LJ)	L	29	1	1	.500	0	14	0	0	17	13	8	11	0	4.76
1 Rich Batchelor	R	30	1	1	.500	0	10	0	0	16	21	7	8	0	4.50
Rigo Beltran	L	27	1	2	.333	1	35	4	0	54	47	17	50	0	3.48
Brady Raggio	R	24	1	2	.333	0	15	4	0	31	44	16	21	0	6.89
1 Danny Jackson (VJ)	L	35	1	2	.333	0	4	4	0	19	26	8	13	0	7.71
Dennis Eckersley	R	42	1	5	.167	36	57	0	0	53	49	8	45	0	3.91
2 Jose Bautista	R	32	0	0	—	0	11	0	0	12	15	2	4	0	6.57
Rick Honeycutt (SJ)	L	43	0	0	—	0	5	0	0	2	5	1	2	0	13.50
Tom McGraw	L	29	0	0	—	0	2	0	0	0.1	0	0	0	0	0.00
Gary Gaetti	R	38	0	0	—	0	2	0	0	2	1	0	0	0	0.00
1 Eric Ludwick	R	25	0	1	.000	0	5	0	0	7	12	6	7	0	9.45
Sean Lowe	R	26	0	2	.000	0	6	4	0	17	27	10	8	0	9.35
2 Mike Busby	R	24	0	3	.000	0	5	5	0	14	24	4	6	0	8.79
2 Fernando Valenzuela	L	36	0	4	.000	0	5	5	0	23	22	14	10	0	5.56

CHICAGO 5th 68-94 .420 16 — JIM RIGGLEMAN

Name	G by Pos	B	AGE	G	AB	R	H	2B	3B	HR	RBI	BB	SO	SB	BA	SA
TOTALS			29	162	5489	687	1444	269	39	127	642	451	1003	116	.263	.396
Mark Grace	1B148	L	33	162	555	87	177	32	5	13	78	88	45	2	.319	.465
Ryne Sandberg	2B126	R	37	135	447	54	118	26	4	12	64	28	94	7	.264	.403
1 Shawon Dunston	SS108 OF7	R	34	114	419	57	119	18	4	9	41	8	64	29	.284	.411
Kevin Orie	3B112 SS3	R	24	114	364	40	100	23	5	8	44	39	57	2	.275	.431
Sammy Sosa	OF161	R	28	162	642	90	161	31	4	36	119	45	174	22	.251	.480
1 Brian McRae	OF107	B	29	108	417	63	100	27	5	6	28	52	62	14	.240	.372
Doug Glanville	OF138	R	26	146	474	79	142	22	5	4	35	24	46	19	.300	.392
Scott Servais	C118 1B1	R	30	122	385	36	100	21	0	6	45	24	56	0	.260	.361
Jose Hernandez	3B47 SS21 2B20 OF6 1B1	R	27	121	183	33	50	8	5	7	26	14	42	2	.273	.486
Dave Clark	OF25	L	34	102	143	19	43	8	0	5	32	19	34	1	.301	.462
1 Rey Sanchez	SS63 2B32 3B1	R	29	97	205	14	51	9	0	1	12	11	26	4	.249	.307
Dave Hansen	3B51 1B4 2B1	L	28	90	151	19	47	8	2	3	21	31	32	1	.311	.450
Tyler Houston	C41 3B12 1B2 2B1 SS1	L	26	72	196	15	51	10	0	2	28	9	35	1	.260	.342
Brant Brown	OF27 1B12	L	26	46	137	15	32	7	1	5	15	7	28	2	.234	.409
2 Lance Johnson	OF39	L	33	39	145	17	44	6	2	4	15	9	10	5	.303	.455
Brooks Kieschnick	OF27	L	25	39	90	9	18	2	0	4	12	12	21	1	.200	.356
2 Manny Alexander	SS28 2B4	R	26	33	99	11	29	3	1	1	7	8	16	2	.293	.374
Mike Hubbard	C20 3B1	R	26	29	64	4	13	0	0	1	2	2	15	0	.203	.250
Miguel Cairo	2B9 SS2	R	23	16	29	7	7	1	0	0	3	2	6	0	.241	.276
Robin Jennings	OF5	L	25	9	18	1	3	1	0	0	2	1	5	0	.167	.222
Terrell Lowery	OF6	R	26	9	14	2	4	0	0	0	0	0	3	1	.286	.286

NAME	T	AGE	W	L	PCT	SV	G	GS	CG	IP	H	BB	SO	SHO	ERA
TOTALS		28	68	94	.420	37	162	162	6	1429	1451	590	1072	4	4.44
Jeremi Gonzalez	R	22	11	9	.550	0	23	23	1	144	126	69	93	1	4.25
Kevin Foster	R	28	10	7	.588	0	26	25	1	146	141	66	118	0	4.61
Kevin Tapani (RJ)	R	33	9	3	.750	0	13	13	1	85	77	23	55	1	3.39
Steve Trachsel	R	26	8	12	.400	0	34	34	0	201	225	69	160	0	4.51
2 Mark Clark	R	29	6	1	.857	0	9	9	2	63	55	12	51	0	2.86
1 Frank Castillo	R	28	6	9	.400	0	20	19	0	98	113	44	67	0	5.42
1 Terry Mulholland	L	34	6	12	.333	0	25	25	1	157	162	45	74	0	4.07
Marc Pisciotta	R	26	3	1	.750	0	24	0	0	28	20	16	21	0	3.18
1 Turk Wendell	R	30	3	5	.375	1	52	0	0	60	53	39	54	0	4.20
Kent Bottenfield	R	28	2	3	.400	2	64	0	0	84	82	35	74	0	3.86
Terry Adams	R	24	2	9	.182	18	74	0	0	74	91	40	64	0	4.62
Ramon Tatis	L	24	1	1	.500	0	56	0	0	56	66	29	33	0	5.34
Bob Patterson	L	38	1	6	.143	0	76	0	0	59	47	10	58	0	3.34
Rodney Myers	R	28	0	0	—	0	9	0	0	12	7	6	6	0	6.00
2 Ramon Morel	R	22	0	0	—	0	3	0	0	4	3	3	3	0	4.91
1 Larry Casian	L	31	0	1	.000	0	12	0	0	10	16	2	7	0	7.45
Dave Swartzbaugh	R	29	0	1	.000	0	8	1	0	8	12	7	4	0	9.00
2 Dave Stevens	R	27	0	2	.000	0	10	0	0	13	18	7	11	0	9.64
Amaury Telemaco	R	23	0	0	—	0	10	5	0	38	47	11	29	0	6.16
1 Mel Rojas	R	30	0	4	.000	13	54	0	0	59	54	30	61	0	4.42
Miguel Batista	R	26	1	1	.500	0	11	6	0	36	36	24	27	0	5.70

WEST DIVISION

SAN FRANCISCO 1st 90-72 .556 — DUSTY BAKER

Name	G by Pos	B	AGE	G	AB	R	H	2B	3B	HR	RBI	BB	SO	SB	BA	SA
TOTALS			30	162	5485	784	1415	266	37	172	746	642	1120	121	.258	.414
J.T. Snow	1B156	B	29	157	531	81	149	36	1	28	104	96	124	6	.281	.510
Jeff Kent	2B148 1B13	R	29	155	580	90	145	38	2	29	121	48	133	11	.250	.472
Jose Vizcaino	SS147 2B5	B	29	151	568	77	151	19	7	5	50	49	87	8	.266	.350
Bill Mueller	3B122	R	26	130	390	51	114	26	3	7	44	44	71	4	.292	.428
Glenallen Hill	OF97	R	32	128	398	47	104	28	4	11	64	19	87	7	.261	.435
Darryl Hamilton	OF118	L	32	125	460	78	124	23	3	5	43	61	61	15	.270	.365
Barry Bonds	OF159	L	32	159	532	123	155	26	5	40	101	145	87	37	.291	.585
2 Brian Johnson	C55 1B2	R	29	56	179	19	50	7	2	11	27	14	26	0	.279	.525
Stan Javier	OF130 1B3	B	33	142	440	69	126	16	4	8	50	56	70	25	.286	.395
Mark Lewis	3B69 2B29	R	27	118	341	50	91	14	6	10	42	23	62	3	.267	.431
Marvin Benard	OF36	L	27	84	114	13	26	4	0	1	13	13	29	3	.228	.289
Damon Berryhill	C51 1B1	B	33	73	167	17	43	8	0	3	23	20	29	0	.257	.359
1 Rick Wilkins	C57	L	30	68	190	18	37	5	0	6	23	17	65	1	.195	.316
Rich Aurilia	SS36	R	25	46	102	16	28	8	0	5	19	8	15	1	.275	.500
1 Marcus Jensen	C28	B	24	30	74	5	11	2	0	1	3	7	23	0	.149	.216
Dante Powell	OF22	R	23	27	39	8	12	1	0	1	3	4	11	3	.308	.410
Jacob Cruz	OF11	L	24	16	25	3	4	0	0	0	3	4	4	0	.160	.200
Wilson Delgado	2B3 SS1	B	22	8	7	1	1	1	0	0	0	0	3	0	.143	.286
Doug Mirabelli	C6	R	26	7	7	0	1	0	0	0	0	0	3	0	.143	.143

NAME	T	AGE	W	L	PCT	SV	G	GS	CG	IP	H	BB	SO	SHO	ERA
TOTALS		29	90	72	.556	45	162	162	5	1446	1494	578	1044	9	4.39
Shawn Estes	L	24	19	5	.792	0	32	32	3	201	162	100	181	2	3.18
Kirk Rueter	L	26	13	6	.684	0	32	32	0	191	194	51	115	0	3.45
Mark Gardner	R	35	12	9	.571	0	30	30	2	180	188	57	136	1	4.29
Rod Beck	R	28	7	4	.636	37	73	0	0	70	67	8	53	0	3.47
Julian Tavarez	R	24	6	4	.600	0	89	0	0	88	91	34	38	0	3.87
2 Roberto Hernandez	R	32	5	2	.714	4	20	0	0	33	29	14	35	0	2.48
1 Wilson Alvarez	L	27	4	3	.571	0	11	11	0	66	54	36	69	0	4.48
Rich Rodriguez	L	34	3	5	.571	1	71	0	0	65	65	21	32	0	3.17
Doug Henry	R	33	4	5	.444	3	75	0	0	71	70	41	69	0	4.71
William VanLandingham	R	26	4	7	.364	0	18	17	0	89	80	59	52	0	4.96
Jim Poole	L	31	3	1	.750	0	63	0	0	49	73	25	26	0	7.11
Osvaldo Fernandez (EJ)	R	28	3	4	.429	0	11	11	0	56	74	15	31	0	4.95
Joe Roa	R	25	2	5	.286	0	28	3	0	66	86	20	34	0	5.21
1 Pat Rapp	R	29	1	2	.333	0	8	8	0	33	37	21	28	0	6.00
Doug Creek	L	28	1	2	.333	0	3	3	0	13	12	14	14	0	6.75
2 Danny Darwin	R	41	1	2	.250	0	10	7	0	44	51	14	30	0	4.91
1 Keith Foulke	R	24	1	5	.167	0	11	8	0	45	60	18	33	0	8.26
2 John Johnstone	R	28	0	0	—	0	13	0	0	19	15	7	15	0	7.63
Dan Carlson	R	27	0	0	—	0	6	0	0	15	20	8	14	0	7.63
Rene Arocha	R	31	0	0	—	0	6	0	0	10	17	5	7	0	11.32
1 Rich DeLucia	R	29	0	0	—	0	2	0	0	3	2	1	1	0	10.80
2 Terry Mulholland	L	34	0	1	.000	0	15	0	0	30	28	6	25	0	5.16
Cory Bailey	R	26	0	1	.000	0	7	0	0	10	15	4	5	0	8.31

LOS ANGELES 2nd 88-74 .543 2 — BILL RUSSELL

Name	G by Pos	B	AGE	G	AB	R	H	2B	3B	HR	RBI	BB	SO	SB	BA	SA
TOTALS			30	162	5544	742	1488	242	33	174	706	498	1079	131	.268	.418
Eric Karros	1B162	R	29	162	628	86	167	28	0	31	104	61	116	15	.266	.459
Wilton Guerrero	2B90 SS5	R	22	111	357	39	104	10	9	4	32	8	52	6	.291	.403
Greg Gagne	SS143	R	35	144	514	49	129	20	3	9	57	31	120	2	.251	.354
Todd Zeile	3B160	R	31	160	575	89	154	17	0	31	90	85	112	8	.268	.459
Raul Mondesi	OF159	R	26	159	616	95	191	42	5	30	87	44	105	32	.310	.541
Brett Butler	OF91	L	40	105	343	52	97	8	3	0	18	42	40	15	.283	.324
Todd Hollandsworth	OF99	L	24	106	296	39	73	24	3	4	31	17	60	5	.247	.368
Mike Piazza	C139	R	28	152	556	104	201	32	1	40	124	69	77	5	.362	.638
Roger Cedeno (PJ-BT)	OF71	B	22	80	194	31	53	10	2	3	17	25	44	9	.273	.392
Nelson Liriano	2B17 1B2 3B1 SS1	B	33	76	88	10	20	6	0	1	11	6	12	0	.227	.330
Billy Ashley	OF35	R	26	71	131	12	32	7	0	6	19	8	46	0	.244	.435
Tom Prince	C45	R	32	47	100	17	22	5	0	3	14	5	15	0	.220	.360
Eric Anthony	OF21	L	29	47	74	8	18	3	2	2	5	12	18	2	.243	.419
Wayne Kirby	OF26	L	33	46	65	6	11	2	0	0	4	10	12	0	.169	.200
2 Otis Nixon (KJ)	OF42	B	38	42	175	30	48	6	2	1	18	13	24	12	.274	.349
Juan Castro (KJ)	SS22 2B14 3B3	R	25	40	75	3	11	3	1	0	4	7	20	0	.147	.213
2 Eric Young	2B37	R	30	37	154	28	42	4	2	2	16	14	17	13	.273	.364
Tripp Cromer (EJ)	2B17 SS10 3B1	R	29	28	86	8	25	4	0	4	20	6	16	0	.291	.465
2 Darren Lewis	OF25	R	29	26	77	7	23	3	1	1	10	6	11	3	.299	.403
Karim Garcia	OF12	L	21	15	39	5	5	0	0	1	2	6	14	0	.128	.205
Chip Hale	3B2	L	32	14	12	0	1	0	0	0	1	4	3	0	.083	.083
Garey Ingram	OF7	R	26	12	9	2	4	0	0	0	2	1	1	0	.444	.444
Adam Riggs	2B8	R	24	9	4	0	1	0	0	0	1	0	2	0	.250	.250
1 Chad Fonville	2B3	B	26	9	14	1	2	1	0	0	2	0	5	0	.143	.143
2 Eddie Murray		R	41	9	7	0	2	0	0	0	1	1	6	0	.286	.286
1 Eddie Williams		R	32	8	7	0	1	0	0	0	1	1	1	0	.143	.143
Paul Konerko	1B3 3B1	R	21	6	7	1	1	0	0	0	1	1	1	0	.143	.143
Henry Blanco	1B1 3B1	R	25	3	1	1	1	0	0	0	0	0	0	0	.400	1.000

NAME	T	AGE	W	L	PCT	SV	G	GS	CG	IP	H	BB	SO	SHO	ERA
TOTALS		29	88	74	.543	45	162	162	6	1459	1325	546	1232	6	3.62
Chan Ho Park	R	24	14	8	.636	0	32	29	2	192	149	70	166	0	3.38
Hideo Nomo	R	28	14	12	.538	0	33	33	1	207	193	92	233	0	4.25
Ramon Martinez (SJ)	R	29	10	5	.667	0	22	22	1	134	123	68	120	0	3.64
Tom Candiotti	R	39	10	7	.588	0	41	18	0	135	128	40	89	0	3.60
Ismael Valdes	R	23	10	11	.476	0	30	30	0	197	171	47	140	0	2.65
1 Pedro Astacio	R	27	7	9	.438	0	26	24	2	154	151	47	115	1	4.10
Scott Radinsky	L	29	5	1	.833	3	75	0	0	62	54	21	44	0	2.89
Darren Dreifort (EJ)	R	25	5	2	.714	4	48	0	0	63	45	34	63	0	2.86
Darren Hall	R	32	3	2	.600	2	50	0	0	55	58	26	39	0	2.30
Antonio Osuna	R	24	3	4	.429	0	48	0	0	62	46	19	68	0	2.19
Dennis Reyes	L	20	2	3	.400	0	14	5	0	47	51	18	36	0	3.83
Todd Worrell	R	37	2	6	.250	35	65	0	0	60	60	23	61	0	5.28
Mike Harkey	R	30	1	0	1.000	0	10	0	0	15	12	5	6	0	4.50
Rick Gorecki	R	23	1	0	1.000	0	6	1	0	6	6	6	6	0	15.00
Mark Guthrie	L	31	1	4	.200	1	62	0	0	69	71	30	42	0	5.32
Mike Judd	R	22	0	0	—	0	1	0	0	2	2	0	0	0	0.00

COLORADO — 3rd 83-79 .512 7 — DON BAYLOR

Name	G by Pos	B	AGE	G	AB	R	H	2B	3B	HR	RBI	BB	SO	SB	BA	SA
TOTALS			31	162	5603	923	1611	269	40	239	869	562	1060	137	.288	.478
Andres Galarraga	1B154	R	36	154	600	120	191	31	3	41	140	54	141	15	.318	.585
1 Eric Young	2B117	R	30	118	468	78	132	29	6	6	45	57	37	32	.282	.408
1 Walt Weiss	SS119	B	33	121	393	52	106	23	5	4	38	66	56	5	.270	.384
Vinny Castilla	3B157	R	29	159	612	94	186	25	2	40	113	44	108	2	.304	.547
Larry Walker	OF151 1B3	L	30	153	568	143	208	46	4	49	130	78	90	33	.366	.720
Ellis Burks (GJ)	OF112	R	32	119	424	91	123	19	2	32	82	47	75	7	.290	.571
Dante Bichette	OF139	R	33	151	561	81	173	31	2	26	118	30	90	6	.308	.510
Kirt Manwaring	C100	R	31	104	337	22	76	6	4	1	27	30	78	1	.226	.276
Quinton McCracken	OF132	B	27	147	325	69	95	11	1	3	36	42	62	28	.292	.360
Jeff Reed	C78	L	34	90	256	43	76	10	0	17	47	35	55	2	.297	.535
Neifi Perez	SS45 2B41 3B2	B	24	83	313	46	91	13	10	5	31	21	43	4	.291	.444
John Vander Wal	OF9 1B5	L	31	76	92	7	16	2	0	1	11	10	33	1	.174	.228
Jason Bates	2B22 SS16 3B6	B	26	62	121	17	29	10	0	3	11	15	27	1	.240	.397
Harvey Pulliam	OF33	R	29	59	67	15	19	3	0	3	9	5	15	0	.284	.463
Todd Helton	OF15 1B8	L	23	35	93	13	26	2	1	5	11	8	11	0	.280	.484
Darnell Coles (JL)	3B3 OF2	R	35	21	22	1	7	1	0	1	2	0	6	0	.318	.500
Angel Echevarria (MJ)	OF7	R	26	15	20	4	5	2	0	0	2	0	5	0	.250	.350
2 Brian Raabe	2B1	R	29	2	3	0	1	0	0	0	0	0	1	0	.333	.333
Rene Gonzales	3B1	R	36	2	2	0	1	0	0	0	1	0	0	0	.500	.500
1 Craig Counsell		L	26	1	0	0	0	0	0	0	0	0	0	0	—	—

NAME	T	AGE	W	L	PCT	SV	G	GS	CG	IP	H	BB	SO	SHO	ERA
TOTALS		28	83	79	.512	38	162	162	9	1433	1697	566	870	5	5.25
Darren Holmes	R	31	9	2	.818	3	42	6	0	89	113	36	70	0	5.34
Roger Bailey	R	26	9	10	.474	0	29	29	5	191	210	70	84	2	4.29
Jamey Wright	R	22	8	12	.400	0	26	26	1	150	198	71	59	0	6.25
John Thomson	R	23	7	9	.438	0	27	27	2	166	193	51	106	1	4.71
2 Frank Castillo	R	28	6	3	.667	0	14	14	0	86	107	25	59	0	5.42
Kevin Ritz (SJ)	R	32	6	8	.429	0	18	18	1	107	142	46	56	0	5.87
2 Pedro Astacio	R	27	5	1	.833	0	7	7	0	49	49	14	51	0	4.25
Jerry Dipoto	R	29	5	3	.625	16	74	0	0	96	108	33	74	0	4.70
Curtis Leskanic	R	29	4	0	1.000	2	55	0	0	58	59	24	53	0	5.55
Bill Swift (TJ)	R	35	4	6	.400	0	14	13	0	65	85	26	29	0	6.34
Steve Reed	R	32	4	6	.400	6	63	0	0	62	49	27	43	0	4.04
Mike Munoz	L	31	3	3	.500	2	64	0	0	46	52	13	26	0	4.53
Mark Thompson (SJ)	R	26	3	3	.500	0	6	6	0	30	40	13	9	0	7.89
John Burke	R	27	2	5	.286	0	17	9	0	59	83	26	39	0	6.56
Bryan Rekar	R	25	1	0	1.000	0	2	2	0	9	11	6	4	0	5.79
Bobby Jones	L	25	1	1	.500	0	4	4	0	19	30	12	5	0	8.38
Jeff McCurry	R	27	1	4	.200	0	33	0	0	41	43	20	19	0	4.43
2 Tim Scott	R	30	0	0	—	0	3	0	0	3	5	2	2	0	10.13
Nate Minchey	R	27	0	0	—	0	2	2	0	2	5	1	1	0	13.50
Robbie Beckett	L	24	0	0	—	0	2	0	0	2	1	1	2	0	5.40
2 Mark Hutton	R	27	0	1	.000	0	8	1	0	13	22	7	10	0	7.11
Bruce Ruffin (EJ)	L	33	0	2	.000	7	23	0	0	22	18	18	31	0	5.32

SAN DIEGO — 4th 76-86 .469 14 — BRUCE BOCHY

Name	G by Pos	B	AGE	G	AB	R	H	2B	3B	HR	RBI	BB	SO	SB	BA	SA
TOTALS			32	162	5609	795	1519	275	16	152	761	604	1129	140	.271	.407
Wally Joyner	1B131	L	35	135	455	59	149	29	2	13	83	51	51	3	.327	.486
Quilvio Veras	2B142	B	26	145	539	74	143	23	1	3	45	72	84	33	.265	.328
Chris Gomez	SS149	R	26	150	522	62	132	19	2	5	54	53	114	5	.253	.326
Ken Caminiti	3B133	B	34	137	486	92	141	28	0	26	90	80	118	11	.290	.508
Tony Gwynn	OF143	L	37	149	592	97	220	49	2	17	119	43	28	12	.372	.547
Steve Finley	OF140	L	32	143	560	101	146	26	5	28	92	43	92	15	.261	.475
Greg Vaughn	OF94	R	31	120	361	60	78	10	0	18	57	56	110	7	.216	.393
John Flaherty	C124	R	29	129	439	38	120	21	1	9	46	33	62	4	.273	.387
Chris Jones	OF61	R	31	92	152	24	37	9	0	7	25	16	45	7	.243	.441
Archi Cianfrocco	1B39 3B38 2B12 SS5 OF2	R	30	89	220	25	54	12	0	4	26	25	80	7	.245	.355
1 Rickey Henderson	OF78	R	38	88	288	63	79	11	0	6	27	71	62	29	.274	.375
2 Mark Sweeney	OF20 1B7	L	27	71	103	11	33	4	0	2	19	11	18	2	.320	.417
Craig Shipley (LJ)	SS21 2B16 1B4 3B2	R	34	63	139	22	38	9	0	5	19	7	20	1	.273	.446
Carlos Hernandez (LJ)	C44 1B4	R	30	50	134	15	42	7	1	3	14	3	27	0	.313	.448
Trey Beamon	OF20	L	23	43	65	5	18	3	0	0	7	2	17	1	.277	.323
1 Scott Livingstone	3B3 1B2 2B1	L	31	23	26	1	4	1	0	0	3	2	1	0	.154	.192
Derrek Lee	1B21	R	21	22	54	9	14	3	0	1	4	9	24	0	.259	.370
Mandy Romero	C19	B	29	21	48	7	10	0	0	2	4	2	18	1	.208	.333
Don Slaught	C6	R	38	20	20	2	0	0	0	0	0	5	4	0	.000	.000
2 Ruben Rivera (SJ)	OF7	R	23	17	20	2	5	1	0	1	2	9	2		.250	.300
Jorge Velandia	SS6 2B5 3B3	R	22	14	29	0	3	2	0	0	1	0	7	0	.103	.172
Terry Shumpert (LJ)	2B7 OF3 3B2	R	30	13	33	4	9	3	0	1	6	3	4	0	.273	.455
2 George Arias	3B8	R	25	11	22	2	5	1	0	0	2	0	1	0	.227	.273
1 Phil Plantier (UJ)	OF3	L	28	10	8	0	1	0	0	0	0	2	3	0	.125	.125

NAME	T	AGE	W	L	PCT	SV	G	GS	CG	IP	H	BB	SO	SHO	ERA
TOTALS		27	76	86	.469	43	162	162	5	1450	1581	596	1059	2	4.98
Joey Hamilton	R	26	12	7	.632	0	31	29	1	193	199	69	124	0	4.25
Sterling Hitchcock	L	26	10	11	.476	0	32	28	1	161	172	55	106	0	5.20
Andy Ashby	R	29	9	11	.450	0	30	30	2	201	207	49	144	0	4.13
Pete Smith	R	31	7	6	.538	1	37	15	0	118	120	52	68	0	4.81
Will Cunnane	R	23	6	3	.667	0	54	8	0	91	114	49	79	0	5.81
Trevor Hoffman	R	29	6	4	.600	37	70	0	0	81	59	24	111	0	2.66
Jim Bruske	R	32	4	1	.800	0	28	0	0	45	37	25	32	0	3.63
Tim Worrell	R	29	4	8	.333	3	60	10	0	106	116	50	81	0	5.16
Doug Bochtler	R	26	3	6	.333	2	54	0	0	60	51	50	46	0	4.77
Todd Erdos	R	23	2	0	1.000	0	11	0	0	14	17	4	13	0	5.27
2 Rich Batchelor	R	30	2	0	1.000	0	13	0	0	13	19	7	10	0	7.82
Dario Veras (SJ)	R	24	2	1	.667	0	23	0	0	25	28	12	21	0	5.11
Paul Menhart	R	28	2	3	.400	0	9	8	0	44	42	13	22	0	4.70
Sean Bergman	R	27	2	4	.333	0	44	9	0	99	126	38	74	0	6.09
1 Fernando Valenzuela	L	36	2	8	.200	0	13	13	1	66	84	32	51	0	4.75
1 Tim Scott	R	30	1	1	.500	0	14	0	0	18	25	5	14	0	7.85
Heath Murray	L	24	1	2	.333	0	17	3	0	33	50	21	16	0	6.75
2 Danny Jackson	L	35	1	7	.125	0	13	9	0	49	72	20	19	0	7.53
Joey Long	R	26	0	0	—	0	10	0	0	11	17	8	8	0	8.18
Marc Kroon	R	24	0	1	.000	0	12	0	0	11	14	5	12	0	6.35
Terry Burrows	L	28	0	2	.000	0	13	0	0	10	12	8	8	0	10.45

DIVISION SERIES

LINE SCORES

DIVISION SERIES: FLORIDA 3 : SAN FRANCISCO 0

Game 1 — September 30 at Florida

Team	1	2	3	4	5	6	7	8	9	10	R	H	E
SF	0	0	0	0	0	0	1	0	0		0	4	0
FLA	0	0	0	0	0	1	0	1			2	7	0

Rueter, **Tavarez** (8), Hernandez (9)   Brown, **Cook** (8)

Game 2 — October 1 at Florida

Team	1	2	3	4	5	6	7	8	9	10	R	H	E
SF	1	1	1	1	0	0	1	0	1		6	11	0
FLA	2	0	1	2	0	1	0	0	1		7	10	2

Estes, Henry (4), Tavarez (6), Rodriguez (8), **Hernandez** (9)   Leiter, Hernandez (5), **Nen** (9)

Game 3 — October 3 at San Francisco

Team	1	2	3	4	5	6	7	8	9	10	R	H	E
FLA	0	0	0	0	0	4	0	2	0		6	10	2
SF	0	0	0	1	0	1	0	0	0		2	7	0

Fernandez, Cook (8), Nen (9)   Alvarez, Tavarez (7), Hernandez (8), Rodriguez (8), **Beck** (8)

COMPOSITE BATTING

NAME	POS	G	AB	R	H	2B	3B	HR	RBI	BA
FLORIDA										
TOTALS		3	99	15	27	5	0	4	14	.273
Alou	LF	3	14	1	3	1	0	0	1	.214
Renteria	SS	3	13	1	2	0	0	0	1	.154
Bonilla	3B	3	12	1	4	0	0	1	3	.333
Conine	1B	3	11	3	4	1	0	0	4	.364
White	CF	3	11	1	2	0	0	1	4	.182
Sheffield	RF	3	9	3	5	1	0	1		.556
Abbott	2B	3	8	0	2	0	0	0		.250
Johnson		3	8	5	2	1	0	1	2	.250
Counsell	2B	3	5	0	2	1	0	0	1	.400
Brown	P	2	2	0	0	0	0	0	0	.000
Fernandez	P	1	2	0	0	0	0	0	0	.000
Arias	PH	1	1	0	1	0	0	0	1	1.000
Cangelosi	PH	1	1	0	0	0	0	0	0	.000
Hernandez	P	1	1	0	0	0	0	0	0	.000
Leiter	P	1	1	0	0	0	0	0	0	.000
Eisenreich	PH	2	0	0	0	0	0	0	0	—
Cook	P	2	0	0	0	0	0	0	0	—
Nen	P	2	0	0	0	0	0	0	0	—
Wehner	RF	1	0	0	0	0	0	0	0	—
SAN FRANCISCO										
TOTALS		3	98	9	22	4	0	4	8	.224
Javier	RF-CF	3	12	2	5	1	0	0	1	.417
Bonds	LF	3	12	0	3	2	0	0	2	.250
Mueller	3B	3	12	1	3	0	0	1	1	.250
Vizcaino	SS	3	11	1	2	1	0	0	0	.182
Kent	2B-1B	3	10	2	3	0	0	2	2	.300
Johnson	C	3	10	2	1	0	0	1	0	.100
Hill	RF	3	7	0	0	0	0	0	0	.000
Snow	1B	3	6	0	1	0	0	0	1	.167
Lewis	2B	1	5	0	3	0	0	0	1	.600
Hamilton	CF	2	5	1	0	0	0	0	0	.000
Rueter	P	1	2	0	1	0	0	0	0	.500
Benard	PH	1	2	0	0	0	0	0	0	.000
Alvarez	P	1	2	0	0	0	0	0	0	.000
Berryhill	PH	1	1	0	0	0	0	0	0	.000
Estes	P	1	1	0	0	0	0	0	0	.000
Tavarez	P	3	0	0	0	0	0	0	0	—
Hernandez	P	2	0	0	0	0	0	0	0	—
Rodriguez	P	2	0	0	0	0	0	0	0	—
Powell	CF	1	0	0	0	0	0	0	0	—
Henry	P	1	0	0	0	0	0	0	0	—
Beck	P	1	0	0	0	0	0	0	0	—

COMPOSITE PITCHING

NAME	G	IP	H	BB	SO	W	L	SV	ERA
FLORIDA									
TOTALS	3	27	22	6	21	3	0	0	2.67
Brown	1	7	4	0	5	0	0	0	1.29
Fernandez	1	7	7	0	5	1	0	0	2.57
Hernandez	1	4	3	0	3	0	0	0	2.25
Leiter	1	4	7	3	0	0	0	0	9.00
Cook	2	3	0	1	3	1	0	0	0.00
Nen	2	2	1	2	2	1	0	0	0.00
SAN FRANCISCO									
TOTALS	3	25.2	27	19	16	0	3	0	5.26
Rueter	1	7	4	3	5	0	0	0	1.29
Alvarez	1	6	6	4	4	0	1	0	6.00
Tavarez	3	4	4	2	0	0	1	0	4.50
Estes	1	3	5	4	3	0	0	0	15.00
Henry	1	3	1	2	0	0	0	0	0.00
Beck	1	1.1	0	1	0	0	0	0	0.00
Hernandez	3	1.1	5	3	1	0	1	0	20.25
Rodriguez	2	1	1	0	0	0	0	0	0.00

LINE SCORES

Team	1	2	3	4	5	6	7	8	9	10	11		R	H	E

DIVISION SERIES: ATLANTA 3 : HOUSTON 0

Game 1   September 30 at Atlanta

| HOU | 0 | 0 | 0 | 0 | 1 | 0 | 0 | 0 | 0 | | | | 1 | 7 | 1 |
| ATL | 1 | 1 | 0 | 0 | 0 | 0 | 0 | 0 | x | | | | 2 | 2 | 0 |

Kile, Springer (8), Martin (8)   **Maddux**

Game 2   October 1 at Atlanta

| HOU | 0 | 0 | 0 | 3 | 0 | 0 | 0 | 0 | 0 | | | | 3 | 6 | 2 |
| ATL | 0 | 0 | 3 | 0 | 3 | 5 | 0 | 2 | x | | | | 13 | 10 | 1 |

Hampton, Magnante (5), Garcia (6),   **Glavine**, Cather (7), Wohlers (9)
Lima (7), Wagner (8)

Game 3   October 3 at Houston

| ATL | 1 | 1 | 0 | 0 | 0 | 0 | 1 | 1 | 0 | | | | 4 | 8 | 2 |
| HOU | 0 | 0 | 0 | 0 | 0 | 1 | 0 | 0 | | | | | 1 | 3 | 1 |

Smoltz   Reynolds, Springer (7), Martin (8),
Garcia (8), Magnante (9)

CHAMPIONSHIP: FLORIDA 4 : ATLANTA 2

Game 1   October 7 at Atlanta

| FLA | 3 | 0 | 2 | 0 | 0 | 0 | 0 | 0 | 0 | | | | 5 | 6 | 0 |
| ATL | 1 | 0 | 1 | 0 | 0 | 1 | 0 | 0 | 0 | | | | 3 | 5 | 2 |

Brown, Cook (7), Powell (8), Nen (9)   **Maddux**, Neagle (7)

Game 2   October 8 at Atlanta

| FLA | 0 | 0 | 0 | 0 | 0 | 0 | 0 | 1 | 0 | | | | 1 | 3 | 1 |
| ATL | 3 | 0 | 2 | 0 | 0 | 0 | 0 | 2 | x | | | | 7 | 13 | 0 |

Fernandez, Leiter (3), Heredia (6),   **Glavine**, Cather (8), Wohlers (9)
Vosberg (7)

Game 3   October 10 at Florida

| ATL | 0 | 0 | 0 | 1 | 0 | 1 | 0 | 0 | 0 | | | | 2 | 6 | 1 |
| FLA | 0 | 0 | 0 | 1 | 0 | 4 | 0 | 0 | x | | | | 5 | 8 | 1 |

Smoltz, Cather (7), Ligtenberg (8)   Saunders, **Hernandez** (6),
Cook (8), Nen (9)

Game 4   October 11 at Florida

| ATL | 1 | 0 | 1 | 0 | 2 | 0 | 0 | 0 | 0 | | | | 4 | 11 | 0 |
| FLA | 0 | 0 | 0 | 0 | 0 | 0 | 0 | 0 | 0 | | | | 0 | 4 | 0 |

Neagle   Leiter, Heredia (7), Vosberg (9)

Game 5   October 12 at Florida

| ATL | 0 | 1 | 0 | 0 | 0 | 0 | 0 | 0 | 0 | | | | 1 | 3 | 0 |
| FLA | 1 | 0 | 0 | 0 | 0 | 0 | 1 | 0 | x | | | | 2 | 5 | 0 |

Maddux, Cather (8)   **Hernandez**

Game 6   October 14 at Atlanta

| FLA | 4 | 0 | 0 | 0 | 0 | 3 | 0 | 0 | | | | | 7 | 10 | 1 |
| ATL | 1 | 2 | 0 | 0 | 0 | 0 | 0 | 0 | 1 | | | | 4 | 11 | 1 |

Brown   Glavine, Cather (6), Ligtenberg (7), Embree (9)

COMPOSITE BATTING

DIVISION SERIES

ATLANTA

NAME	POS	G	AB	R	H	2B	3B	HR	RBI	BA
TOTALS		3	92	19	20	4	0	3	15	.217
Lofton	CF	3	13	2	2	1	0	0	0	.154
Blauser	SS	3	10	2	3	0	0	1	4	.300
McGriff	1B	3	9	4	2	0	0	1	2	.222
C. Jones	3B	3	8	3	4	0	0	1	2	.500
Klesko	LF	3	8	2	2	1	0	1	1	.250
Lopez	C	2	7	3	2	2	0	0	1	.286
Tucker	RF	2	6	0	1	0	0	0	1	.167
Lockhart	2B	2	6	0	0	0	0	0	0	.000
A. Jones	RF	3	5	1	0	0	0	0	1	.000
Smotz	P	1	4	0	0	0	0	0	0	.000
Glavine	P	1	3	2	2	0	0	0	0	.667
Bautista	LF	3	3	0	1	0	0	0	2	.333
Graffanino	2B	2	3	0	0	0	0	0	0	.000
Perez	C	1	3	0	0	0	0	0	0	.000
Maddux	P	1	2	0	0	0	0	0	0	.000
Colbrunn	PH	1	1	0	1	0	0	0	2	1.000
Cather	P	1	1	0	0	0	0	0	0	.000
Wohlers	P	1	0	0	0	0	0	0	0	—

HOUSTON

NAME	POS	G	AB	R	H	2B	3B	HR	RBI	BA
TOTALS		3	96	5	16	1	0	1	5	.167
Bell	RF	3	13	0	0	0	0	0	0	.000
Gonzalez	LF	3	12	0	4	0	0	0	0	.333
Bagwell	1B	3	12	0	1	0	0	0	0	.083
Biggio	2B	3	12	0	1	0	0	0	0	.083
Spiers	3B	3	11	1	0	0	0	0	0	.000
Gutierrez	SS	3	8	0	1	0	0	0	0	.125
Ausmus	C	2	5	1	2	1	0	0	2	.400
Hidalgo	CF	2	5	1	0	0	0	0	0	.000
Carr	CF	2	4	1	1	0	0	1	1	.250
Eusebio	C	1	3	1	2	0	0	0	0	.667
Abreu	PH	3	3	0	1	0	0	0	0	.333
Kile	P	1	2	0	2	0	0	0	1	1.000
Hampton	P	1	2	0	1	0	0	0	1	.500
Howard	PH	2	1	0	0	0	0	0	0	.000
Berry	PH	1	1	0	0	0	0	0	0	.000
Johnson	PH	1	1	0	0	0	0	0	0	.000
Reynolds	P	1	1	0	0	0	0	0	0	.000
Pena	C	2	0	0	0	0	0	0	0	—
Magnante	P	2	0	0	0	0	0	0	0	—
Springer	P	2	0	0	0	0	0	0	0	—
Garcia	P	2	0	0	0	0	0	0	0	—
Martin	P	2	0	0	0	0	0	0	0	—
Lima	P	1	0	0	0	0	0	0	0	—
Wagner	P	1	0	0	0	0	0	0	0	—

NATIONAL LEAGUE CHAMPIONSHIP

FLORIDA

NAME	POS	G	AB	R	H	2B	3B	HR	RBI	BA
TOTALS		6	181	20	36	8	0	1	20	.199
Bonilla	3B	6	23	3	6	1	0	0	4	.261
Renteria	SS	6	22	4	5	1	0	0	1	.227
White	CF	6	21	4	4	1	0	0	1	.190
Conine	1B	6	18	1	2	0	0	0	1	.111
Sheffield	RF	6	17	6	4	0	0	1	1	.235
Johnson	C	6	17	1	2	2	0	0	5	.118
Alou	LF	5	15	0	1	1	0	0	5	.067
Counsell	2B	5	14	0	6	0	0	0	2	.429
Abbott	2B	2	8	0	3	1	0	0	0	.375
Brown	P	2	6	0	0	0	0	0	0	.000
Cangelosi	LF	3	5	0	1	0	0	0	0	.200
Daulton	1B	3	4	1	1	1	0	0	1	.250
Hernandez	P	2	3	0	0	0	0	0	0	.000
Eisenreich	LF	1	1	0	0	0	0	0	0	.000
Saunders	P	1	2	0	0	0	0	0	0	.000
Arias	3B	3	1	0	1	0	0	0	0	1.000
Leiter	P	2	1	0	0	0	0	0	0	.000
Fernandez	P	1	1	0	0	0	0	0	0	.000
Cook	P	2	0	0	0	0	0	0	0	—
Heredia	P	2	0	0	0	0	0	0	0	—
Nen	P	2	0	0	0	0	0	0	0	—
Vosberg	P	2	0	0	0	0	0	0	0	—
Powell	P	1	0	0	0	0	0	0	0	—
Zaun	C	1	1	0	0	0	0	0	0	—

ATLANTA

NAME	POS	G	AB	R	H	2B	3B	HR	RBI	BA
TOTALS		6	194	21	49	5	2	6	21	.253
Lofton	CF	6	27	3	5	0	1	0	1	.185
C. Jones	3B	6	24	5	7	1	0	2	4	.292
McGriff	1B	6	21	0	7	1	0	0	4	.333
Blauser	SS	6	20	5	6	0	0	1	1	.300
Klesko	LF	5	17	2	4	0	0	2	4	.235
Lopez	C	5	17	0	1	1	0	0	2	.059
Lockhart	2B	5	16	4	8	1	1	0	3	.500
Tucker	RF	5	10	1	1	0	0	1	1	.100
A. Jones	RF	5	9	0	4	0	0	0	1	.444
Graffanino	2B	3	8	1	2	1	0	0	0	.250
Bautista	LF	2	4	0	1	0	0	0	0	.250
Gregg	PH	4	4	0	0	0	0	0	0	.000
Colbrunn	PH	3	3	0	2	0	0	0	0	.667
Glavine	P	2	3	0	1	0	0	0	0	.333
Maddux	P	2	3	0	0	0	0	0	0	.000
Neagle	P	2	3	0	0	0	0	0	0	.000
Perez	C	2	3	0	0	0	0	0	0	.000
Smoltz	P	1	2	0	0	0	0	0	0	.000
Cather	P	4	0	0	0	0	0	0	0	—
Ligtenberg	P	2	0	0	0	0	0	0	0	—
Embree	P	1	0	0	0	0	0	0	0	—
Wohlers	P	1	0	0	0	0	0	0	0	—

COMPOSITE PITCHING

ATLANTA

NAME	G	IP	H	BB	SO	W	L	SV	ERA
TOTALS	3	27	16	8	24	3	0	0	1.67
Maddux	1	9	7	1	6	1	0	0	1.00
Smoltz	1	9	3	1	11	1	0	0	1.00
Glavine	1	6	5	4	1	1	0	0	4.50
Cather	1	2	0	1	2	0	0	0	4.50
Wohlers	1	1	1	0	1	0	0	0	0.00

HOUSTON

NAME	G	IP	H	BB	SO	W	L	SV	ERA
TOTALS	3	25	20	15	20	0	3	0	5.04
Kile	1	7	2	2	4	0	1	0	2.57
Reynolds	1	6	5	1	5	0	1	0	3.00
Hampton	1	4.2	8	2	1	0	1	0	11.57
Magnante	2	4	4	2	2	0	0	0	4.50
Springer	2	1.2	2	1	3	0	0	0	5.40
Garcia	2	1	1	1	1	0	0	0	0.00
Lima	1	1	0	1	1	0	0	0	0.00
Wagner	1	1	3	0	2	0	0	0	18.00
Martin	2	.2	1	1	0	0	0	0	0.00

FLORIDA

NAME	G	IP	H	BB	SO	W	L	SV	ERA
TOTALS	6	53	49	16	49	4	2	2	3.57
Brown	2	15	16	5	11	2	0	0	4.20
Hernandez	2	10.2	5	2	16	2	0	0	0.84
Leiter	2	8.1	13	2	6	0	1	0	4.32
Saunders	1	5.1	4	3	3	0	0	0	3.38
Heredia	2	3.1	3	2	4	0	0	0	5.40
Vosberg	2	2.2	2	1	3	0	0	0	0.00
Fernandez	1	2.2	6	1	3	0	1	0	16.88
Cook	2	2.1	0	2	0	0	0	0	0.00
Nen	2	2	0	0	0	0	0	2	0.00
Powell	1	0.2	0	1	0	0	0	0	0.00

ATLANTA

NAME	G	IP	H	BB	SO	W	L	SV	ERA
TOTALS	6	52	36	23	52	2	4	0	2.60
Glavine	2	13.1	13	11	9	1	1	0	5.40
Maddux	2	13	9	4	16	0	2	0	1.38
Neagle	2	12	5	1	9	1	0	0	0.00
Smoltz	1	6	5	9	0	1	0	0	7.50
Ligtenberg	2	3.1	0	4	0	0	0	0	0.00
Cather	4	2.2	3	0	3	0	0	0	0.00
Embree	1	1	0	1	1	0	0	0	0.00
Wohlers	1	1	0	1	1	0	0	0	0.00

LINE SCORES

Team	1	2	3	4	5	6	7	8	9	10	11		R	H	E

WORLD SERIES: FLORIDA (NL) 4 : CLEVELAND (AL) 3

Game 1   October 18 at Florida

	1	2	3	4	5	6	7	8	9	10	11	R	H	E
CLE	1	0	0	0	1	1	0	1	0			4	11	0
FLA	0	0	1	4	2	0	0	x				7	7	1

Hershiser, Juden (5), Plunk (6),   **Hernandez**, Cook (6), Powell (8), Nen (9)
Assenmacher (8)

Game 2   October 19 at Florida

	1	2	3	4	5	6	7	8	9	R	H	E
CLE	1	0	0	0	3	2	0	0	0	6	14	0
FLA	1	0	0	0	0	0	0	0	0	1	8	0

Ogea, Jackson (7), Mesa (9)   Brown, Heredia (7), Alfonseca (8)

Game 3   October 21 at Cleveland

	1	2	3	4	5	6	7	8	9	R	H	E
FLA	1	0	1	1	0	2	2	0	7	14	16	3
CLE	2	0	0	3	2	0	0	0	4	11	10	3

Leiter, Heredia (5), **Cook** (8), Nen (9)   Nagy, Anderson (7), Jackson (7),
                                              Assenmacher (8), Plunk (8), Morman (9), Mesa (9)

Game 4   October 22 at Cleveland

	1	2	3	4	5	6	7	8	9	R	H	E
FLA	0	0	0	1	0	2	0	0	0	3	6	2
CLE	3	0	3	0	0	1	1	2	x	10	15	0

Saunders, Alfonseca (3), Vosberg (6), **Wright**, Anderson (7)
Powell (8)

Game 5   October 23 at Cleveland

	1	2	3	4	5	6	7	8	9	R	H	E
FLA	0	2	0	0	0	4	0	1	1	8	15	2
CLE	0	1	3	0	0	0	0	3		7	9	0

Hernandez, Nen (9)   Hershiser, Morman (6), Plunk (6), Juden (7),
                          Assenmacher (8), Mesa (9)

Game 6   October 25 at Florida

	1	2	3	4	5	6	7	8	9	R	H	E
CLE	0	2	1	0	1	0	0	0	0	4	7	0
FLA	0	0	0	0	1	0	0	0	0	1	8	0

Ogea, Jackson (6), Assenmacher (8), Brown, Heredia (6), Powell (8), Vosberg (9)
Mesa (9)

Game 7   October 26 at Florida

	1	2	3	4	5	6	7	8	9	10	11	R	H	E
CLE	0	0	2	0	0	0	0	0	0	0	0	2	6	2
FLA	0	0	0	0	0	1	0	1	0	1	0	3	8	0

Wright, Assenmacher (7), Jackson (8), Leiter, Cook (7), Alfonseca (8), Heredia (9),
Anderson (8), Mesa (9), **Nagy** (10)   Nen (9), **Powell** (11)

COMPOSITE BATTING

NAME	POS	G	AB	R	H	2B	3B	HR	RBI	BA
FLORIDA										
TOTALS		7	250	37	68	12	1	8	34	.272
White	CF	7	33	0	8	3	1	0	2	.242
Renteria	SS	7	31	3	9	2	0	0	3	.290
Bonilla	3B	7	29	5	6	0	0	1	3	.207
Johnson	C	7	28	4	10	0	0	1	3	.357
Alou	LF	7	28	6	9	2	0	3	9	.321
Sheffield	RF	7	24	4	7	1	0	1	5	.292
Counsell	2B	7	22	4	4	1	0	0	2	.182
Daulton	1B-DH	7	18	7	7	2	0	1	2	.389
Conine	1B	6	13	1	3	0	0	0	2	.231
Eisenreich	DH-1B	5	8	1	4	0	0	1	5	.500
Cangelosi	PH	3	3	0	1	0	0	0	0	.333
Abbott	DH	3	3	0	0	0	0	0	0	.000
Brown	P	2	3	0	0	0	0	0	0	.000
Hernandez	P	2	2	0	0	0	0	0	0	.000
Floyd	DH	4	2	1	0	0	0	0	0	.000
Zaun	C	2	2	0	0	0	0	0	0	.000
Arias	3B	2	1	1	0	0	0	0	0	.000
Heredia	P	4	0	0	0	0	0	0	0	—
Nen	P	4	0	0	0	0	0	0	0	—
Powell	P	4	0	0	0	0	0	0	0	—
Alfonseca	P	3	0	0	0	0	0	0	0	—
Cook	P	3	0	0	0	0	0	0	0	—
Leiter	P	2	0	0	0	0	0	0	0	—
Vosberg	P	2	0	0	0	0	0	0	0	—
Saunders	P	1	0	0	0	0	0	0	0	—
CLEVELAND										
TOTALS		7	247	44	72	12	1	7	42	.291
Alomar	C	7	30	5	11	1	0	2	10	.367
Vizquel	SS	7	30	5	7	2	0	0	1	.233
Thome	1B	7	28	8	8	0	1	2	4	.286
Justice	LF-DH	7	27	4	5	0	0	0	4	.185
Williams	3B	7	26	8	10	1	0	1	3	.385
Ramirez	RF	7	26	3	4	0	0	2	6	.154
Grissom	CF	7	25	5	9	1	0	0	2	.360
Roberts	2B-LF	6	22	3	6	4	0	0	2	.273
Fernandez	2B	5	17	1	8	1	0	0	4	.471
Giles	LF	5	4	1	2	1	0	0	2	.500
Ogea	P	2	4	1	2	1	0	0	2	.500
Hershiser	P	2	4	0	0	0	0	0	0	.000
Jackson	P	4	2	0	0	0	0	0	0	.000
Wright	P	2	2	0	0	0	0	0	0	.000
Branson	PH	1	1	0	0	0	0	0	0	.000
Seitzer	PH	1	1	0	0	0	0	0	0	.000
Anderson	P	3	0	0	0	0	0	0	0	—
Mesa	P	5	0	0	0	0	0	0	0	—
Assenmacher	P	5	0	0	0	0	0	0	0	—
Plunk	P	3	0	0	0	0	0	0	0	—
Nagy	P	2	0	0	0	0	0	0	0	—
Juden	P	2	0	0	0	0	0	0	0	—
Morman	P	2	0	0	0	0	0	0	0	—

COMPOSITE PITCHING

NAME	G	IP	H	BB	SO	W	L	SV	ERA
FLORIDA									
TOTALS	7	64	72	40	51	4	3	2	5.48
Hernandez	2	13.2	15	10	7	2	0	0	5.27
Brown	2	11	15	5	6	0	2	0	8.18
Leiter	2	10.2	10	10	10	0	0	0	5.06
Alfonseca	3	6.1	6	1	5	0	0	0	0.00
Heredia	4	5.1	2	1	5	0	0	0	0.00
Nen	4	4.2	8	2	7	0	0	2	7.71
Powell	4	3.2	4	2	1	0	0	0	7.36
Cook	3	3.2	1	1	5	1	0	0	0.00
Vosberg	2	3	3	3	2	0	0	0	6.00
Saunders	1	2	7	3	2	0	1	0	27.00
CLEVELAND									
TOTALS	7	63.2	68	36	48	3	4	2	4.52
Wright	2	12.1	7	10	12	1	0	0	2.92
Ogea	2	11.2	11	3	5	2	0	0	1.54
Hershiser	2	10	15	6	5	0	2	0	11.70
Nagy	2	7	8	5	5	0	1	0	6.43
Mesa	5	5	10	1	5	0	0	1	5.40
Jackson	4	4.2	5	3	4	0	0	0	1.93
Assenmacher	5	4	5	0	6	0	0	0	0.00
Anderson	3	3.2	2	0	2	0	0	1	2.45
Plunk	3	3	3	4	3	0	1	0	9.00
Juden	2	2	2	2	0	0	0	0	4.50
Morman	2	0.1	0	2	1	0	0	0	0.00

MISCELLANEOUS 1997 INDIVIDUAL LEADERS

BATTING

On Base Average

	American League			National League	
1	Thomas, Chi.	.456	1	Walker, Col.	.452
	Martinez, Sea.	.456	2	Bonds, S.F.	.446
3	Thome, Cle.	.423	3	Piazza, L.A.	.431
4	Vaughn, Bos.	.420	4	Bagwell, Hou.	.425
5	Justice, Cle.	.418	5	Sheffield, Fla.	.424
6	Ramirez, Cle.	.415	6	Biggio, Hou.	.415
7	Williams, N.Y.	.408	7	Lankford, St.L.	.411
8	Greer, Tex.	.405	8	Lofton, Atl.	.409
9	O'Neill, N.Y.	.399		Gwynn, S.D.	.409
10	Salmon, Ana.	.394		Grace, Chi.	.409

On Base Average plus Slugging Average

	American League			National League	
1	Thomas, Chi.	1.067	1	Walker, Col.	1.172
2	Griffey, Sea.	1.028	2	Piazza, L.A.	1.070
3	Justice, Cle.	1.013	3	Bonds, S.F.	1.031
4	Martinez, Sea.	1.009	4	Bagwell, Hou.	1.017
5	Thome, Cle.	1.001	5	Lankford, St.L.	.996
6	Vaughn, Bos.	.980	6	Galarraga, Col.	.974
7	Ramirez, Cle.	.953	7	Gwynn, S.D.	.957
8	Williams, N.Y.	.952	8	Hundley, N.Y.	.943
9	Martinez, N.Y.	.948	9	Biggio, Hou.	.916
10	Greer, Tex.	.936	10	Castilla, Col.	.904

McGwire, Oak.-St.L. 1.039

Total Bases

	American League			National League	
1	Griffey, Sea.	393	1	Walker, Col.	409
2	Garciaparra, Bos.	365	2	Piazza, L.A.	355
3	Martinez, N.Y.	343	3	Galarraga, Col.	351
4	Thomas, Chi.	324	4	Bagwell, Hou.	335
5	Greer, Tex.	319	5	Castilla, Col.	335
6	Gonzalez, Tex.	314	6	Mondesi, L.A.	333
7	Belle, Chi.	311	7	Gwynn, S.D.	324
8	Ramirez, Cle.	302	8	Bonds, S.F.	311
9	Salmon, Ana.	301	9	Biggio, Hou.	310
10	Martinez, Sea.	300	10	Sosa, Chi.	308

McGwire, Oak.-St.L. 349

Caught Stealing

	American League			National League	
1	Hunter, Det.	18	1	Lofton, Atl.	20
2	Durham, Chi.	16	2	Mondesi, L.A.	15
	Goodwin, K.C.-Tex.	16		Renteria, Fla.	15
4	Burnitz, Mil.	13	4	DeShields, St.L.	14
	Easley, Det.	13		Young, Col.-L.A.	14
	Grissom, Cle.	13			

Stolen Base Percentage
(Minimum 20 Attempts)

	American League			National League	
1	Cameron, Chi.	91	1	Womack, Pit.	90
2	Knoblauch, Min.	86	2	Javier, S.F.	89
3	Roberts, K.C.-Cle	86	3	Henderson, S.D.	88
4	Rodriguez, Sea.	83	4	Biggio, Hou.	83
5	Nixon, Tor.	83	5	Bonds, S.F.	82

Extra Base Hits

	American League			National League	
1	Griffey, Sea.	93	1	Walker, Col.	99
2	Garciaparra, Bos.	85	2	Bagwell, Hou.	85
3	Martinez, N.Y.	77	3	Mondesi, L.A.	77
4	Belle, Chi.	76	4	Galarraga, Col.	75
5	Delgado, Tor.	75	5	Piazza, L.A.	73

McGwire, Oak.-St.L. 85

PITCHING

Fewest Hits Per 9 Innings Pitched

	American League			National League	
1	Johnson, Sea.	6.21	1	Martinez, Mon.	5.89
2	Clemens, Tor.	6.95	2	Park, L.A.	6.98
3	Cone, N.Y.	7.15	3	Estes, S.F.	7.25
4	Thompson, Det.	7.58	4	Kile, Hou.	7.32
5	Gordon, Bos.	7.64	5	Schilling, Phi.	7.36
6	Mussina, Bal.	7.89	6	Glavine, Atl.	7.39
7	Appier, K.C.	8.21	7	An. Benes, St.L.	7.58
8	Finley, Ana.	8.34	8	Stottlemyre, St.L.	7.71
9	Hentgen, Tor.	8.63	9	Maddux, Atl.	7.74
10	Wakefield, Bos.	8.63	10	Valdes, L.A.	7.83

Fewest Bases on Balls Per 9 Innings Pitched

	American League			National League	
1	Burkett, Tex.	1.43	1	Maddux, Atl.	0.77
2	Tewksbury, Min.	1.65	2	Reed, N.Y.	1.34
3	Radke, Min.	1.80	3	Neagle, Atl.	1.89
4	Wells, N.Y.	1.86	4	Schilling, Phi.	2.05
5	Moyer, Sea.	2.05	5	Perez, Mon.	2.09
6	Mussina, Bal.	2.16	6	Valdes, L.A.	2.15
7	Clemens, Tor.	2.32	7	Ashby, S.D.	2.20
8	Blair, Det.	2.37	8	Smoltz, Atl.	2.21
9	Hentgen, Tor.	2.42	9	Reynolds, Hou.	2.34
10	Pettitte, N.Y.	2.43	10	Rueter, S.F.	2.41

Strikeouts Per 9 Innings Pitched

	American League			National League	
1	Johnson, Sea.	12.30	1	Martinez, Mon.	11.37
2	Cone, N.Y.	10.25	2	Schilling, Phi.	11.29
3	Clemens, Tor.	9.95	3	Nomo, L.A.	10.11
4	Mussina, Bal.	8.73	4	An. Benes, St.L.	8.90
5	Finley, Ana.	8.51	5	Smoltz, Atl.	8.47
6	Gordon, Bos.	7.83	6	Estes, S.F.	8.10
7	Appier, K.C.	7.49	7	Stottlemyre, St.L.	7.96
8	Fassero, Sea.	7.26	8	Park, L.A.	7.78
9	Wakefield, Bos.	6.75	9	Brown, Fla.	7.77
10	Burkett, Tex.	6.61	10	Lieber, Pit.	7.65

Lowest Batting Average Allowed

	American League			National League	
1	Johnson, Sea.	.194	1	Martinez, Mon.	.184
2	Clemens, Tor.	.213	2	Park, L.A.	.213
3	Cone, N.Y.	.218	3	Estes, S.F.	.223
4	Gordon, Bos.	.226	4	Schilling, Phi.	.224
5	Thompson, Det.	.233	5	Kile, Hou.	.225

	American League			National League	
1	Watson, Ana.	37	1	Trachsel, Chi.	32
2	Witt, Tex.	33	2	Gardner, S.F.	28
3	Dickson, Ana.	32	3	Bailey, Col.	27
	Springer, Ana.	32	4	Foster, Chi.	27
5	Eldred, Mil.	31	5	Beech, Phi.	25
	Belcher, K.C.	31		Schilling, Phi.	25
	Williams, Tor.	31		Leiter, Phi.	25
	Hentgen, Tor.	31		Fernandez, Fla.	25
				Castillo, Chi.-Col.	25

Home Runs Allowed per 9 IP
(Minimum 10 Home Runs Allowed)

	American League			National League	
1	Johnson, Bal.	2.72	1	Tatis, Chi.	2.10
2	Irabu, N.Y.	2.53	2	Burke, Col.	1.98
3	Aldred, Min.	2.33	3	Schourek, Cin.	1.91
4	Jarvis, Min.-Det.	2.14	4	Worrell, L.A.	1.81
5	Guzman, Tor.	2.10	5	Foster, Chi.	1.66

1998: McGwire 70, Sosa 66

The 1998 season will be remembered as the year of the home run duel. Five players topped 50 round-trippers for the season, but what captured the fans' attention, lifted ratings, and filled ballparks was the race between Cardinal Mark McGwire and Cub Sammy Sosa to break Roger Maris' thirty-seven year-old record of 61 homers.

McGwire got off to a wonderful start and was several games ahead of Maris' pace by the All-Star break, assuring fan focus. McGwire didn't slow down, but Sosa speeded up. Their competition, conducted with mutual admiration and respect, was both intense and heartwarming, rekindling a love for the game in the hearts of many fans who had become disgruntled in the last few years. By September, the question was no longer "will the record be broken?", but "by which slugger and by how much?" Although Sosa twice drew even with McGwire, the big Cardinal first baseman was unstoppable. He broke Maris' record in fewer than 154 games, eliminating any talk of an asterisk. Then, by hitting five homers in his last three games, he set the bar at an improbable 70. Sosa, who also surpassed Maris, emerged as an equal hero. All along, he maintained that getting the Cubs to the playoffs was his most important task. That job he accomplished.

In the long run, perhaps the most important event of the season may prove to be that Bud Selig finally agreed to become full-time commissioner, but actions on the field made more headlines. Cubs' rookie Kerry Wood excited fans with big strikeout numbers; the Blue Jays' Roger Clemens put together another Cy Young-worthy season as did Pedro Martinez with his new Red Sox team. Curt Schilling struck out 300 batters for the Phillies. David Wells of the Yankees threw a perfect game; veterans David Cone and Tom Glavine returned to the 20-win club.

The near-daily individual accomplishments made up for an absence of exciting pennant races. By the All-Star Game break, four of the six divisional titles – the N.L. and A.L. East and Central Divisions – had been decided, if not mathematically, certainly in the minds of all but the most die-hard fans. A fifth race – the N.L. West – flickered into late August before being resolved. Only the A.L. West with its duel between the Anaheim Angels and the Texas Rangers went down to the wire. And even there, both teams struggled with records inferior to Boston, the second-place team in the A.L. East. By September, the only race that had any real suspense was the N.L.'s Wild Card chase. The Cubs, Giants, and the Mets staggered to the end in pursuit of a short stay in the playoffs. The Mets dropped

out by losing their last five games. On the final day of the regular season, th Cubs blew a lead, apparently ending their hopes. Then the Giants gave up a even bigger lead to the Rockies to plunge them into a tie with Chicago. The nex day, Chicago won a single-game playoff at home to earn the dubious honor o facing Atlanta in the playoffs.

In the National League East, Atlanta got a big boost with the acquisition o Andres Galarraga and the maturing of Andruw Jones and Javy Lopez. Chippe Jones also had another fine year. The Braves' bullpen was shaky but thei starters – Maddux, Glavine, Smoltz, Neagle, and Kevin Millwood – wer baseball's top rotation. The defending champion Florida Marlins went on a austerity drive and sold or traded away all their big contracts, and, unfortu nately, the players who went with them. The Fish lost 104 games. The Met hoped their acquisition of Mike Piazza would help them overcome the Braves It didn't. Houston got better results from their mid-season pickup of fireballin Randy Johnson, whose 10-1 performance helped them break away from th Cubs in the Central. In the West, San Diego built such an imposing lead the were able to overcome a September hitting dearth.

The American League focus was on the Yankees and the question of whethe they could set a new team record for victories. Although Bernie Williams wo the A.L. batting title, New York was not a team of superstars. Instead, they wo with a roster that was unusually solid and deep. Their 114 wins brok Cleveland's 1954 mark but fell short of the major league record of 116 set b the 1906 Cubs. The Bombers jumped so far out in front that Boston's second best league record went almost unnoticed. Baltimore won the cardboard rin as the most disappointing team. With baseball's biggest payroll, the Birds spen much of the year under .500 with only a remarkable comeback from life threatening cancer by Eric Davis as a bright spot. Before the Orioles' fina home game, iron man Cal Ripken Jr. voluntarily ended his consecutive gam streak at 2,633. Cleveland appeared weaker than in the last few seasons but ha no real competition in the Central. Out West, Texas knocked off the Angels i their last five meetings to edge Anaheim in baseball's only real race for division title. Juan Gonzalez proved an RBI machine for the Rangers, and wa actually ahead of Hack Wilson's 68-year-old record for half the season.

By October, some were calling 1998 "the best season ever." History wil make the final judgment, but it was certainly an interesting season and thoroughly enjoyable season – one that made baseball, for this summer at least once more America's national game.

1998 AMERICAN LEAGUE — EAST DIVISION

Name	G by Pos	B	AGE	G	AB	R	H	2B	3B	HR	RBI	BB	SO	SB	BA	SA
NEW YORK	1st 114-48 .704		JOE TORRE													
TOTALS			32	162	5643	965	1625	290	31	207	907	653	1025	153	.288	.460
Tino Martinez	1B142	L	30	142	531	92	149	33	1	28	123	61	83	2	.281	.505
Chuck Knoblauch	2B149 DH1	R	29	150	603	117	160	25	4	17	64	76	70	31	.265	.405
Derek Jeter	SS324	R	24	149	626	127	203	25	8	19	84	57	119	30	.324	.481
Scott Brosius	3B150 1B3 OF1	R	31	152	530	86	159	34	0	19	98	52	97	11	.300	.472
Paul O'Neill	OF150 DH1	L	35	152	602	95	191	40	2	24	116	57	103	15	.317	.510
Bernie Williams (KJ)	OF123 DH5	B	29	128	499	101	169	30	5	26	97	74	81	15	.339	.575
Chad Curtis	OF148 DH2	R	29	151	456	79	111	21	1	10	56	75	80	21	.243	.360
Jorge Posada	C99 DH6 1B1	B	26	111	358	56	96	23	0	17	63	47	92	0	.268	.475
Chili Davis (NJ)	DH34	B	38	35	103	11	30	7	0	3	9	14	18	0	.291	.447
Tim Raines	DH56 OF47	B	38	109	321	53	93	13	1	5	47	55	49	8	.290	.383
Darryl Strawberry	DH81 OF16	L	36	101	295	44	73	11	2	24	57	46	90	8	.247	.542
Joe Girardi	C78	R	33	78	254	31	70	11	4	3	31	14	38	2	.276	.386
Luis Sojo (BH)SS20 1B19 2B8 3B6		R	33	54	147	16	34	3	1	0	14	4	15	1	.231	.265
Homer Bush	2B24 DH13 3B3 SS2	R	25	45	71	17	27	3	0	1	5	5	19	6	.380	.465
Ricky Ledee	OF42	L	24	42	79	13	19	5	2	1	12	7	29	3	.241	.392
Dale Sveum (RC)	1B21 3B6 DH3	B	34	30	58	6	9	0	0	0	3	4	16	0	.155	.155
Shane Spencer	OF22 DH4 1B1	R	26	27	67	18	25	6	0	10	27	5	12	0	.373	.910
Mike Lowell	3B7 DH1	R	24	8	15	1	4	0	0	0	0	0	1	0	.267	.267
Mike Figga	C1	R	27	1	4	1	1	0	0	0	0	0	1	0	.250	.250

NAME	T	AGE	W	L	PCT	SV	G	GS	CG	IP	H	BB	SO	SHO	ERA
		30	114	48	.704	48	162	162	22	1457	1357	466	1080	16	3.8
David Cone	R	35	20	7	.741	0	31	31	3	208	186	59	209	0	3.5
David Wells	L	35	18	4	.818	0	30	30	8	214	195	29	163	5	3.4
Andy Pettitte	L	26	16	11	.593	0	33	32	5	216	226	87	146	0	4.2
Hideki Irabu	R	29	13	9	.591	0	29	28	2	173	148	76	126	1	4.0
Orlando Hernandez	R	32	12	4	.750	0	21	21	3	141	113	52	131	1	3.1
Ramiro Mendoza	R	26	10	2	.833	1	41	14	1	130	131	30	56	1	3.2
Jeff Nelson (XJ)	R	31	5	3	.625	3	45	0	0	40	44	22	35	0	3.7
Mike Stanton	L	31	4	1	.800	6	67	0	0	79	71	26	69	0	5.4
Mike Buddie	R	27	4	1	.800	0	24	2	0	42	46	13	20	0	5.6
Mariano Rivera	R	28	3	0	1.000	36	54	0	0	61	48	17	36	0	1.9
Graeme Lloyd	L	31	3	0	1.000	0	50	0	0	38	26	6	20	0	1.6
Ryan Bradley	R	22	2	1	.667	0	5	1	0	13	12	9	13	0	5.6
Joe Borowski	R	27	1	0	1.000	0	8	0	0	10	11	4	7	0	6.52
3 Jim Bruske	R	33	1	0	1.000	0	3	1	0	9	9	1	3	0	3.0
Jay Tessmer	R	26	1	0	1.000	0	7	0	0	9	4	4	6	0	3.12
1 Willie Banks	R	29	1	1	.500	0	9	0	0	14	20	12	8	0	10.0
Todd Erdos	R	24	0	0	—	0	2	0	0	5	1	0	0	0	9.00
Mike Jerzembeck	R	26	0	1	.000	0	2	2	0	6	9	4	1	0	12.71
Darren Holmes (XJ)	R	32	0	0	1.000	2	34	0	0	51	53	14	31	0	3.33

Name	G by Pos	B	AGE	G	AB	R	H	2B	3B	HR	RBI	BB	SO	SB	BA	SA
BOSTON	2nd 92-70 .567 22 (Wild Card)		JIMY WILLIAMS													
TOTALS			29	162	5601	876	1568	338	35	205	827	541	1049	72	.280	.463
Mo Vaughn	1B142 DH12	L	30	154	609	107	205	31	2	40	115	61	144	0	.337	.591
Mike Benjamin	2B87 SS20 3B11 1B10 DH2	R	32	124	349	46	95	23	0	4	39	15	73	3	.272	.372
Nomar Garciaparra	SS143	R	24	143	604	111	195	37	8	35	122	33	62	12	.323	.584
John Valentin	3B153 2B1	R	31	153	588	113	145	44	1	23	73	77	82	4	.247	.442
Darren Bragg	OF124 DH4	L	28	129	409	51	114	29	3	8	57	42	99	5	.279	.423
Darren Lewis	OF152 DH1	R	30	155	585	95	157	25	3	8	63	70	94	29	.268	.362
Troy O'Leary	OF155	L	28	156	611	95	165	36	8	23	83	36	108	2	.270	.468
Scott Hatteberg	C108	L	28	112	359	46	99	23	1	12	43	43	58	0	.276	.446
Reggie Jefferson (XJ)	DH48 1B7	L	29	62	196	24	60	16	1	8	31	21	40	0	.306	.520
Jason Varitek	C75 DH3	B	26	86	221	31	56	13	0	7	33	17	45	2	.253	.407
Damon Buford	OF67 DH15 2B1 3B1	R	28	86	216	37	61	14	4	10	42	22	43	5	.282	.523
Midre Cummings (WJ)	DH31 OF17	L	26	67	120	20	34	8	0	5	15	17	19	3	.283	.475
Donnie Sadler	2B50 SS4 DH4	R	23	58	124	21	28	4	4	3	15	6	28	4	.226	.395
1 Jim Leyritz	DH39 C1 1B1	R	34	52	129	17	37	6	0	8	24	21	34	0	.287	.519
2 Mike Stanley	DH34 1B13	R	35	47	156	25	45	12	0	7	32	26	43	1	.288	.500
Lou Merloni (KJ)	2B32 3B5 SS1	R	27	39	96	10	27	6	0	1	15	7	20	1	.281	.375
Mark Lemke (YJ)	2B31	B	32	31	91	10	17	4	0	0	7	6	15	0	.187	.231
Keith Mitchell	DH12 OF10	R	28	23	33	4	9	2	0	0	6	7	5	1	.273	.333
Trot Nixon	OF7 DH4	L	24	13	37	3	7	1	0	1	3	0	8	0	.259	.296
Billy Ashley	DH5 1B2 OF2	R	27	13	24	3	7	3	0	2	7	3	11	0	.292	.792
2 Mandy Romero	C4 DH3	B	30	12	13	2	3	1	0	0	3	5	3	0	.231	.308
2 Orlando Merced	OF1 DH1	L	31	5	8	0	0	0	0	0	0	1	1	0	.000	.000
2 Chris Snopek	2B3 3B3	R	27	8	12	2	2	0	0	0	0	2	4	0	.167	.167
Keith Johns	2B1 DH1	R	26	2	1	0	0	0	0	0	0	0	1	0	.000	.000
Jeff Frye (KJ) 31, Tim Naehring (EJ) 31																

NAME	T	AGE	W	L	PCT	SV	G	GS	CG	IP	H	BB	SO	SHO	ERA
		30	92	70	.568	53	162	162	5	1436	1406	504	1025	8	4.18
Pedro Martinez	R	26	19	7	.731	0	33	33	3	234	188	67	251	2	2.89
Tim Wakefield	R	31	17	8	.680	0	36	33	2	216	211	79	146	0	4.58
Bret Saberhagen	R	34	15	8	.652	0	31	31	0	175	181	29	100	0	3.96
Steve Avery	L	28	10	7	.588	0	34	23	0	124	128	64	57	0	5.02
Tom Gordon	R	30	7	4	.636	46	73	0	0	79	55	25	78	0	2.72
John Wasdin	R	25	6	4	.600	0	47	8	0	96	111	27	59	0	5.25
Dennis Eckersley (SJ)	R	43	4	1	.800	1	50	0	0	40	46	8	22	0	4.76
Jim Corsi	R	36	3	2	.600	0	59	0	0	68	58	23	49	0	2.59
Derek Lowe	R	25	3	9	.250	4	63	10	0	123	126	42	77	0	4.02
2 Greg Swindell	L	33	2	3	.400	0	29	0	0	24	25	13	18	0	3.38
Carlos Valdez	R	26	1	0	1.000	0	4	0	0	3	1	5	4	0	0.00
Rich Garces (EJ)	R	27	1	1	.500	1	30	0	0	46	36	27	34	0	3.33
2 Carlos Reyes	R	29	1	1	.500	0	24	0	0	38	35	14	23	0	3.52
Ron Mahay	L	27	1	1	.500	1	29	0	0	26	26	15	14	0	3.46
2 Pete Schourek	R	29	1	4	.250	0	10	8	0	44	45	14	36	0	4.30
Brian Rose (AJ)	R	22	1	4	.200	0	8	8	0	38	43	14	18	0	6.93
Brian Barkley	L	22	0	0	—	0	1	1	0	16	16	9	2	0	9.82
Butch Henry (KJ)	L	29	0	0	—	0	2	0	0	9	8	3	6	0	4.00
David West	L	33	0	0	—	0	3	0	0	2	7	4	1	0	27.00
Brian Shouse	L	29	0	1	.000	0	5	0	0	4	8	3	1	0	5.63
Dario Veras	R	25	0	0	.000	0	7	0	0	6	12	2	6	0	10.13
Robinson Checo	R	26	0	0	.000	0	2	0	0	8	11	5	5	0	9.39
Jin Ho Cho	R	23	0	0	—	0	4	4	0	19	28	3	15	0	8.20
Kerry Lacy (SJ) 25															

TORONTO — 3rd 88-74 .543 26 — TIM JOHNSON

Name	G by Pos	B	AGE	G	AB	R	H	2B	3B	HR	RBI	BB	SO	SB	BA	SA
TOTALS			29	163	5580	816	1482	316	19	221	776	564	1132	184	.266	.448
Carlos Delgado	1B141 DH1	L	26	142	530	94	155	43	1	38	115	73	139	3	.292	.592
Tony Fernandez	2B82 3B54 DH1	B	36	138	486	71	156	36	2	9	72	45	53	13	.321	.459
Alex Gonzalez	SS158	R	25	158	568	70	136	28	1	13	51	28	121	21	.239	.361
1 Ed Sprague	3B105	R	30	105	382	49	91	20	0	17	51	24	73	0	.238	.424
Shawn Green	OF157	L	25	158	630	106	175	33	4	35	100	50	142	35	.278	.510
Jose Cruz	OF105	R	24	105	352	55	89	14	3	11	42	57	99	11	.253	.403
Shannon Stewart	OF144	R	24	144	516	90	144	29	3	12	55	67	77	51	.279	.417
Darrin Fletcher	C121 DH1	L	31	124	407	37	115	23	1	9	52	25	39	0	.283	.410
Jose Canseco	DH78 OF73	R	33	151	583	98	138	26	0	46	107	65	159	29	.237	.518
Craig Grebeck	2B91 SS6 3B4	R	33	102	301	33	77	17	2	2	27	29	42	2	.256	.346
1 Mike Stanley	DH73 1B22 OF1	R	35	98	341	49	82	13	0	22	47	56	86	2	.240	.472
Felipe Crespo	OF42 2B8 3B2 DH2 1B1	B	25	66	130	11	34	8	1	1	15	15	27	4	.262	.362
Kevin Brown	C52	R	25	52	110	17	29	7	1	2	15	9	31	0	.264	.400
Juan Samuel	DH11 OF10 1B3 2B2	R	37	43	50	14	9	2	0	1	2	7	13	13	.180	.280
Mark Dalesandro	C18 3B8 1B2 OF1	R	30	32	67	8	20	5	0	2	14	1	6	0	.299	.463
Benito Santiago (KJ)	C15	R	33	15	29	3	9	5	0	0	4	1	6	0	.310	.483
1 Tony Phillips	OF13	B	39	13	48	9	17	5	0	1	7	9	6	0	.354	.521
Tom Evans	3B7	R	23	7	10	0	0	0	0	0	0	0	2	0	.000	.000
Tomas Perez	SS4 2B1	B	24	6	9	1	1	0	0	0	0	0	3	0	.111	.111
Kevin Witt	1B1	L	22	5	7	0	1	0	0	0	0	0	3	0	.143	.143
Patrick Lennon	OF2	R	30	2	4	1	2	2	0	0	0	0	1	0	.500	1.000

NAME	T	AGE	W	L	PCT	SV	G	GS	CG	IP	H	BB	SO	SHO	ERA
		30	88	74	.543	47	163	163	10	1465	1443	587	1154	11	4.28
Roger Clemens	R	35	20	6	.769	0	33	33	5	235	169	88	271	3	2.65
Chris Carpenter	R	23	12	7	.632	0	33	24	1	175	177	61	136	1	4.37
Pat Hentgen	R	29	12	11	.522	0	29	29	0	178	208	69	94	0	5.17
Woody Williams	R	31	10	9	.526	0	32	32	1	210	196	81	151	1	4.46
Kelvim Escobar	R	22	7	2	.700	0	22	10	0	80	72	35	72	0	3.73
1 Juan Guzman	R	31	6	12	.333	0	22	22	2	145	133	65	113	0	4.41
Dan Plesac	R	36	4	3	.571	4	78	0	0	50	41	16	55	0	3.78
Robert Person	R	28	3	1	.750	0	27	0	0	38	45	22	31	0	7.04
Paul Quantrill	R	29	3	4	.429	7	82	0	0	80	88	22	59	0	2.59
Bill Risley	R	31	3	4	.429	0	44	0	0	55	52	34	42	0	5.27
1 Randy Myers	L	35	3	4	.429	28	44	0	0	44	44	19	32	0	4.46
Carlos Almanzar	R	24	2	2	.500	0	25	0	0	29	34	8	20	0	5.34
Roy Halladay	R	21	1	0	1.000	0	2	2	1	14	9	2	13	0	1.93
2 Nerio Rodriguez	R	27	1	0	1.000	0	7	0	0	8	10	8	3	0	9.72
Dave Stieb	R	40	1	2	.333	2	19	3	0	50	58	17	27	0	4.83
Luis Andujar	R	25	0	0	—	0	5	0	0	6	12	1	0	0	9.53
Shannon Withem	R	25	0	0	—	1	3	0	0	3	3	2	2	0	3.00
3 Ben VanRyn	L	26	0	1	.000	0	10	0	0	4	6	2	3	0	9.00
Steve Sinclair	L	26	0	2	.000	0	24	0	0	15	13	5	8	0	3.60
Erik Hanson	R	33	0	3	.000	0	11	8	0	49	73	29	21	0	6.24

* Guzman, also with Baltimore, tied for league lead in losses with 16

BALTIMORE — 4th 79-83 .487 35 — RAY MILLER

Name	G by Pos	B	AGE	G	AB	R	H	2B	3B	HR	RBI	BB	SO	SB	BA	SA
TOTALS			34	162	5565	817	1520	303	11	214	783	593	903	86	.273	.447
Rafael Palmeiro	1B159 DH3	L	33	162	619	98	183	36	1	43	121	79	91	11	.296	.565
Roberto Alomar	2B144 DH3	B	30	147	588	86	166	36	1	14	56	59	70	18	.282	.418
Mike Bordick	SS150	R	32	151	465	59	121	29	1	13	51	39	65	6	.260	.411
Cal Ripken	3B161	R	37	161	601	65	163	27	1	14	61	51	68	0	.271	.389
Eric Davis	OF72 DH54	R	36	131	452	81	148	29	1	28	89	44	108	7	.327	.582
Brady Anderson	OF130 DH1	L	34	133	479	84	113	28	3	18	51	75	78	21	.236	.420
B.J. Surhoff	OF157 1B1	L	33	162	573	79	160	34	1	22	92	49	81	9	.279	.457
Lenny Webster	C102 DH4	R	33	108	309	37	88	16	0	10	46	15	38	0	.285	.434
Harold Baines	DH80	L	39	104	293	40	88	17	0	9	57	32	40	0	.300	.451
Chris Hoiles	C83 1B6 DH6	R	33	97	267	36	70	12	0	15	56	38	50	0	.262	.476
1 Joe Carter	OF50 DH32 1B1	R	38	85	283	36	70	15	1	11	34	18	48	3	.247	.424
Jeff Reboulet	2B28 SS28 3B23	R	34	79	126	20	31	6	0	1	8	19	34	0	.246	.317
2 Rich Becker	OF60 DH2	R	26	79	113	22	23	1	0	3	11	22	34	2	.204	.292
1 Jeffrey Hammonds (XJ)	OF53 DH7	R	27	63	171	36	46	12	1	6	28	26	38	7	.269	.456
1 Willie Greene	OF14 DH1	L	26	24	40	8	6	1	0	1	5	13	10	1	.150	.250
Lyle Mouton	OF16 DH2	R	29	18	39	5	12	2	0	2	7	4	8	0	.308	.513
Charlie Greene	C13	R	27	13	21	1	4	1	0	0	0	0	6	0	.190	.238
1 Ozzie Guillen	SS6 3B1	L	34	12	16	2	1	0	0	0	3	1	4	0	.063	.063
Danny Clyburn	OF8 DH1	R	24	11	25	6	7	0	1	1	3	0	10	0	.280	.400
Eugene Kingsale	OF4 DH1	B	21	11	2	1	0	0	0	0	0	0	0	0	.000	.000
Calvin Pickering	1B5 DH3	L	21	9	21	4	5	0	0	2	3	3	4	1	.238	.524
Ryan Minor	3B6 1B3 DH1	R	24	9	14	3	6	1	0	0	1	0	4	0	.429	.500
P.J. Forbes	2B7 SS1 3B1	R	30	9	10	0	1	0	0	0	2	0	0	0	.100	.100
Jesus Tavarez	OF8	R	25	8	11	2	2	0	0	1	1	2	3	0	.182	.455
Jerry Hairston	2B4	R	22	6	7	2	0	0	0	0	0	0	1	0	.000	.000
Willis Otanez (BW)	OF2	R	25	3	5	0	1	0	0	0	1	0	2	0	.200	.200

NAME	T	AGE	W	L	PCT	SV	G	GS	CG	IP	H	BB	SO	SHO	ERA
		31	79	83	.488	37	162	162	16	1431	1505	535	1065	10	4.74
Scott Erickson	R	30	16	13	.552	0	36	36	11	251	284	69	186	2	4.01
Mike Mussina	R	29	13	10	.565	0	29	29	4	206	189	41	175	2	3.49
Sidney Ponson	R	21	8	9	.471	1	31	20	0	135	157	42	85	0	5.27
Jimmy Key (SJ)	L	37	6	3	.667	0	25	11	0	79	77	23	53	0	4.20
Doug Drabek (LJ)	R	35	6	11	.353	0	23	21	1	109	138	29	55	0	7.29
Armando Benitez	R	25	5	6	.455	22	71	0	0	68	48	39	87	0	3.82
Jesse Orosco	L	41	4	1	.800	7	69	0	0	57	46	28	50	0	3.18
Arthur Rhodes (EJ)	L	28	4	4	.500	4	45	0	0	77	65	34	83	0	3.51
2 Juan Guzman	R	31	4	4	.500	0	11	11	0	66	60	33	55	0	4.23
Doug Johns	L	30	3	3	.500	1	31	10	0	87	108	32	34	0	4.57
Alan Mills	R	31	3	4	.429	2	72	0	0	77	55	50	57	0	3.74
1 Norm Charlton	L	35	2	6	.667	0	35	0	0	35	46	25	41	0	6.94
2 Pete Smith	R	31	2	6	.400	0	27	4	0	45	57	16	29	0	6.20
Scott Kamieniecki (ZJ-XJ)	R	34	2	6	.250	0	12	11	0	55	67	26	25	0	6.75
1 Nerio Rodriguez (SJ)	R	27	1	3	.250	0	6	1	0	16	16	7	13	0	5.17
Rocky Coppinger	R	24	0	0	—	0	1	0	0	1	6	1	0	0	9.75
Bobby Munoz	R	30	0	0	—	0	2	0	0	12	18	6	9	0	9.75
Richie Lewis	R	32	0	0	—	0	3	0	0	5	5	4	0	0	15.43
Joel Bennett	R	28	0	0	—	0	2	2	0	9	11	2	7	0	4.50
Radhames Dykhoff	L	23	0	0	—	0	1	0	0	2	5	1	2	0	18.00
Terry Mathews	R	33	0	1	.000	0	17	0	0	26	26	8	10	0	6.20
Chris Fussell	R	22	0	1	.000	0	3	2	0	10	11	9	8	0	8.38

* Guzman, also with Toronto, tied for league lead in losses with 16

TAMPA BAY — 5th 63-99 .388 51 — LARRY ROTHSCHILD

Name	G by Pos	B	AGE	G	AB	R	H	2B	3B	HR	RBI	BB	SO	SB	BA	SA
TOTALS			29	162	5555	620	1450	267	43	111	579	473	1107	120	.261	.385
Fred McGriff	1B135 DH14	L	34	151	564	73	160	33	0	19	81	79	118	7	.284	.443
Miguel Cairo	2B148 DH2	R	24	150	515	49	138	26	5	5	46	24	44	19	.268	.367
Kevin Stocker (BW)	SS110	B	28	112	336	37	70	11	3	6	25	27	80	5	.208	.313
Bobby Smith	3B97 SS7 DH7 2B6	R	24	117	370	44	102	15	3	11	55	34	110	5	.276	.422
Dave Martinez (LJ)	OF86 1B1 DH1	L	33	90	309	31	79	11	0	3	20	35	52	8	.256	.320
Quinton McCracken	OF153	R	28	155	614	77	179	38	7	7	59	41	107	19	.292	.410
Mike Kelly	OF93 DH6	R	28	106	279	39	67	11	2	10	33	24	88	6	.240	.401
John Flaherty	C91	R	30	91	304	21	63	11	0	3	24	22	46	0	.207	.273
Paul Sorrento	DH86 1B27 OF18	L	32	137	435	40	98	27	0	17	57	54	133	2	.225	.405
Wade Boggs	3B78 DH33	L	40	123	435	51	122	23	4	7	52	46	54	3	.280	.400
Randy Winn	OF96 DH4	B	24	109	338	51	94	9	9	1	17	29	69	26	.278	.367
Aaron Ledesma	SS58 2B19 3B7 DH6 1B2	R	27	95	299	30	97	16	3	0	29	9	51	9	.324	.398
Mike DiFelice	C84	R	28	84	248	17	57	12	3	3	23	15	56	0	.230	.339
Rich Butler (BH)	OF61	L	25	72	217	25	49	3	3	7	20	15	37	4	.226	.364
Bubba Trammell	OF37 DH19	R	26	59	199	28	57	18	1	12	35	16	45	0	.286	.568
Jerome Walton	OF8 DH3	R	32	12	34	4	11	3	0	0	3	2	6	0	.324	.412
Scott McClain	1B5 3B3	R	26	9	20	2	2	0	0	0	0	0	5	0	.100	.100
Dave Silvestri	3B3 2B2 DH2 SS1	R	30	8	14	0	1	0	0	0	0	1	5	0	.071	.071
1 Tim Laker	C2 DH1	R	28	3	5	1	1	0	0	0	0	0	2	0	.200	.200
Kerry Robinson	OF2	L	24	2	1	0	0	0	0	0	0	0	1	0	.000	.000
Hebert Perry (KJ) 28																

NAME	T	AGE	W	L	PCT	SV	G	GS	CG	IP	H	BB	SO	SHO	ERA
		28	63	99	.389	28	162	162	7	1443	1425	643	1008	7	4.35
Rolando Arrojo	R	29	14	12	.538	0	32	32	2	202	195	65	152	2	3.56
Jim Mecir	R	28	7	2	.778	0	68	0	0	84	68	33	77	0	3.11
Albie Lopez	R	26	7	4	.636	1	54	0	0	80	73	32	62	0	2.60
Wilson Alvarez (SJ)	L	28	6	14	.300	0	25	25	0	143	130	68	107	0	4.73
Tony Saunders	L	24	6	15	.286	0	31	31	2	192	191	111	172	0	4.12
Esteban Yan	R	23	4	4	.556	1	64	0	0	89	78	41	77	0	3.86
2 Julio Santana	R	25	5	6	.455	0	32	19	1	140	144	58	60	0	4.23
Dennis Springer	R	33	3	11	.214	0	29	17	1	116	120	60	46	0	5.45
Jason Johnson (XJ)	R	24	2	5	.286	0	13	13	0	60	74	27	36	0	5.70
Roberto Hernandez	R	33	2	6	.250	26	67	0	0	71	55	41	55	0	4.04
Rick White	R	29	2	6	.250	0	38	3	0	69	66	23	39	0	3.80
Bryan Rekar (XJ)	R	26	2	8	.200	0	16	15	1	87	95	21	55	0	4.98
1 Terrell Wade (SJ)	L	25	1	1	.500	2	23	0	0	11	14	2	8	0	5.06
Rick Gorecki (AJ)	R	24	1	2	.333	0	3	3	0	17	15	10	7	0	4.86
Scott Aldred	L	30	0	0	—	0	48	0	0	31	33	12	21	0	3.73
Dan Carlson	R	25	0	0	—	0	10	0	0	18	25	8	16	0	7.64
Ramon Tatis (EJ)	L	25	0	0	—	0	22	0	0	23	28	16	5	0	13.89
Eddie Gaillard (EJ)	R	27	0	0	—	0	6	0	0	5	4	1	1	0	5.87
Mike Duvall	L	23	0	0	—	0	6	0	0	3	4	3	1	0	6.75
Brad Pennington	L	29	0	1	.000	0	1	0	0	1	1	3	1	0	20.25
Dave Eiland	R	31	0	1	.000	0	1	1	0	3	9	1	1	0	20.25
Matt Ruebel	L	28	0	2	.000	0	9	0	0	9	11	4	6	0	6.23
Vaughn Eshelman (SJ) 29																

CENTRAL DIVISION

CLEVELAND — 1st 89-73 .549 — MIKE HARGROVE

Name	G by Pos	B	AGE	G	AB	R	H	2B	3B	HR	RBI	BB	SO	SB	BA	SA
TOTALS			29	162	5616	850	1530	334	30	198	811	630	1061	143	.272	.448
Jim Thome (BG)	1B117 DH6	L	27	123	440	89	129	34	2	30	85	89	141	1	.293	.584
2 David Bell	2B101 3B6 1B1 SS1	R	25	107	340	37	89	21	2	10	41	22	54	0	.262	.424
Omar Vizquel	SS151	R	31	151	576	86	166	30	6	2	50	62	64	37	.288	.372
Travis Fryman	3B144 SS3 DH2	R	29	146	557	74	160	33	2	28	96	44	105	10	.287	.504
Manny Ramirez	OF148 DH2	R	26	150	571	108	168	35	2	45	145	76	121	5	.294	.599
Kenny Lofton	OF154	L	31	154	600	101	169	31	6	12	64	87	80	54	.282	.413
Brian Giles (NJ)	OF101 DH6	L	27	112	350	56	94	19	0	16	66	73	75	10	.269	.460
Sandy Alomar	C111 DH3	R	32	117	409	45	96	26	2	6	44	18	45	0	.235	.352
David Justice	DH123 OF21	L	32	146	540	94	151	39	2	21	88	76	98	3	.280	.476
Mark Whiten	OF72 DH5 P1	B	31	88	226	31	64	14	0	6	29	29	60	2	.283	.425
Jeff Branson (LJ)	2B31 3B20 1B3 SS2	L	31	63	100	6	20	4	1	1	9	3	21	0	.200	.290
1 Shawon Dunston	2B24 SS14 OF12 DH7	R	35	62	156	26	37	11	3	3	12	6	18	9	.237	.404
Pat Borders	C53 3B1	R	35	54	160	12	38	6	0	6	10	4	40	0	.238	.275
Richie Sexson	1B45 OF3 DH2	R	23	49	174	28	54	14	1	11	35	6	42	1	.310	.592
Enrique Wilson (RJ)	2B22 SS10 3B2	B	24	32	90	13	29	5	2	0	12	4	8	2	.322	.456
2 Joey Cora	2B28	L	33	24	83	16	19	4	0	0	6	11	9	2	.229	.277
1 Geronimo Berroa (FJ)	OF14 DH5	R	33	20	65	6	13	3	0	3	7	3	17	1	.200	.277
Einar Diaz	C17	R	25	17	48	8	11	1	0	0	4	3	4	0	.229	.375
1,3 Jeff Manto	3B8 1B7 2B1	R	33	15	37	8	8	1	0	2	10	4	11	0	.216	.405
2 Cecil Fielder	DH10 1B3	R	34	14	35	1	5	1	0	1	4	4	10	0	.143	.111
Torey Lovullo	2B5 3B1	B	32	8	19	4	4	0	0	0	3	3	5	0	.211	.263
Alex Ramirez	OF3	R	23	5	6	1	1	0	0	0	0	0	2	0	.125	.125
2 Matt Luke		L	27	4	1	0	0	0	0	0	0	0	1	0	.000	.000
Russell Branyan	3B1	L	22	3	3	0	0	0	0	0	0	0	3	0	.000	.000
Jolbert Cabrera	SS1	R	25	3	1	1	0	0	0	0	0	0	0	0	.000	.000
2 Jacob Cruz		L	25	1	1	0	0	0	0	0	0	0	0	0	.000	.000

NAME	T	AGE	W	L	PCT	SV	G	GS	CG	IP	H	BB	SO	SHO	ERA
		31	89	73	.549	47	162	162	9	1460	1552	563	1037	4	4.44
Charles Nagy	R	31	15	10	.600	0	33	33	2	210	250	66	120	0	5.22
Dave Burba	R	31	15	10	.600	0	32	31	0	204	210	69	132	0	4.11
Bartolo Colon	R	25	14	9	.609	0	31	31	6	204	205	79	158	2	3.71
Jaret Wright	R	22	12	10	.545	0	32	32	1	193	207	87	140	1	4.72
Dwight Gooden (SJ)	R	33	8	6	.571	0	23	23	0	134	135	51	83	0	3.76
Chad Ogea (TJ-RJ)	R	27	5	4	.556	0	19	9	0	69	74	25	43	0	5.61
Paul Shuey (GJ)	R	27	5	4	.556	2	43	0	0	51	44	25	58	0	3.00
1 Eric Plunk	R	34	3	1	.750	0	37	0	0	41	44	15	38	0	4.83
1 Jose Mesa	R	32	3	4	.429	1	44	0	0	54	61	20	35	0	5.17
1 Rick Krivda	L	28	2	0	1.000	0	11	1	0	25	24	16	10	0	3.24
2 Steve Reed	R	33	2	2	.500	0	20	0	0	26	26	8	23	0	6.66
Paul Assenmacher	L	37	2	3	.286	3	69	0	0	47	54	19	43	0	3.26
Mike Jackson	R	33	1	1	.500	40	69	0	0	64	43	13	55	0	1.55
Tom Martin	L	28	1	1	.500	0	14	0	0	15	29	12	9	0	12.89
2 Doug Jones	R	41	1	2	.333	1	23	0	0	31	34	6	28	0	3.45
Ron Villone	L	28	0	0	—	0	25	0	0	30	22	15	6	0	6.00
2 Jim Poole	L	31	0	0	—	0	9	0	0	5	3	1	11	0	5.14
2 Tim Worrell	R	30	0	0	—	0	9	0	0	9	11	3	11	0	5.06
Jason Rakers	R	31	0	0	—	0	9	0	0	9	9	3	9	0	9.00
Mark Whiten	R	31	0	0	—	0	1	0	0	3	1	6	1	0	3.00
1 Alvin Morman	L	27	0	0	—	0	31	0	0	22	21	16	16	0	5.32
Jason Jacome	L	27	0	0	—	0	5	3	0	25	5	10	3	0	14.40
Steve Karsay	R	26	0	0	—	0	11	4	0	24	31	6	13	0	5.92
John Smiley (BA) 33																

CHICAGO 2nd 80-82 .493 9   JERRY MANUEL

Name	G by Pos	B	AGE	G	AB	R	H	2B	3B	HR	RBI	BB	SO	SB	BA	SA
TOTALS			28	163	5585	861	1516	291	38	198	806	551	916	127	.271	.444
Wil Cordero	1B83 OF11	R	26	96	341	58	91	18	2	13	49	22	66	2	.267	.446
Ray Durham	2B158	R	26	158	635	126	181	35	8	19	67	73	105	36	.285	.455
Mike Caruso	SS131	L	21	133	523	81	160	17	6	5	55	14	38	22	.306	.390
Robin Ventura	3B161	L	30	161	590	84	155	31	4	21	91	79	111	1	.263	.436
Magglio Ordonez	OF145	R	24	145	535	70	151	25	2	14	65	28	53	9	.282	.415
Mike Cameron	OF138	R	25	141	396	53	84	16	5	8	43	37	101	27	.210	.336
Albert Belle	OF159 DH4	R	31	163	609	113	200	48	2	49	152	81	84	6	.328	.655
1 Chad Kreuter	C91	B	33	93	245	26	62	9	1	2	33	32	45	1	.253	.322
Frank Thomas	DH146 1B14	R	30	160	585	109	155	35	2	29	109	110	93	7	.265	.480
Greg Norton	1B79 3B11 DH2 2B1	B	25	105	299	38	71	17	2	9	36	26	77	3	.237	.398
Jeff Abbott	OF76 DH2	R	25	89	244	33	68	14	1	12	41	9	28	3	.279	.492
1 Charlie O'Brien	C57	R	38	57	164	12	43	9	0	4	18	9	31	0	.262	.390
1 Chris Snopek	SS33 2B12 3B3 1B1 OF1 DH1	R	27	53	125	17	26	2	0	1	4	14	24	3	.208	.248
Robert Machado	C34	R	25	34	111	14	23	6	0	3	15	7	22	0	.207	.342
Ruben Sierra	OF14 DH5	R	32	27	74	7	16	4	1	4	11	3	11	2	.216	.459
Craig Wilson	SS8 2B4 3B2	R	27	13	47	14	22	5	0	3	10	3	6	1	.468	.766
Mark Johnson	C7	L	22	7	23	2	2	0	0	0	1	1	8	0	.087	.261
Lou Frazier	OF3 DH1	B	33	7	7	0	0	0	0	0	0	2	0	4	.000	.000
Brian Simmons	OF5	B	24	5	19	4	7	0	0	2	6	0	2	0	.368	.684

NAME	T	AGE	W	L	PCT	SV	G	GS	CG	IP	H	BB	SO	SHO	ERA
		26	80	82	.494	42	163	163	8	1439	1569	580	911	4	5.22
Mike Sirotka	L	27	14	15	.483	0	33	33	5	212	255	47	128	0	5.06
James Baldwin	R	26	13	6	.684	0	37	24	1	159	176	60	108	0	5.32
Jaime Navarro	R	31	8	16	.333	1	37	27	1	173	223	77	71	0	6.36
John Snyder	R	23	7	2	.778	0	15	14	1	86	96	23	52	0	4.80
Jim Parque	L	23	7	5	.583	0	21	21	0	113	135	49	77	0	5.10
Carlos Castillo	R	23	6	4	.600	2	54	2	0	100	94	35	64	0	5.11
Jim Abbott	L	30	5	0	1.000	0	5	5	0	32	35	12	14	0	4.55
Bill Simas	R	26	3	3	.571	18	60	0	0	71	54	22	56	0	3.57
Keith Foulke (SJ)	R	25	3	2	.600	1	54	0	0	65	51	20	57	0	4.13
1 Jason Bere	R	27	3	7	.300	0	18	15	0	84	98	58	53	0	6.45
Scott Eyre	R	26	3	8	.273	0	33	17	0	107	114	64	73	0	5.38
Chad Bradford	R	23	2	1	.667	1	29	0	0	31	27	7	11	0	3.23
1 Matt Karchner	R	31	2	4	.333	11	32	0	0	37	33	19	30	0	5.15
Tom Fordham	L	24	1	2	.333	0	29	5	0	48	51	42	23	0	6.75
Bryan Ward	L	26	1	2	.333	0	28	0	0	27	30	7	17	0	3.33
Tony Castillo	L	35	1	2	.333	0	25	0	0	27	38	11	14	0	8.00
Todd Rizzo	L	27	0	0	—	0	9	0	0	7	12	6	3	0	13.50
Larry Casian	L	32	0	0	—	0	4	0	0	4	8	1	3	0	11.25
Mike Heathcott	R	29	0	0	—	0	2	0	0	3	2	1	3	0	3.00
Bob Howry	R	24	0	3	.000	9	44	0	0	54	37	19	51	0	3.15

KANSAS CITY 3rd 72-89 .447 16.5   TONY MUSER

Name	G by Pos	B	AGE	G	AB	R	H	2B	3B	HR	RBI	BB	SO	SB	BA	SA
TOTALS			29	161	5546	714	1459	274	40	134	686	475	984	135	.263	.399
Jeff King	1B112 DH16 3B4	R	33	131	486	83	128	17	1	24	93	42	73	10	.263	.451
Jose Offerman	2B152 DH6	B	29	158	607	102	191	28	13	7	66	89	96	45	.315	.438
Mendy Lopez	SS72 3B2	R	24	74	206	18	50	10	2	1	15	12	40	5	.243	.325
Dean Palmer	3B129 DH21	R	29	152	572	84	159	27	2	34	119	48	134	8	.278	.510
Jermaine Dye (LJ)	OF59	R	24	60	214	24	50	5	1	5	23	11	46	2	.234	.336
Johnny Damon	OF158	L	24	161	642	104	178	30	10	18	66	58	84	26	.277	.439
Jeff Conine (MJ)	OF80 1B12 DH3	R	32	93	309	30	79	26	0	8	43	26	68	3	.256	.417
Mike Sweeney	C91	R	24	92	282	32	73	18	0	8	35	24	38	2	.259	.408
Hal Morris	1B46 OF39 DH39	R	33	127	472	50	146	27	2	1	40	32	52	1	.309	.381
Larry Sutton	OF79 1B6 DH3	L	28	111	310	29	76	14	2	5	42	29	46	3	.245	.352
Shane Halter	SS66 OF9 3B8 2B6 1B1 P1	R	28	86	204	17	45	10	2	3	13	12	38	2	.221	.309
Terry Pendleton (VJ)	DH40 3B23	R	37	79	237	17	61	10	0	3	29	15	49	1	.257	.338
Sal Fasano (LJ)	C70 1B5 3B1	R	26	74	216	21	49	10	0	8	31	10	56	1	.227	.384
2 Shane Mack (XJ)	OF32 DH21	R	34	66	207	30	58	15	1	6	29	15	36	8	.280	.449
Luis Rivera	SS30 2B6 3B6	R	34	42	89	14	22	4	0	0	7	7	17	1	.247	.292
Felix Martinez	SS32 2B2	B	24	34	85	7	11	1	1	0	5	5	21	5	.129	.165
Jermaine Allensworth	OF27	R	26	30	73	15	15	5	0	0	3	9	17	1	.205	.274
Ernie Young	OF24	R	28	25	53	2	10	3	0	1	3	2	9	2	.189	.302
Jeremy Giambi	OF9 DH7	L	23	18	58	6	13	4	0	2	8	11	9	0	.224	.397
Scott Leius	3B15 SS2 DH1	R	32	17	46	2	8	0	0	0	4	1	6	0	.174	.174
Carlos Beltran	OF14	B	21	14	58	12	16	5	3	0	7	3	12	3	.276	.466
Carlos Febles	2B11	R	22	11	25	5	10	1	2	0	2	4	2	2	.400	.600
2 Tim Spehr	C11	R	31	11	25	6	6	2	0	1	2	8	3	0	.240	.440
Chris Hatcher	DH3	R	29	8	15	0	1	0	0	0	0	0	6	0	.067	.067
Dee Brown	DH3 OF2	L	20	5	3	2	0	0	0	0	0	0	0	0	.000	.000
Chris Turner	C4	L	29	4	9	0	0	0	0	0	0	1	4	0	.000	.000
Hector Ortiz	C3 1B1	R	28	4	4	1	0	0	0	0	0	0	0	0	.000	.000
Jed Hansen	2B2	R	24	4	3	0	0	0	0	0	0	0	3	0	.000	.000
1 Mike Macfarlane	C3	R	34	3	11	1	1	0	0	0	1	0	0	0	.091	.091
Joe Vitiello (GJ)	DH2	R	29	3	7	0	1	0	0	0	0	0	1	0	.143	.143
Rod Myers (SJ) 25																

NAME	T	AGE	W	L	PCT	SV	G	GS	CG	IP	H	BB	SO	SHO	ERA
		29	72	89	.447	46	161	161	6	1436	1590	568	999	5	5.15
Tim Belcher	R	36	14	14	.500	0	34	34	2	234	247	73	130	0	4.54
Pat Rapp	R	30	12	13	.480	0	32	32	1	188	208	107	132	1	5.30
Jose Rosado	L	23	8	11	.421	0	38	25	2	175	180	57	135	1	4.69
Hipolito Pichardo (EJ)	R	28	7	8	.467	1	27	18	0	112	126	43	55	0	5.13
Scott Service	R	31	4	4	.600	4	73	0	0	83	70	34	95	0	3.48
1 Chris Haney	R	29	6	6	.500	0	33	12	0	97	125	36	51	0	7.03
Glendon Rusch (SJ)	L	23	6	15	.286	0	29	24	1	155	191	50	94	1	5.88
Brian Bevil (SJ)	R	26	3	1	.750	0	39	0	0	40	47	22	47	0	6.30
Matt Whisenant	R	27	2	1	.667	2	70	0	0	61	61	33	45	0	4.90
Ricky Bones	R	29	2	2	.500	1	32	0	0	53	49	24	38	0	3.04
Brian Barber	R	25	2	4	.333	0	8	8	0	42	45	23	34	0	6.00
Jeff Montgomery	R	36	2	5	.286	36	56	0	0	56	58	22	54	0	4.98
Jim Pittsley	R	25	1	1	.500	0	39	2	0	68	88	37	44	0	6.59
Kevin Appier (SJ)	R	30	1	2	.333	0	3	3	0	15	21	5	9	0	7.80
2 Jeff Suppan	R	23	0	0	—	0	13	9	1	9	12	9	12	0	0.71
Bart Evans (NJ)	R	27	0	0	—	0	8	0	0	9	7	7	7	0	2.00
Allen McDill	L	26	0	0	—	0	7	0	0	6	9	3	6	0	10.50
Jose Santiago	R	23	0	0	—	0	2	0	0	2	4	0	2	0	9.00
Tim Byrdak	L	24	0	0	—	0	1	0	0	1	1	0	0	0	5.40
Shane Halter	R	28	0	0	—	0	1	0	0	1	0	0	0	0	0.00
Jamie Walker (SJ)	L	27	0	1	.000	0	16	0	0	17	30	3	15	0	9.87
Danny Rios	R	25	0	1	.000	0	7	0	0	9	6	6	6	0	6.14

MINNESOTA 4th 70-92 .432 19   TOM KELLY

Name	G by Pos	B	AGE	G	AB	R	H	2B	3B	HR	RBI	BB	SO	SB	BA	SA
TOTALS			29	162	5641	734	1499	285	32	115	691	506	915	112	.266	.389
David Ortiz	1B70 DH10	L	22	86	278	47	77	20	0	9	46	39	72	1	.277	.446
Todd Walker	2B140 DH1	L	25	143	528	85	167	41	3	12	62	47	65	19	.316	.473
Pat Meares	SS149	R	29	149	543	56	141	26	3	9	70	24	86	7	.260	.368
Ron Coomer	3B75 1B54 DH13 OF3	R	31	131	532	55	146	22	1	15	72	18	72	2	.274	.406
Matt Lawton	OF151	R	26	152	557	91	155	36	6	21	77	86	64	16	.278	.478
Otis Nixon (BJ)	OF108	B	39	110	448	71	133	6	6	1	20	44	56	37	.297	.344
Marty Cordova	OF115 DH4	R	28	119	438	52	111	20	2	10	69	50	103	3	.253	.377
Terry Steinbach	C119 DH4	R	36	124	422	45	102	25	2	14	54	38	89	0	.242	.410
Paul Molitor	DH115 1B9	R	41	126	502	75	141	29	5	4	69	45	41	9	.281	.382
Denny Hocking	2B47 SS28 OF24 3B11 1B2 DH2	B	28	110	198	32	40	6	1	3	15	16	44	2	.202	.288
Brent Gates	3B77 2B21 DH2 1B1 SS1	B	28	107	333	31	83	15	0	3	42	36	46	3	.249	.321
Alex Ochoa	OF74 DH8	R	26	94	249	35	64	14	2	2	25	10	35	6	.257	.353
1 Orlando Merced	1B38 OF13 DH8	L	31	63	204	22	59	12	0	5	33	17	29	1	.289	.422
Javier Valentin	C53 DH1	B	22	55	162	11	32	7	1	3	18	11	30	0	.198	.309
Chris Latham	OF32	B	25	34	94	14	15	1	0	1	5	13	36	4	.160	.202
Jon Shave	3B15 1B1 SS1 DH1	R	30	19	40	7	10	3	0	1	5	3	10	1	.250	.400
Corey Koskie	3B10	L	25	11	29	2	4	0	0	1	2	2	10	0	.138	.241
Scott Stahoviak	1B4 OF1	L	28	9	19	1	2	1	0	0	1	0	7	0	.105	.263
Doug Mientkiewicz	1B8	L	24	8	25	1	5	1	0	0	2	4	3	1	.200	.240
A.J. Pierzynski	C6	L	21	9	7	10	1	3	0	0	1	1	2	0	.300	.300
Torii Hunter	OF6	R	22	6	17	0	4	1	0	0	2	2	6	0	.235	.294

NAME	T	AGE	W	L	PCT	SV	G	GS	CG	IP	H	BB	SO	SHO	ERA
		29	70	92	.432	42	162	162	7	1448	1622	457	952	8	4.75
Brad Radke	R	25	12	14	.462	0	32	32	5	214	238	43	146	1	4.30
Eric Milton	L	22	8	14	.364	0	32	32	1	172	195	70	107	0	5.64
Dan Serafini	L	24	7	4	.636	0	28	9	0	75	95	29	46	0	6.48
Bob Tewksbury (SJ)	R	37	7	13	.350	0	26	25	1	148	174	20	60	0	4.79
LaTroy Hawkins	R	25	7	14	.333	0	33	33	0	190	227	61	105	0	5.25
Mike Trombley	R	31	6	5	.545	1	77	1	0	97	90	41	89	0	3.63
1 Mike Morgan (MJ)	R	38	4	7	.364	0	18	17	0	98	108	24	50	0	3.49
Hector Carrasco	R	28	4	2	.667	1	63	0	0	75	73	51	46	0	4.38
Frankie Rodriguez	R	25	4	4	.500	0	20	11	0	70	88	30	62	0	6.56
Rick Aguilera	R	36	4	9	.308	38	68	0	0	74	75	15	57	0	4.24
Eddie Guardado	L	27	3	3	.500	2	52	0	0	66	66	28	53	0	4.52
1 Greg Swindell	L	33	3	3	.500	0	52	0	0	66	67	18	45	0	3.66
Benj Sampson	L	23	1	0	1.000	0	15	0	0	17	16	6	16	0	1.56
Todd Ritchie	R	26	0	1	.000	0	15	0	0	24	30	9	21	0	5.63
Travis Baptist	L	26	0	1	.000	0	13	0	0	27	34	11	11	0	5.67
Dan Naulty (GJ)	R	28	0	1	.000	0	19	0	0	23	25	10	23	0	4.94
Travis Miller	L	25	0	0	—	0	14	0	0	23	25	11	23	0	3.86

DETROIT 5th 65-97 .401 24   BUDDY BELL 52-85 .380 LARRY PARRISH 13-12 .520

Name	G by Pos	B	AGE	G	AB	R	H	2B	3B	HR	RBI	BB	SO	SB	BA	SA
TOTALS			27	162	5664	722	1494	306	29	165	691	455	1070	122	.264	.415
Tony Clark	1B142 DH15	B	26	157	602	84	175	37	0	34	103	63	128	3	.291	.522
Damion Easley	2B140 SS30 DH2	R	28	153	594	84	161	38	2	27	100	39	112	15	.271	.478
Deivi Cruz	SS135	R	25	135	454	52	118	22	3	5	45	13	55	3	.260	.355
Joe Randa	3B118 2B20 1B1 DH1	R	28	138	460	56	117	21	2	9	50	41	70	8	.254	.367
Bobby Higginson	OF153 DH2	L	27	157	612	92	174	37	4	25	85	63	101	3	.284	.480
Brian Hunter	OF139	R	27	142	461	71	131	29	3	4	36	36	94	42	.284	.380
Luis Gonzalez	OF132 DH19	L	30	154	547	84	146	35	5	23	71	57	62	12	.267	.475
Paul Bako	C94	R	26	96	305	23	83	12	1	3	30	23	82	1	.272	.348
2 Geronimo Berroa	DH37 OF4	R	33	52	126	17	30	4	1	1	10	17	27	0	.238	.310
Frank Catalanotto	2B31 DH23 1B18 3B3	L	24	89	213	23	60	13	2	6	25	12	39	3	.282	.446
Gabe Alvarez	3B55 DH2	R	24	58	199	16	46	11	0	5	29	18	65	1	.231	.362
Kimera Bartee	OF29 DH10	B	25	57	98	20	19	5	1	3	5	6	36	9	.194	.357
1 Joe Oliver	C48 1B2 DH1	R	32	50	155	8	35	8	0	4	22	7	33	0	.226	.355
Juan Encarnacion (BF)	OF39 DH1	R	22	40	164	30	54	9	4	7	21	7	31	7	.329	.561
1 Bip Roberts	DH29 OF2 3B1	B	34	34	113	17	28	6	0	0	9	16	14	6	.248	.301
Andy Tomberlin	DH22 OF5	L	31	32	69	8	15	2	0	2	13	3	25	1	.217	.333
Joe Siddall	C27 OF1	L	30	29	65	3	12	3	1	0	7	4	15	0	.185	.277
Trey Beamon (BC)	DH11 OF4	L	24	28	42	4	11	3	0	0	1	2	13	1	.262	.357
Billy Ripken (KJ)	SS21 1B2 2B2 3B2 DH1	R	33	27	74	8	20	3	0	0	5	3	10	0	.270	.311
Raul Casanova	C14	B	25	16	42	4	6	0	0	1	3	5	10	0	.143	.262
2 Jeff Manto	1B10 DH6 OF1	R	33	16	30	6	8	2	1	1	3	11	11	0	.267	.433
2 Jason Wood	1B6 DH3 SS1	R	28	13	40	3	12	1	0	1	7	4	11	0	.300	.425
Gabe Kapler	OF6 DH1	R	22	7	25	3	5	1	0	0	1	1	5	0	.200	.280
Robert Fick	C3 DH2 1B1	L	24	7	11	3	4	0	1	0	3	7	1	2	.364	.818
1 Pete Incaviglia	DH4 OF1	R	34	7	14	0	1	0	0	1	1	1	6	0	.071	.071

NAME	T	AGE	W	L	PCT	SV	G	GS	CG	IP	H	BB	SO	SHO	ERA
		27	65	97	.401	32	162	162	9	1446	1551	595	947	4	4.93
Brian Moehler	R	26	14	13	.519	0	33	33	4	221	220	56	123	0	3.90
Justin Thompson	L	25	11	15	.423	0	34	34	5	222	227	79	149	0	4.05
Bryce Florie	R	28	8	9	.471	0	42	16	0	133	141	59	97	0	4.80
Seth Greisinger	R	22	6	9	.400	0	21	21	0	130	142	48	66	0	5.12
Matt Anderson	R	21	5	1	.833	0	42	0	0	44	38	31	44	0	3.27
Doug Brocail	R	31	5	2	.714	0	60	0	0	63	47	18	55	0	2.73
A.J. Sager	R	33	4	2	.667	2	31	3	0	59	79	23	23	0	6.52
Brian Powell	R	24	3	8	.273	0	18	16	0	84	110	36	46	0	6.35
Frank Castillo	R	29	3	9	.250	1	27	19	0	116	150	44	81	0	6.83
Dean Crow	R	25	2	2	.500	0	30	0	0	46	55	16	18	0	3.94
1 Tim Worrell	R	30	2	6	.250	0	15	9	0	62	66	19	47	0	5.98
Todd Jones	R	30	1	4	.200	28	65	0	0	63	58	37	64	0	4.97
Sean Runyan	L	24	1	1	.200	0	88	0	0	50	47	28	39	0	3.58
Mariano Santana	R	26	0	0	—	0	7	0	0	9	9	10	3	0	3.68
2 Will Brunson	L	28	0	0	—	0	7	2	0	9	7	1	4	0	0.00
Roberto Duran (SJ)	L	25	0	1	.000	0	15	0	0	17	17	17	12	0	5.87
Doug Bochtler	R	27	0	1	.000	0	51	0	0	67	73	42	45	0	6.15
1 Scott Sanders	R	29	0	2	.000	0	10	0	0	24	6	16	0		17.69
Denny Harriger	R	27	0	3	.000	0	7	6	0	39	46	20	25	0	6.75
Greg Keagle	R	27	0	5	.000	0	39	46				20	25	0	5.59

TEXAS — 1st 88-74 .543 — JOHNNY OATES

Name	G by Pos	B	AGE	G	AB	R	H	2B	3B	HR	RBI	BB	SO	SB	BA	SA
TOTALS			30	162	5672	940	1637	314	32	201	894	595	1045	82	.289	.462
Will Clark	1B134 DH15	L	34	149	554	98	169	41	1	23	102	72	97	1	.305	.507
Mark McLemore	2B122 DH2	B	33	126	461	79	114	15	1	5	53	89	64	12	.247	.317
Kevin Elster	SS84	R	33	84	297	33	69	10	1	8	37	33	66	0	.232	.354
Fernando Tatis	3B94	R	23	95	330	41	89	17	2	3	32	12	66	6	.270	.361
Juan Gonzalez	OF116 DH38	R	28	154	606	110	193	50	2	45	157	46	126	2	.318	.630
Tom Goodwin	OF150 DH1	L	29	154	520	102	151	13	3	2	33	73	90	38	.290	.338
Rusty Greer	OF154	L	29	155	598	107	183	31	5	16	108	80	93	2	.306	.455
Ivan Rodriguez	C139 DH6	R	26	145	579	88	186	40	4	21	91	32	88	9	.321	.513
Lee Stevens	DH72 1B37 OF7	L	30	120	344	52	91	17	4	20	59	31	93	0	.265	.512
Luis Alicea	2B45 3B26 DH18 OF2	B	32	101	259	51	71	15	3	6	33	37	40	4	.274	.425
Mike Simms	OF43 DH26 1B16	R	31	86	186	36	55	11	0	16	46	24	47	0	.296	.613
Roberto Kelly (LJ)	OF71 DH2	R	33	82	187	32	60	7	3	16	46	8	46	0	.323	.560
Domingo Cedeno	SS35 DH15 2B7	B	29	61	141	19	37	9	1	2	21	10	32	2	.262	.383
Royce Clayton	SS28	R	28	52	186	30	53	12	1	5	24	13	32	5	.285	.441
Todd Zeile	3B52	R	32	52	180	26	47	14	1	6	28	28	32	1	.261	.450
Bill Haselman	C36 DH3	R	32	40	105	11	33	6	0	6	17	3	17	0	.314	.543
Warren Newson	OF6 DH3	L	33	10	21	1	4	1	0	0	2	1	5	0	.190	.244
Scott Sheldon	3B3 SS2 1B1 DH1	R	29	7	16	0	2	0	0	0	1	1	6	0	.125	.125
Milt Cuyler	OF3 DH3	B	29	7	6	3	3	2	0	1	3	1	0	0	.500	1.333
Chris Tremie	DH2	R	28	2	3	2	1	1	0	0	0	0	1	0	.333	.667
Rob Sasser		R	23	1	1	0	0	0	0	0	0	0	0	0	.000	.000

NAME	T	AGE	W	L	PCT	SV	G	GS	CG	IP	H	BB	SO	SHO	ERA
		30	88	74	.543	46	162	162	10	1431	1624	519	994	8	4.99
Rick Helling	R	27	20	7	.741	0	33	33	4	216	209	78	164	2	4.41
Aaron Sele	R	28	19	11	.633	0	33	33	3	213	239	84	167	2	4.23
John Burkett	R	33	9	13	.409	0	32	32	0	195	230	46	131	0	5.68
Tim Crabtree	R	28	6	1	.857	0	64	0	0	85	86	35	60	0	3.59
Xavier Hernandez (SJ)	R	32	6	6	.500	1	46	0	0	58	43	30	41	0	3.73
1 Darren Oliver	L	27	6	7	.462	0	19	19	2	103	140	43	58	0	6.53
1 Bobby Witt	R	34	5	4	.556	0	14	13	0	69	95	33	30	0	7.66
2 Todd Stottlemyre	R	33	5	4	.556	0	10	10	0	60	68	30	57	0	4.33
John Wetteland	R	31	3	1	.750	42	63	0	0	62	47	14	72	0	2.03
2 Esteban Loaiza	R	26	3	6	.333	0	14	14	1	79	103	22	55	0	5.90
Danny Patterson	R	27	2	5	.286	2	56	0	0	61	64	19	33	0	4.45
Scott Bailes (SJ)	L	36	1	0	1.000	0	46	0	0	40	61	11	30	0	6.47
1 Tony Fossas	L	40	1	0	1.000	0	10	0	0	7	3	4	7	0	0.00
Roger Pavlik (BG)	R	30	1	1	.500	0	5	0	0	14	16	5	8	0	3.86
1 Todd Van Poppel	R	26	1	2	.333	0	4	0	0	19	26	10	10	0	8.84
2 Gred Cadaret	L	36	1	2	.333	0	11	0	0	8	11	3	5	0	4.70
1 Julio Santana	R	25	0	0	—	0	3	0	0	5	7	4	1	0	8.44
Jonathan Johnson	R	23	0	0	—	0	1	1	0	4	5	3	0	0	8.31
Al Levine	R	30	0	1	.000	0	30	0	0	58	68	16	19	0	4.50
Matt Perisho	L	23	0	2	.000	0	2	2	0	5	15	8	2	0	27.00
Eric Gunderson	L	30	0	3	.000	0	68	0	0	68	88	19	41	0	5.19
Mark Brandenburg (TJ) 27															

ANAHEIM — 2nd 85-77 .524 3 — TERRY COLLINS

Name	G by Pos	B	AGE	G	AB	R	H	2B	3B	HR	RBI	BB	SO	SB	BA	SA
TOTALS			28	162	5630	787	1530	314	27	147	739	510	1028	93	.272	.415
Cecil Fielder	1B72 DH31	R	34	103	381	48	92	16	1	17	68	52	98	0	.241	.423
Randy Velarde (EJ-AJ)	2B51	R	35	51	188	29	49	13	1	4	26	34	42	7	.261	.404
Gary DiSarcina	SS157	R	30	157	551	73	158	39	3	3	56	21	51	11	.287	.385
Dave Hollins (SJ)	3B91 1B7 DH2	B	32	101	363	60	88	16	2	11	39	44	69	11	.242	.388
Garret Anderson	OF155	L	26	156	622	62	183	41	5	15	79	29	80	8	.294	.455
Jim Edmonds	OF153	L	28	154	599	115	184	42	1	25	91	57	114	7	.307	.506
Darin Erstad	OF72 1B70 DH2	L	24	133	537	84	159	39	3	19	82	43	77	20	.296	.486
Matt Walbeck	C104 DH2	B	28	115	338	41	87	15	2	6	46	30	68	1	.257	.367
Tim Salmon	DH111 OF19	R	29	136	463	84	139	28	1	26	88	90	100	0	.300	.533
Norberto Martin	2B54 DH10 3B5 OF5 SS2	R	31	79	195	20	42	8	0	1	13	6	29	3	.215	.241
Craig Shipley	3B48 2B11 1B8 SS5 OF2 DH1	R	35	77	147	18	38	7	1	2	17	5	22	0	.259	.361
Phil Nevin	C69 DH3 1B2	R	27	75	237	27	54	8	1	8	27	17	67	0	.228	.371
Orlando Palmeiro	OF54 DH3	L	29	75	165	28	53	7	2	0	21	20	11	5	.321	.388
Justin Baughman	2B59 SS3 DH1	R	23	63	196	24	50	9	1	1	20	6	36	10	.255	.327
Troy Glaus	3B48	R	21	48	165	19	36	9	0	1	23	15	51	1	.218	.291
Damon Mashore	OF35 DH7	R	28	43	98	13	23	6	0	2	11	9	22	1	.235	.357
Chris Pritchett (EJ)	1B29	L	28	31	80	12	23	2	1	2	8	4	16	2	.288	.413
Todd Greene (SJ)	OF12 DH4 1B2	R	27	29	71	3	18	4	0	1	7	2	20	0	.254	.352
Reggie Williams	OF24 DH2	B	32	29	36	7	13	1	0	1	5	7	11	3	.361	.472
Frank Bolick	DH9 3B7 1B1 OF1	B	32	21	45	3	7	2	0	1	2	11	8	0	.156	.267
Gregg Jefferies	OF15 1B3	B	30	19	72	7	25	6	0	1	10	0	5	1	.347	.472
2 Carlos Garcia (LJ)	2B11 SS5 DH1	R	30	19	35	4	5	1	0	0	3	0	11	2	.143	.171
Mark Johnson	1B5 DH2	L	30	10	14	1	1	0	0	0	0	0	6	0	.071	.071
2 Charlie O'Brien (BG)	C5	R	38	5	11	1	2	0	0	0	0	1	2	0	.182	.182
2 Chad Kreuter	C3	B	33	3	7	1	1	1	0	0	1	0	4	0	.143	.286
Bengie Molina	C2	R	23	2	1	0	0	0	0	0	0	0	0	0	.000	.000

NAME	T	AGE	W	L	PCT	SV	G	GS	CG	IP	H	BB	SO	SHO	ERA
		29	85	77	.525	52	162	162	3	1444	1481	630	1091	5	4.49
Chuck Finley	L	35	11	9	.550	0	34	34	1	223	210	109	212	1	3.39
Jason Dickson	R	25	10	10	.500	0	27	18	0	122	147	41	61	0	6.05
Steve Sparks	R	32	9	4	.692	0	22	20	0	129	130	58	90	0	4.34
Ken Hill (EJ)	R	32	9	6	.600	0	19	19	0	103	123	47	57	0	4.98
Omar Olivares	R	30	9	9	.500	0	37	26	1	183	189	91	112	0	4.03
Shigetoshi Hasegawa	R	29	8	3	.727	5	61	0	0	97	86	32	73	0	3.14
Jarrod Washburn	R	23	6	3	.667	0	15	11	0	74	70	27	48	0	4.62
Allen Watson (EJ)	L	27	6	7	.462	0	28	14	1	92	122	34	64	0	6.04
Jack McDowell (EJ)	R	32	5	3	.625	0	14	14	0	76	96	19	45	0	5.09
Pep Harris	R	25	3	1	.750	0	49	0	0	60	55	23	34	0	4.35
Mike Holtz	L	25	2	2	.500	1	53	0	0	30	38	15	29	0	4.75
Rich DeLucia	R	33	2	6	.250	3	61	0	0	72	56	46	73	0	4.27
Troy Percival	R	28	2	7	.222	42	67	0	0	67	45	37	87	0	3.65
1 Greg Cadaret	L	36	1	2	.333	1	39	0	0	37	38	15	37	0	4.14
2 Mike Fetters	R	33	1	2	.333	0	12	0	0	11	14	4	9	0	5.56
2 Jeff Juden	R	27	1	3	.250	0	8	6	0	40	33	18	39	0	6.75
Mike James (AJ)	R	30	0	0	—	0	11	0	0	14	10	7	12	0	1.93
Trevor Wilson	L	32	0	0	—	0	15	0	0	8	8	5	6	0	3.52
Rich Robertson	L	29	0	0	—	0	5	0	0	5	6	11	2	3	15.88

SEATTLE — 3rd 76-85 .472 11.5 — LOU PINIELLA

Name	G by Pos	B	AGE	G	AB	R	H	2B	3B	HR	RBI	BB	SO	SB	BA	SA
TOTALS			30	161	5628	859	1553	321	28	234	822	558	1081	115	.276	.468
David Segui	1B134 OF1	B	31	161	522	79	159	36	1	19	84	49	80	3	.305	.487
1 Joey Cora	2B130	B	33	131	519	95	147	23	6	6	26	62	50	13	.283	.385
Alex Rodriguez	SS160 DH1	R	22	161	686	123	213	35	5	42	124	45	121	46	.310	.560
Russ Davis	3B137 OF3	R	28	141	502	68	130	30	1	20	82	34	134	4	.259	.442
Jay Buhner (KJ)	OF70 DH1	R	33	72	244	33	59	7	1	15	45	38	71	0	.242	.463
Ken Griffey Jr.	OF158 DH3 1B1	L	28	161	633	120	180	33	3	56	146	76	121	20	.284	.611
1 Glenallen Hill	OF71	R	33	74	259	37	75	20	2	12	33	14	45	1	.290	.521
Dan Wilson (NJ)	C94	R	29	96	325	39	82	17	1	9	44	24	56	2	.252	.394
Edgar Martinez	DH147 1B4	R	35	154	556	86	179	46	1	29	102	106	96	1	.322	.565
Rob Ducey	OF83	L	33	97	217	30	52	18	2	5	23	23	61	4	.240	.410
Rich Amaral	OF52 2B11 1B7 DH5 3B1	R	36	73	134	25	37	6	0	1	4	13	24	11	.276	.343
Shane Monahan	OF62	L	23	62	211	17	51	8	1	4	28	8	53	1	.242	.346
John Marzano	C48 DH1	R	35	50	133	13	31	7	1	4	12	9	24	0	.233	.391
Charles Gipson	OF36 3B4 DH1	R	25	44	51	11	12	1	0	0	2	5	9	2	.235	.255
Raul Ibanez	OF17 1B16 DH1	L	26	37	98	12	25	7	1	2	12	5	22	0	.255	.408
Rico Rossy	3B25 2B6 SS4 DH1	R	34	37	81	12	16	6	0	1	5	6	13	0	.198	.309
Jeff Huson	2B8 3B8 SS1 OF1 DH1	L	33	31	49	8	8	1	0	1	4	5	5	1	.163	.245
2 Joe Oliver	C29	R	32	29	85	12	19	3	0	2	10	10	15	1	.224	.329
3 Ryan Radmanovich	OF24 1B1	L	26	25	69	5	15	4	0	2	10	4	25	1	.217	.362
3 David Bell	2B14 1B5 3B5 OF1	R	25	21	80	11	24	8	0	1	6	4	14	0	.325	.425
4 Rick Wilkins	C6 1B6 DH2	L	31	19	41	5	8	1	1	4	14	0		0	.195	.341
Robert Perez	OF17	R	29	17	35	3	6	1	0	0	6	0	5	0	.171	.371
Giomar Guevara (KJ)	2B5 SS5 DH1	B	25	11	13	4	3	2	0	0	0	4	4	0	.231	.385
Carlos Guillen	2B10	B	22	10	39	9	13	1	0	1	5	3	9	2	.333	.410
Dave McCarty	OF5 1B2	R	28	8	18	1	5	0	0	0	2	5	4	1	.278	.444
Rickey Cradle	OF4	R	25	5	7	0	1	0	0	0	0	2	4	1	.143	.143
Raul Chavez	C1	R	25	4	4	0	0	0	0	0	0	0	0	0	.000	.000

NAME	T	AGE	W	L	PCT	SV	G	GS	CG	IP	H	BB	SO	SHO	ERA
		31	76	85	.472	31	161	161	17	1424	1530	528	1156	7	4.93
Jamie Moyer	L	35	15	9	.625	0	34	34	2	234	234	42	158	3	3.53
Jeff Fassero	L	35	13	12	.520	0	32	32	7	225	223	66	176	0	3.97
Bill Swift	R	36	11	9	.550	0	29	26	0	145	183	51	77	0	5.85
1 Randy Johnson	L	34	9	10	.474	0	23	23	6	160	146	60	213	2	4.33
Ken Cloude	R	23	8	10	.444	0	30	30	0	155	187	80	114	0	6.37
Paul Spoljaric	L	27	4	6	.400	0	53	6	0	83	85	55	89	0	6.48
Paul Abbott	R	30	3	1	.750	0	4	4	0	25	24	10	22	0	4.01
Mike Timlin	R	32	3	3	.500	19	70	0	0	79	78	16	60	0	2.95
Jose Paniagua	R	24	2	0	1.000	1	18	0	0	21	15	5	16	0	2.05
Bob Wells (MJ)	R	31	2	2	.500	0	30	0	0	52	54	16	29	0	6.10
Heathcliff Slocumb	R	32	2	5	.286	3	57	0	0	68	72	44	51	0	5.32
Felipe Lira	R	26	1	0	1.000	0	16			22	25	16	5	0	4.60
Mac Suzuki	R	23	1	2	.333	0	6	5	0	26	34	15	19	0	7.18
Greg McCarthy	L	29	1	2	.333	0	29	0	0	23	18	17	25	0	5.01
Bobby Ayala	R	28	1	10	.091	8	62	0	0	75	100	28	68	0	7.29
Steve Gajkowksi	R	28	0	0	—	0	7	0	0	7	6	4	3	0	7.27
David Holdridge	R	29	0	0	—	0	6	0	0	8	11	4	4	0	4.05
Andrew Lorraine	L	25	0	0	—	0	1	0	0	2	6	2	2	0	2.45
Jim Bullinger	R	32	0	3	.000	0	6	3	0	13	15	8	10	0	15.88
1 Tony Fossas	L	40	0	0	—	0	3	0	0	2	1	19	6	10	8.74
Rafael Carmona (BA) 25 Tim Davis (EJ) 27															

* Johnson, also with Houston, major league leader in SO with 329 and ShO with 6

OAKLAND — 4th 74-88 .456 14 — ART HOWE

Name	G by Pos	B	AGE	G	AB	R	H	2B	3B	HR	RBI	BB	SO	SB	BA	SA
TOTALS			29	162	5604	804	1413	295	13	149	755	633	1122	131	.257	.397
Jason Giambi	1B148 DH7	L	27	153	562	92	166	28	0	27	110	81	102	2	.295	.489
Scott Spiezio (KJ)	2B112 DH1	B	25	114	406	54	105	19	1	9	50	44	56	1	.259	.377
Miguel Tejada (BG)	SS104	R	22	105	365	53	85	20	1	11	45	28	86	5	.233	.384
Mike Blowers	3B120 1B8 DH2	R	33	129	409	56	97	24	2	11	71	39	116	1	.237	.386
Ben Grieve	OF151 DH3	L	22	155	583	94	168	41	2	18	89	85	123	2	.288	.458
Ryan Christenson	OF116	R	24	117	353	55	92	25	2	5	40	36	106	5	.257	.368
Rickey Henderson	OF151	R	39	152	542	101	128	16	1	14	57	118	114	66	.236	.347
A.J. Hinch	C102 DH7	R	24	120	337	34	78	10	0	9	35	32	89	3	.231	.341
Matt Stairs	DH120 OF12 1B6	L	30	149	523	88	154	33	1	26	106	59	93	8	.294	.511
Rafael Bournigal	2B48 SS38 DH1	R	32	85	209	23	47	11	0	1	19	10	11	6	.225	.292
2 Mike Macfarlane	C70	R	34	78	207	28	52	12	0	7	34	12	34	1	.251	.411
2 Jason McDonald (YJ)	OF60 DH1	B	26	70	175	25	44	9	0	1	16	27	33	10	.251	.320
2 Bip Roberts	2B30 OF22 3B3	B	34	61	182	28	51	11	0	1	15	15	24	10	.280	.357
Jack Voigt	1B27 OF20 DH3 3B2	R	32	53	72	7	10	4	0	1	10	6	19	5	.139	.236
Kevin Mitchell (EJ)	DH23 OF10 1B2	R	36	51	127	14	29	7	1	2	21	9	26	0	.228	.346
1 Kurt Abbott	SS28 OF5 DH3 3B1	R	29	35	137	17	33	7	1	2	9	10	34	2	.268	.390
Dave Magadan (HJ)	3B30 1B7	L	35	35	109	12	35	8	0	0	13	13	12	0	.321	.422
2 Ed Sprague	3B23 1B7	R	30	35	87	8	13	5	0	2	17	1	19	0	.149	.310
Eric Chavez	3B13	L	20	16	45	6	14	4	0	0	6	3	5	1	.311	.444
Mark Bellhorn	3B5 SS2 DH2 2B1	B	23	11	12	1	1	1	0	0	1	4	4	2	.083	.167
Jorge Velandia	SS7 2B1	R	23	8	8	1	2	0	0	0	1	0	4	0	.250	.250
Brian Lesher	OF4 1B1 DH1	R	27	8	14	2	2	0	0	0	1	0	4	0	.143	.286
Mike Neill (SJ)	OF6	L	28	6	15	2	4	0	0	0	2	4	4	0	.267	.333
Izzy Molina	C5 DH1	R	26	6	10	0	5	0	0	0	5	0	5	0	.500	.500
1 Shane Mack		R	34	3	2	1	1	0	0	0	0	1	0	0	.500	.500
1 Jason Wood	SS2 3B1	R	28	3	8	1	1	0	0	0	1	0	5	0	.125	.125
George Williams (SJ) 29																

NAME	T	AGE	W	L	PCT	SV	G	GS	CG	IP	H	BB	SO	SHO	ERA
		31	74	88	.457	39	162	162	12	1434	1555	529	922	4	4.81
Kenny Rogers	L	33	16	8	.667	0	34	34	7	239	215	67	138	1	3.17
Jimmy Haynes	R	25	11	9	.550	0	33	33	1	194	229	88	134	1	5.09
Tom Candiotti	R	40	11	16	.407	0	33	33	3	201	222	63	98	0	4.84
T.J. Mathews	R	28	7	4	.636	1	66	0	0	73	71	29	53	0	4.58
Mike Oquist	R	30	7	11	.389	0	31	29	0	175	210	57	112	0	6.22
Blake Stein	R	24	5	9	.357	0	24	20	1	117	117	71	89	1	6.37
Billy Taylor	R	36	4	9	.308	33	70	0	0	73	71	22	58	0	3.58
Buddy Groom	L	32	3	1	.750	0	75	0	0	57	62	20	36	0	4.24
Mike Mohler	L	29	3	3	.500	0	57	0	0	61	70	26	42	0	5.16
Gil Heredia	R	32	3	3	.500	0	8	6	0	43	43	3	27	0	2.74
Mark Holzemer	L	28	1	0	1.000	0	13	0	0	10	13	3	3	0	5.59
1 Aaron Small	R	26	1	1	.500	0	24	0	0	36	51	14	19	0	7.25
Jay Witasick	R	25	1	3	.250	0	7	3	0	27	36	15	29	0	6.33
1 Mike Fetters	R	33	1	5	.143	5	48	0	0	48	47	23	34	0	3.99
Steve Connelly	R	24	0	0	—	0	5	0	0	5	10	4	1	0	1.93
3 Tim Worrell	R	30	0	0	—	0	25	0	0	36	34	8	33	0	4.00
Dave Telgheder (KJ)	R	31	0	1	.000	0	8	2	0	17	25	6	9	0	3.60
Ariel Prieto	R	28	0	3	.000	0	9	4	0	22	17	7	8	0	11.88
Jim Dougherty	R	30	0	2	.000	0	12	0	0	17	7	3	6	0	8.25
Willie Adams (SJ) 25															

LINE SCORES

Team	1	2	3	4	5	6	7	8	9	10	11	12	R	H	E

DIVISION SERIES: NEW YORK 3 : TEXAS 0

Game 1 September 29 at New York

	1	2	3	4	5	6	7	8	9	R	H	E
TEX	0	0	0	0	0	0	0	0	0	0	5	0
NYY	0	2	0	0	0	0	0	0	x	2	6	0

Stottlemyre   Wells, Rivera (9)

Game 2 September 30 at New York

	1	2	3	4	5	6	7	8	9	R	H	E
TEX	0	0	0	0	0	1	0	0	0	1	5	0
NYY	0	1	0	2	0	0	0	0	x	3	8	0

Helling, Crabtree (7)   Pettitte, Nelson (8), Rivera (8)

Game 3 October 2 at Texas

	1	2	3	4	5	6	7	8	9	R	H	E
NYY	0	0	0	0	0	4	0	0	0	4	9	1
TEX	0	0	0	0	0	0	0	0	0	0	3	1

Cone, Lloyd (6), Nelson (7), Rivera (9)   Sele, Crabtree (7), Wetteland (9)

DIVISION SERIES: CLEVELAND 3 : BOSTON 1

Game 1 September 29 at Cleveland

	1	2	3	4	5	6	7	8	9	R	H	E
BOS	3	0	0	0	3	2	0	3	0	11	12	0
CLE	0	0	0	0	2	1	0	0		3	7	0

Martinez, Corsi (8)   Wright, Jones (5), Reed (8). Poole (8), Shuey (8), Assenmacher (9)

Game 2 September 30 at Cleveland

	1	2	3	4	5	6	7	8	9	R	H	E
BOS	2	0	1	0	0	2	0	0	0	5	10	0
CLE	1	5	1	0	0	1	0	1	x	9	9	1

Wakefield, Wasdin (2), Lowe (4), Swindell (6), Gordon (8)   Gooden, Burba (1), Shuey (6), Assenmacher (8), Jackson (8)

Game 3 October 2 at Boston

	1	2	3	4	5	6	7	8	9	R	H	E
CLE	0	0	0	0	1	1	1	0	1	4	5	0
BOS	0	1	0	0	0	0	2			3	6	0

Nagy, Jackson (9)   Saberhagen, Corsi (8), Eckersley (9)

Game 4 October 3 at Boston

	1	2	3	4	5	6	7	8	9	R	H	E
CLE	0	0	0	0	0	0	0	2	0	2	5	0
BOS	0	0	0	1	0	0	0	0	0	1	6	0

Colon, Poole (6), Reed (7), Assenmacher (8), Shuey (8), Jackson (9)   Schourek, Lowe (6), Gordon (8)

CHAMPIONSHIP: NEW YORK 4 : CLEVELAND 2

Game 1 October 6 at New York

	1	2	3	4	5	6	7	8	9	R	H	E
CLE	0	0	0	0	0	0	0	2		2	5	0
NYY	5	0	0	0	0	1	1	0	x	7	11	0

Wright, Ogea (1), Poole (7), Reed (7), Shuey (8)   Wells, Nelson (9)

Game 2 October 7 at New York

	1	2	3	4	5	6	7	8	9	10	11	12	R	H	E
CLE	0	0	0	1	0	0	0	0	0	0	0	3	4	7	1
NYY	0	0	0	0	0	1	0	0	0	0	0	1	1	7	1

Nagy, Reed (7), Poole (8), Shuey (8), Assenmacher (10), Burba (11), Jackson (12)   Cone, Rivera (9), Stanton (11), Nelson (11), Lloyd (12)

Game 3 October 9 at Cleveland

	1	2	3	4	5	6	7	8	9	R	H	E
NYY	1	0	0	0	0	0	0	0	0	1	4	0
CLE	0	2	0	0	4	0	0	0	x	6	12	0

Pettitte, Mendoza (5), Stanton (7)   Colon

Game 4 October 10 at Cleveland

	1	2	3	4	5	6	7	8	9	R	H	E
NYY	1	0	0	2	0	0	0	0	1	4	4	0
CLE	0	0	0	0	0	0	0	0	0	0	4	3

Hernandez, Stanton (8), Rivera (9)   Gooden, Poole (5), Burba (6), Shuey (9)

Game 5 October 11 at Cleveland

	1	2	3	4	5	6	7	8	9	R	H	E
NYY	3	1	0	0	0	0	1	0	0	5	6	0
CLE	2	0	0	0	0	1	0	0	0	3	8	0

Wells, Nelson (8), Rivera (8)   Ogea, Wright (2), Reed (8), Assenmacher (8), Shuey (9)

Game 6 October 13 at New York

	1	2	3	4	5	6	7	8	9	R	H	E
CLE	0	0	0	0	5	0	0	0	0	5	8	3
NYY	2	1	3	0	0	3	0	0	x	9	11	1

Cone, Mendoza (6), Rivera (9)   Nagy, Burba (4), Poole (6), Shuey (6), Assenmacher (8)

DIVISION SERIES

COMPOSITE BATTING

NEW YORK

NAME	POS	G	AB	R	H	2B	3B	HR	RBI	BA
TOTALS		3	91	9	23	6	0	4	8	.253
O'Neill	RF	3	11	1	4	2	0	1	0	.364
Martinez	1B	3	11	1	3	2	0	0	0	.273
Knoblauch	2B	3	11	0	1	0	0	0	0	.091
Williams	CF	3	11	0	0	0	0	0	0	.000
Brosius	3B	3	10	1	4	0	0	1	3	.400
Jeter	SS	3	9	0	1	0	0	0	0	.111
Girardi	C	2	7	0	3	0	0	0	0	.429
Spencer	LF	2	6	3	3	0	0	2	4	.500
Davis	DH	2	6	0	1	0	0	0	0	.167
Raines	DH	2	4	1	1	1	0	0	0	.250
Curtis	LF	3	3	1	2	1	0	0	0	.667
Posada	C	1	2	1	0	0	0	0	0	.000
Bush	DH	1	0	0	0	0	0	0	0	—

TEXAS

NAME	POS	G	AB	R	H	2B	3B	HR	RBI	BA
TOTALS		3	92	1	13	3	0	0	1	.141
Gonzalez	RF	3	12	1	1	1	0	0	0	.083
Clark	1B	3	11	0	1	0	0	0	0	.091
Greer	LF	3	11	0	1	0	0	0	0	.091
McLemore	2B	3	10	0	1	1	0	0	0	.100
Rodriguez	C	3	10	0	1	0	0	0	1	.100
Zeile	3B	3	9	0	3	0	0	0	0	.333
Clayton	SS	3	9	0	2	0	0	0	0	.222
Kelly	CF	2	7	0	1	1	0	0	0	.143
Simms	DH	2	5	0	1	0	0	0	0	.200
Goodwin	CF	2	4	0	1	0	0	0	0	.250
Stevens	DH	1	3	0	0	0	0	0	0	.000
Alicea	DH	1	1	0	0	0	0	0	0	.000

CLEVELAND

NAME	POS	G	AB	R	H	2B	3B	HR	RBI	BA
TOTALS		4	126	18	26	12	0	7	17	.206
Lofton	CF	4	16	5	6	1	0	2	4	.375
Justice	DH-LF	4	16	2	5	4	0	1	6	.313
Thome	1B-DH	4	15	2	2	0	0	2	2	.133
Vizquel	SS	4	15	1	1	0	0	0	0	.067
Ramirez	RF	4	14	2	5	2	0	2	3	.357
Alomar	C	4	13	2	3	3	0	0	2	.231
Fryman	3B	4	13	1	2	1	0	0	0	.154
Giles	LF-RF	3	10	1	2	1	0	0	0	.200
Cora	2B	4	10	2	0	0	0	0	0	.000
Sexson	1B	3	2	0	0	0	0	0	0	.000
Wilson	2B	1	2	0	0	0	0	0	0	.000

BOSTON

NAME	POS	G	AB	R	H	2B	3B	HR	RBI	BA
TOTALS		4	135	20	34	6	0	5	19	.252
Vaughn	1B	4	17	3	7	2	0	2	7	.412
O'Leary	LF	4	16	0	1	0	0	0	0	.063
Valentin	3B	4	15	5	7	1	0	0	0	.467
Garciaparra	SS	4	15	4	5	1	0	3	11	.333
Stanley	DH	4	15	1	4	0	0	0	0	.267
Lewis	CF	4	14	4	5	2	0	0	0	.357
Bragg	RF	3	12	0	1	0	0	0	0	.083
Benjamin	2B-1B	4	11	1	1	0	0	0	0	.091
Hatteberg	C	3	9	0	1	0	0	0	0	.111
Varitek	C	1	4	0	1	0	0	0	0	.250
Nixon	RF	2	3	0	1	0	0	0	0	.333
Cummings	PH	3	3	0	0	0	0	0	0	.000
Buford	CF-DH	3	1	2	0	0	0	0	0	.000
Sadler	2B	3	0	0	0	0	0	0	0	—

COMPOSITE PITCHING

NEW YORK

NAME	G	IP	H	BB	SO	W	L	SV	ERA
TOTALS	3	27	13	4	27	3	0	2	0.33
Wells	1	8	5	1	9	1	0	0	0.00
Pettitte	1	7	3	0	8	1	0	0	1.29
Cone	1	5.2	2	1	6	1	0	0	0.00
Rivera	3	3.1	1	1	2	0	0	2	0.00
Nelson	2	2.2	2	1	2	0	0	0	0.00
Lloyd	1	0.1	0	0	0	0	0	0	0.00

TEXAS

NAME	G	IP	H	BB	SO	W	L	SV	ERA
TOTALS	3	25	23	7	24	0	3	0	3.24
Stottlemyre	1	8	6	4	8	0	1	0	2.25
Helling	1	6	8	1	9	0	1	0	4.50
Sele	1	6	8	1	4	0	1	0	6.00
Crabtree	2	4	1	0	2	0	0	0	0.00
Wetteland	1	1	0	1	1	0	0	0	0.00

CLEVELAND

NAME	G	IP	H	BB	SO	W	L	SV	ERA
TOTALS	4	36	34	14	28	3	1	3	5.00
Nagy	1	8	4	0	3	1	0	0	1.13
Colon	1	5.2	5	3	3	0	0	0	1.59
Burba	1	5.1	4	2	4	1	0	0	5.06
Wright	1	4.1	7	2	6	0	1	0	12.46
Jackson	3	4	3	1	1	0	0	3	4.50
Shuey	3	3	3	1	4	0	0	0	0.00
Jones	1	2.2	3	1	1	0	0	0	6.75
Assenmacher	3	1	2	0	2	0	0	0	0.00
Poole	2	1	1	1	2	0	0	0	0.00
Reed	2	0.2	1	1	1	1	0	0	40.50
Gooden	1	0.1	2	1	0	0	0	0	54.00

BOSTON

NAME	G	IP	H	BB	SO	W	L	SV	ERA
TOTALS	4	35	26	15	26	1	3	0	4.63
Martinez	1	7	6	0	8	1	0	0	3.86
Saberhagen	1	7	4	1	7	0	1	0	3.86
Schourek	1	5.1	2	4	1	0	0	0	0.00
Lowe	2	4.1	3	1	2	0	0	0	2.08
Corsi	2	3	1	1	2	0	0	0	0.00
Gordon	2	3	4	4	1	0	1	0	9.00
Wasdin	1	1.2	2	1	2	0	0	0	10.80
Swindell	1	1.1	0	1	1	0	0	0	0.00
Wakefield	1	1.1	3	2	1	0	1	0	33.75
Eckersley	1	1	1	0	1	0	0	0	9.00

AMERICAN LEAGUE CHAMPIONSHIP

COMPOSITE BATTING

NEW YORK

NAME	POS	G	AB	R	H	2B	3B	HR	RBI	BA
TOTALS		6	197	27	43	8	1	4	25	.218
O'Neill	RF	6	25	6	7	2	0	1	3	.280
Jeter	SS	6	25	3	5	1	1	0	2	.200
Knoblauch	2B	6	25	4	5	1	0	0	2	.200
Williams	CF	6	21	4	8	1	0	0	5	.381
Brosius	3B	6	20	2	6	1	0	1	6	.300
Martinez	1B	6	19	1	2	1	0	0	1	.105
Davis	DH	5	14	2	4	1	0	1	5	.286
Posada	C	5	11	1	2	0	0	1	2	.182
Raines	DH-LF	3	10	1	1	0	0	0	1	.100
Spencer	LF	3	10	1	1	0	0	0	0	.100
Girardi	C	3	8	2	2	0	0	0	0	.250
Ledee	LF-DH	3	5	0	0	0	0	0	0	.000
Curtis	LF	2	4	0	0	0	0	0	0	.000
Bush	DH	2	0	1	0	0	0	0	0	—
Sojo	1B	1	0	0	0	0	0	0	0	—

CLEVELAND

NAME	POS	G	AB	R	H	2B	3B	HR	RBI	BA
TOTALS		6	205	20	45	3	1	9	19	.220
Lofton	CF	6	27	2	5	1	0	1	3	.185
Vizquel	SS	6	25	2	11	1	0	1	0	.440
Thome	DH-1B	6	23	4	7	0	0	4	8	.304
Fryman	3B	6	23	2	4	0	0	0	0	.174
Ramirez	RF	6	21	2	7	1	0	2	4	.333
Justice	LF-DH	6	19	2	3	0	1	2	2	.158
Alomar	C	5	16	1	1	0	0	0	0	.063
Wilson	2B	5	14	2	3	0	0	0	4	.214
Giles	LF	2	12	0	1	0	0	0	0	.083
Whiten	LF	2	7	2	2	1	0	1	1	.286
Cora	2B	2	7	1	1	0	0	0	0	.143
Sexson	1B	3	6	0	0	0	0	0	0	.000
Diaz	C	4	4	0	0	0	0	0	0	.000
Branson	PH	1	1	0	0	0	0	0	0	.000

COMPOSITE PITCHING

NEW YORK

NAME	G	IP	H	BB	SO	W	L	SV	ERA
TOTALS	6	56	45	16	51	4	2	1	3.21
Wells	2	15.2	12	2	18	2	0	0	2.87
Cone	2	13	12	6	13	1	0	0	4.15
Hernandez	1	7	3	2	6	1	0	0	0.00
Rivera	4	5.2	0	1	5	0	0	1	0.00
Pettitte	1	4.2	8	3	1	0	1	0	11.57
Mendoza	2	4.1	4	0	1	0	0	0	0.00
Stanton	3	3.2	2	1	4	0	0	0	0.00
Nelson	3	1.1	3	1	3	0	1	0	20.26
Lloyd	1	0.2	1	0	0	0	0	0	0.00

CLEVELAND

NAME	G	IP	H	BB	SO	W	L	SV	ERA
TOTALS	6	55	43	35	42	2	4	1	3.60
Nagy	2	9.2	13	1	6	0	1	0	3.72
Colon	2	9	4	4	3	1	0	0	1.00
Ogea	2	6.2	9	5	4	0	1	0	8.10
Wright	2	6.2	7	8	4	0	1	0	8.10
Shuey	5	6.1	4	7	7	0	0	0	0.00
Burba	3	6	3	5	8	1	0	0	3.00
Gooden	1	4.2	3	3	3	0	1	0	5.79
Assenmacher	3	2	0	3	0	0	0	0	0.00
Reed	3	1.2	0	1	2	0	0	0	0.00
Poole	4	1.1	0	1	2	0	0	0	0.00
Jackson	1	1	0	0	2	0	0	1	0.00

ATLANTA — 1st 106-56 .654 — BOBBY COX

Name	G by Pos	B	AGE	G	AB	R	H	2B	3B	HR	RBI	BB	SO	SB	BA	SA
TOTALS		29		162	5484	826	1489	297	26	215	794	548	1062	98	.272	.453
Andres Galarraga	1B149	R	37	153	555	103	169	27	1	44	121	63	146	7	.305	.595
Keith Lockhart	2B97 3B1	L	33	109	366	50	94	21	0	9	37	29	37	2	.257	.388
Walt Weiss	SS96	B	34	96	347	64	97	18	2	0	27	59	53	7	.280	.343
Chipper Jones	3B158	B	26	160	601	123	188	29	5	34	107	96	93	16	.313	.547
Michael Tucker	OF118	L	27	130	414	54	101	27	3	13	46	49	112	8	.244	.418
Andruw Jones	OF159	R	21	159	582	89	158	33	8	31	90	40	129	27	.271	.515
Ryan Klesko	OF120 1B7	L	27	129	427	69	117	29	1	18	70	56	66	5	.274	.473
Javy Lopez	C128	R	27	133	489	73	139	21	1	34	106	30	85	5	.284	.540
Gerald Williams	OF120	R	31	129	266	46	81	19	2	10	44	17	48	11	.305	.504
Tony Graffanino	2B93 SS2 3B1	R	26	105	289	32	61	14	1	5	22	24	68	1	.211	.318
2 Ozzie Guillen	SS71 2B2 1B1 3B1	L	34	83	264	35	73	15	1	1	22	24	25	1	.277	.352
Danny Bautista	OF58	R	26	82	144	17	36	11	0	3	17	7	21	1	.250	.389
Curtis Pride	OF22	L	29	70	107	19	27	6	1	3	9	9	29	4	.252	.411
Eddie Perez	C45 1B8	R	30	61	149	18	50	12	0	6	32	15	28	1	.336	.537
2 Greg Colbrunn	1B9 OF1	R	28	28	44	6	13	3	0	1	10	2	11	1	.295	.432
Marty Malloy	2B10	L	25	11	28	3	5	1	0	1	1	2	2	0	.179	.321
1 Ray Holbert	SS7	R	27	8	15	2	2	0	0	0	1	2	4	0	.133	.133
Rafael Belliard (LJ)	SS7	R	36	7	20	1	5	0	0	0	1	0	1	0	.250	.250
Randall Simon	1B4	L	22	7	16	2	3	0	0	0	4	0	1	0	.188	.188
Wes Helms	3B4	R	22	7	13	2	4	1	0	1	2	0	4	0	.308	.615
George Lombard	OF2	L	22	6	6	2	2	0	0	1	1	0	1	1	.333	.833
Mark DeRosa	SS4	R	23	5	3	2	1	0	0	0	0	1	1	0	.333	.333
1 Damon Hollins	OF3	R	24	3	6	0	1	0	0	0	0	0	1	0	.167	.167

NAME	T	AGE	W	L	PCT	SV	G	GS	CG	IP	H	BB	SO	SHO	ERA
TOTALS		29	106	56	.654	45	162	162	24	1439	1291	466	1232	23	3.25
Tom Glavine	L	32	20	6	.769	0	33	33	4	229	202	74	157	3	2.47
Greg Maddux	R	32	18	9	.667	0	34	34	9	251	201	45	204	5	2.22
John Smoltz	R	31	17	3	.850	0	26	26	2	168	145	44	173	2	2.90
Kevin Millwood	R	23	17	8	.680	0	31	29	3	174	175	56	163	1	4.08
Denny Neagle	L	29	16	11	.593	0	32	31	5	210	196	60	165	2	3.55
Rudy Seanez	R	29	4	1	.800	2	34	0	0	36	25	15	50	0	2.75
Dennis Martinez	R	43	4	6	.400	2	53	5	1	91	109	19	62	1	4.45
Kerry Ligtenberg	R	27	3	2	.600	30	75	0	0	73	51	24	79	0	2.71
Bruce Chen	L	21	2	0	1.000	0	4	4	0	20	23	9	17	0	3.98
Mike Cather	R	27	2	2	.500	0	36	0	0	41	39	12	33	0	3.92
1 Alan Embree	L	28	1	0	1.000	0	20	0	0	19	23	10	19	0	4.34
1 Russ Springer	R	29	1	1	.500	0	22	0	0	20	22	16	19	0	4.05
John Rocker	L	23	1	3	.250	2	47	0	0	38	22	22	42	0	2.13
2 Norm Charlton	L	35	0	0	—	0	13	0	0	13	7	8	6	0	1.38
1 Paul Byrd	R	27	0	0	—	0	1	0	0	2	4	1	1	0	13.50
Mark Wohlers	R	28	0	1	.000	8	27	0	0	20	18	33	22	0	10.18
1 Brian Edmondson	R	25	0	0	—	0	10	0	0	17	14	8	4	0	4.32
Odalis Perez	L	21	0	1	.000	0	10	0	0	11	10	4	5	0	4.22
Adam Butler	L	24	0	1	.000	0	8	0	0	5	6	7	10	0	10.80

Pedro Borbon (EJ) 30

NEW YORK — 2nd 88-74 .543 18 — BOBBY VALENTINE

Name	G by Pos	B	AGE	G	AB	R	H	2B	3B	HR	RBI	BB	SO	SB	BA	SA
TOTALS		29		162	5510	706	1425	289	24	136	671	572	1049	62	.259	.394
John Olerud	1B157	L	29	160	557	91	197	36	4	22	93	96	73	2	.354	.551
Carlos Baerga	2B144	B	29	147	511	46	136	27	1	7	53	24	55	0	.266	.364
Rey Ordonez	SS151	R	27	153	505	46	124	20	2	1	42	23	60	3	.246	.299
Edgardo Alfonzo	3B144 SS1	R	24	144	557	94	155	28	2	17	78	65	77	8	.278	.427
Butch Huskey	OF103	R	26	113	369	43	93	18	0	13	59	26	66	7	.252	.407
Brian McRae	OF154	B	30	159	552	79	146	36	5	21	79	90	90	20	.264	.462
1 Bernard Gilkey	OF77	R	31	82	264	33	60	15	0	4	28	32	66	5	.227	.330
3 Mike Piazza	C99	R	29	109	394	67	137	33	0	23	76	47	53	1	.348	.607
Luis Lopez	2B50 SS39 3B11 OF9	B	27	117	266	37	67	13	2	2	22	20	60	1	.252	.338
Matt Franco	3B13 OF13 1B11	L	28	103	161	20	44	7	2	1	13	23	26	0	.273	.360
1 Lenny Harris	OF65 3B10 2B2 1B1 P1	L	33	75	168	18	39	7	0	6	17	9	12	5	.232	.381
Todd Hundley (SJ)	OF34 C2	B	29	53	124	8	20	4	0	3	12	16	55	1	.161	.266
2 Tony Phillips	OF51	B	39	52	188	25	42	11	0	3	14	38	44	1	.223	.330
1 Rich Becker	OF41	L	26	49	100	15	19	4	2	3	10	21	42	3	.190	.360
Todd Pratt (SJ)	C16 1B3	R	31	41	69	9	19	9	1	2	18	2	20	0	.275	.522
Alberto Castillo	C35	R	28	38	83	13	17	4	0	2	7	9	17	0	.205	.325
Jim Tatum	1B9 C4 OF4 3B3	R	30	35	50	4	9	1	2	2	13	3	19	0	.180	.400
3 Jermaine Allensworth	OF31	R	26	34	54	9	11	2	0	2	4	2	16	0	.204	.352
Wayne Kirby	OF19	L	34	26	31	5	6	0	1	0	1	9	5	1	.194	.258
1 Tim Spehr (BW)	C21 1B1	R	31	21	51	3	7	1	0	0	3	7	16	1	.137	.157
1 Jorge Fabregas	C12	L	28	20	32	3	6	0	0	1	5	1	6	0	.188	.281
Jay Payton	OF9	R	25	15	22	2	7	1	0	0	1	0	4	0	.318	.364
Benny Agbayani	OF9	R	26	11	15	1	2	0	0	0	1	5	1	0	.133	.133
Ralph Milliard	2B5 SS1	R	24	10	1	3	0	0	0	0	0	0	0	1	0	.000	.000
1 Preston Wilson	OF7	R	23	8	20	3	6	2	0	0	2	2	8	1	.300	.400
Craig Paquette (NJ)	3B4 1B2 OF1	R	29	7	19	3	5	2	0	0	0	0	6	1	.263	.368
2 Rick Wilkins	C4	L	31	5	15	3	2	0	0	0	1	2	2	0	.133	.133
1 Shawn Gilbert	3B1	R	33	3	3	1	0	0	0	0	0	0	1	0	.000	.000
Todd Haney	2B1 OF1	R	32	3	3	0	0	0	0	0	0	0	0	0	.000	.000
Mike Kinkade	3B1	R	25	3	2	2	0	0	0	0	0	0	0	0	.000	.000

NAME	T	AGE	W	L	PCT	SV	G	GS	CG	IP	H	BB	SO	SHO	ERA
TOTALS		31	88	74	.543	46	162	162	9	1458	1381	532	1129	16	3.76
Al Leiter	L	32	17	6	.739	0	28	28	4	193	151	71	174	2	2.47
Rick Reed	R	33	16	11	.593	0	31	31	2	212	208	29	153	1	3.48
Bobby Jones	R	28	9	9	.500	0	30	30	0	195	192	53	115	0	4.05
Dennis Cook	L	35	8	4	.667	1	73	0	0	68	60	27	79	0	2.38
Armando Reynoso (SJ)	R	32	7	3	.700	0	11	11	0	68	64	32	40	0	3.82
Masato Yoshii	R	33	6	8	.429	0	29	29	1	172	166	53	117	0	3.93
Turk Wendell	R	31	5	1	.833	4	66	0	0	77	62	33	58	0	2.93
Mel Rojas	R	31	5	2	.714	2	50	0	0	58	68	30	41	0	6.05
13 Greg McMichael	R	31	5	3	.625	1	52	0	0	54	64	29	44	0	4.02
1 Hideo Nomo	R	29	4	5	.444	0	17	16	1	90	73	56	94	0	4.82
1 Brian Bohanon	L	29	2	4	.333	0	25	4	0	54	47	21	39	0	3.15
2 Willie Blair	R	32	1	1	.500	0	11	2	0	29	23	10	21	0	3.14
Jeff Tam	R	27	1	1	.500	0	15	0	0	14	13	4	8	0	6.28
1 Dave Mlicki	R	30	1	4	.200	0	10	10	1	57	68	25	39	0	5.68
1 John Hudek	R	31	1	4	.200	0	28	0	0	27	23	19	28	0	4.00
1 Bill Pulsipher	L	24	0	0	—	0	15	1	0	14	23	5	13	0	6.91
Rigo Beltran	L	28	0	0	—	0	7	0	0	9	4	2	9	0	3.38
2 Brad Clontz	R	27	0	0	—	0	3	0	0	4	2	2	0	0	9.00
2 Lenny Harris	R	33	0	0	—	0	1	0	0	1	0	1	0	0	9.00
John Franco	L	37	0	8	.000	38	61	0	0	65	66	29	59	0	3.62

Paul Wilson (SJ) 25   Jason Isringhausen (EJ) 25

PHILADELPHIA — 3rd 75-87 .462 31 — TERRY FRANCONA

Name	G by Pos	B	AGE	G	AB	R	H	2B	3B	HR	RBI	BB	SO	SB	BA	SA
TOTALS		26		162	5617	713	1482	286	36	126	672	508	1080	97	.264	.395
Rico Brogna	1B151	L	28	153	565	77	150	36	3	20	104	49	125	7	.265	.446
Mark Lewis	2B140	R	28	142	518	52	129	21	2	9	54	48	111	3	.249	.349
Desi Relaford	SS137	B	24	142	494	45	121	25	3	5	41	33	87	9	.245	.338
Scott Rolen	3B159	R	23	160	601	120	174	45	4	31	110	93	141	14	.290	.532
Bobby Abreu	OF146	L	24	151	497	68	155	29	6	17	74	84	133	19	.312	.497
Doug Glanville	OF158	R	27	158	678	106	189	28	7	8	49	42	89	23	.279	.376
Gregg Jefferies	OF121	B	30	125	483	65	142	22	3	8	48	29	27	11	.294	.402
Mike Lieberthal (MJ)	C83	R	26	86	313	39	80	15	3	8	45	17	44	2	.256	.399
Kevin Jordan	1B24 2B22 3B6	R	28	112	250	23	69	13	0	2	27	8	30	0	.276	.352
Kevin Sefcik	OF60 3B2 2B1	R	27	104	169	27	53	7	2	3	20	25	32	4	.314	.432
Ruben Amaro	OF51	B	33	92	107	7	20	5	0	1	10	6	15	0	.187	.262
Alex Arias	SS38 3B5 2B1	R	30	56	133	17	39	8	0	1	16	13	18	2	.293	.376
Bobby Estalella	C47	R	23	47	165	16	31	6	1	8	20	13	49	0	.188	.382
Jon Zuber	OF5 1B4	L	28	38	45	6	11	3	0	1	6	6	9	0	.244	.489
Mark Parent	C34	R	36	34	113	7	25	4	0	1	13	10	30	1	.221	.283
Rex Hudler	OF9 1B1	R	37	25	41	2	5	1	0	0	2	4	12	0	.122	.146
Wendell Magee	OF19	R	25	20	75	9	22	6	1	1	11	7	11	0	.293	.440
Marlon Anderson	2B9	L	24	17	43	4	14	3	0	1	4	1	6	2	.326	.465
Gary Bennett	C9	R	26	9	31	4	9	0	0	0	3	5	5	0	.290	.290

Lenny Dykstra (XJ) 35

NAME	T	AGE	W	L	PCT	SV	G	GS	CG	IP	H	BB	SO	SHO	ERA
TOTALS		29	75	87	.463	32	162	162	21	1463	1476	544	1176	11	4.64
Curt Schilling	R	31	15	14	.517	0	35	35	15	269	236	61	300	2	3.25
Mark Portugal (KJ)	R	35	10	5	.667	0	26	26	3	166	186	32	104	0	4.44
Wayne Gomes	R	25	9	6	.600	1	71	0	0	93	94	35	86	0	4.24
Mark Leiter	R	35	7	5	.583	23	69	0	0	89	67	47	84	0	3.55
Carlton Loewer	R	24	7	8	.467	0	21	21	1	123	154	39	58	0	6.09
Tyler Green (EJ)	R	28	6	12	.333	0	27	27	0	159	142	85	113	0	5.03
2 Paul Byrd	R	27	5	2	.714	0	8	8	2	55	41	17	38	1	2.29
Jerry Spradlin	R	30	4	4	.500	1	69	0	0	82	63	20	76	0	3.53
Mike Grace	R	28	4	7	.364	0	21	15	0	90	116	30	46	0	5.48
Matt Beech	L	26	3	9	.250	0	21	21	0	117	126	63	113	0	5.15
Darrin Winston	L	31	2	2	.500	1	27	0	0	25	31	6	11	0	6.12
Robert Dodd	L	25	1	0	1.000	0	4	0	0	5	7	1	4	0	7.20
Matt Whiteside	R	30	1	1	.500	0	10	0	0	18	27	5	14	0	8.50
Ricky Bottalico (EJ)	R	28	1	5	.167	6	39	0	0	43	54	25	27	0	6.44
Ken Ryan (SJ)	R	29	0	0	—	0	17	1	0	23	21	20	16	0	4.37
Toby Borland	R	29	0	0	—	0	6	0	0	9	8	5	9	0	5.00
Ryan Nye	R	25	0	0	—	0	1	0	0	1	3	0	1	0	27.00
Billy Brewer (EJ)	L	30	0	1	.000	0	2	0	0	0.1	3	2	1	0	108.00
Yorkis Perez	L	31	0	2	.000	0	57	0	0	52	40	25	42	0	3.81
Garrett Stephenson	R	26	0	2	.000	0	6	6	0	23	31	19	17	0	9.00
Mike Welch	R	25	0	2	.000	0	10	0	0	21	26	7	15	0	8.27

MONTREAL — 4th 65-97 .401 41 — FELIPE ALOU

Name	G by Pos	B	AGE	G	AB	R	H	2B	3B	HR	RBI	BB	SO	SB	BA	SA
TOTALS		26		162	5418	644	1348	280	32	147	602	439	1058	91	.249	.394
Brad Fullmer	1B137	L	23	140	505	58	138	44	2	13	73	39	70	6	.273	.446
2 Wilton Guerrero	2B52	B	23	52	222	29	63	10	6	2	20	5	30	3	.284	.410
1 Mark Grudzielanek	SS105	R	28	105	396	51	109	15	1	8	41	21	55	11	.275	.379
Shane Andrews	3B147	R	26	150	492	48	117	30	1	25	69	58	137	1	.238	.455
Vladimir Guerrero	OF157	R	22	159	623	108	202	37	7	38	109	42	95	11	.324	.589
Rondell White (BG)	OF96	R	26	97	357	54	107	21	2	17	58	30	57	16	.300	.513
F.P. Santangelo	OF92 2B35 3B1	B	30	122	383	53	82	18	4	2	24	52	72	7	.214	.292
Chris Widger	C123	R	27	125	417	36	97	18	1	15	53	29	85	6	.233	.388
Ryan McGuire	1B78 OF46	L	26	130	210	17	39	9	0	1	10	32	55	0	.186	.243
Derrick May	OF48	L	29	85	180	13	43	8	0	5	15	11	24	0	.239	.367
Jose Vidro	2B56 3B7	B	23	83	205	24	45	12	0	6	18	27	33	2	.220	.278
Orlando Cabrera	SS52 2B8 3B7	B	23	79	261	44	73	16	5	3	22	18	27	6	.280	.414
Scott Livingstone	3B17 1B3	L	32	76	110	1	23	6	0	0	12	5	15	1	.209	.264
Mike Mordecai	SS30 2B21 3B11 1B1	R	30	73	119	12	24	4	2	3	10	9	20	1	.202	.345
DaRond Stovall	OF47	B	25	62	78	11	16	2	1	2	9	10	26	1	.205	.333
Terry Jones	OF60	B	27	60	212	30	46	7	2	1	15	21	46	16	.217	.283
2 Robert Perez	OF29	R	29	52	106	9	25	7	0	1	8	2	20	0	.236	.274
Bob Henley (AJ)	C35	R	25	41	115	16	35	8	1	3	18	11	26	3	.304	.470
Mike Hubbard	C24 2B1	R	32	32	55	3	8	1	5	1	4	11	15	0	.145	.218
Fernando Seguignol	OF9 1B7	B	23	16	42	6	11	4	0	2	8	3	15	0	.262	.500
Michael Barrett	C3 3B3	R	21	8	23	3	7	2	0	0	5	2	4	0	.304	.522
2 Ray Holbert	2B1	R	27	2	5	0	0	0	0	0	0	0	0	0	.000	.000

NAME	T	AGE	W	L	PCT	SV	G	GS	CG	IP	H	BB	SO	SHO	ERA
TOTALS		27	65	97	.401	39	162	162	4	1427	1448	533	1017	5	4.38
Dustin Hermanson	R	25	14	11	.560	0	32	30	1	187	163	56	154	0	3.13
1 Carlos Perez	L	27	11	14	.440	0	23	23	3	163	177	33	82	0	3.75
Ugueth Urbina	R	24	6	3	.667	34	64	0	0	69	37	33	94	0	1.30
Carl Pavano	R	22	6	9	.400	0	24	23	0	135	130	43	83	0	4.21
Shayne Bennett	R	26	5	5	.500	1	62	0	0	92	97	45	59	0	5.50
Javier Vazquez	R	22	5	15	.250	0	33	32	0	172	196	68	139	0	6.06
Mike Thurman	R	24	4	5	.444	0	14	13	0	67	60	26	32	0	4.70
Mike Maddux (EJ)	R	36	3	4	.429	1	51	0	0	56	50	15	33	0	3.72
Miguel Batista	R	27	3	8	.375	0	56	13	0	135	141	65	92	0	3.80
Anthony Telford	R	32	3	6	.333	1	77	0	0	91	85	36	59	0	3.86
Steve Kline	L	25	3	6	.333	1	78	0	0	72	62	41	76	0	2.76
Trey Moore (SJ)	L	25	2	5	.286	0	13	11	0	61	78	17	35	0	5.02
Kirk Bullinger	R	28	1	0	1.000	0	7	0	0	7	14	0	2	0	9.00
Marc Valdes	R	26	1	3	.250	0	20	4	0	36	41	21	28	0	7.43
Shawn Boskie	R	31	1	3	.250	0	5	0	0	18	34	4	10	0	9.17
Jeremy Powell	R	22	1	5	.167	0	7	7	0	36	49	11	14	0	7.92
Rick DeHart	L	27	0	0	—	1	26	0	0	28	34	13	14	0	4.82
Tim Young	L	25	0	0	—	0	10	0	0	6	9	6	6	0	6.00
Mike Johnson	R	22	0	2	.000	0	7	2	0	7	16	2	4	0	14.73

Batting / Pitching — EAST DIVISION

FLORIDA 5th 54-108 .333 52 JIM LEYLAND

Name	G by Pos	B	AGE	G	AB	R	H	2B	3B	HR	RBI	BB	SO	SB	BA	SA
TOTALS			26	162	5558	667	1381	277	36	114	621	525	1120	115	.248	.373
Derrek Lee	1B132	R	22	141	454	62	106	29	1	17	74	47	120	5	.233	.414
Craig Counsell (BJ)	2B104	L	27	107	335	43	84	19	5	4	40	51	47	3	.251	.373
Edgar Renteria	SS129	R	22	133	517	79	146	18	2	3	31	48	78	41	.282	.342
2 Todd Zeile	3B65	R	32	66	234	37	68	12	1	6	39	31	34	2	.291	.427
Mark Kotsay	OF145 1B3	L	22	154	578	72	161	25	7	11	68	34	61	10	.279	.403
Todd Dunwoody	OF111	L	23	116	434	53	109	27	7	5	28	21	113	5	.251	.380
Cliff Floyd	OF146	L	25	153	588	85	166	45	3	22	90	47	112	27	.282	.481
Gregg Zaun	C88 2B1	B	27	106	298	19	56	12	2	5	29	35	52	5	.188	.292
Ryan Jackson	1B44 OF32	L	26	111	260	26	65	15	1	5	31	20	73	1	.250	.373
John Cangelosi	OF45	B	35	104	171	19	43	8	0	1	10	30	23	2	.251	.316
Dave Berg	2B27 3B25 SS17	R	27	81	182	18	57	11	0	2	21	26	46	3	.313	.407
John Wehner	OF23 3B8	R	31	53	88	10	20	2	0	0	5	7	12	1	.227	.250
2 Kevin Orie	3B48	R	25	48	175	23	46	8	1	6	17	14	24	1	.263	.423
Luis Castillo	2B44	B	22	44	153	21	31	3	2	1	10	22	33	3	.203	.268
1 Gary Sheffield	OF37	R	29	40	136	21	37	11	1	6	28	26	16	4	.272	.500
Mike Redmond	C37	R	27	37	118	10	39	9	0	2	12	5	16	0	.331	.458
4 Charles Johnson	C31	R	26	31	113	13	25	5	0	7	23	16	30	0	.221	.451
1 Jim Eisenreich	1B10 OF8	L	39	30	64	9	16	1	0	1	7	4	14	2	.250	.313
1 Bobby Bonilla	3B26	B	35	28	97	11	27	5	0	4	15	12	22	0	.278	.454
Alex Gonzalez	SS25	R	21	25	86	11	13	2	0	3	7	9	30	0	.151	.279
Randy Knorr	C15	R	29	15	49	4	10	4	1	2	11	1	10	0	.204	.449
2 Preston Wilson	OF11	R	23	14	31	4	2	0	0	1	1	4	13	0	.065	.161
Brian Daubach	1B4	L	26	10	15	0	3	1	0	0	3	1	6	0	.200	.267
John Roskos	1B1	R	23	10	10	1	1	0	0	0	1	0	5	0	.100	.100
Josh Booty	3B7	R	23	7	19	0	3	1	0	0	3	0	8	0	.158	.211
2 Mike Piazza	C4	R	29	5	18	1	5	0	1	0	5	0	0	0	.278	.389
Kevin Millar (BW)	3B2	R	26	2	2	1	1	0	0	0	0	0	0	0	.500	.500

NAME	T	AGE	W	L	PCT	SV	G	GS	CG	IP	H	BB	SO	SHO	ERA
		25	54	108	.333	24	162	162	11	1450	1617	715	1016	3	5.18
Brian Meadows	R	22	11	13	.458	0	31	31	1	174	222	46	88	0	5.21
Livan Hernandez	R	23	10	12	.455	0	33	33	9	234	265	104	162	0	4.72
Jesus Sanchez	L	23	7	9	.438	0	35	29	0	173	178	91	137	0	4.47
2 Brian Edmondson	R	25	4	3	.571	0	43	0	0	59	62	29	32	0	3.79
1 Jay Powell	R	26	4	4	.500	3	33	0	0	36	36	22	24	0	4.21
Antonio Alfonseca	R	26	4	6	.400	8	58	0	0	71	75	33	46	0	4.08
Matt Mantei	R	24	3	4	.429	9	42	0	0	55	38	23	63	0	2.96
Andy Larkin	R	24	3	8	.273	0	17	14	0	75	101	55	43	0	9.64
Rob Stanifer	R	26	2	4	.333	1	38	0	0	48	54	22	30	0	5.63
Rafael Medina (SJ)	R	23	2	6	.250	0	12	12	0	67	76	52	49	0	6.01
Kirt Ojala	L	29	2	7	.222	0	41	13	1	125	128	59	75	0	4.25
Eric Ludwick (BA-HJ)	R	26	1	4	.200	0	13	6	0	33	46	17	27	0	7.44
Ryan Dempster	R	21	1	5	.167	0	14	11	0	55	72	38	35	0	7.08
Oscar Henriquez	R	24	0	0	—	0	15	0	0	20	26	12	19	0	8.55
1 Manuel Barrios	R	23	0	0	—	0	2	0	0	3	4	2	1	0	3.38
Gabe Gonzalez	L	26	0	0	—	0	3	0	0	1	1	1	0	0	9.00
Donn Pall	R	36	0	1	.000	0	23	0	0	33	42	7	26	0	5.13
Chris Hammond	L	32	0	2	.000	0	14	0	0	14	20	8	8	0	6.59
1 Felix Heredia	L	23	0	3	.000	2	41	0	0	41	38	32	38	0	5.49
2 Justin Speier	R	24	0	3	.000	0	18	0	0	19	25	12	15	0	8.38
Vic Darensbourg	L	27	0	7	.000	1	59	0	0	71	52	30	74	0	3.68
Joe Fontenot (SJ)	R	21	0	7	.000	0	8	8	0	43	56	20	24	0	6.33
Alex Fernandez (SJ) 28															

CENTRAL DIVISION

HOUSTON 1st 102-60 .629 LARRY DIERKER

Name	G by Pos	B	AGE	G	AB	R	H	2B	3B	HR	RBI	BB	SO	SB	BA	SA
TOTALS			29	162	5641	874	1578	326	28	166	818	621	1122	155	.280	.436
Jeff Bagwell	1B147	R	30	147	540	124	164	33	1	34	111	109	90	19	.304	.557
Craig Biggio	2B159	R	32	160	646	123	210	51	2	20	88	64	113	50	.325	.503
Ricky Gutierrez	SS141	R	28	141	491	55	128	24	3	2	46	54	84	13	.261	.334
Bill Spiers	3B99 2B9 1B7 2B2	L	32	123	384	66	105	27	4	4	43	45	62	11	.273	.396
Derek Bell	OF154	R	29	156	630	111	198	41	2	22	108	51	126	13	.314	.490
Carl Everett	OF123	B	27	133	467	72	138	34	4	15	76	44	102	14	.296	.482
Moises Alou	OF154	R	31	159	584	104	182	34	5	38	124	84	87	11	.312	.582
Brad Ausmus	C124	R	29	128	412	62	111	10	4	6	45	53	60	10	.269	.357
Sean Berry	3B87	R	32	102	299	48	94	17	1	13	52	31	50	3	.314	.508
Dave Clark	OF22	L	35	93	131	12	27	7	0	4	14	14	45	1	.206	.260
Tim Bogar	SS55 2B11 3B11	R	31	79	156	12	24	4	1	1	8	16	32	2	.154	.212
Richard Hidalgo (SJ)	OF72	R	23	74	211	31	64	15	0	7	35	17	37	3	.303	.474
Tony Eusebio	C54	R	31	62	182	13	46	6	1	1	36	18	31	1	.253	.313
J.R. Phillips	1B12 OF6	L	28	36	58	4	11	0	0	2	9	7	22	0	.190	.293
Jack Howell (WJ)	1B10 3B2	L	36	24	38	4	11	5	0	1	7	4	12	0	.289	.500
2 Pete Incaviglia	OF3	R	34	13	16	0	2	1	0	0	2	1	4	0	.125	.188
Russ Johnson	3B5 2B1	R	25	8	13	2	3	1	0	0	1	1	5	1	.231	.308
Mitch Meluskey	C3	B	24	8	8	1	2	1	0	0	2	1	0	0	.250	.375
Ray Montgomery (XJ)	OF2	R	28	6	5	2	2	0	0	0	0	1	2	0	.400	.400
Daryle Ward		L	23	4	3	1	1	0	0	0	0	1	2	0	.333	.333

NAME	T	AGE	W	L	PCT	SV	G	GS	CG	IP	H	BB	SO	SHO	ERA
		28	102	60	.630	44	162	162	12	1471	1435	465	1187	11	3.50
Shane Reynolds	R	30	19	8	.704	0	35	35	3	233	257	53	209	1	3.51
Jose Lima	R	25	16	8	.667	0	33	33	3	233	229	32	169	1	3.70
Sean Bergman	R	28	12	9	.571	0	31	27	1	172	183	42	100	0	3.72
Mike Hampton	L	25	11	7	.611	0	32	32	1	212	227	81	137	1	3.36
2 Randy Johnson	L	34	10	1	.909	0	11	11	4	84	57	26	116	4	1.28
Doug Henry	R	34	8	2	.800	2	59	0	0	71	55	35	59	0	3.04
1 Pete Schourek	L	29	7	6	.538	0	15	15	0	80	82	36	59	0	4.50
Billy Wagner	L	26	4	3	.571	30	58	0	0	60	46	25	97	0	2.70
Mike Magnante	L	33	4	7	.364	2	48	0	0	52	56	26	39	0	4.88
C.J. Nitkowski	L	25	3	3	.500	3	43	0	0	60	49	23	44	0	3.77
2 Jay Powell	R	26	3	3	.500	4	29	0	0	34	22	15	38	0	2.38
Trever Miller	L	25	2	0	1.000	1	37	1	0	53	57	20	30	0	3.04
Scott Elarton	R	22	2	1	.667	1	28	2	0	57	40	20	56	0	3.32
John Halama	L	26	1	1	.500	0	6	6	0	32	37	13	21	0	5.85
Reggie Harris	R	29	0	0	—	0	6	0	0	6	6	2	2	0	6.00
Jose Cabrera (SJ)	R	26	0	0	—	0	4	0	0	4	8	2	1	0	8.31
Mike Grzanich	R	25	0	0	—	0	1	0	0	1	1	2	1	0	18.00
Bob Scanlan	R	31	0	1	.000	0	27	0	0	26	24	13	9	0	3.08
Ramon Garcia (EJ) 28 Chris Holt (SJ) 26															

* Johnson, also with Seattle, major league leader in SO with 329 and ShO with 6.

CHICAGO 2nd 90-73 .552 12.5 (Wild Card) JIM RIGGLEMAN

Name	G by Pos	B	AGE	G	AB	R	H	2B	3B	HR	RBI	BB	SO	SB	BA	SA
TOTALS			30	163	5649	831	1494	250	34	212	788	601	1223	65	.264	.433
Mark Grace	1B156	L	34	158	595	92	184	39	3	17	89	93	56	4	.309	.471
Micky Morandini	2B152	L	32	154	582	93	172	20	4	8	53	72	84	13	.296	.385
Jeff Blauser	SS106	R	32	119	361	49	79	11	3	4	26	60	93	2	.219	.299
Jose Hernandez	3B72 OF54 SS45 1B3 2B2	R	28	149	488	76	124	23	7	23	75	40	140	4	.254	.471
Sammy Sosa	OF159	R	29	159	643	134	198	20	0	66	158	73	171	18	.308	.647
Lance Johnson (HJ)	OF78	L	34	85	304	51	85	8	4	2	18	10	38	10	.280	.352
Henry Rodriguez	OF114	L	30	128	415	56	104	21	1	31	85	54	113	1	.251	.530
Scott Servais	C110 1B1	R	31	113	325	35	72	15	1	7	36	26	51	1	.222	.338
Brant Brown	OF102 1B7	L	27	124	347	56	101	17	7	14	48	30	95	4	.291	.501
Manny Alexander	SS50 2B27 3B19 OF1	R	27	108	264	34	60	10	1	5	25	18	66	4	.227	.330
Tyler Houston	C63 3B12 1B7	L	27	95	255	26	65	7	1	9	33	13	53	2	.255	.396
Matt Mieske		R	30	77	97	16	29	7	0	1	12	11	17	0	.299	.402
1 Kevin Orie	3B57	R	25	64	204	24	37	14	0	2	21	18	35	1	.181	.279
1 Glenallen Hill	OF34	R	33	48	131	26	46	5	0	8	23	14	34	0	.351	.573
Sandy Martinez	C33	L	27	45	87	7	23	9	1	0	7	13	21	1	.264	.391
2 Gary Gaetti	3B36 P1	R	39	37	128	21	41	11	0	8	27	12	23	0	.320	.594
Terrell Lowery	OF22	R	27	24	15	2	3	1	0	0	2	3	7	0	.200	.267
Jason Hardtke	3B7 OF1	B	26	18	21	2	5	0	0	0	2	2	6	0	.238	.238
Pedro Valdes (FJ)	OF7	R	25	14	23	1	5	1	1	0	2	1	3	0	.217	.348
3 Orlando Merced	OF4	L	31	12	10	2	3	0	0	1	5	1	0	0	.300	.600
1 Derrick White	OF1	R	28	11	10	1	1	0	0	0	2	0	5	0	.100	.100
Jason Maxwell	2B1	R	26	7	3	2	1	0	0	0	0	2	0	0	.333	.333
Jose Nieves	SS1	R	23	4	3	0	0	0	0	0	0	0	1	0	.000	.000
Robin Jennings (WJ) 26																

NAME	T	AGE	W	L	PCT	SV	G	GS	CG	IP	H	BB	SO	SHO	ERA
		29	90	73	.552	56	163	163	7	1477	1528	575	1207	7	4.47
Kevin Tapani	R	34	19	9	.679	0	35	34	2	219	244	62	136	2	4.85
Steve Trachsel	R	27	15	8	.652	0	33	33	1	208	204	84	149	0	4.46
Kerry Wood	R	21	13	6	.684	0	26	26	1	167	117	85	233	1	3.40
Mark Clark	R	30	9	14	.391	0	33	33	2	214	236	48	161	1	4.84
Jeremi Gonzalez (EJ)	R	23	7	7	.500	0	20	20	1	110	124	41	70	1	5.32
Terry Adams	R	25	7	7	.500	1	63	0	0	73	72	41	73	0	4.33
Terry Mulholland	L	35	6	5	.545	3	70	6	0	112	100	39	72	0	2.89
1 Felix Heredia	L	23	1	0	1.000	0	30	0	0	18	19	6	16	0	4.00
2 Matt Karchner	R	31	3	1	.750	0	29	0	0	28	30	14	22	0	5.14
Rod Beck	R	29	3	4	.429	51	81	0	0	80	86	20	81	0	3.02
1 Amaury Telemaco	R	24	1	1	.500	0	14	0	0	28	23	13	18	0	3.90
Bob Patterson	L	39	1	1	.500	1	33	0	0	20	16	12	17	0	7.53
Marc Pisciotta	R	27	1	2	.333	0	43	0	0	44	44	32	31	0	4.09
Dave Stevens	R	28	1	2	.333	0	31	0	0	38	42	17	31	0	4.74
2 Don Wengert	R	28	1	5	.167	0	21	6	0	50	55	23	41	0	5.07
Rodney Myers	R	28	0	0	—	0	12	0	0	18	26	6	15	0	7.00
1 Ben VanRyn	L	26	0	0	—	0	4	0	0	5	5	4	4	0	7.20
2 Chris Haney	L	29	0	0	—	0	3	0	0	4	4	1	4	0	9.00
Kurt Miller	R	25	0	0	—	0	4	0	0	4	8	4	4	0	9.00
2 Tony Fossas (SJ)	L	40	0	0	—	0	3	0	0	3	4	3	3	0	9.00
Kevin Foster (SJ)	R	29	0	0	—	0	3	1	0	5	8	3	4	0	16.20
Kennie Steenstra	R	27	0	0	—	0	2	0	0	1	4	1	1	0	10.80
1 Justin Speier	R	24	0	1	.000	0	2	0	0	1	2	1	1	0	13.50
2 Mike Morgan	R	38	0	1	.000	0	5	0	0	23	30	15	10	0	7.15

ST. LOUIS 3rd 83-79 .512 19 TONY LaRUSSA

Name	G by Pos	B	AGE	G	AB	R	H	2B	3B	HR	RBI	BB	SO	SB	BA	SA
TOTALS			31	163	5593	810	1444	292	30	223	781	676	1179	133	.258	.441
Mark McGwire	1B151	R	34	155	509	130	152	21	0	70	147	162	155	1	.299	.752
Delino DeShields (KJ)	2B111 1B1	L	29	117	420	74	122	21	8	7	44	56	61	26	.290	.429
1 Royce Clayton	SS89	R	28	90	355	59	83	19	1	4	29	40	51	19	.234	.327
1 Gary Gaetti	3B83 1B3 2B1 OF1 P1	R	39	91	306	39	81	23	1	11	43	31	39	1	.265	.454
Brian Jordan	OF141 3B1	R	31	150	564	100	178	34	7	25	91	40	66	17	.316	.534
Ray Lankford	OF145	L	31	154	533	94	156	37	1	31	105	86	151	26	.293	.540
Ron Gant	OF104	R	33	121	383	60	92	17	1	26	67	51	92	8	.240	.493
Eli Marrero	C73 1B2	R	24	83	254	28	62	18	1	4	20	28	42	6	.244	.370
John Mabry	OF80 3B38 1B16	L	27	142	377	41	94	22	0	9	46	30	76	0	.249	.379
Willie McGee	OF88 1B1	B	39	123	269	27	68	10	1	3	34	14	49	7	.253	.331
Tom Lampkin	C62 OF5 1B2	L	34	93	216	25	50	12	1	6	28	24	32	3	.231	.380
Brian Hunter	OF25 1B10	R	32	102	112	11	23	9	1	4	13	7	23	1	.205	.411
Luis Ordaz	SS54 3B2 2B1	R	22	57	153	9	31	5	0	0	8	12	18	2	.203	.235
2 Fernando Tatis	3B55 SS3	R	23	55	202	28	56	18	2	8	26	24	57	7	.287	.505
Pat Kelly	2B41 OF3 SS2	R	30	53	153	18	33	4	0	2	14	13	48	5	.216	.327
Tom Pagnozzi	C44	R	35	51	160	7	35	9	0	1	12	14	37	0	.219	.294
David Howard (SJ)	2B19 SS16 3B14 OF4	B	31	46	102	15	25	1	1	2	12	12	22	0	.245	.333
Placido Polanco	SS28 2B14 3B11	R	22	45	114	10	29	3	2	1	5	3	13	4	.254	.342
J.D. Drew	OF11	L	22	14	36	9	15	3	1	5	13	4	10	0	.417	.972
Joe McEwing	2B6 OF3	R	25	8	20	1	5	0	0	0	2	0	3	1	.250	.250
Mark Little	OF7	R	25	7	12	0	1	0	0	0	2	0	3	1	.083	.083
1 David Bell	3B4 2B1	R	25	4	9	1	2	0	0	0	3	0	1	1	.222	.333
2 Shawn Gilbert	2B2	R	33	4	2	1	1	0	0	0	0	0	1	0	.500	.500

NAME	T	AGE	W	L	PCT	SV	G	GS	CG	IP	H	BB	SO	SHO	ERA
		29	83	79	.512	44	163	163	6	1470	1513	558	972	10	4.31
Kent Mercker	L	30	11	11	.500	0	30	29	0	162	199	53	72	0	5.07
1 Todd Stottlemyre	R	33	9	9	.500	0	23	23	3	161	146	51	147	0	3.51
Juan Acevedo	R	28	8	6	.727	15	50	9	0	98	83	29	56	0	2.56
Mark Petkovsek	R	32	7	4	.636	0	48	10	0	106	131	36	55	0	4.77
Matt Morris (SJ)	R	23	7	5	.583	0	17	17	2	114	101	42	79	1	2.53
Manny Aybar	R	26	6	6	.500	0	20	14	0	81	90	42	57	5	5.98
Mike Busby (EJ)	R	25	5	2	.714	0	20	7	0	46	45	15	33	0	4.09
Donovan Osborne (SJ)	L	29	3	4	.556	0	14	14	1	84	84	22	60	1	4.09
Lance Painter	L	30	4	0	1.000	1	65	0	0	47	42	28	39	0	3.99
2 Darren Oliver	L	27	4	4	.500	0	10	10	0	57	64	23	29	0	4.26
Kent Bottenfield	R	29	4	6	.400	4	44	17	0	134	128	57	98	0	4.44
Jose Jimenez	R	24	1	1	1.000	0	3	3	0	12	12	4	2	0	2.95
John Frascatore	R	28	3	4	.429	0	69	0	0	96	95	36	49	0	4.14
Curtis King	R	27	2	1	.000	0	36	0	0	36	37	25	22	0	3.53
1 Cliff Politte	R	24	2	3	.400	0	8	8	0	37	45	18	22	0	6.45
2 Bobby Witt	R	34	2	5	.286	0	17	17	0	47	55	20	28	0	4.94
Brady Raggio	R	25	1	1	.500	0	9	7	0	22	33	6	6	0	15.43
Bryan Eversgerd	L	29	0	0	—	0	9	0	0	9	9	4	4	0	9.00
1 Gary Gaetti	R	39	0	0	—	0	1	0	0	0	1	0	0	0	—
Braden Looper	R	23	0	0	—	0	12	0	0	16	14	10	17	0	5.40
Rich Croushore	R	27	0	0	—	0	24	0	0	29	24	29	47	0	4.97
Sean Lowe	R	27	0	0	—	0	4	0	0	7	13	6	6	0	15.19
Jeff Brantley	R	34	0	0	.000	14	48	0	0	51	40	18	48	0	4.44
Alan Benes (SJ) 26															

CINCINNATI — 4th 77-85 .475 25 — JACK McKEON

Name	G by Pos	B	AGE	G	AB	R	H	2B	3B	HR	RBI	BB	SO	SB	BA	SA
TOTALS			27	162	5496	750	1441	298	28	138	723	608	1107	95	.262	.402
Sean Casey (IJ)	1B86	L	23	96	302	44	82	21	1	7	52	43	45	1	.272	.417
Bret Boone	2B156	R	29	157	583	76	155	38	1	24	95	48	104	6	.266	.458
Barry Larkin	SS145	R	34	145	538	93	166	34	10	17	72	79	69	26	.309	.504
Willie Greene	3B76 OF28 SS2	L	26	111	356	57	96	18	1	14	49	56	80	6	.270	.444
Jon Nunnally	OF70	L	26	74	174	29	36	9	0	7	20	34	38	3	.207	.379
Reggie Sanders	OF131	R	30	135	481	83	129	18	6	14	59	51	137	20	.268	.418
Dmitri Young	OF105 1B44	B	24	140	536	81	166	48	1	14	83	47	94	2	.310	.481
Eddie Taubensee	C126	L	29	130	431	61	120	27	0	11	72	52	93	1	.278	.418
Chris Stynes	OF80 3B22 2B11 SS2	R	25	123	347	52	88	10	1	6	27	32	36	15	.254	.340
Eduardo Perez	1B51 3B1 OF1	R	28	84	172	20	41	4	0	4	30	21	45	0	.238	.331
Pat Watkins	OF77	R	25	83	147	11	39	8	1	2	15	8	21	1	.265	.374
Melvin Nieves (XJ)	OF25	B	26	83	119	8	30	4	0	2	17	26	42	0	.252	.336
Pokey Reese (RJ)	3B32 SS18 2B3	R	25	59	133	20	34	2	2	1	16	14	28	3	.256	.323
Aaron Boone	3B52 2B1 SS1	R	25	58	181	24	51	13	2	2	28	15	36	6	.282	.409
Brook Fordyce	C54	R	28	57	146	8	37	9	0	3	14	11	28	0	.253	.377
Lenny Harris	OF32 P1	L	33	57	122	12	36	8	0	0	10	8	9	1	.295	.361
Roberto Petagine	1B15 OF15	L	27	34	62	14	16	2	1	3	7	16	11	1	.258	.468
Mike Frank	OF28	L	24	28	89	14	20	6	0	0	7	7	12	0	.225	.292
Jeffrey Hammonds	OF25	R	27	26	86	14	26	4	1	0	11	13	18	1	.302	.372
Paul Konerko	3B9 1B7 OF7	R	22	26	73	7	16	3	0	3	13	6	10	0	.219	.384
Tony Tarasco	OF7	L	27	15	24	5	5	2	0	1	4	3	5	0	.208	.417
Damian Jackson	SS10 OF3	R	24	13	38	4	12	5	0	0	7	6	4	2	.316	.447
Guillermo Garcia	C11	R	26	12	36	3	7	2	0	2	4	2	13	0	.194	.417
Stephen Larkin	1B1	L	24	1	3	0	1	0	0	0	0	0	1	0	.333	.333

NAME	T	AGE	W	L	PCT	SV	G	GS	CG	IP	H	BB	SO	SHO	ERA
TOTALS		28	77	85	.475	42	162	162	6	1441	1400	573	1098	8	4.44
Pete Harnisch	R	31	14	7	.667	0	32	32	2	209	176	64	157	1	3.14
Brett Tomko	R	25	13	12	.520	0	34	34	1	211	198	64	162	0	4.44
Mike Remlinger	L	32	8	15	.348	0	35	28	1	164	164	87	144	1	4.82
Steve Parris	R	30	6	5	.545	0	18	16	1	99	89	32	77	1	3.73
Scott Sullivan	R	27	5	5	.500	1	67	0	0	102	98	36	86	0	5.21
Gabe White	L	26	5	5	.500	9	69	3	0	99	86	27	83	0	4.01
2 John Hudek	R	31	4	2	.667	0	30	0	0	37	27	28	40	0	2.43
Stan Belinda (XJ)	R	31	4	8	.333	1	40	0	0	61	46	28	57	0	3.23
2 Dennis Reyes	L	21	3	1	.750	0	8	7	0	39	35	27	44	0	4.42
2 Jason Bere	R	27	3	2	.600	0	9	7	0	44	39	20	31	0	4.12
Scott Winchester	R	25	3	6	.333	0	16	16	1	79	101	27	40	0	5.81
Danny Graves	R	25	2	1	.667	8	62	0	0	81	76	28	44	0	3.32
1 David Weathers	R	28	2	4	.333	0	16	9	0	62	86	27	51	0	6.21
1 Jeff Shaw	R	31	2	4	.333	23	39	0	0	50	40	12	29	0	1.81
Steve Cooke	L	28	1	0	1.000	0	1	1	0	6	4	0	3	0	1.50
Ricardo Jordan	L	28	1	0	1.000	0	6	0	0	3	4	7	1	0	24.30
Scott Klingenbeck	R	27	1	3	.250	0	4	4	0	23	26	7	13	0	5.96
Keith Glauber (SJ)	R	26	0	0	—	0	3	0	0	8	6	1	4	0	2.35
2 Marc Kroon (SJ)	R	25	0	0	.000	0	4	0	0	5	7	8	4	0	13.50
Mark Hutton	R	28	0	1	.000	0	10	2	0	17	24	17	3	0	7.41
Todd Williams	R	27	0	0	.000	0	6	0	0	9	15	6	4	0	7.71
Eddie Priest	L	24	0	1	.000	0	2	2	0	6	12	1	1	0	10.50
2 Rick Krivda	R	28	0	2	.000	0	16	1	0	26	41	19	19	0	11.28

MILWAUKEE — 5th 74-88 .456 28 — PHIL GARNER

Name	G by Pos	B	AGE	G	AB	R	H	2B	3B	HR	RBI	BB	SO	SB	BA	SA
TOTALS			28	162	5541	707	1439	266	17	152	673	532	1039	81	.260	.396
John Jaha (FJ)	1B57	R	32	73	216	29	45	6	1	7	38	49	66	1	.208	.343
Fernando Vina	2B158	L	29	159	637	101	198	39	7	7	45	54	46	22	.311	.427
Jose Valentin	SS139	B	28	151	428	65	96	24	0	16	49	63	105	10	.224	.393
Jeff Cirillo	3B149 1B6	R	28	156	604	97	194	31	1	14	68	79	88	10	.321	.445
Jeromy Burnitz	OF161	L	29	161	609	92	160	28	1	38	125	70	158	7	.263	.499
Marquis Grissom	OF137	R	31	142	542	57	147	28	1	10	60	24	78	13	.271	.382
Dave Nilsson (KJ)	1B49 OF37 C7	L	28	102	309	39	83	14	1	12	56	33	48	2	.269	.437
Mike Matheny	C107	R	27	108	320	24	76	13	0	6	27	11	63	1	.238	.334
Mark Loretta	1B70 SS56 3B22 2B13 OF1	R	26	140	434	55	137	29	0	6	54	42	47	9	.316	.424
Darrin Jackson	OF94	R	35	114	204	20	49	13	1	4	20	9	37	1	.240	.373
Bob Hamelin	1B51	L	30	109	146	15	32	6	0	7	22	16	30	0	.219	.404
Marc Newfield	OF55	R	25	93	186	15	44	7	0	3	25	19	29	0	.237	.323
Bobby Hughes	C72 OF3	R	27	85	218	28	50	7	2	9	29	16	54	1	.229	.404
Geoff Jenkins	OF81	L	23	84	262	33	60	12	1	9	28	20	61	1	.229	.385
Eric Owens	OF16 2B4	R	27	34	40	5	5	2	0	1	4	2	6	0	.125	.250
Brian Banks	C5 1B2 3B1 OF1	B	27	24	24	3	7	2	0	1	5	4	7	0	.292	.500
Jesse Levis (SJ)	C14	L	30	22	37	4	13	0	0	0	4	7	6	1	.351	.351
Greg Martinez	OF6	B	26	13	3	2	0	0	0	0	0	1	2	0	.000	.000
Ron Belliard	2B1	R	23	8	5	1	1	0	0	0	0	3	0	0	.200	.200
Marcus Jensen	C1	B	25	2	0	0	0	0	0	0	0	0	0	0	.000	.000

NAME	T	AGE	W	L	PCT	SV	G	GS	CG	IP	H	BB	SO	SHO	ERA
TOTALS		29	74	88	.457	39	162	162	2	1451	1538	550	1063	2	4.63
Scott Karl	L	26	10	11	.476	0	33	33	0	192	219	66	102	0	4.40
Steve Woodard	R	23	10	12	.455	0	34	26	0	166	170	33	135	0	4.18
Brad Woodall	L	29	7	9	.438	0	31	20	0	138	145	47	85	0	4.96
1 Jeff Juden	R	27	7	11	.389	0	24	24	2	138	149	66	109	0	5.53
Bob Wickman	R	29	6	9	.400	25	72	0	0	82	79	39	71	0	3.72
Alberto Reyes (EJ)	R	27	5	1	.833	0	50	0	0	57	55	31	58	0	3.95
Bronswell Patrick	R	27	4	1	.800	0	32	3	0	79	83	29	49	0	4.69
2 David Weathers	R	28	4	1	.800	0	28	0	0	48	44	14	43	0	3.21
Rafael Roque	L	26	4	2	.667	0	9	9	0	48	42	24	34	0	4.88
Cal Eldred (EJ)	R	30	4	8	.333	0	23	23	0	133	157	61	86	0	4.80
2 Bill Pulsipher	L	24	3	4	.429	0	11	10	0	58	63	26	38	0	4.66
1 Doug Jones	R	41	3	4	.429	12	46	0	0	54	65	11	43	0	5.17
Mike Myers	L	29	2	2	.500	1	70	0	0	50	44	22	40	0	2.70
Jose Mercedes (SJ)	R	27	2	2	.500	0	7	5	0	32	42	9	11	0	6.75
2 Eric Plunk	R	34	1	3	.333	1	26	0	0	32	33	15	36	0	3.69
Chad Fox (SJ)	R	27	1	4	.200	0	49	0	0	57	56	20	64	0	3.95
Paul Wagner	R	30	1	5	.167	0	13	9	0	56	67	31	37	0	7.11
Valerio De Los Santos	L	25	0	0	—	0	13	0	0	22	11	2	18	0	2.91
Rod Henderson	R	27	0	0	—	0	1	0	0	4	5	0	1	0	9.82
1 Bobby Chouinard	R	26	0	0	—	0	1	0	0	3	5	0	1	0	3.00
Travis Smith (EJ)	R	25	0	0	—	0	1	0	0	1	1	1	0	0	0.00
Greg Mullins	L	26	0	0	—	0	2	0	0	1	1	0	1	0	0.00
Joe Hudson	R	27	0	0	—	0	1	0	0	0.1	2	4	0	0	162.00
Jeff D'Amico (SJ) 22															

PITTSBURGH — 6th 69-93 .425 33 — GENE LAMONT

Name	G by Pos	B	AGE	G	AB	R	H	2B	3B	HR	RBI	BB	SO	SB	BA	SA
TOTALS			27	163	5650	650	1395	271	35	107	613	393	1060	159	.254	.374
Kevin Young	1B157	R	29	159	592	88	160	40	2	27	108	44	127	15	.270	.481
Tony Womack	2B152 OF5 SS2	L	28	159	655	85	185	26	7	3	45	38	94	58	.282	.357
Lou Collier	SS107	R	24	110	334	30	82	13	6	2	34	31	70	2	.246	.338
Aramis Ramirez (SJ)	3B71	R	20	72	251	23	59	9	1	6	24	18	72	0	.235	.351
Jose Guillen	OF151	R	22	153	573	60	153	38	2	14	84	21	100	3	.267	.414
Jermaine Allensworth	OF66	R	26	69	233	30	72	13	3	3	24	17	43	8	.309	.429
Al Martin	OF114	L	30	125	440	57	105	15	2	12	47	32	91	20	.239	.364
Jason Kendall	C144	R	24	149	535	95	175	36	3	12	75	51	61	26	.327	.473
Turner Ward	OF97	B	33	123	282	33	74	13	3	9	46	27	40	5	.262	.426
Doug Strange	3B42 2B9 1B3	B	34	90	185	9	32	8	0	0	14	10	39	1	.173	.216
Kevin Polcovich	SS54 2B15 3B8	R	28	81	212	18	40	12	0	0	14	15	33	4	.189	.245
Manny Martinez	OF62	R	27	73	180	21	45	11	2	6	24	9	44	0	.250	.433
Mark Smith	OF24 1B6	R	28	59	128	18	25	6	0	2	13	10	26	7	.195	.289
Freddy Garcia	3B47 1B4	R	25	56	172	27	44	11	1	9	26	18	45	0	.256	.488
Adrian Brown	OF38	B	24	41	152	20	43	4	1	0	5	9	18	4	.283	.322
Keith Osik	C26 3B7	R	29	39	98	8	21	4	0	0	7	13	16	1	.214	.255
Abraham Nunez	SS23	B	22	24	52	6	10	2	0	1	2	12	14	4	.192	.288
Chance Sanford	3B5 2B1 SS1	L	26	14	28	3	4	1	1	0	3	1	6	0	.143	.250
Tim Laker	1B4 C1	R	28	14	24	2	9	1	0	1	2	1	3	0	.375	.542
Emil Brown	OF10	R	23	13	39	2	10	1	0	0	3	1	11	0	.256	.282
Steve Bieser	OF1	L	30	13	11	2	3	1	0	0	1	2	2	0	.273	.364

NAME	T	AGE	W	L	PCT	SV	G	GS	CG	IP	H	BB	SO	SHO	ERA
TOTALS		27	69	93	.426	41	163	163	7	1449	1433	530	1112	10	3.91
Francisco Cordova	R	26	13	14	.481	0	33	33	3	220	204	69	157	2	3.31
Jason Schmidt	R	25	11	14	.440	0	33	33	0	214	228	71	158	0	4.07
Chris Peters	L	26	8	10	.444	1	39	21	1	148	142	55	103	0	3.47
Jon Lieber	R	28	8	14	.364	1	29	28	2	171	182	40	138	0	4.11
1 Esteban Loaiza	R	26	6	5	.545	0	21	14	0	92	96	30	53	0	4.52
Jose Silva (BA)	R	24	6	7	.462	0	18	18	1	100	104	30	64	0	4.40
Mike Williams	R	29	4	2	.667	37	61	0	0	51	39	16	59	0	1.94
Jason Christiansen	L	28	3	3	.500	6	60	0	0	65	51	27	71	0	2.51
Sean Lawrence	L	27	2	1	.667	0	7	3	0	25	30	12	12	0	7.32
Jeff Tabaka (BJ)	L	34	2	2	.500	0	37	0	0	51	37	22	40	0	3.02
Elmer Dessens	R	27	2	6	.250	0	43	5	0	75	90	25	43	0	5.67
Rich Loiselle	R	26	2	7	.222	19	54	0	0	55	56	36	48	0	3.44
2 Todd Van Poppel	R	26	1	2	.333	0	18	7	0	47	53	18	32	0	5.36
Jeff McCurry	R	28	1	3	.250	0	16	0	0	19	24	9	11	0	6.52
Marc Wilkins (SJ)	R	27	0	0	—	0	15	0	0	15	13	9	17	0	3.52
Javier Martinez	R	21	0	0	—	0	41	0	0	41	39	34	42	0	4.83
Ricardo Rincon	L	28	0	2	.000	14	60	0	0	65	50	29	64	0	2.91
Jeff Wallace (EJ) 22															

WEST DIVISION

SAN DIEGO — 1st 98-64 .604 — BRUCE BOCHY

Name	G by Pos	B	AGE	G	AB	R	H	2B	3B	HR	RBI	BB	SO	SB	BA	SA
TOTALS			31	162	5490	749	1390	292	30	167	715	604	1072	79	.253	.409
Wally Joyner	1B127	L	36	131	439	58	131	30	1	12	80	51	44	1	.298	.453
Quilvio Veras	2B131	B	27	138	517	79	138	24	2	6	45	84	78	24	.267	.356
Chris Gomez	SS143	R	27	145	449	55	120	32	3	4	39	51	87	1	.267	.379
Ken Caminiti	3B126	B	35	131	452	87	114	29	0	29	82	71	108	6	.252	.509
Tony Gwynn	OF116	L	38	127	461	65	148	35	0	16	69	35	18	3	.321	.501
Steve Finley	OF157	L	33	159	619	92	154	40	6	14	67	45	103	12	.249	.401
Greg Vaughn	OF151	R	32	158	573	112	156	28	4	50	119	79	121	11	.272	.597
Carlos Hernandez	C122 1B1	R	31	129	390	34	102	15	0	9	52	16	54	2	.262	.369
Mark Sweeney	OF34 1B21	L	28	122	192	17	45	8	3	2	15	26	37	1	.234	.339
Ruben Rivera	OF91	R	24	95	172	31	36	7	2	6	29	28	52	5	.209	.378
Ed Giovanola	3B37 2B36 SS1	L	29	92	139	19	32	3	3	1	9	22	22	1	.230	.317
Andy Sheets	SS39 3B23 2B22 1B2	R	26	88	194	31	47	5	3	7	29	21	62	7	.242	.407
Greg Myers (WJ)	C52	L	32	69	171	19	42	10	0	4	20	17	36	0	.246	.374
Jim Leyritz	C24 1B20 3B1 OF1	R	34	62	143	17	38	10	0	4	18	21	40	0	.266	.420
James Mouton	OF33	R	29	55	63	8	12	2	1	0	7	7	11	4	.190	.254
Archi Cianfrocco	1B19 3B13 2B8 OF1	R	31	41	72	4	9	3	1	0	3	3	16	0	.125	.208
George Arias	3B14 1B1	R	26	20	36	4	7	1	0	1	4	3	16	0	.194	.361
John Vander Wal	OF5 1B3	L	32	20	23	3	6	1	0	0	5	2	8	0	.240	.360
Eddie Williams	1B7	R	33	17	28	1	4	0	0	0	1	1	4	0	.143	.143
Mandy Romero	C6	B	30	6	9	1	0	0	0	0	0	2	4	0	.000	.000
Ben Davis	C1	B	21	1	1	0	0	0	0	0	0	0	0	0	.000	.000

NAME	T	AGE	W	L	PCT	SV	G	GS	CG	IP	H	BB	SO	SHO	ERA
TOTALS		30	98	64	.605	59	162	162	14	1455	1384	501	1217	11	3.63
Kevin Brown	R	33	18	7	.720	0	36	35	7	257	225	49	257	3	2.38
Andy Ashby	R	30	17	9	.654	0	33	33	5	227	223	58	151	1	3.34
Joey Hamilton	R	27	13	13	.500	0	34	34	0	217	220	106	147	0	4.27
Dan Miceli	R	27	10	5	.667	2	67	0	0	73	64	27	70	0	3.22
Sterling Hitchcock	L	27	9	7	.563	1	39	27	2	176	169	48	158	1	3.93
Brian Boehringer	R	29	4	2	.714	0	56	1	0	76	75	45	67	0	4.35
Donne Wall	R	30	5	4	.556	1	46	1	0	70	50	32	56	0	2.43
Trevor Hoffman	R	30	4	2	.667	53	66	0	0	73	41	21	86	0	1.48
Mark Langston	L	37	4	6	.400	0	22	16	0	81	107	41	56	0	5.86
2 Scott Sanders	R	29	3	1	.750	0	23	0	0	31	33	5	26	0	4.11
1 Pete Smith	R	32	3	2	.600	0	10	8	0	43	45	18	36	0	4.78
Matt Clement	R	23	2	0	1.000	0	4	2	0	14	15	7	13	0	4.61
1 Carlos Reyes	R	29	2	2	.500	1	22	0	0	28	26	8	24	0	3.58
Stan Spencer	R	29	1	0	1.000	0	6	6	0	31	29	4	31	0	4.70
Roberto Ramirez	L	25	1	0	1.000	0	12	0	0	12	12	17	6	0	6.14
2 Randy Myers	L	35	0	4	.000	3	21	0	0	14	15	7	9	0	6.28
1 Don Wengert	R	28	0	0	—	0	10	0	0	14	15	5	5	0	5.93
2 Jim Bruske	R	33	0	0	—	0	7	0	0	7	10	4	4	0	3.86
Will Cunnane (EJ)	R	24	0	0	—	0	3	0	0	2	5	4	6	0	6.00
1 Marc Kroon	R	25	0	0	—	0	5	0	0	3	4	6	5	0	0.00
2 Ben VanRyn	L	26	0	1	.000	0	3	0	0	3	3	4	1	0	10.13
Ed Vosberg (SJ) 36															

SAN FRANCISCO 2nd 89-74 .546 9.5 DUSTY BAKER

Name	G by Pos	B	AGE	G	AB	R	H	2B	3B	HR	RBI	BB	SO	SB	BA	SA
TOTALS			30	163	5628	845	1540	292	26	161	800	678	1040	102	.274	.421
J.T. Snow	1B136	B	30	138	435	65	108	29	1	15	79	58	84	1	.248	.423
Jeff Kent (KJ)	2B134 1B1	R	30	137	526	94	156	37	3	31	128	48	110	9	.297	.555
Rich Aurilia	SS120	R	26	122	413	54	110	27	2	9	49	31	62	3	.266	.407
Bill Mueller	3B137 2B10	B	27	145	534	93	157	27	0	9	59	79	83	2	.294	.395
Stan Javier	OF121	B	34	135	417	63	121	13	5	4	49	65	63	21	.290	.374
1 Darryl Hamilton	OF96	L	33	97	367	65	108	19	2	1	26	59	53	9	.294	.365
Barry Bonds	OF155	L	33	156	552	120	167	44	7	37	122	130	92	28	.303	.609
Brian Johnson	C95 OF1	R	30	99	308	34	73	8	1	13	34	28	67	0	.237	.396
Marvin Benard	OF79	L	28	121	286	41	92	21	1	3	36	34	39	11	.322	.434
Charlie Hayes	3B46 1B45	R	33	111	329	39	94	8	0	12	62	34	61	2	.286	.419
Rey Sanchez	SS76 2B36	R	30	109	316	44	90	14	2	2	30	16	47	3	.285	.361
Brent Mayne	C88	L	30	94	275	26	75	15	0	3	32	37	47	2	.273	.360
2 Chris Jones	OF29	R	32	45	90	14	17	2	1	2	10	8	28	2	.189	.300
2 Ellis Burks	OF41	R	33	42	147	22	45	6	1	5	22	19	31	8	.306	.463
2 Joe Carter	OF17 1B16	R	38	41	105	15	31	7	0	7	29	6	13	1	.295	.562
2 Shawon Dunston	SS9 OF6 2B1	R	35	36	51	10	9	2	0	3	8	0	10	2	.176	.392
Alex Diaz	OF21	B	29	34	62	5	8	2	0	0	5	0	15	1	.129	.161
Ramon Martinez	2B14	R	25	19	19	4	6	1	0	0	4	2	2	0	.316	.368
Armando Rios	OF5	L	26	12	7	3	4	0	0	2	3	3	2	0	.571	.429
Doug Mirabelli	C10	R	27	10	17	2	4	2	0	1	4	2	6	0	.235	.529
Wilson Delgado	SS6	B	25	10	12	1	2	1	0	0	1	1	3	0	.167	.250
Dante Powell	OF8	R	24	8	4	2	2	0	0	1	1	3	0	0	.500	1.250
1 Jacob Cruz		L	25	3	3	0	0	0	0	0	0	0	0	0	.000	.000
Jeff Ball	1B1	R	29	2	4	0	1	0	0	0	0	0	0	0	.250	.250

NAME	T	AGE	W	L	PCT	SV	G	GS	CG	IP	H	BB	SO	SHO	ERA
TOTALS		31	89	74	.546	44	163	163	6	1477	1457	562	1089	6	4.1
Kirk Rueter	L	27	16	9	.640	0	33	33	1	188	193	57	102	1	4.3
Mark Gardner	R	36	13	6	.684	0	33	33	4	212	203	65	151	2	4.3
Orel Hershiser	R	39	11	10	.524	0	34	34	0	202	200	85	126	0	4.4
Danny Darwin	R	42	8	10	.444	0	33	25	0	149	176	49	81	0	5.5
Robb Nen	R	28	7	7	.500	40	78	0	0	89	59	25	110	0	1.5
Shawn Estes (SJ)	L	25	7	12	.368	0	25	25	1	149	150	80	136	1	5.0
John Johnstone	R	29	6	5	.545	0	70	0	0	88	72	38	86	0	3.0
Julian Tavarez	R	25	5	3	.625	1	60	0	0	85	96	36	52	0	3.0
2 Jose Mesa	R	32	5	3	.625	0	32	0	0	31	30	18	28	0	3.5
Rich Rodriguez	L	35	4	0	1.000	2	68	0	0	66	69	20	44	0	3.7
Russ Ortiz	R	24	4	4	.500	0	22	13	0	88	90	46	75	0	4.9
1 Steve Reed	R	33	2	1	.667	1	50	0	0	55	30	19	50	0	1.4
1 Jim Poole	L	32	1	3	.250	0	26	0	0	32	38	9	16	0	5.2
Chris Brock	R	28	0	0	—	0	13	0	0	28	31	7	19	0	3.9
Dean Hartgraves	L	31	0	0	—	0	5	0	0	6	10	4	4	0	9.5
Cory Bailey	R	27	0	0	—	0	5	0	0	3	2	1	2	0	2.7
Alvin Morman	L	29	0	1	.000	0	9	0	0	7	8	3	7	0	5.1

Osvaldo Fernandez (EJ) 29

LOS ANGELES 3rd 83-79 .512 15 BILL RUSSELL 36-38 .486 GLENN HOFFMAN 47-41 .534

Name	G by Pos	B	AGE	G	AB	R	H	2B	3B	HR	RBI	BB	SO	SB	BA	SA
TOTALS			28	162	5459	669	1374	209	27	159	630	447	1056	137	.252	.387
Eric Karros	1B136	R	30	139	507	59	150	20	1	23	87	47	93	7	.296	.475
Eric Young	2B113	R	31	117	452	78	129	24	1	8	43	45	32	42	.285	.396
Jose Vizcaino (NJ)	SS66	B	30	67	237	30	62	9	0	3	29	17	35	5	.262	.338
Adrian Beltre	3B74 SS2	R	19	77	195	18	42	9	0	7	22	14	37	3	.215	.369
2 Gary Sheffield	OF89	R	29	90	301	52	95	16	1	16	57	69	30	18	.316	.535
Raul Mondesi	OF148	R	27	148	580	85	162	26	5	30	90	30	112	16	.279	.497
Todd Hollandsworth (SJ)	OF51	L	25	55	175	23	47	6	4	3	20	9	42	4	.269	.400
2 Charles Johnson	C100	R	26	102	346	31	75	13	0	12	35	29	99	0	.217	.358
Roger Cedeno	OF77	B	23	105	240	33	58	11	1	2	17	27	57	8	.242	.321
13 Matt Luke	OF63 1B18	L	27	102	237	34	56	12	1	12	34	17	60	2	.236	.447
Trenidad Hubbard (KJ)	OF81 3B1	R	34	94	208	29	62	9	1	7	18	18	46	9	.298	.452
Juan Castro	SS47 2B38 3B12	R	26	89	220	25	43	7	0	2	14	15	37	0	.195	.255
2 Jim Eisenreich	OF24 1B9	L	39	75	127	12	25	2	0	6	12	4	12	4	.197	.244
2 Bobby Bonilla	3B59 OF12	B	35	72	236	28	56	6	1	7	30	29	37	1	.237	.360
1 Wilton Guerrero	2B32 SS14 OF12	B	23	64	180	21	51	4	2	4	33	5	23	5	.283	.339
2 Mark Grudzielanek	SS51	R	28	51	193	11	51	6	0	2	21	5	23	7	.264	.326
1 Paul Konerko	1B23 3B11 OF11	R	22	49	144	14	31	1	0	4	16	10	30	0	.215	.306
Thomas Howard	OF29	L	33	47	76	9	14	4	1	2	9	4	15	1	.184	.316
1 Todd Zeile	3B40 1B1	R	32	40	158	22	40	6	1	7	27	10	24	1	.253	.437
1 Mike Piazza	C37	R	29	37	149	20	42	5	0	9	30	11	27	0	.282	.497
Tom Prince	C32	R	33	37	81	7	15	5	1	0	5	7	24	0	.185	.272
Alex Cora	SS21 2B4	L	22	29	33	1	4	0	0	0	2	6	2	0	.121	.182
Mike Devereaux	OF5	R	35	9	13	0	4	1	0	0	1	3	2	0	.308	.385
Paul LoDuca	C4	R	26	6	14	2	4	1	0	0	1	0	0	0	.286	.357
Angel Pena	C4	R	23	6	13	1	3	0	0	0	0	0	6	0	.231	.231
Tripp Cromer (EJ)		R	30	6	6	1	1	0	0	1	1	0	2	0	.167	.667
2 Damon Hollins	OF4	R	24	5	9	1	2	0	0	0	2	0	2	0	.222	.222
Mike Metcalfe	2B1	R	25	4	1	0	0	0	0	0	0	0	1	2	.000	.000

NAME	T	AGE	W	L	PCT	SV	G	GS	CG	IP	H	BB	SO	SHO	ERA
TOTALS		28	83	79	.512	47	162	162	16	1447	1332	587	1178	10	3.8
Chan Ho Park	R	25	15	9	.625	0	34	34	2	221	199	97	191	0	3.7
Ismael Valdes (VJ)	R	24	11	10	.524	0	27	27	2	174	171	66	122	2	3.9
Darren Dreifort	R	26	8	12	.400	0	32	26	1	180	171	57	168	1	4.0
Antonio Osuna (EJ)	R	25	7	1	.875	6	54	0	0	65	50	32	72	0	3.0
2 Dave Mlicki	R	30	7	3	.700	0	20	20	2	124	120	38	78	1	4.0
Ramon Martinez (SJ)	R	30	7	3	.700	0	15	15	1	102	76	41	91	0	2.8
Scott Radinsky	L	30	6	6	.500	13	62	0	0	62	63	20	45	0	2.6
2 Brian Bohanon	L	29	5	7	.417	0	14	14	2	97	74	36	72	0	2.4
Carlos Perez	L	27	4	4	.500	0	11	11	4	78	67	30	46	2	3.2
1 Jim Bruske	R	33	3	0	1.000	1	35	0	0	44	47	19	31	0	3.4
1 Brad Clontz	R	27	2	0	1.000	0	18	0	0	21	15	10	14	0	5.6
Eric Weaver	R	24	2	0	1.000	0	7	0	0	10	5	6	5	0	0.9
Mark Guthrie	L	32	2	1	.667	0	53	0	0	54	56	24	45	0	3.5
1 Hideo Nomo	R	29	2	7	.222	0	12	12	2	68	57	38	73	0	5.0
Jeff Kubenka	L	23	1	0	1.000	0	9	0	0	9	4	8	10	0	0.9
2 Jeff Shaw	R	31	1	4	.200	25	34	0	0	35	35	7	26	0	2.5
Mike Judd	R	23	0	0	—	0	3	0	0	11	19	9	14	0	15.0
Gary Rath	L	25	0	0	—	0	3	0	0	3	3	2	4	0	10.8
Manuel Barrios	R	23	0	0	—	0	1	0	0	2	2	1	0	0	0.0
2 Greg McMichael	R	31	0	1	.000	1	12	0	0	14	17	6	11	0	4.4
Sean Maloney	R	27	0	1	.000	0	11	0	0	13	13	5	11	0	4.9
1 Will Brunson	L	28	0	1	.000	0	7	0	0	2	3	1	1	0	11.5
Frank Lankford	R	27	0	2	.000	0	12	0	0	20	23	7	7	0	5.9
Darren Hall	R	33	0	3	.000	0	11	0	0	11	17	5	8	0	10.3
1 Dennis Reyes	L	21	0	4	.000	0	11	3	0	29	27	20	33	0	4.7

COLORADO 4th 77-85 .475 21 DON BAYLOR

Name	G by Pos	B	AGE	G	AB	R	H	2B	3B	HR	RBI	BB	SO	SB	BA	SA
TOTALS			31	162	5632	826	1640	333	36	183	791	469	949	67	.291	.461
Todd Helton	1B146	L	24	152	530	78	167	37	1	25	97	53	54	3	.315	.530
Mike Lansing	2B153 3B1	R	30	153	584	73	161	39	2	12	66	39	88	10	.276	.411
Neifi Perez	SS162 C1	B	25	162	647	80	177	25	9	9	59	38	70	5	.274	.382
Vinny Castilla	3B162 SS1	R	30	162	645	108	206	28	4	46	144	40	89	5	.319	.589
Larry Walker	OF123 2B1 3B1	L	31	130	454	113	165	46	3	23	67	64	61	14	.363	.630
1 Ellis Burks	OF98	R	33	100	357	54	102	22	5	16	54	40	55	8	.286	.510
Dante Bichette	OF156	R	34	161	662	97	219	48	2	22	122	28	76	14	.331	.509
Kirt Manwaring	C108	R	32	110	291	30	72	12	3	2	26	38	49	1	.247	.330
Curtis Goodwin	OF91	L	25	119	159	27	39	7	0	1	6	16	40	5	.245	.308
Jeff Reed	C99	L	35	113	259	43	75	17	1	9	39	37	57	0	.290	.467
1 John Vander Wal	OF25 1B2	L	32	89	104	18	30	10	1	5	20	16	29	0	.288	.548
1 Greg Colbrunn	1B27 OF5 C1	R	28	62	122	12	38	8	2	3	13	8	23	3	.311	.459
Jason Bates	2B17 SS3 3B3	B	27	53	74	10	14	3	0	3	8	21	20	0	.189	.230
2 Darryl Hamilton	OF48	L	33	51	194	30	65	9	1	5	25	23	20	4	.335	.469
2 Kurt Abbott	OF9 2B7 SS7 3B3	R	29	42	71	9	18	6	0	3	15	2	19	0	.254	.465
Terry Shumpert	2B6	R	31	23	26	3	6	1	0	1	2	3	8	0	.231	.385
Angel Echevarria	1B4 OF4	R	27	19	29	7	11	3	0	1	9	2	8	0	.379	.586
Jeff Barry	OF10	R	29	15	34	4	6	1	0	0	3	3	11	0	.176	.206
Nelson Liriano	2B3 SS1	B	34	12	17	0	0	0	0	0	0	0	7	0	.000	.000
Edgard Clemente	OF7	R	22	11	17	2	6	0	1	0	2	2	8	0	.353	.471
2 Derrick White	OF2	R	28	9	9	0	0	0	0	0	0	0	4	0	.000	.000
Derrick Gibson	OF7	R	23	7	21	4	9	1	0	1	4	0	9	0	.429	.476
Mark Strittmatter	C3	R	29	4	4	0	0	0	0	0	0	0	2	0	.000	.000

NAME	T	AGE	W	L	PCT	SV	G	GS	CG	IP	H	BB	SO	SHO	ERA
TOTALS		28	77	85	.475	36	162	162	9	1433	1583	562	951	5	4.9
Pedro Astacio	R	28	13	14	.481	0	35	34	0	209	245	74	170	0	6.2
Darryl Kile	R	29	13	17	.433	0	36	35	4	230	257	96	158	1	5.2
Jamey Wright	R	23	9	14	.391	0	34	34	1	206	235	95	86	0	5.6
John Thomson	R	24	8	11	.421	0	26	26	2	161	174	49	106	0	4.8
Bobby Jones	L	26	7	8	.467	0	35	20	1	141	153	66	109	0	5.2
Curtis Leskanic	R	30	6	4	.600	2	66	0	0	76	75	40	55	0	4.4
Chuck McElroy	L	30	6	4	.600	2	78	0	0	68	68	24	61	0	2.9
Dave Veres	R	31	3	1	.750	8	63	0	0	76	67	27	74	0	2.9
Mike DeJean	R	27	3	1	.750	2	59	1	0	74	78	24	27	0	3.0
Jerry Dipoto	R	30	3	4	.429	19	68	0	0	71	61	25	49	0	3.0
Mike Munoz	L	32	3	2	.600	3	40	0	0	41	53	16	24	0	5.8
Mark Brownson	R	23	1	0	1.000	0	2	1	0	13	16	2	8	1	4.7
Dave Wainhouse	R	30	1	0	1.000	0	10	0	0	11	15	5	3	0	4.9
Jim Stoops	R	26	1	0	1.000	0	10	0	0	6	6	6	9	0	8.9
Mark Thompson (SJ)	R	27	1	2	.333	0	6	6	0	23	36	12	14	0	7.7
Fred Rath	R	25	0	0	—	0	2	0	0	2	2	1	2	0	1.6
Lariel Gonzalez	R	22	0	0	—	0	1	0	0	2	1	1	0	0	9.0
Mike Saipe	R	25	0	2	.000	0	2	2	0	10	22	6	2	0	10.8
Kevin Ritz (SJ)	R	33	0	2	.000	0	2	2	0	9	17	2	3	0	11.0

Roger Bailey (XJ-ZJ) 27 John Burke (EJ) 28

ARIZONA 5th 65-97 .401 33 BUCK SHOWALTER

Name	G by Pos	B	AGE	G	AB	R	H	2B	3B	HR	RBI	BB	SO	SB	BA	SA
TOTALS			27	162	5491	665	1353	235	46	159	621	489	1239	73	.246	.393
Travis Lee	1B146	L	23	146	562	71	151	20	2	22	72	67	123	8	.269	.429
Andy Fox	2B60 OF48 3B26 1B12	L	27	139	502	67	139	21	6	9	44	43	97	14	.277	.396
Jay Bell	SS138 2B15	R	32	155	549	79	138	29	5	20	67	81	129	3	.251	.432
Matt Williams	3B134	R	32	135	510	72	136	26	1	20	71	43	102	5	.267	.439
Karim Garcia	OF103	L	22	113	333	39	74	10	8	9	43	18	75	5	.222	.381
Devon White	OF144	B	35	146	563	84	157	32	4	22	85	42	102	22	.279	.456
Dave Dellucci	OF117	L	24	124	416	43	109	19	12	5	51	33	103	3	.260	.399
Kelly Stinnett	C86	R	28	92	274	35	71	14	1	11	34	35	74	0	.259	.438
Tony Batista	2B41 SS34 3B15	R	24	106	293	46	80	16	1	18	41	18	52	1	.273	.519
Brent Brede	OF58 1B12	L	26	98	212	23	48	9	3	2	17	24	43	1	.226	.325
Yamil Benitez	OF62	R	25	91	206	17	41	7	1	9	30	14	66	2	.199	.374
Andy Stankiewicz	2B61	R	33	77	145	9	30	5	0	0	7	33	11	0	.207	.241
Damian Miller	C46 OF2 1B1	R	28	57	168	17	48	14	2	3	14	11	43	1	.286	.446
1 Jorge Fabregas (NJ)	C41	L	28	50	151	8	30	4	0	1	15	13	26	0	.199	.245
Danny Klassen	2B29	R	22	29	108	12	21	2	1	3	9	9	33	1	.194	.315
2 Bernard Gilkey	OF27	R	31	29	101	8	25	0	0	5	11	14	4		.248	.277
2 Chris Jones	OF32	R	32	20	83	8	20	3	1	3	6	1	49	0	.194	.326
Hanley Frias (HJ)	2B3 SS2 3B2	B	24	15	23	4	3	0	1	1	2	0	5	0	.130	.348
Mike Robertson		L	27	11	13	0	2	0	0	0	1	1	3	0	.154	.154
Hensley Meulens	OF4	R	31	9	15	1	1	0	0	0	1	0	4	0	.067	.267
Edwin Diaz	2B3	R	23	9	11	0	0	0	0	0	0	0	5	0	.000	.000

NAME	T	AGE	W	L	PCT	SV	G	GS	CG	IP	H	BB	SO	SHO	ERA
TOTALS		28	65	97	.401	37	162	162	7	1432	1463	489	908	6	4.6
Andy Benes	R	30	14	13	.519	0	34	34	1	231	221	74	164	0	3.9
Brian Anderson	L	26	12	13	.480	0	32	32	2	208	221	41	95	1	4.3
Omar Daal	L	26	8	12	.400	0	33	23	3	163	146	51	132	1	2.8
2 Amaury Telemaco	R	24	6	9	.400	0	27	18	0	121	127	33	60	0	3.9
1 Russ Springer	R	29	4	3	.571	0	26	0	0	33	29	14	37	0	4.1
1 Willie Blair	R	32	4	15	.211	0	23	23	0	147	165	51	71	0	5.3
2 Aaron Small	R	26	3	1	.750	0	23	0	0	32	32	8	14	0	3.6
2 Alan Embree	L	28	2	2	.600	1	35	0	0	35	33	13	24	0	4.1
Gregg Olson	R	31	3	4	.429	30	64	0	0	69	56	25	55	0	3.0
Clint Sodowsky	R	25	3	6	.333	0	45	6	0	78	86	39	42	0	5.6
Scott Brow	R	29	1	0	1.000	0	13	0	0	21	22	14	13	0	7.1
Barry Manuel	R	32	1	0	1.000	0	13	0	0	16	17	14	12	0	3.0
2 Willie Banks	R	29	1	2	.333	1	33	0	0	44	34	25	32	0	3.0
Bob Wolcott	R	24	1	5	.250	0	6	6	0	33	32	13	21	0	7.0
1 Jeff Suppan	R	23	1	7	.125	0	13	13	1	66	82	21	39	0	6.6
Ben Ford	R	22	0	0	—	0	10	0	0	10	13	3	5	0	6.5
Vladimir Nunez	R	23	0	0	—	0	4	0	0	5	5	2	4	0	10.1
Chris Michalak	L	27	0	0	—	0	4	0	0	4	5	3	6	0	11.8
Efrain Valdez	L	31	0	0	—	0	3	0	0	4	4	1	3	0	4.1
Bryan Corey	R	25	0	0	—	0	2	0	0	3	4	3	1	0	9.0
Neil Weber	L	25	0	0	—	0	2	0	0	4	4	6	2	0	11.5
Ricky Pickett	L	28	0	0	—	0	6	0	0	0.2	3	4	1	0	81.0
Felix Rodriguez (PJ)	R	25	0	2	.000	5	43	0	0	44	44	29	36	0	6.1
2 Bobby Chouinard	R	26	0	3	.000	0	26	2	0	38	41	15	26	0	4.2
Joel Adamson (SJ)	L	26	0	3	.000	0	5	1	0	23	11	1	4	0	6.1

Cory Lidle (SJ) 26

LINE SCORES

Team	1	2	3	4	5	6	7	8	9	10	11		R	H	E

DIVISION SERIES: ATLANTA 3 : CHICAGO 0

Game 1   September 30 at Atlanta

CHN	0	0	0	0	0	0	0	1	0		1	5	1
ATL	0	2	0	0	0	1	4	0	x		7	8	0

Clark, Heredia (7), Karchner (7),   **Smoltz**, Rocker (8), Ligtenberg (9)
Morgan (8)

Game 2   October 1 at Atlanta

CHN	0	0	0	0	0	1	0	0	0	0		1	4	1
ATL	0	0	0	0	0	0	0	0	1	1		2	6	0

Tapani, **Mulholland** (10)   Glavine, Rocker (8), Seanez (9),
     Ligtenberg (10), **O. Perez** (10)

Game 3   October 3 at Chicago

ATL	0	0	1	0	0	0	0	5	0		6	9	0
CHN	0	0	0	0	0	0	0	2	0		2	8	2

Maddux, Ligtenberg (8)   Wood, Mulholland (6), Beck (8), Morgan (9)

DIVISION SERIES: SAN DIEGO 3 : HOUSTON 1

Game 1   September 29 at Houston

SD	0	0	0	0	0	1	0	1	0		2	9	1
HOU	0	0	0	0	0	0	0	0	1		1	4	0

Brown, Hoffman (9)   Johnson, Powell (9), Henry (9)

Game 2   October 1 at Houston

SD	0	0	0	0	0	2	0	0	2		4	8	1
HOU	1	0	2	0	0	0	1	1			5	11	1

Ashby, Hamilton (5), Wall (8),   Reynolds, Powell (8), **Wagner** (9)
Miceli (9), Hoffman (9)

Game 3   October 3 at San Diego

HOU	0	0	0	0	0	0	1	0	0		1	4	0
SD	0	0	0	0	0	1	1	0	x		2	3	0

Hampton, **Elarton** (7)   Brown, **Miceli** (7), Hoffman (9)

Game 4   October 4 at San Diego

HOU	0	0	0	1	0	0	0	0		1	3	1
SD	0	1	0	0	0	1	0	4	x		6	7	1

Johnson, Miller (7), Henry (7),   **Hitchcock**, Hamilton (7), Miceli (7), Hoffman (9)
Powell (8)

COMPOSITE BATTING

DIVISION SERIES

NAME	POS	G	AB	R	H	2B	3B	HR	RBI	BA
ATLANTA										
TOTALS		3	101	15	23	2	0	4	14	.228
Weiss	SS	3	13	2	2	0	0	0	0	.154
Lockhart	2B	3	12	2	4	0	0	0	0	.333
Galarraga	1B	3	12	1	3	0	0	0	0	.250
Klesko	LF	3	11	1	3	0	0	1	4	.273
C. Jones	3B	3	10	2	2	0	0	0	1	.200
A. Jones	CF	3	9	2	0	0	0	0	1	.000
Tucker	RF	3	8	1	2	0	0	1	2	.250
Lopez	C	2	7	1	2	0	0	1	1	.286
E. Perez	C	2	5	1	1	0	0	1	4	.200
Maddux	P	1	4	1	1	1	0	0	0	.250
Bautista	LF	2	2	0	1	1	0	0	0	.500
Williams	RF	2	2	1	1	0	0	0	1	.500
Smoltz	P	2	2	0	1	0	0	0	0	.500
Colbrunn	PH	2	2	0	0	0	0	0	0	.000
Glavine	P	1	1	0	0	0	0	0	0	.000
Guillen	PH	1	1	0	0	0	0	0	0	.000
Ligtenberg	P	3	0	0	0	0	0	0	0	—
Rocker	P	2	0	0	0	0	0	0	0	—
Graffanino	PH	1	0	0	0	0	0	0	0	—
O. Perez	P	1	0	0	0	0	0	0	0	—
Seanez	P	1	0	0	0	0	0	0	0	—
CHICAGO										
TOTALS		3	94	4	17	2	0	1	4	.181
Johnson	CF	3	12	0	2	0	0	0	0	.167
Grace	1B	3	12	0	1	0	0	0	1	.083
Sosa	RF	3	11	0	2	1	0	0	0	.182
Gaetti	3B	3	11	0	1	0	0	0	0	.091
Morandini	2B	3	9	1	2	0	0	0	1	.222
Hernandez	SS	3	7	1	2	0	0	0	0	.286
Rodriguez	LF	3	7	0	1	1	0	0	0	.143
Houston	C	3	6	1	1	0	0	1	1	.167
Alexander	SS	2	5	0	0	0	0	0	0	.000
Servais	C	1	3	0	2	0	0	0	0	.667
Hill	LF	1	3	0	1	0	0	0	0	.333
Clark	P	2	2	0	1	0	0	0	0	.500
Blauser	PH	2	2	0	0	0	0	0	0	.000
Martinez	C	1	1	1	1	0	0	0	0	1.000
Brown	PH	1	1	0	0	0	0	0	0	.000
Tapani	P	1	1	0	0	0	0	0	0	.000
Wood	P	1	1	0	0	0	0	0	0	.000
Morgan	P	2	0	0	0	0	0	0	0	—
Mulholland	P	2	0	0	0	0	0	0	0	—
Beck	P	1	0	0	0	0	0	0	0	—
Heredia	P	1	0	0	0	0	0	0	0	—
Karchner	P	1	0	0	0	0	0	0	0	—
SAN DIEGO										
TOTALS		4	125	14	27	4	1	5	13	.216
Vaughn	LF	4	15	2	5	1	0	1	1	.333
Gwynn	RF	4	15	1	3	2	0	0	2	.200
Veras	2B	4	15	1	2	0	0	0	0	.133
Caminiti	3B	4	14	2	2	0	0	0	0	.143
Hernandez	C	4	12	0	5	0	0	0	0	.417
Gomez	SS	4	11	1	3	0	0	0	0	.273
Leyritz	1B-C	4	10	3	4	0	0	3	5	.400
Finley	CF	4	10	2	1	1	0	0	1	.100
Joyner	1B	4	6	1	1	0	0	1	2	.167
Rivera	RF-CF	3	6	0	0	0	0	0	0	.000
Vander Wal	PH	3	3	1	1	0	1	0	2	.333
Brown	P	2	3	0	0	0	0	0	0	.000
Hitchcock	P	1	2	0	0	0	0	0	0	.000
Sweeney	PH	2	1	0	0	0	0	0	0	.000
Ashby	P	1	1	0	0	0	0	0	0	.000
Arias	PH	1	1	0	0	0	0	0	0	.000
Hoffman	P	4	0	0	0	0	0	0	0	—
Miceli	P	3	0	0	0	0	0	0	0	—
Hamilton	P	2	0	0	0	0	0	0	0	—
Sheets	2B	2	0	0	0	0	0	0	0	—
G. Myers	C	1	0	0	0	0	0	0	0	—
Wall	P	1	0	0	0	0	0	0	0	—
HOUSTON										
TOTALS		4	121	8	22	5	0	1	7	.182
Alou	LF	4	16	0	3	0	0	0	0	.188
Bell	RF	4	16	1	2	0	0	1	1	.125
Spiers	3B	4	14	2	4	3	0	0	1	.286
Bagwell	1B	4	14	0	2	0	0	0	4	.143
Everett	CF	4	13	1	2	0	0	0	0	.154
Biggio	2B	4	11	3	2	1	0	0	1	.182
Gutierrez	SS	4	10	1	3	0	0	0	0	.300
Ausmus	C	4	9	0	2	0	0	0	0	.222
Johnson	P	2	4	0	0	0	0	0	0	.000
Hidalgo	CF	1	4	0	1	0	0	0	0	.250
Eusebio	C	1	3	0	1	1	0	0	0	.333
Berry	3B	1	2	0	0	0	0	0	0	.000
Hampton	P	1	2	0	0	0	0	0	0	.000
Reynolds	P	1	2	0	0	0	0	0	0	.000
Incaviglia	PH	1	1	0	0	0	0	0	0	.000
Powell	P	3	0	0	0	0	0	0	0	—
Clark	PH	2	0	0	0	0	0	0	0	—
Henry	P	2	0	0	0	0	0	0	0	—
Elarton	P	1	0	0	0	0	0	0	0	—
Miller	P	1	0	0	0	0	0	0	0	—
Wagner	P	1	0	0	0	0	0	0	0	—

COMPOSITE PITCHING

NAME	G	IP	H	BB	SO	W	L	SV	ERA
ATLANTA									
TOTALS	3	28	17	5	24	3	0	0	1.29
Smoltz	1	7.2	5	0	6	1	0	0	1.17
Glavine	1	7	5	3	1	0	0	0	1.29
Maddux	1	7	7	0	4	1	0	0	2.57
Ligtenberg	3	3.1	1	4	3	0	0	0	0.00
Rocker	2	1.1	1	0	2	0	0	0	0.00
Seanez	1	1	0	0	1	0	0	0	0.00
O. Perez	1	0.2	0	1	1	0	0	0	0.00
CHICAGO									
TOTALS	3	26.1	23	14	20	0	3	0	4.44
Tapani	1	9	5	3	6	0	0	0	1.00
Clark	1	6	7	1	4	0	1	0	3.00
Wood	1	5	3	4	5	0	1	0	1.80
Mulholland	2	2.1	2	2	2	0	1	0	11.57
Beck	1	1.2	5	1	1	0	0	0	16.20
Morgan	2	1.1	0	0	1	0	0	0	0.00
Karchner	1	0.2	1	0	1	0	0	0	13.50
Heredia	1	0.1	0	2	0	0	0	0	54.00
SAN DIEGO									
TOTALS	4	35.1	22	11	49	3	1	2	1.78
Brown	2	14.2	5	7	21	1	0	0	0.61
Hitchcock	1	6	3	0	11	1	0	0	1.50
Ashby	1	4	6	1	4	0	0	0	6.75
Hamilton	2	3.1	1	2	3	0	0	0	0.00
Miceli	3	3.1	2	0	4	1	1	0	2.70
Hoffman	4	3	3	1	4	0	0	2	0.00
Wall	1	1	2	0	2	0	0	0	9.00
HOUSTON									
TOTALS	4	34	27	9	32	1	3	0	3.44
Johnson	2	14	12	2	17	0	2	0	1.93
Reynolds	1	7	4	1	5	0	0	0	2.57
Hampton	1	6	2	1	2	0	0	0	1.50
Powell	3	2.1	2	3	3	0	0	0	11.57
Elarton	1	2	1	1	3	0	1	0	4.50
Henry	1	1.2	2	0	1	0	0	0	5.40
Wagner	1	1	4	0	1	1	0	0	18.00
Miller	1	0	0	1	0	0	0	0	—

LINE SCORES

Team	1	2	3	4	5	6	7	8	9	10	11		R	H	E

CHAMPIONSHIP: SAN DIEGO 4 : ATLANTA 2

Game 1   October 7 at Atlanta

| SD | 0 0 0 0 0 1 0 0 1 0 1 | | 3 7 0 |
| ATL | 0 0 1 0 0 0 0 0 1 0 | | 2 8 3 |

Ashby, Myers (8), Miceli (8),   Smoltz, Rocker (8), Martinez (8), **Ligtenberg** (9)
Hoffman (8), Wall (10)

Game 2   October 8 at Atlanta

| SD | 0 0 0 0 0 0 1 0 0 2 | | 3 11 0 |
| ATL | 1 0 0 0 0 0 0 0 x | | 4 7 0 |

Brown   **Glavine**, Rocker (7), Seanez (8), Perez (9),
Ligtenberg (9)

Game 3   October 10 at San Diego

| ATL | 0 0 1 0 0 0 0 0 0 | | 1 8 2 |
| SD | 0 0 0 0 2 0 0 2 x | | 4 7 0 |

Maddux, Martinez (6), Rocker (7),   **Hitchcock**, Wall (6), Miceli (8), Myers (8),
Seanez (8)   Hoffman (8)

Game 4   October 11 at San Diego

| ATL | 0 0 0 1 0 1 6 0 0 | | 8 12 0 |
| SD | 0 0 2 0 0 1 0 0 0 | | 3 8 0 |

Neagle, **Martinez** (6), Rocker (7),   Hamilton, Myers (7), Miceli (7),
Perez (8), Seanez (8), Ligtenberg (9)   Boehringer (8), Langston (9)

Game 5   October 12 at San Diego

| ATL | 0 0 0 1 0 1 0 5 0 | | 7 14 1 |
| SD | 2 0 0 0 0 2 0 0 2 | | 6 10 1 |

Smoltz, **Rocker** (7), Seanez (8),   Ashby, Langston (7), **Brown** (7),
Ligtenberg (9), Maddux (9)   Wall (8), Boehringer (9), Myers (9)

Game 6   October 14 at Atlanta

| SD | 0 0 0 0 0 5 0 0 0 | | 5 10 0 |
| ATL | 0 0 0 0 0 0 0 0 0 | | 0 2 1 |

Hitchcock, Boehringer (6),   **Glavine**, Rocker (6), Martinez (6), Neagle (8)
Langston (7), Hamilton (7), Hoffman (9)

COMPOSITE BATTING

NAME	POS	G	AB	R	H	2B	3B	HR	RBI	BA
SAN DIEGO										
TOTALS		6	208	24	53	7	0	5	20	.255
Gwynn	RF	6	26	1	6	1	0	0	2	.231
Veras	2B	6	24	2	6	1	0	0	2	.250
Caminiti	3B	6	22	3	6	0	0	2	4	.273
Finley	CF	6	21	3	7	1	0	0	2	.333
Gomez	SS	6	20	2	3	1	0	0	0	.150
Hernandez	C	6	18	2	6	1	0	0	0	.333
Joyner	1B	6	16	3	5	0	0	0	2	.313
Rivera	LF-RF	6	13	1	3	2	0	0	0	.231
Leyritz	1B-C	5	12	1	2	0	0	1	4	.167
Vaughn	LF	3	8	1	2	0	0	0	0	.250
Vander Wal	LF	3	7	1	3	0	0	1	2	.429
Hitchcock	P	2	5	1	1	0	0	0	0	.200
Brown	P	2	4	1	2	0	0	0	0	.500
Ashby	P	2	4	0	0	0	0	0	0	.000
Sheets	SS	3	3	0	0	0	0	0	0	.000
Sweeney	PH	3	2	1	0	0	0	0	0	.000
Hamilton	P	2	2	0	0	0	0	0	0	.000
G. Myers	PH	2	1	1	1	0	0	1	2	1.000
R. Myers	P	4	0	0	0	0	0	0	0	—
Boehringer	P	3	0	0	0	0	0	0	0	—
Hoffman	P	3	0	0	0	0	0	0	0	—
Langston	P	3	0	0	0	0	0	0	0	—
Miceli	P	3	0	0	0	0	0	0	0	—
Wall	P	3	0	0	0	0	0	0	0	—
ATLANTA										
TOTALS		6	200	18	47	4	1	4	17	.235
C. Jones	3B	6	24	2	5	1	0	0	1	.208
A. Jones	CF	6	22	3	6	0	0	1	2	.273
Galarraga	1B	6	21	1	2	0	0	1	4	.095
Lopez	C	6	20	2	6	0	0	1	1	.300
Lockhart	2B	6	17	2	4	1	1	0	0	.235
Weiss	SS	4	15	0	3	0	0	0	0	.200
Tucker	RF	6	13	1	5	1	0	1	5	.385
Williams	LF-RF	5	13	0	2	0	0	0	0	.154
Guillen	SS	4	12	1	5	0	0	0	1	.417
Klesko	LF	5	12	2	1	0	0	0	1	.083
Colbrunn	PH	6	6	0	2	0	0	0	0	.333
Smoltz	P	2	5	0	1	0	0	0	0	.200
Bautista	LF	3	5	0	0	0	0	0	0	.000
E. Perez	C	3	4	0	3	0	0	0	0	.750
Glavine	P	3	4	0	1	0	0	0	0	.250
Graffanino	2B	2	3	2	1	1	0	0	1	.333
Neagle	P	2	2	0	0	0	0	0	0	.000
Malloy	2B	2	1	1	0	0	0	0	0	.000
Maddux	P	2	1	0	0	0	0	0	0	.000
Rocker	P	6	0	1	0	0	0	0	0	—
Ligtenberg	P	4	0	0	0	0	0	0	0	—
Seanez	P	4	0	0	0	0	0	0	0	—
Martinez	P	4	0	0	0	0	0	0	0	—
O. Perez	P	2	0	0	0	0	0	0	0	—

COMPOSITE PITCHING

NAME	G	IP	H	BB	SO	W	L	SV	ERA
SAN DIEGO									
TOTALS	6	55	47	26	54	4	2	2	2.78
Hitchcock	2	10	5	8	14	2	0	0	0.90
Brown	2	10.1	5	4	12	1	1	0	2.61
Hamilton	2	7.1	7	3	6	0	1	0	4.91
Ashby	2	13	14	2	5	0	0	0	2.08
Hoffman	3	4.1	2	2	7	1	0	1	2.08
Boehringer	3	3	3	1	1	0	0	0	0.00
Wall	3	3	4	4	0	0	1	0	3.00
R. Myers	4	2	3	2	3	0	0	0	13.50
Langston	3	1.1	1	0	1	0	0	0	0.00
Miceli	3	0.2	4	0	1	0	0	0	13.50
ATLANTA									
TOTALS	6	54	53	27	48	2	4	1	3.50
Smoltz	2	13.2	13	6	13	0	0	0	3.95
Glavine	2	11.2	13	9	8	0	2	0	2.31
Neagle	2	7.2	8	2	9	0	0	0	3.52
Maddux	2	6	5	3	4	0	1	1	3.00
Rocker	6	4.2	3	1	5	1	0	0	0.00
Ligtenberg	4	3.2	3	2	5	0	1	0	7.36
Martinez	4	3.1	1	1	0	0	0	0	0.00
Seanez	4	3	2	1	4	0	0	0	6.00
O. Perez	2	0.1	5	2	0	0	0	0	54.00

MISCELLANEOUS 1998 INDIVIDUAL LEADERS

BATTING

On Base Average

#	American League		#	National League	
1	Martinez, Sea.	.429	1	McGwire, St.L.	.470
2	Williams, N.Y.	.422	2	Olerud, N.Y.	.447
3	Thome, Cle.	.413	3	Walker, Col.	.445
4	Salmon, Ana.	.410	4	Bonds, S.F.	.438
5	Offerman, K.C.	.403	5	Sheffield, Fla.-L.A.	.428
6	Vaughn, Bos.	.402	6	Bagwell, Hou.	.424
7	Belle, Chi.	.399	7	Kendall, Pit.	.411
8	Davis, Bal.	.388	8	Abreu, Phi.	.409
9	Fernandez, Tor.	.387	9	C. Jones, Atl.	.404
10	Lawton, Min.	.387	10	Biggio, Hou.	.403

On Base Average plus Slugging Average

#	American League		#	National League	
1	Belle, Chi.	1.055	1	McGwire, St.L.	1.222
2	Thome, Cle.	.997	2	Walker, Col.	1.075
3	Williams, N.Y.	.997	3	Bonds, S.F.	1.047
4	Gonzalez, Tex.	.997	4	Sosa, Chi.	1.024
5	Martinez, Sea.	.995	5	Olerud, N.Y.	.998
6	Vaughn, Bos.	.993	6	Galarraga, Atl.	.991
7	Delgado, Tor.	.978	7	Alou, Hou.	.981
8	Griffey, Sea.	.977	8	Bagwell, Hou.	.981
9	Ramirez, Cle.	.976	9	Piazza, L.A.-Fla.-N.Y.	.960
10	Davis, Bal.	.970	10	Vaughn, S.D.	.960

Total Bases

#	American League		#	National League	
1	Belle, Chi.	399	1	Sosa, Chi.	416
2	Griffey, Sea.	387	2	McGwire, St.L.	383
3	Rodriguez, Sea.	384	3	Castilla, Col.	380
4	Gonzalez, Tex.	382	4	V. Guerrero, Mon.	367
5	Vaughn, Bos.	360	5	Vaughn, S.D.	342
6	Garciaparra, Bos.	353	6	Alou, Hou.	340
7	Palmeiro, Bal.	350	7	Bichette, Col.	337
8	Ramirez, Cle.	342	8	Bonds, S.F.	336
9	Green, Tor.	321	9	Galarraga, Atl.	330
10	Martinez, Sea.	315	10	C. Jones, Atl.	329

Caught Stealing

#	American League		#	National League	
1	Goodwin, Tex.	20	1	Renteria, Fla.	22
2	Stewart, Tor.	18	2	Vina, Mil.	16
3	Canseco, Tor.	17	3	Floyd, Fla.	14
4	Rodriguez, Sea.	13	4	Young, L.A.	13
5	Henderson, Oak.	13	5	Everett, Hou.	12
				Bonds, S.F.	12

Stolen Base Percentage
(Minimum 20 Attempts)

#	American League		#	National League	
1	Lofton, Cle.	84	1	Larkin, Cin.	90
2	Nixon, Min.	84	2	Womack, Pit.	88
3	Henderson, Oak.	84	3	A. Jones, Atl.	87
4	Jeter, N.Y.	83	4	Martin, Pit.	87
5	Curtis, N.Y.	81	5	Biggio, Hou.	86

Extra Base Hits

#	American League		#	National League	
1	Belle, Chi.	99	1	McGwire, St.L.	91
2	Gonzalez, Tex.	97	2	Bonds, S.F.	88
3	Griffey, Sea.	92	3	Sosa, Chi.	86
4	Delgado, Tor.	82	4	V. Guerrero, Mon.	82
	Ramirez, Cle.	82		Vaughn, S.D.	82
	Rodriguez, Sea.	82			

PITCHING

Fewest Hits Per 9 Innings Pitched

#	American League		#	National League	
1	Clemens, Tor.	6.48	1	Wood, Chi.	6.32
2	Martinez, Bos.	7.24	2	Leiter, N.Y.	7.04
3	Irabu, N.Y.	7.70	3	Maddux, Atl.	7.21
4	Cone, N.Y.	8.06	4	Harnisch, Cin.	7.58
5	Rogers, Oak.	8.11	5	Smoltz, Atl.	7.78
6	Wells, N.Y.	8.19	6	Hermanson, Mon.	7.84
7	Guzman, Tor.-Bal.	8.23	7	Brown, S.D.	7.88
8	Mussina, Bal.	8.24	8	Schilling, Phi.	7.91
9	Williams, Tor.	8.41	9	Glavine, Atl.	7.93
10	Finley, Ana.	8.46	10	Daal, Ari.	8.08

Fewest Bases on Balls Per 9 Innings Pitched

#	American League		#	National League	
1	Wells, N.Y.	1.22	1	Anderson, Ari.	1.04
2	Saberhagen, Bos.	1.49	2	Lima, Hou.	1.23
3	Moyer, Sea.	1.61	3	Reed, N.Y.	1.23
4	Mussina, Bal.	1.79	4	Maddux, Atl.	1.61
5	Radke, Min.	1.81	5	Brown, S.D.	1.72
6	Sirotka, Chi.	2.00	6	Portugal, Phi.	1.73
7	Burkett, Tex.	2.12	7	Woodard, Mil.	1.79
8	Moehler, Det.	2.28	8	Clark, Chi.	2.02
9	Erickson, Bal.	2.47	9	Reynolds, Hou.	2.04
10	Rogers, Oak.	2.53	10	Schilling, Phi.	2.04

Strikeouts Per 9 Innings Pitched

#	American League		#	National League	
1	Clemens, Tor.	10.39	1	Wood, Chi.	12.58
2	Martinez, Bos.	9.67	2	Schilling, Phi.	10.05
3	Cone, N.Y.	9.06	3	Smoltz, Atl.	9.29
4	Finley, Ana.	8.54	4	Brown, S.D.	9.00
5	Saunders, T.B.	8.05	5	Millwood, Atl.	8.41
6	Mussina, Bal.	7.63	6	Dreifort, L.A.	8.40
7	Guzman, Tor.-Bal.	7.17	7	Leiter, N.Y.	8.11
8	Sele, Tex.	7.07	8	Hitchcock, S.D.	8.06
9	Fassero, Sea.	7.05	9	Reynolds, Hou.	8.06
10	Carpenter, Tor.	6.99	10	Remlinger, Cin.	7.89

Lowest Batting Average Allowed

#	American League		#	National League	
1	Clemens, Tor.	.197	1	Wood, Chi.	.196
2	Martinez, Bos.	.217	2	Leiter, N.Y.	.216
3	Irabu, N.Y.	.233	3	Maddux, Atl.	.220
4	Cone, N.Y.	.237	4	Harnisch, Cin.	.228
5	Wells, N.Y.	.239	5	Smoltz, Atl.	.231

Home Runs Allowed

#	American League		#	National League	
1	Belcher, K.C.	37	1	Anderson, Ari.	39
2	Williams, Tor.	36	2	Astacio, Col.	39
3	Nagy, Cle.	34	3	Hernandez, Fla.	37
4	Fassero, Sea.	33	4	Lima, Hou.	34
5	Moehler, Det.	30	5	Blair, Ari.-N.Y.	31
	Wakefield, Bos.	30		Vazquez, Mon.	31
	Candiotti, Oak.	30			
	Burba, Cle.	30			
	Sirotka, Chi.	30			
	Navarro, Chi.	30			

Home Runs Allowed per 9 IP
(Minimum 10 Home Runs Allowed)

#	American League		#	National League	
1	Bochtler, Det.	2.28	1	Jones, Mil.	2.50
2	Wells, Sea.	2.09	2	Brantley, St.L.	2.13
3	Eyre, Chi.	2.02	3	Anderson, Ari.	1.69
4	Hanson, Tor.	1.84	4	Astacio, Col.	1.68
5	Powell, Det.	1.83	5	Woodall, Mil.	1.63

ALL HAIL THE YANKEES

The 1998 Playoffs had its share of surprises, but form held in the World Series as the New York Yankees – the season's best team – demonstrated their superiority by outhitting, outpitching, and outfielding the San Diego Padres. The Bombers four-game sweep lent credence to those arguing that they were the greatest baseball team ever.

The opening round of the National League Playoffs produced a surprise when the Padres, a tem that had struggled down the stretch, upset the Houston Astros, the league's best hitting team, winning three of four games. Two of the wins came at the expense of the Astros' Randy Johnson. Meanwhile, the Atlanta Braves wrote a Grinch ending to Chicago's fairy tale season by sweeping the Cubs. The superb Braves' pitching allowed only one earned run in the three games.

Over in the American League, the Yankees' pitching was even more dominant in their sweep of the powerful Texas Rangers. New York hurlers allowed just one run of any kind during the three games. The Boston Red Sox got off to a strong start against the Cleveland Indians in their series, winning the opening game decisively 11-3. Then The Curse of the Bambino kicked in and the Sox meekly lost the next three.

The playoffs' biggest upset came with San Diego's surprise trouncing of Atlanta. Billed as a test of the Braves' starting pitching versus the Padres' relievers, San Diego came up stronger in both departments. Padre lefthander Sterling Hitchcock earned MVP honors with a pair of wins. The Braves, with the N.L.'s best regular season record, lost the first three games of the best-of-seven set. With their backs scraping the wallpaper down to the plaster, Atlanta rallied to take two in a row. Surprisingly, the wins went to the little-respected Brave relievers. Hitchcock and the Padres' relievers were brilliant in winning the deciding game 5-0.

New York had a mini-scare in their series against Cleveland as the Indians led two games to one after three. Cleveland's Game Two win was highlighted by a memorable goof when two Indians scored while New York second baseman Chuck Knoblauch left a ball unattended on the ground to argue with the umpire. But the Yankees showed their class by winning two straight in Cleveland to move back in front. Series MVP David Wells, winner of Game One, was the victor in Game Five. When the series returned to New York, the Yankees clinched the franchise's 34th pennant. The Yanks batted a mere .218 for the series, but their hitting was timely and their fine pitching and defense carried the day.

In the David-Goliath World Series matchup, the Padres' left his slingshot in his other league. Disappointed San Diego fans and confirmed Yankee-haters had nothing on the Fox TV folks. The ease and inevitability of the New York win produced the lowest World Series ratings ever and the lack of a fifth game cost the network $15 million in ad revenues. The big boys from the Bronx cared not a whit. They simply treated the World Championship as an inherited right. It was, after all, the team's 24th of the century.

In Game One, they overcame a three-run Padre lead to win going away, 9-6. In Game Two, they battered the Padres for seven runs in the first three innings to coast to a 9-3 victory. For Game Three, they showed their ability to win a close game on the road: San Diego led into the eighth inning, but the Yankees came on to win 5-4. Finally, Andy Petitte and the reliable bullpen tossed a shutout for all the marbles in Game Four, 3-0. Third baseman Scott Brosius, who hit .471 with two timely homers and six RBIs, was named Series MVP.

WORLD SERIES

LINE SCORES

Team	1	2	3	4	5	6	7	8	9	10	11		R	H	E

WORLD SERIES: NEW YORK (AL) 4 : SAN DIEGO (NL) 0

Game 1   October 17 at New York

	1	2	3	4	5	6	7	8	9		R	H	E
SD	0	0	2	0	3	0	0	1	0		6	8	1
NYY	0	2	0	0	0	0	7	0	x		9	9	1

Brown, **Wall** (7), Langston (7), Boehringer (8), Myers (8)   **Wells**, Nelson (8), Rivera (8)

Game 2   October 18 at New York

	1	2	3	4	5	6	7	8	9		R	H	E
SD	0	0	0	0	1	0	0	2	0		3	10	1
NYY	3	3	1	0	2	0	0	0	x		9	16	0

Ashby, Boehringer (3), Wall (5), Miceli (8)   **Hernandez**, Stanton (8), Nelson (8)

Game 3   October 20 at San Diego

	1	2	3	4	5	6	7	8	9		R	H	E
NYY	0	0	0	0	0	0	2	3	0		5	9	1
SD	0	0	0	0	3	0	1	0	0		4	7	1

Cone, Lloyd (7), **Mendoza** (7), Rivera (8)   Hitchcock, Hamilton (7), Myers (8), Hoffman (8)

Game 4   October 21 at San Diego

	1	2	3	4	5	6	7	8	9		R	H	E
NYY	0	0	0	0	0	1	0	2	0		3	9	0
SD	0	0	0	0	0	0	0	0	0		0	7	0

Pettitte, Nelson (8), Rivera (8)   Brown, Miceli (9), Myers (9)

COMPOSITE BATTING

NAME	POS	G	AB	R	H	2B	3B	HR	RBI	BA
NEW YORK										
TOTALS		4	139	26	43	5	0	6	25	.309
O'Neill	RF	4	19	3	4	1	0	0	0	.211
Brosius	3B	4	17	3	8	1	0	2	6	.471
Jeter	SS	4	17	4	6	0	0	0	1	.353
Knoblauch	2B	4	16	3	6	0	0	1	3	.375
Williams	CF	4	16	2	1	0	0	1	3	.063
Martinez	1B	4	13	4	5	0	0	1	4	.385
Ledee	LF	4	10	1	6	3	0	0	4	.600
Posada	C	3	9	2	3	0	0	1	2	.333
Davis	DH	3	7	3	2	0	0	0	2	.286
Girardi	C	2	6	0	0	0	0	0	0	.000
Spencer	LF	1	3	1	1	1	0	0	0	.333
Cone	P	1	2	0	1	0	0	0	0	.500
Pettitte	P	1	2	0	0	0	0	0	0	.000
Rivera	P	3	1	0	0	0	0	0	0	.000
Mendoza	P	1	1	0	0	0	0	0	0	.000
Nelson	P	3	0	0	0	0	0	0	0	—
Bush	DH	2	0	0	0	0	0	0	0	—
Hernandez		1	0	0	0	0	0	0	0	—
Lloyd	P	1	0	0	0	0	0	0	0	—
Stanton	P	1	0	0	0	0	0	0	0	—
Wells	P	1	0	0	0	0	0	0	0	—
SAN DIEGO										
TOTALS		4	134	13	32	7	1	3	11	.239
Gwynn	RF	4	16	2	8	0	0	1	3	.500
Veras	2B	4	15	3	3	2	0	0	1	.200
Vaughn	LF-DH	4	15	3	2	0	0	2	4	.133
Caminiti	3B	4	14	1	2	1	0	0	1	.143
Finley	CF	3	12	0	1	1	0	0	0	.083
Gomez	SS	4	11	2	4	0	1	0	0	.364
Hernandez	C	4	10	0	2	0	0	0	0	.200
Leyritz	1B-DH-C	4	10	0	0	0	0	0	0	.000
Joyner	1B	3	8	0	0	0	0	0	0	.000
Rivera	CF-LF-RF	3	5	1	4	2	0	0	1	.800
VanderWal	LF	4	5	0	2	1	0	0	0	.400
G. Myers	C	2	4	0	0	0	0	0	0	.000
Sweeney	PH	3	3	0	2	0	0	0	1	.667
Brown	P	2	2	1	1	0	0	0	0	.500
Hitchcock	P	1	2	1	1	0	0	0	0	.500
Sheets	SS	2	2	0	0	0	0	0	0	.000
R. Myers	P	3	0	0	0	0	0	0	0	—
Boehringer	P	2	0	0	0	0	0	0	0	—
Miceli	P	2	0	0	0	0	0	0	0	—
Wall	P	2	0	0	0	0	0	0	0	—
Ashby	P	1	0	0	0	0	0	0	0	—
Hamilton	P	1	0	0	0	0	0	0	0	—
Langston	P	1	0	0	0	0	0	0	0	—
Hoffman	P	1	0	0	0	0	0	0	0	—

COMPOSITE PITCHING

NAME	G	IP	H	BB	SO	W	L	SV	ERA
NEW YORK									
TOTALS	4	36	32	12	29	4	0	3	2.75
Pettitte	1	7.1	5	3	4	1	0	0	0.00
Hernandez	1	7	6	3	7	1	0	0	1.29
Wells	1	7	7	2	4	1	0	0	6.43
Cone	1	6	2	3	4	0	0	0	3.00
Rivera	3	4.1	5	0	4	0	0	3	0.00
Nelson	3	2.1	2	1	4	0	0	0	0.00
Mendoza	1	1	2	0	1	1	0	0	9.00
Stanton	1	0.2	3	0	1	0	0	0	27.00
Lloyd	1	0.1	0	0	0	0	0	0	0.00
SAN DIEGO									
TOTALS	4	34	43	20	29	0	4	0	5.82
Brown	2	14.1	14	6	13	0	1	0	4.40
Hitchcock	1	6	7	1	7	0	0	0	1.50
Wall	2	2.2	3	3	1	0	1	0	6.75
Ashby	1	2.2	10	1	1	0	1	0	13.50
Boehringer	2	2	4	2	3	0	0	0	9.00
Hoffman	1	2	2	1	0	0	1	0	9.00
Miceli	2	1.2	2	2	1	0	0	0	0.00
Hamilton	1	1	1	1	1	0	0	0	0.00
R. Myers	3	1	0	1	2	0	0	0	9.00
Langston	1	0.2	1	2	0	0	0	0	40.50

1999: A SATISFACTORY FINISH

Although the last baseball season of the millennium produced few surprises, it nevertheless represented a satisfactory windup to a decade that saw the National Pastime achieve wondrous highs and dreary lows. The offensive firepower of the past few seasons continued unabated, delighting all but baseball purists who mourned the decline of pitching. Most of the same teams that had won in 1998 finished on top again, but there was still plenty of excitement from Opening Day until the final pitch.

Most of the pennant-race suspense came in the National League where both Atlanta and Houston eked out narrow division victories despite potentially crippling player losses. The Braves, with their usual strong pitching and emerging superstars in Chipper Jones and Andruw Jones, overcame the full-season absence of Andres Galarraga and half-season loss of Javy Lopez to overcome a gutsy Mets team. Indeed, in September, New York led by Mike Piazza, Edgardo Alfonzo, and Robin Ventura seemed on the verge of overtaking Atlanta. Then Chipper Jones blasted the Braves to a three-game sweep of the Mets. Reeling, New York immediately dropped four more games. Just when New York was about to be counted out of any post-season play, Bobby Valentine's crew righted itself with a run explosion in a return match against Atlanta's Greg Maddux. From there, the Mets went on to tie Cincinnati for the Wild Card playoff berth.

Houston, which lost Moises Alou for the season to a non-baseball injury, also fell on hard times in September and allowed surprising Cincinnati to edge past them. The Reds boasted an able bullpen and the hitting of Greg Vaughn, Barry Larkin, and Sean Casey. Strong pitching by Mike Hampton, Jose Lima, and Billy Wagner plus the ever-dependable bat of Jeff Bagwell brought the Astros back to the lead in the final week of the regular season. After a great run, the Reds ran out of gas, eventually losing a one-game playoff for the Wild Card slot to the Mets.

The only new kids to reach the playoffs on the National League block were in Arizona. In only their second season, the Diamondbacks parlayed an intelligent expansion draft, clever trading, and wise use of free-agency to win the Western Division with room to spare. Luis Gonzalez, Jay Bell, Matt Williams, and Tony Womack produced runs and Randy Johnson was a devastating stopper.

The American League races went as expected. The New York Yankees were not quite as unstoppable as in 1998. Derek Jeter, Bernie Williams, Paul O'Neill, and Tino Martinez still royally supported a strong pitching staff that included David Cone, Orlando Hernandez, Roger Clemens, Andy Pettitte, and Mariano Rivera. The Boston Red Sox sported baseball's premier pitcher in Pedro Martinez and the A.L.'s top hitter in Nomar Garciaparra. Martinez led baseball in victories, percentage, topped the American League in strikeouts and dazzled with an ERA almost three runs below the league average. But he couldn't pitch every day; Boston had to be content with second place and a Wild Card berth.

Despite so-so pitching, the Cleveland Indians had no trouble hamstringing the otherwise weak Central Division. The Tribe had so much batting power, it seemed almost as though they'd clinched their title in April. Chief among a war party of big bats were RBI-machine Manny Ramirez and All-Star second baseman Roberto Alomar. The Texas Rangers had their own big hitters in Rafael Palmeiro and Juan Gonzalez. They easily withstood early competition from an unexpectedly strong Oakland club.

Although the Athletics and Reds challenged, all the playoff berths went to teams with high payrolls. Underdogs derived some satisfaction from watching free-spenders like the Dodgers and Orioles fall on their faces.

Individual honors went to Tony Gwynn and Wade Boggs, each of whom surpassed 3,000 career hits. Minnesota's Eric Milton and St. Louis' Jose Jimenez threw no-hitters, and the Yankees' David Cone did it up brown with a perfect game against Toronto.

Colorado's Larry Walker cruised to the N.L. batting crown, and Seattle's Ken Griffey, Jr. added another A.L. home run title to his growing list of achievements. Mark McGwire and Sammy Sosa waged a reprise home run race, but while they drew large crowds and both topped the once-magic 61, the contest couldn't quite recapture the excitement of their 1998 quest. The public's somewhat "been there-done-that" attitude was partially due to the fact that the Cardinals and Cubs were so far out of contention that their home runs seldom meant anything more than just more home runs.

The years' looniest exploit was left to the umpires. In an effort to bring major league baseball to the bargaining table before their present contract expired, major league umpires launched a kamikaze attack by voting to resign en masse in September. Baseball responded by accepting the resignations and began hiring replacements. The Union split when a large segment of umpires, mostly American Leaguers, either refused to resign or attempted to rescind their already-accepted resignations. The upshot found 22 umpires, including many veterans, out of work and nursing the bullet holes they'd shot in their own feet.

Perhaps the season's most hopeful sign was baseball's seemingly never ending ability to produce new stars. Even non-contenders could derive thrill from the work of Todd Helton, Brian Giles, Fernando Tatis, Wayne Morris, Vladimir Guerrero, Bobby Abreu, Doug Glanville, Carlos Beltran, Shawn Green, Carlos Delgado, Jason Giambi, Freddy Garcia, Russ Ortiz, and many other youngsters who will carry the game into the next millennium.

1999 AMERICAN LEAGUE — EAST DIVISION

NEW YORK — 1st 93-64 .605 — JOE TORRE

Name	G by Pos	B	AGE	G	AB	R	H	2B	3B	HR	RBI	BB	SO	SB	BA	SA
TOTALS	TOTALS		31	162	5568	900	1568	302	36	193	855	718	978	104	.282	.453
Tino Martinez	1B158	L	31	159	589	95	155	27	2	28	105	69	86	3	.263	.458
Chuck Knoblauch	2B150	R	30	150	603	120	176	36	4	18	68	83	57	28	.292	.454
Derek Jeter	SS158	R	25	158	627	134	219	37	9	24	102	91	116	19	.349	.552
Scott Brosius	3B132 DH1	R	32	133	473	64	117	26	1	17	71	39	74	4	.247	.414
Paul O'Neill	OF151	L	36	153	597	70	170	39	4	19	110	66	89	11	.285	.459
Bernie Williams	OF155 DH2	B	30	158	591	116	202	28	6	25	115	100	95	9	.342	.536
Ricky Ledee	OF77 DH5	L	25	88	250	45	69	13	5	9	40	28	73	4	.276	.476
Jorge Posada	C109 1B1 DH1	B	27	112	379	50	93	19	2	12	57	53	91	1	.245	.401
Chili Davis	DH132	R	39	146	476	59	128	25	1	19	78	73	100	4	.269	.445
Chad Curtis	OF81 DH14	R	30	96	195	37	51	6	0	5	24	43	35	8	.262	.369
Shane Spencer	OF64 DH8	R	27	71	205	25	48	8	0	8	20	18	51	0	.234	.390
Joe Girardi	C65	R	34	65	209	23	50	16	1	2	27	10	26	3	.239	.354
Luis Sojo	3B20 2B16 SS6 1B4 DH2	R	34	49	127	20	32	6	0	2	16	4	17	1	.252	.346
Clay Bellinger	3B16 1B8 DH4 OF2 2B1 SS1	R	30	32	45	12	9	2	0	1	2	1	10	1	.200	.311
2 Jim Leyritz	DH14 1B9 C1 3B1	R	35	31	66	8	15	4	1	0	5	13	17	0	.227	.318
Darryl Strawberry (SD)	DH17	L	37	24	49	10	16	5	0	3	6	17	16	2	.327	.612
Tony Tarasco	OF12 DH1	L	28	14	31	5	5	2	0	0	3	3	5	1	.161	.226
Alfonso Soriano	DH6 SS1	R	23	9	8	2	1	0	0	1	1	0	3	0	.125	.500
D'Angelo Jimenez	3B6 2B1	B	21	7	20	3	8	2	0	0	4	3	4	0	.400	.500
2 Jeff Manto	1B3 3B1	R	34	6	8	0	1	0	0	0	0	0	4	0	.125	.125
1 Mike Figga	C2	R	28	2												

NAME	T	AGE	W	L	PCT	SV	G	GS	CG	IP	H	BB	SO	SHO	ERA
		31	98	64	.605	50	162	162	6	1440	1402	581	1111	10	4.1
Orlando Hernandez	R	33	17	9	.654	0	33	33	2	214	187	87	157	1	4.1
Roger Clemens	R	36	14	10	.583	0	30	30	1	188	185	90	163	1	4.6
Andy Pettitte	L	27	14	11	.560	0	31	31	0	192	216	89	121	0	4.7
David Cone	R	36	12	9	.571	0	31	31	1	193	164	90	177	1	3.4
Hideki Irabu	R	30	11	7	.611	0	32	27	2	169	180	46	133	1	4.8
Ramiro Mendoza	R	27	9	9	.500	3	53	6	0	124	141	27	80	0	4.2
Jason Grimsley	R	31	7	2	.778	1	55	0	0	75	66	40	49	0	3.6
3 Allen Watson	L	28	4	0	1.000	0	21	0	0	34	30	10	30	0	2.1
Mariano Rivera	R	29	4	3	.571	45	66	0	0	69	43	18	52	0	1.8
Jeff Nelson (EJ)	R	32	2	1	.667	1	39	0	0	30	27	22	35	0	4.3
Mike Stanton	L	32	2	2	.500	1	73	1	0	62	71	18	59	0	4.3
Dan Naulty	R	29	1	0	1.000	0	33	0	0	49	40	22	25	0	4.3
Ed Yarnall	L	23	1	0	1.000	0	5	2	0	17	17	10	13	0	3.7
Todd Erdos	R	25	0	0	—	0	7			5	4	4	0		3.8
Jay Tessmer	R	27	0	0	—	0	6	0	0	7	16	4	3	0	14.8
Mike Buddie	R	27	0	0	—	0	2	0	0	2	3	0	1	0	4.5
Tony Fossas	L	41	0	0	—	0	5	0	0	1	6	1	0	0	36.0
Jeff Juden	R	28	0	0	.000	0	2	1	0	5	3	9	10	0	1.5

BOSTON — 2nd 94-68 .580 4 (Wild Card) — JIMY WILLIAMS

Name	G by Pos	B	AGE	G	AB	R	H	2B	3B	HR	RBI	BB	SO	SB	BA	SA
TOTALS			29	162	5579	836	1551	334	42	176	808	597	928	67	.278	.448
Mike Stanley	1B111 DH20	R	36	136	427	59	120	22	0	19	72	70	94	0	.281	.466
Jose Offerman	2B128 DH17 1B8	B	30	149	586	107	172	37	11	8	69	96	79	18	.294	.435
Nomar Garciaparra	SS134	R	25	135	532	103	190	42	4	27	104	51	39	14	.357	.603
John Valentin	3B111 DH1	R	32	129	450	58	114	27	1	12	70	40	68	0	.253	.398
Trot Nixon	OF121	L	25	124	381	67	103	22	5	15	52	53	75	3	.270	.472
Darren Lewis	OF130 DH2	R	31	135	470	63	113	14	6	2	40	45	52	16	.240	.309
Troy O'Leary	OF157	L	29	157	596	84	167	36	4	28	103	56	91	1	.280	.495
Jason Varitek	C140 DH2	B	27	144	483	70	130	39	2	20	76	46	85	1	.269	.482
Brian Daubach	1B61 DH43 OF2 3B1	L	27	110	381	61	112	33	3	21	73	36	92	0	.294	.562
Damon Buford	OF84 DH5	R	29	91	297	39	72	15	2	6	38	21	74	9	.242	.367
Reggie Jefferson	DH58 1B2	L	30	83	206	21	57	13	1	5	17	17	54	0	.277	.422
Donnie Sadler	SS14 2B10 3B9 OF8 DH4	R	24	97	107	18	30	5	1	0	4	5	20	2	.280	.346
2 Butch Huskey	DH37 OF4 3B2	R	27	45	124	18	33	6	0	7	28	7	20	0	.266	.484
Lou Merloni	SS24 3B9 2B8 DH3 1B1 OF1	R	28	43	126	18	32	7	0	1	13	8	16	0	.254	.333
Jeff Frye (KJ)	2B26 3B7 SS2 DH2	R	32	41	114	14	32	3	0	1	12	14	11	2	.281	.333
Wilton Veras	3B35	R	21	36	118	14	34	5	1	2	13	5	14	0	.288	.398
Scott Hatteberg (EJ)	C23 DH6	L	29	30	80	12	22	5	1	0	11	14	14	0	.275	.375
Creighton Gubanich	C14 DH2 3B1	R	27	24	47	4	13	1	1	3	11	3	13	0	.277	.426
Jon Nunnally	DH3 OF2	L	27	10	14	4	4	0	0	1	0	6	0		.286	.357
2 Lenny Webster	C6	R	34	6	14	0	0	0	0	0	0	1	2	0	.000	.000
Chad Fonville	2B2	B	28	3	3	1	1	0	0	0	0	0	1	0	.333	.333
Michael Coleman	OF2	R	23	2	5	1	1	0	0	0	0	0	2	0	.200	.200
Steve Lomasney	C1	R	21	1	2	0	0	0	0	0	0	0	2	0	.000	.000

NAME	T	AGE	W	L	PCT	SV	G	GS	CG	IP	H	BB	SO	SHO	ERA
		31	94	68	.580	50	162	162	6	1437	1396	469	1131	12	4.0
Pedro Martinez	R	27	23	4	.852	0	31	29	5	213	160	37	313	1	2.0
Bret Saberhagen	R	35	10	6	.625	0	22	22	0	119	122	11	81	0	2.9
John Wasdin	R	26	8	3	.727	2	45	0	0	74	66	18	57	0	4.8
Brian Rose	R	23	7	6	.538	0	22	18	0	98	112	29	51	0	4.8
Mark Portugal	R	36	7	12	.368	0	31	27	1	150	179	41	79	0	5.5
Derek Lowe	R	26	6	3	.667	15	74	0	0	109	84	25	80	0	2.6
Pat Rapp	R	31	6	7	.462	0	37	26	0	146	147	69	90	0	4.1
Tim Wakefield	R	32	6	11	.353	15	49	17	0	140	146	72	104	0	5.0
Rich Garces	R	28	5	1	.833	2	30	0	0	41	25	18	33	0	1.5
Rheal Cormier	L	32	2	0	1.000	0	60	0	0	63	61	18	39	0	3.6
2 Bryce Florie	R	29	2	0	1.000	0	14	2	0	30	33	15	25	0	4.3
2 Kent Mercker	L	31	2	0	1.000	0	5	5	0	26	23	13	17	0	3.5
Juan Pena (SJ)	R	22	2	0	1.000	0	2	2	0	13	9	3	15	0	0.6
Ramon Martinez (SJ)	R	31	2	1	.667	0	4	4	0	21	14	8	15	0	3.0
Jin Ho Cho	R	23	2	3	.400	0	7	7	0	39	45	8	16	0	5.7
1 Mark Guthrie	L	33	1	1	.500	2	46	0	0	46	50	20	36	0	5.8
Tim Harikkala	R	28	1	0	1.000	0	1	0	0	13	15	6	7	0	6.1
1 Jim Corsi	R	37	1	2	.333	0	23	0	0	24	25	19	14	0	5.5
Tomokazu Ohka (SJ)	R	23	1	0	1.000	0	1	1	0	7	8	3	6	0	6.0
Bob Wolcott	R	25	0	1	.000	0	7	0	0	8	3	0	2	0	6.1
Marino Santana	R	26	0	0	—	0	3	0	0	4	5	1	5	0	7.0
Kirk Bullinger	R	29	0	0	—	0	4	0	0	5	6	4	1	0	9.0
2 Rod Beck	R	30	0	2	.000	11	21	0	0	18	17	12	24	0	5.5
Tom Gordon (EJ)	R	31	0	1	.000	11	21	0	0	16	11	6	20	0	5.1
Kip Gross	R	34	0	0	—	0	11	1	0	13	15	5	6	0	4.5
2 Julio Santana (SJ) 26															

TORONTO 3rd 84-78 .518 14 JIM FERGOSI

Name	G by Pos	B	AGE	G	AB	R	H	2B	3B	HR	RBI	BB	SO	SB	BA	SA
TOTALS			28	162	5642	883	1580	337	14	212	856	578	1077	119	.280	.457
Carlos Delgado	1B147 DH5	L	27	152	573	113	156	39	0	44	134	86	141	1	.272	.571
Homer Bush (RJ)	2B109 SS18	R	26	128	485	69	155	26	4	5	55	21	82	32	.320	.421
Alex Gonzalez (SJ)	SS37 DH1	R	26	38	154	22	45	13	0	2	12	16	23	4	.292	.416
Tony Fernandez	3B132 DH9 2B1	R	37	142	485	73	159	41	0	6	75	77	62	6	.328	.449
Shawn Green	OF152	L	26	153	614	134	190	45	0	42	123	66	117	20	.309	.588
Jose Cruz	OF106	R	25	106	349	63	84	19	3	14	45	64	91	14	.241	.483
Shannon Stewart	OF142 DH2	R	25	145	608	102	185	28	2	11	67	59	83	37	.304	.411
Darrin Fletcher	C113	L	32	115	412	48	120	26	0	18	80	26	47	0	.291	.485
Willie Greene	DH51 3B7 OF3	L	27	81	226	22	46	7	0	12	41	20	56	0	.204	.394
Tony Batista	SS98	R	25	98	375	61	107	25	1	26	79	22	79	2	.285	.565
Jacob Brumfield	OF53 DH6	R	34	62	170	25	40	8	3	2	19	19	39	1	.235	.353
Mike Matheny	C57	R	28	57	163	16	35	6	0	3	17	12	37	0	.215	.307
Willis Otanez (AJ)	3B24 1B13 DH2	R	26	42	127	21	32	8	0	5	13	9	30	0	.252	.433
Pat Kelly	2B35 DH2	R	31	37	116	17	31	7	0	6	20	10	23	0	.267	.483
Craig Grebeck (FJ)	2B17 DH10 SS4 3B2	R	34	34	113	18	41	7	0	0	10	15	13	0	.363	.425
David Segui	DH15 1B4	R	32	31	95	14	30	5	0	5	13	8	17	0	.316	.526
Brian McRae	DH15 DH1	R	31	31	82	11	16	3	1	3	11	16	22	0	.195	.366
Dave Hollins (BH)	DH23	R	33	27	99	12	22	5	0	2	6	5	22	0	.222	.333
Vernon Wells	OF24	R	20	24	88	8	23	5	0	1	8	4	18	1	.261	.352
Geronimo Berroa (VJ)	DH17 OF2	R	34	22	62	11	12	3	0	1	6	9	15	0	.194	.290
Mark Dalesandro	C8 DH5 3B2	R	31	16	27	3	5	0	0	1	0	2	1	0	.185	.185
Kevin Witt	DH11	L	23	15	34	3	7	1	0	1	5	2	9	0	.206	.324
Casey Blake	3B14	R	25	14	39	6	10	2	0	1	1	2	7	0	.256	.385
Chris Woodward	SS10 3B2	R	22	14	26	1	6	1	0	0	2	2	6	0	.231	.269
Patrick Lennon	OF8	R	31	9	29	3	6	2	0	1	6	2	12	0	.207	.379
Norberto Martin	2B8 SS1	R	32	9	27	3	6	2	0	0	0	4	4	0	.222	.296
Rob Butler (XJ)	DH3 OF2	L	29	8	7	1	1	0	0	0	1	0	0	0	.143	.143
Pat Borders	C3 DH3	R	36	6	14	1	3	0	0	0	3	1	2	0	.214	.429
Anthony Sanders	DH2 OF1	R	25	3	7	1	2	1	0	0	2	0	2	0	.286	.429
Kevin Brown	C2	R	26	2	9	1	4	2	0	0	1	0	1	0	.444	.667
Curtis Goodwin	OF2	L	26	3	4	0	0	0	0	0	0	0	3	0	.000	.000

NAME	T	AGE	W	L	PCT	SV	G	GS	CG	IP	H	BB	SO	SHO	ERA
TOTALS		28	84	78	.519	39	162	162	14	1439	1582	575	1009	9	4.92
David Wells	L	36	17	10	.630	0	34	34	7	232	246	62	169	1	4.82
Kelvin Escobar	R	23	14	11	.560	0	33	30	1	174	203	81	129	0	5.69
Pat Hentgen	R	30	11	12	.478	0	34	34	1	199	225	65	118	0	4.79
Chris Carpenter	R	24	9	8	.529	0	24	24	4	150	177	48	106	1	4.38
Roy Halladay	R	22	8	7	.533	1	36	18	1	149	156	79	82	1	3.92
2 John Frascatore	R	29	7	1	.875	0	33	0	0	37	42	9	22	0	3.41
Joey Hamilton (SJ)	R	28	7	8	.467	0	22	18	0	98	118	39	56	0	6.52
Graeme Lloyd	L	32	5	3	.625	3	74	0	0	72	68	23	47	0	3.63
Paul Quantrill (BL)	R	30	3	2	.600	0	41	0	0	49	53	17	28	0	3.33
2 Paul Spoljaric	L	28	2	2	.500	0	37	2	0	62	62	32	63	0	4.65
1 Tom Davey	R	25	1	1	.500	1	29	0	0	44	40	26	42	0	4.70
1 Steve Sinclair	L	27	1	0	.000	0	0	0	0	6	7	4	3	0	12.71
Mike Romano	R	27	0	0	.000	0	0	0	0	3	5	3	1	0	11.81
3 John Hudek	R	32	0	0	.000	0	4	0	0	4	8	1	2	0	12.27
John Bale	L	25	0	0	.000	0	1	0	0	1	2	2	4	0	13.50
Gary Glover	R	22	0	0	.000	0	1	0	0	1	1	0	0	0	0.00
Eric Ludwick	R	27	0	0	.000	0	2	0	0	2	2	2	2	0	27.00
Nerio Rodriguez	R	23	0	0	.000	0	2	2	0	2	2	0	2	0	13.50
Peter Munro	R	23	0	2	.000	0	31	2	0	55	70	23	38	0	6.02
1 Robert Person	R	29	0	2	.000	0	11	9	0	11	9	15	12	0	9.82
1 Dan Plesac	L	37	0	3	.000	0	30	0	0	23	28	9	26	0	8.34
Billy Koch	R	24	0	5	.000	31	56	0	0	64	55	30	57	0	3.39
Bill Risley (XJ) 32															

BALTIMORE 4th 78-84 .481 20 RAY MILLER

Name	G by Pos	B	AGE	G	AB	R	H	2B	3B	HR	RBI	BB	SO	SB	BA	SA
TOTALS			33	162	5637	851	1572	299	21	203	804	615	890	107	.279	.447
Will Clark (BF-EJ)	1B63 DH3	L	35	77	251	40	76	15	0	10	29	38	42	2	.303	.482
Delino DeShields (LJ)	2B93	L	30	96	330	46	87	11	2	6	34	37	52	11	.264	.364
Mike Bordick	SS159	R	33	160	631	93	175	35	7	10	77	54	102	14	.277	.403
Cal Ripken (XJ)	3B85	R	38	86	332	51	113	27	0	18	57	13	31	0	.340	.584
Albert Belle	OF154 DH7	R	32	161	610	108	181	36	1	37	117	101	82	17	.297	.541
Brady Anderson	OF136 DH10	L	35	150	564	109	159	28	5	24	81	96	105	36	.282	.477
B.J. Surhoff	OF148 DH13 3B2	L	34	162	673	104	207	38	1	28	107	43	78	5	.308	.492
Charles Johnson	C135	R	27	135	426	58	107	19	1	16	54	55	107	0	.251	.413
Harold Baines	DH96	L	40	107	345	57	111	16	1	24	81	43	38	1	.322	.583
Jeff Conine	1B99 DH20 OF13 3B4	R	33	139	444	54	129	31	1	13	75	30	40	0	.291	.453
Jeff Reboulet	3B56 2B36 SS10	R	35	99	154	25	25	4	0	4	33	29	1		.162	.188
Rich Amaral	OF50 DH18 1B2 2B2 3B1	R	37	91	137	21	38	8	1	0	11	15	20	9	.277	.350
Jerry Hairston	2B50 DH26 3B2	R	23	50	175	26	47	12	1	4	17	11	24	9	.269	.417
Ryan Minor	3B45 1B1	R	25	46	124	13	24	7	0	3	10	8	43	1	.194	.323
Mike Figga	C41	R	28	41	86	12	19	4	0	1	5	2	27	0	.221	.302
Willis Otanez	3B22 1B5 DH3	R	26	29	80	7	17	3	0	2	11	6	16	0	.213	.325
Eugene Kingsale	OF24 DH2	B	22	28	85	9	21	2	0	0	7	5	13	1	.247	.271
Derrick May	DH9 OF5	L	30	26	49	5	13	0	0	4	12	4	6	0	.265	.510
Calvin Pickering	1B8 DH7	L	22	23	40	4	5	1	0	1	5	11	16	0	.125	.225
Jesse Garcia	SS7 2B6 3B2 DH1	R	25	17	29	6	6	0	0	0	2	2	3	2	.207	.414
Lenny Webster (NJ)	C12 DH2	R	34	16	36	1	6	1	0	0	3	8	5	0	.167	.194
Tommy Davis	C4 1B1	R	26	5	6	0	1	0	0	0	0	0	2	0	.167	.167

NAME	T	AGE	W	L	PCT	SV	G	GS	CG	IP	H	BB	SO	SHO	ERA
TOTALS		31	78	84	.481	33	162	162	17	1435	1468	647	982	11	4.77
Mike Mussina	R	30	18	7	.720	0	31	31	4	203	207	52	172	0	3.50
Scott Erickson	R	31	15	12	.556	0	34	34	6	230	244	99	106	3	4.81
Sidney Ponson	R	22	12	12	.500	0	32	32	6	210	227	80	112	0	4.71
Jason Johnson	R	25	8	7	.533	0	22	20	0	115	120	55	71	0	5.46
Doug Johns	L	31	6	4	.600	0	32	5	0	87	81	25	50	0	4.47
1 Juan Guzman	R	32	5	9	.357	0	21	21	1	123	124	61	95	1	4.18
Arthur Rhodes	L	29	3	4	.429	3	43	0	0	53	43	45	59	0	5.43
Mike Timlin	R	33	3	9	.250	27	62	0	0	63	51	23	50	0	3.57
2 Alberto Reyes	R	28	2	3	.400	0	27	0	0	33	31	16	28	0	4.85
Scott Kamieniecki (LJ)	R	35	2	4	.333	2	43	3	0	56	52	29	39	0	4.95
Mike Fetters (EJ)	R	34	1	1	1.000	0	27	0	0	31	35	22	22	0	5.81
B.J. Ryan	L	23	1	0	1.000	0	18	0	0	18	9	12	28	0	2.95
Gabe Molina	R	24	1	2	.333	0	20	0	0	23	22	16	14	0	6.65
Doug Linton	R	34	1	4	.200	0	14	8	0	59	69	25	31	0	5.95
Matt Riley	L	19	1	2	.333	0	3	3	0	11	17	13	6	0	7.36
1 Heathcliff Slocumb	R	33	0	0	.000	0	10	0	0	9	15	9	12	0	12.46
Brian Falkenborg	R	21	0	0	.000	0	3	0	0	5	9	2	1	0	0.00
1 Rocky Coppinger	R	25	0	1	.000	0	22	0	0	22	25	19	17	0	8.31
2 Jim Corsi	R	37	0	1	.000	0	13	0	0	13	15	1	8	0	2.70
Jesse Orosco	L	42	0	3	.000	0	65	0	0	32	28	20	35	0	5.34
Ricky Bones	R	30	0	3	.000	0	32	0	0	44	59	19	26	0	5.98

TAMPA BAY 5th 69-93 .426 29 LARRY ROTHSCHILD

Name	G by Pos	B	AGE	G	AB	R	H	2B	3B	HR	RBI	BB	SO	SB	BA	SA
TOTALS			30	162	5586	772	1531	272	29	145	728	544	1042	73	.274	.411
Fred McGriff	1B125 DH18	L	35	144	529	75	164	30	1	32	104	86	107	1	.310	.552
Miguel Cairo	2B117 DH12	R	25	120	465	51	138	15	5	3	36	24	46	22	.295	.368
Kevin Stocker (KJ)	SS76	R	29	79	254	39	76	11	2	1	27	24	41	9	.299	.370
Wade Boggs	3B74 DH7 1B4	L	41	90	292	40	88	14	1	2	29	38	23	1	.301	.377
Dave Martinez	OF140	L	34	143	514	79	146	25	5	6	66	60	76	13	.284	.387
Randy Winn	OF77	R	25	79	303	44	81	16	4	2	24	17	63	9	.267	.366
Quinton McCracken (KJ)	OF40	R	29	40	148	20	37	6	1	1	18	14	33	6	.250	.324
John Flaherty	C115 DH1	R	31	117	446	53	124	19	0	14	71	19	64	0	.278	.415
Jose Canseco (XJ)	DH106 OF6	R	34	113	430	75	120	18	1	34	95	58	135	3	.279	.563
Paul Sorrento	OF57 1B27 DH9	L	33	99	294	40	69	14	1	11	42	49	101	1	.235	.401
Aaron Ledesma (RJ)	SS50 3B26 2B17 1B4 DH1	R	28	93	294	32	78	15	0	0	30	14	35	1	.265	.316
Bubba Trammell	OF74 DH6	R	27	82	283	49	82	19	0	14	39	43	37	0	.290	.505
Bobby Smith	3B59 2B13	R	25	68	199	18	36	4	1	3	19	16	64	4	.181	.256
Herbert Perry (VJ)	3B42 1B14 OF6 DH5	R	29	66	209	29	53	10	1	6	32	16	42	0	.254	.397
Terrell Lowery	OF60 DH1	R	28	66	185	25	48	15	1	2	17	19	53	0	.259	.384
David Lamb	SS35 2B15 DH3	B	23	55	124	18	28	5	1	1	13	10	19	0	.226	.306
Mike DiFelice	C51	R	30	51	179	21	55	11	0	6	27	8	23	0	.307	.469
Jose Guillen	OF47	R	23	47	168	24	41	10	0	2	13	10	36	0	.244	.339
Tony Graffanino	2B17 SS17 3B1 DH1	R	27	39	130	20	41	9	4	2	19	9	22	3	.315	.492
Danny Clyburn	OF24 DH4	R	25	28	81	8	16	4	0	3	5	7	21	0	.198	.358
Rich Butler	OF6	L	26	7	20	2	3	1	0	0	1	4	0		.150	.200
Steve Cox	1B4 OF2	L	24	6	19	0	4	1	0	0	0	2	5	0	.211	.263
Julio Franco	1B1	R	40	1	1	0	0	0	0	0	0	0	0	0	.000	.000

NAME	T	AGE	W	L	PCT	SV	G	GS	CG	IP	H	BB	SO	SHO	ERA
TOTALS		29	69	93	.426	45	162	162	6	1433	1606	695	1055	5	5.06
Wilson Alvarez	L	29	9	9	.500	0	28	28	1	160	159	79	128	0	4.22
Ryan Rupe	R	24	8	9	.471	0	24	24	0	142	136	57	97	0	4.55
Rolando Arrojo (SJ)	R	30	7	12	.368	0	24	24	2	141	162	60	107	0	5.18
Bobby Witt	R	35	7	15	.318	0	32	32	3	180	213	96	123	2	5.84
Bryan Rekar	R	27	6	6	.500	0	27	12	0	95	121	41	55	0	5.80
Rick White	R	30	5	3	.625	0	63	1	0	108	132	38	81	0	4.08
Dave Eiland	R	32	4	8	.333	0	15	15	0	80	98	27	53	0	5.60
Albie Lopez (MJ)	R	27	3	2	.600	1	51	0	0	64	66	34	37	0	4.64
1 Scott Aldred	L	31	4	6	.400	0	37	0	0	24	26	14	22	0	5.18
Tony Saunders (BA)	R	25	3	3	.500	0	9	9	0	42	53	29	30	0	6.43
Esteban Yan	R	24	3	4	.429	0	51	1	0	61	77	32	46	0	5.90
Alan Newman	L	29	2	2	.500	0	18	0	0	9	20	9	20	0	6.89
Roberto Hernandez	R	34	2	3	.400	43	72	0	0	73	68	33	69	0	3.07
Norm Charlton	L	36	2	3	.400	0	42	0	0	51	49	36	45	0	4.44
Eddie Gaillard	R	28	1	0	1.000	0	8	0	0	9	12	4	7	0	2.08
Cory Lidle (EJ)	R	27	1	0	1.000	0	7	0	0	7	7	2	6	0	7.20
Mike Duvall	L	24	1	1	.500	0	40	0	0	40	46	27	18	0	4.05
Mickey Callaway	R	24	1	2	.333	0	5	4	0	19	30	14	11	0	7.45
1 Julio Santana	R	26	1	4	.200	0	22	5	0	55	66	32	34	0	7.32
Jeff Sparks	R	27	0	0	.000	0	15	0	0	12	9	17	18	0	5.40
Jim Morris	L	35	0	0	.000	0	5	0	0	5	3	2	3	0	5.79
Wade Boggs	R	41	0	0	.000	0	1	0	0	1	0	0	0	0	6.75
Jim Mecir (BE)	R	29	0	0	.000	0	0	0	0	23	26	15	15	0	2.61
Dan Wheeler	R	21	0	4	.000	0	11	5	0	31	35	13	32	0	5.87
Rick Gorecki (SJ) 25															

CENTRAL DIVISION

CLEVELAND 1st 97-65 .599 MIKE HARGROVE

Name	G by Pos	B	AGE	G	AB	R	H	2B	3B	HR	RBI	BB	SO	SB	BA	SA
TOTALS			29	162	5634	1009	1629	309	32	209	960	743	1099	147	.289	.467
Jim Thome	1B111 DH34	L	28	146	494	101	137	27	2	33	108	127	171	0	.277	.540
Roberto Alomar	2B156 DH2	B	31	159	563	138	182	40	3	24	120	99	96	37	.323	.533
Omar Vizquel	SS143 OF1	B	32	144	574	112	191	36	4	5	66	65	50	42	.333	.436
Travis Fryman (KJ)	3B85	R	30	85	452	45	82	16	2	10	48	25	72	1	.255	.410
Manny Ramirez	OF145 DH2	R	27	147	522	131	174	34	3	44	165	96	131	2	.333	.663
Kenny Lofton	OF119 DH1	L	32	120	465	110	140	28	7	7	39	79	84	25	.301	.432
David Justice	OF93 DH34	L	33	133	429	75	123	18	0	21	88	94	90	1	.287	.476
Sandy Alomar (KJ)	C35 DH1	R	33	37	137	19	42	13	0	6	25	2	30	3	.307	.533
Richie Sexson	1B61 OF49 DH24	R	24	134	479	72	122	17	7	31	116	34	117	3	.255	.514
Einar Diaz	C119	R	26	119	392	43	110	21	1	3	32	23	41	11	.281	.362
Enrique Wilson	3B61 SS35 2B21 DH1	B	25	113	332	41	87	22	1	2	24	25	41	5	.262	.352
Wil Cordero (BW)	DH23 OF7	R	27	54	194	35	58	15	0	8	32	15	37	2	.299	.500
Alex Ramirez	OF29 DH14	R	24	48	97	11	29	6	1	3	18	3	26	1	.299	.474
Dave Roberts	OF39	L	27	41	143	26	34	4	2	0	12	9	16	11	.238	.308
Jacob Cruz (RJ)	OF24 DH2	L	26	32	88	14	29	5	0	2	13	10	13	0	.330	.511
Jolbert Cabrera	OF16 2B6 DH5	R	26	31	45	2	8	1	0	0	1	3	8	0	.178	.222
2 Harold Baines	DH25	L	40	28	85	6	23	4	0	3	22	11	10	0	.271	.329
2 Carlos Baerga	3B15 2B8 DH4	B	30	27	65	4	13	0	0	1	5	4	10	1	.228	.281
John McDonald	2B7 SS6	R	24	18	21	2	7	0	0	0	1	0	5	0	.333	.333
2 Tyler Houston	3B10 C1	L	28	12	30	1	6	1	0	1	4	1	11	0	.200	.400
3 Jeff Manto	3B10 1B1	R	34	12	25	5	5	0	0	1	3	5	8	0	.200	.320
Chris Turner	C13	R	30	12	21	2	5	1	0	0	3	1	5	0	.238	.286
Russell Branyan	3B8 DH3	L	23	11	38	4	9	2	0	5	10	3	19	0	.237	.684
Jesse Levis	C9	L	31	11	31	1	5	0	0	0	0	8	5	0	.154	.154
Mark Whiten (FJ)	OF7	B	32	9	25	4	9	2	0	0	3	4	9	0	.160	.320
Pat Borders	C5 3B1	R	36	6	20	2	4	2	0	0	3	0	3	0	.300	.400

NAME	T	AGE	W	L	PCT	SV	G	GS	CG	IP	H	BB	SO	SHO	ERA
TOTALS		31	97	65	.599	46	162	162	3	1450	1503	634	1120	6	4.89
Bartolo Colon	R	26	18	5	.783	0	32	32	1	205	185	76	161	1	3.95
Charles Nagy	R	32	17	11	.607	0	33	32	1	202	238	59	126	0	4.95
Dave Burba	R	32	15	9	.625	0	34	34	1	220	211	96	174	0	4.25
Steve Karsay	R	27	10	2	.833	1	50	3	0	79	71	30	68	0	2.97
Paul Shuey	R	28	5	5	.615	6	72	0	0	82	68	40	103	0	3.53
Jaret Wright (XJ)	R	23	8	10	.444	0	26	26	0	134	144	77	91	0	6.06
Jim Brower	R	26	3	3	.750	0	24	2	0	26	27	10	18	0	4.56
Steve Reed	R	34	3	2	.600	0	63	0	0	62	69	20	44	0	4.23
Dwight Gooden	R	34	3	4	.429	0	26	22	0	115	127	67	88	0	6.26
Mike Jackson	R	34	3	4	.429	39	72	0	0	69	60	26	55	0	4.06
Paul Assenmacher	L	38	2	1	.667	0	55	0	0	33	50	17	29	0	8.18
Ricardo Rincon (EJ)	L	29	2	3	.400	0	59	0	0	45	41	24	30	0	4.43
Paul Wagner	R	31	2	0	1.000	0	3	0	0	4	5	3	4	0	4.15
2 Tom Candiotti	R	41	1	0	1.000	2	19	0	0	15	19	7	11	0	11.05
David Riske	R	22	1	1	.500	0	3	0	0	6	10	3	8	0	4.63
Mark Langston	L	38	1	2	.333	0	25	6	0	62	69	29	43	0	5.25
Sean DePaula	R	25	0	0	.000	0	11	0	0	11	5	8	14	0	4.63
Dave Stevens	R	29	0	0	.000	0	5	0	0	6	10	8	6	0	10.00
1 Jerry Spradlin	R	31	0	0	.000	0	1	0	0	1	2	0	0	0	18.00
Jason Rakers (GJ)	R	28	0	0	.000	0	1	0	0	0.1	0	1	0	0	4.50
1 Jeff Tam	R	28	0	0	.000	0	1	0	0	0.1	0	1	0	0	81.00
Rich DeLucia	R	34	0	1	.000	0	20	0	0	23	16	12	13	0	6.75
Tom Martin (SJ)	L	29	0	1	.000	0	15	0	0	13	15	9	8	0	8.68
Chris Haney	L	30	0	1	.000	0	11	0	0	40	43	16	22	0	4.69

CHICAGO 2nd 75-86 .466 21.5 JERRY MANUEL

Name	G by Pos	B	AGE	G	AB	R	H	2B	3B	HR	RBI	BB	SO	SB	BA	SA
TOTALS			26	162	5644	777	1563	298	37	162	742	499	810	110	.277	.429
Paul Konerko	1B92 DH46 3B1	R	23	142	513	71	151	31	4	24	81	45	68	1	.294	.511
Ray Durham	2B148 DH4	R	27	153	612	109	181	30	4	13	60	73	105	34	.296	.435
Mike Caruso	SS132 DH2	L	22	136	529	60	132	11	4	2	35	20	36	12	.250	.297
Greg Norton	3B120 1B26 DH1	B	26	132	436	62	111	26	0	16	50	69	93	4	.255	.424
Magglio Ordonez	OF153 DH2	R	25	157	624	100	188	34	3	30	117	47	64	13	.301	.510
Chris Singleton	OF127 DH2	L	26	133	496	72	149	31	6	17	72	22	45	20	.300	.490
Carlos Lee	OF105 DH16 1B5	R	23	127	492	66	144	32	2	16	84	13	72	4	.293	.463
Brook Fordyce	C103	R	29	105	333	36	99	25	1	9	49	21	48	2	.297	.459
Frank Thomas (NJ)	DH82 1B49	R	31	135	486	74	148	36	0	15	77	87	66	3	.305	.471
Craig Wilson	3B72 SS22 2B7 1B1 DH1	R	28	98	252	28	60	8	1	4	26	23	22	1	.238	.325
Mark Johnson	C72 DH1	L	23	73	207	27	47	11	0	4	16	36	58	3	.227	.338
Darrin Jackson	OF64 DH3	R	36	73	149	22	41	9	1	4	16	3	20	4	.275	.430
Brian Simmons	OF46 DH3	B	25	54	126	14	29	3	3	4	17	9	30	4	.230	.397
Jeff Liefer	OF17 1B15 DH7	L	24	45	113	8	28	7	1	0	14	8	28	2	.248	.327
Liu Rodriguez	2B22 SS14 DH2 3B1	B	22	93	93	8	22	2	2	1	12	12	11	0	.237	.333
McKay Christensen	OF27	L	23	28	53	10	12	1	0	1	6	4	7	2	.226	.302
Jeff Abbott	OF17	R	26	17	57	5	9	0	0	2	6	5	12	1	.158	.263
Jason Dellaero	SS11	B	22	11	33	1	3	0	0	0	2	1	13	0	.091	.091
Josh Paul	C6	R	24	6	18	2	4	1	0	0	1	0	4	0	.222	.278

NAME	T	AGE	W	L	PCT	SV	G	GS	CG	IP	H	BB	SO	SHO	ERA
		26	75	86	.466	39	162	162	6	1438	1608	596	968	3	4.9
James Baldwin	R	27	12	13	.480	0	35	33	1	199	219	81	123	0	5.1
Mike Sirotka	L	28	11	13	.458	0	32	32	3	209	236	57	125	1	4.0
John Snyder	R	24	9	12	.429	0	25	25	1	129	167	49	67	0	6.6
Jim Parque	L	24	9	15	.375	0	31	30	1	174	210	79	111	0	5.1
Jaime Navarro	R	32	8	13	.381	0	32	27	0	160	206	71	74	0	6.0
Bill Simas	R	27	6	3	.667	2	70	0	0	72	73	32	41	0	3.7
Bob Howry	R	25	5	3	.625	28	69	0	0	68	58	38	80	0	3.5
Sean Lowe	R	28	4	1	.800	0	64	0	0	96	90	46	62	0	3.5
Kip Wells	R	22	4	1	.800	0	7	7	0	36	33	15	29	0	4.0
Keith Foulke	R	26	3	3	.500	9	67	0	0	105	72	21	123	0	2.2
Carlos Castillo	R	24	2	2	.500	0	18	2	0	41	45	14	23	0	5.7
Scott Eyre	L	27	1	1	.500	0	21	0	0	25	38	15	17	0	7.1
David Lundquist	R	24	1	1	.500	0	17	0	0	22	28	12	18	0	8.5
Jesus Pena	L	24	0	0	—	0	26	0	0	20	21	23	20	0	5.3
Pat Daneker	R	24	0	0	—	0	3	2	0	15	14	6	5	0	4.2
Tanyon Sturtze	R	28	0	0	—	0	1	1	0	6	4	2	2	0	0.0
Chad Bradford	R	24	0	0	—	0	3	0	0	4	9	5	0	0	19.8
Joe Davenport	R	23	0	0	—	0	3	0	0	2	1	2	0	0	0.0
Bryan Ward	L	27	0	1	.000	0	40	0	0	39	63	11	35	0	7.5
Aaron Myette	R	21	0	2	.000	0	4	3	0	16	17	14	11	0	6.3
Todd Rizzo	L	23	0	2	.000	0	1	0	0	4	4	3	2	0	
Darren Hall (SJ) 34															

DETROIT 3rd 69-92 .429 27.5 LARRY PARRISH

Name	G by Pos	B	AGE	G	AB	R	H	2B	3B	HR	RBI	BB	SO	SB	BA	SA
TOTALS			27	161	5481	747	1433	289	34	212	704	458	1049	108	.261	.443
Tony Clark	1B132 DH11	B	27	143	536	74	150	29	0	31	99	64	133	2	.280	.507
Damion Easley	2B147 SS19	R	29	151	549	83	146	30	1	20	65	51	124	11	.266	.434
Deivi Cruz	SS155	R	26	155	518	64	147	35	0	13	58	12	57	1	.284	.427
Dean Palmer	3B141 DH9	R	30	150	560	92	147	25	2	38	100	57	153	3	.263	.518
Bobby Higginson (FJ)	OF88 DH17	L	28	107	377	51	90	18	0	12	46	64	66	4	.239	.382
Gabe Kapler	OF128 DH2	R	23	132	416	60	102	22	4	18	49	42	74	11	.245	.447
Juan Encarnacion	OF131	R	23	132	509	62	130	30	6	19	74	14	113	33	.255	.450
Brad Ausmus	C127	R	30	127	458	62	126	25	6	9	54	51	71	12	.275	.415
Luis Polonia	DH43 OF40	L	34	87	333	46	108	21	8	10	32	16	32	17	.324	.526
Frank Catalanotto	1B32 2B32 3B21 DH9	L	25	100	286	41	79	19	0	11	35	15	49	3	.276	.458
Karim Garcia	OF81 DH7	L	23	96	288	38	69	10	3	14	32	20	67	2	.240	.441
Gregg Jefferies (LJ)	DH45 1B3 2B2 OF2	B	31	70	205	22	41	9	0	6	18	13	11	3	.200	.327
Bill Haselman	C39 DH9	R	33	48	143	13	39	8	0	4	14	10	26	2	.273	.413
Kimera Bartee	OF38 DH1	R	26	41	77	11	15	1	3	0	3	9	20	3	.195	.286
Jason Wood (BA)	SS9 3B9 1B5 2B1 DH1	R	29	27	44	5	7	1	0	1	8	2	13	0	.159	.250
Gabe Alvarez	DH12 OF5 3B2	R	25	22	53	5	11	3	0	2	4	3	9	0	.208	.377
1 Brian Hunter	OF18	R	28	18	55	8	13	2	1	0	5	11	0	.236	.309
Robert Fick (SJ)	DH8 C4	L	25	15	41	6	9	0	0	3	10	7	6	1	.220	.439
Luis Garcia	SS7 2B1	R	24	8	9	0	1	0	0	0	1	0	5	0	.111	.222
Jose Macias	2B1	B	27	5	4	2	1	0	0	0	0	0	1	.250	1.000

NAME	T	AGE	W	L	PCT	SV	G	GS	CG	IP	H	BB	SO	SHO	ERA
		27	69	92	.429	33	161	161	4	1421	1528	583	976	6	5.1
2 Dave Mlicki	R	31	14	12	.538	0	31	31	2	192	209	70	119	0	4.6
Brian Moehler	R	27	10	16	.385	0	32	32	2	196	229	59	106	2	5.0
Justin Thompson (SJ)	L	26	9	11	.450	0	24	24	0	143	152	59	83	0	5.1
Jeff Weaver	R	22	9	12	.429	0	30	29	0	164	176	56	114	0	5.5
Doug Brocail	R	32	4	4	.500	2	70	0	0	82	60	25	78	0	2.5
Todd Jones	R	31	4	4	.500	30	65	0	0	66	64	35	64	0	3.8
C.J. Nitkowski	L	26	4	5	.444	0	68	7	0	82	63	45	66	0	4.3
Willie Blair	R	33	3	11	.214	0	39	16	0	134	169	44	82	0	6.8
1 Bryce Florie (SJ)	R	29	2	1	.667	0	27	3	0	51	61	20	40	0	4.5
Matt Anderson	R	22	2	1	.667	0	37	0	0	38	33	35	32	0	5.6
Francisco Cordero	R	24	2	2	.500	0	20	0	0	19	19	18	19	0	3.3
Nelson Cruz	R	26	2	5	.286	0	29	6	0	67	74	23	46	0	5.6
Dave Borkowski	R	22	2	6	.250	0	17	12	0	77	86	40	50	0	6.2
Masao Kida	R	30	1	0	1.000	1	49	0	0	65	73	30	50	0	6.2
Will Brunson	L	29	1	0	1.000	0	17	0	0	12	18	6	9	0	6.0
Erik Hiljus	R	26	0	0	—	0	9	7	5	1	0	5.3
2 Mel Rojas	R	32	0	0	—	0	5	0	0	6	12	4	6	0	22.7
Felipe Lira	R	27	0	0	—	0	2	0	0	3	7	2	3	0	10.8
Willis Roberts	R	24	0	1	.000	0	3	0	0	13	0	0	3	0	13.5
Sean Runyan (SJ)	L	25	0	0	—	0	12	0	0	11	9	3	6	0	3.3
Beiker Graterol	R	24	0	1	.000	1	1	0	4	4	4	2	0	15.7
Seth Greisinger (EJ) 23															

KANSAS CITY 4th 64-97 .392 32.5 TONY MUSER

Name	G by Pos	B	AGE	G	AB	R	H	2B	3B	HR	RBI	BB	SO	SB	BA	SA
TOTALS			26	161	5624	856	1584	294	52	151	800	535	932	127	.282	.433
Mike Sweeney	1B74 DH71 C4	R	25	150	575	101	185	44	2	22	102	54	48	6	.322	.520
Carlos Febles	2B122	R	23	123	453	71	116	22	9	10	53	47	91	20	.256	.411
Rey Sanchez	SS134	R	31	134	479	66	141	18	6	2	56	22	48	11	.294	.370
Joe Randa	3B156	R	29	156	628	92	197	36	8	16	84	50	80	5	.314	.473
Jermaine Dye	OF157 DH2	R	25	158	608	96	179	44	8	27	119	58	119	2	.294	.526
Carlos Beltran	OF154 DH2	B	22	156	663	112	194	27	7	22	108	46	123	27	.293	.454
Johnny Damon	OF140 DH4	L	25	145	583	101	179	39	9	14	77	67	50	36	.307	.477
Chad Kreuter	C101 DH1	B	34	107	324	31	73	15	0	5	35	34	65	0	.225	.318
Jeremy Giambi (LJ)	DH48 1B26 OF5	L	24	90	288	34	82	13	1	3	34	40	67	0	.285	.368
Scott Pose	OF25 DH18	L	32	86	137	27	39	3	0	0	12	21	22	6	.285	.307
Tim Spehr	C59	R	32	60	155	26	32	7	0	9	26	22	47	1	.206	.426
Jed Hansen	2B21 SS10 3B4 DH3 OF2 1B1	R	26	49	79	16	16	1	0	3	5	10	32	0	.203	.329
Steve Scarsone	SS16 1B12 2B9 3B3 DH1	R	33	46	68	2	14	5	0	0	6	9	24	1	.206	.279
Larry Sutton (LJ)	1B30 DH5 OF1	L	29	43	102	14	23	6	0	2	15	13	17	1	.225	.343
Scott Leius (SJ)	1B13 3B10 DH6 SS2 2B1	R	33	37	74	8	15	1	0	1	10	4	11	1	.203	.257
Ray Holbert	SS22 2B11 3B1	R	28	34	100	14	28	3	0	5	8	20	7	.280	.310
Sal Fasano	C23	R	27	23	60	11	14	2	0	5	16	7	17	0	.233	.517
Jeff King (VR)	1B20 DH1	R	34	21	72	14	17	2	0	3	11	15	10	2	.236	.389
Mark Quinn	OF15 DH1	R	25	17	60	11	20	4	1	6	18	4	11	1	.333	.733
Joe Vitiello	1B10 DH2	R	30	13	41	4	6	1	0	1	4	2	9	0	.146	.244
Dee Brown	OF3 DH2	L	21	12	25	1	2	0	0	0	2	0	7	0	.080	.080
Mendy Lopez	2B6 SS1	R	25	7	20	2	8	0	1	0	3	0	5	0	.400	.500
Felix Martinez	SS2 2B1	B	25	6	7	1	1	0	0	0	0	0	6	0	.143	.143

NAME	T	AGE	W	L	PCT	SV	G	GS	CG	IP	H	BB	SO	SHO	ERA
		28	64	97	.398	29	161	161	11	1421	1607	643	831	3	5.3
Jeff Suppan	R	24	10	12	.455	0	32	32	4	209	222	62	103	1	4.5
Jose Rosado	L	24	10	14	.417	0	33	33	5	208	197	72	141	0	3.8
1 Kevin Appier	R	31	9	9	.500	0	22	22	1	140	153	51	78	0	4.8
Jay Witasick	R	26	9	12	.429	0	32	28	1	158	191	83	102	1	5.5
Scott Service	R	32	5	5	.500	8	68	0	0	75	87	42	68	0	6.0
1 Matt Whisenant	L	28	4	4	.500	1	48	0	0	40	40	26	27	0	6.3
Jose Santiago (XJ)	R	24	3	4	.429	2	34	0	0	47	46	14	15	0	5.3
Terry Mathews (SJ)	R	34	2	1	.667	1	24	1	0	39	44	17	19	0	4.3
Dan Reichert (EJ)	R	22	2	2	.500	0	8	7	0	37	48	32	20	0	5.9
2 Mac Suzuki	R	24	2	3	.400	0	22	9	0	68	77	30	36	0	5.1
Alvin Morman	L	30	2	4	.333	1	49	0	0	53	66	23	31	0	4.0
Ken Ray	R	24	1	0	1.000	0	13	0	0	11	23	6	0	0	8.7
2 Blake Stein	R	25	1	3	.333	0	12	11	0	70	59	41	43	0	4.0
1 Jim Pittsley	R	25	1	2	.333	0	5	5	0	23	33	15	7	0	6.9
2 Brad Rigby	R	26	1	2	.333	0	20	1	0	21	33	5	10	0	7.1
Brian Barber	R	26	1	3	.250	1	8	3	0	19	31	10	7	0	6.9
Jeff Montgomery (PJ)	R	37	1	4	.200	12	49	0	0	51	72	21	27	0	6.8
2 Dan Murray	R	25	0	0	—	0	4	1	0	5	7	4	1	0	5.6
Orber Moreno (AJ)	R	22	0	0	—	0	2	0	0	1	4	3	1	0	5.6
Chad Durbin	R	21	0	0	—	0	1	0	0	4	5	3	2	0	9.2
Don Wengert	R	29	0	1	.000	0	11	1	0	24	41	5	10	0	9.2
Derek Wallace	R	27	0	1	.000	0	8	7	5	3	3	0	7.5
Lance Carter	R	24	0	1	.000	0	1	0	4	4	3	0	5.6
1 Glendon Rusch	L	24	0	1	.000	0	8	7	0	5	4	4	0	15.7
Marc Pisciotta	R	28	0	2	.000	1	33	0	0	25	32	20	17	0	8.6
Tim Byrdak	L	25	0	0	—	0	8	0	0	12	3	3	8	0	9.9
Chris Fussell	R	23	0	5	.000	0	8	0	0	56	72	36	37	0	7.3
Hipolito Pichardo (EJ) 29															

MINNESOTA 5th 63-97 .394 33 TOM KELLY

Name	G by Pos	B	AGE	G	AB	R	H	2B	3B	HR	RBI	BB	SO	SB	BA	SA
TOTALS			27	161	5495	686	1450	285	30	105	643	500	978	118	.264	.384
Doug Mientkiewicz	1B110	L	25	118	327	34	75	21	3	2	32	43	51	1	.229	.330
Todd Walker	2B103 DH34	L	26	143	531	62	148	37	4	6	46	52	83	18	.279	.397
Cristian Guzman	SS131	B	21	131	420	47	95	12	3	1	26	22	90	9	.226	.276
Corey Koskie	3B79 OF25 DH12	L	26	117	342	42	106	21	0	11	58	40	72	4	.310	.468
Matt Lawton (IJ)	OF109 DH6	L	27	118	406	58	105	18	0	7	54	57	42	26	.259	.355
Torii Hunter	OF130	R	23	135	384	52	98	17	2	9	35	26	72	10	.255	.380
Chad Allen	OF133 DH2	R	24	137	481	69	133	21	3	10	46	37	89	14	.277	.395
Terry Steinbach	C96 DH1	R	37	101	338	35	96	16	4	11	42	38	54	2	.284	.391
Marty Cordova	DH85 OF29	R	29	124	425	62	121	28	3	14	70	48	96	13	.285	.464
Denny Hocking	SS61 2B56 OF38 3B6 1B2	B	29	136	386	47	103	18	2	7	41	22	54	11	.267	.378
Ron Coomer	1B71 3B57 DH7 OF1	R	32	127	467	53	123	25	1	16	65	30	69	2	.263	.424
Brent Gates	3B61 2B47 1B5 SS1 DH1	B	29	110	306	40	78	13	2	3	38	34	56	1	.255	.340
Jacque Jones	OF93	L	24	95	322	54	93	24	2	9	44	17	63	3	.289	.460
Javier Valentin	C76	B	23	78	218	22	54	12	1	5	28	22	39	0	.248	.381
Midre Cummings	OF5 DH5	L	27	16	38	1	10	0	0	1	2	2	3	0	.263	.342
Chris Latham	OF14	B	26	14	22	1	2	0	0	0	3	0	13	0	.091	.091
Cleatus Davidson	2B6 SS4	1 B	22	8	22	1	3	0	0	0	1	5	0	.136	.136
David Ortiz	DH5 1B1	L	23	10	20	1	0	0	0	0	0	5	12	0	.000	.000
A.J. Pierzynski	C9	L	22	9	24	1	6	0	0	1	3	2	4	0	.273	.364

NAME	T	AGE	W	L	PCT	SV	G	GS	CG	IP	H	BB	SO	SHO	ERA
		27	63	97	.394	34	161	161	12	1423	1591	487	927	8	5.0
Brad Radke	R	26	12	14	.462	0	33	33	4	219	239	44	121	0	3.7
LaTroy Hawkins	R	26	10	14	.417	0	33	33	1	174	238	60	103	0	6.6
Bob Wells	R	32	8	3	.727	1	76	0	0	87	79	28	44	0	4.6
Eric Milton	L	23	7	11	.389	0	34	34	5	206	190	63	163	2	4.4
Joe Mays	R	23	6	11	.353	0	49	20	2	171	179	67	115	1	4.3
1 Rick Aguilera	R	37	1	3	.750	6	17	0	0	21	10	2	13	0	1.2
Benj Sampson	L	24	3	2	.600	0	30	4	0	71	107	34	56	0	8.1
Mike Lincoln	R	24	3	10	.231	0	18	15	0	76	102	26	27	0	6.8
Travis Miller	L	26	2	2	.500	0	52	0	0	50	55	16	40	0	2.7
Hector Carrasco (AJ)	R	29	2	3	.400	1	39	0	0	49	48	18	35	0	4.9
2 Eddie Guardado (EJ)	L	28	2	5	.286	2	63	0	0	48	37	25	50	0	4.5
Mike Trombley	R	32	2	8	.200	24	75	0	0	87	93	28	82	0	4.3
Mark Redman	L	25	1	0	1.000	0	5	1	0	13	17	7	11	0	4.9
Jay Ryan	R	23	1	4	.200	0	8	1	0	41	46	17	15	0	4.8
Dan Perkins	R	23	1	7	.125	0	29	12	0	87	117	43	44	0	6.5
J.C. Romero	L	23	0	0	—	0	10	13	0	4	3	0	12.4
Rob Radlosky	R	25	0	0	—	0	5	1	0	15	15	4	3	0	12.4
Gary Rath	L	26	0	0	—	0	5	1	0	6	13	6	6	0	11.5

TEXAS — 1st 95-67 .586 — JOHNNY OATES

Name	G by Pos	B	AGE	G	AB	R	H	2B	3B	HR	RBI	BB	SO	SB	BA	SA
TOTALS			31	162	5651	945	1653	304	29	230	897	611	937	111	.293	.479
Lee Stevens	1B133 DH8	L	31	146	517	76	146	31	1	24	81	52	132	2	.282	.485
Mark McLemore	2B135 OF11 DH1	B	34	144	566	105	155	20	7	6	45	83	79	16	.274	.366
Royce Clayton	SS133	R	29	133	465	69	134	21	5	14	52	39	100	8	.288	.445
Todd Zeile	3B155 1B1 DH1	R	33	156	588	80	172	41	1	24	98	56	94	1	.293	.468
Juan Gonzalez	OF131 DH14	R	29	144	562	114	183	36	1	39	128	51	105	3	.326	.601
Tom Goodwin (PJ)	OF107	L	30	109	405	63	105	12	6	3	33	40	61	39	.259	.341
Rusty Greer	OF145 DH1	L	30	147	556	107	167	41	3	20	101	96	67	2	.300	.493
Ivan Rodriguez	C141 DH1	R	27	144	600	116	199	29	1	35	113	24	64	25	.332	.558
Rafael Palmeiro	DH128 1B28	L	34	158	565	96	183	30	1	47	148	97	69	2	.324	.630
Roberto Kelly	OF85	R	34	87	290	41	87	17	1	8	37	21	57	6	.300	.448
Luis Alicea	2B37 3B10 DH7 OF1	B	33	68	164	33	33	10	0	3	17	28	32	2	.201	.317
Gregg Zaun	C37 DH2	B	28	43	93	12	23	2	1	1	12	10	7	1	.247	.323
Jon Shave	SS24 1B9 3B6 DH3 2B1	R	31	43	73	10	21	4	0	0	9	5	17	1	.288	.342
Ruben Mateo (BW)	OF31 DH1	R	21	32	122	16	29	9	1	5	18	4	28	3	.238	.451
Scarborough Green	OF9 DH4	R	25	18	13	4	4	0	0	0	1	2	0	.308	.308
Kelly Dransfeldt	SS16	R	24	16	53	3	10	1	0	1	5	3	12	0	.189	.264
Mike Simms (LJ)	DH2 1B1 OF1	R	32	4	2	0	1	0	0	0	0	0	1	0	.500	.500
Scott Sheldon	3B2	R	30	2	1	0	0	0	0	0	0	0	0	0	.000	.000

NAME	T	AGE	W	L	PCT	SV	G	GS	CG	IP	H	BB	SO	SHO	ERA
		30	95	67	.586	47	162	162	6	1436	1626	509	979	9	5.07
Aaron Sele	R	29	18	9	.667	0	33	33	2	205	244	70	186	2	4.79
Mike Morgan	R	39	13	10	.565	0	34	25	1	140	184	48	61	0	6.24
Rick Helling	R	28	13	11	.542	0	35	35	3	219	228	85	131	0	4.84
Jeff Zimmerman	R	26	9	3	.750	3	65	0	0	88	50	23	67	0	2.36
Esteban Loaiza (BH)	R	27	9	5	.643	0	30	15	0	120	128	40	77	0	4.56
John Burkett	R	34	9	8	.529	0	30	25	0	147	184	46	96	0	5.62
Tim Crabtree	R	29	5	1	.833	0	68	0	0	65	71	18	54	0	3.46
John Wetteland	R	32	4	4	.500	43	62	0	0	66	67	19	60	0	3.68
Mike Venafro	L	25	3	2	.600	0	65	0	0	68	63	22	37	0	3.29
Mark Clark (EJ)	R	31	3	7	.300	0	15	15	0	74	103	34	44	0	8.60
Danny Patterson	R	28	2	0	1.000	0	53	0	0	60	77	19	43	0	5.67
Mike Munoz	L	33	2	1	.667	1	56	0	0	53	52	18	27	0	3.93
Danny Kolb	R	24	2	1	.667	0	16	0	0	31	33	15	15	0	4.65
Ryan Glynn	R	24	2	4	.333	0	13	10	0	55	71	35	39	0	7.24
2 Jeff Fassero	L	36	1	0	1.000	0	7	3	0	17	20	10	13	0	5.71
Matt Perisho	L	24	0	0	—	0	4	1	0	10	8	2	17	0	2.61
Eric Gunderson (SJ)	L	33	0	0	—	0	11	0	0	10	20	2	6	0	7.20
Jonathan Johnson	R	24	0	0	—	0	1	0	0	3	3	2	3	0	15.00
Doug Davis	L	23	0	0	—	0	2	0	0	3	12	0	3	0	33.75
Corey Lee	L	24	0	1	.000	0	1	1	0	1	3	1	1	0	27.00

OAKLAND — 2nd 87-75 .537 8 — ART HOWE

Name	G by Pos	B	AGE	G	AB	R	H	2B	3B	HR	RBI	BB	SO	SB	BA	SA
TOTALS			29	162	5519	893	1430	287	20	235	845	770	1129	70	.259	.446
Jason Giambi	1B142 DH15 3B1	L	28	158	575	115	181	36	1	33	123	105	106	1	.315	.553
Tony Phillips (BL)	2B66 OF62 3B2 SS1 DH1	B	40	146	406	76	99	24	4	15	49	71	94	11	.244	.433
Miguel Tejada	SS159	R	23	159	593	93	149	33	4	21	84	57	94	8	.251	.427
Eric Chavez	3B105 DH4 SS2	L	21	115	356	47	88	21	2	13	50	46	56	1	.247	.427
Matt Stairs	OF139 DH5 1B1	L	31	146	531	94	137	26	3	38	102	89	124	2	.258	.533
Ryan Christenson	OF104 DH1	R	25	106	268	41	56	12	1	4	24	38	58	7	.209	.306
Ben Grieve	OF137 DH4	L	23	148	486	80	129	21	0	28	86	63	108	4	.265	.481
Mike Macfarlane	C79 DH1	R	35	81	226	24	55	17	0	4	31	13	52	0	.243	.372
John Jaha	DH121 1B8	R	33	142	457	93	126	23	0	35	111	101	129	2	.276	.556
Jason McDonald	OF89 DH5 2B1	B	27	100	187	26	39	2	1	3	8	25	48	6	.209	.278
Olmedo Saenez	3B56 1B28 DH8	R	28	97	255	41	70	18	0	11	41	22	47	1	.275	.475
Scott Spiezio	2B42 3B31 1B10 DH6	B	26	89	247	31	60	24	0	8	33	29	36	0	.243	.437
A.J. Hinch	C73	R	25	76	205	26	44	4	1	7	24	11	41	6	.215	.346
Jorge Velandia (NJ)	2B52 SS8 3B2 DH1	R	24	63	48	4	9	1	0	0	2	2	13	2	.188	.208
2 Randy Velarde	2B61	R	36	61	255	48	85	10	3	7	28	27	42	11	.333	.478
Tim Raines (IL)	OF38 DH3	B	39	58	135	20	29	5	0	4	17	26	17	4	.215	.341
Ramon Hernandez (KJ)	C40	R	23	40	136	13	38	7	0	3	21	18	11	1	.279	.397
2 Rich Becker	OF39 DH1	L	27	40	125	21	33	3	0	1	10	25	43	3	.264	.312
Frank Menechino	SS5 DH3 3B1	R	28	9	9	0	2	0	0	0	0	0	3	0	.222	.222

NAME	T	AGE	W	L	PCT	SV	G	GS	CG	IP	H	BB	SO	SHO	ERA
		30	87	75	.537	48	162	162	6	1438	1537	569	967	5	4.69
Gil Heredia	R	33	13	8	.619	0	33	33	1	200	228	34	117	0	4.81
Tim Hudson	R	23	11	2	.846	0	21	21	1	136	121	62	132	0	3.23
T.J. Mathews	R	29	9	5	.643	3	50	0	0	59	46	20	42	0	3.81
Mike Oquist	R	31	9	10	.474	0	28	24	0	141	158	64	89	0	5.37
2 Omar Olivares	R	31	7	2	.778	0	12	12	1	75	82	32	36	0	4.34
2 Kevin Appier	R	31	7	5	.583	0	12	12	0	69	77	33	53	0	5.77
Jimmy Haynes	R	26	7	12	.368	0	30	25	0	142	158	80	93	0	6.34
1 Kenny Rogers	L	34	5	3	.625	0	19	19	3	119	135	41	68	0	4.30
Doug Jones	R	42	5	5	.500	0	70	0	0	104	106	24	63	0	3.55
Buddy Groom	L	33	3	2	.600	0	76	0	0	46	48	18	32	0	5.09
1 Brad Rigby	R	26	3	4	.429	0	29	0	0	62	69	26	26	0	4.33
1 Tom Candiotti	R	41	3	5	.375	0	11	11	0	57	67	23	30	0	6.35
Ron Mahay	L	28	2	0	1.000	1	6	1	0	19	8	3	15	0	1.86
Tim Worrell	R	31	2	2	.500	0	53	0	0	69	69	34	62	0	4.15
1 Billy Taylor	R	37	1	5	.167	26	43	0	0	43	48	14	38	0	3.98
2 Greg McMichael	R	32	0	0	—	0	17	0	0	15	15	12	3	0	5.40
Tim Kubinski	L	27	0	0	—	0	14	0	0	12	14	5	7	0	5.84
Luis Vizcaino	R	24	0	0	—	0	3	0	0	3	3	2	0	5.40
1 Blake Stein	R	25	0	0	—	0	1	1	0	3	6	6	4	0	16.88
3 Jason Isringhausen	R	26	0	1	.000	8	20	0	0	25	21	12	20	0	2.13
Kevin Jarvis (RJ)	R	29	0	1	.000	0	14	1	0	14	28	6	11	0	11.57
Brett Laxton	R	25	0	1	.000	0	3	2	0	10	12	7	9	0	7.45
Chad Harville	R	22	0	2	.000	0	15	0	0	14	18	10	15	0	6.91

Ariel Prieto (EJ) 29

SEATTLE — 3rd 79-83 .488 16 — LOU PINIELLA

Name	G by Pos	B	AGE	G	AB	R	H	2B	3B	HR	RBI	BB	SO	SB	BA	SA
TOTALS			30	162	5572	859	1499	263	21	244	825	610	1095	130	.269	.455
1 David Segui	1B90	B	32	90	345	43	101	22	3	9	39	42	43	1	.293	.452
David Bell	2B154 1B4 SS1	R	26	157	597	92	160	31	2	21	78	58	90	7	.268	.432
Alex Rodriguez (KJ)	SS129	R	23	129	502	110	143	25	0	42	111	56	109	21	.285	.586
Russ Davis	3B124 SS2	R	29	124	432	55	106	17	1	21	59	32	111	3	.245	.435
Jay Buhner (LJ)	OF85 1B1	R	34	87	266	37	59	11	0	14	38	69	100	0	.222	.421
Ken Griffey Jr.	OF158 DH6	L	29	160	606	123	173	26	3	48	134	91	108	24	.285	.576
2 Brian Hunter	OF121	R	28	121	484	71	112	11	5	4	34	32	80	44	.231	.300
Dan Wilson	C121 1B5	R	30	123	414	46	110	23	2	7	38	29	83	5	.266	.382
Edgar Martinez	DH134 1B5	R	36	142	502	86	169	35	1	24	86	97	99	1	.337	.554
John Mabry (KJ)	OF43 3B24 1B20 DH1	L	28	87	262	34	64	14	0	9	33	20	60	2	.244	.401
Raul Ibanez	OF57 1B21 C1 DH1	L	27	87	209	23	54	7	0	9	27	17	32	5	.258	.421
Tom Lampkin	C56 OF2 DH2	L	35	76	206	29	60	11	2	9	34	13	52	1	.291	.495
1 Butch Huskey	OF53 1B10 DH7 3B1	R	27	74	262	44	76	9	0	15	49	27	45	3	.290	.496
Rafael Bournigal	SS28 2B17 3B8 OF1 DH1	R	33	55	95	16	26	5	0	2	14	7	6	0	.274	.389
Charles Gipson (SJ)	OF28 3B17 DH4 2B3 SS3	R	26	55	80	16	18	5	2	0	9	6	13	3	.225	.338
Ryan Jackson	1B29 OF1	L	27	32	68	4	16	3	0	0	10	6	19	3	.235	.279
Ozzie Timmons	OF17 DH5 1B1	R	28	26	44	4	5	2	0	1	3	4	12	0	.114	.227
1 Matt Mieske	OF20 DH1	R	31	24	41	11	15	4	0	4	7	2	9	0	.366	.659
1 Domingo Cedeno	SS20 2B1 3B1	B	30	21	42	4	9	2	0	2	8	5	9	1	.214	.405
Mike Blowers	1B14 3B4 DH1	R	34	19	46	2	11	1	0	2	7	4	12	0	.239	.391
Shane Monahan	OF9 DH3	L	24	16	15	3	2	0	0	0	0	0	6	0	.133	.133
Giomar Guevara	SS9	B	26	10	12	2	3	2	0	0	2	0	2	0	.250	.417
Carlos Guillen (KJ)	SS3 2B2	B	23	5	19	1	3	0	0	0	3	1	6	0	.158	.158

NAME	T	AGE	W	L	PCT	SV	G	GS	CG	IP	H	BB	SO	SHO	ERA
		28	79	83	.488	40	162	162	7	1434	1613	684	980	6	5.24
Freddy Garcia	R	24	17	8	.680	0	33	33	2	201	205	90	170	1	4.07
Jamie Moyer	L	36	14	8	.636	0	32	32	4	228	235	48	137	0	3.87
John Halama	L	27	11	10	.524	0	38	24	1	179	193	56	105	1	4.22
Gil Meche	R	20	8	4	.667	0	16	15	0	86	73	57	47	0	4.73
Paul Abbott	R	31	6	2	.750	0	25	7	0	73	50	32	68	0	3.10
Jose Paniagua	R	25	6	11	.353	3	59	0	0	78	75	52	74	0	4.06
Ken Cloude	R	24	4	4	.500	1	31	6	0	72	106	46	35	0	7.96
1 Jeff Fassero	L	36	4	14	.222	0	30	24	0	139	188	73	101	0	7.38
Jose Mesa	R	33	3	6	.333	33	68	0	0	69	84	40	42	0	4.98
Butch Henry (SJ)	L	30	2	0	1.000	0	7	4	0	25	30	10	15	0	5.04
Frankie Rodriguez	R	26	2	3	.333	3	28	5	0	73	94	30	47	0	5.65
2 Tom Davey	R	25	1	0	1.000	0	16	0	0	21	22	14	17	0	4.71
Rafael Carmona (AJ)	R	27	1	0	1.000	0	9	0	0	11	18	9	6	0	7.94
Ryan Franklin	R	26	0	0	—	0	11	0	0	11	18	4	6	0	4.76
Melvin Bunch	R	27	0	0	—	0	10	0	0	11	10	7	4	0	11.70
Todd Williams	R	28	0	0	—	0	13	0	0	11	17	7	4	0	4.66
Jordan Zimmerman (NJ)	L	24	0	0	—	0	12	0	0	8	14	4	3	0	7.88
Dennis Stark	R	23	0	0	—	0	6	0	0	8	8	4	3	0	9.95
Aaron Scheffer	R	23	0	0	—	0	3	0	0	1	2	1	1	0	1.93
Sean Spencer	L	24	0	0	—	0	14	0	0	9	9	8	5	0	6.75
Mark Leiter (SJ)	R	36	0	0	—	0	1	0	0	1	2	1	1	0	6.75
2 Steve Sinclair	L	27	0	1	.000	0	14	0	0	15	16	10	15	0	3.95
Eric Weaver (EJ)	R	25	0	1	.000	0	8	0	0	18	14	8	14	0	10.61
Damaso Marte	L	24	0	1	.000	0	9	0	0	16	8	3	9	0	9.35
2 Allen Watson	L	28	0	1	.000	0	16	4	0	42	47	34	32	0	9.43
Mac Suzuki	R	24	0	2	.000	0	14	2	0	18	23	9	11	0	6.38
Robert Ramsay	L	25	0	2	.000	0	3	1	0	4	4	3	4	0	6.38
Brett Hinchliffe	R	24	0	4	.000	0	11	3	0	31	41	11	14	0	8.80

ANAHEIM — 4th 70-92 .432 25 — TERRY COLLINS 51-82 .383 — JOE MADDON 19-10 .655

Name	G by Pos	B	AGE	G	AB	R	H	2B	3B	HR	RBI	BB	SO	SB	BA	SA
TOTALS			29	162	5494	711	1404	248	22	158	673	511	1022	71	.256	.395
Darin Erstad	1B78 OF69 DH2	L	25	142	585	84	148	22	5	13	53	47	101	13	.253	.374
1 Randy Velarde	2B95	R	36	95	376	57	115	15	4	9	48	43	56	13	.306	.439
Gary DiSarcina (BA)	SS81	R	31	81	271	32	62	7	1	1	29	15	32	2	.229	.273
Troy Glaus	3B153 DH1	R	22	154	551	85	132	29	0	29	79	71	143	5	.240	.450
Tim Salmon (WJ)	OF89 DH7	R	30	98	353	60	94	24	2	17	69	63	82	4	.266	.490
Jim Edmonds (SJ)	OF42 DH9 1B2	L	29	55	204	34	51	17	2	5	23	28	45	5	.250	.426
Garret Anderson	OF153 DH4	L	27	157	620	88	188	36	2	21	80	34	81	3	.303	.469
Matt Walbeck	C97 DH1	R	29	107	288	26	69	8	1	3	24	20	40	1	.240	.306
Mo Vaughn	1B72 DH67	L	31	139	524	63	147	20	0	33	108	54	127	0	.281	.508
Orlando Palmeiro	OF92 DH10	L	30	109	317	46	88	12	1	1	23	39	30	5	.278	.331
Todd Greene	DH44 OF30 C12	R	28	97	321	36	78	20	0	14	42	12	63	1	.243	.436
Jeff Huson	2B41 SS22 3B9 1B8 DH7 OF2	L	34	97	225	21	59	7	1	0	18	16	27	10	.262	.302
Andy Sheets	SS76 2B7 3B1	R	27	87	244	22	48	10	0	3	29	14	59	1	.197	.275
Trent Durrington	2B41 DH1	R	23	43	122	14	22	2	0	0	2	4	40	4	.180	.197
Bengie Molina	C30	R	24	31	101	8	26	5	0	1	10	6	6	0	.257	.337
Reggie Williams	OF24 DH3	B	33	30	63	8	14	1	2	1	6	5	21	2	.222	.349
Steve Decker	C17 1B6 DH3	R	33	28	65	5	15	6	0	1	9	5	13	0	.231	.369
Charlie O'Brien (FJ)	C27	R	38	27	62	3	6	0	0	1	4	1	10	0	.097	.145
Tim Unroe	OF12 DH8 3B3 2B1	R	28	27	54	5	13	2	0	1	6	4	16	0	.241	.333
Chris Pritchett	1B15 DH1	L	29	20	45	3	7	1	0	1	2	2	8	0	.156	.244
Matt Luke (VJ)	OF6 1B4	L	28	18	30	4	9	0	0	2	6	2	10	0	.300	.600
Bret Hemphill	C12	B	24	12	30	4	4	1	0	0	2	6	9	0	.143	.143
Jeff DaVanon	OF5 DH2	B	25	7	20	4	4	0	1	1	4	2	4	1	.200	.450
Dave Silvestri	2B1 SS1 1B1	R	31	3	11	0	1	0	0	0	0	1	5	0	.091	.182
Mike Colangelo (RJ)	OF1	R	22	2	2	0	1	0	0	0	0	0	1	0	.500	.500

Justin Baughman (BL) 24

NAME	T	AGE	W	L	PCT	SV	G	GS	CG	IP	H	BB	SO	SHO	ERA
		31	70	92	.432	37	162	162	4	1431	1472	624	877	7	4.79
Chuck Finley	L	36	12	11	.522	0	33	33	1	213	197	94	200	0	4.43
Mark Petkovsek	R	33	10	4	.714	1	64	0	0	83	85	21	43	0	3.47
1 Omar Olivares	R	31	8	9	.471	0	20	20	3	131	135	49	49	0	4.05
Tim Belcher (BG)	R	37	6	8	.429	0	24	24	0	132	168	46	52	0	6.73
Mike Magnante	L	34	5	2	.714	0	53	0	0	69	68	29	44	0	3.38
Steve Sparks	R	33	5	11	.313	0	28	26	0	148	165	82	73	0	5.42
Jarrod Washburn	L	24	5	4	.444	0	16	10	0	62	61	26	39	0	5.25
Shigetoshi Hasegawa	R	30	4	6	.400	2	44	0	0	77	80	34	44	0	4.91
Troy Percival	R	29	4	6	.400	31	60	0	0	57	38	22	58	0	3.79
Ken Hill	R	33	4	11	.267	0	26	22	0	128	129	76	76	0	4.77
Ramon Ortiz	R	26	2	3	.400	0	9	9	0	48	50	25	44	0	6.52
Mike Holtz	L	26	2	3	.400	0	28	0	0	22	26	15	17	0	8.06
Al Levine	R	31	1	1	.500	0	50	1	0	85	76	29	37	0	3.39
Scott Schoeneweis	L	25	1	1	.500	0	32	0	0	30	31	12	20	0	5.49
Lou Pote	R	27	1	1	.500	0	20	0	0	29	23	12	20	0	2.15
Brian Cooper	R	24	1	1	.500	0	5	5	0	28	23	18	15	0	4.88
Steve Mintz	R	30	0	0	—	0	4	0	0	5	8	2	9	0	3.60
Juan Alvarez	L	25	0	0	—	0	7	0	0	4	6	1	2	0	3.00
Mike Fyhrie	R	29	0	1	.000	0	16	0	0	21	31	5	12	0	5.05
Jack McDowell (SJ)	R	33	0	4	.000	0	5	5	0	19	31	5	12	0	8.05

Jason Dickson (SJ) 26, Pep Harris (EJ) 26, Mike James (SJ) 31

LINE SCORES

Team	1	2	3	4	5	6	7	8	9	10	11	12	R	H	E

DIVISION SERIES: NEW YORK 3 : TEXAS 0

Game 1   October 5 at New York

														R	H	E
TEX	0	0	0	0	0	0	0	0	0				0	2	1
NYA	0	1	0	0	2	4	0	1	X				8	10	0

Sele, Crabtree (6), Venafro (6),   **Hernandez**, Nelson (9)
Patterson (7), Fassero (8)

Game 2   October 7 at New York

														R	H	E
TEX	0	0	0	1	0	0	0	0	0				1	7	0
NYA	0	0	0	0	1	0	1	1	X				3	7	2

Helling, Crabtree (7), Venafro (8)   **Pettitte**, Nelson (8), Rivera (9)

Game 3   October 9 at Texas

														R	H	E
NYA	3	0	0	0	0	0	0	0	0				3	6	0
TEX	0	0	0	0	0	0	0	0	0				0	5	1

Clemens, Nelson (8), Rivera (8)   Loaiza, Zimmerman (8), Wetteland (9)

DIVISION SERIES: BOSTON 3 : CLEVELAND 2

Game 1   October 6 at Cleveland

														R	H	E
BOS	0	1	0	1	0	0	0	0	0				2	5	1
CLE	0	0	0	0	0	0	2	0	1				3	6	1

P. Martinez, Lowe (5), Cormier (9), Garces (9)   Colon, **Shuey** (9)

Game 2   October 7 at Cleveland

														R	H	E
BOS	0	0	1	0	0	0	0	0	0				1	6	0
CLE	0	0	6	5	0	0	0	0	X				11	8	0

Saberhagen, Wasdin (3), Wakefield (5),   **Nagy**, Karsay (8), Jackson (9)
Gordon (7), Beck (8)

Game 3   October 9 at Boston

														R	H	E
CLE	0	0	0	1	0	1	1	0	0				3	9	1
BOS	0	0	0	0	2	1	6	0	X				9	11	2

Burba, **Wright** (5), Rincon (7), DePaula (7),   R. Martinez, **Lowe** (6), Beck (9),
Reed (8)

Game 4   October 10 at Boston

														R	H	E
CLE	1	1	0	0	4	0	0	0	1				7	8	0
BOS	2	5	3	5	3	0	0	3	2	X			23	24	0

Colon, Karsay (2), Reed (4), DePaula (5),   Mercker, **Garces** (2), Wakefield (5),
Assenmacher (7), Shuey (8)   Wasdin (5), Cormier (5), Gordon (9)

Game 5   October 11 at Cleveland

														R	H	E
BOS	2	0	5	1	0	0	3	0	1				12	10	0
CLE	3	2	3	0	0	0	0	0	0				8	7	1

Saberhagen, Lowe (2), **P. Martinez** (4)   Nagy, DePaula (4), **Shuey** (7),
Jackson (9)

CHAMPIONSHIP: NEW YORK 4 : BOSTON 1

Game 1   October 13 at New York

														R	H	E
BOS	2	1	0	0	0	0	0	0	0	0			3	8	3
NYY	0	2	0	0	0	1	0	0	1	1			4	10	1

Mercker, Garces (5), Lowe (7),   Hernandez, **Rivera** (9)
Cormier (9), **Beck** (10)

Game 2   October 14 at New York

														R	H	E
BOS	0	0	0	0	0	2	0	0	0				2	10	0
NYY	0	0	1	0	0	2	0	X					3	7	0

R. Martinez, Gordon (7), Cormier (7)   **Cone**, Stanton (8), Nelson (8), Watson (8),
Mendoza (8), Rivera (9)

Game 3   October 16 at Boston

														R	H	E
NYY	0	0	0	0	0	0	0	1	0				1	3	3
BOS	2	2	2	1	4	0	X						13	21	1

Clemens, Irabu (3), Stanton (7),   **P. Martinez**, Gordon (8), Rapp (9)
Watson (8)

Game 4   October 17 at Boston

														R	H	E
NYY	0	1	0	2	0	0	0	0	6				9	11	0
BOS	0	1	1	0	0	0	0	0	0				2	10	4

Pettitte, Rivera (8)   Saberhagen, Lowe (7), Cormier (8), Garces (8),
Beck (9)

Game 5   October 18 at Boston

														R	H	E
NYY	2	0	0	0	0	0	2	0	2				6	11	1
BOS	0	0	0	0	0	0	1	0					1	5	2

Hernandez, Stanton (8), Nelson (8),   Mercker, Lowe (4), Cormier (7), Gordon (9)
Watson (8), Mendoza (8)

COMPOSITE BATTING

NAME	POS	G	AB	R	H	2B	3B	HR	RBI	BA

DIVISION SERIES

NEW YORK

NAME	POS	G	AB	R	H	2B	3B	HR	RBI	BA
TOTALS		3	98	14	23	6	1	2	13	.235
Knoblauch	2B	3	12	1	2	0	0	0	0	.167
Jeter	SS	3	11	3	5	1	1	0	0	.455
Williams	CF	3	11	2	4	1	0	1	6	.364
Ledee	LF-RF	3	11	1	3	2	0	0	2	.273
Martinez	1B	3	11	2	2	0	0	0	0	.182
Brosius	3B	3	10	0	1	0	0	0	1	.100
O'Neill	RF	2	8	2	2	0	0	0	0	.250
Strawberry	DH	2	6	2	2	0	0	1	3	.333
Girardi	C	2	6	0	0	0	0	0	0	.000
Posada	C	1	4	0	1	1	0	0	0	.250
Curtis	LF	3	3	1	0	0	0	0	0	.000
Davis	DH	1	3	0	1	0	0	0	0	.333
Leyritz	DH	2	2	0	0	0	0	0	0	.000
Bellinger	DH	1	0	0	0	0	0	0	0	—

TEXAS

NAME	POS	G	AB	R	H	2B	3B	HR	RBI	BA
TOTALS		3	92	1	14	2	0	1	1	.152
Rodriguez	C	3	12	0	3	1	0	0	0	.250
Palmeiro	DH	3	11	0	3	0	0	0	0	.273
Gonzalez	RF	3	11	1	2	0	0	1	1	.182
McLemore	2B	3	10	0	1	0	0	0	0	.100
Zeile	3B	3	10	0	1	0	0	0	0	.100
Clayton	SS	3	10	0	0	0	0	0	0	.000
Greer	LF	3	9	0	1	0	0	0	0	.111
Stevens	1B	3	9	0	1	1	0	0	0	.111
Goodwin	CF	3	7	0	1	0	0	0	0	.143
Kelly	CF	1	3	0	1	0	0	0	0	.333

BOSTON

NAME	POS	G	AB	R	H	2B	3B	HR	RBI	BA
TOTALS		5	176	47	56	17	1	10	47	.318
Valentin	3B	5	22	6	7	2	0	3	12	.318
Varitek	C	5	21	7	5	3	0	1	3	.238
Stanley	1B	5	20	4	10	2	1	0	2	.500
O'Leary	LF	5	20	4	4	0	0	2	7	.200
Offerman	2B	5	18	4	7	1	0	1	6	.389
Lewis	CF	4	16	5	6	1	0	0	2	.375
Daubach	DH-1B	4	16	3	4	2	0	1	3	.250
Nixon	RF	5	14	5	3	3	0	0	6	.214
Garciaparra	SS	4	12	6	5	2	0	2	4	.417
Merloni	SS	3	6	1	2	0	0	0	1	.333
Huskey	DH	2	5	0	1	0	0	0	0	.200
Buford	CF	1	3	0	0	0	0	0	0	.000
Sadler	3B-DH	2	2	1	1	1	0	0	0	.500
Hatteberg	C	1	1	1	1	0	0	0	1	1.000

CLEVELAND

NAME	POS	G	AB	R	H	2B	3B	HR	RBI	BA
TOTALS		5	163	32	38	7	1	7	31	.233
Vizquel	SS	5	21	3	5	1	1	0	3	.238
R. Alomar	2B	5	19	4	7	4	0	0	3	.368
Ramirez	RF	5	18	1	1	1	0	0	1	.056
Thome	1B	5	17	7	6	0	0	4	10	.353
Lofton	CF	5	16	5	2	1	0	0	1	.125
Fryman	3B	5	15	2	4	0	0	1	4	.267
S. Alomar	C	5	14	1	2	0	0	0	1	.143
Baines	DH	4	14	1	5	0	0	1	4	.357
Cordero	DH-LF	3	9	3	5	0	0	1	2	.556
Justice	LF	3	8	0	0	0	0	0	0	.000
Sexson	1B-LF	3	6	1	1	0	0	0	0	.167
Roberts	CF	2	3	0	0	0	0	0	0	.000
Wilson	2B	3	2	0	0	0	0	0	0	.000
Diaz	C	2	1	0	0	0	0	0	0	.000

AMERICAN LEAGUE CHAMPIONSHIP

NEW YORK

NAME	POS	G	AB	R	H	2B	3B	HR	RBI	BA
TOTALS		5	176	23	42	4	1	8	21	.239
O'Neill	RF	5	21	2	6	0	0	0	1	.286
Jeter	SS	5	20	3	7	1	0	1	3	.350
Williams	CF	5	20	4	5	1	0	1	3	.250
Martinez	1B	5	19	3	5	1	0	1	3	.263
Knoblauch	2B	5	18	3	6	1	0	0	1	.333
Brosius	3B	5	18	3	4	0	1	2	3	.222
Davis	DH	5	11	0	1	0	0	0	0	.091
Posada	C	3	10	1	1	0	0	1	2	.100
Spencer	DH	3	9	1	1	0	0	1	1	.111
Girardi	C	3	8	2	2	0	0	0	0	.250
Ledee	LF-RF-DH	3	8	2	2	0	0	1	4	.250
Strawberry	DH	3	6	1	2	0	0	1	1	.333
Curtis	LF-CF-DH	3	6	1	0	0	0	0	0	.000
Bellinger	SS-DH	3	1	0	0	0	0	0	0	.000
Sojo	2B	2	1	0	0	0	0	0	0	.000

BOSTON

NAME	POS	G	AB	R	H	2B	3B	HR	RBI	BA
TOTALS		5	184	21	54	13	2	5	19	.293
Offerman	2B	5	24	4	11	4	1	0	2	.458
Valentin	3B	5	23	3	8	2	0	1	6	.348
Garciaparra	SS	5	20	2	8	2	0	2	5	.400
O'Leary	LF	5	20	2	7	3	0	0	1	.350
Varitek	C	5	20	1	4	1	1	1	1	.200
Stanley	1B	5	18	1	4	0	0	0	2	.222
Daubach	DH-1B	5	17	2	3	1	0	0	3	.176
Lewis	CF-RF	5	17	2	2	1	0	0	1	.118
Nixon	RF	4	14	2	4	2	0	0	0	.286
Buford	CF	4	5	1	2	0	0	0	0	.400
Huskey	DH	4	5	1	1	0	0	1	3	.200
Hatteberg	C	3	1	0	0	0	0	0	0	.000
Sadler	RF-DH	2	1	0	0	0	0	0	0	—
Merloni	PH	1	0	0	0	0	0	0	0	—

COMPOSITE PITCHING

NAME	G	IP	H	BB	SO	W	L	SV	ERA

DIVISION SERIES

NEW YORK

NAME	G	IP	H	BB	SO	W	L	SV	ERA
TOTALS	3	27	14	9	17	3	0	2	0.33
Hernandez	1	8	2	6	4	1	0	0	0.00
Pettitte	1	7.1	7	0	5	1	0	0	1.23
Clemens	1	7	3	2	2	1	0	0	0.00
Rivera	2	3	1	0	3	0	0	2	0.00
Nelson	3	1.2	1	1	3	0	0	0	0.00

TEXAS

NAME	G	IP	H	BB	SO	W	L	SV	ERA
TOTALS	3	25	23	10	19	0	3	0	3.60
Loaiza	1	7	5	1	4	0	1	0	3.86
Helling	1	6.1	5	1	8	0	1	0	2.84
Sele	1	5	6	5	3	0	1	0	5.40
Crabtree	2	1.2	1	1	1	0	0	0	5.40
Venafro	2	1	2	1	0	0	0	0	0.00
Patterson	1	1	0	0	0	0	0	0	0.00
Wetteland	1	1	0	0	1	0	0	0	0.00
Zimmerman	1	1	1	0	1	0	0	0	0.00
Fassero	1	1	3	1	1	0	0	0	9.00

BOSTON

NAME	G	IP	H	BB	SO	W	L	SV	ERA
TOTALS	5	43.1	38	28	43	3	2	0	6.02
P. Martinez	2	10	3	4	11	1	0	0	0.00
Lowe	3	8.1	6	1	7	1	1	0	4.32
R. Martinez	1	5.2	5	3	6	0	0	0	3.18
Cormier	2	4.2	1	4	0	0	0	0	0.00
Saberhagen	2	3.2	9	4	2	0	1	0	27.00
Garces	2	2.1	2	3	2	1	0	0	3.86
Beck	2	2	2	0	2	0	0	0	0.00
Gordon	2	2	1	1	3	0	0	0	4.50
Wakefield	2	2	3	4	3	0	0	0	13.50
Mercker	1	1.2	3	3	1	0	0	0	10.80
Wasdin	2	1.2	4	1	4	1	0	0	27.00

CLEVELAND

NAME	G	IP	H	BB	SO	W	L	SV	ERA
TOTALS	5	43	56	19	35	2	3	0	9.63
Nagy	2	10	11	2	6	1	0	0	7.20
Colon	2	9	11	4	12	0	1	0	9.00
DePaula	3	5	2	3	5	0	0	0	1.80
Burba	1	4	1	1	0	0	0	0	0.00
Shuey	3	4	4	5	1	1	0	0	11.25
Karsay	2	3	5	1	3	0	0	0	9.00
Reed	2	2.1	9	1	1	0	0	0	30.86
Wright	1	2	2	1	1	0	1	0	22.50
Jackson	2	2	2	1	1	0	0	0	4.50
Assenmacher	1	1	5	0	0	0	0	0	27.00
Rincon	1	0.2	2	1	1	0	0	0	40.50

NEW YORK

NAME	G	IP	H	BB	SO	W	L	SV	ERA
TOTALS	5	45	54	15	38	4	1	3	3.80
Hernandez	2	15	12	6	13	1	0	0	1.80
Pettitte	1	7.1	8	1	5	1	0	0	2.45
Cone	1	7	7	3	9	1	0	0	2.57
Rivera	3	4.2	5	0	3	1	0	2	0.00
Irabu	1	4.2	13	0	3	0	0	0	13.50
Mendoza	2	2.1	0	2	0	0	0	1	0.00
Clemens	1	2	6	2	2	0	1	0	22.50
Watson	3	1	2	1	0	0	0	0	0.00
Nelson	2	0.2	0	0	0	0	0	0	0.00
Stanton	3	0.1	1	1	0	0	0	0	0.00

BOSTON

NAME	G	IP	H	BB	SO	W	L	SV	ERA
TOTALS	5	44	42	18	44	1	4	0	3.68
Mercker	2	7.2	12	4	5	0	1	0	4.70
P. Martinez	1	7	2	3	12	1	0	0	0.00
R. Martinez	1	6.2	6	3	5	0	1	0	4.05
Lowe	3	6.1	6	2	7	0	0	0	1.42
Saberhagen	1	6	5	1	5	0	1	0	1.50
Cormier	4	3.2	3	3	4	0	0	0	0.00
Garces	2	3	3	1	2	0	0	0	12.00
Gordon	3	3	1	3	3	0	0	0	13.50
Rapp	1	1	0	0	0	0	0	0	0.00
Beck	2	0.2	0	1	0	1	0	0	27.00

ATLANTA 1st 103-59 .636   BOBBY COX

Name	G by Pos	B	AGE	G	AB	R	H	2B	3B	HR	RBI	BB	SO	SB	BA	SA
TOTALS			30	162	5569	840	1481	309	23	197	791	608	962	148	.266	.436
Ryan Klesko	1B75 OF53	L	28	133	404	55	120	28	2	21	86	53	69	5	.297	.532
Bret Boone	2B151	R	30	152	608	102	153	38	1	20	63	47	112	14	.252	.416
Walt Weiss	SS102	B	35	110	279	38	63	13	4	2	29	35	48	7	.226	.323
Chipper Jones	3B156 SS1	B	27	157	567	116	181	41	1	45	110	126	94	25	.319	.633
Brian Jordan	OF150	R	32	153	576	100	163	28	4	23	115	51	81	3	.283	.465
Andruw Jones	OF162	R	22	162	592	97	163	35	5	26	84	76	103	24	.275	.483
Gerald Williams	OF139	R	32	143	422	76	116	24	1	17	68	33	67	19	.275	.457
Javy Lopez (KJ)	C60	R	28	65	246	34	78	18	1	11	45	20	41	0	.317	.533
Brian Hunter	1B101 OF8	R	31	114	181	28	45	12	1	6	30	31	40	0	.249	.425
Keith Lockhart	2B25 3B10	L	34	108	161	20	42	3	1	5	21	19	21	3	.261	.311
Eddie Perez	C98 1B2	R	31	104	309	30	77	17	0	7	30	17	40	0	.249	.372
Ozzie Guillen	SS53 3B6 2B1	L	35	92	232	21	56	16	0	1	20	15	17	4	.241	.323
Randall Simon	1B70	L	24	90	218	26	69	16	0	5	25	17	25	2	.317	.459
Otis Nixon (ZJ)	OF52	B	40	84	151	31	31	2	1	0	8	23	15	26	.205	.232
2 Jose Hernandez	SS45 1B1 OF1	R	29	48	166	22	42	8	0	4	19	12	44	4	.253	.373
2 Greg Myers	C31	L	33	34	72	10	16	2	0	2	9	13	16	0	.222	.333
Howard Battle	3B6	R	27	15	17	2	6	0	0	1	5	2	3	0	.353	.529
Mark DeRosa	SS2	R	24	7	8	0	0	0	0	0	0	0	2	0	.000	.000
2 Jorge Fabregas	C4 1B1	L	29	6	8	0	0	0	0	0	0	0	0	0	.000	.000
Pascual Matos	C5	R	24	6	8	0	1	0	0	0	2	0	1	0	.125	.125
George Lombard	OF4	L	23	6	6	1	2	0	0	0	0	0	1	2	.333	.333
2 Freddy Garcia	OF1	R	26	6	2	1	1	0	0	0	1	1	1	0	.500	2.000

Andres Galarraga (IL) 38

NAME	T	AGE	W	L	PCT	SV	G	GS	CG	IP	H	BB	SO	SHO	ERA
		28	103	59	.636	45	162	162	9	1471	1398	507	1197	9	3.63
Greg Maddux	R	33	19	9	.679	0	33	33	4	219	258	37	136	0	3.57
Kevin Millwood	R	24	18	7	.720	0	33	33	2	228	168	59	205	2	2.68
Tom Glavine	L	33	14	11	.560	0	35	35	2	234	259	83	138	0	4.12
John Smoltz	R	32	11	8	.579	0	29	29	1	186	168	40	156	1	3.19
Mike Remlinger	L	33	10	1	.909	1	73	0	0	84	66	35	81	0	2.37
Kevin McGlinchy	R	22	7	3	.700	0	64	0	0	70	66	30	67	0	2.82
Rudy Seanez (EJ)	R	30	6	1	.857	3	56	0	0	54	47	21	41	0	3.35
2 Terry Mulholland	L	36	4	2	.667	1	16	8	0	60	64	13	39	0	2.98
John Rocker	L	24	4	5	.444	38	74	0	0	72	47	37	104	0	2.49
Odalis Perez (EJ)	L	22	4	6	.400	0	18	17	0	93	100	53	82	0	6.00
Russ Springer (XJ)	R	30	2	1	.667	1	49	0	0	47	31	22	49	0	3.42
Bruce Chen	L	22	2	2	.500	0	16	7	0	51	38	27	45	0	5.47
2 Sean Bergman	R	29	1	0	1.000	0	6	0	0	6	5	3	6	0	2.84
Mike Cather	R	28	1	0	1.000	0	4	0	0	3	5	1	0	0	10.13
Justin Speier	R	25	0	0	—	0	19	0	0	29	28	13	22	0	5.65
Dave Cortes	R	27	0	0	—	0	4	0	0	4	3	4	2	0	4.91
Everett Stull	R	27	0	0	—	0	1	0	0	1	2	2	0	0	13.50
1 Mark Wohlers	R	29	0	0	—	0	2	0	0	1	1	6	0	0	27.00
Joe Winkelsas	R	25	0	0	—	0	1	0	0	0.1	4	1	0	0	54.00
2 John Hudek (RJ)	R	32	0	1	.000	0	15	0	0	17	21	11	18	0	6.48
Derrin Ebert	L	22	0	1	.000	1	5	0	0	8	9	5	4	0	5.63
1 Micah Bowie	L	24	0	1	.000	0	4	0	0	4	8	4	2	0	13.50

Kerry Ligtenberg (EJ) 28

NEW YORK 2nd 97-66 .595 6.5 (Wild Card)   BOBBY VALENTINE

Name	G by Pos	B	AGE	G	AB	R	H	2B	3B	HR	RBI	BB	SO	SB	BA	SA
TOTALS			30	163	5572	853	1553	297	14	181	814	717	994	150	.279	.434
John Olerud	1B160	L	30	162	581	107	173	39	0	19	96	125	66	3	.298	.463
Edgardo Alfonzo	2B158	R	25	158	628	123	191	41	1	27	108	85	85	9	.304	.502
Rey Ordonez	SS154	R	27	154	520	49	134	24	2	1	60	49	59	8	.258	.317
Robin Ventura	3B160 1B1	L	31	161	588	88	177	38	0	32	120	74	109	1	.301	.529
Roger Cedeno	OF149 2B1	B	24	155	453	90	142	23	4	4	36	60	100	66	.313	.408
Brian McRae	OF87	B	31	96	298	35	66	12	1	8	36	39	57	2	.221	.349
Rickey Henderson	OF116	R	40	121	438	89	138	30	0	12	42	82	82	37	.315	.466
Mike Piazza	C137	R	30	141	534	100	162	25	0	40	124	51	70	2	.303	.575
Matt Franco	1B19 OF18 3B12	L	29	122	132	18	31	5	0	4	21	28	21	0	.235	.364
Benny Agbayani	OF80	R	27	101	276	42	79	18	3	14	42	32	60	6	.286	.525
Todd Pratt	C52 1B1 OF1	R	32	71	140	18	41	4	0	3	21	15	32	2	.293	.386
Luis Lopez	SS33 2B16 3B9	B	28	68	104	11	22	4	0	2	13	12	33	1	.212	.308
Melvin Mora	OF45 2B4 3B3 SS1	R	27	66	31	6	5	0	0	1	4	7	7	2	.161	.161
Bobby Bonilla (KJ)	OF25 1B4	B	36	60	119	12	19	5	0	4	18	19	16	0	.160	.303
2 Darryl Hamilton	OF52	L	34	55	168	19	57	8	1	5	21	19	18	2	.339	.488
2 Shawon Dunston	OF27 3B1	R	36	42	93	12	32	6	1	0	16	0	16	4	.344	.430
Jermaine Allensworth	OF33	R	27	40	73	14	16	2	0	3	9	9	23	2	.219	.370
Mike Kinkade	OF17 3B3 C1 1B1	R	26	28	46	3	9	2	1	2	8	3	9	1	.196	.413
Jay Payton	OF6	R	26	13	8	1	2	1	0	0	1	0	2	1	.250	.375
Shane Halter	OF2 SS1	R	29	7	0	0	0	0	0	0	0	0	0	0	—	—
Jorge Toca	1B1	R	32	4	3	0	1	0	0	0	0	0	0	0	.333	.333
Terrence Long		R	23	3	3	0	0	0	0	0	0	0	2	0	.000	.000
Vance Wilson (BA)	C1	R	26	1	1	0	0	0	0	0	0	0	1	0	—	—

NAME	T	AGE	W	L	PCT	SV	G	GS	CG	IP	H	BB	SO	SHO	ERA
		32	97	66	.595	49	163	163	5	1457	1372	617	1172	7	4.27
Al Leiter	L	33	13	12	.520	0	32	32	1	213	209	93	162	1	4.23
Orel Hershiser	R	40	13	12	.520	0	32	32	0	179	175	77	89	0	4.58
Masato Yoshii	R	34	12	8	.600	0	31	29	1	174	168	58	105	0	4.40
Rick Reed (RJ)	R	34	11	5	.688	0	26	26	1	149	163	47	104	1	4.58
Dennis Cook	L	36	10	5	.667	3	71	0	0	63	50	27	68	0	3.86
Pat Mahomes	R	28	8	0	1.000	0	39	0	0	64	44	37	51	0	3.68
Octavio Dotel	R	25	8	3	.727	0	19	14	0	85	69	49	85	0	5.38
2 Kenny Rogers	L	34	5	1	.833	0	12	12	2	76	71	28	58	1	4.03
Turk Wendell	R	32	5	4	.556	3	80	0	0	86	80	37	77	0	3.05
Armando Benitez	R	26	4	3	.571	22	77	0	0	78	40	41	128	0	1.85
Bobby Jones (SJ)	R	29	3	3	.500	0	12	9	0	59	69	11	31	0	5.61
Allen Watson	L	28	2	2	.500	1	14	4	0	40	36	22	32	0	4.08
Rigo Beltran	L	29	1	1	.500	0	21	0	0	31	30	12	35	0	3.48
Greg McMichael (SJ)	R	32	1	1	.500	0	19	0	0	19	20	8	18	0	4.82
Jason Isringhausen	R	26	1	3	.250	2	13	5	0	39	43	22	31	0	6.41
Josias Manzanillo	R	31	0	0	—	0	12	0	0	19	19	4	25	0	5.79
Chuck McElroy	L	31	0	0	—	0	15	0	0	13	12	8	7	0	3.38
Jeff Tam	R	28	0	0	—	0	9	0	0	14	16	4	3	0	3.18
Dan Murray	R	25	0	0	—	0	2	0	0	2	4	2	1	0	13.50
Matt Franco	R	29	0	0	—	0	2	0	0	1	3	2	2	0	13.50
Glendon Rusch	L	24	0	0	—	0	1	0	0	1	0	0	0	0	0.00
1 Billy Taylor	R	37	0	1	.000	0	18	0	0	13	20	9	14	0	8.10
John Franco (RJ)	L	38	0	2	.000	19	46	0	0	41	40	19	41	0	2.88

Paul Wilson (EJ) 26

PHILADELPHIA 3rd 77-85 .475 26   TERRY FRANCONA

Name	G by Pos	B	AGE	G	AB	R	H	2B	3B	HR	RBI	BB	SO	SB	BA	SA
TOTALS			28	162	5598	841	1539	302	44	161	797	631	1081	125	.275	.431
Rico Brogna	1B157	L	29	157	619	90	172	29	4	24	102	54	132	8	.278	.454
Marlon Anderson	2B121	L	25	129	404	48	114	26	4	5	54	24	61	13	.282	.361
Desi Relaford (WJ)	SS63	R	25	65	211	31	51	11	2	1	28	19	34	4	.242	.327
Scott Rolen (XJ)	3B112	R	24	112	421	74	113	28	1	26	77	67	114	12	.268	.525
Bob Abreu	OF146	L	25	152	546	118	183	35	11	20	93	109	113	27	.335	.549
Doug Glanville	OF148	R	28	150	628	101	204	38	6	11	73	48	82	34	.325	.457
Ron Gant	OF133	R	34	138	516	107	134	27	5	17	77	85	112	13	.260	.430
Mike Lieberthal	C143	R	27	145	510	84	153	33	1	31	96	44	86	0	.300	.551
Kevin Jordan	3B62 2B33 1B13	R	29	120	347	36	99	17	3	4	51	24	34	0	.285	.386
Alex Arias	SS95 3B2 2B1	R	31	114	347	43	105	20	1	4	48	36	31	2	.303	.401
Kevin Sefcik	OF64 2B15	R	28	111	209	28	58	15	3	1	11	29	24	9	.278	.392
Rob Ducey	OF58	L	34	104	188	29	49	10	2	8	33	38	57	2	.261	.463
David Doster	2B77 3B6 SS5	R	28	99	97	9	19	2	0	3	10	12	23	1	.196	.309
Gary Bennett	C32	R	27	36	88	7	24	4	0	1	21	4	11	0	.273	.352
2 Domingo Cedeno	SS19 2B1	B	30	32	66	5	10	4	0	1	5	5	22	0	.152	.258
Torey Lovullo	1B6 2B6	B	33	17	38	3	8	0	0	2	5	3	11	0	.211	.368
Wendell Magee	OF4	R	26	12	14	4	5	1	0	2	5	1	4	0	.357	.857
Bobby Estalella	C7	R	24	9	18	2	3	0	0	0	1	4	7	0	.167	.167
Tom Prince (WJ)	C4	R	34	4	6	1	1	0	0	0	1	1	1	0	.167	.167

NAME	T	AGE	W	L	PCT	SV	G	GS	CG	IP	H	BB	SO	SHO	ERA
		29	77	85	.475	32	162	162	11	1438	1494	627	1030	6	4.92
Curt Schilling	R	32	15	6	.714	0	24	24	8	180	159	44	152	1	3.54
Paul Byrd	R	28	15	11	.577	0	32	32	1	200	205	70	106	0	4.60
2 Robert Person	R	29	10	5	.667	0	31	22	0	137	130	70	127	0	4.27
Randy Wolf	L	22	6	9	.400	0	22	21	0	122	126	67	116	0	5.55
Chad Ogea	R	28	6	12	.333	0	36	28	0	168	192	61	77	0	5.63
Wayne Gomes	R	26	5	5	.500	19	73	0	0	74	70	56	58	0	4.26
2 Amaury Telemaco	R	25	3	0	1.000	0	44	0	0	47	45	20	41	0	5.55
Yorkis Perez (EJ)	L	31	3	1	.750	0	35	0	0	32	29	15	26	0	3.94
Joel Bennett	R	29	2	1	.667	0	5	3	0	17	26	7	13	0	9.00
Carlton Loewer (BA)	R	25	2	6	.250	0	20	13	2	90	100	26	48	1	5.12
Cliff Politte	R	25	2	1	.667	0	13	0	0	18	19	15	15	0	7.13
1 Jim Poole	L	33	1	1	.500	1	51	0	0	35	48	15	22	0	4.33
1 Scott Aldred	L	31	1	1	.500	1	29	0	0	32	33	15	19	0	3.90
Billy Brewer	L	31	1	1	.500	2	25	0	0	26	30	14	28	0	7.01
Ken Ryan	R	30	1	2	.333	0	15	0	0	16	16	11	9	0	6.32
Jeff Brantley (SJ)	R	35	1	3	.333	5	10	0	0	9	5	8	11	0	5.19
Steve Schrenk	R	30	1	3	.250	1	32	2	0	51	44	14	36	0	4.29
Mike Grace	R	29	1	4	.200	0	27	5	0	55	80	30	28	0	7.69
Joe Grahe	R	31	1	4	.200	0	13	5	0	33	40	17	16	0	3.86
Steve Montgomery	R	28	1	5	.167	3	53	0	0	65	54	31	55	0	3.34
Anthony Shumaker	L	26	0	3	.000	0	8	4	0	21	23	14	17	0	5.96
1 Paul Spoljaric	L	28	0	3	.000	1	11	0	0	11	23	7	10	0	15.09

Matt Beech (EJ) 27, Tyler Green (SJ) 29

MONTREAL 4th 68-94 .420 35   FELIPE ALOU

Name	G by Pos	B	AGE	G	AB	R	H	2B	3B	HR	RBI	BB	SO	SB	BA	SA
TOTALS			26	162	5559	718	1473	320	47	163	680	438	939	70	.265	.427
Brad Fullmer	1B94	L	24	100	347	38	98	34	2	9	47	22	35	2	.277	.464
Jose Vidro	2B121 1B14 OF3 3B2	R	24	140	494	67	150	45	2	12	59	29	51	0	.304	.476
Orlando Cabrera (NJ)	SS102	R	24	104	382	48	97	23	5	8	39	18	38	2	.254	.403
Shane Andrews	3B82 1B18	R	27	98	281	28	51	8	0	11	37	43	88	1	.181	.327
Vladimir Guerrero	OF160	R	23	160	610	102	193	37	5	42	131	55	62	14	.316	.600
Manny Martinez	OF126	R	28	137	331	48	81	12	7	2	26	17	51	19	.245	.341
Rondell White	OF135	R	27	138	539	83	168	26	6	22	64	32	85	10	.312	.505
Chris Widger	C117	R	28	124	383	42	101	24	1	14	56	28	86	1	.264	.441
Wilton Guerrero	2B54 OF22	B	24	132	315	42	92	15	7	2	31	13	38	7	.292	.403
Michael Barrett	3B66 C59 SS2	R	22	126	433	53	127	32	3	8	52	32	39	0	.293	.436
Mike Mordecai	2B38 SS38 3B32 1B1	R	31	109	226	29	53	10	2	5	25	20	31	2	.235	.363
James Mouton	OF56	R	30	95	122	18	32	5	1	2	13	18	31	6	.262	.369
Orlando Merced	OF44 1B7	L	32	93	194	25	52	12	1	8	26	26	27	2	.268	.464
Ryan McGuire	1B58 OF23	L	27	88	140	17	31	7	2	0	18	27	33	1	.221	.343
Geoff Blum	SS42 2B2	B	26	45	133	21	32	7	2	8	17	25	21	1	.241	.504
Fernando Seguignol (LJ)	1B23 OF8	B	24	35	105	14	27	9	0	5	10	5	33	0	.257	.486
Terry Jones	OF17	B	28	17	63	4	17	1	1	0	3	6	14	1	.270	.317
Trace Coquillette	3B11 2B6	R	25	17	49	2	13	3	0	0	4	4	11	1	.265	.327
Robert Machado	C17	R	26	17	45	6	11	2	0	1	5	0	5	0	.182	.227
Peter Bergeron	OF13	L	21	16	45	12	11	2	0	0	1	9	6	5	.244	.289
Darron Cox (KJ)	C14	R	31	15	25	2	6	1	0	2	5	2	9	0	.240	.400
Jose Fernandez	3B6	R	24	8	24	0	5	2	0	0	4	1	8	0	.208	.292
Chris Stowers	OF2	L	24	4	2	0	0	0	0	0	0	1	0	0	.000	.000

Bob Henley (EJ) 26

NAME	T	AGE	W	L	PCT	SV	G	GS	CG	IP	H	BB	SO	SHO	ERA
		26	68	94	.420	44	162	162	6	1434	1505	572	1043	4	4.69
Javier Vazquez	R	23	9	8	.529	0	26	26	3	155	154	52	113	1	5.00
Dustin Hermanson	R	26	9	14	.391	0	34	34	0	216	225	69	145	0	4.20
Miguel Batista	R	28	8	7	.533	1	39	17	2	135	146	58	95	1	4.88
Steve Kline	L	26	7	4	.636	0	82	0	0	70	56	33	69	0	3.75
Mike Thurman	R	25	7	11	.389	0	29	27	0	147	140	52	85	0	4.05
Ugueth Urbina	R	25	6	6	.500	41	71	0	0	76	59	36	100	0	3.69
Carl Pavano (EJ)	R	23	6	8	.429	0	19	18	1	104	117	35	70	1	5.63
Anthony Telford	R	33	4	5	.556	2	79	0	0	98	112	38	69	0	3.94
Jeremy Powell	R	23	4	8	.333	0	17	17	0	97	113	44	44	0	4.73
Dan Smith	R	23	4	9	.308	0	20	17	0	90	104	39	72	0	6.02
Guillermo Mota	R	25	2	4	.333	0	51	0	0	55	54	25	27	0	2.93
1 Bobby Ayala	R	29	1	6	.143	0	53	0	0	66	60	34	64	0	3.68
Mike Johnson	R	23	1	0	1.000	0	8	0	0	8	12	7	6	0	8.64
1 Mike Maddux	R	37	1	0	1.000	1	18	0	0	18	13	4	17	0	3.82
Rick DeHart	L	29	0	0	—	0	8	0	0	8	8	5	9	0	16.88
3 Mel Rojas	R	32	0	0	—	0	5	0	0	5	8	6	3	0	21.60
J.D. Smart	R	25	0	0	—	0	29	0	0	52	56	17	21	0	5.02
Ted Lilly	L	23	0	0	—	0	3	0	0	8	9	2	7	0	7.81
Scott Strickland	R	23	0	0	—	0	17	0	0	18	15	11	23	0	4.50
Shayne Bennett	R	27	0	1	.000	1	24	0	0	30	38	14	24	0	14.29
Tony Armas	R	21	0	1	.000	0	5	1	0	8	8	2	6	0	1.50

Trey Moore (SJ) 26

FLORIDA — 5th 64-98 .395 39 — JOHN BOLES

Name	G by Pos	B	AGE	G	AB	R	H	2B	3B	HR	RBI	BB	SO	SB	BA	SA
TOTALS			25	162	5578	691	1465	266	44	128	655	479	1145	92	.263	.395
Kevin Millar	1B94 3B1 OF1	R	27	105	351	48	100	17	4	9	67	40	64	1	.285	.433
Luis Castillo	2B126	B	23	128	487	76	147	23	4	0	28	67	85	50	.302	.366
Alex Gonzalez	SS135	R	22	136	560	81	155	28	8	14	59	15	113	3	.277	.430
Mike Lowell (IL)	3B83	R	25	97	308	32	78	15	0	12	47	26	69	0	.253	.419
Mark Kotsay	OF129 1B19	L	23	148	495	57	134	23	9	8	50	29	50	7	.271	.402
Preston Wilson	OF136	R	24	149	482	67	135	4	4	26	71	46	156	11	.280	.502
Cliff Floyd (LJ)	OF62	L	26	69	251	37	76	19	1	11	49	30	47	5	.303	.518
Mike Redmond	C82	R	28	84	242	22	73	9	0	1	27	26	34	0	.302	.351
Bruce Aven	OF102	R	27	137	381	57	110	19	2	12	70	44	82	3	.289	.444
Dave Berg	SS37 2B29 3B19 OF3	R	28	109	304	42	87	18	1	3	25	27	59	2	.286	.382
1 Jorge Fabregas	C78	L	29	82	223	20	46	10	2	3	21	26	27	0	.206	.309
Kevin Orie (LJ)	3B64 1B1	R	26	77	240	26	61	16	0	6	29	22	43	1	.254	.396
Derrek Lee	1B66	R	23	70	218	21	45	9	1	5	20	17	70	2	.206	.326
Danny Bautista	OF60	R	27	70	205	32	59	10	1	5	24	4	30	3	.288	.420
Todd Dunwoody	OF55	L	24	64	186	20	41	6	3	2	20	12	41	3	.220	.317
Tim Hyers	OF15 1B14	L	27	58	81	8	18	4	1	2	12	14	11	0	.222	.370
1 Craig Counsell	2B12	L	28	37	66	4	10	1	0	0	2	5	10	0	.152	.167
Chris Clapinski	3B9 SS6 OF3 2B2	B	27	36	56	6	13	1	2	0	2	9	12	1	.232	.321
Ramon Castro	C24	R	23	24	67	4	12	4	0	2	4	10	14	0	.179	.328
Julio Ramirez	OF11	R	21	15	21	3	3	1	0	0	2	1	6	0	.143	.190
John Roskos	C1	R	24	13	12	0	2	2	0	0	1	1	7	0	.167	.333
Amaury Garcia	2B8	R	24	10	24	6	6	0	1	2	2	3	11	0	.250	.583
Guillermo Garcia	C3	R	27	4	4	0	1	0	0	0	0	0	0	0	.250	.250

NAME	T	AGE	W	L	PCT	SV	G	GS	CG	IP	H	BB	SO	SHO	ERA
		26	64	98	.395	33	162	162	6	1436	1560	655	943	5	4.90
Brian Meadows	R	26	11	15	.423	0	31	31	0	178	214	57	72	0	5.60
Ryan Dempster	R	22	7	8	.467	0	25	25	0	147	146	93	126	0	4.71
Alex Fernandez	R	29	7	8	.467	0	24	24	1	141	135	41	91	0	3.38
Dennis Springer	R	34	6	16	.273	1	38	29	3	196	231	64	83	2	4.86
Jesus Sanchez	L	24	5	7	.417	0	59	10	0	76	84	60	62	0	6.01
Brian Edmondson	R	26	5	8	.385	1	68	0	0	94	106	44	58	0	5.84
1 Livan Hernandez	R	24	5	9	.357	0	20	20	2	136	161	55	97	0	4.76
A.J. Burnett	R	22	4	2	.667	0	7	7	0	41	37	25	33	0	3.48
Antonio Alfonseca	R	27	4	5	.444	21	73	0	0	78	79	29	46	0	3.24
2 Vladimir Nunez	R	24	4	8	.333	0	17	12	0	75	66	34	58	0	4.58
Braden Looper	R	24	3	3	.500	2	72	0	0	83	96	31	50	0	3.80
Reid Cornelius	R	29	1	0	1.000	0	5	2	0	19	16	5	12	0	3.26
Rafael Medina	R	24	1	1	.500	0	20	0	0	23	20	20	16	0	5.79
1 Matt Mantei	R	25	1	2	.333	10	35	0	0	36	24	25	50	0	2.72
Brent Billingsley	L	24	0	0	—	0	8	0	0	8	11	10	3	0	16.43
Michael Tejera	L	22	0	0	—	0	3	1	0	10	5	5	7	0	11.37
Vic Darensbourg	L	28	0	1	.000	0	56	0	0	35	50	21	16	0	8.83
Archie Corbin (VJ)	R	31	0	1	.000	0	17	0	0	21	25	15	30	0	7.29
Armando Almanza	L	26	0	1	.000	0	14	0	0	16	8	9	20	0	1.72
Kirt Ojala	L	30	0	1	.000	0	8	1	0	11	21	6	5	0	14.34
Hector Almonte	R	23	0	2	.000	0	15	0	0	15	20	6	8	0	4.20

CENTRAL DIVISION

HOUSTON — 1st 97-65 .599 — LARRY DIERKER

Name	G by Pos	B	AGE	G	AB	R	H	2B	3B	HR	RBI	BB	SO	SB	BA	SA
TOTALS			30	162	5485	823	1463	293	23	168	784	728	1138	166	.267	.420
Jeff Bagwell	1B161	R	31	162	562	143	171	35	0	42	126	149	127	30	.304	.591
Craig Biggio	2B155 OF6	R	33	160	639	123	188	56	0	16	73	88	107	28	.294	.457
Ricky Gutierrez (BH-BW)	SS80 3B1	R	29	85	268	33	70	7	5	1	25	37	45	2	.261	.336
Ken Caminiti (LJ)	3B75	R	36	78	273	45	78	11	1	13	56	46	58	6	.286	.476
Derek Bell	OF126	R	30	128	509	61	120	22	0	12	66	50	129	18	.236	.350
Carl Everett	OF121	B	28	123	464	86	151	33	3	25	108	50	94	27	.325	.571
Richard Hidalgo (KJ)	OF108	R	24	108	383	49	87	25	2	15	56	56	73	8	.227	.420
Tony Eusebio	C98	R	32	103	323	31	88	15	0	4	33	40	67	0	.272	.356
Bill Spiers	3B71 OF31 SS13 2B4 1B1	L	33	127	393	56	113	18	5	4	39	47	45	10	.288	.389
Tim Bogar	SS90 3B12 2B1	R	32	106	309	44	74	16	2	4	31	38	52	3	.239	.343
Russ Johnson	3B36 2B15 SS2	R	26	83	156	24	44	10	0	5	23	10	21	1	.282	.442
Glen Barker	OF57	R	28	81	73	23	21	2	0	1	11	11	19	17	.288	.356
Paul Bako	C71	L	27	73	215	16	55	14	1	2	17	26	57	1	.256	.358
Daryle Ward	OF31 1B10	L	24	64	150	11	41	6	0	8	30	9	31	0	.273	.473
2 Matt Mieske	OF36	R	31	54	109	13	31	5	0	5	22	6	22	0	.284	.468
Jack Howell (GJ-WJ)	1B5 3B3	L	37	33	33	2	7	2	0	1	8	9	0		.212	.364
Lance Berkman	OF27 1B1	B	23	34	93	10	22	2	0	4	15	12	21	5	.237	.387
Alex Diaz (SJ)	OF8	R	30	30	50	3	11	2	0	1	7	3	13	2	.220	.320
2 Stan Javier	OF18	B	35	20	64	12	21	4	1	0	4	9	8	3	.328	.422
Carlos Hernandez	2B7 SS2	R	23	16	14	4	2	0	0	0	1	0	3	1	.143	.143
Randy Knorr	C11	R	30	13	30	2	5	1	0	0	0	1	8	0	.167	.200
Ryan Thompson	OF10	R	31	12	20	2	4	1	0	1	5	2	7	0	.200	.400
Mitch Meluskey (SJ)	C10	B	25	10	24	7	7	1	0	1	3	5	6	1	.212	.333
Moises Alou (KJ) 32																

NAME	T	AGE	W	L	PCT	SV	G	GS	CG	IP	H	BB	SO	SHO	ERA
		28	97	65	.599	48	162	162	12	1459	1485	478	1204	8	3.83
Mike Hampton	L	28	22	4	.846	0	34	34	3	239	206	101	177	2	2.90
Jose Lima	R	26	21	10	.677	0	35	35	3	246	256	44	187	0	3.58
Shane Reynolds	R	31	16	14	.533	0	35	35	4	232	250	37	197	2	3.85
Scott Elarton	R	23	9	5	.643	1	42	15	0	124	111	43	121	0	3.48
Jay Powell	R	27	5	4	.556	0	75	0	0	75	82	40	77	0	4.32
Chris Holt	R	27	5	13	.278	1	32	26	0	164	193	57	115	0	4.66
Jose Cabrera	R	27	4	0	1.000	0	26	0	0	29	21	9	28	0	2.15
Billy Wagner	L	27	4	1	.800	39	66	0	0	75	35	23	124	0	1.57
1 Sean Bergman (AJ)	R	29	4	6	.400	0	19	16	2	99	130	26	38	1	5.36
Trever Miller	L	26	3	2	.600	1	47	0	0	50	58	29	37	0	5.07
Brian Williams	R	30	2	1	.667	0	50	0	0	67	69	35	53	0	4.41
Doug Henry (EJ)	R	35	2	3	.400	2	35	0	0	41	45	24	36	0	4.65
Joe Slusarski	R	32	0	0	—	0	3	0	0	4	1	3	3	0	0.00
Wade Miller	R	22	0	1	.000	0	5	0	0	10	17	5	8	0	9.58
Jeff McCurry	R	29	0	1	.000	0	5	0	0	4	11	2	3	0	15.75

CINCINNATI — 2nd 96-67 .589 1.5 — JACK McKEON

Name	G by Pos	B	AGE	G	AB	R	H	2B	3B	HR	RBI	BB	SO	SB	BA	SA
TOTALS			28	163	5649	865	1536	312	37	209	820	569	1125	164	.272	.451
Sean Casey	1B148	L	24	151	594	103	197	42	3	25	99	61	88	0	.332	.539
Pokey Reese	2B146 SS16	R	26	149	585	85	167	37	5	10	52	35	81	38	.285	.417
Barry Larkin	SS161	R	35	161	583	108	171	30	4	12	75	93	57	30	.293	.420
Aaron Boone	3B136 SS6	R	26	139	472	56	132	25	5	14	72	30	79	17	.280	.445
Michael Tucker	OF114	L	28	133	296	55	75	8	5	11	44	37	81	11	.253	.426
Mike Cameron	OF146	R	26	146	542	93	139	34	9	21	66	80	145	38	.256	.469
Greg Vaughn	OF144	R	33	153	550	104	135	20	2	45	118	85	137	15	.245	.535
Eddie Taubensee	C124	L	30	126	424	58	132	22	2	21	87	30	67	0	.311	.521
Dmitri Young	OF91 1B9	B	25	127	373	63	112	30	2	14	56	30	71	3	.300	.504
Jeffrey Hammonds	OF106	R	28	123	262	43	73	13	0	17	41	27	64	3	.279	.523
Mark Lewis	3B52 2B2	R	29	88	173	18	44	16	0	6	28	7	24	0	.254	.451
Hal Morris (BW)	1B25 OF4	L	33	80	102	10	29	9	0	0	16	10	21	0	.284	.373
Chris Stynes	2B43 3B8 OF4	R	26	73	113	18	27	1	0	2	14	12	13	5	.239	.301
Brian Johnson (KJ)	C39	R	31	45	117	12	27	7	0	5	18	9	31	0	.231	.419
Mark Sweeney	1B1 OF1	L	29	37	31	6	11	3	0	2	7	4	9	0	.355	.645
Jason LaRue	C35	R	25	36	90	12	19	7	0	3	10	11	32	4	.211	.389
Kerry Robinson	OF2	L	25	9	1	4	0	0	0	0	0	0	1	0	.000	.000
Gookie Dawkins	SS7	R	20	7	7	1	1	0	0	0	0	0	4	0	.143	.143
Ralph Milliard (XJ) 25																

NAME	T	AGE	W	L	PCT	SV	G	GS	CG	IP	H	BB	SO	SHO	ERA
		28	96	67	.589	55	163	163	6	1462	1309	636	1081	11	3.98
Pete Harnisch	R	32	16	10	.615	0	33	33	2	198	190	57	120	2	3.68
Scott Williamson	R	23	12	7	.632	19	62	0	0	93	54	43	107	0	2.41
Steve Parris (SJ)	R	31	11	4	.733	0	22	21	2	129	124	52	86	1	3.50
Denny Neagle (SJ)	L	30	9	5	.643	0	20	19	0	112	95	40	76	0	4.27
Ron Villone	L	29	9	7	.563	2	29	22	0	143	114	73	97	0	4.23
Danny Graves	R	26	8	7	.533	27	75	0	0	111	90	49	69	0	3.08
2 Juan Guzman	R	32	6	3	.667	0	12	12	1	77	70	21	60	0	3.03
Steve Avery (SJ)	L	29	6	7	.462	0	19	19	0	96	75	78	51	0	5.16
Scott Sullivan	R	28	5	4	.556	3	79	0	0	114	88	47	78	0	3.01
Brett Tomko	R	26	5	7	.417	0	33	26	1	172	175	60	132	0	4.92
1 Jason Bere (EJ)	R	28	3	0	1.000	0	12	10	0	43	56	40	28	0	6.85
Stan Belinda (EJ)	R	32	3	1	.750	2	29	0	0	43	42	18	40	0	5.27
Dennys Reyes	L	22	2	2	.500	2	65	1	0	62	53	39	72	0	3.79
Gabe White	L	27	1	2	.333	0	50	0	0	61	68	14	61	0	4.43
Rick Greene	R	28	0	0	—	0	1	0	0	6	7	1	3	0	4.76
1 B.J. Ryan	L	23	0	0	—	0	1	0	0	1	4	1	1	0	4.50
John Hudek	R	32	0	1	.000	0	2	0	0	4	3	0	0	0	27.00

2 Mark Wohlers (IL-EJ) 29, Scott Winchester (SJ) 26

PITTSBURGH — 3rd 78-83 .484 18.5 — GENE LAMONT

Name	G by Pos	B	AGE	G	AB	R	H	2B	3B	HR	RBI	BB	SO	SB	BA	SA
TOTALS			27	162	5468	775	1417	282	40	171	735	573	1197	112	.259	.419
Kevin Young	1B155	R	30	156	584	103	174	41	6	26	106	75	124	22	.298	.522
Warren Morris	2B144	L	25	147	511	65	147	20	3	15	73	59	88	3	.288	.427
Pat Meares (HJ)	SS21	R	30	21	91	15	28	4	0	0	9	9	20	0	.308	.352
Ed Sprague	3B134	R	31	137	490	71	131	27	2	22	81	50	93	3	.267	.465
Adrian Brown	OF96	B	25	116	226	34	61	5	2	4	17	33	39	5	.270	.363
Brian Giles	OF138	L	28	141	521	109	164	33	4	39	115	95	80	6	.315	.614
Al Martin	OF133	L	31	143	541	97	150	36	8	24	63	49	119	20	.277	.506
Jason Kendall (BN)	C75	R	25	78	280	61	93	20	2	8	41	38	32	22	.332	.511
Brant Brown	OF82 1B7	L	28	130	341	49	79	20	3	16	58	22	114	3	.232	.449
Mike Benjamin	SS93 2B12 3B6	R	33	110	368	42	91	26	7	1	37	20	90	10	.247	.364
Abraham Nunez	SS65 2B14	B	23	90	259	25	57	8	0	2	17	28	54	9	.220	.251
Keith Osik	C50	R	30	66	167	12	31	3	1	2	13	11	30	0	.186	.251
1 Freddy Garcia	OF24 3B9 1B1	R	26	55	130	16	30	5	0	6	23	4	41	0	.231	.408
1 Turner Ward	OF34	L	34	49	91	2	19	2	0	0	8	13	9	2	.209	.231
Dale Sveum	3B12 1B4 SS4 2B2 OF1	L	35	49	71	7	15	5	1	3	13	7	28	0	.211	.437
Joe Oliver	C44	R	33	41	134	10	27	8	0	3	13	8	22	1	.201	.284
1 Jose Guillen	OF37	R	23	40	120	18	32	6	1	0	18	10	21	1	.267	.342
John Wehner	OF17 SS2 3B2 2B1	R	32	39	65	6	12	2	0	0	6	5	13	0	.185	.262
Chad Hermansen	OF18	R	21	19	60	5	14	3	0	1	7	7	19	2	.233	.333
Aramis Ramirez	3B17	R	21	18	44	1	11	4	0	0	5	5	21	0	.179	.250
Chris Tremie	C8	R	29	9	14	1	1	0	0	0	0	1	4	0	.071	.071
Emil Brown	OF6	R	24	6	14	0	2	1	0	0	0	0	2	0	.143	.214
Tim Laker	C2	R	29	6	3	1	1	0	0	0	0	0	2	0	.333	.333
Ivan Cruz (VJ)	1B1 OF1	L	31	5	10	3	4	1	0	0	0	0	3	0	.400	.700
Yamid Haad		R	21	1	1	0	0	0	0	0	0	0	0	0	.000	.000
Doug Strange (EJ) 35																

NAME	T	AGE	W	L	PCT	SV	G	GS	CG	IP	H	BB	SO	SHO	ERA
		27	78	83	.484	34	161	161	8	1433	1444	633	1083	3	4.33
Todd Ritchie	R	27	15	9	.625	0	28	26	2	173	169	54	107	0	3.49
Jason Schmidt	R	26	13	11	.542	0	33	33	2	213	219	85	148	0	4.19
Kris Benson	R	24	11	14	.440	0	31	31	2	197	184	83	139	0	4.07
Francisco Cordova (SJ)	R	27	8	10	.444	0	27	27	2	161	166	59	98	0	4.43
Chris Peters	L	27	4	5	.444	0	19	11	0	71	98	27	46	0	6.59
Scott Sauerbeck	L	27	4	1	.800	0	65	0	0	68	53	38	55	0	2.00
Pete Schourek (SJ)	L	30	4	7	.364	0	30	17	0	113	128	49	94	0	5.34
Rich Loiselle (EJ)	R	27	4	2	.600	0	13	0	0	15	16	9	14	0	5.28
Mike Williams	R	30	3	4	.429	23	58	0	0	58	63	37	76	0	5.09
Jimmy Anderson	L	23	2	1	.667	0	13	4	0	29	25	16	13	0	3.99
Marc Wilkins	R	28	3	4	.400	0	46	0	0	51	49	26	44	0	4.24
Jason Christiansen (ZJ)	L	29	2	1	.667	0	39	0	0	38	26	22	35	0	4.06
Jose Silva	R	25	2	8	.200	4	34	12	0	97	108	39	77	0	5.73
Jeff Wallace	L	23	1	0	1.000	0	41	0	0	39	26	38	41	0	3.69
Mike Garcia	R	31	1	1	.500	0	30	0	0	23	25	9	19	0	1.29
Brad Clontz	R	28	1	0	.250	2	56	0	0	49	49	24	40	0	2.74
Greg Hansell	R	28	1	1	.250	0	43	0	0	39	42	11	34	0	3.89
Jason Phillips	R	25	0	0	—	0	5	0	0	7	11	6	7	0	11.57
Jason Boyd	R	26	0	1	.000	0	6	0	0	7	9	6	6	0	3.38
Jim Dougherty	R	31	0	0	—	0	4	0	0	7	4	4	6	0	9.00
Keith Osik	R	30	0	0	—	0	1	0	0	1	0	0	0	0	36.00

Javier Martinez (EJ) 22, Jeff Tabaka (EJ) 35

ST. LOUIS — 4th 75-86 .466 21.5 — TONY LaRUSSA

Name	G by Pos	B	AGE	G	AB	R	H	2B	3B	HR	RBI	BB	SO	SB	BA	SA
TOTALS			29	161	5570	809	1461	274	27	194	763	613	1202	134	.262	.426
Mark McGwire	1B151	R	35	153	521	118	145	21	1	65	147	133	141	0	.278	.697
Joe McEwing	2B96 OF66 3B6 1B2 SS1	R	26	152	513	65	141	28	4	9	44	41	87	7	.275	.398
Edgar Renteria	SS151	R	23	154	585	92	161	31	2	11	63	53	81	37	.275	.400
Fernando Tatis	3B147	R	24	149	537	104	160	31	2	34	107	82	128	21	.298	.553
Eric Davis (SJ)	OF51	R	37	58	191	27	49	9	2	5	30	30	49	5	.257	.403
J.D. Drew	OF98	L	23	104	368	72	89	16	6	13	39	50	77	19	.242	.424
Ray Lankford	OF106	L	32	122	422	77	129	32	1	15	63	49	110	14	.306	.493
Eli Marrero	C96 1B20	R	25	114	317	32	61	13	1	6	34	18	56	11	.192	.297
Willie McGee	OF89 1B3	B	40	132	271	25	68	7	0	0	20	17	60	7	.251	.277
Thomas Howard	OF48	L	34	98	195	16	57	10	0	6	28	17	26	1	.292	.436
Darren Bragg (KJ)	OF88	L	29	93	273	38	71	12	1	6	26	44	67	3	.260	.377
Alberto Castillo	C91	R	29	93	255	21	67	8	0	4	31	24	48	0	.263	.341
Placido Polanco	2B66 SS9 3B9	R	23	88	220	24	61	9	3	1	19	15	24	1	.277	.359
Shawon Dunston	OF23 1B8 SS7 3B5	R	36	62	150	23	46	5	2	5	25	2	23	6	.307	.467
David Howard (LJ)	SS13 1B9 2B9 OF5 3B4	B	31	52	82	3	17	4	0	1	6	7	27	0	.207	.293
Craig Paquette	OF27 3B10 2B7 1B6	R	30	48	157	21	45	6	0	10	37	6	38	1	.287	.516
Adam Kennedy	2B29	L	23	33	102	12	26	10	1	1	16	3	8	0	.255	.402
Eduardo Perez	OF6 1B5	R	29	21	32	6	11	2	0	1	9	7	6	0	.344	.500
Marcus Jensen	C14	R	26	16	34	5	8	5	0	1	6	1	12	0	.235	.471
Luis Ordaz	SS8 2B1 3B1	R	23	10	9	3	1	0	0	0	2	1	2	1	.111	.111

NAME	T	AGE	W	L	PCT	SV	G	GS	CG	IP	H	BB	SO	SHO	ERA
TOTALS		29	75	86	.466	38	161	161	5	1445	1519	667	1025	3	4.74
Kent Bottenfield	R	30	18	7	.720	0	31	31	0	190	197	89	124	3	3.97
Darren Oliver	L	28	9	9	.500	0	30	30	2	196	197	74	119	1	4.26
Garrett Stephenson	R	27	6	3	.667	0	18	12	0	85	90	29	59	0	4.22
1 Kent Mercker	L	31	6	5	.545	0	25	18	0	104	125	51	64	0	5.12
Juan Acevedo	R	29	6	8	.429	4	50	12	0	102	115	48	52	0	5.89
Jose Jimenez	R	25	5	14	.263	0	29	28	2	163	173	71	113	2	5.85
Manny Aybar	R	27	4	5	.444	3	65	1	0	97	104	36	74	0	5.47
Lance Painter	L	31	4	5	.444	1	56	4	0	63	63	25	56	0	4.83
2 Heathcliff Slocumb	R	33	3	2	.600	2	40	0	0	53	49	30	48	0	2.36
Larry Luebbers	R	29	3	3	.500	0	8	8	1	46	46	16	16	0	5.12
Ricky Bottalico	R	29	3	7	.300	20	68	0	0	73	83	49	66	0	4.91
Rick Croushore	R	29	3	7	.300	3	59	0	0	72	68	43	88	0	4.14
Scott Radinsky (SJ)	L	31	2	1	.667	3	43	0	0	28	27	18	17	0	4.88
Mike Mohler	L	30	1	1	.500	1	48	0	0	49	47	23	31	0	4.38
Donovan Osborne (SJ)	L	30	1	3	.250	0	6	6	0	29	34	10	21	0	5.52
Mark Thompson	R	28	1	3	.250	0	5	5	0	29	26	17	22	0	2.76
Rick Heiserman	R	26	0	—		0	3	0	0	4	8	4	4	0	8.31
Alan Benes (SJ)	R	27	0	0	—	0	2	2	0	2	2	0	2	0	0.00
Curtis King (SJ)	R	28	0	0	—	0	2	0	0	1	3	0	1	0	18.00
Rick Ankiel	L	19	0	1	.000	0	9	5	0	33	26	14	39	0	3.27
Mike Busby	R	26	0	1	.000	0	15	0	0	18	21	14	7	0	7.13
Clint Sodowky	R	26	0	1	.000	0	3	0	0	6	15	6	2	0	15.63
Matt Morris (EJ) 24															

MILWAUKEE — 5th 74-87 .460 22.5 — PHIL GARNER 52-60 .464 JIM LEFEBVRE 22-27 .449

Name	G by Pos	B	AGE	G	AB	R	H	2B	3B	HR	RBI	BB	SO	SB	BA	SA
TOTALS			28	161	5582	815	1524	299	30	165	777	658	1065	81	.273	.426
Mark Loretta	SS74 1B66 2B17 3B14	R	27	153	587	93	170	34	5	5	67	52	59	4	.290	.390
Fernando Vina (LJ)	2B37	L	30	37	154	19	41	7	0	1	16	14	6	3	.266	.331
Jose Valentin (RJ)	SS85	B	29	89	256	45	58	9	5	10	38	48	52	3	.227	.418
Jeff Cirillo	3B155	R	29	157	607	98	198	35	1	15	88	75	83	7	.326	.461
Jeromy Burnitz (BH)	OF127	L	30	130	467	87	126	33	2	33	103	91	124	7	.270	.561
Marquis Grissom	OF149	R	32	154	603	92	161	27	1	20	83	49	109	24	.267	.415
Geoff Jenkins	OF128	L	24	135	447	70	140	43	3	21	82	35	87	5	.313	.564
Dave Nilsson (BF)	C101	L	29	115	343	58	108	19	1	21	62	53	64	1	.309	.554
Ron Belliard	2B119 SS1 3B1	R	24	124	457	60	135	29	4	8	58	64	59	4	.295	.429
Alex Ochoa	OF85	R	27	119	277	47	83	16	3	8	40	45	43	6	.300	.466
Sean Berry	1B64	R	33	106	259	26	59	11	1	2	23	17	50	0	.228	.301
Brian Banks	1B44 C40 OF5	B	28	105	219	34	53	7	1	5	22	25	59	6	.242	.352
Rich Becker	OF50	L	27	89	139	15	35	5	2	5	16	33	38	5	.252	.424
Lou Collier	SS31 OF10 3B7 2B4	R	25	74	135	18	35	9	0	2	14	4	32	3	.259	.370
Bobby Hughes (EJ)	C44	R	28	48	101	10	26	2	0	3	6	5	28	0	.257	.366
Kevin Barker	1B31	L	23	38	117	13	33	3	0	3	23	9	19	1	.282	.385
Charlie Greene	C31	R	28	32	42	4	8	1	0	1	5	1	11	0	.190	.214
Robinson Cancel	C15	R	23	15	44	5	8	2	0	0	5	2	12	0	.182	.227
Lyle Mouton	OF3	R	30	14	17	2	3	1	0	1	3	2	3	0	.176	.412
Eddie Zosky	3B4 2B2	R	31	8	7	1	1	0	0	0	0	1	2	0	.143	.143

NAME	T	AGE	W	L	PCT	SV	G	GS	CG	IP	H	BB	SO	SHO	ERA
TOTALS		28	74	87	.460	40	161	161	2	1443	1618	616	987	5	5.07
Hideo Nomo	R	30	12	8	.600	0	28	28	0	176	173	78	161	0	4.54
Steve Woodard (BW)	R	24	11	8	.579	0	31	29	2	185	219	36	119	0	4.52
Scott Karl	L	27	11	11	.500	0	33	33	0	198	246	69	74	0	4.78
David Weathers	R	29	7	4	.636	2	63	0	0	93	102	38	74	0	4.65
2 Rocky Coppinger	R	25	5	3	.625	0	29	0	0	37	35	23	39	0	3.68
Bill Pulsipher (XJ)	L	25	5	8	.455	0	19	16	0	87	100	36	42	0	5.98
Eric Plunk	R	35	4	4	.500	0	68	0	0	75	71	43	63	0	5.02
Kyle Peterson	R	23	4	7	.364	0	17	12	0	77	87	25	34	0	4.56
Bob Wickman	R	30	3	8	.273	37	71	0	0	74	75	38	60	0	3.39
1 Alberto Reyes	R	28	2	0	1.000	0	26	0	0	36	27	25	39	0	4.25
Jason Bere	L	30	2	0	1.000	0	71	0	0	23	23	10	19	0	4.63
Mike Myers	L	30	2	1	.667	0	71	0	0	41	46	13	35	0	5.23
Jim Abbott	L	31	2	8	.200	0	20	15	0	82	110	42	37	0	6.91
Cal Eldred (AJ)	R	31	2	8	.200	0	20	15	0	82	101	46	60	0	7.79
Hector Ramirez	R	27	1	2	.333	0	15	0	0	21	19	11	9	0	3.43
Rafael Roque	L	27	1	6	.143	1	43	9	0	84	96	42	66	0	5.34
Reggie Harris	R	30	0	0	—	0	12	8	7	11	0			0	3.00
Steve Falteisek	R	27	0	0	—	0	10	0	1	14	5			0	7.50
Horacio Estrada	L	23	0	0	—	0	5	7	10	4	5			0	7.36
Chad Fox (EJ)	R	28	0	0	—	0	7	11	4	12	0			0	10.80
Jeff D'Amico (SJ)	R	23	0	0	—	0	1	1	0	1	0			0	0.00
2 Jim Pittsley	R	25	0	1	.000	0	15	0	0	19	20	10	13	0	4.82
Valerio De Los Santos (XJ)	L	26	0	1	.000	0	7	0	0	8	12	7	5	0	6.48
Carl Dale	R	26	0	1	.000	0	4	0	0	4	8	6	4	0	20.25

CHICAGO — 6th 67-95 .414 30 — JIM RIGGLEMAN

Name	G by Pos	B	AGE	G	AB	R	H	2B	3B	HR	RBI	BB	SO	SB	BA	SA
TOTALS			32	162	5482	747	1411	255	35	189	717	571	1170	60	.257	.420
Mark Grace	1B160	L	35	161	593	107	183	44	5	16	91	83	44	3	.309	.481
Mickey Morandini	2B132	L	33	144	456	60	110	18	5	4	37	48	61	6	.241	.329
Jose Hernandez	SS92 OF20 1B1	R	29	109	342	57	93	12	2	15	43	40	101	7	.272	.450
Gary Gaetti	3B81 1B8 SS1	R	40	113	280	22	57	9	1	9	46	21	51	0	.204	.339
Sammy Sosa	OF162	R	30	162	625	114	180	24	2	63	141	78	171	7	.288	.635
Lance Johnson (MJ)	OF91	L	35	95	335	46	87	11	6	1	21	37	20	13	.260	.337
Henry Rodriguez	OF122	L	31	130	447	72	136	29	0	26	87	56	113	2	.304	.544
Benito Santiago	C107 1B1	R	34	109	350	28	87	18	3	7	36	32	71	1	.249	.377
Jeff Blauser	2B25 SS22 3B18 OF1	R	34	100	200	41	48	5	2	9	26	26	52	2	.240	.420
Tyler Houston	3B63 C18 1B2 OF1	L	28	100	249	26	58	9	1	9	27	28	67	1	.233	.386
Glenallen Hill	OF62	R	34	99	253	43	76	9	1	20	55	22	61	5	.300	.581
Manny Alexander	SS30 3B22 2B17 OF2	R	28	90	177	17	48	11	2	0	15	10	38	4	.271	.356
Curtis Goodwin	OF76	L	26	89	157	15	38	6	1	0	9	13	38	2	.242	.293
Jeff Reed	C49 3B1	L	36	57	150	18	39	11	2	1	17	28	34	1	.260	.380
Jose Nieves	SS52	R	24	54	181	16	45	9	1	2	18	8	25	0	.249	.343
Chad Meyers	2B32 OF14	R	23	43	142	17	33	9	0	0	4	9	27	4	.232	.296
Roosevelt Brown	OF18	L	23	33	64	6	14	6	1	1	10	2	14	1	.219	.391
Bo Porter	OF21	R	26	24	26	2	5	1	0	0	2	2	13	0	.192	.231
Shane Andrews	3B19 1B1	R	27	19	67	13	17	4	0	5	14	7	21	0	.254	.537
Sandy Martinez (KJ)	C12	L	28	17	30	1	5	0	0	1	0	1	11	0	.167	.267
Cole Liniak	3B10	L	22	12	29	3	7	2	0	0	2	1	4	0	.241	.310
Jose Molina	C10	R	24	10	19	3	5	1	0	0	1	2	4	0	.263	.316
Robin Jennings (HJ)		L	27	8	5	0	1	0	0	0	0	0	2	0	.200	.200

NAME	T	AGE	W	L	PCT	SV	G	GS	CG	IP	H	BB	SO	SHO	ERA
TOTALS		29	67	95	.414	32	162	162	11	1431	1619	529	980	6	5.27
Jon Lieber	R	29	10	11	.476	0	31	31	3	203	226	46	186	1	4.07
Steve Trachsel	R	28	8	18	.308	0	34	34	4	206	226	64	149	0	5.56
Terry Adams (EJ)	R	26	6	3	.667	13	52	0	0	65	60	28	57	0	4.02
2 Rick Aguilera	R	37	6	3	.667	8	44	0	0	46	44	10	32	0	3.69
1 Terry Mulholland	L	36	6	6	.500	0	26	16	0	110	137	32	44	0	5.15
Kevin Tapani (XJ)	R	35	6	12	.333	0	23	23	1	136	151	33	73	0	4.83
Kyle Farnsworth	R	23	5	9	.357	0	27	21	1	130	140	52	70	1	5.05
Scott Sanders	R	30	4	7	.364	2	67	6	0	104	112	53	89	0	5.52
Rodney Myers	R	30	3	1	.750	0	46	0	0	64	71	25	41	0	4.38
Felix Heredia	L	23	3	1	.750	1	69	0	0	52	56	25	50	0	4.85
1 Rod Beck (EJ)	R	30	2	4	.333	7	31	0	0	30	41	13	13	0	7.80
Andrew Lorraine	L	26	2	5	.286	0	11	11	0	62	71	22	40	1	5.55
2 Micah Bowie	L	24	2	6	.250	0	11	11	0	47	59	30	39	0	9.96
Matt Karchner (GJ)	R	32	1	0	1.000	0	16	0	0	18	16	9	9	0	2.50
Ray King	L	25	0	0	—	0	10	0	0	11	11	10	5	0	5.91
Doug Creek	L	30	0	0	—	0	5	0	0	6	6	4	3	0	10.50
Richard Barker	R	26	0	0	—	0	5	0	0	5	6	4	0	0	7.20
Kurt Miller (VJ)	R	26	0	0	—	0	6	0	0	9	12	6	0	0	18.00
Gary Gaetti	R	40	0	0	—	0	1	0	0	1	2	1	1	0	18.00
2 Bobby Ayala	R	29	0	1	.000	0	13	0	0	16	11	5	15	0	2.81
Brad Woodall	L	30	0	1	.000	0	8	0	0	16	17	6	7	0	5.63
Steve Rain	R	24	0	1	.000	0	15	0	0	15	28	7	12	0	9.20
2 Mark Guthrie	L	33	0	2	.000	0	11	0	0	11	15	7	12	0	6.75
Brian McNichol	L	24	0	2	.000	0	4	0	0	11	15	7	12	0	6.75
Jeremi Gonzalez (EJ) 24, Kerry Wood (EJ) 22															

WEST DIVISION

ARIZONA — 1st 100-62 .617 — BUCK SHOWALTER

Name	G by Pos	B	AGE	G	AB	R	H	2B	3B	HR	RBI	BB	SO	SB	BA	SA
TOTALS			30	162	5658	908	1566	289	46	216	865	588	1045	137	.277	.459
Travis Lee	1B114 OF2	L	24	120	375	57	89	16	2	9	50	58	50	17	.237	.363
Jay Bell	2B148 SS1	R	33	151	589	132	170	32	6	38	112	82	132	7	.289	.557
Andy Fox	SS82 3B12	L	28	99	274	34	70	12	2	6	33	33	61	4	.255	.380
Matt Williams	3B153	R	33	154	627	98	190	37	2	35	142	41	93	2	.303	.536
Tony Womack	OF123 2B19 SS19	L	29	144	614	111	170	25	10	4	41	52	68	72	.277	.370
Steve Finley	OF155	L	34	156	590	100	156	32	10	34	103	63	94	8	.264	.525
Luis Gonzalez	OF148	L	31	153	614	112	206	45	4	26	111	66	63	9	.336	.549
Kelly Stinnett	C86	R	29	88	284	36	66	13	0	14	38	24	83	2	.232	.426
Bernard Gilkey	OF53	R	32	94	204	28	60	16	1	8	39	29	42	2	.294	.500
Damian Miller	C86	R	29	86	296	35	80	19	0	11	47	19	78	0	.270	.446
Hanley Frias	SS53 2B8	B	25	69	150	27	41	3	2	1	16	29	18	4	.273	.340
Greg Colbrunn	1B39 3B2	R	29	67	135	20	44	5	3	5	24	12	23	1	.326	.519
Dave Dellucci (WJ)	OF31	L	25	63	109	24	43	7	1	1	15	11	24	2	.394	.505
Erubiel Durazo	1B44	L	25	52	155	31	51	4	2	11	30	26	43	1	.329	.594
Tony Batista	SS43	R	25	44	144	16	37	5	0	5	21	16	17	2	.257	.396
Dante Powell	OF15	R	25	22	25	4	4	3	0	0	1	2	6	2	.160	.280
Rob Ryan	OF5	R	26	20	29	4	7	1	0	2	5	1	8	0	.241	.483
Lenny Harris	3B5 OF2	L	34	19	29	2	11	1	0	1	7	0	1	1	.379	.517
Turner Ward	OF5	R	34	10	23	6	8	1	0	2	7	2	6	0	.348	.652
Ernie Young	OF4	R	29	6	11	1	2	0	0	0	3	2	3	0	.182	.182
Rod Barajas	C5	R	23	5	16	3	4	1	0	1	3	1	1	0	.250	.500
Edwin Diaz	2B2 SS2	R	24	4	5	2	2	0	0	0	1	1	2	0	.400	.800
Danny Klassen		R	23	1	1	0	1	0	0	0	0	0	1	0	1.000	1.000

NAME	T	AGE	W	L	PCT	SV	G	GS	CG	IP	H	BB	SO	SHO	ERA
TOTALS		30	100	62	.617	42	162	162	16	1467	1387	543	1198	9	3.77
Randy Johnson	L	35	17	9	.654	0	35	35	12	272	207	70	364	2	2.48
Omar Daal	L	27	16	9	.640	0	32	32	2	215	188	79	148	1	3.65
Andy Benes	R	31	13	12	.520	0	33	33	0	198	216	82	141	0	4.81
Armando Reynoso	R	33	10	6	.625	0	31	27	0	167	178	67	79	0	4.37
Gregg Olson	R	32	9	4	.692	14	61	0	0	61	54	25	45	0	3.71
Brian Anderson	L	27	8	2	.800	1	31	19	2	130	144	28	75	1	4.57
Todd Stottlemyre (SJ)	R	34	6	3	.667	17	10	0	40	74	40	0	4.09			
Bobby Chouinard	R	27	5	2	.714	1	32	0	0	45	54	21	51	0	2.68
Greg Swindell	L	34	2	0	1.000	1	63	0	0	65	54	21	51	0	2.51
Vladimir Nunez	R	33	4	3	.571	0	44	0	0	49	50	25	35	0	3.70
1 Dan Plesac	L	37	2	2	.500	1	27	0	0	34	29	20	28	0	2.91
2 Amaury Telemaco (SJ)	R	25	1	0	1.000	0	26	0	0	37	20	20	31	0	4.61
1 John Frascatore	R	29	1	4	.200	0	26	0	0	10	12	6	6	0	6.52
Erik Sabel	R	25	0	0	—	0	9	0	0	29	34	19	49	0	9.00
Dan Carlson	R	29	0	0	—	0	6	0	0	6	6	4	3	0	9.00
2 Matt Mantei	R	25	0	1	.000	22	30	0	0	29	20	19	49	0	2.79
Vicente Padilla	R	20	0	0	—	0	34	0	0	7	6	4	3	0	16.88
2 Ed Vosberg	L	37	0	0	—	0	28	0	0	4	6	4	3	0	3.38

SAN FRANCISCO 2nd 86-76 .531 14   DUSTY BAKER

Name	G by Pos	B	AGE	G	AB	R	H	2B	3B	HR	RBI	BB	SO	SB	BA	SA
TOTALS			31	153	5563	872	1507	307	18	188	828	696	1028	109	.271	.434
J.T. Snow	1B160	L	31	161	570	93	156	25	2	24	98	86	121	0	.274	.451
Jeff Kent	2B133 1B1	R	31	138	511	86	148	40	2	23	101	61	112	13	.290	.511
Rich Aurilia	SS150	R	27	152	558	68	157	23	1	22	80	43	71	2	.281	.444
Bill Mueller (BT)	3B108 2B3	B	28	116	414	61	120	24	0	3	36	65	52	4	.290	.362
Ellis Burks	OF107	R	34	120	390	73	110	19	0	31	96	69	86	7	.282	.569
Marvin Benard	OF142	L	29	149	562	100	163	36	5	16	64	55	97	27	.290	.457
Barry Bonds (EJ)	OF96	L	34	102	355	91	93	20	2	34	83	73	62	15	.262	.617
Brent Mayne	C105	L	31	117	322	39	97	32	0	2	39	43	65	2	.301	.419
F.P. Santangelo	OF81 2B11 3B3 SS1	B	31	113	254	49	66	17	3	3	26	53	54	12	.260	.386
1 Stan Javier	OF94	B	35	112	333	49	92	15	1	3	30	29	55	13	.276	.354
Charlie Hayes	3B55 1B20 OF1	R	34	95	264	33	54	9	1	6	48	33	41	3	.205	.314
Armando Rios (SJ)	OF53	L	27	72	150	32	49	9	0	7	29	24	35	7	.327	.527
Scott Servais	C62 1B1	R	32	69	198	21	54	10	0	5	21	13	31	0	.273	.399
Ramon Martinez	2B27 SS12 3B11	R	26	61	144	21	38	6	0	5	19	14	17	1	.264	.410
Wilson Delgado	2B20 2B15	R	26	35	71	7	18	2	1	0	3	5	9	1	.254	.310
Doug Mirabelli	C30	R	28	33	87	10	22	6	0	1	10	9	25	0	.253	.356
Calvin Murray	OF9	R	27	15	19	1	5	2	0	0	5	2	4	1	.263	.368
Edwards Guzman	3B5 C1	L	22	14	15	0	0	0	0	0	0	0	4	0	.000	.000
Jay Canizaro	2B4	R	25	12	18	5	8	2	0	1	9	1	2	1	.444	.722

NAME	T	AGE	W	L	PCT	SV	G	GS	CG	IP	H	BB	SO	SHO	ERA
		29	86	76	.531	42	162	162	6	1456	1486	655	1076	3	4.71
Russ Ortiz	R	25	18	9	.667	0	33	33	2	208	189	125	164	0	3.81
Kirk Rueter	L	28	15	10	.600	0	33	33	1	185	219	55	94	0	5.41
Shawn Estes	L	26	11	11	.500	0	32	32	1	203	209	112	159	1	4.92
Joe Nathan	R	24	7	4	.636	0	19	14	0	90	84	46	54	0	4.18
Chris Brock (KJ)	R	29	6	8	.429	0	19	19	0	107	124	41	76	0	5.48
Mark Gardner	R	37	5	11	.313	0	29	21	1	139	142	57	86	0	6.47
John Johnstone	R	30	4	6	.400	3	62	0	0	66	48	20	56	0	2.60
Rich Rodriguez	L	36	3	0	1.000	0	62	0	0	57	60	28	44	0	5.24
2 Jerry Spradlin	R	31	3	1	.750	0	59	0	0	58	59	29	52	0	4.19
Alan Embree	L	29	3	2	.600	0	68	0	0	59	42	26	53	0	3.38
2 Livan Hernandez	R	24	3	3	.500	0	10	10	0	64	66	21	47	0	4.38
Robb Nen	R	29	3	8	.273	37	72	0	0	72	79	27	77	0	3.98
Julian Tavarez	R	26	2	0	1.000	0	47	0	0	55	65	25	33	0	5.93
Felix Rodriguez	R	26	2	3	.400	0	47	0	0	66	67	29	55	0	3.80
Bronswell Patrick	R	28	1	0	1.000	0	6	0	0	5	9	3	6	0	10.13
Miguel Del Toro	R	26	0	0	—	0	14	0	0	24	24	11	20	0	4.18

LOS ANGELES 3rd 77-85 .475 23   DAVEY JOHNSON

Name	G by Pos	B	AGE	G	AB	R	H	2B	3B	HR	RBI	BB	SO	SB	BA	SA
TOTALS			29	162	5567	793	1480	253	23	187	761	594	1030	167	.266	.420
Eric Karros	1B151	R	31	153	578	74	176	40	0	34	112	53	119	8	.304	.550
Eric Young	2B116	R	32	119	456	73	128	24	2	4	41	63	26	51	.281	.355
Mark Grudzielanek (BH)	SS119	R	29	123	488	72	159	23	5	7	46	31	65	6	.326	.436
Adrian Beltre	3B152	R	20	152	538	84	148	27	5	15	67	61	105	18	.275	.428
Raul Mondesi	OF158	R	28	159	601	98	152	29	5	33	99	71	134	36	.253	.483
Devon White	OF128	B	36	134	474	60	127	20	4	14	68	39	88	19	.268	.407
Gary Sheffield	OF145	R	30	152	549	103	165	20	0	34	101	101	64	11	.301	.523
Todd Hundley	C108	B	30	114	376	49	78	14	0	24	55	44	113	2	.207	.436
Dave Hansen	1B20 3B13 OF2	L	30	100	107	14	27	8	1	2	17	26	20	0	.252	.402
Jose Vizcaino	SS44 2B30 3B9 OF1	B	31	94	266	27	67	9	1	0	29	20	23	2	.252	.297
Todd Hollandsworth	OF67 1B13	L	26	92	261	39	74	12	2	9	32	24	61	5	.284	.448
Trenidad Hubbard	OF51 C1 2B1	R	35	82	105	23	33	5	0	1	13	13	24	4	.314	.390
2 Craig Counsell	2B38 SS2	L	28	50	108	20	28	6	0	0	9	9	14	1	.259	.315
Angel Pena	C43	R	24	43	120	14	25	6	0	4	21	12	24	0	.208	.358
Paul LoDuca	C34	R	27	36	95	11	22	1	0	3	11	10	9	1	.232	.337
Tripp Cromer (IL)	2B9 SS9 3B2 OF2 1B1	R	31	33	52	5	10	0	0	2	8	5	10	0	.192	.308
1 Jacob Brumfield	OF11	R	34	18	17	4	5	0	1	0	1	0	5	0	.294	.412
Alex Cora (BH)	SS8 2B3	L	23	11	30	2	5	1	0	0	3	0	4	0	.167	.200
Chance Sanford	2B2	L	27	5	8	1	2	0	0	0	2	0	1	0	.250	.250
Brent Cookson	OF3	R	29	3	5	0	1	0	0	0	0	0	1	0	.200	.200
Rick Wilkins	C1	L	32	3	4	0	0	0	0	0	0	0	1	0	.000	.000
Juan Castro	2B1 SS1	R	27	2	1	0	0	0	0	0	0	0	1	0	.000	.000

NAME	T	AGE	W	L	PCT	SV	G	GS	CG	IP	H	BB	SO	SHO	ERA
		29	77	85	.475	37	162	162	8	1453	1438	594	1077	6	4.45
Kevin Brown	R	34	18	9	.667	0	35	35	5	252	210	59	221	1	3.00
Chan Ho Park	R	26	13	11	.542	0	33	33	0	194	208	100	174	0	5.23
Darren Dreifort	R	27	13	13	.500	0	30	29	1	179	177	76	140	1	4.79
Ismael Valdes	R	25	9	14	.391	0	32	32	2	203	213	58	143	1	3.98
Pedro Borbon	L	31	4	3	.571	1	70	0	0	51	39	29	33	0	4.09
Mike Judd	R	24	3	1	.750	0	7	4	0	28	30	12	22	0	5.46
Alan Mills	R	32	3	4	.429	0	68	0	0	72	70	43	49	0	3.73
Jeff Williams	L	27	2	0	1.000	0	9	3	0	18	12	9	7	0	4.08
Robinson Checo (GJ)	R	27	2	2	.500	0	9	2	0	16	24	13	11	0	10.34
Jamie Arnold	R	25	2	4	.333	1	36	3	0	69	81	34	26	0	5.48
Jeff Shaw	R	32	3	4	.333	34	64	0	0	68	64	15	43	0	2.78
Onan Masaoka	L	21	1	1	.333	1	54	0	0	67	55	47	61	0	4.32
Carlos Perez	L	28	2	10	.167	0	17	16	0	90	116	39	40	0	7.43
2 Mike Maddux	R	37	1	1	.500	0	49	0	0	55	54	19	41	0	3.29
Eric Gagne	R	23	1	1	.500	0	5	5	0	30	18	15	30	0	2.10
Doug Bochtler	R	28	0	0	—	0	12	0	0	13	11	6	7	0	5.54
1 Mel Rojas	R	32	0	0	—	0	5	0	0	5	5	3	3	0	12.60
Antonio Osuna (EJ)	R	26	0	0	—	0	5	0	0	5	5	3	4	0	7.71
Jeff Kubenka	L	24	0	1	.000	0	6	0	0	8	13	4	2	0	11.74
1 Dave Mlicki	R	31	0	0	—	0	7	0	0	7	10	2	1	0	4.91
Matt Herges	R	29	0	0	—	0	17	0	0	24	24	8	18	0	4.07

SAN DIEGO 4th 74-88 .457 26   BRUCE BOCHY

Name	G by Pos	B	AGE	G	AB	R	H	2B	3B	HR	RBI	BB	SO	SB	BA	SA
TOTALS			30	162	5394	710	1360	256	22	153	671	631	1169	174	.252	.393
Wally Joyner (SJ)	1B105	L	37	110	323	34	80	14	2	5	43	58	54	0	.248	.350
Quilvio Veras	2B118	B	28	118	475	95	133	25	2	6	41	65	88	30	.280	.379
Chris Gomez (KJ)	SS75	R	28	76	234	20	59	8	1	1	15	27	49	1	.252	.308
Phil Nevin	3B67 C31 OF13 1B11	R	28	128	383	52	103	27	0	24	85	51	82	1	.269	.527
Tony Gwynn (LJ)	OF104	L	39	111	411	59	139	27	0	10	62	29	14	7	.338	.477
Ruben Rivera	OF143	R	25	144	411	65	80	16	1	23	48	55	143	16	.195	.406
Reggie Sanders	OF129	R	31	133	478	92	136	24	7	26	72	65	108	36	.285	.527
Ben Davis	C22	B	22	76	266	29	65	14	1	5	30	25	70	2	.244	.361
Eric Owens	OF116 1B12 3B4 2B1	R	28	149	440	55	117	22	3	9	61	38	50	33	.266	.391
Damian Jackson	SS100 2B21 OF3	R	25	133	388	56	87	20	2	9	39	53	105	34	.224	.356
John Vander Wal	OF48 1B28	L	33	132	246	26	67	18	0	6	41	37	59	2	.272	.419
Dave Magadan	3B52 1B42	L	36	116	248	20	68	12	1	2	30	45	36	1	.274	.355
Ed Giovanola	3B25 2B19 SS7	L	30	56	50	10	11	0	0	1	3	9	8	2	.190	.224
George Arias (RJ)	3B50	R	27	55	164	20	40	8	0	7	20	6	54	0	.244	.421
1 Jim Leyritz (BH)	C24 1B19 3B1	R	35	134	17	32	5	0	8	21	15	37	0	.239	.455
1 Greg Myers	C41	L	33	50	128	9	37	4	0	3	15	13	14	0	.289	.391
1 Carlos Baerga	2B13 3B13 1B2	B	30	33	80	6	20	1	0	2	5	6	14	1	.250	.338
David Newhan	2B19 1B1 3B1	L	25	32	43	7	6	1	0	2	6	1	11	2	.140	.302
Wiki Gonzalez	C17	R	25	30	83	7	21	2	1	3	12	1	8	0	.253	.410
Mike Darr	OF22	L	23	25	48	6	13	1	0	2	3	5	18	2	.271	.417
Gary Matthews	OF17	B	24	23	36	4	8	0	0	1	7	9	9	2	.222	.222
Carlos Garcia	3B4 1B1	R	31	6	11	1	2	0	0	0	1	3	1	0	.182	.182
Carlos Hernandez (LJ) 32																

NAME	T	AGE	W	L	PCT	SV	G	GS	CG	IP	H	BB	SO	SHO	ERA
		29	74	88	.457	43	162	162	5	1420	1454	529	1078	6	4.47
Andy Ashby	R	31	14	10	.583	0	31	31	4	206	204	54	132	3	3.80
Woody Williams	R	32	12	12	.500	0	33	33	0	208	213	73	137	0	4.41
Sterling Hitchcock	L	28	12	14	.462	0	33	33	1	206	202	76	194	0	4.11
Matt Clement	R	24	10	12	.455	0	31	31	0	181	190	86	135	0	4.48
Donne Wall	R	31	4	3	.636	0	55	0	0	70	58	23	53	0	3.07
Brian Boehringer (SJ)	R	30	6	5	.545	0	33	11	0	94	97	35	64	0	3.24
Dan Miceli	R	28	5	4	.444	2	66	0	0	69	67	36	59	0	4.46
Will Cunnane	R	25	2	1	.667	0	24	0	0	31	34	12	22	0	5.23
Trevor Hoffman	R	31	2	3	.400	40	64	0	0	67	48	15	73	0	2.14
Carlos Reyes	R	30	2	4	.333	1	65	0	0	77	76	24	57	0	3.72
Matt Whiteside	R	31	1	0	1.000	0	11	0	0	11	19	5	9	0	13.91
Roberto Rivera	L	26	1	2	.333	0	12	0	0	7	7	3	3	0	3.86
Buddy Carlyle	R	21	0	1	.000	0	7	7	0	38	36	17	29	0	5.97
Carlos Almanzar (XJ)	R	25	0	0	—	0	4	0	0	4	8	4	15	30	7.47
1 Ed Vosberg	L	37	0	0	—	0	15	0	0	8	16	3	6	0	9.72
Ed Giovanola	R	30	0	0	—	0	15	0	0	0	8	3	4	0	0.00
2 Matt Whisenant	L	28	0	1	.000	0	19	0	0	15	10	10	10	0	3.68
Domingo Guzman	R	24	0	1	.000	0	3	0	0	5	13	3	4	0	21.60
Heath Murray	L	26	0	0	—	0	22	0	0	50	66	25	36	0	5.76
Stan Spencer	R	30	0	7	.000	0	9	8	0	38	56	11	36	0	9.16
Randy Myers (SJ) 36																

COLORADO 5th 72-90 .444 28   JIM LEYLAND

Name	G by Pos	B	AGE	G	AB	R	H	2B	3B	HR	RBI	BB	SO	SB	BA	SA
TOTALS			29	162	5717	906	1644	305	39	223	863	508	863	70	.288	.472
Todd Helton	1B156	L	25	159	578	114	185	39	5	35	113	68	77	7	.320	.587
Mike Lansing (XJ)	2B35	R	31	35	145	24	45	9	0	4	15	7	22	2	.310	.455
Neifi Perez	SS157	B	26	157	690	108	193	27	11	12	70	28	54	13	.280	.403
Vinny Castilla	3B157	R	31	158	615	83	169	24	1	33	102	53	75	2	.275	.472
Larry Walker	OF114	L	32	127	438	108	166	26	4	37	115	57	52	11	.379	.710
1 Darryl Hamilton	OF82	L	34	91	337	65	103	11	3	4	24	38	21	4	.303	.389
Dante Bichette	OF144	R	35	151	593	104	177	38	2	34	133	54	84	6	.298	.541
Kirt Manwaring (RJ)	C44	R	33	48	137	14	41	7	1	2	14	12	23	0	.299	.409
Angel Echevarria	OF49 1B10	R	28	102	191	28	56	7	0	11	35	17	34	1	.293	.503
Kurt Abbott	2B66 1B8 OF4 SS3	R	30	96	286	41	78	17	2	8	41	16	69	3	.273	.430
Terry Shumpert	2B54 OF19 3B14 SS2	R	32	92	262	58	91	26	3	10	37	31	41	14	.347	.584
1 Lenny Harris	2B24 OF14 3B2	L	34	91	158	15	47	12	0	0	13	6	6	1	.297	.373
Henry Blanco	C86 OF1	R	27	88	263	30	61	12	3	6	28	34	38	1	.232	.369
Jeff Barry	OF56	R	30	74	168	19	45	16	0	5	26	19	29	4	.268	.452
Edgard Clemente	OF49	R	23	50	142	18	36	4	0	8	25	7	46	0	.253	.488
1 Jeff Reed	C36	L	36	46	106	11	27	5	0	2	11	17	24	0	.255	.358
Chris Sexton	OF13 2B10 SS6	R	27	35	59	9	14	0	1	1	7	11	10	4	.237	.322
J.R. Phillips	OF7 1B4	L	29	25	39	5	9	4	0	0	4	0	13	0	.231	.487
Ben Petrick	C19	R	22	19	62	13	20	3	0	4	12	10	13	1	.323	.565
Pat Watkins	OF10	R	26	16	19	2	1	0	0	0	0	1	4	0	.053	.053
Juan Sosa	OF6 SS2	R	23	14	9	3	2	0	0	0	0	2	3	2	.222	.222
Derrick Gibson	OF10	R	24	10	28	2	5	0	0	1	2	0	5	0	.179	.429
2 Brian McRae	OF7	B	31	7	23	1	6	1	0	1	2	2	5	0	.261	.478
Chris Petersen	2B6 SS1	R	24	7	13	0	2	0	0	0	0	3	2	1	.154	.154
John Cangelosi	OF1	B	36	5	6	0	1	0	0	0	0	3	1	0	.167	.333
Mike Kelly	OF1	R	29	2	2	0	1	0	0	0	0	0	0	0	.500	1.000

NAME	T	AGE	W	L	PCT	SV	G	GS	CG	IP	H	BB	SO	SHO	ERA
		29	72	90	.444	33	162	162	12	1429	1700	737	1032	2	6.01
Pedro Astacio	R	29	17	11	.607	0	34	34	7	232	258	75	210	0	5.04
Brian Bohanon	L	30	12	12	.500	0	33	33	3	197	236	92	120	1	6.20
Darryl Kile	R	30	8	13	.381	0	32	32	1	191	225	109	116	0	6.61
Curtis Leskanic	R	31	6	3	.750	0	30	20	0	85	87	49	77	0	5.08
Bobby Jones	R	26	6	10	.375	0	30	20	0	112	132	77	74	0	6.33
Jamey Wright	R	24	4	3	.571	0	16	16	0	94	110	54	49	0	4.87
Jerry Dipoto	R	31	4	5	.444	1	63	0	0	87	91	44	69	0	4.26
Dave Veres	R	32	4	8	.333	31	73	0	0	77	88	37	71	0	5.14
1 Chuck McElroy	L	31	3	1	.750	0	41	0	0	41	48	28	37	0	6.20
David Lee	R	26	3	2	.600	0	36	0	0	49	43	29	38	0	3.67
Mike DeJean	R	28	2	4	.333	0	56	0	0	61	83	32	31	0	8.41
Luther Hackman	R	24	2	1	.333	0	5	3	0	16	12	10	10	0	10.69
Roberto Ramirez	L	26	1	3	.250	0	32	4	0	40	68	22	32	0	8.26
John Thomson	R	25	1	10	.091	0	14	13	1	63	85	36	34	0	8.04
Dave Wainhouse	R	31	0	0	—	0	19	0	0	29	37	16	16	0	6.91
Mike Porzio	L	26	0	0	—	0	9	0	0	21	31	10	10	0	8.59
2 Rigo Beltran	L	29	0	0	—	0	12	0	0	11	20	7	15	0	7.36
Mark Brownson	R	24	0	2	.000	0	7	0	0	30	42	8	21	0	7.89
Kevin Ritz (SJ) 34																

LINE SCORES

Team	1	2	3	4	5	6	7	8	9	10	11		R	H	E

DIVISION SERIES: ATLANTA 3 : HOUSTON 1

Game 1   October 5 at Atlanta

	1	2	3	4	5	6	7	8	9		R	H	E
HOU	0	1	0	0	0	1	0	0	4		6	13	0
ATL	0	0	0	0	0	1	0	0	0		1	7	0

Reynolds, Miller (7), Henry (7), Wagner (9)   **Maddux**, Remlinger (8)

Game 2   October 6 at Atlanta

	1	2	3	4	5	6	7	8	9		R	H	E
HOU	0	1	0	0	0	0	0	0	0		1	1	1
ATL	1	0	0	0	0	1	3	0	X		5	11	1

Lima, Elarton (7), Powell (9)   **Millwood**

Game 3   October 8 at Houston

	1	2	3	4	5	6	7	8	9	10	11	12		R	H	E
ATL	0	0	0	0	0	3	0	0	0	0	0	2		5	12	0
HOU	2	0	0	0	0	0	1	0	0	0	0	0		3	9	2

Glavine, Mulholland (7), Maddux (7), Remlinger (7), Springer (9), **Rocker** (10), Millwood (12)   Hampton, Cabrera (8), Henry (10), **Powell** (12)

Game 4   October 9 at Houston

	1	2	3	4	5	6	7	8	9		R	H	E
ATL	1	0	1	0	0	5	0	0	0		7	15	1
HOU	0	0	0	0	0	0	1	4	0		5	8	1

Smoltz, Mulholland (8), McGlinchy (8), Rocker (8)   **Reynolds**, Holt (6), Elarton (6), Miller (8), Powell (9)

DIVISION SERIES: NEW YORK 3 : ARIZONA 1

Game 1   October 5 at Arizona

	1	2	3	4	5	6	7	8	9		R	H	E
NYN	1	0	2	1	0	0	0	0	4		8	10	0
ARI	0	0	1	1	0	2	0	0	0		4	7	0

Yoshii, Cook (6), **Wendell** (8), Benitez (9)   **Johnson**, Chouinard (9)

Game 2   October 6 at Arizona

	1	2	3	4	5	6	7	8	9		R	H	E
NYN	0	0	1	0	0	0	0	0	0		1	5	0
ARI	0	0	3	0	2	0	2	0	X		7	9	1

Rogers, Mahomes (5), Dotel (7), J. Franco (7)   **Stottlemyre**, Olson (7), Swindell (8)

Game 3   October 8 at New York

	1	2	3	4	5	6	7	8	9		R	H	E
ARI	0	0	0	0	0	2	0	0	0		2	5	3
NYN	0	1	2	0	0	6	0	0	X		9	11	0

Daal, Holmes (5), Plesac (6), Chouinard (6), Swindell (8)   **Reed**, Wendell (7), J. Franco (8), Hershiser (9)

Game 4   October 9 at New York

	1	2	3	4	5	6	7	8	9	10		R	H	E
ARI	0	0	0	0	1	0	0	2	0	0		3	5	1
NYN	0	0	0	1	0	1	0	1	0	1		4	8	0

Anderson, Olson (8), Swindell (8), **Mantei** (8)   Leiter, Benitez (8), **J. Franco** (10)

COMPOSITE BATTING

DIVISION SERIES

ATLANTA

NAME	POS	G	AB	R	H	2B	3B	HR	RBI	BA
TOTALS		4	148	18	45	5	0	1	18	.304
Boone	2B	4	19	3	9	1	0	0	1	.474
Williams	LF	4	18	2	7	1	0	0	3	.389
A. Jones	CF	4	18	1	4	1	0	0	2	.222
Jordan	RF	4	17	2	8	1	0	1	7	.471
Perez	C	4	16	1	4	0	0	0	3	.250
C. Jones	3B	4	13	2	3	0	0	0	1	.231
Klesko	1B	4	12	3	4	0	0	0	1	.333
Hernandez	SS	4	11	1	1	0	0	0	0	.091
Weiss	SS	3	6	1	1	0	0	0	0	.167
Hunter	1B	3	4	0	0	0	0	0	0	.000
Millwood	P	2	4	0	1	0	0	0	0	.250
Smoltz	P	1	3	1	2	1	0	0	0	.667
Glavine	P	1	2	0	0	0	0	0	0	.000
Lockhart	PH	3	1	0	0	0	0	0	0	.000
Nixon	LF	1	1	1	1	0	0	0	0	1.000
Battle	PH	1	1	0	0	0	0	0	0	.000
Guillen	PH	1	1	0	0	0	0	0	0	.000
Maddux	P	1	1	0	0	0	0	0	0	.000
Mulholland	P	2	0	0	0	0	0	0	0	—
Remlinger	P	2	0	0	0	0	0	0	0	—
Rocker	P	2	0	0	0	0	0	0	0	—
McGlinchy	P	1	0	0	0	0	0	0	0	—
Springer	P	1	0	0	0	0	0	0	0	—

HOUSTON

NAME	POS	G	AB	R	H	2B	3B	HR	RBI	BA
TOTALS		4	141	15	31	2	0	5	15	.220
Biggio	2B	4	19	1	2	0	0	0	0	.105
Caminiti	3B	4	17	3	8	0	0	3	8	.471
Eusebio	C	4	15	2	4	0	0	1	3	.267
Everett	CF-RF	4	15	2	2	0	0	0	1	.133
Bagwell	1B	4	13	3	2	0	0	0	0	.154
Javier	LF-RF	4	11	1	3	0	0	0	0	.273
Spiers	RF-LF	4	11	0	3	0	0	0	1	.273
Gutierrez	SS	3	10	0	0	0	0	0	0	.000
Ward	LF	3	7	1	1	0	0	1	1	.143
Bogar	SS	2	4	0	3	1	0	0	1	.750
Reynolds	P	2	4	0	1	0	0	0	0	.250
Mieske	LF	2	4	1	0	0	0	0	0	.000
Bell	RF	2	3	0	1	0	0	0	0	.333
Barker	CF	2	3	1	0	0	0	0	0	.000
Hampton	P	1	2	0	0	0	0	0	0	.000
Lima	P	1	2	0	0	0	0	0	0	.000
Johnson	PH	2	1	0	1	1	0	0	0	1.000
Powell	P	3	0	0	0	0	0	0	0	—
Elarton	P	2	0	0	0	0	0	0	0	—
Henry	P	2	0	0	0	0	0	0	0	—
Miller	P	2	0	0	0	0	0	0	0	—
Cabrera	P	1	0	0	0	0	0	0	0	—
Holt	P	1	0	0	0	0	0	0	0	—
Wagner	P	1	0	0	0	0	0	0	0	—

NEW YORK

NAME	POS	G	AB	R	H	2B	3B	HR	RBI	BA
TOTALS		4	134	22	34	5	0	5	22	.254
Olerud	1B	4	16	3	7	0	0	1	6	.438
Alfonzo	2B	4	16	4	4	1	0	3	6	.250
Henderson	LF	4	15	5	6	0	0	0	1	.400
Ordonez	SS	4	14	1	4	1	0	0	2	.286
Ventura	3B	4	14	1	3	2	0	0	1	.214
Agbayani	RF	4	10	1	3	1	0	0	1	.300
Piazza	C	2	9	0	2	0	0	0	0	.222
Hamilton	CF	4	8	0	1	0	0	0	2	.125
Pratt	C	3	8	2	1	0	0	1	1	.125
Cedeno	RF-CF	4	7	1	2	0	0	0	2	.286
Dunston	CF	4	6	0	1	0	0	0	0	.167
Leiter	P	1	3	0	0	0	0	0	0	.000
Rogers	P	1	2	0	0	0	0	0	0	.000
Yoshii	P	1	2	0	0	0	0	0	0	.000
Mora	CF-LF	3	1	1	0	0	0	0	0	.000
Bonilla	PH	2	1	1	0	0	0	0	0	.000
Wendell	P	2	1	0	0	0	0	0	0	.000
Reed	P	1	1	0	0	0	0	0	0	.000
J. Franco	P	3	0	0	0	0	0	0	0	—
Benitez	P	2	0	0	0	0	0	0	0	—
Cook	P	1	0	0	0	0	0	0	0	—
Dotel	P	1	0	0	0	0	0	0	0	—
M. Franco	PH	1	0	0	0	0	0	0	0	—
Hershiser	P	1	0	0	0	0	0	0	0	—
Mahomes	P	1	0	0	0	0	0	0	0	—

ARIZONA

NAME	POS	G	AB	R	H	2B	3B	HR	RBI	BA
TOTALS		4	126	16	26	7	1	4	16	.206
Womack	RF-SS	4	18	2	2	0	1	0	0	.111
Williams	3B	4	16	3	6	1	0	0	0	.375
Bell	2B	4	14	3	4	1	0	0	3	.286
Stinnett	C	4	14	1	2	1	0	0	0	.143
Finley	CF	4	13	0	5	1	0	0	5	.385
Gonzalez	LF	4	10	3	2	1	0	1	2	.200
Frias	SS	4	7	0	0	0	0	0	0	.000
Durazo	1B	2	7	1	1	0	0	1	1	.143
Gilkey	RF	2	6	0	0	0	0	0	0	.000
Colbrunn	1B	2	5	1	2	1	0	1	2	.400
Johnson	P	1	3	0	1	1	0	0	0	.333
Stottlemyre	P	1	3	0	0	0	0	0	0	.000
Fox	SS	1	3	0	0	0	0	0	0	.000
Ward	PH	3	2	2	1	0	0	1	3	.500
Harris	3B	2	2	0	0	0	0	0	0	.000
Anderson	P	1	2	0	0	0	0	0	0	.000
Daal	P	1	1	0	0	0	0	0	0	.000
Swindell	P	3	0	0	0	0	0	0	0	—
Chouinard	P	2	0	0	0	0	0	0	0	—
Olson	P	2	0	0	0	0	0	0	0	—
Holmes	P	1	0	0	0	0	0	0	0	—
Mantei	P	1	0	0	0	0	0	0	0	—
Plesac	P	1	0	0	0	0	0	0	0	—

COMPOSITE PITCHING

ATLANTA

NAME	G	IP	H	BB	SO	W	L	SV	ERA
TOTALS	4	39	31	17	33	3	1	2	3.46
Millwood	2	10	1	0	9	1	0	1	0.90
Maddux	2	7	10	5	5	0	1	0	2.57
Smoltz	1	7	6	3	3	1	0	0	5.14
Glavine	1	6	5	3	6	0	0	0	3.00
Remlinger	2	3.2	4	3	4	0	0	0	9.82
Rocker	2	3.1	0	2	5	1	0	1	0.00
Springer	1	1	2	1	1	0	0	0	0.00
Mulholland	2	0.2	3	0	0	0	0	0	27.00
McGlinchy	1	0.1	0	0	0	0	0	0	0.00

HOUSTON

NAME	G	IP	H	BB	SO	W	L	SV	ERA
TOTALS	4	38	45	11	35	1	3	0	4.26
Reynolds	2	11	16	3	5	1	1	0	4.09
Hampton	1	7	6	1	9	0	0	0	3.86
Lima	1	6.2	9	2	4	0	1	0	5.40
Henry	2	3.2	1	3	2	0	0	0	0.00
Powell	3	3	3	1	3	0	1	0	6.00
Elarton	2	2.1	4	1	3	0	0	0	3.86
Cabrera	1	2	2	0	6	0	0	0	0.00
Miller	2	1.1	1	0	2	0	0	0	0.00
Wagner	1	1	0	0	1	0	0	0	0.00
Holt	1	0	3	0	0	0	0	0	∞

NEW YORK

NAME	G	IP	H	BB	SO	W	L	SV	ERA
TOTALS	4	36	26	14*	22	3	1	0	4.00
Leiter	1	7.2	3	3	4	0	0	0	3.52
Reed	1	6	4	3	2	1	0	0	3.00
Yoshii	1	5.1	6	0	3	0	0	0	6.75
Rogers	1	4.1	5	2	6	0	1	0	8.31
J. Franco	3	3.2	1	0	2	1	0	0	0.00
Benitez	2	2.1	2	1	2	0	0	0	0.00
Wendell	2	2	0	2	1	0	1	0	0.00
Cook	1	1.2	1	1	1	0	0	0	0.00
Mahomes	1	1.2	3	0	1	0	0	0	5.40
Hershiser	1	1	0	0	1	0	0	0	0.00
Dotel	1	0.1	1	2	0	0	0	0	54.00

ARIZONA

NAME	G	IP	H	BB	SO	W	L	SV	ERA
TOTALS	4	35.1	34	21	28	1	3	0	5.35
Johnson	1	8.1	8	3	11	0	1	0	7.56
Anderson	1	7	7	0	4	0	0	0	2.57
Stottlemyre	1	6.2	4	5	6	1	0	0	1.35
Daal	1	4	6	3	4	0	1	0	6.75
Swindell	3	3.1	1	3	1	0	0	0	0.00
Chouinard	2	2	3	0	1	0	0	0	4.50
Mantei	2	2	1	3	1	0	1	0	4.50
Holmes	1	1.1	1	3	0	0	0	0	27.00
Olson	2	0.1	0	1	0	0	0	0	0.00
Plesac	1	0.1	3	0	0	0	0	0	54.00

LINE SCORES

Team	1	2	3	4	5	6	7	8	9	10	11	12	13	14	15	R	H	E

CHAMPIONSHIP: ATLANTA 4 : NEW YORK 2

Game 1   October 12 at Atlanta

| NYN | 0 | 0 | 0 | 1 | 0 | 0 | 0 | 0 | 1 | | | | | | | 2 | 6 | 2 |
| ATL | 1 | 0 | 0 | 1 | 1 | 0 | 1 | X | | | | | | | | 4 | 8 | 2 |

Yoshii, Mahomes (5), Cook (7), Wendell (8)   Maddux, Remlinger (8), Rocker (8)

Game 2   October 13 at Atlanta

| NYN | 0 | 1 | 0 | 0 | 1 | 0 | 0 | 1 | 0 | | | | | | | 3 | 5 | 1 |
| ATL | 0 | 0 | 0 | 0 | 4 | 0 | 0 | X | | | | | | | | 4 | 9 | 1 |

Rogers, Wendell (6), Benitez (8)   Millwood, Rocker (8), Smoltz (9)

Game 3   October 15 at New York

| ATL | 1 | 0 | 0 | 0 | 0 | 0 | 0 | 0 | 0 | | | | | | | 1 | 3 | 1 |
| NYN | 0 | 0 | 0 | 0 | 0 | 0 | 0 | 0 | 0 | | | | | | | 0 | 7 | 2 |

Glavine, Remlinger (8), Rocker (9)   Leiter, J. Franco (8), Benitez (8)

Game 4   October 16 at New York

| ATL | 0 | 0 | 0 | 0 | 0 | 0 | 0 | 2 | 0 | | | | | | | 2 | 3 | 0 |
| NYN | 0 | 0 | 0 | 0 | 0 | 1 | 0 | 2 | X | | | | | | | 3 | 5 | 0 |

Smoltz, Remlinger (8), Rocker (8)   Reed, Wendell (8), Benitez (9)

Game 5   October 17 at New York

| ATL | 0 | 0 | 0 | 2 | 0 | 0 | 0 | 0 | 0 | 0 | 0 | 0 | 0 | 1 | | 3 | 13 | 2 |
| NYN | 0 | 0 | 0 | 0 | 0 | 0 | 0 | 0 | 0 | 0 | 0 | 0 | 2 | 4 | | 11 | 1 | 1 |

Maddux, Mulholland (8), Remlinger (10), Springer (12), Rocker (13), McGlinchy (14)   Yoshii, Hershiser (4), Wendell (7), Cook (7), Mahomes (7), J. Franco (8), Benitez (10), Rogers (11), Dotel (13)

Game 6   October 19 at Atlanta

| NYN | 0 | 0 | 0 | 0 | 3 | 4 | 1 | 0 | 1 | 0 | | | | | | 9 | 15 | 2 |
| ATL | 5 | 0 | 0 | 0 | 0 | 1 | 0 | 1 | 0 | 1 | 1 | | | | | 10 | 10 | 1 |

Leiter, Mahomes (1), Wendell (5), Cook (6), Hershiser (7), J. Franco (8), Benitez (9), Rogers (11)   Millwood, Mulholland (6), Smoltz (7), Remlinger (7), Rocker (9), Springer (11)

COMPOSITE BATTING

ATLANTA

NAME	POS	G	AB	R	H	2B	3B	HR	RBI	BA
TOTALS		6	206	24	46	9	1	5	22	.223
Williams	LF	6	28	4	5	2	0	0	1	.179
Jordan	RF	6	25	3	5	0	0	2	5	.200
A. Jones	CF	6	23	5	5	0	0	0	1	.217
Boone	2B	6	22	2	4	1	0	0	1	.182
Weiss	SS	6	21	2	6	2	0	0	1	.286
Perez	C	6	20	2	10	2	0	2	5	.500
C. Jones	3B	6	19	3	5	2	0	0	1	.263
Hunter	1B	6	10	1	1	0	0	0	2	.100
Klesko	1B	4	8	1	1	0	0	1	1	.125
Lockhart	2B	3	5	0	2	0	1	0	1	.400
Maddux	P	2	5	0	0	0	0	0	0	.000
Millwood	P	2	4	0	0	0	0	0	0	.000
Guillen	SS	3	3	0	1	0	0	0	1	.333
Hernandez	PH	2	2	0	1	0	0	0	2	.500
Battle	1B	3	2	0	0	0	0	0	0	.000
Smoltz	P	3	2	0	0	0	0	0	0	.000
Fabregas	PH	2	2	0	0	0	0	0	0	.000
Myers	C	2	2	0	0	0	0	0	0	.000
Glavine	P	1	2	0	0	0	0	0	0	.000
McGlinchy	P	1	1	0	0	0	0	0	0	.000
Rocker	P	6	0	0	0	0	0	0	0	—
Remlinger	P	5	0	0	0	0	0	0	0	—
Mulholland	P	2	0	0	0	0	0	0	0	—
Nixon	PR	2	0	1	0	0	0	0	0	—
Springer	P	2	0	0	0	0	0	0	0	—

NEW YORK

NAME	POS	G	AB	R	H	2B	3B	HR	RBI	BA
TOTALS		6	225	21	49	9	0	4	21	.218
Olerud	1B	6	27	4	8	0	0	2	6	.296
Alfonzo	2B	6	27	2	6	4	0	0	1	.222
Ventura	3B	6	25	2	3	1	0	0	1	.120
Piazza	C	6	24	1	4	0	0	1	4	.167
Ordonez	SS	6	24	0	1	0	0	0	1	.042
Henderson	LF	6	23	2	4	1	0	0	1	.174
Hamilton	CF	5	17	0	6	1	0	0	2	.353
Mora	LF-CF-RF	6	14	3	6	0	0	1	2	.429
Cedeno	RF	5	12	2	6	1	0	0	1	.500
Dunston	CF	5	7	2	1	0	0	0	1	.143
Agbayani	RF-LF	4	7	2	1	0	0	0	0	.143
Bonilla	PH	3	3	0	1	0	0	0	0	.333
Yoshii	P	2	3	0	0	0	0	0	0	.000
M. Franco	PH	5	2	1	1	1	0	0	0	.500
Pratt	C	4	2	0	1	0	0	0	3	.500
Mahomes	P	3	2	0	0	0	0	0	0	.000
Leiter	P	2	2	0	0	0	0	0	0	.000
Reed	P	1	2	0	0	0	0	0	0	.000
Rogers	P	3	1	0	0	0	0	0	0	.000
Hershiser	P	2	1	0	0	0	0	0	0	.000
Benitez	P	5	0	0	0	0	0	0	0	—
Wendell	P	5	0	0	0	0	0	0	0	—
Cook	P	3	0	0	0	0	0	0	0	—
J. Franco	P	3	0	0	0	0	0	0	0	—
Dotel	P	1	0	0	0	0	0	0	0	—

COMPOSITE PITCHING

ATLANTA

NAME	G	IP	H	BB	SO	W	L	SV	ERA
TOTALS	6	60.1	49	14	49	4	2	3	2.69
Maddux	2	14	12	1	7	1	0	0	1.93
Millwood	2	12.2	13	1	9	1	0	0	3.55
Smoltz	3	8.2	8	0	8	0	0	1	6.23
Glavine	1	7	1	8	1	0	0	0.00
Rocker	6	6.2	3	2	9	0	0	2	0.00
Remlinger	5	5.2	3	4	0	1	0	3.18
Mulholland	2	2.2	1	1	2	0	0	0	0.00
Springer	2	2	0	1	1	1	0	0	0.00
McGlinchy	1	1	2	4	1	0	1	0	18.00

NEW YORK

NAME	G	IP	H	BB	SO	W	L	SV	ERA
TOTALS	6	59.1	46	31	47	2	4	1	3.49
Rogers	3	7.2	11	7	2	0	2	0	5.87
Yoshii	2	7.2	9	3	4	0	1	0	4.70
Leiter	2	7	5	4	5	0	1	0	6.43
Reed	1	7	3	0	5	0	0	0	2.57
Benitez	5	6.2	3	2	9	0	0	1	1.35
Mahomes	3	6.1	4	3	3	0	0	0	1.42
Wendell	5	5.2	2	4	5	1	0	0	4.76
Hershiser	2	4.1	1	3	5	0	0	0	0.00
Dotel	1	3	4	5	2	1	0	0	3.00
J. Franco	3	2.2	3	1	3	0	0	0	3.38
Cook	3	1.1	1	2	1	0	0	0	0.00

MISCELLANEOUS 1999 INDIVIDUAL LEADERS

BATTING

On Base Average

	American League			National League	
1	Martinez, Sea.	.447	1	Walker, Col.	.458
2	M. Ramirez, Cle.	.442	2	Bagwell, Hou.	.454
3	Jeter, N.Y.	.438	3	Abreu, Phi.	.446
4	Williams, N.Y.	.435	4	C. Jones, Atl.	.441
5	Fernandez, Tor.	.427	5	Olerud, N.Y.	.427
6	Thome, Cle.	.426	6	McGwire, St.L.	.424
7	R. Alomar, Cle.	.422	7	Henderson, N.Y.	.423
	Giambi, Oak.	.422	8	Giles, Pit.	.418
9	Palmeiro, Tex.	.420	9	Sheffield, L.A.	.407
10	Garciaparra, Bos.	.418	10	Tatis, St.L.	.407

On Base Average plus Slugging Average

	American League			National League	
1	M. Ramirez, Cle.	1.105	1	Walker, Col.	1.168
2	Palmeiro, Tex.	1.050	2	McGwire, St.L.	1.120
3	Garciaparra, Bos.	1.022	3	C. Jones, Atl.	1.074
4	Martinez, Sea.	1.001	4	Bagwell, Hou.	1.045
5	Jeter, N.Y.	.989	5	Giles, Pit.	1.032
6	Gonzalez, Tex.	.980	6	Sosa, Chi.	1.002
7	Giambi, Oak.	.975	7	Abreu, Phi.	.995
8	Green, Tor.	.972	8	Helton, Col.	.981
9	Williams, N.Y.	.971	9	V. Guerrero, Mon.	.978
10	Jaha, Oak.	.970	10	Everett, Hou.	.969

Total Bases

	American League			National League	
1	Green, Tor.	361	1	Sosa, Chi.	397
2	Palmeiro, Tex.	356	2	V. Guerrero, Mon.	366
3	Griffey Jr., Sea.	359	3	McGwire, St.L.	363
4	M. Ramirez, Cle.	346	4	C. Jones, Atl.	359
5	Jeter, N.Y.	346	5	Helton, Col.	339
6	Gonzalez, Tex.	338	6	Gonzalez, Ari.	337
7	Rodriguez, Tex.	335	7	Williams, Ari.	336
8	Surhoff, Bal.	331	8	Bagwell, Hou.	332
9	Belle, Bal.	330	9	Bell, Ari.	328
10	Delgado, Tor.	327	10	Bichette, Col.	321

Caught Stealing

	American League			National League	
1	Stewart, Tor.	17	1	Young, L.A.	22
2	Caruso, Chi.	14	2	Castillo, Fla.	17
3	Encarnacion, Det.	12		Cedeno, N.Y.	17
	Offerman, Bos.	12		Veras, S.D.	17
	Rodriguez, Tex.	12	5	Benard, S.F.	14
				Biggio, Hou.	14
				Henderson, N.Y.	14

Stolen Base Percentage
(Minimum 20 Attempts)

	American League			National League	
1	Lawton, Min.	87	1	Glanville, Phi.	94
2	R. Alomar, Cle.	86	2	C. Jones, Atl.	89
	Damon, K.C.	86	3	Kendall, Pit.	88
4	Belle, Bal.	85	4	Martin, Pit.	87
	Hunter, Det.-Sea.	85	5	Drew, St.L.	86

Extra Base Hits

	American League			National League	
1	Green, Tor.	87	1	Sosa, Chi.	89
2	Delgado, Tor.	83	2	C. Jones, Atl.	87
3	M. Ramirez, Cle.	81		McGwire, St.L.	87
4	Dye, K.C.	79	4	V. Guerrero, Mon.	84
5	Palmeiro, Tex.	78	5	Helton, Col.	79

PITCHING

Fewest Hits Per 9 Innings Pitched

	American League			National League	
1	P. Martinez, Bos.	6.75	1	Millwood, Atl.	6.63
2	Cone, N.Y.	7.63	2	Johnson, Ari.	6.86
3	Hernandez, N.Y.	7.85	3	Brown, L.A.	7.49
4	Colon, Cle.	8.12	4	Hampton, Hou.	7.76
5	Milton, Min.	8.29	5	Daal, Ari.	7.88
6	Finley, Ana.	8.31	6	Schilling, Phi.	7.94
7	Rosado, K.C.	8.52	7	Smoltz, Atl.	8.11
8	Burba, Cle.	8.63	8	Ortiz, S.F.	8.19
9	Clemens, N.Y.	8.87	9	Benson, Pit.	8.42
10	Garcia, Sea.	9.16	10	Harnisch, Cin.	8.62
	Mussina, Bal.	9.16			

Fewest Bases on Balls Per 9 Innings Pitched

	American League			National League	
1	Heredia, Oak.	1.53	1	Reynolds, Hou.	1.44
2	P. Martinez, Bos.	1.56	2	Maddux, Atl.	1.52
3	Radke, Min.	1.81	3	Lima, Hou.	1.61
4	Moyer, Sea.	1.89	4	Woodard, Mil.	1.75
5	Mussina, Bal.	2.30	5	Smoltz, Atl.	1.93
6	Wells, Tor.	2.41	6	Lieber, Chi.	2.04
7	Irabu, N.Y.	2.44	7	Brown, L.A.	2.10
8	Sirotka, Chi.	2.45	8	Schilling, Phi.	2.20
9	Nagy, Cle.	2.63	9	Johnson, Ari.	2.32
10	Suppan, K.C.	2.67	10	Millwood, Atl.	2.33

Strikeouts Per 9 Innings Pitched

	American League			National League	
1	P. Martinez, Bos.	13.20	1	Johnson, Ari.	12.06
2	Finley, Ana.	8.44	2	Hitchcock, S.D.	8.49
3	Cone, N.Y.	8.24	3	Lieber, Chi.	8.23
4	Sele, Tex.	8.17	4	Nomo, Mil.	8.22
5	Clemens, N.Y.	7.82	5	Astacio, Col.	8.15
6	Mussina, Bal.	7.61	6	Millwood, Atl.	8.09
7	Garcia, Sea.	7.60	7	Park, L.A.	8.06
8	Burba, Cle.	7.12	8	Brown, L.A.	7.88
9	Milton, Min.	7.11	9	Reynolds, Hou.	7.65
10	Colon, Cle.	7.07	10	Schilling, Phi.	7.59
	Irabu, N.Y.	7.07			

Lowest Batting Average Allowed

	American League			National League	
1	P. Martinez, Bos.	.205	1	Millwood, Atl.	.202
2	Cone, N.Y.	.229	2	Johnson, Ari.	.208
3	Hernandez, N.Y.	.233	3	Brown, L.A.	.222
4	Colon, Cle.	.242	4	Daal, Ari.	.236
5	Milton, Min.	.243	5	Schilling, Phi.	.237

Home Runs Allowed

	American League			National League	
1	Helling, Tex.	41	1	Astacio, Col.	38
2	Fassero, Sea.-Tex.	35	2	Ogea, Phi.	36
	Ponson, Bal.	35	3	Benes, Ari.	34
	Baldwin, Chi.	34		Byrd, Phi.	34
5	Hentgen, Tor.	32	5	Kile, Col.	33
	Wells, Tor.	32		Williams, S.D.	33

Home Runs Allowed per 9 IP
(Minimum 10 Home Runs Allowed)

	American League			National League	
1	Hinchcliffe, Sea.	2.93	1	Bennett, Phi.	5.29
2	Ward, Chi.	2.29	2	Spencer, S.D.	2.58
3	Castillo, Chi.	2.20	3	Belinda, Cin.	2.32
4	Sampson, Min.	2.15	4	Perez, L.A.	2.31
5	Linton, Bal.	2.14	5	Peters, Pit.	2.15

STILL THE ONE

The New York Yankees had a harder row to hoe in the 1999 season than in '98, but once they got to the playoffs, it was business as usual. Their World Series sweep of the Atlanta Braves cemented their place as the Team of the Decade. And certainly, the Yanks twenty-fifth championship over-qualified them as the Franchise of the Century. An oddity was that, unlike other Yankees champions going back to the time of Babe Ruth, this edition did not live by the home run. In a season that saw balls flying out of parks in greater quantities than ever before, Tino Martinez led New York with a modest 28 four-baggers. This Yankee team could hit home runs, but it could also grind out victories with timely hitting, smooth fielding, smart baserunning, and impenetrable pitching.

Yankee pitching was all-but-perfect in the American League Division Series as the Texas Rangers eked out only one run in losing three straight to Hernandez, Pettitte, and Clemens. Meanwhile, a distinct lack of pitching proved Cleveland's downfall against Wild Card Boston. After winning the first two games of their series, the Indians yielded 44 runs in the next three to fall to the Red Sox. Cleveland's disappointing loss cost manager Mike Hargrove his job.

Pitching also proved the key in the National League. Atlanta's strong starting staff proved too much for Houston's bats. Kevin Millwood's one-hitter in the second game spurred the Braves to win three straight after dropping the opener. The New York Mets' pitchers lacked Atlanta starters awesome reputations, but they earned respect in stopping the Arizona Diamondbacks in four games. The Mets also showed timely hitting right from the beginning when Arizona's Randy Johnson struck out eleven but was knicked by New York for seven earned runs.

The NLCS began as romp for the Braves as Maddox, Millwood, Glavine and reliever John Rocker closed down the Mets in the first three games. Then the gutty Mets rallied to take two. The fifth game went 15 innings. The Braves scored in the top of that stanza, then New York came back to win in the bottom of the inning. Robin Ventura hit what would have been a grand slam but when teammates mobbed him on the bases his hit was recorded as a two-run, game-winning single. Game Six was a classic. The Braves jumped off to a 5-0 lead in the first inning, but the Mets pecked away and tied on a Mike Piazza homer. In both the eighth and tenth innings, New York took leads only to have Atlanta re-tie the game. The Braves finally scored the winning run on Andruw Jones' bases-loaded walk.

Yankee pitching continued strong through the first two games of the ALCS. The New York defense slipped and Boston bats woke up to win Game Three 13-1, but New York immediately returned to form and earned another World Series berth with two more wins over the BoSox.

The final World Series of the century was more notable for its historical significance than for suspense. In three of the four consecutive victories, the Yankees followed the same script. In Games One, Two, and Four, the New York starters held the Braves in check while an opportunistic cadre of hitters built a lead. Then the staunch Yankees bullpen, led by World Series MVP Mariano Rivera took over to nail down the victory. Only Game Three departed from that scenario. The Braves, in a virtual do-or-die situation, jumped off to a 5-1 first inning lead. Atlanta's Tom Glavine who'd missed starting Game One with the flu, pitched seven strong innings, but Atlanta could not add to its lead. Although he'd thrown only 73 pitches going into the eighth inning, Glavine weakened. Joe Girardi singled and Chuck Knoblauch followed with a drive to right. Brian Jordan leaped but the ball popped off his glove and over the fence to tie the score. Chad Curtis, who'd homered in the first inning, won the game with his second home run in the tenth.

WORLD SERIES

LINE SCORES

Team	1	2	3	4	5	6	7	8	9	10	11		R	H	E

WORLD SERIES: NEW YORK (AL) 4 : ATLANTA (NL) 0

Game 1 October 23 at Atlanta

NYA	0	0	0	0	0	0	0	4	0				4	6	0
ATL	0	0	0	1	0	0	0	0	0				1	2	2

Hernandez, Nelson (8), Stanton (8), Maddux, Rocker (8), Remlinger (9)
Rivera (8)

Game 2 October 24 at Atlanta

NYA	3	0	2	1	1	0	0	0	0				7	14	1
ATL	0	0	0	0	0	0	0	0	2				2	5	1

Cone, Mendoza (8), Nelson (9) Millwood, Mulholland (3), Springer (6), McGlinchy (8)

Game 3 October 26 at New York

ATL	1	0	3	1	0	0	0	0	0	0			5	14	1
NYA	1	0	0	0	1	0	1	2	0	1			6	9	0

Glavine, Rocker (8), Remlinger (10) Pettitte, Grimsley (4), Nelson (7), Rivera (9)

Game 4 October 27 at New York

ATL	0	0	0	0	0	0	0	1	0				1	5	0
NYA	0	0	3	0	0	0	0	1	X				4	8	0

Smoltz, Mulholland (8), Springer (8) Clemens, Nelson (8), Rivera (8)

COMPOSITE BATTING

NAME	POS	G	AB	R	H	2B	3B	HR	RBI	BA
NEW YORK										
TOTALS		4	137	21	37	5	0	5	20	.270
Jeter	SS	4	17	4	6	1	0	0	1	.353
Brosius	3B	4	16	2	6	1	0	0	1	.375
Knoblauch	2B	4	16	5	5	1	0	1	3	.313
Martinez	1B	4	15	3	4	0	0	1	5	.267
O'Neill	RF	4	15	0	3	0	0	0	4	.200
Williams	CF	4	13	2	3	0	0	0	0	.231
Ledee	LF	3	10	0	2	1	0	0	1	.200
Posada	C	2	8	0	2	1	0	0	1	.250
Girardi	C	2	7	1	2	0	0	0	0	.286
Curtis	LF	3	6	3	2	0	0	2	2	.333
Cone	P	1	4	0	0	0	0	0	0	.000
Davis	DH	1	4	0	0	0	0	0	0	.000
Strawberry	DH	2	3	0	1	0	0	0	0	.333
Leyritz	DH	2	1	1	1	0	0	1	2	1.000
Hernandez	P	1	1	0	0	0	0	0	0	.000
Mendoza	P	1	1	0	0	0	0	0	0	.000
Clemens	P	1	0	0	0	0	0	0	0	—
Grimsley	P	1	0	0	0	0	0	0	0	—
Nelson	P	4	0	0	0	0	0	0	0	—
Pettitte	P	1	0	0	0	0	0	0	0	—
Rivera	P	3	0	0	0	0	0	0	0	—
Sojo	2B	1	0	0	0	0	0	0	0	—
Stanton	P	1	0	0	0	0	0	0	0	—
ATLANTA										
TOTALS		4	130	9	26	5	1	1	9	.200
Williams	LF	4	17	2	3	0	1	0	0	.176
Boone	2B	4	13	1	7	4	0	0	0	.538
C. Jones	3B	4	13	2	3	0	0	1	2	.231
A. Jones	CF	4	13	1	1	0	0	0	0	.077
Jordan	RF	4	13	1	1	0	0	0	1	.077
Klesko	1B	4	12	0	2	0	0	0	0	.167
Weiss	SS	3	9	1	2	0	0	0	0	.222
Perez	C	3	8	0	1	0	0	0	0	.125
Lockhart	2B-DH	4	7	1	1	0	0	0	0	.143
Myers	C	4	6	0	2	0	0	0	1	.333
Hernandez	SS-DH	2	5	0	1	1	0	0	2	.200
Guillen	SS-DH	3	5	0	0	0	0	0	0	.000
Hunter	1B	2	4	0	1	0	0	0	0	.250
Nixon	CF	2	2	0	1	0	0	0	0	.500
Maddux	P	1	2	0	0	0	0	0	0	.000
Fabregas	PH	1	1	0	0	0	0	0	0	.000
Battle	PH	1	0	0	0	0	0	0	0	—
Mulholland	P	2	0	0	0	0	0	0	0	—
Rocker	P	2	0	0	0	0	0	0	0	—
Springer	P	2	0	0	0	0	0	0	0	—
Remlinger	P	2	0	0	0	0	0	0	0	—
Smoltz	P	1	0	0	0	0	0	0	0	—
Glavine	P	1	0	0	0	0	0	0	0	—
McGlinchy	P	1	0	0	0	0	0	0	0	—
Millwood	P	1	0	0	0	0	0	0	0	—

COMPOSITE PITCHING

NAME	G	IP	H	BB	SO	W	L	SV	ERA
NEW YORK									
TOTALS	4	37	26	15	26	4	0	2	2.19
Clemens	1	7.2	4	2	4	1	0	0	1.17
Cone	1	7	1	5	4	1	0	0	0.00
Hernandez	1	7	1	2	10	1	0	0	1.29
Rivera	3	4.2	3	1	3	1	0	2	0.00
Pettitte	1	3.2	10	1	1	0	0	0	12.27
Nelson	4	2.2	2	1	3	0	0	0	0.00
Grimsley	1	2.1	2	2	0	0	0	0	0.00
Mendoza	1	1.2	3	1	0	0	0	0	10.80
Stanton	1	0.1	0	0	1	0	0	0	0.00
ATLANTA									
TOTALS	4	35	37	13	31	0	4	0	4.37
Maddux	1	7	5	3	5	0	1	0	2.57
Smoltz	1	7	6	3	11	0	1	0	3.86
Glavine	1	7	7	0	3	0	0	0	5.14
Mulholland	2	3.2	5	1	3	0	0	0	7.36
Rocker	2	3	2	2	4	0	0	0	0.00
Springer	2	2.1	0	1	0	0	0	0	0.00
McGlinchy	1	2	2	1	2	0	0	0	0.00
Millwood	1	2	8	2	2	0	1	0	18.00
Remlinger	2	1	1	1	0	0	0	0	9.00

2000:NEW MILLENIUM, OLD GAME

The home run continued to rule in the 21st Century's inaugural season. In fact, by the All-Star Game - ironically won by a homerless American League, 6-3 - predictions raged that as many as a half-dozen sluggers would surpass the once-sacrosanct 60 mark. Eventually injuries, cautious pitching, and the law of averages held the foremost homer-hitters to more traditional totals for the year. The Cubs' Sammy Sosa was the only player to reach 50. Many fans believed the floodtide for long balls had passed, but in truth the major league total of 5,693 home runs set a new all-time record, soaring majestically past the 5,528 of 1999.

With no nail-biting McGwire-Sosa home run duel and less than compelling division races, fans were left with home runs, three new stadiums, and close wild-card chases to entice them to the ball parks. Apparently, those were more than enough as the major leagues set a new total attendance record of 72,748,970 and averaged 30,099 per game.

The National League East was expected to be a close race between the Braves and the Mets. Despite a marvelous season by Mike Piazza, New York could not overcome injuries and early pitching problems. An inability to beat the Braves in Atlanta confined the Mets to second place and the wild card. Meanwhile, led by Chipper and Andruw Jones and Andres Galarraga (making a strong comeback after missing a full season for cancer treatment), Atlanta won its ninth straight division crown. Although ace John Smoltz missed the season with arm miseries and Kevin Millwood struggled, Lefty Tom Glavine returned to the 20-win circle and Greg Maddux won 19. Braves' reliever John Rocker was a major story because of controversial anti-minority remarks he made in a *Sports Illustrated* interview.

In the Central, Jeff Bagwell had a terrific season and Moises Alou came back nicely from an injury that kept him out all 1999, but two-time champ Houston collapsed under an overload of poor pitching. Cincinnati acquired Ken Griffey Jr. but that wasn't enough to mount a successful challenge to eventual division champ St. Louis. Although the Cardinals lost Mark McGwire to a knee injury for nearly the whole second half of the season, slugger Jim Edmonds and a rebuilt pitching staff took up the slack. In the West, Barry Bonds and Jeff Kent gave San Francisco the firepower to win over Arizona and their strikeout ace Randy Johnson. For much of 2000, Colorado's Todd Helton was one of the league's best-kept secrets as he flirted with becoming the first .400-hitter since 1941.

The Yankees were not the American League dominators of the previous two seasons, but midseason trades for David Justice and Glenallen Hill helped a so-so offense when Derek Jeter, Paul O'Neill, Tino Martinez, and Bernie Williams had - by their standards - very ordinary seasons. Starter Andy Pettitte and stopper Mariano Rivera held together an erratic pitching staff. Although the Bombers had enough to fight off an early challenge by Boston and a later attack by Toronto, they staggered badly in the final weeks of the regular season. Boston was handicapped when ace Pedro Martinez, the league's top pitcher, was sidelined for a period with a sore shoulder. Toronto's David Wells and Oakland's Tim Hudson each won 20 games but sported ERAs over 4.00; Martinez checked in with 1.74. Carlos Delgado and Tony Batista led the Blue Jays' potent attack while Carl Everett and Nomar Garciaparra, who led the A.L. in hitting, provided fireworks for the Red Sox.

The cream of the American League was the Chicago White Sox. Frank Thomas re-emerged as one of baseball's best hitters and Magglio Ordonez, Paul Konerko, Carlos Lee and other young sluggers boosted the Sox to the A.L.'s best record. After years of treating the Central Division as its own, Cleveland was dethroned by injuries and its own poor pitching. The loss of Manny Ramirez for a spell early in the season put the Indians in a hole from which they never recovered. Nevertheless, Cleveland finished second to the White Sox in league scoring and led the majors in attendance with 3,456,278.

The closest race in the majors came in the A.L. West. The Oakland Athletics used a happy combination of home runs, bases on balls, and strong pitching to eke out a division crown. Jason Giambi put up MVP numbers and Miguel Tejada emerged as a star. Seattle fought Oakland down to the last day before settling for the A.L. wild card. Supposedly doomed by the loss of Ken Griffey, Jr., the Mariners came on strong behind Alex Rodriguez, Edgar Martinez, John Olerud, and improved pitching.

A strength of the American League was its quality shortstops. Perhaps at no time in baseball's history were so many exceptional shortstops gathered in one league. Entering the season, Jeter, Rodriguez, and Garciaparra were well established as capable fielders with super bats. In 2000, Oakland's Tejada joined that group, while Cleveland veteran Omar Vizquel, though not their match as a hitter, was generally viewed as the best with a glove.

2000 AMERICAN LEAGUE — EAST DIVISION

Name	G by Pos	B	AGE	G	AB	R	H	2B	3B	HR	RBI	BB	SO	SB	BA	SA
NEW YORK	1st 87-74 .540		JOE TORRE													
TOTALS			31	161	5556	871	1541	294	25	205	833	631	1007	99	.277	.450
Tino Martinez	1B154	L	32	155	569	69	147	37	4	16	91	52	74	4	.258	.422
Chuck Knoblauch (EJ)	2B82 DH20	R	31	102	400	75	113	22	2	5	26	46	45	15	.283	.385
Derek Jeter	SS148	R	26	148	593	119	201	31	4	15	73	68	99	22	.339	.481
Scott Brosius	3B134 1B2 OF2 DH1	R	33	135	470	57	108	20	0	16	64	45	73	0	.230	.374
Paul O'Neill	OF140 DH2	L	37	142	566	79	160	26	0	18	100	51	90	14	.283	.424
Bernie Williams	OF137 DH4	B	31	141	537	108	165	37	6	30	121	71	84	13	.307	.566
2 David Justice	OF60 DH18	L	34	78	275	43	84	17	0	20	60	39	42	1	.305	.585
Jorge Posada	C142 1B12 DH4	B	28	151	505	92	145	35	1	28	86	107	151	2	.287	.527
Shane Spencer (KJ)	OF40 DH33	R	28	73	248	33	70	11	3	9	40	19	45	1	.282	.460
Clay Bellinger	OF46 2B21 3B18 1B10 SS6	R	31	98	184	33	38	8	2	6	21	17	48	5	.207	.370
2 Jose Vizcaino	2B62 3B6 DH4 SS2	B	32	73	174	23	48	8	1	0	10	12	28	5	.276	.333
1 Ricky Ledee	OF49 DH10	L	26	62	191	23	46	11	1	7	31	16	39	7	.241	.419
2 Glenallen Hill	DH24 OF12	R	35	40	132	22	44	5	0	16	29	9	33	0	.333	.735
2 Jose Canseco	DH26 OF5	R	35	37	111	16	27	3	0	6	19	23	37	0	.243	.432
Chris Turner	C36 1B1	R	31	37	89	9	21	3	0	1	7	10	21	0	.236	.303
2 Luis Polonia	OF28 DH7	L	35	37	77	11	22	4	0	1	5	7	7	4	.286	.377
2 Luis Sojo	2B25 3B10 1B7 SS2	R	35	34	125	19	36	7	1	2	17	6	6	1	.288	.408
Ryan Thompson		R	32	33	50	12	13	3	0	3	14	5	12	0	.260	.500
1 Wilson Delgado	2B14 SS11 3B5	B	27	31	45	6	11	1	0	1	4	5	9	1	.244	.333
1 Jim Leyritz	DH15 C2 1B1	R	36	24	55	2	12	0	0	1	4	7	14	0	.218	.273
Alfonso Soriano	3B10 SS9 2B1 DH1	R	24	22	50	5	9	3	0	2	3	1	15	2	.180	.360
Felix Jose (GJ)	OF14 DH2	B	35	20	29	4	7	0	0	1	5	2	9	0	.241	.345
Lance Johnson	OF4 DH3	L	36	18	30	6	9	1	0	0	2	0	7	2	.300	.333
Roberto Kelly (EJ)	OF10	R	35	10	25	4	3	1	0	1	1	1	6	0	.120	.280
BOSTON	2nd 85-77 .525 2.5		JIMY WILLIAMS													
TOTALS			29	162	5630	792	1503	316	32	167	755	611	1019	43	.267	.423
Brian Daubach	1B83 DH41 OF8 3B1	L	28	142	495	55	123	32	2	21	76	44	130	1	.248	.448
Jose Offerman	2B80 1B38 DH9	B	31	116	451	73	115	14	3	9	41	70	70	0	.255	.359
Nomar Garciaparra	SS136 DH1	R	26	140	529	104	197	51	3	21	96	61	50	5	.372	.599
John Valentin (KJ)	3B10	R	33	10	35	6	9	1	0	2	5	2	5	0	.257	.457
Trot Nixon (LJ)	OF118 DH1	L	26	123	427	66	118	27	8	12	60	63	85	8	.276	.461
Carl Everett	OF126 DH5	B	29	137	496	82	149	32	4	34	108	52	113	11	.300	.587
Troy O'Leary	OF137	L	30	138	513	68	134	30	4	13	70	44	76	0	.261	.411
Jason Varitek	C128 DH1	R	28	139	448	55	111	31	1	10	65	60	84	1	.248	.388
2 Dante Bichette	DH30	R	36	30	114	13	33	5	0	7	14	8	22	0	.289	.518
Manny Alexander	3B63 SS20 2B7 DH3	R	29	101	194	30	41	4	3	4	19	13	41	2	.211	.325
Darren Lewis	OF89 DH5	R	32	97	270	44	65	12	0	2	17	22	34	10	.241	.307
Scott Hatteberg	C48 DH20 3B1	L	30	92	230	21	61	15	0	8	36	38	39	0	.265	.435
1 Jeff Frye	2B52 OF15 3B8 DH3	R	33	69	239	35	69	13	0	1	13	28	18	1	.289	.356
1 Mike Stanley	1B39 DH18	R	37	58	185	22	41	5	0	10	28	30	44	0	.222	.411
Wilton Veras	3B49	R	22	49	164	21	40	7	1	0	14	7	20	0	.244	.299
2 Mike Lansing	2B49 3B1	R	32	49	139	10	27	4	0	0	13	7	26	0	.194	.223
Donnie Sadler	SS19 OF17 2B12 3B3 DH2	R	25	49	99	14	22	5	0	1	10	5	18	3	.222	.303
2 Rico Brogna	1B37 DH2	L	30	43	56	8	11	3	0	1	8	3	13	0	.196	.304
Lou Merloni	3B40	R	29	40	128	10	41	11	2	0	18	4	22	1	.320	.438
2 Bernard Gilkey	OF22 DH8	R	33	36	91	11	21	5	1	1	9	10	12	0	.231	.341
2 Ed Sprague	3B30 1B3 DH3	R	32	33	111	11	24	4	0	2	12	12	18	0	.216	.306
Morgan Burkhart	DH19 1B5 OF1	B	28	25	73	16	21	3	0	4	18	17	25	0	.288	.493
Israel Alcantara	DH8 OF7 1B5	R	27	22	51	9	15	2	0	5	13	4	19	0	.289	.578
2 Midre Cummings	OF4 DH1	L	28	21	25	1	7	2	0	0	2	6	3	0	.280	.280
Andy Sheets	SS10 DH1	R	28	21	25	1	7	1	0	0	6	1	5	0	.095	.095
Curtis Pride	OF9 DH1	L	31	9	20	4	5	1	0	0	5	0	7	0	.250	.300
Gary Gaetti	DH5	R	41	5	7	0	0	0	0	0	0	0	1	0	.000	.000
2 Sean Berry	3B1	R	34	1	4	0	0	0	0	0	0	0	0	0	.000	.000

NAME	T	AGE	W	L	PCT	SV	G	GS	CG	IP	H	BB	SO	SHO	ERA
		32	87	74	.540	40	161	161	9	1424	1458	577	1040	6	4.76
Andy Pettitte	L	28	19	9	.679	0	32	32	3	205	219	80	125	1	4.35
Roger Clemens	R	37	13	8	.619	0	32	32	1	204	184	84	188	0	3.70
Orlando Hernandez	R	34	12	13	.480	0	29	29	3	196	186	51	141	0	4.51
Jeff Nelson	R	33	8	4	.667	0	73	0	0	70	44	45	71	0	2.45
Mariano Rivera	R	30	7	4	.636	36	66	0	0	76	58	25	58	0	2.85
Ramiro Mendoza (SJ)	R	28	7	4	.636	0	14	9	1	66	66	20	30	1	4.25
2 Denny Neagle	L	31	7	7	.500	0	16	15	1	91	99	31	58	0	5.81
3 Dwight Gooden	R	35	4	2	.667	2	18	5	0	64	66	21	31	0	3.36
David Cone	R	37	4	14	.222	0	30	29	0	155	192	82	120	0	6.91
Jason Grimsley	R	32	3	2	.600	1	63	4	0	96	100	42	53	0	5.04
Mike Stanton	L	33	2	3	.400	0	69	0	0	68	68	24	75	0	4.10
Randy Keisler	L	24	1	0	1.000	0	4	1	0	11	16	8	6	0	11.81
1 Todd Erdos	R	26	0	0	—	1	14	0	0	25	31	11	18	0	5.04
Allen Watson (UJ-SJ)	L	29	0	0	—	0	17	0	0	22	30	18	20	0	10.23
Darrell Einertson	R	27	0	0	—	0	11	0	0	13	16	4	3	0	3.55
Craig Dingman	R	26	0	0	—	0	10	0	0	11	18	3	8	0	6.55
Ted Lilly	L	24	0	0	—	0	7	0	0	8	8	5	11	0	5.63
Jay Tessmer	R	28	0	0	—	0	7	0	0	7	9	1	5	0	6.75
Ed Yarnall	L	24	0	0	—	0	2	1	0	3	3	1	1	0	15.00
Randy Choate	L	24	0	1	.000	0	22	0	0	17	14	8	12	0	4.76
Ben Ford	R	24	0	1	.000	0	11	0	0	11	14	7	5	0	9.00
2 Jake Westbrook	R	22	0	2	.000	0	3	2	0	7	15	4	1	0	13.50
		30	85	77	.525	46	162	162	7	1453	1433	498	1121	12	4.23
Pedro Martinez	R	28	18	6	.750	0	29	29	7	217	128	32	284	4	1.74
Ramon Martinez (KJ)	R	32	10	8	.556	0	27	27	0	128	143	67	89	0	6.13
Rich Garces	R	29	8	1	.889	1	64	0	0	75	64	23	69	0	3.25
Jeff Fassero	L	37	8	8	.500	0	38	23	0	130	153	50	97	0	4.78
Hipolito Pichardo	R	30	6	3	.667	1	38	1	0	65	63	26	37	0	3.46
Tim Wakefield	R	33	6	10	.375	0	51	17	0	159	170	65	102	0	5.48
2 Rolando Arrojo	R	31	5	2	.714	0	13	13	0	71	67	22	44	0	5.05
Derek Lowe	R	27	4	4	.500	42	74	0	0	91	90	22	79	0	2.56
Rod Beck (ZJ)	R	31	3	0	1.000	0	34	0	0	41	34	12	35	0	3.10
Rheal Cormier	L	33	3	3	.500	0	64	0	0	68	74	17	43	0	4.61
1 Brian Rose	R	24	3	5	.375	0	15	12	0	53	58	21	24	0	6.11
Tomo Ohka	R	24	3	6	.333	0	13	12	0	69	70	26	40	0	3.12
Pete Schourek (SJ)	L	31	3	10	.231	0	21	21	0	107	116	38	63	0	5.11
Paxton Crawford	R	22	2	1	.667	0	7	4	0	29	25	13	17	0	3.41
2 Hector Carrasco	R	30	1	1	.500	0	7	0	0	7	15	5	7	0	9.45
Steve Ontiveros	R	39	1	1	.500	0	5	0	0	9	4	1	0	0	10.13
1 John Wasdin	R	27	1	3	.250	1	45	48	15	36	0	5.04
Rob Stanifer	R	28	0	0	—	0	13	22	4	3	0	7.62
Sang-Hoon Lee	L	29	0	0	—	0	12	11	4	6	0	3.09
Tim Young	L	26	0	0	—	0	7	2	6	4	0	6.43
Dan Smith	R	24	0	0	—	0	8	8	1	0	8.10
2 Jesus Pena	L	25	0	0	—	0	5	5	5	4	0	5.79
2 Rick Croushore	R	29	0	0	.000	1	7	7	10	5	0	4.56
Bryce Florie (GJ)	R	29	4	4	49	57	19	34	0	4.56

Tom Gordon (KJ) 32 Juan Pena (EJ) 23 Bret Saberhagen (SJ) 36

TORONTO — 3rd 83-79 .512 4.5 — JIM FREGOSI

Name	G by Pos	B	AGE	G	AB	R	H	2B	3B	HR	RBI	BB	SO	SB	BA	SA
TOTALS			29	162	5677	861	1562	328	21	244	826	526	1026	89	.275	.469
Carlos Delgado	1B162	L	28	162	569	115	196	57	1	41	137	123	104	0	.344	.664
Homer Bush (BH)	2B75	R	27	76	297	38	64	8	0	1	18	18	60	4	.215	.253
Alex Gonzalez	SS141	R	27	141	527	68	133	31	2	15	69	43	113	4	.252	.404
Tony Batista	3B154	R	26	154	620	96	163	32	2	41	114	35	121	5	.263	.519
Raul Mondesi (EJ)	OF96	R	29	96	388	78	105	22	2	24	67	32	73	9	.271	.523
Jose Cruz	OF162	B	26	162	603	91	146	32	5	31	76	71	129	15	.242	.466
Shannon Stewart	OF136	R	26	136	583	107	186	43	5	21	69	37	79	20	.319	.518
Darrin Fletcher	C117 DH2	L	33	122	416	43	133	19	1	20	58	20	45	1	.320	.514
Brad Fullmer	DH129 1B1	L	25	133	482	76	142	29	1	32	104	30	68	3	.295	.558
Craig Grebeck	2B56 SS8	R	35	66	241	38	71	19	0	3	23	25	33	0	.295	.411
Alberto Castillo	C66	R	30	66	185	14	39	7	0	1	16	21	36	0	.211	.265
Marty Cordova	OF41 DH15	R	30	62	200	23	49	7	0	4	18	18	35	1	.245	.340
Dave Martinez	OF47	L	35	47	180	29	56	10	1	2	22	24	28	4	.311	.411
Chris Woodward	SS22 3B9 1B3 2B3	R	23	37	104	16	19	7	0	3	14	10	28	1	.183	.337
Mickey Morandini	2B35	L	34	35	107	10	29	2	1	0	7	7	23	1	.271	.308
Todd Greene	DH23 C2 OF1	R	29	34	85	11	20	2	0	5	10	5	18	0	.235	.435
Dewayne Wise (FJ)	OF18 DH1	L	22	28	22	3	3	0	0	0	0	1	5	1	.136	.136
Rob Ducey	OF3	L	35	5	13	2	2	1	0	0	1	2	2	0	.154	.231
Chad Mottola	OF3	R	28	3	9	1	2	0	0	0	2	0	4	0	.222	.222
Charlie Greene	C3	R	29	3	9	0	1	0	0	0	0	0	5	0	.111	.111
Vernon Wells	OF3	R	21	3	2	0	0	0	0	0	0	0	0	0	.000	.000
Andy Thompson	OF2	R	24	2	6	2	1	0	0	0	1	3	2	0	.167	.167
Josh Phelps	C1	R	22	1	1	0	0	0	0	0	0	0	0	0	.000	.000

NAME	T	AGE	W	L	PCT	SV	G	GS	CG	IP	H	BB	SO	SHO	ERA
		29	83	79	.512	37	162	162	15	1437	1615	560	978	4	5.14
David Wells	L	37	20	8	.714	0	35	35	9	230	266	31	166	1	4.11
Frank Castillo (EJ)	R	31	10	5	.667	0	25	24	0	138	112	56	104	1	3.59
Chris Carpenter	R	25	10	12	.455	0	34	27	2	175	204	83	113	0	6.26
Kelvim Escobar	R	24	10	15	.400	2	43	24	3	180	186	85	142	1	5.35
Billy Koch	R	25	9	3	.750	33	68	0	0	79	78	18	60	0	2.63
2 Esteban Loaiza	R	28	5	7	.417	0	14	14	1	92	95	26	62	1	3.62
Roy Halladay	R	23	4	7	.364	0	19	13	0	68	107	42	44	0	10.64
Lance Painter	L	32	2	2	1.000	0	42	2	0	67	69	22	53	0	4.73
Joey Hamilton (SJ)	R	29	2	1	.667	0	6	6	0	33	28	12	15	0	3.55
John Frascatore	R	30	2	4	.333	0	60	0	0	73	87	33	30	0	5.42
Paul Quantrill	R	31	2	5	.286	1	68	0	0	84	100	25	47	0	4.52
2 Steve Trachsel	R	29	2	5	.286	0	11	11	0	63	72	25	32	0	5.29
1 Darwin Cubillan	R	27	1	0	1.000	0	16	0	0	16	20	11	14	0	8.04
Matt DeWitt (BA)	R	23	1	0	1.000	0	8	0	0	14	20	9	6	0	8.56
Pedro Borbon	L	32	1	1	.500	0	59	0	0	42	45	38	24	0	6.48
Peter Munro	R	24	1	1	.500	0	9	3	0	26	38	16	16	0	9.56
Clayton Andrews	L	22	1	2	.333	0	8	2	0	21	34	9	12	0	10.02
Leo Estrella	R	25	0	0	—	0	2	0	0	5	9	0	3	0	5.79
Pasqual Coco	R	22	0	0	—	0	1	1	0	4	5	5	2	0	9.00
John Bale	L	26	0	0	—	0	1	0	0	4	5	3	6	0	14.73
Eric Gunderson	L	34	0	1	.000	0	6	0	0	6	15	2	2	0	7.11
3 Mark Guthrie	L	34	0	1	.000	0	23	0	0	21	20	9	20	0	4.79

BALTIMORE — 4th 74-88 .457 13.5 — MIKE HARGROVE

Name	G by Pos	B	AGE	G	AB	R	H	2B	3B	HR	RBI	BB	SO	SB	BA	SA
TOTALS			32	162	5549	794	1508	310	22	184	750	558	900	126	.272	.435
Will Clark	1B72 DH6	L	36	79	256	49	77	15	1	9	28	47	45	4	.301	.473
Delino DeShields	2B96 OF41 DH10	L	31	151	581	84	166	43	5	10	86	69	82	37	.296	.444
Mike Bordick	SS100	R	34	100	391	70	116	22	1	16	59	34	71	6	.297	.481
Cal Ripken (XJ)	3B73 DH10	R	39	83	309	43	79	16	0	15	56	23	37	0	.256	.453
Albert Belle	OF110 DH31	R	33	141	559	71	157	37	1	23	103	52	68	0	.281	.453
B.J. Surhoff	OF102 DH11	L	35	103	411	56	120	27	0	13	57	29	46	7	.292	.453
Charles Johnson	C83 DH1	R	28	84	286	52	84	16	0	21	55	32	69	2	.294	.570
Harold Baines	DH62	L	41	72	222	24	59	8	0	10	30	29	39	0	.266	.437
Jeff Conine	3B44 1B39 DH20 OF19	R	34	119	409	53	116	20	2	13	46	36	53	4	.284	.438
Luis Matos	OF69 DH3	R	21	72	182	21	41	6	3	1	17	12	30	13	.225	.308
Mark Lewis	3B29 2B21 SS14 DH4	R	30	71	163	19	44	17	0	2	11	12	31	7	.270	.411
Chris Richard	1B53 OF1 DH1	L	26	56	199	38	55	14	2	13	36	15	38	7	.276	.563
Melvin Mora	SS52 2B1	R	28	53	199	25	58	9	1	4	17	17	32	5	.291	.397
Brook Fordyce	C52	R	30	53	177	23	57	11	0	9	28	11	27	0	.322	.537
Jerry Hairston	2B49	R	24	49	180	27	46	5	0	5	19	21	22	8	.256	.367
Greg Myers	C28 DH9	L	34	43	125	9	28	6	0	3	12	8	29	0	.224	.344
Ryan Minor	3B26 1B5	R	26	32	84	4	11	1	0	3	3	3	20	0	.131	.143
Trenidad Hubbard	OF24 DH6	R	36	31	27	3	5	1	0	0	3	2	5	1	.185	.259
Rich Amaral (LJ)	OF19 DH5 1B1	R	38	30	60	10	13	1	1	0	6	7	8	6	.217	.267
Eugene Kingsale (LJ)	OF24 DH1	B	23	26	88	13	21	2	1	0	9	2	14	1	.239	.284
Ivanon Coffie	3B15 SS4 DH1	R	23	23	60	6	13	4	1	0	6	5	11	1	.217	.317
Jesse Garcia	2B6 SS5	R	26	14	17	2	1	0	0	0	0	2	3	0	.059	.059
Fernando Lunar	C9	R	23	9	16	0	2	0	0	0	1	0	4	0	.125	.125
Karim Garcia	DH4 OF2	L	24	8	16	0	0	0	0	0	0	0	6	0	.000	.000
Willie Morales	C3	R	27	3	11	1	3	1	0	0	0	3	4	0	.273	.364
Mike Kinkade	DH2 1B1	R	27	3	7	0	3	1	0	0	1	0	0	0	.429	.571
Carlos Casimiro	DH2	R	23	2	8	0	1	0	0	0	0	3	0	2	.125	.250

NAME	T	AGE	W	L	PCT	SV	G	GS	CG	IP	H	BB	SO	SHO	ERA
		29	74	88	.457	33	162	162	14	1433	1547	665	1017	6	5.37
Jose Mercedes	R	29	14	7	.667	0	36	20	1	146	150	64	70	0	4.02
Mike Mussina	R	31	11	15	.423	0	34	34	6	238	236	46	210	1	3.79
Pat Rapp	R	32	9	12	.429	0	31	30	0	174	203	83	106	0	5.90
Sidney Ponson	R	23	9	13	.409	0	32	32	6	222	223	83	152	1	4.82
Buddy Groom	L	34	6	3	.667	4	70	0	0	59	63	21	44	0	4.85
Scott Erickson (EJ)	R	32	5	8	.385	0	16	16	1	93	127	48	41	0	7.87
Mike Trombley	R	34	5	4	.444	4	75	0	0	72	67	38	72	0	4.13
Chuck McElroy	L	32	3	0	1.000	0	43	2	0	63	60	34	50	0	4.69
2 Alan Mills	R	33	2	0	1.000	1	23	0	0	24	25	19	18	0	6.46
1 Tim Worrell	R	32	2	2	.500	0	7	12	5					0	7.36
B.J. Ryan	L	24	2	3	.400	0	42	0	0	43	36	31	41	0	5.91
1 Mike Timlin	R	34	2	4	.333	11	37	0	0	35	37	15	26	0	4.89
John Parrish	L	22	2	4	.333	0	8	8	0	36	40	35	28	0	7.18
1 Alberto Reyes	R	29	1	0	1.000	0	13	0	0	13	13	11	10	0	6.92
Jay Spurgeon	R	24	1	1	.500	0	4	4	0	24	26	15	11	0	6.00
Jason Johnson	R	26	1	10	.091	0	25	13	0	108	119	61	79	0	7.02
Calvin Maduro (EJ)	R	25	0	0	—	0	15	2	0	23	29	16	18	0	9.64
1 Gabe Molina	R	25	0	0	—	0	9	0	0	13	25	9	8	0	9.00
2 Darren Holmes	R	34	0	0	—	0	5	0	0	5	13	5	6	0	25.07
2 Luis Rivera	R	22	0	0	—	0	1	0	0	0.2	1	1	0	0	0.00
Ryan Kohlmeier	R	23	0	1	.000	13	25	0	0	26	30	15	17	0	2.39
Leslie Brea	R	26	0	1	.000	0	6	1	0	9	12	10	5	0	11.00

TAMPA BAY — 5th 69-92 .429 18 — LARRY ROTHSCHILD

Name	G by Pos	B	AGE	G	AB	R	H	2B	3B	HR	RBI	BB	SO	SB	BA	SA
TOTALS			30	161	5505	733	1414	253	22	162	692	558	1022	90	.257	.399
Fred McGriff	1B144 DH10	L	36	158	566	82	157	18	0	27	106	91	120	2	.277	.452
Miguel Cairo	2B108 DH2	R	26	119	375	49	98	18	2	1	34	24	34	28	.261	.328
Felix Martinez	SS106	B	26	108	299	42	64	11	4	2	17	32	68	9	.214	.298
Vinny Castilla (XJ)	3B83	R	32	85	331	22	73	9	1	6	42	14	41	1	.221	.308
Jose Guillen	OF99	R	24	105	316	40	80	16	5	10	41	18	65	3	.253	.430
Gerald Williams	OF138 DH7	R	34	146	632	87	173	30	2	21	89	34	103	12	.274	.427
Greg Vaughn	OF72 DH52	R	34	127	461	83	117	27	1	28	74	80	128	8	.254	.499
John Flaherty	C108	R	32	109	394	36	103	15	0	10	39	20	57	0	.261	.376
Jose Canseco (FJ)	DH60	R	35	61	218	31	56	15	0	9	30	41	65	2	.257	.450
Steve Cox	OF56 1B24 DH17	L	25	116	318	44	90	19	1	11	35	46	47	1	.283	.453
Russ Johnson	3B49 2B18 SS11	R	27	74	185	28	47	8	0	2	17	25	30	4	.254	.330
Bubba Trammell	OF48 DH9	R	28	66	189	19	52	11	2	7	33	21	30	3	.275	.466
Ozzie Guillen	SS42 3B11 1B5 2B2	L	36	63	107	22	26	6	1	0	12	6	7	1	.243	.336
Mike DiFelice	C59	R	31	60	204	23	49	13	1	6	19	12	40	0	.240	.402
Randy Winn	OF47 DH1	B	26	51	159	28	40	5	0	1	16	26	25	6	.252	.302
Bobby Smith (KJ)	2B45 3B5	R	26	49	175	21	41	8	0	6	26	14	59	2	.234	.383
Kevin Stocker	SS40	R	30	40	114	20	30	7	1	2	8	19	27	1	.263	.395
Aubrey Huff	3B37	L	23	39	122	12	35	7	0	4	14	5	18	0	.287	.443
Jason Tyner	OF31 DH1	L	23	37	83	6	20	2	0	0	4	4	12	6	.241	.265
Dave Martinez	OF28	L	35	29	104	12	27	4	2	1	12	10	17	1	.260	.365
Quinton McCracken	OF11	R	30	15	31	5	4	0	0	0	2	6	4	0	.129	.129
Tony Graffanino	2B6 3B3 SS1	R	28	13	20	8	6	1	0	0	1	6	4	0	.300	.350
Ozzie Timmons	OF9 DH1	R	29	12	41	9	14	3	0	4	13	1	7	0	.341	.707
Herbert Perry	3B7 1B1	R	30	7	28	2	6	1	0	0	1	2	2	0	.214	.250
Toby Hall	C4	R	24	4	12	1	2	0	0	1	1	1	0	0	.167	.417
Damian Rolls (SJ)	3B1 DH1	R	22	2	3	1	1	0	0	0	0	0	1	0	.333	.333
Kenny Kelly	DH1	R	21	2	1	0	0	0	0	0	0	0	0	0	.000	.000

NAME	T	AGE	W	L	PCT	SV	G	GS	CG	IP	H	BB	SO	SHO	ERA
		31	69	92	.429	38	161	161	10	1431	1553	533	955	8	4.86
Albie Lopez	R	28	11	13	.458	2	45	24	4	185	199	70	96	1	4.13
1 Jim Mecir	R	30	7	2	.778	1	38	0	0	50	35	22	33	0	3.08
Esteban Yan	R	25	7	8	.467	0	43	20	0	138	158	42	111	0	6.21
Bryan Rekar	R	28	7	10	.412	0	30	27	2	173	200	39	95	0	4.41
1 Steve Trachsel	R	29	6	10	.375	0	23	23	3	138	160	49	78	1	4.58
Ryan Rupe	R	25	5	6	.455	0	18	18	0	91	121	31	61	0	6.92
2 Tanyon Sturtze (UJ)	R	29	4	0	1.000	0	19	5	0	53	47	14	38	0	2.56
Cory Lidle	R	28	4	6	.400	0	31	11	0	97	114	29	92	0	5.03
Roberto Hernandez	R	35	4	7	.364	32	68	0	0	73	76	23	61	0	3.19
1 Rick White	R	31	3	6	.333	2	44	0	0	71	57	26	47	0	3.41
Dave Eiland (PJ)	R	33	2	3	.400	0	17	10	0	55	77	18	17	0	7.24
2 Dwight Gooden	R	35	2	3	.400	0	8	7	0	37	47	20	23	0	6.63
2 Mark Guthrie	L	34	1	1	.500	0	34	0	0	32	33	18	26	0	4.50
Dan Wheeler	R	22	1	1	.500	0	11	2	0	15	21	9	8	0	5.48
Tony Fiore	R	28	1	1	.500	0	11	0	0	15	21	9	8	0	8.40
Travis Harper	R	24	1	1	.333	0	5	1	0	32	30	15	14	1	4.78
Doug Creek	L	31	1	3	.250	0	45	0	0	61	49	39	73	0	4.60
Billy Taylor	R	38	1	3	.250	0	14	0	0	13	13	9	13	0	8.58
Paul Wilson	R	27	1	1	.200	0	11	7	0	51	38	16	40	0	3.35
Jim Morris	L	36	0	0	—	0	16	0	0	10	10	7	10	0	4.35
Mike Duvall	R	25	0	0	—	0	2	0	0	5	1	0	7	0	7.71
Jeff Sparks	R	26	0	1	.000	0	15	0	0	20	13	18	24	0	3.54
Trevor Enders	L	25	0	0	—	0	8	0	0	9	14	5	5	0	10.61
Juan Guzman (SJ)	R	33	0	1	.000	0	1	1	0	1	1	2	3	0	43.20
Wilson Alvarez (SJ) 30		Tony Saunders (BA-VT) 26													

CENTRAL DIVISION

CHICAGO — 1st 95-67 .586 — JERRY MANUEL

Name	G by Pos	B	AGE	G	AB	R	H	2B	3B	HR	RBI	BB	SO	SB	BA	SA
TOTALS			27	162	5646	978	1615	325	33	216	926	591	960	119	.286	.470
Paul Konerko	1B122 3B7 DH7	R	24	143	524	84	156	31	2	21	97	47	72	1	.298	.481
Ray Durham	2B151	R	28	151	614	121	172	35	9	17	75	75	105	23	.280	.450
Jose Valentin	SS141 OF1	B	30	144	568	107	155	37	6	25	92	59	106	19	.273	.491
Herbert Perry	3B104 1B3 DH3	R	30	109	383	69	118	29	1	12	61	22	64	4	.308	.483
Magglio Ordonez	OF152	R	26	152	588	102	185	34	3	32	126	60	64	18	.315	.546
Chris Singleton	OF145 DH1	L	27	147	511	83	130	22	5	11	62	35	85	22	.254	.382
Carlos Lee	OF149 DH1	R	24	152	572	107	172	29	2	24	92	38	94	13	.301	.484
Brook Fordyce (BF)	C40	R	30	40	125	18	34	7	1	5	21	6	23	0	.272	.464
Frank Thomas	DH127 1B30	R	32	159	582	115	191	44	0	43	143	112	94	1	.328	.625
Jeff Abbott	OF65 DH7	R	27	80	215	31	59	15	1	3	29	21	38	2	.274	.395
Mark Johnson	C74 DH1	L	24	75	213	29	48	11	0	3	23	27	40	1	.225	.319
Greg Norton	3B47 1B17 DH3	B	27	71	201	25	49	6	1	6	28	26	47	1	.244	.373
Tony Graffanino	SS21 2B19 3B12 DH3	R	28	54	148	25	40	5	2	1	16	21	25	7	.270	.358
Charles Johnson	C43	R	28	44	135	24	44	8	0	10	36	20	37	0	.326	.607
Josh Paul	C34 OF1	R	25	36	71	15	20	3	0	2	9	5	17	1	.282	.423
McKay Christensen	OF29	L	24	32	19	4	2	1	0	0	1	1	6	1	.105	.105
Jeff Wilson (XJ)	3B15 SS10 2B4	R	29	28	73	12	19	3	0	1	9	7	11	0	.260	.301
Harold Baines	DH16	L	41	24	61	2	13	6	0	2	9	7	11	0	.213	.344
Joe Crede	3B6 DH1	R	22	7	14	2	5	1	0	1	4	0	2	0	.357	.429
Jeff Liefer	OF5 1B1	L	25	5	11	0	2	1	0	0	0	0	2	0	.182	.182
Brian Simmons (LJ) 26																

NAME	T	AGE	W	L	PCT	SV	G	GS	CG	IP	H	BB	SO	SHO	ERA
		26	95	67	.586	43	162	162	5	1450	1509	614	1037	7	4.66
Mike Sirotka	L	29	15	10	.600	0	32	32	1	197	203	69	128	0	3.79
James Baldwin	R	28	14	7	.667	0	29	29	2	178	185	59	116	1	4.65
Jim Parque	L	25	13	6	.684	0	33	32	0	187	208	71	111	0	4.28
Cal Eldred (EJ)	R	32	10	2	.833	0	20	20	2	112	103	59	97	1	4.58
Kelly Wunsch	L	27	6	3	.667	1	83	0	0	61	50	29	51	0	2.93
Kip Wells	R	23	6	9	.400	0	23	20	0	99	126	58	71	0	6.02
Sean Lowe	R	29	4	1	.800	0	54	5	0	71	78	39	53	0	5.48
Mark Buehrle	L	21	4	1	.800	0	28	3	0	51	55	19	37	0	4.21
Lorenzo Barcelo	R	22	4	2	.667	0	22	1	0	39	34	9	26	0	3.69
Jon Garland	R	20	4	8	.333	0	15	13	0	70	82	40	42	0	6.46
Keith Foulke	R	27	3	1	.750	34	72	0	0	88	66	22	91	0	2.97
1 Jesus Pena	L	25	2	1	.667	1	20	0	0	23	25	16	19	0	5.40
Bill Simas	R	28	2	3	.400	0	60	0	0	68	69	22	48	0	3.46
Bob Howry	R	26	2	4	.333	7	65	0	0	71	54	29	60	0	3.17
Chad Bradford	R	25	1	0	1.000	0	12	0	0	14	13	1	9	0	1.98
Matt Ginter	R	22	1	0	1.000	0	4	0	0	8	10	5	2	0	13.50
Scott Eyre	L	28	1	1	.500	0	13	1	0	19	29	12	16	0	6.63
Rocky Biddle	R	24	1	2	.333	0	4	1	0	8	11	5	8	0	8.34
1 Tanyon Sturtze	R	29	1	3	.333	0	10	1	0	16	25	15	6	0	12.06
Kevin Beirne	R	25	1	2	.333	0	11	0	0	50	50	20	41	0	6.70
Aaron Myette (BH)	R	22	0	0	—	0	2	0	0	2	1	1	0	0	0.00
2 Ken Hill	R	34	0	1	.000	0	3	0	0	3	5	6	0	0	24.00

CLEVELAND — 2nd 90-72 .556 5 — CHARLIE MANUEL

Name	G by Pos	B	AGE	G	AB	R	H	2B	3B	HR	RBI	BB	SO	SB	BA	SA
TOTALS			30	162	5683	950	1639	310	30	221	889	685	1057	113	.288	.470
Jim Thome	1B107 DH48	R	29	158	557	106	150	33	1	37	106	118	171	1	.269	.531
Roberto Alomar	2B155	B	32	155	610	111	189	40	2	19	89	64	82	39	.310	.475
Omar Vizquel	SS156	B	33	156	613	101	176	27	3	7	66	87	72	22	.287	.375
Travis Fryman	3B154 1B1 DH1	R	31	155	574	93	184	38	4	22	106	73	111	1	.321	.516
Manny Ramirez (LJ)	OF93 DH25	R	28	118	439	92	154	34	2	38	122	86	117	1	.351	.697
Kenny Lofton	OF135 DH1	L	33	137	543	107	151	23	5	15	73	79	72	30	.278	.422
1 Richie Sexson	OF58 1B27 DH10	R	25	91	333	45	83	16	1	16	44	25	96	1	.256	.460
Sandy Alomar	C95 DH1	R	34	97	356	44	103	16	2	7	42	16	41	2	.289	.404
1 David Justice	OF47 DH20	L	34	68	249	46	66	14	1	21	58	38	49	1	.265	.582
Jolbert Cabrera	OF74 2B19 SS8 DH2	R	27	100	175	27	44	3	1	2	15	8	15	6	.251	.314
Einar Diaz	C74 3B1	R	27	75	250	29	68	14	2	4	25	11	29	4	.272	.392
Russell Branyan	OF33 DH23 3B1	L	24	67	193	32	46	7	2	16	38	22	76	0	.238	.544
2 David Segui	1B35 DH16 OF7	B	33	57	223	41	74	13	0	8	46	19	33	1	.332	.498
1 Alex Ramirez	OF31 DH6	R	25	41	112	13	32	5	1	5	12	5	17	1	.286	.482
1 Enrique Wilson	3B12 DH8 2B7 SS7	B	26	40	117	16	38	9	0	2	12	7	11	2	.325	.453
1 Wil Cordero	OF38	R	28	38	148	18	39	11	2	0	17	7	18	0	.264	.365
Bill Selby	OF10 2B6 DH6 3B4	L	30	30	46	8	11	1	0	0	4	1	9	0	.239	.261
Dave Roberts	OF17	L	28	19	10	1	2	0	0	0	0	2	1	2	.200	.200
2 Ricky Ledee	OF7 DH4 1B1	L	26	17	63	13	14	2	1	2	8	8	9	0	.222	.381
Chan Perry	OF7 DH4 1B1	R	27	13	14	1	1	0	0	0	0	0	5	0	.071	.071
Jacob Cruz (KJ)	OF9 DH2	L	27	11	29	3	7	3	0	0	5	5	4	1	.241	.345
John McDonald	SS7 2B2	R	25	9	9	0	4	0	0	0	0	0	1	0	.444	.444
Mark Whiten	OF5	B	33	6	7	2	2	1	0	0	1	3	2	0	.286	.429

NAME	T	AGE	W	L	PCT	SV	G	GS	CG	IP	H	BB	SO	SHO	ERA
		30	90	72	.556	34	162	162	6	1442	1511	666	1213	5	4.84
Dave Burba	R	33	16	6	.727	0	32	32	0	191	199	91	180	0	4.47
Chuck Finley	L	37	16	11	.593	0	34	34	3	218	211	101	189	0	4.17
Bartolo Colon	R	27	15	8	.652	0	30	30	2	188	163	98	212	1	3.88
2 Jason Bere	R	29	6	3	.667	0	11	10	0	54	65	26	44	0	6.63
Justin Speier	R	26	5	2	.714	0	47	0	0	68	57	28	69	0	3.29
Steve Karsay	R	28	5	9	.357	20	72	0	0	77	79	25	66	0	3.76
Paul Shuey (PJ)	R	29	4	2	.667	0	57	0	0	64	51	30	69	0	3.39
Jamie Brewington	R	28	3	0	1.000	0	26	0	0	45	56	19	34	0	5.36
2 Steve Woodard	R	25	3	3	.500	0	13	11	0	54	57	11	35	0	5.67
Jaret Wright (SJ)	R	24	3	4	.429	0	9	9	1	52	44	28	36	1	4.70
Steve Reed	R	35	2	0	1.000	0	57	0	0	56	58	21	39	0	4.34
Ricardo Rincon (EJ)	L	30	2	0	1.000	0	35	0	0	20	17	13	20	0	2.70
Jim Brower	R	27	2	3	.400	0	17	11	0	62	80	31	32	0	6.24
Charles Nagy (EJ)	R	33	2	7	.222	0	11	11	0	57	71	21	41	0	8.21
Tom Martin (SJ)	L	30	1	0	1.000	0	33	0	0	33	32	15	21	0	4.05
Cameron Cairncross	L	28	1	0	1.000	0	15	0	0	9	11	3	8	0	3.86
Tim Drew	R	21	1	0	1.000	0	3	3	0	9	7	5	3	0	10.00
1 Paul Rigdon	R	24	1	1	.500	0	5	4	0	18	21	9	15	0	7.64
1 Scott Kamieniecki	R	36	1	3	.250	0	26	0	0	33	42	20	29	0	5.67
2 Bob Wickman	R	31	1	3	.250	14	26	0	0	27	27	12	11	0	3.38
2 Brian Williams	R	31	0	0	—	0	7	0	0	18	23	8	6	0	4.00
Sean DePaula (EJ)	R	26	0	0	—	0	13	0	0	17	20	14	16	0	5.94
2 Andrew Lorraine	L	27	0	0	—	0	10	0	0	9	8	5	5	0	3.86
Chris Nichting	R	34	0	0	—	0	7	0	0	9	13	5	7	0	7.00
Willie Martinez	R	22	0	0	—	0	1	0	0	3	1	1	1	0	3.00
Alan Newman	L	30	0	0	—	0	1	0	0	1	1	0	0	0	20.25
Chris Haney	L	31	0	0	—	0	1	0	0	1	1	1	0	0	9.00
Bobby Witt	R	36	0	1	.000	0	7	2	0	15	28	6	6	0	7.63
2 Jaime Navarro	R	33	0	1	.000	0	7	2	0	15	20	5	9	0	7.98
Mark Watson	L	26	0	1	.000	0	6	0	0	6	12	4	4	0	8.53
2 Mike Mohler	R	31	0	1	.000	0	2	0	0	1	1	2	3	0	9.00
1 Kane Davis	R	25	0	0	—	0	5	2	0	11	20	8	2	0	14.73

2 Jake Westbrook (VJ) 22 David Riske (XJ) 23

DETROIT — 3rd 79-83 .488 16 — PHIL GARNER

Name	G by Pos	B	AGE	G	AB	R	H	2B	3B	HR	RBI	BB	SO	SB	BA	SA
TOTALS			29	162	5644	823	1553	307	41	177	785	562	982	83	.275	.438
Tony Clark (VJ-XJ)	1B58 DH1	B	28	60	208	32	57	14	0	13	37	24	51	0	.274	.529
Damion Easley	2B125	R	30	126	464	76	120	27	2	14	58	55	79	13	.259	.416
Deivi Cruz	SS156	R	27	156	583	68	176	46	5	10	82	13	43	1	.302	.449
Dean Palmer	3B115 1B20 DH14	R	31	145	524	73	134	22	2	29	102	66	146	4	.256	.471
Juan Gonzalez	OF66 DH48	R	30	115	461	69	133	30	2	22	67	32	84	1	.289	.505
Juan Encarnacion	OF141	R	24	141	547	75	158	25	6	14	72	29	90	16	.289	.433
1 Bobby Higginson	OF145 DH10	L	29	154	597	104	179	44	4	30	102	74	99	15	.300	.538
Brad Ausmus	C150 1B1 2B1 3B1	R	31	150	523	75	139	25	3	7	51	69	79	11	.266	.365
1 Luis Polonia	DH44 OF27	L	35	80	267	37	73	10	5	6	25	22	25	8	.273	.416
Shane Halter	3B55 1B29 SS17 2B10 OF8 C2 P1	R	30	105	238	26	62	12	2	3	27	14	49	5	.261	.366
2 Rich Becker	OF80 DH4	L	28	92	238	48	58	12	0	7	34	56	70	1	.244	.382
Wendell Magee	OF76 DH6	R	27	91	186	31	51	4	2	7	31	10	28	1	.274	.430
Jose Macias	2B39 3B26 OF3 SS1 DH1	B	28	73	173	25	44	3	5	2	24	18	24	2	.254	.364
Robert Fick (SJ)	1B34 C16 DH12	L	26	66	163	18	41	7	2	3	22	22	39	2	.252	.374
Billy McMillon	DH24 OF15	L	28	46	123	20	37	7	1	4	24	19	19	1	.301	.472
Gregg Jefferies (LJ)	1B20 2B14 3B6 DH2 OF1	B	32	41	142	18	39	8	0	2	14	16	10	0	.275	.373
1 Hal Morris (BG)	1B38 OF1	L	34	40	106	15	33	7	0	1	8	19	16	0	.311	.406
Javier Cardona	C26	R	24	26	40	1	7	1	0	1	2	0	9	0	.175	.275
2 Dusty Allen	1B17 3B1 OF1	R	27	18	16	5	7	2	0	2	2	2	7	0	.438	.938
Rodney Lindsey	OF7	R	24	11	1	3	0	0	0	0	0	0	2	0	2	.333	.667
1 Karim Garcia	OF7 DH1	L	24	8	17	1	3	0	0	0	0	1	6	0	.176	.176
Eric Munson	1B3	L	22	3	5	0	0	0	0	0	1	0	1	0	.000	.000
1 Gabe Alvarez	DH1	R	26	1	1	0	0	0	0	0	0	0	0	0	.000	.000

NAME	T	AGE	W	L	PCT	SV	G	GS	CG	IP	H	BB	SO	SHO	ERA
		30	79	83	.488	44	162	162	6	1443	1583	496	978	4	4.71
Brian Moehler	R	28	12	9	.571	0	29	29	2	178	222	40	103	0	4.50
Jeff Weaver	R	23	11	15	.423	0	31	30	2	200	205	52	136	0	4.32
Willie Blair	R	34	10	6	.625	0	47	17	0	157	185	35	74	0	4.88
Hideo Nomo	R	31	8	12	.400	0	32	31	1	190	191	89	181	0	4.74
Steve Sparks	R	34	7	5	.583	1	20	15	1	104	108	29	53	1	4.07
Dave Mlicki (IL)	R	32	6	11	.353	0	24	21	0	119	143	44	57	0	5.58
Danny Patterson	R	29	5	1	.833	0	58	0	0	57	69	14	29	0	3.97
Nelson Cruz	R	27	5	2	.714	0	29	0	0	41	39	13	34	0	3.07
Doug Brocail	R	33	5	4	.556	0	49	0	0	51	57	14	41	0	4.09
C.J. Nitkowski	L	27	4	9	.308	0	67	11	0	110	124	49	81	0	5.25
Matt Anderson	R	23	3	2	.600	1	69	0	0	74	61	45	71	0	4.72
Todd Jones	R	32	4	4	.333	42	67	0	0	64	67	25	67	0	3.52
1 Jim Poole	L	34	1	0	1.000	0	18	0	0	9	13	1	5	0	7.27
Allen McDill	L	28	0	0	—	0	13	0	0	10	13	1	7	0	7.20
Brandon Villafuerte	R	24	0	0	—	0	5	0	0	4	4	4	1	0	10.38
Erik Hiljus	R	27	0	0	—	0	3	0	0	5	5	3	3	0	7.36
Kevin Tolar	L	29	0	0	—	0	5	0	0	3	1	1	3	0	3.00
Sean Runyan (SJ)	L	26	0	0	—	0	3	0	0	3	2	2	1	0	6.00
Masao Kida (JL)	R	31	0	0	—	0	2	0	0	3	5	0	0	0	10.13
Shane Halter	R	30	0	0	—	0	1	0	0	1	1	1	0	0	—
Adam Bernero	R	23	0	1	.000	0	12	4	0	34	33	13	20	0	4.19
Mark Johnson (XJ)	R	25	0	1	.000	0	9	3	0	24	25	16	11	0	7.50
Dave Borkowski	R	23	0	1	.000	0	2	1	0	5	11	7	1	0	21.94

Seth Greisinger (EJ) 24

KANSAS CITY — 4th 77-85 .475 18 — TONY MUSER

Name	G by Pos	B	AGE	G	AB	R	H	2B	3B	HR	RBI	BB	SO	SB	BA	SA
TOTALS			28	162	5709	879	1644	281	27	150	831	511	840	121	.288	.425
Mike Sweeney	1B114 DH45	R	26	159	618	105	206	30	0	29	144	71	67	8	.333	.523
Carlos Febles (SJ)	2B99	R	24	100	339	59	87	12	1	2	29	36	48	17	.257	.316
Rey Sanchez	SS156	R	32	143	509	68	139	18	2	1	38	28	55	7	.273	.322
Joe Randa	3B156 DH1	R	30	158	612	88	186	29	4	15	106	36	66	6	.304	.438
Jermaine Dye	OF146 DH10	R	26	157	601	107	193	41	2	33	118	69	99	0	.321	.561
Carlos Beltran (KJ)	OF88 DH7	B	23	98	372	49	92	15	4	7	44	35	69	13	.247	.366
Johnny Damon	OF133 DH25	L	26	159	655	136	214	42	10	16	88	65	60	46	.327	.495
Gregg Zaun (EJ)	C76 1B1 2B1	B	29	83	234	36	64	11	0	7	33	43	34	2	.274	.410
Mark Quinn	OF81 DH48	R	26	135	500	76	147	33	2	20	78	35	91	5	.294	.488
Dave McCarty	1B63 OF11 DH7	R	30	103	270	34	75	14	2	12	53	22	68	0	.278	.478
Jeff Reboulet	2B50 3B11 SS5 DH1	R	36	66	182	29	44	7	0	0	14	23	32	3	.242	.280
Luis Ordaz	SS38 2B22	R	24	65	104	17	23	2	0	0	11	5	10	4	.221	.240
Todd Dunwoody (NJ)	OF40 DH11	L	25	61	178	12	37	9	0	1	23	8	42	3	.208	.275
Scott Pose	OF11 DH4	L	33	47	48	6	9	0	0	0	1	6	13	0	.188	.188
Jorge Fabregas (EJ)	C39 DH1	L	30	43	142	13	40	4	0	3	17	8	11	1	.282	.373
Brian Johnson	C37	R	32	37	105	9	26	6	0	4	18	4	28	0	.248	.362
2 Wilson Delgado	2B19 SS12 3B3	B	27	33	83	15	22	1	0	0	7	6	17	1	.265	.277
Hector Ortiz	C26	R	30	26	88	15	34	6	0	0	15	8	5	0	.386	.455
Dee Brown	OF5	L	22	15	25	4	4	1	0	0	4	3	9	0	.160	.200
Ray Holbert	2B1 3B1 SS1	R	29	3	4	0	1	0	0	0	0	0	2	0	.250	.250

NAME	T	AGE	W	L	PCT	SV	G	GS	CG	IP	H	BB	SO	SHO	ERA
		26	77	85	.475	29	162	162	10	1439	1585	693	927	6	5.48
Jeff Suppan	R	25	10	9	.526	0	35	33	3	217	240	84	128	1	4.94
Ricky Bottalico	R	30	9	6	.600	16	62	0	0	73	65	41	56	0	4.83
Blake Stein (BA)	R	26	8	5	.615	0	17	17	1	108	98	57	78	0	4.68
Jose Santiago	R	25	8	6	.571	2	45	0	0	69	70	26	44	0	3.91
Mac Suzuki	R	25	8	10	.444	0	32	29	1	189	195	94	135	1	4.34
Dan Reichert	R	23	8	10	.444	2	44	18	1	153	157	91	94	1	4.70
2 Brian Meadows	R	24	6	2	.750	0	11	10	2	72	84	14	26	0	4.77
Chris Fussell (EJ)	R	24	5	3	.625	0	20	9	0	70	76	44	46	0	6.30
1 Jerry Spradlin	R	32	4	4	.500	7	50	0	0	75	81	27	54	0	5.52
1 Jay Witasick	R	27	3	8	.273	0	22	14	2	89	109	38	67	0	5.94
Jason Rakers	R	27	2	0	1.000	0	11	0	0	22	33	7	16	0	9.14
Jose Rosado (SJ)	L	25	2	2	.500	0	9	9	0	70	69	15	55	0	5.86
Chad Durbin	R	22	2	5	.286	0	16	16	0	72	91	43	37	0	8.21
2 Miguel Batista	R	29	2	6	.250	0	14	9	0	57	66	34	30	0	7.74
Dan Murray	R	25	0	0	—	0	11	0	0	19	20	10	16	0	4.66
Scott Mullen	L	25	0	0	—	0	13	0	0	11	9	3	6	0	4.35
Paul Spoljaric	L	29	0	0	—	0	13	0	0	9	19	5	3	0	9.00
1 Brad Rigby	R	23	0	1	.000	0	20	0	0	34	38	11	17	0	4.19
Kris Wilson	R	24	0	0	—	0	7	0	0	17	23	10	14	0	8.10
Brett Laxton	R	26	0	0	—	0	4	1	0	8	9	5	9	0	9.22
Jeff D'Amico	R	25	0	1	.000	0	19	0	0	16	19	15	9	0	9.12
Tim Byrdak	L	26	0	1	.000	0	12	0	0	6	11	4	8	0	11.37
Doug Bochtler	R	29	0	2	.000	0	8	0	0	13	10	4	6	0	6.48
2 Andy Larkin	R	25	0	0	—	0	18	0	0	19	11	17	0	8.84

Orber Moreno (EJ) 23

MINNESOTA — 5th 69-93 .426 26 — TOM KELLY

Name	G by Pos	B	AGE	G	AB	R	H	2B	3B	HR	RBI	BB	SO	SB	BA	SA
TOTALS			27	162	5615	748	1516	325	49	116	711	556	1021	90	.270	.407
Ron Coomer	1B124 DH9 3B5	R	33	144	544	64	147	29	1	16	82	36	50	2	.270	.415
Jay Canizaro	2B90 DH2	R	26	102	346	43	93	21	1	7	40	24	57	4	.269	.396
Cristian Guzman	SS151 DH1	B	22	156	631	89	156	25	20	8	54	46	101	28	.247	.388
Corey Koskie	3B139 DH1	L	27	146	474	79	142	32	4	9	65	77	104	5	.300	.441
Matt Lawton	OF143 DH16	L	28	156	561	99	160	44	2	13	88	91	63	23	.305	.460
Torii Hunter	OF99	R	24	99	336	44	94	14	7	5	44	18	68	4	.280	.408
Jacque Jones	OF147	L	25	154	523	66	149	26	5	19	76	26	111	7	.285	.463
Matt LeCroy	C49 1B3 DH3	R	24	58	167	18	29	10	0	5	17	17	38	0	.174	.323
David Ortiz	DH88 1B27	L	24	130	415	59	117	36	1	10	63	57	81	1	.282	.446
Denny Hocking	OF51 2B47 3B16 SS15 1B12 DH2	B	30	134	373	52	111	24	4	4	47	48	77	7	.298	.416
1 Midre Cummings	OF40 DH15	L	28	77	181	28	50	10	0	4	22	11	25	0	.276	.398
1 Butch Huskey	DH39 OF15 1B9	R	28	64	215	22	48	13	0	5	27	25	49	0	.223	.353
Jason Maxwell	2B30 3B19 DH7 SS5 OF2	R	28	64	111	14	27	6	0	1	11	9	32	2	.243	.324
Marcus Jensen	C49 DH1	B	27	52	133	16	29	7	1	3	14	24	36	0	.218	.353
Chad Moeller	C48	R	25	48	128	13	27	3	1	1	9	9	33	1	.211	.273
A.J. Pierzynski	C32	L	23	33	110	9	34	8	0	2	11	5	14	1	.307	.455
Brian Buchanan	OF25 DH2	R	26	30	82	10	19	4	0	0	10	6	25	0	.232	.305
1 Todd Walker	2B19 DH2	L	27	25	81	14	18	6	1	0	3	7	10	0	.234	.325
Luis Rivas	2B14 SS2	R	20	16	58	8	14	4	0	0	6	2	4	2	.310	.414
Chad Allen	OF15	R	25	15	40	4	9	1	0	1	7	3	10	0	.300	.360
Danny Ardoin	C15	R	25	15	32	4	4	1	0	0	1	3	9	0	.125	.250
John Barnes	OF11	R	24	11	37	5	13	4	0	0	6	2	6	0	.351	.459
Casey Blake	3B5 1B1 DH1	R	26	7	16	1	3	0	0	0	2	0	5	0	.188	.313
Doug Mientkiewicz	1B3	L	26	3	14	0	4	0	0	0	0	2	2	0	.429	.429

NAME	T	AGE	W	L	PCT	SV	G	GS	CG	IP	H	BB	SO	SHO	ERA
		27	69	93	.426	35	162	162	6	1433	1634	516	1042	4	5.14
Eric Milton	L	24	13	10	.565	0	33	33	0	200	205	44	160	0	4.86
Mark Redman	L	26	12	9	.571	0	32	24	0	151	168	45	117	0	4.76
Brad Radke	R	27	12	16	.429	0	34	34	4	227	261	51	141	1	4.45
Eddie Guardado	L	29	7	4	.636	9	70	0	0	62	55	25	52	0	3.94
Joe Mays	R	24	7	15	.318	0	31	28	2	160	193	67	102	1	5.56
1 Hector Carrasco	R	30	4	3	.571	1	61	0	0	72	75	33	57	0	4.25
Sean Bergman	R	30	4	5	.444	0	15	14	0	68	111	33	35	0	9.66
Matt Kinney	R	23	2	2	.500	0	8	8	0	42	41	25	24	0	5.10
Johan Santana	L	21	2	3	.400	0	30	5	0	86	102	54	64	0	6.49
Travis Miller	L	27	1	3	.250	0	62	0	0	67	83	32	62	0	3.90
LaTroy Hawkins	R	27	2	5	.286	14	66	0	0	88	85	32	59	0	3.39
J.C. Romero (SJ)	L	24	2	7	.222	0	11	10	0	58	72	30	50	0	7.02
Jack Cressend	R	25	0	0	—	0	11	0	0	14	20	6	6	0	5.27
Danny Mota	R	24	0	0	—	0	5	0	0	8	13	8	8	0	8.44
Jay Ryan	R	25	0	1	.000	0	16	1	0	26	37	10	19	0	7.62
Mike Lincoln (EJ)	R	25	0	4	.000	0	14	6	0	36	49	8	15	0	10.89
Bob Wells	R	33	0	7	.000	10	76	0	0	86	80	15	76	0	3.65

OAKLAND — 1st 91-70 .565 — ART HOWE

Name	G by Pos	B	AGE	G	AB	R	H	2B	3B	HR	RBI	BB	SO	SB	BA	SA
TOTALS			28	161	5560	947	1501	281	23	239	908	750	1159	40	.270	.458
Jason Giambi	1B124 DH24	L	29	152	510	108	170	29	1	43	137	137	96	2	.333	.647
Randy Velarde (KJ)	2B122	R	37	122	485	82	135	23	0	12	41	54	95	9	.278	.400
Miguel Tejada	SS160	R	24	160	607	105	167	32	1	30	115	66	102	6	.275	.479
Eric Chavez	3B146 SS2 DH1	L	22	153	501	89	139	23	4	26	86	62	94	2	.277	.495
Matt Stairs	OF103 DH37 1B1	L	32	143	476	74	108	26	0	21	81	78	122	5	.227	.414
Terrence Long	OF137	L	24	138	584	104	168	34	4	18	80	43	77	5	.288	.452
Ben Grieve	OF144 DH12	L	24	158	594	92	166	40	1	27	104	73	130	3	.279	.487
Ramon Hernandez	C142	R	24	143	419	52	101	19	0	14	62	38	64	1	.241	.387
John Jaha (SJ)	DH30	R	34	33	97	14	17	1	0	1	5	33	38	1	.175	.216
Ryan Christenson	OF114	R	26	121	129	31	32	2	2	4	18	19	33	1	.248	.388
Jeremy Giambi	OF55 DH21 1B15	L	25	104	260	42	66	10	2	10	50	32	61	0	.254	.423
Olmedo Saenz (LJ)	DH27 3B18 1B17	R	29	76	214	40	67	12	2	9	33	25	40	1	.313	.514
Frank Menechino	2B51 SS5 3B4 DH4 P1	R	29	66	145	31	37	9	1	6	26	20	45	1	.255	.455
Adam Piatt	OF29 3B13 DH13 1B3	R	24	60	157	24	47	5	5	5	23	23	44	0	.299	.490
Sal Fasano	OF19 DH2	R	28	52	121	21	27	6	0	7	19	14	47	0	.214	.429
Mike Stanley	1B19 DH8	R	37	32	97	11	26	7	0	4	18	14	21	0	.268	.464
Rich Becker	OF19 DH2	L	28	23	47	11	11	2	0	1	5	11	17	1	.234	.340
Jorge Velandia	2B14 SS4	R	25	18	24	1	3	1	0	0	2	0	6	1	.125	.167
Bo Porter	OF16	R	27	13	13	3	2	0	0	1	2	2	5	0	.154	.385
Eric Byrnes	OF4 DH2	R	24	10	10	5	3	0	0	0	0	0	1	2	.300	.300
Mark Bellhorn	2B2 3B2 SS1	B	25	9	13	2	2	0	0	0	0	2	6	0	.154	.154
Jose Ortiz	DH4 2B3	R	23	7	11	4	2	0	0	0	1	2	3	0	.182	.182
A.J. Hinch	C5 DH1	R	26	8	8	1	2	0	0	0	0	0	5	0	.250	.250
Mario Valdez	1B4	L	25	5	12	0	0	0	0	0	0	0	3	0	.000	.000

NAME	T	AGE	W	L	PCT	SV	G	GS	CG	IP	H	BB	SO	SHO	ERA
TOTALS		31	91	70	.565	43	161	161	7	1435	1535	615	963	11	4.58
Tim Hudson	R	24	20	6	.769	0	32	32	2	202	169	82	169	2	4.14
Gil Heredia	R	34	15	11	.577	0	32	32	2	199	214	66	101	4	4.12
Kevin Appier	R	32	15	11	.577	0	31	31	1	195	200	102	129	1	4.52
Mark Mulder	L	22	9	10	.474	0	27	27	0	154	191	69	88	0	5.44
Barry Zito	L	22	7	4	.636	0	14	14	1	93	64	45	78	1	2.72
Jason Isringhausen	R	27	6	4	.600	33	66	0	0	69	67	32	57	0	3.78
Doug Jones	R	43	4	2	.667	2	54	0	0	73	86	18	54	0	3.93
Omar Olivares (SJ)	R	32	4	8	.333	0	21	16	1	108	134	60	57	0	6.75
2 Jim Mecir	R	30	3	1	.750	4	25	0	0	35	35	14	37	0	2.80
Jeff Tam	R	29	3	3	.500	3	72	0	0	86	86	23	46	0	2.63
T.J. Mathews	R	30	2	3	.400	0	50	0	0	60	73	25	42	0	6.03
Mike Magnante (LJ)	L	35	1	1	.500	0	55	0	0	40	50	19	17	0	4.31
Scott Service	R	33	1	2	.333	1	20	0	0	37	45	19	35	0	6.38
Ariel Prieto	R	30	1	2	.333	1	8	6	0	32	42	13	19	0	5.12
Rich Sauveur	L	36	0	0	---	0	10	0	0	10	13	1	7	0	4.35
Todd Belitz	L	24	0	0	---	0	5	0	0	3	4	4	3	0	2.70
Marcus Jones	R	25	0	0	---	0	1	1	0	2	5	3	1	0	15.43
Jon Ratliff	R	28	0	0	---	0	1	0	0	1	1	0	0	0	0.00
Frank Menechino	R	29	0	0	---	0	1	0	0	1	6	0	0	0	36.00
Luis Vizcaino	R	25	0	1	.000	0	12	0	0	19	25	11	18	0	7.45
1 Ron Mahay	L	29	0	1	.000	0	5	2	0	16	26	9	5	0	9.00

SEATTLE — 2nd 91-71 .562 .5 (Wild Card) — LOU PINIELLA

Name	G by Pos	B	AGE	G	AB	R	H	2B	3B	HR	RBI	BB	SO	SB	BA	SA
TOTALS			32	162	5648	907	1481	300	26	198	869	775	1073	122	.269	.442
John Olerud	1B158	L	31	159	565	84	161	45	0	14	103	102	96	0	.285	.439
Mark McLemore	2B129 OF14	B	35	138	481	72	118	23	1	3	46	81	78	30	.245	.316
Alex Rodriguez	SS148	R	24	148	554	134	175	34	2	41	132	100	121	15	.316	.606
David Bell	3B93 2B48 SS1 DH1	R	27	143	454	57	112	24	2	11	47	42	66	2	.247	.381
Jay Buhner	OF104 DH1	R	35	112	364	50	92	20	0	26	82	59	98	0	.253	.522
Mike Cameron	OF155	R	27	155	543	96	145	28	4	19	78	78	133	24	.267	.438
Rickey Henderson	OF88 DH2	R	41	92	324	58	77	13	2	4	30	63	55	31	.238	.327
Dan Wilson (UJ)	C88 1B1 3B1	R	31	90	268	31	63	12	0	5	27	22	51	1	.235	.336
Edgar Martinez	DH146 1B2	R	37	153	556	100	180	31	0	37	145	96	95	3	.324	.579
Stan Javier	OF88 DH4 1B3	B	36	105	342	61	94	18	5	5	40	42	64	4	.275	.401
Raul Ibanez	OF76 DH4 1B3	L	28	92	140	21	32	8	0	2	15	14	25	2	.229	.329
Carlos Guillen	3B68 SS23	B	24	90	288	45	74	15	2	7	42	28	53	1	.257	.396
Joe Oliver	C66 1B1 DH1	R	34	69	200	33	53	13	1	10	35	14	38	2	.265	.490
Charles Gipson	OF48 3B5 SS5 DH1	R	27	59	29	7	9	1	1	0	3	4	9	2	.310	.414
John Mabry	3B22 OF19 DH5 1B3 P1	L	29	48	103	18	25	5	0	1	7	10	31	0	.243	.320
Al Martin	OF35 DH2	L	32	42	134	19	31	2	4	4	9	8	31	4	.231	.396
Tom Lampkin (EJ)	C28 DH3	L	36	36	103	15	26	6	1	7	23	9	17	0	.252	.534
2 Chris Widger	C6 1B2 DH2 DH1	R	29	10	11	1	1	0	0	1	1	1	2	0	.091	.364
Robert Machado	C8	R	27	8	14	2	3	0	0	1	1	1	4	0	.214	.429
Brian Lesher	1B4 DH1	R	29	5	5	1	4	1	0	0	3	1	0	1	.800	1.400
Carlos Hernandez	3B2	R	24	2	1	0	0	0	0	0	0	0	0	0	.000	.000
Anthony Sanders	OF1	R	26	1	1	1	1	0	0	0	0	0	0	0	1.000	1.000

NAME	T	AGE	W	L	PCT	SV	G	GS	CG	IP	H	BB	SO	SHO	ERA
TOTALS		29	91	71	.562	44	162	162	4	1442	1442	634	998	10	4.49
Aaron Sele	R	30	17	10	.630	0	34	34	2	212	221	74	137	2	4.51
John Halama	L	28	14	9	.609	0	30	30	1	167	206	56	87	1	5.08
Jamie Moyer (SJ)	L	37	13	10	.565	0	26	26	0	154	173	53	98	0	5.49
Freddy Garcia (BA)	R	25	9	5	.643	0	21	20	0	124	112	64	79	0	3.91
Paul Abbott	R	32	9	7	.563	0	35	27	0	179	164	80	100	0	4.22
Brett Tomko	R	27	7	5	.583	1	32	8	0	92	92	40	59	0	4.68
Arthur Rhodes	L	30	5	8	.385	0	72	0	0	69	51	29	77	0	3.78
Gil Meche (SJ)	R	21	4	4	.500	0	15	15	1	86	75	40	60	1	3.78
Jose Mesa	R	34	4	6	.400	1	66	0	0	81	89	41	84	0	5.36
Jose Paniagua	R	26	3	1	.750	0	69	0	0	80	68	38	71	0	3.47
Frankie Rodriguez (SJ)	R	27	2	1	.667	0	23	0	0	57	63	22	19	0	6.27
Kazuhiro Sasaki	R	32	2	5	.286	37	63	0	0	63	42	31	78	0	3.16
Joel Pineiro	R	21	1	0	1.000	0	8	1	0	19	25	13	10	0	5.59
Robert Ramsay	L	26	1	1	.500	0	37	1	0	50	43	40	32	0	3.40
Kevin Hodges	R	27	0	0	---	0	13	0	0	17	18	12	7	0	5.19
John Mabry	L	29	0	0	---	0	1	0	0	0.2	3	1	0	0	27.00

ANAHEIM — 3rd 82-80 .506 9.5 — MIKE SCIOSCIA

Name	G by Pos	B	AGE	G	AB	R	H	2B	3B	HR	RBI	BB	SO	SB	BA	SA
TOTALS			28	162	5628	864	1574	309	34	236	837	608	1024	93	.280	.472
Mo Vaughn	1B147 DH14	L	32	161	614	93	167	31	0	36	117	79	181	2	.272	.498
Adam Kennedy	2B155	L	24	156	598	82	159	33	11	9	72	28	73	22	.266	.403
Gary DiSarcina (SJ)	SS12	R	32	12	36	6	15	2	0	1	1	1	5	0	.395	.526
Troy Glaus	3B156 SS6 DH4	R	23	159	563	120	160	37	1	47	102	112	163	14	.284	.604
Tim Salmon	OF124 DH33	R	31	158	568	108	165	36	2	34	97	104	139	0	.290	.540
Garret Anderson	OF148 DH10	L	28	159	647	92	185	40	3	35	117	24	87	7	.286	.519
Darin Erstad	OF136 DH20 1B3	L	26	157	676	121	240	39	6	25	100	64	82	28	.355	.541
Bengie Molina	C127 DH2	R	25	130	473	59	133	20	2	14	71	23	33	1	.281	.421
Scott Spiezio	DH50 1B29 3B15 OF10 2B2	B	27	123	297	47	72	11	2	17	49	40	56	1	.242	.465
Benji Gil	SS94 2B7 DH6 1B3	R	27	110	301	28	72	14	1	6	23	30	59	10	.239	.352
Orlando Palmeiro	OF72 DH19	L	31	108	243	38	73	20	2	0	25	38	20	4	.300	.399
2 Kevin Stocker	SS69	B	30	70	229	21	45	13	3	0	16	32	54	0	.197	.279
Matt Walbeck	C44 1B2 DH1	B	30	47	146	17	29	5	0	6	12	7	22	0	.199	.356
Edgard Clemente	OF32 DH11	R	24	46	78	4	17	2	0	0	5	0	27	0	.218	.244
2 Ron Gant	OF21 DH12	R	35	34	82	15	19	3	1	6	16	20	18	1	.232	.512
Justin Baughman	2B5 SS5 DH4	R	25	16	22	4	5	2	0	0	3	2	7	2	.227	.318
Shawn Wooten	C4 1B3	R	27	7	9	2	5	1	0	0	1	0	0	0	.556	.667
Keith Luuloa	SS4 2B3	R	25	6	18	3	6	0	0	0	1	1	4	0	.333	.333
Keith Johnson	1B3 2B2 SS1	R	29	6	4	2	2	0	0	0	0	1	2	0	.500	.500
Trent Durrington	2B1	R	24	4	3	0	0	0	0	0	0	0	0	0	.000	.000
Jeff DaVanon (SJ) 26																

NAME	T	AGE	W	L	PCT	SV	G	GS	CG	IP	H	BB	SO	SHO	ERA
TOTALS		29	82	80	.506	46	162	162	5	1448	1534	662	846	3	5.00
Shigetoshi Hasegawa	R	31	10	5	.667	9	66	0	0	96	100	38	59	0	3.48
Ramon Ortiz	R	27	8	6	.571	0	18	18	2	111	96	55	73	0	5.09
Jarrod Washburn (SJ)	R	25	7	2	.778	0	14	14	0	84	64	37	49	0	3.74
Kent Bottenfield	R	31	7	8	.467	0	21	21	0	128	144	56	75	0	5.71
Scott Schoeneweis (VJ)	L	26	7	10	.412	0	27	27	1	170	183	67	78	1	5.45
Seth Etherton (SJ)	R	23	5	1	.833	0	11	11	0	60	68	22	32	0	5.52
Troy Percival	R	30	5	5	.500	32	54	0	0	50	42	30	49	0	4.50
Ken Hill (VJ)	R	34	5	7	.417	0	16	16	0	79	102	53	50	0	6.52
Mark Petkovsek	R	34	4	2	.667	2	64	1	0	81	86	23	31	0	4.33
Tim Belcher (SJ-EJ)	R	38	4	5	.444	0	7	7	0	41	45	22	22	0	6.86
Brian Cooper	R	25	3	8	.333	0	15	15	1	87	105	35	36	1	5.90
Matt Wise	R	24	3	3	.500	0	8	8	0	37	40	13	20	0	5.54
Mike Holtz	L	27	3	4	.429	0	61	0	0	41	37	18	40	0	5.05
Al Levine	R	32	3	4	.429	2	51	5	0	95	98	49	42	0	3.87
Jason Dickson (PJ)	R	27	2	2	.500	0	8	8	0	28	39	7	18	0	6.11
2 Scott Karl	L	28	2	2	.500	0	12	12	0	72	93	37	43	0	6.65
2 Ben Weber	R	30	1	1	1.000	0	15	0	0	15	12	9	8	0	1.84
Lou Pote	R	30	1	1	.500	0	32	1	0	50	44	26	42	0	3.40
Kent Mercker (IL)	L	32	1	3	.250	0	7	7	0	48	57	29	30	0	6.52
Mike Fyhrie	R	30	0	0	---	0	32	0	0	53	54	15	43	0	2.39
Derrick Turnbow	R	22	0	0	---	0	24	1	0	38	36	36	25	0	4.74
2 Bryan Ward	L	28	0	0	---	0	7	0	0	7	8	2	3	0	5.63
Juan Alvarez	L	26	0	0	---	0	11	0	0	6	14	7	2	0	13.50
Brett Hinchliffe	R	25	0	0	---	0	1	0	0	5	4	1	0	0	5.40
Eric Weaver	R	26	0	2	.000	0	18	0	0	20	16	8	0		6.87

TEXAS — 4th 71-91 .438 20.5 — JOHNNY OATES

Name	G by Pos	B	AGE	G	AB	R	H	2B	3B	HR	RBI	BB	SO	SB	BA	SA
TOTALS			29	162	5648	848	1601	330	35	173	806	580	922	69	.283	.446
Rafael Palmeiro	1B108 DH46	L	35	158	565	102	163	29	3	39	120	103	77	2	.288	.558
Luis Alicea	2B129 3B8 DH4 SS2	B	34	139	540	85	159	25	8	6	63	59	75	1	.294	.404
Royce Clayton	SS148	R	30	148	513	70	124	21	5	14	54	42	92	11	.242	.384
Mike Lamb	3B135 DH2	L	24	138	493	65	137	25	2	6	47	34	60	0	.278	.373
Gabe Kapler (LJ)	OF116	R	24	116	444	59	134	32	1	14	66	42	57	8	.302	.473
Ruben Mateo (BL)	OF52	R	22	52	206	32	60	11	0	7	19	10	34	6	.291	.447
Rusty Greer (LJ)	OF97 DH2	L	31	105	394	65	117	34	3	8	65	51	61	4	.297	.459
Ivan Rodriguez (BG)	C87 DH1	R	28	91	363	66	126	27	4	27	83	19	48	5	.347	.667
1 David Segui	DH52 1B38	B	33	93	351	52	118	29	1	11	57	34	51	0	.336	.519
Chad Curtis	OF80 DH16	R	31	108	335	48	91	25	1	8	48	37	71	3	.272	.424
Frank Catalanotto	2B49 DH20 1B17 OF1	L	26	103	282	55	82	13	2	10	42	33	36	6	.291	.457
Scarborough Green	OF65 DH6	B	26	79	124	21	29	1	1	0	9	16	26	10	.234	.258
Bill Haselman	C62	R	34	62	193	23	53	18	0	6	26	15	36	0	.275	.461
3 Ricky Ledee	OF57	L	26	58	213	23	50	6	3	4	38	25	50	6	.235	.347
Scott Sheldon	SS22 3B15 2B12 1B10 C3 OF2 P1 DH1	R	31	58	124	21	35	11	0	4	19	10	37	0	.282	.468
3 Dave Martinez	OF35 1B4	L	35	38	119	14	32	4	1	2	12	14	20	2	.269	.370
Jason McDonald	OF32 DH1	B	28	38	94	15	22	3	0	3	13	17	25	4	.234	.383
Pedro Valdes	OF14 DH4	L	27	30	54	4	15	5	0	1	5	6	7	0	.278	.426
B.J. Waszgis	C23 1B3	R	29	24	45	6	10	1	0	0	4	4	10	0	.222	.244
Tom Evans (SJ)	3B21 1B1 DH1	R	25	23	54	10	15	4	0	0	7	4	9	1	.278	.352
Ruben Sierra	DH14	R	34	20	60	5	14	0	0	2	7	4	9	1	.233	.383
Kelly Dransfeldt	SS14 2B2	R	25	16	26	2	3	1	0	0	2	1	14	0	.115	.192
Randy Knorr	C15	R	31	15	34	5	10	2	0	2	6	1	9	0	.294	.529
Michael Young	2B1	R	23	2	2	0	0	0	0	0	0	0	1	0	.000	.000

NAME	T	AGE	W	L	PCT	SV	G	GS	CG	IP	H	BB	SO	SHO	ERA
TOTALS		28	71	91	.438	39	162	162	4	1429	1683	661	918	4	5.52
Rick Helling	R	29	16	13	.552	0	35	35	0	217	212	99	146	0	4.48
Kenny Rogers	L	35	13	13	.500	0	34	34	2	227	257	78	127	0	4.55
Doug Davis	L	24	7	6	.538	0	30	13	1	99	109	58	66	0	5.38
John Wetteland	R	33	6	5	.545	34	62	0	0	60	67	24	43	0	4.20
Esteban Loaiza	R	28	5	6	.455	1	20	17	0	107	133	31	75	0	5.37
Ryan Glynn	R	25	5	7	.417	0	16	16	0	89	107	41	33	0	5.58
Jeff Zimmerman	R	27	4	5	.444	1	65	0	0	70	80	34	74	0	5.30
Mike Venafro	L	26	3	1	.750	1	77	0	0	56	64	21	32	0	3.83
Mark Clark	R	32	3	5	.375	0	12	8	0	44	66	24	16	0	7.98
Matt Perisho	L	25	2	7	.222	0	34	13	0	105	136	67	74	0	7.37
Tim Crabtree	R	30	2	7	.222	2	68	0	0	80	86	31	54	0	5.15
Darren Oliver (SJ)	L	29	2	9	.182	0	21	21	0	108	151	42	49	0	7.42
Jonathan Johnson	R	25	1	1	.500	0	10	4	0	29	34	19	23	0	6.21
Francisco Cordero	R	25	1	2	.333	0	56	0	0	77	87	48	49	0	5.35
Brian Sikorski	R	25	1	3	.250	0	38	0	0	46	25	32	0		5.73
2 Darwin Cubillan (EJ)	R	27	0	0	---	0	13	0	0	18	32	14	13	0	10.70
Danny Kolb (EJ)	R	25	0	0	---	0	2	0	0	0.2	5	2	0	0	67.50
Scott Sheldon	R	31	0	0	---	0	1	0	0	0.1	0	1	0	0	0.00
Mike Munoz (EJ)	L	34	0	0	.000	0	13	0	0	1	4	6	0	0	13.50
Justin Thompson (SJ) 27																

LINE SCORES

Team	1	2	3	4	5	6	7	8	9	10	11	12	R	H	E

COMPOSITE BATTING										
NAME	POS	G	AB	R	H	2B	3B	HR	RBI	BA

COMPOSITE PITCHING										
NAME	G	IP	H	BB	SO	W	L	SV	ERA

DIVISION SERIES

DIVISION SERIES: NEW YORK 3 : OAKLAND 2

Game 1 October 3 at Oakland

	1	2	3	4	5	6	7	8	9	R	H	E
NYA	0	2	0	0	0	1	0	0	0	3	7	0
OAK	0	0	0	3	1	0	1	X		5	10	2

Clemens, Stanton (7), Nelson (8) Heredia, Tam (7), Mecir (7), Isringhausen (9)

Game 2 October 4 at Oakland

	1	2	3	4	5	6	7	8	9	R	H	E
NYA	0	0	0	0	0	3	0	0	1	4	8	1
OAK	0	0	0	0	0	0	0	0	0	0	6	1

Pettitte, Rivera (8) Appier, Magnante (7), Tam (8), Jones (8)

Game 3 October 6 at New York

	1	2	3	4	5	6	7	8	9	R	H	E
OAK	0	1	0	0	1	0	0	0	0	2	4	2
NYA	0	2	0	1	0	0	0	1	X	4	6	1

Hudson Hernandez, Rivera (8)

Game 4 October 7 at New York

	1	2	3	4	5	6	7	8	9	R	H	E
OAK	3	0	0	0	0	3	0	1	4	11	11	0
NYA	0	0	0	0	0	1	0	0	0	1	8	0

Zito, Mecir (6), Magnante (7), Jones (9) Clemens, Stanton (6), Choate (7), Gooden (8)

Game 5 October 8 at Oakland

	1	2	3	4	5	6	7	8	9	R	H	E
NYA	6	0	0	1	0	0	0	0	0	7	12	0
OAK	0	2	1	2	0	0	0	0	0	5	13	0

Pettitte, Stanton (4), Nelson (6), Hernandez (8), Rivera (8) Heredia, Tam (1), Appier (2), Mecir (6), Isringhausen (9)

DIVISION SERIES: SEATTLE 3 : CHICAGO 0

Game 1 October 3 at Chicago

	1	2	3	4	5	6	7	8	9	10	R	H	E
SEA	2	1	0	0	0	0	0	1	0	3	7	13	0
CHI	0	2	2	0	0	0	0	0	0	0	4	9	0

Garcia, Tomko (4), Paniagua (7), Rhodes (9), Mesa (9), Sasaki (10) Parque, Howry (7), Bradford (7), Wunsch (8), Simas (8), Foulke (10)

Game 2 October 4 at Chicago

	1	2	3	4	5	6	7	8	9	R	H	E
SEA	0	2	0	1	1	0	0	0	1	5	9	1
CHI	1	0	1	0	0	0	0	0	0	2	5	1

Abbott, Rhodes (6), Mesa (7), Sasaki (9) Sirotka, Barcelo (6), Wunsch (8), Simas (8), Buehrle (9)

Game 3 October 6 at Seattle

	1	2	3	4	5	6	7	8	9	R	H	E
CHI	0	1	0	0	0	0	0	0	0	1	3	1
SEA	0	0	0	1	0	0	0	0	1	2	6	0

Baldwin, Howry (7), Wunsch (9), Foulke (9) Sele, Rhodes (8), Paniagua (9)

AMERICAN LEAGUE CHAMPIONSHIP

CHAMPIONSHIP: NEW YORK 4 : SEATTLE 2

Game 1 October 10 at New York

	1	2	3	4	5	6	7	8	9	R	H	E
SEA	0	0	0	0	1	1	0	0	0	2	5	0
NYA	0	0	0	0	0	0	0	0	0	0	6	1

Garcia, Paniagua (7), Rhodes (8), Sasaki (9) Neagle, Nelson (6), Choate (9), Grimsley (9)

Game 2 October 11 at New York

	1	2	3	4	5	6	7	8	9	R	H	E
SEA	0	0	1	0	0	0	0	0	0	1	7	2
NYA	0	0	0	0	0	0	0	7	X	7	14	0

Halama, Paniagua (7), Rhodes (8), Mesa (8) Hernandez, Rivera (9)

Game 3 October 13 at Seattle

	1	2	3	4	5	6	7	8	9	R	H	E
NYA	0	2	1	0	0	1	0	0	4	8	13	0
SEA	1	0	0	1	0	0	0	0	0	2	10	1

Pettitte, Nelson (7), Rivera (8) Sele, Tomko (7), Ramsay (9)

Game 4 October 14 at Seattle

	1	2	3	4	5	6	7	8	9	R	H	E
NYA	0	0	0	0	3	0	0	2	0	5	5	0
SEA	0	0	0	0	0	0	0	0	0	0	1	0

Clemens Abbott, Ramsay (6), Mesa (7), Paniagua (9)

Game 5 October 15 at Seattle

	1	2	3	4	5	6	7	8	9	R	H	E
NYA	0	0	0	2	0	0	0	0	0	2	8	0
SEA	1	0	0	0	5	0	0	0	X	6	8	0

Neagle, Nelson (5), Grimsley (5), Gooden (5), Cone (8) Garcia, Paniagua (6), Rhodes (7), Sasaki (8)

Game 6 October 17 at New York

	1	2	3	4	5	6	7	8	9	R	H	E
SEA	2	0	0	2	0	0	0	3	0	7	10	0
NYA	0	0	3	0	0	6	0	X		9	11	0

Halama, Tomko (4), Paniagua (7), Rhodes (7), Mesa (7) Hernandez, Rivera (8)

DIVISION SERIES — COMPOSITE BATTING

NEW YORK

NAME	POS	G	AB	R	H	2B	3B	HR	RBI	BA
TOTALS		5	168	19	41	12	0	1	19	.244
Williams	CF	5	20	3	5	3	0	0	1	.250
Martinez	1B	5	19	2	8	2	0	0	4	.421
Jeter	SS	5	19	1	4	0	0	0	2	.211
O'Neill	RF	5	19	4	4	1	0	0	0	.211
Justice	LF	5	18	2	4	0	0	1	1	.222
Posada	C	5	17	2	4	2	0	0	1	.235
Brosius	3B	5	17	3	3	1	0	0	1	.176
Sojo	2B	5	16	2	3	2	0	0	5	.188
Hill	DH	4	12	1	1	0	0	0	2	.083
Knoblauch	DH	3	9	1	3	0	0	0	1	.333
Bellinger	LF	2	1	0	1	1	0	0	1	1.000
Polonia	PH	1	1	0	1	0	0	0	0	1.000
Vizcaino	2B	1	0	1	0	0	0	0	0	—

OAKLAND

NAME	POS	G	AB	R	H	2B	3B	HR	RBI	BA
TOTALS		5	167	23	44	9	0	2	22	.263
Chavez	3B	5	21	4	7	3	0	0	4	.333
Tejada	SS	5	20	5	7	2	0	0	1	.350
Velarde	2B	5	20	2	5	1	0	0	3	.250
Long	CF	5	19	2	3	0	0	1	1	.158
Grieve	LF	5	17	1	2	0	0	0	2	.118
Hernandez		5	16	3	6	2	0	0	3	.375
Ja. Giambi	1B	5	14	2	4	0	0	0	1	.286
Saenz	DH	4	13	1	3	0	0	1	4	.231
Je. Giambi	DH-RF	4	9	1	3	0	0	0	1	.333
Stairs	RF	3	9	0	1	1	0	0	0	.111
Piatt	RF-DH	3	6	2	1	0	0	0	0	.167
Christenson	LF-RF	2	2	0	1	0	0	0	1	.500
Porter	RF-CF	2	1	0	1	0	0	0	1	1.000
Menechino	2B	1	1	0	0	0	0	0	0	.000
Fasano	C	1	1	0	0	0	0	0	0	—

SEATTLE

NAME	POS	G	AB	R	H	2B	3B	HR	RBI	BA
TOTALS		3	99	14	28	2	0	4	14	.283
Rodriguez	SS	3	13	0	4	0	0	0	2	.308
Cameron	CF	3	12	2	3	0	0	0	2	.250
Bell	3B	3	11	0	4	1	0	0	1	.364
Martinez	DH	3	11	2	4	1	0	1	2	.364
Olerud	1B	3	10	2	3	0	0	1	2	.300
McLemore	2B	3	9	1	1	0	0	0	0	.111
Ibanez	RF-LF	3	8	2	3	0	0	0	0	.375
Javier	LF	3	6	0	1	0	0	0	1	.167
Henderson	LF	3	5	3	2	0	0	0	0	.400
Buhner	RF	2	5	1	1	0	0	1	1	.200
Oliver	C	2	4	1	1	0	0	1	1	.250
Wilson	C	2	3	0	0	0	0	0	0	.000
Guillen	PH	1	1	0	1	0	0	0	1	1.000
Martin	PH	1	1	0	0	0	0	0	0	.000

CHICAGO

NAME	POS	G	AB	R	H	2B	3B	HR	RBI	BA
TOTALS		3	92	7	17	6	2	1	6	.185
Ordonez	RF	3	11	0	2	0	1	0	1	.182
Lee	LF	3	11	0	1	1	0	0	1	.091
Valentin	SS	3	10	2	3	2	0	0	1	.300
Durham	2B	3	10	2	2	1	0	1	1	.200
Perry	3B	3	9	0	4	1	0	0	1	.444
Johnson		3	9	0	3	0	0	0	0	.333
Singleton	CF	3	9	1	1	0	1	0	1	.111
Konerko	1B	3	9	1	0	0	0	0	0	.000
Thomas	DH-1B	3	9	0	0	0	0	0	0	.000
Baines	DH	2	4	1	1	1	0	0	0	.250
Abbott	CF	1	1	0	0	0	0	0	0	.000
Christensen	CF	1	0	0	0	0	0	0	0	—
Graffanino	3B	1	0	0	0	0	0	0	0	—
Paul	C	1	0	0	0	0	0	0	0	—

DIVISION SERIES — COMPOSITE PITCHING

NEW YORK

NAME	G	IP	H	BB	SO	W	L	SV	ERA
TOTALS	5	44	44	19	31	3	2	3	4.70
Pettitte	2	11.1	15	3	7	1	0	0	3.97
Clemens	2	11	13	8	10	0	2	0	8.18
Hernandez	2	7.1	5	5	5	1	0	0	2.45
Rivera	3	5	2	0	2	0	0	3	0.00
Stanton	3	4.1	5	1	3	1	0	0	2.08
Nelson	2	2	0	2	0	0	0	0	0.00
Gooden	1	1.2	4	1	1	0	0	0	21.60
Choate	1	1.1	0	1	1	0	0	0	6.75

OAKLAND

NAME	G	IP	H	BB	SO	W	L	SV	ERA
TOTALS	5	44	41	16	35	2	3	1	3.48
Appier	2	10.1	10	6	13	0	1	0	3.48
Hudson	1	8	6	4	5	0	1	0	3.38
Heredia	2	6.1	11	3	3	1	1	0	12.79
Zito	1	5.2	7	2	5	1	0	0	1.59
Mecir	3	5.1	1	0	2	0	0	0	0.00
Magnante	2	3	1	0	2	0	0	0	0.00
Tam	3	2	3	1	0	0	0	0	0.00
Isringhausen	2	2	1	0	3	0	0	1	0.00
Jones	2	1.1	0	1	0	0	0	0	0.00

SEATTLE

NAME	G	IP	H	BB	SO	W	L	SV	ERA
TOTALS	3	28	17	15	16	3	0	2	1.93
Sele	1	7.1	3	3	1	0	0	0	1.23
Abbott	1	5.2	5	3	1	1	0	0	1.59
Garcia	1	3.1	6	3	2	0	0	0	10.80
Rhodes	3	2.2	0	2	2	0	0	0	0.00
Tomko	1	2.1	1	0	0	0	0	0	0.00
Paniagua	2	2.1	1	2	3	1	0	0	0.00
Mesa	2	2	1	2	1	0	0	0	0.00
Sasaki	2	2	1	0	5	0	0	2	0.00

CHICAGO

NAME	G	IP	H	BB	SO	W	L	SV	ERA
TOTALS	3	27.1	28	12	13	0	3	0	3.95
Baldwin	1	6	3	3	2	0	0	0	1.50
Parque	1	6	6	1	2	0	0	0	4.50
Sirotka	1	5.2	7	2	0	0	1	0	4.76
Howry	2	2.2	2	4	0	0	0	0	3.38
Foulke	2	2.1	4	2	2	0	1	0	11.57
Barcelo	1	1.2	0	1	0	0	0	0	0.00
Simas	1	1.1	0	1	2	0	0	0	6.75
Wunsch	3	0.2	0	0	0	0	1	0	0.00
Bradford	1	0.2	0	0	0	0	0	0	0.00
Buehrle	1	0.1	2	0	1	0	0	0	0.00

AMERICAN LEAGUE CHAMPIONSHIP — COMPOSITE BATTING

NEW YORK

NAME	POS	G	AB	R	H	2B	3B	HR	RBI	BA
TOTALS		6	204	31	57	10	0	6	31	.279
Justice	LF-RF	6	26	4	6	2	0	2	8	.231
Martinez	1B	6	25	8	8	2	0	1	1	.320
Knoblauch	DH	6	23	1	6	1	0	0	2	.261
Sojo	2B-3B	6	23	1	6	1	0	0	2	.261
Williams	CF	6	23	5	10	1	0	1	3	.435
Jeter	SS	6	22	6	7	0	0	2	5	.318
O'Neill	RF	6	20	0	5	0	0	0	5	.250
Posada	C	6	19	2	3	1	0	0	3	.158
Brosius	3B	6	18	2	4	0	0	0	0	.222
Vizcaino	2B	4	2	3	2	0	0	0	2	1.000
Hill	PH	2	1	0	0	0	0	0	0	.000
Bellinger	LF	5	1	0	0	0	0	0	0	.000

SEATTLE

NAME	POS	G	AB	R	H	2B	3B	HR	RBI	BA
TOTALS		6	191	18	41	12	0	5	18	.215
Rodriguez	SS	6	22	4	9	2	0	2	5	.409
Martinez	DH	6	21	2	5	1	0	1	4	.238
Olerud	1B	6	20	3	7	3	0	1	2	.350
Cameron	CF	6	18	3	2	0	0	0	1	.111
Bell	3B	6	18	0	4	0	0	0	2	.222
McLemore	2B	5	16	2	4	3	0	0	2	.250
Javier	RF-CF-LF	4	14	0	1	0	0	0	0	.071
Wilson	C	4	11	0	1	1	0	0	0	.091
Buhner	RF	4	11	0	2	0	0	0	0	.182
Martin	LF	4	11	1	2	0	0	0	0	.182
Ibanez	LF-RF	6	9	0	0	0	0	0	0	.000
Henderson	LF	3	9	2	2	1	0	0	1	.222
Oliver	C	4	6	0	1	0	0	0	1	.167
Guillen	3B	2	5	1	1	0	0	1	2	.200
Gipson	LF	2	1	0	0	0	0	0	0	.000

AMERICAN LEAGUE CHAMPIONSHIP — COMPOSITE PITCHING

NEW YORK

NAME	G	IP	H	BB	SO	W	L	SV	ERA
TOTALS	6	53	41	21	48	4	2	1	3.06
Hernandez	2	15	13	8	14	2	0	0	4.20
Neagle	2	10	6	7	7	0	2	0	4.50
Clemens	1	9	1	2	15	1	0	0	0.00
Pettitte	1	6.2	9	1	2	1	0	0	2.70
Rivera	3	4.2	4	0	1	0	0	1	1.93
Nelson	3	3	5	0	6	0	0	0	9.00
Gooden	1	2.1	0	1	0	0	0	0	0.00
Grimsley	2	1	2	3	1	0	0	0	0.00
Cone	1	1	0	0	0	0	0	0	0.00
Choate	1	0.1	0	1	0	0	0	0	0.00

SEATTLE

NAME	G	IP	H	BB	SO	W	L	SV	ERA
TOTALS	6	52	57	25	41	2	4	1	5.37
Garcia	2	11.2	10	4	11	2	0	0	1.54
Halama	2	9.1	10	5	3	0	0	0	2.89
Sele	1	6	9	0	4	0	1	0	6.00
Tomko	2	5	3	4	4	0	0	0	7.20
Abbott	1	5	3	3	3	1	0	0	5.40
Paniagua	5	4.1	4	1	4	0	1	0	4.15
Mesa	3	4.1	5	3	3	0	0	0	12.46
Sasaki	2	2.2	3	1	2	0	1	0	0.00
Rhodes	4	2	8	4	5	0	1	0	31.50
Ramsay	2	1.2	2	0	1	0	0	0	0.00

ATLANTA — 1st 95-67 .586 — BOBBY COX

Name	G by Pos	B	AGE	G	AB	R	H	2B	3B	HR	RBI	BB	SO	SB	BA	SA
TOTALS			32	162	5489	810	1490	274	26	179	758	595	1010	148	.271	.429
Andres Galarraga	1B132	R	39	141	494	67	149	25	1	28	100	36	126	3	.302	.526
Quilvio Veras (KJ)	2B82	B	29	84	298	56	92	15	0	4	37	51	50	25	.309	.409
Rafael Furcal	SS110 2B31	B	22	131	455	87	134	20	4	4	37	73	80	40	.295	.382
Chipper Jones	3B152 SS6	B	28	156	579	118	180	38	1	36	111	95	64	14	.311	.566
Brian Jordan	OF130	R	33	133	489	71	129	26	0	17	77	38	80	10	.264	.421
Andruw Jones	OF161	R	23	161	656	122	199	36	6	36	104	59	100	21	.303	.541
Reggie Sanders	OF96	R	32	103	340	43	79	23	1	11	37	32	78	21	.232	.403
Javy Lopez	C132	R	29	134	481	60	138	21	1	24	89	35	80	0	.287	.484
Wally Joyner	1B55	L	38	119	224	24	63	12	0	5	32	31	31	0	.281	.402
Bobby Bonilla	OF64 3B1	B	37	114	239	23	61	13	3	5	28	37	51	0	.255	.397
Keith Lockhart	2B74 3B18	L	36	124	275	32	73	12	3	2	32	29	31	4	.265	.353
Walt Weiss	SS69	B	36	80	192	29	50	6	2	0	18	26	32	1	.260	.313
1 Trenidad Hubbard	OF44	R	36	61	81	15	15	5	2	1	6	11	20	2	.185	.272
2 B.J. Surhoff	OF32	L	35	44	128	13	37	9	2	1	11	12	12	3	.289	.414
George Lombard	OF15	L	24	27	39	8	4	0	0	0	2	1	14	4	.103	.103
Steve Sisco	OF6 2B5 3B2	R	30	25	27	4	5	0	0	1	2	3	4	0	.185	.296
3 Paul Bako	C23 1B1	L	28	24	58	8	11	4	0	2	6	5	15	0	.190	.362
1 Fernando Lunar	C22	R	23	22	54	5	10	1	0	0	3	2	15	0	.185	.204
Mark DeRosa	SS10	R	25	22	13	9	4	1	0	0	3	2	1	0	.308	.385
Eddie Perez (SJ)	C7	R	32	7	22	0	4	1	0	0	3	0	2	0	.182	.227
Wes Helms	3B5	R	24	6	5	0	1	0	0	0	0	0	0	0	.200	.200
Tim Unroe	1B2 OF1	L	29	4	5	0	0	0	0	0	0	0	1	0	.000	.000
Pete Swann	OF3	L	29	4	2	0	0	0	0	0	0	0	0	0	.000	.000
1 Brian Hunter		R	32	2	2	1	1	0	0	1	0	1	0	0	.500	2.000
Mike Hubbard	C1	R	29	2	1	0	0	0	0	0	0	0	0	0	.000	.000

NAME	T	AGE	W	L	PCT	SV	G	GS	CG	IP	H	BB	SO	SHO	ERA
TOTALS		31	95	67	.586	53	162	162	13	1440	1428	484	1093	9	4.05
Tom Glavine	L	34	21	9	.700	0	35	35	4	241	222	65	152	2	3.40
Greg Maddux	R	34	19	9	.679	0	35	35	3	249	225	42	190	3	3.00
John Burkett	R	35	10	6	.625	0	31	22	0	134	162	51	110	0	4.89
Kevin Millwood	R	25	10	13	.435	0	36	35	0	213	213	62	168	0	4.66
Terry Mulholland	L	37	9	9	.500	1	54	20	1	157	198	41	78	0	5.11
2 Andy Ashby	R	32	8	6	.571	0	15	15	2	98	103	23	55	1	4.13
Mike Remlinger	L	34	5	3	.625	12	71	0	0	73	55	37	72	0	3.47
1 Bruce Chen	L	23	4	0	1.000	0	22	0	0	40	35	19	32	0	2.50
2 Scott Kamieniecki	R	36	2	1	.667	2	26	0	0	25	22	22	17	0	5.47
Kerry Ligtenberg	R	29	2	3	.400	12	59	0	0	52	43	24	51	0	3.61
Rudy Seanez (EJ)	R	31	2	3	.333	2	23	0	0	21	15	9	20	0	4.29
Jason Marquis	R	21	1	0	1.000	0	15	0	0	23	23	12	17	0	5.01
1 Luis Rivera	R	22	1	0	1.000	0	7	4	5	9					1.35
John Rocker	L	25	1	2	.333	24	59	0	0	53	42	48	77	0	2.89
Greg McMichael (SJ)	R	33	0	0	—	0	15	0	0	16	12	4	14	0	4.41
2 Stan Belinda	R	33	0	1	.000	0	10	0	0	11	16	5	11	0	9.82
Kevin McGlinchy (SJ)	R	23	0	0	—	0	10	0	0	8	11	6	9	0	2.16
Dave Stevens	R	30	0	0	—	0	2	0	0	3	5	1	4	0	12.00
Ismael Villegas	R	23	0	0	—	0	2	0	0	3	2	1	2	0	13.50
2 Gabe Molina	R	25	0	0	—	0	3	0	0	3	4	3	3	0	9.00
Don Wengert	R	30	0	1	.000	0	10	0	0	10	12	5	7	0	7.20
Chris Seelbach	R	23	0	0	—	0	2	0	0	1	2	2	1	0	10.80

Odalis Perez (EJ) 23 John Smoltz (EJ) 33

NEW YORK — 2nd 94-68 .580 1 (Wild Card) — BOBBY VALENTINE

Name	G by Pos	B	AGE	G	AB	R	H	2B	3B	HR	RBI	BB	SO	SB	BA	SA
TOTALS			30	162	5486	807	1445	281	20	198	761	675	1037	66	.263	.430
Todd Zeile	1B151	R	34	153	544	67	146	36	3	22	79	74	85	3	.268	.467
Edgardo Alfonzo	2B146	R	26	150	544	109	176	40	2	25	94	95	70	3	.324	.542
Rey Ordonez (BA)	SS44	R	28	45	133	10	25	5	0	0	9	17	16	0	.188	.226
Robin Ventura	3B137 1B1	L	32	141	469	61	109	23	1	24	84	75	91	3	.232	.439
Derek Bell	OF143 P1	R	31	144	546	87	145	31	1	18	69	65	125	8	.266	.425
Jay Payton	OF146	R	27	149	488	63	142	23	1	17	62	30	60	5	.291	.447
Benny Agbayani	OF110	R	28	119	350	59	101	19	1	15	60	54	68	5	.289	.477
Mike Piazza	C124	R	31	136	482	90	156	26	0	38	113	58	69	4	.324	.614
Matt Franco	1B28 3B22 OF3 2B1	L	30	101	134	9	32	4	0	2	14	21	22	0	.239	.313
Joe McEwing	OF52 3B19 2B16 SS4	L	27	87	153	20	34	14	1	2	19	5	29	3	.222	.366
Todd Pratt	C71	R	33	80	160	33	44	6	0	8	25	22	31	0	.275	.463
1 Melvin Mora	SS44 OF28 2B4 3B4	R	28	79	215	35	56	13	2	6	30	18	48	7	.260	.423
Kurt Abbott	SS39 2B23 3B2 OF2	R	31	79	157	22	34	7	1	6	12	14	51	1	.217	.389
2 Lenny Harris	3B16 OF11 1B10 2B3	L	35	76	138	22	42	6	3	3	13	17	17	8	.304	.457
2 Mike Bordick	SS56	R	34	56	192	18	50	8	0	4	21	15	28	3	.260	.365
Jon Nunnally (JL)	OF34	L	28	48	74	16	14	5	1	2	6	15	26	3	.189	.365
Darryl Hamilton (FJ)	OF33	L	35	43	105	20	29	4	1	1	6	14	20	2	.276	.362
Bubba Trammell	OF25	R	28	36	56	9	13	2	0	3	12	8	19	1	.232	.429
1 Rickey Henderson	OF29	R	41	31	96	17	21	1	0	0	2	25	20	5	.219	.229
Timo Perez	OF19	L	25	24	49	11	14	4	1	1	3	3	5	1	.286	.469
Mark Johnson	1B4 OF1	L	32	21	22	4	4	0	0	1	6	5	9	0	.182	.318
2 Jorge Velandia	2B7 SS7 3B3	R	25	15	7	1	0	0	0	0	0	2	2	0	.000	.000
1 Jason Tyner	OF12	L	23	13	8	3	8	2	0	0	5	1	4	1	.195	.244
Jorge Toca	1B5 OF1	R	25	8	7	1	3	1	0	0	0	0	1	0	.429	.571
David Lamb	3B3 2B2 SS2	B	25	7	5	1	1	0	0	0	0	1	0	0	.200	.200
Vance Wilson	C3	R	27	4	4	0	0	0	0	0	0	0	0	0	.000	.000
1 Mike Kinkade	OF1	R	27	2	2	0	0	0	0	0	0	0	1	0	.000	.000
Ryan McGuire	OF1	L	28	1	1	0	0	0	0	0	0	0	1	0	.000	.000

NAME	T	AGE	W	L	PCT	SV	G	GS	CG	IP	H	BB	SO	SHO	ERA
TOTALS		32	94	68	.580	49	162	162	8	1450	1398	574	1164	10	4.16
Al Leiter	L	34	16	8	.667	0	31	31	2	208	176	76	200	1	3.20
Mike Hampton	R	27	15	10	.600	0	33	33	3	218	194	99	151	1	3.14
Rick Reed	R	35	11	5	.688	0	30	30	0	184	192	34	121	0	4.11
Bobby J. Jones (LJ)	R	30	11	6	.647	0	27	27	1	155	171	49	85	0	5.06
Glendon Rusch	L	25	11	11	.500	0	31	30	2	191	196	44	157	0	4.01
Turk Wendell	R	33	8	6	.571	1	77	0	0	83	60	41	73	0	3.59
Dennis Cook	L	37	6	3	.667	2	68	0	0	59	63	31	53	0	5.34
Pat Mahomes	R	29	5	3	.625	0	53	5	0	94	96	66	76	0	5.46
John Franco	L	39	5	4	.556	4	62	0	0	56	46	26	56	0	3.40
Armando Benitez	R	27	4	4	.500	41	76	0	0	76	39	38	106	0	2.61
2 Rick White	R	31	3	2	.400	1	28	0	0	28	26	12	20	0	3.81
Eric Cammack	R	24	0	0	—	0	7	0	0	10	7	10	9	0	6.30
Grant Roberts	R	22	0	1	.000	0	7		1	11	4	6	0		11.57
Jim Mann	R	25	0	0	—	0	2	0	0	2	1	3	1	0	10.13
Jerrod Riggan	R	26	0	0	—	0	3	0	0	4	4	1	6	0	0.00
Derek Bell	R	31	0	0	—	0	1	0	0	1	1	0	0	0	36.00
Rich Rodriguez	L	37	0	1	.000	0	32	0	0	37	59	15	18	0	7.78
Bobby M. Jones	R	30	0	1	.000	0	11	1	0	22	18	14	20	0	4.15
Dennis Springer	R	35	0	1	.000	0	2	2	0	11	20	5	5	0	8.74
Bill Pulsipher	L	26	0	2	.000	0	7	1	2	7	12	7	2	0	12.15

FLORIDA — 3rd 79-82 .491 15.5 — JOHN BOLES

Name	G by Pos	B	AGE	G	AB	R	H	2B	3B	HR	RBI	BB	SO	SB	BA	SA
TOTALS			27	161	5509	731	1441	274	29	160	691	540	1184	168	.262	.409
Derek Lee	1B147	R	24	158	477	70	134	18	3	28	70	63	123	0	.281	.507
Luis Castillo	2B136	B	24	136	539	101	180	17	3	2	17	78	86	62	.334	.388
Alex Gonzalez (KJ)	SS104	R	23	109	385	35	77	17	4	7	42	13	77	7	.200	.319
Mike Lowell	3B136	R	26	140	508	73	137	38	4	22	91	54	75	4	.270	.474
Mark Kotsay	OF142 1B2	L	24	152	530	87	158	31	5	12	57	42	46	19	.298	.443
Preston Wilson	OF158	R	25	161	605	94	160	35	3	31	121	55	187	36	.264	.486
Cliff Floyd (KJ)	OF108	L	27	121	420	75	126	30	0	22	91	50	82	24	.300	.529
Mike Redmond	C85	R	29	87	210	17	53	8	1	0	15	13	19	0	.252	.300
Kevin Millar	1B34 OF18 3B13	R	28	123	259	36	67	14	3	14	42	36	47	0	.259	.498
Mark Smith	OF49	R	30	104	192	22	47	8	1	5	27	17	54	2	.245	.375
Dave Berg	SS49 3B13 2B11	R	29	82	210	23	53	14	1	1	21	25	46	3	.252	.343
2 Andy Fox	SS33 OF14 3B12 2B2	L	29	104	164	19	40	4	2	3	10	18	37	8	.244	.348
2 Paul Bako	C50	R	24	50	138	10	33	4	0	2	14	16	36	0	.239	.312
Ramon Castro	C56	R	24	54	89	9	17	4	0	4	12	5	20	1	.191	.371
1 Danny Bautista	OF13 1B5	R	29	41	73	4	14	6	0	2	6	3	33	1	.192	.356
1 Brant Brown	OF32	L	29	36	108	10	29	9	0	2	10	14	23	0	.269	.380
2 Henry Rodriguez	C32	R	32	36	56	9	13	2	0	3	12	8	19	1	.232	.429
Chris Clapinski	2B14 3B3 OF3 SS1	B	28	34	49	12	15	4	1	1	7	5	7	0	.306	.490
Pablo Ozuna	2B7	B	25	14	24	2	8	1	0	0	0	0	2	1	.333	.375
Sandy Martinez	C9	L	29	10	18	1	4	1	0	0	2	1	4	0	.222	.333
Nate Rolison	1B4	L	23	8	13	0	1	0	0	0	0	2	1	0	.077	.077
Mendy Lopez		R	26	4	3	0	0	0	0	0	0	0	1	1	0	.000

NAME	T	AGE	W	L	PCT	SV	G	GS	CG	IP	H	BB	SO	SHO	ERA
TOTALS		28	79	82	.491	48	161	161	5	1430	1477	650	1051	4	4.59
Ryan Dempster	R	23	14	10	.583	0	33	33	2	226	210	97	209	1	3.66
Jesus Sanchez	L	25	9	12	.429	0	32	32	2	182	197	76	123	2	5.34
Brad Penny (SJ)	R	22	8	7	.533	0	23	22	0	120	120	60	80	0	4.81
Dan Miceli (AJ)	R	29	6	4	.600	0	45	0	0	49	45	18	40	0	4.25
Chuck Smith	R	30	6	6	.500	0	19	19	1	123	111	54	118	0	3.23
Braden Looper	R	25	4	3	.571	2	73	0	0	67	71	36	29	0	4.41
Vic Darensbourg	L	29	5	3	.625	0	62	0	0	61	61	28	59	0	4.06
Antonio Alfonseca	R	28	5	6	.455	45	68	0	0	70	82	24	47	0	4.24
Armando Almanza	L	27	4	2	.667	0	67	0	0	46	38	43	46	0	4.86
Alex Fernandez (SJ)	R	30	4	4	.500	0	8	8	0	52	59	16	27	0	4.13
Reid Cornelius	R	30	4	10	.286	0	22	21	0	125	135	50	50	0	4.82
A.J. Burnett (RJ)	R	23	3	7	.300	0	13	13	0	83	80	44	57	0	4.79
Ricky Bones	R	31	2	3	.400	0	56	0	0	77	94	27	59	0	4.54
3 Manny Aybar	R	28	1	0	1.000	0	21	0	0	27	18	13	14	0	2.63
2 Ron Mahay	L	29	1	0	1.000	0	18	0	0	25	31	16	27	0	6.04
Jason Grilli	R	23	1	1	.500	0	1	1	0	7	11	2	3	0	5.40
Joe Strong	R	37	1	1	.500	1	18	0	0	20	16	12	18	0	7.32
Vladimir Nunez	R	25	0	6	.000	0	17	12	0	68	88	34	45	0	7.90

Brian Edmondson (SJ) 27 Michael Tejera (EJ) 23

MONTREAL — 4th 67-95 .414 28 — FELIPE ALOU

Name	G by Pos	B	AGE	G	AB	R	H	2B	3B	HR	RBI	BB	SO	SB	BA	SA
TOTALS			27	162	5535	738	1475	310	35	178	705	476	1048	58	.266	.432
Lee Stevens	1B123	L	32	150	449	60	119	27	2	22	75	48	105	0	.265	.481
Jose Vidro	2B153	B	25	153	606	101	200	51	2	24	97	49	69	5	.330	.540
Orlando Cabrera (SJ)	SS124 2B1	R	25	125	422	47	100	25	1	13	55	25	28	4	.237	.393
Geoff Blum	3B55 SS44 2B13 1B11	B	27	124	343	40	97	20	2	11	45	26	60	1	.283	.449
Vladimir Guerrero	OF151	R	24	154	571	101	197	28	11	44	123	58	74	9	.345	.664
Peter Bergeron	OF146	L	22	148	518	80	127	25	7	5	31	50	98	11	.245	.349
1 Rondell White	OF74	R	28	75	290	52	89	24	0	11	54	28	67	5	.307	.503
1 Chris Widger	C85	R	29	86	281	31	67	17	2	12	34	29	61	1	.238	.441
Wilton Guerrero	OF75 2B1	R	25	127	288	30	77	7	2	2	23	19	41	8	.267	.326
Terry Jones	OF78	B	29	108	168	30	42	8	2	0	13	10	32	7	.250	.321
Michael Barrett	3B55 C28	R	23	89	271	28	58	15	1	1	22	23	35	0	.214	.288
Mike Mordecai	3B58 SS10 2B9 1B3	R	32	86	169	20	48	16	0	4	16	12	34	2	.284	.450
Andy Tracy	3B34 1B27	L	26	83	192	29	50	8	1	11	32	22	61	1	.260	.484
Fernando Seguignol	OF30 1B30	B	25	76	162	22	45	8	0	10	22	9	46	0	.278	.512
Brian Schneider	C43	L	23	45	115	6	27	6	0	0	11	7	24	0	.235	.287
Milton Bradley	OF40	B	22	42	154	20	34	8	1	2	15	14	32	2	.221	.325
Lenny Webster	C32	R	35	39	81	6	17	5	0	2	5	9	10	0	.210	.247
Trace Coquillette	3B19 2B8 OF2	R	26	34	59	6	12	4	0	1	8	7	19	0	.203	.322
Tomas de la Rosa	SS29	R	24	22	32	6	7	1	0	2	6	2	11	2	.219	.469
Talmadge Nunnari	1B14	L	25	18	5	2	1	0	0	0	0	6	4	0	.200	.200
Charlie O'Brien (FJ)	C9	R	40	9	19	1	4	1	0	0	3	0	6	0	.211	.421
Yohanny Valera	C7	R	23	10	7	1	0	0	0	0	0	0	1	0	.000	.000

Bob Henley (EJ) 27

NAME	T	AGE	W	L	PCT	SV	G	GS	CG	IP	H	BB	SO	SHO	ERA
TOTALS		26	67	95	.414	39	162	162	4	1425	1575	579	1011	7	5.13
Dustin Hermanson	R	27	12	14	.462	4	38	30	2	198	226	75	94	1	4.77
Javier Vazquez	R	24	11	9	.550	0	33	33	3	218	247	61	196	1	4.05
Carl Pavano (AJ)	R	24	8	4	.667	0	15	15	0	97	89	34	64	0	3.06
Tony Armas (AJ)	R	22	7	9	.438	0	17	17	0	95	74	50	59	0	4.36
Anthony Telford	R	34	4	4	.556	3	64	0	0	78	76	23	68	0	3.79
Mike Johnson	R	24	5	6	.455	0	41	13	0	101	107	53	70	0	6.39
Felipe Lira	R	28	5	8	.385	0	53	7	0	102	129	36	51	0	5.40
Scott Strickland (SJ)	R	24	4	3	.571	9	49	0	0	48	38	16	48	0	3.02
Mike Thurman (EJ)	R	26	4	9	.308	0	17	17	0	88	112	46	52	0	6.42
Hideki Irabu (KJ-EJ)	R	31	2	5	.286	0	11	11	0	55	77	14	42	0	7.24
Guillermo Mota	R	26	1	1	.500	0	29	0	0	30	27	12	24	0	6.00
Steve Kline	L	27	5	1	.167	14	83	0	0	77	84	27	64	0	3.50
Julio Santana	R	27	1	1	.167	0	36	4	0	67	69	33	58	0	5.67
Trey Moore (SJ)	L	27	1	5	.167	0	35	5	0	55	55	21	24	0	6.62
Sean Spencer	L	25	0	0	—	0	9	0	0	5	4	5	2	0	5.40
Yovanny Lara (AJ)	R	27	0	0	—	0									6.35
2 Brad Rigby	R	27	0	0	—	0	13	0	0	17	28	5	5	0	5.06
1 Matt Skrmetta	R	24	0	0	—	0	3	0	0	3	3	3	1	0	15.19
2 Scott Downs (EJ)	L	24	0	1	.000	0	4	1	0	9	12	5	4	0	9.00
2 Jim Poole	L	38	0	0	—	0	5	0	0	3	6	3	2	0	27.00
1 David Moraga	L	24	0	0	—	0	4	0	0	1	2	4	3	0	37.80
Scott Forster	L	27	0	0	—	0	4	0	0	3	5	3	1	0	7.88
Matt Blank (AJ)	L	24	0	0	—	0	13	0	0	14	12	5	4	0	5.14
1 Ugueth Urbina (AJ)	R	26	0	0	—	0	11	0	0	11	9	3	22	0	4.99
1 Miguel Batista	R	29	0	0	—	0	4	0	0	9	19	3	4	0	14.04
T.J. Tucker	R	21	0	1	.000	0	3	1	0	11	11	3	2	0	11.57
Jeremy Powell	R	24	0	0	—	0	11	0	0	26	35	9	19	0	7.96

Graeme Lloyd (SJ) 33

PHILADELPHIA — 5th 65-97 .401 30 — TERRY FRANCONA

Name	G by Pos	B	AGE	G	AB	R	H	2B	3B	HR	RBI	BB	SO	SB	BA	SA
TOTALS			28	162	5511	708	1386	304	40	144	668	611	1117	102	.251	.400
1 Rico Brogna (BA)	1B34	L	30	38	129	12	32	14	0	1	13	7	28	1	.248	.380
1 Mickey Morandini	2B85	L	34	91	302	31	76	13	3	0	22	29	54	5	.252	.315
1 Desi Relaford	SS81	B	26	83	253	29	56	12	3	3	30	48	45	1	.221	.328
Scott Rolen	3B128	R	25	128	483	88	144	32	6	26	89	51	99	8	.298	.551
Bobby Abreu	OF152	L	26	154	576	103	182	42	10	25	79	100	116	28	.316	.554
Doug Glanville	OF150	R	29	154	637	89	175	27	6	8	52	31	76	31	.275	.374
1 Ron Gant	OF84	R	35	89	343	54	87	16	2	20	38	36	73	5	.254	.487
Mike Lieberthal	C106	R	28	108	389	55	108	30	0	15	71	40	53	2	.278	.470
1,3 Rob Ducey	OF33	L	35	112	152	24	30	4	1	6	25	29	47	1	.197	.355
Pat Burrell	1B58 OF48	R	23	111	408	57	106	27	1	18	79	63	139	0	.260	.463
Kevin Jordan	2B47 3B39 1B9	R	30	109	337	30	74	16	2	5	36	17	41	0	.220	.323
Kevin Sefcik	OF50	R	29	99	153	15	36	6	2	0	10	13	19	4	.235	.301
2 Brian Hunter	1B40 OF9	R	32	85	138	13	29	5	0	7	22	20	39	0	.210	.399
Alex Arias	SS39 3B10 2B1	R	32	70	155	17	29	9	0	2	15	16	28	1	.187	.284
2 Travis Lee	1B47 OF16	L	25	56	180	19	43	11	1	1	14	40	33	3	.239	.328
Tom Prince	C46	R	35	46	122	14	29	9	0	2	16	13	31	1	.238	.361
Tomas Perez	SS44	B	26	45	140	17	31	7	1	1	13	11	30	1	.221	.307
Marlon Anderson	2B41	L	26	41	162	10	37	8	1	1	15	12	22	2	.228	.309
Gary Bennett	C31	R	28	31	74	8	18	5	0	2	5	13	15	0	.243	.392
Jimmy Rollins	SS13	B	21	14	53	5	17	1	1	0	5	2	7	3	.321	.377
2 David Newhan	2B5	L	26	10	17	3	3	0	0	0	0	2	6	0	.176	.176
Reggie Taylor	OF3	L	23	9	11	1	1	0	0	0	0	0	0	1	.091	.091
Chris Pritchett	1B3	L	30	5	11	0	1	0	0	0	0	0	3	0	.091	.091
Clemente Alvarez	C2	R	32	2	5	1	1	0	0	0	0	0	1	0	.200	.200

NAME	T	AGE	W	L	PCT	SV	G	GS	CG	IP	H	BB	SO	SHO	ERA
		29	65	97	.401	34	162	162	8	1439	1458	640	1123	6	4.77
Randy Wolf	L	23	11	9	.550	0	32	32	1	206	210	83	160	1	4.36
Robert Person (SJ)	R	30	9	7	.563	0	28	28	1	173	144	95	164	1	3.63
Chris Brock	R	30	7	8	.467	1	63	5	0	93	85	41	69	0	4.34
1 Curt Schilling	R	33	6	6	.500	0	16	16	4	113	110	32	96	1	3.91
Cliff Politte	R	26	4	3	.571	0	12	8	0	59	55	27	50	0	3.66
Wayne Gomes (EJ)	R	27	4	6	.400	7	65	0	0	74	72	35	49	0	4.40
1 Andy Ashby	R	32	4	7	.364	0	16	16	1	101	113	38	51	0	5.68
1 Bruce Chen	L	23	3	4	.429	0	15	15	0	94	81	27	80	0	3.63
Dave Coggin	R	23	2	0	1.000	0	5	5	0	27	35	12	17	0	5.33
Steve Schrenk	R	31	2	3	.400	0	20	0	0	23	25	13	19	0	7.33
2 Vicente Padilla	R	22	2	6	.250	2	28	0	0	30	40	18	21	0	5.34
Jeff Brantley (AJ)	R	36	2	7	.222	23	55	0	0	55	64	29	57	0	5.86
Paul Byrd (SJ)	R	29	2	9	.182	0	17	15	0	83	89	35	53	0	6.51
2 Omar Daal	L	28	2	9	.182	0	12	12	0	71	81	30	51	0	4.69
Mark Brownson	R	25	1	0	1.000	0	2	0	0	5	7	3	3	0	7.20
Ed Vosberg	L	38	1	1	.500	0	31	0	0	24	21	18	23	0	4.13
2 Kent Bottenfield	R	31	1	2	.333	0	8	8	1	44	41	21	31	1	4.50
Amaury Telemaco	R	26	1	3	.250	0	13	2	0	24	25	14	22	0	6.66
Scott Aldred (SJ)	L	32	1	3	.250	0	20	3	0	23	23	10	21	0	5.75
1 Bryan Ward	L	28	0	0	—	0	20	0	0	19	14	8	11	0	2.33
1 Trever Miller	L	27	0	0	—	0	14	0	0	14	19	9	10	0	8.34
Thomas Jacquez	L	24	0	0	—	1	9	0	0	7	10	3	6	0	11.05
Kirk Bullinger (XJ)	R	30	0	0	—	0	3	0	0	3	4	4	0	0	5.40
Doug Nickle	R	25	0	0	—	0	4	0	0	3	5	2	0	0	13.50
Jason Boyd (SJ-BH)	R	27	0	1	.000	0	30	0	0	34	39	24	32	0	6.55
Mark Holzemer	L	30	0	1	.000	0	25	0	0	26	36	8	19	0	7.71
1 Carlos Reyes	R	31	0	1	.000	0	10	0	0	10	15	5	4	0	5.23

Mike Jackson (SJ) 35
*Daal, also with Arizona, league leader in L with 19

CENTRAL DIVISION

ST. LOUIS — 1st 95-67 .586 — TONY La RUSSA

Name	G by Pos	B	AGE	G	AB	R	H	2B	3B	HR	RBI	BB	SO	SB	BA	SA
TOTALS			31	162	5478	887	1481	259	25	235	841	675	1253	87	.270	.455
Mark McGwire (KJ)	1B70	R	36	89	236	60	72	8	0	32	73	76	78	1	.305	.746
Fernando Vina	2B122	L	31	123	487	81	146	24	6	4	31	36	36	10	.300	.398
Edgar Renteria	SS149	R	24	150	562	94	156	32	1	16	76	63	71	21	.278	.423
Fernando Tatis (GJ)	3B91 1B1	R	25	96	324	59	82	21	1	18	64	57	94	2	.253	.491
J.D. Drew	OF127	L	24	135	407	73	120	17	2	18	57	67	99	17	.295	.479
Jim Edmonds	OF146 1B6	L	30	152	525	129	155	25	0	42	108	103	167	10	.295	.583
Ray Lankford	OF117	L	33	128	392	73	99	16	3	26	65	70	148	5	.253	.508
Mike Matheny	C124 1B8	R	29	128	417	43	109	22	1	6	47	32	96	0	.261	.362
Craig Paquette	3B86 OF31 1B28 2B13	R	31	134	384	47	94	24	2	15	61	27	83	4	.245	.435
Placido Polanco	2B51 3B35 SS29 1B1	R	24	118	323	50	102	12	3	5	39	16	26	4	.316	.418
Shawon Dunston	OF58 SS8 1B6 3B5	R	37	98	216	28	54	11	2	12	43	6	47	3	.250	.486
Eric Davis	OF69	R	38	92	254	38	77	14	0	6	40	36	60	1	.303	.429
Thomas Howard	OF27 1B1	B	35	86	133	13	28	4	1	6	28	7	34	1	.211	.391
Eli Marrero (RJ)	C38 1B7	R	26	53	102	21	23	3	1	5	17	9	16	5	.225	.422
2 Will Clark	1B50	L	36	51	171	29	59	15	1	12	42	22	24	1	.345	.655
Eduardo Perez	1B24 OF4 3B2	R	30	35	91	9	27	4	0	3	10	5	19	1	.297	.440
Larry Sutton	1B6 OF4	L	30	23	25	5	8	0	0	1	6	5	7	0	.320	.440
2 Carlos Hernandez	C16	R	33	17	51	7	14	4	0	1	10	5	9	1	.275	.412
Luis Saturria	OF9	R	24	12	5	1	0	0	0	0	0	0	3	0	.000	.000
1 Chris Richard	OF3 1B2	L	26	6	16	1	2	0	0	1	1	2	4	0	.125	.313
Keith McDonald	C4	R	27	6	7	3	3	0	0	2	5	2	1	0	.429	1.714
Rick Wilkins	C3	L	33	4	11	3	3	1	0	0	0	2	4	0	.273	.273

NAME	T	AGE	W	L	PCT	SV	G	GS	CG	IP	H	BB	SO	SHO	ERA
		30	95	67	.586	37	162	162	10	1434	1403	606	1100	7	4.38
Darryl Kile	R	31	20	9	.690	0	34	34	5	232	215	58	192	1	3.91
Garrett Stephenson	R	28	16	9	.640	0	32	31	3	200	209	63	123	2	4.49
Pat Hentgen	R	31	15	12	.556	0	33	33	1	194	202	89	118	1	4.72
Andy Benes	R	32	12	9	.571	0	30	27	1	166	174	68	137	0	4.88
Rick Ankiel	L	20	11	7	.611	0	31	30	0	175	137	90	194	0	3.50
2 Mike Timlin	R	34	3	1	.750	1	30	0	0	30	30	20	26	0	3.34
Matt Morris (EJ)	R	25	3	3	.500	4	31	0	0	53	53	17	34	0	3.57
Dave Veres	R	33	3	5	.375	29	71	0	0	76	65	25	67	0	2.85
Britt Reames	R	26	2	1	.667	0	8	7	0	41	30	23	31	0	2.88
Mike James	R	32	2	1	.667	0	51	0	0	51	40	24	41	0	3.16
Alan Benes	R	28	2	2	.500	0	30	0	0	48	54	23	26	0	5.67
1 Heathcliff Slocumb	R	34	2	3	.400	1	43	0	0	50	50	24	34	0	5.44
Gene Stechschulte	R	26	1	0	1.000	0	20	0	0	26	24	17	12	0	6.31
2 Jason Christiansen	L	30	1	1	.500	0	21	0	0	10	13	2	12	0	5.40
Mark Thompson (GJ)	R	29	1	1	.500	0	20	0	0	25	24	15	19	0	5.04
1 Mike Mohler	L	31	1	1	.500	0	22	0	0	19	26	15	8	0	9.00
Mike Matthews (BH)	R	26	0	0	—	0	14	0	0	9	15	10	8	0	11.57
Justin Brunette	L	24	0	0	—	0	6	0	0	5	8	5	2	0	5.79
Jose Rodriguez	R	25	0	0	—	0	6	0	0	4	8	1	3	0	9.00
Luther Hackman	R	25	0	0	—	0	7	0	0	4	4	4	0	0	10.13
Jesse Orosco (EJ)	L	43	0	0	—	0	6	0	0	4	3	1	6	0	3.86
Scott Radinsky (EJ)	L	32	0	1	.000	0	10	0	0	8	7	8	4	0	—
Dave Wainhouse (SJ)	R	32	0	1	.000	0	9	0	0	9	13	4	5	0	9.35
2 Darren Holmes	R	34	0	1	.000	0	9	0	0	9	12	3	5	0	9.72

CINCINNATI — 2nd 85-77 .525 10 — JACK McKEON

Name	G by Pos	B	AGE	G	AB	R	H	2B	3B	HR	RBI	BB	SO	SB	BA	SA
TOTALS			30	163	5635	825	1545	302	36	200	794	559	995	100	.274	.447
Sean Casey	1B129	L	25	133	480	69	151	33	2	20	85	52	80	1	.315	.517
Pokey Reese	2B133	R	27	135	518	76	132	20	6	12	46	45	86	29	.255	.386
Barry Larkin (RJ)	SS102	R	36	102	396	71	124	26	5	11	41	48	31	14	.313	.487
Aaron Boone (KJ)	3B84 SS2	R	27	84	291	44	83	18	0	12	43	24	52	6	.285	.471
1 Dante Bichette	OF121	R	36	125	461	67	136	27	2	16	76	41	69	5	.295	.466
Ken Griffey Jr.	OF141	L	30	145	520	100	141	22	3	40	118	94	117	6	.271	.556
Dmitri Young	OF111 1B36	B	26	152	548	90	166	37	6	18	88	36	80	0	.303	.491
Eddie Taubensee (XJ)	C76	L	31	81	266	29	71	12	0	6	24	21	44	0	.267	.380
Michael Tucker	OF120 2B1	L	29	148	270	55	72	13	4	15	36	44	64	13	.267	.511
Chris Stynes	3B77 2B15 OF8	R	27	119	380	71	127	24	1	6	40	32	54	5	.334	.497
Alex Ochoa	OF95	R	28	118	244	50	77	21	3	13	58	24	27	8	.316	.586
Benito Santiago	C84	R	35	89	252	22	66	11	1	8	45	19	45	2	.262	.409
Juan Castro	SS57 2B21 3B7	R	28	82	224	20	54	12	2	4	23	14	33	0	.241	.366
1 Hal Morris	1B16 OF1	L	34	59	63	9	14	2	1	2	6	12	10	0	.222	.381
Chris Sexton	SS14 2B12 3B3	R	28	35	100	9	21	4	0	0	10	13	12	4	.210	.250
D.T. Cromer	1B13	L	29	35	47	7	16	4	0	2	8	1	14	0	.340	.553
2 Brian Hunter	OF25	R	29	32	40	11	9	1	0	0	1	6	9	5	.225	.250
Jason LaRue	C31	R	26	31	98	12	23	9	0	3	12	5	19	0	.235	.418
Mike Bell	3B13	R	25	19	27	5	6	0	0	2	4	4	7	0	.222	.444
Gookie Dawkins	SS14	R	21	14	41	5	9	2	0	0	3	2	12	2	.220	.268
Brooks Kieschnick	1B1	L	28	14	12	0	0	0	0	0	0	1	5	0	.000	.000
1 Mark Lewis	3B5	R	30	11	19	1	2	1	0	0	3	0	2	0	.105	.158
Brady Clark	OF5	R	27	11	11	1	3	1	0	0	2	0	2	0	.273	.364
Kimera Bartee	OF3	R	27	11	2	1	0	0	0	0	0	0	2	0	.000	.000

NAME	T	AGE	W	L	PCT	SV	G	GS	CG	IP	H	BB	SO	SHO	ERA
		28	85	77	.525	42	163	163	8	1456	1446	659	1015	7	4.33
Steve Parris	R	32	12	17	.414	0	33	33	0	193	227	71	117	0	4.81
Elmer Dessens	R	29	11	5	.688	1	40	16	1	147	170	43	85	0	4.28
Danny Graves	R	27	10	5	.667	30	66	0	0	91	81	42	53	0	2.56
Ron Villone	L	30	10	10	.500	0	35	23	2	141	154	78	77	0	5.43
1 Denny Neagle	L	31	8	2	.800	0	18	18	0	118	111	50	88	0	3.52
Pete Harnisch (SJ)	R	33	8	6	.571	0	22	22	3	131	133	46	71	1	4.74
Rob Bell	R	23	7	8	.467	0	26	26	1	140	130	73	112	0	5.00
Scott Williamson	R	24	5	8	.385	6	44	10	0	112	92	75	136	0	3.29
Osvaldo Fernandez (EJ)	R	31	4	3	.571	0	15	14	1	80	69	31	36	0	3.62
John Riedling	R	24	3	1	.750	1	13	0	0	15	11	8	18	0	2.35
Scott Sullivan	R	29	3	6	.333	1	79	0	0	106	87	38	96	0	3.47
Dennys Reyes	L	23	2	1	.667	0	62	0	0	44	43	29	36	0	4.53
2 Manny Aybar	R	28	1	1	.500	0	32	0	0	50	51	22	31	0	4.83
Mark Wohlers	R	30	1	2	.333	2	20	0	0	28	19	17	20	0	4.50
Hector Mercado	L	26	0	0	—	0	12	0	0	14	12	6	13	0	4.50
Keith Glauber	R	27	0	0	—	0	4	0	0	7	6	5	7	0	3.68
Scott Winchester	R	27	0	0	—	0	3	0	0	3	5	1	3	0	3.68
1 Andy Larkin	R	26	0	0	—	0	3	0	0	3	6	5	7	0	5.40
Norm Charlton	L	37	0	0	—	0	3	0	0	3	1	0	1	0	27.00
1 Gabe White	L	28	0	0	—	0	3	0	0	3	6	1	1	0	18.00
Larry Luebbers	R	30	0	0	—	0	1	0	0	2	0	1	1	0	6.20

MILWAUKEE — 3rd 73-89 .451 22 — DAVEY LOPES

Name	G by Pos	B	AGE	G	AB	R	H	2B	3B	HR	RBI	BB	SO	SB	BA	SA
TOTALS			29	163	5563	740	1366	297	25	177	708	620	1245	72	.246	.403
2 Richie Sexson	1B57	R	25	57	213	44	63	11	0	14	47	34	55	1	.296	.559
Ron Belliard	2B151	R	25	152	571	83	150	30	9	8	54	82	84	7	.263	.389
Mark Loretta (BF)	3B81	R	28	91	352	49	99	21	1	7	40	37	38	0	.281	.406
Jose Hernandez	3B95 SS37 OF2	R	30	124	446	51	109	22	1	11	59	41	125	3	.244	.372
Jeromy Burnitz	OF158	L	31	161	564	91	131	29	2	31	98	99	121	6	.232	.456
Marquis Grissom	OF142	R	33	146	595	67	145	18	2	14	62	39	99	20	.244	.351
Geoff Jenkins	OF131	L	25	135	512	100	155	36	4	34	94	33	135	11	.303	.588
Henry Blanco	C88	R	28	93	284	29	67	24	0	7	31	36	60	0	.236	.394
Charlie Hayes	3B59 1B57	R	35	121	370	46	93	17	0	9	46	57	84	1	.251	.370
Tyler Houston	1B35 3B28 C23	L	29	101	284	30	71	15	0	18	43	17	72	2	.250	.493
James Mouton	OF45	R	31	87	159	28	37	7	1	2	17	30	43	13	.233	.327
Raul Casanova	C72	B	27	86	231	20	57	13	3	6	36	26	48	1	.247	.420
Luis Lopez	SS45 2B22 3B6	B	29	78	201	24	53	14	0	6	27	9	35	1	.264	.423
Mark Sweeney (KJ)	OF3 1B2	L	30	71	73	9	16	6	0	1	6	12	18	0	.219	.342
Lyle Mouton	OF27	R	31	42	97	14	27	7	1	2	16	10	29	1	.278	.433
Kevin Barker	1B32	L	24	40	100	14	22	9	1	2	9	20	21	1	.220	.330
1 Sean Berry	3B34	R	34	32	46	1	7	2	0	1	4	4	13	0	.152	.261
2 Angel Echevarria	1B9 OF5	R	29	31	42	3	9	2	0	1	4	7	9	0	.214	.333
Santiago Perez	SS20	B	25	31	52	8	9	2	0	1	4	7	19	4	.173	.212
Lou Collier	OF10 3B1	R	26	14	32	4	7	1	0	0	2	1	9	1	.219	.344
Chris Jones	OF2	R	34	12	16	3	3	1	0	0	3	0	6	0	.188	.313
Kevin Brown	C5	R	27	11	17	1	4	0	0	1	2	1	6	0	.235	.412

Robinson Cancel (SJ) 24

NAME	T	AGE	W	L	PCT	SV	G	GS	CG	IP	H	BB	SO	SHO	ERA
		28	73	89	.451	29	163	163	2	1466	1501	728	967	7	4.63
Jeff D'Amico	R	24	12	7	.632	0	23	23	1	162	143	46	101	1	2.66
Jimmy Haynes	R	27	12	13	.480	0	33	33	0	199	228	100	88	0	5.33
Curtis Leskanic	R	32	9	3	.750	12	73	0	0	77	58	51	75	0	4.30
Jamey Wright (SJ)	R	25	9	4	.438	0	28	25	0	165	157	88	96	0	4.10
1 Jason Bere	R	29	9	6	.462	0	20	20	0	115	115	63	98	0	4.93
2 Paul Rigdon	R	24	4	4	.500	0	12	12	0	70	68	26	48	0	4.52
Horacio Estrada	L	24	3	0	1.000	0	7	4	0	24	30	20	13	0	6.29
Ray King	L	26	3	3	.500	0	69	0	0	29	18	10	19	0	1.26
David Weathers	R	30	3	5	.375	1	69	0	0	78	73	32	50	0	3.07
Juan Acevedo	R	30	3	7	.300	0	62	0	0	83	77	31	51	0	3.81
John Snyder (UJ)	R	25	3	10	.231	0	23	23	0	127	147	77	69	0	6.17
1 Bob Wickman	R	31	2	5	.286	16	44	0	0	46	37	20	44	0	2.93
Valerio De Los Santos	L	25	2	4	.333	0	66	2	0	74	72	33	70	0	5.13
Everett Stull	R	23	2	4	.333	0	13	4	0	43	41	30	33	0	5.82
Jim Bruske (EJ)	R	35	1	0	1.000	0	15	0	0	17	22	12	8	0	6.48
1 Steve Woodard	R	25	1	5	.125	0	27	11	1	94	125	33	65	0	5.96
Matt Williams	L	29	0	0	—	0	11	0	0	9	13	7	7	0	7.00
Mike Buddie	R	29	0	1	.000	0	8	0	0	9	9	8	4	0	5.40
Rafael Roque	L	28	0	0	—	0	7	4	0	14	9	4	4	0	10.13
2 Kane Davis	R	25	0	0	—	0	6	0	0	7	7	4	7	0	6.75
Bob Scanlan	R	33	0	0	—	0	6	0	0	5	10	2	6	0	27.00
Allen Levrault	R	23	0	0	—	0	5	1	0	12	10	7	9	0	8.00
Hector Ramirez	R	28	0	0	—	0	1	0	0	0	0	1	0	0	10.00
1 Jaime Navarro	R	32	0	0	—	0	6	0	0	19	34	18	7	0	12.54

Rocky Coppinger (EJ) 26   Chad Fox (EJ) 29   Kyle Peterson (SJ) 24

HOUSTON 4th 72-90 .444 23 LARRY DIERKER

Name	G by Pos	B	AGE	G	AB	R	H	2B	3B	HR	RBI	BB	SO	SB	BA	SA
TOTALS			29	162	5570	938	1547	289	36	249	900	673	1129	114	.278	.477
Jeff Bagwell	1B158	R	32	159	590	152	183	37	1	47	132	107	116	9	.310	.615
Craig Biggio (KJ)	2B100	R	34	101	377	67	101	13	5	8	35	61	73	12	.268	.393
Julio Lugo	SS60 2B45 OF6	R	24	116	420	78	119	22	5	10	40	37	93	22	.283	.431
Ken Caminiti (WJ)	3B58	B	37	59	208	42	63	13	0	15	45	42	37	3	.303	.582
Moises Alou	OF121	R	33	126	454	82	161	28	2	30	114	52	45	3	.355	.623
Richard Hidalgo (BF)	OF150	R	25	153	558	118	175	42	3	44	122	56	110	13	.314	.636
Roger Cedeno (BF)	OF67	R	25	74	259	54	73	2	5	6	26	43	47	25	.282	.398
Mitch Meluskey	C103 3B1	B	26	117	337	47	101	21	0	14	69	55	74	1	.300	.487
Bill Spiers	3B51 SS27 2B26 OF10	L	34	124	355	41	107	17	3	3	43	49	38	7	.301	.392
Daryle Ward	OF47 1B19	L	25	119	264	36	68	10	2	20	47	15	61	0	.258	.538
Lance Berkman	OF96 1B2	B	24	114	353	76	105	28	1	21	67	56	73	6	.297	.561
Tim Bogar	SS95 P2 2B2 3B1	R	33	110	304	32	63	9	2	7	33	35	56	1	.207	.319
Glen Barker	OF69	R	29	84	67	18	15	2	1	2	6	7	23	9	.224	.373
Chris Truby	3B74	R	26	78	258	28	67	15	4	11	59	10	56	2	.260	.477
Tony Eusebio (SJ)	C68	R	33	74	218	24	61	18	0	7	33	25	45	0	.280	.459
1 Matt Mieske	OF18	R	32	62	81	7	14	1	2	1	5	7	17	0	.173	.272
1 Russ Johnson	SS5 3B4 2B3	R	27	26	45	4	8	0	0	0	3	2	3	0	.178	.178
Raul Chavez	C14	R	27	14	43	3	11	2	0	1	5	3	6	0	.256	.372
Tripp Cromer (PP)	3B2 2B1 SS1	R	32	9	8	2	1	0	0	0	0	1	1	0	.125	.125
Keith Ginter	2B2	R	24	5	8	3	2	0	0	1	3	1	3	0	.250	.625
Frank Charles	C1	R	31	4	7	1	3	1	0	0	2	0	2	0	.429	.571
Morgan Ensberg	3B1	R	24	4	7	0	2	0	0	0	0	0	1	0	.286	.286
Eddie Zosky	C1	R	32	4	4	0	0	0	0	0	0	0	0	0	.000	.000
1 Paul Bako	C1	L	28	1	2	0	0	0	0	0	0	0	0	0	.000	.000

NAME	T	AGE	W	L	PCT	SV	G	GS	CG	IP	H	BB	SO	SHO	ERA
		29	72	90	.444	30	162	162	8	1438	1596	598	1064	2	5.42
Scott Elarton	R	29	17	7	.708	0	30	30	2	193	198	84	131	0	4.81
Chris Holt	R	28	8	16	.333	0	34	32	3	207	247	75	136	1	5.35
Shane Reynolds (XJ)	R	32	7	8	.467	0	22	22	0	131	150	45	93	0	5.22
Jose Lima	R	27	7	16	.304	0	33	33	0	196	251	68	124	0	6.65
Wade Miller	R	23	6	6	.500	0	16	16	2	105	104	42	89	0	5.14
Marc Valdes	R	28	5	5	.500	2	51	0	0	57	69	25	35	0	5.08
Tony McKnight	R	23	4	1	.800	0	5	5	0	35	35	9	23	0	3.86
Octavio Dotel	R	26	3	7	.300	16	50	16	0	125	127	61	142	0	5.40
Brian Powell	R	26	2	1	.667	0	9	5	0	31	34	13	14	0	5.74
Yorkis Perez	L	32	2	1	.667	0	33	0	0	23	25	14	21	0	5.16
Mike Maddux	R	38	2	2	.500	0	21	0	0	27	31	12	17	0	6.26
Jose Cabrera	R	28	2	3	.400	2	52	0	0	59	74	17	41	0	5.92
Billy Wagner (EJ)	L	28	2	4	.333	6	28	0	0	28	28	18	28	0	6.18
Joe Slusarski	R	33	2	7	.222	1	54	0	0	77	80	22	54	0	4.21
Jay Powell (SJ)	R	28	1	1	.500	0	29	0	0	27	29	19	16	0	5.67
Jason Green	R	25	1	1	.500	0	14	0	0	18	15	20	19	0	6.62
1 Doug Henry	R	36	1	3	.250	1	45	0	0	53	39	28	46	0	4.42
Wayne Franklin	L	26	0	0	—	0	25	0	0	21	24	12	21	0	5.48
2 Scott Linebrink	R	23	0	0	—	0	8	0	0	10	11	6	6	0	4.66
Rusty Meacham	R	32	0	0	—	0	5	0	0	5	8	2	3	0	11.57
1 Dwight Gooden	R	35	0	0	—	0	1	1	0	4	6	3	1	0	9.00
Tim Bogar	R	33	0	0	—	0	1	0	0	1	4	1	0	0	4.50
Kip Gross	R	35	0	1	.000	0	2	1	0	4	9	2	3	0	10.38

PITTSBURGH 5th 69-93 .426 26 GENE LAMONT

Name	G by Pos	B	AGE	G	AB	R	H	2B	3B	HR	RBI	BB	SO	SB	BA	SA
TOTALS			29	162	5643	793	1506	320	31	168	749	564	1032	86	.267	.424
Kevin Young	1B129	R	31	132	496	77	128	27	0	20	88	32	96	8	.258	.433
Warren Morris	2B134	L	26	144	528	68	137	31	2	3	43	65	78	7	.259	.343
Pat Meares	SS126	R	31	132	462	55	111	22	2	13	47	36	91	1	.240	.381
Aramis Ramirez (SJ)	3B72	R	22	73	254	19	65	15	2	6	35	10	36	0	.256	.402
Brian Giles	OF155	L	29	156	559	111	176	37	5	35	123	114	69	6	.315	.594
Adrian Brown (LJ)	OF92	R	26	104	308	64	97	18	3	4	28	29	34	13	.315	.432
1 Wil Cordero	OF85	R	28	89	348	46	98	24	3	16	51	25	58	1	.282	.506
Jason Kendall	C147	R	26	152	579	112	185	33	6	14	58	79	79	22	.320	.470
John Vander Wal	OF78 1B33	L	34	134	384	74	115	29	0	24	94	72	92	11	.299	.563
Mike Benjamin	3B34 SS30 2B27 1B1	R	34	93	233	28	63	18	2	9	17	12	45	5	.270	.391
1 Bruce Aven	OF41	R	28	72	148	18	37	11	0	5	25	5	31	2	.250	.426
1 Luis Sojo	3B50 2B1	R	35	61	176	14	50	11	0	3	20	11	16	1	.284	.432
Emil Brown (IL)	OF38	R	25	50	119	13	26	5	0	3	16	11	34	3	.218	.336
Keith Osik	C26 3B12 1B5 P1	R	31	46	123	11	36	6	1	4	22	14	11	3	.293	.455
2 Alex Hernandez	OF31 1B1	R	25	43	115	13	24	6	1	4	18	7	32	1	.209	.383
1 Enrique Wilson	3B16 2B11 SS8	B	26	40	122	11	32	6	1	3	15	11	13	0	.262	.402
Abraham Nunez	SS21 2B6	B	24	40	91	10	20	1	0	1	8	4	16	1	.220	.264
Chad Hermansen	OF31	R	22	33	108	12	20	4	1	2	6	8	37	0	.185	.296
John Wehner	3B16 OF1	R	33	21	50	10	15	3	0	1	9	4	6	0	.300	.420
Alex Hernandez	1B12 OF5	L	25	20	60	4	12	3	0	1	5	0	13	1	.200	.300
Adam Hyzdu	OF5	R	28	12	18	2	7	2	0	1	4	3	0	0	.389	.667
Tike Redman	OF6	L	23	9	18	2	6	1	0	1	1	1	3	1	.333	.556
Ivan Cruz	1B1	L	32	8	11	1	1	0	0	0	0	4	5	0	.091	.091

NAME	T	AGE	W	L	PCT	SV	G	GS	CG	IP	H	BB	SO	SHO	ERA
		27	69	93	.426	27	162	162	5	1449	1554	711	1070	7	4.94
Jose Silva	R	26	11	9	.550	0	51	19	1	136	178	50	98	0	5.56
Kris Benson	R	25	10	12	.455	0	32	32	2	218	206	86	184	1	3.85
Todd Ritchie	R	28	9	8	.529	0	31	31	1	187	208	51	124	1	4.81
Francisco Cordova (EJ)	R	28	6	8	.429	0	18	17	0	95	107	38	66	0	5.21
Scott Sauerbeck	L	28	5	4	.556	1	75	0	0	76	76	61	83	0	4.04
Jimmy Anderson	L	24	5	11	.313	0	27	26	1	144	169	58	73	0	5.25
Marc Wilkins	R	29	4	2	.667	0	52	0	0	65	54	43	37	0	5.07
Mike Williams	R	31	4	3	.429	24	72	0	0	72	56	40	71	0	3.50
Jeff Wallace	L	24	2	0	1.000	0	38	0	0	36	42	34	27	0	7.07
Josias Manzanillo	R	32	2	2	.500	0	43	0	0	59	50	32	39	0	3.38
2 Matt Skrmetta	R	27	2	2	.500	0	9			13					9.64
Rich Loiselle (EJ-SJ)	R	27	2	3	.400	0	42			42	43	30	35	0	5.10
Jason Schmidt (SJ)	R	27	2	5	.286	0	11	11	0	63	71	41	51	0	5.40
2 Dan Serafini	L	26	2	5	.286	0	11	11	0	62	70	26	32	0	4.91
Bronson Arroyo	R	23	2	6	.250	0	20	12	0	72	88	36	50	0	6.40
1 Jason Christiansen	L	30	2	8	.200	1	49	0	0	38	28	25	41	0	4.97
Brian O'Connor	L	23	0	0	—	0	6	1	0	12	12	11	7	0	5.11
Brad Clontz (EJ)	R	29	0	0	—	0	7	0	0	7	11	8	5	0	5.71
Brian Smith	R	27	0	0	—	0	3	0	0	4	5	3	2	0	10.38
Steve Sparks	R	25	0	0	—	0	4	0	0	4	5	0	1	0	6.75
Keith Osik	R	31	0	0	—	0	1	0	0	1	5	1	0	0	45.00
Chris Peters (EJ)	L	28	0	1	.000	1	18	0	0	28	23	14	16	0	2.86
Jose Parra	R	27	0	1	.000	0	6	2	0	12	17	7	9	0	6.94
Mike Garcia	R	32	0	2	.000	0	13	0	0	11	21	7	9	0	11.12

CHICAGO 6th 65-97 .401 30 DON BAYLOR

Name	G by Pos	B	AGE	G	AB	R	H	2B	3B	HR	RBI	BB	SO	SB	BA	SA
TOTALS			32	162	5577	764	1426	272	23	183	722	632	1120	93	.256	.411
Mark Grace	1B140	L	36	143	510	75	143	41	1	11	82	95	28	1	.280	.429
Eric Young	2B150	R	33	153	607	98	180	40	2	6	47	63	39	54	.297	.399
Ricky Gutierrez	SS121	R	30	125	449	73	124	19	2	11	56	66	58	8	.276	.401
Shane Andrews (XJ)	3B58 1B6	R	26	92	192	25	44	5	0	14	39	27	59	1	.229	.474
Sammy Sosa	OF156	R	31	156	604	106	193	38	1	50	138	91	168	7	.320	.634
Damon Buford	OF148	R	30	150	495	64	124	18	3	15	48	47	118	4	.251	.390
1 Henry Rodriguez	OF70	R	32	76	259	37	65	15	1	18	51	22	76	1	.251	.525
Joe Girardi	C103	R	35	106	363	47	101	15	1	6	40	32	61	1	.278	.375
Willie Greene	3B90	L	28	105	299	34	60	15	2	10	37	36	69	4	.201	.365
Jeff Reed	C71	L	37	90	229	26	49	10	0	4	25	44	68	0	.214	.310
Jose Nieves	3B39 SS24 2B7	R	25	82	198	17	42	6	3	5	24	11	43	1	.212	.348
Gary Matthews	OF61	B	25	80	158	24	30	1	2	4	14	15	28	3	.190	.297
Jeff Huson	3B18 2B17 SS17 1B1	L	35	70	130	19	28	7	1	0	11	13	9	2	.215	.285
1 Glenallen Hill	OF29	R	35	64	168	23	44	4	1	11	29	10	43	0	.262	.494
2 Brant Brown	OF28 1B7	L	29	54	89	7	14	1	0	3	10	10	29	2	.157	.270
Roosevelt Brown	OF28	L	24	45	91	11	32	8	0	3	14	4	22	0	.352	.538
Chad Meyers	2B8 3B8	R	24	36	52	8	9	2	0	0	5	3	11	1	.173	.212
Julio Zuleta	1B14 OF6	R	25	30	68	13	20	8	0	3	12	2	19	0	.294	.544
Augie Ojeda	SS25 2B4	B	25	28	77	10	17	3	1	0	8	10	9	0	.221	.364
2 Rondell White (SJ)	OF29	R	28	19	67	7	22	2	0	2	7	5	12	0	.328	.448
2 Dave Martinez	OF10 1B9	L	35	18	54	5	10	1	1	0	1	2	3	10	.185	.241
Ross Gload	OF8 1B2	L	24	18	31	4	6	1	1	0	3	3	10	0	.194	.355
Tarrik Brock	OF10	L	26	13	12	1	2	0	0	0	0	0	6	1	.167	.167
Corey Patterson	OF11	L	20	11	42	9	7	1	0	2	3	2	14	1	.167	.333
Mike Mahoney	C4	R	27	4	7	1	2	1	0	0	1	0	1	0	.286	.429
Cole Liniak		R	23	3	2	0	0	0	0	0	0	0	2	0	.000	.000
Raul Gonzalez	OF2	R	26	3	2	0	0	0	0	0	0	0	0	0	.000	.000

NAME	T	AGE	W	L	PCT	SV	G	GS	CG	IP	H	BB	SO	SHO	ERA
		28	65	97	.401	39	162	162	10	1455	1505	658	1143	5	5.25
Jon Lieber	R	30	12	11	.522	0	35	35	6	251	248	54	192	1	4.41
Kerry Wood (EJ)	R	23	8	7	.533	0	23	23	1	137	112	87	132	0	4.80
Kevin Tapani	R	36	8	12	.400	0	30	30	2	196	208	47	150	0	5.01
Felix Heredia	L	25	7	3	.700	2	74	0	0	59	46	33	52	0	4.76
1 Scott Downs	L	24	4	3	.571	0	18	18	0	94	117	37	63	0	5.17
Todd Van Poppel	R	28	4	5	.444	2	51	2	0	86	80	48	77	0	3.75
2 Tim Worrell	R	32	4	4	.429	3	54	0	0	62	60	24	52	0	2.47
Steve Rain	R	25	3	4	.429	0	37	0	0	50	46	27	54	0	4.35
Ruben Quevedo	R	21	3	10	.231	0	21	15	1	88	96	54	65	0	7.47
1 Mark Guthrie	L	34	2	3	.400	0	19	0	0	19	17	10	17	0	4.82
1 Ismael Valdes (SJ)	R	26	2	4	.333	0	12	12	0	67	71	27	45	0	5.37
Daniel Garibay	L	27	2	8	.200	0	30	8	0	75	88	39	46	0	6.03
Kyle Farnsworth	R	24	2	9	.182	1	46	5	0	77	90	50	74	0	6.43
Will Ohman	L	22	1	0	1.000	0	4	0	0	3	4	4	2	0	8.10
1 Brian Williams	R	31	1	1	.500	1	22	0	0	24	28	23	14	0	9.62
Matt Karchner	R	33	1	1	.500	0	13	0	0	15	19	11	5	0	6.14
Rick Aguilera	R	38	1	2	.333	29	54	0	0	48	47	18	38	0	4.91
1 Andrew Lorraine	L	27	1	2	.333	0	8	5	0	32	36	18	25	0	6.47
Oswaldo Mairena	L	26	0	0	—	0	5	0	0	4	5	6	6	0	18.00
2 Jerry Spradlin	R	32	0	1	.000	2	15	0	0	15	20	5	13	0	8.40
Phil Norton	L	24	0	1	.000	0	3	0	0	1	5	6	0	0	9.00
Danny Young	L	28	0	0	—	0	9	0	0	2	3	6	0	0	21.00
Joey Nation	L	21	0	2	.000	0	2	2	0	12	12	8	4	0	6.94
2 Jamie Arnold	R	26	0	4	.000	0	12	4	0	33	34	19	13	0	6.61
Jeremi Gonzalez (EJ) 25															

WEST DIVISION

SAN FRANCISCO 1st 97-65 .599 DUSTY BAKER

Name	G by Pos	B	AGE	G	AB	R	H	2B	3B	HR	RBI	BB	SO	SB	BA	SA
TOTALS			30	162	5519	925	1535	304	44	226	889	709	1032	79	.278	.472
J.T. Snow	1B153	B	32	155	536	82	152	33	2	19	96	66	129	1	.284	.459
Jeff Kent	2B150 1B16	R	32	159	587	114	196	41	7	33	125	90	107	12	.334	.596
Rich Aurilia	SS140	B	28	141	509	67	138	24	2	20	79	54	90	1	.271	.444
Bill Mueller	3B145 2B2	B	29	153	560	90	150	29	4	10	55	52	62	4	.268	.388
Ellis Burks	OF108	R	35	122	393	74	135	21	5	24	96	56	49	5	.344	.606
Marvin Benard	OF141	L	30	149	560	102	147	27	6	12	55	63	97	22	.263	.396
Barry Bonds	OF141	L	35	143	480	129	147	28	4	49	106	117	77	11	.306	.688
Bobby Estalella	C106	R	25	106	299	45	70	22	3	14	53	57	92	3	.234	.468
Armando Rios	OF93 1B1	L	28	115	233	38	62	15	5	10	50	31	43	3	.266	.502
Calvin Murray	OF28	R	28	108	194	33	47	12	1	2	22	29	33	9	.242	.345
Felipe Crespo	OF26 1B11 2B7	B	27	89	131	17	38	6	1	4	29	10	23	1	.290	.443
Ramon Martinez	SS44 2B32 1B2 3B2	R	27	88	189	30	57	13	2	6	25	15	22	2	.302	.487
Doug Mirabelli	C80	R	29	82	230	23	53	10	2	6	28	36	57	1	.230	.370
Russ Davis	3B43 1B6	R	30	80	180	27	47	5	0	9	24	9	29	0	.261	.439
Terrell Lowery	OF20	R	29	24	34	13	15	4	0	1	5	7	8	1	.441	.647
Juan Melo	2B6	B	24	11	13	0	1	0	0	0	0	0	2	0	.077	.077
Damon Minor	1B4	L	26	10	9	3	4	0	0	0	6	2	1	0	.444	1.444
Pedro Feliz	3B4	R	25	8	7	1	2	0	0	0	0	0	2	0	.286	.286
2 Scott Servais	C6	R	33	7	8	1	2	0	0	0	1	0	1	0	.250	.250

Name	T	AGE	W	L	PCT	SV	G	GS	CG	IP	H	BB	SO	SHO	ERA
		29	97	65	.599	47	162	162	9	1444	1452	623	1076	15	4.21
Livan Hernandez	R	25	17	11	.607	0	33	33	5	240	254	73	165	2	3.75
Shawn Estes	L	27	15	6	.714	0	30	30	4	190	194	108	136	2	4.26
Russ Ortiz	R	26	14	12	.538	0	33	32	0	196	192	112	167	0	5.01
Mark Gardner	R	38	11	7	.611	0	30	20	0	149	155	42	92	0	4.05
Kirk Rueter	L	29	11	9	.550	0	32	31	0	184	205	62	71	0	3.96
Joe Nathan (SJ)	R	25	5	2	.714	0	20	15	0	93	89	63	61	0	5.21
Aaron Fultz	L	26	5	2	.714	0	58	0	0	69	67	28	62	0	4.67
Felix Rodriguez	R	27	4	4	.667	3	76	0	0	82	65	42	95	0	2.64
Robb Nen	R	30	4	3	.571	41	68	0	0	66	37	19	92	0	1.50
2 Doug Henry	R	36	3	1	.750	0	27	0	0	25	18	21	16	0	2.49
John Johnstone (XJ)	R	31	3	4	.429	0	47	0	0	50	64	13	37	0	6.30
Alan Embree	L	30	3	5	.375	2	63	0	0	60	62	25	49	0	4.95
Miguel Del Toro	R	27	2	1	1.000	0	17	0	0	17	17	6	16	0	5.19
Ryan Vogelsong	R	22	0	0	—	0	2	1	0	7	7	2	6	0	0.00
Chad Zerbe	L	28	0	0	—	0	7	0	0	7	2	6	3	0	0.00
1 Scott Linebrink	R	23	0	0	—	0	2	0	0	6	8	1	6	0	11.57
1 Ben Weber	R	30	0	1	.000	0	8	0	0	16	14	6	9	0	14.63

LOS ANGELES — 2nd 86-76 .531 11 — DAVEY JOHNSON

Name	G by Pos	B	AGE	G	AB	R	H	2B	3B	HR	RBI	BB	SO	SB	BA	SA
TOTALS			30	162	5481	798	1408	265	28	211	756	668	1083	95	.257	.431
Eric Karros	1B153	R	32	155	584	84	146	29	0	31	106	63	122	4	.250	.459
Mark Grudzielanek	2B148 SS1	R	30	148	617	101	172	35	6	7	49	45	81	12	.279	.389
Alex Cora	SS101 2B8	L	24	109	353	39	84	18	6	4	32	26	53	4	.238	.357
Adrian Beltre	3B138 SS1	R	21	138	510	71	148	30	2	20	85	56	80	12	.290	.475
Shawn Green	OF161	L	27	162	610	98	164	44	4	24	99	90	121	24	.269	.472
Devon White (SJ)	OF40	B	37	47	158	26	42	5	1	4	13	9	30	5	.266	.386
Gary Sheffield	OF139	R	31	141	501	105	163	24	3	43	109	101	71	4	.325	.643
Todd Hundley	C84	B	31	90	299	49	85	16	0	24	70	45	69	0	.284	.579
Dave Hansen	1B16 3B16 OF3	L	31	102	121	18	35	6	2	8	26	26	32	0	.289	.570
Todd Hollandsworth	OF77	L	27	81	261	42	61	12	0	8	24	30	61	11	.234	.372
F.P. Santangelo (RJ)	OF50 2B7	B	32	81	142	19	28	4	0	1	9	21	33	3	.197	.246
Kevin Elster	SS55 3B8 1B1	R	35	80	220	29	50	8	0	14	32	38	52	0	.227	.455
Chad Kreuter	C78	B	35	80	212	32	56	13	0	6	28	54	48	1	.264	.410
Tom Goodwin	OF55	L	31	56	211	29	53	3	1	1	11	18	41	16	.251	.289
Jim Leyritz	1B8 OF6 C3	R	36	41	60	3	12	1	0	1	8	7	12	0	.200	.267
Jose Vizcaino	SS19 3B12 2B8	B	32	40	93	9	19	2	1	0	4	10	15	1	.204	.247
Paul LoDuca	C20 OF8 3B1	R	28	34	65	6	16	2	0	2	8	6	8	0	.246	.369
Chris Donnels	OF6 1B4 3B2 2B1	L	34	27	34	8	10	3	0	4	9	6	7	0	.294	.735
Geronimo Berroa (FJ)	OF6 1B2	R	35	24	31	2	8	0	0	1	6	1	6	0	.258	.323
Jeff Branson	SS7 2B3 3B3	L	33	18	17	3	4	1	0	0	0	1	6	0	.235	.294
Shawn Gilbert	OF14	R	35	15	20	5	3	1	0	1	3	2	7	0	.150	.350
Bruce Aven	OF9	R	28	9	20	2	5	0	0	2	4	3	8	0	.250	.550
Hiram Bocachica	2B2	R	24	8	10	2	3	0	0	0	0	2	3	0	.300	.300
Mike Metcalfe	OF4 2B1	R	27	4	12	0	1	0	0	0	0	1	2	0	.083	.083
Adam Melhuse		B	28	1	1	0	0	0	0	0	0	0	0	0	.000	.000

NAME	T	AGE	W	L	PCT	SV	G	GS	CG	IP	H	BB	SO	SHO	ERA
		29	86	76	.531	36	162	162	9	1445	1379	600	1154	11	4.10
Chan Ho Park	R	27	18	10	.643	0	34	34	3	226	173	124	217	1	3.27
Kevin Brown	R	35	13	6	.684	0	33	33	5	230	181	47	216	1	2.58
Darren Dreifort	R	28	12	9	.571	0	32	32	1	193	175	87	164	1	4.16
Matt Herges	L	30	11	3	.786	1	59	4	0	100	100	40	75	0	3.17
Mike Fetters	R	35	6	2	.750	5	51	0	0	50	35	25	40	0	3.24
Terry Adams	R	27	6	9	.400	2	66	0	0	84	80	39	56	0	3.52
Carlos Perez	L	29	5	8	.385	0	30	22	0	144	192	33	64	0	5.56
Eric Gagne	R	24	4	6	.400	0	20	19	0	101	106	60	79	0	5.15
Jeff Shaw	R	33	4	3	.429	27	60	0	0	57	61	16	39	0	4.24
Antonio Osuna (EJ)	R	27	3	6	.333	0	46	0	0	67	57	35	70	0	3.74
Alan Mills	R	33	2	1	.667	1	18	0	0	26	31	16	18	0	4.21
Onan Masaoka	L	22	1	1	.500	0	29	0	0	27	23	15	27	0	4.00
Luke Prokopec	R	22	1	1	.500	0	5	3	0	21	19	9	12	0	3.00
Orel Hershiser (VR)	R	41	1	5	.167	0	10	6	0	25	42	14	13	0	13.14
Alberto Reyes	R	29	0	0	—	0	6	0	0	7	2	1	8	0	0.00
Jamie Arnold	L	26	0	0	—	0	2	0	0	7	4	5	3	0	4.50
Jeff Williams (WJ)	L	28	0	0	—	0	7	0	0	6	12	8	3	0	15.88
Trever Miller	L	27	0	0	—	0	2	0	0	2	8	3	1	0	23.14
Gregg Olson (AJ)	R	33	0	1	.000	0	13	0	0	18	21	7	15	0	5.09
Mike Judd	R	25	0	1	.000	0	1	1	0	4	4	1	5	0	15.75
Ismael Valdes	R	26	0	3	.000	0	9	8	0	40	53	13	29	0	4.50

ARIZONA — 3rd 85-77 .525 12 — BUCK SHOWALTER

Name	G by Pos	B	AGE	G	AB	R	H	2B	3B	HR	RBI	BB	SO	SB	BA	SA
TOTALS			30	162	5527	792	1466	282	44	179	756	535	975	97	.265	.429
Erubiel Durazo (WJ)	1B60	L	26	67	196	35	52	11	0	8	33	34	43	1	.265	.444
Jay Bell	2B149	R	34	149	565	87	151	30	6	18	68	70	88	7	.267	.437
Tony Womack	SS143 OF2	L	30	146	617	95	167	21	14	7	57	30	74	45	.271	.384
Matt Williams (BF)	3B94	R	34	96	371	43	102	18	2	12	47	20	51	1	.275	.431
Danny Bautista	OF82	R	28	87	262	45	83	16	7	7	47	20	51	0	.317	.511
Steve Finley	OF148	L	35	152	539	100	151	27	5	35	96	65	87	12	.280	.544
Luis Gonzalez	OF162	L	32	162	618	106	192	47	2	31	114	78	85	2	.311	.544
Damian Miller	C97 1B2 SS1	R	30	100	324	43	89	24	0	10	44	36	74	2	.275	.441
Greg Colbrunn	1B99 3B1	R	30	116	329	48	103	22	1	15	57	43	45	0	.313	.523
Kelly Stinnett	C74	R	30	76	240	22	52	7	0	8	33	19	56	0	.217	.346
Hanley Frias	SS22 2B15 3B7	B	26	75	112	18	23	5	0	2	6	17	18	2	.205	.304
Travis Lee	OF55 1B23 3B7	L	25	72	224	34	52	13	0	8	40	25	46	5	.232	.397
Craig Counsell	2B25 3B23 SS6	L	29	67	152	23	48	8	1	2	11	20	18	3	.316	.421
Jason Conti	OF35	L	25	47	91	11	21	4	3	1	15	7	30	3	.231	.374
Bernard Gilkey	OF17	R	33	38	73	6	8	1	0	2	6	7	16	0	.110	.205
Lenny Harris	3B20 OF3	L	35	36	85	9	16	1	0	1	13	3	5	5	.188	.259
Dave Dellucci	OF12	L	26	34	50	2	15	3	0	0	2	4	9	0	.300	.360
Andy Fox	3B20 OF6 1B1	L	29	31	86	10	18	4	0	1	10	4	16	2	.209	.291
Alex Cabrera	1B15 OF12	R	28	31	80	10	21	2	1	5	14	4	21	0	.263	.500
Danny Klassen (FJ)	3B25 SS3	R	24	29	76	13	18	3	0	2	8	8	24	1	.237	.355
Rob Ryan	OF2	R	27	27	27	4	8	1	0	0	2	4	7	0	.296	.407
Turner Ward	OF15	B	35	15	52	5	9	4	0	0	4	5	7	1	.173	.250
Matt Mieske	OF1	R	32	11	8	3	2	0	0	1	2	1	1	0	.250	.625
Rod Barajas	C5	R	24	5	13	1	3	1	0	0	3	0	4	0	.231	.462

NAME	T	AGE	W	L	PCT	SV	G	GS	CG	IP	H	BB	SO	SHO	ERA
		31	85	77	.525	38	162	162	16	1444	1441	500	1220	8	4.35
Randy Johnson	L	36	19	7	.731	0	35	35	8	249	202	76	347	3	2.64
Brian Anderson	L	28	11	7	.611	0	33	32	2	213	226	39	104	0	4.05
Armando Reynoso	R	34	11	12	.478	0	31	30	2	171	179	52	89	0	5.27
Todd Stottlemyre (EJ)	R	35	9	6	.600	0	18	18	0	95	98	36	76	0	4.91
Byung-Hyun Kim	R	21	6	6	.500	14	61	1	0	71	52	46	111	0	4.46
Dan Plesac	L	38	5	1	.833	0	62	0	0	34	26	45	0	3.15
Geraldo Guzman	R	27	5	4	.556	0	13	10	0	66	66	22	52	0	5.37
Mike Morgan	R	40	5	5	.500	1	60	0	0	102	123	40	56	0	4.87
Curt Schilling	R	33	5	6	.455	0	13	13	4	98	94	13	72	1	3.69
Vicente Padilla	R	22	2	1	.667	0	27	0	0	55	32	10	30	0	2.31
Russ Springer	R	31	2	4	.333	0	52	0	0	62	63	34	59	0	5.08
Greg Swindell	L	35	2	6	.250	1	64	0	0	76	71	20	64	0	3.20
Omar Daal	L	28	2	10	.167	0	20	16	0	96	127	42	45	0	7.22
Matt Mantei	R	26	1	1	.500	17	47	0	0	45	31	35	53	0	4.57
Johnny Ruffin (GJ)	R	26	0	0	—	0	9	0	0	14	3	5	6	0	9.00
Darren Holmes	R	34	0	0	—	0	8	0	0	6	12	1	5	0	8.53
Nelson Figueroa	R	26	0	1	.000	0	3	0	0	16	13	7	7	0	7.47

*Daal, also with Philadelphia, league leader in L with 19

COLORADO — 4th 82-80 .506 15 — BUDDY BELL

Name	G by Pos	B	AGE	G	AB	R	H	2B	3B	HR	RBI	BB	SO	SB	BA	SA
TOTALS			29	162	5660	968	1664	320	53	161	905	601	907	131	.294	.455
Todd Helton	1B160	L	26	160	580	138	216	59	2	42	147	103	61	5	.372	.698
Mike Lansing	2B88	R	32	90	365	62	94	14	6	11	47	31	49	8	.258	.419
Neifi Perez	SS162	B	27	162	651	92	187	39	11	10	71	30	63	3	.287	.427
Jeff Cirillo	3B155	R	30	157	598	111	195	53	2	11	115	67	72	3	.326	.477
Larry Walker (EJ)	OF83	L	33	87	314	64	97	21	7	9	51	46	40	5	.309	.506
Tom Goodwin	OF88	L	31	91	317	65	86	8	5	5	47	50	76	39	.271	.394
Jeffrey Hammonds	OF118	R	29	122	454	94	152	24	2	20	106	44	83	14	.335	.529
Brent Mayne	C105 P1	L	32	117	335	36	101	21	0	6	64	47	48	1	.301	.418
Terry Shumpert	OF40 2B23 3B15 SS7 1B6	R	33	115	263	52	68	11	7	9	40	28	40	8	.259	.456
Brian Hunter	OF63	R	29	72	200	36	55	4	1	1	13	21	31	15	.275	.320
Darren Bragg	OF43	L	30	71	149	16	33	7	1	3	21	17	41	4	.221	.342
Todd Walker	2B52	L	27	57	171	28	54	10	4	7	36	20	19	4	.316	.544
Todd Hollandsworth	OF48	L	27	56	167	39	54	8	0	11	23	11	38	7	.323	.569
Ben Petrick	C48	R	23	52	146	32	47	10	1	3	20	20	33	1	.322	.466
Juan Pierre	OF50	L	22	51	200	26	62	2	0	0	20	13	15	7	.310	.320
Butch Huskey	OF23 1B8	R	28	45	92	18	32	8	0	4	18	16	14	1	.348	.565
Jeff Frye	2B27 3B1	R	33	37	87	14	31	6	0	0	8	7	4	0	.356	.425
Scott Servais (LJ)	C32	R	33	33	101	6	22	4	0	1	13	7	16	0	.218	.287
Aaron Ledesma	3B5 1B3	R	29	32	40	4	9	2	0	0	4	3	5	0	.225	.275
Adam Melhuse	1B3 C1 OF1	B	28	23	23	3	4	0	0	1	4	3	6	0	.174	.261
Bubba Carpenter	OF6	L	31	15	27	4	6	0	0	3	4	0	13	0	.222	.556
Carlos Mendoza	OF3	R	25	13	10	0	1	0	0	0	1	4	0	0	.100	.100
Elvis Pena	SS3 2B1	B	25	10	9	1	3	1	0	0	1	1	1	1	.333	.444
Angel Echevarria	1B2 OF1	R	29	10	9	0	1	0	0	0	1	1	2	0	.111	.111
Jeff Manto	1B1 3B1	R	35	7	5	2	4	2	0	0	4	2	2	0	.800	1.800

NAME	T	AGE	W	L	PCT	SV	G	GS	CG	IP	H	BB	SO	SHO	ERA
		29	82	80	.506	33	162	162	7	1430	1568	588	1001	2	5.26
Pedro Astacio	R	30	12	9	.571	0	32	32	3	196	217	77	193	0	5.27
Brian Bohanon	L	31	12	10	.545	0	34	26	2	177	189	71	98	1	4.68
Gabe White	L	28	11	2	.846	5	67	0	0	83	62	14	82	0	2.17
Julian Tavarez	R	27	11	5	.688	1	51	12	1	120	124	53	62	0	4.43
Masato Yoshii	R	35	6	15	.286	0	29	29	0	167	201	53	88	0	5.86
Jose Jimenez	R	26	5	2	.714	24	72	0	0	71	63	28	44	0	3.18
Rolando Arrojo	R	31	5	9	.357	0	19	19	0	101	120	46	80	0	6.04
Mike DeJean	R	29	4	4	.500	0	54	0	0	53	54	30	40	0	4.89
Brian Rose	R	24	4	5	.444	0	12	12	0	64	72	30	40	0	5.51
Kevin Jarvis (XJ)	R	30	3	4	.429	0	24	19	0	115	138	33	60	0	5.95
Rick Croushore	R	29	2	0	1.000	0	30	0	0	31	30	35	29	0	3.86
Bobby Chouinard	R	28	2	2	.500	0	31	0	0	33	35	9	23	0	5.33
Scott Karl	L	28	2	3	.400	0	17	9	0	66	95	33	29	0	7.68
Brent Mayne	C	32	1	0	1.000	0	1	0	0	1	1	0	1	0	0.00
Craig House	R	22	1	1	.500	0	16	0	0	14	13	17	18	0	7.24
Stan Belinda	R	33	1	3	.250	1	46	0	0	39	37	40	40	0	7.07
Jerry Dipoto (ZJ)	R	32	1	0	1.000	0	17	0	0	14	16	5	9	0	3.95
David Lee	R	27	0	0	—	0	6	0	0	6	6	4	2	0	11.12
Pete Walker	R	31	0	0	—	0	4	0	0	6	6	2	0	17.36
Rigo Beltran	L	30	0	0	—	0	6	0	0	4	4	3	5	0	40.50
David Moraga	R	24	0	0	—	0	3	0	0					0	45.00
Mike Myers	L	31	0	0	—	1	78	0	0	45	24	23	41	0	1.99
Giovanni Carrara (EJ)	R	32	0	0	—	0	8	0	0	13	21	11	15	0	12.83
Manny Aybar	R	28	0	0	.000	0	2	0	0	2	5	0	0	0	16.20
John Wasdin	R	27	0	1	.000	0	14	3	0	36	42	9	35	0	5.80
John Thomson (SJ) 26															

SAN DIEGO — 5th 76-86 .469 21 — BRUCE BOCHY

Name	G by Pos	B	AGE	G	AB	R	H	2B	3B	HR	RBI	BB	SO	SB	BA	SA
TOTALS			29	162	5560	752	1413	279	37	157	714	602	1177	131	.254	.402
Ryan Klesko	1B136 OF4	L	29	145	494	88	140	33	2	26	92	91	81	23	.283	.516
Bret Boone (KJ)	2B126	R	31	127	463	61	116	18	2	19	74	50	97	8	.251	.421
Damian Jackson	SS88 2B36 OF17	R	26	138	470	68	120	27	6	6	37	62	108	28	.255	.377
Phil Nevin	3B142	R	29	143	538	87	163	34	1	31	107	59	121	2	.303	.543
Tony Gwynn (KJ)	OF26	L	40	36	127	17	41	10	0	1	17	9	4	0	.323	.441
Ruben Rivera	OF132	R	26	135	423	62	88	18	6	17	57	44	137	16	.208	.400
Eric Owens	OF144 2B1	R	29	145	583	87	171	16	7	6	51	45	63	29	.293	.381
Wiki Gonzalez	C87	R	26	95	284	25	66	15	1	5	30	30	31	1	.232	.345
Dave Magadan	3B29 1B8 SS2	L	37	95	132	13	36	7	0	2	21	32	23	0	.273	.371
Al Martin	OF89	L	32	93	346	62	106	13	6	11	27	28	54	6	.306	.474
Kory DeHaan	OF60	L	23	90	103	19	21	7	0	2	13	5	39	4	.204	.330
Ed Sprague	1B25 3B10 OF7 2B1	R	32	73	157	19	41	12	0	10	27	13	40	0	.261	.529
Mike Darr	OF57	L	24	58	205	21	55	14	4	1	30	23	45	9	.268	.390
Carlos Hernandez	C54 1B1	R	33	58	191	16	48	11	0	2	25	16	26	1	.251	.340
John Mabry	OF32 1B2	L	29	48	123	17	28	6	0	7	25	5	38	0	.228	.463
Desi Relaford	SS45	B	26	45	157	26	32	6	2	2	16	27	26	5	.204	.255
Ben Davis	C38	B	23	43	130	12	29	6	0	3	14	14	35	1	.223	.338
Joe Vitiello	1B17 OF1	R	30	39	52	7	13	3	0	2	8	6	14	0	.250	.423
Kevin Nicholson	SS30 2B4	B	24	37	97	7	21	6	1	3	11	6	31	1	.216	.330
Chris Gomez (KJ)	SS17 2B3	R	29	33	54	4	12	3	0	0	2	5	13	0	.222	.222
John Roskos	OF6 1B2	R	25	14	27	4	1	1	0	0	0	1	6	0	.037	.074
David Newhan	OF5 2B3 3B2	L	26	14	20	5	3	1	0	1	2	4	6	0	.150	.350
Greg LaRocca	3B8 SS4 2B2	R	27	14	9	2	2	1	0	0	4	1	2	0	.222	.296
George Williams	C6	B	31	11	16	2	3	1	0	0	3	4	1	0	.188	.375
Gabe Alvarez	3B3 OF2	R	26	11	13	1	2	1	0	0	1	1	6	0	.154	.231
Dusty Allen	OF2 1B1	R	27	9	12	0	0	0	0	0	0	1	6	0	.000	.000
Xavier Nady		R	21	1	1	1	1	1	0	0	0	0	1	0	1.000	1.000

NAME	T	AGE	W	L	PCT	SV	G	GS	CG	IP	H	BB	SO	SHO	ERA
		28	76	86	.469	46	162	162	5	1459	1443	649	1071	5	4.52
Matt Clement	R	25	13	17	.433	0	34	34	0	205	194	125	170	0	5.14
Woody Williams (SJ)	R	33	10	8	.556	0	23	23	4	168	152	54	111	0	3.75
Kevin Walker	L	23	7	1	.875	0	70	0	0	67	49	38	56	0	4.19
Adam Eaton	R	22	7	4	.636	0	22	22	0	135	134	61	90	0	4.13
Brian Meadows	R	24	7	8	.467	0	22	22	0	125	150	50	53	0	5.34
Donne Wall (SJ)	R	32	5	4	.556	4	44	0	0	54	36	21	59	0	3.58
Brian Tollberg	R	26	4	5	.444	0	19	19	1	118	126	35	76	0	3.58
Carlos Almanzar	R	26	4	5	.444	0	62	0	0	70	73	25	56	0	4.39
Trevor Hoffman	R	32	4	7	.364	43	70	0	0	72	61	11	85	0	2.99
Jay Witasick	R	27	3	8	.600	0	11	11	0	61	69	35	54	0	5.46
Tom Davey	R	26	1	1	.667	0	11	0	0	13	12	2	7	0	0.71
Stan Spencer (EJ)	R	31	2	0	.500	0	10	10	0	44	44	19	40	0	3.26
Matt Whisenant	L	29	2	2	.500	0	21	0	0	21	16	17	12	0	3.80
Matt Whiteside	R	32	1	3	.400	0	20	0	0	30	32	17	27	0	4.14
Dave Maurer	L	25	1	0	1.000	0	14	0	0	15	15	5	13	0	3.68
Will Cunnane	R	26	1	1	.500	0	38	0	0	35	38	21	34	0	4.23
Carlos Reyes	R	31	1	1	.500	0	21	0	0	18	15	13	10	0	6.00
Sterling Hitchcock (EJ)	L	29	1	6	.143	0	11	9	0	49	69	26	61	0	4.93
Todd Erdos	R	26	0	1	—	0	22	0	0	30	32	17	16	0	6.67
Dan Serafini	L	26	0	0	—	0	2	0	0	6	6	3	3	0	18.00
Buddy Carlyle	R	22	0	1	.000	0	1	1	0	4	9	6	1	0	21.00
Rodney Myers (SJ-KJ)	R	31	0	0	—	0	6	0	0	10	12	4	9	0	4.50
Domingo Guzman	R	25	0	0	—	0	3	0	0					0	9.00
Heathcliff Slocumb	R	34	0	0	—	0	6	0	0	12	13	7	5	0	3.79
Brandon Kolb	R	26	0	0	—	0	4	0	0					0	4.50
Vicente Palacios	R	36	0	1	.000	0	5	0	0					0	6.75
Steve Montgomery (SJ)	R	29	0	1	.000	0	8	0	0					0	7.94
Rodrigo Lopez	R	24	0	1	.000	0	5	0	0	25	40	13	17	0	8.76
Brian Boehringer (SJ)	R	31	0	3	.000	0	10	1	0	18	18	10	9	0	5.74

Carlton Loewer (BL) 26   Randy Myers (SJ) 37

LINE SCORES

Team	1	2	3	4	5	6	7	8	9	10	11	12	13	R	H	E

DIVISION SERIES: NEW YORK 3 : SAN FRANCISCO 1

Game 1 October 4 at San Francisco

	1	2	3	4	5	6	7	8	9		R	H	E
NYN	0	0	1	0	0	0	0	0	0		1	5	0
SF	1	0	4	0	0	0	0	0	X		5	10	0

Hampton, Wendell (6), Cook (7),   **Hernandez**, Rodriguez (8), Nen (9)
White (7), Rusch (8)

Game 2 October 5 at San Francisco

	1	2	3	4	5	6	7	8	9	10	R	H	E
NYN	0	2	0	0	0	0	0	0	2	1	5	10	0
SF	0	1	0	0	0	0	0	3	0		4	8	0

Leiter, **Benitez** (9), J. Franco (10)   Estes, Rueter (4), Henry (8), **Rodriguez** (9)

Game 3 October 7 at New York

	1	2	3	4	5	6	7	8	9	10	11	12	13	R	H	E
SF	0	0	0	2	0	0	0	0	0	0	0	0	0	2	11	0
NYN	0	0	0	0	0	1	0	1	0	0	0	0	1	3	9	0

Ortiz, Embree (6), Henry (7), Nen (8),   Reed, Cook (7), Wendell (7), J. Franco (9)
Rodriguez (10), Fultz (12)   Benitez (10), **White** (12)

Game 4 October 8 at New York

	1	2	3	4	5	6	7	8	9		R	H	E
SF	0	0	0	0	0	0	0	0	0		0	1	1
NYN	2	0	0	0	2	0	0	0	X		4	6	0

Gardner, Henry (5), Embree (7), Del Toro (8)   **B.J. Jones**

DIVISION SERIES: ST. LOUIS 3 : ATLANTA 0

Game 1 October 3 at St. Louis

	1	2	3	4	5	6	7	8	9		R	H	E
ATL	0	0	4	0	0	0	0	0	1		5	8	3
STL	6	0	0	1	0	0	0	0	X		7	11	1

Maddux, Remlinger (5), Mulholland (6),   Ankiel, **James** (3), Timlin (6),
Rocker (8), Ligtenberg (8)   Reames (7), Veres (9)

Game 2 October 5 at St. Louis

	1	2	3	4	5	6	7	8	9		R	H	E
ATL	2	0	0	0	0	0	0	2	0		4	7	1
STL	3	1	3	1	0	1	0	1	X		10	9	0

Glavine, Ashby (3), Burkett (5), Mulholland (6),   **Kile**, Christiansen (8), Timlin (8),
Ligtenberg (8), Remlinger (9)   Morris (9)

Game 3 October 7 at Atlanta

	1	2	3	4	5	6	7	8	9		R	H	E
STL	1	0	2	0	1	3	0	0	0		7	8	0
ATL	1	0	0	0	0	0	0	0	0		1	3	1

Stephenson, **Reames** (4), James (6),   **Millwood**, Mulholland (5),
Morris (8), Veres (9)   Ligtenberg (6), Remlinger (6), Ashby (8)

COMPOSITE BATTING

DIVISION SERIES

NAME	POS	G	AB	R	H	2B	3B	HR	RBI	BA

NEW YORK

NAME	POS	G	AB	R	H	2B	3B	HR	RBI	BA
TOTALS		4	143	13	30	7	0	3	13	.210
Alfonzo	2B	4	18	1	5	2	0	1	5	.278
Perez	RF	4	17	2	5	1	0	0	3	.294
Payton	CF	4	17	1	3	0	0	0	2	.176
Agbayani	LF	4	15	1	5	1	0	1	1	.333
Piazza	C	4	14	1	3	1	0	0	0	.214
Ventura	3B-1B	4	14	1	2	0	0	1	2	.143
Zeile	1B	4	14	0	1	1	0	0	0	.071
Bordick	SS	4	12	3	2	0	0	0	0	.167
Hamilton	RF-LF	3	4	1	2	1	0	0	0	.500
B.J. Jones	P	1	4	1	0	0	0	0	0	.000
Leiter	P	1	4	0	0	0	0	0	0	.000
Harris	PH	2	2	1	0	0	0	0	0	.000
Hampton	P	1	2	0	1	0	0	0	0	.500
Abbott	SS	1	2	0	0	0	0	0	0	.000
McEwing	LF-3B	4	1	0	1	0	0	0	0	1.000
Bell	RF	1	1	0	0	0	0	0	0	.000
Pratt	C	1	1	0	0	0	0	0	0	.000
Reed	P	1	1	0	0	0	0	0	0	.000
Benitez	P	2	0	0	0	0	0	0	0	—
Cook	P	2	0	0	0	0	0	0	0	—
J. Franco	P	2	0	0	0	0	0	0	0	—
Wendell	P	2	0	0	0	0	0	0	0	—
White	P	2	0	0	0	0	0	0	0	—
Rusch	P	1	0	0	0	0	0	0	0	—

SAN FRANCISCO

NAME	POS	G	AB	R	H	2B	3B	HR	RBI	BA
TOTALS		4	146	11	30	6	1	2	11	.205
Mueller	3B	4	20	2	5	2	0	0	0	.250
Bonds	LF	4	17	2	3	1	1	0	1	.176
Kent	2B-1B	4	16	3	6	1	0	0	1	.375
Aurilia	SS	4	15	2	2	1	0	0	0	.133
Benard	CF-RF	4	14	0	1	0	0	0	1	.071
Burks	RF	4	13	2	3	1	0	1	4	.231
Estalella	C	4	12	1	1	0	0	0	1	.083
Snow	1B	4	10	1	4	0	0	1	3	.400
Martinez	2B-SS	2	6	0	2	0	0	0	0	.333
Murray	CF	3	5	0	1	0	0	0	0	.200
Crespo	PH	4	4	0	1	0	0	0	0	.250
Hernandez	P	1	3	0	0	0	0	0	0	.000
Ortiz	P	1	3	0	0	0	0	0	0	.000
Rios	PH	2	2	0	1	0	0	0	0	.500
Davis	PH	2	2	0	0	0	0	0	0	.000
Mirabelli	C	2	2	0	0	0	0	0	0	.000
Gardner	P	1	2	0	0	0	0	0	0	.000
Henry	P	3	0	0	0	0	0	0	0	—
Rodriguez	P	3	0	0	0	0	0	0	0	—
Embree	P	2	0	0	0	0	0	0	0	—
Nen	P	2	0	0	0	0	0	0	0	—
Del Toro	P	1	0	0	0	0	0	0	0	—
Estes	P	1	0	0	0	0	0	0	0	—
Fultz	P	1	0	0	0	0	0	0	0	—
Rueter	P	1	0	0	0	0	0	0	0	—

ST. LOUIS

NAME	POS	G	AB	R	H	2B	3B	HR	RBI	BA
TOTALS		3	102	24	28	5	0	6	23	.275
Edmonds	CF	3	14	5	8	4	0	2	7	.571
Vina	2B	3	13	3	4	0	0	1	3	.308
Clark	1B	3	12	3	3	0	0	1	4	.250
Hernandez	C	3	11	3	3	0	0	1	1	.273
Polanco	3B	3	10	1	3	0	0	0	3	.300
Lankford	LF	3	10	2	2	1	0	0	3	.200
Renteria	SS	3	10	5	2	0	0	0	0	.200
Drew	RF	2	6	1	1	0	0	0	0	.167
Davis	RF	2	4	0	0	0	0	0	1	.000
Kile	P	2	3	0	0	0	0	0	0	.000
McGwire	PH	3	2	1	1	0	0	1	1	.500
Paquette	LF-3B	2	2	0	0	0	0	0	0	.000
James	P	2	1	0	0	0	0	0	0	.000
Reames	P	2	1	0	0	0	0	0	0	.000
Dunston	PH	1	1	0	1	0	0	0	0	1.000
Ankiel	P	1	1	0	0	0	0	0	0	.000
Stephenson	P	1	1	0	0	0	0	0	0	.000
Morris	P	2	0	0	0	0	0	0	0	—
Timlin	P	2	0	0	0	0	0	0	0	—
Veres	P	2	0	0	0	0	0	0	0	—
Christiansen	P	1	0	0	0	0	0	0	0	—

ATLANTA

NAME	POS	G	AB	R	H	2B	3B	HR	RBI	BA
TOTALS		3	95	10	18	5	0	1	9	.189
C. Jones	3B	3	12	2	4	1	0	0	1	.333
Jordan	RF	3	11	1	4	1	0	0	4	.364
Furcal	SS-2B	3	11	2	1	0	0	0	0	.091
Lopez	C	3	11	0	1	0	0	0	0	.091
Galarraga	1B	3	10	1	2	1	0	0	0	.200
A. Jones	CF	3	9	3	1	0	0	1	1	.111
Sanders	LF	3	9	0	0	0	0	0	0	.000
Lockhart	2B	3	8	1	1	0	0	0	0	.125
Joyner	PH	3	3	0	1	1	0	0	0	.333
Weiss	SS	1	3	0	2	1	0	0	2	.667
Bonilla	LF	3	2	0	0	0	0	0	0	.000
Surhoff	PH	2	2	0	1	0	0	0	0	.500
Bako	C	2	1	0	0	0	0	0	0	.000
Glavine	P	1	1	0	0	0	0	0	0	.000
Maddux	P	2	1	1	0	0	0	0	0	.000
Millwood	P	1	1	0	0	0	0	0	0	.000
Ligtenberg	P	3	0	0	0	0	0	0	0	—
Mulholland	P	3	0	0	0	0	0	0	0	—
Remlinger	P	3	0	0	0	0	0	0	0	—
Ashby	P	3	0	0	0	0	0	0	0	—
Burkett	P	1	0	0	0	0	0	0	0	—
Rocker	P	1	0	0	0	0	0	0	0	—

COMPOSITE PITCHING

NAME	G	IP	H	BB	SO	W	L	SV	ERA

NEW YORK

NAME	G	IP	H	BB	SO	W	L	SV	ERA
TOTALS	4	40	30	16	36	3	1	1	2.48
B.J. Jones	1	9	1	2	5	1	0	0	0.00
Leiter	1	8	5	3	6	0	0	0	2.25
Reed	1	6	7	2	6	0	0	0	3.00
Hampton	1	5.1	6	3	2	0	1	0	8.44
Benitez	2	3	4	1	3	1	0	0	6.00
White	2	2.2	6	2	4	1	0	0	0.00
J. Franco	2	2	1	0	2	0	0	1	0.00
Wendell	2	2	0	1	5	0	0	0	0.00
Cook	2	1.1	0	2	1	0	0	0	0.00
Rusch	1	0.2	0	0	2	0	0	0	0.00

SAN FRANCISCO

NAME	G	IP	H	BB	SO	W	L	SV	ERA
TOTALS	4	39.1	30	20	30	1	3	0	2.97
Hernandez	1	7.2	5	5	5	1	0	0	1.17
Ortiz	1	5.1	2	4	4	0	0	0	1.69
Rodriguez	3	4.1	6	1	6	0	1	0	6.23
Rueter	1	4.1	3	1	1	0	0	0	0.00
Gardner	1	4.1	4	2	5	0	1	0	8.31
Henry	3	4	1	3	1	0	0	0	2.25
Estes	1	3	3	2	1	0	0	0	6.00
Nen	2	2.1	2	1	3	0	0	0	0.00
Embree	2	1.2	0	0	0	0	0	0	0.00
Fultz	1	1.1	3	0	0	0	1	0	6.75
Del Toro	1	1	1	0	2	0	0	0	0.00

ST. LOUIS

NAME	G	IP	H	BB	SO	W	L	SV	ERA
TOTALS	3	27	18	16	20	3	0	1	3.00
Kile	1	7	4	2	6	1	0	0	2.57
James	2	4.1	1	1	1	1	0	0	0.00
Stephenson	1	3.2	3	2	2	0	0	0	2.45
Reames	2	3.1	0	3	2	1	0	0	0.00
Ankiel	1	2.2	4	6	3	0	0	0	13.50
Morris	2	2	1	0	4	0	0	1	0.00
Veres	2	2	1	0	4	0	0	1	0.00
Timlin	2	1.2	5	1	2	0	0	0	10.80
Christiansen	1	0.1	0	0	0	0	0	0	0.00

ATLANTA

NAME	G	IP	H	BB	SO	W	L	SV	ERA
TOTALS	3	25	28	14	19	0	3	0	7.92
Millwood	1	4.2	4	3	3	0	1	0	7.71
Maddux	1	4	9	3	2	0	1	0	11.25
Ashby	2	3.2	1	3	5	0	0	0	2.45
Remlinger	3	3.1	6	0	3	0	0	0	2.70
Mulholland	3	3.1	2	1	0	0	0	0	5.40
Glavine	1	2.1	6	1	2	0	1	0	27.00
Ligtenberg	3	1.2	0	1	3	0	0	0	5.40
Burkett	1	1.1	1	0	0	0	0	0	6.75
Rocker	1	0.2	0	1	0	0	0	0	0.00

LINE SCORES

CHAMPIONSHIP: NEW YORK 4 : ST. LOUIS 1

Team	1	2	3	4	5	6	7	8	9	10	11	12	13	14	15	R	H	E

Game 1   October 11 at St. Louis

| NYN | 2 | 0 | 0 | 0 | 1 | 0 | 0 | 0 | 3 | | | | | | | 6 | 8 | 3 |
| STL | 0 | 0 | 0 | 0 | 0 | 0 | 0 | 0 | 2 | | | | | | | 2 | 9 | 0 |

Hampton, J. Franco (8), Benitez (9)   Kile, James (8), Christiansen (9)

Game 2   October 12 at St. Louis

| NYN | 2 | 0 | 1 | 0 | 0 | 0 | 0 | 2 | 1 | | | | | | | 6 | 9 | 0 |
| STL | 0 | 1 | 0 | 0 | 2 | 0 | 0 | 2 | 0 | | | | | | | 5 | 10 | 3 |

Leiter, J. Franco (8), **Wendell** (8), Benitez (9)   Ankiel, Reames (1), Morris (6), Veres (8), **Timlin** (9)

Game 3   October 14 at New York

| STL | 2 | 0 | 2 | 1 | 3 | 0 | 0 | 0 | 0 | | | | | | | 8 | 14 | 0 |
| NYN | 1 | 0 | 0 | 1 | 0 | 0 | 0 | 0 | 0 | | | | | | | 2 | 7 | 1 |

An. Benes, James (9), Veres (9)   Reed, Rusch (4), White (5), Cook (8), Wendell (9)

Game 4   October 15 at New York

| STL | 2 | 0 | 0 | 1 | 3 | 0 | 0 | 0 | 0 | | | | | | | 6 | 11 | 2 |
| NYN | 4 | 3 | 0 | 1 | 0 | 2 | 0 | 0 | X | | | | | | | 10 | 9 | 0 |

Kile, James (4), Timlin (5), Morris (7),   B.J. Jones, **Rusch** (5), J. Franco (8), Christiansen (8)   Benitez (9)

Game 5   October 16 at New York

| STL | 0 | 0 | 0 | 0 | 0 | 0 | 0 | 0 | 0 | | | | | | | 0 | 3 | 2 |
| NYN | 3 | 0 | 0 | 3 | 0 | 0 | 1 | 0 | X | | | | | | | 7 | 10 | 0 |

Hentgen, Timlin (4), Reames (5),   **Hampton** Ankiel (7), James (7), Veres (8)

COMPOSITE BATTING

NAME	POS	G	AB	R	H	2B	3B	HR	RBI	BA
NEW YORK										
TOTALS		5	164	31	43	12	1	4	27	.262
Perez	RF-CF	5	23	8	7	2	0	0	0	.304
Zeile	1B	5	19	1	7	3	0	1	8	.368
Payton	CF	5	19	1	3	0	0	1	3	.158
Alfonzo	2B	5	18	5	8	1	1	0	4	.444
Piazza	C	5	17	7	7	3	0	2	4	.412
Agbayani	LF	5	17	0	6	2	0	0	3	.353
Ventura	3B	5	14	4	3	1	0	0	5	.214
Bordick	SS	5	13	2	1	0	0	0	0	.077
Hampton	P	2	6	1	1	0	0	0	0	.167
Trammell	PH	3	3	0	0	0	0	0	0	.000
Abbott	SS	2	3	0	0	0	0	0	0	.000
M. Franco	1B	2	3	0	0	0	0	0	0	.000
Leiter	P	1	3	0	0	0	0	0	0	.000
Hamilton	PH	3	2	0	0	0	0	0	0	.000
B.J. Jones	P	1	2	0	0	0	0	0	0	.000
Harris	P	2	1	0	0	0	0	0	0	.000
Reed	P	1	1	0	0	0	0	0	0	.000
McEwing	LF-3B-RF	4	0	2	0	0	0	0	0	—
Benitez	P	3	0	0	0	0	0	0	0	—
J. Franco	P	3	0	0	0	0	0	0	0	—
Rusch	P	2	0	0	0	0	0	0	0	—
Wendell	P	2	0	0	0	0	0	0	0	—
Cook	P	1	0	0	0	0	0	0	0	—
White	P	1	0	0	0	0	0	0	0	—

NAME	POS	G	AB	R	H	2B	3B	HR	RBI	BA
ST. LOUIS										
TOTALS		5	177	21	47	11	0	2	18	.266
Vina	2B	5	23	3	6	1	0	0	1	.261
Edmonds	CF	5	22	1	5	1	0	1	5	.227
Renteria	SS	5	20	4	6	1	0	0	4	.300
Clark	1B	5	17	3	7	2	0	1	1	.412
Hernandez	C	5	16	3	4	0	0	0	1	.250
Tatis	3B	5	13	1	3	2	0	0	2	.231
Drew	LF-RF	5	12	2	4	1	0	0	1	.333
Lankford	LF	5	12	1	4	1	0	0	1	.333
Davis	RF	4	10	1	2	1	0	0	0	.200
Dunston	LF-RF	4	6	2	2	1	0	0	0	.333
Paquette	3B-LF-RF	4	6	0	1	0	0	0	0	.167
Polanco	3B	4	5	0	1	0	0	0	0	.200
Marrero	C	4	4	0	0	0	0	0	1	.000
An. Benes	P	2	3	1	1	0	0	0	0	.333
Kile	P	3	2	0	0	0	0	0	0	.000
McGwire	PH	3	2	0	0	0	0	0	0	.000
Wilkins	PH	2	2	0	0	0	0	0	0	.000
Reames	P	2	1	0	0	0	0	0	0	.000
Hentgen	P	1	1	0	1	0	0	0	0	1.000
James	P	4	0	0	0	0	0	0	0	—
Timlin	p	3	0	0	0	0	0	0	0	—
Veres	p	3	0	0	0	0	0	0	0	—
Ankiel	P	2	0	0	0	0	0	0	0	—
Christiansen	P	2	0	0	0	0	0	0	0	—
Morris	P	2	0	0	0	0	0	0	0	—

COMPOSITE PITCHING

NAME	G	IP	H	BB	SO	W	L	SV	ERA
NEW YORK									
TOTALS	5	45	47	11	39	4	1	1	3.60
Hampton	2	16	9	4	12	2	0	0	0.00
Leiter	1	7	8	0	9	0	0	0	3.86
B.J. Jones	1	4	6	0	2	0	0	0	13.50
Rusch	2	3.2	3	0	3	1	0	0	0.00
Reed	1	3.1	8	1	4	0	1	0	10.80
Benitez	3	3	3	2	2	0	0	1	0.00
White	1	3	5	1	1	0	0	0	9.00
J. Franco	3	2.2	3	2	2	0	0	0	6.75
Wendell	2	1.1	1	1	2	1	0	0	0.00
Cook	1	1	1	0	2	0	0	0	0.00

NAME	G	IP	H	BB	SO	W	L	SV	ERA
ST. LOUIS									
TOTALS	5	43	43	27	24	1	4	0	5.86
Kile	2	10	13	5	3	0	2	0	9.00
An. Benes	1	8	6	3	5	1	0	0	2.25
Reames	2	6.1	5	4	6	0	0	0	1.42
Morris	2	3.2	3	2	2	0	0	0	4.91
Hentgen	1	3.2	7	5	2	0	1	0	14.73
Timlin	3	3.1	1	2	0	0	1	0	0.00
James	4	2.1	5	1	0	0	0	0	15.43
Veres	3	2.1	2	0	3	0	0	0	0.00
Christiansen	2	2	0	0	1	0	0	0	0.00
Ankiel	2	1.1	1	5	2	0	0	0	20.25

MISCELLANEOUS 2000 INDIVIDUAL LEADERS

BATTING

On Base Average

	American League			National League	
1	Ja. Giambi, Oak.	.476	1	Helton, Col.	.463
2	Delgado, Tor.	.470	2	Bonds, S.F.	.440
3	M. Ramirez, Cle.	.457	3	Sheffield, L.A.	.438
4	Thomas, Chi.	.436	4	Giles, Pit.	.432
5	Garciaparra, Bos.	.434	5	Alfonzo, N.Y.	.425
6	Martinez, Sea.	.423	6	Kent, S.F.	.424
7	Rodriguez, Sea.	.420		Bagwell, Hou.	.424
8	Posada, N.Y.	.417	8	Castillo, Fla.	.418
9	Jeter, N.Y.	.416	9	Abreu, Phi.	.416
10	Erstad, Ana.	.409		Alou, Hou.	.416
				Clark, Bal.-St.L.	.418

On Base Average plus Slugging Average

	American League			National League	
1	M. Ramirez, Cle.	1.154	1	Helton, Col.	1.162
2	Delgado, Tor.	1.134	2	Bonds, S.F.	1.127
3	Ja. Giambi, Oak.	1.123	3	Sheffield, L.A.	1.081
4	Thomas, Chi.	1.061	4	V. Guerrero, Mon.	1.074
5	Garciaparra, Bos.	1.033	5	Sosa, Chi.	1.040
6	Rodriguez, Sea.	1.026	6	Bagwell, Hou.	1.039
7	Glaus, Ana.	1.008	7	Alou, Hou.	1.039
8	Martinez, Sea.	1.002	8	Hidalgo, Hou.	1.028
9	Justice, Cle.-N.Y.	.961	9	Giles, Pit.	1.026
10	Everett, Bos.	.959	10	Kent, S.F.	1.021

Total Bases

	American League			National League	
1	Delgado, Tor.	378	1	Helton, Col.	405
2	Erstad, Ana.	366	2	Sosa, Chi.	383
3	Thomas, Chi.	364	3	V. Guerrero, Mon.	379
4	Glaus, Ana.	340	4	Bagwell, Hou.	363
5	Dye, K.C.	337	5	Hidalgo, Hou.	355
6	Rodriguez, Sea.	336	6	A. Jones, Atl.	355
	Anderson, Ana.	336	7	Kent, S.F.	350
8	Ja. Giambi, Oak.	330	8	Gonzalez, Ari.	336
9	Damon, K.C.	324	9	Giles, Pit.	332
10	Sweeney, K.C.	323	10	Bonds, S.F.	330

Caught Stealing

	American League			National League	
1	McLemore, Sea.	14	1	Castillo, Fla.	22
2	Durham, Chi.	13	2	Owens, S.D.	14
3	Williams, T.B.	12		Wilson, Fla.	14
4	Glaus, Ana.	11		Furcal, Atl.	14
5	DeShields, Bal.	10	5	Renteria, St.L.	13
	Guzman, Min.	10		Bergeron, Mon.	13
	Vizquel, Cle.	10			

Stolen Base Percentage
(Minimum 20 Attempts)

	American League			National League	
1	R. Alomar, Cle.	91	1	Reese, Cin.	91
2	Valentine, Chi.	91	2	Floyd, Fla.	89
3	Jeter, N.Y.	85	3	Goodwin, Col.-L.A.	89
4	Damon, K.C.	84	4	Hunter, Col.-Cin.	87
5	Ordonez, Chi.	82	5	Sanders, Atl.	84

Extra Base Hits

	American League			National League	
1	Delgado, Tor.	99	1	Helton, Col.	103
2	Thomas, Chi.	87	2	Hidalgo, Hou.	89
3	Glaus, Ana.	85	3	Sosa, Chi.	89
4	Anderson, Ana.	78	4	Bagwell, Hou.	85
5	Higginson, Det.	78	5	V. Guerrero, Mon.	83

PITCHING

Fewest Hits Per 9 Innings Pitched

	American League			National League	
1	P. Martinez, Bos.	5.31	1	Park, L.A.	6.89
2	Hudson, Oak.	7.52	2	Ankiel, St.L.	7.05
3	Colon, Cle.	7.80	3	Brown, L.A.	7.08
4	Clemens, N.Y.	8.10	4	Johnson, Ari.	7.31
5	Abbott, Sea.	8.25	5	Person, Phi.	7.48
6	Hernandez, N.Y.	8.56	6	Leiter, N.Y.	7.62
7	Finley, Tex.	8.71	7	D'Amico, Mil.	7.93
8	Helling, Tex.	8.79	8	Hampton, N.Y.	8.02
9	Mussina, Bal.	8.94	9	Maddux, Atl.	8.12
10	Ponson, Bal.	9.04	10	Williams, S.D.	8.14

Fewest Bases on Balls Per 9 Innings Pitched

	American League			National League	
1	Wells, Tor.	1.21	1	Maddux, Atl.	1.52
2	P. Martinez, Bos.	1.33	2	Anderson, Ari.	1.65
3	Mussina, Bal.	1.74	3	Reed, N.Y.	1.66
4	Milton, Min.	1.98	4	Brown, L.A.	1.84
5	Moehler, Det.	2.02	5	Schilling, Phi.-Ari.	1.93
6	Radke, Min.	2.03	6	Lieber, Chi.	1.94
7	Rekar, T.B.	2.03	7	Rusch, N.Y.	2.08
8	Weaver, Det.	2.34	8	Tapani, Chi.	2.16
9	Hernandez, N.Y.	2.35	9	Kile, St.L.	2.25
10	Loaiza, Tex.-Tor.	2.57	10	Glavine, Atl.	2.43

Strikeouts Per 9 Innings Pitched

	American League			National League	
1	P. Martinez, Bos.	11.78	1	Johnson, Ari.	12.56
2	Colon, Cle.	10.15	2	Ankiel, St.L.	9.98
3	Nomo, Det.	8.57	3	Astacio, Col.	8.85
4	Burba, Cle.	8.47	4	Leiter, N.Y.	8.65
5	Clemens, N.Y.	8.28	5	Park, L.A.	8.64
6	Mussina, Bal.	7.95	6	Person, Phi.	8.52
7	Finley, Tex.	7.80	7	Brown, L.A.	8.45
8	Hudson, Oak.	7.52	8	Dempster, Fla.	8.31
9	Milton, Min.	7.20	9	Vazquez, Mon.	8.10
10	Escobar, Tor.	7.10	10	Ortiz, S.F.	7.68

Lowest Batting Average Allowed

	American League			National League	
1	P. Martinez, Bos.	.167	1	Brown, L.A.	.213
2	Hudson, Oak.	.227	2	Park, L.A.	.214
3	Colon, Cle.	.233	3	Ankiel, St.L.	.219
4	Clemens, N.Y.	.236	4	Johnson, Ari.	.224
5	Abbott, Sea.	.243	5	Leiter, N.Y.	.228

Home Runs Allowed

	American League			National League	
1	Suppan, K.C.	36	1	Lima, Hou.	48
2	Milton, Min.	35	2	Anderson, Ari.	38
3	Baldwin, Chi.	34	3	Lieber, Chi.	36
	Hernandez, N.Y.	34	4	Tapani, Chi.	35
5	Wakefield, Bos.	31	5	Kile, St.L.	33
	Nomo, Det.	31			

Home Runs Allowed per 9 IP
(Minimum 10 Home Runs Allowed)

	American League			National League	
1	Lincoln, Min.	4.35	1	Belinda, Col.-Atl.	2.70
2	Etherton, Ana.	2.39	2	Lima, Hou.	2.20
3	Bergman, Min.	2.38	3	Quevedo, Chi.	2.15
4	Nagy, Cle.	2.37	4	Aguilera, Chi.	2.08
5	Mercker, Ana.	2.23	5	Bell, Cin.	2.05
				Batista, Mon.-K.C.	2.62

DEJA 26

A year after being crowned "The Team of the 20th Century," the New York Yankees began their assault on the 21st by winning their 26th World Series and fourth in the last five years. Joe Torre's Bombers struggled at times during the regular season and first playoff round. But they picked up momentum in the ALCS and peaked against the Mets in the first "Subway Series" since 1951. The prospect of watching two New York teams play for the championship delighted New York fans but left most of the nation apathetic and brought the lowest television ratings ever.

Atlanta, sporting its one-two, Maddux-Glavine pitching punch, was favored to win the National League pennant. Instead, the Cardinals pummeled the two aces at St. Louis in the first two division playoff games, then made it a sweep with a 7-1 victory before the Braves' home fans. Shoddy Atlanta fielding aided the Cardinals no end.

The Mets' less heralded pitchers proved far more effective. After dropping the opening game of their series, New York blazed through the next three to top suddenly punchless San Francisco. Led by Barry Bonds' 3-for-17, the Giants went scoreless through the final 18 innings. Bobby Jones' one-hitter delivered the final game to the Mets.

The Cardinals' pitching fell apart against the Mets in their duel for the N.L. pennant. Most disastrous were the appearances of 21-year-old lefthander Rick Ankiel. In four post-season innings, he walked 11 and threw 7 wild pitches. St. Louis only win in five games came in the third when righthander Andy Benes gave them a good effort. Second baseman Elgardo Alfonzo was outstanding for New York.

In the American League Divisional Playoff, the Mariners made short work of the White Sox. The key hit of the series sweep came in the bottom of the ninth inning of the third game when Carlos Guillan, making his first appearance, pinch-hit a squeeze bunt single to give Seattle a 2-1 win.

The Yankees had all they could handle through the first four games of their series with Oakland. An 11-1 thrashing of New York in Game 4 appeared to give the A's momentum going into the final game, but the next day the Yankees sank Gil Heredia with a six-run, first-inning salvo. Then New York's sterling bullpen held off Oakland as the invulnerable Mariano Rivera earned his third save of the series.

The four-day layoff between their playoff win over the White Sox and their first ALCS game with the Yankees cooled off the Mariners who were quickly down three games to one. Seattle managed to force the series back to Yankee Stadium with a Game 5 win behind Freddy Garcia and its strong bullpen. After 48 hours and 3,000 miles, the Yankees ended the Mariners' hope of becoming the first A.L. wild card team to reach the World Series. David Justice who smashed the go-ahead home run in the Yankees' big seventh inning, was named ALCS MVP.

The first "Subway Series" since the Giants were in New York may not have excited most of the country, but all five games were close. Yankees' second baseman Jose Vizcaino singled home the winning run in the 12th inning to win the opener. The next day, Roger Clemens shut out the Mets for eight innings. A five run Mets' rally in the ninth fell one run short. The main topic of conversation afterward was Clemens' provocative tossing of a piece of broken bat at Met Mike Piazza. Piazza had accused Clemens of intentionally beaning him in a midseason, interleague game.

When the Series moved to Shea Stadium, the Mets ended the Yankees' streak of 14 straight World Series wins in Game 3 as Benny Agbayani drove in the winning run in the eighth. The Yankees started a new streak the next day on Derek Jeter's offense coupled with a brilliant bullpen. Jeter was named Series MVP. Mets' hurler Al Leiter was excellent through 8 2/3 innings of the fifth and final game, but with the score tied 2-2, two outs and none on, he lost it. A walk, a single, and Luis Sojo's single produced two runs and, with Joe Torre's bullpen, the Yankees could begin their celebration.

WORLD SERIES

LINE SCORES

Team	1	2	3	4	5	6	7	8	9	10	11	12	R	H	E

WORLD SERIES: NEW YORK (AL) 4 : NEW YORK (NL) 1

Game 1   October 21 at Yankee Stadium

	1	2	3	4	5	6	7	8	9	10	11	12	R	H	E
NYN	0	0	0	0	0	0	3	0	0	0	0	0	3	10	0
NYA	0	0	0	0	0	2	0	0	1	0	0	1	4	12	0

Leiter, J. Franco (8), Benitez (9), Cook (10), Rusch (10), **Wendell** (11)

Pettitte, Nelson (7), Rivera (9), Stanton (11)

Game 2   October 22 at Yankee Stadium

	1	2	3	4	5	6	7	8	9	R	H	E
NYN	0	0	0	0	0	0	0	0	5	5	7	3
NYA	2	1	0	0	1	0	1	1	X	6	12	1

Hampton, Rusch (7), White (7), Cook (8)

Clemens, Nelson (9), Rivera (9)

Game 3   October 24 at Shea Stadium

	1	2	3	4	5	6	7	8	9	R	H	E
NYA	0	0	1	1	0	0	0	0	0	2	8	0
NYN	0	1	0	0	0	1	0	2	X	4	9	0

Hernandez, Stanton (8)

Reed, **Wendell** (7), Cook (7), J. Franco (8), Benitez (9)

Game 4   October 25 at Shea Stadium

	1	2	3	4	5	6	7	8	9	R	H	E
NYA	1	1	1	0	0	0	0	0	0	3	8	0
NYN	0	0	2	0	0	0	0	0	0	2	6	1

Neagle, Cone (5), **Nelson** (6), Stanton (7), Rivera (8)

B. J. Jones, Rusch (6), J. Franco (8), Benitez (9)

Game 5   October 26 at Shea Stadium

	1	2	3	4	5	6	7	8	9	R	H	E
NYA	0	1	0	0	0	1	0	0	2	4	7	1
NYN	0	2	0	0	0	0	0	0	0	2	8	1

Pettitte, Stanton (8), Rivera (9)

Leiter, J. Franco (9)

COMPOSITE BATTING

NAME	POS	G	AB	R	H	2B	3B	HR	RBI	BA
NEW YORK (A)										
TOTALS		5	179	19	47	8	3	4	18	.263
Jeter	SS	5	22	6	9	2	1	2	2	.409
Martinez	1B	5	22	3	8	1	0	0	2	.364
O'Neill	RF	5	19	2	9	2	2	0	2	.474
Justice	LF	5	19	1	3	2	0	0	3	.158
Posada	C	5	18	2	4	1	0	0	1	.222
Williams	CF	5	18	2	2	0	0	1	1	.111
Vizcaino	2B	4	17	0	4	0	0	0	1	.235
Brosius	3B	5	13	2	4	0	0	1	3	.308
Knoblauch	DH	4	10	1	1	0	0	0	1	.100
Sojo	3B-2B	4	7	0	2	0	0	0	2	.286
Hill	LF	3	3	0	0	0	0	0	0	.000
Pettitte	P	2	3	0	0	0	0	0	0	.000
Polonia	PH	2	2	0	1	0	0	0	0	.500
Hernandez	P	1	2	0	0	0	0	0	0	.000
Neagle	P	1	2	0	0	0	0	0	0	.000
Rivera	P	4	1	0	0	0	0	0	0	.000
Canseco	PH	1	1	0	0	0	0	0	0	.000
Bellinger	LF	4	0	0	0	0	0	0	0	—
Stanton	P	4	0	0	0	0	0	0	0	—
Nelson	P	3	0	0	0	0	0	0	0	—
Clemens	P	1	0	0	0	0	0	0	0	—
Cone	P	1	0	0	0	0	0	0	0	—

NAME	POS	G	AB	R	H	2B	3B	HR	RBI	BA
NEW YORK (N)										
TOTALS		5	175	16	40	8	0	4	15	.229
Piazza	C-DH	5	22	3	6	2	0	2	4	.273
Payton	CF	5	21	3	7	0	0	1	3	.333
Alfonzo	2B	5	21	1	3	0	0	0	1	.143
Zeile	1B	5	20	1	8	2	0	0	1	.400
Ventura	3B	5	20	1	3	1	0	1	1	.150
Agbayani	LF	5	18	2	5	2	0	0	2	.278
Perez	RF	5	16	1	2	0	0	0	0	.125
Abbott	SS	5	8	0	2	1	0	0	0	.250
Bordick	SS	2	8	0	1	0	0	0	0	.125
Trammell	RF	4	5	1	2	0	0	0	3	.400
Harris	DH	3	4	1	0	0	0	0	0	.000
Hamilton	PH	4	3	0	0	0	0	0	0	.000
Leiter	P	2	2	0	0	0	0	0	0	.000
B. J. Jones	P	1	2	0	0	0	0	0	0	.000
Pratt	C	2	1	0	0	0	0	0	0	.000
McEwing	LF	3	1	1	0	0	0	0	0	.000
Reed	P	1	1	0	1	0	0	0	0	1.000
M. Franco	1B	1	1	0	0	0	0	0	0	.000
J. Franco	P	4	0	0	0	0	0	0	0	—
Benitez	P	3	0	0	0	0	0	0	0	—
Cook	P	3	0	0	0	0	0	0	0	—
Rusch	P	3	0	0	0	0	0	0	0	—
Wendell	P	2	0	0	0	0	0	0	0	—
Hampton	P	1	0	0	0	0	0	0	0	—
White	P	1	0	0	0	0	0	0	0	—

COMPOSITE PITCHING

NAME	G	IP	H	BB	SO	W	L	SV	ERA
NEW YORK (A)									
TOTALS	5	47	40	11	48	4	1	2	2.68
Pettitte	2	13.2	16	4	9	0	0	0	1.98
Clemens	1	8	2	0	9	1	0	0	0.00
Hernandez	1	7.1	9	3	12	0	1	0	4.91
Rivera	4	6	4	1	7	0	0	2	3.00
Neagle	1	4.2	4	2	3	0	0	0	3.86
Stanton	4	4.1	0	0	7	2	0	0	0.00
Nelson	3	2.2	5	1	1	1	0	0	10.13
Cone	1	0.1	0	0	0	0	0	0	0.00

NAME	G	IP	H	BB	SO	W	L	SV	ERA
NEW YORK (N)									
TOTALS	5	46.2	47	25	40	1	4	1	3.47
Leiter	2	15.2	12	6	16	0	1	0	2.87
Reed	1	6	6	1	8	0	0	0	3.00
Hampton	1	6	8	5	4	0	1	0	6.00
B.J. Jones	1	5	4	3	3	0	1	0	5.40
Rusch	3	4	6	2	2	0	0	0	2.25
Franco	4	3.1	3	0	1	1	0	0	0.00
Benitez	3	3	3	2	2	0	0	1	3.00
Wendell	2	1.2	3	2	2	0	1	0	5.40
White	1	1.1	1	0	1	0	0	0	6.75
Cook	3	0.2	1	3	1	0	0	0	0.00

2001: STOCKS DOWN, BONDS UP

The 2001 baseball season was played amid a slipping economy and dire warnings by TV-talking heads that it would get worse. Then came the attack of September 11 to remind everyone that baseball was still just a game. Nevertheless, all things considered, baseball had a good season. If the pennant races weren't scintillating, at least there were several unexpected early season competitors. Barry Bonds, Rickey Henderson, Ichiro Suzuki, Roger Clemens, Sammy Sosa either set or nearly set records, and two all-time greats announced their retirements.

Bonds' pursuit and ultimate accomplishment of a new single-season home run record did not create the stir that Mark McGwire did, in part because Bonds' 73 followed McGwire's 70 by only three years. Two other factors: most of his games were played too late for many fans in eastern time zones to follow pitch-by-pitch, and no other player ever got quite close enough to turn the homer pursuit into a horse race. But if the reaction was slightly subdued, Bonds' season was perhaps the greatest offensive display ever. Not only did he set a new home run mark, he also set season records for bases on balls and slugging percentage.

Sosa became the first player to hit more than 60 homers three times. Suzuki cracked out 242 hits, the most since 1930. Clemens ran his record to 20-1 before two late-season losses dropped him below a record winning percentage. Henderson cracked out his 3,000th career hit. Even more impressively, the great lead-off man set the all-time record for runs scored in a career. Cal Ripken Jr. and Tony Gwynn enjoyed final seasons, taking well-deserved bows in each league park.

In the American League, three of the 2000 top teams returned to playoffs. Seattle moved past Oakland for the Western Division crown, recording 116 wins to match the regular-season record of the 1906 Chicago Cubs. Rather than Tinker, Evers, and Chance, the Mariners had their marvelous rookie Suzuki, who led in batting, and Bret Boone, who drove in 141 runs. Edgar Martinez and Mike Cameron also topped 100 RBI's each. Jamie Moyer became the oldest first-time 20-game winner. Ironically, shortstop Alex Rodriguez left Seattle so he could play for a winner. In Texas, he experienced a rich contract, a great personal year, and a last place team. Oakland slipped to second in the West but still won 102 games to gain the playoffs. The Athletics thrived on the slugging of Jason Giambi and the pitching of Tim Hudson, Mark Mulder and Barry Zito.

Minnesota challenged Cleveland for half a season but couldn't hold the pace. The Twins biggest loss may have come at season's end when Tom Kelly announced his retirement as manager. The Indians slugged their way to the division title. Amid the hitting of Jim Thome, Juan Gonzalez and Roberto Alomar, they discovered a pitcher in rookie C.C. Sabathia. Chicago, wounded by injuries, started 14-29 but recovered to eke out a winning record.

The Yankees won as usual, but it might have been harder if the Red Sox hadn't self-destructed. Injuries to Boston ace Pedro Martinez and shortstop Nomar Garciaparra didn't help. Then GM Dan Duquette fired manager Jimy Williams. Under replacement Joe Kerrigan, the team dissolved into back-biting punctuated by Carl Everett's boorishness. New York walked away from the Sox and was only minimally challenged by Toronto. Clemens and free agent pick-up Mike Mussina gave them great pitching that helped overcome arm troubles for Orlando Hernandez and Ramiro Mendoza. Ironically, the terrorist attack of September 11 caused many fans outside New York to root for the Yanks for perhaps the first time in their lives.

In the National League East, the Mets collapsed for lack of hitting and the Phillies weren't quite ready. That enabled the Braves to win the division for the tenth consecutive year. Once more, Greg Maddux and Tom Glavine were the backbone of the pitching staff. A new closer was discovered in veteran John Smoltz. The pitching had to be good in Atlanta because the hitting wasn't. Houston won the Central Division with St. Louis finishing second. Led by Jeff Bagwell and Moises Alou, the Astros didn't lack for big bats. Closer Billy Wagner came back strong from elbow surgery to save the pitching - literally. The Cardinals' Mark McGwire was injured much of the season, but rookie Albert Pujois gave the lineup unexpected punch, and righthander Matt Morris had a terrific season. In Chicago, Sammy Sosa had perhaps his greatest season with 160 RBI and Jon Lieber won 20 games. But, as usual, the Cubs looked like "the team to beat" early and ended as the team that was beaten.

Out West, the Diamondbacks boasted twin aces in Randy Johnson and Curt Schilling. Luis Gonzalez had a career year. It was enough to offset poor seasons by Jay Bell and Matt Williams. The San Francisco Giants were more than Barry Bonds. Shortstop Rich Aurilia had a breakthrough year, and Jeff Kent continued to drive in runs. Still, the best moments of 2001 came when Bonds swung and the ball went up... up... up.

2001 AMERICAN LEAGUE — EAST DIVISION

Name	G by Pos	B	AGE	G	AB	R	H	2B	3B	HR	RBI	BB	SO	SB	BA	SA
NEW YORK 1st 95-65 .594 JOE TORRE																
TOTALS			31	161	5577	804	1488	289	20	203	774	519	1035	161	.267	.435
Tino Martinez	1B149 DH3	L	33	154	589	89	165	24	2	34	113	42	89	1	.280	.501
Alfonso Soriano	2B156 DH2	R	25	158	574	77	154	34	3	18	73	29	125	43	.268	.432
Derek Jeter	SS150	R	27	150	614	110	191	35	3	21	74	56	99	27	.311	.480
Scott Brosius (BG)	3B120 OF2	R	34	120	428	57	123	25	2	13	49	34	83	3	.287	.446
Paul O'Neill	OF130 DH6	L	38	137	510	77	136	33	1	21	70	48	59	22	.267	.459
Bernie Williams	OF144 DH1	B	32	146	540	102	166	38	0	26	94	78	67	11	.307	.522
Chuck Knoblauch	OF108 DH24	R	32	137	521	66	130	20	3	9	44	58	73	38	.250	.351
Jorge Posada	C131 DH6 1B2	B	29	138	484	59	134	28	1	22	95	62	132	2	.277	.475
David Justice (GJ)	DH85 OF25	L	35	111	381	58	92	16	1	18	51	54	83	1	.241	.430
Shane Spencer	OF68 DH14	R	29	80	283	40	73	14	2	10	46	21	58	4	.258	.428
Clay Bellinger	OF25 3B17 1B6 SS2 DH1	R	32	51	81	12	13	1	1	5	12	4	23	1	.160	.383
2 Enrique Wilson	2B7	R	27	48	99	10	24	5	1	1	12	6	14	0	.242	.343
Luis Sojo	3B17 1B8 2B7 SS5 DH1	R	36	39	79	5	13	2	0	0	9	4	12	1	.165	.190
2 Gerald Williams	OF26 DH7	R	34	38	47	12	8	1	0	0	2	5	13	3	.170	.191
Todd Greene	C34 DH2	R	30	35	96	9	20	4	0	1	11	3	21	0	.208	.281
Nick Johnson	1B15 DH6	L	22	23	67	6	13	2	0	2	8	7	15	0	.194	.313
2 Randy Velarde	3B7 DH5 OF3 1B1	R	38	15	46	4	7	3	0	0	1	5	13	2	.152	.217
Michael Coleman	OF9 DH3	R	25	12	38	5	8	0	0	1	7	0	15	0	.211	.289
1 Joe Oliver	C12	R	35	12	36	3	9	1	0	1	2	1	12	0	.250	.361
Erick Almonte	SS4 DH3	R	23	8	4	0	2	1	0	0	0	0	1	2	.500	.750
1 Robert Perez	OF5 DH1	R	32	6	15	1	4	1	0	0	0	1	7	0	.267	.333
Henry Rodriguez (XJ)	DH1	L	33	5	8	0	0	0	0	0	0	0	6	0	.000	.000
2 Darren Bragg	OF3	L	31	5	4	1	1	1	0	0	0	1	0	1	.250	.500
Donzell McDonald	OF3	B	26	5	3	1	0	0	0	0	0	3	0	1	.333	.333
2 Bobby Estalella	C3	R	26	3	4	1	0	0	0	0	0	1	2	0	.000	.000
Juan Rivera	OF3	R	22	3	1	0	0	0	0	0	0	0	0	0	.000	.000
Scott Seabol	DH1	R	26	1	1	0	0	0	0	0	0	0	0	0	.000	.000
BOSTON 2nd 82-79 .509 13.5 JIMY WILLIAMS 65-53 .551 JOE KERRIGAN 17-26 .395																
TOTALS			30	161	5605	772	1493	316	29	198	739	520	1131	46	.266	.439
Brian Daubach	1B106 OF14	L	29	122	404	54	107	28	3	22	71	53	108	1	.263	.509
Jose Offerman	2B91 1B43	B	32	128	524	76	140	23	3	9	49	61	97	5	.267	.374
Nomar Garciaparra (WJ)	SS21	R	27	21	83	13	24	3	0	4	8	7	9	0	.289	.470
Shea Hillenbrand	3B129 1B6 DH1	R	25	139	468	52	123	20	2	12	49	13	61	3	.263	.391
Trot Nixon	OF145 DH1	L	27	148	535	100	150	31	4	27	88	79	113	7	.280	.505
Carl Everett (KJ)	OF93 DH7	B	30	102	409	61	105	24	4	14	58	27	104	9	.257	.438
Manny Ramirez	DH87 OF55	R	29	142	529	93	162	33	2	41	125	81	147	0	.306	.609
Jason Varitek (EJ)	C50	R	29	51	174	19	51	11	1	7	25	21	35	0	.293	.489
Dante Bichette	OF53 DH46	R	37	107	391	45	112	30	1	12	49	20	76	2	.286	.460
Mike Lansing	SS76 2B31	R	33	106	352	45	88	23	0	8	34	22	50	3	.250	.384
Troy O'Leary	OF89 DH4	L	31	104	341	50	82	16	6	13	50	25	73	1	.240	.437
Chris Stynes	3B46 2B43 OF12	R	28	96	361	52	101	19	2	8	33	20	56	4	.280	.410
Scott Hatteberg	C72 DH8	L	31	94	278	34	68	19	0	3	25	33	26	1	.245	.345
Darren Lewis	OF69 DH6	R	33	82	164	18	46	9	1	1	12	8	25	5	.280	.366
2 Doug Mirabelli	C52 DH1	R	30	54	141	16	38	8	0	9	26	17	36	0	.270	.518
Lou Merloni	SS45 2B5 3B1	R	30	52	146	21	39	10	0	3	13	6	31	2	.267	.397
Craig Grebeck (FJ)	SS23	R	36	23	41	1	2	1	0	0	2	2	9	0	.049	.073
John Valentin (KJ-FJ)	SS18 3B3	R	34	20	60	8	12	2	0	1	5	9	8	0	.200	.283
2 Calvin Pickering	1B120 DH2	L	24	17	50	4	14	1	0	3	7	8	13	0	.280	.480
Israel Alcantara	OF8 1B4 DH1	R	28	14	38	3	10	1	0	3	3	3	13	1	.263	.289
Morgan Burkhart	DH6 1B5	B	29	11	33	3	6	1	0	1	3	6	6	0	.182	.303
Angel Santos	2B6	B	21	9	16	2	2	1	0	0	1	0	5	0	.125	.188
James Lofton	SS7	B	27	7	11	4	2	1	0	0	1	3	2	2	.192	.231
2 Joe Oliver	C5	R	35	5	12	1	3	1	0	0	0	0	0	0	.250	.333
1 Marcus Jensen	C1	B	28	1	4	0	1	0	0	0	0	0	1	0	.250	.250

NAME	T	AGE	W	L	PCT	SV	G	GS	CG	IP	H	BB	SO	SHO	ERA
		31	95	65	.594	57	161	161	7	1451	1429	465	1266	9	4.02
Roger Clemens	R	38	20	3	.870	0	33	33	0	220	205	72	213	0	3.51
Mike Mussina	R	32	17	11	.607	0	34	34	4	229	202	42	214	3	3.15
Andy Pettitte	L	29	15	10	.600	0	31	31	2	201	224	41	164	0	3.99
Mike Stanton	L	34	9	4	.692	0	76	0	0	80	80	29	78	0	2.58
Ramiro Mendoza	R	29	8	4	.667	6	56	2	0	101	89	23	70	0	3.75
Ted Lilly	L	25	5	6	.455	0	26	21	0	121	126	51	112	0	5.37
3 Sterling Hitchcock	L	30	4	4	.500	0	10	9	1	51	67	18	28	0	6.49
Mariano Rivera	R	31	4	6	.400	50	71	0	0	81	61	12	83	0	2.34
Orlando Hernandez (FJ)	R	35	4	7	.364	0	17	16	0	95	90	42	77	0	4.85
2 Jay Witasick	R	28	3	0	1.000	0	32	0	0	40	47	18	53	0	4.69
Randy Choate	L	25	3	1	.750	0	37	0	0	48	34	27	35	0	3.35
2 Mark Wohlers	R	31	1	0	1.000	0	31	0	0	36	33	18	33	0	4.54
Todd Williams (MJ)	R	30	1	0	1.000	0	15	0	0	15	22	9	13	0	4.70
Randy Keisler	L	25	1	2	.333	0	10	10	0	51	52	34	36	0	6.22
Brandon Knight	R	25	0	0	—	0	4	0	0	11	18	3	7	0	10.13
1 Brian Boehringer	R	32	0	1	.000	0	22	0	0	35	35	12	33	0	3.12
Carlos Almanzar	R	27	0	1	.000	0	10	0	0	11	14	2	6	0	4.63
Christian Parker (SJ)	R	25	0	1	.000	0	1	1	0	3	8	1	1	0	21.00
1 Brett Jodie	R	24	0	1	.000	0	1	1	0	2	7	1	0	0	27.00
Adrian Hernandez	R	26	0	3	.000	0	6	3	0	22	15	10	10	0	3.68
Allen Watson (SJ) 30															
		30	82	79	.509	48	161	161	3	1448	1412	544	1259	9	4.15
Hideo Nomo	R	32	13	10	.565	0	33	33	2	198	171	96	220	2	4.50
Frank Castillo (XJ)	R	32	10	9	.526	0	26	26	0	137	138	35	89	0	4.31
David Cone (SJ)	R	38	9	7	.563	0	25	25	0	136	148	57	115	0	4.31
Tim Wakefield	R	34	9	12	.429	3	45	17	0	169	156	73	148	0	3.90
Pedro Martinez (SJ)	R	29	7	3	.700	0	18	18	1	117	84	25	163	0	2.39
Rich Garces	R	30	6	1	.857	1	62	0	0	67	55	25	51	0	3.90
Rod Beck	R	32	6	4	.600	6	68	0	0	81	77	28	63	0	3.90
Rolando Arrojo	R	32	5	4	.556	5	41	9	0	103	88	35	78	0	3.48
Derek Lowe	R	28	5	10	.333	24	67	3	0	92	103	29	82	0	3.53
Paxton Crawford	R	23	3	0	1.000	0	8	7	0	36	40	13	25	0	4.75
Casey Fossum	L	23	3	2	.600	0	13	7	0	44	44	20	26	0	4.87
Hipolito Pichardo (EJ-VR)	R	31	2	1	.667	0	30	0	0	35	42	10	17	0	4.93
1 Tomo Ohka	R	25	2	5	.286	0	12	11	0	52	69	19	37	0	6.19
Bret Saberhagen (SJ)	R	37	1	2	.333	0	3	3	0	15	19	0	10	0	6.00
Pete Schourek	L	32	1	5	.167	0	33	0	0	30	35	15	20	0	4.45
1 Bill Pulsipher	L	27	0	0	—	0	6	0	0	16	25	14	6	0	5.32
Todd Erdos	R	27	0	0	—	0	5	0	0	16	15	8	7	0	4.96
Allen McDill	L	29	0	0	—	0	11	0	0	13	7	16	5	0	5.52
Willie Banks	R	32	0	0	—	0	5	0	0	11	5	4	10	0	6.00
Carlos Castillo	R	26	0	0	—	0	9	0	0	16	16	5	8	0	6.00
2 Ugueth Urbina	R	27	0	0	.000	9	19	0	0	20	16	3	32	0	2.25
Bryce Florie (IJ)	R	31	0	0	.000	0	9	0	0	12	12	12	9	0	11.42
Sun-Woo Kim	R	23	0	0	.000	0	20	2	0	42	54	21	27	0	5.65
Juan Pena (EJ) 24															

TORONTO — 3rd 80-82 .494 16 — BUCK MARTINEZ

Name	G by Pos	B	AGE	G	AB	R	H	2B	3B	HR	RBI	BB	SO	SB	BA	SA
TOTALS			28	162	5663	767	1489	287	36	195	728	470	1094	156	.263	.430
Carlos Delgado	1B161	L	28	162	574	102	160	31	1	39	102	111	136	3	.279	.540
Homer Bush (RJ-LJ)	2B78	R	28	78	271	32	83	11	1	3	27	8	50	13	.306	.387
Alex Gonzalez	SS154	R	28	154	636	79	161	25	5	17	76	43	149	18	.253	.388
1 Tony Batista	3B72	R	27	72	271	29	56	11	1	13	45	13	66	0	.207	.399
Raul Mondesi	OF149	R	30	149	572	88	144	26	4	27	84	73	128	30	.252	.453
Jose Cruz	OF143 DH1	B	27	146	577	92	158	38	4	34	88	45	138	32	.274	.530
Shannon Stewart	OF142 DH13	R	27	155	640	103	202	44	7	12	60	46	72	27	.316	.463
Darrin Fletcher	C129 DH1	L	34	134	416	36	94	20	0	11	56	24	43	0	.226	.353
Brad Fullmer	DH135 1B1	L	26	146	522	71	143	31	2	18	83	38	88	5	.274	.444
Jeff Frye	2B47 3B27 SS2 OF1	R	34	74	175	24	43	6	1	2	15	12	18	2	.246	.326
Alberto Castillo	C66	R	31	66	131	9	26	4	0	1	4	7	30	1	.198	.252
Brian Simmons	OF37 DH2	B	27	60	107	8	19	5	0	2	8	8	30	0	.178	.280
Felipe Lopez	3B47 SS3	B	21	49	177	21	46	5	4	5	23	12	39	4	.260	.418
2 Tony Fernandez	DH13	B	39	48	59	5	18	4	0	1	12	1	8	0	.305	.424
Cesar Izturis	2B41 SS6	B	21	46	134	19	36	6	2	2	9	2	15	4	.269	.388
Chris Latham	OF31	B	28	43	73	12	20	3	1	2	10	10	28	4	.274	.425
Luis Lopez	3B28 1B5 DH4	R	27	41	119	10	29	4	0	3	10	8	16	0	.244	.353
Chris Woodward	2B17 3B10 SS4 1B2 DH1	R	25	37	63	9	12	3	2	2	5	1	14	0	.190	.397
Vernon Wells	OF30	R	22	30	96	14	30	8	0	1	6	5	15	5	.313	.427
Ryan Freel	2B7 OF1	R	25	9	22	1	6	1	0	0	3	1	4	2	.273	.318
Josh Phelps	C7	R	23	8	12	3	0	0	0	0	1	2	5	1	.000	.000
Andy Thompson (GJ) 25																

NAME	T	AGE	W	L	PCT	SV	G	GS	CG	IP	H	BB	SO	SHO	ERA
		29	80	82	.494	41	162	162	7	1463	1553	490	1041	10	4.28
Paul Quantrill	R	32	11	2	.846	2	80	0	0	83	86	12	58	0	3.04
Chris Carpenter	R	26	11	11	.500	0	34	34	3	216	229	75	157	2	4.09
Esteban Loaiza	R	29	11	11	.500	0	36	30	1	190	239	40	110	1	5.02
1 Chris Michalak	L	30	6	7	.462	0	24	18	0	115	133	49	57	0	4.62
Kelvim Escobar	R	25	6	8	.429	0	59	11	1	126	93	52	121	1	3.50
Roy Halladay	R	24	5	3	.625	0	17	16	1	105	97	25	96	1	3.16
Bob File	R	24	5	3	.625	0	60	0	0	74	57	29	38	0	3.27
Brandon Lyon	R	21	5	4	.556	0	11	11	0	63	63	15	35	0	4.29
1 Joey Hamilton	R	30	5	8	.385	0	22	22	0	122	170	38	82	0	5.89
Dan Plesac	L	39	4	5	.444	1	62	0	0	45	34	24	68	0	3.57
Steve Parris (SJ)	R	33	4	6	.400	0	19	19	1	106	126	41	49	0	4.60
Pedro Borbon	L	33	2	4	.333	0	71	0	0	53	48	12	45	0	3.71
Billy Koch	R	26	2	5	.286	36	69	0	0	69	69	33	55	0	4.80
John Frascatore	R	31	1	0	1.000	0	12	0	0	16	16	4	9	0	2.20
Pasqual Coco	R	23	1	0	1.000	0	7	1	0	14	12	6	9	0	4.40
Scott Eyre	L	29	1	2	.333	2	17	0	0	16	15	7	16	0	3.45
Kevin Beirne	R	27	0	0	—	0	5	0	0	7	13	6	5	0	12.86
Brian Bowles	R	24	0	0	—	0	2	0	0	4	4	1	4	0	0.00
1 Lance Painter (NJ)	L	33	0	1	.000	0	10	0	0	18	27	11	14	0	7.85
Matt DeWitt	R	24	0	0	—	0	6	0	0	19	22	10	13	0	3.79
Mike Sirotka (SJ) 30															

BALTIMORE — 4th 63-98 .391 32.5 — MIKE HARGROVE

Name	G by Pos	B	AGE	G	AB	R	H	2B	3B	HR	RBI	BB	SO	SB	BA	SA
TOTALS			30	162	5472	687	1359	262	24	136	663	514	989	133	.248	.380
Jeff Conine	1B80 OF36 3B17 DH12	R	35	139	524	75	163	23	2	14	97	64	75	12	.311	.443
Jerry Hairston	2B156	R	25	159	532	63	124	25	5	8	47	44	73	29	.233	.344
Mike Bordick (SJ)	SS58	R	35	58	229	32	57	13	0	7	30	17	36	9	.249	.397
Cal Ripken	3B111 DH10	R	40	128	477	43	114	16	0	14	68	26	63	0	.239	.361
Chris Richard	OF96 DH20 1B18	L	27	136	483	74	128	31	3	15	61	45	100	11	.265	.435
Melvin Mora	OF88 SS43 2B1	R	29	128	436	49	109	28	0	7	48	41	91	11	.250	.362
Brady Anderson	OF120 DH4	L	37	131	430	50	87	12	3	8	45	60	77	12	.202	.300
Brook Fordyce	C95	R	31	95	292	30	61	18	0	5	19	21	56	1	.209	.322
Jay Gibbons (WJ)	OF28 DH28 1B7	L	24	73	225	27	53	10	0	15	36	17	39	0	.236	.480
2 Tony Batista	DH33 3B29 SS20	R	27	84	308	41	82	16	5	12	42	19	47	5	.266	.468
David Segui (KJ)	1B65 DH16	B	34	82	292	48	88	18	1	10	46	49	61	0	.301	.473
Brian Roberts	SS51 2B12 DH1	B	23	75	273	42	69	12	3	2	17	13	36	12	.253	.341
Fernando Lunar	C64	R	26	64	167	8	41	7	0	0	16	7	32	0	.246	.287
Mike Kinkade	OF32 3B10 DH10 1B3 C2	R	27	61	160	19	44	5	0	4	16	14	31	2	.275	.381
Delino DeShields	OF47 DH8	L	32	58	188	29	37	8	2	3	21	31	42	11	.197	.309
Larry Bigbie	OF40	L	23	47	131	15	30	6	0	2	11	17	42	4	.229	.321
Luis Matos (SJ)	OF31	R	22	31	98	16	21	7	0	4	12	11	30	7	.214	.408
1 Greg Myers	DH11 C8	L	35	25	74	11	20	2	0	4	18	8	17	0	.270	.459
Geronimo Gil	C17	R	25	17	58	3	17	2	0	0	6	5	7	0	.293	.328
Willie Harris	OF8	L	23	9	24	3	3	1	0	0	0	0	8	1	.125	.167
Tim Raines Jr.	OF7	R	21	7	23	6	4	2	0	0	0	3	7	3	.174	.261
2 Casey Blake	1B5 DH1	R	27	6	15	2	2	0	0	1	2	0	4	0	.133	.333
2 Tim Raines	OF3 DH1	B	41	4	11	1	3	0	1	0	5	0	1	0	.273	.545
1 Eugene Kingsale	OF1	B	24	3	4	0	0	0	0	0	0	0	2	1	.000	.000
Albert Belle (PJ) 34																

NAME	T	AGE	W	L	PCT	SV	G	GS	CG	IP	H	BB	SO	SHO	ERA
		28	63	98	.391	31	162	162	3	1432	1504	528	938	6	4.67
Jason Johnson	R	27	10	12	.455	0	32	32	2	196	194	77	114	0	4.09
Willis Roberts	R	26	9	10	.474	6	46	18	1	132	142	55	95	0	4.91
Josh Towers	R	24	8	10	.444	0	24	20	1	140	165	16	58	1	4.49
Jose Mercedes	R	30	8	17	.320	0	33	31	2	184	219	63	123	0	5.82
Calvin Maduro	R	26	6	6	.455	0	22	12	0	94	83	36	51	0	4.23
Sidney Ponson (AJ)	R	24	5	10	.333	0	23	23	3	138	161	37	84	1	4.94
1 Mike Trombley	R	34	3	4	.429	6	50	0	0	55	38	27	45	0	3.46
Sean Douglass	R	22	2	1	.667	0	4	3	0	20	21	11	17	0	5.31
Pat Hentgen (EJ)	R	32	2	3	.400	0	9	9	1	62	51	19	33	0	3.47
B.J. Ryan	L	25	2	4	.333	2	61	0	0	53	47	30	54	0	4.25
John Bale	L	27	1	0	1.000	0	14	0	0	27	18	17	21	0	3.04
2 John Wasdin	R	28	1	1	.500	0	26	0	0	50	54	16	47	0	4.17
Jorge Julio	R	22	1	1	.500	0	26	0	1	21	25	9	22	0	3.80
Alan Mills (SJ)	R	34	1	1	.500	0	14	0	0	14	20	11	9	0	9.64
1 Chuck McElroy	L	33	1	2	.333	0	18	5	0	45	49	28	22	0	5.36
Ryan Kohlmeier	R	24	1	2	.333	6	34	1	0	41	48	19	29	0	7.30
John Parrish	R	23	1	2	.333	0	16	1	0	22	22	17	20	0	6.14
Chad Paronto	R	25	1	3	.250	0	24	0	0	27	33	11	16	0	5.00
Buddy Groom	L	35	1	4	.200	11	70	0	0	66	64	9	54	0	3.55
Kris Foster	R	26	0	0	—	0	7	0	0	10	9	8	8	0	2.70
Leslie Brea	R	27	0	0	—	0	2	0	0	6	6	6	3	0	18.00
Rick Bauer	R	24	0	5	.000	0	6	6	0	33	35	9	16	0	4.64
Scott Erickson (EJ) 33 Luis Rivera (SJ) 23															

TAMPA BAY — 5th 62-100 .383 34 — LARRY ROTHSCHILD 4-10 .286 HAL McRAE 58-90 .392

Name	G by Pos	B	AGE	G	AB	R	H	2B	3B	HR	RBI	BB	SO	SB	BA	SA
TOTALS			28	162	5524	672	1426	311	21	121	645	456	1116	115	.258	.388
Steve Cox	1B78 OF8 DH4	L	26	108	342	37	88	20	0	12	51	24	75	2	.257	.427
Brent Abernathy	2B79	R	23	79	304	43	82	17	1	5	33	21	35	8	.270	.382
Felix Martinez	SS67 2B10	R	25	77	219	24	54	13	1	1	14	10	46	6	.247	.329
Aubrey Huff	3B73 DH20 1B19	R	24	111	411	42	102	25	1	8	45	23	72	1	.248	.372
Ben Grieve	OF120 DH32	L	25	154	542	72	143	30	2	11	72	87	159	7	.264	.387
Randy Winn	OF117 DH3	B	27	128	429	54	117	25	6	6	50	38	81	12	.273	.401
Jason Tyner	OF100	L	24	105	396	51	111	8	5	0	21	15	42	31	.280	.326
John Flaherty (ZJ)	C78	R	33	78	248	20	59	17	1	4	29	10	33	1	.238	.363
Greg Vaughn	DH76 OF57	R	35	136	485	74	113	25	0	24	82	71	130	11	.233	.433
1 Fred McGriff	1B74 DH17	L	37	97	343	40	109	18	0	19	61	40	69	1	.318	.536
Russ Johnson	3B36 2B33 SS6 DH2	R	28	85	248	32	73	19	2	4	33	34	57	2	.294	.435
Damian Rolls	2B42 OF25 DH6 3B1	R	23	81	237	33	62	11	1	2	12	10	47	12	.262	.342
1 Gerald Williams	OF59	R	34	62	232	30	48	17	0	4	17	13	42	10	.207	.332
2 Chris Gomez	SS58	R	30	58	189	31	57	16	0	8	36	8	24	3	.302	.513
Toby Hall	C46	R	25	49	188	28	56	16	0	4	30	4	16	2	.298	.447
Andy Sheets	SS49	R	29	49	153	10	30	8	0	1	14	12	35	2	.196	.268
1 Mike DiFelice	C48	R	32	48	149	13	31	5	1	2	9	8	39	1	.208	.295
1 Jose Guillen (KJ)	OF36 DH4	R	25	41	135	14	37	5	1	5	11	6	26	2	.274	.378
Jared Sandberg	3B38 2B1	R	23	39	136	13	28	7	0	7	15	10	45	1	.206	.279
1 Vinny Castilla	3B24	R	33	24	93	7	20	6	0	2	9	3	22	0	.215	.344
Bobby Smith	2B6	R	27	6	19	1	2	0	0	0	1	0	3	0	.105	.105
Paul Hoover	C2	R	25	3	4	1	1	0	0	0	0	1	0	0	.250	.250

NAME	T	AGE	W	L	PCT	SV	G	GS	CG	IP	H	BB	SO	SHO	ERA
		27	62	100	.383	30	162	162	1	1424	1513	569	1030	6	4.94
Tanyon Sturtze	R	30	11	12	.478	1	39	27	0	196	200	79	110	0	4.42
Paul Wilson	R	28	8	9	.471	0	37	24	0	151	165	52	119	0	4.88
Joe Kennedy	L	22	7	8	.467	0	20	20	0	118	122	34	78	0	4.44
Victor Zambrano	R	25	2	0	.750	2	36	0	0	51	38	18	58	0	3.16
Ryan Rupe	R	26	5	12	.294	0	28	26	0	143	161	48	123	0	6.59
1 Albie Lopez	R	29	5	12	.294	0	20	20	1	125	152	51	67	1	5.34
Esteban Yan	R	26	4	6	.400	22	54	0	0	62	64	11	64	0	3.90
2 Nick Bierbrodt	L	23	3	4	.429	0	11	11	0	61	71	27	56	0	4.55
Bryan Rekar (SJ)	R	29	3	13	.188	0	25	25	0	141	167	45	87	0	5.89
Travis Phelps	R	23	2	2	.500	5	49	0	0	62	53	24	54	0	3.48
Jesus Colome	R	23	2	3	.400	0	30	0	0	49	37	25	31	0	3.33
Doug Creek	L	32	2	3	.400	0	66	0	0	63	51	49	66	0	4.31
1 Mike Judd	R	26	1	0	1.000	0	13	0	0	20	19	10	11	0	4.05
Dan Wheeler	R	23	1	0	1.000	0	18	0	0	18	30	5	12	0	8.66
Bobby Seay	L	23	1	1	.500	0	12	0	0	13	13	5	12	0	6.23
Rusty Meacham	R	33	1	3	.250	0	24	0	0	35	39	10	13	0	5.60
Jason Standridge	R	22	0	0	—	0	9	1	0	19	19	14	9	0	4.66
Mickey Callaway	R	26	0	0	—	0	2	0	0	5	4	2	2	0	7.20
Ariel Prieto (SJ)	R	31	0	0	—	0	4	0	0	8	4	2	1	0	2.45
1 Tony Fiore	R	30	0	0	—	0	3	0	0	5	5	5	4	0	5.40
Ken Hill	R	35	0	0	—	0	2	0	0	7	10	5	2	0	12.27
2 Brian Rose	R	25	0	2	.000	0	7	2	0	21	31	12	11	0	8.85
Travis Harper	R	25	0	0	—	0	2	1	0	7	15	3	2	0	7.71
Jeff Wallace	L	25	0	0	—	0	29	0	0	50	43	37	38	0	3.40
Wilson Alvarez (SJ) 31 Juan Guzman (SJ) 34															

CENTRAL DIVISION

CLEVELAND — 1st 91-71 .562 — CHARLIE MANUEL

Name	G by Pos	B	AGE	G	AB	R	H	2B	3B	HR	RBI	BB	SO	SB	BA	SA
TOTALS			31	162	5600	897	1559	294	37	212	868	577	1076	79	.278	.458
Jim Thome	1B148 DH6	L	30	156	526	101	153	26	1	49	124	111	185	0	.291	.624
Roberto Alomar	2B157	B	33	157	575	113	193	34	12	20	100	80	71	30	.336	.541
Omar Vizquel	SS154	B	34	155	611	84	156	26	3	7	50	61	72	13	.255	.334
Travis Fryman (EJ)	3B96 DH2 SS1	R	32	98	334	34	88	15	0	3	38	30	63	1	.263	.335
Juan Gonzalez	OF119 DH21	R	31	140	532	97	173	34	1	35	140	41	94	1	.325	.590
Kenny Lofton	OF130	L	34	133	517	91	135	21	4	14	66	47	69	16	.261	.398
Marty Cordova	OF106 DH7	R	31	122	409	61	123	24	2	20	69	23	81	0	.301	.506
Einar Diaz	C134 2B1	R	28	134	437	54	121	34	4	0	56	17	44	1	.277	.387
Ellis Burks	DH102 OF20	R	36	124	439	63	123	29	1	28	74	62	85	5	.280	.542
Jolbert Cabrera	OF83 2B28 3B27 SS14 DH1	R	28	141	287	50	75	16	3	1	38	16	41	10	.261	.348
Russell Branyan	3B72 OF34 DH7	L	25	113	315	48	73	16	2	20	54	38	132	1	.232	.486
Wil Cordero	OF51 1B22 DH14	R	29	89	268	30	67	11	1	4	21	12	50	0	.250	.343
Eddie Taubensee (IL)	C38 DH5 2B1	L	32	52	116	16	29	7	1	3	11	10	19	0	.250	.362
1 Jacob Cruz	DH1	R	28	28	68	12	15	4	0	3	15	9	13	1	.221	.412
Karim Garcia	OF18 1B2	L	25	20	45	8	14	3	0	5	13	3	13	0	.311	.711
John McDonald	SS9 2B3 3B3	R	26	17	22	1	2	1	0	0	2	0	4	0	.091	.136
Tim Laker	C14 P1	R	31	16	33	5	6	0	0	0	2	1	9	0	.182	.273
Dave Roberts	OF13 DH2	L	29	15	13	9	3	0	0	0	0	1	4	0	.333	.417
2 Milton Bradley	OF9 DH1	B	23	10	18	4	4	1	0	0	1	0	6	1	.222	.278
Mark Lewis	3B4 2B3	R	31	6	13	1	1	0	0	0	0	0	2	0	.077	.077
Dave Hollins	DH2	B	35	2	5	1	1	0	0	0	0	0	0	0	.200	.200

NAME	T	AGE	W	L	PCT	SV	G	GS	CG	IP	H	BB	SO	SHO	ERA
		29	91	71	.562	42	162	162	3	1447	1512	573	1218	4	4.64
C.C. Sabathia	L	20	17	5	.773	0	33	33	0	180	149	95	171	0	4.39
Bartolo Colon	R	28	14	12	.538	0	34	34	1	222	220	90	201	0	4.09
Dave Burba	R	34	10	10	.500	0	32	27	1	151	188	54	118	0	6.21
Chuck Finley (ZJ)	L	38	8	7	.533	0	22	22	1	114	131	95	96	0	5.54
Bob Wickman	R	32	5	0	1.000	32	70	0	0	68	61	14	66	0	2.39
Paul Shuey (EJ)	R	30	5	3	.625	2	47	0	0	54	53	26	70	0	2.82
Danys Baez	R	23	5	3	.625	0	43	0	0	50	54	20	52	0	2.50
Charles Nagy (EJ)	R	34	5	6	.455	0	15	13	0	70	102	20	49	0	6.40
Jake Westbrook	R	23	4	4	.500	0	23	6	0	65	79	22	48	0	5.85
Steve Woodard	R	26	3	3	.500	0	19	10	0	97	129	17	53	0	5.20
2 John Rocker	L	26	3	7	.300	4	38	0	0	35	33	25	43	0	5.45
David Riske	R	24	2	0	1.000	1	26	0	0	27	20	18	29	0	1.98
1 Justin Speier	R	27	2	1	.667	0	17	0	0	35	44	21	50	0	6.97
Ricardo Rincon	L	31	2	1	.667	2	67	0	0	54	44	21	50	0	2.83
Rich Rodriguez	L	38	2	2	.500	0	53	0	0	39	41	17	35	0	4.15
Jaret Wright (SJ)	R	25	2	3	.400	0	11	6	0	29	36	22	18	0	6.52
Steve Reed	R	36	1	1	.500	0	30	0	0	37	32	15	24	0	3.62
Ryan Drese	R	25	1	3	.250	0	11	7	0	48	55	24	32	0	3.44
Roy Smith	L	23	0	0	—	0	6	0	0	9	13	4	4	0	9.00
Mike Bacsik	L	23	0	1	.000	0	3	1	0	11	16	3	6	0	6.06
Scott Radinsky	L	33	0	0	—	0	2	0	0	1	1	1	1	0	27.00
Tim Laker	R	31	0	0	—	0	1	0	0	1	1	0	0	0	0.00
1 Steve Karsay	R	29	0	1	.000	1	31	0	0	43	29	8	44	0	1.25
Tim Drew	R	22	0	2	.000	0	7	5	0	36	51	16	15	0	7.97
Cameron Cairncross (SJ) 29															

MINNESOTA 2nd 85-77 .525 6 TOM KELLY

Name	G by Pos	B	AGE	G	AB	R	H	2B	3B	HR	RBI	BB	SO	SB	BA	SA
TOTALS			27	162	5560	771	1514	328	38	164	717	495	1083	146	.272	.433
Doug Mientkiewicz	1B148 DH2	L	27	151	543	77	166	39	1	15	74	67	92	2	.306	.464
Luis Rivas	2B150	R	21	153	563	70	150	21	6	7	47	40	99	31	.266	.362
Cristian Guzman (SJ)	SS118	B	23	118	493	80	149	28	14	10	51	21	78	25	.302	.477
Corey Koskie	3B150 DH2	L	28	153	582	100	155	37	2	26	103	68	118	27	.276	.488
1 Matt Lawton	OF94 DH7	L	29	103	376	71	110	25	0	10	51	63	46	19	.293	.439
Torii Hunter	OF147	R	25	148	564	82	147	32	5	27	92	29	125	9	.261	.479
Jacque Jones	OF140 DH5	L	26	149	475	57	131	25	0	14	49	39	92	12	.276	.417
A.J. Pierzynski	C110 DH1	L	24	114	381	51	110	33	2	7	55	16	57	1	.289	.441
David Ortiz (BW)	DH80 1B8	L	25	89	303	46	71	17	1	18	48	40	68	1	.234	.475
Denny Hocking	SS47 2B17 OF16 1B11 DH10 3B6	B	31	112	327	34	82	16	2	3	25	29	67	6	.251	.339
Brian Buchanan	OF46 DH19	R	27	69	197	28	54	12	0	10	32	19	58	1	.274	.487
Tom Prince	C64	R	36	64	196	19	43	4	1	7	23	12	39	3	.219	.357
Chad Allen (KJ)	OF27 DH23	R	26	57	175	20	46	13	2	4	20	19	37	1	.263	.429
Jason Maxwell (HJ)	SS12 3B11 2B9 DH7	R	29	39	68	4	13	4	0	1	10	9	23	2	.191	.294
Bobby Kielty	OF34 DH1	B	24	37	104	8	26	8	0	2	14	8	25	3	.250	.385
Quinton McCracken	OF10 DH9	B	31	24	64	7	14	2	2	0	3	5	13	0	.219	.313
Dustan Mohr	OF19 DH1	R	25	20	51	6	12	2	0	0	4	5	17	1	.235	.275
Matt LeCroy	DH9 C3 1B2	R	25	15	40	6	17	5	0	3	12	0	8	0	.425	.775
1 Casey Blake	3B5 DH4 1B3	R	27	13	22	1	7	1	0	0	2	3	8	1	.318	.364
John Barnes (KJ)	OF9	R	25	9	21	1	1	0	0	0	0	1	3	0	.048	.048
Michael Cuddyer	1B5 3B2 DH1	R	22	8	18	1	4	2	0	0	1	2	6	1	.222	.333
Jay Canizaro (KJ) 27																

NAME	T	AGE	W	L	PCT	SV	G	GS	CG	IP	H	BB	SO	SHO	ERA
		28	85	77	.525	45	162	162	12	1441	1494	445	965	8	4.51
Joe Mays	R	25	17	13	.567	0	34	34	4	234	205	64	123	3	3.16
Eric Milton	L	25	15	7	.682	0	35	34	2	221	222	61	157	1	4.32
Brad Radke	R	28	15	11	.577	0	33	33	6	226	235	26	137	2	3.94
Bob Wells	R	34	8	5	.615	2	65	0	0	69	72	18	49	0	5.11
Eddie Guardado	L	30	7	1	.875	12	67	0	0	67	47	23	67	0	3.51
Hector Carrasco	R	31	4	3	.571	1	56	0	0	74	77	30	70	0	4.64
2 Rick Reed	R	36	4	6	.400	0	12	12	0	68	92	14	43	0	5.19
Kyle Lohse	R	22	4	7	.364	0	19	16	0	90	102	29	64	0	5.68
1 Mark Redman (SJ)	L	27	2	4	.333	0	9	9	0	49	57	19	29	0	4.22
Johan Santana (EJ)	L	22	1	0	1.000	0	15	4	0	44	50	16	28	0	4.74
2 Todd Jones	R	33	1	0	1.000	2	24	0	0	19	27	7	15	0	3.26
Adam Johnson	R	21	1	2	.333	0	7	4	0	25	32	13	17	0	8.28
J.C. Romero	L	25	1	4	.200	0	14	11	0	65	71	24	39	0	6.23
Travis Miller	L	28	1	4	.200	0	45	0	0	49	54	20	30	0	4.81
LaTroy Hawkins	R	28	1	5	.167	28	62	0	0	51	59	39	36	0	5.96
Juan Rincon	R	22	0	0	—	0	6			7	5	4	6	0	6.35
Mike Duvall	L	26	0	0	—	0	8	0	0	5	7	2	4	0	7.71
Grant Balfour	R	23	0	0	—	0	2	0	0	3	3	2	2	0	13.50
2 Tony Fiore	R	29	0	1	.000	0	5	0	0	8	8	3	5	0	5.68
Brad Thomas	L	23	0	2	.000	0	5	5	0	16	20	14	6	0	9.37

CHICAGO 3rd 83-79 .512 8 JERRY MANUEL

Name	G by Pos	B	AGE	G	AB	R	H	2B	3B	HR	RBI	BB	SO	SB	BA	SA
TOTALS			29	162	5464	798	1483	300	29	214	770	520	998	123	.268	.451
Paul Konerko	1B144 DH11	R	25	156	582	92	164	35	0	32	99	54	89	1	.282	.507
Ray Durham	2B150 DH1	B	29	152	611	104	163	42	10	20	65	54	110	23	.267	.466
Royce Clayton	SS133	R	31	135	433	62	114	21	4	9	60	33	72	10	.263	.393
Jose Valentin	3B66 SS43 DH2	B	31	124	438	74	113	22	2	28	68	50	114	9	.258	.509
Magglio Ordonez	OF155 DH3	R	27	160	593	97	181	40	1	31	113	70	70	25	.305	.533
Chris Singleton	OF133 DH2	L	28	140	392	57	117	21	5	7	45	20	61	12	.298	.439
Carlos Lee	OF130 DH17	R	25	150	558	75	150	33	3	24	84	38	85	17	.269	.468
Sandy Alomar (KJ)	C69	R	35	70	220	17	54	8	1	4	21	12	17	1	.245	.345
Frank Thomas (AJ)	DH16 1B3	R	33	20	68	8	15	3	0	4	10	10	12	0	.221	.441
Hebert Perry	3B68 1B12 DH10	R	31	92	285	38	73	21	1	7	32	23	55	2	.256	.411
Jeff Liefer	OF38 1B15 3B15 DH10	L	26	83	254	36	65	13	0	18	39	20	69	0	.256	.520
Jose Canseco	DH68 OF2	R	36	76	256	46	66	8	0	16	49	45	75	2	.258	.477
Tony Graffanino	3B38 2B20 SS5 OF3 DH2	R	29	74	145	23	44	9	0	2	15	16	29	4	.303	.407
Aaron Rowand	OF61	R	23	63	123	21	36	5	0	4	20	15	28	5	.293	.431
Mark Johnson	C61	L	25	61	139	20	31	8	1	5	18	23	31	2	.223	.382
Josh Paul	C56	R	26	57	139	20	37	11	0	3	18	13	25	6	.266	.410
Harold Baines (PJ)	DH22	L	42	32	84	3	11	1	0	0	6	8	16	0	.131	.143
Julio Ramirez	OF21	R	23	22	37	2	3	0	0	0	1	2	15	2	.081	.081
Joe Crede	3B15	R	23	17	50	1	11	1	1	0	7	3	11	1	.220	.280
1 McKay Christensen	OF6	L	25	7	4	0	1	0	0	0	0	0	2	0	.250	.250
Mark Dalesandro	C1	R	33	1	0	0	0	0	0	0	0	0	0	0	—	—

NAME	T	AGE	W	L	PCT	SV	G	GS	CG	IP	H	BB	SO	SHO	ERA
		28	83	79	.512	51	162	162	8	1433	1465	500	921	7	4.55
Mark Buehrle	L	22	16	8	.667	0	32	32	4	221	188	48	126	2	3.29
Kip Wells	R	24	10	11	.476	0	40	20	0	133	145	61	99	0	4.79
Sean Lowe	R	30	9	4	.692	3	45	11	0	127	123	32	71	0	3.61
1 James Baldwin	R	29	7	5	.583	0	17	16	2	96	109	38	42	1	4.61
Rocky Biddle	R	25	7	8	.467	0	30	21	0	129	137	52	85	0	5.39
Jon Garland	R	21	6	7	.462	1	35	16	0	117	123	55	61	0	3.69
Dan Wright	R	23	5	3	.625	0	13	12	0	66	78	39	36	0	5.70
Gary Glover	R	24	5	5	.500	0	46	11	0	100	98	32	63	0	4.93
David Wells (XJ)	L	38	5	7	.417	0	16	16	1	101	120	21	59	0	4.47
Bob Howry	R	27	4	5	.444	5	69	0	0	79	85	30	64	0	4.69
Keith Foulke	R	28	4	9	.308	42	72	0	0	81	57	22	75	0	2.33
Kelly Wunsch (SJ)	L	28	2	1	.667	0	33	0	0	22	21	9	16	0	7.66
Matt Ginter	R	23	1	0	1.000	0	20	0	0	40	34	14	24	0	5.22
Lorenzo Barcelo (SJ)	R	23	1	0	1.000	0	17	0	0	21	24	8	15	0	4.71
2 Alan Embree	L	31	2	2	.333	0	39	0	0	34	31	7	34	0	5.03
Josh Fogg	R	24	0	0	—	0	11	0	0	13	10	3	17	0	2.03
2 Bill Pulsipher	L	27	0	0	—	0	14	0	0	8	11	7	4	0	7.88
Ken Vining	R	26	0	0	—	0	8	0	0	7	15	7	3	0	17.55
Antonio Osuna (SJ)	R	28	0	0	—	0	2	0	0	6	12	3	6	0	13.50
Cal Eldred (EJ)	R	33	0	1	.000	0	2	2	0	6	8	3	2	0	20.77
Jim Parque (SJ)	L	26	0	3	.000	0	5	5	0	18	36	10	15	0	8.04
Bill Simas 29																

DETROIT 4th 66-96 .407 25 PHIL GARNER

Name	G by Pos	B	AGE	G	AB	R	H	2B	3B	HR	RBI	BB	SO	SB	BA	SA
TOTALS			28	162	5537	724	1439	291	60	139	691	466	972	133	.260	.409
Tony Clark	1B78 DH42	B	29	126	428	67	123	29	3	16	75	62	108	0	.287	.481
Damion Easley	2B153	R	31	154	585	77	146	27	7	11	65	52	90	10	.250	.376
Deivi Cruz (BF)	SS109 3B7	R	28	110	414	39	106	28	1	7	52	17	46	4	.256	.379
Jose Macias	3B89 OF29 2B18 DH2	B	29	137	488	62	131	24	6	8	51	32	54	21	.268	.391
Juan Encarnacion	OF116 DH2	R	25	120	417	52	101	19	7	12	52	25	93	9	.242	.408
Roger Cedeno	OF120 DH7	B	26	131	523	79	153	14	11	6	48	36	83	55	.293	.396
Bobby Higginson	OF142 DH5	L	30	147	541	84	150	28	6	17	71	80	65	20	.277	.445
Robert Fick	C78 1B26 OF8 DH8	L	27	124	401	62	109	21	2	19	61	39	62	0	.272	.476
Dean Palmer (SJ)	DH57	R	32	57	216	34	48	11	0	11	40	27	59	4	.222	.428
Shane Halter	3B74 SS62 1B8 DH1	R	31	136	450	53	128	32	7	12	65	37	100	3	.284	.447
Wendell Magee	OF74 DH11	R	28	90	207	26	44	11	4	5	17	23	44	3	.213	.377
Randall Simon	1B43 DH29	L	26	81	256	28	78	14	2	6	37	15	28	0	.305	.445
Brandon Inge (SJ)	C79	R	24	79	189	13	34	11	0	0	15	9	41	1	.180	.238
Ryan Jackson	1B35 OF34 DH5	L	29	79	118	19	25	4	2	2	11	5	26	3	.212	.331
Javier Cardona	C44 DH1	R	25	46	96	10	25	8	0	1	10	2	12	0	.260	.375
1 Billy McMillon	OF7 DH3	L	29	20	34	1	3	1	0	1	4	2	12	0	.088	.206
Eric Munson	1B17	L	23	17	66	4	10	1	1	1	6	3	21	0	.152	.273
Jarrod Patterson	3B13	L	27	13	41	6	11	1	1	2	4	4	8	0	.268	.488
Chris Wakeland	OF10	L	27	10	36	5	9	2	0	2	6	0	13	0	.250	.472
Mike Rivera	C4	R	24	4	12	2	4	2	0	0	1	0	2	0	.333	.500
Jermaine Clark	DH2	L	24	3	0	1	0	0	0	0	0	2	0	0	—	—
Pedro Santana	2B1	R	26	1	0	0	0	0	0	0	0	0	0	0	—	—
Mitch Meluskey (SJ) 27																

NAME	T	AGE	W	L	PCT	SV	G	GS	CG	IP	H	BB	SO	SHO	ERA
		28	66	96	.407	34	162	162	16	1429	1624	553	859	2	5.01
Steve Sparks	R	35	14	9	.609	0	35	33	8	232	244	64	116	1	3.65
Jeff Weaver	R	24	13	16	.448	0	33	33	5	229	235	68	152	0	4.08
Chris Holt	R	29	9	16	.438	0	30	22	1	151	197	57	80	0	5.77
Danny Patterson	R	30	5	4	.556	1	60	0	0	65	64	12	27	0	3.06
2 Jose Lima	R	28	5	10	.333	0	18	18	2	113	120	22	43	0	4.71
Nate Cornejo	R	21	4	4	.500	0	10	10	0	43	63	28	22	0	7.38
1 Todd Jones	R	33	4	5	.444	11	45	0	0	49	60	22	39	0	4.62
1 Dave Mlicki	R	33	4	8	.333	0	15	15	0	81	118	41	48	0	7.53
Matt Anderson	R	24	3	1	.750	22	62	0	0	56	56	18	52	0	4.82
Victor Santos	R	24	2	2	.500	0	33	7	0	76	62	49	52	0	3.30
Matt Perisho	L	26	2	4	.333	0	30	4	0	39	54	14	19	0	7.53
Willie Blair	R	35	1	2	.200	0	40	0	0	24	38	11	15	0	10.50
Adam Pettyjohn	L	24	1	6	.143	0	16	9	0	65	81	21	40	0	5.82
Heath Murray	L	28	1	1	.125	0	40	4	0	63	82	40	42	0	6.54
Adam Bernero	R	24	0	0	—	0	12	2	0	13	4	8	7	0	7.30
Kevin Tolar	L	30	0	0	—	0	11	0	0	11	7	13	11	0	7.45
Matt Miller	L	26	0	0	—	0	10	0	0	10	16	4	6	0	7.45
Brian Moehler (SJ)	R	29	0	1	—	0	1	1	0	4	9	1	3	0	3.38
Luis Pineda	R	26	0	1	.000	0	18	0	0	18	16	14	13	0	4.91
Dave Borkowski (SJ)	R	24	0	2	.000	0	15	0	0	30	30	15	30	0	6.00
2 Mark Redman (KJ)	L	27	0	0	—	0	2	0	0	4	9	11	4	0	6.00
C.J. Nitkowski	L	28	0	0	—	0	5	0	0	45	51	31	38	0	5.56
Seth Greisinger (EJ) 25																

KANSAS CITY 5th 65-97 .401 26 TONY MUSER

Name	G by Pos	B	AGE	G	AB	R	H	2B	3B	HR	RBI	BB	SO	SB	BA	SA
TOTALS			29	162	5643	729	1503	277	37	152	691	406	898	100	.266	.409
Mike Sweeney	1B108 DH38	R	27	147	559	97	170	46	0	29	99	64	64	10	.304	.542
Carlos Febles (KJ)	2B78	R	25	79	292	45	69	9	2	8	22	22	58	5	.236	.363
1 Rey Sanchez	SS100	R	33	100	390	46	118	14	5	0	28	11	34	9	.303	.364
Joe Randa	3B137 DH14 2B1	R	31	151	581	59	147	34	2	13	83	42	80	3	.253	.386
1 Jermaine Dye	OF93 DH4	R	27	97	367	50	100	14	0	17	47	30	68	7	.272	.417
Carlos Beltran	OF152 DH3	B	24	155	617	106	189	32	12	24	101	52	120	31	.306	.514
Dee Brown (LJ)	OF83 DH20	L	23	108	380	39	93	19	0	7	40	22	81	5	.245	.350
Gregg Zaun (LJ)	C35 DH2	B	30	39	125	15	40	9	0	6	16	16	12	1	.320	.536
Raul Ibanez	OF42 DH33 1B10 3B1	L	29	104	279	44	78	11	5	13	54	32	51	0	.280	.495
Mark Quinn	OF99 DH18	R	27	118	453	57	122	31	2	17	60	12	69	9	.269	.459
Luis Alicea	2B67 DH22 3B18	B	35	113	387	44	106	16	4	4	32	23	56	8	.274	.367
David McCarty	1B68 OF9 DH7	R	31	98	200	26	50	10	0	7	26	24	45	0	.250	.405
Hector Ortiz	C55 DH1	R	31	56	154	12	38	6	1	0	11	9	24	1	.247	.299
2 Donnie Sadler	OF16 3B15 2B13 SS8 DH1	R	26	54	101	16	13	2	0	0	3	9	17	4	.129	.158
2 Brent Mayne	C49	L	33	51	166	13	40	4	1	2	16	11	27	1	.241	.313
2 Neifi Perez	SS46 2B4	B	28	49	199	18	48	7	3	1	12	10	19	3	.241	.302
A.J. Hinch	C43 DH2	R	27	45	121	10	19	3	0	6	15	8	26	1	.157	.331
Endy Chavez	OF28	L	23	29	77	4	16	2	0	0	5	3	8	2	.208	.234
Luis Ordaz (LJ)	2B19 SS8 3B1 DH1	R	25	29	46	5	14	3	0	0	4	3	10	0	.250	.304
Angel Berroa	SS14	R	23	15	53	8	16	2	0	1	3	3	10	2	.302	.340
Wilson Delgado	SS6 3B3 2B2	B	26	11	23	2	3	1	0	0	1	2	5	0	.130	.174
Brandon Berger	OF5 DH1	R	26	6	16	4	5	2	0	2	6	0	6	0	.313	.875
Trenidad Hubbard	OF3	R	37	5	12	4	3	1	0	0	0	4	0	0	.250	.333
Ken Harvey	1B3 DH1	R	23	4	12	1	3	1	0	0	2	0	4	0	.250	.333
2 Sal Fasano	C3	R	29	3	1	0	0	0	0	0	0	0	0	0	.000	.000

NAME	T	AGE	W	L	PCT	SV	G	GS	CG	IP	H	BB	SO	SHO	ERA
		28	65	97	.401	30	162	162	5	1440	1537	576	911	1	4.87
Jeff Suppan	R	26	10	14	.417	0	34	34	1	218	227	74	120	0	4.37
Chad Durbin	R	23	9	16	.360	0	34	29	2	179	201	58	95	0	4.93
Dan Reichert	R	24	8	8	.500	0	27	19	0	123	131	67	77	0	5.63
Blake Stein	R	27	7	8	.467	1	36	15	0	131	112	79	113	0	4.74
Kris Wilson	R	24	6	5	.545	1	29	15	0	109	132	32	67	0	5.19
2 Paul Byrd (SJ)	R	30	6	6	.500	0	16	15	1	93	110	22	49	0	4.05
Roberto Hernandez	R	36	5	6	.455	28	63	0	0	68	69	26	46	0	4.12
Chris George	L	21	4	8	.333	0	13	13	1	74	83	18	32	0	5.59
Doug Henry	R	37	2	2	.500	0	53	0	0	76	75	45	57	0	6.07
1 Jose Santiago	R	26	2	2	.500	0	20	0	0	29	40	9	15	0	6.75
1 Mac Suzuki	R	26	2	5	.286	0	15	9	0	56	61	25	37	0	5.30
Cory Bailey	R	30	1	1	.500	0	53	0	0	57	53	33	61	0	3.48
Mike MacDougal	R	24	1	1	.500	0	3	3	0	15	18	4	7	0	4.70
Jason Grimsley	R	33	1	5	.167	0	73	0	0	80	71	28	61	0	3.02
Brian Meadows	R	25	1	6	.143	0	10	10	0	50	73	12	21	0	6.97
Jeff Austin	R	24	0	0	—	0	13	0	0	14	27	14	7	0	5.54
Scott Mullen (SJ)	L	26	0	0	—	0	17	0	0	10	13	9	3	0	4.50
Brad Voyles	R	24	0	0	—	0	9	0	0	9	5	6	9	0	3.86
Tony Cogan	L	24	0	0	.000	0	39	0	0	25	32	13	17	0	5.84
Jose Rosado (SJ) 26																

SEATTLE 1st 116-46 .716 — LOU PINIELLA

Name	G by Pos	B	AGE	G	AB	R	H	2B	3B	HR	RBI	BB	SO	SB	BA	SA
TOTALS			32	162	5680	927	1637	310	38	169	881	614	989	174	.288	.445
John Olerud	1B158	L	32	159	572	91	173	32	1	21	95	94	70	2	.302	.472
Bret Boone	2B156 DH2	R	32	158	623	118	206	37	3	37	141	40	110	5	.331	.578
Carlos Guillen	SS137 DH1	B	25	140	456	72	118	21	4	5	53	53	89	4	.259	.355
David Bell	3B134 1B2	R	28	135	470	62	122	28	0	15	64	28	59	2	.260	.415
Ichiro Suzuki	OF152 DH4	L	27	157	692	127	242	34	8	8	69	30	53	56	.350	.457
Mike Cameron	OF149 DH1	R	28	150	540	99	144	30	5	25	110	69	155	34	.267	.480
Al Martin	OF73 DH16	L	33	100	283	41	68	15	2	7	42	37	59	9	.240	.382
Dan Wilson	C122 1B2	R	32	123	377	44	100	20	1	10	42	20	69	3	.265	.403
Edgar Martinez	DH127 1B1	R	38	132	470	80	144	40	1	23	116	93	90	4	.306	.543
Mark McLemore	OF68 3B36 SS35 2B9 DH2	B	36	125	409	78	117	16	9	5	57	69	84	39	.286	.406
Charles Gipson	OF65 DH11 3B9 SS6 2B1	R	28	94	64	16	14	2	2	0	5	4	20	1	.219	.313
Stan Javier	OF76 1B6 DH2	B	37	89	281	44	82	14	1	4	33	36	47	11	.292	.391
Tom Lampkin	C71 OF1 DH1	L	37	79	204	28	46	10	0	5	22	18	41	1	.225	.348
Ed Sprague	1B12 OF9 DH9 3B8 C1	R	33	45	94	9	28	7	0	2	16	11	18	0	.298	.436
Jay Buhner (FJ)	OF12 D4	R	36	19	45	4	10	2	0	2	5	8	9	0	.222	.400
Ramon Vazquez	SS10 2B6 3B2 DH1	L	27	17	35	5	8	0	0	0	4	0	3	0	.229	.229
2 Eugene Kingsale	OF9	B	24	10	15	4	5	0	0	0	1	2	2	2	.333	.333
Anthony Sanders	OF9	R	27	9	17	1	3	2	0	0	2	2	3	0	.176	.294
Pat Borders	C5	R	38	5	6	1	3	0	0	0	0	0	1	0	.500	.500
Scott Podsednik	OF5	L	25	5	6	1	1	0	0	1	0	1	1	0	.167	.500
Chris Widger (SJ) 30																

NAME	T	AGE	W	L	PCT	SV	G	GS	CG	IP	H	BB	SO	SHO	ERA
		31	116	46	.716	56	162	162	8	1465	1293	465	1051	14	3.54
Jamie Moyer	L	38	20	6	.769	0	33	33	1	210	187	44	119	0	3.43
Freddy Garcia	R	26	18	6	.750	0	34	34	4	239	199	69	163	3	3.05
Paul Abbott	R	33	17	4	.810	0	28	27	1	163	145	87	118	0	4.25
Aaron Sele	R	31	15	5	.750	0	34	33	2	215	216	51	114	1	3.60
John Halama	L	29	10	7	.588	0	31	17	0	110	132	26	50	0	4.73
Arthur Rhodes	L	31	8	0	1.000	3	71	0	0	68	46	12	83	0	1.72
Joel Pineiro	R	22	6	2	.750	0	17	11	0	75	50	21	56	0	2.03
Ryan Franklin	R	28	5	1	.833	0	38	0	0	78	76	24	60	0	3.56
Norm Charlton (GJ)	L	38	4	2	.667	1	44	0	0	48	36	11	48	0	3.02
Jose Paniagua	R	27	4	3	.571	3	60	0	0	66	59	38	46	0	4.36
Jeff Nelson	R	34	4	3	.571	4	69	0	0	65	30	44	88	0	2.76
Brett Tomko	R	28	3	1	.750	0	11	4	0	35	42	15	22	0	5.19
Dennis Stark	R	26	1	1	.500	0	4	3	0	15	21	4	12	0	9.20
Brian Fuentes	L	25	1	1	.500	0	10	0	0	12	6	8	10	0	4.63
Kazuhiro Sasaki	R	33	0	4	.000	45	69	0	0	67	48	11	62	0	3.24
Gil Meche (SJ) 22															

OAKLAND 2nd 102-60 .630 14 (Wild Card) — ART HOWE

Name	G by Pos	B	AGE	G	AB	R	H	2B	3B	HR	RBI	BB	SO	SB	BA	SA
TOTALS			27	162	5573	884	1469	334	22	199	835	640	1021	68	.264	.439
Jason Giambi	1B136 DH17	L	30	154	520	109	178	47	2	38	120	129	83	2	.342	.660
Frank Menechino	2B136 SS3 3B1 DH1	R	30	139	471	82	114	22	2	12	60	79	97	2	.242	.374
Miguel Tejada	SS162	R	25	162	622	107	166	31	3	31	113	43	89	11	.267	.476
Eric Chavez	3B149 1B1 SS1 OF1 DH1	L	23	151	552	91	159	43	0	32	114	41	95	8	.288	.540
2 Jermaine Dye	OF61	R	27	61	232	41	69	17	1	13	59	27	44	2	.297	.547
Johnny Damon	OF154 1B1	L	27	155	644	108	165	34	4	9	49	61	70	27	.256	.363
Terrence Long	OF162	L	25	162	629	90	178	37	4	12	85	52	103	9	.283	.412
Ramon Hernandez	C135 1B2	R	25	136	453	55	115	25	0	15	60	37	68	1	.254	.408
Jeremy Giambi	DH61 OF47 1B10	L	26	125	371	64	105	26	0	12	57	63	83	0	.283	.450
Olmedo Seanz	DH58 1B28 3B14	R	30	106	305	33	67	21	1	9	32	19	64	0	.220	.384
Mark Bellhorn	2B12 3B9 SS6 DH4 OF1	B	26	38	74	11	10	1	2	1	4	7	37	0	.135	.243
Adam Piatt (IJ)	OF32 DH1	R	25	36	95	9	20	5	1	0	6	13	26	0	.211	.284
2 Ron Gant	DH21 OF11	R	36	34	81	15	21	5	1	2	13	11	24	2	.259	.420
2 Greg Myers	C28 DH2	L	35	33	87	13	16	1	0	7	13	13	21	0	.184	.437
F.P. Santangelo	2B20 OF6 3B3 DH2	B	33	32	71	16	14	4	0	0	8	11	17	1	.197	.254
Mario Valdez (BH)	DH12 OF7 1B6	L	26	32	54	7	15	1	0	1	8	12	18	0	.278	.352
2 Billy McMillon (SJ)	OF16 DH1	L	29	20	58	6	17	7	1	0	10	5	13	1	.293	.448
1 Robin Jennings	OF13 1B6 DH2	L	29	20	52	4	13	3	0	0	4	2	6	0	.250	.308
Eric Byrnes	OF12 DH5	R	25	19	38	9	9	1	0	3	5	4	6	1	.237	.500
John Jaha (SJ-LJ-VR)	DH12	R	35	12	45	2	4	0	0	0	8	6	15	0	.089	.156
1 Jose Ortiz (LJ)	2B10 DH1	R	24	11	42	4	7	0	0	1	3	1	7	1	.167	.190
1 Sal Fasano	C9 DH1	R	29	11	21	2	1	0	0	0	1	0	12	0	.048	.048
Tom Wilson	C9	R	30	9	21	4	4	0	0	0	4	1	5	0	.190	.476
2 Rob Ryan	OF5 DH1	L	28	7	7	0	0	0	0	0	0	0	3	0	.000	.000
1 Ryan Christenson	OF4 DH1	R	27	7	4	1	0	0	0	0	0	0	1	0	.000	.000
Andy Abad	1B1	L	28	3	2	0	0	0	0	0	0	0	2	0	.000	.000

NAME	T	AGE	W	L	PCT	SV	G	GS	CG	IP	H	BB	SO	SHO	ERA
		29	102	60	.630	44	162	162	13	1463	1384	440	1117	9	3.59
Mark Mulder	L	23	21	8	.724	0	34	34	6	229	214	51	153	4	3.45
Tim Hudson	R	25	18	9	.667	0	35	35	3	235	216	71	181	0	3.37
Barry Zito	L	23	17	8	.680	0	35	35	3	214	184	80	205	2	3.49
Cory Lidle	R	29	13	6	.684	0	29	29	1	188	170	47	118	0	3.59
Gil Heredia	R	35	8	7	.467	0	24	18	0	110	144	29	48	0	5.58
Mark Guthrie	L	35	6	2	.750	1	54	0	0	52	49	20	52	0	4.47
Erik Hiljus	R	28	5	0	1.000	0	16	11	0	66	70	21	67	0	3.41
Jason Isringhausen	R	28	4	3	.571	34	65	0	0	71	54	23	74	0	2.65
Mike Magnante	L	36	3	1	.750	0	65	0	0	55	50	13	23	0	2.77
Chad Bradford	R	26	2	1	.667	1	35	0	0	37	41	6	34	0	2.70
Luis Vizcaino	R	26	2	1	.667	1	36	0	0	37	38	12	31	0	4.66
Jeff Tam	R	30	2	4	.333	1	70	0	0	75	68	29	44	0	3.01
Jim Mecir (KJ)	R	31	2	8	.200	3	54	0	0	63	54	26	61	0	3.43
2 Ron [unclear]		R	31	0	0	—	0	5	2	1	5	0	0.00			
Chad Harville (SJ)		R	24	0	0	—	0	3	2	3	1	5	0	0.00		
1 T.J. Mathews	R	31	0	0	.000	1	20	0	0	23	28	11	19	0	5.09

ANAHEIM 3rd 75-87 .463 41 — MIKE SCIOSCIA

Name	G by Pos	B	AGE	G	AB	R	H	2B	3B	HR	RBI	BB	SO	SB	BA	SA
TOTALS			28	162	5551	691	1447	275	26	158	662	494	1001	116	.261	.405
Scott Spiezio	1B105 DH20 OF18 3B10	B	28	139	457	57	124	29	4	13	54	34	65	5	.271	.438
Adam Kennedy	2B131 DH5	L	25	137	478	48	129	25	6	6	40	27	71	12	.270	.372
David Eckstein	SS126 2B14 DH14	R	26	153	582	82	166	26	2	4	41	43	60	29	.285	.357
Troy Glaus	3B159 SS2 DH2	R	24	161	588	100	147	38	2	41	108	107	158	10	.250	.531
Tim Salmon	OF125 DH12	R	32	137	475	63	108	21	1	17	49	96	121	9	.227	.383
Darin Erstad	OF146 1B12 DH4	L	27	157	631	89	163	35	1	9	63	62	113	24	.258	.360
Garret Anderson	OF149 DH12	L	29	161	672	83	194	39	2	28	123	27	100	13	.289	.478
Bengie Molina (LJ)	C94 DH1	R	26	96	325	31	85	11	0	6	40	16	51	0	.262	.351
Shawn Wooten (WJ)	DH27 C25 1B21 3B1	R	28	79	221	24	69	8	1	8	32	5	42	2	.312	.466
Benji Gil	SS44 2B21 1B18 DH14 OF1	R	28	104	260	33	77	15	4	8	39	14	57	3	.296	.477
Orlando Palmeiro	OF59 DH30	L	32	104	230	29	56	10	1	2	23	25	24	6	.243	.322
Wally Joyner (VR)	1B39 DH9	L	39	53	148	14	36	5	1	3	14	13	18	1	.243	.351
Jorge Fabregas	C53	L	31	53	148	9	33	4	2	2	16	3	15	0	.223	.318
Jeff DaVanon	OF29 DH6	B	27	40	88	7	17	2	1	5	9	11	29	1	.193	.409
Jose Nieves	2B11 SS10 DH4 3B2 1B1	R	26	29	53	5	13	3	1	2	3	2	20	0	.245	.453
Glenallen Hill	DH16	R	36	16	66	4	9	0	0	1	2	0	20	0	.136	.182
Larry Barnes	1B16 OF1	L	26	16	40	2	4	0	0	1	2	1	9	0	.100	.175
Jose Molina (BG)	C15	R	26	15	37	8	10	3	0	2	4	2	5	0	.270	.514
Jose Fernandez	DH7 1B2 3B2	R	26	13	25	1	2	1	0	0	2	0	10	0	.080	.120
Jamie Burke	C8 1B1 DH1	R	29	9	5	1	1	0	0	0	0	0	1	0	.200	.200
Gary DiSarcina (SJ) 33 Mo Vaughn (AJ) 33																

NAME	T	AGE	W	L	PCT	SV	G	GS	CG	IP	H	BB	SO	SHO	ERA
		29	75	87	.463	43	162	162	6	1438	1452	525	947	1	4.20
Ramon Ortiz	R	28	13	11	.542	0	32	32	2	209	223	76	135	0	4.36
Jarrod Washburn	L	26	11	10	.524	0	30	30	1	193	196	54	126	0	3.77
Scott Schoeneweis	R	27	10	11	.476	0	32	32	1	205	227	77	104	0	5.08
Ismael Valdes	R	27	9	13	.409	0	27	27	1	164	177	50	100	0	4.45
Al Levine	R	33	8	10	.444	2	64	1	0	76	71	28	40	0	2.38
Ben Weber	R	31	6	2	.750	0	56	0	0	68	66	31	40	0	3.42
Shigetoshi Hasegawa (SJ)	R	32	5	6	.455	0	46	0	0	56	52	20	41	0	4.04
Pat Rapp	R	33	5	12	.294	0	31	28	1	170	169	71	82	0	4.76
Troy Percival	R	31	4	2	.667	39	57	0	0	58	39	18	71	0	2.65
Lou Pote	R	29	2	0	1.000	2	44	1	0	87	88	32	66	0	4.15
Mike Holtz	L	28	1	2	.333	0	63	0	0	37	40	15	38	0	4.86
Matt Wise	R	25	1	4	.200	0	11	9	0	47	48	11	50	0	4.38
Scot Shields	R	25	0	1	.000	0	8	1	0	11	8	7	7	0	0.00
Bart Miadich	R	25	0	0	—	0	10	0	0	6	4	8	11	0	4.50
Steve Green	R	23	0	1	.000	0	1	1	0	4	5	3	3	0	3.00
Brian Cooper	R	26	0	0	—	0	7	1	0	14	10	4	7	0	10.80
Toby Borland	R	32	0	0	—	0	8	0	0	9	25	0	6.04			
Mark Lukasiewicz	L	28	0	0	—	0	24	0	0	9	25	0	6.04			

TEXAS 4th 73-89 .451 43 — JOHNNY OATES 11-17 .393 JERRY NARRON 62-72 .463

Name	G by Pos	B	AGE	G	AB	R	H	2B	3B	HR	RBI	BB	SO	SB	BA	SA
TOTALS			31	162	5685	890	1566	326	23	246	844	548	1093	97	.275	.471
Rafael Palmeiro	1B113 DH46	L	36	160	600	98	164	33	0	47	123	101	90	1	.273	.563
Michael Young	2B104	R	24	106	386	57	96	18	4	11	49	26	91	1	.249	.402
Alex Rodriguez	SS161 DH1	R	25	162	632	133	201	34	1	52	135	75	131	18	.318	.622
Mike Lamb	3B74	L	25	76	284	42	87	18	0	4	35	14	27	2	.306	.412
Ricky Ledee (LJ)	OF72	L	27	78	242	33	56	21	1	2	36	23	58	3	.231	.351
Gabe Kapler	OF133 DH1	R	25	134	483	77	129	29	1	17	72	61	70	23	.267	.437
Rusty Greer (XJ)	OF60 DH1	L	32	62	245	38	67	23	0	7	29	27	32	1	.273	.453
Ivan Rodriguez (KJ)	C106 DH1	R	29	111	442	70	136	24	2	25	65	23	73	10	.308	.541
Ruben Sierra	DH50 OF36	B	35	94	344	55	100	22	1	23	67	19	52	2	.291	.561
Frank Catalanotto	OF92 2B13 3B11 1B5 DH5	L	27	133	463	77	153	31	5	11	54	39	55	15	.330	.490
1 Randy Velarde (LJ)	2B52 1B9 3B7 DH6 OF2	R	38	78	296	46	88	21	3	7	39	29	73	4	.297	.456
1 Andres Galarraga	DH39 1B25	R	40	72	243	33	57	16	0	10	34	18	68	1	.235	.424
Scott Sheldon	3B38 SS16 OF3 C1	R	32	61	120	11	24	5	0	3	11	3	35	1	.200	.317
1 Ken Caminiti	3B53	B	38	54	185	24	43	8	1	9	25	22	41	0	.232	.432
Bo Porter	OF40 DH2	R	28	48	87	18	20	2	0	4	9	8	34	3	.230	.356
Bill Haselman (EJ)	C47	R	35	47	130	12	37	6	0	3	25	8	27	0	.285	.400
Ruben Mateo	OF39	R	23	40	129	18	32	5	2	1	9	3	28	1	.248	.341
Chad Curtis (LJ)	OF33 DH2	R	32	38	115	24	29	3	0	3	10	14	21	7	.252	.357
Craig Monroe	OF24 DH1	R	24	27	52	8	11	1	0	2	5	2	18	2	.212	.346
1 Doug Mirabelli	C23 DH1	R	30	23	49	4	5	2	0	2	3	10	21	0	.102	.265
Carlos Pena	1B16 DH1	L	23	22	62	6	16	4	1	3	12	10	17	0	.258	.500
Chris Magruder	OF12	B	24	17	29	3	5	0	0	0	3	2	6	0	.172	.172
2 Marcus Jensen	C11	B	28	11	25	4	4	1	0	0	3	6	10	0	.160	.200
1 Cliff Brumbaugh	OF6	R	27	10	1	0	0	0	0	0	0	0	5	0	.000	.000
Mike Hubbard (BG)	C5	R	30	5	11	3	3	1	0	0	1	0	6	0	.273	.636
Kelly Dransfeldt	SS3 3B1	R	26	4	1	0	0	0	0	0	0	0	3	0	.000	.000

NAME	T	AGE	W	L	PCT	SV	G	GS	CG	IP	H	BB	SO	SHO	ERA
		29	73	89	.451	37	162	162	4	1438	1670	596	951	3	5.71
Rick Helling	R	30	12	11	.522	0	34	34	2	216	256	63	154	1	5.17
Doug Davis	L	25	11	10	.524	0	30	30	1	186	220	69	115	0	4.45
Darren Oliver	L	30	11	11	.500	0	28	28	1	154	189	65	104	0	6.02
Pat Mahomes	R	30	7	6	.538	0	56	4	0	107	115	55	61	0	5.70
2 Rob Bell	R	24	5	5	.500	0	18	18	0	105	130	47	64	0	7.18
Mike Venafro	L	27	5	5	.500	4	70	0	0	60	54	28	29	0	4.80
Kenny Rogers (SJ)	L	36	5	7	.417	0	20	20	0	121	150	49	74	0	6.19
Jeff Zimmerman	R	28	4	4	.500	28	66	0	0	71	48	16	72	0	2.40
Aaron Myette	R	23	4	5	.444	0	19	15	0	81	94	37	67	0	7.14
Juan Moreno	L	23	3	3	.500	0	45	0	0	41	22	28	36	0	3.92
2 Chris Michalak	L	30	2	2	.500	0	11	0	0	22	24	6	10	0	3.32
Justin Duchscherer	R	23	1	1	.500	0	5	2	0	11				0	12.27
Mark Petkovsek	R	35	1	2	.333	0	55	0	0	77	103	28	42	0	6.69
J.D. Smart (SJ)	R	27	1	2	.333	0	15	0	0	19	4		10	0	6.46
Ryan Glynn (XJ)	R	26	1	5	.167	0	12	6	0	46	59	26	15	0	7.04
Danny Kolb (EJ)	R	26	0	0	—	0	15	0	0	15	10	15	6	0	4.70
Jonathan Johnson	R	26	0	1	.000	0	5	0	0	13	7	11	9	0	9.58
Brandon Villafuerte	R	25	0	0	—	0	6	0	0	3	4	4	1	0	14.29
Joaquin Benoit	R	22	0	0	—	0	5			3	4	4	0	10.80		
Jeff Brantley	R	37	0	0	—	1	11	0	0	12	16	7	7	0	6.75
Kevin Foster	R	32	0	1	.000	0	18	1	0	21	10	16	0	6.62		
R.A. Dickey	R	26	0	0	—	0	4							0	4.38
2 Mike Judd	R	26	0	1	.000	0	9	1	0	15	9	15	5	0	8.00
Francisco Cordero (XJ)	R	26	0	0	—	0	3			2	3	1		0	3.86
Tim Crabtree (SJ)	R	31	0	0	—	0	23	0	0	37	14	16	10	0	6.58
Justin Thompson (SJ) 28															

LINE SCORES

Team	1	2	3	4	5	6	7	8	9	10	11	12	R	H	E

DIVISION SERIES: NEW YORK 3 : OAKLAND 2

Game 1 October 10 at New York

	1	2	3	4	5	6	7	8	9		R	H	E
OAK	1	0	0	1	0	0	1	2	0		5	10	1
NYA	0	0	0	0	0	0	0	2	0		3	10	1

Mulder, Mecir (7), Isringhausen (9) Clemens, Hitchcock (5), Witasick (8), Stanton (8)

Game 2 October 11 at New York

	1	2	3	4	5	6	7	8	9		R	H	E
OAK	0	0	0	1	0	0	0	0	1		2	9	0
NYA	0	0	0	0	0	0	0	0	0		0	7	1

Hudson, Isringhausen (9) Pettitte, Mendoza (7), Rivera (9)

Game 3 October 13 at Oakland

	1	2	3	4	5	6	7	8	9		R	H	E
NYA	0	0	0	0	1	0	0	0	0		1	2	0
OAK	0	0	0	0	0	0	0	0	0		0	6	1

Mussina, Rivera (8) Zito, Guthrie (9)

Game 4 October 14 at Oakland

	1	2	3	4	5	6	7	8	9		R	H	E
NYA	0	2	2	3	0	0	0	0	2		9	11	1
OAK	0	0	0	0	0	0	0	0	2		2	11	1

Hernandez, Stanton (6), Mendoza (8) Lidle, Hiljus (4), Magnante (4), Guthrie (6), Bradford (8), Tam (9)

Game 5 October 15 at New York

	1	2	3	4	5	6	7	8	9		R	H	E
OAK	1	1	0	0	1	0	0	0	0		3	7	3
NYA	0	2	1	1	0	1	0	0	x		5	10	1

Mulder, Hudson (5), Mecir (7) Clemens, Stanton (5), Mendoza (7), Rivera (8)

DIVISION SERIES: SEATTLE 3 : CLEVELAND 2

Game 1 October 9 at Seattle

	1	2	3	4	5	6	7	8	9		R	H	E
CLE	0	0	0	3	0	1	0	1	0		5	11	1
SEA	0	0	0	0	0	0	0	0	0		0	6	1

Colon, Wickman (9) Garcia, Charlton (6), Paniagua (8), Halama (9)

Game 2 October 11 at Seattle

	1	2	3	4	5	6	7	8	9		R	H	E
CLE	0	0	0	0	0	0	1	0	0		1	6	0
SEA	4	0	0	1	0	0	0	X	0		5	6	0

Finley, Riske (5), Shuey (7), Baez (8) Moyer, Nelson (7), Rhodes (8), Sasaki (9)

Game 3 October 13 at Cleveland

	1	2	3	4	5	6	7	8	9		R	H	E
SEA	1	0	0	0	0	0	1	0	0		2	7	3
CLE	2	2	4	0	1	3	0	5	X		17	19	0

Sele, Abbott (3), Halama (6), Paniagua (8) Sabathia, Riske (7), Rincon (7), Burba (8), Rocker (9)

Game 4 October 14 at Cleveland

	1	2	3	4	5	6	7	8	9		R	H	E
SEA	0	0	0	0	0	0	3	1	2		6	11	0
CLE	0	1	0	0	0	0	1	0	0		2	5	2

Garcia, Nelson (7), Rhodes (7), Sasaki (9) Colon, Baez (7), Rincon (8), Shuey (9)

Game 5 October 15 at Seattle

	1	2	3	4	5	6	7	8	9		R	H	E
CLE	0	0	1	0	0	0	0	0	0		1	4	0
SEA	0	2	0	0	0	0	1	0	X		3	9	1

Finley, Riske (5), Rincon (6), Baez (7) Moyer, Nelson (7), Rhodes (8), Sasaki (9)

CHAMPIONSHIP: NEW YORK 4 : SEATTLE 1

Game 1 October 17 at Seattle

	1	2	3	4	5	6	7	8	9		R	H	E
NYA	0	1	0	2	0	0	0	0	1		4	9	0
SEA	0	0	0	0	1	0	0	0	1		2	4	0

Pettitte, Rivera (9) Sele, Charlton (7), Paniagua (8)

Game 2 October 18 at Seattle

	1	2	3	4	5	6	7	8	9		R	H	E
NYA	0	3	0	0	0	0	0	0	0		3	9	1
SEA	0	0	0	2	0	0	0	0	0		2	6	0

Mussina, Mendoza (7), Rivera (8) Garcia, Rhodes (8), Nelson (9)

Game 3 October 20 at New York

	1	2	3	4	5	6	7	8	9		R	H	E
SEA	0	0	0	0	2	7	2	1	2		14	15	0
NYA	2	0	0	0	0	0	0	1	0		3	7	2

Moyer, Paniagua (8), Halama (9) Hernandez, Stanton (6), Wohlers (6), Witasick (7)

Game 4 October 21 at New York

	1	2	3	4	5	6	7	8	9		R	H	E
SEA	0	0	0	0	0	0	1	0	0		1	2	0
NYA	0	0	0	0	0	0	0	1	2		3	4	0

Abbott, Charlton (6), Nelson (6), Rhodes (8), Sasaki (9) Clemens, Mendoza (6), Rivera (9)

Game 5 October 22 at New York

	1	2	3	4	5	6	7	8	9		R	H	E
SEA	0	0	0	0	0	0	3	0	0		3	9	1
NYA	0	0	4	1	0	4	0	3	X		12	13	1

Sele, Halama (5), Pineiro (6) Pettitte, Mendoza (7), Stanton (8), Rivera (9), Paniagua (8)

DIVISION SERIES

COMPOSITE BATTING

NEW YORK

NAME	POS	G	AB	R	H	2B	3B	HR	RBI	BA
TOTALS		5	166	18	40	8	1	3	16	.241
Knoblauch	LF	5	22	1	6	1	0	0	1	.273
Jeter	SS	5	18	2	8	1	0	0	1	.444
Posada	C	5	18	3	8	0	1	2	2	.444
Soriano	2B	5	18	2	4	0	0	0	3	.222
Williams	CF	5	18	4	4	3	0	0	5	.222
Martinez	1B	5	18	1	2	0	0	1	2	.111
Brosius	3B	5	17	0	1	0	0	0	1	.059
Justice	RF-DH	4	13	3	3	0	0	1	1	.231
O'Neill	DH-RF	3	11	1	1	1	0	0	0	.091
Spencer	RF	3	8	1	2	1	0	0	0	.250
Velarde	DH	2	5	0	1	0	0	0	0	.200
Bellinger	PR	1	0	0	0	0	0	0	0	—

OAKLAND

NAME	POS	G	AB	R	H	2B	3B	HR	RBI	BA
TOTALS		5	174	12	43	13	1	4	11	.247
Damon	CF	5	22	3	9	2	1	0	0	.409
Tejada	SS	5	21	1	6	3	0	1	0	.286
Chavez	3B	5	21	0	3	1	0	0	0	.143
Long	LF-RF	5	18	3	7	3	0	2	3	.389
Ja. Giambi	1B	5	17	2	6	0	0	1	4	.353
Je. Giambi	DH	5	13	0	4	1	0	0	2	.308
Dye	RF	4	13	0	3	2	0	0	0	.231
Menechino	2B	4	12	2	1	0	0	0	0	.083
Gant	DH-LF	4	11	1	2	0	0	1	1	.182
Hernandez	C	5	10	0	0	0	0	0	0	.000
Myers	C	3	7	0	1	0	0	0	0	.143
Saenz	PH	3	4	0	0	0	0	0	0	.000
Santangelo	2B	2	3	0	1	0	0	0	0	.333
Byrnes	DH	2	2	0	0	0	0	0	0	.000

SEATTLE

NAME	POS	G	AB	R	H	2B	3B	HR	RBI	BA
TOTALS		5	158	16	39	8	0	4	16	.247
Boone	2B	5	21	1	2	0	0	0	0	.095
Suzuki	RF	5	20	4	12	1	0	0	2	.600
Cameron	CF	5	18	2	4	3	0	1	3	.222
McLemore	SS	5	18	0	3	0	0	0	3	.167
Olerud	1B	5	17	1	3	0	0	0	1	.176
Bell	3B	5	16	2	5	1	0	1	2	.313
Martinez	DH	5	16	3	5	1	0	2	5	.313
Wilson	C	5	15	0	3	1	0	0	0	.200
Javier	LF	4	8	2	2	1	0	0	0	.250
Buhner	LF	2	3	0	0	0	0	0	0	.000
Martin	PH-PR	3	2	1	0	0	0	0	0	.000
Lampkin	C	2	2	0	0	0	0	0	0	.000
Gipson	PH	1	1	0	0	0	0	0	0	.000
Sprague	PH	1	1	0	0	0	0	0	0	.000
Vazquez	SS	1	0	0	0	0	0	0	0	—

CLEVELAND

NAME	POS	G	AB	R	H	2B	3B	HR	RBI	BA
TOTALS		5	173	26	45	9	1	5	25	.260
Gonzalez	RF	5	23	4	8	3	0	2	5	.348
Vizquel	SS	5	22	2	9	1	1	0	6	.409
Alomar	2B	5	21	3	4	3	0	0	3	.190
Burks	DH	5	19	4	6	1	0	1	1	.316
Thome	1B	5	19	2	3	0	0	1	1	.158
Lofton	CF	5	19	2	2	0	0	1	3	.105
Fryman	3B	5	17	4	3	1	0	0	2	.176
Diaz	C	4	16	3	5	0	0	0	2	.313
Cordova	LF	4	9	0	3	0	0	0	1	.333
Cordero	LF	1	4	0	0	0	0	0	0	.000
Branyan	LF	2	3	1	1	0	0	0	0	.333
Cabrera	LF	2	1	1	1	0	0	0	1	1.000

COMPOSITE PITCHING

NEW YORK

NAME	G	IP	H	BB	SO	W	L	SV	ERA
TOTALS	5	45	43	11	31	3	2	2	2.20
Clemens	2	8.1	9	4	6	0	1	0	5.40
Mussina	1	7	4	1	4	1	0	0	0.00
Pettitte	1	6.1	7	2	4	0	1	0	1.42
Hernandez	1	5.2	8	2	5	1	0	0	3.18
Rivera	3	5	4	0	4	0	0	2	0.00
Stanton	3	4.2	3	0	1	1	0	0	0.00
Mendoza	3	4.1	2	1	5	0	0	0	0.00
Hitchcock	1	3	5	0	2	0	0	0	6.00
Witasick	1	0.2	1	1	0	0	0	0	13.50

OAKLAND

NAME	G	IP	H	BB	SO	W	L	SV	ERA
TOTALS	5	44	40	11	29	2	3	2	2.86
Mulder	2	11	14	2	7	1	1	0	2.45
Hudson	2	9.2	8	1	5	1	0	0	0.93
Zito	1	8	2	1	6	0	1	0	1.13
Mecir	3	3.1	4	0	4	0	0	0	5.40
Lidle	1	3.1	5	3	0	0	1	0	10.80
Guthrie	2	3	0	2	2	0	0	0	0.00
Isringhausen	2	2	1	1	3	0	0	2	0.00
Magnante	1	1.1	3	1	1	0	0	0	0.00
Bradford	1	1	0	0	0	0	0	0	0.00
Tam	1	1	3	0	0	0	0	0	18.00
Hiljus	1	0.1	0	2	0	0	0	0	27.00

SEATTLE

NAME	G	IP	H	BB	SO	W	L	SV	ERA
TOTALS	5	44	45	13	43	3	2	1	4.70
Moyer	2	12	8	2	10	2	0	0	1.50
Garcia	2	11.2	13	3	13	1	1	0	3.86
Sasaki	3	3	1	0	5	0	0	1	0.00
Halama	2	3	3	0	0	0	0	0	0.00
Nelson	3	3	1	1	5	0	0	0	0.00
Abbott	1	3	9	5	3	0	0	0	24.00
Rhodes	5	3	2	2	1	0	0	0	0.00
Paniagua	2	2	4	2	1	0	0	0	27.00
Sele	1	2	5	0	0	0	1	0	9.00
Charlton	1	1.2	0	0	2	0	0	0	0.00

CLEVELAND

NAME	G	IP	H	BB	SO	W	L	SV	ERA
TOTALS	5	43	39	18	48	2	3	0	3.35
Colon	2	14.2	12	6	13	1	1	0	1.84
Finley	2	8.2	9	6	10	0	2	0	7.27
Sabathia	1	6	6	5	5	1	0	0	3.00
Baez	3	3.2	4	0	6	0	0	0	2.45
Riske	3	3.2	2	1	5	0	0	0	0.00
Rincon	3	2	2	1	3	0	0	0	9.00
Shuey	2	1.1	3	0	2	0	0	0	6.75
Burba	1	1	0	1	1	0	0	0	0.00
Rocker	1	1	1	0	1	0	0	0	0.00
Wickman	1	1	0	0	0	0	0	0	0.00

AMERICAN LEAGUE CHAMPIONSHIP

COMPOSITE BATTING

NEW YORK

NAME	POS	G	AB	R	H	2B	3B	HR	RBI	BA
TOTALS		5	159	25	42	7	0	7	24	.264
Martinez	1B	5	20	3	5	1	0	1	3	.250
Knoblauch	LF	5	18	0	6	1	0	0	3	.333
Justice	DH	5	18	3	5	1	0	0	4	.278
Williams	CF	5	17	4	4	0	0	3	5	.235
Jeter	SS	5	17	0	2	0	0	0	2	.118
Brosius	3B	5	16	3	3	2	0	0	2	.188
Soriano	2B	5	15	5	6	0	0	1	2	.400
Posada	C	5	14	4	3	1	0	0	0	.214
O'Neill	RF	5	12	2	5	0	0	2	3	.417
Spencer	RF	5	7	1	2	1	0	0	0	.286
Wilson	SS	1	1	0	1	0	0	0	1	1.000
Bellinger	LF	1	1	0	0	0	0	0	0	.000
Greene	C	1	1	0	0	0	0	0	0	.000
Sojo	1B	1	1	0	0	0	0	0	0	.000
Velarde	3B	1	1	0	0	0	0	0	0	.000

SEATTLE

NAME	POS	G	AB	R	H	2B	3B	HR	RBI	BA
TOTALS		5	171	22	36	4	2	5	20	.211
Martinez	DH	5	20	1	3	1	0	0	0	.150
Boone	2B	5	19	2	6	0	0	2	6	.316
Olerud	1B	5	19	2	4	0	0	1	3	.211
Suzuki	RF-LF	5	18	3	4	1	0	0	1	.222
Cameron	CF	5	17	3	3	2	0	0	0	.176
Bell	3B	5	16	1	3	0	0	0	4	.188
Javier	LF	5	14	2	3	0	0	1	2	.214
McLemore	SS-LF-2B	5	14	1	2	0	1	0	3	.143
Wilson	C	5	13	2	2	0	0	0	0	.154
Guillen	SS	3	8	1	2	0	0	0	0	.250
Buhner	LF-RF	3	6	2	2	0	0	0	0	.333
Lampkin	C	2	4	1	1	0	0	0	0	.250
Martin	PH	2	2	1	1	0	1	0	0	.500
Gipson	DH-RF-LF	2	1	0	0	0	0	0	0	.000

COMPOSITE PITCHING

NEW YORK

NAME	G	IP	H	BB	SO	W	L	SV	ERA
TOTALS	5	45	36	18	35	4	1	2	3.80
Pettitte	2	14.1	11	2	8	2	0	0	2.51
Mussina	1	6	5	1	3	1	0	0	3.00
Mendoza	3	5.1	3	2	4	0	0	0	1.69
Clemens	1	5	1	4	7	0	0	0	0.00
Hernandez	1	5	5	5	7	0	1	0	7.20
Rivera	4	4.2	2	1	3	1	0	2	1.93
Witasick	1	3	6	0	2	0	0	0	9.00
Stanton	2	1	1	2	0	0	0	0	27.00
Wohlers	1	0.2	3	1	1	0	0	0	13.50

SEATTLE

NAME	G	IP	H	BB	SO	W	L	SV	ERA
TOTALS	5	43.1	42	23	31	1	4	0	4.36
Sele	2	10	11	4	5	0	2	0	3.60
Garcia	1	7.1	7	4	6	0	1	0	3.68
Moyer	1	7	4	1	5	1	0	0	2.57
Abbott	1	5	0	8	2	0	0	0	0.00
Paniagua	3	3.2	7	1	1	0	0	0	12.27
Nelson	2	2.1	1	3	4	0	0	0	4.50
Rhodes	2	2	2	0	2	0	0	0	4.50
Halama	2	2	3	0	0	0	0	0	13.50
Pineiro	1	2	3	2	5	0	0	0	4.50
Charlton	1	1.2	1	2	0	0	0	0	0.00
Sasaki	1	0.1	0	0	0	0	1	0	54.00

ATLANTA — 1st 88-74 .543 — BOBBY COX

Name	G by Pos	B	AGE	G	AB	R	H	2B	3B	HR	RBI	BB	SO	SB	BA	SA
TOTALS			30	162	5498	729	1432	263	24	174	696	493	1039	85	.260	.412
Rico Brogna (VR)	1B67	L	31	72	206	15	51	9	0	3	21	14	46	3	.248	.335
Quilvio Veras	2B67	B	30	71	258	39	65	14	2	3	25	24	52	7	.252	.357
Rafael Furcal (SJ)	SS79	B	23	79	324	39	89	19	0	4	30	24	56	22	.275	.370
Chipper Jones	3B149 OF8	B	29	159	572	113	189	33	5	38	102	98	82	9	.330	.605
Brian Jordan	OF144	R	34	148	560	82	165	32	3	25	97	31	88	3	.295	.496
Andruw Jones	OF161	R	24	161	625	104	157	25	2	34	104	56	142	11	.251	.461
B.J. Surhoff	OF129	L	36	141	484	68	131	33	1	10	58	38	48	9	.271	.405
Javy Lopez	C127	R	30	128	438	45	117	16	1	17	66	28	82	1	.267	.425
Dave Martinez	OF52 1B10	L	36	120	237	33	68	11	3	2	20	21	44	3	.287	.384
Keith Lockhart	2B47 3B4	L	36	104	178	17	39	6	0	3	12	16	22	1	.219	.303
Wes Helms	1B77 3B17 OF1	R	25	100	216	28	48	10	3	10	36	21	56	1	.222	.435
Bernard Gilkey	OF36	R	34	69	106	8	29	6	0	2	14	11	31	0	.274	.387
Marcus Giles	2B62	R	23	68	244	36	64	10	2	9	31	28	37	2	.262	.430
Mark DeRosa	SS48 2B5 3B1 OF1	R	26	66	164	27	47	8	0	3	20	12	19	2	.287	.390
Ken Caminiti	1B33 3B13	B	38	64	171	12	38	9	0	6	16	21	44	0	.222	.380
Paul Bako	C60	L	29	61	137	19	29	10	1	2	15	20	34	1	.212	.343
Rey Sanchez	SS48	R	33	49	154	10	35	4	1	0	9	4	15	2	.227	.266
Julio Franco	1B23	R	42	25	90	13	27	4	0	3	11	10	20	0	.300	.444
Jesse Garcia	2B4 SS2	R	27	22	5	3	1	0	0	0	0	0	1	6	.200	.200
Cory Aldridge	OF4	L	22	8	5	1	0	0	0	0	0	0	4	0	.000	.000
Wilson Betemit	SS1	B	19	3	1	0	0	0	0	0	0	0	1		.000	.000
Kurt Abbott (MJ)	2B1 SS1	R	32	6	9	0	2	0	0	0	0	0	3	1	.222	.222
Eddie Perez (SJ)	C5	R	33	5	10	0	3	0	0	0	0	0	2		.300	.300
Steve Torrealba	C2	R	23	2	2	0	1	0	0	0	0	0	0		.500	.500

NAME	T	AGE	W	L	PCT	SV	G	GS	CG	IP	H	BB	SO	SHO	ERA
		31	88	74	.543	41	162	162	5	1447	1363	499	1133	13	3.59
Greg Maddux	R	35	17	11	.607	0	34	34	3	233	220	27	173	3	3.05
Tom Glavine	L	35	16	7	.696	0	34	35	1	219	213	97	116	1	3.57
John Burkett	R	36	12	12	.500	0	34	34	1	219	187	70	187	1	3.04
Jose Cabrera	R	29	7	4	.636	2	55	0	0	59	52	25	43	0	2.88
Kevin Millwood (SJ)	R	26	7	7	.500	0	21	21	0	121	121	40	84	0	4.31
Odalis Perez (HJ)	L	24	7	8	.467	0	24	16	0	95	108	34	71	0	4.91
Jason Marquis	R	22	5	6	.455	0	38	16	0	129	143	59	98	0	3.48
Mike Remlinger	L	35	3	3	.500	1	74	0	0	75	67	23	93	0	2.76
Kerry Ligtenberg	R	30	3	3	.500	1	53	0	0	60	50	30	56	0	3.02
John Smoltz (EJ)	R	34	3	3	.500	10	36	5	0	59	53	10	57	0	3.36
Steve Karsay	R	29	3	4	.429	7	43	0	0	45	44	17	39	0	3.43
John Rocker	L	26	2	2	.500	19	30	0	0	32	25	16	36	0	3.09
Steve Reed	R	36	2	2	.500	1	39	0	0	31	30	13	25	0	3.48
Marc Valdes	R	29	1	0	1.000	0	9	0	0	7	7	1	3	0	7.71
Rudy Seanez	R	32	0	0	—	0	12	0	0	12	8	4	17	0	3.00
Damian Moss (AJ)	L	24	0	0	—	0	5	1	0	9	3	9	8	0	3.00
Chris Seelbach	R	28	0	0	—	0	5	0	0	8	9	5	8	0	7.88
Joe Slusarski	R	34	0	0	—	0	4	0	0	6	9	1	5	0	9.00
Trey Moore	L	28	0	0	—	0	3	0	0	4	7	2	1	0	11.25
Joe Nelson (SJ)	R	26	0	0	—	0	2	0	0	2	7	2	0	0	36.00
Scott Sobkowiak (AJ)	R	23	0	0	—	0	1	0	0	1	2	0	0	0	9.00
Matt Whiteside	R	33	0	0	—	0	13	0	0	16	23	7	10	0	7.16
Tim Spooneybarger	R	21	0	0	.000	0	4	0	0	4	5	2	3	0	2.25
Kevin McGlinchy (SJ) 24															

PHILADELPHIA — 2nd 86-76 .531 2 — LARRY BOWA

Name	G by Pos	B	AGE	G	AB	R	H	2B	3B	HR	RBI	BB	SO	SB	BA	SA
TOTALS			26	162	5497	746	1431	295	29	164	708	551	1125	153	.260	.414
Travis Lee	1B156	L	26	157	555	75	143	34	2	20	90	71	109	3	.258	.434
Marlon Anderson	2B140	L	27	147	522	69	153	30	2	11	61	35	74	8	.293	.421
Jimmy Rollins	SS157	B	22	158	656	97	180	29	12	14	54	48	108	46	.274	.419
Scott Rolen	3B151	R	26	151	554	96	160	39	1	25	107	74	127	16	.289	.498
Bobby Abreu	OF162	L	27	162	588	118	170	48	4	31	110	106	137	36	.289	.543
Doug Glanville	OF150	R	30	153	634	74	166	24	3	14	55	19	91	28	.262	.375
Pat Burrell	OF146	R	24	155	539	70	139	29	2	27	89	70	162	2	.258	.469
Mike Lieberthal (KJ)	C33	R	29	34	121	21	28	8	0	2	11	12	21	0	.231	.347
Johnny Estrada	C89	B	25	89	298	26	68	15	0	8	37	16	32	0	.228	.359
Brian Hunter	OF41	R	30	83	145	22	40	6	0	2	16	16	25	14	.276	.359
Kevin Jordan	1B10 2B10 3B10	R	31	68	113	9	27	5	0	1	13	14	21	0	.239	.310
Tomas Perez	2B29 3B9 SS8 OF1	B	27	62	135	11	41	7	1	3	19	7	22	1	.304	.437
Todd Pratt	C34 1B1	R	34	35	93	12	19	3	0	2	7	19	25	0	.204	.301
Felipe Crespo	OF4 1B2 2B1	B	28	33	41	1	7	3	1	0	5	4	8	0	.171	.293
Rob Ducey	OF3	L	36	30	27	4	6	1	0	1	4	6	11	0	.222	.370
Gary Bennett	C24	R	29	26	75	8	16	3	1	1	9	9	19	0	.213	.320
Eric Valent	OF8	L	24	22	41	3	4	2	0	0	1	4	11	0	.098	.146
Turner Ward		B	36	17	15	1	4	1	0	0	3	3	5	0	.267	.333
David Newhan	2B1	L	27	7	6	2	2	1	0	1	1	0	2	0	.333	.500
Jason Michaels	OF1	R	25	6	6	0	1	0	0	0	1	0	2	0	.167	.167
Reggie Taylor	OF2	L	24	5	7	1	0	0	0	0	0	0	1	1	.000	.000
Nick Punto	SS1	R	23	4	5	0	2	0	0	0	0	0	2	0	.400	.400
P.J. Forbes	2B1	R	33	3	7	1	2	0	0	0	0	0	2	0	.286	.286
Matt Walbeck		B	31	3	1	0	1	0	0	0	0	0	2	0	1.000	1.000

NAME	T	AGE	W	L	PCT	SV	G	GS	CG	IP	H	BB	SO	SHO	ERA
		30	86	76	.531	47	162	162	8	1445	1417	527	1086	7	4.15
Robert Person	R	31	15	7	.682	0	33	33	3	208	179	80	183	1	4.19
Omar Daal	L	29	13	7	.650	0	32	32	0	186	199	56	107	0	4.46
Randy Wolf (NJ)	L	24	10	11	.476	0	28	25	4	163	150	51	152	2	3.70
Dave Coggin	R	24	6	7	.462	0	17	17	0	95	99	39	62	0	4.17
Amaury Telemaco	R	27	5	5	.500	0	24	14	1	89	93	32	59	0	5.54
Rheal Cormier	L	34	5	4	.556	1	60	0	0	51	49	17	37	0	4.21
Wayne Gomes	R	28	4	3	.571	1	42	0	0	48	51	22	35	0	4.31
Nelson Figueroa	R	27	4	5	.444	0	19	13	0	89	95	37	61	0	3.94
Bruce Chen	L	24	4	5	.444	0	16	16	0	86	90	31	79	0	5.00
Chris Brock	R	31	3	0	1.000	0	33	3	0	33	35	15	26	0	4.13
Vicente Padilla	R	23	3	1	.750	0	23	0	0	34	36	12	29	0	4.24
Brandon Duckworth	R	25	3	2	.600	0	11	11	0	69	57	29	40	0	3.52
Jose Mesa	R	35	3	3	.500	42	71	0	0	69	65	20	59	0	2.34
Ricky Bottalico	R	31	3	4	.429	3	66	0	0	67	58	25	57	0	3.90
Cliff Politte (AJ)	R	27	2	3	.400	0	23	0	0	26	24	8	23	0	2.42
Jose Santiago	R	26	2	4	.333	0	53	0	0	62	66	13	28	0	3.61
Eddie Oropesa	L	29	1	0	1.000	0	30	0	0	19	16	17	15	0	4.74
Ed Vosberg	L	39	0	0	—	0	18	0	0	13	8	3	11	0	2.84
Dennis Cook	L	38	0	0	—	0	19	0	0	10	13	4	9	0	5.59
Doug Nickle	R	26	0	0	—	0	2	0	0	2	1	0	1	0	0.00
Paul Byrd (SJ)	R	30	0	1	.000	0	3	1	0	10	10	4	3	0	8.10
Turk Wendell	R	34	0	0	.000	0	21	0	0	21	12	15	15	0	7.47

NEW YORK — 3rd 82-80 .506 6 — BOBBY VALENTINE

Name	G by Pos	B	AGE	G	AB	R	H	2B	3B	HR	RBI	BB	SO	SB	BA	SA
TOTALS			29	162	5642	642	1361	273	18	147	608	545	1062	66	.249	.387
Todd Zeile	1B149	R	35	151	531	66	141	25	1	10	62	73	102	1	.266	.373
Edgardo Alfonzo	2B122	R	27	124	457	64	111	22	0	17	49	51	62	5	.243	.403
Rey Ordonez	SS148	R	29	149	461	31	114	24	4	3	44	34	43	3	.247	.336
Robin Ventura	3B139	L	33	142	456	70	108	20	0	21	61	88	101	2	.237	.419
Matt Lawton	OF48	R	29	48	183	24	45	11	1	3	13	22	34	10	.246	.366
Jay Payton (LJ)	OF103	R	28	104	361	44	92	16	1	8	34	18	53	4	.255	.371
Benny Agbayani (BH)	OF84	R	29	91	296	28	82	14	2	6	27	36	73	4	.277	.399
Mike Piazza	C131	R	32	141	503	81	151	29	0	36	94	67	87	0	.300	.573
Tsuyoshi Shinjo	OF119	R	29	123	400	46	107	23	1	10	56	25	70	4	.268	.405
Desi Relaford	2B54 SS25 3B20 P1	B	27	120	301	43	91	27	0	8	36	27	65	13	.302	.472
Joe McEwing	OF62 3B25 SS12 2B5 1B3	R	28	116	283	41	80	17	3	8	30	17	57	8	.283	.449
Lenny Harris	3B11 OF8 1B7 2B1	L	36	110	135	12	30	9	1	5	9	8	9	3	.222	.274
Timo Perez	OF73	L	26	85	239	26	59	9	1	5	22	12	25	1	.247	.356
Mark Johnson	1B21 OF19	L	33	71	118	17	30	6	1	6	23	16	31	0	.254	.475
Darryl Hamilton	OF37	L	36	52	126	15	27	7	1	1	5	19	20	3	.214	.310
Todd Pratt	C31	R	34	45	80	6	13	5	0	2	4	15	36	1	.163	.300
Vance Wilson	C27	R	28	32	57	3	17	3	0	0	6	2	16	0	.298	.351
Darren Bragg	OF16	L	31	18	57	4	15	6	0	0	5	4	23	1	.263	.368
Alex Escobar	OF15	R	22	18	50	3	10	1	0	3	8	3	19	1	.200	.400
Jorge Toca	1B3 OF2	R	26	13	17	3	3	0	0	0	1	0	8	0	.176	.176
Jorge Velandia (VJ)	SS8 3B1	R	26	9	9	1	0	0	0	0	0	2	1	0	.000	.000
Jason Phillips	C5	R	24	6	7	1	1	0	0	0	0	1	0	0	.143	.286
Gary Bennett		R	29	2	1	0	1	0	0	0	0	0	0	0	1.000	1.000

NAME	T	AGE	W	L	PCT	SV	G	GS	CG	IP	H	BB	SO	SHO	ERA
		31	82	80	.506	48	162	162	6	1446	1418	438	1191	14	4.07
Kevin Appier	R	33	11	10	.524	0	33	33	1	207	181	64	172	1	3.57
Al Leiter	L	35	11	11	.500	0	29	29	0	187	178	46	142	0	3.31
Steve Trachsel	R	30	11	13	.458	0	28	28	1	174	168	47	144	1	4.46
Rick Reed	R	36	8	6	.571	0	20	20	3	135	119	17	99	1	3.48
Glendon Rusch	L	26	8	12	.400	0	33	33	1	179	216	43	156	0	4.63
John Franco	L	40	6	2	.750	2	58	0	0	53	55	19	50	0	4.05
Armando Benitez	R	28	6	4	.600	43	73	0	0	76	59	40	93	0	3.77
Turk Wendell	R	34	4	3	.571	1	49	0	0	51	42	22	41	0	3.51
Rick White	R	32	4	5	.444	2	55	0	0	70	71	17	51	0	3.88
Bruce Chen	L	24	3	2	.600	0	11	11	0	60	56	28	47	0	4.68
Dicky Gonzalez	R	22	3	2	.600	0	16	7	0	59	72	17	31	0	4.88
Jerrod Riggan	R	27	3	3	.500	0	35	0	0	48	42	24	41	0	3.40
Grant Roberts	R	23	1	0	1.000	0	16	0	0	26	24	8	29	0	3.81
Tom Martin (SJ)	L	31	1	0	1.000	0	14	0	0	17	23	10	12	0	10.06
C.J. Nitkowski	L	28	1	0	1.000	0	6	3	0	6	3	4	4	0	4.20
Dennis Cook	L	38	1	1	.500	0	43	0	0	36	28	10	34	0	4.25
Pete Walker	R	32	0	0	—	0	2	0	0	2	5	3	3	0	2.70
Mark Corey	R	26	0	0	—	0	18	0	0	25	18	9	26	0	16.20
Desi Relaford															
Brian Rose	R	25	0	1	.000	0	9	1	0	10	10	4	4	0	4.15
Brett Hinchliffe	R	26	0	1	.000	0	1	1	0	2	9	1	2	0	36.00
Donne Wall (SJ)	R	33	0	4	.000	0	32	0	0	43	51	17	31	0	4.85
Bobby Jones (SJ) 29															

FLORIDA — 4th 76-86 .469 12 — JOHN BOLES 22-26 .458 TONY PEREZ 54-60 .474

Name	G by Pos	B	AGE	G	AB	R	H	2B	3B	HR	RBI	BB	SO	SB	BA	SA
TOTALS			27	162	5542	742	1461	325	30	166	713	470	1145	89	.264	.423
Derek Lee	1B156	R	25	158	561	83	158	37	4	21	75	50	126	4	.282	.474
Luis Castillo	2B133	R	25	134	537	76	141	16	10	2	45	67	90	33	.263	.341
Alex Gonzalez	SS142 C1	R	24	145	515	57	129	36	1	9	48	30	107	2	.250	.377
Mike Lowell	3B144	R	27	146	551	65	156	37	4	18	100	43	79	1	.283	.448
Eric Owens	OF106	R	30	119	400	51	101	16	1	5	28	23	48	8	.253	.335
Preston Wilson (RJ)	OF121	R	26	123	468	70	128	30	2	23	71	36	107	20	.274	.494
Cliff Floyd	OF142	L	28	149	555	123	176	44	4	31	103	59	101	18	.317	.578
Charles Johnson	C125	R	29	128	451	51	117	32	0	18	75	38	133	0	.259	.450
Kevin Millar	OF86 1B15 3B10	R	29	144	449	62	141	39	5	20	85	39	70	0	.314	.557
Dave Berg	2B34 SS19 3B16	R	30	82	215	26	52	12	1	4	16	14	39	0	.242	.363
John Mabry (TJ)	OF39 1B1 P1	L	30	82	147	14	32	7	0	6	20	13	44	1	.218	.388
Andy Fox (BG)	SS12 3B9 2B2 OF2	L	30	54	81	8	15	0	1	3	8	13	13	0	.185	.321
Mike Redmond	C47	R	30	48	141	19	44	4	0	1	14	13	13	0	.312	.426
Ryan McGuire	OF9 1B4	L	29	48	54	8	10	2	0	1	8	7	15	1	.185	.278
Jeff Abbott (KJ)	OF17	R	28	28	42	5	11	3	0	0	5	3	7	0	.262	.333
Lyle Mouton	OF11	R	32	21	17	1	1	0	0	1	1	1	5	0	.059	.059
Ryan Thompson	OF16	R	33	18	31	6	9	0	0	1	1	1	9	0	.290	.452
Ramon Castro	C4	R	25	7	11	0	2	1	0	0	1	0	5	0	.182	.182
Mike Gulan	3B1	R	30	6	6	1	0	0	0	0	0	0	2	0	.000	.000
Chad Mottola	OF5	R	29	5	6	1	0	0	0	0	0	1	2	0	.000	.000

NAME	T	AGE	W	L	PCT	SV	G	GS	CG	IP	H	BB	SO	SHO	ERA
		28	76	86	.469	32	162	162	5	1438	1397	617	1119	11	4.32
Ryan Dempster	R	24	15	12	.556	0	34	34	2	211	218	112	171	1	4.94
A.J. Burnett (BF)	R	24	11	12	.478	0	27	27	2	173	145	83	128	1	4.05
Brad Penny	R	23	10	10	.500	0	31	31	1	205	183	54	154	1	3.69
Matt Clement	R	26	9	10	.474	0	31	31	0	169	172	85	134	0	5.05
Chuck Smith (SJ-EJ)	R	31	5	5	.500	0	15	15	0	88	89	35	71	0	4.70
Ricky Bones	R	32	4	4	.500	0	61	0	0	64	71	33	41	0	5.06
Antonio Alfonseca	R	29	4	4	.500	28	58	0	0	62	68	15	40	0	3.06
Vladimir Nunez	R	26	4	5	.444	0	52	0	0	92	79	30	64	0	2.74
Braden Looper	R	26	3	3	.500	3	71	0	0	71	63	30	53	0	3.55
Armando Almanza	L	28	2	2	.500	0	52	0	0	41	34	26	45	0	4.83
Jason Grilli	R	24	2	2	.500	0	5	5	0	27	30	11	17	0	6.08
Josh Beckett	R	21	2	2	.500	0	4	4	0	24	14	11	24	0	1.50
Juan Acevedo	R	31	2	3	.400	0	20	0	0	28	30	16	21	0	2.54
Jesus Sanchez	L	26	2	3	.333	0	16	9	0	63	61	31	46	0	4.74
Vic Darensbourg (SJ)	L	30	1	2	.333	1	58	0	0	49	52	10	33	0	4.25
Kevin Olsen	R	24	1	2	.333	0	8	2	0	15	11	2	13	0	1.20
Benito Baez	R	24	0	0	—	0	6	0	0	6	2	6	14	0	13.50
Joe Strong	R	38	0	1	.000	0	8	0	0	13	6	6	7	0	6.75
Blaine Neal	R	23	0	0	—	0	1	0	0	1	0	0	1	0	1.35
Johnny Ruffin	R	29	0	0	—	0	7	0	0	13	8	3	8	0	4.91
John Mabry	R	30	0	0	—	0	1	0	0	0.1	0	0	3	0	135.00
Gary Knotts	R	30	0	0	.000	0	3	0	0	3	6	3	1	0	6.00
Dan Miceli	R	30	0	5	.000	0	29	0	0	25	29	11	31	0	6.93
Alex Fernandez (SJ-VR) 31															

MONTREAL 5th 68-94 .420 20   FELIPE ALOU 21-32 .396 JEFF TORBORG 47-62 .431

Name	G by Pos	B	AGE	G	AB	R	H	2B	3B	HR	RBI	BB	SO	SB	BA	SA
TOTALS			27	162	5379	670	1361	320	28	131	622	478	1071	101	.253	.396
Lee Stevens	1B152	L	33	152	542	77	133	35	1	25	95	74	157	2	.245	.452
Jose Vidro	2B121	B	26	124	486	82	155	34	1	15	59	31	49	4	.319	.486
Orlando Cabrera	SS162	R	26	162	626	64	173	41	6	14	96	43	54	19	.276	.428
Fernando Tatis (KJ)	3B41	R	26	41	145	20	37	9	0	2	11	16	43	0	.255	.359
Vladimir Guerrero	OF158	R	25	159	599	107	184	45	4	34	108	60	88	37	.307	.566
Peter Bergeron	OF101	L	23	102	375	53	79	11	4	3	24	28	87	10	.211	.285
Mark Smith	OF60 1B1	R	31	80	194	28	47	13	1	6	18	23	38	0	.242	.412
Michael Barrett	C131	R	24	132	472	42	118	33	2	6	38	25	54	2	.250	.367
Geoff Blum	3B72 OF35 2B25 1B14 SS4	B	28	148	453	57	107	25	0	9	50	43	94	9	.236	.351
Mike Mordecai	3B42 2B32 SS4 C1 1B1 OF1	R	33	96	254	28	71	17	2	3	32	19	53	2	.280	.398
1 Milton Bradley	OF65	B	23	67	220	19	49	16	3	1	19	19	62	7	.223	.336
Ryan Minor	3B24 OF2 1B1	R	27	55	95	10	15	2	0	2	13	9	31	0	.158	.242
Brad Wilkerson	OF38	L	24	47	117	11	24	7	2	1	5	17	41	2	.205	.325
1 Tim Raines (SJ)	OF20	B	41	47	78	13	24	8	1	0	4	18	6	1	.308	.436
Fernando Seguignol	OF13 1B7	B	26	46	50	0	7	2	0	0	5	2	17	0	.140	.180
Andy Tracy	3B11 1B3	L	27	38	55	4	6	1	0	2	8	6	26	0	.109	.236
Curtis Pride (WJ)	OF23	L	32	36	76	8	19	3	1	1	9	9	22	3	.250	.355
Randy Knorr	C27	R	32	34	91	13	20	2	0	3	10	8	22	0	.220	.341
Terry Jones (LJ)	OF22	B	30	30	77	8	20	5	0	2	2	11	3	6	.260	.325
2 Rob Ducey (NJ)	OF14	L	36	27	46	6	11	2	0	2	8	10	14	0	.239	.413
Brian Schneider	C14	L	24	27	41	4	13	3	0	1	6	6	3	0	.317	.463
Henry Mateo	2B2	B	24	5	9	1	3	1	0	0	1	0	1	0	.333	.444
Tomas de la Rosa		R	23	1	1	0	0	0	0	0	0	0	0	0	.000	.000
Sandy Martinez (EJ)	C1	L	30	1	1	0	0	0	0	0	0	0	0	0	.000	.000

Name	T	AGE	W	L	PCT	SV	G	GS	CG	IP	H	BB	SO	SHO	ERA
		29	68	94	.420	28	162	162	5	1431	1509	525	1103	11	4.68
Javier Vazquez	R	29	16	11	.593	0	32	32	5	224	197	44	208	3	3.42
Graeme Lloyd	L	34	9	5	.643	0	84	0	0	70	74	21	44	0	4.35
Mike Thurman (BG)	R	27	9	11	.450	0	28	26	0	147	172	50	96	0	5.33
Tony Armas	R	23	9	14	.391	0	34	34	0	197	180	91	176	0	4.03
Masato Yoshii	R	36	4	7	.364	0	42	11	0	113	127	26	63	0	4.78
Britt Reames	R	27	4	8	.333	0	41	13	0	95	101	48	86	0	5.59
Scott Stewart	L	25	3	1	.750	3	62	0	0	48	43	13	39	0	3.78
Troy Mattes	R	25	3	3	.500	0	8	8	0	45	51	21	26	0	6.00
1 Ugueth Urbina	R	27	2	1	.667	15	45	0	0	47	42	21	57	0	4.24
Matt Blank	L	25	2	2	.500	0	5	4	0	23	23	13	11	0	5.16
Chris Peters	L	29	2	4	.333	0	13	6	0	31	47	15	14	0	7.55
Scott Strickland	R	25	2	6	.250	9	77	0	0	81	67	41	85	0	3.21
Guillermo Mota (SJ)	R	27	1	3	.250	0	53	0	0	50	51	18	31	0	5.26
2 Tomo Ohka	R	25	1	4	.200	0	10	10	0	55	65	10	31	0	4.77
Carl Pavano (EJ)	R	25	1	6	.143	0	8	8	0	43	59	16	36	0	6.33
Darwin Cubillan	R	28	0	0	—	0	29	0	0	26	31	12	19	0	4.10
Bob Scanlan	R	34	0	0	—	0	18	0	0	26	37	14	5	0	7.86
Mike Johnson	R	25	0	0	—	0	10	0	0	11	13	4	10	0	4.76
Felipe Lira	R	29	0	0	—	0	4	0	0	5	11	2	3	0	12.60
Joey Eischen	L	31	0	1	.000	0	30	0	0	29	16	19	19	0	4.85
Anthony Telford	R	35	0	1	.000	0	8	0	0	7	14	5	5	0	10.29
Hideki Irabu (KJ-EJ)	R	32	0	2	.000	0	3	3	0	17	22	3	18	0	4.86
Bobby Munoz	R	33	0	4	.000	0	15	7	0	42	53	21	21	0	5.14
Scott Downs (EJ) 25															

CENTRAL DIVISION

HOUSTON 1st (tie) 93-69 .574   LARRY DIERKER

Name	G by Pos	B	AGE	G	AB	R	H	2B	3B	HR	RBI	BB	SO	SB	BA	SA
TOTALS			30	162	5528	847	1500	313	29	208	805	581	1119	64	.271	.451
Jeff Bagwell	1B160	R	33	161	600	126	173	43	4	39	130	106	135	11	.288	.568
Craig Biggio	2B154	R	35	155	617	118	180	35	3	20	70	66	100	7	.292	.455
Julio Lugo	SS133 OF8 2B2	R	25	140	513	93	135	20	3	10	37	46	116	12	.263	.372
2 Vinny Castilla	3B121 SS3	R	33	122	445	62	120	28	1	23	82	32	86	1	.270	.492
Moises Alou	OF130	R	34	136	513	79	170	31	1	27	108	57	57	5	.331	.554
Richard Hidalgo	OF144	R	26	146	512	70	141	29	3	19	80	54	107	3	.275	.455
Lance Berkman	OF155	B	25	156	577	110	191	55	5	34	126	92	121	7	.331	.620
Brad Ausmus	C127	R	32	128	422	40	98	23	4	5	34	50	64	4	.232	.341
Jose Vizcaino	SS53 2B18 3B7	B	33	107	256	38	71	8	3	1	14	15	33	3	.277	.344
Daryle Ward	OF42 1B9	L	26	95	213	21	56	15	0	9	39	19	48	0	.263	.460
Orlando Merced	OF31 3B2 1B1	L	34	94	137	19	36	6	1	6	29	14	32	5	.263	.453
Glen Barker	OF60	R	30	70	24	12	2	0	0	1	3	6	4	9	.083	.083
Tony Eusebio	C48	R	34	59	154	16	39	8	0	5	14	17	34	0	.253	.403
Chris Truby	3B35 1B1	R	27	48	136	11	28	6	1	8	23	13	38	1	.206	.441
Charlie Hayes	3B11 1B2	R	36	31	50	4	10	2	0	0	4	7	16	0	.200	.240
Scott Servais (LJ)	C9	R	34	11	16	1	6	0	0	0	3	0	5	0	.375	.375
1 Mendy Lopez	2B3 3B2 1B1	R	27	10	15	3	4	0	0	1	3	2	4	0	.267	.467
Adam Everett	SS6	R	24	9	3	0	0	0	0	0	0	0	1	1	.000	.000
Bill Spiers (XJ)		L	35	4	3	0	1	0	0	0	0	0	0	0	.333	.333
Keith Ginter		R	25	1	1	0	0	0	0	0	0	0	0	0	.000	.000

Name	T	AGE	W	L	PCT	SV	G	GS	CG	IP	H	BB	SO	SHO	ERA
		29	93	69	.574	48	162	162	7	1455	1453	486	1228	6	4.37
Wade Miller	R	29	16	8	.667	0	32	32	1	212	183	76	183	0	3.40
Roy Oswalt	R	23	14	3	.824	0	28	20	3	142	126	24	144	1	2.73
Shane Reynolds	R	33	14	11	.560	0	28	28	3	183	208	36	102	0	4.34
2 Dave Mlicki	R	33	3	7	.300	0	19	14	0	87	85	33	49	0	5.09
Octavio Dotel	R	27	7	5	.583	2	61	4	0	105	79	47	145	0	2.66
Mike Jackson	R	36	5	3	.625	4	67	0	0	69	68	22	46	0	4.70
2 Ron Villone	L	31	5	7	.417	0	31	6	0	68	77	24	65	0	5.56
Mike Williams	R	32	4	0	1.000	0	25	0	0	22	21	14	16	0	4.03
1 Scott Elarton (AJ)	R	25	4	8	.333	0	20	20	0	110	126	49	76	0	7.14
Tim Redding	R	23	3	1	.750	0	13	9	0	56	62	24	55	0	5.50
Nelson Cruz	R	28	3	3	.500	2	66	0	0	82	72	24	75	0	4.15
2 Pedro Astacio (SJ)	R	31	2	1	.667	0	4	4	0	29	30	4	19	0	3.14
1 Jay Powell	R	29	2	2	.500	0	35	0	0	36	41	19	28	0	3.72
Billy Wagner	L	29	2	5	.286	39	64	0	0	63	44	20	79	0	2.73
Kent Bottenfield (SJ)	R	32	2	5	.286	1	13	9	0	52	61	16	39	0	6.40
1 Tony McKnight	R	24	1	0	1.000	0	3	3	0	18	21	3	14	0	4.00
Carlos Hernandez (SJ)	L	21	1	0	1.000	0	3	1	0	18	11	7	17	0	1.02
1 Jose Lima	R	28	1	2	.333	0	14	9	0	53	77	16	41	0	7.30
Wayne Franklin	L	27	0	0	—	0	11	0	0	12	17	9	9	0	6.75
Scott Linebrink	R	24	0	0	—	0	9	0	0	10	6	6	9	0	2.61
Ricky Stone	R	26	0	0	—	0	6	0	0	8	8	2	4	0	2.35
Jim Mann	R	26	0	0	—	0	4	0	0	5	3	4	5	0	3.38
Wilfredo Rodriguez	L	22	0	0	—	0	2	0	0	3	6	1	3	0	15.00
2 Joe Slusarski	R	34	0	1	.000	0	8	0	0	10	16	3	6	0	9.00
Brian Powell	R	27	0	1	.000	0	3	0	0	3	3	3	3	0	18.00
Doug Brocail (EJ) 34															

ST. LOUIS 1st (tie) 93-69 .574 (Wild Card)   TONY LA RUSSA

Name	G by Pos	B	AGE	G	AB	R	H	2B	3B	HR	RBI	BB	SO	SB	BA	SA
TOTALS			30	162	5450	814	1469	274	32	199	768	529	1089	91	.270	.441
Mark McGwire (KJ)	1B90	R	37	97	299	48	56	4	0	29	64	56	118	0	.187	.492
Fernando Vina	2B151	L	32	154	631	95	191	30	8	9	56	32	35	17	.303	.418
Edgar Renteria	SS137 1B1	R	25	141	493	54	128	19	3	10	57	39	73	17	.260	.371
Placido Polanco	3B103 SS42 2B15	R	25	144	564	87	173	26	4	3	38	25	42	12	.307	.383
J.D. Drew (BH)	OF107	L	25	109	375	80	121	18	5	27	73	57	75	13	.323	.613
Jim Edmonds	OF147 1B2	L	31	150	500	95	152	38	4	30	110	93	136	5	.304	.564
Albert Pujols	OF78 3B55 1B42	R	21	161	590	112	194	47	4	37	130	69	93	1	.329	.610
Mike Matheny	C121 1B2	R	30	121	381	40	83	12	0	7	42	28	76	0	.218	.304
Craig Paquette	OF56 3B33 1B23 2B4	R	32	123	340	47	96	17	0	15	64	18	67	3	.282	.465
Kerry Robinson	OF74	L	27	114	186	34	53	6	1	1	15	12	20	11	.285	.344
Bobby Bonilla	1B33 OF10 P1	B	38	93	174	17	37	7	0	5	21	23	53	1	.213	.339
1 Ray Lankford	OF85	L	34	91	264	38	62	18	3	15	39	44	105	4	.235	.496
Eli Marrero	C65 OF15 1B6	R	27	86	203	37	54	11	3	6	23	15	36	6	.266	.438
Larry Sutton	1B11 OF3	L	31	33	42	3	5	1	0	1	3	1	10	0	.119	.214
2 Miguel Cairo	OF6 2B5 3B3 1B1 SS1	R	27	27	33	5	11	5	0	1	7	2	2	0	.333	.576
Stubby Clapp	2B4 OF4	L	28	23	25	0	5	2	0	0	1	3	5	0	.200	.280
Luis Saturria	OF9	R	25	13	5	0	1	0	0	0	1	0	4	0	.200	.200
1 John Mabry	1B2 OF2	L	30	5	7	0	0	0	0	0	0	0	0	0	.000	.000
Bill Ortega	OF5	L	25	5	5	0	1	0	0	0	0	0	2	0	.200	.200
Keith McDonald	C2	R	28	2	2	0	0	0	0	0	0	0	0	0	.000	.000
Carlos Hernandez (XJ) 34																

Name	T	AGE	W	L	PCT	SV	G	GS	CG	IP	H	BB	SO	SHO	ERA
		30	93	69	.574	38	162	162	8	1435	1389	526	1083	11	3.93
Matt Morris	R	26	22	8	.733	0	34	34	2	216	218	54	185	1	3.16
Darryl Kile	R	32	16	11	.593	0	34	34	2	227	228	65	179	1	3.09
Dustin Hermanson	R	28	14	13	.519	0	33	33	0	192	195	73	123	0	4.45
2 Woody Williams	R	34	7	1	.875	0	11	11	3	75	54	19	52	1	2.28
Andy Benes	R	33	7	7	.500	0	27	19	0	107	122	61	78	0	7.38
Bud Smith	L	21	6	3	.667	0	16	14	1	85	79	24	59	1	3.83
Mike Timlin	R	35	4	5	.444	3	67	0	0	73	78	19	47	0	4.09
Dave Veres	R	34	3	2	.600	15	71	0	0	66	57	28	61	0	3.70
Steve Kline	L	28	3	3	.500	9	89	0	0	75	53	29	54	0	1.80
Mike Matthews	L	27	3	4	.429	1	51	10	0	89	74	33	72	0	3.24
Alan Benes	R	29	2	0	1.000	0	14	5	0	34	30	17	36	0	7.36
2 T.J. Mathews	R	31	1	0	1.000	0	10	0	0	15	11	1	10	0	3.07
1 Jason Christiansen (SJ)	L	31	1	1	.500	3	30	0	0	19	15	10	19	0	4.66
Mike James (SJ)	R	33	1	2	.333	0	40	0	0	38	43	17	26	0	5.21
Luther Hackman (EJ)	R	26	1	2	.333	1	35	0	0	36	28	14	24	0	4.29
Rick Ankiel	L	21	1	2	.333	0	6	6	0	24	25	25	27	0	7.13
Gene Stechschulte	R	27	1	5	.167	0	67	0	0	70	71	30	51	0	3.86
Jason Karnuth	R	25	0	0	—	0	4	0	0	4	6	1	1	0	9.00
Chad Hutchinson	R	24	0	0	—	0	4	0	0	4	9	6	2	0	24.75
Jeff Tabaka (EJ)	L	37	0	0	—	0	3	0	0	3	1	1	6	0	7.36
Bobby Bonilla	R	38	0	0	—	0	1	0	0	1	0	1	1	0	18.00
Garrett Stephenson (EJ) 29															

CHICAGO 3rd 88-74 .543 5   DON BAYLOR

Name	G by Pos	B	AGE	G	AB	R	H	2B	3B	HR	RBI	BB	SO	SB	BA	SA
TOTALS			32	162	5406	777	1409	268	32	194	748	577	1077	67	.261	.430
Matt Stairs	1B89 OF22 2B1	L	33	128	340	48	85	21	0	17	61	52	76	2	.250	.462
Eric Young	2B147	R	34	149	603	98	168	43	4	6	42	45	54	31	.279	.393
Ricky Gutierrez	SS144	R	31	147	528	76	153	23	3	10	66	40	56	4	.290	.402
Bill Mueller	3B64 2B1	B	30	70	210	38	62	12	1	6	23	37	19	1	.295	.448
Sammy Sosa	OF160	R	32	160	577	146	189	34	5	64	160	116	153	0	.328	.737
1 Gary Matthews	OF100	B	26	108	258	41	56	9	9	3	30	38	55	5	.217	.364
Rondell White (GJ)	OF90	R	29	95	323	43	99	19	1	17	50	26	56	1	.307	.529
Todd Hundley (XJ)	C70	B	32	79	246	23	46	10	0	12	31	25	89	0	.187	.374
Ron Coomer	3B76 1B36	R	34	111	349	25	91	19	1	8	53	29	70	0	.261	.390
Joe Girardi	C71	R	36	78	229	22	58	10	1	3	25	21	50	0	.253	.345
Augie Ojeda	3B35 SS31 2B10	B	26	78	144	16	29	5	1	1	12	12	20	1	.201	.271
2 Delino DeShields	OF33 2B16 3B5 1B1	L	32	68	163	26	45	9	3	2	16	28	35	12	.276	.405
1 Miguel Cairo	3B40 2B11 SS1	R	27	66	123	20	35	3	1	2	9	16	21	2	.285	.374
2 Michael Tucker	OF57 1B4	L	30	63	205	31	54	9	7	5	31	23	47	4	.263	.449
Corey Patterson	OF54	L	21	59	131	26	29	3	0	4	14	4	33	4	.221	.336
Robert Machado	C47	R	28	52	135	13	30	10	0	2	13	7	29	0	.222	.341
2 Fred McGriff	1B49	L	37	49	170	27	48	7	2	12	41	26	37	0	.282	.559
Julio Zuleta	1B35	R	26	49	106	11	23	3	0	6	24	8	32	0	.217	.415
Roosevelt Brown	OF22	L	25	39	83	13	22	6	0	2	12	7	10	0	.265	.506
Damon Buford	OF34	R	31	35	85	11	15	5	0	3	8	9	25	0	.176	.306
Todd Dunwoody	OF26	L	26	33	61	6	13	4	0	1	3	3	14	0	.213	.328
Chad Meyers	2B4 OF4 3B1	R	25	18	17	1	2	0	0	0	1	1	5	0	.118	.118
Jason Smith	SS1	L	23	2	1	0	0	0	0	0	0	0	0	0	.000	.000

Name	T	AGE	W	L	PCT	SV	G	GS	CG	IP	H	BB	SO	SHO	ERA
		30	88	74	.543	41	162	162	8	1437	1357	550	1344	6	4.03
Jon Lieber	R	31	20	6	.769	0	34	34	5	232	226	41	148	1	3.80
Kerry Wood (SJ)	R	24	12	6	.667	0	28	28	1	174	127	92	217	1	3.36
Jason Bere	R	30	11	11	.500	0	32	32	2	188	171	77	175	0	4.31
Julian Tavarez	R	28	10	9	.526	0	34	28	0	161	172	69	107	0	4.52
Kevin Tapani	R	37	9	14	.391	0	29	29	0	168	186	40	149	0	4.49
Todd Van Poppel	R	29	4	1	.800	0	59	0	0	75	63	38	90	0	2.52
Jeff Fassero	L	38	4	4	.500	12	82	0	0	74	66	23	79	0	3.42
Kyle Farnsworth	R	25	4	6	.400	2	76	0	0	82	65	29	107	0	2.74
Juan Cruz	R	22	3	1	.750	0	8	8	0	45	40	17	39	0	3.22
Courtney Duncan (SJ)	R	26	3	3	.500	0	36	0	0	43	42	25	49	0	5.06
Manny Aybar	R	26	2	1	.667	0	17	1	0	23	17	16	16	0	6.35
Felix Heredia (SJ)	L	26	2	1	.500	0	48	0	0	35	45	16	28	0	6.17
2 David Weathers	R	31	1	1	.500	0	28	0	0	28	28	9	20	0	3.18
Scott Chiasson	R	23	1	1	.500	0	7	0	0	7	5	2	6	0	2.70
Tom Gordon (AJ)	R	33	1	2	.333	27	47	0	0	45	32	16	67	0	3.38
Carlos Zambrano	R	20	1	2	.333	0	6	0	0	8	11	8	4	0	15.26
Ron Mahay	L	30	0	0	—	0	21	0	0	21	14	15	24	0	2.61
Will Ohman	L	23	0	0	—	0	11	0	0	12	14	6	12	0	7.71
Joe Borowski	R	30	0	0	—	0	11	0	0	14	16	3	13	0	32.40
1 Mike Fyhrie (BA)	R	31	0	0	—	0	15	0	0	15	16	7	6	0	4.20

Name	G by Pos	B	AGE	G	AB	R	H	2B	3B	HR	RBI	BB	SO	SB	BA	SA

MILWAUKEE   4th 68-94 .420 25   DAVEY LOPES

Name	G by Pos	B	AGE	G	AB	R	H	2B	3B	HR	RBI	BB	SO	SB	BA	SA
	TOTALS		30	162	5488	740	1378	273	30	209	712	488	1399	66	.251	.426
Richie Sexson	1B158	R	26	158	598	94	162	24	3	45	125	60	178	2	.271	.547
Ron Belliard (NJ)	2B96	R	26	101	364	69	96	30	3	11	36	35	65	5	.264	.453
Jose Hernandez	SS150 OF2	R	31	152	542	67	135	26	2	25	78	39	185	5	.249	.443
Tyler Houston (BF)	3B62 1B3	L	30	75	235	36	68	7	0	12	38	18	62	0	.289	.472
Jeromy Burnitz	OF153	L	32	154	562	104	141	32	4	34	100	80	150	0	.251	.504
Devon White	OF100	B	38	126	390	52	108	25	2	14	47	29	95	18	.277	.459
Geoff Jenkins (RJ)	OF104	L	26	105	397	60	105	21	1	20	63	36	120	4	.264	.474
Henry Blanco	C102	R	29	104	314	33	66	18	3	6	31	34	72	3	.210	.344
Mark Loretta (RJ)	2B52 3B39 SS9 P1	R	29	102	384	40	111	14	2	2	29	28	46	1	.289	.352
Luis Lopez	3B46 SS17 2B15	B	30	92	222	22	60	8	3	4	18	14	44	0	.270	.387
James Mouton	OF53	R	32	75	138	20	34	8	0	2	10	11	40	7	.246	.348
Angel Echevarria	OF23 1B10	R	30	75	133	12	34	11	0	5	13	8	29	0	.256	.451
Raul Casanova (KJ)	C56	B	28	71	192	21	50	10	0	11	33	12	29	0	.260	.484
Lou Collier	OF23 3B16	R	27	50	127	19	32	8	1	2	14	17	30	5	.252	.378
Jeffrey Hammonds (SJ)	OF46	R	30	49	174	20	43	11	1	6	21	14	42	5	.247	.425
Mark Sweeney	OF20 1B2	L	31	48	89	9	23	3	1	3	11	12	23	2	.258	.416
Mike Coolbaugh	3B27 SS3	R	29	39	70	10	14	6	0	2	7	5	16	0	.200	.371
Alex Sanchez	OF19	L	24	30	68	7	14	3	2	0	4	5	13	6	.206	.309
1 Tony Fernandez	3B13	B	39	28	64	6	18	0	1	1	3	7	9	1	.281	.328
Kevin Brown	C16	R	28	17	43	7	9	0	1	4	12	2	18	0	.209	.535
Elvis Pena	2B11	B	26	15	40	5	9	2	0	0	6	6	6	2	.225	.275
Jesse Levis	C11	L	33	12	33	6	8	2	0	0	3	3	7	0	.242	.303
2 Robert Perez	OF1	R	32	2	5	0	0	0	0	0	0	0	0	0	.000	.000

NAME	T	AGE	W	L	PCT	SV	G	GS	CG	IP	H	BB	SO	SHO	ERA
		28	68	94	.420	28	162	162	3	1436	1452	667	1057	8	4.64
Ben Sheets (SJ)	R	22	11	10	.524	0	25	25	1	151	166	48	94	1	4.76
Jamey Wright	R	26	11	12	.478	0	33	33	1	195	201	98	129	1	4.90
Jimmy Haynes (UJ)	R	28	8	17	.320	0	31	29	0	173	182	78	112	0	4.85
Allen Levrault	R	23	6	10	.375	0	32	20	1	131	146	59	80	0	6.06
Chad Fox	R	30	5	2	.714	0	65	0	0	67	44	36	80	0	1.89
Mike DeJean	R	30	4	2	.667	2	75	0	0	84	75	39	68	0	2.77
Ruben Quevedo	R	22	4	5	.444	0	10	10	0	57	56	30	60	0	4.61
1 David Weathers	R	31	3	4	.429	4	52	0	0	58	37	25	46	0	2.03
Paul Rigdon (EJ)	R	25	3	5	.375	0	15	15	0	79	86	46	49	0	5.79
1 Mac Suzuki	R	26	3	5	.375	0	15	9	0	58	52	37	47	0	5.30
Mark Leiter (AJ)	R	38	2	1	.667	0	20	3	0	36	32	8	29	0	3.75
Jeff D'Amico (EJ)	R	25	2	4	.333	0	10	10	0	47	60	16	32	0	6.08
Curtis Leskanic	R	33	2	6	.250	17	70	0	0	69	63	31	64	0	3.63
Rocky Coppinger	R	27	1	0	1.000	0	8	3	0	23	24	15	15	0	6.75
2 Lance Painter (EJ)	L	33	1	0	1.000	0	13	0	0	11	11	7	6	0	4.22
Nick Neugebauer (SJ)	R	20	1	1	.500	0	2	2	0	6	6	6	11	0	7.50
Kyle Peterson	R	25	1	2	.333	0	3	3	0	15	19	4	12	0	5.52
Gus Gandarillas	R	29	0	0	—	0	16	0	0	20	25	10	7	0	5.49
Brandon Kolb	R	27	0	0	—	0	10	0	0	10	16	8	4	0	13.03
Valerio De Los Santos (EJ)	L	28	0	0	—	0	1	0	0	1	1	1	1	0	9.00
Mark Loretta	R	29	0	0	—	0	1	0	0	1	1	1	1	0	0.00
Mike Buddie	R	30	0	1	.000	2	31	0	0	42	34	17	22	0	3.89
Will Cunnane	R	27	0	3	.000	0	31	1	0	52	66	22	37	0	5.40
Ray King	R	27	0	4	.000	1	82	0	0	55	49	25	49	0	3.60
Everett Stull (SJ) 29															

CINCINNATI   5th 66-96 .407 27   BOB BOONE

Name	G by Pos	B	AGE	G	AB	R	H	2B	3B	HR	RBI	BB	SO	SB	BA	SA
	TOTALS		28	162	5583	735	1464	304	22	176	690	468	1172	103	.262	.419
Sean Casey	1B136	L	26	145	533	69	165	40	0	13	89	43	63	3	.310	.458
Pokey Reese	SS78 2B51	R	28	133	428	50	96	20	9	9	40	34	82	25	.224	.343
Barry Larkin (GJ)	SS44	R	37	45	156	29	40	12	0	2	17	27	25	3	.256	.372
Aaron Boone (BH)	3B103	R	28	103	381	54	112	26	2	14	62	29	71	6	.294	.483
1 Alex Ochoa	OF85	R	29	90	349	48	101	20	4	7	35	24	53	12	.289	.430
Ken Griffey Jr. (LJ)	OF90	L	31	111	364	57	104	20	2	22	65	44	72	2	.286	.533
Dmitri Young	OF87 1B38 3B36	B	27	142	540	68	163	28	3	21	69	37	77	8	.302	.481
Jason LaRue	C107 3B3 OF2 1B1	R	27	121	364	39	86	21	2	12	43	27	106	1	.236	.404
Ruben Rivera	OF99	R	27	117	263	37	67	13	1	10	34	21	83	6	.255	.426
Juan Castro	SS46 2B37 3B19 1B11	R	29	96	242	27	54	10	3	3	13	13	50	0	.223	.302
Brady Clark	OF43	R	28	89	129	22	34	3	0	6	18	22	16	4	.264	.426
1 Michael Tucker	OF70	L	30	86	231	35	56	10	1	7	30	23	55	12	.242	.385
2 Todd Walker	2B65 SS1	L	28	66	261	41	77	17	0	5	32	26	42	0	.295	.418
Adam Dunn	OF63	L	21	66	244	54	64	18	1	19	43	38	74	4	.262	.578
Kelly Stinnett (EJ)	C59	R	31	63	187	27	48	11	0	9	25	17	61	2	.257	.460
Wilton Guerrero	SS16 2B11 OF6 3B4	B	26	60	142	16	48	5	1	1	8	3	17	5	.338	.408
D.T. Cromer	1B8	L	30	50	57	7	16	3	0	5	12	3	19	0	.281	.596
1 Donnie Sadler	2B15 SS12 OF8	R	26	39	84	9	17	3	0	1	9	3	20	2	.202	.274
Bill Selby	2B21 3B8 1B2	L	31	36	92	7	21	7	1	2	12	5	13	0	.228	.391
Deion Sanders	OF16	L	33	32	75	6	13	2	0	1	4	5	11	0	.173	.240
3 Robin Jennings	OF15 1B8	L	29	27	77	10	22	5	2	0	14	5	11	0	.286	.519
Corky Miller	C17	R	25	17	49	5	9	2	0	1	7	4	11	0	.184	.408
Brandon Larson	3B9	R	25	14	33	2	4	0	0	0	0	1	6	0	.121	.182
Raul Gonzalez	OF2	R	27	11	14	0	3	0	0	0	0	1	3	0	.214	.214
1 Calvin Pickering			24	4	4	0	1	0	0	0	0	0	0	0	.250	.250

NAME	T	AGE	W	L	PCT	SV	G	GS	CG	IP	H	BB	SO	SHO	ERA
		28	66	96	.407	35	162	162	2	1443	1572	515	943	2	4.77
Elmer Dessens	R	30	10	14	.417	0	34	34	1	205	221	56	128	1	4.48
Lance Davis	L	24	4	2	.667	0	20	20	1	106	124	34	53	0	4.74
Scott Sullivan	R	30	7	1	.875	0	79	0	0	103	94	36	82	0	3.31
Jim Brower	R	28	7	10	.412	1	46	10	0	129	119	60	94	0	3.97
Chris Reitsma	R	23	7	15	.318	0	36	29	0	182	209	49	96	0	5.29
Danny Graves	R	28	5	6	.545	32	66	0	0	80	83	18	49	0	4.15
Osvaldo Fernandez	R	32	5	6	.455	0	20	14	0	79	103	33	56	0	6.92
Jose Acevedo	R	23	5	7	.417	0	18	18	0	96	101	34	68	0	5.44
1 Mark Wohlers	R	31	3	1	.750	0	30	0	0	32	36	7	27	0	3.94
Hector Mercado	L	27	3	2	.600	0	56	0	0	53	55	30	59	0	4.08
Dennys Reyes (EJ)	L	24	2	6	.250	0	36	8	0	53	51	35	52	0	4.92
John Riedling (SJ)	R	25	1	1	.500	1	29	0	0	34	22	14	23	0	2.41
2 Joey Hamilton	R	30	1	2	.333	0	4	4	0	17	23	6	10	0	6.23
Pete Harnisch (EJ)	R	34	1	3	.250	0	7	7	0	35	48	17	17	0	6.37
Jose Rijo	R	36	0	0	—	0	13	0	0	17	19	9	12	0	2.12
Chris Piersoll	R	29	0	0	—	0	11	0	0	11	12	6	7	0	2.38
Justin Atchley (SJ)	L	27	0	0	—	0	15	0	0	10	12	5	8	0	6.10
Frankie Rodriguez	R	28	0	0	—	0	7	0	0	7	14	5	5	0	11.42
Scott Williamson (EJ)	R	25	0	0	—	0	2	0	0	0.2	1	2	0	0	0.00
Scott MacRae	R	26	0	1	.000	0	34	0	0	31	33	8	18	0	4.02
Jared Fernandez	R	29	0	1	.000	0	5	2	0	12	13	6	5	0	4.38
Scott Winchester (UJ)	R	28	0	1	.000	0	12	1	0	24	29	4	9	0	4.50
1 Chris Nichting	R	35	0	1	.000	0	36	0	0	36	46	8	33	0	4.46
1 Rob Bell	R	24	0	0	—	0	9	8	0	44	46	17	33	0	5.48
Brian Reith	R	23	0	7	.000	0	9	8	0	40	56	16	22	0	7.81

PITTSBURGH   6th 62-100 .383 31   LLOYD McCLENDON

Name	G by Pos	B	AGE	G	AB	R	H	2B	3B	HR	RBI	BB	SO	SB	BA	SA
	TOTALS		28	162	5398	657	1333	256	25	161	618	467	1106	93	.247	.393
Kevin Young	1B137	R	32	142	449	53	104	33	0	14	65	42	119	15	.232	.399
Pat Meares	2B85	R	32	87	270	27	57	11	1	4	25	16	70	1	.211	.304
Jack Wilson	SS107	R	23	108	390	44	87	17	1	3	25	16	70	1	.223	.295
Aramis Ramirez	3B157	R	23	158	603	83	181	40	0	34	112	40	100	5	.300	.536
1 John Vander Wal	OF73 1B13	L	35	97	313	39	87	22	3	11	50	42	84	7	.278	.473
2 Gary Matthews	OF44	B	26	46	147	22	36	6	1	5	14	22	45	3	.245	.401
Brian Giles	OF159	L	30	160	576	116	178	37	7	37	95	90	67	13	.309	.590
Jason Kendall	C133 OF27	R	27	157	606	84	161	22	2	10	53	44	48	13	.266	.358
Abraham Nunez	2B48 SS48 3B1 OF1	B	25	115	301	30	79	11	4	1	21	28	53	8	.262	.336
Craig Wilson	1B26 OF14 C10	R	24	88	158	27	49	3	1	13	32	15	53	2	.310	.589
1 Enrique Wilson	2B10 3B2	B	27	46	129	7	24	3	0	1	8	3	22	2	.186	.233
Rob Mackowiak (KJ)	OF46 2B21 3B2 1B1	L	25	83	214	30	57	15	2	4	21	15	52	4	.266	.411
1 Emil Brown	OF54	R	26	61	123	18	25	4	1	3	15	13	42	10	.203	.325
Keith Osik	C39 1B5 3B3 2B2 OF1	R	32	56	120	9	25	4	0	2	13	13	24	1	.208	.292
Adam Hyzdu	OF27 1B4	R	29	51	72	7	15	1	0	5	9	4	18	0	.208	.431
Warren Morris	2B29 3B1	L	27	48	103	6	21	6	0	2	11	3	9	2	.204	.320
Derek Bell (KJ-LJ)	OF46	R	32	46	156	14	27	5	0	5	13	25	38	0	.173	.288
John Wehner	1B11 OF8 3B6 C1 2B1	R	34	43	51	3	10	1	0	1	2	10	12	2	.196	.216
Tike Redman	OF35	L	24	37	125	8	28	4	1	1	4	4	25	3	.224	.296
Chad Hermansen	OF20	R	23	22	55	5	9	1	0	1	4	3	18	0	.164	.291
2 Mendy Lopez	2B9 SS6 3B4 OF1	R	27	22	43	5	10	3	0	1	4	4	16	0	.233	.349
Andy Barkett	OF10 1B4	L	26	17	46	5	14	2	0	1	3	4	7	1	.304	.413
Adrian Brown (SJ)	OF7	B	27	8	31	3	6	0	0	1	2	3	4	0	.194	.290
Alex Hernandez (XJ)	OF4 1B2	L	24	7	11	0	1	0	0	0	0	0	6	0	.091	.091
Humberto Cota	C3	R	22	7	9	0	2	0	0	0	2	0	2	0	.222	.222
Luis Figueroa	2B3	R	27	4	9	0	0	0	0	0	0	0	0	0	.000	.000
2 Armando Rios (KJ)	OF2	L	29	3	3	1	1	0	0	0	0	0	2	0	.333	.333
Mike Benjamin (EJ) 35																

NAME	T	AGE	W	L	PCT	SV	G	GS	CG	IP	H	BB	SO	SHO	ERA
		29	62	100	.383	36	162	162	8	1416	1493	549	908	9	5.05
Todd Ritchie	R	29	11	15	.423	0	33	33	4	207	211	52	124	2	4.47
Jimmy Anderson	L	25	9	17	.346	0	34	34	1	206	232	83	89	0	5.10
Joe Beimel	L	24	7	11	.389	0	42	15	0	115	131	49	58	0	5.23
1 Jason Schmidt (MJ)	R	28	6	6	.500	0	14	14	1	84	81	28	77	0	4.61
Omar Olivares	R	33	6	9	.400	1	45	12	1	110	123	42	69	0	6.55
Bronson Arroyo	R	24	5	7	.417	0	24	13	1	88	99	34	39	0	5.09
Josias Manzanillo	R	33	3	2	.600	2	71	0	0	80	60	26	80	0	3.39
Jose Silva (BL)	R	27	3	3	.500	0	22	3	0	32	35	9	23	0	6.75
David Williams	L	22	3	7	.300	0	22	18	0	114	100	45	57	0	3.71
Mike Lincoln	R	26	2	1	.667	0	31	0	0	63	61	40	79	0	2.68
Scott Sauerbeck	L	29	2	2	.500	2	70	0	0	63	41	40	79	0	5.60
1 Mike Williams	R	32	2	4	.333	22	46	0	0	42	39	21	43	0	3.67
2 Tony McKnight	R	24	2	6	.250	0	12	12	0	69	88	21	36	0	5.19
2 Mike Fetters	R	36	1	1	.500	0	30	0	0	18	16	13	11	0	4.58
1 Terry Mulholland (BG)	L	38	0	0	—	0	22	1	0	36	38	10	17	0	3.72
Billy Taylor	R	39	0	0	—	0	8	0	0	9	7	3	12	0	4.50
Damaso Marte	L	26	0	1	.000	0	23	0	0	36	34	12	39	0	4.71
Rich Loiselle (SJ)	R	29	0	1	.000	0	18	0	0	18	28	17	9	0	11.50
Marc Wilkins	R	30	0	1	.000	0	14	0	0	17	22	8	11	0	6.75
Don Wengert	R	31	0	3	.000	0	14	0	0	16	16	9	9	0	12.38
Ramon Martinez (VR)	R	33	0	2	.000	0	16	0	0	16	16	9	9	0	8.62
2 Ryan Vogelsong	R	23	0	2	.000	0	6	6	0	19	25	6	7	0	12.00
Kris Benson (EJ) 26 Francisco Cordova (EJ) 29																

WEST DIVISION

ARIZONA   1st 92-70 .568   BOB BRENLY

Name	G by Pos	B	AGE	G	AB	R	H	2B	3B	HR	RBI	BB	SO	SB	BA	SA
	TOTALS		32	162	5595	818	1494	284	35	208	776	587	1052	71	.267	.442
Mark Grace	1B135	L	37	145	476	66	142	31	2	15	78	67	36	1	.298	.466
Jay Bell	2B80 3B40	R	35	129	428	59	106	24	1	13	46	65	79	0	.248	.407
Tony Womack	SS118 OF1	L	31	125	481	66	128	19	5	3	30	23	54	28	.266	.345
Matt Williams (PJ)	3B102 SS2	R	35	106	408	58	112	30	0	16	65	22	70	1	.275	.472
Reggie Sanders	OF119	R	33	126	441	84	116	21	3	33	90	46	126	14	.263	.549
Steve Finley	OF131 P1	L	36	140	495	66	136	21	4	14	73	47	67	11	.275	.430
Luis Gonzalez	OF161	L	33	162	609	128	198	36	7	57	142	100	83	1	.325	.688
Damian Miller	C121	R	31	123	380	45	103	19	0	13	47	35	80	0	.271	.424
Craig Counsell	SS58 2B55 3B38 1B2	L	30	141	468	76	126	22	3	4	38	61	76	6	.275	.362
Dave Dellucci	OF58	L	27	115	217	28	60	10	2	10	40	22	52	2	.276	.479
Danny Bautista	OF61	R	29	100	222	28	67	11	2	5	26	14	31	3	.302	.437
Erubiel Durazo	1B38 OF2	L	27	92	175	34	47	11	0	12	38	28	49	0	.269	.537
Junior Spivey	2B66 SS1	R	26	72	163	33	42	6	3	5	21	23	47	3	.258	.423
Greg Colbrunn (KJ)	1B14 3B10	R	31	59	97	12	28	8	0	4	18	9	14	0	.289	.495
Rod Barajas	C50	R	25	51	106	9	17	3	0	3	9	4	26	0	.160	.274
Chad Moeller	C25	R	26	25	56	8	13	0	1	1	5	2	6	12	.232	.321
Midre Cummings	OF4	L	29	20	20	1	6	1	0	0	1	1	1	0	.300	.350
2 Ryan Christenson	OF5	R	27	19	4	3	1	1	0	0	1	0	1	0	.250	.500
2 Mike DiFelice	C12	R	32	12	21	1	1	0	0	1	0	1	10	0	.048	.048
Alex Cintron	SS7	B	23	11	14	2	4	0	0	0	4	0	3	0	.286	.571
Jason Conti	OF1	L	26	5	4	1	1	1	0	0	1	0	2	0	.250	.500
Jack Cust	OF1	L	22	5	4	1	1	1	0	0	2	1	2	0	.250	.500
Lyle Overbay		L	24	3	2	2	1	1	0	0	0	0	0	0	.500	.500
Juan Sosa	3B1	R	25	3	2	0	0	0	0	0	0	0	1	0	.000	.000
Ken Huckaby	C1	R	30	3	1	0	0	0	0	0	0	0	0	0	.000	.000
1 Rob Ryan		L	28	1	1	0	0	0	0	0	0	0	0	0	.000	.000

NAME	T	AGE	W	L	PCT	SV	G	GS	CG	IP	H	BB	SO	SHO	ERA
		31	92	70	.568	34	162	162	12	1460	1352	461	1297	13	3.87
Curt Schilling	R	34	22	6	.786	0	35	35	6	257	237	39	293	1	2.98
Randy Johnson	L	37	21	6	.778	0	35	34	3	250	181	71	372	2	2.49
Miguel Batista	R	30	11	8	.579	0	48	18	0	139	113	60	90	0	3.36
Robert Ellis (LJ-BA)	R	30	5	4	.545	0	19	17	0	92	106	34	41	0	5.77
Byung-Hyun Kim	R	22	5	6	.455	19	78	0	0	98	58	46	113	0	2.94
Bobby Witt (EJ)	R	37	4	1	.800	0	14	7	0	43	46	25	31	0	4.78
Bret Prinz	R	24	4	1	.800	0	9	0	0	41	33	19	27	0	2.63
2 Albie Lopez	R	29	4	7	.364	0	13	13	2	81	74	24	69	2	4.00
Brian Anderson	L	29	4	9	.308	0	29	22	1	133	156	30	55	0	5.20
Erik Sabel	R	26	3	2	.600	0	42	0	0	51	57	12	25	0	4.38
1 Nick Bierbrodt	L	23	2	2	.500	0	5	3	0	23	29	12	17	0	8.22
Troy Brohawn	L	28	2	3	.400	0	49	0	0	55	55	23	30	0	4.93
Greg Swindell	L	36	2	2	.500	0	64	0	0	54	51	8	42	0	4.53
Mike Morgan (FJ)	R	41	1	0	1.000	0	31	1	0	38	44	11	22	0	4.26
Armando Reynoso (SJ)	R	35	4	0	.143	0	9	7	0	47	58	13	15	0	5.98
Russ Springer (SJ)	R	32	0	0	—	0	13	0	0	13	16	6	16	0	7.13
Mike Mohler	L	32	0	1	.000	0	18	14	14	7	0	7.24				
Geraldo Guzman	R	28	0	0	—	0	6	0	0	7	6	4	12	0	2.89
Matt Mantei (FJ)	R	27	0	0	—	0	4	0	0	3	4	5	4	0	2.57
Steve Finley	L	36	0	0	—	0	1	0	0	1	0	1	0	0	3.60
Mike Koplove	R	24	0	0	—	0	9	0	0	14	9	14	0	3.60	
Eric Knott	L	26	0	0	.000	0	1	0	0	4	2	0	2	0	1.93
Todd Stottlemyre (SJ) 36																

SAN FRANCISCO — 2nd 90-72 .556 2 DUSTY BAKER

Name	G by Pos	B	AGE	G	AB	R	H	2B	3B	HR	RBI	BB	SO	SB	BA	SA
TOTALS			32	162	5612	799	1493	304	40	235	775	625	1090	57	.266	.460
J.T. Snow	1B92	L	33	101	285	43	70	12	1	8	34	55	81	0	.246	.379
Jeff Kent	2B140 1B30	R	33	159	607	84	181	49	6	22	106	65	96	7	.298	.507
Rich Aurilia	SS149	R	29	156	636	114	206	37	5	37	97	47	83	1	.324	.572
Pedro Feliz	3B86	R	26	94	220	23	50	9	1	7	22	10	50	2	.227	.373
1 Armando Rios	OF87	L	29	93	316	38	82	17	3	14	49	34	73	3	.259	.465
Calvin Murray	OF104	R	29	106	326	54	80	14	2	6	25	32	57	8	.245	.356
Barry Bonds	OF143	L	36	153	476	129	156	32	2	73	137	177	93	13	.328	.863
Benito Santiago	C130 1B2	R	36	133	477	39	125	25	4	6	45	23	78	5	.262	.361
Marvin Benard	OF109	L	31	129	392	70	104	19	2	15	44	29	66	10	.265	.439
Ramon Martinez	3B70 2B42 SS24	R	28	128	391	48	99	18	3	5	37	38	52	1	.253	.353
Shawon Dunston	OF60 1B1	R	38	88	186	26	52	10	3	9	25	2	32	3	.280	.511
Eric Davis	OF48	R	39	74	156	17	32	7	3	4	22	13	38	1	.205	.365
Edwards Guzman	C26 1B7 3B7 2B3 OF2	L	24	61	115	8	28	6	0	3	7	5	16	0	.243	.374
Russ Davis	3B46	R	31	53	167	16	43	13	1	7	17	17	49	1	.257	.473
2 Andres Galarraga	1B41	R	40	49	156	17	45	12	1	7	35	13	49	0	.288	.513
1 John Vander Wal	OF41 1B1	L	35	49	139	19	35	6	1	3	20	26	38	1	.252	.374
1 Felipe Crespo (FJ)	1B16 2B2 OF1	B	28	40	66	8	13	1	0	4	10	7	26	1	.197	.394
1 Bobby Estalella	C28	R	26	29	93	11	19	5	1	3	10	11	28	0	.204	.376
Damon Minor	1B11	L	27	19	45	3	7	1	0	0	3	8		0	.156	.178
Dante Powell	OF9	R	27	13	6	5	2	0	0	0	0	0	0	0	.333	.333
Cody Ransom	SS6	R	25	9	7	1	0	0	0	0	0	0	5	0	.000	.000
Jay Leach	OF3	L	32	8	10	0	1	0	0	0	0	1	2	3	.100	.100
Yorvit Torrealba	C3	R	22	3	4	0	2	0	1	0	2	0	0		.500	1.000

NAME	T	AGE	W	L	PCT	SV	G	GS	CG	IP	H	BB	SO	SHO	ERA
		30	90	72	.556	47	162	162	3	1463	1437	579	1080	8	4.18
Russ Ortiz	R	27	17	9	.654	0	33	33	0	219	187	91	169	1	3.29
Kirk Rueter	L	30	14	12	.538	0	34	34	0	195	213	66	83	0	4.42
Livan Hernandez	R	26	13	15	.464	0	34	34	2	227	266	85	138	0	5.24
Felix Rodriguez	R	28	9	1	.900	0	80	0	0	80	53	27	91	0	1.68
Shawn Estes (NJ)	L	28	9	8	.529	0	27	27	0	159	151	77	109	0	4.02
2 Jason Schmidt	R	28	7	1	.875	0	11	11	0	66	57	33	65	0	3.39
Mark Gardner (SJ)	R	39	5	5	.500	0	23	15	0	92	93	34	53	0	5.40
Robb Nen	L	31	4	5	.444	45	79	0	0	78	58	22	93	0	3.01
Chad Zerbe	L	29	3	0	1.000	0	27	1	0	39	41	10	22	0	3.92
Aaron Fultz	R	27	3	1	.750	1	66	0	0	71	70	21	67	0	4.56
2 Wayne Gomes	R	28	2	0	1.000	0	13	0	0	15	21	7	17	0	8.40
Tim Worrell	R	33	2	5	.286	0	73	0	0	78	71	33	63	0	3.45
2 Jason Christiansen	L	31	1	0	1.000	0	25	0	0	17	14	5	12	0	1.59
Ryan Jensen	R	25	1	2	.333	0	10	7	0	42	44	25	26	0	4.25
Kurt Ainsworth	R	22	0	0	—	0	2	0	0	2	3	2	3	0	13.50
1 Alan Embree	L	31	0	2	.000	0	22	0	0	20	34	10	25	0	11.25
2 Brian Boehringer	R	32	0	1	.000	1	29	0	0	34	32	17	27	0	4.19
1 Ryan Vogelsong	R	23	0	3	.000	0	3	3	0	29	29	14	17	0	5.65
John Johnstone (XJ) 32															

LOS ANGELES — 3rd 86-76 .531 6 JIM TRACY

Name	G by Pos	B	AGE	G	AB	R	H	2B	3B	HR	RBI	BB	SO	SB	BA	SA
TOTALS			31	162	5493	758	1399	264	27	206	714	519	1062	89	.255	.425
Eric Karros	1B119	R	33	121	438	42	103	22	0	15	63	41	101	3	.235	.388
Mark Grudzielanek	2B133	R	31	133	539	83	146	21	3	13	55	28	83	4	.271	.393
Alex Cora	SS132 2B1	L	25	134	405	38	88	18	3	4	29	31	58	0	.217	.306
Adrian Beltre (IL)	3B124 SS2	R	22	126	475	59	126	22	4	13	60	22	88	13	.265	.411
Shawn Green	OF159 1B1	L	28	161	619	121	184	31	4	49	125	72	107	20	.297	.598
Marquis Grissom	OF123	R	34	135	448	56	99	17	1	21	60	16	107	7	.221	.404
Gary Sheffield	OF141	R	32	143	515	98	160	28	2	36	100	94	67	10	.311	.583
Paul LoDuca	C99 1B33 OF5	R	29	125	460	71	147	28	0	25	90	39	30	2	.320	.543
Tom Goodwin	OF78	L	32	105	286	51	66	8	5	4	22	33	66	22	.231	.336
Jeff Reboulet	SS56 2B22 3B7 OF2	R	37	94	214	35	57	15	2	3	22	33	48	1	.266	.397
Dave Hansen	1B25 3B21 SS1	L	32	92	140	13	33	10	0	2	20	32	29	0	.236	.350
Hiram Bocachica	2B19 OF13 3B8	R	25	75	133	15	31	11	1	2	9	9	33	4	.233	.376
Chad Kreuter	C70	R	36	73	191	21	41	11	1	6	17	41	52	0	.215	.377
Chris Donnels	3B14 1B7 P1	L	35	66	88	8	15	2	0	3	8	12	25	0	.170	.295
Phil Hiatt	3B17 1B6	R	32	30	50	6	12	3	0	2	6	3	19	0	.240	.420
2 McKay Christensen	OF14	L	25	28	49	7	16	2	0	1	7	3	10	3	.327	.429
Angel Pena	C15	R	26	22	54	3	11	1	0	1	2	1	17	0	.204	.278
Bruce Aven	OF9	R	29	21	24	3	8	2	0	1	2	0	5	0	.333	.542
Jeff Branson	2B6 SS2 3B1	L	34	13	21	3	6	0	0	0	3	1	4	0	.286	.286
Tim Bogar (LJ-FJ)	1B3 SS2 3B1	R	34	12	15	4	5	2	0	2	2	1	1	0	.333	.867
Brian Johnson	C2	R	33	4	4	0	1	0	0	0	1	0	1	0	.250	.250

NAME	T	AGE	W	L	PCT	SV	G	GS	CG	IP	H	BB	SO	SHO	ERA
		32	86	76	.531	46	162	162	3	1451	1387	524	1212	5	4.25
Chan Ho Park	R	28	15	11	.577	0	36	35	2	234	183	91	218	1	3.50
Terry Adams	R	28	12	8	.600	0	43	22	0	166	172	54	141	0	4.33
Kevin Brown (EJ)	R	36	10	4	.714	0	20	19	1	116	94	38	104	0	2.65
Matt Herges	R	31	9	8	.529	1	75	0	0	99	97	46	76	0	3.44
Luke Prokopec	R	23	8	7	.533	0	29	22	0	138	146	40	91	0	4.88
Giovanni Carrara	R	33	6	1	.857	0	47	3	0	85	73	24	70	0	3.16
Eric Gagne	R	25	6	7	.462	0	33	24	0	152	144	46	130	0	4.75
Darren Dreifort (EJ)	R	29	4	7	.364	0	16	16	0	95	89	47	91	0	5.13
Jeff Shaw	R	34	3	5	.375	43	77	0	0	75	63	18	58	0	3.62
2 James Baldwin	R	29	3	6	.333	0	12	12	0	79	82	25	53	0	4.20
Andy Ashby (EJ)	R	33	2	0	1.000	0	2	2	0	12	14	1	7	0	3.86
1 Mike Fetters	R	36	2	1	.667	1	34	0	0	30	33	13	26	0	6.07
Alberto Reyes	R	30	2	1	.667	1	19	0	0	26	28	13	23	0	3.86
Jeff Williams	L	29	2	1	.667	0	15	1	0	24	26	17	9	0	6.29
2 Terry Mulholland	L	38	1	1	.500	0	19	3	0	29	40	7	25	0	5.83
1 Dennis Springer	R	36	1	1	.500	0	4	3	0	19	19	2	7	0	3.32
Chris Donnels	R	35	0	0	—	0	1	0	0	0.1	0	0	0	0	0.00
Gregg Olson	R	34	0	0	—	0	28	0	0	25	26	20	24	0	8.03
Jesse Orosco	L	44	0	1	.000	0	35	0	0	16	17	7	21	0	3.94
1 Jose Nunez	R	22	0	1	.000	0	7	0	0	14	5	11	13	0	13.50
2 Mike Trombley	R	34	0	4	.000	0	11	0	0	23	27	10	27	0	6.56
Carlos Perez (SJ) 30															

SAN DIEGO — 4th 79-83 .488 13 BRUCY BOCHY

Name	G by Pos	B	AGE	G	AB	R	H	2B	3B	HR	RBI	BB	SO	SB	BA	SA
TOTALS			28	162	5482	789	1379	273	26	161	753	678	1273	129	.252	.399
Ryan Klesko	1B145	L	30	146	538	105	154	34	6	30	113	88	89	23	.286	.539
Damian Jackson (BG)	2B118 SS3 OF2	R	27	122	440	67	106	21	6	4	38	44	128	23	.241	.343
D'Angelo Jimenez	SS85	B	23	86	308	45	85	19	0	3	33	49	68	2	.276	.367
Phil Nevin	3B145	R	30	149	546	97	167	31	0	41	126	71	147	4	.306	.588
Bubba Trammell	OF132	R	29	142	490	66	128	29	3	25	92	48	78	2	.261	.467
Mark Kotsay	OF111	L	25	119	406	67	118	29	1	10	58	48	58	13	.291	.441
Rickey Henderson	OF104	R	42	123	379	70	86	17	3	8	42	81	84	25	.227	.351
Ben Davis	C135 1B2	B	24	138	448	56	107	20	0	11	57	66	112	4	.239	.357
Mike Darr (DD)	OF93	L	25	105	289	36	80	13	1	2	34	39	72	6	.277	.349
Dave Magadan	3B22 1B9 2B1 SS1	L	38	91	128	12	32	7	0	1	12	12	20	0	.250	.328
Tony Gwynn (LJ)	OF17	L	41	71	102	5	33	9	1	1	17	10	9	1	.324	.461
Alex Arias	3B18 1B17 2B13 SS13	R	27	90	137	19	31	9	0	2	12	17	28	0	.226	.336
Wiki Gonzalez (NJ)	C47	R	27	64	160	16	44	6	0	8	27	11	28	2	.275	.463
Cesar Crespo	2B34 OF18 3B2 SS1	B	22	55	153	27	32	6	0	4	12	25	50	6	.209	.327
Mike Colangelo	OF40	R	24	50	91	10	22	3	3	2	8	6	30	0	.242	.407
Donaldo Mendez (KJ)	SS46	R	23	46	118	11	18	2	1	1	5	5	37	1	.153	.212
Santiago Perez	OF26 SS8 2B2	B	25	43	81	13	16	1	0	0	4	15	29	5	.198	.210
2 Ray Lankford	OF38	L	34	40	125	20	36	10	1	4	19	18	40	6	.288	.480
1 Chris Gomez	SS36 2B8	R	30	40	112	6	21	3	0	0	9	9	14	1	.188	.214
Kevin Witt	1B9	L	25	14	27	5	5	0	0	2	5	0	7	0	.185	.407
2 Emil Brown	OF11	R	26	13	14	3	1	0	0	0	0	1	7	2	.071	.071
Adam Riggs	2B11 3B1	R	28	12	36	2	7	1	0	1	0	4	13	1	.194	.222
Rick Wilkins	C7 1B1	L	34	12	22	3	4	1	0	1	8	2	9	0	.182	.364

NAME	T	AGE	W	L	PCT	SV	G	GS	CG	IP	H	BB	SO	SHO	ERA
		28	79	83	.488	46	162	162	5	1441	1519	476	1088	6	4.52
Kevin Jarvis	R	31	12	11	.522	0	32	32	1	193	189	49	133	1	4.79
Brian Tollberg (BG)	R	28	10	4	.714	0	19	19	0	117	133	25	71	0	4.30
Adam Eaton (EJ)	R	23	8	5	.615	0	17	17	2	117	108	40	109	0	4.32
1 Woody Williams	R	34	8	8	.500	0	23	23	0	145	170	37	102	0	4.97
Bobby Jones	R	31	8	19	.296	0	33	33	1	195	250	38	113	0	5.12
1 Jay Witasick	R	28	5	2	.714	1	31	0	0	39	31	15	53	0	1.86
Brian Lawrence	R	25	5	5	.500	0	17	15	1	115	107	34	84	0	3.45
2 Jose Nunez	L	22	4	1	.800	0	56	0	0	52	48	20	49	0	3.31
Wascar Serrano	R	24	3	3	.500	0	20	5	0	47	60	21	39	0	6.56
Trevor Hoffman	R	33	3	4	.429	43	62	0	0	60	48	21	63	0	3.43
Jeremy Fikac	R	26	2	0	1.000	0	23	0	0	26	15	5	19	0	1.37
Jason Middlebrook	R	26	2	1	.667	0	4	3	0	19	18	10	10	0	5.12
1 Sterling Hitchcock (EJ)	L	30	2	1	.667	0	9	9	0	43	22	13	15	0	3.32
Tom Davey (SJ)	R	27	2	4	.333	0	39	0	0	38	41	17	37	0	4.50
Junior Herndon	R	22	2	6	.250	0	12	8	0	43	55	25	14	0	6.33
David Lee (AJ)	R	28	1	0	1.000	0	41	0	0	49	52	27	42	0	3.70
2 Chuck McElroy	L	33	1	1	.500	0	30	0	0	30	38	18	25	0	5.16
Rodney Myers (SJ)	R	32	1	2	.333	1	37	0	0	47	53	20	29	0	5.32
Kevin Walker (EJ)	L	24	0	0	—	0	16	0	0	12	5	8	17	0	3.00
Dave Maurer	L	26	0	0	—	0	3	0	0	5	8	4	4	0	10.80
Jimmy Osting	L	24	0	0	—	0	2	0	0	3	2	2	1	0	4.00
2 Brett Jodie	R	24	0	1	.000	0	7	2	0	23	19	12	13	0	4.63
David Lundquist	R	28	0	1	.000	0	20	0	0	21	20	7	19	0	5.95
1 Rudy Seanez	R	32	0	2	.000	1	26	0	0	24	15	15	24	0	2.63
Carlton Loewer (SJ)	R	27	0	2	.000	0	2	0	0	4	13	3	1	0	24.92

COLORADO — 5th 73-89 .451 19 BUDDY BELL

Name	G by Pos	B	AGE	G	AB	R	H	2B	3B	HR	RBI	BB	SO	SB	BA	SA
TOTALS			28	162	5690	923	1663	324	61	213	874	511	1027	132	.292	.483
Todd Helton	1B157	L	27	159	587	132	197	54	2	49	146	98	104	7	.336	.685
1 Todd Walker	2B77	L	28	85	290	52	86	18	2	12	43	25	40	1	.297	.497
1 Neifi Perez	SS87	B	28	97	382	65	114	19	8	7	47	16	49	6	.298	.445
Jeff Cirillo	3B137	R	31	138	528	72	165	26	4	17	83	43	63	12	.313	.473
Larry Walker	OF129	L	34	142	497	107	174	35	3	38	123	82	103	14	.350	.662
Juan Pierre	OF154	L	23	156	617	108	202	26	11	2	55	41	29	46	.327	.415
Todd Hollandsworth (LJ)	OF31	L	28	33	117	21	43	15	1	6	19	8	20	5	.368	.667
Ben Petrick (AJ)	C77 1B2	R	24	85	244	41	58	15	3	11	39	31	67	3	.238	.459
Greg Norton	OF25 3B24 1B13	B	28	117	225	30	60	13	2	13	40	19	65	1	.267	.516
Terry Shumpert	2B41 OF24 3B12 SS4	R	34	114	242	37	70	14	5	4	24	15	44	14	.289	.438
Juan Uribe	SS69	R	21	72	273	32	82	15	11	8	53	8	55	3	.300	.524
1 Ron Gant	OF51	R	36	59	171	31	44	8	2	8	22	24	56	3	.257	.468
2 Alex Ochoa	OF52	R	29	58	187	25	47	10	3	1	17	21	23	5	.251	.353
2 Jose Ortiz	2B51	R	24	53	204	38	52	8	1	13	35	14	36	3	.255	.495
Brent Butler	2B23 SS10 3B9	R	23	53	119	17	29	7	1	1	14	7	7	1	.244	.361
Mark Little (FJ)	OF29	R	28	51	85	18	29	6	0	3	13	7	20	1	.341	.518
1 Brent Mayne	C44 1B1	L	33	49	160	15	53	7	0	0	20	16	24	0	.331	.375
2 Jacob Cruz (LJ)	OF24	L	28	44	76	7	16	1	0	1	7	10	27	0	.211	.263
Adam Melhuse	C23 1B1	B	29	40	71	6	13	2	0	1	8	6	18	1	.183	.254
Brooks Kieschnick	OF12 1B1	L	29	35	42	5	10	2	0	2	9	2	12	0	.238	.548
3 Sal Fasano	C25	R	29	25	63	10	16	5	0	2	9	4	19	0	.254	.476
Mario Encarnacion	OF20	R	23	20	62	6	15	4	1	0	5	14	22	2	.242	.452
2 Gary Bennett	C19	R	29	19	55	7	15	4	0	1	6	6	10	0	.273	.382
2 Cliff Brumbaugh	OF11	R	27	17	36	5	10	3	0	0	5	5	13	0	.278	.417
Kimera Bartee	OF10	R	28	15	10	3	3	0	0	0	1	2	4	1	.300	.300
3 Robin Jennings	OF1	L	29	1	1	0	0	0	0	0	0	0	0	0	.000	.000
Kevin Sefcik		R	30	1	1	0	0	0	0	0	0	0	0	0	.000	.000

NAME	T	AGE	W	L	PCT	SV	G	GS	CG	IP	H	BB	SO	SHO	ERA
		29	73	89	.451	26	162	162	3	1430	1522	598	1058	0	5.29
Mike Hampton	L	28	14	13	.519	0	32	32	2	203	236	85	122	1	5.41
Denny Neagle	L	32	9	8	.529	0	30	30	0	171	192	60	139	0	5.38
Jose Jimenez	R	27	9	7	.562	17	56	0	0	55	56	22	37	0	4.09
Shawn Chacon	R	23	6	10	.375	0	27	27	0	160	157	87	134	0	5.06
1 Pedro Astacio	R	31	6	13	.316	0	23	22	4	141	151	50	125	1	5.49
Brian Bohanon (EJ)	R	32	5	8	.385	0	20	19	0	97	127	47	47	0	7.14
Jason Jennings	R	22	4	1	.800	0	7	7	1	39	42	19	26	1	4.58
2 Justin Speier	R	27	4	3	.571	0	42	0	0	56	47	12	47	0	3.70
John Thomson (SJ)	R	27	4	5	.444	0	14	14	1	94	84	25	68	1	4.04
2 Jay Powell	R	29	3	1	.750	7	39	0	0	39	34	12	26	0	2.79
2 Dan Miceli	R	30	2	0	1.000	1	22	0	0	20	18	5	17	0	2.21
1 John Wasdin	R	28	2	1	.667	0	24	3	0	31	32	8	17	0	7.03
Mike Myers	L	32	2	3	.400	0	73	0	0	40	32	24	36	0	3.60
2 Kane Davis (EJ)	R	26	2	4	.333	0	57	0	0	68	66	32	47	0	4.35
Todd Belitz	L	25	1	1	.500	0	40	0	0	20	19	14	17	0	7.71
Horacio Estrada (SJ)	L	25	1	1	.500	0	4	1	0	4	4	1	4	0	14.54
1 Ron Villone	L	31	1	5	.250	0	22	12	0	66	67	53	47	0	6.36
Gabe White	L	29	1	7	.125	0	69	0	0	68	70	26	47	0	6.25
Joe Davenport	R	25	0	1	.000	0	10	2	0	10	18	7	5	0	3.48
Bobby Chouinard	R	29	0	0	—	0	9	0	0	16	20	5	6	0	4.50
Craig Dingman (SJ)	R	27	0	0	—	0	2	0	0	3	2	1	5	0	13.50
2 Chris Nichting	R	35	0	0	—	0	4	1	0	12	14	8	4	0	4.50
Tim Christman	R	26	0	0	—	0	1	0	0	2	1	0	0	0	4.50
Juan Acevedo (GJ)	R	31	0	2	.000	0	39	0	0	32	37	19	26	0	5.63
Scott Elarton (AJ)	R	25	0	2	.000	0	3	3	0	13	20	10	11	0	6.65
2 Mac Suzuki	R	26	0	3	.000	0	3	1	0	4	11	5	0	0	15.63

LINE SCORES

Team	1	2	3	4	5	6	7	8	9	10	11	12	13	R	H	E

DIVISION SERIES: ARIZONA 3 : ST. LOUIS 2

Game 1 October 9 at Arizona

	1	2	3	4	5	6	7	8	9		R	H	E
STL	0	0	0	0	0	0	0	0	0		0	3	1
ARI	0	0	0	0	1	0	0	0	X		1	8	1

Morris, Stechschulte (8), Veres (8)   **Schilling**

Game 2 October 10 at Arizona

	1	2	3	4	5	6	7	8	9		R	H	E
STL	2	0	1	0	0	0	0	0	1		4	7	0
ARI	0	0	0	0	0	0	1	0			1	5	2

Williams, Kline (8)   **Johnson**, Morgan (9), Swindell (9), Batista (9)

Game 3 October 12 at St. Louis

	1	2	3	4	5	6	7	8	9		R	H	E
ARI	0	0	0	0	0	1	4	0	0		5	9	0
STL	0	0	0	2	0	0	1	0	0		3	6	0

Batista, Anderson (7), Morgan (8), Kim (8)   **Kile**, Matthews (7), Timlin (7), Stechschulte (9), Kline (9)

Game 4 October 13 at St. Louis

	1	2	3	4	5	6	7	8	9		R	H	E
ARI	1	0	0	0	0	0	0	0	0		1	6	0
STL	1	1	2	0	0	0	0	0	X		4	7	1

Lopez, Anderson (4), Swindell (7), Morgan (8)   **Smith**, Hermanson (6), Kline (9)

Game 5 October 14 at Arizona

	1	2	3	4	5	6	7	8	9		R	H	E
STL	0	0	0	0	0	0	0	1	0		1	6	1
ARI	0	0	0	1	0	0	0	0	1		2	9	1

Morris, Veres (9), **Kline** (9)   **Schilling**

DIVISION SERIES: ATLANTA 3 : HOUSTON 0

Game 1 October 9 at Houston

	1	2	3	4	5	6	7	8	9		R	H	E
ATL	1	0	0	1	0	0	0	4	1		7	13	1
HOU	0	0	0	0	0	2	1	0	0	1	4	6	1

Maddux, **Seanez** (7), Smoltz (8)   Miller, Jackson (8), Wagner (8), Williams (9)

Game 2 October 10 at Houston

	1	2	3	4	5	6	7	8	9		R	H	E
ATL	0	1	0	0	0	0	0	0	0		1	7	0
HOU	0	0	0	0	0	0	0	0	0		0	7	2

Glavine, Smoltz (9)   **Mlicki**, Dotel (6), Jackson (8), Cruz (8), Wagner (9)

Game 3 October 12 at Atlanta

	1	2	3	4	5	6	7	8	9		R	H	E
HOU	0	0	0	0	0	0	2	0	0		2	6	0
ATL	0	2	1	1	0	0	0	2	X		6	10	0

Reynolds, Cruz (5), Dotel (7), Smoltz (9)   **Burkett**, Reed (7), Remlinger (7), Karsay (8), Villone (8)

COMPOSITE BATTING

DIVISION SERIES

NAME	POS	G	AB	R	H	2B	3B	HR	RBI	BA
ARIZONA										
TOTALS		5	156	10	37	5	0	3	10	.237
Finley	CF	5	19	1	8	1	0	0	2	.421
Gonzalez	LF	5	19	1	5	0	0	1	1	.263
Womack	SS	5	17	1	5	1	0	0	1	.294
Counsell	2B	5	16	2	3	0	0	1	3	.188
Williams	3B	5	16	0	1	1	0	0	0	.063
Miller	C	5	15	1	4	0	0	0	0	.267
Sanders	RF	5	14	2	5	1	0	1	1	.357
Grace	1B	4	14	0	3	1	0	0	0	.214
Colbrunn	PH	4	6	0	2	0	0	0	1	.333
Bautista	CF-RF	2	6	1	0	0	0	0	1	.000
Schilling	P	2	5	0	0	0	0	0	0	.000
Bell	2B	2	4	0	1	0	0	0	0	.250
Johnson	P	1	2	0	0	0	0	0	0	.000
Batista	P	2	1	0	0	0	0	0	0	.000
Durazo	PH	1	1	0	0	0	0	0	0	.000
Lopez	P	1	1	0	0	0	0	0	0	.000
Morgan	P	3	0	0	0	0	0	0	0	—
Anderson	P	2	0	0	0	0	0	0	0	—
Cummings	PR	2	0	1	0	0	0	0	0	—
Dellucci	PH	2	0	0	0	0	0	0	0	—
Swindell	P	2	0	0	0	0	0	0	0	—
Barajas	C	1	0	0	0	0	0	0	0	—
Morgan	P	1	0	0	0	0	0	0	0	—
ST. LOUIS										
TOTALS		5	152	12	29	3	0	6	12	.191
Vina	2B	5	19	2	6	0	0	1	2	.316
Pujols	LF-1B	5	18	1	2	0	0	1	2	.111
Edmonds	CF	5	17	3	4	1	0	2	3	.235
Renteria	SS	5	17	2	4	1	0	1	1	.235
Polanco	3B	5	15	1	4	0	0	0	1	.267
Drew	RF	5	13	1	2	0	0	1	2	.154
McGwire	1B	4	11	0	1	0	0	0	0	.091
Matheny	C	4	10	0	2	0	0	0	0	.200
Marrero	C	3	7	0	0	0	0	0	0	.000
Paquette	RF-LF-3B	2	7	0	1	0	0	0	0	.143
Cairo	LF	3	5	0	1	0	0	0	0	.200
Morris	P	2	4	0	0	0	0	0	0	.000
Williams	P	1	3	1	1	1	0	0	0	.333
Robinson	LF	4	2	0	1	0	0	0	1	.500
Kile	P	1	2	0	0	0	0	0	0	.000
Hermanson	P	1	1	0	0	0	0	0	0	.000
Smith	P	1	1	1	0	0	0	0	0	.000
Kline	P	4	0	0	0	0	0	0	0	—
Stechschulte	P	2	0	0	0	0	0	0	0	—
Veres	P	2	0	0	0	0	0	0	0	—
Matthews	P	1	0	0	0	0	0	0	0	—
Timlin	P	1	0	0	0	0	0	0	0	—
ATLANTA										
TOTALS		3	99	14	30	6	0	6	13	.303
Franco	1B	3	13	3	4	0	0	1	1	.308
A. Jones	CF	3	12	2	6	0	0	1	1	.500
Giles	2B	3	12	2	3	1	0	0	1	.250
Surhoff	LF	3	11	1	3	1	0	0	0	.273
Jordan	RF	3	11	1	2	0	0	1	2	.182
C. Jones	3B	3	9	2	4	0	0	2	5	.444
Sanchez	SS	3	9	1	2	1	0	0	0	.222
Bako	C	3	7	1	2	1	0	1	3	.286
Glavine	P	1	3	0	1	0	0	0	0	.333
Caminiti	PH	2	2	0	0	0	0	0	0	.000
Lockhart	2B	1	2	1	1	1	0	0	0	.500
Burkett	P	1	2	0	0	0	0	0	0	.000
Maddux	P	1	2	0	0	0	0	0	0	.000
Smoltz	P	3	1	0	0	0	0	0	0	.000
DeRosa	SS	1	1	0	1	0	0	0	0	1.000
Torrealba	C	1	1	0	1	1	0	0	0	1.000
Martinez	PH	1	1	0	0	0	0	0	0	.000
Karsay	P	1	0	0	0	0	0	0	0	—
Reed	P	1	0	0	0	0	0	0	0	—
Remlinger	P	1	0	0	0	0	0	0	0	—
Seanez	P	1	0	0	0	0	0	0	0	—
HOUSTON										
TOTALS		3	95	6	19	2	0	3	6	.200
Alou	RF	3	12	0	2	1	0	0	1	.167
Berkman	LF	3	12	0	2	0	0	0	0	.167
Biggio	2B	3	12	0	2	0	0	0	0	.167
Castilla	3B	3	11	1	3	0	0	1	1	.273
Ausmus	C	3	8	1	2	0	0	1	2	.250
Hidalgo	CF	3	8	1	1	0	0	0	0	.125
Lugo	SS	3	8	1	0	0	0	0	0	.000
Bagwell	1B	3	7	0	3	0	0	0	0	.429
Vizcaino	SS	3	6	0	1	0	0	0	0	.167
Eusebio	C	1	3	1	2	1	0	0	0	.667
Ward	PH	2	2	1	1	0	0	1	2	.500
Miller	P	1	2	0	0	0	0	0	0	.000
Merced	PH	1	1	0	0	0	0	0	0	.000
Mlicki	P	1	1	0	0	0	0	0	0	.000
Reynolds	P	1	1	0	0	0	0	0	0	.000
Truby	PH	1	1	0	0	0	0	0	0	.000
Cruz	P	2	0	0	0	0	0	0	0	—
Dotel	P	2	0	0	0	0	0	0	0	—
Jackson	P	2	0	0	0	0	0	0	0	—
Wagner	P	2	0	0	0	0	0	0	0	—
Villone	P	1	0	0	0	0	0	0	0	—
Williams	P	1	0	0	0	0	0	0	0	—

COMPOSITE PITCHING

NAME	G	IP	H	BB	SO	W	L	SV	ERA
ARIZONA									
TOTALS	5	44	29	12	38	3	2	1	2.45
Schilling	2	18	9	2	18	2	0	0	0.50
Johnson	1	8	6	2	9	0	1	0	3.38
Batista	2	6.2	3	1	4	1	0	0	2.70
Anderson	2	4	3	0	3	0	0	0	2.25
Lopez	1	3	4	3	0	0	1	0	12.00
Swindell	2	1.1	2	1	2	0	0	0	0.00
Morgan	3	1.1	2	2	1	0	0	0	6.75
Kim	1	1.1	1	2	1	0	0	1	0.00
ST. LOUIS									
TOTALS	5	43.2	37	18	29	2	3	2	2.06
Morris	2	15	13	5	12	0	1	0	1.20
Williams	1	7	4	1	9	1	0	0	1.29
Kile	1	6	3	5	5	0	0	0	3.00
Smith	1	5	4	4	2	1	0	0	1.80
Kline	4	4.1	4	2	0	0	1	2	2.08
Hermanson	1	3	0	0	0	0	0	0	0.00
Timlin	1	1.1	0	0	2	0	0	0	0.00
Veres	2	1	1	1	0	0	0	0	0.00
Matthews	1	0.2	4	0	0	0	1	0	40.50
Stechschulte	2	0.1	3	0	0	0	0	0	0.00
ATLANTA									
TOTALS	3	27	19	8	16	3	0	2	1.67
Glavine	1	8	6	2	3	1	0	0	0.00
Burkett	1	6.1	6	2	4	1	0	0	2.84
Maddux	1	6	4	3	5	0	0	0	3.00
Smoltz	3	4	3	0	3	0	0	2	2.25
Karsay	1	1	0	1	0	1	0	0	0.00
Seanez	1	1	0	1	0	1	0	0	0.00
Reed	1	0.1	0	0	0	0	0	0	0.00
Remlinger	1	0.1	0	0	1	0	0	0	0.00
HOUSTON									
TOTALS	3	26	30	4	18	0	3	0	4.15
Miller	1	7	7	0	6	0	0	0	2.57
Mlicki	1	5	4	2	0	0	1	0	0.00
Reynolds	1	4	6	1	1	0	1	0	9.00
Dotel	2	3.1	5	0	5	0	0	0	5.40
Cruz	2	2.2	1	1	1	0	0	0	0.00
Wagner	2	1.2	1	0	3	0	0	0	5.40
Williams	1	1	3	0	1	0	0	0	9.00
Jackson	2	0.2	3	0	1	0	1	0	27.00
Villone	1	0.2	0	0	0	0	0	0	0.00

LINE SCORES

Team	1	2	3	4	5	6	7	8	9	R	H	E

CHAMPIONSHIP: ARIZONA 4 : ATLANTA 1

Game 1 October 16 at Arizona

	1	2	3	4	5	6	7	8	9	R	H	E
ATL	0	0	0	0	0	0	0	0	0	0	3	1
ARI	1	0	0	0	1	0	0	0	X	2	8	0

Maddux, Remlinger (8), Karsay (8)   **Johnson**

Game 2 October 17 at Arizona

	1	2	3	4	5	6	7	8	9	R	H	E
ATL	1	0	0	0	0	0	2	5	0	8	8	0
ARI	0	0	0	0	0	1	0	0	0	1	5	1

Glavine, Karsay (8), Smoltz (9)   **Batista**, Morgan (8), Swindell (8), Witt (8), Kim (9)

Game 3 October 19 at Atlanta

	1	2	3	4	5	6	7	8	9	R	H	E
ARI	0	2	0	3	0	0	0	0	0	5	9	1
ATL	0	0	0	1	0	0	0	0	0	1	4	1

Schilling   Burkett, Reed (5), Remlinger (5), Ligtenberg (6), Seanez (7), Millwood (8), Marquis (9)

Game 4 October 20 at Atlanta

	1	2	3	4	5	6	7	8	9	R	H	E
ARI	0	0	4	2	0	0	0	1	4	11	12	0
ATL	1	1	0	0	0	0	1	1	0	4	13	4

Lopez, **Anderson** (4), Morgan (7), Swindell (7), Batista (8), Kim (8)   **Maddux**, Remlinger (4), Ligtenberg (5), Seanez (7), Karsay (8), Marquis (9)

Game 5 October 21 at Atlanta

	1	2	3	4	5	6	7	8	9	R	H	E
ARI	0	0	0	1	2	0	0	0	0	3	6	1
ATL	0	0	0	1	0	0	1	0	0	2	7	1

Johnson, Kim (8)   **Glavine**, Karsay (6), Smoltz (8)

COMPOSITE BATTING

NAME	POS	G	AB	R	H	2B	3B	HR	RBI	BA
ARIZONA										
TOTALS		5	172	22	40	6	0	2	19	.233
Counsell	2B-SS	5	21	5	8	3	0	0	4	.381
Womack	SS	4	20	4	4	1	0	0	0	.200
Gonzalez	LF	5	19	4	4	0	0	1	4	.211
Williams	3B	5	18	1	5	1	0	0	2	.278
Miller	C	5	17	0	3	0	0	0	0	.176
Sanders	RF	5	17	2	2	0	0	0	1	.118
Grace	1B	5	16	1	6	0	0	0	1	.375
Finley	CF	5	14	1	4	1	0	0	4	.286
Johnson	P	2	6	0	0	0	0	0	0	.000
Bautsita	CF	2	4	1	1	0	0	0	1	.250
Schilling	P	1	4	1	1	0	0	0	0	.250
Bell	2B	1	4	0	0	0	0	0	0	.000
Durazo	PH	2	3	1	1	0	0	1	2	.333
Dellucci	PH	2	2	1	1	0	0	0	0	.500
Batista	P	2	2	0	0	0	0	0	0	.000
Kim	P	3	1	0	0	0	0	0	0	.000
Anderson	P	1	1	0	0	0	0	0	0	.000
Colbrunn	PH	1	1	0	0	0	0	0	0	.000
Cummings	PH	1	1	0	0	0	0	0	0	.000
Lopez	P	1	1	0	0	0	0	0	0	.000
Morgan	P	2	0	0	0	0	0	0	0	—
Swindell	P	2	0	0	0	0	0	0	0	—
Witt	P	1	0	0	0	0	0	0	0	—
ATLANTA										
TOTALS		5	169	15	35	6	0	5	14	.207
Franco	1B	5	23	4	6	0	0	1	2	.261
Jordan	RF	5	21	1	4	2	0	0	3	.190
Giles	2B	5	20	4	4	1	0	1	1	.200
C. Jones	3B	5	19	1	5	1	0	0	2	.263
Sanchez	SS	5	17	1	5	1	0	0	1	.294
A. Jones	CF	5	17	4	3	0	0	1	1	.176
Lopez	C	5	14	1	2	0	0	1	2	.143
Surhoff	LF	4	13	1	3	0	0	1	2	.231
Martinez	LF	4	5	0	1	0	0	0	0	.200
Gilkey	LF	3	5	0	1	0	0	0	0	.200
DeRosa	SS	4	4	0	0	0	0	0	0	.000
Bako	C	3	3	0	0	0	0	0	0	.000
Maddux	P	2	3	0	1	0	0	0	0	.333
Glavine	P	2	2	0	0	0	0	0	0	.000
Lockhart	PH	2	1	0	0	0	0	0	0	.000
Burkett	P	1	1	0	0	0	0	0	0	.000
Karsay	P	4	0	0	0	0	0	0	0	—
Marquis	PR-P	4	0	0	0	0	0	0	0	—
Remlinger	P	3	0	0	0	0	0	0	0	—
Ligtenberg	P	2	0	0	0	0	0	0	0	—
Seanez	P	2	0	0	0	0	0	0	0	—
Smoltz	P	2	0	0	0	0	0	0	0	—
Millwood	P	1	0	0	0	0	0	0	0	—
Reed	P	1	0	0	0	0	0	0	0	—

COMPOSITE PITCHING

NAME	G	IP	H	BB	SO	W	L	SV	ERA
ARIZONA									
TOTALS	5	45	35	11	39	4	1	2	3.00
Johnson	2	16	10	3	19	2	0	0	1.13
Schilling	1	9	4	2	12	1	0	0	1.00
Batista	2	7	5	2	3	0	1	0	5.14
Kim	3	5	0	1	3	0	0	2	0.00
Anderson	1	3.1	4	1	0	1	0	0	2.70
Lopez	1	3	5	1	1	0	0	0	6.00
Morgan	2	1	3	1	1	0	0	0	27.00
Swindell	2	0.1	1	0	0	0	0	0	27.00
Witt	1	0.1	3	0	0	0	0	0	27.00
ATLANTA									
TOTALS	5	44	40	18	32	1	4	0	2.66
Glavine	2	12	10	5	5	1	1	0	1.50
Maddux	2	10	14	1	7	0	2	0	5.40
Karsay	4	4.1	3	1	6	0	0	0	2.08
Burkett	1	4.1	7	2	2	0	1	0	8.31
Ligtenberg	2	3	0	1	2	0	0	0	0.00
Smoltz	2	3	0	1	6	0	0	0	0.00
Remlinger	3	2.1	3	2	2	0	0	0	0.00
Marquis	2	2	2	3	0	0	0	0	0.00
Seanez	2	2	1	3	3	0	0	0	0.00
Millwood	1	1	0	1	0	0	0	0	0.00
Reed	1	0	0	0	0	0	0	0	—

MISCELLANEOUS 2001 INDIVIDUAL LEADERS

BATTING

On Base Average

	American League			National League	
1	Ja. Giambi, Oak.	.477	1	Bonds, S.F.	.515
2	Martinez, Sea.	.423	2	L. Walker, Col.	.449
3	Thome, Cle.	.416	3	Sosa, Chi.	.437
4	Alomar, Cle.	.415	4	Helton, Col.	.432
5	Delgado, Tor.	.408	5	Berkman, Hou.	.430
6	Ramirez, Bos.	.405	6	Gonzalez, Ari.	.429
7	Olerud, Sea.	.401	7	C. Jones, Atl.	.427
8	A. Rodriguez, Tex.	.399	8	Sheffield, L.A.	.417
9	B. Williams, N.Y.	.395	9	Edmonds, St.L.	.410
10	Catalanotto, Tex.	.391	10	Giles, Pit.	.404

On Base Average plus Slugging Average

	American League			National League	
1	Ja. Giambi, Oak.	1.137	1	Bonds, S.F.	1.379
2	Thome, Cle.	1.040	2	Sosa, Chi.	1.174
3	A. Rodriguez, Tex.	1.021	3	Gonzalez, Ari.	1.117
4	Ramirez, Bos.	1.014	4	Helton, Col.	1.116
5	Martinez, Sea.	.966	5	L. Walker, Col.	1.111
6	Gonzalez, Cle.	.960	6	Berkman, Hou.	1.051
7	Alomar, Cle.	.956	7	C. Jones, Atl.	1.032
8	Boone, Sea.	.950	8	Pujols, St.L.	1.013
9	Delgado, Tor.	.948	9	Sheffield, L.A.	1.000
10	Palmeiro, Tex.	.944	10	Giles, Pit.	.994

Total Bases

	American League			National League	
1	A. Rodriguez, Tex.	393	1	Sosa, Chi.	425
2	Boone, Sea.	360	2	Gonzalez, Ari.	419
3	Ja. Giambi, Oak.	343	3	Bonds, S.F.	411
4	Palmeiro, Tex.	338	4	Helton, Col.	402
5	Thome, Cle.	328	5	Green, L.A.	370
6	Ramirez, Bos.	322	6	Aurilia, S.F.	364
7	Anderson, Ana.	321	7	Pujols, St.L.	360
8	Beltran, K.C.	317	8	Berkman, Hou.	358
9	Ordonez, Chi.	316	9	C. Jones, Atl.	346
10	Suzuki, Sea.	316	10	Bagwell, Hou.	341

Caught Stealing

	American League			National League	
1	Cedeno, Det.	15	1	Pierre, Col.	17
2	Soriano, N.Y.	14	2	Castillo, Fla.	16
	Suzuki, Sea.	14		Guerrero, Mon.	16
4	Damon, Oak.	12	4	Abreu, Phi.	14
	Higginson, Det.	12		Kendall, Pit.	14
				Young, Chi.	14

Stolen Base Percentage
(Minimum 20 Attempts)

	American League			National League	
1	Beltran, K.C.	97	1	Reese, Cin.	86
2	Jeter, N.Y.	90	2	Floyd, Fla.	86
3	O'Neill, N.Y.	88	3	White, L.A.	86
4	Eckstein, Ana.	88	4	Klesko, S.D.	85
5	Cameron, Sea.	87	5	Rollins, Phi.	85

DeShields, Bal.-Chi.N 92

Extra Base Hits

	American League			National League	
1	Ja. Giambi, Oak.	87	1	Bonds, S.F.	107
	A. Rodriguez, Tex.	87	2	Helton, Col.	105
3	Glaus, Ana.	81	3	Sosa, Chi.	103
	Palmeiro, Tex.	80	4	Gonzalez, Ari.	100
5	Boone, Sea.	77	5	Berkman, Hou.	94

PITCHING

Fewest Hits Per 9 Innings Pitched

	American League			National League	
1	Sabathia, Cle.	7.44	1	Johnson, Ari.	6.52
2	Garcia, Sea.	7.50	2	Wood, Chi.	6.56
3	Buehrle, Chi.	7.64	3	Park, L.A.	7.04
4	Zito, Oak.	7.73	4	Burnett, Fla.	7.53
5	Nomo, Bos.	7.77	5	Ortiz, S.F.	7.70
6	Mays, Min.	7.90	6	Person, Phi.	7.73
7	Mussina, N.Y.	7.95	7	Miller, Hou.	7.77
8	Abbott, Sea.	8.01	8	Appier, N.Y.	7.88
9	Moyer, Sea.	8.03	9	Vazquez, Mon.	7.93
10	Lidle, Oak.	8.14	10	Penny, Fla.	8.03

Fewest Bases on Balls Per 9 Innings Pitched

	American League			National League	
1	Radke, Min.	1.04	1	Maddux, Atl.	1.04
2	Mussina, N.Y.	1.65	2	Schilling, Ari.	1.37
3	Pettitte, N.Y.	1.84	3	Lieber, Chi.	1.59
4	Moyer, Sea.	1.89	4	Jones, S.D.	1.75
5	Loaiza, Tor.	1.89	5	Vazquez, Mon.	1.77
6	Buehrle, Chi.	1.95	6	Reynolds, Hou.	1.77
7	Mulder, Oak.	2.00	7	Tapani, Chi.	2.14
8	Sele, Sea.	2.13	8	Rusch, N.Y.	2.16
9	Lidle, Oak.	2.25	9	Leiter, N.Y.	2.21
10	Mays, Min.	2.47	10	Morris, St.L.	2.25

Reed, N.Y.N-Min. 1.38

Strikeouts Per 9 Innings Pitched

	American League			National League	
1	Nomo, Bos.	10.00	1	Johnson, Ari.	13.41
2	Clemens, N.Y.	8.70	2	Wood, Chi.	11.20
3	Zito, Oak.	8.61	3	Schilling, Ari.	10.27
4	Sabathia, Cle.	8.53	4	Wolf, Phi.	8.39
5	Mussina, N.Y.	8.42	5	Park, L.A.	8.38
6	Colon, Cle.	8.14	6	Bere, Chi.	8.38
7	Wakefield, Bos.	7.90	7	Vazquez, Mon.	8.37
8	Pettitte, N.Y.	7.36	8	Armas, Mon.	8.05
9	Hudson, Oak.	6.93	9	Tapani, Chi.	7.97
10	Carpenter, Tor.	6.55	10	Person, Phi.	7.91

Lowest Batting Average Allowed

	American League			National League	
1	Garcia, Sea.	.225	1	Wood, Chi.	.202
2	Sabathia, Cle.	.228	2	Johnson, Ari.	.203
3	Zito, Oak.	.230	3	Park, L.A.	.216
4	Buehrle, Chi.	.230	4	Burkett, Atl.	.230
5	Nomo, Bos.	.231	5	Burnett, Fla.	.231

Home Runs Allowed

	American League			National League	
1	Helling, Tex.	38	1	Schilling, Ari.	37
2	Milton, Min.	35	2	Jones, S.D.	37
3	Rupe, T.B.	30	3	Jarvis, S.D.	37
4	Carpenter, Tor.	29	4	Williams, S.D.-St.L.	35
5	Johnson, Bal.	28	5	Hermanson, St.L.	34
				Person, Phi.	34
				Elarton, Hou.-Col.	34

Milicki, Det.-Hou. 37
Lima, Hou.-Det. 35

Home Runs Allowed per 9 IP
(Minimum 10 Home Runs Allowed)

	American League			National League	
1	Kohlmeier, Bal.	2.88	1	Reith, Cin.	2.90
2	Heredia, Oak.	2.22	2	Bottenfield, Hou.	2.77
3	Meadows, K.C.	2.15	3	An. Benes, St.L.	2.52
4	Wilson, K.C.	2.14	4	Reynoso, Ari.	2.51
5	Kiesler, N.Y.	2.13	5	White, Col.	2.39

Jodie, N.Y.A-S.D. 3.55

A baseball truism holds that the team with the best starting pitching has the advantage in a short series. Never was that more true than in the 2001 postseason.

The Atlanta Braves set the tone during the first round of National League playoffs. Although Greg Maddux was only ordinary in the opening game against Houston, three Atlanta home runs bailed him out. Tom Glavine and John Burkett completed a Braves sweep by allowing only two runs in the next two contests.

Arizona's Curt Schilling was sensational in the Division Series against St. Louis, winning the opening and final games while holding the Cardinals to a single run. The Cardinals got fine pitching from Matt Morris and rookie left-hander Bud Smith for their two wins, but a good effort by Miguel Batista in Game Three coupled with Schilling's gems gave the Diamondbacks the series.

The pitchers' dominance continued in the NL Championship Series. The D-backs' Randy Johnson fired a three-hitter and struck out eleven in the opener to best Maddux 2-0. Glavine evened things in Game Two, but Schilling posted his third straight complete game win 5-1 in Game Three. Maddux faltered and the Braves committed three third-inning errors in Game Four to put Arizona up three games-to-one. In Game Five Johnson struck out eight to give the pennant to the Diamondbacks.

In the American League playoffs, Cleveland, best known for its hitting, got a fine pitching performance by Bartolo Colon in Game One against Seattle. When the Indians broke through for 17 runs behind rookie C.C. Sabathia in Game Three, they took a two-to-one lead over the heavily favored Mariners. Then Freddy Garcia and Jamie Moyer, who'd won Game Two, shut down the Cleveland bats to advance to the ALCS.

At Yankee Stadium, the winners of the last three World Series teetered on the verge of elimination after losing the first two games to Oakland. Up 1-0 with two out in the seventh inning of Game Three, Derek Jeter made a play for the all-time highlight reels. With Jeremy Giambi on first, Terrence Long doubled into the right field corner. Shane Spencer fielded the ball, but overthrew both of his cutoff men as Giambi rumbled towards the plate. Jeter, ranging from his shortstop position to the foul line between home and first, fielded the ball in full stride, flipped it like a quarterback in a college football option play to catcher Jorge Posada, who tagged Giambi on the back of his calf as he crossed the plate. Neither team would score after that, and New York had cut the deficit to two-games-to-one. That seemed to deflate the A's, and the Yanks took the next two to become the first team to win a five-game series after losing the first two games at home.

The Mariners had tied the record for wins during the season, but the Yankees showed no respect in winning the first two games of the ALCS at Seattle. Although the Bombers' bats were near-duds, Andy Pettitte, Mussina, and the great reliever Mariano Rivera silenced the Seattle attack. In Game Three, Seattle exploded for a 14-3 win, but New York got back on track the next night when rookie Alfonso Soriano's ninth-inning homer gave them a 3-1 win. The Yankees wrapped up their 38th pennant in Game Five, 12-3. New York became the first team since the advent of Division Play in 1969 to win four straight League Championship Series.

Mussina started for the Yankees in the World Series opener at Arizona, but he wasn't nearly as sharp as he'd been earlier in the playoffs. Schilling, on the other hand, was as good as he'd been in the previous two series, allowing only three hits in the 9-1 victory. Arizona's other big-game pitcher, Randy Johnson, started Game Two and fired another three-hitter to put Arizona two games up.

But this was a Series for home fans, as New York rallied to win three straight at Yankee Stadium. Roger Clemens pitched well in Game Three, and the D-backs imploded with errors, wild pitches, and bad baserunning. Arizona led Game Four by two with two outs in the ninth, before Tino Martinez homered off closer Byung-Hyun Kim to tie the game. Derek Jeter won the game with a walk-off homer in the 10th, also off Kim. The next night, New York was again trailing by two with two out in the ninth. This time, Scott Brosius homered off Kim to tie the game, and the Yankees won in the 12th.

Back in Arizona, the Diamondbacks continued the home field victory streak. With Johnson on the mound, the D-backs scored 15 runs in the first four innings and coasted to victory. That set the stage for a deciding Game Seven. Schilling versus Clemens lived up to expectations. Arizona eked out a run in the sixth, but New York plated single runs in the seventh and eighth to go into the final inning with a 2-1 lead and the heretofore faultless Rivera on the mound. But this time Arizona shocked with a last-ditch rally. When Luis Gonzalez capped a two-run comeback with a bloop single over a drawn-in infield to score Jay Bell, the D-backs became the fastest expansion team to win a World Series. Schilling and Johnson, who got the win in Game Seven with 1 1-3 innings of perfect relief, were named co-MVPs of an outstanding post-season.

WORLD SERIES

LINE SCORES

Team	1	2	3	4	5	6	7	8	9	10	11	12	R	H	E

WORLD SERIES: ARIZONA 4 : NEW YORK 3

Game 1 October 27 at Arizona

	1	2	3	4	5	6	7	8	9				R	H	E
NYA	1	0	0	0	0	0	0	0	0				1	3	2
ARI	1	0	4	4	0	0	0	0	X				9	10	0

Mussina, Choate (4), Hitchcock (5), Stanton (8)   **Schilling**, Morgan (8), Swindell (9)

Game 2 October 28 at Arizona

	1	2	3	4	5	6	7	8	9				R	H	E
NYA	0	0	0	0	0	0	0	0	0				0	3	0
ARI	0	1	0	0	0	0	3	0	X				4	5	0

Pettitte, Stanton (8)   **Johnson**

Game 3 October 30 at New York

	1	2	3	4	5	6	7	8	9				R	H	E
ARI	0	0	0	1	0	0	0	0	0				1	3	3
NYA	0	1	0	0	0	1	0	0	X				2	7	1

Anderson, Morgan (6), Swindell (7)   **Clemens**, Rivera (8)

Game 4 October 31 at New York

	1	2	3	4	5	6	7	8	9	10			R	H	E
ARI	0	0	0	1	0	0	0	2	0	0			3	6	0
NYA	0	0	1	0	0	0	0	0	2	1			4	7	0

Schilling, Kim (8)   Hernandez, Stanton (7), Mendoza (8), **Rivera** (10)

Game 5 November 1 at New York

	1	2	3	4	5	6	7	8	9	10	11	12	R	H	E
ARI	0	0	0	0	2	0	0	0	0	0	0	0	2	8	0
NYA	0	0	0	0	0	0	0	0	2	0	0	1	3	9	1

Batista, Swindell (8), Kim (9), Morgan (9), **Lopez** (12)   Mussina, Mendoza (9), Rivera (10), **Hitchcock** (12)

Game 6 November 3 at Arizona

	1	2	3	4	5	6	7	8	9				R	H	E
NYA	0	0	0	0	0	2	0	0	0				2	7	1
ARI	1	3	8	3	0	0	0	0	X				15	22	0

Pettitte, Witasick (3), Choate (4), Stanton (7)   **Johnson**, Witt (8), Brohawn (9)

Game 7 November 4 at Arizona

	1	2	3	4	5	6	7	8	9				R	H	E
NYA	0	0	0	0	0	0	1	1	0				2	6	3
ARI	0	0	0	0	0	1	0	0	2				3	11	0

Clemens, Stanton (7), Rivera (8)   Schilling, Batista (8), **Johnson** (8)

COMPOSITE BATTING

NAME	POS	G	AB	R	H	2B	3B	HR	RBI	BA
ARIZONA										
TOTALS		7	245	37	65	14	0	6	36	.265
Womack	SS	7	32	3	8	3	0	0	3	.250
Gonzalez	LF	7	27	4	7	2	0	1	5	.259
Williams	3B	7	26	3	7	2	0	1	7	.269
Counsell	2B	6	24	1	2	0	0	1	1	.083
Sanders	RF	6	23	6	7	1	0	0	1	.304
Miller	C	6	20	3	4	2	0	0	2	.200
Finley	CF	7	19	5	7	0	0	1	1	.368
Grace	1B	6	19	1	5	1	0	1	3	.263
Bautista	CF-DH-LF	5	12	1	7	2	0	0	7	.583
Durazo	DH	4	11	0	4	1	0	0	1	.364
Johnson	P	3	7	3	2	1	0	0	1	.143
Bell	2B	3	7	3	1	0	0	0	1	.143
Schilling	P	3	6	0	0	0	0	0	0	.000
Barajas	C	2	5	1	2	0	0	0	1	.400
Colbrunn	1B	1	5	2	2	0	0	0	1	.400
Dellucci	LF	2	2	0	1	0	0	0	0	.500
Morgan	P	3	3	0	0	0	0	0	0	—
Swindell	P	3	0	0	0	0	0	0	0	—
Batista	P	2	0	0	0	0	0	0	0	—
Cummings	DH	2	0	2	0	0	0	0	0	—
Kim	P	2	0	0	0	0	0	0	0	—
Anderson	P	1	0	0	0	0	0	0	0	—
Brohawn	P	1	0	0	0	0	0	0	0	—
Lopez	P	1	0	0	0	0	0	0	0	—
Witt	P	1	0	0	0	0	0	0	0	—
NEW YORK										
TOTALS		7	229	14	42	6	0	6	14	.183
Jeter	SS	7	27	3	4	0	0	1	1	.148
Soriano	2B	7	25	1	6	0	0	1	2	.240
Williams	CF	7	24	2	5	1	0	0	1	.208
Brosius	3B	7	24	1	4	2	0	1	3	.167
Posada	C	7	23	2	4	1	0	1	1	.174
Martinez	1B	6	21	1	4	0	0	1	3	.190
Spencer	RF-LF	7	20	1	4	0	0	1	2	.200
Knoblauch	LF-DH	6	18	1	1	0	0	0	0	.056
O'Neill	RF	5	15	1	5	1	0	0	0	.333
Justice	RF-LF-DH	5	12	0	2	0	0	0	1	.167
Pettitte	P	2	3	0	1	0	0	0	0	.333
Sojo	1B	2	3	0	1	0	0	0	1	.333
Wilson	SS	2	3	0	0	0	0	0	0	.000
Velarde	1B	1	3	0	0	0	0	0	0	.000
Bellinger	LF	2	2	0	0	0	0	0	0	.000
Clemens	P	2	2	0	0	0	0	0	0	.000
Greene	C	2	2	1	1	0	0	0	0	.500
Choate	P	2	1	0	0	0	0	0	0	.000
Mussina	P	2	1	0	0	0	0	0	0	.000
Stanton	P	5	0	0	0	0	0	0	0	—
Rivera	P	4	0	0	0	0	0	0	0	—
Hitchcock	P	2	0	0	0	0	0	0	0	—
Mendoza	P	2	0	0	0	0	0	0	0	—
Hernandez	P	1	0	0	0	0	0	0	0	—
Witasick	P	1	0	0	0	0	0	0	0	—

COMPOSITE PITCHING

NAME	G	IP	H	BB	SO	W	L	SV	ERA
ARIZONA									
TOTALS	7	65	42	16	63	4	3	0	1.94
Schilling	3	21.1	12	2	26	1	0	0	1.69
Johnson	3	17.1	9	3	19	3	0	0	1.04
Batista	2	8	5	5	6	0	0	0	0.00
Anderson	1	5.1	5	3	1	0	1	0	3.38
Morgan	3	4.2	1	0	1	0	0	0	0.00
Kim	2	3.1	6	1	6	0	1	0	13.50
Swindell	3	2.2	1	1	2	0	0	0	0.00
Brohawn	1	1	1	0	1	0	0	0	0.00
Witt	1	1	0	1	1	0	0	0	0.00
Lopez	1	0.1	2	0	0	1	0	0	27.00
NEW YORK									
TOTALS	7	63.1	65	17	70	3	4	1	4.26
Clemens	2	13.1	10	4	19	1	0	0	1.35
Mussina	2	11	11	4	14	0	1	0	4.09
Pettitte	2	9	12	2	9	0	2	0	10.00
Hernandez	1	6.1	4	4	5	0	0	0	1.42
Rivera	4	6.1	6	1	7	1	1	1	2.84
Stanton	5	5.2	3	1	3	0	0	0	3.18
Hitchcock	2	4	1	0	6	1	0	0	0.00
Choate	2	3.2	7	1	2	0	0	0	2.45
Mendoza	2	2.2	1	0	1	0	0	0	0.00
Witasick	1	1.1	10	0	4	0	0	0	54.00

2002 - IN WITH THE OLD, IN WITH THE NEW

The familiar faces and muscles of Barry Bonds, Alex Rodriguez, Greg Maddux, Pedro Martinez, Jason Giambi, Curt Schilling, Manny Ramirez, and other stars of yesteryear were much in evidence during 2002, but many of the season's greatest thrills came from players whose names were unfamiliar to many fans.

Bonds 46 home runs didn't come close to matching his record 73 of 2001, but he still set several batting records. He became the oldest man ever to lead the National League in batting with .370 at 38, and his .582 on-base percentage topped a Ted Williams-record that stood for 61 years. He walked so often that had he gone the whole season without a hit, he would still have had a .338 on-base mark. His 198 walks shattered the record he set last year, and his 68 intentional walks also set a new mark. No doubt his "intentional-unintentional" walks would have been another new record if anyone had been able to count them.

Bonds did all this while trying to wedge his team into the playoffs.. The race for a playoff spot waged by the Giants and Dodgers was the only one left in the N.L. West once Arizona took control of the division. Bonds, with the ample aid of Jeff Kemp, gave reliever Robb Nen enough late leads to protect to edge out L.A.

Meanwhile, there was no stopping the Arizona Diamondbacks who were almost immune to protracted slumps because of their double-edged sword of Randy Johnson and Curt Schilling. Early in the season, Schilling was unbeatable to establish Arizona's lead; down the stretch Johnson was even better to assure another division crown. Nevertheless, an injury to slugger Luis Gonzalez had to worry Diamondback fans on the eve of the playoffs.

Atlanta won the N.L. East and reached the playoffs as they had every season since 1991 except the strike year. The Braves' offense was only so-so despite the efforts of Chipper Jones and Gary Sheffield, but they didn't need scads of runs when they could regularly send Greg Maddux, Tom Glavine, and Kevin Millwood to the mound to hold the fort until baseball's newest superstar fireman, John Smoltz could relieve. The other big story in the east was the total collapse of the Mets, proving a big payroll doesn't always translate into victories..

Houston sputtered, paving the way for St. Louis to win in the central. The Cardinals overcame tragedy. First, Jack Buck their longtime Hall of Fame announcer, died; then even more shocking, ace right-hander Darryl Kyle suffered a heart attack and died in his sleep. Cardinals' Albert Pujols and Jim Edmonds gave the team batting punch, as did the mid-season acquisition of Scott Rolen.

The American League continued to be The Land of Slugging Shortstops as Derek Jeter and Nomar Garciaparra had their usual strong seasons and Alex Rodriguez hi for the kind of numbers that put leftfielders in the Hall of Fame. Nevertheless, th Rangers' shortstop found himself challenged for MVP honors by Oakland's Migue Tejada, who drove in eleven fewer runs. Tejeda's supporters noted that his many clutch hits helped his team win a division title; Rodriguez's fans wondered where hi team would have finished without his big bat.

In the A.L. East, the Yankees put together a successful defense of their divisio championship despite a pitching staff that was beginning to show its age. Jeter an Bernie Williams had their usual seasons, and Jason Giambi put up numbers simila to those that won him the 2001 MVP. Second baseman Alfonse Soriano develope into a valuable slugger. The Red Sox had several fine individual performances particularly from Manny Ramirez who led the league in hitting and Cy Youn contenders Derek Lowe and Pedro Martinez, but they never really threatened th Yankees.

After being tagged for demolition by contraction before the season, the Minne sota Twins proved that rumors of their demise were premature at the very least, as the ran away and hid from everyone else in the A.L. Central. It's likely that only Twins fans could have named the team's starting nine, none of whom hit over .300 or batte in 100 runs. Team effort brought Minnesota victory, that and fact that neithe Cleveland nor Chicago were finished rebuilding and Kansas City and Detroit wer ready for autopsy.

The only real race developed in the far west, as Anaheim, Oakland, and Seattl took shots at the prize. An historic 20-game winning streak moved the Athletics i front in September. Tejada was far from the team's only clutch performer, but the rea strength was in the pitching, particularly starters Barry Zito, Marc Mulder, and Ti Hudson. Anaheim finished a strong second and qualified for the Playoffs. The Angel lined up with almost as many unknowns as the Twins. Surprise teams winning wit new, young players promised well for baseball's future.

All of the year's frustrations were not particular to Chicago Cubs' fans. Lat night comedians got a lot of mileage out of the fact that the All-Star Game ended i a tie. More worrying, for much of the season, most fans expected everything to blo up in another strike. Then, just hours before the strike date set by the players, th owners and owned reached an agreement. Neither side got everything it wanted, bu the new pact provided hope that teams like Minnesota may be able to hold on to thei new stars instead of seeing them migrate to the wealthy teams.

2002 AMERICAN LEAGUE — EAST DIVISION

Name	G by Pos	B	AGE	G	AB	R	H	2B	3B	HR	RBI	BB	SO	SB	BA	SA
NEW YORK	1st 103-58 .640				JOE TORRE											
TOTALS			30	161	5601	897	1540	314	12	223	857	640	1171	100	.275	.455
Jason Giambi	1B92 DH63	L	31	155	560	120	176	34	1	41	122	109	112	2	.314	.598
Alfonso Soriano	2B155 DH1	R	26	156	696	128	209	51	2	39	102	23	157	41	.300	.547
Derek Jeter	SS156 DH1	R	28	157	644	124	191	26	0	18	75	73	114	32	.297	.421
Robin Ventura	3B137 1B5	L	34	141	465	68	115	17	0	27	93	90	101	3	.247	.458
2 Raul Mondesi	OF70 DH1	R	31	71	270	39	65	18	0	11	43	28	46	6	.241	.430
Bernie Williams	OF147 DH7	B	33	154	612	102	204	37	2	19	102	83	97	8	.333	.493
Rondell White	OF113 DH11	R	30	126	455	59	109	21	0	14	62	25	86	1	.240	.378
Jorge Posada	C138 DH5	B	30	143	511	79	137	40	1	20	99	81	143	1	.268	.468
Nick Johnson	1B78 DH50 OF2	L	23	129	378	56	92	15	0	15	58	48	98	1	.243	.402
Shane Spencer	OF91 DH1	R	30	94	288	32	71	15	2	6	34	31	62	0	.247	.375
John Vander Wal	OF57 DH16 1B6	L	36	84	219	30	57	17	1	6	20	23	58	1	.260	.429
Enrique Wilson	3B26 SS14 2B7 DH2 OF1	B	28	60	105	17	19	2	2	1	11	8	22	1	.181	.295
Ron Coomer	3B26 DH15 1B11	R	35	55	148	14	39	7	0	3	17	6	23	0	.264	.372
Gerald Williams	OF30 DH1	R	35	33	17	6	0	0	0	0	0	2	4	2	.000	.000
Juan Rivera (KJ)	OF28	R	23	28	83	9	22	5	0	1	6	6	10	1	.265	.361
Chris Widger	C21	R	31	21	64	4	19	5	0	0	5	2	9	0	.297	.375
Albert Castillo	C14	R	32	15	37	3	5	1	1	0	4	1	12	0	.135	.216
Marcus Thames	OF7	R	25	7	13	2	3	1	0	1	2	0	4	0	.231	.538
Alex Arias	3B4 SS1	R	34	6	7	0	0	0	0	0	0	1	2	0	.000	.000
Drew Henson	DH2	R	22	3	1	0	0	0	0	0	0	0	1	0	.000	.000
1 Karim Garcia	OF2	L	26	2	5	1	1	0	0	0	0	0	1	0	.200	.200

NAME	T	AGE	W	L	PCT	SV	G	GS	CG	IP	H	BB	SO	SHO	ERA
		32	103	58	.640	53	161	161	9	1452	1441	403	1135	11	3.8
David Wells	L	39	19	7	.731	0	31	31	2	206	210	45	137	1	3.7
Mike Mussina	R	33	18	10	.643	0	33	33	2	216	208	48	182	2	4.0
Andy Pettitte (EJ)	L	30	13	5	.722	0	22	22	3	135	144	32	97	1	4.3
Roger Clemens	R	39	13	6	.684	0	29	29	0	180	172	63	192	0	4.3
Ramiro Mendoza	R	30	8	4	.667	4	62	0	0	92	102	16	61	0	3.6
Orlando Hernandez (XJ)	R	36	8	5	.615	1	24	22	0	146	131	36	113	0	3.6
Mike Stanton	L	35	7	1	.875	6	79	0	0	78	73	28	44	0	3.0
Steve Karsay	R	30	6	4	.600	12	78	0	0	88	87	30	65	0	3.2
2 Jeff Weaver	R	25	5	3	.625	2	15	8	0	78	81	15	57	0	4.3
1 Ted Lilly	R	26	3	6	.333	0	16	11	2	77	57	24	59	1	3.4
Mike Thurman	R	28	1	0	1.000	0	12	2	0	33	45	12	23	0	5.1
Sterling Hitchcock (XJ)	L	31	1	2	.333	0	20	5	0	39	57	15	31	0	5.4
Mariano Rivera (SJ)	R	32	1	4	.200	28	45	0	0	46	35	11	41	0	2.7
Randy Choate	L	26	0	0	—	0	18	0	0	22	18	15	17	0	6.0
Brandon Knight	R	26	0	0	—	0	7	0	0	9	11	5	7	0	11.4
Jay Tessmer	R	30	0	0	—	0	2	0	0	1	0	2	0	0	6.7
Adrian Hernandez	R	27	0	1	.000	0	2	1	0	6	10	6	9	0	12.0

Name	G by Pos	B	AGE	G	AB	R	H	2B	3B	HR	RBI	BB	SO	SB	BA	SA
BOSTON	2nd 93-69 .574 10.5				GRADY LITTLE											
TOTALS			31	162	5640	859	1560	348	33	177	810	545	944	80	.277	.444
Tony Clark	1B85 DH2	B	30	90	275	25	57	12	1	3	29	21	57	0	.207	.291
Rey Sanchez (LJ)	2B100 SS10	R	34	107	357	46	102	12	3	1	38	17	31	2	.286	.345
Nomar Garciaparra	SS154	R	28	156	635	101	197	56	5	24	120	41	63	5	.310	.528
Shea Hillenbrand	3B156	R	26	156	634	94	186	43	4	18	83	25	95	4	.293	.459
Trot Nixon	OF152	L	28	152	532	81	136	38	4	24	94	65	109	4	.256	.470
Johnny Damon	OF151 DH1	L	28	154	623	118	178	34	11	14	63	65	70	31	.286	.443
Manny Ramirez (RJ)	OF68 DH1	R	30	120	436	84	152	31	0	33	107	73	85	0	.349	.647
Jason Varitek	C127 DH1	B	30	132	467	58	124	27	1	10	61	41	95	4	.266	.392
Brian Daubach	1B60 OF48 DH28	L	30	137	444	62	118	24	2	20	78	51	126	2	.266	.464
Lou Merloni	2B66 3B8 SS5 1B3 OF2	R	31	84	194	28	48	12	2	4	18	20	35	1	.247	.392
Carlos Baerga	DH32 2B17 3B1	B	33	73	182	17	52	11	0	2	19	7	20	6	.286	.379
1 Jose Offerman	1B41 DH24 OF2	B	33	72	237	39	55	10	0	4	27	33	29	8	.232	.325
Rickey Henderson	OF54 DH5	R	43	72	179	40	40	6	1	5	16	38	47	8	.223	.352
Doug Mirabelli	C50 DH4	R	31	57	151	17	34	7	0	7	25	17	33	0	.225	.411
3 Cliff Floyd	OF26 DH19	L	29	47	171	30	54	21	0	7	18	15	28	4	.316	.561
Bry Nelson	2B11 OF11 DH1	R	28	25	34	6	9	3	0	0	2	4	1	1	.265	.353
2 Benny Agbayani	OF13	R	30	13	37	5	11	1	0	0	8	6	5	0	.297	.324
Freddy Sanchez	2B5 SS5 DH1	R	24	12	16	3	3	0	0	0	2	2	3	0	.188	.188
Shane Andrews	3B4 1B2 OF1 DH1	R	30	7	13	2	1	1	0	0	1	1	3	0	.077	.154
Juan Diaz	1B1 DH1	R	28	4	7	2	2	1	0	1	3	0	2	0	.286	.857
Kevin Brown	C2	R	29	2	1	0	0	0	0	0	0	0	0	0	.000	.000

NAME	T	AGE	W	L	PCT	SV	G	GS	CG	IP	H	BB	SO	SHO	ERA
		31	93	69	.574	51	162	162	5	1446	1339	430	1157	17	3.75
Derek Lowe	R	29	21	8	.724	0	32	32	1	220	166	48	127	1	2.58
Pedro Martinez	R	30	20	4	.833	0	30	30	2	199	144	40	239	0	2.26
John Burkett	R	37	13	8	.619	0	29	29	0	173	199	50	124	1	4.53
Tim Wakefield	R	35	11	5	.688	3	45	15	0	163	121	51	134	0	2.81
Frank Castillo	R	33	6	15	.286	1	36	23	0	163	174	58	112	0	5.07
Casey Fossum	L	24	5	4	.556	1	43	12	0	107	113	30	101	0	3.46
Rolando Arrojo (XJ)	R	33	4	3	.571	1	29	8	0	81	83	27	51	0	4.98
Darren Oliver	L	31	4	5	.444	0	14	9	1	58	70	27	32	1	4.66
1 Sun-Woo Kim	R	24	2	0	1.000	0	15	2	0	29	34	7	18	0	7.45
Willie Banks	R	33	2	1	.667	1	29	0	0	39	32	14	26	0	3.23
Dustin Hermanson (GJ-EJ)	R	29	1	1	.500	0	12	1	0	22	35	7	13	0	7.77
2 Alan Embree	L	32	1	2	.333	2	32	0	0	33	24	11	43	0	2.97
Wayne Gomes	R	29	1	2	.333	1	21	0	0	20	12	15	6	0	4.64
2 Bob Howry	R	28	1	3	.250	1	20	0	0	18	22	4	14	0	5.00
Ugueth Urbina	R	28	1	6	.143	40	61	0	0	60	44	20	71	0	3.00
Chris Haney	L	33	1	0	.000	0	1	0	0	1	0	0	0	0	4.20
Rich Garces	R	31	0	1	.000	0	26	0	0	21	21	12	16	0	7.59
Josh Hancock	R	24	0	1	.000	0	3	1	0	6	8	5	3	0	3.68

Paxton Crawford (SJ) 24, Jeff Wallace (EJ) 26

TORONTO — 3rd 78-84 .481 25.5 — BUCK MARTINEZ 20-33 .377 — CARLOS TOSCA 58-51 .532

Name	G by Pos	B	AGE	G	AB	R	H	2B	3B	HR	RBI	BB	SO	SB	BA	SA
TOTALS			27	162	5581	813	1457	305	38	187	771	522	1142	71	.261	.430
Carlos Delgado	1B140 DH3	L	30	143	505	103	140	34	2	33	108	102	126	1	.277	.549
Orlando Hudson	2B52	B	24	54	192	20	53	10	5	2	23	11	27	0	.276	.443
Chris Woodward	SS79 2B6 1B3 3B2 DH2	R	26	90	312	48	86	13	4	13	45	26	72	3	.276	.468
Eric Hinske	3B148	L	24	151	566	99	158	38	2	24	84	77	138	13	.279	.481
Jose Cruz (NJ)	OF119 DH2	B	28	124	466	64	114	26	5	18	70	51	106	7	.245	.438
Vernon Wells	OF159	R	23	159	608	87	167	34	4	23	100	27	85	9	.275	.457
Shannon Stewart	OF99 DH38	R	28	141	577	103	175	38	6	10	45	54	60	14	.303	.442
Ken Huckaby	C88	R	31	88	273	29	67	6	1	3	22	9	44	0	.245	.308
Josh Phelps	DH71 1B2	R	24	74	265	41	82	20	1	15	58	19	82	0	.309	.562
Dave Berg	2B52 3B20 SS13 OF13 1B10 DH8	R	31	109	374	42	101	26	2	4	39	26	57	0	.270	.382
Tom Wilson	C65 DH12 1B11	R	31	96	265	33	68	10	0	8	37	28	79	0	.257	.385
Felipe Lopez	SS79 3B2 DH1	B	22	85	282	35	64	15	3	8	34	23	90	5	.227	.387
1 Raul Mondesi	OF62 DH13	R	31	75	299	51	67	16	1	15	45	31	57	9	.224	.435
Joe Lawrence	2B49 DH1	R	25	55	150	16	27	4	0	2	15	16	38	2	.180	.247
Darrin Fletcher (VR)	C36 DH4	L	35	45	127	8	28	6	0	3	22	4	13	0	.220	.339
Dewayne Wise	OF33 DH3	L	24	42	112	14	20	4	1	3	13	4	15	5	.179	.313
Brian Lesher	1B12 OF5 DH3	R	31	24	38	2	5	1	0	0	2	4	15	0	.132	.158
1 Homer Bush	2B22 DH1	R	29	23	78	9	18	2	0	1	2	2	12	2	.231	.295
Jayson Werth	OF15	R	23	15	46	4	12	2	1	0	6	6	11	1	.261	.348
Pete Swann	DH3 OF1	L	31	13	12	3	1	0	0	0	1	1	6	0	.083	.083
Kevin Cash	C7	R	24	7	14	1	2	0	0	0	0	0	4	0	.143	.143

NAME	T	AGE	W	L	PCT	SV	G	GS	CG	IP	H	BB	SO	SHO	ERA
TOTALS		28	78	84	.481	41	162	162	6	1438	1504	590	991	6	4.80
Roy Halladay	R	25	19	7	.731	0	34	34	2	239	223	62	168	1	2.93
2 Pete Walker	R	33	10	5	.667	1	37	20	0	139	143	51	80	0	4.33
Justin Miller	R	24	9	5	.643	0	25	18	0	102	103	66	68	0	5.54
Esteban Loaiza (SJ)	R	30	9	10	.474	0	25	25	3	151	192	38	87	1	5.71
Steve Parris	R	34	5	5	.500	0	14	14	0	75	96	35	48	0	5.97
Kelvim Escobar	R	26	5	7	.417	38	76	0	0	78	75	44	85	0	5.28
Chris Carpenter (SJ)	R	27	4	5	.444	0	13	13	1	73	89	27	45	0	5.28
Mark Hendrickson	L	28	3	0	1.000	0	16	4	0	37	25	12	21	0	2.45
Brian Bowles	R	25	2	1	.667	0	17	0	0	20	13	14	19	0	4.05
Corey Thurman	R	23	2	3	.400	0	43	1	0	68	65	45	56	0	4.37
1 Scott Eyre	L	30	2	4	.333	0	49	3	0	63	69	29	51	0	4.97
Luke Prokopec (EJ)	R	24	2	9	.182	0	22	12	0	72	90	25	41	0	6.78
Felix Heredia	L	27	1	2	.333	0	53	0	0	52	51	26	31	0	3.61
1 Dan Plesac	L	40	1	2	.333	0	19	0	0	13	11	6	14	0	3.38
1 Pedro Borbon	L	34	1	2	.333	0	16	0	0	13	12	6	11	0	4.97
1 Cliff Politte	R	28	1	3	.250	1	55	0	0	57	38	19	57	0	3.61
Scott Cassidy	R	26	1	4	.200	0	58	0	0	66	52	32	48	0	5.73
Brandon Lyon	R	22	1	4	.200	0	15	10	0	62	78	19	30	0	6.53
2 Jason Kershner	L	25	0	0	—	0	10	0	0	5	5	4	7	0	1.69
Scott Wiggins	L	26	0	0	—	0	3	0	0	3	5	1	3	0	3.37
Bob File	R	25	0	1	.000	0	5	0	0	3	8	2	2	0	18.90
Pasqual Coco	R	24	0	1	.000	0	2	0	0	1	4	3	0	0	14.04
Brian Cooper	R	27	0	1	.000	0	2	2	0	8	14	4	3	0	6.62
Mike Smith	R	24	0	3	.000	0	4	6	0	35	43	16	16	0	6.62
Mike Sirotka (SJ) 31															

BALTIMORE — 4th 67-95 .414 36.5 — MIKE HARGROVE

Name	G by Pos	B	AGE	G	AB	R	H	2B	3B	HR	RBI	BB	SO	SB	BA	SA
TOTALS			30	162	5491	667	1353	311	27	165	636	452	993	110	.246	.403
Jeff Conine (LJ)	1B103 DH7 OF6	R	36	116	451	44	123	26	4	15	63	25	66	8	.273	.448
Jerry Hairston	2B119	R	26	122	426	55	114	25	3	5	32	34	55	21	.268	.376
Mike Bordick (KJ)	SS117	R	36	117	367	37	85	19	3	8	36	35	63	7	.232	.365
Tony Batista	3B154 DH7	R	28	161	615	90	150	36	1	31	87	50	107	5	.244	.457
Jay Gibbons	OF92 1B30 DH12	L	25	136	490	71	121	29	1	28	69	45	66	1	.247	.482
Chris Singleton	DH11	L	29	138	466	67	122	30	6	9	50	21	83	20	.262	.410
Melvin Mora	OF104 SS41 2B12 DH3	R	30	149	557	86	130	30	4	19	64	70	108	16	.233	.404
Geronimo Gil	C125	R	26	125	422	33	98	19	0	12	45	21	88	2	.232	.363
Marty Cordova	OF72 DH56	R	32	131	458	55	116	25	2	18	64	47	111	1	.253	.434
2 Gary Matthews	OF100 DH2	B	27	109	344	54	95	25	3	7	38	43	69	15	.276	.427
Brook Fordyce	C55	R	32	56	130	7	30	8	0	1	8	9	19	1	.231	.315
2 Luis Lopez	SS22 2B12 1B1 DH1	B	31	52	109	10	23	6	0	2	9	3	20	1	.211	.321
Chris Richard (SJ)	DH36 1B29	L	28	50	155	15	36	11	0	4	21	12	30	0	.232	.381
Brian Roberts	2B25 DH8	B	24	38	128	18	29	6	1	1	11	15	21	9	.227	.297
Jose Leon	1B17 3B12 OF2 DH2	R	25	36	89	8	22	2	0	3	10	3	20	1	.247	.371
David Segui (HJ)	DH19 1B7	B	35	26	95	10	25	4	0	2	16	11	22	0	.263	.368
Luis Matos (WJ)	OF14 DH1	R	23	17	31	0	4	1	0	0	1	1	6	1	.129	.161
Ryan McGuire	1B7 DH1	L	30	17	26	0	2	1	0	0	2	2	7	0	.077	.115
Larry Bigbie	OF12	L	24	16	34	1	6	1	0	0	3	2	11	1	.176	.206
Howie Clark	DH8 OF4 1B1	L	28	14	53	3	16	5	0	0	4	3	6	0	.302	.396
Mike Moriarty	SS4 2B2 3B1	R	28	8	16	0	3	1	0	0	1	0	6	0	.188	.250
Luis Garcia	OF2	R	26	6	3	0	1	0	0	0	0	0	1	0	.333	.333
Eddie Rogers	SS4	R	23	5	3	0	0	0	0	0	0	0	1	0	.000	.000
2 Raul Casanova	C2	B	29	2	1	0	0	0	0	0	0	0	0	0	.000	—
Fernando Lunar	C2	R	27	2	0	0	0	0	0	0	0	0	0	0	—	—
Izzy Molina	C1	R	31	1	3	1	1	0	0	0	0	0	0	0	.333	.333
Albert Belle (PJ) 35																

NAME	T	AGE	W	L	PCT	SV	G	GS	CG	IP	H	BB	SO	SHO	ERA
TOTALS		28	67	95	.414	31	162	162	8	1451	1491	549	967	3	4.46
Rodrigo Lopez	R	26	15	9	.625	0	33	28	1	197	172	62	136	0	3.57
Travis Driskill	R	30	8	8	.500	0	29	19	0	133	150	48	78	0	4.95
Sidney Ponson	R	25	7	9	.438	0	28	28	3	176	172	63	120	0	4.09
Rick Bauer	R	25	6	7	.462	1	56	1	0	84	84	36	45	0	3.98
Willis Roberts	R	27	5	4	.556	1	66	0	0	75	79	32	51	0	3.36
Jorge Julio	R	23	5	6	.455	25	67	0	0	68	55	27	55	0	1.99
Scott Erickson	R	34	5	12	.294	0	29	28	3	161	192	68	74	0	5.55
Jason Johnson (RJ-SJ)	R	28	5	14	.263	0	22	22	1	131	141	41	97	0	4.59
Buddy Groom	L	36	3	2	.600	2	70	0	0	62	44	12	48	0	1.60
B.J. Ryan	L	26	2	1	.667	1	67	0	0	58	51	33	56	0	4.68
Chris Brock (SJ)	R	32	2	1	.667	0	22	0	0	44	52	14	21	0	4.70
Calvin Maduro (EJ)	R	27	2	5	.286	0	12	10	0	54	64	22	29	0	5.56
John Stephens	R	22	2	5	.286	0	12	11	0	65	68	22	56	0	6.09
Yorkis Perez	L	34	0	0	—	0	23	0	0	27	21	14	25	0	3.29
Eric DuBose	L	26	0	0	—	0	3	0	0	6	6	4	3	0	13.50
Steve Bechler (DD)	R	22	0	0	—	0	3	0	0	5	6	4	3	0	13.50
Erik Bedard	L	23	0	0	—	0	2	0	0	0.2	0	1	1	0	13.50
Josh Towers	R	25	0	3	.000	0	5	3	0	27	42	5	13	0	7.90
Pat Hentgen (EJ)	R	33	0	4	.000	0	4	4	0	22	31	10	11	0	7.77
Sean Douglass	R	23	0	5	.000	0	15	8	0	53	58	35	44	0	6.08
Luis Rivera (SJ) 24															

TAMPA BAY — 5th 55-106 .342 48 — HAL McRAE

Name	G by Pos	B	AGE	G	AB	R	H	2B	3B	HR	RBI	BB	SO	SB	BA	SA
TOTALS			27	161	5604	673	1418	297	35	133	640	456	1115	102	.253	.390
Steve Cox	1B110 DH35	L	27	148	560	65	142	30	1	16	72	60	116	5	.254	.396
Brent Abernathy	2B116 DH1	R	24	117	463	46	112	18	4	2	40	25	46	10	.242	.311
Chris Gomez	SS130	R	31	130	461	51	122	31	3	10	46	21	58	1	.265	.410
Jared Sandberg	3B97 1B3 DH4	R	24	102	358	55	82	21	1	18	54	39	139	3	.229	.444
Ben Grieve	OF118 DH16	L	26	136	482	62	121	30	0	19	64	69	121	8	.251	.432
Randy Winn	OF146 DH4	B	28	152	607	87	181	39	9	14	75	55	109	27	.298	.461
Greg Vaughn (SJ)	DH38 OF31	R	36	69	251	28	41	10	2	8	29	41	82	3	.163	.315
Toby Hall	C83	R	26	85	330	37	85	19	1	6	42	17	27	0	.258	.376
Aubrey Huff	DH53 1B45 3B14	L	25	113	454	67	142	25	0	23	59	37	55	4	.313	.520
Jason Conti	OF74	L	27	78	222	26	57	15	2	3	21	18	51	4	.257	.383
John Flaherty	C75	R	34	76	281	27	73	20	0	4	33	15	50	2	.260	.374
Carl Crawford	OF63	L	20	63	259	23	67	11	6	2	30	9	41	9	.259	.371
Felix Escalona	SS26 2B25 3B4 DH1	R	23	59	157	17	34	8	2	0	9	3	44	7	.217	.293
Russ Johnson (PP)	3B27 DH5 SS2 2B1	R	29	45	111	15	24	5	0	1	12	16	22	5	.216	.288
Jason Tyner	OF42 DH1	L	25	44	168	17	36	2	1	0	9	7	19	7	.214	.238
Andy Sheets	2B26 SS11 3B4	R	30	41	149	18	37	4	0	4	22	12	41	2	.248	.356
Jason Smith	3B12 SS9 2B1 DH1	L	24	26	65	9	13	1	2	1	6	2	24	3	.200	.323
Damian Rolls	OF21	R	24	21	89	15	26	6	1	2	6	3	16	2	.292	.382
Bobby Smith	3B10 1B6 OF2 DH1	R	28	18	63	4	11	2	0	1	6	3	25	0	.175	.254
2 David McCarty	OF11	R	32	12	34	2	6	0	0	1	2	4	9	0	.176	.265
Paul Hoover	C4	R	26	5	17	1	3	0	0	0	0	2	4	0	.176	.176

NAME	T	AGE	W	L	PCT	SV	G	GS	CG	IP	H	BB	SO	SHO	ERA
TOTALS		27	55	106	.342	25	161	161	12	1440	1567	620	925	3	5.29
Victor Zambrano	R	26	8	8	.500	1	42	11	0	114	120	68	73	0	5.53
Joe Kennedy	L	23	8	11	.421	0	30	30	5	197	204	55	109	1	4.53
Esteban Yan	R	27	7	8	.467	19	55	0	0	69	70	29	53	0	4.30
Paul Wilson	R	29	6	12	.333	0	30	30	1	194	219	67	111	0	4.83
Travis Harper	R	26	5	9	.357	1	37	7	0	86	101	27	60	0	5.46
Ryan Rupe (KJ)	R	27	5	10	.333	0	15	15	2	90	83	25	67	0	5.60
Tanyon Sturtze	R	31	4	18	.182	0	33	33	4	224	271	89	137	0	5.18
Lance Carter	R	27	2	0	1.000	2	8	0	0	20	15	5	14	0	1.33
1 Doug Creek	L	33	2	1	.667	0	29	0	0	37	39	21	37	0	6.27
Wilson Alvarez (VJ)	L	32	2	3	.400	1	23	10	0	75	80	36	56	0	5.28
Jesus Colome	R	24	2	7	.222	0	42	0	0	41	56	33	33	0	8.27
Jorge Sosa (SJ)	R	25	2	7	.222	0	31	14	0	99	88	54	48	0	5.53
Lee Gardner	R	27	1	1	.500	0	12	0	0	13	12	8	8	0	4.05
Travis Phelps	R	24	1	2	.333	0	26	0	0	38	30	27	36	0	4.78
Brandon Backe	R	24	0	0	—	0	5	0	0	7	9	1	5	0	5.40
1 Jason Jimenez	L	26	0	0	—	0	9	0	0	6	9	3	6	0	5.40
Tom Martin (JJ)	L	32	0	0	—	0	6	0	0	2	5	1	1	0	16.20
Jason Standridge	R	23	0	1	.000	0	7	1	0	7	7	4	1	0	9.00
Dewon Brazelton	R	23	0	1	.000	0	2	2	0	13	12	6	5	0	4.85
Steve Kent	L	23	0	1	.000	0	34	0	0	57	67	38	41	0	5.65
Delvin James	R	24	0	3	.000	0	8	6	0	34	40	15	17	0	6.55
Luis De Los Santos	R	24	0	3	.000	0	8	6	0	14	24	4	7	0	11.57

CENTRAL DIVISION

MINNESOTA — 1st 94-67 .584 — RON GARDENHIRE

Name	G by Pos	B	AGE	G	AB	R	H	2B	3B	HR	RBI	BB	SO	SB	BA	SA
TOTALS			26	161	5582	768	1518	348	36	167	731	472	1089	79	.272	.437
Doug Mientkiewicz	1B143	L	28	143	467	60	122	29	1	10	64	74	69	1	.261	.392
Luis Rivas (BW)	2B93	R	22	93	316	46	81	23	4	4	35	19	51	9	.256	.392
Cristian Guzman	SS147 DH1	B	24	148	623	80	170	31	6	9	59	17	79	12	.273	.385
Corey Koskie	3B138 DH1	L	29	140	490	71	131	37	3	15	69	72	127	10	.267	.447
Dustan Mohr	OF113 DH3	R	26	120	383	55	103	23	2	12	45	31	86	6	.269	.433
Torii Hunter	OF146 DH1	R	26	148	561	89	162	37	4	29	94	35	118	23	.289	.524
Jacque Jones	OF143 DH1	L	27	149	577	96	173	37	2	27	85	37	129	6	.300	.511
A.J. Pierzynski	C124	L	25	130	440	54	132	31	6	6	49	13	61	1	.300	.439
David Ortiz	DH95 1B15	L	26	125	412	52	112	32	1	20	75	43	87	1	.272	.500
Bobby Kielty	OF82 DH11 1B5	B	25	112	289	49	84	14	3	12	46	52	66	4	.291	.484
Denny Hocking	2B56 SS25 3B16 1B6 OF5	B	32	102	260	28	65	13	0	2	25	24	60	5	.250	.323
Matt LeCroy	DH41 1B8 C6	R	26	63	181	19	47	11	1	7	27	13	38	0	.260	.448
Tom Prince	C50	R	37	51	125	14	28	7	1	4	16	14	26	1	.224	.392
1 Brian Buchanan	OF24 DH17	R	28	44	135	19	34	5	1	5	16	6	33	2	.252	.415
Michael Cuddyer	OF25 3B10 1B6 DH3	R	23	41	112	12	29	7	0	4	13	8	30	2	.259	.429
Jay Canizaro	2B30 3B8	R	28	38	112	14	24	4	1	0	11	10	22	0	.214	.304
Casey Blake	3B5 1B3 DH1	R	28	20	28	2	6	1	0	0	1	0	7	1	.200	.250
Michael Restovich	OF5 DH2	R	23	8	13	4	4	1	0	1	4	1	4	0	.308	.538
Todd Sears	1B6	R	26	7	12	2	4	2	0	0	3	3	3	0	.333	.500
Mike Ryan	OF5 DH1	L	24	7	11	3	1	0	0	0	0	1	5	0	.091	.091
David Lamb	SS4 2B2 3B1	B	27	6	10	1	1	0	0	0	0	1	1	0	.100	.100
Warren Morris	2B4	L	28	4	7	0	0	0	0	0	0	0	2	0	.000	.000
Javier Valentin	C4	B	26	4	4	0	2	0	0	0	0	1	0	0	.500	.500

NAME	T	AGE	W	L	PCT	SV	G	GS	CG	IP	H	BB	SO	SHO	ERA
TOTALS		29	94	67	.584	47	161	161	8	1445	1454	439	1026	9	4.12
Rick Reed	R	37	15	7	.682	0	33	32	2	188	192	26	121	1	3.78
Kyle Lohse	R	23	13	8	.619	0	32	31	1	181	181	70	124	1	4.23
Eric Milton	L	26	13	9	.591	0	29	29	2	171	173	30	121	1	4.84
Tony Fiore	R	30	10	3	.769	0	48	2	0	91	74	43	55	0	3.16
J.C. Romero	L	26	9	2	.818	1	81	0	0	81	62	36	76	0	1.89
Brad Radke (GJ)	R	29	9	5	.643	0	21	21	2	118	124	20	62	1	4.72
Johan Santana	L	23	8	6	.571	1	27	14	0	108	84	49	137	0	2.99
LaTroy Hawkins	R	29	6	0	1.000	0	65	0	0	80	63	15	63	0	2.13
Joe Mays (EJ)	R	26	4	8	.333	0	17	17	1	95	113	25	38	1	5.38
Bob Wells (EJ)	R	35	2	1	.667	0	48	0	0	58	78	16	30	0	5.90
Mike Jackson	R	37	2	3	.400	0	58	0	0	55	59	13	29	0	3.27
Matt Kinney (EJ)	R	25	2	7	.222	0	14	12	0	66	78	33	45	0	4.64
Eddie Guardado	L	31	1	3	.250	45	68	0	0	68	53	18	70	0	2.93
Kevin Frederick	R	26	1	0	1.000	0	9	0	0	12	13	10	5	0	10.03
Travis Miller	L	29	0	0	—	0	5	0	0	4	4	1	2	0	4.50
Jack Cressend (SJ)	R	27	1	0	1.000	0	23	0	0	32	40	19	22	0	5.93
Mike Trombley	R	35	0	3	.000	0	23	0	0	4	10	1	3	0	15.75
2 Jose Rodriguez (EJ)	L	27	0	1	.000	0	10	3	0	13	29	4	11	0	14.73
Juan Rincon	R	23	0	2	.000	0	10	3	0	29	44	9	21	0	6.28

CHICAGO — 2nd 81-81 .500 13.5 — JERRY MANUEL

Name	G by Pos	B	AGE	G	AB	R	H	2B	3B	HR	RBI	BB	SO	SB	BA	SA
TOTALS			29	162	5502	856	1475	289	29	217	819	555	952	75	.268	.449
Paul Konerko	1B140 DH7	R	26	151	570	81	173	30	0	27	104	44	72	0	.304	.498
1 Ray Durham	2B92	B	30	96	345	71	103	20	2	9	48	49	59	20	.299	.446
Royce Clayton	SS109	B	32	112	342	51	86	14	2	7	35	20	67	5	.251	.365
Jose Valentin	3B83 SS50 DH1	B	32	135	474	70	118	26	4	25	75	43	99	3	.249	.479
Magglio Ordonez	OF150 DH1	R	28	153	590	116	189	47	1	38	135	53	77	7	.320	.597
1 Kenny Lofton	OF92	L	35	93	352	68	91	20	6	8	42	49	51	22	.259	.418
Carlos Lee	OF137 DH21	R	26	140	492	82	130	26	2	26	80	75	73	1	.264	.484
Mark Johnson	C85	L	26	86	263	31	55	8	1	4	18	30	52	0	.209	.293
Frank Thomas	DH140 1B4	R	34	148	523	77	132	29	1	28	92	88	115	3	.252	.472
Aaron Rowand	OF120	R	24	126	302	41	78	16	2	7	26	19	60	2	.258	.394
Jeff Liefer	OF36 1B31 DH6	L	27	76	204	28	47	8	0	7	26	19	60	0	.230	.373
Tony Graffanino (KJ)	3B35 2B25 SS63	R	30	129	355	60	102	12	4	6	31	22	38	2	.262	.428
Joe Crede	3B53	R	24	53	200	28	57	10	0	12	35	8	40	0	.285	.515
1 Sandy Alomar	C50	R	36	51	167	21	48	10	1	7	25	5	14	0	.287	.485
Willie Harris	2B38 OF6	L	24	49	163	14	38	4	0	2	12	9	21	8	.233	.294
Josh Paul	C32 OF1	R	27	33	104	11	25	4	0	0	11	3	22	2	.240	.279
2 D'Angelo Jimenez	2B17 SS10 3B1	B	24	27	108	22	31	4	3	1	11	16	10	2	.287	.407
Joe Borchard	OF15	B	23	16	36	5	8	0	0	2	5	1	14	0	.222	.389
Miguel Olivo	C6	R	23	6	19	2	4	1	0	1	5	2	5	0	.211	.421

NAME	T	AGE	W	L	PCT	SV	G	GS	CG	IP	H	BB	SO	SHO	ERA
		27	81	81	.500	35	162	162	7	1423	1422	528	945	7	4.53
Mark Buehrle	L	23	19	12	.613	0	34	34	5	239	236	61	134	2	3.58
Dan Wright	R	24	14	12	.538	0	33	33	1	196	200	71	136	1	5.18
Jon Garland	R	22	12	12	.500	0	33	33	1	193	188	83	112	1	4.58
Antonio Osuna	R	29	8	2	.800	11	59	0	0	68	64	28	66	0	3.86
Gary Glover	R	25	7	8	.467	1	41	22	0	138	136	52	70	0	5.20
Todd Ritchie (SJ)	R	30	5	15	.250	0	26	23	0	134	176	52	77	0	4.06
Rocky Biddle (SJ)	R	26	3	4	.429	1	44	7	0	78	72	39	64	0	4.06
Kelly Wunsch (SJ)	L	29	2	1	.667	0	50	0	0	32	26	19	22	0	3.41
Jon Rauch	R	23	2	1	.667	0	8	6	0	29	28	14	19	0	6.59
1 Bob Howry	R	28	2	2	.500	0	47	0	0	51	45	17	31	0	3.91
Mike Porzio	L	29	2	2	.500	0	32	0	0	43	40	23	33	0	4.81
Keith Foulke	R	29	2	4	.333	11	65	0	0	78	65	13	58	0	2.90
Matt Ginter	R	24	1	0	1.000	1	33	0	0	54	59	21	37	0	4.47
Damaso Marte	L	27	1	0	.500	10	68	0	0	60	44	18	72	0	2.83
Jim Parque	L	27	1	4	.200	0	8	4	0	25	34	16	13	0	9.95
Lorenzo Barcelo	R	24	0	1	.000	0	4	0	0	6	9	1	1	0	9.00

CLEVELAND — 3rd 74-88 .457 20.5 — CHARLIE MANUEL 39-47 .453 — JOEL SKINNER 35-41 .461

Name	G by Pos	B	AGE	G	AB	R	H	2B	3B	HR	RBI	BB	SO	SB	BA	SA
TOTALS			30	162	5423	739	1349	255	26	192	706	542	1000	52	.249	.412
Jim Thome	1B128 DH18	L	31	147	480	101	146	19	2	52	118	122	139	1	.304	.677
Ricky Gutierrez (ZJ)	2B93 DH1	R	32	94	353	38	97	13	0	4	38	20	48	0	.275	.344
Omar Vizquel	SS150	B	35	151	582	85	160	31	5	14	72	56	64	18	.275	.418
Travis Fryman	3B113	R	33	118	397	42	86	14	3	11	55	40	82	0	.217	.350
Matt Lawton	OF108 DH3	L	30	114	416	71	98	19	2	15	57	59	34	8	.236	.399
Milton Bradley (IJ)	OF94 DH1	B	24	98	325	48	81	18	3	9	38	32	58	6	.249	.406
Chris Magruder	OF83	B	25	87	258	34	56	15	1	6	29	15	55	2	.217	.353
Einar Diaz	C100	R	29	102	320	34	66	19	0	2	16	17	27	0	.206	.284
Ellis Burks	DH127 OF6	R	37	138	518	92	156	28	0	32	91	44	108	2	.301	.541
John McDonald	2B64 SS21 3B10 DH1	R	27	93	264	35	66	11	3	1	12	10	50	3	.250	.326
Bill Selby	3B33 OF18 2B6	L	32	65	159	15	34	7	2	6	21	15	27	0	.214	.396
2 Lee Stevens	1B25 OF16 DH13	L	34	53	153	22	34	7	1	5	26	15	32	0	.222	.379
2 Karim Garcia	OF51	L	26	51	197	29	59	8	0	16	52	6	40	0	.299	.584
1 Russell Branyan	OF42 3B8 DH1	L	26	50	161	16	33	4	0	8	17	17	65	1	.205	.379
Eddie Perez	C42	R	34	42	117	6	25	9	0	4	5	5	25	0	.214	.291
Ben Broussard	OF32 1B4 DH3	L	25	39	112	10	27	4	0	4	9	7	25	0	.241	.384
1 Jolbert Cabrera (PJ)	OF34 2B3 DH1	R	29	38	72	5	8	1	0	0	7	5	13	1	.111	.125
Brady Anderson	OF29 DH1	L	38	34	80	4	13	4	0	1	5	6	18	4	.163	.250
Covelli Crisp	OF32	B	22	32	127	16	33	9	2	1	9	11	19	4	.260	.386
Josh Bard	C24	B	24	24	90	9	20	5	0	3	12	4	13	0	.222	.378
Greg LaRocca	3B15 2B3 DH1	R	29	21	52	12	14	3	1	0	4	6	6	1	.269	.365
Earl Snyder	1B12 3B2 DH1	R	26	18	55	5	11	2	0	1	4	6	21	0	.200	.291
Victor Martinez	C9 DH1	R	23	12	32	2	9	1	0	1	5	3	2	0	.281	.406
Brandon Phillips	2B11	R	21	11	31	5	8	3	1	0	4	6	9	1	.258	.419
Bruce Aven	OF7	R	30	7	17	1	2	0	0	0	1	2	4	0	.118	.118
1 Wil Cordero	OF4 1B1	R	30	6	18	1	4	0	0	0	3	0	2	0	.222	.222
Chad Allen	OF4	R	27	5	10	0	1	0	0	0	1	0	4	0	.100	.200
Todd Dunwoody (FJ-NJ)	OF2	L	27	2	6	0	0	0	0	0	0	0	3	0	.000	.000
Alex Escobar (KJ) 23, Eddie Taubensee (XJ) 33																

NAME	T	AGE	W	L	PCT	SV	G	GS	CG	IP	H	BB	SO	SHO	ERA
		29	74	88	.457	34	162	162	9	1425	1508	603	1058	4	4.91
C.C. Sabathia	L	21	13	11	.542	0	33	33	2	210	198	88	149	0	4.37
1 Bartolo Colon	R	29	10	4	.714	0	16	16	4	116	104	31	75	2	2.55
Ryan Drese	R	26	10	9	.526	0	26	26	1	137	176	62	102	0	6.55
Danys Baez	R	24	10	11	.476	6	39	26	1	165	160	82	130	0	4.41
1 Chuck Finley	L	39	4	11	.267	0	18	18	1	105	114	48	91	0	4.44
1 Paul Shuey	R	31	3	0	1.000	0	39	0	0	37	31	10	39	0	2.41
2 Terry Mulholland	L	39	3	2	.600	0	16	3	0	47	56	14	21	0	4.60
Mark Wohlers	R	32	3	4	.429	7	64	0	0	71	71	26	46	0	4.79
Jerrod Riggan	R	28	2	1	.667	0	33	0	0	33	53	18	22	0	7.64
David Riske	R	25	2	2	.500	1	51	0	0	51	49	35	65	0	5.26
Ricardo Rodriguez	R	24	2	2	.500	0	7	7	0	41	40	18	24	0	5.66
Jaret Wright (SJ)	R	26	2	3	.400	0	8	6	0	18	40	19	12	0	15.71
2 Dave Burba	R	35	1	0	1.000	0	12	3	0	34	30	17	25	0	4.50
Jason Davis	R	22	1	0	1.000	0	3	2	0	15	12	4	11	0	1.84
Brian Tallet	L	24	1	0	1.000	0	2	2	0	12	9	4	5	1	1.50
Sean DePaula	R	28	1	0	1.000	0	5	0	0	6	11	3	8	0	12.79
Carl Sadler	L	25	1	2	.333	0	24	0	0	20	15	11	23	0	4.43
Bob Wickman (EJ)	R	33	1	3	.250	20	36	0	0	34	42	10	36	0	4.46
Jake Westbrook (EJ)	R	24	1	3	.250	0	11	4	0	42	50	12	20	0	5.83
Jason Phillips (EJ)	R	28	1	3	.250	0	8	6	0	42	41	20	23	0	4.97
1 Ricardo Rincon	R	32	1	4	.200	0	46	0	0	36	49	16	30	0	4.79
Charles Nagy (EJ)	R	35	1	3	.250	0	19	7	0	49	76	13	22	0	8.88
Alex Herrera	L	25	0	0	—	0	4	0	0	5	3	1	5	0	0.00
1 Jason Beverlin	R	28	0	0	—	0	4	0	0	7	9	4	9	0	7.36
Roy Smith	R	26	0	0	—	0	4	0	0	6	9	5	2	0	3.00
1 Nerio Rodriguez	R	31	0	0	—	0	1	0	0	0.1	0	0	0	0	0.00
Cliff Lee	L	23	0	0	—	0	2	0	0	10	6	8	6	0	1.74
Dave Maurer	L	27	0	0	—	0	4	0	0	3	5	1	3	0	13.50
Chad Paronto (EJ)	R	26	0	0	—	0	29	0	0	36	34	11	23	0	4.04
Dave Elder	R	26	0	0	—	0	15	0	0	23	18	14	23	0	3.03
Heath Murray (SJ)	L	29	0	0	.000	0	12	0	0	12	17	7	11	0	7.50

KANSAS CITY — 4th 62-100 .383 32.5 — TONY MUSER 8-15 .348 — JOHN MIZEROCK 5-8 .385 — TONY PENA 49-77 .389

Name	G by Pos	B	AGE	G	AB	R	H	2B	3B	HR	RBI	BB	SO	SB	BA	SA
TOTALS			30	162	5535	737	1415	285	42	140	695	524	921	140	.256	.398
Mike Sweeney (PJ)	1B102 DH24	R	28	126	471	81	160	31	4	24	86	61	46	9	.340	.563
Carlos Febles	2B116 SS1	R	26	119	351	44	86	16	4	4	26	41	63	16	.245	.348
Neifi Perez	SS139 2B5	B	29	145	554	65	131	20	4	3	37	20	53	8	.236	.303
Joe Randa	3B129 DH19	R	32	151	549	63	155	36	5	11	80	46	69	3	.282	.426
Michael Tucker	OF108 DH23 1B5 2B2	L	31	144	475	65	118	27	6	12	56	56	105	23	.248	.406
Carlos Beltran	OF149 DH2	B	25	162	637	114	174	44	7	29	105	71	135	35	.273	.501
Chuck Knoblauch (AJ)	OF74 DH2	R	33	80	300	41	63	9	0	6	22	39	25	19	.210	.300
Brent Mayne	C99	L	34	101	326	35	77	8	2	4	30	34	54	1	.236	.310
Raul Ibanez	OF55 1B49 DH36	L	30	137	497	70	146	37	6	24	103	40	76	5	.294	.537
Luis Alicea	2B32 3B32 DH17 1B2 SS1 OF1	B	36	94	237	28	54	8	2	1	23	32	34	2	.228	.291
A.J. Hinch	C68	R	28	72	197	25	49	7	1	7	27	18	35	3	.249	.401
Aaron Guiel	OF61 DH2	L	29	70	240	30	56	13	0	4	38	19	61	1	.233	.388
Brandon Berger	OF36 DH10 1B1	R	27	51	134	16	27	5	1	6	17	8	52	1	.201	.388
1 Donnie Sadler	OF15 3B11 2B4 SS4 DH3	R	27	35	68	10	13	1	1	0	5	4	12	3	.191	.235
Luis Ordaz	2B28 3B6 SS2	R	26	33	94	11	21	2	0	0	4	12	13	2	.223	.245
Kit Pellow	3B12 1B10 DH5	R	28	29	63	6	15	1	0	1	5	9	21	1	.238	.302
Mark Quinn (BR-LJ)	OF15 DH7	R	28	23	76	9	18	4	0	2	11	5	15	2	.237	.368
Angel Berroa	SS20	R	24	20	75	8	17	7	1	0	5	7	10	3	.227	.347
Dee Brown	OF8 DH5	L	24	16	51	5	12	3	1	1	7	4	20	0	.235	.392
1 David McCarty	1B9 DH2	R	32	13	32	3	3	1	0	0	2	5	10	0	.094	.219
Mike Caruso	SS5 2B4 3B2	L	25	12	20	3	2	0	0	0	0	1	3	0	.100	.100
Donzell McDonald	OF7	R	27	10	22	3	4	2	0	0	1	4	5	2	.182	.273
Juan Brito	C9	R	22	9	23	1	7	2	0	0	4	0	3	0	.304	.391
Chan Perry	1B5	R	29	5	11	0	1	0	0	0	0	0	3	0	.091	.091
Alexis Gomez	OF2	L	23	5	10	2	2	0	0	0	1	2	1	0	.200	.200
Dusty Wathan	C3	R	28	3	5	0	3	0	0	0	1	0	0	0	.600	.600

NAME	T	AGE	W	L	PCT	SV	G	GS	CG	IP	H	BB	SO	SHO	ERA
		28	62	100	.383	30	162	162	12	1441	1587	572	909	6	5.21
Paul Byrd	R	31	17	11	.607	0	33	33	7	228	224	38	129	2	3.90
Jeff Suppan	R	27	9	16	.360	0	33	33	3	208	229	68	109	1	5.32
Runelvys Hernandez	R	24	4	4	.500	0	12	12	0	74	79	22	45	0	4.36
Scott Mullen	L	27	4	5	.444	0	44	0	0	40	40	13	21	0	3.15
Jason Grimsley	R	34	4	7	.364	1	70	0	0	71	64	37	59	0	3.91
Miguel Asencio	R	21	4	7	.364	0	31	21	0	123	136	64	58	0	5.11
Darrell May (GJ)	L	30	4	10	.286	0	30	21	2	131	144	50	95	1	5.35
Cory Bailey	R	31	3	4	.429	1	37	0	0	46	53	31	24	0	4.11
Jeremy Affeldt (RJ)	L	23	3	4	.429	0	34	7	0	78	85	37	67	0	4.64
Dan Reichert	R	25	3	5	.375	0	30	6	0	66	77	25	36	0	5.32
Shawn Sedlacek	R	25	3	5	.375	0	16	14	0	84	99	36	52	0	6.72
Kris Wilson (AJ)	R	25	2	0	1.000	0	12	0	0	19	25	5	10	0	8.20
Ryan Bukvich	R	24	1	0	1.000	0	25	0	0	26	19	20	6	0	6.12
Roberto Hernandez (EJ)	R	37	1	3	.250	26	53	0	0	52	62	12	39	0	4.33
Brian Shouse	L	33	0	0	—	0	10	0	0	15	15	9	11	0	6.14
Jeff Austin	R	25	0	0	—	0	10	0	0	11	14	6	4	0	4.91
Nate Field	R	26	0	0	—	0	5	0	0	5	8	4	7	0	9.00
Jeremy Hill	R	24	0	1	.000	0	8	0	0	13	17	6	5	0	3.86
Mike MacDougal	R	25	0	1	.000	0	8	0	0	13	15	9	11	0	6.54
Chad Durbin	R	24	0	1	.000	0	4	1	0	13	4	5	6	0	11.88
Brad Voyles	R	25	0	2	.000	0	28	0	0	31	18	26	26	0	6.51
Mac Suzuki	R	27	0	0	—	0	7	0	0	21	24	17	15	0	9.00
Wes Obermueller	R	26	0	0	—	0	2	0	0	7	6	3	0	0	11.74
Bryan Rekar	R	30	0	2	.000	0	7	2	0	12	6	2	2	0	15.43
Blake Stein (GJ)	R	28	0	1	.000	0	4	0	0	7	9	7	8	0	7.91
Chris George (RJ)	L	22	0	3	.000	0	8	7	0	27	37	13	10	0	5.02

DETROIT — 5th 55-106 .342 39 — PHIL GARNER 0-6 .000 — LUIS PUJOLS 55-100 .355

Name	G by Pos	B	AGE	G	AB	R	H	2B	3B	HR	RBI	BB	SO	SB	BA	SA
TOTALS			28	161	5406	575	1340	285	37	124	546	363	1035	65	.248	.379
2 Carlos Pena	1B73 DH2	L	24	75	273	31	69	13	4	12	36	26	73	2	.253	.462
Damion Easley (UJ)	2B84 DH1	R	32	85	304	29	68	14	1	8	30	27	43	1	.224	.355
Ramon Santiago (BW)	SS63 DH1	B	22	85	222	33	54	5	5	4	20	13	48	8	.243	.365
Chris Truby	3B89	R	28	89	277	23	55	13	2	2	15	5	71	1	.199	.282
Robert Fick	OF140 DH6	L	28	148	556	66	150	36	2	17	63	46	90	0	.270	.433
Wendell Magee	OF91 DH4	R	29	97	347	34	94	19	1	6	35	16	64	2	.271	.383
Bobby Higginson (LJ)	OF117 DH1	L	31	119	444	50	125	24	3	10	63	41	45	12	.282	.417
Brandon Inge	C94 DH1	R	25	95	321	27	65	15	3	7	24	24	101	1	.202	.333
Randall Simon	DH65 1B59	L	27	130	482	51	145	17	1	19	82	13	30	0	.301	.459
Shane Halter	SS81 3B30 OF8 2B4 DH2 1B1	R	32	122	410	46	98	22	6	10	39	39	92	0	.239	.395
Damian Jackson	2B56 SS6 OF6 DH5 3B2	R	28	81	245	31	63	20	1	1	25	21	56	12	.257	.359
Craig Paquette	3B49 1B14 OF8 DH5	R	33	72	252	20	49	14	1	4	20	10	53	1	.194	.306
2 George Lombard	OF69 DH2	L	26	72	241	34	58	11	3	5	13	20	78	13	.241	.373
Dmitri Young (GJ)	DH35 1B15 3B1 OF1	B	28	54	201	25	57	14	0	7	27	12	39	2	.284	.458
Mike Rivera	C37 DH1	R	25	39	132	11	30	8	0	3	14	4	35	0	.227	.326
Jacob Cruz (EJ)	DH15 OF12 1B4	L	29	35	88	12	24	3	1	2	6	13	20	1	.273	.398
2 Hiram Bocachica	OF32 2B2 DH1	R	26	34	103	14	23	3	0	4	8	5	31	2	.223	.379
1 Jose Macias	2B17 OF10 3B8	B	30	33	107	10	25	6	0	0	8	6	13	0	.234	.271
Matt Walbeck	C27	B	32	30	93	7	22	5	0	0	6	6	17	0	.237	.290
Andres Torres	OF19	B	24	19	70	7	14	1	0	0	2	6	20	2	.200	.243
Omar Infante	SS16 2B2	R	20	18	59	3	11	1	0	0	6	3	10	0	.186	.288
Eric Munson	DH14 1B4	L	24	18	48	4	7	1	0	2	4	5	13	0	.146	.292
Craig Monroe	OF9 DH3	R	25	11	39	5	7	1	0	1	3	1	10	0	.179	.308
Mitch Meluskey (XJ)	C27	B	28	7	24	1	6	2	0	0	1	3	6	0	.250	.333
Oscar Salazar	2B6 SS1 3B1	R	24	8	21	1	4	1	0	0	2	1	6	0	.190	.381
Dean Palmer (ZJ)	DH4	R	33	4	13	0	0	0	0	0	0	0	5	0	.000	.000
Ryan Jackson	OF3	L	29	3	6	0	2	1	1	0	0	0	1	0	.333	.833

NAME	T	AGE	W	L	PCT	SV	G	GS	CG	IP	H	BB	SO	SHO	ERA
		28	55	106	.342	33	161	161	11	1414	1593	463	794	7	4.93
Mark Redman	L	28	8	15	.348	0	30	30	3	203	211	51	109	0	4.21
Steve Sparks	R	36	8	16	.333	0	32	30	3	189	238	67	98	0	5.52
1 Jeff Weaver	R	25	6	8	.429	0	17	17	3	122	112	33	75	3	3.18
Mike Maroth	L	24	6	10	.375	0	21	21	0	129	136	36	58	0	4.48
Jose Lima	R	29	4	6	.400	0	20	12	0	68	86	21	33	0	7.77
Adam Bernero	R	25	4	7	.364	0	28	11	0	102	128	31	69	0	6.20
Julio Santana (EJ)	R	28	3	5	.375	0	38	0	0	57	49	28	38	0	2.84
Matt Anderson (SJ)	R	26	1	2	.667	0	12	0	0	11	17	8	8	0	9.00
Seth Greisinger	R	26	2	2	.500	0	8	8	0	38	46	13	14	0	6.21
Jeff Farnsworth	L	28	2	3	.400	0	7	4	0	21	17	11	21	0	5.79
Eric Eckenstahler	L	25	1	0	1.000	0	7	0	0	8	14	2	13	0	5.63
Franklyn German	R	22	1	0	1.000	1	7	0	0	9	5	6	10	0	3.00
Jamie Walker	L	30	1	1	.500	1	57	0	0	44	32	9	40	0	3.71
Oscar Henriquez	R	28	1	1	.500	2	30	0	0	19	15	23	19	0	6.49
1 Brian Moehler	R	30	1	1	.500	0	3	3	0	14	23	6	12	0	2.29
Fernando Rodney	R	25	1	3	.250	0	20	0	0	28	30	16	23	0	6.07
Andy Van Hekken	L	22	1	3	.250	0	5	5	0	30	38	6	15	1	3.00
Juan Acevedo	R	32	2	7	.222	28	65	0	0	75	68	23	40	0	2.65
Brian Powell	R	28	0	1	.000	0	13	6	0	58	64	21	30	0	4.84
Nate Cornejo	R	22	1	1	.500	0	9	9	0	50	66	18	23	0	5.04
Matt Perisho	L	27	0	0	—	0	16	0	0	9	9	10	6	0	10.50
Terry Pearson	R	30	0	0	—	0	4	0	0	2	5	1	2	0	13.50
Matt Miller (SJ)	R	27	0	0	—	0	3	0	0	2	6	3	3	0	9.00
2 Jason Jimenez	L	26	0	0	—	0	1	0	0	0.2	4	0	3	0	27.00
Kris Keller	R	27	0	0	—	0	1	0	0	1	2	1	1	0	9.00
Erik Sabel	R	27	0	0	—	0	1	0	0	1	1	1	0	0	∞
Jose Paniagua	R	29	0	0	—	0	41	0	0	42	50	15	34	0	5.00
Danny Patterson (EJ)	R	31	0	0	—	0	3	0	0	6	13	1	5	0	15.00
2 Jason Beverlin	R	28	0	3	.000	0	12	1	0	19	22	3	5	0	9.49
Shane Loux	R	22	0	3	.000	0	14	4	0	19	31	8	7	0	9.00

OAKLAND   1st 103-59 .636   ART HOWE

Name	G by Pos	B	AGE	G	AB	R	H	2B	3B	HR	RBI	BB	SO	SB	BA	SA
TOTALS			28	162	5558	800	1450	279	28	205	772	609	1008	46	.261	.432
Scott Hatteberg	1B91 DH42	L	32	136	492	58	138	22	4	15	61	68	56	0	.280	.433
Mark Ellis	2B85 SS8 3B7 DH1	R	25	98	345	58	94	16	4	6	35	44	54	4	.272	.394
Miguel Tejada	SS162	R	26	162	662	108	204	30	0	34	131	38	84	7	.308	.508
Eric Chavez	3B143 DH9 OF1	L	24	153	585	87	161	31	3	34	109	65	119	2	.275	.513
Jermaine Dye	OF111 DH19 OF1	R	28	131	488	74	123	27	1	24	86	52	108	2	.252	.459
Terrence Long	OF162	L	26	162	587	71	141	32	4	16	67	48	96	3	.240	.390
David Justice	OF75 DH37	L	36	118	398	54	106	18	3	11	49	70	66	4	.266	.410
Ramon Hernandez	C135	R	26	136	403	51	94	20	0	7	42	43	64	0	.233	.335
2 Ray Durham	DH43 2B11	B	30	54	219	43	60	14	4	6	22	24	34	6	.274	.457
Eric Byrnes	OF79 DH7	R	26	90	94	24	23	4	2	3	11	4	17	3	.245	.426
2 John Mabry	OF53 1B50	L	31	89	193	27	53	13	1	11	40	14	37	1	.275	.523
Olmedo Seanz	1B34 3B15 DH7	R	31	68	156	15	43	10	1	6	18	13	31	1	.276	.468
Greg Myers	C53 DH1	L	36	65	144	15	32	5	0	6	21	26	36	0	.222	.382
Randy Velarde (BH)	2B38 1B5 DH5 3B3	R	39	56	133	22	30	8	0	2	8	15	32	3	.226	.331
Adam Piatt	OF50 1B1	R	26	55	137	18	32	8	0	5	18	12	33	2	.234	.401
1 Jeremy Giambi	OF40 DH2	L	27	42	157	26	43	7	0	8	17	27	40	0	.274	.471
1 Carlos Pena	1B40	L	24	40	124	12	27	4	0	7	16	15	38	0	.218	.419
Frank Menechino	2B32 3B4 SS2 DH1	R	31	38	132	22	27	7	0	3	15	20	32	0	.205	.326
Mike Colangelo	OF19	R	25	20	23	2	4	1	0	0	1	0	7	0	.174	.217
Esteban German	2B8	R	24	9	35	4	7	0	0	0	0	4	11	1	.200	.200
Larry Sutton	1B6 OF3	L	32	7	19	3	2	0	0	1	3	1	8	0	.105	.263
Jose Flores	2B2 SS1 DH1	R	29	7	3	2	0	0	0	0	0	1	1	0	1.000	.000
Jason Grabowski	OF4	L	26	4	8	3	3	1	1	0	1	3	1	0	.375	.750
Cody McKay	C1	L	28	2	3	0	2	1	0	0	2	0	1	0	.667	.667

NAME	T	AGE	W	L	PCT	SV	G	GS	CG	IP	H	BB	SO	SHO	ERA
		29	103	59	.636	48	162	35	9	1452	1391	474	1021	19	3.68
Barry Zito	L	24	23	5	.821	0	35	35	1	229	182	78	182	0	2.75
Mark Mulder	L	24	19	7	.731	0	30	30	2	207	182	55	159	1	3.47
Tim Hudson	R	26	15	9	.625	0	34	34	4	238	237	62	152	2	2.98
Billy Koch	R	27	11	4	.733	44	84	0	0	94	73	46	93	0	3.27
Cory Lidle	R	30	8	10	.444	0	31	30	2	192	191	39	111	2	3.89
Jim Mecir	R	32	6	4	.600	1	61	0	0	68	68	29	53	0	4.26
Aaron Harang	R	24	5	4	.556	0	16	15	0	78	78	45	64	0	4.83
Chad Bradford	R	27	4	2	.667	2	75	0	0	75	73	14	56	0	3.11
Erik Hiljus	R	29	3	3	.500	0	9	9	0	46	52	21	29	0	6.50
Micah Bowie	L	27	2	0	1.000	0	13	0	0	12	12	8	8	0	1.50
2 Ted Lilly (SJ)	L	26	2	1	.667	0	6	5	0	23	23	7	18	0	4.63
Mike Venafro	L	28	2	1	.500	0	47	0	0	37	45	14	16	0	4.62
Mike Fyhrie	R	32	2	4	.333	0	16	4	0	49	46	20	29	0	4.44
Jeff Tam	R	31	1	2	.333	0	40	0	0	40	56	13	14	0	5.13
2 Ricardo Rincon	L	32	0	0	—	1	25	0	0	20	11	3	9	0	3.10
1 Mike Holtz	L	29	0	0	—	0	16	0	0	14	24	9	7	0	6.43
Mike Magnante	L	37	0	2	.000	0	32	0	0	29	38	11	11	0	5.97

ANAHEIM   2nd 99-63 .611 4 (Wild Card)   MIKE SCIOSCIA

Name	G by Pos	B	AGE	G	AB	R	H	2B	3B	HR	RBI	BB	SO	SB	BA	SA
TOTALS			29	162	5678	851	1603	333	32	152	811	462	805	117	.282	.433
Scott Spiezio	1B143 3B20 OF10 2B1	B	29	153	491	80	140	34	2	12	82	67	52	6	.285	.436
Adam Kennedy	2B139 OF1 DH1	L	26	144	474	65	148	32	6	7	52	19	80	17	.312	.449
David Eckstein	SS147 DH3	R	27	152	608	107	178	22	6	8	63	45	44	21	.293	.388
Troy Glaus	3B156 SS2	R	25	156	569	99	142	24	1	30	111	88	140	10	.250	.453
Tim Salmon	OF111 DH25	R	33	138	483	84	138	37	1	22	88	71	102	6	.286	.503
Darin Erstad	OF143 1B5 DH4	L	28	150	625	99	177	28	4	10	73	27	67	23	.283	.389
Garret Anderson	OF147 DH10	L	29	158	638	93	195	56	3	29	123	30	80	6	.306	.539
Bengie Molina	C121	R	27	122	428	34	105	18	0	5	47	15	34	0	.245	.322
Brad Fullmer	DH94 1B29	L	27	130	429	75	124	35	6	19	59	32	44	10	.289	.531
Orlando Palmeiro	OF86 DH8	L	33	110	263	35	79	12	1	0	31	30	22	7	.300	.354
Benji Gil (NJ)	2B26 SS14 1B10 DH10	R	29	61	130	11	37	8	1	3	20	5	33	2	.285	.431
Shawn Wooten (RJ)	DH26 1B16 C2 3B1	R	29	49	113	13	33	8	0	3	19	6	24	2	.292	.442
Jose Nieves	2B18 SS13 3B5 1B3 OF2 DH2	R	27	45	97	17	28	2	0	0	6	2	14	1	.289	.309
2 Alex Ochoa	OF36	R	30	37	65	8	18	7	0	2	10	10	5	2	.277	.477
1 Jorge Fabregas	C32	L	32	35	88	8	17	1	0	0	8	6	6	0	.193	.205
Jose Molina	C29	R	27	29	70	5	19	3	0	0	5	5	15	0	.271	.314
Julio Ramirez (LJ)	OF23 DH1	R	24	29	32	6	9	0	1	1	7	2	14	5	.281	.438
Jeff DaVanon	OF10 DH4	B	28	16	30	3	5	3	0	1	4	2	6	2	.167	.367
Chone Figgins	2B8	R	24	15	12	6	2	1	0	0	1	0	5	2	.167	.250
Alfredo Amezaga	SS5 DH1	R	24	12	13	3	7	2	0	0	2	0	1	1	.538	.692
Clay Bellinger	1B2	R	33	2	1	0	0	0	0	0	0	0	0	0	.000	.000
Sal Fasano	C2	R	30	2	1	0	0	0	0	0	0	0	0	0	.000	.000

NAME	T	AGE	W	L	PCT	SV	G	GS	CG	IP	H	BB	SO	SHO	ERA
		31	99	63	.611	54	162	162	7	1452	1345	509	999	14	3.69
Jarrod Washburn	L	27	18	6	.750	0	32	32	1	206	183	59	139	0	3.15
Ramon Ortiz	R	29	15	9	.625	0	32	32	4	217	188	68	162	1	3.77
Kevin Appier	R	34	14	12	.538	0	32	32	0	188	191	64	132	0	3.92
John Lackey	R	23	9	4	.692	0	18	18	1	108	113	33	69	0	3.66
Scott Schoeneweis	L	28	9	8	.529	1	54	15	0	118	119	49	65	0	4.88
Aaron Sele (SJ)	R	32	8	9	.471	0	26	26	1	160	190	49	82	0	4.89
Ben Weber	R	32	7	2	.778	7	63	0	0	78	70	22	43	0	2.54
Scot Shields	R	26	5	3	.625	0	29	1	0	49	31	21	30	0	2.20
Troy Percival	R	32	4	1	.800	40	58	0	0	56	38	25	68	0	1.92
Al Levine	R	34	4	4	.500	5	52	0	0	64	61	34	40	0	4.24
Mark Lukasiewicz	L	29	2	0	1.000	0	17	0	0	14	17	9	15	0	3.86
Mickey Callaway	R	27	1	1	.667	0	6	3	0	34	31	11	23	0	4.19
Brendan Donnelly	R	30	1	1	.500	1	46	0	0	50	32	19	54	0	2.17
Dennis Cook (SJ)	L	39	1	1	.500	0	37	0	0	24	21	19	23	0	3.38
Donne Wall	R	34	0	0	—	0	17	0	0	21	17	7	13	0	6.43
Matt Wise	R	26	0	0	—	0	8	7	1	6	9	3	2	1	3.24
Francisco Rodriguez	R	20	0	0	—	0	5	0	0	6	2	3	13	0	0.00
Lou Pote	R	30	0	2	.000	0				50	33	26	32	0	3.22

SEATTLE   3rd 93-69 .574 10   LOU PINIELLA

Name	G by Pos	B	AGE	G	AB	R	H	2B	3B	HR	RBI	BB	SO	SB	BA	SA
TOTALS			32	162	5569	814	1531	285	31	152	771	629	1003	137	.275	.419
John Olerud	1B152 DH2	L	33	154	553	85	166	39	0	22	102	98	66	0	.300	.490
Bret Boone	2B153 DH1	R	33	155	608	88	169	34	3	24	107	53	102	12	.278	.462
Carlos Guillen	SS130 DH3	B	26	134	475	73	124	24	6	9	56	46	91	4	.261	.394
Jeff Cirillo	3B141 1B11	R	32	146	485	51	121	20	0	6	54	31	67	8	.249	.328
Ichiro Suzuki	OF152 DH4	L	28	157	647	111	208	27	8	8	51	68	62	31	.321	.425
Mike Cameron	OF155 DH1	R	29	158	545	84	130	26	5	25	80	79	176	31	.239	.442
Ruben Sierra	OF60 DH52	B	36	122	419	47	113	23	0	13	60	31	66	4	.270	.418
Dan Wilson	C113 1B4	R	33	115	359	35	106	16	1	6	44	18	81	1	.295	.396
Edgar Martinez (LJ)	DH91	R	39	97	328	42	91	23	0	15	59	67	69	1	.277	.485
Desi Relaford	SS40 3B38 OF35 2B11 DH4	B	28	112	329	55	88	13	2	6	43	33	51	10	.267	.374
Mark McLemore	OF88 3B14 DH4 2B2 SS1	L	37	104	337	54	91	17	2	7	41	61	63	18	.270	.395
Ben Davis	C77 1B2	R	25	80	228	24	59	10	1	7	43	18	58	1	.259	.404
Charles Gipson	OF73 3B4 DH3	R	29	79	72	22	17	5	2	0	8	9	14	4	.236	.361
Luis Ugueto	DH16 2B11 SS8 3B1	B	23	62	23	19	5	0	0	1	1	2	8	3	.217	.348
2 Jose Offerman	1B11 OF6 DH4 2B1	B	33	29	47	9	11	2	1	1	4	4	9	1	.234	.383
Scott Podsednik	OF11 DH2	L	26	14	20	2	4	0	0	1	2	0	5	0	.200	.350
Willie Bloomquist	OF7 2B4 DH2	R	24	12	33	11	15	4	0	0	7	5	2	3	.455	.576
Chris Snelling (KJ)	OF8	L	20	8	27	2	4	1	0	1	3	2	4	0	.148	.259
Pat Borders	C2 DH2	R	39	4	4	0	2	1	0	0	2	0	2	0	.500	.750
1 Eugene Kingsale	OF2	B	25	3	3	0	2	0	0	0	0	0	1	0	.667	.667
Ron Wright	DH1	R	26	1	3	0	0	0	0	0	0	0	1	0	.000	.000

NAME	T	AGE	W	L	PCT	SV	G	GS	CG	IP	H	BB	SO	SHO	ERA
		31	93	69	.574	43	162	162	8	1445	1422	441	1063	12	4.07
Freddy Garcia	R	27	16	10	.615	0	34	34	1	224	227	63	181	0	4.39
Joel Pineiro	R	23	14	7	.667	0	37	28	2	194	189	54	136	1	3.24
Jamie Moyer	L	39	13	8	.619	0	34	34	3	231	198	50	147	2	3.32
Arthur Rhodes	L	32	10	4	.714	2	66	0	0	70	45	13	81	0	2.33
Shigetoshi Hasegawa	R	33	8	3	.727	1	53	0	0	70	63	30	39	0	3.20
Ryan Franklin	R	29	7	5	.583	0	41	12	0	119	117	22	65	0	4.02
James Baldwin	R	30	7	10	.412	0	30	23	0	150	179	49	88	0	5.28
John Halama	L	30	6	5	.545	0	31	10	0	100	112	33	70	0	3.56
Kazuhiro Sasaki	R	34	4	5	.444	37	61	0	0	61	44	20	73	0	2.52
Jeff Nelson (EJ)	R	35	3	2	.600	2	41	0	0	46	36	27	55	0	3.94
2 Ismael Valdes	R	28	2	3	.400	0	8	8	1	49	59	11	27	0	4.93
Mark Watson	L	26	1	0	1.000	0	3	0	0	4	8	4	1	0	18.00
2 Doug Creek	L	33	1	1	.500	0	23	0	0	18	18	14	19	0	4.91
Paul Abbott (SJ)	R	34	1	3	.250	0	7	5	0	26	40	20	12	0	11.96
Julio Mateo	R	24	0	0	—	0	12	0	0	21	20	12	15	0	4.29
Brian Fitzgerald	L	27	0	0	—	0	3	0	0	5	6	3	3	0	8.53
Aaron Taylor	R	26	0	0	—	0	5	0	0	5	6	1	3	0	9.00
Justin Kaye	R	26	0	0	—	0	4	0	0	3	6	1	3	0	12.00
Rafael Soriano (SJ)	R	22	0	3	.000	0	10	10	0	47	45	16	32	0	4.56

TEXAS   4th 72-90 .444 31   JERRY NARRON

Name	G by Pos	B	AGE	G	AB	R	H	2B	3B	HR	RBI	BB	SO	SB	BA	SA
TOTALS			30	162	5618	843	1510	304	27	230	806	554	1055	62	.269	.455
Rafael Palmeiro	1B97 DH55	L	37	155	546	99	149	34	0	43	105	104	94	2	.273	.571
Michael Young	2B152 SS11 3B4 DH1	R	25	156	573	77	150	26	4	9	62	41	112	6	.262	.382
Alex Rodriguez	3B162	R	26	162	624	125	187	27	2	57	142	87	122	9	.300	.623
Herbert Perry	3B112 1B12 DH6 OF1	R	32	132	450	64	124	24	1	22	77	34	66	4	.276	.480
Juan Gonzalez (RJ)	OF62 DH8	R	32	70	277	38	78	21	1	8	35	17	56	2	.282	.451
Carl Everett (LJ)	OF83 DH18	B	31	105	374	47	100	16	0	16	62	33	77	2	.267	.439
Kevin Mench	OF106 DH3	R	24	110	366	52	95	20	2	15	60	31	83	1	.260	.448
Ivan Rodriguez (XJ)	C100 DH6	R	30	108	408	67	128	32	2	19	60	25	71	5	.314	.542
Rusty Greer (XJ)	OF26 DH22 1B1	L	33	51	199	24	59	9	2	1	17	19	17	1	.296	.377
Mike Lamb	1B52 DH21 OF16 3B14 C4 2B1	L	26	115	314	54	89	13	0	9	33	33	48	0	.283	.411
1 Gabe Kapler	OF64 1B1 DH1	R	26	72	196	25	51	12	1	0	17	8	30	5	.260	.332
Bill Haselman	C67 DH2	R	36	69	179	16	44	7	0	3	18	11	25	0	.246	.335
Ruben Rivera	OF67 DH2	R	28	69	158	17	33	4	0	8	14	17	45	4	.209	.310
Frank Catalanotto (GJ-XJ-BH)	OF26 2B23 1B15 DH8	L	28	68	212	42	57	16	4	3	23	25	27	1	.269	.443
Hank Blalock	3B46	L	21	49	147	16	31	8	0	3	17	20	43	0	.211	.327
Todd Greene	C15 1B15 DH4 OF1	R	31	42	112	15	30	5	0	10	19	2	28	0	.268	.580
2 Todd Hollandsworth	OF38	L	29	39	132	16	34	4	0	5	19	14	27	1	.258	.417
2 Donnie Sadler	OF18 SS12 3B4 2B2 DH1	R	27	38	30	6	3	1	0	0	2	2	10	4	.100	.133
2 Calvin Murray	OF34 DH2	R	30	37	77	16	13	5	1	1	4	6	14	4	.169	.260
1 Jason Romano	OF18 2B8 DH4 3B1	R	23	29	54	8	11	1	0	0	3	1	7	2	.204	.278
Ryan Ludwick	OF22	R	23	23	81	10	19	6	0	1	2	2	35	0	.235	.346
Travis Hafner	DH13 1B3	L	25	23	62	6	15	4	1	1	6	8	15	0	.242	.387
Jason Hart	OF7 1B2	R	24	10	15	2	4	1	0	0	1	1	7	0	.267	.467
Hector Ortiz	C7	R	32	9	14	1	3	1	0	0	1	0	3	0	.214	.500

NAME	T	AGE	W	L	PCT	SV	G	GS	CG	IP	H	BB	SO	SHO	ERA
		29	72	90	.444	33	162	162	4	1440	1528	669	1030	4	5.15
Kenny Rogers	L	37	13	8	.619	0	33	33	2	211	212	70	107	1	3.84
Chan Ho Park (LJ)	R	28	9	8	.529	0	25	25	0	146	154	78	121	0	5.75
1 Ismael Valdes	R	28	8	9	.400	0	23	23	0	147	135	36	75	0	3.93
Rob Bell	R	25	8	9	.571	0	17	15	0	94	113	35	70	0	6.22
2 Dennys Reyes	R	25	4	3	.571	0	15	5	0	42	55	21	29	0	6.38
1 Dave Burba	R	35	4	4	.444	0	23	18	1	111	125	40	70	0	5.42
Joaquin Benoit	R	24	4	5	.444	1	17	13	0	85	91	58	59	0	5.31
Jay Powell (RJ)	R	30	3	2	.600	0	51	0	0	50	50	24	35	0	3.44
Todd Van Poppel	R	30	3	2	.600	1	50	0	0	73	80	29	85	0	5.45
Rich Rodriguez (SJ)	L	39	3	2	.600	1	36	0	0	17	14	11	12	0	5.40
Doug Davis	L	26	3	5	.375	0	10	10	1	60	67	22	28	1	4.98
Danny Kolb (SJ)	R	27	3	4	.333	1	34	0	0	32	27	22	20	0	4.22
Hideki Irabu (IL)	R	33	3	8	.273	16	38	2	0	47	51	16	30	0	5.74
Francisco Cordero (SJ)	R	27	2	0	1.000	10	39	0	0	45	33	13	41	0	1.79
Anthony Telford	R	36	2	1	.667	1	30	0	0	24	30	13	30	0	6.46
John Rocker (SJ)	R	27	2	3	.400	1	30	0	0	24	29	13	14	0	6.66
Aaron Myette	R	24	2	5	.286	0	15	12	0	48	64	41	48	0	10.06
Rudy Seanez (XJ)	R	33	1	3	.250	0	15	0	0	23	38	24	40	0	5.73
Colby Lewis	R	22	1	3	.250	0	15	4	0	34	42	26	28	0	6.29
1 Randy Flores	L	26	0	0	—	0	3	0	0	4	7	4	4	0	4.50
Steve Woodard	R	27	0	0	—	0	14	0	0	18	20	8	14	0	6.62
Reynaldo Garcia	R	21	0	0	—	0	3	0	0	5	11	6	5	0	31.50
Ben Kozlowski	L	21	0	0	—	0	3	1	0	11	11	6	9	0	6.30
C.J. Nitkowski	L	29	0	0	—	0	13	0	0	13	13	14	12	0	2.63
Chris Michalak	L	31	0	0	—	0	13	0	0	14	20	10	5	0	4.40
Dan Miceli	R	31	0	0	—	0	9	0	0	9	18	7	8	0	8.64
Juan Alvarez	L	28	0	0	—	0	52	0	0	40	35	21	30	0	4.76
Jeff Zimmerman (EJ)		29													

LINE SCORES

Team	1	2	3	4	5	6	7	8	9	10	11	12	R	H	E

DIVISION SERIES ANAHEIM 3 : NEW YORK 1

Game 1   October 1 at New York

ANA 0 0 1 0 2 1 0 1 0   5 12 0
NYA 1 0 0 1 0 0 1 4 x   8 8 1

Washburn, Weber (8), Schoeneweis (8),
Donnelly (8)
Clemens, Mendoza (6), **Karsay** (8),
Rivera (9)

Game 2   October 2 at New York

ANA 1 2 1 0 0 0 0 3 1   8 17 1
NYA 0 0 1 2 0 2 0 0 1   6 12 1

Appier, Rodriguez (6), Weber (8),
Donnelly (8), Percival (8)
Pettitte, **Hernandez** (4), Karsay (8),
Stanton (8), Weaver (9)

Game 3   October 4 at Anaheim

NYA 3 0 3 0 0 0 0 0 0   6 6 0
ANA 0 1 2 1 0 1 1 3 x   9 12 0

Mussina, Weaver (5), **Stanton** (7),
Karsay (8)
Ortiz, Lackey (3), Schoenwesi (6),
Rodriguez (7), Percival (9)

Game 4   October 5 at Anaheim

NYA 0 1 0 0 1 1 1 0 1   5 12 2
ANA 0 0 1 0 8 0 0 0 x   9 15 1

Wells, Mendoza (5), Hernandez (5),
Karsay (8), Stanton (8)
Washburn, Donnelly (6), Schoeneweis (7),
Rodriguez (7), Percival (9)

DIVISION SERIES: MINNESOTA 3 : OAKLAND 2

Game 1   October 1 at Oakland

MIN 0 1 2 0 0 3 1 0 0   7 13 3
OAK 3 2 0 0 0 0 0 0 0   5 12 0

Radke, Santana (6), Romero (7),
Guardado (9)
Hudson, Lilly (6), Lidle (7),
Rincon (8), Mecir (9)

Game 2   October 2 at Oakland

MIN 0 0 0 0 0 0 1 0 0   1 7 1
OAK 3 0 0 5 1 0 0 0 x   9 14 0

Mays, Fiore (4), Lohse (6), Hawkins (8)
Mulder, Bradford (7), Koch (9)

Game 3   October 4 at Minnesota

OAK 2 0 0 1 0 1 2 0 0   6 9 1
MIN 0 0 0 1 2 0 0 0 0   3 8 0

Zito, Rincon (7), Koch (9)
Reed, Santana (6), Jackson (7), Romero (8),
Hawkins (9)

Game 4   October 5 at Minnesota

OAK 0 0 2 0 0 0 0 0 0   2 7 2
MIN 0 0 2 7 0 0 2 0 x 11 12 0

Hudson, Lilly (4), Bowie (7)
Milton, Lohse (8)

Game 5   October 6 at Oakland

MIN 0 1 1 0 0 0 0 0 3   5 12 0
OAK 0 0 1 0 0 0 0 0 3   4 11 0

Radke, Romero (7), Hawkins (8),
Guardado (9)
Mulder, Bradford (8), Koch (9)

CHAMPIONSHIP: ANAHEIM 4 : MINNESOTA 1

Game 1   October 8 at Minnesota

ANA 0 0 1 0 0 0 0 0 0   1 4 0
MIN 0 1 0 0 1 0 0 0 x   2 5 1

Appier, Donnelly (6), Schoeneweis (7),
Weber (8)
Mays, Guardado (9)

Game 2   October 9 at Minnesota

ANA 1 3 0 0 0 2 0 0 0   6 10 0
MIN 0 0 0 0 0 3 0 0 0   3 11 1

Ortiz, Donnelly (6), Rodriguez (7),
Percival (8)
Reed, Santana (6), Romero (8),
Hawkins (8), Jackson (9)

Game 3   October 11 at Anaheim

MIN 0 0 0 0 0 0 1 0 0   1 6 0
ANA 0 1 0 0 0 0 0 1 x   2 8 0

Milton, Hawkins (7), Santana (7),
Jackson (7), **Romero** (7)
Washburn, **Rodriguez** (8), Percival (9)

Game 4   October 12 at Anaheim

MIN 0 0 0 0 0 0 0 0 1   1 6 2
ANA 0 0 0 0 0 0 2 5 x   7 10 0

Radke, Santana (7), Hawkins (8),
Romero (8), Jackson (8), Wells (8)
Lackey, Rodriguez (8), Weber (9)

Game 5   October 13 at Anaheim

MIN 1 1 0 0 0 0 0 0 0   5 9 0
ANA 0 0 1 0 2 0 10 0 x 13 18 0

Mays, **Santana** (6), Hawkins (7),
Romero (7), Wells (7), Lohse (8)
Appier, Donnelly (6), **Rodriguez** (7), Weber (8),
Percival (9)

COMPOSITE BATTING

DIVISION SERIES

NAME	POS	G	AB	R	H	2B	3B	HR	RBI	BA
ANAHEIM										
TOTALS		4	149	31	56	10	0	9	31	.376
Erstad	CF	4	19	4	8	2	0	0	2	.421
Salmon	RF	4	19	3	5	1	0	2	7	.263
Anderson	LF	4	18	5	7	2	0	1	4	.389
Eckstein	SS	4	18	2	5	0	0	0	1	.278
Glaus	3B	4	16	4	5	0	0	3	3	.313
Spiezio	1B	4	15	2	6	1	0	1	6	.400
B. Molina	C	4	15	0	4	2	0	0	2	.267
Wooten	DH	3	9	4	6	0	0	1	2	.667
Kennedy	2B	4	8	4	4	1	0	0	3	.500
Fullmer	DH	3	7	1	2	1	0	0	0	.286
Gil	2B	2	5	1	4	0	0	0	1	.800
Ochoa	RF	1	0	0	0	0	0	0	0	—
Figgins	DH	1	0	1	0	0	0	0	0	—
NEW YORK										
TOTALS		4	135	25	38	4	0	7	24	.281
Posada	C	4	17	2	4	0	0	1	3	.235
Soriano	2B	4	17	2	2	1	0	1	2	.118
Jeter	SS	4	16	6	8	3	0	2	3	.500
Williams	CF	4	15	4	5	1	0	1	3	.333
Giambi	1B-DH	4	14	5	5	0	0	1	3	.357
Ventura	3B	4	14	1	4	2	0	0	4	.286
Rivera	LF	4	12	2	3	0	0	0	3	.250
Mondesi	RF	4	12	1	3	0	0	0	1	.250
Johnson	1B-DH	3	11	1	2	0	0	0	1	.182
White	LF	4	3	1	1	0	0	1	1	.333
Vander Wal	LF	2	2	0	0	0	0	0	0	.000
Coomer	DH	1	2	0	1	0	0	0	0	.500
Spencer	LF	1	0	0	0	0	0	0	0	—
Wilson	PR	1	0	0	0	0	0	0	0	—
MINNESOTA										
TOTALS		5	179	27	52	15	2	5	23	.291
Guzman	SS	5	21	5	6	2	0	1	2	.286
Koskie	3B	5	21	3	3	0	1	1	5	.143
Hunter	CF	5	20	4	6	4	0	0	2	.300
Jones	LF	5	20	3	5	3	0	0	1	.250
Mientkiewicz	1B	5	20	3	5	0	0	2	4	.250
Pierzynski	C	5	16	4	7	0	1	1	4	.438
Cuddyer	RF	5	13	5	5	1	0	0	1	.385
Ortiz	DH	4	13	0	3	2	0	0	2	.231
Rivas	2B	4	12	2	3	1	0	0	0	.250
LeCroy	DH	3	9	1	4	0	0	0	1	.444
Hocking	RF-2B	3	6	0	3	1	0	0	1	.500
Kielty	RF-CF-DH	3	4	0	0	0	0	0	0	.000
Mohr	RF-LF	4	2	1	2	1	0	0	1	1.000
Prince	C	1	2	0	0	0	0	0	0	.000
OAKLAND										
TOTALS		5	184	26	53	13	1	8	25	.288
Chavez	3B	5	21	3	8	0	0	1	5	.381
Durham	DH	5	21	7	7	3	0	2	2	.333
Justice	LF	5	21	2	5	1	1	0	4	.238
Tejada	SS	5	21	3	3	1	0	1	4	.143
Dye	RF	5	20	3	8	2	0	1	1	.400
Ellis	2B	5	19	1	7	2	0	1	4	.368
Long	CF	5	18	3	3	0	0	1	1	.167
Hernandez	C	5	17	0	1	0	0	0	0	.059
Hatteberg	1B	5	14	5	7	2	0	1	3	.500
Velarde	1B-2B	4	5	1	3	1	0	0	1	.600
Piatt	PH	3	3	0	1	1	0	0	0	.333
Mabry	1B-RF	2	2	0	0	0	0	0	0	.000
Byrnes	LF	2	1	0	0	0	0	0	0	.000
Myers	C	2	1	0	0	0	0	0	0	.000
Saenz	1B	1	0	0	0	0	0	0	0	—

AMERICAN LEAGUE CHAMPIONSHIP

NAME	POS	G	AB	R	H	2B	3B	HR	RBI	BA
ANAHEIM										
TOTALS		5	171	29	49	5	2	8	26	.287
Erstad	CF	5	22	4	8	0	0	1	2	.364
Eckstein	SS	5	21	1	6	0	0	0	2	.286
Anderson	LF	5	20	3	5	1	0	1	3	.250
Glaus	3B	5	19	4	6	0	1	2	4	.316
Spiezio	1B	5	17	5	6	2	0	1	5	.353
B. Molina	C	5	14	0	3	0	0	0	2	.214
Salmon	RF	5	14	3	3	0	0	0	0	.214
Kennedy	2B	4	14	5	5	0	0	3	5	.357
Fullmer	DH	4	12	2	4	0	1	0	4	.333
Wooten	DH	3	8	1	2	0	0	0	1	.250
Ochoa	RF	4	4	2	0	0	0	0	0	.000
Palmiero	RF	2	2	0	0	0	0	0	0	.000
Gil	2B	1	2	0	0	0	0	0	0	.000
Figgins	PR	3	1	2	1	0	0	0	1	1.000
J. Molina	C	3	1	0	0	0	0	0	0	.000
MINNESOTA										
TOTALS		5	160	12	37	9	0	0	11	.231
Jones	LF	5	20	0	2	1	0	0	2	.100
Koskie	3B	5	18	3	5	2	0	0	2	.278
Mientkiewicz	1B	5	18	1	5	1	0	0	2	.278
Guzman	SS	5	18	1	3	0	0	0	1	.167
Hunter	CF	5	18	3	3	2	0	0	0	.167
Ortiz	DH	5	16	0	5	1	0	0	2	.313
Pierzynski	C	5	16	1	4	1	0	0	2	.250
Mohr	RF-CF	5	12	3	5	1	0	0	0	.417
Rivas	2B	5	12	0	3	0	0	0	1	.250
Cuddyer	RF	3	5	0	1	0	0	0	0	.200
Kielty	DH-RF	4	3	0	0	0	0	0	0	.000
LeCroy	DH	1	3	0	1	0	0	0	1	.333
Prince	C	1	1	0	0	0	0	0	0	.000
Lamb	2B	2	0	0	0	0	0	0	0	

COMPOSITE PITCHING

NAME	G	IP	H	BB	SO	W	L	SV	ERA
ANAHEIM									
TOTALS	4	35	38	16	25	3	1	2	6.17
Washburn	2	12	12	3	4	1	0	0	3.75
Rodriguez	3	5.2	2	8	2	0	0	0	3.18
Appier	1	5	5	3	3	0	0	0	5.40
Percival	3	3.1	6	0	4	0	0	2	5.40
Lackey	1	3	3	1	3	0	0	0	0.00
Ortiz	1	2.2	3	4	1	0	0	0	20.25
Donnelly	3	2	3	1	2	0	0	0	13.50
Weber	2	1	2	2	0	0	1	0	18.00
Schoenweis	3	0.1	2	0	0	0	0	0	27.00
NEW YORK									
TOTALS	4	34	56	7	18	1	3	1	8.21
Hernandez	2	6.1	5	0	7	0	1	0	2.84
Clemens	1	5.2	8	3	5	0	0	0	6.35
Wells	1	4.2	10	0	0	0	1	0	15.43
Mussina	1	4	6	0	2	0	0	0	9.00
Pettitte	1	3	8	0	1	0	0	0	12.00
Karsay	4	2.2	3	0	1	1	0	0	6.75
Stanton	3	2.2	6	1	1	0	0	0	10.13
Weaver	2	2.2	4	3	1	0	0	0	6.75
Mendoza	2	1.1	5	0	0	0	0	0	13.50
Rivera	1	1	1	0	0	0	0	1	0.00
MINNESOTA									
TOTALS	5	44	53	12	34	3	2	1	4.50
Radke	2	11.2	14	1	7	2	0	0	1.54
Milton	1	7	6	3	1	0	0	0	2.57
Reed	1	5	6	2	8	0	1	0	7.20
Lohse	2	4	2	0	5	0	0	0	0.00
Mays	1	3.2	9	2	1	0	1	0	14.73
Romero	3	3.1	3	1	2	0	0	0	0.00
Santana	2	3	3	2	2	0	0	0	6.00
Hawkins	3	2.1	0	0	5	0	0	0	0.00
Guardado	2	2	5	1	1	0	0	1	13.50
Fiore	1	1.1	4	2	0	0	0	0	20.25
Jackson	1	0.2	1	0	0	0	0	0	0.00
OAKLAND									
TOTALS	5	44	52	14	42	2	3	1	4.50
Mulder	2	13	14	3	12	1	1	0	2.08
Hudson	2	8.2	13	4	8	0	1	0	6.23
Zito	1	6	5	4	8	0	1	0	4.50
Lilly	2	4	10	1	3	0	1	0	13.50
Bradford	2	3	1	0	1	0	0	0	0.00
Koch	3	3	5	2	3	0	0	1	9.00
Rincon	2	3	0	2	0	0	0	0	0.00
Bowie	1	1.1	0	0	0	0	0	0	0.00
Lidle	1	1	2	0	0	0	0	0	9.00
Mecir	1	1	0	2	0	0	0	0	0.00
ANAHEIM									
TOTALS	5	44	37	7	38	4	1	2	2.45
Appier	2	10.1	10	4	3	0	1	0	3.48
Lackey	1	7	3	0	7	1	0	0	0.00
Washburn	1	7	6	0	7	0	0	0	1.29
Ortiz	1	5.1	10	1	3	1	0	0	5.06
Rodriguez	3	4.1	2	2	7	2	0	0	0.00
Percival	3	3.1	0	0	3	0	0	2	0.00
Donnelly	3	3.1	3	0	5	0	0	0	8.10
Weber	3	2.2	3	0	3	0	0	0	3.38
Schoeneweis	1	0.2	0	0	0	0	0	0	0.00
MINNESOTA									
TOTALS	5	42	49	9	26	1	4	1	5.57
Mays	2	13.1	12	0	3	1	0	0	2.02
Radke	1	6.2	5	1	4	0	1	0	2.70
Milton	1	6	6	7	6	0	0	0	1.50
Reed	1	5.1	8	0	0	0	1	0	6.75
Santana	4	3.1	4	0	4	0	1	0	10.80
Romero	4	2	4	2	3	0	1	0	22.50
Hawkins	4	1.1	4	1	1	0	0	0	20.25
Jackson	3	1	5	2	2	0	0	0	27.00
Wells	2	1	2	0	2	0	0	0	9.00
Guardado	1	1	0	0	1	0	0	1	0.00
Lohse	1	1	1	0	0	0	0	0	0.00

ATLANTA — 1st 101-59 .631 — BOBBY COX

Name	G by Pos	B	AGE	G	AB	R	H	2B	3B	HR	RBI	BB	SO	SB	BA	SA
TOTALS			31	161	5495	708	1428	280	25	164	669	558	1028	76	.260	.409
Julio Franco	1B95	R	43	125	338	51	96	13	1	6	30	39	75	5	.284	.382
Mark DeRosa (NJ)	2B32 SS19 OF7 3B4	R	27	72	212	24	63	9	2	5	23	12	24	2	.297	.429
Rafael Furcal	SS150 2B4	B	24	154	636	95	175	31	8	8	47	43	114	27	.275	.387
Vinny Castilla	3B139	R	34	143	543	56	126	23	2	12	61	22	69	4	.232	.348
Gary Sheffield	OF127	R	33	135	492	82	151	26	0	25	84	72	53	12	.307	.512
Andruw Jones	OF154	R	25	154	560	91	148	34	0	35	94	83	135	8	.264	.513
Chipper Jones	OF152	B	30	158	548	90	179	35	1	26	100	107	89	8	.327	.536
Javy Lopez	C103	R	31	109	347	31	81	15	0	11	52	26	63	0	.233	.372
Keith Lockhart	2B89 3B1	L	37	128	296	34	64	13	3	5	32	27	50	0	.216	.331
Darren Bragg	OF63	L	32	109	212	34	57	15	2	3	15	24	52	5	.269	.401
Wes Helms (RJ)	1B45 3B24 OF9	R	26	85	210	20	51	16	0	6	22	11	57	1	.243	.405
Henry Blanco	C79	R	30	81	221	17	45	9	1	6	22	20	51	0	.204	.335
Matt Franco	1B51 OF4	L	32	81	205	25	65	15	4	6	30	27	31	1	.317	.517
Marcus Giles (NJ)	2B52 3B8	R	24	68	213	27	49	10	1	8	23	25	41	1	.230	.399
Jesse Garcia	2B21 SS5 OF4	R	28	39	61	6	12	1	0	0	5	0	14	0	.197	.213
B.J. Surhoff (KJ)	1B11 OF9	L	37	25	75	5	22	5	0	0	9	9	5	1	.293	.360
Steve Torrealba	C12	R	24	13	17	1	1	0	0	0	1	3	4	0	.059	.059
Ryan Langerhans	OF1	L	22	1	1	0	0	0	0	0	0	0	0	0	.000	.000
George Lombard (LJ) 26, Dave Martinez (XJ) 37																

NAME	T	AGE	W	L	PCT	SV	G	GS	CG	IP	H	BB	SO	SHO	ERA
TOTALS		31	101	59	.631	57	161	161	3	1467	1302	554	1058	15	3.13
Kevin Millwood	R	27	18	8	.692	0	35	34	1	217	186	65	178	1	3.24
Tom Glavine	L	36	18	11	.621	0	36	36	2	225	210	78	127	1	2.96
Greg Maddux	R	36	16	6	.727	0	34	34	0	199	194	45	118	0	2.62
Damian Moss	L	25	12	6	.667	0	33	29	0	179	140	89	111	0	3.42
Jason Marquis	R	23	8	9	.471	0	22	22	0	114	127	49	84	0	5.04
Chris Hammond	L	36	7	2	.778	0	63	0	0	76	53	31	63	0	0.95
Mike Remlinger	L	36	7	3	.700	0	73	0	0	68	48	28	69	0	1.99
John Smoltz	R	35	3	2	.600	55	75	0	0	80	59	24	85	0	3.25
Kerry Ligtenberg	R	31	3	4	.429	0	52	0	0	67	52	33	51	0	2.97
Trey Hodges	R	24	2	0	1.000	0	4	0	0	12	16	2	6	0	5.40
Kevin Gryboski	R	28	2	1	.667	0	57	0	0	52	50	37	33	0	3.48
Darren Holmes	R	36	2	2	.500	1	55	0	0	55	41	12	47	0	1.81
Tim Spooneybarger	R	22	1	0	1.000	1	51	0	0	51	38	26	33	0	2.63
John Foster (IL)	L	24	1	0	1.000	0	5	0	0	5	6	6	6	0	10.80
Albie Lopez	R	30	1	4	.200	0	30	4	0	56	66	18	39	0	4.37
Joey Dawley	R	30	0	0	—	0	1	0	0	0.1	0	0	1	0	0.00
John Ennis	R	22	0	0	—	0	1	1	0	4	5	3	1	0	4.50
Andy Pratt	L	22	0	0	—	0	1	0	0	1	1	4	1	0	6.75
Aaron Small	R	30	0	0	—	0	1	0	0	0.1	2	2	1	0	27.00
Jung Bong	L	21	0	1	.000	0	6	0	0	6	8	2	4	0	7.50

MONTREAL — 2nd 83-79 .512 19 — FRANK ROBINSON

Name	G by Pos	B	AGE	G	AB	R	H	2B	3B	HR	RBI	BB	SO	SB	BA	SA
TOTALS			29	162	5479	735	1432	300	36	162	695	575	1104	118	.261	.418
Andres Galarraga	1B89	R	41	104	292	30	76	12	0	9	40	30	81	2	.260	.394
Jose Vidro	2B152	R	27	152	604	103	190	43	3	19	96	60	70	3	.315	.490
Orlando Cabrera	SS153	R	27	153	563	64	148	43	1	7	56	48	53	25	.263	.380
Fernando Tatis	3B99	R	27	114	381	43	87	18	1	15	55	35	90	2	.228	.399
Vladimir Guerrero	OF161	R	26	161	614	106	206	37	2	39	111	84	70	40	.336	.593
Brad Wilkerson	OF129 1B23	L	25	153	507	92	135	27	8	20	59	81	161	7	.266	.469
Troy O'Leary	OF70	L	32	97	273	27	78	12	2	3	37	34	47	1	.286	.377
Michael Barrett	C110 1B6	R	25	117	376	41	99	20	1	12	49	40	65	6	.263	.418
Jose Macias	OF49 3B22 2B6 SS4	B	30	90	231	33	59	17	1	7	33	13	44	5	.255	.429
Brian Schneider	C65 OF2	L	25	73	207	21	57	19	2	5	29	21	41	1	.275	.459
Wil Cordero	OF28 1B10	R	30	66	143	21	39	9	0	6	29	17	26	2	.273	.462
Lee Stevens	1B58	L	34	63	205	28	39	6	1	10	31	39	57	1	.190	.376
Mike Mordecai	3B28 2B4 1B3 SS3 OF1	R	34	55	74	9	15	4	0	0	4	8	14	1	.203	.257
Wilton Guerrero	OF12 2B7 3B2	R	27	44	62	3	12	1	0	0	1	1	9	0	.194	.210
Endy Chavez	OF35	L	24	36	125	20	37	8	5	1	9	5	16	3	.296	.464
Chris Truby	3B31 1B2 OF1	R	28	35	105	12	27	5	2	2	7	5	27	1	.257	.400
Matt Cepicky	OF17	L	24	32	74	7	16	3	0	3	15	4	21	0	.216	.378
Peter Bergeron	OF31	L	24	31	123	24	23	3	2	0	7	22	44	10	.187	.244
Henry Mateo	2B3 SS2	B	25	22	23	1	4	0	1	0	0	2	6	2	.174	.261
Henry Rodriguez		L	34	20	20	1	1	0	0	0	3	4	8	0	.050	.050
Jamey Carroll	3B13 SS3 2B1	R	28	16	71	16	22	5	3	1	6	4	12	1	.310	.507
Cliff Floyd	OF13	L	29	15	53	7	11	2	0	3	4	3	10	1	.208	.415
Lou Collier	OF7 2B2 3B1	R	28	13	11	3	1	1	0	0	1	3	1	0	.091	.182

NAME	T	AGE	W	L	PCT	SV	G	GS	CG	IP	H	BB	SO	SHO	ERA
TOTALS		28	83	79	.512	39	162	162	9	1453	1475	508	1088	3	3.97
Tomo Ohka	R	26	13	8	.619	0	32	31	2	193	194	45	118	0	3.18
Tony Armas	R	24	12	12	.500	0	29	29	0	164	149	78	131	0	4.44
2 Bartolo Colon	R	29	10	4	.714	0	17	17	4	117	115	39	74	1	3.31
Javier Vazquez	R	26	10	13	.435	0	34	34	2	230	243	49	179	3	3.91
Joey Eischen	L	32	6	1	.857	2	59	0	0	54	43	18	51	0	1.34
T.J. Tucker	R	23	6	3	.667	4	57	0	0	61	69	31	42	0	4.11
Zach Day	R	24	4	1	.800	1	9	2	0	37	28	15	25	0	3.62
Scott Stewart	L	26	4	2	.667	17	67	0	0	64	49	22	67	0	3.09
Masato Yoshii	R	37	4	9	.308	0	31	20	1	131	143	32	74	0	4.11
1 Carl Pavano	R	26	3	8	.273	0	15	14	0	74	98	31	51	0	6.30
1 Graeme Lloyd	L	35	2	3	.400	5	41	0	0	31	41	8	17	0	5.87
2 Bruce Chen	L	25	2	3	.400	0	15	5	0	37	47	23	43	0	6.99
Matt Herges	R	32	2	5	.286	6	62	0	0	65	80	26	50	0	4.04
Tim Drew	R	23	1	1	.500	0	7	1	0	16	12	2	10	0	2.81
2 Sun-Woo Kim	R	24	1	0	1.000	0	4	3	0	20	18	7	11	0	0.89
Dan Smith	R	26	1	1	.500	2	33	0	0	47	34	21	34	0	3.47
2 Jim Brower	R	29	1	2	.333	0	30	0	0	41	39	22	33	0	4.83
Britt Reames	R	28	1	4	.200	0	42	6	0	68	70	38	76	0	5.03
Ed Vosberg	L	40	0	0	—	0	4	0	0	1	3	1	0	0	18.00
1 Scott Strickland	R	26	0	0	—	0	1	0	0	1	0	0	2	0	0.00
Scott Downs (EJ) 26															

PHILADELPHIA — 3rd 80-81 .497 21.5 — LARRY BOWA

Name	G by Pos	B	AGE	G	AB	R	H	2B	3B	HR	RBI	BB	SO	SB	BA	SA
TOTALS			27	161	5523	710	1428	325	41	165	676	640	1095	104	.259	.422
Travis Lee	1B148	L	27	153	536	59	142	26	2	13	70	54	104	5	.265	.394
Marlon Anderson	2B143	L	28	145	539	64	139	30	6	8	48	42	71	5	.258	.380
Jimmy Rollins	SS152 2B1	B	23	154	637	82	156	33	10	11	60	54	103	31	.245	.380
Scott Rolen	3B100	R	27	100	375	52	97	21	4	17	66	52	68	5	.259	.472
Bobby Abreu	OF154	L	28	157	572	102	176	50	6	20	85	104	117	31	.308	.521
Doug Glanville	OF117	R	31	144	422	49	105	16	3	6	29	25	57	19	.249	.344
Pat Burrell	OF157	R	25	157	586	96	165	39	2	37	116	89	153	1	.282	.544
Mike Lieberthal	C129	R	30	130	476	46	133	29	2	15	52	38	58	0	.279	.443
Ricky Ledee	OF51	L	28	96	203	33	46	13	1	8	23	35	50	1	.227	.419
Tomas Perez	2B50 3B14 SS13 1B3 P1	B	28	92	212	22	53	13	1	5	20	21	40	1	.250	.392
Jeremy Giambi	1B21 OF20	L	27	82	156	32	38	10	0	12	28	52	54	0	.244	.538
Jason Michaels	OF26 3B1	R	26	81	105	16	28	10	3	2	11	13	33	1	.267	.476
Placido Polanco	3B53	R	26	53	206	28	61	13	1	4	22	14	14	2	.296	.427
Todd Pratt	C34 1B2	R	35	39	106	14	33	11	0	3	16	24	28	1	.311	.500
John Mabry	1B1 OF1	L	31	21	21	1	6	0	0	0	3	1	5	0	.286	.286
Dave Hollins (IL)	1B5	B	36	14	17	1	2	0	0	0	0	0	3	0	.118	.118
Marlon Byrd	OF10	R	24	10	35	2	8	2	0	1	1		8	0	.229	.371
Johnny Estrada	C10	B	26	10	17	0	2	1	0	0	2	2	2	0	.118	.118
Nick Punto	2B1 SS1	B	24	9	6	0	1	0	0	0	0	0	3	0	.167	.167
Eric Valent	OF2 1B1	L	25	7	10	1	2	1	0	0	0	0	3	0	.200	.200

NAME	T	AGE	W	L	PCT	SV	G	GS	CG	IP	H	BB	SO	SHO	ERA
TOTALS		30	80	81	.497	47	161	161	5	1450	1381	570	1075	9	4.17
Vicente Padilla	R	24	14	11	.560	0	32	32	1	206	198	53	128	1	3.28
Randy Wolf	L	25	11	9	.550	0	31	31	3	211	172	63	172	2	3.20
Brandon Duckworth	R	26	8	9	.471	0	30	29	0	163	167	69	167	0	5.41
Terry Adams	R	29	7	9	.438	0	46	19	0	137	132	58	96	0	4.35
Carlos Silva	R	23	5	0	1.000	1	68	0	0	84	88	22	41	0	3.21
Rheal Cormier	L	35	5	6	.455	0	54	0	0	60	61	32	49	0	5.25
Joe Roa	R	30	4	4	.500	0	14	11	0	71	78	13	35	0	4.04
Robert Person (EJ-SJ)	R	32	4	5	.444	0	16	16	0	88	79	51	61	0	5.44
Brett Myers	R	21	4	5	.444	0	12	12	1	72	73	29	34	0	4.25
Jose Mesa	R	36	4	6	.400	45	74	0	0	76	65	39	64	0	2.97
2 Mike Timlin	R	36	3	3	.500	0	36	0	0	36	27	7	15	0	3.79
1 Cliff Politte	R	28	2	0	1.000	0	13	0	0	16	19	9	15	0	3.86
Eric Junge	R	25	2	0	1.000	0	4	1	0	13	14	5	11	0	1.42
2 Dan Plesac	L	40	2	1	.667	1	41	0	0	26	13	12	27	0	4.70
Hector Mercado	L	28	2	1	.500	0	31	3	0	39	32	25	40	0	4.62
Dave Coggin (SJ)	R	25	2	5	.286	0	38	7	0	77	65	51	64	0	4.68
Jose Santiago	R	27	1	3	.250	0	42	0	0	47	56	15	30	0	6.70
1 Doug Nickle	R	27	0	0	—	0	6	0	0	4	4	2	6	0	6.23
Tomas Perez	R	28	0	0	—	0	1	0	0	0.1	0	1	0	0	0.00
Ricky Bottalico (SJ)	R	32	0	0	.000	0	30	0	0	27	33	13	24	0	4.61
Turk Wendell (EJ) 35															

FLORIDA — 4th 79-83 .488 23 — JEFF TORBORG

Name	G by Pos	B	AGE	G	AB	R	H	2B	3B	HR	RBI	BB	SO	SB	BA	SA
TOTALS			29	162	5496	699	1433	280	32	146	653	595	1130	177	.261	.403
Derrek Lee	1B162	R	26	162	581	95	157	35	7	27	86	98	164	19	.270	.494
Luis Castillo	2B144	B	26	146	606	86	185	18	5	2	39	55	76	48	.305	.361
Alex Gonzalez (SJ)	SS42	R	25	42	151	15	34	7	1	2	18	12	32	3	.225	.325
Mike Lowell	3B159	R	28	160	597	88	165	44	0	24	92	65	92	4	.276	.471
Cliff Floyd	OF80	L	29	84	296	49	85	20	0	18	57	58	68	6	.287	.537
Preston Wilson	OF138	R	27	141	510	80	124	22	2	23	65	58	140	20	.243	.429
Kevin Millar	OF108 1B2 3B2	R	30	126	438	58	134	41	0	16	57	40	74	0	.306	.509
Charles Johnson	C82	R	30	83	244	18	53	19	0	6	36	31	61	0	.217	.369
Andy Fox	SS112 2B7 3B4 OF1	L	31	133	435	55	109	14	5	4	41	49	94	31	.251	.333
Eric Owens	OF121	R	31	131	385	44	104	15	5	4	37	31	33	26	.270	.366
Tim Raines	OF14	B	42	98	89	9	17	3	0	1	7	22	19	0	.191	.258
Mike Redmond	C80 1B2	R	31	89	256	19	78	15	0	2	28	21	34	0	.305	.398
Juan Encarnacion	OF67	R	26	69	263	34	69	11	3	8	34	20	50	12	.262	.418
Ramon Castro	C37	R	26	54	101	11	24	4	0	6	18	14	24	0	.238	.455
Homer Bush	2B12 SS4	R	29	40	54	7	12	0	0	0	5	3	13	2	.222	.222
Mike Mordecai	SS24 3B7 1B1	R	34	38	77	10	22	4	0	3	9	6	11	0	.286	.338
Pablo Ozuna	2B10 OF1	R	27	34	47	4	13	2	0	0	3	1	3	1	.277	.404
Marty Malloy	2B3 3B2	L	29	24	25	1	3	0	0	0	0	2	2	0	.120	.120
Brian Banks	OF8 1B3 1B1	B	31	20	28	3	9	1	0	1	6	6	6	0	.321	.464
Abraham Nunez	OF15	B	25	19	17	2	2	0	0	0	1	0	5	0	.118	.118

NAME	T	AGE	W	L	PCT	SV	G	GS	CG	IP	H	BB	SO	SHO	ERA
TOTALS		27	79	83	.488	36	162	162	11	1456	1449	631	1104	12	4.36
A.J. Burnett	R	25	12	9	.571	0	31	29	7	204	153	90	203	5	3.30
Julian Tavarez	R	29	10	12	.455	0	29	27	0	154	188	74	67	0	5.39
Brad Penny (AJ)	R	24	8	7	.533	0	24	24	1	129	148	50	93	1	4.66
Michael Tejera	L	25	8	8	.500	1	47	18	0	140	144	60	95	0	4.45
Vladimir Nunez	R	27	6	5	.545	20	77	0	0	98	80	37	73	0	3.41
Josh Beckett (RJ)	R	22	6	7	.462	0	23	21	0	108	93	44	113	0	4.10
1 Ryan Dempster	R	25	5	8	.385	0	18	18	3	120	126	55	87	0	4.79
Blaine Neal	R	24	3	0	1.000	0	32	0	0	33	32	14	33	0	2.73
Gary Knotts	R	25	3	1	.750	0	28	0	0	31	31	16	21	0	4.40
Armando Almanza (EJ)	L	29	3	2	.600	2	51	0	0	46	36	23	57	0	4.34
2 Carl Pavano	R	26	3	2	.600	0	22	8	0	62	76	14	41	0	3.73
1 Graeme Lloyd	L	35	2	2	.500	0	20	0	0	30	33	21	20	0	4.55
Hansel Izquierdo	R	25	2	2	1.000	0	31	0	0	34	38	12	21	0	5.35
Justin Wayne	R	23	2	3	.400	0	5	4	0	30	38	13	16	0	5.32
Braden Looper	R	27	2	5	.286	13	78	0	0	86	73	28	55	0	3.14
Toby Borland	R	33	1	0	1.000	0	15	0	0	14	5	11	5	0	5.27
Vic Darensbourg	L	31	1	2	.333	0	42	0	0	48	61	26	33	0	6.14
Nate Robertson	L	24	0	1	.000	0	3	1	0	7	13	4	9	0	11.88
Nate Teut	L	26	0	1	.000	0	1	0	0	7	13	3	4	0	9.82
Kevin Olsen	R	25	0	5	.000	0	17	8	0	56	57	31	38	0	4.53

NEW YORK — 5th 75-86 .466 26.5 — BOBBY VALENTINE

Name	G by Pos	B	AGE	G	AB	R	H	2B	3B	HR	RBI	BB	SO	SB	BA	SA
TOTALS			31	161	5496	690	1409	238	22	160	650	486	1044	87	.256	.395
Mo Vaughn	1B134	L	34	139	487	67	126	18	0	26	72	59	145	0	.259	.456
Roberto Alomar	2B147	B	34	149	590	73	157	24	4	11	53	57	83	16	.266	.376
Rey Ordonez	SS142	R	30	144	460	53	117	25	2	1	42	24	46	2	.254	.324
Edgardo Alfonzo	3B134	R	28	135	490	78	151	26	0	16	56	62	55	0	.308	.459
Jeromy Burnitz	OF140	L	33	154	479	65	103	15	0	19	54	58	135	10	.215	.365
Timo Perez	OF122	L	27	136	444	52	131	27	6	8	47	23	36	10	.295	.437
Roger Cedeno	OF132	B	27	149	511	65	133	19	2	7	41	42	92	25	.260	.346
Mike Piazza	C121	R	33	135	478	69	134	23	2	33	98	57	82	0	.280	.544
John Valentin	SS24 1B22 3B18 2B3	R	35	114	208	18	50	15	0	3	30	22	37	0	.240	.356
Joe McEwing	OF35 SS21 1B20 2B13 3B10	R	29	105	196	22	39	8	1	3	26	9	50	4	.199	.296
1 Jay Payton	OF82	R	29	87	275	33	78	6	3	8	31	21	34	4	.284	.415
Vance Wilson	C66 1B1	R	29	74	163	19	40	7	0	5	26	5	32	0	.245	.380
Tony Tarasco	OF29 1B7	L	31	60	96	15	24	5	0	6	15	8	13	2	.250	.490
Ty Wigginton	3B14 1B13 2B12 OF2	R	24	46	116	18	35	8	0	6	18	8	19	2	.302	.526
Mark Johnson	1B15 OF1	L	34	42	51	5	7	4	0	1	4	9	18	0	.137	.275
2 Raul Gonzalez	OF24	R	28	30	81	9	21	2	0	3	11	4	17	2	.259	.395
Marco Scutaro	2B12 SS6 3B3 OF1	R	26	27	36	2	8	0	1	1	6	0	11	0	.222	.361
Esix Snead	OF6	B	26	17	13	3	4	0	0	1	3	1	4	4	.308	.538
Jason Phillips	C7	R	25	11	19	4	7	0	0	1	3	1	1	0	.368	.526
2 Brady Clark	OF6	R	29	10	12	3	5	1	0	0	1	1	2	0	.417	.500
McKay Christensen	OF3	L	26	4	3	1	1	0	0	0	1	1	1	0	.333	.333
2 Mark Little	OF1	R	29	3	3	0	0	0	0	0	0	0	0	0	.000	.000
1 Gary Matthews		B	27	2	1	0	0	0	0	0	0	0	0	0	.000	.000

NAME	T	AGE	W	L	PCT	SV	G	GS	CG	IP	H	BB	SO	SHO	ERA
TOTALS		30	75	86	.466	36	161	161	9	1443	1408	543	1107	10	3.89
Al Leiter	L	36	13	13	.500	0	33	33	2	204	194	69	172	2	3.48
Pedro Astacio	R	32	12	11	.522	0	31	31	3	192	192	63	152	1	4.79
Steve Trachsel	R	31	11	11	.500	0	30	30	1	174	170	69	105	1	3.37
David Weathers	R	32	6	3	.667	0	71	0	0	77	69	36	61	0	2.91
2 Scott Strickland	R	26	6	9	.400	2	68	0	0	68	61	33	67	0	3.59
Jeff D'Amico	R	26	6	10	.375	0	29	22	1	146	152	37	101	1	4.94
Mark Guthrie	L	36	5	3	.625	1	68	0	0	48	35	19	44	0	2.44
1 Shawn Estes	L	29	4	9	.308	0	23	23	1	133	133	66	92	1	4.55
Grant Roberts (SJ)	R	24	3	1	.750	0	34	0	0	45	43	16	51	0	2.20
Mike Bacsik	L	24	3	2	.600	0	11	9	1	56	63	19	30	0	4.37
2 John Thomson	R	28	2	6	.250	0	9	9	0	54	65	17	31	0	4.31
Armando Benitez	R	29	1	0	1.000	33	62	0	0	67	46	25	79	0	2.27
Tyler Walker	R	26	1	0	1.000	0	5	1	0	11	11	5	7	0	5.91
2 Jason Middlebrook	R	27	1	0	1.000	0	3	3	0	16	13	7	14	0	3.94
Kane Davis (XJ)	R	27	1	1	.500	0	16	0	0	14	15	11	24	0	7.07
Jamie Cerda	L	23	0	0	—	0	32	0	0	26	22	14	21	0	2.45
1 Bobby Jones	R	30	0	0	—	0	12	0	0	17	20	11	11	0	5.29
Pedro Feliciano	L	25	0	0	—	0	6	0	0	6	9	1	4	0	7.50
Pat Strange	R	21	0	0	—	0	5	0	0	8	6	1	4	0	1.13
1 Bruce Chen	L	25	0	0	—	0	1	0	0	0.2	1	1	0	0	0.00
Jae Weong Seo	R	25	0	0	—	0	1	0	0	1	0	1	0	0	0.00
1 Pete Walker	R	33	0	0	—	0	1	0	0	1	1	1	1	0	9.00
2 Steve Reed	R	37	0	1	.000	0	24	0	0	26	23	4	14	0	2.08
Satoru Komiyama	R	36	0	3	.000	0	25	0	0	43	53	12	33	0	5.61
1 Mark Corey	R	27	0	0	—	0	10	0	0	10	10	8	9	0	4.50
John Franco (EJ) 41															

CENTRAL DIVISION

ST. LOUIS — 1st 97-65 .599 — TONY LA RUSSA

Name	G by Pos	B	AGE	G	AB	R	H	2B	3B	HR	RBI	BB	SO	SB	BA	SA
TOTALS			29	162	5505	787	1475	285	26	175	758	542	927	86	.268	.425
Tino Martinez	1B149	L	34	150	511	63	134	25	1	21	75	58	71	3	.262	.438
Fernando Vina	2B150	L	33	150	622	75	168	29	5	1	54	44	36	17	.270	.338
Edgar Renteria	SS152	R	26	152	544	77	166	36	2	11	83	49	57	22	.305	.439
1 Placido Polanco	3B78 SS13 2B6	R	26	94	342	47	97	19	1	5	27	12	27	3	.284	.389
J.D. Drew	OF120	L	26	135	424	61	107	19	1	18	56	57	104	8	.252	.429
Jim Edmonds	OF139	L	32	144	476	96	148	31	2	28	83	86	134	4	.311	.561
Albert Pujols	OF118 3B41 1B21 SS1	R	22	157	590	118	185	40	2	34	127	72	69	2	.314	.561
Mike Matheny	C106 1B1	R	31	110	315	31	77	12	1	3	35	32	49	1	.244	.317
Eli Marrero	OF106 C44 1B4	R	28	131	397	63	104	19	1	18	66	40	72	14	.262	.451
Kerry Robinson	OF76	L	28	124	181	27	47	7	4	1	15	11	29	7	.260	.359
Miguel Cairo	OF24 2B18 3B7 SS6 1B4	R	28	108	184	28	46	9	2	2	23	13	36	1	.250	.353
Eduardo Perez	OF35 1B10 3B6	R	32	96	154	22	31	9	0	10	26	17	36	0	.201	.455
Mike DiFelice	C61	R	33	70	174	17	40	11	0	4	19	17	42	0	.230	.362
2 Scott Rolen	3B55	R	27	55	205	37	57	8	4	14	44	20	34	3	.278	.561
So Taguchi	OF14	R	32	19	15	4	6	0	0	0	2	2	1	1	.400	.400
Ivan Cruz	1B7	L	34	17	14	2	5	0	0	1	3	1	3	0	.357	.571
Wilson Delgado	SS8	B	29	12	20	2	4	2	0	2	5	0	6	0	.200	.600
Mike Coolbaugh	3B4	R	30	5	12	0	1	0	0	0	0	1	3	0	.083	.083

NAME	T	AGE	W	L	PCT	SV	G	GS	CG	IP	H	BB	SO	SHO	ERA
TOTALS		31	97	65	.599	42	162	162	4	1446	1355	547	1009	9	3.70
Matt Morris	R	31	17	9	.654	0	32	32	1	210	210	64	171	1	3.42
Jason Simontacchi	R	28	11	5	.688	0	24	24	0	143	134	54	72	0	4.02
Woody Williams (UJ)	R	35	9	4	.692	0	17	17	1	103	84	25	76	0	2.53
2 Chuck Finley	L	39	7	4	.636	0	14	14	1	85	69	30	83	1	3.80
Gene Stechschulte	R	28	6	2	.750	0	29	0	0	32	27	17	21	0	4.78
Luther Hackman	R	27	5	4	.556	0	43	6	0	81	90	39	46	0	4.11
Andy Benes (KJ)	R	34	5	4	.556	0	18	17	1	97	80	51	64	0	2.78
Darryl Kile (DD)	R	33	5	4	.556	0	14	14	0	85	82	28	50	0	3.72
Dave Veres	R	35	5	8	.385	4	71	0	0	83	67	39	68	0	3.48
Travis Smith	R	29	4	2	.667	0	12	10	0	54	69	20	32	0	7.17
Mike Crudale	R	25	3	0	1.000	0	49	1	0	53	43	14	47	0	1.88
2 Jeff Fassero	L	39	3	0	1.000	0	16	0	0	18	16	5	12	0	3.00
2 Rick White	R	33	3	1	.750	0	20	0	0	22	13	3	14	0	0.82
Jason Isringhausen	R	29	3	2	.600	32	60	0	0	65	46	18	68	0	2.48
2 Jamey Wright	R	27	2	1	.667	0	15	15	0	15	15	12	8	0	4.80
Steve Kline (AJ)	L	29	2	1	.667	6	66	0	0	58	54	21	41	0	3.39
1 Mike Matthews	L	28	2	1	.667	0	43	0	0	42	40	22	32	0	3.89
Garrett Stephenson (XJ-LJ)	R	30	2	5	.286	0	12	10	0	45	48	25	34	0	5.40
Gabe Molina	R	27	1	0	1.000	0	12	0	0	11	6	9	4	0	1.59
1 Mike Timlin	R	36	1	3	.250	0	42	1	0	61	48	7	35	0	2.51
Bud Smith	L	22	1	5	.167	0	11	10	0	48	67	22	22	0	6.94
Matt Duff	R	27	0	0	—	0	7	0	0	8	8	4	0	0	4.76
Josh Pearce	R	24	0	0	—	0	3	3	0	13	20	8	1	0	7.62
1 Jose Rodriguez	R	27	0	0	—	0	1	0	0	0.1	4	2	0	0	54.00
2 Nerio Rodriguez	R	31	0	0	—	0	2	0	0	4	4	1	2	0	4.15
Kevin Joseph	R	25	0	1	.000	0	11	0	0	11	16	6	2	0	4.91
Rick Ankiel (EJ) 22															

HOUSTON — 2nd 84-78 .519 13 — JIMY WILLIAMS

Name	G by Pos	B	AGE	G	AB	R	H	2B	3B	HR	RBI	BB	SO	SB	BA	SA
TOTALS			31	162	5503	749	1441	291	32	167	719	589	1120	71	.262	.417
Jeff Bagwell	1B153	R	34	158	571	94	166	33	2	31	98	101	130	7	.291	.518
Craig Biggio	2B142 OF1	R	36	145	577	96	146	36	3	15	58	50	111	16	.253	.404
Julio Lugo (BW)	SS84	R	26	88	322	45	84	15	1	8	35	28	74	9	.261	.388
Geoff Blum	3B104 OF10 SS2 1B2 2B1	B	29	130	368	45	104	20	4	10	52	49	70	2	.283	.440
Richard Hidalgo	OF110	R	27	114	388	54	91	17	4	15	48	43	85	6	.235	.415
Lance Berkman	OF156	B	26	158	578	106	169	35	2	42	128	107	118	8	.292	.578
Daryle Ward	OF122	L	27	136	453	41	125	31	0	12	72	33	82	1	.276	.424
Brad Ausmus	C129	R	33	130	447	57	115	19	3	6	50	38	71	2	.257	.353
Jose Vizcaino	SS58 3B30 2B25 1B5	B	34	125	406	53	123	19	2	5	37	24	40	3	.303	.397
Orlando Merced	OF56 1B7 3B1	L	35	123	251	35	72	13	3	6	30	26	50	4	.287	.434
Brian Hunter (IL)	OF88	R	31	98	201	32	54	16	3	3	20	16	39	5	.269	.423
Gregg Zaun	C44	B	31	76	185	18	41	7	1	3	24	12	36	1	.222	.319
Morgan Ensberg	3B43	R	26	49	132	14	32	7	2	3	19	18	25	2	.242	.394
Jason Lane	OF38	R	25	44	69	12	20	3	1	4	10	10	12	1	.290	.536
Adam Everett	SS34	R	25	40	88	11	17	2	0	0	4	12	19	3	.193	.227
Alan Zinter	1B8 C1	B	34	39	44	5	6	2	0	2	3	0	19	0	.136	.318
2 Mark Loretta	3B10 SS6 2B3	R	30	21	66	10	28	4	0	2	8	9	5	1	.424	.576
Barry Wesson	OF15	R	25	15	20	1	4	0	1	0	1	1	5	0	.200	.300
1 Keith Ginter	3B4 SS1	R	26	7	5	1	1	1	0	0	0	2	1	0	.200	.400
Raul Chavez	C2	R	29	2	4	1	1	0	0	0	1	0	0	0	.250	.250

NAME	T	AGE	W	L	PCT	SV	G	GS	CG	IP	H	BB	SO	SHO	ERA
TOTALS		27	84	78	.519	43	162	162	2	1445	1423	546	1219	11	4.00
Roy Oswalt	R	24	19	9	.679	0	35	34	0	233	215	62	208	0	3.01
Wade Miller (ZJ)	R	25	15	4	.789	0	26	26	1	165	151	62	144	1	3.28
Carlos Hernandez (SJ)	L	22	7	5	.583	0	23	21	0	111	112	61	93	0	4.38
Octavio Dotel	R	28	6	4	.600	6	83	0	0	97	58	27	118	0	1.85
Kirk Saarloos	R	23	6	7	.462	0	17	17	1	85	100	27	54	1	6.01
Peter Munro	R	27	5	5	.500	0	19	14	0	81	89	23	45	0	3.57
Billy Wagner	L	30	4	2	.667	35	70	0	0	75	51	22	88	0	2.52
Dave Mlicki (UJ)	R	34	4	10	.286	0	22	16	0	86	101	34	57	0	5.34
2 Pedro Borbon	L	34	3	2	.600	1	56	0	0	38	41	19	39	0	5.50
Ricky Stone	R	27	3	3	.500	1	78	0	0	77	78	34	63	0	3.61
Brandon Puffer	R	26	3	3	.500	0	69	0	0	67	38	48	48	0	4.43
Tim Redding	R	24	3	6	.333	0	18	14	0	73	78	35	63	0	5.40
Shane Reynolds (XJ)	R	34	3	6	.333	0	13	13	0	74	80	26	47	0	4.86
Nelson Cruz	R	29	2	6	.250	0	43	5	0	78	90	29	61	0	4.48
Brad Lidge	R	25	1	0	1.000	0	6	1	0	9	12	9	12	0	6.23
Scott Linebrink	R	25	0	0	—	0	22	0	0	24	31	13	24	0	7.03
T.J. Mathews (AJ)	R	32	0	0	—	0	12	0	0	18	19	5	13	0	3.44
2 Tom Gordon	R	34	0	2	.000	0	15	0	0	19	15	6	17	0	3.32
Jeriome Robertson	L	25	0	0	—	0	11	0	0	10	13	5	6	0	6.52
Jim Mann	R	27	0	0	—	0	17	0	0	22	19	7	19	0	4.09
Hipolito Pichardo (EJ-VR)	R	32	0	1	.000	0	0	0	0	0.1	3	2	0	0	81.00
Doug Brocail (EJ) 35															

CINCINNATI — 3rd 78-84 .481 19 — BOB BOONE

Name	G by Pos	B	AGE	G	AB	R	H	2B	3B	HR	RBI	BB	SO	SB	BA	SA
TOTALS			28	162	5470	709	1386	297	21	169	678	583	1188	116	.253	.408
Sean Casey	1B108	L	27	120	425	56	111	25	0	6	42	43	47	2	.261	.362
Todd Walker	2B154	L	29	155	612	79	183	42	3	11	64	50	81	8	.299	.431
Barry Larkin	SS135	R	38	145	507	72	124	37	2	7	47	44	57	13	.245	.367
Aaron Boone	3B154 SS16	R	29	162	606	83	146	38	2	26	87	56	111	32	.241	.439
Austin Kearns (LJ)	OF103	R	22	107	372	66	117	24	3	13	56	54	81	6	.315	.500
Ken Griffey Jr. (KJ)	OF55	L	32	70	197	17	52	8	0	8	23	28	39	1	.264	.449
Adam Dunn	OF118 1B44	L	22	158	535	84	133	28	2	26	71	128	170	19	.249	.454
Jason LaRue	C110	R	28	113	353	42	88	17	1	12	52	27	117	1	.249	.405
Reggie Taylor	OF25	L	25	135	271	37	73	15	4	9	38	14	79	11	.254	.429
2 Russell Branyan	OF25 1B18 3B16	L	26	84	217	34	53	9	1	16	39	34	86	3	.244	.516
1 Juan Encarnacion	OF82	R	26	83	321	43	89	11	2	16	51	26	63	9	.277	.474
1 Wilton Guerrero	2B10 SS7 3B3	B	27	59	78	9	19	1	1	0	4	6	13	2	.244	.282
Juan Castro (LJ)	SS25 2B17 1B1 3B1	R	30	54	82	5	18	2	0	1	7	11	18	0	.220	.329
1 Brady Clark	OF22	R	29	51	66	6	10	3	0	0	2	6	10	2	.152	.197
Ruben Mateo	OF24	R	24	46	86	11	22	6	0	2	7	6	20	0	.256	.395
Corky Miller	C38	R	26	39	114	9	29	10	0	3	15	9	20	0	.254	.421
Kelly Stinnett (EJ)	C30	R	32	34	93	10	21	5	0	3	13	15	25	2	.226	.376
2 Jose Guillen	OF27	R	26	31	109	12	27	3	0	4	16	7	18	1	.248	.385
Gookie Dawkins	SS21 2B3	R	23	31	48	2	6	2	0	0	2	3	18	1	.125	.167
Brandon Larson	OF9 3B5 1B2	R	26	23	51	8	14	2	0	4	6	3	18	0	.275	.549
Wily Mo Pena	OF4	R	20	13	18	1	4	0	0	1	1	0	9	0	.222	.389
1 Raul Gonzalez	OF6	R	28	10	23	4	6	0	0	1	2	1	2	2	.261	.304

NAME	T	AGE	W	L	PCT	SV	G	GS	CG	IP	H	BB	SO	SHO	ERA
TOTALS		29	78	84	.481	42	162	162	2	1454	1502	550	980	8	4.27
Jimmy Haynes	R	29	15	10	.600	0	34	34	0	197	210	81	126	0	4.12
Danny Graves	R	29	7	3	.700	32	68	4	0	99	99	25	58	0	3.19
Elmer Dessens	R	31	7	8	.467	0	30	30	0	178	173	49	93	0	3.03
Gabe White (GJ)	L	30	6	1	.857	0	62	0	0	54	56	10	41	0	2.98
Scott Sullivan	R	31	6	5	.545	1	71	0	0	79	93	31	78	0	6.06
Chris Reitsma	R	24	6	12	.333	0	32	21	1	138	144	45	84	1	3.64
Jose Rijo (SJ)	R	37	5	4	.556	0	31	9	0	77	89	20	38	0	5.14
2 Ryan Dempster	R	25	5	5	.500	0	15	15	1	89	102	38	66	0	6.19
Jose Acevedo	R	24	4	2	.667	0	5	5	0	24	28	12	14	0	7.23
Joey Hamilton	R	31	4	10	.286	1	39	17	0	125	136	50	85	0	5.27
Scott Williamson	R	26	3	4	.429	8	63	0	0	74	46	36	84	0	2.92
1 Jim Brower	R	29	2	0	1.000	0	32	0	0	39	38	10	24	0	3.89
John Riedling (SJ)	R	26	2	4	.333	0	33	0	0	47	39	26	30	0	2.70
2 Brian Moehler	R	30	2	4	.333	0	10	9	0	43	61	11	18	0	6.02
Jose Silva (EJ-SJ)	R	28	1	0	1.000	0	12	0	0	23	25	10	6	0	4.24
Luis Pineda (SJ)	R	27	1	3	.250	0	22	0	0	32	25	24	31	0	4.18
Jared Fernandez	R	30	1	3	.250	0	14	8	0	51	59	24	36	0	4.44
2 Shawn Estes	L	29	1	3	.250	0	6	5	0	38	38	17	17	0	7.71
Luke Hudson	R	25	0	0	—	0	6	6	0	30	38	11	17	0	4.50
Carlos Almanzar (BG)	R	28	0	0	—	0	12	0	0	14	8	6	10	0	2.31
3 Bruce Chen	L	25	0	2	.000	0	39	0	0	40	37	20	37	0	4.31

PITTSBURGH   4th 72-89 .447 24.5   LLOYD McCLENDON

Name	G by Pos	B	AGE	G	AB	R	H	2B	3B	HR	RBI	BB	SO	SB	BA	SA
TOTALS			27	161	5330	641	1300	263	20	142	610	537	1109	86	.244	.381
Kevin Young	1B144	R	33	146	468	60	115	26	1	16	51	50	101	4	.246	.408
Pokey Reese	2B117	R	29	119	421	46	111	25	0	4	50	41	81	12	.264	.352
Jack Wilson	SS143	R	24	147	527	77	133	22	4	4	47	37	74	5	.252	.332
Aramis Ramirez	3B131	R	24	142	522	51	122	26	0	18	71	29	95	2	.234	.387
Armando Rios (KJ)	OF56	L	30	76	208	20	55	11	0	1	24	16	39	1	.264	.332
Adrian Brown	OF71	B	28	91	208	20	45	10	2	1	21	19	34	6	.216	.298
Brian Giles	OF151	L	31	153	497	95	148	37	5	38	103	135	42	15	.298	.622
Jason Kendall	C143	R	28	145	545	59	154	25	3	3	44	49	29	15	.283	.356
Rob Mackowiak	OF106 3B26 2B3	L	26	136	385	57	94	22	0	16	48	42	120	9	.244	.426
Craig Wilson	OF75 1B42 C5	R	25	131	368	48	97	16	1	16	57	32	116	2	.264	.443
Abraham Nunez	2B46 SS24	B	26	112	253	28	59	14	1	2	15	27	44	3	.233	.320
Mike Benjamin	3B62 SS15 2B11 1B1 OF1	R	36	108	120	7	18	2	1	0	3	7	31	0	.150	.183
1 Chad Hermansen (IB)	OF60	R	24	65	194	22	40	11	1	7	15	17	68	7	.206	.381
Adam Hyzdu	OF50 1B1	R	30	59	155	24	36	6	0	11	34	21	44	0	.232	.484
Keith Osik	C27 3B4 1B3 2B1 OF1	R	33	55	100	6	16	3	0	2	11	6	25	0	.160	.250
Tony Alvarez	OF8	R	23	14	26	6	8	2	0	1	2	3	5	1	.308	.500
J.J. Davis	OF4	R	23	9	10	1	1	0	0	0	0	0	4	0	.100	.100
Humberto Cota	C7	R	23	7	17	2	5	1	0	0	0	1	4	0	.294	.353
Mendy Lopez		R	28	3	3	0	0	0	0	0	0	0	1	0	.000	.000
Pat Meares (HJ) 33																

NAME	T	AGE	W	L	PCT	SV	G	GS	CG	IP	H	BB	SO	SHO	ERA
		29	72	89	.447	47	161	161	2	1413	1447	572	920	7	4.23
Josh Fogg	R	25	12	12	.500	0	33	33	0	194	199	69	113	0	4.35
Kip Wells	R	25	12	14	.462	0	33	33	1	198	197	71	134	1	3.58
Kris Benson (EJ)	R	27	9	6	.600	0	25	25	0	130	152	50	79	0	4.70
Jimmy Anderson	L	26	8	13	.381	0	28	25	1	141	167	63	47	0	5.44
Scott Sauerbeck	L	30	5	4	.556	0	78	0	0	63	50	27	70	0	2.30
1 Sean Lowe	R	31	4	2	.667	0	43	1	0	69	85	34	57	0	5.35
Brian Boehringer	R	33	4	4	.500	1	70	0	0	80	65	33	65	0	3.39
Ron Villone	L	32	4	6	.400	0	45	7	0	93	95	34	55	0	5.81
Bronson Arroyo	R	25	2	1	.667	0	9	4	0	27	30	15	22	0	4.00
Salomon Torres	R	30	2	1	.667	0	5	5	0	30	28	13	12	0	2.70
Mike Lincoln	R	27	2	4	.333	0	55	0	0	72	80	27	50	0	3.11
Joe Beimel	L	25	2	5	.286	0	53	4	0	85	88	45	53	0	4.64
David Williams (SJ)	L	23	2	5	.286	0	9	9	0	43	38	24	33	0	4.98
Mike Williams	R	33	2	6	.250	46	59	0	0	61	54	21	43	0	2.93
1 Mike Fetters	R	37	1	0	1.000	0	32	0	0	30	25	18	29	0	3.26
Brian Meadows	R	26	1	6	.143	0	11	11	0	63	62	14	31	0	3.88
Al Reyes	R	31	0	0	—	0	15	0	0	17	9	7	21	0	2.65
Josias Manzanillo (EJ)	R	34	0	0	—	0	13	0	0	13	20	5	4	0	7.62
2 Duaner Sanchez	R	22	0	0	—	0	2	0	0	2	3	2	2	0	15.43
Ryan Vogelsong (EJ) 24															

CHICAGO   5th 67-95 .414 30   DON BAYLOR 34-49 .410   RENE LACHEMANN 0-1 .000   BRUCE KIMM 33-45 .423

Name	G by Pos	B	AGE	G	AB	R	H	2B	3B	HR	RBI	BB	SO	SB	BA	SA
TOTALS			30	162	5496	706	1351	259	29	200	676	585	1269	63	.246	.413
Fred McGriff	1B137	L	38	146	523	67	143	27	2	30	103	63	99	1	.273	.505
Mark Bellhorn	2B77 3B36 1B22 SS12 OF1	B	27	146	445	86	115	24	4	27	56	76	144	7	.258	.512
Alex Gonzalez	SS142	R	29	142	513	58	127	27	5	18	61	46	136	5	.248	.425
1 Bill Mueller (KJ)	3B101	B	31	103	353	51	94	19	4	7	37	51	41	0	.266	.402
Sammy Sosa	OF150	R	33	150	556	122	160	19	2	49	108	103	144	2	.288	.594
Corey Patterson	OF147	L	22	153	592	71	150	30	5	14	54	19	142	18	.253	.392
Moises Alou	OF124	R	35	132	484	50	133	23	1	15	61	47	61	8	.275	.419
Todd Hundley	C79	B	33	92	266	32	56	8	0	16	35	32	80	0	.211	.421
Roosevelt Brown	OF64	L	26	111	204	14	43	12	0	3	23	23	50	2	.211	.314
Chris Stynes	3B40 2B20	R	29	98	195	25	47	9	1	5	26	21	29	1	.241	.374
Joe Girardi	C88	R	37	90	234	19	53	10	1	1	13	16	35	1	.226	.291
Delino DeShields	2B41 OF1	L	33	67	146	20	28	6	1	3	10	21	38	10	.192	.308
Bobby Hill	2B55 SS1	B	24	59	190	26	48	7	2	4	20	17	42	6	.253	.374
Darren Lewis (VR)	OF47	R	34	58	79	7	19	3	1	0	7	7	11	1	.241	.304
Angel Echevarria	OF19 1B13	R	31	50	98	14	30	7	0	3	21	8	17	0	.306	.469
2 Chad Hermansen	OF21	R	24	35	43	3	9	3	0	1	3	5	14	0	.209	.349
Augie Ojeda	SS16 2B10 3B5	L	27	30	70	4	13	4	0	0	4	5	5	1	.186	.243
Hee-Seop Choi	1B22	L	23	24	50	6	9	1	0	2	4	7	15	0	.180	.320
1 Robert Machado	C21 1B1	R	29	22	58	5	16	4	0	1	5	5	11	0	.276	.397
Mike Mahoney	C16	R	29	16	29	2	6	3	0	0	3	1	10	0	.207	.310
Kevin Orie	3B12	R	29	13	32	4	9	3	0	0	5	1	4	0	.281	.375
Mario Encarnacion	OF2	R	26	3	7	0	0	0	0	0	0	2	3	0	.000	.000

NAME	T	AGE	W	L	PCT	SV	G	GS	CG	IP	H	BB	SO	SHO	ERA
		28	67	95	.414	23	162	162	11	1441	1373	606	1333	9	4.29
Kerry Wood	R	25	12	11	.522	0	33	33	4	214	169	97	217	1	3.66
Matt Clement	R	27	12	11	.522	0	32	32	3	205	162	85	215	2	3.60
Mark Prior	R	21	6	6	.500	0	19	19	1	117	98	38	147	0	3.32
Jon Lieber (EJ)	R	32	6	8	.429	0	21	21	3	141	153	12	87	0	3.70
1 Jeff Fassero	L	39	5	6	.455	0	57	0	0	51	65	22	44	0	6.18
Joe Borowski	R	31	4	4	.500	2	73	0	0	96	84	29	97	0	2.73
Kyle Farnsworth (BF)	R	26	4	6	.400	1	45	0	0	47	53	24	46	0	7.33
Carlos Zambrano (LJ)	R	21	4	8	.333	0	32	16	0	108	94	63	93	0	3.66
Juan Cruz	R	23	3	11	.214	1	45	9	0	97	84	59	81	0	3.98
Ron Mahay	L	31	2	0	1.000	0	11	0	0	15	13	8	14	0	8.59
Alan Benes	R	30	2	2	.500	0	7	7	0	39	42	12	32	0	4.35
Antonio Alfonseca	R	30	2	5	.286	19	66	0	0	74	73	36	61	0	4.00
1 Tom Gordon (SJ)	R	34	1	1	.500	0	19	0	0	24	27	10	31	0	3.42
Will Cunnane	R	28	1	1	.500	0	16	0	0	26	27	13	30	0	5.47
Pat Mahomes	R	31	1	1	.500	0	4	0	0	33	36	17	23	0	3.86
Steve Smyth	L	24	1	3	.250	0	7	6	0	26	34	10	16	0	9.35
Jason Bere (KJ)	R	31	1	10	.091	0	16	16	0	86	98	28	65	0	5.67
Francis Beltran	R	22	0	0	—	0	11	0	0	12	14	11	9	0	7.50
Jesus Sanchez	L	27	0	0	—	0	8	0	0	9	15	16	6	0	12.96
Scott Chiasson	R	24	0	0	—	0	9	0	0	5	11	6	9	0	23.14
Courtney Duncan	R	27	0	0	—	0	2	0	0	2	1	1	0	0	0.00
Donovan Osborne (UJ)	L	33	0	1	.000	0	16	0	0	19	16	19	13	0	6.19

MILWAUKEE   6th 56-106 .346 41   DAVEY LOPES 3-12 .200   JERRY ROYSTER 53-94 .361

Name	G by Pos	B	AGE	G	AB	R	H	2B	3B	HR	RBI	BB	SO	SB	BA	SA
TOTALS			30	162	5415	627	1369	269	29	139	597	500	1125	94	.253	.390
Richie Sexson	1B154	R	27	157	570	86	159	37	2	29	102	70	136	0	.279	.504
Eric Young	2B123 OF2	R	35	138	496	57	139	29	3	2	29	39	38	31	.280	.369
Jose Hernandez	SS149	R	32	152	525	72	151	24	2	24	73	52	188	3	.288	.478
1 Tyler Houston	3B72 1B1	L	31	76	255	25	77	15	2	7	33	14	41	1	.302	.459
Jeffrey Hammonds	OF125	R	31	128	448	47	115	26	5	9	41	52	86	4	.257	.397
Alex Sanchez	OF100	L	25	112	394	55	114	10	7	1	33	31	62	37	.289	.358
Geoff Jenkins (NJ)	OF66	L	27	67	243	35	59	17	1	10	29	22	60	1	.243	.444
Paul Bako	C76	L	30	87	234	24	55	8	1	4	20	20	46	0	.235	.329
Lenny Harris	OF16 3B14 1B12	L	37	122	197	23	60	8	2	3	17	14	17	4	.305	.411
Matt Stairs	OF84	L	34	107	270	41	66	15	0	16	41	36	50	2	.244	.478
Ron Belliard	2B49 3B42	R	27	104	289	30	61	13	0	3	26	18	46	2	.211	.287
1 Mark Loretta	3B47 SS12 1B5 2B3	R	30	86	217	23	58	14	0	2	19	23	32	0	.267	.359
1 Alex Ochoa	OF72	R	30	85	215	32	55	9	0	6	21	32	30	8	.256	.381
Ryan Thompson	OF51	R	34	62	137	16	34	9	2	8	24	7	38	1	.248	.518
2 Robert Machado	C48 1B2	R	29	51	153	14	39	10	1	2	17	12	30	0	.255	.373
Raul Casanova (EJ)	C28	B	29	31	87	3	16	1	0	1	8	10	18	0	.184	.230
2 Jorge Fabregas	C20	L	32	30	67	5	11	3	0	3	14	2	7	0	.164	.343
Jim Rushford	OF22	L	28	23	77	8	11	2	0	1	6	6	9	0	.143	.208
Ryan Christenson	OF21	R	28	22	58	5	9	4	0	1	5	3	16	0	.155	.276
1 Keith Ginter	3B21	R	26	21	76	6	18	8	0	1	8	15	14	0	.237	.382
Bill Hall	SS13 3B2	R	22	19	36	3	7	1	1	1	5	3	13	0	.194	.361
Marcus Jensen	C15	R	29	16	35	2	4	0	1	0	4	4	11	0	.114	.200
Israel Alcantara	OF7 1B2	R	29	16	32	3	8	1	0	2	5	0	6	0	.250	.469
1 Luis Lopez (LJ)	SS4	B	31	6	8	1	0	0	0	0	0	1	2	0	.000	.000

NAME	T	AGE	W	L	PCT	SV	G	GS	CG	IP	H	BB	SO	SHO	ERA
		28	56	106	.346	32	162	162	7	1432	1468	666	1026	4	4.73
Ben Sheets	R	23	11	16	.407	0	34	34	1	217	237	70	170	0	4.15
Glendon Rusch	L	27	10	16	.385	0	34	34	4	211	227	76	140	1	4.70
Jose Cabrera	R	30	6	10	.375	0	50	11	0	103	131	36	61	0	6.79
Ruben Quevedo	R	23	6	11	.353	0	26	25	1	139	159	68	93	1	5.76
Luis Vizcaino	R	27	5	3	.625	5	76	0	0	81	55	30	79	0	2.99
1 Jamey Wright (SJ)	R	27	5	13	.278	0	19	19	1	114	115	63	69	1	5.35
Ray King	L	28	3	2	.600	0	76	0	0	65	61	24	50	0	3.05
Wayne Franklin	L	28	2	1	.667	0	4	4	0	24	16	17	17	0	2.63
Valerio De Los Santos	L	29	2	3	.400	0	51	0	0	58	42	26	38	0	3.12
Chad Fox (EJ-SJ)	R	31	1	0	1.000	3	6	0	0	6	5	3	9	0	5.79
Jayson Durocher	R	27	1	1	.500	0	39	0	0	48	27	21	44	0	1.88
Mike Buddie	R	31	1	2	.333	0	25	0	0	40	46	21	28	0	4.54
Mike DeJean	R	31	1	5	.167	27	68	0	0	75	66	39	65	0	3.12
Nelson Figueroa	R	28	1	7	.125	0	30	11	0	93	96	37	51	0	5.03
Nick Neugebauer (SJ)	R	21	1	7	.125	0	12	12	0	55	56	44	47	0	4.72
Takahito Nomura	L	33	0	0	—	0	21	0	0	14	11	18	9	0	8.56
Matt Childers	R	23	0	0	—	0	5	0	0	13	8	6	6	0	12.00
Brian Mallette	R	27	0	0	—	0	5	0	0	5	6	3	6	0	10.80
2 Mike Matthews	L	28	0	0	—	0	4	0	0	3	7	2	4	0	4.50
Shane Nance	L	24	0	1	.000	0	9	0	0	4	3	7	4	0	4.26
Andrew Lorraine	L	29	0	1	.000	0	12	0	0	12	22	6	10	0	11.25
Dave Pember	R	24	0	1	.000	0	4	1	0	12	13	6	5	0	5.19
Everett Stull	R	30	0	3	.000	0	10	3	0	10	15	9	8	0	9.20
Jimmy Osting (SJ)	R	25	0	3	.000	0	3	3	0	12	18	10	7	0	7.50
Ben Diggins	R	24	0	4	.000	0	5	5	0	24	28	15	15	0	8.63
Curtis Leskanic (SJ) 34, Paul Rigdon (SJ) 26															

WEST DIVISION

ARIZONA   1st 98-64 .605   BOB BRENLY

Name	G by Pos	B	AGE	G	AB	R	H	2B	3B	HR	RBI	BB	SO	SB	BA	SA
TOTALS			32	162	5508	819	1471	283	41	165	783	643	1016	92	.267	.423
Erubiel Durazo (BW)	1B56 OF2	L	28	76	222	46	58	12	2	16	48	49	60	0	.261	.550
Junior Spivey	2B143	R	27	143	538	103	162	34	6	16	78	65	100	11	.301	.476
Tony Womack	SS149 OF1	L	32	153	590	90	160	23	5	5	57	46	80	29	.271	.353
Matt Williams (BL)	3B56	R	36	60	215	29	56	7	2	12	40	21	41	3	.260	.479
Danny Bautista (SJ)	OF39	R	30	40	154	22	50	6	2	6	23	11	21	4	.325	.500
Steve Finley	OF144	L	37	150	505	82	145	24	4	25	89	65	73	16	.287	.499
Luis Gonzalez	OF146	L	34	148	524	90	151	19	3	28	103	97	76	9	.288	.496
Damian Miller	C100	R	32	102	297	40	74	22	0	11	42	38	88	0	.249	.434
Mark Grace	1B98 P1	L	38	124	298	43	75	19	0	7	48	46	30	2	.252	.386
Quinton McCracken	OF97	B	32	123	349	60	108	27	3	6	40	32	68	5	.309	.458
Craig Counsell (ZJ)	3B94 SS22 2B13	L	31	112	436	63	123	22	1	2	51	45	52	7	.282	.351
Dave Dellucci	OF64	L	28	97	229	34	56	11	2	7	29	28	55	2	.245	.402
Chris Donnels (XJ)	3B26 1B1	L	35	74	80	5	19	4	1	3	16	10	14	0	.238	.425
Greg Colbrunn	1B40 3B5	R	32	72	171	30	57	16	2	10	27	13	19	0	.333	.626
Rod Barajas	C69 1B1	R	26	70	154	12	36	10	0	3	23	10	25	1	.234	.357
1 Jose Guillen	OF37	R	26	54	131	13	30	4	0	4	15	7	25	3	.229	.351
Alex Cintron	2B18 3B9 SS8	B	23	38	75	11	16	6	0	0	12	4	13	0	.213	.293
Chad Moeller	C35	R	27	37	105	10	30	11	1	2	16	17	23	0	.286	.467
Jay Bell (LJ)	3B6 1B5 2B2 SS2	R	36	32	49	3	8	1	0	2	11	5	9	0	.163	.306
3 Mark Little	OF12	R	29	15	22	8	6	1	0	1	0	2	3	0	.273	.364
Felix Jose	OF5	B	37	13	19	5	5	0	0	1	4	4	8	0	.263	.579
Lyle Overbay	1B12	L	25	10	10	1	0	0	0	0	0	0	1	0	.100	.100
Danny Klassen	3B2 SS1	R	26	4	3	0	1	0	0	0	0	0	0	0	.333	.333

NAME	T	AGE	W	L	PCT	SV	G	GS	CG	IP	H	BB	SO	SHO	ERA
		32	98	64	.605	40	162	162	14	1447	1361	421	1303	10	3.92
Randy Johnson	L	38	24	5	.828	0	35	35	8	260	197	71	334	4	2.32
Curt Schilling	R	35	23	7	.767	0	36	35	5	259	218	33	316	1	3.23
Rick Helling	R	31	10	12	.455	0	30	30	0	176	180	48	120	0	4.51
Byung-Hyun Kim	R	23	8	3	.727	36	72	0	0	84	64	26	92	0	2.04
Miguel Batista	R	31	8	9	.471	0	36	29	1	185	172	70	112	0	4.29
Mike Koplove	R	25	6	1	.857	0	55	0	0	62	47	23	46	0	3.36
Brian Anderson	L	30	6	11	.353	0	35	24	0	156	174	32	81	0	4.79
Mike Myers	L	33	4	3	.571	4	69	0	0	37	39	17	31	0	4.18
Eddie Oropesa	L	30	2	0	1.000	0	32	0	0	25	39	15	18	0	10.30
John Patterson	R	24	2	0	1.000	0	7	5	0	31	27	7	31	0	3.23
Matt Mantei (EJ)	R	28	2	2	.500	0	31	0	0	28	28	12	26	0	4.72
2 Mike Fetters	R	37	2	3	.400	0	35	0	0	25	28	19	24	0	5.11
Mike Morgan (KJ)	R	42	1	1	.500	0	29	0	0	34	41	9	13	0	5.29
1 Duaner Sanchez	R	22	0	0	—	0	2	0	0	2	3	1	2	0	0.00
Armando Reynoso (ZJ)	R	36	0	0	—	0	2	0	0	3	1	2	0	0	10.80
Mark Grace	R	38	0	0	—	0	1	0	0	1	1	0	0	0	9.00
Jose Parra	R	29	0	0	—	0	16	0	0	14	13	11	8	0	3.21
Greg Swindell (SJ)	L	37	0	2	.000	0	30	0	0	33	38	5	23	0	6.27
Bret Prinz	R	25	0	2	.000	0	20	0	0	13	23	10	10	0	9.45
Todd Stottlemyre (SJ-EJ)	R	37	0	2	.000	0	2	0	0	20	26	7	12	0	7.52

SAN FRANCISCO 2nd 95-66 .590 2.5 (Wild Card)   DUSTY BAKER

Name	G by Pos	B	AGE	G	AB	R	H	2B	3B	HR	RBI	BB	SO	SB	BA	SA
TOTALS			32	162	5497	783	1465	300	35	198	751	616	961	74	.267	.442
J.T. Snow	1B135	L	34	143	422	47	104	26	2	6	53	59	90	0	.246	.360
Jeff Kent	2B149 1B9	R	34	152	623	102	195	42	2	37	108	52	101	5	.313	.565
Rich Aurilia	SS131	R	30	133	538	76	138	35	2	15	61	37	90	1	.257	.413
David Bell	3B139 2B12 SS3 1B2	R	29	154	552	82	144	29	2	20	73	54	80	1	.261	.429
Reggie Sanders	OF137	R	34	140	505	75	126	23	6	23	85	47	121	18	.250	.455
Tsuyoshi Shinjo	OF117	R	30	116	362	42	86	15	3	9	37	24	46	5	.238	.370
Barry Bonds	OF135	L	37	143	403	117	149	31	2	46	110	198	47	9	.370	.799
Benito Santiago	C125	R	37	126	478	56	133	24	5	16	74	27	73	4	.278	.450
Damon Minor	1B44	L	28	83	173	21	41	6	0	10	24	24	34	0	.237	.445
Tom Goodwin	OF53	L	33	78	154	23	40	5	2	1	17	14	25	16	.260	.338
Ramon Martinez	SS40 2B17 1B4 OF3 3B2	R	29	72	181	26	49	10	2	4	25	14	26	2	.271	.414
Shawon Dunston	OF49 1B1 SS1	R	39	72	147	7	34	5	0	1	9	3	33	1	.231	.286
Pedro Feliz	3B44 SS1 OF1	R	27	67	146	14	37	4	1	2	13	6	27	0	.253	.336
Marvin Benard (KJ)	OF38	L	32	65	123	16	34	9	2	1	13	7	26	5	.276	.407
Yorvit Torrealba	C53	R	23	53	136	17	38	10	0	2	14	14	20	0	.279	.397
2 Kenny Lofton	OF44	L	35	46	180	30	48	10	3	3	9	23	22	7	.267	.406
1 Calvin Murray	OF10	R	30	11	12	0	0	0	0	0	0	1	2	0	.000	.000
2 Bill Mueller	3B3	B	31	8	13	0	2	0	0	0	1	1	1	0	.154	.154
Cody Ransom	SS3	R	26	7	3	2	2	0	0	0	1	1	1	0	.667	.667
Tony Torcato	OF3	L	22	5	11	0	3	1	0	0	0	0	2	0	.273	.364
Trey Lunsford	C3	R	23	3	3	0	2	1	0	0	1	0	1	0	.667	1.000

NAME	T	AGE	W	L	PCT	SV	G	GS	CG	IP	H	BB	SO	SHO	ERA
		29	95	66	.590	43	162	162	10	1437	1349	523	992	13	3.54
Kirk Rueter	L	31	14	8	.636	0	33	33	0	204	204	54	76	0	3.23
Russ Ortiz	R	28	14	10	.583	0	33	33	2	214	191	94	137	0	3.61
Ryan Jensen	R	26	13	8	.619	0	32	30	1	172	183	66	105	0	4.51
Jason Schmidt	R	29	13	8	.619	0	29	29	2	185	148	73	196	2	3.45
Livan Hernandez	R	27	12	16	.429	0	33	33	5	216	233	71	134	3	4.38
Tim Worrell	R	34	8	2	.800	0	72			72	55	30	55	0	2.25
Felix Rodriguez	R	29	8	6	.571	0	71	0	0	69	53	29	58	0	4.17
Robb Nen	R	32	6	2	.750	43	68	0	0	74	64	20	81	0	2.20
Chad Zerbe	L	30	2	0	1.000	0	50	0	0	56	52	21	26	0	3.04
Aaron Fultz	L	28	2	2	.500	0	43	0	0	41	47	19	31	0	4.79
Jay Witasick	R	29	1	0	1.000	0	44	0	0	68	58	21	54	0	2.37
Manny Aybar	R	30	1	0	1.000	0	15	0	0	14	16	3	11	0	2.51
Kurt Ainsworth	R	23	1	1	.333	0	6	4	0	26	22	12	15	0	2.10
2 Scott Eyre	L	30	0	0		0	21	0	0	11	11	7	7	0	1.59
Joe Nathan	R	27	0	0		0	4	0	0	4	1	4	2	0	0.00
Troy Brohawn	L	29	0	1	.000	0	11	0	0	6	5	1	3	0	6.35
Jason Christiansen (EJ)	L	32	0	1	.000	0	6	0	0	5	6	2	1	0	5.40

LOS ANGELES 3rd 92-70 .568 6   JIM TRACY

Name	G by Pos	B	AGE	G	AB	R	H	2B	3B	HR	RBI	BB	SO	SB	BA	SA
TOTALS			29	162	5554	713	1464	286	29	155	693	428	940	96	.264	.409
Eric Karros	1B142	R	34	142	524	52	142	26	1	13	73	37	74	4	.271	.399
Mark Grudzielanek	2B147	R	32	152	543	65	145	23	0	9	50	22	89	4	.271	.364
Cesar Izturis	SS128 2B1	B	22	135	439	43	102	24	2	1	31	14	39	7	.232	.303
Adrian Beltre	3B157	R	23	159	587	70	151	26	5	21	75	37	96	7	.257	.426
Shawn Green	OF156	L	29	158	582	110	166	31	1	42	114	93	112	8	.285	.558
Dave Roberts	OF117	L	30	127	422	63	117	14	7	3	34	48	51	45	.277	.365
Brian Jordan	OF125	R	35	128	471	65	134	27	3	18	80	34	86	2	.285	.469
Paul LoDuca	C137 1B18 OF9	R	30	149	580	74	163	38	1	10	64	34	31	3	.281	.402
Alex Cora	SS61 2B40	L	26	115	258	37	75	14	4	5	28	26	38	7	.291	.434
Marquis Grissom	OF102	R	35	111	343	57	95	21	4	17	60	22	68	5	.277	.510
Dave Hansen	1B27 3B11	L	33	96	120	15	35	6	0	2	17	14	22	1	.292	.392
1 Hiram Bocachica	OF22	R	26	65	112	14	24	6	0	4	9	5	19	1	.215	.446
Chad Kreuter	C41	R	37	41	95	8	25	5	0	2	12	10	31	1	.263	.379
Jeff Reboulet (XJ)	2B11 SS5 3B3	R	38	38	48	3	10	1	0	0	2	6	13	0	.208	.271
Mike Kinkade	1B11 OF8	R	29	37	50	7	19	5	0	2	11	4	10	1	.380	.600
2 Tyler Houston	1B32 3B2	L	31	35	65	9	13	5	1	0	7	2	21	0	.200	.308
Wilkin Ruan	OF5	R	23	12	11	2	3	1	0	0	3	0	2	0	.273	.364
2 Jolbert Cabrera	OF4 3B3 2B1	R	29	10	12	3	4	1	0	0	1	1	2	0	.333	.417
Joe Thurston	2B4	L	22	8	13	1	6	1	0	0	0	0	0	0	.462	.538
David Ross	C6	R	25	8	10	2	2	1	0	1	2	4	2	0	.200	.600
Luke Allen	OF3	L	23	6	7	2	1	1	0	0	0	1	1	0	.143	.286
Chin-Feng Chen	OF1	R	24	3	1	0	0	0	0	0	0	0	1	0	.000	.000

NAME	T	AGE	W	L	PCT	SV	G	GS	CG	IP	H	BB	SO	SHO	ERA
		33	92	70	.568	56	162	162	4	1458	1311	555	1132	15	3.69
Hideo Nomo	R	33	16	6	.727	0	34	34	0	220	189	101	193	0	3.39
Odalis Perez	L	25	15	10	.600	0	32	32	4	222	182	38	155	2	3.00
Kazuhisa Ishii	L	28	14	10	.583	0	28	28	0	154	137	106	143	0	4.27
Omar Daal	L	30	11	9	.550	0	39	23	0	161	142	54	105	0	3.90
Andy Ashby	R	34	9	13	.409	0	30	30	0	182	179	65	107	0	3.91
Giovanni Carrara	R	34	6	3	.667	1	63	0	0	91	83	32	56	0	3.28
2 Paul Shuey	R	31	5	2	.714	1	28	0	0	31	25	21	24	0	4.40
Paul Quantrill	R	33	4	4	.556	1	86	0	0	77	80	25	53	0	2.70
Eric Gagne	R	26	4	1	.800	52	77	0	0	82	55	16	114	0	1.97
Kevin Brown (EJ)	R	37	3	4	.429	0	17	10	0	64	68	23	58	0	4.81
Kevin Beirne	R	28	2	0	1.000	0	12	3	0	29	26	17	17	0	3.41
Jesse Orosco	L	45	1	2	.333	1	56	0	0	27	24	12	22	0	3.00
Guillermo Mota	R	28	1	3	.250	0	43	0	0	61	45	27	49	0	4.15
1 Terry Mulholland (XJ)	L	39	0	0		0	21	0	0	32	45	7	17	0	7.31
Jeff Williams	L	30	0	0		0	10	0	0	10	15	7	11	0	11.70
Bryan Corey	R	28	0	0		0	1	0	0	1	0	0	0	0	0.00
Victor Alvarez	L	25	0	1	.000	0	4	1	0	9	9	2	7	0	4.35
Robert Ellis	R	31	0	1	.000	0	3	0	0	3	6	0	0	0	10.12
Dennis Springer	R	37	0	0		0	1	0	0	1	1	2	1	0	6.75

COLORADO 4th 73-89 .451 25   BUDDY BELL 6-16 .273   CLINT HURDLE 67-73 .479

Name	G by Pos	B	AGE	G	AB	R	H	2B	3B	HR	RBI	BB	SO	SB	BA	SA
TOTALS			29	162	5778	778	1508	283	41	152	726	497	1043	103	.274	.423
Todd Helton	1B156	L	28	156	553	107	182	39	4	30	109	99	91	5	.329	.577
Brent Butler	2B72 3B33 SS13	R	24	113	344	55	89	18	4	9	42	10	40	2	.259	.413
Juan Uribe	SS155	R	22	155	566	69	136	25	7	6	49	34	120	9	.240	.341
Todd Zeile	3B139 P1	R	36	144	506	61	138	23	0	18	87	66	92	1	.273	.425
Larry Walker	OF123	L	35	136	477	95	161	40	4	26	104	65	73	6	.338	.602
Juan Pierre	OF149	L	24	152	592	90	170	20	5	1	35	31	52	47	.287	.343
1 Todd Hollandsworth	OF90	L	29	95	298	39	88	21	1	11	48	26	71	7	.295	.483
Gary Bennett	C90	R	30	90	291	26	77	10	2	4	26	15	45	1	.265	.354
Greg Norton	3B22 1B15 OF2	B	29	113	168	19	37	8	1	7	37	24	52	2	.220	.405
Terry Shumpert	2B60 OF8 SS3 3B1	R	35	106	234	30	55	12	1	6	21	21	41	4	.235	.372
Jose Ortiz (LJ)	2B53 3B1	R	25	65	192	22	48	7	1	1	12	16	30	2	.250	.313
1 Mark Little	OF36	R	29	61	105	20	21	5	2	0	5	13	28	2	.200	.286
1 Benny Agbayani	OF37	R	30	48	117	10	24	5	0	4	19	10	35	1	.205	.333
2 Jay Payton	OF44	R	29	47	170	36	57	14	4	8	28	8	20	3	.335	.606
2 Gabe Kapler	OF38	R	26	40	119	12	37	4	3	2	17	8	23	1	.311	.445
2 Sandy Alomar	C38	R	36	38	116	8	31	4	0	0	12	4	19	0	.267	.302
Bobby Estalella (SJ)	C38	R	27	38	112	17	23	8	0	8	25	14	33	0	.205	.491
Ben Petrick	OF16 C14	R	25	38	95	10	20	3	5	1	11	9	33	0	.211	.421
Jack Cust	OF18	L	23	35	65	8	11	2	0	1	8	12	32	1	.169	.246
Ross Gload	1B4 OF2	L	26	26	31	4	8	1	0	1	4	3	7	0	.258	.387
2 Jason Romano	2B12 SS5 OF3 3B1	R	23	18	37	9	12	0	0	0	1	3	11	4	.324	.378
Walt McKeel	C5	R	30	5	13	1	4	0	0	0	0	0	3	0	.308	.308

NAME	T	AGE	W	L	PCT	SV	G	GS	CG	IP	H	BB	SO	SHO	ERA
		29	73	89	.451	43	162	162	1	1427	1554	582	920	8	5.20
Jason Jennings	R	23	16	8	.667	0	32	32	0	185	201	70	127	0	4.52
Dennis Stark	R	27	11	4	.733	0	32	20	0	128	108	64	64	0	4.00
Denny Neagle	L	33	8	11	.421	0	35	28	1	164	170	63	111	0	5.26
1 John Thomson	R	28	7	8	.467	0	21	21	0	127	136	27	76	0	4.88
Mike Hampton	L	29	7	15	.318	0	30	30	0	179	228	91	74	0	6.15
Justin Speier (KJ)	R	28	5	1	.833	1	63	0	0	62	51	19	47	0	4.33
Shawn Chacon (TJ)	R	24	5	11	.313	0	21	21	0	119	122	60	67	0	5.73
Kent Mercker (HJ)	L	34	3	1	.750	0	58	0	0	44	55	22	37	0	6.14
Brian Fuentes	L	26	2	0	1.000	0	31	0	0	27	25	13	38	0	4.72
Aaron Cook	R	23	2	1	.667	0	9	5	0	36	41	13	14	0	4.54
1 Rick White	R	33	2	6	.250	0	41	0	0	41	49	18	27	0	6.20
Jose Jimenez	R	28	2	10	.167	41	74	0	0	73	76	11	47	0	3.56
Chris Nichting	R	36	1	1	.500	0	29	0	0	36	40	5	25	0	4.46
2 Sean Lowe	R	31	1	1	.500	0	8	0	0	10	16	7	7	0	8.71
Todd Jones	R	34	1	4	.200	1	79	0	0	62	88	23	73	0	4.70
2 Mark Corey	R	27	0	0		0	14	0	0	12	22	8	12	0	12.00
Mike James	R	34	0	0		0	13	0	0	11	5	10	5	0	5.56
Cory Vance	L	23	0	0		0	2	0	0	4	4	1	1	0	6.75
Todd Zeile	R	36	0	0		0	1	0	0	1	1	0	0	0	0.00
1 Dennys Reyes	L	25	0	0		0	43	0	0	40	43	24	30	0	4.24
2 Randy Flores	L	26	0	2	.000	0	8	0	0	9	8	7	7	0	9.53
Victor Santos	L	25	0	3	.000	0	24	2	0	26	41	22	25	0	10.38

Scott Elarton (SJ) 26, Pete Harnisch (EJ) 35

SAN DIEGO 5th 66-96 .407 32   BRUCE BOCHY

Name	G by Pos	B	AGE	G	AB	R	H	2B	3B	HR	RBI	BB	SO	SB	BA	SA
TOTALS			29	162	5515	662	1393	243	29	136	627	547	1062	71	.253	.381
Ryan Klesko	1B112 OF31	L	31	146	540	90	162	39	1	29	95	76	86	6	.300	.537
Ramon Vazquez	2B81 SS41 3B20	L	25	128	423	50	116	21	5	2	32	45	79	7	.274	.362
Deivi Cruz	SS147 1B1	R	29	151	514	49	135	28	2	7	47	22	58	2	.263	.366
Phil Nevin (BA)	3B71 1B36	R	31	107	407	53	116	16	0	12	57	38	87	4	.285	.413
Bubba Trammell	OF122	R	30	133	403	54	98	16	1	17	56	53	71	1	.243	.414
Mark Kotsay	OF147	L	26	153	578	82	169	27	7	17	61	59	89	11	.292	.452
Ron Gant	OF80	R	37	102	309	58	81	14	1	18	59	36	59	4	.262	.489
Wiki Gonzalez (WJ-PJ)	C54	R	28	56	164	16	36	8	1	2	20	27	24	0	.220	.299
Tom Lampkin	C94	L	38	104	281	32	61	10	1	10	37	38	59	4	.217	.367
2 Eugene Kingsale	OF82	B	25	89	216	27	60	10	3	2	28	20	47	9	.278	.380
Trenidad Hubbard	OF57 3B6 2B4	R	38	89	129	16	27	5	0	1	7	14	28	9	.209	.271
1 D'Angelo Jimenez	2B54 3B32 P1	B	24	87	321	39	77	11	4	3	33	34	63	4	.240	.327
Ray Lankford (LJ)	OF59	L	35	81	205	20	46	7	1	6	26	30	61	2	.224	.356
Julius Matos	2B49 3B17 SS4 OF3 1B2	R	27	76	185	19	44	3	0	2	19	9	33	1	.238	.286
Sean Burroughs (SJ)	3B48 2B13	L	21	63	192	18	52	5	1	1	11	12	30	2	.271	.323
2 Brian Buchanan	1B15 OF14	R	28	48	92	12	27	5	0	6	13	9	26	0	.293	.543
Mark Sweeney	1B11 OF5	L	32	48	65	3	11	4	0	0	4	4	19	0	.169	.262
Wil Nieves	C27	R	24	28	72	2	13	3	1	0	3	4	15	1	.181	.250
Cesar Crespo	OF7 2B4 3B4 SS1	B	23	25	29	5	5	3	1	0	3	3	11	0	.172	.241
Javier Cardona	C14	R	26	15	39	2	4	1	0	0	3	0	13	0	.103	.128
Kory DeHaan	OF9	L	25	12	11	1	1	0	0	0	0	1	6	0	.091	.091
Kevin Barker	1B6	L	26	7	19	0	3	0	0	0	1	1	8	0	.158	.158
Alex Pelaez	1B1 2B1 3B1	R	26	5	4	0	1	0	0	0	0	0	2	0	.250	.250

NAME	T	AGE	W	L	PCT	SV	G	GS	CG	IP	H	BB	SO	SHO	ERA
		28	66	96	.407	40	162	162	5	1436	1522	582	1108	10	4.62
Brian Lawrence	R	26	12	12	.500	0	35	31	2	210	230	52	149	2	3.69
Brett Tomko	R	29	10	10	.500	0	32	32	3	204	212	60	126	0	4.49
Bobby Jones	R	32	8	18	.467	0	19	18	0	108	134	21	60	0	5.50
Jake Peavy	R	21	6	7	.462	0	17	17	0	98	106	33	90	0	4.52
Oliver Perez	L	20	4	5	.444	0	16	15	0	90	71	48	94	0	3.50
Jeremy Fikac	R	27	4	7	.364	0	65	0	0	69	74	34	66	0	5.48
1 Alan Embree	L	32	3	4	.429	0	39	0	0	23	3	8	38	0	0.94
2 Mike Holtz	L	29	2	2	.500	0	33	0	0	21	18	21	19	0	4.71
1 Steve Reed	R	37	2	4	.333	1	40	0	0	41	33	10	36	0	1.98
Kevin Jarvis (EJ-PJ)	R	32	2	4	.333	0	7	7	0	35	36	10	24	0	4.37
Trevor Hoffman	R	34	2	3	.286	38	61	0	0	59	52	18	69	0	2.73
Jason Boyd	R	29	1	0	1.000	0	23	0	0	28	33	15	18	0	7.94
Tom Davey (SJ)	R	28	1	0	1.000	0	19	0	0	21	21	21	11	0	5.57
Mike Bynum	L	24	1	0	1.000	0	14	3	0	27	33	15	17	0	5.27
2 Doug Nickle	R	27	1	0	1.000	0	14	0	0	21	29	10	11	0	8.49
Rodney Myers	R	33	1	1	.500	0	14	0	0	21	29	10	11	0	5.91
Adam Eaton (EJ)	R	24	1	1	.500	0	6	6	0	32	29	17	25	0	5.40
Brandon Villafuerte	R	26	1	1	.333	1	31	0	0	32	29	12	25	0	1.41
Jonathan Johnson	R	27	1	2	.333	0	16	0	0	15	15	5	21	0	4.11
Clay Condrey	R	26	1	2	.333	0	7	0	0	27	20	8	16	0	1.69
1 Jason Middlebrook (GJ)	R	27	0	1	.000	0	27	2	0	51	59	40	39	0	5.09
Dennis Tankersley	R	23	0	4	.200	0	7	7	0	31	28	23	28	0	8.06
Brian Tollberg (EJ)	R	30	0	2	.167	0	12	11	0	62	88	19	33	0	6.13
2 Bobby Jones	L	30	0	0		0	26	0	0	10	10	7	7	0	6.52
Juan Moreno	L	27	0	0		0	4	0	0	6	6	10	3	0	7.50
David Lundquist (SJ)	R	29	0	0		0	3	0	0	2	6	3	0		16.87
Jason Shiell	R	25	0	0		0	3	0	0	1	2	1	1	0	27.00
Jason Pearson	L	26	0	0		0	1	0	0	1	1	1	0		0.00
D'Angelo Jimenez	R	24	0	0		0	1	0	0	1	0	0	0	0	0.00
Jose Nunez	L	25	0	0		0	1	0	0	1	0	0	0		0.00
1 Jason Kershner	L	25	0	1	.000	0	15	0	0	19	15	10	11	0	5.79
Kevin Walker (EJ)	L	25	0	0		0	11	0	0	6	12	5	11	0	6.52
Eric Cyr (SJ)	L	23	0	0		0	4	0	0	6	6	4	4	0	10.50
Matt DeWitt (SJ)	R	24	0	1	.000	0	9	0	0	8	9	10	0		1.23
J.J. Trujillo	R	26	0	0		0	4	0	0	4	9	3	0		10.12
Ben Howard	R	23	0	0		0	3	3	0	13	14	10	9	0	6.08
Kevin Pickford	L	27	0	2	.000	0	6	4	0	30	37	20	18	0	6.00

Robert Ramsay (IL) 28

LINE SCORES

Team	1	2	3	4	5	6	7	8	9	10	11	12	13	R	H	E

DIVISION SERIES: SAN FRANCISCO 3 : ATLANTA 2

Game 1   October 2 at Atlanta

SF	0	3	0	3	0	2	0	0	0					8	12	2
ATL	0	2	0	0	0	0	0	3	0					5	10	0

Ortiz, Worrell (8), Eyre (8), Nen (9)   Glavine, Hammond (6), Gryboski (6), Moss (8), Holmes (9)

Game 2   October 3 at Atlanta

SF	0	1	0	0	0	1	0	0	1					3	7	0
ATL	1	3	0	3	0	0	0	0	x					7	8	0

Rueter, Aybar (4), Witasick (6), Rodriguez (8)   Millwood, Remlinger (7), Holmes (8), Smoltz (8)

Game 3   October 5 at San Francisco

ATL	0	0	1	0	0	5	0	0	4					10	10	0
SF	1	0	0	0	0	1	0	0	0					2	5	0

Maddux, Hammond (7), Remlinger (8), Gryboski (9)   Schmidt, Aybar (6), Rodriguez (7), Eyre (8), Worrell (9), Fultz (9), Nen (9), Witasick (9)

Game 4   October 6 at San Francisco

ATL	0	0	0	0	1	2	0	0	0					3	9	0
SF	2	2	3	0	1	0	0	0	x					8	11	0

Glavine, Gryboski (3), Moss (5), Ligtenberg (7)   Hernandez, Eyre (9), Nen (9)

Game 5   October 7 at Atlanta

SF	0	1	0	1	0	0	1	0	0					3	6	2
ATL	0	0	0	0	0	1	0	0	0					1	7	0

Ortiz, Fultz (6), Rodriguez (6), Worrell (7), Nen (9)   Millwood, Hammond (6), Remlinger (7), Holmes (7), Smoltz (8)

DIVISION SERIES: ST. LOUIS 3 : ARIZONA 0

Game 1   October 1 at Arizona

STL	2	0	0	3	0	1	6	0	0					12	14	1
ARI	1	0	1	0	0	0	0	0	0					2	8	2

Morris, Fassero (8), Crudale (9)   Johnson, Mantei (7), Swindell (7), Fetters (7), Helling (8)

Game 2   October 3 at Arizona

STL	0	0	1	0	0	0	0	0	1					2	10	1
ARI	0	0	0	0	0	0	0	1	0					1	6	0

Finley, Kline (7), White (7), Fassero (8), Isringhausen (8)   Schilling, Koplove (8), Myers (9)

Game 3   October 5 at St. Louis

ARI	0	2	0	0	1	0	0	0	0					3	4	0
STL	0	1	1	2	0	0	0	2	x					6	9	0

Batista, Swindell (4), Helling (5), Kim (8)   Benes, Fassero (5), White (7), Kline (8), Myers (7), Isringhausen (9)

COMPOSITE BATTING

DIVISION SERIES

NAME	POS	G	AB	R	H	2B	3B	HR	RBI	BA
SAN FRANCISCO										
TOTALS		5	166	24	41	9	0	6	24	.247
Aurilia	SS	5	21	4	5	1	0	2	7	.238
Santiago	C	5	21	1	5	2	0	0	5	.238
Lofton	CF	5	20	5	7	1	0	0	2	.350
Snow	1B	5	19	3	6	2	0	1	3	.316
Kent	2B	5	19	1	5	2	0	0	1	.263
Sanders	RF	5	18	1	4	1	0	0	1	.222
Bonds	LF	5	17	5	5	0	0	3	4	.294
Bell	3B	5	16	3	3	0	0	0	1	.188
Ortiz	P	2	6	1	1	0	0	0	0	.167
Goodwin	PH	2	2	0	0	0	0	0	0	.000
Hernandez	P	1	2	0	0	0	0	0	0	.000
Schmidt	P	1	2	0	0	0	0	0	0	.000
Dunston	PH	2	1	0	0	0	0	0	0	.000
Feliz	PH	1	1	0	0	0	0	0	0	.000
Rueter	P	1	1	0	0	0	0	0	0	.000
Nen	P	4	0	0	0	0	0	0	0	—
Eyre	P	3	0	0	0	0	0	0	0	—
Rodriguez	P	3	0	0	0	0	0	0	0	—
Worrell	P	3	0	0	0	0	0	0	0	—
Aybar	P	2	0	0	0	0	0	0	0	—
Fultz	P	2	0	0	0	0	0	0	0	—
Witasick	P	2	0	0	0	0	0	0	0	—
Martinez	PH	1	0	0	0	0	0	0	0	—
ATLANTA										
TOTALS		5	170	26	44	4	2	5	25	.259
Furcal	SS	5	24	2	6	1	1	0	2	.250
J. Franco	1B	5	22	2	4	0	0	0	1	.182
A. Jones	CF	5	19	4	6	1	0	0	2	.316
Castilla	3B	5	18	5	7	0	0	1	4	.389
C. Jones	LF	5	17	3	5	0	0	1	1	.294
Sheffield	RF	5	16	3	1	0	0	1	1	.063
Lopez	C	4	15	4	5	1	0	2	4	.333
Lockhart	2B	5	12	1	4	0	0	1	4	.333
DeRosa	2B	4	7	2	3	1	1	0	3	.429
Blanco	C	2	6	0	1	0	0	0	0	.167
Bragg	LF	4	3	0	0	0	0	0	0	.000
Maddux	P	1	3	0	0	0	0	0	0	.000
M. Franco	PH	4	2	0	0	0	0	0	0	.000
Giles	PH	3	2	0	1	0	0	0	0	.500
Glavine	P	2	2	0	1	0	0	0	2	.500
Millwood	P	2	2	0	0	0	0	0	0	.000
Gryboski	P	3	0	0	0	0	0	0	0	—
Hammond	P	3	0	0	0	0	0	0	0	—
Holmes	P	3	0	0	0	0	0	0	0	—
Remlinger	P	3	0	0	0	0	0	0	0	—
Moss	P	2	0	0	0	0	0	0	0	—
Smoltz	P	2	0	0	0	0	0	0	0	—
Helms	1B	1	0	0	0	0	0	0	0	—
Ligtenberg	P	1	0	0	0	0	0	0	0	—
ST. LOUIS										
TOTALS		3	105	20	33	2	1	3	19	.314
Vina	2B	3	15	3	9	0	0	0	1	.600
Renteria	SS	3	12	3	3	0	0	0	0	.250
Edmonds	CF	3	11	1	3	0	0	1	2	.273
Martinez	1B	3	11	2	0	0	0	0	0	.000
Pujols	LF-3B-1B	3	10	3	3	0	1	0	3	.300
Matheny	C	3	9	3	4	1	0	0	2	.444
Drew	RF	2	9	1	2	0	0	1	1	.222
Rolen	3B	2	7	1	3	0	0	1	2	.429
Marrero	RF-LF	2	6	0	0	0	0	0	1	.000
Cairo	3B	2	4	2	4	1	0	0	3	1.000
Morris	P	1	4	1	1	0	0	0	2	.250
Finley	P	1	3	0	0	0	0	0	0	.000
Robinson	PH	2	2	0	1	0	0	0	1	.500
Benes	P	1	1	0	0	0	0	0	1	.000
Perez	PH	1	1	0	0	0	0	0	0	.000
Fassero	P	3	0	0	0	0	0	0	0	—
Isringhausen	P	2	0	0	0	0	0	0	0	—
Kline	P	2	0	0	0	0	0	0	0	—
White	P	2	0	0	0	0	0	0	0	—
Crudale	P	1	0	0	0	0	0	0	0	—
ARIZONA										
TOTALS		3	98	6	18	2	0	2	6	.184
Spivey	2B	3	13	0	2	0	0	0	0	.154
Womack	SS	3	13	1	2	0	0	0	0	.154
Williams	3B	3	12	0	1	0	0	0	0	.083
McCracken	RF	3	11	1	4	1	0	0	2	.364
Finley	CF	3	9	1	2	0	0	0	1	.222
Dellucci	LF	3	7	1	2	0	0	1	2	.286
Moeller	C	3	5	0	2	0	0	0	0	.400
Barajas	C	2	4	1	1	0	0	1	1	.250
Grace	1B	2	4	0	1	0	0	0	0	.250
Durazo	1B	2	4	0	0	0	0	0	0	.000
Little	LF	2	4	0	0	0	0	0	0	.000
Colbrunn	1B	1	3	1	0	0	0	0	0	.000
Donnells	PH	3	2	0	0	0	0	0	0	.000
Miller	C	1	2	0	1	1	0	0	0	.500
Johnson	P	1	2	0	0	0	0	0	0	.000
Schilling	P	1	2	0	0	0	0	0	0	.000
Batista	P	1	1	0	0	0	0	0	0	.000
Cintron	3B	2	0	1	0	0	0	0	0	—
Helling	P	2	0	0	0	0	0	0	0	—
Myers	P	2	0	0	0	0	0	0	0	—
Swindell	P	2	0	0	0	0	0	0	0	—
Fetters	P	1	0	0	0	0	0	0	0	—
Koplove	P	1	0	0	0	0	0	0	0	—
Kim	P	1	0	0	0	0	0	0	0	—
Mantei	P	1	0	0	0	0	0	0	0	—

COMPOSITE PITCHING

NAME	G	IP	H	BB	SO	W	L	SV	ERA
SAN FRANCISCO									
TOTALS	5	44	44	22	30	3	2	2	4.70
Ortiz	2	12.1	9	8	8	2	0	0	2.19
Hernandez	1	8.1	8	2	6	1	0	0	3.24
Schmidt	1	5.1	3	4	5	0	1	0	6.75
Rodriguez	3	3	1	2	2	0	0	0	0.00
Worrell	3	3	7	2	3	0	0	0	12.00
Rueter	1	3	7	2	1	0	1	0	18.00
Nen	4	2.2	4	1	1	0	0	2	0.00
Aybar	2	2.2	1	3	0	0	0	0	6.75
Witasick	2	2.1	0	1	3	0	0	0	0.00
Eyre	3	1.1	1	0	1	0	0	0	0.00
Fultz	2	0	2	0	0	0	0	0	∞
ATLANTA									
TOTALS	5	44	41	18	45	2	3	0	4.91
Millwood	2	11	7	0	14	1	1	0	3.27
Glavine	2	7.2	17	7	4	0	2	0	15.26
Maddux	1	6	5	1	3	1	0	0	3.00
Gryboski	3	3.2	2	3	0	0	0	0	0.00
Smoltz	3	3.1	2	2	7	0	0	0	2.70
Moss	2	3	2	1	3	0	0	0	3.00
Hammond	3	2.2	3	2	3	0	0	0	6.75
Holmes	3	2.2	1	0	5	0	0	0	0.00
Remlinger	3	2	3	2	3	0	0	0	4.50
Ligtenberg	1	2	0	0	1	0	0	0	0.00
ST. LOUIS									
TOTALS	3	27	18	11	21	3	0	2	1.33
Morris	1	7	7	2	3	1	0	0	1.29
Finley	1	6.1	4	2	7	0	0	0	0.00
Benes	1	4.2	2	4	5	0	0	0	5.79
Fassero	3	2.2	3	0	2	2	0	0	0.00
Isringhausen	2	2	0	1	0	0	0	2	0.00
White	2	2	1	1	4	0	0	0	0.00
Kline	2	1.1	1	1	0	0	0	0	0.00
Crudale	1	1	0	1	2	0	0	0	0.00
ARIZONA									
TOTALS	3	26	33	12	17	0	3	0	5.54
Schilling	1	7	7	1	7	0	0	0	1.29
Johnson	1	6	10	2	4	0	1	0	7.50
Helling	2	4	1	0	2	0	0	0	0.00
Batista	1	3.2	5	3	1	0	1	0	9.82
Myers	2	1.2	2	0	1	0	0	0	0.00
Koplove	1	1.1	2	0	1	0	1	0	6.75
Kim	1	1	2	3	0	0	0	0	18.00
Fetters	1	0.2	1	1	1	0	0	0	0.00
Swindell	2	0.1	2	1	0	0	0	0	27.00
Mantei	1	0.1	1	1	0	0	0	0	54.00

LINE SCORES

Team	1	2	3	4	5	6	7	8	9				R	H	E

CHAMPIONSHIP SERIES: SAN FRANCISCO 4 : ST. LOUIS 1

Game 1   October 9 at St. Louis

SF	1	4	1	0	1	2	0	0	0				9	11	0
STL	0	1	0	2	2	0	1	0					6	11	0

Rueter, Rodriguez (6), Worrell (8), Nen (9)   **Morris**, Crudale (5), Veres (7), Kline (9)

Game 2   October 10 at St. Louis

SF	1	0	0	0	2	0	0	0	1				4	7	0
STL	0	0	0	0	0	0	1	0					1	6	0

Schmidt, Eyre (8), Nen (8)   **Williams**, White (7), Fassero (8), Isringhausen (9)

Game 3   October 12 at San Francisco

STL	0	0	2	1	1	1	0	0	0				5	6	1
SF	0	1	0	3	0	0	0	0					4	10	0

Finley, Veres (6), Kline (7), White (8), Isringhausen (9)   Ortiz, Fultz (5), **Witasick** (6), Rodriguez (7), Eyre (8), Worrell (9)

Game 4   October 13 at San Francisco

STL	2	0	0	0	0	0	0	0	1				3	12	0
SF	0	0	0	0	0	2	0	2	x				4	4	1

Benes, **White** (6), Kline (8)   Hernandez, Rodriguez (7), Eyre (8), **Worrell** (8), Nen (9)

Game 5   October 14 at San Francisco

STL	0	0	0	0	0	0	1	0	0				1	9	0
SF	0	0	0	0	0	0	0	1	1				2	7	0

Morris, Kline (9)   Rueter, Rodirguez (7), Eyre (8), **Worrell** (9)

COMPOSITE BATTING

NAME	POS	G	AB	R	H	2B	3B	HR	RBI	BA
SAN FRANCISCO										
TOTALS		5	158	23	39	3	2	7	23	.247
Lofton	CF	5	21	4	5	0	0	1	2	.238
Santiago	C	5	20	2	6	0	0	2	6	.300
Snow	1B	5	20	1	5	1	1	0	2	.250
Kent	2B	5	19	3	5	0	0	0	0	.263
Bell	3B	5	17	4	7	1	0	1	4	.412
Sanders	RF	4	16	0	1	0	0	0	0	.063
Aurilia	SS	5	15	4	5	1	0	2	5	.333
Bonds	LF	5	11	5	3	0	1	1	6	.273
Rueter	P	2	5	0	0	0	0	0	0	.000
Goodwin	PH	2	3	0	0	0	0	0	0	.000
Dunston	RF	2	2	0	1	0	0	0	0	.500
Schmidt	P	1	2	0	0	0	0	0	0	.000
Rodriguez	P	4	1	0	0	0	0	0	0	.000
Nen	P	3	1	0	0	0	0	0	0	.000
Martinez	SS	2	1	0	0	0	0	0	1	.000
Ortiz	P	1	1	0	1	0	0	0	0	1.000
Feliz	PH	1	1	0	0	0	0	0	0	.000
Hernandez	P	1	1	0	0	0	0	0	0	.000
Shinjo	RF-CF	1	1	0	0	0	0	0	0	.000
Eyre	P	4	0	0	0	0	0	0	0	—
Worrell	P	4	0	0	0	0	0	0	0	—
Fultz	P	1	0	0	0	0	0	0	0	—
Witasick	P	1	0	0	0	0	0	0	0	—

NAME	POS	G	AB	R	H	2B	3B	HR	RBI	BA
ST. LOUIS										
TOTALS		5	171	16	44	8	0	7	16	.257
Vina	2B	5	23	2	6	2	0	0	2	.261
Edmonds	CF	5	20	2	8	2	0	1	4	.400
Matheny	C	5	19	2	6	2	0	1	1	.316
Pujols	LF-3B-1B	5	19	2	5	1	0	2	1	.263
Renteria	SS	5	19	0	3	0	0	0	1	.158
Marrero	RF-LF	4	16	1	3	1	0	1	1	.188
Martinez	1B	4	14	1	2	0	0	0	1	.143
Drew	RF	5	13	1	5	0	0	1	1	.385
Cairo	3B	3	13	2	5	0	0	0	1	.385
Perez	RF	3	4	1	1	0	0	1	0	.250
Morris	P	2	4	0	0	0	0	0	0	.000
Robinson	LF	3	2	1	0	0	0	0	0	.000
Benes	P	1	2	0	0	0	0	0	0	.000
Finley	P	1	2	1	0	0	0	0	0	.000
DiFelice	PH	1	1	0	0	0	0	0	0	.000
Kline	P	4	0	0	0	0	0	0	0	—
White	P	3	0	0	0	0	0	0	0	—
Isringhausen	P	2	0	0	0	0	0	0	0	—
Veres	P	2	0	0	0	0	0	0	0	—
Crudale	P	1	0	0	0	0	0	0	0	—
Fassero	P	1	0	0	0	0	0	0	0	—
Williams	P	1	0	0	0	0	0	0	0	—

COMPOSITE PITCHING

NAME	G	IP	H	BB	SO	W	L	SV	ERA
SAN FRANCISCO									
TOTALS	5	45	44	10	23	4	1	3	3.20
Rueter	2	11	15	2	3	1	0	0	4.09
Schmidt	1	7.2	4	1	8	1	0	0	1.17
Hernandez	1	6.1	9	1	0	0	0	0	2.84
Rodriguez	4	4.2	3	2	2	0	0	0	1.93
Ortiz	1	4.2	5	3	3	0	0	0	7.71
Worrell	4	4.1	2	0	3	2	0	0	2.08
Nen	3	3.1	3	1	4	0	0	3	2.70
Eyre	4	1.2	0	0	0	0	0	0	0.00
Witasick	1	1	1	0	0	0	1	0	9.00
Fultz	1	0.1	0	0	0	0	0	0	0.00

NAME	G	IP	H	BB	SO	W	L	SV	ERA
ST. LOUIS									
TOTALS	5	43.2	39	21	36	1	4	1	4.74
Morris	2	13	16	6	6	0	2	0	6.23
Williams	1	6	6	1	7	0	1	0	4.50
Benes	1	5.1	4	5	0	0	0	0	3.38
Finley	1	5	7	3	1	0	1	0	7.20
White	3	4	2	2	5	0	1	0	4.50
Veres	2	3.2	2	1	5	0	0	0	0.00
Kline	4	2.1	2	0	1	0	0	0	0.00
Isringhausen	2	1	3	3	0	0	1	0.00
Crudale	1	1.2	1	1	2	0	0	0	10.80
Fassero	1	0.2	0	1	0	0	0	0	0.00

MISCELLANEOUS 2002 INDIVIDUAL LEADERS

BATTING

On Base Average

American League		National League	
1 Ramirez, Bos.	.450	1 Bonds, S.F.	.582
2 Thome, Cle.	.445	2 Giles, Pit.	.450
3 Giambi, N.Y.	.435	3 C. Jones, Atl.	.435
4 Sweeney, K.C.	.417	4 Helton, Col.	.429
5 B. Williams, N.Y.	.415	5 Walker, Col.	.421
6 Delgado, Tor.	.406	6 Edmonds, St.L.	.420
7 Olerud, Sea.	.403	7 V. Guerrero, Mon.	.417
8 A. Rodriguez, Tex.	.392	8 Abreu, Phi.	.413
9 Palmeiro, Tex.	.391	9 Berkman, Hou.	.405
10 Suzuki, Sea.	.388	10 Sheffield, Atl.	.404

On Base Average plus Slugging Average

American League		National League	
1 Thome, Cle.	1.122	1 Bonds, S.F.	1.381
2 Ramirez, Bos.	1.097	2 Giles, Pit.	1.072
3 Giambi, N.Y.	1.034	3 Walker, Col.	1.023
4 A. Rodriguez, Tex.	1.015	4 V. Guerrero, Mon.	1.010
5 Sweeney, K.C.	.979	5 Helton, Col.	1.006
6 Ordonez, Chi.	.978	6 Sosa, Chi.	.993
7 Palmeiro, Tex.	.962	7 Berkman, Hou.	.982
8 Delgado, Tor.	.955	8 Edmonds, St.L.	.981
9 B. Williams, N.Y.	.908	9 C. Jones, Atl.	.972
10 Burks, Cle.	.903	10 Pujols, St.L.	.955
		Floyd, Fla.-Mon.-Bos. .920	

Total Bases

American League		National League	
1 A. Rodriguez, Tex.	389	1 V. Guerrero, Mon.	364
2 Soriano, N.Y.	381	2 Kent, S.F.	352
3 Ordonez, Chi.	352	3 Berkman, Hou.	334
4 Anderson, Ana.	344	4 Pujols, St.L.	331
5 Tejada, Oak.	336	5 Sosa, Chi.	330
6 Garciaparra, Bos.	335	6 Green, L.A.	325
Giambi, N.Y.	335	7 Bonds, S.F.	322
8 Thome, Cle.	325	8 Burrell, Phi.	319
9 Beltran, K.C.	319	Helton, Col.	319
10 Palmeiro, Tex.	312	10 Giles, Pit.	309

Caught Stealing

American League		National League	
1 Suzuki, Sea.	15	1 V. Guerrero, Mon.	20
2 Eckstein, Ana.	13	2 Castillo, Fla.	15
Guzman, Min.	13	Furcal, Atl.	15
Soriano, N.Y.	13	4 Sanchez, Mil.	14
5 Koskie, Min.	11	5 Rollins, Phi.	13
Lofton, Chi.A-S.F. 11			

Stolen Base Percentage
(Minimum 20 Attempts)

American League		National League	
1 Jeter, N.Y.	91	1 Glanville, Phi.	91
2 Singleton, Bal.	91	2 Cedeno, N.Y.	86
3 Erstad, Ana.	89	3 Patterson, Chi.	86
4 Knoblauch, K.C.	86	4 Roberts, L.A.	82
5 Damon, Bos.	84	5 Fox, Fla.	82

Extra Base Hits

American League		National League	
1 Soriano, N.Y.	92	1 Kent, S.F.	81
2 Anderson, Ana.	88	2 Giles, Pit.	80
3 A. Rodriguez, Tex.	86	3 Berkman, Hou.	79
Ordonez, Chi.	86	Bonds, S.F.	79
5 Garciaparra, Bos.	85	5 Burrell, Phi.	78
		V. Guerrero, Mon.	78

PITCHING

Fewest Hits Per 9 Innings Pitched

American League		National League	
1 Martinez, Bos.	6.50	1 Burnett, Fla.	6.74
2 Wakefield, Bos.	6.67	2 Johnson, Ari.	6.82
3 Lowe, Bos.	6.80	3 Moss, Atl.	7.04
4 Zito, Oak.	7.14	4 Clement, Chi.	7.11
5 Moyer, Sea.	7.73	5 Wood, Chi.	7.12
6 Ortiz, Ana.	7.79	6 Schmidt, S.F.	7.19
7 Lopez, Bal.	7.87	7 Wolf, Phi.	7.35
8 Mulder, Oak.	7.90	8 Perez, L.A.	7.37
9 Washburn, Ana.	8.00	9 Schilling, Ari.	7.57
10 Halladay, Tor.	8.39	10 Millwood, Atl.	7.71

Fewest Bases on Balls Per 9 Innings Pitched

American League		National League	
1 Reed, Min.	1.24	1 Schilling, Ari.	1.15
2 Byrd, K.C.	1.50	2 Perez, L.A.	1.54
3 Milton, Min.	1.58	3 Vazquez, Mon.	1.91
4 Martinez, Bos.	1.81	4 Maddux, Atl.	2.03
5 Lidle, Oak.	1.83	5 Ohka, Mon.	2.10
6 Moyer, Sea.	1.95	6 Thomson, Col.-N.Y.	2.18
7 Wells, N.Y.	1.96	7 Lawrence, S.D.	2.23
8 Lowe, Bos.	1.97	8 Padilla, Phi.	2.32
9 Mussina, N.Y.	2.00	9 Rueter, S.F.	2.39
10 Valdez, Tex.-Sea.	2.16	10 Oswalt, Hou.	2.39

Strikeouts Per 9 Innings Pitched

American League		National League	
1 Martinez, Bos.	10.79	1 Johnson, Ari.	11.56
2 Clemens, N.Y.	9.60	2 Schilling, Ari.	10.97
3 Mussina, N.Y.	7.60	3 Schmidt, S.F.	9.52
4 Wakefield, Bos.	7.38	4 Clement, Chi.	9.44
5 Garcia, Sea.	7.28	5 Duckworth, Phi.	9.22
6 Zito, Oak.	7.14	6 Wood, Chi.	9.14
7 Baez, Cle.	7.08	7 Burnett, Fla.	8.94
8 Mulder, Oak.	6.90	8 Oswalt, Hou.	8.03
9 Ortiz, Ana.	6.71	9 Nomo, L.A.	7.88
10 Burkett, Bos.	6.45	10 Miller, Hou.	7.87
Finley, Cle.-St.L. 8.21			

Lowest Batting Average Allowed

American League		National League	
1 Martinez, Bos.	.198	1 Johnson, Ari.	.208
2 Wakefield, Bos.	.204	2 Burnett, Fla.	.209
3 Lowe, Bos.	.211	3 Clement, Chi.	.215
4 Zito, Oak.	.218	4 Schmidt, S.F.	.218
5 Ortiz, Ana.	.230	5 Moss, Atl.	.221

Home Runs Allowed

1 Ortiz, Ana.	40	1 Astacio, N.Y.	32
2 Byrd, K.C.	36	2 Tomko, S.D.	31
3 Sturtze, T.B.	33	Helling, Ari.	31
4 Reed, Min.	32	4 Rusch, Mil.	30
Suppan, K.C.	32	5 Schilling, Ari.	29
Wright, Chi.	32		

Home Runs Allowed per 9 IP
(Minimum 10 Home Runs Allowed)

American League		National League	
1 Parque, Chi.	3.91	1 Mercker, Col.	2.45
2 Towers, Bal.	3.62	2 Cabrera, Mil.	2.00
3 Prokopec, Tor.	2.38	3 Chacon, Col.	1.89
4 Hiljus, Oak.	2.17	4 Darensbourg, Oak.	1.86
5 Paniagua, Det.	2.16	5 Chen, N.Y.-Mon.-Cin. 1.85

"THE BAD NEWS IS WE'RE FAVORED"

Pre-World Series odds favored the Yankees or A's, the Braves or Diamondbacks, and Barry Bonds never seeing a hittable pitch, but Americans always root for underdogs. They got their fill in the 2002 postseason.

Arizona – the 2001 world champions – were the first favorite to fall. Slugger Luis Gonzalez was sidelined with an injury, but the D-backs still had world-class aces Johnson and Schilling to throw against the pitcher-parched St. Louis Cardinals in the divisional Series. In an unlikely reversal of form, the Redbirds pounded Johnson in Game One, winning two touchdowns to a safety. Two days later, Schilling was excellent but Chuck Finley and his relievers were better, taking a 1-0 lead into the 8th inning. When Arizona tied the score with an unearned run, the Cards bounced back with Miguel Cairo's game-winning single in the 9th. After another day off, the series moved to St. Louis where the Cardinals delivered the *coup de grace*.

The other N.L. Divisional Series matched Atlanta pitching against San Francisco's Barry Bonds and some lesser mortals. At least that's how it was reported going in. Maddux and Millwood pitched well to put the Braves up two games to one. But the Giants' Livan Hernandez, Russ Ortiz, and bullpen out pitched Atlanta's more famous hurlers, to give the Giants the series win. The Braves walked Bonds when they could, but he still hit three home runs in the five games.

The most stunning result in a Divisional Series came in the A.L. where the wild card Anaheim Angels slugged the Yankees' pitching into submission. Propelled by Bernie Williams' three-run homer, New York won the opener. The Angels came from behind to win in each of the next three games, while scoring 26 runs. The Angels' comebacks were cheered by the Rally Monkey, an image of a wildly excited simian flashed on the big screen in Anaheim. The final victory featured an eight-run fifth-inning for the Californians as the Monkey became more excited than King Kong when he saw Fay Wray.

Minnesota committed three errors in the first two innings of their series opener with Oakland but still won. The A's took the next two games, but a seven-run fourth inning in Game Four helped the Twins tie the series. The next day, Brad Radke took a shutout into the seventh inning, and Minnesota survived a three-run, ninth-inning rally by the A's to move on.

The NLCS pitted the heavy-hitting Cardinals against the wild card Giants, but it was three San Francisco homers and Barry Bonds' two-run triple that got the Giants off with a win. Jason Schmidt tamed St. Louis the next day. The Cards won Game Four, but San Francisco took a pair of one-run decisions in the final two games to advance to the World Series. St. Louis walked Bonds often enough to make Benito Santiago the NLCS MVP.

When the playoffs began, Minnesota was hardly a candidate to win it all, but even more unlikely were the Anaheim Angels who had finished 41 games behind their division leader in 2001. After the Twins opened the ALCS with a tight 2-1 victory, behind the stout pitching of Joe Mays, the Angels' bats woke up. Of the four-straight Angels' wins, only Game Three was a nail-biter, turning on Troy Glaus' home run in the eighth. Game Five featured a ten-run seventh inning that included Adam Kennedy's third home run of the day.

Neither the Giants nor the Angels could be labeled the underdog in the first all-wild card World Series but neither fit the role of favorite — the kiss of death thus far in the postseason. The Angels had a lineup that led the American League in hitting, a prime reliever in Troy Percival, and the Rally Monkey; the Giants had a veteran presence, possibly better starting pitching, and Barry Bonds.

The Giants won the opener 4-3. Bonds homered in the second and Reggie Sanders put one in the seats two batters later to give San Francisco the lead. J.T. Snow hit a two-run home run in the sixth. Schmidt tired in the sixth but three relievers picked up the slack. Game two was a slugfest, with the Angels' Tim Salmon going 4-for4 with two home runs and four RBI.

Moving to San Francisco, the Angels put an early kibosh on the celebrations of a sold-out crowd by batting around in both the third and fourth innings to produce eight runs. The 10-4 win put them back into the Series lead, but the Giants evened things the next day while showing that they too were capable of rallying. David Bell's tie-breaking single in the eighth came at the expense of 20-year-old Francisco Rodriguez who had been unscored upon in postseason play until then. San Francisco took a three-games-to-two lead by blowing out the Angels 16-4 in Game Five. Bonds' RBI-double thrust the Giants into the lead and Jeff Kent hit a pair of two-run homers.

By the seventh inning of Game Six, the Giants led 5-0. With San Francisco nine outs away from a world championship, the Angels had finally qualified as Series underdogs. Perhaps that's what it took. Anaheim rallied for three runs in the seventh to close. Then in the eighth, Troy Glaus' base-clearing double was the turn-around hit of the Series.

The Rally Monkey relaxed in Game Seven as the Angels took an early lead on Garret Anderson's base-clearing double in the third. Rookie John Lackey, Rodriguez, and Percival held San Francisco at bay, and the Angels had their first championship in 42 years. For the Series, Bonds hit .471 with four home runs, thirteen walks, and eight runs scored. But "to the victors . . . .;" Glaus was the Series MVP, a final win for an underdog.

WORLD SERIES

LINE SCORES

Team	1	2	3	4	5	6	7	8	9	10	11	12	R	H	E

WORLD SERIES: ANAHEIM 4 : SAN FRANCISCO 3

Game 1 October 19 at Anaheim

	1	2	3	4	5	6	7	8	9				R	H	E
SF	0	2	0	0	0	2	0	0	0				4	6	0
ANA	0	1	0	0	0	2	0	0	0				3	9	0

Schmidt, Rodriguez (6), Worrell (8),   Washburn, Donnelly (6),
Nen (9)   Schoeneweis (8), Weber (8)

Game 2 October 20 at Anaheim

	1	2	3	4	5	6	7	8	9				R	H	E
SF	0	4	1	0	4	0	0	0	1				10	12	1
ANA	5	2	0	0	1	1	0	2	x				11	16	1

Ortiz, Zerbe (2), Witasick (5), Fultz (5),   Appier, Lackey (3), Weber (5), Rodriguez (6),
Rodriguez (7), Worrell (9)   Percival (9)

Game 3 October 22 at San Francisco

	1	2	3	4	5	6	7	8	9				R	H	E
ANA	0	0	4	0	4	0	1	0	1	0			10	16	0
SF	1	0	0	0	3	0	0	0	0				4	6	2

Ortiz, Donnelly (8), Schoeneweis (8)   Hernandez, Witasick (4), Fultz (5), Rodriguez (7),
   Eyre (8)

Game 4 October 23 at San Francisco

	1	2	3	4	5	6	7	8	9				R	H	E
ANA	0	1	2	0	0	0	0	0	0				3	10	1
SF	0	0	0	0	3	0	0	1	x				4	12	1

Lackey, Weber (8), Rodriguez (7)   Rueter, Rodriguez (7), Worrell (8), Nen (9)

Game 5 October 24 at San Francisco

	1	2	3	4	5	6	7	8	9				R	H	E
ANA	0	0	0	0	3	1	0	0	0				4	10	2
SF	3	3	0	0	0	2	4	4	x				16	16	0

Washburn, Donnelly (5), Weber (7),   Schmidt, Zerbe (5), Rodriguez (6),
Shields (7)   Worrell (7), Eyre (9)

Game 6 October 26 at Anaheim

	1	2	3	4	5	6	7	8	9				R	H	E
SF	0	0	0	0	0	3	1	0	0				5	8	1
ANA	0	0	0	0	0	0	3	3	x				6	10	1

Ortiz, Rodriguez (7), Eyre (7),   Appier, Rodriguez (5), Donnelly (8), Percival (9)
Worrell (7), Nen (8)

Game 7 October 27 at Anaheim

	1	2	3	4	5	6	7	8	9				R	H	E
SF	0	1	0	0	0	0	0	0	0				1	6	0
ANA	0	1	3	0	0	0	0	0	x				4	5	0

Hernandez, Zerbe (3), Rueter (4),   Lackey, Donnelly (6), Rodriguez (8),
Worrell (8)   Percival (9)

COMPOSITE BATTING

NAME	POS	G	AB	R	H	2B	3B	HR	RBI	BA
ANAHEIM										
TOTALS		7	245	41	76	15	1	7	38	.310
Anderson	RF	7	32	3	9	1	0	0	6	.281
Erstad	CF	7	30	6	9	3	0	1	3	.300
Eckstein	SS	7	29	6	9	0	0	0	3	.310
Glaus	3B	7	26	7	10	3	0	3	8	.385
Salmon	RF	7	26	9	9	1	0	2	5	.346
Kennedy	2B	7	25	1	7	2	0	2	2	.280
Spiezio	1B	7	23	3	6	1	1	1	8	.261
B. Molina	C	7	21	2	6	2	0	0	2	.286
Fullmer	DH	5	15	3	4	0	0	0	1	.267
Gil	2B	3	5	1	4	1	0	0	0	.800
Palmiero	PH	4	4	1	1	0	0	0	0	.250
Ortiz	P	1	3	0	0	0	0	0	0	.000
Wooten	1B	3	2	0	1	0	0	0	0	.500
Lackey	P	3	2	0	1	0	0	0	0	.500
Ochoa	RF	4	1	0	0	0	0	0	0	.000
Washburn	P	2	1	0	0	0	0	0	0	.000
Donnelly	P	5	0	0	0	0	0	0	0	—
Rodriguez	P	4	0	0	0	0	0	0	0	—
Weber	P	4	0	0	0	0	0	0	0	—
J. Molina	C	3	0	0	0	0	0	0	0	—
Percival	P	3	0	0	0	0	0	0	0	—
Appier	P	2	0	0	0	0	0	0	0	—
Figgins	PR	2	0	1	0	0	0	0	0	—
Schoeneweis	P	2	0	0	0	0	0	0	0	—
Shields	P	1	0	0	0	0	0	0	0	—
SAN FRANCISCO										
TOTALS		7	235	44	66	7	1	14	42	.281
Aurilia	SS	7	32	5	8	2	0	2	5	.250
Lofton	CF	7	31	7	9	1	1	0	2	.290
Kent	2B	7	29	6	8	1	0	3	7	.276
Snow	1B	7	27	6	11	1	0	1	4	.407
Santiago	C	7	26	2	6	0	0	0	5	.231
Bell	3B	7	23	4	7	0	0	1	4	.304
Sanders	RF	7	21	3	5	0	0	2	6	.238
Bonds	LF	7	17	8	8	2	0	4	6	.471
Dunston	DH	5	9	1	2	0	0	1	3	.222
Shinjo	DH-RF	3	6	1	1	0	0	0	0	.167
Feliz	DH	3	5	0	0	0	0	0	0	.000
Goodwin	DH-RF	5	4	0	0	0	0	0	0	.000
Rueter	P	2	2	1	1	0	0	0	0	.500
Martinez	PH	2	2	0	0	0	0	0	0	.000
Schmidt	P	2	1	0	0	0	0	0	0	.000
Rodriguez	P	6	0	0	0	0	0	0	0	—
Worrell	P	6	0	0	0	0	0	0	0	—
Eyre	P	3	0	0	0	0	0	0	0	—
Nen	P	3	0	0	0	0	0	0	0	—
Zerbe	P	3	0	0	0	0	0	0	0	—
Fultz	P	2	0	0	0	0	0	0	0	—
Hernandez	P	2	0	0	0	0	0	0	0	—
Ortiz	P	2	0	0	0	0	0	0	0	—
Witasick	P	2	0	0	0	0	0	0	0	—

COMPOSITE PITCHING

NAME	G	IP	H	BB	SO	W	L	SV	ERA
ANAHEIM									
TOTALS	7	61	66	30	50	4	3	3	5.75
Lackey	3	12.1	15	5	7	1	0	0	4.38
Washburn	2	9.2	12	7	6	0	2	0	9.31
Rodriguez	4	8.2	6	1	13	1	1	0	2.08
Donnelly	5	7.2	1	4	6	1	0	0	0.00
Appier	2	6.1	9	5	4	0	0	0	11.37
Ortiz	1	5	5	4	3	1	0	0	7.20
Weber	4	4.2	10	2	5	0	0	0	13.50
Percival	3	3	2	1	3	0	0	3	3.00
Schoeneweis	2	2	1	1	2	0	0	0	0.00
Shields	1	1.2	5	0	1	0	0	0	5.40
SAN FRANCISCO									
TOTALS	7	60	76	23	38	3	4	2	5.55
Schmidt	2	10.1	16	4	14	1	0	0	5.23
Rueter	2	10	10	1	5	0	0	0	2.70
Ortiz	2	8	13	2	2	0	0	0	10.13
Zerbe	3	6	6	0	0	1	0	0	3.00
Worrell	6	5.2	4	1	4	1	1	0	3.18
Rodriguez	6	5.2	4	1	3	0	1	0	4.76
Hernandez	2	5.2	9	9	4	0	2	0	14.29
Eyre	3	3	5	1	2	0	0	0	0.00
Nen	3	3	2	1	3	0	0	2	0.00
Fultz	2	2.1	4	1	0	0	0	0	3.86
Witasick	2	0.1	3	2	1	0	0	0	54.00

2003: UNRELIABLE

You can't rely on baseball. The Braves and Yankees make the playoffs, Roger Clemens makes strikeouts, and Barry Bonds makes home runs. Sure, some things never change. But this year, four young teams made unexpected incursions into the playoffs, talented youngsters made the New Star List longer than the throw from rightfield, and the Cubs young hurlers made Wrigley Field a pitcher's park. Go figure!

Although not mesmerizing, the pennant races were serviceable. In the A.L. East, the Yankees won again to prove the ultimate virtue of a $185 million payroll. Nevertheless, the Bombers seemed to have more trouble than they should have, giving rise to speculation that the star-studded lineup boasting Alfonso Soriano, Jason Giambi, Bernie Williams, Derek Jeter, and Hideki Matsui might need some serious refurbishing. Certainly that was true of the overage pitching with Roger Clemens and David Wells at 40. Clemens, who surpassed 300 career wins, announced he was retiring, but the cupboard wasn't bare. Andy Pettitte won 21 games, Mike Mussina 17, and Mariano Rivera remained a "lights out" stopper.

As usual, the Red Sox gave the Yankees staunch competition and as usual fell short. Despite having batting champion Bill Mueller and a record six sluggers bashing 25 or more home runs, the Sox needed more pitching than Pedro Martinez to catch the Yankees. They settled for the wild card slot. Toronto's Roy Halladay won more games than any other A.L. pitcher. The best hitting of the year was done by the Blue Jays' Carlos Delgado, the league RBI leader, who blasted four home runs in one game on September 25.

The central belonged to Minnesota. The Team-That-Selig-Forgot overtook the fading White Sox at the beginning of September and cruised into the playoffs. Shannon Stewart, A.J. Pierzynski, Torii Hunter, and Doug Mientkiewicz delivered excellent arguments for keeping baseball in Minnesota. Athough the Twins were a good story, the Tigers were the most discussed Central team: the question being whether the Tabbies could break the '62 Mets mark of 120 losses in a season. Despite their earnest efforts, Detroit fell just short of the record.

The Rally Monkey lost his mojo as 2002 champion Anaheim fell back to also-ran. Oakland and Seattle fought it out for the West crown until a late August ten-game winning streak keyed an Athletics triumph. Shortstop Miguel Tejada had another big year, but the secret of the Oakland's success continued to be strong pitching, with Tim Hudson, Mark Mulder, and Barry Zito all enjoying fine seasons. Alex Rodriguez led the A.L. in home runs and was widely considered the best player in the league, but he couldn't lift the Rangers out of last place by himself.

There was something new in Atlanta. Not victory; that was old stuff as the Braves won their division for the twelfth time since 1991. What was new is they did it with their bats after winning with pitching seemingly forever. Atlanta let Tom Glavine and Kevin Millwood go as free agents, reliever John Smoltz had some arm problems, and Greg Maddux began to look his age. Russ Ortiz won 21 games but overall the Braves' pitching was ordinary. Undaunted, Gary Sheffield, Javy Lopez, Chipper Jones, Andruw Jones, Marcus Giles, Vinnie Castilla, and Rafael Furcal plated more runs than any other N.L. attack.

Millwood no-hit the Giants for the Phillies, and Jim Thome led his new league in home runs, but Philadelphia was aced out as a wild card in the playoffs by the surprising Marlins. Buoyed by pitching phenom Dontrelle Willis, elder citizen Jack McKeon's young team never quite challenged the Braves but they showed that baseball was not yet dead in southern Florida.

Houston fell short in their pursuit of another playoff berth In the Central. Jeff Kent was signed to play second base and Craig Biggio moved to centerfield; Jeff Bagwell continued as a fine slugger, but the Astros couldn't quite bring it off. St. Louis played *Eight Bats in Search of a Pitcher*. Among their near overload of prime batsmen Albert Pujols looked for a time like a triple crown winner and finished high in nearly every offensive category.

Although Harry Carey was gone, the triumphant "Cubs win!" was regularly heard at Wrigley. Sammy Sosa had his usual season, and a transfusion of players from Pittsburgh's fire sale gave the Cubs enough hitting to support their young pitching stars. Kerry Wood and Mark Prior helped Chicago set a new team strikeout record. When Chicago swept a doubleheader from the Pirates on the next-to-last day of the season, fans could once again dream of the first Cubbie world championship since 1908.

Randy Johnson and Curt Schilling, Arizona's great pitching twosome, were injured most of 2003, allowing San Francisco to come on in the West. Along the way, they proved that as Barry Bonds goes, so go the Giants. The Giants leftfielder spent time away from the team when his father, former major leaguer Bobby Bonds, was taken gravely ill and died. Without Bonds' presence, the Giants slumped; with him on the scene, they soared. It made a good argument for an MVP award. Not that Bonds was the whole show. Jason Schmidt emerged as one of the N.L.'s top pitchers.

Much ink was spilled in the past decade on whether America's love affair with baseball was fading, but the news on that was mostly good. A fan poll showed the game slipping lower in "fan dislike" but that news was contradicted by rises in both total attendance and television ratings. One thing just about everyone liked about the season — the average time for a game fell six minutes to 2:46, the fastest since 1989.

2003 AMERICAN LEAGUE — EAST DIVISION

Name	G by Pos	B	AGE	G	AB	R	H	2B	3B	HR	RBI	BB	SO	SB	BA	SA
NEW YORK	**1st 101-61 .623**															
TOTALS			32	163	5605	877	1518	304	14	230	845	684	1042	98	.271	.453
Nick Johnson (BH)	1B60 DH34	L	24	96	324	60	92	19	0	14	47	70	57	5	.284	.472
Alfonso Soriano	2B155	R	27	156	682	114	198	36	5	38	91	38	130	35	.290	.525
Derek Jeter (SJ)	SS118	R	29	119	482	87	156	25	3	10	52	43	88	11	.324	.450
1 Robin Ventura	3B80 DH4 2B1	L	35	89	283	31	71	13	0	9	42	40	62	0	.251	.392
1 Raul Mondesi	OF97 DH1	R	32	98	361	56	93	23	3	16	49	38	66	17	.258	.471
Bernie Williams (KJ)	OF115 DH4	B	34	119	445	77	117	19	1	15	64	71	61	5	.263	.411
Hideki Matsui	OF159 DH4	L	29	163	623	82	179	42	1	16	106	63	86	2	.287	.435
Jorge Posada	C137 DH2	B	31	142	481	83	135	24	0	30	101	93	110	2	.281	.518
Jason Giambi	1B85 DH69	L	32	156	535	97	134	25	0	41	107	129	140	2	.250	.527
1 Todd Zeile	3B30 1B23 DH8	R	37	66	186	29	39	8	0	6	23	24	36	0	.210	.349
2 Ruben Sierra	DH32 OF17	B	37	63	174	19	48	8	1	6	31	13	20	1	.276	.437
Enrique Wilson	SS33 3B17 2B10 DH11	B	29	63	135	18	31	9	0	3	15	7	14	3	.230	.363
Juan Rivera	OF56	R	24	57	173	22	46	14	0	7	26	10	27	0	.266	.468
2 Aaron Boone	3B54	R	30	54	189	31	48	13	0	6	31	11	30	8	.254	.418
2 Karim Garcia	OF50 DH1	L	27	52	151	17	46	5	0	6	21	9	32	0	.305	.457
John Flaherty	C40	R	35	40	105	16	28	8	0	4	14	4	19	0	.267	.457
Erick Almonte	SS31	R	25	31	100	17	26	6	0	1	11	8	24	1	.260	.350
Bubba Trammell (PP)	DH15 OF3	R	31	22	55	4	11	5	0	0	5	6	10	0	.200	.291
2 Dave Dellucci (NJ)	OF18 DH2	L	29	21	51	8	9	1	0	1	4	4	13	3	.176	.255
Charles Gipson	OF8 DH3	R	30	18	10	3	2	0	0	0	2	1	2	2	.200	.200
Drew Henson	3B3	R	23	5	8	2	1	0	0	0	0	0	2	0	.125	.125
Fernando Seguignol	1B3 DH1	B	28	5	7	0	1	0	0	0	0	1	3	0	.143	.143
Michel Hernandez	C5	R	24	5	4	0	1	0	0	0	0	1	1	0	.250	.250
Curtis Pride	OF3	L	34	4	12	1	1	0	0	1	1	0	2	0	.083	.333
Chris Latham (JL)	OF2 DH1	B	30	4	2	3	2	0	0	0	0	0	0	1	11.000	1.000
Luis Sojo	1B1 2B1 DH1	R	38	3	4	0	0	0	0	0	0	0	0	0	.000	.000

NAME	T	AGE	W	L	PCT	SV	G	GS	CG	IP	H	BB	SO	SHO	ERA
		34	101	61	.623	49	163	163	8	1462	1512	375	1119	12	4.02
Andy Pettitte	L	31	21	8	.724	0	33	33	1	208	227	50	180	0	4.02
Mike Mussina	R	34	17	8	.680	0	31	31	2	215	192	40	195	1	3.40
Roger Clemens	R	40	17	9	.654	0	33	33	1	212	199	58	190	1	3.91
David Wells	L	40	15	7	.682	0	31	30	4	213	242	20	101	1	4.14
Jose Contreras (SJ)	R	31	7	2	.778	0	18	9	0	71	52	30	72	0	3.30
Jeff Weaver	R	26	7	9	.438	0	32	24	0	159	211	47	93	0	5.99
Mariano Rivera	R	33	5	2	.714	40	64	0	0	71	61	10	63	0	1.66
Chris Hammond	L	37	3	2	.600	1	62	0	0	63	65	11	45	0	2.86
2 Gabe White	L	31	2	1	.667	0	12	0	0	12	8	2	6	0	4.38
Antonio Osuna	R	30	2	5	.286	0	48	0	0	51	58	20	47	0	3.73
1 Jason Anderson	R	24	1	0	1.000	0	22	0	0	21	23	14	9	0	4.79
2 Jeff Nelson	R	36	1	0	1.000	1	24	0	0	18	17	10	21	0	4.58
Brandon Claussen	L	24	1	1	.500	0	1	1	0	6	8	1	5	0	1.42
1 Armando Benitez	R	30	1	1	.500	0	9	0	0	9	8	6	10	0	1.93
1 Sterling Hitchcock	L	32	1	3	.250	0	27	1	0	50	57	18	36	0	5.49
Al Reyes	R	32	0	0	—	0	13	0	0	17	13	9	9	0	3.18
Jorge DePaula	R	24	0	0	—	0	4	1	0	11	3	1	7	0	0.79
2 Dan Miceli	R	32	0	0	—	1	7	0	0	5	4	3	1	0	5.79
2 Jesse Orosco	L	46	0	0	—	0	15	0	0	4	4	6	4	0	10.38
Randy Choate	L	27	0	0	—	0	5	0	0	4	7	1	0	0	7.36
2 Bret Prinz	R	26	0	0	—	0	2	0	0	2	6	3	2	0	18.00
2 Felix Heredia	L	28	0	1	.000	0	12	0	0	15	13	5	4	0	1.20
1 Juan Acevedo	R	33	0	3	.000	0	25	0	0	26	34	10	19	0	7.71

Steve Karsay (SJ) 31, Jon Leiber (EJ) 33

Name	G by Pos	B	AGE	G	AB	R	H	2B	3B	HR	RBI	BB	SO	SB	BA	SA
BOSTON	**2nd 95-67 .586 6 (Wild Card)**															
TOTALS			30	162	5769	961	1667	371	40	238	932	620	943	88	.289	.491
Kevin Millar	1B101 OF31 DH19	R	31	148	544	83	150	30	1	25	96	60	108	3	.276	.472
Todd Walker	2B139 DH2	L	30	144	587	92	166	38	4	13	85	48	54	1	.283	.428
Nomar Garciaparra	SS156	R	29	156	658	120	198	37	13	28	105	39	61	19	.301	.524
Bill Mueller	3B135 2B10 DH3 SS1	B	32	146	524	85	171	45	5	19	85	59	77	1	.326	.540
Trot Nixon	OF130	L	29	134	441	81	135	24	6	28	87	65	96	4	.306	.578
Johnny Damon	OF144 DH1	L	29	145	608	103	166	32	6	12	67	68	74	30	.273	.405
Manny Ramirez	OF128 DH26	R	31	154	569	117	185	36	1	37	104	97	94	3	.325	.587
Jason Varitek	C137 DH4	B	31	142	451	63	123	31	1	25	85	51	106	3	.273	.512
David Ortiz	DH74 1B45	L	27	128	448	79	129	39	2	31	101	58	83	0	.288	.592
Damian Jackson	2B38 OF38 SS18 DH9 3B1 1B2	R	29	109	161	34	42	7	0	1	13	8	28	16	.261	.323
2 Gabe Kapler	OF61 1B1 DH1	R	27	68	158	29	46	11	1	4	23	14	23	4	.291	.449
Doug Mirabelli	C55 DH4 1B2	R	32	62	163	23	42	13	0	6	18	11	36	0	.258	.448
Jeremy Giambi (SJ)	DH30 OF11	L	28	50	127	15	25	5	0	5	15	26	42	1	.197	.354
Shea Hillenbrand	3B29 1B28 DH2	R	27	45	185	20	56	17	0	3	38	7	26	1	.303	.443
Freddy Sanchez	3B7 SS6 2B3	R	24	20	34	6	8	2	0	0	2	0	8	0	.235	.294
2 Dave McCarty	OF8 1B5 DH1	R	33	16	27	4	11	3	0	1	6	2	7	0	.407	.630
2 Lou Merloni	2B7 3B7 OF1	R	32	15	30	4	7	1	0	0	1	4	8	0	.233	.267
Andy Abad	1B7 OF1	L	30	9	17	1	2	0	0	0	0	2	5	0	.118	.118
Adrian Brown	OF9	R	29	9	15	2	3	0	0	0	1	1	4	2	.200	.200
Bill Haselman	C2 DH2	R	37	3	3	0	0	0	0	0	0	0	0	0	.000	.000
Lou Collier	3B2 OF2	R	29	4	1	0	0	0	0	0	0	0	0	0	.000	.000

NAME	T	AGE	W	L	PCT	SV	G	GS	CG	IP	H	BB	SO	SHO	ERA
		31	95	67	.586	36	162	162	5	1465	1503	488	1141	6	4.48
Derek Lowe	R	30	17	7	.708	0	33	33	1	203	216	72	110	0	4.47
Pedro Martinez	R	31	14	4	.778	0	29	29	3	187	147	47	206	0	2.22
John Burkett	R	38	12	9	.571	0	32	30	1	182	202	47	107	0	5.15
Tim Wakefield	R	36	11	7	.611	1	35	33	0	202	193	71	169	0	4.09
2 Byung-Hyun Kim	R	24	8	5	.615	16	49	5	0	79	70	18	69	0	3.18
Mike Timlin	R	37	6	4	.600	2	72	0	0	84	77	9	65	0	3.55
Casey Fossum (SJ)	L	25	6	5	.545	1	19	14	0	79	82	34	63	0	5.47
Alan Embree	L	33	4	1	.800	1	65	0	0	55	49	16	45	0	4.25
Brandon Lyon (EJ)	R	23	4	6	.400	9	49	0	0	59	73	19	50	0	4.12
2 Jeff Suppan	R	28	3	4	.429	0	11	10	0	63	70	20	32	0	5.57
Ramiro Mendoza (KJ)	R	31	3	5	.375	5	37	5	0	67	98	20	36	0	6.75
Jason Shiell	R	26	2	1	.667	0	17	0	0	23	23	17	23	0	4.63
2 Todd Jones	R	35	2	1	.667	0	26	0	0	29	32	13	31	0	5.52
Steve Woodard	R	28	1	0	1.000	0	7	0	0	18	23	5	12	0	5.09
Ryan Rupe	R	28	1	1	.500	0	4	1	0	17	17	4	11	0	6.30
1 Chad Fox (UJ)	R	32	1	2	.333	3	17	0	0	18	19	17	19	0	4.50
Bronson Arroyo	R	26	0	0	—	0	9	0	0	17	18	8	14	0	2.08
Robert Person (EJ-PJ)	R	33	0	0	—	0	12	11	0	8	10	8	10	0	7.71
Bob Howry (EJ)	R	29	0	0	—	0	4	0	0	11	13	4	9	0	12.46
Kevin Tolar	L	32	0	0	—	0	8	0	0	9	9	5	9	0	9.00
1 Scott Williamson	R	27	0	1	.000	0	24	0	0	20	20	9	21	0	6.20
2 Scott Sauerbeck	L	31	0	1	.000	0	23	0	0	17	17	18	18	0	6.48
2 Bruce Chen	L	26	0	1	.000	0	12	2	0	12	12	2	12	0	5.11
Rudy Seanez	R	34	0	1	.000	0	7	0	0	9	8	5	11	0	6.49
1 Hector Almonte	R	27	0	0	—	0	7	0	0	9	15	7	5	0	8.22
1 Matt White (XJ)	L	25	0	0	—	0	7	0	0	5	5	5	4	0	7.20

TORONTO — 3rd 86-76 .531 15 — CARLOS TOSCA

Name	G by Pos	B	AGE	G	AB	R	H	2B	3B	HR	RBI	BB	SO	SB	BA	SA
TOTALS	TOTALS		29	162	5661	894	1580	357	33	190	853	546	1081	37	.279	.455
Carlos Delgado	1B147 DH14	L	31	161	570	117	172	38	1	42	145	109	137	0	.302	.593
Orlando Hudson	2B139	B	25	142	474	54	127	21	6	9	57	39	87	1	.268	.395
Chris Woodward	SS103	R	27	104	349	49	91	22	2	7	45	28	72	1	.261	.395
Eric Hinske (BH)	3B124	L	25	124	449	74	109	45	3	12	63	59	104	12	.243	.437
Frank Catalanotto	OF100 DH21 1B5	L	29	133	489	83	146	34	6	13	59	35	62	2	.299	.472
Vernon Wells	OF161	R	24	161	678	118	215	49	5	33	117	42	81	4	.317	.550
Shannon Stewart	OF69 DH2	R	29	71	303	47	89	22	2	7	35	27	30	1	.294	.449
Greg Myers	C81 DH22	L	37	121	329	51	101	19	0	15	52	37	57	0	.307	.502
Josh Phelps	DH107 1B8	R	25	119	396	57	106	18	1	20	66	39	115	1	.268	.470
Reed Johnson	OF111 DH2	R	26	114	412	79	121	21	2	10	52	20	67	5	.294	.427
Mike Bordick	SS69 3B22 2B13 DH1	R	37	102	343	39	94	18	2	5	54	33	60	3	.274	.382
Tom Wilson	C76 1B14 OF2 DH1	R	32	96	256	37	66	19	0	5	35	28	80	0	.258	.391
Bobby Kielty	OF60 1B3	B	26	62	189	31	44	13	1	4	25	29	36	2	.233	.376
Dave Berg	2B24 3B17 DH7 OF6 1B2 SS1	R	32	61	161	26	41	6	1	4	18	11	34	0	.255	.379
Howie Clark	3B13 DH7 OF5 2B3 1B2 SS1	L	29	38	70	9	25	3	1	0	7	3	6	0	.357	.429
Kevin Cash	C	R	25	34	106	10	15	3	0	1	8	4	22	0	.142	.198
Jayson Werth	OF20 DH3	R	24	26	48	7	10	4	0	2	10	3	22	1	.208	.417
Ken Huckaby	C4	R	32	5	11	1	2	1	0	0	2	0	2	0	.182	.273

NAME	T	AGE	W	L	PCT	SV	G	GS	CG	IP	H	BB	SO	SHO	ERA
TOTALS		30	86	76	.531	36	162	162	14	1435	1560	485	984	6	4.69
Roy Halladay	R	26	22	7	.759	0	36	36	9	266	253	32	204	2	3.25
Kelvin Escobar	R	27	13	9	.591	0	41	26	1	180	189	78	159	1	4.29
Cory Lidle	R	31	12	15	.444	0	31	31	2	193	216	60	112	0	5.75
Mark Hendrickson	L	29	9	9	.500	0	30	30	1	158	207	40	76	1	5.51
Josh Towers	R	26	8	1	.889	1	14	8	1	64	67	7	42	0	4.48
Tanyon Sturtze	R	32	7	6	.538	0	40	8	0	89	107	43	54	0	5.94
2 Doug Davis	L	27	4	6	.400	0	12	11	0	54	70	26	25	0	5.00
Jason Kershner	L	26	3	3	.500	0	40	0	0	54	43	15	32	0	3.17
Pete Walker (KJ)	R	34	2	2	.500	0	23	7	0	55	59	24	29	0	4.88
Trever Miller	L	30	2	2	.500	0	79	0	0	53	46	28	44	0	4.61
Corey Thurman	R	24	1	1	.500	0	15	2	1				9	0	6.46
2 Juan Acevedo	R	33	1	2	.333	0	14	0	0	13	18	9	10	0	4.26
Aquilino Lopez	R	28	1	3	.250	14	72	0	0	74	58	34	64	0	3.42
Cliff Politte	R	29	1	5	.167	12	54	0	0	49	52	17	40	0	5.66
Dan Reichert	R	26	0	0	—	0	15	0	0	16	28	8	13	0	6.06
2 Scott Service	R	36	0	0	—	0	15	0	0	16	17	6	17	0	4.50
Doug Creek (EJ)	L	34	0	0	—	0	21	0	0	14	14	12	11	0	3.29
Doug Linton	R	38	0	0	—	0	7	0	0	9	7	4	7	0	3.00
Brian Bowles	R	26	0	0	—	0	5	0	0	7	8	2	2	0	2.57
Vinnie Chulk	R	24	0	0	—	0	3	0	0	5	6	3	2	0	5.06
John Wasdin	R	30	0	1	.000	0	3	2	0	5	16	4	5	0	23.40
Jeff Tam	R	32	0	4	.000	0	14	0	0	45	58	25	26	0	5.64
Justin Miller (SJ) 25															

BALTIMORE — 4th 71-91 .438 30 — MIKE HARGROVE

Name	G by Pos	B	AGE	G	AB	R	H	2B	3B	HR	RBI	BB	SO	SB	BA	SA
TOTALS	TOTALS		30	163	5665	743	1516	277	24	152	695	431	902	89	.268	.405
1 Jeff Conine	1B118 OF8 3B1	R	37	124	493	75	143	33	3	15	80	37	60	5	.290	.460
Jerry Hairston (BF)	2B48 DH9	R	27	58	218	25	59	12	2	2	21	23	25	14	.271	.372
Deivi Cruz	SS147 DH5	R	30	152	548	61	137	24	2	14	65	13	49	1	.250	.378
Tony Batista	3B154 DH7	R	29	161	631	76	148	20	1	26	99	28	102	4	.235	.393
Jay Gibbons	OF144 1B13 DH5	L	26	160	625	80	173	39	2	23	100	49	89	0	.277	.456
Luis Matos	OF107 DH2	R	24	109	439	70	133	23	3	13	45	28	90	15	.303	.458
Melvin Mora (HJ)	OF79 SS11 2B6 1B1	R	31	96	344	68	109	17	1	15	48	49	71	6	.317	.503
Brook Fordyce	C107	R	33	108	348	28	95	12	2	6	31	19	44	2	.273	.371
David Segui (WJ)	DH53 1B8	B	36	67	224	26	59	10	1	5	25	26	47	1	.263	.384
Brian Roberts	2B107 DH4 SS2	B	25	112	460	65	124	22	4	5	41	46	58	23	.270	.367
B.J. Surhoff	DH39 OF27 1B22	L	38	93	319	32	94	20	4	5	41	29	29	2	.295	.404
Larry Bigbie (SJ)	OF80	L	25	83	287	43	87	15	1	9	31	29	60	7	.303	.456
Jose Morban	SS14 DH14 2B12 3B1	R	23	61	71	14	10	0	2	2	5	3	21	4	.141	.225
Geronimo Gil	C53	R	27	54	169	22	40	4	0	3	16	12	34	0	.237	.314
1 Gary Matthews	OF40 DH1	R	28	41	162	21	33	12	1	2	20	9	29	0	.204	.327
Jack Cust	DH23 OF1	L	24	27	73	7	19	7	0	4	11	10	25	0	.260	.521
Carlos Mendez	1B9 DH8	R	29	26	45	3	10	2	0	0	5	0	12	0	.222	.267
Jose Leon	3B10 1B7 DH5	R	26	21	54	6	13	1	0	0	6	3	18	0	.241	.259
Tim Raines Jr.	OF18 DH1	R	23	20	43	4	6	1	0	0	2	2	12	1	.140	.209
Robert Machado	C18	R	30	18	49	8	13	1	0	1	3	6	12	0	.265	.347
Marty Cordova (EJ)	DH5 OF4	R	33	9	30	5	7	1	0	1	4	8	5	1	.233	.367
Pete Swann	OF6 DH1	L	32	8	14	3	3	1	0	1	2	1	4	0	.214	.500
Albert Belle (PJ) 36																

NAME	T	AGE	W	L	PCT	SV	G	GS	CG	IP	H	BB	SO	SHO	ERA
TOTALS		30	71	91	.438	41	163	163	3	1450	1579	526	981	3	4.76
1 Sidney Ponson	R	26	14	6	.700	0	21	21	4	148	147	43	100	0	3.77
Jason Johnson	R	29	10	10	.500	0	32	32	0	190	216	80	118	0	4.18
Pat Hentgen	R	34	7	8	.467	1	28	22	1	161	150	58	100	0	4.09
1 Rick Helling	R	32	7	8	.467	0	24	24	0	139	156	40	86	0	5.71
Rodrigo Lopez (UJ)	R	27	7	10	.412	0	26	26	3	147	188	43	103	1	5.82
B.J. Ryan	L	27	4	1	.800	0	76	0	0	50	42	27	63	0	3.40
Kerry Ligtenberg	R	32	4	2	.667	1	68	0	0	59	60	14	47	0	3.34
Omar Daal (SJ)	L	31	4	11	.267	0	19	17	0	94	134	30	53	0	6.34
Willis Roberts (EJ)	R	28	3	1	.750	0	26	0	0	39	41	16	26	0	5.72
Travis Driskill	R	31	3	5	.375	1	20	0	0	48	62	9	33	0	6.00
Eric DuBose	L	27	3	6	.333	0	17	10	1	74	60	25	44	0	3.79
Hector Carrasco	R	33	2	6	.250	1	40	0	0	38	40	20	27	0	4.93
Matt Riley	L	23	1	0	1.000	0	2	2	0	10	7	5	8	0	1.80
Buddy Groom	L	37	1	3	.250	1	60	0	0	45	58	14	34	0	5.36
2 Damian Moss	L	26	1	5	.167	0	10	9	0	51	63	29	22	0	6.02
Rick Bauer	R	26	0	0	—	0	35	0	0	61	58	24	43	0	4.55
Sean Douglass	R	24	0	0	—	0	3	0	0	8	14	6	3	0	13.50
John Parrish	L	25	0	1	.000	0	14	0	0	24	17	8	15	0	1.90
1 Kurt Ainsworth (SJ)	R	24	0	1	.000	0	2	0	0	6		1	1	0	11.57
Jorge Julio	R	24	0	7	.000	36	64	0	0	62	60	34	52	0	4.38
Scott Erickson (SJ) 35															

TAMPA BAY — 5th 63-99 .389 38 — LOU PINIELLA

Name	G by Pos	B	AGE	G	AB	R	H	2B	3B	HR	RBI	BB	SO	SB	BA	SA
TOTALS	TOTALS		27	162	5654	715	1501	298	38	137	678	420	1030	142	.265	.404
Travis Lee	1B142 DH2	L	28	145	542	75	149	37	3	19	70	64	97	6	.275	.459
Marlon Anderson	2B134 DH4 OF3	L	29	145	482	59	130	27	3	6	67	41	60	19	.270	.376
Rey Ordonez (KJ)	SS34	R	31	34	117	14	37	11	0	3	22	2	12	0	.316	.487
Damian Rolls (RJ)	3B73 OF2 2B2	R	25	107	373	43	95	20	0	7	46	19	84	11	.255	.365
Aubrey Huff	OF102 DH33 1B22 3B8	L	26	162	636	91	198	47	3	34	107	53	80	2	.311	.555
Rocco Baldelli	OF154 DH2	R	21	156	637	89	184	32	8	11	78	30	128	27	.289	.416
Carl Crawford	OF146 DH1	L	21	151	630	80	177	18	9	5	54	26	102	55	.281	.362
Toby Hall	C130	R	27	130	463	50	117	23	0	12	47	23	40	0	.253	.380
Ben Grieve (RJ-VJ)	DH37 OF10	L	27	55	165	28	38	7	0	4	17	32	41	0	.230	.345
2 Julio Lugo	SS117	R	27	117	433	58	119	13	4	15	53	35	88	10	.275	.427
Al Martin	DH57 OF13 1B1	L	35	100	238	19	60	12	2	3	26	17	51	2	.252	.357
Terry Shumpert (LJ)	DH17 2B14 OF14 3B11 SS1	R	36	59	84	14	16	5	2	0	7	10	17	1	.190	.369
Jared Sandberg	3B50 1B1 SS1	R	25	55	136	15	29	10	1	6	23	16	52	1	.213	.434
Javier Valentin	C42 DH6	B	27	49	135	13	30	7	1	3	15	5	31	0	.222	.356
Antonio Perez	2B1 SS6 3B6 DH1	R	23	48	125	19	31	6	1	2	12	18	34	4	.248	.360
Jason Tyner	OF32 DH4	L	26	46	90	12	25	7	0	0	6	10	12	2	.278	.344
Damion Easley	3B23 DH8 2B4	R	33	36	107	8	20	3	1	1	7	2	18	0	.187	.262
Pete LaForest	DH12 C4	L	25	19	48	4	8	2	0	0	6	1	14	0	.167	.208
2 Adam Piatt	OF7 DH4	R	27	14	32	5	6	3	0	2	3	3	16	0	.188	.469
Chris Truby	3B13	R	29	13	43	4	12	3	0	0	4	0	13	0	.279	.349
George Lombard	OF13	L	27	13	37	8	8	1	0	1	4	6	13	0	.216	.324
Felix Escalona	SS8 2B1 3B1	R	24	10	27	2	5	2	0	0	2	0	8	0	.185	.259
2 Jeff Liefer	3B6 DH2 OF1	L	28	9	25	4	3	1	0	1	3	3	13	0	.120	.280
Jonny Gomes	DH8	R	22	8	15	1	2	1	0	0	0	0	6	0	.133	.200
Matt Diaz	DH2 OF1	R	25	4	9	2	1	0	0	0	0	0	3	0	.111	.111
1 Brent Abernathy	2B2	R	25	2	7	1	0	0	0	0	0	0	0	1	.000	.000
Jason Smith	3B1	L	25	1	4	0	1	0	0	0	0	0	0	0	.250	.250

NAME	T	AGE	W	L	PCT	SV	G	GS	CG	IP	H	BB	SO	SHO	ERA
TOTALS		26	63	99	.389	30	162	162	7	1437	1454	639	877	7	4.93
Victor Zambrano	R	27	12	10	.545	0	34	28	1	188	165	106	132	0	4.21
Lance Carter	R	28	7	5	.583	26	62	0	0	79	72	19	64	0	4.33
Jeremi Gonzalez	R	28	6	11	.353	0	25	25	2	156	131	69	97	0	3.91
Rob Bell	R	26	5	4	.556	0	19	18	0	101	103	39	44	0	5.52
2 Jorge Sosa	R	26	5	12	.294	0	29	19	1	129	137	60	72	1	4.62
Seth McClung (EJ)	R	22	4	1	.800	0	12	5	0	39	33	25	25	0	5.35
Travis Harper	R	27	4	8	.333	1	61	0	0	93	86	31	64	0	3.77
Doug Waechter	R	22	3	2	.600	0	6	5	1	35	29	15	29	1	3.31
1 Al Levine	R	35	3	7	.300	3	55	0	0	50	45	18	25	0	2.90
Jesus Colome	R	25	3	7	.300	2	54	0	0	74	69	46	69	0	4.50
Joe Kennedy (SJ)	L	24	3	12	.200	1	32	22	1	134	167	47	77	1	6.13
Chad Gaudin	R	20	2	0	1.000	0	15	3	0	40	37	16	23	0	3.60
Mark Malaska	L	25	2	1	.667	0	26	0	0	16	13	12	17	0	2.81
Mike Venafro	L	29	1	0	1.000	0	24	0	0	19	24	3	9	0	4.74
Brandon Backe	R	25	1	1	.500	0	25	0	0	45	40	25	36	0	5.44
Jim Parque (SJ)	L	28	1	1	.500	0	6	5	0	28	37	16	8	0	11.94
Dewon Brazelton	R	23	1	6	.143	0	10	10	0	48	57	23	24	0	6.89
Jon Switzer	L	24	0	0	—	0	10	0	0	13	13	3	7	0	7.45
Bobby Seay (SJ)	L	25	0	0	—	0	9	0	0	10	13	3	7	0	7.00
John Rocker	L	28	0	0	—	0	9	0	0						
1 Nick Bierbrodt	L	25	0	2	.000	0	13	5	0	35	59	23	20	0	9.68
Steve Parris	R	35	0	3	.000	0	10	7	0	44	60	13	14	0	6.18
Carlos Reyes	R	34	0	3	.000	0	10	3	0	40	40	15	13	0	5.22
Jason Standridge	R	24	0	5	.000	0	8	1	1	35	38	16	20	0	6.37

CENTRAL DIVISION

MINNESOTA — 1st 90-72 .556 — RON GARDENHIRE

Name	G by Pos	B	AGE	G	AB	R	H	2B	3B	HR	RBI	BB	SO	SB	BA	SA
TOTALS	TOTALS		28	162	5655	801	1567	318	45	155	755	512	1027	94	.277	.431
Doug Mientkiewicz	1B139 OF3 3B1 DH1	L	28	142	487	67	146	38	1	11	65	74	55	4	.300	.450
Luis Rivas	2B134 DH1	R	23	135	475	69	123	16	9	8	43	30	65	17	.259	.381
Cristian Guzman	SS141	B	25	134	534	78	143	15	14	3	53	30	68	8	.268	.365
Corey Koskie	3B131	L	30	131	469	76	137	29	2	14	69	77	113	11	.292	.452
Dustan Mohr	OF110 DH6	R	27	121	348	50	87	22	0	10	36	33	106	5	.250	.399
Torii Hunter	OF151 DH3	R	27	154	581	83	145	31	4	26	102	50	106	6	.250	.451
Jacque Jones	OF101 DH29	L	28	136	517	76	157	33	1	16	69	21	105	13	.304	.464
A.J. Pierzynski	C135	L	26	137	487	63	152	35	3	11	74	24	55	3	.312	.464
Matt LeCroy	DH64 C22 1B17	R	27	107	345	39	99	19	0	17	64	25	82	0	.287	.490
Denny Hocking	2B25 3B24 SS17 1B10 OF8 DH2	B	33	83	188	22	45	10	2	3	22	15	37	0	.239	.362
1 Bobby Kielty	OF36 DH32	B	26	75	238	40	60	13	0	9	32	42	56	6	.252	.420
2 Shannon Stewart	OF58 DH6	R	29	65	270	43	87	22	6	9	38	25	36	3	.322	.470
Chris Gomez	2B23 3B18 SS17 DH1	R	32	58	175	14	44	9	3	1	15	7	13	2	.251	.354
Justin Morneau	DH23 1B7	L	22	40	106	14	24	4	0	4	16	9	30	0	.226	.377
Michael Cuddyer	OF18 3B7 1B5 DH2 2B1	R	24	35	102	14	25	7	1	4	8	12	19	1	.245	.431
Lew Ford (BA)	OF25 DH4	R	26	34	73	16	24	7	1	2	8	2	13	4	.329	.575
Mike Ryan	OF16 DH4	L	25	26	61	13	24	7	0	5	12	6	12	0	.393	.754
1 Todd Sears	1B14 DH6	L	27	24	65	7	16	2	0	2	11	7	15	0	.246	.369
Michael Restovich	OF17 DH7	R	24	24	53	10	15	3	0	4	10	12	15	0	.283	.415
1 Tom Prince	C22 DH2	R	38	24	40	5	8	2	0	2	5	4	9	0	.200	.400
Alex Prieto	2B5 SS1	R	27	8	11	1	1	0	0	0	0	4	4	0	.091	.091
Rob Bowen	C7	B	22	7	10	0	1	0	0	0	1	3	6	0	.100	.100

NAME	T	AGE	W	L	PCT	SV	G	GS	CG	IP	H	BB	SO	SHO	ERA
TOTALS		29	90	72	.556	45	162	162	7	1462	1526	402	997	8	4.41
Brad Radke	R	30	14	10	.583	0	33	33	2	212	242	28	120	1	4.49
Kyle Lohse	R	24	14	11	.560	0	33	33	2	201	211	45	130	1	4.61
Kenny Rogers	L	38	13	8	.619	0	33	33	0	195	227	50	116	0	4.57
Johan Santana	L	24	12	3	.800	0	45	18	0	158	127	47	169	0	3.07
LaTroy Hawkins	R	30	9	3	.750	2	74	0	0	77	69	15	75	0	1.86
Joe Mays	R	27	8	8	.500	0	31	21	0	130	159	39	50	0	6.30
Rick Reed	R	38	6	12	.333	0	27	21	2	135	155	29	71	1	5.07
Juan Rincon	R	24	5	4	.455	0	58	0	0	86	74	38	63	0	3.68
Eddie Guardado	L	32	3	5	.375	41	66	0	0	65	50	14	60	0	2.89
J.C. Romero	L	27	3	3	.500	0	73	0	0	63	66	42	50	0	5.00
Grant Balfour	R	25	1	0	1.000	0	17	0	0	26	23	14	30	0	4.15
1 Eric Milton (KJ)	L	27	1	1	.500	0	3	3	0	17	15	1	7	0	2.65
Tony Fiore	R	31	1	1	.500	0	21	0	0	36	32	21	23	0	5.50
3 Michael Nakamura	R	26	0	1	.000	0	12	0	0	13	14	7	9	0	7.82
Mike Fetters (LJ)	R	38	0	0	—	0	12	0	0	13	16	8	5	0	5.40
Carlos Pulido	L	31	0	0	—	0	9	0	0	15	21	6	10	0	4.02
James Baldwin	R	31	0	2	.000	0	7	7	0						7.71
Brad Thomas	L	25	0	1	.500	0	6	0	0	7	8	2	0	0	7.71
Adam Johnson	R	23	0	1	.000	0	2								47.25

CHICAGO — 2nd 86-76 .531 4 — JERRY MANUEL

Name	G by Pos	B	AGE	G	AB	R	H	2B	3B	HR	RBI	BB	SO	SB	BA	SA
TOTALS	TOTALS		30	162	5487	791	1445	303	19	220	766	519	916	77	.263	.446
Paul Konerko	1B119 DH14	R	27	137	444	49	104	19	0	18	65	43	50	0	.234	.399
1 D'Angelo Jimenez	2B68 3B2	B	25	73	271	35	69	11	5	7	26	32	46	4	.255	.410
Jose Valentin	SS143	B	33	144	503	79	119	26	2	28	74	54	114	8	.237	.463
Joe Crede	3B151	R	25	151	536	68	140	31	2	19	75	32	75	1	.261	.433
Magglio Ordonez	OF157 DH2	R	29	160	606	95	192	46	3	29	99	57	73	9	.317	.546
2 Carl Everett	OF68 DH3	B	32	73	256	40	77	4	0	10	41	22	36	4	.301	.473
Carlos Lee	OF156 DH1	R	27	158	623	100	181	35	1	31	113	37	91	18	.291	.499
Miguel Olivo	C113	R	24	114	317	37	75	19	1	6	27	19	80	6	.237	.360
Frank Thomas	DH124 1B27	R	35	153	546	87	146	35	0	42	105	100	115	0	.267	.562
Brian Daubach	1B45 DH15 OF12	L	31	95	183	26	42	11	0	6	21	34	54	1	.230	.388
Aaron Rowand	OF87 DH1	R	25	93	157	22	45	8	0	6	24	7	21	0	.287	.452
Tony Graffanino	SS36 2B29 3B20 DH3 1B2	R	31	90	250	51	65	15	3	7	23	24	37	8	.260	.428
Willie Harris	OF61 2B12	L	25	79	137	19	28	3	1	0	5	10	28	12	.204	.241
Sandy Alomar	C75	R	37	75	194	22	52	12	0	5	26	4	17	0	.268	.407
2 Roberto Alomar	2B67	B	35	67	253	42	64	11	1	3	17	30	37	6	.253	.340
Armando Rios	OF32 DH1	L	31	49	104	4	22	3	0	2	11	5	13	0	.212	.298
Joe Borchard	OF16	B	24	16	49	5	9	1	0	1	5	5	18	0	.184	.265
1 Josh Paul	C11 DH1	R	28	13	17	6	6	0	0	0	4	3	3	0	.353	.353
Aaron Miles	2B3 DH2	B	26	8	12	3	4	3	0	0	2	0	0	0	.333	.583
Jamie Burke	C4 1B1 DH1	R	31	6	8	0	3	0	0	0	2	0	1	0	.375	.375

NAME	T	AGE	W	L	PCT	SV	G	GS	CG	IP	H	BB	SO	SHO	ERA
		28	86	76	.531	36	162	162	12	1431	1364	518	1056	4	4.17
Esteban Loaiza	R	31	21	9	.700	0	34	34	1	226	196	56	207	0	2.90
Bartolo Colon	R	30	15	13	.536	0	34	34	9	242	223	67	173	0	3.87
Mark Buehrle	L	24	14	14	.500	0	35	35	2	230	250	61	119	0	4.14
Jon Garland	R	23	12	13	.480	0	32	32	0	192	188	74	109	0	4.51
Tom Gordon	R	35	7	6	.538	12	66	0	0	74	57	31	91	0	3.16
Billy Koch (EJ)	R	28	5	5	.500	11	55	0	0	53	59	28	42	0	5.77
Damaso Marte	L	28	4	2	.667	11	71	0	0	80	50	34	87	0	1.58
Scott Schoeneweis	L	29	2	1	.667	0	20	0	0	26	26	9	27	0	4.50
1 Gary Glover	R	26	1	0	1.000	0	24	0	0	36	43	14	23	0	4.54
Mike Porzio	L	30	1	1	.500	0	3	0	0	14	18	1	9	0	6.43
Neal Cotts	L	23	1	1	.500	0	4	4	0	13	15	17	10	0	8.10
1 Rick White	R	34	1	1	.333	1	34	0	0	48	56	13	37	0	6.61
Josh Stewart	L	24	1	2	.333	0	5	5	0	26	28	16	13	0	5.96
Dan Wright (EJ)	R	25	1	7	.125	0	20	15	0	86	91	46	47	0	6.15
Kelly Wunsch (UJ)	L	30	0	0	—	0	43	0	0	36	17	25	33	0	2.75
David Sanders	L	23	0	0	—	0	20	0	0	22	25	11	14	0	6.14
2 Scott Sullivan	R	32	0	0	—	0	15	0	0	14	9	6	13	0	3.77
Jon Adkins	R	25	0	0	—	0	4	0	0	9	8	7	3	0	4.82
Matt Ginter	R	25	0	0	—	0	3	0	0	3	2	1	0	0	13.50
Jose Paniagua	R	29	0	0	—	0	1	0	0	0.1	3	1	0	0	108.00

KANSAS CITY — 3rd 83-79 .512 7 — TONY PENA

Name	G by Pos	B	AGE	G	AB	R	H	2B	3B	HR	RBI	BB	SO	SB	BA	SA
TOTALS	TOTALS		30	162	5568	836	1526	288	39	162	781	476	926	120	.274	.427
Ken Harvey	1B99 DH32	R	25	135	485	50	129	30	0	13	64	29	94	2	.266	.408
Desi Relaford	2B89 3B33 OF20 SS6 DH5	B	29	141	500	70	127	27	5	8	59	40	70	20	.254	.376
Angel Berroa	SS158	R	25	158	567	92	163	28	7	17	73	29	100	21	.287	.451
Joe Randa	3B129 DH2	R	33	131	502	80	146	31	1	16	72	41	61	1	.291	.452
Aaron Guiel	OF89 DH1	L	30	99	354	49	98	30	0	15	52	27	63	3	.277	.489
Carlos Beltran	OF130 DH8	B	26	141	521	102	160	14	10	26	100	72	81	41	.307	.522
Raul Ibanez	OF131 1B22 DH12	L	31	157	608	95	179	33	4	18	90	49	81	8	.294	.454
Brent Mayne	C112	L	35	113	372	39	91	17	1	6	36	32	59	0	.245	.344
Mike Sweeney (XJ)	DH62 1B45	R	29	108	392	62	115	18	1	16	83	64	56	3	.293	.467
Michael Tucker (BL)	OF85 DH15	L	32	104	389	61	102	20	5	13	55	39	88	8	.262	.440
Carlos Febles	2B67 DH4 SS1	R	27	74	196	31	46	11	1	3	11	13	30	8	.235	.260
Mike DiFelice	C58 DH2	R	34	62	189	29	48	16	1	3	25	9	30	1	.254	.397
Mendy Lopez (LJ)	1B17 3B13 2B11 SS4 OF3	R	29	52	94	13	26	5	1	3	11	4	28	2	.277	.447
Dee Brown (WJ)	OF25	L	25	50	132	16	30	7	0	2	14	8	37	1	.227	.326
Julius Matos	3B13 2B11 SS2 OF1 DH1	R	28	28	57	7	15	1	0	2	7	1	12	1	.263	.386
1 Rondell White	OF17 DH4	R	31	22	75	13	26	6	1	4	21	6	8	0	.347	.613
Brandon Berger	OF11 DH1	R	28	13	32	3	7	0	0	3	5	4	9	0	.219	.219
Jarrod Patterson	3B4 DH4 1B2	L	29	13	22	3	4	0	0	0	3	0	3	0	.182	.182
David DeJesus	OF9	L	23	12	7	0	2	0	0	0	1	0	2	0	.286	.571
2 Brent Abernathy	2B9	R	25	10	27	2	2	0	0	0	1	0	5	0	.074	.074
2 Tom Prince	C7 DH1	R	38	8	8	0	2	0	0	0	2	0	2	0	.250	.250
Rontrez Johnson	OF6 DH2	R	26	8	3	3	1	0	0	0	0	0	0	0	.333	.333
Morgan Burkhart	1B2 DH2	B	31	6	15	1	3	0	0	0	1	2	0	0	.200	.200
Gookie Dawkins	2B3	R	24	3	0	0	0	0	0	0	0	0	0	0	.000	.000

NAME	T	AGE	W	L	PCT	SV	G	GS	CG	IP	H	BB	SO	SHO	ERA
		29	83	79	.512	36	162	162	7	1439	1569	566	865	10	5.05
Darrell May	L	31	10	8	.556	0	35	32	2	210	197	53	115	1	3.77
Chris George	L	23	9	6	.600	0	18	18	0	94	120	44	39	0	7.11
Jose Lima	R	30	8	3	.727	0	14	14	0	73	80	26	32	0	4.91
Runelvys Hernandez (EJ)	R	25	7	5	.583	0	16	16	0	92	87	37	48	0	4.61
Jeremy Affeldt	L	24	7	6	.538	4	36	18	0	126	126	38	98	0	3.93
Kris Wilson	R	26	6	3	.667	0	29	4	0	73	92	16	42	0	5.33
D.J. Carrasco	R	26	6	5	.545	2	50	2	0	80	82	40	57	0	4.82
2 Brian Anderson	L	31	5	1	.833	0	7	7	2	50	50	11	15	1	3.99
Albie Lopez (GJ)	R	31	4	2	.667	0	15	0	0	23	41	17	15	0	12.71
Jimmy Gobble	L	21	4	5	.444	0	9	9	0	53	56	15	31	0	4.61
Mike MacDougal	R	26	3	5	.375	27	68	0	0	64	64	32	57	0	4.08
Jason Gilfillan	R	26	2	0	1.000	0	13	0	0	16	22	10	12	0	7.71
Miguel Asencio (EJ)	R	22	2	1	.667	0	8	8	1	48	54	21	27	0	5.21
Jason Grimsley	R	35	2	6	.250	0	76	0	0	75	88	36	58	0	5.16
2 Curtis Leskanic	R	35	1	0	1.000	0	27	0	0	26	16	11	22	0	1.73
Ryan Bukvich	R	25	1	0	1.000	0	9	0	0	10	12	9	8	0	9.58
Sean Lowe	R	32	1	1	.500	0	28	0	0	45	55	21	28	0	6.25
Nate Field	R	27	1	1	.500	0	19	0	0	22	19	14	19	0	4.15
Paul Abbott	R	35	1	2	.333	0	10	8	0	48	47	26	32	0	5.29
Jamey Wright	R	28	1	2	.333	0	4	2	0	25	23	11	19	1	4.26
2 Kevin Appier (EJ)	R	35	1	2	.333	0	4	4	0	19	15	7	5	0	4.26
Kyle Snyder (SJ)	R	25	1	6	.143	0	15	15	0	85	94	21	39	0	5.17
1 Scott Mullen	L	28	0	0	—	0	2	0	0	1	1	0	5	3	0.00
Jeremy Hill	R	25	0	0	—	0	1	0	0	1	5	3	0	0	16.62
2 Al Levine	R	35	0	1	.000	0	18	0	0	21	22	11	5	0	2.53
Brad Voyles	R	26	0	2	.000	0	11	0	0	31	47	18	24	0	7.18
2 Graeme Lloyd	L	36	0	2	.000	0	16	0	0	12	29	7	8	0	10.95
Les Walrond	L	26	0	2	.000	0	4	0	0	8	11	7	6	0	10.13
Rick DeHart	L	33	0	2	.000	0	4	0	0	4	8	2	1	0	13.50

CLEVELAND — 4th 68-94 .420 22 — ERIC WEDGE

Name	G by Pos	B	AGE	G	AB	R	H	2B	3B	HR	RBI	BB	SO	SB	BA	SA
TOTALS	TOTALS		28	162	5572	699	1413	296	26	158	660	466	1062	86	.254	.401
Ben Broussard	1B114	L	26	116	386	53	96	21	3	16	55	32	75	5	.249	.443
Brandon Phillips	2B109	R	22	112	370	36	77	18	1	6	33	14	77	5	.208	.311
Omar Vizquel	SS64	B	36	64	250	43	61	13	2	2	19	29	20	8	.244	.336
Casey Blake	3B140 1B31	R	29	152	557	80	143	35	0	17	67	38	109	7	.257	.411
Jody Gerut	OF113 DH11	L	25	127	480	66	134	33	2	22	75	35	70	4	.279	.494
Milton Bradley (XJ)	OF93 DH8	B	25	101	377	61	121	34	2	10	56	64	73	17	.321	.501
Matt Lawton (BG)	OF74 DH21	L	31	99	377	57	93	19	0	15	53	47	47	10	.249	.420
Josh Bard	C87 DH1	B	25	91	303	25	74	13	1	8	36	22	53	0	.244	.373
Ellis Burks (EJ)	DH51 OF2	R	38	55	198	27	52	11	1	6	28	27	46	1	.263	.419
Coco Crisp	OF90 DH7	B	23	99	414	55	110	15	6	3	27	23	51	15	.266	.353
Travis Hafner	DH43 1B42	L	26	91	291	35	74	19	3	14	40	22	81	2	.254	.485
John McDonald (KJ)	2B37 SS27 3B23	R	28	82	214	21	46	9	1	1	14	11	31	3	.215	.280
Jhonny Peralta	SS72 3B6	R	21	77	242	24	55	10	1	4	21	20	65	1	.227	.326
1 Shane Spencer	OF43 1B11 DH7	R	31	64	210	23	57	10	0	8	26	18	52	2	.271	.433
Tim Laker	C50 DH2	R	33	52	162	17	39	11	0	3	21	9	38	2	.241	.364
Victor Martinez	C40 DH5	B	24	49	159	15	46	4	0	1	16	13	21	1	.289	.333
2 Ryan Ludwick	OF32 DH4	R	24	39	136	14	36	7	1	7	26	8	39	2	.265	.485
Zach Sorensen	2B14 SS3 3B1 OF1 DH1	B	26	36	37	2	5	1	0	1	2	7	13	0	.135	.243
Angel Santos	2B28 3B4	B	23	32	76	9	17	3	1	3	6	3	18	1	.224	.408
Alex Escobar	OF25	R	24	28	99	16	27	2	0	5	14	7	33	1	.273	.444
Bill Selby	3B10 DH2 1B1 2B1 OF1	L	33	27	39	3	4	1	0	0	5	3	11	0	.103	.128
1 Karim Garcia (WJ)	OF23 DH1	R	27	24	93	8	18	1	0	5	14	5	20	0	.194	.366
Ricky Gutierrez (XJ)	SS9 3B7	R	33	16	50	2	13	3	0	0	3	3	5	0	.260	.320
Chris Magruder	OF8	B	26	9	26	3	9	2	1	1	3	3	6	0	.346	.615
Greg LaRocca	3B2 DH1	R	30	9	9	3	3	1	0	0	1	1	1	0	.333	.444

NAME	T	AGE	W	L	PCT	SV	G	GS	CG	IP	H	BB	SO	SHO	ERA
		27	68	94	.420	34	162	162	5	1459	1477	501	943	7	4.21
C.C. Sabathia	L	22	13	9	.591	0	30	30	2	198	190	66	141	1	3.60
1 Brian Anderson	L	31	9	10	.474	0	25	24	0	148	162	32	72	0	3.71
Jason Davis	R	23	8	11	.421	0	27	27	1	165	172	47	85	0	4.68
Jake Westbrook	R	25	7	10	.412	0	34	22	1	133	142	56	58	0	4.33
Billy Traber	L	23	6	9	.400	0	33	18	1	112	132	40	88	1	5.24
Jason Boyd	R	30	3	1	.750	0	44	0	0	52	38	26	31	0	4.30
Cliff Lee (MJ)	L	24	3	3	.500	0	9	9	0	52	41	20	44	0	3.61
Terry Mulholland	L	40	3	4	.429	0	45	3	0	99	117	37	42	0	4.91
1 Ricardo Rodriguez	R	25	3	9	.250	0	15	15	0	82	89	28	41	0	5.73
Jack Cressend	R	28	2	1	.667	0	33	0	0	43	40	9	28	0	2.51
David Riske	R	26	2	2	.500	8	68	0	0	75	52	20	82	0	2.29
Rafael Betancourt	R	28	2	2	.500	1	33	0	0	38	27	13	36	0	2.13
Danys Baez	R	25	2	9	.182	25	73	0	0	76	65	23	66	0	3.81
David Lee	R	30	1	0	1.000	0	8	0	0	9	4	6	3	0	5.40
2 Dan Miceli	R	32	1	1	.500	0	13	0	0	15	9	6	19	0	1.20
Dave Elder (SJ)	R	27	1	1	.500	0	4	0	0	2	5	4	3	0	19.29
Jason Stanford	R	26	1	3	.250	0	13	8	0	50	48	16	30	0	3.60
Jose Santiago	R	28	1	3	.250	0	13	0	0	32	37	14	15	0	2.84
Carl Sadler	L	26	0	0	—	0	18	0	0	10	11	5	10	0	1.86
2 Nick Bierbrodt	L	25	0	0	—	0	5	0	0	8	9	6	3	0	6.75
Alex Herrera	L	26	0	0	—	0	10	0	0	7	8	5	4	0	9.00
Jason Bere (SJ)	R	32	0	1	.000	0	2	2	0	7	5	2	6	0	9.00
Jerrod Riggan	R	29	0	0	—	0	10	0	0	7	8	2	5	0	4.05
David Cortes	R	29	0	1	.000	0	8	0	0	9	12	3	3	0	12.00
Aaron Myette	R	25	0	0	—	0	3	2	0	8	7	3	2	0	23.62
Chad Durbin	R	25	0	1	.000	0	9	0	0	9	18	3	8	0	7.27
Jason Phillips (JL)	L	25	0	2	.000	0	5	0	0	4	5	3	2	0	9.00
Brian Tallet	L	25	0	2	.000	0	3	0	0	19	23	8	9	0	4.74
Chad Paronto	R	28	0	0	—	0	6	0	0	7	7	3	6	0	9.45

Bob Wickman (EJ) 34, Mark Wohlers (EJ) 33

DETROIT — 5th 43-119 .265 47 — ALAN TRAMMELL

Name	G by Pos	B	AGE	G	AB	R	H	2B	3B	HR	RBI	BB	SO	SB	BA	SA
TOTALS	TOTALS		27	162	5466	591	1312	201	39	153	553	443	1099	98	.240	.375
Carlos Pena	1B128 DH1	L	25	131	452	51	112	21	6	18	50	53	123	4	.248	.440
Warren Morris	2B89	L	29	97	346	37	94	13	2	6	37	23	42	4	.272	.373
Ramon Santiago	SS85 2B53	B	23	141	444	44	100	18	1	2	29	33	66	10	.225	.284
Eric Munson (BG)	3B91 DH3	L	25	99	313	28	75	9	0	18	50	35	61	3	.240	.441
Bobby Higginson	OF118 DH8	L	32	130	469	61	110	13	4	14	52	59	73	8	.235	.369
2 Alex Sanchez	OF99	L	26	101	394	43	114	13	5	2	22	18	46	44	.289	.355
Craig Monroe	OF108 DH13	R	26	128	425	51	102	18	1	23	70	27	89	4	.240	.449
Brandon Inge	C104	R	26	104	330	32	67	15	3	8	30	24	79	2	.203	.339
Dmitri Young	DH75 OF61 3B16 1B1	B	29	155	562	78	167	34	7	29	85	58	130	2	.297	.537
Shane Halter	3B50 SS27 2B24 1B12 DH4 OF2	R	33	114	360	33	78	5	2	12	30	27	77	2	.217	.342
Kevin Witt	DH36 1B27 OF13 3B5	L	27	93	270	25	71	9	0	10	26	15	68	1	.263	.407
Omar Infante	SS63 3B4 2B2	R	21	69	221	24	49	6	1	0	9	18	37	6	.222	.258
Andres Torres	OF50 DH3	B	25	54	154	19	33	4	3	1	9	10	35	5	.220	.298
Matt Walbeck	C55 DH1	B	33	59	138	11	24	4	1	1	9	3	26	0	.174	.239
2 Ben Petrick	OF32 C6 1B2	R	26	43	120	18	27	6	0	4	12	8	30	0	.225	.375
Eugene Kingsale	OF30 DH4	B	26	39	120	11	25	3	1	1	8	10	17	1	.208	.275
A.J. Hinch (GJ)	C27	R	29	27	74	7	15	3	1	3	11	3	18	0	.203	.392
Dean Palmer (SJ)	DH22 1B3 3B1	R	34	26	86	3	12	2	0	0	6	9	28	0	.140	.163
Danny Klassen	3B13 2B4 SS3	R	27	22	73	9	18	3	1	1	7	4	26	0	.247	.336
Craig Paquette	1B5 OF5	R	34	11	33	2	5	0	0	0	0	0	5	0	.152	.152
Hiram Bocachica	OF6	R	27	9	22	3	1	0	0	0	1	5	9	0	.045	.091
Cody Ross	OF6	R	22	6	19	1	4	2	0	0	2	3	3	0	.211	.421
Ernie Young	DH4	R	33	5	11	0	2	0	0	0	0	4	5	0	.182	.182

NAME	T	AGE	W	L	PCT	SV	G	GS	CG	IP	H	BB	SO	SHO	ERA
		27	43	119	.265	27	162	162	3	1439	1616	557	764	5	5.30
Mike Maroth	L	25	9	21	.300	0	33	33	1	193	231	50	87	0	5.73
Nate Cornejo	R	23	6	17	.261	0	32	32	2	195	236	58	46	0	4.67
Jeremy Bonderman	R	20	6	19	.240	0	33	28	0	162	193	58	108	0	5.56
Jamie Walker	L	31	4	3	.571	3	78	0	0	65	61	17	45	0	3.32
Wil Ledezma	L	22	3	7	.300	0	34	8	0	84	99	35	49	0	5.79
Gary Knotts	R	26	3	8	.273	0	20	18	0	95	111	47	51	0	6.04
Steve Avery	L	33	2	0	1.000	0	19	0	0	16	19	7	6	0	5.63
Franklyn German	R	23	2	4	.333	5	45	0	0	45	47	45	41	0	6.04
Brian Schmack	R	29	1	0	1.000	0	11	0	0	13	14	4	4	0	3.46
Shane Loux	R	24	1	1	.500	0	11	4	0	30	37	12	8	0	7.12
Nate Robertson	L	25	1	2	.333	0	8	8	0	45	55	23	33	0	5.44
Chris Spurling	R	26	1	3	.250	0	66	0	0	77	78	22	38	0	4.68
Chris Mears	R	25	1	3	.250	5	29	3	0	41	50	11	21	0	5.44
Fernando Rodney	R	26	1	3	.250	3	27	0	0	30	35	17	33	0	6.07
Matt Roney	R	23	1	9	.100	0	45	11	0	101	102	48	47	0	5.45
1 Adam Bernero	R	26	1	12	.077	0	41	10	0	101	104	41	54	0	6.08
Danny Patterson (EJ)	R	32	0	0	—	0	19	0	0	18	15	4	19	0	4.08
Eric Eckenstahler	L	26	0	1	.000	0	23	0	0	9	6	15	12	0	2.87
Matt Anderson	R	26	0	1	.000	0	23	0	0	23	25	9	13	0	5.40
1 Steve Sparks	R	37	0	6	.000	2	42	0	0	90	95	34	49	0	4.72

OAKLAND — 1st 96-66 .593 — KEN MACHA

Name	G by Pos	B	AGE	G	AB	R	H	2B	3B	HR	RBI	BB	SO	SB	BA	SA
TOTALS			28	162	5497	768	1398	317	24	176	742	556	898	48	.254	.417
Scott Hatteberg	1B128 DH15	L	33	147	541	63	137	34	0	12	61	66	53	0	.253	.383
Mark Ellis	2B153	R	26	154	553	78	137	31	5	9	52	48	94	6	.248	.371
Miguel Tejada	SS162	R	27	162	636	98	177	42	0	27	106	53	65	10	.278	.472
Eric Chavez	3B154	L	25	156	588	94	166	39	5	29	101	62	89	4	.282	.514
Jermaine Dye (KJ-SJ)	OF61 DH3	R	29	65	221	28	38	6	0	4	20	25	42	1	.172	.253
Eric Byrnes	OF117 DH2	R	27	121	414	64	109	27	9	12	51	42	71	10	.263	.459
Terrence Long	OF137 DH1	L	27	140	486	64	119	22	2	14	61	31	67	4	.245	.385
Ramon Hernandez	C139	R	27	140	483	70	132	24	1	21	78	33	79	1	.273	.458
Erubiel Durazo	DH121 1B33	L	29	154	537	92	139	29	0	21	77	100	105	1	.259	.430
Chris Singleton	OF113	L	30	120	306	38	75	24	1	1	36	26	55	7	.245	.340
Billy McMillon	OF37 DH9 1B3	L	31	66	153	15	41	11	0	6	26	19	36	0	.268	.458
1 Adam Piatt	OF38 DH2 1B3	R	27	47	100	6	24	10	0	4	15	6	30	1	.240	.460
2 Jose Guillen	OF44 DH1	R	27	45	170	25	45	7	1	8	23	7	32	0	.265	.459
Frank Menechino	2B22 3B19 SS3 DH1	R	32	43	83	10	16	0	0	2	9	19	16	1	.193	.265
Adam Melhuse	C33 3B2 1B1	B	31	40	77	13	23	7	0	5	14	9	19	0	.299	.584
Ron Gant	OF9 DH6	R	38	17	41	4	6	0	0	1	4	2	9	0	.146	.220
Mark Johnson	C13	R	27	13	27	3	3	1	0	0	3	3	4	0	.111	.148
Bobby Crosby	SS9 DH2	R	23	11	12	1	0	0	0	0	0	1	5	0	.000	.000
1 Dave McCarty	OF5 1B3	R	33	8	26	2	7	2	0	0	2	1	7	0	.269	.346
Jason Grabowski	OF3 3B1 DH1	L	27	8	8	0	0	0	0	0	0	1	5	0	.000	.000
Graham Koonce	1B5	L	28	6	8	0	1	1	0	0	0	1	6	0	.125	.250
Esteban German	2B5	R	25	5	4	0	1	0	0	0	1	0	1	0	.250	.250
Mike Edwards	OF2 DH2	R	26	4	4	0	1	0	0	0	0	0	2	1	.250	.250

NAME	T	AGE	W	L	PCT	SV	G	GS	CG	IP	H	BB	SO	SHO	ERA
TOTALS		28	96	66	.593	48	162	162	16	1442	1336	499	1018	14	3.63
Tim Hudson	R	27	16	7	.696	0	34	34	3	240	197	61	162	2	2.70
Mark Mulder (PJ)	L	25	15	9	.625	0	26	26	9	187	180	40	128	2	3.13
Barry Zito	L	25	14	12	.538	0	35	35	4	232	186	88	146	1	3.30
Ted Lilly	L	27	12	10	.545	0	32	31	0	178	179	58	147	0	4.34
Keith Foulke	R	30	9	1	.900	43	72	0	0	87	57	20	88	0	2.08
Ricardo Rincon	L	33	8	4	.667	0	55	0	0	55	45	32	40	0	3.25
Chad Bradford	R	28	7	4	.636	2	72	0	0	77	67	30	62	0	3.04
Rich Harden	R	21	5	4	.556	0	15	13	0	75	72	40	67	0	4.46
John Halama	L	31	3	5	.375	0	35	13	0	109	117	36	51	0	4.22
Mike Wood	R	23	2	1	.667	0	7	1	0	14	24	7	15	0	10.54
Jim Mecir	R	33	2	3	.400	1	41	0	0	37	40	16	25	0	5.59
Chad Harville	R	26	1	0	1.000	1	21	0	0	22	25	17	18	0	5.82
Justin Duchscherer	R	25	1	1	.500	0	3	1	0	16	17	3	15	0	3.31
1 Aaron Harang	R	25	1	3	.250	0	7	6	0	30	41	9	16	0	5.34
Mike Neu	R	25	0	0	—	1	32	0	0	42	43	26	20	0	3.64
2 Steve Sparks	R	37	0	0	—	0	9	0	0	17	19	3	5	0	5.71
Jeremy Fikac	R	28	0	1	.000	0	14	0	0	16	14	11	9	0	4.50
Micah Bowie (EJ)	L	28	0	1	.000	0	6	0	0	8	13	2	4	0	7.56

SEATTLE — 2nd 93-69 .574 3 — BOB MELVIN

Name	G by Pos	B	AGE	G	AB	R	H	2B	3B	HR	RBI	BB	SO	SB	BA	SA
TOTALS			32	162	5561	795	1509	290	33	139	759	586	989	108	.271	.410
John Olerud	1B152	L	34	152	539	64	145	35	0	10	83	84	67	0	.269	.390
Bret Boone	2B159	R	34	159	622	111	183	35	5	35	117	68	125	16	.294	.535
Carlos Guillen	SS76 3B32 DH1	B	27	109	388	63	107	19	3	7	52	52	64	4	.276	.394
Jeff Cirillo (SJ)	3B85 1B1 DH1	R	33	87	258	24	53	11	0	2	23	24	32	1	.205	.271
Ichiro Suzuki	OF159	L	29	159	679	111	212	29	8	13	62	36	69	34	.312	.436
Mike Cameron	OF147	R	30	147	534	74	135	31	5	18	76	70	137	17	.253	.431
Randy Winn	OF157	B	29	157	600	103	177	37	4	11	75	41	100	23	.295	.425
Dan Wilson	C96	R	34	96	316	32	76	15	2	4	43	15	52	0	.241	.339
Edgar Martinez	DH140	L	40	145	497	72	146	25	0	24	98	92	95	0	.294	.489
Mark McLemore	SS38 3B29 OF16 DH11 2B6	B	38	99	309	34	72	15	2	2	37	38	71	5	.233	.314
Willie Bloomquist	3B37 SS18 DH12 OF11 2B7 1B3	R	25	89	196	30	49	7	2	1	14	19	39	4	.250	.321
Ben Davis	C73 DH1	B	26	80	246	25	58	18	0	6	42	18	61	0	.236	.382
John Mabry	OF22 DH12 1B9	L	32	64	104	12	22	6	0	3	16	15	21	0	.212	.356
2 Rey Sanchez	SS46	R	35	46	170	22	50	5	1	0	11	8	21	1	.294	.335
Greg Colbrunn (WJ)	1B14 DH4	R	33	22	58	7	16	1	1	3	7	4	16	0	.276	.483
Pat Borders	C7 3B2 DH1	R	40	12	14	1	2	1	0	0	1	0	5	0	.143	.214
Luis Ugueto	2B4 DH3 3B1 SS1	B	24	12	5	4	1	0	0	0	1	1	0	2	.200	.200
Jamal Strong	DH7 OF2	R	24	12	2	2	0	0	0	0	0	0	0	2	.000	.000
Chad Meyers	DH6 OF3	R	27	9	1	1	0	0	0	0	0	0	1	0	.000	.000

NAME	T	AGE	W	L	PCT	SV	G	GS	CG	IP	H	BB	SO	SHO	ERA
TOTALS		30	93	69	.574	38	162	162	8	1441	1340	466	1001	15	3.76
Jamie Moyer	L	40	21	7	.750	0	33	33	1	215	199	66	129	0	3.27
Joel Pineiro	R	24	16	11	.593	0	32	32	2	212	192	76	151	2	3.78
Gil Meche	R	24	15	13	.536	0	32	32	1	186	187	63	130	0	4.59
Freddy Garcia	R	28	12	14	.462	0	33	33	1	201	196	71	144	0	4.51
Ryan Franklin	R	30	11	13	.458	0	32	32	2	212	199	61	99	1	3.57
Julio Mateo	R	25	4	0	1.000	1	50	0	0	86	69	13	71	0	3.15
Rafael Soriano	R	23	3	0	1.000	1	40	0	0	53	30	12	68	0	1.53
1 Jeff Nelson	R	36	3	2	.600	7	46	0	0	38	34	14	47	0	3.35
Arthur Rhodes	L	33	3	3	.500	3	67	0	0	54	53	18	48	0	4.17
Giovanni Carrara	R	35	2	0	1.000	0	29	0	0	40	14	13		0	6.83
Shigetoshi Hasegawa	R	34	2	4	.333	16	63	0	0	73	62	18	32	0	1.48
Kazuhiro Sasaki (BR)	R	35	1	1	.500	10	35	0	0	33	31	15	29	0	4.05
3 Armando Benitez	R	30	0	0	—	0	15	0	0	14	10	11	15	0	3.14
Aaron Taylor	R	25	0	0	—	0	10	0	0	13	17	6	9	0	8.53
Brian Sweeney	R	29	0	0	—	0	7	0	0	7	7	2	6	0	1.93
Aaron Looper	R	26	0	0	—	0	7	0	0	7	2	6	1	0	5.14
J.J. Putz	R	26	0	0	—	0	6	0	0	5	5	3	3	0	4.91
2 Matt White	L	25	0	0	—	0	2	0	0	2	4	1	0	0	13.50

ANAHEIM — 3rd 77-85 .475 19 — MIKE SCIOSCIA

Name	G by Pos	B	AGE	G	AB	R	H	2B	3B	HR	RBI	BB	SO	SB	BA	SA
TOTALS			29	162	5487	736	1473	276	33	150	687	476	838	129	.268	.413
Scott Spiezio	1B114 3B52 OF10	B	30	158	521	69	138	36	7	16	83	46	66	6	.265	.453
Adam Kennedy	2B140 DH1	L	27	143	449	71	121	17	1	13	49	45	73	22	.269	.399
David Eckstein	SS116 DH3	R	28	120	452	59	114	22	1	3	31	36	45	16	.252	.325
Troy Glaus (SJ)	3B87 DH4	R	27	91	319	53	79	17	2	16	50	46	73	7	.248	.464
Tim Salmon	OF78 DH68	R	34	148	528	78	145	35	4	19	72	77	93	3	.275	.464
Darin Erstad (LJ)	OF66	L	29	67	258	35	65	7	1	4	17	18	40	9	.252	.333
Garret Anderson	OF144 DH15	L	30	159	638	80	201	49	4	29	116	31	83	6	.315	.541
Bengie Molina	C117	R	28	119	409	37	115	24	0	14	71	13	31	1	.281	.443
Brad Fullmer (KJ)	DH41 1B18	L	28	63	206	32	63	9	2	9	35	26	31	5	.306	.500
Jeff DaVanon	OF115 DH1	B	29	123	330	56	93	16	1	12	43	42	59	17	.282	.445
Eric Owens	OF97 DH3	R	32	111	241	29	65	6	0	1	20	10	24	11	.270	.307
Shawn Wooten	1B32 DH28 C19 3B17	R	30	98	272	25	66	8	0	7	32	24	45	0	.243	.349
Chone Figgins	OF47 2B14 SS8 DH3	B	25	71	240	34	71	9	4	0	27	20	38	13	.296	.367
Benji Gil	2B28 SS20 1B5 3B4 DH2	R	28	62	125	12	24	5	1	1	9	4	33	5	.192	.272
Jose Molina	C53	R	28	53	114	12	21	4	0	0	6	1	26	0	.184	.219
Robb Quinlan	1B33 DH3 OF1	R	26	38	94	13	27	4	2	2	4	6	16	1	.287	.372
Alfredo Amezaga	SS24 3B13 DH1	B	25	37	105	15	22	3	2	1	7	9	23	2	.210	.333
Adam Riggs	1B10 OF8 2B3 DH3	R	30	24	61	11	15	4	1	3	5	9	9	3	.246	.492
2 Wilson Delgado	SS9 3B9 2B1	B	30	19	50	4	16	0	0	0	2	3	6	0	.320	.320
Tom Gregorio	C12	R	26	12	19	1	3	0	0	0	1	3	0	1	.158	.158
Trent Durrington	2B5 3B4 DH2 OF1	R	27	12	14	5	2	0	0	0	1	3	0	1	.143	.143
Barry Wesson	OF9 DH1	R	26	10	11	2	2	0	0	1	3	0	4	1	.182	.455
Julio Ramirez	OF5 DH1	R	25	6	2	1	0	0	0	0	0	0	0	0	.000	.000
Gary Johnson	OF4	L	27	5	8	1	3	1	0	0	1	1	0	0	.375	.500

NAME	T	AGE	W	L	PCT	SV	G	GS	CG	IP	H	BB	SO	SHO	ERA
TOTALS		29	77	85	.475	39	162	162	5	1431	1444	486	980	9	4.28
Ramon Ortiz	R	30	16	13	.552	0	32	32	1	180	209	63	94	0	5.20
Jarrod Washburn	L	28	10	15	.400	0	32	32	2	207	205	54	118	0	4.43
John Lackey	R	24	10	16	.385	0	33	33	2	204	223	66	151	2	4.63
Francisco Rodriguez	R	21	8	3	.727	2	59	0	0	86	50	35	95	0	3.03
1 Kevin Appier	R	35	7	7	.500	0	19	19	0	93	105	36	50	0	5.63
Aaron Sele (SJ)	R	33	7	11	.389	0	25	25	0	122	135	58	53	0	5.77
Ben Weber	R	33	5	1	.833	0	62	0	0	80	84	22	46	0	2.69
Scot Shields	R	27	5	6	.455	1	44	13	0	148	138	38	111	0	2.85
Kevin Gregg	R	25	2	1	.667	0	5	3	0	25	18	6	14	0	3.28
Derrick Turnbow	R	25	2	0	1.000	0	11	0	0	15	7	3	15	0	0.59
Brendan Donnelly	R	31	2	2	.500	3	63	0	0	74	55	24	79	0	1.58
2 Gary Glover	R	26	1	0	1.000	0	18	0	0	27	34	8	14	0	5.00
1 Scott Schoeneweis	L	29	1	1	.500	0	39			37	16	22		0	3.96
1 Mickey Callaway (SJ)	R	28	1	4	.200	0	17	4	0	38	57	16	22	0	6.81
Greg Jones	R	28	0	0	—	0	3	0	0	4	1	3		0	2.45
Rich Rodriguez	L	40	0	0	—	0	3	0	0	4	4	1	3	0	18.00
Bart Miadich	R	30	0	0	—	0	4	0	0	10	16	6	7	0	9.58
Chris Bootcheck	R	24	0	1	.000	0	4	1	0	10	16	6	7	0	9.58
Troy Percival	R	33	0	5	.000	33	52	0	0	49	35	23	48	0	3.47
Matt Wise (EJ) 27															

TEXAS — 4th 71-91 .438 25 — BUCK SHOWALTER

Name	G by Pos	B	AGE	G	AB	R	H	2B	3B	HR	RBI	BB	SO	SB	BA	SA
TOTALS			29	162	5664	826	1506	274	36	**239**	799	488	1052	65	.266	.454
Mark Teixeira	1B116 OF25 3B15 DH15	R	23	146	529	66	137	29	5	26	84	44	120	1	.259	.480
Michael Young	2B159 SS7	R	26	160	666	106	204	33	9	14	72	36	103	13	.306	.446
Alex Rodriguez	SS158 DH1	R	27	161	607	124	181	30	6	47	118	87	126	17	.298	**.600**
Hank Blalock	3B141 2B4	L	22	143	567	89	170	33	3	29	90	44	97	2	.300	.522
Juan Gonzalez (LJ)	OF57 DH24	R	33	82	327	49	96	17	1	24	70	14	73	1	.294	.572
1 Doug Glanville (LJ)	OF52	R	32	52	195	22	53	5	0	4	14	6	25	4	.272	.359
1 Carl Everett	OF72 DH1	B	32	74	270	53	74	13	3	18	51	31	48	4	.274	.544
Einar Diaz	C101	R	30	101	334	30	86	14	1	4	35	9	32	3	.257	.341
Rafael Palmeiro	DH97 1B55	L	38	154	561	92	146	21	2	38	112	84	77	2	.260	.508
Donnie Sadler	OF41 3B23 SS19 2B1	R	28	77	131	27	26	5	2	1	5	13	34	4	.198	.290
Todd Greene	C51 DH3 1B2	R	32	62	205	25	47	10	1	10	20	2	47	0	.229	.434
Ryan Christenson	OF59	R	29	60	165	22	29	7	0	2	16	15	44	2	.176	.255
2 Shane Spencer	OF54 DH1	R	31	55	185	16	42	10	0	4	23	27	40	0	.227	.346
Laynce Nix	OF52 DH1	L	22	50	184	25	47	10	4	8	30	9	53	3	.255	.440
1 Ruben Sierra	OF23 DH15	B	37	43	133	14	35	9	0	3	11	11	26	1	.263	.398
Kevin Mench (BW)	OF35	R	25	38	125	15	40	12	0	2	11	10	17	1	.320	.464
Marcus Thames	OF24 DH4	R	26	30	73	12	15	2	0	3	10	8	18	0	.205	.274
Ramon Nivar	OF27 DH6 1B3	R	23	28	90	9	19	1	2	1	7	4	10	4	.211	.300
Mike Lamb	DH6 1B5 OF2 3B1	L	27	28	38	3	5	1	0	1	6	4	5	0	.132	.132
1,3 Jermaine Clark	OF17 2B7 DH2	L	26	24	46	2	8	2	0	0	6	4	11	2	.174	.217
Gerald Laird	C16	R	23	19	44	9	12	2	1	1	5	1	10	0	.273	.432
Herbert Perry (KJ-SJ)	1B5 3B2	R	33	11	24	1	4	1	0	0	1	4	3	0	.167	.208
1 Ryan Ludwick	OF8	R	24	8	26	4	4	1	0	0	2	2	9	0	.154	.192
Chad Kreuter	C7	B	38	7	18	0	2	0	0	0	1	6	6	0	.111	.167
Rusty Greer (XJ) 34																

NAME	T	AGE	W	L	PCT	SV	G	GS	CG	IP	H	BB	SO	SHO	ERA
TOTALS		28	71	91	.438	43	162	162	4	1433	**1625**	603	1009	3	5.67
John Thomson	R	29	13	14	.481	0	35	35	3	217	234	49	136	1	4.85
Colby Lewis	R	23	10	9	.526	0	26	26	0	127	163	70	88	0	7.30
R.A. Dickey	R	28	9	8	.529	1	38	13	1	117	135	38	94	1	5.09
Joaquin Benoit	R	25	8	5	.615	0	25	17	0	105	99	51	87	0	5.49
Ismael Valdes	R	29	8	8	.500	0	22	22	0	115	148	29	47	0	6.10
Francisco Cordero	R	28	5	8	.385	15	73	0	0	83	70	38	90	0	2.94
Jay Powell	R	31	3	1	1.000	0	51	0	0	59	75	34	40	0	7.82
Erasmo Ramirez	L	27	2	1	.750	0	34	0	0	49	46	9	28	0	3.86
Ron Mahay	L	32	3	3	.500	0	35	0	0	45	33	20	38	0	3.18
Ryan Drese	R	27	2	4	.333	0	11	8	0	46	61	24	26	0	6.85
1 Todd Van Poppel (GJ)	R	31	1	1	1.000	0	20	0	0	28	30	9	9	0	8.53
Robert Ellis	R	32	1	1	.500	0	4	4	0	18	26	10	8	0	8.35
Mario Ramos	L	25	1	1	.500	0	3	3	0	13	11	13	8	0	6.23
Rosman Garcia	R	24	1	2	.333	0	46	0	0	46	63	23	25	0	6.02
Aaron Fultz	L	29	1	3	.250	0	64	0	0	67	75	27	53	0	5.21
Chan Ho Park (XJ)	R	29	1	3	.250	0	7	7	0	34	45	16	27	0	7.58
Tony Mounce	L	28	1	5	.167	0	11	11	0	51	65	25	30	0	7.11
Reynaldo Garcia	R	24	0	1	—	0	6	0	0	10	17	14	15	0	9.00
C.J. Nitkowski	L	30	0	0	—	0	6	0	0	10	17	14	15	0	7.45
1 Doug Davis	L	27	0	0	—	0	7	0	0	6	6	3	6	0	12.00
Brian Shouse	L	34	0	0	—	0	62	0	0	61	62	14	40	0	3.10
1 Esteban Yan	R	28	0	0	—	0	31	0	0	31	26	16	15	0	6.94
Victor Santos	R	26	0	1	.000	0	8	8	0	29	26	15		0	7.01
Juan Dominguez	R	22	1	1	.500	0	8	8	0	22	17	12	12	0	7.16
2 Mickey Callaway	R	28	0	1	.000	0	4	0	0	22	27	19	19	0	6.45
Alan Benes	R	31	0	1	.000	0	5	0	0					0	
1 Ugueth Urbina	R	29				26	39	6		33	35	18	41	0	4.19

2 Ricardo Rodriguez (PJ) 25   Jeff Zimmerman (EJ) 30

LINE SCORES

Team	1	2	3	4	5	6	7	8	9	10	11	12		R	H	E

DIVISION SERIES: NEW YORK 3 : MINNESOTA 1

Game 1   September 30 at New York

	1	2	3	4	5	6	7	8	9	R	H	E
MIN	0	0	1	0	0	2	0	0	0	3	8	0
NYA	0	0	0	0	0	0	0	0	1	1	9	1

Santana, Reed (5), Romero (5), Hawkins (7), Guardado (9)
Mussina, Nelson (8), Heredia (8)

Game 2   October 2 at New York

	1	2	3	4	5	6	7	8	9	R	H	E
MIN	0	0	0	0	0	1	0	0	0	1	4	1
NYA	1	0	0	0	0	0	3	0	x	4	8	1

Radke, Hawkins (7), Romero (7), Rincon (8)
Pettitte, Rivera (8)

Game 3   October 4 at Minnesota

	1	2	3	4	5	6	7	8	9	R	H	E
NYA	0	2	1	0	0	0	0	0	0	3	8	1
MIN	0	0	1	0	0	0	0	0	0	1	5	0

Clemens, Rivera (8)
Lohse, Rogers (6), Romero (7), Rincon (8)

Game 4   October 5 at Minnesota

	1	2	3	4	5	6	7	8	9	R	H	E
NYA	0	0	0	6	0	0	0	1	1	8	13	0
MIN	0	0	0	1	0	0	0	0	0	1	9	1

Wells, White (8)
Santana, Rincon (4), Milton (4), Hawkins (8), Guardado (9)

DIVISION SERIES: BOSTON 3 : OAKLAND 2

Game 1   October 1 at Oakland

	1	2	3	4	5	6	7	8	9	10	11	12	R	H	E
BOS	1	0	0	0	1	0	2	0	0	0	0	0	4	12	2
OAK	0	0	3	0	0	0	0	0	1	0	0	1	5	8	0

Martinez, Timlin (8), Kim (9), Embree (9), Williamson (10), Lowe (11)
Hudson, Rincon (7), Bradford (8), Foulke (9), Harden (12)

Game 2   October 2 at Oakland

	1	2	3	4	5	6	7	8	9	R	H	E
BOS	0	0	1	0	0	0	0	0	0	1	6	1
OAK	0	5	0	0	0	0	0	0	x	5	6	0

Wakefield, Embree (7), Williamson (8)
Zito, Bradford (8), Foulke (9)

Game 3   October 4 at Boston

	1	2	3	4	5	6	7	8	9	10	11	R	H	E
OAK	0	0	0	0	0	1	0	0	0	0	0	1	6	4
BOS	0	1	0	0	0	0	0	0	0	0	2	3	7	2

Lilly, Bradford (8), Rincon (9), Mecir (10), Harden (11)
Lowe, Timlin (8), Williamson (11)

Game 4   October 5 at Boston

	1	2	3	4	5	6	7	8	9	R	H	E
OAK	0	1	0	0	0	3	0	0	0	4	11	1
BOS	0	0	2	0	0	1	0	2	x	5	7	0

Hudson, Sparks (2), Rincon (6), Foulke (8)
Burkett, Wakefield (6), Williamson (8)

Game 5   October 6 at Oakland

	1	2	3	4	5	6	7	8	9	R	H	E
BOS	0	0	0	0	0	4	0	0	0	4	6	0
OAK	0	0	0	1	0	0	1	0	0	3	7	0

Martinez, Embree (8), Timlin (8), Zito, Lilly (7), Williamson (9), Lowe (9)
Bradford (9), Rincon (9)

CHAMPIONSHIP: NEW YORK 4 : BOSTON 3

Game 1   October 8 at New York

	1	2	3	4	5	6	7	8	9	R	H	E
BOS	0	0	0	2	2	0	1	0	0	5	13	0
NYA	0	0	0	0	0	0	0	2	0	2	3	0

Wakefield, Embree (7), Timlin (8), Williamson (9)
Mussina, Heredia (6), Nelson (7), White (7), Contreras (9)

Game 2   October 9 at New York

	1	2	3	4	5	6	7	8	9	R	H	E
BOS	0	1	0	0	0	1	0	0	0	2	10	1
NYA	0	2	1	0	1	0	2	0	x	6	8	0

Lowe, Sauerbeck (7), Arroyo (8)
Pettitte, Contreras (7), Rivera (9)

Game 3   October 11 at Boston

	1	2	3	4	5	6	7	8	9	R	H	E
NYA	0	1	1	2	0	0	0	1	0	4	7	0
BOS	2	0	0	0	0	0	1	0	0	3	6	0

Clemens, Heredia (7), Contreras (7), Rivera (8)
Martinez, Timlin (8), Embree (9)

Game 4   October 13 at Boston

	1	2	3	4	5	6	7	8	9	R	H	E
NYA	0	0	0	0	1	0	0	0	1	2	6	1
BOS	0	0	0	1	1	0	1	0	x	3	6	0

Mussina, Heredia (7), Nelson (8)
Wakefield, Timlin (8), Williamson (9)

Game 5   October 14 at Boston

	1	2	3	4	5	6	7	8	9	R	H	E
NYA	0	3	0	0	0	0	0	1	0	4	7	1
BOS	0	0	0	1	0	0	0	1	0	2	6	1

Wells, Rivera (8)
Lowe, Embree (8), Arroyo (9)

Game 6   October 15 at New York

	1	2	3	4	5	6	7	8	9	R	H	E
BOS	0	0	4	0	0	0	3	0	2	9	16	1
NYA	1	0	1	0	0	0	3	0	1	6	12	2

Burkett, Arroyo (4), Jones (6), Embree (6), Timlin (8), Williamson (9)
Pettitte, Contreras (7), Heredia (7), Nelson (8), White (9)

Game 7   October 16 at New York

	1	2	3	4	5	6	7	8	9	10	11	R	H	E
BOS	0	3	0	1	0	0	0	0	1	0	0	5	11	0
NYA	0	0	0	1	0	1	0	1	3	0	1	6	11	1

Martinez, Embree (8), Timlin (8), Wakefield (10)
Clemens, Mussina (4), Heredia (7), Nelson (7), Wells (8), Rivera (9)

COMPOSITE BATTING

DIVISION SERIES

NEW YORK

NAME	POS	G	AB	R	H	2B	3B	HR	RBI	BA
TOTALS		4	138	16	38	9	0	2	15	.275
Soriano	2B	4	19	2	7	1	0	0	4	.368
Posada	C	4	17	1	3	1	0	0	0	.176
Giambi	DH	4	16	1	4	2	0	0	2	.250
Williams	CF	4	15	3	6	2	0	0	3	.400
Matsui	LF	4	15	2	4	1	0	1	3	.267
Boone	3B	4	15	1	3	1	0	0	0	.200
Jeter	SS	4	14	2	6	0	0	1	1	.429
Johnson	1B	4	13	2	1	1	0	0	2	.077
J. Rivera	RF	4	12	2	4	0	0	0	0	.333
Sierra	RF	1	2	0	0	0	0	0	0	.000
Dellucci	DH	1	0	0	0	0	0	0	0	—

MINNESOTA

NAME	POS	G	AB	R	H	2B	3B	HR	RBI	BA
TOTALS		4	131	6	26	3	1	2	5	.198
Jones	RF	4	16	0	2	0	0	0	0	.125
Stewart	LF	4	15	0	6	2	0	0	0	.400
Koskie	3B	4	15	0	3	1	0	0	0	.200
Mientkiewicz	1B	4	15	0	2	0	0	0	0	.133
Hunter	CF	4	14	3	6	0	1	1	2	.429
Pierzynski	C	4	13	1	3	0	0	0	1	.231
Guzman	SS	4	13	1	2	0	0	0	0	.154
Rivas	2B	4	13	0	0	0	0	0	1	.000
LeCroy	DH	3	11	1	1	0	0	0	0	.091
Cuddyer	DH	1	4	0	1	0	0	0	1	.250
Ford	PH	1	1	0	0	0	0	0	0	.000
Ryan	PH	1	1	0	0	0	0	0	0	.000
Gomez	2B	1	0	0	0	0	0	0	0	—
Hocking	2B	1	0	0	0	0	0	0	0	—

BOSTON

NAME	POS	G	AB	R	H	2B	3B	HR	RBI	BA
TOTALS		5	180	17	38	6	0	8	16	.211
Millar	1B	5	21	0	5	0	0	0	0	.238
Ortiz	DH	5	21	0	2	1	0	0	2	.095
Garciaparra	SS	5	20	2	6	1	0	0	0	.300
Ramirez	LF	5	20	2	4	0	0	1	3	.200
Damon	CF	5	19	2	6	2	0	1	3	.316
Mueller	3B	5	19	0	2	1	0	0	0	.105
Walker	2B	5	16	4	5	0	0	3	4	.313
Varitek	C	5	14	4	4	0	0	2	3	.286
Nixon	RF	4	10	1	2	0	0	1	2	.200
Kapler	RF-DH	4	9	0	0	0	0	0	0	.000
Jackson	2B	4	5	0	0	0	0	0	0	.000
Mirabelli	C	2	4	2	2	1	0	0	0	.500
Brown	RF-CF	4	2	0	0	0	0	0	0	.000
McCarty	DH	1	0	0	0	0	0	0	0	—

OAKLAND

NAME	POS	G	AB	R	H	2B	3B	HR	RBI	BA
TOTALS		5	178	18	38	8	1	1	15	.213
Tejada	SS	5	23	0	2	1	0	0	2	.087
Chavez	3B	5	22	1	1	1	0	0	0	.045
Durazo	DH	5	21	3	5	2	0	0	3	.238
Hatteberg	1B	5	17	3	3	0	0	0	0	.176
Ellis	2B	5	17	2	2	0	0	0	0	.118
Hernandez	C	4	15	1	3	0	0	0	0	.200
Byrnes	LF-CF	5	13	2	6	1	0	0	2	.462
Dye	RF	4	13	3	3	0	0	1	1	.231
Guillen	LF	4	11	1	5	1	0	0	1	.455
Long	LF-RF	4	8	0	2	0	0	0	0	.250
Singleton	CF	2	7	2	2	2	0	0	0	.286
McMillon	LF	3	6	0	1	0	0	0	1	.167
Melhuse	C	2	5	1	3	0	0	0	1	.600
Menechino	2B	1	0	0	0	0	0	0	0	—

AMERICAN LEAGUE CHAMPIONSHIP

NEW YORK

NAME	POS	G	AB	R	H	2B	3B	HR	RBI	BA
TOTALS		7	238	30	54	12	0	8	29	.227
Jeter	SS	7	30	3	7	2	0	1	2	.233
Soriano	2B	7	30	4	4	1	0	1	3	.133
Posada	C	7	27	5	8	4	0	1	6	.296
Matsui	LF	7	26	3	8	3	0	0	4	.308
Giambi	DH	7	26	4	6	0	0	3	3	.231
Johnson	1B	7	26	4	6	0	0	1	3	.231
Williams	CF	7	26	5	5	1	0	0	2	.192
Boone	3B	7	17	2	3	0	0	1	2	.176
Garcia	RF	5	16	1	4	0	0	0	2	.250
Wilson	3B	2	7	0	1	0	0	0	0	.143
Dellucci	DH-RF	3	3	2	1	0	0	0	0	.333
Sierra	RF	3	2	1	1	0	0	1	1	.500
Rivera	RF	2	2	0	0	0	0	0	0	.000

BOSTON

NAME	POS	G	AB	R	H	2B	3B	HR	RBI	BA
TOTALS		7	250	29	68	9	2	12	26	.272
Ramirez	LF	7	29	6	9	1	0	2	4	.310
Garciaparra	SS	7	29	2	7	0	1	0	1	.241
Millar	1B	7	29	3	7	0	0	1	3	.241
Walker	2B	7	27	5	10	1	1	2	2	.370
Mueller	3B	7	27	1	6	2	0	0	0	.222
Ortiz	DH	7	26	4	7	1	0	2	6	.269
Nixon	RF	7	24	3	8	1	0	3	5	.333
Varitek	C	6	20	4	6	2	0	2	3	.300
Damon	CF	5	20	1	4	1	0	0	1	.200
Kapler	CF-DH	3	8	0	1	0	0	0	1	.125
Mirabelli	C	3	7	0	2	0	0	0	0	.286
Jackson	2B	5	3	0	1	0	0	0	0	.333
McCarty	PH	1	1	0	0	0	0	0	0	.000

COMPOSITE PITCHING

DIVISION SERIES

NEW YORK

NAME	G	IP	H	BB	SO	W	L	SV	ERA
TOTALS	4	36	26	9	33	3	1	2	1.50
Wells	1	7.2	8	0	5	1	0	0	1.17
Clemens	1	7	5	1	6	1	0	0	1.29
Pettitte	1	7	4	3	10	1	0	0	1.29
Mussina	1	7	7	3	6	0	1	0	3.86
M. Rivera	2	4	0	0	4	0	0	2	0.00
Heredia	2	1	1	1	0	0	0	0	0.00
White	1	1.1	0	1	0	0	0	0	0.00
Nelson	1	0	0	1	0	0	0	0	∞

MINNESOTA

NAME	G	IP	H	BB	SO	W	L	SV	ERA
TOTALS	4	35	38	14	29	1	3	1	3.86
Santana	2	7.2	9	3	6	0	1	0	7.04
Radke	1	6.1	5	2	4	0	1	0	2.84
Lohse	1	5	6	2	5	0	1	0	5.40
Romero	3	3.1	3	2	1	0	0	0	0.00
Milton	1	3.1	2	0	2	0	0	0	0.00
Hawkins	3	3	5	0	5	1	0	0	6.00
Rincon	3	2.1	4	1	0	0	0	0	0.00
Guardado	2	2	5	0	2	0	0	1	9.00
Rogers	1	1.1	1	3	1	0	0	0	0.00
Reed	1	0.2	1	0	0	0	0	0	0.00

BOSTON

NAME	G	IP	H	BB	SO	W	L	SV	ERA
TOTALS	5	48.2	38	21	37	3	2	1	2.77
Martinez	2	14	13	5	9	1	0	0	3.86
Lowe	2	9.2	7	7	6	0	1	1	0.93
Wakefield	2	7.2	6	3	7	0	1	0	3.52
Burkett	1	5.1	9	2	1	0	0	0	6.75
Williamson	5	5	2	3	8	2	0	0	0.00
Timlin	3	4.1	0	0	5	0	0	0	0.00
Embree	2	3	2	1	0	0	0	0	0.00
Kim	1	0.2	1	1	1	0	0	0	13.50

OAKLAND

NAME	G	IP	H	BB	SO	W	L	SV	ERA
TOTALS	5	48.1	38	18	39	2	3	0	2.98
Zito	2	13	9	4	13	1	1	0	3.46
Lilly	2	9	2	2	7	0	0	0	0.00
Hudson	2	7.2	10	1	6	0	0	0	3.52
Foulke	3	5	4	2	3	0	1	0	3.60
Rincon	4	4	4	1	3	0	0	0	4.50
Sparks	1	4	3	1	0	0	0	0	4.50
Bradford	4	3.2	4	2	5	1	0	0	13.50
Harden	2	1.1	2	1	1	1	1	0	13.50
Mecir	1	0.2	1	1	0	0	0	0	0.00

AMERICAN LEAGUE CHAMPIONSHIP

NEW YORK

NAME	G	IP	H	BB	SO	W	L	SV	ERA
TOTALS	7	64	68	17	60	4	3	2	3.94
Mussina	3	15.1	16	4	17	0	2	0	4.11
Pettitte	2	11.2	17	4	10	1	0	0	4.63
Clemens	2	9	11	2	8	1	0	0	5.00
Rivera	4	8	5	0	6	1	0	2	1.13
Wells	2	7.2	5	2	5	1	0	0	2.35
Contreras	4	4.2	6	2	7	0	1	0	5.79
Nelson	4	3	4	0	3	0	0	0	6.00
Heredia	5	2.2	0	3	3	0	0	0	3.38
White	2	2	4	1	0	0	0	0	4.50

BOSTON

NAME	G	IP	H	BB	SO	W	L	SV	ERA
TOTALS	7	63	54	21	49	3	4	3	4.00
Martinez	2	14.1	16	2	14	0	1	0	5.65
Wakefield	3	14	8	6	10	2	1	0	2.57
Lowe	2	14	14	7	5	0	2	0	6.43
Timlin	5	5.1	1	2	6	0	0	0	0.00
Embree	5	4.2	3	0	1	0	0	0	0.00
Burkett	1	3.2	7	0	1	0	0	0	7.36
Arroyo	3	3.1	2	5	5	0	0	0	2.70
Williamson	3	3	1	0	6	0	0	3	3.00
Jones	1	0.1	1	1	0	0	0	0	0.00
Sauerbeck	1	0.1	1	1	0	0	0	0	0.00

ATLANTA — 1st 101-61 .623 — BOBBY COX

Name	G by Pos	B	AGE	G	AB	R	H	2B	3B	HR	RBI	BB	SO	SB	BA	SA
TOTALS			31	162	5670	907	1608	321	31	235	872	545	933	68	.284	.475
Robert Fick	1B115	L	29	126	409	52	110	26	1	11	80	42	47	1	.269	.418
Marcus Giles	2B139	R	25	145	551	101	174	49	2	21	69	59	80	14	.316	.526
Rafael Furcal	SS155	B	25	156	664	130	194	35	10	15	61	60	76	25	.292	.443
Vinny Castilla	3B147	R	35	147	542	65	150	28	3	22	76	26	86	1	.277	.461
Gary Sheffield	OF154	R	34	155	576	126	190	37	2	39	132	86	55	18	.330	.604
Andruw Jones	OF155	R	26	156	595	101	165	28	2	36	116	53	125	4	.277	.513
Chipper Jones	OF149	B	31	153	555	103	169	33	2	27	106	94	83	2	.305	.517
Javy Lopez	C120	R	32	129	457	89	150	29	3	43	109	33	90	0	.328	.687
Matt Franco	1B15 OF3	L	33	112	134	11	33	5	0	3	15	11	26	0	.246	.351
Darren Bragg	OF78	L	33	104	162	21	39	5	1	0	9	13	38	2	.241	.284
Mark DeRosa	2B29 3B25 SS20 OF2 1B1	R	28	103	266	40	70	14	0	6	22	16	49	1	.263	.383
Julio Franco	1B75	R	44	103	197	28	58	12	2	5	31	25	43	0	.294	.452
Henry Blanco	C18	R	31	55	151	11	30	8	0	1	13	10	21	0	.199	.272
Mike Hessman	OF8 1B4 3B3	R	25	19	21	2	6	2	0	2	3	5	6	0	.286	.667
Johnny Estrada	C14	B	27	16	36	2	11	0	0	0	2	0	3	0	.306	.306
Ryan Langerhans	OF14	L	23	16	15	2	4	0	0	0	0	0	6	0	.267	.267
Jesse Garcia	2B6 SS3 3B2	R	29	13	10	6	4	0	1	0	2	0	1	0	.400	.600

NAME	T	AGE	W	L	PCT	SV	G	GS	CG	IP	H	BB	SO	SHO	ERA
TOTALS		30	101	61	.623	51	162	162	4	1456	1425	555	992	7	4.10
Russ Ortiz	R	29	21	7	.750	0	34	34	1	212	177	102	149	1	3.81
Greg Maddux	R	37	16	11	.593	0	36	36	1	218	225	33	124	0	3.96
Mike Hampton	L	30	14	8	.636	0	31	31	1	190	186	78	110	0	3.84
Horacio Ramirez	L	23	12	4	.750	0	29	29	1	182	181	72	100	0	4.00
Shane Reynolds	R	35	11	9	.550	0	30	29	0	167	191	59	94	0	5.43
Jung Bong	L	22	6	2	.750	1	44	0	0	57	56	31	47	0	5.05
Kevin Gryboski	R	29	6	4	.600	0	64	0	0	44	44	23	32	0	3.86
Roberto Hernandez	R	38	5	3	.625	0	66	0	0	60	61	43	45	0	4.35
Trey Hodges (EJ)	R	25	3	3	.500	0	52	1	0	66	69	31	66	0	4.66
Ray King	L	29	3	4	.429	0	80	0	0	59	46	27	43	0	3.51
Will Cunnane	R	29	2	2	.500	3	20	0	0	20	14	6	20	0	2.70
2 Jaret Wright	R	27	1	0	1.000	0	11	0	0	9	7	3	9	0	2.00
Darren Holmes (SJ)	R	37	1	2	.333	0	48	0	0	42	47	11	46	0	4.29
Jason Marquis	R	24	0	0	—	1	21	2	0	41	43	18	19	0	5.53
2 Kent Mercker	L	35	0	0	—	1	18	0	0	17	15	7	7	0	1.06
Joey Dawley	R	31	0	0	—	0	7	0	0	7	15	3	8	0	18.00
John Smoltz	R	36	0	2	.000	45	62	0	0	64	48	8	73	0	1.12
Paul Byrd (EJ) 32															

FLORIDA — 2nd 91-71 .562 10 (Wild Card) — JEFF TORBORG 16-22 .421 JACK McKEON 75-49 .605

Name	G by Pos	B	AGE	G	AB	R	H	2B	3B	HR	RBI	BB	SO	SB	BA	SA
TOTALS			27	162	5490	751	1459	292	44	157	709	515	978	150	.266	.421
Derrek Lee	1B155	R	27	155	539	91	146	31	2	31	92	88	131	21	.271	.508
Luis Castillo	2B152	B	27	152	595	99	187	19	6	6	39	63	60	21	.314	.397
Alex Gonzalez	SS150	R	26	150	528	52	135	33	6	18	77	33	106	0	.256	.443
Mike Lowell	3B128	R	29	130	492	76	136	27	1	32	105	56	78	3	.276	.530
Juan Encarnacion	OF155	R	27	156	601	80	162	37	6	19	94	37	82	19	.270	.446
Juan Pierre	OF161	L	25	162	668	100	204	28	7	1	41	55	35	65	.305	.373
Miguel Cabrera	OF55 3B34	R	20	87	314	39	84	21	3	12	62	25	84	0	.268	.468
Ivan Rodriguez	C138	R	31	144	511	90	152	36	3	16	85	55	92	10	.297	.474
Todd Hollandsworth	OF64	L	30	93	228	32	58	23	3	9	20	22	55	2	.254	.421
Brian Banks	OF33 1B12	B	32	92	149	14	35	6	2	4	23	25	38	2	.235	.383
Andy Fox	2B15 SS9 3B5 1B2 OF2	L	32	70	108	12	21	5	1	0	8	7	29	1	.194	.259
Mike Mordecai	SS14 2B12 3B12 1B1	R	35	65	89	11	19	4	0	2	8	8	21	0	.213	.326
Mike Redmond	C37 1B1 3B1	R	32	59	125	12	30	7	1	0	11	7	16	0	.240	.312
Ramon Castro	C18	R	27	40	53	6	15	2	0	5	8	4	11	0	.283	.604
Gerald Williams	OF16	R	36	27	31	5	4	1	0	0	3	2	5	3	.129	.161
2 Jeff Conine	OF25	R	37	25	84	13	20	3	0	5	15	13	10	0	.238	.452
2 Lenny Harris	OF4	L	38	13	14	3	4	0	0	0	1	3	1	0	.286	.286
Chad Allen	OF8	R	28	12	24	2	5	1	1	0	5	0	5	0	.208	.333

NAME	T	AGE	W	L	PCT	SV	G	GS	CG	IP	H	BB	SO	SHO	ERA
TOTALS		27	91	71	.562	36	162	162	7	1445	1415	530	1132	11	4.04
Dontrelle Willis	L	21	14	6	.700	0	27	27	2	161	148	58	142	2	3.30
Mark Redman (BF)	L	29	14	9	.609	0	29	29	3	191	172	61	151	0	3.59
Brad Penny	R	25	14	10	.583	0	32	32	0	196	195	56	138	0	4.13
Carl Pavano	R	27	12	13	.480	0	33	32	2	201	204	49	133	0	4.30
Josh Beckett (EJ)	R	23	9	8	.529	0	24	23	0	142	132	56	152	0	3.04
Braden Looper	R	28	6	4	.600	28	74	0	0	81	82	29	56	0	3.68
Nate Bump	R	26	4	0	1.000	0	32	0	0	36	34	20	17	0	4.71
Armando Almanza (EJ)	L	30	4	5	.444	0	51	0	0	50	59	25	49	0	6.08
2 Ugueth Urbina	R	29	3	0	1.000	6	33	0	0	38	23	13	37	0	1.41
Tommy Phelps (EJ)	L	29	3	2	.600	0	27	7	0	63	70	23	43	0	4.00
Michael Tejera	L	26	3	4	.429	2	50	6	0	81	82	36	58	0	4.67
2 Chad Fox	R	32	2	1	.667	0	21	0	0	25	16	14	27	0	2.13
Allen Levrault	R	25	1	0	1.000	0	19	0	0	28	38	15	21	0	3.86
2 Rick Helling	R	32	1	0	1.000	0	11	0	0	16	11	5	12	0	0.55
Tim Spooneybarger (EJ)	R	23	1	2	.333	0	33	0	0	42	27	11	32	0	4.07
Blaine Neal	R	25	0	0	—	0	18	0	0	21	18	9	10	0	8.14
Kevin Olsen (CN)	R	26	0	0	—	1	12	0	0	12	25	4	12	0	12.75
Juan Alvarez	L	29	0	0	—	0	9	0	0	12	8	6	8	0	3.09
Toby Borland (IL)	R	34	0	0	—	0	7	0	0	10	3	8	4	0	1.86
A.J. Burnett (EJ)	R	26	0	2	.000	0	4	4	0	23	18	18	21	0	4.70
Justin Wayne	R	24	0	2	.000	0	4	2	0	5	9	5	1	0	11.81
Vladimir Nunez	R	28	0	3	.000	1	14	0	0	11	21	7	10	0	16.03

PHILADELPHIA — 3rd 86-76 .531 15 — LARRY BOWA

Name	G by Pos	B	AGE	G	AB	R	H	2B	3B	HR	RBI	BB	SO	SB	BA	SA
TOTALS			28	162	5543	791	1448	325	27	166	757	651	1155	72	.261	.419
Jim Thome	1B156	L	32	159	578	111	154	30	3	47	131	111	182	0	.266	.573
Placido Polanco	2B99 3B21	R	27	122	492	87	142	30	3	14	63	42	38	14	.289	.447
Jimmy Rollins	SS154	B	24	156	628	85	165	42	6	8	62	54	113	20	.263	.387
David Bell (XJ)	3B85 2B3	R	30	85	297	32	58	14	0	4	37	41	40	0	.195	.283
Bobby Abreu	OF131	L	29	158	577	99	173	35	1	20	101	109	126	22	.300	.468
Marlon Byrd	OF131	R	25	135	495	86	150	28	4	7	45	44	94	11	.303	.418
Pat Burrell	OF140	R	26	146	522	57	109	31	4	21	64	72	142	0	.209	.404
Mike Lieberthal	C131	R	31	131	508	68	159	30	1	13	81	38	59	0	.313	.453
Tomas Perez	3B58 2B26 1B9 SS4	B	29	125	298	39	79	18	1	5	33	23	54	0	.265	.383
Ricky Ledee	OF71	L	29	121	255	37	63	15	2	13	46	34	59	0	.247	.475
Jason Michaels	OF38	R	27	76	109	20	36	11	0	5	17	15	22	0	.330	.569
Nick Punto	2B16 3B9 SS7	R	25	64	92	14	20	2	1	0	4	7	22	2	.217	.272
Tyler Houston (BF)	3B21 1B1	L	32	54	97	7	27	6	0	2	14	6	19	0	.278	.402
Chase Utley	2B37	L	24	43	134	13	32	10	1	2	21	11	22	2	.239	.373
Todd Pratt	C35 1B6	R	36	43	125	16	34	10	1	4	20	22	38	0	.272	.464
2 Kelly Stinnett	C1	R	33	7	7	3	3	0	0	0	0	0	6	0	.429	.429
Travis Chapman	3B1	R	25	1	1	0	0	0	0	0	0	0	0	0	.000	.000
Andy Machado		B	22	1	0	0	0	0	0	0	0	0	1	0	—	—

NAME	T	AGE	W	L	PCT	SV	G	GS	CG	IP	H	BB	SO	SHO	ERA
TOTALS		30	86	76	.531	33	162	162	9	1444	1386	536	1060	13	4.04
Randy Wolf	L	26	16	10	.615	0	33	33	2	200	176	78	177	2	4.23
Brett Myers	R	22	14	9	.609	0	32	32	1	193	205	76	143	1	4.43
Kevin Millwood	R	28	14	12	.538	0	35	35	5	222	210	68	169	3	4.01
Vicente Padilla	R	25	14	12	.538	0	32	32	1	209	196	62	133	1	3.62
Rheal Cormier	L	36	8	0	1.000	0	65	0	0	85	54	25	67	0	1.70
Jose Mesa	R	37	5	7	.417	24	61	0	0	58	71	31	45	0	6.52
Brandon Duckworth	R	27	4	7	.364	0	24	18	0	93	98	44	68	0	4.94
Carlos Silva	R	24	3	1	.750	1	62	1	0	87	92	37	48	0	4.43
Turk Wendell	R	36	3	3	.500	1	56	0	0	64	54	28	27	0	3.38
Dan Plesac	L	41	2	1	.667	2	58	0	0	33	29	11	37	0	2.70
2 Valerio De Los Santos	L	30	1	0	1.000	0	6	0	0	4	7	3	4	0	9.00
Terry Adams	R	30	1	4	.200	0	66	0	0	68	68	23	51	0	2.65
Amaury Telemaco	R	29	1	4	.200	0	8	8	0	45	41	11	29	0	3.97
Hector Mercado (LJ)	L	29	0	0	—	1	13	0	0	19	18	12	15	0	5.79
Eric Junge	R	26	0	0	—	0	8	5	1	5	5	1	5	0	3.52
Geoff Geary	R	26	0	0	—	0	8	0	0	8	11	2	5	0	4.50
Josh Hancock	R	25	0	0	—	0	4	0	0	4	6	4	4	0	
Ryan Madson	R	22	0	0	—	0	2	0	0	3	4	1	1	0	
1 Joe Roa	R	31	0	2	.000	0	3	0	0	19	28	4	16	0	6.05
2 Mike Williams	R	34	0	4	.000	3	20	0	0	26	24	19	19	0	5.96

MONTREAL — 4th 83-79 .512 18 — FRANK ROBINSON

Name	G by Pos	B	AGE	G	AB	R	H	2B	3B	HR	RBI	BB	SO	SB	BA	SA
TOTALS			28	162	5437	711	1404	294	25	144	682	522	990	100	.258	.401
Wil Cordero	1B123 OF1	R	31	130	436	57	121	27	0	16	71	49	90	1	.278	.450
Jose Vidro	2B137	B	28	144	509	77	158	36	0	15	65	69	50	3	.310	.470
Orlando Cabrera	SS162	R	28	162	626	95	186	47	2	17	80	52	64	24	.297	.460
Fernando Tatis (TJ)	3B49	R	28	53	175	15	34	6	0	2	15	18	40	2	.194	.263
Vladimir Guerrero (XJ)	OF112	R	27	112	394	71	130	20	3	25	79	63	53	9	.330	.586
Endy Chavez	OF135	L	25	141	483	66	121	25	5	5	47	31	59	18	.251	.354
Brad Wilkerson	OF135 1B27	L	26	146	504	78	135	34	4	19	77	89	155	13	.268	.464
Michael Barrett (PJ)	C68	R	26	70	226	33	47	9	2	10	30	21	37	0	.208	.398
Ron Calloway	OF97	L	26	126	340	36	81	17	1	9	52	20	80	9	.238	.374
Jose Macias	OF62 3B25 2B4	B	31	111	272	31	65	15	2	4	22	11	45	4	.239	.353
Brian Schneider	C98	L	26	108	335	34	77	26	1	9	46	37	75	0	.230	.394
Jamey Carroll	3B67 SS14 2B11	R	29	105	227	31	59	11	1	0	19	19	39	5	.260	.326
Henry Mateo	2B43 OF10 SS2	B	26	100	154	29	37	3	1	0	7	11	38	11	.240	.273
Edwards Guzman	3B28 1B13 C4	L	26	52	146	15	35	5	0	1	14	5	17	0	.240	.295
Joe Vitiello	OF15 1B12	R	33	38	76	12	26	6	0	3	13	7	14	0	.342	.539
1 Jeff Liefer	1B21	L	28	35	88	6	17	3	0	3	18	3	26	0	.193	.330
2 Todd Zeile	3B34	R	37	34	113	11	29	2	1	5	19	10	18	1	.257	.442
Matt Cepicky	OF4	L	25	5	8	0	2	1	0	0	0	0	2	0	.250	.375

NAME	T	AGE	W	L	PCT	SV	G	GS	CG	IP	H	BB	SO	SHO	ERA
TOTALS		27	83	79	.512	42	162	162	15	1438	1467	463	1028	10	4.01
Livan Hernandez	R	28	15	10	.600	0	33	33	8	233	225	57	178	0	3.20
Javier Vazquez	R	27	13	12	.520	0	34	34	4	231	198	57	241	1	3.24
Luis Ayala (SJ)	R	25	10	3	.769	0	65	0	0	71	65	13	46	0	2.92
Tomo Ohka	R	27	10	12	.455	0	34	34	2	199	233	45	118	0	4.16
Zach Day (SJ)	R	25	8	9	.529	0	23	23	1	131	132	59	61	1	4.18
Claudio Vargas (SJ)	R	25	6	8	.429	0	23	20	0	114	111	41	62	0	4.34
Rocky Biddle	R	27	8	5	.615	34	73	0	0	72	71	40	54	0	4.65
Scott Stewart (IL)	L	27	3	1	.750	0	57	0	0	43	52	13	29	0	3.98
Tony Armas (SJ)	R	25	2	1	.667	0	5	5	0	31	25	8	23	0	2.61
Joey Eischen	L	33	2	1	.667	0	70	0	0	53	57	13	40	0	3.06
Dan Smith (SJ)	R	27	2	2	.500	0	32	0	0	38	42	18	35	0	5.26
T.J. Tucker	R	24	2	2	.500	0	45	7	0	80	90	20	47	0	4.73
Chad Cordero	R	21	1	0	1.000	0	12	0	0	11	6	4	12	0	1.64
2 Hector Almonte	R	27	1	1	.500	0	29	0	0	29	34	17	26	0	6.83
Julio Manon	R	30	1	2	.333	1	23	0	0	28	26	11	15	0	4.40
Eric Knott	L	28	0	0	—	0	13	1	0	19	23	6	17	0	5.12
Roy Corcoran	R	23	0	0	—	0	5	0	0	7	5	5	3	0	1.23
Jose Mercedes	R	32	0	0	—	0	5	0	0	7	9	7	3	0	
2 Vic Darensbourg	L	32	0	0	—	0	8	0	0	14	14	1	10	0	10.80
Anthony Ferrari	L	25	0	0	—	0	2	0	0	1	1	1	1	0	6.75
Bryan Hebson	R	29	0	0	—	0	1	0	0	1	3	1	1	0	13.50
Britt Reames	R	29	0	0	—	0	1	0	0	1	2	2	0	0	27.00
Sun-Woo Kim	R	25	0	1	.000	0	7	1	0	24	34	5	11	0	8.36
Scott Downs	L	27	0	1	.000	0	3	1	0	3	4	1	0	0	15.00
Tim Drew	R	24	0	2	.000	0	6	1	0	9	12	8	1	0	12.46
Orlando Hernandez (SJ) 37															

Batting

Name	G by Pos	B	AGE	G	AB	R	H	2B	3B	HR	RBI	BB	SO	SB	BA	SA
NEW YORK 5th 66-95 .410 34.5	ART HOWE		30	161	5341	642	1317	262	24	124	607	489	1035	70	.247	.374
	TOTALS		30	161	5341	642	1317	262	24	124	607	489	1035	70	.247	.374
Mo Vaughn (KJ)	1B25	L	35	27	79	10	15	2	0	3	15	14	22	0	.190	.329
1 Roberto Alomar	2B72	B	35	73	263	34	69	17	1	2	22	29	40	6	.262	.357
Jose Reyes	SS69	B	20	69	274	47	84	12	4	5	32	13	36	13	.307	.434
Ty Wigginton	3B155	R	25	156	573	73	146	36	6	11	71	46	124	12	.255	.396
Roger Cedeno	OF128	B	28	148	484	70	129	25	4	7	37	38	86	14	.267	.378
Timo Perez	OF104	L	28	127	346	32	93	21	0	4	42	18	25	5	.269	.364
Cliff Floyd (NJ)	OF95	L	30	108	365	57	106	25	2	18	68	51	66	3	.290	.518
Mike Piazza (GJ)	C65 1B1	R	34	68	234	37	67	13	0	11	34	35	40	0	.286	.483
Tony Clark	1B80 OF1	B	31	125	254	29	59	13	0	16	43	24	73	0	.232	.472
Jason Phillips	1B84 C29	R	26	119	403	45	120	25	0	11	58	39	50	0	.298	.442
Joe McEwing	2B55 SS42 OF18 1B5 3B2	R	30	119	278	31	67	11	0	1	16	25	57	3	.241	.291
Raul Gonzalez	OF88	R	29	107	217	28	50	12	2	2	21	27	34	3	.230	.332
Vance Wilson	C89	R	30	96	269	28	65	9	1	8	39	15	56	1	.242	.372
Jay Bell	2B14 3B14 1B14 SS12	R	37	72	116	11	21	1	0	0	3	22	38	0	.181	.190
1 Jeromy Burnitz (BH)	OF65	L	34	65	234	38	64	18	0	18	45	21	55	1	.274	.581
Tsuyoshi Shinjo	OF54	R	31	62	114	10	22	3	0	1	7	6	12	0	.193	.246
1 Rey Sanchez	SS42 2B12	R	35	56	174	11	36	3	1	0	12	8	18	1	.207	.236
Jeff Duncan	OF52	L	24	56	139	13	27	0	2	1	10	17	41	4	.194	.245
Marco Scutaro	2B39 SS1	R	27	48	75	10	16	4	0	2	6	13	14	2	.213	.347
Jorge Velandia	SS23	R	28	23	58	6	11	3	1	0	8	10	15	0	.190	.276
Danny Garcia	2B17 OF1	L	23	19	56	5	12	2	0	2	6	2	11	0	.214	.357
Prentice Redman	OF10	R	23	15	24	3	3	1	0	1	2	1	9	2	.125	.292
Matt Watson	OF5	L	24	14	22	0	4	2	0	0	2	1	5	0	.182	.273
Mike Glavine	1B3	L	30	6	7	0	1	0	0	0	0	0	2	0	.143	.143
Joe DePastino	C1	R	29	2	2	0	0	0	0	0	0	0	1	0	.000	.000

Pitching

NAME	T	AGE	W	L	PCT	SV	G	GS	CG	IP	H	BB	SO	SHO	ERA
		31	66	95	.410	38	161	161	3	1413	1497	576	907	10	4.48
Steve Trachsel	R	32	16	10	.615	0	33	33	2	205	204	65	111	2	3.78
Al Leiter	L	37	15	9	.625	0	30	30	1	181	176	94	139	1	3.99
Jae Weong Seo	R	26	9	12	.429	0	32	31	0	188	193	46	110	0	3.82
Tom Glavine	L	37	9	14	.391	0	32	32	0	183	205	66	82	0	4.52
Pedro Astacio (SJ)	R	33	3	2	.600	0	7	7	0	37	47	18	20	0	7.36
1 Armando Benitez	R	30	3	3	.500	21	45	0	0	49	41	24	50	0	3.10
Aaron Heilman	R	24	2	7	.222	0	14	13	0	65	79	41	51	0	6.75
Mike Stanton (KJ)	L	36	2	7	.222	5	50	0	0	45	37	19	34	0	4.57
Jamie Cerda	L	24	1	1	.500	0	27	0	0	32	32	20	19	0	5.85
1 Graeme Lloyd	L	36	1	2	.333	0	36	0	0	35	39	7	17	0	3.31
Mike Bacsik	L	25	1	2	.333	0	5	3	0	18	28	8	12	0	10.19
Dan Wheeler	R	25	1	3	.250	2	35	0	0	51	49	17	35	0	3.71
David Cone (PJ-VR)	R	40	1	3	.250	0	5	4	0	18	20	13	13	0	6.50
Jeremy Griffiths	R	25	1	4	.200	0	9	6	0	41	57	19	25	0	7.02
David Weathers	R	33	1	6	.143	7	77	0	0	88	87	40	75	0	3.08
Pedro Feliciano	L	26	0	0	—	0	23	0	0	48	52	21	43	0	3.35
Edwin Almonte	R	26	0	0	—	0	12	0	0	11	21	5	7	0	11.12
2 Jason Anderson	R	24	0	0	—	0	11	0	0	11	10	5	7	0	5.06
Pat Strange	R	22	0	0	—	0	6	0	0	9	13	11	5	0	11.00
Orber Moreno	R	26	0	0	—	0	7	0	0	8	10	3	5	0	7.88
Jason Middlebrook	R	28	0	0	—	0	5	0	0	7	13	4	3	0	10.29
Scott Strickland (EJ)	R	27	0	2	.000	0	19	0	0	20	16	10	16	0	2.25
Jason Roach	R	27	0	2	.000	0	2	2	0	9	14	4	2	0	12.00
John Franco (EJ)	L	42	0	3	.000	2	38	0	0	34	35	13	16	0	2.62
Grant Roberts (AJ)	R	25	0	3	.000	1	18	0	0	19	19	13	10	0	3.79

CENTRAL DIVISION

Batting

Name	G by Pos	B	AGE	G	AB	R	H	2B	3B	HR	RBI	BB	SO	SB	BA	SA
CHICAGO 1st 88-74 .543	DUSTY BAKER		31	162	5519	724	1431	302	24	172	691	492	1158	73	.259	.416
	TOTALS		31	162	5519	724	1431	302	24	172	691	492	1158	73	.259	.416
Eric Karros	1B97	R	35	114	336	37	96	16	1	12	40	24	46	1	.286	.446
Mark Grudzielanek (BH)	2B121	R	32	121	481	73	151	38	1	3	38	30	64	6	.314	.416
Alex Gonzalez	SS150	R	30	152	536	71	122	37	0	20	59	47	123	4	.228	.409
2 Aramis Ramirez	3B63	R	25	63	232	31	60	7	1	15	39	17	31	1	.259	.491
Sammy Sosa	OF137	R	34	137	517	99	144	22	0	40	103	62	143	0	.279	.553
Corey Patterson (KJ)	OF82	L	23	83	329	49	98	17	7	13	55	15	77	16	.298	.511
Moises Alou	OF142	R	36	151	565	83	158	35	1	22	91	63	67	3	.280	.462
Damian Miller	C114	R	33	114	352	34	82	19	1	9	36	39	91	1	.233	.369
Ramon Martinez	2B42 3B37 SS32 1B2	R	30	108	293	30	83	16	1	3	34	24	50	0	.283	.375
Troy O'Leary	OF51	L	33	93	174	18	38	9	0	5	28	14	31	3	.218	.356
Tom Goodwin	OF57	L	34	87	171	26	49	10	0	1	12	11	33	19	.287	.363
Hee-Seop Choi	1B69	L	24	80	202	31	44	17	0	8	28	37	71	1	.218	.421
1 Lenny Harris	3B35 1B2 OF2	L	38	75	131	11	24	3	0	1	7	13	20	1	.183	.229
Paul Bako	C69	L	31	70	188	19	43	13	3	0	17	22	47	0	.229	.330
2 Kenny Lofton	OF55	L	36	56	208	39	68	13	4	3	20	18	22	12	.327	.471
1 Mark Bellhorn	3B42	B	28	51	139	15	29	7	1	2	22	29	46	3	.209	.317
2 Randall Simon	1B29	L	28	33	103	13	29	3	0	6	21	4	7	0	.282	.485
2 Doug Glanville	OF18	R	32	28	51	2	12	0	0	1	2	2	4	0	.235	.294
2 Jose Hernandez	3B17 SS5 OF2 2B1	R	33	23	69	6	13	3	1	2	9	3	26	0	.188	.348
3 Tony Womack	2B14 SS1	L	33	21	51	4	12	2	1	0	2	1	11	2	.235	.314
Augie Ojeda	SS7 2B5 3B1	B	28	12	25	2	3	0	0	0	1	5	3	0	.120	.120
Trenidad Hubbard	OF4	R	39	10	16	2	4	1	0	0	2	4	3	1	.250	.313
Dave Kelton	OF2	R	23	10	12	1	2	1	0	0	1	0	5	0	.167	.250
1 Bobby Hill	2B2	B	25	5	4	0	1	0	0	0	0	0	2	0	.250	.250
2 Josh Paul	C3	R	28	3	6	0	0	0	0	0	0	0	3	0	.000	.000

Pitching

NAME	T	AGE	W	L	PCT	SV	G	GS	CG	IP	H	BB	SO	SHO	ERA
		29	88	74	.543	36	162	162	13	1456	1304	617	1404	14	3.83
Mark Prior	R	22	18	6	.750	0	30	30	3	211	183	50	245	1	2.43
Kerry Wood	R	26	14	11	.560	0	32	32	4	211	152	100	266	2	3.20
Matt Clement	R	28	14	12	.538	0	32	32	2	202	169	79	171	1	4.11
Carlos Zambrano	R	22	13	11	.542	0	32	32	3	214	188	94	168	1	3.11
Shawn Estes	L	30	8	11	.421	0	29	28	1	152	182	83	103	1	5.73
Mike Remlinger	L	37	6	5	.545	0	73	0	0	69	54	39	83	0	3.65
Antonio Alfonseca (LJ)	R	31	3	1	.750	0	60	0	0	66	76	27	51	0	5.83
Kyle Farnsworth	R	27	3	2	.600	0	77	0	0	76	53	36	92	0	3.30
Dave Veres (SJ)	R	36	2	1	.667	1	31	0	0	33	36	5	26	0	4.68
Joe Borowski	R	32	2	2	.500	33	68	0	0	68	53	19	66	0	2.63
Mark Guthrie	L	37	2	3	.400	0	65	0	0	43	40	22	24	0	2.74
Juan Cruz	R	24	2	7	.222	0	25	6	0	61	66	28	65	0	6.05
Todd Wellemeyer	R	24	1	1	.500	1	15	0	0	28	25	19	30	0	6.51
1 Alan Benes	R	31	0	0	—	0	18	6	0	48	48	29	30	0	6.01
1 Phil Norton	L	27	0	0	—	0	4	0	0	3	2	3	0	0	5.40
Felix Sanchez	L	21	0	0	—	0	3	0	0	5	3	2	1	0	10.80
Sergio Mitre	R	22	0	1	.000	0	3	2	0	9	15	4	3	0	8.31

Batting

Name	G by Pos	B	AGE	G	AB	R	H	2B	3B	HR	RBI	BB	SO	SB	BA	SA
HOUSTON 2nd 87-75 .537 1	JIMY WILLIAMS		32	162	5583	805	1466	308	30	191	763	557	1021	66	.263	.431
	TOTALS		32	162	5583	805	1466	308	30	191	763	557	1021	66	.263	.431
Jeff Bagwell	1B158	R	35	160	605	109	168	28	2	39	100	88	119	11	.278	.524
Jeff Kent	2B121	R	35	130	505	77	150	39	1	22	93	39	85	6	.297	.509
Adam Everett	SS128	R	26	128	387	51	99	18	3	8	51	28	66	8	.256	.380
Morgan Ensberg	3B111	R	27	127	385	69	112	15	1	25	60	48	60	7	.291	.530
Richard Hidalgo	OF137	R	28	141	514	91	159	43	4	28	88	58	104	9	.309	.572
Craig Biggio	OF150	R	37	153	628	102	166	44	2	15	62	57	116	8	.264	.412
Lance Berkman	OF153	B	27	153	538	110	155	35	6	25	93	107	108	5	.288	.515
Brad Ausmus	C143	R	34	143	450	43	103	12	2	4	47	46	66	5	.229	.291
Geoff Blum	3B83 2B25 SS11 1B6 OF2	B	30	123	420	51	110	19	0	10	52	20	50	0	.262	.379
Orlando Merced	OF31 1B12 3B2	L	36	123	212	20	49	17	2	3	26	15	33	3	.231	.373
Jose Vizcaino (BW)	SS32 2B20 3B2 1B1	B	35	91	189	14	47	7	3	3	26	8	22	0	.249	.365
1 Gregg Zaun	C31	B	32	59	120	9	26	7	0	1	13	14	14	1	.217	.300
Brian Hunter	OF32	R	32	56	98	13	23	6	1	0	13	6	21	2	.235	.316
Eric Bruntlett	SS10 2B9 OF2 3B1	R	25	31	54	3	14	3	0	1	4	6	10	0	.259	.370
Colin Porter	OF14	L	27	24	32	5	6	0	0	0	0	1	17	1	.188	.188
1 Julio Lugo	SS22	R	27	22	65	6	16	3	0	2	5	2	12	2	.246	.292
Raul Chavez	C16	R	30	19	37	5	10	1	1	1	4	1	6	0	.270	.432
Jason Lane	OF10	R	26	18	27	5	8	2	0	4	10	0	2	0	.296	.815
Mitch Meluskey		B	29	12	9	1	1	1	0	0	2	2	2	0	.111	.222
David Matranga	2B2	R	26	6	5	1	1	0	0	0	1	0	2	0	.200	.800
Tripp Cromer	2B1	R	35	4	4	0	1	0	1	0	1	0	1	0	.250	.750

Pitching

NAME	T	AGE	W	L	PCT	SV	G	GS	CG	IP	H	BB	SO	SHO	ERA
		28	87	75	.537	50	162	162	1	1450	1350	565	1139	5	3.86
Jeriome Robertson	L	26	15	9	.625	0	32	31	0	161	180	64	99	0	5.10
Wade Miller	R	26	14	13	.519	0	33	33	1	187	168	77	161	0	4.13
Roy Oswalt (GJ)	R	25	10	5	.667	0	21	21	0	127	116	29	108	0	2.97
Tim Redding	R	25	10	14	.417	0	33	32	0	176	179	65	116	0	3.68
Brad Lidge	R	26	6	3	.667	1	78	0	0	85	60	42	97	0	3.60
Ocatvio Dotel	R	29	6	4	.600	4	76	0	0	87	53	31	97	0	2.48
Ricky Stone	R	28	6	4	.600	1	65	0	0	83	76	31	43	0	3.69
Ron Villone	L	33	6	6	.500	0	19	19	0	107	91	48	91	0	4.13
Jared Fernandez	R	31	3	3	.500	0	12	6	0	38	37	12	19	0	3.99
Peter Munro	R	28	3	4	.429	0	40	2	0	54	63	26	27	0	4.67
Kirk Saarloos	R	24	2	1	.667	0	36	4	0	49	55	17	43	0	4.93
Mike Gallo	L	26	1	0	1.000	0	32	0	0	30	28	10	16	0	3.00
Rodrigo Rosario (SJ)	R	25	1	0	1.000	0	2	2	0	8	5	3	6	0	1.13
1 Scott Linebrink	R	26	1	1	.500	0	23	0	0	32	38	14	17	0	4.26
4 Dan Miceli	R	32	1	1	.500	0	23	0	0	30	22	7	20	0	2.10
Nate Bland	L	28	1	2	.333	0	22	0	0	20	22	12	18	0	5.75
Billy Wagner	L	31	1	4	.200	44	78	0	0	86	52	23	105	0	1.78
Brandon Puffer	R	28	0	0	—	0	13	0	0	21	24	16	10	0	5.14
2 Rick White	R	34	0	0	—	0	15	0	0	19	18	8	17	0	3.72
Brian Moehler (EJ)	R	31	0	0	—	0	3	0	0	14	22	6	5	0	7.90
1 Bruce Chen	L	26	0	0	—	0	11	0	0	12	14	8	6	0	6.00
Kirk Bullinger	R	34	0	0	—	0	7	0	0	8	7	1	5	0	6.75
Jonathan Johnson	R	28	0	1	.000	0	3	0	0	15	20	15	7	0	5.87
Carlos Hernandez (SJ) 23															

Batting

Name	G by Pos	B	AGE	G	AB	R	H	2B	3B	HR	RBI	BB	SO	SB	BA	SA
ST. LOUIS 3rd 85-77 .525 3	TONY LA RUSSA		32	162	5672	876	1580	342	32	196	827	580	952	82	.279	.454
	TOTALS		32	162	5672	876	1580	342	32	196	827	580	952	82	.279	.454
Tino Martinez	1B126	L	35	138	476	66	130	25	2	15	69	53	71	1	.273	.429
Fernando Vina (LJ)	2B60	L	34	61	259	35	65	14	4	4	23	11	24	4	.251	.382
Edgar Renteria	SS156	R	27	157	587	96	194	47	1	13	100	65	54	34	.330	.480
Scott Rolen	3B153	R	28	154	559	98	160	49	1	28	104	82	104	13	.286	.528
J.D. Drew	OF75	L	27	100	287	60	83	13	3	15	42	36	48	2	.289	.512
Jim Edmonds	OF129	L	33	137	447	89	123	32	2	39	89	77	127	1	.275	.617
Albert Pujols	OF113 1B62	R	23	157	591	137	212	51	1	43	124	79	65	5	.359	.667
Mike Matheny	C138 1B4	R	32	141	444	43	111	18	2	8	47	44	81	1	.252	.356
Orlando Palmeiro	OF112	L	34	141	317	37	86	13	1	3	33	32	31	3	.271	.347
Kerry Robinson	OF88	L	29	116	208	19	52	6	3	1	16	8	27	6	.250	.322
Eduardo Perez	OF71 3B12 1B5	R	33	105	253	47	72	16	0	11	41	29	53	5	.285	.478
Miguel Cairo (BG)	2B40 OF27 3B12 SS7 1B3	R	29	92	261	41	64	15	2	5	32	13	30	4	.245	.375
Bo Hart	2B69 SS3	R	26	77	296	46	82	13	5	4	28	12	64	3	.277	.395
Chris Widger	C41 1B1 OF1	R	32	44	102	9	24	9	0	0	14	6	20	0	.235	.324
1 Wilson Delgado	2B12 SS11 3B11	B	30	43	77	8	13	3	0	0	3	6	10	0	.169	.208
So Taguchi	3B3	R	33	43	54	9	14	3	0	1	5	2	10	1	.259	.519
Eli Marrero (NJ)	OF31 C6 1B2	R	29	41	107	10	24	4	2	2	20	7	18	0	.224	.355
Joe Girardi (XJ)	C13	R	38	16	23	1	3	0	0	0	1	3	4	0	.130	.130

Pitching

NAME	T	AGE	W	L	PCT	SV	G	GS	CG	IP	H	BB	SO	SHO	ERA
		32	85	77	.525	41	162	162	9	1464	1544	508	969	10	4.60
Woody Williams	R	36	18	9	.667	0	34	33	0	221	220	55	153	0	3.87
Brett Tomko	R	30	13	9	.591	0	33	32	2	203	252	57	114	0	5.28
Matt Morris (BG)	R	28	11	8	.579	0	27	27	5	172	164	39	120	3	3.76
Jason Simontacchi	R	29	9	5	.643	1	46	16	1	126	153	41	74	0	5.56
Cal Eldred	R	35	7	4	.636	0	62	0	0	67	62	31	67	0	3.74
Garrett Stephenson	R	31	7	13	.350	0	32	27	1	174	167	60	91	0	4.59
2 Sterling Hitchcock	L	32	5	1	.833	0	8	6	0	38	34	14	32	0	3.79
Steve Kline	L	30	5	5	.500	3	78	0	0	64	56	30	33	0	3.82
Danny Haren	R	22	3	7	.300	0	14	14	0	73	84	22	43	0	5.08
2 Esteban Yan	R	28	2	0	1.000	1	39	0	0	43	53	16	28	0	6.02
Kiko Calero (KJ)	R	28	1	1	.500	1	26	1	0	38	29	20	51	0	2.82
2 Mike DeJean	R	32	1	1	.500	1	18	0	0	18	17	12	13	0	4.00
Russ Springer (EJ)	R	34	1	1	.500	0	17	0	0	17	19	6	11	0	8.31
1 Dustin Hermanson	R	30	1	2	.333	1	23	0	0	30	35	14	12	0	5.46
Jeff Fassero	L	40	1	7	.125	0	78	0	0	78	93	34	55	0	5.68
Jimmy Journell	R	25	0	0	—	0	7	0	0	9	10	11	8	0	6.00
Josh Pearce	R	25	0	0	—	0	3	0	0	1	5	1	0	0	3.00
Kevin Ohme	L	32	0	0	—	0	3	0	0	1	3	1	1	0	0.00
Gabe Molina	R	27	0	0	—	0	3	0	0	2	4	1	1	0	13.50
Jason Pearson	L	27	0	0	—	0	2	0	0	1	4	4	1	0	63.00
Jason Isringhausen (SJ)	R	30	0	1	.000	22	40	0	0	42	31	18	41	0	2.36
Lance Painter (LJ)	L	35	0	1	.000	0	22	0	0	17	18	4	13	0	5.50
1 Mike Crudale	R	26	0	0	—	0	13	0	0	11	11	12	6	0	2.38
Pedro Borbon	L	35	0	0	—	0	3	0	0	4	14	2	1	0	20.25
Chris Carpenter (SJ) 28, Gene Stechsculte (SJ) 29															

PITTSBURGH 4th 75-87 .463 13   LLOYD McCLENDON

Name	G by Pos	B	AGE	G	AB	R	H	2B	3B	HR	RBI	BB	SO	SB	BA	SA
TOTALS			30	162	5581	753	1492	275	45	163	711	529	1049	86	.267	.420
1 Randall Simon	1B80	L	28	91	307	34	84	14	0	10	51	12	30	0	.274	.417
Pokey Reese (RJ)	2B33	R	30	37	107	9	23	4	0	1	12	9	31	6	.215	.262
Jack Wilson	SS149	R	25	150	558	58	143	21	3	9	62	36	74	5	.256	.353
1 Aramis Ramirez	3B96	R	25	96	375	44	105	25	1	12	67	25	68	1	.280	.448
Reggie Sanders	OF120	R	35	130	453	74	129	27	4	31	87	38	110	15	.285	.567
Tike Redman	OF54	L	26	56	230	36	76	16	5	3	19	14	18	7	.330	.483
1 Brian Giles	OF105	L	32	105	388	70	116	30	4	16	70	85	48	0	.299	.521
Jason Kendall	C146	R	29	150	587	84	191	29	3	6	58	49	40	1	.325	.416
Matt Stairs	OF55 1B31	L	35	121	305	49	89	20	1	20	57	45	64	0	.292	.561
Abraham Nunez	2B71 SS23 3B1	B	27	118	311	37	77	8	7	4	35	26	53	9	.248	.357
Craig Wilson	OF46 1B36 C21	R	26	116	309	49	81	15	4	18	48	35	89	3	.262	.511
Jeff Reboulet	2B76 3B7	R	39	93	261	37	63	10	2	3	25	27	47	2	.241	.330
1 Kenny Lofton	OF82	L	36	84	339	58	94	19	4	9	26	28	29	18	.277	.437
Carlos Rivera	1B60	L	25	78	95	12	21	5	0	3	10	8	28	0	.221	.368
Rob Mackowiak	OF30 3B19 2B15	L	27	77	174	20	47	4	4	6	19	15	53	6	.270	.443
3 Jose Hernandez	SS	R	33	58	193	19	43	9	1	3	21	16	56	1	.223	.326
Kevin Young	1B44 OF1	R	34	52	84	8	17	4	0	2	7	12	25	1	.202	.321
Adam Hyzdu	OF31	R	31	51	63	16	13	5	0	1	8	10	21	0	.206	.333
2 Jason Bay	OF26	L	24	27	79	13	23	6	1	3	12	18	28	3	.291	.506
J.J. Davis	OF10	R	24	19	35	1	7	0	0	1	4	3	13	0	.200	.286
Humberto Cota	C4	R	24	10	16	1	4	1	0	0	1	1	5	0	.250	.313
2 Bobby Hill	2B1	B	25	1	3	1	1	0	0	0	0	0	0	0	.333	.333
J.R. House		R	23	1	1	0	1	0	0	0	0	0	0	0	1.000	1.000

Pat Meares (HJ) 34

NAME	T	AGE	W	L	PCT	SV	G	GS	CG	IP	H	BB	SO	SHO	ERA
		29	75	87	.463	44	162	162	7	1444	1527	502	926	10	4.64
1 Jeff Suppan	R	28	10	7	.588	0	21	21	3	141	147	31	78	2	3.57
Kip Wells	R	26	10	9	.526	0	31	31	1	197	171	76	147	0	3.28
Josh Fogg (UJ)	R	26	10	9	.526	0	26	26	1	142	166	40	71	0	5.26
Jeff D'Amico	R	27	9	16	.360	0	29	29	2	175	204	42	100	1	4.77
Salomon Torres	R	31	7	5	.583	2	41	16	0	121	128	42	84	0	4.76
Brian Boehringer	R	34	4	4	.556	0	62			64	64	30	47	0	5.49
Kris Benson (SJ)	R	28	5	9	.357	0	18	18	0	105	127	36	68	0	4.97
Julian Tavarez	R	30	3	3	.500	0	64	0	0	84	75	27	39	0	3.66
1 Scott Sauerbeck	L	31	3	4	.429	0	53	0	0	40	30	25	32	0	4.05
Mike Lincoln (SJ)	R	28	3	4	.429	5	36	0	0	36	38	13	28	0	5.20
Brian Meadows	R	27	2	1	.667	1	34	7	0	76	91	11	38	0	4.72
Nelson Figueroa	R	29	2	1	.667	0	7	3	0	35	28	13	23	0	3.31
Ryan Vogelsong	R	25	2	2	.500	0	6	5	0	22	30	9	15	0	6.55
Duaner Sanchez	R	23	1	0	1.000	0	6	0	0	6	15	1	3	0	16.50
Mark Corey	R	28	1	2	.333	0	22	0	0	30	29	11	27	0	5.34
Joe Beimel	L	26	1	2	.333	0	69	0	0	62	69	33	42	0	5.05
1 Mike Williams	R	34	1	3	.250	25	40	0	0	37	42	22	20	0	6.27
1 Dennys Reyes	L	26	0	0	—	0	12	0	0	10	10	9	11	0	10.45
John Grabow	L	24	0	0	—	0	5	0	0	5	6	0	9	0	3.60
Jim Mann	R	28	0	0	—	0	2	0	0	2	5	1	1	0	10.80
Pat Mahomes	R	32	0	1	.000	0	9	1	0	22	19	12	13	0	4.84
Mike Gonzalez	L	25	0	1	.000	0	16	0	0	8	7	6	6	0	7.56
2 Oliver Perez	L	21	0	3	.000	0	5	5	1	23	24	12	24	0	5.87

CINCINNATI 5th 69-93 .426 19   BOB BOONE 46-58 .442 DAVE MILEY 23-35 .397

Name	G by Pos	B	AGE	G	AB	R	H	2B	3B	HR	RBI	BB	SO	SB	BA	SA
TOTALS			27	162	5509	694	1349	239	21	182	669	524	1326	80	.245	.395
Sean Casey	1B144	L	28	147	573	71	167	19	3	14	80	51	58	4	.291	.408
2 D'Angelo Jimenez	2B73 3B2	B	25	73	290	34	84	13	2	7	31	34	43	7	.290	.421
1 Barry Larkin (RJ)	SS60	R	39	70	241	39	68	16	1	2	18	22	32	2	.282	.382
Aaron Boone	3B83 2B19 SS5	R	30	106	403	61	110	19	3	18	65	35	74	15	.273	.469
Austin Kearns (SJ)	OF80	R	23	82	292	39	71	10	0	15	58	41	68	5	.264	.455
Ken Griffey Jr. (SJ-NJ)	OF43	L	33	53	166	34	41	12	1	13	26	27	44	1	.247	.566
Adam Dunn (RJ)	OF102 1B19	L	23	116	381	70	82	12	1	27	57	74	126	8	.215	.465
Jason LaRue	C114 1B1 OF1	R	29	118	379	52	87	23	1	16	50	33	111	3	.230	.422
Juan Castro	2B56 3B30 SS24 1B1	R	31	113	320	28	81	14	1	9	33	18	58	2	.253	.388
Reggie Taylor (SJ)	OF60	L	26	100	180	17	39	5	2	5	19	11	68	7	.217	.350
Jose Guillen	OF78	R	27	91	315	52	106	21	1	23	63	17	63	1	.337	.629
Wily Mo Pena	OF47 3B1	R	21	80	165	20	36	6	1	5	16	12	53	3	.218	.358
Ray Olmedo	SS51 2B18	B	22	79	230	24	55	6	1	0	17	13	46	1	.239	.274
Ruben Mateo	OF54	R	25	74	207	16	50	9	0	3	18	12	53	0	.242	.329
Russell Branyan (SJ)	3B20 OF17 1B14	L	27	74	176	22	38	12	0	9	26	27	69	0	.216	.438
1 Kelly Stinnett	C50	R	33	60	179	14	41	13	0	3	19	13	51	0	.229	.352
Felipe Lopez	SS50 3B8 2B3	B	23	59	197	28	42	7	2	3	13	28	59	0	.213	.299
Ryan Freel (LJ)	OF24 2B11 3B2	R	27	43	137	23	39	6	1	4	12	9	35	9	.285	.431
Dernell Stenson (DD)	OF22 1B1	L	25	37	81	14	20	5	0	3	13	11	24	0	.247	.420
Brandon Larson (SJ)	3B24 OF3	R	27	32	89	6	9	1	0	1	9	3	33	0	.101	.146
Tim Hummel	3B20 SS2 2B1	R	24	26	84	9	19	5	0	2	10	8	13	0	.226	.357
Steve Smitherman	OF14	R	24	21	44	3	7	2	0	1	6	3	9	1	.159	.273
Eric Valent	OF8	L	26	18	42	3	9	0	0	1	2	9	11	0	.214	.214
Corky Miller	C11	R	27	14	30	4	8	0	0	1	5	7	7	0	.267	.267
Mark Budzinski	OF1	L	29	4	7	0	0	0	0	0	0	0	4	0	.000	.000
Jim Chamblee	3B1	R	28	2	2	0	0	0	0	0	0	0	2	0	.000	.000
Dane Sardinha	C1	R	24	1	2	0	0	0	0	0	0	0	1	0	.000	.000

NAME	T	AGE	W	L	PCT	SV	G	GS	CG	IP	H	BB	SO	SHO	ERA
		28	69	93	.426	38	162	162	4	1446	1578	590	932	5	5.09
Chris Reitsma	R	25	9	5	.643	12	57	3	0	84	92	19	53	0	4.29
Paul Wilson	R	30	8	10	.444	0	28	28	0	167	190	50	93	0	4.64
1 Scott Sullivan	R	32	6	0	1.000	0	50	0	0	50	39	26	43	0	3.62
Felix Heredia	L	28	5	2	.714	1	57	0	0	72	61	28	41	0	3.00
1 Scott Williamson	R	27	5	3	.625	21	42	0	0	49	35	31	61	0	3.19
2 Aaron Harang	R	25	4	3	.571	0	9	9	0	46	48	10	26	0	5.28
Danny Graves	R	30	4	15	.211	2	30	26	2	169	204	41	60	1	5.33
1 Gabe White (GJ)	L	31	3	0	1.000	0	34	0	0	34	36	3	30	0	3.93
Ryan Dempster (EJ)	R	26	3	7	.300	0	22	20	0	116	134	70	84	0	6.54
Jose Acevedo (NJ)	R	25	2	0	1.000	0	5	4	1	27	17	6	23	0	2.67
Ryan Wagner	R	20	2	0	1.000	0	17	0	0	22	13	12	25	0	1.66
2 Todd Van Poppel	R	31	2	0	.667	0	9	4	0	36	31	6	25	0	4.54
John Riedling	R	27	2	3	.400	1	55	8	0	101	107	47	65	0	4.90
Brian Reith	R	25	2	4	.400	1	42	1	0	61	61	36	39	0	4.11
Jeff Austin	R	26	2	3	.400	0	7	7	0	28	28	21	22	0	8.58
Seth Etherton	R	26	2	4	.333	0	7	7	0	30	39	15	17	0	6.90
Scott Randall	R	27	2	5	.286	0	15	2	0	28	34	11	25	0	6.51
Jimmy Haynes (XJ)	R	30	2	12	.143	0	18	18	1	94	118	57	49	0	6.30
Matt Belisle	R	23	1	1	.500	0	6	0	0	10	12	6	5	0	5.19
John Bale	L	29	1	2	.333	0	10	0	0	46	50	12	37	0	4.47
Dan Serafini	L	29	1	3	.250	0	10	4	0	30	41	14	13	0	5.40
Jimmy Anderson	L	27	1	6	.167	0	8	7	0	39	60	14	13	0	8.84
2 Phil Norton	L	27	0	0	—	0	17	0	0	15	7	6	7	0	2.45
Juan Cerros	R	26	0	0	—	0	11	0	0	13	11	5	9	0	4.85
Joey Hamilton	R	32	0	0	—	0	3	0	0	11	15	5	7	0	12.66
Joe Valentine	R	23	0	0	—	0	3	0	0	3	3	4	1	0	18.00
Mark Watson (IL)	L	29	0	0	—	0	2	0	0	2	2	1	2	0	4.50
1 Kent Mercker	L	35	0	2	.000	0	49	0	0	38	31	25	41	0	2.35
Josh Hall	R	22	0	2	.000	0	6	5	0	25	33	15	18	0	6.57
Josias Manzanillo	R	35	0	2	.000	0	11	0	0	11	11	4	12	0	12.66

Luke Prokopec (SJ) 25, Jose Rijo (EJ) 38

MILWAUKEE 6th 68-94 .420 20   NED YOST

Name	G by Pos	B	AGE	G	AB	R	H	2B	3B	HR	RBI	BB	SO	SB	BA	SA
TOTALS			31	162	5548	714	1423	266	24	196	685	547	1221	99	.256	.419
Richie Sexson	1B162	R	28	162	606	97	165	28	2	45	124	98	151	2	.272	.548
1 Eric Young	2B99	R	36	109	404	71	105	18	1	15	39	48	34	25	.260	.421
Royce Clayton	SS141	R	33	146	483	49	110	16	1	11	39	49	92	5	.228	.333
Wes Helms	3B130	R	27	134	476	56	124	21	0	23	67	43	131	0	.261	.450
John Vander Wal	OF89	L	37	117	327	50	84	25	1	14	45	46	104	1	.257	.468
Scott Podsednik	OF139	L	27	154	558	100	175	29	8	9	58	56	91	43	.314	.443
Geoff Jenkins (RJ)	OF123	L	28	124	487	81	144	30	2	28	95	53	128	0	.296	.538
Eddie Perez	C102	R	35	107	350	26	95	17	1	11	45	17	47	0	.271	.420
Brady Clark	OF105	R	30	128	315	33	86	21	1	6	40	21	40	13	.273	.403
Keith Ginter	2B53 3B40 SS2 OF2	R	27	127	358	51	92	15	2	14	44	37	87	1	.257	.427
Keith Osik	C78	R	34	80	241	22	60	12	0	2	21	31	44	0	.249	.324
Brooks Kieschnick	P42 OF3	R	31	69	70	12	21	1	0	7	12	6	13	0	.300	.614
Enrique Cruz	SS13 2B6 3B2	R	21	60	71	6	6	1	0	0	2	4	30	0	.085	.099
Bill Hall	2B18 SS18 3B1	R	23	52	142	23	37	9	2	5	20	7	28	1	.261	.458
1 Alex Sanchez	OF36	L	26	43	163	15	46	10	3	0	10	7	28	8	.282	.380
Mark Smith	OF15	R	33	33	63	8	15	4	0	3	10	4	13	0	.238	.444
Jason Conti	OF20	L	28	30	48	3	11	2	0	2	7	3	12	0	.229	.396
Pete Zoccolillo	OF7	R	26	20	37	4	4	1	0	0	3	2	13	0	.108	.135
1 Jeffrey Hammonds (NJ)	OF10	R	32	10	38	2	6	2	0	1	3	3	7	0	.158	.289
Rickie Weeks	2B4	R	20	7	12	1	2	1	0	0	1	0	6	0	.167	.250

NAME	T	AGE	W	L	PCT	SV	G	GS	CG	IP	H	BB	SO	SHO	ERA
		28	68	94	.420	44	162	162	5	1452	1590	575	1034	3	5.02
Ben Sheets	R	24	11	13	.458	0	34	34	1	221	232	43	157	0	4.45
Wayne Franklin	L	29	10	13	.435	0	36	34	1	195	201	94	116	1	5.50
Matt Kinney	R	26	10	13	.435	0	33	31	1	191	201	80	152	0	5.19
Leo Estrella	R	28	3	1	.700	3	58	0	0	66	75	21	37	0	4.36
1 Curtis Leskanic	R	35	4	0	1.000	0	26	0	0	27	24	10	25	0	2.70
Luis Vizcaino	R	28	4	3	.571	0	75	0	0	62	64	25	61	0	6.39
1 Mike DeJean	R	33	4	7	.364	18	58	0	0	65	69	27	58	0	4.87
1 Doug Davis	L	27	3	2	.600	0	8	8	1	52	49	21	35	0	2.58
1 Valerio De Los Santos (SJ)	L	30	3	3	.500	1	45	0	0	48	38	22	35	0	4.13
John Foster	L	25	2	0	1.000	0	23	0	0	21	30	8	16	0	4.71
Jayson Durocher (EJ-SJ)	R	28	2	0	1.000	0	8	0	0	12	11	10	13	0	11.05
Wes Obermueller	R	26	2	5	.286	0	12	11	0	66	81	25	34	0	5.07
Brooks Kieschnick	L	31	1	1	.500	0	42	0	0	53	66	13	39	0	5.26
Dave Burba	R	36	1	1	.500	0	17	2	0	43	42	19	35	0	3.53
Danny Kolb	R	28	1	3	.333	21	37	0	0	41	34	19	39	0	1.96
Todd Ritchie (SJ)	R	31	1	4	.333	0	5	5	0	28	36	10	15	0	5.08
Ruben Quevedo (SJ)	R	24	1	4	.200	0	9	8	0	43	53	23	19	0	6.75
Glendon Rusch (GJ)	L	28	1	12	.077	1	32	19	1	123	171	45	93	0	6.42
2 Mike Crudale	R	26	0	0	—	0	9	0	0	11	9	7	7	0	2.89
Shane Nance	L	25	0	2	.000	0	26	0	0	24	34	10	25	0	4.81
David Manning	R	30	0	2	.000	0	7	1	0	7	11	8	2	0	16.20
Matt Ford (EJ)	L	22	0	3	.000	0	25	4	0	44	46	21	26	0	4.13
Luis Martinez	L	23	0	4	.000	0	16	15	1	82	92	52	54	0	9.92

Nick Neugebauer (SJ) 22

WEST DIVISION

SAN FRANCISCO 1st 100-61 .621   FELIPE ALOU

Name	G by Pos	B	AGE	G	AB	R	H	2B	3B	HR	RBI	BB	SO	SB	BA	SA
TOTALS			33	161	5456	755	1440	281	29	180	713	593	980	52	.264	.425
J.T. Snow	1B98	L	35	103	330	48	90	18	3	8	51	55	55	1	.273	.418
Ray Durham	2B105	B	31	110	410	61	117	30	5	8	33	50	82	7	.285	.441
Rich Aurilia	SS123	R	31	129	505	65	140	26	1	13	58	36	82	2	.277	.410
Edgardo Alfonzo	3B133 2B6	R	29	142	514	56	133	25	2	13	81	58	41	5	.259	.391
Jose Cruz	OF158	B	29	158	539	90	135	26	1	20	68	102	121	5	.250	.414
Marquis Grissom	OF148	R	36	149	587	82	176	33	4	20	79	20	82	11	.300	.468
Barry Bonds	OF123	L	38	130	390	111	133	22	1	45	90	148	58	7	.341	.749
Benito Santiago	C106	R	38	108	401	53	112	21	2	11	56	29	69	0	.279	.424
Neifi Perez	2B57 SS45 3B2	B	30	120	328	27	84	19	4	1	31	14	23	3	.256	.348
Andres Galarraga	1B69	R	42	110	272	36	82	15	0	12	42	19	61	1	.301	.489
Pedro Feliz	3B49 OF15 1B12	R	28	95	235	31	58	9	3	16	48	10	53	2	.247	.515
Yorvit Torrealba	C66 OF1	R	24	66	200	22	52	10	2	4	29	14	39	1	.260	.390
Marvin Benard (KJ)	OF21	L	33	46	71	5	14	3	1	0	4	4	9	1	.197	.268
2 Jeffrey Hammonds	OF30	R	32	36	94	10	26	10	0	3	10	13	21	1	.277	.479
Ruben Rivera	OF27	R	29	31	50	6	9	2	0	2	4	5	19	1	.180	.340
2 Eric Young	2B18 OF2	R	36	26	71	9	14	2	0	2	5	5	9	2	.197	.225
Cody Ransom	SS12	R	27	20	27	7	6	1	0	1	1	0	11	0	.222	.370
Todd Linden	OF13	B	22	18	38	2	8	1	0	1	1	5	16	0	.211	.316
Tony Torcato	OF16	L	23	14	16	0	3	1	0	0	2	1	4	0	.188	.250
Alberto Castillo (WJ)	OF3 1B1	L	33	11	15	2	3	2	0	0	1	8	4	0	.200	.467
Francisco Santos	OF3	R	28	8	15	2	3	2	0	0	2	0	4	0	.200	.533
Jason Ellison	OF4	R	25	7	10	1	1	0	0	0	1	0	2	1	.100	.100
Carlos Valderrama	OF5	R	25	7	7	1	1	0	0	0	0	0	2	1	.143	.143
Lance Niekro	1B3	R	24	5	5	2	1	0	0	0	2	0	1	0	.200	.400
Trey Lunsford	C1	R	24	1	1	1	0	0	0	0	0	0	0	0	.000	.000

NAME	T	AGE	W	L	PCT	SV	G	GS	CG	IP	H	BB	SO	SHO	ERA
		29	100	61	.621	43	161	161	7	1437	1349	546	1006	10	3.73
Jason Schmidt	R	30	17	5	.773	0	29	29	5	208	152	46	208	3	2.34
Joe Nathan	R	28	12	4	.750	0	78	0	0	79	51	33	83	0	2.96
Kirk Rueter	L	32	10	5	.667	0	27	27	0	147	170	47	41	0	4.53
1 Damian Moss	L	26	9	7	.563	0	21	20	0	115	121	63	57	0	4.70
Felix Rodriguez	R	30	8	2	.800	2	68	0	0	61	59	29	46	0	3.10
Jim Brower	R	30	8	5	.615	2	51	5	0	100	90	39	65	0	3.96
Jesse Foppert (EJ)	R	22	8	9	.471	0	21	21	1	111	103	69	101	0	5.03
Jerome Williams	R	21	7	5	.583	0	21	21	2	131	116	49	88	1	3.30
1 Kurt Ainsworth (SJ)	R	24	5	4	.556	0	11	11	0	66	66	26	48	0	3.82
Tim Worrell	R	35	4	4	.500	38	76	0	0	78	74	28	65	0	2.87
Kevin Correia	R	22	3	1	.750	0	10	7	0	39	41	18	28	0	3.66
2 Sidney Ponson	R	26	3	6	.333	0	10	10	1	68	64	18	34	0	3.71
Scott Eyre	L	31	2	1	.667	1	57	0	0	57	60	26	33	0	3.32
2 Dustin Hermanson	R	30	2	1	.667	0	9	9	0	39	35	10	27	0	3.00
2 Matt Herges	R	33	1	0	1.000	0	9	0	0	9	8	4	5	0	2.31
Chad Zerbe	L	31	1	0	.500	0	33	1	0	50	60	14	17	0	4.71
Jason Christiansen (EJ)	L	33	0	0	—	0	40	0	0	26	25	11	22	0	5.19
Ryan Jensen (XJ)	R	27	0	1	.000	0	13	13	0	21	15	13	9	0	10.80
Noah Lowry	L	22	0	1	.000	0	2	1	0	4	3	2	6	0	0.00
Manny Aybar	R	31	0	1	.000	0	9	0	0	9	9	6	3	0	6.00
Brian Powell	R	29	0	1	.000	0	3	0	0	4	7	3	1	0	13.50

Robb Nen (SJ) 33

LOS ANGELES — 2nd 85-77 .525 15.5 — JIM TRACY

Name	G by Pos	B	AGE	G	AB	R	H	2B	3B	HR	RBI	BB	SO	SB	BA	SA
TOTALS			30	162	5458	574	1328	260	25	124	544	407	985	80	.243	.368
Fred McGriff (GJ)	1B79	L	39	86	297	32	74	14	0	13	40	31	66	0	.249	.428
Alex Cora	2B141 SS15	L	27	148	477	39	119	24	3	4	34	16	59	4	.249	.338
Cesar Izturis	SS158	B	23	158	558	47	140	21	6	1	40	25	70	10	.251	.315
Adrian Beltre	3B157 SS1	R	24	158	559	50	134	30	2	23	80	37	103	2	.240	.424
Shawn Green	OF157	L	30	160	611	84	171	49	2	19	85	68	112	6	.280	.460
Dave Roberts	OF105	L	31	107	388	56	97	6	5	2	16	43	39	40	.250	.307
Brian Jordan (KJ)	OF62	R	36	66	224	28	67	9	0	6	28	23	30	1	.299	.420
Paul LoDuca	C123 1B22 OF6	R	31	147	568	64	155	34	2	7	52	44	54	0	.273	.377
Jolbert Cabrera	OF63 2B59 SS9 1B8 3B5	R	30	128	347	43	98	32	2	6	37	17	62	6	.282	.438
Mike Kinkade	OF36 1B13 3B2	R	30	88	162	25	35	7	0	5	14	13	38	1	.216	.352
Ron Coomer	1B24 3B11	R	36	69	125	11	30	4	0	4	15	10	19	0	.240	.368
2 Jeromy Burnitz	OF60	L	34	61	230	25	47	4	0	13	32	14	57	4	.204	.391
Daryle Ward	1B13 OF11	L	28	52	109	6	20	1	0	0	9	3	19	0	.183	.193
2 Robin Ventura	1B42 3B3	L	35	49	109	11	24	5	1	5	13	18	25	0	.220	.422
David Ross	C38	R	26	40	124	19	32	7	0	10	18	13	42	0	.258	.556
Jason Romano	OF28 2B1	R	24	37	36	3	3	0	0	0	1	4	8	2	.083	.083
Rickey Henderson	OF18	R	44	30	72	7	15	1	0	2	5	11	16	3	.208	.306
Larry Barnes	1B8 OF2	L	28	30	38	2	8	2	0	0	2	1	9	0	.211	.263
Wilkin Ruan	OF20	R	24	21	41	2	9	2	1	0	2	0	7	1	.220	.317
Todd Hundley (XJ)	C10	B	34	21	33	2	6	1	0	2	11	8	13	0	.182	.394
Joe Thurston	2B3	L	23	12	10	2	2	0	0	0	0	1	1	0	.200	.200
Chad Hermansen (SJ)	OF6	R	25	11	25	2	4	1	0	0	2	2	9	0	.160	.200
Bubba Crosby	OF1	L	26	9	12	0	1	0	0	0	0	0	5	0	.083	.083
Koyie Hill		B	24	3	3	0	1	1	0	0	1	0	0	0	.333	.667
Chin-Feng Chen		R	25	1	1	0	0	0	0	0	0	0	0	0	.000	.000

NAME	T	AGE	W	L	PCT	SV	G	GS	CG	IP	H	BB	SO	SHO	ERA
		32	85	77	.525	58	162	162	3	1458	1254	526	1289	17	3.16
Hideo Nomo	R	34	16	13	.552	0	33	33	2	218	175	98	177	2	3.09
Kevin Brown	R	38	14	9	.609	0	32	32	0	211	184	56	185	0	2.39
Odalis Perez	L	26	12	12	.500	0	30	30	0	185	191	46	141	0	4.52
Kazuhisa Ishii (KJ)	L	29	9	7	.563	0	27	27	0	147	129	101	140	0	3.86
Wilson Alvarez	L	33	6	2	.750	1	21	12	1	95	80	23	82	1	2.37
Guillermo Mota	R	29	6	3	.667	1	76	0	0	105	78	26	99	0	1.97
Paul Shuey	R	32	6	4	.600	0	62	0	0	69	50	33	60	0	3.00
Darren Dreifort (KJ)	R	31	4	4	.500	0	10	10	0	60	58	25	67	0	4.03
Andy Ashby	R	35	3	10	.231	0	21	12	0	73	90	17	41	0	5.18
Troy Brohawn (SJ)	L	30	2	0	1.000	0	12	0	0	12	10	4	13	0	3.86
Edwin Jackson	R	19	2	1	.667	0	4	3	0	22	17	11	19	0	2.45
Eric Gagne	R	27	2	3	.400	55	77	0	0	82	37	20	137	0	1.20
Paul Quantrill	R	34	2	5	.286	1	89	0	0	77	61	15	44	0	1.75
Tom Martin	L	33	1	2	.333	0	80	0	0	51	36	24	51	0	3.53
Steve Colyer	L	24	0	0	—	0	13	0	0	20	22	9	16	0	2.75
Rodney Myers	R	34	0	0	—	0	4	0	0	9	10	4	5	0	6.00
2 Scott Mullen	L	28	0	0	—	0	3	0	0	3	2	5	1	0	9.00
Masao Kida	R	34	0	1	.000	0	3	2	0	12	15	3	8	0	3.00
Victor Alvarez	L	26	0	1	.000	0	5	0	0	6	9	6	3	0	12.71

ARIZONA — 3rd 84-78 .519 16.5 — BOB BRENLY

Name	G by Pos	B	AGE	G	AB	R	H	2B	3B	HR	RBI	BB	SO	SB	BA	SA
TOTALS			30	162	5570	717	1467	303	47	152	696	531	1006	76	.263	.417
Lyle Overbay	1B75	L	26	86	254	23	70	20	4	4	28	35	67	1	.276	.402
Junior Spivey (NJ)	2B98 OF1	R	28	106	365	52	93	22	2	13	50	33	95	4	.255	.433
Alex Cintron	SS93 3B16 2B9	B	24	117	448	70	142	26	6	13	51	29	33	2	.317	.489
Craig Counsell (RJ)	3B57 SS26 2B10 1B2	L	32	89	303	40	71	6	3	3	21	41	32	11	.234	.304
Danny Bautista (LJ)	OF79	R	31	88	284	29	78	16	3	4	36	21	50	3	.275	.394
Steve Finley	OF140	L	38	147	516	82	148	24	10	22	70	57	94	15	.287	.500
Luis Gonzalez	OF154	L	35	156	579	92	176	46	4	26	104	94	67	5	.304	.532
Chad Moeller	C76	R	28	78	239	29	64	17	1	7	29	23	59	1	.268	.435
Quinton McCracken	OF55	B	33	115	203	17	46	5	2	0	18	15	34	5	.227	.271
Carlos Baerga	1B19 2B15 3B5	B	34	105	207	31	71	13	0	4	39	18	20	1	.343	.464
2 Shea Hillenbrand	1B56 3B34	R	27	85	330	40	88	18	1	17	59	17	44	0	.267	.482
Rod Barajas	C79	R	27	80	220	19	48	15	0	3	28	14	33	0	.218	.327
Matt Kata	2B52 3B23 SS6	B	25	78	288	42	74	16	5	7	29	25	53	3	.257	.420
1 Dave Dellucci	OF53	L	29	70	165	18	40	11	3	2	19	19	45	9	.242	.382
Mark Grace	1B39	L	39	66	135	13	27	5	0	3	16	16	15	0	.200	.304
Rob Hammock	C36 OF17 3B16	R	26	65	195	30	55	10	2	8	28	17	44	3	.282	.477
1 Tony Womack	SS58	R	33	61	219	30	52	10	3	2	15	8	27	8	.237	.338
2 Raul Mondesi	OF43	R	32	45	162	27	49	8	1	8	22	18	31	5	.302	.512
Matt Williams (VR)	3B42	R	37	44	134	17	33	9	0	4	16	16	26	0	.246	.403
Felix Jose	OF1	B	38	18	18	1	6	1	0	1	6	6	3	0	.333	.556
Luis Terrero	OF3	R	23	16	8	2	2	0	0	0	0	1	1	0	.250	.250

NAME	T	AGE	W	L	PCT	SV	G	GS	CG	IP	H	BB	SO	SHO	ERA
		29	84	78	.519	42	162	162	7	1455	1379	526	1291	11	3.84
Oscar Villarreal	R	21	10	7	.588	0	86	1	0	98	80	46	80	0	2.57
Miguel Batista	R	32	10	9	.526	0	36	29	2	193	197	60	142	1	3.54
Brandon Webb	R	24	10	9	.526	0	29	28	1	181	140	68	172	1	2.84
Steve Randolph	L	29	8	1	.889	0	50	0	0	60	50	43	50	0	4.05
Elmer Dessens	R	32	8	8	.500	0	34	30	0	176	212	57	113	0	5.07
Curt Schilling (BH)	R	36	8	9	.471	0	24	24	3	168	144	32	194	2	2.95
Randy Johnson (KJ)	L	39	6	8	.429	0	18	18	1	114	125	27	125	1	4.26
Matt Mantei (SJ)	R	29	5	4	.556	29	50	0	0	55	37	18	68	0	2.62
Andrew Good	R	23	4	2	.667	0	16	10	0	66	74	16	42	0	5.29
Mike Koplove (SJ)	R	26	3	0	1.000	0	31	0	0	38	31	10	27	0	2.15
Eddie Oropesa	L	31	3	3	.500	0	47	0	0	39	38	27	39	0	5.82
Jose Valverde	R	23	2	1	.667	10	54	0	0	50	24	26	71	0	2.15
Edgar Gonzalez	R	20	2	1	.667	0	9	2	0	18	28	7	14	0	4.91
Chris Capuano	L	24	2	4	.333	0	9	5	0	33	27	11	23	0	4.64
Ricky Bottalico	R	33	1	0	1.000	0	2	0	0	2	3	2	2	0	5.40
John Patterson	R	25	1	4	.200	0	16	8	0	55	61	30	43	0	6.05
1 Byung-Hyun Kim	R	24	1	5	.167	7	7	7	0	44	43	15	33	0	3.56
Brady Raggio	R	30	0	0	—	0	10	0	0	8	9	6	4	0	6.48
2 Dennys Reyes	L	26	0	0	—	0	3	0	0	2	5	1	5	0	11.57
1 Bret Prinz (GJ)	R	26	0	0	—	0	3	0	0	1	1	1	0	0	0.00
Mike Myers	L	34	0	1	.000	0	64	0	0	36	38	21	21	0	5.70
1 Scott Service	R	36	0	2	.000	1	18	0	0	18	21	2	18	0	4.91

COLORADO — 4th 74-88 .457 26.5 — CLINT HURDLE

Name	G by Pos	B	AGE	G	AB	R	H	2B	3B	HR	RBI	BB	SO	SB	BA	SA
TOTALS			30	162	5518	853	1472	330	31	198	814	619	1134	63	.267	.445
Todd Helton	1B159	L	29	160	583	135	209	49	5	33	117	111	72	0	.358	.630
Ron Belliard	2B113	R	28	116	447	73	124	31	2	8	50	49	71	4	.277	.409
Juan Uribe (BF)	SS74 2B31 OF7	R	23	87	316	45	80	19	3	10	33	17	60	7	.253	.427
Chris Stynes	3B119 2B5	R	30	138	443	71	113	31	3	11	73	48	76	3	.255	.413
Larry Walker	OF131	L	36	143	454	86	129	25	7	16	79	98	87	7	.284	.476
Preston Wilson	OF155	R	28	155	600	94	169	43	1	36	141	54	139	14	.282	.537
Jay Payton	OF151	R	30	157	600	93	181	32	5	28	89	43	77	6	.302	.512
Charles Johnson	C107	R	31	108	356	49	82	20	0	20	61	49	84	1	.230	.455
Greg Norton	3B34 1B9 OF3	B	30	114	179	19	47	15	0	6	31	16	47	2	.263	.447
1 Jose Hernandez	SS69 1B1	R	33	69	257	33	61	6	1	8	27	27	95	1	.237	.362
Mark Sweeney	OF17 1B8	L	33	67	97	13	25	9	0	2	14	9	27	0	.258	.412
Rene Reyes	OF36	B	25	53	116	13	30	7	1	2	7	5	19	2	.259	.388
2 Mark Bellhorn	2B20 3B15 SS6 OF5 1B1	B	28	48	110	12	26	3	0	0	13	19	26	2	.236	.264
Bobby Estalella (EJ)	C46	R	28	46	140	17	28	7	0	7	21	19	55	0	.200	.400
1 Gabe Kapler	OF27	R	27	39	67	10	15	2	0	0	4	8	18	2	.224	.254
Brent Butler	2B20 3B8 SS4	R	25	37	90	13	19	3	1	1	7	3	13	0	.211	.300
Garrett Atkins	3B19	R	23	25	69	6	11	2	0	1	6	3	14	0	.159	.188
Greg Vaughn	OF7	R	37	22	37	8	7	3	0	1	5	8	13	0	.189	.514
2 Tony Womack	SS14 2B7 OF1	L	33	21	79	9	15	2	0	0	5	0	9	5	.190	.215
Chris Richard (LJ)	OF3 1B1	L	29	19	27	3	6	1	0	0	4	8	6	0	.222	.444
Pablo Ozuna (KJ)	2B8 OF5 SS3	R	28	17	40	5	8	1	0	0	2	0	6	0	.200	.225
2 Gregg Zaun	C14	B	32	15	46	6	12	1	0	3	8	6	4	0	.261	.478
Clint Barmes	SS12	R	24	12	25	2	8	2	0	0	2	0	2	0	.320	.400
Kit Pellow	C7 1B1 OF1	R	29	11	18	6	8	3	1	1	4	0	4	0	.444	.889
Mandy Romero	C2	B	35	3	7	2	3	1	0	0	1	1	1	0	.429	.571
1 Ben Petrick	OF2 C1	R	26	3	3	0	0	0	0	0	0	0	1	0	.000	.000
Luke Allen		L	24	3	3	0	0	0	0	0	0	0	0	0	.000	.000

NAME	T	AGE	W	L	PCT	SV	G	GS	CG	IP	H	BB	SO	SHO	ERA
		29	74	88	.457	34	162	162	3	1420	1629	552	866	4	5.20
Darren Oliver	L	32	13	11	.542	0	33	32	1	180	201	61	88	0	5.04
Jason Jennings	R	24	12	13	.480	0	32	32	1	181	212	88	119	0	5.11
Shawn Chacon (EJ)	R	25	11	8	.579	0	23	23	0	137	124	58	93	0	4.60
Steve Reed	R	38	5	3	.625	0	67	0	0	63	59	26	39	0	3.27
Javier Lopez	L	25	4	1	.800	1	75	0	0	58	58	12	40	0	3.70
Scott Elarton (SJ)	R	27	4	4	.500	0	11	10	0	52	73	20	20	0	6.27
Aaron Cook	R	24	4	6	.400	0	43	16	1	124	160	57	43	0	6.02
Justin Speier	R	29	3	1	.750	9	72	0	0	73	73	23	66	0	4.05
Dennis Stark (SJ)	R	28	3	3	.500	0	17	13	0	79	98	33	30	0	5.83
Brian Fuentes	L	27	3	3	.500	0	75	0	0	75	64	34	82	0	2.75
Chin-hui Tsao	R	22	3	3	.500	0	9	8	0	43	48	20	29	0	6.02
Nelson Cruz (SJ)	R	30	3	5	.375	0	20	7	0	54	65	11	38	0	7.21
Denny Neagle (EJ)	L	34	2	4	.333	0	7	7	0	35	47	12	21	0	7.90
Jose Jimenez	R	29	2	10	.167	20	63	7	0	102	137	32	45	0	5.22
Cory Vance	L	24	1	3	.250	0	9	0	0	31	30	10	12	0	5.60
1 Todd Jones	R	35	1	4	.200	0	33	1	0	39	61	18	28	0	8.24
Jesus Sanchez	L	28	0	0	—	0	9	0	0	8	11	4	2	0	9.00
2 Joe Roa	R	30	0	0	—	0	4	0	0	7	7	4	4	0	4.05
Matt Miller	L	31	0	0	—	0	4	0	0	4	5	2	5	0	2.08
1 Vic Darensbourg	L	32	0	0	—	0	4	0	0	4	4	4	4	0	0.00
2 Adam Bernero	R	26	0	2	.000	0	31	0	0	33	33	13	26	0	5.23
Jason Young	R	23	0	2	.000	0	3	0	0	21	34	9	18	0	8.44
1 Dan Miceli	R	32	0	2	.000	0	14	0	0	21	24	9	18	0	5.66

SAN DIEGO — 5th 64-98 .395 36.5 — BRUCE BOCHY

Name	G by Pos	B	AGE	G	AB	R	H	2B	3B	HR	RBI	BB	SO	SB	BA	SA
TOTALS			29	162	5531	678	1442	257	32	128	641	565	1073	76	.261	.388
Ryan Klesko	1B111	L	32	121	397	47	100	18	0	21	67	65	83	2	.252	.456
Mark Loretta	2B150 SS3	R	31	154	589	74	185	28	4	13	72	54	62	5	.314	.441
Ramon Vazquez (MJ)	SS108 3B4 2B3	L	26	116	422	56	110	17	4	3	30	52	88	10	.261	.341
Sean Burroughs	3B137	L	22	146	517	62	148	27	6	7	58	44	75	7	.286	.402
Phil Nevin (SJ)	1B31 OF29	R	32	59	226	30	63	8	0	13	46	21	44	2	.279	.487
Mark Kotsay	OF126	L	27	128	482	64	128	28	4	7	38	56	82	6	.266	.384
1 Rondell White	OF104	R	31	115	413	49	115	17	3	18	66	25	71	1	.278	.465
Gary Bennett (KJ)	C91	R	31	96	307	26	73	15	0	2	24	25	42	0	.238	.306
Brian Buchanan	OF43 1B24	R	29	115	198	29	52	10	2	8	29	24	51	6	.263	.455
Xavier Nady	OF105	R	24	110	371	50	99	17	1	9	39	24	74	6	.267	.391
Dave Hansen	1B20 3B11 2B1	L	34	110	135	13	33	4	1	2	15	23	25	1	.244	.333
2 Gary Matthews	OF92	B	28	103	306	50	83	19	1	4	22	34	66	12	.271	.379
1 Lou Merloni	3B25 SS23 2B10 1B2 OF2	R	32	65	151	20	41	7	2	1	22	22	33	2	.272	.364
Keith Lockhart (XJ)	2B27 3B3	L	38	62	95	18	23	5	1	3	8	13	19	0	.242	.411
Miguel Ojeda	C48 1B2	R	28	61	141	13	33	6	0	4	17	18	26	1	.234	.362
Shane Victorino	OF32	R	22	36	73	8	11	2	0	0	4	7	17	7	.151	.178
2 Brian Giles	OF29	L	32	29	104	23	31	4	2	4	18	20	10	4	.298	.490
Donaldo Mendez	SS26	R	25	26	84	10	19	6	0	2	10	5	13	0	.226	.369
Wiki Gonzalez	C23 P1	R	29	24	65	1	13	5	0	0	5	10	13	0	.200	.277
Khalil Greene	SS20	R	23	20	65	8	14	4	1	1	7	7	13	0	.215	.400
Mike Rivera	C19 1B1	R	26	19	65	6	11	3	0	1	5	3	17	0	.170	.262
Humberto Quintero	C11	R	23	12	23	1	5	0	0	0	1	1	6	0	.217	.217
2 Todd Sears	1B1	L	27	7	8	1	2	1	0	0	0	1	3	0	.250	.375
1 Jason Bay (BW)	OF3	R	24	3	8	4	2	0	1	1	5	0	5	0	.250	.750
2 Jermaine Clark	OF1	L	26	3	1	0	0	0	0	0	0	0	2	0	.000	.000

NAME	T	AGE	W	L	PCT	SV	G	GS	CG	IP	H	BB	SO	SHO	ERA
		29	64	98	.395	31	162	162	2	1431	1458	611	1091	10	4.87
Jake Peavy	R	22	12	11	.522	0	32	32	0	195	173	82	156	0	4.11
Brian Lawrence	R	27	10	15	.400	0	33	33	1	211	206	57	116	0	4.19
Adam Eaton	R	25	9	12	.429	0	31	31	1	183	173	68	146	0	4.08
Mike Matthews	L	29	6	4	.600	0	77	0	0	65	65	29	44	0	4.45
1 Oliver Perez	L	21	4	7	.364	0	19	19	0	104	103	65	117	0	5.38
Kevin Jarvis (AJ)	R	33	4	8	.333	0	16	16	0	92	113	32	49	0	5.87
Rod Beck	R	34	3	2	.600	20	36	0	0	35	25	11	32	0	1.78
Jay Witasick (AJ)	R	30	3	7	.300	2	46	0	0	46	42	25	42	0	4.53
2 Scott Linebrink	R	26	2	1	.667	0	43	0	0	61	55	22	51	0	2.82
Luther Hackman	R	28	2	2	.500	0	65	0	0	77	78	36	48	0	5.17
1 Matt Herges	R	33	2	2	.500	0	40	0	0	44	40	20	40	0	2.86
Joe Roa	R	31	1	1	.500	0	18	1	0	25	34	6	18	0	6.75
2 Jesse Orosco	L	46	1	1	.500	2	42	0	0	25	33	10	22	0	7.56
Clay Condrey (UJ)	R	27	1	3	.333	0	8	6	0	34	43	21	25	0	8.47
Carlton Loewer	R	29	1	3	.333	0	5	5	0	28	38	5	11	0	6.65
Ben Howard	R	25	1	4	.200	0	13	5	0	36	44	15	35	0	8.75
Mike Bynum	L	25	1	4	.200	0	13	5	0	30	38	16	19	0	6.50
1 Jaret Wright	R	27	1	5	.167	2	39	0	0	47	69	28	41	0	8.37
Trevor Hoffman (SJ)	R	35	0	2	.000	2	9	0	0	9	7	1	11	0	2.00
Kevin Walker (EJ)	L	26	0	0	—	0	4	0	0	5	5	3	0	0	5.40
Wiki Gonzalez	R	29	0	0	—	0	1	0	0	1	0	0	0	0	0.00
Roger Deago	L	27	0	1	.000	0	9	1	0	20	25	8	15	0	7.84
Randy Keisler	L	27	0	1	.000	0	6	1	0	6	7	7	5	0	12.00
Dennis Tankersley	R	24	0	2	.000	0	3	2	0	9	14	10	7	0	∞
Brandon Villafuerte	R	27	0	0	—	0	2	0	0	4	9	3	4	0	4.20
Charles Nagy	R	36	0	2	.000	0	3	3	0	14	15	4	7	0	4.38
Brian Tollberg	R	30	0	2	.000	0	3	1	0	10	11	4	7	0	6.97

LINE SCORES

Team	1	2	3	4	5	6	7	8	9	10	11	12	13	R	H	E

DIVISION SERIES: FLORIDA 3 : SAN FRANCISCO 1

Game 1   September 30 at San Francisco

	1	2	3	4	5	6	7	8	9		R	H	E
FLA	0	0	0	0	0	0	0	0	0		0	3	1
SF	0	0	0	1	0	0	0	1	x		2	3	2

Beckett, Fox (8)   Schmidt

Game 2   October 1 at San Francisco

	1	2	3	4	5	6	7	8	9		R	H	E
FLA	1	0	0	0	3	3	1	1	0		9	14	0
SF	1	0	3	1	0	0	0	0			5	8	2

Penny, Helling (6), Pavano (5), Fox (6),   Ponson, **Nathan** (6), Christiansen (6),
Willis (8), Looper (8), Urbina (9)   Herges (6), Rodriguez (7), Brower (8),
                                             Worrell (9)

Game 3   October 3 at Florida

	1	2	3	4	5	6	7	8	9	10	11		R	H	E
SF	0	0	0	0	0	2	0	0	0	0	1		3	12	1
FLA	2	0	0	0	0	0	0	0	0	0	2		4	8	1

Rueter, Herges (6), Eyre (7), Nathan (8),   Redman, Fox (7), Urbina (9), Pavano (10),
Rodriguez (8), **Worrell** (10)   **Looper** (11)

Game 4   October 4 at Florida

	1	2	3	4	5	6	7	8	9		R	H	E
SF	0	1	0	0	0	4	0	0	1		6	9	2
FLA	0	1	2	2	0	0	0	2	x		7	12	0

Williams, Brower (3), Hermanson (5),   Willis, Penny (6), **Pavano** (8), Urbina (9)
Herges (6), **Rodriguez** (8)

DIVISION SERIES: CHICAGO 3 : ATLANTA 2

Game 1   September 30 at Atlanta

	1	2	3	4	5	6	7	8	9		R	H	E
CHN	0	0	0	0	0	4	0	0	0		4	10	0
ATL	0	0	1	0	0	0	0	1	0		2	3	1

Wood, Remlinger (8), Farnsworth (8),   Ortiz, King (6), Gryboski (6),
Borowski (9)   Wright (7), Mercker (8),
                                        Hernandez (9)

Game 2   October 1 at Atlanta

	1	2	3	4	5	6	7	8	9		R	H	E
CHN	2	0	0	0	0	0	1	0			3	6	0
ATL	1	0	0	1	0	1	0	2	x		5	13	0

Zambrano, Farnsworth (6), **Veres** (8)   Hampton, King (7), Gryboski (7),
                                           Smoltz (8)

Game 3   October 3 at Chicago

	1	2	3	4	5	6	7	8	9		R	H	E
ATL	0	0	0	0	0	0	0	1	0		1	2	4
CHN	2	0	0	0	0	0	1	x			3	8	0

Maddux, Wright (7), Gryboski (8)   Prior

Game 4   October 5 at Chicago

	1	2	3	4	5	6	7	8	9		R	H	E
ATL	0	0	0	1	3	0	0	2	0		6	12	0
CHN	0	0	1	0	0	1	0	1	1		4	10	0

Ortiz, King (6), Gryboski (6), Wright (7),   Clement, Alfonseca (5), Remlinger (6),
Cunnane (8), Smoltz (9)   Veres (7), Farnsworth (7), Guthrie (8),
                                              Cruz (9)

Game 5   October 6 at Atlanta

	1	2	3	4	5	6	7	8	9		R	H	E
CHN	1	1	0	0	0	2	0	0	1		5	9	0
ATL	0	0	0	0	0	1	0	0			1	5	1

Wood, Borowski (9)   Hampton, Gryboski (7), Wright (8),
                      Cunnane (9), King (9)

COMPOSITE BATTING

DIVISION SERIES

NAME	POS	G	AB	R	H	2B	3B	HR	RBI	BA
FLORIDA										
TOTALS		4	146	20	37	8	1	2	18	.253
Pierre	CF	4	19	5	5	1	0	0	3	.263
Rodriguez	C	4	17	3	6	1	0	1	6	.353
Castillo	2B	4	17	2	5	3	0	0	1	.294
Lee	1B	4	16	2	4	1	0	0	2	.250
Gonzalez	SS	4	16	2	1	0	0	0	0	.063
Encarnacion	RF	4	15	1	2	0	0	1	1	.133
Conine	LF	3	15	2	4	0	0	0	2	.267
Cabrera	3B	4	14	1	4	2	0	0	3	.286
Hollandsworth	PH	3	3	1	1	0	0	0	0	.333
Willis	P	2	3	1	3	0	1	0	0	1.000
Lowell	3B	2	3	0	0	0	0	0	0	.000
Harris	PH	2	2	0	1	0	0	0	0	.500
Banks	PH	2	2	0	0	0	0	0	0	.000
Redman	P	1	2	0	0	0	0	0	0	.000
Penny	P	2	1	0	1	0	0	0	0	1.000
Beckett	P	1	1	0	0	0	0	0	0	.000
Fox	P	3	0	0	0	0	0	0	0	—
Pavano	P	3	0	0	0	0	0	0	0	—
Urbina	P	3	0	0	0	0	0	0	0	—
Looper	P	2	0	0	0	0	0	0	0	—
Helling	P	1	0	0	0	0	0	0	0	—
SAN FRANCISCO										
TOTALS		4	136	16	32	7	1	0	15	.235
Alfonzo	3B	4	17	3	9	4	0	0	5	.529
Durham	2B	4	17	2	4	0	0	0	0	.235
Snow	1B	4	16	0	5	0	0	0	3	.313
Aurilia	SS	4	15	4	2	1	0	0	1	.133
Grissom	CF	4	14	1	2	0	0	0	1	.143
Santiago	C	4	11	0	2	0	0	0	0	.182
Cruz	RF	4	11	0	0	0	0	0	1	.000
Bonds	LF	4	9	3	2	1	0	0	2	.222
Hammonds	RF-CF	3	5	1	2	0	0	0	0	.400
Galarraga	1B	2	5	0	0	0	0	0	0	.000
Feliz	PH	3	3	1	2	0	1	0	1	.667
Perez	2B	3	3	1	1	1	0	0	0	.333
Torrealba	C	2	3	0	0	0	0	0	1	.000
Schmidt	P	1	3	0	0	0	0	0	0	.000
Rueter	P	1	2	0	1	0	0	0	0	.500
Ponson	P	1	1	0	0	0	0	0	0	.000
Williams	P	1	1	0	0	0	0	0	0	.000
Herges	P	3	0	0	0	0	0	0	0	—
Rodriguez	P	3	0	0	0	0	0	0	0	—
Brower	P	2	0	0	0	0	0	0	0	—
Nathan	P	2	0	0	0	0	0	0	0	—
Worrell	P	2	0	0	0	0	0	0	0	—
Christiansen	P	1	0	0	0	0	0	0	0	—
Eyre	P	1	0	0	0	0	0	0	0	—
Hermanson	P	1	0	0	0	0	0	0	0	—
CHICAGO										
TOTALS		5	167	19	43	8	0	4	19	.257
Lofton	CF	5	21	3	6	1	0	0	1	.286
Alou	LF	5	20	3	10	1	0	0	3	.500
Grudzielanek	2B	5	20	2	3	0	0	0	0	.150
Ramirez	3B	5	18	2	5	1	0	1	3	.278
Sosa	RF	5	16	1	3	1	0	0	1	.188
Karros	1B	4	16	4	6	0	0	2	2	.375
Gonzalez	SS	5	12	1	3	0	0	1	1	.250
Miller	C	4	11	0	1	1	0	0	1	.091
Simon	1B	4	7	1	3	1	0	0	2	.429
Wood	P	2	7	1	2	1	0	0	2	.286
Bako	C	3	4	0	0	0	0	0	1	.000
Martinez	SS	2	4	0	0	0	0	0	0	.000
Prior	P	1	3	0	0	0	0	0	0	.000
Zambrano	P	1	3	0	0	0	0	0	0	.000
Clement	P	2	2	0	0	0	0	0	0	.000
Goodwin	PH	2	1	0	1	1	0	0	2	1.000
Glanville	PH-PR	2	1	1	0	0	0	0	0	.000
O'Leary	PH	1	1	0	0	0	0	0	0	.000
Farnsworth	P	3	0	0	0	0	0	0	0	—
Borowski	P	2	0	0	0	0	0	0	0	—
Remlinger	P	2	0	0	0	0	0	0	0	—
Veres	P	2	0	0	0	0	0	0	0	—
Alfonseca	P	1	0	0	0	0	0	0	0	—
Cruz	P	1	0	0	0	0	0	0	0	—
Guthrie	P	1	0	0	0	0	0	0	0	—
ATLANTA										
TOTALS		5	163	15	35	5	0	3	15	.215
Lopez	C	5	21	1	7	2	0	0	0	.333
Furcal	SS	5	19	3	4	0	0	0	0	.211
C. Jones	LF	5	18	3	3	0	0	2	6	.167
A. Jones	CF	5	17	1	1	0	0	0	0	.059
Castilla	3B	5	16	0	4	0	0	0	0	.250
Giles	2B	5	14	3	5	0	0	1	3	.357
Sheffield	RF	4	14	0	2	0	0	0	1	.143
Fick	1B	4	11	0	0	0	0	0	0	.000
J. Franco	1B	4	8	1	4	1	0	0	0	.500
DeRosa	2B-3B	4	7	1	3	2	0	0	2	.429
Ortiz	P	2	5	0	1	0	0	0	0	.200
Bragg	RF	2	5	0	0	0	0	0	1	.000
Hampton	P	2	4	0	1	0	0	0	0	.250
M. Franco	PH	2	2	1	0	0	0	0	0	.000
Maddux	P	1	2	0	0	0	0	0	0	.000
Gryboski	P	5	0	0	0	0	0	0	0	—
King	P	4	0	0	0	0	0	0	0	—
Wright	P	4	0	0	0	0	0	0	0	—
Cunnane	P	2	0	0	0	0	0	0	0	—
Garcia	2B	2	0	1	0	0	0	0	0	—
Smoltz	P	2	0	0	0	0	0	0	0	—
Hernandez	P	1	0	0	0	0	0	0	0	—
Mercker	P	1	0	0	0	0	0	0	0	—

COMPOSITE PITCHING

NAME	G	IP	H	BB	SO	W	L	SV	ERA
FLORIDA									
TOTALS	4	37	32	20	28	3	1	1	3.65
Beckett	1	7	2	5	9	0	1	0	1.29
Redman	1	6	7	3	4	0	0	0	3.00
Penny	2	5.2	5	1	6	0	0	0	6.35
Willis	2	5.2	7	2	3	0	0	0	7.94
Fox	3	5	3	3	3	0	0	0	1.80
Urbina	3	3	4	1	2	0	0	1	3.00
Pavano	3	2.2	1	1	1	2	0	0	0.00
Looper	2	1.2	1	2	0	1	0	0	0.00
Helling	1	0.1	2	2	0	0	0	0	27.00
SAN FRANCISCO									
TOTALS	4	36.2	37	14	25	1	3	0	3.68
Schmidt	1	9	3	0	5	1	0	0	0.00
Rueter	1	5	3	2	2	0	0	0	3.60
Ponson	1	5	7	0	3	0	0	0	7.20
Herges	3	4.1	1	2	5	0	0	0	0.00
Rodriguez	3	4	4	1	5	0	1	0	2.25
Brower	2	3	5	3	3	0	0	0	6.00
Worrell	2	3	2	3	0	0	1	0	0.00
Williams	1	2	5	1	1	0	0	0	13.50
Hermanson	1	1	1	1	1	0	0	0	0.00
Nathan	2	0.1	4	1	1	0	1	0	81.00
Eyre	1	0.1	0	0	0	0	0	0	0.00
Christiansen	1	0	1	0	0	0	0	0	∞
CHICAGO									
TOTALS	5	44	35	21	42	3	2	1	3.07
Wood	2	15.1	7	7	18	2	0	0	1.76
Prior	1	9	2	4	7	1	0	0	1.00
Zambrano	1	5.2	11	4	4	0	0	0	4.76
Clement	1	4.2	8	4	3	0	1	0	7.71
Farnsworth	3	2.2	1	1	2	0	0	0	0.00
Borowski	2	2	0	5	0	0	0	1	0.00
Veres	2	1.1	2	2	0	0	1	0	13.50
Alfonseca	1	1	1	0	0	0	0	0	0.00
Cruz	1	1	0	1	2	0	0	0	0.00
Remlinger	2	0.2	1	1	0	0	0	0	0.00
Guthrie	1	0.2	2	1	0	0	0	0	27.00
ATLANTA									
TOTALS	5	44	43	20	38	2	3	1	3.68
Hampton	2	12.2	11	6	16	0	1	0	4.26
Ortiz	2	10.2	15	7	9	1	1	0	5.06
Maddux	1	6	6	1	1	0	1	0	3.00
Wright	4	4	0	2	4	0	0	0	0.00
Gryboski	5	3	2	2	4	0	0	0	3.00
Smoltz	2	3	4	0	1	1	0	1	6.00
Cunnane	2	1.2	3	0	2	0	0	0	5.40
King	4	1	1	1	0	0	0	0	0.00
Hernandez	1	1	1	0	0	0	0	0	0.00
Mercker	1	1	0	1	1	0	0	0	0.00

LINE SCORES

Team	1	2	3	4	5	6	7	8	9			R	H	E

CHAMPIONSHIP: FLORIDA 4 : CHICAGO 3

Game 1   October 7 at Chicago

FLA	0	0	5	0	0	1	0	0	2	0	1	9	14	1
CHN	4	0	0	0	0	2	0	0	2	0	0	8	11	1

Beckett, Fox (7), Urbina (9), Looper (11)   Zambrano, Remlinger (7), Farnsworth (7), Borowski (9), **Guthrie** (11), Alfonseca (11)

Game 2   October 8 at Chicago

FLA	0	0	0	0	0	2	0	1	0	3	9	1
CHN	2	3	3	0	3	1	0	0	x	12	16	1

Penny, Bump (3), Helling (4), Pavano (7), Tejera (8)   Prior, Veres (8), Guthrie (9)

Game 3   October 10 at Florida

CHN	1	1	0	0	0	0	0	2	0	0	1	5	12	0
FLA	0	1	0	0	2	0	1	0	0	0	0	4	10	0

Wood, Farnsworth (7), Borowski (8), Remlinger (11)   Redman, Fox (7), Urbina (9), **Tejera** (11), Looper (11)

Game 4   October 11 at Florida

CHN	4	0	2	1	0	0	1	0	0	8	8	0
FLA	0	0	0	0	2	0	0	1	0	3	6	1

Clement, Farnsworth (8)   Willis, Helling (3), Bump (5), Penny (8), Pavano (9)

Game 5   October 12 at Florida

CHN	0	0	0	0	0	0	0	0	0	0	2	0
FLA	0	0	0	2	0	0	1	1	x	4	8	0

Zambrano, Veres (6), Alfonseca (7), Remlinger (8)   Beckett

Game 6   October 14 at Chicago

FLA	0	0	0	0	0	0	0	8	0	8	9	0
CHN	1	0	0	0	0	1	1	0	0	3	10	2

Pavano, Willis (6), Fox (7), Urbina (8)   Prior, Farnsworth (8), Remlinger (8), Alfonseca (9)

Game 7   October 15 at Chicago

FLA	3	0	0	0	3	1	2	0	0	9	12	0
CHN	0	3	2	0	0	0	1	0	0	6	6	0

Redman, Penny (4), Beckett (5), Urbina (9)   **Wood**, Farnsworth (6), Veres (7), Remlinger (8), Borowski (8)

COMPOSITE BATTING

NAME	POS	G	AB	R	H	2B	3B	HR	RBI	BA
ARIZONA										
TOTALS		7	256	40	68	12	3	10	39	.266
Pierre	CF	7	33	5	10	1	2	0	1	.303
Lee	1B	7	32	2	6	2	0	1	4	.188
Cabrera	RF-3B-SS	7	30	9	10	0	0	3	6	.333
Rodriguez	C	7	28	5	9	2	0	2	10	.321
Castillo	2B	7	28	3	6	1	0	0	2	.214
Conine	LF	7	24	4	11	1	1	1	3	.458
Gonzalez	SS	7	24	1	3	2	0	0	1	.125
Lowell	3B	7	20	5	4	0	0	2	3	.200
Encarnacion	RF	7	12	1	3	1	0	1	1	.250
Beckett	P	3	8	0	2	0	0	0	0	.250
Mordecai		5	5	1	1	1	0	0	3	.200
Hollandsworth	PH	4	3	2	3	1	0	0	2	1.000
Harris	PH	3	3	0	0	0	0	0	0	.000
Pavano	P	3	2	0	0	0	0	0	0	.000
Redman	P	2	2	0	0	0	0	0	0	.000
Penny	P	3	1	0	0	0	0	0	0	.000
Banks	PH	2	1	1	0	0	0	0	0	.000
Helling	P	2	1	0	0	0	0	0	0	.000
Urbina	P	4	0	0	0	0	0	0	0	—
Fox	P	3	0	0	0	0	0	0	0	—
Bump	P	2	0	0	0	0	0	0	0	—
Looper	P	2	0	0	0	0	0	0	0	—
Tejera	P	2	0	0	0	0	0	0	0	—
Willis	P	2	0	0	0	0	0	0	0	—
Redmond	C	1	0	1	0	0	0	0	0	—
ATLANTA										
TOTALS		7	252	42	65	10	4	13	41	.258
Lofton	CF	7	31	8	10	1	0	0	2	.323
Grudzielanek	2B	7	30	2	6	1	1	0	3	.200
Alou	LF	7	29	4	9	1	0	2	5	.310
Gonzalez	SS	7	28	5	8	2	0	3	7	.286
Sosa	RF	7	26	7	8	1	0	2	6	.308
Ramirez	3B	7	26	4	6	0	1	3	7	.231
Simon	1B	6	17	3	5	2	0	1	4	.294
Bako	C	6	16	4	4	1	0	0	1	.250
Karros	1B	5	13	2	3	0	0	0	0	.231
Miller	C	4	10	0	2	1	0	0	1	.200
Goodwin	RF	5	4	1	1	0	1	0	0	.250
Martinez	SS-2B	4	4	0	0	0	0	0	0	.000
Prior	P	2	4	0	0	0	0	0	0	.000
Clement	P	1	4	0	0	0	0	0	0	.000
O'Leary	LF	3	3	1	1	0	0	0	1	.333
Wood	P	2	3	1	1	0	0	1	3	.333
Zambrano	P	2	3	0	0	0	0	0	0	.000
Glanville	LF	4	1	0	1	0	1	0	1	1.000
Farnsworth	P	5	0	0	0	0	0	0	0	—
Remlinger	P	5	0	0	0	0	0	0	0	—
Alfonseca	P	3	0	0	0	0	0	0	0	—
Borowski	P	3	0	0	0	0	0	0	0	—
Veres	P	3	0	0	0	0	0	0	0	—
Guthrie	P	2	0	0	0	0	0	0	0	—

COMPOSITE PITCHING

NAME	G	IP	H	BB	SO	W	L	SV	ERA
ARIZONA									
TOTALS	7	66	65	23	57	4	3	2	5.59
Beckett	3	19.1	11	2	19	1	0	0	3.26
Redman	2	9.2	13	4	4	0	0	0	6.52
Pavano	3	7.2	8	1	8	0	0	0	2.35
Urbina	4	7	2	0	10	1	0	1	2.57
Helling	2	5.2	7	4	5	0	0	0	6.35
Penny	3	4	9	3	0	1	1	0	15.75
Fox	3	3.1	5	2	2	1	0	0	5.40
Willis	2	3.1	4	6	4	0	1	0	18.90
Bump	2	3	3	0	3	0	0	0	6.00
Looper	2	1.2	1	1	0	0	0	1	0.00
Tejera	2	1.1	2	0	1	0	1	0	6.75
ATLANTA									
TOTALS	7	66	68	28	45	3	4	1	4.77
Prior	2	14.1	14	5	11	1	1	0	3.14
Wood	2	12.1	14	7	13	0	1	0	7.30
Zambrano	2	11	14	5	8	0	1	0	5.73
Clement	1	7.2	5	2	3	1	0	0	3.52
Borowski	3	5.2	5	3	1	1	0	0	1.59
Farnsworth	5	5.1	6	2	7	0	0	0	10.13
Remlinger	5	3.1	3	1	2	0	0	1	2.70
Veres	3	3	4	1	0	0	0	0	3.00
Alfonseca	3	2.1	2	2	0	0	0	0	0.00
Guthrie	2	1	1	0	0	0	1	0	9.00

MISCELLANEOUS 2003 INDIVIDUAL LEADERS

BATTING

On Base Average

	American League				National League	
1	Ramirez, Bos.	.427		1	Bonds, S.F.	.529
2	Delgado, Tor.	.426		2	Helton, Col.	.458
3	Giambi, N.Y.	.412		3	Pujols, St.L.	.439
4	Martinez, Sea.	.406		4	Giles, Pit.-S.D.	.427
5	Posada, N.Y.	.405		5	Walker, Col.	.422
6	Mueller, Bos.	.398		6	Sheffield, Atl.	.419
7	Nixon, Bos.	.396		7	Berkman, Hou.	.412
8	Rodriguez, Tex.	.396		8	Abreu, Phi.	.409
9	Mientkiewicz, Min.	.393		9	C. Jones, Atl.	.402
10	Jeter, N.Y.	.393		10	Gonzalez, Ari.	.402

On Base Average plus Slugging Average

	American League				National League	
1	Delgado, Tor.	1.019		1	Bonds, S.F.	1.278
2	Ramirez, Bos.	1.014		2	Pujols, St.L.	1.106
3	Rodriguez, Tex.	.995		3	Helton, Col.	1.088
4	Nixon, Bos.	.975		4	Sheffield, Atl.	1.023
5	Ortiz, Bos.	.961		5	Edmonds, St.L.	1.002
6	Thomas, Chi.	.952		6	Thome, Phi.	.958
7	Giambi, N.Y.	.939		7	Hidalgo, Hou.	.957
8	Mueller, Bos.	.938		8	Giles, Pit.-S.D.	.941
9	Ordonez, Chi.	.926		9	Gonzalez, Ari.	.934
10	Posada, N.Y.	.922		10	Berkman, Hou.	.927

Guillen, Cin.-Oak. .928

Total Bases

	American League				National League	
1	Wells, Tor.	373		1	Pujols, St.L.	394
2	Rodriguez, Tex.	364		2	Helton, Col.	367
3	Soriano, N.Y.	358		3	Sheffield, Atl.	348
4	Huff, T.B.	353		4	Sexson, Mil.	332
5	Anderson, Ana.	345		5	Thome, Phi.	331
	Garciaparra, Bos.	345		6	Wilson, Col.	322
7	Delgado, Tor.	338		7	Bagwell, Hou.	317
8	Ramirez, Bos.	334		8	Lopez, Atl.	314
9	Boone, Sea.	333		9	Gonzalez, Ari.	308
10	Ordonez, Chi.	331		10	Payton, Col.	307

Caught Stealing

	American League				National League	
1	Sanchez, Det.	18		1	Pierre, Fla.	20
2	Baldelli, T.B.	10		2	Castillo, Fla.	19
	Crawford, T.B.	10		3	Roberts, L.A.	14
	Tucker, K.C.	10		4	Rollins, Phi.	12
5	Blake, Cle.	9			Young, Mil.-S.F.	12
	Crisp, Cle.	9				
	Guzman, Min.	9				
	Kennedy, Ana.	9				

Sanchez, Mil.-Det. 24
Mondesi, N.Y.-Ari. 11

Stolen Base Percentage
(Minimum 20 Attempts)

	American League				National League	
1	Beltran, K.C.	91		1	Furcal, Atl.	93
2	Anderson, T.B.	86		2	Cabrera, Mon.	92
3	Rodriguez, Tex.	85		3	Renteria, St.L.	83
4	Crawford, T.B.	85		4	Sheffield, Atl.	82
5	Damon, Bos.	83		5	Podsednik, Mil.	81
	Relaford, K.C.	83				

Boone, Cin.-N.Y. 88

Extra Base Hits

	American League				National League	
1	Wells, Tor.	87		1	Pujols, St.L.	95
2	Huff, T.B.	84		2	Helton, Col.	87
3	Rodriguez, Tex.	83		3	Thome, Phi.	80
4	Anderson, Ana.	82		4	Wilson, Col.	80
5	Delgado, Tor.	81		5	Rolen, St.L.	78
					Sheffield, Atl.	78

PITCHING

Fewest Hits Per 9 Innings Pitched

	American League				National League	
1	Martinez, Bos.	7.09		1	Wood, Chi.	6.48
2	Zito, Oak.	7.23		2	Schmidt, S.F.	6.59
3	Hudson, Oak.	7.39		3	Webb, Ari.	6.97
4	Loaiza, Chi.	7.79		4	Nomo, L.A.	7.21
5	Zambrano, T.B.	7.88		5	Ortiz, Atl.	7.50
6	Mussina, N.Y.	8.05		6	Clement, Chi.	7.54
7	Pineiro, Sea.	8.16		7	Schilling, Ari.	7.71
8	Colon, Chi.	8.29		8	Vazquez, Mon.	7.73
9	Moyer, Sea.	8.33		9	Prior, Chi.	7.79
10	May, K.C.	8.44		10	Wells, Pit.	7.80

Fewest Bases on Balls Per 9 Innings Pitched

	American League				National League	
1	Wells, N.Y.	0.85		1	Maddux, Atl.	1.36
2	Halladay, Tor.	1.08		2	Schilling, Ari.	1.71
3	Radke, Min.	1.19		3	Sheets, Mil.	1.75
4	Mussina, N.Y.	1.68		4	Schmidt, S.F.	1.99
5	Mulder, Oak.	1.93		5	Morris, St.L.	2.04
6	Anderson, Cle.-K.C.	1.96		6	Ohka, Mon.	2.04
7	Lohse, Min.	2.01		7	Prior, Chi.	2.13
8	Thomson, Tex.	2.03		8	D'Amico, Pit.	2.16
9	Pettitte, N.Y.	2.16		9	Graves, Cin.	2.18
10	Loaiza, Chi.	2.23		10	Pavano, Fla.	2.19

Strikeouts Per 9 Innings Pitched

	American League				National League	
1	Martinez, Bos.	9.93		1	Wood, Chi.	11.35
2	Loaiza, Chi.	8.23		2	Prior, Chi.	10.43
3	Mussina, N.Y.	8.18		3	Schilling, Ari.	10.39
4	Clemens, N.Y.	8.08		4	Vazquez, Mon.	9.40
5	Escobar, Tor.	7.94		5	Schmidt, S.F.	9.01
6	Pettitte, N.Y.	7.78		6	Webb, Ari.	8.57
7	Wakefield, Bos.	7.52		7	Wolf, Phi.	7.97
8	Lilly, Oak.	7.42		8	Brown, L.A.	7.89
9	Halladay, Tor.	6.90		9	Miller, Hou.	7.73
10	Lackey, Ana.	6.66		10	Clement, Chi.	7.63

Lowest Batting Average Allowed

	American League				National League	
1	Martinez, Bos.	.215		1	Schmidt, S.F.	.200
2	Zito, Oak.	.219		2	Wood, Chi.	.203
3	Hudson, Oak.	.223		3	Webb, Ari.	.212
4	Loaiza, Chi.	.233		4	Nomo, L.A.	.223
5	Zambrano, T.B.	.237		5	Ortiz, Atl.	.223

Home Runs Allowed

	American League				National League	
1	Franklin, Sea.	34		1	Franklin, Mil.	36
	Maroth, Det.	34		2	Tomko, St.L.	35
	Washburn, Ana.	34		3	Peavy, S.D.	33
4	Radke, Min.	32		4	Graves, Cin.	30
5	Garcia, Sea.	31			Stephenson, St.L.	30
	Lackey, Ana.	31				
	May, K.C.	31				

Helling, Bal.-Fla. 31

Home Runs Allowed per 9 IP
(Minimum 10 Home Runs Allowed)

	American League				National League	
1	Parris, T.B.	2.47		1	Bynum, S.D.	3.50
2	Reyes, T.B.	2.27		2	Neagle, Col.	3.06
3	Moss, Bal.	2.13		3	Smith, Mon.	2.63
4	George, K.C.	2.11		4	Howard, S.D.	2.60
5	Towers, Tor.	2.10		5	Quevedo, Mil.	2.53

"ANYTHING CAN HAPPEN"

Sooner or later, baseball will break your heart. For a few days in October, fans all over the country warmed to the prospect that the two most angst-driven franchises would meet in a Suffer-a-Thon of historic proportions. Neither the Cubs nor the Red Sox had won a championship in more than eighty years, and the prospect of a World Series meeting forcing one or the other to break its particular jinx appealed to many fans. But, in the end, Chicago and Boston gave way to a team few fans knew much about and a team many said they'd seen much too often.

The wild card Florida Marlins began the playoffs as the least-known and least respected participant. Only a few noted that when 72-year-old Jack McKeon took over as manager on May 11, the Fish stopped floundering and treated the rest of the NL as chum. As a consequence, Florida's three-games-to-one victory over the flat San Francisco Giants came as a surprise to many. Fans discovered veteran Ivan Rodriguez was still baseball's best all-around catcher and youngsters like Juan Pierre, Luis Castillo, Derek Lee and Mike Lowell were worth remembering.

The other NL Division Series produced a lesser surprise. Although Atlanta won more games than any other NL team during the season, the Braves couldn't handle the Cubs and their pitching tandem of Kerry Wood and Mark Prior and Chicago moved on to the NLCS.

The Minnesota Twins had lost 13 straight games to the Yaqnkees when the two opened their series. They broke the skein in the opening game of their playoffs. Then normality returned and the Yankees won three in a row to move on. Pettitte, Clemens, and Wells held the Twins to three runs in three games.

Wild card Boston's big bats trumped Oakland's pitching aces in their first round playoff series. After a surprise bunt by catcher Ramon Hernandez in extra innings and a strong pitching performance by Barry Zito had the Red Sox on the brink of elimination, Boston roared back with enough home runs to win three straight.

The Florida-Chicago NLCS set a new home run record with 23, 13 by the Cubs. Chicago lost the opening game but then took three straight from the Marlins. A 4-0 loss in Game 5 didn't phase Cubs fans. In what looked like a done deal, the teams returned to Wrigley Field with Chicago needing only one more victory and both Wood and Prior ready to throw. By the eighth inning of Game 6, the Cubbies led 3-0 when Castillo lofted a fly down the left field line. It fell perhaps six inches inside the stands. Moises Alou drifted over, but as he reached for the ball, a fan in the stands made a grab for a souvenir and Castillo got a reprieve. He walked, the Cubs shortstop made an error, and the Marlins proceeded to score eight runs. In agony, Cubs fans ignored the error and poor relief pitching and blamed the fan who only tried to catch a foul ball – something every person at Wrigley would have tried. The next night was anticlimactic; Florida was in the Series.

Amid a thousand references to the "Curse of the Bambino," the Red Sox and the Yankees went to the seventh game of the ALCS. Red Sox fans waited for "the other Bucky Dent" to drop. Leading 5-2 and needing only five outs to take his team to the World Series, Red Sox manager Grady Little ignored his bullpen and left a visably tiring Pedro Martinez on the mound until the game was tied. Knuckleballer Tim Wakefield, to that point Boston's hero with two earlier wins, pitched a perfect tenth. Then in the eleventh, Aaron Boone, a defensive replacement, knocked Wakefield's first knuckler deep into the leftfield grandstand. Little was fired two days after the World Series.

Few commentators failed to mention that the World Series pitted the Yankees' $185 million payroll against the Marlins' mere $52 mil. That tended to make Florida a popular rooting choice outside the Big Apple. However, the young, hustling Marlins earned a lot of appreciation on their own with their speed and clutch play.

Florida broke on top by handing the Yankees their first WS home loss since 1996. Marlins centerfielder Juan Pierre scored one run and drove in two in the 3-1 win. Pettite evened things the next day, dominating the Florideans. In Game Three, Josh Beckett pitched well but Mussina kept the game even until the Yankees had the chance to bomb Florida's relievers. Florida tied the Series with Alex Gonzalez' 12th-inning home run in Game Four.

Wells was scheduled to go in Game Five, but a chronic back problem had him out of the game after one inning. Brad Penny earned his second win of the Series when the Marlins jumped on Wells' relievers to score six runs. Astonishingly, the Marlins were one game away from a World Championship.

With a well-rested Pettite on the mound, the Yankees seemed to have an advantage for Game Six. Josh Beckett was a semi-surprise starter for the Marlins in that the 23-year old righthander was going on only three days rest. Pettitte was up to his task, holding Florida to two runs, one unearned. Beckett was even more brilliant, shutting out New York on five hits before an increasingly hushed Yankee Stadium crowd. Afterward McKeon told a roomful of reporters, "I guess you will believe me now anything can happen."

WORLD SERIES

LINE SCORES

Team	1	2	3	4	5	6	7	8	9	10	11	12		R	H	E

WORLD SERIES: FLORIDA 4 : NEW YORK 2

Game 1   October 18 at New York

	1	2	3	4	5	6	7	8	9		R	H	E
FLA	1	0	0	0	2	0	0	0	0		3	7	1
NYA	0	0	1	0	0	1	0	0	0		2	9	0

Penny, Willis (6), Urbina (8)   Wells, Nelson (8), Contreras (9)

Game 2   October 19 at New York

	1	2	3	4	5	6	7	8	9		R	H	E
FLA	0	0	0	0	0	0	0	0	1		1	6	0
NYA	3	1	0	2	0	0	0	0	x		6	10	2

Redman, Helling (3), Fox (5), Pavano (7), Looper (8)   Pettitte, Contreras (9)

Game 3   October 21 at Forida

	1	2	3	4	5	6	7	8	9		R	H	E
NYA	0	0	0	1	0	0	0	1	4		6	6	1
FLA	1	0	0	0	0	0	0	0	0		1	8	0

Mussina, Rivera (8)   Beckett, Willis (8), Fox (8), Looper (9)

Game 4   October 22 at Florida

	1	2	3	4	5	6	7	8	9	10	11	12		R	H	E
NYA	0	1	0	0	0	0	0	2	0	0	0			3	12	0
FLA	3	0	0	0	0	0	0	0	0	0	1			4	10	0

Clemens, Nelson (8), Contreras (9), Weaver (11)   Pavano, Urbina (9), Fox (10), Looper (11)

Game 5   October 23 at Florida

	1	2	3	4	5	6	7	8	9		R	H	E
NYA	1	0	0	0	0	0	1	0	2		4	12	1
FLA	0	3	0	1	2	0	0	0	x		6	9	1

Wells, Contreras (2), Hammond (5), Nelson (7)   Penny, Willis (8), Looper (9), Urbina (9)

Game 6   October 25 at New York

	1	2	3	4	5	6	7	8	9		R	H	E
FLA	0	0	0	0	1	1	0	0	0		2	7	0
NYA	0	0	0	0	0	0	0	0	0		0	5	1

Beckett   Pettitte, Rivera (8)

COMPOSITE BATTING

NAME	POS	G	AB	R	H	2B	3B	HR	RBI	BA
FLORIDA										
TOTALS		6	203	17	47	8	0	2	17	.232
Castillo	2B	6	26	1	4	0	0	0	1	.154
Lee	1B	6	24	2	5	0	0	0	2	.208
Cabrera	LF-RF	6	24	1	4	0	0	1	3	.167
Lowell	3B	6	23	1	5	1	0	0	2	.217
Gonzalez	SS	6	22	3	6	2	0	1	2	.273
Rodriguez	C	6	22	2	6	2	0	0	1	.273
Conine	DH-LF	6	21	4	7	1	0	0	0	.333
Pierre	CF	6	21	2	7	2	0	0	3	.333
Encamacion	RF	6	11	1	2	0	0	0	1	.182
Penny	P	2	2	0	1	0	0	0	2	.500
Beckett	P	2	2	0	0	0	0	0	0	.000
Hollandsworth	PH	2	2	0	0	0	0	0	0	.000
Pavano	P	2	2	0	0	0	0	0	0	.000
Redmond	C	1	1	0	0	0	0	0	0	.000
Looper	P	4	0	0	0	0	0	0	0	—
Fox	P	3	0	0	0	0	0	0	0	—
Urbina	P	3	0	0	0	0	0	0	0	—
Willis	P	3	0	0	0	0	0	0	0	—
Helling	P	1	0	0	0	0	0	0	0	—
Redman	P	1	0	0	0	0	0	0	0	—
NEW YORK										
TOTALS		6	207	21	54	10	1	6	21	.261
Jeter	SS	6	26	5	9	3	0	0	2	.346
Williams	CF	6	25	5	10	2	0	2	5	.400
Matsui	LF	6	23	1	6	0	0	1	4	.261
Soriano	2B-RF	6	22	2	5	0	0	1	2	.227
Boone	3B	6	21	1	3	0	0	1	2	.143
Posada	C	6	19	3	3	1	0	0	1	.158
Johnson	1B	6	17	3	5	1	0	0	0	.294
Giambi	DH-1B	6	17	2	4	1	0	1	1	.235
Garcia	RF	5	14	1	4	0	0	0	0	.286
J. Rivera	RF	4	6	0	1	1	0	0	1	.167
Sierra	RF	5	4	0	1	0	1	0	2	.250
Wilson	2B-3B	2	4	0	2	1	0	0	1	.500
Mussina	P	1	3	0	0	0	0	0	0	.000
Dellucci	RF	4	2	1	0	0	0	0	0	.000
Clemens	P	1	2	0	1	0	0	0	0	.500
Flaherty	C	1	2	0	0	0	0	0	0	.000
Contreras	P	4	0	0	0	0	0	0	0	—
Nelson	P	3	0	0	0	0	0	0	0	—
Pettitte	P	2	0	0	0	0	0	0	0	—
M. Rivera	P	2	0	0	0	0	0	0	0	—
Wells	P	2	0	0	0	0	0	0	0	—
Hammond	P	1	0	0	0	0	0	0	0	—
Weaver	P	1	0	0	0	0	0	0	0	—

COMPOSITE PITCHING

NAME	G	IP	H	BB	SO	W	L	SV	ERA
FLORIDA									
TOTALS	6	56	54	22	49	4	2	2	3.21
Beckett	2	16.1	8	5	19	1	1	0	1.10
Penny	2	12.1	15	5	7	2	0	0	2.19
Pavano	2	9	8	1	6	0	0	0	1.00
Looper	4	3.2	6	0	4	1	0	0	9.82
Willis	3	3.2	4	2	3	0	0	0	0.00
Fox	3	3	4	4	4	0	0	0	6.00
Urbina	3	3	2	3	2	0	0	2	6.00
Helling	1	2.2	2	0	2	0	0	0	6.75
Redman	1	2.1	5	2	2	0	1	0	15.43
NEW YORK									
TOTALS	6	55	47	14	48	2	4	1	2.13
Pettitte	2	15.2	12	4	14	1	1	0	0.57
Wells	2	8	6	2	1	0	1	0	3.38
Mussina	1	7	7	1	9	1	0	0	1.29
Clemens	1	7	8	0	5	0	0	0	3.86
Contreras	4	6.1	5	5	10	0	1	0	5.68
Nelson	3	4	4	2	5	0	0	0	0.00
MRivera	2	4	2	0	4	0	0	1	0.00
Hammond	1	2	2	0	0	0	0	0	0.00
Weaver	1	1	1	0	0	0	1	0	9.00

2004: THE LINE ON THE CHART RISES

After years of slippage in both prestige and attendance, baseball rebounded in 2004. There seemed to be fewer carping essays predicting baseball's destiny as a minor sport, and the total regular season attendance of 72,968,953 set an all-time record. The pennant races were enjoyable if not barnburning. In Ichiro Suzuki and Barry Bonds, each league had a hero pursuing an all-time hitting record, while Randy Johnson tossed a perfect game and Roger Clemens added to his strikeout trove. One thorn was removed from baseball's side when at season's end, the commissioner announced that the Montreal Expos, a ward of the league for two seasons, would be relocated under new owners in Washington, D.C.

As they have so often, the Yankees dominated pre-season speculation. Pundits pondered the Bombers' pitching losses against their improved batting. Andy Pettitte had opted for free agency and Clemens retired (only to later un-retire to join his buddy Pettitte in Houston). On the plus side, New York added Alex Rodriguez and Gary Sheffield to create a potentially irresitable offense. Meanwhile, the Red Sox, after failing to get A-Rod, concentrated on pitching by adding Curt Schilling. The Yankee-Red Sox rivalry got so much pre-season ink that at times it seemed the American League consisted only of New York and Boston, but the race didn't live up to the hype. After staggering a bit early, the Yankees took the lead in the A.L. East and led the rest of the way. Despite strong pitching by Schilling and the usual fence-busting by Manny Ramirez and David Ortiz, the Red Sox could only scramble for a wild card berth.

The Minneapolis Twins, led by Cy Young candidate Johan Santana, had the Central Division under control most of the season and finished comfortably ahead of Chicago and Cleveland. Santana put up a streak of thirteen straight wins during the season and led all A.L. pitchers in strikeouts.

The A.L.'s best pennant race was in the west where the Rangers, Angels and Athletics went into the final week. The challenge by Texas came as a surprise to many after Rodriguez was subtracted from their last-place finisher of 2003. Oakland also lost an MVP shortstop to free agency as Miguel Tejada jumped to Baltimore where he led the league with an impressive 150 RBIs. The Angels' Mike Scioscia made a bold decision in late September when he suspended outfielder Jose Guillen, the Angels' second-leading home run and RBI man. Rather than weakened, Anaheim seemed to draw strength from the move. On the next-to-last day of the season, Anaheim rebuffed Oakland's try for a fifth straight playoff appearance. Vladimir Guerrero, the five-tool outfielder obtained from Montreal, was the Angels' top slugger and one of the best in the league.

Although Seattle finished dead last in its division, Mariners' outfielder Ichiro Suzuki enjoyed a record-breaking year, by advancing Hall-of-Famer George Sisler's season hit record from 257 to 262. His .372 led the A.L. in batting.

The biggest pre-season question in the National League was which eastern team would replace Atlanta. The Braves seemed certain to miss the playoffs for the first time in thirteen seasons after free agency stripped them of Sheffield, Javy Lopez and Greg Maddux. Once the season got started, however, the Braves moved in front early and coasted while the Marlins floundered, the Phillies flopped, and the Mets met disaster. Although the Braves' lineup wasn't at potent as usual, Chipper Jones and Andruw Jones blended nicely with newcomer J.D. Drew and several youngsters, while John Smoltz remained a reliable closer.

St. Louis was generally favored to come in third in the Central, well behind powerful Houston and improved Chicago. Then the Astros started so slowly that manager Jimy Williams was replaced by Phil Garner, and the Cubs finished so flat they made Kansas look like Colorado. Meanwhile, Tony LaRussa's Cardinals kept on truckin' with the most devastating lineup in the league. Albert Pujols, Jim Edmonds, Scott Rolen, and mid-season acquisition Larry Walker assured the Cards' surprisingly effective pitching of run support. Garner, with the help of Jeff Kent and the "Killer Bees" — Lance Berkman, Jeff Bagwell, Craig Biggio, and Carlos Beltran — came on strong at the end to gain the wild card slot. Although Pettitte was laid low by injury, Clemens was brilliant and Roy Oswalt won twenty games.

If baseball's stock rose in 2004, its Bonds rose even higher – Barry Bonds that is. At age 40, he remained the most feared hitter of the era and perhaps ever. How else to explain the 232 walks he was awarded to break the record he set in 2002? Even though he was limited to a paltry 373 at bats, the Giants' slugger blasted 45 homers and drove in 101 runs while leading the N.L. with a .362 average. Even more breathtaking were his league-leading .812 slugging average and .609 on-base percentage. Obviously, to restore balance, pitchers must be allowed to throw him kryptonite instead of baseballs.

Despite Bonds' wonders and strong pitching by Jeff Schmidt, San Francisco was knocked out of the playoffs at season's end, thanks to a seven-run, ninth inning rally by the Dodgers, capped by Steve Finley's walk-off grand slam home run. Los Angeles grabbed Finley from Arizona just before the trading deadline, and he gave them an important bat to go with N.L. home run leader Adrian Beltre throughout the final month.

Like Sinatra used to say, "It was a very good year."

2004 AMERICAN LEAGUE — EAST DIVISION

Name	G by Pos	B	AGE	G	AB	R	H	2B	3B	HR	RBI	BB	SO	SB	BA	SA
NEW YORK	1st 101-61 .623			JOE TORRE												
TOTALS			33	162	5527	897	1483	281	20	242	863	670	982	84	.268	.458
Jason Giambi (IL)	1B47 DH28	L	33	80	264	33	55	9	0	12	40	47	62	0	.208	.379
Miguel Cairo	2B113 3B8 SS3 1B1	R	30	122	360	48	105	17	5	6	42	18	49	11	.292	.417
Derek Jeter	SS154	R	30	154	643	111	188	44	1	23	78	46	99	23	.292	.471
Alex Rodriguez	3B155 SS2	R	28	155	601	112	172	24	2	36	106	80	131	28	.286	.512
Gary Sheffield	OF136 DH18 3B2	R	35	154	573	117	166	30	1	36	121	92	83	5	.290	.534
Bernie Williams	OF97 DH50	B	35	148	561	105	147	29	1	22	70	85	96	1	.262	.435
Hideki Matsui	OF160	L	30	162	584	109	174	34	2	31	108	88	103	3	.298	.522
Jorge Posada	C134	B	32	137	449	72	122	31	0	21	81	88	92	1	.272	.481
Ruben Sierra	DH56 OF29	B	38	107	307	40	75	12	1	17	65	25	55	1	.244	.456
Tony Clark	1B99 DH1	B	32	106	253	37	56	12	0	16	49	26	92	0	.221	.458
Enrique Wilson	2B80 SS16	B	30	93	240	19	51	9	0	6	31	15	20	1	.213	.325
Kenny Lofton	OF74 DH4	L	37	83	276	51	76	10	7	3	18	31	27	7	.275	.395
Bubba Crosby	OF45 DH2	L	27	55	53	8	8	2	0	2	7	2	13	2	.151	.302
2 John Olerud	1B47	L	35	49	164	16	46	7	0	4	26	21	20	0	.280	.396
John Flaherty	C46	R	36	47	127	11	32	9	0	6	16	5	25	0	.252	.465
Homer Bush	2B4 DH2	R	31	9	7	2	0	0	0	0	0	0	2	1	.000	.000
Travis Lee (SJ)	1B6	L	29	7	19	1	2	1	0	0	2	1	3	0	.105	.158
Andy Phillips	3B4	R	27	5	8	1	2	0	0	1	2	0	1	0	.250	.625
Felix Escalona	SS4 3B1	R	25	5	8	1	0	0	0	0	0	0	2	0	.000	.000
Dioner Navarro	C4	B	20	5	7	2	3	0	0	0	1	0	1	0	.429	.429
BOSTON	2nd 98-64 .605 3 (Wild Card)			TERRY FRANCONA												
TOTALS			30	162	5720	949	1613	373	25	222	912	659	1189	68	.282	.472
Kevin Millar	OF74 1B69 DH8	R	32	150	508	74	151	36	0	18	74	57	91	1	.297	.474
Mark Bellhorn	2B124 3B16 SS1	B	29	138	523	93	138	37	3	17	82	88	177	6	.264	.444
1 Nomar Garciaparra (LJ)	SS38	R	30	38	156	24	50	7	3	5	21	8	16	2	.321	.500
Bill Mueller (KJ)	3B96 2B14	B	33	110	399	75	113	27	1	12	57	51	56	2	.283	.446
Trot Nixon (XJ-LJ)	OF40 DH3	L	30	48	149	24	47	9	1	6	23	15	31	0	.315	.510
Johnny Damon	OF148 DH1	L	30	150	621	123	189	35	6	20	94	76	71	19	.304	.477
Manny Ramirez	OF132 DH19	R	32	152	568	108	175	44	0	43	130	82	124	2	.308	.613
Jason Varitek	C130 DH1	B	32	137	463	67	137	30	1	18	73	62	126	10	.296	.482
David Ortiz	DH115 1B34	L	28	150	582	94	175	47	3	41	139	75	133	0	.301	.603
Gabe Kapler	OF127 DH12	R	28	136	290	51	79	14	1	6	33	15	49	5	.272	.390
Pokey Reese (VJ)	SS71 2B30	R	31	96	244	32	54	7	2	3	29	17	60	6	.221	.303
Dave McCarty	1B67 OF17 P3 DH3	R	34	91	151	24	39	8	1	4	17	14	40	1	.258	.404
Kevin Youkilis	3B65 DH2	R	25	72	208	38	54	11	0	7	35	33	45	0	.260	.413
Doug Mirabelli	C53 DH4	R	33	59	160	27	45	12	0	9	32	19	46	0	.281	.525
2 Orlando Cabrera	SS57	R	29	58	228	33	67	19	1	6	31	11	23	4	.294	.465
Cesar Crespo	SS27 OF19 2B11	B	25	52	79	6	13	2	1	0	2	0	20	2	.165	.215
2 Doug Mientkiewicz	1B47 2B1	L	30	49	107	13	23	6	1	1	10	16	18	0	.215	.318
2 Dave Roberts	OF38 DH1	L	32	45	86	19	22	10	0	2	14	10	17	5	.256	.442
Brian Daubach	1B14 OF7	L	32	30	75	9	17	2	0	2	8	10	21	0	.227	.413
2 Ricky Gutierrez	2B14 SS6	R	34	21	40	6	11	1	0	0	3	2	6	1	.275	.300
Adam Hyzdu	OF14 DH2	R	32	17	10	3	3	2	0	0	1	3	6	0	.300	.800
Ellis Burks (KJ)	DH9	R	39	11	33	6	6	0	0	1	6	2	8	0	.182	.273
Andy Dominique	1B5 C1	R	28	7	11	0	2	0	0	0	1	0	4	0	.182	.182
2 Sandy Martinez	C3	L	33	3	4	0	0	0	0	0	0	0	1	0	.000	.000
Earl Snyder	3B1	R	28	1	4	0	1	0	0	0	0	0	0	0	.250	.250

NAME	T	AGE	W	L	PCT	SV	G	GS	CG	IP	H	BB	SO	SHO	ERA
NEW YORK		33	101	61	.623	59	162	162	1	1444	1532	445	1058	5	4.69
Jon Lieber (GJ)	R	34	14	8	.636	0	27	27	0	177	216	18	102	0	4.33
Javier Vazquez	R	28	14	10	.583	0	32	32	0	198	195	60	150	0	4.91
Mike Mussina (EJ)	R	35	12	9	.571	0	27	27	1	165	178	40	132	0	4.59
Kevin Brown (XJ)	R	39	10	6	.625	0	22	22	0	132	132	35	83	0	4.09
Tom Gordon	R	36	9	4	.692	4	80	0	0	90	56	23	96	0	2.21
Orlando Hernandez (SJ)	R	38	8	2	.800	0	15	15	0	85	73	36	84	0	3.30
1 Jose Contreras	R	32	8	5	.615	0	18	18	0	96	93	42	82	0	5.64
Paul Quantrill	R	35	7	3	.700	1	86	0	0	95	124	20	37	0	4.72
Tanyon Sturtze	R	33	6	2	.750	1	28	3	0	77	75	33	56	0	5.47
Mariano Rivera	R	34	4	2	.667	53	74	0	0	79	65	20	66	0	1.94
Donovan Osborne	L	35	2	0	1.000	0	9	2	0	18	25	5	10	0	7.13
Scott Proctor	R	27	2	1	.667	0	26	0	0	25	29	14	21	0	5.40
Bret Prinz	R	27	1	0	1.000	0	26	0	0	28	28	14	22	0	5.08
Felix Heredia (RJ)	L	29	1	1	.500	0	47	0	0	39	44	20	25	0	6.28
2 C.J. Nitkowski	L	31	1	1	.500	0	19	0	0	13	18	6	10	0	7.62
2 Esteban Loaiza (EJ)	R	32	1	2	.333	0	10	6	0	42	61	26	34	0	8.50
Brad Halsey	L	23	1	3	.250	0	8	7	0	32	41	14	25	0	6.47
Steve Karsay (SJ)	R	32	0	0	—	0	7	5	2	4	4	0	2	0	2.70
1 Juan Padilla	R	27	0	0	—	0	6	0	0	11	16	4	5	0	3.97
Alex Graman	L	26	0	0	—	0	3	2	0	5	14	2	4	0	19.80
Sam Marsonek (KJ)	R	25	0	0	—	0	1	0	0	2	2	0	0	0	0.00
1 Gabe White	L	32	0	1	.000	0	24	0	0	21	33	7	8	0	8.27
Jorge DePaula (EJ)	R	25	0	1	.000	0	3	1	0	9	9	4	2	0	5.00
BOSTON		32	98	64	.605	36	162	162	4	1451	1430	447	1132	12	4.18
Curt Schilling	R	37	21	6	.778	0	32	32	3	227	206	35	203	0	3.26
Pedro Martinez	R	32	16	9	.640	0	33	33	1	217	193	61	227	1	3.90
Derek Lowe	R	31	14	12	.538	0	33	33	0	183	224	71	105	0	5.42
Tim Wakefield	R	37	12	10	.545	0	32	30	0	188	197	63	116	0	4.87
Bronson Arroyo	R	27	10	9	.526	0	32	29	0	179	171	47	142	0	4.03
Keith Foulke	R	31	5	3	.625	32	72	0	0	83	63	15	79	0	2.17
Mike Timlin	R	38	5	4	.556	1	76	0	0	76	75	19	56	0	4.13
2 Curtis Leskanic	R	36	3	2	.600	2	32	0	0	28	24	16	22	0	3.58
2 Terry Adams	R	31	2	0	1.000	0	19	0	0	27	35	6	21	0	6.00
Ramiro Mendoza (SJ)	R	32	2	1	.667	0	27	0	0	31	25	7	13	0	3.52
Anastacio Martinez	R	25	2	1	.667	0	11	0	0	11	13	6	5	0	8.44
Byung-hyun Kim	R	25	2	1	.667	0	7	3	0	17	17	7	6	0	6.23
Alan Embree	L	34	2	2	.500	0	71	0	0	52	49	11	37	0	4.13
2 Mike Myers	L	35	1	0	1.000	0	25	0	0	15	16	6	9	0	4.20
Mark Malaska	L	26	1	1	.500	0	19	0	0	20	21	12	12	0	4.50
Lenny DiNardo (RJ)	L	24	0	0	—	0	22	0	0	28	34	21	21	0	4.23
2 Jimmy Anderson	L	28	0	0	—	0	6	0	0	6	10	3	6	0	6.00
Pedro Astacio	R	34	0	0	—	0	5	5	0	23	28	14	12	0	10.38
Jamie Brown	R	27	0	0	—	0	8	0	0	8	15	4	6	0	5.87
Dave McCarty	L	34	0	0	—	0	3	0	0	4	3	1	0	0	2.45
Joe Nelson	R	29	0	0	—	0	2	0	0	3	6	3	1	0	16.87
Frank Castillo	R	35	0	0	—	0	2	0	0	3	3	0	0	0	0.00
Phil Seibel	L	25	0	0	—	0	2	0	0	2	2	1	1	0	0.00
Scott Williamson (AJ)	R	28	0	0	—	1	28	0	0	29	11	18	28	0	1.26
Bobby Jones	L	32	0	0	1.000	0	4	0	0	5	4	3	3	0	5.40
Abe Alvarez	L	21	0	1	.000	0	1	1	0	5	8	5	2	0	9.00
2 Brad Thomas (EJ) 26, Reynoldo Garcia (EJ) 30, Jason Shiell (EJ) 27															

714

BALTIMORE — 3rd 78-84 .481 23 — LEE MAZZILLI

Name	G by Pos	B	AGE	G	AB	R	H	2B	3B	HR	RBI	BB	SO	SB	BA	SA
TOTALS			30	162	5736	842	1614	319	18	169	803	528	949	101	.281	.432
Rafael Palmeiro	1B130 DH20	L	39	154	550	68	142	29	0	23	88	86	61	2	.258	.436
Brian Roberts	2B150 DH6	B	26	159	641	107	175	50	2	4	53	71	95	29	.273	.376
Miguel Tejada	SS162	R	28	162	653	107	203	40	2	34	150	48	73	4	.311	.534
Melvin Mora	3B137 SS1 DH1	R	32	140	550	111	187	41	0	27	104	66	95	11	.340	.562
Jay Gibbons (PJ)	OF66 DH16 1B14	L	27	97	346	36	85	14	1	10	47	29	64	1	.246	.379
Luis Matos (LJ)	OF89	R	25	89	330	36	74	18	0	6	28	19	60	12	.224	.333
Larry Bigbie	OF134 DH2	L	26	139	478	76	134	23	1	15	68	45	113	8	.280	.427
Javy Lopez	C132 DH21	R	33	150	579	83	183	33	3	23	86	47	97	0	.316	.503
David Newhan	OF42 DH32 3B17 1B2	L	30	95	373	66	116	15	7	8	54	27	72	11	.311	.453
B.J. Surhoff (LJ)	OF70 DH18 1B10	L	39	100	343	49	106	12	1	8	50	30	46	2	.309	.420
Jerry Hairston (RJ-BN)	OF52 DH21 2B123 3B1	R	28	86	287	43	87	19	1	2	24	29	29	13	.303	.397
Luis Lopez	SS14 3B11 DH8 1B6 2B6	B	33	56	88	7	16	5	0	1	8	3	20	0	.182	.227
Tim Raines Jr.	OF38 DH4	R	24	48	94	14	24	6	0	0	5	4	16	7	.255	.319
Robert Machado	C35	R	31	37	73	5	11	3	0	1	3	4	18	0	.151	.233
Jose Leon	1B16 3B6 DH5	R	27	31	66	4	12	2	0	2	8	2	19	0	.182	.303
2 Karim Garcia	OF19 1B1	R	28	23	66	9	14	0	0	3	11	4	15	0	.212	.348
David Segui (KJ)	DH15 1B2	B	37	18	59	8	20	3	0	1	7	5	13	0	.339	.441
Darnell McDonald	OF13 DH1	R	25	17	32	3	5	1	0	0	1	2	6	1	.156	.188
1 Jose Bautista	OF6 3B4 DH2	R	23	16	11	3	3	0	0	0	0	1	3	0	.273	.273
Geronimo Gil	C11	R	28	12	32	1	9	2	0	0	4	3	5	0	.281	.344
Keith Osik	C11	R	35	11	25	0	2	0	0	0	0	0	7	0	.080	.080
Val Majewski	OF4 DH3	L	23	9	13	3	2	1	0	0	1	0	1	0	.154	.231
2 Ken Huckaby	C8	R	33	8	12	1	2	1	0	0	1	0	0	0	.167	.250
Chad Mottola	OF5	R	32	6	14	2	2	1	0	0	3	2	3	0	.143	.429
Jack Cust		L	25	1	1	0	0	0	0	0	0	0	1	0	.000	.000
Marty Cordova (EJ) 34																

NAME	T	AGE	W	L	PCT	SV	G	GS	CG	IP	H	BB	SO	SHO	ERA
		28	78	84	.481	27	162	162	8	1455	1488	687	1090	10	4.70
Rodrigo Lopez	R	28	14	9	.609	0	37	23	1	171	164	54	121	1	3.59
Daniel Cabrera	R	23	12	8	.600	0	28	27	1	148	145	89	76	1	5.00
Sidney Ponson	R	27	11	15	.423	0	33	33	5	216	265	69	115	2	5.30
John Parrish	L	26	6	3	.667	1	56	1	0	78	68	55	71	0	3.46
Erik Bedard	L	25	6	10	.375	0	27	26	0	137	149	71	121	0	4.59
Buddy Groom	L	38	4	1	.800	0	53	0	0	53	67	16	32	0	4.78
B.J. Ryan	L	28	4	6	.400	3	76	0	0	87	64	35	122	0	2.28
Eric DuBose (SJ)	L	28	4	6	.400	0	14	14	0	75	76	44	48	0	6.39
Dave Borkowski	R	27	3	4	.429	0	17	8	0	56	65	15	45	0	5.14
Matt Riley	L	24	3	4	.429	0	14	13	0	64	60	44	60	0	5.63
Todd Williams	R	33	2	0	1.000	0	29	0	0	31	26	9	13	0	2.87
Rick Bauer	R	27	2	1	.667	0	23	2	0	54	49	20	37	0	4.70
Bruce Chen	L	27	2	1	.667	0	8	7	1	48	39	16	32	0	3.02
2 Jason Grimsley	R	36	2	4	.333	0	41	0	0	36	37	20	21	0	4.21
Jorge Julio	R	25	2	5	.286	22	65	0	0	69	59	39	70	0	4.57
Eddy Rodriguez	R	22	1	0	1.000	0	29	0	0	43	36	30	37	0	4.78
Darwin Cubillan	R	31	0	0	—	0	7	0	0	10	13	7	8	0	5.40
Aaron Rakers	R	27	0	0	—	0	3	0	0	4	5	2	5	0	4.15
1 Denny Bautista	R	23	0	0	—	0	2	0	0	2	6	2	1	0	36.00
Kurt Ainsworth (EJ)	R	25	0	1	.000	0	7	7	0	31	39	20	20	0	9.68
John Maine	R	23	0	1	.000	0	1	1	0	4	7	3	1	0	9.82
1 Mike DeJean	R	33	0	5	.000	0	37	0	0	40	49	28	36	0	6.13
Omar Daal (SJ) 32															

TAMPA BAY — 4th 70-91 .435 30.5 — LOU PINIELLA

Name	G by Pos	B	AGE	G	AB	R	H	2B	3B	HR	RBI	BB	SO	SB	BA	SA
TOTALS			28	161	5483	714	1416	278	46	145	685	469	944	132	.258	.405
Tino Martinez	1B114 DH19	L	36	138	458	63	120	20	1	23	76	66	72	3	.262	.461
Rey Sanchez	2B87 SS4	R	36	91	285	23	70	14	3	2	26	12	28	0	.246	.337
Julio Lugo	SS143 2B8 DH5	R	28	157	581	83	160	41	4	7	75	54	106	21	.275	.396
Aubrey Huff	3B86 1B38 DH34 OF9	L	27	157	600	92	178	27	2	29	104	56	74	5	.297	.493
Jose Cruz	OF152	R	30	153	545	76	132	25	8	21	78	76	117	11	.242	.433
Carl Crawford	OF145 DH5	L	22	152	626	104	185	26	19	11	55	35	81	59	.296	.450
Rocco Baldelli	OF124 DH13	R	22	136	518	79	145	27	3	16	74	30	88	17	.280	.436
Toby Hall	C119	R	28	119	404	35	103	21	0	8	60	24	41	0	.255	.366
1 Robert Fick	DH34 OF21 1B10 C3	L	30	76	214	12	43	5	2	6	26	20	32	0	.201	.327
Geoff Blum	3B59 2B52 OF7 1B2 DH2 SS1	B	31	112	339	38	73	21	0	8	35	24	58	2	.215	.348
Brook Fordyce	C51 DH1	R	34	54	151	14	31	6	0	2	9	9	34	0	.205	.285
Damian Rolls (TJ)	OF24 3B19 DH5 2B2 1B1	R	26	53	117	12	19	5	0	0	9	10	36	2	.162	.205
Jorge Cantu	2B33 3B11 DH4 SS1	R	22	50	173	25	52	20	1	2	17	9	44	0	.301	.462
B.J. Upton	SS16 DH14 3B13 OF1	R	19	45	159	19	41	8	2	4	12	18	58	2	.258	.409
Fred McGriff	DH14 1B6	L	40	27	72	7	13	2	0	2	7	9	19	0	.181	.306
Midre Cummings	DH12 OF2	L	32	22	54	10	15	4	0	2	7	5	12	1	.278	.463
Joey Gathright	OF16 DH1	L	23	19	52	11	13	0	0	0	1	2	14	6	.250	.250
Eduardo Perez (LJ)	1B5 OF3 DH3 3B1	R	34	13	38	2	8	2	0	1	7	4	9	0	.211	.342
2 Jose Bautista	OF8 3B2	R	23	12	12	1	2	0	0	0	0	3	7	0	.167	.167
Matt Diaz	OF4 DH4	R	26	10	21	3	4	1	1	1	3	1	5	0	.190	.476
1 Randall Simon	DH6 1B1	R	29	8	17	2	2	0	0	0	3	2	1	0	.118	.118
Jonny Gomes	DH4	R	23	5	14	0	1	0	0	0	1	1	6	0	.071	.071
Charles Gipson	SS2 OF2 DH1	R	31	5	4	1	2	0	0	0	0	1	2	1	.500	.500
1 Jason Romano	2B1 OF1	R	25	4	8	0	1	0	0	0	1	0	2	0	.125	.125

NAME	T	AGE	W	L	PCT	SV	G	GS	CG	IP	H	BB	SO	SHO	ERA
		27	70	91	.435	35	161	161	3	1417	1459	580	923	5	4.81
Mark Hendrickson	L	30	10	15	.400	0	32	30	2	183	211	46	87	0	4.81
1 Victor Zambrano	R	28	9	7	.563	0	23	22	0	128	107	96	109	0	4.43
Rob Bell	R	27	8	8	.500	0	24	19	1	123	121	41	57	0	4.48
John Halama	L	32	7	6	.538	0	34	14	0	119	134	27	59	0	4.70
Travis Harper	R	28	6	2	.750	0	52	0	0	79	69	23	59	0	3.89
Dewon Brazelton	R	24	6	8	.429	0	22	21	0	121	121	53	64	0	4.77
Doug Waechter (RJ)	R	23	5	7	.417	0	14	14	0	70	68	33	36	0	6.01
Danys Baez	R	26	4	4	.500	30	62	0	0	68	60	29	52	0	3.57
Jorge Sosa	R	27	4	7	.364	1	43	8	0	99	100	54	94	0	5.53
Lance Carter	R	29	3	3	.500	0	56	0	0	80	77	23	36	0	3.47
Jesus Colome	R	26	2	2	.500	3	33	0	0	41	28	18	40	0	3.27
Scott Kazmir	L	20	2	3	.400	0	8	8	0	33	33	21	41	0	5.67
1 Paul Abbott	R	36	2	5	.286	0	10	9	0	47	49	27	25	0	6.70
Trever Miller	L	31	1	1	.500	1	60	0	0	49	48	15	43	0	3.12
Chad Gaudin	R	21	1	2	.333	0	26	4	0	43	59	16	30	0	4.65
Bobby Seay	L	26	0	0	—	0	21	0	0	23	21	5	17	0	2.38
Dicky Gonzalez (JL)	R	25	0	0	—	0	7	0	0	9	7	2	6	0	6.14
John Webb	R	25	0	0	—	0	2	0	0	9	12	7	9	0	7.00
1 Bartolome Fortunato	R	29	0	0	—	0	3	0	0	7	4	4	7	0	9.00
Jason Standridge (SJ)	R	25	0	1	.000	0	10	1	4	7	0				9.00
Damian Moss	L	27	0	1	.000	0	8	3	0	13	15	6	6	0	16.88
Todd Ritchie	R	32	0	0	—	0	3	0	0	8	4	0	4	0	9.00
Franklin Nunez	R	23	0	0	—	0	11	0	0	11	7	7	14	0	5.91
Jeremi Gonzalez	R	29	0	5	.000	0	18	8	0	50	72	20	22	0	6.97
Seth McClung (EJ) 23															

TORONTO — 5th 67-94 .416 33.5 — CARLOS TOSCA 47-64 .423 JOHN GIBBONS 20-30 .400

Name	G by Pos	B	AGE	G	AB	R	H	2B	3B	HR	RBI	BB	SO	SB	BA	SA
TOTALS			28	161	5531	719	1438	290	34	145	680	513	1083	58	.260	.403
Carlos Delgado (VJ)	1B120 DH8	L	32	128	458	74	123	26	0	32	99	69	115	0	.269	.535
Orlando Hudson	2B133	B	26	135	489	73	132	32	7	12	58	51	98	7	.270	.438
Chris Gomez	SS77 1B19 3B5 DH5 2B3	R	33	109	341	41	96	11	1	3	37	28	41	3	.282	.346
Eric Hinske	3B153 DH1	L	26	155	570	66	140	23	3	15	69	54	109	12	.246	.375
Alex Rios	OF111	R	23	111	426	55	122	24	7	1	28	31	84	15	.286	.383
Vernon Wells (LJ)	OF131 DH5	R	25	134	536	82	146	34	2	23	67	51	83	9	.272	.472
Reed Johnson	OF137 DH4	R	27	141	537	68	145	25	2	10	61	24	88	6	.270	.393
Gregg Zaun	C97 DH6	B	33	107	338	46	91	24	0	6	36	47	61	0	.269	.393
1 Josh Phelps	DH65 1B12	R	26	79	295	38	70	13	2	12	51	18	73	0	.237	.417
Frank Catalanotto (GJ)	OF41 DH29	L	30	75	249	27	73	19	1	1	26	17	33	1	.293	.390
2 Frank Menechino	2B30 DH19 SS14 3B7 P1	R	33	72	236	40	71	13	4	9	25	36	44	0	.301	.504
Chris Woodward	SS64 DH2	R	28	69	213	21	50	13	4	1	24	14	46	1	.235	.347
Kevin Cash	C60	R	26	60	181	18	35	9	4	2	21	10	59	0	.193	.309
Dave Berg	OF31 1B7 DH7 2B4 3B3	R	33	58	154	13	39	4	0	3	23	4	27	0	.253	.338
Gabe Gross	OF38 DH7	L	24	44	129	18	27	4	0	3	16	19	31	2	.209	.310
Howie Clark	OF19 1B11 DH4 2B1 3B1	L	30	40	115	17	25	6	0	3	12	13	15	0	.217	.348
Russ Adams	SS21	R	23	22	72	10	22	4	1	0	5	5	5	1	.306	.528
Guillermo Quiroz	C15 DH2	R	22	17	52	2	11	2	0	0	6	2	15	0	.212	.250
Simon Pond	OF9 DH6	L	27	16	49	4	8	2	0	0	6	5	12	0	.163	.265
Eric Crozier	DH8 1B5	L	25	14	33	5	5	2	0	1	2	6	19	0	.152	.394
Greg Myers (NJ)	C4 DH1	L	38	8	18	0	4	2	0	0	2	2	4	0	.222	.333
2 Bobby Estalella (NJ)	C3 DH2	R	29	5	13	1	3	0	0	0	3	0	5	0	.231	.231
Chad Hermansen	OF4	R	26	4	7	0	0	0	0	0	0	0	3	0	.000	.000

NAME	T	AGE	W	L	PCT	SV	G	GS	CG	IP	H	BB	SO	SHO	ERA
		29	67	94	.416	37	161	161	6	1421	1505	608	956	11	4.91
Ted Lilly	L	28	12	10	.545	0	32	32	2	197	171	89	168	1	4.06
Miguel Batista	R	33	10	13	.435	5	38	31	2	199	206	96	104	1	4.80
Josh Towers	R	27	9	9	.500	0	21	21	0	116	148	26	51	0	5.11
Roy Halladay (SJ)	R	27	8	8	.500	0	21	21	1	133	140	39	95	1	4.20
Dave Bush	R	24	5	4	.556	0	16	16	1	98	95	25	64	1	3.69
1 Terry Adams	R	31	4	4	.500	3	42	0	0	43	49	22	35	0	3.98
Jason Frasor	R	26	4	6	.400	17	63	0	0	68	64	36	54	0	4.08
Justin Miller (LJ)	R	26	3	4	.429	0	19	15	0	82	101	42	47	0	6.06
Justin Speier	R	30	3	8	.273	7	63	0	0	69	61	25	52	0	3.91
Pat Hentgen (VR)	R	35	2	9	.182	0	18	16	0	80	90	42	33	0	6.95
Bob File (SJ)	R	27	1	0	1.000	0	24	0	0	34	45	12	15	0	4.81
Ryan Glynn	R	29	1	0	1.000	0	6	2	0	20	19	8	14	0	4.05
Brandon League	R	21	1	0	1.000	0	18	0	0	21	21	13	13	0	6.00
Aquilino Lopez	R	29	1	1	.500	0	18	0	0	21	21	13	13	0	6.00
Gustavo Chacin	L	23	1	1	.500	0	2	2	0	14	8	5	9	0	2.57
Vinnie Chulk	R	25	1	3	.250	2	47	0	0	56	59	27	44	0	4.66
Kerry Ligtenberg	R	33	1	6	.143	3	57	0	0	55	73	25	49	0	6.38
Valerio De Los Santos (SJ)	L	31	0	0	—	0	17	0	0	12	11	10	10	0	6.17
Dave Maurer	L	29	0	0	—	0	1	0	0	1	6	5	1	0	54.00
Adam Peterson	R	25	0	0	—	0	7	0	0	7	8	5	3	0	16.87
Frank Menechino	R	33	0	0	—	0	1	0	0	1	1	1	0	0	0.00
Jason Kershner	L	27	0	1	.000	0	24	0	0	22	30	8	15	0	6.04
Kevin Frederick	R	27	0	2	.000	0	16	0	0	22	32	16	22	0	6.59
Sean Douglass	R	25	0	4	.000	0	14	3	0	39	37	28	36	0	6.92
Michael Nakamura	R	27	0	1	.000	0	19	0	0	26	27	7	24	0	7.36

CENTRAL DIVISION

MINNESOTA — 1st 92-70 .568 — RON GARDENHIRE

Name	G by Pos	B	AGE	G	AB	R	H	2B	3B	HR	RBI	BB	SO	SB	BA	SA
TOTALS			28	162	5623	780	1494	310	24	191	735	513	982	116	.266	.431
Justin Morneau	1B61 DH11	L	23	74	280	39	76	17	0	19	58	28	54	0	.271	.536
Luis Rivas	2B109	R	24	109	336	44	86	19	5	10	34	13	53	15	.256	.432
Cristian Guzman	SS145	R	26	145	576	84	158	31	4	8	46	30	64	10	.274	.384
Corey Koskie	3B115 DH1	L	31	118	422	68	106	24	2	25	71	49	103	9	.251	.495
Jacque Jones	OF142 DH3	L	29	151	555	69	141	22	1	24	80	40	117	13	.254	.427
Torii Hunter	OF126 DH10	R	28	138	520	79	141	37	0	23	81	40	101	21	.271	.475
Shannon Stewart (FJ)	OF71 DH21	R	30	92	378	46	115	17	2	11	47	47	44	6	.304	.447
Joe Mauer (SJ)	C32 DH1	L	21	35	107	18	33	8	1	6	17	11	14	1	.308	.570
Matt LeCroy (VJ)	DH30 C26 1B23	R	28	88	264	25	71	14	0	9	39	16	60	0	.269	.424
Lew Ford	OF126 DH26	R	27	154	569	89	170	31	4	15	72	67	75	20	.299	.446
Michael Cuddyer	2B48 3B43 OF15 1B10 DH5	R	25	115	339	49	89	22	1	12	45	37	74	5	.263	.440
Henry Blanco	C114	R	32	114	315	36	65	19	1	10	37	21	56	0	.206	.368
1 Doug Mientkiewicz	1B77	L	30	78	284	34	70	18	0	5	25	38	38	2	.246	.363
Jose Offerman	DH39 1B7 2B3	B	35	77	172	22	44	14	2	2	22	29	31	1	.256	.395
Nick Punto (UJ-BC)	2B19 SS11 DH3 3B2 OF1	B	26	38	91	17	23	0	0	2	12	12	19	6	.253	.319
Mike Ryan (SJ)	OF15 DH11	L	26	36	71	9	17	2	0	1	4	4	16	1	.239	.296
Augie Ojeda	2B20 SS7 3B4	B	29	30	59	16	20	1	0	2	7	10	3	1	.339	.458
Michael Restovich	OF19 DH5	R	25	29	47	9	12	3	0	2	6	4	10	0	.255	.447
Jason Kubel	OF10 DH9	L	22	23	60	10	18	2	0	2	7	6	9	1	.300	.433
2 Pat Borders	C19	R	41	19	42	3	12	4	0	0	5	2	8	0	.286	.381
Terry Tiffee	3B12 1B1 DH1	B	25	17	44	7	12	4	0	0	3	2	6	0	.273	.500
Rob Bowen	C15	R	23	15	27	3	3	0	0	0	1	4	7	0	.111	.111
Alex Prieto	2B8 3B5 SS3 DH1	R	28	16	32	4	8	1	0	0	2	2	6	0	.250	.375
Jason Bartlett	SS5 2B1 DH1	R	24	8	12	1	1	0	0	0	0	1	3	0	.083	.083

NAME	T	AGE	W	L	PCT	SV	G	GS	CG	IP	H	BB	SO	SHO	ERA
		28	92	70	.568	48	162	162	4	1476	1523	431	1123	9	4.03
Johan Santana	L	25	20	6	.769	0	34	34	1	228	156	54	265	1	2.61
Carlos Silva	R	25	14	8	.636	0	33	33	1	203	255	35	76	1	4.21
Juan Rincon	R	25	11	6	.647	2	77	0	0	82	52	32	106	0	2.63
Brad Radke	R	31	11	8	.579	0	34	34	1	220	229	26	143	1	3.48
Kyle Lohse	R	25	9	13	.409	0	35	34	1	194	240	76	111	1	5.34
J.C. Romero	L	28	7	4	.636	1	74	0	0	74	61	38	69	0	3.51
Terry Mulholland	L	41	5	9	.357	0	39	15	0	123	163	33	60	0	5.18
Grant Balfour (SJ)	R	26	4	1	.800	0	36	0	0	39	35	21	42	0	4.35
Jesse Crain	R	22	3	0	1.000	0	22	0	0	27	17	12	14	0	2.00
Aaron Fultz	L	30	3	3	.500	1	55	0	0	50	50	23	37	0	5.04
Joe Roa	R	32	2	3	.400	0	48	0	0	70	84	24	47	0	4.50
Seth Greisinger	R	28	2	5	.286	0	12	5	0	55	68	15	36	0	6.18
Joe Nathan	R	29	1	2	.333	44	73	0	0	72	48	23	89	0	1.62
Carlos Pulido	L	32	0	0	—	0	11	0	0	16	14	4	9	0	8.74
Joe Beimel	L	27	0	0	—	0	2	0	0	3	7	1	0	0	43.20
1 Brad Thomas	L	26	0	0	—	0	3	1	0	6	11	4	6	0	16.87
Matt Guerrier	R	25	0	0	—	0	2	0	0	9	12	6	11	0	5.68
J.D. Durbin	R	22	0	0	—	0	4	0	0	4	4	4	6	0	7.36
Joe Mays (SJ) 28															

CHICAGO — 2nd 83-79 .512 9 — OZZIE GUILLEN

Name	G by Pos	B	AGE	G	AB	R	H	2B	3B	HR	RBI	BB	SO	SB	BA	SA
TOTALS			28	162	5534	865	1481	284	19	242	823	499	1030	78	.268	.457
Paul Konerko	1B139 DH16	R	28	155	563	84	156	22	0	41	117	69	107	1	.277	.535
Juan Uribe	2B77 SS38 3B27 DH2	R	24	134	502	82	142	31	6	23	74	32	96	1	.283	.506
Jose Valentin	SS122 DH2	B	34	125	450	73	97	20	3	30	70	43	139	8	.216	.473
Joe Crede	3B144	R	26	144	490	67	117	25	0	21	69	34	81	1	.239	.418
Magglio Ordonez (KJ)	OF43 DH7	R	30	52	202	32	59	8	2	9	37	16	22	0	.292	.485
Aaron Rowand	OF137	R	26	140	487	94	151	38	2	24	69	30	91	17	.310	.544
Carlos Lee	OF148 DH5	R	28	153	591	103	180	37	0	31	99	54	86	11	.305	.525
2 Ben Davis	C53	R	27	54	160	21	37	9	0	6	16	9	40	1	.231	.400
Frank Thomas (NJ)	DH65 1B4	R	36	74	240	53	65	16	0	18	49	64	57	0	.271	.563
Willie Harris	2B92 OF30 DH2	L	26	129	409	68	107	15	2	2	27	51	79	19	.262	.323
Ross Gload	1B42 OF39 DH13	L	28	110	234	28	75	16	0	7	44	20	37	3	.321	.479
Timo Perez	OF80 DH6	L	29	103	293	38	72	12	0	5	40	15	29	3	.246	.338
Joe Borchard	OF56 DH4	B	25	63	201	26	35	4	1	9	20	19	57	1	.174	.338
Jamie Burke	C45 DH3 1B2 3B2 OF2	R	32	57	120	22	40	9	0	0	15	10	13	0	.333	.408
Sandy Alomar	C49 DH1	R	38	50	146	15	35	4	0	2	14	11	13	0	.240	.308
1 Miguel Olivo	C46	R	25	46	141	21	38	7	2	7	26	10	29	5	.270	.496
2 Carl Everett	DH41 OF1	B	33	43	154	21	41	7	1	5	21	8	26	1	.266	.422
Wilson Valdez	SS12 2B5	R	26	19	43	8	10	1	0	1	4	2	5	1	.233	.326
2 Roberto Alomar	2B13 DH5	B	36	18	61	4	11	1	0	1	8	2	13	0	.180	.246
Kelly Dransfeldt	SS8 3B3 DH1	R	29	15	30	5	10	1	0	0	4	0	6	0	.333	.333
2 Alex Escobar (BF) 25																

NAME	T	AGE	W	L	PCT	SV	G	GS	CG	IP	H	BB	SO	SHO	ERA
TOTALS		29	83	79	.512	34	162	162	8	1432	1505	527	1013	8	4.91
Mark Buehrle	L	29	16	10	.615	0	35	35	4	245	257	51	165	1	3.89
Jon Garland	R	24	12	11	.522	0	34	33	1	217	223	76	113	0	4.89
2 Freddy Garcia	R	29	9	4	.692	0	16	16	0	103	96	32	102	0	4.46
1 Esteban Loaiza	R	32	9	5	.643	0	21	21	2	141	156	45	83	1	4.86
Shingo Takatsu	R	35	6	4	.600	19	59	0	0	62	40	21	50	0	2.31
Damaso Marte	L	29	6	5	.545	6	74	0	0	74	56	34	68	0	3.42
Scott Schoeneweis (EJ)	L	30	6	9	.400	0	20	20	0	113	129	49	69	0	5.59
2 Jose Contreras	R	32	5	4	.556	0	13	13	0	75	73	42	68	0	5.30
Neal Cotts	L	24	4	4	.500	0	56	1	0	65	61	30	58	0	5.65
Mike Jackson	R	39	3	0	1.000	0	45	0	0	47	55	15	26	0	5.01
Jon Adkins	R	26	2	3	.400	0	50	0	0	62	75	20	44	0	4.65
Jason Grilli	R	27	2	3	.400	0	8	8	1	45	52	20	26	0	7.40
Felix Diaz	R	23	2	5	.286	0	18	7	0	49	62	16	33	0	6.75
1 Billy Koch	R	29	1	1	.500	8	24	0	0	23	24	16	25	0	5.40
1 Jon Rauch	R	25	1	1	.500	0	2	2	0	9	16	4	4	0	6.23
Kelly Wunsch (SJ)	L	31	0	0	---	0	3	0	0	2	1	1	1	0	0.00
1 Vic Darensbourg	L	33	0	0	---	0	1	0	0	1	1	1	0	0	0.00
Arnie Munoz	L	22	0	1	.000	0	11	1	0	14	20	12	11	0	10.05
Jeff Bajenaru	R	26	0	1	.000	0	9	0	0	8	15	6	8	0	10.80
Josh Stewart	L	26	0	1	.000	0	3	2	0	8	16	5	5	0	15.26
Cliff Politte (IL)	R	30	0	3	.000	1	54	0	0	51	52	22	48	0	4.38
Dan Wright	R	26	0	4	.000	0	4	4	0	18	24	11	6	0	8.15

CLEVELAND — 3rd 89-82 .494 12 — ERIC WEDGE

Name	G by Pos	B	AGE	G	AB	R	H	2B	3B	HR	RBI	BB	SO	SB	BA	SA
TOTALS			29	162	5676	858	1565	345	29	184	820	606	1009	94	.276	.444
Ben Broussard	1B133	L	27	139	418	57	115	28	5	17	82	52	95	4	.275	.488
Ron Belliard	2B151 DH1	R	29	152	599	78	169	48	1	12	70	60	98	3	.282	.426
Omar Vizquel	SS147	B	37	148	567	82	165	28	3	7	59	57	62	19	.291	.388
Casey Blake	3B152 1B8	R	30	152	587	93	159	36	3	28	88	68	139	5	.271	.486
Jody Gerut	OF131 DH6	L	26	134	481	72	121	31	5	11	51	54	59	3	.252	.405
Coco Crisp	OF128 DH6	B	24	139	491	78	146	24	2	15	71	36	69	20	.297	.446
Matt Lawton	OF142 DH3	L	32	153	591	109	164	25	0	20	70	74	84	23	.277	.421
Victor Martinez	C132 DH8	B	25	141	520	77	147	38	1	23	108	60	69	0	.283	.492
Travis Hafner	DH128 1B11	L	27	140	482	96	150	41	3	28	109	68	111	3	.311	.583
Lou Merloni (EJ)	1B42 3B10 2B7 OF4 DH3	R	33	71	190	25	55	12	1	4	28	14	41	1	.289	.426
John McDonald	SS30 2B12 3B9 DH8	R	29	66	93	17	19	5	1	2	7	4	11	0	.204	.344
1 Alex Escobar	OF42 DH3	R	25	46	152	20	32	8	2	1	12	23	42	1	.211	.309
Tim Laker	C41 P1	R	34	44	117	12	25	2	0	3	17	7	28	0	.214	.308
Grady Sizemore	OF42	L	21	43	138	15	34	6	2	4	24	14	34	2	.246	.449
2 Josh Phelps	DH16 1B8	R	26	24	76	13	23	6	0	5	10	4	20	0	.303	.579
Ryan Ludwick (KJ)	OF15	R	25	15	50	3	11	2	0	2	4	2	14	0	.220	.380
Mark Little	OF11	R	31	11	20	0	4	1	0	0	0	0	6	0	.200	.200
Jhonny Peralta	SS7 3B2	R	22	8	25	2	6	1	0	0	2	3	6	0	.240	.280
Josh Bard (GJ)	C7	B	26	7	19	5	8	2	0	1	4	3	0	0	.421	.684
Raul Gonzalez	OF4	R	30	7	11	0	1	0	0	0	0	0	4	0	.091	.091
Brandon Phillips	2B6	R	23	6	22	1	4	2	0	0	1	0	5	0	.182	.273
Ernie Young	DH2	R	34	3	4	0	2	0	0	0	0	0	1	0	.500	.500
1 Sandy Martinez	C1	L	33	2	2	0	0	0	0	0	0	0	0	0	.000	.000
Aaron Boone (KJ) 31																

NAME	T	AGE	W	L	PCT	SV	G	GS	CG	IP	H	BB	SO	SHO	ERA
TOTALS		28	80	82	.494	32	162	162	8	1467	1553	579	1115	8	4.81
Cliff Lee	L	25	14	8	.636	0	33	33	0	179	188	81	161	5	5.43
Jake Westbrook	R	26	14	9	.609	0	33	30	5	216	208	61	116	1	3.38
C.C. Sabathia	L	23	11	10	.524	0	30	30	1	188	176	72	139	1	4.12
David Riske	R	27	7	3	.700	5	72	0	0	77	69	41	78	0	3.72
Rick White	R	35	5	5	.500	1	59	0	0	78	88	29	44	0	5.29
Rafael Betancourt	R	29	5	6	.455	4	68	0	0	67	71	18	76	0	3.91
1 Chad Durbin	R	26	5	6	.455	0	17	8	1	51	63	24	38	0	6.66
Matt Miller	R	32	4	1	.800	1	57	0	0	55	42	23	55	0	3.09
Bob Howry	R	30	4	2	.667	0	37	0	0	43	37	12	39	0	2.74
2 Scott Elarton	R	28	3	5	.375	0	21	21	1	117	107	42	80	1	4.53
Jason Davis	R	24	2	7	.222	0	26	19	0	114	148	51	72	0	5.51
1 Cliff Bartosh	L	24	1	0	1.000	0	34	0	0	19	22	11	25	0	4.66
Kazuhito Tadano	R	24	1	1	.500	0	14	4	0	50	55	18	39	0	4.65
Jeriome Robertson	L	27	1	1	.500	0	8	0	0	14	22	9	6	0	12.21
Jeff D'Amico (XJ)	R	28	1	2	.333	0	7	3	0	31	45	6	16	0	7.63
Kyle Denney	R	26	1	2	.333	0	4	4	0	16	32	8	13	0	9.56
Jose Jimenez	R	30	1	7	.125	8	31	0	0	36	45	14	21	0	8.42
Jeremy Guthrie	R	25	0	0	---	0	6	0	0	6	12	6	4	0	4.63
Fernando Cabrera	R	22	0	0	---	0	6	0	0	5	3	1	6	0	3.38
David Lee	R	31	0	0	---	0	2	0	0	4	8	6	4	0	10.38
Joey Dawley (EJ)	R	32	0	0	---	0	2	0	0	3	7	8	0	0	5.40
Lou Pote	R	32	0	0	---	0	2	0	0	2	5	9	0	0	9.00
Jake Robbins	R	25	0	0	---	0	2	0	0	3	4	1	5	0	5.40
Jason Anderson	R	25	0	0	---	0	1	0	0	1	1	4	1	0	45.00
Tim Laker	R	34	0	0	---	0	1	0	0	1	1	1	0	0	0.00
Jack Cressend	R	29	0	1	.000	0	11	0	0	16	22	10	8	0	6.32
Francisco Cruceta	R	22	0	1	.000	0	2	2	0	8	10	4	9	0	9.39
Jason Stanford (AJ)	L	27	0	1	.000	0	2	2	0	11	12	5	5	0	6.82
Bob Wickman (EJ)	R	35	0	2	.000	13	30	0	0	30	33	10	26	0	4.25
1 Scott Stewart	L	28	0	2	.000	0	14	0	0	14	23	6	18	0	7.24

Brian Tallet (EJ) 26, Billy Traber (EJ) 24

DETROIT — 4th 72-90 .444 20 — ALAN TRAMMELL

Name	G by Pos	B	AGE	G	AB	R	H	2B	3B	HR	RBI	BB	SO	SB	BA	SA
TOTALS			28	162	5623	827	1531	284	54	201	800	518	1144	86	.272	.449
Carlos Pena	1B135 DH5	L	26	142	481	89	116	22	4	27	82	70	146	7	.241	.472
Fernando Vina (LJ)	2B29	L	35	29	115	21	26	9	1	0	9	9	2	2	.226	.270
Carlos Guillen	SS135	B	28	136	522	97	166	37	10	20	97	52	87	12	.318	.542
Eric Munson	3B94 DH7 C1	L	26	109	321	36	68	14	2	19	49	29	90	1	.212	.445
Bobby Higginson	OF115 DH10	L	33	131	448	63	110	24	2	12	64	70	84	5	.246	.388
Alex Sanchez (LJ)	OF78	L	27	79	332	41	107	9	3	2	26	7	50	19	.322	.386
Rondell White	OF74 DH43	R	32	121	448	76	121	21	2	19	67	39	77	1	.270	.453
Ivan Rodriguez	C124 DH8	R	32	135	527	72	176	32	2	19	86	41	91	7	.334	.510
Dmitri Young (BL)	DH74 1B25 OF2 3B1	B	30	104	389	72	106	23	2	18	60	33	71	0	.272	.481
Omar Infante	2B105 SS23 3B10 OF5	R	22	142	503	69	133	27	9	16	55	40	112	13	.264	.449
Brandon Inge	3B73 C39 OF26	R	27	131	408	43	117	15	7	13	64	32	72	5	.287	.453
Craig Monroe	OF125 DH2	R	27	128	447	65	131	27	3	18	72	29	79	3	.293	.488
Marcus Thames	OF52 DH5	R	27	61	165	24	42	12	0	10	33	16	42	0	.255	.509
Jason Smith	OF46	B	26	61	155	20	37	7	4	5	19	8	37	1	.239	.432
Nook Logan	OF46	B	24	47	133	12	37	5	2	0	10	13	24	8	.278	.346
Greg Norton (KJ)	3B18 1B7 DH7 OF6	B	31	41	86	9	15	1	0	2	12	2	21	0	.174	.256
Chris Shelton (FJ)	DH11 1B8 C6 OF1	R	24	27	46	6	9	1	0	1	3	9	14	0	.196	.283
1 Mike DiFelice	C12 DH1	R	35	13	22	3	3	0	0	0	2	3	3	0	.136	.227
Ryan Raburn	2B11	R	23	12	29	4	4	1	0	0	1	2	15	1	.138	.172
Curtis Granderson	OF8	L	23	9	25	2	6	1	1	0	0	3	8	0	.240	.360
Andres Torres	DH2 OF1	B	26	3	0	1	0	0	0	0	0	0	0	0	.---	.---

NAME	T	AGE	W	L	PCT	SV	G	GS	CG	IP	H	BB	SO	SHO	ERA
TOTALS		28	72	90	.444	35	162	162	7	1440	1542	530	995	9	4.93
Nate Robertson	L	26	12	10	.545	1	34	32	1	197	210	66	155	0	4.90
Jeremy Bonderman	R	21	11	13	.458	0	33	32	2	184	168	73	168	2	4.89
Mike Maroth	L	26	11	13	.458	0	33	33	2	217	244	59	108	1	4.31
Jason Johnson	R	30	8	15	.348	0	33	33	2	197	222	60	125	1	5.13
Gary Knotts	R	27	6	7	.538	2	36	19	0	135	142	58	81	0	5.25
Wil Ledezma	L	23	4	3	.571	0	15	8	0	53	55	18	29	0	4.39
Ugueth Urbina (PP)	R	30	4	6	.400	21	54	0	0	54	38	32	56	0	4.50
Jamie Walker	L	32	3	4	.429	1	70	0	0	65	69	12	53	0	3.20
Al Levine	R	36	3	4	.429	0	65	0	0	71	83	24	32	0	4.58
Esteban Yan	R	29	3	6	.333	7	69	0	0	87	92	32	69	0	3.83
Craig Dingman	R	30	2	2	.500	0	24	0	0	29	33	22	16	0	6.75
Steve Colyer	L	25	1	0	1.000	0	41	0	0	32	33	24	31	0	6.47
Franklyn German	R	24	1	0	1.000	0	16	0	0	15	17	11	8	0	7.36
Roberto Novoa	R	24	1	1	.500	0	16	0	0	21	25	6	15	0	5.57
Nate Cornejo (SJ)	R	24	0	1	.250	0	5	5	0	26	42	11	12	0	8.42
John Ennis	R	24	0	0	---	0	12	0	0	16	20	5	13	0	8.44
Lino Urdaneta (EJ)	R	24	0	0	---	0	5	0	0	5	5	1	0	0	∞
Danny Patterson	R	33	0	0	.000	2	37	0	0	42	44	16	24	0	4.75

Fernando Rodney (EJ) 27, Chris Spurling (EJ) 27

KANSAS CITY — 5th 58-104 .358 34 — TONY PENA

Name	G by Pos	B	AGE	G	AB	R	H	2B	3B	HR	RBI	BB	SO	SB	BA	SA
TOTALS			29	162	5538	720	1432	261	29	150	675	461	1057	67	.259	.397
Ken Harvey	1B73 DH41 OF4	R	26	120	456	47	131	20	1	13	55	28	89	1	.287	.421
Tony Graffanino (KJ)	2B75	R	32	75	278	32	73	11	0	3	25	27	38	10	.263	.335
Angel Berroa	SS133	B	26	134	512	72	134	27	6	8	43	23	87	14	.262	.385
Joe Randa	3B119 DH6 1B3	R	34	128	485	65	139	31	2	8	56	40	77	0	.287	.408
Juan Gonzalez (XJ)	OF29 DH4	R	34	33	127	17	35	4	1	5	17	9	19	0	.276	.441
David DeJesus	OF94	L	24	96	363	58	104	15	3	7	39	33	53	8	.287	.402
Matt Stairs	OF71 1B30 DH22	L	36	126	439	48	117	21	3	18	66	49	92	1	.267	.451
Benito Santiago (BH)	C49	R	39	49	175	15	48	10	0	6	23	8	22	0	.274	.434
Mike Sweeney (XJ)	1B55 DH48	R	30	106	411	56	118	23	0	22	79	33	44	3	.287	.504
Desi Relaford	3B42 2B36 OF32 SS12	B	30	114	380	45	84	14	0	6	34	34	56	5	.221	.305
John Buck	C68 DH3	R	23	71	238	36	56	9	0	12	30	15	79	1	.235	.424
1 Carlos Beltran	OF69	B	27	69	266	51	74	19	2	15	51	37	44	14	.278	.534
2 Abraham Nunez	OF57 DH2	B	27	59	221	31	50	9	0	4	21	25	48	0	.226	.335
Dee Brown	OF53 DH1	L	26	59	195	19	49	7	0	4	24	11	50	2	.251	.349
Ruben Gotay	2B42	B	21	44	152	17	41	7	3	1	16	9	36	0	.270	.375
Aaron Guiel (IJ)	OF39 DH2	L	31	42	135	15	21	5	0	5	13	17	42	1	.156	.296
Calvin Pickering	DH27 1B8	L	27	35	122	21	30	8	1	7	26	18	42	0	.246	.500
2 Ruben Mateo	OF30	R	26	32	93	9	18	4	0	2	7	3	20	1	.194	.301
Alberto Castillo	C49	R	34	29	89	12	24	6	0	1	11	14	10	0	.270	.371
Wilton Guerrero	2B8 SS3 OF3 1B2 3B2 DH2	R	29	24	32	7	7	1	0	0	5	1	1	1	.219	.281
Byron Gettis	OF21	R	24	21	39	7	7	1	0	1	6	3	8	0	.179	.256
Kelly Stinnett (EJ)	C20	R	34	20	59	10	18	0	0	3	6	6	15	0	.305	.458
Andres Blanco	SS20	B	20	19	60	9	19	2	2	0	5	6	9	1	.317	.417
Mendy Lopez (JL)	2B6 SS4 3B4 OF4 1B2	R	30	18	38	4	4	0	0	0	1	1	10	0	.105	.184
2 Damian Jackson	OF5 DH2 2B1 SS1	R	30	14	15	1	2	1	0	0	0	2	6	1	.133	.267
Alexis Gomez	OF12	L	25	13	29	1	8	1	0	0	0	0	5	0	.276	.310
3 Jose Bautista	3B11 OF1	R	23	12	29	4	7	1	0	0	3	1	15	0	.200	.240
Brandon Berger	OF11	R	29	11	35	5	7	2	0	1	4	5	10	0	.200	.257
Donnie Murphy	2B7	R	21	7	27	3	8	1	0	1	1	1	5	1	.185	.296
Rich Thompson	OF3	R	25	6	1	1	0	0	0	0	0	0	0	0	1.000	.000
Adrian Brown	OF5	B	30	6	11	3	3	0	0	0	0	0	1	0	.273	.273
Paul Phillips	C4	R	27	4	5	0	1	0	0	0	0	0	1	0	.200	.200
Mike Tonis	C2	R	25	2	4	0	0	0	0	0	0	0	2	0	.000	.000

NAME	T	AGE	W	L	PCT	SV	G	GS	CG	IP	H	BB	SO	SHO	ERA
TOTALS		29	58	104	.358	25	162	162	6	1420	1638	518	887	3	5.15
Jimmy Gobble	L	22	9	8	.529	0	25	24	1	148	157	43	49	0	5.35
Darrell May	L	32	9	19	.321	0	31	31	3	186	234	55	120	1	5.61
Zach Greinke	R	20	8	11	.421	0	24	24	0	145	143	26	100	0	3.97
Brian Anderson	L	32	6	12	.333	0	35	26	2	166	217	53	70	1	5.64
Dennys Reyes	L	27	4	8	.333	0	40	12	0	108	114	50	91	0	4.75
1 Jason Grimsley	R	36	4	3	.500	0	32	0	0	27	24	15	18	0	3.37
Scott Sullivan (XJ)	R	33	3	4	.429	0	49	0	0	60	73	24	43	0	4.77
Jeremy Affeldt (VJ)	L	25	3	4	.429	13	38	6	0	76	91	32	49	0	4.95
Mike Wood	R	24	3	8	.273	0	17	17	0	100	112	28	54	0	5.94
Shawn Camp	R	28	2	2	.500	2	42	0	0	67	74	16	51	0	3.91
D.J. Carrasco	R	27	2	2	.500	0	30	0	0	35	41	15	23	0	4.84
Nate Field	R	28	2	2	.500	3	43	0	0	44	40	19	30	0	4.26
Mike MacDougal	R	27	1	1	.500	1	13	0	0	11	16	9	14	0	5.56
Chris George	L	24	1	2	.333	0	10	7	0	42	60	25	15	0	7.47
Jimmy Serrano	R	25	1	2	.333	0	10	1	0	16	25	8	8	0	4.68
Jamie Cerda	L	25	1	4	.200	0	53	0	0	46	41	30	33	0	3.15
Justin Huisman	R	25	0	0	---	1	14	0	0	25	36	8	13	0	6.84
Ryan Bukvich	R	26	0	0	---	0	3	0	0	4	4	1	4	0	3.68
Jorge Vasquez	R	25	0	0	---	0	2	0	0	3	4	1	4	0	8.10
1 Rudy Seanez	R	35	0	1	.000	0	23	0	0	25	21	13	23	0	3.91
2 Matt Kinney	R	27	0	4	.000	0	11	0	0	16	27	7	21	0	7.16
Kevin Appier (EJ)	R	36	0	1	.000	0	3	3	0	8	6	7	3	0	4.98
Eduardo Villacis	R	24	0	1	.000	0	2	2	0	8	8	4	5	0	13.50
Curtis Leskanic	R	36	0	0	---	0	13	0	0	16	23	16	9	0	8.04
1 Denny Bautista	R	23	0	3	.000	0	5	5	0	28	38	11	18	0	6.51

Miguel Asencio (EJ) 23, Runelvys Hernandez (EJ) 26, Kyle Snyder (SJ) 26

ANAHEIM 1st 92-70 .568 — MIKE SCIOSCIA

Name	G by Pos	B	AGE	G	AB	R	H	2B	3B	HR	RBI	BB	SO	SB	BA	SA
TOTALS			29	162	5675	836	1603	272	37	162	783	450	942	143	.282	.429
Darin Erstad (LJ)	1B124	L	30	125	495	79	146	29	1	7	69	37	74	16	.295	.400
Adam Kennedy	2B144	L	28	144	468	70	130	20	5	10	48	41	92	15	.278	.406
David Eckstein	SS138 DH1	R	29	142	566	92	156	24	1	2	35	42	49	16	.276	.332
Troy Glaus (SJ)	DH39 3B19	R	27	58	207	47	52	11	1	18	42	31	52	2	.251	.575
Vladimir Guerrero	OF143 DH13	R	28	156	612	124	206	39	2	39	126	52	74	15	.337	.598
Garret Anderson (XJ)	OF94 DH18	L	32	112	442	57	133	20	1	14	75	29	75	2	.301	.446
Jose Guillen	OF136 DH10	R	28	148	565	88	166	28	3	27	104	37	92	5	.294	.497
Bengie Molina	C89 DH5	R	29	97	337	36	93	13	0	10	54	18	35	0	.276	.404
Tim Salmon (KJ-SJ)	DH39 OF8	R	35	60	186	15	47	7	0	2	23	14	41	1	.253	.323
Chone Figgins	3B92 OF57 2B20 SS13 DH1	B	26	148	577	83	171	22	17	5	60	49	94	34	.296	.419
Jeff DaVanon	OF81 DH19	B	30	108	285	41	79	11	4	7	34	46	54	18	.277	.418
Jose Molina	C70 1B2	R	29	73	203	26	53	10	2	3	25	10	52	4	.261	.374
Alfredo Amezaga	SS32 3B26 2B16	B	26	73	93	12	15	2	0	2	11	3	24	3	.161	.247
Robb Quinlan (VJ)	3B32 1B13 OF9 DH4	R	27	56	160	23	55	14	0	5	23	14	26	3	.344	.525
Shane Halter	3B33 2B6 1B4 SS3 DH3	R	34	46	114	10	23	5	0	4	13	7	30	1	.202	.351
Josh Paul	C37 OF4 DH2	R	29	46	70	11	17	3	0	2	10	7	17	2	.243	.371
Casey Kotchman	1B34 DH2	L	21	38	116	7	26	6	0	0	15	7	11	3	.224	.276
Curtis Pride	OF24 DH2	L	35	35	40	5	10	3	0	0	3	3	11	1	.250	.325
Dallas McPherson	3B14	L	23	16	40	5	9	1	0	3	6	3	17	1	.225	.475
Adam Riggs	OF8 DH4 1B1 2B1	R	31	16	36	2	7	3	0	0	3	1	10	1	.194	.278
2 Raul Mondesi (LJ)	OF7 DH1	R	33	8	34	2	4	1	0	1	1	2	4	0	.118	.235
Andres Galarraga	DH4 1B1	R	43	7	10	1	3	0	0	1	3	0	3	0	.300	.600

NAME	T	AGE	W	L	PCT	SV	G	GS	CG	IP	H	BB	SO	SHO	ERA
		29	92	70	.568	50	162	162	2	1454	1476	502	1164	11	4.28
Bartolo Colon	R	31	18	12	.600	0	34	34	0	208	215	71	158	0	5.01
John Lackey	R	25	14	13	.519	0	33	32	1	198	215	60	144	1	4.67
Jarrod Washburn (VJ)	L	29	11	8	.579	0	25	25	1	149	159	40	86	1	4.64
Kelvim Escobar	R	28	11	12	.478	0	33	33	0	208	192	76	191	0	3.93
Aaron Sele	R	34	9	4	.692	0	28	24	0	132	163	51	51	0	5.05
Scot Shields	R	28	8	2	.800	0	60	0	0	105	97	40	109	0	3.33
Kevin Gregg	R	26	5	2	.714	1	55	0	0	88	86	28	84	0	4.21
Brendan Donnelly (BZ)	R	32	5	2	.714	0	40	0	0	42	34	15	56	0	3.00
Ramon Ortiz	R	31	5	7	.417	0	34	14	0	128	139	38	82	0	4.43
Francisco Rodriguez	R	22	4	1	.800	12	69	0	0	84	51	33	123	0	1.82
Troy Percival	R	34	2	3	.400	33	52	0	0	50	43	19	33	0	2.90
Derrick Turnbow	R	26	0	0	—	0	4	0	0	6	2	5	3	0	0.00
Scott Dunn	R	26	0	0	—	0	3	0	0	3	7	1	2	0	9.00
Dusty Bergman	L	26	0	0	—	0	1	0	0	3	2	0	3	0	13.50
Ben Weber	R	34	0	2	.000	0	18	0	0	22	37	15	11	0	8.06
Matt Hensley	R	25	0	2	.000	0	16	0	0	28	32	7	30	0	4.88
Greg Jones (SJ) 27															

OAKLAND 2nd 91-71 .562 1 — KEN MACHA

Name	G by Pos	B	AGE	G	AB	R	H	2B	3B	HR	RBI	BB	SO	SB	BA	SA
TOTALS			30	162	5728	793	1545	336	15	189	752	608	1061	47	.270	.433
Scott Hatteberg	1B148 DH2	L	34	152	550	87	156	30	0	15	82	72	48	0	.284	.420
Marco Scutaro	2B123 SS16 3B1	R	28	137	455	50	124	32	1	7	43	16	58	0	.273	.393
Bobby Crosby	SS151	R	24	151	545	70	130	34	1	22	64	58	141	7	.239	.426
Eric Chavez (BH)	3B125 OF1	L	26	125	475	87	131	20	0	29	77	95	99	6	.276	.501
Jermaine Dye	OF134 DH7	R	30	137	532	87	141	29	4	23	80	49	128	4	.265	.464
Mark Kotsay	OF141 DH1	R	28	148	606	78	190	37	3	15	63	55	70	8	.314	.459
Eric Byrnes	OF143 DH1	R	28	143	569	91	161	39	3	20	73	46	111	17	.283	.467
Damian Miller	C109	R	34	110	397	39	108	25	0	9	58	39	87	0	.272	.403
Erubiel Durazo	DH132 1B4	L	30	142	511	80	164	35	1	22	88	56	104	3	.321	.523
Bobby Kielty	OF67 DH11	B	27	83	238	29	51	14	1	7	31	35	47	1	.214	.370
Mark McLemore (KJ)	2B47 3B27 OF1	B	39	77	250	29	62	14	0	2	21	41	33	0	.248	.328
Adam Melhuse	C64 3B3 1B1	B	32	69	214	23	55	11	0	11	31	16	47	0	.257	.463
Billy McMillon (XJ)	OF21 DH6 1B3	L	32	52	92	10	17	4	0	3	11	8	22	0	.185	.326
Eric Karros	1B22 DH10	R	36	40	103	8	20	6	0	2	11	7	16	1	.194	.311
Esteban German (UJ)	3B15 2B10 DH2	R	26	31	60	9	15	1	1	0	7	4	13	0	.250	.300
Nick Swisher	OF16 1B3 DH2	B	24	20	60	11	15	4	0	2	8	8	11	0	.250	.417
1 Frank Menechino	2B12	R	33	13	33	0	3	0	0	0	1	1	8	0	.091	.091
Ramon Castro	3B6 SS1 DH1	B	24	9	15	2	2	1	0	0	1	1	3	1	.133	.200
Mike Rose	C2	B	27	3	2	1	0	0	0	0	0	0	0	0	.000	.000
Mark Ellis (SJ) 27																

NAME	T	AGE	W	L	PCT	SV	G	GS	CG	IP	H	BB	SO	SHO	ERA
		30	91	71	.562	35	162	162	10	1471	1466	544	1034	8	4.17
Mark Mulder	L	26	17	8	.680	0	33	33	5	226	223	83	140	1	4.43
Tim Hudson (UJ)	R	28	12	6	.667	0	27	27	3	189	194	44	103	2	3.53
Rich Harden	R	22	11	7	.611	0	31	31	0	190	171	81	167	0	3.99
Barry Zito	L	26	11	11	.500	0	34	34	0	213	216	81	163	0	4.48
Mark Redman	L	30	11	12	.478	0	32	32	2	191	218	68	102	0	4.71
Justin Duchscherer	R	26	7	6	.538	0	53	0	0	96	85	32	59	0	3.27
2 Octavio Dotel	R	30	6	2	.750	22	45	0	0	51	41	18	72	0	4.09
Chad Bradford	R	29	5	7	.417	1	68	0	0	59	51	24	34	0	4.42
Chris Hammond (SJ)	L	38	4	1	.800	1	41	0	0	54	56	13	34	0	2.68
Arthur Rhodes (XJ)	L	34	3	3	.500	9	37	0	0	39	46	21	34	0	5.12
Kirk Saarloos (EJ)	R	25	2	1	.667	0	6	5	0	24	27	12	10	0	4.44
Ricardo Rincon	L	34	1	1	.500	0	67	0	0	44	45	22	40	0	3.68
Justin Lehr	R	26	1	1	.500	0	27	0	0	33	35	14	16	0	5.23
Jairo Garcia	R	20	0	0	—	0	3	0	0	6	5	6	5	0	12.71
Joe Blanton	R	23	0	0	—	0	3	0	0	3	3	1	2	0	5.63
1 Chad Harville	R	28	0	0	—	0	3	0	0	3	3	0	1	0	3.37
Jim Mecir	R	34	0	5	.000	2	65	0	0	48	45	19	49	0	3.59

TEXAS 3rd 89-79 .549 3 — BUCK SHOWALTER

Name	G by Pos	B	AGE	G	AB	R	H	2B	3B	HR	RBI	BB	SO	SB	BA	SA
TOTALS			28	162	5615	860	1492	323	34	227	825	500	1099	69	.266	.457
Mark Teixeira	1B142 OF7 DH2	B	24	145	545	101	153	34	2	38	112	68	117	4	.281	.560
Alfonso Soriano	2B142 DH3	R	28	145	608	77	170	32	4	28	91	33	121	18	.280	.484
Michael Young	SS158 DH2	R	27	160	690	114	216	33	9	22	99	44	99	12	.313	.483
Hank Blalock	3B159	L	23	159	624	107	172	38	3	32	110	75	149	2	.276	.500
Kevin Mench	OF109 DH14	R	26	125	438	69	122	30	3	26	71	33	63	0	.279	.539
Laynce Nix	OF114	L	23	115	371	58	92	20	4	14	46	23	113	1	.248	.437
Dave Dellucci	OF94 DH9	L	30	107	331	59	80	13	1	17	61	47	88	9	.242	.441
Rod Barajas	C105 1B2	R	28	108	358	50	89	26	1	15	58	13	63	0	.249	.453
Brad Fullmer (KJ)	DH66 1B4	L	29	76	258	41	60	19	1	11	33	27	30	1	.233	.442
Eric Young	OF53 DH23 2B20 SS8 3B1	R	37	104	344	55	99	25	2	7	27	43	28	14	.288	.381
Gary Matthews	OF85	B	29	87	280	37	77	17	1	11	36	33	64	5	.275	.461
Brian Jordan (KJ)	OF44 DH17	R	37	61	212	27	47	13	1	5	23	16	35	2	.222	.363
Gerald Laird (RJ)	C49	R	24	49	147	20	33	6	0	1	16	12	35	0	.224	.286
Herbert Perry	DH21 1B15 3B6	R	34	49	134	13	30	2	1	5	17	14	19	0	.224	.366
Jason Conti	OF21	L	29	22	55	6	10	3	0	0	4	5	19	0	.182	.236
Manny Alexander	2B11 SS7 3B3	R	33	21	21	3	5	2	0	0	3	1	7	0	.238	.333
Chad Allen	OF13 DH5	R	29	20	58	4	14	4	1	0	6	2	13	0	.241	.345
Adrian Gonzalez	1B11 DH1	L	22	16	42	7	10	3	0	1	7	2	6	0	.238	.381
1 Ken Huckaby	C16	R	33	16	38	3	5	2	0	0	0	5	12	0	.132	.184
2 Andy Fox	2B3 3B2 OF2 DH1	L	33	13	12	2	1	0	0	0	1	3	0	0	.083	.083
Ramon Nivar	OF6	R	24	7	18	3	4	1	0	0	4	0	7	1	.222	.222
Danny Ardoin	C6	R	29	6	8	1	1	0	0	0	0	1	5	0	.125	.125
Rusty Greer (SJ) 35																

NAME	T	AGE	W	L	PCT	SV	G	GS	CG	IP	H	BB	SO	SHO	ERA
		31	89	73	.549	52	162	162	2	1440	1536	547	979	3	4.53
Kenny Rogers	L	39	18	9	.667	0	35	35	2	212	248	66	126	1	4.76
Ryan Drese	R	28	14	10	.583	0	34	33	2	208	233	58	98	0	4.20
Carlos Almanzar	R	30	3	1	.700	0	67	0	0	73	66	19	44	0	3.72
R.A. Dickey	R	29	6	7	.462	1	25	15	0	104	136	33	57	0	5.61
Frank Francisco	R	24	1	0	.833	0	45	0	0	51	36	28	60	0	3.33
Erasmo Ramirez	L	28	5	3	.625	0	34	0	0	36	34	7	21	0	4.29
Doug Brocail	R	37	4	1	.800	1	43	0	0	52	54	20	43	0	4.13
Chan Ho Park (XJ)	R	31	4	7	.364	0	16	16	0	96	105	33	63	0	5.46
Ron Mahay	L	33	3	0	1.000	0	60	0	0	67	60	29	54	0	2.55
Ricardo Rodriguez (BE)	R	26	3	1	.750	0	5	4	1	27	28	12	15	1	2.02
Chris Young	R	25	3	2	.600	0	7	7	0	36	36	10	27	0	4.71
Francisco Cordero	R	29	2	3	.429	49	67	0	0	72	60	32	79	0	2.13
Joaquin Benoit	R	26	3	5	.375	0	28	15	0	103	113	31	95	0	5.68
Brian Shouse (SJ)	L	35	2	0	1.000	0	53	0	0	44	36	18	34	0	2.23
John Wasdin	R	31	2	4	.333	0	15	10	0	65	83	23	36	0	6.78
Jay Powell (EJ)	R	32	1	1	.500	0	23	0	0	24	24	11	17	0	3.38
Nick Bierbrodt	L	26	1	1	.500	0	4	3	0	16	16	11	6	0	5.82
Mike Bacsik	L	26	1	1	.500	0	3	0	0	16	16	1	4	0	4.60
Colby Lewis (SJ)	R	24	1	1	.500	0	3	3	0	15	13	13	11	0	4.11
Jeff Nelson (KJ-AJ)	R	37	1	2	.333	1	29	0	0	24	17	19	22	0	5.32
Juan Dominguez (ZJ)	R	24	1	2	.333	0	4	4	0	23	25	5	14	0	3.91
2 Scott Erickson	R	36	1	3	.250	0	4	4	0	19	23	16	6	0	6.16
2 Michael Tejera	L	27	0	0	—	0	4	0	0	5	4	3	7	0	10.13
Rosman Garcia	R	25	0	0	—	0	9	0	0	9	5	5	5	0	5.40
Travis Hughes	R	26	0	0	—	0	2	0	0	2	1	6	3	0	13.50
Kameron Loe	R	22	0	0	—	0	2	0	0	4	6	3	0	0	5.40
Sam Narron	L	23	0	0	—	0	1	0	0	2	5	1	3	0	13.50
Ryan Snare	L	25	0	0	—	0	1	0	0	1	5	2	0	0	10.80
Mickey Callaway (EJ-SJ)	R	29	0	1	.000	0	4	1	0	11	18	7	9	0	7.94
Nick Regilio	R	26	0	1	.000	0	6	4	0	19	20	15	12	0	6.05
Jeff Zimmerman (EJ) 31																

SEATTLE 4th 63-99 .389 29 — BOB MELVIN

Name	G by Pos	B	AGE	G	AB	R	H	2B	3B	HR	RBI	BB	SO	SB	BA	SA
TOTALS			32	162	5722	698	1544	276	20	136	658	492	1058	110	.270	.396
1 John Olerud	1B77	L	35	78	261	29	64	13	1	5	22	40	41	0	.245	.360
Bret Boone	2B148	R	35	148	593	74	149	30	0	24	83	56	135	10	.251	.423
1 Rich Aurilia	SS73	R	32	73	261	27	63	13	0	4	28	22	43	1	.241	.337
Scott Spiezio	3B66 1B42 DH2	B	31	112	367	38	79	12	3	10	41	36	60	4	.215	.346
Ichiro Suzuki	OF158 DH3	L	30	161	704	101	262	24	5	8	60	49	63	36	.372	.455
Randy Winn	OF154 DH2	B	30	157	626	84	179	34	6	14	81	53	98	21	.286	.427
Raul Ibanez (LJ)	OF112 1B10 DH2	L	32	123	481	67	146	31	1	16	62	36	72	1	.304	.472
Dan Wilson	C103	R	35	103	319	23	80	13	0	2	33	26	57	0	.251	.310
Edgar Martinez	DH122 3B1	R	41	141	486	45	128	23	0	12	63	58	107	1	.263	.385
Jolbert Cabrera	3B36 1B23 OF23 2B18 SS14 DH5	R	31	113	359	38	97	19	2	6	47	16	70	10	.270	.384
Willie Bloomquist	3B31 SS20 1B19 OF9 DH6 2B1	R	26	93	188	27	46	10	0	2	18	10	48	13	.245	.330
Jose Lopez	SS57 3B1	R	20	57	207	28	48	13	0	5	22	8	31	0	.232	.367
1 Dave Hansen	DH8 1B7 3B6	L	35	57	78	14	22	5	0	2	12	18	16	0	.282	.423
2 Miguel Olivo	C49	R	25	50	160	25	32	8	2	6	14	10	55	2	.200	.388
Hiram Bocachica	OF44 DH3	R	28	50	90	9	22	5	0	3	6	12	27	5	.244	.400
Bucky Jacobson	1B21 DH20	R	28	42	160	17	44	9	0	9	28	14	47	0	.275	.500
Justin Leone (BH)	3B28 SS2 DH1	R	26	31	102	15	22	5	0	6	13	9	32	1	.216	.441
1 Pat Borders	C19	R	41	19	53	6	10	2	0	1	5	1	12	0	.189	.283
Ramon Santiago	SS16 DH2	B	24	19	39	8	7	1	0	2	4	3	9	0	.179	.205
1 Quinton McCracken	OF8 DH6	B	34	18	20	6	3	0	0	0	5	7	1	3	.150	.150
Jeremy Reed	OF16	L	23	18	58	11	23	4	0	0	5	7	4	3	.397	.517
Greg Dobbs	3B14 DH1	L	25	18	53	4	12	3	0	0	3	2	4	0	.226	.302
1 Ben Davis	C14	B	27	14	33	1	3	0	0	0	1	5	8	0	.091	.091
Mickey Lopez	2B3 DH3	R	30	6	4	1	1	0	0	0	2	0	0	0	.250	.250
Rene Rivera	C2	R	20	4	7	0	0	0	0	0	0	0	1	0	.000	.000
Chris Snelling (WJ) 22																

NAME	T	AGE	W	L	PCT	SV	G	GS	CG	IP	H	BB	SO	SHO	ERA
		30	63	99	.389	28	162	162	7	1459	1498	575	1036	7	4.76
Ron Villone	L	34	8	6	.571	0	56	10	0	117	102	64	86	0	4.08
Gil Meche	R	25	7	7	.500	0	23	23	1	128	139	47	99	1	5.01
Jamie Moyer	L	41	7	13	.350	0	34	33	1	202	217	63	125	0	5.21
Bobby Madritsch	L	28	6	3	.667	0	15	11	1	88	74	33	60	0	3.27
Joel Pineiro (EJ)	R	25	6	11	.353	0	21	21	1	141	144	43	111	0	4.67
1 Mike Myers	L	35	4	1	.800	0	68	0	0	29	29	17	23	0	4.88
Shigetoshi Hasegawa	R	35	5	5	.500	8	60	0	0	68	67	31	46	0	5.16
1 Freddy Garcia	R	29	4	7	.364	0	15	15	1	107	96	32	82	0	3.20
Ryan Franklin	R	31	4	16	.200	0	32	32	2	200	224	61	104	1	4.90
George Sherrill	L	27	2	1	.667	0	21	0	0	24	24	9	16	0	3.80
Eddie Guardado (SJ)	L	33	2	2	.500	18	41	0	0	45	31	14	45	0	2.78
Scott Atchison	R	28	2	3	.400	0	25	0	0	31	29	14	18	0	3.52
Cha-Seung Baek	R	24	2	4	.333	0	7	5	0	31	35	11	20	0	5.52
1 Kevin Jarvis	R	34	1	1	1.000	0	7	0	0	9	18	3	8	0	8.31
Julio Mateo (EJ)	R	26	1	1	.333	1	45	0	0	58	56	16	43	0	4.68
Matt Thornton	L	27	1	1	.333	0	19	1	0	34	33	29	32	0	4.13
Travis Blackley	L	21	1	3	.250	0	6	6	0	26	35	22	16	0	10.04
Clint Nageotte (XJ)	R	23	1	6	.143	0	7	6	0	30	35	23	27	0	7.36
2 Masao Kida	R	35	0	0	—	0	10	0	0	15	15	5	6	0	8.38
Randy Williams	L	28	0	0	—	0	5	0	0	6	9	4	4	0	5.79
Aaron Taylor (SJ)	R	26	0	0	—	0	4	0	0	4	6	2	4	0	9.82
J.J. Putz	R	27	0	3	.000	9	54	0	0	63	66	24	47	0	4.71
Rafael Soriano (EJ)	R	24	0	0	—	0	6	0	0	3	6	1	5	0	13.50

		LINE SCORES																
Team	1	2	3	4	5	6	7	8	9	10	11	12	13	14	R	H	E

COMPOSITE BATTING

NAME	POS	G	AB	R	H	2B	3B	HR	RBI	BA

COMPOSITE PITCHING

NAME	G	IP	H	BB	SO	W	L	SV	ERA

DIVISION SERIES

DIVISION SERIES: BOSTON 3 : ANAHEIM 0

Game 1   October 5 at Anaheim

```
BOS   1 0 0 7 0 0 0 1 0            9 11 1
ANA   0 0 0 1 0 0 2 0 0            3  9 1
```
Schilling, Embree (7), Timlin (8)   Washburn, Shields (4), Gregg (6), Ortiz (8)

Game 2   October 6 at Anaheim

```
BOS   0 1 0 0 0 2 1 0 4            8 12 0
ANA   0 1 0 0 2 0 0 0 0            3  7 0
```
Martinez, Timlin (8), Myers (8), Foulke (8)   Colon, Rodriguez (7), Donnelly (9)

Game 3   October 8 at Boston

```
ANA   0 0 0 1 0 0 5 0 0 0         6  8 2
BOS   0 0 2 3 1 0 0 0 2           8 12 0
```
Escobar, Shields (4), Donnelly (5), Rodriguez (8), Washburn (10)   Arroyo, Myers (7), Timlin (8), Embree (8), Foulke (8), Lowe (10)

BOSTON

			TOTALS	3	116	25	35	6	0	4	23	.302
Damon	CF	3	15	4	7	1	0	0	4	.467
Ramirez	LF	3	13	3	5	2	0	1	7	.385
Cabrera	SS	3	13	1	2	1	0	0	3	.154
Mueller	3B	3	12	3	4	0	0	0	0	.333
Varitek	C	3	12	3	2	0	0	1	2	.167
Ortiz	DH	3	11	4	6	2	0	1	4	.545
Bellhorn	2B	3	11	2	1	0	0	0	0	.091
Millar	1B	3	10	2	3	0	0	1	4	.300
Nixon	RF	2	8	0	2	0	0	0	0	.250
Kapler	RF	3	5	2	1	0	0	0	0	.200
Mientkiewicz	1B	3	4	0	2	0	0	0	1	.500
Youkilis	3B	1	2	0	0	0	0	0	0	.000
Reese	2B	3	0	1	0	0	0	0	0	—
Roberts	PR	1	0	0	0	0	0	0	0	—

ANAHEIM

			TOTALS	3	106	12	24	3	0	4	12	.226
Figgins	3B-2B	3	14	0	2	0	0	0	0	.143
Anderson	CF	3	13	1	2	0	0	0	0	.154
Eckstein	SS	3	12	2	4	0	0	0	0	.333
Guerrero	RF	3	12	1	2	0	0	1	6	.167
Glaus	DH	3	11	3	4	2	0	2	3	.364
Erstad	1B	3	10	2	5	1	0	1	2	.500
DaVanon	LF	3	10	1	2	0	0	0	0	.200
McPherson	3B	3	9	0	1	0	0	0	1	.111
B. Molina	C	3	6	0	1	0	0	0	0	.167
J. Molina	C	2	3	2	1	0	0	0	0	.333
Amezaga	2B	2	2	0	0	0	0	0	0	.000
Pride	PH	2	2	0	0	0	0	0	0	.000
Kotchman	PH	2	1	0	0	0	0	0	0	.000
Riggs	LF	2	1	0	0	0	0	0	0	.000

BOSTON

	TOTALS	3	28	24	11	28	3	0	1	3.54
Martinez	1	7	6	2	6	1	0	0	3.86
Schilling	1	6.2	9	2	4	1	0	0	2.70
Arroyo	1	6	3	2	7	0	0	0	3.00
Timlin	3	3	3	1	1	0	0	0	9.00
Foulke	2	3	2	1	5	0	0	1	0.00
Embree	2	1	1	0	0	0	0	0	0.00
Lowe	1	1	1	1	1	0	0	0	0.00
Myers	2	0.1	1	1	1	0	0	0	27.00

ANAHEIM

	TOTALS	3	27.2	35	20	23	0	3	0	5.86
Colon	1	6	7	3	3	0	0	0	4.50
Rodriguez	2	4.2	4	3	5	0	2	0	3.86
Donnelly	2	3.1	3	2	5	0	0	0	10.80
Washburn	2	3.1	6	3	3	0	1	0	10.80
Escobar	1	3.1	5	4	0	0	0	0	8.10
Shields	2	3	5	2	3	0	0	0	6.00
Gregg	1	2	3	1	0	0	0	0	0.00
Ortiz	1	2	2	1	0	0	0	0	4.50

DIVISION SERIES: NEW YORK 3 : MINNESOTA 1

Game 1   October 5 at New York

```
MIN   0 0 1 0 0 1 0 0 0            2 7 0
NYA   0 0 0 0 0 0 0 0 0            0 9 0
```
Santana, Rincon (8), Nathan (9)   Mussina, Gordon (8), Rivera (9)

Game 2   October 6 at New York

```
MIN   1 2 0 0 0 0 0 2 0 0          6 12 0
NYA   1 0 2 0 1 0 1 0 0 0          7  9 0
```
Radke, Balfour (7), Rincon (8), Nathan (10), Romero (12)   Lieber, Gordon (7), Rivera (8), Sturtze (10), Quantrill (12)

Game 3   October 8 at Minnesota

```
NYA   0 3 0 0 0 4 1 0 0            8 14 1
MIN   1 0 0 0 0 0 0 0 3            4 12 1
```
Brown, Quantrill (7), Heredia (8), Sturtze (9), Rivera (9)   Silva, Romero (6), Crain (6), Mulholland (7)

Game 4   October 9 at Minnesota

```
NYA   0 0 1 0 0 0 0 4 0 0          6 11 0
MIN   1 0 0 1 3 0 0 0 0 0          5 12 1
```
Vazquez, Loaiza (6), Gordon (8), Rivera (10)   Santana, Balfour (6), Rincon (8), Nathan (8), Lohse (10)

NEW YORK

			TOTALS	4	154	21	43	10	0	6	20	.279
Rodriguez	3B	4	19	3	8	3	0	1	3	.421
Jeter	SS	4	19	3	6	1	0	1	4	.316
Williams	CF	4	18	2	5	1	0	1	3	.278
Posada	C	4	18	2	4	0	0	0	2	.222
Sheffield	RF	4	18	2	4	1	0	1	2	.222
Matsui	LF	4	17	3	7	1	0	1	3	.412
Cairo	2B	4	14	3	3	1	0	0	1	.214
Olerud	1B	4	14	2	3	2	0	0	0	.214
Sierra	DH	3	12	1	2	0	0	1	3	.167
Lofton	DH	1	4	0	1	0	0	0	0	.250
Clark	1B	1	1	0	0	0	0	0	0	.000
Crosby	RF	2	0	0	0	0	0	0	0	—

MINNESOTA

			TOTALS	4	152	17	43	7	0	4	17	.283
Jones	RF	4	20	3	6	1	0	2	2	.300
Stewart	LF-DH	4	20	1	4	0	0	0	2	.200
Hunter	CF	4	17	5	6	1	0	1	2	.353
Morneau	1B	4	17	1	4	2	0	0	2	.235
Cuddyer	2B-1B	4	15	1	7	0	0	0	2	.467
Guzman	SS	4	15	2	5	0	0	0	0	.333
Koskie	3B	4	13	2	4	1	0	0	2	.308
Ford	LF-DH	3	11	3	3	1	0	0	2	.273
Blanco	C	4	8	1	2	0	0	1	2	.250
Kubel	DH	3	7	0	1	1	0	0	0	.143
LeCroy	1B-C	3	3	0	1	0	0	0	0	.333
Offerman	PH	3	3	0	0	0	0	0	1	.000
Borders	C	2	2	0	0	0	0	0	0	.000
Rivas	2B	3	1	0	0	0	0	0	0	.000

NEW YORK

	TOTALS	4	41	43	7	28	3	1	0	3.73
Mussina	1	7	7	1	7	0	1	0	2.57
Lieber	1	6.2	7	1	4	0	0	0	4.05
Brown	1	6	8	0	1	1	0	0	1.50
Rivera	4	5.2	2	0	2	1	0	0	0.00
Vazquez	1	5	7	2	6	0	0	0	9.00
Gordon	3	3.2	5	3	0	0	0	0	4.91
Sturtze	2	2.2	4	3	4	0	0	0	6.75
Quantrill	2	2	2	0	1	1	0	0	0.00
Loaiza	1	2	4	0	0	0	0	0	0.00
Heredia	1	0.1	0	0	0	0	0	0	54.00

MINNESOTA

	TOTALS	4	40.2	43	15	30	1	3	1	4.65
Santana	2	12	14	4	12	1	0	0	0.75
Radke	1	6.1	8	3	0	0	0	0	7.11
Nathan	3	5	2	5	6	0	1	1	3.60
Silva	1	5	10	0	4	0	1	0	10.80
Rincon	3	3.1	4	2	5	0	0	0	10.80
Mulholland	1	3	3	0	1	0	0	0	3.00
Balfour	2	2.2	0	2	2	0	0	0	0.00
Lohse	1	2	1	0	3	0	0	0	4.50
Romero	2	1	0	1	1	0	0	0	9.00
Crain	1	0.1	1	0	0	0	0	0	0.00

AMERICAN LEAGUE CHAMPIONSHIP

CHAMPIONSHIP: BOSTON 4 : NEW YORK 3

Game 1   October 12 at New York

```
BOS   0 0 0 0 0 0 5 2 0            7 10 1
NYA   2 0 4 0 0 2 0 2 x           10 14 0
```
Schilling, Leskanic (4), Mendoza (5), Wakefield (6), Embree (7), Timlin (8), Foulke (8)   Mussina, Sturtze (7), Gordon (8), Rivera (8)

Game 2   October 13 at New York

```
BOS   0 0 0 0 0 0 0 1 0            1 5 0
NYA   1 0 0 0 0 2 0 0 x            3 7 0
```
Martinez, Timlin (7), Embree (7), Foulke (8)   Lieber, Gordon (8), Rivera (8)

Game 3   October 16 at Boston

```
NYA   3 0 3 5 2 0 4 0 2          19 22 1
BOS   0 4 2 0 0 0 2 0 0           8 15 0
```
Brown, Vazquez (3), Quantrill (7), Gordon (9)   Arroyo, Mendoza (3), Leskanic (4), Wakefield (4), Embree (7), Myers (8)

Game 4   October 17 at Boston

```
NYA   0 0 2 0 0 2 0 0 0 0          4 12 1
BOS   0 0 0 0 3 0 0 1 0 2          6  8 0
```
Hernandez, Sturtze (6), Rivera (8), Gordon (10), Quantrill (12)Myers (11), Leskanic (11)   Lowe, Timlin (6), Foulke (7), Embree (10)

Game 5   October 18 at Boston

```
NYA   0 1 0 0 0 3 0 0 0 0 0 0 0 0   4 12 1
BOS   2 0 0 0 0 0 0 1 0 0 0 0 5 1 3  13 11 ?
```
Mussina, Sturtze (7), Gordon (7), Rivera (8), Heredia (10), Quantrill (10), Loaiza (11)   Martinez, Timlin (6), Foulke (8), Arroyo (10), Myers (11), Embree (11), Wakefield (12)

Game 6   October 19 at New York

```
BOS   0 0 0 4 0 0 0 0 0            4 11 0
NYA   0 0 0 0 0 0 0 1 1 0          2  6 0
```
Schilling, Arroyo (8), Foulke (9)   Lieber, Heredia (8), Quantrill (8), Sturtze (9)

Game 7   October 20 at New York

```
BOS   2 4 0 2 0 0 0 1 1           10 13 0
NYA   0 0 1 0 0 0 2 0 0            3  5 1
```
Lowe, Martinez (7), Timlin (8), Embree (9)   Brown, Vazquez (2), Loaiza (4), Heredia (7), Gordon (8), Rivera (9)

BOSTON

			TOTALS	7	271	41	75	12	1	10	40	.277
Damon	CF	7	35	6	6	0	1	2	7	.171
Ortiz	DH	7	31	6	12	0	0	3	11	.387
Ramirez	LF	7	30	3	9	1	0	0	5	.300
Mueller	3B	7	30	4	8	1	0	0	1	.267
Cabrera	SS	7	29	5	11	2	0	0	5	.379
Nixon	RF	7	29	4	6	1	0	1	3	.207
Varitek	C	7	28	5	9	1	0	2	7	.321
Bellhorn	2B	7	26	3	5	2	0	2	4	.192
Millar	1B	7	24	4	6	3	0	0	2	.250
Mientkiewicz	1B	4	4	0	2	1	0	0	0	.500
Kapler	RF	2	3	0	1	0	0	0	0	.333
Reese	2B	3	1	0	0	0	0	0	0	.000
Mirabelli	C	1	1	0	0	0	0	0	0	.000
Roberts	PR	2	0	0	0	0	0	0	0	—

NEW YORK

			TOTALS	7	277	45	78	21	2	9	44	.282
Williams	CF	7	36	4	11	3	0	2	10	.306
Matsui	LF	7	34	9	14	6	1	2	10	.412
Rodriguez	3B	7	31	8	8	2	0	2	5	.258
Sheffield	RF	7	30	7	10	3	0	1	5	.333
Jeter	SS	7	30	5	6	1	0	0	5	.200
Posada	C	7	27	4	7	1	0	0	2	.259
Cairo	2B	7	25	4	7	3	0	0	0	.280
Sierra	DH	5	21	1	7	1	1	0	2	.333
Clark	1B	5	21	0	3	1	0	0	1	.143
Olerud	1B	4	12	1	2	0	0	0	0	.167
Lofton	DH	3	10	1	3	0	0	1	2	.300
Crosby	RF	1	0	1	0	0	0	0	0	—

BOSTON

	TOTALS	7	69	78	33	51	4	3	1	5.87
Martinez	3	13	14	9	14	0	1	0	6.23
Lowe	2	11.1	7	4	6	1	0	0	3.18
Schilling	2	10	12	5	1	1	0	0	6.30
Wakefield	3	7.1	9	3	6	1	0	0	8.59
Foulke	5	6	1	6	6	0	0	1	0.00
Timlin	5	5.2	10	5	2	0	0	0	4.76
Embree	6	4.2	9	1	2	0	0	0	3.86
Arroyo	3	4	8	3	3	0	0	0	15.75
Leskanic	3	2.2	3	3	2	1	0	0	10.12
Myers	3	2.1	5	1	4	0	0	0	7.71
Mendoza	2	2	2	1	0	0	1	0	4.50

NEW YORK

	TOTALS	7	69.2	75	28	53	3	4	2	5.17
Lieber	2	14.1	12	1	5	1	1	0	3.14
Mussina	2	12.2	10	2	15	1	0	0	4.26
Rivera	5	7	6	2	6	0	0	2	1.29
Gordon	6	6.2	10	2	8	0	1	0	8.10
Loaiza	2	6.1	5	3	5	0	1	0	1.42
Vazquez	2	6.1	9	7	4	1	0	0	9.95
Hernandez	1	5	3	5	6	0	0	0	5.40
Sturtze	4	3.1	2	2	2	0	0	0	2.70
Quantrill	3	3.1	8	0	2	0	1	0	5.40
Brown	2	3.1	9	4	2	0	1	0	21.60
Heredia	3	1.1	1	0	1	0	0	0	0.00

ATLANTA — 1st 96-66 .593 — BOBBY COX

Name	G by Pos	B	AGE	G	AB	R	H	2B	3B	HR	RBI	BB	SO	SB	BA	SA
TOTALS			29	162	5570	803	1503	304	37	178	767	587	1158	86	.270	.434
Adam LaRoche (SJ)	1B98	L	24	110	324	45	90	27	1	13	45	27	78	0	.278	.488
Marcus Giles (BC)	2B97	R	26	102	379	61	118	22	2	8	48	36	70	17	.311	.443
Rafael Furcal	SS131 2B1	B	26	143	563	103	157	24	5	14	59	58	71	29	.279	.414
Chipper Jones	3B96 OF29	B	32	137	472	69	117	20	1	30	96	84	96	2	.248	.485
J.D. Drew	OF142	L	28	145	518	118	158	28	8	31	93	118	116	12	.305	.569
Andruw Jones	OF154	R	27	154	570	85	149	34	4	29	91	71	147	6	.261	.488
Eli Marrero (IL)	OF73	R	30	90	250	37	80	18	1	10	40	23	50	4	.320	.520
Johnny Estrada	C133	B	28	134	462	56	145	36	0	9	76	39	66	0	.314	.450
Julio Franco	1B84	R	45	125	320	37	99	18	3	6	57	36	68	4	.309	.441
Mark DeRosa	3B72 SS11 2B5 OF3	R	29	118	309	33	74	16	0	3	31	23	53	1	.239	.320
Nick Green	2B75 3B5 OF1	R	25	95	264	40	72	15	3	3	26	12	63	1	.273	.386
Charles Thomas	OF71	L	25	83	236	35	68	4		7	31	21	45	3	.288	.445
Dewayne Wise	OF56	L	26	77	162	24	37	9	4	6	17	9	28	6	.228	.444
Eddie Perez	C66 1B1	R	36	74	170	14	39	12	0	3	13	11	29	0	.229	.353
Jesse Garcia	SS25 2B11 3B3	R	30	50	115	14	29	4	1	1	10	1	16	1	.252	.330
Mike Hessman	1B16 3B7 OF3	R	26	29	69	8	9	3	0	2	5	1	24	0	.130	.261
Wilson Betemit	SS11 3B7	B	22	22	47	2	8	0	0	0	3	4	16	0	.170	.170
Damon Hollins	OF6	R	30	7	22	3	8	2	0	0	5	0	4	0	.364	.455

NAME	T	AGE	W	L	PCT	SV	G	GS	CG	IP	H	BB	SO	SHO	ERA
		30	96	66	.593	48	162	162	4	1450	1475	523	1025	13	3.74
Jaret Wright	R	28	15	8	.652	0	32	32	0	186	168	70	159	0	3.28
Russ Ortiz	R	30	15	9	.625	0	34	34	2	205	197	112	143	1	4.13
John Thomson	R	30	14	8	.636	0	33	33	0	198	210	52	133	0	3.72
Mike Hampton	L	31	13	9	.591	0	29	29	1	172	198	65	87	0	4.28
Paul Byrd (EJ)	R	33	8	7	.533	0	19	19	0	114	123	19	79	0	3.94
Juan Cruz	R	25	6	2	.750	0	50	0	0	72	59	30	70	0	2.75
Chris Reitsma	R	26	6	4	.600	2	84	0	0	80	89	20	60	0	4.07
Antonio Alfonseca	R	32	6	4	.600	0	79	0	0	74	71	28	45	0	2.57
Kevin Gryboski	R	30	3	2	.600	2	69	0	0	51	54	23	24	0	2.84
Roman Colon	R	24	2	1	.667	0	18	0	0	19	18	8	15	0	3.32
Travis Smith	R	31	2	3	.400	0	16	4	0	41	48	12	26	0	6.20
Horacio Ramirez (SJ)	L	24	2	4	.333	0	10	9	1	60	51	30	31	0	2.39
C.J. Nitkowski	L	31	1	0	1.000	0	22	0	0	20	22	10	16	0	4.50
Sam McConnell	R	28	1	0	1.000	0	10	0	0	9	11	4	4	0	3.86
Armando Almanza (EJ)	L	31	1	1	.500	0	12	0	0	12	9	7	13	0	6.17
Will Cunnane	R	30	1	1	.500	0	9	0	0	12	18	4	11	0	7.30
Tim Drew	R	25	1	1	.500	0	11	0	0	16	21	5	7	0	4.50
Dan Meyer	L	22	0	0	—	0	2	0	0	2	1	1	1	0	0.00
John Smoltz	R	37	0	1	.000	44	73	0	0	82	75	13	85	0	2.76
2 Tom Martin	L	34	0	1	.000	0	17	0	0	17	17	5	12	0	3.71
Jose Capellan	R	23	0	1	.000	0	3	2	0	8	14	5	4	0	11.25

PHILADELPHIA — 2nd 86-76 .531 10 — LARRY BOWA 85-75 .531 GARY VARSHO 1-1 .500

Name	G by Pos	B	AGE	G	AB	R	H	2B	3B	HR	RBI	BB	SO	SB	BA	SA
TOTALS			29	162	5643	840	1505	303	23	215	802	645	1133	100	.267	.443
Jim Thome	1B134	L	33	143	508	97	139	28	4	42	105	104	144	0	.274	.581
Placido Polanco (LJ)	2B109 3B13	R	28	126	503	74	150	21	0	17	55	27	39	7	.298	.441
Jimmy Rollins	SS154	B	25	154	657	119	190	43	12	14	73	57	73	30	.289	.455
David Bell	3B142	R	31	143	533	67	155	33	1	18	77	53	73	1	.291	.458
Bobby Abreu	OF158	L	30	159	574	118	173	47	1	30	105	127	116	40	.301	.544
Marlon Byrd	OF92	R	26	106	346	48	79	13	2	5	33	22	68	2	.228	.321
Pat Burrell (WJ)	OF122	R	27	127	448	66	115	17	0	24	84	78	130	2	.257	.455
Mike Lieberthal	C129	R	32	131	476	58	129	31	1	17	61	37	69	1	.271	.447
Jason Michaels	OF78	R	28	115	299	44	82	12	0	10	40	42	68	2	.274	.415
Chase Utley	2B50 1B13	L	25	94	267	36	71	11	2	13	57	15	40	4	.266	.468
Doug Glanville	OF68	R	33	87	162	21	34	1	1	2	14	8	21	8	.210	.265
Tomas Perez	3B22 2B17 SS10 1B2	R	30	86	176	22	38	13	2	6	21	9	44	0	.216	.415
1 Ricky Ledee	OF22	L	30	73	123	19	35	7	0	7	26	22	27	1	.285	.512
Todd Pratt	C43	R	37	45	128	16	33	5	0	3	16	18	38	0	.258	.367
Shawn Wooten	1B11 3B4	R	31	33	53	2	9	3	0	0	2	6	9	0	.170	.226
Lou Collier	OF8 3B1	R	31	32	36	7	10	1	0	1	4	5	10	1	.278	.389
Ryan Howard	1B8	L	24	19	39	5	11	5	0	2	5	2	13	0	.282	.564
A.J. Hinch	C4	R	30	4	11	1	2	1	0	0	1	1	3	0	.182	.273

NAME	T	AGE	W	L	PCT	SV	G	GS	CG	IP	H	BB	SO	SHO	ERA
		30	86	76	.531	43	162	162	4	1463	1488	502	1070	5	4.45
Eric Milton	L	28	14	6	.700	0	34	34	0	201	196	75	161	0	4.75
Brett Myers	R	23	11	11	.500	0	32	31	1	176	196	62	116	1	5.52
Ryan Madson (RJ)	R	23	9	3	.750	1	52	1	0	77	68	19	55	0	2.34
Kevin Millwood (EJ)	R	29	9	6	.600	0	25	25	0	141	155	51	125	0	4.85
Vicente Padilla (AJ)	R	26	7	7	.500	0	20	20	0	115	119	36	82	0	4.53
Cory Lidle	R	32	5	2	.714	0	10	10	2	62	54	17	33	*2	3.90
Tim Worrell	R	36	5	6	.455	19	77	0	0	78	71	24	64	0	3.68
Randy Wolf (EJ)	L	27	5	8	.385	0	23	23	1	137	145	36	89	1	4.28
Billy Wagner (GJ-SJ)	L	32	4	0	1.000	21	45	0	0	48	31	6	59	0	2.42
Rheal Cormier	L	37	4	5	.444	0	81	0	0	81	70	26	46	0	3.56
2 Todd Jones	R	36	3	3	.500	1	27	0	0	55	35	8	22	0	4.97
Roberto Hernandez	R	39	5	3	.375	0	63	0	0	57	66	29	44	0	4.76
Gavin Floyd	R	21	2	0	1.000	0	8	3	0	28	25	16	24	0	3.49
2 Felix Rodriguez	R	31	3	4	.300	1	21	0	0	21	18	10	28	0	3.00
Geoff Geary	R	27	1	0	1.000	0	33	0	0	45	52	16	30	0	5.44
Brian Powell (ZJ-AJ)	R	30	1	1	.333	0	17	2	0	39	39	16	24	0	5.03
2 Paul Abbott	R	36	1	6	.143	0	10	10	0	49	57	31	21	0	6.24
Elizardo Ramirez	R	21	0	0	—	0	7	0	0	15	17	5	9	0	4.80
Jim Crowell	L	30	0	0	—	0	3	0	0	4	3	1	1	0	3.00
1 Josh Hancock	R	26	0	1	.000	0	13	0	0	8	13	3	5	0	9.00
Amaury Telemaco (SJ)	R	30	0	2	.000	0	42	0	0	54	51	19	32	0	4.31

* Lidle, also with Cincinnati, tied for league lead in ShO with 3

FLORIDA — 3rd 83-79 .512 13 — JACK McKEON

Name	G by Pos	B	AGE	G	AB	R	H	2B	3B	HR	RBI	BB	SO	SB	BA	SA
TOTALS			29	162	5486	718	1447	275	32	148	677	499	968	96	.264	.406
1 Hee-Seop Choi	1B89	L	25	95	281	48	76	16	1	15	40	52	78	1	.270	.495
Luis Castillo	2B148	B	28	150	564	91	164	12	7	2	47	75	68	21	.291	.348
Alex Gonzalez	SS158	R	27	159	561	67	130	30	3	23	79	27	126	3	.232	.419
Mike Lowell	3B142	R	30	158	598	87	175	44	1	27	85	64	77	5	.293	.505
Miguel Cabrera	OF158	R	21	160	603	101	177	31	1	33	112	68	148	5	.294	.512
Juan Pierre	OF162	L	26	162	678	100	221	22	12	3	49	45	35	45	.326	.407
Jeff Conine	OF83 1B57	R	38	140	521	55	146	35	1	14	83	48	78	5	.280	.432
Mike Redmond	C79	R	33	81	246	19	63	15	0	2	25	14	28	1	.256	.341
Damion Easley	2B25 1B18 SS15 3B6 OF5	R	34	98	223	26	53	20	1	9	43	24	36	4	.238	.457
Lenny Harris	OF14 3B3	L	39	79	95	7	20	5	0	1	17	3	9	0	.211	.295
Mike Mordecai	3B19 2B4 SS3 C1	R	36	69	84	7	19	3	0	1	5	6	18	0	.226	.298
1 Abraham Nunez	OF48	B	27	58	64	9	11	1	1	1	9	2	11	0	.172	.266
2 Paul LoDuca	C49	R	32	52	186	27	48	11	1	3	14	14	22	2	.258	.376
1 Juan Encarnacion	OF48	R	28	49	160	21	38	12	1	3	19	17	33	2	.238	.381
Ramon Castro (FJ)	C31	R	28	32	96	9	13	3	0	3	8	11	30	0	.135	.260
Matt Treanor	C27	R	28	29	55	7	13	2	0	0	4	4	13	0	.236	.273
Chris Aguila	OF20	R	25	29	45	10	10	2	1	0	5	2	10	0	.222	.311
Wil Cordero (KJ)	1B13 OF3	R	32	27	66	6	13	3	0	1	6	3	19	1	.197	.288
Josh Willingham	C5 OF3	R	25	12	25	2	5	0	0	1	1	4	8	0	.200	.320
Larry Sutton	1B1	L	34	8	5	0	1	0	0	0	1	2	1	0	.200	.200

NAME	T	AGE	W	L	PCT	SV	G	GS	CG	IP	H	BB	SO	SHO	ERA
		29	83	79	.512	53	162	162	6	1439	1395	513	1116	14	4.10
Carl Pavano	R	28	18	8	.692	0	31	31	2	222	212	49	139	2	3.00
Dontrelle Willis	L	22	10	11	.476	0	32	32	2	197	210	61	139	0	4.02
Josh Beckett	R	24	9	9	.500	0	26	26	1	157	137	54	152	1	3.79
1 Brad Penny	R	26	8	8	.500	0	21	21	0	131	124	39	105	0	3.15
A.J. Burnett (EJ)	R	27	7	6	.538	0	20	19	1	120	102	38	113	0	3.68
Matt Perisho	R	29	5	3	.625	0	66	0	0	47	45	26	42	0	4.40
2 Ismael Valdez	R	30	5	3	.625	0	11	11	0	56	61	18	30	0	4.50
2 Rudy Seanez	R	35	3	1	.750	0	23	0	0	23	18	8	25	0	2.74
Josias Manzanillo	R	36	3	3	.500	1	26	0	0	32	38	15	27	0	6.12
Justin Wayne	R	25	3	3	.500	0	19	1	0	33	35	18	20	0	5.79
Armando Benitez	R	31	2	2	.500	47	64	0	0	70	36	21	62	0	1.29
1 Darren Oliver	L	33	2	3	.400	0	18	8	0	59	75	17	33	0	6.44
Nate Bump	R	27	2	4	.333	1	50	2	0	74	86	32	44	0	5.01
3 David Weathers	R	34	1	0	1.000	0	17	0	0	17	13	7	10	0	2.70
Ben Howard	R	25	1	0	.500	0	31	0	0	38	37	21	33	0	5.50
Tommy Phelps	L	29	1	0	.500	0	18	0	0	14	18	12	14	0	5.40
Toby Borland	R	35	1	2	.500	0	18	0	0	18	12	8	18	0	4.76
Billy Koch (PP)	R	29	1	3	.333	2	26	0	0	26	24	10	20	0	3.51
2 Guillermo Mota	R	30	1	4	.200	3	26	0	0	46	42	14	33	0	4.81
Aaron Small	R	32	0	0	—	0	1	0	0	1	4	2	2	0	8.27
Mike Neu	R	26	0	0	—	0	7	0	0	4	5	2	8	0	4.50
Chad Fox (EJ)	R	33	0	1	.000	0	12	0	0	11	9	8	17	0	6.75
Franklyn Gracesqui	L	24	0	0	—	0	11	0	0	6	4	8	3	0	11.25
Logan Kensing	R	21	0	1	.000	0	5	3	0	19	19	9	7	0	9.88
1 Michael Tejera	L	27	0	2	.000	0	13	0	0	9	14	7	7	0	18.00
Tim Spooneybarger (EJ) 24															

NEW YORK — 4th 71-91 .438 25 — ART HOWE

Name	G by Pos	B	AGE	G	AB	R	H	2B	3B	HR	RBI	BB	SO	SB	BA	SA
TOTALS			29	162	5532	684	1376	289	20	185	658	512	1159	107	.249	.409
Mike Piazza	1B68 C50	R	35	129	455	47	121	21	0	20	54	68	78	0	.266	.444
Jose Reyes (LJ)	2B43 SS10	B	21	53	220	33	56	16	2	2	14	5	31	19	.255	.373
Kaz Matsui (XJ)	SS110 2B3	B	28	114	460	65	125	32	2	7	44	40	97	14	.272	.396
David Wright	3B69	R	21	69	263	41	77	17	1	14	40	14	40	6	.293	.525
2 Richard Hidalgo	OF86	R	29	86	324	46	74	11	1	21	52	27	76	3	.228	.463
Mike Cameron	OF135	R	31	140	493	76	114	30	1	30	76	57	143	22	.231	.479
Cliff Floyd (LJ)	OF106	L	31	113	396	55	103	26	0	18	63	47	103	11	.260	.462
Jason Phillips	C87 1B38	R	27	128	362	34	79	18	0	7	34	35	61	0	.218	.326
Todd Zeile	1B67 3B46 C2 P1	R	38	137	348	30	81	16	0	9	35	44	83	0	.233	.356
Eric Valent	OF46 1B27	L	27	130	270	39	72	15	2	13	34	28	61	0	.267	.481
1 Ty Wigginton	3B66 2B25 1B5	R	26	86	312	46	89	23	2	12	42	23	48	6	.285	.487
Vance Wilson	C69	R	31	79	157	18	43	10	1	4	21	11	24	1	.274	.427
Joe McEwing (BL)	2B34 OF15 SS13 1B11 3B1	R	31	75	138	17	35	3	1	1	16	9	32	4	.254	.312
Shane Spencer	OF62 1B1	R	32	74	185	21	52	10	1	4	26	13	37	1	.281	.411
1 Karim Garcia	OF51	L	28	62	192	24	45	7	2	7	22	10	35	2	.234	.401
Danny Garcia	2B44	R	24	58	138	23	32	7	1	3	17	22	34	3	.232	.362
Gerald Williams	OF45	R	37	57	129	17	30	8	2	4	11	8	26	2	.233	.419
Wilson Delgado	SS39	B	31	42	130	11	38	4	1	2	13	15	29	1	.292	.385
Jeff Keppinger	2B32	R	24	33	116	9	33	2	0	0	9	6	7	2	.284	.379
1 Ricky Gutierrez	2B18 3B2	R	34	24	63	2	11	2	0	0	5	4	8	0	.175	.206
Craig Brazell	1B7	L	24	24	34	3	9	2	0	1	4	0	8	0	.265	.412
Victor Diaz	OF14	R	22	15	51	8	15	3	0	3	11	2	15	0	.294	.529
Jeff Duncan	OF4	L	25	13	15	2	1	0	0	0	0	4	6	0	.067	.067
1 Tom Wilson	C3	R	33	4	8	0	2	0	0	0	0	2	5	0	.250	.250
2 Brian Buchanan	1B1	R	30	4	4	0	0	0	0	0	0	1	3	0	.000	.000
Joe Hietpas	C1	R	25	1	1	0	0	0	0	0	0	0	0	0		
Esix Snead	OF1	B	28	4	0											
Mo Vaughn (KJ) 36																

NAME	T	AGE	W	L	PCT	SV	G	GS	CG	IP	H	BB	SO	SHO	ERA
		31	71	91	.438	31	162	162	2	1449	1452	592	977	6	4.09
Steve Trachsel	R	33	12	13	.480	0	33	33	0	203	203	83	117	0	4.00
Tom Glavine	L	38	11	14	.440	0	33	33	1	212	204	70	109	1	3.60
Al Leiter	L	38	10	8	.556	0	30	30	0	174	138	97	117	0	3.21
3 David Weathers	R	34	5	3	.625	0	32	0	0	34	41	15	25	0	4.28
Jae Weong Seo	R	27	5	10	.333	0	24	21	0	118	133	50	54	0	4.90
2 Kris Benson	R	29	4	4	.500	0	11	11	0	68	65	17	51	1	4.50
Orber Moreno (SJ)	R	27	3	1	.750	0	33	0	0	35	29	11	29	0	3.37
1 Dan Wheeler	R	26	3	1	.750	0	32	1	0	51	65	17	46	0	4.80
Ricky Bottalico	R	34	3	1	.600	0	60	0	0	69	54	34	61	0	3.38
2 Victor Zambrano (EJ)	R	28	2	0	1.000	0	3	3	0	18	15	14	10	0	3.86
Tyler Yates	R	26	3	4	.333	0	21	7	0	83	86	16	60	0	6.36
Braden Looper	R	29	2	9	.286	29	71	0	0	83	93	16	60	0	2.70
Mike Stanton	L	37	2	6	.250	0	83	0	0	77	70	33	58	0	3.16
John Franco	L	43	2	7	.222	0	52	0	0	46	46	24	36	0	5.28
2 Bartolome Fortunato	R	29	1	0	1.000	0	19	0	0	14	14	13	20	0	3.86
Jose Parra (PJ)	R	31	1	0	1.000	0	13	0	0	14	14	4	14	0	3.21
Pedro Feliciano	L	27	1	1	.500	0	12	0	0	14	13	9	17	0	5.40
Matt Ginter	R	26	1	3	.250	0	15	14	0	69	82	20	38	0	4.54
Aaron Heilman	R	25	2	7	.222	0	18	13	0	66	74	22	42	0	5.46
2 Mike DeJean (LJ)	R	33	0	0	—	0	17	0	0	21	15	15	24	0	1.69
Grant Roberts (SJ)	R	26	0	1	.000	0	2	0	0	3	4	2	6	0	4.50
Todd Zeile	R	38	0	0	—	0	1	0	0	1	2	1	0	0	45.00
1 Scott Erickson (LJ)	R	36	1	1	.500	0	10	6	0	22	31	15	9	0	7.88
2 Vic Darensbourg	L	33	0	0	—	0	6	0	0	8	12	4	6	0	7.94
Heath Bell	R	26	1	0	1.000	0	17	0	0	24	28	5	27	0	3.33
James Baldwin	R	32	0	1	.000	0	2	2	0	8	14	5	6	0	15.00
Scott Strickland (EJ) 28															

MONTREAL 5th 67-95 .414 29 FRANK ROBINSON

Name	G by Pos	B	AGE	G	AB	R	H	2B	3B	HR	RBI	BB	SO	SB	BA	SA
TOTALS			28	162	5474	635	1361	276	27	151	605	496	925	109	.249	.392
Nick Johnson (XJ-BY)	1B73	L	25	73	251	35	63	16	0	7	33	40	58	6	.251	.398
Jose Vidro (KJ)	2B105	B	29	110	412	51	121	24	0	14	60	49	43	3	.294	.454
1 Orlando Cabrera	SS101	R	29	103	390	41	96	19	2	4	31	28	31	12	.246	.336
Tony Batista	3B155	R	30	157	606	76	146	30	2	32	110	26	78	14	.241	.455
Juan Rivera	OF121	R	25	134	391	48	120	24	1	12	49	34	45	4	.307	.465
Endy Chavez	OF127	L	26	132	502	65	139	20	6	5	34	30	40	32	.277	.371
Brad Wilkerson	1B86 OF80	L	27	160	572	112	146	39	2	32	67	106	152	13	.255	.498
Brian Schneider	C133	L	27	135	436	40	112	20	3	12	49	42	63	0	.257	.399
Termmel Sledge	OF114 1B10	L	27	133	398	45	107	20	6	15	62	40	66	3	.269	.462
Jamey Carroll	2B51 3B13 SS10 OF2	R	30	102	218	36	63	14	2	0	16	32	21	5	.289	.372
Einar Diaz	C44 3B1	R	31	55	139	9	31	6	1	1	11	11	10	2	.223	.302
Ron Calloway	OF20	R	27	46	84	4	14	2	0	1	10	5	22	2	.167	.226
Henry Mateo	2B9 OF1	R	27	40	44	3	12	2	0	0	1	1	9	2	.273	.318
1 Carl Everett (SJ)	OF33	B	33	39	127	8	32	10	0	2	14	8	19	0	.252	.378
1 Alex Gonzalez	SS33	R	31	35	133	19	32	7	0	4	16	8	21	1	.241	.383
1 Andy Fox	SS5 2B3 3B3 1B1	L	33	34	43	2	4	0	0	1	1	0	16	0	.093	.163
Maicer Izturis	SS23 2B10	R	23	32	107	10	22	5	2	1	4	10	10	4	.206	.318
Valentino Pascucci	OF17 1B5	R	25	32	62	6	11	1	0	2	6	10	22	1	.177	.290
Matt Cepicky	OF11	L	26	32	60	4	13	4	0	1	3	1	18	1	.217	.333
Ryan Church	OF18	L	25	30	63	6	11	1	0	1	6	7	16	0	.175	.238
2 Brendan Harris	2B11 3B4	R	23	20	50	4	8	2	0	1	2	2	11	0	.160	.260
Peter Bergeron (VJ)	OF11	L	26	11	42	2	9	0	0	0	1	2	16	2	.214	.214
Luis Lopez	1B8	R	30	11	26	0	4	0	0	0	0	0	9	0	.154	.154
Josh Labandeira	SS3 2B1	R	25	7	14	0	0	0	0	0	0	0	4	0	.000	.000

NAME	T	AGE	W	L	PCT	SV	G	GS	CG	IP	H	BB	SO	SHO	ERA
TOTALS		26	67	95	.414	31	162	162	11	1447	1477	582	1032	11	4.33
Livan Hernandez	R	29	11	15	.423	0	35	35	9	255	234	83	186	2	3.60
Chad Cordero	R	22	7	3	.700	14	69	0	0	83	68	43	83	0	2.94
Luis Ayala	R	26	6	12	.333	2	81	0	0	90	92	15	63	0	2.69
Claudio Vargas	R	26	5	5	.500	0	45	14	0	118	120	64	89	0	5.25
Zach Day (BG)	R	26	5	10	.333	0	19	19	1	117	117	45	61	1	3.93
Joe Horgan	L	27	4	1	.800	2	47	0	0	40	35	22	30	0	3.15
T.J. Tucker	R	25	4	2	.667	0	54	1	0	68	73	17	44	0	3.72
Sun-Woo Kim	R	26	4	6	.400	0	43	17	0	136	145	55	87	0	4.58
John Patterson (GJ)	R	26	4	7	.364	0	19	19	0	98	100	46	99	0	5.03
Rocky Biddle	R	28	4	8	.333	11	47	9	0	78	98	31	51	0	6.92
2 Jon Rauch (UJ)	R	25	3	0	1.000	0	9	2	0	23	14	7	18	0	1.54
Scott Downs	L	28	3	6	.333	0	12	12	1	63	79	23	38	1	5.14
Tomo Ohka (BA)	R	28	3	7	.300	0	15	15	0	85	98	20	38	0	3.40
Tony Armas (SJ)	R	26	2	4	.333	0	16	16	0	72	66	45	54	0	4.88
Jeremy Fikac	R	29	1	2	.333	0	19	0	0	25	26	13	22	0	5.40
Shawn Hill	R	23	1	2	.333	0	3	3	0	9	17	7	10	0	16.00
2 Francis Beltran	R	24	0	0	—	1	11	0	0	14	20	5	8	0	7.53
Roy Corcoran	R	24	0	0	—	0	5	0	0	5	7	5	4	0	6.75
Rigo Beltran (UJ)	L	34	0	0	—	0	2	0	0	1	1	0	0	0	13.50
Joey Eischen (EJ)	L	34	0	1	.000	0	21	0	0	18	16	8	17	0	3.93
Gary Majewski	R	24	0	1	.000	0	16	0	0	21	28	5	12	0	3.86
Chad Bentz	L	24	0	3	.000	0	36	0	0	28	23	23	18	0	5.86
Dan Smith (SJ) 28															

CENTRAL DIVISION

ST. LOUIS 1st 105-57 .648 TONY LA RUSSA

Name	G by Pos	B	AGE	G	AB	R	H	2B	3B	HR	RBI	BB	SO	SB	BA	SA
TOTALS			31	162	5555	855	1544	319	24	214	817	548	1085	111	.278	.460
Albert Pujols	1B150	R	24	154	592	133	196	51	2	46	123	84	52	5	.331	.657
Tony Womack	2B133	L	34	145	553	91	170	22	3	5	38	36	60	26	.307	.385
Edgar Renteria	SS149	R	28	149	586	84	168	37	4	10	72	39	78	17	.287	.401
Scott Rolen	3B141	R	29	142	500	109	157	32	4	34	124	72	92	4	.314	.598
Reggie Sanders	OF119	R	36	135	446	64	116	27	3	22	67	33	118	21	.260	.482
Jim Edmonds	OF146 1B1	L	34	153	498	102	150	38	3	42	111	101	150	8	.301	.643
Ray Lankford (WJ)	OF70	L	37	92	200	36	51	14	1	6	22	29	55	2	.255	.425
Mike Matheny	C122 1B1	R	33	122	385	28	95	22	1	5	50	23	83	0	.247	.348
Marlon Anderson	2B37 OF36 1B2	L	30	113	253	31	60	12	0	8	28	12	38	6	.237	.379
So Taguchi	OF103	R	34	109	179	26	52	10	2	3	25	12	23	6	.291	.419
Roger Cedeno (LJ)	OF54	B	29	95	200	22	53	9	2	3	23	19	41	5	.265	.375
John Mabry	OF57 3B20 1B14	L	33	87	240	32	71	11	0	13	40	26	63	0	.296	.504
Hector Luna	SS24 2B19 3B16 OF10	R	24	83	173	25	43	7	2	3	22	13	37	6	.249	.364
Yadier Molina	C51	R	21	51	135	12	36	6	0	2	15	13	20	0	.267	.356
1 Larry Walker	OF41	L	37	44	150	29	42	7	1	11	27	24	34	4	.280	.540
Cody McKay	C18 3B7 P1 1B1	L	30	53	74	7	17	2	0	0	6	2	14	0	.230	.257
Colin Porter	OF14	L	28	23	35	3	11	1	0	1	2	0	13	0	.314	.429
Bo Hart	2B4 SS1	R	27	11	13	0	2	0	0	0	2	1	3	0	.154	.154

NAME	T	AGE	W	L	PCT	SV	G	GS	CG	IP	H	BB	SO	SHO	ERA
TOTALS		31	105	57	.648	57	162	162	4	1454	1378	440	1041	12	3.75
Jeff Suppan	R	29	16	9	.640	0	31	31	0	188	192	65	110	0	4.16
Chris Carpenter	R	29	15	5	.750	0	28	28	1	182	169	38	152	0	3.46
Jason Marquis	R	25	15	7	.682	0	32	32	0	201	215	70	138	0	3.71
Matt Morris	R	29	15	10	.600	0	32	32	2	202	205	56	131	2	4.72
Woody Williams	R	37	11	8	.579	0	31	31	0	190	193	58	131	0	4.18
Julian Tavarez	R	31	7	4	.636	4	77	0	0	64	57	19	48	0	2.38
Ray King	L	30	5	4	.714	0	86	0	0	62	43	24	40	0	2.61
Jason Isringhausen	R	31	4	2	.667	47	74	0	0	75	55	23	71	0	2.87
Cal Eldred	R	36	4	2	.667	1	52	0	0	67	71	17	54	0	3.76
Kiko Calero	R	29	3	1	.750	2	41	0	0	45	27	10	47	0	2.78
Mike Lincoln (EJ)	R	29	3	2	.600	0	13	0	0	17	10	6	14	0	5.19
Danny Haren	R	23	3	3	.500	0	14	5	0	46	45	17	32	0	4.50
Steve Kline (GJ)	L	31	2	2	.500	3	67	0	0	50	37	17	35	0	1.79
Randy Flores	L	28	1	0	1.000	0	9	1	0	14	13	3	7	0	1.93
Rick Ankiel (EJ)	R	24	1	0	1.000	0	5	0	0	10	9	2	9	0	5.40
Jason Simontacchi	R	30	0	0	—	0	13	0	0	15	17	7	3	0	5.40
Al Reyes	R	33	0	0	—	0	12	2	0	12	3	2	11	0	0.75
Carmen Cali	L	25	0	0	—	0	10	0	0	7	13	6	9	0	3.86
Josh Pearce	R	26	0	0	—	0	1	0	0	2	3	0	0	0	3.86
Cody McKay	R	30	0	0	—	0	1	0	0	1	0	0	0	0	0.00

HOUSTON 2nd 92-70 .568 13 (Wild Card) JIMY WILLIAMS 44-44 .500 PHIL GARNER 48-26 .649

Name	G by Pos	B	AGE	G	AB	R	H	2B	3B	HR	RBI	BB	SO	SB	BA	SA
TOTALS			31	162	5468	803	1458	294	36	187	756	590	999	89	.267	.436
Jeff Bagwell	1B152	R	36	156	572	104	152	29	2	27	89	96	131	6	.266	.465
Jeff Kent	2B139	R	36	145	540	96	156	34	8	27	107	49	96	7	.289	.531
Adam Everett (BW)	SS99	R	27	104	384	66	105	15	2	8	31	17	56	13	.273	.385
Morgan Ensberg	3B118 SS1	R	28	131	411	51	113	20	3	10	66	36	46	6	.275	.411
Lance Berkman	OF160 1B4	B	28	160	544	104	172	40	3	30	106	127	101	9	.316	.566
2 Carlos Beltran	OF89	B	27	90	333	70	86	17	7	23	53	55	57	28	.258	.559
Craig Biggio	OF149	R	38	156	633	100	178	47	2	24	63	40	94	7	.281	.469
Brad Ausmus	C128	R	35	129	403	38	100	14	1	5	31	33	56	2	.248	.325
Jose Vizcaino	SS64 2B37 3B21 1B8	B	36	138	358	34	98	21	3	3	33	20	39	1	.274	.374
Mike Lamb	3B57 1B10 2B7	L	28	112	278	38	80	14	3	14	58	31	63	1	.288	.511
Jason Lane	OF76 1B3	R	27	107	136	21	37	10	2	4	19	16	33	1	.272	.463
Orlando Palmeiro	OF37	L	35	102	133	19	32	5	0	3	12	18	19	2	.241	.346
Raul Chavez	C61	R	31	64	162	9	34	8	0	0	23	10	38	0	.210	.259
1 Richard Hidalgo	OF56	R	29	58	199	21	51	15	2	4	30	17	53	1	.256	.412
Eric Bruntlett	SS33 2B5 OF2	R	26	45	52	14	13	2	0	4	8	7	13	4	.250	.519
Chris Burke	2B7	R	24	17	17	2	1	0	0	0	0	0	6	0	.059	.059
Willy Taveras	OF7	R	22	10	1	2	0	0	0	0	0	0	1	1	1.000	.000
Jason Alfaro	SS3	R	26	9	11	1	2	0	0	0	0	0	5	0	.182	.182
Chris Tremie	C1	R	34	1	0	0	0	0	0	0	0	0	0	0	—	—

NAME	T	AGE	W	L	PCT	SV	G	GS	CG	IP	H	BB	SO	SHO	ERA
TOTALS		30	92	70	.568	47	162	162	2	1443	1416	525	1282	13	4.05
Roy Oswalt	R	26	20	10	.667	0	36	35	2	237	233	62	206	2	3.49
Roger Clemens	R	41	18	4	.818	0	33	33	0	214	169	79	218	0	2.98
Wade Miller (SJ)	R	27	7	7	.500	0	15	15	0	89	76	44	74	0	3.35
Andy Pettitte (AJ-EJ)	L	32	6	4	.600	0	15	15	0	83	71	31	79	0	3.90
Brad Lidge	R	27	6	5	.545	29	80	0	0	95	57	30	157	0	1.90
Dan Miceli	R	33	6	6	.500	2	74	0	0	78	74	27	83	0	3.59
Brandon Backe	R	26	5	3	.625	0	33	9	0	67	75	27	54	0	4.30
Tim Redding	R	26	5	7	.417	0	27	17	0	101	125	43	56	0	5.72
Chad Qualls	R	25	4	0	1.000	1	25	0	0	33	34	8	24	0	3.55
Peter Munro	R	29	4	7	.364	0	21	19	0	100	120	26	63	0	5.15
2 Chad Harville	R	27	3	2	.600	0	56	0	0	53	54	26	46	0	4.75
Mike Gallo	L	27	2	0	1.000	0	69	0	0	49	55	20	34	0	4.74
Kirk Bullinger	R	34	1	0	1.000	1	27	0	0	31	36	10	11	0	6.16
2 Darren Oliver (SJ)	R	33	1	0	1.000	0	9	4	0	14	12	4	13	0	3.86
1 Ricky Stone	R	29	1	0	1.000	0	16	0	0	19	26	7	16	0	5.60
Brandon Duckworth	R	28	1	2	.333	0	19	6	0	39	55	13	23	0	6.86
Carlos Hernandez	L	24	1	3	.250	0	9	9	0	42	50	23	26	0	4.78
2 David Weathers	R	34	1	4	.200	0	32	0	0	32	31	13	26	0	4.78
2 Dan Wheeler	R	26	0	0	—	0	14	0	0	14	11	3	9	0	2.51
Jared Fernandez	R	32	0	0	—	0	2	1	0	5	8	1	2	0	54.00
Jeremy Griffiths	R	26	0	0	—	0	1	1	0	4	4	3	5	0	10.38
Russ Springer	R	35	0	0	—	0	16	0	0	14	15	6	9	0	2.63
1 Octavio Dotel	R		0	0	—	14	32	0	0	35	27	15	50	0	3.12

CHICAGO 3rd 89-73 .549 16 DUSTY BAKER

Name	G by Pos	B	AGE	G	AB	R	H	2B	3B	HR	RBI	BB	SO	SB	BA	SA
TOTALS			31	162	5628	789	1508	308	29	235	755	489	1080	66	.268	.458
Derrek Lee	1B161	R	28	161	605	90	168	39	4	32	98	68	128	12	.278	.504
Todd Walker	2B89 1B5 OF1	L	31	129	372	60	102	19	4	15	50	43	52	0	.274	.468
Alex Gonzalez (BW)	SS37	R	31	37	129	15	28	10	0	3	4	4	26	1	.217	.364
Aramis Ramirez	3B144	R	26	145	547	99	174	32	1	36	103	49	68	0	.318	.578
Sammy Sosa (XJ)	OF124	R	35	126	478	69	121	21	0	35	80	56	133	0	.253	.517
Corey Patterson	OF157	L	24	157	631	91	168	33	6	24	72	45	168	32	.266	.452
Moises Alou	OF154	R	37	155	601	106	176	36	3	39	106	68	80	3	.293	.557
Michael Barrett	C130	R	27	134	456	55	131	32	6	16	65	33	64	1	.287	.489
Ramon Martinez	SS73 3B24 2B6	R	31	102	260	22	64	15	1	3	30	26	40	1	.246	.346
Jose Macias	OF28 3B18 2B16	B	32	98	194	23	52	6	3	3	22	5	38	4	.268	.376
Mark Grudzielanek (LJ)	2B76	R	34	81	257	32	79	12	1	6	23	15	32	1	.307	.432
Tom Goodwin	OF28	L	35	77	105	11	21	8	0	0	8	8	22	5	.200	.276
Todd Hollandsworth (LJ)	OF36 1B3	L	31	57	148	28	47	6	2	8	22	17	26	1	.318	.547
Paul Bako	C47	L	32	49	138	13	28	8	0	1	10	15	29	1	.203	.283
2 Nomar Garciaparra	SS42	R	30	43	165	28	49	14	0	4	20	16	14	2	.297	.455
2 Neifi Perez	SS19 2B2	B	31	23	62	12	23	5	0	2	6	3	6	1	.371	.548
Rey Ordonez	SS22	R	32	23	61	2	10	3	0	1	5	2	14	0	.164	.262
Jason Dubois	OF5 1B1	R	25	20	23	2	5	0	1	1	5	1	7	0	.217	.435
2 Ben Grieve	OF4	L	28	15	16	2	4	2	0	1	6	0	5	0	.250	.563
Calvin Murray	OF8	R	32	11	5	2	1	0	0	0	1	1	0	0	.200	.200
Dave Kelton	OF3	R	24	8	10	1	1	0	0	0	0	1	6	0	.100	.100
Damian Jackson	2B5	R	30	7	15	1	1	0	0	0	1	0	6	1	.067	.267
2 Mike DiFelice	C4	R	35	4	7	1	1	0	0	0	0	0	3	0	.000	.000
1 Brendan Harris	3B3	R	23	3	9	1	2	0	0	0	2	0	3	0	.222	.333

NAME	T	AGE	W	L	PCT	SV	G	GS	CG	IP	H	BB	SO	SHO	ERA
TOTALS		29	89	73	.549	42	162	162	3	1465	1363	545	1346	6	3.81
Carlos Zambrano	R	23	16	8	.667	0	31	31	1	210	174	81	188	1	2.75
Greg Maddux	R	38	16	11	.593	0	33	33	2	213	218	33	151	1	4.02
Matt Clement	R	29	9	13	.409	0	30	30	0	181	155	77	190	0	3.68
Kerry Wood (AJ)	R	27	8	9	.471	0	22	22	0	140	127	51	144	0	3.72
Glendon Rusch	L	29	6	2	.750	2	32	16	0	130	127	33	90	0	3.47
Mark Prior (LJ)	R	23	6	4	.600	0	21	21	0	119	112	48	139	0	4.02
Jon Leicester	R	25	5	1	.833	0	32	0	0	42	40	15	35	0	3.89
LaTroy Hawkins	R	31	5	4	.556	25	77	0	0	82	72	14	69	0	2.63
Kyle Farnsworth	R	28	4	5	.444	0	72	0	0	67	67	33	78	0	4.72
Kent Mercker	L	36	3	1	.750	0	71	0	0	53	39	27	51	0	2.55
Todd Wellemeyer (SJ)	R	25	2	2	.667	0	34	0	0	35	27	20	40	0	5.92
1 Francis Beltran	R	24	2	0	1.000	0	11	0	0	14	20	5	8	0	4.63
Joe Borowski (SJ)	R	33	2	4	.333	9	22	0	0	39	35	17	40	0	8.02
Sergio Mitre	R	23	2	4	.333	0	12	6	0	52	71	20	37	0	6.62
Mike Wuertz	R	25	1	0	1.000	0	13	0	0	15	10	10	15	0	4.34
Ryan Dempster (EJ)	R	27	1	1	.500	2	23	0	0	21	16	13	18	0	4.94
Mike Remlinger (SJ)	R	38	1	2	.333	2	47	0	0	37	33	16	35	0	3.44
1 Jimmy Anderson	L	28	0	0	—	0	9	1	0	10	9	3	3	0	4.63
Andy Pratt	L	24	0	1	.000	0	4	0	0	2	5	7	1	0	21.60

CINCINNATI — 4th 76-86 .4693 29 — DAVE MILEY

Name	G by Pos	B	AGE	G	AB	R	H	2B	3B	HR	RBI	BB	SO	SB	BA	SA
TOTALS			28	162	5518	750	1380	287	28	194	713	599	1335	77	.250	.418
Sean Casey	1B145	L	29	146	571	101	185	44	2	24	99	46	36	2	.324	.534
D'Angelo Jimenez	2B146 SS5	B	26	152	563	76	152	28	3	12	67	82	99	13	.270	.394
Barry Larkin	SS85	R	40	111	346	55	100	15	3	8	44	34	39	2	.289	.419
Ryan Freel	OF89 3B56 2B15	R	28	143	505	74	140	21	8	3	28	67	88	37	.277	.368
Austin Kearns (RJ)	OF60	R	24	64	217	28	50	10	2	9	32	28	71	2	.230	.419
Ken Griffey Jr. (LJ)	OF77	L	34	83	300	49	76	18	0	20	60	44	67	1	.253	.513
Adam Dunn	OF156 1B10	L	24	161	568	105	151	34	0	46	102	108	195	6	.266	.569
Jason LaRue	C111 OF1	R	30	114	390	46	98	24	2	14	55	26	108	1	.251	.431
Juan Castro	3B78 SS31 2B12 1B4	R	32	111	299	36	73	21	2	5	26	14	51	1	.244	.378
Wily Mo Pena	OF91	R	22	110	336	45	87	10	1	26	66	22	108	5	.259	.527
Jacob Cruz	OF29 1B6	L	31	96	147	22	33	8	0	3	28	16	43	0	.224	.340
Javier Valentin	C55 1B7	B	28	82	202	18	47	10	1	6	20	17	36	0	.233	.381
Felipe Lopez	SS51 3B24 2B2	B	24	79	264	35	64	18	2	7	31	25	81	1	.242	.405
Tim Hummel	3B32 1B13 2B1 SS1	R	25	56	110	10	24	4	0	1	7	8	17	1	.218	.282
John Vander Wal (KJ)	OF7 1B4	L	38	42	51	2	6	2	0	2	4	4	20	0	.118	.275
Brandon Larson (LJ)	3B35	R	28	40	118	13	25	6	0	3	14	14	35	1	.212	.339
2 Darren Bragg	OF26	L	34	38	94	11	18	3	1	4	9	8	29	1	.191	.372
2 Jason Romano (LJ)	OF11	R	25	22	26	3	4	0	0	1	3	2	10	0	.154	.269
Andy Machado	SS17	B	23	17	56	6	15	5	1	0	4	10	26	3	.268	.393
Jermaine Clark	OF8 2B2	L	27	14	30	4	4	1	0	0	2	1	8	1	.133	.167
Corky Miller	C12	R	28	13	39	2	1	0	0	0	0	3	6	0	.026	.026
Ray Olmedo	SS7	B	23	8	1	0	0	0	0	0	0	0	1	0	.000	.000

NAME	T	AGE	W	L	PCT	SV	G	GS	CG	IP	H	BB	SO	SHO	ERA
		29	76	86	.469	47	162	162	5	1444	1595	572	992	8	5.19
Paul Wilson	R	31	11	6	.647	0	29	29	0	184	192	63	117	0	4.36
Aaron Harang	R	26	10	9	.526	0	28	28	1	161	177	53	125	1	4.86
1 Todd Jones	R	36	8	2	.800	1	51	0	0	57	49	25	37	0	3.79
Cory Lidle	R	32	7	10	.412	0	24	24	3	149	170	44	93	*1	5.32
2 Josh Hancock	R	26	5	1	.833	0	12	9	0	55	60	25	31	0	4.45
John Riedling	R	28	5	3	.625	0	70	0	0	78	90	40	46	0	5.10
Jose Acevedo	R	26	5	12	.294	0	39	27	0	158	188	45	117	0	5.94
Luke Hudson	R	27	4	2	.667	0	9	9	0	48	36	25	38	0	2.42
Todd Van Poppel	R	32	4	6	.400	0	48	11	0	115	136	32	72	0	6.09
Ryan Wagner	R	21	3	2	.600	0	49	0	0	52	59	27	37	0	4.70
Mike Matthews (EJ)	L	30	2	1	.667	0	35	0	0	30	31	16	15	0	6.30
Brian Reith	R	26	2	2	.500	0	22	0	0	26	30	19	24	0	7.27
Joe Valentine	R	24	2	3	.400	4	24	1	0	29	23	25	29	0	5.22
Phil Norton	L	28	2	5	.286	0	69	0	0	66	71	38	48	0	5.07
Brandon Claussen	L	25	2	8	.200	0	14	14	0	66	80	35	45	0	6.14
2 Juan Padilla	R	27	1	0	1.000	0	12	0	0	14	23	8	12	0	10.67
Jung Bong	L	24	1	1	.500	0	3	3	0	15	17	10	11	0	4.70
2 Gabe White	L	32	1	2	.333	1	40	0	0	39	39	5	33	0	6.23
Danny Graves	R	31	1	6	.143	41	68	0	0	68	77	13	40	0	3.95
Aaron Myette	R	26	0	0	—	0	3	0	0	4	3	6	4	0	8.31
Jesus Sanchez	L	29	0	2	.000	0	3	0	0	14	18	9	8	0	7.53
Jimmy Haynes	R	31	0	3	.000	0	3	3	0	15	26	7	8	0	9.60
Josh Hall (SJ) 23															

* Lidle, also with Philadelphia, tied for league lead in ShO with 3

PITTSBURGH — 5th 72-89 .447 32.5 — LLOYD McCLENDON

Name	G by Pos	B	AGE	G	AB	R	H	2B	3B	HR	RBI	BB	SO	SB	BA	SA
TOTALS			28	161	5483	680	1428	267	39	142	648	415	1066	63	.260	.401
Craig Wilson	OF100 1B65 C4	R	27	155	561	97	148	35	5	29	82	50	169	2	.264	.499
Jose Castillo	2B123 SS2	R	23	129	383	44	98	15	2	8	39	23	92	3	.256	.368
Jack Wilson	SS156	R	26	157	652	82	201	41	12	11	59	26	71	8	.308	.459
2 Ty Wigginton	3B56	R	26	58	182	17	40	7	0	5	24	22	34	1	.220	.341
Rob Mackowiak	OF118 3B55 1B1	L	27	155	491	65	121	22	6	17	75	50	114	13	.246	.442
Tike Redman	OF147	L	27	155	546	65	153	19	4	8	51	23	52	18	.280	.374
Jason Bay (SJ)	OF119	R	25	120	411	61	116	24	4	26	82	41	129	4	.282	.550
Jason Kendall	C146	R	30	147	574	86	183	32	0	3	51	60	41	11	.319	.390
Bobby Hill	2B40 3B25	B	26	126	233	28	62	7	2	2	27	20	39	0	.266	.339
Abraham Nunez	2B32 SS13 3B6 P1	B	28	112	182	17	43	9	0	2	13	10	36	1	.236	.319
Daryle Ward (RJ)	1B71 OF12	L	29	79	293	39	73	17	2	15	57	22	45	0	.249	.474
Chris Stynes	3B71	R	31	74	162	16	35	10	0	1	16	9	23	0	.216	.296
1 Randall Simon (LJ)	1B46	L	29	61	175	14	34	6	0	3	14	15	17	0	.194	.280
Humberto Cota (UJ)	C24	R	25	36	66	10	15	1	1	5	8	3	20	0	.227	.500
Raul Mondesi	OF26	R	33	26	99	8	28	8	0	2	14	11	27	0	.283	.424
J.J. Davis (RJ-PJ)	OF17	R	25	25	35	4	5	1	0	3	4	10	2		.143	.171
Tony Alvarez	OF16	R	25	24	38	5	8	2	0	1	8	4	7	2	.211	.342
4 Jose Bautista	OF12	R	23	23	40	1	8	2	0	0	2	1	18	0	.200	.250
1 Ruben Mateo	OF10	R	26	19	33	4	8	0	0	3	7	5	6	0	.242	.515
Freddy Sanchez (NJ)	SS4 2B3 3B1	R	26	7	15	1	3	0	0	0	0	0	3	0	.200	.200
Carlos Rivera	1B7	L	26	7	15	1	3	0	0	0	2	0	4	0	.200	.200
J.R. House	C3	R	24	5	9	1	1	1	0	0	0	0	2	0	.111	.222

NAME	T	AGE	W	L	PCT	SV	G	GS	CG	IP	H	BB	SO	SHO	ERA
		28	72	89	.447	46	161	161	3	1428	1451	576	1079	8	4.29
Oliver Perez	L	22	12	10	.545	0	30	30	2	196	145	81	239	1	2.98
Josh Fogg	R	27	11	10	.524	0	32	32	0	178	193	66	82	0	4.64
1 Kris Benson	R	29	8	8	.500	0	20	20	0	132	137	44	83	0	4.22
Salomon Torres	R	32	7	7	.500	0	84	0	0	92	87	22	62	0	2.64
Ryan Vogelsong	R	26	6	13	.316	0	31	26	0	133	148	67	92	0	6.50
Jose Mesa	R	38	5	2	.714	43	70	0	0	69	78	20	37	0	3.25
Sean Burnett (EJ)	L	21	5	5	.500	0	13	13	1	72	86	28	30	1	5.02
Kip Wells	R	27	5	7	.417	0	24	24	0	138	145	66	116	0	4.55
Mike Gonzalez	L	25	3	1	.750	1	47	0	0	43	32	6	55	0	1.25
David Williams	L	25	2	3	.400	0	10	6	0	39	31	13	33	0	4.42
Brian Meadows	R	28	2	4	.333	1	68	0	0	78	76	19	46	0	3.58
John Grabow	L	25	2	5	.286	0	68	0	0	62	81	28	64	0	5.11
Jason Boyd	R	31	1	0	1.000	0	12	0	0	13	13	8	12	0	5.54
Brian Boehringer (SJ)	R	35	1	1	.500	0	21	0	0	25	27	17	20	0	4.62
Mark Corey	R	30	1	2	.333	0	31	0	0	36	39	19	28	0	4.54
John Van Benschoten	R	24	1	3	.250	0	5	5	0	29	33	19	18	0	6.91
Willis Roberts	R	29	0	0	—	0	1	0	0	12	12	9	7	0	5.25
Abraham Nunez	R	28	0	0	—	0	1	0	0	0	0	0	0	0	0.00
Frank Brooks	L	25	0	1	.000	0	11	1	0	17	13	9	18	0	4.67
Ian Snell	R	22	0	1	.000	0	2	2	0	12	14	9	9	0	7.50
Mike Johnston (EJ)	L	25	0	4	.000	0	24	0	0	23	29	15	18	0	4.37
Nelson Figueroa	R	30	0	0	.000	0	10	3	0	28	32	11	10	0	5.72

MILWAUKEE — 6th 67-94 .416 37.5 — NED YOST

Name	G by Pos	B	AGE	G	AB	R	H	2B	3B	HR	RBI	BB	SO	SB	BA	SA
TOTALS			29	161	5483	634	1358	295	32	135	601	540	1312	138	.248	.387
Lyle Overbay	1B158	L	27	159	579	83	174	53	1	16	87	81	128	2	.301	.478
Keith Ginter (WJ)	2B54 3B47 OF2	R	28	113	386	47	101	23	2	19	60	37	100	8	.262	.479
Craig Counsell	SS129 3B1	L	33	140	473	59	114	19	5	2	23	59	88	17	.241	.315
Wes Helms (KJ)	3B66 1B10	R	28	92	274	24	72	13	1	4	28	24	60	0	.263	.361
Brady Clark	OF133	R	31	138	353	41	99	18	1	7	46	43	45	15	.280	.397
Scott Podsednik	OF153	L	28	154	640	85	156	27	7	12	39	58	105	70	.244	.364
Geoff Jenkins	OF156	L	29	157	617	88	163	36	6	27	93	46	152	3	.264	.473
Chad Moeller	C100	R	29	101	317	25	66	13	1	5	27	21	74	0	.208	.303
Bill Hall	2B50 SS37 3B11	R	24	126	390	43	93	20	3	9	53	20	119	12	.238	.374
1 Ben Grieve	OF65	L	28	108	234	28	61	15	0	7	29	39	65	0	.261	.415
Brooks Kieschnick (SJ)	P32	L	32	77	63	2	17	3	0	1	7	5	16	0	.270	.365
Gary Bennett	C75	R	32	75	219	18	49	14	0	3	20	22	32	1	.224	.329
Junior Spivey (SJ)	2B58 SS1	R	29	59	228	33	62	13	0	7	28	25	48	5	.272	.421
Chris Magruder	OF24	B	27	56	89	11	21	6	1	2	10	8	21	0	.236	.393
Trent Durrington	3B11 2B6 P1	R	28	53	82	13	19	4	2	4	4	4	23	4	.232	.402
Russell Branyan	3B44 1B2	L	28	51	158	21	37	11	1	11	27	20	68	1	.234	.525
Dave Krynzel	OF12	L	22	16	41	6	9	1	0	0	3	3	15	0	.220	.244
Jeff Liefer	OF3	L	29	16	28	2	6	2	0	1	5	2	8	0	.214	.393
Mark Johnson	C5	L	29	8	11	1	1	0	0	0	2	3	2	0	.091	.091
Matt Erickson	2B1 SS1	L	28	4	6	0	1	0	0	0	0	1	0	0	.167	.167
Corey Hart		R	22	1	1	1	0	0	0	0	0	0	0	0	.000	.000

NAME	T	AGE	W	L	PCT	SV	G	GS	CG	IP	H	BB	SO	SHO	ERA
		28	67	94	.416	42	161	161	6	1442	1440	476	1098	10	4.24
Doug Davis	L	28	12	12	.500	0	34	34	0	207	192	79	166	0	3.39
Ben Sheets	R	25	12	14	.462	0	34	34	5	237	201	32	264	0	2.70
Victor Santos	R	27	11	12	.478	0	31	28	0	154	169	57	115	0	4.97
Wes Obermueller	R	27	6	8	.429	0	25	20	1	118	138	42	59	1	5.80
Chris Capuano (LJ-EJ)	L	25	6	8	.429	0	17	17	0	88	91	37	80	0	4.99
Luis Vizcaino	R	29	4	4	.500	1	73	0	0	72	61	24	63	0	3.75
1 Dave Burba	R	37	3	1	.750	2	41	5	0	71	63	24	47	0	4.08
1 Matt Kinney	R	27	3	4	.429	0	32	6	0	62	77	23	52	0	5.78
Gary Glover	R	27	2	1	.667	0	3	0	0	18	18	8	8	0	3.50
Mike Adams	R	25	2	3	.400	0	46	0	0	53	50	14	39	0	3.40
Chris Saenz	R	22	1	0	1.000	0	1	1	0	6	2	3	7	0	0.00
Brooks Kieschnick (SJ)	R	32	1	1	.500	0	32	0	0	43	44	13	26	0	3.77
Ben Ford (SJ)	R	28	1	1	.500	0	24	0	0	24	25	10	13	0	6.38
Matt Wise	R	28	1	2	.333	0	30	3	0	53	51	15	30	0	4.44
Jeff Bennett	R	24	1	5	.167	0	60	0	0	71	78	26	45	0	4.79
Ben Hendrickson	R	23	1	8	.111	0	11	11	0	46	58	20	29	0	6.22
Pedro Liriano	R	23	0	0	—	0	11	0	0	16	15	3	10	0	4.02
Trent Durrington	R	28	0	0	—	0	1	0	0	0	0	0	0	0	0.00
Travis Phelps	R	26	0	1	.000	0	4	0	0	8	3	3	3	0	10.50
Adrian Hernandez	R	28	0	2	.000	0	6	1	0	16	20	14	14	0	8.44
Jorge de la Rosa	L	23	0	3	.000	0	23	1	0	23	29	14	15	0	6.35
Danny Kolb	R	29	0	4	.000	39	64	0	0	57	50	15	21	0	2.98

WEST DIVISION

LOS ANGELES — 1st 93-69 .574 — JIM TRACY

Name	G by Pos	B	AGE	G	AB	R	H	2B	3B	HR	RBI	BB	SO	SB	BA	SA
TOTALS			29	162	5542	761	1450	226	30	203	731	536	1092	102	.262	.423
Shawn Green	1B111 OF52	L	31	157	590	92	157	28	1	28	86	71	114	5	.266	.459
Alex Cora	2B138	L	28	138	405	47	107	9	4	10	47	47	41	3	.264	.380
Cesar Izturis	SS159	R	24	159	670	90	193	32	9	4	62	43	70	25	.288	.381
Adrian Beltre	3B155 SS1	R	25	156	598	104	200	32	0	48	121	53	87	7	.334	.629
1 Juan Encarnacion	OF85	R	28	86	324	42	76	18	1	13	43	21	53	5	.235	.420
Milton Bradley	OF138	B	26	141	516	72	138	24	0	19	67	71	123	15	.267	.424
Jayson Werth (UJ)	OF79	R	25	89	290	56	76	11	3	16	47	30	85	4	.262	.486
1 Paul LoDuca	C81 OF9 1B3	R	32	91	349	41	105	18	1	10	49	22	27	2	.301	.444
Jason Grabowski	OF31 1B3	L	28	113	173	18	38	0	0	7	20	19	50	0	.220	.382
Robin Ventura	1B40 3B10 P1	L	36	102	152	19	37	3	0	5	28	22	31	0	.243	.362
Jose Hernandez	2B50 SS13 3B12 OF9 1B8	R	34	95	211	32	61	12	1	13	29	26	61	3	.289	.540
Olmedo Saenz	3B25 3B2	R	33	77	111	19	31	8	0	8	22	12	33	0	.279	.505
David Ross	C67	R	27	70	165	13	28	3	1	5	15	15	62	0	.170	.291
1 Dave Roberts	OF62	L	32	68	233	45	59	4	7	2	21	28	31	33	.253	.356
2 Steve Finley	OF55	L	39	58	224	31	59	12	0	13	46	21	30	1	.263	.491
2 Brent Mayne	C47	L	36	47	96	5	18	4	0	0	11	14	13	0	.188	.188
2 Hee-Seop Choi	1B23	L	25	31	62	5	10	5	0	0	6	11	18	0	.161	.242
Joe Thurston	2B4	L	24	17	17	1	3	1	0	0	0	0	5	0	.176	.353
Antonio Perez	2B2 SS1	R	24	13	13	1	3	1	0	0	1	1	4	0	.231	.308
2 Tom Wilson	C7	R	33	9	8	1	2	1	0	0	3	1	2	0	.250	.375
Jose Flores	2B1 3B1	R	31	9	4	2	1	0	0	0	0	3	0	0	.250	.250
Chin-Feng Chen	OF3	R	26	8	4	0	0	0	0	0	0	0	3	0	.000	.000
Todd Hundley (XJ) 35																

NAME	T	AGE	W	L	PCT	SV	G	GS	CG	IP	H	BB	SO	SHO	ERA
		30	93	69	.574	51	162	162	2	1453	1386	521	1066	6	4.01
Jose Lima	R	31	13	5	.722	0	36	24	0	170	178	34	93	0	4.07
Kazuhisa Ishii	L	30	13	8	.619	0	31	31	2	172	155	98	99	2	4.71
Jeff Weaver	R	27	13	13	.500	0	34	34	0	220	219	67	153	0	4.01
1 Guillermo Mota	R	30	4	4	.667	1	52	0	0	63	51	27	52	0	2.14
Eric Gagne	R	28	7	3	.700	45	70	0	0	82	51	22	114	0	2.19
Wilson Alvarez	L	34	7	6	.538	1	40	15	0	121	109	31	102	0	4.03
Odalis Perez	L	27	7	6	.538	0	31	31	0	196	180	44	128	0	3.25
Yhency Brazoban	R	24	6	2	.750	0	33			25	15	27		0	2.48
Giovanni Carrara	R	36	5	2	.714	2	42	0	0	54	46	20	48	0	2.18
Hideo Nomo (SJ)	R	35	4	11	.267	0	18	18	0	84	105	42	54	0	8.25
Duaner Sanchez	R	24	3	1	.750	0	80		81	27	44			0	3.38
Edwin Jackson (AJ)	R	20	2	1	.667	0	9		25	31	11	16		0	7.30
2 Elmer Dessens	R	33	2	1	.667	0				25	31	11	16	0	3.20
2 Scott Stewart	L	28	1	0	1.000	0	12	0	0	12	20	6	18	0	5.84
Brian Falkenborg	R	26	1	0	1.000	0	14	0	0	19	19	11	13	0	7.53
2 Brad Penny (AJ)	R	26	3		.333	0			3	12	6	6		0	3.09
Darren Dreifort (KJ)	L				.200	1	60	0	0	51	43	36	63	0	4.44
Mike Venafro	L	30								9	11	3	6	0	4.00
1 Masao Kida	R	35													
Rodney Myers	R	35													
Robin Ventura	R	36													
1 Tom Martin	L	34	0	0	.000	0	47	0	0	28	32	14	18	0	4.13
Paul Shuey (RJ) 33															

SAN FRANCISCO 2nd 91-71 .562 2 — FELIPE ALOU

Name	G by Pos	B	AGE	G	AB	R	H	2B	3B	HR	RBI	BB	SO	SB	BA	SA
TOTALS			31	162	5546	850	1500	314	33	183	805	705	874	43	.270	.438
J.T. Snow (KJ)	1B100	L	36	107	346	62	113	32	1	12	60	58	61	0	.327	.529
Ray Durham	2B118	B	32	120	471	95	133	28	8	17	65	57	60	10	.282	.484
Deivi Cruz	SS104 2B2 3B1	R	31	127	397	46	116	30	2	7	55	17	32	1	.292	.431
Edgardo Alfonzo	3B129 2B5	R	30	139	519	66	150	26	1	11	77	46	40	1	.289	.407
Michael Tucker	OF124	L	33	140	464	77	119	21	6	13	62	70	106	5	.256	.412
Marquis Grissom	OF142	R	37	145	562	78	157	26	2	22	90	37	83	3	.279	.450
Barry Bonds	OF133	L	39	147	373	129	135	27	3	45	101	232	41	6	.362	.812
A.J. Pierzynski	C118	L	27	131	471	45	128	28	2	11	77	19	27	1	.272	.410
Pedro Feliz	1B70 3B51 SS20 OF4	R	29	144	503	72	139	33	3	22	84	23	85	5	.276	.485
Dustan Mohr	OF95	R	28	117	263	52	72	20	1	7	28	46	64	0	.274	.437
1 Neifi Perez	SS57 2B39 3B2	B	31	103	319	28	74	12	1	2	33	21	35	0	.232	.295
Cody Ransom	SS45 2B16 3B1 OF1	R	28	78	68	13	17	6	0	1	11	6	20	2	.250	.382
Yorvit Torrealba	C59	R	25	64	172	19	39	7	1	6	23	17	31	2	.227	.407
Jeffrey Hammonds	OF28	R	33	40	95	14	20	5	0	3	6	15	22	1	.211	.358
2 Ricky Ledee	OF15	L	30	31	53	6	6	2	0	0	4	5	20	1	.113	.151
Damon Minor	1B17	L	30	24	58	8	14	2	0	0	6	12	18	0	.241	.276
Brian Dallimore	2B9 3B6	R	30	20	43	8	12	2	0	1	7	4	7	0	.279	.395
Todd Linden	OF11	B	24	16	32	6	5	1	0	0	1	5	7	0	.156	.188
Tony Torcato			24	13	9	1	5	0	0	0	2	1	0	0	.556	.556
Jason Ellison	OF4	R	26	13	4	4	2	0	0	0	1	0	1	2	.500	1.250
Justin Knoedler	C1	R	23	1	1	0	0	0	0	0	0	0	1	0	.000	.000

NAME	T	AGE	W	L	PCT	SV	G	GS	CG	IP	H	BB	SO	SHO	ERA
		30	91	71	.562	46	162	162	8	1457	1481	548	1020	8	4.29
Jason Schmidt	R	31	18	7	.720	0	32	32	4	225	165	77	251	3	3.20
Brett Tomko	R	31	11	7	.611	0	32	31	2	194	196	64	108	1	4.04
Jerome Williams (AJ)	R	22	10	7	.588	0	22	22	0	129	123	44	80	0	4.24
Kirk Rueter	L	33	9	12	.429	0	33	33	0	190	225	66	56	0	4.73
Jim Brower	R	31	7	7	.500	1	89	0	0	93	90	36	63	0	3.29
Noah Lowry	L	23	6	0	1.000	0	16	14	2	92	96	28	72	1	3.82
Dustin Hermanson	R	31	6	9	.400	17	47	18	0	131	132	46	102	0	4.53
Tyler Walker	R	28	5	1	.833	1	52	0	0	64	69	24	48	0	4.24
Jason Christiansen	L	34	4	3	.571	3	60	0	0	36	34	26	22	0	4.50
Matt Herges	L	34	4	5	.444	23	70	0	0	65	90	21	39	0	5.23
1 Felix Rodriguez	R	31	3	5	.375	0	53	0	0	45	43	19	31	0	3.43
Wayne Franklin	L	30	2	1	.667	0	43	2	0	51	55	22	40	0	6.39
Scott Eyre	L	32	2	2	.500	1	83	0	0	53	43	27	49	0	4.10
Brad Hennessey	R	24	2	2	.500	0	7	7	0	34	42	15	25	0	4.98
David Aardsma	R	22	1	0	1.000	0	11	0	0	11	20	10	5	0	6.75
3 Dave Burba	R	37	1	0	1.000	0	6	0	0	7	6	2	3	0	5.68
Kevin Walker	L	27	0	0	—	0	2	0	0	2	3	2	1	0	16.20
Leo Estrella	R	29	0	0	—	0	5	0	0	6	9	2	1	0	6.75
Merkin Valdez	R	22	0	0	—	0	2	0	0	2	4	3	2	0	27.00
Jesse Foppert	R	23	0	0	—	0	1	1	0	2	2	2	0	0	27.00
Kevin Correia	R	23	0	1	.000	0	12	1	0	19	25	10	14	0	8.05
Brian Cooper	R	29	0	2	.000	0	2	2	0	13	15	5	7	0	8.78
Robb Nen (SJ) 34															

SAN DIEGO 3rd 87-75 .537 6 — BRUCE BOCHY

Name	G by Pos	B	AGE	G	AB	R	H	2B	3B	HR	RBI	BB	SO	SB	BA	SA
TOTALS			29	162	5573	768	1521	304	32	139	722	566	910	52	.273	.414
Phil Nevin	1B144 C1	R	33	147	547	78	158	31	1	26	105	66	121	0	.289	.492
Mark Loretta	2B154	R	32	154	620	108	208	47	2	16	76	58	45	5	.335	.495
Khalil Greene	SS136	R	24	139	484	67	132	31	4	15	65	53	94	4	.273	.446
Sean Burroughs	3B125	L	23	130	523	76	156	28	3	2	47	31	52	5	.298	.365
Brian Giles	OF159	L	33	159	609	97	173	33	7	23	94	89	80	10	.284	.475
Jay Payton	OF137	R	31	143	458	57	119	17	4	8	55	43	56	2	.260	.367
Ryan Klesko	OF104 1B18	L	33	127	402	58	117	32	2	9	66	73	67	3	.291	.448
Ramon Hernandez (KJ)	C108	R	28	111	384	45	106	23	0	18	63	35	45	1	.276	.477
Terrence Long	OF87	L	28	136	288	31	85	19	4	3	28	19	51	3	.295	.420
Kerry Robinson	OF49	L	30	90	92	20	27	4	0	0	5	5	8	11	.293	.337
Miguel Ojeda	C50	R	29	62	156	23	40	3	0	8	26	15	34	0	.256	.429
Ramon Vazquez (UJ)	SS22 2B10 3B9 1B3	L	27	52	115	12	27	3	2	1	13	11	24	1	.235	.322
2 Rich Aurilia	3B29 2B7 SS6 1B1	R	32	51	138	22	35	8	2	2	16	15	28	0	.254	.384
1 Brian Buchanan	OF18 1B3	R	30	38	60	7	12	4	0	2	6	6	19	0	.200	.333
Xavier Nady	OF22	R	25	34	77	7	19	4	0	3	9	5	13	0	.247	.416
Jeff Cirillo (BG)	3B11 1B10 2B4 OF1	R	34	33	75	12	16	3	0	1	7	5	14	0	.213	.293
2 Dave Hansen	1B7 3B2	L	35	29	28	1	4	0	0	0	3	5	8	0	.143	.143
Humberto Quintero	C21	R	24	23	72	7	18	3	0	2	10	5	16	0	.250	.375
Freddy Guzman	OF17	R	23	20	76	8	16	0	0	0	3	6	13	5	.211	.250
2 Robert Fick	1B1	L	30	13	12	2	2	0	0	0	2	0	6	0	.167	.167
3 Alex Gonzalez	SS11	R	31	11	23	2	4	1	0	0	3	2	6	0	.174	.304
Jon Knott	OF5	R	25	9	14	1	3	2	0	0	1	1	5	0	.214	.357
1 Darren Bragg		L	34	9	7	2	1	0	0	0	0	3	3	0	.143	.143

NAME	T	AGE	W	L	PCT	SV	G	GS	CG	IP	H	BB	SO	SHO	ERA
		30	87	75	.537	44	162	162	3	1441	1460	422	1079	8	4.03
Jake Peavy (AJ)	R	23	15	6	.714	0	27	27	0	166	146	53	173	0	2.27
Brian Lawrence	R	28	15	14	.517	0	34	34	2	203	226	55	121	1	4.12
David Wells	L	41	12	8	.600	0	31	31	0	196	203	20	101	1	3.73
Adam Eaton	R	26	11	14	.440	0	33	33	0	199	204	52	153	0	4.61
Ismael Valdez	R	30	9	6	.600	0	23	20	1	114	141	31	37	1	5.53
Akinori Otsuka	R	32	7	2	.778	2	73	0	0	77	56	26	87	0	1.75
Scott Linebrink	R	27	7	3	.700	0	73	0	0	84	61	26	83	0	2.14
Trevor Hoffman	R	36	3	3	.500	41	55	0	0	55	42	8	53	0	2.30
Antonio Osuna (EJ)	R	31	2	1	.667	0	37	0	0	31	32	11	36	0	2.45
Eddie Oropesa	L	32	2	1	.667	0	16	0	0	9	6	13	6	0	11.00
Brian Sweeney	R	30	1	1	.500	0	20	2	0	35	42	10	18	0	5.65
Blaine Neal	R	26	1	1	.500	0	40	0	0	42	49	11	36	0	4.07
2 Ricky Stone	R	29	1	1	.500	0	27	0	0	33	40	9	22	0	6.89
Justin Germano	R	21	1	2	.333	0	5	2	0	21	31	14	16	0	8.86
Steve Watkins	R	25	0	0	—	0	1	1	0	4	4	7	0	0	6.28
Jason Szuminski	R	25	0	0	—	0	10	0	0	10	12	11	5	0	7.20
Marty McLeary	R	29	0	0	—	0	2	0	0	2	4	2	2	0	14.73
Andy Ashby (EJ)	R	36	0	0	—	0	1	0	0	2	2	1	0	0	0.00
Jay Witasick (UJ)	R	31	0	1	.000	1	44	0	0	62	57	26	57	0	3.21
Brandon Puffer	R	28	0	1	.000	0	14	0	0	18	24	11	12	0	5.50
Mike Bynum	L	26	0	1	.000	0	4	2	0	14	13	9	9	0	54.00
Rod Beck (PP)	R	35	0	0	—	0	26	0	0	24	27	9	15	0	6.38
Sterling Hitchcock (UJ-EJ-VR)	L	33	0	0	.000	0	4	0	0	21	22	8	14	0	6.33
Dennis Tankersley	R	25	0	5	.000	0	9	6	0	35	35	17	29	0	5.14

COLORADO 4th 68-94 .420 25 — CLINT HURDLE

Name	G by Pos	B	AGE	G	AB	R	H	2B	3B	HR	RBI	BB	SO	SB	BA	SA
TOTALS			31	162	5577	833	1531	331	34	202	795	568	1181	44	.275	.455
Todd Helton	1B153	L	30	154	547	115	190	49	2	32	96	127	72	3	.347	.620
Aaron Miles	2B128	B	27	134	522	75	153	15	3	6	47	29	53	12	.293	.368
Royce Clayton	SS144	R	34	146	574	95	160	36	4	8	54	48	125	10	.279	.397
Vinny Castilla	3B148	R	36	148	583	93	158	43	3	35	131	51	113	0	.271	.535
1 Larry Walker (GJ)	OF34	L	37	38	108	22	35	9	3	6	20	25	23	2	.324	.630
Preston Wilson (KJ)	OF52	R	29	58	202	24	50	11	0	6	29	17	49	2	.248	.391
Jeromy Burnitz	OF143	L	35	150	540	94	153	30	4	37	110	58	124	5	.283	.559
Charles Johnson	C91	R	32	109	305	42	72	20	0	13	47	49	91	2	.236	.430
Mark Sweeney	OF28 1B15	L	34	122	177	25	47	12	2	9	40	32	51	1	.266	.508
Matt Holliday	OF115	R	24	121	400	65	116	31	3	14	57	31	86	3	.290	.488
Luis Gonzalez	2B40 OF29 3B18 SS10	R	25	102	322	42	94	17	2	12	46	15	67	1	.292	.469
Todd Greene	C53	R	33	75	195	23	55	14	0	10	35	13	38	0	.282	.508
Kit Pellow	OF36 1B5 C4 3B4	R	30	59	121	15	29	5	1	2	10	8	43	1	.240	.347
Denny Hocking	OF30 SS13 2B8 3B2	B	34	55	94	7	19	2	0	0	4	7	20	0	.202	.223
Choo Freeman	OF41	R	24	45	90	15	17	3	2	1	11	14	21	1	.189	.300
Brad Hawpe	OF34	L	25	42	105	12	26	3	2	3	9	11	34	1	.248	.400
Jorge Piedra	OF34	L	25	38	91	15	27	8	0	3	6	5	19	0	.297	.484
J.D. Closser	C32	B	24	36	113	5	36	6	0	1	10	6	22	0	.319	.398
Rene Reyes	OF21	B	26	28	61	5	9	2	0	1	6	3	17	0	.148	.180
Clint Barmes	2B9 SS9	R	25	20	71	14	20	5	2	2	10	3	10	0	.282	.437
Garrett Atkins	3B4 1B3 OF3	R	24	15	28	3	10	2	0	1	8	4	3	0	.357	.536
Andy Tracy	3B1	L	30	15	16	1	3	1	0	0	1	1	8	0	.188	.250

NAME	T	AGE	W	L	PCT	SV	G	GS	CG	IP	H	BB	SO	SHO	ERA
		29	68	94	.420	36	162	162	3	1435	1634	697	947	2	5.54
Shawn Estes	L	31	15	8	.652	0	34	34	2	202	223	105	117	0	5.84
Jason Jennings	R	25	11	12	.478	0	33	33	0	201	194	101	133	0	5.51
Joe Kennedy (SJ)	L	25	9	7	.563	0	27	27	1	162	163	67	117	0	3.66
Aaron Cook (IL)	R	25	6	4	.600	0	16	16	1	97	112	39	40	0	4.28
Tim Harikkala	R	32	6	6	.500	0	55	0	0	63	55	23	30	0	4.74
Jeff Francis	L	23	3	6	.333	0	7	7	0	37	42	13	32	0	5.15
Vladimir Nunez	R	29	3	3	.500	0	22	0	0	26	26	14	22	0	7.01
Steve Reed	R	39	3	8	.273	0	65	0	0	66	72	17	38	0	3.68
1 Jeff Fassero	L	41	3	8	.273	0	40	12	0	111	136	44	59	0	5.51
Allan Simpson	R	26	2	1	.667	0	32	0	0	39	44	20	46	0	5.08
Jamey Wright	R	29	2	3	.400	0	14	14	0	79	82	45	41	0	4.12
Brian Fuentes (XJ)	L	28	2	4	.333	0	47	0	0	45	46	19	48	0	5.64
Adam Bernero (SJ)	R	27	1	1	.500	0	16	2	0	32	36	17	21	0	5.57
Javier Lopez	L	26	1	2	.333	0	64	0	0	41	45	26	20	0	5.64
Shawn Chacon	R	26	1	9	.100	35	66	0	0	63	71	52	52	0	7.11
Turk Wendell (SJ)	R	37	0	0	—	0	12	0	0	9	21	11	11	0	7.02
Chin-hui Tsao	R	23	0	0	—	0	10	0	0	9	9	2	11	0	3.86
Marc Kroon	R	31	0	0	—	0	9	0	0	9	7	6	11	0	6.48
Travis Driskill	R	32	0	0	—	0	5	0	0	8	13	3	6	0	6.48
2 Kevin Jarvis	R	34	0	1	—	0	1	0	0	2	4	1	1	0	27.00
Chris Gissell	R	24	0	1	.000	0	3	0	0	3	11	0	3	0	14.54
Jason Young (VJ)	R	24	0	1	.000	0	8	1	0	17	30	11	10	0	12.96
Scott Dohmann	R	26	0	3	.000	0	41	0	0	46	41	19	49	0	4.91
Dennis Stark (GJ)	R	29	0	5	.000	0	8	6	0	26	53	18	10	0	11.42
1 Scott Elarton	R	28	0	0	—	0	8	0	0	41	57	20	23	0	9.80
Denny Neagle (EJ) 35															

ARIZONA 5th 51-111 .315 42 — BOB BRENLY 29-50 .367 — AL PEDRIQUE 22-61 .265

Name	G by Pos	B	AGE	G	AB	R	H	2B	3B	HR	RBI	BB	SO	SB	BA	SA
TOTALS			28	162	5544	615	1401	295	38	135	582	441	1022	53	.253	.393
Richie Sexson (SJ)	1B23	R	29	23	90	20	21	4	0	9	23	14	21	0	.233	.578
1 Roberto Alomar (BH)	2B36	B	36	38	110	14	34	5	2	3	16	12	18	0	.309	.473
Alex Cintron	SS133 2B19 3B1	R	25	154	564	56	148	31	7	4	49	31	59	3	.262	.363
Chad Tracy	3B135 1B11 OF1	L	24	143	481	45	137	29	3	8	53	45	60	2	.285	.407
Danny Bautista	OF137	R	32	141	539	64	154	27	1	11	65	35	66	6	.286	.401
1 Steve Finley	OF103	L	39	104	404	61	111	16	1	23	48	40	52	6	.275	.490
Luis Gonzalez (EJ)	OF105	L	36	105	379	69	98	28	5	17	48	68	58	2	.259	.493
Robby Hammock (KJ)	C46 OF12 3B1	R	27	62	195	22	47	16	2	4	18	13	39	1	.241	.405
Shea Hillenbrand	1B131 3B17	R	28	148	562	68	174	36	3	15	80	24	49	2	.310	.464
Scott Hairston	2B85 OF3	R	24	101	339	39	84	15	6	13	29	21	88	3	.248	.442
Carlos Baerga (LJ)	1B6	B	35	79	85	6	20	2	0	0	6	6	12	0	.235	.329
Luis Terrero	OF61	R	24	62	150	20	35	7	0	4	14	20	78	10	.245	.358
2 Quinton McCracken	OF37	L	34	55	156	20	45	11	1	2	13	13	23	2	.288	.410
Juan Brito	C54	R	24	54	171	17	35	7	0	3	13	4	31	1	.205	.298
Doug DeVore	OF31	L	26	50	107	5	24	7	0	1	13	7	31	1	.224	.374
Tim Olson	3B19 SS17 OF4	R	25	48	97	8	18	7	0	1	5	16	18	1	.186	.320
Andy Green	3B18 2B14 OF9	R	26	46	109	13	22	2	1	1	4	5	17	1	.202	.266
Matt Kata (SJ)	2B38 3B3 SS1	B	26	42	162	17	40	9	0	3	14	13	29	4	.247	.364
1 Brent Mayne (XJ)	C30 1B1	L	36	36	94	9	24	6	1	0	10	13	17	1	.255	.340
Chris Snyder	C23	R	23	29	96	10	23	6	0	5	13	15	25	0	.240	.458
Jerry Gil	SS28	R	21	29	86	3	15	3	0	0	0	0	33	2	.174	.221
Alan Zinter (FJ)	1B8	B	36	28	34	4	9	2	0	1	6	5	15	0	.265	.353
Josh Kroeger	OF19	L	21	22	54	5	9	2	0	0	5	2	21	0	.167	.222
Greg Colbrunn (WJ)	3B4	R	34	20	27	1	3	0	0	0	1	3	6	0	.111	.111
Donnie Sadler	OF6 SS3 2B2 3B2	R	29	18	23	4	4	0	0	0	3	2	8	1	.174	.174
Koyie Hill (NJ)	C11	B	25	13	36	3	9	2	0	0	3	2	6	1	.250	.361
1 Bobby Estalella	C6	R	29	7	14	2	2	0	0	1	3	4	5	0	.143	.571

NAME	T	AGE	W	L	PCT	SV	G	GS	CG	IP	H	BB	SO	SHO	ERA
		29	51	111	.315	33	162	162	5	1436	1480	668	1153	6	4.98
Randy Johnson	L	40	16	14	.533	0	35	35	4	246	177	44	290	2	2.60
Brandon Webb	R	25	7	16	.304	0	35	35	4	208	194	119	164	0	3.59
Mike Koplove	R	27	4	4	.500	2	76	0	0	87	86	37	55	0	4.05
Casey Fossum (SJ)	L	26	4	15	.211	0	27	27	0	142	171	63	117	0	6.65
Brian Bruney (EJ)	R	22	3	4	.429	0	30	0	0	31	20	27	34	0	4.31
Steve Sparks	R	38	3	7	.300	0	29	18	0	121	139	45	57	0	6.04
Casey Daigle	R	23	2	4	.333	0	10	10	0	49	63	27	17	0	7.16
Randy Choate	L	28	2	4	.333	0	74	0	0	51	52	28	49	0	4.62
Steve Randolph	L	30	2	5	.286	0	45	6	0	82	73	76	62	0	5.51
Scott Service (XJ)	R	37	1	1	.500	0	21	0	0	20	24	10	17	0	7.08
Shane Nance (EJ)	L	26	1	1	.500	0	19	0	0	12	19	12	9	0	5.84
2 Chad Durbin	R	26	1	1	.500	0	9	7	0	9	11	10	8	0	8.68
Mike Gosling	L	23	1	1	.500	0	6	5	0	26	33	16	14	0	6.42
Jose Valverde (SJ)	R	24	1	2	.333	8	29	0	0	30	23	17	38	0	4.25
Andrew Good (EJ)	R	24	1	2	.333	0	6	4	0	32	43	13	26	0	8.14
Lance Cormier	R	23	1	2	.333	0	14	5	0	45	62	25	24	0	8.14
1 Elmer Dessens	R	33	1	6	.143	2	38	9	0	85	107	23	55	0	4.75
2 Jeff Fassero	L	41	0	0	—	0	2	0	0	1	0	2	1	0	0.00
Mike Fetters	R	39	0	1	.000	0	20	0	0	19	24	14	14	0	4.50
Shane Reynolds (SJ-KJ)	R	36	0	1	.000	0	5	0	0	9	11	4	6	0	4.50
Greg Aquino	R	26	0	2	.000	16	34	0	0	35	24	17	26	0	3.06
Oscar Villarreal (AJ)	R	22	0	1	.000	0	10	0	0	20	20	15	13	0	7.00
Brandon Villafuerte	R	28	0	1	.000	0	20	0	0	20	24	14	13	0	4.05
Matt Mantei (SJ)	R	30	0	4	.000	0	14	0	0	11	8	7	14	0	11.81
Edgar Gonzalez	R	21	0	9	.000	0	10	10	0	46	72	18	31	0	9.32
Brandon Lyon (EJ) 24															

LINE SCORES

Team	1	2	3	4	5	6	7	8	9	10	11	12	13	R	H	E

DIVISION SERIES: ST. LOUIS 3 : LOS ANGELES 1

Game 1   October 5 at St. Louis

	1	2	3	4	5	6	7	8	9		R	H	E
LA	0	0	0	0	1	1	0	0	1		3	9	1
STL	1	0	5	1	0	0	1	0	x		8	9	0

Perez, Dessens (3), Sanchez (5), Venafro (6), Carrara (7), Brazoban (8)

Williams, Calero (7), King (8), Isringhausen (9)

Game 2   October 7 at St. Louis

	1	2	3	4	5	6	7	8	9		R	H	E
LA	1	0	0	2	0	0	0	0	0		3	6	1
STL	0	3	0	0	3	0	2	0	x		8	11	0

Weaver, Sanchez (5), Alvarez (6), Carrara (7), Gagne (8)

Marquis, Eldred (4), **Haren** (5), King (7), Tavarez (8), Kline (9)

Game 3   October 9 at Los Angeles

	1	2	3	4	5	6	7	8	9		R	H	E
STL	0	0	0	0	0	0	0	0	0		0	5	0
LA	0	0	2	1	0	1	0	0	x		4	7	0

Morris, Eldred (8), Kline (8)

Lima

Game 4   October 10 at Los Angeles

	1	2	3	4	5	6	7	8	9		R	H	E
STL	0	1	1	3	0	0	1	0	0		6	8	0
LA	1	0	1	0	0	0	0	0	0		2	3	1

Suppan, Tavarez (8), King (8), Isringhausen (9)

Perez, **Alvarez** (3), Brazoban (5), Venafro (7), Carrara (7), Gagne (8)

DIVISION SERIES: HOUSTON 3 : ATLANTA 2

Game 1   October 6 at Atlanta

	1	2	3	4	5	6	7	8	9		R	H	E
HOU	0	0	4	0	3	0	1	0	1		9	13	1
ATL	1	0	0	1	0	0	1	0	0		3	7	0

Clemens, Qualls (8), Gallo (9)

Wright, Gryboski (5), Cruz (6), Alfonseca (8), Reitsma (9)

Game 2   October 7 at Atlanta

	1	2	3	4	5	6	7	8	9	10		R	H	E
HOU	1	0	1	0	0	0	0	0	0	0		2	4	1
ATL	0	0	0	0	0	1	0	1	0	2		4	14	0

Oswalt, Lidge (7), **Miceli** (10)

Hampton, Gryboski (7), Smoltz (8), **Alfonseca** (11)

Game 3   October 9 at Houston

	1	2	3	4	5	6	7	8	9		R	H	E
ATL	0	0	0	2	0	0	0	3	0		5	8	0
HOU	0	0	2	0	2	3	1	0	x		8	11	0

Thomson, **Byrd** (1), Gryboski, (5), Alfonseca (6), Martin (6), Reitsma (6), Cruz (8)

Backe, Qualls (7), Springer (8), Lidge (9)

Game 4   October 10 at Houston

	1	2	3	4	5	6	7	8	9		R	H	E
ATL	0	2	0	0	0	3	0	0	1		6	10	0
HOU	0	5	0	0	0	0	0	0			5	13	0

Ortiz, Gryboski (4), Alfonseca (6), Hampton (7), **Smoltz** (8)

Clemens, Qualls (6), Gallo (7), Miceli (8), Lidge (8), **Springer** (9)

Game 5   October 11 at Atlanta

	1	2	3	4	5	6	7	8	9		R	H	E
ATL	0	2	1	0	0	1	5	3	0		12	17	1
HOU	0	0	0	0	2	0	1	0	0		3	9	1

Oswalt, Qualls (6), Gallo (7), Harville (7), Miceli (8), Wheeler (9)

Wright, Gryboski (6), Reitsma (7), Martin (7), Cruz (8), Byrd (8)

COMPOSITE BATTING

DIVISION SERIES

ST. LOUIS

NAME	POS	G	AB	R	H	2B	3B	HR	RBI	BA
TOTALS		4	130	22	33	3	1	7	21	.254
Womack	2B	4	19	2	3	0	1	0	1	.158
Pujols	1B	4	15	4	5	0	0	2	5	.333
Walker	RF	4	15	6	5	1	0	2	3	.333
Edmonds	CF	4	15	1	4	0	0	1	2	.267
Sanders	LF	4	14	3	4	0	0	1	1	.286
Matheny	C	4	14	1	4	0	0	1	5	.286
Rolen	3B	4	12	1	0	0	0	0	0	.000
Renteria	SS	4	11	4	5	2	0	0	4	.455
Anderson	PH	3	3	0	0	0	0	0	0	.000
Suppan	P	1	3	0	2	0	0	0	0	.667
Cedeno	PH	2	2	0	1	0	0	0	0	.500
Morris	P	1	2	0	0	0	0	0	0	.000
Williams	P	1	2	0	0	0	0	0	0	.000
Haren	P	1	1	0	0	0	0	0	0	.000
Mabry	PH	1	1	0	0	0	0	0	0	.000
Marquis	P	1	1	0	0	0	0	0	0	.000
King	P	3	0	0	0	0	0	0	0	—
Eldred	P	2	0	0	0	0	0	0	0	—
Isringhausen	P	2	0	0	0	0	0	0	0	—
Kline	P	2	0	0	0	0	0	0	0	—
Tavarez	P	2	0	0	0	0	0	0	0	—
Calero	P	1	0	0	0	0	0	0	0	—
Taguchi	LF	1	0	0	0	0	0	0	0	—

LOS ANGELES

NAME	POS	G	AB	R	H	2B	3B	HR	RBI	BA
TOTALS		4	126	12	25	4	1	7	12	.198
Izturis	SS	4	17	1	3	1	0	0	0	.176
Green	1B	4	16	3	4	0	0	3	3	.250
Finley	CF	4	16	0	2	1	0	0	2	.125
Beltre	3B	4	15	1	4	0	0	0	1	.267
Cora	2B	4	15	1	2	0	1	0	1	.133
Werth	LF	4	14	3	4	1	0	2	3	.286
Bradley	RF	4	11	1	3	1	0	1	1	.273
Mayne	C	4	6	1	2	0	0	0	0	.333
Ventura	PH	3	3	0	0	0	0	0	0	.000
Ross	C	2	3	0	0	0	0	0	0	.000
Grabowski	PH	3	2	0	0	0	0	0	0	.000
Perez	P	2	2	0	0	0	0	0	0	.000
Lima	P	1	2	0	0	0	0	0	0	.000
Weaver	P	1	2	0	0	0	0	0	0	.000
Wilson	C	2	1	1	1	0	0	1	1	1.000
Choi	PH	1	1	0	0	0	0	0	0	.000
Carrara	P	3	0	0	0	0	0	0	0	—
Alvarez	P	2	0	0	0	0	0	0	0	—
Brazoban	P	2	0	0	0	0	0	0	0	—
Gagne	P	2	0	0	0	0	0	0	0	—
Sanchez	P	2	0	0	0	0	0	0	0	—
Venafro	P	2	0	0	0	0	0	0	0	—
Dessens	P	1	0	0	0	0	0	0	0	—
Hernandez	PH	1	0	0	0	0	0	0	0	—

HOUSTON

NAME	POS	G	AB	R	H	2B	3B	HR	RBI	BA
TOTALS		5	180	36	58	12	0	11	36	.322
Beltran	CF	5	22	9	10	2	0	4	9	.455
Berkman	RF-CF	5	22	5	9	1	0	1	3	.409
Bagwell	1B	5	22	5	7	2	0	2	5	.318
Kent	2B	5	22	3	5	3	0	0	3	.227
Biggio	LF	5	20	5	8	2	0	1	4	.400
Ensberg	3B	5	19	1	7	2	0	0	5	.368
Vizcaino	SS	5	19	2	2	0	0	0	1	.105
Ausmus	C	5	9	3	3	0	0	1	1	.333
Lane	LF-RF	5	5	2	3	0	0	1	2	.600
Chavez	C	2	5	1	3	0	0	1	1	.600
Palmeiro	LF	5	4	0	1	0	0	0	0	.250
Lamb	PH	4	3	0	0	0	0	0	1	.000
Clemens	P	2	3	0	0	0	0	0	0	.000
Oswalt	P	2	3	0	0	0	0	0	0	.000
Bruntlett	SS	2	1	0	0	0	0	0	0	.000
Backe	P	1	1	0	0	0	0	0	0	.000
Qualls	P	4	0	0	0	0	0	0	0	—
Gallo	P	3	0	0	0	0	0	0	0	—
Lidge	P	3	0	0	0	0	0	0	0	—
Miceli	P	3	0	0	0	0	0	0	0	—
Everett	SS	2	0	0	0	0	0	0	0	—
Springer	P	2	0	0	0	0	0	0	0	—
Wheeler	P	1	0	0	0	0	0	0	0	—
Harville	P	1	0	0	0	0	0	0	0	—

ATLANTA

NAME	POS	G	AB	R	H	2B	3B	HR	RBI	BA
TOTALS		5	180	21	48	4	1	7	20	.267
Giles	2B	5	24	1	3	0	0	0	1	.125
Furcal	SS	5	21	5	8	0	1	2	4	.381
Drew	RF	5	20	1	4	0	0	0	0	.200
C. Jones	3B	5	20	4	4	0	0	0	0	.200
A. Jones	CF	5	19	4	10	2	0	2	5	.526
Estrada	C	5	17	3	6	0	0	2	4	.353
LaRoche	1B	5	17	1	4	1	0	1	4	.235
Thomas	LF	5	16	1	4	0	0	0	0	.250
Wise	LF	5	5	1	1	1	0	0	0	.200
Marrero	LF	3	5	0	1	0	0	0	0	.200
Franco	1B	3	4	0	0	0	0	0	0	.000
Perez	C	2	3	0	0	0	0	0	0	.000
Wright	P	2	3	0	0	0	0	0	0	.000
Byrd	P	2	2	0	1	0	0	0	1	.500
Hampton	P	2	2	0	1	0	0	0	0	.500
Smoltz	P	2	1	0	1	0	0	0	0	1.000
Ortiz	P	1	1	0	0	0	0	0	0	.000
Gryboski	P	5	0	0	0	0	0	0	0	—
Alfonseca	P	4	0	0	0	0	0	0	0	—
Cruz	P	3	0	0	0	0	0	0	0	—
Reitsma	P	3	0	0	0	0	0	0	0	—
Green	PR	2	0	0	0	0	0	0	0	—
Martin	P	2	0	0	0	0	0	0	0	—
Betemit	PR	1	0	0	0	0	0	0	0	—
Thomson	P	1	0	0	0	0	0	0	0	—

COMPOSITE PITCHING

ST. LOUIS

NAME	G	IP	H	BB	SO	W	L	SV	ERA
TOTALS	4	35	25	15	20	3	1	0	3.09
Suppan	1	7	2	3	2	1	0	0	2.57
Morris	1	7	6	2	5	0	1	0	5.14
Williams	1	6	8	1	2	1	0	0	3.00
Marquis	1	3.1	4	4	0	0	0	0	8.10
King	3	2.1	0	0	1	0	0	0	0.00
Tavarez	2	2.1	2	0	3	0	0	0	0.00
Isringhausen	2	2	1	2	2	0	0	0	4.50
Haren	1	2	1	1	3	1	0	0	0.00
Kline	2	1.1	0	0	0	0	0	0	0.00
Calero	1	1	0	0	2	0	0	0	0.00
Eldred	2	0.2	1	2	0	0	0	0	0.00

LOS ANGELES

NAME	G	IP	H	BB	SO	W	L	SV	ERA
TOTALS	4	34	33	15	26	1	3	0	5.82
Lima	1	9	5	1	4	1	0	0	0.00
Perez	2	5	8	7	3	0	1	0	14.40
Weaver	1	4.2	8	2	4	0	1	0	11.57
Alvarez	2	3.1	4	0	4	0	1	0	10.80
Gagne	2	3	1	1	3	0	0	0	0.00
Brazoban	2	3	1	2	2	0	0	0	3.00
Carrara	3	2	4	1	1	0	0	0	9.00
Sanchez	2	2	1	1	3	0	0	0	0.00
Dessens	1	1.1	1	0	1	0	0	0	6.75
Venafro	2	0.2	0	1	0	0	0	0	0.00

HOUSTON

NAME	G	IP	H	BB	SO	W	L	SV	ERA
TOTALS	5	46.2	48	19	45	3	2	1	3.86
Clemens	2	12	12	8	12	1	0	0	3.00
Oswalt	2	11.1	15	4	8	1	0	0	2.38
Backe	1	6	5	2	5	1	0	0	3.00
Lidge	3	4.1	4	1	6	0	0	1	2.08
Qualls	4	4	4	1	3	0	0	0	6.75
Miceli	3	3.1	2	1	2	0	1	0	5.40
Gallo	3	2	3	1	4	0	0	0	4.50
Springer	2	2	3	1	5	0	1	0	18.00
Wheeler	1	1	0	0	0	0	0	0	0.00
Harville	1	0.2	0	0	0	0	0	0	0.00

ATLANTA

NAME	G	IP	H	BB	SO	W	L	SV	ERA
TOTALS	5	46	58	21	30	2	3	0	7.04
Wright	2	9.2	14	1	7	0	2	0	9.31
Hampton	2	7.1	4	4	6	0	0	0	2.45
Byrd	2	5.2	8	3	3	0	1	0	6.35
Smoltz	2	5	4	2	4	1	0	0	0.00
Gryboski	5	4.1	3	1	3	0	0	0	2.08
Alfonseca	4	3.2	2	2	0	1	0	0	4.91
Cruz	3	3.2	6	4	4	0	0	0	9.82
Reitsma	3	3	5	1	2	0	0	0	18.00
Ortiz	1	3	7	1	1	0	0	0	15.00
Martin	2	0.1	4	1	0	0	0	0	54.00
Thomson	1	0.1	1	1	0	0	0	0	0.00

LINE SCORES

Team	1	2	3	4	5	6	7	8	9	10	11	12	R	H	E

CHAMPIONSHIP: ST. LOUIS 4 : HOUSTON 3

Game 1   October 13 at St. Louis

| HOU | 2 | 0 | 0 | 2 | 0 | 0 | 0 | 2 | 1 | | | | 7 | 10 | 1 |
| STL | 2 | 0 | 0 | 0 | 2 | 6 | 0 | 0 | x | | | | 10 | 12 | 0 |

Backe, **Qualls** (5), Harville (6), Wheeler (7)   **Williams**, Calero (7), Haren (8), King (8), Tavarez (8), Isringhausen (9)

Game 2   October 14 at St. Louis

| HOU | 1 | 0 | 0 | 1 | 1 | 0 | 1 | 0 | 0 | | | | 4 | 10 | 1 |
| STL | 0 | 0 | 0 | 0 | 0 | 4 | 0 | 2 | x | | | | 6 | 9 | 0 |

Munro, Harville (5), Wheeler (6), **Miceli** (8)   Morris, Kline (6), Calero (6), **Tavarez** (8), Isringhausen (9)

Game 3   October 16 at Houston

| STL | 1 | 1 | 0 | 0 | 0 | 0 | 0 | 0 | 0 | | | | 2 | 5 | 0 |
| HOU | 3 | 0 | 0 | 0 | 0 | 0 | 2 | x | | | | | 5 | 8 | 0 |

Suppan, Haren (7), King (8), Eldred (8)   **Clemens**, Lidge (8)

Game 4   October 17 at Houston

| STL | 3 | 0 | 1 | 1 | 0 | 0 | 0 | 0 | 0 | | | | 5 | 9 | 0 |
| HOU | 1 | 0 | 2 | 0 | 0 | 2 | 1 | 0 | x | | | | 6 | 9 | 0 |

Marquis, Calero (5), King (6), **Tavarez** (7), Isringhausen (8)   Oswalt, **Wheeler** (7), Lidge (8)

Game 5   October 18 at Houston

| STL | 0 | 0 | 0 | 0 | 0 | 0 | 0 | 1 | 0 | | | | 0 | 1 | 0 |
| HOU | 0 | 0 | 0 | 0 | 0 | 0 | 0 | 0 | 3 | | | | 3 | 3 | 0 |

Williams, **Isringhausen** (8)   **Backe**, Lidge (9)

Game 6   October 20 at St. Louis

| HOU | 1 | 0 | 1 | 1 | 0 | 0 | 0 | 0 | 1 | 0 | 0 | 0 | 4 | 10 | 0 |
| STL | 2 | 0 | 2 | 0 | 0 | 0 | 0 | 0 | 2 | 0 | 0 | 0 | 6 | 15 | 0 |

Munro, Harville (3), Qualls (4), Wheeler (7), Lidge (9), **Miceli** (12)   Morris, King (6), Calero (6), Isringhausen (8), **Tavarez** (11)

Game 7   October 21 at St. Louis

| HOU | 1 | 0 | 1 | 0 | 0 | 0 | 0 | 0 | 0 | | | | 2 | 3 | 0 |
| STL | 0 | 0 | 1 | 0 | 0 | 3 | 0 | 1 | x | | | | 5 | 9 | 1 |

Clemens, Oswalt (7)   **Suppan**, Calero (7), Tavarez (8), Isringhausen (9)

COMPOSITE BATTING

NAME	POS	G	AB	R	H	2B	3B	HR	RBI	BA
ST. LOUIS										
TOTALS		7	235	34	60	12	1	11	33	.255
Rolen	3B	7	29	6	9	2	0	3	6	.310
Walker	RF	7	29	6	7	1	1	2	5	.241
Pujols	1B	7	28	10	14	2	0	4	9	**.500**
Womack	2B	7	26	5	7	1	0	0	1	.269
Edmonds	CF	7	24	2	7	2	0	2	7	.292
Renteria	SS	7	24	1	4	0	0	0	2	.167
Sanders	LF	6	21	1	4	2	0	0	0	.190
Matheny	C	7	19	0	2	0	0	0	1	.105
Cedeno	LF	6	6	1	1	0	0	0	1	.167
Mabry	LF	4	6	0	1	0	0	0	1	.167
Williams	P	2	4	1	1	1	0	0	0	.250
Luna	2B-SS	4	4	0	0	0	0	0	0	.000
Molina	C	1	4	0	1	0	0	0	0	.250
Anderson	2B	3	3	1	1	1	0	0	0	.333
Taguchi	LF	3	2	0	0	0	0	0	0	.000
Morris	P	2	2	0	0	0	0	0	0	.000
Suppan	P	2	2	0	0	0	0	0	1	.000
Marquis	P	1	2	0	1	0	0	0	0	.500
Isringhausen	P	6	0	0	0	0	0	0	0	—
Calero	P	5	0	0	0	0	0	0	0	—
Tavarez	P	5	0	0	0	0	0	0	0	—
King	P	4	0	0	0	0	0	0	0	—
Haren	P	2	0	0	0	0	0	0	0	—
Eldred	P	1	0	0	0	0	0	0	0	—
Kline	P	1	0	0	0	0	0	0	0	—
HOUSTON										
TOTALS		7	233	31	53	10	0	14	30	.227
Biggio	LF	7	32	3	6	1	0	1	1	.188
Vizcaino	SS-2B	7	28	1	7	1	0	0	0	.250
Bagwell	1B	7	27	1	7	2	0	0	3	.259
Kent	2B	7	25	3	6	2	0	3	7	.240
Beltran	CF	7	24	12	10	1	0	4	5	.417
Berkman	RF	7	24	7	7	2	0	3	9	.292
Ensberg	3B	7	22	2	3	0	0	1	1	.136
Ausmus	C	7	19	0	2	0	0	0	0	.105
Palmeiro	LF	7	6	0	2	1	0	0	0	.333
Backe	P-PH	3	5	0	0	0	0	0	0	.000
Lamb	3B	5	5	2	2	0	0	2	2	.400
Chavez	C	2	4	0	1	0	0	0	1	.250
Clemens	P	2	4	0	0	0	0	0	0	.000
Bruntlett	SS	4	2	0	0	0	0	0	0	.000
Munro	P	2	2	0	0	0	0	0	0	.000
Oswalt	P	2	2	0	0	0	0	0	0	.000
Everett	SS	3	1	0	0	0	0	0	0	.000
Lane	RF-LF	2	1	0	0	0	0	0	0	.000
Lidge	P	4	0	0	0	0	0	0	0	—
Wheeler	P	4	0	0	0	0	0	0	0	—
Harville	P	3	0	0	0	0	0	0	0	—
Miceli	P	2	0	0	0	0	0	0	0	—
Qualls	P	2	0	0	0	0	0	0	0	—

COMPOSITE PITCHING

NAME	G	IP	H	BB	SO	W	L	SV	ERA
ST. LOUIS									
TOTALS	7	63.1	53	25	42	4	3	3	4.26
Williams	2	13	5	3	9	1	0	0	2.77
Suppan	2	12	8	4	9	1	1	0	3.00
Morris	2	10	11	8	6	0	0	0	5.40
Isringhausen	6	7.2	4	3	0	1	3	3	4.70
Calero	5	7	8	1	7	0	0	0	3.86
Tavarez	5	6	3	2	3	2	1	0	3.00
Marquis	1	4	5	2	2	0	0	0	6.75
King	4	1.2	4	0	1	0	0	0	10.80
Haren	2	1.2	3	0	2	0	0	0	10.80
Eldred	1	0.1	0	1	0	0	0	0	0.00
Kline	1	0	2	0	0	0	0	0	—
HOUSTON									
TOTALS	7	62.1	60	17	56	3	4	2	4.91
Clemens	2	13	10	2	9	1	1	0	4.15
Backe	2	12.2	6	4	10	0	0	0	2.84
Lidge	4	8	1	2	14	1	0	2	0.00
Oswalt	2	8	11	4	2	0	0	0	6.75
Wheeler	4	4	0	9	1	0	0	0	0.00
Munro	2	7	14	1	5	0	0	0	9.00
Qualls	2	8	8	2	4	0	1	0	11.25
Harville	3	1.1	3	1	3	0	0	0	13.50
Miceli	2	1.1	3	1	0	0	2	0	27.00

MISCELLANEOUS 2004 INDIVIDUAL LEADERS

BATTING

On Base Average

	American League			National League	
1	Mora, Bal.	.419	1	Bonds, S.F.	.609
2	Suzuki, Sea.	.414	2	Helton, Col.	.469
3	Hafner, Cle.	.410	3	Berkman, Hou.	.450
4	Posada, N.Y.	.400	4	Drew, Atl.	.436
5	Chavez, Oak.	.397	5	Abreu, Phi.	.428
6	Ramirez, Bos.	.397	6	Edmonds, St.L.	.418
7	Durazo, Oak.	.396	7	Pujols, St.L.	.415
8	Sheffield, N.Y.	.393	8	Rolen, St.L.	.409
9	Guerrero, Ana.	.391	9	Kendall, Pit.	.399
10	Varitek, Bos.	.390	10	Thome, Phi.	.396

On Base Average plus Slugging Average

	American League			National League	
1	Ramirez, Bos.	1.009	1	Bonds, S.F.	1.422
2	Hafner, Cle.	.993	2	Helton, Col.	1.088
3	Guerrero, Ana.	.989	3	Pujols, St.L.	1.072
4	Ortiz, Bos.	.983	4	Edmonds, St.L.	1.061
5	Mora, Bal.	.981	5	Beltre, L.A.	1.017
6	Teixeira, Tex.	.929	6	Berkman, Hou.	1.016
7	Sheffield, N.Y.	.927	7	Rolen, St.L.	1.007
8	Guillen, Det.	.921	8	Drew, Atl.	1.006
9	Durazo, Oak.	.919	9	Thome, Phi.	.977
10	Matsui, N.Y.	.912	10	Abreu, Phi.	.971
				Beltran, K.C.-Hou. .915	

Total Bases

	American League			National League	
1	Guerrero, Ana.	366	1	Pujols, St.L.	389
2	Ortiz, Bos.	351	2	Beltre, L.A.	376
3	Tejada, Bal.	349	3	Helton, Col.	339
4	Ramirez, Bos.	348	4	Alou, Chi.	335
5	M. Young, Tex.	333	5	Dunn, Cin.	323
6	Suzuki, Sea.	320	6	Edmonds, St.L.	320
7	Blalock, Tex.	312	7	Ramirez, Chi.	316
8	Lee, Chi.	310	8	Abreu, Phi.	312
9	Mora, Bal.	309	9	Castilla, Col.	312
10	Rodriguez, N.Y.	308	10	Cabrera, Fla.	309
				Beltran, K.C.-Hou. 328	

Stolen Base Percentage
(Minimum 20 Attempts)

	American League			National League	
1	Ford, Min.	91	1	Reyes, N.Y.	90
2	Rodriguez, N.Y.	88	2	Abreu, Phi.	89
3	DaVanon, Ana.	86	3	Podsednik, Mil.	84
4	Jeter, N.Y.	85	4	Castillo, Fla.	84
5	Baldelli, T.B.	81	5	Womack, St.L.	84
				Beltran, K.C.-Hou. 93	
				Roberts, L.A.-Bos. 93	

Extra Base Hits

	American League			National League	
1	Ortiz, Bos.	91	1	Pujols, St.L.	99
2	Ramirez, Bos.	87	2	Edmonds, St.L.	83
3	Guerrero, Ana.	80	3	Helton, Col.	83
4	Tejada, Bal.	76	4	Castilla, Col.	81
5	Teixeira, Tex.	74	5	Beltre, L.A.	80
				Dunn, Cin.	80
				Beltran, K.C.-Hou. 83	

Caught Stealing

	American League			National League	
1	Crawford, T.B.	15	1	Pierre, Fla.	24
2	Crisp, Cle.	13	2	Podsednik, Mil.	13
	Figgins, Ana.	13	3	Bradley, L.A.	11
	Sanchez, Det.	13		Renteria, St.L.	11
5	Roberts, Bal.	12	5	Freel, Cin.	10

PITCHING

Fewest Hits Per 9 Innings Pitched

	American League			National League	
1	Santana, Min.	6.16	1	Johnson, Ari.	6.48
2	Lilly, Tor.	7.80	2	Schmidt, S.F.	6.60
3	P. Martinez, Bos.	8.00	3	Perez, Pit.	6.66
4	Harden, Oak.	8.11	4	Clemens, Hou.	7.10
5	Schilling, Bos.	8.18	5	Leiter, N.Y.	7.15
6	Bonderman, Det.	8.22	6	Zambrano, Chi.	7.47
7	Garcia, Sea.-Chi.	8.23	7	Sheets, Mil.	7.63
8	Escobar, Ana.	8.29	8	Clement, Chi.	7.71
9	Sabathia, Cle.	8.43	9	Peavy, S.D.	7.90
10	Arroyo, Bos.	8.61	10	Ishii, L.A.	8.11

Fewest Bases on Balls Per 9 Innings Pitched

	American League			National League	
1	Lieber, N.Y.	0.92	1	Wells, S.D.	0.92
2	Radke, Min.	1.07	2	Sheets, Mil.	1.22
3	Schilling, Bos.	1.39	3	Maddux, Chi.	1.40
4	Silva, Min.	1.55	4	Johnson, Ari.	1.61
5	Buehrle, Chi.	1.87	5	Lima, L.A.	1.80
6	Hudson, Oak.	2.10	6	Carpenter, St.L.	1.88
7	Santana, Min.	2.13	7	Pavano, Fla.	1.98
8	Mussina, N.Y.	2.19	8	Perez, L.A.	2.02
9	Hendrickson, T.B.	2.26	9	Eaton, S.D.	2.35
10	Arroyo, Bos.	2.37	10	Oswalt, Hou.	2.35

Strikeouts Per 9 Innings Pitched

	American League			National League	
1	Santana, Min.	10.46	1	Perez, Pit.	10.97
2	P. Martinez, Bos.	9.41	2	Johnson, Ari.	10.62
3	Escobar, Ana.	8.25	3	Schmidt, S.F.	10.04
4	Bonderman, Det.	8.22	4	Sheets, Mil.	10.03
5	C. Lee, Cle.	8.09	5	Clement, Chi.	9.45
6	Schilling, Bos.	8.06	6	Peavy, S.D.	9.36
7	Contreras, N.Y.-Chi.	7.93	7	Clemens, Hou.	9.15
8	Harden, Oak.	7.92	8	Zambrano, Chi.	8.07
9	Garcia, Sea.-Chi.	7.89	9	Oswalt, Hou.	7.82
10	Lilly, Tor.	7.66	10	Wright, Atl.	7.68

Lowest Batting Average Allowed

	American League			National League	
1	Santana, Min.	.192	1	Johnson, Ari.	.197
2	Lilly, Tor.	.230	2	Schmidt, S.F.	.202
3	P. Martinez, Bos.	.238	3	Perez, Pit.	.207
4	Schilling, Bos.	.239	4	Clemens, Hou.	.217
5	Garcia, Sea.-Chi.	.242	5	Leiter, N.Y.	.218

Home Runs Allowed

	American League			National League	
1	Moyer, Sea.	44	1	Milton, Phi.	43
2	Colon, Ana.	38	2	Maddux, Chi.	35
	May, K.C.	38		Morris, St.L.	35
4	Garland, Chi.	34	4	Lima, L.A.	33
	Anderson, K.C.	33	4	Valdez, S.D.-Fla.	33
	Buehrle, Chi.	33			
	Franklin, Sea.	33			
	Vazquez, N.Y.	33			
	Elarton, Col.-Cle. 33				

Home Runs Allowed per 9 IP
(Minimum 10 Home Runs Allowed)

	American League			National League	
1	Waechter, T.B.	2.56	1	Gonzalez, Ari.	2.91
2	Wasdin, Tex.	2.49	2	Smith, Atl.	2.66
3	Diaz, Chi.	2.37	3	Cormier, Ari.	2.58
4	Grilli, Chi.	2.20	4	Duckworth, Phi.	2.52
5	Greisinger, Min.	2.12	5	Hancock, Phi.-Cin.	2.40

Three more outs. So near. Only three more outs and the ancient curse would once more be fulfilled. The Curse of the Bambino began in 1920 when the Red Sox sold Babe Ruth to the Yankees for a mess of pottage. Ever after, the Sox were doomed to either be barred from the World Series (see Bucky Dent) or to lose it in some absurd way (see Bill Buckner). Now in 2004, Mariano Rivera, the greatest post-season stopper of all time, needed only to negotiate the ninth inning to doom Red Soxers to another winter of discontent.

Until that moment, the playoffs had gone more or less predictably. In the National League, the Dodgers came into the playoffs red hot, but the Cardinals tied a post-season record with five home runs in the opening game and scored eight runs on lesser hits in the second. Dodger righthander Jose Lima put off the inevitable with a five-hit shutout in Game Three, but the next night Albert Pujols' home run and four RBI's helped St. Louis wrap things up. In Houston's series with the Braves, Roger Clemens and four home runs started the wild card Astos off with a win. After that, the teams alternated victories until the Astros had collected the necessary three to give Houston a shot at its first N.L. pennant.

Meanwhile, many Red Sox fans believed the American League playoffs were following a plan laid out by the malicious gods of baseball – build up Bosox hopes, then crush them. It wasn't just that the Red Sox had not won a World Series in 86 years. Worse, they had come heartbreakingly close so many times. The annual glimmer of hope surfaced this year when the Sox annihilated Anaheim in three straight. Yet at the same time, Boston's particular Darth Vader, the New York Yankees, also won their playoff series in dashing style. After losing the opener to Johan Santana's 2-0 shutout, the Yankees won Game Two with an 11th-inning rally, coasted through a Game Three victory, and then wrapped things up with a four-run eighth-inning rally to tie followed by an eleventh-inning win. Beantowners nodded; the curse was taking shape.

The Cardinals and Astros met in an exciting series that would have been the gem of the fall in most years. Led by Albert Pujols, the heavy-hitting Cardinals outslugged Houston in the first two games. Then Roger Clemens put a stop to that sort of stuff, limiting the Cards to four hits in seven innings and starting the Astros on a three-game win streak. Jeff Kent's walk-off home run in Game Five brought Houston to the brink of a pennant. It took an extra-inning homer by Jim Edmonds to keep St. Louis alive for a seventh game. There, the Cardinals finally downed Clemens to move into the World Series.

In the American League, just what all Red Sox fans feared and many expected was happening. The Yankees outhit the Bosox in Game One. Worse, Curt Schilling was suffering from a torn tendon in his ankle. Then New York righthander Jon Lieber outpitched Pedro Martinez for the Yankees' second win. Game Three was the worst. New York humiliated the Sox 19-8 in a new Boston Massacre. Hideki Matsui went 5-for-6 and batted in five runs. Only three outs from extinction, the Sox regained a smatch of honor when they shocked Rivera by tying the Yankees in the ninth and winning Game Four in twelve innings on series MVP David Ortiz's walk-off four-bagger. The Yankees had been within three outs of another pennant; surely they could win one more game. When Boston won again the next night in 14 innings and again on an Ortiz hit, the smart guys reminded everyone that no team had ever come back from being 3-down in a playoff. Never!

In Game Six, Schilling showed up with his torn tendon sutured in place and stitched the Red Sox into a series tie. Three games apiece! Was it possible? The Red Sox? Do what had never been done before? It wasn't even close. The Red Sox roared to a 10-3, pennant-winning, don't-fire-till-you-see-the-blue-of-their-pinstripes, this-was-worth-waiting-86-years-for, impossible victory. Take *that*, Bambino!

But Boston's World Series history against the Cardinals was 0-for-2. In 1946, Enos Slaughter's mad dash home had conquered Ted Williams' team. In 1967, Bob Gibson won three games to upend Carl Yastrzemski and Co. The Yankees were dead, but the Bambino still lurked.

The curse seemed to be out in full force as the Red Sox clutzed four errors in the opening game of the World Series, but Boston used clutch hitting to have the last laugh on the heavy-hitting Cardinals. In the bottom of the eighth, Mark Bellhorn snapped a 9-9 tie with a two-run homer. The next night, Schilling ignored the pain in his ankle and the pain his teammates caused him with four more errors to go six gutty innings. The inspirational win was his third of the post-season. The Red Sox stood halfway home as the Series shifted to St. Louis. Boston's pitching kept getting better. Martinez threw seven scoreless innings in a 4-1, third game victory. Now the question being asked was "Could St. Louis do a 'Boston' and come back from three games down?"

Not with Derek Lowe on the mound for Boston. From the first inning when Johnny Damon homered to put his team in front 1-0, the Sox were never behind. Among the happy Bostonians who celebrated were an 86-year-old fan born in 1918, the year of the last Red Sox World Series win, and Johnny Pesky, shortstop on the 1946 Red Sox. For them, victory may have been long delayed, but maybe that made it sweeter.

WORLD SERIES

LINE SCORES

Team	1	2	3	4	5	6	7	8	9	10	11	12		R	H	E

WORLD SERIES: BOSTON 4 : ST. LOUIS 0

Game 1   October 23 at Boston

	1	2	3	4	5	6	7	8	9		R	H	E
STL	0	1	1	3	0	2	0	2	0		9	11	1
BOS	4	0	3	0	0	0	2	2	x		11	13	4

Williams, Haren (3), Calero (7), King (7), Eldred (7), **Tavarez** (8)   Wakefield, Arroyo (4), Timlin (7), Embree (8), **Foulke** (8)

Game 2   October 24 at Boston

	1	2	3	4	5	6	7	8	9		R	H	E
STL	0	0	0	1	0	0	0	1	0		2	5	0
BOS	2	0	0	2	0	2	0	0	x		6	8	4

Morris, Eldred (5), King (6), Marquis (7), Reyes (8)   **Schilling**, Embree (7), Timlin (8), Foulke (8)

Game 3   October 26 at St. Louis

	1	2	3	4	5	6	7	8	9		R	H	E
BOS	1	0	0	1	2	0	0	0	0		4	9	0
STL	0	0	0	0	0	0	0	0	1		1	4	0

Martinez, Timlin (8), Foulke (9)   **Suppan**, Reyes (5), Calero (6), King (7), Tavarez (9)

Game 4   October 27 at St. Louis

	1	2	3	4	5	6	7	8	9		R	H	E
BOS	1	0	2	0	0	0	0	0	0		3	9	0
STL	0	0	0	0	0	0	0	0	0		0	4	0

Lowe, Arroyo (8), Embree (8), Foulke (9)   **Marquis**, Haren (7), Isringhausen 8)

COMPOSITE BATTING

NAME	POS	G	AB	R	H	2B	3B	HR	RBI	BA
BOSTON										
TOTALS		4	138	24	39	11	2	4	24	.283
Damon	CF	4	21	4	6	2	1	1	2	.286
Ramirez	LF	4	17	2	7	0	0	1	4	.412
Cabrera	SS	4	17	3	4	1	0	0	3	.235
Mueller	3B	4	14	3	6	2	0	0	2	.429
Nixon	RF	4	14	1	5	3	0	0	3	.357
Ortiz	DH-1B	4	13	3	4	1	0	1	4	.308
Varitek	C	4	13	2	2	0	1	0	2	.154
Bellhorn	2B	4	10	3	3	1	0	1	4	.300
Millar	1B	4	8	2	1	1	0	0	0	.125
Mirabelli	C	1	3	1	1	0	0	0	0	.333
Kapler	RF-LF	4	2	0	0	0	0	0	0	.000
Lowe	P	1	2	0	0	0	0	0	0	.000
Martinez	P	1	2	0	0	0	0	0	0	.000
Mientkiewicz	1B	4	1	0	0	0	0	0	0	.000
Reese	2B	4	1	0	0	0	0	0	0	.000
Foulke	P	4	0	0	0	0	0	0	0	—
Embree	P	3	0	0	0	0	0	0	0	—
Arroyo	P	2	0	0	0	0	0	0	0	—
Schilling	P	1	0	0	0	0	0	0	0	—
Timlin	P	1	0	0	0	0	0	0	0	—
Wakefield	P	1	0	0	0	0	0	0	0	—
ST. LOUIS										
TOTALS		4	126	12	24	8	0	2	8	.190
Pujols	1B	4	15	1	5	2	0	0	0	.333
Renteria	SS	4	15	2	5	3	0	0	1	.333
Edmonds	CF	4	15	2	1	0	0	0	0	.067
Rolen	3B	4	15	0	0	0	0	0	0	.000
Walker	RF	4	14	2	5	2	0	2	3	.357
Womack	2B	4	11	1	2	0	0	0	0	.182
Sanders	LF-DH	4	9	1	0	0	0	0	0	.000
Matheny	C	4	8	0	2	1	0	0	2	.250
Anderson	DH-2B	4	6	0	1	0	0	0	0	.167
Cedeno	LF	3	4	1	1	0	0	0	1	.250
Taguchi	LF-DH	2	4	1	1	0	0	0	1	.250
Mabry	LF	2	4	0	0	0	0	0	0	.000
Molina	C	3	3	0	0	0	0	0	0	.000
Marquis	P-PR	3	1	0	0	0	0	0	0	.000
Suppan	P	1	1	0	1	0	0	0	0	1.000
Luna	2B	1	1	0	0	0	0	0	0	.000
King	P	3	0	0	0	0	0	0	0	—
Calero	P	2	0	0	0	0	0	0	0	—
Eldred	P	2	0	0	0	0	0	0	0	—
Haren	P	2	0	0	0	0	0	0	0	—
Reyes	P	2	0	0	0	0	0	0	0	—
Tavarez	P	2	0	0	0	0	0	0	0	—
Isringhausen	P	1	0	0	0	0	0	0	0	—
Morris	P	1	0	0	0	0	0	0	0	—
Williams	P	1	0	0	0	0	0	0	0	—

COMPOSITE PITCHING

NAME	G	IP	H	BB	SO	W	L	SV	ERA
BOSTON									
TOTALS	4	36	24	12	32	4	0	1	2.50
Lowe	1	7	3	1	4	1	0	0	0.00
Martinez	1	7	3	2	6	1	0	0	0.00
Schilling	1	6	4	1	4	1	0	0	0.00
Foulke	4	5	4	1	8	1	0	1	1.80
Wakefield	1	3.2	3	5	2	0	0	0	12.27
Timlin	3	3	2	1	0	0	0	0	6.00
Arroyo	2	2.2	4	1	4	0	0	0	6.75
Embree	3	1.2	1	0	4	0	0	0	0.00
ST. LOUIS									
TOTALS	4	34	39	24	20	0	4	0	6.09
Marquis	2	7	6	7	4	0	1	0	3.86
Haren	2	4.2	4	3	2	0	0	0	0.00
Suppan	1	4.2	8	1	4	0	1	0	7.71
Morris	1	4.1	4	3	0	0	1	0	8.31
King	3	2.2	1	1	1	0	0	0	0.00
Williams	1	2.1	8	3	1	0	0	0	27.00
Tavarez	2	2	1	0	1	0	1	0	4.50
Isringhausen	1	2	1	1	2	0	0	0	0.00
Eldred	2	1.2	4	0	2	0	0	0	10.80
Reyes	2	1.1	0	0	0	0	0	0	0.00
Calero	2	1.1	2	4	0	0	0	0	13.50

2005: FOR IT'S A LONG, LONG WHILE FROM APRIL TO OCTOBER

It's a long season. In May, predictions buzzed that the Yankees wouldn't pull out of their doldrums this time. Too much of their obese budget had gone into hitting while pitching languished, the pundits said. A rumor was even blogged that Joe Torre might be on his way out as manager. But, it is indeed a long season, and when September ended the Yankees were once again on top of the American League East. The powerful bats of A-Rod, Gary Sheffield, Hideki Matsui, Derek Jeter and Jason Giambi provided enough punch to resurrect the Bombers. New bellweather Randy Johnson struggled at times and the starting pitching remained spotty until journeyman Aaron Small and Shawn Chacon pitched well down the stretch. And, of course, Mariano Rivera was his usual unhittable self out of the bullpen.

Meanwhile, Boston, the 2004 World Champions, had a strong crop of starters and a bullpen filled with gasoline. It got so bad that for a time starter Kurt Schilling was pressed into service as a stopper. Fortunately, Johnny Damon, David Ortiz, and Manny Ramirez hit a ton, outweighing a peck of late-inning poundings. The Red Sox ended with the same win-loss record as New York but lost the division championship to the Yankees who had the better head-to-head record. That put them in the playoffs as the wild card, the entry that had worked well for them in 2004.

Who would have guessed that the best win-loss mark in the A.L. would be built by the Chicago White Sox? Even more surprising, they did it with little contribution from injured Frank Thomas, the owner of just about every franchise batting record that deals with accumulating runs. A strong and deep pitching staff, speed, Paul Konerko's power hitting, and great team chemistry put the White Sox out front. The Sox held a fifteen-game lead on August 1. Then the Cleveland got red hot while Chicago settled for luke warm down the stretch. Just as the obituary writers had their pens poised to record the greatest crash since the Hindenburg, the Sox righted themselves, thrashed Cleveland, and pocketed the Central Division.

Out West in the A.L., the Los Angeles Angels collected the division diadem almost in secret to much of the eastern part of the country. Had easterners read afternoon newspapers instead of morning editions, they would have known that Vladimir Guerrero had put together an MVP-worthy season and Bartolo Colon was the league's top-winning starter. Down the stretch, while the Angels held off a challenge by Oakland, Colon was 10-3 and Francisco Rodriguez was 14 for 14 in save opportunities.

Before the long season began, the Atlanta Braves were expected finally, after thirteen straight titles, to miss the National League East championship. Gone were most of the pitchers who'd kept Atlanta on top season after season and the whole roster was filled with rookies. All good things must end, but not this year. With Andruw Jones having a breakout season as a slugger and a talented crew of youngsters that bode well for the future, Atlanta wrapped up N.L. East championship number fourteen without breathing hard. One unexpected development was the play of the new Washington Nationals. Under the steady hand of Frank Robinson, the former Montreal orphans finished at .500. More unexpected, every other N.L. East team did better than that, but only Atlanta made the playoffs.

In the Central, the St. Louis Cardinals brandished an explosive line-up even after Scott Rolen sat down with an injury. Jim Edmonds, Reggie Sanders, and Larry Walker supported Albert Puljos who set a record by becoming the first player ever to hit 30-or-more home runs in each of his first five seasons. Chris Carpenter was a 21-game winner to lead a strong starting staff. Houston had great pitching with Roy Oswalt, Andy Pettitte, and Roger Clemens who decided to return for one more season. The Astros lost their chance to catch the Cardinals when veteran slugger Jeff Bagwell was injured, but they rallied to earn the N.L. wild card.

Until the last couple days of the season, there was a very strong possiblilty that the N.L. West champion would finish with a losing record. The San Diego Padres with the N.L.'s best closer in Trevor Hoffman avoided the ignominy of being a "loser" winner and scraped in at 82-80, but as Manager Bruce Bochy pointed out, "In the playoffs, you only have to win one more than your opponent." Ironically, three Eastern Division teams – Philadelphia, the Mets, and Florida – all had better records than the Padres but couldn't get in the playoffs.

Like every long season, 2005 had great hitting, marvelous pitching, and amazing fielding, but too often the headlines went to a West Coast investigation of steroid providers and a Washington inquest into their use. Rafael Palmiero, baseball's most recent collector of 3000 hits, swore to the gathered senators that he never used them. In August, he was suspended for failing a steroids test as baseball belatedly attacked the barn door. Some things more than others made it a very long season.

2005 AMERICAN LEAGUE — EAST DIVISION

Name	G by Pos	B	AGE	G	AB	R	H	2B	3B	HR	RBI	BB	SO	SB	BA	SA
NEW YORK	1st (tie) 95-67 .586			**JOE TORRE**												
TOTALS			33	162	5624	886	1552	259	16	229	847	637	989	84	.276	.450
Tino Martinez	1B122 DH1	L	37	131	303	43	73	9	0	17	49	38	54	2	.241	.439
Robinson Cano	2B131	L	22	132	522	78	155	34	4	14	62	16	68	1	.297	.458
Derek Jeter	SS157 DH1	R	31	159	654	122	202	25	5	19	70	77	117	14	.309	.450
Alex Rodriguez	3B161 SS3 DH1	R	29	162	605	124	194	29	1	48	130	91	139	21	.321	.610
Gary Sheffield	OF131 DH23	R	36	154	584	104	170	27	0	34	123	78	76	10	.291	.512
Bernie Williams	OF112 DH23	B	36	141	485	53	121	19	1	12	64	53	75	1	.249	.367
Hideki Matsui	OF142 DH19	L	31	162	629	108	192	45	3	23	116	63	78	2	.305	.496
Jorge Posada	C133 DH3	B	33	142	474	67	124	23	0	19	71	66	94	1	.262	.430
Jason Giambi	1B78 DH60	L	34	139	417	74	113	14	0	32	87	108	109	0	.271	.535
Tony Womack	OF66 2B24 DH11	L	35	108	329	46	82	8	1	0	15	12	49	27	.249	.280
Bubba Crosby	OF67 DH4	L	28	76	98	15	27	0	1	1	6	4	14	4	.276	.327
Ruben Sierra (LJ)	DH30 OF18	B	39	61	170	14	39	12	0	4	29	9	41	0	.229	.371
John Flaherty	C45 1B1	R	37	47	127	10	21	5	0	2	11	6	26	0	.165	.252
Andy Phillips	1B19 DH6 3B1 OF1	R	28	27	40	7	6	4	0	1	4	1	13	0	.150	.325
Rey Sanchez (XJ)	SS10 2B9 DH2 3B1	R	37	23	43	7	12	1	0	0	2	2	3	0	.279	.302
Russ Johnson	3B8 1B7 OF3 DH3 2B1	R	32	22	18	5	4	2	0	0	1	4	0	0	.222	.333
3 Matt Lawton	DH19	L	33	21	48	6	6	0	0	2	4	7	8	1	.125	.250
Felix Escalona	SS5 3B3 1B1 2B1	R	26	10	14	0	4	1	0	0	2	1	4	0	.286	.357
2 Mark Bellhorn	3B4 2B2 SS2	B	30	9	17	2	2	0	0	1	2	3	3	0	.118	.294
Melky Cabrera	OF6	B	20	6	19	1	4	0	0	0	0	0	2	0	.211	.211
Wil Nieves	C3	R	27	3	4	0	0	0	0	0	0	0	1	0	.000	.000
Mike Vento	OF2	R	27	2	2	0	0	0	0	0	0	0	1	0	.000	.000
Kevin Reese	OF2	L	27	2	1	0	1	0	0	0	0	1	1	0	.000	.000

NAME	T	AGE	W	L	PCT	SV	G	GS	CG	IP	H	BB	SO	SHO	ERA
		35	95	67	.586	46	162	162	8	1431	1495	463	985	14	4.52
Randy Johnson	L	41	17	8	.680	0	34	34	4	226	207	47	211	0	3.79
Mike Mussina	R	36	13	8	.619	0	30	30	2	180	199	47	142	2	4.41
Aaron Small	R	33	10	0	1.000	0	15	9	1	76	71	24	37	1	3.20
Chien-Ming Wang (SJ)	R	25	8	5	.615	0	18	17	0	116	113	32	47	0	4.02
2 Shawn Chacon	R	27	7	3	.700	0	14	12	0	79	66	30	40	0	2.85
Mariano Rivera	R	35	7	4	.636	43	71	0	0	78	50	18	80	0	1.38
Tanyon Sturtze	R	34	5	3	.625	1	64	1	0	78	76	27	45	0	4.73
Tom Gordon	R	37	5	4	.556	2	79	0	0	81	59	29	69	0	2.57
Jaret Wright (SJ)	R	29	5	5	.500	0	13	13	0	64	81	32	34	0	6.08
2 Al Leiter	L	39	4	5	.444	0	16	10	0	62	66	38	45	0	5.49
Carl Pavano (SJ)	R	29	4	6	.400	0	17	17	1	100	129	18	56	1	4.77
Kevin Brown (XJ)	R	40	4	7	.364	0	13	13	0	73	107	19	50	0	6.50
Scott Proctor	R	28	1	0	1.000	0	29	1	0	45	46	17	36	0	6.04
1 Buddy Groom	L	39	1	0	1.000	0	24	0	0	26	32	7	13	0	4.91
1 Paul Quantrill	R	36	1	0	1.000	0	22	0	0	32	48	7	11	0	6.75
Jason Anderson	R	26	1	0	1.000	0	3	0	0	6	4	7	2	0	7.94
2 Alan Embree	L	35	1	1	.500	0	24	0	0	14	20	3	8	0	7.53
1 Mike Stanton	L	38	1	2	.333	0	28	0	0	14	17	6	12	0	7.07
Felix Rodriguez (KJ)	R	32	0	0	—	0	34	0	0	32	33	20	18	0	5.01
1 Steve Karsay	R	33	0	0	—	0	6	0	0	6	6	2	5	0	6.00
Jorge DePaula	R	26	0	0	—	0	3	0	0	7	8	3	3	0	8.10
Alex Graman	L	27	0	0	—	0	2	0	0	1	3	2	0	0	13.50
Colter Bean	R	28	0	0	—	0	1	0	0	2	1	2	2	0	4.50
Ramiro Mendoza	R	33	0	0	—	0	1	0	0	1	2	0	1	0	18.00
Wayne Franklin	L	31	0	1	.000	0	13	0	0	13	11	8	10	0	6.39
2 Darrell May	L	33	0	1	.000	0	2	1	0	7	14	3	3	0	16.71
2 Tim Redding	R	27	0	1	.000	0	1	1	0	1	4	4	2	0	54.00
Sean Henn	L	24	0	3	.000	0	3	3	0	11	18	11	3	0	11.12

Name	G by Pos	B	AGE	G	AB	R	H	2B	3B	HR	RBI	BB	SO	SB	BA	SA
BOSTON	1st (tie) 95-67 .586 (Wild Card)			**TERRY FRANCONA**												
TOTALS			32	162	5626	910	1579	339	21	199	863	653	1044	45	.281	.454
Kevin Millar	1B110 OF34	R	33	134	449	57	122	28	1	9	50	54	74	0	.272	.399
1 Mark Bellhorn (RJ)	2B83 SS1	B	30	85	283	41	61	20	0	7	28	49	109	3	.216	.360
Edgar Renteria	SS153	R	29	153	623	100	172	36	4	8	70	55	100	9	.276	.385
Bill Mueller	3B142 2B5	B	34	150	519	69	153	34	3	10	62	59	74	0	.295	.430
Trot Nixon	OF118 DH2	L	31	124	408	64	112	29	1	13	67	53	59	2	.275	.446
Johnny Damon	OF147 DH1	L	31	148	624	117	197	35	6	10	75	53	69	18	.316	.439
Manny Ramirez	OF149 DH2	R	33	152	554	112	162	30	1	45	144	80	119	1	.292	.594
Jason Varitek	C130	B	33	133	470	70	132	30	1	22	70	62	117	2	.281	.489
David Ortiz	DH148 1B10	L	29	159	601	119	180	40	1	47	148	102	124	1	.300	.604
John Olerud	1B80	L	36	87	173	18	50	7	0	7	37	16	20	0	.289	.451
1 Jay Payton	OF53	R	32	55	133	24	35	7	0	5	21	10	14	0	.263	.429
2 Tony Graffanino	OF51	R	33	51	188	39	60	12	1	4	20	19	24	3	.319	.457
Doug Mirabelli	C43 DH5	R	34	50	136	16	31	7	0	6	18	14	48	2	.228	.412
2 Alex Cora	2B35 SS11 3B5	L	29	47	104	14	28	3	2	1	16	6	12	1	.269	.394
Kevin Youkilis	3B24 1B9 2B2	R	26	44	79	11	22	7	0	1	9	14	19	0	.278	.405
Gabe Kapler	OF36	R	29	36	97	15	24	7	0	1	9	3	15	1	.247	.351
Adam Stern (BG)	OF21	L	25	36	15	4	2	0	0	1	3	0	4	1	.133	.333
1 Ramon Vazquez	SS12 3B8 2B4 DH1	L	28	27	61	6	12	2	0	0	4	3	14	0	.197	.230
Roberto Petagine	1B10 DH3 OF2	L	34	18	32	4	9	2	0	1	9	4	5	0	.281	.438
Dave McCarty	1B12 OF1	R	35	13	4	2	1	0	0	0	0	3	1	0	.250	.313
2 Adam Hyzdu	OF12	R	33	12	16	1	4	1	0	0	2	0	5	0	.250	.313
Alejandro Machado	OF6 2B3 SS1	R	23	10	5	4	1	0	0	0	1	1	1	0	.200	.400
Kelly Shoppach	C7 DH2	R	25	8	14	2	3	1	0	0	0	0	3	0	.000	.000
2 Jose Cruz	OF4	B	31	4	12	0	3	1	0	0	1	2	4	0	.250	.333
Hanley Ramirez	SS2	R	21	2	2	1	0	0	0	0	0	0	1	0	.000	.000
Shawn Wooten	C1	R	32	1	1	0	0	0	0	0	0	0	0	0	.000	.000

NAME	T	AGE	W	L	PCT	SV	G	GS	CG	IP	H	BB	SO	SHO	ERA
		33	95	67	.586	38	162	162	6	1429	1550	440	959	8	4.74
Tim Wakefield	R	38	16	12	.571	0	33	33	3	225	210	68	151	0	4.15
David Wells	L	42	15	7	.682	0	30	30	2	184	220	21	107	0	4.45
Bronson Arroyo	R	28	14	10	.583	0	35	32	0	205	213	54	100	0	4.51
Matt Clement	R	30	13	6	.684	0	32	32	1	191	192	68	146	0	4.57
Curt Schilling (NJ)	R	38	8	8	.500	9	32	11	0	93	121	22	87	0	5.69
Mike Timlin	R	39	7	3	.700	13	81	0	0	80	86	20	59	0	2.24
Keith Foulke (KJ)	R	32	5	5	.500	15	43	0	0	46	53	18	34	0	5.91
Wade Miller (SJ)	R	28	4	4	.500	0	16	16	0	91	96	47	64	0	4.95
Mike Myers	L	36	1	1	.750	0	65	0	0	37	30	13	21	0	3.13
Jonathan Papelbon	R	24	3	1	.750	0	17	3	0	34	33	17	34	0	2.65
2 Chad Bradford	R	30	2	1	.667	0	31	0	0	23	29	4	10	0	3.86
Jeremi Gonzalez	R	30	2	1	.667	0	28	3	0	56	64	16	28	0	6.11
Matt Mantei (NJ)	R	31	1	1	1.000	0	30	0	0	23	23	24	22	0	6.49
1 John Halama	L	33	1	1	.500	0	30	1	0	44	56	9	26	0	6.18
1 Alan Embree	L	35	1	4	.200	1	43	0	0	38	42	11	30	0	7.65
Manny Delcarmen	R	23	0	0	—	0	10	0	0	9	8	7	9	0	3.00
2 Mike Remlinger	L	39	0	0	—	0	8	0	0	7	15	5	5	0	14.85
Craig Hansen	R	21	0	0	—	0	4	0	0	4	6	2	4	0	6.00
Cla Meredith	R	22	0	0	—	0	2	0	0	4	9	1	1	0	27.00
Abe Alvarez	L	22	0	0	—	0	1	1	0	6	7	0	3	0	15.43
1 Scott Cassidy	R	29	0	0	—	0	1	0	0	0	2	0	1	0	40.50
2 Matt Perisho	L	30	0	0	—	0	1	0	0	0	1	0	0	0	*
3 Mike Stanton	L	38	0	0	—	0	6	0	0	5	4	1	2	0	0.00
Lenny DiNardo	L	25	0	1	.000	0	15	1	0	15	12	5	15	0	1.84
1 Blaine Neal	R	27	0	1	.000	0	8	0	0	8	15	3	3	0	9.00
2 Chad Harville	R	28	0	1	.000	0	5	0	0	7	10	8	6	0	6.43

TORONTO — 3rd 80-82 .494 15   JOHN GIBBONS

Name	G by Pos	B	AGE	G	AB	R	H	2B	3B	HR	RBI	BB	SO	SB	BA	SA
TOTALS	TOTALS		28	162	5581	775	1480	307	39	136	735	486	955	72	.265	.407
Eric Hinske	1B100 DH43	L	27	147	477	79	125	31	2	15	68	46	121	8	.262	.430
Orlando Hudson	2B130	B	27	131	461	62	125	25	5	10	63	30	65	7	.271	.412
Russ Adams	SS132	L	24	139	481	68	123	27	5	8	63	50	57	11	.256	.383
Corey Koskie (BG)	3B76 DH19	L	32	97	354	49	88	20	0	11	36	44	90	4	.249	.398
Alex Rios	OF142 DH1	R	24	146	481	71	126	23	6	10	59	28	101	14	.262	.397
Vernon Wells	OF155 DH2	R	26	156	620	78	167	30	3	28	97	47	86	8	.269	.463
Frank Catalanotto	OF111 DH15	L	31	130	419	56	126	29	5	8	59	37	53	0	.301	.451
Gregg Zaun	C132	B	34	133	434	61	109	18	1	11	61	73	70	2	.251	.373
Shea Hillenbrand	1B67 3B54 DH33	R	29	152	594	91	173	36	2	18	82	26	79	5	.291	.449
Reed Johnson	OF139	R	28	142	398	55	107	21	6	8	58	22	82	5	.269	.412
Aaron Hill	3B35 DH34 2B22 SS16	R	23	105	361	49	99	25	3	3	40	34	41	2	.274	.385
Frank Menechino	2B26 DH25 3B9 SS1	R	34	70	148	22	32	7	0	4	13	25	33	0	.216	.345
Gabe Gross	OF37 DH2	L	25	40	92	11	23	4	1	1	7	10	21	1	.250	.348
1 John McDonald	SS32 2B5	R	30	37	93	8	27	3	0	0	12	6	12	5	.290	.323
Ken Huckaby	C35	R	34	35	87	8	18	4	0	0	6	5	19	0	.207	.253
Guillermo Quiroz	C10 DH2	R	23	12	36	3	7	2	0	0	4	2	13	0	.194	.250
John-Ford Griffin	DH4	L	25	7	13	3	4	2	0	1	6	0	4	0	.308	.692
Greg Myers	C4	L	39	6	12	0	1	0	0	0	1	1	1	0	.083	.083
Andy Dominique	C1	R	29	2	2	0	0	0	0	0	0	0	0	0	.000	.000

NAME	T	AGE	W	L	PCT	SV	G	GS	CG	IP	H	BB	SO	SHO	ERA
		28	80	82	.494	35	162	162	9	1447	1475	444	958	8	4.06
Gustavo Chacin	L	28	13	9	.591	0	34	34	0	203	213	70	121	0	3.72
Josh Towers	R	28	13	12	.520	0	33	33	3	209	237	29	112	1	3.71
Roy Halladay (BL)	R	28	12	4	.750	0	19	19	5	142	118	18	108	2	2.41
Ted Lilly (AJ)	L	29	10	11	.476	0	25	25	0	126	135	58	96	0	5.56
Pete Walker	R	36	6	6	.500	2	41	4	0	84	81	33	43	0	3.54
Miguel Batista	R	34	5	8	.385	31	71	0	0	75	80	27	54	0	4.10
Dave Bush	R	25	5	11	.313	0	25	24	2	136	142	29	75	0	4.49
Scott Downs	L	29	4	3	.571	0	26	13	0	94	93	34	75	0	4.31
Justin Speier	R	31	3	2	.600	0	65	0	0	67	48	15	56	0	2.56
Scott Schoeneweis	L	31	3	4	.429	1	80	0	0	57	54	25	43	0	3.32
Jason Frasor	R	27	3	5	.375	1	67	0	0	75	67	28	62	0	3.25
Brandon League	R	22	1	0	1.000	0	20	0	0	36	42	20	17	0	6.56
Dustin McGowan	R	23	1	3	.250	0	13	7	0	45	49	17	34	0	6.35
Chad Gaudin	R	22	1	3	.250	0	5	3	0	13	31	6	12	0	13.15
Shaun Marcum	R	23	0	0	—	0	5	0	0	7	8	4	5	0	5.59
Matt Whiteside	R	37	0	0	—	0	2	0	0	4	6	5	5	0	19.64
Justin Miller	R	27	0	0	—	0	1	0	0	2	5	0	2	0	15.43
Vinnie Chulk	R	26	0	0	.000	0	62	0	0	72	68	26	39	0	3.88

BALTIMORE — 4th 74-88 .457 21   LEE MAZZILLI 51-56 .477   SAM PERLOZZO 23-32 .418

Name	G by Pos	B	AGE	G	AB	R	H	2B	3B	HR	RBI	BB	SO	SB	BA	SA
TOTALS	TOTALS		32	162	5551	729	1492	296	27	189	700	447	902	83	.269	.434
Rafael Palmeiro (KJ-NJ)	1B93 DH15	L	40	110	369	47	98	13	0	18	60	43	43	2	.266	.447
Brian Roberts	2B141	B	27	143	561	92	176	45	7	18	73	67	83	27	.314	.515
Miguel Tejada	SS160 DH2	R	29	162	654	89	199	50	5	26	98	40	83	5	.304	.515
Melvin Mora	3B148 DH1	R	33	149	593	86	168	30	1	27	88	50	112	7	.283	.474
Sammy Sosa (FJ)	OF66 DH35	R	36	102	380	39	84	15	1	14	45	39	84	1	.221	.376
Luis Matos (BG)	OF120	R	26	121	389	53	109	20	2	4	32	27	58	17	.280	.373
1 Larry Bigbie (BH)	OF62	L	27	67	206	22	51	9	1	5	21	21	49	3	.248	.374
Javy Lopez (BH)	C75 DH28 1B1	R	34	103	395	47	110	24	1	15	49	19	68	0	.278	.458
Jay Gibbons	OF71 DH42 1B22	L	28	139	488	72	135	33	3	26	79	28	56	0	.277	.516
David Newhan	OF73 3B8 DH7	L	31	96	218	31	44	9	0	5	21	22	45	9	.202	.312
B.J. Surhoff	OF60 1B18 DH7	L	40	91	303	30	78	11	2	5	34	11	32	0	.257	.356
Chris Gomez	1B42 2B18 3B17 SS10 DH6	R	34	89	219	27	61	11	0	1	18	27	17	2	.279	.342
Sal Fasano	C60 DH3 1B1	R	34	64	160	25	40	3	0	11	20	9	41	0	.250	.475
Geronimo Gil (RJ)	C62	R	29	64	125	7	24	3	0	4	17	5	23	0	.192	.312
3 Eric Byrnes	OF51	R	29	52	167	17	32	7	1	3	11	11	33	3	.192	.299
Alejandro Freire	1B16 DH9 OF1	R	30	25	65	7	16	3	0	1	4	6	17	0	.246	.338
Bernie Castro	2B11 DH9 OF1	L	25	24	80	14	23	3	1	0	7	9	10	6	.288	.350
2 Eli Marrero (RJ)	OF16	R	31	22	50	8	11	3	2	3	10	4	20	0	.220	.540
Walter Young	1B10 DH3	L	25	14	33	2	10	1	0	1	3	4	7	0	.303	.424
Jeff Fiorentino	OF12	L	22	13	44	7	11	2	0	1	5	2	10	1	.250	.364
Eli Whiteside	C9	R	25	9	12	1	3	0	0	0	1	0	2	0	.250	.250
Eddie Rogers	DH2 SS1	R	26	8	1	4	1	0	0	0	0	0	0	0	1.000	4.000
Ramon Nivar	OF4	R	25	7	13	1	4	0	0	0	1	0	2	0	.308	.308
Keith Reed	OF6	R	26	6	5	1	1	0	0	0	1	1	2	0	.200	.200
Napoleon Calzado	OF2	R	28	4	5	0	1	0	0	0	0	0	1	0	.200	.200
Midre Cummings	OF1	L	33	2	0	1	0	0	0	0	0	0	0	0	.000	.000

NAME	T	AGE	W	L	PCT	SV	G	GS	CG	IP	H	BB	SO	SHO	ERA
		30	74	88	.457	38	162	162	2	1428	1458	580	1052	9	4.56
Rodrigo Lopez	R	29	15	12	.556	0	35	35	0	209	232	63	118	0	4.90
Bruce Chen	L	28	13	10	.565	0	34	32	1	197	187	63	133	0	3.83
Daniel Cabrera	R	24	10	13	.435	0	29	29	0	161	144	87	157	0	4.52
Sidney Ponson	R	28	7	11	.389	0	23	23	1	130	177	48	68	0	6.21
Erik Bedard (KJ)	L	26	6	8	.429	0	24	24	0	142	139	57	125	0	4.00
Todd Williams	R	34	5	5	.500	1	72	0	0	76	72	26	38	0	3.30
Hayden Penn	R	20	3	2	.600	0	8	8	0	38	46	21	18	0	6.34
Jorge Julio	R	26	3	5	.375	0	67	0	0	72	76	24	58	0	5.90
Eric DuBose	L	29	2	3	.400	0	15	3	0	29	28	19	17	0	5.52
John Maine	R	24	2	3	.400	0	10	8	0	40	39	24	24	0	6.30
Steve Kline	L	32	2	4	.333	0	67	0	0	61	59	30	36	0	4.28
John Parrish (EJ)	L	27	1	0	1.000	0	14	0	0	17	19	17	25	0	3.12
Aaron Rakers	R	28	1	0	1.000	0	10	0	0	14	11	3	11	0	3.29
Steve Reed	R	40	1	2	.333	0	30	0	0	33	41	11	15	0	6.61
Jason Grimsley (EJ)	R	37	1	2	.333	0	22	0	0	22	24	9	10	0	5.73
Chris Ray	R	23	1	2	.250	0	41	0	0	41	34	18	43	0	2.66
B.J. Ryan	L	29	1	4	.200	36	69	0	0	70	54	26	100	0	2.43
1,3 James Baldwin	R	33	0	0	—	0	20	0	0	39	36	9	20	0	3.20
Rick Bauer	R	28	0	0	.000	0	5	0	0	8	13	4	5	0	9.72
Tim Byrdak	L	31	0	1	.000	0	41	0	0	27	27	21	31	0	4.05
Kurt Ainsworth (SJ) 26															

TAMPA BAY — 5th 67-95 .414 28   LOU PINIELLA

Name	G by Pos	B	AGE	G	AB	R	H	2B	3B	HR	RBI	BB	SO	SB	BA	SA
TOTALS	TOTALS		27	162	5552	750	1519	289	40	157	717	412	990	151	.274	.425
Travis Lee	1B124	L	30	129	404	54	110	22	2	12	49	35	66	7	.272	.426
Jorge Cantu	2B80 3B62 DH13	R	23	150	598	73	171	40	1	28	117	19	83	1	.286	.497
Julio Lugo	SS156	R	29	158	616	89	182	36	6	6	57	61	72	39	.295	.403
Alex Gonzalez	3B98 SS12	R	32	109	349	47	94	20	1	9	38	26	74	2	.269	.410
Aubrey Huff	OF97 DH33 1B25 3B4	L	28	154	575	70	150	26	2	22	92	49	88	8	.261	.428
Damon Hollins	OF116	R	31	120	342	44	85	17	1	13	46	23	63	8	.249	.418
Carl Crawford	OF154 DH1	L	23	156	644	101	194	33	15	15	81	27	84	46	.301	.469
Toby Hall	C135 1B2	R	29	135	432	28	124	20	0	5	48	16	39	0	.287	.368
Jonny Gomes	OF50 DH49	R	24	101	348	61	98	13	6	21	54	39	113	9	.282	.534
Nick Green	2B91 3B13 OF1	R	26	111	318	53	76	15	2	5	29	33	86	3	.239	.346
Eduardo Perez	1B49 DH7 OF4 3B3	R	35	77	161	23	41	6	0	11	28	26	30	0	.255	.497
Joey Gathright	OF70 DH1	L	24	76	203	29	56	7	3	0	13	10	39	20	.276	.340
Josh Phelps	DH42 1B1	R	27	47	158	21	42	10	0	5	26	12	48	0	.266	.424
1 Alex Sanchez	OF31 DH7	L	28	43	133	18	46	8	1	2	13	7	25	6	.346	.466
Chris Singleton	OF19 DH4	L	32	28	59	9	16	5	0	0	11	6	14	0	.271	.356
Pete LaForest	C21 DH2 1B1	L	27	25	64	5	11	3	0	1	4	6	23	0	.172	.266
Charles Johnson	C19	R	33	19	46	5	9	1	0	2	5	9	11	0	.196	.283
Kevin Cash (VJ)	C13	R	27	13	31	4	5	1	0	2	2	1	13	0	.161	.387
Reggie Taylor	OF10	L	28	11	22	2	4	0	0	0	1	2	7	2	.182	.273
Eric Munson (VJ)	DH3 3B2 1B1 OF1	L	27	11	18	2	3	1	0	0	2	4	3	0	.167	.222
Fernando Cortez	2B3 SS2 3B1	L	23	8	13	0	1	0	0	0	1	1	3	0	.077	.077
Tim Laker	C1	R	35	1	1	0	0	0	0	0	0	0	0	0	.000	.000
Rocco Baldelli (KJ-EJ) 23																

TAMPA BAY	T	AGE	W	L	PCT	SV	G	GS	CG	IP	H	BB	SO	SHO	ERA
		28	67	95	.414	43	162	162	1	1422	1570	615	949	4	5.39
Mark Hendrickson	L	31	11	8	.579	0	31	31	1	178	227	49	89	0	5.90
Scott Kazmir	L	21	10	9	.526	0	32	32	0	186	172	100	174	0	3.77
Casey Fossum	L	27	8	12	.400	0	36	25	0	163	170	60	128	0	4.92
Seth McClung	R	24	7	11	.389	0	34	17	0	109	106	62	92	0	6.59
Danys Baez	R	27	4	5	.556	41	67	0	0	72	66	30	51	0	2.86
Hideo Nomo	R	36	5	8	.385	0	19	19	0	101	127	51	59	0	7.24
Doug Waechter	R	24	5	12	.294	0	29	25	0	157	191	38	87	0	5.62
Travis Harper	R	29	4	6	.400	0	52	0	0	73	88	24	40	0	6.75
Chad Orvella	R	24	3	3	.500	1	37	0	0	50	47	23	43	0	3.60
Trever Miller	L	32	2	2	.500	0	61	0	0	44	45	29	35	0	4.06
Jesus Colome (SJ)	R	27	2	3	.400	0	36	0	0	45	54	18	28	0	4.57
Franklin Nunez (SJ)	R	28	1	0	1.000	0	5	0	0	5	4	2	2	0	10.80
Rob Bell (PP)	R	28	1	1	.500	0	8	3	0	25	41	12	13	0	8.28
Lance Carter	R	30	1	2	.333	1	39	0	0	57	61	15	22	0	4.89
2 Joe Borowski	R	34	1	5	.167	0	32	0	0	35	26	11	16	0	3.82
Dewon Brazelton	R	25	1	8	.111	0	20	8	0	71	87	60	43	0	7.61
Tim Corcoran	R	27	0	0	—	0	10	1	0	23	19	12	13	0	5.96
Joe Beimel	L	28	0	0	—	0	7	0	0	11	15	4	3	0	3.27
Lee Gardner	R	30	0	0	—	0	7	0	0	7	12	2	4	0	4.91
Jon Switzer	L	25	0	0	—	0	4	0	0	4	5	7	5	0	6.75
John Webb	R	26	0	0	.000	0	1	0	0	4	6	4	2	0	18.00

CENTRAL DIVISION

CHICAGO — 1st 99-63 .611   OZZIE GUILLEN

Name	G by Pos	B	AGE	G	AB	R	H	2B	3B	HR	RBI	BB	SO	SB	BA	SA
TOTALS			29	162	5529	741	1450	253	23	200	713	435	1002	137	.262	.425
Paul Konerko	1B146 DH11	R	29	158	575	98	163	24	0	40	100	81	109	0	.283	.534
Tadahito Iguchi	2B133	R	30	135	511	74	142	25	6	15	71	47	114	15	.278	.438
Juan Uribe	SS146	R	25	146	481	58	121	23	3	16	71	34	77	4	.252	.412
Joe Crede	3B130 SS1 DH1	R	27	132	432	54	109	21	0	22	62	25	66	1	.252	.454
Jermaine Dye	OF140 1B1 SS1 DH1	R	31	145	529	74	145	29	2	31	86	39	99	11	.274	.512
Aaron Rowand	OF157	R	27	157	578	77	156	30	5	13	69	32	116	16	.270	.407
Scott Podsednik	OF127	L	29	129	507	80	147	28	1	0	25	47	75	59	.290	.349
A.J. Pierzynski	C128	L	28	128	460	61	118	21	0	18	56	23	68	0	.257	.420
Frank Thomas (NJ-BF)	DH28	R	37	34	105	19	23	3	0	12	26	16	31	0	.219	.590
Carl Everett	DH107 OF22	B	34	135	490	58	123	17	2	23	87	42	99	4	.251	.435
Timo Perez	OF50 DH11 1B2	L	30	76	179	13	39	8	0	2	15	12	25	2	.218	.296
Pablo Ozuna	3B32 SS15 OF10 2B6 DH4 1B2	R	30	70	203	27	56	7	2	0	11	7	26	14	.276	.330
Willie Harris	2B32 DH9 SS5	L	27	56	121	17	31	2	1	1	8	13	25	10	.256	.314
Chris Widger	C42 1B1 3B1 DH1	R	34	45	141	18	34	8	0	4	11	10	22	0	.241	.383
2 Geoff Blum	1B12 3B12 SS6 2B2	B	32	31	95	6	19	2	1	1	3	4	15	0	.200	.274
Ross Gload (SJ)	1B24 OF3	L	29	28	42	2	7	2	0	1	5	2	9	0	.167	.214
Brian Anderson	OF12	R	23	13	34	3	6	1	0	2	3	0	12	1	.176	.382
Joe Borchard	DH3 OF2	B	27	10	12	1	5	1	0	0	2	0	3	0	.417	.583
Raul Casanova	C6	B	32	6	5	0	1	0	0	0	2	1	0	0	.200	.200
Pedro Lopez	2B1 SS1	R	21	2	7	1	2	0	0	0	1	0	1	0	.286	.286
Jamie Burke	1B1	R	33	1	1	0	0	0	0	0	0	0	0	0	.000	.000

NAME	T	AGE	W	L	PCT	SV	G	GS	CG	IP	H	BB	SO	SHO	ERA
		30	99	63	.611	54	162	162	9	1476	1392	459	1040	10	3.61
Jon Garland	R	25	18	10	.643	0	32	32	3	221	212	47	115	3	3.50
Mark Buehrle	L	26	16	8	.667	0	33	33	3	237	240	40	149	1	3.12
Jose Contreras	R	33	15	7	.682	0	32	32	1	205	177	75	154	0	3.61
Freddy Garcia	R	30	14	8	.636	0	33	33	2	228	225	60	146	0	3.87
Orlando Hernandez (SJ)	R	39	9	9	.500	1	24	22	0	128	137	50	91	0	5.12
Cliff Politte	R	31	7	1	.875	1	68	0	0	67	42	21	57	0	2.00
Luis Vizcaino	R	30	6	5	.545	0	65	0	0	70	74	29	43	0	3.73
Neal Cotts	L	25	4	0	1.000	0	69	0	0	60	38	29	58	0	1.94
Brandon McCarthy	R	21	3	2	.600	0	12	10	0	67	62	17	48	0	4.03
Damaso Marte	L	30	3	4	.429	4	60	0	0	45	45	33	54	0	3.77
Dustin Hermanson	R	32	2	4	.333	34	57	0	0	57	46	17	33	0	2.04
Bobby Jenks	R	24	1	1	.500	6	32	0	0	39	34	15	50	0	2.75
1 Shingo Takatsu	R	36	1	2	.333	8	31	0	0	29	30	16	32	0	5.97
Jeff Bajenaru	R	27	0	0	—	0	2	0	0	3	1	1	3	0	6.23
David Sanders	L	25	0	0	—	0	2	0	0	3	3	1	3	0	13.50
Kevin Walker	L	28	0	1	.000	0	8	0	0	7	8	5	7	0	9.00
Jon Adkins	R	28	0	0	—	0	18	0	0	28	29	6	13	0	8.64
Felix Diaz (XJ) 24															

CLEVELAND 2nd 93-69 .574 6 MIKE HARGROVE

Name	G by Pos	B	AGE	G	AB	R	H	2B	3B	HR	RBI	BB	SO	SB	BA	SA
TOTALS			28	162	5609	790	1522	337	30	207	760	503	1093	62	.271	.453
Ben Broussard	1B138 DH2	L	28	142	466	59	119	30	5	19	68	32	98	2	.255	.464
Ron Belliard	2B141	R	30	145	536	71	152	36	1	17	78	35	72	1	.284	.450
Jhonny Peralta	SS141	R	23	141	504	82	147	35	4	24	78	58	128	0	.292	.520
Aaron Boone	3B142 DH1	R	32	143	511	61	124	19	1	16	60	35	92	9	.243	.378
Casey Blake	OF138 3B6 1B4	R	31	143	523	72	126	32	1	23	58	43	116	4	.241	.438
Grady Sizemore	OF155	L	22	158	640	111	185	37	11	22	81	52	132	22	.289	.484
Coco Crisp	OF145	B	25	145	594	86	178	42	4	16	69	44	81	15	.300	.465
Victor Martinez	C142 DH2	B	26	147	547	73	167	33	0	20	80	63	78	0	.305	.475
Travis Hafner	DH130 1B1	L	28	137	486	94	148	42	0	33	108	79	123	0	.305	.595
Jose Hernandez	1B45 3B21 OF6 2B4 SS1 DH1	R	35	84	234	28	54	7	0	6	31	14	60	1	.231	.338
1 Alex Cora	SS24 2B15 OF1	L	29	49	146	11	30	5	2	1	8	5	18	6	.205	.288
1 Jody Gerut (KJ)	OF38 DH3	L	27	44	138	12	38	9	1	1	12	18	14	1	.275	.377
Josh Bard	C31	B	27	34	83	6	16	4	0	1	9	9	11	0	.193	.277
Jeff Liefer	DH9 1B5 OF3	L	30	19	56	5	11	2	0	1	8	1	15	0	.196	.286
Ryan Ludwick	OF15 DH3	R	26	19	41	8	9	0	0	4	5	7	13	0	.220	.512
2 Jason Dubois	OF7 DH7	R	26	14	45	6	10	0	0	2	2	5	25	0	.222	.356
2 Ramon Vazquez	2B8 SS2	L	28	12	24	1	6	3	0	0	1	2	3	0	.250	.375
Franklin Gutierrez	DH3 OF2	R	22	7	1	2	0	0	0	0	0	0	1	0	.000	.000
Brandon Phillips	2B2 SS1 DH1	R	24	6	9	1	0	0	0	0	0	0	4	0	.000	.000
Ryan Garko	DH1	R	24	1	1	0	0	0	0	0	0	0	1	0	.000	.000
Juan Gonzalez (LJ)		R	35	1	1	0	0	0	0	0	0	0	0	0	.000	.000

NAME	T	AGE	W	L	PCT	SV	G	GS	CG	IP	H	BB	SO	SHO	ERA
		30	93	69	.574	51	162	162	6	1453	1363	413	1050	10	3.61
Cliff Lee	L	26	18	5	.783	0	32	32	1	202	194	52	143	0	3.79
C.C. Sabathia	L	24	15	10	.600	0	31	31	1	197	185	62	161	0	4.03
Jake Westbrook	R	27	15	15	.500	0	34	34	2	211	218	56	119	0	4.49
Scott Elarton	R	29	11	9	.550	0	31	31	1	182	189	48	103	0	4.61
Kevin Millwood	R	30	9	11	.450	0	30	30	1	192	182	52	146	0	2.86
Bob Howry	R	31	7	4	.636	0	79	0	0	73	49	16	48	0	2.47
Jason Davis	R	25	4	2	.667	0	11	4	0	40	44	20	32	0	4.69
Rafael Betancourt	R	30	4	3	.571	1	54	0	0	68	57	17	73	0	2.79
Arthur Rhodes (KJ)	L	35	3	1	.750	0	47	0	0	43	33	12	43	0	2.08
David Riske	R	28	3	4	.429	1	58	0	0	73	55	15	48	0	3.10
Fernando Cabrera	R	23	2	1	.667	0	15	0	0	31	24	11	29	0	1.47
Scott Sauerbeck	L	33	1	0	1.000	0	58	0	0	36	35	16	35	0	4.04
Matt Miller (AJ)	R	33	1	0	1.000	1	23	0	0	30	22	10	23	0	1.82
Brian Tallet	L	27	0	0	—	0	2	0	0	5	6	3	2	0	7.71
Jeremy Guthrie	R	26	0	0	—	0	1	0	0	6	9	2	3	0	6.00
Kazuhito Tadano	R	25	0	0	—	0	1	0	0	4	4	0	1	0	2.25
Bob Wickman	R	36	0	4	.000	45	64	0	0	62	57	21	41	0	2.47
Jason Stanford (EJ) 28															

MINNESOTA 3rd 83-79 .512 16 RON GARDENHIRE

Name	G by Pos	B	AGE	G	AB	R	H	2B	3B	HR	RBI	BB	SO	SB	BA	SA
TOTALS			27	162	5564	688	1441	269	32	134	644	485	978	102	.259	.391
Justin Morneau	1B138 DH1	L	24	141	490	62	117	23	4	22	79	44	94	0	.239	.437
Nick Punto (LJ)	2B73 SS34 3B12 DH5 OF3	B	27	112	394	45	94	18	4	4	26	36	66	13	.239	.335
Jason Bartlett	SS68 DH5	R	25	74	224	33	54	10	1	3	16	21	37	4	.241	.335
Michael Cuddyer	3B95 OF20 2B11 1B8	R	26	126	422	55	111	25	3	12	42	41	93	3	.263	.422
Jacque Jones	OF132 DH9	L	30	142	523	74	130	22	4	23	73	51	120	13	.249	.438
Torii Hunter (NJ)	OF93 DH5	R	29	98	372	63	100	24	1	14	56	34	65	23	.269	.452
Shannon Stewart	OF125 DH5	R	31	132	551	69	151	27	3	10	56	34	73	7	.274	.388
Joe Mauer	C116 DH13	L	22	131	489	61	144	26	2	9	55	61	64	13	.294	.411
Matt LeCroy	DH63 1B23 C1	R	29	101	304	33	79	5	0	17	50	41	85	0	.260	.444
Lew Ford	OF95 DH44	R	28	147	522	70	138	30	4	7	53	45	85	13	.264	.377
Juan Castro	SS73 3B22 2B5	R	33	97	272	27	70	18	1	5	33	9	39	0	.257	.386
Luis Rodriguez	2B40 3B27 SS10 DH3	B	25	79	175	21	47	10	2	2	20	18	23	2	.269	.383
Luis Rivas	2B53 SS6	R	25	59	136	21	35	3	1	1	12	9	17	4	.257	.316
Mike Ryan	OF25 DH13 3B1	L	27	57	117	7	27	5	0	2	13	9	22	1	.231	.325
Terry Tiffee	3B24 1B13 DH10	B	26	54	150	9	31	8	1	1	15	8	15	1	.207	.293
Mike Redmond	C45	R	34	45	148	17	46	9	0	1	26	6	14	0	.311	.392
Brent Abernathy	2B17 OF5 DH2	R	27	24	67	5	16	1	0	1	6	7	9	2	.239	.299
Jason Tyner	OF15 DH3	L	28	18	56	8	18	1	1	0	5	4	4	2	.321	.375
2 Bret Boone	2B14	R	36	14	53	3	9	0	0	0	3	4	13	0	.170	.170
Glenn Williams (SJ)	3B12	B	27	13	40	3	17	1	0	0	3	2	7	1	.425	.450
Chris Heintz	C8	R	30	8	25	1	5	3	0	0	2	1	6	0	.200	.320
Corky Miller	C4 DH1	R	29	5	12	0	0	0	0	0	0	0	2	0	.000	.000

NAME	T	AGE	W	L	PCT	SV	G	GS	CG	IP	H	BB	SO	SHO	ERA
		29	83	79	.512	44	162	162	9	1464	1458	348	965	8	3.71
Johan Santana	L	26	16	7	.696	0	33	33	3	232	180	45	238	2	2.87
Jesse Crain	R	23	12	5	.706	1	75	0	0	80	61	29	25	0	2.71
Carlos Silva	R	26	9	8	.529	0	27	27	2	188	212	9	71	0	3.44
Brad Radke	R	32	9	12	.429	0	31	31	3	201	214	23	117	1	4.04
Kyle Lohse	R	26	9	13	.409	0	31	30	0	179	211	44	86	0	4.18
Joe Nathan	R	30	7	4	.636	43	69	0	0	70	46	22	94	0	2.70
Juan Rincon	R	26	6	6	.500	0	75	0	0	77	63	30	84	0	2.45
Joe Mays	R	29	6	10	.375	0	31	26	1	156	203	41	59	1	5.65
J.C. Romero	L	29	4	3	.571	0	68	0	0	57	50	39	48	0	3.47
Scott Baker	R	23	3	3	.500	0	10	9	0	54	48	14	32	0	3.35
Dave Gassner	R	26	1	0	1.000	0	2	2	0	9	9	1	2	0	5.87
Francisco Liriano	L	21	1	2	.333	0	6	4	0	24	19	7	33	0	5.70
Travis Bowyer	R	23	0	1	.000	0	6	0	0	10	10	3	12	0	5.59
Terry Mulholland	L	42	0	2	.000	0	49	0	0	59	61	17	18	0	4.27
Matt Guerrier	R	26	0	3	.000	0	43	0	0	72	71	24	46	0	3.39
Grant Balfour (EJ) 27															

DETROIT 4th 71-92 .438 28 ALAN TRAMMELL

Name	G by Pos	B	AGE	G	AB	R	H	2B	3B	HR	RBI	BB	SO	SB	BA	SA
TOTALS			28	162	5602	723	1521	283	45	168	678	384	1038	66	.272	.428
Chris Shelton	1B84 DH15 OF1	R	25	107	388	61	116	22	3	18	59	34	87	0	.299	.510
2 Placido Polanco	2B84 3B1	R	29	86	343	58	116	26	2	6	36	21	16	4	.338	.461
Carlos Guillen (KJ)	SS75 DH10	B	29	87	334	48	107	15	4	5	23	24	45	2	.320	.434
Brandon Inge	3B160 OF2	R	28	160	616	75	161	31	9	16	72	63	140	7	.261	.419
Magglio Ordonez (GJ)	OF81 DH1	R	31	82	305	38	92	17	0	8	46	30	35	0	.302	.436
Nook Logan	OF123 DH3	B	25	129	322	47	83	12	5	1	17	21	52	23	.258	.335
Craig Monroe	OF156 DH1	R	28	157	567	69	157	30	3	20	89	40	95	8	.277	.446
Ivan Rodriguez	C123 DH3	R	33	129	504	71	139	33	5	14	50	11	93	7	.276	.444
Dmitri Young	DH71 1B30 OF20	B	31	126	469	61	127	25	3	21	72	29	100	1	.271	.471
Omar Infante	2B69 SS50	R	23	121	406	36	90	28	2	9	43	16	73	8	.222	.367
Rondell White (SJ)	OF65 DH30	R	33	97	374	49	117	24	3	12	53	17	48	1	.313	.489
Carlos Pena	1B51 DH24	L	27	79	260	37	61	9	0	18	44	31	95	0	.235	.477
Vance Wilson	C60	R	32	61	152	18	30	4	0	3	19	11	26	0	.197	.283
Curtis Granderson	OF45	L	24	47	162	18	44	6	3	8	20	10	43	1	.272	.494
Marcus Thames	OF31 DH4	R	28	38	107	11	21	2	0	7	16	9	38	0	.196	.411
2 John McDonald	SS22 2B8 3B1	R	30	31	73	10	19	3	1	0	4	5	12	1	.260	.329
Jason Smith	SS15 2B6 3B3 1B1 DH1	L	27	27	58	4	11	1	2	0	2	0	16	2	.190	.276
1 Ramon Martinez	SS12 2B4 1B2 3B1	R	32	19	56	4	15	1	0	0	5	3	4	0	.268	.286
Tony Giarratano	SS13	B	22	15	42	4	6	0	0	1	4	5	7	1	.143	.214
Bobby Higginson (EJ)	OF7 DH1	L	34	10	26	1	2	0	0	0	1	1	5	0	.077	.077
Alexis Gomez	OF9	L	26	9	16	2	3	0	0	0	1	2	2	0	.188	.188
Kevin Hooper	OF3 SS2 2B1	R	28	6	5	0	1	0	0	0	0	0	2	0	.200	.200
Fernando Vina (LJ) 36																

NAME	T	AGE	W	L	PCT	SV	G	GS	CG	IP	H	BB	SO	SHO	ERA
		30	71	91	.438	37	162	162	7	1436	1504	461	907	2	4.51
Jeremy Bonderman	R	22	14	13	.519	0	29	29	4	189	199	57	145	0	4.57
Mike Maroth	L	27	14	14	.500	0	34	34	0	209	235	51	115	0	4.74
Jason Johnson	R	31	8	13	.381	0	33	33	1	210	233	49	93	0	4.54
Nate Robertson	R	27	7	16	.304	0	32	32	2	197	202	65	122	0	4.48
Sean Douglass	R	26	5	5	.500	0	18	16	0	87	92	33	55	0	5.56
Franklyn German	R	25	4	0	1.000	1	58	0	0	59	63	34	38	0	3.66
Jamie Walker	L	33	4	3	.571	0	66	0	0	49	49	13	30	0	3.70
Chris Spurling	R	28	3	4	.429	0	56	0	0	71	58	22	26	0	3.44
Fernando Rodney (SJ)	R	28	3	4	.400	9	39	0	0	44	39	17	42	0	2.86
Craig Dingman	R	31	2	3	.400	4	34	0	0	32	32	12	24	0	7.07
Wil Ledezma	L	24	2	4	.333	0	10	10	0	50	61	24	30	0	7.07
1 Kyle Farnsworth	R	29	1	1	.500	6	46	0	0	43	29	20	55	0	2.32
Vic Darensbourg	L	34	1	1	.500	0	22	0	0	22	24	7	9	0	2.82
2 Roman Colon	R	25	1	1	.500	0	12	3	0	25	35	7	17	0	6.12
Jason Grilli	R	28	1	0	1.000	0	3	2	0	16	14	7	6	0	3.38
Troy Percival (AJ)	R	35	1	3	.250	8	26	0	0	25	19	11	20	0	5.76
1 Ugueth Urbina	R	31	0	0	—	9	25	0	0	27	21	14	31	0	2.63
Doug Creek	L	36	0	0	—	0	20	0	0	22	27	7	18	0	6.85
Jason Karnuth	R	29	0	0	—	0	2	0	0	2	4	3	0	0	5.40
Mark Woodyard	R	26	0	0	—	0	1	0	0	1	3	3	0	0	1.50
Andrew Good	R	25	0	0	—	0	2	0	0	5	8	0	6	0	5.40
Matt Ginter	R	27	0	1	.000	0	14	1	0	35	45	9	15	0	6.17
Justin Verlander	R	22	0	2	.000	0	2	2	0	11	15	5	7	0	7.15
Gary Knotts (SJ) 28 Colby Lewis (SJ) 25															

KANSAS CITY 5th 56-106 .346 43 TONY PENA 8-25 .242 BOB SCHAEFER 5-12 .294 BUDDY BELL 43-69 .422

Name	G by Pos	B	AGE	G	AB	R	H	2B	3B	HR	RBI	BB	SO	SB	BA	SA
TOTALS			29	162	5503	701	1445	289	34	126	653	424	1008	53	.263	.396
Matt Stairs	1B64 DH40 OF15	L	37	127	396	55	109	26	1	13	66	60	69	1	.275	.444
Ruben Gotay	2B81 DH2	B	22	86	282	32	64	14	2	5	29	22	51	2	.227	.344
Angel Berroa	SS159	R	27	159	608	68	164	21	5	11	55	18	108	7	.270	.375
Mark Teahen	3B128	L	23	130	447	60	110	29	4	7	55	40	107	7	.246	.376
Emil Brown	OF139 DH10	R	30	150	545	75	156	31	5	17	86	48	108	10	.286	.455
David DeJesus	OF119	L	25	122	461	69	135	31	6	9	56	42	76	5	.293	.445
Terrence Long	OF121 DH4	L	29	137	455	62	127	31	3	6	53	30	56	3	.279	.378
John Buck	C117	R	24	118	401	40	97	21	1	12	47	23	94	2	.242	.389
Mike Sweeney	DH73 1B49	R	31	122	470	63	141	39	0	21	83	33	61	3	.300	.517
Joe McEwing	3B29 1B20 2B11 SS6 DH6 OF5	R	32	83	180	16	43	7	0	1	6	6	35	4	.239	.294
1 Tony Graffanino	1B22 2B22 3B17 SS1 DH1	R	33	59	191	29	57	5	2	3	18	22	29	1	.298	.393
Chip Ambres	OF47 DH2	R	25	53	145	25	35	8	0	4	9	16	32	3	.241	.379
1 Alberto Castillo	C34	R	35	34	100	13	21	5	1	1	14	12	21	1	.210	.310
Matt Diaz (UJ)	OF21 DH7	R	27	34	89	7	25	4	2	1	9	4	15	0	.281	.404
Aaron Guiel	OF30	L	32	33	109	18	32	5	0	4	7	6	21	1	.294	.450
1 Eli Marrero	OF20 1B9 DH2	R	31	32	88	11	14	4	0	4	9	6	18	1	.159	.341
Donnie Murphy	2B29 SS2 DH1	R	22	32	77	4	12	5	0	1	8	9	23	0	.156	.260
Shane Costa	OF20 DH4	L	23	27	81	13	19	2	0	0	5	5	11	0	.235	.333
Andres Blanco	2B24 SS7	B	21	26	79	6	17	0	1	0	5	0	15	0	.215	.241
Justin Huber	1B19 DH4	R	22	25	78	6	17	3	0	2	18	6	21	0	.218	.256
Paul Phillips	C20 DH2	R	28	23	67	6	18	4	0	0	7	1	6	0	.269	.403
Denny Hocking	2B13 3B1 SS1	B	35	23	60	14	16	1	0	0	7	10	10	0	.267	.283
Ken Harvey (XJ)	DH7 1B5	R	27	12	45	4	10	1	0	0	3	3	12	0	.222	.356
Calvin Pickering	DH7	L	28	7	27	4	4	0	0	1	3	3	14	0	.148	.259
Chris Truby (BW) 31																

NAME	T	AGE	W	L	PCT	SV	G	GS	CG	IP	H	BB	SO	SHO	ERA
		25	56	106	.346	25	162	162	4	1413	1640	580	924	4	5.49
Runelvys Hernandez	R	27	8	14	.364	0	29	29	0	160	172	70	88	0	5.52
D.J. Carrasco	R	28	8	12	.429	0	21	20	1	115	129	51	49	0	4.79
Mike MacDougal	R	28	5	6	.455	21	68	0	0	70	69	24	72	0	3.33
Mike Wood	R	25	5	8	.385	2	47	10	0	115	129	52	60	0	4.46
Jose Lima	R	32	5	16	.238	0	32	32	1	169	219	61	80	0	6.99
Zach Greinke	R	21	5	17	.227	0	33	33	2	183	233	53	114	0	5.80
Leo Nunez	R	21	3	2	.600	0	41	0	0	54	73	18	32	0	7.55
Ryan Jensen	R	29	3	5	.375	0	9	5	0	25	31	7	18	0	7.11
Ambiorix Burgos	R	21	3	5	.375	2	59	0	0	63	31	31	65	0	3.98
J.P. Howell	L	22	3	5	.375	0	15	15	0	73	73	39	54	0	6.19
Denny Bautista (SJ)	R	24	2	2	.500	0	7	7	0	36	36	17	23	0	5.80
Andy Sisco	L	22	2	5	.286	0	67	0	0	75	68	42	76	0	3.11
Chris Demaria	R	24	1	0	1.000	0	14	0	0	14	15	11	9	0	9.00
Jimmy Gobble	L	23	1	0	1.000	0	28	4	0	54	64	30	38	0	5.70
Brian Anderson (EJ)	L	33	1	2	.333	0	6	3	0	31	39	4	17	0	6.75
Kyle Snyder (SJ)	R	27	1	3	.250	0	13	3	0	36	55	10	19	0	6.75
Shawn Camp	R	29	1	4	.200	0	69	0	0	69	69	13	28	0	6.43
Jamie Cerda	L	26	1	4	.200	0	20	0	0	19	21	11	18	0	6.63
Jonah Bayliss	R	24	0	1	.000	0	11	0	0	12	14	4	10	0	4.63
Nate Field	R	29	0	0	—	0	7	0	0	7	13	5	4	0	5.06
Steve Stemle (XJ)	R	28	0	0	—	0	11	0	0	11	10	4	9	0	5.06
Jeremy Affeldt (GJ)	L	26	0	1	.000	0	49	0	0	50	56	29	39	0	5.26
Scott Sullivan (XJ) 34															

LOS ANGELES OF ANAHEIM 1st 95-67 .586 — MIKE SCIOSCIA

Name	G by Pos	B	AGE	G	AB	R	H	2B	3B	HR	RBI	BB	SO	SB	BA	SA
TOTALS			30	162	5624	761	1520	278	30	147	726	447	848	161	.270	.409
Darin Erstad	1B147 DH5	L	31	153	609	86	166	33	3	7	66	47	109	10	.273	.371
Adam Kennedy (KJ)	2B127	L	29	129	416	49	125	23	0	2	37	29	64	19	.300	.370
Orlando Cabrera	SS140	R	30	141	540	70	139	28	3	8	57	38	50	21	.257	.365
Dallas McPherson (PJ)	3B60	L	24	61	205	29	50	14	2	8	26	14	64	3	.244	.449
Vladimir Guerrero	OF120 DH19	R	29	141	520	95	165	29	2	32	108	61	48	13	.317	.565
Steve Finley	OF104 DH5	L	40	112	406	41	90	20	3	12	54	26	71	4	.222	.374
Garret Anderson	OF106 DH36	L	32	142	575	68	163	34	1	17	96	23	84	1	.283	.435
Bengie Molina	C105 DH11	R	30	119	410	45	121	17	0	15	69	27	41	0	.295	.446
Juan Rivera	OF74 DH28	R	26	106	350	46	95	17	1	15	59	23	44	1	.271	.454
Chone Figgins	OF72 3B56 2B42 DH7 SS4	B	27	158	642	113	186	25	10	8	57	64	101	62	.290	.397
Jeff DaVanon	OF63 DH30	B	31	108	225	42	52	10	1	2	15	39	44	11	.231	.311
Maicer Izturis (KJ)	3B45 SS29 2B1 OF1	B	24	77	191	18	47	8	4	1	15	17	21	9	.246	.346
Jose Molina	C65 DH5 1B4	R	30	75	184	14	42	4	0	6	25	13	41	2	.228	.348
Robb Quinlan (ZJ-SJ)	3B33 1B9 OF6	R	28	81	254	34	71	12	2	5	14	7	26	0	.231	.403
Casey Kotchman	1B20 DH20	L	22	47	126	16	35	5	0	7	22	15	18	1	.278	.484
Josh Paul	C29 OF2	R	30	34	37	4	7	1	0	2	4	2	9	0	.189	.378
Zach Sorensen	2B5 3B1	B	28	12	12	3	2	1	0	0	0	0	2	0	.167	.250
Curtis Pride	OF4 DH3	L	36	11	11	2	1	1	0	0	0	0	4	0	.091	.182
Lou Merloni (NJ)	3B4 1B1	R	34	5	5	1	0	0	0	0	1	1	2	0	.000	.000
Jeff Mathis	C3 DH2	R	22	5	3	1	1	0	0	0	0	0	1	0	.333	.333
Chris Prieto	OF2	L	32	2	2	0	0	0	0	0	0	0	0	0	.000	.000
David Matranga	2B1	R	28	1	1	0	0	0	0	0	0	0	0	0	.000	.000
Tim Salmon (KJ-SJ) 36																

NAME	T	AGE	W	L	PCT	SV	G	GS	CG	IP	H	BB	SO	SHO	ERA
TOTALS		28	95	67	.586	54	162	162	7	1464	1419	443	1126	11	3.68
Bartolo Colon	R	32	21	8	.724	0	33	33	2	223	215	43	157	0	3.48
John Lackey	R	26	14	5	.737	0	33	33	1	209	208	71	199	0	3.44
Ervin Santana	R	22	12	8	.600	0	23	23	1	134	139	47	99	1	4.65
Paul Byrd	R	34	12	11	.522	0	31	31	2	204	216	28	102	1	3.74
Scot Shields	R	29	10	11	.476	7	78	0	0	92	66	37	98	0	2.75
Brendan Donnelly	R	33	9	3	.750	0	65	0	0	65	60	19	53	0	3.72
Jarrod Washburn	L	30	8	8	.500	0	29	29	1	177	184	51	94	1	3.20
Kelvim Escobar (EJ)	R	29	3	2	.600	1	16	7	0	60	45	21	63	0	3.02
Francisco Rodriguez	R	23	2	5	.286	45	66	0	0	67	45	32	91	0	2.67
Joel Peralta	R	29	1	0	1.000	0	28	0	0	35	28	14	30	0	3.89
Esteban Yan	R	30	1	1	.500	0	49	0	0	67	66	30	45	0	4.59
Jake Woods	L	23	1	1	.500	0	28	0	0	28	30	8	20	0	4.55
Kevin Gregg	R	27	1	2	.333	0	33	2	0	64	70	29	52	0	5.04
2 Jason Christiansen	L	35	0	0	—	0	12	0	0	4	7	2	4	0	2.45
Greg Jones	R	28	0	0	—	0	6	0	0	5	7	2	6	0	6.75
Joe Saunders	L	24	0	0	—	0	2	2	0	9	10	4	4	0	7.71
Chris Bootcheck	R	26	0	1	.000	1	5	2	0	19	19	4	8	0	3.37
Bret Prinz (SJ)	R	28	0	1	.000	0	4	0	0	4	1	1	1	0	3.00

OAKLAND 2nd 88-74 .543 7 — KEN MACHA

Name	G by Pos	B	AGE	G	AB	R	H	2B	3B	HR	RBI	BB	SO	SB	BA	SA
TOTALS			29	162	5627	772	1476	310	20	155	739	537	819	31	.262	.407
Dan Johnson	1B101 DH5	L	25	109	375	54	103	21	0	15	58	50	52	0	.275	.451
Mark Ellis	2B115 SS7 1B2 DH1	R	28	122	434	76	137	21	5	13	52	44	51	1	.316	.477
Bobby Crosby (VJ)	SS84	R	25	84	333	66	92	25	4	9	38	35	54	0	.276	.456
Eric Chavez	3B153 DH6	L	27	160	625	92	168	40	1	27	101	58	129	6	.269	.466
Nick Swisher	OF121 1B21	B	25	131	462	66	109	32	1	21	74	55	110	0	.236	.446
Mark Kotsay	OF137 DH21	L	29	139	582	75	163	35	1	15	82	40	51	5	.280	.421
Bobby Kielty	OF98 DH17	B	28	116	377	55	99	20	0	10	57	50	67	3	.263	.395
Jason Kendall	C147 DH1	R	31	150	601	70	163	28	1	0	53	50	39	8	.271	.321
Erubiel Durazo (EJ)	DH39 1B1	L	31	41	152	15	36	6	1	4	16	14	24	1	.237	.368
Scott Hatteberg	DH79 1B53	L	35	134	464	52	119	19	0	7	59	51	54	0	.256	.343
Marco Scutaro	SS81 2B30 3B5 1B3	R	29	118	381	48	94	22	3	9	37	36	48	5	.247	.391
2 Jay Payton	OF69	R	32	69	275	38	74	9	1	13	42	14	33	0	.269	.451
1 Eric Byrnes	OF54 DH4	R	29	59	195	30	51	15	2	7	24	14	27	2	.262	.467
Keith Ginter	2B25 3B12 DH9 OF2	R	29	51	137	12	22	5	0	3	25	13	25	0	.161	.263
Adam Melhuse	C24 DH8	B	33	39	97	11	24	7	0	2	12	5	28	0	.247	.381
Charles Thomas	OF27	R	26	30	46	4	5	0	0	0	1	5	8	0	.109	.109
Matt Watson	OF17	L	26	19	48	4	9	3	0	0	5	2	4	0	.188	.250
Hiram Bocachica	OF6 3B2 DH1	R	29	9	19	2	2	0	0	0	1	0	6	0	.105	.105
Freddie Bynum	2B3 OF2	L	25	7	7	0	2	1	0	0	1	0	3	0	.286	.429
Jermaine Clark	2B2 OF1	L	28	4	0	2	0	0	0	0	0	0	1	0	—	—
2 Alberto Castillo	C1	R	35	1	1	0	0	0	0	0	0	0	1	0	.000	.000

NAME	T	AGE	W	L	PCT	SV	G	GS	CG	IP	H	BB	SO	SHO	ERA
TOTALS		28	88	74	.543	38	162	162	9	1450	1315	504	1075	12	3.69
Danny Haren	R	24	14	12	.538	0	34	34	3	217	212	53	163	0	3.73
Barry Zito	L	27	14	13	.519	0	35	35	0	228	185	89	171	0	3.86
Joe Blanton	R	24	12	12	.500	0	33	33	2	201	178	67	116	0	3.53
Rich Harden (UJ)	R	23	10	5	.667	0	22	19	2	128	93	43	121	1	2.53
Kirk Saarloos	R	26	10	9	.526	0	29	27	2	160	170	54	53	1	4.17
Justin Duchscherer	R	27	7	4	.636	5	65	0	0	86	67	19	85	0	2.21
Huston Street	R	21	5	1	.833	23	67	0	0	78	53	26	72	0	1.72
Keiichi Yabu	R	36	4	0	1.000	1	40	0	0	58	64	26	44	0	4.50
Kiko Calero	R	30	4	1	.800	1	58	0	0	56	45	18	52	0	3.23
2 Joe Kennedy	L	26	4	5	.444	0	19	8	0	61	64	20	45	0	4.45
Ricardo Rincon	L	35	1	1	.500	0	67	0	0	37	34	20	27	0	4.34
2 Jay Witasick	R	32	1	1	.500	1	28	0	0	28	26	17	33	0	3.25
Seth Etherton	R	28	1	1	.500	0	3	3	0	18	16	5	16	0	6.62
Ocatvio Dotel (EJ)	R	31	1	2	.333	7	15	0	0	15	11	4	16	0	3.52
Ron Flores	L	26	0	0	—	0	11	0	0	9	8	6	6	1	1.04
Tim Harikkala	R	33	0	0	—	0	3	0	0	4	6	4	7	0	6.39
Jairo Garcia	R	25	0	0	—	0	3	0	0	3	4	5	1	0	3.00
Britt Reames	R	31	0	0	—	0	5	0	0	6	5	3	9	0	9.53
Juan Cruz	R	26	0	0	.000	0	28	0	0	33	38	22	34	0	7.44
Ryan Glynn	R	30	0	4	.000	0	5	3	0	17	24	7	15	0	6.88
1 Chad Bradford (XJ) 30															

TEXAS 3rd 79-83 .488 16 — BUCK SHOWALTER

Name	G by Pos	B	AGE	G	AB	R	H	2B	3B	HR	RBI	BB	SO	SB	BA	SA
TOTALS			28	162	5716	865	1528	311	29	260	834	495	1112	67	.267	.465
Mark Teixeira	1B155 DH8	R	25	162	644	112	194	41	3	43	144	72	124	4	.301	.575
Alfonso Soriano	2B153 DH2	R	29	156	637	102	171	43	2	36	104	33	125	30	.268	.512
Michael Young	SS155 DH4	R	28	159	668	114	221	40	5	24	91	58	91	5	.331	.513
Hank Blalock	3B158 DH2	L	24	161	647	80	170	34	0	25	92	51	132	1	.263	.431
Richard Hidalgo (WJ)	OF85 DH1	R	30	88	308	43	68	12	0	16	43	26	74	1	.221	.416
Laynce Nix (SJ)	OF42	L	24	63	229	28	55	12	3	6	32	9	45	2	.240	.397
Kevin Mench	OF148 DH1	R	27	150	557	71	147	33	3	25	73	50	68	4	.264	.469
Rod Barajas	C119 1B1	R	29	120	410	53	104	24	0	21	60	26	70	0	.254	.466
Dave Dellucci	DH67 OF52	L	31	128	435	97	109	17	5	29	65	76	121	4	.251	.513
Gary Matthews	OF123 DH1	B	30	131	475	72	121	25	5	17	55	47	90	9	.255	.436
Mark DeRosa	OF25 2B17 SS16 3B5 DH4 1B1	R	30	66	148	26	36	5	0	8	20	16	35	1	.243	.439
Sandy Alomar	C46	R	39	46	128	11	35	7	0	0	14	5	12	0	.273	.328
Adrian Gonzalez	DH32 1B10 OF1	L	23	43	150	17	34	7	1	6	17	10	37	0	.227	.407
1 Phil Nevin	DH25 1B3 3B1	R	34	29	99	15	18	5	0	3	8	8	30	2	.182	.323
Chad Allen	OF18	R	30	21	53	5	15	1	1	0	5	2	13	0	.283	.340
Marshall McDougall	3B5 OF3 2B2 DH2 SS1	R	26	18	18	3	3	1	0	0	0	0	10	0	.167	.222
Gerald Laird	C13 OF1	R	25	13	40	7	9	2	0	1	4	2	7	0	.225	.350
Jason Botts	OF7 DH3	B	24	10	27	4	8	0	0	1	3	3	13	0	.296	.296
Andres Torres	OF5	R	27	8	19	2	3	1	0	0	1	1	6	1	.158	.211
Esteban German	2B1 3B1	R	27	4	4	3	3	1	0	0	0	0	1	2	.750	1.000
Greg Colbrunn (WJ-AJ) 35																

NAME	T	AGE	W	L	PCT	SV	G	GS	CG	IP	H	BB	SO	SHO	ERA
TOTALS		30	79	83	.488	46	162	162	2	1440	1589	522	932	6	4.96
Kenny Rogers	L	40	14	8	.636	0	30	30	1	195	205	53	87	1	3.46
Chris Young	R	26	12	7	.632	0	31	31	0	165	162	45	137	0	4.26
Kameron Loe	R	23	9	6	.600	1	48	8	0	92	89	31	45	0	3.42
1 Chan Ho Park	R	32	8	5	.615	0	20	20	0	110	130	54	80	0	5.66
Doug Brocail	R	38	5	3	.625	1	61	0	0	73	90	34	61	0	5.52
Joaquin Benoit (SJ)	R	27	4	4	.500	0	32	9	0	87	69	38	78	0	3.72
Juan Dominguez	R	25	4	6	.400	0	22	10	0	70	78	25	45	0	4.22
1 Ryan Drese	R	29	4	4	.400	0	12	12	1	70	96	24	20	0	6.46
Francisco Cordero	R	30	3	1	.750	37	69	0	0	69	61	30	79	0	3.39
Brian Shouse	L	36	3	2	.600	0	64	0	0	53	55	18	35	0	5.23
John Wasdin	R	32	3	2	.600	4	31	6	0	76	77	20	44	0	4.28
Ricardo Rodriguez (SJ)	L	27	2	3	.400	0	12	10	0	57	67	17	24	0	5.53
1 Pedro Astacio	R	35	2	8	.200	0	12	12	0	67	79	11	45	0	6.04
Matt Riley	L	25	1	0	1.000	0	3	3	0	13	16	10	4	0	9.95
Josh Rupe	R	22	1	0	1.000	0	11	0	0	17	4	6	7	0	2.79
2 Kevin Gryboski	R	31	1	1	.500	0	11	0	0	17	18	8	2	0	11.17
Nick Regilio (EJ)	R	26	1	2	.333	0	18	22	7	14	0	4.58				
R.A. Dickey (AJ)	R	30	1	2	.333	0	9	4	0	30	29	11	15	0	6.67
C.J. Wilson	L	24	1	7	.125	1	24	6	0	48	63	18	30	0	6.94
Erasmo Ramirez (RJ)	L	24	0	0	—	0	16	0	0	23	24	3	6	0	3.97
Carlos Almanzar (EJ)	R	31	0	0	—	0	5	0	0	5	10	7	3	0	14.40
Ryan Bukvich (EJ)	R	28	0	0	—	0	5	0	0	4	7	8	1	0	11.25
Michael Tejera	L	28	0	0	—	0	3	0	0	2	5	1	2	0	13.50
1 Jason Standridge	R	26	0	0	—	0	7	0	0	7	14	6	3	0	11.57
Justin Thompson	L	32	0	0	—	0	3	0	0	1	4	1	1	0	21.60
2 Steve Karsay	R	33	0	1	.000	0	14	0	0	16	26	5	9	0	7.47
Scott Feldman	R	22	0	0	—	0	8	0	0	9	10	1	6	0	0.96
Ron Mahay	L	34	0	2	.000	1	30	0	0	36	47	16	30	0	6.81
2 James Baldwin	R	33	0	0	—	0	3	0	0	17	18	7	9	0	5.19
Edinson Volquez	R	21	0	4	.000	0	3	3	0	13	25	10	11	0	14.21
Frank Francisco (EJ) 25															

SEATTLE 4th 69-93 .426 26 — BOB MELVIN

Name	G by Pos	B	AGE	G	AB	R	H	2B	3B	HR	RBI	BB	SO	SB	BA	SA
TOTALS			28	162	5507	699	1408	289	34	130	657	466	986	102	.256	.391
Richie Sexson	1B151 DH5	R	30	156	558	99	147	36	1	39	121	89	167	1	.263	.541
1 Bret Boone	2B74	R	36	74	273	30	63	15	3	7	34	24	52	4	.231	.385
Mike Morse	SS55 DH9 OF8	R	23	72	230	27	64	10	1	3	21	18	50	3	.278	.370
Adrian Beltre	3B155 DH6	R	26	156	603	69	154	36	1	19	87	38	108	3	.255	.413
Ichiro Suzuki	OF158 DH3	L	31	162	679	111	206	21	12	15	68	48	66	33	.303	.436
Jeremy Reed	OF137	L	24	141	488	61	124	33	3	3	45	48	74	12	.254	.352
1 Randy Winn	OF96 DH2	B	31	103	386	46	106	25	1	6	37	37	53	12	.275	.391
1 Miguel Olivo	C54	R	26	54	152	14	23	4	0	5	18	4	49	1	.151	.276
Raul Ibanez	DH101 OF58 1B4	L	33	162	614	92	172	32	2	20	89	71	99	9	.280	.436
Willie Bloomquist (LJ)	2B32 SS24 OF15 3B6 1B1 DH1	R	27	82	249	27	64	15	2	0	22	11	38	14	.257	.333
Yuniesky Betancourt	SS53 2B9	R	23	60	211	24	54	11	5	1	15	11	24	1	.256	.370
Dave Hansen	1B9 3B7 DH5	L	36	60	75	5	13	0	2	1	8	13	9	1	.173	.253
Greg Dobbs	DH24 1B5 OF4 3B2	L	26	59	142	8	35	7	1	1	20	5	23	1	.246	.331
Jose Lopez	2B51 3B1	R	21	54	190	18	47	19	0	2	25	6	25	2	.247	.379
1 Wilson Valdez	SS42	R	27	42	126	9	25	5	1	0	8	6	25	2	.198	.254
2 Yorvit Torrealba	C41	R	26	42	108	14	26	4	0	2	13	6	25	0	.241	.333
Pat Borders	C39	R	42	39	117	12	23	7	0	1	7	4	22	0	.197	.265
Scott Spiezio (UJ)	3B6 DH5 1B4 2B1	B	32	29	47	2	3	1	0	1	2	8	13	0	.064	.149
Rene Rivera	C15	R	21	16	48	3	19	3	0	1	5	1	11	0	.396	.521
2 Miguel Ojeda	C16	R	30	16	29	2	5	3	0	0	2	3	6	0	.172	.276
Jamal Strong	OF11 DH3	R	26	16	20	6	5	0	0	0	2	2	5	2	.250	.350
Chris Snelling (KJ)	OF10	L	23	15	29	5	8	1	0	1	1	2	6	0	.276	.448
Wiki Gonzalez (LJ)	C14	R	31	14	45	7	12	5	0	0	2	2	6	0	.267	.378
Dan Wilson (KJ)	C11	R	36	11	29	1	5	0	0	0	1	3	6	0	.185	.185
Jaime Bubela	OF7 DH1	R	27	11	19	3	2	1	0	0	1	1	5	0	.105	.105
Shin-Soo Choo	OF5	L	22	10	18	1	1	0	0	0	1	2	5	0	.056	.056
Ramon Santiago	2B2 SS2	B	25	8	8	1	1	0	0	0	0	1	4	0	.125	.125
Bucky Jacobson (KJ) 29 Pokey Reese (SJ) 32																

NAME	T	AGE	W	L	PCT	SV	G	GS	CG	IP	H	BB	SO	SHO	ERA
TOTALS		32	69	93	.426	39	162	162	6	1428	1483	496	892	7	4.49
Jamie Moyer	L	42	13	7	.650	0	32	32	1	200	225	52	102	0	4.28
Gil Meche (KJ)	R	26	10	8	.556	0	29	26	1	143	153	72	83	0	5.09
Ryan Franklin	R	32	8	15	.348	0	32	30	2	191	212	62	93	1	5.10
Joel Pineiro	R	26	7	11	.389	0	30	30	2	189	224	56	107	0	5.62
J.J. Putz	R	28	6	5	.545	1	64	0	0	60	58	23	45	0	3.60
Aaron Sele	R	35	6	12	.333	0	21	21	1	116	147	41	53	1	5.66
George Sherrill	L	28	4	3	.571	0	29	0	0	19	13	7	24	0	5.21
Felix Hernandez	R	19	4	4	.500	0	12	12	0	84	61	23	77	0	2.67
Julio Mateo	R	27	3	3	.333	0	55	1	0	88	79	17	52	0	3.06
Eddie Guardado	L	34	2	3	.400	36	58	0	0	56	52	15	48	0	2.72
1 Ron Villone	L	35	2	4	.400	1	52	0	0	40	33	23	41	0	2.45
Jeff Harris	R	30	2	5	.286	0	11	8	0	54	48	20	25	0	4.19
Jeff Nelson	R	38	1	3	.250	1	37	0	0	37	32	22	34	0	3.93
Shigetoshi Hasegawa	R	36	1	3	.250	0	46	0	0	67	66	16	30	0	4.18
Rafael Soriano (EJ)	R	25	0	0	—	0	6	0	0	9	9	6	9	0	2.45
Scott Atchison (EJ)	R	29	0	0	—	0	6	0	0	2	1	1	1	0	6.75
Clint Nageotte	R	24	0	0	—	0	2	1	0	7	6	5	4	0	6.75
Jorge Campillo (EJ)	R	26	0	0	—	0	2	0	0	2	2	1	1	0	0.00
Masao Kida	R	36	0	0	—	0	4	0	0	4	5	2	3	0	4.50
Bobby Madritsch (SJ)	L	29	0	1	.000	0	2	2	0	9	16	7	6	0	6.23
Matt Thornton	L	28	0	0	.000	0	55	0	0	57	54	42	57	0	5.21

LINE SCORES

Team	1	2	3	4	5	6	7	8	9	10	11	12	13	14	R	H	E

DIVISION SERIES: CHICAGO 3 : BOSTON 0

Game 1   October 4 at Chicago

| BOS | 0 0 0 2 0 0 0 0 0 | 2 9 0 |
| CHI | 5 0 1 2 0 4 0 2 x | 14 11 1 |

Clement, Bradford (4), Gonzalez (5), Arroyo (8)   **Contreras**, Cotts (8), Politte (9)

Game 2   October 5 at Chicago

| BOS | 2 0 2 0 0 0 0 0 0 | 4 9 1 |
| CHI | 0 0 0 0 5 0 0 0 x | 5 9 0 |

Wells, Papelbon (7)   **Buehrle**, Jenks (8)

Game 3   October 7 at Boston

| CHI | 0 0 2 0 0 2 0 0 1 | 5 8 0 |
| BOS | 0 0 0 2 0 1 0 0 0 | 3 7 1 |

Garcia, Marte (6), Hernandez (6), Jenks (9)   **Wakefield**, Bradford (6), Myers (6), Papelbon (6), Timlin (9)

DIVISION SERIES: LOS ANGELES 3 : NEW YORK 2

Game 1   October 4 at Los Angeles

| NYA | 3 1 0 0 0 0 0 1 0 | 4 9 0 |
| LAA | 0 0 0 0 0 0 1 0 1 | 2 7 0 |

Mussina, Leiter (6), Sturtze (7), Gordon (7), Rivera (9)   **Colon**, Shields (8)

Game 2   October 5 at Los Angeles

| NYA | 0 1 0 0 1 0 0 0 1 | 3 6 3 |
| LAA | 0 0 1 1 2 1 x | 5 7 0 |

Wang, Leiter (7), Proctor (8)   Lackey, Shields (6), **Escobar** (7), Rodriguez (9)

Game 3   October 7 at New York

| LAA | 3 0 2 0 0 2 2 2 0 | 11 19 1 |
| NYA | 0 0 0 4 2 0 0 1 0 | 7 12 2 |

Byrd, Donnelly (4), **Shields** (5), Escobar (7), Rodriguez (9)   Johnson, **Small** (4), Sturtze (6), Gordon (7), Leiter (7), Proctor (8)

Game 4   October 9 at New York

| LAA | 0 0 0 0 0 2 0 0 0 | 2 4 0 |
| NYA | 0 0 0 0 0 1 2 0 x | 3 4 1 |

Lackey, **Shields** (6), Escobar (7)   Chacon, **Leiter** (7), Rivera (8)

Game 5   October 10 at Los Angeles

| NYA | 0 2 0 0 0 0 1 0 0 | 3 11 0 |
| LAA | 0 3 2 0 0 0 0 0 x | 5 9 0 |

Mussina, Johnson (3), Gordon (8)   Colon, **Santana** (2), Escobar (7), Rodriguez (8)

CHAMPIONSHIP: CHICAGO 4 : LOS ANGELES 1

Game 1   October 11 at Chicago

| LAA | 0 1 2 0 0 0 0 0 0 | 3 7 1 |
| CHI | 0 0 1 1 0 0 0 0 0 | 2 7 0 |

Byrd, Shields (7), Rodriguez (9)   **Contreras**, Cotts (9)

Game 2   October 12 at Chicago

| LAA | 0 0 0 0 1 0 0 0 0 | 1 5 3 |
| CHI | 1 0 0 0 0 0 0 0 1 | 2 7 1 |

Washburn, Donnelly (5), Shields (6), **Escobar** (7)   **Buehrle**

Game 3 October 14 at Los Angeles

| CHI | 3 0 1 0 1 0 0 0 0 | 5 11 0 |
| LAA | 0 0 0 0 0 2 0 0 0 | 2 4 0 |

Garland   **Lackey**, Gregg (6), Donnelly (8)

Game 4 October 15 at Los Angeles

| CHI | 3 0 1 1 1 0 0 2 0 | 8 8 1 |
| LAA | 0 1 0 1 0 0 0 0 0 | 2 6 1 |

Garcia   **Santana**, Shields (5), Donnelly (7), Yan (8)

Game 5 October 16 at Los Angeles

| CHI | 0 1 0 0 1 0 1 1 2 | 6 8 1 |
| LAA | 0 0 1 0 2 0 0 0 0 | 3 5 2 |

Contreras   Byrd, Shields (5), **Escobar** (7), Rodriguez (8)

COMPOSITE BATTING

DIVISION SERIES

CHICAGO

NAME	POS	G	AB	R	H	2B	3B	HR	RBI	BA
TOTALS		3	97	24	28	6	0	7	24	.289
Iguchi	2B	3	12	1	3	0	0	1	4	.250
Konerko	1B	3	12	3	3	0	0	2	4	.250
Everett	DH	3	11	2	3	0	0	0	0	.273
Podsednik	LF	3	11	3	3	1	0	1	4	.273
Rowand	CF	3	10	3	4	2	0	0	2	.400
Uribe	SS	3	10	4	4	1	0	1	4	.400
Dye	RF	3	10	1	2	0	0	0	0	.200
Pierzynski	C	3	9	5	4	2	0	2	4	**.444**
Crede	3B	3	9	2	1	0	0	0	1	.111
Harris	2B	1	1	0	1	0	0	0	1	1.000
Blum	1B	1	1	0	0	0	0	0	0	.000
Perez	RF	1	1	0	0	0	0	0	0	.000

BOSTON

NAME	POS	G	AB	R	H	2B	3B	HR	RBI	BA
TOTALS		3	104	9	25	9	0	3	8	.240
Damon	CF	3	13	2	3	1	0	0	0	.231
Renteria	SS	3	13	1	3	2	0	0	0	.231
Ortiz	DH	3	12	2	4	2	0	1	1	.333
Graffanino	2B	3	12	0	3	2	0	0	0	.250
Mueller	3B	3	11	0	0	0	0	0	0	.000
Nixon	RF	2	11	1	3	0	0	0	1	.273
Ramirez	LF	3	10	2	3	0	0	2	4	.300
Varitek	C	3	10	1	3	0	0	0	1	.300
Olerud	1B	3	7	0	2	1	0	0	0	.286
Millar	1B	2	3	0	1	0	0	0	1	.333
Mirabelli	C	1	2	0	0	0	0	0	0	.000
Cora	SS	1	0	0	0	0	0	0	0	—
Hyzdu	CF	1	0	0	0	0	0	0	0	—
Machado	PR	1	0	0	0	0	0	0	0	—

LOS ANGELES

NAME	POS	G	AB	R	H	2B	3B	HR	RBI	BA
TOTALS		5	167	25	46	7	3	6	25	.275
Cabrera	SS	5	21	3	5	2	0	0	3	.238
Figgins	3B-CF	5	21	2	3	1	1	0	2	.143
Erstad	1B	5	20	1	6	2	0	0	3	.300
Anderson	LF	5	19	2	5	0	1	2	7	.263
B. Molina	C	5	18	5	8	0	0	3	5	**.444**
Guerrero	RF	5	18	5	6	0	0	0	0	.333
Rivera	DH	5	17	3	6	1	0	1	1	.353
Kennedy	2B	5	17	0	4	0	1	0	2	.235
Finley	CF	5	11	2	1	1	0	0	1	.091
Quinlan	3B-DH	2	2	0	1	0	0	0	0	.500
Kotchman	DH	2	2	0	0	0	0	0	0	.000
J. Molina	C	1	1	1	1	0	0	0	1	1.000
DaVanon	DH	1	0	1	0	0	0	0	0	—
Paul	PR	1	0	0	0	0	0	0	0	—

NEW YORK

NAME	POS	G	AB	R	H	2B	3B	HR	RBI	BA
TOTALS		5	166	20	42	11	0	4	20	.253
Jeter	SS	5	21	4	7	0	0	2	5	.333
Sheffield	RF	5	21	1	6	0	0	0	2	.286
Matsui	LF-CF	5	20	4	4	1	0	1	1	.200
Giambi	1B-DH	5	19	1	8	3	0	0	2	.421
Cano	2B	5	19	5	5	3	0	0	5	.263
Williams	DH-CF	5	19	2	4	2	0	0	1	.211
Rodriguez	3B	5	15	2	2	1	0	0	0	.133
Posada	C	5	13	3	3	1	0	1	2	.231
Martinez	1B	4	8	0	0	0	0	0	0	.000
Crosby	CF	3	8	0	2	0	0	0	1	.250
Sierra	LF	3	3	0	1	0	0	0	1	.333
Womack	PR	2	0	0	0	0	0	0	0	—
Bellhorn	PR	1	0	0	0	0	0	0	0	—
Flaherty	C	1	0	0	0	0	0	0	0	—
Rivera	P	1	1	0	0	0	0	0	0	—

AMERICAN LEAGUE CHAMPIONSHIP

CHICAGO

NAME	POS	G	AB	R	H	2B	3B	HR	RBI	BA
TOTALS		5	165	23	41	10	1	5	23	.248
Konerko	1B	5	21	2	6	1	0	2	7	.286
Everett	DH	5	20	2	5	0	0	0	3	.250
Crede	3B	5	19	2	7	2	0	2	7	.368
Dye	RF	5	19	3	5	2	0	0	3	.263
Pierzynski	C	5	18	1	3	0	0	1	2	.167
Rowand	CF	5	18	3	3	3	0	0	1	.167
Iguchi	2B	5	17	4	3	1	0	0	1	.176
Podsednik	LF	5	17	4	5	0	1	0	0	.294
Uribe	SS	5	16	1	4	1	0	0	0	.250
Ozuna	DH	2	0	1	0	0	0	0	0	—

LOS ANGELES

NAME	POS	G	AB	R	H	2B	3B	HR	RBI	BA
TOTALS		5	154	11	27	5	0	3	11	.175
Cabrera	SS	5	20	1	4	1	0	1	3	.200
Guerrero	RF-DH	5	20	0	1	0	0	0	1	.050
Anderson	LF-CF	5	17	2	3	0	0	1	2	.176
Erstad	1B	5	17	1	4	1	0	0	0	.235
Figgins	3B-CF	5	17	1	2	1	0	0	1	.118
B. Molina	C-DH	5	17	0	2	0	0	0	0	.118
Kennedy	2B	5	14	3	4	0	0	0	1	.286
Finley	CF	3	9	1	2	0	0	0	0	.222
Rivera	RF-LF-DH	3	9	1	1	1	0	0	0	.111
Kotchman	DH	2	7	0	2	1	0	0	1	.286
J. Molina	C	1	3	0	1	0	0	0	0	.333
Quinlan	3B	1	3	1	1	0	0	1	1	.333
DaVanon	DH	3	1	0	0	0	0	0	0	.000
Izturis	SS	1	0	0	0	0	0	0	0	—
Paul	C	1	0	0	0	0	0	0	0	—

COMPOSITE PITCHING

NAME	G	IP	H	BB	SO	W	L	SV	ERA

DIVISION SERIES

CHICAGO

NAME	G	IP	H	BB	SO	W	L	SV	ERA
TOTALS	3	27	25	8	14	3	0	2	3.00
Contreras	2	7.2	8	0	6	1	0	0	2.35
Buehrle	1	7	8	1	2	1	0	0	5.14
Garcia	1	5	5	4	1	1	0	0	5.40
Jenks	2	3	1	1	1	0	0	2	0.00
Hernandez	1	3	1	0	4	0	0	0	0.00
Politte	1	1	1	0	0	0	0	0	0.00
Cotts	1	0.1	0	0	0	0	0	0	0.00
Marte	1	0	1	2	0	0	0	0	—

BOSTON

NAME	G	IP	H	BB	SO	W	L	SV	ERA
TOTALS	3	25	28	5	11	0	3	0	7.56
Wells	1	6.2	7	0	2	0	1	0	2.70
Wakefield	1	5.1	6	1	4	0	1	0	6.75
Papelbon	2	4	2	0	2	0	0	0	0.00
Clement	1	3.1	7	0	0	0	1	0	21.60
Gonzalez	1	2.1	2	1	0	0	0	0	15.43
Bradford	2	1.1	1	0	1	0	0	0	0.00
Timlin	1	1	1	0	1	0	0	0	9.00
Arroyo	1	1	2	2	1	0	0	0	18.00
Myers	1	0	0	1	0	0	0	0	—

LOS ANGELES

NAME	G	IP	H	BB	SO	W	L	SV	ERA
TOTALS	5	44	42	24	32	3	2	2	3.89
Lackey	2	11.1	7	9	9	0	0	0	2.38
Colon	2	8	10	2	7	0	1	0	4.50
Escobar	4	7	2	5	5	1	0	0	1.29
Santana	1	5.1	5	2	2	1	0	0	5.06
Shields	4	5	4	3	5	1	1	0	3.60
Byrd	1	3.2	7	2	2	0	0	0	9.82
Rodriguez	3	3.1	5	0	2	0	0	2	2.70
Donnelly	1	0.1	2	1	0	0	0	0	27.00

NEW YORK

NAME	G	IP	H	BB	SO	W	L	SV	ERA
TOTALS	5	43	46	5	26	2	3	2	4.40
Mussina	2	8.1	11	1	7	1	1	0	5.40
Johnson	2	7.1	12	1	4	0	0	0	6.14
Wang	1	6.2	6	0	1	0	1	0	1.35
Chacon	1	6.1	4	1	5	0	0	0	2.84
Leiter	4	3.2	2	1	2	1	0	0	7.36
Rivera	3	3	1	1	2	0	0	2	3.00
Small	1	2.2	4	0	2	0	1	0	6.75
Gordon	3	2.1	2	0	2	0	0	0	3.86
Proctor	2	2	3	0	1	0	0	0	0.00
Sturtze	2	0.2	1	0	0	0	0	0	13.50

CHICAGO

NAME	G	IP	H	BB	SO	W	L	SV	ERA
TOTALS	5	45	27	4	22	4	1	0	2.20
Contreras	2	17.1	12	2	6	1	1	0	3.12
Buehrle	1	9	5	0	4	1	0	0	1.00
Garcia	1	9	6	1	5	1	0	0	2.00
Garland	1	9	4	1	7	1	0	0	2.00
Cotts	1	0.2	0	0	0	0	0	0	0.00

LOS ANGELES

NAME	G	IP	H	BB	SO	W	L	SV	ERA
TOTALS	5	44.2	41	16	36	1	4	1	3.43
Byrd	2	10.2	10	2	2	1	0	0	3.38
Shields	4	6	4	1	5	0	0	0	0.00
Lackey	1	5	8	1	3	0	1	0	9.00
Washburn	1	4.2	4	1	1	0	0	0	0.00
Escobar	2	4.1	4	2	10	0	2	0	2.08
Santana	1	4.1	3	3	2	0	1	0	10.38
Donnelly	2	3.1	2	1	5	0	0	0	0.00
Rodriguez	2	2.1	3	3	3	0	0	1	0.00
Gregg	1	2	1	1	3	0	0	0	0.00
Yan	1	2	3	1	2	0	0	0	9.00

ATLANTA — 1st 90-72 .556 — BOBBY COX

Name	G by Pos	B	AGE	G	AB	R	H	2B	3B	HR	RBI	BB	SO	SB	BA	SA
TOTALS			28	162	5486	769	1453	308	37	184	733	534	1084	92	.265	.435
Adam LaRoche	1B125	L	25	141	451	53	117	28	0	20	78	39	87	0	.259	.455
Marcus Giles	2B149 3B1	R	27	152	577	104	168	45	4	15	63	64	108	16	.291	.461
Rafael Furcal	SS152	B	27	154	616	100	175	31	11	12	58	62	78	46	.284	.429
Chipper Jones (FJ)	3B101	B	33	109	358	66	106	30	0	21	72	72	56	5	.296	.556
Jeff Francoeur	OF67	R	21	70	257	41	77	20	1	14	45	11	58	3	.300	.549
Andruw Jones	OF159	R	28	160	586	95	154	24	3	51	128	64	112	4	.263	.575
Brian Jordan (KJ)	OF62	R	38	76	231	25	57	8	2	3	24	14	46	2	.247	.338
Johnny Estrada	C104	B	29	105	357	31	93	26	0	4	39	20	38	0	.261	.367
Ryan Langerhans	OF114	L	25	128	326	48	87	22	3	8	42	37	75	0	.267	.426
Wilson Betemit	3B63 SS25 2B1	B	23	115	246	36	75	12	4	4	20	22	55	1	.305	.435
Pete Orr	2B25 3B12 OF3 SS1	L	26	112	150	32	45	8	1	1	8	6	23	7	.300	.387
Julio Franco	1B62	R	46	108	233	30	64	12	1	9	42	27	57	4	.275	.451
Kelly Johnson	OF79	L	23	87	290	46	70	12	3	9	40	40	75	2	.241	.397
Brian McCann	C57	L	21	59	180	20	50	7	0	5	23	18	26	1	.278	.400
Raul Mondesi	OF40	R	34	41	142	17	30	7	1	4	17	12	35	0	.211	.359
Andy Marte	3B17	R	21	24	57	3	8	2	1	0	4	7	13	0	.140	.211
2 Todd Hollandsworth	OF9 1B1	L	32	24	35	3	6	0	0	1	1	5	13	0	.171	.257
Brayan Pena	C15	B	23	18	39	2	7	2	0	0	4	1	7	0	.179	.231
Eddie Perez (SJ)	C13	R	37	16	38	3	8	2	0	2	6	1	5	0	.211	.421

NAME	T	AGE	W	L	PCT	SV	G	GS	CG	IP	H	BB	SO	SHO	ERA
TOTALS		28	90	72	.556	38	162	162	8	1444	1487	520	929	12	3.98
John Smoltz	R	28	14	7	.667	0	33	33	3	230	210	53	169	1	3.06
Tim Hudson (UJ)	R	29	14	9	.609	0	29	29	2	192	194	65	115	0	3.52
Jorge Sosa	R	28	13	3	.813	0	44	20	0	134	122	64	85	0	2.55
Horacio Ramirez	L	25	11	9	.550	0	33	32	1	202	214	67	80	1	4.63
Kyle Davies	R	21	7	6	.538	0	21	14	0	88	98	49	62	0	4.93
Mike Hampton (AJ-EJ-XJ)	L	32	5	3	.625	0	12	12	1	69	74	18	27	1	3.50
John Foster	L	27	4	2	.667	1	62	0	0	35	27	19	32	0	4.15
Blaine Boyer	R	23	4	2	.667	0	43	0	0	38	32	17	33	0	3.11
Adam Bernero	R	28	4	3	.571	0	36	0	0	47	61	12	37	0	6.51
John Thomson (RJ)	R	31	4	6	.400	0	17	17	1	99	111	28	61	0	4.47
Chris Reitsma	R	27	3	6	.333	15	76	0	0	73	79	14	42	0	3.93
Danny Kolb	R	30	3	8	.273	11	65	0	0	58	78	29	39	0	5.93
Macay McBride	L	22	1	0	1.000	1	23	0	0	14	18	7	22	0	5.79
Jorge Vasquez	R	26	1	0	1.000	0	7	0	0	9	11	5	9	0	3.00
2 Jim Brower	R	32	1	2	.333	0	37	0	0	30	33	17	28	0	4.20
1 Roman Colon	R	25	1	5	.167	0	23	4	0	44	47	14	30	0	5.28
1 Kevin Gryboski	R	31	0	0	—	0	31	0	0	21	24	12	8	0	2.95
2 Kyle Farnsworth	R	29	0	0	—	10	26	0	0	27	15	7	32	0	1.98
Anthony Lerew	R	22	0	0	—	0	7	0	0	9	8	5	5	0	5.63
Jay Powell (BA)	R	33	0	0	—	0	5	0	0	3	1	4	1	0	0.00
Tom Martin	L	35	0	0	—	0	4	0	0	2	6	2	0	0	19.29
Matt Childers	R	26	0	0	—	0	4	0	0	4	5	3	2	0	4.50
Chuck James	L	23	0	0	—	0	2	0	0	6	4	3	5	0	1.59
Frank Brooks	L	26	0	0	—	0	1	0	0	0	0	0	0	0	0.00
Seth Greisinger	R	29	0	0	—	0	1	1	0	5	7	1	2	0	3.60
Joey Devine	R	21	0	1	.000	0	5	0	0	5	6	5	3	0	12.60

PHILADELPHIA — 2nd 88-74 .543 2 — CHARLIE MANUEL

Name	G by Pos	B	AGE	G	AB	R	H	2B	3B	HR	RBI	BB	SO	SB	BA	SA
TOTALS			31	162	5542	807	1494	282	35	167	760	639	1083	116	.270	.423
Jim Thome (EJ)	1B52	L	34	59	193	26	40	7	0	7	30	45	59	0	.207	.352
Chase Utley	2B135 1B8	L	26	147	543	93	158	39	6	28	105	69	109	16	.291	.540
Jimmy Rollins	SS157	B	26	158	677	115	196	38	11	12	54	47	71	41	.290	.431
David Bell	3B150	R	32	150	557	53	138	31	1	10	61	47	69	0	.248	.361
Bobby Abreu	OF158	L	31	162	588	104	168	37	1	24	102	117	134	31	.286	.474
Kenny Lofton	OF97	L	38	110	367	67	123	15	5	2	36	32	41	22	.335	.420
Pat Burrell	OF153	R	28	154	562	78	158	27	1	32	117	99	160	1	.281	.504
Mike Lieberthal	C117	R	33	118	392	48	103	25	0	12	47	35	35	0	.263	.418
Jason Michaels	OF91	R	29	105	289	54	88	16	2	4	31	44	45	3	.304	.415
Tomas Perez	1B24 3B15 SS14	B	31	94	159	17	37	7	0	2	22	11	27	1	.233	.277
2 Endy Chavez	OF51	L	27	91	107	17	23	3	3	0	10	4	13	2	.215	.299
Ryan Howard	1B84	L	25	88	312	52	90	17	2	22	63	33	100	0	.288	.567
Todd Pratt	C57	R	38	60	175	17	44	4	0	7	23	19	50	0	.251	.394
1 Placido Polanco	2B29 3B8 OF5 SS1	R	29	43	158	26	50	7	0	3	20	12	9	0	.316	.418
2 Ramon Martinez	1B10 3B3 SS3 2B1	R	32	33	56	7	16	2	0	1	9	3	7	0	.286	.375
Jose Offerman	1B4	R	36	33	33	6	6	1	1	1	3	5	6	0	.182	.364
2 Michael Tucker	OF1	L	34	22	18	3	4	0	0	0	3	3	4	0	.222	.222
Shane Victorino	OF12	R	24	21	17	5	5	0	0	2	8	1	3	0	.294	.647
2 Matt Kata	2B3 SS1 OF1	B	27	10	6	1	1	0	0	0	0	0	2	0	.167	.167
1 Marlon Byrd	OF5	R	27	5	13	0	4	0	0	0	0	0	3	0	.308	.308
Danny Sandoval	SS1	B	26	3	2	1	0	0	0	0	0	0	0	0	.000	.000

NAME	T	AGE	W	L	PCT	SV	G	GS	CG	IP	H	BB	SO	SHO	ERA
TOTALS		31	88	74	.543	40	162	162	4	1435	1379	487	1159	6	4.21
Jon Lieber	R	35	17	13	.567	0	35	35	1	218	223	41	149	0	4.20
Brett Myers	R	24	13	8	.619	0	34	34	2	215	193	68	208	0	3.72
Cory Lidle	R	33	13	11	.542	0	31	31	1	185	210	40	121	0	4.53
Vicente Padilla	R	27	9	12	.429	0	27	27	0	147	146	74	103	0	4.71
Randy Wolf (EJ)	L	28	4	4	.600	0	13	13	0	80	87	26	61	0	4.39
Ryan Madson	R	24	6	5	.545	0	78	0	0	87	84	25	79	0	4.14
Aaron Fultz	L	31	4	0	1.000	0	62	0	0	72	47	23	54	0	2.24
Rheal Cormier	L	38	4	2	.667	0	57	0	0	47	56	16	34	0	5.89
Billy Wagner	L	33	4	3	.571	38	75	0	0	78	45	20	87	0	1.51
2 Ugueth Urbina	R	31	4	3	.571	1	56	0	0	52	35	25	66	0	4.13
Robinson Tejada	R	23	4	3	.571	0	26	13	0	86	67	51	72	0	3.57
Geoff Geary	R	28	2	1	.667	0	40	0	0	58	54	21	42	0	3.72
Gavin Floyd	R	22	1	2	.333	0	7	4	0	26	30	16	17	0	10.04
Eude Brito	L	26	1	2	.333	0	5	4	0	22	20	11	15	0	9.68
Pedro Liriano	R	24	0	0	—	0	5	0	0	8	10	6	6	0	10.57
1 Tim Worrell (PP)	R	37	0	1	.000	1	19	0	0	17	29	3	17	0	7.41
2 Aquilino Lopez	R	30	0	1	.000	0	10	0	0	13	13	7	16	0	2.13
Amaury Telemaco	R	31	0	1	.000	0	7	0	0	11	5	4	8	0	4.22
Terry Adams	R	32	0	2	.000	0	13	0	0	13	25	10	4	0	12.83

NEW YORK — 3rd (tie) 83-79 .512 7 — WILLIE RANDOLPH

Name	G by Pos	B	AGE	G	AB	R	H	2B	3B	HR	RBI	BB	SO	SB	BA	SA
TOTALS			29	162	5505	722	1421	279	32	175	683	486	1075	153	.258	.416
Doug Mientkiewicz	1B83	L	31	87	275	36	66	13	0	11	29	32	39	0	.240	.407
Kaz Matsui (KJ)	2B71	R	29	87	267	31	68	9	4	3	24	14	43	6	.255	.352
Jose Reyes	SS161	B	22	161	696	99	190	24	17	7	58	27	78	60	.273	.386
David Wright	3B160	R	22	160	575	99	176	42	1	27	102	72	113	17	.306	.523
Mike Cameron (WJ-CJ)	OF76	R	32	76	308	47	84	23	2	12	39	29	85	13	.273	.477
Carlos Beltran	OF150	B	28	151	582	83	155	34	2	16	78	56	96	17	.266	.414
Cliff Floyd	OF150	L	32	150	550	85	150	22	2	34	98	63	98	12	.273	.505
Mike Piazza	C101	R	36	113	398	41	100	23	0	19	62	41	67	0	.251	.452
Marlon Anderson	1B23 OF23 2B20	L	31	123	235	31	62	9	0	7	19	18	45	6	.264	.391
Miguel Cairo	2B82 1B8 3B3 OF3	R	31	100	327	31	82	18	0	2	19	19	31	13	.251	.324
Ramon Castro	OF81	R	29	99	209	26	51	16	0	8	41	25	58	1	.244	.435
Victor Diaz	OF81	R	23	89	280	41	72	17	3	12	38	30	82	6	.257	.468
Chris Woodward	1B34 OF23 SS7 3B6 2B5	R	29	81	173	16	49	10	0	3	18	13	46	0	.283	.393
2 Jose Offerman	1B11 2B1	B	36	53	72	5	18	2	0	1	10	6	11	0	.250	.319
Gerald Williams	OF27	R	38	39	30	9	7	2	0	1	3	1	7	2	.233	.400
Mike Jacobs	1B28	L	24	30	100	19	31	7	0	11	23	10	22	0	.310	.710
Eric Valent	OF12	L	28	28	43	4	8	3	0	0	1	7	17	0	.186	.256
Brian Daubach	1B6	L	33	15	25	4	3	2	0	1	3	7	5	0	.120	.320
Mike DiFelice	C11	R	36	11	17	0	2	0	0	0	0	0	8	0	.118	.118
Anderson Hernandez	2B5 SS2	B	22	6	18	1	1	0	0	0	0	0	4	0	.056	.056

NAME	T	AGE	W	L	PCT	SV	G	GS	CG	IP	H	BB	SO	SHO	ERA
TOTALS		32	83	79	.512	38	162	162	8	1436	1390	491	1012	11	3.76
Pedro Martinez	R	33	15	8	.652	0	31	31	4	217	159	47	208	1	2.82
Tom Glavine	L	39	13	13	.500	0	33	33	2	211	227	61	105	1	3.53
Kris Benson (UJ)	R	30	10	8	.556	0	28	28	0	174	171	49	95	0	4.13
Jae Weong Seo	R	28	8	2	.800	0	14	14	1	90	84	16	59	0	2.59
Roberto Hernandez	R	40	8	6	.571	4	67	0	0	70	57	28	61	0	2.58
Victor Zambrano	R	29	7	12	.368	0	31	27	0	166	170	77	112	0	4.17
Aaron Heilman	R	26	5	3	.625	5	53	7	1	108	87	37	106	1	3.17
Braden Looper	R	30	4	7	.364	28	60	0	0	59	65	22	27	0	3.94
1 Mike DeJean	R	34	3	1	.750	0	26	0	0	36	18	17	0	6.31	
Juan Padilla	R	28	3	1	.750	1	24	0	0	36	24	13	17	0	1.49
Kazuhisa Ishii	L	31	3	9	.250	0	19	16	0	91	87	49	53	0	5.14
2 Shingo Takatsu	R	36	1	0	1.000	0	9	0	0	6	5	4	2	0	2.35
Mike Matthews	L	31	1	0	1.000	0	42	0	0	5	9	4	2	0	10.80
Heath Bell	R	27	1	3	.250	0	42	0	0	47	56	13	43	0	5.59
Steve Trachsel (XJ)	R	34	1	4	.200	0	7	6	0	37	37	12	24	0	4.14
Dae-Sung Koo	L	35	0	0	—	0	33	0	0	23	12	13	23	0	3.91
Manny Aybar	R	33	0	0	—	0	22	0	0	25	31	7	27	0	6.04
2 Danny Graves	R	32	0	0	—	0	20	0	0	29	8	12	0	5.75	
Tim Hamulack	L	28	0	0	—	0	7	0	0	8	9	4	8	0	23.14
Jose Santiago	R	30	0	0	—	0	6	0	0	7	11	2	10	0	3.18
Felix Heredia (SJ)	L	30	0	1	—	0	11	0	0	11	10	10	8	0	5.06
Royce Ring	L	24	0	2	.000	0	9	0	0	11	10	10	8	0	5.06

FLORIDA — 3rd (tie) 83-79 .512 7 — JACK McKEON

Name	G by Pos	B	AGE	G	AB	R	H	2B	3B	HR	RBI	BB	SO	SB	BA	SA
TOTALS			30	162	5502	717	1499	306	32	128	678	512	918	96	.272	.409
Carlos Delgado	1B141	L	33	144	521	81	157	41	3	33	115	72	121	0	.301	.582
Luis Castillo	2B120	B	29	122	439	72	132	12	4	4	30	65	32	10	.301	.374
Alex Gonzalez	SS124	R	28	130	435	45	115	30	0	5	45	31	81	5	.264	.368
Mike Lowell	3B135 2B9	R	31	150	500	56	118	36	1	8	58	46	58	4	.236	.360
Juan Encarnacion	OF139	R	29	141	506	59	145	27	3	16	76	41	104	6	.287	.447
Juan Pierre	OF160	L	27	162	656	96	181	19	13	2	47	41	45	57	.276	.354
Miguel Cabrera	OF134 3B29	R	22	158	613	106	198	43	2	33	116	64	125	1	.323	.561
Paul LoDuca	C128	R	33	132	445	45	126	23	1	6	57	34	31	4	.283	.380
Jeff Conine	OF61 1B45	R	39	131	335	42	102	20	2	3	33	38	58	2	.304	.403
Damion Easley	2B46 SS30 3B10	R	35	102	267	37	64	19	1	9	30	26	47	2	.240	.419
Lenny Harris	3B2 OF2 1B1	L	40	83	70	5	22	4	0	1	13	7	11	0	.314	.414
Chris Aguila	OF42	R	26	65	78	11	19	3	0	0	4	3	19	0	.244	.282
Matt Treanor	C55	R	29	58	134	10	27	8	0	0	13	16	28	0	.201	.261
Dontrelle Willis	P34	L	23	39	92	14	24	4	0	1	11	1	18	0	.261	.337
Joe Dillon	2B4 OF3 3B2 1B1	R	29	27	36	6	6	1	0	1	1	1	8	0	.167	.278
Jeremy Hermida	OF14	L	21	23	41	9	12	2	0	1	6	6	12	0	.293	.634
Robert Andino	SS17	R	21	17	44	4	7	1	0	0	1	1	9	0	.159	.250
Josh Willingham (BA)	C8 OF1	R	26	16	23	3	7	1	0	2	4	6	6	0	.304	.348
Josh Wilson	SS6 2B4	R	24	11	10	2	1	0	0	0	2	0	4	0	.100	.200
Ryan Jorgensen	C3	R	26	4	4	0	0	0	0	0	0	1	1	0	.000	.000
Mike Mordecai	2B1 SS1	R	37	2	2	0	0	0	0	0	0	0	0	0	.000	.000

NAME	T	AGE	W	L	PCT	SV	G	GS	CG	IP	H	BB	SO	SHO	ERA
TOTALS		30	83	79	.512	42	162	162	14	1442	1459	563	1125	15	4.16
Dontrelle Willis	L	23	22	10	.688	0	34	34	7	236	213	55	170	5	2.63
Josh Beckett	R	25	15	8	.652	0	29	29	2	179	153	58	166	1	3.37
A.J. Burnett	R	28	12	12	.500	0	32	32	4	209	184	79	198	2	3.44
Brian Moehler	R	33	6	12	.333	0	37	25	0	158	198	42	95	0	4.55
Jason Vargas	L	22	5	5	.500	0	17	13	1	74	71	31	59	0	4.03
John Riedling (SJ)	R	29	4	1	.800	0	29	0	0	28	34	13	16	0	7.16
2 Ron Villone	L	35	3	2	.600	0	27	0	0	24	24	12	29	0	6.85
1 Al Leiter (SJ)	L	39	3	7	.300	0	17	16	0	80	88	60	52	0	6.64
1 Matt Perisho	L	30	2	0	1.000	0	24	0	0	14	12	11	10	0	1.93
Chris Resop	R	22	2	0	1.000	0	15	0	0	17	12	8	12	0	8.47
Guillermo Mota (EJ)	R	31	2	2	.500	2	56	0	0	67	65	32	60	0	4.70
Ismael Valdez (BL)	R	31	2	2	.500	0	14	7	0	51	64	22	27	0	5.33
Antonio Alfonseca (EJ)	R	33	1	1	.500	0	33	0	0	27	29	14	16	0	4.94
Scott Olsen	L	21	1	1	.500	0	5	2	0	20	21	10	21	0	3.98
Valerio De Los Santos	L	32	1	2	.333	0	27	0	0	22	25	12	16	0	6.14
Jim Mecir	R	35	1	4	.200	0	52	0	0	43	39	17	34	0	3.12
Todd Jones	R	37	1	5	.167	40	68	0	0	73	61	14	62	0	2.10
Randy Messenger	R	23	0	0	—	0	29	0	0	37	39	30	29	0	5.35
Travis Smith	R	32	0	0	—	0	9	0	0	14	16	4	9	0	4.94
Chad Bentz	L	25	0	0	—	0	3	0	0	1	4	2	1	0	31.50
Jim Crowell	L	30	0	0	—	0	2	0	0	1	2	0	1	0	21.60
Josh Johnson (EJ)	R	21	0	0	—	0	4	0	0	12	11	10	10	0	3.65
Logan Kensing (EJ)	R	22	0	0	—	0	4	4	0	21	21	14	13	0	11.12
Yorman Bazardo	R	20	0	0	—	0	2	0	0	3	6	2	0	0	21.60
3 Paul Quantrill	R	36	0	1	.000	0	22	0	0	22	38	4	1	0	8.44
Frank Castillo	R	36	0	2	.000	0	5	1	0	11	14	4	4	0	10.38
Nate Bump (SJ)	R	28	0	3	.000	0	31	0	0	38	43	12	18	0	4.03
Tim Spooneybarger (EJ)		25													

WASHINGTON — 5th 81-81 .500 9 — FRANK ROBINSON

Name	G by Pos	B	AGE	G	AB	R	H	2B	3B	HR	RBI	BB	SO	SB	BA	SA
TOTALS			29	162	5426	639	1367	311	32	117	615	491	1090	45	.252	.386
Nick Johnson	1B129	L	26	131	453	66	131	35	3	15	74	80	87	3	.289	.479
Jose Vidro (NJ)	2B79	B	30	87	309	38	85	21	2	7	32	31	30	0	.275	.424
Cristian Guzman	SS142	R	27	142	456	39	100	19	6	4	31	25	76	7	.219	.314
Vinny Castilla	3B138	R	37	142	494	53	125	36	1	12	66	43	82	4	.253	.403
Jose Guillen	OF142	R	29	148	551	81	156	32	2	24	76	31	102	1	.283	.479
2 Preston Wilson	OF68	R	30	68	253	34	66	14	1	10	43	20	71	3	.261	.443
Brad Wilkerson	OF129 1B25	L	28	148	565	76	140	42	7	11	57	84	147	8	.248	.405
Brian Schneider	C113	L	28	116	369	38	99	20	1	10	44	29	48	1	.268	.409
Jamey Carroll	2B63 SS41 3B12	R	31	113	303	44	76	8	1	0	22	34	55	3	.251	.284
Ryan Church	OF85	L	26	102	268	41	77	15	3	9	42	24	70	3	.287	.466
Carlos Baerga	3B20 1B11 2B7	B	36	93	158	18	40	7	0	2	19	7	17	0	.253	.335
2 Marlon Byrd	OF65	R	27	74	216	20	57	15	2	2	26	18	47	5	.264	.380
Gary Bennett	C64	R	33	68	199	11	44	7	0	1	21	21	37	0	.221	.271
Tony Blanco	OF11 3B5 1B3	R	23	56	62	7	11	3	0	1	7	2	19	1	.177	.274
Wil Cordero (KJ)	1B12	R	33	29	51	2	6	2	0	0	2	3	14	0	.118	.157
2 Junior Spivey (BW)	2B22	R	30	28	77	15	17	7	0	2	7	11	26	2	.221	.390
Brandon Watson	OF13	L	23	25	40	8	7	1	1	1	5	4	8	0	.175	.325
Ryan Zimmerman	3B14 SS1	R	20	20	58	6	23	10	0	0	6	3	12	0	.397	.569
2 Deivi Cruz	2B16 SS8	R	32	20	51	2	13	1	0	0	1	3	0	0	.255	.275
Terrmel Sledge (LJ)	OF13	L	28	20	37	7	9	0	1	1	8	7	8	2	.243	.378
2 Kenny Kelly	OF2	R	26	17	4	3	1	1	0	0	0	1	3	1	.250	.500
J.J. Davis	OF10	R	26	14	26	0	6	0	0	0	2	2	7	1	.231	.231
Jeffrey Hammonds (VR)	OF11	R	34	13	32	3	7	1	0	0	1	2	4	0	.219	.250
Matt Cepicky	OF6	L	27	11	25	1	6	3	0	0	3	0	4	0	.240	.360
Rick Short	2B6 1B1	R	32	11	15	4	6	2	0	2	4	1	1	0	.400	.933
1 Endy Chavez	OF6	L	27	7	9	2	2	1	0	0	1	3	1	0	.222	.333
Keith Osik	C5	R	36	6	4	0	0	0	0	0	0	0	2	0	.000	.000
Brendan Harris	2B2 3B1	R	24	4	9	1	3	1	0	1	3	0	1	0	.333	.778
Tyrell Godwin		L	25	3	3	0	0	0	0	0	0	0	1	0	.000	.000
Henry Mateo (SJ)	2B1	B	28	1	0	0	0	0	0	0	0	1	0	0	.000	.000
Alex Escobar (LJ) 26																

NAME	T	AGE	W	L	PCT	SV	G	GS	CG	IP	H	BB	SO	SHO	ERA
		29	81	81	.500	51	162	162	4	1458	1456	539	997	9	3.87
Livan Hernandez	R	30	15	10	.600	0	35	35	2	246	268	84	147	0	3.98
Esteban Loaiza	R	33	12	10	.545	0	34	34	0	217	227	55	173	0	3.77
John Patterson	R	27	9	7	.563	0	31	31	2	198	172	65	185	1	3.13
Luis Ayala	R	27	8	7	.533	1	68	0	0	71	75	14	40	0	2.66
Tony Armas (GJ-SJ)	R	27	7	7	.500	0	19	19	0	101	100	54	59	0	4.97
Hector Carrasco	R	35	5	4	.556	2	64	5	0	88	59	38	75	0	2.04
1 Tomo Ohka	R	29	4	3	.571	0	10	9	0	54	44	27	17	0	3.33
Gary Majewski	R	25	4	4	.500	1	79	0	0	86	80	37	50	0	2.93
2 Ryan Drese (SJ)	R	29	3	6	.333	0	11	11	0	60	66	22	26	0	4.98
Jason Bergmann	R	23	2	1	1.000	0	15	1	0	20	14	11	21	0	2.75
Joey Eischen (BA)	L	35	2	1	.667	0	57	0	0	36	34	19	30	0	3.22
2 Mike Stanton	L	38	2	1	.667	0	30	0	0	28	31	9	14	0	3.58
Chad Cordero	R	23	2	4	.333	47	74	0	0	74	55	17	61	0	1.82
Jon Rauch (SJ)	R	26	2	4	.333	0	15	1	0	30	24	11	23	0	3.60
T.J. Tucker (GJ-EJ)	R	26	1	0	1.000	0	13	0	0	13	20	2	5	0	6.39
Travis Hughes	R	27	1	1	.500	0	14	0	0	13	18	8	8	0	5.54
1 Zach Day (BW)	R	27	1	2	.333	0	12	5	0	36	41	25	16	0	6.75
1 Sun-Woo Kim	R	27	1	2	.333	0	12	2	0	29	41	8	17	0	6.14
Joe Horgan	L	28	0	0	—	0	8	0	0	6	19	4	5	0	21.00
C.J. Nitkowski	L	32	0	0	—	0	7	0	0	3	5	2	2	0	8.10
Antonio Osuna (SJ)	R	32	0	0	—	0	4	0	0	2	9	7	0	0	42.43
Darrell Rasner	R	24	0	1	.000	0	5	1	0	7	5	2	4	0	3.68
Matt White	R	27	0	1	.000	0	1	1	0	4	4	3	3	0	9.00
2 John Halama	L	33	0	3	.000	0	10	3	0	21	23	8	11	0	4.64
1 Claudio Vargas (EJ)	R	27	0	3	.000	0	4	4	0	13	22	7	5	0	9.24
Francis Beltran (EJ) 25															

CENTRAL DIVISION

ST. LOUIS — 1st 100-62 .617 — TONY LA RUSSA

Name	G by Pos	B	AGE	G	AB	R	H	2B	3B	HR	RBI	BB	SO	SB	BA	SA
TOTALS			32	162	5538	805	1494	287	26	170	757	534	947	83	.270	.423
Albert Pujols	1B157	R	25	161	591	129	195	38	2	41	117	97	65	16	.330	.609
Mark Grudzielanek	2B137	R	35	137	528	64	155	30	3	8	59	26	81	8	.294	.407
David Eckstein	SS156	R	30	158	630	90	185	26	7	8	61	58	44	11	.294	.395
Scott Rolen (SJ)	3B56	R	30	56	196	28	46	12	1	5	28	25	28	1	.235	.383
Larry Walker	OF83	L	38	100	315	66	91	20	1	15	52	41	64	2	.289	.502
Jim Edmonds	OF139	L	35	142	467	88	123	37	1	29	89	91	139	5	.263	.533
Reggie Sanders (BL)	OF81	R	37	93	295	49	80	14	2	21	54	28	75	14	.271	.546
Yadier Molina (BH)	C114 1B1	R	22	114	385	36	97	15	1	8	49	23	30	2	.252	.358
So Taguchi	OF131	R	35	143	396	45	114	21	2	8	53	20	62	11	.288	.412
Abraham Nunez	3B98 2B22 SS21	B	29	139	421	64	120	13	2	5	44	37	63	0	.285	.361
John Mabry	3B34 1B12	L	34	112	246	26	59	15	1	8	32	20	63	0	.240	.407
Hector Luna	OF25 2B22 3B7 SS6	R	25	64	137	26	39	10	2	1	18	9	25	5	.285	.409
Scott Seabol	3B20 2B8 1B5 OF4	R	30	59	105	11	23	5	0	1	10	8	23	0	.219	.295
Einar Diaz	C50 1B3	R	32	58	130	14	27	6	0	1	17	5	12	0	.208	.277
John Rodriguez	OF45	L	27	56	149	15	44	6	0	5	24	19	45	2	.295	.436
Jason Marquis	P33	R	26	43	87	10	27	8	1	1	10	2	11	0	.310	.460
Roger Cedeno	OF16	B	30	37	57	4	9	1	0	0	8	2	6	1	.158	.175
Skip Schumaker	OF21	L	25	27	24	9	6	1	0	0	1	2	6	1	.250	.292
Mike Mahoney	C25	R	32	26	64	5	10	1	0	1	6	4	10	0	.156	.219
John Gall	OF10	R	27	22	37	5	10	3	0	2	10	1	8	0	.270	.514
Chris Duncan	1B2 OF1	L	24	9	10	2	2	1	0	0	3	0	5	0	.200	.600

NAME	T	AGE	W	L	PCT	SV	G	GS	CG	IP	H	BB	SO	SHO	ERA
		30	100	62	.617	48	162	162	15	1446	1399	443	974	14	3.49
Chris Carpenter	R	30	21	5	.808	0	33	33	7	242	204	51	213	4	2.83
Mark Mulder	L	27	16	8	.667	0	32	32	3	205	212	70	111	2	3.64
Jeff Suppan	R	30	16	10	.615	0	32	32	0	194	206	63	114	0	3.57
Matt Morris	R	30	14	10	.583	0	31	31	2	193	209	37	117	0	4.11
Jason Marquis	R	26	13	14	.481	0	33	32	3	207	206	69	100	1	4.13
Brad Thompson	R	23	4	0	1.000	1	40	0	0	55	46	15	29	0	2.95
Al Reyes	R	34	4	2	.667	3	65	0	0	63	38	20	67	0	2.15
Ray King	L	31	4	4	.500	0	77	0	0	40	46	16	23	0	3.38
Randy Flores	L	29	3	1	.750	1	50	0	0	42	37	13	43	0	3.46
Julian Tavarez	R	32	2	3	.400	4	74	0	0	66	68	19	47	0	3.43
Cal Eldred (IL)	R	37	1	0	1.000	0	31	1	0	37	35	18	29	0	2.19
Anthony Reyes	R	23	1	1	.500	0	4	3	0	13	6	4	12	0	2.70
Jason Isringhausen	R	32	1	2	.333	39	63	0	0	59	43	27	51	0	2.14
Carmen Cali	L	26	0	0	—	0	6	0	0	6	10	6	5	0	10.50
Gabe White	L	33	0	0	—	0	8	0	0	8	14	1	1	0	12.00
Tyler Johnson	L	24	0	0	—	0	5	0	0	3	3	3	4	0	0.00
Bill Pulsipher	L	31	0	0	—	0	5	0	0	4	5	2	1	0	6.75
Adam Wainwright	R	23	0	0	—	0	2	0	0	2	0	1	1	0	13.50
Jimmy Journell	R	27	0	0	—	0	2	0	0	4	6	5	5	0	10.38
Kevin Jarvis	R	35	0	1	.000	0	3	0	0	3	3	2	1	0	13.50

HOUSTON — 2nd 89-73 .549 11 (Wild Card) — PHIL GARNER

Name	G by Pos	B	AGE	G	AB	R	H	2B	3B	HR	RBI	BB	SO	SB	BA	SA
TOTALS			31	163	5462	693	1400	281	32	161	654	481	1037	115	.256	.408
Jeff Bagwell (SJ)	1B24	R	37	39	100	11	25	4	0	3	19	18	21	0	.250	.380
Craig Biggio	2B141	R	39	155	590	94	156	40	1	26	69	37	90	11	.264	.468
Adam Everett	SS150	R	28	152	549	58	136	27	2	11	54	26	103	21	.248	.364
Morgan Ensberg	3B148	R	29	150	526	86	149	30	3	36	101	85	119	6	.283	.557
Jason Lane	OF141	R	28	145	517	65	138	34	4	26	78	32	105	6	.267	.499
Willy Taveras	OF148	R	23	152	592	82	172	13	4	3	29	25	103	34	.291	.341
Lance Berkman (KJ)	1B96 OF49	B	29	132	468	76	137	34	1	24	82	91	72	4	.293	.524
Brad Ausmus	C134 2B1 SS1	R	36	134	387	35	100	19	0	3	47	51	48	5	.258	.331
Mike Lamb	1B68 3B15 OF13	L	29	125	322	41	76	13	5	12	53	22	65	1	.236	.419
Orlando Palmeiro	OF36	L	36	114	204	22	58	17	2	3	20	15	23	3	.284	.431
Chris Burke	OF84 2B18	R	25	108	318	49	79	19	2	5	26	23	62	11	.248	.368
Jose Vizcaino	2B23 SS17 1B13 3B8	B	37	98	187	15	46	10	2	1	23	15	40	2	.246	.337
Eric Bruntlett	2B28 OF26 SS10 3B8 1B1	R	27	91	109	19	24	5	2	4	14	10	25	7	.220	.413
Raul Chavez	C36	R	32	37	90	6	17	3	0	2	6	4	18	1	.172	.263
Luke Scott	OF24	L	27	34	80	6	15	4	2	0	4	9	23	1	.188	.288
Todd Self	OF15	L	26	21	45	7	9	2	0	1	4	4	13	0	.200	.311
Charles Gipson	OF13	R	32	19	11	2	2	1	0	1	1	3	4	1	.182	.273
Humberto Quintero (IL)	C16 1B1	R	25	18	54	6	10	1	0	1	8	1	10	0	.185	.259
Charlton Jimerson	OF1	R	25	1	0	0	0	0	0	0	0	0	0	0	—	—

NAME	T	AGE	W	L	PCT	SV	G	GS	CG	IP	H	BB	SO	SHO	ERA
		30	89	73	.549	45	163	163	6	1443	1336	440	1164	11	3.51
Roy Oswalt	R	27	20	12	.625	0	35	35	4	242	243	48	184	1	2.94
Andy Pettitte	L	33	17	9	.654	0	33	33	0	222	188	41	171	0	2.39
Roger Clemens	R	42	13	8	.619	0	32	32	1	211	151	62	185	0	1.87
Brandon Backe (UJ)	R	27	10	8	.556	0	26	25	1	149	151	67	97	1	4.76
Wandy Rodriguez	B	26	10	10	.500	0	25	22	0	129	135	53	80	0	5.53
Chad Qualls	R	26	6	4	.600	0	77	0	0	80	73	23	60	0	3.28
Brad Lidge	R	28	4	4	.500	42	70	0	0	71	58	23	103	0	2.29
Russ Springer	R	36	4	4	.500	0	62	0	0	59	49	21	54	0	4.73
Ezequiel Astacio	R	25	3	6	.333	0	22	14	0	81	100	25	66	0	5.67
Dan Wheeler	R	27	2	3	.400	3	71	0	0	73	53	19	69	0	2.21
Mike Burns	R	26	0	0	—	0	7	2	0	31	29	8	20	0	4.94
Scott Strickland	R	29	0	0	—	0	5	0	0	4	4	0	2	0	6.75
Travis Driskill	R	33	0	0	—	0	5	0	0	4	4	2	1	0	0.00
Mike Gallo	L	28	0	1	.000	0	36	0	0	20	18	10	12	0	2.66
John Franco	L	44	0	1	.000	0	31	0	0	15	23	9	16	0	7.20
Brandon Duckworth	R	29	0	1	.000	0	7	2	0	16	24	7	10	0	11.02
1 Chad Harville	R	28	0	2	.000	0	37	0	0	38	36	24	33	0	4.46

MILWAUKEE — 3rd 81-81 .500 19 — NED YOST

Name	G by Pos	B	AGE	G	AB	R	H	2B	3B	HR	RBI	BB	SO	SB	BA	SA
TOTALS			29	162	5448	726	1413	327	19	175	689	531	1162	79	.259	.423
Lyle Overbay	1B154	L	28	158	537	80	148	34	1	19	72	78	98	1	.276	.449
Rickie Weeks	2B95	R	22	96	360	56	86	13	2	13	42	40	96	15	.239	.394
J.J. Hardy	SS119	R	22	124	372	46	92	22	1	9	50	44	48	0	.247	.384
Russell Branyan (BG)	3B59 1B5 OF3	L	29	85	202	23	52	11	0	12	31	39	80	1	.257	.490
Geoff Jenkins	OF144	R	30	148	538	87	157	42	4	25	86	56	138	0	.292	.513
Brady Clark	OF145	R	32	145	599	94	183	31	1	13	53	47	55	10	.306	.426
Carlos Lee	OF162	R	29	162	618	85	164	41	0	32	114	57	87	13	.265	.487
Damian Miller	C111	R	35	114	385	50	105	25	1	9	43	37	94	0	.273	.413
Bill Hall	SS66 3B59 2B23	R	25	146	501	69	146	39	6	17	62	39	103	18	.291	.495
Chris Magruder	OF45	B	28	100	138	16	28	9	0	2	13	7	33	3	.203	.312
Wes Helms	3B35 1B16	R	29	95	168	18	50	13	1	4	24	14	30	0	.298	.458
Jeff Cirillo (BH)	3B53 2B3 1B1	R	35	77	185	29	52	15	0	4	23	22	23	4	.281	.427
Chad Moeller	C65	R	30	66	199	23	41	9	1	7	23	13	48	0	.206	.367
1 Junior Spivey	2B48	R	30	49	182	22	43	8	1	5	17	18	57	7	.236	.374
Prince Fielder	1B7	L	21	39	59	2	17	4	0	2	10	2	17	0	.288	.458
Trent Durrington	3B1	R	29	28	14	3	3	1	0	0	2	1	3	5	.214	.286
Corey Hart	OF16	R	23	21	57	9	11	2	1	2	7	6	11	2	.193	.368
Nelson Cruz	OF8	R	24	8	5	2	1	0	0	0	0	0	2	0	.200	.400
Dave Krynzel	OF1	L	23	5	7	0	0	0	0	0	0	1	4	0	.000	.000
Julio Mosquera		R	33	1	0	0	0	0	0	0	0	0	0	0	—	—

NAME	T	AGE	W	L	PCT	SV	G	GS	CG	IP	H	BB	SO	SHO	ERA
		28	81	81	.500	46	162	162	7	1438	1382	569	1173	6	3.97
Chris Capuano	L	26	18	12	.600	0	35	35	0	219	212	91	176	0	3.99
Doug Davis	L	29	11	11	.500	0	35	35	2	223	196	93	208	1	3.84
Ben Sheets (IL-XJ)	R	26	10	9	.526	0	22	22	3	157	142	25	141	0	3.33
Derrick Turnbow	R	27	7	1	.875	39	69	0	0	67	49	24	64	0	1.74
2 Tomo Ohka	R	29	7	6	.538	0	22	20	1	126	145	38	81	1	4.35
Gary Glover	R	28	5	4	.556	0	15	11	0	65	74	20	58	0	5.57
Matt Wise	R	29	4	4	.500	1	49	0	0	64	37	25	62	0	3.36
Victor Santos	R	28	4	13	.235	0	29	24	1	142	153	60	89	0	4.57
Rick Helling	R	34	3	1	.750	0	15	7	0	49	39	18	42	0	2.39
Julio Santana (EJ)	R	31	3	5	.375	1	41	0	0	42	49	19	49	0	4.50
Ricky Bottalico	R	35	2	2	.500	0	40	0	0	42	43	19	29	0	4.54
Jorge de la Rosa	L	24	2	2	.500	0	38	0	0	42	38	23	42	0	4.46
Dana Eveland	L	21	1	1	.500	0	27	0	0	32	40	18	23	0	5.97
Justin Lehr	R	27	1	1	.500	0	17	0	0	35	32	18	13	0	3.89
Jose Capellan	R	24	1	1	.500	0	17	0	0	16	17	5	14	0	2.87
Kane Davis	R	30	1	1	.500	0	15	0	0	17	10	10	9	0	2.70
Wes Obermueller	R	28	1	4	.200	0	23	8	0	65	74	36	33	0	5.26
Mike Adams	R	26	0	1	.000	0	13	0	0	13	12	10	14	0	2.70
Tommy Phelps	L	31	0	2	.000	0	29	0	0	23	25	12	14	0	4.63

CHICAGO — 4th 79-83 .488 21 — DUSTY BAKER

Name	G by Pos	B	AGE	G	AB	R	H	2B	3B	HR	RBI	BB	SO	SB	BA	SA
TOTALS			30	162	5584	703	1506	323	23	194	674	419	920	65	.270	.440
Derek Lee	1B158	R	29	158	594	120	199	50	3	46	107	85	109	15	.335	.662
Todd Walker (KJ)	2B97 1B4	L	32	110	397	50	121	25	3	12	40	31	40	1	.305	.474
Nomar Garciaparra (GJ)	3B34 SS26	R	31	62	230	28	65	12	0	9	30	12	24	0	.283	.452
Aramis Ramirez (LJ)	3B119	R	27	123	463	72	140	30	0	31	92	35	60	0	.302	.568
Jeromy Burnitz	OF160	L	36	160	605	84	156	31	2	24	87	57	109	5	.258	.435
Corey Patterson	OF122	L	25	126	451	47	97	15	3	13	34	23	118	15	.215	.348
1 Todd Hollandsworth	OF95 1B1	L	32	107	268	23	68	17	2	5	35	18	53	4	.254	.388
Michael Barrett	C122	R	28	133	424	48	117	32	3	16	61	40	61	0	.276	.479
Neifi Perez	SS130 2B26 3B4	B	32	154	572	59	157	33	1	9	54	18	47	8	.274	.383
Jerry Hairston	OF62 2B44 SS1	R	29	114	380	51	99	25	2	4	30	31	46	1	.261	.368
Jose Macias	3B23 2B20 OF20	B	33	112	177	15	45	8	0	1	13	6	24	4	.254	.316
Henry Blanco	C54	R	33	54	161	16	39	6	0	6	25	11	24	0	.242	.391
Jason Dubois	OF38	R	26	52	142	16	34	12	0	7	22	7	49	0	.239	.472
Matt Murton	OF43	R	23	51	140	19	45	3	2	7	14	16	22	2	.321	.521
Ronny Cedeno	SS29 2B1	R	22	41	80	13	24	3	0	1	6	5	11	1	.300	.375
Carlos Zambrano	P33	R	24	33	80	8	24	6	2	1	6	0	25	0	.300	.463
Ben Grieve	OF1	L	29	23	20	1	5	0	0	0	1	5	7	0	.250	.250
2 Matt Lawton		L	33	19	78	8	19	2	0	1	5	4	8	1	.244	.308
Enrique Wilson	2B5 1B3 SS3 3B1	B	31	15	22	1	3	2	0	0	5	4	8	1	.136	.227
Scott McClain	1B4 3B3	R	33	13	14	1	2	1	0	0	1	2	2	0	.143	.214
1 Jody Gerut	OF5	L	27	11	14	1	1	1	0	0	0	0	3	0	.071	.143
Ryan Theriot	2B3	R	25	9	13	3	2	1	0	0	0	1	6	0	.154	.231
Mike Fontenot		L	25	7	2	4	0	0	0	0	0	0	0	0	.000	.000
Geovany Soto		R	22	1	1	0	0	0	0	0	0	0	0	0	.000	.000
Adam Greenberg		L	24	1	0	0	0	0	0	0	0	0	0	0	—	—

NAME	T	AGE	W	L	PCT	SV	G	GS	CG	IP	H	BB	SO	SHO	ERA
		28	79	83	488	39	162	162	8	1440	1357	576	1256	10	4.19
Carlos Zambrano	R	24	14	6	.700	0	33	33	3	223	170	86	202	10	3.26
Greg Maddux	R	39	13	15	.464	0	35	35	3	225	239	36	136	0	4.24
Mark Prior	R	24	11	7	.611	0	27	27	1	167	143	59	188	0	3.67
Glendon Rusch	L	30	9	8	.529	0	46	19	1	145	175	53	111	1	4.52
2 Jerome Williams	R	23	6	8	.429	0	18	17	0	106	98	45	59	0	3.91
Ryan Dempster	R	28	5	3	.625	33	63	6	0	92	83	49	89	0	3.13
Roberto Novoa	R	25	4	5	.444	0	49	0	0	45	47	25	47	0	4.43
Kerry Wood (SJ)	R	28	3	4	.429	0	21	10	0	66	52	26	77	0	4.23
Todd Wellemeyer	R	26	2	1	.667	1	22	0	0	32	32	22	32	0	6.12
Will Ohman	L	27	2	2	.500	0	69	0	0	43	32	24	45	0	2.91
Sergio Mitre	R	24	2	5	.286	0	21	7	1	60	62	23	37	1	5.37
John Koronka	L	24	1	2	.333	0	4	3	0	16	19	8	10	0	7.47
LaTroy Hawkins	R	32	1	4	.200	4	21	0	0	19	18	7	13	0	3.32
Scott Williamson (EJ)	R	29	0	0	—	0	17	0	0	14	15	6	23	0	5.65
1 Joe Borowski (WJ)	R	34	0	0	—	0	11	0	0	11	12	1	11	0	6.55
Chad Fox (EJ)	R	34	0	0	—	1	11	0	0	8	8	8	11	0	6.75
Cliff Bartosh	L	25	0	2	.000	0	19	0	0	20	23	11	15	0	5.49
Rich Hill	R	25	0	2	.000	0	10	4	0	24	25	17	21	0	9.13
Jon Leicester	R	26	0	2	.000	0	6	1	0	9	11	9	7	0	9.00
Jermaine Van Buren	R	24	0	2	.000	0	6	0	0	6	2	9	3	0	3.00
1 Mike Remlinger	L	39	0	0	.000	0	35	0	0	33	31	12	30	0	4.91

CINCINNATI — 5th 73-89 .451 27 — DAVE MILEY 27-43 .386 — JERRY NARRON 46-46 .500

Name	G by Pos	B	AGE	G	AB	R	H	2B	3B	HR	RBI	BB	SO	SB	BA	SA
TOTALS			29	162	5565	820	1453	335	15	222	784	611	1303	72	.261	.446
Sean Casey	1B134	L	30	137	529	75	165	32	0	9	58	48	48	2	.312	.423
Ryan Freel (FJ)	OF51 2B48 3B10	R	29	103	369	69	100	19	3	4	21	51	59	36	.271	.371
Felipe Lopez	SS140 2B	B	25	148	580	97	169	34	5	23	85	57	111	15	.291	.486
1 Joe Randa	3B84	R	35	92	332	44	96	26	1	13	48	33	52	0	.289	.491
Austin Kearns	OF107	R	25	112	387	62	93	26	1	18	67	48	107	0	.240	.452
Ken Griffey Jr.	OF124	L	35	128	491	85	148	30	0	35	92	54	93	0	.301	.576
Adam Dunn	OF133 1B33	L	25	160	543	107	134	35	2	40	101	114	168	4	.247	.540
Jason LaRue	C109 OF1	R	31	110	361	38	94	27	0	14	60	41	101	0	.260	.452
Rich Aurilia	2B68 SS30 3B18	R	33	114	426	61	120	23	2	14	68	37	67	2	.282	.444
Jacob Cruz	OF20 1B5 3B2	L	33	110	127	12	30	10	0	4	18	16	46	0	.236	.409
Wily Mo Pena (LJ)	OF83	R	23	99	311	42	79	17	0	19	51	20	116	2	.254	.492
Javier Valentin	C62 1B2	B	29	76	221	36	62	11	0	14	50	30	37	0	.281	.520
Edwin Encarnacion	3B56	R	22	69	211	25	49	16	0	9	31	20	60	3	.232	.436
Ray Olmedo (EJ)	2B31 SS5 3B5	B	24	54	77	10	17	4	1	1	4	6	22	4	.221	.338
D'Angelo Jimenez	2B27	B	27	35	105	14	24	7	0	0	5	14	23	2	.229	.295
Aaron Holbert	2B4 1B2 3B2	R	32	22	27	3	6	3	0	0	1	1	3	1	.222	.333
Jason Romano	OF14	R	26	19	30	3	8	2	0	0	3	0	6	1	.267	.433
Chris Denorfia	OF12	R	24	18	38	8	10	3	0	0	1	0	6	2	.263	.421
William Bergolla	2B9 SS1	R	22	17	38	3	5	0	0	0	1	0	10	0	.132	.132
Luis Lopez (LJ)	3B6 2B4	L	34	17	27	0	6	3	0	0	2	2	3	0	.222	.333
1 Kenny Kelly	OF4	R	26	7	7	1	2	0	0	0	0	0	4	0	.333	.333
Miguel Perez	C1	R	22	2	3	0	0	0	0	0	0	0	1	0	.000	.000
1 Andy Machado (KJ)		B	24	2	3	0	0	0	0	0	0	0	0	0	.000	.000
Dane Sardinha	C1	R	26	1	3	0	0	0	0	0	0	0	1	0	.000	.000

NAME	T	AGE	W	L	PCT	SV	G	GS	CG	IP	H	BB	SO	SHO	ERA
		28	73	89	451	31	163	163	2	1433	1657	492	955	1	5.15
Aaron Harang	R	27	11	13	.458	0	32	32	1	212	217	51	163	0	3.83
Brandon Claussen	L	26	10	11	.476	0	29	29	0	167	178	57	121	0	4.21
Ramon Ortiz	R	32	9	11	.450	0	30	30	1	171	206	51	96	0	5.36
Eric Milton	L	29	8	15	.348	0	34	34	0	186	237	52	123	0	6.47
David Weathers	R	35	7	4	.636	15	73	0	0	78	71	29	61	0	3.94
Luke Hudson (SJ)	R	28	6	9	.400	0	19	16	0	85	83	50	53	0	6.38
Todd Coffey	R	24	4	1	.800	1	57	0	0	58	84	11	24	0	4.50
Matt Belisle	R	25	4	8	.333	1	60	5	0	86	101	26	59	0	4.41
Kent Mercker	L	37	3	1	.750	0	78	0	0	62	64	19	45	0	3.65
Ryan Wagner (SJ)	R	22	3	2	.600	0	42	0	0	46	56	17	39	0	6.11
Randy Keisler	L	29	2	1	.667	0	24	4	0	56	64	28	43	0	6.27
2 Jason Standridge	R	26	2	2	.500	0	32	1	0	31	38	16	17	0	4.06
Brian Shackelford	L	28	1	0	1.000	0	30	0	0	30	21	9	17	0	2.43
Josh Hancock (GJ)	R	27	1	0	1.000	0	11	0	0	14	11	1	5	0	1.93
1 Danny Graves	R	32	1	1	.500	10	20	0	0	18	30	12	8	0	7.36
Paul Wilson (SJ)	R	32	1	5	.167	0	9	9	0	46	68	17	30	0	7.77
Ricky Stone	R	30	0	0	—	0	23	0	0	31	48	7	15	0	6.75
Ben Weber (ZJ)	R	35	0	0	—	0	10	0	0	12	20	9	8	0	8.03
Chris Booker	R	28	0	0	—	0	6	0	0	3	4	6	6	0	31.50
Joe Valentine	R	25	0	0	—	0	16	0	0	14	18	11	9	0	8.16
2 Allan Simpson	R	27	0	1	.000	0	6	0	0	7	3	5	6	0	6.75
Elizardo Ramirez	R	22	0	3	.000	0	6	3	0	33	33	10	9	0	8.46

PITTSBURGH — 6th 67-95 .414 33 — LLOYD McCLENDON 55-81 .404 — PETE MACKANIN 12-14 .462

Name	G by Pos	B	AGE	G	AB	R	H	2B	3B	HR	RBI	BB	SO	SB	BA	SA
TOTALS			27	162	5573	680	1445	292	38	139	656	471	1092	73	.259	.400
Daryle Ward	1B109	L	30	133	407	46	106	21	1	12	63	37	60	0	.260	.405
Jose Castillo (KJ)	2B100	R	24	101	370	49	99	16	3	11	53	23	59	2	.268	.416
Jack Wilson	SS163	R	27	158	587	60	151	24	7	8	52	31	58	7	.257	.363
Freddy Sanchez	3B65 2B58 SS11	R	26	132	453	54	132	26	4	5	35	27	36	3	.291	.400
1 Matt Lawton	OF98	L	34	101	374	53	102	28	1	10	44	58	61	16	.273	.433
Tike Redman	OF85	L	28	135	319	33	80	12	4	2	26	19	27	4	.251	.332
Jason Bay	OF162	R	26	162	599	110	183	44	6	32	101	95	142	21	.306	.559
Humberto Cota	C87	R	26	93	297	29	72	20	1	7	43	17	80	0	.242	.387
Rob Mackowiak	3B65 OF63 2B20 1B3	L	29	142	463	57	126	21	3	9	58	43	100	8	.272	.389
Ryan Doumit	C50 OF3	R	24	75	231	25	59	13	1	6	35	11	48	2	.255	.398
Craig Wilson (RJ-BH)	OF47 1B15	R	28	59	197	23	52	14	1	5	22	30	69	3	.264	.421
Bobby Hill	3B24 2B1	R	27	58	93	12	25	6	0	0	11	9	17	0	.269	.333
Ty Wigginton	3B40 1B3 2B1	R	27	57	155	20	40	9	1	7	25	14	30	0	.258	.465
Brad Eldred	1B50	R	24	55	190	23	42	9	0	12	27	13	77	1	.221	.458
2 Michael Restovich	OF31	R	26	52	84	10	18	3	1	3	8	8	24	0	.214	.345
Nate McLouth	OF29	L	23	41	109	20	24	8	0	2	15	6	24	0	.222	.380
1 David Ross	C35	R	28	40	108	9	24	8	0	3	15	6	34	0	.222	.389
Chris Duffy (LJ)	OF34	L	25	39	126	22	43	4	2	1	9	7	22	2	.341	.429
J.J. Furmaniak	2B9 SS2	R	25	25	26	5	5	1	1	0	1	4	7	0	.192	.308
Jose Bautista	3B8	R	24	11	28	3	4	1	0	0	1	3	7	1	.143	.179
Benito Santiago	C6	R	40	6	23	1	6	1	0	0	3	0	3	0	.261	.391
Alfredo Amezaga	3B1 SS1	B	27	5	6	2	1	0	0	0	1	0	3	0	.167	.167
3 Jody Gerut (KJ)	OF4	R	28	4	18	2	4	1	0	0	0	2	2	0	.222	.278
Ray Sadler	OF3	R	24	3	8	2	2	0	0	0	0	1	1	0	.250	.625
Ronny Paulino	C2	R	24	2	4	1	2	0	0	0	0	0	1	0	.500	.500

NAME	T	AGE	W	L	PCT	SV	G	GS	CG	IP	H	BB	SO	SHO	ERA
		29	67	95	414	35	162	162	4	1436	1456	612	958	14	4.42
David Williams	L	29	10	11	.476	0	25	25	1	139	137	58	88	1	4.41
Zach Duke	L	22	8	2	.800	0	14	14	0	85	79	23	58	1	1.81
Kip Wells	R	28	8	18	.308	0	33	33	1	182	186	99	132	1	5.09
Oliver Perez (BT)	L	23	7	5	.583	0	20	20	0	103	102	70	97	0	5.85
Josh Fogg	R	28	6	11	.353	0	34	28	0	169	196	53	85	0	5.05
Salomon Torres	R	33	5	5	.500	3	78	0	0	95	76	36	55	0	2.76
Mark Redman	L	31	5	15	.250	0	30	30	2	178	188	56	101	1	4.90
Rick White	R	36	4	7	.364	2	71	0	0	75	90	29	40	0	3.72
Brian Meadows	R	29	1	3	.750	0	65	0	0	75	84	21	44	0	4.58
Paul Maholm	L	23	3	1	.750	0	6	6	0	41	31	17	26	0	2.18
Ryan Vogelsong	R	27	2	2	.500	0	44	0	0	81	82	40	52	0	4.43
John Grabow	L	26	2	3	.400	0	63	0	0	52	46	25	42	0	4.85
Jose Mesa	R	39	2	8	.200	27	55	0	0	57	61	26	37	0	4.76
Ian Snell	R	23	1	2	.333	0	15	5	0	42	43	24	34	0	5.14
Mike Gonzalez (KJ)	L	27	1	3	.250	3	51	0	0	50	35	31	58	0	2.70
Matt Capps	R	21	0	0	—	0	4	0	0	4	5	3	2	0	4.50
Bryan Bullington	R	24	0	0	—	0	1	0	0	1	1	1	1	0	13.50
Mike Johnston	L	26	0	0	—	0	1	0	0	0	2	5	0	0	36.00
Tom Gorzelanny	L	22	0	1	.000	0	3	1	0	6	10	3	2	0	12.00
Sean Burnett (EJ)	L	22													

WEST DIVISION

SAN DIEGO — 1st 82-80 .506 — BRUCE BOCHY

Name	G by Pos	B	AGE	G	AB	R	H	2B	3B	HR	RBI	BB	SO	SB	BA	SA
TOTALS			31	162	5502	684	1416	269	39	130	655	600	977	99	.257	.391
1 Phil Nevin	1B71 C2	R	34	73	281	31	72	11	1	9	47	19	67	1	.256	.399
Mark Loretta (RJ)	2B105 3B1	R	33	105	404	54	113	16	1	3	38	45	34	8	.280	.347
Khalil Greene	SS121	R	25	121	436	51	109	30	2	15	70	25	93	5	.250	.431
Sean Burroughs	3B78 SS1 P1	R	24	93	284	20	71	7	2	1	17	24	41	4	.250	.299
Brian Giles	OF155	L	34	158	545	92	164	38	8	15	83	119	64	13	.301	.483
Dave Roberts	OF109	L	33	115	411	65	113	19	10	8	38	53	59	23	.275	.428
Ryan Klesko	OF121 1B1	L	34	137	443	61	110	19	1	18	58	75	80	3	.248	.410
Ramon Hernandez (WJ)	C97	R	29	99	369	36	107	19	2	12	58	18	40	1	.290	.450
Mark Sweeney	1B53 OF6	L	35	135	221	31	65	12	1	8	40	40	58	4	.294	.466
Xavier Nady	OF68 1B44 3B3	R	26	124	326	40	85	15	2	13	43	22	67	2	.261	.479
Damian Jackson	OF52 2B35 SS26 3B8	R	31	118	275	44	70	9	0	5	23	30	45	15	.255	.342
Robert Fick	1B29 C28 OF13 3B1	L	31	93	230	25	61	10	2	3	30	26	33	0	.265	.365
1 Geoff Blum	3B34 2B19 SS14 1B2	B	32	78	224	26	54	13	1	5	22	24	28	2	.241	.375
2 Joe Randa	3B58	R	35	58	223	27	57	17	1	4	20	14	20	0	.256	.395
Eric Young (SJ)	OF25 2B14	R	38	56	142	22	39	9	0	2	12	18	12	7	.275	.380
1 Miguel Ojeda	C25 OF5	R	30	43	73	6	13	5	1	1	6	14	17	0	.178	.356
2 Miguel Olivo	C37	R	26	37	115	16	35	7	1	4	16	4	31	0	.304	.487
Ben Johnson	OF29	R	24	31	75	10	16	8	1	3	13	11	23	0	.213	.467
Paul McAnulty	OF6 1B1	L	24	18	27	1	7	1	0	0	5	7	5	0	.208	.208
1 Adam Hyzdu	OF12	R	33	17	20	1	3	1	0	0	2	2	3	0	.150	.200
Jesse Garcia	SS13 2B2	R	31	16	16	4	4	0	0	0	0	0	5	0	.167	.333
2 David Ross	C7	R	28	11	17	2	6	2	0	1	5	2	6	0	.353	.471
Manny Alexander	SS4 1B3 3B1	R	34	10	9	1	1	0	0	0	1	2	1	0	.111	.167
2 Wilson Valdez	SS8	R	27	9	13	0	3	2	0	0	1	2	1	0	.231	.385
Freddy Guzman (EJ)	24															

NAME	T	AGE	W	L	PCT	SV	G	GS	CG	IP	H	BB	SO	SHO	ERA
		31	82	80	506	45	162	162	4	1455	1452	503	1133	8	4.13
Jake Peavy	R	24	13	7	.650	0	30	30	3	203	162	50	216	3	2.88
Adam Eaton (RJ)	R	27	11	5	.688	0	24	22	0	129	140	44	100	0	4.27
Woody Williams (UJ)	R	38	9	12	.429	0	28	28	0	160	174	51	106	0	4.85
Scott Linebrink	R	28	8	1	.889	1	73	0	0	74	55	23	70	0	1.83
Rudy Seanez (SJ)	R	36	7	1	.875	0	57	0	0	60	49	22	84	0	2.69
Brian Lawrence	R	29	7	15	.318	0	33	33	1	196	211	57	109	0	4.83
Chris Hammond	L	39	5	1	.833	0	55	0	0	51	54	14	34	0	3.84
2 Pedro Astacio	R	35	4	2	.667	0	12	10	0	60	54	26	33	0	3.17
2 Chan Ho Park	R	32	4	3	.571	0	10	9	0	65	68	34	53	0	5.91
Dennys Reyes	L	28	2	2	.500	0	36	1	0	44	57	32	35	0	5.15
Tim Stauffer	R	23	3	6	.333	0	15	14	0	81	92	29	49	0	5.33
Akinori Otsuka	R	33	2	8	.200	1	66	0	0	63	55	34	60	0	3.59
1 Randy Williams	L	29	1	0	1.000	0	24	0	0	12	17	8	9	0	12.46
Clay Hensley	R	25	1	1	.500	0	24	1	0	48	33	17	28	0	1.70
2 Paul Quantrill	R	36	1	1	.500	0	22	0	0	12	15	3	12	0	3.41
2 Scott Cassidy	R	30	1	0	1.000	0	10	0	0	12	15	3	12	0	6.57
1 Darrell May	R	33	1	0	1.000	0	11	1	0	31	39	20	32	0	5.61
Trevor Hoffman	R	37	1	6	.143	43	60	0	0	58	52	12	54	0	2.97
Craig Breslow	L	24	0	0	—	0	14	0	0	15	13	14	14	0	2.20
Brian Falkenborg	R	27	0	0	—	0	9	0	0	11	17	6	11	0	8.18
Chris Oxspring	R	28	0	0	—	0	4	0	0	8	13	6	7	0	3.75
Sean Burroughs	R	24	0	0	—	0	1	0	0	1	1	0	0	0	27.00
1 Tim Redding (SJ)	R	27	0	5	.000	0	9	9	0	30	40	13	17	0	9.10

ARIZONA   2nd 77-85 .475 5   BOB MELVIN

Name	G by Pos	B	AGE	G	AB	R	H	2B	3B	HR	RBI	BB	SO	SB	BA	SA
TOTALS			31	162	5550	696	1419	291	27	191	670	606	1094	67	.256	.421
Chad Tracy	1B80 OF51	L	25	145	503	73	155	34	4	27	72	35	78	3	.308	.553
Craig Counsell	2B143 SS1	L	34	150	578	85	148	34	4	9	42	78	69	26	.256	.375
Royce Clayton	SS141	R	35	143	522	59	141	28	4	2	44	38	105	13	.270	.351
Troy Glaus	3B145	R	28	149	538	78	139	29	1	37	97	84	145	4	.258	.522
Shawn Green	OF155	L	32	158	581	87	166	37	4	22	73	62	95	8	.286	.477
Luis Terrero	OF77	R	25	88	161	23	37	6	1	4	20	14	40	4	.230	.354
Luis Gonzalez	OF152	L	37	155	579	90	157	37	0	24	79	78	90	4	.271	.459
Chris Snyder	C113	R	24	115	326	24	66	14	0	6	28	40	87	0	.202	.301
Quinton McCracken	OF59	B	35	134	215	23	51	4	3	1	13	23	35	4	.237	.298
Tony Clark	1B83	R	33	130	349	47	106	22	2	30	87	37	88	0	.304	.636
Alex Cintron	SS39 3B32 2B23	B	26	122	330	36	90	19	2	8	48	12	33	1	.273	.415
1 Jose Cruz	OF58	B	31	64	202	23	43	9	0	12	28	42	54	0	.213	.436
Kelly Stinnett	C56	R	35	59	129	15	32	4	0	6	12	12	32	0	.248	.419
Conor Jackson	1B20 OF1	R	23	40	85	8	17	3	0	2	8	12	11	0	.200	.306
Koyie Hill	C32	B	26	34	78	6	17	5	0	0	6	11	27	0	.218	.282
1 Matt Kata	2B7	B	27	30	31	6	6	2	1	0	5	4	9	0	.194	.323
Andy Green	2B5 SS2 OF2	R	27	31	31	5	7	1	0	0	2	7	3	0	.226	.258
Scott Hairston (SJ)	OF4	R	25	15	20	0	2	1	0	0	0	0	6	0	.100	.150

NAME	T	AGE	W	L	PCT	SV	G	GS	CG	IP	H	BB	SO	SHO	ERA
		28	77	85	.475	45	162	162	6	1456	1580	537	1038	10	4.84
Brandon Webb	R	26	14	12	.538	0	33	33	1	229	229	59	172	0	3.54
Javier Vazquez	R	29	11	15	.423	0	33	33	3	216	223	46	192	1	4.42
2 Claudio Vargas	R	27	9	6	.600	0	21	19	0	120	124	40	90	0	4.81
Brad Halsey	L	24	8	12	.400	0	28	26	0	160	191	39	82	0	4.61
Lance Cormier	R	24	7	3	.700	0	67	0	0	79	86	43	63	0	5.11
Shawn Estes (NJ)	L	32	7	8	.467	0	21	21	2	124	132	45	63	0	4.80
Russ Ortiz (BR)	R	31	5	11	.313	0	22	22	0	115	147	65	46	0	6.89
Brandon Medders	R	25	5	0	.800	0	27	0	0	30	21	11	31	0	1.78
Jose Valverde (AJ)	R	25	3	4	.429	15	61	0	0	66	51	20	75	0	2.44
Oscar Villarreal (SJ)	R	23	2	0	1.000	0	11	0	0	14	11	6	5	0	5.27
Mike Koplove	R	28	2	1	.667	0	44	0	0	50	48	20	28	0	5.07
Jason Bulger	R	26	1	0	1.000	0	9	0	0	14	14	5	9	0	5.40
Dustin Nippert	R	24	1	0	1.000	0	3	3	0	15	10	13	11	0	5.52
1 Tim Worrell	R	37	1	1	.500	0	32	0	0	32	30	9	22	0	2.27
1 Javier Lopez	L	27	1	1	.500	2	29	0	0	14	19	11	11	0	9.42
Brian Bruney	R	23	1	3	.250	12	47	0	0	46	56	35	51	0	7.43
Randy Choate	L	29	0	0	—	0	8	0	0	7	8	5	4	0	9.00
2 Matt Herges	L	35	0	0	—	0	7	0	0	8	12	5	3	0	13.50
Kerry Ligtenberg	R	34	0	0	—	0	7	0	0	10	16	4	5	0	13.97
Armando Almanza	L	32	0	0	—	0	6	0	0	4	5	3	2	0	2.25
Edgar Gonzalez	R	22	0	0	—	0	1	0	0	2	2	1	0	0	108.00
Greg Aquino (EJ)	R	27	0	1	.000	1	35	0	0	31	42	17	34	0	7.76
2 Buddy Groom	L	39	0	1	.000	1	15	0	0	15	19	5	7	0	4.70
Brandon Lyon (EJ)	R	25	0	2	.000	14	32	0	0	29	44	10	17	0	6.44
Mike Gosling	L	24	0	3	.000	0	13	5	0	32	40	19	14	0	4.45

SAN FRANCISCO   3rd 75-87 .463 7   FELIPE ALOU

Name	G by Pos	B	AGE	G	AB	R	H	2B	3B	HR	RBI	BB	SO	SB	BA	SA
TOTALS			32	162	5462	649	1427	299	26	128	617	431	901	71	.261	.396
J.T. Snow	1B108	L	37	117	367	40	101	17	2	4	40	32	61	1	.275	.365
Ray Durham	2B133 OF1	B	33	142	497	67	144	33	0	12	62	48	59	6	.290	.429
Omar Vizquel	SS150	B	38	152	568	66	154	28	4	3	45	56	58	24	.271	.350
Edgardo Alfonzo (LJ)	3B97 2B2	R	31	109	368	36	102	17	1	2	43	27	34	2	.277	.345
Moises Alou	OF117	R	38	123	427	67	137	21	3	19	63	56	43	5	.321	.518
Marquis Grissom (LJ)	OF36	R	38	44	137	8	29	4	0	2	15	7	18	1	.212	.285
Barry Bonds (KJ)	OF13	L	40	14	42	8	12	1	0	5	10	9	6	0	.286	.667
Mike Matheny	C132	R	34	134	443	42	107	34	0	13	59	29	91	0	.242	.406
Pedro Feliz	3B79 OF75 1B15	R	30	156	569	69	142	30	4	20	81	38	102	0	.250	.422
Jason Ellison	OF122	R	27	131	352	49	93	18	2	4	24	24	44	14	.264	.361
Lance Niekro	1B74	R	26	113	278	32	70	16	3	12	46	17	53	0	.252	.460
1 Michael Tucker	OF72	L	34	104	250	32	60	16	1	5	33	28	48	4	.240	.372
1 Deivi Cruz	2B33 SS16 3B5	R	32	81	209	26	56	10	1	5	19	10	31	0	.268	.397
Todd Linden	OF52	B	24	60	171	20	37	8	0	4	13	10	54	3	.216	.333
2 Randy Winn	OF55	B	31	58	231	39	83	22	5	14	26	11	38	7	.359	.680
1 Yorvit Torrealba	C27	R	26	34	93	18	21	8	0	1	7	9	25	2	.226	.344
2 Alex Sanchez	OF10	L	28	19	43	4	11	3	0	0	3	1	9	2	.256	.326
Yamid Haad	C16	R	27	17	28	0	2	1	0	0	1	3	6	0	.071	.107
Dan Ortmeier	OF7	B	24	15	22	1	3	0	0	0	3	1	9	0	.136	.136
Julio Ramirez	OF6	R	27	12	4	3	1	0	0	0	1	0	2	0	.250	.250
Tony Torcato	OF1	R	25	11	11	1	3	0	0	0	0	1	0	0	.273	.273
Angel Chavez	2B5 SS4 3B1	R	23	10	19	1	5	1	0	0	1	0	3	0	.263	.316
Justin Knoedler	C4	R	24	8	10	0	1	0	0	0	0	0	2	0	.100	.100
Doug Clark		L	29	8	5	2	0	0	0	0	0	0	1	0	.000	.000
Brian Dallimore	2B2 SS1	R	31	7	7	1	1	0	0	0	0	0	0	0	.143	.286
Adam Shabala	OF5	L	27	4	5	0	1	0	0	0	0	0	5	0	.200	.200

NAME	T	AGE	W	L	PCT	SV	G	GS	CG	IP	H	BB	SO	SHO	ERA
		30	75	87	.463	46	162	162	4	1444	1456	592	972	8	4.33
Noah Lowry	L	24	13	13	.500	0	33	33	0	205	193	76	172	0	3.78
Jason Schmidt	R	32	12	7	.632	0	29	29	0	172	160	85	165	0	4.40
Brett Tomko	R	32	8	15	.348	1	33	30	3	191	205	57	114	0	4.48
1 Jason Christiansen	L	35	6	1	.857	0	56	0	0	42	48	15	17	0	5.36
Tyler Walker	R	29	6	4	.600	23	67	0	0	62	68	27	54	0	4.23
Brad Hennessey	R	25	5	8	.385	0	21	21	0	118	127	52	64	0	4.64
Jeff Fassero	L	42	4	7	.364	0	48	6	0	91	92	31	60	0	4.05
Scott Munter	R	25	2	1	1.000	0	45	0	0	39	40	12	11	0	2.56
Jack Taschner	L	27	2	0	1.000	0	24	0	0	23	15	13	19	0	1.59
Matt Kinney	R	28	2	0	1.000	0	5	1	0	12	18	6	3	0	6.00
1 Jim Brower	R	32	2	1	.667	1	32	0	0	40	40	15	25	0	6.53
Matt Cain	R	20	2	1	.667	0	7	7	1	46	24	19	30	0	2.33
Scott Eyre	L	33	2	2	.500	0	86	0	0	68	48	26	65	0	2.63
Armando Benitez (LJ)	R	32	3	4	.400	19	30	0	0	30	25	16	23	0	4.50
Kevin Correia	R	24	2	5	.286	0	16	11	0	58	61	31	44	0	4.63
Kirk Rueter	L	34	2	7	.222	0	20	18	0	107	131	46	44	0	5.95
1 Matt Herges	L	35	1	1	.500	0	21	0	0	23	7	6	4	0	4.71
2 LaTroy Hawkins	R	32	1	1	.500	0	20	0	0	37	40	17	30	0	4.10
Jeremy Accardo	R	23	1	1	.167	0	28	0	0	30	30	9	16	0	3.94
Al Levine	R	37	0	0	—	0	10	0	0	16	4	4	6	0	9.58
Jesse Foppert (ZJ)	R	24	0	0	—	0	3	0	0	10	11	13	6	0	5.23
Brandon Puffer	R	29	0	0	—	0	7	0	0	7	9	2	1	0	10.29
Brian Cooper	R	30	0	1	.000	0	3	0	0	11	13	3	6	0	3.06
1 Jerome Williams	R	23	0	2	.000	0	11	11	0	17	21	4	11	0	6.48

LOS ANGELES   4th 71-91 .438 11   JIM TRACY

Name	G by Pos	B	AGE	G	AB	R	H	2B	3B	HR	RBI	BB	SO	SB	BA	SA
TOTALS			28	162	5433	685	1374	284	21	149	653	541	1094	58	.253	.395
Hee Seop Choi	1B83	L	26	133	320	40	81	15	2	15	42	34	80	1	.253	.453
Jeff Kent	2B140 1B14	R	37	149	553	100	160	36	2	29	105	72	85	6	.289	.512
Cesar Izturis (XJ-EJ)	SS106	B	25	106	444	48	114	19	2	2	31	25	51	8	.257	.322
Jose Valentin (KJ)	3B29 OF22 SS1	B	35	56	147	13	25	4	2	2	14	31	38	0	.170	.265
J.D. Drew (BW)	OF72	L	29	72	252	48	72	12	1	15	36	51	50	6	.286	.520
Milton Bradley (RJ-KJ)	OF72	B	27	75	283	49	82	14	1	13	38	25	47	6	.290	.484
Jayson Werth (BW)	OF101	R	26	102	337	46	79	22	2	7	43	48	114	11	.234	.374
Jason Phillips	C93 1B21	R	28	121	399	38	95	20	0	10	55	25	50	0	.238	.363
Jason Repko	OF118	R	24	129	276	43	61	15	3	8	30	16	80	5	.221	.384
Oscar Robles	SS54 3B40 2B1	L	29	110	364	44	99	18	1	5	34	33	40	2	.272	.368
Olmedo Saenz	1B66 3B17	R	34	109	319	39	84	24	0	15	63	27	63	0	.263	.480
Ricky Ledee (LJ)		L	31	102	237	31	66	16	1	7	39	20	55	0	.278	.443
Antonio Perez (LJ)	3B35 2B29 SS9 OF1	R	25	98	259	28	77	13	2	3	23	21	61	11	.297	.398
Mike Edwards	3B39 OF34 SS1	R	28	88	239	23	59	9	2	3	15	16	34	1	.247	.339
Jason Grabowski	OF32 1B3	L	29	65	112	14	18	0	0	4	12	10	29	1	.161	.268
Dioner Navarro	C50	B	21	50	176	21	48	9	0	3	14	20	21	0	.273	.375
3 Jose Cruz	OF45	B	31	47	156	23	47	14	2	6	22	23	43	0	.301	.532
Willy Aybar	3B20 2B6	B	22	26	86	12	28	8	0	1	10	18	11	3	.326	.453
Brian Myrow	1B5	L	28	17	17	3	4	1	0	0	1	3	2	0	.200	.250
Norihiro Nakamura	3B10 1B4 SS2 2B1	R	31	17	39	1	5	2	0	0	2	5	7	0	.128	.179
Mike Rose	C13	B	28	15	43	2	9	2	0	1	3	6	0	0	.209	.326
Cody Ross	OF9	R	24	14	25	1	4	1	0	0	1	0	10	0	.160	.200
Paul Bako (KJ)	C13	L	33	13	40	1	10	2	0	0	4	7	12	0	.250	.300
Chin-Feng Chen	OF3	R	27	7	8	1	2	0	0	0	2	0	4	0	.250	.250

NAME	T	AGE	W	L	PCT	SV	G	GS	CG	IP	H	BB	SO	SHO	ERA
		29	71	91	.438	40	162	162	6	1427	1434	471	1004	9	4.38
Jeff Weaver	R	28	14	11	.560	0	34	34	3	224	220	43	157	2	4.22
Derek Lowe	R	32	12	15	.444	0	35	35	2	222	223	55	146	2	3.61
Giovanni Carrara	R	37	7	4	.636	0	72	0	0	76	65	38	56	0	3.93
Odalis Perez (SJ-UJ)	L	28	7	8	.467	0	19	19	0	109	109	28	74	0	4.56
Brad Penny	R	27	7	9	.438	0	29	29	1	175	185	41	122	0	3.90
D.J. Houlton	R	25	6	9	.400	0	35	19	0	129	145	52	90	0	5.16
Duaner Sanchez	R	25	7	4	.364	8	79	0	0	82	75	36	71	0	3.73
Yhancy Brazoban	R	25	4	10	.286	21	74	0	0	73	70	32	61	0	5.33
Steve Schmoll	R	25	2	2	.500	3	48	0	0	47	47	22	29	0	5.01
Edwin Jackson	R	21	2	2	.500	0	7	6	0	29	31	17	13	0	6.28
Jonathan Broxton	R	21	1	1	.500	0	14	0	0	14	13	12	22	0	5.93
Eric Gagne (EJ)	R	29	1	0	1.000	8	14	0	0	13	13	4	22	0	2.70
Kelly Wunsch (NJ)	L	32	1	1	.500	0	45	0	0	24	20	14	22	0	4.56
Elmer Dessens (SJ)	R	34	1	2	.333	0	28	7	0	66	63	19	37	0	3.56
Wilson Alvarez (SJ)	L	35	4	3	.200	0	21	3	0	24	31	7	16	0	5.63
Scott Erickson	R	37	1	4	.200	0	19	8	0	55	62	25	15	0	6.02
Buddy Carlyle	R	27	0	0	—	0	10	0	0	14	16	4	13	0	8.36
Derek Thompson	L	24	0	0	—	0	5	0	0	10	13	3	10	0	3.50
Hong-Chih Kuo	L	23	0	0	.000	0	5	0	0	5	5	10	16	0	6.75
Franquelis Osoria	R	23	0	0	.000	0	8	0	0	18	18	8	15	0	3.94
Darren Dreifort (SJ) 33															

COLORADO   5th 67-95 .414 15   CLINT HURDLE

Name	G by Pos	B	AGE	G	AB	R	H	2B	3B	HR	RBI	BB	SO	SB	BA	SA
TOTALS			27	162	5542	740	1477	280	34	150	704	509	1103	65	.267	.411
Todd Helton	1B144	L	31	144	509	92	163	45	2	20	79	106	80	3	.320	.534
Aaron Miles (UJ)	2B79 SS1	B	28	99	324	37	91	12	3	2	28	8	38	4	.281	.355
Clint Barmes (BC)	SS80	R	26	81	350	55	101	19	1	10	46	16	36	6	.289	.434
Garrett Atkins	3B136	R	25	138	519	62	149	31	1	13	89	45	72	0	.287	.426
Brad Hawpe (LJ)	OF89	L	26	101	305	38	80	10	3	9	47	43	70	2	.262	.403
Cory Sullivan	OF114	L	25	139	378	64	111	15	4	4	30	28	83	12	.294	.386
Matt Holliday (BG)	OF123	R	25	125	479	68	147	24	7	19	87	36	79	14	.307	.505
Danny Ardoin	C80	R	30	80	210	28	48	10	0	6	22	20	69	1	.229	.362
Luis Gonzalez	2B83 SS17 3B12 1B10 OF8	R	26	128	404	51	118	25	0	9	44	20	63	3	.292	.421
Dustan Mohr	OF76	R	29	98	266	34	57	10	3	17	38	23	94	1	.214	.466
J.D. Closser	C80	B	25	92	237	31	52	12	2	7	27	32	48	1	.219	.376
Desi Relaford	SS37 3B21 2B11 OF4	B	31	73	210	24	47	13	1	1	16	22	48	3	.224	.319
1 Preston Wilson	OF69	R	30	71	267	39	69	15	1	15	47	25	77	3	.258	.491
Jorge Piedra	OF26	L	26	61	112	19	35	8	1	6	16	10	15	2	.313	.563
Eddy Garabito	2B18 SS2	R	28	42	88	15	27	5	0	1	9	4	13	0	.307	.398
Omar Quintanilla	SS31 2B6	L	23	39	128	16	28	1	1	0	7	4	20	1	.219	.242
Todd Greene (LJ)	C33	R	34	38	126	10	32	4	0	7	23	7	21	0	.254	.452
Ryan Shealy	1B19	R	25	35	91	14	30	7	0	2	16	13	22	1	.330	.473
2 Larry Bigbie	OF15	L	27	23	66	5	14	1	1	0	3	3	18	2	.212	.258
Choo Freeman	OF6	R	25	15	53	2	10	2	0	0	5	7	11	2	.273	.409
2 Eric Byrnes	OF14	R	29	15	53	2	10	2	0	0	5	7	11	2	.189	.226
1 Michael Restovich	OF8	R	26	14	40	5	9	3	0	0	5	6	12	0	.290	.452
Jeff Baker	3B10	R	24	12	37	5	8	2	1	3	8	5	12	0	.211	.395
2 Andy Machado	SS4	B	28	4	10	1	0	0	0	0	0	1	0	0	.000	.000
Tim Olson		R	26	3	4	0	0	0	0	0	0	1	2	0	.000	.000
Ryan Spilborghs	OF1	R	25	1	4	0	2	0	0	0	1	1	0	0	.500	.500

NAME	T	AGE	W	L	PCT	SV	G	GS	CG	IP	H	BB	SO	SHO	ERA
		28	67	95	.414	37	162	162	4	1419	1600	604	981	4	5.13
Jeff Francis	L	24	14	12	.538	0	33	33	0	184	228	70	128	0	5.68
Jamey Wright	R	30	8	16	.333	0	34	27	0	171	201	81	101	0	5.46
Aaron Cook (IL)	R	26	7	2	.778	0	13	13	2	83	101	16	24	0	3.67
Jason Jennings (BG)	R	26	6	9	.400	0	20	21	1	122	130	62	75	0	5.02
2 Sun-Woo Kim	R	27	5	1	.833	0	12	8	1	53	56	13	38	1	4.22
Byung-Hyun Kim	R	26	5	12	.294	0	22	22	0	148	156	71	115	0	4.86
1 Joe Kennedy	L	26	4	8	.333	0	16	16	0	92	128	44	52	0	7.04
David Cortes	R	31	2	0	1.000	2	50	0	0	53	50	10	36	0	4.10
Scott Dohmann	R	27	2	1	.667	0	31	0	0	33	33	19	35	0	6.10
2 Randy Williams	L	29	2	1	.667	0	30	0	0	22	26	9	19	0	3.65
Ryan Speier	R	25	2	1	.667	0	22	0	0	22	26	9	19	0	3.19
2 Mike DeJean	R	34	2	3	.400	0	38	0	0	37	26	12	35	0	3.19
Jose Acevedo (GJ)	R	27	2	4	.333	1	35	5	0	61	86	16	31	0	6.47
Brian Fuentes	L	29	2	4	.286	31	78	0	0	74	59	34	91	0	2.91
Chin-hui Tsao (SJ)	R	24	1	0	1.000	0	3	0	0	4	4	2	4	0	6.55
Dan Miceli (FJ)	R	34	1	3	.333	0	19	0	0	19	18	13	19	0	5.89
2 Blaine Neal (EJ)	R	27	1	0	1.000	0	9	0	0	12	12	6	6	0	6.14
1 Shawn Chacon (LJ)	R	27	1	7	.125	0	12	12	0	73	69	36	39	0	4.09
Bobby Seay (TJ)	L	27	1	1	.500	0	12	0	0	10	18	8	11	0	8.44
Matt Anderson	R	28	0	0	—	0	12	0	0	11	11	4	4	0	12.60
1 Javier Lopez	L	27	0	0	—	0	12	0	0	12	19	11	4	0	10.38
Allan Simpson	R	27	0	0	—	0	1	0	0	1	2	2	0	0	67.50
1 Aquilino Lopez	R	27	0	0	—	0	9	0	0	16	23	8	9	0	6.75
Zach Day	R	27	1	1	.500	0	11	20	0	1	7	0	7	0	7.15
Marcos Carvajal	R	20	0	0	—	0	53	0	0	53	52	21	47	0	5.09
Mike Esposito	R	23	0	1	.000	0	5	1	0	15	21	6	8	0	9.00
1 Jay Witasick	R	32	0	4	.000	0	32	0	0	36	27	12	40	0	2.52

LINE SCORES

Team	1	2	3	4	5	6	7	8	9	10	11	12	13	R	H	E

DIVISION SERIES: HOUSTON 3 : ATLANTA 1

Game 1   October 5 at Atlanta

| HOU | 1 | 0 | 2 | 1 | 0 | 0 | 1 | 5 | 0 | | | | | 10 | 11 | 1 |
| ATL | 1 | 0 | 0 | 2 | 0 | 0 | 0 | 1 | 1 | | | | | 5 | 9 | 0 |

Pettitte, Wheeler (8), Springer (9), Gallo (9)   **Hudson**, Devine (7), Reitsma (8), Foster (8), Brower (8), McBride (9)

Game 2   October 6 at Atlanta

| HOU | 1 | 0 | 0 | 0 | 0 | 0 | 0 | 0 | 0 | | | | | 1 | 8 | 1 |
| ATL | 0 | 3 | 2 | 0 | 0 | 0 | 0 | 2 | x | | | | | 7 | 11 | 0 |

Clemens, Backe (6), Qualls (7), Lidge (8)   **Smoltz**, Reitsma (8), Farnsworth (9)

Game 3   October 8 at Houston

| ATL | 0 | 2 | 0 | 0 | 0 | 0 | 0 | 1 | 0 | | | | | 3 | 8 | 0 |
| HOU | 2 | 0 | 1 | 0 | 0 | 0 | 4 | 0 | x | | | | | 7 | 12 | 1 |

Sosa, Reitsma (7), Foster (7), Devine (7), Brower (7)   **Oswalt**, Wheeler (8), Gallo (8), Lidge (9)

Game 4   October 9 at Houston

| ATL | 0 | 0 | 4 | 0 | 1 | 0 | 0 | 1 | 0 | 0 | 0 | 0 | 0 | 6 | 13 | 0 |
| HOU | 0 | 0 | 0 | 0 | 1 | 0 | 0 | 4 | 1 | 0 | 0 | 0 | 1 | 7 | 10 | 1 |

Hudson, Farnsworth (8), Reitsma (10), Thomson (12), Brower (14), **Devine** (17)   Backe, Gallo (5), Springer (6), Rodriguez (8), Qualls (9), Lidge (11), Wheeler (13), **Clemens** (16)

DIVISION SERIES: ST. LOUIS 3 : SAN DIEGO 0

Game 1   October 4 at St. Louis

| SD | 0 | 0 | 0 | 0 | 0 | 0 | 1 | 1 | 3 | | | | | 5 | 13 | 1 |
| STL | 1 | 0 | 3 | 0 | 4 | 0 | 0 | 0 | x | | | | | 8 | 10 | 1 |

Peavy, Hensley (5), Lawrence (6), Otsuka (7), Linebrink (8)   **Carpenter**, Thompson (7), Flores (7), Eldred (8), Isringhausen (9)

Game 2   October 6 at St. Louis

| SD | 0 | 0 | 0 | 0 | 0 | 0 | 1 | 1 | 0 | | | | | 2 | 10 | 1 |
| STL | 0 | 0 | 2 | 2 | 0 | 0 | 2 | 0 | x | | | | | 6 | 6 | 0 |

Astacio, Hensley (5), Seanez (7), Otsuka (8)   **Mulder**, Tavarez (7), Flores (8), Isringhausen (9)

Game 3   October 8 at San Diego

| STL | 1 | 4 | 0 | 0 | 2 | 0 | 0 | 0 | 0 | | | | | 7 | 13 | 1 |
| SD | 0 | 0 | 0 | 0 | 2 | 0 | 1 | 1 | 0 | | | | | 4 | 9 | 0 |

Morris, Thompson (7), Flores (7), Tavarez (8), Isringhausen (8)   **Williams**, Lawrence (2), Hensley (4), Seanez (6), Otsuka (8), Hoffman (9)

COMPOSITE BATTING

DIVISION SERIES

NAME	POS	G	AB	R	H	2B	3B	HR	RBI	BA
HOUSTON										
TOTALS		4	155	25	41	12	0	4	24	.265
Biggio	2B	4	19	6	6	4	0	0	1	.316
Ensberg	3B	4	18	2	5	2	0	0	7	.278
Ausmus	C-1B	4	18	3	4	1	0	1	1	.222
Lane	RF	4	17	1	4	1	0	0	3	.235
Berkman	1B-LF	4	14	4	5	1	0	1	5	.357
Taveras	CF	4	14	2	5	1	0	0	0	.357
Everett	SS	4	14	1	3	0	0	0	1	.214
Palmeiro	LF	4	7	0	1	0	0	0	3	.143
Bruntlett	CF-2B-SS	3	6	1	1	0	0	0	0	.167
Lamb	1B	2	6	1	3	0	0	1	1	.500
Vizcaino	2B-SS-1B	2	5	0	0	0	0	0	0	.000
Burke	LF-CF	3	3	1	2	1	0	1	1	.667
Clemens	P-PH	2	3	0	0	0	0	0	0	.000
Oswalt	P	1	3	0	0	0	0	0	0	.000
Bagwell	PH	2	2	1	1	0	0	0	1	.500
Scott	RF-LF	2	2	1	0	0	0	0	0	.000
Pettitte	P	1	2	1	1	1	0	0	0	.500
Backe	P	2	1	0	0	0	0	0	0	.000
Chavez	C-1B	1	1	0	0	0	0	0	0	.000
Gallo	P	3	0	0	0	0	0	0	0	—
Lidge	P	3	0	0	0	0	0	0	0	—
Wheeler	P	3	0	0	0	0	0	0	0	—
Qualls	P	2	0	0	0	0	0	0	0	—
Springer	P	2	0	0	0	0	0	0	0	—
Rodriguez	P	1	0	0	0	0	0	0	0	—
ATLANTA										
TOTALS		4	161	21	41	11	1	5	21	.255
Giles	2B	4	20	5	4	1	0	0	0	.200
Furcal	SS	4	20	1	3	0	0	0	0	.150
A. Jones	CF	4	17	5	8	3	0	1	5	.471
Francoeur	RF	4	17	2	4	1	1	0	1	.235
C. Jones	3B	4	17	3	3	2	0	1	2	.176
McCann	C	3	16	2	3	0	0	2	5	.188
Langerhans	LF	4	12	1	4	1	0	0	0	.333
Franco	1B	3	9	0	2	0	0	0	0	.222
LaRoche	1B	3	8	2	4	1	0	1	6	.500
Hudson	P	2	6	0	2	1	0	0	0	.333
Jordan	LF	3	5	0	1	1	0	0	0	.200
Estrada	C	1	4	0	1	0	0	0	1	.250
Johnson	PH	4	2	0	0	0	0	0	0	.000
Orr	PH-PR	3	2	1	0	0	0	0	0	.000
Betemit	PH	2	2	0	1	0	0	0	0	.500
Sosa	P	1	2	0	1	0	0	0	1	.500
Smoltz	P	1	2	0	0	0	0	0	0	.000
Reitsma	P	4	0	0	0	0	0	0	0	—
Brower	P	3	0	0	0	0	0	0	0	—
Devine	P	3	0	0	0	0	0	0	0	—
Farnsworth	P	2	0	0	0	0	0	0	0	—
Foster	P	2	0	0	0	0	0	0	0	—
McBride	P	1	0	0	0	0	0	0	0	—
Thomson	P	1	0	0	0	0	0	0	0	—
ST. LOUIS										
TOTALS		3	102	21	29	7	0	3	20	.284
Eckstein	SS	3	13	3	5	0	0	1	4	.385
Molina	C	3	13	1	3	0	0	0	3	.231
Grudzielanek	2B	3	13	2	2	0	0	0	0	.154
Sanders	LF	3	12	1	4	2	0	1	10	.333
Edmonds	CF	3	11	5	4	2	0	1	1	.364
Nunez	3B	3	11	3	4	1	0	0	0	.364
Pujols	1B	3	9	4	5	2	0	0	2	.556
Walker	RF	3	9	1	0	0	0	0	0	.000
Carpenter	P	1	3	0	0	0	0	0	0	.000
Mabry	LF-RF	2	2	0	1	0	0	0	0	.500
Morris	P	1	2	1	1	0	0	0	0	.500
Taguchi	LF-RF	3	1	0	0	0	0	0	0	.000
Gall	PH	1	1	0	0	0	0	0	0	.000
Mulder	P	1	1	0	0	0	0	0	0	.000
Rodriguez	PH	1	1	0	0	0	0	0	0	.000
Flores	P	3	0	0	0	0	0	0	0	—
Isringhausen	P	3	0	0	0	0	0	0	0	—
Tavarez	P	2	0	0	0	0	0	0	0	—
Thompson	P	2	0	0	0	0	0	0	0	—
Eldred	P	1	0	0	0	0	0	0	0	—
SAN DIEGO										
TOTALS		3	106	11	32	4	0	3	11	.302
Loretta	2B	3	15	0	4	0	0	0	2	.267
Giles	RF-CF	3	13	0	3	0	0	0	0	.231
Hernandez	C	3	11	2	5	0	0	1	1	.455
Randa	3B	3	11	1	4	1	0	0	0	.364
Greene	SS	3	10	2	4	2	0	0	1	.400
Klesko	LF	3	10	1	2	0	0	0	0	.200
Roberts	CF	3	9	1	2	0	0	1	1	.222
Young	CF-LF	3	6	2	2	0	0	1	3	.333
Fick	1B	2	5	0	1	0	0	0	0	.200
Jackson	CF	3	3	1	2	0	0	0	0	.667
Sweeney	1B	3	3	1	2	1	0	0	0	.667
Nady	1B	2	3	0	1	0	0	0	2	.333
Johnson	RF	2	2	0	0	0	0	0	0	.000
Peavy	P	1	2	0	0	0	0	0	0	.000
Burroughs	PH	1	1	0	0	0	0	0	0	.000
Astacio	P	1	1	0	0	0	0	0	0	.000
Olivo	PH	1	1	0	0	0	0	0	0	.000
Hensley	P	3	0	0	0	0	0	0	0	—
Otsuka	P	3	0	0	0	0	0	0	0	—
Lawrence	P	2	0	0	0	0	0	0	0	—
Seanez	P	2	0	0	0	0	0	0	0	—
Hoffman	P	1	0	0	0	0	0	0	0	—
Linebrink	P	1	0	0	0	0	0	0	0	—
Williams	P	1	0	0	0	0	0	0	0	—

COMPOSITE PITCHING

NAME	G	IP	H	BB	SO	W	L	SV	ERA
HOUSTON									
TOTALS	4	44	41	21	36	3	1	0	4.30
Clemens	2	8	7	3	6	1	1	0	5.63
Oswalt	1	7.1	6	2	7	1	0	0	3.68
Pettitte	1	7	4	2	6	1	0	0	3.86
Backe	2	5.1	6	3	3	0	0	0	8.44
Wheeler	3	4.1	4	3	5	0	0	0	2.08
Lidge	3	4	2	4	5	0	0	0	0.00
Qualls	2	3	5	2	1	0	0	0	6.00
Springer	2	2.1	5	1	1	0	0	0	3.86
Gallo	3	1.2	1	1	0	0	0	0	0.00
Rodriguez	1	1	1	0	2	0	0	0	9.00
ATLANTA									
TOTALS	4	43.1	41	19	30	1	3	0	5.19
Hudson	2	13.2	13	6	8	0	1	0	5.27
Smoltz	1	7	7	1	5	1	0	0	1.29
Sosa	1	6	7	2	3	0	1	0	4.50
Brower	3	5.1	0	3	2	0	0	0	0.00
Reitsma	4	3.1	7	2	0	0	0	0	16.20
Farnsworth	2	3	2	1	4	0	0	0	9.00
Thomson	1	2	0	1	3	0	0	0	0.00
Devine	3	1.2	3	1	3	0	1	0	10.80
McBride	1	1	0	0	1	0	0	0	0.00
Foster	2	0.1	2	2	1	0	0	0	54.00
ST. LOUIS									
TOTALS	3	27	32	10	17	3	0	1	3.67
Mulder	1	6.2	8	1	2	1	0	0	1.35
Carpenter	1	6	3	3	3	1	0	0	0.00
Morris	1	6	7	3	3	1	0	0	3.00
Isringhausen	3	3	5	1	4	0	0	1	3.00
Flores	3	2	2	0	3	0	0	0	4.50
Tavarez	2	1.1	4	1	0	0	0	0	13.50
Thompson	2	1.1	3	0	1	0	0	0	13.50
Eldred	1	0.2	2	1	0	0	0	0	27.00
SAN DIEGO									
TOTALS	3	25	29	13	17	0	3	0	6.84
Hensley	3	4.2	4	3	1	0	0	0	3.86
Peavy	1	4.1	8	3	3	0	1	0	16.62
Astacio	1	4	3	3	4	0	1	0	4.50
Otsuka	3	3	1	1	0	0	0	0	0.00
Seanez	2	3	3	1	4	0	0	0	6.00
Lawrence	2	2.1	3	1	4	0	0	0	0.00
Williams	1	1.2	6	2	2	0	1	0	27.00
Hoffman	1	1	0	0	0	0	0	0	0.00
Linebrink	1	1	2	0	1	0	0	0	0.00

LINE SCORES

Team	1	2	3	4	5	6	7	8	9	10	11	12	R	H	E

CHAMPIONSHIP: HOUSTON 4 : ST LOUIS 2

Game 1   October 12 at St. Louis

| HOU | 0 | 0 | 0 | 0 | 0 | 0 | 0 | 2 | 0 | 1 | | | 3 | 7 | 0 |
| STL | 2 | 1 | 0 | 0 | 2 | 0 | 0 | 0 | x | | | | 5 | 8 | 1 |

Pettitte, Springer (7), Astacio (8)   Carpenter, Isringhausen (9)

Game 2   October 13 at St. Louis

| HOU | 0 | 1 | 0 | 0 | 1 | 0 | 0 | 2 | 0 | | | | 4 | 11 | 1 |
| STL | 0 | 0 | 0 | 0 | 0 | 1 | 0 | 0 | 0 | | | | 1 | 6 | 0 |

Oswalt, Lidge (8)   Mulder, Tavarez (8), Marquis (9)

Game 3   October 15 at Houston

| STL | 0 | 0 | 0 | 0 | 1 | 1 | 0 | 0 | 1 | | | | 3 | 7 | 1 |
| HOU | 0 | 0 | 0 | 2 | 0 | 2 | 0 | 0 | x | | | | 4 | 11 | 0 |

Morris, Thompson (6), Flores (7), Tavara (8)   Clemens, Qualls (7), Lidge (9)

Game 4   October 16 at Houston

| STL | 0 | 0 | 0 | 1 | 0 | 0 | 0 | 0 | 0 | | | | 1 | 5 | 1 |
| HOU | 0 | 0 | 0 | 1 | 0 | 1 | 0 | x | | | | | 2 | 6 | 0 |

Suppan, Marquis (6)   Backe, Gallo (6), Qualls (7), Wheeler (8), Lidge (9)

Game 5   October 17 at Houston

| STL | 0 | 0 | 2 | 0 | 0 | 0 | 0 | 0 | 3 | | | | 5 | 9 | 1 |
| HOU | 0 | 1 | 0 | 0 | 0 | 0 | 3 | 0 | 0 | | | | 4 | 9 | 2 |

Carpenter, Isringhausen (8)   Pettitte, Qualls (7), Gallo (8), Wheeler (9), Lidge (9)

Game 6   October 19 at St. Louis

| HOU | 0 | 0 | 2 | 1 | 0 | 1 | 1 | 0 | 0 | | | | 5 | 11 | 0 |
| STL | 0 | 0 | 0 | 0 | 0 | 0 | 0 | 0 | 0 | | | | 1 | 4 | 1 |

Oswalt, Qualls (8), Wheeler (9)   Mulder, Thompson (5), Marquis (6), Flores (7), Tavarez (7), Isringhausen (9)

COMPOSITE BATTING

NAME	POS	G	AB	R	H	2B	3B	HR	RBI	BA
HOUSTON										
TOTALS		6	198	22	55	7	2	5	19	.278
Biggio	2B	6	24	2	8	0	0	0	3	.333
Everett	SS	6	23	2	7	1	1	0	2	.304
Ausmus	C	6	22	3	7	2	0	0	1	.318
Berkman	LF-1B	6	21	2	6	2	0	1	3	.286
Ensberg	3B	6	21	1	5	1	0	0	3	.238
Lane	RF	6	21	3	5	0	0	2	3	.238
Burke	LF-CF	6	20	5	6	0	1	1	3	.300
Lamb	1B	4	16	3	3	1	0	1	2	.188
Taveras	CF	6	14	1	5	0	0	0	0	.357
Palmeiro	PH	4	3	0	1	0	0	0	0	.333
Oswalt	P	2	3	0	1	0	0	0	0	.333
Pettitte	P	2	2	0	0	0	0	0	0	.000
Vizcaino	PH	2	2	0	0	0	0	0	0	.000
Clemens	P	1	2	0	1	0	0	0	0	.500
Backe	P	1	2	0	0	0	0	0	0	.000
Bruntlett	2B-SS	5	1	0	0	0	0	0	0	.000
Bagwell	PH	1	1	0	0	0	0	0	0	.000
Lidge	P	4	0	0	0	0	0	0	0	—
Qualls	P	4	0	0	0	0	0	0	0	—
Wheeler	P	3	0	0	0	0	0	0	0	—
Gallo	P	2	0	0	0	0	0	0	0	—
Astacio	P	1	0	0	0	0	0	0	0	—
Springer	P	1	0	0	0	0	0	0	0	—
ST. LOUIS										
TOTALS		6	187	16	39	6	0	3	16	.209
Pujols	1B	6	23	3	7	0	0	2	6	.304
Molina	C	6	22	1	7	3	0	0	1	.318
Grudzielanek	2B	6	22	2	5	0	0	0	2	.227
Eckstein	SS	6	20	5	4	0	0	0	2	.200
Edmonds	CF	6	19	2	4	1	0	0	0	.211
Walker	RF	6	19	0	3	1	0	0	1	.158
Sanders	LF	5	18	1	3	0	0	1	2	.167
Nunez	3B	4	13	1	5	0	0	0	0	.385
Mabry	3B-RF-LF	5	8	0	1	1	0	0	1	.125
Taguchi	LF-RF-CF	6	6	0	0	0	0	0	0	.000
Carpenter	P	2	4	0	0	0	0	0	0	.000
Luna	3B	2	4	0	0	0	0	0	0	.000
Mulder	P	2	3	0	0	0	0	0	0	.000
Rodriguez	PH	5	2	1	0	0	0	0	1	.000
Suppan	P	1	2	0	0	0	0	0	0	.000
Marquis	P	3	1	0	0	0	0	0	0	.000
Morris	P	1	1	0	0	0	0	0	0	.000
Isringhausen	P	3	0	0	0	0	0	0	0	—
Tavarez	P	3	0	0	0	0	0	0	0	—
Flores	P	2	0	0	0	0	0	0	0	—
Thompson	P	2	0	0	0	0	0	0	0	—

COMPOSITE PITCHING

NAME	G	IP	H	BB	SO	W	L	SV	ERA
HOUSTON									
TOTALS	6	53	39	16	42	4	2	3	2.72
Oswalt	2	14	8	4	12	2	0	0	1.29
Pettitte	2	12.1	15	4	6	0	1	0	5.11
Clemens	1	6	6	2	1	1	0	0	3.00
Backe	1	5.2	3	7	0	0	0	0	1.59
Lidge	4	5	6	2	7	0	1	3	7.20
Qualls	4	4.2	0	0	4	1	0	0	0.00
Wheeler	3	2.2	0	0	2	0	0	0	0.00
Astacio	1	1	0	2	0	0	0	0	0.00
Springer	1	1	0	1	1	0	0	0	0.00
Gallo	2	0.2	0	0	0	0	0	0	0.00
ST. LOUIS									
TOTALS	6	52	55	15	33	2	4	1	2.94
Carpenter	2	15	14	4	9	1	0	0	3.00
Mulder	2	11.2	14	3	8	0	2	0	3.09
Marquis	3	5.1	6	3	4	0	1	0	3.38
Morris	1	5.1	8	1	3	0	1	0	5.06
Suppan	1	5	3	5	0	0	0	0	1.80
Isringhausen	3	4	3	0	2	1	0	1	0.00
Tavarez	3	3.1	5	0	2	0	0	0	5.40
Flores	2	1.1	0	1	0	0	0	0	0.00
Thompson	2	1	2	0	0	0	0	0	0.00

MISCELLANEOUS 2005 INDIVIDUAL LEADERS

BATTING

On Base Average

American League		National League	
1 Giambi, N.Y.	.440	1 Helton, Col.	.445
2 Rodriguez, N.Y.	.421	2 Pujols, St.L.	.430
3 Hafner, Cle.	.408	3 Giles, S.D.	.423
4 Ortiz, Bos.	.397	4 Lee, Chi.	.418
5 Guerrero, L.A.	.394	5 Berkman, Hou.	.411
6 Jeter, N.Y.	.389	6 Johnson, Was.	.408
7 Ramirez, Bos.	.388	7 Abreu, Phi.	.405
8 Roberts, Bal.	.387	8 Bay, Pit.	.402
9 Young, Tex.	.385	9 Delgado, Fla.	.399
10 Sheffield, N.Y.	.379	10 Castillo, Fla.	.391
Teixeira, Tex.	.379		

On Base Average plus Slugging Average

American League		National League	
1 Rodriguez, N.Y.	1.031	1 Lee, Chi.	1.080
2 Hafner, Cle.	1.003	2 Pujols, St.L.	1.039
3 Ortiz, Bos.	1.001	3 Delgado, Fla.	.981
4 Ramirez, Bos.	.982	4 Helton, Col.	.979
5 Giambi, N.Y.	.975	5 Bay, Pit.	.961
6 Guerrero, L.A.	.959	6 Cabrera, Fla.	.947
7 Teixeira, Tex.	.954	7 Griffey, Cin.	.946
8 Sexson, Sea.	.910	8 Ensberg, Hou.	.945
9 Konerko, Chi.	.909	9 Berkman, Hou.	.934
10 Roberts, Bal.	.903	10 Dunn, Cin.	.927

Total Bases

American League		National League	
1 Teixeira, Tex.	370	1 Lee, Chi.	393
2 Rodriguez, N.Y.	369	2 Pujols, St.L.	360
3 Ortiz, Bos.	363	3 Cabrera, Fla.	344
4 Young, Tex.	343	4 A. Jones, Atl.	337
5 Tejada, Bal.	337	5 Bay, Pit.	335
6 Ramirez, Bos.	329	6 Delgado, Fla.	303
7 Soriano, Tex.	326	7 Lee, Mil.	301
8 Matsui, N.Y.	312	Wright, N.Y.	301
9 Sizemore, Cle.	310	9 Dunn, Cin.	293
10 Konerko, Chi.	307	Ensberg, Hou.	293
		Utley, Phi.	293
Winn, Sea.-S.F. 308			

Caught Stealing

American League		National League	
1 Podsednik, Chi.	23	1 Pierre, Fla.	17
2 Figgins, L.A.	17	2 Reyes, N.Y.	15
3 Lugo, T.B.	11	3 Clark, Mil.	13
Reed, Sea.	11	4 Roberts, S.D.	12
5 Roberts, Bal.	10	5 Taveras, Hou.	11
Sizemore, Cle.	10		
		Winn, Sea.-S.F. 11	

Stolen Base Percentage
(Minimum 20 Attempts)

American League		National League	
1 Soriano, Tex.	94	1 Bay, Pit.	95
2 Cabrera, L.A.	91	2 Lofton, Phi.	88
3 Crawford, T.B.	85	3 Rollins, Phi.	87
4 Womack, N.Y.	84	4 Furcal, Atl.	82
5 Suzuki, Sea.	80	5 Reyes, N.Y.	80

Extra Base Hits

American League		National League	
1 Ortiz, Bos.	88	1 Lee, Chi.	99
2 Teixeira, Tex.	87	2 Bay, Pit.	82
3 Soriano, Tex.	81	3 Pujols, St.L.	81
Tejada, Bal.	81	4 Cabrera, Fla.	78
5 Rodriguez, N.Y.	78	A. Jones, Atl.	78

PITCHING

Fewest Hits Per 9 Innings Pitched

American League		National League	
1 Santana, Min.	6.99	1 Clemens, Hou.	6.43
2 Zito, Oak.	7.29	2 Martinez, N.Y.	6.59
3 Contreras, Chi.	7.78	3 Zambrano, Chi.	6.85
4 Blanton, Oak.	7.96	4 Peavy, S.D.	7.18
5 Johnson, N.Y.	8.26	5 Carpenter, St.L.	7.60
6 Kazmir, T.B.	8.32	6 Pettitte, Hou.	7.61
7 Wakefield, Bos.	8.39	7 Beckett, Fla.	7.71
8 Sabathia, Cle.	8.47	8 Prior, Chi.	7.72
9 Chen, Bal.	8.53	9 Patterson, Was.	7.81
Millwood, Cle.	8.53	10 Burnett, Fla.	7.92
		Davis, Mil.	7.92

Fewest Bases on Balls Per 9 Innings Pitched

American League		National League	
1 Silva, Min.	0.43	1 Maddux, Chi.	1.44
2 Radke, Min.	1.03	2 Pettitte, Hou.	1.66
3 Wells, Bos.	1.03	3 Lieber, Phi.	1.69
4 Byrd, L.A.	1.23	4 Morris, St.L.	1.73
5 Towers, Tor.	1.25	Weaver, L.A.	1.73
6 Buehrle, Chi.	1.52	6 Oswalt, Hou.	1.79
7 Colon, L.A.	1.74	7 Carpenter, St.L.	1.90
8 Santana, Min.	1.75	8 Vazquez, Ari.	1.92
9 Johnson, N.Y.	1.87	9 Lidle, Phi.	1.95
10 Garland, Chi.	1.91	10 Martinez, N.Y.	1.95

Strikeouts Per 9 Innings Pitched

American League		National League	
1 Santana, Min.	9.25	1 Prior, Chi.	10.15
2 Lackey, L.A.	8.57	2 Peavy, S.D.	9.58
3 Johnson, N.Y.	8.42	3 Myers, Phi.	8.69
4 Kazmir, T.B.	8.42	4 Martinez, N.Y.	8.63
5 Young, Tex.	7.49	Schmidt, S.F.	8.63
6 Sabathia, Cle.	7.37	6 Burnett, Fla.	8.53
7 Mussina, N.Y.	7.11	7 Davis, Mil.	8.41
8 Fossum, T.B.	7.08	8 Patterson, Was.	8.39
9 Bonderman, Det.	6.90	9 Beckett, Fla.	8.36
10 Clement, Bos.	6.88	10 Zambrano, Chi.	8.14

Lowest Batting Average Allowed

American League		National League	
1 Santana, Min.	.210	1 Clemens, Hou.	.198
2 Zito, Oak.	.221	2 Martinez, N.Y.	.204
3 Contreras, Chi.	.232	3 Zambrano, Chi.	.212
4 Blanton, Oak.	.236	4 Peavy, S.D.	.217
5 Johnson, N.Y.	.243	5 Prior, Chi.	.227

Home Runs Allowed

American League		National League	
1 Wakefield, Bos.	35	1 Milton, Cin.	40
2 Chen, Bal.	33	2 Vazquez, Ari.	35
Radke, Min.	33	Weaver, L.A.	35
4 Elarton, Cle.	32	4 Ortiz, Cin.	34
Johnson, N.Y.	32	5 Lieber, Phi.	33

Home Runs Allowed per 9 IP
(Minimum 10 Home Runs Allowed)

American League		National League	
1 Thornton, Sea.	2.05	1 Astacio, Hou.	2.56
2 Proctor, N.Y.	2.01	2 Erickson, L.A.	1.95
3 Ledezma, Det.	1.81	3 Wilson, Cin.	1.94
4 Julio, Bal.	1.77	4 Milton, Cin.	1.93
5 McCarthy, Chi.	1.75	5 Wood, Chi.	1.91
		Takatsu, Chi.A -N.Y.N. 2.72	
		Colon, Atl.-Det. 2.21	

First the Curse of the Babe; then the Curse of Shoeless Joe. The Chicago White Sox had not won a pennant since 1959, but worse, there had been no World Series flag flown on the South Side since 1917. Superstitious fans whispered that the Sox were doing penance for the 1919 "Black Sox," who for a proffered 30 pieces of silver gained eternal damnation by throwing the Series. Hopeful fans prayed that more than four score years without a championship had been sufficient atonement.

The White Sox shook off the ennui that had put their Central Division title at risk and won the last five games of their regular season. That was only the warm-up. They opened the playoffs with a 14-2 crushing of the Boston Red Sox, and having established their superiority, took the 2004 champions out with two well-pitched wins. Meanwhile, the Los Angeles Angels used the full five games to eliminate the New York Yankees. Boston and New York had hogged the nation's baseball headlines for several seasons. With both of them out, many casual fans across the country lost any rooting interest in the playoffs and television ratings fell.

In the National League, the St. Louis Cardinals brushed off the San Diego Padres in three straight. Although Scott Rolen was injured and Larry Walker was hurting, Albert Pujols and Reggie Sanders provided ample firepower. The Houston Astros knocked off the Atlanta Braves in four games, but the final was a gem. Houston trailed by five in the eighth when Lance Berkman hit a grand slam. Then with two out in the ninth, Brad Ausmus homered to send the contest into the longest postseason game in history. It ended on Chris Burke's eighteenth-inning home run as 43-year-old Roger Clemens got the win in relief.

The Angels defeated the White Sox in the opening game for the A.L. championship and seemed to have a good shot at Game Two when A.J. Pierzynski swung and missed a third strike with two out in the bottom of the ninth of a 1-1 tie. But the ball was ruled to have bounced, and Pierzynski ran to first untagged. A pinch-runner stole second and scored on Joe Crede's double. With the second game win, the White Sox began a streak of four-straight complete-game playoff victories – something not done since the 1956 Yankees. Mark Buehrle, Jon Garland, Freddy Garcia, and Jose Contreras gave up only eight runs in the last four games. Additionally, Contreras, nicked for two runs in Game One, came within two-thirds of an inning of opening with a complete game.

St. Louis won the NLCS opener as Sanders homered again, but the Astros fought back to take Game Two behind Roy Oswalt. Clemens gave his hometown six shutout innings as the Astros went one up in the third game. Perhaps more injurious to Cardinals' hopes, Reggie Sanders, their hottest hitter, injured his back when he fell awkwardly on the warning track while chasing a line drive. The Astros won their third game the next day. In Game 4, Berkman's three-run homer in the seventh gave the Astros a 4-2 lead. With three wins in the bank, the Houston crowd roared with anticipation, Brad Lidge, who already had three saves in the playoffs, got the first two Cardinals out in the ninth. Then a single and a walk brought up Pujols who shocked the Astros with a game-winning home run. The Redbirds joy was short lived. Two days later, with the series back in St. Louis, Oswalt was ready and won his second NLCS game and third win of the playoffs.

Clemens opened the World Series for the Astros but left after two innings with a hamstring injury. White Sox third baseman Joe Crede hit a go-ahead home run and saved two runs with a pair of diving stops in Chicago's 5-3 win. On a drizzly, dreary night in Chicago, the White Sox took Game Two in a 7-6 slugfest. Houston's Andy Pettitte left after six innings with a 4-2 lead, but Paul Konerko hit a grand slam to put Chicago in front. The Astros fought back and tied the game. Then Scott Podsednik, who had not homered during the regular season, smashed a walk-off homer for the victory.

Game Three set a record for the longest World Series game – five hours and 41 minutes – and tied the record for number of innings – 14. When it finally ended, the White Sox had their third victory and a choke hold on the championship. Houston gave Roy Oswalt a 4-0 lead, but the White Sox moved in front with a five-run rally in the fifth. The Astros Jason Lane tied the game with a run-scoring double in the eighth. The tie held until former Astro Geoff Blum smacked a two-out home run in the 14th. With that, the Astros bullpen fell apart and eventually walked in an insurance run to make the final 7-5.

Trailing three games to none, the Astros refused to roll over. Brandon Backe pitched seven shutout innings in Game Four, allowing the White Sox only four hits. Unfortunately, Freddy Garcia gave Houston the same number of runs on five hits over the same seven innings. In the eighth, Willie Harris, batting for Garcia, singled. He was sacrificed to second and moved to third on a ground out. Jermaine Dye, voted the Series MVP, singled up the middle to drive in the run. It took staunch relief by the Chicago bullpen and a couple of standout defensive plays by White Sox shortstop Juan Uribe to hold the win.

Last year, the Red Sox ended an 86-year championship dearth; this year, the White Sox won after 88. Can the Cubs be next?

WORLD SERIES

LINE SCORES

Team	1	2	3	4	5	6	7	8	9	10	11	12	13	14	R	H	E

WORLD SERIES: CHICAGO 4 ; HOUSTON 0

Game 1   October 22 at Chicago

	1	2	3	4	5	6	7	8	9						R	H	E
HOU	0	1	2	0	0	0	0	0	0						3	7	1
CHI	1	2	0	1	0	0	0	1	x						5	10	0

Clemens, Rodriguez (3), Qualls (6), Springer (8)

Contreras, Cotts (8), Jenks (8)

Game 2   October 23 at Chicago

	1	2	3	4	5	6	7	8	9						R	H	E
HOU	0	1	1	0	2	0	0	0	2						6	9	0
CHI	0	2	0	0	4	0	0	0	1						7	12	0

Pettitte, Wheeler (7), Qualls (7), Gallo (8), **Lidge** (9)

Buehrle, Politte (8), Jenks (9), **Cotts** (9)

Game 3   October 25 at Houston

	1	2	3	4	5	6	7	8	9	10	11	12	13	14	R	H	E
CHI	0	0	0	0	5	0	0	0	0	0	0	0	0	2	7	14	3
HOU	1	0	2	1	0	0	0	1	0	0	0	0	0	0	5	8	1

Garland, Politte (8), Cotts (8), Hermanson (8), Hernandez (9), Vizcaino (10), Jenks (11), **Marte** (13), Buehrle (14)

Oswalt, Springer (7), Wheeler (8), Gallo (9), Lidge (9), Qualls (11), **Astacio** (14), Rodriguez (14)

Game 4   October 26 at Houston

	1	2	3	4	5	6	7	8	9						R	H	E
CHI	0	0	0	0	0	0	0	1	0						1	8	0
HOU	0	0	0	0	0	0	0	0	0						0	5	0

Garcia, Politte (8), Cotts (8), Jenks (9)

Backe, **Lidge** (8)

COMPOSITE BATTING

NAME	POS	G	AB	R	H	2B	3B	HR	RBI	BA
CHICAGO										
TOTALS		4	154	20	44	9	2	6	20	.286
Podsednik	LF	4	21	2	6a	0	2	1	2	.286
Iguchi	2B	4	18	2	3	0	0	0	1	.167
Crede	3B	4	17	2	5	1	0	2	3	.294
Rowand	CF	4	17	2	5	1	0	0	0	.294
Dye	RF	4	16	3	7	1	0	1	3	.438
Konerko	1B	4	16	1	4	1	0	1	4	.250
Uribe	SS	4	16	2	4	3	0	0	2	.250
Pierzynski	C	4	15	3	4	2	0	0	3	.267
Everett	DH	4	9	1	4	0	0	0	0	.444
Garland	P	1	3	0	0	0	0	0	0	.000
Garcia	P	1	2	0	0	0	0	0	0	.000
Harris	2B	2	1	1	1	0	0	0	0	1.000
Blum	2B	1	1	1	1	0	0	1	1	1.000
Perez	PH	1	1	0	0	0	0	0	0	.000
Widger	C	1	1	0	0	0	0	0	1	.000
Cotts	P	4	0	0	0	0	0	0	0	—
Jenks	P	4	0	0	0	0	0	0	0	—
Politte	P	3	0	0	0	0	0	0	0	—
Buehrle	P	2	0	0	0	0	0	0	0	—
Contreras	P	1	0	0	0	0	0	0	0	—
Hermanson	P	1	0	0	0	0	0	0	0	—
Hernandez	P	1	0	0	0	0	0	0	0	—
Marte	P	1	0	0	0	0	0	0	0	—
Vizcaino	P	1	0	0	0	0	0	0	0	—
HOUSTON										
TOTALS		4	143	14	29	8	1	3	14	.203
Biggio	2B	4	18	3	4	1	0	0	1	.222
Lane	RF	4	18	1	4	1	0	1	2	.222
Ensberg	3B	4	18	2	2	0	0	1	2	.111
Ausmus	C	4	16	1	4	1	0	0	0	.250
Taveras	CF	4	15	2	5	2	1	0	0	.333
Everett	SS	4	15	2	1	0	0	0	0	.067
Berkman	LF-1B	4	13	0	5	2	0	0	6	.385
Lamb	1B	4	10	1	2	1	0	1	1	.200
Bagwell	DH	4	8	1	1	0	0	0	0	.125
Burke	LF-2B	4	5	1	0	0	0	0	0	.000
Vizcaino	SS-2B-1B	3	2	0	1	0	0	0	2	.500
Palmeiro	LF	2	2	0	0	0	0	0	0	.000
Backe	P	1	2	0	0	0	0	0	0	.000
Oswalt	P	1	1	0	0	0	0	0	0	—
Lidge	P	3	0	0	0	0	0	0	0	—
Qualls	P	3	0	0	0	0	0	0	0	—
Bruntlett	2B-LF	2	0	0	0	0	0	0	0	—
Gallo	P	2	0	0	0	0	0	0	0	—
Rodriguez	P	2	0	0	0	0	0	0	0	—
Springer	P	2	0	0	0	0	0	0	0	—
Wheeler	P	2	0	0	0	0	0	0	0	—
Astacio	P	1	0	0	0	0	0	0	0	—
Clemens	P	1	1	0	0	0	0	0	0	—
Pettitte	P	1	1	0	0	0	0	0	0	—

COMPOSITE PITCHING

NAME	G	IP	H	BB	SO	W	L	SV	ERA
CHICAGO									
TOTALS	4	41	29	17	36	4	0	3	2.63
Buehrle	2	7.1	7	0	6	0	0	1	4.91
Contreras	1	7	6	0	2	1	0	0	3.86
Garcia	1	7	4	3	7	1	0	0	0.00
Garland	1	7	7	2	4	0	0	0	2.57
Jenks	4	5	3	2	7	0	0	2	3.60
Politte	3	2.1	0	2	2	0	0	0	3.86
Marte	1	1.2	0	2	3	1	0	0	0.00
Cotts	4	1.1	1	1	2	1	0	0	0.00
Hernandez	1	1	0	4	2	0	0	0	0.00
Vizcaino	1	1	0	1	0	0	0	0	0.00
Hermanson	1	0.1	0	1	1	0	0	0	0.00
HOUSTON									
TOTALS	4	39.1	44	15	30	0	4	0	4.58
Backe	1	7	5	0	7	0	0	0	0.00
Oswalt	1	6	8	5	3	0	0	0	7.50
Pettitte	1	6	8	0	4	0	0	0	3.00
Qualls	3	5.1	3	2	5	0	0	0	1.69
Lidge	3	3.2	4	0	6	0	2	0	4.91
Rodriguez	3	3.2	4	5	2	0	1	0	2.45
Clemens	1	2	4	1	1	0	0	0	13.50
Springer	2	2	2	0	1	0	0	0	4.50
Wheeler	2	2	2	1	1	0	0	0	13.50
Gallo	2	1	0	0	0	0	0	0	0.00
Astacio	1	0.2	4	2	0	0	1	0	27.00

TIGER, TIGER, BURNING BRIGHT

Detroit had not made the playoffs since Reagan was president, but in their first year under supposedly "burned-out" manager Jim Leyland, the Tigers jumped out to a Central Division lead and then spent the summer fending off the 2005 World Series champion Chicago White Sox. The Tigers held a two-game division lead at the All-Star break. With Chicago's Jim Thome and Jermaine Dye cranking out home runs, the Sox appeared poised to take over the division, but Leyland's Tigers kept the lead with pitching and defense, winning 19 games in which they scored three or fewer runs. In September, the Tigers' strong starting pitching began to slump. Aces Kenny Rogers and Justin Verlander gave signs of exhaustion. On the final day of the regular season, Detroit was passed but not by Chicago. Detroit slipped to second place behind the charging Minnesota Twins — eleven games back on July 8. The Twins' Joe Mauer was the first catcher ever to win an A.L. batting championship, but sluggers Justin Morneau, Torii Hunter, and Michael Cuddyer pushed more runs across the plate. The strength of the team was pitching, particularly the exceptional Johan Santana who made a strong bid for a second consecutive Cy Young Award.

The battle in the A.L. East was less than expected. The Red Sox wasted a great year by David Ortiz and collapsed from age, injuries, and lack of pitching. The Yankees won again, but the team was not as strong as usual. Gary Sheffield and Hideki Matsui missed more than half the season with injuries. Nevertheless, Derek Jeter, Alex Rodriguez, Jason Giambi, and Robinson Cano gave the Pinstripers enough fire power, and Mariano Rivera remained an exceptional closer. Some Yankee fans grew tired of A-Rod being merely exceptional and began booing him when he was less than godlike.

After several injury-spoiled seasons, Frank Thomas seemed at the end of the road in Chicago, but he was reborn in Oakland to lead the A's to the Western Division title. With strong hitting from Vladimir Guerrero and saves leader Francisco Rodriguez in the bullpen, the Los Angeles Angels finished four games behind.

Accusations of steroid use made many of baseball's 2006 headlines and brought some recent player achievements into question. Nevertheless, when 34 players hit at least 30 home runs, the indication was that more than pills were responsible. That three division races were not decided until the last day of the season, that a new season attendance record was set, and the emergence of so many new young stars all proved that, despite a good deal of bad publicity, baseball was still alive and well in America.

Entering the season, perhaps the most lethal lineup belonged to the St. Louis Cardinals, but injuries nearly ruined their pursuit of the Central Division title. Both Jim Edmonds and Scott Rolen missed stretches of games, but the worst period was the more than three weeks superstar Albert Pujols was sidelined. Despite missing an eighth of the season, Pujols finished third in batting and second in both home runs and runs batted in. With poor starting pitching, St. Louis needed every run it could get. Fortunately for the Cardinals, the other teams in the division had their own injury absences. Runner-up Houston had an outstanding hitter in Lance Berkman. Roger Clemens came out of retirement again to give the Astros a boost in the second half of the season, but it wasn't quite enough.

The lowly Pittsburgh Pirates, who barely edged the injury-stricken Chicago Cubs to escape last place in the central, provided a popular human interest story. Infielder Freddy Sanchez began the season hoping just to make the Pirates' roster. He stepped in for an injured teammate, got a hot bat, became the regular third baseman, and ended up leading the N.L. in batting.

The National League's best-balanced team was the New York Mets. Carlos Beltran, Carlos Delgado, and David Wright each had more than 100 rbi's; Tom Glavine, Steve Trachsel, and, when he was healthy, Pedro Martinez gave them solid starters, and Billy Wagner was a reliable closer. The Mets had little trouble in topping the Phillies for the Eastern Division crown despite a massive 58 home-run, 149 run-batted-in year for Phillies' first baseman Ryan Howard in his first full season.

Out west, San Diego won with a lineup that was less than terrorizing. Although the Padres fielded such veteran sluggers as Brian Giles and Mike Piazza, no San Diego hitter topped 83 rbi's. The Padres' strength was in its bullpen where Trevor Hoffman, arguably the greatest stopper ever, saved 46 of San Diego's 88 victories. Los Angeles put together a lineup of mostly first and second-year Dodgers to end up with San Diego at the top of the division. New with L.A. were Rafael Furcal, Kenny Lofton, and Nomar Garciaparra. J.D. Drew and Jeff Kent were in their second year of Dodger blue.

2006 AMERICAN LEAGUE — EAST DIVISION

Name	G by Pos	B	AGE	G	AB	R	H	2B	3B	HR	RBI	BB	SO	SB	BA	SA
NEW YORK	**1st 97-65 .599**			**JOE TORRE**												
TOTALS	TOTALS		31	162	5651	930	1608	327	21	210	902	649	1053	139	.285	.461
Andy Phillips	1B94 3B10 DH4 2B1	R	29	110	246	30	59	11	3	7	29	15	56	3	.240	.394
Robinson Cano (LJ)	2B118 DH4	L	23	122	482	62	165	41	1	15	78	18	54	5	.342	.525
Derek Jeter	SS150 DH9	R	32	154	623	118	214	39	3	14	97	69	102	34	.343	.483
Alex Rodriguez	3B151 DH3	R	30	154	572	113	166	26	1	35	121	90	139	15	.290	.523
Gary Sheffield (WJ)	OF21 1B9 DH9	R	37	39	151	22	45	5	0	6	25	13	16	5	.298	.450
Johnny Damon	OF131 DH16 1B1	L	32	149	593	115	169	35	5	24	80	67	85	25	.285	.482
Hideki Matsui (BW)	OF36 DH13	L	32	51	172	32	52	9	0	8	29	27	23	1	.302	.494
Jorge Posada	C134 DH2 1B1	B	34	143	465	65	129	27	2	23	93	64	97	3	.277	.492
Jason Giambi	DH70 1B68	L	35	139	446	92	113	25	0	37	113	110	106	2	.253	.558
Bernie Williams	OF89 DH31	B	37	131	420	65	118	29	0	12	61	33	53	2	.281	.436
Melky Cabrera	OF127	B	21	130	460	75	129	26	2	7	50	56	59	12	.280	.391
Miguel Cairo (LJ)2B45 1B16 SS14 3B8 DH2 OF1		R	32	81	222	28	53	12	3	0	30	13	31	13	.239	.320
Bubba Crosby	OF62 DH1	L	29	65	87	9	18	3	1	1	6	4	21	3	.207	.299
2 Bobby Abreu	OF57 DH1	L	32	58	209	37	69	16	0	7	42	*33	52	10	.330	.507
2 Nick Green	2B19 3B17 SS10 1B1 DH1	R	27	46	75	8	18	5	0	2	4	5	29	1	.240	.387
2 Aaron Guiel	OF27 1B15 DH1	L	33	44	82	16	21	3	0	4	11	7	20	2	.256	.439
2 Craig Wilson	1B35 OF2 DH1	R	29	40	104	15	22	4	0	4	8	4	34	0	.212	.365
1 Kelly Stinnett	C34	R	36	34	79	6	18	3	0	1	9	5	29	0	.228	.304
2 Sal Fasano	C27 DH1	R	34	28	49	3	7	4	0	1	5	2	14	0	.143	.286
Kevin Thompson	OF15 DH2	R	26	19	30	5	9	3	0	1	6	6	9	2	.300	.500
Andy Cannizaro	SS10 2B2 3B2	R	27	13	8	5	2	0	0	1	1	1	1	0	.250	.625
Terrence Long	OF10 DH1	L	30	12	36	6	6	1	0	0	2	4	8	0	.167	.194
Kevin Reese	OF4 DH2	L	28	10	12	2	5	0	0	0	1	1	1	0	.417	.417
Wil Nieves	C6	R	28	6	6	0	0	0	0	0	0	0	1	0	.000	.000

*Abreu, also with Philadelphia, major league leader in BB with 124

NAME	T	AGE	W	L	PCT	SV	G	GS	CG	IP	H	BB	SO	SHO	ERA
		32	97	65	.599	43	162	162	5	1444	1463	496	1019	8	4.43
Chien-Ming Wang	R	26	19	6	.760	1	34	33	2	218	233	52	76	1	3.63
Randy Johnson	L	42	17	11	.607	0	33	33	2	205	194	60	172	0	5.00
Mike Mussina	R	37	15	7	.682	0	32	32	1	197	184	35	172	0	3.51
Jaret Wright	R	30	11	7	.611	0	30	27	0	140	157	57	84	0	4.49
Scott Proctor	R	29	6	4	.600	1	83	0	0	102	89	33	89	0	3.52
1 Shawn Chacon	R	28	5	3	.625	0	17	11	0	63	77	36	35	0	7.00
Mariano Rivera	R	36	5	5	.500	34	63	0	0	75	61	11	55	0	1.80
2 Cory Lidle	R	34	4	3	.571	0	10	9	0	45	49	19	32	0	5.16
Darrell Rasner (SJ)	R	25	3	1	.750	0	6	3	0	20	18	5	11	0	4.43
Ron Villone	L	36	3	3	.500	0	70	0	0	80	75	51	72	0	5.04
Kyle Farnsworth	R	30	3	6	.333	1	72	0	0	66	62	28	75	0	4.36
T.J. Beam	R	25	2	0	1.000	0	20	0	0	18	26	6	12	0	3.80
Jeff Karstens	R	23	2	1	.667	0	8	6	0	43	40	11	16	0	3.80
Brian Bruney	R	24	1	1	.500	0	19	0	0	21	14	15	25	0	0.87
Mike Myers	L	37	1	2	.333	0	62	0	0	31	29	10	22	0	3.23
1 Matt Smith	L	27	0	0	—	0	12	0	0	12	4	8	9	0	0.00
Scott Erickson	R	38	0	0	—	0	9	0	0	11	13	7	2	0	7.94
Jose Veras	R	25	0	0	—	1	12	0	0	11	8	5	6	0	4.09
Tanyon Sturtze (SJ)	R	35	0	0	—	0	18	0	0	11	17	6	6	0	7.59
Octavio Dotel (EJ)	R	32	0	0	—	0	14	0	0	10	18	11	7	0	10.80
Kris Wilson	R	29	0	0	—	0	5	1	0	8	14	4	6	0	8.64
Colter Bean	R	29	0	0	—	0	2	0	0	2	2	1	1	0	9.00
2 Sidney Ponson	R	29	0	1	.000	0	5	3	0	16	26	7	15	0	10.47
Sean Henn	L	25	0	1	.000	0	4	1	0	9	11	5	7	0	4.82
Aaron Small	R	34	0	3	.000	1	3	0	0	28	42	12	12	0	8.46
Carl Pavano (XJ-BR) 30															

TORONTO	2nd 87-75 .537 10				JOHN GIBBONS											
TOTALS	TOTALS		30	162	5596	809	1591	348	27	199	778	514	906	65	.284	.463
Lyle Overbay	1B145 DH11	L	29	157	581	82	181	46	1	22	92	55	96	5	.312	.508
Aaron Hill	2B112 SS63 DH1	R	24	155	546	70	159	28	3	6	50	42	66	5	.291	.386
John McDonald	SS90 2B10 3B2 DH1	R	31	104	260	35	58	7	3	3	23	16	41	7	.223	.308
Troy Glaus	3B145 SS8 DH4	R	29	153	540	105	136	27	0	38	104	86	134	3	.252	.513
Armando Rios (LJ)	OF125	L	34	128	450	68	136	33	6	17	82	35	89	15	.302	.516
Vernon Wells	OF150 DH4	R	27	154	611	91	185	40	5	32	106	54	90	17	.303	.542
Frank Catalanotto	OF102 DH20	L	32	128	460	72	131	36	2	7	56	52	37	1	.300	.439
Bengie Molina	C99 DH16	R	31	117	433	44	123	20	1	19	57	19	47	1	.284	.467
1 Shea Hillenbrand	DH44 1B19 3B17	R	30	81	296	40	89	15	1	12	39	14	40	1	.301	.480
Reed Johnson	OF133 DH1	R	29	134	461	86	147	34	2	12	49	33	81	8	.319	.479
Gregg Zaun	C72 DH19	B	35	99	290	39	79	19	0	12	40	41	42	0	.272	.462
Russ Adams	2B50 SS36 DH1	L	25	90	251	31	55	14	1	3	28	22	41	1	.219	.319
1 Eric Hinske	OF30 DH19 3B10 1B4	L	28	78	197	35	52	9	2	12	29	27	49	1	.264	.513
Jason Phillips	C9 DH9 1B6	R	29	25	48	4	12	6	0	0	6	1	5	0	.250	.375
Adam Lind	DH15 OF2	L	22	18	60	8	22	8	0	2	8	5	12	0	.367	.600
John Hattig	3B10	B	26	13	24	2	8	1	0	0	3	4	6	0	.333	.375
2 Edgardo Alfonzo	3B15 2B12 1B2 DH1	R	32	12	37	4	6	1	0	0	4	5	1	0	.162	.189
Kevin Barker	DH5 1B2 OF1	L	30	12	17	3	4	1	0	1	1	1	10	0	.235	.471
Chad Mottola	OF5 DH2	R	34	10	16	3	4	2	0	0	0	0	3	0	.250	.375
Ryan Roberts	2B8 DH1	R	25	9	13	1	1	0	0	1	1	1	4	0	.077	.308
Luis Figueroa	2B5 SS2	R	32	8	9	1	1	0	0	0	1	0	0	0	.111	.222

	T	AGE	W	L	PCT	SV	G	GS	CG	IP	H	BB	SO	SHO	ERA
		28	87	75	.537	42	162	162	6	1428	1447	504	1076	6	4.37
Roy Halladay	R	29	16	5	.762	0	32	32	4	220	208	34	132	0	3.19
Ted Lilly	L	30	15	13	.536	0	32	32	0	182	179	81	160	0	4.31
A.J. Burnett (EJ)	R	29	10	8	.556	0	21	21	2	136	138	39	118	1	3.98
Gustavo Chacin (EJ)	L	25	9	4	.692	0	17	17	0	87	90	38	47	0	5.05
Scott Downs	L	30	6	2	.750	1	59	5	0	77	73	30	61	0	4.09
Casey Janssen	R	24	6	10	.375	0	19	17	0	94	103	21	44	0	5.07
Brian Tallet	L	28	3	0	1.000	0	44	1	0	54	45	31	37	0	3.81
Jason Frasor	R	28	2	2	.500	1	51	0	0	50	47	17	51	0	4.33
Shaun Marcum	R	24	3	4	.429	0	21	14	0	78	87	38	65	0	5.06
Justin Speier (AJ)	R	32	2	1	.667	0	58	0	0	51	47	21	55	0	2.98
B.J. Ryan	L	30	2	2	.500	38	65	0	0	72	42	20	86	0	1.37
1 Scott Schoeneweis	L	32	2	2	.500	1	55	0	0	37	39	16	18	0	6.51
Josh Towers	R	29	2	10	.167	0	15	12	0	62	93	17	35	0	8.42
1 Vinnie Chulk	R	27	1	0	1.000	0	20	0	0	24	29	5	18	0	5.25
Davis Romero	L	23	1	0	1.000	0	7	0	0	16	19	6	10	0	4.88
Pete Walker (SJ)	R	37	1	1	.500	1	23	0	0	30	37	13	27	0	5.40
2 Jeremy Accardo	R	24	1	1	.500	0	27	0	0	29	38	9	14	0	5.97
Brandon League	R	23	1	4	.333	1	33	0	0	43	34	9	29	0	2.53
Dustin McGowan	R	24	1	2	.333	0	16	3	0	27	35	25	22	0	7.24
Francisco Rosario	R	25	1	2	.333	0	17	1	0	23	24	16	21	0	6.65
Ty Taubenheim	R	23	1	5	.167	0	12	7	0	35	40	18	26	0	4.89

BOSTON — 3rd 86-76 .531 11 — TERRY FRANCONA

Name	G by Pos	B	AGE	G	AB	R	H	2B	3B	HR	RBI	BB	SO	SB	BA	SA
TOTALS			30	162	5619	820	1510	327	16	192	777	672	1056	51	.269	.435
Kevin Youkilis	1B127 OF18 3B16	R	27	147	569	100	159	42	2	13	72	91	120	5	.279	.429
Mark Loretta	2B138 1B11 DH6	R	34	155	635	75	181	33	0	5	59	49	63	4	.285	.361
Alex Gonzalez	SS111	R	29	111	388	48	99	24	2	9	50	22	67	1	.255	.397
Mike Lowell	3B153	R	32	153	573	79	163	47	1	20	80	47	61	2	.284	.475
Trot Nixon (AJ)	OF110	L	32	114	381	59	102	24	0	8	52	60	56	0	.268	.394
Coco Crisp (BG)	OF103	R	26	105	413	58	109	22	2	8	36	31	67	22	.264	.385
Manny Ramirez	OF123 DH5	R	34	130	449	79	144	27	1	35	102	100	102	0	.321	.619
Jason Varitek (KJ)	C99	B	34	103	365	46	87	19	2	12	55	46	87	1	.238	.400
David Ortiz	DH138 1B10	L	30	151	558	115	160	29	2	54	137	119	117	1	.287	.636
Alex Cora	SS63 2B18 3B11 DH2	L	30	96	235	31	56	7	2	1	18	19	29	6	.238	.298
Wily Mo Pena (WJ)	OF76 DH5	R	24	84	276	36	83	15	2	11	42	20	90	1	.301	.489
Gabe Kapler (NJ)	OF68 DH1	R	30	72	130	21	33	7	0	2	12	14	15	1	.254	.354
2 Doug Mirabelli	C57 DH2	R	35	59	161	12	31	6	0	6	25	11	54	0	.193	.342
Willie Harris	OF36 2B1	L	28	47	45	17	7	2	0	0	1	4	11	6	.156	.200
J.T. Snow	1B26 DH1	L	38	38	44	5	9	0	0	0	4	8	8	0	.205	.205
Dustin Pedroia	2B7 SS6	R	22	31	89	5	17	4	0	2	7	7	7	0	.191	.303
2 Eric Hinske	OF15 1B12 DH1	L	28	31	80	8	23	8	0	1	5	8	30	1	.288	.425
Dustan Mohr	OF20	R	30	21	40	5	7	1	0	2	3	3	20	0	.175	.350
David Murphy	OF16 DH1	L	24	20	22	4	5	1	0	1	3	4	5	0	.227	.409
2 Javy Lopez	C17	R	35	18	63	6	12	5	0	0	4	2	16	0	.190	.270
Carlos Pena	1B17 OF1	L	28	18	33	3	9	2	0	1	3	4	10	0	.273	.424
Adam Stern (LJ)	OF10	L	26	10	20	3	3	1	0	0	4	1	4	1	.150	.200
Ken Huckaby	C8	R	35	8	5	0	1	0	0	0	1	0	0	0	.200	.200
1 Josh Bard	C7	B	28	7	18	2	5	1	0	0	3	0	3	0	.278	.333
Corky Miller	C1	R	30	4	0	0	0	0	0	0	0	0	0	0	.000	.000

NAME	T	AGE	W	L	PCT	SV	G	GS	CG	IP	H	BB	SO	SHO	ERA
		31	86	76	.531	46	162	162	3	1441	1570	509	1070	6	4.83
Josh Beckett	R	26	16	11	.593	0	33	33	0	205	191	74	158	0	5.01
Curt Schilling	R	39	15	7	.682	0	31	31	0	204	220	28	183	0	3.97
Jon Lester (IL)	L	22	7	2	.778	0	15	15	0	81	91	43	60	0	4.76
Tim Wakefield (BR)	R	39	7	11	.389	0	23	23	1	140	135	51	90	0	4.63
Mike Timlin	R	40	6	6	.500	9	68	0	0	64	78	16	30	0	4.36
Julian Tavarez	R	33	5	4	.556	1	58	6	1	99	110	44	56	0	4.47
Matt Clement (SJ)	R	31	5	5	.500	0	12	12	0	65	77	38	43	0	6.61
Jonathan Papelbon (SJ)	R	25	4	2	.667	35	59	0	0	68	40	13	75	0	0.92
2 Kyle Snyder	R	28	4	5	.444	0	16	10	0	58	77	19	55	0	6.02
Keith Foulke (EJ)	R	33	3	1	.750	0	44	0	0	50	52	7	36	0	4.35
Manny Delcarmen	R	24	2	0	1.000	0	50	0	0	53	68	17	45	0	5.06
1 Rudy Seanez	R	37	2	1	.667	0	41	0	0	47	51	26	48	0	4.82
Craig Hansen	R	22	2	2	.500	0	38	0	0	38	46	15	30	0	6.63
1 David Wells (KJ)	L	43	2	3	.400	0	8	8	0	47	64	8	24	0	4.98
2 Bryan Corey	R	32	1	0	1.000	0	16	0	0	22	20	7	15	0	4.57
Javier Lopez	L	28	1	0	1.000	1	27	0	0	17	13	10	11	0	2.70
Jermaine Van Buren	R	25	1	0	1.000	0	10	0	0	13	14	15	8	0	11.77
Devern Hansack	R	28	1	1	.500	0	2	2	1	10	6	1	8	1	2.70
Lenny DiNardo (ZJ)	L	26	1	2	.333	0	13	6	0	39	61	20	17	0	7.85
Kason Gabbard	L	24	1	3	.250	0	7	4	0	26	24	16	15	0	3.51
2 Mike Burns	R	27	0	0	—	0	7	0	0	8	10	1	7	0	4.70
Abe Alvarez	L	23	0	0	—	0	1	1	0	3	5	2	2	0	12.00
Mike Holtz (EJ)	L	33	0	0	—	0	4	0	0	5	3	5	2	0	16.20
2 Kevin Jarvis	R	36	0	1	.000	0	4	3	0	17	22	6	7	0	4.86
1 David Riske (XJ)	R	29	0	1	.000	0	10	0	0	8	3	5	5	0	3.72
David Pauley (AJ)	R	23	0	2	.000	0	3	3	0	16	31	6	10	0	7.88
Craig Breslow	L	25	0	2	.000	0	13	0	0	12	12	6	12	0	3.75
2 Jason Johnson	R	32	0	6	.000	0	8	8	0	29	41	13	18	0	7.36

BALTIMORE — 4th 70-92 .432 27 — SAM PERLOZZO

Name	G by Pos	B	AGE	G	AB	R	H	2B	3B	HR	RBI	BB	SO	SB	BA	SA
TOTALS			30	162	5610	768	1556	288	20	164	727	474	878	121	.277	.424
Kevin Millar	1B98 DH30	R	34	132	430	64	117	26	0	15	64	59	74	1	.272	.437
Brian Roberts	2B137 DH1	B	28	138	563	85	161	34	3	10	55	55	66	36	.286	.410
Miguel Tejada	SS150 DH12	R	30	162	648	99	214	37	2	24	100	46	79	6	.330	.498
Melvin Mora	3B154 2B1 DH1	R	34	155	624	96	171	25	0	16	83	54	99	11	.274	.391
Nick Markakis	OF145 DH1	L	22	147	491	72	143	25	2	16	62	43	72	2	.291	.448
Corey Patterson	OF134	R	26	135	463	75	128	19	5	16	53	21	94	45	.276	.443
1 Jeff Conine	1B73 OF57 DH3 3B1	R	40	114	389	43	103	20	3	9	49	35	53	3	.265	.401
Ramon Hernandez	C135 DH6 1B2	R	30	144	501	66	138	29	2	23	91	43	79	1	.275	.479
Jay Gibbons (KJ)	DH46 OF44	L	29	90	343	34	95	23	0	13	46	32	48	0	.277	.458
Brandon Fahey	OF54 SS17 2B13 3B1 DH1	L	25	91	251	36	59	8	2	2	23	23	48	8	.235	.307
1 Javy Lopez	DH53 C21	R	35	76	279	30	74	15	1	8	31	18	60	0	.265	.412
Chris Gomez (BH)	1B27 2B15 SS6 3B5 DH2	R	35	55	132	14	45	7	0	2	17	7	11	1	.341	.439
1 Luis Matos	OF47 DH1	R	27	55	121	14	25	7	1	2	5	10	21	7	.207	.331
David Newhan (BL)	OF37 1B1 DH1	L	32	39	131	14	33	4	0	4	18	7	22	4	.252	.374
Fernando Tatis	DH9 3B5 1B4 OF4 2B1	R	31	28	56	7	14	6	1	2	8	6	17	0	.250	.500
Luis Terrero	OF23 DH1	R	26	27	40	4	8	1	0	1	6	1	7	0	.200	.300
Jeff Fiorentino	OF17 DH2	L	23	19	39	8	10	2	0	0	7	3	1	1	.256	.308
Eddie Rogers	2B4 3B4 OF4 SS1 DH1	R	27	17	25	1	5	0	0	0	4	0	5	0	.200	.200
Raul Chavez	C15	R	33	16	28	1	5	0	0	0	2	2	4	0	.179	.179
2 Chris Widger	C6 DH1	R	35	9	17	0	2	0	0	0	2	2	4	0	.118	.118
Howie Clark	3B1 DH1	L	32	7	7	1	1	0	0	0	0	0	2	0	.143	.143
2 Danny Ardoin	C5	R	31	5	13	2	1	0	0	0	1	1	6	0	.077	.077

NAME	T	AGE	W	L	PCT	SV	G	GS	CG	IP	H	BB	SO	SHO	ERA
		70	92	.432	35	162	162	5	1419	1579	613	1016	9	5.35		
Erik Bedard	L	27	15	11	.577	0	33	33	0	196	196	69	171	0	3.76
Kris Benson	R	31	11	12	.478	0	30	30	3	183	199	58	88	0	4.82
Daniel Cabrera	R	25	9	10	.474	0	26	26	2	148	130	104	157	1	4.74
Rodrigo Lopez	R	30	9	18	.333	0	36	29	0	189	234	59	136	0	5.90
Adam Loewen	L	22	6	6	.500	0	22	19	0	112	111	62	98	0	5.37
Kurt Birkins (EJ)	L	25	5	2	.714	0	35	0	0	31	25	16	27	0	4.94
Chris Ray	R	24	4	4	.500	33	61	0	0	66	45	27	51	0	2.73
John Halama	L	34	3	1	.750	0	17	1	0	29	38	13	12	0	6.14
LaTroy Hawkins	R	33	3	2	.600	0	60	0	0	60	73	15	27	0	4.48
Todd Williams	R	35	3	4	.333	1	62	0	0	57	76	19	24	0	4.74
Tim Byrdak (EJ)	L	32	1	0	1.000	0	16	0	0	7	14	8	2	0	12.86
Sendy Rleal	R	26	1	0	1.000	0	42	0	0	47	48	23	19	0	4.44
Eddy Rodriguez	R	24	1	1	.500	0	15	0	0	17	10	11	11	0	7.20
Winston Abreu	R	29	0	0	—	0	7	0	0	10	6	6	9	0	10.13
Brian Burres	L	25	0	0	—	0	11	0	0	8	1	6	5	0	2.25
Eric DuBose	L	30	0	0	—	0	2	0	0	1	3	2	0	0	9.64
Julio Manon	R	33	0	1	.000	0	5	0	0	5	6	3	2	0	5.40
1 Jim Brower	R	33	0	1	.000	0	12	0	0	12	21	13	9	0	13.86
Jim Hoey	R	23	0	1	.000	0	14	0	0	10	14	5	6	0	10.24
Jim Johnson	R	23	0	1	.000	0	1	1	0	4	5	1	3	0	24.00
Chris Britton	R	23	0	2	.000	1	52	0	0	54	46	17	41	0	3.35
2 Russ Ortiz	R	32	0	3	.000	0	20	5	0	40	59	18	23	0	8.48
Hayden Penn (IL)	R	21	0	6	.000	0	6	6	0	20	38	13	8	0	15.10
Bruce Chen	L	29	0	7	.000	0	40	12	0	99	137	35	70	0	6.93
John Parrish (EJ) 28															

TAMPA BAY — 5th 61-101 .377 36 — JOE MADDON

Name	G by Pos	B	AGE	G	AB	R	H	2B	3B	HR	RBI	BB	SO	SB	BA	SA
TOTALS			28	162	5474	689	1395	267	33	190	650	441	1106	134	.255	.420
Travis Lee	1B112	L	31	114	343	35	77	11	2	11	31	42	73	5	.224	.364
Jorge Cantu (BF)	2B103 DH2	R	24	107	413	40	103	18	2	14	62	26	65	1	.249	.404
Julio Lugo (MJ)	SS73	R	30	73	289	53	89	17	1	12	27	27	47	18	.308	.498
1 Aubrey Huff	3B60 DH3	L	29	63	230	26	65	15	1	8	28	24	25	0	.283	.461
Damon Hollins	OF115 DH3	R	32	121	333	37	76	20	0	15	33	19	64	3	.228	.423
Rocco Baldelli (LJ)	OF91	R	24	92	364	59	110	24	6	16	57	14	70	10	.302	.533
Carl Crawford	OF148 DH3	L	24	151	600	89	183	20	16	18	77	37	85	58	.305	.482
1 Toby Hall	C61 DH2 3B1	R	30	64	221	15	51	13	0	8	23	8	17	0	.231	.398
Jonny Gomes (SJ)	DH101 OF8	R	25	117	385	53	83	21	1	20	59	61	116	1	.216	.431
Ty Wigginton (BW)	1B45 2B43 3B34 OF12 DH1	R	28	122	444	55	122	25	1	24	79	32	97	4	.275	.498
Tomas Perez	3B40 SS36 2B22 OF5 1B1	B	32	99	241	31	51	12	0	2	16	5	44	1	.212	.286
Greg Norton	OF31 DH31 1B25	B	33	98	294	47	87	15	0	17	45	35	69	1	.296	.520
1 Russell Branyan	OF55 3B5 1B2	L	30	64	169	23	34	10	0	12	27	19	62	2	.201	.473
Josh Paul	C52 OF1 DH1	R	31	58	146	15	38	9	0	1	8	14	39	1	.260	.342
2 Dioner Navarro	C54	B	22	56	193	23	47	7	0	4	20	20	33	1	.244	.342
1 Joey Gathright	OF54	L	25	55	154	25	31	6	0	0	13	20	20	12	.201	.240
Ben Zobrist	SS52	B	25	52	183	10	41	6	2	2	18	10	26	2	.224	.311
B.J. Upton	SS50	R	21	50	175	20	43	9	1	1	10	13	40	11	.246	.291
Delmon Young	OF30	R	20	30	126	16	40	9	1	3	10	1	24	2	.317	.476
Kevin Witt	DH10 1B5	L	30	19	61	5	9	2	0	2	5	2	20	0	.148	.279
1 Nick Green	SS10 2B4 OF1 DH1	R	27	17	39	4	3	0	0	0	0	6	11	0	.077	.077
Shawn Riggans	C8 DH1	R	25	10	29	3	5	1	0	0	1	4	5	0	.172	.207
Sean Burroughs	3B7	L	25	8	21	3	4	1	0	0	2	3	5	1	.190	.238
Luis Ordaz (KJ)	SS1	R	30	1	1	0	0	0	0	0	0	0	1	0	.000	.000

NAME	T	AGE	W	L	PCT	SV	G	GS	CG	IP	H	BB	SO	SHO	ERA
		27	61	101	.377	33	162	162	1	1420	1600	606	979	7	4.97
Scott Kazmir (SJ)	L	22	10	8	.556	0	24	24	1	145	132	52	163	1	3.24
Shawn Camp	R	30	7	4	.636	4	75	0	0	75	93	19	53	0	4.68
Casey Fossum (SJ)	L	28	6	6	.500	0	25	25	0	130	136	63	88	0	5.33
James Shields	R	24	6	8	.429	0	21	21	1	125	141	38	104	0	4.84
Seth McClung	R	25	6	12	.333	6	39	15	0	103	120	68	59	0	6.29
Tim Corcoran	R	28	5	9	.357	0	21	16	0	90	92	48	59	0	4.38
1 Mark Hendrickson	L	32	4	8	.333	0	13	13	1	90	81	34	51	1	3.81
Brian Meadows	R	30	3	6	.333	8	53	0	0	70	90	15	35	0	5.17
Travis Harper (SJ)	R	30	2	2	.500	0	42	0	0	62	63	13	32	0	4.93
Jon Switzer	L	26	2	2	.500	0	40	0	0	34	38	19	18	0	4.54
Ruddy Lugo	R	26	2	4	.333	0	64	0	0	85	75	37	48	0	3.81
Brian Stokes	R	26	1	0	1.000	0	5	4	0	24	31	9	15	0	4.88
Scott Dunn	R	28	1	0	1.000	0	5	0	0	8	17	4	4	0	11.74
Dan Miceli (SJ)	R	35	1	1	.333	4	33	0	0	35	25	20	18	0	3.94
J.P. Howell	L	23	1	3	.250	0	8	8	0	40	52	14	33	0	5.10
2 Tyler Walker (EJ)	R	30	1	3	.250	10	20	0	0	20	18	7	16	0	4.95
Doug Waechter	R	25	1	4	.200	0	11	5	0	53	67	19	25	0	6.62
Chad Orvella	R	25	0	1	.167	0	22	0	0	24	36	20	17	0	7.40
2 Jae Weong Seo	R	29	0	2	.000	0	13	7	0	36	42	25	27	0	5.45
Edwin Jackson	R	22	0	0	—	0	23	1	0	36	42	25	27	0	5.45
Juan Salas	R	27	0	0	—	0	1	0	0	10	13	3	8	0	5.40
Jesus Colome	R	28	0	0	—	0	1	0	0	0.1	0	1	0	0	27.00
Jason Childers	R	32	0	0	—	1	1	0	0	12	4	1	5	0	4.70
Chad Harville	R	29	0	0	—	0	41	0	0	41	44	24	30	0	5.93
Jason Hammel	R	23	0	0	—	0	9	6	0	44	61	21	32	0	7.77

CENTRAL DIVISION

MINNESOTA — 1st 96-66 .593 — RON GARDENHIRE

Name	G by Pos	B	AGE	G	AB	R	H	2B	3B	HR	RBI	BB	SO	SB	BA	SA
TOTALS			29	162	5602	801	1608	275	34	143	754	490	872	101	.287	.425
Justin Morneau	1B153 DH4	L	25	157	592	97	190	37	1	34	130	53	93	3	.321	.559
Luis Castillo	2B142	B	30	142	584	84	173	22	6	3	49	56	58	25	.296	.370
Jason Bartlett	SS99	R	26	99	333	44	103	18	2	2	32	24	46	10	.309	.393
Nick Punto	3B89 SS26 2B17 OF3 DH2	B	28	135	459	73	133	21	7	1	45	47	68	17	.290	.373
Michael Cuddyer	OF143 1B6 DH2	R	27	150	557	102	158	41	5	24	109	62	130	6	.284	.504
Torii Hunter	OF143 DH4	R	30	147	557	86	155	21	2	31	98	45	108	12	.278	.490
Shannon Stewart (FJ)	OF34 DH10	R	32	44	174	21	51	5	1	2	14	14	19	3	.293	.368
Joe Mauer	C120 DH17	L	23	140	521	86	181	36	4	13	84	79	54	8	.347	.507
Rondell White	DH54 OF38	R	34	99	337	32	83	17	1	7	38	11	54	1	.246	.365
Lew Ford	OF92 DH5	R	29	104	234	40	53	6	1	4	18	16	43	5	.226	.312
Jason Kubel	OF37 DH30	L	24	73	220	23	53	8	0	8	26	12	45	2	.241	.386
Jason Tyner	OF50 DH12	L	29	62	218	29	68	5	2	0	18	11	18	4	.312	.353
Luis Rodriguez	3B29 2B14 DH3 SS2 1B1	B	26	59	115	11	27	3	0	1	14	16	16	0	.235	.322
Tony Batista	3B50	R	32	50	178	24	42	12	0	5	21	15	27	0	.236	.388
1 Juan Castro	SS50	R	34	50	156	10	36	5	0	2	14	6	23	1	.231	.308
Mike Redmond	C43 DH2	R	35	47	179	20	61	13	0	0	23	4	18	0	.341	.413
Josh Rabe	DH12 OF11	R	27	24	49	8	14	1	0	0	5	5	6	0	.286	.490
Terry Tiffee	3B6 DH5 1B3	B	27	20	45	4	11	1	0	2	5	0	5	0	.244	.400
3 Phil Nevin	DH10 1B5	R	35	18	52	8	10	3	0	0	4	2	15	0	.190	.286
Ruben Sierra (AJ)	DH7	B	40	14	28	3	5	1	0	0	4	0	9	0	.179	.214
Alexi Casilla	2B4 SS2 DH2	B	21	9	16	1	4	0	0	0	0	1	4	0	.250	.250
Chris Heintz	C2	R	31	2	0	0	0	0	0	0	0	0	0	0	.000	.000

NAME	T	AGE	W	L	PCT	SV	G	GS	CG	IP	H	BB	SO	SHO	ERA
		27	96	66	.593	40	162	162	1	1439	1490	356	1164	6	3.95
Johan Santana	L	27	19	6	.760	0	34	34	1	234	186	47	245	0	2.77
Francisco Liriano (EJ)	L	22	12	3	.800	0	28	16	0	121	89	32	144	0	2.16
Brad Radke (SJ)	R	33	12	9	.571	0	28	28	0	162	197	32	83	0	4.32
Carlos Silva	R	27	11	15	.423	0	36	31	0	180	246	32	70	0	5.94
Joe Nathan	R	31	7	0	1.000	36	64	0	0	68	38	16	95	0	1.58
Boof Bonser	R	24	7	6	.538	0	18	18	0	100	104	24	84	0	4.22
Dennys Reyes	L	29	5	0	1.000	0	66	0	0	51	35	15	49	0	0.89
Scott Baker	R	24	5	8	.385	0	16	16	0	83	114	16	62	0	6.37
Pat Neshek	R	25	4	2	.667	0	32	0	0	37	23	6	53	0	2.19
Jesse Crain	R	24	4	5	.444	1	68	0	0	77	79	18	60	0	3.52
Juan Rincon	R	27	3	1	.750	1	75	0	0	74	76	24	65	0	2.91
Matt Garza	R	22	3	6	.333	0	10	9	0	50	62	23	38	0	5.76
1 Kyle Lohse	R	27	2	5	.286	0	22	8	0	64	80	25	46	0	7.07
Matt Guerrier (BG)	R	27	1	1	.500	1	39	1	0	70	78	21	37	0	3.36
Willie Eyre	R	27	0	1	.000	0	42	0	0	59	75	22	26	0	5.11
Glen Perkins	L	23	0	0	—	0	4	0	0	5	3	1	6	0	1.59
Mike Smith	R	28	0	0	—	0	1	0	0	3	5	3	1	0	12.00

DETROIT — 2nd 95-67 .586 1 (Wild Card)   JIM LEYLAND

Name	G by Pos	B	AGE	G	AB	R	H	2B	3B	HR	RBI	BB	SO	SB	BA	SA
TOTALS			29	162	5642	822	1548	294	40	203	785	430	1133	60	.274	.449
Chris Shelton	1B115	R	26	115	373	50	102	16	4	16	47	34	107	1	.273	.466
Placido Polanco (SJ)	2B108	R	30	110	461	58	136	18	1	4	52	17	27	1	.295	.364
Carlos Guillen	SS145 1B8 DH4	B	30	153	543	100	174	41	5	19	85	71	87	20	.320	.519
Brandon Inge	3B159	R	29	159	542	83	137	29	2	27	83	43	128	7	.253	.463
Magglio Ordonez	OF148 DH6	R	32	155	593	82	177	32	1	24	104	45	87	1	.298	.477
Curtis Granderson	OF157	L	25	159	596	90	155	31	9	19	68	66	174	8	.260	.438
Craig Monroe	OF116 DH30	R	29	147	541	89	138	35	2	28	92	37	126	2	.255	.482
Ivan Rodriguez	C123 1B7 DH5 2B1	R	34	136	547	74	164	28	4	13	69	26	86	8	.300	.437
Marcus Thames	OF59 DH46	R	29	110	348	61	89	20	2	26	60	37	92	1	.256	.549
Omar Infante	2B37 DH17 SS10 3B7 OF4	R	24	78	224	35	62	11	4	4	25	14	45	3	.277	.415
Alexis Gomez	OF52 DH7	L	27	62	103	17	28	5	2	1	6	6	21	4	.272	.388
Vance Wilson	C55	R	33	56	152	18	43	9	0	5	18	2	33	0	.283	.441
2 Sean Casey	1B51	L	31	53	184	17	45	7	0	5	30	10	21	0	.245	.364
Dmitri Young (LJ)	DH44 1B3	B	32	48	172	19	43	4	1	7	23	11	39	1	.250	.407
Ramon Santiago	SS27 2B12 3B1 DH1	B	26	43	80	9	18	1	1	0	3	1	14	2	.225	.263
Brent Clevlen	OF29	R	22	31	39	9	11	1	2	3	6	2	15	0	.282	.641
2 Neifi Perez	2B14 SS7 3B1 DH1	B	33	21	65	4	13	1	0	0	5	3	4	1	.200	.215
3 Matt Stairs	DH14	L	38	14	41	5	10	3	0	2	8	3	12	0	.244	.463
Kevin Hooper	2B3 3B2 DH1	R	29	8	3	1	0	0	0	0	0	1	1	0	.000	.000
Jack Hannahan	1B1 DH1	L	26	3	9	0	0	0	0	0	0	0	1	0	.000	.000
Mike Rabelo	DH1	B	26	1	1	0	0	0	0	0	0	0	1	0	.000	.000

NAME	T	AGE	W	L	PCT	SV	G	GS	CG	IP	H	BB	SO	SHO	ERA
		28	95	67	.586	46	162	162	3	1448	1420	489	1003	16	3.85
Kenny Rogers	L	41	17	8	.680	0	34	33	0	204	195	62	99	0	3.84
Justin Verlander	R	23	17	9	.654	0	30	30	1	186	187	60	124	1	3.63
Jeremy Bonderman	R	23	14	8	.636	0	34	34	0	214	214	64	202	0	4.08
Nate Robertson	R	29	13	13	.500	0	32	32	1	209	206	67	137	0	3.84
Fernando Rodney	R	29	7	4	.636	7	63	0	0	72	51	34	65	0	3.52
Zach Miner	R	24	7	6	.538	0	27	16	1	93	100	32	59	0	4.84
Joel Zumaya	R	21	6	3	.667	1	62	0	0	83	56	42	97	0	1.94
Mike Maroth (EJ)	L	28	5	2	.714	0	13	9	0	54	64	16	24	0	4.19
Wil Ledezma	L	25	3	3	.500	0	24	7	0	60	60	23	39	0	3.58
Roman Colon (ZJ)	R	26	2	0	1.000	1	20	1	0	39	46	14	25	0	4.89
Jason Grilli	R	29	2	3	.400	0	51	0	0	62	61	25	31	0	4.21
Todd Jones	R	38	2	6	.250	37	62	0	0	64	70	11	28	0	3.94
Bobby Seay	L	28	0	0	—	0	14	0	0	15	14	9	12	0	6.46
Jordan Tata	R	24	0	0	—	0	8	0	0	15	14	7	6	0	6.14
1 Chris Spurling	R	29	0	0	—	0	9	0	0	11	13	4	4	0	3.18
Chad Durbin	R	28	0	0	—	0	3	0	0	6	6	0	3	0	1.50
Colby Lewis	R	26	0	0	—	0	3	0	0	3	8	1	5	0	3.00
Jamie Walker	L	34	0	0	.000	1	56	0	0	48	47	8	37	0	2.81
Andrew Miller	L	21	0	1	.000	0	8	0	0	8	10	6	6	0	6.10
Craig Dingman (IL) 32 Troy Percival (EJ) 36															

CHICAGO — 3rd 90-72 .556 6   OZZIE GUILLEN

Name	G by Pos	B	AGE	G	AB	R	H	2B	3B	HR	RBI	BB	SO	SB	BA	SA
TOTALS			29	162	5657	868	1586	291	20	236	839	502	1056	93	.280	.464
Paul Konerko	1B140 DH12	R	30	152	566	97	177	30	0	35	113	60	104	1	.313	.551
Tadahito Iguchi	2B136 DH1	R	31	138	555	97	156	24	0	18	67	59	110	11	.281	.422
Juan Uribe	SS132	R	26	132	463	53	109	28	2	21	71	13	82	1	.235	.441
Joe Crede	3B149	R	28	150	544	76	154	31	0	30	94	28	58	0	.283	.506
Jermaine Dye	OF146	R	32	146	539	103	170	27	3	44	120	59	118	7	.315	.622
Brian Anderson	OF134	R	24	134	365	46	82	23	1	8	33	30	90	4	.225	.359
Scott Podsednik	OF135 DH2	L	30	139	524	86	137	27	6	3	45	54	96	40	.261	.353
A.J. Pierzynski	C132	L	29	140	509	65	150	24	0	16	64	22	72	1	.295	.436
Jim Thome	DH136 1B3	L	35	143	490	108	141	26	0	42	109	107	147	0	.288	.598
Rob Mackowiak	OF96 3B6 DH2	L	30	112	255	31	74	12	1	5	23	28	59	5	.290	.404
Alex Cintron	SS41 2B26 3B11 DH8	B	27	91	288	35	82	10	3	5	41	10	35	0	.285	.392
Pablo Ozuna	OF39 3B17 DH9 2B6	R	31	79	189	25	62	12	2	2	17	7	16	6	.328	.444
Ross Gload	1B49 OF19 DH1	L	30	77	156	22	51	8	2	3	18	6	15	6	.327	.462
1 Chris Widger	C22 DH4	R	35	27	76	6	14	3	0	1	7	9	20	0	.184	.263
2 Sandy Alomar	C17 DH2	R	40	19	46	5	10	3	0	1	5	1	7	0	.217	.348
Ryan Sweeney	OF15 DH1	L	21	18	35	1	8	0	0	0	5	0	7	0	.229	.229
Jerry Owens	DH6 OF5	L	25	12	9	4	3	0	0	0	0	0	2	1	.333	.444
Josh Fields	3B6 DH2 OF1	R	23	11	20	4	3	2	0	1	5	0	6	0	.150	.400
Chris Stewart	C5 DH1	R	24	6	8	0	0	0	0	0	0	0	0	0	.000	.000

NAME	T	AGE	W	L	PCT	SV	G	GS	CG	IP	H	BB	SO	SHO	ERA
		28	90	72	.556	46	162	162	5	1449	1534	433	1012	11	4.61
Jon Garland	R	26	18	7	.720	0	33	32	1	211	247	41	112	1	4.51
Freddy Garcia	R	31	17	9	.654	0	33	33	1	216	228	48	135	0	4.53
Jose Contreras	R	34	13	9	.591	0	30	30	1	196	194	55	134	1	4.27
Mark Buehrle	L	27	12	13	.480	0	32	32	1	204	247	48	98	0	4.99
Javier Vazquez	R	30	11	12	.478	0	33	33	1	203	206	56	184	0	4.84
Matt Thornton	L	29	5	3	.625	2	63	0	0	54	46	21	49	0	3.33
Brandon McCarthy	R	22	4	7	.364	0	53	2	0	85	77	33	69	0	4.68
Bobby Jenks	R	25	3	4	.429	41	67	0	0	70	66	31	80	0	4.00
Cliff Politte	R	32	2	2	.500	0	30	0	0	47	56	15	15	0	8.70
Augustin Montero	R	28	1	0	1.000	0	11	0	0	14	15	2	7	0	5.14
2 David Riske	R	29	1	1	.500	0	33	0	0	34	32	14	23	0	3.93
2 Mike MacDougal	R	29	1	1	.500	0	25	0	0	25	19	6	19	0	1.80
Charlie Haeger	R	22	1	1	.500	1	7	1	0	18	12	13	19	0	3.44
Neal Cotts	L	26	1	2	.333	1	70	0	0	54	64	24	43	0	5.17
Boone Logan	L	21	0	0	—	0	21	0	0	17	21	15	15	0	8.31
Sean Tracey	R	25	0	0	—	0	7	0	0	8	4	5	3	0	3.38
Dustin Hermanson (XJ)	R	33	0	0	—	0	6	0	0	7	6	1	5	0	4.05
Jeff Nelson (EJ)	R	39	0	0	—	0	6	0	0	6	9	4	3	0	3.37

CLEVELAND — 4th 78-84 .481 18   ERIC WEDGE

Name	G by Pos	B	AGE	G	AB	R	H	2B	3B	HR	RBI	BB	SO	SB	BA	SA
TOTALS			28	162	5619	870	1576	351	27	196	839	556	1204	55	.280	.457
1 Ben Broussard	1B80	L	29	88	268	44	86	14	0	13	46	17	58	0	.321	.519
1 Ron Belliard	2B108	R	31	93	350	43	102	21	0	8	44	21	45	2	.291	.420
Jhonny Peralta	SS147 DH1	R	24	149	569	84	146	28	3	13	68	56	152	0	.257	.385
Aaron Boone	3B101 2B1 DH1	R	33	104	354	50	89	19	1	7	46	27	62	5	.251	.353
Casey Blake (UJ)	OF93 1B9 DH8	R	32	160	401	63	113	20	1	19	68	45	93	6	.282	.479
Grady Sizemore	OF160 DH1	L	23	162	655	134	190	53	11	28	76	78	153	22	.290	.533
Jason Michaels	OF118 DH2	R	30	123	494	77	132	32	1	9	55	43	101	9	.267	.391
Victor Martinez	C133 1B22 DH3	B	27	153	572	82	181	37	0	16	93	71	78	0	.316	.465
Travis Hafner (BH)	DH122 1B4	L	29	129	454	100	140	31	1	42	117	100	111	0	.308	.659
Joe Inglett	2B53 OF9 SS1 DH1	L	28	64	201	26	57	8	3	2	21	14	39	5	.284	.383
1 Todd Hollandsworth	OF44 DH1	L	33	56	156	21	37	12	1	6	27	4	33	0	.237	.442
Ryan Garko	1B45 DH2	R	25	50	185	28	54	12	0	7	45	14	37	0	.292	.470
Andy Marte	3B50	R	22	50	164	20	37	15	1	5	23	13	38	0	.226	.421
2 Shin-Soo Choo	OF39 DH1	L	23	45	146	23	43	11	3	3	22	18	46	5	.295	.473
Franklin Gutierrez	OF42	R	23	43	136	21	37	9	0	1	8	3	28	0	.272	.360
Kelly Shoppach	C40	R	26	41	110	7	27	6	0	3	16	8	45	0	.245	.382
2 Hector Luna	2B20 SS10 3B2 DH2 OF1	R	26	37	127	14	35	7	1	2	17	6	26	0	.276	.394
1 Eduardo Perez	1B29 OF5	R	36	37	99	16	30	9	0	8	22	5	11	0	.303	.636
Ramon Vazquez	3B14 2B7 SS7	L	29	34	67	11	14	2	0	1	6	6	18	0	.209	.284
Kevin Kouzmanoff	DH14 3B2	R	24	16	56	4	12	2	0	3	11	5	12	0	.214	.411
Lou Merloni	2B3 3B3 SS3 DH1	R	35	9	19	1	4	1	0	0	2	4	3	0	.211	.263
Tim Laker	C4	R	36	4	13	1	4	0	0	0	2	0	4	0	.308	.385

NAME	T	AGE	W	L	PCT	SV	G	GS	CG	IP	H	BB	SO	SHO	ERA
		29	78	84	.481	24	162	162	13	1423	1583	429	948	13	4.43
Jake Westbrook	R	28	15	10	.600	0	32	32	3	211	247	55	109	2	4.17
Cliff Lee	L	27	14	11	.560	0	33	33	1	201	224	58	129	0	4.40
C.C. Sabathia	L	25	12	11	.522	0	28	28	6	193	182	44	172	2	3.22
Paul Byrd	R	35	10	9	.526	0	31	31	1	179	232	38	88	0	4.88
Jeremy Sowers	L	23	7	4	.636	0	14	14	2	88	85	20	35	2	3.57
Jason Davis	R	26	3	2	.600	1	39	0	0	55	67	14	37	0	3.74
Fernando Cabrera	R	24	3	3	.500	0	51	0	0	61	53	32	71	0	5.19
Rafael Betancourt	R	31	3	4	.429	3	50	0	0	57	52	11	48	0	3.81
1 Jason Johnson	R	32	3	8	.273	0	14	14	0	77	108	22	32	0	5.96
2 Brian Sikorski	R	31	2	1	.667	0	17	0	0	20	20	4	24	0	4.58
David Riske	R	33	2	1	.667	0	13	0	0	14	18	5	3	0	5.79
Matt Miller (EJ)	R	34	1	0	1.000	0	4	0	0	16	11	9	12	0	3.45
1 Guillermo Mota	R	32	1	3	.250	0	34	0	0	38	45	19	27	0	6.21
2 Bob Wickman	R	37	1	5	.200	15	29	0	0	28	29	11	17	0	4.18
Fausto Carmona	R	22	1	10	.091	0	38	7	0	75	88	31	58	0	5.42
Jeremy Guthrie	R	27	0	0	—	0	9	1	0	19	24	15	14	0	5.60
Brian Slocum	R	25	0	0	—	0	9	0	0	9	11	9	11	0	5.60
Rafael Perez	L	24	0	0	—	0	10	0	0	12	10	6	15	0	4.38
Andrew Brown	R	25	0	0	—	0	9	0	0	10	6	8	7	0	3.60
Juan Lara	L	25	0	0	—	0	9	0	0	5	4	1	2	0	1.80
Edward Mujica	R	22	0	0	.000	0	9	0	0	18	25	0	12	0	2.95
Thomas Mastny	R	25	0	1	.000	0	15	0	0	16	17	8	14	0	5.51
1 Scott Sauerbeck	L	34	0	1	.000	0	24	0	0	13	9	11	6	0	6.23

KANSAS CITY — 5th 62-100 .383 34   BUDDY BELL

Name	G by Pos	B	AGE	G	AB	R	H	2B	3B	HR	RBI	BB	SO	SB	BA	SA
TOTALS			30	162	5589	757	1515	335	37	124	718	474	1040	65	.271	.411
Doug Mientkiewicz (XJ)	1B90	L	32	91	314	37	89	24	2	4	43	35	50	3	.283	.411
Mark Grudzielanek	2B132 SS4	R	36	134	548	85	163	32	4	7	52	28	69	3	.297	.409
Angel Berroa	SS131	R	28	132	474	45	111	18	1	9	54	14	88	3	.234	.333
Mark Teahen	3B109	L	24	109	393	70	114	21	7	18	69	40	85	10	.290	.517
Reggie Sanders (KJ)	OF73 DH1	R	38	88	325	45	80	23	1	11	49	28	86	7	.246	.425
David DeJesus (LJ)	OF119	L	26	119	491	83	145	36	7	8	56	43	70	6	.295	.446
Emil Brown	OF134 DH2	R	31	147	527	77	151	21	2	15	81	59	95	6	.287	.457
John Buck	C112	R	25	114	371	37	91	21	1	11	50	26	84	0	.245	.396
Mike Sweeney (XJ)	DH59	R	32	60	217	23	56	15	0	8	33	28	48	2	.258	.438
Esteban German	2B26 3B24 OF25 DH25	R	28	106	279	44	91	18	5	3	34	40	49	7	.326	.459
	1B1 SS1															
2 Joey Gathright	OF76 DH1	L	25	79	229	34	60	6	3	1	28	22	45	10	.262	.328
1 Matt Stairs	DH54 1B11 OF2	L	38	77	226	31	59	14	0	8	32	31	52	0	.261	.429
Shane Costa	OF65 DH1	L	24	72	237	23	65	20	1	3	23	6	29	2	.274	.405
1 Tony Graffanino	3B27 1B16 2B10 SS9 DH6	R	34	69	220	34	59	16	0	5	32	25	31	3	.268	.409
Paul Bako (UJ)	C53 DH1	L	34	56	153	7	32	3	0	0	10	11	46	0	.209	.229
2 Ryan Shealy	DH26 1B15	R	26	51	193	29	54	10	1	7	36	15	50	1	.280	.451
Andres Blanco	SS25 2B7 DH2	B	22	33	87	9	21	4	1	0	9	6	14	0	.241	.310
Paul Phillips	C13 1B5 DH2	R	29	23	65	8	18	3	0	1	5	4	9	0	.277	.369
Jeff Keppinger	3B12 1B4 DH3 2B1 OF1	R	26	22	60	11	16	2	0	2	5	6	6	0	.267	.400
1 Aaron Guiel	OF14 DH3	L	33	19	50	9	11	3	0	2	7	7	11	0	.220	.460
Kerry Robinson	OF16	L	32	18	64	8	17	2	1	0	5	1	9	2	.266	.328
Angel Sanchez	2B4 SS4	R	22	12	9	2	2	0	0	0	0	0	4	0	.222	.222
Mitch Maier	OF4 DH1	L	24	5	13	3	2	0	0	0	0	0	4	0	.154	.154
Justin Huber	DH4	R	23	5	10	1	2	1	0	0	1	0	0	0	.200	.300

NAME	T	AGE	W	L	PCT	SV	G	GS	CG	IP	H	BB	SO	SHO	ERA
		28	62	100	.383	35	162	162	3	1426	1648	637	904	5	5.67
Mark Redman	L	32	11	10	.524	0	29	29	2	167	202	63	76	1	5.71
Luke Hudson	R	29	7	6	.538	0	26	15	0	102	109	38	64	0	5.12
Runelvys Hernandez	R	28	6	10	.375	0	21	21	1	110	145	48	50	1	6.48
1 Elmer Dessens	R	35	5	7	.417	2	43	0	0	54	63	13	36	0	4.50
Ambiorix Burgos	R	22	4	5	.444	18	68	1	0	73	83	37	72	0	5.52
Jimmy Gobble	L	24	4	6	.400	2	60	6	0	84	95	29	80	0	5.14
1 Jeremy Affeldt	L	27	4	6	.400	0	27	9	0	70	71	42	28	0	5.91
Scott Elarton (SJ)	R	30	4	9	.308	0	20	20	0	115	117	52	49	0	5.34
Mike Wood (XJ)	R	26	3	3	.500	0	23	7	0	65	86	23	29	0	5.71
2 Jorge de la Rosa	L	25	3	4	.429	0	10	10	0	49	49	32	36	0	5.18
2 Odalis Perez	L	29	2	4	.333	0	12	12	0	67	80	18	48	0	5.64
2 Adam Bernero (EJ)	R	29	2	0	1.000	0	3	2	0	13	15	0	12	0	1.38
Zach Greinke (PP)	R	22	1	0	1.000	0	6	7	3	6	7	3	6	0	4.26
Joe Nelson	R	31	1	1	.500	9	43	0	0	45	37	24	44	0	4.43
Seth Etherton	R	29	1	1	.500	0	2	1	0	8	10	6	4	0	9.39
1 Todd Wellemeyer	R	27	1	2	.333	1	28	0	0	57	48	37	57	0	3.63
Joel Peralta	R	30	1	2	.333	1	64	0	0	74	74	17	57	0	4.40
Andy Sisco	L	23	1	3	.250	0	58	0	0	66	60	40	52	0	7.10
2 Scott Dohmann	R	28	1	3	.250	0	21	0	0	24	33	18	22	0	7.99
Brandon Duckworth (EJ)	R	30	1	5	.167	0	10	8	0	46	62	24	27	0	6.11
Leo Nunez	R	22	0	0	—	0	13	15	5	7	0	4	0	4.73
Joselo Diaz	R	26	0	0	—	0	7	10	0	4	0	10.80
Steve Andrade	R	28	0	0	—	0	3	5	6	6	0	9.64
1 Mike MacDougal (SJ)	R	29	0	0	—	0	3	3	1	2	0	0.00
1 Kyle Snyder	R	28	0	1	.000	0	3	2	0	4	10	1	2	0	22.50
2 Chris Booker	R	29	0	1	.000	0	2	0	0	2	6	5	6	0	54.00
Ryan Braun	R	25	0	1	.000	0	11	13	3	6	0	6.75
Steve Stemle (EJ)	R	28	0	1	.000	0	6	9	15	0	15.00
1 Denny Bautista	R	25	0	3	.000	0	9	35	38	17	22	0	5.66
Bobby Keppel	R	24	0	3	.000	0	9	34	45	15	20	0	5.50
1 Joe Mays	R	30	0	4	.000	0	6	24	38	14	9	0	10.27

OAKLAND — 1st 93-69 .574 — KEN MACHA

Name	G by Pos	B	AGE	G	AB	R	H	2B	3B	HR	RBI	BB	SO	SB	BA	SA
	TOTALS		30	162	5500	771	1429	266	22	175	735	650	976	61	.260	.412
Nick Swisher	1B90 OF80 DH2	B	26	157	556	106	141	24	2	35	95	97	152	1	.254	.493
Mark Ellis (BG)	2B123 1B1	R	29	124	441	64	110	25	1	11	52	40	76	4	.249	.385
Bobby Crosby (XJ)	SS95	R	26	96	358	42	82	12	0	9	40	36	76	3	.229	.338
Eric Chavez	3B134 DH3	L	28	137	485	74	117	24	2	22	72	84	100	3	.241	.435
Milton Bradley (KJ)	OF94 DH1	B	28	96	351	43	97	14	2	14	52	51	65	10	.276	.447
Mark Kotsay	OF127 1B4 DH1	L	30	129	502	57	138	29	3	7	59	44	55	6	.275	.386
Jay Payton	OF137 DH4	R	33	142	557	78	165	32	3	10	59	22	52	8	.296	.419
Jason Kendall	C141 DH1	R	32	143	552	76	163	23	0	1	50	53	54	11	.295	.342
Frank Thomas	DH135	R	38	137	466	77	126	11	0	39	114	81	81	0	.270	.545
Marco Scutaro	SS69 2B37 3B12 OF2	R	30	117	365	52	97	21	6	5	41	50	66	5	.266	.397
Dan Johnson	1B85 DH2	L	26	91	286	30	67	13	1	9	37	40	45	0	.234	.381
Bobby Kielty	OF73 DH3	B	29	81	270	35	73	20	1	8	36	22	49	2	.270	.441
Antonio Perez	3B27 DH21 SS4 2B2	R	26	57	98	10	10	5	1	1	8	10	44	0	.102	.204
Adam Melhuse	C24 DH15 3B3 1B2	B	34	49	128	10	28	8	0	4	18	9	34	0	.219	.375
Mike Rouse	2B7	L	26	8	24	2	7	3	0	0	2	1	4	1	.292	.417
2 D'Angelo Jimenez	3B3 SS3 2B2	B	28	8	14	1	1	0	0	0	0	6	7	0	.071	.071
Hiram Bocachica	OF8	R	30	8	13	3	3	0	0	0	0	3	4	1	.231	.231
Doug Clark	OF1	L	30	6	6	0	1	0	0	0	0	0	3	1	.167	.167
Jeremy Brown	DH4 C1	R	26	5	10	1	3	2	0	0	0	1	1	0	.300	.500

NAME	T	AGE	W	L	PCT	SV	G	GS	CG	IP	H	BB	SO	SHO	ERA
		28	93	69	.574	54	162	162	5	1452	1525	529	1003	11	4.22
Barry Zito	L	28	16	10	.615	0	34	34	0	221	211	99	151	0	3.83
Joe Blanton	R	25	16	12	.571	0	32	31	1	194	241	58	107	1	4.82
Danny Haren	R	25	14	13	.519	0	34	34	2	223	224	45	176	0	4.12
Esteban Loaiza (SJ)	R	34	11	9	.550	0	26	26	2	155	179	40	97	1	4.89
Kirk Saarloos	R	27	7	7	.500	2	35	16	0	121	149	53	52	0	4.75
Brad Halsey	L	25	5	4	.556	0	52	7	0	94	108	46	53	0	4.67
Rich Harden (XJ-EJ)	R	24	4	0	1.000	0	9	9	0	47	31	26	49	0	4.24
Joe Kennedy (SJ)	L	27	4	1	.800	1	39	0	0	35	34	13	29	0	2.31
Chad Gaudin	R	23	4	2	.667	2	55	0	0	64	51	42	36	0	3.09
Huston Street	R	22	4	4	.500	37	69	0	0	71	64	13	67	0	3.31
Kiko Calero	R	31	3	2	.600	2	70	0	0	58	50	24	67	0	3.41
Justin Duchscherer (EJ)	R	28	2	1	.667	9	53	0	0	56	52	9	51	0	2.91
Jay Witasick (NJ)	R	33	1	0	1.000	0	20	0	0	23	25	21	23	0	6.75
Steve Karsay (VR)	R	34	1	0	1.000	0	9	0	0	9	13	3	5	0	5.79
Ron Flores	L	27	1	2	.333	1	25	0	0	30	28	10	20	0	3.34
2 Scott Sauerbeck	L	34	0	0	—	0	22	0	0	12	13	9	6	0	3.65
Randy Keisler	L	30	0	0	—	0	11	0	0	10	14	2	5	0	4.50
Shane Komine	R	25	0	0	—	0	2	2	0	9	10	8	1	0	5.00
Santiago Casilla	R	26	0	0	—	0	2	0	0	2	2	2	2	0	11.57
Jason Windsor	R	23	0	1	.000	0	4	3	0	14	21	5	6	0	6.59
Matt Roney	R	26	0	1	.000	0	4	0	0	4	5	1	0	0	4.50

LOS ANGELES OF ANAHEIM — 2nd 89-73 .549 4 — MIKE SCIOSCIA

Name	G by Pos	B	AGE	G	AB	R	H	2B	3B	HR	RBI	BB	SO	SB	BA	SA
	TOTALS		29	162	5609	766	1539	309	29	159	737	486	914	148	.274	.425
Kendry Morales	1B56	B	23	57	197	21	46	10	1	5	22	17	28	1	.234	.371
Adam Kennedy	2B133 DH2	L	30	139	451	50	123	26	6	4	55	39	72	16	.273	.384
Orlando Cabrera	SS152	R	31	153	607	95	171	45	1	9	72	51	58	27	.282	.404
Maicer Izturis (LJ)	3B87 SS10 2B4 DH2	B	25	104	352	64	103	21	3	5	44	38	35	14	.293	.412
Vladimir Guerrero	OF126 DH30	R	30	156	607	92	200	34	1	33	116	50	68	15	.329	.552
Darin Erstad (NJ)	OF27 1B13	L	32	40	95	8	21	8	1	0	5	6	18	1	.221	.326
Garret Anderson	OF94 DH45	L	33	141	543	63	152	28	2	17	85	38	95	1	.280	.433
Mike Napoli	C94 DH1	R	24	99	268	47	61	13	0	16	42	51	90	2	.228	.455
Tim Salmon	DH54 OF4	R	37	76	211	30	56	8	2	9	27	29	44	0	.265	.450
Chone Figgins	OF112 3B34 2B9 DH6 SS2	B	28	155	604	93	161	23	8	9	62	65	100	52	.267	.376
Juan Rivera	OF127 1B4	R	27	124	448	65	139	27	0	23	85	33	59	0	.310	.525
Robb Quinlan	1B54 3B18 OF16 DH2	R	29	86	234	28	75	11	1	9	32	7	28	2	.321	.491
Jose Molina	C76 1B3	R	31	78	225	18	54	17	0	4	22	9	49	1	.240	.369
Howie Kendrick	1B44 2B28 DH2 3B1	R	22	72	267	25	76	21	1	4	30	9	44	6	.285	.416
Tommy Murphy	OF42 DH2	B	25	48	70	12	16	4	1	1	6	5	21	4	.229	.357
Dallas McPherson (XJ)	3B31 1B6 DH2	L	25	40	115	16	30	4	0	7	13	6	40	1	.261	.478
Erick Aybar	SS19 DH5 2B3	B	22	34	40	5	10	1	1	0	2	0	8	1	.250	.325
Casey Kotchman (IL)	1B26	L	23	29	79	6	12	2	1	1	6	7	13	0	.152	.215
Reggie Willits	OF20 DH2	B	25	28	45	12	12	1	0	0	2	11	10	4	.267	.289
Jeff Mathis	C20 DH2	R	23	23	55	9	8	2	0	2	6	1	14	0	.145	.291
Curtis Pride	OF11 DH4	L	37	22	27	6	6	2	0	1	6	6	8	0	.222	.407
1 Edgardo Alfonzo		R	32	18	50	1	5	1	0	0	5	3	6	0	.100	.120

NAME	T	AGE	W	L	PCT	SV	G	GS	CG	IP	H	BB	SO	SHO	ERA
		29	89	73	.549	50	162	162	5	1453	1410	471	1164	12	4.04
Ervin Santana	R	23	16	8	.667	0	33	33	0	204	181	70	141	0	4.28
John Lackey	R	27	13	11	.542	0	33	33	3	218	203	72	190	2	3.56
Jered Weaver	R	23	11	2	.846	0	19	19	0	123	94	33	105	0	2.56
Kelvim Escobar	R	30	11	14	.440	0	30	30	1	189	192	50	147	0	3.61
Hector Carrasco	R	36	7	3	.700	0	56	3	0	100	93	27	72	0	3.41
Joe Saunders	L	25	7	3	.700	0	13	13	0	71	71	29	51	0	4.71
Scot Shields	R	30	7	7	.500	2	74	0	0	88	70	24	84	0	2.87
Brendan Donnelly	R	34	6	0	1.000	0	62	0	0	64	58	28	53	0	3.94
Kevin Gregg	R	28	3	4	.429	0	32	3	0	78	88	21	71	0	4.14
1 Jeff Weaver	R	29	3	10	.231	0	16	16	0	89	114	21	62	0	6.29
Francisco Rodriguez	R	24	2	3	.400	47	69	0	0	73	52	28	98	0	1.73
Dustin Moseley	R	24	1	0	1.000	0	3	2	0	11	22	2	3	0	9.00
J.C. Romero	L	30	1	2	.333	0	65	0	0	48	57	28	31	0	6.70
Bartolo Colon (SJ)	R	33	1	5	.167	0	10	10	1	56	71	11	31	1	5.11
1 Esteban Yan	R	31	0	0	—	0	13	0	0	22	19	13	16	0	6.85
Greg Jones	R	29	0	0	—	0	6	0	0	6	8	2	1	0	6.00
Jason Bulger	R	27	0	0	—	0	3	1	0	3	4	3	1	0	16.20
Chris Bootcheck	R	27	0	1	.000	0	7	0	0	10	16	9	7	0	10.45

TEXAS — 3rd 80-82 .494 13 — BUCK SHOWALTER

Name	G by Pos	B	AGE	G	AB	R	H	2B	3B	HR	RBI	BB	SO	SB	BA	SA
	TOTALS		29	162	5659	835	1571	357	23	183	799	505	1061	53	.278	.446
Mark Teixeira	1B159 DH3	R	26	162	628	99	177	45	1	33	110	89	128	2	.282	.514
Ian Kinsler (RJ)	2B119	R	24	120	423	65	121	27	1	14	55	40	64	11	.286	.454
Michael Young	SS155 DH7	R	29	162	691	93	217	52	3	14	103	48	96	7	.314	.459
Hank Blalock	3B122 DH29	L	25	152	591	76	157	26	3	16	89	51	98	1	.266	.401
Mark DeRosa	OF64 3B40 2B26 SS7 DH1 3B1	R	31	136	520	78	154	40	2	13	74	44	102	4	.296	.456
Gary Matthews	OF145 DH1	B	31	147	620	102	194	44	6	19	79	58	99	10	.313	.495
Brad Wilkerson (SJ)	OF82 DH12	L	29	99	320	56	71	15	2	15	44	37	116	3	.222	.422
Rod Barajas	C94 1B5	R	30	97	344	49	88	20	0	11	41	17	51	0	.256	.410
1 Phil Nevin	DH44 1B11	R	35	46	176	26	38	8	0	9	31	21	39	0	.216	.415
1 Kevin Mench	OF72 DH15	R	28	87	320	36	91	18	1	12	50	23	42	1	.284	.459
Gerald Laird	C71 OF1 DH1	R	26	78	243	46	72	20	1	7	22	12	54	3	.296	.473
2 Jerry Hairston	OF52 SS3 DH3 2B1 3B1	R	30	63	88	17	18	3	1	0	6	9	20	2	.205	.261
2 Carlos Lee	OF51 DH8	R	30	59	236	42	76	19	1	9	35	20	26	7	.322	.525
Nelson Cruz	OF39	R	25	41	130	15	29	5	0	6	22	7	32	1	.223	.385
2 Matt Stairs	DH19 1B1 OF1	L	38	81	6	17	4	0	3	11	6	22	0	.210	.370
Adrian Brown	OF24	B	32	25	36	6	7	1	0	0	2	2	9	1	.194	.222
1 D'Angelo Jimenez	2B16 3B2	B	28	20	57	7	12	3	0	1	8	10	6	0	.211	.316
Jason Botts	DH13 OF1	R	25	20	50	8	11	4	0	1	6	8	18	0	.220	.360
1 Laynce Nix	OF9	L	25	9	32	1	3	1	0	0	4	0	17	0	.094	.125
Freddy Guzman	OF4 DH1	B	25	9	7	1	2	0	0	0	0	0	1	0	.286	.286
Joaquin Arias	SS5 3B1	R	21	6	11	4	6	1	0	0	1	1	0	0	.545	.636
Drew Meyer	2B3 SS1 OF1	L	24	5	14	1	3	0	0	0	0	0	8	0	.214	.214
2 Miguel Ojeda	C5	R	31	5	13	0	4	2	0	0	4	0	3	0	.308	.462
1 Eric Young	2B1 OF1 DH1	R	39	4	10	1	2	1	0	0	2	1	1	0	.200	.500
Adam Hyzdu	OF1 DH1	R	34	2	4	0	1	0	0	0	0	0	1	0	.250	.250

NAME	T	AGE	W	L	PCT	SV	G	GS	CG	IP	H	BB	SO	SHO	ERA
		28	80	82	.494	42	162	162	3	1431	1558	496	972	8	4.61
Kevin Millwood	R	31	16	12	.571	0	34	34	2	215	228	53	157	0	4.52
Vicente Padilla	R	28	15	10	.600	0	33	33	0	200	206	70	156	0	4.50
Adam Eaton (RJ)	R	28	7	4	.636	0	13	13	0	65	78	24	43	0	5.12
1 Francisco Cordero	R	31	7	4	.636	49	69	0	0	49	49	16	54	0	4.81
John Koronka	L	25	7	7	.500	0	23	23	0	125	145	47	61	0	5.69
Robinson Tejeda	R	24	5	5	.500	0	14	14	0	74	83	32	40	0	4.28
John Rheinecker	L	27	4	6	.400	0	21	13	0	71	104	19	28	0	5.86
Rick Bauer	R	29	3	1	.750	2	58	1	0	71	73	25	35	0	3.55
Kameron Loe (EJ)	R	24	3	6	.333	0	15	15	1	78	105	22	34	1	5.86
Wes Littleton	R	23	1	1	.667	1	33	0	0	36	23	13	17	0	1.73
John Wasdin	R	33	2	2	.500	0	9	5	0	30	33	13	16	0	5.10
Akinori Otsuka	R	34	2	4	.333	32	63	0	0	60	53	11	47	0	2.11
C.J. Wilson	L	25	2	4	.333	1	44	0	0	44	39	18	43	0	4.06
2 Kip Wells (FJ)	R	29	1	0	1.000	0	2	2	0	8	5	3	4	0	5.63
Joaquin Benoit	R	28	1	1	.500	0	56	0	0	80	68	38	85	0	4.86
1 Bryan Corey	R	32	1	1	.500	0	15	0	0	15	18	3	12	0	2.60
Ron Mahay	L	35	1	3	.250	0	62	0	0	57	54	28	56	0	3.95
Edinson Volquez	R	22	1	6	.143	0	8	8	0	33	52	17	15	0	7.29
Antonio Alfonseca	R	34	0	0	—	0	19	0	0	16	23	7	5	0	5.63
Nick Masset	R	24	0	0	—	0	4	0	0	6	6	7	6	0	4.15
1 Fabio Castro (GJ)	L	21	0	0	—	0	7	0	0	6	7	5	6	0	4.32
1 Brian Shouse	L	37	0	0	—	0	16	0	0	19	20	4	19	0	3.41
Josh Rupe (EJ)	R	23	0	1	.000	0	16	0	0	29	33	9	14	0	3.41
Frank Francisco (EJ)	R	26	0	1	.000	0	7	0	0	7	8	2	6	0	4.91
R.A. Dickey	R	31	0	1	.000	0	1	1	0	4	9	2	2	0	18.90
Scott Feldman	R	23	0	0	—	0	36	0	0	41	42	10	30	0	3.92

SEATTLE — 4th 78-84 .481 15 — MIKE HARGROVE

Name	G by Pos	B	AGE	G	AB	R	H	2B	3B	HR	RBI	BB	SO	SB	BA	SA
	TOTALS		29	162	5670	756	1540	266	42	172	703	404	974	106	.272	.424
Richie Sexson	1B150 DH8	R	31	158	591	75	156	40	0	34	107	64	154	1	.264	.504
Jose Lopez	2B150	R	22	151	603	78	170	28	8	10	79	26	80	5	.282	.405
Yuniesky Betancourt	SS157	R	24	157	558	68	161	28	6	8	47	17	54	11	.289	.403
Adrian Beltre	3B155 2B1 DH1	R	27	156	620	88	166	39	4	25	89	47	118	11	.268	.465
Ichiro Suzuki	OF159 DH2	L	32	161	695	110	224	20	9	9	49	49	71	45	.322	.416
Jeremy Reed (BG)	OF64	L	25	67	212	27	46	6	5	6	17	11	31	2	.217	.377
Raul Ibanez	OF157 DH1	L	34	159	626	103	181	33	5	33	123	65	115	2	.289	.516
Kenji Johjima	C144	R	30	144	506	61	147	25	1	18	76	20	46	3	.291	.451
Carl Everett	DH80 OF2	B	35	92	308	37	70	8	0	11	33	29	57	1	.227	.360
Willie Bloomquist	OF59 SS17 2B15 3B12 1B4 DH2	R	28	102	251	36	62	6	2	1	15	24	40	16	.247	.299
2 Ben Broussard	DH45 1B10	L	29	56	164	17	39	7	0	8	17	9	45	2	.238	.427
2 Eduardo Perez	DH36 1B5	R	36	43	87	6	17	1	0	1	11	13	22	0	.195	.241
Chris Snelling (KJ)	OF34	L	24	36	96	14	24	6	1	3	8	13	38	2	.250	.427
Rene Rivera	C35	R	22	35	99	8	15	4	0	2	4	3	29	1	.152	.253
Adam Jones	OF26 DH1	R	20	32	74	6	16	4	0	1	8	2	22	2	.216	.311
Roberto Petagine	1B9	L	35	31	27	3	5	2	0	1	2	4	10	0	.185	.370
Greg Dobbs	DH5 1B3 OF3 3B2	L	27	33	27	4	10	3	0	3	9	1	5	0	.370	.556
Mike Morse	OF9 DH4 3B5 1B2 SS1	R	24	21	43	5	16	5	0	0	11	3	7	1	.372	.488
T.J. Bohn	OF8	R	26	18	14	2	2	0	0	0	1	2	4	0	.143	.357
Matt Lawton	OF7 DH2	L	34	11	27	5	7	0	0	0	1	7	1	0	.259	.259
1 Joe Borchard	OF3 DH1	B	27	9	3	2	0	0	0	0	2	2	0	0	.222	.222
1 Shin-Soo Choo	OF4	L	23	4	11	0	1	0	0	0	1	0	3	0	.091	.182
Oswaldo Navarro	SS2 DH1	R	21	4	3	0	0	0	0	0	0	0	1	0	.667	.667
Guillermo Quiroz	C1	R	24	1	2	0	0	0	0	0	0	0	0	0	.000	.000

NAME	T	AGE	W	L	PCT	SV	G	GS	CG	IP	H	BB	SO	SHO	ERA
		27	78	84	.481	47	162	162	6	1447	1500	560	1067	6	4.60
Felix Hernandez	R	20	12	14	.462	0	31	31	2	191	195	60	176	1	4.52
Gil Meche	R	27	11	8	.579	0	32	32	1	187	183	84	156	0	4.48
Julio Mateo (BH)	R	28	4	2	.692	0	48	0	0	54	62	22	31	0	4.19
Joel Pineiro	R	27	8	13	.381	1	40	25	1	166	209	64	87	0	6.36
Jarrod Washburn	L	31	8	14	.364	0	31	31	0	187	198	55	103	0	4.67
Jake Woods	L	25	4	4	.636	1	37	8	0	105	115	53	66	0	4.20
1 Jamie Moyer	L	43	6	12	.333	0	25	25	2	160	179	44	82	1	4.39
J.J. Putz	R	29	4	1	.800	36	72	0	0	78	59	13	104	0	2.30
Cha-Seung Baek	R	26	4	1	.800	0	6	6	0	34	26	13	23	0	3.67
Jon Huber	R	24	1	0	1.000	0	16	0	0	17	10	6	11	0	1.08
Emiliano Fruto	R	22	2	2	.500	1	23	0	0	36	34	24	34	0	5.50
George Sherrill	L	29	2	4	.333	1	72	0	0	40	30	27	42	0	4.28
Mark Lowe (EJ)	R	23	1	0	1.000	0	15	0	0	19	12	9	20	0	1.93
Rafael Soriano (CN)	R	26	2	3	.333	2	53	0	0	60	44	21	65	0	2.25
1 Eddie Guardado	L	35	1	3	.250	5	28	0	0	23	29	11	22	0	5.48
Sean Green	R	27	0	0	—	0	24	0	0	32	34	13	15	0	4.50
Eric O'Flaherty	L	21	0	0	—	0	15	0	0	8	6	7	5	0	4.50
Cesar Jimenez	L	21	0	0	—	0	5	0	0	4	7	2	3	0	14.73
Francisco Cruceta	R	24	0	0	—	0	2	0	0	3	9	4	3	0	10.80
Travis Chick	R	22	0	0	—	0	2	2	0	6	13	6	4	0	12.60
Bobby Livingston	L	23	0	1	.000	0	2	2	0	9	16	3	4	0	18.00
Jeff Harris	R	31	0	0	—	0	3	0	0	5	11	2	1	0	5.40
Jorge Campillo	R	27	0	0	—	0	1	0	0	2	3	0	1	0	15.43
Clint Nageotte	R	25	0	0	—	0	2	0	0	4	5	4	3	0	27.00
Ryan Feierabend	L	20	0	1	.000	0	4	4	0	17	15	7	11	0	3.71

LINE SCORES

Team	1	2	3	4	5	6	7	8	9	10	11	12	13	14	R	H	E

DIVISION SERIES: DETROIT 3 : NEW YORK 1

Game 1   October 3 at New York

	1	2	3	4	5	6	7	8	9		R	H	E
DET	0	0	0	0	0	3	0	1	0	0	4	12	1
NYA	0	0	5	0	0	2	0	1	x		8	14	0

Robertson, Grilli (6), Walker (7)   **Wang**, Myers (7), Proctor (7), Farnsworth (8), Rivera (9)

Game 2   October 5 at New York

	1	2	3	4	5	6	7	8	9		R	H	E
DET	0	0	1	0	0	1	1	1	0	0	4	8	0
NYA	0	0	0	3	0	0	0	0	0		3	8	1

Verlander, **Walker** (6), Zumaya (7), Jones (9)   **Mussina**, Proctor (8), Bruney (9)

Game 3   October 6 at Detroit

	1	2	3	4	5	6	7	8	9	R	H	E
NYA	0	0	0	0	0	0	0	0	0	0	5	0
DET	0	3	0	0	0	2	1	0	x	6	10	0

Johnson, Bruney (6), Villone (8)   **Rogers**, Zumaya (8), Jones (9)

Game 4   October 7 at Detroit

	1	2	3	4	5	6	7	8	9	R	H	E
NYA	0	0	0	0	0	0	1	0	2	3	6	1
DET	0	3	1	0	3	1	0	0	x	8	13	0

Wright, Lidle (3), Bruney (5), Proctor (5), Farnsworth (8)   **Bonderman**, Walker (9)

DIVISION SERIES: OAKLAND 3 : MINNESOTA 0

Game 1   October 3 at Minnesota

	1	2	3	4	5	6	7	8	9	R	H	E
OAK	0	2	0	0	0	0	0	0	1	3	7	0
MIN	0	0	0	0	0	0	1	0	1	2	5	2

Zito, Street (9)   **Santana**, Crain (9), Neshek (9)

Game 2   October 4 at Minnesota

	1	2	3	4	5	6	7	8	9	R	H	E
OAK	0	0	0	0	2	0	0	2	1	5	11	0
MIN	0	0	0	0	0	2	0	0	0	2	9	0

Loaiza, **Calero** (6), Duchscherer (7), Street (9)   Bonser, **Neshek** (7), Reyes (7), Rincon (8), Nathan (9)

Game 3   October 6 at Oakland

	1	2	3	4	5	6	7	8	9	R	H	E
MIN	0	0	0	1	0	1	0	1	0	3	12	3
OAK	0	2	2	0	0	0	4	0	x	8	8	1

Radke, Perkins (5), Rincon (7), Reyes (7), Crain (7), Guerrier (8)   **Haren**, Duchscherer (7), Street (9)

CHAMPIONSHIP: DETROIT 4 : OAKLAND 0

Game 1   October 10 at Oakland

	1	2	3	4	5	6	7	8	9	R	H	E
DET	0	0	2	3	0	0	0	0	0	5	11	1
OAK	0	0	0	0	0	0	0	1	0	1	8	1

Robertson, Rodney (6), Zumaya (8), Jones (9)   **Zito**, Gaudin (4), Kennedy (6), Calero (7), Blanton (8)

Game 2   October 11 at Oakland

	1	2	3	4	5	6	7	8	9	R	H	E
DET	0	1	0	4	0	2	0	0	1	8	11	0
OAK	1	0	2	0	0	1	1	0	0	5	11	1

Verlander, Ledezma (6), Grilli (7), Rodney (8), Jones (9)   **Loaiza**, Gaudin (7), Kennedy (7), Street (9)

Game 3   October 13 at Detroit

	1	2	3	4	5	6	7	8	9	R	H	E
OAK	0	0	0	0	0	0	0	0	0	0	2	0
DET	2	0	0	1	0	0	0	0	x	3	6	0

Harden, Gaudin (6), Kennedy (8), Calero (8)   **Rogers**, Rodney (8), Jones (9)

Game 4   October 14 at Detroit

	1	2	3	4	5	6	7	8	9	R	H	E
OAK	2	0	0	1	0	0	0	0	0	3	8	1
DET	0	0	0	0	0	2	1	0	3	6	11	0

Haren, Kennedy (6), Calero (7), **Street** (7)   **Bonderman**, Walker (7), Grilli (8), **Ledezma** (8)

COMPOSITE BATTING

DIVISION SERIES

DETROIT

NAME	POS	G	AB	R	H	2B	3B	HR	RBI	BA
TOTALS		4	139	22	43	12	1	6	22	.309
Polanco	2B	4	17	3	7	1	0	0	2	.412
Casey	1B	4	17	1	6	3	0	0	4	.353
Granderson	CF	4	17	3	5	0	1	2	5	.294
Monroe	LF	4	16	3	3	1	0	2	3	.188
Thames	DH	4	15	2	5	2	0	0	1	.333
Ordonez	RF	4	15	3	4	1	0	1	2	.267
Inge	3B	4	15	1	2	0	0	0	0	.133
Guillen	SS	4	14	3	8	3	0	1	2	**.571**
Rodriguez	C	4	13	3	3	1	0	0	3	.231

NEW YORK

NAME	POS	G	AB	R	H	2B	3B	HR	RBI	BA
TOTALS		4	134	14	33	7	0	4	14	.246
Damon	CF	4	17	3	4	0	0	1	3	.235
Jeter	SS	4	16	4	8	4	0	1	1	.500
Matsui	LF-DH	4	16	1	4	1	0	0	1	.250
Abreu	RF	4	15	2	5	1	0	0	4	.333
Cano	2B	4	15	0	2	0	0	0	0	.133
Posada	C	4	14	2	7	1	0	1	2	.500
Rodriguez	3B	4	14	0	1	0	0	0	0	.071
Sheffield	1B	3	12	1	1	0	0	0	1	.083
Giambi	DH-1B	3	8	1	1	0	0	1	2	.125
Cabrera	LF	2	3	0	0	0	0	0	0	.000
Williams	DH	1	3	0	0	0	0	0	0	.000
Phillips	1B	1	1	0	0	0	0	0	0	.000

OAKLAND

NAME	POS	G	AB	R	H	2B	3B	HR	RBI	BA
TOTALS		3	106	16	26	9	0	5	15	.245
Kendall	C	3	14	1	3	1	0	0	1	.214
Kotsay	CF	3	14	2	2	0	0	1	2	.143
Bradley	RF	3	13	1	1	0	0	1	2	.077
Scutaro	SS	3	12	1	4	4	0	0	6	.333
Payton	LF	3	12	3	4	0	0	0	0	.333
Thomas	DH	3	10	3	5	1	0	2	2	**.500**
Swisher	1B	3	10	3	3	2	0	0	1	.300
Chavez	3B	3	10	2	2	1	0	1	1	.200
Ellis	2B	2	7	0	2	0	0	0	0	.286
Jimenez	2B	2	4	0	0	0	0	0	0	.000

MINNESOTA

NAME	POS	G	AB	R	H	2B	3B	HR	RBI	BA
TOTALS		3	101	7	26	4	1	5	7	.257
White	LF	3	12	1	5	1	0	1	2	.417
Morneau	1B	3	12	3	5	1	0	2	2	.417
Cuddyer	RF	3	12	2	3	0	1	1	1	.250
Punto	3B	3	12	0	2	0	0	0	0	.167
Castillo	2B	3	11	0	3	0	0	0	0	.273
Hunter	CF	3	11	1	3	1	0	1	2	.273
Bartlett	SS	3	11	0	3	1	0	0	0	.273
Mauer	C	3	11	0	2	0	0	0	0	.182
Tyner	DH	2	6	0	0	0	0	0	0	.000
Nevin	DH	1	3	0	0	0	0	0	0	.000
Ford	PR	1	0	0	0	0	0	0	0	—

AMERICAN LEAGUE CHAMPIONSHIP

DETROIT

NAME	POS	G	AB	R	H	2B	3B	HR	RBI	BA
TOTALS		4	137	22	39	7	0	7	22	.285
Polanco	2B	4	17	2	9	1	0	0	2	.529
Ordonez	RF	4	17	3	4	0	0	2	6	.235
Guillen	1B-SS	4	16	1	3	1	0	0	0	.188
Rodriguez	C	4	16	2	2	0	0	1	1	.125
Granderson	CF	4	15	4	5	2	0	1	2	.333
Monroe	LF	4	14	5	6	2	0	1	4	.429
Inge	3B	4	12	3	4	1	0	1	3	.333
Gomez	DH	3	9	1	4	0	0	0	4	.444
Santiago	SS	2	7	0	0	0	0	0	0	.000
Thames	DH	2	5	1	0	0	0	0	0	.000
Perez	SS	1	4	0	0	0	0	0	0	.000
Casey	1B	1	3	0	1	0	0	0	0	.333
Infante	DH	1	2	0	1	0	0	0	0	.500

OAKLAND

NAME	POS	G	AB	R	H	2B	3B	HR	RBI	BA
TOTALS		4	131	9	29	7	0	4	9	.221
Bradley	RF	4	18	4	9	2	0	2	5	.500
Kendall	C	4	17	0	5	0	0	0	0	.294
Kotsay	CF	4	16	3	4	2	0	0	0	.250
Scutaro	SS	4	15	0	1	0	0	0	0	.067
Payton	LF	4	14	1	4	2	0	1	2	.286
Chavez	3B	4	13	1	3	1	0	1	1	.231
Thomas	DH	4	13	0	0	0	0	0	0	.000
Jimenez	2B	4	12	0	2	0	0	0	0	.167
Swisher	1B	4	10	0	1	0	0	0	0	.100
Kielty	PH	2	2	0	0	0	0	0	0	.000
Melhuse	PH	1	1	0	0	0	0	0	0	.000
Kiger	2B	2	0	0	0	0	0	0	0	—

COMPOSITE PITCHING

DIVISION SERIES

DETROIT

NAME	G	IP	H	BB	SO	W	L	SV	ERA
TOTALS	4	35	33	8	24	3	1	1	3.60
Bonderman	1	8.1	5	1	4	1	0	0	2.16
Rogers	1	7.2	5	2	8	1	0	0	0.00
Robertson	1	5.2	12	0	1	0	0	1	11.12
Verlander	1	5.1	7	4	5	0	0	0	5.06
Walker	3	3.2	3	1	1	0	0	0	4.91
Jones	2	2	1	0	2	0	0	1	0.00
Zumaya	2	2	0	0	3	0	0	0	0.00
Grilli	1	0.1	0	0	0	0	0	0	0.00

NEW YORK

NAME	G	IP	H	BB	SO	W	L	SV	ERA
TOTALS	4	34	43	7	22	1	3	0	5.29
Mussina	1	7	8	0	5	0	1	0	5.14
Wang	1	6.2	8	1	4	1	0	0	4.05
Johnson	1	5.2	8	2	4	0	0	1	7.94
Proctor	3	4	5	1	1	0	0	0	2.25
Bruney	3	2.2	1	0	4	0	0	0	3.38
Wright	1	2.2	5	1	1	0	0	1	10.12
Farnsworth	2	2	1	1	1	0	0	0	0.00
Lidle	1	1.1	4	0	1	0	0	0	20.25
Villone	1	1	1	1	1	0	0	0	0.00
Rivera	1	1	1	0	0	0	0	0	0.00
Myers	1	0	1	0	0	0	0	0	∞

OAKLAND

NAME	G	IP	H	BB	SO	W	L	SV	ERA
TOTALS	3	27	26	6	11	3	0	2	2.33
Zito	1	8	4	3	1	1	0	0	**1.13**
Haren	1	6	9	1	2	1	0	0	3.00
Loaiza	1	5	8	0	2	0	0	0	3.60
Duchscherer	2	4	1	0	4	0	0	0	2.25
Street	3	3	4	1	1	0	0	2	3.00
Calero	1	1	0	1	1	1	0	0	0.00

MINNESOTA

NAME	G	IP	H	BB	SO	W	L	SV	ERA
TOTALS	3	26	26	6	19	0	3	0	3.81
Santana	1	8	5	1	8	0	1	0	2.25
Bonser	1	6	7	1	3	0	0	0	3.00
Radke	1	4	5	1	2	0	1	0	6.75
Rincon	2	1	0	3	0	0	0	0	3.00
Crain	2	1	3	1	1	0	0	0	9.00
Reyes	2	1	1	2	0	0	0	0	9.00
Neshek	2	1	1	0	1	0	1	0	9.00
Guerrier	1	1	0	0	0	0	0	0	0.00
Nathan	1	0.2	1	0	1	0	0	0	0.00
Perkins	1	0.1	2	0	0	0	0	0	0.00

AMERICAN LEAGUE CHAMPIONSHIP

DETROIT

NAME	G	IP	H	BB	SO	W	L	SV	ERA
TOTALS	4	36	29	14	28	4	0	2	2.25
Rogers	1	7.1	2	2	6	1	0	0	0.00
Bonderman	1	6.2	6	2	3	0	0	0	4.05
Verlander	1	5.1	7	1	6	1	0	0	6.75
Robertson	1	5	6	3	4	1	0	0	0.00
Rodney	3	3.2	1	1	2	0	0	0	0.00
Jones	3	3	3	1	2	0	0	2	0.00
Ledezma	2	2.2	2	1	1	1	0	0	3.38
Grilli	2	1	1	3	1	0	0	0	9.00
Zumaya	1	1	1	0	0	0	0	0	9.00
Walker	1	0.1	0	1	0	0	0	0	0.00

OAKLAND

NAME	G	IP	H	BB	SO	W	L	SV	ERA
TOTALS	4	34.2	39	19	25	0	4	0	5.71
Loaiza	1	6	9	1	5	0	1	0	10.50
Harden	1	5.2	5	4	4	0	1	0	4.76
Haren	1	5	7	2	7	0	0	0	5.40
Kennedy	4	3.2	2	2	2	0	0	0	0.00
Zito	1	3.2	7	3	0	0	1	0	12.27
Gaudin	3	3.1	2	3	1	0	0	0	0.00
Street	3	3.1	4	0	3	0	1	0	10.80
Blanton	1	2	0	2	2	0	0	0	0.00
Calero	3	2	3	1	1	0	0	0	9.00

NEW YORK — 1st 97-65 .599 — WILLIE RANDOLPH

Name	G by Pos	B	AGE	G	AB	R	H	2B	3B	HR	RBI	BB	SO	SB	BA	SA
TOTALS			30	162	5559	834	1469	323	41	200	800	547	1071	146	.264	.445
Carlos Delgado	1B141	L	34	144	524	89	139	30	2	38	114	74	120	0	.265	.548
Jose Valentin	2B94 OF7 1B1 3B1	B	36	137	384	56	104	24	3	18	62	37	71	6	.271	.490
Jose Reyes	SS149	B	23	153	647	122	194	30	17	19	81	53	81	64	.300	.487
David Wright	3B153	R	23	154	582	96	181	40	5	26	116	66	113	20	.311	.531
1 Xavier Nady	OF71 1B1	R	27	75	265	37	70	15	1	14	40	19	51	2	.264	.487
Carlos Beltran	OF136	B	29	140	510	127	140	38	1	41	116	95	99	18	.275	.594
Cliff Floyd	OF92	L	33	97	332	45	81	19	1	11	44	29	58	6	.244	.407
Paul LoDuca	C118	R	34	124	512	80	163	39	1	5	49	24	38	3	.318	.428
Endy Chavez	OF120	L	28	133	353	48	108	22	5	4	42	24	44	12	.306	.431
Julio Franco	1B27 3B3	R	47	95	165	14	45	10	0	2	26	13	49	6	.273	.370
Chris Woodward	2B39 SS13 OF9 3B11 1B1	R	30	83	222	25	48	10	1	3	25	23	55	1	.216	.311
Lastings Milledge	OF50	R	21	56	166	14	40	7	2	4	22	12	39	1	.241	.380
Ramon Castro (UJ)	C37	R	30	40	126	13	30	7	0	4	12	15	40	0	.238	.389
1 Kaz Matsui	2B31	B	30	38	130	10	26	6	0	1	7	6	19	2	.200	.269
Michael Tucker	OF18 1B1	L	35	56	56	3	11	4	0	1	6	16	14	2	.196	.321
2 Shawn Green	OF31 1B1	L	33	34	113	14	29	9	0	4	15	8	18	0	.257	.442
2 Ricky Ledee	OF4	L	32	27	32	4	3	1	0	1	4	6	0		.094	.219
Anderson Hernandez (XJ)	2B23 SS10	B	23	25	66	4	10	1	1	1	3	1	12	0	.152	.242
2 Eli Marrero	OF7 C2 1B1 3B1	R	32	25	33	4	6	1	0	2	5	4	15	2	.182	.394
Mike DiFelice	C15	R	37	15	25	3	2	1	0	0	1	3	5	10	.080	.120
Kelly Stinnett	C7	R	36	7	12	0	1	0	0	0	0	0	4	0	.083	.083
Victor Diaz	OF4	R	24	6	11	0	2	1	0	0	2	0	5	0	.182	.273

NAME	T	AGE	W	L	PCT	SV	G	GS	CG	IP	H	BB	SO	SHO	ERA
		32	97	65	.599	43	162	162	5	1461	1402	527	1161	12	4.16
Tom Glavine	L	40	15	7	.682	0	32	32	0	198	202	62	131	0	3.82
Steve Trachsel	R	35	15	8	.652	0	30	30	1	165	185	78	79	0	4.97
2 Orlando Hernandez	R	40	9	7	.563	0	20	20	1	117	103	41	112	0	4.09
Pedro Martinez (LJ)	R	34	9	8	.529	0	23	23	0	133	108	39	137	0	4.48
Pedro Feliciano	L	29	7	2	.778	0	64	0	0	60	56	20	54	0	2.09
John Maine (RJ)	R	25	6	5	.545	0	16	15	1	90	69	33	71	1	3.60
Duaner Sanchez (SJ)	R	26	5	1	.833	0	49	0	0	55	43	24	44	0	2.60
Darren Oliver	L	35	4	1	.800	0	45	0	0	81	70	21	60	0	3.44
Chad Bradford	R	31	4	2	.667	2	70	0	0	62	59	13	45	0	2.90
Aaron Heilman	R	27	4	5	.444	0	74	0	0	87	73	28	73	0	3.62
2 Guillermo Mota	R	32	3	0	1.000	0	18	0	0	18	10	5	19	0	1.00
2 David Williams	L	27	3	1	.750	0	6	5	0	29	39	4	16	0	5.59
Billy Wagner	L	34	3	2	.600	40	70	0	0	72	59	21	94	0	2.24
Brian Bannister (LJ)	R	25	2	1	.667	0	8	6	0	38	34	22	19	0	4.26
Mike Pelfrey	R	22	2	1	.667	0	4	4	0	21	25	12	13	0	5.48
Alay Soler	R	26	2	3	.400	0	8	8	1	45	50	21	23	1	6.00
Bartolome Fortunato	R	31	1	0	1.000	0	3	0	0	3	7	2	0	0	27.00
1 Jorge Julio	R	27	1	2	.333	1	18	0	0	21	21	10	33	0	5.06
Victor Zambrano (EJ)	R	30	1	2	.333	0	5	5	0	21	25	11	15	0	6.75
2 Oliver Perez	R	24	1	3	.250	0	7	7	1	37	41	17	41	1	6.38
Heath Bell	R	28	0	0	—	0	22	0	0	37	51	11	35	0	5.11
2 Roberto Hernandez	R	41	0	0	—	0	22	0	0	21	15	8	15	0	3.48
1 Jeremi Gonzalez	R	31	0	0	—	0	3	3	0	14	21	6	9	0	7.71
Royce Ring	L	25	0	0	—	0	11	0	0	13	7	3	8	0	2.13
Henry Owens	R	27	0	0	—	0	3	0	0	4	4	2	9	0	9.00
Philip Humber	R	23	0	0	—	0	2	0	0	2	1	2	0	0	9.00
Jose Lima	R	33	0	4	.000	0	4	4	0	17	25	10	12	0	9.87
Juan Padilla (EJ) 29															

PHILADELPHIA — 2nd 85-77 .525 12 — CHARLIE MANUEL

Name	G by Pos	B	AGE	G	AB	R	H	2B	3B	HR	RBI	BB	SO	SB	BA	SA
TOTALS			30	162	5687	865	1518	294	41	216	823	626	1203	92	.267	.447
Ryan Howard	1B159	L	26	159	581	104	182	25	1	58	149	108	181	0	.313	.659
Chase Utley	2B156 1B2	L	27	160	658	131	203	40	4	32	102	63	132	15	.309	.527
Jimmy Rollins	SS157	B	27	158	689	127	191	45	9	25	83	57	80	36	.277	.478
1 David Bell	3B90	R	33	92	324	39	90	17	2	6	34	32	38	1	.278	.398
1 Bobby Abreu	OF97	L	32	98	339	61	94	25	2	8	65	*91	86	20	.277	.434
Aaron Rowand (BN)		R	28	109	405	59	106	24	3	12	47	18	76	10	.262	.425
Pat Burrell	OF126	R	29	144	462	80	119	24	1	29	95	98	131	0	.258	.502
Mike Lieberthal (PJ)	C60	R	34	67	209	22	57	14	0	9	36	8	19	0	.273	.469
Shane Victorino	OF122	R	25	153	415	70	119	19	8	6	46	24	54	4	.287	.414
Dave Dellucci	OF67	L	32	132	264	41	77	14	5	13	39	28	62	1	.292	.530
Abraham Nunez	SS3 3B74	B	30	123	322	42	68	10	2	2	32	41	58	1	.211	.273
Chris Coste	C54 1B2	R	33	65	198	25	65	14	0	7	32	10	31	0	.328	.505
Chris Roberson	OF45	B	26	57	41	9	8	0	1	0	1	0	9	3	.195	.244
Sal Fasano	C50	R	34	50	140	9	34	8	0	4	10	5	47	0	.243	.386
2 Jeff Conine	OF26	R	40	28	100	11	28	6	1	1	17	5	12	0	.280	.390
Danny Sandoval	2B8 SS6	R	27	38	38	1	8	1	0	0	4	4	3	0	.211	.237
Carlos Ruiz	C24	R	27	27	69	5	18	1	1	3	10	5	8	0	.261	.435
Randall Simon		L	31	23	21	0	5	0	0	0	2	2	6	0	.238	.238
Alex Gonzalez (VR)	1B3 SS3 3B2 OF1	R	33	20	36	4	4	0	0	0	2	1	6	0	.111	.111
2 Jose Hernandez	3B7 SS2 OF2 1B1	R	36	18	32	4	8	2	0	1	7	1	11	0	.250	.406
Joe Thurston	2B4 OF3	L	26	18	18	3	4	1	0	0	0	1	3	1	.222	.278
Michael Bourn	OF15	L	23	17	8	2	1	0	0	0	1	0	6	1	.125	.125

*Abreu, also with New York AL, major league leader in BB with 124

NAME	T	AGE	W	L	PCT	SV	G	GS	CG	IP	H	BB	SO	SHO	ERA
		31	85	77	.525	42	162	162	4	1460	1561	512	1138	6	4.61
Brett Myers	R	25	12	7	.632	0	31	31	1	198	194	63	189	0	3.91
Ryan Madson	R	25	11	9	.550	2	50	17	0	134	176	50	99	0	5.69
Cole Hamels	L	22	9	8	.529	0	23	23	0	132	117	48	145	0	4.08
Jon Lieber (GJ)	R	36	9	11	.450	0	27	27	2	168	196	24	100	1	4.93
1 Cory Lidle	R	34	8	7	.533	0	21	21	0	125	132	39	98	0	4.74
Geoff Geary	R	29	7	1	.875	1	81	0	0	91	103	20	60	0	2.96
2 Jamie Moyer	L	43	5	2	.714	0	8	8	0	51	49	7	26	0	4.03
Randy Wolf (EJ)	L	29	4	0	1.000	0	12	12	0	57	63	33	44	0	5.56
Gavin Floyd	R	23	4	3	.571	0	11	11	1	54	70	32	34	1	7.29
Aaron Fultz	L	32	3	1	.750	0	66	1	0	71	80	28	62	0	4.54
2 Rick White	R	37	3	1	.750	0	37	0	0	37	38	15	23	0	4.34
Tom Gordon	R	38	3	4	.429	34	59	0	0	59	53	22	68	0	3.34
1 Rheal Cormier	L	39	2	2	.500	0	43	0	0	34	27	13	13	0	1.59
Clay Condrey	R	30	2	2	.500	0	21	0	0	29	35	9	16	0	3.14
Eude Brito	L	27	1	2	.333	0	5	2	0	18	21	12	9	0	7.36
Scott Mathieson (EJ)	R	22	1	4	.200	0	9	8	0	37	48	16	28	0	7.47
1 Ryan Franklin	R	33	1	5	.167	0	46	0	0	53	59	17	25	0	4.58
Brian Sanches	R	27	0	0	—	0	18	0	0	21	23	13	22	0	5.91
Julio Santana (EJ)	R	32	0	0	—	0	7	0	0	8	8	4	7	0	7.56
2 Fabio Castro	L	21	0	0	.000	1	16	0	0	23	12	6	13	0	1.54
Matt Smith	L	27	0	0	.000	0	14	0	0	9	3	4	12	0	2.08
1 Adam Bernero	R	29	0	0	—	0	1	1	0	2	3	0	1	0	36.00
Arthur Rhodes	L	36	0	5	.000	0	55	0	0	46	47	30	48	0	5.32
1 Chris Booker (KJ) 29															

ATLANTA — 3rd 79-83 .488 18 — BOBBY COX

Name	G by Pos	B	AGE	G	AB	R	H	2B	3B	HR	RBI	BB	SO	SB	BA	SA
TOTALS			27	162	5583	849	1510	312	26	222	818	526	1169	52	.270	.455
Adam LaRoche	1B142	L	27	149	492	89	140	38	1	32	90	55	128	0	.285	.561
Marcus Giles	2B134	R	28	141	550	87	144	32	2	11	60	62	105	10	.262	.387
Edgar Renteria	SS146	R	30	149	598	100	175	40	2	14	70	62	89	17	.293	.436
Chipper Jones	3B105	B	34	110	411	87	133	28	3	26	86	61	73	6	.324	.596
Jeff Francoeur	OF162	R	22	162	651	83	169	24	6	29	103	23	132	1	.260	.449
Andruw Jones	OF153	R	29	156	565	107	148	29	0	41	129	82	127	4	.262	.531
Ryan Langerhans	OF119	L	26	131	315	46	76	16	3	7	28	50	91	1	.241	.378
Brian McCann	C124	L	22	130	442	61	147	34	0	24	93	41	54	2	.333	.572
Matt Diaz	OF99	R	28	124	297	37	97	15	4	7	32	11	49	5	.327	.475
Pete Orr	2B32 3B10	L	27	102	154	22	39	3	4	1	8	5	30	2	.253	.344
1 Wilson Betemit	3B30 SS18 2B10	B	24	88	199	30	56	16	0	9	29	19	57	2	.281	.497
Todd Pratt	C54	R	39	62	135	14	28	6	0	4	19	12	43	1	.207	.341
Scott Thorman	OF21 1B18	L	24	55	128	13	30	11	0	5	14	5	21	1	.234	.430
Brian Jordan (SJ)	1B25 OF6	R	39	48	91	11	21	2	0	3	10	7	23	0	.231	.352
Tony Pena	SS22 3B1	R	24	40	44	12	10	2	0	1	3	2	10	0	.227	.341
1 Willy Aybar	3B32	B	23	36	115	17	36	6	0	1	8	10	19	0	.313	.391
Martin Prado	2B11 3B8	R	22	24	42	3	11	1	1	1	9	5	7	0	.262	.405
Brayan Pena	C15 3B1	B	24	23	41	9	11	2	1	0	5	2	5	0	.268	.390
2 Daryle Ward	1B4 OF2	L	31	20	26	2	4	1	0	1	7	3	6	0	.308	.462
Kelly Johnson (EJ) 24																	

NAME	T	AGE	W	L	PCT	SV	G	GS	CG	IP	H	BB	SO	SHO	ERA
		30	79	83	.488	38	162	162	6	1441	1529	572	1049	6	4.60
John Smoltz	R	39	16	9	.640	0	35	35	3	232	221	55	211	1	3.49
Tim Hudson	R	30	13	12	.520	0	35	35	2	218	235	79	141	1	4.86
Chuck James (LJ)	L	24	11	4	.733	0	25	18	0	119	101	47	91	0	3.78
Oscar Villarreal	R	24	9	1	.900	0	58	4	0	92	93	27	55	0	3.61
Horacio Ramirez (LJ-RJ)	L	26	5	5	.500	0	14	14	0	76	85	31	37	0	4.48
Macay McBride (AJ)	L	23	4	1	.800	1	71	0	0	57	53	32	46	0	3.65
Lance Cormier	R	25	4	4	.500	0	29	9	0	74	90	39	43	0	4.89
Kyle Davies (GJ)	R	22	3	7	.300	0	14	14	1	63	90	33	51	0	8.38
1 Jorge Sosa	R	29	3	10	.231	0	26	13	0	87	105	32	58	0	5.46
Chad Paronto	R	30	2	3	.400	0	65	0	0	57	53	19	41	0	3.18
Mike Remlinger	L	40	2	4	.333	2	36	0	0	22	27	19	19	0	4.03
Tyler Yates	R	28	2	5	.286	1	56	0	0	50	42	31	46	0	3.96
John Thomson (SJ)	R	32	2	7	.222	0	18	15	0	80	93	32	46	0	4.82
Ken Ray	R	31	1	1	.500	5	69	0	0	68	66	38	50	0	5.61
Kevin Barry	R	27	1	0	1.000	0	8	1	0	26	24	14	19	0	5.61
Chris Reitsma (EJ)	R	28	1	2	.333	8	27	0	0	28	46	8	13	0	8.68
Peter Moylan	R	27	0	0	—	0	15	0	0	15	18	5	14	0	4.80
Wayne Franklin	L	32	0	0	—	0	11	0	0	11	9	5	10	0	7.04
Joey Devine (LJ)	R	22	0	0	—	0	10	0	0	4	8	9	10	0	9.95
Phil Stockman (LJ)	R	26	0	0	—	0	4	0	0	4	3	4	9	0	2.25
Anthony Lerew	R	23	0	0	—	0	2	0	0	4	1	0	1	0	22.50
Blaine Boyer (SJ)	R	24	0	0	—	0	1	0	0	2	4	1	0	0	40.50
2 Danys Baez (IL)	R	28	0	0	—	0	10	7	0	10	7	6	10	0	5.40
Travis Smith	R	33	0	1	.000	0	4	0	0	4	5	1	1	0	4.15
2 Bob Wickman	R	37	0	0	.000	18	20	0	0	24	24	2	25	0	1.04
Jason Shiell	R	29	0	0	.000	0	4	3	0	16	19	3	14	0	8.62
John Foster (EJ) 28 Mike Hampton (EJ) 33															

FLORIDA — 4th 78-84 .481 19 — JOE GIRARDI

Name	G by Pos	B	AGE	G	AB	R	H	2B	3B	HR	RBI	BB	SO	SB	BA	SA
TOTALS			26	162	5502	759	1454	309	42	182	713	497	1249	110	.264	.435
Mike Jacobs	1B124	L	25	136	469	54	123	37	1	20	77	45	105	3	.262	.473
Dan Uggla	2B151	R	26	154	611	105	172	26	7	27	90	48	123	6	.282	.480
Hanley Ramirez	SS154	R	22	158	633	119	185	46	11	17	59	56	128	51	.292	.480
Miguel Cabrera	3B157	R	23	158	576	112	195	50	2	26	114	86	108	9	.339	.568
Jeremy Hermida (PJ)	OF89	L	22	99	307	37	77	19	1	5	28	33	70	4	.251	.368
Reggie Abercrombie	OF93	R	25	111	255	39	54	12	2	5	24	18	78	6	.212	.333
Josh Willingham	OF132 C2 1B2	R	27	142	502	62	139	28	2	26	74	54	109	2	.277	.496
Miguel Olivo	C124 1B5	R	27	127	430	52	113	22	3	16	58	9	103	2	.263	.440
Wes Helms	1B88 3B24 OF1	R	30	140	240	30	79	19	5	10	47	21	55	0	.329	.575
Alfredo Amezaga	OF78 2B23 SS11 3B4 1B2	B	28	132	334	42	87	9	3	3	19	24	46	20	.260	.332
2 Joe Borchard	OF63 1B1	B	27	108	230	30	53	7	1	10	28	28	66	0	.230	.400
3 Cody Ross	OF79	R	25	91	250	30	53	11	1	11	37	22	51	5	.212	.396
Matt Treanor	C61	R	30	67	157	12	36	6	1	2	14	19	34	0	.229	.318
Chris Aguila	OF31	R	27	47	95	5	22	8	1	0	7	3	26	2	.232	.337
Eric Reed	OF32	L	25	42	41	6	4	0	0	0	0	2	10	3	.098	.098
Jason Wood	1B5 2B1	R	36	22	13	3	6	2	0	0	1	1	2	0	.462	.615
Robert Andino	SS9	R	22	11	24	0	4	1	0	0	5	0	8	0	.167	.208
Matt Cepicky	OF6	L	28	9	18	0	2	1	0	0	0	0	0	0	.111	.111
Paul Hoover	C3	R	30	4	5	0	2	0	0	0	2	0	0	0	.400	.400

NAME	T	AGE	W	L	PCT	SV	G	GS	CG	IP	H	BB	SO	SHO	ERA
		25	78	84	.481	41	162	162	6	1433	1465	622	1088	6	4.37
Josh Johnson	R	22	12	7	.632	0	31	24	0	157	136	68	133	0	3.10
Scott Olsen	L	22	12	10	.545	0	31	31	0	181	160	75	166	0	4.04
Dontrelle Willis	L	24	12	12	.500	0	34	34	4	223	234	83	160	1	3.87
Ricky Nolasco	R	23	11	11	.500	0	35	22	0	140	157	41	99	0	4.82
Anibal Sanchez	R	22	10	3	.769	0	18	17	2	114	90	46	72	1	2.83
Brian Moehler	R	34	7	11	.389	0	29	21	0	122	164	38	58	0	6.57
Joe Borowski	R	35	3	3	.500	36	72	0	0	70	63	33	64	0	3.75
Taylor Tankersley	L	23	3	1	.667	3	49	0	0	41	33	26	46	0	2.85
Matt Herges	R	36	2	3	.400	0	66	0	0	71	94	28	36	0	4.31
Randy Messenger	R	24	2	7	.222	0	59	0	0	60	72	24	45	0	5.67
Yusmeiro Petit	R	21	1	1	.500	0	15	1	0	26	46	9	20	0	9.57
Jason Vargas	L	23	1	2	.333	0	6	5	0	43	50	30	25	0	7.33
Chris Resop	R	23	2	2	.333	0	22	0	0	26	16	10	33	0	3.38
Logan Kensing (WJ)	R	23	1	3	.250	1	37	0	0	38	30	19	45	0	4.54
Sergio Mitre (SJ)	R	25	1	5	.167	0	15	7	0	51	51	17	36	0	5.71
Renyel Pinto	L	23	0	0	—	0	27	0	0	30	20	27	36	0	3.03
Franklyn German	R	26	0	0	—	0	7	0	0	5	7	14	6	0	9.00
Jose Garcia	R	21	0	0	—	0	5	0	0	11	10	5	8	0	4.91
Jeff Fulchino	R	26	0	0	—	0	1	0	0	0.1	0	1	0	0	0.00
Carlos Martinez (EJ)	R	24	0	0	—	0	5	0	0	6	8	6	11	0	7.14
1 Todd Wellemeyer	R	27	0	2	.000	0	18	0	0	21	20	13	17	0	5.48

WASHINGTON — 5th 71-91 .438 26 — FRANK ROBINSON

Name	G by Pos	B	AGE	G	AB	R	H	2B	3B	HR	RBI	BB	SO	SB	BA	SA
TOTALS			29	162	5495	746	1437	322	22	164	695	594	1156	123	.262	.418
Nick Johnson	1B147	L	27	147	500	100	145	46	6	23	77	110	99	10	.290	.520
Jose Vidro (LJ)	2B107 1B8	B	31	126	463	52	134	26	1	7	47	41	48	1	.289	.395
1 Royce Clayton	SS86	R	36	87	305	36	82	22	1	0	27	19	53	6	.269	.348
Ryan Zimmerman	3B157	R	21	157	614	84	176	47	3	20	110	61	120	11	.287	.471
Jose Guillen (EJ)	OF68	R	30	69	241	28	52	15	1	9	40	15	48	1	.216	.398
Marlon Byrd	OF71	R	28	78	197	28	44	8	1	5	18	22	47	3	.223	.350
Alfonso Soriano	OF158	R	30	159	647	119	179	41	2	46	95	67	160	41	.277	.560
Brian Schneider	C123 1B1	L	29	124	410	30	105	18	0	4	55	38	67	2	.256	.329
1 Marlon Anderson	2B32 OF17 1B2	L	32	109	215	31	59	13	2	5	23	18	41	2	.274	.423
1 Daryle Ward	OF12 1B6	L	31	78	104	15	32	9	0	6	19	14	21	0	.308	.567
2 Felipe Lopez	SS71	B	26	71	274	43	77	13	2	2	22	34	60	21	.281	.365
Ryan Church	OF62	L	27	71	196	22	54	17	1	10	35	26	60	6	.276	.526
Damian Jackson	OF26 SS16 2B11 3B6	R	32	67	116	16	23	6	1	4	10	12	39	1	.198	.371
2 Austin Kearns	OF60	R	26	63	212	33	53	12	1	8	36	41	50	2	.250	.429
Robert Fick (EJ)	C26 1B13 OF6	L	32	60	128	14	34	4	0	2	9	10	24	1	.266	.344
Bernie Castro	2B29 OF2	B	26	42	110	18	25	1	3	0	10	9	18	7	.227	.291
Matt LeCroy	C13 1B6	R	30	39	67	5	16	3	0	2	9	11	17	0	.239	.373
Alex Escobar (LJ-SJ)	OF23	R	27	33	87	14	31	3	2	4	18	8	18	2	.356	.575
Nook Logan	OF26	B	26	27	90	13	27	3	1	1	8	6	20	2	.300	.389
Henry Mateo	SS3 3B2 OF1	R	29	22	26	5	4	2	0	1	3	2	3	0	.154	.346
George Lombard	OF8	L	30	20	21	2	3	0	0	1	1	5	10	2	.143	.286
Brandon Harper	C14	R	30	18	41	6	12	3	0	2	6	4	4	0	.293	.512
1 Brendan Harris	SS5 2B4 3B3	R	25	17	32	3	8	2	0	0	2	3	3	0	.250	.313
Melvin Dorta	3B3 SS3	B	24	15	19	3	4	1	0	0	0	1	2	0	.211	.263
2 Luis Matos	OF4	R	27	14	15	2	3	2	0	0	0	0	2	0	.200	.333
Wiki Gonzalez	C12	R	32	12	35	3	8	0	0	0	4	1	5	0	.229	.229
2 Brandon Watson	OF8	L	24	9	28	0	5	0	0	0	0	1	3	0	.179	.179
Mike Vento	OF8	R	28	9	18	3	5	1	0	0	1	0	5	0	.278	.333

Cristian Guzman (SJ) 28

NAME	T	AGE	W	L	PCT	SV	G	GS	CG	IP	H	BB	SO	SHO	ERA
TOTALS		29	71	91	.438	32	162	162	1	1436	1535	584	960	3	5.03
Ramon Ortiz	R	33	11	16	.407	0	33	33	0	191	230	64	104	0	5.57
1 Livan Hernandez	R	31	9	8	.529	0	24	24	0	147	176	52	89	0	5.34
Tony Armas	R	28	9	12	.429	0	30	30	0	154	167	64	97	0	5.03
Chad Cordero	R	24	7	4	.636	29	68	0	0	73	59	22	69	0	3.19
Pedro Astacio (AJ)	R	36	5	5	.500	0	17	17	1	90	109	31	42	1	5.98
Billy Traber	L	26	4	3	.571	0	15	8	0	43	53	14	25	0	6.44
Jon Rauch	R	27	4	5	.444	2	85	0	0	91	78	36	86	0	3.35
Saul Rivera	R	28	3	0	1.000	1	54	0	0	60	59	32	41	0	3.43
1 Gary Majewski	R	26	3	2	.600	0	46	0	0	55	49	25	34	0	3.58
Ryan Wagner	R	23	3	3	.500	0	26	0	0	31	36	15	20	0	4.70
1 Mike Stanton	L	39	3	5	.375	0	56	0	0	44	47	21	30	0	4.47
Mike O'Connor	L	25	3	8	.273	0	21	20	0	105	96	45	59	0	4.80
Beltran Perez	R	24	2	1	.667	0	8	3	0	21	16	13	9	0	3.86
Felix Rodriguez (SJ)	R	33	1	1	.500	0	31	0	0	29	32	16	15	0	7.67
1 Bill Bray	L	23	1	1	.500	0	19	0	0	23	24	9	16	0	3.91
John Patterson (AJ)	R	28	1	2	.333	0	8	8	0	41	36	9	42	0	4.43
Shawn Hill (EJ)	R	25	1	3	.250	0	6	6	0	37	43	12	16	0	4.66
2 Zach Day (EJ)	R	28	1	3	.250	0	5	5	0	27	29	11	13	0	4.72
Travis Hughes	R	28	0	0	—	0	11	0	0	11	13	6	4	0	6.35
3 Chris Booker	R	29	0	0	—	0	10	0	0	7	5	1	7	0	3.68
Kevin Gryboski	R	32	0	0	—	0	6	0	0	6	14	2	4	0	14.29
Brett Campbell	R	24	0	0	—	0	4	0	0	4	4	2	4	0	10.38
Santiago Ramirez (EJ)	R	27	0	0	—	0	4	0	0	4	4	2	4	0	8.10
Micah Bowie (SJ)	R	31	0	1	.000	0	15	0	0	20	11	7	11	0	1.37
Joey Eischen (EJ)	L	36	0	1	.000	0	22	0	0	15	18	19	18	0	8.59
Roy Corcoran	R	26	0	1	.000	0	6	0	0	6	12	4	6	0	11.12
Jason Bergmann	R	24	0	2	.000	0	29	6	0	65	81	27	54	0	6.68
Chris Schroder	R	27	0	2	.000	0	21	0	0	28	23	15	39	0	6.35
Ryan Drese (EJ)	R	30	0	2	.000	0	2	2	0	9	9	8	5	0	5.19

Luis Ayala (EJ) 28   Brian Lawrence (SJ) 30

CENTRAL DIVISION

ST. LOUIS — 1st 83-78 .516 — TONY LA RUSSA

Name	G by Pos	B	AGE	G	AB	R	H	2B	3B	HR	RBI	BB	SO	SB	BA	SA
TOTALS			30	161	5522	781	1484	292	27	184	745	531	922	59	.269	.431
Albert Pujols	1B143	R	26	143	535	119	177	33	1	49	137	92	50	7	.331	.671
Aaron Miles	2B88 SS39 3B1	B	29	135	426	48	112	20	5	2	30	38	42	2	.263	.347
David Eckstein (UJ)	SS120	R	31	123	500	68	146	18	1	2	23	31	41	7	.292	.344
Scott Rolen	3B142	R	31	142	521	94	154	48	1	22	95	56	69	7	.296	.518
Juan Encarnacion	OF148	R	30	153	557	74	155	25	5	19	79	30	86	6	.278	.443
Jim Edmonds	OF99 1B6	L	36	110	350	52	90	18	0	19	70	53	101	4	.257	.471
Chris Duncan	OF70 1B14	L	25	90	280	60	82	11	3	22	43	30	69	0	.293	.589
Yadier Molina	C127 1B4	R	23	129	417	29	90	26	0	6	49	26	41	1	.216	.321
So Taguchi	OF123 2B1	R	36	134	316	46	84	19	1	2	31	32	48	11	.266	.351
Scott Spiezio	3B38 OF35 1B13 2B8	B	33	119	276	44	75	15	4	13	52	37	66	1	.272	.496
John Rodriguez	OF51	L	28	102	183	31	55	12	3	2	19	21	45	0	.301	.443
1 Hector Luna	2B41 OF18 SS14 1B6 3B2	R	26	76	222	27	65	14	1	4	21	21	34	5	.291	.417
Gary Bennett	C56 1B1	R	34	60	157	13	35	5	0	4	22	11	30	0	.223	.331
2 Ron Belliard	2B54	R	31	54	194	20	46	9	1	5	23	15	36	0	.237	.371
Jason Marquis	P33	R	27	45	78	8	14	4	1	0	5	2	14	0	.179	.256
2 Preston Wilson	OF28	R	31	33	111	18	27	3	0	8	17	7	27	6	.243	.486
Skip Schumaker	OF25	L	26	28	54	3	10	1	0	1	2	5	9	2	.185	.259
Timo Perez	OF7	L	31	23	31	3	6	1	0	1	3	3	4	0	.194	.323
Larry Bigbie (LJ-GJ)	OF12	L	28	17	25	2	6	1	0	0	1	3	9	0	.240	.280
2 Jose Vizcaino	SS7 2B2 1B1	B	38	16	23	3	8	3	0	1	3	1	4	0	.348	.609
Mike Rose	C4	R	29	10	9	0	2	0	0	0	1	0	4	0	.222	.222
John Gall	OF2 1B1	R	28	8	12	1	3	0	0	0	1	0	3	0	.250	.250
John Nelson	1B1 SS1	R	27	8	5	2	0	0	0	0	0	0	4	0	.000	.000

NAME	T	AGE	W	L	PCT	SV	G	GS	CG	IP	H	BB	SO	SHO	ERA
TOTALS		28	83	78	.516	38	161	161	0	1430	1475	504	970	9	4.54
Chris Carpenter	R	31	15	8	.652	0	32	32	5	222	194	43	184	3	3.09
Jason Marquis	R	27	14	16	.467	0	33	33	0	194	221	75	96	0	6.02
Jeff Suppan	R	31	12	7	.632	0	32	32	0	190	207	69	104	0	4.12
Braden Looper	R	31	9	3	.750	0	69	0	0	73	76	20	41	0	3.56
Mark Mulder (SJ)	L	28	6	7	.462	0	17	17	0	93	124	35	50	0	7.14
2 Jeff Weaver	R	29	4	4	.556	0	15	15	0	83	99	26	45	0	5.18
Anthony Reyes	R	24	5	8	.385	0	17	17	1	85	84	34	72	0	5.06
1 Sidney Ponson	R	29	4	4	.500	0	14	13	0	69	82	29	33	0	5.24
Jason Isringhausen	R	33	4	8	.333	33	59	0	0	58	47	38	52	0	3.55
Josh Hancock	R	28	3	3	.500	1	62	0	0	77	70	23	50	0	4.09
Adam Wainwright	R	24	2	1	.667	3	61	0	0	75	64	22	72	0	3.12
Tyler Johnson	L	25	4	3	.571	0	56	0	0	36	33	23	37	0	4.95
Randy Flores	L	30	1	1	.500	0	65	0	0	42	49	22	40	0	5.62
Brad Thompson	R	24	1	2	.333	0	43	1	0	57	58	20	32	0	3.34
Josh Kinney	R	27	1	0	1.000	0	21	0	0	25	17	8	22	0	3.24
Chris Narveson	L	24	0	0	—	0	5	1	0	9	6	5	12	0	4.82
Ricardo Rincon (SJ)	L	36	0	0	—	0	23	0	0	15	11	6	11	0	10.80
2 Jorge Sosa	R	29	0	1	.000	1	19	0	0	31	33	8	17	0	5.28
Brian Falkenborg	R	28	0	0	—	0	5	0	0	6	5	0	5	0	2.84

HOUSTON — 2nd 82-80 .506 1.5 — PHIL GARNER

Name	G by Pos	B	AGE	G	AB	R	H	2B	3B	HR	RBI	BB	SO	SB	BA	SA
TOTALS			30	162	5535	735	1407	275	27	174	708	585	1076	79	.255	.409
Lance Berkman	1B112 OF44	B	30	152	536	95	169	29	0	45	136	98	106	3	.315	.621
Craig Biggio	2B129	R	40	145	548	79	135	33	0	21	62	40	84	3	.246	.422
Adam Everett	SS149	R	29	150	514	52	123	28	6	6	59	34	71	9	.239	.352
Morgan Ensberg	3B117	R	30	127	387	67	91	17	1	23	58	101	96	1	.235	.463
Jason Lane	OF98 1B1	R	29	112	288	44	58	10	0	15	45	49	75	1	.201	.392
Willy Taveras	OF138	R	24	149	529	83	147	19	5	1	30	34	88	33	.278	.338
1 Preston Wilson	OF100	R	31	102	390	40	105	22	2	9	55	22	94	6	.269	.405
Brad Ausmus	C138 2B2 1B1	R	37	139	439	37	101	16	1	2	39	45	71	3	.230	.285
Mike Lamb	1B68 3B36 2B2	L	30	126	381	70	117	22	3	12	45	35	55	2	.307	.475
Chris Burke	2B69 OF61 SS8	R	26	133	366	58	101	23	1	9	40	27	77	11	.276	.418
Orlando Palmeiro	OF23	L	37	103	119	12	30	6	1	0	17	6	17	0	.252	.319
Eric Bruntlett	2B23 OF18 3B2	R	28	73	119	11	33	8	0	0	10	13	21	3	.277	.345
2 Aubrey Huff	OF37 3B30 1B3	L	29	68	224	31	56	10	1	13	38	26	39	0	.250	.478
Luke Scott	OF60	L	28	65	214	31	72	19	6	10	37	30	43	2	.336	.621
Eric Munson	C37 1B4	L	28	53	141	10	28	6	0	5	19	11	32	0	.199	.348
Charlton Jimerson	OF9	R	26	17	6	2	0	0	0	1	1	0	4	0	.333	.833
Humberto Quintero	C10	R	26	11	21	2	7	2	0	0	2	1	5	0	.333	.429
Joe McEwing	2B2	R	33	7	6	0	0	0	0	0	0	0	1	0	.000	.000
J.R. House	C3 1B2	R	26	4	9	0	0	0	0	0	0	0	2	0	.000	.000
Hector Gimenez		B	23	1	0	0	0	0	0	0	0	0	0	0	.000	.000

Jeff Bagwell (SJ) 38

NAME	T	AGE	W	L	PCT	SV	G	GS	CG	IP	H	BB	SO	SHO	ERA
TOTALS		30	82	80	.506	42	162	162	5	1469	1425	480	1160	12	4.09
Roy Oswalt	R	28	15	8	.652	0	33	32	2	221	220	38	166	0	2.98
Andy Pettitte	L	34	14	13	.519	0	36	35	2	214	238	70	178	1	4.20
Wandy Rodriguez	L	27	9	10	.474	0	30	24	0	136	154	63	98	0	5.64
Chad Qualls	R	27	7	3	.700	0	81	0	0	89	76	28	56	0	3.76
Roger Clemens (VR)	R	43	7	6	.538	0	19	19	0	113	89	29	102	0	2.30
Taylor Buchholz	R	24	6	10	.375	0	22	19	1	113	107	34	77	1	5.89
Dave Borkowski	R	29	3	2	.600	0	40	0	0	71	70	23	52	0	4.69
Brandon Backe (EJ)	R	28	3	2	.600	0	8	8	0	43	43	18	19	0	5.73
Fernando Nieve	R	23	3	3	.500	0	40	11	0	96	87	41	70	0	4.20
Jason Hirsh	R	24	3	4	.429	0	9	9	0	45	44	22	29	0	6.04
Dan Wheeler	R	28	3	5	.375	9	75	0	0	71	58	24	68	0	2.52
Ezequiel Astacio	R	26	2	0	1.000	0	8	7	0	6	7	6	7	0	11.12
Chris Sampson	R	28	2	1	.667	0	12	3	0	34	25	5	15	0	2.12
Trever Miller	L	33	2	3	.400	1	70	0	0	51	42	13	56	0	3.02
Russ Springer	R	37	1	1	.500	0	72	0	0	60	46	16	46	0	3.47
Mike Gallo	L	29	1	2	.333	0	23	0	0	16	28	7	7	0	6.06
Brad Lidge	R	29	1	5	.167	32	78	0	0	75	69	36	104	0	5.28
Philip Barzilla	R	27	0	0	—	0	4	0	0	0.1	0	1	0	0	0.00
Matt Albers	R	23	0	2	.000	0	4	2	0	15	17	7	11	0	6.00

CINCINNATI — 3rd 80-82 .494 3.5 — JERRY NARRON

Name	G by Pos	B	AGE	G	AB	R	H	2B	3B	HR	RBI	BB	SO	SB	BA	SA
TOTALS			29	162	5515	749	1419	291	12	217	718	614	1192	124	.257	.432
Scott Hatteberg	1B131	L	36	141	456	62	132	28	0	13	51	74	41	2	.289	.436
Brandon Phillips	2B142 SS3	R	25	149	536	65	148	28	1	17	75	35	88	25	.276	.427
1 Felipe Lopez	SS84	B	26	85	349	55	92	14	1	9	30	47	66	23	.268	.394
Edwin Encarnacion	3B111 1B2	R	23	117	406	60	112	33	1	15	72	41	70	6	.276	.473
1 Austin Kearns	OF85	R	26	87	325	53	89	21	1	16	50	35	85	5	.274	.492
Ken Griffey Jr.	OF100	R	36	109	428	62	108	19	0	27	72	39	78	0	.252	.486
Adam Dunn	OF156 1B2	L	26	160	561	99	131	24	0	40	92	112	194	7	.234	.490
David Ross	C75	R	29	90	247	37	63	15	1	21	52	37	75	0	.255	.579
Ryan Freel	OF105 2B13 3B13	R	30	132	454	67	123	30	2	8	27	57	98	37	.271	.399
Rich Aurilia	3B52 1B47 SS26 2B10	R	34	122	440	61	132	25	1	23	70	34	51	3	.300	.518
Javier Valentin	C46 1B2	B	30	92	186	24	50	6	1	8	27	13	29	0	.269	.441
Jason LaRue	C63	R	32	52	191	22	37	5	0	8	21	27	51	1	.194	.346
2 Juan Castro	SS27 3B20 2B1	R	34	54	95	8	27	5	1	2	14	5	13	0	.284	.421
2 Royce Clayton	SS43	R	36	50	149	13	35	8	0	2	13	11	32	6	.235	.329
Chris Denorfia	OF37	R	25	49	106	14	30	6	0	1	7	11	21	1	.283	.368
Quinton McCracken	OF15	B	36	45	53	5	11	1	1	1	7	3	9	2	.208	.321
2 Todd Hollandsworth	OF20	L	33	34	68	6	18	6	0	2	6	8	19	0	.265	.397
Dewayne Wise	OF15	B	28	31	38	3	7	2	0	0	6	1	9	1	.184	.237
Ray Olmedo	2B5 SS4 3B3 OF1	B	25	30	44	5	9	2	0	1	4	1	9	1	.205	.318
Norris Hopper	OF15	R	27	21	39	6	14	1	0	1	3	2	4	2	.359	.462
1 Tony Womack	2B5	L	36	9	11	2	3	0	0	0	2	0	3	0	.222	.500
2 Brendan Harris	2B3	R	25	9	10	2	2	1	0	0	1	1	4	0	.200	.500
Andy Abad		L	33	5	4	0	0	0	0	0	0	1	1	0	.000	.000
2 Cody Ross	OF1	R	25	2	2	1	0	0	0	0	0	0	1	0	.200	.200
2 Brandon Watson		L	24	1	5	0	0	0	0	0	0	0	0	0	—	—

NAME	T	AGE	W	L	PCT	SV	G	GS	CG	IP	H	BB	SO	SHO	ERA
TOTALS		31	80	82	.494	36	162	162	9	1446	1576	464	1053	10	4.53
Aaron Harang	R	28	16	11	.593	0	36	35	6	234	242	56	216	2	3.76
Bronson Arroyo	R	29	14	11	.560	0	35	35	3	241	222	64	184	1	3.29
Eric Milton (KJ)	L	30	8	8	.500	0	26	26	0	153	163	42	90	0	5.19
Todd Coffey	R	25	6	7	.462	0	81	0	0	78	85	27	60	0	3.58
2 Ryan Franklin	R	33	5	2	.714	0	20	0	0	24	27	16	18	0	4.44
David Weathers	R	36	4	4	.500	12	67	0	0	74	61	34	50	0	3.54
Elizardo Ramirez	R	23	4	9	.308	0	21	19	0	104	123	29	69	0	5.37
2 Kyle Lohse	R	27	3	5	.375	0	12	11	0	63	70	19	51	0	4.57
Brandon Claussen (SJ)	R	27	2	3	.273	0	14	11	0	77	93	28	57	0	6.19
Matt Belisle (XJ)	R	26	2	0	1.000	0	30	2	0	40	43	19	26	0	3.60
2 Scott Schoeneweis	L	32	2	0	1.000	3	16	0	0	14	8	8	11	0	0.63
2 Bill Bray	R	23	1	1	.667	0	28	0	0	28	33	9	23	0	4.23
David Williams	L	27	2	3	.400	0	14	14	0	54	62	16	16	0	7.20
Chris Michalak	L	35	4	0	1.000	0	36	0	0	35	42	16	10	0	4.89
1 Rick White	R	37	1	0	1.000	0	26	0	0	27	16	10	15	0	6.26
Brian Shackelford	L	29	1	0	1.000	0	16	0	0	16	19	10	15	0	7.16
2 Esteban Yan	R	31	1	0	1.000	0	19	0	0	19	22	9	13	0	3.60
Chris Hammond	L	40	1	0	1.000	0	29	0	0	36	42	16	23	0	6.91
Kent Mercker (EJ)	L	38	1	1	.500	1	37	0	0	28	28	11	17	0	4.13
Jason Standridge	R	27	1	1	.500	0	21	0	0	19	17	14	18	0	4.82
2 Gary Majewski	R	26	1	2	.333	0	19	0	0	14	23	13	11	0	8.40
2 Eddie Guardado (EJ)	L	35	0	0	—	0	15	0	0	14	15	2	17	0	1.29
Mike Burns	R	27	0	0	—	0	11	0	0	13	30	7	9	0	8.78
2 Jason Johnson	R	32	0	1	.000	0	4	1	0	11	11	6	3	0	3.12
Mike Gosling	L	26	0	1	.000	0	4	0	0	4	5	6	4	0	13.50
2 Joe Mays	R	30	0	2	.000	0	8	8	0	34	43	10	20	0	7.33
2 Rheal Cormier (EJ)	L	39	0	0	—	0	21	0	0	14	21	4	6	0	4.50
Justin Germano	R	23	0	0	—	0	5	1	0	7	13	0	4	0	5.40
2 Sun-Woo Kim	R	28	0	0	—	0	7	0	0	7	8	4	6	0	5.40

Grant Balfour (EJ) 28   Paul Wilson (SJ) 33

MILWAUKEE — 4th 75-87 .463 8.5 — NED YOST

Batting

Name	G by Pos	B	AGE	G	AB	R	H	2B	3B	HR	RBI	BB	SO	SB	BA	SA
TOTALS			30	162	5433	730	1400	301	20	180	695	502	1233	71	.258	.420
Prince Fielder	1B152	L	22	157	569	82	154	35	1	28	81	59	125	7	.271	.483
Rickie Weeks (WJ)	2B92	R	23	95	359	73	100	15	3	8	34	30	92	19	.279	.404
Bill Hall	SS127 3B11 OF7 2B4	R	26	148	537	101	145	39	4	35	85	63	162	8	.270	.553
Corey Koskie (CN)	3B70	L	33	76	257	29	67	23	0	12	33	29	58	1	.261	.490
Geoff Jenkins	OF133	L	31	147	484	62	131	26	1	17	70	56	129	4	.271	.434
Brady Clark	OF119	R	33	138	415	51	109	14	2	4	29	43	60	3	.263	.335
Carlos Lee	OF98	R	30	102	388	60	111	18	0	28	81	38	71	12	.286	.549
Damian Miller	C98	R	36	101	331	34	83	28	0	6	38	33	86	0	.251	.390
Gabe Gross	OF59	L	26	117	208	42	57	15	0	9	38	36	60	1	.274	.476
Jeff Cirillo	3B42 1B13 2B12 SS3	R	36	112	263	33	84	16	0	3	23	21	33	1	.319	.414
Corey Hart	OF61 1B2	R	24	87	237	32	67	13	2	9	33	17	58	5	.283	.468
Tony Graffanino	2B57 SS4	R	34	60	236	34	66	17	3	2	27	20	37	3	.280	.403
David Bell	3B53	R	33	53	180	21	46	10	2	4	29	18	30	2	.256	.400
Mike Rivera	C44	R	29	46	142	16	38	9	0	6	24	10	21	0	.268	.458
Kevin Mench	OF38	R	28	40	126	9	29	6	1	1	18	4	17	0	.230	.317
J.J. Hardy	SS32	R	23	35	128	13	31	5	0	5	14	10	23	1	.242	.398
Tony Gwynn	OF19	L	23	32	77	5	20	2	1	0	4	2	15	3	.260	.312
Chad Moeller	C29	R	31	29	98	9	18	3	0	2	5	4	26	0	.184	.276
Chris Barnwell	SS5 2B3 3B3	R	27	13	30	2	2	0	0	1	1	1	6	1	.067	.067
Laynce Nix	OF9	L	25	10	35	2	8	1	0	1	6	0	11	0	.229	.343
Vinny Rottino	3B3 OF2 C1	R	26	9	14	1	3	1	0	0	1	1	2	1	.214	.286
Drew Anderson	OF2	L	25	9	9	3	1	0	0	0	0	1	4	0	.111	.111

Pitching

NAME	T	AGE	W	L	PCT	SV	G	GS	CG	IP	H	BB	SO	SHO	ERA
		29	75	87	.463	43	162	162	7	1426	1454	514	1145	8	4.83
Dave Bush	R	26	12	11	.522	0	34	32	3	210	201	38	166	2	4.41
Doug Davis	L	30	11	11	.500	0	34	34	1	203	206	102	159	1	4.91
Chris Capuano	L	27	11	12	.478	0	34	34	3	221	229	47	174	2	4.03
Ben Sheets (SJ)	R	27	6	7	.462	0	17	17	0	106	105	11	116	0	3.82
Matt Wise (EJ)	R	30	5	6	.455	0	40	0	0	44	45	14	27	0	3.86
Jose Capellan	R	25	4	2	.667	0	61	0	0	72	65	31	58	0	4.40
2 Jeremi Gonzalez	R	31	4	2	.667	0	21	1	0	42	50	17	36	0	5.14
Tomo Ohka	R	30	4	5	.444	0	18	18	0	97	98	35	50	0	4.82
Derrick Turnbow	R	28	4	9	.308	24	64	0	0	56	56	39	69	0	6.87
2 Francisco Cordero	R	31	3	1	.750	16	28	0	0	27	20	16	30	0	1.69
Justin Lehr	R	28	2	1	.667	0	16			24		7	12		8.62
Carlos Villanueva	R	22	2	2	.500	0	10	6	0	54	43	11	39	0	3.69
Danny Kolb	R	31	2	2	.500	1	53	0	0	48	53	20	26	0	4.84
Zach Jackson	L	23	2	2	.500	0	8	7	0	38	48	14	22	0	5.40
1 Jorge de la Rosa (RJ)	L	25	2	2	.500	0	18	3	0	30	32	22	31	0	8.60
2 Brian Shouse	L	37	1	3	.250	2	59	0	0	34	34	17	20	0	3.97
2 Chris Spurling	R	29	0	0	—	0	7	0	0	10	12	4	3	0	7.20
Dennis Sarfate	R	25	0	0	—	0	8	0	0	9	8	4	11	0	4.32
Jared Fernandez	R	34	0	0	—	0	6	1	0	6	11	1	1	0	9.95
Allan Simpson	R	28	0	0	—	0	2	0	0	3	1	4	5	0	3.37
Mike Adams	R	27	0	0	—	0	2	0	0	2	4	2	1	0	11.57
Chris Mabeus	R	27	0	0	—	0	1	0	0	2	4	3	2	0	21.60
Chris Demaria	R	25	0	1	.000	0	10	0	0	14	10	9	11	0	5.93
Joe Winkelsas	R	32	0	1	.000	0	7	0	0	7	9	4	4	0	7.71
Rick Helling (EJ)	R	35	0	2	.000	0	20	2	0	35	25	15	32	0	4.11
Ben Hendrickson	R	25	0	2	.000	0	4	3	0	12	21	9	8	0	12.00
Dana Eveland	L	22	0	3	.000	0	9	5	0	28	39	16	32	0	8.13

PITTSBURGH — 5th 67-95 .414 16.5 — JIM TRACY

Batting

Name	G by Pos	B	AGE	G	AB	R	H	2B	3B	HR	RBI	BB	SO	SB	BA	SA
TOTALS			28	162	5558	691	1462	286	17	141	656	459	1200	68	.263	.397
Sean Casey (XJ)	1B55	L	31	59	213	30	63	15	0	3	29	23	22	0	.296	.408
Jose Castillo	2B145	R	25	142	518	54	131	25	0	14	65	32	98	6	.253	.382
Jack Wilson	SS131	R	28	142	543	70	148	27	1	8	35	33	65	4	.273	.370
Freddy Sanchez	3B99 SS28 2B23	R	27	157	582	85	200	53	2	6	85	31	52	3	.344	.473
Jeromy Burnitz	OF84	L	37	111	313	35	72	12	0	16	49	22	74	1	.230	.422
Chris Duffy	OF77	L	26	84	314	46	80	14	3	2	18	19	71	26	.255	.338
Jason Bay	OF157	R	27	159	570	101	163	29	3	35	109	102	156	11	.286	.532
Ronny Paulino	C124	R	25	129	442	37	137	19	0	6	55	34	79	0	.310	.394
Jose Bautista	OF85 3B33 2B3	R	25	117	400	58	94	20	3	16	51	46	110	2	.235	.420
Nate McLouth (NJ)	OF75	L	24	106	270	36	63	16	2	7	16	18	59	10	.233	.385
Joe Randa (FJ)	3B42 1B15	R	36	89	206	23	55	13	0	4	28	16	26	0	.267	.388
Craig Wilson	OF29	R	29	85	235	38	68	11	2	13	41	24	88	1	.267	.419
Jose Hernandez	1B18 OF10 SS9 3B4 2B3	R	36	67	120	8	32	2	1	2	12	11	29	0	.267	.350
Ryan Doumit (LJ)	1B28 C11	R	25	54	149	15	31	9	0	6	17	15	42	0	.208	.389
2 Xavier Nady	1B34 OF28	R	27	55	203	20	61	13	0	3	23	11	34	1	.300	.409
Humberto Cota	C33	R	27	38	100	5	19	1	0	0	5	8	26	0	.190	.200
Rajai Davis	OF1	R	25	20	14	1	2	1	0	0	0	2	3	1	.143	.214
Mike Edwards	3B3	R	29	14	16	1	3	0	0	0	1	0	3	0	.188	.188
Carlos Maldonado	C8	R	27	8	19	0	2	0	0	0	0	1	10	0	.105	.105
Yurendell de Caster		R	26	3	2	0	0	0	0	0	0	0	2	0	.000	.000
Jody Gerut (KJ) 28																

Pitching

NAME	T	AGE	W	L	PCT	SV	G	GS	CG	IP	H	BB	SO	SHO	ERA
		28	67	95	.414	39	162	162	2	1435	1545	620	1060	10	4.55
Ian Snell	R	24	14	11	.560	0	32	32	0	186	198	74	169	0	4.74
Zach Duke	L	23	10	15	.400	0	34	34	2	215	255	68	117	1	4.47
Matt Capps	R	22	9	1	.900	1	85	0	0	81	81	12	56	0	3.79
Paul Maholm	L	24	8	10	.444	0	30	30	0	176	202	81	117	0	4.76
Victor Santos	R	29	5	9	.357	0	25	19	0	115	150	42	81	0	5.70
John Grabow	L	27	4	2	.667	0	72	0	0	70	68	30	66	0	4.13
Mike Gonzalez (AJ)	L	28	3	4	.429	24	54	0	0	54	42	31	64	0	2.17
Salomon Torres	R	34	3	6	.333	12	94	0	0	93	98	38	72	0	3.28
Marty McLeary	R	31	2	0	1.000	0	8	1	0	18	17	6	8	0	2.04
2 Shawn Chacon	R	28	2	3	.400	0	9	9	0	46	47	27	27	0	5.48
Tom Gorzelanny (EJ)	L	23	2	5	.286	0	11	11	0	62	50	31	40	0	3.79
1 Oliver Perez	L	24	2	10	.167	0	15	15	0	76	88	51	61	0	6.63
Jonah Bayliss	R	25	1	1	.500	0	11	0	0	15	11	15	15	0	4.30
1 Kip Wells (IL)	R	29	1	5	.167	0	7	7	0	36	46	18	16	0	6.69
Damaso Marte	L	31	1	7	.125	0	75	0	0	58	51	31	63	0	3.70
Ryan Vogelsong	R	28	0	0	—	0	20	0	0	38	44	16	27	0	6.39
Josh Sharpless	R	25	0	0	—	0	14	0	0	12	7	11	7	0	1.50
Brian Rogers	R	23	0	0	—	0	10	0	0	9	11	2	7	0	8.31
Britt Reames	R	32	0	0	—	0	6	0	0	7	11	5	6	0	9.82
Juan Perez	L	27	0	1	.000	0	7	0	0	3	5	1	3	0	8.10
Shane Youman	L	26	0	2	.000	0	5	3	0	22	15	10	5	0	2.91
1 Roberto Hernandez	R	41	0	3	.000	0	46	0	0	43	46	24	33	0	2.93

CHICAGO — 6th 66-96 .407 17.5 — DUSTY BAKER

Batting

Name	G by Pos	B	AGE	G	AB	R	H	2B	3B	HR	RBI	BB	SO	SB	BA	SA
TOTALS			30	162	5587	716	1496	271	46	166	677	395	928	121	.268	.422
Derrek Lee (BW)	1B47	R	30	50	175	30	50	9	0	8	30	25	41	8	.286	.474
Todd Walker	2B46 1B37	L	33	94	318	38	88	16	1	6	40	38	27	0	.277	.390
Ronny Cedeno	SS134 2B15	R	23	151	534	51	131	18	7	6	41	17	109	8	.245	.384
Aramis Ramirez	3B156	R	28	157	594	93	173	38	4	38	119	50	63	2	.291	.561
Jacque Jones	OF143	L	31	149	533	73	152	31	1	27	81	35	116	9	.285	.499
Juan Pierre	OF162	L	28	162	699	87	204	32	13	3	40	32	38	58	.292	.388
Matt Murton	OF133	R	24	144	455	70	135	22	3	13	62	45	62	5	.297	.444
Michael Barrett	C102	R	29	107	375	54	115	25	3	16	53	33	41	0	.307	.517
John Mabry	1B51 OF11 3B2	L	35	107	210	16	43	8	1	5	25	23	57	0	.205	.324
Neifi Perez	2B53 SS21 3B10	B	33	87	236	27	60	13	1	2	24	5	21	0	.254	.343
Angel Pagan (LJ)	OF58	B	24	77	170	28	42	6	2	5	18	15	28	4	.247	.394
Henry Blanco	C69 1B6	R	34	74	241	23	64	15	2	6	37	14	38	0	.266	.419
Freddie Bynum (SJ)	OF22 2B15	L	26	71	136	20	35	5	5	4	12	9	44	8	.257	.456
2 Phil Nevin	1B38 OF10 C1	R	35	67	179	26	49	4	0	12	33	17	52	0	.274	.453
Ryan Theriot	2B39 SS2 3B1	R	26	53	134	34	44	11	3	1	16	17	19	13	.328	.522
1 Jerry Hairston	2B24 OF8 1B1	R	30	38	82	8	17	3	0	0	4	4	14	3	.207	.244
Carlos Zambrano	P33	R	25	35	73	9	17	2	0	6	11	1	27	1	.151	.397
2 Cesar Izturis	SS21	B	26	22	73	4	17	2	0	0	5	2	4	1	.233	.260
2 Tony Womack	2B16	L	36	19	50	6	14	1	0	0	2	4	4	3	.280	.360
Buck Coats	OF4	L	24	18	18	2	3	1	0	1	1	0	6	0	.167	.389
Scott Moore	1B6 3B5	L	22	16	38	6	10	2	0	2	5	2	10	0	.263	.474
Geovany Soto	C7	R	23	11	25	1	5	1	0	0	1	0	5	0	.200	.240
Michael Restovich	OF3	R	27	10	12	0	2	1	0	0	1	1	5	0	.167	.250
Jose Reyes	C2	B	23	4	5	0	1	0	0	0	1	0	2	0	.200	.200

Pitching

NAME	T	AGE	W	L	PCT	SV	G	GS	CG	IP	H	BB	SO	SHO	ERA
		28	66	96	.407	29	162	162	2	1439	1396	687	1250	7	4.74
Carlos Zambrano	R	25	16	7	.696	0	33	33	0	214	162	115	210	0	3.41
1 Greg Maddux	R	40	9	11	.450	0	22	22	0	136	153	23	81	0	4.69
Rich Hill	L	26	6	7	.462	0	17	16	2	99	83	39	90	1	4.17
Sean Marshall (UJ)	L	23	6	9	.400	0	24	24	0	126	132	59	77	0	5.59
Carlos Marmol	R	23	5	7	.417	0	19	13	0	77	71	59	59	0	6.08
Bob Howry	R	32	3	5	.444	0	84	0	0	77	70	17	71	0	3.17
David Aardsma	R	24	3	0	1.000	0	45	0	0	53	41	28	49	0	4.08
Mike Wuertz	R	27	3	0	.750	0	41	0	0	41	35	16	42	0	2.66
Glendon Rusch	L	31	3	8	.273	0	25	9	0	66	86	33	59	0	7.46
Roberto Novoa	R	26	2	1	.667	0	66	0	0	76	77	32	53	0	4.26
1 Scott Williamson	R	30	2	3	.400	0	31	0	0	28	27	16	32	0	5.08
Will Ohman	L	28	1	1	.500	0	78	0	0	65	51	34	74	0	4.13
Ryan O'Malley (EJ)	L	26	1	1	.500	0	2	2	1	10	7	4	2	0	2.13
Kerry Wood (SJ)	R	29	1	2	.333	0	4	4	0	20	19	8	13	0	4.12
Scott Eyre	L	34	1	3	.250	0	74	0	0	61	61	30	73	0	3.38
Juan Mateo	R	23	1	2	.333	0	10	10	0	46	51	23	35	0	5.32
Mark Prior (SJ)	R	26	1	6	.143	0	9	9	0	44	46	28	38	0	7.21
Ryan Dempster	R	29	1	9	.100	24	74	0	0	75	74	36	67	0	4.80
Les Walrond	L	29	0	1	.000	0	10	2	0	15	19	12	21	0	6.23
Jae Kuk Ryu	R	23	0	1	.000	0	1	0	0	15	23	6	17	0	8.40
Wade Miller (SJ)	R	29	0	5	.000	0	5	5	0	21	18	20	14	0	4.57
Jerome Williams	R	24	0	2	.000	0	12	12	0	56	68	37	60	0	7.30
Angel Guzman	R	24	0	6	.000	0	15	10	0	56	68	37	60	0	7.39

WEST DIVISION

SAN DIEGO — 1st (tie) 88-74 .543 — BRUCE BOCHY

Batting

Name	G by Pos	B	AGE	G	AB	R	H	2B	3B	HR	RBI	BB	SO	SB	BA	SA
TOTALS			31	162	5576	731	1465	298	38	161	698	564	1104	123	.263	.416
Adrian Gonzalez	1B155	L	24	156	570	83	173	38	1	24	82	52	113	0	.304	.500
Josh Barfield	2B143	R	23	159	539	72	151	32	3	13	58	30	81	21	.280	.423
Khalil Greene	SS113	R	26	121	412	56	101	26	2	15	55	39	87	5	.245	.427
1 Vinny Castilla	3B69	R	38	72	254	24	59	10	0	4	23	9	40	0	.232	.319
Brian Giles	OF158	L	35	158	604	87	159	37	1	14	83	104	60	9	.263	.397
Mike Cameron	OF141	R	33	144	552	88	148	34	9	22	83	71	142	25	.268	.482
Dave Roberts	OF127	L	34	129	499	80	146	18	13	2	44	51	61	49	.293	.393
Mike Piazza	C99	R	37	126	399	39	113	19	1	22	68	34	66	0	.283	.501
Mark Bellhorn	3B50 1B18 2B11 OF1	B	31	115	253	26	48	11	2	8	27	32	90	0	.190	.344
Geoff Blum	SS49 3B34 1B2 2B1 OF1	B	33	109	276	27	70	17	1	4	34	17	51	0	.254	.366
Rob Bowen	C65 1B1	B	25	94	94	22	23	5	1	3	13	13	26	0	.245	.394
2 Josh Bard	C71	B	28	93	231	28	78	19	0	9	40	27	39	1	.338	.537
Ben Johnson	OF43	R	25	58	120	19	30	5	2	4	12	14	36	3	.250	.425
1 Eric Young	OF39 2B1	R	39	52	128	19	26	5	0	3	13	11	18	8	.203	.313
2 Todd Walker	3B23 2B14 1B3	L	33	44	124	18	35	6	1	3	13	17	11	2	.282	.419
Termmel Sledge	OF22	L	29	37	70	7	16	3	0	2	9	6	15	0	.229	.357
2 Russell Branyan	3B26	L	30	27	72	14	21	3	0	7	15	9	27	0	.292	.542
Manny Alexander	3B13 SS9	R	35	22	34	2	6	1	1	0	3	2	4	0	.176	.265
Paul McAnulty	OF1	L	25	16	13	3	3	1	0	1	3	2	5	0	.231	.538
1 Doug Mirabelli	C9	R	35	14	22	1	4	1	0	0	2	2	6	0	.182	.227
Ryan Klesko (SJ)	OF1	L	35	6	4	0	3	1	0	0	2	0	1	0	.750	1.000
Jack Cust	OF1	L	27	4	3	1	1	0	0	0	0	3	1	0	.333	.333
Jon Knott		R	27	3	3	0	0	0	0	0	0	1	1	0	.000	.000
Justin Leone		R	28	1	1	0	0	0	0	0	0	0	1	0	.000	.000

Pitching

NAME	T	AGE	W	L	PCT	SV	G	GS	CG	IP	H	BB	SO	SHO	ERA
		31	88	74	.543	50	162	162	4	1464	1385	468	1097	11	3.88
Woody Williams (LJ)	R	39	12	5	.706	0	25	24	0	145	152	35	72	0	3.65
Chris Young	R	27	11	5	.688	0	31	31	0	179	134	69	164	3	3.46
Clay Hensley	R	26	11	12	.478	0	37	29	1	187	174	76	122	1	3.71
Jake Peavy	R	25	11	14	.440	0	32	32	2	202	187	62	215	0	4.09
Scott Linebrink	R	29	7	4	.636	2	73	0	0	76	70	22	68	0	3.57
Chan Ho Park (IL)	R	32	7	7	.500	0	24	21	1	137	146	44	96	1	4.81
Scott Cassidy	R	30	6	4	.600	0	42	0	0	43	39	19	49	0	2.53
Cla Meredith	R	23	5	1	.833	0	45	0	0	51	30	6	37	0	1.07
Alan Embree	L	36	4	3	.571	0	73	0	0	52	50	15	53	0	3.27
Mike Thompson	R	25	4	5	.444	0	19	16	0	92	103	30	35	0	4.99
Brian Sweeney	R	32	2	0	1.000	0	37	0	0	56	53	16	23	0	3.20
Jon Adkins	R	28	2	1	.667	0	55	0	0	54	55	20	30	0	3.98
Doug Brocail (IL)	R	39	2	2	.500	0	25	0	0	28	27	8	19	0	4.76
Tim Stauffer	R	24	1	0	1.000	0	6	1	0	8	11	3	2	0	1.50
1 Brian Sikorski	R	31	1	1	.500	0	13	0	0	14	16	7	13	0	5.65
2 David Wells	L	43	1	2	.333	0	5	5	0	28	33	4	14	0	3.49
2 Rudy Seanez	R	37	1	2	.333	0	53	0	0	50	43	24	59	0	5.68
2 Jim Brower	R	33	0	0	—	0	4	0	0	5	9	2	1	0	9.39
2 Scott Williamson (EJ)	R	30	0	0	—	0	8	0	0	6	4	4	10	0	7.36
Shawn Estes (EJ)	L	33	0	1	.000	0	3	1	0	5	7	4	4	0	4.50
Trevor Hoffman	R	38	0	2	.000	46	65	0	0	63	48	13	50	0	2.14
Dewon Brazelton	R	26	0	2	.000	0	18	1	0	28	28	16	9	0	12.00

LOS ANGELES — 1st (tie) 88-74 .543 (Wild Card) — GRADY LITTLE

Name	G by Pos	B	AGE	G	AB	R	H	2B	3B	HR	RBI	BB	SO	SB	BA	SA
TOTALS			31	162	5628	820	1552	307	58	153	787	601	959	128	.276	.432
Nomar Garciaparra	1B118	R	32	122	469	82	142	31	2	20	93	42	30	3	.303	.505
Jeff Kent	2B108 1B9	R	38	115	407	61	119	27	3	14	68	55	69	1	.292	.477
Rafael Furcal	SS156	B	28	159	654	113	196	32	9	15	63	73	98	37	.300	.445
Bill Mueller (KJ)	3B30	R	35	32	107	12	27	7	0	3	15	17	9	1	.252	.402
J.D. Drew	OF135	L	30	146	494	84	140	34	6	20	100	89	106	2	.283	.498
Kenny Lofton	OF120	L	39	129	469	79	141	15	12	3	41	45	42	32	.301	.403
Andre Ethier	OF109	L	24	126	396	50	122	20	7	11	55	34	77	5	.308	.477
Russell Martin	C117	R	23	121	415	65	117	26	4	10	65	45	57	10	.282	.436
Olmedo Saenz	1B30 3B16	R	35	103	179	30	53	15	0	11	48	14	47	0	.296	.564
Jose Cruz	OF71	R	32	86	223	34	52	16	1	5	17	43	54	5	.233	.381
Ramon Martinez	2B39 3B20 SS12 1B1 OF1	R	33	82	176	20	49	7	1	2	24	15	20	0	.278	.364
Jason Repko (NJ)	OF62	R	25	69	130	21	33	5	1	3	16	15	24	10	.254	.377
2 Wilson Betemit	3B49	R	24	54	174	19	42	7	0	9	24	17	45	1	.241	.437
Matt Kemp	OF46	R	21	52	154	30	39	7	1	7	23	9	53	6	.253	.448
2 Julio Lugo	2B29 3B16 SS8 OF3	R	30	49	146	16	32	5	1	0	10	12	29	6	.219	.297
James Loney	1B39 OF2	L	22	48	102	20	29	6	5	4	18	8	10	1	.284	.559
1 Willy Aybar	3B29 2B15	B	23	43	128	15	32	12	0	3	22	18	17	1	.250	.414
1 Ricky Ledee (GJ)	OF9	L	32	43	53	4	13	5	0	1	8	2	10	1	.245	.396
1 Cesar Izturis (EJ)	3B28 SS2 2B1	R	26	32	119	10	30	7	1	1	12	7	6	1	.252	.353
Oscar Robles	2B13 3B6	L	30	29	33	6	5	0	1	0	0	5	5	0	.152	.212
1 Sandy Alomar	C18	R	40	27	62	3	20	5	0	0	9	0	7	0	.323	.403
1 Dioner Navarro (WJ)	C24	B	22	25	75	5	21	2	0	2	8	11	18	1	.280	.387
2 Marlon Anderson	OF15 2B1	L	32	25	64	12	24	3	2	7	15	7	8	2	.375	.813
2 Toby Hall	C21	R	30	21	57	2	21	4	0	0	3	0	4	0	.368	.439
Joel Guzman	3B6 1B1 OF1	R	21	8	19	2	4	0	0	0	3	3	2	0	.211	.211
1 Cody Ross	OF3	R	25	8	14	4	7	1	1	2	9	0	2	1	.500	1.143
Delwyn Young	OF2	B	24	5	5	0	0	0	0	0	0	0	2	0	.000	.000
Einar Diaz	C1	R	33	3	3	0	2	1	0	0	1	0	0	0	.667	.667
Jayson Werth (WJ) 27																

NAME	T	AGE	W	L	PCT	SV	G	GS	CG	IP	H	BB	SO	SHO	ERA
TOTALS		30	88	74	.543	40	162	162	1	1460	1524	492	1068	10	4.23
Derek Lowe	R	33	16	8	.667	0	35	34	1	218	221	55	123	0	3.63
Brad Penny	R	28	16	9	.640	0	34	33	0	189	206	54	148	0	4.33
Aaron Sele	R	36	8	6	.571	0	28	15	0	103	120	30	57	0	4.53
Brett Tomko (UJ)	R	33	8	7	.533	0	44	15	0	112	123	29	76	0	4.73
Chad Billingsley	R	21	7	4	.636	0	18	16	0	90	92	58	59	0	3.80
Takashi Saito	R	36	6	2	.750	24	72	0	0	78	48	23	107	0	2.07
2 Greg Maddux	R	40	6	3	.667	0	12	12	0	74	66	14	36	0	3.30
1 Danys Baez	R	28	5	5	.500	9	46	0	0	50	53	11	29	0	4.35
Jonathan Broxton	R	22	4	1	.800	3	68	0	0	76	61	33	97	0	2.59
1 Odalis Perez	L	29	4	4	.500	0	20	8	0	59	89	13	33	0	6.83
Joe Beimel	L	29	2	1	.667	2	62	0	0	70	70	21	30	0	2.96
1 Jae Weong Seo	R	29	2	4	.333	0	19	10	0	67	75	25	49	0	5.78
2 Mark Hendrickson	L	32	2	7	.222	0	18	12	0	75	92	28	48	0	4.22
Eric Stults	L	26	1	0	1.000	0	6	2	0	18	17	7	5	0	5.60
Hong-Chih Kuo	L	24	1	5	.167	0	28	5	0	60	54	33	71	0	4.22
Yhancy Brazoban (EJ)	R	26	0	0	—	0	5	0	0	5	7	2	4	0	5.40
Eric Gagne (EJ)	R	30	0	0	—	1	2	0	0	2	1	3	0	0	0.00
Giovanni Carrara	R	38	0	1	.000	1	25	0	0	28	27	7	25	0	4.55
2 Elmer Dessens	R	35	0	1	.000	0	19	0	0	23	23	9	16	0	4.70
Lance Carter	R	31	0	1	.000	0	10	0	0	12	17	8	5	0	8.49
Franquelis Osoria	R	24	0	2	.000	0	12	0	0	18	27	9	13	0	7.13
Tim Hamulack	L	29	0	3	.000	0	33	0	0	34	36	22	34	0	6.35

SAN FRANCISCO — 3rd 76-85 .472 11.5 — FELIPE ALOU

Name	G by Pos	B	AGE	G	AB	R	H	2B	3B	HR	RBI	BB	SO	SB	BA	SA
TOTALS			34	161	5472	746	1418	297	52	163	711	494	891	58	.259	.422
Lance Niekro (SJ)	1B58	R	27	66	199	27	49	9	2	5	31	11	32	0	.246	.387
Ray Durham	2B133	B	34	137	498	79	146	30	7	26	93	51	61	7	.293	.538
Omar Vizquel	SS152	B	39	153	579	88	171	22	10	4	58	56	51	24	.295	.389
Pedro Feliz	3B159 OF3 SS2	R	31	160	603	75	147	35	5	22	98	33	112	1	.244	.428
Moises Alou (NJ)	OF92	R	39	98	345	52	104	25	1	22	74	28	31	2	.301	.571
Steve Finley	OF130	L	41	139	426	66	105	21	12	6	40	46	55	7	.246	.394
Barry Bonds	OF116	L	41	130	367	74	99	23	0	26	77	115	51	3	.270	.545
Mike Matheny (CN)	C46	R	35	47	160	10	37	8	0	3	18	9	30	0	.231	.338
Randy Winn	OF141	B	32	149	573	82	150	34	5	11	56	48	63	10	.262	.396
Mark Sweeney	1B53 OF21	L	36	114	259	32	65	15	2	5	37	28	50	0	.251	.382
Eliezer Alfonzo	C84	R	27	87	286	27	76	17	2	12	39	9	74	1	.266	.465
Jason Ellison	OF64	R	28	84	81	14	18	5	1	2	4	5	14	2	.222	.383
1 Jose Vizcaino	SS19 2B16 1B10 3B2	B	38	64	119	16	25	3	0	1	5	16	10	0	.210	.261
Todd Greene	C42 1B5	R	35	61	116	16	46	12	2	2	17	10	45	0	.289	.428
Todd Linden	OF47	R	25	61	77	15	21	4	2	2	5	9	20	1	.273	.455
2 Shea Hillenbrand	1B58 3B8	R	30	60	233	33	58	12	0	9	29	7	40	0	.248	.415
Kevin Frandsen	2B28 SS3	R	24	41	93	12	20	4	0	2	7	3	14	0	.215	.323
Tomas de la Rosa	SS8 2B2 3B2	R	28	16	16	1	5	0	0	0	2	0	3	0	.313	.313
Fred Lewis	OF6	L	25	13	11	5	5	1	0	0	1	0	6	0	.455	.545
Travis Ishikawa	1B10	L	22	12	24	1	7	3	1	0	4	1	6	0	.292	.500
Dan Ortmeier	OF3	L	25	9	12	0	3	1	0	0	2	0	4	0	.250	.333
Justin Knoedler	C5	R	25	5	7	0	1	0	0	0	0	0	2	0	.143	.143
Chad Santos	1B3	L	25	3	7	2	3	0	0	1	2	0	3	0	.429	.857

NAME	T	AGE	W	L	PCT	SV	G	GS	CG	IP	H	BB	SO	SHO	ERA
TOTALS		29	76	85	.472	37	161	161	7	1430	1422	584	992	9	4.64
Matt Cain	R	21	13	12	.520	0	32	31	1	191	157	87	179	1	4.15
Jason Schmidt	R	33	11	9	.550	0	32	32	3	213	189	80	180	1	3.59
Matt Morris	R	31	10	15	.400	0	33	33	2	208	218	63	117	0	4.98
Noah Lowry (UJ)	L	25	7	10	.412	0	27	27	1	159	166	56	84	1	4.74
Jamey Wright	R	31	6	10	.375	0	34	21	0	156	167	64	79	0	5.19
Brad Hennessey	R	26	5	6	.455	1	34	12	0	99	92	42	42	0	4.26
Armando Benitez	R	33	4	2	.667	17	41	0	0	38	39	21	31	0	3.52
2 Mike Stanton	L	39	4	2	.667	8	26	0	0	23	23	6	18	0	3.09
Steve Kline	L	33	4	3	.571	1	72	0	0	52	53	26	33	0	3.66
Jonathan Sanchez	L	23	3	1	.750	0	27	4	0	40	39	33	33	0	4.95
Tim Worrell (XJ)	R	38	3	2	.600	6	23	0	0	28	28	7	12	0	7.52
Kevin Correia	R	25	2	1	1.000	0	48	0	0	70	64	22	57	0	3.49
Brian Wilson	R	24	2	3	.400	1	31	0	0	30	32	21	23	0	5.40
Jeff Fassero	L	43	1	1	.500	0	10	1	0	15	23	8	7	0	7.80
1 Jeremy Accardo	R	24	1	3	.250	3	38	0	0	40	38	11	40	0	4.91
Billy Sadler	R	24	0	0	—	0	5	0	0	4	5	2	4	0	6.75
Patrick Misch	L	22	0	0	—	0	1	0	0	1	1	2	0	0	0.00
Scott Munter	R	26	0	1	.000	0	27	0	0	23	30	18	7	0	8.74
Jack Taschner	L	28	0	1	.000	0	24	0	0	19	31	7	15	0	8.38
1 Tyler Walker	R	30	0	1	.000	0	6	0	0	5	5	3	5	0	15.19
2 Vinnie Chulk	R	27	0	3	.000	0	28	0	0	22	17	15	25	0	5.24

ARIZONA — 4th (tie) 76-86 .469 12 — BOB MELVIN

Name	G by Pos	B	AGE	G	AB	R	H	2B	3B	HR	RBI	BB	SO	SB	BA	SA
TOTALS			29	162	5645	773	1506	331	38	160	743	504	965	76	.267	.424
Conor Jackson	1B129	R	24	140	485	75	141	26	1	15	79	54	73	1	.291	.441
Orlando Hudson	2B157	B	28	157	579	87	166	34	9	15	67	61	78	9	.287	.454
Craig Counsell (BR)	SS88 3B7 2B2	L	35	105	372	56	95	14	4	4	30	31	47	15	.255	.347
Chad Tracy	3B147 1B8	L	26	154	597	91	168	41	0	20	80	54	129	5	.281	.451
1 Shawn Green	OF100 1B12	L	33	115	417	59	118	22	3	11	51	37	64	4	.283	.429
Eric Byrnes	OF137	R	30	143	562	82	150	37	3	26	79	34	68	25	.267	.482
Luis Gonzalez	OF150	L	38	153	586	93	159	52	2	15	73	69	58	0	.271	.444
Johnny Estrada	C108	B	30	115	414	43	125	26	0	11	71	13	40	0	.302	.444
Damion Easley	SS27 3B20 2B9 1B3 OF1	R	36	90	189	24	44	6	1	9	28	21	30	1	.233	.418
Jeff DaVanon (NJ)	OF58	B	32	87	221	38	64	12	4	5	35	31	42	10	.290	.448
Tony Clark (SJ)	1B53	R	34	79	132	13	26	4	0	6	16	13	40	0	.197	.364
Andy Green	3B7 OF7 2B6 SS2	R	28	73	86	15	16	4	0	1	6	13	20	1	.186	.267
Chris Snyder	C60	R	25	81	184	19	51	9	0	6	32	22	39	0	.277	.424
Stephen Drew	SS56	L	23	59	209	27	66	13	7	5	23	14	50	2	.316	.517
Carlos Quentin	OF46	R	23	57	166	23	42	13	3	9	32	15	34	1	.253	.530
Chris Young	OF24	R	22	30	70	10	17	4	2	2	10	6	12	2	.243	.386
Alberto Callaspo	SS4 2B3 3B2	B	23	23	42	2	10	1	1	0	2	4	5	0	.238	.310
Scott Hairston (SJ)	OF5	R	26	9	15	2	6	2	0	0	2	1	5	0	.400	.533
Miguel Montero	C5	L	22	6	16	0	4	1	0	0	2	0	4	0	.250	.313
Robby Hammock	1B1	R	29	1	2	0	1	0	0	0	0	0	0	0	.500	1.000

NAME	T	AGE	W	L	PCT	SV	G	GS	CG	IP	H	BB	SO	SHO	ERA
TOTALS		28	76	86	.469	34	162	162	8	1460	1503	536	1115	9	4.49
Brandon Webb	R	27	16	8	.667	0	33	33	5	235	216	50	178	3	3.10
Claudio Vargas	R	28	12	10	.545	0	31	30	0	168	185	52	123	0	4.83
Miguel Batista	R	35	11	8	.579	0	34	33	3	206	231	84	110	1	4.58
Brandon Medders	R	26	5	3	.625	0	60	0	0	72	76	28	47	0	3.64
Juan Cruz	R	27	5	6	.455	0	31	15	0	95	80	47	88	0	4.18
2 Livan Hernandez	R	31	4	5	.444	0	10	10	0	79	76	26	39	0	3.76
Luis Vizcaino	R	31	4	6	.400	0	70	0	0	65	51	29	72	0	3.58
Edgar Gonzalez	R	23	3	4	.429	0	11	5	0	43	45	9	28	0	4.22
Tony Pena	R	24	3	4	.429	1	25	0	0	31	36	8	21	0	5.58
Enrique Gonzalez	R	23	3	7	.300	0	22	18	0	106	114	34	66	0	5.67
Greg Aquino	R	28	2	0	1.000	0	42	0	0	48	54	24	51	0	4.47
Jose Valverde	R	26	2	3	.400	18	44	0	0	49	50	22	69	0	5.84
Brandon Lyon	R	26	2	4	.333	0	68	0	0	69	68	22	46	0	3.89
1 Orlando Hernandez	R	40	2	4	.333	0	11	5	0	55	52	20	52	0	6.11
2 Jorge Julio	R	27	1	2	.333	15	44	0	0	45	31	25	55	0	3.83
Jason Grimsley	R	38	1	2	.333	0	19	0	0	28	30	13	20	0	4.88
Casey Daigle	R	25	0	0	—	0	10	0	0	12	14	6	7	0	3.65
Doug Slaten	L	26	0	0	—	0	22	0	0	18	21	7	13	0	3.00
Mike Koplove	R	29	0	0	—	0	8	0	0	8	13	2	3	0	3.00
Terry Mulholland (EJ)	L	43	0	0	—	0	26	0	0	31	37	6	10	0	9.00
Randy Choate	L	30	0	0	—	0	30	0	0	16	21	13	12	0	3.94
1 Kevin Jarvis	R	36	0	1	.000	0	11	3	0	11	18	5	6	0	11.91
1 Jeff Bajenaru	R	28	0	0	—	0	1	0	0	1	1	4	0	0	36.00
Dustin Nippert	R	25	0	0	—	0	2	0	0	10	15	7	9	0	11.70
1 Russ Ortiz (LJ)	R	32	0	5	.000	0	6	6	0	23	27	22	21	0	7.54

COLORADO — 4th (tie) 76-86 .469 12 — CLINT HURDLE

Name	G by Pos	B	AGE	G	AB	R	H	2B	3B	HR	RBI	BB	SO	SB	BA	SA
TOTALS			28	162	5562	813	1504	325	54	157	761	561	1108	85	.270	.433
Todd Helton	1B145	L	32	145	546	94	165	40	5	15	81	91	64	3	.302	.476
Jamey Carroll	2B109 SS10 3B8	R	32	136	463	84	139	23	5	5	36	56	66	10	.300	.404
Clint Barmes	SS125 2B4	R	27	131	478	57	105	26	4	7	58	22	72	5	.220	.335
Garrett Atkins	3B157 1B3	R	26	157	602	117	198	48	1	29	120	79	76	4	.329	.556
Brad Hawpe	OF145	R	27	150	499	67	146	36	4	22	84	74	123	5	.293	.515
Cory Sullivan	OF114	L	26	126	386	47	103	26	10	2	30	32	100	5	.267	.402
Matt Holliday	OF153	R	26	156	602	119	196	45	5	34	114	47	110	10	.326	.586
Yorvit Torrealba (SJ)	C63	R	27	65	223	23	55	16	3	7	43	11	49	4	.247	.439
Choo Freeman	OF51	R	26	88	173	24	41	6	3	2	18	14	42	5	.237	.341
Ryan Spilborghs	OF46	R	26	67	167	26	48	6	3	4	30	14	30	5	.287	.431
Luis Gonzalez	2B32 1B7 OF7 3B3	R	27	61	149	7	36	9	1	2	14	4	27	1	.242	.356
Jason Smith	2B18 1B6 3B3 SS1	L	28	49	99	9	26	3	1	5	14	6	29	1	.263	.424
Jorge Piedra	OF5	L	27	43	59	4	10	2	0	3	10	3	12	1	.169	.356
1 Danny Ardoin (KJ)	C35	R	31	35	109	12	21	5	1	0	8	8	27	0	.193	.257
2 Kaz Matsui	2B21 SS3	B	30	32	113	22	39	9	3	2	19	10	27	8	.345	.504
J.D. Closser	C29	B	26	32	97	10	19	3	1	2	11	12	23	0	.196	.309
1 Eli Marrero	1B7 OF6 C5	R	32	30	60	7	13	3	0	4	10	11	16	3	.217	.467
Troy Tulowitzki	SS25	R	21	25	96	15	23	6	1	1	6	10	25	2	.240	.292
1 Miguel Ojeda	C24	R	31	25	74	5	17	3	0	2	12	10	17	0	.230	.378
Chris Iannetta	C21	R	23	21	77	12	20	4	0	2	10	13	15	0	.260	.390
Jeff Salazar	OF14	L	25	19	53	13	15	4	0	1	5	8	10	2	.283	.415
Jeff Baker	OF12 1B1	R	25	18	57	13	21	7	0	2	9	1	14	2	.368	.825
2 Vinny Castilla	1B7 3B1	R	38	21	53	6	14	3	0	1	7	4	7	0	.264	.377
Omar Quintanilla	SS8 2B3	L	24	11	34	3	6	1	0	0	1	6	9	0	.176	.265
1 Ryan Shealy (EJ)	1B2	R	26	5	9	2	2	0	0	0	2	1	1	0	.222	.444
Alvin Colina	C1	R	24	2	5	0	1	0	0	0	0	1	2	0	.200	.200

NAME	T	AGE	W	L	PCT	SV	G	GS	CG	IP	H	BB	SO	SHO	ERA
TOTALS		29	76	86	.469	34	162	162	5	1447	1549	553	952	8	4.66
Jeff Francis	L	25	13	11	.542	0	32	32	1	199	187	69	117	1	4.16
Josh Fogg	R	29	11	9	.550	0	31	31	1	172	206	60	93	1	5.49
Jason Jennings	R	27	9	13	.409	0	32	32	3	212	206	85	142	2	3.78
Aaron Cook	R	27	9	15	.375	0	32	32	0	213	242	55	92	0	4.23
Byung-Hyun Kim	R	27	8	12	.400	0	27	26	0	155	179	61	129	0	5.57
2 Jeremy Affeldt	L	27	4	2	.667	1	27	6	0	27	31	13	20	0	6.91
Ramon Ramirez	R	24	4	3	.571	0	61	0	0	58	58	27	61	0	3.46
David Cortes	R	32	3	1	.750	0	29	0	0	29	35	6	14	0	4.30
Brian Fuentes	L	30	3	4	.429	30	66	0	0	65	50	26	73	0	3.44
Tom Martin	L	36	2	0	1.000	0	68	0	0	60	62	25	46	0	5.07
Justin Hampson	L	26	1	0	1.000	1	12	0	0	19	15	9	7	0	7.50
Miguel Asencio	R	25	1	0	1.000	0	4	1	0	4	11	9	4	0	4.70
Mike Venafro	L	32	1	0	1.000	0	8	0	0	4	6	1	2	0	2.45
Mike DeJean (SJ)	R	35	1	0	1.000	0	20	0	0	21	22	18	17	0	5.40
1 Scott Dohmann	R	28	1	1	.500	1	27	0	0	25	26	15	22	0	6.20
Nate Field	R	31	1	1	.500	0	14	0	0	14	9	4	9	0	4.50
Manuel Corpas	R	23	1	1	.333	0	32	0	0	32	36	8	27	0	3.62
2 Zach Day	R	28	1	2	.333	0	3	3	0	13	19	6	5	0	10.80
Ray King	L	32	1	4	.200	0	79	0	0	45	56	20	23	0	4.43
Jose Mesa	R	40	1	5	.167	1	79	0	0	72	73	36	39	0	3.86
Ubaldo Jimenez	R	22	0	0	—	0	2	1	0	7	8	4	9	0	3.52
Sun-Woo Kim (LJ)	R	28	0	2	.000	0	8	5	0	45	62	19	23	0	4.91
Juan Morillo	R	22	0	1	.000	0	3	1	0	4	8	5	3	0	15.75
2 Denny Bautista	R	25	0	2	.000	0	6	4	0	25	27	22	21	0	5.40
Chin-hui Tsao (SJ) 25															

LINE SCORES

Team	1	2	3	4	5	6	7	8	9	10	11	12	R	H	E

DIVISION SERIES: ST LOUIS 3 : SAN DIEGO 1

Game 1   October 3 at San Diego

| STL | 0 0 0 3 1 1 0 0 0 | 5 12 0 |
| SD | 0 0 0 0 0 0 1 0 0 | 1 6 0 |

Carpenter, Johnson (7), Wainwright (9)   Peavy, Seanez (6), Park (8)

Game 2   October 5 at San Diego

| STL | 0 0 0 2 0 0 0 0 0 | 2 10 0 |
| SD | 0 0 0 0 0 0 0 0 0 | 0 4 0 |

Weaver, Flores (6), Kinney (6), (8),   Wells, Meredith (6), Hensley (8),
Johnson (8), Wainwright   Linebrink (9)

Game 3   October 7 at St. Louis

| SD | 0 0 0 3 0 0 0 0 0 | 3 10 0 |
| STL | 0 0 0 0 0 0 0 1 0 | 1 5 2 |

Young, Embree (7), Linebrink (8), Hoffman (9)   Suppan, Hancock (5), Flores (7),
                                                  Looper (7), Johnson (9), Thompson (9)

Game 4   October 8 at St. Louis

| SD | 2 0 0 0 0 0 0 0 0 | 2 9 1 |
| STL | 2 0 0 0 4 0 0 x | 6 7 0 |

Williams, Meredith (6), Hensley (8)   Carpenter, Johnson (8), Kinney (8),
                                              Wainwright (9)

DIVISION SERIES: NEW YORK 3 : LOS ANGELES 0

Game 1   October 4 at New York

| LA | 0 1 0 0 0 0 3 0 1 | 5 11 1 |
| NYN | 0 0 0 2 0 2 2 0 x | 6 9 1 |

Lowe, Hendrickson (6), **Penny** (7), Broxton (8)   Maine, Feliciano (5), Bradford (5),
                                                       Mota (6), Heilman (8), Wagner (9)

Game 2   October 5 at New York

| LA | 0 0 0 0 0 0 0 1 0 | 1 5 1 |
| NYN | 0 0 1 0 1 2 0 0 x | 4 7 0 |

Kuo, Tomko (5), Hendrickson (6),   **Glavine**, Feliciano (7),
Billingsley (7), Saito (8)   Heilman (8), Wagner (9)

Game 3   October 7 at Los Angeles

| NYN | 3 0 1 0 0 3 0 2 0 | 9 14 2 |
| LA | 0 0 0 2 3 0 0 0 0 | 5 16 2 |

Trachsel, Oliver (4), Bradford (5),   Maddux, Hendrickson (5), **Broxton** (6),
Feliciano (5), Mota (6), Heilman (8),   Billingsley (7), Tomko (8), Saito (8)
Wagner (9)

COMPOSITE BATTING

DIVISION SERIES

ST. LOUIS

NAME	POS	G	AB	R	H	2B	3B	HR	RBI	BA
TOTALS		3	125	14	34	5	1	2	13	.272
Pujols	1B	4	15	3	5	1	0	1	3	.333
Eckstein	SS	4	15	1	2	0	0	0	1	.133
Encarnacion	RF	4	14	1	4	0	1	0	2	.286
Belliard	2B	4	13	2	6	1	0	0	2	.462
Edmonds	CF	4	13	2	4	0	0	0	2	.308
Molina	C	4	13	0	4	1	0	0	1	.308
Rolen	3B	3	11	0	1	1	0	0	0	.091
Wilson	LF	2	8	2	2	1	0	0	0	.250
Duncan	LF	2	6	1	1	0	0	0	0	.167
Carpenter	P	2	5	0	1	0	0	0	0	.200
Spiezio	3B	2	5	1	1	0	0	0	1	.200
Miles	2B	2	2	0	1	0	0	0	0	.500
Weaver	P	1	2	0	1	0	0	0	0	.500
Taguchi	LF	2	1	1	1	0	0	1	1	1.000
Rodriguez	PH	1	1	0	0	0	0	0	0	.000
Suppan	P	1	1	0	0	0	0	0	0	.000
Johnson	P	4	0	0	0	0	0	0	0	—
Wainwright	P	3	0	0	0	0	0	0	0	—
Flores	P	2	0	0	0	0	0	0	0	—
Kinney	P	2	0	0	0	0	0	0	0	—
Bennett	C	1	0	0	0	0	0	0	0	—
Hancock	P	1	0	0	0	0	0	0	0	—
Looper	P	1	0	0	0	0	0	0	0	—
Thompson	P	1	0	0	0	0	0	0	0	—

SAN DIEGO

NAME	POS	G	AB	R	H	2B	3B	HR	RBI	BA
TOTALS		3	129	6	29	7	2	0	6	.225
Roberts	LF	4	16	1	7	0	1	0	0	.438
Gonzalez	1B	4	14	2	5	0	0	0	0	.357
Giles	RF	4	14	1	4	1	0	0	1	.286
Cameron	CF	4	14	1	2	1	0	0	1	.143
Branyan	3B	4	13	1	3	1	1	0	3	.231
Piazza	C	4	10	0	1	1	0	0	0	.100
Walker	2B	3	9	0	0	0	0	0	0	.000
Barfield	2B	4	8	0	2	1	0	0	0	.250
Blum	SS-3B	4	8	0	1	1	0	0	1	.125
Bard	C	3	7	0	1	0	0	0	0	.143
Greene	SS	3	4	0	0	0	0	0	0	.000
Klesko	PH	3	3	0	2	1	0	0	0	.667
Young	P	1	3	0	0	0	0	0	0	.000
Williams	P	1	2	0	0	0	0	0	0	.000
Bellhorn	3B	2	1	0	0	0	0	0	0	.000
Bowen	C	2	1	0	1	0	0	0	0	1.000
Peavy	P	1	1	0	0	0	0	0	0	.000
Wells	P	1	1	0	0	0	0	0	0	.000
Hensley	P	2	0	0	0	0	0	0	0	—
Linebrink	P	2	0	0	0	0	0	0	0	—
Meredith	P	2	0	0	0	0	0	0	0	—
Embree	P	1	0	0	0	0	0	0	0	—
Hoffman	P	1	0	0	0	0	0	0	0	—
Park	P	1	0	0	0	0	0	0	0	—
Seanez	P	1	0	0	0	0	0	0	0	—

NEW YORK

NAME	POS	G	AB	R	H	2B	3B	HR	RBI	BA
TOTALS		3	102	19	30	6	0	2	18	.294
Delgado	1B	3	14	3	6	0	0	1	2	.429
Wright	3B	3	12	1	4	2	0	0	4	.333
Reyes	SS	3	12	2	2	0	0	0	3	.167
Lo Duca	C	3	11	2	5	1	0	0	3	.455
Floyd	LF	3	9	3	4	0	0	1	2	.444
Beltran	CF	3	9	2	2	0	0	0	1	.222
Valentin	2B	3	9	0	0	0	0	0	0	.000
Green	RF	2	9	1	3	2	0	0	2	.333
Chavez	LF-RF	3	8	1	3	0	0	0	0	.375
Franco	PH	2	2	0	0	0	0	0	1	.000
Trachsel	P	1	2	0	0	0	0	0	0	.000
Mota	P	2	1	0	0	0	0	0	0	.000
Tucker	PH	2	1	1	0	0	0	0	0	.000
Woodward	PH	1	1	1	1	1	0	0	0	1.000
Glavine	P	1	1	0	0	0	0	0	0	.000
Maine	P	1	1	0	0	0	0	0	0	.000
Feliciano	P	3	0	0	0	0	0	0	0	—
Heilman	P	3	0	0	0	0	0	0	0	—
Wagner	P	3	0	0	0	0	0	0	0	—
Bradford	P	2	0	0	0	0	0	0	0	—
Oliver	P	1	0	0	0	0	0	0	0	—

LOS ANGELES

NAME	POS	G	AB	R	H	2B	3B	HR	RBI	BA
TOTALS		3	110	11	32	6	0	2	11	.291
Kent	2B-1B	3	13	2	8	1	0	1	2	.615
Anderson	LF-RF	3	13	2	4	1	0	0	1	.308
Drew	RF	3	13	1	2	0	0	0	0	.154
Lofton	CF	3	13	0	1	0	0	0	0	.077
Martin	C	3	12	2	4	0	0	0	0	.333
Furcal	SS	3	11	1	2	0	0	0	1	.182
Garciaparra	1B	3	9	0	2	1	0	0	2	.222
Betemit	3B	3	8	3	4	1	0	1	1	.500
Lugo	3B-2B	2	4	0	1	1	0	0	0	.250
Loney	1B	1	4	0	3	0	0	0	3	.750
Martinez	PH	3	3	0	1	0	0	0	0	.333
Saenz	PH	2	2	0	0	0	0	0	0	.000
Kuo	P	1	2	0	0	0	0	0	0	.000
Ethier	LF	2	1	0	0	0	0	0	0	.000
Lowe	P	1	1	0	0	0	0	0	0	.000
Maddux	P	1	1	0	0	0	0	0	0	.000
Hendrickson	P	3	0	0	0	0	0	0	0	—
Billingsley	P	2	0	0	0	0	0	0	0	—
Broxton	P	2	0	0	0	0	0	0	0	—
Saito	P	2	0	0	0	0	0	0	0	—
Tomko	P	2	0	0	0	0	0	0	0	—
Penny	P	1	0	0	0	0	0	0	0	—
Repko	PR	1	0	0	0	0	0	0	0	—

COMPOSITE PITCHING

ST. LOUIS

NAME	G	IP	H	BB	SO	W	L	SV	ERA
TOTALS	4	36	29	16	34	3	1	1	1.50
Carpenter	2	13.1	12	4	12	2	0	0	2.03
Weaver	1	5	2	3	3	1	0	0	0.00
Suppan	1	4.1	6	3	3	0	1	0	6.23
Wainwright	3	3.2	3	0	6	0	0	1	0.00
Johnson	4	2.2	2	1	6	0	0	0	0.00
Kinney	2	2	0	1	1	0	0	0	0.00
Looper	1	1.2	1	0	0	0	0	0	0.00
Hancock	1	1.2	1	2	1	0	0	0	0.00
Flores	2	1	2	1	1	0	0	0	0.00
Thompson	1	0.2	0	1	1	0	0	0	0.00

SAN DIEGO

NAME	G	IP	H	BB	SO	W	L	SV	ERA
TOTALS	4	35	34	7	21	1	3	1	3.09
Young	1	6.2	4	2	9	1	0	0	0.00
Williams	1	5.1	5	2	1	0	1	0	6.75
Peavy	1	5.1	11	1	2	0	1	0	8.44
Wells	1	5	7	0	2	0	1	0	3.60
Meredith	2	3.2	3	0	3	0	0	0	0.00
Hensley	2	2.2	2	1	0	0	0	0	0.00
Park	1	2	1	0	0	0	0	0	0.00
Seanez	1	1.2	0	1	2	0	0	0	0.00
Linebrink	2	1.1	1	1	0	0	0	0	6.75
Hoffman	1	1	0	1	0	0	0	1	0.00
Embree	1	0.1	0	0	1	0	0	0	0.00

NEW YORK

NAME	G	IP	H	BB	SO	W	L	SV	ERA
TOTALS	3	27	32	8	21	3	0	2	3.67
Glavine	1	6	4	2	2	1	0	0	0.00
Maine	1	4.1	6	2	5	0	0	0	2.08
Mota	2	4	6	0	5	1	0	0	6.75
Trachsel	1	3.1	6	1	2	0	0	0	5.40
Wagner	3	3	3	0	4	0	0	2	3.00
Heilman	3	3	3	0	1	0	0	0	3.00
Feliciano	3	1.2	0	2	2	1	0	0	0.00
Oliver	1	1.1	3	0	0	0	0	0	20.25
Bradford	2	0.1	1	1	0	0	0	0	0.00

LOS ANGELES

NAME	G	IP	H	BB	SO	W	L	SV	ERA
TOTALS	3	25	30	13	22	0	3	0	5.76
Lowe	1	5.1	6	2	6	0	0	0	6.75
Kuo	1	4.1	4	2	4	0	1	0	4.15
Maddux	1	4	7	2	0	0	0	0	9.00
Hendrickson	3	2.2	1	1	1	0	0	0	0.00
Saito	2	2.2	0	4	4	0	0	0	0.00
Billingsley	2	2	1	0	3	0	0	0	0.00
Broxton	2	2	5	2	3	0	1	0	13.50
Tomko	2	1	4	2	0	0	0	0	9.00
Penny	1	1	2	2	1	0	1	0	18.00

LINE SCORES

Team	1	2	3	4	5	6	7	8	9	10	11	12	R	H	E

CHAMPIONSHIP SERIES: ST LOUIS 4 : NEW YORK 3

Game 1   October 12 at New York

| STL | 0 | 0 | 0 | 0 | 0 | 0 | 0 | 0 | 0 | | | | 0 | 4 | 0 |
| NYN | 0 | 0 | 0 | 0 | 0 | 2 | 0 | 0 | x | | | | 2 | 6 | 0 |

Weaver, Johnson (6), Thompson (7), Looper (8)   **Glavine**, Mota (8), Wagner (9)

Game 2   October 13 at New York

| STL | 0 | 2 | 2 | 0 | 0 | 0 | 2 | 0 | 3 | | | | 9 | 10 | 1 |
| NYN | 3 | 1 | 0 | 0 | 1 | 1 | 0 | 0 | 0 | | | | 6 | 9 | 2 |

Carpenter, Hancock (6), Flores (6), **Kinney** (8), Johnson (9), Wainwright (9)   Maine, Bradford (5), Feliciano (6), Mota (7), Heilman (7), **Wagner** (9), Hernandez (9)

Game 3   October 14 at St. Louis

| NYN | 0 | 0 | 0 | 0 | 0 | 0 | 0 | 0 | 0 | | | | 0 | 3 | 0 |
| STL | 2 | 3 | 0 | 0 | 0 | 0 | 0 | 0 | x | | | | 5 | 8 | 0 |

Trachsel, Oliver (2), Hernandez (8)   **Suppan**, Kinney (9)

Game 4   October 15 at St. Louis

| NYN | 0 | 0 | 2 | 0 | 3 | 6 | 1 | 0 | 0 | | | | 12 | 14 | 1 |
| STL | 0 | 1 | 1 | 0 | 1 | 2 | 0 | 0 | 0 | | | | 5 | 11 | 1 |

Perez, Bradford (6), Feliciano (8), Mota (9)   Reyes, **Thompson** (5), Flores (5), Hancock (6), Johnson (6), Looper (7)

Game 5   October 17 at St. Louis

| NYN | 0 | 0 | 0 | 2 | 0 | 0 | 0 | 0 | 0 | | | | 2 | 8 | 0 |
| STL | 0 | 0 | 0 | 2 | 1 | 1 | 0 | 0 | x | | | | 4 | 10 | 0 |

Glavine, Bradford (5), Feliciano (5), Hernandez (7), Mota (8)   **Weaver**, Kinney (7), Flores (8), Wainwright (8)

Game 6   October 18 at New York

| STL | 0 | 0 | 0 | 0 | 0 | 0 | 0 | 0 | 2 | | | | 2 | 7 | 1 |
| NYN | 1 | 0 | 0 | 1 | 0 | 0 | 2 | 0 | x | | | | 4 | 10 | 0 |

Carpenter, Looper (7), Johnson (7)   **Maine**, Bradford (6), Mota (7), Heilman (8), Wagner (9)

Game 7   October 19 at New York

| STL | 0 | 1 | 0 | 0 | 0 | 0 | 0 | 0 | 2 | | | | 3 | 6 | 1 |
| NYN | 1 | 0 | 0 | 0 | 0 | 0 | 0 | 0 | 0 | | | | 1 | 4 | 1 |

Suppan, **Flores** (8), Wainwright (9)   Perez, Bradford (7), **Heilman** (8)

COMPOSITE BATTING

NAME	POS	G	AB	R	H	2B	3B	HR	RBI	BA
ST. LOUIS										
TOTALS		7	226	28	56	7	4	9	27	.248
Eckstein	SS	7	26	3	6	1	0	1	1	.231
Belliard	2B	7	25	0	6	0	0	0	1	.240
Molina	C	7	23	2	8	1	0	2	6	**.348**
Pujols	1B	7	22	5	7	1	0	1	1	.318
Edmonds	CF	7	22	5	5	0	0	2	4	.227
Encarnacion	RF	6	22	1	4	0	1	0	2	.182
Rolen	3B	7	21	4	5	1	0	0	0	.238
Spiezio	LF-3B	6	17	3	4	1	2	0	5	.235
Wilson	LF-RF	6	17	2	3	1	0	0	0	.176
Duncan	LF	5	8	1	1	0	0	1	1	.125
Rodriguez	PH	4	4	0	0	0	0	0	0	.000
Weaver	P	2	4	0	1	0	0	0	0	.250
Carpenter	P	2	4	0	0	0	0	0	0	.000
Taguchi	LF-CF	5	3	1	3	1	0	1	3	1.000
Miles	2B	2	3	0	2	0	1	0	0	.667
Suppan	P	2	3	1	1	0	0	0	1	.333
Bennett	C	2	1	0	0	0	0	0	0	.000
Reyes	P	1	1	0	0	0	0	0	0	.000
Flores	P	4	0	0	0	0	0	0	0	—
Johnson	P	4	0	0	0	0	0	0	0	—
Kinney	P	3	0	0	0	0	0	0	0	—
Looper	P	3	0	0	0	0	0	0	0	—
Wainwright	P	3	0	0	0	0	0	0	0	—
Hancock	P	2	0	0	0	0	0	0	0	—
Thompson	P	2	0	0	0	0	0	0	0	—
NEW YORK										
TOTALS		3	234	27	54	12	1	8	27	.231
Reyes	SS	7	32	5	9	1	1	1	2	.281
Lo Duca	C	7	29	3	6	1	0	0	3	.207
Beltran	CF	7	27	8	8	1	0	3	4	.296
Chavez	LF	7	27	1	5	2	0	0	0	.185
Wright	3B	7	25	2	4	1	0	1	2	.160
Valentin	2B	7	24	0	6	2	0	0	5	.250
Delgado	1B	7	23	5	7	3	0	3	9	.304
Green	RF	7	23	2	7	1	0	0	2	.304
Tucker	PH	6	5	1	2	0	0	0	0	.400
Perez	P	2	5	0	0	0	0	0	0	.000
Glavine	P	2	4	0	0	0	0	0	0	.000
Floyd	LF	3	3	0	0	0	0	0	0	.000
Franco	PH	3	2	0	0	0	0	0	0	.000
Maine	P	2	2	0	0	0	0	0	0	.000
Oliver	P	1	2	0	0	0	0	0	0	.000
A. Hernandez	PH-PR	2	1	0	0	0	0	0	0	.000
Bradford	P	5	0	0	0	0	0	0	0	—
Mota	P	5	0	0	0	0	0	0	0	—
Feliciano	P	3	0	0	0	0	0	0	0	—
Heilman	P	3	0	0	0	0	0	0	0	—
R. Hernandez	P	3	0	0	0	0	0	0	0	—
Wagner	P	3	0	0	0	0	0	0	0	—
Trachsel	P	1	0	0	0	0	0	0	0	—

COMPOSITE PITCHING

NAME	G	IP	H	BB	SO	W	L	SV	ERA
ST. LOUIS									
TOTALS	7	61	54	24	36	4	3	2	3.84
Suppan	2	15	5	6	11	0	0	0	0.60
Weaver	2	11.2	10	4	2	1	1	0	3.09
Carpenter	2	11	13	4	5	0	1	0	5.73
Looper	3	4.2	7	0	1	0	0	0	5.79
Reyes	1	4	3	4	4	0	0	0	4.50
Flores	4	3.2	2	0	3	1	0	0	0.00
Johnson	4	3.2	2	1	5	0	0	0	2.45
Kinney	3	3.1	3	1	4	1	0	0	0.00
Wainwright	3	3	2	1	4	0	0	2	0.00
Thompson	2	0.2	3	0	1	0	1	0	27.00
Hancock	2	0.1	4	3	1	0	0	0	162.00
NEW YORK									
TOTALS	7	61	56	29	33	3	4	1	3.98
Perez	2	11.2	13	3	7	1	0	0	4.63
Glavine	2	11	11	5	4	1	0	0	2.45
Maine	2	9.1	4	9	8	1	0	0	2.89
Oliver	1	6	3	1	3	0	0	0	0.00
Bradford	5	5.1	3	0	2	0	0	0	0.00
Mota	5	4.1	4	2	2	0	0	0	4.15
Heilman	3	4.1	4	1	5	0	1	0	4.15
Feliciano	3	3	2	0	1	0	1	0	3.00
Wagner	3	2.7	7	1	0	0	1	1	16.87
Hernandez	3	2.1	0	2	0	0	0	0	0.00
Trachsel	1	1	5	5	1	0	1	0	45.00

MISCELLANEOUS 2006 INDIVIDUAL LEADERS

BATTING

On Base Average

	American League			National League	
1	Ramirez, Bos.	.439	1	Pujols, St.L.	.431
2	Hafner, Cle.	.439	2	Cabrera, Fla.	.430
3	Mauer, Min.	.429	3	Johnson, Was.	.428
4	Jeter, N.Y.	.417	4	Howard, Phi.	.425
5	Thome, Chi.	.416	5	Berkman, Hou.	.420
6	Giambi, N.Y.	.413	6	Atkins, Col.	.409
7	Ortiz, Bos.	.413	7	Helton, Col.	.404
8	Guillen, Det.	.400	8	Bay, Pit.	.396
9	Rodriguez, N.Y.	.392	9	Drew, L.A.	.393
10	Martinez, Cle.	.391	10	Hatteberg, Cin.	.389
				Abreu, Phi.N.-N.Y.A.	.424

On Base Average plus Slugging Average

	American League			National League	
1	Hafner, Cle.	1.098	1	Pujols, St.L.	1.102
2	Ramirez, Bos.	1.058	2	Howard, Phi.	1.084
3	Ortiz, Bos.	1.049	3	Berkman, Hou.	1.041
4	Thome, Chi.	1.014	4	Cabrera, Fla.	.998
5	Dye, Chi.	1.007	5	Beltran, N.Y.	.982
6	Giambi, N.Y.	.971	6	Holliday, Col.	.973
7	Mauer, Min.	.936	7	Atkins, Col.	.965
8	Morneau, Min.	.934	8	Johnson, Was.	.948
9	Guerrero, L.A.	.934	9	Bay, Pit.	.928
10	Konerko, Chi.	.932	10	LaRoche, Atl.	.915

Total Bases

	American League			National League	
1	Ortiz, Bos.	355	1	Howard, Phi.	383
2	Sizemore, Cle.	349	2	Soriano, Was.	362
3	Dye, Chi.	335	3	Pujols, St.L.	359
	Guerrero, L.A.	335	4	Holliday, Col.	353
5	Morneau, Min.	331	5	Utley, Phi.	347
	Wells, Tor.	331	6	Berkman, Hou.	335
7	Ibanez, Sea.	323	7	Berkman, Hou.	333
	Teixeira, Tex.	323		Ramirez, Chi.	333
	Tejada, Bal.	323	9	Rollins, Phi.	329
10	Young, Tex.	317	10	Cabrera, Fla.	327
				Lee, Mil.N.-Tex.A.	337

Caught Stealing

	American League			National League	
1	Podsednik, Chi.	19	1	Pierre, Chi.	20
2	Figgins, L.A.	16	2	Reyes, N.Y.	17
3	Castillo, Min.	11		Soriano, Was.	17
4	Damon, N.Y.	10	4	Ramirez, Fla.	15
	Kennedy, L.A.	10	5	Furcal, L.A.	13

Stolen Base Percentage
(Minimum 20 Attempts)

	American League			National League	
1	Suzuki, Sea.	96	1	Phillips, Cin.	93
2	Cabrera, L.A.	90	2	Rollins, Phi.	90
3	Jeter, N.Y.	87	3	Byrnes, Ari.	89
4	Crawford, T.B.	87	4	Roberts, S.D.	89
5	Roberts, Bal.	84	5	Lofton, L.A.	86
				Lee, Mil.N.-Tex.A.	90

Extra Base Hits

	American League			National League	
1	Sizemore, Cle.	92	1	Soriano, Was.	89
2	Ortiz, Bos.	85	2	Holliday, Col.	84
3	Teixeira, Tex.	79		Howard, Phi.	84
4	Wells, Tor.	77	4	Pujols, St.L.	83
5	Dye, Chi.	74	5	Beltran, N.Y.	80
	Hafner, Cle.	74		Ramirez, Chi.	80
	Sexson, Sea.	74		Lee, Mil.N.-Tex.A.	75

PITCHING

Fewest Hits Per 9 Innings Pitched

	American League			National League	
1	Santana, Min.	7.16	1	Young, S.D.	6.72
2	Santana, L.A.	7.99	2	Zambrano, Chi.	6.81
3	Mussina, N.Y.	8.39	3	Cain, S.F.	7.41
4	Lackey, L.A.	8.39	4	Carpenter, St.L.	7.88
5	Beckett, Bos.	8.40	5	Olsen, Fla.	7.97
6	Sabathia, Cle.	8.50	6	Schmidt, S.F.	7.97
7	Halladay, Tor.	8.51	7	Webb, Ari.	8.27
8	Johnson, N.Y.	8.52	8	Arroyo, Cin.	8.30
9	Zito, Oak.	8.59	9	Peavy, S.D.	8.32
10	Rogers, Det.	8.60	10	Hensley, S.D.	8.37

Fewest Bases on Balls Per 9 Innings Pitched

	American League			National League	
1	Schilling, Bos.	1.24	1	Lieber, Phi.	1.29
2	Halladay, Tor.	1.39	2	Oswalt, Hou.	1.55
3	Mussina, N.Y.	1.60	3	Maddux, Chi.-L.A.	1.59
4	Silva, Min.	1.60	4	Bush, Mil.	1.63
5	Garland, Chi.	1.75	5	Carpenter, St.L.	1.75
6	Radke, Min.	1.77	6	Capuano, Mil.	1.91
7	Santana, Min.	1.81	7	Webb, Ari.	1.91
8	Haren, Oak.	1.82	8	Smoltz, Atl.	2.13
9	Byrd, Cle.	1.91	9	Harang, Cin.	2.15
10	Garcia, Chi.	2.00	10	Lowe, L.A.	2.27

Strikeouts Per 9 Innings Pitched

	American League			National League	
1	Santana, Min.	9.44	1	Peavy, S.D.	9.56
2	Bonderman, Det.	8.50	2	Hernandez, Ari.-N.Y.	9.09
3	Hernandez, Sea.	8.29	3	Zambrano, Chi.	8.83
4	Vazquez, Chi.	8.17	4	Myers, Phi.	8.59
5	Schilling, Bos.	8.07	5	Cain, S.F.	8.45
6	Sabathia, Cle.	8.03	6	Harang, Cin.	8.30
7	Lilly, Tor.	7.93	7	Olsen, Fla.	8.27
8	Lackey, L.A.	7.86	8	Young, S.D.	8.23
9	Mussina, N.Y.	7.84	9	Smoltz, Atl.	8.19
10	Bedard, Bal.	7.84	10	Snell, Pit.	8.18

Lowest Batting Average Allowed

	American League			National League	
1	Santana, Min.	.216	1	Young, S.D.	.206
2	Santana, L.A.	.241	2	Zambrano, Chi.	.208
3	Mussina, N.Y.	.241	3	Cain, S.F.	.222
4	Beckett, Bos.	.245	4	Carpenter, St.L.	.235
5	Lackey, L.A.	.246	5	Schmidt, S.F.	.238

Home Runs Allowed

	American League			National League	
1	Silva, Min.	38	1	Marquis, St.L.	35
2	Beckett, Bos.	36	2	Arroyo, Cin.	31
	Buehrle, Chi.	36		Ortiz, Was.	31
4	Benson, Bal.	33	4	Sosa, Atl.-St.L.	30
5	Garcia, Chi.	32	5	Capuano, Mil.	29
	Lopez, Bal.	32		Hernandez, Was.-Ari.	29
				Milton, Cin.	29
				Myers, Phi.	29
				Snell, Pit.	29

Weaver, L.A.A.-St.L.N. 34
Moyer, Sea.A.-Phi.N. 33
Seo, L.A.N.-T.B.A. 31
Lidle, Phi.N.-N.Y.A. 30

Home Runs Allowed per 9 IP
(Minimum 10 Home Runs Allowed)

	American League			National League	
1	Chen, Bal.	2.55	1	Rusch, Chi.	2.85
2	Towers, K.C.	2.47	2	Floyd, Phi.	2.32
3	Elarton, K.C.	2.04	3	Sosa, Atl.-St.L.	2.29
4	Cotts, Chi.	2.00	4	Hirsh, Hou.	2.22
5	Burgos, K.C.	1.96	5	Wolf, Phi.	2.06
				Ortiz, Ari.N.-Bal.A.	2.57
				Guardado, Sea.A.-Cin.N.	2.43

The "losingest" team won! The St. Louis Cardinals went into the playoffs with a record only two wins above .500. Twelve teams had better records, including five excluded from the post-season. No team with so few regular season victories had ever won a World Series. In September, they nearly collapsed.

Small wonder many consider the playoffs a new season.

In the National League, the New York Mets were favored by many to go to the World Series. They reinforced those opinions with a quick sweep of the Los Angeles Dodgers. Although the Cardinals staggered home losing seven of their last ten games, they wrapped up the San Diego Padres in four games to reach the NLCS for the third straight year.

In the American League, the Detroit Tigers had been the feel good story all season, but as the playoffs began, they appeared to be out of wind. At season's end, a five-game loss cost them their division title. They opened their division series by dropping their first game with the Yankees. A TV ad proclaimed that, "October is the time to root against the Yankees," but Yankee-haters had little chance to do it. The Tigers showed they were not done yet by bouncing back for three straight wins to eliminate New York. Meanwhile, the Oakland A's surprised the Minnesota Twins, the most red-hot team at the end of the season, and cooled them with a three-game division series sweep.

The Tigers' resurrection against New York set rumors flying that Manager Joe Torre would be fired. He wasn't. Instead, the A's fired their manager, Ken Macha, when Detroit continued its rampage by knocking off Oakland in another sweep to take the A.L. pennant. Tiger second baseman Placido Polanco was the series MVP, but it was Magglio Ordonez's walk-off, three-run homer that cinched it for the Tigers.

The N.L. pennant was more of a battle. The Cardinals and Mets split the first six games. In the final, NLCS MVP Jeff Suppan allowed the Mets only two hits in seven-plus innings. Yadier Molina smashed a two-run ninth-inning homer to give the Cards their 3-1 victory.

The Cardinals had to work hard right up to the World Series, while the Tigers, as a consequence of their ALCS sweep had a week off to relax, enjoy their pennant, bask in the glory, and go flat. St. Louis took the World Series opener 7-2 on the arm of rookie pitcher Anthony Reyes and home runs by Albert Puljos and Scott Rolen. Three Tigers errors didn't help their cause.

The story of Game Two was Kenny Rogers. The veteran lefty held the Cards to two hits and ran his post-season scoreless streak to 23 straight innings. His mastery came under some suspicion as a few observers suggested that slight dark area on his hand might be more than a dirt smudge. Nothing came of the accusation, no doubt because the very idea of a major league player going outside the rules to win is so foreign to fans. Craig Monroe cracked his fifth home run of the playoffs. Almost overlooked was an excellent performance by Cardinal pitcher Jeff Weaver.

When the Series moved to Busch Stadium, the Cardinals jumped out in front on the dominant pitching of Chris Carpenter. Jim Edmonds made the big hit of the game, a two-run double in the fourth inning. Detroit's success was mainly due to strong pitching and defense. Ominously, in the first three games, the pitching had been erratic and the Tigers pitchers had made three errors.

A rainout of Game Four gave the Tigers a chance to relax, regroup, and rearm. When Detroit built a 3-0 lead in Game Four, the day off seemed to have done the trick. Then the Tigers fielding slipped again as Curtis Granderson took a misstep in center and Fernando Rodney committed the Tigers' fourth error by a pitcher. That set a record and they would add a fifth in Game Five. In the seventh inning, Cardinal Preston Wilson tied the score at 4-4 with an RBI single. Then in the eighth, David Eckstein's fourth hit and third double of the day drove in the winning run to give the Cardinals an overpowering 3-1 lead in the Series.

Of course, 3-1 was the game count for the Cardinals over the Tigers in 1968 when Mickey Lolich stepped in to turn the series around. Justin Verlander was no Lolich, but he held the Cardinals to one earned run through six innings. Unfortunately for Jim Leyland's team, Jeff Weaver was even more effective for Tony LaRussa's Cardinals. He struck out nine while limiting the Tigers to a single run in eight innings. There were more than enough heros in redbird uniforms. Yadier Molina had three hits and scored twice in Game Five, but the MVP for the Series was David Eckstein who added two RBIs and scored one to add to his series total.

WORLD SERIES

LINE SCORES

Team	1	2	3	4	5	6	7	8	9	10	11	12	R	H	E

WORLD SERIES: ST LOUIS 4 : DETROIT 1

Game 1   October 21 at Detroit

	1	2	3	4	5	6	7	8	9				R	H	E
STL	0	1	3	0	0	3	0	0	0				7	8	2
DET	1	0	0	0	0	0	0	0	1				2	4	3

Reyes, Looper (9)   Verlander, Grilli (6), Rodney (7), Ledezma (8), Jones (9), Walker (9)

Game 2   October 22 at Detroit

	1	2	3	4	5	6	7	8	9				R	H	E
STL	0	0	0	0	0	0	0	0	1				1	4	1
DET	0	0	1	0	0	2	0	0	x				3	10	1

Weaver, Johnson (6), Kinney (6), Flores (7), Thompson (8), Wainwright (8)   Rogers, Jones (9)

Game 3   October 24 at St. Louis

	1	2	3	4	5	6	7	8	9				R	H	E
DET	0	0	0	0	0	0	0	0	0				0	3	1
STL	0	0	0	2	0	0	2	1	x				5	7	0

Robertson, Ledezma (6), Zumaya (6), Grilli (7), Rodney (8), Miner (8)   Carpenter, Looper (9)

Game 4   October 26 at St. Louis

	1	2	3	4	5	6	7	8	9				R	H	E
DET	0	1	2	0	0	0	0	1	0				4	10	1
STL	0	0	1	1	0	0	2	1	x				5	9	0

Bonderman, Rodney (6), Zumaya (8)   Suppan, Kinney (7), Johnson (7), Looper (8), Wainwright (8)

Game 5   October 27 at St. Louis

	1	2	3	4	5	6	7	8	9				R	H	E
DET	0	0	0	2	0	0	0	0	0				2	5	2
STL	0	1	0	2	0	0	1	0	x				4	8	1

Verlander, Rodney (7), Zumaya (8)   Weaver, Wainwright (9)

COMPOSITE BATTING

NAME	POS	G	AB	R	H	2B	3B	HR	RBI	BA
ST. LOUIS										
TOTALS		5	158	22	36	12	0	2	16	.228
Eckstein	SS	5	22	3	8	3	0	0	4	.364
Rolen	3B	5	19	5	8	3	0	1	2	.421
Molina	C	5	17	3	7	2	0	1	1	.412
Edmonds	CF	5	17	1	4	2	0	0	4	.235
Pujols	1B	5	15	3	3	1	0	1	2	.200
Belliard	2B	3	12	0	0	0	0	0	0	.000
Taguchi	LF-RF	4	11	3	2	0	0	0	0	.182
Wilson	LF-DH	5	10	1	2	0	0	0	1	.200
Duncan	RF-DH	3	8	1	1	1	0	0	1	.125
Encarnacion	RF	3	8	0	0	0	0	0	1	.000
Miles	2B	2	6	2	1	0	0	0	0	.167
Spiezio	DH	2	4	0	0	0	0	0	0	.000
Weaver	P	2	3	0	0	0	0	0	0	.000
Carpenter	P	1	3	0	0	0	0	0	0	.000
Suppan	P	1	2	0	0	0	0	0	0	.000
Rodriguez	PH	1	1	0	0	0	0	0	0	.000
Looper	P	3	0	0	0	0	0	0	0	—
Wainwright	P	3	0	0	0	0	0	0	0	—
Johnson	P	2	0	0	0	0	0	0	0	—
Kinney	P	2	0	0	0	0	0	0	0	—
Flores	P	1	0	0	0	0	0	0	0	—
Reyes	P	1	0	0	0	0	0	0	0	—
Thompson	P	1	0	0	0	0	0	0	0	—
DETROIT										
TOTALS		5	161	11	32	8	1	4	11	.199
Granderson	CF	5	21	1	2	1	0	0	0	.095
Monroe	LF	5	20	3	3	1	0	2	2	.150
Rodriguez	C	5	19	1	3	1	0	0	1	.158
Ordonez	RF	5	19	2	2	0	0	0	0	.105
Casey	1B-DH	5	17	2	9	2	0	2	5	.529
Guillen	SS-1B	5	17	2	6	1	1	0	2	.353
Inge	3B	5	17	0	6	2	0	0	1	.353
Polanco	2B	5	17	0	0	0	0	0	0	.000
Santiago	SS	3	5	0	1	0	0	0	0	.200
Gomez	PH	3	3	0	0	0	0	0	0	.000
Verlander	P	2	2	0	0	0	0	0	0	.000
Bonderman	P	1	2	0	0	0	0	0	0	.000
Thames	LF	2	2	0	0	0	0	0	0	.000
Infante	PH	1	1	0	0	0	0	0	0	.000
Rodney	P	4	0	0	0	0	0	0	0	—
Zumaya	P	3	0	0	0	0	0	0	0	—
Grilli	P	2	0	0	0	0	0	0	0	—
Jones	P	2	0	0	0	0	0	0	0	—
Ledezma	P	2	0	0	0	0	0	0	0	—
Perez	SS-3B	2	0	0	0	0	0	0	0	—
Miner	P	1	0	0	0	0	0	0	0	—
Robertson	P	1	0	0	0	0	0	0	0	—
Rogers	P	1	0	0	0	0	0	0	0	—
Walker	P	1	0	0	0	0	0	0	0	—

COMPOSITE PITCHING

NAME	G	IP	H	BB	SO	W	L	SV	ERA
ST. LOUIS									
TOTALS	5	44	32	8	37	4	1	1	2.05
Weaver	2	13	13	2	14	1	1	0	2.77
Carpenter	1	8	3	0	6	1	0	0	0.00
Reyes	1	8	4	1	4	1	0	0	2.25
Suppan	1	6	8	2	4	0	0	0	4.50
Wainwright	3	3	2	1	5	1	0	1	0.00
Looper	3	2.1	1	0	1	0	0	0	3.86
Johnson	2	1	0	1	1	0	0	0	0.00
Kinney	2	1	0	2	1	0	0	0	0.00
Flores	1	1	1	0	0	0	0	0	0.00
Thompson	1	0.2	0	0	1	0	0	0	0.00
DETROIT									
TOTALS	5	42	36	23	34	1	4	1	3.00
Verlander	2	11	12	5	12	0	2	0	5.73
Rogers	1	8	2	3	5	1	0	0	0.00
Bonderman	1	5.1	6	4	4	0	0	0	3.38
Robertson	1	5	5	3	3	0	1	0	3.60
Rodney	4	4	5	4	5	0	0	0	4.50
Zumaya	3	3	1	3	3	0	1	0	3.00
Grilli	2	1.2	0	1	0	0	0	0	0.00
Jones	2	1.2	3	0	0	0	0	1	0.00
Ledezma	2	1.1	2	0	1	0	0	0	0.00
Miner	1	0.2	0	0	0	0	0	0	0.00
Walker	1	0.1	0	0	0	0	0	0	0.00

USE NAME - GIVEN NAMES (NICKNAMES)	TEAM BY YEAR	BIRTH DATE	BIRTH PLACE	DEATH DATE	B	T	HGT	WGT	G	AB	R	H	2B	3B	HR	RBI	BB	SO	SB	BA	SA
Abad, Andy-Fausto Andres	01OakA 03BosA 06CinN	08-25-72	West Palm Beach, Fla.		L	L	6'1	184	15	21	1	2	0	0	0	0	4	5	0	.095	.095
Abbott, Jeff-Jeffrey William	97-00ChiA 01FlaN	08-17-72	Atlanta, Ga.		R	L	6'2	200	233	596	82	157	33	2	18	83	38	91	6	.263	.416
Abbott, Kurt-Kurt Thomas	93OakA 94-97FlaN 98OakA 98-99ColN 00NYN 01AtlN	06-02-69	Zanesville, Ohio		R	R	6'	195	702	2044	273	523	109	23	62	242	133	571	22	.256	.423
Abercrombie, Reggie-Reginald Demascus	06FlaN	07-15-80	Columbus, Ga.		R	R	6'3	225	111	255	39	54	12	2	5	24	18	78	6	.212	.333
Abernathy, Brent-Michael Brent	01-03TBA 03KCA 05MinA	09-23-77	Atlanta, Ga.		R	R	6'	185	232	868	97	212	36	5	8	79	60	93	21	.244	.325
Abner, Shawn-Shawn Wesley	87-91SDN 91CalA 92ChiA	06-17-66	Hamilton, Ohio		R	R	6'1	190	392	840	89	191	39	4	11	71	43	153	6	.227	.323
Abreu, Bobby-Bob Kelly	96-97HouN 98-06PhiN 06NYA	03-11-74	Aragua, Venezuela		L	R	6'	200	1485	5276	951	1595	375	44	205	883	1003	1181	271	.302	.507
Adams, Bob-Robert Melvin	77DetA	01-06-52	Pittsburgh, Pa.		R	R	6'1	195	15	24	2	6	1	0	2	2	0	5	0	.250	.542
Adams, Glenn-Glenn Charles	75-76SFN 77-81MinA 82TorA	10-04-47	Northbridge, Mass.		L	R	6'	185	661	1617	152	452	79	5	34	225	111	183	6	.280	.398
Adams, Mike-Robert Michael	72-73MinA 76-77ChiN 78OakA	07-24-48	Cincinnati, Ohio		R	R	5'9	180	100	118	27	23	5	0	3	9	32	29	2	.195	.314
Adams, Rick-Ricky Lee	82-83CalA 85SFN	01-21-59	Upland, Cal.		R	R	6'1	180	120	247	35	53	5	1	4	16	10	37	3	.215	.291
Adams, Russ-Russ Moore	04-06TorA	08-30-80	Laurinburg, N.C.		L	R	6'1	180	251	804	109	200	43	7	15	101	77	103	13	.249	.376
Adduci, Jim-James David	83StLN 86MilA 87JL 88MilA 89PhiN	08-09-59	Chicago, Ill.		L	L	6'4	200	70	144	11	34	8	1	1	15	2	27	0	.236	.326
Afenir, Troy-Michael Troy	87HouN 90-91OakA 92CinN	09-21-63	Escondido, Cal.		R	R	6'4	185	45	79	4	15	2	2	0	7	5	32	0	.190	.266
Agbayani, Benny-Benny Peter	98-01NYN 02ColN 02BosA	12-28-71	Honolulu, Hawaii		R	R	6'0	225	383	1091	145	299	57	6	39	156	139	246	16	.274	.445
Aguayo, Luis-Luis [Muriel]	80-88PhiN 88NYA 89CleA	03-13-59	Vega Baja, P.R.		R	R	5'9	190	568	1104	142	260	43	10	37	109	94	220	7	.236	.393
Aguila, Chris-Christopher Louis	04-06FlaN	02-23-79	Redwood City, Cal.		R	R	5'11	180	141	218	26	51	13	2	3	16	14	57	2	.234	.353
Aikens, Willie-Willie Mays (Ack-Ack)	77,79CalA 80-83KCA 84-85TorA	10-14-54	Seneca, S.C.		L	R	6'2	220	774	2492	301	675	125	2	110	415	319	444	3	.271	.455
Ainge, Danny-Daniel Ray (81-94 played in N.B.A.)	79-81TorA 82RB	03-17-59	Eugene, Ore.		R	R	6'4	185	211	665	57	146	19	4	2	37	37	128	12	.220	.269
Alberts, Butch-Francis Burt	78TorA	05-04-50	Williamsport, Pa.		R	R	6'2	205	6	18	1	5	1	0	0	0	0	2	0	.278	.333
Alcantara, Israel-Israel [Cristosomo] (Izzy)	00-01BosA 02MilIN	05-06-73	Bani, Dom. Rep.		R	R	6'2	180	51	115	15	31	3	0	6	15	6	26	1	.270	.452
Aldrete, Mike-Michael Peter	86-88SFN 89-90MonN 91SDN 91CleA 93-95OakA 95-96CalA 96NYA	01-29-61	Carmel, Cal.		L	L	5'11	185	930	2147	277	565	104	9	41	271	314	381	19	.263	.377
Aldridge, Cory-Cory Jerome	01AtlN	06-13-79	San Angelo, Tex.		R	R	6'	210	8	5	1	0	0	0	0	0	0	4	0	.000	.000
Alexander, Gary-Gary Wayne (Sleepy)	75-77SFN 78OakA 78-80CleA 81PitN	03-27-53	Los Angeles, Cal.		R	R	6'2	195	432	1276	169	293	45	11	55	202	154	381	9	.230	.411
Alexander (DeJesus), Manny-Manuel DeJesus [Alexander]	92-93,95-96BalA 97NYN 97-99CinN 00BosA 04TexA 05-06SDN	03-20-71	San Pedro de Mac.,D.R.		R	R	5'10	180	594	1271	166	293	50	12	15	115	86	276	37	.231	.324
Alexander, Matt-Matthew (Sonny)	73-74ChiN 75-77OakA 78-81PitN	01-03-47	Shreveport, La.		B	R	5'11	170	374	168	111	36	4	2	0	4	18	26	103	.214	.262
Alfaro, Jason-Jason	04HouN	11-29-77	San Antonio, Tex.		R	R	5'10	165	7	11	1	2	0	0	0	0	0	5	0	.182	.182
Alfonzo, Edgardo-Edgardo Antonio	95-02NYN 03-05SFN 06LAA 06HouN	11-08-73	Santa Teresa, Venez.		R	R	5'11	195	1506	5385	777	1532	282	18	146	744	596	617	53	.284	.425
Alfonzo, Eliezer-Eliezer Jesus	06SFN	02-07-79	Puerto La Cruz, Venez.		R	R	6'0	225	87	286	27	76	17	2	12	39	9	74	1	.266	.465
Alicea, Luis-Luis Rene [DeJesus]	88,91-94StLN 95BosA 96StLN 97AnaA 98-00TexA 01-02KCA	07-29-65	Santurce, P.R.		B	R	5'9	175	1341	3971	551	1031	189	53	47	422	500	624	81	.260	.369
Allanson, Andy-Andrew Neal	86-89CleA 91DetA 92MilA 93SFN 94BG 95CalA	12-22-61	Richmond, Va.		R	R	6'5	255	512	1486	145	357	48	4	16	140	87	223	23	.240	.310
Allen, Chad-John Chad	99-01MinA 02CleA 03FlaN 04-05TexA	02-06-75	Dallas, Texas		R	R	6'1	195	267	851	102	229	44	8	14	84	63	173	15	.269	.389
Allen, Dusty-Dustin Rock	00SDN 00DetA	08-09-72	Oklahoma City, Okla.		R	R	6'4	215	27	28	5	7	2	0	2	4	2	12	0	.250	.536
Allen, Jamie-James Bradley	83SeaA	05-29-58	Yakima, Wash.		R	R	5'11	205	86	273	23	61	10	0	4	21	33	52	6	.223	.304
Allen, Kim-Kim Bryant	80-81SeaA	04-05-53	Fontana, Cal.		R	R	5'10	165	42	54	10	12	3	0	0	3	8	5	12	.222	.278
Allen, Luke-Lucas Gale	02LAN 03ColN	08-04-78	Covington, Ga.		L	R	6'2	220	8	9	2	1	1	0	0	0	0	3	0	.111	.222
Allen, Rod-Roderick Bernet	83SeaA 84DetA 88CleA	10-05-59	Los Angeles, Cal.		R	R	6'1	185	31	50	5	11	4	0	1	3	2	11	1	.220	.360
Allenson, Gary-Gary Martin (Mugs, Hardrock)	79-84BosA 85TorA	02-04-55	Culver City, Cal.		R	R	5'11	190	416	1061	114	235	49	2	19	131	130	192	3	.221	.325
Allensworth, Jermaine-Jermaine Lamont	96-98PitN 98KCA 98-99NYN	01-11-72	Anderson, Ind.		R	R	6'	190	342	1031	155	268	49	8	15	114	104	228	42	.260	.367
Allietta, Bob-Robert George	75CalA	05-01-52	New Bedford, Mass.		R	R	6'	178	21	45	4	8	1	0	1	2	1	6	0	.178	.267
Allred, Beau-Dale LeBeau	89-91CleA	06-04-65	Mesa, Ariz.		L	L	6'3	193	65	165	19	38	7	0	4	15	29	48	2	.230	.345
Almon, Bill-William Francis (Bats Both part of 80)	74-79SDN 80MonN 80NYN 81-82ChiN 83-84OakA 85-87PitN 87NYN 88PhiN	11-21-52	Providence, R.I.		R	R	6'3	190	1236	3330	390	846	138	25	36	296	250	636	128	.254	.343
Almonte, Erick-Erick R.	01,03NYA	02-01-78	Santo Domingo, D.R.		R	R	6'2	180	39	104	17	28	7	0	1	11	8	25	3	.269	.365
Alomar, Roberto-Roberto [Velazquez] (Bats Left part of 97)	88-90SDN 91-95TorA 96-98BalA 99-01CleA 02-03NYN 04AriN 04ChiA	02-05-68	Ponce, P.R.		B	R	6'	185	2379	9073	1508	2724	504	80	210	1134	1032	1140	474	.300	.443
Alomar, Sandy-Santos [Velazquez] Jr.	88-89SDN 90-00CleA 01-02ChiA 02ColN 03-04ChiA 05TexA 06LAN 06ChiA	06-18-66	Salinas, P.R.		R	R	6'5	225	1369	4508	519	1233	248	10	112	588	212	496	25	.274	.407
Alou, Moises-Moises Rojas	90PitN 90MonN 91SJ 92-96MonN 97FlaN 98HouN 99KJ 00-01HouN 02-04ChiN 05-06SFN	07-03-66	Atlanta, Ga.		R	R	6'3	210	1840	6660	1054	2005	400	38	319	1229	708	860	102	.301	.516
Alston, Dell-Wendell	77-78NYA 78OakA 79-80CleA	09-22-52	Valhalla, N.Y.		L	R	6'	180	189	332	48	79	7	4	3	35	28	44	20	.238	.310
Alvarez, Clemente-Clemente Rafael	00PhiN	05-18-68	Anzoategui, Venezuela		R	R	5'11	180	2	5	1	1	0	0	0	0	0	1	0	.200	.200
Alvarez, Gabe-Gabriel DeJesus	98-00DetA 00SDN	03-06-74	Navajoa, Mexico		R	R	6'1	195	92	266	22	59	15	0	7	33	24	76	1	.222	.357
Alvarez, Orlando-Jesus Manuel Orlando [Monge]	73-75LAN 76CalA	02-28-52	Rio Grande, P.R.		R	R	6'1	175	25	51	4	8	2	0	2	6	0	5	0	.157	.314
Alvarez, Tony-Antonio Enrique	02,04PitN	05-10-79	Caracas, Venezuela		R	R	6'1	202	38	64	11	16	4	0	2	10	7	12	1	.250	.406
Amaral, Rich-Richard Louis	91-98SeaA 99-00BalA	04-01-62	Visalia, Cal.		R	R	6'	175	727	1788	305	493	82	10	11	159	176	277	112	.276	.351
Amaro, Ruben-Ruben Jr.	91CalA 92-93PhiN 94-95CleA 96-98PhiN	02-12-65	Philadelphia, Pa.		B	R	5'10	175	485	927	99	218	43	9	16	100	88	128	15	.235	.353
Ambres, Chip-Raymond Payne	05KCA	12-19-79	Beaumont, Tex.		R	R	6'1	190	53	145	25	35	8	4	0	9	16	32	3	.241	.379
Amelung, Ed-Edward Allen	84,86LAN	04-13-59	Fullerton, Cal.		L	L	6'	180	42	57	7	11	0	0	0	4	2	8	3	.193	.193
Amezaga, Alfredo-Alfredo [Delgado]	02-04AnaA 05PitN 06FlaN	01-16-78	Ciudad Obregon, Mex.		B	R	5'10	165	259	551	74	132	16	5	7	39	46	94	27	.240	.325
Anderson, Brady-Brady Kevin	88BosA 88-01BalA 02CleA	01-18-64	Silver Spring, Md.		L	L	6'1	195	1834	6499	1062	1661	338	67	210	761	960	1190	315	.256	.425
Anderson, Brian-Brian Nikola	05-06ChiA	03-11-82	Tucson, Ariz.		R	R	6'2	205	147	399	49	88	24	1	10	36	30	102	5	.221	.361
Anderson, Dave-David Carter	83-89LAN 90-91SFN 92LAN	08-01-60	Louisville, Ky		R	R	6'2	190	873	2026	244	490	73	12	19	143	206	331	49	.242	.318
Anderson, Drew-Drew Thomas	06MilN	06-09-81	Kearney, Neb.		L	R	6'2	195	9	9	3	1	0	0	0	1	0	4	0	.111	.111
Anderson, Garret-Garret Joseph	94-96CalA 97-04AnaA 05-06LAA	06-30-72	Los Angeles, Cal.		L	L	6'3	225	1760	7015	891	2081	431	31	241	1128	341	986	70	.297	.470
Anderson, Jim-James Lea	78-79CalA 80-81SeaA 83-84TexA	02-23-57	Los Angeles,Cal.		R	R	5'11	180	419	970	107	211	35	2	13	86	81	130	9	.218	.298
Anderson, Kent-Kent McKay	89-90CalA	08-12-63	Florence, S.C.		R	R	6'1	185	135	366	43	95	12	1	1	22	30	61	1	.260	.311
Anderson, Marlon-Marlon Ordell	98-02PhiN 03TBA 04StLN 05NYN 06WasN 06LAN	01-06-74	Montgomery, Ala.		L	R	5'11	192	994	2897	359	792	161	20	59	334	210	426	65	.267	.394
Anderson, Mike-Michael Allen	71-75PhiN 76-77StLN 78BalA 79PhiN	06-22-51	Florence, S.C.		R	R	6'2	200	721	1490	159	367	67	11	28	134	161	343	8	.246	.362
Andino, Robert-Robert Lazaro	05-06FlaN	04-25-84	Miami, Fla.		R	R	6'	170	28	68	4	11	5	0	0	3	6	14	2	.162	.235
Andrew, Kim-Kim Darnell	75BosA	11-14-53	Burbank, Cal.		R	R	5'11	165	2	2	0	1	0	0	0	0	0	0	0	.500	.500
Andrews, Fred-Fred (Smokey)	76-77PhiN	05-04-52	Lafayette, La.		R	R	5'8	165	16	29	4	8	0	1	0	2	3	5	2	.276	.345
Andrews, Rob-Robert Patrick	75-76HouN 77-79SFN	12-11-52	Santa Monica, Cal.		R	R	5'11	180	493	1454	174	365	30	15	3	91	148	121	33	.251	.298
Andrews, Shane-Darrell Shane	95-99MonN 99-00ChiN 02BosA	08-28-71	Dallas, Tex.		R	R	6'1	220	569	1704	196	375	76	4	86	263	191	515	7	.220	.421
Anthony, Eric-Eric Todd	89-93HouN 94SeaA 94-95CinN 96ColN 97LAN	11-08-67	San Diego, Cal.		L	L	6'2	195	682	1999	249	462	81	8	78	269	217	491	24	.231	.397
Ardoin, Danny-Daniel Wayne	00MinA 04TexA 05-06ColN 06BalA	07-08-74	Mamou, La.		R	R	6'	215	141	372	47	75	18	1	7	31	40	114	1	.202	.306
Arias, Alex-Alejandro	92ChiN 93-97FlaN 98-00PhiN 01SDN 02NYA	11-20-67	New York, N.Y.		R	R	6'3	200	775	1773	203	470	84	6	18	196	181	211	10	.265	.350
Arias, George-George Albert	96CalA 97AnaA 97-99SDN	03-12-72	Tucson, Ariz.		R	R	5'11	190	173	480	46	114	18	2	14	55	25	121	2	.238	.371
Arias, Joaquin-Joaquin	06TexA	09-21-84	Santo Domingo, D.R.		R	R	6'1	165	6	11	4	6	1	0	0	1	1	0	0	.545	.636
Armas, Marcos-Marcos Rafael [Ruiz]	93OakA	08-05-69	Puerto Piritu, Venez.		R	R	5'11	205	15	31	7	6	2	0	1	5	1	12	1	.194	.355
Armas, Tony-Antonio Rafael [Machado]	76PitN 77-82OakA 83-86BosA 87-89CalA	07-12-53	Anzoategui,Venezuela		R	R	5'11	205	1432	5164	614	1302	204	39	251	815	260	1201	18	.252	.453
Armbrister, Ed-Edson Rosando	73-77CinN	07-04-58	Nassau, Bahamas		R	R	6'	175	224	265	46	65	11	6	4	19	24	71	15	.245	.377
Arndt, Larry-Larry Wayne	89OakA	02-25-63	Fremont, Ohio		R	R	6'2	195	2	6	1	1	0	0	0	1	0	1	0	.167	.167
Arnold, Chris-Christopher Paul	71-76SFN	11-06-47	Long Beach, Cal.		R	R	5'11	185	273	435	47	103	12	5	4	51	42	76	1	.237	.315
Asadoor, Randy-Randall Carl	86SDN	10-20-62	Fresno, Cal.		R	R	6'1	185	15	55	9	20	5	0	0	7	3	13	1	.364	.455
Ashby, Alan-Alan Dean (Bats Left 75, 79, part of 77-78)	73-76CleA 77-78TorA 79-89HouN	07-08-51	Long Beach, Cal.		B	R	6'	190	1370	4123	397	1010	183	13	90	513	461	622	7	.245	.361
Ashford, Tucker-Thomas Steven	76-78SDN 80TexA 81NYA 83NYN 84KCA	12-04-54	Memphis, Tenn.		R	R	6'1	185	222	510	50	111	31	1	6	55	47	75	5	.218	.318
Ashley, Billy-Billy Manual	92-97LAN 98BosA	07-11-70	Trenton, Mich.		R	R	6'7	225	281	618	56	144	23	1	28	84	63	236	0	.233	.409
Asselstine, Brian-Brian Hanly	76-81AtlN	09-23-53	Santa Barbara, Cal.		L	R	6'1	185	284	574	52	146	27	4	12	68	38	74	5	.254	.378
Atkins, Garrett-Garrett Bernard	03-06ColN	12-12-79	Orange, Cal.		R	R	6'2	210	335	1218	188	368	83	2	43	221	131	165	4	.302	.479
Aude, Rich-Richard Thomas	93,95-96PitN	07-13-71	Van Nuys, Cal.		R	R	6'5	220	62	151	11	34	9	0	2	24	7	35	1	.225	.325
Auerbach, Rick-Frederick Steven (Reindeer)	71-73MilA 74-76LAN 77-80CinN 80TexA 81SeaA	02-15-50	Glendale, Cal.		R	R	6'1	175	624	1407	167	309	56	5	9	86	127	198	36	.220	.286
Augustine, Dave-David Ralph (Augie)	73-74PitN	11-28-49	Follansbee, W.Va.		R	R	6'2	178	29	29	4	6	1	0	0	1	1	8	0	.207	.241
Ault, Doug-Douglas Reagan	76TexA 77-78,80TorA	03-09-50	Beaumont, Tex.	12-22-04	R	L	6'2	205	256	713	66	168	29	5	17	86	71	108	4	.236	.362
Aurilia, Rich-Richard Santo	95-03SFN 04SeaA 04SDN 05-06CinN	09-02-71	Brooklyn, N.Y.		R	R	5'11	180	1353	4863	682	1352	259	19	169	655	390	736	22	.278	.443
Ausmus, Brad-Bradley David	93-96SDN 96DetA 97HouN 98-00DetA 01-06HouN	04-14-69	New Haven, Conn.		R	R	5'11	195	1716	5556	652	1408	240	31	73	547	560	883	95	.253	.347
Aven, Bruce-David Bruce	97CleA 99FlaN 00PitN 00-01LAN 02CleA	03-04-72	Orange, Tex.		R	R	5'9	180	259	609	85	166	33	2	20	100	57	135	6	.273	.432
Aviles, Ramon-Ramon Antonio [Miranda]	77BosA 79-81PhiN	01-22-52	Manati, P.R.		R	R	5'9	170	117	190	21	51	9	0	1	24	21	22	0	.268	.347
Ayala, Benny-Benigno [Felix]	74,76NYN 77StLN 79-84BalA 85CleA	02-07-51	Yauco, P.R.		R	R	6'1	195	425	865	114	217	42	1	38	145	71	136	2	.251	.434

USE NAME - GIVEN NAMES (NICKNAMES)	TEAM BY YEAR	BIRTH DATE	BIRTH PLACE	DEATH DATE	B	T	HGT	WGT	G	AB	R	H	2B	3B	HR	RBI	BB	SO	SB	BA	SA
Aybar, Erick-Erick Johan	06LAA	01-14-84	Bani, Dom. Rep.		B	R	5'10	170	34	40	5	10	1	1	0	2	0	8	1	.250	.325
Aybar, Willy-Willy Del Jesus	05-06LAN 06AtlN	03-09-83	Bani, Dom. Rep.		B	R	6'	175	105	329	44	96	26	0	5	40	46	47	4	.292	.416
Ayrault, Joe-Joseph Allen	96AtlN	10-08-71	Rochester, Mich.		R	R	6'3	190	7	5	0	1	0	0	0	0	0	1	0	.200	.200
Azocar, Oscar-Oscar Gregorio [Azocar]	90NYA 91-92SDN	02-21-65	Soro, Venez.		L	L	6'1	170	202	439	38	99	16	0	5	36	12	36	10	.226	.296
Babitt, Shooty-Mack Neal	81OakA	03-09-59	Oakland, Cal.		B	R	5'8	175	54	156	10	40	4	1	3	14	13	13	5	.256	.301
Backman, Wally-Walter Wayne	80-88NYN 89MinA 90PitN 91-92PhiN 93SeaA	09-22-59	Hillsboro, Ore.		B	R	5'8	165	1102	3245	482	893	138	19	10	240	371	480	117	.275	.339
Baerga,Carlos-Carlos Obed [Ortiz]	90-96CleA 96-98NYN 99SDN 02BosA 03-04AriN 05WasN	11-04-68	Santurce, P.R. Bats Left part of 97		B	R	5'11	210	1630	5439	731	1583	279	17	134	774	291	580	59	.291	.423
Baez (Mota), Jose-Antonio [Baez]	77-78SeaA	12-31-53	San Christobal, D.R.		R	R	5'9	160	114	355	47	87	14	2	1	19	25	27	7	.245	.304
Baez, Kevin-Kevin Richard	90, 92-93NYN	01-10-67	Brooklyn, N.Y.		R	R	6'	170	63	151	10	27	10	0	0	7	13	17	0	.179	.245
Bagwell, Jeff-Jeffrey Robert	91-05HouN 06SJ	05-27-68	Boston, Mass.		R	R	6'	205	2150	7797	1517	2314	488	32	449	1529	1401	1558	202	.297	.540
Bailey, Mark-John Mark	84-88HouN 90, 92SFN	11-04-61	Springfield, Mo.		B	R	6'5	215	340	949	101	209	37	1	24	101	166	222	2	.220	.337
Bailor, Bob-Robert Michael (Buzz)	75-76BalA 77-80TorA 81-83NYN 84-85LAN	07-10-51	Connellsville, Pa.		R	R	5'10	165	955	2937	339	775	107	23	9	222	187	164	90	.264	.325
Baines, Harold-Harold Douglas	80-89ChiA 90-92OakA 93-95BalA 96-97ChiA 97-99BalA 99CleA 00BalA 00-01ChiA	03-15-59	Easton, Md.		L	L	6'2	190	2830	9908	1299	2866	488	49	384	1628	1062	1441	34	.289	.465
Baker, Chuck-Charles Joseph	78,80SDN 81MinA	12-06-52	Seattle, Wash.		B	R	5'11	175	93	146	14	27	2	3	0	9	3	27	0	.185	.240
Baker, Dave-David Glenn	82TorA	11-25-57	Lacona, Iowa		L	R	6'	185	9	20	3	5	1	0	0	2	3	3	0	.250	.300
Baker, Doug-Douglas Lee	84-87DetA 88-90MinA	04-03-61	Fullerton, Cal.		B	R	5'9	165	136	246	38	51	11	2	0	22	18	62	3	.207	.268
Baker, Dusty-Johnnie B.	68-75AtlN 76-83LAN 84SFN 85-86OakA M93-02SFN M03-06ChiN	06-15-49	Riverside, Cal.		R	R	6'	195	2039	7117	964	1981	320	23	242	1013	762	926	137	.278	.432
Baker, Jack-Jack Edward (Buck)	76-77BosA	05-04-50	Birmingham, Ala.		R	R	6'5	220	14	26	1	3	0	0	1	2	1	6	0	.115	.231
Baker, Jeff-Jeffrey Glen	05-06ColN	06-21-81	Bad Kissagen, Germany		R	R	6'2	210	30	95	19	29	11	2	6	25	6	26	2	.305	.653
Bako, Paul-Gabor Paul	98DetA 99-00HouN 00FlaN 00-01AtlN 02MilN 03-04ColN 05LAN 06KCA	06-20-72	Lafayette, La.		L	R	6'2	210	586	1631	140	385	80	8	14	143	171	417	4	.236	.321
Balaz, John-John Larry (Blazer)	74-75CalA	09-26-51	Toronto, Canada		R	R	6'3	185	59	162	14	39	8	1	2	15	7	35	0	.241	.340
Balboni, Steve-Stephen Charles (Bye-Bye)	81-83NYA 84-88KCA 88SeaA 89-90NYA 93TexA	01-16-57	Brockton, Mass.		R	R	6'3	230	960	3120	351	714	127	11	181	495	273	856	1	.229	.451
Baldelli, Rocco-Rocco Dan	03-04TBA 05KJ 06TBA	09-25-81	Woonsocket, R.I.		R	R	6'4	190	384	1519	227	439	83	17	43	209	74	286	54	.289	.451
Baldwin, Billy-Robert Harvey	75DetA 76NYN	06-09-51	Tazewell, Va.		L	L	6'	180	39	117	12	27	4	1	5	13	6	16	2	.231	.410
Baldwin, Jeff-Jeffrey Allen	90HouN	09-05-65	Milford, Del.		L	L	6'1	180	7	8	1	0	0	0	0	0	1	2	0	.000	.000
Baldwin, Reggie-Reginald Conrad	78-79HouN	08-19-54	River Rouge, Mich.		R	R	6'	195	52	87	5	21	6	0	1	12	3	4	0	.241	.345
Ball, Jeff-Jeffery D.	98SFN	04-17-69	Merced, Cal.		R	R	5'10	185	2	4	0	1	0	0	0	0	0	2	0	.250	.250
Bando, Chris-Christopher Michael (C.B.)	81-88CleA 88DetA 89OakA	02-04-56	Cleveland, Ohio		B	R	6'	195	498	1284	134	292	46	2	27	142	138	197	1	.227	.329
Bando, Sal-Salvatore Leonard	66-67KCA 68-76OakA 77-81MilA	02-13-44	Cleveland, Ohio		R	R	6'	210	2019	7060	982	1790	289	38	242	1039	1031	923	75	.254	.408
Banister, Jeff-Jeffery Todd	91PitN	01-15-65	Weatherford, Okla.		R	R	6'2	200	1	1	0	1	0	0	0	0	0	0	0	1.000	1.000
Banks, Brian-Brian Glen	96-97MilA 98-99MilN 00JL 02-03FlaN	09-28-70	Mesa, Ariz.		B	R	6'3	205	273	495	65	122	19	3	13	64	62	129	8	.246	.376
Bannister, Alan-Alan	74-75PhiN 76-80ChiA 80-83CleA 84HouN 84-85TexA	09-03-51	Montebello, Cal.		R	R	5'11	175	972	3007	430	811	143	28	19	288	292	318	106	.270	.355
Barajas, Rod-Rodrigo Richard	99-03AriN 04-06TexA	09-05-75	Ontario, Calif.		R	R	6'2	220	536	1621	196	389	99	1	58	225	85	283	1	.240	.410
Barberie, Bret-Bret Edward	91-92MonN 93-94FlaN 95BalA 96ChiN	08-16-67	Long Beach, Cal.		B	R	5'11	185	479	1434	163	388	73	6	16	133	164	268	16	.271	.363
Bard, Josh-Joshua David	02-05CleA 06BosA 06SDN	03-30-78	Ithaca, N.Y.		B	R	6'3	210	256	744	75	204	44	1	22	101	68	119	1	.270	.421
Barfield, Jesse-Jesse Lee	81-89TorA 89-92NYA	10-29-59	Joliet, Ill.		R	R	6'1	200	1428	4759	715	1219	216	30	241	716	551	1234	66	.256	.466
Barfield, Josh-Joshua LaRoy	06SDN	12-17-82	Barquisimeto, Venez.		R	R	6'	185	150	539	72	151	32	3	13	58	30	81	21	.280	.423
Barker, Glen-Glen Franklin	99-01HouN	05-10-71	Albany, N.Y.		R	R	5'10	180	235	164	53	38	4	1	3	18	21	48	30	.232	.323
Barker, Kevin-Kevin Stewart	99-00MilN 02SDN 06TorA Bats Both 99	07-26-75	Bristol, Va.		L	L	6'3	205	97	253	30	62	9	0	6	33	31	56	3	.245	.352
Barkett, Andy-Andrew Jon	01PitN	09-05-74	Miami, Fla.		L	L	6'1	205	17	46	5	14	2	0	1	3	4	7	1	.304	.413
Barmes, Clint-Clint Harold	03-06ColN	03-06-79	Vincennes, Ind.		R	R	6'	175	244	924	128	234	50	6	19	114	41	128	11	.253	.382
Barnes, John-John Delbert	00-01MinA	04-24-76	San Diego, Cal.		R	R	6'2	205	20	58	6	14	4	0	0	4	2	4	0	.241	.310
Barnes, Larry-Larry Richard Jr.	01AnaA 03LAN	07-24-76	Bakersfield, Cal.		L	L	6'1	195	46	78	4	12	2	0	1	4	4	18	0	.154	.244
Barnes, Skeeter-William Henry	83-84CinN 85MonN 87StlN 89CinN 91-94DetA	03-07-57	Cincinnati, Ohio		R	R	5'11	180	353	614	95	159	30	4	14	83	41	74	20	.259	.389
Barnwell, Chris-Christopher Edward	06MilN	03-01-79	Jacksonville, Fla.		R	R	5'10	180	13	30	2	2	0	0	0	1	1	6	1	.067	.067
Barranca, German-German [Costales]	79-80KCA 81-82CinN	10-19-56	Veracruz, Mexico		L	R	6'	170	67	62	19	18	2	3	0	3	2	9	5	.290	.419
Barrett, Marty-Martin Glenn (Bubble)	82-90BosA 91SDN	06-23-58	Arcadia, Cal.		R	R	5'10	170	941	3378	418	938	163	9	18	314	304	209	57	.278	.347
Barrett, Michael-Michael Patrick	98-03MonN 04-06ChiN	10-22-76	Atlanta, Ga.		R	R	6'3	200	916	3056	357	819	200	21	86	372	250	402	9	.268	.432
Barrett, Tommy-Thomas Loren	88-89PhiN 90KJ 92BosA	04-02-60	San Fernando, Cal.		B	R	5'10	165	54	84	9	17	1	0	0	4	10	15	0	.202	.214
Barrios, Jose-Jose Manuel	82SFN	06-26-57	New York, N.Y.		R	R	6'4	200	10	19	2	3	0	0	0	0	1	4	0	.158	.158
Barron, Tony-Anthony Dirk	96MonN 97PhiN	08-17-66	Portland, Ore.		R	R	6'	185	58	190	22	54	12	1	4	24	12	39	0	.284	.421
Barry, Jeff-Jeffrey Finas	95NYN 98-99ColN	09-22-68	San Diego, Cal.		R	R	6'1	200	104	217	25	53	18	0	5	28	22	48	0	.244	.396
Bartee, Kimera-Kimera Anotchi	96-99DetA 00CinN 01ColN Bats Both 98	07-21-72	Omaha, Neb.		R	R	6'	200	243	416	69	90	12	5	4	33	36	141	36	.216	.298
Bartlett, Jason-Jason Alan	04-06MinA	10-30-79	Mountain View, Cal.		R	R	6'	180	181	569	79	158	28	3	5	49	44	84	16	.278	.364
Bass, Kevin-Kevin Charles (K.B.)	82MilA 82-89HouN 90-92SFN 92NYN 93-94HouN 95BalA	05-12-59	Menlo Park, Cal.		B	R	6'	190	1571	4839	609	1308	248	40	118	611	357	668	151	.270	.411
Bass, Randy-Randy William (Oak)	77MinA 78KCA 79MonN 80-82SDN 82TexA	03-13-54	Lawton, Okla.		L	R	6'1	210	130	325	24	69	6	2	9	42	30	51	0	.212	.326
Bates, Billy-William Derrick	89-90MilA 90CinN	12-07-63	Houston, Tex.		L	R	5'7	155	29	48	11	6	1	0	0	2	4	10	8	.125	.146
Bates, Jason-Jason Charles	95-98ColN	01-05-71	Downey, Cal.		B	R	5'11	170	319	677	88	162	38	5	12	69	88	152	5	.239	.363
Bathe, Bill-William David	86OakA 89-90SFN	10-14-60	Downey, Cal.		R	R	6'2	195	121	183	15	39	4	1	8	29	9	39	0	.213	.377
Batista, Rafael-Rafael [Sanchez]	73,75HouN	11-21-45	San Pedro de Mac,D.R.		L	L	6'1	190	22	25	2	7	1	0	0	2	1	10	0	.280	.320
Batista,Tony-Leocadio Francisco	96-97OakA 98-99AriN 99-01TorA 01-03BalA 04MonN 05JL 06MinA	12-09-73	Puerto Plata, D.R.		R	R	6'	205	1229	4467	615	1120	223	17	219	702	275	776	47	.251	.455
Batiste, Kevin-Kevin Wade	89TorA	10-21-66	Galveston, Tex.		R	R	6'1	185	6	8	1	2	0	0	0	0	0	5	0	.250	.250
Batiste, Kim-Kimothy Emil	91-94PhiN 96SFN	03-15-68	New Orleans, La.		R	R	6'	200	251	658	59	154	23	1	10	64	14	120	4	.234	.318
Battle, Allen-Allen Zelmo	95StlN 96OakA	11-29-68	Grantham, N.C.		B	R	6'	170	108	248	33	57	8	0	1	7	32	52	13	.230	.314
Battle, Howard-Howard Dion	95TorA 96PhiN 99AtlN	03-25-72	Biloxi, Miss.		R	R	6'	200	29	37	5	9	0	0	1	5	6	13	1	.243	.324
Baughman, Justin-Justin Reis	98AnaA 99BBL 00AnaA	08-01-74	Mountain View, Cal.		R	R	5'11	175	79	218	28	55	11	1	1	20	7	38	13	.252	.326
Bautista, Danny-Daniel [Alcantara]	93-96DetA 96-98AtlN 99-00FlaN 00-04AriN	05-24-72	Santo Domingo, D.R.		R	R	5'11	215	895	2517	317	685	121	19	62	319	149	409	37	.272	.409
Bautista, Jose-Jose Antonio	04BalA 04TBA 04KCA 04-06PitN	10-19-80	Santo Domingo, D. R.		R	R	6'	192	192	516	67	116	24	3	16	54	56	157	3	.225	.376
Bay, Jason-Jason Raymond	03SDN 03-06PitN	09-20-78	Trail, Canada		R	R	6'2	200	471	1667	287	487	104	14	97	306	257	456	39	.292	.546
Baylor, Don-Don Edward (Groove)	70-75BalA 76OakA 77-82CalA 83-85NYA 86-87BosA 87MinA 88OakA M93-98ChiA M00-02ChiN	06-28-49	Austin, Tex.		R	R	6'1	200	2292	8198	1236	2135	366	28	338	1276	805	1069	285	.260	.436
Beall, Bob Robert Brooks	75,78-79AtlN 80PitN	04-24-48	Portland, Ore.		B	L	5'11	180	148	234	32	54	12	0	1	18	45	41	4	.231	.295
Beamon, Charlie-Charles Alonzo	78-79SeaA 81TorA	12-04-53	Oakland, Cal.		L	L	6'1	185	45	51	8	10	2	0	0	0	3	8	1	.196	.235
Beamon, Trey-Clifford III	96PitN 97SDN 98DetA	02-11-74	Dallas, Tex.		L	L	6'3	195	95	158	16	40	9	0	0	15	11	36	3	.253	.310
Bean, Billy-William Daro	87-89DetA 89LAN 92JL 93-95SDN	05-11-64	Santa Ana, Cal.		L	L	6'	190	272	478	42	108	20	2	5	53	25	84	3	.226	.308
Beane, Billy-William Lamar	84-85NYN 86-87MinA 88DetA 89OakA	03-29-62	Orlando, Fla.		R	R	6'4	205	148	301	30	66	14	0	3	29	11	80	5	.219	.296
Beasley, Lew-Lewis Paige	77TexA	08-27-48	Sparta, Va.		L	R	5'9	178	25	32	5	7	1	0	0	3	2	12	1	.219	.250
Becker, Rich-Richard Godhard	93-95,97MinA 98NYN 98BalA 99MilN 99-00OakA 00DetA Bats Both 93-95	02-01-72	Aurora, Ill.		L	L	5'10	190	789	2227	345	570	100	12	45	243	350	616	66	.256	.372
Belanger, Mark-Mark Henry	65-81BalA 82LAN	06-08-44	Pittsfield, Mass.	10-06-98	R	R	6'2	185	2016	5784	676	1316	175	33	20	389	576	839	167	.228	.280
Belcher, Kevin-Kevin Donnell	90TexA	06-08-67	Waco, Tex.		R	R	6'	170	16	15	4	2	1	0	0	0	2	8	0	.133	.200
Belk, Tim-Timothy William	96CinN	04-06-70	Cincinnati, Ohio		R	R	6'3	200	7	15	2	3	1	0	0	1	0	2	0	.200	.200
Bell, Buddy-David Gus	72-78CleA 79-85TexA 85-88CinN 88HouN 89TexA M96-98DetA M00-02ColN M05-06KCA	08-27-51	Pittsburgh,Pa.		R	R	6'2	185	2405	8995	1151	2514	425	56	201	1106	836	776	55	.279	.406
Bell, David-David Michael	95CleA 95-98StlN 98CleA 98-01SeaA 02SFN 03-06PhiN 06MilN	09-14-72	Cincinnati, Ohio		R	R	5'10	185	1403	4826	587	1239	267	18	123	589	428	687	19	.257	.396
Bell, Derek-Derek Nathaniel	91-92TorA 93-94SDN 95-99HouN 00NYN 01PitN	12-11-68	Tampa, Fla.		R	R	6'2	215	1210	4578	664	1262	202	33	134	668	377	955	170	.276	.421
Bell, George-Jorge Antonio [Mathey]	81,83-90TorA 91ChiN 92-93ChiA	10-21-59	San Pedro de Mac.D.R.		R	R	6'1	200	1587	6123	814	1702	308	34	265	1002	331	771	67	.278	.469
Bell, Jay-Jay Stuart	86-88CleA 89-96PitN 97KCA 98-02AriN 03NYN	12-11-65	Eglin A.F.B., Fla.		R	R	6'1	185	2063	7398	1123	1963	394	67	195	860	853	1443	91	.265	.416
Bell, Juan-Juan [Mathey]	89-91BalA 92-93PhiN 93MilA 94MonN 95BosA Bats right 89	03-29-68	San Pedro de Mac,D.R.		R	R	5'11	175	329	836	107	177	30	6	10	71	84	189	16	.212	.298
Bell, Kevin-Kevin Robert	76-80ChiA 82OakA	07-13-55	Los Angeles, Cal.		R	R	6'	195	297	726	74	161	22	9	13	64	70	165	5	.222	.331
Bell, Mike-Michael Allen	90-91AtlN	04-22-68	Lewiston, N.Y.		L	L	6'	175	53	75	12	15	5	2	0	6	4	16	1	.200	.373
Bell, Mike-Michael John	00CinN	12-07-74	Cincinnati, Ohio		R	R	6'	195	19	27	5	6	2	0	0	2	4	7	0	.222	.444
Bell, Terry-Terence William	86KCA 87AtlN	12-07-62	Dayton, Ohio		R	R	6'	195	9	4	0	0	0	0	0	0	0	1	0	.000	.000
Belle, Albert-Albert Jojuan	89-96CleA 97-98ChiA 99-00BalA 01-03PJ 89-90 known as Joey Belle	08-25-66	Shreveport, La.		R	R	6'2	220	1539	5853	974	1726	389	21	381	1239	683	961	88	.295	.564
Bellhorn, Mark-Mark Christian	97-98,00-01OakA 02-03ChiN 03ColN 04-05BosA 05NYA 06SDN	08-23-74	Boston, Mass.		B	R	6'1	200	718	2093	322	483	113	13	69	245	342	718	30	.231	.396
Belliard, Rafael-Rafael Leonidas [Matias]	82-90PitN 91-98AtlN Bats Both 82	10-24-61	Pueblo Nuevo, D.R.		R	R	5'6	160	1155	2301	217	508	55	14	2	142	136	384	43	.221	.259

USE NAME - GIVEN NAMES (NICKNAMES)	TEAM BY YEAR	BIRTH DATE	BIRTH PLACE	DEATH DATE	B	T	HGT	WGT	G	AB	R	H	2B	3B	HR	RBI	BB	SO	SB	BA	SA
Belliard, Ron-Ronald	98-02MilN 03ColN 04-06CleA 06StLN	04-07-75	New York, N.Y.		R	R	5'9	190	1049	3812	528	1036	247	21	80	439	379	576	32	.272	.411
Bellinger, Clay-Clayton Daniel	99-01NYA 02AnaA	11-18-68	Oneonta, N.Y.		R	R	6'3	205	183	311	57	60	11	3	12	35	22	82	7	.193	.363
Belloir, Rob-Robert Edward	75-78AtlN	07-13-48	Heidelberg, Germany		R	R	5'10	165	81	167	18	36	5	1	0	13	12	15	0	.216	.257
Beltran, Carlos-Carlos Ivan	98-04KCA 04HouN 05-06NYN	04-24-77	Manati, P.R.		B	R	6'0	190	1176	4559	826	1280	245	55	203	763	522	836	227	.281	.492
Beltre, Adrian-Adrian [Perez]	98-04LAN 05-06SeaA	04-07-79	Santo Domingo, D.R.		R	R	5'11	220	1278	4685	613	1269	251	23	191	686	371	816	76	.271	.457
Beltre, Esteban-Esteban [Valera]	91-92ChiA 94-95TexA 96BosA	12-26-67	Ingenio Quisqueya,D.R.		R	R	5'10	170	186	401	46	95	17	0	1	35	28	73	5	.237	.287
Benard, Marvin-Marvin Larry	95-03SFN	01-20-70	Bluefields, Nicaragua		L	L	5'10	185	891	2630	441	714	138	21	54	260	265	454	105	.271	.402
Benavides, Freddie-Alfredo III	91-92CinN 93ColN 94MonN	04-07-66	Laredo, Tex.		R	R	6'2	185	219	534	53	135	26	5	4	52	20	91	4	.253	.343
Bench, Johnny-Johnny Lee	67-83CinN	12-07-47	Oklahoma City, Okla.		R	R	6'1	205	2158	7658	1091	2048	381	24	389	1376	891	1278	68	.267	.476
Benedict, Bruce-Bruce Edwin	78-89AtlN	08-18-55	Birmingham, Ala.		R	R	6'1	185	982	2878	214	696	98	6	18	260	328	251	12	.242	.299
Beniquez, Juan-Juan Jose [Torres]	71-72,74-75BosA 76-78TexA 79NYA 80SeaA 81-85CalA 86BalA 87KCA 87-88TorA	05-13-50	San Sebastian, P.R.		R	R	5'11	170	1500	4651	610	1274	190	30	79	476	349	551	104	.274	.379
Benitez, Yamil-Yamil Antonio	95-96MonN 97KCA 98AriN	10-05-72	San Juan, P.R.		R	R	6'2	195	169	448	47	109	16	3	19	60	25	106	4	.243	.420
Benjamin, Mike-Michael Paul	89-95SFN 96PhiN 97-98BosA 99-00PitN 01EJ 02PitN	11-22-65	Euclid, Ohio		R	R	6'	172	818	1926	227	442	109	15	24	169	106	429	44	.229	.339
Bennett, Gary-Gary David Jr.	95-96,98-01PhiN 01NYN 01-02ColN 03SDN 04MilN 05WasN 06StLN	04-17-72	Waukegan, Ill.		R	R	6'	205	518	1514	128	364	66	3	19	171	129	254	5	.240	.326
Benton, Butch-Alfred Lee	78,80NYN 82ChiN 85CleA	08-24-57	Tampa, Fla.		R	R	6'1	195	51	99	6	16	4	0	0	10	5	14	0	.162	.202
Benzinger, Todd-Todd Eric	87-88BosA 89-91CinN 91KCA 92LAN 93-95SFN	02-11-63	Dayton, Ky.		B	R	6'1	195	924	2856	316	733	135	18	66	376	181	552	21	.257	.386
Berblinger, Jeff-Jeffrey James	97StLN	11-19-70	Wichita, Kans.		R	R	6'0	190	7	5	1	0	0	0	0	0	0	1	0	.000	.000
Berg, Dave-David Scott	98-01FlaN 02-04TorA	09-03-70	Roseville, Cal.		R	R	5'11	195	582	1600	190	430	91	6	21	163	133	308	8	.269	.378
Berger, Brandon-Brandon Charles	01-04KCA	02-21-75	Covington, Ky.		R	R	5'11	205	81	217	28	46	8	2	8	24	15	45	2	.212	.378
Bergeron, Peter-Peter Francis	99-02,04MonN	11-09-77	Greenfield, Mass.		L	R	6'2	185	308	1103	171	249	41	13	8	56	119	252	31	.226	.308
Bergman, Dave-David Bruce	75,77NYA 78-81HouN 81-83SFN 84-92DetA	06-06-53	Evanston, Ill.		L	L	6'2	185	1349	2679	312	690	100	16	54	289	380	347	19	.258	.367
Bergolla, William-William Jose	05CinN	02-04-83	Carabobo, Venezuela		R	R	6'	175	17	38	3	5	0	0	0	1	0	10	0	.132	.132
Berkman, Lance-William Lance	99-06HouN	02-10-76	Waco, Texas		B	L	6'1	205	1059	3687	687	1120	258	18	225	753	690	720	47	.304	.567
Bernazard, Tony-Antonio [Garcia]	79-80MonN 81-83ChiA 83SeaA 84-87CleA 87OakA 88-90JL 91DetA	08-24-56	Caguas, P.R.		B	R	5'9	165	1071	3700	523	970	177	30	75	391	428	606	113	.262	.387
Bernhardt, Juan-Juan Ramon [Coradin] (Moncho)	76NYA 77-79SeaA	08-31-53	San Pedro de Mac,D.R.		R	R	6'	175	154	492	46	117	19	2	9	43	14	40	3	.238	.339
Berra, Dale-Dale Anthony	77-84PitN 85-86NYA 87HouN	12-13-56	Ridgewood, N.J.		R	R	6'	190	853	2553	236	603	109	9	49	278	210	422	32	.236	.344
Berroa, Angel-Angel Maria [Selmo]	01-06KCA	01-27-78	Santo Domingo, D.R.		R	R	5'11	175	618	2289	293	605	103	20	45	234	94	403	54	.264	.386
Berroa (Letta), Geronimo-Geronimo Emiliano [Letta]	89-90AtlN 92CinN 93FlaN 94-97OakA 97BalA 98CleA 98DetA 99TorA 00LAN	03-18-65	Santo Domingo, D.R.		R	R	6'	205	779	2506	379	692	113	9	101	382	276	510	19	.276	.449
Berry, Sean-Sean Robert	90-91KCA 92-95MonN 96-98HouN 99-00MilN 00BosA	03-22-66	Santa Monica, Cal.		R	R	6'	200	860	2413	310	657	153	10	81	369	206	438	47	.272	.445
Berryhill, Damon-Damon Scott	87-91ChiN 91-93AtlN 94BosA 95CinN 97SFN	12-03-63	South Laguna, Cal.		B	R	6'	210	683	2030	175	488	106	6	47	257	139	409	3	.240	.368
Beswick, Jim-James William	78SDN	02-12-58	Wilkinsburg, Pa.		B	R	6'2	190	17	20	2	1	0	0	0	0	1	7	0	.050	.050
Betancourt, Yuniesky-Yuniesky [Perez]	05-06SeaA	01-31-82	Santa Clara, Cuba		R	R	5'10	190	217	769	92	215	39	11	9	62	28	78	12	.280	.394
Betemit, Wilson-Wilson Antonio	01,04-06AtlN 06LAN	11-02-81	Santo Domingo, D.R.		B	R	6'2	190	288	669	88	181	35	4	22	76	64	176	5	.271	.433
Bevacqua, Kurt-Kurt Anthony (Dirty)	71-72CleA 73-74KCA 74PitN 75-76MilA 77-78TexA 79-80SDN 80-81PitN 82-85SDN	01-23-47	Miami Beach, Fla.		R	R	6'1	190	970	2117	214	499	90	11	27	275	221	329	12	.236	.327
Biancalana, Buddy-Roland Americo	82-87KCA 87HouN	02-02-60	Greenbrae, Cal.		B	R	5'11	160	311	550	70	113	16	7	6	30	41	157	8	.205	.293
Bianco, Tommy-Thomas Anthony (Toby)	75MilA	12-16-52	Rockville Centre, N.Y.		B	R	5'11	190	18	34	6	6	1	0	0	3	3	7	0	.176	.206
Bichette, Dante-Alphonse Dante	88-90CalA 91-92MilA 93-99ColN 00CinN 00-01BosA	11-18-63	West Palm Beach,Fla.		R	R	6'3	230	1704	6381	934	1906	401	27	274	1141	355	1078	152	.299	.499
Bieser, Steve-Steven Ray	97NYN 98PitN	08-04-67	Perryville, Mo.		L	R	5'10	170	60	80	18	20	4	0	0	5	9	22	2	.250	.300
Bigbie, Larry-Larry Robert	01-05BalA 05ColN 06StLN	11-04-77	Hobart, Ind.		L	R	6'4	205	392	1227	164	328	56	4	31	137	119	302	25	.267	.395
Biggio, Craig-Craig Alan	88-06HouN	12-14-65	Smithtown, N.Y.		R	R	5'11	185	2709	10359	1776	2930	637	52	281	1125	1137	1641	410	.283	.436
Biittner, Larry-Lawrence David (Butch)	70-71WasA 72-73TexA 74-76MonA 76-80ChiN 81-82CinN 83TexA	07-25-45	Fort Dodge, Iowa		L	L	6'2	195	1217	3151	310	861	144	20	29	354	236	287	10	.273	.358
Bilardello, Dann-Dann James	83-85CinN 86MonN 89-90PitN 91-92SDN	05-26-59	Santa Cruz, Cal.		R	R	6'	190	382	949	79	194	39	1	18	91	65	170	4	.204	.305
Bishop, Mike-Michael David	83NYN	11-05-58	Santa Maria, Cal.	02-08-05	R	R	6'2	200	3	8	2	1	1	0	0	3	0	4	0	.125	.250
Bjorkman, George-George Anton	83NYN	08-26-56	Ontario, Cal.		R	R	6'2	190	29	75	8	17	4	0	2	14	16	29	0	.227	.360
Blackwell, Tim-Timothy P.	74-75BosA 76-77PhiN 77MonN 78-81ChiN 82-83MonN	08-19-52	San Diego, Cal.		B	R	5'11	180	426	1044	91	238	40	11	6	80	154	183	3	.228	.305
Bladt, Rick-Richard Alan	69ChiN 75NYA	12-09-46	Santa Cruz, Cal.		R	R	6'1	160	62	130	14	28	3	1	1	12	11	13	6	.215	.277
Blake, Casey-William Casey	99TorA 00-01MinA 01BalA 02MinA 03-06CleA	08-23-73	Des Moines, Iowa		R	R	6'2	205	609	2180	320	567	129	5	89	288	205	490	25	.260	.446
Blalock, Hank-Hank Joe	02-06TexA	11-21-80	San Diego, Cal.		L	R	6'1	192	664	2576	368	700	139	9	105	398	241	519	6	.272	.455
Blanco, Andres-Andres Eloy [Perez]	04-06KCA	04-11-84	Urama, Venezuela		B	R	5'10	155	78	226	24	57	6	4	0	19	10	25	1	.252	.314
Blanco, Damie-Damaso [Caripe]	72-74SFN	11-12-41	Curlepe, Venezuela		R	R	5'9	160	72	33	9	7	1	0	0	2	5	6	3	.212	.242
Blanco, Henry-Henry Ramon	97LAN 99ColN 00-01MilN 02-03AtlN 04MinN 05-06ChiN	08-29-71	Caracas, Venezuela		R	R	5'11	220	666	1955	196	439	111	10	49	255	180	361	4	.225	.367
Blanco, Tony-Tony Hemiphere [Cabrera]	05WasN	11-10-81	San Juan de la Maguana, D.R.		R	R	6'1	175	56	62	7	11	3	0	1	7	2	19	1	.177	.274
Blankenship, Lance-Lance Robert	88-93OakA 94SJ	12-06-63	Portland, Ore.		R	R	6'	185	461	1050	171	233	48	3	9	92	200	218	54	.222	.299
Blanks, Larvell-Larvell (Sugar Bear, Scotter)	72-75AtlN 76-78CleA 79TexA 80AtlN	01-28-50	Del Rio, Tex.		R	R	5'8	165	629	1766	203	446	57	14	20	172	132	178	9	.253	.335
Blauser, Jeff-Jeffrey Michael	87-97AtlN 98-99ChiN	11-08-65	Los Gatos, Cal.		R	R	6'	185	1407	4522	691	1187	217	33	122	513	569	937	65	.262	.406
Blocker, Terry-Terry Fennell	85NYN 88-89AtlN	08-18-59	Columbia, S.C.		L	L	6'2	195	110	244	15	50	5	2	2	11	12	27	2	.205	.266
Blomberg, Ron-Ronald Mark (Boomer)	69,71-76NYA 77KJ 78ChiA	08-23-48	Atlanta, Ga.		L	R	6'1	205	461	1333	184	391	67	8	52	224	140	134	6	.293	.473
Bloomquist, Willie-William Paul	02-06SeaA	11-27-77	Bremerton, Wash.		R	R	5'11	185	378	917	131	236	42	6	4	76	69	167	50	.257	.329
Blosser, Greg-Gregory Brent	93-94BosA	06-26-71	Manatee, Fla.		L	L	6'3	200	22	39	3	3	1	0	0	3	3	15	1	.077	.103
Blowers, Mike-Michael Roy	89-91NYA 92-95SeaA 96LAN 97SeaA 98OakA 99SeaA	04-24-65	Wurzburg, Germany		R	R	6'2	190	761	2300	290	591	116	8	78	365	248	610	7	.257	.416
Blum, Geoff-Geoffrey Edward	99-01MonN 02-03HouN 04TBA 05SDN 05ChiA 06SDN	04-26-73	Redwood City, Calif.		B	R	6'3	200	900	2651	311	666	144	11	66	311	224	451	18	.251	.389
Bocachica, Hiram-Hiram Colon	00-02LAN 02-03DetA 04SeaA 05-06OakA	03-04-76	Ponce, P.R.		R	R	5'11	180	239	455	58	99	24	1	13	32	34	121	13	.218	.360
Bochte, Bruce-Bruce Anton	74-77CalA 77CleA 78-82SeaA 83VR 84-86OakA	11-12-50	Pasadena, Cal.		L	L	6'3	195	1538	5233	643	1478	250	21	100	658	653	662	43	.282	.396
Bochy, Bruce-Bruce Douglas	78-80HouN 82NYN 83-87,M95-05SDN	04-16-55	Landes de Bussac,Fr.		R	R	6'4	225	358	802	75	192	37	2	26	93	67	177	1	.239	.388
Bogar, Tim-Timothy Paul	93-96NYN 97-00HouN 01LAN	10-28-66	Indianapolis, Ind.		R	R	6'2	198	701	1516	180	345	69	9	24	161	143	272	13	.228	.332
Bogener, Terry-Terrence Wayne (Bogle)	82TexA	09-28-55	Hannibal, Mo.		L	L	6'	200	24	60	6	13	2	1	1	4	4	8	2	.217	.333
Boggs, Wade-Wade Anthony	82-92BosA 93-97NYA 98-99TBA	06-15-58	Omaha, Neb.		L	R	6'2	195	2440	9180	1513	3010	578	61	118	1014	1412	745	24	.328	.443
Bohn, T.J.-Thomas Joseph	06SeaA	01-17-80	St. Louis Park, Minn.		R	R	6'5	210	18	14	2	2	0	0	1	2	2	8	0	.143	.357
Boisclair, Bruce-Bruce Armand (Bo)	74,76-79NYN	12-09-52	Putnam, Conn.		L	L	6'3	195	410	917	114	241	47	6	10	77	86	183	18	.263	.360
Bolick, Frank-Frank Charles	93MonN 98AnaA	06-28-66	Ashland, Pa.		B	R	5'10	177	116	258	28	52	15	0	5	26	34	45	1	.202	.318
Bonds, Barry-Barry Lamar	86-92PitN 93-06SFN	07-24-64	Riverside, Cal.		L	L	6'2	205	2860	9507	2152	2841	587	77	734	1930	2426	1485	509	.299	.608
Bonds, Bobby-Bobby Lee	68-74SFN 75NYA 76-77CalA 78ChiA 78TexA 79CleA 80StLN 81CchN	03-15-46	Riverside, Cal.	08-23-03	R	R	6'1	195	1849	7043	1258	1886	302	66	332	1024	914	1757	461	.268	.471
Bonilla, Bobby-Roberto Martin Antonio	86ChiA 86-91PitN 92-94NYN 95-96BalA 97-98FlaN 98LAN 99NYN 00AtlN 01StLN	02-23-63	Bronx, N.Y.		B	R	6'3	230	2113	7213	1084	2010	408	61	287	1173	912	1204	45	.279	.472
Bonilla, Juan-Juan Guillermo [Urania]	81-83SDN 85NYA 86BalA 87NYA	02-12-55	Santurce, P.R.		R	R	5'9	170	429	1462	145	375	59	9	7	101	116	108	7	.256	.317
Bonnell, Barry-Robert Barry	77-79AtlN 80-83TorA 84-86SeaA	10-27-53	Mariemont, Ohio		R	R	6'3	205	976	3068	363	833	143	24	56	355	229	387	64	.272	.389
Bonner, Bob-Robert Averill	80-83BalA	08-13-56	Uvalde, Tex.		R	R	6'	185	61	108	15	21	5	1	0	8	4	16	1	.194	.259
Booker, Rod-Roderick Stewart	87-89StLN 90-91PhiN	09-04-58	Los Angeles, Cal.		L	R	6'	173	274	38	68	10	3	0	28	27	44	7	.248	.307
Boone, Aaron-Aaron John	97-03CinN 03NYA 04KJ 05-06CleA	03-09-73	La Mesa, Cal.		R	R	6'2	200	969	3437	469	907	192	16	115	499	264	612	105	.264	.429
Boone, Bob-Robert Raymond	72-81PhiN 82-88CalA 89-90,M95-97KCA M01-03CinN	11-19-47	San Diego, Cal.		R	R	6'2	200	2264	7245	679	1838	303	26	105	826	663	608	38	.254	.346
Boone, Bret-Bret Robert	92-93SeaA 94-98CinN 99SDN 00SDN 01-05SeaA 05MinA	04-06-69	El Cajon, Cal.		R	R	5'10	185	1780	6683	927	1775	366	28	252	1021	552	1295	94	.266	.442
Booty, Josh-Joshua Gibson	96-98FlaN	04-29-75	Starkville, Miss.		R	R	6'3	210	13	26	3	7	1	0	0	4	4	9	0	.269	.308
Borchard, Joe-Joseph Edward	02-05ChiA 06SeaA 06FlaN	11-25-78	Panorama City, Cal.		B	R	6'5	220	216	537	69	112	14	2	22	58	53	162	1	.209	.365
Borders, Pat-Patrick Lance	88-94TorA 95KCA 95HouN 96StLN 96CalA 96ChiA 97-99ClaN 97TorA 01-04SeaA 04-06MinN 05SeaA	05-14-63	Columbus, Ohio		R	R	6'2	200	1099	3282	289	831	168	12	69	368	155	557	9	.253	.375
Bordick, Mike-Michael Todd	90-96OakA 97-00BalA 00NYN 01-02BalA 03TorA	07-21-65	Marquette, Mich.		R	R	5'11	175	1720	5770	676	1500	257	30	91	626	500	800	96	.260	.362
Borgmann, Glenn-Glenn Dennis	72-79MinA 80ChiA	05-25-50	Paterson, N.J.		R	R	6'3	208	474	1294	137	296	42	4	16	151	191	191	4	.229	.304
Bosetti, Rick-Richard Alan	76PhiN 77StLN 78-81TorA 81-82OakA	08-05-53	Redding, Cal.		R	R	6'1	185	445	1543	172	385	70	8	17	133	79	188	30	.250	.338
Bosley, Thad-Thaddis Jr.	77CalA 78-80ChiA 81MilA 82SeaA 83-86ChiN 87-88KCA 88CalA 89-90TexA	09-17-56	Oceanside, Cal.		L	L	6'3	175	784	1581	183	430	50	12	20	158	143	275	47	.272	.357
Bostock, Lyman-Lyman Wesley	75-77MinA 78CalA	11-12-50	Birmingham, Ala.	09-24-78	L	R	6'1	175	526	2004	305	624	103	30	23	250	171	174	45	.311	.427
Boston, Daryl-Daryl Lamont	84-90ChiA 90-92NYN 93ColN 94NYA	01-04-63	Cincinnati, Ohio		L	L	6'3	200	1058	2629	378	655	131	22	83	278	237	469	98	.249	.410
Botts, Jason-Jason Carl	05-06TexA	07-26-80	Paso Robles, Cal.		B	R	6'5	250	30	77	12	18	0	0	3	11	11	31	0	.234	.338
Bourjos, Chris-Christopher (Taz)	80SFN	10-16-55	Chicago, Ill.		R	R	6'	185	13	22	4	5	1	0	0	1	1	4	0	.227	.409
Bourn, Michael-Michael Ray	06PhiN	12-27-82	Houston, Tex.		L	R	5'11	180	17	8	3	1	0	0	0	1	1	5	1	.125	.125
Bournigal, Rafael-Rafael Antonio [Pelletier]	92-94LAN 96-98OakA 99SeaA	05-12-66	Azua, Dom. Rep.		R	R	5'11	170	365	932	104	234	44	3	4	85	59	64	12	.251	.318
Bourque, Pat-Patrick Daniel	71-73ChiN 73-74OakA 74MinA	03-23-47	Worcester, Mass.		L	L	6'	220	201	405	36	87	17	2	12	61	58	73	1	.215	.356

USE NAME - GIVEN NAMES (NICKNAMES)	TEAM BY YEAR	BIRTH DATE	BIRTH PLACE	DEATH DATE	B	T	HGT	WGT	G	AB	R	H	2B	3B	HR	RBI	BB	SO	SB	BA	SA
Bowa, Larry-Lawrence Robert	70-81PhiN 82-85ChiN 85NYN M87-88SDN M01-04PhiN	12-06-45	Sacramento, Cal.		B	R	5'10	155	2247	8418	987	2191	262	99	15	525	474	569	318	.260	.320
Bowen, Rob-Robert McClure	03-04MinA 06SDN	02-24-81	Bedford, Texas		R	R	6'2	216	118	131	23	27	5	0	4	16	17	40	0	.206	.336
Bowen, Sam-Samuel Thomas	77-78,80BosA	09-18-52	Brunswick, Ga.		R	R	5'9	167	16	22	3	3	0	0	0	1	3	7	1	.136	.273
Bowers, Brent-Brent Raymond	96BalA	05-02-71	Bridgeview, Ill.		L	R	6'3	200	21	39	6	12	2	0	0	3	0	7	0	.308	.359
Bowie, Jim-James R.	94OakA	02-17-65	Tokyo, Japan		L	L	6'	205	6	14	0	3	0	0	0	0	0	2	0	.214	.214
Bowling, Steve-Stephen Shaddon	76MilA 77TorA	06-26-52	Tulsa, Okla.		R	R	6'	185	103	236	21	47	10	1	1	15	39	47	2	.199	.263
Boyland, Doe-Dorian Scott [Costales]	78-79,81PitN	01-06-55	Chicago, Ill.		L	L	6'4	205	21	19	1	2	0	0	0	1	1	6	0	.105	.105
Bradley, Mark-Mark Allen (Slo Mo)	81-82LAN 83NYN	12-03-56	Elizabethtown, Ky.		R	R	6'	185	90	113	13	23	5	0	3	5	11	36	4	.204	.327
Bradley, Milton-Milton Obelle Jr.	00-01MonN 01-03CleA 04-05LAN 06OakA	04-15-78	Los Angeles, Cal.		B	R	6'	190	630	2244	325	606	129	12	68	285	278	463	64	.270	.429
Bradley, Phil-Philip Poole	83-87SeaA 88PhiN 89-90BalA 90ChiA	03-11-59	Bloomington, Ind.		R	R	6'	185	1022	3695	565	1058	179	43	78	376	432	718	155	.286	.421
Bradley, Scott-Scott William	84-85NYA 86ChiA 86-92SeaA 92CinN	03-22-60	Glen Ridge, N.J.		L	R	5'11	190	604	1648	149	424	75	6	18	184	104	110	3	.257	.343
Bradshaw, Terry-Terry Leon	95-96StlN	02-03-69	Franklin, Va.		L	R	6'	180	34	65	10	17	2	1	0	5	5	12	1	.262	.323
Brady, Brian-Brian Phelan	89CalA	07-11-62	Queens, N.Y.		L	L	5'11	185	2	2	0	1	1	0	0	1	0	1	0	.500	1.000
Brady, Doug-Stephen Douglas	95ChiA	11-23-69	Jacksonville, Ill.		B	R	5'11	165	12	21	4	4	1	0	0	3	2	4	0	.190	.238
Bragg, Darren-Darren William	94-96SeaA 96-98BosA 99StlN 00ColN 01NYN 01NYA 02-03AtlN 04SDN 04CinN	09-07-69	Waterbury, Conn.		L	R	5'9	180	916	2461	341	627	145	14	46	260	304	570	56	.255	.381
Braggs, Glenn-Glenn Erick	86-90MilA 90-92CinN	10-17-62	San Bernardino, Cal.		R	R	6'3	210	692	2336	308	601	102	16	70	321	211	472	58	.257	.405
Branson, Jeff-Jeffery Glenn	92-97CinN 97-98CleA 00-01LAN	01-26-67	Waynesboro, Miss.		L	R	6'	180	694	1555	173	383	72	11	34	156	122	312	9	.246	.372
Brant, Marshall-Marshall Lee	80NYA 83OakA	09-17-55	Garberville, Cal.		R	R	6'5	215	8	20	2	2	0	0	0	2	0	6	0	.100	.100
Brantley, Mickey-Michael Charles	86-89SeaA	06-17-61	Catskill, N.Y.		R	R	5'10	185	302	1138	154	295	56	8	32	125	67	136	34	.259	.407
Branyan, Russell-Russell Oles	98-02CleA 02-03CinN 04-05MilN 06TBA 06SDN	12-19-75	Warner Robins, Ga.		L	R	6'3	195	627	1705	237	395	83	6	111	274	234	686	9	.232	.483
Braun, Steve-Stephen Russell	71-76MinA 77-78SeaA 78-80KCA 80TorA 81-85StlN	05-08-48	Trenton, N.J.		L	R	5'10	180	1425	3650	466	989	155	19	52	388	579	433	45	.271	.367
Brazell, Craig-Craig Walter	04NYN	05-10-80	Montgomery, Ala.		R	R	6'3	211	24	34	3	9	2	0	1	3	1	7	0	.265	.412
Bream, Sid-Sidney Eugene	83-85LAN 85-90PitN 91-93AtlN 94HouN	08-03-60	Carlisle, Pa.		L	L	6'4	220	1088	3108	351	819	191	12	90	455	346	450	47	.264	.420
Brede, Brent-Brent David	96-97MinA 98AriN	09-13-71	Belleville, Ill.		L	L	6'4	190	169	422	50	106	20	5	5	40	46	86	8	.251	.358
Breeden, Hal-Harold Noel	71ChiN 72-75MonN	06-28-44	Albany, Ga.		L	L	6'2	205	273	608	61	148	28	6	21	76	69	107	0	.243	.413
Brenly, Bob-Robert Earl	81-88SFN 89TorA 89SFN M01-04AriN	02-25-54	Coshocton, Ohio		R	R	6'2	210	871	2615	321	647	119	7	91	333	318	438	45	.247	.403
Brett, George-George Howard	73-93KCA	05-15-53	Glen Dale, W.Va.		L	R	6'1	200	2707	10349	1583	3154	665	137	317	1595	1096	908	201	.305	.487
Brewer, Mike-Michael Quinn	86KCA	10-24-59	Shreveport, La.		R	R	6'5	190	12	18	0	3	1	0	0	1	0	6	0	.167	.222
Brewer, Rod-Rodney Lee	90-93StlN	02-24-66	Eustis, Fla.		L	R	6'3	210	172	288	30	80	15	0	2	33	25	47	1	.278	.351
Brewer, Tony-Anthony Bruce	84LAN	11-25-57	Coushatta, La.		R	R	5'11	175	24	37	3	4	1	0	1	4	4	9	1	.108	.216
Briggs, Dan-Daniel Lee	75-77CalA 78CleA 79SDN 81MonN 82CinN	11-18-52	Scotia, Cal.		L	L	6'	180	325	688	67	134	20	6	12	53	45	133	2	.195	.294
Briley, Greg-Gregory (Pee Wee)	88-92SeaA 93FlaN	05-24-65	Greenville, N.C.		L	R	5'8	175	598	1518	172	384	75	9	29	135	124	260	65	.253	.372
Brito, Bernardo-Bernardo [Perez]	92-93,95MinA	12-04-63	San Cristobal, D.R.		R	R	6'1	190	40	73	10	16	5	0	3	12	1	27	0	.219	.466
Brito, Jorge-Jorge Manuel [Uceta]	95-96ColN	06-22-66	Moncion, Dom. Rep.		R	R	6'1	190	26	65	6	12	3	0	0	7	3	25	1	.185	.231
Brito, Juan-Juan Ramon	02KCA 04AriN	11-07-79	Santiago, Dom.Rep.		R	R	5'11	205	63	194	18	42	9	0	3	13	9	44	1	.216	.309
Brito, Tilson-Tilson Manuel [Jiminez]	96-97TorA 97OakA	05-28-72	Santo Domingo, D.R.		R	R	6'	175	92	252	27	60	12	1	3	21	20	56	2	.238	.329
Brock, Greg-Gregory Allen	82-86LAN 87-91MilA	06-14-57	McMinnville, Ore.		L	R	6'3	205	1013	3202	420	794	141	6	110	462	434	469	41	.248	.399
Brock, Tarrik-Tarrik Jumaan	00ChiN	12-25-73	Goleta, Cal.		L	L	6'3	170	13	12	1	2	0	0	0	0	4	4	1	.167	.167
Brogna, Rico-Rico Joseph	92DetA 94-96NYN 97-00PhiN 00BosA 01AtlN	04-18-70	Turners Falls, Mass.		L	L	6'2	200	848	2958	379	795	176	13	106	458	227	655	32	.269	.445
Brohamer, Jack-John Anthony (Hammer)	72-75CleA 76-77ChiA 78-80BosA 80CleA. Bats Both part 72	02-26-50	Maywood, Cal.		L	R	5'9	166	805	2500	262	613	91	12	30	227	222	178	9	.245	.327
Brookens, Tom-Thomas Dale	79-88DetA 89NYA 90CleA	08-10-53	Chambersburg, Pa.		R	R	5'10	180	1336	3865	477	950	175	40	71	431	281	605	86	.246	.403
Brooks, Hubie-Hubert	80-84NYN 85-89MonN 90LAN 91NYN 92CalA 93-94KCA	09-24-56	Los Angeles, Cal.		R	R	6'	195	1645	5974	656	1608	290	31	149	824	387	1015	64	.269	.403
Brooks, Jerry-Jerome Edward	93LAN 96FlaN	03-23-67	Syracuse, N.Y.		R	R	6'	195	17	14	4	4	1	1	1	4	1	3	0	.286	.714
Brosius, Scott-Scott David	91-97OakA 98-01NYA	08-15-66	Hillsboro, Ore.		R	R	6'1	200	1146	3889	544	1001	200	8	141	531	348	699	57	.257	.422
Brouhard, Mark-Mark Steven	80-85MilA	05-22-56	Burbank, Cal.		R	R	6'	210	304	909	108	235	40	7	25	104	53	183	2	.259	.400
Broussard, Ben-Benjamin Isaac	02-06CleA 06SeaA	09-24-76	Beaumont, Texas		L	L	6'3	220	580	1814	240	482	104	13	77	277	149	396	13	.266	.465
Brower, Bob-Robert Richard	86-88TexA 89NYA	01-10-60	Queens, N.Y.		R	R	5'11	190	256	582	104	141	21	3	17	60	69	118	29	.242	.376
Brown, Adrian-Adrian Demond	97-02PitN 03BosA 04KCA 06TexA	02-07-74	McComb, Miss.		B	R	6'0	195	447	1134	166	293	44	8	11	86	109	161	45	.258	.340
Brown, Bobby-Rodgers Lee	79TorA 79-81NYA 82SeaA 83-85SDN	05-24-54	Norfolk, Va.		B	R	6'1	210	502	1277	183	313	38	12	26	130	94	238	110	.245	.355
Brown, Brant-Brant Michael	96-98ChiN 99PitN 00FlaN 00ChiN	06-22-71	Porterville, Cal.		L	L	6'3	220	424	1056	142	261	52	11	45	146	74	316	15	.247	.445
Brown, Chris-John Christopher	84-87SFN 87-88SDN 89DetA	08-15-61	Jackson, Miss.		R	R	6'	200	449	1523	164	410	61	6	38	184	120	252	21	.269	.392
Brown, Curt-Curtis (Bubba)	86KCA	09-14-45	Sacramento, Cal.		R	R	6'	183	1	1	0	0	0	0	0	0	0	0	0	.000	.000
Brown, Darrell-Darrell Wayne (Downtown)	81DetA 82OakA 83-84MinA	10-29-55	Oklahoma City, Okla.		B	R	6'	185	210	591	82	162	15	6	1	44	25	47	9	.274	.325
Brown, Dee-Dermal Bram	98-04KCA	03-27-78	Bronx, N.Y.		L	R	5'11	215	263	811	86	190	37	1	14	89	50	205	8	.234	.334
Brown, Emil-Emil Quincy	97-01PitN 01SDN 05-06KCA	12-29-74	Chicago, Ill.		R	R	6'2	195	506	1476	204	388	85	4	40	205	145	332	30	.263	.414
Brown, Jake-Jerald Ray	75SFN	03-22-48	Sumrall, Miss.	12-18-81	R	R	6'2	200	41	43	6	9	3	0	0	4	5	13	0	.209	.279
Brown, Jarvis-Jarvis Ardel	91-92MinA 93SDN 94AtlN 95BalA	03-26-67	Waukegan, Ill.		R	R	5'7	165	155	227	44	46	11	2	1	10	26	49	13	.203	.282
Brown, Jeremy-Jeremy Scott	06OakA	10-25-79	Birmingham, Ala.		R	R	5'10	225	5	10	1	3	2	0	0	1	0	1	0	.300	.500
Brown, Kevin-Kevin Lee	96-97TexA 98-99TorA 00-01MilN 02BosA	04-21-73	Valparaiso, Ind.		R	R	6'2	220	85	189	30	48	12	2	7	31	14	59	0	.254	.450
Brown, Leon-Leon (Super Bee)	76NYN	11-16-49	Sacramento, Cal.		R	R	6'	180	64	70	11	15	3	0	0	2	4	14	2	.214	.257
Brown, Marty-Marty Leo	88-89CinN 90BalA	01-23-63	Lawton, Okla.		R	R	6'1	190	35	61	3	11	2	0	0	6	6	18	0	.180	.213
Brown, Mike-Michael Charles	83-85CalA 85-86PittN 88CalA	12-29-59	San Francisco, Cal.		R	R	6'2	195	315	903	105	239	49	7	23	113	77	135	5	.265	.411
Brown, Roosevelt-Roosevelt Lawayne	99-02ChiN	08-03-75	Vicksburg, Miss.		L	R	5'11	195	228	442	44	111	32	2	11	69	36	98	3	.251	.407
Browne, Jerry-Jerome Austin	86-88TexA 89-91CleA 92-93OakA 94-95FlaN	02-13-66	Christiansted, V.I.		B	R	5'10	170	982	3190	431	866	135	25	23	288	393	325	73	.271	.351
Bruett, J. T.-Joseph Timothy	92-93MinA	10-08-67	Milwaukee, Wis.		L	L	5'11	175	73	96	9	24	6	0	0	3	7	16	6	.250	.313
Brumbaugh, Cliff-Clifford Michael	01TexA 01ColN	04-21-74	Wilmington, Del.		R	R	6'2	205	21	46	6	10	2	0	1	4	3	14	0	.217	.326
Brumfield, Jacob-Jacob Donnell	92-94CinN 95-96PitN 96-97TorA 99LAN 99TorA	05-27-65	Bogalusa, La.		R	R	6'	185	568	1575	260	404	91	14	32	162	137	290	74	.257	.393
Brumley, Mike-Anthony Michael	87ChiN 89DetA 90SeaA 91-92BosA 93HouN 94OakA 95HouN	04-09-63	Oklahoma City, Okla.		B	R	5'10	165	295	635	78	131	17	4	3	38	46	136	20	.206	.272
Brummer, Glenn-Glenn Edward	81-84StlN 85TexA	11-23-54	Olney, Ill.		R	R	6'	200	178	347	29	87	16	0	1	27	25	54	0	.251	.305
Brunansky, Tom-Thomas Andrew (Bruno)	81CalA 82-88MinA 88-90StlN 90-92BosA 93-94MilA 94BosA	08-20-60	Covina, Cal.		R	R	6'5	215	1800	6289	804	1543	306	33	271	919	770	1187	69	.245	.434
Bruntlett, Eric-Eric Kevin	03-06HouN	03-29-78	Lafayette, Ind.		R	R	6'	200	240	334	47	84	18	2	6	36	30	69	14	.251	.398
Bryant, Derek-Derek Roszell	79OakA	10-09-51	Lexington, Ky.		R	R	5'11	185	39	106	8	19	2	1	0	13	10	10	0	.179	.217
Bryant, Ralph-Ralph Wendell	85-87LAN	05-20-61	Fort Gaines, Ga.		L	R	6'2	205	79	150	22	38	6	3	8	24	15	51	2	.253	.493
Brye, Steve-Stephen Robert	70-76MinA 77MilA 78PitN	02-04-49	Alameda, Cal.		R	R	6'	190	697	1997	237	515	97	13	30	193	144	276	16	.258	.365
Bubela, Jaime-Jaime Lee	05SeaA	06-06-78	Houston, Tex.		L	R	6'1	200	11	19	3	2	0	0	0	0	1	4	1	.105	.105
Buchanan, Brian-Brian James	00-02MinA 02-04SDN 04NYN	07-21-73	Miami, Fla.		R	R	6'4	230	346	767	105	198	37	3	32	103	73	210	9	.258	.439
Buck, John-Johnathan R.	04-06KCA	07-07-80	Kemmerer, Wyo.		R	R	6'3	210	303	1010	113	244	51	2	35	127	64	257	3	.242	.400
Buckley, Kevin-Kevin John	84TexA	01-16-59	Quincy, Mass.		R	R	6'1	195	5	7	1	2	1	0	0	0	2	0	0	.286	.429
Buckner, Bill-William Joseph	69-76LAN 77-84ChiN 84-87BosA 87-88CalA 88-89KCA 90BosA	12-14-49	Vallejo, Cal.		L	L	6'	185	2517	9397	1077	2715	498	49	174	1208	450	453	183	.289	.408
Budaska, Mark-Mark David	78,81OakA	12-27-52	Sharon, Pa.		B	L	6'	185	13	36	3	6	2	0	0	2	5	12	0	.167	.222
Budzinski, Mark-Mark Joseph	03CinN	08-26-73	Baltimore, Md.		L	L	6'2	180	4	7	0	0	0	0	0	0	0	4	0	.000	.000
Buechele, Steve-Steven Bernard	85-91TexA 91-92PitN 92-95ChiN 95TexA 00-01ChiN	09-26-61	Lancaster, Cal.		R	R	6'2	200	1334	4266	501	1046	183	21	137	547	408	842	17	.245	.394
Buford, Damon-Damon Jackson	93-95BalA 95NYN 96-97TexA 98-99BosA 00-01ChiN	06-12-70	Baltimore, Md.		R	R	5'10	180	699	1853	280	448	86	9	54	218	173	430	56	.242	.385
Buhner, Jay-Jay Campbell	87-88NYA 88-01SeaA	08-13-64	Louisville, Ky.		R	R	6'3	215	1472	5013	798	1273	233	19	310	965	792	1406	6	.254	.494
Bullett, Scott-Scott Douglas	91,93PitN 95-96ChiN	12-25-68	Martinsburg, W. Va.		L	L	6'2	200	247	374	49	87	10	8	10	42	25	102	19	.233	.356
Bulling, Terry-Terry Charles (Bud)	77MinA 81-83SeaA	12-15-52	Lynwood, Cal.		R	R	6'	200	138	345	34	77	11	0	3	28	45	41	2	.223	.281
Bullock, Eric-Eric Gerald	85-86HouN 88MinA 89PhiN 90-92MonN	02-16-60	Los Angeles, Cal.		L	L	5'11	185	131	146	13	30	1	0	0	12	13	23	9	.205	.267
Bumbry, Al-Alonza Benjamin (Bumble Bee)	72-84BalA 85SDN	04-21-47	Fredericksburg, Va.		L	R	5'8	175	1496	5053	778	1422	220	52	54	402	471	709	254	.281	.378
Burke, Chris-Christopher Allen	04-06HouN	03-11-80	Houston, Tex.		R	R	5'11	180	248	701	109	181	42	3	14	66	53	142	22	.258	.387
Burke, Glenn-Glenn Lawrence (Mandingo, Mad Hatter)	76-78LAN 78-79OakA 80KCJ	11-16-52	Oakland, Cal.	05-30-95	R	R	5'11	195	225	523	50	124	18	2	3	41	55	77	35	.237	.291
Burke, Jamie-James Eugene	01AnaA 03-05CinN	09-24-71	St. Louis, Mo.		R	R	6'	195	73	134	23	34	4	1	4	15	10	15	3	.254	.396
Burkhart, Morgan-Morgan	00-01BosA 02JL 03KCA	01-29-72	St. Louis, Mo.		B	L	5'11	225	42	121	20	30	7	0	4	23	19	38	0	.248	.405
Burks, Ellis-Ellis Rena	87-92BosA 93ChiA 94-98ColN 98-00SFN 01-03CleA 04BosA	09-11-64	Vicksburg, Miss.		R	R	6'2	205	2000	7232	1253	2107	402	63	352	1206	793	1340	181	.291	.510
Burleson, Rick-Richard Paul (The Rooster)	74-80BosA 81-84,86CalA 85SJ 87BalA	04-19-51	Lynwood, Cal.		R	R	5'10	160	1346	5139	656	1401	256	23	50	449	420	477	72	.273	.361

USE NAME - GIVEN NAMES (NICKNAMES)	TEAM BY YEAR	BIRTH DATE	BIRTH PLACE	DEATH DATE	B	T	HGT	WGT	G	AB	R	H	2B	3B	HR	RBI	BB	SO	SB	BA	SA
Burnitz, Jeromy-Jeromy Neal	93-94NYN 95-96CleA 96-97MilA 98-01MilN 02-03NYN 04LAN 05ColN 06PitN	04-15-69	Westminster, Cal.		L	R	6'	210	1694	5710	917	1447	298	29	315	981	739	1376	74	.253	.481
Burrell, Pat-Patrick Brian (Pat the Bat)	00-06PhiN	10-10-76	Eureka Springs, Ark.		R	R	6'4	230	994	3527	504	911	194	11	188	644	569	1017	5	.258	.479
Burroughs, Jeff-Jeffrey Alan	70-71WasA 72-76TexA 77-80AtlN 81SeaA 82-84OakA 85TorA	03-07-51	Long Beach, Cal.		R	R	6'2	200	1689	5536	720	1443	230	20	240	882	831	1135	16	.261	.439
Burroughs, Sean-Sean Patrick	02-05SDN 06TBA	09-12-80	Atlanta, Ga.		L	R	6'2	200	440	1537	179	431	63	12	11	134	115	205	19	.280	.358
Busch, Mike-Michael Anthony	95-96LAN	07-07-68	Davenport, Iowa		R	R	6'5	240	51	100	11	22	4	0	7	23	5	40	0	.220	.470
Bush, Homer-Homer Giles	97-98NYA 99-02TorA 02FlaN 04NYA	11-12-72	East St. Louis, Ill.		R	R	5'11	200	409	1274	176	363	50	5	11	115	57	238	65	.285	.358
Bush, Randy-Robert Randall	82-93MinA	10-05-58	Dover, Del.		L	R	6'1	190	1219	3045	388	763	154	26	96	409	348	505	33	.251	.413
Buskey, Mike-Michael Thomas	77PhiN	01-13-49	San Francisco, Cal.		R	R	5'11	160	6	7	1	2	0	1	0	1	0	1	0	.286	.571
Busse, Ray-Raymond Edward	71HouN 73StlN 73-74HouN	09-25-48	Daytona Beach, Fla.		R	R	6'4	185	68	155	12	23	8	2	2	9	11	54	0	.148	.265
Butera, Sal-Salvatore Philip	80-82MinA 83DetA 84-85MonN 86-87CinN 87MinA 88TorA	09-25-52	Queens, N.Y.		R	R	6'	185	359	801	63	182	24	3	8	76	86	85	0	.227	.295
Butler, Brent-Justin Brent	01-03ColN	02-11-78	Laurinburg, N.C.		R	R	6'	180	203	553	85	137	28	6	11	60	24	60	4	.248	.380
Butler, Brett-Brett Morgan	81-83AtlN 84-87CleA 88-90SFN 91-94LAN 95NYN 95-97LAN	06-15-57	Los Angeles, Cal.		L	L	5'10	160	2213	8180	1359	2375	277	131	54	578	1129	907	558	.290	.376
Butler, Rich-Richard Dwight	97TorA 98-99TBA	05-01-73	Toronto, Canada		L	R	6'1	205	86	251	30	56	5	3	7	22	19	44	4	.223	.351
Butler, Rob-Robert Frank John	93-94TorA 97PhiN 99TorA	04-10-70	East York, Canada		L	L	5'11	185	93	218	32	53	13	2	0	21	19	28	3	.243	.321
Bynum, Freddie-Freddie Lee	05OakA 06ChiN	03-15-80	Wilson, N.C.		L	R	6'1	180	78	143	20	37	6	5	4	13	9	47	8	.259	.455
Byers, Randy-Randell Parker	87-88SDN	10-02-64	Bridgeton, N.J.		L	R	6'2	180	21	26	1	7	2	0	0	1	1	10	1	.269	.346
Byrd, Jim-James Edward	93BosA	10-03-68	Wewahitchka, Fla.		R	R	6'1	185	2	0	0	0	0	0	0	0	0	0	0	—	—
Byrd, Marlon-Marlon Jerrard	02-05PhiN 05-06WasN	08-30-77	Boynton Beach, Fla.		R	R	6'	225	408	1302	184	342	66	9	20	123	108	267	21	.263	.373
Byrnes, Eric-Eric James	00-05OakA 05ColN 05BalA 06AriN	02-16-76	Redwood City, Cal.		R	R	6'2	210	652	2102	324	548	132	20	74	259	162	365	65	.261	.448
Cabell, Enos-Enos Milton (Big E)	72-74BalA 75-80HouN 81SFN 82-83DetA 84-85HouN 85-86LAN	10-08-49	Fort Riley, Kans.		R	R	6'5	190	1688	5952	753	1647	263	56	60	596	259	691	238	.277	.370
Cabrera, Alex-Alexander Alberto	00AriN	12-24-71	Caripito, Venezuela		R	R	6'2	220	31	80	10	21	2	1	5	14	4	21	0	.263	.500
Cabrera, Francisco-Francisco [Paulino]	89TorA 89-93AtlN	10-10-66	Santo Domingo, D.R.		R	R	6'4	195	196	351	32	89	17	1	17	62	21	69	2	.254	.453
Cabrera, Jolbert-Jolbert Alexis	98-02CleA 02-03LAN 04SeaA	12-08-72	Cartagena, Colombia		R	R	6'0	177	561	1291	172	333	73	8	15	145	65	212	36	.258	.362
Cabrera, Melky-Melky	05-06NYA	08-11-84	Santo Domingo, D. R.		B	L	5'11	170	136	479	76	133	26	2	7	50	56	61	12	.278	.384
Cabrera, Miguel-Jose Miguel [Torres]	03-06FlaN	04-18-83	Maracay, Venezuela		R	R	6'2	200	563	2106	358	654	145	8	104	404	243	465	15	.311	.535
Cabrera, Orlando-Orlando Luis	97-04MonN 04BosA 05-06LAA	11-02-74	Cartagena, Colombia		R	R	5'11	180	1256	4663	605	1254	306	27	89	541	333	429	145	.269	.403
Cacek, Craig-Craig Thomas	77HouN	09-10-54	Hollywood, Cal.		R	R	6'2	200	7	20	0	1	0	0	0	1	1	3	0	.050	.050
Caceres, Edgar-Edgar Fidel	95KCA	06-06-64	Barquisimeto, Venez.		B	R	6'	180	55	117	13	28	6	2	1	17	8	15	2	.239	.350
Cage, Wayne-Wayne Levell	78-79CleA	11-23-51	Jonesboro, La.		L	L	6'4	210	65	154	17	37	8	1	5	19	14	44	1	.240	.403
Cairo, Miguel-Miguel Jesus	96TorA 97ChiN 98-00TBA 01ChiN 01-03StlN 04NYA 05NYN 06NYA	05-04-74	Anaco, Venezuela		R	R	6'	200	1010	2921	372	782	141	25	27	280	175	336	113	.268	.361
Calderon, Ivan-Ivan [Perez]	84-85SeaA 86-90ChiA 91-92MonN 93BosA 93ChiA	03-19-62	Fajardo, P.R.	12-27-03	R	R	6'1	220	924	3312	470	901	200	25	104	444	306	556	97	.272	.442
Callaspo, Alberto-Alberto Jose	06AriN	04-19-83	Maracay, Venezuela		B	R	5'10	175	23	42	2	10	1	1	0	6	4	2	0	.238	.310
Calloway, Ron-Ronald Isiah	03-04MonN	09-04-76	San Jose, Cal.		L	L	6'1	210	172	424	40	95	19	1	10	62	25	102	11	.224	.344
Calzado, Napoleon-Napoleon	05BalA	02-09-77	Santo Domingo, D. R.		R	R	6'3	200	4	5	0	1	0	0	0	0	0	0	0	.200	.200
Cameron, Mike-Michael Terrance	95-98ChiA 99CinN 00-03SeaA 04-05NYN 06SDN	01-08-73	La Grange, Ga.		R	R	6'1	195	1409	4881	778	1228	272	48	195	708	629	1340	254	.252	.447
Caminiti, Ken-Kenneth Gene	87-94HouN 95-98SDN 99-00HouN 01TexA 01AtlN	04-21-63	Hanford, Cal.	10-10-04	B	R	6'	200	1760	6288	894	1710	348	17	239	983	727	1163	88	.272	.447
Campusano, Sil-Silvestre [Diaz]	88TorA 90-91PhiN	12-31-65	Mano Guayabo, D.R.		R	R	6'	175	154	262	26	53	11	3	5	23	16	59	1	.202	.324
Canale, George-George Anthony	89-91MilA	08-11-65	Memphis, Tenn.		L	R	6'1	190	44	73	15	12	4	0	4	13	12	15	0	.164	.384
Canate, Willie-Emisael William [Librada]	93TorA	12-11-71	Maracaibo, Venez.		R	R	6'	170	38	47	12	10	0	0	1	3	6	15	1	.213	.277
Cancel, Robinson-Robinson Castro	99MilN 00SJ	05-04-76	Lajas, P.R.		R	R	6'	175	15	44	5	8	2	0	0	5	2	12	0	.182	.227
Candaele, Casey-Casey Todd	86-88MonN 88,90-93HouN 96-97CleA	01-12-61	Lompoc, Cal.		B	R	5'9	165	754	1934	206	483	86	20	11	139	161	211	37	.250	.332
Cangelosi, John-John Anthony	85-86ChiA 87-90PitN 92TexA 94NYN 95-96HouN 97-98FlaN 99ColN	03-10-63	Brooklyn, N.Y.		B	L	5'7	155	1038	2004	328	501	73	15	12	134	358	322	154	.250	.319
Canizaro, Jay-Jason Kyle	96,99SFN 00MinA 01KJ 02MinA	07-04-73	Beaumont, Tex.		R	R	5'9	175	195	596	73	149	35	3	10	68	44	119	5	.250	.369
Cannizaro, Andy-Andrew Lee	06NYA	12-19-78	New Orleans, La.		R	R	5'10	170	13	8	5	2	0	0	1	1	1	4	0	.250	.625
Cannon, Joe-Joseph Jerome (J.J.)	77-78HouN 79-80TorA	07-13-53	Camp Lejeune, N.C.		L	R	6'2	185	148	227	34	40	3	1	1	11	1	54	15	.176	.211
Cano, Robinson-Robinson Jose [Mercedes]	05-06NYA	10-22-82	San Pedro de Mac., D.R.		L	R	6'	175	254	1004	140	320	75	5	29	140	34	122	6	.319	.490
Canseco, Jose-Jose Jr. [Capas]	85-92OakA 92-94TexA 95-96BosA 97OakA 98TorA 99-00TBA 00NYA 01ChiA	07-02-64	Havana, Cuba		R	R	6'3	235	1887	7057	1186	1877	340	14	462	1407	906	1942	200	.266	.515
Canseco, Ozzie-Osvaldo [Capas]	90OakA 92-93StlN	07-02-64	Havana, Cuba		R	R	6'2	220	24	65	8	13	6	0	0	4	9	17	0	.200	.292
Cantu, Jorge-Jorge Luis [Guzman]	04-06TBA	01-30-82	McAllen, Tex.		R	R	6'1	184	307	1184	138	326	78	4	44	196	54	218	2	.275	.459
Capra, Nick-Nick Lee	82-83,85TexA 88KCA 91TexA	03-08-58	Denver, Colo.		R	R	5'8	165	45	54	9	9	1	0	1	6	7	3	3	.167	.241
Caraballo, Ramon-Ramon [Sanchez]	93AtlN 95StlN	05-23-69	Rio San Juan, D.R.		B	R	5'7	150	40	99	10	20	4	1	2	13	6	33	3	.202	.323
Carbo, Bernie-Bernardo	69-72CinN 72-73StlN 74-76BosA 76MilA 77-78BosA 78CleA 79-80StlN 80PitN	08-05-47	Detroit, Mich.		L	R	6'	185	1010	2733	372	722	140	9	96	358	538	611	51	.264	.427
Cardona, Javier-Javier Peterson	00-01DetA 02SDN	09-15-75	Santurce, P.R.		R	R	6'1	185	87	175	13	36	10	0	2	14	4	31	0	.206	.297
Carew, Rod-Rodney Cline	67-78MinA 79-85CalA	10-01-45	Gatun, Canal Zone		L	R	6'	180	2469	9315	1424	3053	445	112	92	1015	1018	1028	353	.328	.429
Carey, Paul-Paul Stephen	93BalA 94BalA	01-08-68	Boston, Mass.		L	L	6'4	215	18	47	1	10	1	0	0	3	5	14	0	.213	.234
Carpenter, Bubba-Charles Sydney	00ColN	07-23-68	Dallas, Tex.		L	L	6'1	195	15	27	4	6	0	0	0	5	4	13	0	.222	.556
Carr, Chuck-Charles Lee Glenn	90-91NYN 92StlN 93-95FlaN 96-97MilA 97HouN	08-10-67	San Bernardino, Cal.		B	R	5'10	165	507	1713	254	435	81	7	13	123	149	273	144	.254	.332
Carreon, Mark-Mark Steven	87-91NYN 92DetA 93-96SFN 96CleA	07-19-63	Chicago, Ill.		R	L	6'	195	738	2012	246	557	108	5	69	289	140	246	12	.277	.438
Carrillo, Matias-Matias [Garcia]	91MilA 93-94FlaN	02-24-63	Los Mochis, Mexico		L	L	5'11	190	107	191	17	48	13	0	0	12	10	38	3	.251	.319
Carroll, Jamey-Jamey Blake	02-04MonN 05WasN 06ColN	02-18-74	Evansville, Ind.		R	R	5'10	175	472	1282	211	359	60	12	7	90	145	193	24	.280	.362
Carter, Gary-Gary Edmund (Kid)	74-84MonN 85-89NYN 90SFN 91LAN 92MonN	04-08-54	Culver City, Cal.		R	R	6'2	210	2296	7971	1025	2092	371	31	324	1225	848	997	39	.262	.439
Carter, Joe-Joseph Chris	83ChiN 84-89CleA 90SDN 91-97TorA 98BalA 98SFN	03-07-60	Oklahoma City, Okla.		R	R	6'3	220	2189	8422	1170	2184	432	53	396	1445	527	1387	231	.259	.464
Carter, Steve-Steven Jerome	89-90PitN	12-03-64	Charlottesville, Va.		L	R	6'4	190	14	21	2	3	1	0	1	3	2	6	0	.143	.333
Caruso, Mike-Michael John	98-99ChiA 02KCA	05-27-77	Queens, N.Y.		L	R	6'1	172	281	1072	144	294	28	10	7	90	35	76	34	.274	.339
Casanova, Raul-Raul	96-98DetA 99XJ 00-02MilN 02BalA 05ChiA	08-23-72	Humacao, P.R.		B	R	6'	225	338	947	81	220	37	4	28	115	83	173	2	.232	.369
Casey, Sean-Sean Thomas	97CleA 98-05CinN 06PitN 06DetA	07-02-74	Willingboro, N.J.		L	L	6'4	225	1193	4414	636	1333	278	11	126	664	421	510	15	.302	.456
Cash, Dave-David	69-73PitN 74-76PhiN 77-79MonN 80SDN	06-11-48	Utica, N.Y.		R	R	6'	175	1422	5554	732	1571	243	56	21	426	424	309	120	.283	.358
Cash, Kevin-Kevin Forrest	02-04TorA 05TBA	12-06-77	Tampa, Fla.		R	R	6'	185	114	332	33	57	13	0	7	31	16	98	0	.172	.274
Cash, Ron-Ronald Forrest	73-74DetA	11-20-49	Atlanta, Ga.		R	R	6'	185	34	101	14	30	3	1	0	11	5	16	0	.297	.347
Casilla, Alexi-Alexi [Lora]	06MinA	07-20-84	San Cristobal, Dom. Rep.		B	R	5'9	160	9	4	1	1	0	0	0	0	1	1	0	.250	.250
Casimiro, Carlos-Carlos Rafael	00BalA	11-08-76	San Pedro de Mac.,D.R.		R	R	5'11	175	2	8	0	1	0	0	0	3	0	2	0	.125	.250
Castellano, Pedro-Pedro Orlando [Arrieta]	93,95-96ColN	03-11-70	Lara, Venezuela		R	R	6'1	175	51	93	13	15	2	0	3	12	3	25	1	.161	.280
Castilla, Vinny-Vinicio [Soria]	91-92AtlN 93-99ColN 00-01TBA 01HouN 02-03AtlN 04ColN 05WasN 06SDN 06ColN	07-04-67	Oaxaca, Mexico		R	R	6'1	205	1854	6822	902	1884	349	28	320	1105	423	1069	33	.276	.476
Castillo, Alberto-Alberto Terrero	95-98NYN 99StlN 00-01TorA 03SFN 04-05KCA 06OakA	02-10-70	San Juan de la Mag. D.R.		R	R	6'	200	407	995	93	221	37	2	11	98	100	209	3	.222	.359
Castillo (Medrano), Braulio-Braulio Robinson [Castillo]	91-92PhiN	05-13-68	Elias Pina, Dom. Rep.		R	R	6'	160	56	128	15	24	6	1	2	9	5	30	2	.188	.297
Castillo, Carmen-Monte Carmelo	82-88CleA 89-91MinA	06-08-58	San Pedro de Mac.,D.R.		R	R	6'	185	631	1519	190	383	71	8	55	197	90	291	15	.252	.418
Castillo, Jose-Jose [Rondon]	04-06PitN	03-19-81	Las Mercedes, Venez.		R	R	6'1	200	378	1271	147	328	56	5	33	157	78	249	11	.258	.388
Castillo, Juan-Juan [Brayas]	86-89MilA	01-25-62	San Pedro de Mac., D.R.		B	R	6'1	182	199	469	60	101	11	5	3	35	41	104	18	.215	.279
			Bats Right 88																		
Castillo, Luis-Luis Antonio [Donato]	96-05FlaN 06MinA	09-12-75	San Pedro de Mac.,D.R.		B	R	5'11	195	1270	4931	759	1446	152	48	23	320	589	687	306	.293	.358
Castillo, Manny-Esteban Manuel Antonio [Cabrera]	80KCA 82-83SeaA	04-01-57	Santo Domingo, D.R.		R	R	5'9	165	236	719	63	174	35	4	3	73	29	55	3	.242	.314
Castillo, Marty-Martin Horace (The Grinch)	81-85DetA	01-16-57	Long Beach, Cal.		R	R	6'	205	201	352	31	67	11	2	8	32	19	76	3	.190	.301
Castillo, Tony-Anthony Beltran	78SDN	06-14-57	San Jose, Cal.		R	R	6'3	210	5	8	0	1	0	0	0	0	1	0	0	.125	.125
Castino, John-John Anthony (Clams)	79-84MinA 85XJ	10-23-54	Evanston, Ill.		R	R	5'11	175	666	2320	293	646	86	34	41	249	177	298	22	.278	.398
Castle, Don-Donald Hardy	73TexA	02-01-50	Kokomo, Ind.		L	L	6'2	195	4	13	0	4	1	0	0	2	1	3	0	.308	.384
Castro, Bernie-Bernabel	05BalA 06WasN	07-14-79	Santo Domingo, D. R.		B	R	5'10	165	66	190	32	48	4	4	0	17	18	28	13	.253	.316
Castro, Juan-Juan Gabriel	95-99LAN 00-04CinN 05-06MinA 06CinN	06-20-72	Los Mochis, Mexico		R	R	5'10	190	869	2122	205	494	103	13	33	190	119	371	5	.233	.340
Castro, Ramon-Ramon Abraham	99-04FlaN 05-06NYN	03-01-76	Vega Baja, P.R.		R	R	6'2	255	346	801	79	180	40	0	30	106	96	214	1	.225	.387
Castro, Ramon-Ramon Alfredo [Munoz]	04OakA	10-23-79	Valencia, Venez.		B	R	6'3	200	9	12	2	2	1	0	0	1	1	6	0	.133	.200
Catalanotto, Frank-Frank John	97-99DetA 00-02TexA 03-06TorA	04-27-74	Smithtown, N.Y.		L	R	6'0	195	972	3076	462	915	212	29	70	382	268	398	40	.297	.454
Cedeno, Andujar-Andujar [Donastorg]	90-94HouN 95-96SDN 96DetA 96HouN	08-21-69	La Romana, D.R.	10-28-00	R	R	6'1	170	616	2051	221	485	98	13	47	223	143	488	26	.236	.366
Cedeno, Cesar-Cesar Eugenio [Encarnacion]	70-81HouN 82-85CinN 85StlN 86LAN	02-25-51	Santo Domingo, D.R.		R	R	6'2	195	2006	7310	1084	2087	436	60	199	976	664	938	550	.285	.443
Cedeno, Domingo-Domingo Antonio [Donastorg]	93-96TorA 96ChiA 97-98TexA 99SeaA 99PhiN	11-04-68	La Romana, Dom. Rep.		B	R	6'1	170	429	1219	160	306	54	13	15	121	83	280	14	.251	.354

USE NAME - GIVEN NAMES (NICKNAMES)	TEAM BY YEAR	BIRTH DATE	BIRTH PLACE	DEATH DATE	B	T	HGT	WGT	G	AB	R	H	2B	3B	HR	RBI	BB	SO	SB	BA	SA
Cedeno, Roger-Roger Leandro	95-98LAN 99NYN 00HouN 01DetA 02-03NYN 04-05StLN	08-16-74	Valencia, Venezuela		B	R	6'1	205	1100	3174	478	865	127	32	40	274	319	613	213	.273	.371
Cedeno, Ronny-Ronny Alexander	05-06ChiN	02-02-83	Carabobo, Venezuela		R	R	6'	180	192	614	64	155	21	7	7	47	22	120	9	.252	.344
Cepicky, Matt-Matthew William	02-04MonN 05WasN 06FlaN	11-10-77	St. Louis, Mo.		L	R	6'2	215	89	185	12	39	11	0	4	21	7	53	1	.211	.335
Cerone, Rick-Richard Aldo	75-76CleA 77-79TorA 80-84NYA 85AtlN 86MilA 87NYA 88-89BosA 90NYA 91NYN 92MonN	05-19-54	Newark, N.J.		R	R	5'11	190	1329	4069	393	998	190	15	59	436	320	450	6	.245	.343
Cey, Ron-Ronald Charles (The Penguin)	71-82LAN 83-86ChiN 87OakA	02-15-48	Tacoma, Wash.		R	R	5'10	185	2073	7162	977	1868	328	21	316	1139	1012	1235	24	.261	.445
Chalk, David-David Lee (Shaver)	73-79CalA 79TexA 79OakA 80-81KCA	08-30-50	Del Rio, Tex.		R	R	5'10	175	903	2910	292	733	107	9	15	243	295	327	36	.252	.310
Chamberlain, Wes-Wesley Polk	90-94PhiN 94-95BosA	04-13-66	Chicago, Ill.		R	R	6'2	215	385	1263	144	322	72	6	43	167	77	249	20	.255	.424
Chambers, Al-Albert Eugene	83-85SeaA	03-24-61	Harrisburg, Pa.		L	L	6'4	217	57	120	21	25	4	0	2	11	21	34	2	.208	.292
Chamblee, Jim-James Nathaniel	03CinN	05-06-75	Denton, Texas		R	R	6'4	186	2	2	0	0	0	0	0	0	0	2	0	.000	.000
Chambliss, Chris-Carroll Christopher	71-74CleA 74-79NYA 80-86AtlN 87RC 88NYA	12-26-48	Dayton, Ohio		L	R	6'2	210	2173	7571	912	2103	392	42	185	972	632	926	40	.279	.415
Champion, Mike-Robert Michael	76-78SDN	02-10-55	Montgomery, Ala.		R	R	6'	185	193	598	42	137	16	8	2	49	33	101	3	.229	.293
Chaney, Darrel-Darrel Lee (Nort)	69-75CinN 76-79AtlN	03-09-48	Hammond, Ind.		B	R	6'2	188	915	2113	237	458	75	17	14	190	238	471	19	.217	.288
				Bats Left 74-75, part of 73																	
Chant, Charlie-Charles Joseph	75OakA 76StLN	08-07-51	Bell Gardens, Cal.		R	R	6'	190	20	19	1	2	0	0	0	0	0	4	0	.105	.105
Chapman, Kelvin-Kelvin Keith	79,84-85NYN	06-02-56	Willits, Cal.		R	R	5'11	180	172	421	50	94	17	2	3	34	33	60	13	.223	.295
Chapman, Travis-Travis Adrian	03PhiN	06-05-78	Jacksonville, Fla.		R	R	6'2	185	1	1	0	0	0	0	0	0	0	0	0	.000	.000
Chappas, Harry-Harry Perry	78-80ChiA	10-26-57	Mount Rainier, Md.		B	R	5'3	155	72	184	26	45	4	0	1	12	15	26	2	.245	.283
Charboneau, Joe-Joseph (Super Joe)	80-82CleA	06-17-55	Belvidere, Ill.		R	R	6'2	200	201	647	97	172	26	4	29	114	61	99	3	.266	.453
Charles, Frank-Franklin Scott	00HouN	02-23-69	Fontana, Cal.		R	R	6'4	210	4	7	1	3	1	0	0	2	0	2	0	.429	.571
Chavez, Angel-Angel Aristides [Castro]	05SFN	07-22-81	David, Panama		R	R	6'1	195	10	19	1	5	1	0	0	1	0	3	0	.263	.316
Chavez, Endy-Endy DeJesus	01KCA 02-04MonN 05WasN 05PhiN 06NYN	02-07-78	Valencia, Venezuela		L	L	6'	175	569	1656	222	446	81	24	15	148	100	181	67	.269	.374
Chavez, Eric-Eric Cesar	98-06OakA	12-07-77	Los Angeles, Cal.		L	R	6'1	205	1166	4212	667	1143	245	18	212	716	516	790	43	.271	.489
Chavez, Raul-Raul Alexander	96-97MonN 98SeaA 00,02-05HouN 06BalA	03-18-73	Valencia, Venezuela		R	R	5'11	205	170	405	26	86	15	1	4	40	21	78	3	.212	.284
Chen, Chin-Feng-Chin-Feng	02-05LAN	10-28-77	Tainan City, Taiwan		R	R	6'1	189	19	22	3	2	0	0	0	3	3	10	0	.091	.091
Chiles, Rich-Richard Francis	71-72HouN 73NYN 76HouN 77-78MinA	11-22-49	Sacramento, Cal.		L	L	5'11	170	284	618	68	157	37	2	6	76	50	65	1	.254	.350
Chism, Tom-Thomas Raymond	79BalA	05-09-55	Chester, Pa.		L	L	6'1	195	6	3	0	0	0	0	0	0	0	0	0	.000	.000
Choi, Hee-Seop-Hee-Seop	02-03ChiN 04FlaN 04-05LAN	03-16-79	Chun-Nam, South Korea		L	L	6'5	235	363	915	130	220	54	3	40	120	141	262	3	.240	.437
Choo, Shin-Soo-Shin-Soo	05-06SeaA 06CleA	07-13-82	Pusan, South Korea		L	L	5'11	180	59	175	24	45	12	3	3	23	21	54	5	.257	.411
Christensen, John-John Lawrence	84-85NYN 87SeaA 88MinA	09-05-60	Downey, Cal.		R	R	6'	190	132	294	36	66	16	2	5	33	35	58	3	.224	.344
Christensen, McKay-McKay Andrew	99-01ChiA 01LAN 02NYN	08-14-75	Uplands, Cal.		L	L	5'11	180	99	128	22	32	3	0	2	14	10	26	6	.250	.320
Christensen, Ryan-Ryan Alan	98-01OakA 01AriN 02MilN 03TexA	03-28-74	Redlands, Cal.		R	R	5'11	205	452	998	159	222	48	5	16	102	114	256	16	.222	.329
Christmas, Steve-Stephen Randall	83CinN 84ChiA 86ChiN	12-09-57	Orlando, Fla.		L	R	6'	190	24	37	1	6	2	0	1	7	1	6	0	.162	.297
Church, Ryan-Ryan Matthew	04MonN 05-06WasN	10-14-78	Santa Barbara, Cal.		L	L	6'1	190	203	527	69	142	33	4	20	83	57	146	9	.269	.461
Cianfrocco, Archi-Angelo Dominic	92-93MonN 93-98SDN	10-06-66	Rome, N.Y.		R	R	6'5	215	500	1276	136	308	59	7	34	185	80	360	16	.241	.395
Cias, Darryl-Darryl Richard	83OakA	04-23-57	New York, N.Y.		R	R	5'11	190	20	18	1	6	1	0	0	1	2	4	1	.333	.389
Cintron, Alex-Alexander	01-05AriN 06ChiA	12-17-78	Humacao, P.R.		B	R	6'1	200	530	1712	208	480	92	19	30	193	94	173	16	.280	.409
Cirillo, Jeff-Jeffrey Howard	94-97MilA 98-99MilN 00-01ColN 02-03SeaA 04SDN 05-06MilN	09-23-69	Pasadena, Cal.		R	R	6'2	195	1539	5203	776	1550	330	19	110	700	544	675	61	.298	.432
Clapinski, Chris-Christopher Alan	99-00FlaN	08-20-71	Buffalo, N.Y.		R	R	6'	175	70	105	18	28	5	3	1	9	14	19	1	.267	.400
Clapp, Stubby-Richard Keith	01StLN	02-24-73	Windsor, Canada		L	R	5'8	175	23	25	0	5	2	0	0	1	1	7	0	.200	.280
Clarey, Doug-Douglas William	76StLN	04-20-54	Los Angeles, Cal.		R	R	6'	180	9	4	2	1	0	0	1	2	0	1	0	.250	1.000
Clark, Bobby-Robert Cale	79-83CalA 84-85MilA	05-13-56	Sacramento, Cal.		R	R	6'	195	396	967	97	231	34	7	19	100	55	199	4	.239	.347
Clark, Brady-Brady William	00-02CinN 02NYN 03-06MilN	04-18-73	Portland, Ore.		R	R	6'2	195	710	1900	251	529	92	5	36	198	193	232	46	.278	.384
Clark, Dave-David Earl	86-89CleA 90ChiN 91KCA 92-96PitN 96LAN 97ChiN 98HouN	09-03-62	Tupelo, Miss.		L	R	6'2	200	905	1964	248	518	81	8	62	284	222	451	19	.264	.408
Clark, Doug-Douglas Dwyer	05SFN 06OakA	03-05-76	Springfield, Mass.		L	R	6'2	205	14	11	2	1	0	0	0	0	1	5	1	.091	.091
Clark, Howie-Howard Roddy	02BalA 03-04TorA 06BalA	02-13-74	San Diego, Cal.		L	R	5'10	191	99	245	30	67	14	1	3	23	21	29	0	.273	.376
Clark, Jack-Jack Anthony (Jack the Ripper)	75-84SFN 85-87StLN 88NYA 89-90SDN 91-92BosA	11-10-55	New Brighton, Pa.		R	R	6'3	205	1994	6847	1118	1826	332	39	340	1180	1262	1441	77	.267	.476
Clark, Jerald-Jerald Dwayne	88-92SDN 93ColN 94JL 95MinA	08-10-63	Crockett, Tex.		R	R	6'4	205	516	1609	170	414	79	16	44	208	83	295	17	.257	.408
Clark, Jermaine-Jermaine Marcel	01DetA 03TexA 03SDN 03TexA 04CinN 05OakA	09-29-76	Berkeley, Cal.		L	R	5'10	175	46	78	9	12	3	0	0	9	8	13	3	.154	.192
Clark, Phil-Phillip Benjamin	92DetA 93-95SDN 96BosA	05-06-68	Crockett, Tex.		R	R	6'	200	264	543	62	150	30	0	17	65	27	76	4	.276	.425
Clark, Tony-Anthony Christopher	95-01DetA 02BosA 03NYN 04NYA 05-06AriN	06-15-72	Newton, Kans.		B	R	6'7	240	1302	4094	579	1087	219	10	227	738	464	1071	6	.266	.490
Clark, Will-William Nuschler (The Thrill)	86-93SFN 94-98TexA 99-00BalA 00StLN	03-13-64	New Orleans, La.		L	L	6'2	200	1976	7173	1186	2176	440	47	284	1205	937	1190	67	.303	.497
Clayton, Royce-Royce Spencer	91-95SFN 96-98StLN 98-00TexA 01-02ChiA 03MilN 04ColN 05AriN 06WasN 06CinN	01-02-70	Burbank, Cal.		R	R	6'	180	2031	7184	911	1856	349	55	109	711	551	1362	229	.258	.368
Clemente, Edgard-Edgard Alexis [Velazquez]	98-99ColN 00AnaA	12-15-75	Santurce, P.R.		R	R	6'0	185	114	257	30	64	12	3	8	32	9	81	0	.249	.412
Clevlen, Brent-Brent Aaron	06DetA	10-27-83	Austin, Tex.		R	R	6'2	190	31	39	9	11	1	2	3	6	3	17	0	.282	.641
Cliburn, Stan-Stanley Gene (Ank)	80CalA	12-19-56	Jackson, Miss.		R	R	6'	195	54	56	7	10	2	0	2	6	3	9	0	.179	.321
Clines, Gene-Eugene Anthony (Road Runner)	70-74PitN 75NYN 76TexA 77-79ChiN	10-06-46	San Pablo, Cal.		R	R	5'9	175	870	2328	314	645	85	24	5	187	169	291	71	.277	.341
Closser, J.D.-Jeffrey Darrin	04-06ColN	01-15-80	Beech Grove, Ind.		B	R	5'10	176	160	447	46	107	21	3	10	48	50	93	1	.239	.367
Clyburn, Danny-Danny	97-98BalA 99TBA	04-06-74	Lancaster, S.C.		R	R	6'3	220	41	109	14	23	4	0	4	8	8	33	0	.211	.358
Coachman, Pete-Bobby Dean	90CalA	11-11-61	Cottonwood, Ala.		R	R	5'9	175	16	45	3	14	3	0	0	5	3	8	0	.311	.378
Coats, Buck-Buck	06CinN	06-09-82	Fort Benning, Ga.		L	R	6'3	195	18	18	2	3	1	0	1	1	0	6	0	.167	.389
Cochrane, Dave - David Carter	86ChiA 89-92SeaA	01-31-63	Riverside, Cal.		B	R	6'2	180	215	514	43	121	24	1	8	43	40	129	1	.235	.333
Cockrell, Alan-Atlee Alan	96ColN	12-05-62	Kansas City, Kans.		R	R	6'2	210	9	8	0	2	1	0	0	1	0	4	0	.250	.375
Coffie, Ivanon-Ivanon Angelino	00BalA	05-16-77	Willemstad, Curacao		L	R	6'1	190	23	60	6	13	4	1	0	6	5	11	1	.217	.317
Coggins, Rich-Richard Allen	72-74BalA 75MonN 75-76NYA 76ChiA	12-07-50	Indianapolis, Ind.		L	L	5'9	170	342	1083	125	287	42	13	12	90	72	100	50	.265	.361
Colangelo, Mike-Michael Gus	99AnaA 01SDN 02OakA	10-22-76	Teaneck, N.J.		R	R	6'1	185	71	116	12	27	4	3	2	8	10	32	0	.233	.371
Colbern, Mike-Michael Malloy	78-79ChiA	04-19-55	Santa Monica, Cal.		R	R	6'3	205	80	224	16	58	10	2	2	28	5	61	0	.259	.348
Colbert, Craig-Craig Charles	92-93SFN	02-13-65	Iowa City, Iowa		R	R	6'2	205	72	163	12	35	7	2	2	21	12	35	1	.215	.319
Colbrunn, Greg-Gregory Joseph	92-93MonN 94-96FlaN 97MinA 97AtlN 98ColN 98AtlN 99-02AriN 03SeaA 04AriN 05WJ	07-26-69	Fontana, Cal.		R	R	6'	205	992	2769	337	801	155	12	98	422	170	444	29	.289	.460
Cole, Alex-Alexander	90-91CleA 92PitN 93ColN 94-95MinA 96BosA	08-17-65	Fayetteville, N.C.		L	L	6'2	180	573	1760	286	493	58	26	5	117	217	296	148	.280	.351
Cole, Stu-Stewart Bryan	91KCA	07-07-66	Charlotte, N.C.		R	R	6'1	175	9	7	1	1	0	0	0	0	2	3	0	.143	.143
Coleman, Dave-David Lee (Moe)	77BosA	10-26-50	Dayton, Ohio		R	R	6'1	197	11	12	1	0	0	0	0	1	0	3	0	.000	.000
Coleman, Michael-Michael Donnell	97,99BosA 01NYA	08-16-75	Nashville, Tenn.		R	R	5'11	215	22	67	8	13	5	1	1	8	1	26	1	.194	.254
Coleman, Vince-Vincent Maurice	85-90StLN 91-93NYN 94-95KCA 95SeaA 96CinN 97DetA	09-22-60	Jacksonville, Fla.		B	R	6'	185	1371	5406	849	1425	176	89	28	346	477	960	752	.264	.345
Coles, Darnell-Darnell	83-85SeaA 86-87DetA 87-88PitN 88-90SeaA 90DetA 91SFN 92CinN 93-94TorA 95StLN 96JL 97ColN	06-02-62	San Bernardino, Cal.		R	R	6'1	185	957	2891	333	709	142	14	75	368	237	445	20	.245	.382
Colina, Alvin-Alvin Enrique	06ColN	12-26-81	Puerto Cabello, Venezuela		R	R	6'3	210	2	5	0	1	0	0	0	1	0	1	0	.200	.200
Collier, Lou-Louis Keith	97-98PitN 99-02MilN 03BosA 04PhiN	08-21-73	Chicago, Ill.		R	R	5'10	182	315	713	89	172	33	7	8	78	75	160	12	.241	.341
Collins, Dave-David Scott	75-76CinN 77SeaA 78-81CinN 82NYA 83-84TorA 85OakA 86DetA 87-89CinN 90StLN	10-20-52	Rapid City, S.D.		B	L	5'11	175	1701	4907	667	1335	187	52	32	373	467	660	395	.272	.351
Colon, Cris-Cristobal [Martinez]	92TexA	01-03-69	La Guaira, Venez.		B	R	6'2	180	14	36	5	6	0	0	0	0	1	8	0	.167	.167
Colucci, Bob-Robert Pasquali (The Macaroni Pony)	73-75MilA 75,77ChiA 78StLN	10-02-51	Centralia, Wash.		R	R	5'11	185	370	1095	141	241	38	15	26	114	128	202	33	.220	.353
Concepcion, Dave-David Ismael [Benitez]	70-88CinN	06-17-48	Ocumare de la Costa, Venez.		R	R	6'2	185	2488	8723	993	2326	389	48	101	950	736	1186	321	.267	.357
Concepcion, Onix-Onix Cardona [Cardona]	80-85KCA 87PitN	10-05-57	Dorado, P.R.		R	R	5'7	180	1041	108	249	34	7	3	80	47	93	25		.239	.294
Conine, Jeff-Jeffrey Guy	90,92KCA 93-97FlaN 98KCA 99-03BalA 03-05FlaN 06BalA 06PhiN	06-26-66	Tacoma, Wash.		R	R	6'1	220	1923	6701	845	1917	372	35	208	1034	644	1132	50	.286	.445
Connally, Fritz-Fritzie Lee	83ChiN 85BalA	05-19-58	Bryan, Tex.		R	R	6'3	210	58	122	16	27	8	1	5	15	19	26	0	.221	.328
Conti, Jason-Stanley Jason	00-01AriN 02TBA 03MilN 04TexA	01-27-75	Pittsburgh, Pa.		L	R	5'11	180	182	420	47	100	24	5	6	47	33	124	7	.238	.362
Cookson, Brent-Brent Adam	95KCA 99LAN	09-07-69	Van Nuys, Cal.		R	R	5'11	200	25	40	2	6	1	0	0	5	2	8	1	.150	.175
Coolbaugh, Mike-Michael Robert	01MilN 02StLN	06-05-72	Binghamton, N.Y.		R	R	6'1	185	44	82	10	15	6	0	2	9	3	20	0	.183	.329
Coolbaugh, Scott-Scott Robert	89-90TexA 91SDN 94StLN	06-13-66	Binghamton, N.Y.		R	R	5'11	190	167	432	44	93	15	1	8	41	39	108	1	.215	.319
Coomer, Ron-Ronald Bryan	95-00MinA 01ChiN 02NYA 03LAN	11-18-66	Crest Hill, Ill.		R	R	5'11	205	911	3019	333	827	151	8	92	449	177	429	13	.274	.421
Cooper, Cecil-Cecil Celester	71-76BosA 77-87MilA	12-20-49	Brenham, Tex.		L	L	6'2	188	1896	7349	1012	2192	415	47	241	1125	448	911	89	.298	.466
Cooper, Gary-Gary Clifton	91HouN	03-13-64	Lynwood, Cal.		R	R	6'	200	9	16	1	4	1	0	0	0	0	4	0	.250	.313
Cooper, Gary-Gary Nathaniel (Easy)	80AtlN	12-22-56	Savannah, Ga.		B	R	5'11	160	21	2	0	0	0	0	0	0	0	0	0	.000	.000
Cooper, Scott-Scott Kendrick	90-94BosA 95StLN 96JL 97KCA	10-13-67	St. Louis, Mo.		L	R	6'3	205	592	1801	197	478	94	12	33	211	193	299	1	.265	.384
Coquillette, Trace-Trace Robert	99-00MonN	06-04-74	Carmichael, Calif.		R	R	5'11	185	51	108	14	25	5	2	1	12	11	26	1	.231	.324
Cora, Alex-Jose Alexander	98-04LAN 05CleA 05-06BosA	10-18-75	Caguas, Puerto Rico		L	R	6'0	180	876	2446	259	596	99	27	31	215	178	320	31	.244	.344

USE NAME - GIVEN NAMES (NICKNAMES)	TEAM BY YEAR	BIRTH DATE	BIRTH PLACE	DEATH DATE	B	T	HGT	WGT	G	AB	R	H	2B	3B	HR	RBI	BB	SO	SB	BA	SA
Cora, Joey-Jose Manuel [Amaro] (The Rooster)	87,89-90SDN 91-94ChiA 95-98SeaA 98CleA	05-14-65	Caguas, P.R.		B	R	5'7	155	1118	3733	624	1035	171	41	30	294	380	335	117	.277	.369
Corcoran, Tim-Timothy Michael	77-80DetA 81MinA 83-85PhiN 86NYN	03-19-53	Glendale, Cal.		L	L	5'11	175	509	1050	120	283	46	4	12	128	130	102	4	.270	.355
Cordero, Wil-Wilfredo [Nieva]	92-95MonN 96-97BosA 98ChiA 99CleA 00PitN 00-02CleA 02-03MonN 04FlaN 05WasN	10-03-71	Mayaguez, P.R.		R	R	6'2	200	1247	4311	587	1178	261	19	122	566	325	775	49	.273	.428
Cordova, Marty-Martin Keevin	95-98MinN 99MinA 00TorA 01CleA 02-03BalA 04EJ	07-10-69	Las Vegas, Nev.		R	R	6'	205	952	3419	480	938	192	18	122	540	329	730	57	.274	.448
Corey, Mark-Mark Mundell	79-81BalA	11-03-55	Tucumcari, N.M.		R	R	6'2	210	59	57	10	12	2	0	1	3	7	13	1	.211	.298
Correia, Rod-Ronald Douglas	93-95CalA	09-13-67	Providence, R.I.		R	R	5'11	170	84	166	19	43	7	1	0	12	6	25	2	.259	.313
Correll, Vic-Victor Crosby	72BosA 74-77AtlN 78-80CinN	02-05-46	Washington, D.C.		R	R	5'10	185	410	1132	124	259	60	4	29	125	128	220	2	.229	.366
Cortez, Fernando-Fernando Allen	05TBA	08-10-81	Stockton, Cal.		L	R	6'1	175	8	13	0	1	0	0	0	0	1	3	0	.077	.077
Cosey, Ray-Donald Ray	80OakA	02-15-56	San Rafael, Cal.		L	L	5'10	180	9	9	0	1	0	0	0	0	0	0	0	.111	.111
Costa, Shane-Shane Jeremy	05-06KCA	12-12-81	Visalia, Cal.		L	R	6'	220	99	318	36	84	22	1	5	30	11	40	2	.264	.387
Coste, Chris-Christopher Robert	06PhiN	02-04-73	Fargo, N.D.		R	R	6'1	200	65	198	25	65	14	0	7	32	10	31	0	.328	.505
Costo, Tim-Timothy Roger	92-93CinN	02-16-69	Melrose Park, Ill.		R	R	6'5	220	43	134	16	30	7	0	3	14	9	23	0	.224	.343
Cota, Humberto-Humberto Figueroa	01-06PitN	02-07-79	San Luis Rio Colorado, Mexico		R	R	6'	210	191	505	47	117	24	2	12	58	30	140	0	.232	.358
Cotto, Henry-Henry [Suarez]	84ChiN 85-87NYA 88-93SeaA 93FlaN	01-05-61	Bronx, N.Y.		R	R	6'2	180	884	2178	296	569	87	9	44	210	107	352	130	.261	.370
Counsell, Craig-Craig John	95,97ColN 97-99FlaN 99LAN 00-03AriN 04MilN 05-06AriN	08-21-70	South Bend, Ind.		L	R	6'	180	1053	3446	489	896	160	28	31	283	419	470	90	.260	.350
Cowens, Al-Alfred Edward	74-79KCA 80CalA 80-81DetA 82-86SeaA	10-25-51	Los Angeles, Cal.	03-11-02	R	R	6'2	205	1584	5534	704	1494	276	68	108	717	389	659	120	.270	.403
Cox, Darron-James Darron	99MonN	11-21-67	Oklahoma City, Okla.		R	R	6'1	215	15	25	2	6	1	0	1	2	0	5	0	.240	.400
Cox, Jeff-Jeffrey Lindon (Wally)	80-81OakA	11-09-55	Los Angeles, Cal.		R	R	5'11	170	61	169	20	36	3	0	0	9	14	23	8	.213	.231
Cox, Jim-James Charles	73-76MonN	05-28-50	Bloomington, Ill.		R	R	5'11	175	110	307	33	66	11	2	3	33	27	44	3	.215	.293
Cox, Larry-Larry Eugene	73-75PhiN 77SeaA 78ChiN 79-80SeaA 81TexA 82ChiN	09-11-47	Bluffton, Ohio	02-17-90	R	R	5'11	190	348	825	72	182	31	5	12	85	70	117	5	.221	.314
Cox, Steve-Charles Steven	99-02TBA	10-31-74	Delano, Calif.		L	L	6'4	225	378	1239	146	324	72	2	39	158	130	240	8	.262	.417
Cox, Ted-William Ted	77BosA 78-79CleA 80SeaA 81TorA	01-24-55	Oklahoma City, Okla.		R	R	6'3	200	272	771	65	189	29	1	10	79	57	98	3	.245	.324
Cradle, Rickey-Rickey Nelson	98SeaA	06-20-73	Norfolk, Va.		R	R	6'2	180	5	7	0	1	0	0	0	2	1	5	1	.143	.143
Craig, Rodney-Rodney Paul	79-80SeaA 82CleA 86ChiA	01-12-58	Los Angeles, Cal.		B	R	6'1	195	145	367	49	94	25	2	3	27	24	48	7	.256	.360
Crawford, Carl-Carl Demonte	02-06TBA	08-05-81	Houston, Texas		L	L	6'2	219	673	2759	397	806	108	65	51	297	134	393	227	.292	.434
Crede, Joe-Joseph Antonio	00-06ChiA	04-26-78	Jefferson City, Mo.		R	R	6'3	195	654	2266	296	593	120	3	104	345	130	334	4	.262	.455
Crespo, Cesar-Cesar Antonio	01-02SDN 04BosA	05-23-79	Rio Piedras, P.R.		B	R	5'11	170	132	261	38	50	10	1	4	18	28	76	11	.192	.284
Crespo, Felipe-Felipe Javier [Clausio]	96-98TorA 00-01SFN 01PhiN	03-05-73	Rio Piedras, P.R.		B	R	5'11	200	262	445	46	109	22	4	10	68	50	101	9	.245	.380
Cripe, Dave-David Gordon (Grip)	78KCA	04-07-51	Ramona, Cal.		R	R	6'	185	7	13	1	2	0	0	0	1	0	1	0	.154	.154
Criscione, Dave-David Gerald (Cris)	77BalA	09-02-51	Dunkirk, N.Y.		R	R	5'8	185	7	9	1	3	0	0	0	1	0	1	0	.333	.667
Crisp, Coco-Covelli Loyce	02-05CleA 06BosA	11-01-79	Los Angeles, Cal.		B	R	6'	185	520	2039	293	576	112	16	43	212	145	287	76	.282	.416
Cromartie, Warren-Warren Livingston (Cro)	74,76-83MonN 84-90JL 91KCA	09-29-53	Miami Beach, Fla.		L	L	6'	190	1107	3927	459	1104	229	32	61	391	325	403	50	.281	.402
Cromer, D.T.-David Thomas	00-01CinN	03-19-71	Lake City, S.C.		L	R	6'2	220	85	104	14	32	7	0	7	24	4	33	0	.308	.577
Cromer, Tripp-Roy Bunyan	93-95StlN 97-99LAN 00,03HouN	11-21-67	Lake City, S.C.		R	R	6'2	165	196	524	54	118	22	1	12	48	27	101	0	.225	.340
Crosby, Bobby-Robert Edward	03-06OakA	01-12-80	Lakewood, Cal.		R	R	6'3	195	342	1248	179	304	71	5	40	142	130	276	15	.244	.405
Crosby, Bubba-Richard Stephen	03LAN 04-06NYA	08-11-76	Houston, Texas		L	L	5'11	185	205	250	32	54	5	2	4	20	10	51	9	.216	.300
Crosby, Ed-Edward Carlton (Spider)	70,72-73StlN 73CinN 74-76CleA	05-26-49	Long Beach, Cal.		L	R	6'2	175	297	677	67	149	22	4	0	44	55	74	1	.220	.264
Cron, Chris-Christopher John	91CalA 92ChiA	03-31-64	Albuquerque, N.M.		R	R	6'2	200	12	25	0	2	0	0	0	0	2	9	0	.080	.080
Crow, Don-Donald LeRoy	82LAN	08-18-58	Yakima, Wash.		R	R	6'4	200	4	4	0	0	0	0	0	0	0	3	0	.000	.000
Crowley, Terry-Terrence Michael	69-73BalA 74-75CinN 76AtlN 76-82BalA 83MonN	02-16-47	Staten Island, N.Y.		L	L	6'	180	865	1518	174	379	62	1	42	229	222	181	3	.250	.375
Crozier, Eric-Eric LeRoi	04TorA	08-11-78	Columbus, Ohio		L	L	6'4	200	14	33	5	5	2	0	2	4	6	19	0	.152	.394
Cruz, Deivi-Deivi [Garcia]	97-01DetA 02SDN 03BalA 04-05SFN 05WasN	11-06-72	Bani, Dom. Rep.		R	R	5'11	195	1234	4424	442	1109	250	16	70	464	132	429	16	.269	.384
Cruz, Enrique-Enrique Michael	03MilN	11-21-81	Santo Domingo, D.R.		R	R	6'1	180	60	71	6	6	1	0	0	2	4	30	0	.085	.099
Cruz, Fausto-Fausto Santiago	93-95OakA 96DetA	05-01-72	Montecristi, D.R.		R	R	5'10	165	39	89	7	17	2	0	0	5	8	22	1	.191	.213
Cruz, Heity-Hector Louis [Dilan]	73,75-77StlN 78ChiN 78-79SFN 79-80CinN 81-82ChiN	04-02-53	Arroyo, P.R.		R	R	5'11	180	624	1607	186	361	71	9	39	200	176	317	7	.225	.353
Cruz, Henry-Henry [Acosta] (Papo)	75-76LAN 77-78ChiA	02-27-52	Christiansted, V.I.		L	L	6'	175	171	280	32	64	7	3	8	34	25	31	1	.229	.361
Cruz, Ivan-Luis Ivan	97NYA 99-00PitN 01JL 02StlN	05-03-68	Fajardo, P.R.		L	L	6'3	215	41	55	5	15	1	0	2	8	3	17	0	.273	.400
Cruz, Jacob-Jacob Antonio	96-98SFN 98-01CleA 01ColN 02DetA 04-05CinN	01-28-73	Oxnard, Cal.		L	L	6'2	205	409	729	95	176	38	2	19	105	85	207	4	.241	.377
Cruz, Jose-Jose Javier [Dilan] (Cheo)	70-74StlN 75-87HouN 88NYA	08-08-47	Arroyo, P.R.		L	L	6'	180	2353	7917	1036	2251	391	94	165	1077	898	1031	317	.284	.420
Cruz, Jose-Jose Luis (Cheito)	97SeaA 97-02TorA 03SFN 04TBA 05AriN 05BosA 05-06LAN	04-19-74	Arroyo, P.R.		B	R	6'0	205	1259	4419	670	1101	239	33	198	602	616	1073	107	.249	.453
Cruz, Julio-Julio Luis (The Cruiser, Juice)	77-83SeaA 83-86ChiA	12-02-54	Brooklyn, N.Y.		B	R	5'9	175	1156	3859	557	916	113	27	23	279	478	508	343	.237	.299
Cruz, Nelson-Nelson Ramon [Martinez]	05MilN 06TexA	07-01-80	Monte Cristi, Dom. Rep.		R	R	6'3	175	49	135	16	30	4	0	6	22	9	32	1	.222	.385
Cruz, Todd-Todd Ruben (T.C., Caribbean)	78PhiN 79KCA 80CalA 80ChiA 81XJ 82-83SeaA 83-84BalA	11-23-55	Highland Park, Mich.		R	R	6'	180	544	1526	133	336	58	6	34	154	59	317	9	.220	.333
Cruz, Tommy-Cirilio T. [Dilan] (Cuki)	73StlN 77ChiA	02-15-51	Arroyo, P.R.		L	L	5'9	170	7	7	1	0	0	0	0	0	0	0	0	.000	.000
Cubbage, Mike-Michael Lee	74-76TexA 76-80MinA 81,M91NYN	07-21-50	Charlottesville, Va.		L	R	6'	182	703	1951	218	503	74	20	34	251	215	233	6	.258	.369
Cuddyer, Michael-Michael Brent	01-06MinA	03-27-79	Norfolk, Va.		R	R	6'2	220	475	1550	233	416	98	12	56	218	162	352	18	.268	.455
Culmer, Wil-Wilfred Hillard	83CleA	11-11-57	Nassau, Bahamas	10-14-03	R	R	6'4	210	7	19	0	2	0	0	0	1	0	4	0	.105	.105
Cummings, Midre-Midre Almeric	93-97PitN 97PhiN 98BosA 99-00MinA 00BosA 01AriN 04TBA 05BalA	10-14-71	St. Croix, V.I.		L	R	6'1	195	460	1113	136	286	60	8	22	124	94	200	9	.257	.385
Curtis, Chad-Chad David	92-94CalA 95-96DetA 96LAN 97CleA 97-99NYA 00-01TexA	11-06-68	Marion, Ind.		R	R	5'10	185	1204	4017	648	1061	195	16	101	461	510	676	212	.264	.396
Cust, Jack-John Joseph Jr.	01AriN 02ColN 03-04BalA 06SDN	01-16-79	Flemington, N.J.		L	R	6'1	205	70	144	16	32	9	0	5	19	23	59	0	.222	.389
Cuyler, Milt-Milton	90-95DetA 96BosA 98TexA	10-07-68	Macon, Ga.		B	R	5'10	185	490	1386	227	329	47	23	10	119	121	273	77	.237	.326
Dade, Paul-Lonnie Paul (Executioner)	75-76CalA 77-79CleA 79-80SDN	12-07-51	Seattle, Wash.		R	R	6'	190	439	1313	166	355	54	7	10	107	113	193	57	.270	.345
Dalena, Pete-Peter Martin	89CleA	06-26-60	Fresno, Cal.		L	R	5'11	205	5	7	0	1	0	0	0	0	0	3	0	.143	.286
Dalesandro, Mark-Mark Anthony	94-95CalA 98-99TorA 01ChiA	05-14-68	Chicago, Ill.		R	R	6'	195	79	129	17	31	7	0	3	17	3	14	1	.240	.364
Dallimore, Brian-Brian Scott	04-05SFN	11-15-73	Las Vegas, Nev.		R	R	6'1	180	27	50	9	13	0	0	1	7	4	7	0	.260	.380
Damon, Johnny-Johnny David	95-00KCA 01OakA 02-05BosA 06NYA	11-05-73	Fort Riley, Kans.		L	L	6'	190	1704	6766	1188	1958	361	85	154	780	665	789	306	.289	.436
Daniels, Kal-Kalvoski	86-89CinN 89-92LAN 92ChiN	08-20-63	Vienna, Ga.		L	L	5'11	195	727	2338	391	666	125	8	104	360	365	493	87	.285	.479
Darr, Mike-Michael Curtis	99-01SDN	03-21-76	Corona, Calif.	02-15-02	L	R	6'3	205	188	542	63	148	28	5	5	67	67	135	17	.273	.371
Darwin, Bobby-Arthur Bobby Lee (See P 61-72)	62LAA 69,71LAN 72-75MinA 75-76MilA 76-77BosA 77CinN	02-16-43	Los Angeles, Cal.		R	R	6'2	190	646	2224	250	559	76	16	83	328	160	577	15	.251	.412
Dascenzo, Doug-Douglas Craig	88-92ChiN 93TexA 96SDN	06-30-64	Cleveland, Ohio		B	L	5'7	160	540	1225	156	287	42	10	5	90	103	117	49	.234	.297
Datz, Jeff-Jeffrey William	89DetA	11-28-59	Camden, N.J.		R	R	6'4	210	7	10	0	2	0	0	0	0	1	1	0	.200	.200
Daubach, Brian-Brian Michael	98FlaN 99-02BosA 03ChiA 04BosA 05NYN	02-11-72	Belleville, Ill.		L	R	6'1	200	661	2025	271	525	139	10	93	333	236	541	5	.259	.476
Dauer, Rich-Richard Fremont	76-85BalA	07-27-52	San Bernardino, Cal.		R	R	6'	180	1140	3829	448	984	193	3	43	372	297	219	6	.257	.343
Daugherty, Jack-John Michael	87MonN 89-92TexA 93HouN 93CinN	07-03-60	Hialeah, Fla.		B	L	6'	188	355	759	80	194	39	6	10	87	76	132	5	.256	.362
Daulton, Darren-Darren Arthur (Dutch)	83,85-97PhiN 97FlaN	01-03-62	Arkansas City, Kans.		L	R	6'2	190	1161	3630	511	891	197	25	137	588	629	726	50	.245	.427
DaVanon, Jeff-Jeffrey Graham	99AnaA 01-04AnaA 05LAA 06AriN	12-08-73	San Diego, Calif.		B	R	6'	190	489	1199	191	314	54	12	33	144	173	241	58	.262	.410
DaVanon, Jerry-Frank Gerald	69SDN 69-70StlN 71BalA 73CalA 74StlN 75-76HouN 77StlN	08-21-45	Oceanside, Cal.		R	R	5'11	175	262	499	73	117	21	5	3	50	68	80	3	.234	.315
David, Andre-Andre Anter	84,86MinA	05-18-58	Hollywood, Cal.		L	L	6'	170	38	53	5	13	0	4	1	5	7	13	0	.245	.340
Davidson, Cleatus-Cleatus LaVon	99MinA	11-01-76	Bartow, Fla.		B	R	5'10	170	22	23	3	3	0	0	0	3	1	3	0	.136	.136
Davidson, Mark-John Mark	86-88MinA 89-91HouN	02-15-61	Knoxville, Tenn.		R	R	6'2	190	413	661	88	149	27	3	6	57	58	128	15	.225	.303
Davis, Alvin-Alvin Glenn	84-91SeaA 92CalA	09-09-60	Riverside, Cal.		L	R	6'	190	1206	4240	568	1189	220	10	160	683	685	558	7	.280	.450
Davis, Ben-Benjamin Matthew	98-01SDN 02-04SeaA 04ChiA	03-10-77	Chester, Pa.		B	R	6'4	220	486	1512	168	358	77	2	38	204	153	385	9	.237	.366
Davis, Bob-Robert John Eugene (Stinger)	73,75-78SDN 79-80TorA 81CalA	03-01-52	Pryor, Okla.		R	R	6'1	190	290	665	50	131	19	3	6	51	40	118	0	.197	.262
Davis, Butch-Wallace McArthur	83-84KCA 87PitN 88-89BalA 91LAN 93-94TexA	06-19-58	Williamston, N.C.		R	R	6'1	190	166	453	56	110	23	2	7	50	20	83	13	.243	.380
Davis, Chili-Charles Theodore	81-87SFN 88-90CalA 91-92MinN 93-96CalA 97KCA 98-99NYA	01-17-60	Kingston, Jamaica		B	R	6'2	220	2436	8673	1240	2380	424	30	350	1372	1194	1698	142	.274	.451
Davis, Dick-Richard Earl	77-80MilA 81-82PhiN 82TorA 82PitN	09-25-53	Long Beach, Cal.		R	R	6'1	185	403	1217	160	323	62	7	27	141	50	152	13	.265	.394
Davis, Doug-Douglas Raymond	88CalA 92TexA	09-24-62	Bloomsburg, Pa.		R	R	6'	185	7	13	0	1	0	0	0	0	0	3	0	.077	.077
Davis, Eric-Eric Keith	84-91CinN 92-93LAN 93-94DetA 95ZJ 96CinN 97-98BalA 99-00StlN 01SFN	05-29-62	Los Angeles, Cal.		R	R	6'2	195	1626	5321	938	1430	239	26	282	934	740	1398	349	.269	.482
Davis, Glenn-Glenn Earle	84-90HouN 91-93BalA	03-28-61	Jacksonville, Fla.		R	R	6'3	210	1015	3719	510	965	177	13	190	603	370	613	28	.259	.467
Davis, Jerry-Jerry Edward	83,85NYA	12-25-58	Trenton, N.J.		R	R	6'1	185	49	73	13	22	3	1	1	9	11	11	0	.301	.397
Davis, J.J.-Jerry C.	02-04PitN 05WasN	10-25-78	Glendora, Cal.		R	R	6'5	250	67	106	6	19	1	0	4	9	7	34	3	.179	.217
Davis, Jody-Jody Richard	81-88ChiN 88-90AtlN	11-12-56	Gainesville, Ga.		R	R	6'3	210	1082	3585	364	877	164	11	127	490	333	712	7	.245	.403
Davis, Mark-Mark Anthony	91CalA	11-25-64	San Diego, Cal.		R	R	6'	180	3	2	0	0	0	0	0	0	0	0	0	.000	.000

USE NAME - GIVEN NAMES (NICKNAMES)	TEAM BY YEAR	BIRTH DATE	BIRTH PLACE	DEATH DATE	B	T	HGT	WGT	G	AB	R	H	2B	3B	HR	RBI	BB	SO	SB	BA	SA
Davis, Mike-Michael Dwayne (Greyhound)	80-87OakA 88-89LAN	06-11-59	San Diego, Cal.		L	L	6'3	185	963	2999	419	778	161	16	91	371	236	537	134	.259	.415
Davis, Odie-Odie Ernest (O.D.)	80TexA	08-13-55	San Antonio, Tex.		R	R	6'1	176	17	8	0	1	0	0	0	0	0	2	0	.125	.125
Davis, Rajai-Rajai Lavae	06PitN	10-19-80	Norwich, Conn.		R	R	5'11	195	20	14	1	2	1	0	0	0	2	3	1	.143	.214
Davis, Russ-Russell Stuart	94-95NYA 96-99SeaA 00-01SFN	09-13-69	Birmingham, Ala.		R	R	6'	195	612	1980	261	508	108	6	84	276	146	503	16	.257	.444
Davis, Steve-Steven Michael	79ChiN	12-30-53	Oakland, Cal.		R	R	6'1	195	3	4	0	0	0	0	0	1	0	0	0	.000	.000
Davis, Tommy-Thomas James	99BalA	05-21-73	Mobile, Ala.		R	R	6'1	210	5	6	0	1	0	0	0	0	0	2	0	.167	.167
Davis, Trench-Trench Neal	85-86PitN 87AtlN	09-12-60	Baltimore, Md.		L	L	6'1	185	23	33	3	4	0	0	0	1	0	5	1	.121	.121
Dawkins, Gookie-Travis Sentell	99-00,02CinN 03KCA	05-12-79	Newberry, S.C.		R	R	6'1	180	55	98	8	16	4	0	0	3	9	34	2	.163	.204
Dawson, Andre-Andre Nolan (Hawk)	76-86MonN 87-92ChiN 93-94BosA 95-96FlaN	07-10-54	Miami, Fla.		R	R	6'2	195	2627	9927	1373	2774	503	98	438	1591	589	1509	314	.279	.482
Dayett, Brian-Brian Kelly	83-84NYA 85-87ChiN	01-22-57	New London, Conn.		R	R	5'10	185	218	426	45	110	26	2	14	68	37	71	0	.258	.427
de Caster, Yurendell-Yurendell Eithel	06PitN	09-26-79	Brevengat, Curacao		R	R	6'1	205	3	2	0	0	0	0	0	0	0	2	0	.000	.000
DeCinces, Doug-Douglas Vernon	73-81BalA 82-87CalA 87StLN	08-29-50	Burbank, Cal.		R	R	6'2	193	1649	5809	778	1505	312	29	237	879	618	904	58	.259	.445
Decker, Steve-Steven Michael	90-92SFN 93,95FlaN 96SFN 96ColN 99AnaA	10-25-65	Rock Island, Ill.		R	R	6'3	210	263	688	60	152	21	2	13	72	76	124	2	.221	.314
Deer, Rob-Robert George	84-85SFN 86-90MilA 91-93DetA 93BosA 94JL 96SDN	09-29-60	Orange, Cal.		R	R	6'3	220	1155	3881	578	853	148	13	230	600	575	1409	43	.220	.442
DeFreitas, Arturo-Arturo Marcelino [Simon] (Toro)	78-79CinN	04-26-53	San Pedro de Mac,D.R.		R	R	6'2	190	32	53	3	11	3	0	1	6	1	20	0	.208	.321
DeHaan, Kory-Korwin Jay	00,02SDN	07-16-76	Pella, Iowa		L	R	6'2	187	102	114	20	22	7	0	2	13	5	45	4	.193	.307
Deidel, Jim-James Lawrence	74NYA	06-06-49	Denver, Colo.		R	R	6'2	215	2	2	0	0	0	0	0	0	0	0	0	.000	.000
DeJesus, David-David Christopher	03-06KCA	12-20-79	Brooklyn, N.Y.		L	L	6'	175	349	1322	210	386	82	17	24	151	119	201	19	.292	.434
DeJesus, Ivan-Ivan [Alverez]	74-76LAN 77-81ChiN 82-84PhiN 85StLN 86NYA 87SFN 88DetA	01-09-53	Santurce, P.R.		R	R	5'11	180	1371	4602	595	1167	175	48	21	324	466	664	194	.254	.326
DeJohn, Mark-Mark Stephen (D.J.)	82DetA	09-18-53	Middletown, Conn.		B	R	5'11	175	24	21	1	4	2	0	0	1	4	4	1	.190	.286
de la Rosa, (de los Santos), Jesus-Jesus [de la Rosa]	75HouN	08-05-53	Santo Domingo, D.R.		R	R	6'1	185	3	3	1	1	0	0	0	0	0	0	0	.333	.667
de la Rosa, Tomas-Tomas Agramonte	00-01MonN 06SFN	01-28-78	La Victoria, Dom. Rep.		R	R	5'10	165	49	83	8	24	3	1	2	10	8	14	2	.289	.422
Delgado, Alex-Alexander	96BosA	01-11-71	Palmarejo, Venezuela		R	R	6'	160	26	20	5	5	0	0	0	1	3	3	0	.250	.250
Delgado, Carlos-Carlos Juan [Hernandez]	93-04TorA 05FlaN 06NYN	06-25-72	Aguadilla, P.R.		L	R	6'3	225	1711	6053	1059	1709	414	16	407	1287	973	1483	9	.282	.558
Delgado, Luis-Luis Felipe [Robles] (Puchy)	77SeaA	02-02-54	Hatillo, P.R.		B	L	5'11	170	13	22	4	4	0	0	0	2	1	8	0	.182	.182
Delgado, Wilson-Wilson [Duran]	96-99SFN 00NYA 00-01KCA 02-03StLN 03AnaA 04NYN	07-15-75	Santo Domingo, D.R.		B	R	5'11	165	253	542	59	136	15	2	5	43	47	108	5	.251	.314
Dellaero, Jason-Jason Christopher	99ChiA	12-17-76	Mount Kisco, N.Y.		B	R	6'2	195	11	33	1	3	0	0	0	2	1	11	0	.091	.091
Dellucci, Dave-David Michael	97BalA 98-03AriN 03NYA 04-05TexA 06PhiN	10-31-73	Baton Rouge, La.		L	L	5'10	195	908	2294	360	603	107	31	86	328	276	579	36	.263	.449
de los Santos, Luis-Luis Manuel [Martinez]	88-89KCA 91DetA	12-29-66	San Cristobal,D.R.		R	R	6'5	205	55	139	8	29	6	2	0	7	11	22	0	.209	.281
Dempsey, Rick-John Rikard	69-72MinA 73-76NYA 76-86BalA 87CleA 88-90LAN 91MilA 92BalA	09-13-49	Fayetteville, Tenn.		R	R	6'	180	1766	4692	525	1093	223	12	96	471	592	736	20	.233	.347
Denorfia, Chris-Christopher Anthony	05-06CinN		Bats Both part of 82																		
		07-15-80	Bristol, Conn.		R	R	6'	195	67	144	22	40	8	0	2	9	17	30	2	.278	.382
Denson, Drew-Andrew Jr.	89AtlN 93ChiA	11-16-65	Cincinnati, Ohio		R	R	6'5	210	16	41	1	10	1	0	0	5	3	11	1	.244	.268
Dent (O'Dey), Bucky-Russell Earl	73-76ChiA 77-82NYA 82-83TexA 84KCA M89-90NYA	11-25-51	Savannah, Ga.		R	R	5'9	180	1392	4512	451	1114	196	23	40	423	292	349	17	.247	.321
DePastino, Joe-Joseph Bernard	03NYN	09-04-73	Philadelphia, Pa.		R	R	6'2	210	2	2	0	0	0	0	0	0	0	0	0	.000	.000
Dernier, Bob-Robert Eugene (Deer)	80-83PhiN 84-87ChiN 88-89PhiN	01-05-57	Kansas City, Mo.		R	R	6'	165	904	2483	374	634	92	16	23	152	222	301	218	.255	.333
DeRosa, Mark-Mark Thomas	98-04AtlN 05-06TexA		Bats Both part of 83																		
		02-26-75	Passaic, N.J.		R	R	6'1	200	595	1643	239	449	93	4	38	193	125	286	11	.273	.404
DeSa, Joe-Joseph	80StLN 85ChiA	07-27-59	Honolulu, Hawaii	12-20-86	L	L	5'11	180	35	55	5	11	2	0	2	7	3	8	0	.200	.345
DeShields, Delino-Delino Lamont	90-93MonN 94-96LAN 97-98StLN 99-01BalA 01-02ChiN	01-15-69	Seaford, Del.		L	R	6'1	175	1615	5779	872	1548	244	74	80	561	754	1061	463	.268	.377
Destrade, Orestes-Orestes [Cucuas]	87NYA 88PitN 89-92JL 93-94FlaN	05-08-62	Santiago de Cuba,Cuba		B	R	6'4	230	237	765	80	184	25	3	26	106	87	184	1	.241	.383
Detherage, Bobby-Robert Wayne (Dr. Death)	80KCA	09-20-54	Springfield, Mo.		R	R	6'	180	20	26	2	8	0	1	1	4	1	1	0	.308	.500
Devarez, Cesar-Cesar Salvatore [Santana]	95-96BalA	09-22-69	San Fran. de Mac., D.R.		R	R	5'10	175	16	22	3	2	0	1	0	0	1	3	0	.091	.182
Devereaux, Mike-Michael	87-88LAN 89-94BalA 95ChiA 95AtlN 96BalA 97TexA 98LAN	04-10-63	Casper, Wyo.		R	R	6'	195	1086	3740	491	949	170	33	105	480	296	635	85	.254	.401
DeVore, Doug-Douglas Rinehart	04AriN	12-14-77	Columbus, Ohio		L	L	6'4	217	50	107	5	24	3	2	1	3	7	31	1	.224	.374
DeWillis, Jeff-Jeffrey Allen	87TorA	04-13-65	Houston, Tex.		R	R	6'2	170	13	25	2	3	0	1	0	2	2	12	0	.120	.280
Diaz, Alex-Alexis	92-94MilA 95-96SeaA 97TexA 98SFN 99HouN	10-05-68	Brooklyn, N.Y.		B	R	5'11	185	366	816	102	195	31	7	8	75	33	107	41	.239	.324
Diaz, Bo-Baudillo Jose [Seijas]	77BosA 78-81CleA 82-85PhiN 85-89CinN	03-23-53	Cua, Venezuela	11-23-90	R	R	6'	200	993	3274	327	834	162	5	87	452	198	429	9	.255	.387
Diaz, Carlos-Carlos Francisco	90TorA	12-24-64	Jersey City, N.J.		R	R	6'3	195	9	3	1	1	0	0	0	0	0	2	0	.333	.333
Diaz, Eddie-Edgar [Serrano]	86,90MilA	02-08-64	Santurce, P.R.		R	R	6'	165	91	231	27	62	2	2	0	14	22	35	3	.268	.294
Diaz, Eddy-Eddy Javier	97MilA	09-29-71	Barquisimeto, Venez.		R	R	5'10	160	16	50	4	11	2	1	0	7	1	5	0	.220	.300
Diaz, Edwin-Edwin [Rosario]	98-99AriN	01-15-75	Bayamon, P.R.		R	R	5'11	170	7	12	2	2	0	0	0	1	3	3	0	.167	.333
Diaz, Einar-Einar Antonio	96-02CleA 03TexA 04MonN 05StLN 06LAN	12-28-72	Chiriqui, Panama		R	R	5'10	195	673	2061	222	523	116	6	21	202	96	199	21	.254	.346
Diaz, Juan-Juan Carlos	02BosA	02-19-74	San Jose de las Lajas, Cuba		R	R	6'2	269	4	7	2	2	1	0	1	2	1	2	0	.286	.857
Diaz, Mario-Mario Rafael [Torres]	87-89SeaA 90NYN 91-93TexA 94-95FlaN	01-10-62	Humacao, P.R.		R	R	5'10	160	374	773	84	198	31	4	5	84	41	70	1	.256	.326
Diaz, Matt-Matthew Edward	03-04TBA 05KCA 06AtlN	03-03-78	Portland, Ore.		R	R	6'1	200	172	416	49	127	20	7	9	44	17	73	5	.305	.452
Diaz, Mike-Michael Anthony (Rambo)	83ChiN 86-88PitN 88ChiA	07-15-60	San Francisco, Cal.		R	R	6'2	220	293	683	70	169	27	2	31	102	71	128	1	.247	.429
Diaz, Victor-Victor Israel III	04-06NYN	12-10-81	Santo Domingo, D. R.		R	R	6'	200	110	342	49	89	21	3	15	48	31	102	6	.260	.471
DiFelice, Mike-Michael William	96-97StLN 98-01TBA 01AriN 02StLN 03KCA 04DetA 04ChiN 05-06NYN	05-28-69	Philadelphia, Pa.		R	R	6'2	205	527	1498	143	352	88	2	38	158	98	321	3	.235	.355
Dillard, Steve-Stephen Bradley	75-77BosA 78DetA 79-81ChiN 82ChiA	02-17-51	Memphis, Tenn.		R	R	6'1	180	438	1013	148	246	50	6	13	102	76	147	15	.243	.333
Dillon, Joe-Joseph William	05FlaN	08-02-75	Modesto, Cal.		R	R	6'2	215	27	36	6	6	0	1	1	8	1	9	0	.167	.278
Dilone, Miguel-Miguel Angel [Reyes] (Evelo)	74-77PitN 77-79OakA 79ChiN 80-83CleA 83ChiA 83PitN 84-85MonN 85SDN	11-01-54	Santiago, D. R.		B	R	5'11	165	800	2000	314	530	67	25	6	129	142	197	267	.265	.333
Dimmel, Mike-Michael Wayne	77-78BalA 79StLN	10-16-54	Albert Lea, Minn.		R	R	6'	180	39	8	11	1	0	0	0	0	0	1	1	.125	.125
Dineen, Kerry-Kerry Michael	75-76NYA 78PhiN	05-01-52	Englewood, N.J.		L	L	5'11	167	16	37	3	12	2	0	0	2	4	3	1	.324	.378
DiSarcina, Gary-Gary Thomas	89-96CalA 97-00AnaA 01SJ	11-19-67	Malden, Mass.		R	R	6'1	190	1086	3744	444	966	186	20	28	355	154	306	47	.258	.354
Distefano, Benny-Benito James	84,86,88-89PitN 90JL 92HouN	01-23-62	Brooklyn, N.Y.		L	L	6'2	205	240	360	35	82	13	5	7	42	31	66	1	.228	.350
Dobbs, Greg-Gregory Stuart	04-06SeaA	07-02-78	Los Angeles, Cal.		L	R	6'1	205	100	222	16	57	11	2	2	32	10	43	1	.257	.351
Dodd, Tom-Thomas Marion	86BalA	08-15-58	Portland, Ore.		R	R	6'	190	8	13	1	3	0	0	1	2	2	2	0	.231	.462
Dodson, Pat-Patrick Neal	86-88BosA	11-19-59	Santa Monica, Cal.		L	L	6'4	220	52	99	12	20	8	1	4	10	17	33	0	.202	.424
Doherty, John-John Michael (Pup)	74-75CalA	08-22-51	Auburn, Mass.		L	L	6'3	185	104	317	27	76	17	1	4	27	16	25	3	.240	.338
Dominique, Andy-Andrew John	04BosA 05TorA	10-30-75	Tarzana, Cal.		R	R	6'	220	9	13	0	2	0	0	1	0	3	0	.154	.154
Donnels,Chris-Chris Barton	91-92NYN 93-95HouN 95BosA 96-99JL 00-01LAN 02AriN	04-21-66	Los Angeles, Cal.		L	R	6'	185	450	798	83	186	36	5	17	86	103	165	5	.233	.355
Donohue, Tom-Thomas James (Digger)	79-80CalA	11-15-52	Mineola, N.Y.		R	R	6'	192	122	325	31	65	7	2	5	28	10	92	7	.200	.280
Doran, Bill-William Donald	82-90HouN 90-92CinN 93MilA	05-28-58	Cincinnati, Ohio		B	R	5'11	175	1453	5131	727	1366	220	39	84	497	709	600	209	.266	.373
Dorsett, Brian-Brian Richard	87CleA 88CalA 89-90NYA 91SDN 93-94CinN 96ChiN	04-09-61	Terre Haute, Ind.		R	R	6'3	215	163	411	38	92	15	0	9	51	32	73	0	.224	.326
Dorta, Melvin-Melvin A.	06WasN	05-18-82	Valencia, Venezuela		R	R	5'11	160	15	19	3	4	1	0	0	0	1	2	0	.211	.263
Doster, David-David Eric	96,99PhiN	08-07-70	Fort Wayne, Ind.		R	R	5'10	185	138	202	23	47	10	0	4	18	19	44	1	.233	.342
Doumit, Ryan-Ryan Matthew	05-06PitN	04-03-81	Moses Lake, Wash.		B	R	6'	200	136	380	40	90	22	1	12	52	26	90	2	.237	.395
Dowell, Ken-Kenneth Allen	87PhiN	01-19-61	Sacramento, Cal.		R	R	5'9	160	15	39	4	5	0	0	0	1	2	5	0	.128	.128
Downing, Brian-Brian Jay (The Incredible Hulk)	73-77ChiA 78-90CalA 91-92TexA	10-09-50	Los Angeles, Cal.		R	R	5'10	195	2344	7853	1188	2099	360	28	275	1073	1197	1127	50	.267	.425
Doyle, Brian-Brian Reed	78-80NYA 81OakA	01-26-54	Glasgow, Ky.		L	R	5'10	170	110	199	18	32	3	0	0	13	10	13	1	.161	.191
Doyle, Denny-Denny Robert Dennis	70-73PhiN 74-75CalA 75-77BosA	01-17-44	Glasgow, Ky.		L	R	5'10	160	944	3290	357	823	113	28	16	237	205	310	38	.250	.316
Doyle, Jeff-Jeffrey Donald	83StLN	10-02-56	Havre, Mont.		B	R	5'9	160	13	37	4	11	1	0	0	2	1	3	0	.297	.432
Dozier, D.J.-William Henry	87-91 played in N.F.L.	92NYN	09-21-65	Norfolk, Va.		R	R	6'	204	25	47	4	9	2	0	0	4	2	19	4	.191	.234
Dransfeldt, Kelly-Kelly Daniel	99-01TexA 04ChiA	04-16-75	Joliet, Ill.		R	R	6'2	195	51	112	10	23	8	0	1	11	4	32	0	.205	.259
Drew, Cameron-Cameron Steward	88HouN	02-12-64	Boston, Mass.		L	R	6'5	215	7	16	1	3	1	0	0	1	0	1	0	.188	.313
Drew, J.D.-David Jonathan	98-03StLN 04AtlN 05-06LAN	11-20-75	Valdosta, Ga.		L	R	6'1	195	960	3161	605	905	160	33	162	509	529	685	74	.286	.512
Drew, Stephen-Stephen Oris	06AriN	03-16-83	Valdosta, Ga.		L	R	6'1	185	59	209	27	66	13	7	5	23	14	50	2	.316	.517
Driessen, Dan-Daniel (The Cobra)	73-84CinN 84-85MonN 85-86SFN 86HouN 87StLN	07-29-51	Hilton Head Island, S.C.		L	R	5'11	195	1732	5479	746	1464	282	23	153	763	761	719	154	.267	.411
Drumright, Keith-Keith Alan (Drummer)	78HouN 81OakA	10-21-54	Springfield, Mo.		L	R	5'10	160	48	141	13	34	1	1	0	13	7	6	1	.241	.262
Dubois, Jason-Jason Bradford	04-05ChiN 05CleA	03-26-79	Virginia Beach, Va.		R	R	6'5	220	86	210	23	49	11	0	10	29	13	61	0	.233	.443
Ducey, Rob-Robert Thomas	87-92TorA 92CalA 93-94TexA 95-96JL 97-98SeaA 99-00PhiN 00TorA 00-01PhiN 01MonN	05-24-65	Toronto, Canada		L	R	6'2	180	703	1279	190	309	78	11	31	146	166	346	22	.242	.396
Duffy, Chris-Christopher Ellis	04-20-80	Brattleboro, Vt.		L	L	5'10	185	133	440	68	123	27	26	93	.280	.364									
Duffy, Frank-Frank Thomas	70-71CinN 71SFN 72-77CleA 78-79BosA	10-14-46	Oakland, Cal		R	R	6'	180	915	2665	248	619	104	14	26	240	171	342	49	.232	.334
Dunbar, Tommy-Thomas Jerome	83-85TexA	05-05-59	Graniteville, S.C.		L	L	6'2	180	91	225	19	52	5	2	3	18	23	32	4	.231	.298
Duncan, Chris-Christopher Edward	05-06StLN	05-05-81	Tucson, Ariz.		L	R	6'5	210	99	290	62	84	12	3	23	46	30	74	0	.290	.590
Duncan, Jeff-Jeffrey Matthew	03-04NYN	12-09-78	Harvey, Ill.		L	L	6'2	185	69	154	15	28	4	1	0	11	18	46	7	.182	.227

USE NAME - GIVEN NAMES (NICKNAMES)	TEAM BY YEAR	BIRTH DATE	BIRTH PLACE	DEATH DATE	B	T	HGT	WGT	G	AB	R	H	2B	3B	HR	RBI	BB	SO	SB	BA	SA
Duncan, Mariano-Mariano [Nalasco]	85-87,89LAN 89-91CinN 92-95CinN 95CinN 96-97NYA 97TorA	03-13-63	San Pedro de Mac.,D.R.		R	R	6'	195	1279	4677	619	1247	233	37	87	491	201	913	174	.267	.388
			Bats Both 85-86, part of 87																		
Duncan, Taylor-Taylor McDowell	77StLN 78OakA	05-12-53	Memphis, Tenn.	01-03-04	R	R	6'	185	112	331	27	86	15	2	3	39	21	39	1	.260	.344
Dunn, Adam-Adam Troy	01-06CinN	11-09-79	Houston, Tex.		L	R	6'6	240	821	2832	519	695	151	6	198	466	574	927	48	.245	.513
Dunn, Ron-Ronald Ray	74-75CinN	01-24-50	Oklahoma City, Okla.		R	R	5'11	180	55	112	8	27	10	0	3	21	18	25	0	.241	.411
Dunn, Steve-Steven Robert	94-95MinA	04-18-70	Champaign, Ill.		L	L	6'4	225	19	41	2	8	5	0	0	4	2	15	0	.195	.317
Dunn, Todd-Todd Kent	96-97MilA	07-29-70	Tulsa, Okla.		R	R	6'5	220	50	128	19	30	6	0	3	10	2	42	3	.234	.352
Dunston, Shawon-Shawon Donnell	85-95ChiN 96SFN 97ChiN 97PitN 98CleA 98SFN 99StLN 99CinN 00StLN 01-02SFN	03-21-63	Brooklyn, N.Y.		R	R	6'1	180	1814	5927	736	1597	292	62	150	668	203	1000	212	.269	.416
Dunwoody, Todd-Todd Franklin	97-99FlaN 00KCA 01ChiN 02CleA	04-11-75	Lafayette, Ind.		L	L	6'1	205	295	915	98	213	48	12	11	81	51	234	13	.233	.348
Duran, Dan-Daniel James	81TexA	03-16-54	Palo Alto, Cal.		L	L	6'	195	13	16	1	4	0	0	0	1	1	1	0	.250	.263
Durant, Mike-Michael Joseph	96MinA	09-14-69	Columbus, Ohio		R	R	6'2	200	40	81	15	17	3	0	0	5	10	15	3	.210	.247
Durazo, Erubiel-Erubiel [Cardenas]	99-02AriN 03-05OakA	01-23-74	Hermosillo, Mexico		L	L	6'3	235	624	1948	333	547	108	6	94	330	307	428	7	.281	.487
Durham, Leon-Leon (Bull)	80StLN 81-88ChiN 88CinN 89StLN	07-31-57	Cincinnati, Ohio		L	L	6'1	220	1067	3527	522	992	192	40	147	530	444	679	106	.277	.475
Durham, Ray-Ray	95-02ChiA 02OakA 03-06SFN	11-30-71	Charlotte, N.C.		B	R	5'8	180	1709	6574	1129	1846	384	77	175	759	714	1054	255	.281	.443
Durrington, Trent-Trent John	99-00,03AnaA 04-05MinN	08-27-75	Sydney, Australia		R	R	5'10	185	140	235	35	46	5	3	2	9	17	54	14	.196	.268
Dwyer, Jim-James Edward	73-75StLN 75-76MonN 76NYN 77-78StLN 78SFN 79-80BosA 81-88BalA 88-89MinA 89MonN 90MinA	01-03-50	Evergreen Park, Ill.		L	L	5'10	175	1327	2761	409	719	115	17	77	349	402	402	26	.260	.398
Dybzinski, Jerry-Jerome Matthew	80-82CleA 83-84ChiA 85PitN	07-07-55	Cleveland, Ohio		R	R	6'2	185	468	909	108	213	32	5	3	93	70	109	32	.234	.290
Dye, Jermaine-Jermaine Terrell	96AtlN 97-01KCA 01-04OakA 05-06ChiA	01-28-74	Oakland, Cal.		R	R	6'4	200	1330	4886	742	1352	269	22	236	817	444	989	41	.277	.486
Dyer, Duffy-Don Robert	68-74NYN 75-78PitN 79MonN 80-81DetA	08-15-45	Dayton, Ohio		R	R	6'	200	722	1993	151	441	74	11	30	173	228	415	10	.221	.315
Dykstra, Lenny-Leonard Kyle (Nails, The Kamikaze Kid)	85-89NYN 89-96PhiN 97-98XJ	02-10-63	Santa Ana, Cal.		L	L	5'10	190	1278	4559	802	1298	281	43	81	404	640	503	283	.285	.419
Earl, Scott-William Scott (Scottie)	84DetA	09-18-60	Seymour, Ind.		R	R	5'11	165	14	35	3	4	0	1	0	1	0	9	1	.114	.171
Easler, Mike-Michael Anthony (Hit Man)	73-75HouN 76CalA 77,79-83PitN 84-85BosA, 86NYA 87PhiN 87NYA	11-29-50	Cleveland, Ohio		L	L	6'	195	1151	3677	465	1078	189	25	118	522	321	696	20	.293	.454
Easley, Damion-Jacinto Damion	92-96CalA 96-02DetA 03TBA 04-05FlaN 06AriN	11-11-69	New York, N.Y.		R	R	5'11	185	1517	4975	678	1247	271	25	147	614	472	862	114	.251	.404
Echevarria, Angel-Angel Santos	96-00ColN 00-01MilN 02CinN	05-25-71	Bridgeport, Conn.		R	R	6'4	225	328	543	70	152	32	0	21	90	46	104	1	.280	.455
Eckstein, David-David Mark	01-04AnaA 05-06StLN	01-20-75	Sanford, Fla.		R	R	5'8	170	848	3338	498	945	138	18	27	254	255	283	100	.283	.359
Eden, Mike-Edward Michael	76AtlN 78ChiA	05-22-49	Ft. Clayton, Canal Zone		B	R	5'11	175	15	25	1	2	0	0	0	1	4	0	0	.080	.080
Edler, Dave-David Delmar	80-83SeaA	08-05-56	Sioux City, Iowa		R	R	6'	195	126	334	34	72	7	3	6	36	35	53	12	.216	.308
Edmonds, Jim-James Patrick	93-96CalA 97-99AnaA 00-06StLN	06-27-70	Fullerton, Cal.		L	L	6'1	210	1697	5907	1115	1709	380	21	350	1068	878	1512	63	.289	.539
Edwards, Dave-David Leonard	77-80MinA 81-82SDN	03-24-54	Los Angeles, Cal.		R	R	6'	175	321	640	95	152	26	2	14	73	55	147	12	.238	.350
Edwards, Marshall-Marshall Lynn (Flea)	81-83MilA	08-27-52	Fort Lewis, Wash.		L	L	5'9	160	160	310	48	80	6	3	2	23	5	19	21	.258	.316
Edwards, Mike-Michael Donald	03OakA 05LAN 06PitN	11-24-76	Goshen, N.Y.		R	R	6'1	185	106	259	24	63	9	2	3	15	19	40	1	.243	.328
Edwards, Mike-Michael Lewis	77PitN 78-80OakA	08-27-52	Fort Lewis, Wash.		R	R	5'9	155	317	879	94	220	28	4	2	49	32	77	38	.250	.298
Eenhoorn, Robert-Robert Franciscus	94-96NYA 96CalA 97AnaA	02-09-68	Rotterdam, Neth.		R	R	6'3	170	37	67	7	16	3	0	1	10	3	10	0	.239	.328
Eisenreich, Jim-James Michael (Ike)	82-84MinA 85-86IL 87-92KCA 93-96PhiN 97-98FlaN 98LAN	04-18-59	St. Cloud, Minn.		L	L	5'11	195	1422	3995	492	1160	221	39	52	477	324	435	105	.290	.404
Eldred, Brad-Bradley Ross (Big Country)	05PitN	07-12-80	Ft. Lauderdale, Fla.		R	R	6'5	270	55	190	23	42	9	0	12	27	13	77	1	.221	.458
Elliott, Randy-Randy Lee	72,74SDN 77SFN 80OakA	06-05-51	Oxnard, Cal.		R	R	6'2	200	114	288	31	62	12	2	8	35	18	57	0	.215	.354
Ellis, Johnny-John Charles	69-72NYA 73-75CleA 76-81TexA	08-21-48	New London, Conn.		R	R	6'2	220	883	2672	259	699	116	13	69	391	190	403	6	.262	.392
Ellis, Mark-Mark William	02-03OakA 04SJ 05-06OakA	06-06-77	Rapid City, S.D.		R	R	5'11	180	498	1773	276	478	93	15	39	191	176	275	15	.270	.405
Ellis, Rob-Robert Walker	71,74-75MilA	07-03-50	Grand Rapids, Mich.		R	R	5'11	180	64	166	16	38	4	0	0	16	16	35	0	.229	.253
Ellison, Jason-Jason Jerome	03-06SFN	04-04-78	Quincy, Cal.		R	R	5'10	180	235	447	68	114	23	3	7	31	29	60	18	.255	.367
Elster, Kevin-Kevin Daniel	86-96NYN 94-95NYA 95PhiN 96TexA 97PitN 98TexA 00LAN	08-03-64	San Pedro, Cal.		R	R	6'2	190	940	2844	332	648	136	12	88	376	295	562	14	.228	.377
Encarnacion, Angelo-Angelo Benjamin	95-96PitN 97AnaA	04-18-69	Santo Domingo, D.R.		R	R	5'8	180	76	198	23	50	10	2	3	15	13	34	3	.253	.369
Encarnacion, Edwin-Edwin Elpidio	05-06CinN	01-07-83	La Romana, Dom. Rep.		R	R	6'1	195	186	617	85	161	49	1	24	103	61	138	9	.261	.460
Encarnacion, Juan-Juan de Dios	97-01DetA 02CinN 02-03FlaN 04LAN 04-05FlaN 06StLN	03-08-76	Las Matas,D.R.		R	R	6'2	210	1181	4402	575	1184	225	45	147	620	270	810	125	.269	.441
Encarnacion (Gonzalez), Mario-Mario Gonzalez [Encarnacion]	01ColN 02ChiN	09-24-75	Bani, Dom. Rep.	10-03-05	R	R	6'2	210	23	69	3	14	1	0	0	3	7	17	2	.203	.217
Engle, Dave-Ralph David	81-85MinA 86DetA 87-88MonN 89MilA	11-30-56	San Diego, Cal.		R	R	6'3	215	594	1643	201	431	88	13	31	181	120	190	5	.262	.388
Enright, George-George Albert	76ChiA	05-09-54	New Britain, Conn.		R	R	5'11	175	2	1	0	0	0	0	0	0	0	0	0	.000	.000
Ensberg, Morgan-Morgan Paul	00,02-06HouN	08-26-75	Redondo Beach, Cal.		R	R	6'2	210	588	1848	287	499	89	10	97	304	288	347	22	.270	.486
Eppard, Jim-James Gerhard	87-89CalA 90TorA	04-27-60	South Bend, Ind.		L	L	6'2	180	82	139	9	39	3	1	0	16	14	21	0	.281	.317
Erickson, Matt-Matthew R.	04MilN	07-30-75	Appleton, Wis.		L	R	5'11	190	4	6	1	1	0	0	0	0	0	1	0	.167	.167
Erstad, Darin-Darin Charles	96CalA 97-04AnaA 05-06LAA	06-04-74	Jamestown, N.D.		L	L	6'2	210	1320	5258	818	1505	279	30	114	625	419	796	170	.286	.416
Esasky, Nick-Nicholas Andrew	83-88CinN 89BosA 90AtlN 91-92IL	02-24-60	Hialeah, Fla.		R	R	6'3	215	810	2703	336	677	120	21	122	427	314	712	18	.250	.446
Escalona, Felix-Felix Eduardo	02-03TBA 04-05NYA	06-27-79	Puerto Cabello, Venez.		R	R	6'	190	84	206	20	43	11	2	0	13	6	56	8	.209	.282
Escobar, Alex-Alexander Jose	01NYN 02KJ 03-04CleA 04ChiA 05LJ 06WasN	09-06-78	Valencia, Venezuela		R	R	6'1	185	125	388	53	100	14	4	13	52	41	112	5	.258	.415
Escobar, Angel-Angel Rubenque [Rivas]	88SFN	05-12-65	La Sabana, Venez.		B	R	6'	160	3	3	1	1	0	0	0	0	0	0	0	.333	.333
Escobar, Jose-Jose Elias [Sanchez]	91CleA	10-30-60	Las Flores, Venez.		R	R	5'10	140	10	15	0	3	0	0	0	1	1	4	0	.200	.200
Espino, Juan-Juan [Reyes]	82-83,85-86NYA	03-16-56	Bonao, Dom. Rep.		R	R	6'	185	49	73	2	16	2	0	1	8	3	15	0	.219	.288
Espinoza, Alvaro-Alvaro Alberto [Ramirez]	84-86MinA 89-91NYA 93-96CleA 96NYN 97SeaA	02-19-62	Valencia, Venezuela		R	R	6'	190	942	2478	252	630	105	9	22	201	76	324	13	.254	.331
Espy, Cecil-Cecil Edward	83LAN 87-90TexA 91-92PitN 93CinN	01-20-63	San Diego, Cal.		B	R	6'3	195	546	1248	160	304	43	16	7	108	104	277	103	.244	.321
Essian, Jim-James Sarkis	73-75PhiN 76-77ChiA 78-80OakA 81ChiA 82SeaA 83CleA 84OakA M91ChiN	01-02-51	Detroit, Mich.		R	R	6'1	187	710	1855	194	453	85	3	33	207	231	171	9	.244	.347
Estalella, Bobby-Robert M.	96-99PhiN 00-01SFN 01NYA 02-03ColN 04AriN 04TorA	08-23-74	Hialeah, Fla.		R	R	6'1	220	310	904	126	195	49	5	48	147	130	290	6	.216	.440
Estrada, Johnny-Johnny Pulado III	01PhiN 02NYN 03-05AtlN 06AriN	06-27-76	Hayward, Cal.		B	R	5'11	209	469	1584	158	444	104	0	32	227	90	181	0	.280	.407
Ethier, Andre-Andre Everett	06LAN	04-10-82	Phoenix, Ariz.		L	L	6'2	210	126	396	50	122	20	7	11	55	34	77	5	.308	.477
Eusebio (Bare), Tony-Raul Antonio [Eusebio]	91,94-01HouN	04-27-67	San Jose de los Llamos, D.R.		R	R	6'2	210	598	1739	179	479	87	5	30	241	182	324	1	.275	.383
Evans, Barry-Barry Steven	78-81SDN 82NYA	11-30-56	Atlanta, Ga.		R	R	6'1	185	224	501	40	126	17	3	2	41	41	62	3	.251	.309
Evans, Darrell-Darrell Wayne (Dee)	69-76AtlN 76-83SFN 84-88DetA 89AtlN	05-26-47	Pasadena, Cal.		L	R	6'2	200	2687	8973	1344	2223	329	36	414	1354	1605	1410	98	.248	.431
Evans, Dwight-Dwight Michael (Dewey)	72-90BosA 91BalA	11-03-51	Santa Monica, Cal.		R	R	6'3	210	2606	8996	1470	2446	483	73	385	1384	1391	1697	78	.272	.470
Evans, Tom-Thomas John	97-98TorA 00TexA	07-09-74	Kirkland, Wash.		R	R	6'1	180	42	102	17	26	6	0	1	7	13	25	0	.255	.343
Everett, Adam-Jeffrey Adam	01-06HouN	02-02-77	Austell, Ga.		R	R	6'	170	583	1925	239	480	91	13	33	199	117	316	55	.249	.362
Everett, Carl-Carl Edward	93-94FlaN 95-97NYN 98-99HouN 00-01BosA 02-03TexA 03ChiA 04MonN 04-05ChiA 06SeaA	06-03-71	Tampa, Fla.		B	R	6'	205	1405	4809	707	1304	258	26	202	792	442	1021	107	.271	.462
Ewing, Sam-Samuel James	73,76ChiA 77-78TorA	04-09-49	Lewisburg, Tenn.		L	R	6'3	205	167	361	31	92	11	3	6	47	28	65	1	.255	.352
Fabregas, Jorge-Jorge	94-96CalA 97AnaA 97ChiA 98AriN 98NYN 99FlaN 99AtlN 00KCA 01-02AnaA 02MilN	03-17-70	Miami, Fla.		L	R	6'3	210	646	1827	153	441	56	5	23	211	114	217	4	.241	.315
Faedo, Lenny-Leonard Lago	80-84MinA	05-13-60	Tampa, Fla.		R	R	5'11	180	174	529	42	133	17	1	5	52	25	49	1	.251	.316
Fahey, Bill-William Roger	71WasA 72,74-77TexA 78-80SDN 81-83DetA	06-14-50	Detroit, Mich.		L	R	6'	200	383	934	75	225	26	2	7	83	74	93	9	.241	.296
Fahey, Brandon-Brandon Wade	06BalA	01-18-81	Dallas, Tex.		L	R	6'2	160	91	251	36	59	8	2	2	23	23	48	3	.235	.307
Faneyte, Rikkert-Rikkert	93-95SFN 96TexA	05-31-69	Amsterdam, Neth.		R	R	6'1	170	80	132	10	23	7	0	0	9	16	42	1	.174	.242
Faries, Paul-Paul Tyrrell	90-92SDN 93FlaN	02-20-65	Berkeley, Cal.		R	R	5'10	170	96	214	26	43	7	2	0	14	20	34	5	.201	.252
Fariss, Monty-Monty Ted	91-92TexA 93FlaN	10-13-67	Cordell, Okla.		R	R	6'4	200	104	226	22	49	10	2	4	29	29	75	0	.217	.332
Fasano, Sal-Salvatore Frank	96-99KCA 00-01OakA 01KCA 01ColN 02AnaA 05BalA 06PhiN 06NYA	08-10-71	Chicago, Ill.		R	R	6'2	230	396	1018	126	225	42	0	46	130	67	291	2	.221	.398
Febles, Carlos-Carlos Manuel	98-03KCA	05-24-76	Santa Cruz de El Seibe, D.R.		R	R	5'11	185	506	1656	255	414	65	18	24	146	163	297	68	.250	.354
Felder, Mike-Michael Otis	85-90MilA 91-92SFN 93SeaA 94HouN	11-18-61	Vallejo, Cal.		B	R	5'8	175	899	2262	318	564	59	32	14	173	168	217	161	.249	.322
Felix, Junior-Junior Francisco [Sanchez]	89-90TorA 91-92CalA 93FlaN 94DetA	10-03-67	Laguna Salada, D.R.		B	R	5'11	185	585	2132	309	562	105	24	55	280	158	509	49	.264	.413
Feliz, Pedro-Pedro Julio	00-06SFN	04-27-75	Azua, Dom. Rep.		R	R	6'1	200	724	2283	285	575	120	17	89	346	120	430	10	.252	.436
Ferguson, Joe-Joseph Vance	70-76LAN 76StLN 77-78HouN 78-81LAN 81-83CalA	09-16-46	San Francisco, Cal.		R	R	6'2	210	1013	3001	407	719	121	11	122	445	562	607	22	.240	.429
Fermin, Felix-Felix Jose [Minaya]	87-88PitN 89-93CleA 94-95SeaA 96ChiN	10-09-63	Mao, Dom. Rep.		R	R	5'11	170	903	2767	294	718	86	11	4	207	166	147	27	.259	.303
Fernandez, Osvaldo-Osvaldo	99MonN 01AnaA	11-02-74	La Vega, Dom. Rep.		R	R	6'2	210	21	49	1	7	3	0	0	3	1	16	0	.143	.204
Fernandez (Fernando),Tony-Octavio Antonio [Castro]	83-90TorA 91-92SDN 93TorA 94CinN 95NYA 96BE 97CleA 98-99TorA 00JL 01MilN 01TorA	06-30-62	San Pedro de Mac.,D.R.		B	R	6'1	185	2158	7911	1057	2276	414	92	94	844	690	784	246	.288	.399
Ferrer, Sergio-Sergio [Marrero] (Cucho)	74-75MinA 78-79NYN	01-29-51	Santurce, P.R.		B	R	5'7	145	125	178	41	43	3	4	0	3	17	27	7	.242	.303
Fiala, Neil-Neil Stephen	81StLN 81CinN	08-24-56	St. Louis, Mo.		R	R	6'1	187	5	10	0	2	0	0	0	0	2	5	0	.200	.200
Fick, Robert-Robert Charles John	98-02DetA 03AtlN 04TBA 04-05SDN 06WasN	03-15-74	Torrance, Cal.		L	L	6'1	200	728	2176	263	567	110	11	67	308	216	344	6	.261	.414
Fielder, Cecil-Cecil Grant	85-88TorA 89JL 90-96DetA 96NYA 98AnaA 98CleA	09-21-63	Los Angeles, Cal.		R	R	6'3	255	1470	5157	744	1313	200	7	319	1008	693	1316	2	.255	.482
Fielder, Prince-Prince Semien Grant	05-06MilN	05-09-84	Ontario, Cal.		L	R	6'	260	196	628	84	171	39	1	30	91	61	142	7	.272	.481

USE NAME - GIVEN NAMES (NICKNAMES)	TEAM BY YEAR	BIRTH DATE	BIRTH PLACE	DEATH DATE	B	T	HGT	WGT	G	AB	R	H	2B	3B	HR	RBI	BB	SO	SB	BA	SA
Fields, Bruce-Bruce Alan	86DetA 88-89SeaA	10-06-60	Cleveland, Ohio		L	R	6'	185	58	113	14	31	7	1	1	11	5	18	1	.274	.381
Fields, Josh-Joshua Dean	06ChiA	12-14-82	Ada, Okla.		R	R	6'1	215	11	20	4	3	2	0	1	2	5	8	0	.150	.400
Figga, Mike-Michael Anthony	97-99NYA 99BalA	07-31-70	Tampa, Fla.		R	R	6'0	200	46	94	13	20	4	0	1	5	2	31	0	.213	.287
Figgins, Chone-Desmond DeChone	02-04AnaA 05-06LAA	01-22-78	Leary, Ga.		B	R	5'8	160	547	2075	329	591	80	39	22	207	198	338	163	.285	.393
Figueroa, Bien-Bienvenido [DeLeon]	92StlN	02-07-64	Santo Domingo, D.R.		R	R	5'10	170	12	11	1	2	1	0	0	4	1	2	0	.182	.273
Figueroa, Jesus-Jesus Maria (Figueroa) (Chits)	80ChiN	02-20-57	Santo Domingo, D.R		L	L	5'9	160	115	198	20	50	5	0	1	11	14	16	2	.253	.293
Figueroa, Luis-Luis R.	01PitN 06TorA	02-16-74	Bayamon, P.R.		B	R	5'9	152	12	11	1	1	1	0	0	0	0	2	0	.091	.182
Fimple, Jack-John Joseph	83-84,86LAN 87CalA	02-10-59	Darby, Pa.		R	R	6'2	195	92	197	21	45	9	1	2	28	19	53	1	.228	.315
Finley, Steve-Steven Allen	89-90BalA 91-94HouN 95-98SDN 99-04AriN 04LAN 05LAA 06SFN	03-12-65	Union City, Tenn.		L	L	6'2	190	2540	9303	1434	2531	446	124	303	1165	836	1295	320	.272	.444
Fiorentino, Jeff-Jeffrey Philip	05-06BalA	04-14-83	Pembroke Pines, Fla.		L	R	6'1	190	32	83	15	21	4	1	1	12	9	13	2	.253	.337
Firova, Dan-Daniel Michael	81-82SeaA 88CleA	10-16-56	Refugio, Tex.		R	R	6'	185	17	7	0	0	0	0	0	0	0	1	0	.000	.000
Fischlin, Mike-Michael Thomas (Fish)	77-78,80HouN 81-85CleA 86NYA 87AtlN	09-13-55	Sacramento, Cal.		R	R	6'1	165	517	941	109	207	29	6	3	68	92	142	24	.220	.273
Fishel, John-John Alan (Fish)	88HouN	11-08-62	Fullerton, Cal.		R	R	5'11	185	19	26	1	6	0	0	1	2	3	6	0	.231	.346
Fisk, Carlton-Carlton Ernest (Pudge)	69,71-80BosA 81-93ChiA	12-26-47	Bellows Falls, Vt.		R	R	6'2	215	2499	8756	1276	2356	421	47	376	1330	849	1386	128	.269	.457
Fitzgerald, Mike-Michael Patrick	88StlN	03-28-64	Savannah, Ga.		R	R	6'1	200	13	46	4	9	1	0	0	1	0	9	0	.196	.217
Fitzgerald, Mike-Michael Roy	83-84NYN 85-91MonN 92CalA	07-13-60	Long Beach, Cal.		R	R	6'	190	848	2316	220	545	95	9	48	293	292	432	31	.235	.346
Flaherty, John-John Timothy	92-93BosA 94-96DetA 96-97SDN 98-02TBA 03-05NYA	10-21-67	New York, N.Y.		R	R	6'1	200	1047	3372	319	849	176	3	80	395	175	514	10	.252	.377
Flannery, John-John Michael (Father)	77ChiA	01-25-57	Long Beach, Cal.		R	R	6'3	170	7	2	1	0	0	0	0	0	1	1	0	.000	.000
Flannery, Tim-Timothy Earl	79-89SDN	09-29-57	Tulsa, Okla.		L	R	5'11	175	972	2473	255	631	77	25	9	209	277	293	22	.255	.317
Fletcher, Darrin-Darrin Glen	89-90LAN 90-91PhiN 92-97MonN 98-02TorA	10-03-66	Elmhurst, Ill.		L	R	6'2	200	1245	3902	377	1048	214	8	124	583	255	399	2	.269	.423
Fletcher, Scott-Scott Brian (Scooter)	81-82ChiN 83-85ChiA 86-89TexA 89-91ChiA 93MilA 93-94BosA 95DetA	07-30-58	Ft Walton Beach, Fla.		R	R	5'11	172	1612	5258	688	1376	243	38	34	510	514	541	99	.262	.342
Flora, Kevin-Kevin Scot	91,95CalA 95PhiN	06-10-69	Fontana, Cal.		R	R	6'	180	29	84	14	17	3	0	2	7	5	28	2	.202	.310
Flores, Gil-Gilberto [Garcia]	77CalA 78-79NYN	10-27-52	Ponce, P.R.		R	R	6'	183	185	464	58	121	20	6	2	37	34	61	15	.261	.343
Flores, Jose-Jose Carlos	02OakA 04LAN	06-28-73	New York, N.Y.		R	R	5'11	180	16	7	2	1	0	0	0	0	2	2	1	.143	.143
Floyd, Cliff-Cornelius Clifford	93-96MonN 97-01FlaN 02MonN 02BosA 03-06NYN	12-05-72	Chicago, Ill.		L	L	6'5	240	1423	4775	752	1331	317	22	213	781	537	952	147	.279	.488
Flynn, Doug-Robert Douglas	75-77CinN 77-81NYN 82TexA 82-85MonN 85DetA	04-18-51	Lexington, Ky.		R	R	5'11	170	1308	3853	288	918	115	39	7	284	151	320	20	.238	.294
Foley, Marv-Marvis Edwin	78-80,82ChiA 84TexA	08-29-53	Stanford, Ky.		L	R	6'	195	203	419	37	94	10	0	12	51	41	61	0	.224	.334
Foley, Tom-Thomas Michael	83-85CinN 85-86PhiN 86-92MonN 93-94PitN 95MonN	09-09-59	Columbus, Ga.		L	R	6'1	180	1108	2708	248	661	134	20	32	263	232	387	32	.244	.344
Foli, Tim-Timothy John (Crazy Horse)	70-71NYN 72-77MonN 77SFN 78-79NYN 79-81PitN 82-83CalA 84NYA 85PitN	12-08-50	Culver City, Cal.		R	R	6'	180	1696	6047	576	1515	241	20	25	501	265	399	81	.251	.309
Fontenot, Mike-Michael Eugene	05ChiN	06-09-80	Slidell, La.		L	R	5'8	165	7	2	4	0	0	0	0	0	2	0	0	.000	.000
Fonville, Chad-Chad Everette	95MonN 95-97LAN 97ChiA 99BosA	03-05-71	Jacksonville, N.C.		B	R	5'6	155	226	546	80	133	10	2	0	31	45	77	30	.244	.269
Foote, Barry-Barry Clifton	73-77MonN 77-78PhiN 79-81CinN 81-82NYA	02-16-52	Smithfield, N.C.		R	R	6'3	210	687	2127	191	489	103	10	57	230	136	287	10	.230	.368
Forbes, P.J.-Patrick Joseph	98BalA 01PhiN	09-22-67	Pittsburg, Kan.		R	R	5'10	160	12	17	1	3	0	0	0	3	0	2	0	.176	.176
Ford, Curt-Curtis Glenn	85-88StlN 89-90PhiN	10-11-60	Jackson, Miss.		L	R	5'10	150	406	742	88	182	37	8	7	89	66	126	36	.245	.345
Ford, Dan-Darnell Glenn (Disco Dan)	75-78MinA 79-81CalA 82-85BalA	05-19-52	Los Angeles, Cal.		R	R	6'	185	1153	4163	598	1123	214	38	121	566	303	722	61	.270	.427
Ford, Lew-Jon Lewis	03-06MinA	08-12-76	Beaumont, Texas		R	R	6'	190	439	1398	215	385	74	10	29	158	136	212	44	.275	.405
Fordyce, Brook-Brook Alexander	95NYN 96-98CinN 99-00ChiA 00BalA 04TBA	05-07-70	New London, Conn.		R	R	6'1	190	623	1807	172	467	103	4	41	188	119	295	8	.258	.388
Fosse, Ray-Raymond Earl	67-72CleA 73-75OakA 76-77CleA 77SeaA 78KJ 79MilA	04-04-47	Marion, Ill.		R	R	6'2	215	924	2957	299	758	117	13	61	324	203	363	15	.256	.367
Foster, George- George Arthur (The Destroyer)	69-71SFN 71-81CinN 82-86NYN 86ChiA	12-01-48	Tuscaloosa, Ala.		R	R	6'2	195	1977	7023	986	1925	307	47	348	1239	666	1419	51	.274	.480
Foster, Leo-Leonard Norris (Bananas)	71,73-74AtlN 76-77NYN	02-02-51	Covington, Ky.		R	R	5'11	162	144	262	35	52	8	2	1	26	22	44	7	.198	.275
Fox, Andy-Andrew Junipero	96-97NYA 98-00AriN 00-03FlaN 04MonN 04TexA	01-12-71	Sacramento, Cal.		L	R	6'4	205	776	1925	248	461	65	17	30	168	197	407	74	.239	.338
Fox, Eric-Eric Hollis	92-94OakA 95TexA	08-15-63	LeMoore, Cal.		B	L	5'10	180	116	258	40	51	8	2	5	19	21	48	5	.198	.302
Franco (Robles), Julio-Juilo Cesar Robles [Franco] (Junior)	82PhiN 82-88CleA 89-93TexA 94ChiA 95JL 96-97CleA 97MilA 98JL 99TBA 01-05AtlN 06NYN	08-23-58	Hato Mayor, Dom.Rep.		R	R	6'1	195	2472	8587	1277	2566	404	54	172	1178	903	1318	279	.299	.419
Franco, Matt-Matthew Neil	95ChiN 96-00NYN 02-03AtlN	08-19-69	Santa Monica, Cal.		L	R	6'2	210	661	977	110	261	43	6	22	117	124	158	2	.267	.391
Francona, Terry-Terry Jon	81-85MonN 86ChiN 87CinN 88CleA 89-90MilA M97-00PhiN M04-06BosA	04-22-59	Aberdeen, S.D.		L	L	6'1	182	708	1731	163	474	74	6	16	143	65	119	12	.274	.351
Francoeur, Jeff-Jeffrey Braden	05-06AtlN	01-08-84	Atlanta, Ga.		R	R	6'4	220	232	908	124	246	44	7	43	148	34	190	4	.271	.477
Frandsen, Kevin-Kevin Vincent	06SFN	05-24-82	San Jose, Cal.		R	R	6'	175	41	93	12	20	4	0	2	7	3	14	0	.215	.323
Frank, Mike-Stephen Michael	98CinN	01-14-74	Pomona, Cal.		L	L	6'2	195	28	89	14	20	6	0	0	7	7	12	0	.225	.292
Franklin, Micah-Micah Ishanti	97StlN	04-25-72	San Francisco, Cal.		B	R	6'0	205	17	34	6	11	0	0	2	2	3	10	0	.324	.500
Frazier, Lou-Arthur Louis	93-95MonN 95-96TexA 98AtlN	01-26-65	St. Louis, Mo.		B	R	6'2	175	309	548	82	138	16	3	1	46	59	95	58	.252	.297
Freed, Roger-Roger Vernon	70BalA 71-72PhiN 74CinN 76MonN 77-79StlN	06-02-46	Los Angeles, Cal.	01-09-96	R	R	6'	210	344	717	49	176	27	2	22	109	95	166	1	.245	.351
Freel, Ryan-Ryan Paul	01TorA 03-06CinN	03-08-76	Jacksonville, Fla.		R	R	5'10	185	430	1487	234	408	77	14	19	91	185	262	121	.274	.383
Freeman, Choo-Raphael Desepition	04-06ColN	10-20-79	Pine Bluff, Ark.		R	R	6'2	200	151	285	45	64	10	6	3	29	28	68	6	.225	.333
Freeman, LaVel-LaVel Maurice	89MilA	02-18-63	Oakland, Cal.		L	L	5'9	170	2	3	1	0	0	0	0	0	0	2	0	.000	.000
Freire, Alejandro-Alejandro	05BalA	08-23-74	Caracas, Venezuela		R	R	6'2	225	25	65	7	16	3	0	1	6	4	17	0	.246	.338
Frias, Hanley-Hanley [Acevedo]	97TexA 98-00AriN	12-05-73	Villa Altagracia, D.R.		B	R	6'0	165	173	311	53	72	9	4	3	25	47	45	6	.232	.318
Frias, Pepe-Jesus Maria [Andujar]	73-78MonN 79AtlN 80TexA 80-81LAN	07-14-48	San Pedro de Mac.,D.R.	Bats Right 73-75,80-81	B	R	5'9	165	723	1346	132	323	49	8	1	108	49	136	12	.240	.290
Fritz, Larry-Lawrence Joseph (Zeb)	75PhiN	02-14-49	East Chicago, Ind.		L	L	6'2	220	1	1	0	0	0	0	0	0	0	0	0	.000	.000
Frobel, Doug-Douglas Steven	82-85PitN 85MonN 87CleA	06-06-59	Ottawa, Canada		L	R	6'4	196	268	542	70	109	21	4	20	58	55	155	13	.201	.365
Fry, Jerry-Jerry Ray	78MonN	02-29-56	Salinas, Cal.		R	R	6'	185	4	9	0	0	0	0	0	0	1	0	0	.000	.000
Frye, Jeff-Jeffrey Dustin	92TexA 93KJ 94-95TexA 96-97BosA 98KJ 99-00BosA 00ColN 01TorA	08-31-66	Oakland, Cal.		R	R	5'9	180	667	2155	316	626	135	11	16	194	212	279	56	.290	.386
Fryman, Travis-David Travis	90-97DetA 98-02CleA	03-25-69	Lexington, Ky.		R	R	6'1	195	1698	6481	895	1776	345	40	223	1022	602	1369	72	.274	.443
Fuentes, Mike-Michael Jay	83-84MonN	07-11-58	Miami, Fla.		R	R	6'3	190	9	8	1	2	0	0	0	1	0	4	0	.250	.250
Fuller, Jim-James Hardy	73-74BalA 77HouN	11-28-50	Bethesda, Md.		R	R	6'4	220	107	315	24	61	17	0	11	41	19	130	1	.194	.352
Fuller, John-John Edward (Turkey)	74AtlN	01-29-50	Lynwood, Cal.		R	R	6'3	185	3	3	1	1	0	0	0	0	0	0	0	.333	.333
Fullmer, Brad-Bradley Ryan	97-99MonN 00-01TorA 02-03AnaA 04TexA	01-17-75	Los Angeles, Cal.		L	R	6'1	215	807	2789	395	778	203	16	114	442	216	373	32	.279	.486
Funderburk, Mark-Mark Clifford (Thunder)	81,85MinA	05-16-57	Charlotte, N.C.		R	R	6'5	230	31	85	9	25	8	0	2	15	7	13	0	.294	.482
Furcal, Rafael-Rafael Antoni	00-05AtlN 06LAN	10-24-77	Loma de Cabrera, D.R.		B	R	5'10	165	976	3912	667	1120	192	47	72	355	393	573	226	.286	.415
Furmaniak, J.J.-Jason Joseph	05PitN	07-31-79	Naperville, Ill.		R	R	6'3	190	13	26	3	5	1	1	0	1	4	4	0	.192	.308
Gaetti, Gary-Gary Joseph (G-Man)	81-91MinA 92-93CalA 93-95KCA 96-98StlN 98-99ChiN 00BosA	08-19-58	Centralia, Ill.		R	R	6'	200	2507	8951	1130	2280	443	39	360	1341	634	1602	96	.255	.434
Gagne, Greg-Gregory Carpenter	83-92MinA 93-95KCA 96-97LAN	11-12-61	Fall River, Mass.		R	R	5'11	185	1798	5673	712	1440	296	50	111	604	367	1121	108	.254	.382
Gainer, Jay-Jonathan Keith	93ColN	10-08-66	Panama City, Fla.		L	L	6'	190	23	44	4	7	0	0	3	6	4	12	1	.171	.390
Gainey, Ty-Tyrone Matthew	85-87HouN	12-25-60	Cheraw, S.C.		L	L	6'1	190	57	111	12	24	3	1	1	7	10	37	4	.216	.288
Galarraga (Padovani), Andres-Andres Jose [Galarraga] (The Big Cat)	85-91MonN 92StlN 93-97ColN 98AtlN 99IL 00AtlN 01TexA 01SFN 02MonN 03SFN 04AnaA	06-18-61	Caracas, Venezuela		R	R	6'3	235	2257	8096	1195	2333	444	32	399	1425	583	2003	128	.288	.499
Gall, John-John Christopher	05-06StlN	04-02-78	Stanford, Cal.		R	R	6'	195	30	49	6	13	2	0	1	11	1	13	0	.265	.449
Gallagher, Bob-Robert Collins	72BosA 73-74HouN 75NYN	07-07-48	Newton, Mass.		L	R	6'4	190	213	255	34	56	6	1	2	13	16	56	1	.220	.275
Gallagher, Dave-David Thomas	87CleA 88-90ChiA 90BalA 91CalA 92-93NYN 94AtlN 95PhiN 95CalA	09-20-60	Trenton, N.J.		R	R	6'	180	794	2081	273	564	100	10	17	190	187	251	20	.271	.353
Gallego, Mike-Michael Anthony	85-91OakA 92-94NYA 95OakA 96-97StlN	10-31-60	Whitier, Cal.		R	R	5'7	170	1111	2931	374	700	111	12	42	282	326	465	24	.239	.328
Gamble, Oscar-Oscar Charles	69ChiN 70-72PhiN 73-75CleA 76 NYA 77ChiA 78SDN 79TexA 79-84NYA 85ChiA	12-20-49	Ramer, Ala.		L	R	5'11	180	1584	4502	656	1195	188	31	200	666	610	546	47	.265	.454
Gant, Ron-Ronald Edwin	87-93AtlN 94BL 95CinN 96-98StlN 99-00PhiN 00AnaA 01ColN 01OakA 02SDN 03OakA	03-02-65	Victoria, Tex.		R	R	6'	190	1832	6449	1080	1651	302	50	321	1008	770	1411	243	.256	.468
Gantner, Jim-James Elmer	76-92MilA	01-05-53	Fond du Lac, Wis.		L	R	6'	180	1801	6189	726	1696	262	38	47	568	383	501	137	.274	.351
Garabito, Eddy-Eddy Jorge	05ColN	12-02-76	Manreza, Dom. Rep.		B	R	5'8	190	42	88	15	27	5	0	1	8	8	17	0	.307	.398
Garbey, Barbaro-Barbaro [Garbey]	84-85DetA 88TexA	12-04-56	Santiago de Cuba, Cuba		R	R	5'10	170	226	626	76	167	28	2	11	86	36	83	9	.267	.371
Garcia, Amaury-Amaury Paula Migiel (Paula)	99FlaN	05-20-75	Santo Domingo, D.R.		R	R	5'10	160	10	8	3	2	0	0	0	1	0	1	0	.250	.250
Garcia, Carlos-Carlos Jesus (Guerrero)	90-96PitN 97TorA 98AnaA 99SDN	10-15-67	Tachira, Venez.		R	R	6'1	190	610	2178	274	580	102	17	33	197	115	340	73	.266	.374
Garcia, Damaso-Damaso Domingo (Sanchez) (Damo)	78-79NYA 80-86TorA 87SDN 87KJ 88AtlN 89MonN	02-07-55	Moca, Dom. Rep.		R	R	6'	185	1032	3914	490	1108	183	27	36	323	130	322	203	.283	.371
Garcia, Danny-Daniel Joseph	03-04NYN	04-12-80	Riverside, Cal.		R	R	6'1	175	77	194	28	44	9	1	5	23	24	45	3	.227	.361
Garcia, Danny-Daniel Raphael	81KCA	04-29-54	Brooklyn, N.Y.		R	R	6'1	175	12	14	3	2	0	0	0	2	0	5	1	.143	.143
Garcia, Freddy-Freddy Adrian (Felix)	95,97-99PhiN 99AtlN	08-01-72	La Romana, Dom. Rep.		R	R	6'2	215	120	271	37	59	13	2	13	33	29	80	0	.218	.424
Garcia, Guillermo-Guillermo Antonio [Morel]	98CinN 99FlaN	04-04-72	Santiago, Dom. Rep.		R	R	6'3	215	16	40	3	8	1	0	2	4	2	15	0	.200	.400
Garcia, Jesse-Jesus Jesse Jr.	99-00BalA 01-04AtlN 05SDN	09-24-73	Corpus Christi, Tex.		R	R	5'10	170	171	273	41	59	9	1	1	23	6	48	7	.216	.304

USE NAME - GIVEN NAMES (NICKNAMES) / TEAM BY YEAR	BIRTH DATE	BIRTH PLACE	DEATH DATE	B	T	HGT	WGT	G	AB	R	H	2B	3B	HR	RBI	BB	SO	SB	BA	SA
Garcia, Karim-Gustavo Karim — 95-97LAN 98AriN 99-00DetA 00BalA 01CleA 02NYA 02-03CleA 03NYA 04NYN 04BalA	10-29-75	C. Obregon, Mexico		L	L	6'	205	488	1463	180	352	44	13	66	212	81	330	10	.241	.424
Garcia, Kiko-Alfonso Raphael — 76-80OakA 81-82HouN 83-85PhiN	10-14-53	Martinez, Cal.		R	R	5'10	175	619	1470	162	351	56	16	12	112	95	285	34	.239	.323
Garcia, Leo-Leonardo Antonio [Peralta] — 87-88CinN	11-06-62	Santiago, Dom. Rep.		L	L	5'8	165	54	58	10	10	1	0	1	2	8	13	3	.172	.241
Garcia, Luis-Luis Carlos — 02BalA	09-22-75	Hermosillo, Mexico		R	R	6'3	208	6	3	0	1	0	0	0	0	0	1	0	.333	.333
Garcia, Luis-Luis Rafael — 99DetA	05-20-75	San Francisco de Mac., D.R.		R	R	6'	175	8	9	0	1	1	0	0	0	0	0	0	.111	.222
Garcia, Pete-Pedro Modesto [Delfi] (Chicken) — 73-76MilA 76DetA 77TorA	04-17-50	Guayama, P.R.		R	R	5'11	175	558	1797	196	395	89	15	37	184	102	329	35	.220	.348
Garciaparra, Nomar-Anthony Nomar — 96-04BosA 04-05ChiN 06LAN	07-23-73	Whittier, Cal.		R	R	6'	185	1193	4832	847	1537	336	52	211	833	349	474	89	.318	.540
Gardenhire, Ron-Ronald Clyde — 81-85NYN M02-06MinA	10-24-57	Butzbach, Germany		R	R	6'	175	285	710	57	165	27	3	4	49	46	122	13	.232	.296
Gardner, Art-Arthur Junior — 75,77HouN 78SFN	09-21-52	Madden, Miss.		L	R	5'11	175	86	99	12	16	0	0	0	5	4	25	1	.162	.162
Gardner, Jeff-Jeffrey Scott — 91NYN 92-93SDN 94MonN	02-04-64	Newport Beach, Cal.		L	R	5'11	175	186	492	60	121	21	8	1	26	53	88	2	.246	.327
Garko, Ryan-Ryan F. — 05-06CleA	01-02-81	Pittsburgh, Pa.		R	R	6'2	225	51	186	28	54	12	0	7	45	14	38	0	.290	.468
Garner, Phil-Philip Mason — 73-76OakA 77-81PitN 81-87HouN 87LAN 88SFN M92-97MilA M98-99MilN M00-02DetA M04-06HouN	04-30-49	Jefferson City, Tenn.		R	R	5'10	180	1860	6136	780	1594	299	82	109	738	564	842	225	.260	.389
Garr, Ralph-Ralph Allen (Flip, Road Runner) — 68-75AtlN 76-79ChiA 79-80CalA	12-12-45	Monroe, La.		L	R	5'11	190	1317	5108	717	1562	212	64	75	408	246	445	172	.306	.416
Garrett, Adrian-Henry Adrian — 66AtlN 70ChiA 71-72OakA 73-75ChiN 75-76CalA	01-03-43	Brooksville, Fla.		L	R	6'3	185	163	276	30	51	8	0	11	37	31	87	4	.185	.333
Garrett, Wayne-Ronald Wayne (Red) — 69-76NYN 76-78MonN 78StLN	12-03-47	Brooksville, Fla.		L	R	6'	175	1092	3285	438	786	107	22	61	340	561	529	38	.239	.341
Garrison, Webster-Webster Leotis — 96OakA	08-24-65	Marrero, La.		R	R	5'11	170	5	9	0	1	0	0	0	0	1	0	0	.000	.000
Garvey, Steve-Steven Patrick (Mr. Clean) — 69-82LAN 83-87SDN	12-22-48	Tampa, Fla.		R	R	5'10	192	2232	8835	1143	2599	440	43	272	1308	479	1003	83	.294	.446
Gaston, Cito-Clarence Edward — 67AtlN 69-74SDN 76-78AtlN 78PitN M89-96TorA	03-17-44	San Antonio, Tex.		R	R	6'3	210	1026	3120	314	799	106	30	91	387	185	693	13	.256	.397
Gates, Brent-Brent Robert — 93-96OakA 97SeaA 99-99MinA	03-14-70	Grandville, Mich.		B	R	6'1	190	685	2329	268	616	119	11	25	279	225	349	18	.264	.357
Gates, Joe-Joesph Daniel — 78-79ChiA	10-03-54	Gary, Ind.		B	R	5'8	175	24	40	11	7	0	1	0	2	6	9	2	.175	.225
Gates, Mike-Michal Grant (Gator) — 81-82MonN	09-20-56	Culver City, Cal.		R	R	6'	165	37	123	17	29	2	4	0	9	9	20	0	.236	.317
Gathright, Joey-Joey Renard — 04-06TBA 06KCA	04-27-81	Hattiesburg, Miss.		L	R	5'10	170	229	638	99	160	19	6	1	55	54	128	48	.251	.304
Gaudet, Jim-James Jennings (Go) — 78-79KCA	06-03-55	New Orleans, La.		R	R	6'	183	6	14	0	1	0	0	0	0	0	3	0	.071	.071
Gedman, Rich-Richard Leo — 80-90BosA 90HouN 91-92StLN	09-26-59	Worcester, Mass.		L	R	6'	215	1033	3159	331	795	176	12	88	382	236	509	3	.252	.399
Gerber, Craig-Craig Stuart — 85CalA	01-08-59	Chicago, Ill.		R	R	6'	175	65	91	8	24	1	2	0	6	2	3	0	.264	.319
Geren, Bob-Robert Peter — 88-91NYA 93SDN	09-22-61	San Diego, Cal.		R	R	6'2	210	307	765	62	178	21	1	22	76	49	179	0	.233	.349
Gerhart, Ken-Harold Kenneth — 86-88BalA	05-19-61	Charleston, S.C.		R	R	6'	195	215	615	72	136	22	3	24	64	42	128	16	.221	.384
German, Esteban-Esteban [Guridi] — 02-04OakA 05TexA 06KCA	01-26-78	Haina, Dom.Rep.		R	R	5'9	165	156	382	60	117	20	6	3	43	48	75	10	.306	.414
Geronimo, Cesar-Cesar Francisco [Zorilla] (Chief) — 69-71HouN 72-80CinN 81-83KCA	03-11-48	Santa Cruz de El Seibo, D. R.		L	L	6'1	170	1522	3780	460	977	158	50	51	392	354	746	82	.258	.368
Gerut, Jody-Joseph Diego — 03-05CleA 05ChiN 05PitN 06KJ	09-18-77	Elmhurst, Ill.		L	L	6'	190	320	1131	153	298	75	8	34	140	109	149	18	.263	.434
Gettis, Byron-Byron Earl — 05DetA	03-13-80	Centreville, Ill.		R	R	6'	240	21	39	7	7	1	1	0	1	8	14	0	.179	.256
Giambi, Jason-Jason Gilbert — 95-01OakA 02-06NYA	01-08-71	West Covina, Cal.		L	R	6'2	235	1622	5620	1017	1639	335	8	350	1144	1089	1131	15	.292	.541
Giambi, Jeremy-Jeremy Dean — 98-99KCA 00-02OakA 02PhiN 03BosA	09-30-74	San Jose, Cal.		L	R	6'0	200	511	1417	219	372	75	3	52	209	251	356	1	.263	.430
Giannelli, Ray-Raymond John — 91TorA 95StLN	02-05-66	Brooklyn, N.Y.		L	R	6'	195	18	35	2	5	1	0	0	0	8	13	1	.143	.171
Giarratano, Tony-Anthony J. — 05DetA	11-29-82	Queens, N.Y.		B	R	6'	180	15	42	4	6	0	0	1	4	5	7	1	.143	.214
Gibbons, Jay-Jay Jonathan — 01-06BalA	03-02-77	Rochester, Mich.		L	L	6'	200	695	2517	320	662	148	7	115	377	200	362	2	.263	.464
Gibbons, John-John Michael — 84,86NYN M04-06TorA	06-08-62	Great Falls, Mont.		R	R	5'11	187	18	50	5	11	4	0	1	2	6	16	0	.220	.360
Gibralter, Steve-Stephan Benson — 95-96CinN	10-09-72	Dallas, Tex.		R	R	6'	185	6	5	1	1	0	0	0	0	0	2	0	.200	.200
Gibson, Derrick-Derrick Lamont — 98-99ColN	02-05-75	Winter Haven, Fla.		R	R	6'2	240	17	49	6	14	2	0	2	8	1	11	0	.286	.449
Gibson, Kirk-Kirk Harold — 79-87DetA 88-90LAN 91KCA 92PitN 93-95DetA	05-28-57	Pontiac, Mich.		L	L	6'3	220	1635	5798	985	1553	260	54	255	870	718	1285	284	.268	.463
Gil, Benji-Romar Benjamin — 93,95-97TexA 00-03AnaA	10-06-72	Tijuana, Mexico		R	R	6'2	185	604	1610	158	381	75	12	32	171	102	448	24	.237	.358
Gil, Geronimo-Geronimo — 01-05BalA	08-07-75	Estacion Laguna, Mex.		R	R	6'2	225	272	806	66	188	30	0	19	88	46	157	2	.233	.341
Gil, Jerry-Jerry Bienvenido [Manzanillo] — 04-06AriN	10-14-82	San Pedro de Mac., D.R.		R	R	6'3	183	29	86	3	15	2	1	0	8	0	33	2	.174	.221
Gilbert, Mark-Mark David — 85ChiA	08-22-56	Atlanta, Ga.		B	R	6'	175	7	22	3	6	1	0	0	3	4	5	0	.273	.318
Gilbert, Shawn-Albert Shawn — 97-98NYN 98StLN 00LAN	03-12-65	Camden, N.J.		R	R	5'9	170	51	47	9	7	1	0	2	4	3	17	2	.149	.298
Gilbreath, Rod-Rodney Joe — 72-78AtlN	09-24-52	Laurel, Miss.		R	R	6'1	180	500	1436	164	356	45	15	14	125	147	212	25	.248	.329
Bats Both part of 75																				
Giles, Brian-Brian Jeffrey — 81-83NYN 85MilA 86ChiA 90SeaA	04-27-60	Manhattan, Kan.		R	R	6'1	165	287	709	74	162	27	0	10	50	70	151	27	.228	.309
Giles, Brian-Brian Stephen — 95-98CinN 99-03PitN 03-06SDN	01-20-71	El Cajon, Cal.		L	L	5'11	200	1518	5260	950	1552	334	48	260	941	1006	691	102	.295	.525
Giles, Marcus-Marcus William — 01-06AtlN	05-18-78	San Diego, Cal.		R	R	5'8	180	676	2534	416	717	168	13	72	294	274	441	60	.283	.448
Gilkey, Bernard-Otis Bernard — 90-95StLN 96-98NYN 98-00AriN 00BosA 01AtlN	09-24-66	St. Louis, Mo.		R	R	6'	195	1239	4061	606	1115	244	24	118	546	466	708	115	.275	.434
Gimenez, Hector-Hector C. — 06HouN	09-28-82	San Felipe, Venezuela		B	R	5'10	180	2	0	0	0	0	0	0	0	0	1	0	.000	.000
Ginter, Keith-Keith Michael — 00-02HouN 02-04MilN 05OakA	05-05-76	Norwalk, Cal.		R	R	5'10	195	325	971	120	236	52	4	38	140	105	230	9	.243	.422
Giovanola, Ed-Edward Thomas — 95-97AtlN 98-99SDN	03-04-69	Los Gatos, Cal.		L	R	5'10	175	218	301	41	65	5	4	1	19	44	49	4	.216	.269
Gipson, Charles-Charles Wells Jr. — 98-02SeaA 03NYA 04TBA 05HouN	12-16-72	Orange, Cal.		R	R	6'0	188	373	321	78	76	15	7	0	30	30	71	16	.237	.327
Girardi, Joe-Joseph Elliott — 89-92ChiN 93-95ColN 96-99NYA 00-02ChiN 03StLN M06FlaN	10-14-64	Peoria, Ill.		R	R	5'11	195	1277	4127	454	1100	186	26	36	422	279	607	44	.267	.350
Gladden, Dan-Clinton Daniel — 83-86SFN 87-91MinA 92-93DetA	07-07-57	San Jose, Cal.		R	R	5'11	180	1197	4501	663	1215	203	40	74	446	337	625	222	.270	.382
Glanville, Doug-Douglas Metunwa — 96-97ChiN 98-02PhiN 03TexA 03ChiN 04PhiN	08-25-70	Hackensack, N.J.		R	R	6'2	170	1115	3964	553	1100	166	32	59	333	208	502	168	.277	.380
Glaus, Troy-Troy Edward — 98-05AnaA 06TorA	08-03-76	Tarzana, Cal.		R	R	6'5	235	1129	4040	706	1023	221	8	257	716	640	1063	56	.253	.503
Glavine, Mike-Michael Patrick — 03NYN	01-24-73	Concord, Mass.		L	L	6'3	210	6	7	0	1	0	0	0	0	0	2	0	.143	.143
Gload, Ross-Ross Peter — 00,02ChiN 04-06ChiA	04-05-76	Brooklyn, N.Y.		L	L	6'2	185	259	494	60	147	27	3	12	74	34	78	6	.298	.437
Godby, Danny-Danny Ray — 74StLN	11-04-46	Logan, W. Va.		R	R	6'	185	13	13	2	2	0	0	0	1	3	4	0	.154	.154
Godwin, Tyrell-Carlton Tyrell — 05WasN	07-10-79	Wilmington, N.C.		R	R	6'	200	3	3	0	0	0	0	0	0	0	1	0	.000	.000
Goff, Jerry-Jerry Leroy — 90,92MonN 93-94PitN 95-96HouN	04-12-64	San Rafael, Cal.		L	R	6'3	205	90	214	22	46	5	0	7	19	33	73	0	.215	.336
Goggin, Chuck-Charles Francis — 72-73PitN 73AtlN 74BosA	07-07-45	Pompano Beach, Fla.		B	R	5'11	165	72	99	19	29	5	0	0	7	10	21	0	.293	.343
Gomes, Jonny-Jonny Johnson — 03-06TBA	11-22-80	San Francisco, Cal.		R	R	6'1	205	231	762	115	184	35	7	41	114	101	241	10	.241	.467
Gomez, Alexis-Alexis DeJesus — 02,04KCA 05-06DetA	08-08-78	Dajabon, Dom. Rep.		L	L	6'2	180	89	158	20	41	6	2	1	10	13	33	4	.259	.342
Gomez, Chris-Christopher Cory — 93-96DetA 96-01SDN 01-02TBA 03MinA 04TorA 05-06BalA	06-16-71	Los Angeles, Cal.		R	R	6'1	195	1333	4199	470	1090	214	17	58	446	385	694	34	.260	.360
Gomez, Leo-Leonardo [Velez] — 90-95BalA 96ChiN	03-02-66	Canovanas, P.R.		R	R	6'	200	611	1916	241	466	92	2	79	259	255	399	4	.243	.417
Gomez, Luis-Jose Luis [Sanchez] — 74-77MinA 78-79TorA 80-81AtlN	08-19-51	Guadalajara, Mexico		R	R	5'9	150	609	1251	108	363	26	5	0	90	86	129	6	.210	.239
Gomez, Randy-Randall Mark — 84SFN	02-04-57	San Mateo, Cal.		R	R	5'9	180	14	30	0	5	1	0	0	0	0	3	0	.167	.200
Gonzales, Larry-Lawrence Christopher — 93CalA	03-28-67	Covina, Cal.		R	R	6'	200	1	0	0	0	0	0	0	0	0	0	0	.500	.500
Gonzales, Rene-Rene Adrian — 84,86MonN 87-90BalA 91TorA 92-93CalA 94CalN 95CalA 96TexN 97ColN	09-03-60	Austin, Tex.		R	R	6'3	210	705	1539	185	368	59	4	19	136	161	230	23	.239	.320
Gonzalez, Adrian-Adrian Sabin — 04-05TexA 06SDN	05-08-82	San Diego, Cal.		L	L	6'2	220	215	762	107	217	48	2	31	106	64	156	0	.285	.475
Gonzalez, Alex-Alexander Luis — 98-05FlaN 06BosA	02-15-77	Cagua, Venezuela		R	R	6'0	195	1007	3609	411	887	207	25	90	425	192	739	24	.246	.392
Gonzalez, Alex-Alexander Scott — 94-01TorA 02-04ChiN 04MonN 04SDN 05TBA 06FlaN	04-08-73	Miami, Fla.		R	R	6'	200	1396	4977	623	1209	274	27	137	536	392	1165	97	.243	.391
Gonzalez, Dan-Daniel David (Gonzo) — 79-80DetA	09-30-53	Whittier, Cal.		L	R	6'1	190	5	5	1	1	0	0	0	1	0	0	0	.200	.240
Gonzalez, Denny-Denio Mariano [Manzueta] — 84-85,87-88PitN 89CalN	07-22-63	Sabana Grande, D.R.		R	R	5'11	185	98	262	29	54	9	1	4	18	27	64	3	.206	.294
Gonzalez, Fernando-Jose Fernando [Quinones] — 72-73PitN 74KCA 74NYA 77-78PitN 78-79SDN	06-19-50	Arecibo, P.R.		R	R	5'10	170	404	1038	85	244	40	7	17	104	58	114	8	.235	.332
Gonzalez, Jose (See Jose Uribe)																				
Gonzalez, Jose-Jose Rafael [Gutierrez] — 85-91LAN 91PitN 91CleA 92CalA	11-23-64	Puerto Plata, D.R.		R	R	6'3	195	461	676	95	144	30	7	9	42	60	186	33	.213	.318
Gonzalez, Juan-Juan Alberto [Vazquez] (Igor) — 89-99TexA 00DetA 01CleA 02-03TexA 04KCA 05CleA	10-16-69	Vega Baja, P.R.		R	R	6'3	220	1689	6556	1061	1936	388	25	434	1404	457	1273	26	.295	.561
Gonzalez, Julio-Julio Cesar [Hernandez] (July) — 77-80HouN 81-82StLN 83DetA	12-25-52	Caguas, P.R.		R	R	5'11	162	370	969	90	228	32	8	4	66	36	132	13	.235	.297
Gonzalez, Luis-Luis Alberto — 04-06ColN	06-26-79	Maracay, Venezuela		R	R	5'11	170	291	875	100	248	51	3	23	98	39	157	5	.283	.427
Gonzalez, Luis-Luis Emilio — 90-95HouN 95-96ChiN 97HouN 98DetA 99-06AriN	09-03-67	Tampa, Fla.		L	R	6'2	195	2316	8352	1312	2373	547	65	331	1324	1058	1119	121	.284	.484
Gonzalez, Orlando-Orlando Eugene — 76CleA 78PhiN 80OakA	11-15-51	Havana, Cuba		L	L	6'2	180	79	164	16	39	7	2	0	15	16	16	1	.238	.250
Gonzalez, Raul-Victor Raul — 00-02ChiN 02-03NYN 04CleA	12-27-73	Santurce, P.R.		R	R	5'9	190	168	348	41	81	15	2	5	33	34	65	7	.233	.330
Gonzalez, Wiki-Wiklenman Vicente — 99-03SDN 05SeaA 06WasN	05-17-74	Aragua, Venezuela		R	R	5'11	200	295	836	75	200	41	3	17	103	78	112	3	.239	.356
Goodson, Ed-James Edward — 70-75SFN 75AtlN 76-77LAN	01-25-48	Pulaski, Va.		L	R	6'1	185	515	1266	108	329	51	2	30	170	63	135	1	.260	.374
Goodwin, Curtis-Curtis LaMar — 95BalA 96-97CinN 98ColN 99ChiN 99TorA	09-30-72	Oakland, Cal.		L	L	5'11	180	431	1014	129	251	38	4	9	56	87	221	66	.248	.302
Goodwin, Tom-Thomas Jones — 91-93LAN 94-97KCA 97-99TexA 00ColN 00-01LAN 02SFN 03-04ChiN	07-27-68	Fresno, Cal.		L	R	6'1	180	1288	3846	636	1029	125	39	24	284	365	660	369	.268	.339
Goodwin, Danny-Danny Kay — 75,77-78CalA 79-81MinA 82OakA	09-02-53	St. Louis, Mo.		L	R	6'1	195	252	636	72	150	32	8	13	81	61	137	0	.236	.373
Gordon, Keith-Keith Bradley — 95CinN	01-22-69	Bethesda, Md.		R	R	6'	200	4	6	1	1	0	0	0	0	0	0	0	.167	.167
Gordon, Mike-Michael William — 77-78ChiN	09-11-53	Leominster, Mass.		B	R	6'3	212	12	28	0	2	0	0	0	2	5	10	0	.071	.071
Gorinski, Bob-Robert John (Tiger) — 77MinA	01-07-52	Latrobe, Pa.		R	R	6'2	218	54	118	14	23	4	1	2	22	5	29	1	.195	.322
Gotay, Ruben-Ruben Bruce — 04-05KCA	12-25-82	Rio Piedras, P.R.		B	R	5'11	160	131	434	49	105	24	1	6	45	31	87	2	.242	.355

USE NAME - GIVEN NAMES (NICKNAMES)	TEAM BY YEAR	BIRTH DATE	BIRTH PLACE	DEATH DATE	B	T	HGT	WGT	G	AB	R	H	2B	3B	HR	RBI	BB	SO	SB	BA	SA
Grabowski, Jason-Jason William	02-03OakA 04-05LAN	05-24-76	New Haven, Conn.		L	R	6'3	200	190	301	35	59	8	1	7	33	33	85	1	.196	.339
Grace, Mark-Mark Eugene	88-00ChiN 01-03AriN	06-28-64	Winston-Salem, N.C.		L	L	6'2	195	2245	8065	1179	2445	511	45	173	1146	1075	642	70	.303	.442
Grace, Mike-Michael Lee	78CinN	06-14-56	Pontiac, Mich.		R	R	6'	175	5	3	0	0	0	0	0	0	0	2	0	.000	.000
Graffanino, Tony-Anthony Joseph	96-98AtlN 99-00TBA 00-03ChiA 04-05KCA 05BosA 06KCA 06MilN	06-07-72	Amityville, N.Y.		R	R	6'1	195	888	2556	407	688	136	21	49	272	250	437	53	.269	.396
Graham, Dan-Daniel Jay	79MinA 80-81BalA	07-19-54	Ray, Ariz.		L	R	6'1	210	143	412	39	99	10	1	17	65	27	72	0	.240	.393
Graham, Lee-Lee Williard	83BosA	09-22-59	Summerfield, Fla.		L	L	5'10	170	6	2	0	0	0	0	0	1	0	0	0	.000	.000
Granderson, Curtis-Curtis	04-06DetA	03-16-81	Blue Island, Ill.		L	R	6'1	185	215	783	110	205	38	13	27	88	79	225	9	.262	.447
Grant, Tom-Thomas Raymond	83ChiN	05-28-57	Worcester, Mass.		R	R	6'2	190	16	20	2	3	1	0	0	2	3	4	0	.150	.200
Gray, Gary-Gary George	77-79TexA 80CleA 81-82SeaA	09-21-52	New Orleans, La.		R	R	6'	200	211	625	65	150	23	3	24	71	34	137	5	.240	.402
Gray, Lorenzo-Lorenzo (Greyhound)	82-83ChiA	03-04-58	Mound Bayou, Miss.		R	R	6'2	190	58	106	22	22	4	0	1	4	10	20	2	.208	.274
Grebeck, Craig-Craig Allen	90-95ChiA 96FlaN 97AnaA 98-00TorA 01BosA	12-29-64	Johnstown, Pa.		R	R	5'8	160	752	1988	239	518	116	8	19	187	228	274	4	.261	.356
Green, Andy-Andrew Mulligan	04-06AriN	07-07-77	Lexington, Ky.		R	R	5'9	180	136	226	33	45	7	1	2	12	25	40	2	.199	.265
Green, David-David Alejandro [Casaya]	81-84StLN 85SFN 86JL 87StLN	12-04-60	Managua, Nicaragua		R	R	6'3	185	489	1398	168	374	48	18	31	180	84	278	68	.268	.394
Green, Gary-Gary Allan	86,89SDN 90-91TexA 92CinN	01-14-62	Pittsburgh, Pa.		R	R	6'3	175	106	180	19	40	9	0	0	11	9	38	1	.222	.272
Green, Nick-Nicholas Anthony	04AtlN 05-06TBA 06NYA	09-10-78	Pensacola, Fla.		R	R	6'	178	269	696	105	169	35	5	10	59	56	189	5	.243	.351
Green, Scarborough-Bertrum Scarborough	97StLN 99-00TexA	06-09-74	Creve Coeur, Mo.		B	R	5'10	175	117	168	30	36	1	1	0	10	13	33	10	.214	.232
	Bats Right 97, 99																				
Green, Shawn-Shawn David	93-99TorA 00-04LAN 05-06AriN 06NYN	11-10-72	Des Plaines, Ill.		L	L	6'4	200	1821	6636	1067	1873	415	34	318	1024	707	1253	151	.282	.499
Greenberg, Adam-Adam Daniel	05ChiN	02-21-81	New Haven, Conn.		L	L	5'9	180	1	0	0	0	0	0	0	0	0	0	0	—	—
Greene, Al-Altar Alphonse	79DetA	11-09-54	Detroit, Mich.		L	R	5'11	190	29	59	9	8	1	0	3	6	10	15	0	.136	.305
Greene, Charlie-Charles Patrick	96NYN 97-98BalA 99MilN 00TorA	01-23-71	Miami, Fla.		R	R	6'1	190	55	75	5	13	2	0	2	5	25	0	.173	.200
Greene, Khalil-Khalil Thabit	03-06SDN	10-21-79	Butler, Pa.		R	R	5'11	210	401	1397	182	356	91	6	47	196	121	293	14	.255	.434
Greene,Todd-Todd Anthony	96CalA 97-99AnaA 00TorA 01NYA 02-03TexA 04-05ColN 06SFN	05-08-71	Augusta, Ga.		R	R	5'9	205	536	1573	181	397	82	3	71	217	67	332	5	.252	.444
Greene, Willie-Willie Louis	92-98CinN 98BalA 99TorA 00ChiN	09-23-71	Milledgeville, Ga.		L	R	5'11	190	655	1902	254	446	76	12	86	307	260	477	17	.234	.423
Greenwell, Mike-Michael Lewis	85-96BosA	07-18-63	Louisville, Ky.		L	R	6'	205	1269	4623	657	1400	275	38	130	726	460	364	80	.303	.463
Greer, Brian-Brian Keith	77,79 SDN	05-14-59	Lynwood, Cal.		R	R	6'2	205	5	4	0	0	0	0	0	0	0	2	0	.000	.000
Greer, Rusty-Thurman Clyde III	94-02TexA 03XJ 04SJ	01-21-69	Fort Rucker, Ala.		L	L	6'	190	1027	3829	643	1166	258	25	119	614	519	555	31	.305	.478
Gregg, Tommy-William Thomas	87-88PitN 88-92AtlN 93CinN 95FlaN 97AtlN	07-29-63	Boone, N.C.		L	L	6'1	190	446	880	86	214	41	2	20	88	71	158	14	.243	.363
Gregorio, Tom-Thomas Andrew	03AnaA	05-05-77	Brooklyn, N.Y.		R	R	6'2	215	12	19	1	3	0	0	0	2	1	8	0	.158	.158
Grich, Bobby-Robert Anthony	70-76BalA 77-86Cal A	01-15-49	Muskegon, Mich.		R	R	6'2	185	2008	6890	1033	1833	320	47	224	864	1087	1278	104	.266	.424
Grieve, Ben-Benjamin	97-00OakA 01-03TBA 04-05ChiN	05-04-76	Arlington, Tex.		L	R	6'4	230	976	3215	471	864	192	5	118	492	466	784	24	.269	.442
Grieve, Tommy-Thomas Alan	70WasA 72-77TexA 78NYN 79StLN	03-04-48	Pittsfield, Mass.		R	R	6'2	195	485	1756	278	492	108	3	76	303	234	386	9	.280	.475
Griffey, Ken-George Kenneth Sr.	73-81CinN 82-86NYA 86-88AtlN 88-90CinN 90-91SeaA	04-10-50	Donora, Pa.		L	L	6'	195	2097	7229	1129	2143	364	77	152	859	719	898	200	.296	.431
Griffey, Ken-George Kenneth Jr. (Junior)	89-99SeaA 00-06CinN	11-21-69	Donora, Pa.		L	L	6'3	205	2234	8298	1467	2412	449	36	563	1608	1077	1494	178	.291	.557
Griffin (Baptist), Alfredo-Alfredo Claudino [Griffin]	76-78CleA 79-84TorA 85-87OakA 88-91LAN 92-93TorA	10-06-57	Santo Domingo, D.R		B	R	5'11	165	1962	6780	759	1688	245	78	24	527	338	664	192	.249	.319
Griffin, Doug-Douglas Lee	70CalA 71-77BosA	06-04-47	South Gate, Cal.		R	R	6'1	160	632	2136	209	524	70	12	7	165	158	204	33	.245	.299
Griffin, John-Ford-John-Ford David	05TorA	11-19-79	Sarasota, Fla.		L	L	6'2	215	7	13	3	4	2	0	0	6	0	4	0	.308	.692
Grissom, Marquis-Marquis Deon	89-94MonN 95-96AtlN 97CleA 98-00MilN 01-02LAN 03-05SFN	04-17-67	Atlanta, Ga.		R	R	5'11	192	2165	8275	1187	2251	386	56	227	967	553	1240	429	.272	.415
Gross, Gabe-Gabriel Jordan	04-05TorA 06MilN	10-21-79	Baltimore, Md.		L	R	6'3	209	201	429	71	107	23	1	13	61	65	112	4	.249	.399
Gross, Greg-Gregory Eugene	73-76 HouN 77-78 ChiN 79-88PhiN 89HouN	08-01-52	York, Pa.		L	L	5'11	175	1809	3745	449	1073	130	46	7	308	523	250	39	.287	.351
Gross, Wayne-Wayne Dale	76-83OakA 84-85BalA 86OakA	01-14-52	Riverside, Cal.		L	R	6'2	200	1106	3125	373	727	126	9	121	396	482	496	24	.233	.395
Grotewald, Jeff-Jeffrey Scott	92PhiN 95KCA	12-08-65	Madera, Cal.		L	R	6'	215	87	101	11	23	4	0	1	18	18	23	0	.228	.376
Grubb, Johnny-John Maywood	72-76SDN 77-78CleA 78-82TexA 83-87DetA	08-04-48	Richmond, Va.		L	R	6'3	185	1424	4154	553	1153	207	29	99	475	566	558	27	.278	.413
Gruber, Kelly-Kelly Wayne	84-92TorA 93CalA	02-26-62	Houston, Tex.		R	R	6'1	185	939	3159	431	818	148	24	117	443	197	504	80	.259	.432
Grudzielanek, Mark-Mark James	95-98MonN 98-02LAN 03-04ChiN 05StLN 06KCA	06-30-70	Milwaukee, Wis.		R	R	6'1	185	1570	6158	830	1774	335	33	81	554	314	843	128	.288	.393
Gubanich, Creighton-Creighton Wade	99BosA	03-27-72	Belleville, N.J.		R	R	6'3	200	18	47	4	13	2	1	1	11	3	13	0	.277	.426
Guerrero, Juan-Juan Antonio [de la Cruz]	92HouN	02-01-67	San Pedro de Mac., D.R.		R	R	5'11	160	79	125	8	25	4	1	1	14	10	32	1	.200	.288
Guerrero, Mike-Mario Miguel [Abud] (Mickey)	73-74BosA 75StLN 76-77CalA 78-80OakA	09-28-49	Santo Domingo, D.R.		R	R	5'9	160	697	2251	166	578	79	12	7	170	84	152	8	.257	.312
Guerrero, Pedro-Pedro (Pete, Tito)	78-88LAN 88-92StLN	06-29-56	San Pedro de Mac., D.R.		R	R	6'	200	1536	5392	730	1618	267	29	215	898	609	862	97	.300	.480
Guerrero, Vladimir-Vladimir Alvino	96-03MonN 04AnaA 05-06LAA	02-09-76	Nizao, Dom. Rep.		R	R	6'2	215	1457	5502	952	1786	328	39	338	1052	544	674	166	.325	.583
Guerrero, Wilton-Wilton Alvaro	96-98LAN 98-00MonN 01-02CinN 02MonN 04KCA	10-24-74	Don Gregorio, Dom. Rep.		B	R	5'11	175	678	1678	197	473	53	30	11	127	64	249	42	.282	.369
	Bats Right 96																				
Guevara, Giomar-Giomar Antonio [Diaz]	97-99SeaA	10-23-72	Guatire Miranda, Venez.		B	R	5'9	158	26	29	6	6	4	0	0	2	4	8	1	.207	.345
Guiel, Aaron-Aaron Colin	02-06KCA 06NYA	10-05-72	Vancouver, Canada		L	R	5'10	200	307	970	151	239	58	0	35	128	83	218	8	.246	.414
Guillen, Carlos-Carlos Alfonso	98-03SeaA 04-06DetA	09-30-75	Maracay, Venezuela		B	R	6'1	195	864	3064	509	886	173	35	73	416	330	531	49	.289	.440
Guillen, Jose-Jose Manuel	97-99PitN 99-01TBA 02AriN 02-03CinN 03OakA 04AnaA 05-06WasN	05-17-76	San Cristobal, D.R.		R	R	5'11	195	1115	3892	513	1058	205	20	143	574	203	716	22	.272	.445
Guillen, Ozzie-Oswaldo Jose [Barrios]	85-97ChiA 98BalA 98-99AtlN 00TBA M04-06ChiA	01-20-64	Ocumare del Tuy, Venez.		L	R	5'10	160	1993	6686	773	1764	275	69	28	619	239	511	169	.264	.338
Gulan, Mike-Michael Watts	97StLN 01FlaN	12-18-70	Steubenville, Ohio		R	R	6'1	192	11	15	3	0	0	0	0	1	3	7	0	.000	.000
Gulden, Brad-Bradley Lee	78LAN 79-80NYA 81SeaA 82MonN 84CinN 86SFN	06-10-56	New Ulm, Minn.		L	R	5'10	180	182	435	45	87	14	2	5	43	45	61	2	.200	.276
Gulliver, Glenn-Glenn James (Gully)	82-83BalA	10-15-54	Detroit, Mich.		L	R	5'11	175	73	192	29	39	10	0	1	7	46	23	0	.203	.271
Gutierrez, Franklin-Franklin Rafael	05-06CleA	02-21-83	Caracas, Venezuela		R	R	6'2	180	50	137	23	37	9	0	1	8	4	28	0	.270	.358
Gutierrez, Jackie-Joaquin Fernando [Hernandez]	83-85BosA 86-87BalA 88PhiN	06-27-60	Cartagena, Colombia		R	R	5'11	180	356	957	106	227	24	5	4	63	33	123	25	.237	.385
Gutierrez, Ricky-Ricardo	93-94SDN 95-99HouN 00-01ChiN 02-03CleA 04NYN 04BosA	05-23-70	Miami, Fla.		R	R	6'1	190	1119	3632	471	967	141	25	38	357	364	586	50	.266	.350
Guzman, Cristian-Cristian Antonio	99-04MinA 05WasN 06SJ	03-21-78	Santo Domingo, D.R.		B	R	6'	195	983	3733	497	971	161	67	43	320	191	567	109	.260	.374
Guzman, Edwards-Edwards G.	99,01SFN 03MonN	09-11-76	Bayamon, P.R.		L	R	5'11	170	127	276	23	63	11	0	4	21	10	37	0	.228	.312
Guzman, Freddy-Freddy Antonio	04SDN 05EJ J06TexA	01-20-81	Santo Domingo, D.R.		B	R	5'10	165	29	83	9	18	3	0	0	5	4	14	5	.217	.253
Guzman, Joel-Irvin Joel [Vigo]	06LAN	11-24-84	Quisqueya, Dom. Rep.		R	R	6'6	250	8	19	2	4	0	0	0	3	0	9	0	.211	.211
Gwosdz, Doug-Douglas Wayne	81-84SDN	06-20-60	Houston, Tex.		R	R	5'11	180	69	104	9	15	3	0	1	8	14	37	0	.144	.202
Gwynn, Chris-Christopher Karlton	87-91LAN 92-93KCA 94-95LAN 96SDN	10-13-64	Los Angeles, Cal.		L	L	6'	210	599	1007	119	263	36	11	17	118	71	171	2	.261	.369
Gwynn, Tony-Anthony Keith	82-01SDN	05-09-60	Los Angeles, Cal.		L	L	5'11	205	2440	9288	1383	3141	543	85	135	1138	790	434	319	.338	.459
Gwynn, Tony-Anthony Keith	06MilN	10-04-82	Long Beach, Cal.		L	R	6'	185	32	77	5	20	2	1	0	4	2	15	3	.260	.312
Haad, Yamid-Yamid Salcedo	99PitN 05SFN	09-02-77	Cartagena, Colombia		R	R	6'2	204	18	29	0	2	1	0	0	1	3	7	0	.069	.103
Hafner, Travis-Travis Lee (Pronk)	02TexA 03-06CleA	06-03-77	Jamestown, N.D.		L	R	6'3	240	520	1775	331	527	137	8	118	380	277	441	5	.297	.583
Hairston, Jerry-Jerry Wayne (Popeye)	73-77ChiA 77PitN 81-89ChiA	02-16-52	Birmingham, Ala.		B	R	5'10	185	859	1699	216	438	91	6	30	205	282	240	4	.258	.371
Hairston, Jerry-Jerry Wayne Jr.	98-04BalA 05-06ChiN 06TexA	05-29-76	Des Moines, Iowa		R	R	5'10	180	745	2375	317	611	129	15	30	200	206	309	107	.257	.362
Hairston, Scott-Scott Alexander	04-06AriN	05-25-80	Fort Worth, Tex.		R	R	6'	188	125	374	41	92	18	6	13	31	22	99	3	.246	.430
Hajek, Dave-David Vincent	95-96HouN	10-14-67	Roseville, Cal.		R	R	5'11	165	13	12	3	3	1	0	0	1	1	2	0	.250	.333
Hale, Chip-Walter William	89-90,93-96MinA 97LAN	12-02-64	San Jose, Cal.		L	R	5'11	190	333	575	62	159	27	1	7	78	58	68	2	.277	.363
Hale, John-John Steven	74-77LAN 78-79SeaA	08-05-53	Fresno, Cal.		L	R	6'2	190	359	681	66	137	25	2	14	72	103	183	10	.201	.305
Hall, Albert-Albert	81-88AtlN 89PitN	03-07-59	Birmingham, Ala.		B	R	5'11	155	375	805	125	202	37	8	5	53	89	115	67	.251	.335
Hall, Bill-William	02-06MilN	12-28-79	Nettleton, Miss.		R	R	6'	175	491	1606	239	428	108	16	67	225	132	425	39	.267	.479
Hall, Joe-Joseph Geroy	94ChiA 95,97DetA	03-06-66	Paducah, Ky.		R	R	6'	180	26	47	9	15	4	0	1	8	4	9	0	.319	.468
Hall, Mel-Melvin	81-84ChiN 84-88CleA 89-92NYA 93-95JL 96SFN	09-16-60	Lyons, N.Y.		L	L	6'	200	1276	4237	568	1171	229	25	134	620	267	575	31	.276	.437
Hall, Toby-Toby Jason	00-06TBA 06LAN	10-21-75	Tacoma, Wash.		R	R	6'3	230	607	2107	196	559	116	1	44	259	95	185	2	.265	.384
Halter, Shane-Shane David	97-98KCA 99NYN 00-03DetA 04AnaA	11-08-69	La Plata, Md.		R	R	5'10	185	690	1899	201	468	93	18	45	197	146	414	17	.246	.385
Hamelin, Bob-Robert James (Hammer)	93-96KCA 97DetA 98MilN	11-29-67	Elizabeth, N.J.		L	L	6'	230	497	1272	179	313	70	3	67	209	206	293	11	.246	.464
Hamilton, Darryl-Darryl Quinn	88,90-95MilA 96TexA 97-98SFN 98-99ColN 99-01NYN	12-03-64	Baton Rouge, La.		L	R	6'1	185	1328	4577	707	1333	204	37	51	454	493	494	163	.291	.385
Hamilton, Jeff-Jeffrey Robert	86-91LAN	03-19-64	Flint, Mich.		R	R	6'3	215	416	1205	111	282	61	31	24	124	43	211	0	.234	.349
Hammock, Robby-Robert Wade	03-04,06AriN	05-13-77	Macon, Ga.		R	R	5'11	185	128	392	53	103	27	4	12	46	30	83	6	.263	.444
Hammond, Steve-Steven Benjamin	82KCA	05-09-57	Atlanta, Ga.		L	L	6'2	185	46	126	14	29	5	1	1	11	4	18	0	.230	.310
Hammonds, Jeffrey-Jeffrey Brian	93-98BalA 98-99CinN 00ColN 01-03MilN 03-04SFN 05WasN	03-05-71	Plainfield, N.J.		R	R	6'	200	957	3032	475	824	172	17	110	423	292	596	67	.272	.449
Hampton, Ike-Isaac Bernard	74NYN 75-79CalA	08-22-51	Camden, S.C.		R	R	6'	185	113	135	15	32	4	0	2	18	11	38	1	.207	.341
	Bats Right 78																				
Hancock, Garry-Ronald Garry	78,80-82BosA 83-84OakA	01-23-54	Tampa, Fla.		L	L	6'	190	273	570	57	141	21	3	12	66	42	42	3	.247	.358
Haney, Todd-Todd Michael	92MonN 94-96ChiN 98NYN	07-30-65	Galveston, Tex.		R	R	5'9	165	101	205	28	50	10	1	2	12	18	29	0	.244	.337
Hannahan, Jack-John Joseph	06DetA	03-04-80	St. Paul, Minn.		L	R	6'2	205	3	7	1	0	0	0	0	0	0	1	0	.000	.000
Hansen, Bob-Robert Joseph	74,76MilA	05-26-48	Boston, Mass.		L	L	6'	195	82	149	12	36	13	0	2	13	9	24	2	.242	.329

USE NAME - GIVEN NAMES (NICKNAMES)	TEAM BY YEAR	BIRTH DATE	BIRTH PLACE	DEATH DATE	B	T	HGT	WGT	G	AB	R	H	2B	3B	HR	RBI	BB	SO	SB	BA	SA
Hansen, Dave-David Andrew	90-96LAN 97ChiN 98JL 99-02LAN 93SDN 04SeaA 05SDN 05SeaA	11-24-68	Long Beach, Cal.		L	R	6'	195	1230	1793	187	466	79	6	35	222	283	332	5	.260	.369
Hansen, Jed-Jed Ramon	97-99KCA	08-19-72	Tacoma, Wash.		R	R	6'1	195	87	176	27	45	7	1	4	19	23	64	3	.256	.375
Hardtke, Jason-Jason Robert	96-97NYN 98ChiN	09-15-71	Milwaukee, Wis.		B	R	5'10	175	67	134	14	31	7	0	2	16	8	24	1	.231	.328
Hardy, J.J.-James Jerry	05-06MilN	08-19-82	Tucson, Ariz.		R	R	6'2	180	159	500	59	123	27	1	14	64	54	71	1	.246	.388
Hare, Shawn-Shawn Robert	91-92DetA 94NYN 95TexA	03-26-67	St. Louis, Mo.		L	L	6'2	190	64	109	9	19	4	1	0	9	12	22	0	.174	.229
Hargis, Gary-Gary Lynn	79DetN	11-02-56	Minneapolis, Minn		R	R	5'11	165	1	0	0	0	0	0	0	0	0	0	0	—	—
Hargrove, Mike-Dudley Michael (The Human Rain Delay)	74-78TexA 79SDN 79-85,M91-99CleA M00-03BalA M05-06SeaA	10-26-49	Perryton, Tex.		L	L	6'	195	1666	5564	783	1614	266	28	80	686	965	550	24	.290	.391
Harlow, Larry-Larry Duane (Hawk)	75,77-79BalA 79-81CalA	11-13-51	Colorado Springs,Colo.		L	L	6'2	185	449	1094	159	271	48	8	12	72	156	205	26	.248	.339
Harper, Brandon-Brandon Scott	06WasN	04-29-76	Odessa, Tex.		R	R	6'4	200	18	41	6	12	3	0	2	6	4	4	0	.293	.512
Harper, Brian-Brian David	79,81CalA 82-84PitN 85StLN 86DetA 87OakA 88-93MinA 94MilA 95OakA	10-16-59	Los Angeles, Cal.		R	R	6'2	200	1001	3151	339	931	186	7	63	428	133	188	8	.295	.419
Harper, Terry-Terry Joe	80-86AtlN 87DetA 87PitN	08-19-55	Douglasville, Ga.		R	R	6'2	200	540	1467	147	371	55	5	36	180	144	248	37	.253	.391
Harrah, Toby-Colbert Dale	69,71WasA 72-78TexA 79-83CleA 84NYA 85-86,M92TexA	10-26-48	Sissonville, W. Va.		R	R	6'	185	2155	7402	1115	1954	307	40	195	918	1153	868	238	.264	.395
Harris, Brendan-Brendan Michael	04ChiN 04MonN 05-06WasN 06CinN	08-26-80	Queensbury, N.Y.		R	R	6'1	200	52	110	10	23	6	0	3	9	7	19	0	.209	.345
Harris, Donald-Donald	91-93TexA	11-12-67	Waco, Tex.		R	R	6'1	185	82	117	17	24	3	0	2	11	6	36	2	.205	.282
Harris, John-John Thomas	79-81CalA	09-13-54	Portland, Ore.		L	L	6'3	215	56	120	13	31	8	0	5	16	10	15	0	.258	.450
Harris, Lenny-Leonard Anthony	88CinN 88-93LAN 94-98CinN 98NYN 99ColN 99-00AriN 02MilN 03ChiN 03-05FlaN	10-28-64	Miami, Fla.		L	R	5'10	210	1903	3924	460	1055	161	21	37	369	279	337	131	.269	.349
Harris, Vic-Victor Lanier	72-73TexA 74-75ChiN 76StLN 77-78SFN 80MilA	03-27-50	Los Angeles, Cal.		B	R	6'	170	579	1610	168	349	57	15	13	121	160	281	36	.217	.295
Harris, Willie-William Charles	01BalA 02-05ChiA 06BosA	06-22-78	Cairo, Ga.		L	R	5'9	175	369	899	138	214	27	4	5	53	87	171	55	.238	.294
Hart, Bo-Bodhi J.	03-04StLN	09-27-76	Creswell, Ore.		R	R	5'11	170	88	309	46	84	13	5	4	30	13	67	3	.272	.385
Hart, Corey-Jon Corey	04-06MilN	03-24-82	Bowling Green, Ky.		R	R	6'6	200	109	295	41	78	15	3	11	40	23	70	7	.264	.447
Hart, Jason-Jason Wyatt	02TexA	09-05-77	Walnut Creek, Cal.		R	R	6'4	237	10	15	2	4	3	0	0	2	2	7	0	.267	.467
Hart, Mike-James Michael	80TexA	12-20-51	Kalamazoo, Mich.		B	R	6'2	180	5	4	1	1	0	0	0	0	1	1	0	.250	.250
Hart, Mike-Michael Lawrence	84MinA 87BalA	02-17-58	Milwaukee, Wis.		L	L	5'11	185	47	105	7	17	2	0	4	17	7	21	1	.162	.295
Harts, Greg-Gregory Rudolph	73NYN	04-21-50	Atlanta, Ga.		R	L	6'	168	3	2	0	1	0	0	0	0	0	0	0	.500	.500
Harvey, Ken-Kenneth Eugene	01,03-05KCA	03-01-78	Los Angeles, Cal.		R	R	6'2	240	271	998	102	273	54	1	27	126	60	200	3	.274	.411
Haselman, Bill-William Joseph	90TexA 92-94SeaA 95-97BosA 98TexA 99DetA 00-02TexA 03BosA	05-25-66	Long Branch, N.J.		R	R	6'3	220	589	1606	185	416	94	3	47	210	114	300	9	.259	.409
Hassey, Ron-Ronald William	78-84CleA 84ChiN 85-86NYA 86-87ChiA 88-90OakA 91MonN	02-27-53	Tucson, Ariz.		L	R	6'2	200	1192	3440	348	914	172	7	71	438	385	378	14	.266	.382
Hatcher, Billy-William Augustus	84-85ChiN 86-89HouN 89PitN 90-92CinN 92-94BosA 94PhiN 95TexA	10-04-60	Williams, Ariz.		R	R	5'9	190	1233	4339	586	1146	210	30	54	399	267	476	218	.264	.364
Hatcher, Chris-Christopher Kenneth	98KCA	01-07-69	Anaheim, Cal.		R	R	6'3	220	8	15	0	1	0	0	0	1	1	7	0	.067	.067
Hatcher, Mickey-Michael Vaughn	79-80LAN 81-86MinA 87-90LAN	03-15-55	Cleveland, Ohio		R	R	6'2	195	1130	3377	348	946	172	20	38	375	164	246	11	.280	.377
Hatteberg, Scott-Scott Allen	95-01BosA 02-05OakA 06CinN	12-14-69	Salem, Ore.		L	R	6'1	205	1164	3813	485	1032	219	6	96	473	506	461	3	.271	.407
Hattig, John-John Duane	06TorA	02-27-80	Tamuning, Guam		B	R	6'2	230	13	24	2	8	1	0	0	3	5	8	0	.333	.375
Hawpe, Brad-Bradley Bonte	04-06ColN	06-22-79	Fort Worth, Tex.		L	L	6'3	200	293	909	117	252	46	11	34	140	128	227	8	.277	.464
Hayes, Bill-William Ernest	80-81ChiN	10-24-57	Cheverly, Md.		R	R	6'1	195	5	9	0	2	1	0	0	0	0	3	0	.222	.333
Hayes, Charlie-Charles DeWayne	88-89SFN 89-91PhiN 92NYA 93-94ColN 95PhiN 96-97NYA 98-99SFN 00MilN 01HouN	05-29-65	Hattiesburg, Miss.		R	R	6'	215	1547	5262	580	1379	251	16	144	740	420	918	47	.262	.398
Hayes, Von-Von Francis	81-82CleA 83-91PhiN 92CalN	08-31-58	Stockton, Cal.		L	R	6'4	185	1495	5249	767	1402	282	36	143	696	712	804	253	.267	.416
Hazewood, Drungo-Drungo Larue	80BalA	09-02-59	Molle, Ala.		R	R	6'3	205	6	5	1	0	0	0	0	0	0	4	0	.000	.000
Healy, Fran-Francis Xavier	69KCA 71-72SFN 73-76KCA 76-78NYA	09-06-46	Holyoke, Mass.		R	R	6'5	220	470	1326	144	332	60	6	20	141	154	242	30	.250	.350
Hearn, Ed-Edward John	86NYN 87-88KCA	08-23-60	Stuart, Fla.		R	R	6'3	215	62	171	19	45	9	0	4	14	16	22	0	.263	.350
Hearron, Jeff-Jeffrey Vernon	85-86TorA	11-19-61	Long Beach, Cal.		R	R	6'1	195	16	30	2	6	1	0	0	4	3	9	0	.200	.233
Heath, Kelly-Kelly Mark (Pee Wee)	82KCA	09-04-57	Plattsburg, N.Y.		R	R	5'7	155	1	0	0	0	0	0	0	0	0	0	0	.000	.000
Heath, Mike-Michael Thomas	78NYA 79-85OakA 86SFN 86-90DetA 91AtlN	02-05-55	Tempa, Fla.		R	R	5'11	185	1325	4212	462	1061	173	27	86	469	278	616	54	.252	.367
Hebner, Richie-Richard Joseph	68-76PitN 77-78PhiN 79NYN 80-82DetA 82-83PitN 84-85ChiN	11-26-47	Brighton, Mass.		L	R	6'1	195	1908	6144	865	1694	273	57	203	890	687	741	38	.276	.438
Heep, Danny-Daniel William	79-82HouN 83-86NYN 87-88LAN 89-90BosA 91AtlN	07-03-57	San Antonio, Tex.		L	L	5'11	188	883	1961	208	503	96	6	30	229	220	242	12	.257	.357
Heffernan, Bert-Bertram Alexander	92SeaA	03-03-65	Centereach, N.Y.		L	R	5'10	185	8	11	0	1	1	0	0	1	0	1	0	.091	.182
Hegman, Bob-Robert Hilmer	85KCA	02-26-58	Springfield, Minn.		R	R	6'1	180	1	0	0	0	0	0	0	0	0	0	0	—	—
Heintz, Chris-Christopher John	05-06MinA	08-06-74	Syosset, N.Y.		R	R	6'1	210	10	26	1	5	3	0	0	2	1	2	0	.192	.308
Heintzelman, Tom-Thomas Kenneth	73-74StLN 77-78SFN	11-03-46	St. Charles, Mo.		R	R	6'	185	90	140	17	34	5	0	3	12	14	22	0	.243	.343
Helfand, Eric-Eric James	93-95OakA	03-25-69	Erie, Pa.		L	R	6'1	195	53	105	11	18	2	1	0	9	11	27	0	.171	.210
Helms, Wes-Wesley Ray	98,00-02AtlN 03-05MilN 06FlaN	05-12-76	Gastonia, N.C.		R	R	6'4	230	659	1602	178	429	93	10	58	246	134	395	2	.268	.447
Helton, Todd-Todd Lynn	97-06ColN	08-20-73	Knoxville, Tenn.		L	L	6'2	205	1424	5106	1018	1700	413	29	286	996	864	686	36	.333	.593
Hemond, Scott-Scott Mathew	89-92OakA 92ChiA 93-94OakA 95StLN	11-18-65	Taunton, Mass.		R	R	6'1	205	298	607	79	132	30	0	12	58	65	162	23	.217	.326
Hemphill, Bret-Bret Ryan	99AnaA	04-29-75	Inglewood, Calif.		B	R	6'2	196	12	21	3	3	0	0	0	2	4	4	0	.143	.143
Henderson, Dave-David Lee	81-86SeaA 86-87BosA 87SFN 88-93OakA 94KCA	07-21-58	Merced, Cal.		R	R	6'2	215	1538	5130	710	1324	286	17	197	708	465	1105	50	.258	.436
Henderson, Ken-Kenneth Joseph	65-72SFN 73-75ChiA 76AtlN 77TexA 78NYA 79-80ChiN	06-15-46	Carroll, Iowa		B	R	6'2	185	1444	4553	595	1168	216	26	122	576	589	763	86	.257	.396
Henderson, Rickey-Rickey Henley	79-84OakA 85-89NYA 89-93OakA 93TorA 94-95OakA 96-97SDN 97AnaA 98OakA 99-00NYN 00SeaA 01SDN 02BosA 03LAN	12-25-58	Chicago, Ill.		R	L	5'10	190	3081	10961	2295	3055	510	66	297	1115	2190	1694	1406	.279	.419
Henderson, Steve-Stephen Curtis	77-80NYN 81-82ChiN 83-84SeaA 85-87OakA 88HouN	11-18-52	Houston, Tex		R	R	6'1	190	1085	3484	459	976	162	49	68	428	386	677	79	.280	.413
Hendrick, George-George Andrew	71-72OakA 73-76CleA 77-78SDN 78-84StLN 85PitN 85-88CalA	10-18-49	Los Angeles, Cal.		R	R	6'3	195	2048	7129	941	1980	343	27	267	1111	567	1013	59	.278	.446
Hengel,Dave-David Lee	86-88SeaA 89CleA	12-18-61	Oakland, Cal.		R	R	6'	195	69	167	10	31	3	0	4	18	4	36	0	.186	.275
Henley, Bob-Robert Clifton	98MonN 99-00EJ	01-30-73	Mobile, Ala.		R	R	6'2	205	41	115	16	35	8	1	3	18	11	26	3	.304	.470
Henson, Drew-Drew Daniel 04 played in the NFL	02-03NYA	02-13-80	San Diego, Cal.		R	R	6'5	222	8	9	3	1	0	0	0	0	0	6	0	.111	.111
Hermansen, Chad-Chad Bruce	99-01PitN 02ChiN 03LaN 04TorA	09-10-77	Salt Lake City, Utah		R	R	6'2	190	189	492	49	96	23	2	13	34	38	168	9	.195	.329
Hermida, Jeremy-Jeremy Ryan	05-06FlaN	01-30-84	Atlanta, Ga.		L	R	6'4	200	122	348	46	89	21	1	9	39	39	82	6	.256	.399
Hernandez, Alex-Alexander [Vargas]	00-02PitN	05-28-77	San Juan, P.R.		L	L	6'4	190	27	71	4	13	3	0	1	5	0	15	1	.183	.268
Hernandez, Anderson-Anderson Mejia	05-06NYN	10-30-82	Santo Domingo, D. R.		B	R	5'9	170	31	84	5	11	1	1	1	3	2	16	0	.131	.202
Hernandez, Carlos-Carlos Alberto [Almeida]	90-96LAN 97-98SDN 99LJ 00SDN 00StLN 01XJ	05-24-67	San Felix, Venez.		R	R	5'11	210	488	1244	102	315	51	1	24	141	63	196	5	.253	.354
Hernandez, Carlos-Carlos Eduardo	99HouN 00SeaA	12-12-75	Caracas, Venezuela		R	R	5'9	175	18	15	4	2	0	0	0	1	0	3	0	.133	.133
Hernandez, Cesar-Cesar Dario [Perez]	92-93ChiN	09-28-66	Yamasa, D.R.		R	R	6'	160	61	75	9	16	4	0	0	5	1	18	4	.213	.267
Hernandez, Enzo-Enzo Octavio [Martinez]	71-77SDN 78LAN	02-12-49	Valle de Guanape,Venez.		R	R	5'9	165	714	2327	241	522	66	13	2	113	189	151	129	.224	.266
Hernandez, Jose-Jose Antonio [Figueroa]	91TexA 92CleA 94-98ChiN 99AtlN 00-02MilN 03ColN 03PitN 04LAN 05CleA 06PitN 06PhiN	07-14-69	Rio Piedras, P.R.		R	R	6'1	185	1587	4618	623	1166	193	33	168	603	384	1391	41	.252	.427
Hernandez, Keith-Keith	74-83StLN 83-89NYN 90CleA 91XJ	10-20-53	San Francisco, Cal.		L	L	6'	195	2088	7370	1124	2182	426	60	162	1071	1070	1012	98	.296	.436
Hernandez, Leo-Leonardo Jesus [Trapera]	82-83,85BalA 86NYA	11-06-59	Santa Lucia, Venez.		R	R	5'11	190	85	249	23	56	8	1	7	30	13	33	1	.225	.349
Hernandez, Michel-Michel	03NYA	08-12-78	Havana, Cuba		R	R	6'	210	5	4	0	1	0	0	0	0	0	1	0	.250	.250
Hernandez (Montas), Pedro-Pedro Julio Montas [Hernandez]	79,82 TorA	04-04-59	La Romana, D.R.		R	R	6'1	160	11	9	2	1	0	0	0	0	0	0	0	.111	.111
Hernandez, Ramon-Ramon Jose [Marin]	99-03OakA 04-05SDN 06BalA	05-20-76	Caracas, Venezuela		R	R	6'	225	949	3148	388	831	166	5	113	475	265	450	6	.264	.428
Hernandez, Toby-Rafael Tobias [Montas]	84TorA	11-30-58	Calabozo, Venez.		R	R	5'11	180	3	2	1	1	0	0	0	0	0	0	0	.500	.500
Herndon, Larry-Larry Darnell (Hondo)	74StLN 76-81SFN 82-88DetA	11-03-53	Sunflower, Miss.		R	R	6'3	195	1537	4877	605	1334	186	76	107	550	353	793	92	.273	.409
Herr, Tommy-Thomas Mitchell (T-Bird)	79-88StLN 88MinA 89-90PhiN 90-91NYN 91SFN	04-04-56	Lancaster, Pa.		B	R	6'	190	1514	5349	676	1450	254	41	28	574	627	584	188	.271	.350
Herrera, Jose-Jose Ramon [Catalino]	95-96OakA	08-30-72	Santo Domingo, D.R.		L	R	5'11	160	141	390	53	103	16	3	6	32	26	70	9	.264	.367
Herrmann, Ed-Edward Martin	67,69-74ChiA 75NYA 76CalA 76-78HouN 78MonN	08-27-46	San Diego, Cal.		L	R	6'1	205	922	2729	247	654	92	4	80	320	260	361	6	.240	.364
Hessman, Mike-Michael Steven	03-04AtlN	03-05-78	Fountain Valley, Cal.		R	R	6'5	215	48	90	10	15	5	0	4	8	6	30	0	.167	.356
Hiatt, Phil-Philip Farrell	93-95KCA 96DetA 97JL 01LAN	05-01-69	Pensacola, Fla.		R	R	6'2	200	170	422	50	91	21	2	13	55	30	149	7	.216	.367
Hidalgo, Richard-Richard Jose	97-04HouN 04NYN 05TexA	06-28-75	Caracas, Venezuela		R	R	6'3	215	987	3459	531	929	214	19	171	560	358	737	48	.269	.490
Hietpas, Joe-Joseph Carl	04NYN	05-01-79	Appleton, Wis.		R	R	6'3	220	1	0	0	0	0	0	0	0	0	0	0	—	—
Higgins, Kevin-Kevin Wayne	93SDN	01-22-67	San Gabriel, Cal.		L	R	5'11	185	71	181	17	40	4	1	0	13	16	17	0	.221	.254
Higgins, Mark-Mark Douglas	89CleA	07-09-63	Miami, Fla.		R	R	6'2	215	9	10	1	1	0	0	0	0	0	4	0	.100	.100
Higginson, Bobby-Robert Leigh	95-06DetA	08-18-70	Philadelphia, Pa.		L	R	5'11	185	1362	4910	736	1336	270	33	187	709	649	796	91	.272	.455
Hill, Aaron-Aaron Walter	05-06TorA	03-21-82	Visalia, Cal.		R	R	5'11	195	260	907	119	258	53	6	9	90	76	107	7	.284	.386
Hill, Bobby-William Robert	02-03ChiN 03-05PitN	04-03-78	San Jose, Cal.		B	R	5'10	190	249	523	67	137	20	4	6	58	48	100	6	.262	.350

USE NAME - GIVEN NAMES (NICKNAMES)	TEAM BY YEAR	BIRTH DATE	BIRTH PLACE	DEATH DATE	B	T	HGT	WGT	G	AB	R	H	2B	3B	HR	RBI	BB	SO	SB	BA	SA
Hill, Donnie-Donald Earl	83-86OakA 87-88ChiA 90-91CalA 92MinA	11-12-60	Pomona, Cal.		B	R	5'10	165	756	2307	276	594	91	14	26	228	175	225	22	.257	.343
Hill, Glenallen-Glenallen	89-90TorA 91-93CleA 93-94ChiN 95-97SFN 98SeaA 98-00ChiN 00NYA 01AnaA	03-22-65	Santa Cruz, Cal.		R	R	6'2	225	1162	3715	528	1005	187	21	186	586	270	845	96	.271	.482
Hill, Koyie-Koyie Dolan	03LAN 04-05AriN	03-09-79	Tulsa, Okla.		B	R	6'	190	50	117	9	27	7	0	1	12	13	35	1	.231	.316
Hill, Marc-Marc Kevin (The Booter)	73-74StLN 75-80SFN 80SeaA 81-86ChiA	02-18-52	Elsberry, Mo.		R	R	6'3	225	737	1809	146	404	62	3	34	198	185	243	1	.223	.317
Hillenbrand, Shea-Shea Matthew	01-03BosA 03-04AriN 05-06TorA 06SFN	07-27-75	Mesa, Ariz.		R	R	6'1	210	870	3303	438	947	197	13	104	459	133	434	16	.287	.449
Hilton, Dave-John David	72-75SDN	09-15-50	Uvalde, Tex.		R	R	6'	180	161	506	40	108	19	3	6	43	35	69	6	.213	.298
Hinch, A.J.-Andrew Jay	98-00OakA 01-02KCA 03DetA 04PhiN	05-15-74	Waverly, Iowa		R	R	6'1	205	350	953	104	209	28	3	32	112	71	214	13	.219	.356
Hinshaw, George-George Addison	82-83SDN	10-23-59	Los Angeles, Cal.		R	R	6'	185	13	31	2	11	1	0	0	5	3	9	1	.355	.387
Hinske, Eric-Eric Scott	02-06TorA 06BosA	08-05-77	Menasha, Wis.		L	R	6'2	225	686	2339	361	607	154	12	79	318	271	551	47	.260	.437
Hinzo, Tommy-Thomas Lee	87,89CleA	06-18-64	San Diego, Cal.		B	R	5'10	170	85	274	35	68	9	3	3	21	12	53	10	.248	.336
Hiser, Gene-Gene Taylor	71-75ChiN	12-11-48	Baltimore, Md.		L	L	5'11	170	206	263	34	53	7	0	1	18	32	43	6	.202	.240
Hisle, Larry-Larry Eugene	68-71PhiN 73-77MinA 78-82MilA	05-04-47	Portsmouth, Ohio		R	R	6'1	190	1197	4205	652	1146	193	32	166	674	462	941	128	.273	.452
Hobson, Butch-Clell Lavern	75-80BosA 81CalA 82NYA M92-93BosA	08-17-51	Tuscaloosa, Ala.		R	R	6'1	190	738	2556	314	634	107	23	98	397	183	569	8	.248	.423
Hocking, Denny-Dennis Lee	93-03MinA 04ColN 05KCA	04-02-70	Torrance, Cal.		B	R	5'10	180	954	2358	294	591	112	17	25	226	205	442	36	.251	.344
Hodges, Ron-Ronald Wray	73-84NYN	06-22-49	Rocky Mount, Va.		L	R	6'1	185	666	1426	119	342	56	2	19	147	224	217	10	.240	.322
Hodgson, Paul-Paul Joseph Denis	80TorA	04-14-60	Montreal, Canada		R	R	6'	185	20	41	5	9	0	1	1	5	3	12	0	.220	.341
Hoffman, Glenn-Glenn Edward	80-87BosA 87LAN 89CalA M98LAN	07-07-58	Orange, Cal.		R	R	6'2	190	766	2163	247	524	106	9	23	210	136	309	5	.242	.331
Hoiles, Chris-Christopher Allen	89-98BalA	03-20-65	Bowling Green, Ohio		R	R	6'	210	894	2820	415	739	147	2	151	449	435	616	5	.262	.467
Holbert, Aaron-Aaron Keith	96StLN 05CinN	01-09-73	Torrance, Cal.		R	R	6'	160	23	30	3	6	3	0	0	2	3	8	1	.200	.300
Holbert, Ray-Ray Arthur	94-95SDN 98AtlN 98MonN 99-00KCA	09-25-70	Torrance, Cal.		R	R	6'	180	115	202	28	45	5	1	2	11	18	51	11	.223	.287
Hollandsworth, Todd-Todd Mathew	95-00LAN 00-02ColN 02TexA 03FlaN 04-05ChiN 05AtlN 06CleA 06CinN	04-20-73	Dayton, Ohio		L	L	6'2	215	1118	3191	451	871	192	22	98	401	262	701	75	.273	.439
Holle, Gary-Gary Charles	79TexA	08-11-54	Albany, N.Y.		R	L	6'6	210	5	6	0	1	1	0	0	0	1	0	0	.167	.333
Holliday, Matt-Matthew Thomas	04-06ColN	01-15-80	Stillwater, Okla.		R	R	6'4	235	401	1481	252	459	100	15	67	258	114	275	27	.310	.533
Hollins, Damon-Damon Jamall	98AtlN 98LAN 04AtlN 05-06TBA	06-12-74	Fairfield, Cal.		R	R	5'11	180	256	712	85	172	39	1	28	86	42	134	11	.242	.417
Hollins, Dave-David Michael (Bats right part of 96)	90-95PhiN 95BosA 96MinA 96SeaA 97-98AnaA 99TorA 01CleA 02PhiN	05-25-66	Buffalo, N.Y.		B	R	6'1	220	983	3346	578	870	166	17	112	482	464	687	47	.260	.420
Holt, Roger-Roger Boyd	80NYA	04-08-56	Daytona Beach, Fla.		B	R	5'11	168	2	6	0	1	0	0	0	1	1	2	0	.167	.167
Hooper, Kevin-Kevin J.	05-06DetA	12-07-76	Lawrence, Kans.		R	R	6'	160	14	8	1	1	0	0	0	0	1	2	0	.125	.125
Hoover, Paul-Paul Chester	01-02TBA 06FlaN	04-14-76	Columbus, Ohio		R	R	6'1	210	12	26	2	6	0	0	0	3	0	6	0	.231	.231
Hopkins, Don-Donald (Hoppy)	75-76OakA	01-09-52	West Point, Miss.		L	R	5'11	185	85	6	25	1	0	0	0	0	0	0	21	.167	.167
Hopper, Norris-Norris Stephen	06CinN	03-24-79	Shelby, N.C.		R	R	5'10	198	21	39	6	14	1	0	1	5	6	4	2	.359	.462
Horn, Sam-Samuel Lee	87-89BosA 90-92BalA 93CleA 95TexA	11-02-63	Dallas, Tex.		L	R	6'5	240	389	1040	132	250	49	1	62	179	132	323	0	.240	.468
Horner, Bob-James Robert	78-86AtlN 87JL 88StLN	08-06-57	Junction City, Kans.		R	R	6'1	220	1020	3777	560	1047	169	8	218	685	369	512	14	.277	.499
Hosey, Dwayne-Dwayne Samuel	95-96BosA	03-11-67	Sharon, Pa.		B	R	5'10	175	52	146	33	40	10	3	4	10	15	33	12	.274	.466
Hosey, Steve-Steven Bernard	92-93SFN	04-02-69	Oakland, Cal.		R	R	6'3	215	24	58	6	15	2	0	1	7	1	16	1	.259	.345
Hosley, Tim-Timothy Kenneth	70-71DetA 73-74OakA 75-76ChiN 76-78,81OakA	05-10-47	Spartanburg, S.C.		R	R	5'11	190	207	368	43	79	11	0	12	53	57	73	1	.215	.342
Hostetler, Dave-David Alan (Hoss)	81MonN 82-84TexA 86-87JL 88PhiN	03-27-56	Pasadena, Cal.		R	R	6'5	220	255	818	92	187	23	6	37	124	97	248	2	.229	.407
House, J.R.-James Rodger	03-04PitN 06HouN	11-11-79	Charleston, W.Va.		R	R	5'10	202	10	19	1	2	1	0	0	0	4	4	0	.105	.158
Householder, Paul-Paul Wesley (House)	80-84CinN 84StLN 85-86MilA 87HouN	09-04-58	Columbus, Ohio		B	R	6'	185	466	1326	146	313	60	11	29	144	126	250	36	.236	.363
Housie, Wayne-Wayne Tyrone	91BosA 93NYN	05-20-65	Hampton, Va.		B	R	5'9	165	29	24	4	5	2	0	0	1	2	4	1	.208	.292
Houston, Tyler-Tyler Sam	96AtlN 96-99ChiN 99CleA 00-02MilN 02LAN 03PhiN	01-17-71	Las Vegas, Nev.		L	R	6'2	210	700	1805	197	479	84	6	63	253	119	408	10	.265	.423
Howard, Chris-Christopher Hugh	91,93-94SeaA	02-27-66	San Diego, Cal.		R	R	6'2	200	22	32	3	6	2	0	0	2	2	8	0	.188	.250
Howard, David-David Wayne	91-97KCA 98-99StLN	02-26-67	Sarasota, Fla.		B	R	6'	175	645	1583	169	362	57	14	11	148	137	311	23	.229	.303
Howard, Doug-Douglas Lynn	72-74CalA 75StLN 76CleA	02-06-48	Salt Lake City, Utah		R	R	6'3	185	97	217	19	46	5	1	1	22	7	30	2	.212	.258
Howard, Matt-Matthew Christopher	96NYA	09-22-67	Fall River, Mass.		R	R	5'10	170	35	54	9	11	1	0	1	9	2	8	1	.204	.278
Howard, Mike-Michael Frederic (Mad Dog)	81-83NYN	04-02-58	Seattle, Wash.		B	R	6'2	185	48	66	4	12	1	0	1	7	10	14	4	.182	.242
Howard, Ryan-Ryan James	04-06PhiN	11-19-79	St. Louis, Mo.		L	L	6'4	230	266	932	161	283	47	3	82	217	143	294	0	.304	.624
Howard, Steve-Steven Bernard	90OakA	12-07-63	Oakland, Cal.		R	R	6'2	185	21	52	5	12	1	0	0	1	4	17	0	.231	.308
Howard, Thomas-Thomas Sylvester (Bats Left 96-99)	90-92SDN 92-93CleA 93-96CinN 97HouN 98LAN 99-00StLN	12-11-64	Middletown, Ohio		B	R	6'2	205	1015	2483	297	655	123	22	44	264	165	432	66	.264	.384
Howard, Wilbur-Wilbur Leon (Willie Whistle)	73MilA 74-78HouN	01-08-49	Lowell, N.C.		B	R	6'2	180	466	1068	149	267	37	11	6	71	44	175	60	.250	.322
Howe, Art-Arthur Henry	74-75PitN 76-82HouN 83EJ-NJ 84-85StLN M89-93HouN M96-02OakA M03-04NYN	12-15-46	Pittsburgh, Pa.		R	R	6'2	185	891	2626	268	682	139	23	43	293	275	287	10	.260	.379
Howell, Jack-Jack Robert	85-91CalA 91SDN 92-95JL 96CalA 97AnaA 98-99HouN	08-18-61	Tucson, Ariz.		L	R	6'1	190	941	2639	345	632	129	16	108	337	300	626	14	.239	.423
Howell, Pat-Patrick O'Neal	92NYN	08-31-68	Mobile, Ala.		B	R	5'11	155	31	75	9	14	1	0	0	1	2	15	4	.187	.200
Howell, Roy-Roy Lee	74-77TexA 77-80TorA 81-84MilA	12-18-53	Lompoc, Cal.		L	R	6'	195	1112	3791	422	991	183	31	80	454	318	675	9	.261	.389
Howitt, Dann-Dann Paul John	89-92OakA 92-93SeaA 94ChiA	12-13-64	Battle Creek, Mich.		L	R	6'5	205	115	242	25	47	7	1	5	22	17	60	1	.194	.326
Hrbek, Kent-Kent Alan	81-94MinA	05-21-60	Minneapolis, Minn.		L	R	6'4	245	1747	6192	903	1749	312	18	293	1086	838	798	37	.282	.481
Hubbard, Glenn-Glenn Dee (Bam Bam)	78-87AtlN 88-89OakA	09-25-57	Hahn AFB, Germany		R	R	5'8	168	1354	4441	545	1084	214	22	70	448	539	640	35	.244	.349
Hubbard, Mike-Michael Wayne	95-97ChiN 98MonN 00AtlN 01TexA	02-16-71	Lynchburg, Va.		R	R	6'	195	104	192	11	32	3	2	0	11	4	60	0	.167	.240
Hubbard, Trenidad-Trinidad Aviel	94-96ColN 96SFN 97CleA 98-99LAN 00AtlN 00BalA 01KCA 02SDN 03ChiN	05-11-64	Chicago, Ill.		R	R	5'8	195	476	762	124	196	33	7	16	72	83	166	33	.257	.382
Huber, Justin-Justin Patrick	05-06KCA	07-01-82	Melbourne, Australia		R	R	6'2	200	30	88	7	19	4	0	3	7	6	24	1	.216	.261
Huckaby, Ken-Kenneth Paul	01AriN 02-03TorA 04TexA 04BalA 05TorA 06BosA	01-27-71	San Leandro, Cal.		R	R	6'1	205	161	427	42	95	14	1	3	31	19	78	0	.222	.281
Hudgens, Dave-David Mark	83OakA	12-05-56	Oroville, Cal.		L	L	6'2	210	6	7	0	1	0	0	0	0	0	3	0	.143	.143
Hudler, Rex-Rex Allen	84-85NYA 86BalA 88-90MonN 90-92StLN 93JL 94-96CalA 97-98PhiN	09-02-60	Tempe, Ariz.		R	R	6'	190	774	1767	261	461	96	10	56	169	77	325	107	.261	.422
Hudson, Orlando-Orlando Thill	02-05TorA 06AriN	12-12-77	Darlington, S.C.		B	R	6'	185	619	2195	296	603	122	32	50	268	192	355	28	.275	.428
Huff, Aubrey-Aubrey Lewis	00-06TBA 06HouN	12-20-76	Marion, Ohio		L	R	6'4	220	867	3252	431	926	182	10	141	487	273	451	20	.285	.477
Huff, Mike-Michael Kale	89LAN 91CleA 91-93ChiA 94-96TorA	08-11-63	Honolulu, Hawaii		R	R	6'1	190	369	801	113	198	42	7	9	75	109	146	19	.247	.351
Hughes, Bobby-Robert E.	98-99MilN	03-10-71	Burbank, Cal.		R	R	6'4	205	133	319	38	76	9	2	12	37	21	82	1	.238	.392
Hughes, Keith-Keith Wills	87NYA 87PhiN 88BalA 90NYN 93CinN	09-12-63	Bryn Mawr, Pa.		L	L	6'3	210	93	201	18	41	6	2	2	24	23	44	1	.204	.284
Hughes, Terry-Terry Wayne	70ChiN 73StLN 74BosA	05-13-49	Spartanburg, S.C.		R	R	6'	185	54	86	6	18	3	0	1	7	7	22	0	.209	.279
Hulett, Tim-Timothy Craig	83-87ChiA 89-94BalA 95StLN	01-12-60	Springfield, Ill.		R	R	6'	195	720	2128	245	529	90	13	48	220	145	438	14	.249	.371
Hulse, David-David Lindsey	92-94TexA 95-96MilA	02-25-68	San Angelo, Tex.		L	L	5'11	170	423	1265	207	336	35	20	5	103	76	204	69	.266	.337
Hummel, Tim-Timothy Robert	03-04CinN	11-18-78	Goshen, N.Y.		R	R	6'2	195	82	194	19	43	9	0	3	17	16	30	1	.222	.314
Humphrey, Terry-Terryal Gene	71-74MonN 75DetA 76-79CalA	08-04-49	Chickasha, Okla.		R	R	6'3	190	415	1055	69	223	39	1	6	85	68	75	5	.211	.267
Humphreys, Mike-Michael Butler	91-93NYA	04-10-67	Dallas, Tex.		R	R	5'11	175	35	46	10	8	1	2	1	9	13	19	4	.176	.259
Hundley, Todd-Todd Randolph (Bats Left part of 99-00)	90-98NYN 99-00LAN 01-02ChiN 03LAN 04XJ	05-27-69	Martinsville, Va.		B	R	5'11	195	1225	3769	495	883	167	7	202	599	453	988	14	.234	.443
Hunt, Randy-James Randall	85StLN 86MonN	01-03-60	Prattville, Ala.		R	R	6'	195	35	67	5	13	0	0	2	6	5	21	0	.194	.284
Hunter, Brian-Brian Lee	94-96HouN 97-99DetA 99SeaA 00ColN 00CinN 01PhiN 02-03HouN	03-05-71	Portland, Ore.		R	R	6'4	180	1000	3347	500	882	146	28	25	241	243	581	260	.264	.346
Hunter, Brian-Brian Ronald	91-93AtlN 94PitN 94-95CinN 96SeaA 98StLN 99-00AtlN 00PhiN	03-04-68	Torrance, Cal.		R	L	6'	220	699	1555	187	364	90	4	67	259	141	335	4	.234	.430
Hunter, Buddy-Harold James	71,73,75BosA	08-09-47	Omaha, Neb.		R	R	5'10	178	22	17	5	5	0	2	0	2	5	2	0	.294	.412
Hunter, Torii-Torii Kedar	97-06MinA	07-18-75	Pine Bluff, Ark.		R	R	6'2	205	1074	3892	578	1046	214	25	164	604	279	769	108	.269	.463
Huppert, Dave-David Blain	83BalA 85MilA	04-17-57	South Gate, Cal.		R	R	6'1	190	17	21	1	1	0	0	0	0	2	7	0	.048	.048
Hurdle, Clint-Clinton Merrick	77-81KCA 82CinN 83,85NYN 86StLN 87NYN M02-06ColN	07-30-57	Big Rapids, Mich.		R	R	6'3	195	515	1391	162	360	81	12	32	193	176	261	1	.259	.403
Hurst, Jimmy-Jimmy O'Neal	97DetA	03-01-72	Tuscaloosa, Ala.		R	R	6'6	225	13	17	1	3	1	0	0	1	2	6	0	.176	.412
Huskey, Butch-Robert Leon	93,95-98NYN 99SeaA 99BosA 00MinN 00ColN	11-10-71	Anadarko, Okla.		R	R	6'3	245	642	2078	259	555	98	4	86	336	164	384	21	.267	.442
Huson, Jeff-Jeffrey Kent	88-89MonN 90-93TexA 94KJ 95-96BalA 97MilA 98SeaA 99AnaA 00ChiN	08-15-64	Scottsdale, Ariz.		L	R	6'3	183	827	1879	242	439	65	13	8	150	191	228	64	.234	.295
Hutton, Tommy-Thomas George	66,69LAN 72-77PhiN 78TorA 78-81MonN	04-20-46	Los Angeles, Cal.		L	L	5'11	180	952	1655	196	410	63	7	22	186	234	140	15	.248	.334
Hyers, Tim-Timothy James	94-95SDN 96DetA 99FlaN	10-03-71	Atlanta, Ga.		L	L	6'2	195	133	230	22	50	8	1	2	19	27	32	3	.217	.287
Hyzdu, Adam-Adam Davis	00-03PitN 04BosA 05SDN 05BosA 06DetA	12-06-71	San Jose, Cal.		R	R	6'2	220	221	358	54	82	19	0	9	61	41	98	1	.229	.439
Iannetta, Chris-Christopher Domenic	06ColN	04-08-83	Providence, R.I.		R	R	5'11	195	21	77	12	20	4	0	2	10	13	17	0	.260	.390
Ibanez, Raul-Raul Javier	96-00SeaA 01-03KCA 04-06SeaA	06-02-72	New York, N.Y.		L	R	6'2	210	1073	3583	530	997	234	26	138	579	329	580	22	.278	.470
Iguchi, Tadahito-Tadahito	05-06ChiA	12-04-74	Tokyo, Japan		R	R	5'10	185	273	1066	171	298	49	6	33	138	106	224	26	.280	.430
Incaviglia, Pete-Peter Joseph (Inky)	86-90TexA 91DetA 92HouN 92NYA 93PhiN 95JL 96PhiN 96-97BalA 97DetA 98HouN	04-02-64	Pebble Beach, Cal.		R	R	6'1	230	1284	4233	546	1043	194	21	206	655	360	1277	26	.246	.448
Infante, Alex-Fermin Alexis [Carpio]	87-89TorA 90AtlN	12-04-61	Barquisimeto, Venez.		R	R	5'10	175	60	55	11	6	1	0	0	3	0	12	1	.109	.127
Infante, Omar-Omar Rafael	02-06DetA	12-26-81	Puerto la Cruz, Venez.		R	R	5'9	150	428	1426	169	358	75	16	30	137	91	277	30	.251	.389

USE NAME - GIVEN NAMES (NICKNAMES)	TEAM BY YEAR	BIRTH DATE	BIRTH PLACE	DEATH DATE	B	T	HGT	WGT	G	AB	R	H	2B	3B	HR	RBI	BB	SO	SB	BA	SA
Inge, Brandon-Charles Brandon	01-06DetA	05-19-77	Lynchburg, Va.		R	R	5'11	190	728	2406	273	581	116	24	71	288	195	561	25	.241	.398
Inglett, Joe-Joseph Steven	06CleA	06-29-78	Sacramento, Cal.		L	R	5'10	180	64	201	26	57	8	3	2	21	14	39	5	.284	.383
Ingram, Garey-Garey Lamar	94-95,97LAN	07-25-70	Columbus, Ga.		R	R	5'11	180	82	142	17	37	3	0	3	12	17	33	4	.261	.345
Ingram, Riccardo-Riccardo Benay	94DetA 95MinA	09-10-66	Douglas, Ga.		R	R	6'	205	16	31	3	6	0	0	0	3	3	3	0	.194	.194
Iorg, Dane-Dane Charles	77PhiN 77-84StLN 84-85KCA 86SDN	05-11-50	Eureka, Cal.		L	R	6'	180	743	1647	149	455	103	11	14	216	107	180	5	.276	.378
Iorg, Garth-Garth Ray	78,80-87TorA	10-12-54	Arcata, Cal.		R	R	5'11	170	931	2450	251	633	125	16	20	238	114	298	22	.258	.347
Ireland, Tim-Timothy Neal Christopher	81-82KCA	03-14-53	Oakland, Cal.		B	R	6'	180	11	7	3	1	0	0	0	0	1	1	0	.143	.143
Isales, Orlando-Orlando [Pizarro] (Bambino)	80PhiN	12-22-59	Santurce, P.R.		R	R	5'11	190	3	5	1	2	0	1	0	3	1	0	0	.400	.800
Ishikawa, Travis-Travis Takashi	06SFN	09-24-83	Seattle, Wash.		L	L	6'3	200	12	24	1	7	3	1	0	4	1	6	0	.292	.500
Ivie, Mike-Michael Wilson (Moose)	71,74-77SDN 78-81SFN 81-82HouN 82-83DetA	08-08-52	Atlanta, Ga.		R	R	6'3	210	857	2694	309	724	133	17	81	411	214	402	22	.269	.421
Izturis, Cesar-Cesar David	01TorA 02-06LAN 06CinN	02-10-80	Barquisimeto, Venez.		B	R	5'9	175	658	2437	261	632	111	22	11	191	121	259	59	.259	.336
Izturis, Maicer-Maicer E.	04MonN 05-06LAA	09-12-80	Barquisimeto, Venez.		B	R	5'8	155	213	650	92	172	34	9	7	63	65	76	27	.265	.377
Jackson, Bo-Vincent Edward	87-90 played in N.F.L. 86-90KCA 91ChiA 92PJ 93ChiA 94CalA	11-30-62	Bessemer, Ala.		R	R	6'1	222	694	2393	341	598	86	14	141	415	200	841	82	.250	.474
Jackson, Chuck-Charles Leo	87-88HouN 94TexA	03-19-63	Seattle, Wash.		R	R	6'	185	82	156	10	34	8	1	2	14	14	35	2	.218	.321
Jackson, Conor-Conor Sims	05-06AriN	05-07-82	Austin, Tex.		R	R	6'2	225	180	570	83	158	29	1	17	87	66	84	1	.277	.421
Jackson, Damian-Damian Jacques	96-97SDN 97-98CinN 99-01SDN 02DetA 03BosA 04ChiN 04KCA 05SDN 06WasN	08-16-73	Los Angeles, Cal.		R	R	5'10	185	827	2209	332	536	121	17	32	198	245	517	133	.243	.356
Jackson, Darrin-Darrin Jay (D.J.)	85,87-89SDN 93TorA 93NYN 94ChiA 95-96JL 97MinA 97MilA 98MinA 99ChiA	08-22-62	Los Angeles, Cal.		R	R	6'	185	960	2629	311	676	114	15	80	317	131	480	43	.257	.400
Jackson, Ken-Kenneth Bernard	87PhiN	08-21-63	Shreveport, La.		R	R	6'1	190	8	16	1	4	2	0	0	2	1	4	0	.250	.375
Jackson, Reggie-Reginald Martinez (Mr. October)	67KCA 68-75OakA 76BalA 77-81NYA 82-86CalA 87OakA	05-18-46	Wyncote, Pa.		L	L	6'	200	2820	9864	1551	2584	463	49	563	1702	1375	2597	228	.262	.490
Jackson, Ron-Ronnie Damien (Pop, Papa Jack)	75-78CalA 79-81MinA 81DetA 82-84CalA 84BalA	05-09-53	Birmingham, Ala.		R	R	6'	215	926	2986	356	774	165	22	56	342	213	329	23	.259	.385
Jackson, Ryan-Ryan Dewitte	98FlaN 99SeaA 01-02DetA	11-15-71	Orlando, Fla.		L	L	6'2	196	226	452	49	108	23	4	7	52	32	120	7	.239	.354
Jacobs, Mike-Michael James	05NYN 06FlaN	10-30-80	Chula Vista, Cal.		L	R	6'2	200	166	569	73	154	44	1	31	100	55	127	3	.271	.515
Jacobson, Bucky-Larry William	04SeaA 05KJ	08-30-75	Riverton, Wyo.		R	R	6'4	255	42	160	17	44	9	0	9	28	14	47	0	.275	.500
Jacoby, Brook-Brook Wallace (Jake)	81,83AtlN 84-91CleA 91OakA 92CleA	11-23-59	Philadelphia, Pa.		R	R	5'11	185	1311	4520	535	1220	201	24	120	545	439	764	16	.270	.405
Jaha, John-John Emil	92-97MilA 98MilN 99-01OakA	05-27-66	Portland, Ore.		R	R	6'1	210	826	2775	470	730	126	5	141	490	430	686	36	.263	.465
James, Art-Arthur (Spider)	75DetA 76FJ	08-02-52	Detroit, Mich.		L	L	6'	170	11	40	2	9	2	0	0	1	1	7	1	.225	.275
James, Chris-Donald Christopher	86-89PhiN 89SDN 90-91CleA 92SFN 93HouN 93-94TexA 95KCA 95BosA	10-04-62	Rusk, Tex.		R	R	6'1	200	946	3040	343	794	145	24	90	386	193	490	27	.261	.413
James, Dion-Dion	83-85MilA 87-89AtlN 89-90CleA 92-93NYA 94JL 95-96NYA	11-09-62	Philadelphia, Pa.		L	L	6'1	185	917	2708	362	781	142	21	32	266	318	307	43	.288	.392
James, Skip-Phillip Robert	77-78SFN	10-21-49	Elmhurst, Ill.		L	L	6'	185	51	36	8	6	2	0	0	6	6	8	1	.167	.222
Javier (Wilkes), Al-Ignacio Alfredo Wilkes [Javier]	76HouN	02-04-54	San Pedro de Mac, D.R.		B	R	5'11	170	8	24	1	5	0	0	0	2	5	0	0	.208	.208
Javier, Stan-Stanley Julian Antonio [Negrin]	84NYA 86-90OakA 90-91LAN 92PhiN 93CalA 94-95OakA 96-99SFN 99HouN 00-01SeaA	01-09-64	San Fran de Mac, D.R.		B	R	6'	190	1763	5047	781	1358	225	40	57	503	578	839	246	.269	.363
Jefferies, Gregg-Gregory Scott	87-91NYN 92KCA 93-94StLN 95-98PhiN 98-00DetA	08-01-67	Burlingame, Cal.		B	R	5'11	185	1465	5520	761	1593	300	27	126	663	472	348	196	.289	.421
Jefferson, Reggie-Reginald Jirod	91CinN 91-93CleA 94SeaA 95-99BosA	09-25-68	Tallahassee, Fla.		L	L	6'4	215	680	2123	285	637	131	11	72	300	146	452	2	.300	.474
Jefferson, Stan-Stanley Bats Both 91-94	86NYN 87-88SDN 89NYA 89-90BalA 90CleA 91CinN	12-04-62	New York, NY		B	R	5'11	175	296	832	125	180	25	9	16	67	65	177	60	.216	.326
Jelic, Chris-Christopher John	90NYN	12-16-63	Bethlehem, Pa.		R	R	5'11	185	4	11	2	1	0	0	1	1	0	3	0	.091	.364
Jelks, Greg-Gregory Dion	87PhiN	08-16-61	Cherokee, Ala.		R	R	6'2	190	10	11	2	1	1	0	0	0	3	4	0	.091	.182
Jeltz, Steve-Larry Steven Bats Right 83-85	83-89PhiN 90KCA	05-28-59	Paris, France		B	R	5'11	160	727	1749	183	367	46	20	5	130	248	342	18	.210	.268
Jenkins, Geoff-Geoffrey Scott	98-06MilN	07-21-74	Olympia, Wash.		L	R	6'1	210	1102	3987	616	1114	263	20	191	640	362	1002	29	.279	.499
Jennings, Doug-James Douglas	88-91OakA 93ChiN	09-30-64	Atlanta, Ga.		L	L	5'10	175	189	322	36	65	16	3	5	37	43	90	0	.202	.317
Jennings, Robin-Robin Christopher	96-97ChiN 98WJ 99ChiN 01OakA 01ColN 01CinN	04-11-72	Singapore		L	L	6'2	205	93	213	22	52	14	2	3	24	10	31	1	.244	.371
Jensen, Marcus-Marcus Christian	96-97SFN 97DetA 98MilN 99StLN 00MinN 01BosA 01TexA 02MilN	12-14-72	Oakland, Cal.		B	R	6'4	200	145	343	33	63	16	1	6	29	50	106	0	.184	.289
Jeter, Derek-Derek Sanderson	95-06NYA	06-26-74	Pequannock, N.J.		R	R	6'3	195	1679	6790	1277	2150	347	50	183	860	705	1191	249	.317	.463
Jeter, Shawn-Shawn Darrell	92ChiA	06-28-66	Shreveport, La.		L	R	6'2	185	13	18	1	2	0	0	0	0	0	7	0	.111	.111
Jiminez, D'Angelo-D'Angelo	99NYA 01-02SDN 02-03ChiA 03-05CinN 06TexA 06OakA	12-21-77	Santo Domingo, D.R.		B	R	6'	190	568	2057	276	543	98	17	34	218	270	369	34	.264	.378
Jimenez, Houston-Alfonso [Gonzalez]	83-84MinA 87PitN 88CleA	10-30-57	Mexico City, Mexico		R	R	5'8	145	158	411	34	76	16	2	0	29	20	49	0	.185	.234
Jimerson, Charlton-Charlton Maxwell	05-06HouN	09-22-79	San Leandro, Cal.		R	R	6'3	210	18	6	2	2	0	0	1	1	0	3	2	.333	.833
Johjima, Kenji-Kenji	06SeaA	06-08-76	Nagasaki, Japan		R	R	6'	200	144	506	61	147	25	1	18	76	20	46	3	.291	.451
Johns, Keith-Robert Keith	98BosA	07-19-71	Callahan, Fla.		R	R	6'1	175	2	0	0	0	0	0	0	0	1	0	0	—	—
Johnson, Ben-Benjamin Joseph	05-06SDN	06-18-81	Memphis, Tenn.		R	R	6'1	200	89	195	29	46	13	3	7	25	25	59	3	.236	.441
Johnson, Bobby-Bobby Earl	81-83TexA	07-31-59	Dallas, Tex.		R	R	6'3	195	98	249	24	49	8	1	9	27	20	80	3	.197	.345
Johnson, Brian-Brian David	94-96SDN 97DetA 97-98SFN 99CinN 00KCA 01LAN	01-08-68	Oakland, Cal.		R	R	6'2	210	471	1415	132	351	60	6	49	196	80	268	1	.248	.403
Johnson, Charles-Charles Edward Jr.	94-98FlaN 98LAN 99-00BalA 00ChiA 01-02FlaN 03-04ColN 05TBA	07-20-71	Fort Pierce, Fla.		R	R	6'2	220	1188	3836	465	940	211	4	167	570	475	997	6	.245	.445
Johnson, Cliff-Clifford (Top Cat, Boomer, Heathcliff)	72-77HouN 77-79NYA 79-80CleA 80ChiN 81-82OakA 83-84TorA 85TexA 85-86TorA	07-22-47	San Antonio, Tex.		R	R	6'4	225	1369	3945	539	1016	188	10	196	699	568	719	4	.258	.459
Johnson, Dan-Daniel Ryan	05-06OakA	08-10-79	Coon Rapids, Minn.		L	R	6'2	220	200	661	84	170	34	1	24	95	90	97	0	.257	.421
Johnson, Erik-Erik Anthony	93-94SFN	10-11-65	Oakland, Cal.		R	R	5'11	175	9	18	1	4	2	0	0	0	0	5	0	.222	.333
Johnson, Gary-Gerald Clyde	03AnaA	10-29-75	Palo Alto, Cal.		L	L	6'3	210	5	8	1	3	1	0	0	1	0	1	0	.375	.500
Johnson, Howard-Howard Michael (HoJo)	82-84DetA 85-93NYN 94ColN 95ChiN	11-29-60	Clearwater, Fla.		B	R	5'11	190	1531	4940	760	1229	247	22	228	760	692	1053	231	.249	.446
Johnson, Keith-Keith	00AnaA	04-17-71	Hanford, Cal.		R	R	5'11	200	6	4	2	2	0	0	0	0	2	0	0	.500	.500
Johnson, Kelly-Kelly Andrew	05AtlN 06EJ	02-22-82	Austin, Tex.		L	R	6'1	205	87	290	46	70	12	3	9	40	40	75	2	.241	.397
Johnson, Lamar-Lamar	74-81ChiA 82TexA	09-02-50	Bessemer, Ala.		R	R	6'2	225	792	2631	294	755	122	12	64	381	211	307	22	.287	.415
Johnson, Lance-Kenneth Lance	87StLN 88-95ChiA 96-97NYN 97-99ChiN 00NYA	07-06-63	Cincinnati, Ohio		L	L	5'11	160	1447	5379	767	1565	175	117	34	486	352	384	327	.291	.386
Johnson, Larry-Larry Doby	72,74CleA 75-76MonN 78ChiA	04-17-55	Cleveland, Ohio		R	R	6'	184	12	26	1	5	2	0	0	1	2	8	0	.192	.269
Johnson, Mark-Mark Landon	98-02ChiA 03OakA 04MilN	09-12-75	Wheat Ridge, Colo.		L	R	6'0	185	322	917	114	199	37	4	16	81	123	195	8	.217	.318
Johnson, Mark-Mark Patrick	95-97PitN 98AnaA 99JL 00-02NYN	10-17-67	Worcester, Mass.		L	L	6'4	205	428	988	142	229	50	2	38	157	154	272	12	.232	.402
Johnson, Nick-Nicholas Robert	01-03NYA 04MonN 05-06WasN	09-19-78	Sacramento, Cal.		L	R	6'3	224	599	1973	323	536	133	3	76	297	355	414	25	.272	.458
Johnson, Randy-Randall Glenn (Rags)	82-84AtlN	06-10-56	Escondido, Cal.		R	R	6'1	185	204	484	55	129	21	0	6	53	47	52	5	.267	.347
Johnson, Randy-Randall Stuart	80ChiA 82MinA	08-18-58	Miami, Fla.		L	L	6'2	190	101	254	26	62	10	0	10	36	32	50	0	.244	.402
Johnson, Reed-Reed Cameron	03-06TorA	12-08-76	Riverside, Cal.		R	R	5'10	180	531	1808	280	520	101	12	40	220	103	328	24	.288	.423
Johnson, Ron-Ronald David (R.J.)	82-83KCA 84MonN	03-23-56	Long Beach, Cal.		R	R	6'3	215	22	46	4	12	2	0	0	2	7	6	0	.261	.304
Johnson, Ron-Rondin Allen	86KCA	12-16-58	Bremerton, Wash.		B	R	5'10	160	11	31	1	8	0	0	0	2	0	3	2	.258	.323
Johnson, Rontrez-Rontrez DeMon	03KCA	12-08-76	Marshall, Texas		R	R	5'10	160	8	3	3	1	0	0	0	0	0	2	0	.333	.333
Johnson, Roy-Roy Edward	82,84-85MonN	06-27-59	Parkin, Ark.		L	L	6'5	225	36	70	4	12	4	0	1	4	8	19	1	.171	.271
Johnson, Russ-William Russell	97-00HouN 00-02TBA 05NYA	02-22-73	Baton Rouge, La.		R	R	5'10	180	364	836	117	221	46	2	14	97	105	173	16	.264	.374
Johnson, Tim-Timothy Evald	73-78MilA 78-79TorA M98TorA	07-22-49	Grand Forks, N.D.		B	R	6'1	180	515	1269	116	283	27	13	0	84	88	231	18	.223	.265
Johnson, Tony-Anthony Clair (Ambee)	81MonN 82TorA	06-23-56	Memphis, Tenn.		R	R	6'3	195	72	99	19	23	2	1	3	14	11	26	3	.232	.364
Johnson, Wallace-Wallace Darnell	81-83MonN 83SFN 84,86-90MonN	12-25-56	Gary, Ind.		B	R	6'	185	428	569	52	145	17	6	5	59	52	58	19	.255	.332
Johnston, Greg-Gregory Bernard	79SFN 80-81MinN	02-12-55	Los Angeles, Cal.		L	L	6'	170	63	117	10	22	5	0	1	8	6	26	0	.188	.256
Johnstone, Jay-John William (Moon Man) Bats Both 66	66-70CalA 71-72ChiA 73OakA 74-78PhiN 78-79NYA 79SDN 80-82LAN 82-84ChiN 85LAN	11-20-45	Manchester, Conn.		L	R	6'1	185	1748	4703	578	1254	215	38	102	531	429	632	50	.267	.394
Jones, Adam-Adam LaMarque	06SeaA	08-01-85	San Diego, Cal.		R	R	6'2	200	32	74	6	16	4	0	1	8	2	22	3	.216	.311
Jones, Andruw-Andruw Rudolf	96-06AtlN	04-23-77	Willemstad, Curacao		R	R	6'1	210	1607	5836	962	1556	303	32	342	1023	647	1256	133	.267	.505
Jones, Bobby-Robert Oliver	74-75TexA 76-77CalA 79-80JL 81,83-86TexA	10-11-49	Elkton, Md.		L	L	6'	185	314	603	55	133	17	0	20	86	50	117	5	.221	.348
Jones, Chipper-Larry Wayne	93AtlN 94KJ 95-06AtlN	04-24-72	DeLand, Fla.		B	R	6'3	210	1761	6385	1188	1944	383	30	357	1197	1070	1006	129	.304	.542
Jones, Chris-Christopher Carlos	91CinN 92HouN 93-94ColN 95-96NYN 97SDN 98AriN 98SFN 00MilN	12-16-65	Utica, N.Y.		R	R	6'2	215	548	1021	155	257	43	11	30	131	74	287	26	.252	.404
Jones, Chris-Christopher Dale	85HouN 86SFN	07-13-57	Los Angeles, Cal.		L	L	6'	183	34	26	0	5	0	0	0	6	0	3	7	.192	.192
Jones, Darryl-Darryl Lee (D.J.)	79NYA	06-05-51	Meadville, Pa.		R	R	5'10	190	18	47	6	12	1	0	0	6	4	9	0	.255	.404
Jones, Dax-Dax Xenos	96SFN	04-25-70	San Diego, Calif.		R	R	5'10	195	34	58	7	10	0	2	0	2	3	11	3	.172	.293
Jones, Jacque-Jacque Dewayne	99-05MinA 06ChiN	04-25-75	San Diego, Cal.		L	L	5'10	195	1125	4025	565	1126	220	16	159	557	266	853	76	.280	.461
Jones, Jason-Jason Dewey	03TexA	10-17-76	Marietta, Ga.		B	R	6'3	210	40	107	11	23	4	0	0	11	10	21	0	.215	.355
Jones, Jeff-Jeffrey Raymond	83ChiN	10-22-57	Philadelphia, Pa.		R	R	6'	200	18	44	6	10	3	0	0	5	11	13	2	.227	.295
Jones, Lynn-Lynn Morris	79-83DetA 84-86KCA	01-01-53	Meadville, Pa.		R	R	5'9	175	527	947	109	239	34	5	9	91	73	86	13	.252	.321

USE NAME - GIVEN NAMES (NICKNAMES)	TEAM BY YEAR	BIRTH DATE	BIRTH PLACE	DEATH DATE	B	T	HGT	WGT	G	AB	R	H	2B	3B	HR	RBI	BB	SO	SB	BA	SA
Jones, Ricky-Ricky Miron	86BalA	06-04-58	Tupelo, Miss.		R	R	6'3	186	16	33	2	6	2	0	0	4	6	8	0	.182	.242
Jones, Ron-Ronald Glen	88-91PhiN	06-11-64	Seguin, Tex.	06-04-06	L	R	5'10	200	97	239	27	65	10	1	13	40	22	33	1	.272	.485
Jones, Ross-Ross A.	84NYN 86SeaA 87KCA	01-14-60	Miami, Fla.		R	R	6'2	185	67	145	12	32	5	2	0	11	8	23	1	.221	.283
Jones, Ruppert-Ruppert Sanderson	76KCA 77-79SeaA 80NYA 81-83SDN 84DetA 85-87CalA	03-12-55	Dallas, Tex.		L	L	5'10	170	1331	4415	643	1103	215	38	147	579	534	817	143	.250	.416
Jones, Terry-Terry Lee	96ColN 98-01MonN	02-15-71	Birmingham, Ala.		B	R	5'10	165	227	530	78	128	21	5	1	34	36	106	27	.242	.306
Jones, Tim-William Timothy	88-93StLN	12-01-62	Sumter, S.C.		L	R	5'10	175	252	685	45	113	25	1	1	28	45	81	15	.233	.295
Jones, Tracy-Tracy Donald	86-88CinN 88MonN 89SFN 89-90DetA 90-91SeaA	03-31-61	Inglewood, Cal.		R	R	6'3	210	493	1303	173	356	56	6	27	164	100	140	62	.273	.388
Jordan, Brian-Brian O'Neal 89-91 played in N.F.L.	92-98StLN 99-01AtlN 02-03LAN 04TexA 05-06AtlN	03-29-67	Baltimore, Md.		R	R	5'11	215	1456	5160	755	1454	267	37	184	821	353	842	119	.282	.455
Jordan, Kevin-Kevin Wayne	95-01PhiN	10-09-69	San Francisco, Cal.		R	R	6'1	200	560	1409	138	363	70	5	23	175	73	181	2	.258	.363
Jordan, Ricky-Paul Scott	88-94PhiN 96SeaA	05-26-65	Richmond, Cal.		R	R	6'3	210	677	2104	261	592	116	10	55	304	77	303	10	.281	.424
Jordan, Scott-Scott Alan	88CleA	05-27-63	Waco, Tex.		R	R	6'	178	14	18	0	2	0	0	0	2	0	6	1	.111	.111
Jorgensen, Mike-Michael	68,70-71NYN 72-77MonN 77OakA 78-79TexA 80-83NYN 83-84AtlN 84-85,M95StLN	08-16-48	Passaic, N.J.		L	L	6'	195	1633	3421	429	833	132	13	95	426	532	589	58	.243	.373
Jorgensen, Ryan-Ryan Wayne	05FlaN	05-04-79	Jacksonville, Fla.		R	R	6'2	220	4	4	0	0	0	0	0	0	0	3	0	.000	.000
Jorgensen, Terry-Terry Allen	89,92-93MinA	09-02-66	Kewaunee, Wis.		R	R	6'4	210	91	233	21	56	9	0	1	19	17	37	2	.240	.292
Jose (Andujar), Felix-Domingo Felix [Jose]	88-90OakA 90-92StLN 93-95KCA 00NYA 02-03AriN	05-08-65	Santo Domingo, D.R.		B	R	6'1	220	747	2527	322	708	135	14	54	324	203	507	102	.280	.409
Joshua, Von-Von Everett	69-71,73-74LAN 75-76SFN 76-77MilA 79LAN 80SDN	05-01-48	Oakland, Cal.		L	L	5'10	170	822	2234	277	610	87	31	30	184	108	338	55	.273	.380
Joyner, Wally-Wallace Keith	86-91CalA 92-95KCA 96-99SDN 00AtlN 01AnaA	06-16-62	Atlanta, Ga.		L	L	6'2	200	2033	7127	973	2060	409	26	204	1106	833	825	60	.289	.440
Jurak, Ed-Edward James (Lizard)	82-85BosA 88OakA 89SFN	10-24-57	Hollywood, Cal.		R	R	6'2	185	193	302	35	80	11	5	1	33	38	49	1	.265	.344
Justice, David-David Christopher	89-96AtlN 97-00CleA 00-01NYA 02OakA	04-14-66	Cincinnati, Ohio		L	L	6'3	200	1610	5625	929	1571	280	24	305	1017	903	999	53	.279	.500
Jutze, Skip-Alfred Henry	72StLN 73-76HouN 77SeaA	05-28-46	Queens, NY		R	R	6'	195	254	656	45	141	14	3	3	51	34	86	0	.215	.259
Kapler, Gabe-Gabriel Stefan	98-99DetA 00-02TexA 02-03ColN 03-06BosA	08-31-75	Hollywood, Cal.		R	R	6'2	205	850	2425	362	655	140	13	64	302	216	378	68	.270	.418
Karkovice, Ron-Ronald Joseph	86-97ChiA	08-08-63	Union, N.J.		R	R	6'1	215	939	2597	336	574	120	6	96	335	233	749	24	.221	.383
Karros, Eric-Eric Peter	91-02LAN 03ChiN 04OakA	11-04-67	Hackensack, N.J.		R	R	6'4	220	1755	6441	797	1724	324	11	284	1027	552	1167	59	.268	.454
Kata, Matt-Matthew John	03-05AriN 05PhiN	03-14-78	Avon Lake, Ohio		B	R	6'1	185	160	487	66	121	27	8	9	42	43	88	7	.248	.392
Kearney, Bob-Robert Henry (Buckshot, Sarge)	79SFN 81-83OakA 84-87SeaA	10-03-56	San Antonio, Tex.		R	R	6'	185	479	1356	131	316	66	3	27	133	67	235	9	.233	.346
Kearns, Austin-Austin Ryan	02-06CinN 06WasN	05-20-80	Lexington, Ky.		R	R	6'3	235	515	1805	281	479	104	8	79	299	247	462	22	.265	.463
Keatley, Greg-Gregory Steven (Keat)	81KCA	09-12-53	Princeton, W. Va.		R	R	6'2	200	2	0	0	0	0	0	0	0	0	0	0	—	—
Keedy, Pat-Charles Patrick	85CalA 87ChiA 89CleA	01-10-58	Birmingham, Ala.		R	R	6'4	220	29	59	10	12	4	0	3	4	4	19	1	.203	.424
Kelleher, Mick-Michael Dennis	72-73StLN 74HouN 75StLN 76-80ChiN 81-82DetA 82CalA	07-25-47	Seattle, Wash.		R	R	5'9	176	622	1081	106	230	32	6	0	65	74	133	9	.213	.253
Kelly, Kenny-Kenneth Alphonso	00TBA 05CinN	01-26-79	Plant City, Fla.		R	R	6'3	180	26	14	5	4	1	0	0	1	2	6	1	.286	.357
Kelly, Mike-Michael Raymond	94-95AtlN 96-97CinN 98TBA 99OakA	06-02-70	Los Angeles, Cal.		R	R	6'4	195	327	684	111	165	45	6	22	86	54	187	30	.241	.421
Kelly, Pat-Dale Patrick	80TorA	08-27-55	Santa Maria, Cal.		R	R	6'3	210	3	7	0	2	0	0	0	0	0	4	0	.286	.286
Kelly, Pat-Harold Patrick	67-68MinA 69-70KCA 71-76ChiA 77-80BalA 81-82NYA	07-30-44	Philadelphia, Pa.	10-02-05	L	L	6'1	190	1385	4338	620	1147	189	35	76	418	588	768	250	.264	.377
Kelly, Pat-Patrick Franklin	91-97NYA 98StLN 99TorA	10-14-67	Philadelphia, Pa.		R	R	6'	180	681	1988	253	495	109	11	36	217	145	425	61	.249	.369
Kelly, Roberto-Roberto Conrado [Gray] (93 known as Bobby Kelly)	87-92NYA 93-94CinN 94AtlN 95MonN 95LAN 96-97MinA 97SeaA 98-99TexA 00NYA	10-01-64	Panama City, Panama		R	R	6'2	200	1337	4797	687	1390	241	30	124	585	317	862	235	.290	.430
Kelly, Tom-Jay Thomas (Red)	75,M86-01MinA	08-15-50	Graceville, Minn.		L	L	5'11	185	49	127	11	23	5	0	1	11	15	22	0	.181	.244
Kelton, Dave-David Wayne	03-04ChiN	12-17-79	Dothan, Ala.		R	R	6'3	200	18	22	2	3	2	0	0	1	0	8	0	.136	.227
Kemp, Matt-Matthew Ryan	06LAN	09-23-84	Midwest City, Okla.		R	R	6'2	230	52	154	30	39	7	1	7	23	9	53	6	.253	.448
Kemp, Steve-Steven F.	77-81DetA 82ChiA 83-84NYA 85-86PitN 88CinN	08-07-54	San Angelo, Tex.		L	L	6'	195	1168	4068	581	1128	179	25	130	634	576	605	39	.278	.431
Kendall, Fred-Fred Lyn	69-76SDN 77CleA 78BosA 79-80SDN	01-31-49	Torrance, Cal.		R	R	6'1	180	877	2576	170	603	86	11	31	244	189	240	5	.234	.312
Kendall, Jason-Jason Daniel	96-04PitN 05-06OakA	06-26-74	San Diego, Cal.		R	R	6'	195	1545	5759	852	1735	307	30	68	574	557	496	159	.301	.400
Kendrick, Howie-Howard Joseph	06LAA	07-12-83	Jacksonville, Fla.		R	R	5'10	195	72	267	25	76	21	1	4	30	9	44	6	.285	.416
Kennedy, Adam-Adam Thomas	99StLN 00-04AnaA 05-06LAA	01-10-76	Riverside, Calif.		L	R	6'1	180	1025	3436	447	961	186	33	52	369	231	533	123	.280	.398
Kennedy, Junior-Junior Raymond	74,78-81CinN 82-83ChiN	08-09-50	Fort Gibson, Okla.		R	R	6'	185	447	1041	114	258	29	6	4	95	124	142	12	.248	.299
Kennedy, Terry-Terrence Edward	78-80StLN 81-86SDN 87-88BalA 89-91SFN	06-04-56	Euclid, Ohio		L	R	6'4	225	1491	4979	474	1313	244	12	113	628	365	855	6	.264	.386
Kent, Jeff-Jeffrey Franklin	92TorA 92-96NYN 96CleA 97-02SFN 03-04HouN 05-06LAN	03-07-68	Bellflower, Cal.		R	R	6'1	205	2041	7564	1200	2189	501	45	345	1380	719	1409	93	.289	.504
Keppinger, Jeff-Jeffrey Scott	04NYN 06KCA	04-21-80	Miami, Fla.		R	R	6'1	181	55	176	20	49	4	0	5	17	11	13	2	.278	.386
Kessinger, Keith-Keith Keith	93CinN	02-19-67	Forrest City, Ark.		B	R	6'2	185	11	27	4	7	1	0	1	3	4	4	0	.259	.407
Khalifa, Sammy-Sam	85-87PitN	12-05-63	Fontana, Cal.		R	R	5'10	170	164	488	39	107	20	3	2	37	53	86	5	.219	.285
Kiefer, Steve-Steven George	84-85OakA 86-88MilA 89NYA	10-18-60	Chicago, Ill.		R	R	6'	185	105	229	34	44	7	3	7	30	12	68	2	.192	.341
Kielty, Bobby-Robert Michael	01-03MinA 03TorA 04-06OakA	08-05-76	Fontana, Cal.		B	R	6'1	215	566	1705	247	437	102	6	52	241	238	346	21	.256	.415
Kieschnick, Brooks-Michael Brooks (See P73-03)	96-97ChiN 00CinN 01ColN 03-04MilN	06-06-72	Robstown, Tex.		L	L	6'4	220	485	1435	212	364	82	5	44	205	216	297	19	.254	.410
Kiger, Mark-Mark Winston (06OakA played in ALCS)		05-30-80	San Diego, Cal.		R	R	5'10	190													
Kimm, Bruce-Bruce Edward (Gamer)	76-77DetA 79ChiN 80ChiA M02ChiN	06-29-51	Cedar Rapids, Iowa		R	R	5'11	175	186	439	35	104	19	1	1	26	32	50	5	.237	.292
King, Jeff-Jeffrey Wayne	89-96PitN 97-99KCA	12-26-64	Marion, Ind.		R	R	6'1	180	1201	4262	600	1091	222	18	154	709	442	584	75	.256	.425
Kingery, Mike-Michael Scott	86KCA 87-89SeaA 90-91SFN 92OakA 94-95ColN 96PitN	03-29-61	St. James, Minn.		L	L	6'	180	819	2034	292	546	108	26	30	219	191	248	45	.268	.391
Kingman, Dave-David Arthur (Kong, Sky King, Big Bird)	71-74SFN 75-77NYN 77SDN 77CalA 77NYA 78-80ChiN 81-83NYN 84-86OakA	12-21-48	Pendleton, Ore.		R	R	6'6	210	1941	6677	901	1575	240	25	442	1210	608	1816	85	.236	.478
Kingsale, Eugene-Eugene Humphrey	96,98-01BalA 02SeaA 02SDN 03DetA	08-20-76	Solito, Aruba		B	R	6'3	190	211	533	65	134	17	5	3	53	39	96	15	.251	.319
Kinkade, Mike-Michael Arthur	98-00NYN 00-01BalA 02-03LAN	05-06-73	Livonia, Mich.		R	R	6'1	210	222	429	56	110	20	1	13	48	34	89	5	.256	.399
Kinsler, Ian-Ian Michael	06TexA	06-22-82	Tucson, Ariz.		R	R	6'	200	120	423	65	121	27	1	14	55	40	64	11	.286	.454
Kirby, Wayne-Wayne Leonard	91-96CleA 96-97LAN 98NYN	01-22-64	Williamsburg, Va.		L	R	5'11	185	516	1198	183	302	51	9	9	119	98	168	44	.252	.345
Kittle, Ron-Ronald Dale	82-86ChiA 86-87NYA 88CleA 89-90ChiA 90BalA 91ChiA	01-05-58	Gary, Ind.		R	R	6'4	215	843	2708	356	648	100	3	176	460	236	744	16	.239	.473
Klassen, Danny-Daniel Victor	98-00,02AriN 03DetA	09-22-75	Leamington, Canada		R	R	6'0	175	85	261	34	59	8	2	6	23	21	84	2	.226	.341
Klesko, Ryan-Ryan Anthony	92-99AtlN 00-06SDN	06-12-71	Westminster, Cal.		L	L	6'3	220	1620	5249	823	1470	316	30	272	943	771	1009	86	.280	.507
Kleven, Jay-Jay Allen	76NYN	12-04-49	Oakland, Cal.		R	R	6'2	200	2	5	0	1	0	0	0	0	0	0	0	.200	.200
Klutts, Mickey-Gene Ellis	76-78NYA 78-82OakA 83TorA	09-30-54	Montebello, Cal.		R	R	6'	190	199	536	49	129	26	1	14	59	34	101	1	.241	.371
Kmak, Joe-Joseph Robert	93MilA 95CinN	05-03-63	Napa, Cal.		R	R	6'	185	70	163	16	37	8	0	1	13	20	25	6	.227	.294
Knicely, Alan-Alan Lee (Nasty)	79-82HouN 83-85CinN 85PhiN 86StLN	05-19-55	Harrisonburg, Va.		R	R	6'	205	228	521	48	111	18	0	12	61	68	128	1	.213	.315
Knight, Ray-Charles Ray (Night Train)	74,77-81CinN 82-84HouN 84-86NYN 87BalA 88DetA M96-97,03CinN	12-28-52	Albany, Ga.		R	R	6'2	195	1495	4829	490	1311	266	27	84	595	343	579	14	.271	.390
Knoblauch, Chuck-Edward Charles	91-97MinA 98-01NYA 02KCA	07-07-68	Houston, Tex.		R	R	5'9	180	1632	6366	1132	1839	322	64	98	615	804	730	407	.289	.406
Knoedler, Justin-Justin Joseph	04-06SFN	07-17-80	Springfield, Ill.		R	R	6'2	210	14	18	0	2	0	0	0	1	1	6	0	.111	.111
Knorr, Randy-Randy Duane	91-95TorA 96-97HouN 98FlaN 99HouN 00TexA 01MonN	11-12-68	San Gabriel, Cal.		R	R	6'2	215	253	676	82	153	27	3	24	88	47	161	0	.226	.382
Knott, Jon-Jonathan David	04,06SDN	08-04-78	Menassas, Va.		R	R	6'3	220	12	17	1	3	2	0	0	1	1	6	0	.176	.294
Knox, John-John Clinton	72-75DetA	07-26-48	Newark, N.J.		R	R	6'	170	124	219	21	60	4	1	0	11	20	27	7	.274	.301
Koelling, Brian-Brian Wayne	93CinN	06-11-69	Cincinnati, Ohio		R	R	6'1	187	7	15	2	1	0	0	0	0	1	4	0	.067	.067
Komminsk, Brad-Brad Lynn	83-86AtlN 87MilA 89CleA 90SFN 90BalA 91OakA	04-04-61	Lima, Ohio		R	R	6'2	205	376	986	140	215	37	5	23	105	114	258	39	.218	.336
Konerko, Paul-Paul Henry	97-98LAN 98CinN 99-06ChiA	03-05-76	Providence, R.I.		R	R	6'3	210	1275	4561	677	1292	226	5	245	805	460	713	5	.283	.496
Koonce, Graham-Graham Clinton	03OakA	05-15-75	El Cajon, Cal.		L	L	6'4	225	6	8	0	1	0	0	0	0	1	5	0	.125	.250
Koskie, Corey-Cordel Leonard	98-04MinA 05TorA 06MilN	06-28-73	Anola, Canada		L	R	6'3	215	989	3399	516	936	223	13	124	506	458	795	71	.275	.458
Koslofski, Kevin-Kevin Craig	92-94KCA 96MilA	09-24-66	Decatur, Ill.		L	L	5'8	175	97	205	31	50	3	4	4	21	22	41	2	.244	.356
Kotchman, Casey-Casey John	04AnaA 05-06LAA	02-22-83	St. Petersburg, Fla.		L	L	6'3	210	114	321	29	73	13	0	8	43	29	42	4	.227	.343
Kotsay, Mark-Mark Steven	97-00FlaN 01-03SDN 04-06OakA	12-02-75	Whittier, Cal.		L	L	6'0	200	1284	4811	644	1369	265	41	102	540	411	569	88	.285	.420
Kouzmanoff, Kevin-Kevin	06CleA	07-25-81	Newport Beach, Cal.		R	R	6'2	210	16	56	4	12	2	0	3	11	5	12	0	.214	.411
Kowitz, Brian-Brian Mark	95AtlN	08-07-69	Baltimore, Md.		L	L	5'10	180	10	24	3	4	1	0	0	2	6	5	0	.167	.208
Kremers, Jimmy-James Edward	90AtlN	10-08-65	Little Rock, Ark.		L	R	6'3	205	29	73	7	8	1	0	0	2	6	20	0	.110	.192
Krenchicki, Wayne-Wayne Richard	79-81BalA 82-83CinN 83DetA 84-85CinN 86MonN	09-17-54	Trenton, N.J.		L	R	6'1	175	550	1063	107	283	46	5	15	124	106	141	7	.266	.359
Kreuter, Chad-Chadden Michael Bats Right 90 and part of 89	88-91TexA 92-94DetA 95SeaA 96-97ChiA 97AnaA 98ChiA 98AnaA 99KCA 00-02LAN 03TexA	08-26-64	Greenbrae, Cal.		B	R	6'2	195	944	2525	291	593	123	8	54	274	361	593	5	.237	.357
Kroeger, Josh-Joshua Jerez	04AriN	08-31-82	Davenport, Iowa		L	L	6'2	200	22	54	5	9	3	0	2	1	2	21	0	.167	.222
Krug, Gary-Gary Eugene (Gene)	81ChiN	02-15-55	Garden City, Kans.		L	L	6'4	207	7	15	2	6	1	0	0	2	1	0	0	.400	.400
Kruk, John-John Martin	86-89SDN 89-94PhiN 95ChiA	02-09-61	Charleston, W. Va.		L	L	5'10	220	1200	3897	582	1170	199	34	100	592	649	701	58	.300	.446
Krynzel, Dave-David Benjamin	04-05MilN	11-07-81	Dayton, Ohio		L	L	6'2	180	21	48	6	9	3	0	0	3	3	18	0	.188	.208
Kubel, Jason-Jason James	04,06MinA	05-25-82	Belle Fourche, S.D.		L	R	5'11	200	96	280	33	71	10	0	10	33	18	54	3	.254	.396

USE NAME - GIVEN NAMES (NICKNAMES) / TEAM BY YEAR	BIRTH DATE	BIRTH PLACE	DEATH DATE	B	T	HGT	WGT	G	AB	R	H	2B	3B	HR	RBI	BB	SO	SB	BA	SA
Kubski, Gil-Gilbert Thomas — 80CalA	10-12-54	Longview, Tex.		L	R	6'3	195	22	63	11	16	3	0	0	6	6	10	1	.254	.302
Kuiper, Duane-Duane Eugene — 74-81CleA 82-85SFN	06-19-50	Racine, Wis.		L	R	6'	173	1057	3379	329	917	91	29	1	263	248	255	52	.271	.316
Kunkel, Jeff-Jeffrey William — 84-90TexA 91KJ 92ChiN	03-25-62	West Palm Beach, Fla.		R	R	6'2	175	357	867	88	192	44	9	18	73	37	234	9	.221	.355
Kuntz, Rusty-Russell Jay — 79-83ChiA 83MinA 84-85DetA	02-04-55	Orange, Cal.		R	R	6'3	190	277	441	75	104	23	0	5	38	60	106	5	.236	.322
Kusick, Craig-Craig Robert — 73-79MinA 79TorA	09-30-48	Milwaukee, Wis.	09-27-06	R	R	6'3	225	497	1238	155	291	50	3	46	171	194	228	11	.235	.392
Kusyner, Art-Arthur William — 70ChiA 71-73CalA 76MilA 78KCA	12-19-45	Akron, Ohio		R	R	6'2	200	139	313	21	55	6	1	3	21	21	51	1	.176	.230
Kutcher, Randy-Randy Scott — 86-87SFN 88-90BosA	04-20-60	Anchorage, Alaska		R	R	5'10	175	244	448	83	102	25	6	10	40	36	112	13	.228	.377
Labandeira, Josh-John Joshua — 04MonN	02-25-79	Tulare, Cal.		R	R	5'7	180	7	14	0	0	0	0	0	0	0	4	0	.000	.000
LaCock, Pete-Ralph Pierre — 72-76ChiN 77-80KCA	01-17-52	Burbank, Cal.		L	L	6'2	205	715	1729	214	444	86	11	27	224	182	171	8	.257	.366
Lacy, Lee-Leondaus — 72-75LAN 76AtlN 76-78LAN 79-84PitN 85-87BalA	04-10-48	Longview, Tex.		R	R	6'1	190	1523	4549	650	1303	207	42	91	458	372	657	185	.286	.410
LaForest, Pete-Pierre Luc — 03,05TBA	01-27-78	Hull, Canada		L	R	6'2	210	44	112	5	19	5	0	1	10	7	37	0	.170	.241
LaFrancois, Roger-Roger Victor — 82BosA	08-02-56	Norwich, Conn.		R	R	6'2	210	8	10	1	4	1	0	0	1	0	0	0	.400	.500
Laga, Mike-Michael Russell — 82-86DetA 86-88StLN 89-90SFN	06-14-60	Ridgewood, N.J.		L	L	6'3	210	188	423	39	84	18	0	16	55	22	115	1	.199	.355
Lahoud, Joe-Joseph Michael — 68-71BosA 72-73MilA 74-76CalA 76TexA 77-78KCA	04-14-47	Danbury, Conn.		L	L	6'1	198	791	1925	239	429	68	12	65	218	309	339	20	.223	.372
Laird, Gerald-Gerald Lee — 03-06TexA	11-13-79	Westminster, Cal.		R	R	6'2	200	159	474	82	126	30	2	10	46	31	107	3	.266	.401
Lake, Steve-Steven Michael — 83-86ChiN 86-88StLN 89-92PhiN 93ChiN	03-14-57	Inglewood, Cal.		R	R	6'1	190	476	1125	89	267	41	5	18	108	43	159	1	.237	.331
Laker, Tim-Timothy John — 92-93,95MonN 96EJ 97BalA 98TBA 98-99PitN 01,03-04CleA 05TBA 06CleA	11-27-69	Encino, Cal.		R	R	6'2	215	282	651	66	147	28	2	11	79	44	162	5	.226	.326
Lamb, David-David Christian — 99TBA 00NYN 02MinA	06-06-75	West Hills. Calif.		B	R	6'2	165	69	139	19	30	5	1	1	13	11	21	0	.216	.288
Lamb, Mike-Michael Robert — 00-03TexA 04-06HouN	08-09-75	West Covina, Cal.		L	R	6'1	195	720	2110	313	591	105	13	57	273	171	325	7	.280	.423
Lampkin, Tom-Thomas Michael — 88CleA 90-92SDN 93MilA 95-96SFN 99SDN 99-01SeaA 02SDN	03-04-64	Cincinnati, Ohio		L	R	5'11	190	777	1796	224	422	78	8	56	236	193	286	23	.235	.381
Lancellotti, Rick-Richard Anthony (Lance) — 82SDN 86SFN 87-88JL 90BosA	07-05-56	Providence, R.I.		L	L	6'3	200	36	65	4	11	2	0	2	11	2	18	0	.169	.292
Landestoy, Rafael Silvaldo Camilo [Santana] — 77LAN 78-81HouN 81-83CinN 83-84LAN	05-28-53	Bani, Dom. Rep. Bats Right 77,79		B	R	5'10	180	596	1230	134	291	32	17	4	83	100	123	54	.237	.300
Landreaux, Ken-Kenneth Francis (General) — 77-78CalA 79-80MinA 81-87LAN	12-22-54	Los Angeles, Cal.		L	L	5'11	185	1264	4101	522	1099	180	45	91	479	299	421	142	.268	.400
Landrum, Ced-Cedric Bernard — 91ChiN 93NYN	09-03-63	Butler, Ala.		L	R	5'9	167	78	105	30	25	3	1	0	7	10	23	27	.238	.286
Landrum, Tito-Terry Lee — 80-83StLN 83BalA 84-87StLN 87LAN 88BalA	10-25-54	Joplin, Mo.		R	R	5'11	185	607	995	120	248	40	12	13	111	85	196	17	.249	.353
Lane, Jason-Jason Dean — 02-06HouN	12-22-76	Santa Rosa, Cal.		R	L	6'2	216	426	1037	147	261	59	7	53	162	107	227	9	.252	.475
Lane, Marvin-Marvin — 71-74,76DetA	01-18-50	Sandersville, Ga.		L	L	5'11	180	90	149	23	37	5	1	3	17	28	42	2	.207	.296
Langerhans, Ryan-Ryan David — 02-03,05-06AtlN	02-20-80	San Antonio, Texas		L	L	6'3	195	276	657	96	167	38	6	15	70	87	172	1	.254	.399
Lankford, Ray-Raymond Lewis — 90-01StLN 01-02SDN 04StLN	06-05-67	Los Angeles, Cal.		L	L	5'11	200	1701	5747	968	1561	356	54	238	874	828	1550	258	.272	.477
Lansford, Carney-Carney Ray — 78-80CalA 81-82BosA 83-92OakA	02-07-57	San Jose, Cal.		R	R	6'2	195	1862	7158	1007	2074	332	40	151	874	553	719	224	.290	.411
Lansford, Jody-Joseph Dale (Joe D) — 82-83SDN	01-15-61	San Jose, Cal.		R	R	6'5	225	25	30	7	6	0	0	1	5	0	7	0	.200	.300
Lansing, Mike-Michael Thomas — 93-97MonN 98-00ColN 00-01BosA	04-03-68	Rawlins, Wyo.		R	R	6'	190	1110	4150	554	1124	254	17	84	440	299	570	119	.271	.401
Larkin, Barry-Barry Louis — 86-04CinN	04-28-64	Cincinnati, Ohio		R	R	6'	195	2180	7937	1329	2340	441	76	198	960	939	817	379	.295	.444
Larkin, Gene-Eugene Thomas — 87-93MinA	10-24-62	Queens, N.Y.		B	R	6'3	212	758	2321	275	618	131	12	32	266	268	278	23	.266	.374
Larkin, Stephen-Stephen Karari — 98CinN	07-24-73	Cincinnati, Ohio		L	L	6'0	190	1	2	0	0	0	0	0	0	0	1	0	.333	.333
LaRocca, Greg-Gregory Mark — 00SDN 02-03CleA	11-10-72	Oswego, N.Y.		R	R	5'11	185	39	88	16	23	6	1	0	6	8	11	1	.261	.352
LaRoche, Adam-David Adam — 04-06AtlN	11-06-79	Orange Co., Cal.		L	L	6'3	180	400	1267	187	347	93	2	65	213	121	293	0	.274	.504
Larson, Brandon-Brandon John — 01-04CinN	05-24-76	San Angelo, Tex.		R	R	6'	210	109	291	29	52	11	0	8	37	35	86	4	.179	.299
LaRue, Jason-Michael Jason — 99-06CinN	03-19-74	Houston, Texas		R	R	5'11	200	715	2226	263	532	127	6	84	303	197	645	12	.239	.415
Latham, Chris-Christopher Joseph — 97-99MinA 01TorA 03NYA	05-26-73	Coeur D'Alene, Idaho		B	R	6'0	205	110	213	34	43	5	1	3	19	23	85	9	.202	.277
Laudner, Tim-Timothy Jon — 81-89MinA	06-07-58	Mason City, Iowa		R	R	6'3	212	734	2038	221	458	97	5	77	263	190	1053	3	.225	.391
Lawrence, Joe-Joseph Dudley — 02TorA	02-13-77	Lake Charles, La.		R	R	6'2	190	55	150	16	27	4	0	2	15	16	38	2	.180	.247
LaValliere, Mike-Michael Eugene (Spanky) — 84PhiN 85-86StLN 87-93PitN 93-95ChiA	08-18-60	Charlotte, N.C.		L	R	5'10	205	879	2473	185	663	109	5	18	294	321	244	5	.268	.338
Law, Rudy-Rudy Karl — 78,80LAN 82-85ChiA 86KCA	10-07-56	Waco, Tex.	Bats Both part of 87	L	L	6'2	175	749	2421	379	656	101	37	18	198	184	210	228	.271	.366
Law, Vance-Vance Aaron — 80-81PitN 82-84ChiA 85-87MonN 88-89ChiN 90JL 91OakA	10-01-56	Boise, Idaho		R	R	6'2	190	1212	3802	453	972	193	26	71	442	408	602	34	.256	.376
Lawless, Tom-Thomas James — 82,84ChiN 84MonN 85-88StLN 89-90TorA	12-19-56	Erie, Pa.		R	R	5'10	170	343	531	78	110	17	2	2	24	41	85	53	.207	.258
Lawton, Marcus-Marcus Dwayne — 89NYA	08-18-65	Gulfport, Miss.		B	R	6'1	163	10	14	1	3	0	0	0	0	3	1	1	.214	.214
Lawton, Matt-Matthew Hanks III — 95-01MinA 01NYN 02-04CleA 05PitN 05ChiN 05NYA 06SeaA	11-30-71	Gulfport, Miss.		L	L	5'9	185	1334	4763	756	1273	267	17	138	631	681	613	165	.267	.417
Leach, Jay-Jalal Donnell — 01SFN	03-14-69	San Francisco, Cal.		L	L	6'2	200	8	10	0	1	0	0	0	1	2	3	0	.100	.100
Leach, Rick-Richard Max — 81-83DetA 84-88TorA 89TexA 90SFN	05-04-57	Ann Arbor, Mich.		L	L	6'1	194	799	1719	205	460	100	10	18	183	176	217	8	.268	.369
LeCroy, Matt-Matthew Hanks — 00-05MinA 06WasN	12-13-75	Belton, S.C.		R	R	6'2	225	469	1368	145	358	67	1	60	218	123	328	0	.262	.444
Ledee, Ricky-Ricardo Alberto — 98-00NYA 00CleA 00-01TexA 02-04PhiN 04SFN 05-06LAN 06NYN	11-22-73	Ponce, Puerto Rico		L	L	6'2	200	838	1994	284	486	117	17	62	312	239	485	28	.244	.413
Ledesma, Aaron-Aaron David — 95NYN 97BalA 98-99TBA 00ColN	06-03-71	Union City, Cal.		R	R	6'2	210	284	754	94	223	38	4	2	76	44	111	11	.296	.365
Lee, Carlos-Carlos [Noriel] — 99-04ChiA 05-06MilN 06TexA	06-20-76	Aguadulce, Panama		R	R	6'2	230	1203	4570	720	1308	270	11	221	782	370	653	96	.286	.495
Lee, Derek-Derek Gerald — 93MinA	07-28-66	Chicago, Ill.		L	R	6'1	200	15	33	3	5	1	0	0	1	4	6	0	.152	.182
Lee, Derek-Derrek Leon — 97SDN 98-03FlaN 04-06ChiN	09-06-75	Sacramento, Cal.		R	R	6'5	240	1235	4258	671	1177	260	22	216	656	550	1036	86	.276	.500
Lee, (Lora), Manny-Manuel Lora [Lee] — 85-92TorA 93-94TexA 95StLN (92-95 known as Manuel Lee)	06-17-65	San Pedro de Mac. D.R.		B	R	5'9	170	922	2693	304	686	88	20	19	249	201	531	31	.255	.323
Lee, Terry-Terry James — 90-91CinN	03-13-62	San Francisco, Cal.		R	R	6'5	215	15	25	1	4	1	0	0	3	2	6	0	.160	.200
Lee, Travis-Travis Reynolds — 98-00AriN 00-02PhiN 03TBA 04NYA 05-06TBA	05-26-75	San Diego, Cal.		L	L	6'3	220	1099	3740	476	958	191	16	115	488	457	704	59	.256	.408
Leeper, Dave-Dave Dale — 84-85KCA	10-30-59	Santa Ana, Cal.		L	R	5'11	170	19	40	2	3	0	0	0	4	4	0	0	.075	.075
Lefebvre, Joe-Joseph Henry — 80NYA 81-83SDN 83-84PhiN 85KJ 86PhiN	02-22-58	Concord, N.H.		L	R	5'10	180	447	1091	139	281	52	13	31	130	139	204	11	.258	.414
LeFlore, Ron-Ronald A. — 74-79DetA 80MonN 81-82ChiA	06-16-48	Detroit, Mich.		R	R	6'	198	1099	4458	731	1283	172	57	59	353	363	888	455	.288	.392
Legg,Greg-Gregory Lynn — 86-87PhiN	04-21-60	San Jose, Cal.		R	R	6'1	180	14	22	3	9	1	0	0	1	0	4	0	.409	.545
Leius, Scott-Scott Thomas — 90-95MinA 96CleA 98-99KCA	09-24-65	Yonkers, N.Y.		R	R	6'3	195	557	1536	214	375	63	10	28	172	161	236	16	.244	.353
LeMaster, Johnnie-Johnnie Lee (Peanut, Bones) — 75-85SFN 85CleA 85PitN 870akA	06-19-54	Portsmouth, Ohio		R	R	6'2	180	1039	3191	320	709	109	19	22	229	241	564	94	.222	.289
Lemke, Mark-Mark Alan — 88-97AtlN 98BosA	08-13-65	Utica, N.Y.		B	R	5'9	165	1069	3230	349	795	125	15	32	270	348	341	11	.246	.324
Lemon, Chet-Chester Earl — 75-81ChiA 82-90DetA	02-12-55	Jackson, Miss.		R	R	6'	190	1988	6868	973	1875	396	61	215	884	749	1024	58	.273	.442
Lentine, Jim-James Matthew — 78-80StLN 80DetA	07-16-54	Los Angeles, Cal.		R	R	5'11	175	95	205	22	54	9	1	1	20	31	38	3	.263	.332
Lennon, Patrick-Patrick Orlando — 91-92SeaA 96KCA 97OakA 98-99TorA	04-27-68	Whiteville, N.C.		R	R	6'2	220	91	189	25	50	14	1	2	22	27	59	0	.265	.381
Leon, Jose-Jose Geraldo [Vega] — 02-04BalA	12-08-76	Caguas, P.R.		R	R	6'	213	88	209	18	47	5	0	5	18	8	57	1	.225	.321
Leonard, Jeff-Jeffrey (Hac Man) — 77LAN 78-81HouN 81-88SFN 88MilA 89-90SeaA	09-22-55	Philadelphia, Pa.		R	R	6'3	200	1415	5045	614	1342	223	37	144	723	342	1000	163	.266	.411
Leonard, Mark-Mark David — 90-92SFN 93BalA 94-95SFN	08-14-64	Mountain View, Cal.		L	R	6'1	205	168	321	37	73	18	2	8	41	42	75	0	.227	.371
Leone, Justin-Justin Paul — 04SeaA 06SDN	07-09-77	Las Vegas, Nev.		R	R	6'1	210	32	103	15	22	5	0	6	13	9	32	1	.214	.437
Lesher, Brian-Brian Herbert — 96-98OakA 00SeaA 02TorA	03-05-71	Belgium		R	L	6'5	225	108	263	31	59	10	2	9	38	19	65	5	.224	.380
Levis, Jesse-Jesse — 92-95CleA 96-97MilA 98MilN 99CleA 01MilN	04-16-68	Philadelphia, Pa.		L	R	5'9	195	319	654	66	167	23	1	6	60	76	66	2	.255	.307
Lewis, Darren-Darren Joel — 90OakA 91-95SFN 95CinN 96-97ChiA 97LAN 98-01BosA 02ChiN	08-28-67	Berkeley, Cal.		R	R	6'	185	1354	4081	607	1021	137	37	27	342	403	514	247	.250	.322
Lewis, Fred-Frederick Deshaun — 06SFN	12-09-80	Hattiesburg, Miss.		L	L	6'1	195	13	11	5	5	1	0	0	2	0	3	0	.455	.545
Lewis, Mark-Mark David — 91-94CleA 95CinN 96DetA 97SFN 98PhiN 99-00CinN 00BalA 01CleA	11-30-69	Hamilton, Ohio		R	R	6'1	195	902	2795	320	736	155	13	48	306	196	511	29	.263	.380
Leyritz, Jim-James Joseph (The King) — 90-96NYA 97AnaA 97TexA 98BosA 98-99SDN 99-00NYA 00LAN	12-27-63	Lakewood, Ohio		R	R	6'	205	903	2527	325	667	107	2	90	387	337	581	7	.264	.415
Lezcano, Carlos-Carlos Manuel [Rubio] — 80-81ChiN	09-30-55	Arecibo, P.R.		R	R	6'2	185	49	102	16	19	4	1	3	14	11	33	1	.186	.333
Lezcano, Sixto-Sixto Joaquin [Curras] (Tato) — 74-80MilA 81StLN 82-83SDN 83-84PhiN 85PitN	11-28-53	Arecibo, P.R.		R	R	5'11	190	1291	4134	560	1122	184	34	148	591	576	768	37	.271	.440
Lickert,John-John Wilbur (Lick) — 81BosA	04-04-60	Pittsburgh, Pa.		R	R	5'10	182	1	0	0	0	0	0	0	0	0	0	0	—	—
Liddell, Dave-David Alexander — 90NYN	06-15-66	Glendale, Cal.		R	R	6'2	195	1	1	1	1	0	0	0	0	0	0	0	1.000	1.000
Lieberthal, Mike-Michael Scott — 94-06PhiN	01-18-72	Glendale, Cal.		R	R	6'	190	1174	4141	528	1137	255	10	150	609	331	560	8	.275	.450
Liefer, Jeff-Jeffery David — 99-02ChiA 03MonN 03TBA 04MilN 05CleA	08-17-74	Fontana, Calif.		L	R	6'2	205	288	779	80	179	36	1	31	113	56	223	2	.230	.398
Linares (de la Cruz), Ruffino-Ruffino [Linares] — 81-82,84AtlN 85CalA	02-28-51	San Pedro de Mac. D.R	05-16-98	R	R	6'	170	207	545	66	147	21	3	11	63	24	74	15	.270	.380
Lind, Adam-Adam Alan — 06TorA	07-17-83	Anderson, Ind.		L	L	6'2	195	18	60	6	8	3	0	2	8	5	12	0	.367	.600
Lind, Jack-Jackson Hugh — 74-75MilA	06-08-46	Denver, Colo.		B	R	6'	170	26	37	5	5	2	0	0	1	5	14	1	.135	.189
Lind, Jose-Jose [Salgado] (Chico) — 87-92PitN 93-95KCA 95ChiA 93HouN	05-01-64	Toabaja, P.R.		R	R	5'11	180	1044	3677	368	935	145	27	9	324	215	370	62	.254	.316
Lindeman, Jim-James William (Lindy) — 86-89StLN 90DetA 91-92PhiN 93HouN 94NYN	01-10-62	Evanston, Ill.		R	R	6'1	200	351	676	82	165	34	1	21	89	42	173	4	.244	.391

USE NAME - GIVEN NAMES (NICKNAMES)	TEAM BY YEAR	BIRTH DATE	BIRTH PLACE	DEATH DATE	B	T	HGT	WGT	G	AB	R	H	2B	3B	HR	RBI	BB	SO	SB	BA	SA
Linden, Todd-Todd Anthony	03-06SFN	06-30-80	Edmonds, Wash.		B	R	6'3	210	155	318	43	71	14	2	7	25	25	89	4	.223	.346
Lindsey, Bill-William Donald	87ChiA	04-12-60	Staten Island, N.Y.		R	R	6'3	195	9	16	2	3	0	0	0	1	0	3	0	.188	.188
Lindsey, Doug-Michael Douglas	91,93PhiN 93ChiA	09-22-67	Austin, Tex.		R	R	6'2	220	5	6	0	1	0	0	0	0	0	4	0	.167	.167
Lindsey, Rodney-Rodney Lee	00DetA	01-28-76	Opelika, Ala.		R	R	5'8	175	11	3	6	1	1	0	0	0	0	1	2	.333	.667
Liniak, Cole-Cole Edward	99-00CinN	08-23-76	Encinitas, Calif.		R	R	6'1	190	15	32	3	7	2	0	0	2	1	6	0	.219	.281
Lintz, Larry-Larry C. (Candy Man)	73-75MonN 75StLN 76-77OakA 78CleA	10-10-49	Martinez, Cal.		B	R	5'10	150	350	616	137	140	13	1	0	27	97	101	128	.227	.252
Liriano, Nelson-Nelson Arturo [Bonilla]	87-90TorA 90MinA 91KCA 93-94ColN 95-96PitN 97LAN 98ColN	06-03-64	Puerto Plata, D.R.		B	R	5'10	165	823	2216	296	576	105	27	25	240	212	300	59	.260	.366
Lis, Joe-Joseph Anthony	70-72PhiN 73-74MinA 74-76CleA 77SeaA	08-15-46	Somerville, N.J.		R	R	6'	195	356	780	96	182	31	1	32	92	106	209	1	.233	.399
Lisi, Rick-Riccardo Patrick Emilio	81TexA	03-17-56	Halifax, Canada		R	R	6'	180	9	16	4	5	0	0	0	1	4	0	0	.313	.313
Listach, Pat-Patrick Alan	92-96MilA 96NYA 97HouN	09-12-67	Natchitoches, La.		B	R	5'9	170	503	1772	250	444	63	13	5	143	167	338	116	.251	.309
Little, Bryan-Bryan Alan	85-86ChiA 86NYA	10-08-59	Houston, Tex.		B	R	5'11	155	327	922	126	226	37	5	3	77	120	79	8	.245	.306
Little, Mark-Mark Travis	98StLN 01-02ColN 02NYN 02AriN 04CleA	07-11-72	Edwardsville, Ill.		R	R	6'0	195	148	247	46	61	11	3	3	22	18	66	8	.247	.352
Little, Scott-Dennis Scott	89PitN	01-19-63	East St. Louis, Ill.		R	R	6'	190	3	4	1	1	0	0	0	0	0	1	0	.250	.250
Littlejohn, Dennis-Dennis Gerald (Johnny)	78-80SFN	10-04-54	Santa Monica, Cal.		R	R	6'2	205	78	222	17	45	7	1	1	15	28	53	0	.203	.257
Littleton, Larry-Larry Marvin	81CleA	04-03-54	Charlotte, N.C.		R	R	6'	190	26	23	2	0	0	0	0	1	3	6	0	.000	.000
Litton, Greg-Jon Gregory	89-92SFN 93SeaA 94BosA	07-13-64	New Orleans, La.		R	R	6'	175	374	809	78	195	43	5	13	97	58	167	1	.241	.355
Livingstone, Scott-Scott Louis	91-94DetA 94-97SDN 97StLN 98MonN	07-15-65	Dallas, Tex.		L	R	6'	195	673	1533	163	431	76	4	17	177	89	189	10	.281	.369
Lockhart, Keith-Keith Virgil	94SDN 95-96KCA 97-02AtlN 03SDN	11-10-64	Whittier, Cal.		L	R	5'10	170	979	2268	290	591	117	17	44	268	195	268	30	.261	.385
Locklear, Gene-Gene (Chief)	73CinN 73-76SDN 76-77NYA	07-19-49	Lumberton, N.C.		L	R	5'10	170	292	595	76	163	24	4	9	66	55	87	13	.274	.373
LoDuca, Paul-Paul Anthony	98-04LAN 04-05FlaN 06NYN	04-12-72	Brooklyn, N.Y.		R	R	5'10	193	896	3274	421	949	195	7	71	412	227	251	17	.290	.419
Lofton, James-James O'Neal	01BosA	03-06-74	Los Angeles, Cal.		B	R	5'9	170	8	26	1	5	0	0	0	1	1	4	2	.192	.231
Lofton, Kenny-Kenneth	91HouN 92-96CleA 97AtlN 98-01CleA 02ChiA 02SFN 03PitN 03ChiN 04NYA 05PhiN 06LAN	05-31-67	East Chicago, Ind.		L	L	6'	180	1967	7630	1442	2283	358	110	123	743	889	965	599	.299	.423
Logan, Nook-Exavier Prente	04-05DetA 06WasN	11-28-79	Natchez, Miss.		B	R	6'2	180	203	545	72	147	20	8	2	35	40	96	33	.270	.347
Lois (Louis), Albert-Alberto [Pie]	78-79PhiN	05-06-56	Hato Mayor, Dom. Rep.		R	R	5'9	175	14	4	6	1	0	1	0	0	0	1	1	.250	.750
Loman, Doug-Douglas Edward	84-85MilA	05-09-58	Bakersfield, Cal.		L	L	6'	185	47	142	23	35	7	2	2	19	16	19	0	.246	.366
Lomasney, Steve-Steven James	99BosA	08-29-77	Melrose, Mass.		R	R	6'	185	1	2	0	0	0	0	0	0	0	1	0	.000	.000
Lombard, George-George Paul	98-00,02AtlN 02DetA 03TBA 06WasN	09-14-75	Atlanta		L	R	6'0	208	144	350	55	77	12	3	8	21	27	111	23	.220	.340
Lombardi, Phil-Phillip Arden	86-87NYA 89NYN	02-20-63	Abilene, Tex.		R	R	6'	200	43	92	10	22	4	0	3	9	9	17	0	.239	.380
Lombardozzi, Steve-Stephen Paul	85-88MinA 89-90HouN	04-26-60	Malden, Mass.		R	R	6'	180	446	1264	153	294	61	12	20	107	131	206	13	.233	.347
Loney, James-James Anthony	06LAN	05-07-84	Houston, Tex.		L	L	6'2	220	48	102	20	29	6	5	4	18	8	10	1	.284	.559
Long, Ryan-Ryan Marcus	97KCA	02-07-73	Houston, Tex.		R	R	6'2	215	6	9	2	2	0	0	0	2	0	1	0	.222	.222
Long, Terrence-Terrence Deon	99NYN 00-03OakA 04SDN 05KCA 06NYA	02-29-76	Montgomery, Ala.		L	L	6'1	200	890	3068	428	824	166	21	69	376	227	460	27	.269	.404
Longmire, Tony-Anthony Eugene	93-95PhiN 96BW	08-12-68	Vallejo, Cal.		L	R	6'1	197	139	256	32	73	13	0	3	37	21	47	3	.285	.391
Lopes, Davey-David Earl	72-81LAN 82-84OakA 84-86ChiN 86-87HouN M00-02MilN	05-03-45	East Providence, R.I.		R	R	5'9	175	1812	6354	1023	1671	232	50	155	614	833	852	557	.263	.388
Lopez, Carlos-Carlos Antonio [Morales] (The Merry Mariner from Mazatlan)	76CalA 77SeaA 78BalA	09-27-48	Mazatlan, Mexico		R	R	6'	190	237	500	61	130	24	1	12	54	25	98	23	.260	.384
Lopez, Felipe-Felipe Jr.	01-02TorA 03-06CinN 06WasN	05-12-80	Bayamon, P.R.		B	R	6'1	185	576	2117	314	554	106	19	56	238	226	506	77	.262	.409
Lopez, Javy-Javier [Torres]	92-03AtlN 04-06BalA 06BosA	11-05-70	Ponce, P.R.		R	R	6'3	210	1503	5319	674	1527	267	19	260	864	357	969	8	.287	.491
Lopez, Jose-Jose Celestino	04-06SeaA	11-24-83	Barcelona, Venezuela		R	R	6'2	170	262	1000	124	265	60	8	17	126	40	136	9	.265	.392
Lopez, Luis-Luis Antonio	90LAN 91CleA	09-01-64	Brooklyn, N.Y.		R	R	6'1	190	41	88	7	18	4	1	0	7	4	9	0	.205	.273
Lopez, Luis Manuel [Santos]	93-94SDN 95EJ 96SDN 97-99NYN 00-02MilN 02,04BalA 05CinN	09-04-70	Cidra, P.R.		B	R	5'11	175	721	1620	171	390	85	7	22	151	100	343	10	.241	.343
Lopez, Luis-Luis Jr.	01TorA 04MonN	10-05-73	Brooklyn, N.Y.		R	R	6'	205	52	145	10	33	4	0	3	10	8	25	0	.228	.317
Lopez, Mendy-Mendy [Aude]	98-99KCA 00FlaN 01HouN 01-02PitN 03-04KCA	10-15-73	Santo Domingo, D.R.		R	R	6'2	195	190	422	45	102	18	5	6	40	27	106	7	.242	.351
Lopez, Mickey-Raymond Michael	04SeaA	11-17-73	Miami, Fla.		R	R	5'9	170	6	4	1	1	0	0	0	0	1	0	0	.250	.250
Lopez, Pedro-Pedro Michel	05ChiA	04-28-84	Moca, Dom. Rep.		R	R	6'1	160	2	7	1	2	0	0	0	2	0	1	0	.286	.286
Loretta, Mark-Mark David	95-97MilA 98-02MilN 02HouN 03-05SDN 06BosA	08-14-71	Santa Monica, Cal.		R	R	6'	190	1385	4910	670	1466	263	20	68	525	462	513	45	.299	.402
Loucks, Scott-Scott Gregory (Scotty)	80-83HouN 85PitN	11-11-56	Anchorage, Alaska		R	R	5'11	180	73	80	15	21	4	0	0	4	7	28	7	.263	.313
Loviglio, Jay-John Paul	80PhiN 81-82ChiA 83CinN	05-30-56	Freeport, N.Y.		B	R	5'9	160	46	52	17	10	0	0	0	4	3	6	5	.192	.192
Lovitto, Joe-Joseph	72-75TexA	01-06-51	San Pedro, Cal.	05-19-01	B	R	6'	190	306	763	70	165	22	4	4	53	80	113	22	.216	.271
Lovullo, Torey-Salvatore Anthony	88-89DetA 91NYA 93CalA 94SeaA 96OakA 98CleA 99PhiN	07-25-65	Santa Monica, Cal.		B	R	6'	185	303	737	80	165	35	1	15	60	80	121	9	.224	.335
Lowell, Mike-Michael Averett	98NYA 99-05FlaN 06BosA	02-24-74	San Juan, P.R.		R	R	6'4	205	1142	4142	557	1132	288	4	163	658	401	590	23	.273	.463
Lowenstein, John-John Lee (Steiner)	70-77CleA 78Tex 79-85BalA	01-27-47	Wolf Point, Mont.		L	R	6'1	175	1368	3476	510	881	137	18	116	441	446	596	128	.253	.403
Lowery, Terrell-Quenton Terrell	97-98ChiN 99TBA 00SFN	10-25-70	Oakland, Cal.		R	R	6'3	195	123	248	42	70	20	1	3	23	32	71	2	.282	.407
Lowry (Lowrey), Dwight-Dwight	84,86-87DetA 88MinA	10-23-57	Lumberton, N.C.	07-10-97	L	R	6'3	210	108	227	29	62	8	0	5	26	20	38	0	.273	.374
Lozado, Willie-William	84MilA	05-12-59	Brooklyn, N.Y.		R	R	6'	166	43	107	15	29	8	1	0	20	12	23	0	.271	.411
Lubratich, Steve-Steven George	81,83CalA	05-01-55	Oakland, Cal.		R	R	6'	170	64	177	14	37	10	0	0	8	4	19	1	.209	.266
Ludwick, Ryan-Ryan Andrew	02-03TexA 03-05CleA	07-13-78	Satellite Beach, Fla.		R	R	6'3	205	104	334	38	79	16	1	14	44	28	99	4	.237	.416
Lugo, Julio-Julio Cesar	00-03HouN 03-06TBA 06LAN	11-16-75	Santa Cruz de Barahona, D.R.		R	R	6'1	170	920	3385	521	936	172	25	68	336	309	637	139	.277	.402
Lukachyk, Rob-Robert James	96MonN	07-24-68	Jersey City, N.J.		L	R	6'	185	2	2	0	0	0	0	0	1	0	0	0	.000	.000
Luke, Matt-Matthew Clifford	96NYA 98LAN 98CleA 98LAN 99AnaA	02-26-71	Long Beach, Cal.		L	L	6'5	220	123	269	39	65	12	1	15	40	19	70	2	.242	.461
Lum, Mike-Michael Ken-Wai	67-75AtlN 76-78CinN 79-81AtlN 81ChiN	10-27-45	Honolulu, Hawaii		L	L	6'	180	1517	3554	404	877	128	20	90	431	366	506	13	.247	.385
Luna, Hector-Hector Adrien	04-06StLN 06CleA	02-01-80	Monte Cristi, D.R.		R	R	6'1	170	260	660	92	182	38	6	10	78	49	122	21	.276	.397
Lunar, Fernando-Fernando Jose	00AtlN 00-02BalA	05-25-77	Cantaura, Venezuela		R	R	6'1	190	97	237	13	53	8	0	2	22	10	51	0	.224	.257
Lunsford, Trey-James Lewis III	02-03SFN	05-25-79	Odessa, Texas		R	R	6'1	195	4	4	0	2	0	0	0	1	0	1	0	.500	.750
Lunstedt, Tom-Thomas Robert	73-74ChiN 75MinA	04-10-49	Davenport, Iowa		L	L	5'10	165	35	52	4	6	1	0	0	2	4	13	0	.115	.135
Lusader, Scott-Scott Edward	87-90DetA 91NYA	09-30-64	Chicago, Ill.		L	R	5'10	180	86	213	24	54	9	2	4	21	16	42	0	.254	.371
Luuloa, Keith-Keith H.M.	00AnaA	12-24-74	Honolulu, Hawaii		R	R	6'	185	6	18	3	6	0	0	0	2	0	3	0	.333	.333
Luzinski, Greg-Gregory Michael (Bull)	70-80PhiN 81-84ChiA	11-22-50	Chicago, Ill.		R	R	6'1	225	1821	6505	880	1795	344	24	307	1128	845	1495	37	.276	.478
Lyden, Mitch-Mitchell Scott	93FlaN	12-14-64	Portland, Ore.		R	R	6'3	225	6	10	2	3	0	0	1	1	0	3	0	.300	.600
Lydy, Scott-Donald Scott	93OakA	10-26-68	Mesa, Ariz.		R	R	6'5	195	41	102	11	23	4	0	1	7	8	39	2	.225	.333
Lynn, Fred-Fredric Michael	74-80BosA 81-84CalA 85-88BalA 88-89DetA 90SDN	02-03-52	Chicago, Ill.		L	L	6'1	190	1969	5589	1063	1960	388	43	306	1111	857	1116	72	.283	.484
Lyons, Barry-Barry Stephen	86-90NYN 90-91LAN 91CalA 95ChiA	06-03-60	Biloxi, Miss.		R	R	6'1	205	253	628	53	150	26	2	15	89	29	92	0	.239	.358
Lyons, Billy-William Allen	83-84StLN	04-26-58	Alton, Ill.		R	R	6'1	175	88	133	16	26	4	1	0	10	24	6	0	.195	.241
Lyons, Steve-Stephen John	85-86BosA 86-90ChiA 91BosA 92AtlN 92MonN 92-93BosA	06-03-60	Tacoma, Wash.		L	R	6'3	200	853	2162	264	545	100	17	19	196	156	364	42	.252	.340
Maas, Kevin-Kevin Christian	90-93NYA 95MinA	01-20-65	Castro Valley, Cal.		L	L	6'3	205	406	1248	171	287	43	1	65	169	182	310	10	.230	.422
Mabry, John-John Steven	94-98StLN 99-00SeaA 00SDN 01StLN 01FlaN 02PhiN 02OakA 03SeaA 04-05StLN 06CinN	10-17-70	Wilmington, Del.		L	R	6'4	205	1294	3375	378	894	182	6	95	441	279	707	7	.265	.407
Macfarlane, Mike-Michael Andrew	87-94KCA 95BosA 96-98KCA 98-99OakA	04-12-64	Stockton, Cal.		R	R	6'1	205	1164	3602	458	906	221	17	129	514	295	700	12	.252	.430
Macha, Ken-Kenneth Edward	74,77-78PitN 79-80MonN 81TorA M03-06OakA	09-29-50	Monroeville, Pa.		R	R	6'3	210	180	380	30	98	17	1	1	35	39	68	4	.258	.324
Macha, Mike-Michael William	79AtlN 80TorA	02-17-54	Victoria, Tex.		R	R	5'11	215	11	21	2	2	0	0	0	1	1	6	0	.095	.095
Machado, Alejandro-Alejandro Jose	05BosA	04-26-82	Caracas, Venezuela		B	R	6'	185	10	5	4	1	1	0	0	0	6	12	0	.200	.400
Machado, Andy-Anderson Javier	03PhiN 04-06CinN 05ColN	01-25-81	Caracas, Venezuela		B	R	5'11	165	24	68	7	15	6	0	1	6	12	32	1	.221	.324
Machado, Robert-Robert Alexis	96-98ChiA 99MonN 00SeaA 01-02ChiN 02MilN 03-04BalA	06-03-73	Puerto Cabello, Venez.		R	R	6'1	212	253	636	66	146	36	2	11	61	45	135	0	.230	.344
Machemer, Dave-David Ritchie (Mac)	78CalA 79DetA	05-24-51	St. Joseph, Mich.		R	R	5'10	170	29	48	14	11	4	0	0	4	5	3	0	.229	.333
Macias, Jose-Jose Prado [Salazar]	99-02DetA 02-03MonN 04-05ChiN	01-25-72	Panama City, Panama		B	R	5'10	185	659	1646	201	422	77	17	26	173	93	243	43	.256	.377
Mack, Quinn-Quinn David		09-11-65	Los Angeles, Cal.		L	L	5'10	185	3	21	1	5	0	0	0	2	1	3	2	.238	.381
Mack, Shane-Shane Lee	87-88SDN 90-94MinA 95-96JL 97BosA 98OakA 98KCA	12-07-63	Los Angeles, Cal.		R	R	6'	190	923	2857	436	853	155	28	80	398	256	509	90	.299	.456
Mackanin, Pete-Peter	73-74TexA 75-77MonN 78-79PhiN 80-81MinA M05PitN	08-01-51	Chicago, Ill.		R	R	6'2	190	548	1570	161	355	63	12	30	141	76	290	27	.226	.339
Macko, Steve-Steven Joseph (L'il Mac)	79-80ChiN 81IL	09-06-54	Burlington, Iowa	11-15-81	R	R	5'10	165	25	60	4	15	3	1	0	5	4	11	0	.250	.300
Mackowiak, Rob-Robert William	01-05PitN 06ChiA	06-20-76	Oak Lawn, Ill.		L	R	5'10	190	705	1982	260	519	96	16	57	244	193	498	45	.262	.413
Maclin, Lonnie-Lonnie Lee	93StLN	02-17-67	Clayton, Mo.		L	L	5'11	185	11	13	3	1	0	0	0	1	0	6	2	.077	.077
Maddox, Elliott-Elliott	70DetA 71WasA 72-73TexA 74-76NYA 77BalA	12-21-47	East Orange, N.J.		R	R	5'10	180	1029	2843	340	742	121	16	18	234	409	358	60	.261	.334
Maddox, Garry-Garry Lee (The Secretary of Defense)	72-75SFN 75-86PhiN	09-01-49	Cincinnati, Ohio		R	R	6'3	190	1749	6331	777	1802	337	62	117	754	323	781	248	.285	.413
Maddox, Jerry-Jerry Glenn (Dog)	78AtlN	07-28-53	Whittier, Cal.		R	R	6'2	200	7	14	1	3	0	0	0	1	1	2	0	.214	.214
Madison, Scotti-Charles Scott	85-86DetA 87-88KCA 89CinN	09-12-59	Pensacola, Fla.		R	R	5'11	185	55	135	11	22	5	0	1	8	11	30	0	.163	.253
Madlock, Bill-Bill (Mad Dog)	73TexA 74-76ChiN 77-79SFN 79-85PitN 85-87LAN 87DetA	01-12-51	Memphis, Tenn.		R	R	5'11	200	1806	6594	920	2008	348	34	163	860	605	510	174	.305	.442
Magadan, Dave-David Joseph	86-92NYN 93SeaA 93FlaN 95HouN 96ChiN 97-98OakA 99-01SDN	09-30-62	Tampa, Fla.		L	R	6'3	205	1582	4159	516	1197	218	13	42	495	718	546	11	.288	.377

USE NAME - GIVEN NAMES (NICKNAMES)	TEAM BY YEAR	BIRTH DATE	BIRTH PLACE	DEATH DATE	B	T	HGT	WGT	G	AB	R	H	2B	3B	HR	RBI	BB	SO	SB	BA	SA
Magallanes, Ever-Everardo [Espinoza]	91CleA	11-06-65	El Sauz, Mexico		L	R	5'10	165	3	2	0	0	0	0	0	0	0	1	1	0	.000	.000
Magee, Wendell-Wendell Errol Jr.	96-99PhiN 00-02DetA	08-03-72	Hattiesburg, Miss.		R	R	6'	225	386	1086	120	268	52	8	24	122	69	204	7	.247	.376
Magrann, Tom-Thomas Joseph	89CleA	12-09-63	Hollywood, Fla.		R	R	6'3	180	9	10	0	0	0	0	0	0	0	4	0	.000	.000
Magruder, Chris-Christopher James	01TexA 02-03CleA 04-05MilN	04-26-77	Tacoma, Wash.		B	R	5'11	200	270	540	67	119	32	3	11	56	34	120	5	.220	.352
Mahay, Ron-Ronald Matthew (See P73-06)	95,97-98BosA 99-00OakA 00FlaN 01-02ChiN 03-06TexA	06-28-71	Crestwood, Ill.		L	L	6'2	185	117	27	3	6	3	0	0	3	1	8	0	.222	.444
Mahlberg, Greg-Gregory John	78-79TexA	08-08-52	Milwaukee, Wis.		R	R	5'10	178	8	18	2	2	0	0	1	1	2	4	0	.111	.278
Mahoney, Mike-Michael John	00,02ChiN 05StlN	12-05-72	Des Moines, Iowa		R	R	6'1	200	46	100	8	18	5	0	1	6	6	20	0	.180	.260
Maier, Mitch-Mitchell William	06KCA	06-30-82	Petoskey, Mich.		L	R	6'2	210	5	13	3	2	0	0	0	0	0	4	0	.154	.154
Majewski, Val-Walter V.	04BalA	06-19-81	New Brunswick, N.J.		L	L	6'2	200	9	13	3	2	1	0	0	0	2	4	0	.154	.231
Maksudian, Mike-Michael Bryant	92ToraA 93MinA 94ChiN	05-28-66	Belleville, Ill.		L	R	5'11	220	34	41	8	9	3	0	0	6	14	6	0	.220	.293
Malave, Jose-Jose Francisco	96-97BosA	05-31-71	Cumana, Venezuela		R	R	6'2	212	45	106	12	24	3	0	4	17	2	27	0	.226	.368
Maldonado, Candy-Candido [Guadarrama]	81-85LAN 86-89SFN 90CleA 91MilA 91-92ToraA 93ChiN 93-94CleA 95ToraA 95TexA	09-05-60	Humacao, P.R.		R	R	5'11	195	1410	4106	498	1042	227	17	146	618	391	864	34	.254	.424
Maldonado, Carlos-Carlos Luis	06PitN	01-03-79	Maracaibo, Venezuela		R	R	6'1	250	8	19	0	2	0	0	0	0	1	10	1	.105	.105
Maler, Jim-James Michael	81-83SeaA	08-16-58	New York, N. Y.		R	R	6'4	228	102	310	24	70	10	3	5	31	19	47	1	.226	.326
Malloy, Marty-Marty Thomas	98AtlN 02FlaN	07-06-72	Gainesville, Fla.		R	R	5'10	160	35	53	4	8	1	0	1	2	4	10	0	.151	.226
Mallory, Sheldon-Sheldon (Shell)	77OakA	07-16-53	Argo, Ill.		L	L	6'2	180	64	126	19	27	4	1	0	5	11	18	12	.214	.262
Mangual, Angel-Angel Luis [Guilbe]	69PitN 71-76OakA	03-19-47	Juana Diaz, P.R.		R	R	5'1	178	450	1241	122	304	44	8	22	125	59	187	5	.245	.346
Mangual, Pepe-Jose Manuel [Guilbe]	72-76MonN 76-77NYN	05-23-52	Ponce, P.R.		R	R	5'9	170	319	972	155	235	35	6	16	83	147	238	64	.242	.340
Mankowski, Phil-Phillip Anthony	76-79DetA 80-82NYN	01-09-53	Buffalo, N.Y.		L	R	6'	180	269	739	72	195	23	4	8	64	55	103	3	.264	.338
Mann, Kelly-Kelly John	89-90AtlN	08-17-67	Santa Monica, Cal.		R	R	6'3	215	18	52	3	9	3	0	1	3	0	12	0	.173	.288
Manning, Rick-Richard Eugene	75-83CleA 83-87MilA	09-02-54	Niagara Falls, N.Y.		L	R	6'1	180	1555	5248	664	1349	189	43	56	458	471	616	168	.257	.341
Manrique, Fred-Fred Eloy [Reyes]	81,84ToraA 85MonN 86StlN 87-89ChiA 89TexA 90MinA 91OakA	11-05-61	Edo, Venezuela		R	R	6'1	175	498	1337	151	340	59	11	20	151	65	239	18	.254	.360
Manto, Jeff-Jeffrey Paul	90-91CleA 93PhiN 95BalA 96BosA 96SeaA 96-98CleA 98DetA 99NYA 99CleA 00ColN	08-23-64	Bristol, Pa.		R	R	6'3	210	289	713	97	164	35	2	31	97	97	182	3	.230	.415
Manuel, Jerry-Jerry Lindsey	75-76DetA 80-81MonN 82StlN M98-03ChiA	12-23-53	Hahira, Ga.		B	R	6'	165	96	127	14	19	6	1	3	13	10	26	1	.150	.283
Manwaring, Kirt-Kirt Dean	87-96SFN 96HouN 97-99ColN	07-15-65	Elmira, N.Y.		R	R	5'11	200	1008	2982	248	733	111	20	21	278	243	505	10	.246	.318
Markakis, Nick-Nicholas Pacheco	06BalA	11-17-83	Woodstock, Ga.		L	L	6'2	195	147	491	72	143	25	2	16	62	43	72	2	.291	.448
Marquez, Gonzalo-Gonzalo Enrique [Moya]	72-73OakA 73-74ChiN	03-31-46	Carupano, Venezuela	12-19-84	L	L	5'11	190	76	115	9	27	3	0	1	10	7	14	1	.235	.287
Marrero, Eli-Elieser	97-03StlN 04AtlN 05KCA 05BalA 06ColN 06NYN	11-17-73	Havana, Cuba		R	R	6'1	180	724	1906	262	463	99	12	66	261	168	372	56	.243	.411
Marrero, Oreste-Oreste Vilato [Vasquez]	93MonN 96LAN	10-31-69	Bayamon, P.R.		L	L	6'	200	42	89	12	20	6	1	1	5	15	19	1	.225	.348
Marsh, Tom-Thomas Owen	92,94-95PhiN	12-27-65	Toledo, Ohio		R	R	6'2	180	93	252	23	62	7	4	5	34	7	49	0	.246	.365
Marshall, Keith-Keith Alan	73KCA	07-21-51	San Francisco, Cal.		R	R	6'2	185	8	9	0	2	0	0	0	3	1	4	0	.222	.333
Marshall, Mike-Michael Allen	81-89LAN 90NYN 90-91BosA 91CalA	01-12-60	Libertyville, Ill.		R	R	6'5	235	1035	3593	433	971	173	8	148	530	247	810	26	.270	.446
Marte, Andy-Andy Manuel	05AtlN 06CleA	10-21-83	Valla Tapia, Dom. Rep.		R	R	6'1	185	74	221	23	45	17	2	5	27	20	51	0	.204	.367
Martin, Al-Albert Lee	92-99PitN 00SDN 00-01SeaA 03TBA	11-24-67	West Covina, Cal.		L	L	6'2	220	1232	4242	664	1172	220	48	132	485	390	879	173	.276	.444
Martin, Jerry-Jerry Lindsey	74-78PhiN 79-80ChiN 81SFN 82-83KCA 84NYN	05-11-49	Columbia, S.C.		R	R	6'1	195	1018	2652	337	666	130	17	85	345	207	574	38	.251	.409
Martin, Mike-Joseph Michael	86ChiN	12-03-58	Portland, Ore.		L	R	6'2	190	8	13	1	1	0	1	0	0	2	4	0	.077	.154
Martin, Norberto-Norberto Enrique [McDonald] (Paco)	93-97ChiA 98AnaA 99TexA	12-10-66	San Pedro de Mac., D.R.		R	R	5'10	180	354	880	116	245	32	6	7	89	35	123	23	.278	.352
Martin, Russell-Russell Nathan Coltrane Jeanson	06LAN	02-15-83	East York, Canada		R	R	5'10	210	121	415	65	117	26	4	10	65	45	57	10	.282	.436
Martinez, Buck-John Albert	69-71,73-77KCA 78-80MilA 81-86,M01-02TorA	11-07-48	Redding, Cal.		R	R	5'10	195	1049	2743	245	618	128	10	66	321	230	419	5	.225	.343
Martinez (Escobar), Carlos-Carlos Alberto [Martinez]	88-90ChiA 91-93CleA 95CalA	08-11-65	LaGuaira, Venezuela	01-24-06	R	R	6'5	215	465	1485	145	383	63	6	25	161	74	209	10	.258	.359
Martinez, Carmelo-Carmelo [Salgado] (Bitu)	83ChiN 84-89SDN 90PhiN 90-91PitN 91KCA 91CinN	07-28-60	Dorado, P.R.		R	R	6'2	220	1003	2906	350	713	134	7	108	424	404	528	10	.245	.408
Martinez, Chito-Reynaldo Ignacio	91-93BalA	12-19-65	Belize City, Belize		L	L	5'10	185	158	429	58	111	22	2	18	58	46	102	1	.259	.445
Martinez, Dave-David	86-88ChiN 88-91MonN 92CinN 93-94SFN 95-97ChiA 98-00TBA 00ChiN 00TexA 00ToraA 01AtlN 02XJ	09-26-64	New York, N.Y.		L	L	5'10	185	1919	5795	795	1599	238	72	91	580	567	893	183	.276	.389
Martinez, Domingo-Domingo Emilio [LaFontaine]	92-93ToraA	08-04-65	Santo Domingo, D.R.		R	R	6'2	215	15	22	4	9	0	0	2	7	1	8	0	.409	.682
Martinez, Edgar-Edgar	87-04SeaA	01-02-63	New York, N.Y.		R	R	6'	200	2055	7213	1219	2247	514	15	309	1261	1283	1202	49	.312	.515
Martinez, Felix-Felix [Mata]	97-99KCA 00-01TBA	05-18-74	Nagua, Dom. Rep.		B	R	6'0	180	239	641	77	137	26	7	3	39	53	143	18	.214	.290
Martinez, Greg-Gregory Alfred	98MilN	01-27-72	Las Vegas, Nev.		S	R	5'10	168	13	3	2	0	0	0	0	0	1	2	2	.000	.000
Martinez, Manny-Manuel [DeJesus]	96SeaA 98PhiN 98PitN 99MonN	10-03-70	San Pedro de Mac.,D.R.		R	R	6'2	180	232	564	74	138	25	12	8	53	30	111	23	.245	.374
Martinez, Pablo-Pablo Made [Valera]	96AtlN	08-26-69	Sabana Grande, D.R.		R	R	5'10	155	4	2	1	1	0	0	0	0	0	1	0	.500	.500
Martinez, Ramon-Ramon E.	98-02SFN 03-04ChiN 05DetA 05PhiN 06LAN	10-10-72	Philadelphia, Pa.		R	R	6'1	185	712	1765	212	476	89	10	29	208	156	240	8	.270	.381
Martinez, Sandy-Angel Sandy [Martinez]	95-97ToraA 98-99ChiN 00FlaN 01MonN 04CleA 04BosA	10-08-70	Villa Mella, Dom.Rep.		L	R	6'2	210	218	564	39	130	32	4	6	51	37	147	1	.230	.333
Martinez, Ted-Teodoro Noel [Encarnacion]	70-74NYN 75StlN 75OakA 77-79LAN	12-10-47	Santa Cruz de Barahona, D.R. Bats Both part of 73		R	R	6'	170	657	1480	165	355	50	16	7	108	55	213	29	.240	.309
Martinez, Tino-Constantino	90-95SeaA 96-01NYA 02-03StlN 04TBA 05NYA	12-07-67	Tampa, Fla.		L	R	6'2	220	2023	7111	1008	1925	365	21	339	1271	780	1069	27	.271	.471
Martinez, Victor-Victor Jesus	02-06CleA	12-23-78	Ciudad Bolivar, Venez.		B	R	6'2	190	502	1830	249	550	113	1	61	302	210	248	1	.301	.463
Martz, Gary-Gary Arthur (Sugar Bear)	75KCA	01-10-51	Spokane, Wash.		R	R	6'4	210	1	0	0	0	0	0	0	0	0	0	0	.000	.000
Marzano, John-John Robert	87-92BosA 95TexA 96-98SeaA	02-14-63	Philadelphia, Pa.		R	R	5'11	195	301	794	79	191	45	2	11	72	39	138	0	.241	.344
Mashore, Damon-Damon Wayne	96-97OakA 98AnaA	10-31-69	Ponce, P.R.		R	R	5'11	195	185	482	88	120	23	3	8	41	75	135	10	.249	.359
Mason, Jim-James Percy	71WasA 72-73TexA 74-76NYA 77ToraA 77-78TexA 79MonN	04-14-50	Mobile, Ala.		L	R	6'2	190	633	1584	140	322	53	12	12	114	124	316	2	.203	.274
Masteller, Dan-Dan Patrick	95MinA	03-17-68	Lyndhurst, Ohio		L	L	6'	185	71	198	21	47	12	0	3	21	18	19	1	.237	.348
Mata, Vic-Victor Jose [Abreu]	84-85NYA	06-17-61	Santiago, Dom. Rep.		R	R	6'1	165	36	77	9	24	5	0	1	6	0	12	1	.312	.442
Mateo, Henry-Henry Antonio [Valera]	01-04MonN 05-06WasN	10-14-76	Santo Domingo, D.R.		B	R	5'11	180	190	257	39	60	8	2	1	10	17	57	15	.233	.292
Mateo, Ruben-Ruben Amaury	99-01TexA 02-03CinN 04PitN 04KCA	02-10-78	San Cristobal, D.R.		R	R	6'	185	295	876	106	219	44	6	21	89	49	189	11	.250	.388
Matheny, Mike-Michael Scott	94-97MilA 98MilN 99ToraA 00-04StlN 05-06SFN	09-22-70	Columbus, Ohio		R	R	6'3	215	1305	3877	353	925	190	9	67	443	266	795	8	.239	.344
Mathis, Jeff-Jeffrey Stephen	05-06LAA	03-31-83	Marianna, Fla.		R	R	6'	180	28	58	10	9	2	0	1	6	7	15	0	.155	.293
Matos, Francisco-Francisco Aguirre [Mancebo]	94OakA	07-23-69	Santo Domingo, D.R.		R	R	6'	160	14	28	1	7	1	0	0	2	1	2	1	.250	.286
Matos, Julius-Julius	02SDN 03KCA	12-14-72	New York, N.Y.		R	R	5'11	175	104	242	26	59	4	0	4	20	10	45	2	.244	.310
Matos, Luis-Luis David	00-06BalA 06WasN	10-30-78	Bayamon, P.R.		R	R	6'	200	508	1605	212	410	84	9	30	140	108	297	72	.255	.375
Matos, Pascual-Pascual [Cuevas]	99AtlN	12-23-74	Santa Cruz de Barahona, D.R.		R	R	6'2	180	8	8	0	1	0	0	0	0	0	2	0	.125	.125
Matranga, David-David Michael	03HouN 05LAA	01-08-77	Orange, Cal.		R	R	6'	170	7	6	1	1	0	0	1	0	0	2	0	.167	.667
Matsui, Hideki-Hideki (Godzilla)	03-06NYA	06-12-74	Ishikawa, Japan		L	R	6'1	210	538	2008	331	597	130	6	78	359	241	290	8	.297	.485
Matsui, Kaz-Kazuo	04-06NYN 06ColN	10-23-75	Osaka, Japan		B	R	5'10	183	271	970	128	258	53	9	13	94	70	186	30	.266	.379
Matthews, Gary-Gary Nathaniel (Sarge)	72-76SFN 77-80AtlN 81-83PhiN 84-87ChiN 87SeaA	07-05-50	San Fernando, Cal.		R	R	6'2	200	2033	7147	1083	2011	319	51	234	978	940	1125	183	.281	.439
Matthews, Gary-Gary Nathaniel Jr.	99SDN 00-01ChiN 01PitN 02NYN 02-03BalA 03SDN 04-06TexA	08-25-74	San Francisco, Calif.		B	R	6'3	215	875	2787	427	733	158	21	78	315	308	554	64	.263	.419
Mattingly, Don-Donald Arthur	82-95NYA	04-20-61	Evansville, Ind.		L	L	5'11	190	1785	7003	1007	2153	442	20	222	1099	588	444	14	.307	.471
Matuszek, Len-Leonard James	81-84PhiN 85ToraA 85-87LAN	09-27-54	Toledo, Ohio		L	R	6'2	205	379	820	113	192	40	5	30	119	88	168	8	.234	.405
Mauer, Joe-Joseph Patrick	04-06MinA	04-19-83	St. Paul, Minn.		L	R	6'4	220	306	1117	165	358	70	7	28	156	151	132	22	.321	.419
Maurer, Rob-Robert John	91-92TexA 93KJ	01-07-67	Evansville, Ind.		L	L	6'3	210	21	25	1	3	1	0	0	3	3	8	0	.120	.160
Maxwell, Jason-Jason Ramond	98ChiN 00-01MinA	03-26-72	Lewisburg, Tenn.		R	R	6'0	185	110	182	20	41	10	0	3	23	18	57	4	.225	.330
May, Carlos-Carlos	68-76ChiA 76-77NYA 77CalA	05-17-48	Birmingham, Ala.		L	R	5'11	210	1165	4120	545	1127	172	23	90	536	512	565	85	.274	.392
May, Dave-David LaFrance (Chopper)	67-70BalA 70-74MilA 75-76AtlN 77-78TexA 78MilA 78PitN	12-23-43	New Castle, Del.		L	R	5'10	195	1252	3670	462	920	130	20	96	422	344	501	60	.251	.375
May, Derrick-Derrick Brant	90-94ChiN 95MilA 95-96HouN 97PhiN 98MonN 99BalA	07-14-68	Rochester, N.Y.		L	R	6'4	220	797	2200	244	584	103	10	52	310	156	254	30	.271	.398
May, Lee-Lee Andrew (Mo, The Big Bopper)	65-71CinN 72-74HouN 75-80BalA 81-82KCA	03-23-43	Birmingham, Ala.		R	R	6'3	215	2071	7609	959	2031	340	31	354	1244	487	1570	39	.267	.459
May, Milt-Milton Scott	70-73PitN74-75HouN76-79DetA79CalA80-83SFN83-84PitN	08-01-50	Gary, Ind.		L	R	6'	190	1192	3693	313	971	147	11	77	443	305	361	4	.263	.392
Mayberry, John-John Claiborn	68-71HouN 72-77KCA 78-82TorA 82NYA	02-18-49	Detroit, Mich.		L	L	6'3	220	1620	5447	733	1379	211	19	255	879	881	810	20	.253	.439
Mayne, Brent-Brent Danem	90-95KCA 96NYN 97OakA 98-99SFN 00-01ColN 01-03KCA 04AriN 04LAN	04-19-68	Loma Linda, Cal.		L	R	6'1	195	1279	3614	359	951	178	8	38	403	370	580	18	.263	.348
Mazzilli, Lee-Lee Louis (The Italian Stallion)	76-81NYN 82TexA 82NYA 83-86PitN 86-89NYN 89ToraA M04-05BalA	03-25-55	New York, N.Y.		B	R	6'1	190	1475	4124	571	1068	191	24	93	460	642	627	197	.259	.385
McAnulty, Paul-Paul Michael	05-06SDN	02-24-81	Oxnard, Cal.		L	R	5'10	220	30	37	7	8	1	0	1	4	5	11	1	.216	.324
McBride, Bake-Arnold Ray	73-77StlN 77-81PhiN 82-83CleA	02-03-49	Fulton, Mo.		L	R	6'2	195	1071	3853	548	1153	167	55	63	430	248	457	183	.299	.424
McCann, Brian- Brian Michael	05-06AtlN	02-20-84	Athens, Ga.		L	R	6'3	210	189	622	81	197	41	0	29	116	59	80	1	.317	.523
McCarty, Dave-David Andrew	93-95MinA 95-96SFN 98SeaA 00-02KCA 02TBA 03OakA 03-05BosA	11-23-69	Houston, Tex.		R	L	6'5	210	632	1493	182	362	68	8	36	175	126	367	9	.242	.371
McClain, Scott-Scott Michael	98TBA 05ChiN	05-19-72	Simi Valley, Cal.		R	R	6'4	220	22	14	1	2	0	0	0	1	2	2	0	.143	.214

USE NAME - GIVEN NAMES (NICKNAMES)	TEAM BY YEAR	BIRTH DATE	BIRTH PLACE	DEATH DATE	B	T	HGT	WGT	G	AB	R	H	2B	3B	HR	RBI	BB	SO	SB	BA	SA
McClendon, Lloyd-Lloyd Glenn	87-88CinN 89-90ChiN 90-94,M01-05PitN	01-11-59	Gary, Ind.		R	R	5'10	200	570	1204	150	294	54	3	35	154	143	165	15	.244	.381
McCormack, Don-Donald Ross	80-81PhiN	09-18-55	Omak, Wash.		R	R	6'3	205	5	5	0	2	0	0	0	0	0	1	0	.400	.400
McCracken, Quinton-Quinton Antoine	95-97ColN 98-00TBA 01MinA 02-03AriN 04SeaA 04-05AriN 06CinN	03-16-70	Wilmington, N.C.		B	R	5'8	180	999	2462	359	675	118	32	21	244	229	445	89	.274	.374
McCray, Rodney-Rodney Duncan	90-92ChiA 92NYN	09-13-63	Detroit, Mich.		R	R	5'10	175	67	14	13	3	0	0	0	1	1	6	9	.214	.214
McDaniel, Terry-Terrence Keith	91NYN	12-06-66	Kansas City, Mo.		B	R	5'9	195	23	29	3	6	1	0	0	2	1	11	2	.207	.247
McDavid, Ray-Ray Darnell	94-95SDN	07-20-71	San Diego, Cal.		L	R	6'3	190	20	45	4	10	1	0	0	2	3	14	2	.222	.244
McDonald, Darnell-Darnell Tyrone	04BalA	11-17-78	Fort Collins, Colo.		R	R	5'11	210	17	32	3	5	1	0	0	1	2	6	1	.156	.188
McDonald, Donzell-Donzell	01NYA 02KCA	02-20-75	Long Beach, Cal.		B	R	5'11	180	15	25	3	5	2	0	0	1	4	7	1	.200	.280
McDonald, Jason-Jason Adam	97-99OakA 00TexA	03-20-72	Modesto, Cal.		B	R	5'8	180	286	692	113	167	27	5	11	51	105	155	33	.241	.342
McDonald, John-John Joseph	99-04CleA 05TorA 05DetA 06TorA	09-24-74	New London, Conn.		R	R	5'11	175	457	1049	129	248	39	9	7	72	53	168	19	.236	.311
McDonald, Keith-William Keith	00-01StlN	02-08-73	Yokosuka, Japan		R	R	6'2	215	8	9	3	3	0	0	3	5	2	2	0	.333	1.333
McDougall, Marshall-Marshall James	05TexA	12-19-78	Jacksonville, Fla.		R	R	6'1	200	18	18	3	3	1	0	0	0	0	10	0	.167	.222
McDowell, Oddibe-Oddibe	85-88TexA 89CleA 89-90AtlN 94TexA	08-25-62	Hollywood, Fla.		L	L	5'9	170	830	2829	458	715	125	28	74	266	294	500	169	.253	.395
McEwing, Joe-Joseph Earl	98-99StlN 00-04NYN 05KCA 06HouN	10-19-72	Bristol, Pa.		R	R	5'10	195	754	1767	217	443	89	10	25	158	113	352	33	.251	.355
McGee, Willie-Willie Dean	82-90StlN 90OakA 91-94SFN 95BosA 96-99StlN	11-02-58	San Francisco, Cal.		B	R	6'2	180	2201	7649	1010	2254	350	94	79	856	448	1238	352	.295	.396
McGinnis, Russ-Russell Brent	92TexA 95KCA	06-18-63	Coffeyville, Kans.		R	R	6'3	225	17	38	3	8	4	0	0	4	4	8	0	.211	.316
McGriff, Fred-Frederick Stanley (Prime Dog)	86-90TorA 91-93SDN 93-97AtlN 98-01TBA 01-02ChiN 03LAN 04TBA	10-31-63	Tampa, Fla.		L	L	6'3	215	2460	8757	1349	2490	441	24	493	1550	1305	1882	72	.284	.509
McGriff, Terry-Terence Roy	87-90CinN 90HouN 93FlaN 94StlN	09-23-63	Fort Pierce, Fla.		R	R	6'2	200	126	326	26	67	12	0	3	23	24	58	1	.206	.270
McGuire, Bill-William Patrick	88-89SeaA	02-14-64	Omaha, Neb.		R	R	6'3	195	23	44	3	8	0	0	1	6	5	8	0	.182	.250
McGuire, Ryan-Ryan Byron	97-99MonN 00NYN 01FlaN 02BalA	11-23-71	Bellflower, Cal.		L	L	6'1	215	368	631	64	133	34	4	7	55	88	144	3	.211	.311
McGwire, Mark-Mark David (Big Mac)	86-97OakA 97-01StlN	10-01-63	Pomona, Cal.		R	R	6'5	250	1874	6187	1167	1626	252	6	583	1414	1317	1596	12	.263	.588
McHenry, Vance-Vance Loren	81-82SeaA	07-10-56	Chico, Cal.		R	R	5'9	165	18	19	3	4	0	0	0	2	1	1	0	.211	.211
McIntosh, Tim-Timothy Allen	90-93MilA 93MonN 95JL 96NYA	03-21-65	Minneapolis, Minn.		R	R	5'11	195	71	117	12	21	5	0	2	10	3	22	1	.179	.274
McKay, Cody-Cody Dean	02OakA 04StlN	01-11-74	Vancouver, Canada		L	R	6'	208	37	77	7	19	2	0	0	8	2	15	0	.247	.273
McKay, Dave-David Lawrence	75-76MinA 77-79TorA 80-82OakA	03-14-50	Vancouver, Canada		B	R	6'2	195	645	1928	191	441	70	15	21	170	86	337	20	.229	.313
Bats Both 80-81, part of 77-78																					
McKeel, Walt-Walter Thomas	96-97BosA 02ColN	01-17-72	Wilson, N.C.		R	R	6'2	200	11	16	1	4	0	0	0	0	0	5	0	.250	.250
McKinney, Rich-Charles Richard	70-71ChiA 72NYA 73-75,77OakA	11-24-46	Piqua, Ohio		R	R	5'11	187	341	886	79	199	28	2	20	100	77	124	4	.225	.328
McKnight, Jeff-Jefferson Alan	89NYN 90-91BalA 92-94NYN	02-18-63	Conway, Ark.		B	R	6'	180	218	404	45	94	10	2	5	34	28	76	1	.233	.304
McLemore, Mark-Mark Tremell	86-90CalA 90CleA 91HouN 92-94BalA 95-99TexA 00-03SeaA 04OakA	10-04-64	San Diego, Cal.		B	R	5'11	200	1832	6192	943	1602	255	47	53	615	875	983	272	.259	.341
McLouth, Nate-Nathan Richard	05-06PitN	10-28-81	Muskegon, Mich.		L	R	5'11	185	147	379	70	91	28	2	12	28	21	79	12	.240	.404
McMillian, Tommy-Thomas Erwin	77SeaA	09-13-51	Richmond, Va.		R	R	5'9	165	2	5	0	0	0	0	0	0	0	0	0	.000	.000
McMillon, Billy-William Edward	96-97FlaN 97PhiN 00PitN 01DetA 01,03-04OakA	11-17-71	Alamogordo, N.M.		L	L	5'11	185	269	601	66	149	35	3	16	93	64	140	4	.248	.396
McNamara, Jim-James Patrick	92-93SFN	06-10-65	Nashua, N.H.		L	R	6'4	220	34	81	6	17	1	0	1	10	6	26	0	.210	.259
McNealy, Rusty-Robert Lee	83OakA	08-12-58	Sacramento, Cal.		L	L	5'8	165	15	4	5	0	0	0	0	0	0	0	0	.000	.000
McNeely, Jeff-Jeffrey Lavern	93BosA	10-18-69	Monroe, N.C.		R	R	6'2	190	21	37	10	11	1	1	0	5	3	9	6	.297	.378
McPherson, Dallas-Dallas Lyle	04AnaA 05-06LAA	07-23-80	Greensboro, N.C.		L	R	6'4	230	117	360	50	89	19	2	18	45	23	121	5	.247	.461
McRae, Brian-Brian Wesley	90-94KCA 95-97ChiN 97-99NYN 99ColN 99TorA	08-27-67	Bradenton, Fla.		B	R	6'	190	1354	5114	734	1336	264	58	103	532	488	824	196	.261	.396
McRae, Hal-Harold Abraham	68CinN 69BL 70-72CinN 73-87,M91-94KCA M01-02TBA	07-10-45	Avon Park, Fla.		R	R	5'11	180	2084	7218	940	2091	484	66	191	1097	648	779	109	.290	.454
McReynolds, Kevin-Walter Kevin	83-86SDN 87-91NYN 92-93KCA 94NYN	10-16-59	Little Rock, Ark.		R	R	6'	220	1502	5423	727	1439	284	35	211	807	522	707	93	.265	.447
Meacham, Bobby-Robert Andres	83-88NYA	08-25-60	Los Angeles, Cal.		B	R	6'1	180	457	1371	202	324	18	8	8	114	140	276	58	.236	.308
Bats Right 87																					
Meadows, Louie-Michael Ray	86,88-90HouN 90PhiN	04-29-61	Maysville, N.C.		L	L	5'11	190	102	127	15	22	0	1	5	13	10	28	6	.173	.307
Meares, Pat-Patrick James	93-98MinA 99-01PitN 02-03HJ	09-06-68	Salina, Kans.		R	R	6'	185	982	3287	401	849	157	24	58	382	150	588	43	.258	.374
Medina, Luis-Luis Main	88-89,91CleA	03-26-63	Santa Monica, Cal.		R	L	6'3	190	51	150	18	31	1	0	10	16	9	60	0	.207	.413
Meier, Dave-David Keith	84-85MinA 87TexA 88ChiN	08-08-59	Helena, Mont.		R	R	6'	195	145	277	37	70	15	1	1	22	24	26	0	.253	.325
Mejia, Miguel-Miguel	96StlN	03-25-75	San Pedro de Mac.,D.R.		R	R	6'1	155	45	23	10	2	0	0	0	0	0	10	6	.087	.087
Mejia, Roberto-Roberto Antonio [Diaz]	93-95ColN 97StlN	04-14-72	Hato Mayor, Dom. Rep.		R	R	5'11	165	133	411	47	90	24	6	10	40	28	118	7	.219	.380
Mejias, Sammy-Samuel Elias	76StlN 77-78MonN 79ChiN 79-81CinN	05-09-52	Santiago, Dom. Rep.		R	R	6'	165	334	348	51	86	13	2	4	31	16	51	8	.247	.330
Melendez, Francisco-Francisco Javier [Villegas]	84,86PhiN 87-88SFN 89BalA	01-25-64	Rio Piedras, P.R.		L	L	6'	185	74	84	4	18	0	0	0	9	5	14	0	.214	.250
Melendez, Luis-Luis Antonio [Santana]	70-76StlN 76-77SDN	08-11-49	Aibonito, P.R.		R	R	5'10	165	641	1477	167	366	50	13	9	122	109	175	18	.248	.318
Melhuse, Adam-Adam Michael	00LAN 00-01ColN 03-06OakA	03-27-72	Santa Clara, Cal.		B	R	6'2	195	261	611	65	147	35	1	23	87	48	152	1	.241	.414
Melo, Juan-Juan Esteban	00SFN	10-11-76	Bani, Dom. Rep.		R	R	6'3	206	11	13	0	1	0	0	0	1	0	5	0	.077	.077
Melton, Bill-William Edward	68-75ChiA 76CalA 77CleA	07-07-45	Gulfport, Miss.		R	R	6'2	200	1144	3971	496	1004	162	9	160	591	479	669	23	.253	.419
Meluskey, Mitch-Mitchell Wade	98-00HouN 01SJ 02DetA 03HouN	09-18-73	Yakima, Wash.		B	R	6'0	185	155	414	56	117	24	0	15	75	68	89	2	.283	.449
Melvin, Bob-Robert Paul	85DetA 86-88SFN 89-91BalA 92KCA 93BosA 94NYA 94ChiA M03-04SeaA M05-06AriN	10-28-61	Palo Alto, Cal.		R	R	6'4	205	692	1955	174	456	81	6	35	212	98	396	4	.233	.335
Mench, Kevin-Kevin Ford	02-06TexA 06MilN	01-07-78	Wilmington, Del.		R	R	6'	230	550	1932	252	524	119	10	81	283	151	290	7	.271	.469
Mendez, Carlos-Carlos Alberto [Castillo]	03BalA	06-18-74	Caracas, Venezuela		R	R	6'	210	26	45	3	10	2	0	0	5	0	12	0	.222	.267
Mendez, Donaldo-Donaldo Alfonso	01,03SDN	06-07-78	Barquisimeto, Venez.		R	R	6'1	155	72	202	19	37	8	1	3	14	12	69	2	.183	.277
Mendoza, Carlos-Carlos Ramon	97NYN 00ColN	11-04-74	Bolivar, Venezuela		L	L	5'11	160	28	22	6	4	0	0	0	1	5	6	0	.182	.182
Mendoza, Mario-Mario [Aizpuru] (Coruco)	74-78PitN 79-80SeaA 81-82TexA	12-26-50	Chihuahua, Mexico		R	R	5'11	185	686	1337	106	287	33	9	4	102	52	219	12	.215	.262
Menechino, Frank-Frank	99-04OakA 04-05TorA	01-07-71	Staten Island, N.Y.		R	R	5'9	185	450	1257	207	302	58	7	36	149	200	279	3	.240	.384
Meoli, Rudy-Rudolph Batholomew	71,73-75CalA 78CinN 79PhiN	05-01-51	Troy, N.Y.		L	R	5'9	165	310	626	69	133	20	4	7	40	69	83	10	.212	.267
Mercado, Orlando-Orlando [Rodriguez]	82-84SeaA 86TexA 87DetA 87LAN 88OakA 89MinA 90NYN 90MonN	11-07-61	Arecibo, P.R.		R	R	6'	185	253	562	40	112	17	4	7	45	42	82	4	.199	.291
Merced, Orlando-Orlando Luis [Villanueva]	90-96PitN 97TorA 98MinA 98BosA 98ChiN 99MonN 01-03HouN	11-02-66	Hato Rey, P.R.		L	R	6'	190	1391	3998	564	1108	229	28	103	585	487	661	57	.277	.426
Bats Both 90-92, part of 93																					
Mercedes, Henry-Henry Felipe [Perez]	92-93OakA 95-96KCA 97TexA	07-23-69	Santo Domingo, D.R.		R	R	5'11	185	79	146	18	36	8	1	0	17	16	55	1	.247	.315
Mercedes, Luis-Luis Roberto [Santana]	91-93BalA 93SFN	02-15-68	San Pedro de Mac., D.R.		R	R	6'	180	70	153	19	29	5	1	0	9	18	25	1	.190	.242
Merchant, Andy-James Anderson	75-76BosA	08-30-50	Mobile, Ala.		L	R	5'11	190	3	6	1	2	0	0	0	0	1	0	0	.333	.333
Merloni, Lou-Louis William	98-02BosA 03SDN 03BosA 04CleA 05LAA 06CleA	04-06-71	Framingham, Mass.		R	R	5'10	195	423	1085	138	294	67	7	14	125	88	213	9	.271	.384
Merullo, Matt-Matthew Bates	89,91-93ChiA 94CleA 95MinA	08-04-65	Winchester, Mass.		L	R	6'2	200	223	496	37	116	17	2	7	59	32	69	0	.234	.319
Metcalfe, Mike-Michael Henry	98,00LAN	01-02-73	Quantico, Va.		R	R	6'	180	13	13	0	1	0	0	0	0	1	3	2	.077	.077
Metzger, Roger-Roger Henry	70ChiN 71-78HouN 78-80SFN	10-10-47	Fredericksburg, Tex.		B	R	6'	165	1219	4201	453	972	101	71	5	254	355	449	83	.231	.293
Bats Left 70,80 (after severing tips of 4 fingers)																					
Meulens, Hensley-Hensley Filemon Acasio (Bam-Bam)	89-93NYA 94-96JL 97MonN 98AriN	06-23-67	Willemstad, Curacao		R	R	6'4	210	182	496	67	109	17	2	15	53	42	165	4	.220	.353
Meyer, Dan-Daniel Thomas	74-76DetA 77-81SeaA 82-85OakA	08-03-52	Hamilton, Ohio		L	R	5'11	180	1118	3734	411	944	153	31	86	459	220	277	61	.253	.379
Meyer, Drew-Drew Edward	06TexA	08-29-81	Charleston, S.C.		L	R	5'10	200	5	14	1	3	0	0	0	0	0	4	0	.214	.214
Meyer, Joey-Tanner Joe	88-89MilA	05-10-62	Honolulu, Hawaii		R	R	6'3	260	156	474	35	119	24	0	18	74	35	124	1	.251	.416
Meyer, Scott-Scott William	78OakA	08-19-57	Evergreen Park, Ill.		R	R	6'1	200	8	9	1	1	0	0	0	0	0	1	0	.111	.222
Meyers, Chad-Chad William	99-01ChiN 03SeaA	08-08-75	Omaha, Neb.		R	R	6'	190	106	212	27	44	9	1	0	9	14	43	4	.208	.259
Michaels, Jason-Jason Drew	01-05PhiN 06CleA	05-04-76	Tampa, Fla.		R	R	6'	204	506	1302	211	367	81	6	30	155	157	283	15	.282	.422
Mientkiewicz, Doug-Douglas Andrew (Mint)	98-04MinA 04BosA 05NYN 06KCA	06-19-74	Toledo, Ohio		L	R	6'2	200	870	2843	359	768	189	9	59	348	377	415	14	.270	.405
Mieske, Matt-Matthew Todd	93-97MilA 98ChiN 99SeaA 99-00HouN 00AriN	02-13-68	Midland, Mich.		R	R	6'	190	663	1547	225	406	78	10	56	226	124	313	7	.262	.434
Milbourne, Larry-Lawrence William	74-76HouN 77-80SeaA 81-82NYA 82MinA 82CleA 83PhiN 83NYA 84SeaA 85WJ	02-14-51	Port Norris, N.J.		B	R	6'	165	989	2448	290	623	71	24	11	184	133	176	41	.254	.317
Miles, Aaron-Aaron Wade	03ChiA 04-05ColN 06StlN	12-15-76	Pittsburg, Cal.		B	R	5'8	170	376	1284	163	360	50	11	10	107	75	133	18	.280	.340
Miley, Mike-Michael Wilfred	75-76CalA	03-30-53	Yazoo City, Miss.	01-06-77	R	R	5'11	190	84	262	21	46	5	2	4	30	20	62	1	.176	.256
Millar, Kevin-Kevin Charles	98-02FlaN 03-05BosA 06BalA	09-24-71	Los Angeles, Cal.		R	R	6'1	205	1064	3430	483	983	231	14	126	535	386	602	6	.287	.472
Milledge, Lastings-Lastings Darnell	06NYN	04-05-85	Bradenton, Fla.		R	R	6'1	185	56	56	16	14	4	0	2	12	12	39	1	.241	.380
Miller, Bruce-Charles Bruce	73-76SFN	03-04-47	Fort Wayne, Ind.		R	R	6'1	185	196	553	43	136	14	4	1	51	30	49	1	.246	.291
Miller, Corky-Abraham Philip	01-04CinN 05MinA 06BosA	03-18-76	Yucaipa, Cal.		R	R	6'1	225	89	248	20	47	12	0	6	29	24	58	1	.190	.310
Miller, Damian-Damian Donald	97MinA 98-02AriN 03ChiN 04OakA 05-06MilN	10-13-69	La Crosse, Wis.		R	R	6'3	210	931	2996	342	790	196	4	83	382	289	733	4	.264	.415
Miller, Darrell-Darrell Keith	84-88CalA	02-26-58	Washington D.C.		R	R	6'2	205	224	394	54	95	13	2	7	37	27	69	3	.241	.350
Miller, Eddie-Edward Lee	77TexA 78-81AtlN 82DetA 84SDN	06-29-57	San Pablo, Cal.		B	R	5'9	175	138	332	63	79	5	2	1	17	19	71	49	.238	.274
Miller, Keith-Keith Alan	87-91NYN 92-95KCA	06-12-63	Midland, Mich.		R	R	5'11	180	465	1326	190	347	67	8	12	92	100	205	63	.262	.351
Miller, Keith-Neal Keith	88-89PhiN	03-07-63	Dallas, Tex.		B	R	5'11	175	55	58	4	11	4	0	0	0	0	16	0	.190	.259
Miller, Lemmie-Lemmie Earl	84LAN	06-02-60	Dallas, Tex.		R	R	6'1	190	9	12	1	2	0	0	0	0	1	2	0	.167	.167

USE NAME - GIVEN NAMES (NICKNAMES)	TEAM BY YEAR	BIRTH DATE	BIRTH PLACE	DEATH DATE	B	T	HGT	WGT	G	AB	R	H	2B	3B	HR	RBI	BB	SO	SB	BA	SA
Miller, Orlando-Orlando Salmon [Dixon]	94-96HouN 97DetA	01-13-69	Changuinola, Panama		R	R	6'1	180	297	943	95	244	53	5	24	113	43	223	8	.259	.402
Miller, Rick-Richard Alan	71-77BosA 78-80CalA 81-85BosA	04-19-48	Grand Rapids, Mich.		L	L	6'1	185	1482	3887	552	1046	161	35	28	369	454	583	78	.269	.350
Millette, Joe-Joseph Anthony	92-93PhiN	08-12-66	Walnut Creek, Cal.		R	R	6'1	180	42	88	8	18	0	0	0	4	6	12	1	.205	.205
Milliard, Ralph-Ralph Gregory	96-97FlaN 98NYN 99XJ	12-30-73	Willemstad, Curacao		R	R	5'11	170	43	93	12	16	2	0	0	3	17	20	3	.172	.194
Milligan, Randy-Randy Andre (Moose)	87NYN 88PitN 89-92BalA 93CinN 93CleA 94MonN	11-27-61	San Diego, Cal.		R	R	6'1	230	703	2118	305	553	106	10	70	284	447	431	16	.261	.415
Mills, Brad-James Bradley	80-83MonN	01-19-57	Exeter, Cal.		L	R	195	106	168	11	43	5	0	1	12	14	21	0	.256	.304
Milner, Brian-Brian Tate	78TorA	11-17-59	Fort Worth, Tex.		R	R	6'2	200	9	9	3	4	0	1	0	2	0	1	0	.444	.667
Milner, Eddie-Eddie James (Greyhound)	80-86CinN 87SFN 88CinN	05-21-55	Columbus, Ohio		L	L	6'	173	804	2395	376	607	111	28	42	195	286	280	145	.253	.376
Milner, John-John David (The Hammer)	71-77NYN 78-81PitN 81-82MonN 82PitN	12-28-49	Atlanta, Ga.	01-04-00	L	L	6'	185	1215	3436	455	855	140	16	131	498	504	473	31	.249	.413
Minor, Damon-Damon Reed	00-02,04SFN	01-05-74	Canton, Ohio		L	L	6'7	230	136	285	35	66	9	0	13	39	41	61	0	.232	.400
Minor, Ryan-Ryan Dale	98-00BalA 01MonN	01-05-74	Canton, Ohio		R	R	6'7	245	142	317	30	56	11	0	5	27	20	97	1	.177	.259
Mirabelli, Doug-Douglas Anthony	96-00SFN 01TexA 01-05BosA 06SDN 06BosA	10-18-70	Kingman, Ariz.		R	R	6'1	215	518	1342	153	314	75	2	53	190	154	374	3	.234	.411
Mitchell, Bobby-Robert Van	80-81LAN 82-83MinA	04-07-55	Salt Lake City, Utah		L	L	5'9	175	202	617	75	150	15	8	3	43	84	78	9	.243	.308
Mitchell, Bobby-Robert Vance	70NYA 71,73-75MilA	10-22-43	Norristown, Pa.		R	R	6'3	195	273	609	86	143	29	6	21	91	56	168	14	.235	.406
Mitchell, Keith-Keith Alexander	91AtlN 94SeaA 96CinN 98BosA	08-06-69	San Diego, Cal.		R	R	5'10	180	128	242	38	63	5	0	8	29	34	42	4	.260	.380
Mitchell, Kevin-Kevin Darnell	84,86NYN 87SDN 87-91SFN 92SeaA 93-94CinN 95JL 96BosA 96CinN 97CleA 98OakA	01-13-62	San Diego, Cal.		R	R	5'10	233	1223	4134	630	1173	224	25	234	760	491	719	30	.284	.520
Mitterwald, George-George Eugene (The Baron)	66,68-73MinA 74-77ChiN	06-07-45	Berkeley, Cal.		R	R	6'2	205	887	2645	251	623	93	7	76	301	222	607	14	.236	.362
Mizerock, John-John Joseph	83HouN 84EJ 85-86HouN 89AtlN M02KCA	06-07-45	Punxsutawney, Pa.		L	R	190	103	231	24	43	9	2	2	24	38	42	0	.186	.268
Moates, Dave-David Allen (Motor)	74-76TexA	01-30-48	Great Lakes, Ill.		L	L	5'9	170	140	312	42	81	16	1	3	27	24	33	15	.260	.346
Moeller, Chad-Chad Edward	00MinA 01-03AriN 04-06MilN	02-18-75	Upland, Cal.		R	R	6'3	207	384	1142	117	259	56	6	25	111	93	275	2	.227	.352
Mohr, Dustan-Dustan Kyle	01-03MinA 04SFN 05ColN 06BosA		Hattiesburg, Miss.		R	R	6'	210	497	1351	202	338	78	6	48	154	141	387	13	.250	.423
Molina, Bengie-Benjamin Jose [Matta]	98-04AnaA 05LAA 06TorA	07-20-74	Rio Piedras, P.R.		R	R	5'11	215	833	2917	294	801	128	3	84	419	137	278	3	.275	.407
Molina, Izzy-Islay	96-98OakA 02BalA	06-03-71	New York, N.Y.		R	R	6'	200	69	141	8	29	5	1	3	8	4	20	0	.206	.319
Molina, Jose-Jose Benjamin [Matta]	99CinN 01-04AnaA 05-06LAA	06-03-71	Bayamon, P.R.		R	R	6'1	215	352	852	86	204	42	2	15	88	43	195	7	.239	.346
Molina, Yadier-Yadier B. [Matta]	04-06StLN	07-13-82	Bayamon, P.R.		R	R	5'11	225	294	937	77	223	47	1	16	113	62	91	3	.238	.342
Molinaro, Bob-Robert Joseph	75,77DetA 77-78ChiA 79BalA 80-81ChiA 82ChiA 82-83PhiN 83DetA	05-21-50	Newark, N.J.		L	R	6'	185	401	803	106	212	25	11	14	90	65	57	46	.264	.375
Molitor, Paul-Paul Leo (The Ignitor)	78-92MilA 93-95TorA 96-98MinA	08-22-56	St. Paul, Minn.		R	R	6'	185	2683	10835	1782	3319	605	114	234	1307	1094	1244	504	.306	.448
Monahan, Shane-Shane Hartland	98-99SeaA	08-12-74	Syosset, N.Y.		L	R	6'0	195	78	226	20	53	8	1	4	28	8	59	1	.235	.332
Monday, Rick-Robert James	66-67KCA 68-71OakA 72-76ChiN 77-84LAN	11-20-45	Batesville, Ark.		L	L	6'3	195	1986	6136	950	1619	248	64	241	775	924	1513	98	.264	.443
Mondesi, Raul-Raul Ramon (Avelino)	93-99LAN 00-02TorA 02-03NYA 03AriN 04PitN 04AnaA 05AtlN	03-12-71	San Cristobal, D.R.		R	R	5'11	230	1525	5814	909	1589	319	49	271	860	475	1130	229	.273	.485
Money, Don-Donald Wayne	68-72PhiN 73-83MilA 84IL	06-07-47	Washington D.C.		R	R	6'1	190	1720	6215	798	1623	302	36	176	729	600	866	80	.261	.406
Monroe, Craig-Craig Keystone	01TexA 02-06DetA	02-27-77	Texarkana, Tex.		R	R	6'1	190	600	2057	285	542	112	9	92	329	139	412	19	.263	.461
Montanez, Willie-Guillermo [Naranjo]	66CalA 70-75PhiN 75-76SFN 76-77AtlN 78-79NYN 79TexA 80SDN 80-81MonN 81-82PitN 82PhiN	04-01-48	Catano, P.R.		L	L	6'	190	1632	5843	645	1604	279	25	139	802	465	751	32	.275	.402
Montero, Miguel-Miguel Angel	06AriN	07-09-83	Caracas, Venezuela		L	R	5'11	195	6	16	0	4	1	0	0	3	1	3	0	.250	.313
Montgomery, Bob-Robert Edward	70-79BosA	04-16-44	Nashville, Tenn.		R	R	6'2	200	387	1185	125	306	50	8	23	156	64	268	6	.258	.372
Montgomery, Ray-Raymond James	96-98HouN	08-08-69	Bronxville, N.Y.		R	R	6'3	195	47	87	14	21	5	1	1	8	6	23	0	.241	.356
Montoyo, Charlie-Jose Carlos [Diaz]	93MonN	10-17-65	Manati, P.R.		R	R	5'10	170	4	5	1	2	1	0	0	1	1	0	0	.400	.600
Monzon, Dan-Daniel Francisco	72-73MinA	05-17-46	Bronx, N.Y.	01-21-96	R	R	5'10	182	94	131	23	32	2	1	0	9	19	21	2	.244	.275
Moore, Billy-William Ross	86MonN	10-10-60	Los Angeles, Cal.		R	L	6'1	185	6	12	0	4	0	0	0	0	0	4	0	.167	.167
Moore, Bobby-Robert Vincent	91KCA	10-27-65	Cincinnati, Ohio		R	R	5'11	165	18	14	3	5	1	0	0	1	0	3	0	.357	.429
Moore, Charlie-Charles William (Butch)	73-86MilA 87TorA	06-21-53	Birmingham, Ala.		R	R	5'11	190	1334	4033	456	1052	187	43	36	408	346	470	51	.261	.355
Moore, Junior-Alvin Earl	76-77AtlN 78-80ChiA	01-25-53	Waskom, Tex.		R	R	5'11	195	289	774	83	204	20	7	7	73	62	71	5	.264	.335
Moore, Kelvin-Kelvin Orlando	81-83OakA	09-26-57	Le Roy, Ala.		R	L	6'1	195	76	238	23	53	5	2	8	25	18	77	3	.223	.361
Moore, Kerwin-Kerwin Lamar	96OakA	10-29-70	Detroit, Mich.		B	R	190	22	16	4	1	1	0	0	0	2	6	1	.063	.125
Moore, Scott-Scott Alan Boyd	06ChiN	11-17-83	Long Beach, Cal.		L	R	6'2	180	16	38	6	10	2	0	2	5	2	10	0	.263	.474
Mora, Andres-Andres [Ibarra]	76-78BalA 80CleA	05-25-55	Rio Bravo, Mexico		R	R	6'	182	235	700	71	156	27	2	27	83	31	149	1	.223	.383
Mora, Melvin-Melvin	99-00NYN 00-06BalA	02-02-72	Aguas Negras, Venez.		R	R	5'10	190	1015	3549	562	993	193	11	119	483	369	663	76	.280	.441
Morales, Jerry-Julio Ruben [Torres]	69-73SDN 74-77ChiN 78StLN 79DetA 80NYN 81-83ChiN	02-18-49	Yabucoa, P.R.		R	R	5'10	170	1441	4528	516	1173	199	36	95	570	366	567	37	.259	.382
Morales, Jose-Jose Manuel [Hernandez] (Shady)	73OakA 73-77MonN 78-80MinA 81-82BalA 82-84LAN	12-30-44	Frederiksted, V.I.		R	R	5'11	205	733	1305	126	375	68	6	26	207	89	182	0	.287	.408
Morales, Kendry-Kendry	06LAA	06-20-83	Fomento, Cuba		B	R	6'1	220	57	197	21	46	10	1	5	22	17	28	1	.234	.371
Morales, Willie-William Anthony	00BalA	09-07-72	Tucson, Ariz.		B	R	5'10	182	3	11	1	3	1	0	0	0	0	3	0	.273	.364
Morandini, Mickey-Michael Robert	90-97PhiN 98-99ChiN 00PhiN 00TorA	04-22-66	Kittanning, Pa.		L	R	5'11	180	1298	4558	597	1222	209	54	32	351	437	714	123	.268	.359
Morban, Jose-Jose	03BalA	10-02-79	Santiago, Dom. Rep.		R	R	5'11	170	61	71	14	10	0	2	0	5	3	21	8	.141	.197
Mordecai, Mike-Michael Howard	94-97AtlN 98-02MonN 02-05FlaN	12-13-67	Birmingham, Ala.		R	R	5'11	180	793	1362	157	333	75	7	24	132	112	261	13	.244	.363
Moreland, Keith-Bobby Keith (Zonk)	78-81PhiN 82-87ChiN 88SDN 89DetA 89BalA	05-02-54	Dallas, Tex.		R	R	6'	200	1306	4581	511	1279	214	14	121	674	405	515	28	.279	.411
Moreno (Mauricio), Jose-Jose de los Santos Mauricio [Moreno]	80NYN 81SDN 82CalA	11-01-57	Santo Domingo, D.R.		B	R	6'	190	82	97	14	20	4	1	2	6	6	20	5	.206	.330
Moreno, Omar-Omar Renan (Quintero)	75-82PitN 83HouN 83-85NYA 86AtlN 86KCA	10-24-52	Puerto Armuellus, Pan.		L	L	6'3	185	1382	4992	699	1257	171	87	37	386	387	885	487	.252	.343
Morgan, Joe-Joe Leonard	63-71HouN 72-79CinN 80HouN 81-82SFN 83PhiN 84OakA	09-19-43	Bonham, Tex.		L	R	5'7	160	2649	9277	1650	2517	449	96	268	1133	1865	1015	689	.271	.427
Morgan, Kevin-Kevin Lee	97NYN	12-03-70	Lafayette, La.		R	R	170	1	1	0	0	0	0	0	0	0	0	0	.000	.000
Moriarty, Mike-Michael Thomas	02BalA	03-08-74	Camden, N.J.		R	R	6'	188	8	16	0	3	1	0	0	3	0	2	0	.188	.250
Morman, Russ-Russell Lee	86,88-89ChiA 90-91KCA 94-97FlaN	04-28-62	Independence, Mo.		R	R	6'4	215	207	470	51	117	17	4	10	43	35	102	3	.249	.366
Morneau, Justin-Justin Ernest George	03-06MinA	05-15-81	New Westminster, Canada		L	R	6'4	220	412	1468	212	407	81	5	79	283	134	271	3	.277	.491
Moronko, Jeff-Jeffrey Robert	84CleA 87NYA	08-17-59	Houston, Tex.		R	R	6'2	185	14	30	1	4	1	0	0	3	2	7	0	.133	.167
Morris, Hal-William Harold	88-89NYA 90-97CinN 98KCA 99-00CinN 00DetA	04-09-65	Fort Rucker, Ala.		L	L	6'4	210	1246	3998	535	1216	246	21	76	513	356	548	45	.304	.433
Morris, John-John Daniel	86-90StLN 91PhiN 92CalA	02-23-61	North Bellmore, N.Y.		L	L	6'1	185	402	614	60	145	15	8	8	63	42	108	15	.236	.326
Morris, Warren-Warren Randall	99-01PitN 02MinA 03DetA	01-11-74	Alexandra, La.		L	R	5'11	184	440	1495	176	399	70	7	26	164	150	218	16	.267	.375
Morrison, Jim-James Forrest	77-78PhiN 79-82ChiA 82-87PitN 87-88DetA 88AtlN	09-23-52	Pensacola, Fla.		R	R	5'11	180	1089	3375	371	876	170	16	112	435	213	521	50	.260	.419
Morse, Mike-Michael John	05-06SeaA	03-22-82	Ft. Lauderdale, Fla.		R	R	6'4	205	93	273	32	80	15	1	3	34	21	57	4	.293	.388
Moseby, Lloyd-Lloyd Anthony (Shaker)	80-90TorA 90-91DetA	11-05-59	Portland, Ark.		L	R	6'3	205	1588	5815	869	1494	273	66	169	737	616	1135	280	.257	.414
Moses, John-John William	82-87SeaA 88-90MinA 91DetA 92SeaA	08-09-57	Los Angeles, Cal.		B	L	5'9	170	769	1723	247	438	69	17	11	145	143	226	101	.254	.333
Mosquera, Julio-Julio Alberto [Cervantes]	96-97TorA 05MilN	01-29-72	Panama City, Panama		R	R	6'	185	32	31	2	7	3	0	0	3	2	6	0	.226	.323
Mota, Andy-Andres Alberto [Matos]	91HouN	03-04-66	Santo Domingo, D.R.		R	R	5'10	180	27	90	4	17	2	0	1	6	1	17	2	.189	.244
Mota, Jose-Jose Manuel [Matos]	91SDN 95KCA	03-16-65	Santo Domingo, D.R.		B	R	5'9	155	19	38	4	8	0	0	0	1	2	4	1	.211	.211
Motley, Darryl-Darryl DeWayne	81,83-86KCA 86-87AtlN	01-21-60	Muskogee, Okla.		R	R	5'9	196	413	1333	156	324	58	10	44	159	67	186	19	.243	.401
Mottola, Chad-Charles Edward	96CinN 00TorA 01FlaN 04BalA 06TorA	10-15-71	Augusta, Ga.		R	R	6'3	220	59	125	17	25	6	0	4	12	10	28	2	.200	.344
Mouton, James-James Raleigh	94-97HouN 98SDN 99MonN 00-01MilN	12-29-68	Denver, Colo.		R	R	5'9	175	723	1570	223	386	75	7	18	147	174	338	109	.246	.337
Mouton, Lyle-Lyle Joseph	95-97ChiA 98BalA 99DetA 89PhiN	05-13-69	Lafayette, La.		R	R	6'4	240	328	805	96	225	43	2	22	116	71	209	9	.280	.420
Mueller, Bill-William Richard	96-00SFN 01-02ChiN 02SFN 03-05BosA 06LAN	03-17-71	Maryland Heights, Mo.		B	R	5'10	180	1216	4223	663	1229	265	22	85	493	543	571	20	.291	.425
Mulligan, Sean-Sean Patrick	96SDN	04-25-70	Lynwood, Cal.		R	R	6'2	210	2	1	0	0	0	0	0	0	0	0	0	.000	.000
Mulliniks, Rance-Steven Rance	77-79CalA 80-81KCA 82-92TorA	01-15-56	Tulare, Cal.		L	R	5'11	175	1325	3569	445	972	226	17	73	435	460	555	15	.272	.407
Mullins, Fran-Francis Joseph	80ChiA 84SFN 86CleA	05-14-57	Oakland, Cal.		R	R	6'	180	106	212	20	43	16	0	3	18	20	48	3	.203	.307
Mumphrey, Jerry-Jerry Wayne	74-79StLN 80SDN 81-83NYA 83-85HouN 86-88ChiN	09-09-52	Tyler, Tex.		B	R	6'2	195	1585	4993	660	1442	217	55	70	575	478	688	174	.289	.396
Munoz, Jose-Jose Luis	96ChiA	11-11-67	Chicago, Ill.		B	R	5'11	165	17	27	7	7	0	1	0	3	4	2	0	.259	.259
Munoz, Noe-Noe	95LAN	11-11-67	San Cristobal, Mexico		R	R	5'11	180	2	1	0	0	0	0	0	0	0	0	0	.000	.000
Munoz, Pedro-Pedro Javier [Gonzalez]	90-95MinA 96OakA	09-19-68	Ponce, P.R.		R	R	5'11	200	517	1708	203	467	75	8	67	252	100	418	11	.273	.444
Munson, Eric-Eric Walter	00-04DetA 05TBA 06HouA	10-03-77	San Diego, Cal.		L	R	6'3	220	310	802	94	181	33	3	45	132	88	219	1	.226	.416
Munson, Thurman-Thurman Lee	69-79NYA	06-07-47	Akron, Ohio	08-02-79	R	R	5'11	190	1423	5344	696	1558	229	32	113	701	438	571	48	.292	.410
Murcer, Bobby-Bobby Ray	65-66NYA 67-68MS 69-74NYA 75-76SFN 77-79ChiN 79-83NYA	05-20-46	Oklahoma City, Okla.		L	R	5'11	175	1908	6730	972	1862	285	45	252	1043	862	841	127	.277	.445
Murphy, Dale-Dale Bryan	76-90AtlN 90-92PhiN 93ColN	03-12-56	Portland, Ore.		R	R	6'4	215	2180	7960	1197	2111	350	39	398	1266	986	1748	161	.265	.469
Murphy, David-David Matthew	06BosA	10-18-81	Houston, Tex.		L	L	6'2	180	24	4	4	1	0	0	0	0	0	2	0	.227	.409
Murphy, Donnie-Donald Rex	04-05KCA	03-10-83	Lakewood, Cal.		R	R	5'10	180	39	104	5	17	4	0	1	9	6	30	1	.163	.269
Murphy, Dwayne-Dwayne Keith	78-87OakA 88DetA 89PhiN	03-18-55	Merced, Cal.		L	L	6'1	190	1360	4347	648	1069	139	20	166	609	747	953	100	.246	.402
Murphy, Tommy-Thomas Christian	06LAA	08-27-79	Suffern, N.Y.		B	R	6'	185	48	70	12	16	4	1	0	4	3	18	4	.229	.357
Murray, Calvin-Calvin Duane	99-02SFN 02TexA 04ChiN	07-30-71	Dallas, Texas		R	R	5'11	190	288	633	108	146	33	4	8	54	71	111	22	.231	.333
Murray, Eddie-Eddie Clarence	77-88BalA 89-91LAN 92-93NYN 94-96CleA 96BalA 97AnaA 97LAN	02-24-56	Los Angeles, Cal.		B	R	6'2	210	3026	11336	1627	3255	560	35	504	1917	1333	1516	110	.287	.476

USE NAME - GIVEN NAMES (NICKNAMES)	TEAM BY YEAR	BIRTH DATE	BIRTH PLACE	DEATH DATE	B	T	HGT	WGT	G	AB	R	H	2B	3B	HR	RBI	BB	SO	SB	BA	SA
Murray, Glenn-Glenn Everett	96PhiN	11-23-70	Manning, S.C.		R	R	6'2	225	38	97	8	19	3	0	2	6	7	36	1	.196	.289
Murray, Larry-Larry (Slick)	74-76NYA 77-79OakA	04-01-53	Chicago, Ill.		B	R	6'	178	226	412	49	73	16	4	3	31	48	74	20	.177	.257
Murray, Rich-Richard Dale	80,83SFN	07-06-57	Los Angeles, Cal.		R	R	6'4	205	57	204	19	44	8	2	4	25	11	51	2	.216	.333
Murton, Matt-Matthew Henry	05-06ChiN	10-03-81	Ft. Lauderdale, Fla.		R	R	6'1	215	195	595	89	180	25	5	20	76	61	84	7	.303	.462
Muser, Tony-Anthony Joseph	69BosA 71-72ChiA 75-77BalA 78MilA M97-02KCA	08-01-47	Van Nuys, Cal.		L	L	6'2	185	663	1268	123	329	41	9	7	117	95	138	14	.259	.323
Myers, Greg-Gregory Richard	87,89-92TorA 92-95CalA 96-97MinA 97AtlN 98-99SDN 99BalA 00-01BalA 01-02OakA 03-05TorA	04-14-66	Riverside, Cal.		L	R	6'1	215	1108	3042	333	776	150	7	87	396	268	539	3	.255	.395
Myers, Rod-Roderick Demond	96-97KCA 98SJ	01-14-73	Conroe, Tex.		L	L	6'	190	53	164	23	44	14	0	3	20	24	38	7	.268	.409
Myrow, Brian-Brian Shawn	05LAN	09-04-76	Fort Worth, Tex.		L	R	5'11	190	19	20	2	4	1	0	0	0	5	8	0	.200	.250
Nady, Xavier-Xavier Clifford	00,03-05SDN 06NYN 06PitN	11-14-78	Salinas, Cal.		R	R	6'2	220	399	1243	155	335	64	4	42	154	81	239	11	.270	.429
Naehring, Tim-Timothy James	90-97BosA 98EJ	02-01-67	Cincinnati, Ohio		R	R	6'2	200	547	1872	254	527	104	4	49	250	236	312	5	.282	.420
Nahorodny, Bill-William Gerard	76PhiN 77-79ChiA 80-81AtlN 82CleA 83DetA 84SeaA	08-31-53	Hamtramck, Mich.		R	R	6'2	195	308	844	74	203	41	3	25	109	56	118	1	.241	.385
Nakamura, Norihiro-Norihiro	05LAN	07-24-73	Osaka, Japan		R	R	5'10	203	17	39	1	5	2	0	0	3	2	7	0	.128	.179
Napoli, Mike-Michael Anthony	06LAA	10-31-81	Hollywood, Fla.		R	R	6'	205	99	268	47	61	13	0	16	42	51	90	2	.228	.455
Narron, Jerry-Jerry Austin	79NYA 80-81SeaA 83-86CalA 87SeaA M01-02TexA M05-06CinN	11-15-56	Goldsboro, N. C.		L	R	6'3	205	392	840	64	177	23	2	21	96	67	127	0	.211	.318
Natal, Bob-Robert Marcel	92MonN 93-97FlaN	11-13-65	Long Beach, Cal.		R	R	5'11	190	120	289	13	57	10	3	4	19	30	68	2	.197	.294
Navarro, Dioner-Dioner Favian Navarro [Vivas]	04NYA 05-06LAN 06TBA	02-09-84	Caracas, Venezuela		B	R	5'10	190	136	451	51	119	18	0	9	43	51	72	2	.264	.364
Navarro, Oswaldo-Oswaldo Ramses	06SeaA	10-02-84	Villa de Cura, Venezuela		R	R	6'	155	4	3	0	2	0	0	0	0	0	1	0	.667	.667
Navarro, Tito-Noberto [Rodriguez]	93NYN	09-12-70	Rio Piedras, P.R.		B	R	5'10	165	12	17	1	1	0	0	0	1	0	4	0	.059	.059
Neel, Troy-Troy Lee	92-94OakA	09-14-65	Freeport, Tex.		L	R	6'4	215	230	758	110	212	37	0	37	120	92	177	5	.280	.475
Neill, Mike-Michael Robert	98OakA	04-27-70	Martinsville, Va.		L	L	6'2	190	6	15	2	4	1	0	0	0	2	4	0	.267	.333
Nelson, Bry-Bryant Lawrence	02BosA	01-27-74	Crossett, Ark.		R	R	5'10	205	25	34	6	9	3	0	2	0	2	4	1	.265	.353
Nelson, Dave-David Earl	68-69CleA 70-71WasA 72-75TexA 76-77KCA	06-20-44	Fort Sill, Okla.		R	R	5'10	160	813	2578	340	630	77	19	20	211	220	392	187	.244	.312
			Bats Both 68																		
Nelson, Jamie-James Victor	83SeaA	09-05-59	Clinton, Okla.		R	R	5'11	185	40	96	9	21	3	0	1	5	13	12	4	.219	.281
Nelson, John-John Clark	06StLN	03-03-79	Denton, Tex.		R	R	6'1	190	8	5	2	0	0	0	0	0	0	4	0	.000	.000
Nelson, Ricky-Ricky Lee	83-86SeaA	05-08-59	Eloy, Ariz.		L	R	6'	200	123	320	38	79	13	3	6	39	19	59	8	.247	.363
Nelson, Rob-Robert Augustus	86-87OakA 87-90SDN	05-17-64	Pasadena, Cal.		L	L	6'4	215	76	152	12	27	2	1	4	11	24	66	1	.178	.283
Nettles, Graig-Graig	67-69MinA 70-72CleA 73-83NYA 84-86SDN 87AtlN 88MonN	08-20-44	San Diego, Cal.		L	R	6'	185	2700	8986	1193	2225	328	28	390	1314	1088	1209	32	.248	.421
Nettles, Morris-Morris	74-75CalA	01-26-52	Los Angeles, Cal.		L	L	6'2	175	168	489	77	116	15	0	3	31	42	95	42	.247	.279
Nevin, Phil-Phillip Joseph	95HouN 95-97DetA 98AnaA 99-05SDN 05-06TexA 06ChiN 06MinA	01-19-71	Fullerton, Cal.		R	R	6'2	225	1217	4188	584	1131	209	6	208	743	449	1019	18	.270	.472
Newfield, Marc-Marc Alexander	93-95SeaA 95-96SDN 96-97MilA 98MilN	10-19-72	Sacramento, Cal.		R	R	6'4	205	355	957	98	238	53	1	22	132	69	162	1	.249	.375
Newman, David-David Matthew	99-00SDN 00-01PhiN 04-06BalA	09-07-73	Fullerton, Calif.		L	R	5'10	180	293	808	128	207	31	7	20	102	66	163	26	.256	.386
Newman, Al-Albert Dwayne	85-86MonN 87-91MinA 92TexA	06-30-60	Kansas City, Mo.		B	R	5'9	190	854	2107	264	476	68	7	1	156	236	212	91	.226	.266
Newman, Jeff-Jeffrey Lynn	76-82OakA 83-84BosA M86OakA	09-11-48	Fort Worth, Tex.		R	R	6'2	215	735	2123	189	475	85	4	65	233	116	369	7	.224	.357
Newson, Warren-Warren Dale	91-95ChiA 95SeaA 96-98TexA	07-03-64	Newnan, Ga.		L	L	5'7	200	489	992	156	248	40	4	34	120	196	292	14	.250	.401
Nichols, Carl-Carl Edward	86-88BalA 89-91HouN	10-14-62	Los Angeles, Cal.		R	R	6'	205	96	186	16	38	8	0	4	18	18	49	0	.204	.247
Nichols, Reid-Thomas Reid	80-85BosA 85-86ChiA 87MonN	08-05-58	Ocala, Fla.		R	R	5'11	178	540	1160	156	306	63	8	22	131	99	149	27	.266	.391
Nicholson, Kevin-Kevin Ronald	00SDN	03-29-76	Vancouver, Canada		B	R	5'10	190	37	97	7	21	6	1	1	8	4	31	1	.216	.330
Nicosia, Steve-Steven Richard (Nick)	78-83PitN 83-84SFN 85MonN 85TorA	08-06-55	Paterson, N.J.		R	R	5'10	185	358	938	86	233	52	3	11	88	86	90	5	.248	.345
Niekro, Lance-Lance Joseph	03,05-06SFN	01-29-79	Winter Haven, Fla.		R	R	6'3	210	184	482	61	120	26	5	17	79	28	86	0	.249	.429
Nieto, Tom-Thomas Andrew	84-85StLN 86MonN 87-88MinA 89-90PhiN	10-27-60	Downey, Cal.		R	R	6'1	205	251	619	37	127	24	4	5	69	55	135	0	.205	.281
Nieves, Jose-Jose Miguel [Pinto]	98-00CinN 01-02AnaA	06-16-75	Guacara, Venezuela		R	R	6'1	180	212	530	55	128	20	5	9	51	23	102	2	.242	.349
Nieves, Melvin-Melvin [Ramos]	92AtlN 93-95SDN 96-97DetA 98CinN	12-28-71	San Juan, P.R.		B	R	6'2	200	458	1228	163	284	53	6	63	187	136	483	4	.231	.438
Nieves, Wil-Wilbert	02SDN 05-06NYA	09-25-77	San Juan, P.R.		R	R	5'11	190	37	82	2	13	3	1	0	3	4	17	1	.159	.220
Nilsson, Dave-David Wayne	92-97MilA 98-99MilN	12-14-69	Brisbane, Australia		L	R	6'3	225	837	2779	389	789	157	10	105	470	320	424	15	.284	.461
Nivar, Ramon-Ramon A. [Martinez]	03-04TexA 05BalA	02-22-80	San Cristobal,D.R.		R	R	5'10	170	42	121	13	27	1	2	0	12	4	19	5	.223	.264
Nix, Laynce-Laynce Michael	03-06TexA 06MilN	10-30-80	Houston, Texas		L	L	6'	190	250	851	114	205	44	7	29	118	41	239	6	.241	.411
Nixon, Donell-Robert Donell	87SeaA 88-89SFN 90BalA	12-31-61	Evergreen, N.C.		R	R	6'1	185	208	396	56	109	11	0	4	35	35	77	47	.275	.333
Nixon, Otis-Otis Junior	83NYA 84-87CleA 88-90MonN 91-93AtlN 94BosA 95TexA 96-97TorA 97LAN 98MinA 99AtlN	01-09-59	Evergreen, N.C.		B	R	6'2	180	1709	5115	878	1379	142	27	11	318	585	694	620	.270	.314
Nixon, Trot-Christopher Trotman	96,98-06BosA	04-11-74	Durham, N.C.		L	L	6'1	210	982	3285	547	912	204	28	133	523	454	621	29	.278	.478
Noboa, Junior-Milciades Arturo [Diaz]	84,87CleA 88CalA 89-91MonN 92NYN 94OakA 94PitN	11-10-64	Azua, Dom. Rep.		R	R	5'10	175	71	181	17	42	9	3	1	14	6	49	5	.232	.354
Noce, Paul-Paul David	87ChiN 90CinN	12-16-59	San Francisco, Cal.		R	R	5'10	175	71	181	17	42	9	2	3	14	6	49	5	.232	.354
Nokes, Matt-Matthew Dodge	85SFN 86-90DetA 90-94NYA 95BalA 95ColN	10-31-63	San Diego, Cal.		L	R	6'1	200	902	2735	310	695	96	4	136	422	200	395	8	.254	.441
Nolan, Joe-Joseph William (Juice)	72NYN 75,77-80AtlN 80-81CinN 82-85BalA	05-12-51	St. Louis, Mo.		L	R	6'	190	621	1454	156	382	66	10	27	178	164	183	7	.263	.378
Nordbrook, Tim-Timothy Charles	74-76BalA 76CalA 77ChiA 77-78TorA 78-79MilA	08-12-53	Baltimore, Md.		R	R	6'1	178	126	169	27	30	1	1	0	3	25	33	4	.178	.195
Nordhagen, Wayne-Wayne Oren	76-81ChiA 82TorA 82PitN 82CubA 83ChiN	07-04-48	Thief River Falls, Minn.		R	R	6'2	210	502	1423	147	401	77	8	39	205	54	162	1	.282	.429
Norman, Dan-Daniel Edmund (Chauffer)	77-80NYN 82MonN	01-11-55	Los Angeles, Cal.		R	R	6'2	200	192	346	29	94	8	3	11	37	29	76	8	.227	.362
			Bats both part of 80																		
Norman, Les-Leslie Eugene	95-96KCA	02-25-69	Warren, Mich.		R	R	6'1	185	78	89	15	15	0	1	0	4	12	20	1	.169	.191
Norman, Nelson-Nelson Augusto [Martin] (Nellie)	78-81TexA 82PitN 87MonN	05-23-58	San Pedro de Mac.,D.R.		B	R	6'2	162	198	429	42	95	12	3	0	25	21	50	4	.221	.263
			Bats both 87, part of 79																		
Norris, Jim-James Francis	77-79CleA 80TexA	12-20-48	Brooklyn, N.Y.		L	L	5'11	190	489	1282	173	338	57	17	7	110	173	126	59	.264	.351
North, Billy-William Alex	71-72ChiN 73-78OakA 78LAN 79-81SFN	05-15-48	Seattle, Wash.		B	R	5'11	185	1169	3900	640	1016	120	31	20	230	627	665	395	.261	.323
			Bats Right 71																		
Norton, Greg-Gregory Blakemoor	96-00ChiA 01-03ColN 04DetA 06TBA	07-06-72	San Leandro, Cal.		B	R	6'1	205	820	1945	258	491	103	8	78	273	233	485	14	.252	.434
Norwood, Willie-Willie	77-80MinA	11-07-50	Greene Co., Ala.		R	R	6'	185	294	854	109	207	40	6	18	93	57	145	41	.242	.367
Nunez, Abraham-Abraham Orlando [Adames]	97-04PitN 05StLN 06PhiN	03-16-76	Santo Domingo, D.R.		B	R	5'11	185	892	2232	262	542	78	18	18	193	220	399	36	.243	.318
Nunez, Abraham-Abraham	02,04FlaN 04KCA	02-05-77	Haina, Dom. Rep.		B	R	6'3	210	136	302	42	63	10	1	6	35	34	74	1	.209	.308
Nunnally, Jon-Jonathan Keith	95-97KCA 97-98CinN 99BosA 00NYN	11-09-71	Pelham, N.C.		L	R	5'10	190	364	885	162	218	47	12	42	125	146	239	19	.246	.469
Nunnari, Talmadge-Talmadge Raphael	00MonN	04-08-75	Pensacola, Fla.		L	L	6'1	205	18	5	2	1	0	0	0	1	6	2	0	.200	.200
Nyman, Chris-Christopher Curtis	82-83ChiA	06-06-55	Pomona, Cal.		R	R	6'4	200	49	93	18	24	1	0	2	6	7	16	5	.258	.333
Nyman, Nyls-Nyls Wallace Rex	74-77ChiA	03-07-54	Detroit, Mich.		L	R	6'	185	120	357	43	85	9	4	2	33	11	38	12	.238	.303
Oates, Johnny-Johnny Lane	70,72BalA 73-75AtlN 75-76PhiN 77-79LAN 80-81NYA M91-94BalA M95-01TexA	01-21-46	Sylva, N.C.	12-24-04	L	R	5'11	185	593	1637	146	410	56	2	14	126	141	149	11	.250	.313
Obando, Sherman-Sherman Omar [Gainor]	93,95BalA 96-97MonN	01-23-70	Bocas del Toro,Panama		R	R	6'4	215	177	355	41	85	13	0	13	49	34	100	3	.239	.386
Oberkfell, Ken-Kenneth Ray (Obie)	77-84StLN 84-88AtlN 88-89PitN 89SFN 90-91HouN 92CalA	05-04-56	Highland, Ill.		L	R	6'1	200	1602	4874	558	1354	237	44	29	446	546	356	62	.278	.364
O'Berry, Mike-Preston Michael	79BosA 80ChiN 81-82CinN 83CalA 84NYA 85MonN	04-20-54	Birmingham, Ala.		R	R	6'2	195	197	376	38	72	10	1	4	27	43	77	1	.191	.247
Obradovich, Jim-James Thomas	78HouN	09-13-49	Fort Campbell, Ky.		L	L	6'1	200	10	17	3	3	0	1	0	2	1	3	0	.176	.294
O'Brien, Charlie-Charles Hugh	85OakA 87-90MilA 90-93NYN 94-95AtlN 96-97TorA 98ChiA 98-99AnaA 00MonN	05-01-60	Tulsa, Okla.		R	R	6'2	195	800	2232	216	493	119	4	56	261	209	354	1	.221	.353
O'Brien, Pete-Peter Michael (O'B)	82-88TexA 89CleA 90-93SeaA	02-09-58	Santa Monica, Cal.		L	L	6'1	200	1567	5437	654	1421	254	21	169	736	641	563	24	.261	.409
Ochoa, Alex-Alex	95-97NYN 98MinA 99MilN 00-01CinN 01ColN 02MilN 02AnaA	03-29-72	Miami Lakes, Fla.		R	R	6'	195	807	2143	320	597	131	19	46	261	203	288	55	.279	.422
Oester, Ron-Ronald John (O)	78-90CinN	05-05-56	Cincinnati, Ohio		B	R	6'2	190	1276	4214	458	1118	190	33	42	344	369	681	40	.265	.356
Offerman, Jose-Jose Antonio (Dono)	90-95LAN 96-98KCA 99-02BosA 02SeaA 04MinN 05PhiN 05NYN	11-08-68	San Pedro de Mac.,D.R.		B	R	6'	185	1651	5681	840	1551	252	72	57	537	772	914	172	.273	.373
Office, Rowland-Rowland Johnie	72,74-79AtlN 80-82 MonN 83NYA	10-25-52	Sacramento, Cal.		L	L	6'	170	899	2413	259	626	101	11	32	242	189	311	27	.259	.350
Oglivie, Ben-Benjamin Ambrosio [Palmer] (Junie)	71-73BosA 74-77DetA 78-86MilA	02-11-49	Colon, Panama		L	L	6'2	175	1754	5913	784	1615	277	33	235	901	560	852	87	.273	.450
O'Halloran, Greg-Gregory Joseph	94FlaN	05-21-68	Toronto, Canada		L	R	6'2	205	12	11	1	2	0	0	0	1	0	1	0	.182	.182
Ojeda, Augie-Octavio Augie	00-03ChiN 04MinA	12-20-74	Los Angeles, Cal.		B	R	5'9	170	178	375	48	82	13	2	5	31	38	42	3	.219	.304
Ojeda, Miguel-Miguel Arturo	03-05SDN 05SeaA 06ColN 06TexA	01-29-75	Guaymas, Mexico		R	R	6'2	190	212	486	49	109	17	1	15	72	56	103	2	.224	.356
Olander, Jim-James Bentley	91MilA	02-21-63	Tucson, Ariz.		R	R	6'2	185	12	9	2	0	0	0	0	0	2	5	0	.000	.000
O'Leary, Troy-Troy Franklin	93-94MilA 95-01BosA 02MonN 03ChiN	08-04-69	Compton, Cal.		L	L	6'	200	1198	4010	547	1100	234	40	127	591	334	661	17	.274	.448
Olerud, John-John Garrett	89-96TorA 97-99NYN 00-04SeaA 04NYA 05BosA	08-05-68	Seattle, Wash.		L	L	6'5	215	2234	7592	1139	2239	500	13	255	1230	1275	1016	11	.295	.465
Oliva, Jose-Jose [Galvez]	94-95AtlN 95StLN	03-03-71	San Pedro de Mac.,D.R.	12-22-97	R	R	6'1	215	89	242	24	43	10	0	13	31	19	56	0	.178	.380
Oliver, Al-Albert (Scoop)	68-77PitN 78-81TexA 82-83MonN 84SFN 84PhiN 85LAN 85TorA	10-14-46	Portsmouth, Ohio		L	L	6'	195	2368	9049	1189	2743	529	77	219	1326	535	756	84	.303	.451
Oliver, Dave-David Jacob (Ollie)	77CleA	04-07-51	Stockton, Cal.		R	R	5'11	175	7	22	2	7	0	0	0	3	0	0	0	.318	.409
Oliver, Joe-Joseph Melton	89-94CinN 95MilA 96-97CinN 98DetA 98SeaA 99PitN 00SeaA 01NYA 01BosA	07-24-65	Memphis, Tenn.		R	R	6'3	215	1076	3367	320	831	174	3	102	476	248	637	13	.247	.391

USE NAME - GIVEN NAMES (NICKNAMES)	TEAM BY YEAR	BIRTH DATE	BIRTH PLACE	DEATH DATE	B	T	HGT	WGT	G	AB	R	H	2B	3B	HR	RBI	BB	SO	SB	BA	SA
Olivo, Miguel-Miguel Eduardo [Pena]	02-04ChiA 04-05SeaA 05SDN 06FlaN	07-15-78	Villa Vasquez,Dom.Rep.		R	R	6'	215	434	1334	167	320	68	9	45	164	58	352	22	.240	.406
Olmedo, Ray-Rainer Gustavo	03-06CinN	05-31-81	Maracay, Venezuela		B	R	5'11	155	171	352	39	81	12	2	2	25	24	72	6	.230	.293
Olson, Greg-Gregory William	89MinA 90-93AtlN	09-06-60	Marshall, Minn.		R	R	6'	200	414	1275	132	309	61	3	20	131	137	151	5	.242	.342
Olson, Tim-Timothy Lane	04AriN 05ColN	08-01-78	Grand Forks, N.D.		R	R	6'2	200	51	99	8	18	7	0	2	5	17	20	1	.182	.313
O'Malley, Tom-Thomas Patrick	82-84SFN 84ChiA 85-86BalA 87TexA 88MonN 89-90NYN	12-25-60	Orange, N.J.		L	R	6'	190	466	1213	117	310	54	5	13	131	133	151	2	.256	.340
O'Neill, Paul-Paul Andrew	85-92CinN 93-01NYA	02-25-63	Columbus, Ohio		L	L	6'4	215	2053	7318	1041	2105	451	21	281	1269	892	1166	141	.288	.470
Ontiveros, Steve-Steven Robert	73-76SFN 77-80ChiN	10-26-51	Bakersfield, Cal.		B	R	6'	190	732	2193	230	600	111	10	24	224	309	290	5	.274	.366
Oquendo, Jose-Jose Manuel [Contreras] (Cheo)	83-84NYN 86-95StlN	07-04-63	Rio Piedras, P.R.	Bats Right 83-84	B	R	5'9	170	1190	3202	339	821	104	24	14	254	448	376	35	.256	.317
Ordaz, Luis-Luis Javier	97-99StlN 00-02KCA 06TBA	08-12-75	Maracaibo, Venezuela		R	R	5'11	170	206	440	51	96	13	0	0	30	34	53	12	.218	.248
Ordonez, Magglio-Magglio [Delgado] (Mags)	97-04ChiA 05-06DetA	01-28-74	Caracas, Venezuela		R	R	5'11	205	1238	4705	744	1436	289	16	219	853	408	553	83	.305	.513
Ordonez, Rey-Reynaldo	96-02NYN 03TBA 04ChiN	01-11-71	Havana, Cuba		R	R	5'9	160	973	3115	291	767	129	17	12	287	191	339	28	.246	.310
Orie, Kevin-Kevin Leonard	97-98ChiN 98-99FlaN 02ChiN	09-01-72	West Chester, Pa.		R	R	6'4	215	316	1015	117	253	64	6	22	116	94	163	5	.249	.389
Orr, Pete-Peterson Thomas Gordon	05-06AtlN	06-08-79	Richmond Hill, Canada		L	R	6'1	175	214	304	54	84	11	5	2	16	11	53	9	.276	.365
Orsulak, Joe-Joseph Michael	83-86PitN 88-92BalA 93-95NYN 96FlaN 97MonN	05-31-62	Parsippany, N.J.		L	L	6'1	200	1494	4293	559	1173	186	37	57	405	318	402	93	.273	.374
Orta, Jorge-Jorge [Nunez]	72-79ChiA 80-81CleA 82LAN 83TorA 84-87KCA	11-26-50	Mazatlan, Mexico		L	R	5'10	175	1755	5829	733	1619	267	63	130	745	500	715	79	.278	.412
Ortega, Bill-William [Bobadilla]	01StlN	07-24-75	Havana, Cuba		R	R	6'4	205	5	5	0	1	0	0	0	0	0	1	0	.200	.200
Ortenzio, Frank-Frank Joseph (Moose)	73KCA	02-24-51	Fresno, Cal.		R	R	6'	220	9	25	1	7	2	0	1	6	2	6	0	.280	.480
Ortiz, David-David Americo [Arias] (Big Papi)	97-02MinA 03-06BosA	11-18-75	Santo Domingo, D.R.		L	L	6'4	235	1043	3666	622	1037	263	11	231	763	540	796	6	.283	.570
Ortiz, Hector-Hector Jr, [Montanez]	98KCA 00-01KCA 02TexA	10-14-69	Rio Piedras, P.R.		R	R	6'0	205	93	260	29	75	13	1	1	18	18	33	1	.288	.358
Ortiz, Javier-Javier Victor	90-91HouN	01-22-63	Boston, Mass.		R	R	6'4	220	77	160	14	44	9	2	2	15	26	25	1	.275	.394
Ortiz, Jose-Jose Daniel	00-01OakA 01-02ColN	06-13-77	Santo Domingo, D.R.		R	R	5'9	160	136	449	68	109	15	2	14	51	35	74	6	.243	.379
Ortiz, Junior-Adalberto [Colon]	82-83PitN 83-84NYN 85-89PitN 90-91MinA 92-93CleA 94TexA	10-24-59	Humacao, P.R.		R	R	5'10	175	749	1894	142	484	71	4	5	186	121	222	8	.256	.305
Ortiz, Luis-Luis Alberto [Galarza]	93-94BosA 95-96TexA	05-25-70	Santo Domingo, D.R.		R	R	6'	190	60	145	14	33	7	3	2	26	7	26	0	.228	.359
Ortmeier, Dan-Daniel David	05-06SFN	05-11-81	Chattanooga, Tenn.		B	L	6'4	220	24	34	1	6	1	0	0	3	3	9	1	.176	.206
Orton, John-John Andrew	89-93CalA	12-08-65	Santa Cruz, Cal.		R	R	6'1	195	156	401	35	80	18	0	4	29	31	121	2	.200	.274
Osik, Keith-Keith Richard	96-02PitN 03MilN 04BalA 05WasN	10-22-68	Port Jefferson, N.Y.		R	R	6'	200	456	1123	96	259	55	4	13	108	111	202	6	.231	.321
Otanez, Willis-Willis Alexander	98-99BalA 99TorA	04-19-73	La Vega , Dom. Rep.		R	R	6'1	215	74	212	28	50	11	0	7	24	15	48	0	.236	.387
Otero, Ricky-Ricardo [Figueroa]	95NYN 96-97PhiN	04-15-72	Vega Baja, P.R.		B	R	5'7	150	189	613	79	157	19	9	2	36	56	55	18	.256	.326
Ostrosser, Brian-Brian Leonard	73NYN	05-17-49	Hamilton, Canada		L	R	6'1	175	4	5	0	0	0	0	0	0	2	0	0	.000	.000
Otis, Amos-Amos Joseph	67-69NYN 70-83KCA 84PitN	04-26-47	Mobile, Ala.		R	R	5'11	170	1998	7299	1092	2020	374	66	193	1007	757	1008	341	.277	.425
Ott, Ed-Nathan Edward	74-80PitN 81CalA 82-83SJ	07-11-51	Muncy, Pa.		L	R	5'11	190	567	1792	196	465	76	10	33	195	138	254	14	.259	.368
Ouellette, Phil-Phillip Roland	86SFN	11-10-61	Salem, Ore.		B	R	6'	190	10	23	1	4	0	0	0	0	3	3	0	.174	.174
Overbay, Lyle-Lyle Stefan	01-03AriN 04-05MilN 06TorA	01-28-77	Centralia, Wash.		L	L	6'2	225	572	1963	268	575	153	3	61	280	249	395	9	.293	.467
Owen, Dave-Dave	83-85ChiN 88KCA	04-25-58	Cleburne, Tex.		B	R	6'1	175	92	139	15	27	2	3	1	16	11	30	3	.194	.273
Owen, Larry-Lawrence Thomas (Buck)	81-83,85AtlN 87-88KCA	03-31-55	Cleveland, Ohio		R	R	5'11	190	171	352	30	68	11	0	8	30	34	98	0	.193	.293
Owen, Spike-Spike Dee	83-86SeaA 86-88BosA 89-92MonN 93NYA 94-95CalA	04-19-61	Cleburne, Tex.		B	R	5'9	165	1544	4930	587	1211	215	59	46	439	569	519	82	.246	.341
Owens, Eric-Eric Blake	95-97CinN 98MilN 99-00SDN 01-02FlaN 03AnaA	02-03-71	Danville, Va.		R	R	6'1	195	806	2353	305	621	86	16	26	214	182	284	126	.264	.347
Owens, Jayhawk-Claude Jayhawk	93-96CinN	02-10-69	Cincinnati, Ohio		R	R	6'1	200	130	323	54	75	16	2	11	36	38	104	5	.232	.396
Owens, Jerry-Jerry Lee	06ChiA	02-16-81	Los Angeles, Cal.		L	L	6'3	195	12	9	4	3	1	0	0	0	0	2	1	.333	.444
Ozuna, Pablo-Pablo Jose	00,02FlaN 03ColN 05-06ChiA	08-25-74	Santo Domingo, D.R.		R	R	6'	160	214	503	63	147	23	6	2	33	17	53	25	.292	.394
Paciorek, Jim-James Joseph	87MilA	06-07-60	Detroit, Mich.		R	R	6'3	203	48	101	16	23	5	1	0	10	12	20	1	.228	.317
Paciorek, Tom-Thomas Marian	70-75LAN 76-78AtlN 78-81SeaA 82-85ChiA 85NYN 86-87TexA	11-02-46	Detroit, Mich.		R	R	6'4	215	1392	4121	494	1162	232	30	86	503	245	704	55	.282	.415
Pagan, Angel-Angel Anthony	06ChiN	07-02-81	Rio Piedras, P.R.		B	R	6'1	180	77	170	28	42	6	2	5	18	15	28	4	.247	.394
Page, Mitchell-Mitchell Otis	77-83OakA 84PitN	10-15-51	Los Angeles, Cal.		L	R	6'2	210	673	2104	297	560	84	21	72	259	245	449	104	.266	.429
Pagel, Karl-Karl Douglas	78-79ChiN 81-83CleA	03-29-55	Madison, Wis.		L	L	6'2	195	48	56	7	13	0	0	2	1	7	11	0	.232	.357
Pagliarulo, Mike-Michael Timothy (Pags)	84-89NYA 89-90SDN 91-93MinA 93BalA 94JL 95TexA	03-15-60	Medford, Mass.	Bats Both part of 85	L	R	6'2	205	1246	3901	462	942	206	18	134	505	343	785	18	.241	.407
Pagnozzi, Tom-Thomas Alan	87-98StlN	07-30-62	Tucson, Ariz.		R	R	6'1	190	927	2896	247	733	153	11	44	320	189	450	18	.253	.359
Palacios, Rey-Robert Rey	88-90KCA	05-14-62	Brooklyn, N.Y.		R	R	5'10	190	101	114	22	22	5	0	3	17	7	42	2	.193	.316
Palmeiro, Orlando-Orlando	95-96CalA 97-02AnaA 03StlN 04-06HouN	01-19-69	Hoboken, N.J.		L	R	5'11	175	1105	2232	294	616	110	14	12	220	249	222	37	.276	.354
Palmeiro,Rafael-Rafael [Corrales]	86-88ChiN 89-93TexA 94-98BalA 99-03TexA 04-05BalA	09-24-64	Havana, Cuba		L	L	6'	195	2831	10472	1663	3020	585	38	569	1835	1353	1348	97	.288	.515
Palmer, Dean-Dean William	89,91-97TexA 97-98KCA 99-03DetA	12-27-68	Tallahassee, Fla.		R	R	6'1	205	1357	4902	734	1229	231	15	275	849	502	1332	48	.251	.472
Pankovits, Jim-James Franklin	84-88HouN 90BosA	08-06-55	Pennington Gap, Va.		R	R	5'10	175	318	567	62	142	25	2	9	55	44	115	8	.250	.349
Pape, Ken-Kenneth Wayne	76TexA	10-01-51	San Antonio, Tex.		R	R	5'11	195	21	23	7	5	1	0	1	4	3	2	0	.217	.391
Papi, Stan-Stanley Gerard	74StlN 75IL 77-78MonN 79-80BosA 80-81DetA	02-04-51	Fresno, Cal.		R	R	6'	175	225	523	49	114	26	6	7	51	24	99	2	.218	.331
Pappas, Erik-Erik Daniel	91ChiN 93-94StlN	04-25-66	Chicago, Ill.		R	R	6'1	190	104	289	34	70	13	0	1	35	46	53	1	.242	.298
Paquette, Craig-Craig Howard	93-95OakA 96-97KCA 98NYN 99-01StlN 02-03DetA	03-28-69	Long Beach, Cal.		R	R	6'	190	814	2591	304	620	128	10	99	377	120	620	27	.239	.414
Pardo, Al-Alberto Judas	85-86BalA 88-89PhiN	09-08-62	Oviedo, Spain		B	R	6'2	195	53	129	6	17	2	0	1	4	3	31	0	.132	.171
Paredes, Johnny-Johnny Alfonso [Isambert]	88MonN 89ElJ 90DetA 90MonN 91DetA	09-02-62	Maracaibo, Venez.		R	R	5'11	165	60	123	12	26	3	0	1	11	11	18	6	.211	.260
Parent, Mark-Mark Alan	86-90SDN 91TexA 92-93BalA 94ChiN 95PitN 95ChiA 96DetA 96BalA 97-98PhiN	09-16-61	Ashland, Ore.		R	R	6'5	220	474	1303	112	279	50	0	53	168	98	319	3	.214	.375
Paris, Kelly-Kelly Jay	82StlN 83CinN 85-86BalA 88CinA	10-17-57	Encino, Cal.		R	R	6'1	173	92	212	20	46	6	0	3	14	15	39	8	.217	.288
Parker, Dave-David Gene (The Cobra)	73-83PitN 84-87CinN 88-89OakA 90MilA 91CalA 91TorA	06-09-51	Grenada, Miss.		L	R	6'5	235	2466	9358	1272	2712	526	75	339	1493	683	1537	154	.290	.471
Parker, Rick-Richard Alan	90-91SFN 93HouN 94-96LAN	03-20-63	Kansas City, Mo.		R	R	6'	185	163	225	36	55	9	1	2	24	16	36	9	.244	.347
Parks, Derek-Derek Gavin	92-94MinA	09-29-68	Covina, Cal.		R	R	6'	210	45	115	10	23	6	0	1	10	6	23	0	.200	.278
Parrish, Lance-Lance Michael	77-86DetA 87-88PhiN 89-92CalA 92-93CleA 94PitN 95TorA M98-99DetA	06-15-56	McKeesport, Pa.		R	R	6'3	220	1988	7067	856	1782	305	27	324	1070	612	1527	28	.252	.440
Parrish, Larry-Larry Alton (Gov)	74-81MonN 82-88TexA 88BosA	11-10-53	Winter Haven, Fla.		R	R	6'3	210	1891	6792	850	1789	360	33	256	992	529	1359	3	.263	.439
Parsons, Casey-Casey Robert	81SeaA 83-84 ChiA 87CleA	04-14-54	Wenatchee, Wash.		L	R	6'	185	63	53	9	10	1	0	2	3	3	11	0	.189	.321
Pascucci, Valentino-Valentino Martin	04MonN	11-17-78	Bellflower, Cal.		R	R	6'6	235	32	62	6	11	2	0	3	10	10	22	1	.177	.290
Pasley, Kevin-Kevin Patrick	74,76-77LAN 77-78SeaA	07-22-53	Bronx, N.Y.		R	R	6'	190	55	122	8	31	7	0	1	9	6	13	0	.254	.336
Pasqua, Dan-Daniel Anthony	85-87NYA 88-94ChiA	10-17-61	Yonkers, N.Y.		L	L	6'	215	905	2620	341	638	129	15	117	390	335	642	7	.244	.438
Pastornicky, Cliff-Clifford Scott	83KCA	11-18-58	Seattle, Wash.		R	R	5'10	170	9	32	4	4	0	0	0	5	0	3	0	.125	.125
Pate, Bob-Robert Wayne	80-81MonN	12-03-53	Los Angeles, Cal.		R	R	6'3	200	31	45	3	12	2	0	0	5	4	5	0	.267	.311
Patek, Freddie-Frederick Joseph (The Flea, Moochie)	68-70PitN 71-79KCA 80-81CalA	10-09-44	Seguin, Tex.		R	R	5'4	160	1650	5530	736	1340	216	55	41	490	523	757	385	.242	.324
Patterson, Corey-Donald Corey	00-05ChiN 06BalA	08-13-79	Atlanta, Ga.		L	R	5'10	180	724	2639	368	677	118	26	86	284	132	646	131	.257	.439
Patterson, Jarrod-Jarrod Lane	01DetA 03KCA	09-07-73	Montgomery, Ala.		L	R	6'1	195	26	63	9	15	1	1	2	4	3	10	0	.238	.381
Patterson, John-John Allen	92-95SFN	01-11-67	Key West, Fla.		B	R	5'9	165	228	564	74	121	16	5	5	52	35	113	22	.215	.287
Patterson, Mike-Michael Lee (Buck)	81OakA 81-82NYA	01-26-58	Santa Monica, Cal.		L	R	6'	185	27	48	9	13	2	0	1	2	4	11	1	.271	.396
Paul, Josh-Joshua William	99-03ChiA 03ChiN 04AnaA 05LAA 06TBA	05-19-75	Evanston, Ill.		R	R	6'1	195	286	608	84	154	32	2	9	64	53	139	12	.253	.357
Paulino, Ronny-Ronny Leonel	05-06PitN	04-21-81	Santo Domingo, D.R.		R	R	6'3	235	131	446	38	139	19	0	6	55	35	79	0	.312	.395
Payton, Jay-Jason Lee	98-02NYN 02-03ColN 04SDN 05AtlN 06OakA	11-22-72	Zanesville, Ohio		R	R	5'10	185	981	3347	469	952	158	22	105	422	210	404	33	.284	.439
Pecota, Bill-William Joseph	86-92KCA 92NYN 93-94AtlN	02-16-60	Redwood City, Cal.		R	R	6'2	195	698	1527	223	380	72	11	22	148	160	216	52	.249	.354
Pedre, George-Jorge Enrique	91KCA 92ColN	10-12-66	Culver City, Cal.		R	R	5'11	210	14	23	2	5	1	0	0	3	3	6	0	.217	.348
Pederson, Stu-Stuart Russell	85LAN	01-28-60	Palo Alto, Cal.		L	L	6'	190	8	4	1	0	0	0	0	1	0	2	0	.000	.000
Pedrique, Al-Alfredo Jose [Garcia]	87NYN 87-88PitN 89DetA M04AriN	08-11-60	Valencia, Venezuela		R	R	6'	155	174	449	32	111	18	1	1	36	29	61	5	.247	.298
Pedroia, Dustin-Dustin Luis	06BosA	08-17-83	Woodland, Cal.		R	R	5'9	180	31	89	5	17	4	0	2	7	7	7	0	.191	.303
Peguero, Julio-Julio Cesar [Santana]	92PhiN	09-07-68	San Isidro, D.R.		B	R	6'	160	14	9	3	2	0	0	0	0	3	2	0	.222	.222
Pegues, Steve-Steven Antone	94CinN 94-95PitN	05-21-68	Pontotoc, Miss.		R	R	6'2	190	100	207	19	55	10	0	6	18	6	41	2	.266	.401
Pelaez, Alex-Alejandro	02SDN	04-06-76	San Diego, Cal.		R	R	5'9	190	3	4	0	1	0	0	0	0	0	1	0	.250	.250
Pellow, Kit-Kit Donovan	02KCA 03-04ColN	08-28-73	Kansas City, Mo.		R	R	6'	205	99	202	27	52	9	2	4	19	17	68	2	.257	.411
Peltier, Dan-Daniel Edward	92-93TexA 96SFN	06-30-68	Clifton Park, N.Y.		L	L	6'1	200	108	243	27	62	9	1	4	28	27	39	0	.255	.313
Pemberton, Brock-Brock S.	74-75NYN	11-05-53	Tulsa, Okla.		B	L	6'2	195	13	24	0	4	0	0	0	1	0	5	0	.167	.167
Pemberton, Rudy-Rudy Hector [Perez]	95DetA 96-97BosA	12-17-69	San Pedro de Mac.,D.R.		R	R	6'1	185	52	134	22	45	13	1	3	19	6	34	3	.336	.515
Pena, Angel-Angel Maria	98-99,01LAN	02-16-75	San Pedro de Mac,D.R.		R	R	5'10	230	71	187	18	39	7	0	5	23	13	47	0	.209	.326

USE NAME - GIVEN NAMES (NICKNAMES)	TEAM BY YEAR	BIRTH DATE	BIRTH PLACE	DEATH DATE	B	T	HGT	WGT	G	AB	R	H	2B	3B	HR	RBI	BB	SO	SB	BA	SA
Pena, Bert-Adalberto [Rivera]	81,83-87HouN	07-11-59	Santurce, P.R.		R	R	5'11	165	88	153	18	31	4	0	1	10	13	28	1	.203	.248
Pena, Brayan-Brayan Eduardo	05-06AtlN	01-07-82	Havana, Cuba		B	R	5'11	210	41	80	11	18	4	0	1	9	3	12	0	.225	.313
Pena, Carlos-Carlos Felipe	01TexA 02OakA 02-05DetA 06BosA	05-17-78	Santo Domingo, D. R.		L	L	6'2	210	507	1685	229	410	75	15	86	243	209	502	13	.243	.459
Pena, Elvis-Elvis [Mendez]	00ColN 01MilN	08-15-74	San Pedro de Mac.,D.R.		B	R	5'11	164	25	49	6	12	3	0	0	7	7	7	3	.245	.306
Pena, Geronimo-Geronimo [Martinez]	90-95StLN 96CleA	03-29-67	Los Alcarrizos, D.R.		B	R	6'1	195	378	1010	162	265	60	8	30	124	112	255	54	.262	.427
Pena, Tony-Antonio Francisco [Padilla]	80-86PitN 87-89StLN 90-93BosA 94-97CleA 97HouN M02-05KCA	06-04-57	Montecristi, Dom. Rep.		R	R	5'11	185	1988	6489	667	1687	298	27	107	708	455	846	80	.260	.364
Pena, Tony-Tony Francisco	06AtlN	03-23-81	Santiago, Dom. Rep.		R	R	6'1	180	40	44	12	10	2	0	1	3	2	10	0	.227	.341
Pena, Wily Mo-Wily Modesto	02-05CinN 06BosA	01-23-82	Laguna Salada, D.R.		R	R	6'3	215	386	1106	144	289	48	4	62	176	74	378	10	.261	.480
Pendleton, Terry-Terry Lee	84-90StLN 91-94AtlN 95-96FlaN 96AtlN 97CinN 98KCA	07-16-60	Los Angeles, Cal.		B	R	5'9	195	1893	7032	851	1897	356	39	140	946	486	979	127	.270	.391
Penn, Shannon-Shannon Dion	95-96DetA	09-11-69	Cincinnati, Ohio		B	R	5'10	160	9	23	6	4	0	0	0	1	1	5	0	.174	.174
Pennyfeather, Will-William Nathaniel	92-94PitN	05-25-68	Perth Amboy, N.J.		R	R	6'2	210	40	46	6	9	1	0	1	2	0	6	0	.196	.217
Peralta, Jhonny-Jhonny Antonio	03-06CleA	05-28-82	Santiago, Dom. Rep.		R	R	6'1	180	375	1340	192	354	74	8	41	169	137	351	1	.264	.423
Perconte, Jack-John Patrick	80-81LAN 82-83CleA 84-85SeaA 86ChiA	08-31-54	Joliet, Ill.		L	R	5'10	165	433	1441	191	389	47	16	2	76	149	123	78	.270	.329
Perez, Antonio-Antonio Miguel	03TBA 04-05LAN 06OakA	01-26-80	Bani, Dom. Rep.		R	R	5'11	170	216	495	62	121	25	4	6	43	49	144	16	.244	.347
Perez, Danny-Daniel	96MilA	02-16-71	El Paso, Tex.		R	R	5'10	188	4	4	0	0	0	0	0	0	0	0	0	.000	.000
Perez, Eddie-Eduardo Rafael	95-01AtlN 02CleA 03MilN 04-05AtlN 04-05TBA 06CleA 06SeaA	05-04-68	Ciudad Ojeda, Venez.		R	R	6'1	210	564	1525	137	386	85	2	40	172	84	234	1	.253	.390
Perez, Eduardo-Eduardo Atanacio	93-95CalA 96-98CinN 99-00StLN 01JL 02-03StLN 04-05TBA 06CleA 06SeaA	09-11-69	Cincinnati, Ohio		R	R	6'4	230	754	1800	238	445	88	3	79	294	194	393	19	.247	.431
Perez, Marty-Martin Roman	69-70CalA 71-76AtlN 76SFN 77NYA 77-78OakA	02-28-46	Visalia, Cal.		R	R	5'11	160	931	3131	313	771	108	22	22	241	245	369	11	.246	.316
Perez, Miguel-Miguel Angel	96MilA	09-25-83	Caracas, Venezuela		R	R	6'3	190	2	3	0	0	0	0	0	0	0	1	0	.000	.000
Perez, Neifi-Neifi Neftali [Diaz]	96-01ColN 01-02KCA 03-04SFN 04-06ChiN 06DetA	06-02-73	Villa Mella, Dom. Rep.		B	R	6'	175	1370	5063	635	1359	235	61	63	483	227	495	57	.268	.376
Perez, Robert-Robert Alexander [Jimenez]	94-97TorA 98SeaA 98MonN 99JL 01NYA 01MilN	06-04-69	Bolivar, Venez.		R	R	6'3	220	221	497	48	126	19	1	8	44	11	74	3	.254	.344
Perez, Santiago-Santiago Alberto	00MilN 01SDN	12-30-75	Santo Domingo, D.R.		B	R	6'2	185	67	133	21	25	3	0	0	6	23	38	9	.188	.211
Perez, Timo-Timoniel David	00-03NYN 04-05ChiA 06StLN	04-08-75	Bani, Dom. Rep.		L	L	5'9	167	574	1581	175	414	82	8	26	172	86	153	22	.262	.373
Perez, Tomas-Tomas Orlando	95-98TorA 00-05PhiN 06TBA	12-29-73	Barquisimeto, Venez.		B	R	5'11	180	781	1886	205	453	96	13	24	180	131	339	6	.240	.343
Perez, Tony-Atanasio [Rigal]	64-76CinN 77-79MonN 80-82BosA 83PhiN 84-86CinN, M93CinN M01FlaN	05-14-42	Ciego de Avila, Cuba		R	R	6'2	205	2777	9778	1272	2732	505	79	379	1652	925	1867	49	.279	.463
Perezchica, Tony-Antonio Llamas [Gonzales]	88,90-91SFN 91-92CleA	04-20-66	Mexicali, Mexico		R	R	5'11	165	69	101	10	23	7	1	0	5	10	26	0	.228	.317
Perkins, Broderick-Broderick Phillip (Outfield Patrol)	78-82SDN 83-84CleA	11-23-54	Pittsburg, Cal.		L	L	5'10	180	516	1255	127	340	62	8	8	157	80	116	9	.271	.352
Perlozzo, Sam-Samuel Benedict	77MinA 79SDN M05-06BalA	03-04-51	Cumberland, Md.		R	R	5'9	170	12	26	6	7	0	0	0	0	3	3	0	.269	.423
Perry, Chan-Chan Everett	00CleA 02KCA	09-13-72	Live Oak, Fla.		R	R	6'2	200	18	25	1	2	0	0	0	6	0	5	0	.080	.080
Perry, Gerald-Gerald June	83-89AtlN 90KCA 91-95StLN	10-30-60	Savannah, Ga.		L	R	5'11	195	1193	3144	383	832	150	11	59	396	328	374	142	.265	.376
Perry, Herbert-Herbert Edward Jr.	94-96CleA 97-98KJ 99-00TBA 00-01ChiA 02-04TexA	09-15-69	Live Oak, Fla.		R	R	6'2	220	529	1696	241	461	102	6	55	246	128	291	12	.272	.436
Petagine, Roberto-Roberto Antonio [Guerra]	94HouN 95SDN 96-97NYN 98CinN 05BosA 06SeaA	06-07-71	Nueva Esparta, Venez.		L	L	6'1	170	242	366	48	83	11	1	12	54	63	103	1	.227	.377
Peters, Rickey-Richard Devin	79-81DetA 82EJ 83,86OakA	11-21-55	Lynwood, Cal.		B	R	5'9	165	307	919	135	255	34	10	2	80	107	107	20	.277	.343
Petersen, Chris-Christopher Ronald	99ColN	11-06-70	Boston, Mass.		R	R	5'11	180	7	13	1	2	0	0	0	2	2	3	0	.154	.154
Petralli, Geno-Eugene James	82-84TorA 85-93TexA	09-25-59	Sacramento, Cal.		B	R	6'1	185	809	1874	184	501	83	9	24	192	216	263	8	.267	.360
Petrick, Ben-Benjamin Wayne	99-03ColN 03DetA	04-07-77	Salem, Ore.		R	R	6'	205	240	669	114	172	37	5	27	94	78	177	5	.257	.448
Pettini, Joe-Joseph Paul	80-83SFN	01-26-55	Wheeling, W. Va.		R	R	5'9	165	188	344	38	70	7	1	0	20	33	53	10	.203	.238
Pettis, Gary-Gary George	82-87CalA 88-89DetA 90-91TexA 92SDN 92DetA	04-03-58	Oakland, Cal.		B	R	6'1	165	1183	3629	568	855	109	49	21	259	521	958	354	.236	.310
Pevey, Marty-Marty Ashley	89MonN	09-18-61	Statesboro, Ga.		L	R	6'1	185	13	41	2	9	1	1	0	3	0	8	0	.220	.293
Phelps, Josh-Joshua Lee	00-04TorA 04CleA 05TBA	05-12-78	Anchorage, Alaska		R	R	6'3	220	352	1203	173	323	67	4	57	212	94	344	2	.268	.473
Phelps, Ken-Kenneth Allen (Big Red)	80-81KCA 82MonN 83-88SeaA 88-89NYA 89-90OakA 90CleA	08-06-54	Seattle, Wash.		L	L	6'1	205	761	1854	308	443	64	7	123	313	390	449	10	.239	.480
Phillips, Andy-George Andrew	04-06NYA	04-06-77	Tuscaloosa, Ala.		R	R	6'	205	142	294	38	67	15	3	9	35	16	70	3	.228	.391
Phillips, Brandon-Brandon Emil	02-05CleA 06CinN	06-28-81	Raleigh, N.C.		R	R	5'11	185	284	968	108	237	51	3	23	113	54	180	29	.245	.375
Phillips, J.R.-Charles Gene	93-96SFN 96PhiN 97-98HouN 99ColN	04-29-70	West Covina, Cal.		L	L	6'1	185	242	501	52	94	19	1	23	67	38	180	2	.188	.367
Phillips, Jason-Jason Lloyd (J.P.)	01-04NYN 05LAN 06TorA	09-27-76	La Mesa, Cal.		R	R	6'1	177	410	1238	127	314	70	0	29	156	101	149	0	.254	.380
Phillips, Mike-Michael Dwayne	73-75SFN 75-77NYN 77-80StLN 81SDN 81-83MonN	08-19-50	Beaumont, Tex.		L	R	6'	185	712	1719	166	412	46	24	11	145	133	242	12	.240	.314
Phillips, Paul-Paul Anthony	04-06KCA	04-15-77	Demopolis, Ala.		R	R	5'11	185	50	137	16	37	7	1	2	14	1	14	0	.270	.380
Phillips, Tony-Keith Anthony	82-89OakA 90-94DetA 95CalA 96-97ChiA 97AnaA 98TorA 98NYN 99OakA	04-25-59	Atlanta, Ga.		B	R	5'10	170	2161	7617	1300	2023	360	50	160	819	1319	1499	177	.266	.389
Piatt, Adam-Adam David	00-03OakA 03TBA	02-08-76	Chicago, Ill.		R	R	6'2	195	212	521	62	129	31	6	16	65	57	149	3	.248	.422
Piazza, Mike-Michael Joseph	92-98LAN 98FlaN 98-05NYN 06SDN	09-04-68	Norristown, Pa.		R	R	6'3	215	1829	6602	1015	2042	327	7	419	1291	741	1052	17	.309	.551
Picciolo, Rob-Robert Michael	77-82OakA 82-83MilA 84CalA 85OakA	02-04-53	Santa Monica, Cal.		R	R	6'	185	730	1628	192	381	56	10	17	109	25	254	9	.234	.312
Pickering, Calvin-Calvin Elroy	98-99BalA 01CinN 01BosA 04-05KCA	09-29-76	St. Thomas, V.I.		L	R	6'5	280	95	264	37	59	10	1	14	45	43	91	1	.223	.428
Pierce, Jack-Lavern Jack	73-74AtlN 75DetA	06-02-49	Laurel, Miss.		R	R	6'2	215	70	199	20	42	6	1	8	22	22	48	0	.211	.372
Piedra, Jorge-Jorge Moises	04-06ColN	04-17-79	Sun Valley, Cal.		L	L	6'	190	142	262	38	72	18	1	12	36	18	56	3	.275	.489
Pierre, Juan-Juan D'Vaughn	00-02ColN 03-05FlaN 06ChiN	08-14-77	Mobile, Ala.		L	L	6'	180	1007	4110	607	1244	149	61	13	287	258	249	325	.303	.377
Pierzynski, A.J.-Anthony John	98-03MinA 04SFN 05-06ChiA	12-30-76	Bridgehampton, N.Y.		L	R	6'3	218	829	2868	355	826	179	14	71	390	124	360	7	.288	.434
Piniella, Lou-Louis Victor	64BalA 68CleA 69-73KCA 74-84,M86-88NYA M90-92CinN M93-02SeaA M03-05TBA	08-28-43	Tampa, Fla.		R	R	6'	195	1747	5867	651	1705	305	41	102	766	368	541	32	.291	.409
Pirkl, Greg-Gregory Daniel	93-96SeaA 96BosA	08-07-70	Long Beach, Cal.		R	R	6'5	245	45	116	12	26	4	0	8	16	2	27	0	.224	.466
Pittaro, Chris-Christopher Francis	85DetA 86-87MinA	08-07-61	Trenton, N.J.		B	R	5'11	170	52	95	16	21	3	1	0	7	6	21	2	.221	.274
Pittman, Joe-Joseph Wayne (Shoes)	81-82HouN 82SDN 84SFN	01-01-54	Houston, Tex.		R	R	6'1	180	169	285	29	75	7	2	0	16	20	37	13	.263	.302
Pitts, Gaylen-Gaylen Richard	74-75OakA	06-07-46	Wichita, Kans.		R	R	6'	190	28	44	5	11	4	0	0	4	5	4	0	.250	.341
Plantier, Phil-Phillip Alan	90-92BosA 93-94SDN 95HouN 95SDN 96OakA 97SDN 97StLN	01-27-69	Manchester, N.H.		L	R	5'11	195	610	1883	260	457	90	3	91	292	237	476	13	.243	.439
Plummer, Bill-William Francis	68ChiN 70-77CinN 78,M92SeaA	03-21-47	Oakland, Cal.		R	R	6'2	200	367	892	72	168	37	1	14	82	95	191	4	.188	.277
Pocoroba, Biff-Benedict	75-84AtlN	07-25-53	Burbank, Cal.		B	R	5'10	180	596	1457	132	374	71	2	21	172	182	109	6	.257	.351
	Bats Left 82-84, most of 77, Bats Right most of 75																				
Podsednik, Scott-Scott Eric	01-02SeaA 03-04MilN 05-06ChiA	03-18-76	West, Texas		L	L	6'	180	595	2255	354	620	111	23	25	175	219	374	212	.275	.378
Poepping, Mike-Michael Harold	75MinA	08-07-50	Little Falls, Minn.		R	R	6'6	230	14	37	0	5	1	0	0	1	5	7	0	.135	.162
Poff, John-John William	79PhiN 80MilA	10-23-52	Chillicothe, Ohio		L	L	6'2	200	31	87	9	19	2	2	1	8	4	11	0	.218	.322
Polanco, Placido-Placido Enrique	98-02StLN 02-05PhiN 05-06DetA	10-10-75	Santo Domingo, D.R.		R	R	5'10	180	1029	3726	549	1117	178	20	63	382	206	272	50	.300	.409
Polcovich, Kevin-Kevin Michael	97-98PitN	06-28-70	Auburn, N.Y.		R	R	5'9	170	165	457	55	107	28	1	4	35	36	78	6	.234	.326
Polidor, Gus-Gustavo Adolfo [Gonzalez]	85-88CalA 89-90MilA 93FlaN	10-26-61	Caracas, Venezuela	04-28-95	R	R	6'	180	229	434	33	90	15	0	2	35	12	47	3	.207	.256
Polonia, Luis-Luis Andrew [Almonte]	87-89OakA 89-90NYA 90-93CalN 94-95NYA 95AtlN 96BalA 96AtlN 99-00DetA 00NYA	10-12-63	Santiago, Dom. Rep.		L	L	5'8	155	1379	4840	728	1417	189	70	36	405	369	543	321	.293	.383
Ponce, Carlos-Carlos Antonio [Diaz]	85MilA	02-07-59	Rio Piedras, P.R.		R	R	5'10	170	21	62	4	10	2	0	1	5	1	9	0	.161	.242
Pond, Simon-Simon Emilio	04TorA	10-27-76	North Vancouver, Canada		L	R	6'1	205	16	49	4	8	2	0	1	6	5	12	0	.163	.265
Poquette, Tom-Thomas Arthur	73,76-79KCA 79BosA 80SJ 81BosA 81TexA 82KCA	10-30-51	Eau Claire, Wis.		L	R	5'11	178	452	1226	127	329	62	18	10	136	81	82	13	.268	.373
Porter, Bo-Marquis Donnell	99ChiN 00OakA 01TexA	07-05-72	Newark, N.J.		R	R	6'2	195	89	126	23	27	5	2	3	8	13	52	3	.214	.333
Porter, Bob-Robert Lee	81-82AtlN	07-22-59	Yuma, Ariz.		L	L	5'10	180	41	41	3	7	1	0	0	4	3	10	1	.171	.195
Porter, Colin-Colin Frederick	03HouN 04StLN	11-23-75	Tucson, Ariz.		L	L	6'2	210	47	67	8	17	2	1	0	3	2	30	1	.254	.284
Porter, Darrell-Darrell Ray (Dee)	71-76MilA 77-80KCA 81-85StLN 86-87TexA	01-17-52	Joplin, Mo.	08-05-02	L	R	6'	193	1782	5539	765	1369	237	48	188	826	905	1025	39	.247	.409
Posada, Jorge-Jorge Rafael III [Villeta]	95-06NYA	08-17-71	Santurce, P.R.		B	R	6'2	205	1288	4308	653	1163	262	7	198	771	692	1041	14	.270	.472
Pose, Scott-Scott Vernon	93FlaN 97NYA 99-00KCA	02-11-67	Davenport, Iowa		L	R	5'11	180	202	313	52	75	7	1	0	21	38	50	9	.240	.268
Potter, Mike-Michael Gary	76-77StLN	05-16-51	Montebello, Cal.		R	R	6'1	190	14	23	0	0	0	0	0	0	3	9	0	.000	.000
Powell, Alonzo-Alonzo Sidney	87MonN 91SeaA	12-16-64	San Francisco, Cal.		R	R	6'2	195	71	152	19	32	9	1	3	16	16	41	0	.211	.342
Powell, Dante-LeJon Dante	97-98SFN 99AriN 01SFN	08-25-73	Long Beach, Cal.		R	R	6'2	185	70	74	19	20	4	1	3	5	9	17	3	.270	.405
Powell, Hosken-Hosken	78-81MinA 82-83TorA	04-14-55	Selma, Ala.		L	L	6'1	185	594	1816	241	470	78	17	17	160	144	164	43	.259	.349
Powell, Paul-Paul Ray	71MinA 73,75LAN	03-19-48	San Angelo, Tex.		R	R	5'11	185	30	42	9	7	1	0	0	2	4	15	0	.167	.262
Pozo, Arquimedez-Arquimedez [Ortiz]	95SeaA 96-97BosA	08-24-73	Santo Domingo, D.R.		R	R	5'10	160	26	74	4	14	2	0	1	6	2	15	0	.189	.311
Prado, Martin-Martin Manual	06AtlN	10-27-83	Maracay, Venezuela		R	R	6'1	170	24	42	3	11	1	1	0	5	4	5	0	.262	.405
Pratt, Todd-Todd Alan	92-94PhiN 95ChiN 97-01NYN 01-05PhiN 06AtlN	02-09-67	Bellevue, Neb.		R	R	6'3	225	662	1612	194	404	84	3	49	224	208	454	4	.251	.398
Presley, Jim-James Arthur	84-89SeaA 90AtlN 91SDN	10-23-61	Pensacola, Fla.		R	R	6'1	200	959	3546	413	875	181	14	135	495	210	859	9	.247	.420
Pride, Curtis-Curtis John	93,95MonN 96-97DetA 97BosA 98AtlN 00BosA 01MonN 03NYA 04AnaA 05-06LAA	12-17-68	Washington, D.C.		L	R	6'	205	421	796	132	199	48	7	20	82	85	211	29	.250	.405
Prieto, Alex-Alejandro Antonio	03-04MinA	06-19-76	Caracas, Venezuela		R	R	5'10	200	24	43	5	9	2	0	0	5	1	5	0	.209	.302
Prieto, Chris-Christian Michael	05LAA	08-24-72	Carmel, Cal.		L	L	5'11	180	2	4	0	0	0	0	0	0	0	0	0	.000	.000
Prince, Tom-Thomas Albert	87-93PitN 94-98LAN 99-00PhiN 01-03MinA 03KCA	08-13-64	Kankakee, Ill.		R	R	5'11	200	519	1190	113	248	66	4	24	140	105	252	9	.208	.331
Prichett, Chris-Christopher Davis	96CalA 98-99AnaA 00PhiN	01-13-70	Merced, Cal.		L	R	6'4	210	61	149	16	33	7	1	1	11	7	31	3	.221	.315

USE NAME - GIVEN NAMES (NICKNAMES)	TEAM BY YEAR	BIRTH DATE	BIRTH PLACE	DEATH DATE	B	T	HGT	WGT	G	AB	R	H	2B	3B	HR	RBI	BB	SO	SB	BA	SA
Pruitt, Ron-Ronald Ralph	75TexA 76—80CleA 80ChiA 81CleA 82-83SFN	10-21-51	Flint, Mich.		R	R	6'1	185	341	795	88	214	28	4	12	92	94	90	8	.269	.360
Pryor, Greg-Gregory Russell	76TexA 78-81ChiA 82-86KCA	10-02-49	Marietta, Ohio		R	R	6'	185	789	1883	204	471	85	9	14	146	104	185	11	.250	.327
Puckett, Kirby-Kirby	84-95MinA 96-97IJ	03-14-60	Chicago, Ill.	03-06-06	R	R	5'8	210	1783	7244	1071	2304	414	57	207	1085	450	965	134	.318	.477
Puhl, Terry-Terry Stephen (T.P.)	77-90HouN 91KCA	07-08-56	Melville, Canada		L	R	6'2	200	1531	4855	676	1361	226	56	62	435	505	507	217	.280	.388
Puig, Rich-Richard Gerald	74NYA	03-16-53	Tampa, Fla.		L	R	5'10	165	4	10	0	0	0	0	0	0	1	2	0	.000	.000
Pujols, Albert-Jose Alberto	01-06StLN	01-16-80	Santo Domingo, D.R.		R	R	6'3	225	933	3489	748	1159	260	12	250	758	493	394	36	.332	.629
Pujols, Luis-Luis Bienvenido [Toribio]	77-83HouN 84KCA 85TexA M02DetA	11-18-55	Santiago, Dom.Rep.		R	R	6'	205	316	850	50	164	27	6	6	81	52	164	1	.193	.260
Pulliam, Harvey-Harvey Jerome	91-93KCA 95-97ColN	10-20-67	San Francisco, Cal.		R	R	6'	210	123	187	31	49	11	0	8	22	13	49	0	.262	.449
Punto, Nick-Nicholas Paul	01-03PhiN 04-06MinA	11-08-77	San Diego, Cal.		B	R	5'9	170	362	1047	149	273	41	11	8	87	102	198	38	.261	.344
Putman, Ed-Eddy William	76,78ChiN 79DetA	09-25-53	Los Angeles, Cal.		R	R	6'1	190	43	71	6	17	3	0	2	7	8	18	0	.239	.366
Putnam, Pat-Patrick Edward	77-82TexA 83-84SeaA 84MinA	12-03-53	Bethel, Vt.		L	R	6'	210	677	1989	223	508	95	8	63	255	144	260	10	.255	.406
Pye, Eddie-Robert Edward	94-95LAN	02-13-67	Columbia, Tenn.		R	R	5'10	175	14	18	2	1	0	0	0	0	1	8	0	.056	.056
Pyznarski, Tim-Timothy Matthew	86SDN	02-04-60	Chicago, Ill.		R	R	6'2	200	15	42	3	10	1	0	0	0	4	11	2	.238	.262
Quentin, Carlos-Carlos Jose	06AriN	08-28-82	Bellflower, Cal.		R	R	6'2	225	57	166	23	42	13	3	9	32	15	34	1	.253	.530
Quinlan, Robb-Robb William	03-04AnaA 05-06LAA	03-17-77	St. Paul, Minn.		R	R	6'1	200	234	622	81	188	37	3	19	73	34	96	6	.302	.463
Quinlan, Tom-Thomas Raymond	90,92TorA 94PhiN 96MinA	03-27-68	St. Paul, Minn.		R	R	6'3	200	42	58	8	9	3	0	1	5	5	26	0	.155	.259
Quinn, Mark-Mark David	99-02KCA	05-21-74	La Mirada, Calif.		R	R	6'1	195	293	1089	153	307	72	5	45	167	56	186	17	.282	.481
Quinones, Luis-Luis Raul [Torruellas]	83OakA 86SFN 87ChiN 88-91CinN 92MinA	04-28-62	Ponce, P.R.		B	R	5'11	175	442	1003	102	227	36	11	19	106	75	154	9	.226	.341
Quinones, Rey-Rey Francisco [Santiago]	86BosA 86-89SeaA 89PitN	11-11-63	Rio Piedras, P.R.		R	R	5'11	185	451	1533	173	373	75	6	29	159	89	240	5	.243	.357
Quintana, Carlos-Carlos Narcis [Hernandez]	88-91BosA 92AnaA 93BosA	08-26-65	Estado Miranda,Venez.		R	R	6'	200	438	1376	163	380	59	1	19	165	153	207	3	.276	.362
Quintanilla, Omar-Omar	05-06ColN	10-24-81	El Paso, Tex.		L	R	5'9	190	50	162	19	34	2	2	0	10	12	24	3	.210	.247
Quintero, Humberto-Humberto	03-04SDN 05-06HouN	08-02-79	Maracaibo, Venezuela		R	R	5'9	215	64	170	16	40	6	0	3	22	8	35	0	.235	.324
Quirk, Jamie-James Patrick	75-76KCA 77MilA 78-82KCA 83StLN 84ChiA 84CleA 85-88KCA 89NYA 89OakA 89BalN 90-92OakA	10-22-54	Whittier, Cal.		R	L	6'4	200	984	2266	193	544	100	7	43	247	177	435	5	.240	.347
Quiroz, Guillermo-Guillermo Antonio	04-05TorA 06SeaA	11-29-81	Maracaibo, Venezuela		R	R	6'1	202	30	90	5	18	4	0	0	10	4	23	1	.200	.244
Raabe, Brian-Brian Charles	95-96MinA 97SeaA 97ColN	11-05-67	New Ulm, Minn.		R	R	5'9	175	17	29	4	6	0	0	0	2	2	4	0	.207	.207
Rabb, John-John Andrew	82-84SFN 85AtlN 88SeaA	06-23-60	Los Angeles, Cal.		R	R	6'1	180	108	204	22	46	12	1	4	27	19	53	2	.225	.353
Rabe, Josh-Joshua Wayne	06MinA	10-15-78	Quincy, Ill.		R	R	6'3	215	24	49	8	14	1	0	3	7	2	11	0	.286	.490
Rabelo, Mike-Michael Gregory	06DetA	01-17-80	New Port Richey, Fla.		B	R	6'1	200	1	1	0	0	0	0	0	0	1	0	0	.000	.000
Raburn, Ryan-Ryan Neil	04DetA	04-17-81	Tampa, Fla.		R	R	6'	185	12	29	4	4	1	0	0	1	2	15	1	.138	.172
Rader, Dave-David Martin	71-76SFN 77StLN 78ChiN 79PhiN 80BosA	12-26-48	Claremore, Okla.		L	R	5'11	170	846	2405	254	619	107	12	30	235	245	180	8	.257	.349
Radmanovich, Ryan-Ryan Ashley	98SeaA	08-09-71	Calgary, Canada		L	R	6'2	185	25	69	5	15	4	0	2	10	4	25	1	.217	.362
Raines, Tim-Timothy Sr. (Rock)	79-90MonN 91-95ChiA 96-98NYA 99OakA 00IL 01MonN 01BalA 02FlaN	09-16-59	Sanford, Fla.		B	R	5'8	180	2502	8872	1571	2605	430	113	170	980	1330	966	808	.294	.425
Raines, Tim Jr.-Timothy Jr.	01,03-04BalA	08-31-79	Memphis, Tenn.		R	R	5'10	183	75	160	24	34	9	1	0	7	9	36	10	.213	.281
Rajsich, Gary-Gary Louis (Cowboy)	82-83NYN 84StLN 85SFN	10-28-54	Youngstown, Ohio		L	L	6'2	200	149	296	28	70	17	3	3	27	39	64	1	.236	.345
Ramirez, Alex-Alexander Ramon	98-00CleA 00PitN	10-03-74	Caracas, Venezuela		R	R	5'11	180	135	332	38	86	17	3	12	48	15	78	3	.259	.437
Ramirez, Aramis-Aramis [Nin]	98-03PitN 03-06ChiN	06-25-78	Santo Domingo, D.R.		R	R	6'1	215	1047	3897	517	1089	224	11	196	669	279	596	11	.279	.493
Ramirez, Hanley-Hanley	05-06BosA	12-23-83	Samana, Dom. Rep.		R	R	6'3	195	160	635	119	185	46	11	17	59	56	130	51	.291	.479
Ramirez, Julio-Julio Cesar [Figueroa]	99FlaN 01ChiA 02-03AnaA 05SFN	08-10-77	San Juan de la Maguana, D.R.		R	R	5'11	170	84	96	15	16	1	1	1	11	5	36	2	.167	.229
Ramirez, Manny-Manuel Aristides [Onelcida]	93-00CleA 01-06BosA	05-30-72	Santo Domingo, D.R.		R	R	6'	205	1817	6575	1258	2066	438	16	470	1516	1054	1451	34	.314	.600
Ramirez, Mario-Mario [Torres] (Nato)	80NYN 81-85SDN	09-12-57	Yauco, P.R.		B	R	5'9	170	184	286	33	55	8	3	4	28	41	64	0	.192	.283
Ramirez, Orlando-Orlando [Leal]	74-77,79CalA	12-18-51	Cartagena, Columbia		R	R	5'9	175	143	281	24	53	5	1	0	16	24	65	16	.189	.214
Ramirez, Rafael-Rafael Emilio [Peguero] (Raffy)	80-87AtlN 88-92HouN	02-18-58	San Pedro de Mac, D.R.		R	R	5'11	165	1539	5494	562	1432	224	31	53	484	264	621	112	.261	.342
Ramos, Bobby-Roberto (The Hawk)	78,80-81MonN 82NYA 83-84MonN	11-05-55	Calabazar de Sagua, Cuba		R	R	6'	205	103	232	20	44	7	1	4	17	22	38	0	.190	.280
Ramos, Domingo-Domingo Antonio [de Ramos]	78NYA 80TorA 82-87SeaA 88CleA 88CalA 89-90ChiN	03-29-58	Santiago, Dom. Rep.		R	R	5'11	165	507	1086	109	261	34	2	8	85	92	138	6	.240	.297
Ramos, John-John Joseph	91NYA 92EJ	08-06-65	Tampa, Fla.		R	R	6'	190	10	26	4	8	1	0	0	3	1	3	0	.308	.346
Ramos, Ken-Kenneth Cecil	97HouN	06-06-67	Sidney, Neb.		L	L	6'1	185	14	12	0	0	0	0	0	0	2	0	0	.000	.000
Ramsey, Fernando-Fernando David [Ramsey]	92ChiN	12-20-65	Rainbow City, Panama		R	R	6'2	180	18	25	0	3	0	0	0	2	0	6	0	.120	.120
Ramsey, Mike-Michael James	87LAN	07-08-60	Thomson, Ga.		R	R	6'	170	48	125	18	29	4	2	0	12	10	32	2	.232	.296
Ramsey, Mike-Michael Jeffrey	78,80-84StLN 84MonN 85LAN	03-29-54	Roanoke, Va.		B	R	5'11	175	394	786	81	189	26	6	2	57	48	111	14	.240	.296
Randa, Joe-Joseph Gregory (The Joker)	95-96KCA 97PitN 98DetA 99-04KCA 05CinN 05SDN 06PitN	12-18-69	Milwaukee, Wis.		R	R	5'11	190	1522	5428	697	1543	327	36	123	739	432	738	42	.284	.453
Randall, Bob-Robert Lee	76-80MinA	06-10-48	Norton, Kans.		R	R	6'2	180	460	1325	154	341	50	9	1	91	83	102	11	.257	.311
Randall, Sap-James Odell	88ChiA	08-19-60	Mobile, Ala.		B	R	5'11	195	8	24	2	0	0	0	0	0	2	4	6	0	.000	.000
Randle, Lenny-Leonard Shenoff	71WasA 72-76TexA 77-78NYN 79NYA 80ChiN 81-82SeaA	02-12-49	Long Beach, Cal.	Bats Right 71, part of 72	B	R	5'10	175	1138	3950	488	1016	145	40	27	322	372	505	156	.257	.335
Randolph, Willie-Willie Larry	75PitN 76-88NYA 89-90LAN 90OakA 91MilA 92,M05-06NYN	07-06-54	Holly Hill, S.C.		R	R	5'11	165	2202	8018	1239	2210	316	65	54	687	1243	675	271	.276	.351
Ransom, Cody-Bryan Cody	01-04SFN	02-17-76	Mesa, Ariz.		R	R	6'2	190	114	105	23	25	7	0	2	13	8	37	2	.238	.362
Ransom, Jeff-Jeffery Dean (Sheriff)	81-83SFN	11-11-60	Fresno, Cal.		B	R	5'11	185	26	79	10	15	1	0	1	6	11	15	0	.190	.241
Ray, Johnny-John Cornelius	81-87PitN 87-90CalA	03-01-57	Chouteau, Okla.		B	R	5'11	185	1353	5188	604	1502	294	36	53	594	353	329	80	.290	.391
Ray, Larry-Larry Dale	82HouN	03-11-58	Madison, Ind.		L	R	6'	190	9	6	1	1	0	0	0	1	0	4	0	.167	.167
Rayford, Floyd-Floyd Kinnard (Honey Bear)	80,82BalA 83StLN 84-87BalA	07-27-57	Memphis, Tenn.		R	R	5'11	195	390	1044	112	255	43	1	38	117	55	225	4	.244	.397
Ready, Randy-Randy Max	83-86MilA 86-89SDN 89-91PhiN 92OakA 93MonN 94-95PhiN	01-08-60	San Mateo, Cal.		R	R	5'11	180	777	2110	312	547	107	21	40	239	326	276	27	.259	.387
Reboulet, Jeff-Jeffrey Allen	92-96MinA 97-99BalA 00KCA 01-02LAN 03PitN	04-30-64	Dayton, Ohio		R	R	6'	167	1018	2229	310	536	100	6	20	202	292	401	22	.240	.318
Redfield, Joe-Joseph Randall	88CalA 91PitN	01-14-61	Doylestown, Pa.		R	R	6'2	185	12	20	1	4	2	0	0	0	4	1	0	.200	.300
Redman, Prentice-Prentice Montezz	03NYN	08-23-79	Tuscaloosa, Ala.		R	R	6'3	185	15	24	3	3	1	0	1	0	1	9	2	.125	.292
Redman, Tike-Julian Jawonn	00-01,04-05PitN	03-10-77	Tuscaloosa, Ala.		L	L	5'11	172	392	1238	144	343	52	14	15	101	61	129	33	.277	.392
Redmon, Glenn-Glenn Vincent (Red)	74SFN	11-11-48	Detroit, Mich.		R	R	5'11	178	121	362	32	112	18	0	3	39	31	50	0	.311	.386
Redmond, Mike-Michael Patrick	98-04FlaN 05-06MinA	05-05-71	Seattle, Wash.		R	R	6'	200	577	1665	155	487	89	2	12	181	109	192	1	.292	.370
Redus, Gary-Gary Eugene (Pockets)	82-85CinN 86PhiN 87-88ChiA 88-92PitN 93-94TexA	11-01-56	Tanner, Ala.		R	R	6'1	185	1159	3513	591	886	183	51	90	352	481	688	322	.252	.410
Reece, Bob-Robert Scott	78MonN	06-01-62	Sacramento, Cal.		R	R	6'1	190	9	11	2	2	1	0	0	3	0	0	0	.182	.273
Reed, Darren-Darren A. Douglas	90NYN 91BA 92MonN 92MinA	10-16-65	Ojai, Cal.		R	R	6'1	195	82	153	17	28	8	1	6	16	11	45	1	.183	.366
Reed, Eric-Eric Shane	06FlaN	12-02-80	Little Rock, Ark.		L	L	5'11	170	42	41	6	4	0	0	0	0	2	10	3	.098	.098
Reed, Jeff-Jeffrey Scott	84-86MinA 87-88MonN 88-92CinN 93-95ColN 96-99ChiN 00-01ChiA	11-12-62	Joliet, Ill.		L	R	6'2	190	234	3101	311	774	144	10	61	323	391	566	7	.250	.367
Reed, Jeremy-Jeremy Thomas	04-06SeaA	06-15-81	San Dimas, Cal.		L	L	6'	185	226	758	99	193	43	8	17	67	66	109	17	.255	.368
Reed, Jody-Jody Eric	87-92BosA 93LAN 94MilA 95-96SDN 97DetA	07-26-62	Tampa, Fla.		R	R	5'9	170	1284	4554	566	1231	263	10	27	392	542	407	40	.270	.350
Reed, Keith-Keith A.	05BalA	10-08-78	Yarmouth Port, Mass.		R	R	6'4	205	6	5	1	1	0	0	0	1	1	2	0	.200	.200
Reese, Kevin-Kevin Patrick	05-06NYA	03-11-78	San Diego, Cal.		L	L	5'11	195	12	13	2	5	0	0	0	1	2	1	0	.385	.385
Reese, Pokey-Calvin Jr.	97-01CinN 02-03PitN 04BosA 05SJ	06-10-73	Columbia, S.C.		R	R	5'11	180	856	2833	366	704	128	17	44	271	226	531	144	.248	.352
Reid, Jessie-Jessie Thomas	87-88SFN	06-01-62	Honolulu, Hawaii		L	L	6'1	200	8	10	1	1	0	0	0	1	1	6	0	.100	.400
Reimer, Kevin-Kevin Michael	88-92TexA 93MilA	06-28-64	Macon, Ga.		L	R	6'2	220	488	1455	162	376	85	4	52	204	115	297	7	.258	.430
Reinbach, Mike-Michael Wayne (Rhino)	74BalA	08-06-49	San Diego, Cal.	05-20-89	L	R	6'2	195	12	20	2	5	1	0	0	2	2	5	0	.250	.300
Reitz, Ken-Kenneth John (The Zamboni Machine)	72-75StLN 76SFN 77-80StLN 81ChiN 82PitN	06-24-51	San Francisco, Cal.		R	R	6'	186	1344	4777	366	1243	243	12	68	548	184	518	10	.260	.383
Relaford, Desi-Desmond Lamont	96-00PhiN 00SDN 01NYN 02SeaA 03-04KCA 05ColN	09-16-73	Valdosta, Ga.		B	R	5'8	170	925	2913	373	711	147	19	40	308	291	491	81	.244	.349
Remy, Jerry-Gerald Peter	75-77CalA 78-84BosA 85KJ	11-08-52	Fall River, Mass.		L	R	5'9	165	1154	4455	605	1226	140	38	7	329	356	404	178	.275	.328
Renteria, Edgar-Edgar Enrique	96-98FlaN 99-04StLN 05BosA 06AtlN	08-07-75	Barranquilla, Colombia		R	R	6'1	195	1598	6143	934	1770	340	23	105	705	551	864	263	.288	.402
Renteria, Rich-Richard Avina	86PitN 87-88SeaA 93-94FlaN	12-25-61	Harbor City, Cal.		R	R	5'9	172	184	422	42	100	20	2	4	41	25	49	2	.237	.322
Repko, Jason-Jason Edward	05-06LAN	12-27-80	East Chicago, Ind.		R	R	5'11	195	198	406	64	94	20	4	11	46	31	104	15	.232	.382
Restovich, Michael-Michael Jerome	02-04MinA 05ColN 05PitN 06ChiN	01-03-79	Rochester, Minn.		R	R	6'4	245	137	240	37	60	12	3	6	20	27	60	1	.250	.400
Rettenmund, Merv-Mervin Weldon	68-73BalA 74-75CinN 76-77SDN 78-80CalA	06-06-43	Flint, Mich.		R	R	5'11	195	1023	2555	393	693	114	16	66	329	445	382	66	.271	.406
Revering, Dave-David Alvin	78-81OakA 81-82NYA 82TorA 82SeaA	02-12-53	Roseville, Cal.		L	R	6'4	210	557	1832	205	472	83	16	62	234	148	240	2	.265	.430
Reyes, Gil-Gilberto Rolando [Polanco]	83-85,87-88LAN 89,91MonN 92DR	12-10-63	Santo Domingo, D.R.		R	R	6'2	200	122	258	13	52	11	0	0	24	20	64	2	.202	.244
Reyes, Jose-Jose Ariel [Ramirez]	06CinN	02-26-83	Barahona, Dom. Rep.		B	R	5'11	180	2	5	0	1	0	0	0	0	0	0	0	.200	.200
Reyes, Jose-Jose Bernabe	03-06NYN	06-11-83	Gonzalez, Dom. Rep.		B	R	6'	160	436	1837	301	524	82	40	33	185	98	226	156	.285	.427
Reyes, Rene-Rene	03-04ColN	02-21-78	Margarita, Venezuela		B	R	5'11	210	81	177	18	39	9	1	2	13	14	34	3	.220	.314
Reynolds, Craig-Gordon Craig	75-76PitN 77-78SeaA 79-89HouN	12-27-52	Houston, Tex.		L	R	6'1	175	1491	4466	480	1142	143	95	42	377	227	406	58	.256	.356
Reynolds, Don-Donald Edward (King Cobra)	78-79SDN	04-16-53	Arkadelphia, Ark.		R	R	5'9	180	87	132	14	32	3	2	0	16	22	20	1	.242	.295
Reynolds, Harold-Harold Craig	83-92SeaA 93BalA 94CalA	11-26-60	Eugene, Ore.		B	R	5'11	165	1374	4782	640	1233	230	53	21	353	480	417	250	.258	.341

USE NAME - GIVEN NAMES (NICKNAMES)	TEAM BY YEAR	BIRTH DATE	BIRTH PLACE	DEATH DATE	B	T	HGT	WGT	G	AB	R	H	2B	3B	HR	RBI	BB	SO	SB	BA	SA
Reynolds, R.J.-Robert James	83-85LAN 85-90PitN	04-19-59	Sacramento, Cal.		R	R	6'	190	786	2270	288	605	121	17	35	294	190	419	109	.267	.381
Reynolds, Ronn-Ronn Dwayne	82-83,85NYN 86PhiN 87HouN 90SDN	09-28-58	Wichita, Kans.		R	R	6'	200	143	356	22	67	12	0	4	21	18	96	0	.188	.256
Rhodes, Karl-Karl Derrick (Tuffy)	90-93HouN 93-95ChiN 95BosA	08-21-68	Cincinnati, Ohio		L	L	5'11	195	225	590	74	132	29	3	13	44	74	121	14	.224	.349
Rhomberg, Kevin-Kevin Jay	82-84CleA	11-22-55	Dubuque, Iowa		R	R	5'11	175	41	47	5	18	0	0	1	3	4	11	1	.383	.447
Rice, Jim-James Edward	74-89BosA	03-08-53	Anderson, S.C.		R	R	6'1	205	2089	8225	1249	2452	373	79	382	1451	670	1423	58	.298	.502
Richard, Chris-Christopher Robert	00StLN 00-02BalA 03ColN	06-07-74	San Diego, Cal.		L	L	6'2	185	267	880	131	227	57	6	34	122	77	176	18	.258	.452
Richard, Lee-Lee Edward (Bee Bee)	71-72, 74-75ChiA 76StLN	09-18-48	Lafayette, La.		R	R	5'11	165	239	492	71	103	12	6	2	29	33	77	12	.209	.270
Richards, Gene-Eugene	77-83SDN 84SFN	09-29-53	Monticello, S.C.		L	L	6'	175	1026	3549	502	1028	127	63	26	255	356	436	247	.290	.383
Richardson, Jeff-Jeffrey Scott	89CinN 91PitN 93BosA	08-26-65	Grand Island, Neb.		R	R	6'2	175	74	153	13	27	6	0	2	13	11	29	1	.176	.255
Richardt, Mike-Michael Anthony (Rudy)	80,82-84TexA 84HouN 85SJ	05-24-58	N.Hollywood, Cal.		R	R	5'11	170	186	580	46	131	15	1	4	60	27	62	11	.226	.276
Richie, Rob-Robert Eugene	89DetA	09-05-65	Reno, Nev.		L	R	6'3	185	19	49	6	13	4	2	1	10	5	10	0	.265	.490
Riesgo, Nikco-Damon Nikco	91MonN	01-11-67	Long Beach, Cal.		R	R	6'2	185	4	7	1	1	0	0	0	0	3	1	0	.143	.143
Riggans, Shawn-Shawn Willis	06TBA	07-25-80	Fort Lauderdale, Fla.		R	R	6'2	190	10	29	3	5	1	0	0	1	4	7	0	.172	.207
Riggs, Adam-Adam David	97LAN 01SDN 03-04AnaA	10-04-72	Steubenville, Ohio		R	R	6'	195	61	153	18	33	9	1	3	10	16	30	6	.216	.346
Riles, Ernest-Ernest A.	85-88MilA 88-90SFN 91OakA 92HouN 93BosA	10-02-60	Cairo, Ga.		L	R	6'	180	919	2504	309	637	92	20	48	284	244	409	20	.254	.365
Rios, Alex-Alexis Israel	04-05TorA	02-18-81	Coffee, Ala.		R	R	6'5	194	257	907	126	248	47	13	11	87	59	185	29	.273	.390
Rios, Armando-Armando	98-01SFN 01-02PitN 03ChiA 06TorA	09-13-71	Santurce, P.R.		L	L	5'9	185	547	1471	203	411	88	14	53	249	150	295	29	.279	.466
Ripken, Billy-William Oliver	87-92BalA 93-94TexA 95CleA 96BalA 97TexA 98DetA	12-16-64	Havre de Grace, Md.		R	R	6'1	185	912	2729	287	674	121	6	20	229	174	332	25	.247	.318
Ripken, Cal-Calvin Edwin Jr.	81-01BalA	08-24-60	Havre de Grace, Md.		R	R	6'4	225	3001	11551	1647	3184	603	44	431	1695	1129	1305	36	.276	.447
Rivas, Luis-Luis Wilfredo	00-05MinA	08-30-79	La Guaira, Venezuela		R	R	5'10	185	565	1884	258	493	86	26	30	177	113	289	78	.262	.383
Rivera, Bombo-Jesus Manuel [Torres]	75-76MonN 78-79MinA 82KCA	08-02-52	Ponce, D.R.		R	R	5'9	187	335	831	100	220	39	11	10	83	71	144	11	.265	.374
Rivera, Carlos-Carlos Alberto	03-04PitN	06-10-78	Fajardo, P.R.		L	L	5'11	230	85	110	13	24	5	0	3	11	9	31	0	.218	.345
Rivera, German-German [Diaz]	83-84LAN 85HouN	07-06-59	Santurce, P.R.		R	R	6'2	195	120	280	24	72	15	3	2	19	27	40	1	.257	.354
Rivera, Juan-Juan Luis	01-03NYA 04MonN 05-06LAA	07-03-78	Guarenas, Venezuela		R	R	6'2	185	452	1449	190	422	87	2	58	225	106	185	8	.291	.474
Rivera, Luis-Luis Antonio [Pedraza]	86-88MonN 89-93BosA 94NYN 97HouN 98KCA	01-03-64	Cidra, P.R.		R	R	5'9	175	781	2215	249	516	114	12	28	209	171	443	20	.233	.333
Rivera, Mike-Michael R.	01-02DetA 03SDN 06MilN	09-08-76	Rio Piedras, P.R.		R	R	6'	190	108	339	31	81	20	1	8	38	19	69	0	.239	.375
Rivera, Rene-Rene [Rivera]	04-06SeaA	07-31-83	Bayamon, P.R.		R	R	5'10	190	53	150	11	34	7	0	3	10	4	41	1	.227	.333
Rivera, Ruben-Ruben [Moreno]	95-97NYA 97-00SDN 01CinN 02TexA 03SFN	11-14-73	La Chorrera, Panama		R	R	6'3	205	662	1586	237	343	67	11	64	203	185	510	50	.216	.393
Rivers, Mickey-John Milton (Mick the Quick, Swift)	70-75CalA 76-79NYA 79-84TexA	10-31-48	Miami, Fla.		L	L	5'10	165	1468	5629	785	1660	237	71	61	499	266	471	267	.295	.397
Roberson, Chris-Christopher William	06PhiN	08-23-79	Oakland, Cal.		B	R	6'2	180	57	41	9	8	0	1	0	1	0	9	3	.195	.244
Roberson, Kevin-Kevin Lynn	93-95ChiN 96NYN	01-29-68	Decatur, Ill.		B	R	6'4	210	165	309	44	61	11	0	20	51	27	93	0	.197	.430
Roberts, Bip-Leon Joseph	86,88-91SDN 92-93CinN 94-95SDN 96-97KCA 97CleA 98DetA 98OakA	10-27-63	Berkeley, Cal.		B	R	5'7	160	1202	4147	663	1220	203	31	30	352	396	548	264	.294	.380
Roberts, Brian-Brian Michael	01-06BalA	10-09-77	Durham, N.C.		B	R	5'9	175	665	2626	409	734	169	19	40	250	267	359	136	.280	.404
Roberts, Dave-David Ray	99-01CinN 02-04LAN 04bSDN 05-06SDN	05-31-72	Okinawa, Japan		L	L	5'10	172	666	2204	358	594	76	42	21	181	245	278	207	.270	.371
Roberts, Dave-David Wayne	72-75,77-78SDN 79-80TexA 81HouN 82PhiN	02-17-51	Lebanon, Ore.		L	R	6'3	205	709	2019	194	483	77	7	49	208	128	361	27	.239	.357
Roberts, Leon-Leon Kauffman	74-75DetA 76-77HouN 78-80SeaA 81-82TexA 82TorA 83-84KCA	01-22-51	Vicksburg, Mich.		R	R	6'3	200	901	2737	342	731	126	28	78	328	256	428	26	.267	.419
Roberts, Ryan-Ryan Alan	06TorA	09-19-80	Fort Worth, Tex.		R	R	5'11	190	9	13	1	1	0	0	1	1	1	4	0	.077	.308
Robertson, Andre-Andre Levett	81-85NYA	10-02-57	Orange, Tex.		R	R	5'10	160	254	724	80	182	32	4	5	54	26	120	4	.251	.327
Robertson, Bob-Robert Eugene	67PitN 68IL 69-76PitN 77XJ 78SeaA 79TorA	10-02-46	Frostburg, Md.		R	R	6'1	210	829	2385	283	578	93	10	115	368	317	546	7	.242	.434
Robertson, Mike-Michael Francis	96ChiA 97PhiN 98AriN	10-09-70	Norwich, Conn.		L	L	6'	180	39	58	3	11	3	1	0	4	0	9	1	.190	.276
Robidoux, Billy Jo-William Joseph	85-88MilA 89ChiA 90BosA	01-13-64	Ware, Mass.		L	R	6'2	200	173	468	43	98	21	0	5	43	71	106	1	.209	.286
Robinson, Bill-William Henry	66AtlN 67-69NYA 72-74PhiN 75-82PitN 82-83PhiN	06-26-43	McKeesport, Pa.		R	R	6'2	190	1472	4364	536	1127	229	29	166	641	263	819	71	.258	.438
Robinson, Bruce-Bruce Phillip	78OakA 79-80NYA 81SJ	04-16-54	LaJolla, Cal.		L	R	6'2	200	38	101	5	23	3	0	1	10	4	12	0	.228	.277
Robinson, Craig-Craig George	72-73PhiN 74-75AtlN 75-76SFN 76-77AtlN	08-21-48	Abington, Pa.		R	R	5'9	185	292	718	80	157	15	6	0	42	42	107	12	.219	.256
Robinson, Kerry-Kerry Keith	98TBA 99CinN 01-03StLN 04SDN 06KCA	10-03-73	St. Louis, Mo.		L	L	6'0	175	463	735	112	196	25	9	3	56	37	93	36	.267	.337
Robles, Oscar-Oscar Manuel [Arenas]	05-06LAN	04-09-76	Tijuana, Mexico		L	R	5'11	155	139	397	50	104	18	2	5	34	36	38	0	.262	.355
Robles, Sergio-Sergio [Valenzuela]	72-73BalA 76LAN	04-16-46	Magdalena de Kino, Mex.		R	R	6'1	190	16	21	0	2	0	0	0	0	3	3	0	.095	.143
Robson, Tom-Thomas James	74-75TexA	01-15-46	Rochester, N.Y.		R	R	6'4	220	23	48	5	10	1	0	0	4	5	6	0	.208	.229
Rockett, Pat-Patrick Edward	76-78AtlN	01-09-55	San Antonio, Tex.		R	R	5'11	170	152	411	33	88	12	0	1	28	40	45	2	.214	.251
Rodriguez, Alex-Alexander Emmanuel (A-Rod)	94-00SeaA 01-03TexA 04-06NYA	07-27-75	New York, N.Y.		R	R	6'3	210	1746	6767	1358	2067	364	26	464	1347	820	1404	241	.305	.573
Rodriguez, Aurelio-Aurelio [Ituarte] (Chi-Chi)	67-70CalA 70WasA 71-79DetA 80SDN 80-81NYA 82ChiA 83BalA 83ChiA	12-28-47	Cananea, Mexico	09-23-00	R	R	5'10	180	2017	6611	612	1570	287	46	124	648	324	943	35	.237	.351
Rodriguez, Carlos-Carlos [Marquez]	91NYA 94-95BosA	11-01-67	Mexico City, Mexico		B	R	5'9	160	85	241	21	67	16	1	1	20	14	17	1	.278	.365
Rodriguez, Eddie-Edwin [Morales]	82NYA 83,85SDN	08-14-60	Ponce, P.R.		R	R	5'10	175	21	22	3	5	1	0	0	1	2	4	0	.227	.273
Rodriguez, Henry-Henry Anderson [Lorenzo]	92-95LAN 95-97MonN 98-00ChiN 00FlaN 01NYA 02MonN	11-08-67	Santo Domingo, D.R.		L	L	6'1	215	950	3031	389	784	176	9	160	523	276	803	10	.259	.481
Rodriguez, Ivan-Ivan [Torres] (Pudge)	91-02TexA 03FlaN 04-06DetA	11-27-71	Manati, P.R.		R	R	5'9	205	2023	7745	1159	2354	473	42	277	1119	437	1125	112	.304	.483
Rodriguez, John-John Joseph	05-06StLN	01-20-78	New York, N.Y.		L	L	6'	205	332	46	99	18	3	7	43	40	90	2		.298	.434
Rodriguez, Liu-Liubiemithz	99ChiA	11-05-76	Caracas, Venezuela		B	R	5'9	170	39	93	8	22	4	1	0	12	12	11	0	.237	.333
Rodriguez, Luis-Luis Orlando	05-06MinA	06-27-80	San Carlos, Venezuela		B	R	5'9	180	138	290	32	74	14	2	4	26	32	39	2	.255	.359
Rodriguez, Ruben-Ruben Dario [Martinez]	86,88PitN	08-04-64	Cabrera, Dom. Rep.		R	R	6'	170	4	8	1	1	0	0	0	1	0	3	0	.125	.375
Rodriguez, Steve-Steven James	95BosA 95DetA	11-29-67	Las Vegas, Nev.		R	R	5'8	170	18	39	5	7	1	0	0	6	6	10	2	.179	.205
Rodriguez, Tony-Luis Antonio	96BosA	08-15-70	Rio Piedras, P.R.		R	R	5'11	165	27	67	7	16	1	0	1	9	4	8	0	.239	.299
Rodriguez, Vic-Victor Manuel [Rivera]	84BalA 89MinA	07-14-61	New York, N.Y.		R	R	5'11	160	17	28	6	12	5	0	2	3	0	5	0	.429	.607
Roenicke, Gary-Gary Steven (Rhino)	76MonN 78-85BalA 86NYA 87-88AtlN	12-05-54	Covina, Cal.		R	R	6'3	205	1063	2708	367	670	135	4	121	410	406	428	16	.247	.434
Roenicke, Ron-Ronald Jon	81-83LAN 83SeaA 84SDN 85SFN 86-87PhiN 88CinN	08-29-56	Covina, Cal.		B	R	6'	180	527	1076	141	256	51	3	17	113	190	195	24	.238	.338
Rogers, Eddie-Edward Antonio	02,05-06BalA	08-29-78	San Pedro de Mac., D.R		R	R	6'1	172	30	29	5	6	0	0	1	4	0	3	0	.207	.310
Rogodzinski, Mike-Michael George	73-75PhiN	02-22-48	Evanston, Ill.		L	R	6'	185	99	114	17	25	4	0	2	12	17	23	0	.219	.307
Rohde, Dave-David Grant	90-91HouN 92CleA	05-08-64	Los Altos, Cal.		B	R	6'2	180	93	146	11	23	4	0	0	5	16	31	0	.158	.185
Rohn, Dan-Daniel Jay	83-84ChiN 86CleA	01-10-56	Alpena, Mich.		L	R	5'8	165	54	72	5	18	3	2	1	11	4	9	1	.250	.389
Rohrmeier, Dan-Daniel	97SeaA	09-27-65	Cincinnati, Ohio		R	R	6'0	185	7	9	4	3	0	0	0	2	2	4	0	.333	.333
Rolen, Scott-Scott Bruce	96-02PhiN 02-06StLN	04-04-75	Evansville, Ind.		R	R	6'4	230	1393	5106	899	1454	356	30	253	954	681	1041	99	.285	.515
Rolison, Nate-Nathan Mardis	00FlaN	03-27-77	Hattiesburg, Miss.		L	R	6'6	240	8	13	0	1	0	0	0	2	1	4	0	.077	.077
Rollins, Jimmy-James Calvin	00-06PhiN	11-27-78	Oakland, Cal.		B	R	5'8	165	952	3997	630	1095	231	61	84	391	319	555	207	.274	.425
Rolls, Damian-Damian Michael	00-04TBA	09-15-77	Manhattan, Kans.		R	R	6'2	205	266	819	103	203	42	2	9	73	42	184	27	.248	.337
Romano, Jason-Jason Anthony	02TexA 02ColN 03LAN 04TBA 04-05CinN	06-24-79	Tampa, Fla.		R	R	6'	185	129	191	26	39	6	1	2	12	13	53	8	.204	.277
Romano, Tom-Thomas Michael	87MonN	10-25-58	Syracuse, N.Y.		R	R	5'11	170	7	3	1	0	0	0	0	0	0	1	0	.000	.000
Romero, Ed-Edgardo Ralph [Rivera]	77,80-85MilA 86-89BosA 89AtlN 89MilA 90DetA	12-09-57	Santurce, P.R.		R	R	5'11	170	730	1912	218	473	79	1	8	155	140	159	9	.247	.302
Romero, Mandy-Armando	97-98SDN 98BosA 03ColN	10-29-67	Miami, Fla.		B	R	5'11	200	42	77	12	16	2	0	2	5	6	25	1	.208	.312
Romine, Kevin-Kevin Andrew	85-91BosA	05-23-61	Exeter, N.H.		R	R	5'11	190	331	630	89	158	30	1	5	55	49	124	11	.251	.325
Ronan, Marc-Edward Marcus	93StLN	09-19-68	Ozark, Ala.		L	R	6'2	190	6	12	0	1	0	0	0	1	1	3	0	.083	.083
Roof, Gene-Eugene Lawrence (Geno)	81-83StLN 83MonN	01-13-58	Paducah, Ky.		B	R	6'2	195	48	90	17	24	8	0	0	6	14	23	7	.267	.356
Roomes, Rolando-Rolando Audley (Rollie)	88ChiN 89-90CinN 90MonN	02-15-62	Kingston, Jamaica		R	R	6'3	180	170	406	45	103	18	6	9	42	14	130	12	.254	.394
Rooney, Pat-Patrick Eugene	81MonN	11-28-57	Chicago, Ill.		R	R	6'	195	4	5	0	0	0	0	0	0	0	2	0	.000	.000
Rosado, Luis-Luis [Robles] (Papo)	77,80NYN	12-06-55	Santurce, P.R.		R	R	5'11	185	11	28	1	5	0	0	0	3	1	4	0	.179	.214
Rosario, Mel-Melvin Gregario	97BalA	05-23-73	Santo Domingo, D.R.		B	R	6'0	191	4	3	0	0	0	0	0	0	0	2	0	.000	.000
Rosario, Victor-Victor Manuel [Rivera]	90AtlN	08-26-66	Hato Mayor, D.R.		R	R	5'11	155	9	7	3	1	0	0	0	0	0	4	1	.143	.143
Rose, Bobby-Robert Richard	89-92CalA	03-15-67	Covina, Cal.		R	R	6'	172	73	200	24	49	11	3	5	23	15	33	1	.245	.405
Rose, Mike-Michael John Ferrero	04OakA 05LAN 06StLN	08-25-76	Sacramento, Cal		B	R	6'1	185	27	54	3	11	4	0	1	3	3	12	0	.204	.296
Rose, Pete-Peter Edward Sr. (Charlie Hustle)	63-78CinN 79-83PhiN 84MonN 84-86,M84-89CinN	04-14-41	Cincinnati, Ohio		B	R	5'11	195	3562	14053	2165	4256	746	135	160	1314	1566	1143	198	.303	.409
Rose, Pete-Peter Edward Jr.	97CinN	11-16-69	Cincinnati, Ohio		L	R	6'1	180	11	14	2	2	0	0	0	1	0	5	0	.143	.143
Rosello, Dave-David [Rodriguez]	72-77ChiN 79-81CleA	06-26-50	Mayaguez, P.R.		R	R	5'11	160	422	873	114	206	31	3	10	76	108	145	5	.236	.313
Roskos, John-John Edward	98-99FlaN 00SDN	11-08-74	Victorville, Cal.		L	R	6'	190	37	49	4	5	1	0	1	4	4	19	0	.102	.143
Ross, Cody-Cody Joseph	03DetA 05-06LAN 06CinN 06FlaN	12-23-80	Portales, N.M.		R	L	5'11	180	121	313	36	69	14	2	14	52	24	78	1	.220	.412
Ross, David-David Wade	02-04LAN 05PitN 05SDN 06CinN	03-19-77	Bainbridge, Ga.		R	R	6'2	205	259	671	82	155	34	3	40	102	73	211	0	.231	.469
Rossy, Rico-Elam Jose [Ramos]	91AtlN 92-93KCA 98SeaA	02-16-64	San Juan, P.R.		R	R	5'10	175	147	317	43	67	18	1	4	28	35	45	0	.211	.312
Rottino, Vinny-Vincent Antonio	06MilN	04-07-80	Racine, Wis.		R	R	6'	195	9	14	5	3	1	0	0	2	1	5	1	.214	.286
Rouse, Mike-Michael Gregory	06OakA	25-80	San Jose, Cal.		L	R	5'11	190	14	24	2	7	3	0	0	1	2	5	0	.292	.417

USE NAME - GIVEN NAMES (NICKNAMES)	TEAM BY YEAR	BIRTH DATE	BIRTH PLACE	DEATH DATE	B	T	HGT	WGT	G	AB	R	H	2B	3B	HR	RBI	BB	SO	SB	BA	SA
Rowand, Aaron-Aaron Ryan	01-05ChiA 06PhiN	08-29-77	Portland, Ore.		R	R	6'1	200	688	2052	314	572	121	12	66	258	114	386	48	.279	.446
Rowdon, Wade-Wade Lee	84-86CinN 87ChiN 88BalA	09-07-60	Riverhead, N.Y.		R	R	6'2	180	78	157	14	34	6	2	1	16	14	35	3	.217	.299
Rowland, Rich-Richard Garnet	90-93DetA 94-95BosA	02-25-64	Cloverdale, Cal.		R	R	6'1	210	98	230	22	49	8	0	9	26	22	71	0	.213	.365
Royer, Stan-Stanley Dean	91-94StLN 94BosA	08-31-67	Olney, Ill.		R	R	6'3	215	89	164	14	41	10	0	4	21	4	41	0	.250	.384
Royster, Jerry-Jeron Kennis	73-75LAN 76-84AtlN 85-86SDN 87ChiA 87NYA 88AtlN M02MilN	10-18-52	Sacramento, Cal.		R	R	6'	165	1428	4208	552	1049	165	33	40	352	411	534	189	.249	.333
Royster, Willie-Willie Arthur	81BalA	04-11-54	Clarksville, Va.		R	R	5'10	185	4	4	0	0	0	0	0	0	0	2	0	.000	.000
Ruan, Wilkin-Wilkin Chal	02-03LAN	10-18-78	Guaymate, Dom. Rep.		R	R	6'	170	33	52	4	12	3	1	0	5	0	9	1	.231	.327
Rudi, Joe-Joseph Oden	67KCA 68-76OakA 77-80CalA 81BosA 82OakA	09-07-46	Modesto, Cal.		R	R	6'2	200	1547	5556	684	1468	287	39	179	810	369	870	25	.264	.427
Rudolph, Ken-Kenneth Victor	69-73ChiN 74SFN 75-76StLN 77SFN 77BalA	12-29-46	Rockford, Ill.		R	R	6'1	185	328	743	55	158	23	2	6	64	52	121	2	.213	.273
Ruiz, Carlos-Carlos Joaquin	06PhiN	01-22-79	David, Panama		R	R	5'10	200	27	69	5	18	1	1	3	10	5	8	0	.261	.435
Ruiz, Chico-Manuel [Cruz]	78,80AtlN	11-01-51	Santurce, P.R.		R	R	5'11	175	43	72	6	21	5	1	0	4	5	11	0	.292	.389
Runge, Paul-Paul William	81-88AtlN	05-21-58	Kingston, N.Y.		R	R	6'	165	183	345	43	80	13	1	4	26	54	75	5	.232	.310
Runnells, Tom-Thomas William	85-86CinN M91-92MonN	04-17-55	Greeley, Colo.		B	R	6'	175	40	46	4	8	2	0	0	0	3	6	0	.174	.217
Rushford, Jim-James Thomas	02MilN	03-24-74	Chicago, Ill.		L	L	6'1	190	23	77	8	11	2	0	1	6	6	9	0	.143	.208
Russell, Bill-William Ellis	69-86,M96-98LAN	10-21-48	Pittsburg, Kans.		R	R	6'	180	2181	7318	796	1926	293	57	46	627	483	667	167	.263	.338
							Bats Both 71														
Russell, John-John William	84-88PhiN 89AtlN 90-93TexA	01-05-61	Oklahoma City, Okla.		R	R	6'	200	448	1087	113	245	50	3	34	129	84	355	3	.225	.371
Ryal, Mark-Mark Dwayne	82KCA 85ChiA 86-87CalA 89PhiN 90PitN	04-28-60	Henryetta, Okla.		L	L	6'1	195	127	223	19	47	11	0	7	31	10	34	1	.211	.354
Ryan, Mike-Michael Sean	02-05MinA	07-06-77	Indiana, Pa.		R	R	5'10	190	127	260	32	69	14	1	7	33	19	52	4	.265	.408
Ryan, Rob-Robert James	99-01AriN 01OakA	06-24-73	Havre, Mont.		L	L	5'11	190	55	64	8	15	2	1	2	7	5	21	0	.234	.391
Sabo, Chris-Christopher Andrew (Spuds)	88-93CinN 94BalA 95ChiA 95StLN 95CinN 96CinN	01-19-62	Detroit, Mich.		R	R	6'	185	911	3354	494	898	214	17	116	426	274	460	120	.268	.445
Sadek, Mike-Michael George	73,75-81SFN	05-30-46	Minneapolis, Minn.		R	R	5'10	165	383	813	88	184	30	4	5	74	108	97	6	.226	.292
							Bats Both part of 79														
Sadler, Donnie-Donnie Lamont	98-99BosA 00BosA 01CinN 01-02KCA 02-03TexA 04AriN	06-17-75	Clifton, Texas		R	R	5'6	175	417	767	125	155	29	8	6	46	55	163	25	.202	.284
Sadler, Ray-Raymond Lee	05PitN	09-19-80	Clifton, Tex.		R	R	6'1	200	3	8	1	2	0	0	1	1	0	1	0	.250	.625
Saenez, Olmedo-Olmedo [Sanchez]	94ChiA 99-02OakA 04-06LAN	10-08-70	Chitre, Panama		R	R	6'2	210	641	1553	217	417	101	5	69	257	132	330	3	.269	.473
Sagmoen, Marc-Marc Richard	97TexA	04-16-71	Seattle, Wash.		L	L	5'11	185	21	43	2	6	1	0	1	4	2	13	0	.140	.256
Sakata, Lenn-Lenn Haruki (Cat)	77-79MilA 80-85BalA 86OakA 87NYA	06-08-54	Honolulu, Hawaii		R	R	5'9	160	565	1289	163	296	46	4	25	109	97	158	30	.230	.330
Salas, Mark-Mark Bruce	84StLN 85-86MinA 87NYA 88ChiA 89CleA 90DetA	03-08-61	Montebello, Cal.		L	R	6'	200	509	1292	142	319	49	10	38	143	89	163	3	.247	.389
Salazar, Angel-Argenis Antonio [Yepez]	83-84MonN 86-87KCA 88ChiN	11-04-61	Anaco, Venezuela		R	R	6'	180	383	886	69	188	33	6	2	59	19	150	6	.212	.270
Salazar, Jeff-Jeffrey Dewan	06ColN	11-24-80	Oklahoma City, Okla.		L	L	6'	190	19	53	13	15	4	0	1	8	11	16	2	.283	.415
Salazar, Luis-Luis Ernesto [Garcia]	80-84SDN 85-86ChiA 87SDN 88DetA 89SDN 89-92ChiN	05-19-56	Barcelona, Venezuela		R	R	5'9	185	1302	4101	438	1070	144	33	94	455	179	653	117	.261	.381
Salazar, Oscar-Oscar Enrique	02DetA	06-27-78	Maracay, Venezuela		R	R	5'11	178	8	21	2	4	1	0	0	3	1	2	0	.190	.381
Salmon, Tim-Timothy James	92-96CalA 97-04AnaA 05KCA J06LAA	08-24-68	Long Beach, Cal.		R	R	6'3	225	1672	5934	986	1674	339	24	299	1016	970	1360	48	.282	.498
Sample, Billy-William Amos	78-84TexA 85NYA 86AtlN	04-02-55	Roanoke, Va.		R	R	5'9	175	826	2516	371	684	127	9	46	230	195	230	98	.272	.384
Samuel (Romero), Juan-Juan Milton Romero [Samuel]	83-89PhiN 89NYN 90-92LAN 92KCA 93CinN 94-95DetA 95KCA 96-98TorA	12-09-60	San Pedro de Mac. D.R.		R	R	5'11	170	1720	6081	873	1578	287	102	161	703	440	1442	396	.259	.420
Sanchez, Alex-Alejandro [Pimental]	82-83PhiN 84SFN 85DetA 86MinA 87OakA	02-26-59	San Pedro de Mac.D.R.		R	R	6'	190	109	214	28	49	7	3	8	21	1	66	4	.229	.402
Sanchez, Alex-Alexis	01-03MilN 03-04DetA 05TBA 05SFN	08-26-76	Havana, Cuba		L	L	5'10	180	427	1527	193	452	56	21	6	111	76	233	122	.296	.372
Sanchez, Angel-Angel Luis	06KCA	08-23-83	Humacao, P.R.		R	R	6'2	185	8	27	2	6	0	0	1	0	4	0	2	.222	.222
Sanchez, Freddy-Frederick Philip	02-03BosA 04-06PitN	12-21-78	Los Angeles, Cal.		R	R	5'11	190	330	1104	150	346	81	6	11	126	60	102	5	.313	.484
Sanchez, Orlando-Orlando [Marquez]	81-83StLN 84KCA 84BalA	11-04-57	Canovanas, P.R.		L	R	6'	185	74	110	11	24	3	2	0	12	7	19	1	.218	.282
Sanchez, Rey-Rey Francisco [Guadalupe]	91-97ChiN 97NYA 98SFN 99-01KCA 01AtlN 02BosA 03NYN 03SeaA 05NYA	10-05-67	Rio Piedras, P.R.		R	R	5'10	180	1490	4850	549	1317	193	32	15	389	229	508	55	.272	.334
Sandberg, Jared-Jared Lawrence	01-03TBA	03-02-78	Olympia, Wash.		R	R	6'3	210	196	630	83	139	38	2	25	92	65	236	4	.221	.406
Sandberg, Ryne-Ryne Dee (Ryno)	81PhiN 82-94ChiN 95VR 96-97ChiN	09-18-59	Spokane, Wash.		R	R	6'1	185	2164	8385	1318	2386	403	76	282	1061	761	1260	344	.285	.452
Sanders, Anthony-Anthony Marcus	99TorA 00-01SeaA	03-22-74	Tucson, Ariz.		R	R	6'2	205	13	25	3	6	3	0	0	4	2	5	0	.240	.360
Sanders, Deion-Deion Luwynn (Neon, Prime Time)	89-90NYA 91-94AtlN 89-00,04-04 Played in NFL 94-95CinN 95SFN 97CinN 01CinN	08-09-67	Ft. Myers, Fla.		L	L	6'1	195	641	2123	308	558	72	43	39	168	159	352	186	.263	.392
Sanders, Reggie-Reginald Jerome (Doctor)	74DetA	09-09-49	Birmingham, Ala.		R	R	6'2	210	26	99	12	27	7	0	3	10	5	20	0	.273	.434
Sanders, Reggie-Reginald Laverne	91-98CinN 99SDN 00AtlN 01AriN 02SFN 03PitN 04-05StLN 06KCA	12-01-67	Florence, S.C.		R	R	6'1	200	1753	6168	1025	1643	334	60	303	972	663	1599	304	.266	.487
Sandoval, Danny-Daniel A. [Escalona]	05-06PhiN	04-07-79	Lara, Venezuela		B	R	5'11	190	31	40	2	8	1	0	0	4	4	4	0	.200	.225
Sands, Charlie-Charles Duane	67NYA 71-72PitN 73-74CalA 75OakA	12-17-47	Newport News, Va.		L	R	6'3	220	93	145	15	31	6	1	6	23	36	35	0	.214	.393
Sandt, Tommy-Thomas James (Mr. Bout)	75-76OakA	12-22-50	Brooklyn, N.Y.		R	R	5'11	180	42	67	6	14	1	0	0	3	7	9	0	.209	.224
Sanford, Chance-Chance Steven	98PitN 99LAN	06-02-72	Houston, Texas		L	R	5'10	175	19	36	4	6	1	1	0	5	1	7	0	.167	.250
Sanguillen, Manny-Manuel DeJesus [Magan]	67,69-76PitN 77OakA 78-80PitN	03-21-44	Colon, Panama		R	R	6'	193	1448	5062	566	1500	205	57	65	585	223	331	35	.296	.398
Santana, Andres-Andres Confesor [Belonis]	90SFN 92SJ	05-25-68	San Pedro de Mac.D.R.		B	R	5'11	160	6	2	0	0	0	0	0	0	0	0	0	.000	.000
Santana, Pedro-Pedro C.	01DetA	12-21-74	San Pedro de Mac., D.R.		R	R	5'11	180	1	0	0	0	0	0	0	0	0	0	0	—	—
Santana, Rafael-Rafael Francisco [de la Cruz]	83StLN 84-87NYN 88NYA 89EJ 90CleA	01-31-58	La Romana, Dom.Rep.		R	R	6'1	165	668	2021	188	497	74	5	13	156	138	234	3	.246	.307
Santangelo, F. P.-Frank Paul	95-98MonN 99SFN 00LAN 01OakA	10-24-67	Livonia, Mich.		B	R	5'10	185	665	1691	258	415	87	14	21	162	240	319	37	.245	.351
Santiago, Benito-Benito [Rivera]	86-92SDN 93-94FlaN 95CinN 96PhiN 97-98TorA 99ChiN 00CinN 01-03SFN 04KCA 05PitN	03-09-65	Ponce, P.R.		R	R	6'1	190	1978	6951	755	1830	323	41	217	920	430	1270	91	.263	.415
Santiago, Ramon-Ramon D.	02-03DetA 04-05SeaA 06DetA	08-31-79	Las Matas, D.R.		B	R	5'11	160	276	793	93	180	25	7	6	54	51	133	20	.227	.299
Santo Domingo, Rafael-Rafael [Molina]	79CinN	11-24-55	Orocovis, P.R.		B	R	6'	165	7	6	0	1	0	0	0	0	1	3	0	.167	.167
Santos, Angel-Angel Ramon	01BosA 03CleA	08-14-79	Rio Piedras, P.R.		B	R	5'11	178	41	92	11	19	4	1	3	7	5	25	1	.207	.370
Santos, Chad-Chad Roque	06SFN	04-28-81	Honolulu, Hawaii		L	L	6'2	220	3	7	2	3	0	0	1	2	1	0	0	.429	.857
Santos, Francisco-Francisco Alejandro	03SFN	03-09-74	Santo Domingo, D.R.		L	L	6'1	170	8	15	2	3	2	0	1	3	0	3	0	.200	.533
Santovenia, Nelson-Nelson Gil [Mayol]	87-91MonN 92ChiA 93KCA	07-27-61	Pinar del Rio, Cuba		R	R	6'3	220	297	884	77	206	42	4	22	116	59	165	4	.233	.364
Sardinha, Dane-Dane K. A. A.	03,05CinN	04-08-79	Honolulu, Hawaii		R	R	6'2	215	2	5	0	0	0	0	0	0	0	0	0	.000	.000
Sasser, Mackey-Mack Daniel	87SFN 87PitN 88-92NYN 93-94SeaA 95PitN	08-03-62	Fort Gaines, Ga.		L	R	6'1	210	534	1189	103	317	69	7	16	156	55	104	1	.267	.384
Sasser, Rob-Robert Doffell	98TexA	03-25-75	Philadelphia, Pa.		R	R	6'3	205	1	1	0	0	0	0	0	0	0	0	0	.000	.000
Saturria, Luis-Luis Arturo	00-01StLN	07-21-75	San Pedro de Mac.,D.R.		R	R	6'2	165	25	10	1	1	1	0	0	1	1	4	1	.100	.200
Saunders, Doug-Douglas Long	93NYN	12-13-69	Lakewood, Cal.		R	R	6'	172	28	67	8	14	2	0	0	4	3	4	0	.209	.239
Sax, Dave-David John	82-83LAN 85-87BosA	09-22-58	Sacramento, Cal.		R	R	6'	190	37	60	3	16	4	0	1	8	3	5	0	.267	.383
Sax, Steve-Stephen Louis	81-88LAN 89-91NYA 92-93ChiA 94OakA	01-29-60	Sacramento, Cal.		R	R	5'11	185	1769	6940	913	1949	278	47	54	550	556	584	444	.281	.358
Scanlon, Pat-James Patrick	74-76MonN 77SDN	09-23-52	Minneapolis, Minn.		L	R	6'1	180	120	219	17	41	7	1	4	22	28	51	0	.187	.283
Scarsone, Steve-Steven Wayne	92PhiN 92BalA 93-96SFN 97StLN 99KCA	04-11-66	Anaheim, Cal.		R	R	6'2	190	350	830	103	198	44	4	20	86	70	266	7	.239	.373
Schaefer, Jeff-Jeffrey Scott	89ChiA 90-92SeaA 94OakA	05-31-60	Patchogue, N.Y.		R	R	5'10	170	225	359	37	73	12	1	2	20	10	49	8	.203	.259
Schall, Gene-Eugene David	95-96PhiN	06-05-70	Abington, Pa.		R	R	6'3	190	52	131	9	33	7	1	2	15	18	31	0	.252	.366
Schmidt, Dave-David Frederick	81BosA	12-22-56	Mesa, Ariz.		R	R	6'1	205	15	42	6	10	1	0	2	3	5	17	0	.238	.405
Schmidt, Mike-Michael Jack	72-89PhiN	09-27-49	Dayton, Ohio		R	R	6'2	195	2404	8352	1506	2234	408	59	548	1595	1507	1883	174	.267	.527
Schneck, Dave-David Lee	72-74NYN	06-18-49	Allentown, Pa.		L	L	6'	195	143	413	31	82	14	4	8	35	27	73	4	.199	.310
Schneider, Brian-Brian Duncan	00-04MonN 05-06WasN	11-26-76	Jacksonville, Fla.		L	R	6'1	200	628	1913	173	490	112	7	41	240	180	321	4	.256	.386
Schofield, Dick-Richard Craig	83-92CalA 92NYN 93-94TorA 95LAN 95-96CalA	11-21-62	Springfield, Ill.		R	R	5'10	180	1368	4299	505	989	137	32	56	353	446	684	120	.230	.316
Schroeder, Bill-Alfred William	83-88MilA 89-90CalA	09-07-58	Baltimore, Md.		R	R	6'2	210	376	1262	153	303	49	1	61	152	58	343	6	.240	.426
Schu, Rick-Richard Spencer (Rich)	84-87PhiN 88-89BalA 89DetA 90CalA 91PhiN 93-94JL 96MonN	01-26-62	Philadelphia, Pa.		R	R	6'	185	580	1568	189	386	67	13	41	134	139	282	17	.246	.384
Schulz, Jeff-Jeffrey Alan	89-90KCA 91PitN	06-02-61	Evansville, Ind.		L	R	6'1	190	40	78	5	19	5	1	0	7	6	17	0	.244	.333
Schumaker, Skip-Jared Michael	02-03-80	Torrance, Cal.		L	R	5'10	175	55	75	8	12	16	2	0	1	5	3	3	1	.205	.269
Scioscia, Mike-Michael Lorri	80-92LAN 93SJ M00-04AnaA M05-06LAA	11-27-58	Upper Darby, Pa.		L	R	6'2	220	1441	4373	398	1131	198	12	68	446	567	307	29	.259	.356
Sconiers, Daryl-Daryl Anthony	81-85CalA	10-03-58	San Bernardino, Cal.		L	L	6'3	195	234	637	83	169	30	5	15	84	48	87	7	.265	.399
Scott, Dick-Richard Edward	89OakA	07-19-62	Ellsworth, Maine		R	R	6'	165	3	2	0	0	0	0	0	0	0	0	0	.000	.000
Scott, Donnie-Donald Malcolm	83-84TexA 85SeaA 91CinN	08-16-61	Dunedin, Fla.		B	R	5'11	185	173	443	34	96	22	0	7	43	35	87	1	.217	.314
Scott, Gary-Gary Thomas	91-92ChiN	08-22-68	New Rochelle, N.Y.		R	R	6'	175	67	175	16	28	5	0	3	18	18	28	0	.160	.240
Scott, John-John Henry	74-75SDN 77TorA	01-24-52	Tunica, Miss.		R	R	6'1	185	118	257	35	57	8	3	4	22	24	45	13	.222	.280
Scott, Luke-Luke Brandon	05-06HouN	06-25-78	De Leon Springs, Fla.		L	L	6'	210	99	294	37	87	23	8	10	41	39	66	3	.296	.531
Scott, Rodney-Rodney Darrell (Cool Breeze)	75KCA 76MonN 77OakA 78ChiN 79-82MonN 82NYA	10-16-53	Indianapolis, Ind.		B	R	6'	180	690	2132	316	504	43	26	3	150	281	291	205	.236	.285
							Bats Right 75														
Scott, Tony-Anthony	73-75MonN 77-81StLN 81-84HouN 84MonN	09-18-51	Cincinnati, Ohio		B	R	6'	190	991	2803	331	699	111	28	17	253	186	464	125	.249	.327

USE NAME - GIVEN NAMES (NICKNAMES)	TEAM BY YEAR	BIRTH DATE	BIRTH PLACE	DEATH DATE	B	T	HGT	WGT	G	AB	R	H	2B	3B	HR	RBI	BB	SO	SB	BA	SA
Scranton, Jim-James Dean	84-85KCA	04-05-60	Torrance, Cal.		R	R	6'	185	8	6	1	0	0	0	0	0	0	0	0	.000	.000
Scrivener, Chuck-Wayne Allison	75-77DetA	10-03-47	Alexandria, Va.		R	R	5'9	170	145	310	38	59	8	1	2	18	24	44	2	.190	.242
Scruggs, Tony-Anthony Raymond	91TexA	03-19-66	Riverside, Cal.		R	R	6'1	210	5	6	1	0	0	0	0	0	0	1	0	.000	.000
Scutaro, Marco-Marcos L.	02-03NYN 04-06OakA	10-30-75	San Felipe, Venezuela		R	R	5'10	170	447	1312	162	339	79	11	24	133	115	197	12	.258	.390
Seabol, Scott-Scott Anthony	01NYA 05StLN	05-17-75	McKeesport, Pa.		R	R	6'4	200	60	106	11	23	5	0	1	10	8	23	0	.217	.292
Sears, Todd-Todd Andrew	02-03MinA 03SDN	10-23-75	Des Moines, Iowa		R	R	6'5	215	40	85	11	22	5	0	2	11	7	19	0	.259	.388
See, Larry-Ralph Laurence	86LAN 88TexA	06-20-60	Norwalk, Cal.		R	R	6'	195	26	43	1	8	2	0	0	2	3	15	0	.186	.233
Sefcik, Kevin-Kevin John	95-00PhiN 01ColN	02-10-71	Oak Lawn, Ill.		R	R	5'11	180	425	771	92	212	36	10	6	56	80	102	21	.275	.371
Segui, David-David Vincent	90-93BalA 94-95NYN 95-97MonN 98-99SeaA 99TorA 00TexA 00CleA 01-04BalA	07-19-66	Kansas City, Kans.		B	L	6'1	200	1456	4847	683	1412	284	16	139	684	524	687	17	.291	.443
Seguignol, Fernando-Fernando Alfredo	98-01MonN 02JL 03NYA	01-19-75	Bocas del Toro, Panama		B	R	6'5	225	178	366	42	91	23	0	17	40	20	114	0	.249	.451
Seibert, Kurt-Kurt Elliott	79ChiN	10-16-55	Cheverly, Md.		B	R	6'	160	7	2	2	0	0	0	0	0	0	1	0	.000	.000
Seilheimer, Ricky-Ricky Allen (Cowboy)	80ChiA	08-30-60	Brenham, Tex.		L	R	5'11	185	21	52	4	11	3	1	1	3	4	15	1	.212	.365
Seitzer, Kevin-Kevin Lee	86-91KCA 92MilA 93OakA 93-96MilA 96-97CleA	03-26-62	Springfield, Ill.		R	R	5'11	185	1439	5278	739	1557	285	35	74	613	669	617	80	.295	.404
Selby, Bill-William Frank	96BosA 97JL 00CleA 01CinN 02-03CleA	06-11-70	Monroeville, Ala.		L	R	5'9	190	198	431	45	96	20	3	11	48	33	71	1	.223	.360
Self, Todd-Todd Douglas	05HouN	11-09-78	Shreveport, La.		L	R	6'5	215	21	45	7	9	2	0	1	4	3	9	0	.200	.311
Sember, Mike-Michael David	77-78ChiN	02-24-53	Hammond, Ind.		R	R	6'	185	12	7	2	0	0	0	0	0	1	3	0	.286	.286
Serna, Paul-Paul David (Ponch)	81-82SeaA	11-16-58	El Centro, Cal.		R	R	5'7	173	95	263	26	62	5	0	7	17	7	24	2	.236	.335
Servais, Scott-Scott Daniel	91-95HouN 95-98ChiN 99SFN 00ColN 00SFN 01HouN	06-04-67	La Crosse, Wis.		R	R	6'2	205	820	2493	243	611	130	2	63	319	183	407	3	.245	.375
Sexson, Richie-Richmond Lockwood	97-00CleA 00-03MilN 04AriN 05-06SeaA	12-29-74	Portland, Ore.		R	R	6'7	225	1150	4214	661	1135	230	17	273	844	494	1127	12	.269	.508
Sexton, Chris-Christopher Philip	99ColN 00CinN	08-03-71	Cincinnati, Ohio		R	R	5'11	180	70	159	16	35	4	1	1	17	24	22	8	.220	.277
Sexton, Jimmy-Jimmy Dale	77SeaA 78-79HouN 81-82OakA 83StLN	12-15-51	Mobile, Ala.		R	R	5'10	175	236	372	53	81	9	3	5	24	32	71	36	.218	.298
Shabala, Adam-Adam Jason	05SFN	02-06-78	Streator, Ill.		L	R	6'1	190	6	15	1	3	0	0	0	4	1	5	0	.200	.200
Sharon, Dick-Richard Louis	73-74DetA 75SDN	04-15-50	San Mateo, Cal.		R	R	6'2	210	242	467	46	102	20	0	13	46	50	95	6	.218	.345
Sharp, Bill-William Howard	73-75ChiA 75-76MilA	01-18-50	Lima, Ohio		L	L	5'10	178	398	1104	122	281	52	8	9	95	75	109	3	.255	.341
Sharperson, Mike-Michael Tyrone	87TorA 87-93LAN 95AtlN	10-04-61	Orangesburg, S.C.	05-26-96	R	R	6'3	200	557	1203	149	337	61	5	10	123	139	154	22	.280	.364
Shave, Jon-Jonathan Taylor	93TexA 98MinA 99TexA	11-04-67	Waycross, Ga.		R	R	6'	185	79	160	20	46	9	0	1	21	8	35	3	.288	.363
Sheaffer, Danny-Danny Todd	87BosA 89CleA 93-94ColN 95-97StLN	06-02-61	Jacksonville, Fla.		R	R	6'	185	389	946	87	219	38	5	13	110	60	122	6	.232	.323
Shealy, Ryan-Ryan Nelson	05-06ColN 06KCA	08-29-79	Ft. Lauderdale, Fla.		R	R	6'5	240	92	293	45	86	19	1	9	53	28	76	2	.294	.457
Sheets, Andy-Andrew Mark	96-97SeaA 98SDN 99AnaA 00BosA 01-02TBA	11-19-71	Baton Rouge, La.		R	R	6'2	180	356	960	118	207	38	3	19	113	76	275	16	.216	.321
Sheets, Larry-Larry Kent	84-89BalA 90DetA 92JL 93SeaA	12-06-59	Staunton, Va.		L	R	6'4	220	748	2284	273	607	98	5	94	339	175	351	18	.266	.437
Sheffield, Gary-Gary Antonian	88-91MilA 92-93SDN 93-98FlaN 98-01LAN 02-03AtlN 04-06NYA	11-18-68	Tampa, Fla.		R	R	5'11	200	2229	8037	1433	2390	418	24	455	1501	1293	971	220	.297	.525
Shelby, John-John T. (T-Bone)	81-87BalA 87-90LAN 90-91DetA	02-23-58	Lexington, Ky.		B	R	6'1	175	1036	3090	389	739	128	24	70	313	182	671	98	.239	.364
Sheldon, Bobby-Bob Mitchell	74-75,77MilA	11-27-50	Montebello, Cal.		R	R	6'	170	94	262	30	67	8	5	0	17	23	25	0	.256	.324
Sheldon, Scott-Scott Patrick	97OakA 98-01TexA	11-28-68	Hammond, Ind.		R	R	6'3	210	141	285	34	67	16	0	8	33	15	84	1	.235	.375
Shelton, Ben-Benjamin Davis	93PitN	09-21-69	Chicago, Ill.		L	L	6'3	210	15	24	3	6	1	0	2	7	3	3	0	.250	.542
Shelton, Chris-Christopher Bob	04-06DetA	06-26-80	Salt Lake City, Utah		R	R	6'	225	249	807	117	227	39	7	35	109	77	208	1	.281	.477
Shepherd, Ron-Ronald Wayne	84-86TorA	10-27-60	Longview, Tex.		R	R	6'4	190	115	108	23	18	6	0	2	5	5	37	3	.167	.278
Sheridan, Pat-Patrick Arthur	81,83-85KCA 86-89DetA 89SFN 91NYA	12-04-57	Ann Arbor, Mich.		L	R	6'3	175	876	2419	319	611	91	21	51	257	236	501	86	.253	.371
Sherman, Darrell-Darrell Edward	93SDN	12-04-67	Los Angeles, Cal.		L	L	5'9	160	37	63	8	14	1	0	0	2	6	8	2	.222	.238
Sherrill, Denny-Dennis Lee	78,80NYA	03-03-56	Miami, Fla.		R	R	6'	165	5	5	1	1	0	0	0	0	0	1	0	.200	.200
Shields, Tommy-Thomas Charles	92BalA 93ChiN	08-14-64	Fairfax, Va.		R	R	6'	180	22	34	4	6	1	0	0	1	2	10	1	.176	.206
Shines, Razor-Anthony Raymond (Ray)	83-85,87MonN	07-18-56	Durham, N.C.		B	R	6'1	210	68	81	0	15	1	0	0	5	5	12	1	.185	.198
Shinjo, Tsuyoshi-Tsuyoshi	01NYN 02SFN 03NYN	01-28-72	Osaka, Japan		R	R	6'1	185	303	876	98	215	41	4	20	100	55	128	9	.245	.370
Shipley, Craig-Craig Barry	86-87LAN 89NYN 91-94SDN 95HouN 96-97SDN 98AnaA	01-07-63	Parramatta, Australia		R	R	6'1	185	582	1345	155	364	63	6	20	138	47	191	33	.271	.371
Bats Both - 86																					
Shoppach, Kelly-Kelly Brian	05BosA 06CleA	04-29-80	Fort Worth, Tex.		R	R	5'11	210	50	125	9	27	6	0	3	16	8	52	0	.216	.336
Short, Rick-Richard Ryan	05WasN	12-06-72	Elgin, Ill.		R	R	6'	190	11	15	4	6	2	0	2	4	1	1	0	.400	.933
Shumpert, Terry-Terrance Darnell	90-94KCA 95BosA 96ChiN 97SDN 98-02ColN 03TBA	08-16-66	Paducah, Ky.		R	R	5'11	190	854	1969	295	497	109	26	49	223	166	369	85	.252	.409
Siddall, Joe-Joseph Todd	93,95MonN 96FlaN 98DetA	10-25-67	Windsor, Canada		L	R	6'1	197	73	142	7	24	5	0	1	11	13	41	0	.169	.225
Sierra, Ruben-Ruben Angel [Garcia]	86-92TexA 92-95OakA 95-96NYA 96DetA 97TorA 97CinN 98ChiA 00-01TexA 02SeaA 03TexA 03-05NYA 06MinA	10-06-65	Rio Piedras, P.R.		B	R	6'1	200	2186	8044	1084	2152	428	59	306	1322	610	1239	142	.268	.450
Silverio, Luis-Luis Pascual [Delmonte]	78KCA	10-23-56	Villa Gonzalez, D.R.		R	R	5'11	165	8	11	7	6	2	1	0	3	2	3	1	.545	.909
Silvestri, Dave-David Joseph	92-95NYA 95-96MonN 97TexA 98TBA 99AnaA	09-29-67	St. Louis, Mo.		R	R	6'	190	181	336	42	68	12	3	6	36	56	96	4	.202	.310
Simmons, Brian-Brian Lee	98-99ChiA 00LJ 01TorA	09-04-73	Lebanon, Pa.		B	R	6'2	190	119	252	26	55	8	3	8	31	17	58	5	.218	.369
Simmons, Nelson-Nelson Bernard	84-85DetA 87BalA	06-27-63	Washington D.C.		B	B	6'1	195	100	330	38	86	14	4	11	40	31	54	2	.261	.427
Simmons, Ted-Ted Lyle (Simba)	68-80StLN 81-85MilA 86-88AtlN	08-09-49	Highland Park, Mich.		B	R	5'11	193	2456	8680	1074	2472	483	47	248	1389	855	694	21	.285	.437
Simms, Mike-Michael Howard	90-92,94-96HouN 97-99TexA	01-12-67	Orange, Cal.		R	R	6'4	220	330	660	92	163	33	1	36	121	69	175	4	.247	.464
Simon, Randall-Randall Carlito	97-99AtlN 01-02DetA 03PitN 03ChiN 04PitN 04TBA 06PhiN	05-26-75	Willemstad, Curacao		L	L	6'0	225	537	1609	172	455	71	3	49	237	82	148	2	.283	.422
Simpson, Joe-Joe Allen	75-78LAN 79-82SeaA 83KCA	12-31-51	Purcell, Okla.		L	L	6'3	180	607	1397	166	338	54	12	9	124	90	190	45	.242	.374
Sinatro, Matt-Matthew Stephen	81-84AtlN 87-88OakA 89DetA 90-92SeaA	03-22-60	Hartford, Conn.		R	R	5'10	185	140	252	20	48	6	1	1	21	17	35	2	.190	.234
Singleton, Chris-Christopher Verdell	99-01ChiA 02BalA 03OakA 05TBA	08-15-72	Martinez, Calif.		L	R	6'2	195	704	2230	326	609	133	23	45	276	130	343	81	.273	.414
Singleton, Duane-Duane Earl	94-95MilA 96DetA	08-06-72	Staten Island, N.Y.		L	R	6'	170	33	87	5	11	1	0	0	3	5	25	1	.126	.138
Singleton, Ken-Kenneth Wayne	70-71NYN 72-74MonN 75-84BalA	06-10-47	New York, N.Y.		B	R	6'4	215	2082	7189	985	2029	317	25	246	1065	1263	1246	21	.282	.436
Sisco, Steve-Steven Michael	00AtlN	12-02-69	Thousand Oaks, Cal.		R	R	5'10	190	29	27	4	5	0	0	0	2	3	4	0	.185	.296
Sizemore, Grady-Grady III	04-06CleA	08-02-82	Seattle, Wash.		L	L	6'2	200	363	1433	260	409	96	24	54	181	144	319	46	.285	.499
Sizemore, Ted-Ted Crawford	69-70LAN 71-75StLN 76LAN 77-78PhiN 79ChiN 79-80BosA	04-15-45	Gadsden, Ala.		R	R	5'10	170	1411	5011	577	1311	188	21	23	430	469	350	59	.262	.321
Skaggs, Dave-David Lindsey	77-80BalA 80CalA	06-12-51	Santa Monica, Cal.		R	R	6'2	200	205	510	44	123	18	2	3	49	51	76	0	.241	.302
Skinner, Joel-Joel Patrick	83-86ChiA 86-88NYA 89-91CleA 92-93SJ M02CleA	02-21-61	La Jolla, Cal.		R	R	6'4	205	564	1441	119	329	62	3	17	136	80	387	3	.228	.311
Skube, Bob-Robert Jacob (Skub)	82-83MilA	09-11-58	Northridge, Cal.		L	L	6'	182	16	28	2	7	1	1	0	4	4	7	0	.250	.357
Slaught, Don-Donald Martin	82-84KCA 85-87TexA 88-89NYA 90-95PitN 96CalA 96ChiA 97SDN	09-11-58	Long Beach, Cal.		R	R	6'	190	1327	4063	415	1151	235	28	77	476	311	559	18	.283	.412
Sledge, Termel-Terrmel	04MonN 05WasN 06SDN	03-18-77	Fayetteville, N.C.		L	L	6'	185	191	505	59	132	23	7	18	77	55	91	6	.261	.442
Smajstrla, Craig-Craig Lee	88HouN	06-19-62	Houston, Tex.		B	R	5'8	160	8	3	2	0	0	0	0	0	0	0	0	.000	.000
Small, Hank-George Henry	78AtlN	07-31-53	Atlanta, Ga.		R	R	6'	200	1	4	0	0	0	0	0	0	0	1	0	.000	.000
Smalley, Roy-Roy Frederick III	75-76TexA 76-82MinA 82-84NYA 84ChiA 85-87MinA	10-25-52	Los Angeles, Cal.		B	R	6'1	190	1653	5657	745	1454	244	25	163	694	771	908	27	.257	.395
Smith, Billy-Billy Edward (Billy the Kid)	75-76CalA 77-79BalA 81SFN	07-14-53	Jonesboro, La.		B	R	6'2	183	370	1018	107	234	38	9	17	111	96	189	8	.230	.335
Smith, Bobby-Robert Eugene	98-02TBA	04-10-74	Oakland, Cal.		R	R	6'3	190	258	826	88	192	29	4	21	107	70	268	11	.232	.354
Smith, Brick-Brick Dudley	87-88SeaA	05-02-59	Charlotte, N.C.		L	R	6'4	225	9	18	2	2	0	0	0	1	2	5	0	.111	.111
Smith, Chris-Christopher William	81-82MinN 83SFN	05-02-58	Torrance, Cal.		B	L	6'	185	31	76	13	23	5	1	4	11	7	15	0	.289	.434
Smith, Dwight-John Dwight	89-93ChiN 94CalA 94BalA 95-96AtlN	11-08-63	Tallahassee, Fla.		L	R	5'11	180	813	1807	244	497	88	20	46	226	150	334	42	.275	.422
Smith, Greg-Gregory Alan	89-90ChiN 91LAN	04-05-67	Baltimore, Md.		B	R	5'11	170	27	52	6	11	2	0	1	5	7	2	1	.212	.288
Smith, Jason-Jason William	01ChiN 02-03TBA 04-05DetA 06ColN	07-24-77	Meridian, Miss.		L	R	6'3	195	166	382	42	88	10	8	11	40	17	107	9	.230	.385
Smith, Jimmy-James Lorne	82DetA	09-08-54	Santa Monica, Cal.		R	R	6'3	185	42	42	5	10	2	1	0	4	5	9	0	.238	.333
Smith, Keith-Keith Lavarne (The Guy)	77TexA 79-80StLN	05-03-53	Palmetto, Fla.		R	R	5'9	180	53	111	17	23	5	0	2	8	6	10	2	.207	.306
Smith, Keith-Keith Patrick	84-85NYA	10-20-61	Los Angeles, Cal.		B	R	6'	180	6	4	1	0	0	0	0	0	5	0	1	0	.000	.000
Smith, Ken-Kenneth Earl (High Rise)	81-83AtlN	02-12-58	Youngstown, Ohio		L	R	6'2	195	83	56	8	15	0	0	2	5	5	7	1	.268	.357
Smith, Lonnie-Lonnie	78-81PhiN 82-85StLN 85-87KCA 88-92AtlN 93PitN 93-94BalA	12-22-55	Chicago, Ill.		R	R	5'9	185	1613	5170	909	1488	273	58	98	533	623	849	370	.288	.420
Smith, Mark-Mark Edward	94-96BalA 97-98PhiN 99JL 00FlaN 01MonN 03MilN	05-07-70	Pasadena, Cal.		R	R	6'3	220	414	959	125	233	51	3	32	130	97	211	15	.243	.403
Smith, Ozzie-Osborne Earl (The Wizard of Oz)	78-81SDN 82-96StLN	12-26-54	Mobile, Ala.		B	R	5'10	160	2573	9396	1257	2460	402	69	28	793	1072	589	580	.262	.328
Smith, Ray-Raymond Edward (Quality)	81-83MinA	09-18-55	Glendale, Cal.		B	R	6'	188	83	215	16	47	6	1	1	10	11	18	1	.219	.270
Smith, Reggie-Carl Reginald	66-73BosA 74-76StLN 76-81LAN 82SFN	04-02-45	Shreveport, La.		B	R	6'	195	1987	7033	1123	2020	363	57	314	1092	890	1030	137	.287	.489
Smith, Tommy-Tommy Alexander	73-76CleA 77SeaA	08-01-48	Albemarle, N.C.		R	R	6'4	225	121	271	28	63	7	2	3	22	12	32	4	.232	.317
Smitherman, Steve-Stephen Lydell	03CinN	09-01-78	McAlester, Okla.		R	R	6'4	230	21	44	3	7	2	0	1	6	3	9	1	.159	.273
Snead, Esix-Esix Jr.	02,04NYN	06-07-76	Fort Myers, Fla.		B	R	5'10	175	18	13	4	4	0	0	0	3	1	5	4	.308	.538
Snelling, Chris-Christopher Doyle	02SeaA 04WJ 05-06SeaA	12-03-81	North Miami, Fla.		L	R	5'9	185	59	162	20	36	7	1	4	20	21	40	0	.222	.401
Snider, Van-Van Voorhees	88-89CinN	08-11-63	Birmingham, Ala.		L	R	6'3	185	19	35	5	7	1	0	2	6	6	10	0	.200	.314
Snopek, Chris-Christopher Charles	95-98ChiA 98BosA	09-20-70	Cynthiana, Ky.		R	R	6'	180	215	607	76	142	27	1	13	66	49	108	7	.234	.346
Snow, J.T.-Jack Thomas	92NYA 93-96CalA 97-05SFN 06BosA	02-26-68	Long Beach, Cal.		B	L	6'2	200	1715	5641	798	1509	293	19	189	877	760	1142	20	.268	.427
Bats Left 99-04																					

USE NAME - GIVEN NAMES (NICKNAMES)	TEAM BY YEAR	BIRTH DATE	BIRTH PLACE	DEATH DATE	B	T	HGT	WGT	G	AB	R	H	2B	3B	HR	RBI	BB	SO	SB	BA	SA
Snyder, Chris-Christopher Ryan	04-06AriN	02-12-81	Houston Tex.		R	R	6'3	220	205	606	53	140	29	0	17	75	75	151	0	.231	.363
Snyder, Cory-James Cory	85-90CleA 91ChiA 91TorA 92SFN 93-94LAN	11-11-62	Inglewood, Cal.		R	R	6'4	200	1068	3658	439	902	178	13	149	488	226	992	28	.247	.425
Snyder, Earl-Earl Clifford	02CleA 04BosA	05-06-76	New Britain, Conn.		R	R	6'	207	19	59	5	12	2	0	1	4	6	22	0	.203	.288
Soderholm, Eric-Eric Thane	71-75MilA 76KJ 77-79ChiA 79TexA 80NYA 81KJ	09-24-48	Cortland, N.Y.		R	R	6'	195	894	2894	402	764	120	14	102	383	295	359	18	.264	.421
Sofield, Rick-Richard Michael	79-81MilA	12-16-56	Cheyenne, Wyo.		L	R	6'1	195	217	612	69	149	25	4	9	66	44	141	9	.243	.342
Sojo, Luis-Luis Beltran [Sojo]	90TorA 91-92CalA 93TorA 94-96SeaA 96-99NYA 00PitN 00-01,03NYA	01-03-65	Barquisimeto, Venez.		R	R	5'11	180	848	2571	300	671	103	12	36	261	124	198	28	.261	.352
Solaita, Tony-Tolia	68NYA 74-76KCA 76-78CalA 79MonN 79TorA	01-15-47	Nuuuli, Amer. Samoa	02-10-90	L	L	6'	210	525	1316	164	336	66	1	50	203	214	345	2	.255	.421
Sorensen, Zach-Zach Hart	03CleA 05LAA	01-07-77	Salt Lake City, Utah		B	R	6'	190	48	49	5	7	2	0	1	2	7	15	0	.143	.245
Soriano, Alfonso-Alfonso Guilleard	99-03NYA 04-05TexA 06WasN	01-07-76	San Pedro de Mac., D.R.		R	R	6'1	180	961	3902	624	1091	240	18	208	560	224	836	210	.280	.510
Sorrento, Paul-Paul Anthony	89-91MinA 92-95CleA 96-97SeaA 98-99TBA	11-17-65	Somerville, Mass.		L	R	6'2	220	1093	3412	454	876	176	5	166	565	426	844	8	.257	.457
Sosa, Juan-Juan Luis [Encarnacion]	99ColN 01AriN	08-19-75	San Francisco de Mac., D.R.		R	R	6'1	175	13	10	3	2	0	0	0	0	2	3	0	.200	.200
Sosa, Sammy-Samuel Kevin [Peralta]	89TexA 89-91ChiA 92-04ChiN 05BalA	11-12-68	San Pedro de Mac., D.R.		R	R	6'	215	2240	8401	1422	2304	355	44	588	1575	895	2194	234	.274	.537
Soto, Geovany-Geovany [Ponce]	05-06ChiN	01-20-83	San Juan, P.R.		R	R	6'1	230	12	26	1	5	1	0	0	2	0	5	0	.192	.231
Speed, Horace-Horace Arthur	75SFN 78-79CleA	01-28-51	Los Angeles, Cal.		R	R	6'1	180	113	135	21	28	5	1	0	6	20	46	4	.207	.259
Spehr, Tim-Timothy Joseph	91KCA 93-96MonN 97KCA 97AtlN 98NYN 98-99KCA	07-02-66	Excelsior Springs, Mo.		R	R	6'2	205	363	556	76	110	31	1	19	72	67	153	9	.198	.360
Speier, Chris-Chris Edward	71-77SFN 77-84MonN 84StLN 84MinA 85-86ChiN 87-89SFN	06-28-50	Alameda, Cal.		R	R	6'1	180	2260	7156	770	1759	302	50	112	720	847	988	42	.246	.449
Spencer, Jim-James Lloyd	68-73CalA 73-75TexA 76-77ChiA 78-81NYA 81-82OakA	07-30-47	Hanover, Pa.	02-10-02	L	L	6'2	195	1553	4908	541	1227	179	27	46	599	407	582	11	.250	.387
Spencer, Shane-Michael Shane	98-02NYA 03CleA 03TexA 04NYN	02-20-72	Key West, Fla.		R	R	5'11	210	538	1671	208	438	84	6	59	242	152	357	13	.262	.428
Spencer, Tom-Hubert Thomas (Sporty)	78ChiA	02-28-51	Gallipolis, Ohio		R	R	6'	170	29	65	3	12	1	0	0	4	2	9	0	.185	.200
Sperring, Rob-Robert Walter	74-76ChiN 77HouN	10-10-49	San Francisco, Cal.		R	R	6'2	185	208	473	48	100	13	1	3	30	46	107	1	.211	.262
Spiers, Bill-William James III	89-94MilA 95HouN 96-01HouN	06-05-66	Orangeburg, S.C.		L	R	6'2	190	1252	3408	477	922	158	35	37	388	355	496	97	.271	.370
Spiezio, Scott-Scott Edward	96-99OakA 00-03AnaA 04-05SeaA 06StLN	09-21-72	Joliet, Ill.		B	R	6'2	220	1192	3676	486	936	211	27	115	518	385	554	33	.255	.421
Spikes, Charlie-Leslie Charles (The Bogalusa Bomber)	72NYA 73-77CleA 78DetA 79-80AtlN	01-23-51	Bogalusa, La.		R	R	6'3	213	670	2039	240	502	72	12	65	256	154	388	27	.246	.389
Spilborghs, Ryan-Ryan Adam Rene Jean	05-06ColN	09-05-79	Santa Barbara, Cal.		R	R	6'1	190	68	171	26	50	6	3	4	22	14	31	5	.292	.433
Spilman, Harry-William Harry	78-81CinN 81-85HouN 86DetA 86-88SFN 88-89HouN	07-18-54	Albany, Ga.		L	R	6'	190	563	810	96	192	34	1	18	117	81	126	1	.237	.348
Spivey, Junior-Ernest Lee Jr.	01-03AriN 04-05MilN 05WasN	01-28-75	Oklahoma City, Okla.		R	R	6'1	195	457	1553	258	419	90	12	48	201	175	373	32	.270	.436
Sprague, Ed-Edward Nelson Jr.	91-98TorA 98OakA 99PitN 00SDN 00BosA 00SDN 01SeaA	07-25-67	Castro Valley, Cal.		R	R	6'2	215	1203	4095	506	1010	225	12	152	558	358	833	6	.247	.419
Springer, Steve-Steven Michael	90CleA 92NYN	02-11-61	Long Beach, Cal.		R	R	6'	190	8	17	1	4	1	0	0	1	0	7	0	.235	.294
Squires, Mike-Michael Lynn (Spanky)	75,77-85ChiA	03-05-52	Kalamazoo, Mich.		L	L	5'11	195	779	1580	211	411	53	10	6	141	143	106	45	.260	.318
Staggs, Steve-Stephen Robert	77TorA 78OakA	05-06-51	Anchorage, Alaska		R	R	5'9	155	119	368	47	94	13	8	2	28	55	55	7	.255	.350
Stahoviak, Scott-Scott Edmund	93,95-98MinA	03-06-70	Waukegan, Ill.		L	R	6'5	220	344	1019	135	261	70	3	27	119	116	277	13	.256	.410
Staiger, Roy-Roy Joseph (Linus)	75-77NYN 79NYA	06-26-50	Tulsa, Okla.		R	R	6'2	200	152	457	42	104	19	1	4	38	30	59	4	.228	.300
Stairs, Matt-Matthew Wade	92-93MonN 95BosA 96-00OakA 01ChiN 02MilN 03PitN 04-06KCA 06TexA 06DetA	02-27-68	St. John, Canada		L	R	5'9	215	1416	4243	633	1125	243	11	220	751	588	881	25	.265	.483
Stanicek, Pete-Peter Louis	87-88BalA	04-16-63	Harvey, Ill.		B	R	5'11	190	113	374	38	91	10	1	4	26	36	64	20	.243	.307
Stanicek, Steve-Stephen Blair	87MilA 89PhiN	06-19-61	Lake Forest, Ill.		R	R	6'	190	13	16	2	3	0	0	0	1	0	5	0	.188	.188
Stankiewicz, Andy-Andrew Neal	92-93NYA 94-95HouN 96-97MonN 98AriN	08-10-64	Inglewood, Cal.		R	R	5'9	165	429	844	105	203	45	3	4	59	80	141	17	.241	.315
Stanley, Fred-Frederick Blair (Chicken)	69SeaA 70MilA 71-72CleA 72SDN 73-80NYA 81-82OakA	08-13-47	Farnhamville, Iowa		R	R	5'10	175	815	1650	197	356	38	5	10	120	196	243	11	.216	.263
Bats Both 69-71																					
Stanley, Mike-Robert Michael	86-91TexA 92-95NYA 96-97BosA 97NYA 98TorA 98-00BosA 00OakA	06-23-63	Fort Lauderdale, Fla.		R	R	6'	195	1467	4222	625	1138	220	7	187	702	652	929	13	.270	.458
Stanton, Lee-Leroy Bobby (Baby Bull)	70-71NYN 72-76CalA 77-78SeaA 80-86BosA	04-10-46	Latta, S.C.		R	R	6'1	200	829	2575	294	628	114	13	77	358	236	636	36	.244	.388
Stapleton, Dave-David Leslie	80-86BosA	01-16-54	Fairhope, Ala.		R	R	6'1	185	582	2028	238	550	118	8	41	224	114	162	6	.271	.398
Stark, Matt-Matthew Scott	87TorA 90ChiA	01-21-65	Whittier, Cal.		R	R	6'4	225	13	28	0	5	1	0	0	3	1	6	0	.179	.214
Staton, Dave-David Alan	93-94SDN	04-12-68	Seattle, Wash.		R	R	6'5	225	46	108	13	23	5	0	9	15	13	30	0	.213	.509
Staton, Joe-Joseph	72-73DetA	03-08-48	Seattle, Wash.		L	L	6'4	178	15	19	3	4	0	0	0	3	0	4	1	.211	.211
Staub, Rusty-Daniel Joseph (Le Grande Orange)	63-68HouN 69-71MonN 72-75NYN 76-79DetA 79MonN 80TexA 81-85NYN	04-01-44	New Orleans, La.		L	R	6'2	205	2951	9720	1189	2716	499	47	292	1466	1255	888	47	.279	.431
Stearns, John-John Hardin (Dude)	74PhiN 75-84NYN	08-21-51	Denver, Colo.		R	R	5'11	185	810	2681	334	696	152	10	46	312	323	294	91	.260	.375
Steels, James-James Earl	87SDN 88TexA 89SFN	05-30-61	Bentonia, Miss.		L	L	5'10	185	111	133	13	24	2	1	0	11	13	33	5	.180	.211
Stefero, John-John Robert	83,86BalA 87MonN	09-22-59	Sumter, S.C.		L	R	5'8	185	79	187	20	44	3	0	3	20	22	44	0	.235	.299
Stegman, Dave-David William	78-80DetA 82NYA 83-84ChiA	01-30-54	Inglewood, Cal.		R	R	6'	190	171	320	39	66	10	2	8	32	31	55	5	.206	.325
Stein, Bill-William Allen	72-73StLN 74-76ChiA 77-80SeaA 81-85TexA	01-21-47	Battle Creek, Mich.		R	R	5'10	175	959	2811	268	751	122	18	44	311	186	413	16	.267	.377
Steinbach, Terry-Terry Lee	86-96OakA 97-99MinA	03-02-62	New Ulm, Minn.		R	R	6'1	205	1546	5369	638	1453	273	21	162	745	418	938	23	.271	.420
Stelmaszek, Dick-Richard Francis (Rick)	71WasA 73TexA 73CalA 74CinN	10-08-48	Chicago, Ill.		L	R	6'1	200	60	88	4	15	3	0	1	10	17	18	0	.170	.239
Stenhouse, Mike-Michael Steven	82-84MonN 85MinA 86BosA	05-29-58	Pueblo, Colo.		L	R	6'1	195	207	416	40	79	15	0	9	40	71	66	1	.190	.291
Stennett, Rennie-Renaldo Antonio [Porte]	71-79PitN 80-81SFN	04-05-51	Colon, Panama		R	R	5'11	178	1237	4521	500	1239	177	41	41	432	207	348	75	.274	.359
Stenson, Dernell-Dernell Renauld	03CinN	06-17-78	La Grange, Ga.	11-05-03	L	L	6'1	230	37	81	14	20	5	0	3	13	11	24	0	.247	.420
Stephens, Ray-Carl Ray	90-91StLN 92TexA	09-20-62	Houston, Tex.		R	R	6'	190	40	35	2	6	1	1	0	1	1	11	0	.171	.286
Stephenson, Phil-Phillip Raymond	89ChiN 89-92SDN	09-19-60	Guthrie, Okla.		L	L	6'1	195	194	298	35	60	11	2	6	29	47	62	3	.201	.312
Stern, Adam-Adam James	05-06BosA	02-12-80	London, Canada		L	R	5'11	180	46	35	7	5	1	0	0	6	0	8	2	.143	.257
Stevens, Lee-DeWain Lee	90-92CalA 94-95JL 96-99TexA 00-02MonN 02CleA	07-10-67	Kansas City, Mo.		L	L	6'4	225	1012	3332	440	847	185	15	144	531	345	832	9	.254	.448
Steverson, Todd-Todd Anthony	95DetA 96SDN	11-15-71	Los Angeles, Cal.		R	R	6'2	195	90	43	11	11	0	0	2	6	6	11	2	.256	.395
Stewart, Andy-Andrew David	97KCA	12-05-70	Oshawa, Canada		R	R	5'11	205	5	8	1	2	1	0	0	0	0	0	0	.250	.375
Stewart, Chris-Christopher David	06ChiA	02-19-82	Fontana, Cal.		R	R	6'4	205	6	8	0	0	0	0	0	0	0	0	0	.000	.000
Stewart, Shannon-Shannon Harold	95-03TorA 03-06MinA	02-25-74	Cincinnati, Ohio		R	R	6'	205	1188	4823	760	1444	289	38	102	518	435	606	182	.299	.459
Stillman, Royle-Royle Eldon	75-76BalA 77ChiA	01-03-51	Santa Monica, Cal.		L	L	5'10	175	89	155	19	33	7	1	3	15	21	28	2	.213	.329
Stillwell, Kurt-Kurt Andrew (Opie)	86-87CinN 88-91KCA 92-93SDN 93CalA 96TexA	06-04-65	Glendale, Cal.		B	R	5'11	180	998	3125	362	779	151	30	34	310	274	455	38	.249	.349
Stimac, Craig-Craig Steven (Steamer)	80-81SDN	11-18-54	Oak Park, Ill.		R	R	6'2	190	29	59	5	12	2	0	0	7	1	9	0	.203	.237
Stinnett, Kelly-Kelly Lee	94-95NYN 96-97MilA 98-00AriN 01-03CinN 03PhiN 04KCA 05AriN 06NYA 06NYN	02-14-70	Lawton, Okla.		R	R	5'11	215	708	1951	221	463	88	4	64	225	191	545	10	.237	.385
Stinson, Bob-Gorrell Robert	69-70LAN 71StLN 72HouN 73-74MonN 75-76KCA 77-80SeaA	10-11-45	Elkin, N.C.		B	R	5'11	180	652	1634	166	408	61	7	33	180	201	254	8	.250	.356
Bats Right 69																					
Stocker, Kevin-Kevin Douglas	93-97PhiN 98-00TBA 00AnaA	02-13-70	Spokane, Wash.		B	R	6'1	175	846	2773	340	703	124	28	23	248	313	541	45	.254	.343
Stone, Jeff-Jeffrey Glen	83-87PhiN 88BalA 89TexA 89-90BosA	12-26-60	Kennett, Mo.		L	R	6'	180	372	941	129	261	23	18	11	72	60	186	75	.277	.375
Stovall, DaRond-DaRond Tyrone	98MonN	01-03-73	St. Louis, Mo.		B	L	6'1	185	62	78	11	16	0	2	1	6	8	29	1	.205	.333
Stowers, Chris-Christopher James	99MonN	08-18-74	St. Louis, Mo.		L	L	6'3	195	4	2	0	0	0	0	0	0	0	0	0	.000	.000
Strain, Joe-Joseph Allan	79-80SFN 81CinN	04-30-54	Denver, Colo.		R	R	5'10	165	169	520	60	130	15	1	1	29	28	38	9	.250	.288
Strange, Doug-Joseph Douglas	89DetA 91-92ChiN 93-94TexA 95-96SeaA 97MonN 98PitN 99EJ	04-13-64	Greenville, S.C.		B	R	6'2	170	707	1859	194	434	87	7	31	211	155	330	14	.233	.338
Strawberry, Darryl-Darryl Eugene (Straw Man)	83-90NYN 91-94LAN 94SFN 95-99NYA 00SD	03-12-62	Los Angeles, Cal.		L	L	6'6	210	1583	5418	898	1401	256	38	335	1000	816	1352	221	.259	.505
Strittmatter, Mark-Mark Arthur	98ColN	04-04-69	Huntington, N.Y.		R	R	6'	200	4	4	0	0	0	0	0	0	0	0	0	.000	.000
Strong, Jamal-Jamal Najar	03,05SeaA	08-05-78	Pasadena, Cal.		R	R	5'10	180	28	22	4	5	0	0	0	2	2	6	0	.227	.227
Stroughter, Steve-Stephen Lewis	82SeaA	03-15-52	Visalia, Cal.		R	R	6'2	190	26	47	4	8	1	0	0	3	3	9	0	.170	.255
Stubbs, Franklin-Franklin Lee	84-89LAN 90HouN 91-92MilA 95DetA	10-21-60	Richland, N.C.		L	L	6'2	215	945	2591	323	602	109	12	104	348	260	626	74	.232	.404
Stynes, Chris-Christopher Desmond	95-96KCA 97-00CinN 01BosA 02-03ChiN 04PitN	01-19-73	Queens, N.Y.		R	R	5'9	195	828	2326	351	640	118	9	51	265	191	308	49	.275	.399
Suero, William-Williams [Urban]	92-93MilA	11-07-66	Santo Domingo, D.R.	11-30-95	R	R	5'9	175	33	30	4	7	1	0	0	3	4	1	1	.233	.267
Sularz, Guy-Guy Patrick (G-Man)	80-83SFN	11-07-55	Minneapolis, Minn.		R	R	5'11	170	108	206	21	45	4	1	1	12	23	23	4	.218	.262
Sullivan, Cory-Cory	05-06ColN	08-20-79	Tulsa, Okla.		L	L	6'	180	265	764	111	214	41	14	6	60	60	183	22	.280	.394
Sullivan, Marc-Marc Cooper	82,84-87BosA	07-25-58	Quincy, Mass.		R	R	6'4	210	137	360	37	67	11	0	5	28	18	92	0	.186	.258
Summers, Champ-John Junior	74OakA 75-76ChiN 77-79CinN 79-81DetA 82-83SFN 84SDN	06-15-46	Bremerton, Wash.		L	R	6'2	205	698	1371	199	350	63	4	54	218	188	244	16	.255	.425
Sundberg, Jim-James Howard (Sunny)	74-83TexA 84MilA 85-86KCA 87-88ChiN 88-89TexA	05-18-51	Galesburg, Ill.		R	R	6'	195	1962	6021	621	1493	243	36	95	624	699	963	20	.248	.389
Surhoff, B.J.-William James	87-95MilA 96-00BalA 00-02AtlN 03-05BalA	08-04-64	Bronx, N.Y.		L	L	6'1	195	2313	8258	1062	2326	440	42	188	1153	640	839	141	.282	.413
Sutton, Larry-Larry James	97-99KCA 00-01StLN 02OakA 04FlaN	05-14-70	West Covina, Cal.		L	L	5'11	185	252	572	63	135	23	2	12	78	55	102	4	.236	.346
Sutherland, Leo-Leonardo [Cantin]	80-81ChiA	08-14-58	Santiago de Cuba, Cuba		L	R	6'1	195	45	101	15	25	3	0	0	5	4	12	6	.248	.277
Sutko, Glenn-Glenn Edward	90-91CinN	05-09-68	Atlanta, Ga.		R	R	6'3	225	11	11	0	1	0	0	0	1	2	7	0	.091	.091
Suzuki, Ichiro-Ichiro	01-06SeaA	10-22-73	Kasugai, Japan		L	R	5'9	170	957	4096	671	1354	155	50	61	359	280	384	235	.331	.438
Sveum, Dale-Dale Curtis	86-88MilA 89BL 90-91MilA 92PhiN 92ChiA 93OakA 94SeaA 96-97PitN 98NYN 99PitN	11-23-63	Richmond, Cal.		B	R	6'3	200	862	2526	305	597	128	13	69	340	227	656	10	.236	.378
Swann, Pete-Pedro Maurice	00AtlN 02TorA 03BalA	10-27-70	Wilmington, Del.		L	R	6'	195	25	28	4	4	1	0	0	3	2	10	1	.143	.286

USE NAME - GIVEN NAMES (NICKNAMES)	TEAM BY YEAR	BIRTH DATE	BIRTH PLACE	DEATH DATE	B	T	HGT	WGT	G	AB	R	H	2B	3B	HR	RBI	BB	SO	SB	BA	SA
Sweeney, Mark-Mark Patrick	95-97StLN 97-98SDN 99CinN 00-01MilN 02SDN 03-04ColN 05SDN 06SFN	10-28-69	Framingham, Mass.		L	L	6'1	205	1014	1615	198	420	89	9	40	232	230	368	14	.260	.401
Sweeney, Mike-Michael John	95-06KCA	07-22-73	Orange, Cal.		R	R	6'1	215	1208	4404	674	1329	282	4	190	799	467	526	50	.302	.497
Sweeney, Ryan-Ryan Joseph	06ChiA	02-20-85	Cedar Rapids, Iowa		L	L	6'4	200	18	35	1	8	0	0	0	5	0	7	0	.229	.229
Sweet, Rick-Ricky Joe	78SDN 82NYN 82-83SeaA	09-07-52	Longview, Wash.		B	R	6'1	190	272	736	62	172	23	1	6	57	60	73	6	.234	.292
Swisher, Nick-Nicholas Thompson	04-06OakA	01-25-80	Columbus, Ohio		B	L	6'	194	308	1078	183	265	60	3	58	177	160	273	1	.246	.468
Swisher, Steve-Steven Eugene	74-77ChiN 78-80StLN 81-82SDN	08-09-51	Parkersburg, W.Va.		R	R	6'2	205	509	1414	108	305	49	7	20	124	118	322	4	.216	.303
Tabb, Jerry-Jerry Lynn	76ChiN 77-78OakA	03-17-52	Altus, Okla.		L	R	6'2	195	74	177	10	40	3	0	6	20	15	33	0	.226	.345
Tabler, Pat-Patrick Sean	81-82ChiN 83-88CleA 88-90KCA 90NYN 91-92TorA	02-02-58	Hamilton, Ohio		R	R	6'2	195	1202	3911	454	1101	190	25	47	512	375	559	16	.282	.379
Tabor, Greg-Gregory Steven	87TexA	05-21-61	Castro Valley, Cal.		R	R	6'	185	9	9	4	1	1	0	0	1	0	4	0	.111	.222
Tackett, Jeff-Jeffrey Wilson	91-94BalA	12-01-65	Fresno, Cal.		R	R	6'2	205	136	327	35	71	14	2	7	42	37	71	0	.217	.336
Taguchi, So-So	02-06StLN	07-02-69	Hyogo Prefecture, Japan		R	R	5'10	163	448	960	130	270	53	6	16	124	70	145	29	.281	.399
Tamargo, John-John Felix	76-78StLN 78-79SFN 79-80MonN	11-07-51	Tampa, Fla.		B	R	5'10	173	135	244	19	59	12	1	4	33	34	27	1	.242	.348
Tarasco, Tony-Anthony Giacinto	93-94AtlN 95MonN 96-97BalA 98CinN 99NYA 00JL 02NYN	12-09-70	New York, N.Y.		L	R	6'	200	457	1006	151	241	46	5	34	118	106	171	39	.240	.397
Tartabull, Danny-Danilo [Mora]	84-86SeaA 87-91KCA 92-95NYA 95OakA 96ChiA 97PhiN	10-30-62	San Juan, P.R.		R	R	6'1	205	1406	5011	756	1366	289	22	262	925	768	1362	37	.273	.496
Tarver, LaSchelle-LaSchelle	86BosA	01-30-59	Modesto, Cal.		L	L	5'11	165	13	25	3	3	0	0	0	1	1	4	0	.120	.120
Tatis, Fernando-Fernando Jr.	97-98TexA 98-00StLN 01-03MonN 06BalA	01-01-75	San Pedro de Mac.,D.R.		B	R	5'10	180	691	2373	346	618	133	9	92	347	264	577	43	.260	.440
Tatum, Jim-James Ray	92MilA 93,95ColN 96BosA 96SDN 97JL 98NYN	10-09-67	San Diego, Cal.		R	R	6'2	200	173	201	16	39	7	3	3	29	10	58	0	.194	.303
Taubensee, Eddie-Edward Kenneth	91CleA 92-94HouN 94-00CinN 01CleA 02XJ	10-31-68	Beeville, Tex.		L	R	6'4	220	975	2874	351	784	151	9	94	419	255	258	11	.273	.430
Tavarez, Jesus-Jesus Rafael [Alcantaras]	94-96FlaN 97BosA 98BalA	03-26-71	Santo Domingo, D.R.		B	R	6'	170	228	423	63	101	12	3	3	33	30	62	13	.239	.303
Taveras, Alex-Alejandro Antonio [Betances]	76HouN 82-83LAN	10-09-55	Santiago, Dom. Rep.		R	R	5'9	165	35	53	4	11	1	0	0	4	2	3	1	.208	.226
Taveras, Frank-Frank Crisostomo [Fabian] (The Pittsburgh Stealer)	71-72,74-79PitN 79-81NYN 82MonN	12-24-49	Villa Vasquez, D.R.		R	R	6'	165	1150	4043	503	1029	144	44	2	214	249	474	300	.255	.313
Taveras, Willy-Willy	04-06HouN	12-25-81	Tenares, Dom. Rep.		R	R	6'	160	311	1122	167	319	32	9	4	59	59	192	68	.284	.340
Taylor, Dwight-Dwight Bernard	86KCA 88MonN	03-24-60	Los Angeles, Cal.		L	L	5'9	165	4	2	1	0	0	0	0	0	0	0	0	.000	.000
Taylor, Reggie-Reginald Tremain	00-01PhiN 02-03CinN 05TBA	01-12-77	Newberry, S.C.		L	R	6'1	175	260	507	62	117	22	6	14	58	28	163	21	.231	.381
Teahen, Mark-Mark Thomas	05-06KCA	09-06-81	Redlands, Cal.		L	R	6'3	210	239	840	130	224	50	11	25	124	80	192	17	.267	.442
Teixeira, Mark-Mark Charles	03-06TexA	04-11-80	Annapolis, Md.		B	R	6'2	215	615	2346	378	661	149	11	140	450	273	489	11	.282	.534
Tejada, Miguel-Miguel Odalis [Martinez]	97-03OakA 04-06BalA	05-25-76	Bani, Dom. Rep.		R	R	5'10	195	1422	5539	869	1584	318	18	240	952	421	777	64	.286	.480
Tejada, Wil-Wilfredo Aristides [Andujar]	86,88MonN	11-12-62	Santo Domingo, D.R.		B	R	6'	185	18	40	2	10	3	0	0	4	2	12	0	.250	.325
Templeton, Garry-Garry Lewis (Jump Steady)	76-81StLN 82-91SDN 91NYN	03-24-56	Lockney, Tex.		B	R	5'11	185	2079	7721	893	2096	329	106	70	728	375	1092	242	.271	.369
Tenace (Tennaci), Gene (Fiore Gino)-Fury Gene	69-76OakA 77-80SDN 81-82StLN 83PitN	10-10-46	Russellton, Pa.		R	R	6'	195	1555	4390	653	1060	179	20	201	674	984	998	36	.241	.429
Terrell, Jerry-Jerry Wayne	73-77MinA 78-80KCA	07-13-46	Waseca, Minn.	Bats Both most of 74	R	R	6'	165	657	1626	218	412	48	14	4	125	76	160	50	.253	.304
Terrero, Luis-Luis Enrique	03-05AriN 06BalA	05-18-80	Santa Cruz de Barahona, D.R.		R	R	6'	200	182	434	48	102	21	1	9	40	35	126	13	.235	.350
Tettleton, Mickey-Mickey Lee	84-87OakA 88-90BalA 91-94DetA 95-97TexA	09-16-60	Oklahoma City, Okla.		B	R	6'1	205	1485	4698	711	1132	210	16	245	732	949	1307	23	.241	.449
Teufel, Tim-Timothy Shawn	83-85MinA 86-91NYN 91-93SDN	07-07-58	Greenwich, Conn.		R	R	6'	175	1073	3112	415	789	185	12	86	379	387	531	23	.254	.404
Thames, Marcus-Marcus Markey	02NYA 03TexA 04-06DetA	03-06-77	Louisville, Miss.		R	R	6'2	205	246	706	110	170	37	2	45	115	70	194	1	.241	.490
Theodore, George-George Basil (The Stork)	73-74NYN	11-13-46	Salt Lake City, Utah		R	R	6'5	195	105	192	21	42	5	0	2	16	18	27	1	.219	.276
Theriot, Ryan-Ryan Stewart	05-06ChiN	12-07-79	Baton Rouge, La.		R	R	5'11	175	102	147	37	46	12	3	3	16	18	20	13	.313	.497
Thomas (Perez), Andres-Andres Perez [Thomas]	85-90AtlN	11-10-63	Boca Chica,Dom.Rep.		R	R	6'1	185	577	2103	182	493	76	4	42	228	59	301	22	.234	.334
Thomas, Charles-Charles Wesley	04AtlN 05OakA	04-23-79	Fairfield, Cal.		L	L	6'	190	113	282	39	73	8	4	7	32	26	53	3	.259	.390
Thomas, Danny-Danny Lee (Big Dog, The Sundown Kid)	76-77MilA	05-09-51	Birmingham, Ala.	06-12-80	R	R	6'2	195	54	175	24	48	8	3	6	26	22	39	1	.274	.457
Thomas, Derrel-Derrel Osbon	71HouN 72-74SDN 75-77SFN 78SDN 79-83LAN 84MonN 84CalA 85PhiN	01-14-51	Los Angeles, Cal.		B	R	6'	160	1597	4677	585	1163	154	54	43	370	456	593	140	.249	.332
Thomas, Frank-Frank Edward (The Big Hurt)	90-05ChiA 06OakA	05-27-68	Columbus, Ga.		R	R	6'5	255	2096	7422	1404	2262	458	11	487	1579	1547	1246	32	.305	.566
Thomas, Gorman-James Gorman	73-76,78-83MilA 83CleA 84-86SeaA 86MilA	12-12-50	Charleston, S.C.		R	R	6'2	210	1435	4677	681	1051	212	13	268	782	697	1339	50	.225	.448
Thome, Jim-James Howard	91-02CleA 03-05PhiN 06ChiA	08-27-70	Peoria, Ill.		L	R	6'3	235	1881	6409	1259	1806	350	24	472	1302	1364	1909	18	.282	.565
Thomasson, Gary-Gary Leah	72-77SFN 78OakA 78NYA 79-80LAN	07-29-51	San Diego, Cal.		L	L	6'2	190	901	2373	315	591	103	25	61	294	291	463	50	.249	.391
Thompson, Andy-Andrew John	00-01TorA	10-08-75	Oconomowoc, Wis.		R	R	6'3	210	2	6	2	1	0	0	0	1	3	2	0	.167	.167
Thompson, Bobby-Bobby LaRue	78TexA	11-03-53	Charlotte, N.C.		B	R	5'10	175	64	120	23	27	3	3	2	12	9	26	7	.225	.350
Thompson, Danny-Danny Leon	70-76MinA 76TexA	02-01-47	Wichita, Kans.	12-10-76	R	R	6'	180	694	2218	189	550	70	11	15	194	120	235	8	.248	.310
Thompson, Jason-Jason Dolph	76-80DetA 80CalA 81-85PitN 86MonN	07-06-54	Hollywood, Cal.		L	L	6'4	210	1418	4802	640	1253	204	12	208	782	816	862	8	.261	.438
Thompson, Jason-Jason Michael	96SDN	06-13-71	Orlando, Fla.		L	L	6'4	200	13	49	4	11	4	0	2	6	1	14	0	.224	.429
Thompson, Kevin-Kevin Deshawn	06NYA	09-18-79	Fort Worth, Tex.		R	R	5'10	185	19	30	5	9	3	0	1	6	6	9	2	.300	.500
Thompson, Milt-Milton Bernard	84-85AtlN 86-88PhiN 89-92StLN 93-94PhiN 94-95HouN 96LAN 96ColN	01-05-59	Washington D.C.		L	R	5'10	190	1359	3761	491	1029	156	37	47	357	336	635	214	.274	.372
Thompson, Rich-Richard Charles	04KCA	04-23-79	Reading, Pa.		L	R	6'3	180	6	1	1	0	0	0	0	0	0	0	1	.000	.000
Thompson, Robby-Robert Randall	86-96SFN	05-10-62	West Palm Beach, Fla.		R	R	5'11	170	1304	4612	671	1187	238	39	119	458	439	987	103	.257	.403
Thompson, Ryan-Ryan Orlando	92-95NYN 96CleA 98JL 99HouN 00NYA 01FlaN 02MilN	11-04-67	Chestertown, Md.		R	R	6'3	220	416	1257	165	305	71	6	52	176	90	347	9	.243	.433
Thompson, Scot-Vernon Scot	78-83ChiN 84-85SFN 85MonN	12-07-55	Grove City, Pa.		L	L	6'2	190	626	1273	132	333	52	9	5	110	97	141	17	.262	.328
Thon, Dickie-Richard William	79-80CalA 81-87HouN 88SDN 89-91PhiN 92TexA 93MilA	06-20-58	South Bend, Ind.		R	R	5'11	175	1387	4449	496	1176	193	42	71	435	348	658	167	.264	.374
Thorman, Scott-Scott Robert	06AtlN	01-06-82	Cambridge, Canada		R	R	6'3	235	55	128	13	30	11	0	5	14	5	21	1	.234	.438
Thornton, Andre-Andre (Thunder)	73-76ChiN 76MonN 77-79CleA 80KJ 81-87CleA	08-13-49	Tuskegee, Ala.		R	R	6'2	205	1565	5291	742	1342	244	22	253	895	876	951	48	.254	.452
Thornton, Lou-Louis	85,87-88TorA 89-90NYN	04-26-63	Montgomery, Ala.		L	R	6'	175	95	89	29	22	2	1	1	9	3	25	3	.247	.326
Thornton, Otis-Otis Benjamin	73HouN	06-30-45	Docena, Ala.		R	R	6'1	200	2	3	0	0	0	0	0	0	0	1	0	.000	.000
Thurman, Gary-Gary Montez	87-92KCA 93DetA 95SeaA 97NYN	11-12-64	Indianapolis, Ind.		R	R	5'10	175	424	798	121	194	27	6	2	64	61	187	65	.243	.299
Thurston, Joe-Joseph William	02-04LAN 06PhiN	09-29-79	Fairfield, Cal.		L	R	5'11	175	55	58	7	15	3	1	0	3	2	9	1	.259	.345
Tiffee, Terry-Terry Ronald	04-06MinA	04-21-79	North Little Rock, Ark.		B	R	6'3	210	91	239	20	54	13	1	5	29	15	26	1	.226	.351
Tillman, Rusty-Kerry Jerome	82NYN 86OakA 88SFN	08-29-60	Jacksonville, Fla.		R	R	6'	190	38	56	11	13	2	0	2	5	2	12	0	.232	.375
Timmons, Ozzie-Osborne Llewellyn	95-96ChiN 97CinN 99SeaA 00TBA	09-18-70	Tampa, Fla.		R	R	6'2	215	186	405	62	95	20	1	20	60	33	82	4	.235	.437
Tingley, Ron-Ronald Irvin	82SDN 88CleA 89-93CalA 94FlaN 94ChiA 95DetA	05-27-59	Presque Isle, Maine		R	R	6'2	190	278	563	52	110	27	3	10	55	54	165	2	.195	.307
Tinsley, Lee-Lee Owen	93SeaA 94-95BosA 96PhiN 96BosA 97BosA	03-04-69	Shelbyville, Ky.		B	R	5'10	185	361	870	131	210	34	4	13	79	88	231	41	.241	.334
Toca, Jorge-Jorge Luis	99-01NYN	01-07-75	Remedios, Cuba		R	R	6'3	220	25	27	4	7	0	0	1	5	0	11	0	.259	.296
Tolentino(Franco), Jose-Jose Franco [Tolentino]	91HouN	06-03-61	Mexico City, Mexico		L	L	6'1	195	44	54	6	14	4	1	0	6	9	6	0	.259	.389
Tolleson, Wayne-Jimmy Wayne	81-85TexA 86ChiA 86-90NYA	11-22-55	Spartanburg, S.C.		B	R	5'9	165	863	2322	301	559	60	17	9	133	219	384	108	.241	.294
Tolman, Tim-Timothy Lee	81-85HouN 86-87DetA	04-20-56	Santa Monica, Cal.		R	R	6'	195	132	196	21	33	10	0	5	24	24	31	1	.168	.342
Tomberlin, Andy-Andy Lee	93PitN 94BosA 95OakA 96-97NYN 98DetA	11-07-66	Monroe, N.C.		L	L	5'11	160	192	305	40	71	8	4	9	40	26	103	6	.233	.374
Tonis, Mike-Michael Timothy	04KCA	02-09-79	Sacramento, Cal.		R	R	6'3	220	2	6	0	0	0	0	0	0	0	3	0	.000	.000
Torcato, Tony-Anthony Dale	02-05SFN	10-25-79	Woodland, Cal.		L	R	6'2	195	43	47	2	14	2	0	0	3	2	6	0	.298	.340
Torrealba, Steve-Steven Alexander	01-02AtlN	11-28-77	Barquisimeto, Venez.		R	R	6'	175	19	19	1	2	0	0	0	2	1	5	0	.105	.105
Torrealba, Yorvit-Yorvit Adolfo	01-05SFN 05SeaA 06ColN	07-19-78	Caracas, Venezuela		R	R	5'11	190	327	936	113	233	55	9	22	126	72	189	6	.249	.395
Torres, Andres-Andres Vungo [Feliciano]	02-04DetA 05TexA	01-26-78	Aguadilla, P.R.		B	R	5'10	189	89	257	33	54	6	4	1	13	17	57	9	.210	.276
Torres, Rusty-Rosendo [Hernandez]	71-72NYA 73-74CleA 76-77CalA 78-79ChiA 80KCA	09-30-48	Aguadilla, P.R.		B	R	5'11	180	654	1314	159	279	45	5	35	126	164	246	13	.212	.334
Torve, Kelvin-Kelvin Curtis	88MinA 90-91NYN	01-10-60	Rapid City, S.D.		L	R	6'3	205	42	62	1	14	4	0	1	4	5	12	0	.226	.339
Traber, Jim-James Joseph	84,86,88-89BalA	12-26-61	Columbus, Ohio		L	L	6'	220	264	819	70	208	21	0	27	117	58	118	0	.227	.352
Tracy, Andy-Andrew Michael	00-01MonN 04ColN	12-11-73	Bowling Green, Ohio		L	R	6'3	230	136	263	34	59	10	1	13	41	29	95	1	.224	.418
Tracy, Chad-Chad Austin	04-06AriN	05-22-80	Charlotte, N.C.		L	R	6'2	200	442	1581	209	460	104	7	55	205	134	267	10	.291	.470
Tracy, Jim-James Edwin (Trace)	80-81ChiN M01-05LAN M06PitN	12-31-55	Hamilton, Ohio		L	L	6'3	195	87	185	18	46	5	4	3	22	25	51	3	.249	.368
Trammell, Alan-Alan Stuart	77-96,M03-05DetA	02-21-58	Garden Grove, Cal.		R	R	6'	180	2293	8288	1231	2365	412	55	185	1003	850	874	236	.285	.415
Trammell, Bubba-Thomas Bubba	97DetA 98-00TBA 00NYN 01-02SDN 03NYA	11-06-71	Knoxville, Tenn.		R	R	6'2	220	584	1798	243	469	96	7	82	285	210	325	10	.261	.459
Traxler, Brian-Brian Lee	90LAN	09-26-67	Waukegan, Ill.	11-19-04	L	L	5'10	203	8	11	0	1	0	0	0	0	2	1	0	.091	.182
Treadway, Jeff-Hugh Jeffery	87-88CinN 89-92AtlN 93CleA 94-95LAN 95MonN	01-22-63	Columbus, Ga.		L	R	5'11	175	762	2119	244	596	103	14	28	208	140	184	14	.281	.383
Treanor, Matt-Matthew Aaron	04-06FlaN	03-03-76	Garden Grove, Cal.		R	R	6'2	210	154	346	29	76	16	1	2	28	39	75	0	.220	.289
Tremie, Chris-Christopher James	95ChiA 98TexA 99PitN 04HouN	10-17-69	Houston, Tex.		R	R	6'	210	22	41	3	6	1	0	1	4	1	9	0	.146	.171
Trevino, Alex-Alejandro [Castro]	78-81NYN 82-84CinN 84AtlN 85SFN 86-87LAN 88-90HouN 90NYN 90CinN	08-26-57	Monterrey, Mexico		R	R	5'10	170	939	2430	245	604	117	10	23	244	205	317	19	.249	.333
Trillo (Marcano), Manny-Jesus Manuel Marcano [Trillo]	73-74OakA 75-78ChiN 79-82PhiN 83CleA 83MonN 84-85SFN 86-88ChiN 89CinN	12-25-50	Caripito, Venezuela		R	R	6'1	160	1780	5950	598	1562	239	33	61	571	452	742	35	.263	.345
Truby, Chris-Christopher John	00-01HouN 02MonN 02DetA 03TBA 05BW	12-09-73	Palm Springs, Cal.		R	R	6'2	190	263	819	78	189	42	6	19	107	38	205	5	.231	.388
Tubbs, Greg-Gregory Alan	93CinN	08-31-62	Smithville, Tenn.		R	R	5'9	165	35	59	10	11	0	0	0	2	4	10	3	.186	.237

USE NAME - GIVEN NAMES (NICKNAMES) / TEAM BY YEAR	BIRTH DATE	BIRTH PLACE	DEATH DATE	B	T	HGT	WGT	G	AB	R	H	2B	3B	HR	RBI	BB	SO	SB	BA	SA
Tucker, Michael-Michael Anthony 95-96KCA 97-98AtlN 99-01CinN 01ChiN 02-03KCA 04-05SFN 05PhiN 06NYN	06-25-71	South Boston, Va.		L	R	6'2	190	1417	4083	625	1047	208	49	125	528	490	960	114	.256	.423
Tucker, Scooter-Eddie Jack 92-93,95HouN 95CleA	11-18-66	Greenville, Miss.		R	R	6'2	205	51	103	9	13	2	0	1	7	10	20	1	.126	.175
Tulowitzki, Troy-Troy-Trever 06ColN	10-10-84	Santa Clara, Cal.		R	R	6'3	205	25	96	15	23	2	0	1	6	10	25	3	.240	.292
Turang, Brian-Brian Craig 93-94SeaA	06-14-67	Long Beach, Cal.		R	R	5'10	170	78	252	31	56	16	2	1	15	24	45	9	.222	.313
Turner, Chris-Christopher Wan 93-96CalA 97AnaA 98KCA 99CleA 00NYA	03-23-69	Bowling Green, Ky.		R	R	6'1	195	158	379	49	90	16	2	4	36	36	89	5	.237	.322
Turner, Jerry-John Webber 74-81SDN 81ChiA 82DetA 83SDN	01-17-54	Texarkana, Ark.		L	L	5'9	180	733	1742	222	448	73	9	45	238	159	245	45	.257	.387
Turner, Shane-Shane Lee 88PhiN 91BalA 92SeaA	01-08-63	Los Angeles, Cal.		L	R	5'10	180	56	110	9	26	5	0	0	6	14	24	2	.236	.282
Tyner, Jason-Jason Renyt 00NYN 00-03TBA 05-06MinA	04-23-77	Beaumont, Tex.		L	L	6'1	170	325	1052	126	286	27	9	0	72	52	111	53	.272	.315
Tyrone, Jim-James Vernon 72,74-75ChiN 77OakA	01-29-49	Alice, Tex.		R	R	6'	185	177	405	52	92	11	3	8	32	32	77	6	.227	.328
Tyrone, Wayne-Oscar Wayne 76ChiN	08-01-50	Alice, Tex.		R	R	6'	185	30	57	3	13	1	0	1	3	3	21	0	.228	.298
Tyson, Mike-Michael Ray (Rocky) 72-79StlN 80-81ChiN	01-13-50	Rocky Mount, N.C.		R	R	5'9	175	1017	2959	281	714	98	28	27	269	175	411	23	.241	.327
								Bats Both parts of 72, 79, 80												
Uggla, Dan-Daniel Cooley 06FlaN	03-11-80	Louisville, Ky.		R	R	5'10	200	154	611	105	172	26	1	27	90	48	123	6	.282	.480
Ugueto, Luis-Luis Enrique 02-03SeaA	02-15-79	Caracas, Venezuela		B	R	5'11	170	74	28	23	6	0	0	1	2	3	8	10	.214	.321
Ullger, Scott-Scott Matthew 83MinA	06-10-55	New York, N.Y.		R	R	6'3	196	35	79	8	15	4	0	0	5	5	21	0	.190	.241
Unroe, Tim-Timothy Brian 95-97MilA 99AnaA 00AtlN	10-07-70	Round Lake Beach, Ill.		R	R	6'3	200	79	95	13	21	3	0	3	11	11	32	2	.221	.347
Unser, Del-Delbert Bernard 68-71WasA 72CleA 73-74PhiN 75-76NYN 76-78MonN 79-82PhiN	12-09-44	Decatur, Ill.		L	L	6'1	180	1799	5215	617	1344	179	42	87	481	481	675	64	.258	.358
Upshaw, Willie-Willie Clay 78,80-87TorA 88CleA	04-27-57	Blanco, Tex.		L	L	6'	190	1264	4203	596	1103	199	45	123	528	452	642	88	.262	.419
Upton, B.J.-Melvin Emanuel 04,06TBA	08-21-84	Norfolk, Va.		R	R	6'3	180	95	334	39	84	13	2	5	22	28	86	15	.251	.347
Uribe (Gonzalez), Jose-Jose Altagracia Gonzalez [Uribe] played as Jose Gonzalez 84 84StlN 85-92SFN 93HouN	01-21-59	San Cristobal, D.R.		B	R	5'10	165	1038	3064	307	738	99	34	19	219	256	425	74	.241	.314
Uribe, Juan-Juan C. [Tena] 01-03ColN 04-06ChiA	07-22-79	Bani, Dom. Rep.		R	R	5'11	173	726	2601	339	670	141	32	84	351	138	490	33	.258	.433
Utley, Chase-Chase Cameron 03-06PhiN	12-17-78	Pasadena, Cal.		L	R	6'1	180	444	1602	273	464	100	13	75	285	158	303	37	.290	.509
Vail, Mike-Michael Lewis 75-77NYN 78CleA 78-80ChiN 81-82CinN 83SFN 83MonN 84LAN	11-10-51	San Francisco, Cal.		R	R	6'	190	665	1604	146	447	71	11	34	219	81	273	3	.279	.400
Valderrama, Carlos-Carlos Alberto [Cordero] 03SFN	11-30-77	Bachaquero, Venez.		R	R	6'	180	7	7	0	1	0	0	0	0	0	3	1	.143	.143
Valdes, Pedro-Pedro Jose [Manzo] 96,98ChiN 00TexA	06-29-73	Fajardo, P.R.		L	L	6'1	180	53	85	7	21	7	1	1	8	8	15	0	.247	.388
Valdez (Castillo), Julio-Julio Julian [Valdez] 80-83BosA	06-03-56	San Cristobal, P.R.		B	R	6'2	175	65	87	11	18	2	0	1	8	1	18	3	.207	.264
								Bats Right 80												
Valdez, Mario-Mario A. 97ChiA 00TexA 01OakA	11-19-74	Ciudad Obregon, Mex.		L	R	6'2	205	91	181	18	43	8	0	2	21	29	60	1	.238	.315
Valdez, Wilson-Wilson Antonio 04ChiA 05SeaA 05SDN	05-20-78	Nizao, Dom. Rep.		R	R	5'11	160	70	182	17	38	8	1	1	13	10	31	3	.209	.280
Valent, Eric-Eric Christian 01-02PhiN 03CinN 04-05NYN	04-04-77	La Mirada, Cal.		L	L	6'	191	205	406	50	95	20	2	13	37	41	101	0	.234	.389
Valentin, Javier-Jose Javier [Rosario] 97-99MinA 02MinA 03TBA 04-06CinN	09-19-75	Manati, P.R.		B	R	5'10	191	440	1135	125	279	53	5	39	158	98	205	0	.246	.404
Valentin, John-John William 92-01BosA 02NYN	02-18-67	Mineola, N.Y.		R	R	6'	180	1105	3917	614	1093	281	17	124	558	463	524	47	.279	.454
Valentin, Jose-Jose Antonio [Rosario] 92-97MilA 98-99MilN 00-04ChiA 05LAN 06NYN	10-12-69	Manati, P.R.		B	R	5'10	185	1627	5373	854	1308	291	40	246	798	615	1266	134	.243	.450
Valentine, Bobby-Robert John 69,71-72LAN 73-75CalA 75-77SDN 77-78NYN 78SeaA M85-92TexA M96-02NYN	05-13-50	Stamford, Conn.		R	R	5'10	185	639	1698	176	441	59	9	12	157	140	134	27	.260	.326
Valentine, Ellis-Ellis Clarence (Bubba) 75-81MonN 81-82NYN 83CalA 84FJ 85TexA	07-30-54	Helena, Ark.		R	R	6'4	215	894	3166	380	881	169	15	123	474	180	462	59	.278	.458
Valera, Yohanny-Yohanny 00MonN	03-17-74	Santo Domingo, D.R.		R	R	6'1	196	7	10	1	0	0	0	0	1	1	5	0	.000	.000
Valle, Dave-David 84-93SeaA 94BosA 94MilA 95-96TexA	10-30-60	Queens, N.Y.		R	R	6'2	215	970	2775	314	658	121	12	77	350	258	413	5	.237	.373
Van Burkleo, Ty-Tyler Lee 93CalA 94ColN	10-07-63	Oakland, Cal.		L	L	6'5	225	14	38	2	5	3	0	1	1	6	10	1	.132	.289
Vander Wal, John-John Henry 91-93MonN 94-98ColN 98-99SDN 00-01PitN 01SFN 02NYA 03MilN 04CinN	04-29-66	Grand Rapids, Mich.		L	L	6'1	190	1372	2751	374	717	170	18	97	430	385	698	38	.261	.441
Van Gorder, Dave-David Thomas 82,84-86CinN 87BalA	03-27-57	Los Angeles, Cal.		R	R	6'2	205	183	420	30	89	12	1	3	38	39	63	1	.212	.267
Van Slyke, Andy-Andrew James 83-86StlN 87-94PitN 95BalA 95PhiN	12-21-60	Utica, N.Y.		L	R	6'1	195	1658	5711	835	1562	293	91	164	792	667	1063	245	.274	.443
Vargas, Hedi-Hediberto [Rodriguez] 82,84PitN	02-23-59	Guanica, P.R.		R	R	6'4	215	26	39	4	10	3	0	0	5	3	7	0	.256	.333
Varitek, Jason-Jason Andrew 97-06BosA	04-11-72	Rochester, Minn.		B	R	6'2	220	1068	3543	479	952	231	10	131	543	406	780	24	.269	.443
Varney, Pete-Richard Fred 73-76ChiA 76AtlN	04-10-49	Roxbury, Mass.		R	R	6'	235	69	190	19	47	7	1	5	15	10	47	2	.247	.374
Varsho, Gary-Gary Andrew 88-90ChiN 91-92PitN 93CinN 94PhiN 95,M04PhiN	06-20-61	Marshfield, Wis.		L	R	5'11	190	571	837	101	204	41	11	10	84	55	146	27	.244	.355
Vatcher, Jim-James Ernest 90PhiN 90AtlN 91-92SDN	05-27-65	Santa Monica, Cal.		R	R	5'9	165	87	109	11	27	3	1	1	11	12	27	1	.248	.321
Vaughn, Greg-Gregory Lamont 89-96MilA 96-98SDN 99CinN 00-02TBA 03ColN	07-03-65	Sacramento, Cal.		R	R	6'	200	1731	6103	1017	1475	284	23	355	1072	865	1513	121	.242	.470
Vaughn, Mo-Maurice Samuel 91-98BosA 99-00AnaA 01AJ 02-03NYN 04KJ	12-15-67	Norwalk, Conn		L	R	6'1	250	1512	5532	861	1620	270	10	328	1064	725	1429	30	.293	.523
Vazquez, Ramon-Ramon Luis 01SeaA 02-04SDN 05BosA 05-06CleA	08-21-76	Aibonito, P.R.		L	R	5'11	170	386	1147	141	293	48	11	7	92	119	229	18	.255	.335
Vega, Jesus-Jesus Antonio [Morales] 79-80,82MinA	10-14-55	Bayamon, P.R.		R	R	6'	190	87	236	26	58	6	0	5	33	11	28	7	.246	.381
Velandia, Jorge-Jorge Luis [Macias] 97SDN 98-00OakA 00-01,03NYN	10-15-75	Caracas, Venezuela		R	R	5'9	185	150	179	13	27	7	1	0	12	17	45	2	.151	.201
Velarde, Randy-Randy Lee 87-95NYA 96CalA 97-99AnaA 99-00OakA 01TexA 01NYA 02OakA	11-24-62	Midland, Tex.		R	R	6'	195	1273	4244	633	1171	214	23	100	445	463	853	78	.276	.408
Velasquez, Guillermo-Guillermo [Burgara] 92-93SDN	04-23-68	Mexicali, Mexico		L	R	6'3	220	94	166	8	37	0	0	4	25	14	42	0	.223	.307
Velazquez, Freddy-Federico Antonio [Velazquez] 69SeaA 73AtlN	12-06-37	Santo Domingo, D.R.		R	R	6'1	190	21	39	3	10	3	0	0	5	2	6	0	.256	.333
Velez, Otto-Otoniel [Franceschi] 73-76NYA 77-82TorA 83CleA	11-29-50	Ponce, P.R.		R	R	6'	190	637	1802	244	452	87	11	78	272	336	414	6	.251	.441
Venable, Max-William McKinley 79-83SFN 84MonN 85-87CinN 89-91CalA	06-06-57	Phoenix, Ariz.		L	L	5'10	185	727	1397	176	337	57	17	18	128	120	218	64	.241	.349
Vento, Mike-Michael 05NYA 06WasN	05-25-78	Albuquerque, N.M.		R	R	6'	195	11	20	3	5	1	0	0	1	4	6	0	.250	.300
Ventura, Robin-Robin Mark 89-98ChiA 99-03NYN 03-04LAN	07-14-67	Santa Maria, Cal.		L	R	6'1	195	2079	7064	1006	1885	338	14	294	1182	1075	1179	24	.267	.444
Veras, Quivlio-Quilvio Alberto [Perez] 95-96FlaN 97-99SDN 00-01AtlN	04-03-71	Santo Domingo, D.R.		B	R	5'9	180	700	2780	469	750	129	15	32	239	427	462	183	.270	.362
Veras, Wilton-Wilton Andres 99-00BosA	01-19-78	Montecristi, Dom. Rep.		R	R	6'2	198	85	282	35	74	12	2	2	27	12	34	0	.262	.340
Veryzer, Tom-Thomas Martin 73-77DetA 78-81CleA 82NYN 83-84CinN 85ChiN	02-11-53	Port Jefferson, N.Y.		R	R	6'1	180	996	2848	250	687	84	12	14	231	143	329	11	.241	.294
Victorino, Shane-Shane Patrick 03SDN 05-06PhiN	11-30-80	Wailuku, Hawaii		B	R	5'9	160	210	505	83	135	21	8	8	58	31	74	11	.267	.388
Vidro, Jose-Jose Angel [Cetty] 97-04MonN 05-06WasN	08-27-74	Mayaguez, P.R.		B	R	5'11	190	1186	4257	614	1280	304	12	115	550	397	463	21	.301	.459
Villanueva, Hector-Hector [Balasquide] 90-92ChiN 93CinN	10-02-64	Rio Piedras, P.R.		R	R	6'1	235	191	453	53	109	21	2	25	72	40	98	1	.230	.442
Vina, Fernando-Fernando 93SeaA 94NYN 95-97MilA 98-99MilN 00-03StlN 04DetA 05LJ	04-16-69	Sacramento, Cal.		L	R	5'9	175	1148	4240	627	1196	194	49	40	343	288	292	116	.282	.379
Virgil, Ozzie-Osvaldo Jose [Lopez] 80-85PhiN 86-88AtlN 89-90TorA	12-07-56	Mayaguez, P.R.		R	R	6'1	205	739	2258	258	549	84	6	98	307	248	453	4	.243	.416
Vitiello, Joe-Joseph David 95-99KCA 00SDN 01JL 03MonN	04-11-70	Cambridge, Mass.		R	R	6'2	225	282	693	76	172	35	1	26	104	80	165	2	.248	.414
Vizcaino, Jose-Jose Luis [Pimental] 89-90LAN 91-93ChiN 94-96NYN 96CleA 97SFN 98-00LAN 00NYA 01-05HouN 06SFN 06StlN	03-26-68	San Cristobal, D.R.		B	R	6'1	180	1820	5379	633	1453	204	47	36	480	378	729	74	.270	.346
								Bats Left part of 93												
Vizquel, Omar-Omar Enrique [Gonzalez] 89-93SeaA 94-04CleA 05-06SFN	04-24-67	Caracas, Venezuela		B	R	5'9	175	2443	8966	1283	2472	398	68	73	818	897	903	366	.276	.360
Voigt, Jack-John David 92-95BalA 95-96TexA 97MilA 98OakA	05-17-66	Sarasota, Fla.		R	R	6'1	170	294	588	84	138	32	3	20	83	78	129	7	.235	.401
Vukovich, George-George Stephen 80-82PhiN 83-85CleA	06-24-56	Chicago, Ill.		L	R	6'	195	628	1602	164	428	76	10	27	203	127	229	9	.268	.399
Vukovich, John-John Christopher 70-71PhiN 73-74MilA 75CinN 76-81PhiN M86ChiN M88PhiN 02-03PhiN	07-31-47	Sacramento, Cal.		R	R	6'1	190	277	559	37	90	14	1	6	44	29	109	4	.161	.222
Wagner, Mark-Mark Duane (Wags) 76-80DetA 81-83TexA 84OakA	03-04-54	Conneaut, Ohio		R	R	6'	175	414	843	81	205	20	9	3	71	61	130	8	.243	.299
Wakamatsu, Don-Wilbur Donald 91ChiA	02-22-63	Hood River, Ore.		R	R	6'2	200	18	31	2	7	0	0	0	0	1	6	0	.226	.226
Wakeland, Chris-Christopher Robert 01DetA	06-15-74	Huntington Beach, Cal.		L	L	6'	180	10	36	5	9	2	0	2	6	0	13	0	.250	.472
Walbeck, Matt-Matthew Lovick 93ChiN 94-96MinA 97DetA 98-00AnaA 01PhiN 02-03DetA	10-02-69	Sacramento, Cal.		B	R	5'11	195	682	2109	215	492	79	5	28	208	133	343	13	.233	.315
Walewander, Jim-James Lee 87-88DetA 90NYA 93CalA	05-02-62	Chicago, Ill.		B	R	5'10	165	162	242	50	52	9	1	1	14	24	33	15	.215	.277
Walker, Chico-Cleotha (Lee) 80-81,83-84BosA 85-87ChiN 88CalA 91-92ChiN 92-93NYN	11-25-57	Jackson, Miss.		B	R	5'9	175	526	1217	150	299	37	7	17	116	109	212	67	.246	.329
Walker, Duane-Duane Allen (Weiner) 82-85CinN 85TexA 88StlN	03-13-57	Pasadena, Tex.		L	L	6'	185	392	861	95	197	37	5	24	99	103	190	25	.229	.367
Walker, Greg-Gregory Lee 82-90ChiA 90BalA	10-06-59	Douglas, Ga.		L	R	6'3	210	855	2864	368	746	164	19	113	444	268	520	19	.260	.449
Walker, Larry-Larry Kenneth Robert 89-94MonN 95-04ColN 04-05StlN	12-01-66	Maple Ridge, Canada		L	R	6'3	227	1988	6907	1355	2160	471	62	383	1311	913	1231	230	.313	.565
Walker, Todd-Todd Arthur 96-00MinA 00ColN 01-02CinN 03BosA 04-06ChiN 06SDN	05-25-73	Bakersfield, Cal.		L	R	6'	180	1270	4506	642	1303	283	30	107	541	419	567	66	.289	.437
Walker, Tony-Anthony Bruce 86HouN	07-01-59	San Diego, Cal.		R	R	6'2	204	84	90	19	20	7	0	2	10	11	15	11	.222	.367
Wallach, Tim-Timothy Charles 80-92MonN 93-95LAN 96CalA 96LAN	09-14-57	Huntington Park, Cal.		R	R	6'3	215	2212	8099	908	2085	432	36	260	1125	649	1307	51	.257	.416
Waller, Ty-Elliott Tyrone 80StlN 81-82ChiN 87HouN	03-14-57	Fresno, Cal.		R	R	6'	190	63	110	18	26	3	1	3	14	7	31	2	.236	.364
Walling, Denny-Dennis Martin 75-76OakA 78-88HouN 88-90StlN 91TexA 92HouN	04-17-54	Neptune, N.J.		L	R	6'	185	1271	2945	372	799	142	30	49	380	308	316	44	.271	.390
Wallis, Joe-Harold Joseph (Tarzan) 75-78ChiN 78-79OakA	01-09-52	East St. Louis, Ill.		B	R	5'10	185	329	886	115	216	36	9	16	68	95	174	7	.244	.359
Walters, Dan-Daniel Gene 92-93SDN	08-15-66	Brunswick, Maine		R	R	6'4	225	84	273	20	64	14	1	5	32	17	41	1	.234	.348
Walton, Jerome-Jerome O'Terrell 89-92ChiN 93CalA 94-95CinN 96AtlN 97BalA 98TBA	07-08-65	Newnan, Ga.		R	R	6'1	185	598	1573	241	423	77	8	25	132	138	280	58	.269	.376
Walton, Reggie-Reginald Sherard 80-81SeaA 82PitN	10-24-52	Kansas City, Mo.		R	R	6'3	200	56	104	10	26	7	0	0	9	5	13	2	.250	.375
Ward, Chris-Chris Gilbert 72,74ChiN	08-25-50	Oakland, Cal.		R	R	6'	175	93	138	8	28	8	0	1	10	21	20	0	.203	.254
Ward, Daryle-Daryle Lamar 98-02HouN 03LAN 04-05PitN 06WasN 06AtlN	06-27-75	Lynwood, Cal.		L	L	6'2	230	780	2022	218	530	111	5	83	343	154	375	1	.262	.446
Ward, Gary-Gary Lamell (Waldo) 79-83MinA 84-87TexA 87-89NYA 90-91DetA	12-06-53	Los Angeles, Cal.		R	R	6'1	205	1287	4479	594	1236	196	41	130	597	351	775	83	.276	.425
Ward, Kevin-Kevin Michael 91-92SDN	09-28-61	Lansdale, Pa.		R	R	6'1	195	125	254	25	55	12	2	7	20	21	78	7	.217	.339

USE NAME - GIVEN NAMES (NICKNAMES)	TEAM BY YEAR	BIRTH DATE	BIRTH PLACE	DEATH DATE	B	T	HGT	WGT	G	AB	R	H	2B	3B	HR	RBI	BB	SO	SB	BA	SA
Ward, Turner-Turner Max	90-91CleA 91-93TorA 94-96MilA 97-99PitN 99-00AriN 01PhiN	04-11-65	Orlando, Fla.		B	R	6'2	200	626	1548	210	389	73	11	39	219	186	247	33	.251	.388
Washington, Claudell-Claudell	74-76OakA 77-78TexA 78-80ChiA 80NYN 81-86AtlN 86-88NYA 89-90CalA 90NYA	08-31-54	Los Angeles, Cal.		L	L	6'1	195	1912	6787	926	1884	334	69	164	824	468	1266	312	.278	.420
Washington, Herb-Herbert Lee	74-75OakA	11-16-51	Flint, Mich.		R	R	6'1	170	105	0	33	0	0	0	0	0	0	0	31	—	—
Washington, LaRue-LaRue	78-79TexA	09-07-53	Long Beach, Cal.		R	R	6'	170	28	21	5	5	0	0	0	2	4	1	2	.238	.238
Washington, Ron-Ronald (Sweetwater)	77LAN 81-86MinA 87BalA 88CleA 89HouN	04-29-52	New Orleans, La.		R	R	5'11	160	564	1586	190	414	65	22	20	146	65	266	28	.261	.368
Washington, U.L.-U.L. (Sweetstick)	77-84KCA 85MonN 86-87PitN	10-27-53	Atoka, Okla.		B	R	5'11	175	907	2797	358	703	103	36	27	255	261	409	132	.251	.343
Wasinger, Mark-Mark Thomas	86SDN 87-88SFN	08-04-61	Monterey, Cal.		R	R	6'	170	50	90	17	22	3	0	1	4	8	16	2	.244	.311
Waszgis, B.J.-Robert Michael	00TexA	08-24-70	Omaha, Neb.		R	R	6'2	215	24	45	6	10	1	0	0	4	4	10	0	.222	.244
Wathan, Dusty-Dustin James	02KCA	08-22-73	Jacksonville, Fla.		R	R	6'4	215	3	5	1	3	1	0	0	1	0	1	0	.600	.800
Wathan, John-John David (Duke)	76-85,M87-91KCA	10-04-49	Cedar Rapids, Iowa		R	R	6'2	205	860	2505	305	656	90	25	21	261	199	265	105	.262	.343
Watkins, Pat-William Patrick	97-98CinN 99ColN	09-02-72	Raleigh, N.C.		R	R	6'2	195	116	195	15	46	10	1	2	15	10	36	2	.236	.328
Watson, Bob-Robert Jose (Bull)	66-79HouN 79BosA 80-82NYA 82-84AtlN	04-10-46	Los Angeles, Cal.		R	R	6'1	205	1832	6185	802	1826	307	41	184	989	653	796	27	.295	.447
Watson, Brandon-Brandon Eric	05-06WasN 06CinN	09-30-81	Los Angeles, Cal.		L	R	6'1	170	35	68	8	12	1	1	1	5	5	11	1	.176	.265
Watson, Matt-Matthew Kyle	03NYN 05OakA	11-05-78	Lancaster, Pa.		L	R	5'11	200	33	70	4	13	5	0	0	7	3	9	0	.186	.257
Weaver, Jim-James Francis	85DetA 87SeaA 89SFN	10-10-59	Kingston, N.Y.		L	L	6'4	200	31	31	6	5	4	0	0	2	3	14	2	.161	.290
Webster, Lenny-Leonard Irell	89-93MinA 94MonN 95PhiN 96MonN 97-99BalA 99BosA 00MonN	02-10-65	New Orleans, La.		R	R	5'9	195	587	1450	157	368	73	4	33	176	140	209	1	.254	.375
Webster, Mitch-Mitchell Dean	83-85TorA 85-88MonN 88-89ChiN 90-91CleA 91PitN 91-95LAN	05-16-59	Larned, Kans.		B	L	6'1	190	1265	3419	504	900	150	55	70	342	325	578	160	.263	.401
Wedge, Eric-Eric Michael	91-92BosA 93ColN 94BosA M03-06CleA	01-27-68	Fort Wayne, Ind.		R	R	6'2	210	39	86	13	20	2	0	5	12	14	25	0	.233	.430
Weeks, Rickie-Rickie Darnell	03,05-06MilN	09-13-82	Altamonte Springs, Fla.		R	R	6'	195	198	731	130	188	29	5	21	76	71	194	34	.257	.397
Wehner, John-John Paul	91-96PitN 97-98FlaN 99-01PitN	06-29-67	Pittsburgh, Pa.		R	R	6'3	205	461	804	99	200	33	4	4	54	73	136	15	.249	.315
Weiss, Gary-Gary Lee	80-81LAN	09-06-59	Brenham, Tex.		B	R	5'9	170	22	19	4	2	0	0	0	1	1	4	0	.105	.105
Weiss, Walt-Walter William	87-92OakA 93FlaN 94-97ColN 98-00AtlN	11-28-63	Tuxedo, N.Y.		B	R	6'	180	1495	4686	623	1207	182	31	25	386	658	658	96	.258	.326
Wellman, Brad-Brad Eugene	82-86SFN 87LAN 88-89KCA	08-17-59	Lodi, Cal.		R	R	6'	170	441	927	97	214	30	2	6	77	59	176	26	.231	.287
Wells, Greg-Gregory DeWayne (Boomer)	81TorA 82MinA	04-25-54	McIntosh, Ala.		R	R	6'6	220	47	127	12	29	8	2	0	8	6	20	0	.228	.307
Wells, Vernon-Vernon M. III	99-06TorA	12-08-78	Shreveport, La.		R	R	6'1	225	821	3239	478	933	200	19	141	501	230	457	53	.288	.492
Werner, Don-Donald Paul	75-78,80CinN 81-82TexA	03-08-53	Appleton, Wis.		R	R	6'1	185	118	279	17	49	7	1	2	24	27	53	2	.176	.229
Werth, Dennis-Dennis Dean	79-81NYA 82KCA	12-29-52	Lincoln, Ill.		R	R	6'1	200	117	139	28	29	4	0	3	15	24	33	1	.209	.302
Werth, Jayson-Jayson Richard Gowan	02-03TorA 04-05LAN 06WlJ	05-20-79	Springfield, Ill.		R	R	6'5	215	232	721	113	177	39	6	25	106	87	232	17	.245	.420
Wessinger, Jim-James Michael	79AtlN	09-25-55	Utica, N.Y.		R	R	5'11	170	10	7	2	0	0	0	0	0	1	4	0	.000	.000
Wesson, Barry-Barry Jarvis	02HouN 03AnaA	04-06-77	Tupelo, Miss.		R	R	6'2	225	25	31	3	6	0	1	1	4	1	9	1	.194	.355
Wetherby, Jeff-Jeffrey Barret	89AtlN	10-18-63	Granada Hills, Cal.		L	L	6'2	200	52	48	5	10	2	1	1	7	4	6	1	.208	.354
Whisenton, Larry-Larry	77-79,81-82AtlN	07-03-56	St. Louis, Mo.		L	L	6'	195	116	205	27	48	10	3	4	21	29	42	3	.234	.371
Whitaker, Lou-Louis Rodman (Sweet Lou)	77-95DetA	05-12-57	Brooklyn, N.Y.		L	R	5'11	170	2390	8570	1386	2369	420	65	244	1084	1197	1099	143	.276	.426
White, Derrick-Derrick Ramon	93MonN 95DetA 98ChiN 98ColN	10-12-69	San Rafael, Cal.		R	R	6'1	220	76	116	10	21	5	0	3	8	2	28	3	.181	.302
White, Devon-Devon Markes	85-91CalA 91-95TorA 96-97FlaN 98AriN 99-00LAN 01MilN	12-29-62	Kingston, Jamaica		B	R	6'	185	1941	7344	1125	1934	378	71	208	846	541	1526	346	.263	.419
White, Frank-Frank (Academy Frank)	73-90KCA	09-04-50	Greenville, Miss.		R	R	5'11	180	2324	7859	912	2006	407	58	160	886	412	1035	178	.255	.383
White, Jerry-Jerome Cardell	74-78MonN 78ChiN 79-83MonN 84-85JL 86StLN	08-23-52	Shirley, Mass.		B	R	5'10	170	646	1196	155	303	50	9	21	109	148	174	57	.253	.363
White, Myron-Myron Alan (Whitehead)	78LAN	08-01-57	Long Beach, Cal.		L	L	5'11	185	7	4	1	2	0	0	0	1	0	1	0	.500	.500
White, Rondell-Rondell Bernard	93-00MonN 00-01ChiN 02NYA 03SDN 03KCA 04-05DetA 06MinA	02-23-72	Milledgeville, Ga.		R	R	6'1	210	1436	5248	748	1500	292	34	194	748	354	906	94	.286	.465
Whited, Ed-Edward Morris	89AtlN	02-09-64	Bristol, Pa.		R	R	6'3	195	36	74	5	12	3	0	1	4	6	15	1	.162	.243
Whiten, Mark-Mark Anthony	90-91TorA 91-92CleA 93-94StLN 95BosA 95-96PhiN 96AtlN 96SeaA 97NYA 98-00CleA	11-25-66	Pensacola, Fla.		B	R	6'3	220	940	3104	465	804	129	20	105	423	378	712	78	.259	.415
Whiteside, Eli-Dustin Eli	05BalA	10-22-79	New Albany, Miss.		R	R	6'2	210	9	12	1	3	0	0	0	1	0	2	0	.250	.250
Whitfield, Terry-Terry Bertland	74-76MinA 77-80SFN 81-83JL 84-86LAN	01-12-53	Blythe, Cal.		L	R	6'1	195	730	1913	233	537	93	12	33	179	138	288	18	.281	.394
Whitmer, Dan-Daniel Charles	80CalA 81TorA	11-23-55	Redlands, Cal.		R	R	6'3	200	49	96	8	22	4	0	0	7	5	23	1	.229	.271
Whitmore, Darrell-Darrell Lamont	93-95FlaN	11-18-68	Front Royal, Va.		L	R	6'2	210	112	330	31	67	11	2	5	21	18	92	4	.203	.294
Whitt, Ernie-Leo Ernest	76BosA 77-78,80-89TorA 90AtlN 91BalA	06-13-52	Detroit, Mich.		L	R	6'2	200	1328	3774	447	938	176	15	134	534	436	491	22	.249	.410
Widger, Chris-Christopher Jon	95-96SeaA 97-00MonN 00SeaA 01SJ 02NYA 03StLN 05-06ChiA 06BalA	05-21-71	Pennsauken, N.J.		R	R	6'3	210	613	1826	180	435	104	7	55	222	141	384	10	.238	.393
Wiedenbauer, Tom-Thomas John	79HouN	11-05-58	Menomonie, Wis.		R	R	6'1	180	4	6	0	4	1	0	0	2	0	2	0	.667	.833
Wieghaus, Tom-Thomas Robert	81,83MonN 84HouN	02-01-57	Chicago Heights, Ill.		R	R	6'	195	8	11	0	0	0	0	0	1	1	3	0	.000	.000
Wiggins, Alan-Alan Anthony	81-85SDN 85-87BalA	02-17-58	Los Angeles, Cal.	01-06-91	B	R	6'2	165	631	2247	346	581	61	19	5	118	235	193	242	.259	.309
Wigginton, Ty-Ty Allen	02-04NYN 04-05PitN 06TBA	10-11-77	San Diego, Cal.		R	R	6'	220	525	1782	229	472	108	10	65	259	145	352	25	.265	.446
Wilborn, Ted-Thaddeus Inglehart	79TorA 80NYA	12-16-58	Waco, Tex.		B	R	5'11	170	30	20	5	2	0	0	0	1	1	6	2	.100	.100
Wilfong, Rob-Robert Donald (Fong)	77-82MinA 82-86CalA 87SFN	09-01-53	Pasadena, Cal.		L	R	6'1	185	959	2690	318	668	97	23	39	261	205	387	54	.248	.345
Wilhelm, Jim-James Webster	78-79SDN	09-20-52	San Rafael, Cal.		R	R	6'3	190	49	122	10	32	6	3	0	12	2	14	2	.262	.361
Wilkerson, Brad-Stephen Bradley	01-04MonN 05WasN 06TexA	06-01-77	Owensboro, Ky.		L	L	6'	200	749	2585	425	651	164	25	98	309	414	772	46	.252	.448
Wilkerson, Curt-Curtis Vernon	83-88TexA 89-90ChiN 91PitN 92-93KCA	04-26-61	Petersburg, Va.		B	R	5'9	165	972	2452	272	600	78	23	8	179	138	403	81	.245	.305
Wilkins, Rick-Richard David	91-95ChiN 95-96HouN 96-97SFN 97-98SeaA 98StLN 99LAN 00StLN 01SDN	06-04-67	Jacksonville, Fla.		L	R	6'2	210	720	2114	280	515	95	7	81	275	278	571	9	.244	.410
Willard, Jerry-Gerald Duane	84-85CleA 86-87OakA 90ChiA 91-92AtlN 92MonN 94SeaA	03-14-60	Oxnard, Cal.		L	R	6'2	200	346	783	82	195	29	1	25	114	83	161	1	.249	.384
Williams, Bernie-Bernabe [Figueroa]	91-06NYA	09-13-68	San Juan, P.R.		B	R	6'2	200	2076	7869	1366	2336	449	55	287	1257	1069	1212	147	.297	.477
Williams, Dallas-Dallas McKinley	81BalA 83CinN	02-28-58	Brooklyn, N.Y.		L	L	5'11	168	20	38	2	3	0	0	0	1	3	6	0	.079	.079
Williams, Dana-Dana Lamont	89BosA	03-20-63	Weirton, W Va.		R	R	5'9	170	8	5	1	1	1	0	0	0	0	1	0	.200	.400
Williams, Earl-Earl Craig	70-72AtlN 73-74BalA 75-76AtlN 76MonN 77OakA	07-14-48	Newark, N.J.		R	R	6'4	220	889	3058	361	756	115	6	138	457	298	574	2	.247	.424
Williams, Eddie-Edward Laquan	86-88CleA 89ChiA 90SDN 91JL 94-95SDN 96DetA 97LAN 97PitN 98SDN	11-01-64	Shreveport, La.		R	R	5'11	175	395	1145	146	288	47	2	39	150	101	216	2	.252	.398
Williams, George-George Erik	95-97OakA 98SJ 00SDN	04-22-69	La Crosse, Wis.		B	R	5'10	190	128	428	62	104	19	2	10	48	74	103	0	.243	.367
Williams, Gerald-Gerald Floyd (Ice)	92-96NYA 96-97MilA 98-99AtlN 00-01TBA 01-02NYA 03FlaN 04-05NYN	08-10-66	New Orleans, La.		R	R	6'2	190	1168	3059	474	780	183	18	85	365	180	530	106	.255	.410
Williams, Glenn-Glenn David	05MinA	07-18-77	Gosford, Australia		B	R	6'2	195	13	40	3	17	1	0	0	3	2	7	1	.425	.450
Williams, Keith-David Keith	96SFN	04-21-72	Bedford, Pa.		R	R	6'	190	9	20	0	5	0	0	0	0	0	4	0	.250	.250
Williams, Kenny-Kenneth Royal	86-88ChiA 89-90DetA 90-91TorA 91MonN	04-06-64	Berkeley, Cal.		R	R	6'2	187	451	1154	136	252	42	8	27	119	56	290	49	.218	.339
Williams, Mark-Mark Westley	77OakA	07-28-53	Elmira, N.Y.		L	L	5'11	175	3	2	0	0	0	0	0	1	1	1	0	.000	.000
Williams, Matt-Matthew Derrick	87-96SFN 97CleA 98-03AriN	11-28-65	Bishop, Cal.		R	R	6'2	215	1866	7000	997	1878	338	35	378	1218	469	1363	53	.268	.489
Williams, Reggie-Reginald Bernard	92CalA 95CalA 98-99AnaA	05-05-66	Laurens, S.C.		B	R	6'1	185	88	136	22	34	3	3	2	14	15	45	5	.250	.360
Williams, Reggie-Reggie DeWayne	85-87LAN 88CleA	08-29-60	Memphis, Tenn.		R	R	5'11	185	200	379	52	98	16	2	5	39	28	76	11	.259	.351
Williamson, Antone-Anthony Joseph	97MilA	07-18-73	Harbor City, Cal.		L	R	6'1	195	24	54	2	11	3	0	0	6	4	8	0	.204	.259
Willingham, Josh-Joshua David	04-06FlaN	02-17-79	Florence, Ala.		R	R	6'1	200	170	550	67	151	29	2	27	79	60	122	2	.275	.482
Willits, Reggie-Reggie Gene	06LAA	05-03-80	Chickasha, Okla.		B	R	5'11	185	28	45	12	12	1	0	0	2	11	10	4	.267	.289
Wills, Bump-Elliott Taylor	77-81TexA 82ChiN	07-27-52	Washington D.C.		B	R	5'9	175	831	3030	472	807	128	24	36	302	310	441	196	.266	.360
Wilson, Craig-Craig Alan	89-92StLN 93KCA	11-28-64	Annapolis, Md.		R	R	5'11	190	203	362	31	91	11	0	1	37	32	50	2	.251	.290
Wilson, Craig-Craig Alan	01-06PitN 06NYA	11-30-76	Fountain Valley, Cal.		R	R	6'2	217	674	1952	297	517	98	14	98	290	190	618	14	.265	.480
Wilson, Craig-Craig Franklin	98-00ChiA	09-03-70	Chicago, Ill.		R	R	6'0	185	139	372	54	101	16	1	7	40	31	39	3	.272	.376
Wilson, Dan-Daniel Allen	92-93CinN 94-05SeaA	03-25-69	Arlington Heights, Ill.		R	R	6'3	210	1299	4386	441	1097	211	13	88	519	280	763	23	.250	.382
Wilson, Desi-Desi Bernard	96SFN	05-09-68	Glen Cove, N.Y.		L	L	6'7	230	41	118	10	32	2	0	2	12	12	27	0	.271	.339
Wilson, Enrique-Enrique [Martes]	97-00CleA 00-01PitN 01-04NYA 05ChiN	07-27-73	Santo Domingo, D.R.		B	R	5'11	190	555	1406	155	343	73	5	22	141	89	169	14	.244	.350
Wilson, Glenn-Glenn Dwight (Tex)	82-83DetA 84-87PhiN 88SeaA 88-89PitN 89-90HouN 93PitN	12-22-58	Baytown, Tex.		R	R	6'1	195	1151	4151	451	1098	209	26	98	521	253	672	27	.265	.398
Wilson, Jack-Jack Eugene	01-06PitN	12-29-77	Westlake Village, Cal.		R	R	6'	190	862	3257	391	863	152	28	43	280	179	412	30	.265	.398
Wilson, Jim-James George	85CleA 89SeaA	12-29-60	Corvallis, Ore.		R	R	6'3	230	9	22	2	5	0	0	0	4	1	6	0	.227	.227
Wilson, Josh-Joshua Aaron	05FlaN	03-26-81	Pittsburgh, Pa.		R	R	5'11	185	10	10	2	1	1	0	0	0	0	2	0	.100	.200
Wilson, Mookie-William Hayward	80-89NYN 89-91TorA	02-09-56	Bamberg, S.C.		B	R	5'9	170	1403	5094	731	1397	227	71	67	438	282	866	327	.274	.386
Wilson, Nigel-Nigel Edward	93FlaN 95CinN 96CleA	01-12-70	Oshawa, Canada		L	L	6'1	185	22	35	2	3	0	0	2	6	1	17	0	.086	.257
Wilson, Preston-Preston James Richard	98NYN 98-02FlaN 03-05ColN 05WasN 06HouN 06StLN	07-19-74	Bamberg, S.C.		R	R	6'2	210	1083	3939	567	1041	218	16	188	663	346	1068	122	.264	.471
Wilson, Tack-Michael	83MinA 87CalA	05-16-56	Shreveport, La.		R	R	5'10	192	12	6	6	2	1	0	0	1	1	0	0	.333	.500
Wilson, Tom-Thomas Leroy	01OakA 02-03TorA 04NYN 04LAN	12-19-70	Fullerton, Cal.		R	R	6'3	220	214	554	75	140	29	0	15	76	58	169	0	.253	.396
Wilson, Vance-Vance Allen	99-04NYN 05-06DetA	03-17-73	Mesa, Ariz.		R	R	5'11	190	403	954	104	238	42	2	25	129	46	189	2	.249	.376
Wilson, Willie-Willie James	76-90KCA 91-92OakA 93-94ChiN	07-09-55	Montgomery, Ala.		B	R	6'3	195	2154	7731	1169	2207	281	147	41	585	425	1144	668	.285	.376

Bats Right 76

USE NAME - GIVEN NAMES (NICKNAMES)	TEAM BY YEAR	BIRTH DATE	BIRTH PLACE	DEATH DATE	B	T	HGT	WGT	G	AB	R	H	2B	3B	HR	RBI	BB	SO	SB	BA	SA
Wine, Robbie-Robert Paul	86-87HouN	07-13-62	Norristown, Pa.		R	R	6'2	200	23	41	3	6	2	0	0	0	2	14	0	.146	.195
Winfield, Dave-David Mark (The Rave)	73-80SDN 81-88NYA 89XJ 90NYA 90-91CalA 92TorA 93-94MinA 95CleA	10-03-51	St. Paul, Minn.		R	R	6'6	225	2973	11003	1669	3110	540	88	465	1833	1216	1686	223	.283	.475
Winn, Randy-Dwight Randolph	98-02TBA 03-05SeaA 05-06SFN	06-09-74	Los Angeles, Cal.		B	R	6'2	190	1142	4252	618	1208	246	49	80	457	355	707	153	.284	.421
Winningham, Herm-Herman Son	84NYN 85-88MonN 88-91CinN 92BosA	12-01-61	Orangeburg, S.C.		L	R	5'11	185	868	1888	212	452	69	26	19	147	157	417	105	.239	.334
Winters, Matt-Matthew Littleton	89KCA	03-18-60	Buffalo, N.Y.		L	R	5'11	185	42	107	14	25	6	0	2	9	14	23	0	.234	.364
Wise, Dewayne-Larry Dewayne	00,02TorA 04AtlN 06CinN	02-24-78	Columbia, S.C.		L	L	6'1	180	178	334	44	67	15	5	9	31	14	54	12	.201	.356
Witmeyer, Ron-Ronald Herman	91OakA	06-28-67	West Islip, N.Y.		L	L	6'3	215	11	19	0	1	0	0	0	0	0	5	0	.053	.053
Witt, Kevin-Kevin Joseph	98-99TorA 01SDN 03DetA 06TBA	01-05-76	High Point, N.C.		L	R	6'4	210	146	399	38	93	12	0	15	41	19	108	1	.233	.376
Wockenfuss, John-John Bilton (Fuss)	74-83DetA 84-85PhiN	02-27-49	Welch, W. Va		R	R	6'	190	795	2072	267	543	73	11	86	310	277	278	5	.262	.432
Wohlford, Jim-James Eugene (Wolfie)	72-76KCA 77-79MilA 80-82SFN 83-86MonN	02-28-51	Visalia, Cal.		R	R	5'10	175	1220	3049	349	793	125	33	21	305	241	376	89	.260	.343
Wolfe, Larry-Laurence Marcy	77-78MinA 79-80BosA	03-02-53	Melbourne, Fla.		R	R	5'11	180	161	361	43	83	16	1	7	50	54	53	0	.230	.338
Womack, Tony-Anthony Darrell	93-94,96-98PitN 99-03AriN 03ColN 03ChiN 04StlN 05NYA 06CinN 06ChiN	09-25-69	Danville, Va.		L	R	5'9	165	1303	4963	739	1353	190	59	36	368	308	649	363	.273	.356
Wood, Jason-Jason William	98OakA 98-99DetA 06FlaN	12-16-69	San Bernardino, Cal.		R	R	6'1	170	52	81	14	21	5	0	2	10	6	20	1	.259	.395
Wood, Ted-Edward Robert	91-92SFN 93MonN	01-04-67	Mansfield, Ohio		L	L	6'2	185	47	109	9	20	3	0	1	7	11	29	0	.183	.239
Woodard, Darrell-Darrell Lee	78OakA	12-10-56	Wilma, Ark.		R	R	5'11	160	33	9	10	0	0	0	0	0	1	1	3	.000	.000
Woodard, Mike Michael Cary	85-87SFN 88ChiA	03-02-60	Melrose Park, Ill.		L	R	5'9	160	100	225	29	50	4	2	1	19	16	18	14	.222	.271
Woods, Al-Alvis	77-82TorA 86MinA	08-08-53	Oakland, Cal.		L	L	6'3	200	609	1986	233	538	98	14	35	196	167	180	23	.271	.387
Woods, Gary-Gary Lee	76OakA 77-78TorA 80-81HouN 82-85ChiN	07-20-54	Santa Barbara, Cal.		R	R	6'2	190	525	1032	117	251	50	4	13	110	86	187	19	.243	.337
Woodson, Tracy-Tracy Michael	87-89LAN 92-93StlN	10-05-62	Richmond, Va.		R	R	6'3	215	215	506	42	125	22	2	5	50	20	78	2	.247	.328
Woodward, Chris-Christopher Michael	99-04TorA 05-06NYN	06-27-76	Covina, Calif.		R	R	6'	180	515	1462	185	361	79	13	32	178	117	339	7	.247	.384
Wooten, Shawn-William Shawn	00-03AnaA 04PhiN 05BosA	07-24-72	Glendora, Cal.		R	R	5'10	215	267	669	66	182	28	1	18	86	37	120	4	.272	.398
Worthington, Craig-Craig Richard	88-91BalA 92CleA 95CinN 95-96TexA	04-17-65	Los Angeles, Cal.		R	R	6'	200	393	1234	126	284	50	0	33	144	162	264	3	.230	.351
Wotus, Ron-Ronald Allan	83-84PitN 85SJ	03-03-61	Colchester, Conn.		R	R	6'1	175	32	58	4	12	6	0	0	2	6	9	0	.207	.310
Wright, David-David Allen	04-06NYN	12-20-82	Norfolk, Va.		R	R	6'	200	383	1420	236	434	99	7	67	258	152	266	43	.306	.527
Wright, George-George DeWitt (Gee)	82-86TexA 86MonN	12-22-58	Oklahoma City, Okla.		B	R	5'11	185	627	2160	231	529	88	18	42	208	126	314	19	.245	.361
Wright, Ron-Ronald Wade	02SeaA	01-21-76	Delta, Utah		R	R	6'1	230	1	3	0	0	0	0	0	0	0	1	0	.000	.000
Wrona, Rick-Richard James	88-90ChiN 92CinN 93ChiA 94MilA	12-10-63	Tulsa, Okla.		R	R	6'1	185	79	168	16	41	6	1	3	18	5	41	1	.244	.345
Wynegar, Butch-Harold Delano	76-82MinA 82-86NYA 87-88CalA	03-14-56	York, Pa.		B	R	6'1	195	1301	4330	498	1102	176	15	65	506	626	428	10	.255	.347
Wynne, Marvell-Marvell N.	83-85PitN 86-89SDN 89-90ChiN	12-17-59	Chicago, Ill.		L	L	5'11	185	940	2693	300	664	107	28	40	244	191	398	80	.247	.352
Yancy, Hugh-Hugh Jr.	72,74,76ChiA	10-16-49	Sarasota, Fla.		R	R	5'11	180	7	19	0	2	1	0	0	0	0	3	0	.105	.158
Yeager, Steve-Stephen Wayne	72-85LAN 86SeaA	11-24-48	Huntington, W. Va.		R	R	6'	200	1269	3584	357	816	118	16	102	410	342	726	14	.228	.355
Yelding, Eric-Eric Gerard	89-92HouN 93ChiN	02-22-65	Montrose, Ala.		R	R	5'11	170	368	993	122	242	27	7	3	67	70	177	89	.244	.294
Yost, Ned-Edgar Frederick	80-83MilA 84TexA 85MonN M03-06MilN	08-19-54	Eureka, Cal.		R	R	6'1	190	219	605	54	128	15	4	16	64	21	117	5	.212	.329
Youkilis, Kevin-Kevin Edmund	04-06BosA	03-15-79	Cincinnati, Ohio		R	R	6'1	220	263	856	149	235	60	2	21	116	138	184	5	.275	.423
Youmg, Chris-Christopher Brandon	06AriN	09-05-83	Houston, Tex.		R	R	6'2	180	30	70	10	17	4	0	2	10	6	12	2	.243	.386
Young, Delmon-Delmon Damarcus	06TBA	09-14-85	Birmingham, Ala.		R	R	6'3	205	30	126	16	40	9	1	3	10	1	24	2	.317	.476
Young, Delwyn-Delwyn Rudy	06LAN	06-30-82	Los Angeles, Cal.		B	R	5'8	210	8	5	0	0	0	0	0	0	0	1	0	.000	.000
Young, Dmitri-Dmitri Dell	96-97StlN 98-01CinN 02-06DetA	10-11-73	Vicksburg, Miss.		B	R	6'2	230	1178	4152	576	1200	257	28	154	599	335	769	25	.289	.476
Young, Eric-Eric Orlando	92LAN 93-97ColN 97-99LAN 00-01ChiN 02MilN 03MilN 03SFN 04TexA 05-06SDN 06TexA	05-18-67	New Brunswick, N.J.		R	R	5'9	180	1730	6119	996	1731	327	46	79	543	660	462	464	.283	.390
Young, Ernie-Ernest Wesley	94-97OakA 98KCA 99AriN 03DetA 04CleA	07-08-69	Chicago, Ill.		R	R	6'1	220	288	796	108	179	33	4	27	90	90	213	10	.225	.378
Young, Gerald-Gerald Anthony	87-92HouN 93ColN 94StlN	10-22-64	Tele, Honduras		B	R	6'2	185	640	1815	259	446	58	19	3	113	227	213	155	.246	.304
Young, Kevin-Kevin Stacey	92-95PitN 96KCA 97-03PitN	06-16-69	Alpena, Mich.		R	R	6'3	220	1205	3897	536	1007	235	17	144	606	336	882	83	.258	.438
Young, Michael-Michael Brian	00-06TexA	10-19-76	Covina, Cal.		R	R	6'	190	965	3676	561	1104	202	38	94	476	253	583	46	.300	.453
Young, Mike-Michael Darren	82-87BalA 88MilA 88PhiN 89CleA	03-20-60	Oakland, Cal.		B	R	6'3	200	635	1840	244	454	80	6	72	235	237	465	22	.247	.414
Young, Walter-Walter Ernest	05BalA	02-18-80	Hattiesburg, Miss.		L	R	6'5	320	14	33	2	10	1	0	1	3	4	7	0	.303	.424
Youngblood, Joel-Joel Randolph	76CinN 77StlN 77-82NYN 82MonN 83-88SFN 89CinN	08-28-51	Houston, Tex.		R	R	6'	175	1408	3659	453	969	180	23	80	422	332	588	60	.265	.392
Yount, Robin-Robin R.	74-93MilA	09-16-55	Danville, Ill.		R	R	6'	180	2856	11008	1632	3142	583	126	251	1406	966	1350	271	.285	.430
Yurak, Jeff-Jeffrey Lynn (Yak)	78MilA	02-26-54	Pasadena, Cal.		B	R	6'2	195	5	5	0	0	0	0	0	0	1	0	0	.000	.000
Zambrano, Eddie-Eduardo Jose [Guerra]	92-93ChiN	02-01-66	Maracaibo, Venez.		R	R	6'2	195	75	133	18	35	7	0	6	20	17	32	2	.263	.451
Zaun, Gregg-Gregory Owen	95-96BalA 96-98FlaN 99TexA 00-01KCA 02-03HouN 03ColN 04-06TorA	04-14-71	Glendale, Cal.		B	R	5'10	190	918	2549	320	645	134	8	62	323	348	391	21	.253	.385
Zdeb, Joe-Joseph Edmund (Mad Dog)	77-79KCA	06-27-53	Compton, Ill.		R	R	5'11	185	180	345	47	94	8	6	2	34	25	45	10	.272	.348
Zeber, George-George William	77-78NYA	08-29-50	Ellwood City, Pa.		B	R	6'	180	28	71	8	21	3	0	3	10	9	11	0	.296	.465
Zeile, Todd-Todd Edward	89-95StlN 95ChiN 96PhiN 96BalA 97-98LAN 98FlaN 98-99TexA 00-01NYN 02ColN 03NYA 03MonN 04NYN	09-09-65	Van Nuys, Cal.		R	R	6'1	195	2158	7573	986	2004	397	23	253	1110	945	1279	53	.265	.423
Zimmerman, Ryan-Ryan Wallace	05-06WasN	09-28-84	Virginia Beach, Va.		R	R	6'3	220	177	672	90	199	57	3	20	116	64	132	11	.296	.479
Zinter, Alan-Alan Michael	02HouN 04AriN	05-19-68	El Paso, Texas		B	R	6'2	200	67	78	7	13	4	0	3	9	5	34	0	.167	.308
Zisk, Richie-Richard Walter	71-76PitN 77ChiA 78-80TexA 81-83SeaA 84KJ	02-06-49	Brooklyn, N.Y.		R	R	6'1	215	1453	5144	681	1477	245	26	207	792	533	910	8	.287	.466
Zobrist, Ben-Benjamin T.	06TBA	05-26-81	Eureka, Ill.		B	R	6'3	200	52	183	10	41	6	2	2	18	10	26	2	.224	.311
Zoccolillo, Pete-Peter Jude	03MilN	02-06-77	Bronx, N.Y.		L	R	6'2	200	20	37	0	4	1	0	0	3	2	13	0	.108	.135
Zosky, Eddie-Edward James	91-92TorA 93EJ 95FlaN 99MilN 00HouN	02-10-68	Whittier, Cal.		R	R	6'	175	44	50	4	8	1	2	0	3	1	13	0	.160	.260
Zuber, Jon-Jon Edward	96,98PhiN	12-10-69	Encino, Cal.		L	L	6'	190	68	136	13	34	7	1	3	16	12	20	1	.250	.382
Zuleta, Julio-Julio Ernesto [Tapia]	00-01ChiN	03-28-75	Panama City, Panama		R	R	6'6	235	79	174	24	43	11	0	9	36	10	51	0	.247	.466
Zupcic, Bob-Robert	91-94BosA 94ChiA	08-18-66	Pittsburgh, Pa.		R	R	6'4	220	319	795	99	199	47	4	7	80	57	137	7	.250	.346
Zuvella, Paul-Paul (Zu)	82-85AtlN 86-87NYA 88-89CleA 91KCA	10-31-58	San Mateo, Cal.		R	R	6'	173	209	491	41	109	17	2	2	20	34	50	2	.222	.277

USE NAMES - GIVEN NAMES (NICKNAMES) / TEAM BY YEAR	BIRTH DATE	BIRTHPLACE	DEATH DATE	B	T	HGT	WGT	W	L	Pct.	SV	G	GS	CG	IP	H	BB	SO	ShO	ERA
Aardsma, David-David Allan 04SFN 06ChiN	12-27-81	Denver, Colo.		R	R	6'5	200	4	0	1.000	0	56	0	0	64	61	38	54	0	4.52
Aase, Don-Donald William 77BosA 78-82CalA 83EJ 84CalA 85-88BalA 89NYN 90LAN	09-08-54	Orange, Cal.		R	R	6'3	215	39	24	.619	0	132	85	1	577	529	309	418	0	4.63
Abbott, Glenn-William Glenn 73-76OakA 77-78SeaA 82EJ 83SeaA 83-84DetA	02-16-51	Little Rock, Ark		R	R	6'6	210	62	83	.428	0	248	206	37	1285	1405	352	484	5	4.39
Abbott, Jim-James Anthony 89-92CalA 93-94NYA 95CalA 95-96ChiA 99MilN	09-19-67	Flint, Mich.		L	L	6'3	210	87	108	.446	0	263	254	31	1674	1779	620	888	6	4.25
Abbott, Kyle-Lawrence Kyle 91CalA 92PhiN 94JL 95PhiN 96CalA	02-18-68	Newburyport, Mass.		L	L	6'4	210	4	17	.190	0	57	22	0	185	207	79	124	0	5.20
Abbott, Paul-Paul David 90-92MinA 93CleA 98-02SeaA 03KCA 04TBA 04PhiN	09-15-67	Van Nuys, Cal.		R	R	6'3	195	43	37	.538	0	162	112	1	721	682	393	496	0	4.92
Abrego, Johnny-Johnny Ray 85ChiN	07-04-62	Corpus Christi, Tex		R	R	6'	185	1	1	.500	0	6	5	0	24	32	12	13	0	6.38
Abreu, Winston-Winston Leonardo 06BalA	04-05-77	Cotui, Dom. Rep.		R	R	6'2	170	0	0	—	0	7	0	0	8	10	6	6	0	10.13
Accardo, Jeremy-Jeremy Lee 05-06SFN 06TorA	12-18-81	Phoenix, Ariz.		R	R	6'2	190	3	9	.250	3	93	0	0	99	102	29	70	0	4.93
Acevedo, Jose-Jose Omar 01-04CinN 05ColN	12-18-77	Santo Domingo, D.R.		R	R	6'	185	18	25	.419	1	104	59	1	368	420	113	253	0	5.74
Acevedo, Juan-Juan Carlos [Lara] 95ColN 97NYN 98-99StLN 00MilN 01ColN 01FlaN 02DetA 03NYA 03TorA	05-05-70	Juarez, Mexico		R	R	6'2	230	28	40	.412	53	367	34	0	570	597	226	350	0	4.33
Acker, Jim-James Justin 83-86TorA 86-89AtlN 89-91TorA 92SeaA	09-24-58	Freer, Tex		R	R	6'2	212	33	49	.402	30	467	32	0	904	918	329	482	0	3.97
Acosta, Cy-Cecilio [Miranda] 72-74ChiA 75PhiN	11-20-46	El Sabino, Mexico		R	R	5'10	175	13	9	.591	27	107	0	0	187	143	77	109	0	2.65
Acre, Mark-Mark Robert 94-97OakA	09-16-68	Concord, Cal.		R	R	6'8	235	9	6	.600	2	114	0	0	127	135	68	98	0	5.17
Adams, Mike-Jon Michael 04-06MilN	07-29-78	Corpus Christi, Tex.		R	R	6'5	190	2	4	.333	1	61	0	0	69	66	26	54	0	3.54
Adams, Terry-Terry Wayne 95-99ChiN 00-01LAN 02-03PhiN 04TorA 04BosA 05PhiN	03-06-73	Mobile, Ala.		R	R	6'3	185	51	62	.451	42	574	41	0	869	890	380	691	0	4.17
Adams, Willie-William Edward 96-97OakA 98SJ	10-08-72	Gallup, N.M.		R	R	6'7	225	6	9	.400	0	25	24	1	135	149	55	105	1	5.81
Adamson, Joel-Joel Lee 96FlaN 97MilA 98AriN	07-02-71	Lakewood, Cal.		L	L	6'4	185	5	6	.455	0	44	11	0	110	121	37	77	0	4.89
Adkins, Jon-Jonathan Scott 03-05ChiA 06SDN	08-30-77	Huntington, W.Va.		L	R	6'	200	4	5	.444	0	114	0	0	134	151	51	78	0	4.63
Adkins, Steve-Steven Thomas 90NYA	10-26-64	Chicago, Ill.		R	L	6'6	210	1	2	.333	0	5	5	0	24	19	29	14	0	6.38
Affeldt, Jeremy-Jeremy David 02-06KCA 06ColN	06-06-79	Phoenix, Ariz.		L	L	6'4	205	21	24	.467	18	211	42	0	427	460	191	301	0	4.91
Agosto, Juan-Juan Roberto [Gonzalez] 81-86ChiA 86MinA 87-90HouN 91-92StLN 92SeaA 93HouN	02-23-58	Rio Piedras, P.R.		L	L	6'2	190	40	33	.548	29	543	2	0	627	639	248	307	0	4.01
Aguilera, Rick-Richard Warren (Aggie) 85-89NYN 89-95MinA 95BosA 96-99MinA 99-00ChiN	12-31-61	San Gabriel, Cal.		R	R	6'4	205	86	81	.515	318	732	89	0	1291	1233	351	1030	0	3.57
Ahearne, Pat-Patrick Howard 95DetA	12-10-69	San Francisco, Cal.		R	R	6'3	195	0	2	.000	0	4	3	0	10	20	5	4	0	11.70
Ainsworth, Kurt-Kurt Harold 01-03SFN 03-04BalA 05SJ	09-09-78	Baton Rouge, La.		R	R	6'3	192	6	8	.429	0	29	22	0	127	136	61	90	0	5.19
Akerfelds, Darrel-Darrel Wayne 86OakA 87CleA 89TexA 90-91PhiN	06-12-62	Denver, Colo.		R	R	6'2	210	9	10	.474	3	125	13	1	224	216	127	129	0	5.31
Alba, Gibson-Gibson Alberto [Rosado] 88StLN	01-18-60	Santiago, Dom. Rep.		L	L	6'1	150	0	0	—	0	3	0	0	3	1	2	3	0	2.70
Alberro, Jose-Jose Edgardo 95-97TexA	06-29-69	San Juan, P.R.		R	R	6'	190	0	4	.000	0	27	5	0	58	77	36	23	0	7.41
Albers, Matt-Matthew James 06HouN	01-20-83	Houston, Tex.		L	R	6'	205	0	2	.000	0	4	2	0	15	17	7	11	0	6.00
Albury, Vic-Victor 73-76MinA	05-12-47	Key West, Fla.		L	L	6'	192	18	17	.514	1	101	37	6	372	338	220	193	1	4.11
Alcala , Santo-Santo Anibol [Alcala] 76-77CinN 77MonN	12-23-52	San Pedro de Mac., D.R.		R	R	6'6	210	14	11	.560	2	68	33	3	249	257	121	140	1	4.76
Aldred, Scott-Scott Phillip 90-92DetA 93ColN 93MonN 96DetA 96-97MinA 98-99TBA 99-00PhiN	06-12-68	Flint, Mich.		L	L	6'4	215	20	39	.339	1	229	67	1	500	581	230	312	0	6.02
Aldrich, Jay-Jay Robert 87,89MilA 89AtlN 90BalA	04-14-61	Alexandria, La		R	R	6'3	210	6	5	.545	2	62	0	0	109	119	39	46	0	4.72
Alexander, Doyle-Doyle Lafayette 71LAN 72-76BalA 77-79TexA 80AtlN 81SFN 82-83NYA 83-86TorA 86-87AtlN 87-89DetA	09-05-50	Cordova, Ala.		R	R	6'3	200	194	174	.527	3	561	464	98	3367	3376	978	1528	18	3.76
Alexander, Gerald-Gerald Paul 90-92TexA	03-26-68	Baton Rouge, La.		R	R	6'3	235	1	3	.250	0	17	0	0	26	36	10	19	0	4.91
Alfonseca, Antonio-Antonio 97-00-01FlaN 02-03CinN 04AtlN 05FlaN 06TexA	04-16-72	La Romana, Dom. Rep.		R	R	6'5	250	30	35	.462	121	531	0	0	563	612	223	376	0	3.99
Allard, Brian-Brian Marshall 79-80TexA 81SeaA 82EJ	01-03-58	Spring Valley, Ill.		R	R	6'2	185	4	6	.400	0	19	13	3	95	97	31	44	0	4.26
Allen, Neil-Neil Patrick (Napalm Neil) 79-83NYN 83-85StLN 85NYA 86-87ChiA 87-88NYA 89CleA	01-24-58	Kansas City, Kans.		R	R	6'2	190	58	70	.453	75	434	59	7	989	985	417	611	6	3.88
Allison, Dana-Dana Eric 91OakA	08-14-66	Front Royal, Va.		R	L	6'3	215	1	1	.500	0	11	0	0	11	16	5	4	0	7.36
Almanza, Armando-Armando N. 99-03FlaN 04AtlN 05AriN	10-26-72	El Paso, Texas		L	L	6'3	230	14	13	.519	2	254	0	0	215	189	136	232	0	4.82
Almanzar, Carlos-Carlos Manuel [Giron] 97-98TorA 99-00SDN 01NYA 02CinN 04-05TexA	11-06-73	Santiago, Dom. Rep.		R	R	6'2	200	13	13	.500	0	239	0	1	239	252	82	170	0	4.82
Almonte, Edwin-Edwin Sanchez 03NYN	12-17-76	Santiago, Dom. Rep.		R	R	6'3	200	0	0	—	0	12	0	0	11	11	5	7	0	11.12
Almonte, Hector-Hector Radhames [Moreta] 99FlaN 01-02JL 03BosA 03MonN	10-17-75	Santo Domingo, D.R.		R	R	6'2	190	1	4	.200	0	50	0	0	52	63	30	40	0	6.27
Alston, Garvin-Garvin James 96ColN	12-08-71	Mt. Vernon, N.Y.		R	R	6'2	185	1	0	1.000	0	6	0	0	6	3	5	5	0	9.00
Altamirano, Porfi-Porfirio [Ramirez] 82-83PhiN 84ChiN	05-17-52	Esteli, Nicaragua		R	R	5'11	177	7	4	.636	2	65	0	0	92	87	30	57	0	4.03
Alvarez, Abe-Abraham 04-06BosA	10-17-82	Los Angeles, Cal.		L	L	6'2	190	0	1	.000	0	4	1	0	10	19	7	5	0	11.32
Alvarez, Jose-Jose Lino (Ho-Hose) 81-82, 88-89AtlN 90AJ	04-12-56	Tampa, Fla.		R	R	5'10	170	8	9	.471	5	98	0	0	162	140	79	134	0	2.99
Alvarez, Juan-Juan M. 99-00AnaA 02TexA 03FlaN	08-09-73	Coral Gables, Fla.		L	L	6'1	180	0	5	.000	0	80	0	0	60	58	40	42	0	5.22
Alvarez, Tavo-Cesar Octavo 95-96MonN	11-25-71	Obregon, Mexico		R	R	6'3	245	3	6	.333	0	19	13	0	58	65	26	26	0	5.40
Alvarez, Victor-Victor Aurelio 02-03LAN	11-08-76	Culiacan, Mexico		L	L	5'10	150	0	2	.000	0	9	1	0	16	18	8	10	0	7.31
Alvarez, Wilson-Wilson Eduardo [Fuenmayor] 89TexA 91-97ChiA 97SFN 98-99TBA 00SJ 01SJ 02TBA 03-05LAN	03-24-70	Maracaibo, Venez.		L	L	6'1	240	102	92	.526	4	355	263	12	1748	1624	805	1330	5	3.96
Andersen, Larry-Larry Eugene 75,77,79SeaA 81-82SeaA 83-86PhiN 86-90HouN 90BosA 91-92SDN 93-94PhiN	05-06-53	Portland, Ore.		R	R	6'3	205	40	39	.506	49	699	1	0	996	932	311	758	0	3.14
Anderson, Allan-Allan Lee 86-91MinA	01-07-64	Lancaster, Ohio		L	L	5'11	178	49	54	.476	0	148	128	15	819	901	211	339	3	4.11
Anderson, Brian-Brian James 93-95CalA 96-97CleA 98-02AriN 03CleA 03-05KCA	04-26-72	Geneva, Ohio		B	L	6'1	190	82	83	.497	1	291	245	12	1547	1743	337	723	4	4.74
Anderson, Bud-Karl Adam 82-83CleA	05-27-56	Westbury, N.Y.		R	R	6'2	215	4	10	.286	0	64	6	1	149	148	62	76	0	3.68
Anderson, Jason-Jason Roger 03NYA 03NYN 04CleA 05NYA	06-09-79	Danville, Ill.		L	R	6'	188	2	0	1.000	0	32	0	0	38	38	30	19	0	6.39
Anderson, Jimmy-James Drew Jr. 99-02PitN 03CinN 04ChiN 04BosA	01-22-76	Portsmouth, Va.		L	L	6'1	215	25	47	.347	0	122	96	3	575	672	240	241	0	5.42
Anderson, Larry-Lawrence Dennis 74-75MilA 77ChiA	12-03-52	Maywood, Cal.		R	R	6'4	200	2	3	.400	0	16	1	1	41	48	22	23	1	5.71
Anderson, Matt-Matthew Jason 98-03DetA 05ColN	08-17-76	Louisville, Ky.		R	R	6'4	200	15	7	.682	26	257	0	0	257	249	157	224	0	5.19
Anderson, Mike-Michael James 93CinN	07-30-66	Austin, Tex.		R	R	6'3	200	0	0	—	0	3	0	0	5	12	3	4	0	18.56
Anderson, Rick-Richard Arlen 87NYN 87AtlN	11-29-56	Everett, Wash.		R	R	6'	180	4	4	.500	1	28	10	0	97	112	29	42	0	4.75
Anderson, Rick-Richard Lee (Andy) 79NYA 80SeaA	12-25-53	Inglewood, Cal.	06-23-89	R	R	6'2	210	0	0	—	0	12	0	0	12	9	14	7	0	3.75
Anderson, Scott-Scott Richard 87TexA 90MonN 91-92JL 95KCA	08-01-62	Corvallis, Ore		R	R	6'6	190	1	2	.333	0	18	7	0	55	58	21	28	0	5.43
Andrade, Steve-Stephen Michael 06KCA	02-06-78	Woodland, Cal.		R	R	6'1	220	0	0	—	0	4	0	0	5	4	5	5	0	9.64
Andrews, Clayton-Clayton John 00TorA	05-15-78	Dunedin, Fla.		L	L	5'11	175	1	2	.333	0	8	2	0	21	34	9	12	0	10.02
Andrews, John-John Richard 73StLN	02-09-49	Monterey, Cal.		L	L	5'10	180	1	1	.500	0	16	0	0	18	16	11	5	0	4.50
Andujar, Joaquin-Joaquin (One Tough Dominican) 76-81HouN 81-85StLN 86-87OakA 88HouN	12-21-52	San Pedro de Mac., D.R.		B	R	5'11	185	127	118	.518	9	405	305	68	2154	2016	731	1032	19	3.58
Bats left only against certain pitchers and only with men on base																				
Andujar, Luis-Luis [Sanchez] 95-96ChiA 96-98TorA	11-22-72	Bani, Dom. Rep.		R	R	6'2	175	3	10	.231	0	35	20	0	123	160	53	49	0	5.98
Ankiel, Rick-Richard Alexander 99-01StLN 02EJ 04StLN	07-19-79	Fort Pierce, Fla.		L	L	6'1	210	13	10	.565	1	51	41	0	242	198	130	269	0	3.90
Apodaca, Bob-Robert John 73-77NYN 78-79EJ	01-31-50	Los Angeles, Cal.		R	R	5'10	175	16	25	.390	26	184	11	1	362	312	131	197	0	2.86
Aponte, Luis-Luis Eduardo [Yuripe] (Expedito) 80-83BosA 84CleA	06-14-53	El Tigre, Venezuela		R	R	6'	185	9	6	.600	7	110	0	0	220	222	68	113	0	3.27
Appier, Kevin-Robert Kevin 89-99KCA 99-00OakA 01NYN 02-03AnaA 03-04KCA	12-06-67	Lancaster, Cal.		R	R	6'2	205	169	137	.552	0	414	402	34	2595	2425	933	1994	12	3.74
Aquino, Greg-Gregori Emilio (Valera) 04-06AriN	01-11-78	Palenque, Dom. Rep.		R	R	6'2	188	2	3	.400	17	111	0	0	115	120	58	111	0	4.93
Aquino, Luis-Luis Antonio (Colon) 86TorA 88-92KCA 93-94FlaN 95MonN 95SFN	05-19-64	Santurce, P.R.		R	R	6'	195	31	32	.492	5	222	69	5	678	698	224	318	3	3.68
Armas, Tony-Antonio Jose Jr. 99-04MonN 05-06WasN	04-29-78	Puerto Piritu, Venezuela		R	R	6'4	215	48	60	.444	0	151	151	4	820	769	392	601	0	4.45
Armstrong, Jack-Jack William 88-91CinN 92CleA 93FlaN 94TexA	03-07-65	Englewood, N.J.		R	R	6'5	220	40	45	.471	0	152	130	4	787	807	319	510	1	4.58
Armstrong, Mike-Michael Dennis 80-81SDN 82-83KCA 84-85NYA	03-07-54	Glen Cove, N.Y.		R	R	6'3	205	19	17	.528	11	197	1	0	338	300	155	221	0	4.10
Arnold, Jamie-James Lee 99-00LAN 00ChiN	03-24-74	Dearborn, Mich.		R	R	6'2	190	2	7	.222	2	50	7	0	108	119	58	42	0	5.73
Arnold, Scott-Scott Gentry 88StLN	08-18-62	Lexington, Ky.		R	R	6'	210	0	0	—	0	6	0	0	7	9	4	8	0	5.40
Arnold, Tony-Tony Dale 86-87BalA	05-03-59	El Paso, Tex.		R	R	6'	175	0	2	.000	0	38	0	0	78	96	28	35	0	5.06
Arnsberg, Brad-Bradley James 86-87NYA 88EJ 89-91TexA 92CleA	08-20-63	Seattle, Wash.		R	R	6'4	205	9	6	.600	6	94	4	0	158	159	85	100	0	4.25
Arocha, Rene-Rene [Magaly] 93-95StLN 97SFN	02-24-66	Regla, Cuba		R	R	6'	180	18	17	.514	11	124	36	2	331	363	75	190	1	4.11
Arrojo, Rolando-Luis Rolando 98-99TBA 00ColN 00-02BosA	07-18-68	Santa Clara, Cuba		R	R	6'4	220	40	42	.488	6	158	105	4	700	715	255	512	2	4.55
Arroyo, Bronson-Bronson Anthony 00-02PitN 03-05BosA 06CinN	02-24-77	Key West, Fla.		R	R	6'5	180	47	44	.516	1	161	125	4	829	833	254	551	1	4.21
Arroyo, Fernando-Fernando (Freddie) 75,77-79DetA 80-82MinA 82,86OakA	03-21-52	Sacramento, Cal.		R	R	6'2	190	24	37	.393	0	121	60	12	534	589	160	172	2	4.45
Asencio, Miguel-Miguel [DePaula] 02-03KCA 04EJ 06ColN	09-29-80	Villa Mella, Dom. Rep.		R	R	6'2	190	7	8	.467	0	42	30	1	179	199	89	92	0	5.12
Ashby, Andy-Andrew Jason 91-92PhiN 93ColN 93-99SDN 00PhiN 00AtlN 01-03LAN 04SDN	07-11-67	Kansas City, Mo.		R	R	6'1	200	98	110	.471	1	309	285	21	1811	1857	540	1173	7	4.12
Assenmacher, Paul-Paul Andre 86-89AtlN 89-93ChiN 93NYA 94CleA 95-99CleA	12-10-60	Detroit, Mich.		L	L	6'3	210	61	44	.581	56	884	1	0	856	817	315	807	0	3.53
Astacio, Ezequiel-Ezequiel F. 05-06HouN	11-04-79	Hato Mayor, Dom. Rep.		R	R	6'3	150	5	8	.455	0	28	14	0	87	107	31	72	0	6.02
Astacio, Pedro-Pedro Julio [Pura] 92-97LAN 97-01ColN 01HouN 02-03NYN 04BosA 05TexA 05SDN 06WasN	11-28-69	Hato Mayor, D.R.		R	R	6'2	205	129	124	.510	0	392	343	31	2197	2292	726	1664	12	4.67

USE NAMES - GIVEN NAMES (NICKNAMES)	TEAM BY YEAR	BIRTH DATE	BIRTHPLACE	DEATH DATE	B	T	HGT	WGT	W	L	Pct.	SV	G	GS	CG	IP	H	BB	SO	ShO	ERA
Atchison, Scott-Scott Barham	04-05SeaA	03-29-76	Denton, Tex.		R	R	6'2	180	2	3	.400	0	31	0	0	37	36	15	45	0	4.10
Atchley, Justin-Justin Scott	01CinN	09-05-73	Sedro-Woolley, Wash.		L	L	6'3	215	0	0	—	0	15	0	0	10	12	5	8	0	6.10
Atherton, Keith-Keith Rowe	83-86OakA 86-88MinA 89CleA	02-19-59	Mathews, Va.		R	R	6'4	200	33	41	.446	26	342	0	0	566	546	215	349	0	3.99
Atkinson, Bill-William Cecil Glenn	76-79MonN	10-04-54	Chatham, Canada		R	R	5'8	165	11	4	.733	11	98	0	0	147	129	62	99	0	3.43
Aucoin, Derek-Derek Alfred	96MonN	03-27-70	Lachine, Canada		R	R	6'7	235	0	1	.000	0	2	0	0	3	3	1	1	0	3.38
August, Don-Donald Glenn (Augie)	88-91MilA	07-03-63	Inglewood, Cal.		R	R	6'3	190	34	30	.531	0	88	70	9	440	491	158	181	3	4.64
Augustine, Jerry-Gerald Lee	75-84MilA	07-24-52	Green Bay, Wis.		L	L	6'	185	55	59	.482	11	279	104	27	944	1028	340	348	6	4.23
Ausanio, Joe-Joseph John	94-95NYA	12-09-65	Kingston, N.Y.		R	R	6'1	205	4	1	.800	1	41	0	0	53	58	29	51	0	5.57
Austin, Jeff-Jeffrey Wellington	01-02KCA 03CinN	10-19-76	San Bernardino, Cal.		R	R	6'	185	2	3	.400	0	38	7	0	65	69	41	55	0	6.75
Austin, Jim-James Parker	91-93MilA	12-07-63	Farmville, Va.		R	R	6'2	200	6	4	.600	0	83	0	0	100	73	56	48	0	3.06
Autry, Al-Albert (Hustle)	76AtlN	02-29-52	Modesto, Cal.		R	R	6'5	225	1	0	1.000	0	1	1	0	5	4	3	3	0	5.40
Avery, Steve-Steven Thomas	90-96AtlN 97-98BosA 99CinN 03DetA	04-14-70	Trenton, Mich.		L	L	6'4	205	96	83	.536	0	297	261	14	1555	1529	569	980	6	4.19
Ayala, Bobby-Robert Joseph	92-93CinN 94-98SeaA 99MonN 99CinN	07-08-69	Ventura, Cal.		R	R	6'2	205	37	44	.457	59	406	14	0	576	581	245	541	0	4.78
Ayala, Luis-Luis Ignacio	03-04MonN 05WasN 06EJ	01-12-78	Los Mochis, Mexico		R	R	6'2	185	24	22	.522	8	214	0	0	232	232	42	149	0	2.75
Aybar, Manny-Manuel Antonio	97-99StLN 00ColN 00CinN 00FlaN 01ChiN 02-03SfN 04NYN	05-04-72	Bani, Dom. Rep.		R	R	6'1	205	17	18	.486	3	208	28	0	391	413	172	273	0	5.11
Ayrault, Bob-Robert Cunningham	92-93PhiN 93SeaA	04-27-66	South Lake Tahoe, Cal.		R	R	6'4	230	5	3	.625	0	54	0	0	73	68	33	42	0	4.05
Babcock, Bob-Robert Ernest	79-81TexA	08-25-49	New Castle, Pa.		R	R	6'2	205	2	3	.440	0	39	0	0	57	48	31	39	0	3.95
Backe, Brandon-Brandon Allen	02-03TBA 04-06HouN	04-05-78	Galveston, Texas		R	R	6'	188	19	14	.576	0	104	42	1	317	324	144	212	1	4.71
Bacsik, Mike-Michael Joseph	01CleA 02-03NYN 04TexA	11-11-77	Dallas, Tex.		L	L	6'3	190	5	5	.500	0	22	15	1	98	120	31	52	0	5.88
Bacsik, Mike-Michael James	75-77TexA 79-80MinA	04-01-52	Dallas, Tex.		R	R	6'2	190	8	6	.571	1	73	3	0	173	190	75	77	0	4.42
Baek, Cha-Seung-Cha-Seung	04,06SeaA	05-29-80	Pusan, South Korea		R	R	6'4	190	6	5	.545	0	13	11	0	65	61	24	43	0	4.55
Baez(Ceri), Benito-Benito Ceri [Baez]	01FlaN	05-06-77	Bonao, Dom. Rep.		L	L	6'	160	0	0	—	0	8	0	0	9	22	6	14	0	13.50
Baez, Danys-Danys Joseph	01-03CleA 04-05TBA 06LAN 06AtlN	09-10-77	Pinar Del Rio, Cuba		R	R	6'3	225	31	37	.456	111	341	26	1	491	445	201	390	0	3.79
Bahnsen, Stan-Stanley Raymond	66,68-71NYA 72-75ChiA 75-77OakA 77-81MonN 82CalN 82PhiN	12-15-44	Council Bluffs, Iowa		R	R	6'2	195	146	149	.495	20	574	327	73	2528	2440	924	1359	16	3.61
Bailes, Scott-Scott Alan	86-89CleA 90-92CalA 97-98TexA	12-18-61	Chillicothe, Ohio		L	L	6'2	175	39	44	.470	13	343	59	5	680	758	256	351	2	4.95
Bailey, Cory-Phillip Cory	93-94BosA 95-96StLN 97-98SFN 01-02KCA	01-24-71	Herrin, Ill.		R	R	6'1	210	9	10	.474	1	172	0	0	207	208	116	150	0	3.96
Bailey, Howard-Howard Lee	81-83DetA	07-31-57	Grand Haven, Mich.		R	L	6'1	195	6	9	.400	1	50	8	0	119	120	40	41	0	5.22
Bailey, Roger-Charles Roger	95-97ColN 98XJ-ZJ	10-03-70	Chattahoochee, Fla.		R	R	6'1	180	18	19	.486	1	92	46	5	356	392	161	162	2	4.90
Bair, Doug-Charles Douglas	76PitN 77OakA 78-81CinN 81-83StLN 83-85DetA 85StLN 86OakA 87PhiN 88TorA 89-90PitN	08-22-49	Defiance, Ohio		R	R	6'	190	55	43	.561	81	584	5	0	909	839	405	689	0	3.63
Bajenaru, Jeff-Jeffrey Michael	04-05ChiA 06AriN	03-21-78	Pomona, Cal.		R	R	6'1	190	0	2	.000	0	14	0	0	14	23	6	11	0	11.20
Baker, Scott-Scott	95OakA	05-18-70	San Jose, Cal.		L	L	6'2	175	0	0	—	0	5	0	0	5	5	3	3	0	9.82
Baker, Scott-Timothy Scott	05-06MinA	09-19-81	Shreveport, La.		R	R	6'4	220	8	11	.421	0	26	25	0	137	162	30	94	0	5.19
Baker, Steve-Steven Byrne	78-79DetA 82-83OakA 83StLN	08-30-56	Eugene, Ore.		R	R	6'	200	7	16	.304	6	84	26	0	237	262	127	131	0	5.13
Baldwin, James-James Jr.	95-01ChiA 01LAN 02SeaA 03MinA 04NYN 05BalA 05TexA 05BalA	07-15-71	Southern Pines, N.C.		R	R	6'3	235	79	74	.516	2	266	202	7	1323	1443	486	844	2	5.01
Baldwin, Rick-Rickey Alan	75-77NYN	06-01-53	Fresno, Cal.		L	R	6'3	175	4	7	.364	7	105	0	0	183	173	75	86	0	3.59
Bale, John-John Robert	99-00TorA 01BalA 03CinN	05-22-74	Cheverly, Md.		L	L	6'4	205	2	2	.500	0	27	9	0	79	75	34	68	0	4.69
Balfour, Grant-Grant Robert	01,03-04MinA 05-06EJ	12-30-77	Sydney, Australia		R	R	6'2	188	5	1	.833	0	55	1	0	68	61	38	74	0	4.63
Ballard, Jeff-Jeffrey Scott	87-91BalA 93-94PitN	08-13-63	Billings, Mont.		L	L	6'	210	41	53	.436	2	197	118	10	773	914	229	244	2	4.71
Baller, Jay-Jay Scot	82PhiN 85-87ChiN 90KCA 92PhiN	10-06-60	Stayton, Ore.		R	R	6'6	215	4	9	.308	6	94	5	0	156	169	79	117	0	5.24
Bane, Eddie-Edward Norman	73,75-76MinA	03-22-52	Great Lakes, Ill.		R	L	5'10	165	7	13	.350	2	44	25	1	167	182	84	80	0	4.69
Baney, Dick-Richard Lee	69SeaA 73-74CinN	11-01-46	Fullerton, Cal.		R	R	6'	200	4	1	.800	3	42	3	0	91	98	30	36	0	4.25
Bankhead, Scott-Michael Scott	86KCA 87-91SeaA 92CinN 93-94BosA 95NYA	07-31-63	Raleigh, N.C.		R	R	5'10	185	57	48	.543	1	267	110	7	901	867	289	614	3	4.18
Banks, Willie-Willie Anthony	91-93MinA 94-95ChiN 95LAN 95FlaN 97-98NYA 98AriN 99JL 01-02BosA	02-27-69	Jersey City, N.J.		R	R	6'1	202	33	39	.458	2	181	84	1	610	632	302	428	1	4.75
Bannister, Brian-Brian P.	06NYN	02-28-81	Scottsdale, Ariz.		R	R	6'2	200	2	1	.667	0	8	6	0	38	34	22	19	0	4.26
Bannister, Floyd-Floyd Franklin	77-78HouN 79-82SeaA 83-87ChiA 88-89KCA 90JL 91CalA 92TexA	06-10-55	Pierre, S.D.		L	L	6'1	195	134	143	.484	0	431	363	62	2388	2320	846	1723	16	4.06
Baptist, Travis-Travis Steven	98MinA	12-30-71	Forest Grove, Ore.		L	L	6'0	195	0	1	.000	0	13	0	0	27	34	11	11	0	5.67
Barber, Brian-Brian Scott	95-96StLN 98-99KCA	03-04-73	Hamilton, Ohio		R	R	6'1	190	5	8	.385	1	26	16	0	93	111	45	59	0	6.77
Barcelo, Lorenzo-Lorenzo Antonio	00-02ChiA	08-10-77	San Pedro de Mac., D.R.		R	R	6'4	220	5	3	.625	0	43	1	0	66	67	18	42	0	4.50
Bare, Ray-Raymond Douglas	72-74StLN 75-77DetA	04-15-49	Miami, Fla.	03-29-94	R	R	6'2	193	16	26	.381	1	88	49	9	340	398	120	145	3	4.79
Barfield, John-John David	89-91TexA	10-15-64	Pine Bluff, Ark.		L	L	6'1	185	8	8	.500	2	65	11	0	139	153	39	53	0	4.72
Bargar, Greg-Greg Robert	83-84MonN 86StLN	01-27-59	Inglewood, Cal.		R	R	6'2	185	2	3	.400	0	33	4	0	55	67	25	23	0	6.34
Bark, Brian-Brian Stuart	95BosA	08-26-68	Baltimore, Md.		L	L	5'9	170	0	0	—	0	3	0	0	2	2	1	0	0	0.00
Barker, Len-Leonard Harold	76-78TexA 79-83CleA 83-85AtlN 87MilA	07-07-55	Fort Knox, Ky.		R	R	6'5	225	74	76	.493	5	248	194	35	1323	1289	513	975	6	4.35
Barker, Rich-Richard Frank	99ChiN	10-29-72	Revere, Mass.		R	R	6'2	220	0	0	—	0	5	0	0	5	6	4	3	0	7.20
Barkley, Brian-Brian Edward	98BosA	12-08-75	Conroe, Tex.		L	L	6'2	170	0	0	—	0	6	0	0	11	16	9	2	0	9.82
Barkley, Jeff-Jeffrey Carver	84-85CleA	05-31-59	Hickory, N.C.		B	R	6'3	185	0	3	.000	0	24	0	0	45	43	16	34	0	5.40
Barlow, Mike-Michael Roswell	75StLN 76HouN 77-79CalA 80-81TorA	04-30-48	Stamford, N.Y.		L	R	6'6	215	10	6	.625	6	133	2	0	247	279	104	96	0	4.63
Barnes, Brian-Brian Keith	90-93MonN 94CleA 94LAN	03-25-67	Roanoke Rapids, N.C.		L	L	5'9	170	14	22	.389	3	116	56	2	406	364	204	275	0	3.94
Barnes, Rich-Richard Monroe (Rico)	82ChiA 83CleA	07-21-59	Palm Beach, Fla.		B	L	6'1	190	1	3	.250	1	10	4	0	29	39	14	8	0	5.65
Barojas, Salome-Salome [Romero]	82-84ChiA 84-85SeaA 88AtlN	06-16-57	Cordoba, Mexico		R	R	5'9	183	18	21	.462	35	179	18	0	390	374	179	177	0	3.95
Barr, Jim-James Leland	71-78SFN 79-80CalA 82-83SFN	02-10-48	Los Angeles, Cal.		R	R	6'2	215	101	112	.474	12	454	252	64	2065	2170	469	741	20	3.56
Barr, Steve-Steven Charles	74-75BosA 76TexA	09-08-51	St.Louis, Mo.		L	L	6'4	200	3	7	.300	0	24	13	4	84	88	57	32	0	5.14
Barrett, Tim-Timothy Wayne	88-89MonN	01-24-61	Huntingburg, Ind.		R	R	6'1	185	0	0	—	1	4	0	0	9	10	2	5	0	5.79
Barrios, Francisco-Francisco Javier [Jiminez] (Frankie)	74,76-81ChiA	06-10-53	Hemosillo, Mexico	04-09-82	R	R	6'3	200	38	38	.500	3	129	102	27	718	718	246	323	2	4.15
Barrios, Manuel-Manuel Antonio	97HouN 98FlaN 98LAN	09-21-74	Cabecera, Panama		R	R	6'0	185	0	0	—	0	5	0	0	7	10	7	4	0	6.75
Barry, Kevin-Kevin Thomas	06AtlN	08-18-78	Princeton, N.J.		R	R	6'2	235	1	1	.500	0	19	1	0	26	24	14	19	0	5.61
Barton, Shawn-Shawn Edward	92SeaA 95-96SFN	05-14-63	Los Angeles, Cal.		R	L	6'3	195	4	2	.667	1	73	0	0	65	66	27	29	0	4.71
Bartosh, Cliff-Clifford Paul	04CleA 05ChiN	09-05-79	West, Tex.		L	L	6'2	180	1	2	.333	0	53	0	0	39	45	22	40	0	5.08
Barzilla, Philip-Philip Joseph	05HouN	01-25-79	Houston, Tex.		R	R	6'1	180	0	0	—	0	1	0	0	1	3	1	0	0	0.00
Batchelor, Rich-Richard Anthony	93,96-97StLN 97SDN	04-08-67	Florence, S.C.		R	R	6'1	195	5	1	.833	0	43	0	0	54	63	18	33	0	5.03
Batista, Miguel-Miguel Jerez [Decartes]	92PitN 96FlaN 97ChiN 98-00MonN 00KCA 01-03AriN 04-05TorA 06AriN	02-19-71	Santo Domingo, D.R.		R	R	6'	190	68	79	.463	37	397	185	10	1382	1420	591	870	4	4.46
Batton, Chris-Christopher Sean (Duke)	76OakA	08-24-54	Los Angeles, Cal.		R	R	6'	195	0	0	—	0	2	1	0	4	5	3	4	0	9.00
Bauer, Rick-Richard Edward	01-05BalA 06TexA	01-10-77	Garden Grove, Cal.		R	R	6'6	212	11	14	.440	3	183	0	0	311	312	118	181	0	4.34
Baumgarten, Ross-Ross (Bomber)	78-81ChiA 82PitN	05-27-55	Highland Park, Ill.		L	L	6'1	180	22	36	.379	0	90	84	10	496	492	211	222	4	3.99
Bautista, Denny-Denny M.	04BalA 04-06KCA 06ColN	08-23-80	Sanchez, Dom. Rep.		R	R	6'3	170	2	9	.182	0	26	20	0	107	127	51	69	0	6.48
Bautista, Jose-Jose Joaquin [Arias]	88-91BalA 93-94ChiN 95-96SFN 97DetA 97StLN	07-25-64	Bani, Dom. Rep.		R	R	6'1	177	32	42	.432	3	312	49	4	686	732	171	328	0	4.62
Bayliss, Jonah-Jonah James	05KCA 06PitN	08-13-80	North Adams, Mass.		R	R	6'2	210	1	1	.500	0	22	0	0	26	20	15	25	0	4.44
Bazardo, Yorman-Yorman Michael [Osoric]	05FlaN	07-11-84	Maracay, Venezuela		R	R	6'2	202	0	0	—	0	5	2	0	5	2	2	2	0	21.60
Beam, T.J.-Theodore Lester	06NYA	08-28-80	Scottsdale, Ariz.		R	R	6'7	215	2	0	1.000	0	20	0	0	18	26	6	12	0	8.50
Bean, Colter-Randall Colter	05-06NYA	01-16-77	Anniston, Ala.		R	R	6'6	255	0	0	—	0	3	0	0	4	3	4	3	0	6.75
Beard, Dave-David David	80-83OakA 84SeaA 85ChiN 89DetA	10-02-59	Atlanta, Ga.		R	R	6'5	215	19	20	.487	30	172	3	0	276	274	124	185	0	4.70
Beard, Mike-Michael Richard	74-77AtlN	06-21-50	Little Rock, Ark.		L	L	6'1	185	4	2	.667	1	74	2	0	118	128	45	43	0	3.74
Beare, Gary-Gary Ray	76-77MilA	08-22-52	San Diego, Cal.		R	R	6'4	210	5	6	.455	0	23	11	2	100	106	53	64	0	5.13
Bearse, Kevin-Kevin Gerard	90CleA	11-07-65	Jersey City, N.J.		L	L	6'2	195	0	3	.000	0	8	3	0	16	16	5	2	0	12.91
Beasley, Chris-Christopher Charles	91CalA	06-23-62	Jackson, Tenn.		R	R	6'2	190	0	1	.000	0	22	0	0	27	26	10	14	0	3.38
Beattie, Jim-James Louis	78-79NYA 80-86SeaA	07-04-54	Hampton, Va.		R	R	6'5	220	52	87	.374	0	203	182	31	1149	1174	461	660	7	4.17
Beatty, Blaine-Gordon Blaine	89NYN 90EJ 91NYN	04-25-64	Victoria, Tex.		L	L	6'2	185	0	0	—	0	7	1	0	16	14	6	10	0	2.30
Bechler, Steve-Steven Scott	02BalA	11-18-79	Medford, Ore.	02-17-03	R	R	6'2	239	0	0	—	0	3	0	0	5	5	2	1	0	13.50
Beck, Rod-Rodney Roy	91-97SFN 98-99ChiN 99-01BosA 03-04SDN	08-03-68	Burbank, Cal.		R	R	6'1	235	38	45	.458	286	704	0	0	768	703	191	644	0	3.30
Beckett, Josh-Joshua Patrick	01-05FlaN 06BosA	05-15-80	Spring, Tex.		R	R	6'5	200	57	45	.559	0	139	136	3	814	720	297	765	2	3.85
Beckett, Robbie-Robert Joseph	96-97ColN	07-16-72	Austin, Tex.		R	L	6'5	240	0	0	—	0	7	0	0	7	11	10	8	0	11.57
Beckwith, Joe-Thomas Joseph (Cotton)	79-80LAN 81LJ 82-83LAN 84-85KCA 86LAN	01-28-55	Opelika, Ala.		R	R	6'3	200	18	19	.486	7	229	5	0	422	432	150	319	0	3.54
Bedard, Erik-Erik Joseph	02,04-06BalA	03-05-79	Naum, Canada		L	L	6'1	186	27	29	.482	0	86	83	0	476	486	197	418	0	4.08
Bedrosian, Steve-Stephen Wayne (Bedrock)	81-85AtlN 86-89PhiN 89-90SFN 91MinA 93-95AtlN	12-06-57	Methuen, Mass.		R	R	6'4	205	76	79	.490	184	732	46	0	1191	1026	518	921	0	3.38

USE NAMES - GIVEN NAMES (NICKNAMES) / TEAM BY YEAR	BIRTH DATE	BIRTHPLACE	DEATH DATE	B	T	HGT	WGT	W	L	Pct.	SV	G	GS	CG	IP	H	BB	SO	ShO	ERA
Beech, Matt-Lucas Matthew 96-98PhiN 99EJ	01-20-72	Oakland, Cal.		L	L	6'2	190	8	22	.267	0	53	53	0	295	322	131	266	0	5.37
Beene, Andy-Ramon Andrew 83-84MilA	10-13-56	Freeport, Tex.		R	R	6'3	205	0	2	.000	0	6	3	0	21	31	10	11	0	10.45
Behenna, Rick-Richard Kipp 83AtlN 83-85CleA	03-06-60	Miami, Fla.		R	R	6'2	170	3	10	.231	0	26	17	0	93	105	42	36	0	6.12
Beimel, Joe-Joseph Ronald 01-03PitN 04MinA 05TBA 06LAN	04-19-77	St. Mary's, Pa.		L	L	6'3	215	12	20	.375	2	236	23	0	346	381	154	188	0	4.71
Beirne, Kevin-Kevin Patrick 00ChiA 01TorA 02LAN	01-01-74	Houston, Tex.		L	R	6'4	210	3	3	.500	0	46	4	0	86	89	43	63	0	6.09
Belcher, Tim-Timothy Wayne 87-91LAN 92-93CinN 93ChiA 94DetA 95SeaA 96-98KCA 99-00AnaA	10-19-61	Mount Gilead, Ohio		R	R	6'3	225	146	140	.510	5	394	373	42	2443	2423	860	1519	18	4.16
Belinda, Stan-Stanley Peter 89-93PitN 93-94KCA 95-96BosA 97-99CinN 00ColN 00AtlN	08-06-66	Huntingdon, Pa.		R	R	6'3	210	41	37	.526	79	585	0	0	685	590	285	622	0	4.15
Belisle, Matt-Matthew Thomas 03,05-06CinN	06-06-80	Austin, Texas		B	R	6'3	195	7	9	.438	1	96	7	0	134	154	47	91	0	4.22
Belitz, Todd-Todd Stephen 00OakA 01ColN	10-23-75	Des Moines, Iowa		L	L	6'3	220	1	1	.500	0	13	0	0	13	13	7	8	0	6.39
Bell, Eric-Eric Alvin 85-87BalA 91-92CleA 93HouN	10-27-63	Modesto, Cal.		L	L	6'	175	15	18	.455	0	68	34	2	235	238	112	152	0	5.18
Bell, Heath-Heath Justin 04-06NYN	09-29-77	Oceanside, Cal.		R	R	6'2	244	1	5	.167	0	81	0	0	108	129	30	105	0	4.92
Bell, Jerry-Jerry Houston 71-74MilA	10-06-47	Madison, Tenn.		B	R	6'4	195	17	11	.607	5	69	28	8	284	262	114	89	0	3.26
Bell, Rob-Robert Allen 00-01CinN 01-02TexA 03-05TBA	01-17-77	Newburgh, N.Y.		R	R	6'5	225	30	34	.469	0	121	108	2	633	684	264	393	0	5.69
Beltran, Francis-Francis LeBron 02,04ChiN 04MonN 05EJ	11-29-79	Santo Domingo, D.R.		R	R	6'5	230	2	2	.500	0	56	0	0	61	61	43	59	0	5.87
Beltran, Rigo-Rigoberto 97StLN 98-99NYN 99-00ColN 02JL 04MonN	11-13-69	Tijuana, Mexico		L	L	5'11	195	2	3	.400	1	78	5	0	106	110	43	106	0	4.40
Benes, Alan-Alan Paul 95-97StLN 98SJ 99-01StLN 02-03ChiN 03TexA	01-21-72	Evansville, Ind.		R	R	6'5	235	29	28	.509	0	115	70	5	494	493	220	401	1	4.59
Benes, Andy-Andrew Charles 89-95SDN 95SeaA 96-97StLN 98-99AriN 00-02StLN	08-20-67	Evansville, Ind.		R	R	6'6	240	155	139	.527	1	403	387	21	2505	2377	909	2000	9	3.97
Benitez, Armando-Armando German 94-98BalA 99-03NYN 03NYA 03SeaA 04FlaN 05-06SFN	11-03-72	Ramon Santana, D.R.		R	R	6'4	230	38	38	.500	280	699	0	0	722	492	372	880	0	2.95
Bennett, Erik-Erik Hans 95CalA 96MinA	09-13-68	Yreka, Cal.		R	R	6'2	205	2	0	1.000	1	25	0	0	28	33	16	13	0	7.81
Bennett, Jeff-David Jeffrey 04MilN	06-10-80	Donelson, Tenn.		R	R	6'3	205	1	5	.167	0	60	0	0	71	78	26	45	0	4.79
Bennett, Joel-Joel Todd 98BalA 99PhiN	01-31-70	Binghamton, N.Y.		R	R	6'1	160	2	1	.667	0	7	3	0	19	28	10	13	0	8.53
Bennett, Shayne-Shayne Anthony 97-99MonN	04-10-72	Adelaide, Australia		R	R	6'5	220	5	7	.417	1	83	1	0	126	142	57	71	0	5.87
Benoit, Joaquin-Joaquin Antonio [Pena] 01-06TexA	07-26-77	Santiago, Dom. Rep.		R	R	6'3	205	20	20	.500	1	159	55	0	464	448	219	408	0	5.12
Benson, Kris-Kristen James 99-00PitN 01EJ 02-04PitN 04-05NYN 06BalA	11-07-74	Superior, Wis.		R	R	6'4	200	68	73	.482	0	195	195	8	1207	1241	423	787	2	4.34
Bentz, Chad-Chad Robert 04MonN 05FlaN	05-05-80	Seward, Alaska		R	L	6'2	215	0	3	.000	0	40	0	0	30	31	23	18	0	7.58
Bere, Jason-Jason Phillip 93-98ChiA 98-99CinN 99-00MilN 00CleA 01-03CinN	05-26-71	Cambridge, Mass.		R	R	6'3	210	71	65	.522	0	211	203	4	1111	1095	626	920	0	5.14
Berenguer, Juan-Juan Bautista (Panama Express) 79-80NYN 81KCA 81TorA 82-85DetA 86SFN 87-90MinA 91-92AtlN 92KCA	11-30-54	Aguadulce, Panama		R	R	5'11	215	67	62	.519	32	490	95	5	1206	1034	604	975	2	3.90
Berenyi, Bruce-Bruce Michael 80-84CinN 84-86NYN	08-21-54	Bryan, Ohio		R	R	6'3	215	44	55	.444	0	142	131	13	782	730	425	607	5	4.03
Bergman, Dusty-Dustin Michael 04AnaA	02-01-78	Carson City, Nev.		L	L	6'5	200	0	0	—	0	1	0	0	2	4	1	1	0	13.50
Bergman, Sean-Sean Frederick 93-95DetA 96-97SDN 98-99HouN 99AtlN 00MinA	04-11-70	Joliet, Ill.		R	R	6'4	200	39	47	.453	0	196	117	5	750	912	272	455	2	5.28
Bergmann, Jason-Jason Chris (Jay) 05-06WasN	09-25-81	Manalapan, N.J.		R	R	6'4	205	2	2	.500	0	44	7	0	84	95	38	75	0	5.76
Bernal, Vic-Victor Hugo 77SDN	10-06-53	Los Angeles, Cal.	09-02-06	R	R	6'	177	1	1	.500	0	15	0	0	20	23	9	6	0	5.40
Bernard, Dwight-Dwight Vern (D) 78-79NYN 81-82MilA	05-31-52	Mount Vernon, Ill.		R	R	6'2	170	4	8	.333	6	115	2	0	176	196	86	92	0	4.14
Bernero, Adam-Adam Gino 00-03DetA 03-04ColN 05AtlN 06PhiN 06KCA	11-28-76	San Jose, Cal.		R	R	6'4	205	11	27	.289	0	150	37	0	376	430	133	247	0	5.91
Bertotti, Mike-Michael David 95-97ChiA	01-18-70	Jersey City, N.J.		L	L	6'1	185	3	1	.750	0	28	6	0	46	60	33	38	0	7.63
Berumen, Andres-Andres 95-96SDN	04-05-71	Tijuana, Mexico		R	R	6'2	210	2	3	.400	1	40	0	0	48	40	38	46	0	5.66
Best, Karl-Karl Jon 83-86SeaA 88MinA 89EJ	03-06-59	Aberdeen, Wash.		R	R	6'5	205	5	6	.455	5	61	0	0	91	96	39	73	0	4.04
Betancourt, Rafael-Rafael Jose 03-06CleA	04-29-75	Cumana, Venezuela		R	R	6'2	200	14	15	.483	9	205	0	0	229	207	59	233	0	3.26
Bettendorf, Jeff-Jeffrey Allen 84OakA	12-10-60	Lompoc, Cal.		R	R	6'3	180	0	0	—	0	3	0	0	10	9	5	4	0	4.66
Beverlin, Jason-Jason Robert 02CleA 02DetA	11-27-73	Ashtabula, Ohio		L	R	6'5	220	0	3	.000	0	7	3	0	20	27	9	16	0	8.69
Bevil, Brian-Brian Scott 96-98KCA	09-05-71	Houston, Tex.		R	R	6'3	190	5	3	.625	1	60	1	0	67	72	36	67	0	6.28
Bibby, Jim-James Blair 72-73StLN 73-75TexA 75-77CleA 78-81PitN 82SJ 83PitN 84TexA	10-29-44	Franklinton, N.C.		R	R	6'4	240	111	101	.524	8	340	239	56	1723	1565	723	1079	19	3.76
Biddle, Rocky-Lee Francis 00-02ChiA 03-04MonN	05-21-76	Las Vegas, Nev.		R	R	6'3	230	20	30	.400	46	198	41	0	379	409	170	261	0	5.47
Bielecki, Mike-Michael Joseph 84-87PitN 88-91ChiN 91-92AtlN 93CleA 94AtlN 95CalA 96-97AtlN	07-31-59	Baltimore, Md		R	R	6'3	200	70	73	.490	5	347	178	7	1231	1236	496	783	4	4.18
Bierbrodt, Nick-Nicholas Raymond 01AriN 01,03TBA 03CleA 04TexA	05-16-78	Tarzana, Cal.		L	L	6'5	210	6	9	.400	0	38	25	0	145	178	85	112	0	6.66
Billingham, Jack-John Eugene 68LAN 69-71HouN 72-77CinN 78-80DetA 80BosA	02-21-43	Orlando, Fla.		R	R	6'4	210	145	113	.562	15	476	305	74	2231	2272	750	1141	27	3.83
Billingsley, Brent-Brent Aaron 99FlaN	04-19-75	Downey, Calif.		L	L	6'2	200	0	0	—	0	8	0	0	8	11	10	3	0	16.43
Billingsley, Chad-Chad Ryan 06LAN	07-29-84	Defiance, Ohio		R	R	6'	245	7	4	.636	0	18	16	0	90	92	58	59	0	3.80
Bird, Doug-James Douglas 73-78KCA 79PhiN 80-81NYA 81-82ChiN 83BosA	03-05-50	Corona, Cal.		R	R	6'1	190	73	60	.549	60	432	100	16	1213	1273	296	680	3	3.99
Birkbeck, Mike-Michael Lawrence 86-89MilA 92,95NYN	03-10-61	Orrville, Ohio		R	R	6'1	190	12	19	.387	0	54	51	2	270	319	93	149	0	4.86
Birkins, Kurt-Kurt Daniel 06BalA	08-11-80	West Hills, Cal.		L	L	6'2	190	5	2	.714	0	35	0	0	31	25	16	27	0	4.94
Birtsas, Tim-Timothy Dean (Big Bird) 85-86OakA 88-90CinN	09-05-60	Pontiac, Mich.		L	L	6'7	240	14	14	.500	1	138	30	2	329	324	170	231	0	4.08
Bitker, Joe-Joseph Anthony 90OakA 90-91TexA	02-12-64	Glendale, Cal.		R	R	6'	175	1	0	1.000	0	15	0	0	27	25	12	24	0	4.72
Bittiger, Jeff-Jeffrey Scott 86PhiN 87MinA 88-89ChiA	04-13-62	Jersey City, N.J.		R	R	5'10	175	4	6	.400	0	33	12	0	94	95	42	53	0	4.77
Black, Bud-Harry Ralston (Buddy) 81SeaA 82-88KCA 88-90CleA 90TorA 91-94SFN 95CleA	06-30-57	San Mateo, Cal.		L	L	6'1	180	121	116	.511	11	398	296	12	2053	1978	623	1039	12	3.84
Blackley, Travis-Travis Jarrod 04SeaA	11-04-82	Melbourne, Australia		L	L	6'3	190	1	3	.250	0	6	6	0	26	35	22	16	0	10.04
Blair, Dennis-Dennis Herman 74-76MonN 80SDN	06-05-54	Middletown, Ohio		R	R	6'5	190	19	25	.432	0	62	54	6	339	302	192	178	1	3.69
Blair, Willie-William Allen 90TorA 91CleA 92HouN 93-94ColN 95-96SDN 97DetA 98AriN 98NYN 99-01DetA	12-18-65	Paintsville, Ky.		R	R	6'1	185	60	86	.411	4	418	139	3	1274	1438	415	759	0	5.04
Bland, Nate-Nathan Garrett 03HouN	12-27-74	Birmingham, Ala.		L	L	6'5	190	1	2	.333	0	22	0	0	20	22	12	16	0	5.75
Blank, Matt-Clarence Matthew 00-01MonN	04-05-76	Texarkana, Tex.		L	L	6'2	200	2	3	.400	0	18	4	0	37	35	18	15	0	5.15
Blankenship, Kevin-Kevin DeWayne 88AtlN 88-90ChiN	01-26-63	Anaheim, Cal.		R	R	6'	175	1	3	.250	0	8	5	0	33	31	16	16	0	4.59
Blanton, Joe-Joseph Matthew 04-06OakA	12-11-80	Bowling Green, Ky.		R	R	6'3	225	28	24	.538	0	68	64	3	404	425	127	229	1	4.19
Blazier, Ron-Ronald Patrick 96-97PhiN	07-30-71	Altoona, Pa.		R	R	6'6	215	4	2	.667	0	63	0	0	92	111	31	67	0	5.38
Blomdahl, Ben-Benjamin Earl 95DetA	12-30-70	Long Beach, Cal.		R	R	6'2	185	0	0	—	1	14	0	0	24	36	13	15	0	7.77
Blue, Vida-Vida Rochelle 69-77OakA 78-81SFN 82-83KCA 85-86SFN	07-28-49	Mansfield, La.		B	L	6'	200	209	161	.565	2	502	473	143	3343	2939	1185	2175	37	3.27
Bluma, Jaime-James Andrew 96KCA 97SJ	05-18-72	Beaufort, S.C.		R	R	5'11	195	0	0	—	5	17	0	0	20	18	4	14	0	3.60
Blyleven (Blijleven),Bert-Rik Aalbert 70-76MinA 76-77TexA 78-80PitN 81-85CalA 85-88MinA 89-90CalA 91EJ 92CalA	04-06-51	Zeist, Netherlands		R	R	6'3	210	287	250	.534	0	692	685	242	4970	4632	1322	3701	60	3.31
Bochtler, Doug-Douglas Eugene 95-97SDN 98DetA 99LAN 00KCA	07-05-70	West Palm Beach, Fla.		R	R	6'3	205	9	18	.333	6	220	0	0	260	231	166	215	0	4.57
Bockus, Randy-Randy Walter 86-88SFN 89DetA	10-05-60	Canton, Ohio		L	R	6'2	205	2	3	.400	0	39	0	0	62	66	25	33	0	4.23
Boddicker, Mike-Michael James 80-88BalA 88-90BosA 91-93KCA 93MilA	08-23-57	Cedar Rapids, Iowa		R	R	6'	185	134	116	.536	3	342	309	63	2124	2082	721	1330	16	3.80
Boehringer, Brian-Brian Edward 95-97NYA 98-00SDN 01NYA 01SFN 02-04PitN	01-08-69	St. Louis, Mo.		B	R	6'2	190	26	32	.448	9	356	21	0	535	522	274	432	0	4.36
Boever, Joe-Joseph Martin 85-86StLN 87-90AtlN 90-91PhiN 92HouN 93OakA 93-95DetA 96PitN	10-04-60	Kirkwood, Mo.		R	R	6'1	200	34	45	.430	49	516	0	0	754	751	343	541	0	3.93
Boggs, Tommy-Thomas Winton 76-77TexA 78-83AtlN 85TexA	10-25-55	Poughkeepsie, N.Y.		R	R	6'2	200	20	44	.313	0	114	94	10	587	612	201	278	4	4.23
Bohanon, Brian-Brian Edward Jr. 90-94TexA 95DetA 96TorA 97-98NYN 98LAN 99-01ColN	08-01-68	Denton, Tex.		L	L	6'2	230	54	60	.474	2	304	157	8	1116	1229	489	671	2	5.19
Bohnet, John-John Kelly (Brinks) 82NYA	01-18-61	Pasadena, Cal.		B	L	6'	180	0	0	—	0	3	0	0	12	11	7	4	0	6.94
Boitano, Danny-Danny Jon 78PhiN 79-80MilA 81NYN 82TexA	03-22-53	Sacramento, Cal.		R	R	6'3	190	2	2	.500	2	51	0	0	71	86	28	52	0	5.68
Bolton, Rodney-Rodney Earl 93,95ChiA	09-23-68	Chattanooga, Tenn.		R	R	6'2	190	2	8	.200	0	17	11	0	64	88	30	27	0	7.69
Bolton, Tom-Thomas Edward 87-92BosA 92CinN 93DetA 94BalA	05-06-62	Nashville, Tenn.		L	L	6'3	185	31	34	.477	1	209	56	3	540	614	244	336	0	4.56
Bomback, Mark-Mark Vincent (Bomber) 78MilA 80NYN 81-82TorA	04-14-53	Portsmouth, Va.		R	R	5'11	180	16	18	.471	0	74	45	2	317	367	110	124	1	4.47
Bonderman, Jeremy-Jeremy Allen 03-06DetA	10-28-82	Kennewick, Wash.		R	R	6'2	210	45	53	.459	0	129	123	6	749	774	252	623	2	4.72
Bones, Ricky-Ricardo 91SDN 92-96MilA 96NYA 97CinN 97-98KCA 99BalA 00-01FlaN	04-07-69	Salinas, P.R.		R	R	5'10	200	63	82	.434	11	375	164	11	1278	1422	464	564	1	4.85
Bong, Jung-Jung Kuen 02-03AtlN 04CinN	07-15-80	Seoul, South Korea		L	L	6'3	175	7	4	.636	1	48	4	0	78	81	43	62	0	5.17
Bonham, Bill-William Gordon 71-77ChiN 78-80CinN 81EJ	10-01-48	Glendale, Calif.		R	R	6'3	195	75	83	.475	11	300	214	28	1488	1512	636	985	4	4.00
Bonser, Boof-Boof 06MinA	10-14-81	St. Petersburg, Fla.		R	R	6'4	260	7	6	.538	0	18	18	0	100	104	24	84	0	4.22
Booker, Chris-Christopher Scott 05CinN 06PhiN 06KCA 06WasN	12-09-76	Monroeville, Ala.		R	R	6'3	235	0	0	—	0	14	0	0	10	16	8	9	0	13.94
Booker, Greg-Gregory Scott 83-89SDN 89MinA 90SFN	06-22-60	Lynchburg, Va.		R	R	6'6	240	5	7	.417	1	161	4	0	264	278	118	119	0	3.89
Boone, Dan-Daniel Hugh 81-82SDN 82HouN 90BalA	01-14-54	Long Beach, Cal.		L	L	5'8	132	2	1	.667	4	61	1	0	101	103	31	57	0	3.38
Bootcheck, Chris-Christopher Brandon 03AnaA 05-06LAA	10-24-78	La Porte, Ind.		R	R	6'3	200	0	3	.000	0	39	5	0	51	19	22	28	0	6.86
Borbon, Pedro-Pedro [Rodriguez] 69CalA 70-79CinN 79SFN 80StLN	12-02-46	Valverde de Mao, D.R.		R	R	6'2	195	69	39	.639	80	593	4	0	1026	1098	251	409	0	3.52
Bordon, Pedro-Pedro Felix Jr. [Marte] 92-93,95-96AtlN 97EJ-KJ 98EJ 99LAN 00-02TorA 02HouN 03StLN	11-15-67	Valverde de Mao, D.R.		L	L	6'1	215	16	16	.500	0	368	0	0	271	259	134	224	0	4.68
Bordi, Rich-Richard Albert 80-81OakA 82SeaA 83-84ChiN 85NYA 86BalA 87NYA 88OakA	04-18-59	S. San Francisco, Cal.		R	R	6'7	220	20	20	.500	10	173	17	0	371	383	121	247	0	4.34

USE NAMES - GIVEN NAMES (NICKNAMES)	TEAM BY YEAR	BIRTH DATE	BIRTHPLACE	DEATH DATE	B	T	HGT	WGT	W	L	Pct.	SV	G	GS	CG	IP	H	BB	SO	ShO	ERA
Bordley, Bill-William Clarke	80SFN 81-82EJ	01-09-58	Los Angeles, Cal.		L	L	6'2	195	2	3	.400	0	8	6	0	31	34	21	11	0	4.65
Boris, Paul-Paul Stanley (Bo)	82MinA	12-13-55	Irvington, N.J.		R	R	6'2	200	1	2	.333	0	23	0	0	50	46	19	30	0	3.99
Borkowski, Dave-David Richard	99-01DetA 04BalA 06HouN	02-07-77	Detroit, Mich.		R	R	6'1	200	8	15	.348	0	91	21	0	239	262	100	178	0	5.84
Borland, Toby-Toby Shawn	94-96PhiN 97NYN 97BosA 98PhiN 01AnaA 02-04FlaN	05-29-69	Ruston, La.		R	R	6'6	210	11	9	.550	8	207	0	0	270	263	146	211	0	4.17
Borowski, Joe-Joseph Thomas	95BalA 96-97AtlN 97-98NYA 01-05ChiN 05TBA 06FlaN	05-04-71	Bayonne, N.J.		R	R	6'2	225	17	26	.395	80	336	1	0	372	349	152	305	0	3.87
Bosio, Chris-Christopher Louis	86-92MilA 93-96SeaA	04-03-63	Carmichael, Cal.		R	R	6'3	230	94	93	.503	9	309	246	39	1710	1742	481	1059	9	3.96
Boskie, Shawn-Shawn Kealoha	90-94ChiN 94PhiN 94SeaA 95-96CalA 97BalA 98MonN	03-28-67	Hawthorne, Nev.		R	R	6'3	205	49	63	.438	1	217	132	4	870	982	292	494	0	5.14
Botelho, Derek-Derek Wayne (Bo)	82KCA 85ChiN	08-02-56	Long Beach, Cal.		R	R	6'2	180	2	4	.429	0	19	11	1	68	77	31	35	0	4.90
Bottalico, Ricky-Ricky Paul	94-98PhiN 99StLN 00KCA 01-02PhiN 03AriN 04NYN 05MilN	08-26-69	New Britain, Conn.		L	R	6'1	210	33	42	.440	116	562	0	0	629	561	316	575	0	3.99
Bottenfield, Kent-Kent Dennis	92-93MonN 93-94ColN 94SFN 96-97ChiN 98-99StLN 00AnaA 00PhiN 01HouN (Bats Both 92-93)	11-14-68	Portland, Ore.		R	R	6'3	230	46	49	.484	10	292	116	2	912	950	385	566	1	4.54
Botting, Ralph-Ralph Wayne	79-80CalA	05-12-55	Houlton, Maine		L	L	6'	190	2	3	.400	0	18	7	0	56	86	28	34	0	7.39
Boucher, Denis-Denis	91TorA 91-92CleA 93-94MonN	03-07-68	Montreal, Canada		R	L	6'1	195	6	11	.353	0	35	26	0	146	170	54	77	0	5.42
Bourgeois, Steve-Steven James	96SFN	08-04-72	Lutcher, La.		R	R	6'1	200	1	3	.250	0	15	5	0	40	60	21	17	0	6.30
Bovee, Mike-Michael Craig	97AnaA	08-21-73	San Diego, Cal.		R	R	5'10	200	0	0	—	0	3	0	0	3	3	1	5	0	5.40
Bowen, Ryan-Ryan Eugene	91-92HouN 93-95FlaN	02-10-68	Hanford, Cal.		R	R	6'	185	17	28	.378	0	64	60	3	326	350	184	216	1	5.30
Bowers, Shane-Shane Patrick	97MinA	07-27-71	Glendora, Cal.		R	R	6'4	215	0	3	.000	0	5	5	0	19	27	8	7	0	8.05
Bowie, Micah-Micah Andrew	99AtlN 99ChiN 02-03OakA 06WasN	11-10-74	Humble, Texas		L	L	6'4	210	4	9	.308	0	48	11	0	91	117	51	64	0	6.92
Bowles, Brian-Brian Christopher	01-03TorA	08-18-76	Los Angeles, Cal.		R	R	6'5	220	2	1	.667	0	24	0	0	31	25	17	25	0	3.23
Bowyer, Travis-Travis Charlton	05MinA	08-03-81	Lynchburg, Va.		R	R	6'3	210	0	1	.000	0	8	0	0	10	10	3	12	0	5.59
Boyd, Jason-Jason Pernell	99PitN 00PhiN 02SDN 03CleA 04PitN	02-23-73	St. Clair, Ill.		R	R	6'3	175	5	2	.714	0	113	0	0	133	128	75	97	0	5.74
Boyd, Oil Can-Dennis Ray	82-89BosA 90-91MonN 91TexA	10-06-59	Meridian, Miss.		R	R	6'1	160	78	77	.503	0	214	207	43	1390	1427	368	799	10	4.04
Boyer, Blaine-Blaine Thomas	05-06AtlN	07-11-81	Atlanta, Ga.		R	R	6'3	215	4	2	.667	0	45	0	0	38	36	18	33	0	3.76
Boze, Marshall-Marshall Wayne	96MilA	05-23-71	San Manuel, Ariz.		R	R	6'1	215	0	0	—	1	25	0	0	32	47	25	19	0	7.79
Bradford, Chad-Chadwick Lee	98-00ChiA 01-05OakA 05BosA 06NYN	09-14-74	Jackson, Miss.		R	R	6'5	205	27	18	.600	9	395	0	0	381	369	104	261	0	3.40
Bradford, Larry-Larry	77,79-81AtlN	12-21-49	Chicago, Ill	09-11-98	R	L	6'1	205	6	4	.600	1	104	0	0	104	89	44	58	0	2.51
Bradley, Bert-Steven Bert	83OakA	12-23-56	Athens, Ga.		B	R	6'1	190	0	0	—	0	6	0	0	8	14	4	3	0	6.48
Bradley, Ryan-Ryan James	98NYA	10-26-75	Covina, Cal.		R	R	6'6	225	2	1	.667	0	5	1	0	13	12	9	13	0	5.68
Branch, Roy-Roy	79SeaA	07-12-53	St. Louis, Mo.		R	R	6'	190	0	1	.000	0	2	2	0	11	12	7	6	0	8.18
Brandenburg, Mark-Mark Clay	95-96TexA 96-97BosA 98TJ	07-14-70	Houston, Tex.		R	R	6'	180	5	8	.385	0	97	0	0	144	161	56	121	0	4.49
Brantley, Cliff-Clifford	91-92PhiN	04-12-68	Staten Island, N.Y.		R	R	6'2	215	4	8	.333	0	34	14	0	108	97	77	57	0	4.25
Brantley, Jeff-Jeffrey Hoke	88-93SFN 94-97CinN 98StLN 99-00PhiN 01TexA	09-05-63	Florence, Ala.		R	R	5'10	193	43	46	.483	172	615	18	0	859	754	366	728	0	3.39
Braun, Ryan-Ryan Zachary	06KCA	07-29-80	Kitchener, Canada		R	R	6'5	215	0	1	.000	0	9	0	0	11	13	3	6	0	6.75
Bray, Bill-William Paul	06WasN 06CinN	06-05-83	Virginia Beach, Va.		L	L	6'3	215	3	2	.600	2	48	0	0	51	57	18	39	0	4.09
Brazelton, Dewon-Dewon Cortez	02-05TBA 06SDN	06-16-80	Tullahoma, Tenn.		R	R	6'4	214	8	25	.242	0	63	43	0	271	305	151	145	0	6.38
Brazoban, Yhency-Yhency Jose	04-06LAN	06-11-80	Santo Domingo, D.R.		R	R	6'1	170	10	12	.455	21	110	0	0	110	102	49	92	0	4.49
Brea, Leslie-Leslie Guillermo	00-01BalA	10-12-73	San Pedro de Macoris,D.R.		R	R	5'10	170	0	1	.000	0	8	1	0	11	18	13	5	0	12.27
Breining, Fred-Fred Lawrence	80-83SFN 84MonN	11-15-55	San Francisco, Cal.		R	R	6'4	185	27	20	.574	1	140	42	8	438	426	159	260	0	3.33
Brennan, Tom-Thomas Martin (Gabby The Flamingo)	81-83CleA 84ChiA 85LAN	10-30-52	Chicago, Ill.		R	R	6'1	185	9	10	.474	2	64	20	2	219	255	46	102	1	4.40
Brennan, Bill-William Raymond	88LAN 93ChiN	01-15-63	Tampa, Fla.		R	R	6'3	200	2	2	.500	0	12	3	0	24	29	14	18	0	5.18
Breslow, Craig-Craig Andrew	05SDN 06BosA	08-08-80	New Haven, Conn.		L	L	6'1	180	0	2	.000	0	27	0	0	28	27	19	26	0	2.86
Brett, Ken-Kenneth Alven	67,69-71BosA 72MilA 73PhiN 74-75PitN 76NYA 76-77ChiA 77-78CalA 79MinA 79LAN 80-81KCA	09-18-48	Brooklyn, N.Y.	11-18-03	L	L	6'1	195	83	85	.494	11	349	184	51	1526	1490	562	807	8	3.93
Brewer, Billy-William Robert	93-95KCA 96NYA 97OakA 97PhiN	04-15-68	Fort Worth, Tex.		L	L	6'1	195	11	11	.500	5	203	0	0	178	172	93	137	0	4.79
Brewington, Jamie-Jamie Chancellor	95SFN 00CleA	09-28-71	Greenville, N.C.		R	R	6'4	180	9	4	.692	0	39	13	0	121	124	64	79	0	4.85
Brink, Brad-Bradford Albert	92-93PhiN 94SFN	01-20-65	Roseville, Cal.		R	R	6'2	200	0	4	.000	0	14	7	0	56	60	20	27	0	3.56
Briscoe, John-John Eric	91-96OakA	09-22-67	La Grange, Ill.		R	R	6'3	185	5	5	.500	2	100	2	0	140	124	129	115	0	5.67
Brito, Eude-Eude Ezequiel	05-06PhiN	08-19-78	Sabana de La Mar, D.R.		L	L	5'11	160	2	4	.333	0	11	7	0	40	41	23	24	0	5.36
Britton, Chris-Christopher Daniel	06BalA	12-16-82	Hollywood, Fla.		R	R	6'3	280	0	2	.000	1	52	0	0	54	46	17	41	0	3.35
Brizzolara, Tony-Anthony John	79,83-84AtlN	01-14-57	Santa Monica, Cal.		R	R	6'5	217	8	11	.421	1	44	23	2	156	188	52	98	0	5.07
Broberg, Pete-Peter Sven	71TexA 72-74TexA 75-76MilA 77ChiN 78OakA	03-02-50	West Palm Beach, Fla.		R	R	6'3	205	47	71	.366	1	206	134	8	963	942	478	536	6	4.56
Brocail, Doug-Douglas Keith	92-94SDN 95-96HouN 97-00DetA 01-02EJ 04-05TexA 06SDN	05-16-67	Clearfield, Pa.		L	R	6'5	230	39	42	.481	7	467	42	0	717	735	252	526	0	4.09
Brock, Chris-Terrence Christopher	97AtlN 98-99SFN 00-01PhiN 02BalA	02-05-70	Orlando, Fla.		R	R	6'0	185	18	17	.514	1	148	30	0	335	361	137	227	0	4.81
Brohawn, Troy-Michael Troy	01AriN 02SFN 03LAN	01-14-73	Cambridge, Md.		L	L	6'1	190	4	4	.500	1	82	0	0	82	70	28	46	0	4.86
Bronkey, Jeff-Jacob Jeffery	93TexA 94-95MilA	09-18-65	Kabul, Afghanistan		R	R	6'3	210	2	2	.500	2	45	0	0	69	74	29	56	0	4.04
Brookens, Ike-Edward Dwain	75DetA	01-03-49	Chambersburg, Pa.		R	R	6'3	170	0	0	—	0	3	0	0	10	11	5	8	0	5.40
Brooks, Frank-Frank J.	04PitN 05AtlN	09-06-78	Brooklyn, N.Y.		L	L	6'1	190	0	1	.000	0	12	1	0	18	14	9	18	0	4.58
Bross, Terry-Terrance Paul	91NYN 93SFN	03-30-66	El Paso, Tex.		R	R	6'9	235	0	0	—	0	10	0	0	12	10	4	6	0	3.00
Brow, Scott-Scott John	93-94,96TorA 98AriN	03-17-69	Butte, Mont.		R	R	6'3	200	3	4	.429	0	59	4	0	107	120	68	58	0	6.06
Brower, Jim-James Robert	99-00CleA 01-02CinN 02MonN 03-05SFN 05AtlN 06BalA 06SDN	12-29-72	Edina, Minn.		R	R	6'2	210	33	32	.508	2	351	28	0	571	588	254	396	0	4.62
Brown, Andrew-Andrew Aaron	06CleA	02-17-81	Chardon, Ohio		R	R	6'6	230	0	0	—	0	9	0	0	10	6	8	7	0	3.60
Brown, Curt-Curtis Steven	83CalA 84NYA 86-87MonN	01-15-60	Ft. Lauderdale, Fla.		R	R	6'2	170	2	4	.333	0	34	0	0	52	68	14	27	0	4.18
Brown, Jackie-Jackie Gene	70-71WasA 73-75TexA 75-76CleA 77MonN	05-31-43	Holdenville, Okla.		R	R	6'2	195	47	53	.470	3	214	105	26	894	934	353	516	8	4.18
Brown, Jamie-Jamie Monroe	04BosA	03-31-77	Meridian, Miss.		R	R	6'2	200	0	0	—	0	4	0	0	8	15	4	6	0	5.87
Brown, Keith-Keith Edward	88,90-92CinN	02-14-64	Flagstaff, Ariz.		R	R	6'4	215	2	2	.500	0	25	5	0	48	51	18	23	0	3.40
Brown, Kevin-James Kevin	86,88-94TexA 95BalA 96-97FlaN 98SDN 99-03LAN 04-05NYA	03-14-65	Milledgeville, Ga.		R	R	6'3	205	211	144	.594	0	486	476	72	3256	3079	901	2397	17	3.28
Brown, Kevin-Kevin Dewayne	90NYN 90-91MilA 92SeaA	03-05-66	Oroville, Cal.		L	L	6'1	185	3	5	.375	0	24	13	0	90	86	45	44	0	4.82
Brown, Mark-Mark Anthony	84BalA 85MinA	07-13-59	Bellows Falls, Vt.		B	R	6'2	190	1	2	.333	0	15	0	0	39	43	14	15	0	5.12
Brown, Mike-Michael Gary	82-86BosA 86-87SeaA	03-04-59	Haddon Township, N.J.		R	R	6'2	200	12	20	.375	0	61	42	3	254	324	102	115	1	5.75
Brown, Scott-Scott Edward	81CinN 82EJ	08-30-56	DeQuincy, Ill.		R	R	6'6	225	1	0	1.000	0	10	0	0	13	16	1	7	0	2.77
Brown, Steve-Steven Elbert	83-84CalA	02-12-57	San Francisco, Cal.		R	R	6'5	200	2	4	.333	0	15	7	0	57	61	25	28	1	4.58
Brown, Tom-Thomas Dale	78SeaA	08-10-49	Lafayette, La.		R	R	6'	170	0	0	—	0	13	0	0	13	14	4	8	0	4.15
Browning, Tom-Thomas Leo	84-94CinN 95KCA	04-28-60	Casper, Wyo.		L	L	6'1	195	123	90	.577	0	302	300	31	1921	1931	511	1000	12	3.94
Brownson, Mark-Mark Phillip	98-99ColN 00PhiN	06-17-75	West Palm Beach, Fla.		R	R	6'2	185	2	2	.500	0	11	9	1	48	65	13	32	1	6.94
Broxton, Jonathan-Jonathan Roy	05-06LAN	06-16-84	Augusta, Ga.		R	R	6'4	275	5	1	.833	0	90	0	0	90	74	45	119	0	3.10
Bruhert, Mike-Michael Edwin	78NYN	06-24-51	Queens, N.Y.		R	R	6'6	230	4	11	.267	0	27	22	1	134	171	34	56	1	4.77
Brumley, Duff-Duff Lechaun	94TexA	08-25-70	Cleveland, Tenn.		R	R	6'4	195	0	0	—	0	2	0	0	3	6	5	4	0	16.20
Brummett, Greg-Gregory Scott	93SFN 93MinA	04-20-67	Wichita, Kans.		R	R	6'1	180	4	4	.500	0	13	13	0	73	82	28	30	0	5.08
Brunette, Justin-Justin Thomas	00StLN	10-07-75	Los Alamitos, Cal.		L	L	6'1	200	0	0	—	0	5	0	0	5	8	5	2	0	5.79
Bruney, Brian-Brian Anthony	04-05AriN 06NYA	02-17-82	Astoria, Ore.		R	R	6'3	226	5	8	.385	0	96	0	0	98	90	77	110	0	5.05
Bruno, Tom-Thomas Michael	76KCA 77TorA 78-79StLN	01-26-53	Chicago, Ill.		R	R	6'5	210	7	7	.500	1	69	4	0	123	125	61	80	0	4.24
Brunson, Will-William Donald	98LAN 98-99DetA	03-20-70	Irving, Tex.		L	L	6'4	185	1	1	.500	0	27	0	0	17	23	9	11	0	5.71
Bruske, Jim-James Scott	95-96LAN 97SDN 98LAN 98SDN 98NYA 00MilN	10-07-64	East St. Louis, Ill.		R	R	6'1	185	9	1	.900	0	105	1	0	144	154	68	95	0	4.13
Brusstar, Warren-Warren Scott	77-82PhiN 82ChiA 83-85ChiN	02-01-52	Oakland, Cal.		R	R	6'3	200	28	16	.636	14	340	1	0	485	476	183	273	0	3.51
Bryden, T.R.-Thomas Ray	86CalA	01-17-59	Moses Lake, Wash.		R	R	6'4	190	2	1	.667	0	34	3	0	38	38	21	25	0	6.55
Buchanan, Bob-Robert Gordon	85CinN 89KCA	05-03-61	Ridley Park, Pa.		L	L	6'1	185	1	0	1.000	0	16	0	0	19	30	12	6	0	9.78
Buchholz, Taylor-Taylor	06HouN	10-31-81	Lower Merion Twp., Pa.		R	R	6'4	220	6	10	.375	0	22	19	1	113	107	34	77	0	5.89
Buckels, Gary-Gary Scott	94StLN	07-22-65	La Mirada, Cal.		R	R	6'	185	0	0	—	0	10	0	0	12	8	7	9	0	2.25
Buddie, Mike-Michael Joseph	98-99NYA 00-02MilN	12-12-70	Berea, Ohio		R	R	6'3	215	5	4	.556	2	87	2	0	131	137	52	76	0	4.97
Buehrle, Mark-Mark Alan	00-06ChiA	03-23-79	St. Charles, Mo.		L	L	6'2	200	97	66	.595	0	229	204	19	1428	1473	328	828	6	3.83
Buice, DeWayne-DeWayne Allison	87-88CalA 89TorA	08-20-57	Lynwood, Cal.		R	R	6'	170	9	11	.450	20	96	0	0	172	145	72	157	0	4.23
Bukvich, Ryan-Ryan Adrien	02-04KCA 05TexA	05-13-78	Naperville, Ill.		R	R	6'2	250	1	0	1.000	0	48	0	0	47	44	41	39	0	4.58
Bulger, Jason-Jason Patrick	05AriN 06LAA	12-06-78	Lawrenceville, Ga.		R	R	6'4	215	1	0	1.000	0	11	0	0	12	15	8	10	0	6.94
Bullinger, Jim-James Eric	92-96ChiN 97MonN 98SeaA	08-21-65	New Orleans, La.		R	R	6'2	185	34	41	.453	11	186	89	6	642	651	306	392	4	5.06
Bullinger, Kirk-Kirk Matthew	98MonN 99BosA 00PhiN 03-04HouN	10-28-69	New Orleans		R	R	6'2	170	2	0	1.000	0	49	0	0	51	63	13	22	0	6.53
Bullington, Bryan-Bryan Paul	05PitN	09-30-80	Indianapolis, Ind.		R	R	6'4	220	0	2	.000	0	3	1	0	11	11	1	5	0	13.50

USE NAMES - GIVEN NAMES (NICKNAMES)	TEAM BY YEAR	BIRTH DATE	BIRTHPLACE	DEATH DATE	B	T	HGT	WGT	W	L	Pct.	SV	G	GS	CG	IP	H	BB	SO	ShO	ERA
Bump, Nate-Nathan Louis	03-05FlaN	07-24-76	Towanda, Pa.		R	R	6'2	180	6	7	.462	1	113	2	0	148	163	64	79	0	4.68
Bunch, Melvin-Melvin Lynn	95KCA 99SeaA	11-04-71	Texarkana, Tex.		R	R	6'1	165	1	3	.250	0	18	6	0	50	62	21	23	0	6.84
Burba, Dave-David Allen	90-91SeaA 92-95SFN 95-97CinN 98-01CleA 02TexA 02CleA 03-04MilN 04SFN	07-07-66	Dayton, Ohio		R	R	6'4	240	115	87	.569	3	511	234	8	1778	1777	762	1398	1	4.49
Burgos, Enrique-Enrique [Calles]	93KCA 95SFN	10-07-65	Chorrera, Panama		L	L	6'4	195	0	1	.000	0	10	0	0	13	19	12	18	0	8.78
Burgos, Ambiorix-Ambiorix Wayne	05-06KCA	04-19-84	Nagua, Dom. Rep.		R	R	6'3	235	7	10	.412	20	127	1	0	137	143	68	137	0	4.81
Burgmeier, Tom-Thomas Henry (Bugs)	68CalA 69-73KCA 74-77MinA 78-82BosA 83-84OakA	08-02-43	St Paul, Minn.		L	L	5'11	185	79	55	.590	102	745	3	0	1258	1231	384	584	0	3.23
Burke, John-John C.	96-97ColN 98EJ	02-09-70	Durango, Colo.		B	R	6'4	220	4	6	.400	0	28	9	0	75	104	33	58	0	6.75
Burke, Steve-Steven Michael (Budge)	77-78SeaA	03-05-55	Stockton, Cal.		R	R	6'3	195	0	2	.000	0	24	0	0	65	58	31	22	0	3.32
Burke, Tim-Timothy Philip	85-91MonN 91-92NYN 92NYA	02-19-59	Omaha, Neb.		R	R	6'3	205	49	33	.598	102	498	2	0	699	624	219	444	0	2.72
Burkett, John-John David	87,90-94SFN 95-96FlaN 96-99TexA 00-01AtlN 02-03BosA	11-28-64	New Brighton, Pa.		R	R	6'2	210	166	136	.550	1	445	423	21	2648	2866	700	1766	6	4.31
Burnett, A.J.-Allan James	99-05FlaN 06TorA	01-03-77	North Little Rock, Ark.		R	R	6'5	230	59	58	.504	0	155	152	16	989	857	416	871	9	3.77
Burnett, Sean-Sean Richard	04PitN 05EJ	09-17-82	Dunedin, Fla.		L	L	6'1	190	5	5	.500	0	13	13	1	72	86	28	30	1	5.02
Burns, Britt-Robert Britt	78-85ChiA 86PJ	06-08-59	Houston, Tex.		L	L	6'5	220	70	60	.538	3	193	161	39	1095	1045	362	734	11	3.66
Burns, Mike-Michael John	05HouN 06CinN 06BosA	07-14-78	Westminster, Cal.		R	R	6'	205	0	0	—	0	45	0	0	52	69	12	36	0	5.88
Burns, Todd-Todd Edward	88-91OakA 92-93TexA 93StLN	07-06-63	Maywood, Cal.		R	R	6'2	195	21	23	.477	13	203	33	2	490	439	175	252	0	3.47
Burnside, Sheldon-Sheldon John	78-79DetA 80CinN	12-22-54	South Bend, Ind.		R	L	6'5	205	2	1	.667	0	19	0	0	30	38	11	18	0	6.00
Burres, Brian-Brian James	06BalA	04-08-81	Oregon City, Ore.		L	L	6'1	180	0	0	—	0	11	0	0	8	6	1	6	0	2.25
Burris, Ray-Bertram Ray	73-79ChiN 79NYA 79-80NYN 81-83MonN 84OakA 85MilA 86StLN 87MilA	08-22-50	Idabel, Okla.		R	R	6'5	205	108	134	.446	4	480	302	47	2189	2310	764	1065	10	4.17
Burrows, Terry-Terry Dale	94-95TexA 96MilA 97StLN	11-24-68	Lake Charles, La.		L	L	6'1	185	4	4	.500	1	50	3	0	69	85	38	35	0	6.42
Burton, Jim-Jim Scott (Eric)	75,77BosA	10-27-49	Royal Oak, Mich.		R	L	6'3	195	1	2	.333	1	30	4	0	56	60	20	42	0	2.73
Burtt, Dennis-Dennis Allen	85-86MinA	11-29-57	San Diego, Cal.		B	R	6'	187	2	2	.500	0	8	2	0	30	27	10	10	0	5.64
Busby, Mike-Michael James	96-99StLN	12-27-72	Lomita, Cal.		R	R	6'4	210	5	6	.455	0	45	6	0	82	99	37	50	0	6.48
Busby, Steve-Steven Lee	72-76KCA 77SJ 78-80KCA	09-22-49	Burbank, Cal.		R	R	6'3	205	70	54	.565	0	167	150	53	1060	1003	433	659	7	3.72
Bush, Dave-David T.	04-05TorA 06MilN	11-09-79	Pittsburgh, Pa.		R	R	6'2	212	22	26	.458	0	75	72	6	444	438	92	305	3	4.28
Bushing, Chris-Christopher Shaun	93CinN	11-04-67	Rockville Centre, N.Y.		R	R	6'	183	0	0	—	0	6	0	0	4	9	4	3	0	12.46
Buskey, Tom-Thomas William (Husky)	73-74NYA 74-77CleA 78-80TorA	02-20-47	Harrisburg, Pa.	06-07-98	R	R	6'3	220	21	27	.438	34	258	0	0	480	479	167	212	0	3.66
Butcher, John-John Daniel (Butch)	80-83TexA 84-86MinA 86CleA	03-08-57	Glendale, Cal.		B	R	6'4	190	36	49	.424	0	164	113	23	834	931	229	363	6	4.42
Butcher, Mike-Michael Dana	92-95CalA	05-10-65	Davenport, Iowa		R	R	6'1	200	11	4	.733	9	115	0	0	137	130	82	96	0	4.47
Butler, Adam-Adam Christopher	98AtlN	08-17-63	Fairfax, Va.		L	L	6'2	225	0	1	.000	0	9	0	0	5	5	6	7	0	10.80
Bynum, Mike-Michael Alan	02-04SDN	03-20-78	Tampa, Fla.		L	L	6'4	200	2	5	.286	0	29	8	0	64	78	33	52	0	7.73
Byrd, Jeff-Jeffrey Alan	77TorA	11-11-56	La Mesa, Cal.		R	R	6'3	195	2	13	.133	0	17	17	1	87	98	68	40	0	6.21
Byrd, Paul-Paul Gregory	95-96NYN 97-98AtlN 98-01PhiN 01-02KCA 03EJ 04AtlN 05LAA 06CleA	12-03-70	Louisville, Ky.		R	R	6'1	185	82	73	.529	0	277	189	14	1291	1367	328	742	4	4.32
Byrdak, Tim-Timothy Christopher	98-00KCA 05-06BalA	10-31-73	Oak Lawn, Ill.		L	L	5'11	180	1	5	.167	2	105	0	0	66	89	53	59	0	7.00
Bystrom, Marty-Martin Eugene	80-84PhiN 84-85NYA	07-26-58	Coral Gables, Fla.		R	R	6'3	210	29	26	.527	0	84	79	4	435	454	158	258	2	4.26
Cabrera, Daniel-Daniel Alberto [Cruz]	04-06BalA	05-28-81	San Pedro de Mac.,D.R.		R	R	6'7	230	31	31	.500	1	83	82	3	457	419	280	390	2	4.75
Cabrera, Fernando-Fernando Jose	04-06CleA	11-16-81	Toa, P.R.		R	R	6'4	170	5	4	.556	0	70	0	0	97	80	44	106	0	3.91
Cabrera, Jose-Jose Alberto	97-00HouN 01AtlN 02MilN	03-24-72	La Delgada, Dom. Rep.		R	R	6'0	200	19	17	.528	4	198	11	0	271	291	94	192	0	4.95
Cadaret, Greg-Gregory James	87-89OakA 89-92NYA 93CinN 93KCA 94TorA 94DetA 97-98AnaA 98TexA	02-27-62	Detroit, Mich.		L	L	6'3	215	38	32	.543	14	451	35	4	724	716	403	539	2	3.99
Cain, Matt-Matthew T.	05-06SFN	10-01-84	Dothan, Ala.		R	R	6'3	230	15	13	.536	0	39	38	2	237	181	106	209	1	3.80
Cairncross, Cameron-Cameron	00CleA 01SJ	05-11-72	Cairns, Australia		L	L	6'	195	1	0	1.000	0	15	0	0	9	11	3	8	0	3.86
Caldwell, Mike-Ralph Michael	71-73SDN 74-76SFN 77ChiN 77-84MilA	01-22-49	Tarboro, N.C.		L	L	6'1	185	137	130	.513	18	475	307	98	2408	2581	597	939	23	3.81
Calero, Kiko-Enrique Nomar	03-04StLN 05-06OakA	01-09-75	Santurce, P.R.		R	R	6'1	180	11	5	.688	6	195	1	0	197	151	72	217	0	3.10
Calhoun, Jeff-Jeffrey Wilton	84-86HouN 87-88PhiN	04-11-58	La Grange, Ga.		L	L	6'2	190	6	7	.462	5	118	0	0	151	120	65	104	0	2.51
Cali, Carmen-Carmen Salvatore	04-05StLN	11-04-78	Cleveland, Ohio		L	L	5'10	185	0	0	—	0	16	0	0	13	23	12	13	0	9.45
Callahan, Ben-Benjamin Franklin	83AtlN	05-19-57	Mount Airy, N.C.		R	R	6'7	230	1	2	.330	0	4	2	0	9	18	5	2	0	12.54
Callaway, Mickey-Michael Christopher	99,01TBA 02-03AnaA 03-04TexA	05-13-75	Memphis, Tenn.		R	R	6'2	200	4	11	.267	0	40	20	0	131	166	58	86	0	6.27
Calvert, Mark-Mark	83-84SFN	09-29-56	Tulsa, Okla.		R	R	6'1	200	3	8	.273	0	28	91	1	69	86	43	19	0	5.71
Camacho, Ernie-Ernest Carlos	80OakA 81PitN 83-87CleA 88HouN 89-90SFN 90StLN	02-01-55	Salinas, Cal.		R	R	6'1	180	10	20	.333	45	193	3	0	263	268	128	159	0	4.20
Cammack, Eric-Eric Wade	00NYN	08-14-75	Nederland, Tex.		R	R	6'1	175	0	0	—	0	8	0	0	10	7	10	9	0	6.30
Camp Rick-Rick Lamar	76-78,80-85AtlN	06-05-53	Trion, Ga.		R	R	6'1	195	56	49	.533	57	414	65	5	942	970	336	407	0	3.37
Camp, Shawn-Shawn Anthony	04-05KCA 06TBA	11-18-75	Fairfax, Va.		R	R	6'1	200	10	10	.500	6	146	0	0	191	236	48	132	0	4.88
Campbell Bill-William Richard	73-76MinA 77-81BosA 82-83ChiN 84PhiN 85StLN 86DetA 87MonN 90MinA 90TorA	08-09-48	Highland Park, Mich.		R	R	6'3	195	83	68	.550	126	700	9	2	1229	1139	495	864	1	3.54
Campbell, Brett-Richard Brett	06WasN	10-17-81	Atlanta, Ga.		R	R	6'	175	0	0	—	0	4	0	0	4	4	2	4	0	10.38
Campbell, Dave-David Alan (Chopper)	77-78AtlN	09-03-51	Princeton, Ind.		R	R	6'3	210	4	10	.286	14	109	0	0	158	145	82	87	0	3.82
Campbell, Jim-James Marcus	90KCA	05-19-67	Santa Maria, Cal.		L	L	5'11	175	1	0	1.000	0	2	2	0	10	15	1	2	0	8.38
Campbell, Kevin-Kevin Wade	91-93OakA 94-95MinA	12-06-64	Marianna, Ark.		R	R	6'2	225	4	3	.571	1	77	5	0	138	127	80	83	0	4.55
Campbell, Mike-Michael Thomas	87-89SeaA 92TexA 94SDN 96ChiN	02-17-64	Seattle, Wash.		R	R	6'3	210	12	19	.387	0	51	41	3	233	242	95	135	0	5.86
Camper, Cardell-Cardell (Campy)	77CleA	07-06-52	Boley, Okla.		R	R	6'3	203	1	0	1.000	0	9	7	4	9	9	4	9	0	4.00
Campillo, Jorge-Jorge Hidalgo	05-06SeaA	08-10-78	Tijuana, Mexico		R	R	6'1	190	0	0	—	0	3	1	0	4	5	1	2	0	8.31
Candelaria, John-John Robert (Candy Man)	75-85PitN 85-87CalA 87NYN 88-89NYA 89MonN 90MinA 90TorA 91-92LAN 93PitN	11-06-53	Brooklyn, N.Y.		L	L	6'7	230	177	122	.592	29	600	356	54	2526	2399	592	1673	13	3.33
Candiotti, Tom-Thomas Caesar	83-84MilA 86-91CleA 91TorA 92-97LAN 98-99OakA 99CleA	08-31-57	Walnut Creek, Cal.		R	R	6'3	215	151	164	.479	0	451	410	68	2725	2662	883	1735	11	3.73
Caneira, John-John Cascaes (J.C.)	77-78CalA	10-07-52	Waterbury, Conn.		R	R	6'4	210	2	2	.500	0	8	6	3	37	39	19	17	0	4.62
Cano, Jose-Joselito [Soriano]	89HouN	03-07-62	Boca de Soco, Dom. Rep.		R	R	6'3	175	1	1	.500	0	6	3	1	23	24	7	8	0	5.09
Capel, Mike-Michael Lee	88ChiN 90MilA 91HouN	10-13-61	Marshall, Tex.		R	R	6'2	175	3	4	.429	3	49	0	0	62	73	29	43	0	4.62
Capellan, Jose-Jose Francisco	04AtlN 05-06MilN	01-13-81	Cotui, Dom. Rep.		R	R	6'4	235	5	4	.556	0	81	2	0	95	96	41	76	0	4.72
Capilla, Doug-Douglas Edmund	76-77StLN 77-79CinN 79-81ChiN	01-07-52	Honolulu, Hawaii		L	L	5'9	170	12	18	.400	7	140	18	1	293	273	173	178	0	4.33
Capps, Matt-Matthew Dicus	05-06PitN	09-03-83	Douglasville, Ga.		R	R	6'2	240	9	1	.900	1	89	0	0	85	86	12	59	0	3.83
Cappuzzello, George-George Angelo	81DetA 82HouN	01-15-54	Youngstown, Ohio		R	L	6'	190	1	2	.333	1	35	3	0	53	44	25	32	0	3.21
Capra, Buzz-Lee William	71-73NYN 74-77AtlN	10-01-47	Chicago, Ill.		R	R	5'11	170	31	37	.456	5	142	61	16	543	479	258	362	5	3.88
Capuano, Chris-Christopher Frank	03AriN 04-06MilN	08-19-78	Springfield, Mass.		L	L	6'3	210	37	36	.507	0	95	91	3	562	559	186	453	2	4.20
Carlson, Dan-Daniel Steven	96-97SFN 98TBA 99AriN	01-26-70	Portland, Ore.		R	R	6'1	200	1	0	1.000	0	23	0	0	47	63	18	37	0	6.70
Carlton, Steve-Steven Norman (Lefty)	65-71StLN 72-86PhiN 86SFN 86ChiA 87CleA 87-88MinA	12-22-44	Miami, Fla.		L	L	6'4	210	329	244	.574	2	741	709	254	5217	4672	1833	4136	55	3.22
Carlyle, Buddy-Earl L.	99-00SDN 05LAN	12-21-77	Omaha, Neb.		L	R	6'3	185	1	3	.250	0	21	7	0	55	58	24	44	0	7.41
Carman, Don-Donald Wayne	83-90PhiN 91CinN 92TexA	08-14-59	Oklahoma City, Okla.		L	L	6'3	195	53	54	.495	11	342	102	7	922	849	378	598	3	4.11
Carmona, Fausto-Fausto C.	06CleA	12-07-83	Santo Domingo, D.R.		R	R	6'4	220	1	10	.091	0	38	7	0	75	88	31	58	0	5.42
Carmona, Rafael-Rafael	95-97SeaA 98BalA 99SeaA	10-02-72	Comerio, P.R.		R	R	6'2	185	11	7	.611	2	81	4	0	155	171	100	96	0	4.94
Carpenter, Chris-Christopher John	97-02TorA 03SJ 04-06StLN	04-27-75	Exeter, N.H.		R	R	6'6	225	100	68	.595	0	245	228	25	1516	1551	463	1161	12	4.09
Carpenter, Cris-Cris Howell	88-92StLN 93FlaN 93-94TexA 96MilA	04-05-65	St. Augustine, Fla.		R	R	6'1	195	27	22	.551	7	291	13	1	414	398	131	252	0	3.91
Carrara, Giovanni-Giovanni [Jímenez]	95-96TorA 96-97CinN 98JL 00ColN 01-02LAN 03SeaA 04-06LAN	05-04-68	Edo Anzoategui, Venez.		R	R	6'2	220	29	18	.617	4	313	18	1	472	487	202	338	0	4.69
Carrasco, D.J.-Daniel J.	03-05KCA	04-12-77	Safford, Ariz.		R	R	6'1	210	14	15	.483	2	101	22	1	230	252	106	128	0	4.81
Carrasco, Hector-Hector Pipo [Pacheco]	94-97CinN 97KCA 98-00MinA 00BosA 01MinA 03BalA 05WasN 06LAA	10-22-69	San Pedro de Mac., D.R.		R	R	6'2	215	42	49	.462	19	618	6	0	794	748	364	629	0	3.88
Carreno, Amalio-Amalio Rafael [Adrian]	91PhiN	04-11-64	Chacachacare, Venez.		R	R	6'	170	0	0	—	0	3	0	0	5	3	2	2	0	16.20
Carrithers, Don-Donald George	70-73SFN 74-76MonN 77MinA	09-15-49	Lynwood, Cal.		R	R	6'3	205	28	32	.467	3	165	67	11	565	595	267	275	3	4.46
Carroll, Tom-Thomas Michael	74-75CinN	11-05-52	Utica, N.Y.		R	R	6'4	190	8	4	.667	0	28	20	0	125	120	70	51	0	4.18
Carter, Andy-Andrew Godfrey	94-95PhiN	11-09-68	Philadelphia, Pa.		L	L	6'5	200	0	2	.000	0	42	38	14	24	4	0	4.75
Carter, Jeff-Jeffrey Allen	91ChiA	12-03-64	Tampa, Fla.		R	R	6'3	195	0	1	.000	0	5	0	0	12	8	5	2	0	5.25
Carter, Lance-Lance David	99KCA 02-05TBA 06LAN	12-18-74	Bradenton, Fla.		R	R	6'1	190	13	12	.520	29	181	0	0	254	245	73	127	0	4.15
Carter, Larry-Larry Gene	92SFN	05-28-65	Charleston, W. Va.		R	R	6'5	198	1	5	.167	0	9	6	0	33	34	18	21	0	4.64
Carvajal, Marcos-Marcos Jose	05ColN	08-19-84	Bolivar, Venezuela		R	R	6'4	175	0	2	.000	0	39	0	0	53	52	21	47	0	5.09
Cary, Chuck-Charles Douglas	85-86DetA 87-88AtlN 89-91NYA 92JL 93ChiA	03-03-60	Whittier, Cal.		L	L	6'4	210	14	26	.350	5	168	47	4	410	390	158	322	0	4.17
Casian, Larry-Lawrence Paul	90-94MinA 94CleA 95-97ChiN 97KCA 98ChiA	10-28-65	Lynwood, Cal.		L	L	6'	170	11	13	.458	3	241	286	77	125	0	4.56
Casilla, Santiago-Santiago (played as Jairo Garcia 04-05)	04-06OakA	06-25-80	Don Gregorio, Dom. Rep.		R	R	6'	170	0	0	—	0	11	0	0	9	12	8	8	0	9.82
Caskey, Craig-Craig Douglas	73MonN	12-11-49	Visalia, Cal.		B	L	5'11	180	0	0	—	0	9	1	0	14	15	4	6	0	5.79

USE NAMES - GIVEN NAMES (NICKNAMES) — TEAM BY YEAR	BIRTH DATE	BIRTHPLACE	DEATH DATE	B	T	HGT	WGT	W	L	Pct.	SV	G	GS	CG	IP	H	BB	SO	ShO	ERA
Cassidy, Scott-Scott Robert — 02TorA 05BosA 05-06SDN	10-03-75	Syracuse, N.Y.		R	R	6'2	175	8	9	.471	0	111	0	0	122	110	54	109	0	4.88
Castillo, Bobby-Robert Ernie (Babo) — 77-81LAN 82-84MinA 85LAN	04-18-55	Los Angeles, Cal.		R	R	5'10	180	38	40	.487	18	250	59	9	688	623	327	434	1	3.95
Castillo, Carlos-Carlos — 97-99ChiA 01BosA	04-21-75	Boston, Mass.		R	R	6'2	240	10	7	.588	0	111	6	0	211	210	82	130	0	5.04
Castillo, Frank-Frank Anthony — 91-97ChiN 97ColN 98DetA 00TorA 01-02,04BosA 05FlaN	04-01-69	El Paso, Tex.		R	R	6'1	195	82	104	.441	2	297	268	10	1595	1660	506	1101	3	4.56
Castillo, Juan-Juan Francisco — 94NYN	06-23-70	Caracas, Venez.		R	R	6'5	205	0	0	—	0	2	0	0	12	17	5	1	0	6.94
Castillo, Tony-Anthony Jose [Jimenez] — 88-89TorA 89-91AtlN 91NYN 93-96TorA 96-98ChiA	03-01-63	Quibor, Venez.		R	L	5'10	180	28	23	.549	22	403	6	0	527	555	179	333	0	3.93
Castro, Bill-William Radhames [Checo] — 74-80MilA 81NYA 82-83KCA	12-12-53	Santiago, Dom. Rep.		R	R	6'	170	31	26	.544	45	303	9	0	545	564	145	203	0	3.33
Castro, Fabio-Fabio E. — 06TexA 06PhiN	01-20-85	Monte Cristi, Dom. Rep.		L	L	5'7	175	0	1	.000	1	20	0	0	32	18	13	18	0	2.27
Cather, Mike-Michael Peter — 97-99AtlN	12-17-70	San Diego, Cal.		R	R	6'2	195	5	6	.455	0	75	0	0	82	67	32	62	0	3.42
Cato, Keefe-John Keefe — 83-84CinN	05-06-58	Yonkers, N.Y.		R	R		185	1	1	.500	1	12	0	0	19	24	5	15	0	6.98
Caudill, Bill-William Holland — 79-81ChiN 82-83SeaA 84OakA 85-86TorA 87OakA	07-13-56	Santa Monica, Cal.		R	R	6'2	205	35	52	.402	106	445	24	0	667	587	288	620	0	3.68
Cecena, Jose-Jose Isabel [Lugo] — 88TexA	08-20-63	Ciudad Obregon, Mex.		R	R	5'11	180	0	0	—	1	22	0	0	26	20	23	27	0	4.78
Cerda, Jamie-Jamie M. — 02-03NYN 04-05KCA	10-26-78	Fresno, Cal.		L	L	6'	175	3	9	.250	2	132	0	0	123	116	75	91	0	4.26
Cerros, Juan-Juan R. — 03CinN	09-25-76	Monterrey, Mexico		R	R		200	0	0	—	0	11	0	0	13	11	5	9	0	4.85
Cerutti, John-John Joseph — 85-90TorA 91DetA	04-28-60	Albany, N.Y.	10-03-04	L	L	6'2	200	49	43	.533	4	229	116	8	861	894	291	398	2	3.94
Chacin, Gustavo-Gustavo Adolfo [Gonzalez] — 04-06TorA	12-04-80	Maracaibo, Venezuela		L	L	5'11	193	23	14	.622	0	53	53	0	304	311	111	174	0	4.05
Chacon, Shawn-Shawn Anthony — 01-05ColN 05-06NYA 06PitN	12-23-77	Anchorage, Alaska		R	R	6'3	212	38	54	.413	35	190	115	0	740	733	386	487	0	5.12
Chadwick, Ray-Ray Charles — 86CalA	11-17-62	Durham, N.C.		B	R	6'2	180	0	5	.000	0	7	7	0	27	39	15	9	0	7.24
Chamberlain, Craig-Craig Phillip — 79-80KCA	02-01-57	Hollywood, Cal.		R	R		195	4	5	.444	0	15	10	4	79	78	23	33	0	4.10
Champion, Billy-Buford Billy — 69-72PhiN 73-76MilA	09-18-47	Shelby, N.C.		R	R	6'4	190	34	50	.405	2	202	102	13	805	873	354	360	3	4.68
Chapin, Darrin-Darrin John — 91NYA 92PhiN	02-01-66	Warren, Ohio		R	R	6'	170	0	1	.000	0	4	0	0	7	5	6	6	0	6.14
Charlton, Norm-Norman Wood III (The Genius) — 88-92CinN 93SeaA 94EJ 95PhiN 95-97SeaA 98BalA 98AtlN 99TBA 00CinN 01SeaA	01-06-63	Fort Polk, La.		B	L	6'3	205	51	54	.486	97	605	37	1	899	798	409	808	1	3.71
Chavez, Tony-Anthony Francisco — 97AnaA	10-22-70	Turlock, Cal.		R	R	5'10	180	0	0	—	0	7	0	0	10	7	5	10	0	0.93
Cheadle, Dave-David Baird — 73AtlN	02-19-52	Greensboro, N.C.		L	L	6'3	205	0	2	.000	0	2	0	0	2	2	3	2	0	18.00
Checo, Robinson-Robinson [Perez] — 97-98BosA 99LAN	09-09-71	Santiago, Dom. Rep.		R	R		185	3	5	.375	0	16	6	0	37	47	21	30	0	7.61
Chen, Bruce-Bruce Kastulo — 98-00AtlN 00-01PhiN 01-02NYN 02MonN 02CinN 03HouN 03BosA 04-06BalA	06-19-77	Panama City, Panama		L	L	6'1	205	35	37	.486	0	237	112	2	797	807	308	635	0	4.60
Chevez, (Aguilera),Tony-Silvio Antonio Aguilera [Chevez] — 77BalA	06-20-54	Telica, Nicaragua		R	R	5'11	185	0	0	—	0	4	0	0	8	10	8	7	0	12.38
Chiamparino, Scott-Scott Michael — 90-92TexA 93EJ	08-22-66	San Mateo, Cal.		R	R	6'2	200	2	6	.250	0	15	15	0	85	87	29	40	0	3.27
Chiasson, Scott-Scott Christopher — 01-02ChiN	08-14-77	Norwich, Conn.		R	R	6'3	200	1	1	.500	0	10	0	0	11	16	8	9	0	11.12
Chick, Travis-Travis Cole — 06SeaA	06-10-84	Irving, Tex.		R	R	6'3	215	0	0	—	0	3	0	0	5	7	10	2	0	12.60
Chiffer, Floyd-Floyd John — 82-84SDN	04-20-56	Glen Cove, N.Y.		R	R	6'2	185	5	5	.500	5	81	1	0	130	132	60	83	0	4.02
Childers, Jason-Jason Lee — 06TBA	01-13-75	Statesboro, Ga.		R	R	6'	160	0	0	—	0	5	0	0	8	12	4	5	0	4.70
Childers, Matt-Matthew Wilkie — 02MilN 05AtlN	12-03-78	Douglas, Ga.		R	R	6'5	215	0	0	—	0	11	0	0	13	18	11	8	0	9.69
Childress, Rocky-Rodney Osborne — 85-86PhiN 87-88HouN	02-18-62	Santa Rosa, Cal.		R	R	6'2	195	2	3	.400	0	61	1	0	108	121	37	65	0	4.76
Chitren, Steve-Stephen Vincent — 90-91OakA	06-08-67	Tokyo, Japan		R	R	6'	180	2	4	.333	4	64	0	0	78	66	36	66	0	3.58
Cho, Jin Ho-Jin Ho — 98-99OakA	08-16-75	Jun Ju City, Korea		R	R	6'3	220	2	6	.250	0	13	11	0	58	73	11	31	0	6.52
Choate, Randy-Randol Doyle — 00-03NYA 04-06AriN	09-05-75	San Antonio, Tex.		L	L	6'3	190	5	7	.417	0	194	0	0	165	154	87	129	0	4.64
Chouinard, Bobby-Robert William — 96OakA 98MilN 98-99AriN 00-01ColN	05-01-72	Manila, Philippines		R	R	6'1	188	11	8	.579	1	111	13	0	181	197	65	110	0	4.57
Chris, Mike-Michael — 79DetA 82-83SFN	10-08-57	Santa Monica, Cal.		L	L	6'2	180	3	5	.375	0	29	14	0	78	85	63	46	0	6.43
Christiansen, Jason-Jason Samuel — 95-00PitN 00-01StLN 01-05SFN 05LAA	09-21-69	Omaha, Neb.		R	L	6'5	240	27	26	.509	16	528	0	0	434	409	217	384	0	4.30
Christenson, Gary-Gary Richard — 79-80KCA	05-05-53	Mineola, N.Y.		L	L	6'5	210	3	0	1.000	0	30	0	0	42	45	20	20	0	4.71
Christenson, Larry-Larry Richard — 73-83PhiN 84EJ	11-10-53	Everett, Wash.		R	R	6'4	220	83	71	.539	4	243	220	27	1403	1401	395	781	6	3.79
Christiansen, Clay-Clay C. — 84NYA	06-28-58	Wichita, Kans.		R	R	6'5	215	2	4	.333	2	24	1	0	39	50	12	27	0	6.05
Christman, Tim-Timothy Arthur — 01ColN	03-31-75	Oneonta, N.Y.		L	L	6'	195	0	0	—	0	1	0	0	2	1	1	2	0	4.50
Christopher, Mike-Michael Wayne — 91LAN 92-93CleA 95-96DetA	11-03-63	Petersburg, Va.		R	R	6'5	205	5	1	.833	1	71	0	0	125	151	40	76	0	4.90
Chulk, Vinnie-Charles Vincent — 03-06TorA 06SFN	12-19-78	Miami, Fla.		R	R	6'2	185	2	7	.222	2	160	0	0	180	179	76	128	0	4.51
Ciardi, Mark-Mark Thomas — 87MilA	08-19-61	New Brunswick, N.J.		R	R	6'	180	1	1	.500	0	4	3	0	16	26	9	6	0	9.37
Cimorelli, Frank-Frank Thomas — 94StLN	08-02-68	Poughkeepsie, N.Y.		R	R	6'	175	0	0	—	1	11	0	0	13	20	10	1	0	8.78
Citarella, Ralph-Ralph Alexander — 83-84StLN 87ChiA	02-07-58	East Orange, N.J.		R	R	6'	180	0	1	.000	0	21	2	0	44	41	14	28	0	4.06
Clancy, Jim-James — 77-88TorA 89-91HouN 91AtlN	12-18-55	Chicago, Ill.		R	R	6'4	220	140	167	.456	10	472	381	74	2517	2513	947	1422	11	4.23
Clark, Bryan-Bryan Donald — 81-83SeaA 84TorA 85CleA 86-87ChiA 90SeaA	07-12-56	Madera, Cal.		L	L	6'2	210	20	23	.465	4	186	37	4	516	536	241	259	1	4.15
Clark, Mark-Mark Willard — 91-92StLN 93-95CleA 96-97NYN 97-98ChiN 99-00TexA	05-12-68	Bath, Ill.		R	R	6'5	230	74	71	.510	0	219	197	15	1246	1364	367	728	3	4.61
Clark, Terry-Terry Lee — 88-89CalA 90HouN 95AtlN 95BalA 96KCA 96HouN 97CleA 97TexA	10-18-60	Los Angeles, Cal.		R	R	6'2	190	10	23	.303	1	91	27	2	232	299	89	109	1	5.54
Clarke, Stan-Stanley Marten — 83,85-86TorA 87SeaA 89KCA 90StLN	08-09-60	Toledo, Ohio		R	L	6'1	180	3	6	.333	0	50	2	0	61	78	31	36	0	6.79
Clary, Marty-Martin Keith — 87,89-90AtlN	04-03-62	Detroit, Mich.		R	R	6'4	190	5	14	.263	0	58	32	2	225	251	74	81	1	4.48
Claussen, Brandon-Brandon Allen Falker — 03NYA 04-05,88CinN	05-01-79	Rapid City, S.D.		R	R	6'2	200	16	27	.372	0	58	58	0	316	359	121	228	0	5.04
Clay, Danny-Danny Bruce — 88PhiN	10-24-61	Sun Valley, Cal.		R	R	6'1	190	0	1	.000	0	17	0	0	24	27	21	12	0	6.00
Clay, Ken-Kenneth Earl — 77-79NYA 80TexA 81SeaA	04-06-54	Lynchburg, Va.		R	R	6'2	190	10	24	.294	3	111	36	0	354	389	141	129	0	4.68
Clear, Mark-Mark Alan (Horse) — 79-80CalA 81-85BosA 86-88MilA 90CalA	05-27-56	Los Angeles, Cal.		R	R	6'4	215	71	49	.592	83	481	1	0	804	674	554	804	0	3.83
Clemens, Roger-William Roger (Rocket) — 84-96BosA 97-98TorA 99-03NYA 04-06HouN	08-04-62	Dayton, Ohio		R	R	6'4	230	348	178	.662	0	691	690	118	4818	4086	1549	4604	46	3.10
Clement, Matt-Matthew Paul — 98-00SDN 01FlaN 02-04ChiN 05-06BosA	08-12-74	McCandless Township,Pa.		R	R	6'3	205	86	86	.503	0	238	236	6	1413	1326	650	1217	3	4.47
Clements, Pat-Patrick Brian — 85CalA 85-86PitN 87-88NYA 89-92SDN 92BalA	02-02-62	McCloud,Cal.		R	L	6'	180	17	11	.607	12	288	2	0	360	362	160	158	0	3.77
Clemons, Chris-Christopher Hale — 97ChiA	10-31-72	Baytown, Tex.		R	R	6'4	220	0	2	.000	0	5	2	0	13	19	11	8	0	8.53
Cleveland, Reggie-Reginald Leslie — 69-73StLN 74-78BosA 78TexA 79-81MilA	05-23-48	Swift Current, Canada		R	R	6'1	205	105	106	.496	25	428	203	57	1809	1843	543	930	12	4.01
Cliburn, Stew-Stewart Walker — 84-85,88CalA	12-19-56	Jackson, Miss.		R	R	6'	190	13	5	.722	6	85	1	0	185	173	59	91	0	3.11
Clontz, Brad-John Bradley — 94-97AtlN 98LAN 98NYN 99-00PitN	04-25-71	Stuart, Va.		R	R	6'1	200	22	8	.733	8	272	0	0	278	276	120	210	0	4.34
Cloude, Ken-Kenneth Brian — 97-99SeaA	01-09-75	Baltimore, Md.		R	R	6'1	200	16	16	.500	1	71	45	0	279	334	152	195	0	6.56
Clutterbuck, Bryan-Bryan Richard — 86,89MilA	12-17-59	Detroit, Mich.		R	R	6'4	225	2	6	.250	0	34	11	1	124	141	32	67	0	4.21
Clyde, David-David Eugene — 73-75TexA 78-79CleA	04-22-55	Kansas City, Kans.		L	L	6'1	190	18	33	.353	0	84	73	10	416	457	180	228	0	4.63
Cocanower, Jamie-James Stanley [Geiser] — 83-86MilA	02-14-57	San Juan, P.R.		R	R	6'4	200	16	26	.390	0	79	47	5	366	371	201	139	1	3.98
Coco, Pasqual-Pasqual [Reynoso] — 00-02TorA	09-08-77	Santo Domingo, Dom.Rep.		R	R		185	1	1	.500	0	10	2	0	19	21	14	11	0	6.05
Codiroli, Chris-Christopher Allen (Gabby) — 82-87OakA 88CleA 90KCA	03-26-58	Oxnard, Cal.		R	R	6'1	165	38	47	.447	0	144	108	13	670	711	261	312	2	4.87
Coffey, Todd-Justin Todd — 05-06CinN	09-09-80	Shelby, N.C.		R	R	6'5	230	10	8	.556	9	138	0	0	136	169	38	86	0	3.97
Coffman, Kevin-Kevin Reese — 87-88AtlN	01-19-65	Austin, Tex.		R	R	6'2	205	4	11	.267	0	31	18	0	111	119	95	47	0	6.42
Cogan, Tony-Anthony Michael — 01KCA	12-21-76	Chicago, Ill.		L	L	6'2	205	0	4	.000	0	39	0	0	25	32	13	17	0	5.84
Coggin, Dave-David Raymond — 00-02PhiN	10-30-76	Covina, Cal.		R	R	6'4	200	10	12	.455	0	60	29	0	199	199	102	143	0	4.52
Colborn, Jim-James William — 69-71ChiN 72-76MilA 77-78KCA 78SeaA	05-22-46	Santa Paula, Cal.		R	R	6'	195	83	88	.485	7	301	204	60	1597	1619	475	688	8	3.80
Cole, Victor-Victor Alexander — 92PitN	01-23-68	St. Petersburg, Russia		R	R	5'10	160	0	2	.000	0	8	4	0	23	23	14	12	0	5.48
Collins, Don-Donald Edward — 77AtlN 80CleA	09-15-52	Lyons, Ga.		R	R	6'4	195	3	9	.250	2	44	4	0	77	91	48	27	0	5.26
Colome, Jesus-Jesus [De La Cruz] — 01-06TBA	12-23-77	San Pedro de Mac., D.R.		R	R	6'3	205	5	18	.217	3	186	0	0	251	244	141	201	0	4.73
Colon, Bartolo-Bartolo (Boogie Bear) — 97-02CleA 02MonN 03ChiA 04AnaA 05-06LAA	05-24-73	Altamira, Dom. Rep.		R	R	5'11	240	140	87	.617	0	290	288	31	1876	1823	650	1466	8	3.98
Colon, Roman-Roman Benedicto — 04-05AtlN 05-06DetA	08-13-79	Montecristi, D.R.		R	R	6'6	225	6	7	.462	0	73	8	0	127	146	43	87	0	5.03
Colyer, Steve-Stephen Edward — 03LAN 04DetA	02-22-79	St. Louis, Mo.		L	L	6'4	205	1	0	1.000	0	54	0	0	55	53	47	50	0	5.05
Combe, Geoff-Geoffrey Wade — 80-81CinN	02-01-56	Melrose, Mass.		R	R	6'1	185	1	0	1.000	0	18	0	0	25	36	14	19	0	8.27
Combs, Pat-Patrick Dennis — 89-92PhiN	10-29-66	Newport, R.I.		L	L	6'3	210	17	17	.500	0	56	54	5	305	299	147	190	3	4.22
Comer, Steve-Stephen Michael (Kid) — 77-82TexA 83PhiN 84CleA	01-13-54	Minneapolis, Minn.		B	R	6'3	205	44	37	.543	13	176	83	11	701	762	252	245	3	4.13
Comstock, Keith-Keith Martin — 84MinA 85-86JL 87SFN 87-88SDN 89-91SeaA	12-23-55	San Francisco, Cal.		L	L	6'	175	10	7	.588	3	144	0	0	153	134	75	142	0	4.18
Condrey, Clay-Clayton Lee — 02-03SDN 06PhiN	11-19-75	Beaumont, Texas		R	R	6'3	195	4	6	.400	0	39	9	0	89	98	38	57	0	4.74
Cone, David-David Brian — 86KCA 87-92NYN 92TorA 93-94KCA 95TorA 95-00NYA 01BosA 03NYN	01-02-63	Kansas City, Mo.		L	R	6'1	190	194	126	.606	1	450	419	56	2899	2504	1137	2668	22	3.46
Connelly, Steve-Steven Lee — 98OakA	04-27-74	Long Beach, Cal.		R	R	6'4	210	0	0	—	0	14	0	0	24	30	11	14	0	1.93
Conroy, Tim-Timothy James — 78,82-85OakA 86-87StLN	04-03-60	McKeesport, Pa.		L	L	6'	185	18	32	.360	0	135	71	5	466	438	284	307	1	4.69
Contreras, Jose-Jose Ariel — 03-04NYA 04-06ChiA	12-06-71	Las Martinas, Cuba		R	R	6'4	230	48	27	.640	0	111	102	2	642	589	244	510	1	4.28
Contreras, Nardi-Arnaldo Juan — 80ChiA	09-19-51	Tampa, Fla.		B	R	6'2	195	0	0	—	0				14	18	7	8	0	5.79

USE NAMES - GIVEN NAMES (NICKNAMES)	TEAM BY YEAR	BIRTH DATE	BIRTHPLACE	DEATH DATE	B	T	HGT	WGT	W	L	Pct.	SV	G	GS	CG	IP	H	BB	SO	ShO	ERA
Converse, Jim-James Daniel	93-95SeaA 95KCA 96SJ 97KCA	08-17-71	San Francisco, Cal.		L	R	5'9	180	2	11	.154	1	35	13	0	97	128	75	66	0	7.21
Cook, Aaron-Aaron Lane	02-06ColN	02-06-79	Ft. Campbell, Ky.		R	R	6'3	185	28	28	.500	0	113	82	4	552	656	180	213	0	4.58
Cook, Andy-Andrew Bernard	93NYA	08-30-67	Memphis, Tenn.		R	R	6'5	205	0	1	.000	0	4	0	0	5	4	7	4	0	5.06
Cook, Dennis-Dennis Bryan	88-89SFN 89-90PhiN 90-91LAN 92-93CleA 94ChiA 95CleA 95-96TexA 97FlaN 98-01NYN 01PhiN 02AnaA	10-04-62	LaMarque, Tex.		L	L	6'3	185	64	46	.582	9	665	71	6	1012	950	390	739	3	3.91
Cook, Glen-Glen Patrick	85TexA	09-08-59	Buffalo, N.Y.		R	R	5'11	180	2	3	.400	0	9	7	0	40	53	18	19	0	9.45
Cook, Mike-Michael Horace	86-88CalA 89MinA 93BalA	08-14-63	Charleston, S.C.		R	R	6'2	215	1	6	.143	0	41	2	0	71	74	45	53	0	5.55
Cooke, Steve-Stephen Montague	92-94PitN 95SJ 96-97PitN 98CinN	01-14-70	Lihue, Hawaii		R	L	6'6	225	26	36	.419	0	104	88	5	550	585	191	335	1	4.31
Cooper, Brian-Brian John	99-01AnaA 02TorA 04-05SDN	08-19-74	Los Angeles, Calif.		R	R	6'1	185	5	14	.263	0	42	26	1	168	182	74	75	1	5.80
Cooper, Don-Donald James	81-82MinA 83TorA 85NYA	01-15-56	Queens, N.Y.		R	R	6'	180	1	6	.143	0	44	3	0	86	95	46	47	0	5.25
Coppinger, Rocky-John Thomas	96-99BalA 99MilN 00EJ 01MilN	03-19-74	El Paso, Tex.		R	R	6'5	245	17	11	.607	0	82	32	0	242	247	140	210	0	5.47
Corbett, Doug-Douglas Mitchell (Senator)	80-82MinA 82-86CalA 87BalA	11-04-52	Sarasota, Fla.		R	R	6'1	185	24	30	.444	66	313	1	0	553	497	200	343	0	3.32
Corbett, Sherman-Sherman Stanley	88-90CalA	11-03-62	New Braunfels, Tex.		L	L	6'4	205	2	1	.667	1	42	0	0	56	58	27	33	0	4.50
Corbin, Archie-Archie Ray	91KCA 96BalA 99FlaN	12-30-67	Beaumont, Tex.		R	R	6'4	220	2	1	.667	0	37	0	0	51	50	39	51	0	4.44
Corbin, Ray-Alton Ray	71-75MinA	02-12-49	Live Oak, Fla.		R	R	6'	190	36	38	.486	17	181	63	12	652	638	261	348	3	3.84
Corcoran, Roy-Roy Elliot	03-04MonN 06WasN	05-11-80	Baton Rouge, La.		R	R	5'10	170	0	1	.000	0	16	0	0	18	26	12	12	0	5.89
Corcoran, Tim-Timothy Hugh	05-06TBA	04-15-78	Baton Rouge, La.		R	R	6'2	205	5	9	.357	0	31	17	0	113	111	60	72	0	4.70
Cordero, Chad-Chad Patrick	03-04MonN 05-06WasN	03-18-82	Upland, Cal.		R	R	6'	195	17	11	.607	91	223	0	0	241	186	85	225	0	2.61
Cordero, Francisco-Francisco Javier	99DetA 00-06TexA 06MilN	05-11-75	Santo Domingo, D.R.		R	R	6'2	215	26	23	.531	133	404	0	0	443	402	195	441	0	3.33
Cordova, Francisco-Francisco	96-00PitN 01EJ	04-26-72	Veracruz, Mexico		R	R	5'11	195	42	47	.472	12	166	112	3	754	755	235	537	4	3.96
Corey, Bryan-Bryan Scott	98AriN 02LAN 06TexA 06BosA	10-21-73	Thousand Oaks, Cal.		R	R	6'1	170	2	1	.667	0	36	0	0	44	41	17	29	0	4.09
Corey, Mark-Mark Franklin	01-02NYN 03-04PhiN	11-16-74	Coudersport, Pa.		R	R	6'2	215	2	7	.222	0	81	0	0	90	105	49	79	0	6.02
Cormier, Lance-Lance Robert	04-06AriN	08-19-80	Lafayette, La.		R	R	6'1	192	12	12	.500	0	113	14	0	198	238	107	130	0	5.72
Cormier, Rheal-Rheal Paul	91-94StLN 95BosA 96-97MonN 98EJ 99-00BosA 01-06PhiN 06CinN	04-23-67	Moncton, Canada		L	L	5'10	185	71	64	.526	2	677	108	7	1219	1244	316	759	1	4.02
Cornejo, Mardie-Nieves Mardie (Chief)	78NYN	08-05-51	Wellington, Kans.		R	R	6'4	205	4	2	.667	3	25	0	0	37	37	14	17	0	2.43
Cornejo, Nate-Nathan John	01-04DetA	09-24-79	Wellington, Kans.		R	R	6'5	240	12	29	.293	0	56	56	3	313	404	115	103	0	5.41
Cornelius, Reid-Jonathan Reid	95MonN 95NYN 99-00FlaN	06-02-70	Thomasville, Ala.		R	R	6'6	200	8	17	.320	0	45	33	0	211	226	85	101	0	4.91
Cornell, Jeff-Jeffrey Ray	84SFN	02-10-57	Kansas City, Mo.		B	R	6'	170	1	3	.250	0	23	0	0	38	51	22	19	0	6.10
Cornett, Brad-Brad Byron	94-95TorA	02-04-69	Lamesa, Tex.		R	R	6'2	190	1	3	.250	0	14	4	0	36	49	14	26	0	7.00
Cornutt, Terry-Terry Stanton	77-78SFN	10-02-52	Roseburg, Ore.		R	R	6'2	195	1	2	.333	0	29	1	0	47	39	22	23	0	3.64
Corpas, Manuel-Manuel	06ColN	12-03-82	Panama City, Panama		R	R	6'3	170	1	2	.333	0	35	0	0	32	36	8	27	0	3.62
Correa, Ed-Edwin Jose [Andino]	85ChiA 86-87TexA 88-89SJ	04-29-66	Hato Rey, P.R.		R	R	6'2	205	16	19	.457	0	52	48	4	283	261	188	260	2	5.16
Correia, Kevin-Kevin John	03-06SFN	08-24-80	San Diego, Cal.		R	R	6'3	200	7	7	.500	0	86	19	0	186	191	81	143	0	4.35
Corsi, Jim-James Bernard	88-89OakA 90EJ 91HouN 92OakA 93FlaN 95-96OakA 97-99BosA 99BalA	09-09-61	Newton, Mass.		R	R	6'1	220	22	24	.478	7	368	1	0	481	450	191	290	0	3.25
Cort, Barry-Barry Lee	77MilA	04-15-56	Toronto, Canada		R	R	6'5	213	1	1	.500	0	7	3	1	24	25	9	17	0	3.38
Cortes, David-David [Cardenas]	99AtlN 03CleA 05-06ColN	10-15-73	Mexicali, Mexico		R	R	5'11	195	5	1	.833	2	86	0	0	89	96	20	53	0	4.47
Cosgrove, Mike-Michael John	72-76HouN	02-17-51	Phoenix, Ariz.		L	L	6'1	180	12	11	.522	8	119	20	2	275	271	145	122	1	4.03
Costello, John-John Reilly (Elvis)	88-90StLN 90MonN 91SDN	12-24-60	Bronx, N.Y.		R	R	6'1	190	11	6	.647	4	119	0	0	158	141	64	104	0	2.97
Cotts, Neal-Neal James	03-06ChiA	03-25-80	Belleville, Ill.		L	L	6'2	200	10	7	.588	1	199	5	0	193	178	100	169	0	4.52
Couchee, Mike-Michael Eugene	83SDN	12-04-57	San Jose, Cal.		R	R	6'	190	0	0	.000	0	8	0	0	14	12	6	5	0	5.14
Courtright, John-John Charles	95CinN	05-30-70	Marion, Ohio		L	L	6'2	185	0	0	—	0	1	0	0	1	2	0	0	0	9.00
Cowley, Joe-Joseph Alan	82AtlN 84-85NYA 86ChiA 87PhiN	08-15-58	Lexington, Ky.		R	R	6'5	215	33	25	.569	0	95	76	8	469	414	232	332	1	4.00
Cox, Danny-Danny Bradford	83-88StLN 89-90EJ 91-92PhiN 92PitN 93-95TorA	09-21-59	Northampton, England		R	R	6'4	230	74	75	.497	8	278	174	21	1298	1292	432	723	5	3.64
Crabtree, Tim-Timothy Lyle	95-97TorA 98-01TexA	10-13-69	Jackson, Mich.		R	R	6'4	215	21	22	.488	9	342	0	0	394	434	150	288	0	4.20
Crain, Jesse-Jesse Alan	04-06MinA	07-05-81	Toronto, Canada		R	R	6'1	205	19	10	.655	2	165	0	0	183	157	59	99	0	2.95
Cram, Jerry-Gerald Allen	69KCA 74-75NYN 76KCA	12-09-47	Los Angeles, Cal.		R	R	6'	180	0	3	.000	0	23	2	0	48	52	13	22	0	3.00
Crawford, Carlos-Carlos Lamonte	96PhiN	10-04-71	Charlotte, N.C.		R	R	6'1	190	0	1	.000	0	1	1	0	4	7	2	4	0	4.91
Crawford, Jim-James Frederick (Catfish)	73,75HouN 76-78DetA	09-29-50	Chicago, Ill.		L	L	6'3	200	15	28	.349	13	181	14	1	431	477	182	276	0	4.41
Crawford, Joe-Joseph Randal	97NYN	05-02-70	Gainesville, Fla.		L	L	6'3	225	4	3	.571	0	19	2	0	46	36	13	25	0	3.30
Crawford, Paxton-Paxton Keith	00-01BosA 02SJ	08-04-77	Little Rock, Ark.		R	R	6'3	205	5	1	.833	0	15	11	0	65	65	26	42	0	4.15
Crawford, Steve-Steven Ray (Shag)	80-82,84-87BosA 89-91KCA	04-29-58	Pryor, Okla.		R	R	6'5	225	30	23	.566	19	277	16	2	563	643	186	320	0	4.17
Creek, Doug-Paul Douglas	95StLN 96-97SFN 98JL 99ChiN 00-02TBA 02SeaA 03TorA 05DetA	03-01-69	Winchester, Va.		L	L	5'10	205	7	14	.333	1	279	3	0	289	263	199	292	0	4.51
Creel, Keith-Steven Keith (KC)	82-83KCA 85CleA 87TexA	02-04-59	Dallas, Tex.		R	R	6'3	185	5	14	.363	0	55	24	1	203	244	88	80	0	5.60
Cressend, Jack-John Baptiste III	00-02MinA 03MilN	05-13-75	New Orleans, La.		R	R	6'1	190	5	5	.500	0	122	0	0	161	172	60	104	0	4.20
Crews, Tim-Stanley Timothy	87-92LAN	04-03-61	Tampa, Fla.	03-23-93	R	R	6'	190	11	13	.458	15	281	4	0	424	444	110	293	0	3.44
Crim, Chuck-Charles Robert	87-91MilA 92-93CalA 94ChiN	07-23-61	Van Nuys, Cal.		R	R	6'	180	47	43	.522	45	449	6	0	696	731	209	334	0	3.83
Crosby, Ken-Kenneth Stewart	75-76ChiN	12-16-47	New Denver, Canada		R	R	6'3	188	1	0	1.000	0	16	1	0	20	30	15	11	0	8.55
Crouch, Zach-Zachary Quinn	88BosA	10-26-65	Folsom, Cal.		L	L	6'3	180	0	0	—	0	3	0	0	4	6	4	0	0	6.75
Croushore, Rich-Richard Steven	98-99StLN 00ColN 00BosA	08-07-70	Lakehurst, N.J.		R	R	6'4	210	5	11	.313	11	111	0	0	142	131	83	149	0	4.88
Crow, Dean-Paul Dean	98DetA	08-21-72	Garland, Tex.		R	R	6'3	212	2	2	.500	0	32	0	0	46	55	16	18	0	3.94
Crowell, Jim-James Everett	04PhiN	05-14-74	Minneapolis, Minn.		R	L	6'4	225	0	0	—	0	4	0	0	3	6	0	1	0	4.50
Crowell, Jim-James Everett	97CinN 04PhiN 05FlaN	05-14-74	Minneapolis, Minn.		R	L	6'4	220	0	1	.000	0	11	0	0	13	28	5	6	0	11.37
Cruceta, Francisco-Francisco Alberto	04CleA 06SeaA	07-04-81	Rancho Viejo, D.R.		R	R	6'2	180	0	1	.000	0	6	3	0	14	20	10	11	0	10.05
Crudale, Mike-Michael Christopher	02-03StLN 03MilN	01-03-77	San Diego, Cal.		R	R	6'	205	3	1	.750	0	71	1	0	73	55	32	60	0	2.09
Cruz, Juan-Juan Carlos	01-03ChiN 04AtlN 05OakA 06AriN	10-15-78	Bonao, Dom. Rep.		R	R	6'2	165	19	30	.388	1	187	38	0	402	367	203	377	0	4.32
Cruz, Nelson-Nelson	97ChiA 99-00DetA 01-02HouN 03ColN	09-13-72	Puerta Plata, Dom. Rep.		R	R	6'1	185	15	23	.395	2	204	18	0	348	369	109	277	0	5.04
Cruz (de la Cruz), Victor-Victor Manuel [Gil] (Hill)	78TorA 79-80CleA 81PitN 83TexA	12-24-57	Rancho Viejo, D.R.		R	R	5'10	205	18	23	.439	37	187	0	0	271	218	131	248	0	3.09
Cubillan, Darwin-Darwin Harrikson [Salom]	00TorA 00TexA 01MonN 04BalA	11-15-72	Bobure, Venezuela		R	R	6'2	170	1	0	1.000	0	56	0	0	70	96	44	54	0	6.85
Cuellar, Bobby-Robert	77TexA	08-20-52	Alice, Tex.		R	R	5'11	190	0	0	—	0	4	0	0	7	4	2	3	0	1.29
Cummings, John-John Russell	93-95SeaA 95-96LAN 96-97DetA	05-10-69	Torrance, Cal.		L	L	6'3	200	10	15	.400	1	110	16	1	216	251	106	114	0	5.33
Cummings, Steve-Steven Brent	89-90TorA	07-15-64	Houston, Tex.		B	R	6'2	200	2	0	1.000	0	11	4	0	33	40	16	12	0	3.78
Cunnane, Will-William Joseph	97-00SDN 01MilN 02ChiN 03-04AtlN	04-24-74	Suffern, N.Y.		R	R	6'2	195	13	12	.520	3	184	12	0	274	312	128	234	0	5.26
Currence, Lafayette-DeLancey Lafayette	75MilA	12-03-51	Rock Hill, S.C.		R	L	5'11	175	0	2	.000	0	8	1	0	19	25	14	7	0	7.58
Curry, Steve-Stephen Thomas	88BosA	09-13-65	Winter Park, Fla.		R	R	6'6	217	0	1	.000	0	3	3	0	11	15	14	4	0	8.18
Curtis, John-John Duffield	70-73BosA 74-76StLN 77-79SFN 80-82SDN 82-84CalA	03-09-48	Newton, Mass.		L	L	6'2	190	89	97	.478	11	438	199	42	1641	1695	669	825	14	3.96
Cyr, Eric-Eric	02ColN	02-11-79	Montreal, Canada		R	L	6'2	210	0	1	.000	0	5	0	0	6	6	4	4	0	10.50
Czajkowski, Jim-James Mark	94ColN	12-18-63	Parma, Ohio		B	R	6'4	215	0	0	—	0	5	0	0	6	9	6	2	0	4.15
Daal, Omar-Omar Jesus [Cordero]	93-95LAN 96-97MonN 97TexA 98-00AriN 00-01PhiN 02LAN 03BalA 04SJ	03-01-72	Maracaibo, Venez.		L	L	6'3	195	68	78	.466	1	392	164	5	1199	1250	441	806	2	4.55
D'Acquisto, John-John Francis (D)	73-76SFN 77StLN 77-80SDN 80MonN 81CalA 82OakA	12-24-51	San Diego, Cal.		R	R	6'2	205	34	51	.400	15	266	92	7	780	708	544	600	2	4.56
Daigle, Casey-Sean Casey	04,06AriN	04-04-81	Lake Charles, La.		R	R	6'5	217	2	3	.400	0	20	10	0	61	77	33	24	0	6.46
Dale, Carl-James Carl	99MilN	12-07-72	Indianapolis, Ind.		R	R	6'2	215	0	1	.000	0	4	0	0	8	6	4	6	0	20.25
Dalton, Mike-Michael Edward	91DetA	03-27-63	Palo Alto, Cal.		L	L	6'	215	0	0	—	0	4	0	0	8	12	2	4	0	3.38
D'Amico, Jeff-Jeffrey Charles	96-97MilA 98SJ 99-01MilN 02NYN 03PitN 04CleA	12-27-75	St. Petersburg, Fla.		R	R	6'7	250	45	52	.464	0	139	131	5	784	832	221	498	4	4.61
D'Amico, Jeff-Jeffrey Michael	00KCA	11-09-74	Inglewood, Cal.		R	R	6'3	200	0	1	.000	0	7	1	0	14	19	15	9	0	9.22
Daneker, Pat-Patrick Rees		01-14-76	Williamsport, Pa.		R	R	6'3	195	0	0	—	0	3	0	0	15	14	6	5	0	4.20
Darensbourg, Vic-Victor Anthony	98-02FlaN 03ColN 03MonN 04ChiA 04NYN 05DetA	11-13-70	Los Angeles, Cal.		L	L	5'10	165	8	17	.320	2	309	0	0	303	328	126	229	0	4.96
Darcy, Pay-Patrick Leonard	74-76CinN	05-12-50	Troy, Ohio		L	R	6'4	195	14	8	.636	3	44	28	1	187	192	89	75	0	4.14
Darling, Ron-Ronald Maurice	83-91NYN 91MonN 91-95OakA	08-19-60	Honolulu, Hawaii		R	R	6'3	205	136	116	.540	0	382	364	37	2360	2244	906	1590	13	3.87
Darr, Mike-Michael Edward	77DetA	03-23-56	Pomona, Cal.		R	R	6'	190	0	1	.000	0	4	1	0	3	4	1	1	0	45.00
Darwin, Danny-Daniel Wayne	78-84TexA 85-86MilA 87-90HouN 91-94BosA 95TorA 95TexA 96PitN 96HouN 97ChiA 97-98SFN	10-25-55	Bonham, Tex.		R	R	6'2	205	171	182	.484	32	716	371	53	3017	2951	874	1942	9	3.84
Darwin, Jeff-Jeffrey Scott	94SeaA 96-97ChiA	07-06-69	Sherman, Tex.		R	R	6'3	180	0	2	.000	0	38	0	0	48	50	19	25	0	4.47
Davenport, Joe-Joseph Jonathan	99ChiA 01ColN	03-24-76	Chicago, Ill.		R	R	6'5	225	0	0	—	0	12	0	0	9	9	8	0	0	3.00
Davey, Mike-Michael Gerard	77-78AtlN	06-02-52	Spokane, Wash.		R	L	6'2	200	0	0	—	0	19	0	0	19	20	10	7	0	4.26
Davey, Tom-Thomas Joseph	99TorA 99SeaA 00-02SDN	09-11-73	Garden City, Mich.		R	R	6'7	230	7	6	.538	1	114	0	0	137	138	70	123	0	4.41

USE NAMES - GIVEN NAMES (NICKNAMES)	TEAM BY YEAR	BIRTH DATE	BIRTHPLACE	DEATH DATE	B	T	HGT	WGT	W	L	Pct.	SV	G	GS	CG	IP	H	BB	SO	ShO	ERA
Davidson, Bobby-Robert Banks	89NYA	01-06-63	Bad Kurznach, Germany		R	R	6'	185	0	0	—	0	1	0	0	1	1	1	0	0	18.00
Davies, Kyle-Hiram Kyle	05-06AtlN	09-09-83	Decatur, Ga.		R	R	6'2	205	10	13	.435	0	35	28	1	151	188	82	113	0	6.38
Davis, Doug-Douglas P.	99-03TexA 03TorA 03-06MilN	09-21-75	Sacramento, Calif.		R	L	6'3	190	62	63	.496	0	196	176	7	1089	1125	474	807	3	4.35
Davis, Jason-Jason Thomas	02-06CleA	05-08-80	Chattanooga, Tenn.		R	R	6'6	195	18	22	.450	1	106	52	1	390	443	136	237	0	4.68
Davis, Joel-Joel Clark	85-88ChiA	01-30-65	Jacksonville, Fla.		L	R	6'5	205	8	14	.364	0	49	41	3	248	263	111	126	0	4.91
Davis, John-John Kirk	87KCA 88-89ChiA 90SDN	01-05-63	Chicago, Ill.		R	R	6'7	215	7	9	.438	4	71	1	0	123	120	82	73	0	4.92
Davis, Kane-Kane Thomas	00CleA 00MilN 01ColN 02NYN 05MilN	06-25-75	Ripley, W.Va.		R	R	6'3	194	4	9	.308	0	96	2	0	114	118	66	86	0	5.53
Davis, Lance-Johnny Lance	01CinN	09-01-76	Winter Haven, Fla.		R	L	6'	170	8	4	.667	0	20	20	1	106	124	34	53	0	4.74
Davis, Mark-Mark William	80-81PhiN 83-86SFN 87-89SDN 90-92KCA 92AtlN 93PhiN 93-94SDN 97MilA	10-19-60	Livermore, Cal.		L	L	6'4	210	51	84	.378	96	624	85	4	1145	1068	534	1007	2	4.17
Davis, Ron-Ronald Gene	78-81NYA 82-86MinA 86-87ChiN 87TexA 88SFN	08-06-55	Houston, Tex.		R	R	6'4	205	47	53	.470	130	481	0	0	746	735	300	597	0	4.05
Davis, Steve-Steven Kennon	85-86TorA 89CleA	08-04-60	San Antonio, Tex		L	L	6'1	180	3	2	.600	0	25	7	0	58	65	32	39	0	6.44
Davis, Storm-George Earl	82-86BalA 87SDN 87-89OakA 90-91KCA 92BalA 93OakA 93-94DetA	12-26-61	Dallas, Tex.		R	R	6'4	220	113	96	.541	11	442	239	30	1781	1792	687	1046	5	4.02
Davis, Tim-Timothy Howard	94-97SeaA 98EJ	07-14-70	Marianna, Fla.		L	L	5'11	165	6	5	.545	2	89	6	0	123	136	64	91	0	4.62
Davison, Scott-Scotty Ray	95-96SeaA	10-16-70	Inglewood, Cal.		R	R	6'	190	0	0	—	0	8	0	0	13	18	4	12	0	8.10
Dawley, Bill-William Chester	83-85HouN 86ChiN 87StLN 88PhiN 89OakA	02-06-58	Norwich, Conn.		R	R	6'5	235	27	30	.474	25	275	0	0	471	420	166	292	0	3.42
Dawley, Joey-Joseph Thomas	02-03AtlN 04CleA	09-19-71	Riverside, Cal.		R	R	6'4	205	0	0	—	0	8	2	0	16	22	10	17	0	10.91
Day, Zach-Stephen Zachary	02-04MonN 05WasN 05-06ColN 06KCA	06-15-78	Cincinnati, Ohio		R	R	6'4	210	21	27	.438	1	86	60	2	373	389	172	189	2	4.66
Dayley, Ken-Kenneth Grant (Major)	82-84AtlN 84-90StLN 91TorA 92EJ 93TorA	02-25-59	Jerome, Idaho		L	L	6'	180	33	45	.423	39	385	33	0	574	564	225	406	0	3.64
Deago, Roger-Roger I. (Villarreal)	03SDN	05-04-76	Monagrillo, Panama		R	L	5'8	180	0	1	.000	0	2	2	0	10	11	8	10	0	7.84
DeBarr, Dennis-Dennis Lee (Vulture)	77TorA	01-16-53	Cheyenne, Wyo.		L	L	6'2	195	0	1	.000	0	14	0	0	21	29	8	10	0	6.00
Decker, Joe-George Henry	69-72ChiN 73-76MinA 79SeaA	06-16-47	Storm Lake, Iowa		R	R	6'	180	36	44	.450	1	152	105	19	710	702	377	458	4	4.17
Decker, Marty-Dee Martin	83SDN	06-07-57	Upland, Cal.		R	R	5'10	170	0	0	—	0	4	0	0	9	5	3	9	0	2.08
Dedmon, Jeff-Jeffrey Linden	83-87AtlN 88CleA	03-04-60	Torrance, Cal.		L	R	6'2	200	20	16	.556	12	250	3	0	394	387	186	210	0	3.84
Dedrick, Jim-James Michael	95BalA	04-04-68	Los Angeles, Cal.		B	R	6'	185	0	0	—	0	6	0	0	8	8	6	3	0	2.35
DeHart, Rick-Richard Allen	97-99MonN 03KCA	01-21-70	Topeka, Kans.		L	L	6'1	190	2	3	.400	1	56	0	0	63	81	32	45	0	6.14
DeJean, Mike-Michel Dwain	97-00ColN 01-03MilN 03StLN 04BalA 04-05NYN 05-06ColN	09-28-70	Baton Rouge, La.		R	R	6'2	210	30	33	.476	52	565	1	0	623	649	292	446	0	4.30
DeJesus, Jose-Jose Luis [Velazquez]	88-89KCA 90-91PhiN 92-93SJ 94KCA	01-06-65	Brooklyn, N.Y.		R	R	6'5	210	20	19	.513	1	63	57	6	349	284	227	221	1	3.84
De La Maza, Roland-Roland Robert	97KCA	11-11-71	Granada Hills, Cal.		R	R	6'0	175	0	0	—	0	1	0	0	2	1	1	1	0	4.50
de la Rosa, Francisco-Francisco [Jimenez]	91BalA	03-03-66	La Romana, Dom. Rep.		B	R	5'11	185	0	0	—	0	2	0	0	4	6	2	1	0	4.50
de la Rosa, Jorge-Jorge Alberto [Gonzalez]	04-06MilN 06KCA	04-05-81	Monterrey, Mexico		L	L	6'1	190	7	11	.389	0	71	18	0	144	158	106	114	0	5.87
Delcarmen, Manny-Manuel Anthony	05-06BosA	02-16-82	Boston, Mass.		R	R	6'2	190	2	0	1.000	0	60	0	0	62	76	24	54	0	4.76
DeLeon, Jose-Jose [Chestaro]	83-86PitN 86-87ChiA 88-92StLN 92-93ChiA 95MonN	12-20-60	La Vega, Dom. Rep.		R	R	6'3	220	86	119	.420	6	415	264	21	1897	1556	841	1594	7	3.76
DeLeon, Luis-Luis Antonio [Tricoche]	81StLN 82-85SDN 87BalA 89SeaA	08-19-58	Ponce, P.R.		R	R	6'1	153	17	19	.472	32	207	1	0	334	284	77	248	0	3.13
De Los Santos, Luis-Luis	02TBA	11-01-77	Santo Domingo, D.R.		R	R	6'2	216	0	3	.000	0	3	3	0	14	24	4	7	0	11.57
De Los Santos, Ramon-Ramon [Generol] (Pinta Cora)	74HouN	05-19-49	Santo Domingo, D.R.		L	L	6'2	183	1	1	.500	0	12	0	0	12	11	12	7	0	2.25
De Los Santos, Valerio-Valerio Lorenzo	98-03MilN 03PhiN 04TorA 05FlaN	10-06-72	Las Matas, Dom.Rep.		L	L	6'4	210	9	12	.429	1	233	2	0	248	219	116	197	0	4.54
Del Toro, Miguel-Miguel Angel	99-00SFN	06-22-72	Obregon, Mexico	10-06-01	R	R	6'1	180	2	0	1.000	0	23	1	0	41	41	17	36	0	4.61
DeLucia, Rich-Richard Anthony	90-93SeaA 94CinN 95StLN 96-97SFN 97-98AnaA 99CleA	10-07-64	Reading, Pa.		R	R	6'	185	38	51	.427	7	320	49	1	624	590	299	502	0	4.62
Demaria, Chris-Christopher Neil	05KCA 06MilN	09-28-80	Torrance, Cal.		B	R	6'3	220	1	1	.500	0	18	0	0	23	24	14	22	0	7.15
Demery, Larry-Lawrence Calvin	74-77PitN 78SJ	06-11-53	Bakersfield, Cal.		R	R	6'	172	29	23	.558	7	139	46	7	445	413	199	217	1	3.72
DeMola, Don-Donald John (Mole)	74-75MonN 76AJ	07-05-52	Glen Cove, N.Y.		R	R	6'2	185	5	7	.417	1	85	1	0	156	138	63	110	0	3.75
Dempsey, Mark-Mark Steven	82SFN	12-17-57	Dayton, Ohio		R	R	6'6	225	0	0	—	0	3	1	0	6	11	2	4	0	7.94
Dempster, Ryan-Ryan Scott	98-02FlaN 02-03CinN 04-06CubN	05-03-77	Sechelt, Canada		R	R	6'2	210	57	68	.456	59	321	162	8	1152	1184	601	952	2	4.83
Denman, Brian-Brian John	82BosA	02-12-56	Minneapolis, Minn.		R	R	6'4	210	3	4	.429	0	9	9	2	49	55	9	9	0	4.78
Denney, Kyle-Kyle Dean	04CleA	07-27-77	Prague, Okla.		R	R	6'2	190	1	2	.333	0	4	1	0	16	32	8	13	0	9.56
Denny, John-John Allen	74-79StLN 80-82CleA 82-85PhiN 86CinN	11-08-52	Prescott, Ariz.		R	R	6'3	190	123	108	.532	0	325	322	62	2150	2093	778	1146	18	3.58
DePaula, Jorge-Jorge A.	03-05NYA	11-10-78	Sabana Grande, D.R.		R	R	6'1	160	0	1	.000	0	10	2	0	27	20	8	12	0	4.00
DePaula, Sean-Sean Michael	99-00,02CleA	11-07-73	Newton, Mass.		R	R	6'4	215	1	1	.500	0	29	0	0	35	39	20	42	0	6.75
Deshaies, Jim-James Joseph	84NYA 85-91HouN 92SDN 93MinA 93SFN 94MinA 95PhiN	06-23-60	Massena, N.Y.		L	L	6'5	220	84	95	.469	0	257	253	15	1525	1434	575	951	6	4.14
DeSilva, John-John Reed	93DetA 93LAN	09-30-67	Fort Bragg, Cal.		R	R	6'	195	1	0	1.000	0	6	2	0	15	16	8	7	0	7.20
Dessens, Elmer-Elmer [Jusaino]	96-98PitN 99JL 00-02CinN 03-04AriN 04-05LAN 06KCA 06LAN	01-13-71	Hermosillo, Mexico		R	R	6'	190	46	59	.438	5	339	135	2	1057	1180	306	639	1	4.41
Dettmer, John-John Franklin	94-95TexA	03-04-70	Centreville, Ill.		R	R	6'	185	0	6	.000	0	12	9	0	54	65	20	27	0	4.47
Dettore, Tom-Thomas Anthony	73PitN 74-76ChiN	11-17-47	Canonsburg, Pa.		R	L	6'4	210	8	11	.421	0	68	15	0	180	196	78	106	0	5.20
Devine, Adrian-Paul Adrian	73,75-76AtlN 77TexA 78-79AtlN 80TexA	12-02-51	Galveston, Tex.		R	R	6'4	200	26	22	.542	31	217	12	0	387	455	135	194	0	4.21
Devine, Joey-Joseph N.	05-06AtlN	09-19-83	Junction City, Kan.		R	R	6'	210	0	1	.000	0	15	0	0	11	14	14	13	0	11.12
Dewey, Mark-Mark Alan	90SFN 92NYN 93-94PitN 95-96SFN	01-03-65	Grand Rapids, Mich.		R	R	6'	210	12	7	.632	8	205	0	0	249	243	102	168	0	3.65
DeWitt, Matt-Matthew Brian	00-01TorA 02SDN	09-04-77	San Bernardino, Cal.		R	R	6'4	220	1	3	.250	0	40	48	22	24	0	4.95			
Diaz, Carlos-Carlos Antonio	82AtlN 82-83NYN 84-86LAN	01-07-58	Kaneohe, Hawaii		R	L	6'	170	13	6	.684	4	179	0	0	258	249	97	207	0	3.21
Diaz, Felix-Felix Antonio	04ChiA 05XJ	07-27-80	Las Matas, Dom. Rep.		R	R	6'1	180	2	5	.286	0	18	7	0	49	62	16	33	0	6.75
Diaz, Joselo-Joselo Soriano	06KCA	04-13-80	San Pedro de Mac., D.R.		R	R	6'	240	0	0	—	0	4	0	0	7	10	8	3	0	10.80
Dibble, Rob-Robert Keith	88-93CinN 94SJ 95ChiA 95MilA	01-24-64	Bridgeport, Conn.		L	R	6'4	230	27	25	.519	89	385	0	0	477	332	238	645	0	2.98
Dickey, R.A.-Robert Alan	01,03-06TexA	10-29-74	Nashville, Tenn.		R	R	6'3	205	16	19	.457	2	77	33	1	266	321	96	171	1	5.72
Dickson, Jason-Jason Royce	96CalA 97-98AnaA 99SJ 00AnaA	03-30-73	London, Canada		L	R	6'2	195	26	25	.510	0	73	63	2	397	474	122	214	1	4.99
Dickson, Lance-Lance Michael	90ChiN	10-19-69	Fullerton, Cal.		R	L	6'	185	0	3	.000	0	3	3	0	14	20	4	4	0	7.24
Diggins, Ben-Benjamin Howard	02MilN	06-13-78	Leota, Kans.		R	R	6'7	230	0	4	.000	0	5	5	0	24	28	18	15	0	8.63
Dillard, Gordon-Gordon Lee	88BalA 89PhiN	05-20-64	Salinas, Cal.		L	L	6'1	190	0	0	—	0	7	1	0	7	10	4	4	0	6.43
DiMichele, Frank-Frank Lawrence	88CalA	02-16-65	Philadelphia, Pa.		R	L	6'3	205	0	0	—	0	5	5	0	5	2	1	0	9.64
DiNardo, Lenny-Leonard Edward	04-06BosA	09-19-79	Miami, Fla.		L	L	6'4	195	1	3	.250	0	43	7	0	81	108	37	53	0	5.53
Dingman, Craig-Craig Allen	00NYA 01ColN 04-05DetA 06IL	04-10-74	Wichita, Kans.		R	R	6'4	215	4	5	.444	3	75	0	0	80	92	37	50	0	6.10
Diorio, Ron-Ronald Michael (D.O.)	73-74PhiN	07-15-46	Waterbury, Conn.		R	R	6'6	212	0	0	—	1	25	0	0	20	20	7	11	0	3.15
DiPino, Frank-Frank Michael	81MilA 82-86HouN 86-88ChiN 89-90StLN 91EJ 92StLN 93KCA	10-22-56	Syracuse, N.Y.		L	L	5'11	190	35	38	.479	56	514	6	0	700	673	269	515	0	3.83
Dipoto, Jerry-Gerard Peter	93-94CleA 95-96NYN 97-00ColN	05-24-68	Jersey City, N.J.		R	R	6'2	200	27	24	.529	49	390	0	0	495	527	221	352	0	4.05
Dishman, Glenn-Glenelg Edward	95-96SDN 96PhiN 97DetA	11-05-70	Baltimore, Md.		L	L	6'1	195	5	10	.333	0	33	21	0	135	146	45	66	0	5.25
Dixon, Ken-Kenneth John	84-87BalA	10-17-60	Monroe, Va.		B	R	5'10	190	26	28	.481	6	105	68	5	482	480	178	377	1	4.66
Dixon, Steve-Steven Ross	93-94StLN	08-03-69	Cincinnati, Ohio		R	L	6'	190	0	0	—	0	6	0	0	5	10	13	3	0	28.80
Dixon, Tom-Thomas Earl	77-79HouN 83MonN	04-23-55	Orlando, Fla.		R	R	6'	180	9	14	.391	1	62	24	4	200	225	63	94	2	4.33
Dobson, Pat-Patrick Edward	67-69DetA 70SDN 71-72BalA 73AtlN 73-75NYA 76-77CleA 78XJ	02-12-42	Depew, N.Y.		R	R	6'3	200	122	129	.486	19	414	279	74	2119	2043	665	1301	14	3.54
Dodd, Robert-Robert Wayne	98PhiN	03-14-73	Kansas City, Kan.		L	L	6'3	195	1	0	1.000	0	5	7	1	4	0	7.20			
Doherty, John-John Harold	92-95DetA 96BosA	06-11-67	Bronx, N.Y.		R	R	6'4	210	32	31	.508	3	148	61	5	521	613	140	177	2	4.87
Dohmann, Scott-Christopher Scott	04-06ColN 06KCA	02-13-78	New Orleans, La.		R	R	6'1	181	4	8	.333	1	121	0	0	125	133	71	128	0	5.74
Dominguez, Juan-Juan Ramon	03-05TexA	05-18-80	Sanchez Ramirez, D.R.		R	R	6'2	195	5	10	.333	0	27	20	0	110	119	42	72	0	4.60
Donnelly, Brendan-Brendan Kevin	02-04AnaA 05-06LAA	07-04-71	Washington, D.C.		R	R	6'2	225	23	8	.742	4	276	0	0	295	239	105	295	0	2.87
Dopson, John-John Robert	85,88MonN 89-93BosA 94CalA	07-14-63	Baltimore, Md.		R	R	6'4	220	30	47	.390	1	144	119	4	725	752	264	386	1	4.27
Dorsey, Jim-James Edward	80CalA 84-85BosA	08-02-55	Oak Park, Ill.		R	R	6'3	200	1	3	.250	0	9	5	0	24	43	20	14	0	11.63
Dotel, Octavio-Octavio Eduardo [Diaz]	99NYN 00-04HouN 04-05OakA 06NYA	11-25-73	Santo Domingo, D.R.		R	R	6'	200	37	31	.544	71	395	34	0	610	482	270	732	0	3.75
Dotson, Rich-Richard Elliott	79-87ChiA 88-89NYA 89ChiA 90KCA	01-10-59	Cincinnati, Ohio		R	R	6'	200	111	113	.496	0	305	295	65	1857	1884	740	973	11	4.23
Dougherty, Jim-James E.	95-96HouN 98OakA 99PitN	03-08-68	Brentwood, N.Y.		R	R	6'	210	8	8	.500	0	79	0	0	95	110	46	59	0	5.99
Douglass, Sean-Sean Reed	01-03BalA 04TorA 05DetA	04-28-79	Lancaster, Cal.		R	R	6'6	210	7	13	.350	0	54	31	0	208	222	113	155	0	6.11
Downs, Kelly-Kelly Robert	86-92SFN 92-93OakA	10-25-60	Ogden, Utah		R	R	6'4	205	57	53	.518	4	237	135	11	964	912	373	598	6	3.86
Downs, Scott-Scott Jeremy	00ChiN 00MonN 01-02EJ 03-04MonN 05-06TorA	03-17-76	Louisville, Ky.		L	L	6'2	190	17	15	.531	1	117	50	1	334	372	130	241	1	4.80
Dozier, Tom-Thomas Dean	86BalA	09-05-61	San Pablo, Cal.		R	R	6'2	190	0	0	—	1	2	0	0	5	6	2	4	0	5.68
Drabek, Doug-Douglas Dean	86NYA 87-92PitN 93-96HouN 97ChiA 98BalA	07-25-62	Victoria, Tex.		R	R	6'1	185	155	134	.536	0	398	387	53	2535	2448	704	1594	21	3.73
Drago, Dick-Richard Anthony	69-73KCA 74-75BosA 76-77CalA 77BalA 78-80BosA 81SeaA	06-25-45	Toledo, Ohio		R	R	6'1	195	108	117	.480	58	519	189	62	1876	1901	558	987	10	3.62
Drahman, Brian-Brian Stacy	91-93ChiA 94FlaN	11-07-66	Kenton, Ky.		R	R	6'2	230	3	2	.600	4	47	0	0	56	49	23	29	0	3.54
Draper, Mike-Michael Anthony	93NYN	09-14-66	Hagerstown, Md.		R	R	6'2	195	1	1	.500	0	29	0	0	42	53	14	16	0	4.39

USE NAMES - GIVEN NAMES (NICKNAMES)	TEAM BY YEAR	BIRTH DATE	BIRTHPLACE	DEATH DATE	B	T	HGT	WGT	W	L	Pct.	SV	G	GS	CG	IP	H	BB	SO	ShO	ERA
Dravecky, Dave-David Francis	82-87SDN 87-89SFN	02-14-56	Youngstown, Ohio		R	L	6'1	200	64	57	.529	10	226	146	28	1063	968	315	558	9	3.13
Drees, Tom-Thomas Kent	91ChiA	06-17-63	Des Moines, Iowa		B	L	6'6	210	0	0	—	0	4	0	0	7	10	6	2	0	12.27
Dreifort, Darren-Darren John	94LAN 95EJ 96-01LAN 02EJ 03-04LAN 05SJ	05-03-72	Wichita, Kans.		R	R	6'2	210	48	60	.444	11	274	113	3	873	826	389	802	3	4.36
Drese, Ryan-Ryan Thomas	01-02CleA 03-05TexA 05-06WasN	04-05-76	San Francisco, Cal.		R	R	6'3	220	34	39	.466	0	105	96	4	566	673	213	301	0	5.31
Dressendorfer, Kirk-Kirk Richard	91OakA 92SJ	04-08-69	Houston, Tex.		R	R	5'11	185	3	3	.500	0	7	7	0	35	33	21	17	0	5.45
Dressler, Rob-Robert Alan	75-76SFN 78StLN 79-80SeaA	02-02-54	Portland, Ore.		R	R	6'3	190	11	23	.324	0	82	48	6	390	449	98	129	0	4.18
Drew, Tim-Timothy Andrew	00-01CleA 02-03MonN 04AtlN	08-31-78	Valdosta, Ga.		R	R	6'1	195	2	4	.333	2	35	11	0	85	113	39	40	0	7.02
Dreyer, Steve-Steven William	93-94TexA	11-19-69	Ames, Iowa		R	R	6'3	180	4	4	.500	0	15	9	0	58	67	28	34	0	5.71
Driskill, Travis-Travis Corey	02-03BalA 04ColN 05HouN	08-01-71	Omaha, Neb.		R	R	6'	225	11	13	.458	1	55	19	0	190	226	60	119	0	5.26
Drummond, Tim-Timothy Darnell	87PitN 89-90MinA	12-24-64	La Plata, Md.		R	R	6'3	170	3	5	.375	2	49	4	0	113	125	47	63	0	4.29
DuBois, Brian-Brian Andrew	89-90DetA 90BalA 91SJ	04-18-65	Joliet, Ill.		L	L	5'10	170	3	9	.250	1	18	16	0	94	99	39	47	0	3.82
DuBose, Eric-Eric Ladell	02-06BalA	05-15-76	Bradenton, Fla.		L	L	6'3	231	9	15	.375	0	52	27	1	188	181	92	115	0	5.21
Duchscherer, Justin-Justin Craig	01TexA 03-06OakA	11-19-77	Aberdeen, S.D.		R	R	6'3	190	18	13	.581	14	180	5	0	269	245	67	221	0	3.35
Duckworth, Brandon-Brandon J.	01-03PhiN 04-05HouN 06KCA	01-23-76	Salt Lake City, Utah		B	R	6'2	185	17	26	.395	0	101	74	0	426	463	186	335	0	5.43
Dues, Hal-Hal Joseph	77-78,80MonN	09-22-54	Texas City, Tex.		R	R	6'3	190	6	8	.429	1	37	17	1	134	128	56	47	0	3.09
Duff, Matt-Matthew Clark	02StLN	10-06-74	Clarksdale, Miss.		R	R	6'1	192	0	0	—	0	7	0	0	6	3	8	4	0	4.76
Duke, Zach-Zachary Thomas	05-06PitN	04-19-83	Clifton, Tex.		L	L	6'2	210	18	17	.514	0	48	48	2	300	334	91	175	1	3.72
Dumoulin, Dan-Daniel Lynn (Dummy)	77-78CinN	08-20-53	Kokomo, Ind.		R	R	5'11	180	1	0	1.000	0	8	0	0	10	19	6	7	0	8.10
Dunbar, Matt-Matthew Marshall	95FlaN	10-15-68	Tallahassee, Fla.		L	L	6'	170	0	1	.000	0	8	0	0	7	12	11	5	0	11.57
Duncan, Courtney-Courtney Demond	01-02CinN	10-09-74	Mobile, Ala.		L	R	6'	185	3	3	.500	0	38	0	0	45	44	26	50	0	4.80
Dunn, Scott-Scott Allen	04AnaA 06TBA	05-23-78	San Antonio, Tex.		R	R	6'3	200	1	0	1.000	0	10	0	0	11	24	5	6	0	10.97
Dunne, Mike-Michael Dennis	87-89PitN 89SeaA 90SDN 92ChiA 93EJ	10-27-62	South Bend, Ind.		R	R	6'4	210	25	30	.455	0	85	76	7	474	471	225	205	1	4.08
Dunning, Steve-Steven John	70-73CleA 73-74TexA 76CalA 76MonN 77OakA	05-15-49	Denver, Colo.		R	R	6'2	205	23	41	.359	1	136	84	7	612	604	323	390	1	4.57
Dupree, Mike-Michael Dennis	76SDN	05-29-53	Kansas City, Kans.		R	R	6'1	195	0	0	—	0	12	0	0	16	18	7	5	0	9.00
Duran, Roberto-Roberto Alejandro	97-98DetA	03-06-73	Moca, Dom. Rep.		L	L	6'0	167	0	1	.000	0	31	0	0	26	26	32	23	0	6.58
Durbin, Chad-Chad Griffin	99-02KCA 03-04CleA 04AriN 06DetA	12-03-77	Spring Valley, Ill.		B	R	6'1	195	17	30	.362	0	78	56	3	337	402	144	199	0	6.14
Durbin, J.D.-Joseph Adam	04MinA	02-24-82	Portland, Ore.		R	R	6'	200	1	0	1.000	0	4	1	0	7	12	6	6	0	7.36
Durocher, Jayson-Jayson Paul	02-03MilN	08-14-74	Hartford, Conn.		R	R	6'3	195	3	1	.750	0	45	0	0	55	36	23	51	0	3.09
Duvall, Mike-Michael Alan	98-00TBA 01MinA 02EJ	10-11-74	Warrenton, Va.		L	L	6'1	195	1	1	.500	0	53	0	0	51	62	32	23	0	4.76
Dyer, Mike-Michael Lawrence	89MinA 94-95PitN 96MonN	09-08-66	Upland, Cal.		R	R	6'3	195	14	18	.438	6	155	13	1	237	249	113	154	0	4.60
Dykhoff, Radhames-Radhames Alviro	98BalA	09-27-74	Paradera, Aruba		L	L	6'0	205	0	0	—	0	1	0	0	1	2	1	1	0	18.00
Earley, Bill-William Albert	86StLN	01-30-56	Cincinnati, Ohio		R	L	6'4	200	0	0	—	0	3	0	0	3	0	2	2	0	0.00
Easley, Logan-Kenneth Logan	87,89PitN	11-04-61	Salt Lake City, Utah		R	R	6'1	185	2	1	.667	2	27	0	0	39	31	24	27	0	5.12
Easterly, Jamie-James Morris (Rat)	74-79AtlN 81-83MilA 83-87CleA	02-17-53	Houston, Tex.		L	L	5'9	180	23	33	.411	14	321	36	0	613	663	319	350	0	4.61
Eastwick, Rawley-Rawlins Jackson	74-77CinN 77StLN 78NYA 78-79PhiN 80KCA 81ChiN	10-24-50	Camden, N.J.		R	R	6'2	175	28	27	.509	68	326	1	0	526	519	156	295	0	3.30
Eaton, Adam-Adam Thomas	00-05SDN 06TexA	11-23-77	Seattle, Wash.		R	R	6'2	190	54	45	.545	0	146	144	3	861	865	306	666	0	4.40
Eaton, Craig-Craig Thomas	79KCA	09-07-54	Glendale, Cal.		R	R	6'	180	0	0	—	0	5	0	0	10	8	3	4	0	2.70
Eave, Gary-Gary Louis	88-89AtlN 90SeaA	07-22-63	Monroe, La.		R	R	6'4	200	2	3	.400	0	16	8	0	56	49	35	25	0	3.56
Ebert, Derrin-Derrin Lee	99AtlN	08-21-76	Anaheim, Calif.		R	L	6'2	200	1	0	1.000	1	5	0	0	8	9	5	4	0	5.63
Eckenstahler, Eric-Eric Ryan	02-03DetA	12-17-76	Waukegan, Ill.		L	L	6'7	220	1	0	1.000	0	27	0	0	24	23	17	25	0	3.80
Eckersley, Dennis-Dennis Lee	75-77CleA 78-84BosA 84-86ChiN 87-95OakA 96-97StLN 98BosA	10-03-54	Oakland, Cal.		R	R	6'2	195	197	171	.535	390	1071	361	100	3286	3076	738	2401	20	3.50
Eddy, Chris-Christopher Mark	95OakA	11-27-69	Dallas, Tex.		L	L	6'3	200	0	0	—	0	4	0	0	4	7	2	2	0	7.36
Edelen, Joe-Benny Joe	81StLN 81-82CinN	09-16-55	Durant, Okla.		R	R	6'	180	2	0	1.000	0	27	0	0	45	56	11	26	0	6.75
Edenfield, Ken-Kenneth Edward	95-96CalA	03-18-67	Jesup, Ga.		R	R	6'1	165	0	0	—	0	9	0	0	17	25	7	10	0	5.82
Edens, Tom-Thomas Patrick	87NYN 90MilA 91-92MinA 93-94HouN 94PhiN 95ChiN	06-09-61	Ontario, Ore.		R	R	6'2	185	19	12	.613	4	182	14	0	312	315	123	182	0	3.86
Edge, Butch-Claude Lee	79TorA	07-18-56	Houston, Tex.		R	R	6'3	215	3	4	.429	0	9	9	1	52	60	24	19	0	5.19
Edmondson, Brian-Brian Christopher	98AtlN 98-99FlaN 00SJ	01-29-73	Fontana, Cal.		R	R	6'2	175	9	12	.429	1	121	0	0	170	182	81	98	0	4.98
Edwards, Wayne-Wayne Maurice	89-91ChiA	03-07-64	Burbank, Cal.		L	L	6'5	185	5	5	.500	2	68	5	0	126	110	61	84	0	3.37
Egloff, Bruce-Bruce Edward	91CleA 92EJ	04-10-65	Denver, Colo.		R	R	6'2	215	0	0	—	0	6	0	0	6	8	4	4	0	4.76
Eichelberger, Juan-Juan Tyrone (Ike)	78-82SDN 83CleA 88AtlN	10-21-53	St. Louis, Mo.		R	R	6'2	200	26	36	.419	0	125	79	14	603	575	283	281	1	4.10
Eichhorn, Mark-Mark Anthony (Ike)	82,86-88TorA 89AtlN 90-92CalA 92-93TorA 94BalA 95SJ 96CalA	11-21-60	San Jose, Cal.		R	R	6'4	210	48	43	.527	32	563	7	0	886	825	270	640	0	3.00
Eiland, Dave-David William	88-91NYA 92-93SDN 95NYA 98-00TBA	07-05-66	Dade City, Fla.		R	R	6'3	210	12	27	.308	0	92	70	0	373	465	118	153	0	5.74
Einertson, Darrell-Darrell Lee	00NYA	09-04-72	Rhinelander, Wis.		R	R	6'2	190	0	0	—	0	11	0	0	13	16	4	3	0	3.55
Eischen, Joey-Joseph Raymond	94MonN 95-96LAN 96DetA 97CinN 01-04MonN 05-06WasN	05-25-70	West Covina, Cal.		L	L	6'1	205	11	9	.550	3	324	0	0	296	297	139	244	0	3.67
Elarton, Scott-Vincent Scott	98-01HouN 01ColN 02SJ 03-04ColN 04-05CleA 06KCA	02-23-76	Lamar, Colo.		R	R	6'8	240	54	56	.491	3	215	161	4	1013	1038	388	670	1	5.13
Elder, Dave-David Matthew	02-03CleA	09-23-75	Atlanta, Ga.		R	R	6'	180	1	3	.250	0	19	0	0	25	23	18	26	0	4.62
Eldred, Cal-Calvin John	91-97MilA 98-99MilN 00-01ChiA 03-05StLN	11-24-67	Cedar Rapids, Iowa		R	R	6'4	230	86	74	.538	0	341	192	19	1368	1340	576	939	4	4.42
Ellingsen, Bruce-Harold Bruce	74CleA	04-26-49	Pocatello, Idaho		L	R	6'	180	1	1	.500	0	16	2	0	42	45	17	16	0	3.21
Elliott, Donnie-Donald Glenn	94-95SDN	09-20-68	Pasadena, Tex.		R	R	6'4	220	0	1	.000	0	31	1	0	35	33	22	27	0	3.09
Ellis, Dock-Dock Phillip	68-75PitN 76-77NYA 77OakA 77-79TexA 79NYN 79PitN	03-11-45	Los Angeles, Cal.		B	R	6'3	205	138	119	.537	1	345	317	71	2129	2067	674	1136	14	3.45
Ellis, Robert-Robert Randolph	96CalA 01AriN 02LAN 03TexA	12-15-70	Baton Rouge, La.		R	R	6'5	220	7	7	.500	0	29	21	0	118	138	48	54	0	6.03
Ellsworth, Steve-Steven Clark	88BosA	07-30-60	Chicago, Ill.		R	R	6'8	220	1	6	.143	0	8	7	0	36	47	16	16	0	6.75
Elvira, Narciso-Narciso Chico [Delgado]	90MilA	10-29-67	Veracruz, Mexico		L	L	5'10	170	0	0	—	0	4	0	0	5	6	5	6	0	5.40
Embree, Alan-Alan Duane	92,95-96CleA 97-98AtlN 98AriN 99-01SFN 01ChiA 02SDN 02-05BosA 05NYA 06SDN	01-23-70	The Dalles, Ore.		L	L	6'2	185	34	36	.486	8	708	0	0	620	590	232	571	0	4.56
Encarnacion (Lora), Luis-Luis Martin [Encarnacion]	90KCA	10-20-63	Santo Domingo, D.R.		R	R	5'10	180	0	0	—	0	10	0	0	10	14	4	8	0	7.84
Enders, Trevor-Trevor Hale	00TBA	12-22-74	Milwaukee, Wis.		R	L	6'1	205	0	1	.000	0	9	0	0	9	14	5	5	0	10.61
Engel, Steve-Steven Michael	85ChiN	12-31-61	Cincinnati, Ohio		L	L	6'3	210	1	5	.167	0	11	8	1	52	61	26	29	0	5.57
Engle, Rick-Richard Douglas	81MonN	04-07-57	Corbin, Ky.		R	L	6'3	183	0	0	—	0	1	0	0	2	6	1	2	0	18.00
Ennis, John-John Wayne	02AtlN 04DetA	10-17-79	Montrose, Colo.		R	R	6'5	220	0	0	—	1	13	1	0	20	25	8	14	0	7.65
Enyart, Terry-Terry Gene (Earthquake)	74MonN	10-10-50	Ironton, Ohio		R	R	6'3	220	0	0	—	0	2	1	0	2	4	1	2	0	13.50
Erardi, Greg-Joseph Gregory	77SeaA	05-31-54	Syracuse, N.Y.		R	R	6'1	195	0	1	.000	0	9	0	0	9	12	6	5	0	6.00
Erdos, Todd-Todd Michael	97SDN 98-00NYA 00SDN 01BosA	11-21-73	Washington, Pa.		R	R	6'1	205	2	0	1.000	2	63	0	0	94	105	45	58	0	5.57
Ericks, John-John Edward	95-97PitN	06-16-67	Tinley Park, Ill.		R	R	6'7	220	8	14	.364	14	57	22	1	162	171	73	132	0	4.78
Erickson, Roger-Roger Farrell (Pudge)	78-82MinA 82-83NYA	08-30-56	Springfield, Ill.		R	R	6'1	185	35	53	.398	1	135	117	24	799	868	251	365	0	4.14
Erickson, Scott-Scott Gavin	90-95MinA 95-00BalA 01EJ 02BalA 03SJ 04NYN 04TexA 05LAN 06NYA	02-02-68	Long Beach, Cal.		R	R	6'4	230	142	136	.511	0	389	364	51	2361	2586	865	1252	17	4.59
Escarrega (Acosta), Chico-Ernesto Acosta [Escarrega]	82ChiA	12-27-49	Los Mochis, Mexico		R	R	5'11	195	1	3	.250	1	38	2	0	74	73	16	33	0	3.67
Escobar, Kelvim-Kelvim Jose [Bolivar]	97-03TorA 04AnaA 05-06LAA	04-11-76	La Guaira, Venezuela		R	R	6'1	210	83	83	.500	59	380	171	2	1306	1275	541	1145	3	4.26
Eshelman, Vaughn-Vaughn Michael	95-97BosA 98SJ	05-22-69	Philadelphia, Pa.		L	L	6'3	205	15	9	.625	0	83	30	0	212	256	111	118	0	6.07
Espinosa (Acevedo), Nino-Amulfo Acevedo [Espinosa]	74-78NYN 78-81PhiN 81TorA	08-15-53	Villa Altagracia, D.R.	12-25-87	R	R	6'1	180	44	56	.444	0	140	126	14	821	865	252	338	5	4.17
Esposito, Mike-Michael Anthony	05ColN	09-27-81	Los Angeles, Cal.		R	R	6'	190	0	2	.000	0	3	3	0	15	21	9	5	0	6.75
Esser, Mark-Mark Gerald (Express)	79CinN	04-01-56	Erie, Pa.		R	L	6'	198	0	0	—	0	2	0	0	2	4	1	1	0	13.50
Estes, Shawn-Aaron Shawn (Buck)	95-01SFN 02NYN 02-03CinN 04ColN 05AriN 06SDN	02-18-73	San Bernardino, Cal.		R	L	6'2	195	99	90	.524	0	274	273	14	1635	1658	840	1191	8	4.71
Estrada, Horacio-Horacio [Jimenez]	99-00MilN 01ColN	10-19-75	San Joaquin, Venezuela		L	L	6'1	190	4	1	.800	0	15	4	0	36	48	25	22	0	7.50
Estrella, Leo-Leoncio [Ramirez]	00TorA 03MilN 04SFN	02-20-75	Puerto Plata, Dom. Rep.		R	R	6'1	185	7	3	.700	3	62	0	0	72	92	22	28	0	4.88
Etherton, Seth-Seth Michael	00AnaA 03CinN 05OakA 06KCA	10-17-76	Laguna Beach, Cal.		R	R	6'2	200	9	7	.563	0	23	23	0	116	133	48	63	0	6.30
Ettles, Mark-Mark Edward	93SDN	10-30-66	Perth, Australia		R	R	6'	178	1	0	1.000	1	14	0	0	18	23	4	9	0	6.50
Eufemia, Frank-Frank Anthony	85MinA	12-23-59	Bronx, N.Y.		R	R	5'11	185	4	2	.667	1	39	0	0	60	56	21	30	0	3.79
Evans, Bart-Bart Steven	98KCA	12-30-70	Springfield, Mo.		R	R	6'2	210	0	0	—	0	9	0	0	7	0	7	2	0	2.00
Eveland, Dana-Dana J.	05-06MilN	10-29-83	Olympia, Wash.		L	L	6'1	219	1	4	.200	1	36	5	0	59	79	34	55	0	6.98
Eversgerd, Bryan-Bryan David	94StLN 95MonN 97TexA 98StLN	02-11-69	Centralia, Ill.		L	L	6'1	190	2	5	.286	0	76	1	0	96	111	34	61	0	5.16
Eyre, Scott-Scott Alan	97-00ChiA 01-02TorA 02-05SFN 06ChiN	05-30-72	Inglewood, Cal.		L	L	6'1	200	19	28	.404	4	482	32	0	541	550	274	438	0	4.39
Eyre, Willie-William Mays	06MinA	07-21-78	Fountain Valley, Cal.		R	R	6'2	205	1	0	1.000	0	59	0	0	75	72	28	26	0	5.31
Fajardo, Hector-Hector [Nabaratte]	91PitN 91,93-95TexA	11-06-70	Michoacan, Mexico		R	R	6'4	200	5	9	.357	0	30	17	0	124	149	40	78	0	6.95
Falcone, Pete-Peter Frank	75SFN 76-78StLN 79-82NYN 83-84AtlN	10-01-53	Brooklyn, N.Y.		L	L	6'2	185	70	90	.438	7	325	217	25	1435	1385	671	865	7	4.07
Falkenborg, Brian-Brian Thomas	99BalA 04LAN 05SDN 06StLN	01-18-78	Newport Beach, Calif.		R	R	6'6	195	1	1	.500	0	35	0	0	35	43	16	27	0	6.23

USE NAMES - GIVEN NAMES (NICKNAMES)	TEAM BY YEAR	BIRTH DATE	BIRTHPLACE	DEATH DATE	B	T	HGT	WGT	W	L	Pct.	SV	G	GS	CG	IP	H	BB	SO	ShO	ERA
Fallon, Bob-Robert Joseph	84-85ChiA	02-18-60	Bronx, N.Y.		L	L	6'3	210	0	0	—	0	13	3	0	31	37	20	27	0	4.99
Falteisek, Steve-Steven James	97MonN 99MilN	01-28-72	Mineola, N.Y.		R	R	6'2	200	0	0	—	0	15	0	0	20	26	6	7	0	5.85
Fansler, Stan-Stanley Robert	86PitN	02-12-65	Elkins, W. Va.		R	R	5'11	185	0	3	.000	0	5	5	0	24	20	15	13	0	3.75
Farmer, Ed-Edward Joseph (The Raven)	71-73CleA 73DetA 74PhiN 77BalA 78MilA 79TexA 79-81ChiA 82-83PhiN 83OakA	10-18-49	Evergreen Park, Ill.		R	R	6'5	205	30	43	.411	75	370	21	0	624	611	345	395	0	4.30
Farmer, Howard-Howard Earl	90MonN	11-18-66	Gary, Ind.		R	R	6'3	190	0	3	.000	0	6	4	0	23	26	10	14	0	7.04
Farmer, Mike-Michael Anthony	96ColN	07-03-68	Gary, Ind.		B	L	6'1	193	0	1	.000	0	7	4	0	28	32	13	16	0	7.71
Farnsworth, Jeff-Jeffrey Ellis	02DetA	10-06-75	Wichita, Kans.		R	R	6'2	190	2	3	.400	0	44	0	0	70	100	29	28	0	5.79
Farnsworth, Kyle-Kyle Lynn	99-04ChiN 05DetA 05AtlN 06NYA	04-14-76	Wichita, Kans.		R	R	6'4	230	26	44	.371	26	487	26	1	615	574	279	629	1	4.44
Farr, Jim-James Alfred	82TexA	05-18-56	Waverly, N.Y.		R	R	6'1	190	0	0	—	0	5	0	0	18	20	7	6	0	2.50
Farr, Steve-Steven Michael	84CleA 85-90KCA 91-93NYA 94CleA 94BosA	12-12-56	Cheverly, Md.		R	R	5'10	198	48	45	.516	132	509	28	1	824	751	334	668	1	3.25
Farrell, John-John Edward	87-90CleA 91-92EJ 93-94CalA 95CleA 96DetA	08-04-62	Monmouth Beach, N.J.		R	R	6'4	210	36	46	.439	0	116	109	13	699	732	250	355	2	4.56
Fassero, Jeff-Jeffrey Joseph	91-96MonN 97-99SeaA 99TexA 00BosA 01-02ChiN 03StLN 04ColN 04AriN 05-06SFN	01-05-63	Springfield, Ill.		L	L	6'1	195	121	124	.494	25	720	242	17	2034	2083	724	1643	2	4.11
Feierabend, Ryan-Ryan Robert		08-22-85	Cleveland, Ohio		L	L	6'3	190	0	1	.000	0	4	2	0	17	15	7	11	0	3.71
Feldman, Scott-Scott Wayne	05-06TexA	02-07-83	Kailua, Hawaii		L	R	6'5	225	0	3	.000	0	44	0	0	51	51	12	34	0	3.38
Feliciano, Pedro-Pedro Juan [Molina]	02-04,06NYN	08-25-76	Rio Piedras, P.R.		L	L	5'10	185	8	3	.727	0	115	0	0	133	131	54	115	0	3.25
Felton, Terry-Terry Lane (Smiley)	79-82MinA	10-29-57	Texarkana, Ark.		R	R	6'2	185	0	16	.000	3	55	10	0	138	123	87	108	0	5.53
Fermin, Ramon-Ramon Antonio [Ventura]	95OakA	11-25-72	San Francisco de Mac.,D.R.		R	R	6'3	180	0	0	—	0	1	0	0	4	1	0	1	0	13.50
Fernandez, Alex-Alexander	90-96ChiA 97FlaN 98SJ 99-00FlaN 01SJ	08-13-69	Miami Beach, Fla.		R	R	6'2	220	107	87	.552	0	263	261	33	1760	1693	552	1252	10	3.74
Fernandez, Jared-Jared Wade	01-02HouN 03-04HouN 06MilN	08-13-72	Salt Lake City, Utah		R	R	6'2	223	4	7	.364	0	37	17	0	109	126	48	61	0	5.05
Fernandez, Osvaldo-Osvaldo	96-97SFN 98EJ 00-01CinN	11-04-68	Holguin, Cuba		R	R	6'2	190	19	26	.422	0	76	67	3	387	439	136	208	0	4.93
Fernandez, Sid-Charles Sidney (El Sid)	83LAN 84-93NYN 94-95BalA 95-96PhiN 97HouN	10-12-62	Honolulu, Hawaii		L	L	6'1	230	114	96	.543	1	307	300	25	1867	1421	715	1743	9	3.36
Ferrari, Anthony-Anthony Michael	03MonN	06-22-78	San Francisco, Cal.		L	L	5'9	160	0	0	—	0	4	0	0	4	4	5	1	0	6.75
Ferreira, Tony-Anthony Ross	85KCA	10-04-62	Riverside, Cal.		L	L	6'1	160	0	0	—	0	2	0	0	6	6	2	5	0	7.94
Ferris, Bob-Robert Eugene (Wheel)	79-80CalA	05-07-55	Arlington, Va.		R	R	6'6	220	0	2	.000	0	7	3	0	21	28	12	6	0	4.71
Fetters, Mike-Michael Lee	89-91CalA 92-97MilA 98OakA 98AnaA 99BalA 00-01LAN 01-02PitN 02AriN 03MinA 04AriN	12-19-64	Van Nuys, Cal.		R	R	6'4	220	31	41	.431	100	620	6	0	717	699	351	518	0	3.86
Fidrych, Mark-Mark Steven (Bird)	76-80DetA	08-14-54	Northboro, Mass.		R	R	6'1	175	29	19	.604	0	58	56	34	412	397	99	170	5	3.10
Field, Nate-Nathan Patrick	02-05KCA 06ColN	12-11-75	Denver, Colo.		R	R	6'2	200	4	5	.444	3	88	0	0	87	89	46	70	0	4.88
Fife, Dan-Danny Wayne	73-74MinA	10-05-49	Harrisburg, Ill.		R	R	6'2	190	3	2	.600	0	14	7	1	57	64	33	21	0	5.37
Figueroa, Ed-Eduardo [Padilla]	74-75CalA 76-80NYA 80TexA 81OakA	10-14-48	Ciales, P.R.		R	R	6'1	195	80	67	.544	1	200	179	63	1310	1299	443	571	12	3.51
Figueroa, Nelson-Nelson	00AriN 01PhiN 02MilN 03-04PitN	05-18-74	Brooklyn, N.Y.		B	R	6'1	170	7	17	.292	0	74	33	0	261	268	103	152	0	4.65
Fikac, Jeremy-Jeremy Joseph	01-02SDN 03OakA 04MonN	04-08-75	Shiner, Tex.		R	R	6'1	185	7	10	.412	0	121	0	0	136	129	63	116	0	4.60
File, Bob-Robert Michael	01-02,04TorA		Philadelphia, Pa.		R	R	6'4	215	6	4	.600	0	89	0	0	111	110	43	55	0	4.20
Filer, Tom-Thomas Carson (Files)	82ChiN 85TorA 86EJ 88-90MilA 92NYN	12-01-56	Philadelphia, Pa.		R	R	6'1	198	22	17	.564	0	67	51	2	307	314	107	115	1	4.25
Filson, Pete-William Peter	82-86MinA 86ChiA 87NYA 90KCA	09-28-58	Darby, Pa.		B	L	6'2	190	15	18	.455	1	148	34	1	392	398	150	187	0	4.18
Finch, Joel-Joel D.	79BosA	08-12-56	South Bend, Ind.		R	R	6'2	188	0	3	.000	0	15	7	0	57	65	25	25	0	4.89
Fingers, Rollie-Roland Glen	68-76OakA 77-80SDN 81-82MilA 83EJ 84-85MilA	08-25-46	Steubenville, Ohio		R	R	6'4	195	114	118	.491	341	944	37	4	1701	1474	492	1299	2	2.90
Finley, Chuck-Charles Edward	86-96CalA 97-99AnaA 00-02CleA 02StLN	11-26-62	Monroe, La.		L	L	6'6	215	200	173	.536	0	524	467	63	3197	3069	1332	2610	15	3.85
Finnvold, Gar-Anders Gar	94BosA	03-11-68	Boynton Beach, Fla.		R	R	6'5	200	0	4	.000	0	8	8	0	36	45	15	17	0	5.94
Fiore, Tony-Anthony James	00-01TBA 01-03MinA	10-12-71	Oak Park, Ill.		R	R	6'4	210	12	6	.667	0	87	2	0	152	136	76	94	0	4.39
Fireovid, Steve-Stephen John (Fire)	81,83SDN 84PhiN 85ChiA 86SeaA 92TexA	06-06-57	Bryan, Ohio		B	R	6'2	210	3	1	.750	0	31	5	0	71	93	19	27	0	3.41
Fischer, Jeff-Jeffrey Thomas	87MonN 89LAN	08-17-63	West Palm Beach, Fla.		R	R	6'3	185	0	1	.000	0	6	2	0	17	28	5	8	0	9.53
Fischer, Todd-Todd Richard	86ColN	09-15-60	Columbus, Ohio		R	R	5'10	170	0	0	—	0	9	0	0	17	18	8	7	0	4.24
Fisher, Brian-Brian Kevin	85-86NYA 87-89PitN 90HouN 92SeaA	03-18-62	Honolulu, Hawaii		R	R	6'4	220	36	34	.514	23	222	65	7	640	638	252	370	0	4.39
Fitzgerald, Brian-Brian Michael	02SeaA	12-26-74	Woodbridge, Va.		R	R	5'11	175	0	0	—	0	6	0	0	6	11	2	3	0	8.53
Fitzmorris, Al-Alan James	69-76KCA 77-78CleA 78CalA	03-21-46	Buffalo, N.Y.		B	R	6'2	190	77	59	.566	7	288	159	36	1277	1284	433	458	11	3.65
Flanagan, Mike-Michael Kendall	75-87BalA 87-90TorA 91-92BalA	12-16-51	Manchester, N.H.		L	L	6'	190	167	143	.539	4	526	404	101	2770	2806	890	1491	19	3.90
Fleming, Dave-David Anthony	91-95SeaA 95KCA	11-07-69	Queens, N.Y.		L	L	6'3	200	38	32	.543	0	116	97	9	610	669	248	303	5	4.67
Flener, Huck-Gregory Alan	93,96-97TorA	02-25-69	Austin, Tex.		B	L	5'11	185	3	3	.500	0	29	12	0	95	115	43	55	0	5.51
Fletcher, Paul-Edward Paul	93,95PhiN 96OakA	01-14-67	Gallipolis, Ohio		R	R	6'1	185	1	0	1.000	0	12	0	0	15	21	10	10	0	6.60
Flinn, John-John Richard	78-79BalA 80MilA 82BalA	09-02-54	Merced, Cal.		R	R	6'2	180	5	2	.714	2	42	1	0	69	70	37	36	0	4.15
Florence, Don-Donald Emery	95NYN	03-16-67	Manchester, N.H.		R	L	6'	195	3	0	1.000	0	14	0	0	12	17	6	5	0	1.50
Flores, Randy-Randy Alan	02TexA 02ColN 04-06StLN	07-31-75	Bellflower, Cal.		L	L	6'	180	4	5	.556	2	152	3	0	126	139	54	104	0	4.92
Flores, Ron-Ronald Joel	05-06OakA	08-09-79	Whittier, Cal.		L	L	5'11	190	1	2	.333	1	36	0	0	38	36	10	26	0	2.82
Florie, Bryce-Bryce Bettencourt	94-96SDN 96-97MilA 98-99DetA 99-01BosA	05-21-70	Charleston, S.C.		R	R	6'	190	20	24	.455	2	261	29	0	494	500	243	395	0	4.47
Floyd, Gavin-Gavin Christopher	04-06PhiN	01-27-83	Annapolis, Md.		R	R	6'4	212	7	5	.583	0	24	19	1	109	125	64	75	1	6.96
Fogg, Josh-Joshua Smith	01ChiA 02-05PitN 06ColN	12-13-76	Lynn, Mass.		R	R	6'2	195	50	51	.495	0	167	150	2	869	970	291	461	1	4.89
Folkers, Rich-Richard Nevin	70NYN 72-74StLN 75-76SDN 77MilA	10-17-46	Waterloo, Iowa		L	L	6'2	180	19	23	.452	7	195	28	5	422	416	170	242	0	4.12
Fontenot, Joe-Joseph Daniel	98FlaN	03-20-77	Scott, La.		R	R	6'2	185	0	7	.000	0	8	8	0	43	56	20	24	0	6.33
Fontenot, Ray-Silton Ray	83-84NYA 85-86ChiN 86MinA	08-08-57	Lake Charles, La.		L	L	6'	175	25	26	.490	2	145	62	3	493	561	153	216	1	4.03
Foppert, Jesse-Jesse William	03-05SFN	07-10-80	Reading, Pa.		R	R	6'6	200	8	9	.471	0	27	23	0	122	115	82	109	0	5.00
Ford, Ben-Benjamin Cooper	98AriN 00NYA 04MilN	08-15-75	Cedar Rapids, Iowa		R	R	6'7	225	2	2	.333	0	31	2	0	45	52	20	23	0	7.80
Ford, Dave-David Alan	78-81BalA	12-29-56	Cleveland, Ohio		R	R	6'4	200	5	6	.455	3	51	8	1	155	160	32	46	0	4.01
Ford, Matt-Matthew Lee	03MilN	04-08-81	Plantation, Fla.		B	L	6'1	170	0	3	.000	0	25	4	0	44	46	21	26	0	4.33
Ford, Wenty-Percival Edmund Wentworth	73AtlN	11-25-46	Nassau, Bahamas	07-08-80	R	R	6'	180	1	2	.333	0	4	2	1	16	17	8	4	0	5.62
Fordham, Tom-Thomas James	97-98ChiA	02-20-74	San Diego, Cal.		L	L	6'2	210	1	3	.250	0	36	6	0	65	68	52	33	0	6.61
Forsch, Bob-Robert Herbert	74-88StLN 88-89HouN	01-13-50	Sacramento, Cal.		R	R	6'4	210	168	136	.553	3	498	422	67	2795	2777	832	1133	19	3.76
Forsch, Ken-Kenneth Roth	70-80HouN 81-84CalA 85EJ 86CalA	09-08-46	Sacramento, Cal.		R	R	6'4	210	114	113	.502	51	521	241	70	2126	2071	586	1047	18	3.37
Forster, Scott-Scott Christian	00MonN	10-27-71	Philadelphia, Pa.		R	L	6'1	194	0	1	.000	0	42	0	0	32	28	25	23	0	7.88
Forster, Terry-Terry Jay	71-76ChiA 77PitN 78-82LAN 83-85AtlN 86CalA	01-14-52	Sioux Falls, S.D.		L	L	6'3	190	54	65	.454	127	614	38	5	1105	1034	457	791	0	3.23
Fortugno, Tim-Timothy Shawn	92CalA 94CinN 95ChiA	04-11-62	Clinton, Mass.		L	L	6'1	195	4	4	.429	1	76	5	1	110	99	52	84	1	5.06
Fortunato, Bartolome-Bartolome [Araujo]	04TBA 04,06NYN	08-24-74	Santo Domingo, D.R.		R	R	6'1	197	2	0	1.000	1	20	0	0	29	31	17	25	0	6.21
Fossas, Tony-Emilio Antonio [Morejon]	88TexA 88,90MilA 91-94BosA 95-97StLN 98SeaA 98ChiN 98TexA 99NYA	09-23-57	Havana, Cuba		L	L	6'	195	17	24	.415	7	567	0	0	416	434	180	324	0	3.90
Fossum, Casey-Casey Paul	01-03BosA 04AriN 05-06TBA	01-09-78	Cherry Hill, N.J.		L	L	6'1	160	32	44	.421	2	163	110	0	665	716	270	523	0	5.20
Foster, Kevin-Kevin Christopher	93PhiN 94-98ChiN 01TexA	01-13-69	Evanston, Ill.		R	R	6'1	170	32	30	.516	0	100	83	2	510	500	220	417	0	4.86
Foster, Kris-John Kristian	01BalA	08-30-74	Riverdale, N.J.		R	R	6'5	230	0	0	—	0	7	0	0	10	9	8	7	0	2.70
Foster, John-John Norman	02AtlN 03MilN 05AtlN 06EJ	05-17-78	Stockton, Cal.		L	L	6'	220	7	2	.778	1	90	0	0	61	63	33	54	0	4.90
Foster, Steve-Stephen Eugene	91-93CinN 94EJ	08-16-66	Dallas, Tex.		R	R	6'	180	3	3	.500	2	59	1	0	90	82	22	61	0	2.41
Foucault, Steve-Steven Raymond	73-76TexA 77-78DetA 78KCA	10-03-49	Duluth, Minn.		R	R	6'	210	35	36	.493	52	277	0	0	496	458	190	307	0	3.21
Foulke, Keith-Keith Charles	97SFN 97-02ChiA 03OakA 04-06BosA	10-19-72	San Diego, Cal.		R	R	6'	205	41	34	.547	190	588	8	0	756	624	181	695	0	3.30
Fowlkes, Alan-Alan Kim	82SFN 85CalA	08-08-58	Brawley, Cal.		R	R	6'2	190	4	2	.667	0	23	15	1	92	119	28	56	0	5.48
Fox, Chad-Chad Douglas	97AtlN 98-99MilN 00EJ 01-02MilN 03BosA 03-04FlaN 05ChiN	09-03-70	Coronado, Cal.		R	R	6'3	190	10	11	.476	3	214	0	0	224	193	128	261	0	3.57
Frailing, Ken-Kenneth Douglas	72-73ChiA 74-76ChiN	01-19-48	Marion, Wis.		L	L	6'	187	10	16	.385	2	116	19	1	218	252	82	116	0	3.96
Francis, Jeff-Jeffrey William	04-06ColN	01-08-81	Vancouver, Canada		L	L	6'5	200	30	25	.545	0	72	72	1	457	457	152	277	1	4.91
Francisco, Frank-Franklin	04TexA 05EJ 06TexA	09-11-79	Santo Domingo, D.R.		R	R	6'2	180	5	2	.714	0	53	0	0	59	44	30	66	0	3.53
Franco, John-John Anthony	84-89CinN 90-01NYN 02EJ 03-04NYN 05HouN	09-17-60	Brooklyn, N.Y.		L	L	5'10	185	90	87	.508	424	1119	0	0	1246	1166	495	975	0	2.89
Franklin, Ryan-Ryan Ray	99,01-05SeaA 06PhiN 06CinN	03-05-73	Fort Smith, Ark.		R	R	6'3	185	41	57	.418	0	247	106	6	889	924	271	470	3	4.35
Franklin, Wayne-Gary Wayne Jr.	00-01HouN 02-03MilN 04SFN 05NYA 06AtlN	03-09-74	Wilmington, Del.		L	L	6'2	200	14	16	.467	0	143	40	0	323	332	168	216	1	5.54
Frascatore, John-John Vincent	94-95,97-98StLN 99AriN 99-01TorA	02-04-70	Queens, N.Y.		R	R	6'1	215	20	17	.541	1	274	5	0	371	391	145	206	0	4.00
Fraser, Willie-William Patrick	86-90CalA 91TorA 91StLN 94FlaN 95MonN	05-26-64	New York, N.Y.		R	R	6'1	215	38	40	.487	7	248	57	7	657	640	238	320	1	4.47
Frasor, Jason-Jason Andrew	04-06TorA	08-09-77	Chicago, Ill.		R	R	5'10	170	10	13	.435	18	181	0	0	193	178	81	167	0	3.82
Frazier, George-George Allen	78-80StLN 81-83NYA 84CleA 84-86ChiN 86-87MinA	10-13-54	Oklahoma City, Okla.		R	R	6'5	205	35	43	.448	29	415	0	0	676	653	313	449	0	4.20
Frederick, Kevin-Kevin Albert Francis	02MinA 04TorA		Evanston, Ill.		R	R	6'1	215	0	1	.000	0	30	0	0	40	45	26	27	0	7.59
Fredrickson, Scott-Scott Eric	93ColN 94BK	08-19-67	Manchester, N.H.		R	R	6'3	215	0	1	.000	0	29	0	0	33	17	20		0	6.10
Freeman, Marvin-Marvin	86,88-90PhiN 90-93AtlN 94-96ColN 96ChiA	04-10-63	Chicago, Ill.		R	R	6'7	220	35	28	.556	5	221	78	0	594	616	249	383	0	4.64
Freisleben, Dave-David James	74-78SDN 78CleA 79TorA	10-30-51	Coraopolis, Pa.		R	R	6'	200	34	60	.362	4	202	121	17	866	897	430	430	6	4.29

USE NAMES - GIVEN NAMES (NICKNAMES)	TEAM BY YEAR	BIRTH DATE	BIRTHPLACE	DEATH DATE	B	T	HGT	WGT	W	L	Pct.	SV	G	GS	CG	IP	H	BB	SO	ShO	ERA
Frey, Steve-Steven Francis	89-91MonN 92-93CalA 94-95SFN 95SeaA 95-96PhiN	07-29-63	Meadowbrook, Pa.		R	L	5'9	170	18	15	.545	28	314	0	0	304	297	154	157	0	3.76
Frohwirth, Todd-Todd Gerard	87-90PhiN 91-93BalA 94BosA 96CalA	09-28-62	Milwaukee, Wis.		R	R	6'4	210	20	19	.513	11	284	0	0	418	389	172	259	0	3.60
Frost, Dave-Carl David	77ChiA 78-81CalA 82KCA	11-17-52	Long Beach, Cal.		R	R	6'6	235	33	37	.471	1	99	84	16	550	571	174	222	3	4.11
Fruto, Emiliano-Emiliano Ricardo	06SeaA	06-06-84	Cartagena, Colombia		R	R	6'3	235	2	2	.500	1	23	0	0	36	34	24	50	0	5.50
Fryman, Woody-Woodrow Thompson	66-67PitN 68-72PhiN 72-74DetA 75-76MonN 77CinN 78ChiN 78-83MonN	04-12-40	Ewing, Ky.		R	L	6'3	205	141	155	.476	58	625	322	68	2412	2367	890	1587	27	3.77
Fuentes, Brian-Brian Christopher	01SeaA 02-06ColN	08-09-75	Merced, Cal.		L	L	6'4	220	13	17	.433	65	307	0	0	298	250	134	342	0	3.62
Fulchino, Jeff-Jeffrey Joseph	06FlaN	11-26-79	Titusville, Fla.		R	R	6'5	250	0	0	—	0	1	0	0	0	0	1	0	0	0.00
Fulgham, John-John Thomas	79-80StLN 81SJ	06-09-56	St. Louis, Mo.		R	R	6'2	205	14	12	.538	0	35	33	14	231	189	58	123	3	2.84
Fulton, Bill-William David	87NYA	10-22-63	Pittsburgh, Pa.		R	R	6'3	195	1	0	1.000	0	5	1	0	5	9	1	2	0	11.57
Fultz, Aaron-Richard Aaron	00-02SFN 03TexA 04MinA 05-06PhiN	04-09-73	Memphis, Tenn.		L	L	6'	196	21	12	.636	3	414	1	0	443	436	169	366	0	4.37
Funk, Tom-Thomas James	86HouN	03-13-62	Kansas City, Mo.		L	L	6'2	205	0	0	—	0	8	0	0	8	10	6	2	0	6.48
Fussell, Chris-Christopher Wren	98BalA 99-00KCA	05-19-76	Oregon, Ohio		R	R	6'2	200	5	9	.357	2	40	19	0	136	159	89	91	0	6.90
Fyhrie, Mike-Michael Edwin	96NYN 97JL 99-00AnaA 01ChiN 01-02OakA	12-09-69	Long Beach, Cal.		R	R	6'2	200	2	11	.154	0	84	11	0	175	183	67	109	0	4.00
Gabbard, Kason-Kason Ronald	06BosA	04-08-82	Oxford, Ohio		L	L	6'3	200	1	3	.250	0	7	4	0	26	24	16	15	0	3.51
Gaff, Brent-Brent Allen	82-84NYN 85SJ	10-05-58	Fort Wayne, Ind.		R	R	6'1	195	4	5	.444	1	58	5	0	126	136	47	60	0	4.06
Gagne, Eric-Eric Serge	99-06LAN	01-07-76	Montreal, Canada		R	R	6'2	235	25	21	.543	161	298	48	0	545	423	183	629	0	3.27
Gaillard, Eddie-Julian Edward	97DetA 98-99TBA	08-13-70	Camden, N.J.		R	R	6'2	195	2	0	1.000	1	30	0	0	37	32	17	24	0	4.66
Gajkowski, Steve-Stephen Robert	98SeaA	12-30-69	Seattle, Wash.		R	R	6'2	200	0	0	—	0	9	0	0	9	14	4	3	0	7.27
Gakeler, Dan-Daniel Michael	91DetA 92SJ	05-01-64	Mt Holly, N.J.		R	R	6'6	215	1	4	.200	2	31	7	0	74	73	39	43	0	5.74
Galasso, Bob-Robert Joseph (Biff)	77SeaA 79MilA 81SeaA	01-13-52	Connellsville, Pa.		L	R	6'1	205	4	8	.333	4	56	8	0	118	153	47	63	0	5.87
Gale, Rich-Richard Blackwell (Big Man)	78-81KCA 82SFN 83CinN 84BosA	01-19-54	Littleton, N.H.		R	R	6'7	225	55	56	.495	2	195	144	21	971	997	457	518	5	4.53
Gallo, Mike-Michael Dwain	03-06HouN	04-02-77	Long Beach, Cal.		L	L	6'	175	4	3	.571	0	160	0	0	116	129	47	69	0	4.11
Galvez, Balvino-Balvino [Jerez]	86LAN	03-31-64	San Pedro de Mac, D.R.		R	R	6'	180	0	1	.000	0	10	0	0	21	19	12	11	0	3.92
Gandarillas, Gus-Gustavo	01MilN	07-19-71	Coral Gables, Fla.		R	R	6'	190	0	0	—	0	16	0	0	20	25	10	7	0	5.49
Garagozzo, Keith-Keith John	94MinA	10-25-69	Camden, N.J.		L	L	6'	170	0	0	—	0	7	0	0	9	9	13	3	0	9.64
Garber, Gene-Henry Eugene	69,70,72PitN 73-74KCA 74-78PhiN 78-87AtlN 87-88KCA	11-13-47	Elizabethtown, Pa.		R	R	5'10	175	96	113	.459	218	931	9	4	1509	1464	445	940	0	3.34
Garces, Rich-Richard Aron Jr. [Mendoza] (El Guapo)	90,93MinA 95ChiN 95FlaN 96-01BosA	05-18-71	Maracay, Venez.		R	R	6'	250	23	10	.697	7	287	0	0	341	290	164	296	0	3.74
Garcia, Freddy-Freddy Antonio	99-04SeaA 04-06ChiA	06-10-75	Caracas, Venezuela		R	R	6'4	235	116	71	.620	0	252	251	12	1644	1584	529	1202	4	4.01
Garcia, Jairo	see Santiago Casilla																				
Garcia, Jose-Jose Luis	06FlaN	01-07-85	De Jabon, Dom. Rep.		R	R	5'11	165	0	0	—	0	5	0	0	11	10	5	8	0	4.91
Garcia, Mike-Michael R.	99-00PitN	05-11-68	Riverside, Calif.		R	R	6'2	220	1	2	.333	0	20	0	0	18	23	10	18	0	7.36
Garcia, Miguel-Miguel Angel [Sifontes]	87CalA 87-89PitN	04-03-67	Caracas, Venezuela		L	L	6'1	173	0	2	.000	0	14	0	0	20	31	12	11	0	8.41
Garcia, Ralph-Ralph	72,74SDN	12-14-48	Los Angeles, Cal.		R	R	6'1	195	0	0	—	0	11	0	0	15	19	10	12	0	4.80
Garcia, Ramon-Ramon Antonio [Fortunato]	91ChiA 96MilA 97HouN 98EJ	12-09-69	Guanare, Venez.		R	R	6'2	200	17	16	.515	2	95	37	1	313	318	104	200	1	4.84
Garcia, Reynaldo-Reynaldo	02-03TexA 04EJ	04-15-74	Nagua, Dom. Rep.		R	R	6'3	170	0	0	—	0	20	0	0	20	26	15	17	0	11.25
Garcia, Rosman-Rosman Jose	03-04TexA	01-03-79	Maracay, Venezuela		R	R	6'2	185	1	2	.333	0	50	0	0	53	72	28	30	0	5.94
Gardiner, Mike-Michael James	90SeaA 91-92BosA 93MonN 93-95DetA	10-19-65	Sarnia, Canada		B	R	6'	200	17	27	.386	5	136	46	0	394	420	161	239	0	5.21
Gardner, Chris-Christopher John	91HouN	03-30-69	Long Beach, Cal.		R	R	6'	175	1	2	.333	0	5	4	0	25	19	14	12	0	4.01
Gardner, Lee-Terrence Lee	02,05TBA	01-16-75	Hartland, Mich.		R	R	6'	219	1	1	.500	0	17	0	0	21	24	10	12	0	4.35
Gardner, Mark-Mark Allan	89-92MonN 93KCA 94-95FlaN 96-01SFN	03-01-62	Los Angeles, Cal.		R	R	6'1	210	99	93	.516	1	345	275	15	1765	1752	628	1256	8	4.56
Gardner, Wes-Wesley Brian	84-85NYN 86-90BosA 91SDN 91KCA	04-29-61	Benton, Ark.		R	R	6'4	200	18	30	.375	14	189	44	1	466	476	218	358	0	4.90
Garibay, Daniel-Daniel [Bravo]	00ChiN	02-14-73	Maniadero, Mexico		L	L	5'8	154	2	8	.200	0	30	8	0	75	88	39	46	0	6.03
Garland, Jon-Jon Steven	00-06ChiA	09-27-79	Valencia, Cal.		R	R	6'6	205	82	68	.547	1	214	191	6	1220	1263	416	663	5	4.44
Garland, Wayne-Marcus Wayne	73-76BalA 77-81CleA	10-26-50	Nashville, Tenn.		R	R	6'1	212	55	66	.455	6	190	121	43	1040	1082	328	450	7	3.89
Garman, Mike-Michael Douglas	69,71-73BosA 74-75StLN 76ChiN 77-78LAN 78MonN	09-16-49	Caldwell, Idaho		R	R	6'3	200	22	27	.449	42	303	8	0	434	411	202	213	0	3.63
Garrelts, Scott-Scott William	82-91SFN 92EJ	10-30-61	Champaign, Ill.		R	R	6'4	210	69	53	.566	48	352	89	9	959	815	413	703	4	3.29
Garvin, Jerry-Theodore Jared	77-82TorA	10-21-55	Oakland, Cal.		L	L	6'3	195	20	41	.326	8	195	65	15	607	648	219	320	1	4.42
Garza, Matt-Matthew Scott	06MinA	11-26-83	Selma, Cal.		R	R	6'4	185	3	6	.333	0	10	9	0	50	62	23	38	0	5.76
Gassner, Dave-David Kenneth	05MinA	12-14-78	Hortonville, Wisc.		R	L	6'2	190	1	0	1.000	0	2	2	0	8	9	1	2	0	5.87
Gaudin, Chad-Chad Edward	03-05TBA 06OakA	03-24-83	New Orleans, La.		R	R	5'10	170	8	7	.533	2	101	10	0	160	178	80	101	0	4.51
Geary, Geoff-Geoffrey Michael	03-06PhiN	08-26-76	Buffalo, N.Y.		R	R	6'	170	10	2	.833	1	159	0	0	200	217	60	135	0	3.78
Geddes, Jim-James Lee	72-73ChiA	03-23-49	Columbus,Ohio		R	R	6'2	200	0	0	—	0	11	2	0	26	26	24	10	0	4.50
Geisel, Dave-John David	78-79,81ChiN 82-83TorA 84-85SeaA	01-18-55	Windber, Pa.		L	L	6'3	210	5	5	.500	8	131	8	0	208	209	97	144	0	4.02
George, Chris-Christopher Coleman	01-04KCA	09-16-79	Houston, Tex.		L	L	6'2	200	14	20	.412	0	47	44	1	237	300	95	99	0	6.48
George, Chris-Christopher Sean	91MilA	09-24-66	Pittsburgh, Pa.		R	R	6'2	200	0	0	—	0	2	1	0	6	8	0	2	0	3.00
Gerhardt, Rusty-Allen Russell	74SDN	08-13-50	Baltimore, Md.		B	L	5'9	175	2	1	.667	1	23	1	0	36	44	17	22	0	7.00
German, Franklyn-Franklyn Miguel [Made]	02-05DetA 06FlaN	01-20-80	San Cristobal, Dom. Rep.		R	R	6'4	250	3	4	.667	7	138	0	0	137	137	106	99	0	4.60
Germano, Justin-Justin William	04SDN 06CinN	08-06-82	Pasadena, Cal.		R	R	6'1	190	1	3	.250	0	9	6	0	28	39	17	24	0	8.04
Ghelfi, Tony-Anthony Paul	83PhiN 84SJ	08-23-61	La Crosse, Wis.		R	R	6'2	185	1	1	.500	0	3	3	0	14	15	6	14	0	3.14
Gibson, Bob-Robert Louis	83-86MilA 87NYN	06-19-57	Philadelphia, Pa.		R	R	6'	195	12	18	.400	13	98	18	1	270	241	166	166	1	4.24
Gibson, Paul-Paul Marshall	88-91DetA 92-93NYN 93-94,96NYA	01-04-60	Southampton, N.Y.		L	L	6'	185	22	24	.478	11	319	15	0	557	570	236	345	0	4.07
Gideon, Brett-Byron Brett	87PitN 89-90MonN	08-08-63	Ozona, Tex.		R	R	6'2	200	1	5	.167	3	34	0	0	42	41	19	33	0	4.46
Gideon, Jim-James Leslie	75TexA	09-26-53	Taylor, Tex.		R	R	6'4	190	0	0	—	0	1	1	0	6	7	2	5	0	7.50
Gilbert, Joe-Joe Denis	72-73MonN	04-20-52	Jasper, Tex.		R	L	6'1	165	1	3	.250	1	43	0	0	62	71	37	42	0	6.82
Gilfillan, Jason-Jason Edward	03KCA	08-31-76	Shelby, N.C.		R	R	6'5	220	2	0	1.000	0	13	0	0	16	22	10	12	0	7.71
Gilles, Tom-Thomas Bradford	90TorA	07-02-62	Peoria, Ill.		R	R	6'1	185	1	0	1.000	0	2	0	0	1	2	1	0	0	6.75
Ginter, Matt-Matthew Shane	00-03ChiA 04NYN 05DetA	12-24-77	Lexington, Ky.		R	R	6'2	220	4	4	.500	1	92	15	0	211	244	72	120	0	5.08
Gissell, Chris-Christopher Odell	04ColN	01-04-78	Tacoma, Wash.		R	R	6'5	210	0	1	.000	0	5	1	0	9	20	3	11	0	14.54
Givens, Brian-Brian Alan	95-96MilA	11-06-65	Lompoc, Cal.		R	L	6'6	220	6	10	.375	0	23	23	0	121	148	61	83	0	5.86
Glauber, Keith-Keith Harris	98,00CinN	01-08-72	Brooklyn, N.Y.		R	R	6'2	190	0	0	—	0	7	0	0	15	11	3	8	0	3.00
Glavine, Tom-Thomas Michael	87-02AtlN 03-06NYN	03-25-66	Concord, Mass.		L	L	6'1	190	290	191	.603	0	635	635	55	4150	4012	1399	2481	24	3.46
Gleaton, Jerry Don-Jerry Don (Opie)	79-80TexA 81-82SeaA 84-85ChiA 87-89KCA 90-91DetA 92PitN	09-14-57	Brownwood, Tex.		L	L	6'3	205	15	23	.395	26	307	16	1	447	433	199	265	0	4.25
Glinatsis, George-George	94SeaA	06-29-69	Youngstown, Ohio		R	R	6'4	195	0	1	.000	0	2	2	0	5	9	6	1	0	13.50
Glover, Gary-John Gary II	99TorA 01-03ChiA 03AnaA 04-05MilA	12-03-76	Cleveland, Ohio		R	R	6'5	205	21	18	.538	1	149	47	0	385	403	135	236	0	5.03
Glynn, Ed-Edward Paul (The Flushing Flash)	75-78DetA 79-80NYN 81-83CleA 85MonN	06-03-53	Queens, N.Y.		R	L	6'2	180	12	17	.414	12	175	8	1	265	261	151	184	0	4.25
Glynn, Ryan-Ryan David	99-01TexA 04TorA 05OakA	11-01-74	Portsmouth, Va.		R	R	6'3	195	9	20	.310	0	52	40	0	226	280	117	116	0	6.24
Gobble, Jimmy-Billy James	03-06KCA	07-19-81	Bristol, Tenn.		L	L	6'3	190	18	20	.474	2	122	43	0	338	372	117	198	0	5.24
Gohr, Greg-Gregory James	93-96DetA 96CalA	10-29-67	Santa Ana, Cal.		R	R	6'3	205	8	11	.421	1	66	22	0	183	234	82	131	0	6.21
Goltz, David-David Allan	72-79MinA 80-82LAN 82-83CalA	06-23-49	Pelican Rapids, Minn.		R	R	6'4	210	113	109	.509	8	353	264	83	2039	2104	646	1105	13	3.69
Gomes, Wayne-Wayne Maurice	97-01PhiN 01SFN 02BosA	01-15-73	Hampton, Va.		R	R	6'2	225	30	23	.566	29	321	0	0	368	373	191	284	0	4.60
Gomez, Pat-Patrick Alexander	93SDN 94-95SFN	03-17-68	Roseville, Cal.		R	L	5'11	185	1	3	.250	0	71	1	0	79	74	51	55	0	4.56
Gonzalez, Dicky-Dicky Angel	01NYN 04TBA	12-21-78	Bayamon, P.R.		R	R	5'11	170	3	2	.600	0	20	7	0	66	81	19	38	0	5.02
Gonzalez, Edgar-Edgardo Gerardo [Elizondo]	03-06AriN	02-23-83	San Nicolas de los Garza, Mex.		R	R	6'	220	5	14	.263	0	31	17	0	108	147	36	74	0	6.85
Gonzalez, Enrique-Enrique Cesar	06AriN	04-12-82	Ciudad Bolivar, Venez.		R	R	5'10	210	3	7	.300	0	22	18	0	106	114	34	66	0	5.67
Gonzalez, Gabe-Gabriel	98FlaN	05-24-72	Long Beach, Cal.		B	L	6'1	160	0	0	—	0	1	0	0	1	1	1	0	0	9.00
Gonzalez, German-German Jose [Caraballo]	88-89MinA	03-07-62	Rio Caribe, Venez.		R	R	6'	170	3	2	.600	1	38	0	0	50	52	19	44	0	4.11
Gonzalez, Jeremi-Geremis Segundo [Acosta]	97-98ChiN 99-00EJ 03-04TBA 05BosA 06NYN 06MilN	01-08-75	Maracaibo, Venezuela		R	R	6'2	212	30	35	.462	0	131	83	4	573	588	238	354	2	4.93
Gonzalez, Lariel-Lariel Alfonso	98ColN	05-25-76	San Cristobal, Dom. Rep.		R	R	6'1	220	0	0	—	0	1	0	0	1	0	0	1	0	0.00
Gonzalez, Mike-Michael Vela	03-06PitN	05-23-78	Corpus Christi, Texas		R	L	6'2	213	7	9	.438	28	168	0	0	156	116	74	183	0	2.37
Good, Andrew-Andrew Richard	03-04AriN 05DetA	08-19-79	San Diego, Cal.		R	R	6'2	205	5	4	.556	0	22	12	0	112	121	30	75	0	5.30
Gooden, Dwight-Dwight Eugene (Dr.K, Doc)	84-94NYN 95SD 96-97NYA 98-99CleA 00HouN 00TBA 00NYA	11-16-64	Tampa, Fla.		R	R	6'2	205	194	112	.634	3	430	410	68	2801	2564	954	2293	24	3.51
Gordon, Don-Donald Thomas	86-87TorA 87-88CleA	10-10-59	New York, N.Y.		R	R	6'1	175	3	8	.273	3	78	0	0	132	150	42	56	0	4.72
Gordon, Tom-Thomas (Flash)	88-95KCA 96-99BosA 00EJ 01-02ChiN 02HouN 03ChiA 04-05NYA 06PhiN	11-18-67	Sebring, Fla.		R	R	5'9	185	130	119	.522	150	809	203	18	2037	1815	944	1870	4	3.91

USE NAMES - GIVEN NAMES (NICKNAMES)	TEAM BY YEAR	BIRTH DATE	BIRTHPLACE	DEATH DATE	B	T	HGT	WGT	W	L	Pct.	SV	G	GS	CG	IP	H	BB	SO	ShO	ERA
Gorecki, Rick-Richard John	97LAN 98TBA 99SJ	08-27-73	Evergreen Park, Ill.		R	R	6'3	167	2	2	.500	0	7	4	0	23	24	16	13	0	7.54
Gorman, Tom-Thomas Patrick	81-82MonN 82-85NYN 86PhiN 87SDN	12-16-57	Portland, Ore.		L	L	6'4	200	12	10	.545	0	126	7	0	214	212	66	144	0	4.34
Gorzelanny, Tom-Thomas Stephen	05-06PitN	07-12-82	Evergreen Park, Ill.		L	L	6'2	205	2	6	.250	0	14	12	0	68	60	34	43	0	4.52
Gosling, Mike-Michael Frederick	04-05AriN 06CinN	09-23-80	Madison, Wis.		L	L	6'2	210	1	4	.200	0	20	9	0	59	67	33	29	0	4.73
Gossage, Goose-Richard Michael (Rich)	72-76ChiA 77PitN 78-83NYA 84-87SDN 88ChiN 89SFN 89NYA 90JL 91TexA 92-93OakA 94SeaA	07-05-51	Colorado Springs, Colo.		R	R	6'3		124	107	.537	310	1002	37	16	1809	1497	732	1502	0	3.01
Gott, Jim-James William	82-84TorA 85-87SFN 87-89PitN 90-94LAN 95PitN	08-03-59	Hollywood, Cal.		R	R	6'3	220	56	74	.431	91	554	96	10	1120	1081	466	837	3	3.87
Gozzo, Mauro-Mauro Paul (Goose)	89TorA 90-91CleA 92MinA 93-94NYN	03-07-66	New Britain, Conn.		R	R	6'2	210	7	7	.500	1	48	13	0	124	150	51	55	0	5.30
Grabow, John-John William	03-06PitN	11-04-78	Arcadia, Cal.		L	L	6'2	200	8	10	.444	1	208	0	0	188	201	83	181	0	4.64
Grace, Mike-Michael James	95-99PhiN	06-20-70	Joliet, Ill.		R	R	6'4	215	16	16	.500	0	68	40	2	276	310	90	156	2	4.96
Gracesqui, Franklyn-Franklyn Benjamin	04FlaN	08-20-79	Santo Domingo, D.R.		B	L	6'5	210	0	1	.000	1	7	0	0	4	6	3	1	0	11.25
Grahe, Joe-Joseph Milton	90-94CalA 95ColN 99DetA	08-14-67	West Palm Beach, Fla.		R	R	6'1	200	21	27	.438	45	175	35	1	372	415	169	190	0	4.58
Graman, Alex-Alex Joseph	04-05NYA	11-17-77	Huntingburg, Ind.		L	L	6'4	210	0	0	—	0	5	2	0	6	17	4	4	0	18.47
Granger, Jeff-Jeffrey Adam	93-94,96KCA 97PitN	12-16-71	San Pedro, Cal.		L	L	6'4	200	0	1	.000	0	27	2	0	32	47	26	19	0	9.09
Grant, Mark-Mark Andrew	84,86-87SFN 87-90SDN 90AtlN 91EJ 92SeaA 93HouN 93ColN	10-24-63	Aurora, Ill.		R	R	6'2	215	22	32	.407	8	233	58	2	639	676	235	382	1	4.31
Grapenthin, Dick-Richard Ray	83-85MonN	04-16-58	Linn Grove, Iowa		R	R	6'2	205	1	3	.250	2	19	1	0	34	36	16	16	0	6.35
Grater, Mark-Mark Anthony	91StLN 93DetA	01-19-64	Rochester, Pa.		R	R	5'10	205	0	0	—	0	9	0	0	8	11	6	4	0	3.38
Graterol, Beiker-Beiker		11-09-74	Lara, Venezuela		R	R	6'2	165	1	4	.200	0	13	5	0	33	40	17	16	0	3.86
Graves, Danny-Daniel Peter	96-97CleA 97-05CinN 05NYN 06CleA	08-07-72	Saigon, Vietnam		R	R	5'11	200	43	44	.494	182	518	30	2	808	857	271	429	1	4.05
Gray, Jeff-Jeffrey Edward	88CinN 90-91BosA 92IL	04-10-63	Richmond, Va.		R	R	6'1	190	4	7	.364	10	96	0	0	122	104	29	96	0	3.33
Green, Chris-Christopher De Wayne	84PitN	09-05-60	Los Angeles, Cal.		L	L	6'2	210	0	0	—	0	4	0	0	3	5	1	3	0	6.00
Green, Jason-David Jason	00HouN	06-05-75	Port Hope, Canada		R	R	6'1	205	1	1	.500	0	14	0	0	18	15	20	19	0	6.62
Green, Sean-Sean William	06SeaA	04-20-79	Louisville, Ky.		R	R	6'6	230	0	0	—	0	24	0	0	32	34	13	15	0	4.50
Green, Steve-Steve	01AnaA	01-26-78	Greenfield Parc, Canada		R	R	6'2	195	0	0	—	0	1	1	0	6	4	6	4	0	3.00
Green, Tyler-Tyler Scott	93,95PhiN 96SJ 97-98PhiN 99SJ	02-18-70	Springfield, Ohio		R	R	6'5	200	18	25	.419	0	70	68	4	384	387	201	263	2	5.16
Greene, Rick-Richard Douglas	99CinN	01-02-71	Ft. Knox, Ky.		R	R	6'5	200	0	0	—	0	1	0	0	6	7	1	3	0	4.76
Greene, Tommy-Ira Thomas (Jethro)	89-90AtlN 90-95PhiN 97HouN	04-06-67	Lumberton, N.C.		R	R	6'5	225	38	25	.603	0	119	97	11	628	591	241	461	5	4.14
Greer, Kenny-Kenneth William	93NYN 95SFN	05-12-67	Hull, Mass.		R	R	6'3	210	1	2	.333	0	9	0	0	13	15	5	9	0	4.85
Gregg, Kevin-Kevin Marschall	03-04AnaA 05-06LAA	06-20-78	Corvallis, Ore.		R	R	6'6	225	11	8	.579	1	125	6	0	255	262	86	221	0	4.31
Greif, Bill-William Briley	71HouN 72-76SDN 76StLN	04-25-50	Fort Stockton, Cal.		R	R	6'5	205	31	67	.316	19	231	97	18	715	747	287	442	4	4.42
Bats both part of 76																					
Greinke, Zach-Donald Zackary	04-06KCA	10-21-83	Orlando, Fla.		R	R	6'2	200	14	28	.333	0	60	57	2	334	383	82	219	0	4.98
Greisinger, Seth-Seth Adam	98DetA 99-01EJ 02DetA 04MinA 05AtlN	07-29-75	Kansas City, Kan.		R	R	6'4	200	10	16	.385	0	42	39	0	224	263	77	118	0	5.51
Griffin, Mike-Michael LeRoy	79-81NYA 81ChiN 82SDN 87BalA 89CinN	06-26-57	Colusa, Cal.		R	R	6'5	205	7	15	.318	3	67	24	1	203	235	73	101	0	4.61
Griffin, Tom-Thomas James	69-76HouN 76-77SDN 78CalA 79-81SFN 82PitN	02-22-48	Los Angeles, Cal.		R	R	6'3	210	77	94	.450	5	401	191	29	1493	1407	769	1054	10	4.07
Griffiths, Jeremy-Jeremy Richard	03NYN 04HouN	03-22-78	Fairview, Ohio		R	R	6'6	240	1	4	.200	0	10	7	0	45	61	22	30	0	7.35
Grilli, Jason-Jason Michael	00-01FlaN 04ChiA 05-06DetA	11-17-76	Royal Oak, Mich.		R	R	6'4	185	8	9	.471	0	69	16	1	156	168	64	82	0	5.41
Grilli, Steve-Stephen Joseph	75-77DetA 79TorA	05-02-49	Brooklyn, N.Y.		R	R	6'2	200	4	3	.571	3	70	2	0	148	138	96	91	0	4.50
Grimsley, Jason-Jason Alan	89-91PhiN 93-95CleA 96CalA 99-00NYA 01-04KCA 04-05BalA 06AriN	08-07-67	Cleveland, Tex.		R	R	6'3	200	42	58	.420	4	552	72	3	937	954	498	622	1	4.77
Grimsley, Ross-Ross Albert	71-73CinN 74-77BalA 78-80MonN 80CleA 81VJ 82BalA	01-07-50	Topeka, Kans.		L	L	6'3	200	124	99	.556	3	345	295	79	2038	2105	559	750	15	3.81
Groom, Buddy-Wedsel Gary Jr.	92-95DetA 95FlaN 96-99OakA 00-04BalA 05NYA 05AriN	07-10-65	Dallas, Tex.		L	L	6'2	200	31	32	.492	27	786	15	0	735	825	260	494	0	4.64
Gross, Kevin-Kevin Frank	83-88PhiN 89-90MonN 91-94LAN 95-96TexA 97AnaA	06-08-61	Downey, Cal.		R	R	6'5	225	142	158	.473	5	474	368	42	2488	2519	986	1727	14	4.11
Gross, Kip-Kip Lee	90-91CinN 92-93LAN 94-98JL 99BosA 00HouN	08-24-64	Scottsbluff, Neb.		R	R	6'2	195	7	8	.467	0	73	12	1	148	168	66	81	0	3.90
Grott, Matt-Matthew Allen	95CinN	12-05-67	La Porte, Ind.		L	L	6'1	210	0	0	—	0	2	0	0	2	6	2	2	0	21.60
Grundt, Ken-Kenneth Allan	96-97BosA	08-26-69	Melrose Park, Ill.		L	L	6'4	195	0	0	—	0	3	0	0	3	6	0	0	0	10.80
Gryboski, Kevin-Kevin John	02-05AtlN 05TexA 06WasN	11-15-73	Wilkes-Barre, Pa.		R	R	6'5	235	12	8	.600	2	238	0	0	183	203	105	103	0	4.07
Grzanich, Mike-Michael Edward	98HouN	09-24-72	Canton, Ill.		R	R	6'1	180	0	0	—	0	1	0	0	1	1	2	1	0	18.00
Guante, Cecilio-Cecilio [Magallanes]	82-86PitN 87-88NYA 88-89TexA 90CleA	02-01-60	Villa Mella, D.R.		R	R	6'3	205	29	34	.460	35	363	1	0	595	512	236	503	0	3.48
Guardado, Eddie-Edward Adrian	93-03MinA 04-06SeaA 06CinN	10-02-70	Stockton, Cal.		R	L	6'	195	41	55	.427	183	781	25	0	836	789	310	737	0	4.26
Gubicza, Mark-Mark Steven	84-96KCA 97AnaA	08-14-62	Philadelphia, Pa.		R	R	6'6	225	132	136	.493	2	384	329	42	2223	2239	786	1371	16	3.96
Guerrier, Matt-Matthew Olson	04-06MinA	08-02-78	Cleveland, Ohio		R	R	6'3	185	1	4	.200	0	91	0	0	160	171	51	94	0	3.65
Guetterman, Lee-Arthur Lee	84,86-87SeaA 88-92NYA 92NYN 93StLN 95-96SeaA	11-22-58	Chattanooga, Tenn.		L	L	6'8	225	38	36	.514	25	425	23	3	658	717	222	287	1	4.33
Guidry, Ron-Ronald Ames (Louisiana Lightnin', Ragin' Cajun, Gator)	75-88NYA	08-20-50	Lafayette, La.		L	L	5'11	170	170	91	.651	4	368	323	95	2392	2198	633	1778	26	3.29
Gullett, Don-Donald Edward	70-76CinN 77-78NYA 79-80SL	01-06-51	Lynn, Ky.		R	L	6'	190	109	50	.686	11	266	186	44	1391	1205	501	921	14	3.11
Gullickson, Bill-William Lee	79-85MonN 86-87CinN 87NYA 88-89JL 90HouN 91-94DetA	02-20-59	Marshall, Minn.		R	R	6'3	220	162	136	.544	0	398	390	54	2560	2659	622	1279	11	3.93
Gumpert, Dave-David Lawrence (Gump)	82-83DetA 85-86ChiN 87KCA	05-05-58	South Haven, Mich.		R	R	6'3	190	3	2	.600	5	86	1	0	136	149	50	76	0	4.31
Gunderson, Eric-Eric Andrew	90-91SFN 92SeaA 94-95NYN 95-96BosA 97-99TexA 00TorA	03-29-66	Portland, Ore.		R	L	6'	185	8	11	.421	2	254	5	0	229	274	84	137	0	4.95
Gura, Larry-Lawrence Cyril	70-73ChiN 74-75NYA 76-85KCA 85ChiN	11-26-47	Joliet, Ill.		B	L	6'	185	126	97	.565	14	403	261	71	2047	2020	600	801	15	3.76
Bats Right 70																					
Guthrie, Jeremy-Jeremy Shane	04-06CleA	04-08-79	Rosenburg, Ore.		B	R	6'1	200	0	0	—	0	16	1	0	37	42	23	24	0	6.08
Guthrie, Mark-Mark Andrew	89-95MinA 95-98LAN 99BosA 99-00ChiN 00TBA 00TorA 01OakA 02NYN 03ChiN	09-22-65	Buffalo, N.Y.		R	L	6'4	210	51	54	.486	14	765	43	3	979	989	381	778	1	4.05
Guzman, Angel-Angel Moises	06CinN	12-14-81	Caracas, Venezuela		R	R	6'3	195	0	6	.000	0	15	10	0	56	68	37	60	0	7.39
Guzman, Domingo-Domingo Serrano	99-00SDN	04-05-75	San Cristobal, Dom. Rep.		R	R	6'3	210	0	1	.000	0	8	0	0	6	14	4	4	0	19.50
Guzman, Geraldo-Geraldo Moreno	00-01AriN	11-28-72	Tenares, Dom. Rep.		R	R	6'1	180	5	4	.556	0	17	10	0	70	73	25	56	0	5.04
Guzman, Johnny-Dionini Ramon (Estrella)	91-92OakA	01-21-71	Hatillo Palma, D.R.		R	L	5'10	155	1	0	1.000	0	7	0	0	8	19	2	3	0	10.12
Guzman, Jose-Jose Alberto (Mirabel)	85-88TexA 89-90SJ 91-92TexA 93-94ChiN 95SJ	04-09-63	Santa Isabel, P.R.		R	R	6'3	195	80	74	.519	0	193	186	26	1224	1193	482	889	4	4.05
Guzman, Juan-Juan Andres [Correa]	91-98TorA 98-99BalA 99CinN 00TBA 01SJ	10-28-66	Santo Domingo, D.R.		R	R	5'11	195	91	79	.535	0	240	240	17	1483	1360	667	1243	3	4.08
Haas, Dave-Robert David	91-93DetA	10-19-65	Independence, Mo.		R	R	6'1	200	7	5	.583	0	43	11	1	100	121	36	52	1	4.84
Haas, Moose-Bryan Edmund	76-85MilA 86-87OakA	04-22-56	Baltimore, Md.		R	R	6'	180	100	83	.546	2	266	252	56	1655	1717	436	853	8	4.01
Habyan, John-John Gabriel	85-88BalA 90-93NYA 93KCA 94-95StLN 95CalA 96ColN	01-29-64	Bay Shore, N.Y.		R	R	6'1	195	26	24	.520	12	348	18	0	532	537	186	372	0	3.85
Hackman, Luther-Luther Gean	99ColN 00-02StLN 03SDN	10-10-74	Columbus, Miss.		R	R	6'4	195	9	10	.474	1	149	9	0	212	226	105	128	0	5.09
Haeger, Charlie-Charles Wallis		09-19-83	Livonia, Mich.		R	R	6'1	200	1	1	.500	0	7	1	0	18	12	13	19	0	3.44
Hagen, Kevin-Kevin Eugene	83-84StLN	03-08-60	Renton, Wash.		R	R	6'2	185	3	2	.600	0	13	4	0	30	43	8	9	0	4.25
Halama, John-John Thadeuz	98HouN 99-02SeaA 03OakA 04TBA 05BosA 05WasN 06BalA	02-22-72	Brooklyn, N.Y.		L	L	6'5	210	56	48	.538	0	262	119	2	911	1048	277	492	2	4.65
Halicki, Ed-Edward Louis (Big Ed)	74-80SFN 80CalA	10-04-50	Newark, N.J.		R	R	6'7	228	55	66	.455	1	192	157	36	1063	1007	334	707	13	3.62
Hall, Darren-Michael Darren	94-95TorA 96-98LAN 99SJ	07-11-64	Marysville, Ohio		R	R	6'3	205	5	12	.294	22	130	0	0	126	135	59	98	0	3.93
Hall, Drew-Andrew Clark	86-88ChiN 89TexA 90MonN	03-27-63	Louisville, Ky.		L	L	6'4	200	9	12	.429	5	125	4	1	195	184	95	148	0	5.21
Hall, Josh-Joshua Alan	03CinN 04SJ	12-16-80	Lynchburg, Va.		R	R	6'2	190	0	2	.000	0	6	5	0	25	33	15	18	0	6.57
Halladay, Roy-Harry Leroy III	98-06TorA	05-14-77	Denver, Col.		R	R	6'6	230	95	48	.664	1	216	191	24	1336	1311	333	942	8	3.62
Halsey, Brad-Bradford Alexander	04NYA 05AriN 06OakA	02-14-81	Houston, Tex.		L	L	6'1	180	14	19	.424	0	88	40	0	286	340	99	160	0	4.84
Hamels, Cole-Colbert Richard	06PhiN	12-27-83	San Diego, Cal.		L	L	6'3	190	9	8	.529	0	23	23	0	132	117	48	145	0	4.08
Hamilton, Dave-David Edward	72-75OakA 75-77ChiA 78StLN 78PitN 79-80OakA	12-13-47	Seattle, Wash.		L	L	6'1	190	38	41	.488	31	301	57	4	703	692	317	434	1	3.85
Hamilton, Joey-Johns Joseph	94-98SDN 99-01TorA 01-03CinN	09-09-70	Statesboro, Ga.		R	R	6'4	235	74	73	.503	0	242	209	7	1341	1408	493	894	4	4.44
Hammaker, Atlee-Charlton Atlee (Ham, Chief)	81KCA 82-85SFN 86SJ 87-90SFN 90-91SDN 94-95ChiA	01-24-58	Carmel, Cal.		B	L	6'3	200	59	67	.468	1	249	152	18	1079	1050	287	615	8	3.66
Hammel, Jason-Jason Aaron	06TBA	09-02-82	Greenville, S.C.		R	R	6'6	200	0	6	.000	0	9	6	0	44	61	21	32	0	7.77
Hammond, Chris-Christopher Andrew	90-92CinN 93-96FlaN 97BosA 98FlaN 99-00VR 02AtlN 03NYA 04OakA 05SDN 06CinN	01-21-66	Atlanta, Ga.		L	L	6'1	200	66	62	.516	3	441	136	5	1124	1163	387	712	3	4.14
Hampson, Justin-Justin Michael	06ColN	05-24-80	Belleville, Ill.		L	L	6'1	200	1	0	1.000	0	5	1	0	12	19	5	9	0	7.50
Hampton, Mike-Michael William	93SeaA 94-99HouN 00NYN 01-02ColN 03-05AtlN 06EJ	09-09-72	Brooksville, Fla.		R	L	5'10	190	138	101	.577	1	375	321	21	2074	2156	826	1272	9	3.97
Hamulack, Tim-Timothy William	05NYN 06LAN	11-14-76	Ithaca, N.Y.		R	L	6'4	220	0	3	.000	0	39	0	0	36	43	23	36	0	7.43
Hancock, Josh-Joshua Morgan	02BosA 03-04PhiN 04-05CinN 06StLN	04-11-78	Cleveland, Miss.		R	R	6'3	205	9	6	.600	1	94	12	0	165	161	54	101	0	4.25
Hancock, Lee-Leland David	95-96PitN	06-27-67	North Hollywood, Cal.		L	L	6'4	215	0	0	—	0	24	0	0	32	31	12	19	0	4.45
Hancock, Ryan-Ryan Lee	96CalA	11-11-71	Santa Clara, Cal.		R	R	6'2	220	4	1	.800	0	11	4	0	28	34	17	19	0	7.48

USE NAMES - GIVEN NAMES (NICKNAMES)	TEAM BY YEAR	BIRTH DATE	BIRTHPLACE	DEATH DATE	B	T	HGT	WGT	W	L	Pct.	SV	G	GS	CG	IP	H	BB	SO	ShO	ERA
Haney, Chris-Christopher Deane	91-92MonN 92-98KCA 98ChiN 99-00CleA 01JL 02BosA	11-16-68	Baltimore, Md.		L	L	6'3	205	38	52	.422	1	196	125	8	825	924	286	442	4	5.07
Hanna, Preston-Preston Lee	75-82AtlN 82OakA	09-10-54	Pensacola, Fla.		R	R	6'1	195	17	25	.405	1	156	47	2	436	444	279	253	0	4.62
Hannahs, Gerald-Gerald Ellis (Ark)	76-77MonN 78-79LAN	03-06-53	Binghamton, N.Y.		L	L	6'3	210	3	7	.300	1	16	12	0	71	76	42	42	0	5.07
Hansack, Devern-Devern M.	06BosA	02-05-78	Pearl Lagoon, Nicaragua		R	R	6'2	180	1	1	.500	0	2	2	1	10	6	1	8	1	2.70
Hansell, Greg-Gregory Michael	95LAN 96MinA 97MilA 99PitN	03-12-71	Bellflower, Cal.		R	R	6'5	220	4	4	.500	3	106	0	0	138	159	49	98	0	5.56
Hansen, Craig-Craig R.	05-06BosA	11-15-83	Glen Cove, N.Y.		R	R	6'6	210	2	2	.500	0	42	0	0	41	52	16	33	0	6.59
Hanson, Erik-Erik Brian	88-93SeaA 94CinN 95BosA 96-98TorA	05-18-65	Kinnelon, N.J.		R	R	6'5	215	89	84	.514	0	245	238	26	1555	1604	504	1175	5	4.15
Harang, Aaron-Aaron Michael	02-03OakA 03-06CinN	05-09-78	San Diego, Cal.		R	R	6'7	240	47	43	.522	0	128	125	3	762	803	224	610	3	4.28
Harden, Rich-James Richard	03-06OakA	11-30-81	Victoria, Canada		L	R	6'1	180	30	16	.652	0	77	72	2	439	367	190	404	1	3.67
Hardy, Jack-John Graydon	89ChiA	10-08-59	St. Petersburg, Fla.		R	R	6'2	175	0	0	—	0	5	0	0	12	14	5	4	0	6.57
Hardy, Larry-Howard Lawrence	74-75SDN 76HouN	01-10-48	Goose Creek, Tex.		R	R	5'11	170	9	4	.692	5	94	1	0	127	171	56	70	0	5.24
Haren, Danny-Daniel John	03-04StlN 05-06OakA	09-17-80	Monterey Park, Cal.		R	R	6'5	220	34	35	.493	0	96	87	5	559	565	137	414	0	4.12
Hargesheimer, Alan-Alan Robert	80-81SFN 83ChiN 86KCA	11-21-54	Chicago, Ill.		R	R	6'3	195	5	9	.357	0	31	17	0	111	126	50	55	0	4.70
Harikkala, Tim-Timothy Allan	95-96SeaA 99BosA 04ColN 05OakA	07-15-71	West Palm Beach, Fla.		R	R	6'2	185	7	8	.467	2	72	1	0	96	97	36	46	0	5.91
Harkey, Mike-Michael Anthony	88,90-93ChiN 94ColN 95OakA 95CalA 97LAN	10-25-66	San Diego, Cal.		R	R	6'5	235	36	36	.500	0	131	104	4	656	720	225	316	1	4.49
Harnisch, Pete-Peter Thomas	88-90BalA 91-94HouN 95-97NYN 97MilA 98-01CinN 02EJ	09-23-66	Commack, N.Y.		B	R	6'1	215	111	103	.519	0	321	318	24	1959	1822	716	1368	11	3.89
Harper, Travis-Travis Boyd	00-06TBA	03-21-76	Harrisonburg, Va.		L	R	6'4	195	22	29	.431	2	240	14	1	412	451	136	271	1	4.94
Harriger, Denny-Dennis Scott	98DetA	07-21-69	Kittanning, Pa.		R	R	5'11	185	0	3	.000	0	4	2	0	12	17	8	3	0	6.75
Harris, Gene-Tyrone Eugene	89MonN 89-92SeaA 92-94SDN 94DetA 95PhiN 95BalA	12-05-64	Sebring, Fla.		R	R	5'11	190	12	18	.400	26	183	7	0	241	246	136	170	0	4.71
Harris, Greg-Greg Allen	81NYN 82-83CinN 84MonN 84SDN 85-87TexA 88-89PhiN 89-94BosA 94NYA 95MonN	11-02-55	Lynwood, Cal.		B	R	6'	175	74	90	.451	54	703	98	4	1467	1329	652	1141	0	3.69

Pitched right and left-handed in one game - 9-28-95

USE NAMES - GIVEN NAMES (NICKNAMES)	TEAM BY YEAR	BIRTH DATE	BIRTHPLACE	DEATH DATE	B	T	HGT	WGT	W	L	Pct.	SV	G	GS	CG	IP	H	BB	SO	ShO	ERA
Harris, Greg-Gregory Wade	88-92SDN 93-94ColN 95MinA	12-01-63	Greensboro, N.C.		R	R	6'3	195	45	64	.413	16	243	109	10	909	883	303	605	2	3.98
Harris, Jeff-Jeffrey Austin	05-06SeaA	07-04-74	Alameda, Cal.		R	R	6'1	190	2	5	.286	0	14	8	0	57	51	20	26	0	4.26
Harris, Pep-Hernando Petrocelli	96CalA 97-98AnaA 99EJ	09-23-72	Lancaster, S.C.		R	R	6'2	185	10	5	.667	0	121	3	0	172	168	78	110	0	3.92
Harris, Reggie-Reginald Allen	90-91OakA 96BosA 97PhiN 98HouN 99MilA	08-12-68	Waynesboro, Va.		R	R	6'1	205	2	3	.400	0	86	1	0	121	106	81	95	0	4.91
Harrison,Roric-Roric Edward (Duke)	72BalA 73-75AtlN 75CleA 78MinA	09-20-46	Los Angeles, Cal.		R	R	6'3	200	30	35	.462	0	140	70	12	590	590	257	319	0	4.26
Hartgraves, Dean-Dean Charles	95-96HouN 96AtlN 98SFN	08-12-66	Central Point, Ore.		R	L	6'	185	3	0	1.000	0	84	0	0	80	74	43	58	0	4.41
Hartley, Mike-Michael Edward	89-91LAN 91-92PhiN 93MinA 94JL 95BosA 95BalA	08-31-61	Hawthorne, Cal.		R	R	6'1	192	19	13	.594	4	202	6	1	319	287	139	259	1	3.70
Hartsock, Jeff-Jeffrey Roger	92ChiN	11-19-66	Fairfield, Ohio		R	R	6'	190	0	0	—	0	3	1	0	9	15	4	6	0	6.75
Hartzell, Paul-Paul Franklin	76-78CalA 79MinA 80BalA 84MilA	11-02-53	Bloomsburg, Pa.		R	R	6'5	200	27	39	.409	12	170	77	22	703	766	181	237	2	3.90
Harvey, Bryan-Bryan Stanley	87-92CalA 93-95FlaN 96EJ	06-02-63	Chattanooga, Tenn.		R	R	6'3	230	17	25	.405	177	322	0	0	387	278	144	448	0	2.49
Harville, Chad-Chad Ashley	99,01,03-04OakA 04-05HouN 05BosA 06TBA	09-16-76	Selmer, Tenn.		R	R	5'9	180	2	5	.308	0	175	0	0	181	188	103	147	0	5.22
Hasegawa, Shigetoshi-Shigetoshi (Shiggy)	97-01AnaA 02-05SeaA	08-01-68	Kobe, Japan		R	R	5'11	175	45	43	.511	33	517	8	0	720	691	265	447	0	3.70
Hassler, Andy-Andrew Earl	71,73-76CalA 76-78KCA 78-79BosA 79NYN 80PitN 80-83CalA 84-85StlN	10-18-51	Texas City, Tex.		L	L	6'5	220	44	71	.383	29	387	112	26	1123	1125	520	630	5	3.83
Hathaway, Hilly-Hillary Houston	92-93CalA	09-12-69	Jacksonville, Fla.		L	L	6'4	195	4	3	.571	0	13	12	0	63	79	29	12	0	4.94
Haught, Gary-Gary Allen	97OakA	09-29-70	Tacoma, Wash.		B	R	6'1	190	0	0	—	0	6	0	0	11	12	6	11	0	7.15
Hausman, Tom-Thomas Matthew	75-76MilA 78-82NYN 82AtlN	03-31-53	Mobridge, S.D.		R	R	6'5	200	15	23	.395	3	160	33	2	442	439	121	180	0	3.79
Havens, Brad-Bradley David	81-83MinA 85-86BalA 87-88LAN 88-89ClcA 89DetA	11-17-59	Highland Park, Mich.		L	L	6'1	195	24	37	.393	3	205	61	6	591	624	246	370	2	4.81
Hawblitzel, Ryan-Ryan Wade	96ColN	04-30-71	West Palm Beach, Fla.		R	R	6'2	170	0	1	.000	0	8	0	0	15	18	6	7	0	6.00
Hawkins, Andy-Melton Andrew	82-88SDN 89-91NYA 91OakA	01-21-60	Waco, Tex.		R	R	6'4	215	84	91	.480	0	280	249	27	1558	1574	612	706	10	4.22
Hawkins, LaTroy-LaTroy	95-03MinA 04-05ChiN 05SFN 06BalA	12-21-72	Gary, Ind.		R	R	6'4	210	54	71	.432	75	569	98	2	1017	1159	343	671	0	4.75
Hayes, Ben-Ben Joseph	82-83CinN	08-04-57	Niagara Falls, N.Y.		R	R	6'1	185	6	6	.500	9	86	0	0	115	119	59	82	0	4.70
Haynes, Heath-Heath Burnett	94MonN	11-30-68	Wheeling, W. Va.		L	L	6'	175	0	0	—	0	4	0	0	4	3	3	1	0	0.00
Haynes, Jimmy-Jimmy Wayne	95-96BalA 97-99OakA 00-01MilN 02-04CinN	09-05-72	La Grange, Ga.		R	R	6'4	215	63	89	.414	1	227	203	2	1201	1358	601	762	1	5.37
Hayward, Ray-Raymond Alton	86-87SDN 88TexA	04-27-61	Enid, Okla.		L	L	6'1	190	4	8	.333	0	19	15	1	79	91	42	45	1	6.75
Heathcock, Jeff-Ronald Jeffrey	83,85,87-88HouN	11-18-59	West Covina, Cal.		R	R	6'4	205	9	9	.500	3	56	13	1	158	146	42	64	0	3.76
Heathcott, Mike-Michael Joseph	98ChiA	05-16-69	Chicago, Ill.		R	R	6'3	180	0	0	—	0	1	0	0	3	2	1	3	0	3.00
Heaton, Neal-Neal	82-86CleA 86MinA 87-88MonN 89-91PitN 92KCA 92MilA 93NYA	03-03-60	Queens, N.Y.		L	R	6'1	200	80	96	.455	10	382	202	22	1507	1589	524	699	6	4.37
Heaverlo, Dave-David Wallace (Kojak)	75-77SFN 78-79OakA 80SeaA 81OakA	08-25-50	Ellensburg, Wash.		R	R	6'1	210	26	26	.500	26	356	0	0	539	559	188	288	0	3.41
Hebson, Bryan-Bryan McCall	03MonN	03-12-76	Columbus, Ga.		R	R	6'5	210	0	0	—	0	2	0	0	2	4	1	1	0	13.50
Heflin, Bronson-Bronson Wayne	96PhiN	08-29-71	Clarksville, Tenn.		R	R	6'3	195	0	0	—	0	7	0	0	7	11	3	4	0	6.75
Heilman, Aaron-Aaron Michael	03-06NYN	11-12-78	Logansport, Ind.		R	R	6'5	220	12	18	.400	5	146	25	1	288	266	119	252	1	4.34
Heimueller, Gorman-Gorman John	83-84OakA	09-24-55	Los Angeles, Cal.		L	L	6'4	195	3	6	.333	0	22	14	2	98	114	36	34	1	4.67
Heinkel, Don-Donald Elliott	88DetA 89StlN	10-20-59	Racine, Wis.		R	R	6'1	185	1	1	.500	1	28	5	0	63	70	19	46	0	4.74
Heiserman, Rick-Richard Michael	99StlN	02-22-73	Atlantic, Iowa		R	R	6'7	225	0	0	—	0	4	0	0	4	8	4	4	0	8.31
Helling, Rick-Ricky Allen	94-96TexA 96-97FlaN 97-01TexA 02AriN 03BalA 03FlaN 05-06MilN	12-15-70	Devils Lake, N.D.		R	R	6'3	215	93	81	.534	0	301	234	10	1527	1540	562	1058	4	4.67
Henderson, Joe-Joseph Lee (Fresno Joe)	74ChiA 76-77CinN	07-04-46	Lake Cormorand, Miss.		L	R	6'1	195	3	2	.600	0	16	3	0	35	47	25	27	0	6.69
Hendrickson, Ben-Benjamin John	04,06MilN	02-04-81	St. Cloud, Minn.		R	R	6'4	190	1	10	.091	0	14	12	0	58	79	29	37	0	7.41
Hendrickson, Mark-Mark Allan 96-00 played in N.B.A.	02-03TorA 04-06TBA 06LAN	06-23-74	Mount Vernon, Wash.		L	L	6'9	230	39	47	.453	0	140	120	2	721	843	209	372	2	4.98
Henderson, Rod-Rodney Wood	94MonN 98MilN	03-11-71	Greensburg, Ky.		R	R	6'4	195	0	1	.000	0	5	2	0	10	14	7	4	0	9.58
Henke, Tom-Thomas Anthony (The Terminator, The Canada Goose)	82-84TexA 86-92TorA 93-94TexA 95StlN	12-21-57	Kansas City, Mo.		R	R	6'5	225	41	42	.494	311	642	0	0	790	607	255	861	0	2.67
Henn, Sean-Sean Michael	05-06NYA	04-23-81	Fort Worth, Tex.		R	L	6'5	225	0	4	.000	0	7	4	0	21	29	16	10	0	8.27
Henneman, Mike-Michael Alan	87-95DetA 95HouN 96TexA	12-11-61	St. Charles, Mo.		R	R	6'4	205	57	42	.576	193	561	0	0	733	686	271	533	0	3.21
Hennessey, Brad-Brad Martin	04-06SFN	02-07-80	Toledo, Ohio		R	R	6'2	185	12	16	.429	1	62	40	0	252	261	109	131	0	4.54
Henninger, Rick-Richard Lee	73TexA	01-11-48	Hastings, Neb.		R	R	6'7	225	1	0	1.000	0	6	2	0	23	23	11	6	0	2.74
Hennis, Randy-Randall Philip	90HouN	12-16-65	Clearlake, Cal.		R	R	6'6	220	0	0	—	0	3	1	0	10	4	3	4	0	0.00
Henriquez, Oscar-Oscar Eduardo	97HouN 98FlaN 02DetA	01-28-74	La Guaira, Venezuela		R	R	6'6	220	1	2	.333	2	49	0	0	52	47	30	45	0	6.06
Henry, Butch-Floyd Bluford	92HouN 93ColN 93-95MonN 96SJ 97-98BosA 99SeaA	10-07-68	El Paso, Tex.		L	L	6'1	200	33	33	.500	7	148	91	4	621	677	149	345	2	3.83
Henry, Doug-Richard Douglas	91-94MilA 95-96NYN 97SFN 98-00HouN 00SFN 01KCA	12-10-63	Sacramento, Cal.		R	R	6'4	200	34	42	.447	82	582	0	0	666	611	341	541	0	4.19
Henry, Dwayne-Dwayne Allen	84-88TexA 89-90AtlN 91HouN 92-93CinN 93SeaA 94JL 95DetA	02-16-62	Elkton, Md.		R	R	6'3	225	14	15	.483	14	256	0	0	335	298	216	275	0	4.65
Hensley, Chuck-Charles Floyd	86SFN	03-11-59	Tulare, Cal.		L	L	6'3	185	0	0	—	1	11	0	0	7	5	2	6	0	2.45
Hensley, Clay-Clayton Allen	05-06SDN	08-31-79	Tomball, Tex.		R	R	5'11	190	12	13	.480	0	61	30	1	235	207	93	150	1	3.30
Hensley, Matt-Matthew Davis	04AnaA	08-18-78	San Diego, Cal.		R	R	6'2	220	0	2	.000	0	16	0	0	28	32	7	30	0	4.88
Hentgen, Pat-Patrick George	91-99TorA 00StlN 01-03BalA 04TorA	11-13-68	Detroit, Mich.		R	R	6'2	200	131	112	.539	1	344	306	34	2075	2111	775	1290	10	4.32
Heredia, Felix-Felix Santo [Perez]	96-98FlaN 98-01ChiN 02TorA 03CinN 03-04NYN 05NYN	06-18-75	Santa Cruz de Barahona, D.R.		L	L	6'	180	28	19	.596	6	511	2	0	458	448	232	351	0	4.42
Heredia, Gil-Gilbert	91-92SFN 92-95MonN 96TexA 98-01OakA	10-26-65	Nogales, Ariz.		R	R	6'1	210	57	51	.528	4	267	128	6	954	1079	221	547	0	4.46
Heredia, Ubaldo-Ubaldo Jose [Martinez]	87MonN	05-04-56	Ciudad Bolivar, Venez.		R	R	6'2	180	0	1	.000	0	2	0	0	10	10	3	6	0	5.40
Heredia, Wilson-Wilson	95TexA 96EJ 97TexA	03-30-72	La Romana, Dom. Rep.		R	R	6'	175	1	1	.500	0	16	0	0	32	33	31	14	0	3.41
Herges, Matt-Matthew Tyler	99-01LAN 02MonN 03SDN 03-05SFN 05AriN 06FlaN	04-01-70	Champaign, Ill.		R	R	6'	200	32	29	.525	34	444	4	0	543	588	210	371	0	3.89
Hermanson, Dustin-Dustin Michael	95-96SDN 97-00MonN 01StlN 02BosA 03StlN 04SFN 05-06ChiA	12-21-72	Springfield, Ohio		R	R	6'3	200	73	78	.483	56	357	180	4	1283	1285	460	874	2	4.21
Hernaiz, Jesus-Jesus Rafael [Rodriguez] (Chuito)	74PhiN	01-08-45	Santurce, P.R.		R	R	6'2	175	2	3	.400	1	27	0	0	41	53	25	16	0	5.93
Hernandez, Adrian-Adrian (El Duquecito)	01-02NYA 04MilN	03-25-75	Havana, Cuba		R	R	6'1	185	6	6	.500	0	44	12	0	105	101	45	86	0	6.55
Hernandez, Carlos-Carlos Enrique	01-02HouN 03SJ 04HouN	04-22-80	Guacara, Venezuela		B	L	5'10	180	9	8	.529	0	33	33	0	171	173	91	136	0	4.54
Hernandez, Felix-Felix Abraham (King Felix)	05-06SeaA	04-08-86	Valencia, Venezuela		R	R	6'3	225	16	18	.471	0	43	43	2	275	256	83	253	1	3.96
Hernandez, Fernando-Fernando	97DetA	06-16-71	Santiago, Dom. Rep.		R	R	6'2	185	0	0	—	0	2	0	0	1	5	3	2	0	40.50
Hernandez, Jeremy-Jeremy Stuart	91-93SDN 93CleA 94-95FlaN	07-06-66	Burbank, Cal.		R	R	6'5	195	10	14	.417	20	133	0	0	193	191	67	122	0	3.64
Hernandez, Livan-Eisler Livan	96-99FlaN 99-02SFN 03-04MonN 05-06WasN 06AriN	02-20-75	Villa Clara, Cuba		R	R	6'2	240	123	117	.513	0	318	317	42	2167	2302	751	1456	7	4.18
Hernandez, Manny-Manuel Antonio [Montas]	86-87HouN 89NYN	05-07-61	La Romana, Dom. Rep.		R	R	6'	150	2	7	.222	0	16	7	0	50	58	17	22	0	4.47
Hernandez, Orlando-Orlando P. (El Duque)	98-02NYA 03SJ 04NYA 05ChiA 06AriN 06NYN	10-11-65	Villa Clara, Cuba		R	R	6'2	215	81	60	.574	2	192	187	9	1167	1072	415	958	2	4.19
Hernandez, Roberto-Roberto Manuel [Rodriguez]	91-97ChiA 97SFN 98-00TBA 01-02KCA 03AtlN 04PhiN 05NYN 06PitN 06NYN	11-11-64	Santurce, P.R.		R	R	6'4	240	64	68	.485	326	960	0	0	1025	943	437	914	0	3.32
Hernandez, Runelvys-Runelvys Antonio	02-03KCA 04EJ 05-06KCA	04-27-78	Santo Domingo, D.R.		R	R	6'1	250	25	33	.431	0	78	78	1	435	483	177	231	1	5.38

USE NAMES - GIVEN NAMES (NICKNAMES)	TEAM BY YEAR	BIRTH DATE	BIRTHPLACE	DEATH DATE	B	T	HGT	WGT	W	L	Pct.	SV	G	GS	CG	IP	H	BB	SO	ShO	ERA
Hernandez, Willie-Guillermo [Villanueva] (87-89 known as Guillermo Hernandez)	77-83ChiN 83PhiN 84-89DetA	11-14-54	Aguada, P.R.		L	L	6'2	185	70	63	.526	147	744	11	0	1045	952	349	788	0	3.38
Hernandez, Xavier-Francis Xavier	89TorA 90-93HouN 94NYA 95-96CinN 96HouN 97-98TexA	08-16-65	Port Arthur, Tex.		L	R	6'2	185	40	35	.533	35	463	7	0	671	621	266	562	0	3.90
Herndon, Junior-Harry Francis Jr.	01SDN	09-11-78	Liberal, Kans.		R	R	6'1	190	2	6	.250	0	12	8	0	43	55	25	14	0	6.33
Herrera, Alex-Alexander Jose	02-03CleA	11-05-76	Maracaibo, Venezuela		L	L	5'11	175	0	0	—	0	15	0	0	12	10	9	11	0	5.11
Hershiser, Orel-Orel Leonard (Bulldog)	83-94LAN 95-97CleA 98SFN 99NYN 00LAN	09-16-58	Buffalo, N.Y.		R	R	6'3	195	204	150	.576	5	510	466	68	3130	2939	1007	2014	25	3.48
Hesketh, Joe-Joseph Thomas	84-90MonN 90AtlN 90-94BosA	02-15-59	Lackawana, N.Y.		R	L	6'2	175	60	47	.561	21	339	114	4	962	947	378	726	2	3.78
Hetzel, Eric-Eric Paul	89-90BosA	09-25-63	Crowley, La.		R	R	6'3	175	3	7	.300	1	21	19	0	85	100	49	53	0	6.12
Heydeman, Greg-Gregory George	73LAN	01-02-52	Carmel, Cal.		R	R	6'3	205	0	0	—	0	1	0	0	2	2	1	1	0	4.50
Hibbard, Greg-James Gregory	89-92ChiA 93ChiN 94SeaA 95-97SJ	09-13-64	New Orleans, La.		L	L	6'	185	57	50	.533	1	165	158	11	990	1051	288	408	1	4.05
Hickerson, Bryan-Bryan David	91-94SFN 95ChiN 95ColN	10-13-63	Bemidji, Minn.		L	L	6'2	200	21	21	.500	2	209	36	0	404	451	143	279	0	4.72
Hickey, Kevin-Kevin John (Tug)	81-83ChiA 89-91BalA	02-25-57	Chicago, Ill.		L	L	6'1	180	9	14	.391	17	231	0	0	232	213	101	118	0	3.91
Higuera, Teddy-Teodoro Valenzuela [Valenzuela]	85-91MilA 92SJ 93-94MilA	11-09-58	Los Mochis, Mexico		B	L	5'10	180	94	64	.595	0	213	205	50	1380	1262	443	1081	12	3.61
Hiljus, Erik-Erik Kristian	99-00DetA 01-02OakA	12-25-72	Panorama City, Calif.		R	R	6'5	230	8	3	.727	0	34	20	0	124	134	48	99	0	4.79
Hill, Jeremy-Jeremy Dee	02-03KCA	08-08-77	Dallas, Texas		R	R	5'11	200	0	1	.000	0	11	0	0	10	9	8	7	0	3.48
Hill, Ken-Kenneth Wade (Thrill)	88-91StLN 92-94MonN 95StLN 95CalA 96-97TexA 97-00AnaA 00ChiA 01TBA	12-14-65	Lynn, Mass.		R	R	6'2	210	117	109	.518	0	332	315	19	1973	1938	852	1181	8	4.06
Hill, Milt-Milton Giles	91-93CinN 94AtlN 94SeaA	08-22-65	Atlanta, Ga.		R	R	6'	180	5	1	.833	1	78	0	0	117	133	39	79	0	5.08
Hill, Rich-Richard Joseph	05-06ChiN	03-11-80	Boston, Mass.		L	L	6'5	205	6	9	.400	0	27	26	1	123	108	56	111	1	5.12
Hill, Shawn-Shawn Richard	04MonN 06WasN	04-28-81	Mississauga, Canada		R	R	6'2	185	2	5	.286	0	9	9	0	46	60	19	26	0	6.90
Hillegas, Shawn-Shawn Patrick	87-88LAN 88-90ChiA 91CleA 92NYA 92-93OakA	08-21-64	Dos Palos, Cal.		R	R	6'3	220	24	38	.387	10	181	62	1	515	521	238	332	1	4.61
Hiller, John-John Frederick	65-70DetA 71IL 72-80DetA	04-08-43	Toronto, Canada		R	L	6'1	190	87	76	.534	125	545	43	13	1242	1040	535	1036	6	2.83
Hillman, Eric-John Eric	92-94NYN	04-27-66	Gary, Ind.		L	L	6'10	235	4	14	.222	0	49	36	3	232	285	45	96	1	4.85
Hilton, Howard-Howard James	90StLN	01-03-64	Oxnard, Cal.		R	R	6'3	200	0	0	—	0	2	0	0	3	2	3	2	0	0.00
Hinchliffe, Brett-Brett	99SeaA 00AnaA 01NYN	07-21-74	Detroit, Mich.		R	R	6'5	190	0	5	.000	0	14	5	0	34	51	23	16	0	10.22
Hinds, Sam-Samuel Russell	77MilA	07-11-53	Frederick, Md.		R	R	6'7	210	0	3	.000	0	29	1	0	72	72	40	46	0	4.75
Hinton, Rich-Richard Michael	71ChiA 72NYA 72TexA 75ChiA 76CinN 78-79ChiA 79SeaA	05-22-47	Tucson, Ariz.		L	L	6'2	185	9	17	.346	3	116	13	2	250	283	91	152	0	4.86
Hirsh, Jason-Jason Michael	06HouN	02-20-82	Santa Monica, Cal.		R	R	6'8	250	3	4	.429	0	9	9	0	45	48	22	29	0	6.04
Hitchcock, Sterling-Sterling Alex	92-95NYA 96SeaA 97-01SDN 01-03NYA 03StLN 04SDN	04-29-71	Fayetteville, N.C.		L	L	6'1	200	74	76	.493	3	281	200	10	1286	1374	471	997	2	4.80
Hobbs, Jack-John Douglas	81MinA	11-11-56	Philadelphia, Pa.		R	L	6'3	190	0	0	—	0	4	0	0	6	5	6	1	0	3.00
Hockenberry, Chuck-Charles Marion	75CalA	10-15-50	LaCrosse, Wis.		B	R	6'1	192	0	5	.000	1	16	4	0	41	48	19	15	0	5.27
Hodge, Ed-Ed Oliver	84MinA	04-19-58	Beltflower, Cal.		L	L	6'2	192	4	3	.571	0	25	15	0	100	116	29	59	0	4.77
Hodges, Kevin-Kevin Jon	00SeaA	06-24-73	Houston, Tex.		R	R	6'4	200	0	0	—	0	13	0	0	17	18	12	7	0	5.19
Hodges, Trey-Trey Alan	02-03AtlN	06-23-78	Houston, Texas		R	R	6'3	187	5	3	.625	0	56	1	0	77	85	33	72	0	4.77
Hoey, Jim-James Urban	06BalA	12-30-82	Trenton, N.J.		R	R	6'6	200	0	1	.000	0	12	0	0	10	14	5	6	0	10.24
Hoffman, Guy-Guy Alan	79-80,83ChiA 86ChiN 87CinN 88TexA	07-09-56	Ottawa, Ill.		L	L	5'8	175	17	17	.500	3	137	31	1	339	356	128	187	0	4.25
Hoffman, Trevor-Trevor William	93FlaN 93-06SDN	10-13-67	Bellflower, Cal.		R	R	6'1	205	49	55	.471	482	821	0	0	885	675	250	965	0	2.71
Holdridge, David-David Allen	98SeaA	02-05-69	Wayne, Mich.		R	R	6'3	190	0	0	—	0	7	0	0	7	6	4	6	0	4.05
Holdsworth, Fred-Frederick William	72-74DetA 76-77BalA 77-78MonN 80MilA	05-29-52	Detroit, Mich.		R	R	6'1	190	7	10	.412	3	72	15	0	183	182	86	94	0	4.38
Holland, Al-Alfred Willis	77PitN 79-82SFN 83-85PhiN 85PitN 85CalA 86-87NYA	08-16-52	Roanoke, Va.		R	L	5'11	205	34	30	.531	78	384	11	0	646	548	232	513	0	2.98
Hollins, Jessie-Jessie Edward	92ChiN 93AJ 94SJ	01-27-70	Conroe, Tex.		R	R	6'3	215	0	0	—	0	4	0	0	5	6	5	1	0	13.50
Holly, Jeff-Jeffrey Owen (Hollister)	77-79MinA	03-01-53	San Pedro, Cal.		L	L	6'5	210	3	4	.429	0	39	6	0	89	95	33	49	0	5.66
Holman, Brad-Bradley Thomas	93SeaA	02-09-68	Kansas City, Mo.		R	R	6'5	200	1	3	.250	3	19	0	0	36	27	16	17	0	3.72
Holman, Brian-Brian Scott	88-89MonN 89-91SeaA 92-93SJ	01-25-65	Denver, Colo.		R	R	6'4	185	37	45	.451	0	109	99	15	677	682	254	392	6	3.71
Holman, Scott-Randy Scott (Funky)	80,82-83NYN	09-18-58	Santa Paula, Cal.		R	R	6'2	195	3	8	.273	0	43	14	1	135	119	60	58	0	3.34
Holman, Shawn-Shawn Leroy	89DetA	11-10-64	Sewickley, Pa.		R	R	6'2	185	0	0	—	0	5	0	0	10	8	11	9	0	1.80
Holmes, Darren-Darren Lee	90LAN 91-92MilA 93-97ColN 98NYA 99-00AriN 00StLN 00BalA 00AriN 02-03AtlN	04-25-66	Asheville, N.C.		R	R	6'	195	35	33	.515	59	557	6	0	680	709	256	581	0	4.25
Holt, Chris-Christopher Michael	96-97HouN 98SJ 99-00HouN 01DetA	09-18-71	Dallas, Tex.		R	R	6'4	205	28	51	.354	1	133	112	4	737	853	253	426	1	4.76
Holtz, Mike-Michael James	96CalA 97-01AnaA 02OakA 02SDN 06BosA	10-10-72	Arlington, Va.		L	L	5'9	185	16	20	.444	3	353	0	0	240	245	131	223	0	4.76
Holton, Brian-Brian John	85-88LAN 89-90BalA	11-29-59	McKeesport, Pa.		R	R	6'2	195	20	19	.513	3	185	16	0	371	401	125	210	0	3.62
Holzemer, Mark-Mark Harold	93,95-96CalA 97SeaA 98OakA 00PhiN	08-20-69	Littleton, Colo.		L	L	6'	165	2	5	.286	1	94	4	0	101	138	47	64	0	7.69
Honeycutt, Rick-Frederick Wayne	77-80SeaA 81-83TexA 83-87LAN 87-93OakA 94TexA 95OakA 95NYA 96-97StLN	06-29-54	Chattanooga, Tenn.		L	L	6'1	190	109	143	.433	38	797	268	47	2160	2183	657	1038	11	3.72
Hood, Don-Donald Harris	73-75BalA 75-79CleA 80StLN 82-83KCA	10-16-49	Florence, S.C.		L	L	6'3	192	34	35	.493	6	297	72	6	848	840	364	374	1	3.79
Hook, Chris-Christopher Wayne	95-96SFN	08-04-68	San Diego, Cal.		R	R	6'5	230	5	2	.714	0	55	0	0	66	71	43	44	0	5.89
Hooten, Leon-Michael Leon	74OakA	04-04-48	Downey, Cal.		R	R	5'11	175	0	0	—	0	8	0	0	8	6	4	1	0	3.38
Hooton, Burt-Burt Carlton (Night Owl, Happy)	71-75ChiN 75-84LAN 85TexA	02-07-50	Greenville, Tex.		R	R	6'1	210	151	136	.526	7	480	377	86	2651	2497	799	1491	29	3.38
Hoover, John-John Nicklaus	90TexA	11-22-62	Fresno, Cal.		R	R	6'2	195	0	0	—	0	2	0	0	5	8	3	0	0	11.57
Hope, John-John Alan	93-96PitN	12-21-70	Fort Lauderdale, Fla.		R	R	6'3	200	1	5	.167	0	24	11	0	74	90	27	29	0	5.99
Horgan, Joe-Joseph Paul	04MonN 05WasN	06-07-77	Sacramento, Cal.		L	L	6'1	200	4	1	.800	2	55	0	0	46	54	26	35	0	5.48
Horsman, Vince-Vincent Stanley Joseph	91TorA 92-94OakA 95MinA	03-09-67	Halifax, Canada		R	L	6'2	180	4	2	.667	1	141	0	0	111	107	54	61	0	4.07
Horton, Ricky-Ricky Neal	84-87StLN 88ChiA 88-89LAN 89-90StLN	07-30-59	Poughkeepsie, N.Y.		L	L	6'2	195	32	27	.542	15	325	53	3	673	696	222	319	1	3.76
Hough, Charlie-Charles Oliver (The Hope Diamond)	70-80LAN 80-90TexA 91-92ChiA 93-94FlaN	01-05-48	Honolulu, Hawaii		R	R	6'2	195	216	216	.500	61	858	440	107	3800	3283	1665	2362	13	3.75
Houlton, D.J.-Dennis Sean	05LAN	08-12-79	Fullerton, Cal.		R	R	6'4	220	6	9	.400	0	35	19	0	129	145	52	90	0	5.16
House, Craig-Craig Michael	00ColN	07-08-77	Nash AFB, Okinawa, Japan		R	R	6'2	210	1	1	.500	0	16	0	0	14	13	17	8	0	7.24
House, Tom-Thomas Ross	71-75AtlN 76-77BosA 77-78SeaA	04-29-47	Seattle, Wash.		L	L	5'11	185	29	23	.558	33	289	21	4	536	516	182	261	0	3.79
Howard, Ben-Benjamin Richard	02-03SDN 04FlaN	01-15-79	Danville, Ill.		R	R	6'2	190	2	5	.286	0	40	8	0	83	81	50	67	0	5.20
Howard, Chris-Christian	93ChiA 94BosA 95TexA 96SJ	11-18-65	Lynn, Mass.		R	L	6'	185	2	0	1.000	1	44	0	0	46	40	16	25	0	3.13
Howard, Fred-Fred Irving	79ChiA	09-02-56	Portland, Maine		R	R	6'3	200	1	5	.167	0	28	6	0	68	73	32	36	0	3.57
Howe, Steve-Steven Roy	80-83LAN 84SD 85LAN 85MinA 87TexA 88-89SDN 91-96NYA	03-10-58	Pontiac, Mich.	04-28-06	L	L	5'11	195	47	41	.534	91	497	0	0	606	586	139	328	0	3.03
Howell, J.P.-James Phillip	05KCA 06TBA	04-25-83	Modesto, Cal.		L	L	6'	175	4	8	.333	0	23	23	0	115	125	53	87	0	5.79
Howell, Jay-Jay Canfield	80CinN 81ChiN 82-84NYA 85-87OakA 88-92LAN 93AtlN 94TexA	11-26-55	Miami, Fla.		R	R	6'3	200	58	53	.523	155	568	21	2	844	782	291	666	0	3.34
Howell, Ken-Kenneth	84-88LAN 89-90PhiN 91-92SJ	11-28-60	Detroit, Mich.		R	R	6'3	225	38	48	.442	31	245	54	3	613	534	275	549	1	3.95
Howry, Bob-Bobby Dean	98-02ChiA 02-03BosA 04-05CleA 06ChiN	08-04-73	Phoenix, Ariz.		R	R	6'5	220	29	31	.483	57	518	0	0	537	468	185	462	0	3.52
Hoy, Peter-Peter Alexander	92BosA	06-07-66	Brockville, Canada		R	R	6'7	220	0	0	—	0	4	0	0	8	2	2	0	0	7.36
Hoyt, LaMarr-Dewey LaMarr (The Incredible Hulk)	79-84ChiA 85-86SDN 87SD	01-01-55	Columbia, S.C.		R	R	6'3	235	98	68	.590	10	244	172	48	1312	1313	279	681	8	3.99
Hrabosky, Al-Alan Thomas (The Mad Hungarian)	70-77StLN 78-79KCA 80-82AtlN	07-21-49	Oakland, Cal.		R	L	5'11	185	64	35	.646	97	545	1	0	722	619	315	548	0	3.10
Huber, Jon-Jonathan Lloyd	06SeaA	07-07-81	Sacramento, Cal.		R	R	6'2	195	2	1	.667	0	16	0	0	17	10	6	11	0	1.08
Hudek, John-John Raymond	94-97HouN 98NYN 98CinN 99AtlN 99CinN 99TorA	08-08-66	Tampa, Fla.		B	R	6'1	190	10	15	.400	29	194	0	0	201	176	123	206	0	4.43
Hudson, Charlie-Charles	72StLN 73TexA 75CalA	08-18-49	Ada, Okla.		L	L	6'3	190	1	0	—	1	40	5	1	80	76	42	38	0	5.51
Hudson, Charlie-Charles Lynn	83-86PhiN 87-88NYA 89DetA	03-16-56	Ennis, Tex.		R	R	6'3	190	50	60	.455	2	208	140	14	1008	997	361	580	3	4.14
			(Bats Right 83)																		
Hudson, Joe-Joseph Paul	95-97BosA 98MilN	09-29-70	Philadelphia, Pa.		R	R	6'1	175	6	7	.462	2	102	0	0	127	151	73	62	0	4.82
Hudson, Luke-Luke Stephen	02,04-05CinN 06KCA	05-02-77	Fountain Valley, Cal.		R	R	6'3	205	17	17	.500	0	57	40	0	241	233	119	162	0	5.00
Hudson, Rex-Rex Haughton	74LAN	08-11-53	Tulsa, Okla.		B	R	5'10	170	0	0	—	0	1	0	0	2	6	0	0	0	22.50
Hudson, Tim-Timothy Adam	99-04OakA 05-06AtlN	07-14-75	Columbus, Ga.		R	R	6'	165	119	60	.665	0	247	247	20	1651	1563	526	1155	9	3.53
Huffman, Phil-Phillip Lee	79TorA 85BalA	06-20-58	Freeport, Tex.		R	R	6'1	180	6	18	.250	0	33	32	2	178	227	73	58	1	6.03
Hughes, Jim-James Michael (Blue Gills)	74-77MinA	07-02-51	Los Angeles, Cal.		R	R	6'2	190	25	30	.455	9	76	62	16	441	443	205	226	2	4.19
Hughes, Travis-Travis Wade	04TexA 05-06WasN	05-25-78	Newton, Kan.		R	R	6'5	240	1	1	.500	0	24	0	0	26	35	16	16	0	6.31
Huisman, Justin-Justin Ray	04KCA	04-16-79	Harvey, Ill.		R	R	6'3	195	0	0	—	1	25	0	0	36	38	13	13	0	6.84
Huisman, Rick-Richard Allen	95-96KCA	05-17-69	Oak Park, Ill.		R	R	6'3	200	2	1	.667	1	29	0	0	39	39	19	35	0	5.31
Huismann, Mark-Mark Lawrence	83-86KCA 86-87SeaA 87CleA 88DetA 89BalA 90-91PitN	05-11-58	Littleton, Col.		R	R	6'3	185	13	11	.542	14	152	1	0	296	305	83	219	0	4.40
Humber, Philip-Philip Gregory	06NYN	12-21-82	Nacogdoches, Tex.		R	R	6'4	210	0	0	—	0	2	0	0	2	0	1	0	0	0.00
Hume, Tom-Thomas Hubert	77-85CinN 86-87PhiN 87CinN	03-29-53	Cincinnati, Ohio		R	R	6'1	185	57	71	.445	92	543	55	5	1086	1106	384	536	0	3.85
Hunter, Jim-James MacGregor	91MilA	06-22-64	Jersey City, N.J.		R	R	6'3	205	0	0	—	0	31	0	0	31	45	17	14	0	7.26
Hunter, Rich-Richard Thomas	96PhiN	09-25-74	Pasadena, Cal.		R	R	6'1	185	4	4	.500	0	14	14	0	69	84	33	32	0	6.49
Hurst, Bill-William Hansel	96FlaN	04-28-70	Miami Beach, Fla.		R	R	6'7	220	3	0	—	0	2	2	0	3	6	1	0	0	4.00

USE NAMES - GIVEN NAMES (NICKNAMES)	TEAM BY YEAR	BIRTH DATE	BIRTHPLACE	DEATH DATE	B	T	HGT	WGT	W	L	Pct.	SV	G	GS	CG	IP	H	BB	SO	ShO	ERA
Hurst, Bruce-Bruce Vee (Lefty)	80-88BosA 89-93SDN 93ColN 94TexA	03-24-58	St. George, Utah		L	L	6'4	220	145	113	.562	0	379	359	83	2418	2463	740	1689	23	3.92
Hurst, James-James Lavon	94TexA	06-01-67	Plantation, Fla.		L	L	6'	160	0	0	—	0	8	0	0	11	17	8	5	0	10.13
Hurst, Jonathan-Jonathan	92MonN 94NYN	10-20-66	New York, N.Y.		R	R	6'3	175	1	2	.333	0	10	3	0	26	33	12	10	0	8.20
Hurtado, Edwin-Edwin Amilgar	95TorA 96-97SeaA	02-01-70	Barquisimeto, Venez.		R	R	6'3	215	8	9	.471	2	43	15	1	144	167	85	79	0	6.67
Hutchinson, Chad-Chad Martin 02-04 played in N.F.L.	01StLN	02-21-77	Boulder, Colo.		R	R	6'5	230	0	0	—	0	3	0	0	4	6	6	2	0	24.75
Hutson, Herb-George Herbert	74ChiN	07-17-49	Savannah, Ga.		R	R	6'1	205	0	2	.000	0	29				24	15	22	0	3.41
Hutton, Mark-Mark Steven	93-94,96NYA 96-97FlaN 97ColN 98CinN	02-06-70	South Adelaide, Australia		R	R	6'6	240	9	7	.563	0	84	18	0	190	203	96	111	0	4.75
Ignasiak, Gary-Gary Raymond (Iggy)	73DetA	09-01-49	Mt. Clemens, Mich.		R	L	5'11	185	0	0	—	0	3	0	0	5	5	3	4	0	3.60
Ignasiak, Mike-Michael James	91,93-95MilA	03-12-66	Anchorville, Mich.		B	R	5'11	180	10	4	.714	0	79	6	0	137	141	65	88	0	4.80
Ilsley, Blaise-Blaise Francis	94ChiN	04-09-64	Alpena, Mich.		L	L	6'1	195	0	0	—	0	15	0	0	15	25	9	9	0	7.80
Innis, Jeff-Jeffrey David	87-93NYN	07-05-62	Decatur, Ill.		R	R	6'	170	10	20	.333	5	288	1	0	360	337	121	192	0	3.05
Irabu, Hideki-Hideki	97-99NYA 00-01MonN 02TexA	05-05-69	Hyogo, Japan		R	R	6'4	240	34	35	.493	16	126	80	4	514	547	175	405	2	5.15
Irvine, Daryl-Daryl Keith	90-92BosA	11-15-64	Harrisonburg, Va.		R	R	6'3	210	4	5	.444	0	41	0	0	63	71	33	27	0	5.68
Ishii, Kazuhisa-Kazuhisa	02-04LAN 05NYN	09-09-73	Tokyo, Japan		L	L	6'1	200	39	34	.534	0	105	102	2	564	508	354	435	2	4.44
Isringhausen, Jason-Jason Derik	95-97NYN 98EJ 99NYN 99-01OakA 02-06StLN	09-07-72	Brighton, Ill.		R	R	6'3	220	40	44	.476	249	507	52	3	799	725	339	659	1	3.56
Izquierdo, Hansel-Hansel	02FlaN	01-02-77	Havana, Cuba		R	R	6'1	200	2	0	1.000	0	20	2	0	30	33	21	20	0	4.55
Jackson, Danny-Danny Lynn (Jason)	83-87KCA 88-90CinN 91-92PhiN 92PitN 93-94PhiN 95-97StLN 97SDN	01-05-62	San Antonio, Tex.		R	L	6'	210	112	131	.461	1	353	324	44	2073	2110	816	1225	15	4.01
Jackson, Darrell-Darrell Preston (Glade)	78-82MinA	04-03-56	Los Angeles, Cal.		B	L	5'10	155	20	27	.426	1	102	60	3	411	425	186	229	1	4.38
Jackson, Edwin-Edwin	03-05LAN 06TBA	09-09-83	Neu-Ulm, Germany		R	R	6'3	190	6	4	.600	0	42	15	0	112	121	64	75	0	5.48
Jackson, Grant-Grant Dwight (Buck) (Bats Left 71-78)	65-70PhiN 71-76BalA 76NYA 77-81PitN 81MonN 82KCA 82PitN	09-28-42	Fostoria, Ohio		B	L	6'	195	86	75	.534	79	692	83	16	1358	1272	511	889	5	3.46
Jackson, Mike-Michael Ray	86-87PhiN 88-91SeaA 92-94SFN 95CinN 96SeaA 97-99CleA 00SJ 01HouN 02MinA 04ChiA	12-22-64	Houston, Tex.		R	R	6'2	215	62	67	.481	142	1005	7	0	1188	983	464	1006	0	3.42
Jackson, Roy Lee-Roy Lee	77-80NYN 81-84TorA 85SDN 86MinA	05-01-54	Opelika, Ala.		R	R	6'3	205	28	34	.452	34	280	18	1	559	531	203	351	0	3.77
Jackson, Zach-Zachary Thomas	06MilN	05-13-83	Greensburg, Pa.		L	L	6'5	220	2	2	.500	0	8	7	0	38	48	14	22	0	5.40
Jacome, Jason-Jason James	94-95NYN 95-97KCA 97-98CleA	11-24-70	Tulsa, Okla.		L	L	6'1	175	10	18	.357	1	106	34	2	261	323	98	141	1	5.34
Jacquez, Thomas-Thomas Patrick	00PhiN	12-29-75	Stockton, Cal.		L	L	6'2	195	0	0	—	0	9	0	0	7	10	3	6	0	11.05
James, Bob-Robert Harvey (Beau)	78-79,82MonN 82-83DetA 83-84MonN 85-87ChiA	08-18-58	Glendale, Cal.		R	R	6'4	230	24	26	.480	73	279	2	0	407	377	157	340	0	3.80
James, Chuck-Charles Hamilton	05-06AtlN	11-09-81	Atlanta, Ga.		L	L	6'	170	11	4	.733	0	27	18	0	125	105	50	96	0	3.68
James, Delvin-Delvin DeWayne	02TBA	01-03-78	Nacogdoches, Texas		R	R	6'4	240	0	3	.000	0	8	6	0	34	40	15	17	0	6.55
James, Mike-Michael Elmo	95-96CalA 97-98AnaA 99SJ 00-01StLN 02ColN	08-15-67	Ft. Walton Beach, Fla.		R	R	6'2	215	16	14	.533	11	288	0	0	314	285	149	247	0	3.67
Janssen, Casey-Robert Casey	06TorA	09-17-81	Orange, Cal.		R	R	6'4	205	6	10	.375	0	19	17	0	94	103	21	44	0	5.07
Janzen, Marty-Martin Thomas	96-97TorA	05-31-73	Homestead, Fla.		R	R	6'2	197	6	7	.462	0	27	11	0	99	118	51	64	0	6.39
Jarvis, Kevin-Kevin Thomas	94-97CinN 97MinA 97DetA 98JL 99OakA 00ColN 01-03SDN 04SeaA 04ColN 05ColN 06AriN 06BosA	08-01-69	Lexington, Ky.		L	R	6'2	200	34	49	.410	1	187	118	4	781	937	262	453	3	6.03
Jean, Domingo-Domingo [Luisa]	93NYA	01-09-69	San Pedro de Mac., D.R.		R	R	6'2	175	1	1	.500	0	40	37	1	50	37	19	20	0	4.46
Jeffcoat, Mike-James Michael	83-85CleA 85SFN 87-92TexA 94FlaN	08-03-59	Pine Bluff, Ark.		L	L	6'2	187	25	26	.490	7	255	45	3	500	576	149	242	2	4.37
Jefferson, Jesse-Jesse Harrison	73-75BalA 75-76ChiA 77-80TorA 80PitN 81CalA	03-03-48	Midlothian, Va.		R	R	6'3	205	39	81	.325	1	237	144	25	1086	1151	520	522	4	4.81
Jenkins, Ferguson-Ferguson Arthur (Fergie) (Middle name changed to Ahmad 79-80)	65-66PhiN 66-73ChiN 74-75TexA 76-77BosA 78-81TexA 82-83ChiN	12-13-42	Chatham, Canada		R	R	6'5	210	284	226	.567	7	664	594	267	4501	4142	997	3192	48	3.34
Jenks, Bobby-Robert Scott	05-06ChiA	03-14-81	Mission Hills, Cal.		R	R	6'3	270	4	5	.444	47	99	0	0	109	100	46	130	0	3.55
Jennings, Jason-Jason Ryan	01-06ColN	07-17-78	Dallas, Tex.		R	R	6'2	242	58	56	.509	0	156	156	6	941	1032	425	622	3	4.74
Jensen, Ryan-Larry Ryan	01-03SFN 05KCA	09-17-75	Salt Lake City, Utah		R	R	6'	205	17	12	.586	0	57	42	1	253	279	103	152	0	5.06
Jerzembeck, Mike-Michael Joseph	98NYA	05-18-72	Queens, N.Y.		R	R	6'1	185	0	1	.000	0	3	2	0	6	9	4	1	0	12.79
Jimenez, Cesar-Cesar Enrique	06SeaA	11-12-84	Cumana, Venezuela		L	L	5'11	180	0	0	—	0	4	1	0	7	13	4	3	0	14.73
Jimenez, German-German [Camarena]	88AtlN	12-05-62	Santiago, Mexico		L	L	5'11	200	1	6	.143	0	15	9	0	56	65	12	26	0	5.01
Jimenez, Jason-Jason Jon	02TBA 02DetA	01-10-76	Elk Grove, Cal.		R	L	6'2	208	0	0	—	0	6	0	0	7	12	2	5	0	7.36
Jimenez, Jose-Jose	98-99StLN 00-03ColN 04CleA	07-07-73	San Pedro de Mac., D.R.		R	R	6'3	225	24	44	.353	110	329	38	2	521	572	186	319	2	4.92
Jimenez, Miguel-Miguel Anthony	93-94OakA	08-19-69	New York, N.Y.		R	R	6'2	205	2	4	.333	0	13	11	0	61	65	48	35	0	5.90
Jimenez, Ubaldo-Ubaldo	06ColN	01-22-84	Nagua, Dom. Rep.		R	R	6'4	200	0	0	—	0	2	1	0	8	5	3	3	0	3.52
Jiminez, Juan-Juan Antonio [Martes]	74PitN	03-08-49	La Torre, Dom. Rep.		R	R	6'1	185	0	0	—	0	4	0	0	4	6	2	0		6.75
Jodie, Brett-Brett Paul	01NYA 01SDN	03-25-77	Columbia, S.C.		R	R	6'4	208	0	2	.000	0	8	3	0	25	26	13	13	0	6.39
John, Tommy-Thomas Edward	63-64CleA 65-71ChiA 72-74LAN 76J 76-78LAN 79-82NYA 82-85CalA 85OakA 86-89NYA	05-22-43	Terre Haute, Ind.		R	L	6'3	195	288	231	.555	4	760	700	162	4710	4783	1259	2245	46	3.34
Johns, Doug-Douglas Alan	95-96OakA 98-99BalA	12-19-67	South Bend, Ind.		R	L	6'2	190	20	22	.476	2	114	47	2	386	420	152	180	1	5.13
Johnson, Adam-Adam Bryant	01,03MinA	07-12-79	San Jose, Cal.		R	R	6'2	210	1	3	.250	0	9	4	0	26	40	14	17	0	10.25
Johnson, Bart-Clair Barth	69-74ChiA 75XJ 76-77ChiA	01-03-50	Torrance, Cal.		R	R	6'5	215	43	51	.457	17	185	97	22	810	806	348	520	6	3.93
Johnson, Bill-William Charles	83-84CinN	10-06-60	Wilmington, Del.		R	R	6'5	205	1	0	1.000	0	14	0	0	18	21	4	7	0	3.57
Johnson, Dane-Dane Edward	94ChiA 96TorA 97OakA	02-10-63	Coral Gables, Fla.		R	R	6'5	205	6	2	.750	2	40	0	0	67	70	47	57	0	4.70
Johnson, Dave-David Charles	74-75BalA 76BW 77-78MinA	10-04-48	Abilene, Tex.		R	R	6'2	185	4	10	.286	0	53	7	0	109	126	44	50	0	4.62
Johnson, Dave-David Wayne	87PitN 89-91BalA 93DetA	10-24-59	Baltimore, Md.		R	R	5'10	180	22	25	.468	0	77	57	7	368	439	102	143	0	5.11
Johnson, Jason-Jason Michael	97PitN 98TBA 99-03BalA 04-05DetA 06CleA 06BosA 06CinN	10-27-73	Santa Barbara, Cal.		R	R	6'6	230	55	98	.359	0	239	219	6	1328	1489	486	790	1	4.99
Johnson, Jeff-William Jeffrey	91-93NYA	08-04-66	Durham, N.C.		R	L	6'3	200	8	16	.333	0	38	33	0	182	239	58	76	0	6.52
Johnson, Jerry-Jerry Michael	68-69PhiN 70StLN 70-72SFN 73CleA 74HouN 75-76SDN 77TorA	12-03-43	Miami, Fla.		R	R	6'3	200	48	51	.485	41	365	39	6	771	779	369	489	2	4.28
Johnson, Jim-James Robert	06BalA	06-27-83	Johnson City, N.Y.		R	R	6'5	225	0	1	.000	0	1	1	0	3	9	3	0	0	24.00
Johnson, Joe-Joseph Richard	85-86AtlN 87TorA	10-30-61	Brookline, Mass.		R	R	6'2	195	20	18	.526	0	62	58	3	328	367	99	149	0	4.48
Johnson, Jonathan-Jonathan Kent	98-01TexA 02SDN 03HouN	07-16-74	La Grange, Ga.		R	R	6'	180	2	4	.333	0	42	4	0	77	96	53	68	0	6.63
Johnson, John Henry-John Henry (J.J.)	78-79OakA 79-81TexA 83-84BosA 86-87MilA	08-21-56	Houston, Tex.		L	L	6'2	210	26	33	.441	9	214	61	6	603	585	250	407	2	3.89
Johnson, Josh-Joshua Michael	05-06FlaN	01-31-84	Minneapolis, Minn.		L	R	6'7	240	12	7	.632	0	35	25	0	169	147	78	143	0	3.14
Johnson, Mark-Mark J.	00DetA	05-02-75	Dayton, Ohio		R	R	6'2	226	0	1	.000	0	9	3	0	24	25	16	11	0	7.50
Johnson, Mike-Michael Keith	97BalA 97-01MonN	10-03-75	Edmonton, Canada		R	R	6'2	175	7	14	.333	0	81	32	0	218	254	103	147	0	6.85
Johnson, Mike-Michael Norton	74SDN	03-02-51	Slayton, Minn.		R	R	6'1	190	0	2	.000	0	18	0	0	21	29	15	15	0	4.71
Johnson, Randy-Randall David (The Big Unit)	88-89MonN 89-98SeaA 98HouN 99-04AriN 05-06NYA	09-10-63	Walnut Creek, Cal.		R	L	6'10	225	280	147	.656	2	556	546	98	3799	3013	1409	4544	37	3.22
Johnson, Tom-Thomas Raymond	74-78MinA	04-02-51	St. Paul, Minn.		R	R	6'1	185	23	14	.622	22	129	1	0	274	282	93	166	0	3.38
Johnson, Tyler-Tyler James	05-06StLN	06-07-81	Columbia, Mo.		B	L	6'2	180	2	4	.333	0	61	0	0	39	36	26	41	0	4.62
Johnston, Joel-Joel Raymond	91-92KCA 93-94PitN 95BosA	03-08-67	West Chester, Pa.		R	R	6'5	225	3	5	.375	2	59	0	0	86	66	37	61	0	4.31
Johnston, Mike-Michael Charles	04-05PitN	03-30-79	Philadelphia, Pa.		L	L	6'2	215	0	3	.000	0	24	0	0	24	33	15	20	0	5.70
Johnstone, John-John William	93-95FlaN 96HouN 97OakA 97-00SFN 01XJ	11-25-68	Liverpool, N.Y.		R	R	6'3	205	15	19	.441	3	234	0	0	278	269	115	234	0	4.01
Jones, Al-Alfornia	83-85ChiA	02-10-59	Charleston, Miss.		R	R	5'11	195	2	1	.667	5	27	0	0	29	29	19	16	0	3.77
Jones, Barry-Barry Louis	86-88PitN 88-90ChiA 91MonN 92PhiN 92NYN 93ChiA	02-15-63	Centerville, Ind.		R	R	6'4	225	33	33	.500	23	348	0	0	433	415	194	250	0	3.66
Jones, Bobby-Robert Joseph	93-00NYN 01-02SDN	02-10-70	Fresno, Cal.		R	R	6'4	225	89	83	.517	0	245	241	11	1519	1639	412	887	4	4.36
Jones, Bobby-Robert Mitchell	97-99ColN 00NYN 01SJ 02NYN 02SDN 04BosA	04-11-72	Orange, N.J.		R	L	6'0	175	14	21	.400	0	99	47	1	325	366	195	229	0	5.77
Jones, Calvin-Calvin Douglas	91-92SeaA	09-26-63	Compton, Cal.		R	R	6'3	210	5	7	.417	2	65	1	0	108	83	76	91	0	4.33
Jones, Doug-Douglas Reid	82MilA 86-91CleA 92-93HouN 94PhiN 95BalA 96ChiN 96-97MilA 98MilN 98CleA 99-00OakA	06-24-57	Lebanon, Ind.		R	R	6'3	205	69	79	.466	303	846	4	0	1128	1155	247	909	0	3.30
Jones, Greg-Greg Alan	03AnaA 04SJ 05-06LAA	11-15-76	Clearwater, Fla.		R	R	6'2	190	0	0	—	0	29	0	0	39	44	18	35	0	5.31
Jones, Jeff-Jeffrey Allen	80-84OakA	07-29-56	Detroit, Mich.		R	R	6'3	210	9	9	.500	8	112	3	0	205	201	112	128	0	3.95
Jones, Jimmy-James Condia	86-88SDN 89-90NYA 91-92HouN 93MonN	04-20-64	Dallas, Tex.		R	R	6'2	190	43	39	.524	0	153	118	7	755	809	239	376	3	4.46
Jones, Marcus-Marcus Ray	00OakA	03-29-75	Bellflower, Cal.		R	R	6'3	235	0	0	—	0	1	1	0	2	5	3	1	0	15.43
Jones, Mike-Michael Carl	80-81KCA 82-83AAA 84-85KCA	07-30-59	Penfield, N.Y.		L	L	6'5	225	11	10	.524	0	71	25	0	226	228	108	106	0	4.42
Jones, Odell-Odell (D.D.)	75,77-78PitN 79SeaA 81PitN 83-84TexA 86BalA 88MilA	01-13-53	Tuulare, Cal.		R	R	6'3	175	24	35	.407	4	201	45	4	549	579	213	338	0	4.42
Jones, Randy-Randall Leo	73-80SDN 81-82NYN	01-12-50	Fullerton, Cal.		R	L	6'	177	100	123	.448	2	305	285	73	1932	1915	503	735	19	3.42
Jones, Rick-Thomas Frederick	76BosA 77-78SeaA	04-16-55	Jacksonville, Fla.		L	L	6'5	195	6	9	.400	1	56	16	1	156	197	70	72	0	4.04
Jones, Stacy-Joseph Stacy	91BalA 96ChiA	05-26-67	Gadsden, Ala.		R	R	6'6	225	0	0	—	0	6	0	0	13	11	6	11	0	3.46
Jones, Tim-Timothy Byron	77PitN	01-24-54	Sacramento, Cal.		B	R	6'4	210	1	0	1.000	0	10				4	3	5	0	3.86
Jones, Todd-Todd Barton Givin	93-96HouN 97-01DetA 01MinA 02-03ColN 03BosA 04CinN 04PhiN 05FlaN 06DetA	04-24-68	Marietta, Ga.		R	R	6'3	225	53	58	.477	263	874	2	0	969	958	402	821	0	3.91
Jordan, Ricardo-Ricardo	95TorA 96PhiN 97NYN 98CinN	06-27-70	Delray Beach, Fla.		L	L	5'11	170	5	4	.556	0	69	0	0	70	71	47	47	0	5.25
Joseph, Kevin-Kevin John	02StLN	08-01-76	Camp Hill, Pa.		R	R	6'4	200	0	1	.000	0	11	0	0	11	16	6	2	0	4.91

USE NAMES - GIVEN NAMES (NICKNAMES)	TEAM BY YEAR	BIRTH DATE	BIRTHPLACE	DEATH DATE	B	T	HGT	WGT	W	L	Pct.	SV	G	GS	CG	IP	H	BB	SO	ShO	ERA
Journell, Jimmy-James Richard	03,05StLN	12-29-77	Springfield, Ohio		R	R	6'4	200	0	1	.000	0	12	0	0	13	16	16	13	0	7.43
Judd, Mike-Michael Galen	97-00LAN 01TBA 01TexA	06-30-75	San Diego, Cal.		R	R	6'2	215	4	3	.571	0	28	8	0	75	91	39	61	0	7.20
Juden, Jeff-Jeffrey Daniel	91,93HouN 94-95PhiN 96SFN 96-97MonN 97CleA 98MilN 98AnaA 99NYA	01-19-71	Salem, Mass.		R	R	6'7	255	27	32	.458	0	147	76	6	533	510	247	441	0	4.81
Julio, Jorge-Jorge Dandys	01-05BalA 06NYN 06AriN	03-03-79	Caracas, Venezuela		R	R	6'1	200	13	28	.317	99	343	0	0	358	327	168	345	0	4.28
Junge, Eric-Eric DeBari	02-03PhiN	01-05-77	Manhasset, N.Y.		R	R	6'5	215	2	0	1.000	0	10	1	0	20	19	6	16	0	2.21
Kainer, Don-Donald Wayne	80TexA	09-03-55	Houston, Tex.		R	R	6'2	205	0	0	—	0	4	3	0	20	22	9	10	0	1.80
Kaiser, Jeff-Jeffrey Patrick	85OakA 87-90CleA 91DetA 93CinN 93NYN	07-24-60	Wyandotte, Mich.		R	L	6'3	195	0	2	.000	0	52	0	0	52	68	46	38	0	9.17
Kamieniecki, Scott-Scott Andrew	91-96NYA 97-99BalA 00CleA 00AtlN	04-19-64	Mt. Clemens, Mich.		R	R	6'	195	53	59	.473	5	250	138	8	976	1006	446	542	0	4.52
Kammeyer, Bob-Robert Lynn	78-79NYA	12-02-50	Kansas City, Kans.	01-27-03	R	R	6'4	210	0	0	—	0	8	0	0	22	31	6	11	0	9.00
Karchner, Matt-Matthew Dean	94-98ChiA 98-00ChiN	06-28-67	Berwick, Pa.		R	R	6'4	245	21	13	.618	27	223	0	0	241	242	132	166	0	4.21
Karl, Scott-Randall Scott	95-97MilA 98-99MilN 00ColN 00AnaA	08-09-71	Fontana, Cal.		L	L	6'2	205	54	56	.491	0	180	161	5	1002	1164	369	513	1	4.81
Karnuth, Jason-Jason Andre	01StLN 05DetA	05-15-76	La Grange, Ill.		R	R	6'2	190	0	0	—	0	7	0	0	7	8	4	1	0	2.70
Karp, Ryan-Ryan Jason	95,97PhiN	04-05-70	Los Angeles, Cal.		L	L	6'4	220	1	1	.500	0	16	1	0	17	13	12	20	0	5.29
Karsay, Steve-Stefan Andrew	93-94OakA 95-96EJ 97OakA 98-01CleA 01AtlN 02NYA 03SJ 04-05NYA 05TexA 06OakA	03-24-72	Queens, N.Y.		R	R	6'3	210	32	39	.451	41	357	40	1	603	636	199	458	0	4.01
Karstens, Jeff-Jeffrey Wayne	06NYA	09-24-82	San Diego, Cal.		R	R	6'3	175	2	1	.667	0	8	6	0	43	40	11	16	0	3.80
Kashiwada, Takashi-Takashi	97NYN	05-14-71	Tokyo, Japan		L	L	5'11	165	3	1	.750	0	35	0	0	31	35	18	19	0	4.31
Kaufman, Curt-Curt Gerrard	82-83NYA 84CalA	07-19-57	Omaha, Neb.		R	R	6'2	175	3	3	.500	1	40	1	0	86	87	30	50	0	4.48
Kaye, Justin-Justin Malcolm	02SeaA	06-09-76	Ft. Lauderdale, Fla.		R	R	6'4	185	0	0	—	0	3	0	0	3	6	1	3	0	12.00
Kazmir, Scott-Scott Edward	04-06TBA	01-24-84	Houston, Tex.		L	L	6'	170	22	20	.524	0	64	63	1	364	337	173	378	1	3.73
Keagle, Greg-Gregory Charles	96-98DetA	06-28-71	Corning, N.Y.		R	R	6'1	185	6	16	.273	0	46	23	0	172	208	106	128	0	6.76
Keener, Jeff-Jeffrey Bruce	82-83StLN	01-14-59	Pana, Ill.		L	R	6'	175	1	1	.500	0	23	0	0	27	25	20	29	0	2.70
Keener, Joe-Joseph Donald	76MonN	04-21-53	San Pedro, Cal.		R	R	6'3	198	0	1	.000	0	2	2	0	4	7	8	1	0	11.25
Keeton, Buster-Rickey	80-81MilA	03-18-58	Cincinnati, Ohio		R	R	6'2	190	3	2	.600	0	22	5	0	63	82	20	17	0	5.00
Keisler, Randy-Randy Dean	00-01NYA 03SDN 05CinN 06OakA	02-24-76	Richardson, Tex.		L	L	6'3	190	4	4	.500	0	51	17	0	133	153	79	95	0	6.82
Keller, Kris-Kristopher Shane	02DetA	03-01-78	Williamsport, Pa.		R	R	6'2	200	0	0	—	0	1	0	0	1	2	3	1	0	27.00
Kelly, Bryan-Bryan Keith	86-87DetA	02-24-59	Silver Spring, Md.		R	R	6'2	195	1	3	.250	0	11	4	0	31	33	17	28	0	4.70
Kennedy, Joe-Joseph Darley	01-03TBA 04-05ColN 05-06OakA	05-24-79	La Mesa, Cal.		R	L	6'4	227	39	52	.429	2	183	123	7	798	882	280	507	2	4.79
Kensing, Logan-Logan French	04-06FlaN	07-03-82	San Antonio, Tex.		R	R	6'1	185	1	6	.143	1	45	3	0	57	60	31	56	0	6.47
Kent, Steve-Steven Patrick	02TBA	10-03-78	Frankfurt, Germany		B	L	5'11	168	0	2	.000	1	34	0	0	57	67	38	41	0	5.65
Keough, Matt-Matthew Lon	77-83OakA 83NYA 85StLN 86ChiN 86HouN	07-03-55	Pomona, Cal.		R	R	6'3	185	58	84	.408	0	215	175	53	1190	1190	510	590	5	4.17
Keppel, Bobby-Robert Griffin	06KCA	06-11-82	St. Louis, Mo.		R	R	6'5	205	4	0	.000	0	8	6	0	34	45	15	20	0	5.50
Kepshire, Kurt-Kurt David	84-86StLN	07-03-59	Bridgeport, Conn.		R	R	6'2	195	16	15	.516	0	51	46	2	270	263	119	144	2	4.16
Kerfeld, Charley-Charles Patrick	85-87,90HouN 90AtlN	09-28-63	Knob Noster, Mo.		R	R	6'6	245	18	9	.667	9	123	6	0	202	189	117	155	0	4.20
Kern, Jim-James Lester (The Texas Tornado)	74-78CleA 79-81TexA 82CinN 82-83ChiA 84PhiN 84-85MilA 86CleA	03-15-49	Gladwin, Mich.		R	R	6'5	200	53	57	.482	88	416	14	1	793	670	644	651	0	3.32
Kerrigan, Joe-Joseph Thomas	76-77MonN 78,80BalA M01BosA	11-30-54	Philadelphia, Pa.		R	R	6'5	210	8	12	.400	15	131	2	0	220	221	92	107	0	3.89
Kershner, Jason-Jason Ashley	02SDN 02-04TorA	12-19-76	Scottsdale, Ariz.		L	L	6'2	165	3	5	.375	1	89	2	0	100	93	37	65	0	4.22
Key, Jimmy-James Edward	84-92TorA 93-96NYA 97-98BalA	04-22-61	Huntsville, Ala.		R	L	6'1	190	186	117	.614	10	470	389	34	2592	2518	668	1538	13	3.51
Keyser, Brian-Brian Lee	95-96ChiA	10-31-66	Walnut Creek, Cal.		R	R	6'1	180	6	8	.429	1	51	10	0	152	192	55	67	0	4.97
Kida, Masao-Masao	99-00DetA 03-04LAN 04-05SeaA	09-12-68	Tokyo, Japan		R	R	6'2	209	1	1	.500	1	65	2	0	96	114	39	68	0	5.83
Kiecker, Dana-Dana Ervin	90-91BosA	02-25-61	Sleepy Eye, Minn.		R	R	6'3	185	10	12	.455	0	50	30	0	192	201	77	114	0	4.68
Kiefer, Mark-Mark Andrew	93-96MilA	11-13-68	Orange, Cal.		R	R	6'4	180	5	1	.833	1	44	0	0	80	70	45	61	0	4.29
Kiely, John-John Francis	91-93DetA	10-04-64	Boston, Mass.		R	R	6'3	210	4	5	.444	0	54	0	0	73	70	50	24	0	4.17
Kieschnick, Brooks-Michael Brooks (See B73-04)	03-04MilN	06-06-72	Robstown, Tex.		L	R	6'4	225	2	2	.500	0	74	0	0	96	110	26	67	0	4.59
Kile, Darryl-Darryl Andrew	91-97HouN 98-99ColN 00-02StLN	12-02-68	Garden Grove, Cal.	06-22-02	R	R	6'5	210	133	119	.528	0	359	331	28	2165	2135	918	1668	9	4.12
Kilgus, Paul-Paul Nelson (Killer)	87-88TexA 89CubN 90TorA 91BalA 93StLN 94SJ	02-02-62	Bowling Green, Ky.		L	L	6'1	180	21	34	.382	4	163	68	5	545	546	190	251	3	4.19
Kim, Byung-Hyun-Byung-Hyun	99-03AriN 03-04BosA 05-06ColN	01-21-79	Kwangju, S. Korea		R	R	5'11	176	44	52	.458	86	366	65	0	723	650	308	699	0	4.15
Kim, Sun-Woo-Sun-Woo (Sunny)	01BosA 02BosA 02-04MonN 05WasN 05-06ColN 06CinN	09-04-77	Inchon, S. Korea		R	R	6'2	185	13	13	.500	0	118	38	1	337	396	127	211	1	5.31
King, Curtis-Curtis Albert	97-99StLN	10-25-70	Norristown, Pa.		R	R	6'5	205	6	2	.750	2	68	0	0	81	91	31	42	0	3.43
King, Eric-Eric Steven (Sluggo)	86-88DetA 89-90ChiA 91CleA 92DetA	04-10-64	Oxnard, Cal.		R	R	6'2	215	52	45	.536	16	203	113	8	863	814	333	459	5	3.97
King, Kevin-Kevin Ray	93-95SeaA	02-11-69	Atwater, Cal.		L	L	6'4	200	0	3	.000	0	34	0	0	31	37	22	17	0	7.34
King, Ray-Raymond Keith	99ChiN 00-02MilN 03AtlN 04-05StLN 06ColN	01-15-74	Chicago, Ill.		L	L	6'1	235	19	22	.463	2	514	0	0	365	330	156	252	0	3.28
Kingman, Brian-Brian Paul	79-82OakA 83SFN	07-27-54	Los Angeles, Cal.		R	R	6'1	195	23	45	.338	1	94	82	21	551	275	205	273	3	4.13
Kinney, Dennis-Dennis Paul	78CleA 78-80SDN 81DetA 82OakA	02-26-52	Toledo, Ohio		L	L	6'1	175	4	9	.308	6	97	0	0	155	153	71	75	0	4.53
Kinney, Josh-Joshua Thomas	06StLN	03-31-79	Coudersport, Pa.		R	R	6'1	190	0	0	—	0	21	0	0	25	17	8	22	0	3.24
Kinney, Matt-Matthew John	00,02MinA 03-04MilN 04KCA 05SFN	12-16-76	Bangor, Maine		R	R	6'5	220	19	27	.413	0	103	58	1	360	442	174	297	0	5.73
Kinnunen, Mike-Michael John	80MinA 86-87BalA	04-01-58	Seattle, Wash.		L	L	6'1	200	0	0	—	0	48	0	0	52	64	30	23	0	5.19
Kinzer, Matt-Matthew Roy	87 played in NFL 89StLN 90DetA	06-17-63	Indianapolis, Ind.		R	R	6'3	210	0	2	.000	0	9	1	0	15	28	7	9	0	13.20
Kipper, Bob-Robert Wayne	85CalA 85-91PitN 92MinA	07-07-64	Aurora, Ill.		R	L	6'2	200	27	37	.422	11	271	45	1	562	527	217	369	1	4.34
Kirkwood, Don-Donald Paul (Red)	74-77CalA 77ChiA 78TorA	09-24-49	Pontiac, Mich.		R	R	6'3	190	18	23	.439	8	120	37	7	373	409	135	194	0	4.37
Kiser, Garland-Garland Routhard	91CleA	07-08-68	Charlotte, N.C.		L	L	6'3	190	0	0	—	0	7	0	0	5	7	4	3	0	9.64
Kison, Bruce-Bruce Eugene	71-79PitN 80-84CalA 85BosA	02-18-50	Pasco, Wash.		R	R	6'5	180	115	88	.567	12	380	246	36	1809	1693	662	1073	7	3.66
Klawitter, Tom-Thomas Carl	85MinA	06-24-58	LaCrosse, Wis.		R	L	6'2	195	0	0	—	0	7	2	0	9	7	13	5	0	6.75
Kline, Steve-Steven James	97CleA 97-00MonN 01-04StLN 05BalA 06SFN	08-22-72	Sunbury, Pa.		B	L	6'2	210	33	37	.471	37	728	1	0	636	591	277	476	0	3.42
Klingenbeck, Scott-Scott Edward	94-95BalA 95-96MinA 98ConN	02-03-71	Cincinnati, Ohio		R	R	6'2	205	5	8	.385	0	39	17	0	138	175	63	75	0	6.91
Klink, Joe-Joseph Charles	87MinA 90-91OakA 92EJ 93FlaN 96SeaA	02-03-62	Johnstown, Pa.		L	L	5'11	175	10	6	.625	3	176	0	0	165	171	75	94	0	4.04
Knackert, Brent-Brent Bradley	90SeaA 96BosA	08-01-69	Los Angeles, Cal.		R	R	6'3	185	1	2	.333	1	32	2	0	47	66	28	33	0	7.04
Knapp, Chris-Robert Christian	75-77ChiA 78-80CalA	09-16-53	Cherry Point, N.C.		R	R	6'5	205	36	32	.529	1	122	99	15	603	642	250	355	0	5.00
Knepper, Bob-Robert Wesley	78-80SFN 81-89HouN 89-90SFN	05-25-54	Akron, Ohio		L	L	6'3	210	146	155	.485	1	445	413	78	2708	2737	857	1473	30	3.68
Knight, Brandon-Brandon Michael	01-02NYA	10-01-75	Oxnard, Cal.		R	R	6'	170	0	0	—	0	11	0	0	19	29	8	14	0	10.71
Knott, Eric-Eric James	01AriN 03MonN	09-23-74	Harvey, Ill.		L	L	6'	188	1	3	.250	0	16	2	0	24	31	6	21	0	4.50
Knotts, Gary-Gary Everett	01-02FlaN 03-04DetA 05SJ	02-12-77	Decatur, Ala.		R	R	6'4	235	13	16	.448	2	86	38	0	267	281	122	162	0	5.45
Knudsen, Kurt-Kurt David	92-94DetA	06-10-65	Houston, Tex.		R	R	6'3	200	6	5	.545	7	82	1	0	114	118	68	81	0	5.07
Knudson, Mark-Mark Richard	85-86HouN 86-91MilA 93ColN	10-28-60	Denver, Colo.		R	R	6'5	215	24	29	.453	0	121	59	6	482	563	128	195	2	4.72
Kobel, Kevin-Kevin Richard	73-74,76MilA 78-80NYN	10-02-53	Buffalo, N.Y.		R	L	6'1	190	18	34	.345	4	115	64	5	475	481	152	205	3	3.88
Koch, Billy-William Christopher	99-01TorA 02OakA 03-04ChiA 04FlaN	12-14-74	Rockville Centre, N.Y.		R	R	6'3	218	29	25	.537	163	379	0	0	407	379	191	357	0	3.89
Kohlmeier, Ryan-Ryan Lyle	00-01BalA	06-25-77	Salina, Kans.		R	R	6'2	195	1	3	.250	19	59	1	0	67	78	34	46	0	5.37
Kolb, Brandon-Brandon Charles	00SDN 01MilN	11-20-73	Oakland, Cal.		R	R	6'1	190	0	1	.000	0	21	0	0	24	32	19	20	0	7.99
Kolb, Danny-Daniel Lee	99-02TexA 03-04MilN 05AtlN 06MilN	03-29-75	Sterling, Ill.		R	R	6'4	225	11	23	.324	73	287	0	0	284	295	132	175	0	4.21
Komine, Shane-Shane Kenji	06OakA	10-18-80	Honolulu, Hawaii		R	R	5'9	175	0	0	—	0	2	2	0	9	10	8	1	0	5.00
Komiyama, Satoru-Satoru	02NYN	09-15-65	Chiba, Japan		R	R	6'2	195	0	3	.000	0	25	0	0	43	53	12	33	0	4.21
Konieczny, Doug-Douglas James (Doctor Kono)	73-75,77HouN	09-27-51	Detroit, Mich.		R	R	6'3	215	7	18	.280	0	44	38	4	221	240	111	110	1	4.93
Konuszewski, Dennis-Dennis John	95PitN	02-04-71	Bridgeport, Mich.		R	R	6'3	210	0	0	—	0	1	0	0	0.1	3	1	0	0	54.00
Koo, Dae-Sung-Dae-Sung	05NYN	08-02-69	Daejeon, South Korea		L	L	6'1	187	0	0	—	0	33	0	0	23	32	13	23	0	3.91
Koosman, Jerry-Jerome Martin	67-78NYN 79-81MinA 81-83ChiA 84-85PhiN	12-23-42	Appleton, Minn.		R	L	6'2	210	222	209	.515	17	612	527	140	3839	3635	1198	2556	33	3.36
Koplove, Mike-Michael Paul	01-06AriN	08-30-76	Philadelphia, Pa.		R	R	6'	175	15	7	.682	2	217	0	0	249	225	101	171	0	3.76
Koronka, John-John Vincent	05ChiN 06TexA	07-03-80	Clearwater, Fla.		L	L	6'1	180	8	9	.471	0	27	26	0	141	164	55	71	0	5.59
Kozlowski, Ben-Benjamin Anthony	02TexA	08-16-80	St. Petersburg, Fla.		L	L	6'6	220	1	0	1.000	0	2	2	0	10	11	11	6	0	6.30
Kraemer, Joe-Joseph Wayne	89-90ChiN	09-10-64	Olympia, Wash.		L	L	6'2	185	1	0	1.000	0	19	0	0	29	38	16	21	0	6.91
Kramer, Randy-Randall John	88-90PitN 90ChiN 92SeaA	09-20-60	Palo Alto, Cal.		R	R	6'2	185	6	15	.286	2	66	24	1	184	179	90	92	1	4.51
Kramer, Tommy-Thomas Joseph	91,93CleA	01-09-68	Cincinnati, Ohio		B	R	6'	200	7	3	.700	0	43	16	1	126	136	65	75	0	4.51
Kravec, Ken-Kenneth Peter (Rocky)	75-80ChiA 81-82ChiN	07-28-51	Cleveland, Ohio		L	L	6'2	185	43	56	.434	1	160	128	24	859	814	404	557	6	4.46
Krawczyk, Ray-Raymond Allen	84-86PitN 88CalA 89MilA	10-09-59	Sewickly, Pa.		R	R	6'2	190	0	4	.000	1	39	1	0	52	77	29	42	0	7.19
Kremmel, Jim-James Louis	73-74ChiN 74CinN	09-28-49	Belleville, Ill.		L	L	6'1	185	0	0	—	0	27	0	0	40	52	24	28	0	6.08
Kreuger, Rick-Richard Allen	75-77BosA 78CleA	11-03-48	Grand Rapids, Mich.		R	L	6'2	185	2	2	.500	0	17	4	1	44	42	20	22	0	4.50

USE NAMES - GIVEN NAMES (NICKNAMES)	TEAM BY YEAR	BIRTH DATE	BIRTHPLACE	DEATH DATE	B	T	HGT	WGT	W	L	Pct.	SV	G	GS	CG	IP	H	BB	SO	ShO	ERA
Krivda, Rick-Rick Michael	95-97BalA 98CleA 98CinN	01-19-70	McKeesport, Pa.		R	L	6'1	180	11	16	.407	0	72	36	1	258	297	117	165	0	5.57
Kroon, Marc-Marc Jason	95,97-98SDN 98CinN 04ColN	04-02-73	Bronx, N.Y.		B	R	6'2	195	0	2	.000	0	26	0	0	27	29	26	23	0	7.42
Krueger, Bill-William Culp	83-87OakA 87-88LAN 89-90MilA 91SeaA 92MinA 92MonN 93-94DetA 94-95SDN 95SeaA	04-24-58	Waukegan, Ill.		L	L	6'5	210	68	66	.507	4	301	164	9	1194	1305	493	639	2	4.35
Krukow, Mike-Michael Edward	76-81ChiN 82PhiN 83-89SFN	01-21-52	Long Beach, Cal.		R	R	6'4	205	124	117	.515	1	369	355	41	2190	2188	767	1478	10	3.90
Kubenka, Jeff-Jeffrey Scott	98-99LAN	08-24-74	Weimar, Tex.		R	L	6'2	191	1	1	.500	0	12	0	0	17	17	12	12	0	5.82
Kubinski, Tim-Timothy Mark	97,99OakA	01-20-72	Pullman, Wash.		L	L	6'4	205	0	0	—	0	25	0	0	25	26	11	17	0	5.76
Kucek, Jack-John Andrew Charles	74-79ChiA 79PhiN 80TorA	06-08-52	Warren, Ohio		R	R	6'2	200	7	16	.304	2	58	27	3	207	232	111	121	0	5.10
Kuhaulua, Fred-Fred Mahele (Pineapple)	77CalA 78JL 81SDN	02-23-53	Honolulu, Hawaii		L	L	5'11	180	1	0	1.000	0	8	5	0	35	43	16	19	0	4.89
Kuo, Hong-Chih-Hong Chih	05-06LAN	07-23-81	Tainan City, Taiwan		L	L	6'	235	1	5	.167	0	28	5	0	60	54	33	71	0	4.22
Kurosaki, Ryan-Ryan Yoshitomo	75StlN	07-03-52	Honolulu, Hawaii		R	R	5'10	205	0	0	.000	0	7	0	0	13	15	7	6	0	7.62
Kutzler, Jerry-Jerry Scott	90ChiA	03-25-65	Waukegan, Ill.		L	R	6'1	175	2	1	.667	0	7	7	0	31	38	14	21	0	6.03
Lacey, Bob-Robert Joseph (Beau)	77-80OakA 81CleA 81TexA 83CalA 84SFN	08-25-53	San Jose, Cal.		R	L	6'5	210	20	29	.408	22	284	2	1	452	464	139	251	1	3.67
Lachowitz, Al-Allen Robert	83TexA	09-06-60	Pittsburgh, Pa.		R	R	6'3	198	0	1	.000	0	2	1	0	8	9	2	8	0	2.25
Lackey, John-John Derran	02-04AnaA 05-06CalA	10-23-78	Abilene, Texas		R	R	6'6	225	60	49	.550	0	150	149	8	937	962	302	753	5	4.01
LaCorte, Frank-Frank Joseph	75-79AtlN 79-83HouN 84CalA 85SJ	10-31-51	San Jose, Cal.		R	R	6'1	185	23	44	.343	26	253	32	1	490	457	258	372	0	5.01
LaCoss, Mike-Michael James	78-81CinN 82-84HouN 85KCA 86-91SFN	05-30-56	Glendale, Cal.		R	R	6'5	200	98	103	.488	12	415	243	26	1740	1786	725	783	9	4.02
Lacy, Kerry-Kerry Ardeen	96-97BosA 98SJ	08-07-72	Chattanooga, Tenn.		R	R	6'2	195	3	1	.750	3	44	0	0	56	75	30	27	0	5.59
Ladd, Pete-Peter Linwood (Bigfoot)	79HouN 82-85MilA 86SeaA	07-17-56	Portland, Maine		R	R	6'3	240	17	23	.425	39	205	1	0	287	275	96	209	0	4.14
LaGrow, Lerrin-Lerrin Harris	70,72-75DetA 76StLN 77-79ChiA 79LAN 80PhiN	07-08-48	Phoenix, Ariz.		R	R	6'5	230	34	55	.382	54	309	67	19	778	814	312	375	2	4.12
Lahti, Jeff-Jeffrey Allen	82-86StLN 87SJ	10-08-56	Oregon City, Ore.		R	R	6'	190	17	11	.607	20	205	1	0	286	252	111	137	0	3.12
Lamp, Dennis-Dennis Patrick	77-80ChiN 81-83ChiA 84-86TorA 87OakA 88-91BosA 92PhiN	09-23-52	Los Angeles, Cal.		R	R	6'3	210	96	96	.500	35	639	163	21	1831	1975	549	857	7	3.93
Lancaster, Les-Lester Wayne	87-91ChiN 92DetA 93StlN	04-21-62	Dallas, Tex.		R	R	6'2	205	41	28	.594	22	323	39	3	704	715	261	408	1	4.05
Lance, Gary-Gary Dean	77KCA	09-21-48	Greenville, S.C.		B	R	6'3	192	0	1	.000	0	2	0	0	2	2	2	0	0	4.50
Landreth, Larry-Larry Robert	76-77MonN	03-11-55	Stratford, Canada		R	R	6'1	175	1	4	.200	0	7	4	0	20	29	18	12	0	6.75
Landrum, Bill-Thomas William	86-87CinN 88ChiN 89-91PitN 92MonN 93CinN	08-17-57	Columbia, S.C.		R	R	6'2	200	18	15	.595	58	268	2	0	361	360	124	218	0	3.39
Lang, Chip-Robert David	75-76MonN	08-21-52	Pittsburgh, Pa.		R	R	6'4	210	1	3	.250	0	30	1	0	64	58	37	32	0	4.36
Lange, Dick-Richard Otto	72-75CalA	09-01-48	Harbor Beach, Mich.		R	R	5'10	195	9	15	.375	1	70	31	3	277	298	123	137	0	4.45
Langford, Rick-James Rick	76PitN 77-86OakA	03-20-52	Farmville, Va.		R	R	6'	180	73	106	.408	0	260	196	85	1491	1570	416	671	10	4.01
Langston, Mark-Mark Edward	84-89SeaA 89MonN 90-96CalA 97AnaA 98SDN 99CleA	08-20-60	San Diego, Cal.		R	L	6'2	185	179	158	.531	0	457	428	81	2963	2723	1289	2464	18	3.97
Lankford, Frank-Frank Greenfield	98LAN	03-26-71	Atlanta, Ga.		R	R	6'2	190	0	2	.000	1	12	0	0	20	23	7	7	0	5.95
LaPoint, Dave-David Jeffrey	80MilA 81-84StLN 85SFN 86DetA 86SDN 87StLN 87-88ChiA 88PitN 89-90NYA 91PhiN	07-29-59	Glens Falls, N.Y.		L	L	6'3	225	80	86	.482	1	294	227	11	1487	1598	559	802	4	4.02
Lara, Juan-Juan Manuel	06CleA	01-26-81	Azua, Dom. Rep.		R	L	6'2	190	0	0	—	0	9	0	0	5	4	1	2	0	1.80
Lara, Yovanny-Yovanny B.	00MonN	09-20-75	San Cristobal, Dom. Rep.		R	R	6'4	180	0	0	—	0	6	0	0	6	5	8	3	0	6.35
Larkin, Andy-Andrew Dane	96,98FlaN 00CinN 00KCA	06-27-74	Chelan, Wash.		R	R	6'4	180	3	11	.214	0	39	15	0	106	139	75	69	0	8.86
Larkin, Pat-Patrick Clibborn	83SFN	01-31-60	Arcadia, Cal.		L	L	6'	180	0	0	—	0	5	0	0	10	13	3	6	0	4.35
LaRoche, Dave-David Eugene	70-71CalA 72MinA 73-74ChiN 75-77CleA 77-80CalA 81-83NYA	05-14-48	Colorado Springs, Colo.		L	L	6'2	200	65	58	.528	126	647	15	1	1049	919	459	819	0	3.53
LaRose, John-Henry John	78BosA	10-25-51	Pawtucket, R.I.		L	L	6'1	188	0	0	—	0	1	0	0	2	3	3	0	0	22.50
Larson, Dan-Daniel James	76-77HouN 78-81PhiN 82ChiN	07-04-54	Los Angeles, Cal.		R	R	6'	180	10	25	.286	1	78	43	7	324	331	140	151	0	4.39
Laskey, Bill-William Alan	82-85SFN 85MonN 86SFN 88CleA	12-20-57	Toledo, Ohio		R	R	6'5	195	42	53	.442	0	159	116	10	745	784	210	325	1	4.14
Latham, Bill-William Carol	85NYN 86MilA	08-29-60	Birmingham, Ala		R	L	6'2	190	1	4	.200	0	14	5	0	39	45	13	18	0	5.35
Lavelle, Gary-Gary Robert (Pudge)	74-84SFN 85TorA 86EJ 87TorA 87OakA	01-03-49	Scranton, Pa.		B	L	6'1	200	80	77	.510	136	745	3	0	1086	1004	440	769	0	2.93
Lawrence, Brian-Brian Michael	01-05SDN 06SJ	05-14-76	Fort Collins, Colo.		R	R	6'	195	49	61	.445	0	162	146	7	934	980	255	579	3	4.10
Lawrence, Sean-Sean Christopher	98PitN	09-02-70	Oak Park, Ill.		L	L	6'4	215	2	1	.667	0	7	3	0	20	25	10	12	0	7.32
Laxton, Bill-William Harry	70PhiN 71,74SDN 76DetA 77SeaA 77CleA	01-05-48	Camden, N.J.		L	L	6'2	190	3	10	.231	5	121	4	0	244	212	158	189	0	4.72
Laxton, Brett-Brett William	99OakA 00KCA	10-05-73	Stratford, N.J.		R	R	6'2	205	0	2	.000	0	9	3	0	26	35	17	23	0	7.86
Layana, Tim-Timothy Joseph	90-91CinN 93SFN	03-02-64	Inglewood, Cal.	06-26-99	R	R	6'2	195	5	5	.500	2	78	0	0	103	101	56	68	0	4.56
Lazorko, Jack-Jack Thomas	84MilA 85SeaA 86DetA 87-88CalA	03-30-56	Hoboken, N.J.		R	R	5'11	205	5	8	.385	2	69	15	2	222	213	94	108	0	4.22
Lea, Charlie-Charles William	80-84MonN 85-86SJ 87MonN 88MinA	12-25-56	Orleans, France		R	R	6'5	200	62	48	.564	0	152	144	22	923	864	341	535	3	3.54
Leach, Terry-Terry Hester (Beauregard)	81-82,85-89NYN 89KCA 90-91MinN 92-93ChiA	03-13-54	Selma, Ala.		R	R	6'	200	38	27	.585	10	376	21	3	700	688	197	331	3	3.15
League, Brandon-Brandon Paul	04-06TorA	03-16-83	Sacramento, Cal.		R	R	6'3	192	3	2	.600	1	56	0	0	83	79	30	48	0	4.12
Leal, Luis-Luis Enrique Leal [Alvarado]	80-85TorA	03-21-57	Barquisimeto, Venez.		R	R	6'3	215	51	58	.468	1	165	151	27	946	968	320	491	3	4.14
Leary, Tim-Timothy James	81,83-84NYN 85-86MilA 87-89LAN 89CinN 90-92NYA 92-93SeaA 94TexA	12-23-58	Santa Monica, Cal.		R	R	6'3	215	78	105	.426	1	292	224	25	1491	1570	535	888	9	4.36
Ledezma, Wil-Wilfredo Jose	03-06DetA	01-21-81	Guarico, Venezuela		L	L	6'3	180	12	17	.414	0	83	33	0	247	275	100	147	0	5.20
Lee, Bill-William Francis (Spaceman)	69-78BosA 79-82MonN	12-28-46	Burbank, Cal.		L	L	6'3	205	119	90	.569	19	416	225	72	1944	2122	531	713	10	3.62
Lee, Cliff-Clifton Phifer	02-06CleA	08-30-78	Benton, Ark.		L	L	6'3	190	49	28	.636	0	109	109	2	644	653	219	483	0	4.39
Lee, Corey-Corey Wayne	99TexA	12-26-74	Raleigh, N.C.		B	L	6'2	185	0	1	.000	0	1	0	0	1	2	1	0	0	27.00
Lee, David-David Emmer	99-00ColN 01SDN 03-04CleA	03-12-73	Pittsburgh, Pa.		R	R	6'2	200	5	2	.714	1	96	0	0	115	117	72	97	0	4.37
Lee, Mark-Mark Linden (Vulture)	78-79SDN 80-81PitN	06-14-53	Inglewood, Cal.		R	R	6'4	225	7	8	.467	7	118	1	0	176	184	69	63	0	3.63
Lee, Mark-Mark Owen	88KCA 90-91MilA 95BalA	07-20-64	Williston, N.D.		L	L	6'3	198	5	5	.500	2	116	0	0	127	129	54	84	0	3.82
Lee, Sang-Hoon-Sang Hoon	00BosA	03-11-71	Seoul, South Korea		L	L	6'	190	0	0	—	0	9	0	0	12	11	5	6	0	3.09
Lefferts, Craig-Craig Lindsay	83ChiN 84-87SDN 87-89SFN 90-92SDN 92BalA 93TexA 94CalA	09-29-57	Munich, Germany		L	L	6'1	215	58	72	.446	101	696	45	1	1146	1108	322	719	0	3.43
Leftwich, Phil-Phillip Dale	93-94CalA 95SJ 96CalA	05-19-69	Lynchburg, Va.		R	R	6'5	205	9	17	.346	0	34	34	0	202	220	72	102	0	4.99
Lehr, Justin-Justin Charles Larry	04OakA 05-06MilN	08-17-77	Orange, Cal.		R	R	6'1	200	4	3	.571	0	66	0	0	83	91	39	51	0	5.31
Leibrandt, Charlie-Charles Louis	79-82CinN 84-89KCA 90-92AtlN 93TexA	10-04-56	Chicago, Ill.		R	L	6'3	200	140	119	.541	4	394	346	52	2308	2390	656	1121	18	3.71
Leicester, Jon-Jonathan David	04-05ChiN	02-07-79	Mariposa, Cal.		R	R	6'3	230	5	3	.625	0	38	1	0	51	51	24	42	0	4.80
Leiper, Dave-David Paul	84,86-87OakA 87-89SDN 90IL 94-95OakA 95MonN 96PhiN 96MonN	06-18-62	Whittier, Cal.		L	L	6'1	165	12	8	.600	7	264	0	0	278	282	114	150	0	3.98
Leister, John-John William	87,90BosA	01-03-61	San Antonio, Tex.		R	R	6'2	200	0	7	.000	0	10	7	0	36	56	16	19	0	8.50
Leiter, Al-Alois Terry	87-89NYA 89-95TorA 96-97FlaN 98-04NYN 05FlaN 05NYA	10-23-65	Toms River, N.J.		L	L	6'2	215	162	132	.551	2	419	382	16	2391	2152	1163	1974	10	3.80
Leiter, Mark-Mark Edward	90NYA 91-93DetA 94CalA 95-96SFN 96MonN 97-98PhiN 99SeaA 00SJ 01MilN	04-13-63	Joliet, Ill.		R	R	6'3	215	65	73	.471	26	335	149	15	1184	1205	424	892	1	4.57
Lemanczyk, Dave-David Lawrence (Mule)	73-76DetA 77-80TorA 80CalA	08-17-50	Syracuse, N.Y.		R	R	6'5	230	37	63	.370	4	185	103	30	913	1012	363	429	3	4.62
Lemongello, Mark-Mark	76-78HouN 79TorA	07-21-56	Jersey City, N.J.		R	R	6'1	175	22	38	.367	1	89	74	17	537	564	158	209	1	4.06
Leon, Danny-Danilo Enrique [Lineco]	92TexA	04-03-67	La Concepcion, Venez.		R	R	6'1	185	1	1	.500	0	15	0	0	18	18	10	15	0	5.89
Leon, Max-Maximino [Molina]	73-78AtlN	02-04-50	Ponta Coza Acula, Mex.		R	R	5'9	158	14	18	.438	13	162	13	12	311	315	100	170	1	3.70
Leonard, Dennis-Dennis Patrick	74-83KCA 84KJ 85-86KCA	05-08-51	Brooklyn, N.Y.		R	R	6'1	190	144	106	.576	1	312	302	103	2188	2137	622	1323	23	3.69
Lerch, Randy-Randy Louis	75-80PhiN 81-82MilA 82-83MonN 83-84SFN 86PhiN	10-09-54	Sacramento, Cal.		L	L	6'5	195	60	64	.484	3	253	164	18	1100	1232	432	507	2	4.52
Lerew, Anthony-Anthony Allen	05-06AtlN	10-28-82	Carlisle, Pa.		R	R	6'3	220	0	0	—	0	10	0	0	14	14	8	6	0	9.00
Leroy, John-John Michael	97AtlN	04-19-75	Bellevue, Wash.	06-26-01	R	R	6'3	175	1	0	1.000	0	1	0	0	2	3	3	0	0	0.00
Leskanic, Curtis-Curtis John	93-99ColN 00-01MilN 02SJ 03MilN 03-04KCA 04BosA	04-02-68	Homestead, Pa.		R	R	6'	185	50	34	.595	55	603	11	0	713	678	362	641	0	4.36
Lesley, Brad-Bradley Jay (The Animal)	82-84CinN 85MilA	09-11-58	Turlock, Cal.		R	R	6'6	225	1	3	.250	6	54	0	0	72	61	29	46	0	3.86
Lester, Jon-Jonathan Tyler	06BosA	01-07-84	Tacoma, Wash.		L	L	6'2	190	7	2	.778	0	15	15	0	81	91	43	60	0	4.76
Levine, Al-Alan Brian	96-97ChiA 98TexA 99-02AnaA 03TBA 03KCA 04DetA 05SFN	05-22-68	Park Ridge, Ill.		R	R	6'3	195	24	33	.421	10	416	7	0	575	597	236	278	0	3.96
Levrault, Allen-Allen Harry	00-01MilN 03FlaN	08-15-77	Fall River, Mass.		R	R	6'6	240	7	11	.389	0	56	21	1	171	194	81	110	0	5.59
Lewallyn, Dennis-Dennis Dale	75-79LAN 80TexA 81-82CleA	08-11-53	Pensacola, Fla.		R	R	6'4	200	4	4	.500	1	34	3	0	80	92	22	28	0	4.50
Lewis, Colby-Colby Preston	02-04TexA 05SJ 06DetA	08-02-79	Bakersfield, Cal.		R	R	6'4	230	12	13	.480	0	46	33	0	180	226	110	132	0	6.76
Lewis, Jim-James Martin	79SeaA 82NYA 83MinA 85MinA	10-12-55	Miami, Fla.		R	R	6'2	190	0	1	.000	2	25	0	0	45	45	12	9	0	8.88
Lewis, Jim-Jim Steven	91SDN	07-20-64	Jackson, Mich.		R	R	6'2	200	0	0	—	0	13	0	0	13	14	11	10	0	4.15
Lewis, Richie-Richie Todd	92BalA 93-95FlaN 96DetA 97OakA 97CinN 98BalA	01-25-66	Muncie, Ind.		R	R	5'6	200	14	15	.483	2	217	4	0	293	287	191	244	0	4.88
Lewis, Scott-Scott Allen	90-94CalA	12-05-65	Grants Pass, Ore.		R	R	6'3	190	9	9	.500	0	74	19	1	178	210	59	84	0	5.01
Lidge, Brad-Bradley Thomas	02-06HouN	12-23-76	Sacramento, Cal.		R	R	6'5	210	18	17	.514	104	312	1	0	334	256	140	473	0	3.29
Lidle, Cory-Cory Fulton	97NYN 98SJ 99-00TBA 01-02OakA 03TorA 04CinN 04-06PhiN 06NYN	03-22-72	Hollywood, Cal.	10-11-06	R	R	5'11	185	82	72	.532	2	277	199	11	1322	1400	356	838	5	4.57
Lieber, Jon-Jonathan Ray	94-98PitN 99-02ChiN 03EJ 04NYA 05-06PhiN	04-02-70	Council Bluffs, Iowa		L	R	6'3	225	126	115	.523	2	361	314	24	2073	2238	394	1472	4	4.26
Ligtenberg, Kerry-Kerry Dale	97-98AtlN 99EJ 00-02AtlN 03BalA 04TorA 05BosA	05-11-71	Rapid City, S.D.		R	R	6'2	215	17	20	.459	48	386	0	0	391	357	158	357	0	3.82
Lilliquist, Derek-Derek Jansen (The Georgia Bulldog)	89-90AtlN 90-91SDN 92-94CleA 95BosA 96CinN	02-20-66	Winter Park, Fla.		L	L	6'	210	25	34	.424	17	262	52	1	484	532	134	261	1	4.13

USE NAMES - GIVEN NAMES (NICKNAMES)	TEAM BY YEAR	BIRTH DATE	BIRTHPLACE	DEATH DATE	B	T	HGT	WGT	W	L	Pct.	SV	G	GS	CG	IP	H	BB	SO	ShO	ERA
Lilly, Ted-Theodore Roosevelt	99MonN 00-02NYA 02-03OakA 04-06TorA	01-04-76	Lamita, Calif.		L	L	6'1	185	59	58	.504	0	185	160	4	936	908	382	799	2	4.60
Lima (Rodriguez), Jose-Jose Desiderio Rodriguez [Lima]	94-96DetA 97-01HouN 01-02DetA 03KCA 04LAN 05PhiN 06NYN	09-30-72	Santiago, Dom. Rep.		R	R	6'2	205	89	102	.466	5	348	235	9	1568	1783	393	980	1	5.26
Lincoln, Mike-Michael George	99-00MinA 01-03PitN 04StlN	04-10-75	Carmichael, Calif.		R	R	6'2	210	13	24	.351	5	161	19	0	263	300	96	158	0	5.16
Linebrink, Scott-Scott Cameron	00SFN 00-03HouN 03-06SDN	08-04-76	Austin, Tex.		R	R	6'3	195	25	10	.714	3	313	6	0	372	334	134	328	0	3.12
Linton, Doug-Douglas Warren	92-93TorA 93CalA 94NYN 95-96KCA 99BalA 03TorA	02-09-65	Santa Ana, Cal.		R	R	6'1	190	17	20	.459	0	112	35	0	305	360	125	206	0	5.78
Lira, Felipe-Antonio Felipe	95-97DetA 97-98SeaA 99DetA 00-01MonN	04-26-72	Miranda, Venez.		R	R	6'	170	26	46	.361	1	163	79	4	577	656	222	348	3	5.32
Liriano, Francisco-Francisco Casillas	05-06MinA	10-26-83	San Cristobal, Dom. Rep.		L	L	6'2	185	13	5	.722	1	34	20	0	145	108	39	177	0	2.74
Liriano, Pedro-Pedro Antonio	04MilN 05PhiN	10-23-80	Cotui, Dom. Rep.		R	R	6'2	170	0	0	—	0	16	0	0	23	25	9	16	0	6.17
Littell, Mark-Mark Alan (Country)	73,75-77KCA 78-82StlN	01-17-53	Cape Girardeau, Mo.		L	R	6'3	210	32	31	.508	56	316	19	2	532	416	304	406	0	3.32
Little, Jeff-Donald Jeffrey	80StlN 82MinA	12-25-54	Fremont, Ohio		R	L	6'6	220	3	1	.750	0	40	2	0	55	51	36	43	0	4.07
Littlefield, John-John Andrew	80StlN 81SDN	01-05-54	Covina, Cal.		R	R	6'1	200	7	8	.467	11	94	0	0	130	124	48	43	0	3.39
Littleton, Wes-Wes Avi	06TexA	09-02-82	Hayward, Cal.		R	R	6'2	210	2	1	.667	1	33	0	0	36	23	13	17	0	1.73
Livingston, Bobby-Robert James	06SeaA	09-03-82	St. Louis, Mo.		L	L	6'3	195	0	0	—	0	3	0	0	5	9	6	3	0	18.00
Lloyd, Graeme-Graeme John	93-96MilA 96-98NYA 99TorA 00SJ 01-02MonN 02FlaN 03NYN 03KCA	04-09-67	Geelong, Australia		L	L	6'7	225	30	36	.455	17	568	0	0	533	560	161	304	0	4.04
Loaiza, Esteban-Esteban Antonio [Veyna]	95-98PitN 98-00TexA 00-02TorA 03-04ChiA 04NYA 05WasN 06OakA	12-31-71	Tijuana, Mexico		R	R	6'4	210	123	108	.532	1	360	323	14	2035	2289	579	1352	6	4.62
Lockwood, Skip-Claude Edward (Jaws) (See B61-72)	69SeaA 70-73MilA 74CalA 75-79NYN 80BosA	08-17-46	Roslindale, Miss.		R	R	6'1	195	57	97	.370	68	420	106	16	1236	1130	490	829	5	3.55
Loe, Kameron-Kameron David	04-06TexA	09-10-81	Simi Valley, Cal.		R	R	6'8	225	12	12	.500	1	65	24	1	177	200	59	82	1	4.58
Loewen, Adam-Adam A.	06BalA	04-09-84	Surrey, Canada		L	L	6'5	235	6	6	.500	0	22	19	0	112	111	62	98	0	5.37
Loewer, Carlton-Carlton Ernest	98-99PhiN 00BL 01,03SDN	09-24-73	Lafayette, La.		R	R	6'6	220	10	18	.357	0	48	41	3	238	302	76	118	1	6.12
Logan, Boone-Boone	06ChiA	08-13-84	San Antonio, Tex.		R	L	6'5	200	0	0	—	1	21	0	0	17	21	15	15	0	8.31
Lohse, Kyle-Kyle Matthew	01-06MinA 06CinN	10-04-78	Chico, Cal.		R	R	6'2	195	54	62	.466	0	184	163	4	971	1095	308	612	3	4.86
Loiselle, Rich-Richard Frank	96-01PitN	01-12-72	Neenah, Wis.		R	R	6'5	240	9	18	.333	49	202	3	0	224	241	124	178	0	4.38
Lollar, Tim-William Timothy	80NYA 81-84SDN 85ChiA 85-86BosA	03-17-56	Poplar Bluff, Mo.		L	L	6'3	200	47	52	.475	4	199	131	9	907	841	480	600	4	4.27
Lomon, Kevin-Kevin Dale	95NYN 96AtlN	11-20-71	Fort Smith, Ark.		R	R	6'1	195	0	1	.000	0	12	0	0	17	24	8	7	0	5.94
Long, Bill-William Douglas	85,87-90ChiA 90ChiN 91MonN	02-29-60	Cincinnati, Ohio		R	R	6'	185	27	27	.500	9	159	52	8	519	568	140	247	2	4.37
Long, Bob-Robert Earl (Rapid)	81PitN 85SeaA	11-11-54	Jasper, Tenn.		R	R	6'3	200	1	2	.333	0	33	3	0	58	53	27	37	0	4.47
Long, Joey-Joey J.	97SDN	07-15-70	Sidney, Ohio		R	L	6'2	220	0	0	—	0	10	0	0	11	17	8	8	0	8.18
Looney, Brian-Brian James	93-94MonN 95BosA	09-26-69	New Haven, Conn.		L	L	5'10	180	0	1	.000	0	7	2	0	13	24	6	11	0	11.37
Looper, Aaron-Aaron Joseph	03SeaA	09-07-76	Ada, Okla.		R	R	6'2	180	0	0	—	0	6	0	0	7	7	2	6	0	5.14
Looper, Braden-Braden LaVern	98StlN 99-03FlaN 04-05NYN 06StlN	10-28-74	Weatherford, Okla.		R	R	6'5	225	34	32	.515	103	572	0	0	607	617	213	374	0	3.57
Lopez, Albie-Albert Anthony	93-97CleA 98-01TBA 01AriN 02AtlN 03KCA	08-18-71	Mesa, Ariz.		R	R	6'1	230	47	58	.448	4	297	92	8	841	938	343	558	5	4.94
Lopez, Aquilino-Aquilino Gary [Roa]	03-04TorA 05ColN 05PhiN	04-21-75	Altagracia, Dom. Rep.		R	R	6'2	200	2	5	.286	14	101	0	0	111	95	54	99	0	3.72
Lopez, Aurelio-Aurelio Alejandro [Rios] (Senor Smoke, Yoyo)	74KCA 78StlN 79-85DetA 86-87HouN	09-21-48	Tecamachalco, Mexico	09-22-92	R	R	6'	220	62	36	.633	93	459	9	0	910	785	367	635	0	3.56
Lopez, Javier-Javier Alfonso	03-05ColN 05AriN 06BosA	07-11-77	San Juan, P.R.		L	L	6'4	200	7	4	.636	4	198	0	0	132	142	59	83	0	5.66
Lopez, Rodrigo-Rodrigo [Munoz]	00SDN 02-06BalA	12-14-75	Tlalnepantla, Mexico		R	R	6'1	187	60	61	.496	0	173	147	5	937	1030	294	631	2	4.83
Lorraine, Andrew-Andrew Jason	94CalA 95ChiA 97OakA 98SeaA 99-00ChiN 00CleA 02MilN	08-11-72	Los Angeles, Cal.		L	L	6'3	200	6	11	.353	0	59	26	2	175	218	83	113	1	6.53
Loux, Shane-Shane A.	02-03DetA	08-31-79	Rapid City, S.D.		R	R	6'2	235	1	4	.200	0	14	7	0	44	56	15	15	0	7.71
Lovelace, Vance-Vance Odell	88-89CalA 90SeaA	08-09-63	Tampa, Fla.		L	L	6'5	205	0	0	—	0	5	0	0	5	5	10	2	0	5.79
Lowe, Derek-Derek Christopher	97SeaA 97-04BosA 05-06LAN	06-01-73	Dearborn, Mich.		R	R	6'6	205	100	82	.549	85	466	189	5	1530	1527	442	981	3	3.81
Lowe, Mark-Mark Christopher	06SeaA	06-07-83	Houston, Tex.		R	R	6'3	190	1	0	1.000	0	15	0	0	19	12	9	20	0	1.93
Lowe, Sean-Jonathan Sean	97-98StlN 99-01ChiA 02PitN 02ColN	03-29-71	Dallas, Tex.		R	R	6'2	205	23	15	.605	3	248	22	0	440	485	194	288	0	4.95
Lowry, Noah-Noah Ryan	03-06SFN	10-10-80	Ventura, Cal.		R	L	6'2	200	26	23	.531	0	80	74	3	462	451	162	333	2	4.07
Loynd, Mike-Michael Wallace	86-87TexA	03-26-64	St. Louis, Mo.		R	R	6'4	212	3	7	.300	2	35	16	0	111	131	57	81	0	5.82
Lucas, Gary-Gary Paul	80-83SDN 84-85MonN 86-87CalA	11-08-54	Riverside, Cal.		L	L	6'6	200	29	44	.397	64	409	18	0	669	618	227	410	0	3.01
Ludwick, Eric-Eric David	96-97StlN 97OakA 98FlaN 99TorA	03-05-77	Whiteman AFB, Mo.		R	R	6'5	210	2	10	.167	0	31	12	0	74	104	44	60	0	8.35
Luebber, Steve-Stephen Lee	71-72,76MinA 79TorA 81BalA	07-09-49	Clinton, Mo.		R	R	6'2	195	6	10	.375	3	66	24	2	206	213	106	93	1	4.63
Luebbers, Larry-Larry Christopher	93CinN 99StlN 00CinN	10-11-69	Cincinnati, Ohio		R	R	6'6	205	5	10	.333	1	36	23	1	143	147	66	63	0	4.96
Luecken, Rick-Richard Fred	89KCA 90AtlN 90TorA	11-15-60	McAllen, Tex.		R	R	6'6	210	3	5	.375	2	56	0	0	78	98	44	51	0	5.10
Lugo, Ruddy-Ruddy Joraider	06TBA	05-22-80	Barahona, Dom. Rep.		B	R	5'10	205	2	4	.333	0	64	0	0	85	75	37	48	0	3.81
Lugo, Urbano-Rafael Urbano [Colina]	85-88CalA 89MonN 90DetA	08-12-62	Punta Fijo, Venezuela		R	R	6'	200	6	7	.462	0	50	19	1	163	185	67	91	0	5.31
Lukasiewicz, Mark-Mark Francis	01-02AnaA	03-08-73	Jersey City, N.J.		L	L	6'5	240	2	2	.500	0	41	0	0	36	38	18	40	0	5.20
Lundquist, David-David Bruce Jr.	99ChiA 01-02SDN	06-04-73	Beverly, Mass.		R	R	6'2	200	0	1	.000	0	20	0	0	22	28	12	19	0	7.25
Lyle, Sparky-Albert Walter (The Count)	67-71BosA 72-78NYA 79-80TexA 80-82PhiN 82ChiA	07-22-44	Du Bois, Pa.		L	L	6'1	195	99	76	.566	238	899	0	0	1391	1292	481	873	0	2.88
Lynch, Ed-Edward Francis	80-86NYN 86-87ChiN	02-22-56	Brooklyn, N.Y.		R	R	6'5	220	47	54	.465	8	248	119	8	940	1050	229	396	2	4.00
Lyon, Brandon-Brandon James	01-02TorA 03BosA 04EJ 05-06AriN	08-10-79	Salt Lake City, Utah		R	R	6'1	175	12	20	.375	23	175	21	0	283	326	85	178	0	4.87
Lyons, Curt-Curt Russell	96CinN	10-17-74	Greencastle, Ind.		R	R	6'3	230	2	0	1.000	0	3	3	0	16	17	7	14	0	4.50
Lysander, Rick-Richard Eugene	80OakA 83-85MinA	02-21-53	Huntington Park, Cal.		R	R	6'2	190	9	17	.346	11	137	5	1	257	290	96	111	1	4.31
Mabeus, Chris-Christopher Eugene	06MilN	02-11-79	Peoria, Ill.		R	R	6'3	235	0	0	—	0	1	0	0	2	4	3	2	0	21.60
MacCormick, Frank-Frank Louis (Big Mac)	76DetA 77SeaA	09-21-54	Jersey City, N.J.		R	R	6'4	210	0	5	.000	0	12	11	0	40	39	46	18	0	5.40
MacDonald, Bob-Robert Joseph	90-92TorA 93DetA 95NYA 96NYN	04-27-65	East Orange, N.J.		L	L	6'3	205	8	9	.471	3	197	0	0	234	234	107	142	0	4.34
MacDougal, Mike-Michael Meiklejohn	01-06KCA 06ChiA	03-05-77	Las Vegas, Nev.		B	R	6'4	195	11	15	.423	50	187	3	0	199	193	82	181	0	3.62
Machado, Julio-Julio Segundo [Rondon]	89-90NYN 90-91MilA 92AV	12-01-65	Zulia, Venezuela		R	R	6'	175	7	5	.583	6	101	0	0	147	115	83	151	0	3.12
Mack, Tony-Tony Lynn	85CalA	04-30-61	Lexington, Ky.		R	R	5'10	177	0	1	.000	0	1	1	0	2	8	0	0	0	15.43
MacRae, Scott-Scott Patrick	01CinN	08-13-74	Dearborn, Mich.		R	R	6'3	205	0	1	.000	0	24	0	0	31	33	8	18	0	4.02
MacWhorter, Keith-Keith	80BosA	12-30-55	Worcester, Mass.		R	R	6'4	185	0	3	.000	1	14	2	0	42	46	18	21	0	5.57
Madden, Mike-Michael Anthony	83-86HouN	01-13-58	Denver, Colo.		L	L	6'1	190	12	10	.545	0	71	26	0	195	198	113	119	0	3.94
Madden, Morris-Morris DeWayne	87DetA 88-89PitN	08-31-60	Laurens, S.C.		L	L	6'	155	2	2	.500	0	16	3	0	21	26	23	9	0	5.91
Maddux, Greg-Gregory Alan	86-92ChiN 93-03AtlN 04-06ChiN 06LAN	04-14-66	San Angelo, Tex.		R	R	6'	185	333	203	.621	0	677	673	108	4616	4301	944	3169	35	3.07
Maddux, Mike-Michael Ausley	86-89PhiN 90LAN 91-92SDN 93-94NYN 95PitN 95-96BosA 97SeaA 98-99MonN 99LAN 00HouN	08-27-61	Dayton, Ohio		L	R	6'2	190	39	37	.513	20	472	48	2	862	873	284	564	1	4.05
Madrid, Alex-Alexander	87MilA 88-89PhiN	04-18-63	Springerville, Ariz.		R	R	6'3	200	2	3	.400	0	14	5	1	46	58	21	16	0	5.63
Madritsch, Bobby-Robert A.	04-05SeaA	02-28-76	Oak Lawn, Ill.		L	L	6'3	190	6	4	.600	0	16	12	1	92	78	34	61	0	3.41
Madson, Ryan-Ryan Michael	03-06PhiN	08-28-80	Long Beach, Cal.		R	R	6'6	190	26	17	.605	3	181	18	0	300	328	94	233	0	4.35
Maduro, Calvin-Calvin Gregory	96-97PhiN 00-06BalA	09-05-74	Santa Cruz, Aruba		R	R	6'	180	10	19	.345	0	68	39	0	260	272	118	140	0	5.78
Magnante, Mike-Michael Anthony	91-96KCA 97-98HouN 99AnaA 00-02OakA	06-17-65	Glendale, Cal.		L	L	6'1	190	26	32	.448	3	484	19	0	618	666	234	347	0	4.08
Magrane, Joe-Joseph David	87-90StlN 91EJ 92-93StlN 93-94CalA 96ChiA	07-02-64	Des Moines, Iowa		R	L	6'6	225	57	67	.460	0	190	166	21	1097	1081	391	564	10	3.81
Mahay, Ron-Ronald Matthew (See B73-06)	95,97-98BosA 99-00OakA 00FlaN 01-02ChiN 05-06TexA	06-28-71	Crestwood, Ill.		L	L	6'2	185	16	10	.615	3	301	3	0	352	331	170	299	0	4.12
Mahler, Mickey-Michael James	77-79AtlN 80PitN 81-82CalA 85MonN 85DetA 86TexA 86TorA	07-30-52	Montgomery, Ala.		B	L	6'3	202	14	32	.304	4	122	58	3	406	429	190	262	1	4.68
Mahler, Rick-Richard Keith	79-88AtlN 89-90CinN 91MonN 91AtlN	08-05-53	Austin, Tex.		R	R	6'1	200	96	111	.464	7	392	271	43	1951	2069	606	952	9	3.99
Maholm, Paul-Paul Gurner	05-06PitN	06-25-82	Greenwood, Miss.		L	L	6'2	225	11	11	.500	0	36	36	0	217	233	98	143	0	4.27
Mahomes, Pat-Patrick Lavon	92-96MinA 96-97BosA 98JL 99-00NYN 01TexA 02ChiN 03PitN	08-09-70	Bryan, Tex.		R	R	6'4	212	42	39	.519	5	308	63	0	709	738	392	452	0	5.47
Maine, John-John K.	04-05BalA 06NYN	05-08-81	Fredericksburg, Va.		R	R	6'4	193	8	9	.471	0	27	24	1	134	115	60	96	1	4.58
Mairena, Oswaldo-Oswaldo Antonio	00ChiN 02FlaN	06-30-74	Chinandega, Nicaragua		L	L	5'11	165	2	3	.400	0	33	0	0	36	45	14	21	0	6.06
Majewski, Gary-Gary Wayne	04MonN 05-06WasN 06CinN	02-26-80	Houston, Tex.		R	R	6'1	215	8	9	.471	2	160	0	0	177	187	71	105	0	3.70
Makowski, Tom-Thomas Anthony	75DetA	12-22-50	Buffalo, N.Y.		R	L	5'11	185	0	0	—	0	9	0	0	10	9	3	3	0	5.00
Malaska, Mark-Dennis Mark	03TBA 04BosA	01-17-78	Youngstown, Ohio		L	L	6'3	180	2	2	.500	0	41	0	0	36	34	22	29	0	3.75
Maldonado, Carlos-Carlos Cesar [Delgado]	90-91KCA 93MilA	10-18-66	Chepo, Panama		B	R	6'2	210	2	2	.500	1	38	0	0	51	60	30	28	0	5.65
Mallette, Brian-Brian Drew	02MilN	01-19-75	Dublin, Ga.		R	R	6'	185	0	0	—	0	5	0	0	5	7	3	5	0	10.80
Mallicoat, Rob-Robbin Dale	87,91-92HouN 93SJ	11-16-64	St. Helens, Ore.		L	L	6'3	180	0	2	.000	1	51	1	0	54	56	38	42	0	5.70
Malloy, Bob-Robert William	87TexA 90MonN	11-24-64	Arlington, Tex.		R	R	6'5	200	0	0	—	0	5	2	0	13	14	4	9	0	5.54
Malone, Chuck-Charles Ray	90PhiN	07-08-65	Harrisburg, Ark.		R	R	6'7	250	1	0	1.000	0	7	0	0	7	3	11	7	0	3.68
Maloney, Sean-Sean Patrick	97MilA 98LAN	05-25-71	South Kingstown, R.I.		R	R	6'7	210	0	1	.000	0	14	0	0	20	20	7	16	0	5.03
Mann, Jim-James Joseph	00NYN 01-02HouN 03PitN	11-17-74	Brockton, Mass.		R	R	6'3	225	0	1	.000	0	25	0	0	32	33	13	25	0	4.83

USE NAMES - GIVEN NAMES (NICKNAMES)	TEAM BY YEAR	BIRTH DATE	BIRTHPLACE	DEATH DATE	B	T	HGT	WGT	W	L	Pct.	SV	G	GS	CG	IP	H	BB	SO	ShO	ERA
Manning, David-David Anthony	03MilN	08-14-72	Buffalo, N.Y.		R	R	6'3	210	0	2	.000	0	7	2	0	7	11	8	2	0	16.20
Manon, Julio-Julio Alberto	03MonN 06BalA	06-10-73	Guerra, Dom. Rep.		L	R	6'	200	1	3	.250	1	45	0	0	48	49	33	37	0	4.66
Manon, Ramon-Ramon [Reyes]	90TexA	01-20-68	Santo Domingo, D.R.		R	R	6'	170	0	0	—	0	1	0	0	2	3	3	0	0	13.50
Mantei, Matt-Matthew Bruce	95-96,98-99FlaN 99-04AriN 05BosA	07-07-73	Tampa, Fla.		R	R	6'1	195	14	18	.438	93	315	0	0	323	249	200	396	0	4.07
Manuel, Barry-Barry Paul	91-92TexA 96MonN 97NYN 98AriN	08-12-65	Mamou, La.		R	R	5'11	175	7	2	.778	0	96	0	0	149	135	60	109	0	3.87
Manzanillo, Josias-Josias [Adams] (Manzy)	91BosA 93MilA 93-94NYN 95NYA 97SeaA 99NYN 00-02PitN 03CinN 04FlaN	10-16-67	San Pedro de Mac., D.R.		R	R	6'	200	13	15	.464	6	267	1	0	342	330	153	300	0	4.71
Manzanillo, Ravelo-Ravelo [Adams]	88ChiA 94-95PitN	10-17-63	San Pedro de Mac., D.R.		L	L	5'10	190	4	3	.571	1	53	2	0	63	55	56	50	0	4.43
Marak, Paul-Paul Patrick	90AtlN	08-02-65	Lakenheath, England		R	R	6'2	180	1	2	.333	0	7	7	1	39	39	19	15	1	3.69
Marcum, Shaun-Shaun M.	05-06TorA	12-14-81	Kansas City, Mo.		R	R	6'	180	3	4	.429	0	26	14	0	86	93	42	69	0	4.59
Marmol, Carlos-Carlos Agustin	06ChiN	10-14-82	Bonao, Dom. Rep.		R	R	6'2	180	5	7	.417	0	19	13	0	77	71	59	59	0	6.08
Maroth, Mike-Michael Warren	02-06DetA	08-17-77	Orlando, Fla.		L	L	6'	190	45	60	.429	0	134	130	3	802	910	212	392	1	4.78
Marquez, Isidro-Isidro [Espinoza]	95ChiA	05-14-65	Navojoa, Mexico		R	R	6'3	190	0	1	.000	0	7	0	0	7	9	2	8	0	6.75
Marquis, Jason-Jason Scott	00-03AtlN 04-06StlN	08-21-78	Manhasset, N.Y.		L	R	6'	205	56	52	.519	1	194	137	3	910	948	352	552	1	4.55
Marshall, Mike-Michael Grant	67DetA 69SeaA 70HouN 70-73MonN 74-76LAN 76-77AtlN 77TexA 78-80MinA 81NYN	01-15-43	Adrian, Mich.		R	R	5'10	180	97	112	.464	188	723	24	3	1386	1281	514	880	1	3.14
Marshall, Sean-Sean Christopher	06ChiN	08-30-82	Richmond, Va.		L	L	6'7	205	6	9	.400	0	24	24	0	126	132	59	77	0	5.59
Marsonek, Sam-Samuel R.	04NYA	07-10-78	Tampa, Fla.		R	R	6'6	225	0	0	—	0	1	0	0	1	2	0	0	0	0.00
Marte, Damaso-Damaso [Sabinon]	99SeaA 01PitN 02-05ChiA 06PitN	02-14-75	Santo Domingo, D.R.		L	L	6'	190	15	21	.417	31	382	0	0	362	296	168	386	0	3.28
Martin, John-John Robert	80-83StlN 83DetA	04-11-56	Wyandotte, Mich.		B	L	6'	190	17	14	.548	1	91	32	5	291	255	95	120	0	3.93
Martin, Renie-Donald Renie	79-81KCA 82-84SFN 84PhiN	08-30-55	Dover, Del.		R	R	6'5	190	24	35	.407	12	173	51	3	509	509	256	237	0	4.27
Martin, Tom-Thomas Edgar	97HouN 98-00CleA 01NYN 02TBA 03-04LAN 04-05AtlN 06ColN	05-21-70	Charleston, S.C.		L	L	6'1	200	11	9	.550	3	350	0	0	291	307	134	214	0	4.92
Martinez, Anastacio-Anastacio Euclides	04BosA	11-03-78	Santa Cruz, Dom. Rep.		R	R	6'2	180	2	1	.667	0	11	0	0	11	13	6	5	0	8.44
Martinez, Carlos-Carlos M.	06FlaN	05-26-82	Villa Vasquez, Dom. Rep.		R	R	6'2	170	0	1	.000	0	12	0	0	10	9	6	11	0	1.74
Martinez, Dennis-Jose Dennis [Emilia] (El Presidente)	76-86BalA 86-93MonN 94-96CleA 97SeaA 98AtlN	05-14-55	Granada, Nicaragua		R	R	6'1	185	245	193	.559	8	692	562	122	4000	3897	1165	2149	29	3.70
Martinez, Freddie-Alfredo	80-81CalA	03-15-57	Los Angeles, Cal.		R	R	6'3	180	7	9	.438	0	32	23	4	155	155	62	61	1	4.47
Martinez, Javier-Javier Antonio	98PitN 99EJ	02-05-77	Bayamon, P.R.		R	R	6'2	195	0	1	.000	0	37	0	0	41	39	34	42	0	4.83
Martinez, Jose-Jose Miguel [Martinez]	94SDN	04-01-71	Guayubin, Dom. Rep.		R	R	6'2	180	0	2	.000	0	4	1	0	12	18	5	7	0	6.75
Martinez, Luis-Luis	03MilN	01-20-80	Santo Domingo, D.R.		L	L	6'6	200	0	3	.000	0	4	4	0	16	25	15	10	0	9.92
Martinez (Jaime), Pedro-Pedro Jaime [Martinez]	92-93LAN 94-97MonN 98-04BosA 05-06NYN	10-25-71	Manoguayabo, D.R.		R	R	5'11	175	206	92	.691	3	442	375	46	2646	2013	701	2998	17	2.81
Martinez, Pedro-Pedro [Aquino]	93-94SDN 95HouN 96NYN 96-97CinN	11-29-68	Villa Mella, Dom. Rep.		L	L	6'1	185	7	4	.636	3	122	1	0	143	125	93	114	0	3.97
Martinez (Jaime), Ramon-Ramon Jaime [Martinez]	88-98LAN 99-00BosA 01PitN	03-22-68	Santo Domingo, D.R.		R	R	6'4	180	135	88	.605	0	301	297	37	1896	1691	795	1427	20	3.67
			Bats Right 89																		
Martinez, Silvio-Silvio Ramon [Cabrera]	77ChiA 78-81StlN 82AJ	08-19-55	Santiago, Dom. Rep.		R	R	5'10	170	31	32	.492	1	107	87	14	583	568	237	230	4	3.87
Martinez, Tippy-Felix Anthony	74-76NYA 76-86BalA 87SJ 88MinA	05-31-50	La Junta, Colo.		L	L	5'10	180	55	42	.567	115	546	2	0	835	732	425	632	0	3.45
Martinez, Willie-William Jose	00CleA	01-04-78	Barquisimeto, Venezuela		R	R	6'2	180	0	0	—	0	1	0	0	3	1	1	1	0	3.00
Martz, Randy-Randy Carl	80-82ChiN 83ChiA	05-28-56	Harrisburg, Pa.		L	R	6'4	220	17	19	.472	7	68	45	2	291	292	100	78	0	3.78
Masaoka, Onan-Onan Kainoa Satoshi	99-00LAN	10-27-77	Hilo, Hawaii		R	L	6'	188	3	5	.375	1	83	0	0	94	78	62	88	0	4.23
Masch, Patrick-Theodore Joseph	06SFN	08-18-81	Northbrook, Ill.		R	L	6'	170	0	0	—	0	1	0	0	1	2	0	1	0	9.00
Mason, Mike-Michael Paul (Mase)	82-87TexA 87ChiN 88MinA	11-21-58	Fairbault, Minn.		L	L	6'2	205	29	39	.426	0	140	90	7	606	625	249	363	2	4.53
Mason, Roger-Roger LeRoy	84DetA 85-87SFN 89HouN 91-92PitN 93SDN 93-94PhiN 94NYN	09-18-58	Bellaire, Mich.		R	R	6'6	220	22	35	.386	13	232	23	2	416	385	161	286	1	4.02
Masset, Nick-Nicholas Allen	06TexA	05-17-82	St. Petersburg, Fla.		R	R	6'4	190	0	0	—	0	8	0	0	9	9	2	4	0	4.15
Mastny, Thomas-Thomas Raymond	06CleA	02-04-81	East Bontang, Borneo, Indonesia		R	R	6'6	220	0	1	.000	5	15	0	0	16	17	8	14	0	5.51
Mateo, Juan-Juan Manuel	06ChiN	12-17-82	Bani, Dom. Rep.		R	R	6'2	180	1	3	.250	0	11	10	0	46	51	23	35	0	5.32
Mateo, Julio-Julio Cesar	02-06SeaA	08-02-77	Bani, Dom. Rep.		R	R	6'	177	17	12	.586	2	210	1	0	306	286	80	212	0	3.67
Mathews, Greg-Gregory Inman	86-88StlN 89EJ 90StlN 92PhiN	05-17-62	Harbor City, Cal.		B	L	6'2	180	28	33	.459	0	93	84	4	514	491	202	251	1	4.08
Mathews, Terry-Terry Alan	91-92TexA 94-96FlaN 96-98BalA 99KCA	10-05-64	Alexandria, La.		R	R	6'2	210	22	21	.512	10	324	5	0	422	429	180	300	0	4.25
Mathews, T.J.-Timothy Jay	95-97StlN 97-01OakA 01StlN 02HouN	01-09-70	Belleville, Ill.		R	R	6'2	210	32	26	.552	16	362	5	0	435	406	164	357	0	3.82
Mathieson, Scott-Scott William	06PhiN	02-27-84	Vancouver, Canada		R	R	6'3	190	1	4	.200	0	9	8	0	37	48	16	28	0	7.47
Mathis, Ron-Ronald Vance	85,87HouN	09-25-58	Kansas City, Mo.		R	R	6'	180	3	6	.333	1	31	8	0	82	93	38	42	0	5.93
Matlack, Jon-Jonathan Trumpbour	71-77NYN 78-83TexA	01-19-50	West Chester, Pa.		L	L	6'3	205	125	126	.498	3	361	318	97	2363	2276	638	1516	30	3.18
Mattes, Troy-Troy Walter	01MonN	08-26-75	Champaign, Ill.		R	R	6'8	230	3	3	.500	0	8	8	0	45	51	21	26	0	6.00
Matthews, Mike-Michael Scott	00-02StlN 02MilN 03SDN 04CinN 05NYN	10-24-73	Fredericksburg, Va.		L	L	6'2	190	14	10	.583	1	230	10	0	244	237	121	175	0	4.54
Matula, Rick-Richard Carlton	79-81AtlN	11-22-53	Wharton, Tex.		R	R	6'	195	19	23	.452	0	66	58	4	355	396	126	129	1	4.41
Maurer, Dave-David Charles	00-01SDN 02CleA 04TorA	02-23-75	Minneapolis, Minn.		R	L	6'2	205	1	1	.500	0	22	0	0	22	32	14	18	0	8.87
Mauser, Tim-Timothy Edward	91,93PhiN 93-95SDN	10-04-66	Fort Worth, Tex.		R	R	6'	190	2	6	.250	2	79	0	0	119	123	55	93	0	4.37
Maxcy, Brian-David Brian	95-96DetA	05-04-71	Amory Mass.		R	R	6'1	170	4	5	.444	0	43	0	0	56	69	33	21	0	7.28
May, Darrell-Darrell Kevin	95AtlN 96PitN 96CalA 97AnaA 98-01JL 02-04KCA 05SDN 05NYA	06-13-72	San Bernardino, Cal.		L	L	6'2	175	26	43	.377	0	161	97	7	661	746	212	414	3	5.16
May, Rudy-Rudolph (Mr. Coffeyville)	65CalA 66-67SA 69-74CalA 74-76NYA 76-77BalA 78-79MonN 80-83NYA 84XJ	07-18-44	Coffeyville, Kans.		L	L	6'2	205	152	156	.494	12	535	360	87	2621	2314	958	1760	24	3.46
May, Scott-Scott Francis	88TexA 91ChiN	11-11-61	West Bend, Wis.		R	R	6'1	185	0	0	—	0	5	1	0	9	14	5	5	0	10.61
Mays, Joe-Joseph Emerson	99-03MinA 04SJ 05MinA 06KCA 06CinN	12-10-75	Flint, Mich.		B	R	6'1	185	48	70	.407	0	206	156	10	997	1130	329	512	6	5.05
Maysey, Matt-Matthew Samuel	92MonN 93MilA	01-08-67	Hamilton, Canada		R	R	6'4	225	1	2	.333	1	25	0	0	24	32	13	11	0	5.55
McAndrew, Jamie-James Brian	95MilA 96KJ 97MilA	09-02-67	Williamsport, Pa.		R	R	6'2	190	3	4	.429	0	15	8	0	56	61	35	27	0	5.98
McBride, Macay-Joseph Macay	05-06AtlN	10-24-82	Augusta, Ga.		L	L	5'11	210	5	1	.833	2	94	0	0	71	71	39	68	0	4.08
McCall, Larry-Larry Stephen	77-78NYA 79TexA	09-08-52	Asheville, N.C.		R	R	6'2	195	2	2	.500	0	9	2	0	30	39	10	10	0	5.10
McCament, Randy-Larry Randall	89-90SFN	07-29-62	Albuquerque, N.M.		R	R	6'3	195	1	1	.500	0	28	0	0	43	40	28	17	0	3.80
McCarthy, Brandon-Brandon Patrick	05-06ChiA	07-07-83	Glendale, Cal.		R	R	6'7	190	7	9	.438	0	65	12	0	152	139	50	117	0	4.39
McCarthy, Greg-Gregory O'Neil	96-98SeaA	10-30-68	Norwalk, Conn.		L	L	6'2	195	2	3	.400	0	76	0	0	63	52	37	66	0	4.74
McCarthy, Tom-Thomas Michael	85BosA 88-89ChiA 06HouN	06-18-61	Lundstahl, Germany		R	R	6'	180	3	2	.600	1	40	0	0	85	88	26	34	0	3.61
McCaskill, Kirk-Kirk Edward	85-91CalA 92-96ChiA	04-09-61	Kapuskasing, Canada		R	R	6'1	200	106	108	.495	7	380	242	30	1729	1748	665	1003	11	4.12
McCatty, Steve-Steven Earl	77-85OakA	03-20-54	Detroit, Mich.		R	R	6'3	210	63	63	.500	5	221	161	45	1190	1172	520	541	7	3.99
McClellan, Paul-Paul William	90-91SFN	02-08-66	San Mateo, Cal.		R	R	6'2	185	3	7	.300	0	17	13	1	79	82	31	46	0	5.26
McClung, Seth-Michael Seth	03TBA 04EJ 05-06TBA	02-07-81	Lewisburg, W.Va.		R	R	6'6	230	17	24	.415	6	85	37	0	251	259	155	176	0	6.27
McClure, Bob-Robert Craig	75-76KCA 77-86MilA 86-88MonN 88NYN 89-91CalA 91-92StlN 93PhiN	04-29-52	Oakland, Cal.		B	L	5'11	180	68	57	.544	52	698	73	12	1159	1125	497	701	1	3.81
McConnell, Sam-John Samuel	04AtlN	12-31-75	Middletown, Ohio		L	L	6'5	228	1	0	1.000	0	10	0	0	9	11	4	4	0	3.86
McCullers, Lance-Lance Graye	85-88SDN 89-90NYA 90DetA 92TexA	03-08-64	Tampa, Fla.		B	R	6'1	215	28	31	.475	39	306	9	0	526	427	252	442	0	3.25
McCurry, Jeff-Jeffrey Dee	95PitN 96DetA 97ColN 98PitN 99HouN	01-21-70	Tokyo, Japan		R	R	6'7	215	3	12	.200	1	111	0	0	128	169	63	60	0	5.89
McDill, Allen-Allen Gabriel	97-98KCA 00DetA 01BosA	08-23-71	Greenville, Miss.		L	L	6'	170	0	0	—	0	38	0	0	35	38	18	28	0	7.79
McDonald, Ben-Larry Benard	89-95BalA 96-97MilA	11-24-67	Baton Rouge, La.		R	R	6'7	212	78	70	.527	0	211	198	24	1291	1186	437	894	6	3.91
McDowell, Jack-Jack Burns	87-88,90-94ChiA 95NYA 96-97CleA 98-99AnaA	01-16-66	Van Nuys, Cal.		R	R	6'5	188	127	87	.593	0	277	275	62	1889	1854	606	1311	13	3.85
McDowell, Roger-Roger Alan (Bubbles)	85-89NYN 89-91PhiN 91-94LAN 95TexA 96BalA 97SJ	12-21-60	Cincinnati, Ohio		R	R	6'1	190	70	70	.500	159	723	2	0	1050	1045	410	524	0	3.30
McElroy, Chuck-Charles Dwayne	89-90PhiN 91-93ChiN 94-96CinN 96-97AnaA 97ChiA 98-99ColN 99NYN 00-01BalA 01SDN	10-01-67	Port Arthur, Tex.		L	L	6'	200	38	30	.559	17	654	7	0	739	724	362	604	0	3.90
McEnaney, Will-William Henry	74-76CinN 77MonN 78PitN 79StlN	02-14-52	Springfield, Ohio		L	L	6'	180	12	17	.414	29	269	0	0	350	380	95	148	0	3.75
McGaffigan, Andy-Andrew Joseph	81NYA 82-83SFN 84MonN 84-85CinN 86-89MonN 90SFN 90-91KCA	10-25-56	West Palm Beach, Fla.		R	R	6'3	200	38	33	.535	24	363	62	3	833	773	294	610	1	3.38
McGehee, Kevin-George Kevin	93BalA	01-18-69	Alexandria, La.		R	R	6'	190	0	0	—	0	5	0	0	17	19	7	7	0	5.94
McGilberry, Randy-Randall Kent	77-78KCA	10-29-53	Mobile, Ala.		B	R	6'2	195	0	2	.000	0	21	0	0	33	34	19	13	0	4.64
McGlinchy, Kevin-Kevin Michael	99-00AtlN 01SJ	06-28-77	Malden, Mass.		R	R	6'5	220	7	3	.700	4	74	0	0	79	77	36	76	0	2.75
McGlothen, Lynn-Lynn Everett	72-73BosA 74-76StlN 77-78SFN 78-81ChiN 81ChiA 82NYA	03-27-50	Monroe, La.	08-14-84	L	R	6'2	200	86	93	.480	2	318	201	41	1498	1553	572	939	13	3.98
McGowan, Dustin-Dustin Michael	05-06TorA	03-24-82	Savannah, Ga.		R	R	6'3	220	2	5	.286	0	29	10	0	73	84	42	56	0	6.69
McGraw, Tom-Thomas Virgil	97StlN	12-17-72	Portland, Ore.		R	R	6'3	220	0	0	—	0	5	0	0	2	5	1	0	0	0.00
McGraw, Tug-Frank Edwin	65-67,69-74NYN 75-84PhiN	08-30-44	Martinez, Cal.	01-05-04	R	L	6'	180	96	92	.511	180	824	39	5	1515	1318	582	1109	1	3.14
			Bats both part of 73																		
McGregor, Scott-Scott Houton	76-88BalA	01-18-54	Inglewood, Cal.		B	L	6'	190	138	108	.561	5	356	309	83	2140	2245	518	904	23	3.99
McIntosh, Joe-Joseph Anthony	74-75SDN 76SJ	08-04-51	Billings, Mont.		B	R	6'2	190	8	19	.296	0	44	33	4	220	231	77	93	1	3.68
McKee, Jim-James Marion	72-73PitN	02-01-47	Columbus, Ohio		R	R	6'7	230	1	1	.500	0	12	0	0	32	33	18	17	0	4.78
McKeon, Joel-Joel Jacob	86-87ChiA	02-25-63	Covington, Ky.		L	L	6'	185	4	3	.571	1	43	0	0	54	45	32	32	0	5.17

USE NAMES - GIVEN NAMES (NICKNAMES)	TEAM BY YEAR	BIRTH DATE	BIRTHPLACE	DEATH DATE	B	T	HGT	WGT	W	L	Pct.	SV	G	GS	CG	IP	H	BB	SO	ShO	ERA
McKnight, Tony-Tony Mark	00-01HouN 01PitN	06-29-77	Texarkana, Ark.		R	R	6'5	205	7	7	.500	0	21	21	1	122	144	33	69	0	4.63
McLaughlin, Bo-Michael Duanne	76-79HouN 79AtlN 81-82OakA	10-23-53	Oakland, Cal.		R	R	6'5	210	10	20	.333	9	156	21	5	313	335	123	188	2	3.73
McLaughlin, Byron-Byron Scott	77-80SeaA 82OakA 83CalA	09-29-55	Van Nuys, Cal.		R	R	6'	180	16	25	.390	16	129	35	5	379	403	171	248	0	5.11
McLaughlin, Joey-Joey Richard	77,79AtlN 80-84TorA 84TexA	07-11-56	Tulsa, Okla.		R	R	6'3	215	29	28	.509	36	250	12	0	449	440	198	268	0	3.85
McLeary, Marty-Marty Lee	04SDN 06PitN	10-26-74	Kettering, Ohio		R	R	6'5	230	2	0	1.000	0	8	2	0	21	24	8	12	0	4.22
McMichael, Greg-Gregory Winston	93-96AtlN 97-98NYN 98LAN 98-99NYN 99OakA 00AtlN	12-01-66	Knoxville, Tenn.		R	R	6'3	215	31	29	.517	53	453	0	0	523	483	193	459	0	3.25
McMurtry, Craig-Joe Craig	83-86AtlN 88-90TexA 95HouN	11-05-59	Temple, Tex.		R	R	6'5	195	28	42	.400	4	212	79	6	668	650	336	349	3	4.08
McNichol, Brian-Brian David	99ChiN	05-20-74	Fairfax, Va.		L	L	6'5	225	0	2	.000	0	4	2	0	11	15	7	12	0	6.75
McWilliams, Larry-Larry Dean	78-82AtlN 82-86PitN 87AtlN 88StLN 89PhiN 89-90KCA	02-10-54	Wichita, Kans.		L	L	6'5	185	78	90	.464	3	370	224	34	1558	1548	542	940	13	3.99
Meacham, Rusty-Russell Loren	91DetA 92-95KCA 96SeaA 00HouN 01TBA	01-27-68	Stuart, Fla.		R	R	6'3	175	23	17	.575	9	218	9	0	343	381	93	198	0	4.43
Meadows, Brian-Matthew Brian	98-99FlaN 00-01KCA 02-05PitN 06TBA	11-21-75	Montgomery, Ala.		R	R	6'4	220	47	62	.431	10	336	122	3	961	1146	259	454	0	5.05
Meads, Dave-David Donald	87-88HouN 89EJ	01-07-64	Montclair, N.J.		L	L	6'	175	8	4	.667	0	67	2	0	89	97	30	59	0	4.48
Mears, Chris-Christopher Peter	03DetA	01-20-78	Ottawa, Canada		R	R	6'4	190	1	3	.250	5	29	3	0	41	50	11	21	0	5.44
Meche, Gil-Gilbert Allen	99-00SeaA 01SJ 03-06SeaA	09-08-78	Lafayette, La.		R	R	6'3	200	55	44	.556	0	147	143	4	815	810	363	575	2	4.65
Mecir, Jim-James Jason	95SeaA 96-97NYA 98-00TBA 00-04OakA 05FlaN	05-16-70	Queens, N.Y.		B	R	6'1	220	29	35	.453	12	474	0	0	527	482	225	450	0	3.77
Medders, Brandon-Brandon Edward	05-06AriN	01-26-80	Tuscaloosa, Ala.		R	R	6'2	195	9	4	.692	0	87	0	0	102	97	39	78	0	3.09
Medich, Doc-George Francis	72-75NYA 76PitN 77OoakA 77SeaA 77NYN 78-82TexA 82MilA	12-09-48	Aliquippa, Pa.		R	R	6'5	225	124	105	.541	2	312	287	71	1996	2036	624	955	16	3.78
Medina, Rafael-Rafael Eduardo	98-99FlaN	02-15-75	Panama City, Panama		R	R	6'3	200	3	7	.300	0	32	12	0	91	96	72	65	0	5.96
Medvin, Scott-Scott Howard	88-89PitN 90SeaA	09-16-61	North Olmstead, Ohio		R	R	6'1	195	3	2	.600	0	28	0	0	38	36	16	21	0	5.17
Melendez, Jose-Jose Luis [Garcia]	90SeaA 91-92SDN 93-94BosA	09-02-65	Naguabu, P.R.		R	R	6'2	180	16	14	.533	3	109	12	0	221	197	60	172	0	3.47
Mendoza, Mike-Michael Joseph	79HouN	11-26-55	Inglewood, Cal.		R	R	6'5	215	0	0	—	0	1	0	0	1	0	0	0	0	0.00
Mendoza, Ramiro-Ramiro	96-02NYA 03-04BosA 05NYA	06-15-72	Los Santos, Panama		R	R	6'2	190	59	40	.596	16	342	62	2	797	891	181	463	2	4.30
Menendez, Tony-Antonio Gustavo [Remon]	92CinN 93PitN 94SFN	02-10-65	Havana, Cuba		R	R	6'2	190	3	1	.750	0	23	0	0	29	29	6	20	0	4.97
Menhart, Paul-Paul Gerard	95TorA 96SeaA 97SDN	03-25-69	St. Louis, Mo.		R	R	6'2	190	5	9	.357	0	41	23	1	165	169	85	90	0	5.47
Mercado, Hector-Hector Luis	00-01CinN 02-03PhiN	04-29-74	Catano, P.R.		L	L	6'3	230	5	4	.556	1	112	3	0	125	117	75	127	0	4.55
Mercedes, Jose-Jose Miguel [Santana]	94-97MilA 98MilN 00-01BalA 03MonN	03-05-71	El Seibo, Dom. Rep.		R	R	6'1	180	33	39	.458	0	145	79	5	583	617	223	310	1	4.75
Mercer, Mark-Mark Kenneth	81TexA	05-22-54	Fort Bragg, N.C.		L	L	6'2	220	0	1	.000	0	7	0	0	8	7	7	8	0	4.50
Mercker, Kent-Kent Franklin	89-95AtlN 96BalA 96CleA 97CinN 98-99StLN 99BosA 00AnaA 02ColN 03CinN 03AtlN 04ChiN 05-06CinN	02-01-68	Indianapolis, Ind.		R	L	6'2	195	73	67	.521	25	677	150	2	1312	1294	599	911	1	4.16
Meredith, Cla-Olise C.	05BosA 06SDN	06-04-83	Richmond, Va.		R	R	6'	180	5	1	.833	0	53	0	0	53	36	10	37	0	2.21
Meredith, Ron-Ronald Knox	84-85ChiN 86-87TexA	11-26-56	San Pedro, Cal.		L	L	6'	175	5	2	.714	1	51	0	0	75	86	39	46	0	4.78
Merriman, Brett-Brett Alan	93-94MinA	07-15-66	Jacksonville, Ill.		R	R	6'2	200	1	2	.333	0	34	0	0	44	54	37	24	0	8.39
Mesa (Nova), Jose-Jose Ramon Nova [Mesa]	87,90-92BalA 92-95CleA 98SFN 99-00SeaA 01-03PhiN 04-05PitN 06ColN	05-22-66	Pueblo Viejo, Dom. Rep.		R	R	6'3	225	78	106	.424	320	966	95	6	1498	1576	626	1009	2	4.27
Messenger, Randy-Randall Jerome	05-06FlaN	08-13-81	Reno, Nev.		R	R	6'6	245	2	7	.222	0	97	0	0	111	54	74	0	5.55
Messersmith, Andy-John Alexander	68-72CalA 73-75StLN 76-77AtlN 78NYA 79LAN	08-06-45	Toms River, N.J.		R	R	6'1	200	130	99	.568	15	344	295	98	2230	1719	831	1625	27	2.86
Metzger, Butch-Clarence Edward	74SFN 75-77SDN 77StLN 78NYN	05-23-52	Lafayette, Ind.		R	R	6'1	185	18	9	.667	23	191	1	0	293	289	140	175	0	3.75
Meyer, Brian-Brian Scott	88-90HouN	01-29-63	Camden, N.J.		R	R	6'1	190	0	5	.000	2	34	0	0	51	41	23	29	0	2.84
Meyer, Dan-Daniel Livingston	04DetA	07-03-81	Woodbury, N.J.		R	L	6'2	210	0	0	—	0	2	0	0	2	2	1	1	0	0.00
Miadich, Bart-John Barton	01,03AnaA	02-03-76	Torrance, Cal.		R	R	6'4	205	0	0	—	0	12	0	0	12	11	9	14	0	6.75
Miceli, Dan-Daniel	93-96PitN 97DetA 98-99SDN 00-01FlaN 01ColN 02TexA 03ColN 03CleA 03NYA 03-04HouN 05ColN 06TBA	09-09-70	Newark, N.J.		R	R	6'1	220	43	52	.453	39	631	9	0	701	684	310	632	0	4.48
Michalak, Chris-Christian Matthew	98AriN 01TorA 01-02TexA 06CinN	01-04-71	Joliet, Ill.		L	L	6'2	195	10	15	.400	1	61	24	0	191	228	85	87	0	4.70
Middlebrook, Jason-Jason Douglas	01-02SDN 02-03NYN	06-26-75	Jackson, Mich.		R	R	6'3	215	4	4	.500	0	24	8	0	78	75	36	55	0	5.33
Mielke, Gary-Gary Roger	87,89-90TexA	01-28-63	St. James, Minn.		R	R	6'3	215	2	1	.667	0	4	3	0	19	18	10	10	0	5.12
Milacki, Bob-Robert	88-92BalA 93CleA 94KCA 96SeaA	07-28-64	Trenton, N.J.		R	R	6'4	225	39	47	.453	1	143	125	8	796	817	301	387	5	4.38
Milchin, Mike-Michael Wayne	96MinA 96BalA	02-28-68	Knoxville, Tenn.		L	L	6'3	190	3	1	.750	0	39	0	0	33	44	17	29	0	7.44
Militello, Sam-Sam Salvatore	92-93NYA	11-26-69	Tampa, Fla.		R	R	6'3	200	4	4	.500	0	12	11	0	69	53	39	47	0	3.89
Miller, Andrew-Andrew Mark	06DetA	05-21-85	Gainesville, Fla.		L	L	6'6	210	0	1	.000	0	10	8	0	10	6	9	6	0	6.10
Miller, Dyar-Dyar K. (D)	75-77BalA 77-79CalA 79TorA 80-81NYN	05-29-46	Batesville, Ind.		R	R	6'1	210	23	17	.575	22	251	1	0	465	450	177	235	0	3.23
Miller, Justin-Justin Mark	02TorA 03SJ 04-05TorA	08-27-77	Torrance, Cal.		R	R	6'2	209	12	9	.571	0	45	33	0	186	209	108	117	0	5.89
Miller, Kurt-Kurt Everett	94,96-97FlaN 98-99CinN	08-24-72	Tucson, Ariz.		R	R	6'5	220	2	7	.222	0	44	9	0	81	104	50	55	0	7.47
Miller, Matt-Matt Jacob	03ColN	11-23-71	Greenwood, Miss.		R	R	6'3	215	0	0	—	0	4	0	0	4	5	2	5	0	2.08
Miller, Matt-Matthew Lincoln	01-02DetA 04-06CleA	08-02-74	Lubbock, Tex.		L	L	6'3	175	6	1	.857	2	98	0	0	105	80	44	95	0	2.74
Miller, Paul-Paul Robert	91-93PitN	04-27-65	Burlington, Wis.		R	R	6'5	215	1	0	1.000	0	10	3	0	26	30	6	9	0	4.10
Miller, Randy-Randall Scott	77BosA 78MonN	03-18-53	Oxnard, Cal.		R	R	6'1	180	0	1	.000	0	6	0	0	8	15	3	6	0	12.38
Miller, Roger-Roger Wesley (Killer)	74MilA	08-01-54	Connellsville, Pa.	04-26-93	R	R	6'2	215	0	0	—	0	2	0	0	2	3	0	2	0	13.50
Miller, Travis-Travis Eugene	96-02MinA	11-02-72	Dayton, Ohio		R	L	6'3	210	7	18	.280	1	203	14	0	267	331	113	199	0	5.05
Miller, Trever-Trever Douglas	96DetA 98-99HouN 00PhiN 00LAN 03TorA 04-05TBA 06HouN	05-29-73	Louisville, Ky.		R	L	6'3	195	12	14	.462	8	375	5	0	333	351	155	264	0	4.41
Miller, Wade-Wade T.	99-04HouN 05BosA 06ChiN	09-13-76	Reading, Pa.		R	R	6'2	210	62	45	.579	0	148	144	5	881	814	371	743	1	4.00
Mills, Alan-Alan Bernard	90-91NYA 92-98BalA 99-00LAN 00-01BalA	10-18-66	Lakeland, Fla.		R	R	6'1	190	39	32	.549	15	474	5	0	636	577	395	456	0	4.12
Millwood, Kevin-Kevin Austin	97-02AtlN 03-04PhiN 05CleA 06TexA	12-24-74	Gastonia, N.C.		R	R	6'4	220	123	87	.586	0	292	284	6	1774	1693	527	1437	5	3.85
Milton, Eric-Eric Robert	98-03MinA 04PhiN 05-06CinN	09-04-75	State College, Pa.		L	L	6'3	220	87	80	.521	0	260	259	10	1527	1596	438	1089	4	5.01
Mimbs, Michael-Michael Randall	95-97PhiN	02-13-69	Macon, Ga.		L	L	6'2	180	12	19	.387	1	73	37	2	265	274	143	178	1	5.03
Minchey, Nate-Nathan Derek	93-94,96BosA 97ColN	08-31-69	Austin, Tex.		R	R	6'8	225	3	7	.300	0	15	12	1	64	100	28	38	0	6.75
Miner, Zach-Zachary Charles	06DetA	03-12-82	St. Louis, Mo.		R	R	6'3	200	7	6	.538	0	27	16	1	93	100	32	59	0	4.84
Minetto, (Briceno), Craig-Craig Steven (Crik)	78-81OakA	04-25-54	Stockton, Cal.		R	L	6'1	185	1	7	.125	1	55	15	0	145	162	72	76	0	5.40
Mingori, Steve-Stephen Bernard	70-73CleA 73-79KCA	02-29-44	Kansas City, Mo.		L	L	5'10	170	18	33	.353	42	385	2	0	584	544	225	329	0	3.04
Minor, Blas-Blas	92-94PitN 95-96NYN 96SeaA 97HouN	03-20-66	Merced, Cal.		R	R	6'3	200	13	10	.565	5	157	0	0	225	231	70	184	0	4.40
Minshall, Jim-James Edward (Minnie)	74-75PitN	07-04-47	Covington, Ky.		R	R	6'6	215	0	1	.000	0	6	0	0	5	1	4	5	0	0.00
Minton, Greg-Gregory Brian (Moon Man)	75-87SFN 87-90CalA	07-28-51	Lubbock, Tex.		B	R	6'2	200	59	65	.476	150	710	7	0	1131	1082	483	479	0	3.10
Mintz, Steve-Stephen Wayne	95SFN 99AnaA	11-24-68	Wilmington, N.C.		R	L	5'11	190	1	2	.333	0	17	0	0	24	34	14	9	0	6.66
Minutelli, Gino-Gino Michael	90-91CinN 93SFN	05-23-64	Wilmington, Del.		L	L	6'	185	0	3	.000	0	27	3	0	41	37	35	31	0	5.31
Mirabella, Paul-Paul Thomas (Bells)	78TexA 79NYA 80-81TorA 82TexA 83BalA 84-86SeaA 87-90MilA	03-20-54	Belleville, N.J.		L	L	6'1	195	19	29	.396	13	298	33	3	500	526	239	258	1	4.45
Miranda, Angel-Angel Luis [Andujar]	93-97MilA	11-09-69	Arecibo, P.R.		L	L	6'1	190	17	21	.447	2	116	47	3	363	355	206	243	0	4.46
Misch, Patrick-Patrick Theodore Joseph	06SFN	08-18-81	Northbrook, Ill.		R	L	6'2	170	0	0	—	0	1	0	0	1	2	0	1	0	0.00
Misuraca, Mike-Michael William	97MilA	08-21-68	Long Beach, Cal.		R	R	6'0	190	0	0	—	0	5	0	0	10	15	7	10	0	11.32
Mitchell, Charlie-Charles Ross	84-85BosA	06-24-62	Dickson, Tenn.		R	R	6'3	170	0	0	—	0	12	0	0	18	19	6	9	0	4.00
Mitchell, Craig-Craig Seton	75-77OakA	04-14-54	Santa Ana, Cal.		R	R	6'2	195	0	2	.000	0	13	2	0	18	18	4	3	0	7.61
Mitchell, John-John Kyle	86-89NYN 90BalA	08-11-65	Dickson, Tenn.		R	R	6'2	165	9	14	.391	0	51	37	1	240	272	93	107	0	4.35
Mitchell, Larry-Larry Paul II	96PhiN	10-16-71	Flint, Mich.		R	R	6'1	220	0	0	—	0	7	0	0	12	14	5	7	0	4.50
Mitchell, Paul-Paul Michael	75BalA 76-77CleA 77-79SeaA 79-80MilA	08-19-50	Worcester, Mass.		R	R	6'1	195	32	39	.451	1	125	96	11	621	673	191	277	4	4.45
Mitre, Sergio-Sergio Armando	03-05ChiN 06FlaN	02-16-81	Los Angeles, Cal.		R	R	6'3	210	5	15	.250	0	51	25	1	162	192	67	108	1	6.01
Mlicki, Dave-David John	92-93CleA 95-98NYN 98-99LAN 99-01DetA 01-02HouN	06-08-68	Cleveland, Ohio		R	R	6'4	200	66	80	.452	1	262	193	6	1233	1337	472	834	2	4.72
Mmahat, Kevin-Kevin Paul	89NYA	11-09-64	Memphis, Tenn.		L	L	6'5	220	0	2	.000	0	4	2	0	8	13	8	3	0	12.91
Moehler, Brian-Brian Merritt	96-02DetA 02CinN 03HouN 05-06FlaN	12-31-71	Rockingham, N.C.		R	R	6'3	230	63	79	.444	0	210	189	10	1146	1348	324	622	6	4.78
Moeller, Dennis-Dennis Michael	92KCA 93PitN	09-15-67	Tarzana, Cal.		R	L	6'2	195	1	3	.250	0	15	4	0	34	50	18	19	0	8.39
Moffitt, Randy-Randall James	72-81SFN 82HouN 83TorA	10-13-48	Long Beach, Cal.		R	R	6'3	190	43	52	.453	96	534	1	0	781	766	286	455	0	3.65
Mohler, Mike-Michael Ross	93-98OakA 99-00StLN 00CleA 01AriN	07-26-68	Dayton, Ohio		R	L	6'2	205	14	27	.341	10	347	20	0	417	428	232	281	0	4.99
Mohorcic, Dale-Dale Robert	86-88TexA 88-89NYA 90MonN	01-25-56	Cleveland, Ohio		R	R	6'3	220	16	21	.432	33	254	0	0	364	378	99	174	0	3.49
Molina, Gabe-Cruz Gabriel	99-00BalA 00AtlN 02-03StLN	05-03-75	Denver, Colo.		R	R	5'11	205	2	2	.500	0	46	0	0	52	61	33	28	0	6.58
Monge, Sid-Isidro Pedroza	75-77CalA 77-81CleA 82-83PhiN 83-84SDN 84DetA	04-11-51	Agua Prieta, Mexico		B	L	6'2	195	49	40	.551	56	435	17	4	764	708	366	471	0	3.53
Monroe, Larry-Lawrence James	76ChiA	06-20-56	Detroit, Mich.		R	R	6'4	212	0	1	.000	0	22	0	0	23	13	9	4	0	4.09
Montague, John-John Evans	73-75MonN 75PhiN 77-79SeaA 79-80CalA	09-12-47	Newport News, Va.		R	R	6'2	205	24	26	.480	21	223	17	2	548	595	226	260	0	4.75
Montalvo, Rafael-Rafael Edgardo [Torres]	86HouN	03-31-64	Rio Piedras, P.R.		R	R	6'	185	0	0	—	0	7	0	0	9	8	9	0	0	9.00
Montefusco, John-John Joseph (Count)	74-80SFN 81AtlN 82-83SDN 83-86NYA	05-25-50	Long Branch, N.J.		R	R	6'	190	90	83	.520	2	298	244	32	1652	1604	513	1081	11	3.54
Monteleone, Rich-Richard	87SeaA 88-89CalA 90-93NYA 94SFN 95-96CalA	03-22-63	Tampa, Fla.		R	R	6'2	215	24	17	.585	0	210	0	0	353	344	119	212	0	3.87
Montero, Augustin-Augustin Alcantara	06ChiA	08-26-77	San Pedro de Mac., D.R.		R	R	6'3	210	1	0	1.000	0	11	0	0	14	15	2	7	0	5.14

USE NAMES - GIVEN NAMES (NICKNAMES)	TEAM BY YEAR	BIRTH DATE	BIRTHPLACE	DEATH DATE	B	T	HGT	WGT	W	L	Pct.	SV	G	GS	CG	IP	H	BB	SO	ShO	ERA
Montgomery, Jeff-Jeffrey Thomas	87CinN 88-99KCA	01-07-62	Wellston, Ohio		R	R	5'11	180	46	52	.469	304	700	1	0	869	785	296	733	0	3.27
Montgomery, Steve-Steven Lewis	96-97OakA 99PhiN 00SDN	12-25-70	Westminster, Cal.		R	R	6'4	210	2	8	.200	3	72	0	0	90	88	56	67	0	4.98
Moody, Eric-Eric Lane	97TexA	01-06-71	Greenville, S.C.		R	R	6'	185	0	1	.000	0	10	1	0	19	26	2	12	0	4.26
Mooneyham, Bill-William Craig (Wild'n'Wonderful)	86OakA	08-16-60	Livermore, Cal.		R	R	6'	175	4	5	.444	2	45	6	0	100	103	67	75	0	4.52
Moore, Balor-Balor Libron (Butch)	70,72-74MonN 77CalA 78-80TorA	01-25-51	Smithville, Tex.		L	L	6'2	190	28	48	.368	1	180	98	16	719	704	365	496	4	4.52
Moore, Bobby-Robert Devell (Big Money)	85SFN	11-08-58	Sweetwater, La.		R	R	6'5	215	0	0	—	0	11	0	0	17	18	10	10	0	3.24
Moore, Brad-Bradley Alan	88,90PhiN	06-21-64	Loveland, Colo.		R	R	6'1	185	0	0	—	0	8	0	0	8	8	6	3	0	1.08
Moore, Donnie-Donnie Ray	75,77-79ChiN 80StLN 81MilA 82-84AtlN 85-88CalA	02-13-54	Lubbock, Tex.	07-18-89	L	R	6'	190	43	40	.518	89	416	4	0	657	698	186	416	0	3.66
Moore, Marcus-Marcus Braymont	93-94ColN 96CinN	11-02-70	Oakland, Cal.		B	R	6'5	195	7	5	.583	2	79	0	0	86	79	63	73	0	6.25
Moore, Mike-Michael Wayne	82-88SeaA 89-92OakA 93-95DetA	11-26-59	Carnegie, Okla.		R	R	6'4	210	161	176	.478	2	450	440	79	2832	2858	1156	1667	16	4.39
Moore, Tommy-Tommy Joe	72-73NYN 75StLN 75TexA 77SeaA	07-07-48	Lynwood, Cal.		R	R	5'11	180	2	4	.333	0	42	3	0	88	100	49	40	0	5.42
Moore, Trey-Warren Neal III	98MonN 99SJ 00MonN 01AtlN	10-02-72	Houston, Cal.		L	L	6'2	200	3	10	.231	0	23	19	0	100	140	40	60	0	5.83
Moraga, David-David Michael	00MonN 00ColN	07-08-75	Torrance, Cal.		L	L	6'	184	0	0	—	0	4	0	0	3	10	2	2	0	40.50
Moran, Bill-Carl William (Bugs)	74ChiA	09-26-50	Portsmouth, Va.		R	R	6'4	210	1	3	.250	0	15	5	0	46	57	23	17	0	4.70
Morel, Ramon-Ramon Rafael	95-97PitN 97ChiN	08-15-74	Villa Gonzalez, D.R.		R	R	6'2	175	2	2	.500	0	42	0	0	60	77	28	32	0	4.98
Moreno, Angel-Angel [Veneroso]	81-82CalA	06-06-55	Soledad de Doblado,Mex.		L	L	5'10	170	4	10	.286	1	21	12	3	80	82	37	34	0	4.03
Moreno, Juan-Juan Carlos [Vegas]	01TexA 02SDN	02-28-75	Maiquetia, Venezuela		L	L	6'1	205	3	3	.500	0	49	0	0	47	28	38	39	0	4.37
Moreno, Orber-Orber [Aquiles]	99KCA 00EJ 03-04NYN	04-27-77	Caracas, Venezuela		R	R	6'2	195	3	1	.750	4	47	0	0	51	43	20	41	0	4.44
Moret, Roger-Rogelio [Torrez] (Gallo)	70-75BosA 76AtlN 77-78TexA	09-16-49	Guayama, P.R.		B	L	6'4	170	47	27	.635	12	168	82	24	722	656	339	408	5	3.66
Morgan, Mike-Michael Thomas	78-79OakA 82NYA 83TorA 85-87SeaA 88BalA 89-91LAN 92-95ChiN 95-96StLN 96-97CinN 98MinA 98ChiN 99TexA 00-02AriN	10-08-59	Tulare, Cal.		R	R	6'2	220	141	186	.431	8	597	411	46	2772	2943	938	1403	10	4.23
Morillo, Juan-Juan Bautista		11-05-83	San Pedro de Mac., D.R.		R	R	6'3	190	0	0	—	0	1	1	0	4	8	3	4	0	15.75
Morlan, John-John Glen	73-74PitN	11-12-47	Columbus, Ohio		R	R	5'11	185	2	5	.286	0	49	7	1	106	96	71	61	0	4.16
Morman, Alvin-Alvin	96HouN 97-98CleA 98SFN 99KCA	01-06-69	Rockingham, N.C.		L	L	6'3	210	6	7	.462	3	176	0	0	143	161	75	98	0	4.79
Morogiello, Dan-Daniel Joseph	83BalA	03-26-55	Brooklyn, N.Y.		L	L	6'1	200	0	1	.000	0	22	0	0	38	39	10	15	0	2.39
Morris Jack-John Scott	77-90DetA 91MinA 92-93TorA 94CleA	05-16-55	St. Paul, Minn.		R	R	6'3	205	254	186	.577	0	549	527	175	3825	3567	1390	2478	28	3.90
Morris, Jim-James Samuel	99-00TBA	01-19-64	Brownwood, Texas		L	L	6'3	215	0	0	—	0	21	0	0	15	13	9	13	0	4.80
Morris, Matt-Matthew Christian	97-98StLN 99EJ 00-05StLN 06SFN	08-09-74	Middletown, N.Y.		R	R	6'5	215	111	77	.590	4	270	239	20	1585	1586	441	1103	8	3.79
Morton, Carl-Carl Wendle	69-72MonN 73-76AtlN	01-18-44	Kansas City, Mo.	04-12-83	R	R	6'2	200	87	92	.486	1	255	242	51	1649	1753	565	650	13	3.73
Morton, Kevin-Kevin Joseph	91BosA	08-03-68	Norwalk, Conn.		R	L	6'2	185	6	5	.545	0	16	15	1	86	93	40	45	0	4.59
Moseley, Dustin-Dustin Aaron	06LAA	12-26-81	Texarkana, Tex.		R	R	6'4	190	1	0	1.000	0	3	2	0	11	22	2	3	0	9.00
Moskau, Paul-Paul Richard	77-81CinN 82PitN 83ChiN	12-20-53	St. Joseph, Mo.		R	R	6'2	205	32	27	.542	5	148	92	7	634	650	243	374	4	4.22
Moss, Damian-Damian Joseph	01-02AtlN 03SFN 03BalA 04TBA	11-24-76	Darlinghurst, Australia		R	L	6'	187	22	19	.537	0	74	61	0	362	340	195	204	0	4.50
Mota, Danny-Daniel Avila	00MinA	05-09-74	Seybol, Dom. Rep.		R	R	6'	180	0	0	—	0	5	0	0	5	10	1	3	0	8.44
Mota, Guillermo-Guillermo Reynoso	99-01MonN 02-04LAN 04-05FlaN 06CleA 06NYN	07-25-73	San Pedro de Mac., D.R.		R	R	6'4	205	26	27	.491	7	438	0	0	520	450	201	421	0	3.70
Mounce, Tony-Anthony David	03TexA	02-08-75	Sacramento, Cal.		L	L	6'2	170	1	5	.167	0	11	11	0	51	65	25	30	0	7.11
Moyer, Jamie-Jamie	86-88ChiN 89-90TexA 91StLN 93-95BalA 96BosA 96-06SeaA 06PhiN	11-18-62	Sellersville, Pa.		L	L	6'1	170	216	166	.565	0	571	518	30	3351	3455	946	1992	9	4.17
Moylan, Peter-Peter Michael	06AtlN	12-02-78	Attadale, Australia		R	R	6'3	220	0	0	—	0	15	0	0	15	18	5	14	0	4.80
Mueller (Caceres), Willie-Willard Lawrence	78,81MilA	08-30-56	West Bend, Wis.		R	R	6'4	220	1	0	1.000	0	6	0	0	15	20	6	7	0	6.00
Mujica, Edward-Edward Jose	06CleA	05-10-84	Valencia, Valenzuela		R	R	6'2	220	0	1	.000	0	18	0	0	18	25	0	12	0	2.95
Mulder, Mark-Mark Alan	00-04OakA 05-06StLN	08-05-77	South Holland, Ill.		L	L	6'6	205	103	57	.644	0	199	199	25	1301	1326	403	829	10	4.11
Mulholland, Terry-Terence John	86,88-89SFN 89-93PhiN 94NYA 95SFN 96PhiN 96SeaA 97ChiN 97SFN 98-99ChiN 99-00AtlN 01PitN 01-02LAN 02-03CleA 04-05MinA 06AriN	03-09-63	Uniontown, Pa.		R	L	6'2	215	124	142	.466	5	685	332	46	2576	2833	681	1325	10	4.41
Mullen, Scott-Kenneth Scott	00-03KCA 03LAN	01-17-75	San Benito, Tex.		R	L	6'2	190	4	5	.444	0	75	1	0	68	76	35	35	0	4.66
Mullins, Greg-Gregory Eugene	98MilN	12-13-71	Palatka, Fla.		L	L	5'10	160	0	0	—	0	2	0	0	1	1	0	1	0	0.00
Munninghoff, Scott-Scott Andrew (Money)	80PhiN	12-05-58	Cincinnati, Ohio		R	R	6'	180	0	0	—	0	4	0	0	6	8	5	2	0	4.50
Munoz, Arnie-Arnaldo Rafel	04ChiA	06-21-82	Mao, Dom. Rep.		L	L	5'9	170	0	1	.000	0	11	1	0	14	20	12	11	0	10.05
Munoz, Bobby-Robert [Sbert]	93NYA 94-97PhiN 98BalA 01MonN	03-03-68	Rio Piedras, P.R.		R	R	6'7	235	11	22	.333	1	100	38	1	278	324	119	153	0	5.17
Munoz, Mike-Michael Anthony	89-90LAN 91-93DetA 93-98ColN 99-00TexA	07-12-65	Baldwin Park, Cal.		L	L	6'2	190	18	20	.474	11	453	0	0	364	408	174	240	0	5.19
Munoz, Oscar-Juan Oscar	95MinA	09-25-69	Hialeah, Fla.		R	R	6'3	220	2	1	.667	0	3	0	0	35	40	17	25	0	5.60
Munro, Peter-Peter Daniel	99-00TorA 02-04HouN	06-14-75	Queens, N.Y.		R	R	6'2	210	13	19	.406	0	120	40	0	315	380	114	189	0	4.88
Munter, Scott-Scott Michael	05-06SFN	03-07-80	Norfolk, Neb.		R	R	6'6	235	2	1	.667	0	72	0	0	61	70	30	18	0	4.84
Mura, Steve-Stephen Andrew	78-81SDN 82StLN 83ChiA 85OakA	02-12-55	New Orleans, La.		R	R	6'2	190	30	39	.435	5	167	83	12	633	627	289	360	2	4.00
Murphy, Dan-Daniel Lee	89SDN	09-18-64	Artesia, Cal.		R	R	6'2	196	0	0	—	0	7	0	0	6	6	4	1	0	5.68
Murphy, Rob-Robert Albert	85-88CinN 89-90BosA 91SeaA 92HouN 93-94StLN 94NYA 95LAN 95FlaN	05-26-60	Miami, Fla.		L	L	6'2	210	32	38	.457	30	597	0	0	623	598	247	520	0	3.64
Murphy, Tom-Thomas Andrew	68-72CalA 72KCA 73StLN 74-76MilA 76-77BosA 77-79TorA	12-30-45	Cleveland, Ohio		R	R	6'3	205	68	101	.402	59	439	147	22	1443	1425	493	621	3	3.78
Murray, Dale-Dale Albert (Spud, Tex)	74-76MonN 77-78CinN 78-79NYN 79-80MonN 81-82TorA 83-85NYA 85TexA	02-02-50	Cuero, Tex.		R	R	6'4	205	53	50	.515	60	518	1	0	902	976	329	400	0	3.85
Murray, Dan-Daniel Saffle	99NYN 99-00KCA	11-21-73	Los Alamitos, Calif.		R	R	6'1	193	0	0	—	0	15	0	0	30	33	16	25	0	5.76
Murray, Heath-Heath Robertson	97,99SDN 01DetA 02CleA	04-19-73	Troy, Ohio		L	L	6'4	215	2	15	.118	0	88	15	0	159	204	94	94	0	6.41
Murray, Matt-Matthew Robert	95AtlN 95BosA	09-26-70	Boston, Mass.		R	R	6'6	240	0	3	.000	0	6	2	0	14	21	8	4	0	9.64
Musselman, Jeff-Jeffrey Joseph	86-89TorA 89-90NYN	06-21-63	Doylestown, Pa.		L	L	6'	180	23	15	.605	3	142	19	0	249	249	123	125	0	4.31
Musselman, Ron-Ralph Ronald	82SeaA 84-85TorA	11-11-54	Wilmington, N.C.		R	R	6'1	190	4	2	.667	1	48	4	0	89	95	40	47	0	3.73
Mussina, Mike-Michael Cole [Moose]	91-00BalA 01-06NYA	12-08-68	Williamsport, Pa.		L	R	6'2	185	239	134	.641	0	475	475	57	3210	3058	719	2572	23	3.63
Mutis, Jeff-Jeffrey Thomas	91-93CleA 94FlaN	12-20-66	Allentown, Pa.		L	L	6'2	185	4	11	.267	0	58	18	1	143	191	61	73	1	6.48
Myers, Brett-Brett Allen	02-06PhiN	08-17-80	Jacksonville, Fla.		R	R	6'4	215	54	40	.574	0	141	140	6	854	861	298	690	2	4.34
Myers, Jimmy-James Xavier	96BalA	04-28-69	Oklahoma City, Okla.		R	R	6'1	190	0	0	—	0	11	0	0	14	18	3	6	0	7.07
Myers, Mike-Michael Stanley	95FlaN 95-97DetA 98-99MilN 00-01ColN 02-03AriN 04SeaA 04-05BosA 06NYA	06-26-69	Arlington Heights, Ill.		L	L	6'3	210	21	24	.467	14	811	0	0	487	466	233	402	0	4.23
Myers, Randy-Randall Kirk	85-89NYN 90-91CinN 92SDN 93-95ChiN 96-97BalA 98TorA 98SDN 99-00SDN	09-19-62	Vancouver, Wash.		L	L	6'1	220	44	63	.411	347	728	12	1	885	758	396	884	0	3.19
Myers, Rodney-Rodney Luther	96-99ChiN 00-02SDN 03-04LAN	06-26-69	Rockford, Ill.		R	R	6'1	215	7	5	.583	1	167	1	0	240	265	110	161	0	5.07
Myette, Aaron-Aaron Kenneth	99-00ChiA 01-02TexA 03CleA 04CinN	09-26-77	New Westminster,Canada		R	R	6'4	205	6	12	.333	0	47	30	0	154	185	106	134	0	8.16
Myrick, Bobby-Robert Howard	76-78NYN 79SA	10-01-52	Hattiesburg, Miss.		R	L	6'2	195	3	6	.333	2	82	5	0	140	138	59	73	0	3.47
Nabholz, Chris-Christopher William	90-93MonN 94CleA 94SDN 95ChiN	01-05-67	Harrisburg, Pa.		L	L	6'5	210	37	35	.514	0	141	100	4	612	542	278	405	2	3.94
Nageotte, Clint-Clinton Scott	04-06SeaA	10-25-80	Parma, Ohio		R	R	6'3	200	1	6	.143	0	42	5	0	56	30	26	0	7.78
Nagy, Charles-Charles Harrison	90-02CleA 03SDN	05-05-67	Bridgeport, Conn.		L	R	6'3	200	129	105	.551	0	318	297	31	1955	2188	586	1242	6	4.51
Nakamura, Michael-Michael Yoshihide	03MinA 04TorA	09-06-76	Nara, Japan		R	R	5'10	170	3	0	.000	1	31	0	0	38	47	9	38	0	7.51
Nance, Shane-Joseph Shane	02-03MilN 04AriN	09-07-77	Pasadena, Texas		L	L	5'10	180	1	3	.250	0	49	0	0	43	57	26	39	0	5.02
Narron, Sam-Samuel Franklin	04TexA	07-12-81	Goldsboro, N.C.		L	L	6'7	210	0	0	—	0	7	0	0	8	16	6	7	0	13.50
Narveson, Chris-Christopher Gregg	06StLN	12-20-81	Englewood, Colo.		R	L	6'2	205	0	0	—	0	9	1	0	9	5	12	4	0	4.82
Nastu, Phil-Phillip	78-80SFN	03-08-55	Bridgeport, Conn.		R	L	6'2	180	3	5	.375	0	35	15	1	114	123	48	53	0	4.50
Nathan, Joe-Joseph Michael	99-00,02-03SFN 04-06MinA	11-22-74	Houston, Texas		R	R	6'4	205	39	16	.709	124	327	29	0	477	357	203	478	0	3.17
Nation, Joey-Joseph Paul	00ChiN	09-28-78	Oklahoma City, Okla.		L	L	6'2	175	0	2	.000	0	2	2	0	12	12	8	8	0	6.94
Naulty, Dan-Daniel Donovan	96-98MinA 99NYA	01-06-70	Los Angeles, Cal.		R	R	6'6	220	5	5	.500	3	130	0	0	161	137	77	119	0	4.54
Navarro, Jaime-Jaime [Citron]	89-94MilA 95-96CinN 97-99ChiA 00MilN 00CleA	03-27-67	Bayamon, P.R.		R	R	6'4	235	116	126	.479	9	361	309	32	2055	2313	690	1113	8	4.72
Neagle, Denny-Dennis Edward Jr.	91MinA 92-96PitN 96-98AtlN 99-00CinN 00NYA 01-03ColN 04EJ	09-13-68	Gambrills, Md.		L	L	6'2	210	124	92	.574	3	392	286	20	1890	1887	594	1415	7	4.24
Neal, Blaine-Blaine	01-03FlaN 04SDN 05BosA 05ColN	04-06-78	Marlton, N.J.		L	R	6'5	240	5	4	.556	0	113	0	0	124	161	51	93	0	5.08
Neidlinger, Jim-James Llewellyn	90LAN	09-24-64	Vallejo, Cal.		B	R	6'2	195	5	3	.625	0	12	12	0	74	67	15	46	0	3.28
Nelson, Gene-Wayland Eugene	81NYA 82-83SeaA 84-86ChiA 87-92OakA 93CalA 93TexA	12-03-60	Tampa, Fla.		R	R	6'1	175	53	64	.453	28	493	68	6	1080	1061	418	655	1	4.13
Nelson, Jeff-Jeffrey Allan	92-95SeaA 96-00NYA 01-03SeaA 03NYA 04TexA 05SeaA 06ChiA	11-17-66	Baltimore, Md.		R	R	6'8	235	48	45	.516	33	798	0	0	785	633	428	829	0	3.41
Nelson, Joe-Joseph George	01AtlN 04BosA 06KCA	10-25-74	Alameda, Cal.		R	R	6'2	185	1	1	.500	0	48	0	0	49	48	29	49	0	6.39
Nen, Robb-Robert Allen	93TexA 93-97FlaN 98-02SFN 03-04SJ	11-28-69	San Pedro, Cal.		R	R	6'4	215	45	42	.517	314	643	4	0	715	607	260	793	0	2.98
Neshek, Pat-Patrick J.		09-04-80	Madison, Wis.		B	R	6'3	205	4	2	.667	0	37	0	0	37	23	6	53	0	2.19
Neu, Mike-Michael David	03OakA 04FlaN	03-09-78	Napa, Cal.		R	R	5'10	190	0	1	.000	1	46	0	0	46	48	28	34	0	3.72
Neugebauer, Nick-Nicklaus Donald	01-02MilN 03SJ	07-15-80	Riverside, Cal.		R	R	6'3	235	2	8	.200	0	14	14	0	61	62	50	58	0	4.99

USE NAMES - GIVEN NAMES (NICKNAMES)	TEAM BY YEAR	BIRTH DATE	BIRTHPLACE	DEATH DATE	B	T	HGT	WGT	W	L	Pct.	SV	G	GS	CG	IP	H	BB	SO	ShO	ERA
Newell, Tom-Thomas Dean	87PhiN	05-17-63	Monrovia, Cal.		R	R	6'1	185	0	0	—	0	1	0	0	1	4	3	1	0	108.00
Newhauser, Don-Donald Lewis	72-74BosA	11-07-47	Miami, Fla.		R	R	6'4	215	4	3	.571	5	42	0	0	53	44	42	37	0	2.38
Newman, Alan-Alan Spencer	99TBA 00CleA	10-02-69	La Habra, Calif.		L	L	6'6	240	2	2	.500	0	19	0	0	17	28	10	20	0	7.94
Nichols, Rod-Rodney Lea	88-92CleA 93LAN 95AtlN	12-29-64	Burlington, Iowa		R	R	6'2	190	11	31	.262	1	100	48	6	413	460	121	214	1	4.43
Nichting, Chris-Christopher Thomas	95TexA 96ZJ 00CleA 01CinN 01-02ColN	05-13-66	Cincinnati, Ohio		R	R	6'1	205	1	4	.200	1	92	0	0	112	144	31	78	0	5.22
Nickle, Doug-Douglas Alan	00-02PhiN 02SDN	10-02-74	Sonoma, Cal.		R	R	6'4	210	1	0	1.000	0	20	0	0	21	32	15	10	0	7.84
Nied, David-David Glen	92AtlN 93-96ColN	12-22-68	Dallas, Tex.		R	R	6'2	185	17	18	.486	0	52	41	3	242	262	105	146	1	5.06
Niedenfuer, Tom-Thomas Edward	81-87LAN 87-88BalA 89SeaA 90StlN	08-13-59	St. Louis Park, Minn.		R	R	6'4	220	36	46	.439	97	484	0	0	653	601	226	474	0	3.29
Niekro, Joe-Joseph Franklin	67-69ChiN 69SDN 70-72DetA 73-74AtlN 75-85HouN 85-87NYA 87-88MinA	11-07-44	Martins Ferry, Ohio	10-27-06	R	R	6'1	195	221	204	.520	16	702	500	107	3585	3466	1262	1747	29	3.59
Niekro, Phil-Philip Henry (Knucksie)	64-65MilN 66-83AtlN 84-85NYA 86-87CleA 87TorA 87AtlN	04-01-39	Blaine, Ohio		R	R	6'1	190	318	274	.537	30	864	716	245	5404	5044	1809	3342	45	3.35
Nielsen, Jerry-Gerald Arthur	92NYA 93CalA	08-05-66	Sacramento, Cal.		L	L	6'3	185	1	0	1.000	0	30	0	0	32	35	22	20	0	5.91
Nielsen, Scott-Jeffrey Scott	86NYA 87ChiA 88-89NYA	02-18-58	Salt Lake City, Utah		R	R	6'1	190	9	11	.450	2	38	18	3	143	178	51	47	3	5.49
Niemann,Randy-Randal Harold	79-80HouN 81EJ 82-83PitN 84ChiA 85-86NYN 87MinA	11-15-55	Scotia, Cal.		L	L	6'4	200	7	8	.467	3	122	10	3	200	219	82	102	2	4.63
Nieve, Fernando-Fernando Alexis	06HouN	07-15-82	Puerto Cabello, Venezuela		R	R	6'	195	3	3	.500	0	40	11	0	96	87	41	70	0	4.20
Nieves, Juan-Juan Manuel [Cruz]	86-88MilA 89-90SJ	01-25-65	Los Lomas, P.R.		L	L	6'3	190	32	25	.561	0	94	81	8	491	507	227	352	5	4.71
Nipper, Al-Albert Samuel	83-87BosA 88ChiN 90CleA	04-02-59	San Diego, Cal.		R	R	6'	195	46	50	.479	1	144	124	21	798	846	303	381	0	4.52
Nippert, Dustin-Dustin David	05-06AriN	05-06-81	Wheeling, W.Va.		R	R	6'7	215	1	2	.333	0	5	5	0	25	20	20	20	0	8.03
Nitkowski, C.J.-Christopher John	95CinN 95-96DetA 98HouN 99-01DetA 01NYN 02-03TexA 04AtlN 04NYA 05WasN	03-04-73	Suffern, N.Y.		L	L	6'2	205	18	32	.360	3	336	44	0	479	519	263	347	0	5.37
Nolasco, Ricky-Carlos Enrique	06FlaN	12-13-82	Corona, Cal.		R	R	6'2	220	11	11	.500	0	35	22	0	140	157	41	99	0	4.82
Noles, Dickie-Dickie Ray	79-81PhiN 82-84ChiN 84-85TexA 86CleA 87ChiN 87DetA 88BalA 90PhiN	11-19-56	Charlotte, N.C.		R	R	6'2	190	36	53	.404	11	277	96	3	860	909	338	455	3	4.56
Nolte, Eric-Eric Carl	87-89,91SDN 91TexA	04-28-64	Canoga Park, Cal.		L	L	6'3	205	5	8	.385	0	26	19	1	104	115	58	69	0	5.63
Nomo, Hideo-Hideo	95-98LAN 98NYN 99MilN 00DetA 01BosA 02-04LAN 05TBA	08-31-68	Osaka, Japan		R	R	6'2	220	123	109	.530	0	320	318	16	1972	1758	904	1915	9	4.21
Nomura, Takahito-Takahito	02MilN	01-10-69	Kouchi Prefecture, Japan		L	L	5'7	175	0	0	—	0	21	0	0	14	11	18	9	0	8.56
Norman, Fred-Freddie Hubert	62-63KCA 64,66-67ChiN 70LAN 70-71StlN 71-73SDN 73-79CinN 80MonN	08-20-42	San Antonio, Tex.		B	L	5'8	170	104	103	.502	8	403	268	56	1938	1790	815	1303	15	3.64
Norris, Mike-Michael Kelvin	75-83OakA 84SJ 85SJ-DR 90OakA	03-19-55	San Francisco, Cal.		R	R	6'2	175	58	59	.496	0	201	157	52	1124	972	499	636	7	3.89
Norton, Phil-Phillip Douglas	00,03ChiN 03-04CinN	02-01-76	Texarkana, Tex.		R	L	6'1	200	2	6	.250	0	92	2	0	92	94	54	61	0	5.07
Nosek, Randy-Randall William	89-90DetA	01-08-67	Omaha, Neb.		R	R	6'4	215	1	3	.250	0	5	4	0	12	14	19	7	0	10.22
Novoa, Rafael-Rafael Angel	90SFN 93MilA	10-26-67	New York, N.Y.		L	L	6'	185	0	4	.000	1	22	9	2	75	79	35	31	0	5.06
Novoa, Roberto-Roberto	04DetA 05-06ChiN	08-15-79	Las Matas, Dom. Rep.		R	R	6'5	230	0	7	.500	0	131	0	0	142	149	63	115	0	4.51
Nunez, Edwin-Edwin [Martinez]	82-88SeaA 88NYN 89DetA 91-92MilA 92TexA 93-94OakA	05-27-63	Humacao, P.R.		R	R	6'5	230	28	36	.438	54	427	14	0	652	666	280	508	0	4.19
Nunez, Franklin-Franklin	04-05TBA	01-18-77	Nagua, Dom. Rep.		R	R	6'	175	1	3	.250	0	13	0	0	16	16	11	16	0	7.47
Nunez, Jose-Jose Antonio	01LAN 01-02SDN	03-14-79	Montecristi, Dom. Rep.		L	L	6'2	173	4	2	.667	0	63	0	0	60	62	26	60	0	4.50
Nunez, Jose-Jose [Jimenez]	87-89TorA 90ChiN	01-13-64	Jarabacoa, Dom. Rep.		R	R	6'3	175	9	10	.474	1	77	22	0	198	188	111	171	0	5.05
Nunez, Leo-Leonel	05-06KCA	08-14-83	Jamao Norte, Dom. Rep.		R	R	6'1	160	3	2	.600	0	48	0	0	67	88	23	39	0	6.99
Nunez, Vladimir-Vladimir [Zarabaza]	98-99AriN 99-03FlaN 04ColN	03-15-75	Havana, Cuba		R	R	6'4	235	20	32	.385	21	230	27	0	408	396	178	302	0	4.83
Nye, Ryan-Ryan Craig	97-98PhiN	06-24-73	Biloxi, Miss.		R	R	6'2	195	0	2	.000	0	5	2	0	13	23	9	10	0	9.69
Obermueller, Wes-Wesley Mitchell	02KCA 03-05MilN	12-22-76	Cedar Rapids, Iowa		R	R	6'2	195	9	19	.321	0	62	41	1	256	307	105	131	1	5.65
O'Brien, Dan-Daniel Joseph	78-79StlN	04-22-54	St. Petersburg, Fla.		R	R	6'3	215	1	3	.250	0	13	2	0	29	43	11	17	0	5.90
O'Connor, Brian-Brian Michael	00PitN	01-04-77	Cincinnati, Ohio		L	L	6'2	190	0	0	—	0	6	1	0	12	12	11	7	0	5.11
O'Connor, Jack-Jack William	81-84MinA 85MonN 87BalA	01-02-58	29 Palms, Cal.		L	L	6'3	215	14	17	.452	2	129	28	6	319	343	163	177	1	4.89
O'Connor, Mike-Michael Patrick	06WasN	08-17-80	Dallas, Tex.		L	L	6'3	170	3	8	.273	0	21	20	0	105	96	45	59	0	4.80
O'Donoghue, John-John Preston Jr.	93BalA	05-26-69	Wilmington, Del.		L	L	6'6	198	0	1	.000	0	11	0	0	20	22	10	16	0	4.58
Oelkers, Bryan-Bryan Alois	83MinA 86CleA	03-11-61	Zaragoza, Spain		R	L	6'3	192	3	8	.273	1	45	12	0	103	126	57	46	0	6.01
O'Flaherty, Eric-Eric George	06SeaA	02-05-85	Walla Walla, Wash.		L	L	6'2	185	0	0	—	0	15	0	0	11	18	6	6	0	4.09
Ogea, Chad-Chad Wayne	94-98CleA 99PhiN	11-09-70	Lake Charles, La.		R	R	6'2	215	37	35	.514	0	129	94	3	633	672	214	369	1	4.88
Ohka, Tomo-Tomokazu	99-01BosA 01-04MonN 05WasN 05-06MilN	03-18-76	Kyoto, Japan		R	R	6'1	190	48	58	.453	0	174	162	5	943	1037	261	538	1	4.04
Ohman, Will-William McDaniel	00-01,05-06ChiN	08-13-77	Frankfurt, Germany		L	L	6'2	195	4	4	.500	0	164	0	0	124	101	68	133	0	4.15
Ohme, Kevin-Kevin Arthur	03StlN	04-13-71	Palm Beach, Fla.		L	L	6'1	180	0	0	—	0	2	0	0	4	3	1	2	0	0.00
Ojala, Kirt-Kirt Stanley	97-99FlaN	12-24-68	Kalamazoo, Mich.		L	L	6'2	215	3	10	.231	0	56	19	1	164	177	83	99	0	4.71
Ojeda, Bob-Robert Michael	80-85BosA 86-90NYN 91-92LAN 93CleA 94NYA	12-17-57	Los Angeles, Cal.		L	L	6'	190	115	98	.540	1	351	291	41	1884	1833	676	1128	16	3.65
Olin, Steve-Steven Robert	89-92CleA	10-04-65	Portland, Ore.	03-22-93	R	R	6'3	190	16	19	.457	48	195	1	0	273	272	90	173	0	3.10
Olivares, Omar-Omar [Palqu]	90-94StlN 95ColN 95PhiN 96-97DetA 97SeaA 98-99AnaA 99-00OakA 01PitN	07-06-67	Mayaguez, P.R.		R	R	6'1	200	77	86	.472	4	349	229	16	1592	1678	685	853	2	4.67
Oliver, Darren-Darren Christopher	93-98TexA 98-99StlN 00-01TexA 02BosA 03ColN 04FlaN 04HouN 06NYN	10-06-70	Kansas City, Mo.		R	L	6'1	210	91	80	.532	2	351	228	11	1488	1661	603	894	4	4.98
Oliveras, Francisco-Francisco Javier [Noa]	89MinA 90-92SFN	01-13-63	Santurce, P.R.		R	R	5'10	180	11	15	.423	5	116	18	1	235	221	68	130	0	3.71
Olmsted,Al-Alan Ray	80StlN	03-18-57	St. Louis, Mo.		R	L	6'1	195	1	1	.500	0	5	0	0	35	32	14	14	0	2.83
Olsen, Kevin-Kevin Gary	01-03FlaN	07-26-76	Covina, Cal.		R	R	6'2	200	0	5	.000	0	28	10	0	83	93	37	63	0	5.12
Olsen, Scott-Scott Matthew	01-12-84	05-06FlaN	Kalamazoo, Mich.		L	L	6'4	200	13	11	.542	0	36	35	0	201	181	85	187	0	4.03
Olson, Gregg-Greggory William	88-93BalA 94AtlN 95CleA 95KCA 96DetA 96HouN 97MinA 97KCA 98-99AriN 00-01LAN	10-11-66	Scribner, Neb.		R	R	6'4	210	40	39	.506	217	622	0	0	672	598	330	588	0	3.46
Olwine, Ed-Edward R.	86-88AtlN	05-11-58	Greenville, Ohio		R	L	6'2	165	1	0	1.000	3	80	0	0	90	82	29	54	0	4.52
O'Malley, Ryan-Ryan Joseph	06ChiN	04-09-80	Springfield, Ill.		R	L	6'1	205	1	1	.500	0	2	2	0	13	10	7	4	0	2.13
O'Neal, Randy-Randall Jeffrey	84-86DetA 87AtlN 87-88StlN 89PhiN 90SFN	08-30-60	Ashland, Ky.		R	R	6'2	195	17	19	.472	3	142	46	2	441	461	149	248	0	4.35
Ontiveros, Steve-Steven	86-88OakA 89-90PhiN 91EJ 93SeaA 94-95OakA 96-97EJ 00BosA	03-15-61	Tularosa, N.M.		R	R	6'	180	34	31	.523	19	207	73	6	662	622	207	382	5	3.67
Oquist, Mike-Michael Lee	93-95BalA 96SDN 97-99OakA	05-30-68	La Junta, Colo.		R	R	6'1	185	25	31	.446	0	133	79	1	555	623	243	351	0	5.46
Oropesa, Eddie-Edilberto	01PhiN 02-03AriN 04SDN	11-23-71	Colon, Cuba		L	L	6'3	215	4	2	.667	0	125	0	0	92	99	72	78	0	7.34
Orosco, Jesse-Jesse Russell (Cat)	79,81-87NYN 88LAN 89-91CleA 92-94MilA 95-99BalA 00-02StlN 03SDN 03NYA 03MinA	04-21-57	Santa Barbara, Cal.		R	L	6'1	195	87	80	.521	144	1252	4	0	1295	1055	581	1179	0	3.16
Ortiz, Ramon-Diogenes Ramon [Ortiz]	99-04AnaA 05CinN 06WasN	03-23-73	Cotui, Dom. Rep.		R	R	6'	175	79	76	.510	0	220	200	10	1256	1341	440	790	1	4.85
Ortiz, Russ-Russell Reid	98-02SFN 03-04AtlN 05-06AriN 06BalA	06-05-74	Encino, Cal.		R	R	6'1	210	108	79	.578	0	270	245	9	1520	1456	787	1094	3	4.39
Orvella, Chad-Chad Robert	05-06TBA	10-01-80	Renton, Wash.		R	R	5'11	190	1	2	.333	1	59	0	0	74	83	43	60	0	4.84
Osborn, Danny-Danny Leon (Ozzie)	75ChiA	06-19-46	Springfield, Md.		R	R	6'2	195	3	0	1.000	0	24	0	0	58	57	38	38	0	4.50
Osborne, Donovan-Donovan Alan	92-93StlN 94SJ 95-99StlN 00-01VR 02ChiN 04NYA	06-21-69	Roseville, Cal.		B	L	6'2	195	49	46	.516	0	163	140	4	874	895	246	558	2	4.03
Osburn, Pat-Larry Pat (Oz)	74CinN 75MilA	05-04-49	Murray, Ky.		L	L	6'2	190	0	1	.000	0	12	1	0	21	30	13	5	0	6.43
Osoria, Franquelis-Franquelis Antonio	05-06LAN	09-12-81	Santiago, Dom. Rep.		R	R	6'	165	0	4	.000	0	36	0	0	47	55	17	28	0	5.13
Osting, Jimmy-James Michael	01SDN 02MilN	04-07-77	Louisville, Ky.		R	L	6'5	190	0	2	.000	0	6	3	0	14	19	12	10	0	6.43
Osuna, Al-Alfonso	90-93HouN 94LAN 96SDN	08-10-65	Inglewood, Cal.		R	L	6'3	200	18	10	.643	14	218	0	0	193	156	109	143	0	3.75
Osuna, Antonio-Antonio Pedro	95-00LAN 01-02ChiA 03NYA 04SDN 05WasN	04-12-73	Sinaloa, Mexico		R	R	5'11	200	36	29	.554	21	411	0	0	489	432	209	501	0	3.68
Oswalt, Roy-Roy Edward	01-06HouN	08-29-77	Kosciusko, Miss.		R	R	6'	180	98	47	.676	0	188	177	11	1201	1153	263	1016	4	3.07
Otsuka, Akinori-Akinori	04-05SDN 06TexA	01-13-72	Chiba, Japan		R	R	6'	200	11	14	.440	35	202	0	0	200	164	71	194	0	2.43
Otten, Jim-James Edward	74-76ChiA 80-81StlN	07-01-49	Lewiston, Mont.		R	R	6'2	195	1	6	.143	0	64	6	0	118	150	67	75	0	5.49
Otto, Dave-David Alan	87-90OakA 91-92CleA 93PitN 94ChiN	11-12-64	Chicago, Ill.		R	L	6'7	210	10	22	.313	0	109	41	1	318	377	122	144	0	5.06
Overy, Mike-Harry Michael	76CalA	01-27-51	Clinton, Ill.		R	R	6'2	195	0	2	.000	0	5	0	0	7	6	3	8	0	6.43
Owchinko, Bob-Robert Dennis	76-79SDN 80CleA 81-82OakA 83PitN 84CinN 86MonN	01-11-55	Detroit, Mich.		L	L	6'2	195	37	60	.381	7	275	104	10	889	937	363	490	4	4.29
Owens, Henry-Henry Jay	06NYN	04-23-79	Miami, Fla.		R	R	6'3	230	0	0	—	0	4	0	0	4	4	2	9	0	9.00
Ownbey, Rick-Richard Wayne	82-83NYN 84,86StlN	10-20-57	Coronas, Cal.		R	R	6'3	185	3	11	.214	0	39	19	2	147	145	91	83	0	4.71
Oxspring, Chris-Chris Andrew	05SDN	05-13-77	Ipswich, Australia		R	R	6'	185	0	0	—	0	5	0	0	12	9	4	11	0	3.75
Pacella, John-John Lewis	77,79-80NYN 82NYA 82MinA 84BalA 86DetA	09-15-56	Brooklyn, N.Y.		R	R	6'2	195	4	10	.286	1	74	21	0	192	206	133	116	0	5.73
Pacheco, Alex-Alexander Melchor [Lara]	96MonN	07-19-73	Caracas, Venezuela		R	R	6'2	200	0	0	—	0	6	0	0	8	11	7	1	0	11.12
Pacillo, Pat-Patrick Michael	87-88CinN	07-23-63	Jersey City, N.J.		R	R	6'2	205	4	3	.571	0	18	7	0	51	55	23	34	0	5.82
Pactwa, Joe-Joseph Martin (Packy)	75CalA	06-02-48	Hammond, Ind.		L	L	5'10	185	1	0	1.000	0	8	0	0	23	23	10	3	0	3.94
Padilla, Juan-Juan Miguel	04NYA 04CinN 05NYN 06EJ	02-17-77	Rio Piedras, P.R.		R	R	6'	200	4	1	.800	1	42	0	0	62	63	25	34	0	4.06
Padilla, Vicente-Vicente De La Cruz	99-00AriN 00-05PhiN 06TexA	09-27-77	Chinandega, Nicaragua		R	R	6'2	210	66	61	.520	2	227	144	5	979	980	338	682	2	4.06
Pagan, Dave-David Percy	73-76NYA 76BalA 77SeaA 77PitN	09-15-49	Nipawin, Canada		R	R	6'2	180	4	9	.308	4	85	18	3	232	254	95	147	1	4.97

USE NAMES - GIVEN NAMES (NICKNAMES)	TEAM BY YEAR	BIRTH DATE	BIRTHPLACE	DEATH DATE	B	T	HGT	WGT	W	L	Pct.	SV	G	GS	CG	IP	H	BB	SO	ShO	ERA
Painter, Lance-Lance Telford	93-96ColN 97-99StLN 00-01TorA 01MilN 03StLN	07-21-67	Bedford, England		L	L	6'1	195	25	18	.581	3	314	28	1	450	496	178	331	0	5.24
Palacios, Vicente-Vicente [Diaz]		07-19-63	Veracruz, Mexico		R	R	6'3	195	17	20	.459	7	134	44	2	372	348	158	270	2	4.43
Pall, Donn-Donn Steven	88-93ChiA 93PhiN 94NYA 94ChiN 96-98FlaN	01-11-62	Chicago, Ill.		R	R	6'1	185	24	23	.511	10	328	0	0	505	519	139	278	0	3.63
Palmer, David-David William	78-80MonN 81EJ 82MonN 83EJ 84-85MonN 86-87AtlN 88PhiN 89DetA	10-19-57	Glens Falls, N.Y.		R	R	6'1	205	64	59	.520	2	212	176	10	1086	1036	434	748	4	3.78
Palmer, Jim-James Alvin	65-67BalA 68SA 69-84BalA	10-15-45	New York, N.Y.		R	R	6'3	195	268	152	.638	4	558	521	211	3948	3349	1311	2212	53	2.86
Paniagua, Jose-Jose Luis [Sanchez]	96-97MonN 98-01SeaA 02DetA 03ChiA	08-20-73	San Jose de Ocoa, D.R.		R	R	6'2	190	18	21	.462	13	270	14	0	357	354	188	276	0	4.49
Papelbon, Jonathan-Jonathan R.	05-06BosA	11-23-80	Baton Rouge, La.		R	R	6'4	230	7	3	.700	35	76	3	0	102	73	30	109	0	1.50
Park, Chan Ho-Chan Ho	94-01LAN 02-05TexA 05-06SDN	06-30-73	Kongju, South Korea		R	R	6'2	200	113	87	.565	0	323	274	10	1747	1620	820	1507	3	4.37
Parker, Christian-Christian Michael	01NYA	07-03-75	Albuquerque, N.M.		R	R	6'1	200	0	1	.000	0	1	1	0	3	8	1	1	0	21.00
Parker, Clay-James Clayton	87SeaA 89-90NYA 90DetA 92SeaA	12-19-62	Columbia, La.		R	R	6'1	185	7	10	.412	0	62	27	2	234	249	78	121	0	4.42
Parker, Harry-Harry William	70-71StLN 73-75NYN 75StLN 76CleA	09-14-47	Highland, Ill.		R	R	6'3	190	15	21	.417	12	124	30	1	315	315	128	172	0	3.86
Paronto, Chad-Chad Michael	01BalA 02-03CleA 06AtlN	07-28-75	Woodsville, N.H.		R	R	6'5	255	3	10	.231	0	124	0	0	126	127	44	86	0	4.14
Parque, Jim-Jim Vo	98-02ChiA 03TBA	02-08-75	Norwalk, Cal.		L	L	5'11	165	31	34	.477	0	103	97	2	544	650	241	335	0	5.42
Parra, Jose-Jose Miguel	95LAN 95-96MinA 99JL 00PitN 02AriN 04NYN	11-28-72	Jacagua, Dom. Rep.		R	R	5'11	170	7	12	.368	0	82	19	0	182	225	79	117	0	6.09
Parrett, Jeff-Jeffrey Dale	86-88MonN 89-90PhiN 90-91AtlN 92OakA 93ColN 95-96StLN 96PhiN	08-26-61	Indianapolis, Ind.		R	R	6'4	200	56	43	.566	22	491	11	0	725	672	345	616	0	3.80
Parris, Steve-Steven Mark	95-96PitN 98-00CinN 01-02TorA 03TBA	12-17-67	Joliet, Ill.		R	R	6'	190	44	49	.473	0	139	129	5	753	846	288	479	3	4.75
Parrish, John-John Henry Jr.	00-01,03-05BalA 06EJ	11-26-77	Lancaster, Pa.		L	L	5'11	180	10	10	.500	1	108	10	0	177	166	132	159	0	4.31
Parrott, Mike-Michael Everett Arch (Birdman)	77BalA 77-81SeaA	12-06-54	Oxnard, Cal.		R	R	6'4	205	19	39	.328	5	119	68	14	494	581	190	266	2	4.88
Paschall, Bill-William Herbert	78-79,81KCA	04-22-54	Norfolk, Va.		R	R	6'1	178	0	2	.000	1	10	0	0	24	26	5	9	0	5.25
Pashnick, Larry-Larry John	82-83DetA 84MinA	04-25-56	Lincoln Park, Mich.		R	R	6'3	202	7	8	.467	1	53	20	1	170	196	54	46	0	4.17
Pastore, Frank-Frank Enrico	79-85CinN 86MinA	08-21-57	Alhambra, Cal.		R	R	6'2	210	48	58	.453	6	220	139	32	985	1029	301	541	7	4.29
Patrick, Bronswell-Bronswell Dante	98MilN 99SFN	09-16-70	Greenville, N.C.		R	R	6'1	220	5	1	.833	1	38	3	0	84	92	32	55	0	5.04
Patterson, Bob-Robert Chandler	85SDN 86-87,89,-92PitN 93TexA 94-95CalA 96-98ChiN	05-16-59	Jacksonville, Fla.		R	L	6'2	195	39	40	.494	28	559	21	0	617	619	180	483	0	4.08
Patterson, Danny-Danny Shane	96-99TexA 00-04DetA	02-17-71	San Gabriel, Cal.		R	R	6'	215	24	22	.522	9	350	0	0	384	418	112	250	0	4.14
Patterson, Dave-David Glenn (Opie)	79LAN	07-25-56	Springfield, Mo.		R	R	5'10	165	4	1	.800	6	36	0	0	53	62	22	34	0	5.26
Patterson, Gil-Gilbert Thomas	77NYA	09-05-55	Philadelphia, Pa.		R	R	6'1	200	1	2	.333	1	10	6	0	30	38	20	29	0	5.45
Patterson, Jeff-Jeffrey Simmons	95NYA	10-01-68	Anaheim, Cal.		R	R	6'2	200	0	0	—	0	3	0	0	3	3	3	3	0	2.70
Patterson, John-John Hollis	02-03AriN 04MonN 05-06WasN	01-30-78	Orange, Texas		R	R	6'6	210	17	20	.459	1	81	71	2	423	396	157	400	1	4.09
Patterson, Ken-Kenneth Brian	88-91ChiA 92ChiN 93-94CalA	07-08-64	Costa Mesa, Cal.		L	L	6'4	230	14	8	.636	5	224	4	0	318	290	166	183	0	3.88
Patterson, Reggie-Reginald Allen	81ChiA 83-85ChiN	11-07-58	Birmingham, Ala.		R	R	6'4	190	4	4	.500	0	22	9	1	71	77	24	34	0	5.22
Pattin, Marty-Martin William	68CalA 69SeaA 70-71MilA 72-73BosA 74-80KCA	04-06-43	Charleston, Ill.		R	R	5'11	180	114	109	.511	25	475	224	64	2038	1933	603	1179	14	3.62
Pauley, David-David Wayne	06BosA	06-17-83	Longmont, Col.		R	R	6'2	200	0	2	.000	0	3	3	0	16	31	6	10	0	7.88
Pavano, Carl-Carl Anthony	98-02MonN 02-04FlaN 05NYA 06XJ-BR	01-08-76	New Britain, Conn.		R	R	6'5	235	61	64	.488	0	184	166	6	1038	1114	289	673	4	4.27
Pavlas, Dave-David Lee	90-91ChiN 95-96NYA	08-12-62	Frankfurt, Germany		R	R	6'7	180	2	0	1.000	1	34	0	0	51	57	13	33	0	2.65
Pavlik, Roger-Roger Allen	92-98TexA 99SJ	10-04-67	Houston, Tex.		R	R	6'2	200	47	39	.547	0	131	125	12	743	743	351	526	1	4.58
Pawlowski, John-John	87-88ChiA	09-06-63	Johnson City, N.Y.		R	R	6'2	175	1	0	1.000	0	18	0	0	18	27	6	12	0	7.64
Paxton, Mike-Michael DeWayne	77BosA 78-80CleA	09-03-53	Memphis, Tenn.		R	R	5'11	190	30	24	.556	1	99	63	10	467	536	146	230	3	4.70
Payne, Mike-Michael Earl	84AtlN	11-15-61	Woonsocket, R.I.		R	R	5'11	165	0	1	.000	0	3	1	0	6	7	3	3	0	6.35
Pazik, Mike-Michael Joseph	75-77MinA	01-26-50	Lynn, Mass.		L	L	6'2	190	1	4	.200	0	13	6	0	47	59	20	20	0	5.74
Pearce, Josh-Joshua Ray	02-04StLN	08-20-77	Yakima, Wash.		R	R	6'3	215	0	0	—	0	13	3	0	24	34	10	5	0	5.55
Pearson, Jason-Jason John	02SDN 03StLN	12-29-75	Freeport, Ill.		L	L	6'	195	0	0	—	0	4	0	0	3	5	3	4	0	23.62
Pearson, Terry-Terry Bobby Gene	02DetA	11-10-71	Tuscaloosa, Ala.		R	R	6'	200	0	0	—	0	6	8	2	4	9	0	10.50	
Peavy, Jake-Jacob Edward	02-06SDN	05-31-81	Mobile, Ala.		R	R	6'1	180	57	45	.559	0	138	138	5	864	774	280	850	3	3.51
Pelfrey, Mike-Michael Alan	06NYN	01-14-84	Wright Patterson AFB, Ohio		R	R	6'7	210	2	1	.667	0	4	4	0	21	25	12	13	0	5.48
Pember, Dave-David Randolph	02MilN	05-24-78	Cincinnati, Ohio		R	R	6'5	225	0	1	.000	0	9	7	6	5	5	0	5.19	
Pena, Alejandro-Alejandro [Vasquez]	81-89LAN 90-91NYN 91-92AtlN 93EJ 94PitN 95BosA 95FlaN 95AtlN 96FlaN	06-25-59	Cambiaso, Dom. Rep.		R	R	6'1	210	56	52	.519	74	503	72	12	1058	959	331	839	7	3.11
Pena, Hipolito-Hipolito [Concepcion]	86-87PitN 88NYA	01-30-64	Fantino, Dom. Rep.		L	L	6'3	170	1	7	.125	2	42	0	0	48	33	38	32	0	4.84
Pena, Jesus-Jesus	99-00ChiA 00BosA	03-08-75	Santo Domingo, D.R.		L	L	6'	170	2	1	.667	1	48	0	0	47	49	42	40	0	5.21
Pena, Jim-James Patrick	92SFN	09-17-64	Los Angeles, Cal.		L	L	6'	175	1	1	.500	0	25	2	0	44	49	20	32	0	3.48
Pena, Juan-Juan Francisco	99BosA 00-01EJ	06-27-77	Santo Domingo, D.R.		R	R	6'5	215	2	0	1.000	0	3	3	0	13	9	3	15	0	0.69
Pena, Ramon-Ramon Arturo [Padilla]	89DetA	05-05-62	Santiago, Dom. Rep.		R	R	5'10	155	0	0	—	0	8	0	0	18	26	8	12	0	6.00
Pena, Tony-Ramon Antonio	06AriN	01-09-82	Santo Domingo, D. R.		R	R	6'1	220	3	4	.429	1	25	0	0	31	36	8	21	0	5.58
Penn, Hayden-Hayden Andrew	05-06BalA	10-13-84	Santee, Cal.		R	R	6'3	195	3	6	.333	0	14	14	0	58	84	34	26	0	9.31
Pennington, Brad-Brad Lee	93-95BalA 95CinN 96BosA 96CalA 98TBA	04-14-69	Salem, Ind.		L	L	6'5	205	3	6	.333	1	79	0	0	76	67	89	83	0	7.02
Penny, Brad-Brad Wayne	00-04FlaN 04-06LAN	05-24-78	Broken Arrow, Okla.		R	R	6'4	240	72	62	.537	0	197	195	3	1158	1167	360	846	2	4.06
Pentz, Gene-Eugene David (Ginn)	75DetA 76-78HouN	06-21-53	Johnstown, Pa.		R	R	6'	205	9	8	.471	7	104	4	0	191	177	108	116	0	3.63
Peralta, Joel-Joel [Gutierrez]	05LAA 06KCA	03-23-76	Bonao, Dom. Rep.		R	R	5'11	170	2	3	.400	1	92	0	0	108	102	31	87	0	4.24
Peraza, Oswald-Oswald Jose	88BalA 89SJ	10-19-62	Puerto Cabello, Venez.		R	R	6'4	172	5	7	.417	0	19	15	1	86	98	37	61	0	5.55
Percival, Troy-Troy Eugene	95-96CalA 97-04AnaA 05DetA 06EJ	08-09-69	Fontana, Cal.		R	R	6'3	230	30	41	.423	324	605	0	0	612	412	264	700	0	3.10
Perez, Beltran-Beltran Ogilbio	06WasN	10-24-81	San Francisco de Mac., D.R.		R	R	6'2	180	2	1	.667	0	8	3	0	21	16	13	9	0	3.86
Perez (Gross), Carlos-Carlos Gross [Perez]	95MonN 96SJ 97-98MonN 98-00LAN 01SJ	04-14-71	Nigua, Dom. Rep.		L	L	6'3	205	40	53	.430	0	142	127	17	823	900	211	448	4	4.44
Perez, Juan-Juan P.	06PitN	09-03-78	Villa Rivas, Dom. Rep.		R	L	6'	170	0	1	.000	0	7	0	0	3	5	1	3	0	8.10
Perez (Gross), Melido-Melido Turpen Gross [Perez]	87KCA 88-91ChiA 92-95NYA 96EJ	02-15-66	San Cristobal, D. R.		R	R	6'4	210	78	85	.479	1	243	201	20	1355	1268	551	1092	5	4.17
Perez, Mike-Michael Irvin [Ortega]	90-94StLN 95-96ChiN 97KCA	10-19-64	Yauco, P.R.		R	R	6'	185	24	16	.600	22	313	0	0	346	334	120	224	0	3.56
Perez, Odalis-Odalis Amadol	98-99AtlN 00EJ 01-02AtlN 03-06LAN 06KCA	06-11-77	Las Matas de Farfan,D.R.		L	L	6'0	150	58	59	.496	0	196	165	4	1038	1049	283	737	2	4.33
Perez, Oliver-Oliver Michael [Martinez]	02-03SDN 03-06PitN 06NYN	08-15-81	Culiacan, Mexico		L	L	6'3	180	30	43	.411	0	112	111	3	629	576	344	673	2	4.67
Perez (Gross), Pascual-Pascual Gross [Perez] (Pete)	80-81PitN 82-85AtlN 87-89MonN 90-91NYA 92-93SD	05-17-57	San Cristobal, D. R.		R	R	6'3	170	67	68	.496	0	207	193	21	1244	1167	344	822	4	3.44
Perez, Rafael-Rafael Jerome	06CleA	05-15-82	Santo Domingo, D. R.		L	L	6'3	185	0	0	—	0	18	0	0	12	10	6	15	0	4.38
Perez(Vargas), Yorkis-Yorkis Miguel Vargas [Perez]	91ChiN 92JL 94-96FlaN 97NYN 98-99PhiN 00HouN 02BalA	09-30-67	Bajos de Haina, D.R.		L	L	6'	180	14	15	.483	2	337	0	0	282	251	147	259	0	4.44
Perisho, Matt-Matthew Alan	97AnaA 98-00TexA 01-02DetA 04-05FlaN 05BosA	06-08-75	Burlington, Iowa		L	L	6'0	200	11	17	.393	0	177	28	0	276	346	162	202	0	6.39
Perkins, Dan-Daniel Lee	99MinA	03-15-75	Miami, Fla.		R	R	6'2	193	1	7	.125	0	29	12	0	87	117	43	44	0	6.54
Perkins, Glen-Glen Weston	06MinA	03-02-83	St. Paul, Minn.		L	L	5'11	200	0	0	—	0	4	0	0	6	3	0	6	0	1.59
Perlman, Jon-Jonathan Samuel	85ChiN 87SFN 88CleA	12-13-56	Dallas, Tex.		R	R	6'3	185	1	2	.333	0	26	0	0	40	46	23	17	0	6.35
Perry, Gaylord-Gaylord Jackson	62-71SFN 72-75CleA 75-77TexA 78-79SDN 80TexA 81NYA 81AtlN 82-83SeaA 83KCA	09-15-38	Williamston, N.C.		R	R	6'4	215	314	265	.542	11	777	690	303	5350	4938	1379	3534	53	3.11
Perry, Pat-William Patrick (Atlas)	85-87StLN 87-88CinN 88-89ChiN 90LAN	02-04-59	Taylorville, Ill.		L	L	6'1	190	12	10	.545	9	182	0	0	263	215	99	131	0	3.46
Person, Robert-Robert Alan	95-96NYN 97-99TorA 99-02PhiN 03BosA	10-06-69	St. Louis, Mo.		R	R	6'	190	51	42	.548	0	206	135	4	897	813	438	773	2	4.64
Perzanowski, Stan-Stanley	71,74ChiA 75-76TexA 78MinA	08-25-50	East Chicago, Ind.		R	R	6'3	190	5	11	.313	2	143	16	2	160	60	70	0	5.10	
Peterek, Jeff-Jeffrey Allen	89MilA	09-22-63	Michigan City, Ind.		R	R	6'2	200	0	2	.000	0	7	4	0	31	31	14	16	0	4.02
Peters, Chris-Christopher Michael	96-00PitN 01MonN	01-28-72	Fort Thomas, Ky.		L	L	6'1	170	19	25	.432	1	136	49	1	380	420	157	224	0	4.81
Peters, Steve-Steven Bradley	87-88StLN	11-14-62	Oklahoma City, Okla.		L	L	5'11	173	3	3	.500	1	56	0	0	80	74	28	41	0	5.25
Peterson, Adam-Adam Charles	87-90ChiA 91SDN	12-11-65	Long Beach, Cal.		R	R	6'3	205	5	11	.313	0	39	27	2	155	167	65	75	0	5.46
Peterson, Adam-Adam L.	04TorA	05-18-79	Savannah, Ga.		R	R	6'3	220	0	0	—	0	3	0	0	3	7	3	2	0	16.87
Peterson, Kyle-Kyle Johnathan	99MilN 00SJ 01MilN	04-09-76	Elkhorn, Neb.		L	R	6'3	215	5	9	.357	0	20	14	0	92	106	29	46	0	4.71
Petit, Yusmeiro-Yusmeiro Alberto	06FlaN	11-22-84	Maracaibo, Venezuela		R	R	6'3	230	1	2	.333	0	15	1	0	26	46	9	20	0	9.57
Petkovsek, Mark-Mark Joseph	91TexA 93PitN 95-98StLN 99-00AnaA 01TexA	11-18-65	Beaumont, Tex.		R	R	6'	190	46	28	.622	1	390	41	0	710	797	222	358	1	4.74
Petry, Dan-Daniel Joseph (Peaches)	79-87DetA 88-89CalA 90-91DetA 91AtlN 91BosA	11-13-58	Palo Alto, Cal.		R	R	6'5	210	125	104	.546	1	370	300	52	2081	1984	852	1063	11	3.94
Pettibone, Jay-Harry Jonathan	83MinA	06-21-57	Mt. Clemens, Mich.		R	R	6'4	185	0	4	.000	0	4	4	1	27	28	8	10	0	5.33
Pettitte, Andy-Andrew Eugene	95-03NYA 04-06HouN	06-15-72	Baton Rouge, La.		L	L	6'5	235	186	104	.641	0	367	359	25	2312	2398	721	1703	4	3.81
Pettyjohn, Adam-Adam Christopher	01DetA	06-11-77	Phoenix, Ariz.		R	L	6'2	205	1	6	.143	0	16	9	0	65	81	21	40	0	5.82
Phelps, Tommy-Thomas Allen	03-04FlaN 05MilN	03-04-74	Seoul, South Korea		L	L	6'3	205	5	5	.444	1	75	10	0	120	129	47	85	0	4.34
Phelps, Travis-Travis Howard	01-02TBA 04MilN	07-25-77	Neosho, Mo.		R	R	6'2	195	3	5	.375	5	106	0	0	106	91	54	93	0	4.34
Phillips, Jason-Jason Charles	99PitN 02-03CleA	03-22-74	Williamsport, Pa.		R	R	6'6	225	1	4	.200	0	47	9	0	80	25	0	5.40	

USE NAMES - GIVEN NAMES (NICKNAMES)	TEAM BY YEAR	BIRTH DATE	BIRTHPLACE	DEATH DATE	B	T	HGT	WGT	W	L	Pct.	SV	G	GS	CG	IP	H	BB	SO	ShO	ERA
Phoenix, Steve-Steven Robert	94-95OakA	01-31-68	Phoenix, Ariz.		R	R	6'2	175	0	0	—	0	3	0	0	6	7	5	6	0	13.50
Piatt, Doug-Douglas William	91MonN	09-26-65	Beaver, Pa.		L	R	6'1	185	0	0	—	0	21	0	0	35	29	17	29	0	2.60
Pichardo, Hipolito-Hipolito Antonio [Balbina]	92,94-98KCA 99EJ 00-01BosA 02HouN	08-22-69	Esperanza, D.R.		R	R	6'1	190	50	44	.532	20	350	68	3	770	838	287	394	1	4.44
Pickett, Ricky-Cecil Lee	98AriN	01-19-70	Fort Worth, Tex.		L	L	6'0	185	0	0	—	0	2	0	0	1	3	4	2	0	81.00
Pickford, Kevin-Kevin Patrick	02SDN	03-12-75	Fresno, Cal.		L	L	6'4	200	0	2	.000	0	16	4	0	30	37	20	18	0	6.00
Pico, Jeff-Jeffrey Mark	88-90ChiN	02-12-66	Antioch, Cal.		R	R	6'1	180	13	12	.520	5	113	26	3	295	327	105	132	2	4.24
Pierce, Ed-Edward John	92KCA	10-06-68	Arcadia, Cal.		L	L	6'1	185	0	0	—	0	2	1	0	5	9	4	3	0	3.38
Pierce, Jeff-Jeffrey Charles	95BosA	06-07-69	Poughkeepsie, N.Y.		R	R	6'1	190	0	3	.000	0	12	0	0	15	16	14	12	0	6.60
Piersoll, Chris-Christopher Earl	01CinN	09-25-77	Van Nuys, Cal.		R	R	6'4	195	0	0	—	0	11	0	0	11	12	6	7	0	2.38
Pineda, Luis-Luis A.	01DetA 02CinN	10-17-74	San Cristobal, Dom. Rep.		R	R	6'1	160	1	4	.200	0	42	2	0	51	41	38	44	0	4.44
Pineiro, Joel-Joel Alberto	00-06SeaA	09-25-78	Rio Piedras, P.R.		R	R	6'1	195	58	55	.513	1	185	148	9	996	1033	327	658	3	4.48
Pinto, Renyel-Renyel Eligio	06FlaN	07-08-82	Cupira, Venezuela		L	L	6'4	195	0	0	—	1	27	0	0	30	20	27	36	0	3.03
Pirtle, Gerry-Gerald Eugene	78MonN	12-03-47	Tulsa, Okla.		R	R	6'1	185	0	2	.000	0	19	0	0	26	33	23	14	0	5.88
Pisciotta, Marc-Marc George	97-98ChiN 99KCA	08-07-70	Edison, N.J.		R	R	6'5	240	4	5	.444	0	75	0	0	81	73	58	55	0	4.24
Pitlock, Skip-Lee Patrick Thomas	70SFN 74-75ChiA	11-06-47	Chicago, Ill.		L	L	6'3	190	8	8	.500	1	58	20	1	193	196	103	124	0	4.52
Pittsley, Jim-James Michael	95KCA 96EJ 97-99KCA 99MilN	08-08-71	Danville, Cal.		R	R	6'7	230	7	12	.368	0	81	29	0	226	268	117	116	0	6.02
Pladson, Gordy-Gordon Cecil	79-82HouN	07-31-56	New Westminster, Can.		R	R	6'4	210	0	4	.000	0	20	6	0	50	66	23	18	0	6.08
Plank, Ed-Edward Arthur	78-79SFN	04-09-52	Chicago, Ill.		R	R	6'1	205	0	0	—	0	9	0	0	11	15	4	2	0	4.91
Plantenberg, Erik-Erik John	93-94SeaA 97PhiN	10-30-68	Kenton, Wash.		B	L	6'1	180	0	0	—	1	61	0	0	42	40	31	16	0	4.46
Plesac, Dan-Daniel Thomas	86-92MilA 93-94ChiN 95-96PitN 97-99TorA 99-00AriN 01-02TorA 02-03PhiN	02-04-62	Gary, Ind.		L	L	6'5	210	65	71	.478	158	1064	14	0	1072	977	402	1041	0	3.64
Plunk, Eric-Eric Vaughn	86-89OakA 89-91NYA 92-98CleA 98-99MilN	09-03-63	Wilmington, Cal.		R	R	6'5	220	72	58	.554	35	714	41	0	1151	1009	647	1081	0	3.82
Plympton, Jeff-Jeffrey Hunter	91BosA	11-24-65	Framingham, Mass.		R	R	6'2	205	0	0	—	0	4	0	0	5	6	5	3	0	0.00
Pole, Dick-Richard Henry	73-76BosA 77-78SeaA	10-13-50	Trout Creek, Mich.		R	R	6'3	215	25	37	.403	1	122	77	8	532	607	209	239	1	5.04
Politte, Cliff-Clifford Anthony	98StLN 99-02PhiN 02-03TorA 04-06ChiA	02-27-74	St. Louis, Mo.		R	R	5'9	185	22	23	.489	15	330	16	0	411	393	171	342	0	4.40
Polley, Dale-Ezra Dale	96NYA	08-09-65	Georgetown, Ky.		R	L	6'	165	1	3	.250	0	32	0	0	22	23	11	14	0	7.89
Poloni, John-John Paul	77TexA	02-28-54	Dearborn, Mich.		L	L	6'5	215	1	0	1.000	0	2	1	0	7	8	1	5	0	6.43
Ponson, Sidney-Sidney Alton	98-03BalA 03SFN 04-05BalA 06StLN 06NYA	11-02-76	Noord, Aruba		R	R	6'1	250	80	96	.455	1	252	238	28	1528	1701	519	918	4	4.89
Poole, Jim-James Richard	90LAN 91TexA 91-94BalA 95-96CleA 96-98SFN 98CleA 99PhiN 99CleA 00DetA 00MonN	04-28-66	Rochester, N.Y.		L	L	6'2	200	22	12	.647	4	431	0	0	363	376	156	256	0	4.31
Porter, Chuck-Charles William	81-85MilA	01-12-56	Baltimore Md.		R	R	6'3	187	13	13	.500	0	54	34	7	237	278	54	136	1	4.15
Portugal, Mark-Mark Steven	85-88MinA 89-93HouN 94-95SFN 95-96CinN 97-98PhiN 99BosA	10-30-62	Los Angeles, Cal.		R	R	6'	200	109	95	.534	5	346	283	16	1826	1813	607	1134	4	4.03
Porzio, Mike-Lawrence Michael	99ColN 02-03ChiA	08-20-72	Waterbury, Conn.		L	L	6'3	190	3	3	.500	0	35	3	0	57	58	24	42	0	5.21
Pote, Lou-Louis William	99-02AnaA 03JL 04CinN	08-21-71	Evergreen Park, Ill.		R	R	6'3	205	4	4	.500	6	129	2	0	220	199	88	167	0	3.56
Potts, Mike-Michael Larry	96MilA	09-05-70	Langdale, Ala.		L	L	5'9	170	1	2	.333	1	24	0	0	45	58	30	21	0	7.15
Powell, Brian-William Brian	98DetA 00-01HouN 02DetA 03SFN 04PhiN	10-10-73	Bainbridge, Ga.		R	R	6'2	205	7	18	.280	0	59	34	0	220	251	90	120	0	5.94
Powell, Dennis-Dennis Clay	85-86LAN 87-90SeaA 90MilA 92-93SeaA	08-13-63	Moultrie, Ga.		L	R	6'3	220	11	22	.333	3	207	12	0	340	360	159	199	0	4.95
Powell, Jay-James Willard Jr.	95-98FlaN 98-00-01HouN 01ColN 02-04TexA 05AtlN	01-09-72	Meridian, Miss.		R	R	6'4	220	36	23	.610	22	512	0	0	542	543	272	423	0	4.17
Powell, Jeremy-Jeremy Robert	98-00MonN	06-18-76	Bellflower, Cal.		R	R	6'5	230	5	16	.238	0	35	27	0	148	175	64	77	0	5.84
Powell, Ross-Ross John	93CinN 94HouN 95PitN	01-24-68	Grand Rapids, Mich.		L	L	6'	180	0	5	.000	0	48	4	0	53	55	31	42	0	5.40
Power, Ted-Ted Henry	81-82LAN 83-87CinN 88KCA 88DetA 89StLN 90PitN 91CinN 92-93CleA 93SeaA 94SJ	01-31-55	Guthrie, Okla.		R	R	6'4	220	68	69	.496	70	564	85	5	1160	1159	452	701	3	4.00
Prall, Willie-Wilfred Anthony	75ChiN	04-20-50	Hackensack, N.J.		L	L	6'3	195	0	2	.000	0	3	3	0	15	21	8	7	0	8.40
Pratt, Andy-Andrew Elias	02AtlN 04ChiN	08-27-79	Mesa, Ariz.		L	L	6'	185	0	1	.000	0	5	0	0	3	1	11	2	0	15.00
Price, Joe-Joseph Walter	80-86CinN 87-89SFN 89BosA 90BalA	11-29-56	Inglewood, Cal.		L	L	6'4	220	45	49	.479	13	372	84	10	906	839	337	657	1	3.65
Priest, Eddie-Eddie Lee	98CinN	04-08-74	Boaz, Ala.		R	L	6'1	200	0	1	.000	0	2	2	0	6	12	1	1	0	10.50
Prieto, Ariel-Ariel [Fernandez]	95-98OakA 99EJ 00OakA 01TBA	10-22-69	Havana, Cuba		R	R	6'3	235	15	24	.385	0	70	60	3	352	407	176	231	0	4.85
Prinz, Bret-Bret Randolph	01-03AriN 03-04NYA 05LAA	06-15-77	Chicago Heights, Ill.		R	R	6'3	205	5	4	.556	9	98	0	0	89	95	48	63	0	4.77
Prior, Mark-Mark William	02-06ChiN	09-07-80	San Diego, Cal.		R	R	6'5	230	42	29	.592	0	106	106	5	657	582	223	757	1	3.51
Proctor, Scott-Scott Christopher	04-06NYA	01-02-77	Stuart, Fla.		R	R	6'1	198	9	5	.643	1	138	1	0	172	164	64	146	0	4.45
Prokopec, Luke-Kenneth Luke	00-01LAN 02TorA 03SJ	02-23-78	Blackwood, Australia		R	R	5'11	166	11	17	.393	0	56	37	0	231	255	74	144	0	5.30
Proly, Mike-Michael James	76StLN 78-80ChiA 81PhiN 82-83ChiN	12-15-50	Queens, N.Y.		R	R	5'11	185	22	29	.431	22	267	18	2	546	531	195	185	0	3.19
Puffer, Brandon-Brandon Duane	02-03HouN 04SDN 05SFN	10-05-75	Downey, Cal.		R	R	6'3	190	4	4	.429	0	85	0	0	115	124	67	71	0	5.09
Pugh, Tim-Timothy Dean	92-96CinN 96KCA 96CinN 97DetA	01-26-67	Lake Tahoe, Cal.		R	R	6'6	225	25	28	.472	1	107	58	4	417	479	158	214	1	4.97
Puleo, Charlie-Charles Michael	81-82NYN 83-84CinN 86-89AtlN	02-07-55	Glen Ridge, N.J.		R	R	6'2	200	29	39	.426	2	180	76	3	633	621	319	387	1	4.25
Pulido, Alfonso-Alfonso [Manzo]	83-84PitN 86NYA	01-23-57	Veracruz, Mexico		L	L	5'11	175	1	1	.500	1	12	4	0	35	45	11	16	0	5.19
Pulido, Carlos-Juan Carlos [Valera]	94MinA 03-04MinA	08-05-71	Caracas, Venez.		L	L	6'	195	3	8	.273	0	35	12	0	111	118	47	47	0	5.98
Pulsipher, Bill-William Thomas	95NYN 96-97EJ 98NYN 98-99MilN 00NYN 01BosA 01ChiA 01StLN	10-09-73	Fort Benning, Ga.		L	L	6'3	210	13	19	.406	0	106	46	2	327	361	141	202	0	5.15
Putz, J.J.-Joseph Jason	03-06SeaA	02-22-77	Trenton, Mich.		R	R	6'5	220	10	9	.526	46	193	0	0	205	187	63	199	0	3.47
Qualls, Chad-Chad Michael	04-06HouN	08-17-78	Lomita, Cal.		R	R	6'5	220	17	7	.708	1	183	0	0	201	183	59	140	0	3.53
Quantrill, Paul-Paul John	92-94BosA 94-95PhiN 96-01TorA 02-03LAN 04-05NYA 05SDN 05FlaN	11-03-68	London, Canada		L	R	6'1	190	68	78	.466	21	841	64	1	1256	1442	336	725	1	3.83
Quevedo, Ruben-Ruben Eduardo [Yetez]	00ChiN 01-03MilN	01-05-79	Valencia, Venezuela		R	R	6'1	220	14	30	.318	0	66	58	2	326	364	175	237	1	6.15
Quintana, Luis-Luis Joaquin [Santos]	74-75CalA	12-25-51	Veja Beja, P.R.		L	L	6'2	185	2	3	.400	0	22	0	0	30	20	16		0	4.95
Quirico, Rafael-Rafael Octavio [Dottin]	96PhiN	09-07-69	Santo Domingo, D.R.		L	L	6'1	195	0	1	.000	0	1	0	0	2	4	5	1	0	37.80
Quisenberry, Dan-Daniel Raymond (Quiz)	79-88KCA 88-89StLN 90SFN	02-07-53	Santa Monica, Cal.	09-30-98	R	R	6'2	180	56	46	.549	244	674	0	0	1043	1064	162	379	0	2.76
Raczka, Mike-Michael	92OakA	11-16-62	New Britain, Conn.		L	L	6'2	200	0	0	—	0	8	0	0	6	8	5	2	0	8.53
Radinsky, Scott-Scott David	90-93ChiA 94IL 95ChiA 96-98LAN 99-00StLN 01CinN	03-03-68	Glendale, Cal.		L	L	6'3	210	42	25	.627	52	557	0	0	482	461	209	358	0	3.44
Radke, Brad-Brad William	95-06MinA	10-27-72	Eau Claire, Wis.		R	R	6'2	185	148	139	.516	0	378	377	37	2451	2643	445	1467	10	4.22
Radlosky, Rob-Robert Vincent	99MinA	01-07-74	West Palm Beach, Fla.		R	R	6'2	205	0	1	.000	0	7	0	0	9	15	4	3	0	12.46
Raggio, Brady-Brady John	97-98StLN 03AriN	09-17-72	Los Angeles, Cal.		R	R	6'4	210	2	3	.400	1	29	5	0	47	75	25	32	0	8.10
Raich, Eric-Eric James (Big E)	75-76CleA	11-01-51	Detroit, Mich.		R	R	6'4	220	7	8	.467	0	19	17	2	96	125	31	35	0	5.81
Rain, Steve-Steven Nicholas	99-00ChiN	06-02-75	Los Angeles, Calif.		R	R	6'6	250	3	5	.375	0	53	0	0	64	74	34	66	0	5.46
Rainey, Chuck-Charles David	79-82BosA 83-84ChiN 84OakA	07-14-54	San Diego, Cal.		R	R	5'11	190	43	35	.551	1	141	106	10	670	738	287	300	6	4.50
Rajsich, Dave-David Christopher	78NYA 78-80TexA	09-28-51	Youngstown, Ohio		L	L	6'5	190	3	4	.429	2	55	4	0	115	128	46	76	0	4.62
Rakers, Aaron-Aaron James	04-05BalA	01-22-77	Highland, Ill.		R	R	6'3	205	1	0	1.000	0	13	0	0	18	16	4	14	0	3.50
Rakers, Jason-Jason Paul	98-99CleA 00KCA	06-29-73	Pittsburgh, Pa.		R	R	6'2	197	2	0	1.000	0	13	0	0	25	35	11	16	0	8.76
Ramirez, Allan-Daniel Allan	83BalA	05-01-57	Victoria, Tex.		R	R	6'	190	4	4	.500	0	11	10	1	57	46	30	20	0	3.47
Ramirez, Elizardo-Elizardo [de Palma]	04PhiN 05-06CinN	01-28-83	Villa Mella, Dom. Rep.		R	R	6'	180	4	12	.250	0	34	23	0	141	173	44	87	0	5.79
Ramirez, Erasmo-Erasmo	03-05TexA	04-29-76	Santa Ana, Cal.		L	L	6'	180	8	4	.667	2	84	0	0	108	104	19	55	0	4.01
Ramirez, Hector-Hector Bienvenido	99-00MilN	12-15-71	El Seibo, Dom. Rep.		R	R	6'3	218	1	3	.250	0	30	0	0	30	16	13		0	5.40
Ramirez, Horacio-Horacio	03-06AtlN	11-24-79	Carson, Cal.		L	L	6'1	210	30	22	.577	0	86	84	3	521	531	200	248	1	4.19
Ramirez, Roberto-Roberto Sanchez	98SDN 99ColN	08-17-72	Veracruz, Mexico		L	R	5'11	170	2	5	.286	1	53	4	0	55	80	34	49	0	7.69
Ramirez, Ramon-Ramon Santo	06ColN	08-31-81	Puerto Plata, Dom. Rep.		R	R	5'11	190	4	3	.571	0	61	0	0	68	58	27	61	0	3.46
Ramirez, Santiago-Santiago	06WasN	08-15-78	Bonao, Dom. Rep.		R	R	5'11	210	0	0	—	0	3	0	0	6	6	2	1	0	8.10
Ramos, Edgar-Edgar Jose [Malave]	97PhiN	03-06-75	Cumana, Venezuela		R	R	6'5	190	0	2	.000	0	4	2	0	14	15	6	4	0	5.14
Ramos, Mario-Mario Martin	03TexA	10-19-77	Aurora, Ill.		L	L	6'1	180	1	1	.500	0	3	3	0	13	11	13	8	0	6.23
Ramsay, Robert-Robert Arthur	99-00SeaA 02IL	12-03-73	Vancouver, Wash.		L	L	6'5	230	1	3	.250	0	43	0	0	69	66	49	43	0	4.19
Randall, Scott-Scott Philip	03CinN	10-29-75	Fullerton, Cal.		R	R	6'3	225	2	5	.286	0	15	2	0	28	34	11	25	0	6.51
Randolph, Stephen-Stephen LeCharles	02-04AriN	05-01-74	Okinawa, Japan		L	L	6'3	210	10	6	.625	0	95	6	0	112	109	119	112	0	4.89
Rapp, Pat-Patrick Leland	92SFN 93-97FlaN 97SFN 98KCA 99BosA 00BalA 01AnaA	07-13-67	Jennings, La.		R	R	6'3	210	70	91	.435	0	259	239	9	1387	1468	683	825	5	4.68
Rasmussen, Dennis-Dennis Lee	83SDN 84-87NYA 87-88CinN 88-91SDN 92ChiN 92-93,95KCA	04-18-59	Los Angeles, Cal.		L	L	6'7	230	91	77	.542	0	256	235	21	1461	1424	522	835	5	4.15
Rasmussen, Eric (Harold)-Eric Ralph (The Great Dane)	75-78StLN 78-80SDN 82-83StLN 83KCA	03-22-52	Racine, Wis.		R	R	6'3	205	50	77	.394	5	238	144	27	1018	1033	309	489	12	3.85
Rasner, Darrell-Darrell Wayne	05WasN 06NYA	01-13-81	Carson City, Nev.		R	R	6'2	220	3	2	.600	0	11	4	0	28	23	7	15	0	4.23
Rath, Fred-Frederick Helsher Jr.	98ColN	01-05-73	Dallas, Tex.		R	R	6'3	220	0	0	—	0	5	0	0	5	6	2	2	0	1.69
Rath, Gary-Alfred Gary	98LAN 99MinA	01-10-73	Gulfport, Miss.		L	L	6'2	185	0	1	.000	0	8	1	0	8	9	7	5	0	11.25

USE NAMES - GIVEN NAMES (NICKNAMES)	TEAM BY YEAR	BIRTH DATE	BIRTHPLACE	DEATH DATE	B	T	HGT	WGT	W	L	Pct.	SV	G	GS	CG	IP	H	BB	SO	ShO	ERA
Ratliff, Jon-Jon Charles	00OakA	12-22-71	Syracuse, N.Y.		R	R	6'4	195	0	0	—	0	1	0	0	1	0	0	0	0	0.00
Ratzer, Steve-Stephen Wayne	80-81MonN	09-09-53	Paterson, N.J.		R	R	6'	180	1	1	.500	0	13	1	0	21	32	9	4	0	7.29
Rau, Doug-Douglas James	72-79LAN 80SJ 81CalA	12-15-48	Columbus, Tex.		L	L	6'2	180	81	60	.574	3	222	187	33	1261	1259	382	697	11	3.35
Rauch, Jon-Jon Eirch	02,04ChiA 04MonN 05-06WasN	09-27-78	Louisville, Ky.		R	R	6'11	250	12	11	.522	2	119	11	0	182	160	72	150	0	3.81
Rautzhan, Lance-Clarence George	77-79LAN 79MilA	08-20-52	Pottsville, Pa.		R	L	6'1	200	6	4	.600	7	83	0	0	95	98	47	45	0	3.88
Rawley, Shane-Shane William	78-81SeaA 82-84NYA 84-88PhiN 89MinA	07-07-55	Racine, Wis.		L	L	6'	180	111	118	.485	40	469	230	41	1871	1934	734	991	7	4.02
Ray, Chris-Christopher T.	05-06BalA	01-12-82	Tampa, Fla.		R	R	6'3	200	5	7	.417	33	102	0	0	107	79	45	94	0	2.70
Ray, Ken-Kenneth Alan	99KCA 06AtlN	.11-27-74	Atlanta, Ga.		R	R	6'2	200	2	1	.667	0	82	0	0	79	89	44	50	0	5.13
Raziano, Barry-Barry John	73KCA 74CalA	02-05-47	New Orleans, La.		B	R	5'11	185	1	2	.333	1	15	0	0	22	21	9	9	0	6.14
Reames, Britt-William Britt	00StLN 01-03MonN 05OakA 06PitN	08-19-73	Seneca, S.C.		R	R	5'11	175	7	13	.350	0	101	26	0	218	226	118	204	0	5.28
Reardon, Jeff-Jeffrey James	79-81NYN 81-86MonN 87-89MinA 90-92BosA 92AtlN 93CinN 94NYA	10-01-55	Dalton, Mass.		R	R	6'	200	73	77	.487	367	880	0	1	1132	1000	358	877	0	3.16
Redding, Tim-Timothy James	01-04HouN 05SDN 05NYA	02-12-78	Rochester, N.Y.		R	R	6'	195	21	34	.382	0	101	79	0	436	488	184	309	0	5.16
Redfern, Pete-Pete Irvine (Red)	76-82MinA	08-25-54	Glendale, Cal.		R	R	6'2	195	42	48	.467	3	170	111	9	714	764	306	426	0	4.54
Redman, Mark-Mark Allen	99-01MinA 01-02DetA 03FlaN 04OakA 05PitN 06KCA	01-05-74	San Diego, Calif.		L	L	6'5	235	64	76	.457	0	198	186	12	1152	1244	374	700	2	4.65
Reed, Jerry-Jerry Maxwell	81-82PhiN 82-83,85CleA 86-90SeaA 90BosA	10-08-55	Bryson City, N.C.		R	R		190	20	19	.513	18	238	12	0	480	477	172	248	0	3.94
Reed, Rick-Richard Allen	88-91PitN 92-93KCA 93-94TexA 95CinN 97-01MinA 01-03MinA	08-16-64	Huntington, W. Va.		R	R	6'1	200	93	76	.550	1	273	245	14	1546	1601	285	970	7	4.03
Reed, Ron-Ronald Lee (65-67 played in N.B.A.)	65-75AtlN 75StLN 76-83PhiN 84ChiA	11-02-42	La Porte, Ind.		R	R	6'6	215	146	140	.510	103	751	236	55	2476	2374	633	1481	8	3.46
Reed, Steve-Stephen Vincent	92SFN 93-97ColN 98SFN 98-01CleA 01AtlN 02SDN 02NYN 03-04ColN 05BalA	03-11-65	Los Angeles, Cal.		R	R	6'2	205	49	44	.527	18	833	0	0	871	811	285	630	0	3.63
Regilio, Nick-Nicholas D.	04-05TexA	09-04-78	Miami, Fla.		R	R	6'2	205	1	6	.143	0	7	4	0	37	42	22	26	0	5.35
Reichert, Dan-Daniel Robert	99-02KCA 03TorA	07-12-76	Monterey, Calif.		R	R	6'3	175	21	25	.457	2	124	51	1	395	441	223	240	1	5.55
Reith, Brian-Brian Eric	01,03-04CinN	02-28-78	Fort Wayne, Ind.		R	R	6'5	220	4	12	.250	1	73	9	0	128	147	71	85	0	5.92
Reitsma, Chris-Christopher Michael	01-03CinN 04-06AtlN	12-31-77	Minneapolis, Minn.		R	R	6'5	230	32	44	.421	37	312	53	1	585	659	155	348	1	4.58
Rekar, Bryan-Bryan Robert	95-97ColN 98-01TBA 02KCA	06-03-72	Oak Lawn, Ill.		R	R	6'3	215	25	49	.338	0	131	108	4	655	788	208	383	0	5.62
Remlinger, Mike-Michael John	91SFN 94-95NYN 95-98CinN 99-02AtlN 03-05ChiN 05BosA 06AtlN	03-23-66	Middletown, N.Y.		L	L	6'	200	53	55	.491	20	639	59	4	879	784	430	854	2	3.90
Remmerswaal, Win-Wilhelmus Abraham	79-80BosA	03-08-54	The Hague, Neth.		R	R	6'	162	3	1	.750	0	22	0	0	55	65	21	36	0	5.56
Renfroe, Laddie-Cohen Williams	91ChiN	05-09-62	Nanchez, Miss.		B	R	5'11	200	0	1	.000	0	4	0	0	5	11	2	4	0	13.50
Renko, Steve-Steven	69-76MonN 76-77ChiN 77ChiA 78OakA 79-80BosA 81-82CalA 83KCA	12-10-44	Kansas City, Kans.		R	R	6'6	230	134	146	.479	6	451	365	57	2493	2438	1010	1455	9	4.00
Replogle, Andy-Andrew David	78-79MilA	10-07-53	South Bend, Ind.		R	R	6'6	205	9	5	.643	0	35	18	3	157	190	48	43	2	4.01
Resop, Chris-Christopher Paul	05-06FlaN	11-04-82	Naples, Fla.		R	R	6'3	220	3	2	.600	0	37	0	0	38	48	25	25	0	5.63
Reuschel, Paul-Paul Richard	75-78ChiN 78-79CleA	01-12-47	Quincy, Ill.		R	R	6'3	230	16	16	.500	13	188	9	1	393	440	132	188	0	4.51
Reuschel, Rick-Ricky Eugene (Big Daddy)	72-81ChiN 81NYA 82SJ 83-84ChiN 85-87PitN 87-91SFN	05-16-49	Quincy, Ill.		R	R	6'4	230	214	191	.528	5	557	529	102	3550	3588	935	2015	26	3.37
Reuss, Jerry-Jerry	69-71StLN 72-73HouN 74-78PitN 79-87LAN 87CinN 87CalA 88-89ChiA 89MilA 90PitN	06-19-49	St. Louis, Mo.		L	L	6'5	215	220	191	.535	11	628	547	127	3669	3734	1127	1907	39	3.64
Revenig, Todd-Todd Michael	92OakA 93EJ	06-28-69	Brainerd, Minn.		R	R		185	0	0	—	0	2	0	0	2	2	1	0	0	0.00
Reyes, Al-Rafael Alberto	95-97MilA 98-99MilN 99-00BalA 00-01LAN 02PitN 03NYA 04-05StLN	04-10-71	San Cristobal, D.R.		R	R	6'1	205	19	10	.655	6	297	2	0	345	270	164	333	0	3.60
Reyes, Anthony-Anthony Loza	05-06StLN	10-16-81	Downey, Cal.		R	R	6'2	215	6	9	.400	0	21	18	1	99	90	38	84	0	4.74
Reyes, Carlos-Carlos Alberto	94-97OakA 98SDN 98BosA 99SDN 00PhiN 00SDN 03TBA	04-04-69	Miami, Fla.		R	R	6'1	190	20	36	.357	4	293	29	0	558	576	220	360	0	4.66
Reyes, Dennys-Dennys [Valarde]	97-98LAN 98-02CinN 02TexA 03PitN 03AriN 04KCA 05SDN 06MinA	04-19-77	Higuera de Zaragoza, Mex.		R	L	6'3	246	27	31	.466	2	410	40	0	570	579	320	523	0	4.45
Reynolds, Bob-Robert Allen (Bullet Bob)	69MonN 71StLN 71MilA 72-75BalA 75DetA 75CleA	01-21-47	Seattle, Wash.		R	R	6'	205	14	16	.467	21	140	2	0	254	255	82	167	0	3.15
Reynolds, Shane-Richard Shane	92-02HouN 03AtlN 04AriN	03-26-68	Bastrop, La.		R	R	6'3	210	114	96	.543	0	305	278	20	1792	1935	419	1403	7	4.09
Reynoso, Armando-Martin Armando [Gutierrez]	91-92AtlN 93-96ColN 97-98NYN 99-02AriN	05-01-66	San Luis Potosi, Mex.		R	R	6'	200	68	62	.523	1	198	186	8	1080	1185	376	554	1	4.74
Rheinecker, John-John Philip	06TexA	05-29-79	Belleville, Ill.		L	L	6'2	230	4	6	.400	0	21	13	0	71	104	19	28	0	5.86
Rhoden, Rick-Richard Alan	74-78LAN 79-86PitN 87-88NYA 89HouN	05-16-53	Boynton Beach, Fla.		R	R	6'3	200	151	125	.547	1	413	380	69	2593	2606	801	1419	17	3.60
Rhodes, Arthur-Arthur Lee Jr.	91-99BalA 00-03SeaA 04OakA 05CleA 06PhiN	10-24-69	Waco, Tex.		L	L	6'2	205	75	60	.556	30	653	61	5	1011	896	451	993	3	4.31
Riccelli, Frank-Frank Joseph	76SFN 78-79HouN	02-24-53	Syracuse, N.Y.		L	L	6'3	205	3	3	.500	0	17	5	0	41	39	23	32	0	4.39
Ricci, Chuck-Charles Mark	95PhiN	11-20-68	Abington, Pa.		R	R	6'2	185	1	0	1.000	0	7	0	0	10	9	3	9	0	1.80
Rice, Pat-Patrick Edward	91SeaA	11-02-63	Rapid City, S.D.		R	R	6'2	200	1	1	.500	0	7	2	0	21	18	10	12	0	3.00
Richard, J.R.-James Rodney (High Rise)	71-80HouN 81-83IL	03-07-50	Vienna, La.		R	R	6'8	230	107	71	.601	0	238	221	76	1606	1227	770	1493	19	3.15
Richards, Rusty-Russell Earl	89-90AtlN	01-27-65	Houston, Tex.		L	R	6'4	200	0	0	—	0	3	2	0	10	12	7	4	0	6.97
Richardson, Jeff-Jeffrey Scott	90CalA	08-29-63	Wichita, Kans.		R	R		185	0	0	—	0	1	0	0	0.1	1	0	0	0	0.00
Riedling, John-John Richard Jr.	00-04CinN 05FlaN	08-29-75	Fort Lauderdale, Fla.		R	R	5'11	190	17	13	.567	3	229	0	0	302	303	148	198	0	4.41
Rigby, Brad-Bradley Kenneth	97,99OakA 99-00KCA 00MonN	05-14-73	Milwaukee, Wis.		R	R	6'5	215	5	13	.278	2	73	14	0	175	221	61	75	0	5.49
Rigdon, Paul-Paul David	00CleA 00-01MilN 02SJ	11-02-75	Jacksonville, Fla.		R	R	6'2	235	8	10	.444	0	32	31	0	167	175	81	112	0	5.45
Riggan, Jerrod-Jerrod Ashley	00-01NYN 02-03CleA	05-16-74	Brewster, Wash.		R	R	6'3	200	5	4	.556	2	67	0	0	87	105	43	66	0	5.19
Righetti, Dave-David Allan (Rags)	79,81-90NYA 91-93SFN 94OakA 94TorA 95ChiA 95ChiN	11-28-58	San Jose, Cal.		L	L	6'4	215	82	79	.509	252	718	89	13	1404	1287	591	1112	2	3.46
Rightnowar, Ron-Ronald Gene	95MilA	05-06-66	Toledo, Ohio		R	R	6'	190	2	1	.667	1	34	0	0	37	35	18	22	0	5.40
Rijo, Jose-Jose Antonio [Abreu]	84NYA 85-87OakA 88-95CinN 96-97EJ 90-97VR 01-02CinN 03EJ	05-13-65	San Cristobal, D.R.		R	R	6'2	210	116	91	.560	3	376	269	22	1880	1710	663	1606	4	3.24
Riley, George-George Michael (Heater)	79-80ChiN 84SFN 85MonN	10-06-56	Philadelphia, Pa.		L	L	6'4	210	1	5	.167	0	41	5	0	87	103	41	40	0	4.97
Riley, Matt-Matthew Paul	99BalA 03-04BalA 05TexA	08-02-79	Antioch, Cal.		L	L	6'1	205	5	4	.556	0	26	18	0	98	100	72	78	0	5.99
Rincon, Andy-Andrew John	80-82StLN	03-05-59	Monterey Park, Cal.		R	R	6'2	190	8	5	.615	0	20	15	3	107	85	37	46	1	3.11
Rincon, Juan-Juan Manuel	01-06MinA	01-23-79	Maracaibo, Venezuela		R	R	5'11	190	25	21	.543	3	299	3	0	353	316	138	343	0	3.26
Rincon, Ricardo-Ricardo [Espinoza]	97-98PitN 99-02CleA 02-05OakA 06StLN	04-13-70	Veracruz, Mexico		L	L	5'10	190	21	24	.467	21	557	0	0	440	380	200	397	0	3.58
Rineer, Jeff-Jeffrey Alan	79BalA	07-03-55	Lancaster, Pa.		L	L	6'4	210	0	0	—	0	1	0	0	2	1	1	0	0	0.00
Ring, Royce-Roger Royce	05-06NYN	12-21-80	La Mesa, Cal.		L	L	6'	220	0	2	.000	0	26	0	0	23	17	13	16	0	3.47
Rios, Danny-Daniel	97NYA 98KCA	11-11-72	Madrid, Spain		R	R	6'2	190	0	1	.000	0	10	1	0	8	18	7	9	0	9.31
Ripley, Allen-Allen Stevens	78-79BosA 80-81SFN 82CinN	10-18-52	Norwood, Mass.		R	R	6'3	200	23	27	.460	1	101	67	4	464	521	148	229	0	4.52
Riske, David-David Richard	99CleA 00XJ 01-05CleA 06BosA 06ChiA	10-23-76	Renton, Wash.		R	R	6'2	180	18	14	.563	16	328	0	0	361	305	152	346	0	3.59
Risley, Bill-William Charles	92-93MonN 94-95SeaA 96-98TorA 99XJ	05-29-67	Chicago, Ill.		R	R	6'2	215	15	13	.536	1	157	1	0	221	180	101	203	0	3.98
Ritchie, Todd-Todd Everett	97-98MinA 99-01PitN 02ChiA 03MilN 04TBA	11-07-71	Portsmouth, Va.		R	R	6'3	220	43	54	.443	0	184	120	7	836	929	262	516	3	4.71
Ritchie, Wally-Wallace Reid	87-88,91-92PhiN	07-12-65	Glendale, Cal.		L	L	6'2	180	6	5	.545	4	147	0	0	178	167	80	98	0	3.14
Ritter, Reggie-Reggie Blake	86-87CleA	01-23-60	Malvern, Ark.		R	R	6'2	195	1	1	.500	2	19	0	0	37	47	20	17	0	6.14
Ritz, Kevin-Kevin D.	89-92DetA 93AJ 94-98ColN	06-08-65	Eatontown, N.J.		R	R	6'4	220	45	56	.446	2	151	130	4	753	848	377	462	0	5.35
Rivera, Ben-Bienvenido [Santana]	92AtlN 92-94PhiN	01-11-68	San Pedro de Mac, D.R.		R	R	6'6	235	23	17	.575	0	67	49	5	318	314	152	219	2	4.52
Rivera, Luis-Luis [Gutierrez]	00AtlN 00BalA 01SJ 02BalA	06-21-78	Chihuahua, Mexico		R	R	6'3	163	1	0	1.000	0	7	5	0	7	5	6	5	0	1.23
Rivera, Mariano-Mariano (Mo)	95-06NYA	11-29-69	Panama City, Panama		R	R	6'2	185	59	40	.596	413	720	10	0	882	691	226	783	0	2.29
Rivera, Roberto-Roberto [Diaz]	95ChiN 99SDN	01-01-69	Bayamon, P.R.		L	L	6'	200	1	2	.333	0	19	0	0	12	14	5	9	0	4.50
Rivera, Saul-Saul Rabell	06WasN	12-06-77	San Juan, P.R.		R	R	5'11	150	0	1	.000	0	54	0	0	60	59	32	41	0	3.43
Rizzo, Todd-Todd Michael	98-99ChiA	05-24-71	Media, Pa.		L	L	6'3	220	0	2	.000	0	32	0	0	16	18	9	5	0	12.37
Rleal, Sendy-Sendy [Aquino]	06BalA	06-21-80	San Pedro de Mac., D.R.		R	R	6'1	180	1	1	.500	0	42	0	0	47	48	23	19	0	4.44
Roa, Joe-Joseph Rodger	95-96CleA 97SFN 02-03PhiN 03ColN 03SDN 04MinA	10-11-71	Southfield, Mich.		R	R	6'1	195	9	16	.360	0	100	38	0	266	330	72	154	0	4.94
Roach, Jason-Jason Glenn	03NYN	04-20-76	Kinston, N.C.		R	R	6'4	190	0	2	.000	0	3	2	0	9	14	4	2	0	12.00
Robbins, Bruce-Bruce Duane (Marty)	79-80DetA	09-10-59	Portland, Ind.		L	L	6'2	185	7	5	.583	0	25	14	0	98	105	49	45	0	5.33
Robbins, Jake-Phillip Jacob	05CleA	05-23-76	Charlotte, N.C.		R	R	6'5	190	0	0	—	0	2	0	0	3	3	1	0	0	5.40
Roberge, Bert-Bertrand Roland	79-80,82HouN 84ChiA 85-86MonN	10-03-54	Lewiston, Maine		R	R	6'2	190	12	12	.500	10	146	0	0	219	200	80	119	0	3.99
Roberson, Sid-Sidney Dean	95MilA	09-07-71	Jacksonville, Fla.		L	L	5'9	170	6	4	.600	0	26	13	0	84	102	37	40	0	5.76
Roberts, Dave-David Arthur	69-71SDN 72-75HouN 76-77DetA 77-78ChiN 79SFN 79-80PitN 80SeaA 81NYN	09-11-44	Gallipolis, Ohio		L	L	6'3	190	103	125	.452	15	445	277	77	2098	2188	615	957	20	3.78
Roberts, Grant-Grant William	00-04NYN	09-13-77	El Cajon, Cal.		R	R	6'3	205	4	4	.500	1	102	0	0		106	37		0	4.25
Roberts, Willis-Willis Augusto [DeLeon]	99DetA 01-03BalA 04PitN	06-19-75	San Cristobal, Dom. Rep.		R	R	6'3	230	17	15	.531	7	148	18	1	259	277	112	179	0	4.62
Robertson, Jeriome-Jerome Paul	02-03HouN 04CleA	03-30-77	San Jose, Cal.		L	L	6'1	195	16	12	.571	0	57	32	0	184	215	78	111	0	5.71
Robertson, Nate-Nathan Daniel	02FlaN 03-06DetA	09-03-77	Wichita, Kans.		L	L	6'3	225	41	44	.482	0	112	105	4	655	688	225	450	0	4.56
Robertson, Rich-Richard Wayne	93-94PitN 95-97MinA 98AnaA	09-15-68	Nacogdoches, Tex.		L	R	6'4	175	17	30	.362	0	114	61	6	415	460	233	237	3	5.40
Robinson, Dewey-Dewey Everett	79-81ChiA	04-28-55	Evanston, Ill.		R	R	6'	185	2	2	.500	1	30	0	0	53	42	28	35	0	4.08

USE NAMES - GIVEN NAMES (NICKNAMES)	TEAM BY YEAR	BIRTH DATE	BIRTHPLACE	DEATH DATE	B	T	HGT	WGT	W	L	Pct.	SV	G	GS	CG	IP	H	BB	SO	ShO	ERA
Robinson, Don-Don Allen	78-87PitN 87-91SFN 92CalA 92PhiN	06-08-57	Ashland, Ky.		R	R	6'4	235	109	106	.507	57	524	229	34	1958	1894	643	1251	6	3.79
Robinson, Jeff-Jeffrey Daniel	84-87SFN 87-89PitN 90NYA 91CalA 92CinN	12-13-60	Santa Ana, Cal.		R	R	6'4	200	46	57	.447	39	454	62	2	901	880	349	629	1	3.79
Robinson, Jeff-Jeffrey Mark	87-90DetA 91BalA 92PitN	12-14-61	Ventura, Cal.		R	R	6'6	230	47	40	.540	0	141	117	10	709	672	347	425	5	4.79
Robinson, Ken-Kenneth Neal	95TorA 96KCA 97TorA	11-03-69	Barberton, Ohio		R	R	5'7	175	2	2	.500	0	29	0	0	48	35	26	40	0	3.91
Robinson, Ron-Ronald Dean	84-90CinN 90-92MilA	03-24-62	Exeter, Cal.		R	R	6'5	235	48	39	.552	19	232	102	8	800	819	253	473	2	3.63
Rochford, Mike-Michael Joseph	88-90BosA	03-14-63	Methuen, Mass.		L	L	6'4	205	0	1	.000	0	8	1	0	10	18	9	2	0	9.58
Rocker, John-John Loy	98-01AtlN 01CleA 02TexA 03TBA	10-17-74	Statesboro, Ga.		R	L	6'4	225	13	22	.371	88	280	0	0	255	200	164	332	0	3.42
Rodas, Rich-Richard Martin	83-84LAN	11-07-59	Roseville, Cal.		L	L	6'1	180	0	0	—	0	10	0	0	10	9	4	6	0	3.72
Rodney, Fernando-Fernando	02-03DetA 04EJ 05-06DetA	03-18-77	Santo Domingo, D.R.		R	R	5'11	170	11	13	.458	19	149	0	0	163	150	78	150	0	4.08
Rodriguez, Eddy-Eddy	04,06BalA	08-08-81	San Pedro de Mac., D.R.		R	R	6'1	194	2	1	.667	0	38	0	0	58	53	40	48	0	5.40
Rodriguez, Eduardo-Eduardo [Reyes] (Volanta)	73-78MilA 79KCA	03-06-52	Barceloneta, P.R.		R	R	6'	185	42	36	.538	32	264	39	7	734	681	323	430	1	3.89
Rodriguez, Felix-Felix Antonio	95LAN 97CinN 98AriN 99-04SFN 04PhiN 05NYA 06WasN	09-09-72	Montecristi, D.R.		R	R	6'1	190	38	26	.594	11	563	1	0	586	526	283	512	0	3.71
Rodriguez, Francisco-Francisco Jose (K-Rod)	02-04AnaA 05-06LAA	01-07-82	Caracas, Venezuela		R	R	6'	180	16	12	.571	106	268	0	0	316	201	130	420	0	2.28
Rodriguez, Frankie-Francisco	95BosA 95-98MinA 99-00SeaA 01CinN	12-11-72	Brooklyn, N.Y.		R	R	6'	205	29	39	.426	5	184	82	3	654	737	282	371	0	5.53
Rodriguez, Jose-Jose Ilich [Jose]	00,02StLN 02MinA	12-18-74	Cayey, P.R.		L	L	6'1	205	0	1	.000	0	12	0	0	8	14	9	3	0	9.00
Rodriguez, Nerio-Nerio	96-98BalA 98-99TorA 02CleA 02StLN	03-04-71	San Pedro de Mac., D.R.		R	R	6'1	205	4	6	.400	0	32	7	0	73	80	35	38	0	6.32
Rodriguez, Ricardo-Ricardo Antonio	03-05CleA 03-05TexA	05-21-78	Guayabin, Dom. Rep.		R	R	6'3	195	10	15	.400	0	39	36	1	207	224	75	104	1	5.18
Rodriguez, Rich-Richard Anthony	90-92SDN 93FlaN 94-95StLN 97-99SFN 00NYN 01CleA 02TexA 03AnaA	03-01-63	Downey, Cal.		L	L	6'	200	31	22	.585	8	609	2	0	641	642	261	396	0	3.81
Rodriguez, Rick-Ricardo	86-87OakA 88CleA 90SFN	09-21-60	Oakland, Cal.		R	R	6'3	190	3	4	.429	1	31	8	0	77	97	41	22	0	5.73
Rodriguez, Rosario-Rosario Isabel [Echavarria]	89-90CinN 91PitN	07-08-69	Los Mochis, Mexico		R	L	6'	200	2	2	.500	6	34	0	0	30	32	13	18	0	4.80
Rodriguez, Wandy-Wandy E.	05-06HouN	01-18-79	Santiago Rodriguez, D.R.		B	L	5'11	160	19	20	.487	0	55	46	0	264	289	116	178	0	5.58
Rodriguez, Wilfredo-Wilfredo Jose	01HouN	03-20-79	Ciudad Bolivar, Venezuela		L	L	6'3	180	0	0	—	0	2	0	0	3	6	1	3	0	15.00
Roesler, Mike-Michael Joseph	89CinN 90PitN	09-12-63	Fort Wayne, Ind.		R	R	6'5	195	1	1	.500	0	22	0	0	31	27	11	18	0	3.77
Rogers, Brian-Brian Alan		07-17-82	Dallas, Tex.		R	R	6'4	190	0	0	—	0	10	0	0	9	11	2	7	0	8.31
Rogers, Jimmy-James Randall	95TorA	01-03-67	Tulsa, Okla.		R	R	6'2	190	2	4	.333	1	19	0	0	24	21	18	13	0	5.70
Rogers, Kenny-Kenneth Scott	89-95TexA 96-97NYA 98-99OakA 99NYN 00-02TexA 03MinA 04-05TexA 06DetA	11-10-64	Savannah, Ga.		L	L	6'1	205	207	139	.598	28	721	433	36	3066	3180	1079	1850	9	4.19
Rogers, Kevin-Charles Kevin	92-94SFN 95SJ	08-20-68	Cleveland, Miss.		B	L	6'2	198	2	4	.333	0	79	6	0	125	118	47	95	0	3.17
Rogers, Steve-Stephen Douglas	73-85MonN	10-26-49	Jefferson City, Mo.		R	R	6'1	185	158	152	.510	2	399	393	129	2839	2619	876	1621	37	3.17
Rojas, Mel-Melquiades [Medrano]	90-96MonN 97ChiN 97-98NYN 99LAN 99DetA 99MonN	12-10-66	Haina, Dom. Rep.		R	R	5'11	200	34	31	.523	126	525	0	0	667	591	254	562	0	3.82
Roman, Jose-Jose Rafael [Sarita]	84-86CleA	05-21-63	Puerto Plata, D.R.		R	R	6'	175	1	8	.111	0	14	10	0	44	45	42	24	0	8.12
Romanick, Ron-Ronald James	84-86CalA	11-06-60	Burley, Idaho		R	R	6'4	210	31	29	.517	0	82	82	15	531	574	167	189	4	4.24
Romano, Mike-Michael Desport	99TorA	03-03-72	New Orleans, La.		R	R	6'2	190	0	0	—	0	3	0	0	5	8	5	3	0	11.81
Romero, Davis-Davis Javier [Rodriguez]	06TorA	03-30-83	Aguadulce, Panama		L	L	5'10	170	1	0	1.000	0	7	0	0	16	19	6	10	0	3.86
Romero, J.C.-Juan Carlos	99-05MinA 06LAA	06-04-76	Rio Piedras, P.R.		B	L	5'11	193	26	22	.542	2	392	22	0	456	452	237	367	0	4.60
Romero, Ramon-Ramon [de los Santos]	84-85CleA	01-08-59	San Pedro de Mac, D.R.		L	L	6'4	170	2	3	.400	0	20	10	0	67	69	38	41	0	6.28
Romo, Enrique-Enrique [Navarro] (Huevo)	77-78SeaA 79-82PitN	07-15-47	Santa Rosalia, Mexico		R	R	5'10	180	44	33	.571	52	350	3	0	603	548	203	436	0	3.45
Rondon, Gil-Gilberto	76HouN 79ChiA	11-18-53	Bronx, N.Y.		R	R	6'2	193	2	2	.500	0	23	7	0	64	81	45	24	0	5.34
Roney, Matt-Matthew Stephen	03DetA 06OakA	01-10-80	Tulsa, Okla.		R	R	6'3	230	1	10	.091	0	48	11	0	105	107	49	47	0	5.42
Rooker, Jim-James Phillip	68DetA 69-72KCA 73-80PitN	09-23-42	Lakeview, Ore.		R	L	6'	195	103	109	.486	7	319	255	66	1811	1694	703	976	15	3.46
Roper, John-John Christopher	93-94CinN 95SFN	11-21-71	Southern Pines, N.C.		R	R	6'1	190	8	7	.533	0	35	32	0	180	197	72	111	0	5.35
Roque, Rafael-Rafael Antonio	98-00MilN	01-01-72	Cotui, Dom. Rep.		L	L	6'41	186	5	8	.385	1	56	18	0	138	145	73	104	0	5.36
Rosado, Jose-Jose Antonio	96-00KCA 01SJ	11-09-74	Newark, N.J.		L	L	6'	185	37	45	.451	1	125	112	11	720	715	237	484	2	4.27
Rosario, Francisco-Francisco Alberto [Division]	06TorA	09-28-80	San Rafael del Yuma, D.R.		R	R	6'	195	1	2	.333	0	17	1	0	23	24	16	21	0	6.65
Rosario, Rodrigo-Rodrigo	03HouN	12-14-77	La Romana, D.R.		R	R	6'2	160	1	0	1.000	0	2	2	0	8	5	3	6	0	1.13
Rose, Brian-Brian Leonard	97-00BosA 00ColN 01NYN 01TBA	02-13-76	New Bedford, Mass.		R	R	6'3	215	15	23	.395	0	68	54	0	284	331	110	151	0	5.86
Rosenberg, Steve-Steven Allen	88-90ChiA 91SDN 92SJ	10-31-64	Brooklyn, N.Y.		L	L	6'	185	6	15	.286	1	87	21	2	210	222	87	115	0	4.94
Rosenthal, Wayne-Wayne Scott	91-92TexA	02-19-65	Brooklyn, N.Y.		R	R	6'5	220	1	4	.200	1	42	0	0	75	79	38	62	0	5.40
Ross, Gary-Gary Douglas	68-69ChiN 69-74SDN 75-77CalA	09-16-57	McKeesport,Pa.		R	R	6'1	185	25	47	.347	11	283	59	8	713	764	288	378	2	3.92
Ross, Mark-Mark Joseph	82,84-85HouN 87PitN 88TorA 90PitN	08-08-54	Galveston, Tex.		R	R	6'	195	2	2	.500	1	27	0	0	42	33	10	17	0	3.83
Rosselli, Joe-Joseph Donald	95SFN	05-28-72	Burbank, Cal.		R	L	6'1	170	2	1	.667	0	9	5	0	30	39	20	7	0	8.70
Rothschild, Larry-Lawrence Lee	81-82DetA M98-01TBA	03-12-54	Chicago, Ill.		R	R	6'2	185	0	0	—	0	7	0	0	9	8	8	1	0	5.19
Rowland, Mike-Michael Evan	80-81SFN	01-31-53	Chicago, Ill.		R	R	6'3	205	1	2	.333	0	28	1	0	43	33	14	16	0	2.72
Rozema, Dave-David Scott (Rose)	77-84DetA 85-86TexA	08-05-56	Grand Rapids, Mich.		R	R	6'4	200	60	53	.531	17	248	132	36	1106	1125	258	448	7	3.47
Rucker, Dave-David Michael	81-83DetA 83-84StLN 85-86PhiN 88PitN	09-01-57	San Bernardino, Cal.		L	L	6'1	190	16	20	.444	1	206	10	1	320	337	147	170	0	3.94
Ruebel, Matt-Matthew Alexander	96-97PitN 98TBA	10-16-69	Cincinnati, Ohio		L	L	6'2	180	4	5	.444	1	77	8	0	130	152	56	78	0	5.54
Rueter, Kirk-Kirk Wesley	93-96MonN 96-05SFN	12-01-70	Centralia, Ill.		L	L	6'3	205	130	92	.586	0	340	336	4	1918	2092	582	818	1	4.27
Ruffcorn, Scott-Scott Patrick	93-96ChiA 97PhiN	12-12-69	New Braunfels, Tex.		R	R	6'4	215	0	8	.000	0	30	9	0	70	86	70	46	0	8.57
Ruffin, Bruce-Bruce Wayne	86-91PhiN 92MilA 93-97ColN	10-04-63	Lubbock, Tex.		R	L	6'2	210	60	82	.423	63	469	152	17	1268	1345	565	843	3	4.19
Ruffin, Johnny-Johnny Renando	93-96CinN 97JL 00AriN 01FlaN	07-29-71	Butler, Ala.		R	R	6'3	172	10	6	.625	3	139	0	0	196	187	93	163	0	4.13
Ruhle, Vern-Vernon Gerald	74-77DetA 78-84HouN 85CleA 86CalA	01-25-51	Midland, Mich.		R	R	6'1	190	67	88	.432	11	1327	188	29	1411	1483	348	582	12	3.73
Runyan, Sean-Sean David	98-00DetA	06-21-74	Fort Smith, Ark.		L	L	6'3	210	1	5	.167	1	103	0	0	64	58	33	46	0	3.66
Rupe, Josh-Joshua Matthew	05-06TexA	08-18-82	Portsmouth, Va.		R	R	6'2	190	1	1	.500	0	20	1	0	39	40	13	20	0	3.26
Rupe, Ryan-Ryan Kittman	99-02TBA 03BosA	03-31-75	Houston, Texas		R	R	6'6	240	24	38	.387	0	89	84	2	477	514	162	355	0	5.85
Rusch, Glendon-Glendon James	97-99KCA 99-01NYN 02-03MilN 04-06ChiN	11-07-74	Seattle, Wash.		L	L	6'2	215	60	94	.390	4	296	211	11	1375	1603	432	1020	3	5.01
Ruskin, Scott-Scott Drew	90PitN 90-91MonN 92-93CinN 95-96TexA	06-08-63	Jacksonville, Fla.		R	L	6'1	195	11	9	.550	8	192	0	0	194	191	90	146	0	3.95
Russell, Jeff-Jeffrey Lee	83-84CinN 85-92TexA 92OakA 93-94BosA 94CleA	09-02-61	Cincinnati, Ohio		R	R	6'4	210	56	73	.434	186	589	79	11	1100	1065	415	693	2	3.75
Ruthven, Dick-Richard David	73-75PhiN 76-78AtlN 78-83PhiN 83-86ChiN	03-27-51	Sacramento, Cal.		R	R	6'2	190	123	127	.492	1	355	332	61	2109	2155	767	1145	17	4.14
Ryan, B.J.-Robert Victor Jr. (Bo Junior)	99CinN 99-05BalA 06TorA	12-28-75	Bossier City, La.		L	L	6'6	235	18	21	.462	80	470	0	0	454	349	215	551	0	3.19
Ryan, Jay-Jason Paul	99-00MinA	01-21-76	Long Branch, N.J.		R	R	6'3	195	1	5	.167	0	14	1	0	67	83	27	34	0	5.94
Ryan, Ken-Kenneth Frederick	92-95BosA 96-99PhiN	10-24-68	Pawtucket, R.I.		R	R	6'3	225	14	16	.467	30	240	1	0	286	266	164	225	0	3.91
Ryan, Nolan-Lynn Nolan	66,68-71NYN 72-79CalA 80-88HouN 89-93TexA	01-31-47	Refugio, Tex.		R	R	6'2	205	324	292	.526	3	807	773	222	5386	3923	2795	5714	61	3.19
Ryu, Jae Kuk-Jae Kuk	06ChiN	05-30-83	Choon Chung Do, South Korea		R	R	6'3	220	0	1	.000	0	10	1	0	15	23	6	17	0	8.40
Saarloos, Kirk-Kirk Craig	02-03HouN 04-06OakA	05-23-79	Long Beach, Cal.		R	R	6'	185	27	25	.519	2	123	69	3	440	501	163	212	2	4.79
Sabathia, C.C.-Carsten Charles	01-06CleA	07-21-80	Vallejo, Cal.		L	L	6'7	290	81	56	.591	0	185	185	12	1165	1080	427	933	4	3.95
Sabel, Erik-Erik Douglas	99,01AriN 02DetA	10-14-74	Lafayette, Ind.		R	R	6'3	193	3	2	.600	0	50	0	0	61	71	18	31	0	5.02
Saberhagen, Bret-Bret William	84-91KCA 92-95NYN 95ColN 96SJ 97-99BosA 00SJ 01BosA	04-11-64	Chicago Heights, Ill.		R	R	6'1	195	167	117	.588	1	399	371	76	2563	2452	471	1715	16	3.34
Sackinsky, Brian-Brian Walter	96BalA	06-22-71	Pittsburgh, Pa.		R	R	6'4	220	0	0	—	0	3	0	0	5	5	3	2	0	3.86
Sadler, Billy-William Henry IV	06SFN	09-21-81	Pensacola, Fla.		R	R	6'	190	0	0	—	0	24	0	0	26	23	16	24	0	6.75
Sadler, Carl-William Carl	02-03CleA	10-11-76	Gainesville, Fla.		L	L	6'2	180	1	2	.333	0	42	0	0	30	26	16	33	0	3.60
Sadowski, Jim-James Michael	74PitN	08-07-51	Pittsburgh, Pa.		R	R	6'2	200	0	1	.000	0	9	0	0	9	7	9	1	0	6.00
Saenz, Chris-Christopher Andrew	04MilN	08-14-81	Tucson, Ariz.		R	R	6'1	200	1	0	1.000	0	1	1	0	6	3	1	4	0	1.50
Sager, A.J.-Anthony Joseph	94SDN 95ColN 96-98DetA	03-03-65	Columbus, Ohio		R	R	6'4	220	12	15	.444	5	123	16	0	284	332	99	164	0	5.36
St. Claire, Randy-Randy Anthony	84-88MonN 88CinN 89MinA 91-92AtlN 94TorA	08-23-60	Glens Falls, N.Y.		R	R	6'3	200	12	6	.667	9	162	0	0	252	252	93	160	0	4.14
Saipe, Mike-Michael Eric	98ColN	09-10-73	San Diego, Cali.f		R	R	6'1	190	0	1	.000	0	3	1	0	10	22	0	2	0	10.80
Saito, Takashi-Takashi	06LAN	02-14-70	Miyagi, Japan		R	R	6'2	200	6	2	.750	24	72	0	0	78	48	23	107	0	2.07
Salas, Juan-Juan	06TBA	11-07-78	Santo Domingo, D.R.		R	R	6'2	210	0	0	—	0	10	0	0	13	13	8	8	0	5.40
Salkeld, Roger-Roger William	93-94SeaA 96CinN	03-06-71	Burbank, Cal.		R	R	6'5	215	10	10	.500	0	45	34	1	189	203	103	141	1	5.61
Sambito, Joe-Joseph Charles	76-82HouN 83EJ 84HouN 85NYN 86-87BosA	06-28-52	Brooklyn, N.Y.		L	L	6'	190	37	38	.493	84	461	5	1	629	562	195	489	0	3.03
Sampen, Bill-William Albert	90-92MonN 92-93KCA 94CalA	01-18-63	Lincoln, Ill.		R	R	6'2	190	25	21	.543	2	182	14	0	299	312	133	176	0	3.73
Sampson, Benj-Benjamin Damon	98-99MinA	04-27-75	Des Moines, Iowa		L	L	6'1	205	4	2	.667	0	35	6	0	88	117	40	72	0	6.83
Sampson, Chris-Christopher Keith	06HouN	05-23-78	Pasadena, Tex.		R	R	6'1	190	2	1	.667	0	12	3	0	34	25	5	15	0	2.12
Samuels, Roger-Roger Howard	88SFN 89PitN	01-05-61	San Jose, Cal.		L	L	6'5	208	1	2	.333	1	20	0	0	27	26	11	24	0	4.33
Sanches, Brian-Brian Lee	06TexA	08-08-78	Beaumont, Tex.		R	R	6'2	190	0	0	—	0	10	0	0	16	14	4	9	0	10.13
Sanchez, Alex-Alex Anthony	89TorA	04-08-66	Concord, Cal.		R	R	6'2	195	0	1	.000	0	4	4	0	15	16	14	4	0	10.03
Sanchez, Anibal-Anibal Alejandro	06FlaN	02-27-84	Maracay, Venezuela		R	R	6'	180	10	3	.769	0	18	17	2	114	90	46	72	1	2.83
Sanchez, Duaner-Duaner	02AriN 02-03PitN 04-05LAN 06NYN	10-14-79	Cotui, Dom. Rep.		R	R	6'	190	13	9	.591	8	210	0	0	229	220	95	168	0	3.81
Sanchez, Felix-Felix Antonio	03ChiN	08-03-81	Puerto Plata, Dom. Rep.		R	L	6'3	180	0	0	—	0	3	0	0	2	2	2	2	0	10.80

USE NAMES - GIVEN NAMES (NICKNAMES)	TEAM BY YEAR	BIRTH DATE	BIRTHPLACE	DEATH DATE	B	T	HGT	WGT	W	L	Pct.	SV	G	GS	CG	IP	H	BB	SO	ShO	ERA
Sanchez, Israel-Israel [Matos] (Zip)	88KCA 89EJ 90KCA	08-20-63	Falcon Lasvias, Cuba		L	L	5'9	170	3	2	.600	1	30	1	0	45	52	21	19	0	5.36
Sanchez, Jesus-Jesus Paulino	98-01FlaN 02ChiN 03ColN 04CinN	10-11-74	Nizao, Dom. Rep.		L	L	5'10	160	23	34	.404	0	162	83	2	525	564	281	384	2	5.32
Sanchez, Jonathan-Jonathan O.	06SFN	11-19-82	Mayaguez, P.R.		L	L	6'2	165	3	1	.750	0	27	4	0	40	39	23	33	0	4.95
Sanchez (Escoba), Luis-Luis Mercedes Escoba [Sanchez]	81-85CalA	08-24-53	Cariaco, Venezuela		R	R	6'2	210	28	21	.571	27	194	1	0	370	371	145	216	0	3.75
Sanders, David-David Andrew	03,05ChiA	08-29-79	Oklahoma City, Okla.		L	L	6'	200	0	0	—	0	22	0	0	24	28	12	15	0	6.75
Sanders, Scott-Scott Gerald	93-96SDN 97SeaA 97-98DetA 98SDN 99ChiN	03-25-69	Hannibal, Mo.		R	R	6'4	220	34	45	.430	5	235	88	2	682	674	276	632	1	4.86
Sanderson, Scott-Scott Douglas	78-83MonN 84-89ChiN 90OakA 91-92NYA 93CalA 93SFN 94ChiA 95-96CalA	07-22-56	Dearborn, Mich.		R	R	6'5	200	163	143	.533	5	472	407	43	2562	2580	625	1611	14	3.84
Sanford, Mo-Meredith Leroy	91CinN 93ColN 95MinA	12-24-66	Americus, Ga.		R	R	6'6	225	2	4	.333	0	27	11	0	82	72	58	84	0	4.81
Santana, Ervin-Ervin Ramon	05-06LAA	01-10-83	La Romana, Dom. Rep.		R	R	6'2	160	28	16	.636	0	56	56	1	338	320	117	240	1	4.42
Santana, Johan-Johan Alexander	00-06MinA	03-13-79	Tovar, Venezuela		L	L	6'1	195	78	31	.716	1	218	142	5	1090	885	312	1146	3	3.20
Santana, Julio-Julio Franklin	97-98TexA 98-99TBA 99BosA 00MonN 02DetA 03-04JL 05MilN 06PhiN	01-20-73	San Pedro de Mac, D.R.		R	R	6'0	220	17	31	.354	2	209	42	1	479	518	232	308	0	5.30
Santana, Marino-Marino [Castro]	98DetA 99BosA	05-10-72	San Jose de los Llanos, D.R.		R	R	6'1	190	0	0	—	0	10	0	0	11	17	11	14	0	7.94
Santiago, Jose-Jose Rafael [Fuentes]	97-01KCA 01-02PhiN 03CleA 05NYN	11-05-74	Fajardo, P.R.		R	R	6'3	215	17	22	.436	4	229	0	0	299	336	95	153	0	4.36
Santos, Victor-Victor Irving	01DetA 02ColN 03TexA 04-05MilN 06PitN	10-02-76	San Pedro de Mac., D.R.		R	R	6'3	185	22	42	.344	0	150	84	1	539	604	246	377	0	5.14
Sarfate, Dennis-Dennis Scott	06MilN	04-09-81	Queens, N.Y.		R	R	6'4	210	0	0	—	0	8	0	0	8	9	4	11	0	4.32
Sarmiento, Manny-Manuel Eduardo [Aponte]	76-79CinN 80SeaA 82-83PitN 84EJ	02-02-56	Cagua, Venezuela		R	R	6'	180	26	22	.542	12	228	22	4	514	461	172	283	0	3.48
Sasaki, Kazuhiro-Kazuhiro	00-03SeaA 04JL	02-22-68	Tokyo, Japan		R	R	6'4	209	7	16	.304	129	228	0	0	223	165	77	242	0	3.14
Saucier, Kevin-Kevin Andrew (Hot Sauce)	78-80PhiN 81-82DetA	08-09-56	Pensacola, Fla.		L	R	6'1	190	15	11	.577	19	139	3	0	203	183	104	94	0	3.32
Sauerbeck, Scott-Scott William	99-03PitN 03BosA 05-06CleA 06OakA	11-09-71	Cincinnati, Ohio		R	L	6'3	195	20	17	.541	5	471	0	0	386	344	243	389	0	3.82
Saunders, Joe-Joseph Francis	05-06LAA	06-16-81	Falls Church, Va.		L	L	6'3	210	7	3	.700	0	15	15	0	80	81	33	55	0	5.06
Saunders, Tony-Anthony Scott	97FlaN 98TBA 00BA	04-29-74	Baltimore, Md.		L	L	6'2	205	13	24	.351	0	62	61	2	346	343	204	304	0	4.56
Sauveur, Rich-Richard Daniel	86PitN 88MonN 91NYN 92KCA 96ChiN 00OakA	11-23-63	Arlington, Va.		L	L	6'5	170	0	1	.000	0	34	3	0	46	58	24	28	0	6.07
Savage, Jack-John Joseph	87LAN 90MinA	04-22-64	Louisville, Ky.		R	R	6'1	185	0	2	.000	1	20	0	0	29	41	11	12	0	7.67
Sawyer, Rick-Richard Clyde (Buzz)	75-76NYA 76-77SDN 91-93ChiN 94-95MilA 96DetA 96KCA 98HouN	04-07-48	Bakersfield, Cal.		R	R	6'2	205	12	9	.571	4	74	20	4	201	229	96	82	2	4.48
Scanlan, Bob-Robert Guy	00MilN 01MonN	08-09-66	Los Angeles, Cal.		R	R	6'7	215	20	34	.370	17	290	39	0	537	583	209	245	0	4.63
Scarbery, Randy-Randy James	79-80ChiN	06-22-52	Fresno, Cal.		B	R	6'1	185	3	10	.231	6	60	5	0	130	126	41	63	0	4.50
Scarce, Mac-Guerrant McCurdy	72-74PhiN 75NYN 78KCA	04-08-49	Danville, Va.		L	L	6'3	190	6	19	.240	21	159	0	0	210	192	117	164	0	3.69
Schattinger, Jeff-Jeffrey Charles	81KCA	10-25-55	Fresno, Cal.		L	R	6'5	220	0	0	—	0	1	0	0	3	2	1	1	0	0.00
Schatzeder, Dan-Daniel Ernest	77-79MonN 80-81DetA 82SFN 82-86MonN 86-87PhiN 87MinA 88CleA 88MinA 89-90HouN 90NYN 91KCA	12-01-54	Elmhurst, Ill.		L	L	6'	195	69	68	.504	10	504	121	18	1318	1257	475	748	4	3.74
Scheffer, Aaron-Aaron Alvin Marcus	99SeaA	08-15-75	Ypsilanti, Mich.		L	R	6'2	185	0	0	—	0	4	0	0	5	6	3	4	0	1.93
Scheid, Rich-Richard Paul	92HouN 94-95FlaN	02-03-65	Staten Island, N.Y.		L	L	6'3	185	1	4	.200	0	21	6	0	55	63	21	35	0	4.45
Scherrer, Bill-William Joseph (Cy, Bones)	82-84CinN 84-86DetA 87CinN 88BalA 89PitN 99PhiN	01-20-58	Tonawanda, N.Y.		L	L	6'3	172	8	10	.444	11	228	2	0	311	307	140	207	0	4.08
Schilling, Curt-Curtis Montague	88-90BalA 91HouN 92-00PhiN 00-03AriN 04-06BosA	11-14-66	Anchorage, Alaska		R	R	6'4	225	207	138	.600	22	545	412	82	3110	2833	688	3015	19	3.44
Schiraldi, Calvin-Calvin Drew	84-85NYN 86-87BosA 88-89ChiN 89-90SDN 91TexA	06-16-62	Houston, Tex.		R	R	6'5	215	32	39	.451	21	235	47	2	553	522	267	471	1	4.28
Schmack, Brian-Brian Robert	03DetA	12-07-73	Chicago, Ill.		R	R	6'2	190	1	0	1.000	0	11	0	0	13	14	4	4	0	3.46
Schmidt, Curt-Curtis Allen	95MonN	03-16-70	Miles City, Mont.		R	R	6'6	200	0	0	—	0	10	0	0	10	15	9	7	0	6.97
Schmidt, Dave-David Joseph	81-85TexA 86ChiA 87-89BalA 90-91MonN 92SeaA	04-22-57	Niles, Mich.		R	R	6'1	190	54	55	.495	50	462	63	5	902	962	237	479	3	3.88
Schmidt, Jason-Jason David	95-96AtlN 96-01PitN 01-06SFN	01-29-73	Lewiston, Idaho		R	R	6'5	215	127	90	.585	0	313	304	20	1953	1798	766	1728	9	3.91
Schmidt, Jeff-Jeffrey Thomas	96CalA	02-21-71	Northfield, Minn.		R	R	6'5	205	0	0	1.000	0	9	0	0	8	13	8	2	0	7.88
Schmoll, Steve-Stephen John	05LAN	02-04-80	Silver Spring, Md.		R	R	6'2	200	2	2	.500	3	48	0	0	47	47	22	29	0	5.01
Schneider, Jeff-Jeffrey Theodore	81BalA	12-06-52	Bremerton, Wash.		L	L	6'3	195	0	0	—	1	11	0	0	27	27	12	17	0	4.88
Schoeneweis, Scott-Scott David	99-03AnaA 03-04ChiA 05-06TorA 06CinN	10-02-73	Long Branch, N.J.		L	L	6'	185	43	47	.478	6	374	93	2	819	870	324	466	1	5.01
Schooler, Mike-Michael Ralph	88-92SeaA 93TexA	08-10-62	Anaheim, Cal.		R	R	6'3	220	15	29	.341	98	260	0	0	292	283	103	248	0	3.49
Schourek, Pete-Peter Alan	91-93NYN 94-97CinN 98HouN 98BosA 99PitN 00-01BosA	05-10-69	Austin, Tex.		L	L	6'5	215	66	77	.462	2	288	176	3	1149	1198	420	813	1	4.59
Schrenk, Steve-Steven Wayne	99-00PhiN	11-20-68	Chicago, Ill.		R	R	6'3	215	3	6	.333	1	52	2	0	74	68	27	55	0	5.25
Schroder, Chris-Christopher Keith	06WasN	08-20-78	Okarche, Okla.		R	R	6'3	210	0	2	.000	0	21	0	0	28	23	15	39	0	6.35
Schrom, Ken-Kenneth Marvin	80,82TorA 83-85MinA 86-87CleA	11-23-54	Grangeville, Idaho		R	R	6'2	195	51	51	.500	1	176	137	22	900	963	320	372	3	4.81
Schueler, Ron-Ronald Richard	72-73AtlN 74-76PhiN 77MinA 78-79ChiA	04-18-48	Catherine, Kans.		R	R	6'4	210	40	48	.455	11	291	86	13	914	861	393	563	2	4.08
Schuler, Dave-David Paul	79-80CalA 85AtlN	10-04-53	Framingham, Mass.		R	L	6'3	210	0	1	.000	0	18	0	0	26	34	5	17	0	5.26
Schullstrom, Erik-Erik Paul	94-95MinA	03-25-69	San Diego, Cal.		R	R	6'5	220	0	0	—	1	46	0	0	60	79	27	34	0	6.00
Schulz, Buddy-Charles Budd	75-76ChiN 77-79StLN 80SJ	09-19-50	Cleveland, Ohio		L	R	5'11	170	15	9	.625	12	168	3	0	240	232	88	193	0	3.67
Schulze, Don-Donald Arthur	83-84ChiN 84-86CleA 87NYN 89NYA 89SDN	09-27-62	Roselle, Ill.		R	R	6'4	230	15	25	.375	0	76	59	4	339	422	105	144	0	5.47
Schutz, Carl-Carl James	96AtlN	08-22-71	Hammond, La.		L	L	5'11	205	0	0	—	0	3	0	0	3	3	2	5	0	2.70
Schwabe, Mike-Michael Scott	89-90DetA	07-12-64	Fort Dodge, Iowa		R	R	6'4	200	2	4	.333	0	14	4	0	48	63	16	14	0	5.77
Schwarz, Jeff-Jeffrey William	93-94ChiA	05-20-64	Fort Pierce, Fla.		R	R	6'5	190	2	2	.500	1	54	0	0	69	49	60	59	0	4.17
Scott, Darryl-Darryl Nelson	93CalA	08-06-68	Fresno, Cal.		R	R	6'1	185	1	2	.333	0	10	0	0	20	19	11	13	0	5.85
Scott, Mickey-Ralph Robert	72-73BalA 73MonN 75-77CalA	07-25-47	Weimar, Germany		L	L	6'1	175	8	7	.533	4	133	0	0	172	177	50	70	0	3.71
Scott, Mike-Michael Warren	79-82NYN 83-91HouN	04-26-55	Santa Monica, Cal.		R	R	6'3	215	124	108	.534	3	347	319	45	2068	1858	627	1469	22	3.54
Scott, Tim-Timothy Dale	91-93SDN 93-96MonN 96SFN 97SDN 97ColN	11-16-66	Hanford, Cal.		R	R	6'2	205	24	13	.649	5	276	0	0	314	308	133	253	0	4.13
Scudder, Scott-William Scott	89-91CinN 92-93CleA	02-14-68	Paris, Tex.		R	R	6'2	185	21	34	.382	1	96	64	0	386	395	206	226	0	4.80
Scurry, Rod-Rodney Grant	80-85PitN 85-86NYA 88SeaA	03-17-56	Sacramento, Cal.	11-05-92	L	L	6'2	200	19	32	.373	39	332	7	0	461	384	274	431	0	3.24
Seaman, Kim-Kim Michael	79-80StLN	05-06-57	Pascagoula, Miss.		L	L	6'2	215	3	2	.600	4	27	0	0	26	16	15	13	0	3.12
Seanez, Rudy-Rudy Caballero	89-91CleA 92XJ 93SDN 94-95LAN 98-00AtlN 01SDN 01AtlN 02TexA 03BosA 04FlaN 05SDN 06BosA 06SDN	10-20-68	Brawley, Cal.		R	R	5'10	195	30	23	.566	11	429	0	0	447	399	233	471	0	4.21
Searage, Ray-Raymond Mark	81NYN 84-86MilA 86-87ChiA 89-90LAN	05-01-55	Freeport, N.Y.		L	L	6'	195	11	13	.458	11	254	0	0	288	267	137	193	0	3.50
Searcy, Steve-William Steven	88-91DetA 91-92PhiN	06-04-64	Knoxville, Tenn.		L	L	6'1	190	6	13	.316	0	70	21	1	187	205	119	140	0	5.68
Seaver, Tom-George Thomas (Tom Terrific)	67-77NYN 77-82CinN 83NYN 84-86ChiA 86BosA	11-17-44	Fresno, Cal.		R	R	6'1	200	311	205	.603	1	656	647	231	4783	3971	1390	3640	61	2.86
Seay, Bobby-Robert Michael	01,03-04TBA 05ColN 06DetA	06-20-78	Sarasota, Fla.		L	L	6'3	225	1	1	.500	0	76	0	0	72	73	33	57	0	5.02
Sebra, Bob-Robert Bush	85TexA 86-87MonN 88-89PhiN 89CinN 90MilA	12-11-61	Ridgewood, N.J.		R	R	6'2	200	15	29	.341	0	94	52	7	367	392	149	281	2	4.71
Sedlacek, Shawn-Shawn Patrick	02KCA	06-29-77	Cedar Rapids, Iowa		R	R	6'4	200	3	5	.375	0	84	99	36	52	0	6.72				
Seelbach, Chris-Christopher Don	00-01AtlN	12-18-72	Lufkin, Tex.		R	R	6'4	180	0	1	.000	0	7	0	0	10	12	5	9	0	8.38
Seelbach, Chuck-Charles Frederick	71-74DetA	03-20-48	Lakewood, Ohio		R	R	6'	185	10	8	.556	14	75	3	0	131	118	51	79	0	3.37
Segelke, Herm-Herman Neils	82ChiN	04-24-58	San Mateo, Cal.		R	R	6'4	215	0	0	—	0	3	0	0	4	6	6	4	0	8.31
Segura, Jose-Jose Altagracia [Mota]	88-89ChiA 91SFN	01-26-63	Fundacion, Dom. Rep.		R	R	5'11	180	0	2	.000	0	22	0	0	31	52	16	16	0	9.00
Seibel, Phil-Philip Matthew	04BosA	01-28-79	Louisville, Ky.		L	L	6'1	195	0	0	—	0	2	0	0	4	0	5	1	0	0.00
Sele, Aaron-Aaron Helmer	93-97BosA 98TexA 00-01SeaA 02-04AnaA 05SeaA 06LAN	06-25-70	Golden Valley, Minn.		R	R	6'5	225	145	110	.569	0	370	352	15	2099	2335	777	1378	4	4.59
Sellers, Jeff-Jeffrey Doyle	85-88BosA 89EJ	05-11-64	Compton, Cal.		R	R	6'1	195	13	22	.371	0	61	51	7	330	364	164	226	2	4.97
Sells, Dave-David Wayne	72-75CalA 75LAN	09-18-46	Vacaville, Cal.		R	R	5'11	185	11	7	.611	12	90	0	0	138	146	67	49	0	3.91
Seminara, Frank-Frank Peter	92-93SDN 94NYN	05-16-67	Brooklyn, N.Y.		R	R	6'2	205	12	9	.571	0	47	26	0	164	171	75	90	0	4.12
Senteney, Steve-Stephen Leonard	82TorA	08-07-55	Indianapolis, Ind.	06-18-89	R	R	6'2	205	0	0	—	0	11	0	0	22	23	6	20	0	4.91
Seo, Jae Weong-Jae Weong	02-05NYN 06LAN 06TBA	05-24-77	Kwanju, South Korea		R	R	6'1	215	25	36	.410	0	107	92	1	554	607	168	312	0	4.27
Seoane, Manny-Manuel Modesto	77PhiN 78ChiN	06-26-55	Tampa, Fla.		R	R	6'4	190	1	0	1.000	0	14	22	9	9	0	5.79			
Serafini, Dan-Daniel Joseph	96-98MinA 99ChiN 00SDN 00PitN 03CinN	01-25-74	San Francisco, Cal.		B	L	6'1	195	15	16	.484	1	101	33	1	263	335	116	127	0	5.98
Serrano, Jimmy-James	04KCA	05-09-76	Grand Junction, Colo.		R	R	5'10	170	1	2	.333	0	10	5	0	33	35	12	25	0	4.68
Serrano, Wascar-Wascar Radames	01SDN	06-02-77	Santo Domingo, D.R.		R	R	6'2	178	3	3	.500	0	20	1	0	47	60	21	39	0	6.56
Serum, Gary-Gary Wayne (Truth)	77-79MinA	10-24-56	Fargo, N.D.		R	R	6'2	180	10	12	.455	1	62	28	6	271	303	74	125	1	4.72
Service, Scott-Scott David	88HouN 92MonN 93ColN 93-94CinN 95SFN 96-97CinN 97-99KCA 00OakA 03TorA 04AriN	02-26-67	Cincinnati, Ohio		R	R	6'6	230	20	22	.476	16	338	1	0	416	435	182	413	0	4.99
Shackelford, Brian-Brian Wesley	05-06CinN	08-30-76	McAlester, Okla.		L	L	6'1	195	2	0	1.000	0	63	0	0	46	39	19	32	0	4.11
Shanahan, Greg-Paul Gregory (Shany)	73-74LAN	12-11-47	Eureka, Cal.		R	R	6'2	190	0	0	—	0	23	0	0	39	9	13	0	3.52		
Sharpless, Josh-Joshua David	06PitN	01-26-81	Beaver, Pa.		R	R	6'3	235	0	0	—	0	11	0	0	11	7	11	7	0	1.50
Shaver, Jeff-Jeffrey Thomas (Shave)	88OakA	07-30-63	Beaver, Pa.		R	R	6'3	195	0	0	—	0	1	0	0	3	3	3	0	0.00	
Shaw, Jeff-Jeffrey Lee	90-92CleA 93-95MonN 95ChiA 96-98CinN 98-01LAN	07-07-66	Washington C.H., Ohio		R	R	6'2	195	34	54	.386	203	719	19	0	848	821	234	545	0	3.54
Sheets, Ben-Ben M.	01-06MilN	07-18-78	Baton Rouge, La.		R	R	6'1	215	61	69	.469	0	166	166	11	1088	1083	229	942	1	3.83
Shepherd, Keith-Keith Wayne	92PhiN 93ColN 95BosA 96BalA	01-21-68	Wabash, Ind.		R	R	6'2	205	2	5	.286	3	41	1	0	63	69	30	34	0	6.71
Sherrill, George-George Friederich	04-06SeaA	04-19-77	Memphis, Tenn.		L	L	6'	210	8	8	.500	1	122	0	0	83	67	43	82	0	4.35
Sherrill, Tim-Timothy Shawn	90-91StLN	09-10-65	Harrison, Ark.		L	L	5'11	170	0	0	—	0	18	0	0	19	30	6	10	0	7.71

USE NAMES - GIVEN NAMES (NICKNAMES)	TEAM BY YEAR	BIRTH DATE	BIRTHPLACE	DEATH DATE	B	T	HGT	WGT	W	L	Pct.	SV	G	GS	CG	IP	H	BB	SO	ShO	ERA
Shields, James-James Anthony	06TBA	12-20-81	Newhall, Cal.		R	R	6'4	215	6	8	.429	0	21	21	1	125	141	38	104	0	4.84
Shields, Scot-Robert Scot	01-04AnaA 05-06LAA	07-22-75	Fort Lauderdale, Fla.		R	R	6'1	175	35	29	.547	14	293	14	0	493	410	167	439	0	2.81
Shields, Steve-Stephen Mack	85-86AtlN 86KCA 87SeaA 88NYA 89MinA	11-30-58	Gadsden, Ala.		R	R	6'5	230	8	8	.500	3	10	2	60	219	269	91	126	0	5.26
Shiell, Jason-Jason Alexander	02SDN 03BosA 04EJ 06AtlN	10-19-76	Savannah, Ga.		R	R	6'	180	2	2	.500	1	24	3	0	40	53	29	38	0	6.92
Shifflett, Steve-Stephen Earl	92KCA	01-05-66	Kansas City, Mo.		R	R	6'1	205	1	4	.200	0	34	0	0	52	55	17	25	0	2.60
Shinall, Zak-Zakary Sebastien	93SeaA	10-14-68	St. Louis, Mo.		R	R	6'3	215	0	0	—	0	1	0	0	3	4	2	0	0	3.38
Shipanoff, Dave-David Noel	85PhiN	11-13-59	Edmonton, Canada		R	R	6'2	185	1	2	.333	3	26	0	0	36	33	16	26	0	3.22
Shirley, Bob-Robert Charles	77-80SDN 81StLN 82CinN 83-87NYA 87KCA	06-25-54	Cushing, Okla.		R	L	5'11	185	67	94	.416	18	434	162	16	1431	1432	543	790	2	3.82
Shirley, Steve-Steven Brian	82LAN	10-12-56	San Francisco, Cal.		L	L	6'	175	1	1	.500	0	11	0	0	13	15	7	8	0	4.26
Shouse, Brian-Brian Douglas	93PitN 98BosA 02KCA 03-06TexA 06MilN	09-26-68	Effingham, Ill.		L	L	5'11	180	6	7	.462	3	280	0	0	224	224	83	151	0	3.98
Show, Eric-Eric Vaughn (Django)	81-90SDN 91OakA	05-19-56	Riverside, Cal.	03-16-94	R	R	6'1	190	101	89	.532	7	332	235	35	1655	1526	610	971	11	3.66
Shuey, Paul-Paul Kenneth	94-02CleA 02-03LAN 04RJ	09-16-70	Lima, Ohio		R	R	6'3	215	45	27	.625	22	451	0	0	504	438	256	534	0	3.57
Shumaker, Anthony-Anthony Warren	99PhiN	05-14-73	Tucson, Ariz.		L	L	6'5	225	0	3	.000	0	8	4	0	23	23	14	17	0	5.96
Siebert, Paul-Paul Edward	74-76HouN 77SDN 77-78NYN	06-05-53	Minneapolis, Minn.		L	L	6'2	205	3	8	.273	3	87	7	1	129	130	73	59	1	3.77
Sierra, Candy-Ulises [Pizarro]	88SDN 88CinN	03-27-67	Rio Piedres, P.R.		R	R	6'2	190	0	1	.000	0	16	0	0	28	41	12	24	0	5.53
Sikorski, Brian-Brian Patrick	00TexA 06SDN 06CleA	07-27-74	Detroit, Mich.		R	R	6'1	190	4	5	.444	0	40	5	0	72	82	32	70	0	5.40
Silva, Carlos-Carlos	02-03PhiN 04-06MinA	04-23-79	Bolivar, Venezuela		R	R	6'4	225	42	32	.568	2	226	92	3	743	893	135	306	1	4.35
Silva, Jose-Jose Leonel	96TorA 97-02PitN	12-19-73	Tijuana, Mexico		R	R	6'5	235	25	28	.472	4	154	53	2	427	507	154	298	0	5.41
Simas, Bill-William Anthony	95-00ChiA 01EJ	11-28-71	Hanford, Cal.		L	R	6'3	230	18	19	.486	23	308	0	0	338	332	149	265	0	3.83
Simons, Doug-Douglas Eugene	91NYN 92MonN	09-15-66	Bakersfield, Cal.		L	L	6'	190	2	3	.400	1	49	1	0	66	70	21	44	0	6.68
Simontacchi, Jason-Jason William	02-04StLN 05SJ	11-13-73	Mountain View, Cal.		R	R	6'2	185	20	10	.667	1	83	40	1	285	304	102	149	0	4.77
Simpson, Allan-Larry Allan	04-05ColN 05CinN 06MilN	08-26-77	Springfield, Ill.		R	R	6'4	185	2	2	.500	0	45	0	0	49	51	32	57	0	6.06
Simpson, Wayne-Wayne Kirby	70-72CinN 73KCA 75PhiN 77CalA	12-02-48	Los Angeles, Cal.		R	R	6'3	215	36	31	.537	0	122	107	13	636	606	315	353	2	4.37
Sinclair, Steve-Steven Scott	98-99TorA 99SeaA	08-02-71	Victoria, Canada		L	L	6'2	190	0	3	.000	0	45	0	0	34	35	19	26	0	5.24
Sirotka, Mike-Michael Robert	95-00ChiA 01-02SJ	05-13-71	Chicago, Ill.		L	L	6'1	200	45	42	.517	0	125	111	9	710	803	207	435	1	4.31
Sisco, Andy-Andrew Frank	05-06KCA	01-13-83	Steamboat Springs, Colo.		L	L	6'10	270	3	8	.273	1	132	0	0	134	134	82	128	0	4.85
Sisk, Doug-Douglas Randall	82-87NYN 88BalA 90-91AtlN	09-26-57	Renton, Wash.		R	R	6'2	205	22	20	.524	33	332	0	0	523	527	267	195	0	3.27
Siwy, Jim-James Gerard	82,84ChiA	09-20-58	Pawtucket, R.I.		R	R	6'3	210	0	0	—	0	3	1	0	11	13	7	4	0	7.15
Skalski, Joe-Joseph Douglas	89CleA	09-26-64	Burnham, Ill.		R	R	6'3	190	0	2	.000	0	2	1	0	7	7	4	3	0	6.75
Skok, Craig-Craig Richard	73BosA 76TexA 78-79AtlN	09-01-47	Dobbs Ferry, N.Y.		B	L	6'	190	4	7	.364	5	107	0	0	150	170	58	85	0	4.86
Skrmetta, Matt-Matthew Leland	00MonN 00PitN	11-06-72	Biloxi, Miss.		B	R	6'3	220	2	2	.500	0	14	0	0	15	19	9	11	0	11.66
Slagle, Roger-Roger Lee	79NYA	11-04-53	Wichita, Kans.		B	R	6'3	190	0	0	—	0	3	0	0	3	2	0	2	0	0.00
Slaten, Doug-Douglas	06AriN	02-04-80	Venice, Cal.		L	L	6'5	200	0	0	—	0	9	0	0	6	3	2	3	0	0.00
Slaton, Jim-James Michael	71-77MilA 78DetA 79-83MilA 84-86CalA 86CleA	06-19-50	Long Beach, Cal.		R	R	6'1	190	151	158	.489	14	496	360	86	2683	2773	1004	1191	22	4.03
Slayback, Bill-William Grover	72-74DetA	02-21-48	Hollywood, Cal.		R	R	6'4	200	6	9	.400	0	42	17	3	139	136	51	89	1	3.82
Slocum, Brian-Brian John	06CleA	03-27-81	New Rochelle, N.Y.		R	R	6'4	200	0	0	—	0	8	0	0	18	27	9	11	0	5.60
Slocumb, Heathcliff-Heathcliff	91-92ChiN 93CleA 94-95PhiN 96-97BosA 97-98SeaA 99BalA 99-00StLN 00SDN	06-07-66	Queens, N.Y.		R	R	6'3	220	26	34	.433	97	504	0	0	581	585	334	478	0	3.96
Slusarski, Joe-Joseph Andrew	91-93OakA 95MilA 99-00HouN 01AtlN 01HouN	12-19-66	Indianapolis, Ind.		R	R	6'4	195	13	21	.382	3	118	34	1	306	342	125	173	0	5.18
Small, Aaron-Aaron James	94TorA 95FlaN 96-98OakA 98AriN 02AtlN 04FlaN 05-06NYA	11-23-71	Oxnard, Cal.		R	R	6'5	210	25	13	.658	4	172	15	1	322	380	137	170	1	5.20
Small, Mark-Mark Allen	96HouN	11-12-67	Portland, Ore.		R	R	6'3	205	0	1	.000	0	16	0	0	24	33	13	16	0	5.92
Smart, J.D.-Jon David	99MonN 01TexA	11-12-73	San Saba, Texas		R	R	6'2	185	1	3	.250	0	44	0	0	67	75	21	31	0	5.35
Smiley, John-John Patrick	86-91PitN 92MinA 93-97CinN 97CleA 98BA	03-17-65	Phoenixville, Pa.		L	L	6'5	215	126	103	.550	4	361	280	28	1908	1842	496	1284	8	3.80
Smith, Billy-Billy Lavern (Tex)	81HouN	09-13-54	LaMarque, Tex.		R	R	6'7	220	1	1	.500	1	10	1	0	21	20	3	3	0	3.00
Smith, Brian-Randall Brian	00PitN	07-19-72	Salisbury, N.C.		R	R	5'11	185	0	0	—	0	3	0	0	4	6	2	3	0	10.38
Smith, Bryn-Bryn Nelson	81-89MonN 90-92StLN 93ColN	08-11-55	Marietta, Ga.		R	R	6'2	210	108	94	.535	6	365	255	23	1791	1725	432	1028	8	3.53
Smith, Bud-Robert Allan	01-02StLN 02PhiN	10-23-79	Torrance, Cal.		L	L	6'	170	7	8	.467	0	27	24	1	133	146	46	81	1	4.95
Smith, Chuck-Charles Edward	00-01FlaN	10-21-69	Memphis, Tenn.		R	R	6'1	185	11	11	.500	0	34	34	1	211	200	89	189	0	3.84
Smith, D.W.-David Wayne	84-85CalA	08-30-57	Tomball, Tex.		R	R	6'1	190	0	0	—	0	5	0	0	6	9	1	3	0	9.00
Smith, Dan-Daniel Charles	99MonN 00BosA 02-03MonN 04SJ	09-15-75	Flemington, N.J.		R	R	6'3	210	7	12	.368	2	87	17	0	177	182	81	142	0	5.23
Smith, Dan-Daniel Scott	92,94TexA 95EJ	04-20-69	St. Paul, Minn.		L	L	6'5	190	1	5	.167	0	17	2	0	29	36	20	14	0	4.66
Smith, Daryl-Daryl Clinton	90KCA	07-29-60	Baltimore, Md.		R	R	6'4	185	0	1	.000	0	2	1	0	7	5	4	6	0	4.05
Smith, Dave-David Stanley	80-90HouN 91-92CinN	01-21-55	Richmond, Cal.		R	R	6'1	195	53	53	.500	216	609	1	0	810	700	283	548	0	2.67
Smith, Lee-Lee Arthur	80-87ChiN 88-90BosA 90-93StLN 93NYA 94BalA 95-96CalA 96CinN 97MonN	12-04-57	Shreveport, La.		R	R	6'6	255	71	92	.436	478	1022	6	0	1289	1133	486	1251	0	3.03
Smith, Mark-Mark Christopher	83OakA	11-23-55	Alexandria, Va.		L	R	6'2	215	1	0	1.000	0	8	1	0	15	24	6	10	0	6.75
Smith, Matt-Matthew Joel	06NYA 06PhiN	06-15-79	Las Vegas, Nev.		L	L	6'4	220	0	0	—	0	26	0	0	21	7	12	21	0	0.87
Smith, Mike-Michael Anthony	02TorA 06MinA	09-19-77	Norwood, Mass.		R	R	5'11	195	0	3	.000	0	15	0	0	38	48	23	17	0	7.04
Smith, Mike-Michael Anthony (Mississippi)	84-86CinN 88MonN 89PitN	02-23-61	Jackson, Miss.		B	R	6'1	190	1	1	.500	1	33	1	0	50	55	10	12	0	4.71
Smith, Mike-Michael Anthony (Texas)	89-90BalA	10-31-63	San Antonio, Tex.		R	R	6'3	180	2	0	1.000	0	15	1	0	23	29	15	14	0	8.22
Smith, Pete-Peter John	87-93AtlN 94NYN 95CinN 97-98SDN 98BalA	02-27-66	Abington, Mass.		R	R	6'2	200	47	71	.398	1	231	163	12	1026	1043	404	640	4	4.55
Smith, Roy-Leroy Purdy	84-85CleA 86-90MinA 91BalA	09-06-61	Mt. Vernon, N.Y.		R	R	6'3	205	30	31	.492	1	136	93	4	618	707	202	320	1	4.60
Smith, Roy-Walter Roy	01-02CleA	05-18-76	St. Petersburg, Fla.		R	R	6'6	235	0	0	—	0	13	1	0	22	25	18	19	0	5.24
Smith, Travis-Travis William	98MilN 02StLN 04AtlN 05FlaN 06AtlN	11-07-72	Springfield, Ore.		R	R	5'10	170	6	6	.500	0	42	15	0	112	140	38	69	0	6.53
Smith, Willie-Willie Everett (Big Willie)	94StLN	08-27-67	Savannah, Ga.		R	R	6'5	250	1	1	.500	0	8	0	0	7	9	3	7	0	9.00
Smith, Zane-Zane William	84-89AtlN 89-90MonN 90-94PitN 95BosA 96PitN	12-28-60	Madison, Wis.		L	L	6'2	200	100	115	.465	3	360	291	35	1919	1980	583	1011	16	3.74
Smithberg, Roger-Roger Craig	93-94OakA	03-21-66	Elgin, Ill.		R	R	6'3	205	1	2	.333	3	15	0	0	22	19	8	7	0	4.09
Smithson, Mike-Mike (Snuffy)	82-83TexA 84-87MinA 88-89BosA	01-21-55	Centerville, Tex.		R	R	6'8	215	76	86	.469	2	240	204	41	1357	1473	383	731	6	4.58
Smoltz, John-John Andrew	88-99AtlN 00EJ 01-06AtlN	05-15-67	Detroit, Mich.		R	R	6'3	210	193	137	.585	154	670	429	53	3161	2758	937	2778	16	3.27
Smyth, Steve-Steven Delton	02ChiN	06-03-78	Brawley, Cal.		L	L	6'1	200	1	3	.250	0	8	1	0	26	34	10	16	0	9.35
Snare, Ryan-Ryan Delbert	04TexA	02-08-79	Clearwater, Fla.		L	L	6'	190	0	0	—	0	1	0	0	3	5	2	0	0	10.80
Snell, Ian-Ian Dante	04-06PitN	10-30-81	Dover, Del.		R	R	5'11	170	15	14	.517	0	50	38	0	240	255	107	212	0	4.95
Snell, Nate-Nathaniel	84-86BalA 87DetA	09-02-52	Orangeburg, S.C.		R	R	6'4	190	7	6	.538	5	104	2	0	219	216	72	96	0	3.29
Snook, Frank-Frank Walter (Snooker)	73SDN	03-28-49	Somerville, N.J.		R	R	6'2	180	0	2	.000	1	18	0	0	27	19	18	13	0	3.67
Snyder, Brian-Brian Robert	85SeaA 89OakA	02-20-58	Flemington, N.J.		L	L	6'3	185	1	2	.333	1	17	6	0	36	46	21	24	0	6.75
Snyder, John-John Michael	98-99ChiA 00MilN	08-16-74	Southfield, Mich.		R	R	6'3	200	19	24	.442	0	63	62	2	343	410	149	188	0	6.01
Snyder, Kyle-Kyle Ehren	03KCA 04SJ 05-06KCA 06BosA	09-09-77	Houston, Tex.		R	R	6'8	220	6	14	.300	0	45	29	0	182	236	51	115	0	5.94
Sobkowiak, Scott-Scott	01AtlN	10-26-77	Woodstock, Ill.		R	R	6'5	230	0	0	—	0	1	0	0	1	2	0	0	0	9.00
Soderstrom, Steve-Stephen Andrew	96SFN	04-03-72	Turlock, Cal.		R	R	6'3	215	2	0	1.000	0	3	3	0	14	16	6	9	0	5.27
Sodowsky, Clint-Clint Ray	95-96DetA 97PitN 98AriN 99StLN	07-13-72	Ponca City, Okla.		R	R	6'3	195	8	14	.364	0	106	20	0	184	214	117	118	0	6.17
Soff, Ray-Raymond John	86-87StLN	10-31-58	Adrian, Mich.		R	R	6'	185	2	2	.714	4	42	0	0	54	55	18	31	0	4.19
Solano (Mercado), Julio-Julio Cesar Mercado [Solano]	83-87HouN 88-89SeaA	01-08-60	Agua Blanca, D.R.		R	R	6'1	170	6	8	.429	3	106	1	0	174	162	82	102	0	4.55
Soler, Alay-Alain	06NYN	10-09-79	Pinar Del Rio, Cuba		R	R	6'1	240	2	3	.400	0	8	8	0	45	50	21	23	1	6.00
Solomon, Eddie-Eddie (King) (Played as Buddy Solomon 78-79)	73-74LAN 75CinN 76StLN 77-79AtlN 80-82PitN 82ChiA	02-09-51	Perry, Ga.	01-12-86	R	R	6'3	205	36	42	.462	4	191	95	8	719	764	247	337	0	3.99
Soriano, Rafael-Rafael	02-06SeaA	12-19-79	San Jose, Dom. Rep.		R	R	6'1	175	4	8	.333	4	116	4	0	171	134	53	177	0	2.89
Sorensen, Lary-Lary Alan	77-80MilA 81StLN 82-83CleA 84OakA 85ChiN 87MonN 88SFN	10-04-55	Detroit, Mich.		R	R	6'2	205	93	103	.474	6	346	235	69	1736	1960	402	569	10	4.15
Sosa, Elias-Elias [Martinez]	72-74SFN 75StLN 75-76AtlN 76-77LAN 78OakA 79-81MonN 82DetA 83SDN	06-10-50	La Vega, Dom. Rep.		R	R	6'2	198	59	51	.536	83	601	3	0	919	873	334	538	0	3.32
Sosa, Jorge-Jorge Bolivar	02-04TBA 05-06AtlN 06StLN	04-28-77	Santo Domingo, D.R.		R	R	6'2	180	27	40	.403	5	192	74	1	579	585	272	374	1	4.61
Sosa (Ynocencio), Jose-Jose Ynocencio [Sosa]	75-76HouN	12-28-52	Santo Domingo, D.R.		R	R	6'	190	1	3	.250	1	34	2	0	59	67	29	36	0	4.59
Soto, Mario-Mario Melvin	77-88CinN	07-12-56	Bani, Dom. Rep.		R	R	6'	190	100	92	.521	4	297	224	72	1731	1395	657	1449	13	3.47
Souza, Mark-Kenneth Mark	80OakA	02-01-55	Redwood City, Cal.		L	L	6'2	185	0	0	—	0	7	0	0	9	5	2	7	0	7.71
Sowers, Jeremy-Jeremy Bryan	06CleA	05-17-83	Wheeling, W.Va.		L	L	6'1	180	7	4	.636	0	14	14	2	88	85	20	35	2	3.57
Sparks, Jeff-James Jeffrey	99TBA	04-24-72	Houston, Texas		R	R	6'2	220	0	1	.000	0	23	0	0	30	19	30	41	0	4.15
Sparks, Steve-Steven William	95-96MilA 97EJ 98-99AnaA 00-02DetA 03DetA 03OakA 04AriN	07-02-65	Tulsa, Okla.		R	R	6'	185	59	76	.437	2	270	182	16	1320	1451	520	658	2	4.88
Sparks, Steve-Stephen Lanier	00PitN	03-28-75	Mobile, Ala.		R	R	6'4	210	0	0	—	0	4	0	0	4	5	2	6	0	6.75

USE NAMES - GIVEN NAMES (NICKNAMES)	TEAM BY YEAR	BIRTH DATE	BIRTHPLACE	DEATH DATE	B	T	HGT	WGT	W	L	Pct.	SV	G	GS	CG	IP	H	BB	SO	ShO	ERA
Speck, Cliff-Robert Clifford	86AtlN	08-08-56	Portland, Ore.		R	R	6'4	195	2	1	.667	0	13	1	0	28	25	15	21	0	4.13
Speier, Justin-Justin James	98ChiN 98FlaN 99AtlN 00-01ColN 01-03ColA 04-06TorA	11-06-73	Daly City, Cal.		R	R	6'4	205	27	20	.574	17	459	0	0	517	463	177	446	0	4.02
Speier, Ryan-Ryan Andrew	05ColN	07-24-79	Frankfort, Ky.		R	R	6'7	200	2	1	.667	0	22	0	0	25	26	13	10	0	3.65
Spencer, Sean-Sean James	99SeaA 00MonN	05-29-75	Seattle, Wash.		L	L	5'11	185	0	0	—	0	10	0	0	8	12	6	8	0	8.64
Spencer, Stan-Stanley Roger	98-00SDN	08-02-68	Vancouver, Wash.		R	R	6'4	205	3	9	.250	0	23	21	0	119	129	34	107	0	5.54
Spillner, Dan-Daniel Ray	74-78SDN 78-84CleA 84-85ChiA	11-27-51	Casper, Wyo.		R	R	6'1	195	76	89	.457	50	556	123	19	1493	1585	605	878	5	4.21
Splittorff, Paul-Paul William	70-84KCA	10-08-46	Evansville, Ind.		L	L	6'3	205	166	143	.537	1	429	392	88	2555	2644	780	1057	17	3.81
Spoljaric, Paul-Paul Nikola	94,96-97TorA 97-98SeaA 99PhiN 99TorA 00KCA	09-24-70	Kelowna, Canada		R	L	6'3	205	8	17	.320	4	195	12	0	277	275	163	278	0	5.52
Spooneybarger, Tim-Timothy Floyd	01-02AtlN 03FlaN 04-05EJ	10-21-79	San Diego, Cal.		R	R	6'3	190	2	3	.400	1	88	0	0	97	70	39	68	0	3.24
Spradlin, Jerry-Jerry Carl	93-94,96CinN 97-98PhiN 99CleA 99SFN 00KCA 00ChiN	08-14-67	Fullerton, Cal.		B	R	6'7	240	17	19	.472	11	310	0	0	372	371	122	292	0	4.75
Sprague, Ed-Edward Nelson	68-69OakA 71-73CinN 73StLN 73-76MilA 00NYN 01-02LAN	09-16-45	Boston, Mass.		R	R	6'1	200	17	23	.425	9	198	23	3	409	406	206	188	0	3.83
Springer, Dennis-Dennis Leroy	95PhiN 96CalA 97AnaA 98TBA 99FlaN	02-12-65	Fresno, Cal.		R	R	5'10	185	24	48	.333	1	130	98	9	655	702	258	296	4	5.18
Springer, Russ-Russell Paul	92NYA 93-95CalA 95-96PhiN 97HouN 98AriN 98-00AtlN 01AriN 03StLN 04-06HouN	11-07-68	Alexandria, La.		R	R	6'4	215	25	39	.391	8	518	27	1	681	674	295	605	0	4.94
Sprowl, Bobby-Robert John	78BosA 79-81HouN	04-14-56	Sandusky, Ohio		L	L	6'2	195	0	3	.000	0	22	4	0	47	54	27	34	0	5.36
Spurgeon, Jay-Jay Aaron	00BalA	07-05-76	West Covina, Cal.		R	R	6'6	211	1	1	.500	0	7	4	0	24	26	15	11	0	6.00
Spurling, Chris-Christopher Michael	03DetA 04EJ 05-06DetA 06MilN	06-28-77	Dayton, Ohio		R	R	6'6	240	4	7	.364	3	138	0	0	169	161	52	71	0	4.21
Stablein, George-George Charles	80SDN	10-29-57	Inglewood, Cal.		R	R	6'	190	0	1	.000	0	4	2	0	12	16	3	4	0	3.00
Standridge, Jason-Jason Wayne	01-04TBA 05TexA 05-06CinN	11-09-78	Birmingham, Ala.		R	R	6'4	225	3	8	.273	0	76	9	1	120	140	69	74	0	5.64
Stanfield, Kevin-Kevin Bruce	79MinA	12-09-55	Huron, S.D.		L	L	6'1	190	0	0	—	0	3	0	0	3	2	0	0	0	6.00
Stanford, Jason-Jason John	03-04CleA 05EJ	01-23-77	Tucson, Ariz.		L	L	6'2	200	1	4	.200	0	15	10	0	61	60	21	35	0	3.10
Stanhouse, Don-Donald Joseph	72-74TexA 75-77MonN 78-79BalA 80LAN 82BalA	02-12-51	Du Quoin, Ill.		R	R	6'3	195	38	54	.413	64	294	66	11	760	707	455	408	2	3.84
Stanifer, Rob-Robert Wayne	97-98FlaN 00BosA	03-10-72	Easley, S.C.		R	R	6'3	205	3	6	.333	2	82	0	0	106	119	42	61	0	5.43
Stanley, Bob-Robert William (Big Foot, Steamer)	77-89BosA	11-10-54	Portland, Maine		R	R	6'4	225	115	97	.542	132	637	85	21	1708	1858	471	693	7	3.64
Stanton, Mike-Michael Thomas	75HouN 80-81CleA 82-85SeaA 85ChiA	09-25-52	St. Louis, Mo.		R	R	6'3	200	13	22	.371	31	277	3	0	384	398	182	304	0	4.62
Stanton, Mike-William Michael	89-95AtlN 95-96BosA 96TexA 97-02NYA 03-04NYN 05NYA 05WasN 05BosA 06WasN 06SFN	06-02-67	Houston, Tex.		L	L	6'1	205	67	60	.528	84	1109	1	0	1056	1011	402	855	0	3.81
Stapleton, Dave-David Earl	87-88MilA	10-16-61	Miami, Ariz.		L	L	6'1	185	2	0	1.000	0	10	0	0	28	33	12	20	0	3.81
Stark, Dennis-Dennis James	99,01SeaA 02-04ColN	10-27-74	Hicksville, Ohio		R	R	6'2	210	15	13	.536	0	64	42	0	254	290	123	120	0	5.78
Stauffer, Tim-Timothy James	05-06SDN	06-02-82	Portland, Maine		R	R	6'1	215	4	6	.400	0	16	15	0	87	95	30	51	0	5.07
Stechschulte, Gene-Gene Urban	00-02StLN 03SJ	08-12-73	Lima, Ohio		R	R	6'5	210	8	7	.533	6	116	0	0	128	122	64	84	0	4.58
Steenstra, Kennie-Kenneth Gregory	98ChiN	10-13-70	Springfield, Mass.		R	R	6'5	220	0	0	—	0	4	0	0	3	7	1	4	0	10.80
Stein, Blake-William Blake	98-99OakA 99-02KCA	08-03-73	McComb, Miss.		R	R	6'7	240	21	28	.429	2	117	66	2	476	451	281	369	1	5.41
Stein, Randy-William Randolph	78MilA 79,81SeaA 82ChiN	03-07-53	Pomona, Cal.		R	R	6'4	210	5	6	.455	1	65	2	0	133	151	81	93	0	5.75
Steiner, Rick-Ricky Francis (Sly)	82-84CalA	08-27-56	Baltimore, Md.		R	R	6'	200	4	3	.571	0	30	7	0	91	108	31	41	0	4.85
Stember, Jeff-Jeffrey Alan (Stems)	80SFN	03-02-58	Elizabeth, N.J.		R	R	6'5	220	0	0	—	0	1	1	0	3	2	2	0	0	3.00
Stemle, Steve-Stephen Joseph	05-06KCA	05-20-77	Louisville, Ky.		R	R	6'4	200	1	0	1.000	0	17	0	0	17	25	7	9	0	8.64
Stephens, John-John M.	02BalA	11-15-79	Sydney, Australia		R	R	6'1	204	2	5	.286	0	12	11	0	65	68	22	56	0	6.09
Stephenson, Garrett-Garrett Charles	96BalA 97-98PhiN 99-00StLN 01EJ 02-03StLN	01-02-72	Takoma Park, Md.		R	R	6'4	205	39	39	.500	0	123	104	6	651	662	237	408	2	4.55
Sterling, Randy-Randall Wayne	74NYN	04-21-51	Key West, Fla.		R	R	6'3	195	1	1	.500	0	3	2	0	9	13	3	2	0	5.00
Stevens, Dave-David James	94-97MinA 97-98ChiN 99CleA 00AtlN	03-04-70	Fullerton, Cal.		R	R	6'3	210	15	16	.484	21	183	6	0	251	298	132	170	0	6.02
Stewart, Dave-David Keith (Smoke)	78,81-83LAN 83-85TexA 85-86PhiN 86-92OakA 93-94TorA 95OakA	02-19-57	Oakland, Cal.		R	R	6'2	200	168	129	.566	19	523	348	55	2630	2499	1034	1741	9	3.95
Stewart, Josh-Joshua Craig	03-04ChiA	12-05-78	Paducah, Ky.		L	L	6'3	200	1	3	.250	0	8	7	0	33	44	19	18	0	8.10
Stewart, Sammy-Samuel Lee	78-85BalA 86BosA 87CleA	10-28-54	Asheville, N.C.		R	R	6'3	205	59	48	.551	45	359	25	4	957	863	502	586	1	3.59
Stewart, Scott-Scott Edward	01-03MonN 04CleA 04LAN	08-14-75	Stoughton, Mass.		R	L	6'2	225	11	6	.647	20	214	0	0	181	187	60	161	0	3.99
Stidham, Phil-Phillip Wayne	94DetA	11-18-68	Tulsa, Okla.		R	R	6'	180	0	0	—	0	5	0	0	4	12	4	4	0	24.92
Stieb, Dave-David Andrew	79-92TorA 93ChiA 98TorA	07-22-57	Santa Ana, Cal.		R	R	6'	195	176	137	.562	3	443	412	103	2895	2572	1034	1669	30	3.44
Stockman, Phil-Phillip Matthew	06AtlN	01-25-80	Oldham, England		R	R	6'8	250	0	0	—	0	4	0	0	4	3	4	4	0	2.25
Stoddard, Bob-Robert Lyle	81-84SeaA 85DetA 86SDN 87KCA	03-08-57	San Jose, Cal.		R	R	6'2	200	18	27	.400	3	119	45	5	433	437	160	223	2	4.03
Stoddard, Tim-Timothy Paul (Big Foot)	75ChiA 78-83BalA 84ChiN 85-86SDN 86-88NYA 89CleA	01-24-53	East Chicago, Ind.		R	R	6'7	250	41	35	.539	76	485	0	0	729	680	356	582	0	3.95
Stokes, Brian-Brian Alexander	06TBA	09-07-79	Ponoma, Cal.		R	R	6'3	205	1	0	1.000	0	5	4	0	24	31	9	15	0	4.88
Stone, Ricky-Ricky L.	01-04HouN 04SDN 05CinN	02-28-75	Hamilton, Ohio		R	R	6'1	185	11	9	.550	2	215	0	0	250	276	90	167	0	4.57
Stone, Steve-Steven Michael	71-72SFN 73ChiA 74-76ChiN 77-78ChiA 79-81BalA 82EJ	07-14-47	Euclid, Ohio		R	R	5'10	175	107	93	.535	1	320	269	43	1789	1707	716	1065	7	3.96
Stoops, Jim-James Wellington	98ColN	06-30-72	Edison, N.J.		R	R	6'2	180	1	0	1.000	0	3	0	0	4	5	3	0	0	2.25
Stottlemyre, Mel-Melvin Leon Jr.	90KCA	12-28-63	Prosser, Wash.		R	R	6'	190	0	1	.000	0	13	2	0	31	35	12	14	0	4.88
Stottlemyre, Todd-Todd Vernon	88-94TorA 95OakA 96-98StLN 98TexA 99-00AriN 01SJ 02AriN	05-20-65	Sunnyside, Wash.		L	R	6'3	210	138	121	.533	1	372	339	25	2192	2200	816	1587	6	4.28
Straker, Les-Lester Paul [Bolnalda]	87-88MinA	10-10-59	Ciudad Bolivar, Venez.		R	R	6'1	190	10	15	.400	1	47	40	2	237	236	84	99	1	4.22
Strange, Pat-Patrick Martin	02-03NYN	08-23-80	Springfield, Mass.		R	R	6'5	243	0	0	—	0	11	0	0	17	19	12	9	0	6.35
Street, Huston-Huston Lowell	05-06OakA	08-02-83	Austin, Tex.		R	R	6'	190	9	5	.643	60	136	0	0	149	117	39	139	0	2.48
Strickland, Jim-James Michael	71-73MinA 75CleA	06-12-46	Los Angeles, Cal.		L	L	6'	175	4	2	.667	5	60	0	0	77	63	44	60	0	2.69
Strickland, Scott-Scott Michael	99-02MonN 03NYN 04EJ 05HouN	06-16-76	Houston, Texas		R	R	5'11	180	12	21	.364	20	236	0	0	240	201	111	243	0	3.34
Strom, Brent-Brent Terry	72NYN 73CleA 75-77SDN	10-14-48	San Diego, Cal.		R	L	6'3	190	22	39	.361	0	100	75	16	501	482	180	278	3	3.95
Strong, Joe-Joseph Benjamin	00-01FlaN	09-09-62	Fairfield, Cal.		B	R	6'	200	1	1	.500	1	23	0	0	26	29	15	22	0	5.81
Stull, Everett-Everett James	97MonN 99AtlN 00MilN 01SJ 02MilN	08-24-71	Fort Riley, Kans.		R	R	6'3	200	2	5	.286	0	26	6	0	57	65	45	42	0	6.59
Stults, Eric-Eric William	06LAN	12-09-79	Plymouth, Ind.		L	L	6'	215	1	0	1.000	0	6	2	0	18	17	7	5	0	5.60
Stuper, John-John Anton	82-84StLN 85CinN	05-09-57	Butler, Pa.		R	R	6'2	198	32	28	.533	1	111	76	9	495	528	183	191	1	3.96
Sturtze, Tanyon-Tanyon James	95-96ChiN 97TexA 99-00ChiA 00-02TBA 03TorA 04-06NYA	10-12-70	Worcester, Mass.		R	R	6'5	200	40	44	.476	3	269	84	4	795	885	332	479	0	5.21
Sullivan, Scott-William Scott	95-03CinN 03ChiA 04KCA 05XJ	05-13-71	Carrollton, Ala.		R	R	6'3	210	40	28	.588	9	558	0	0	737	671	281	622	0	3.98
Suppan, Jeff-Jeffrey Scot	95-97BosA 98AriN 98-00-02KCA 03PitN 03BosA 04-06StLN	01-02-75	Oklahoma City, Okla.		R	R	6'1	210	106	101	.512	0	317	301	15	1865	2029	612	1048	5	4.60
Surhoff, Rick-Richard Clifford	85PhiN 85TexA	10-03-62	Bronx, N.Y.		R	R	6'3	215	1	1	.500	2	9	0	0	14	16	3	6	0	6.75
Sutcliffe, Rick-Richard Lee	76,78-81LAN 82-84CleA 84-91ChiN 92-93BalA 94StLN	06-21-56	Independence, Mo.		L	R	6'7	230	171	139	.552	6	457	392	72	2698	2662	1081	1679	18	4.08
Sutter, Bruce-Howard Bruce	76-80ChiN 81-84StLN 85-86AtlN 87SJ 88AtlN 89SJ	01-08-53	Lancaster, Pa.		R	R	6'2	190	68	71	.489	300	661	0	0	1042	879	309	861	0	2.83
Sutton, Don-Donald Howard	66-80LAN 81-82HouN 82-84MilA 85OakA 85-87CalA 88LAN	04-02-45	Clio, Ala.		R	R	6'1	190	324	256	.559	5	774	756	178	5282	4692	1343	3574	58	3.26
Sutton, Johnny-Johnny Ike (Ike)	77StLN 78MinA	11-13-52	Dallas, Tex.		R	R	5'11	185	2	1	.667	0	31	0	0	68	74	24	27	0	3.18
Suzuki, Mac-Makoto	96,98-99SeaA 99-01KCA 01ColN 01MilN 02KCA	05-31-75	Kobe, Japan		R	R	6'3	200	16	31	.340	0	117	67	1	466	501	265	327	1	5.72
Swaggerty, Bill-William David	83-86BalA	12-05-56	Sanford, Fla.		R	R	6'2	190	4	3	.571	0	32	8	0	81	100	30	28	0	4.76
Swan, Craig-Craig Steven	73-84NYN 84CalA	11-30-50	Van Nuys, Cal.		R	R	6'3	215	59	72	.450	2	231	185	25	1234	1199	368	673	7	3.75
Swan, Russ-Russell Howard	89-90SFN 90-93SeaA 94CleA	01-03-64	Fremont, Cal.	04-26-06	L	L	6'4	210	14	22	.389	11	168	20	1	267	282	124	108	0	4.83
Swartzbaugh, Dave-David Theodore	95-97ChiN	02-11-68	Middletown, Ohio		R	R	6'2	195	0	3	.000	0	15	7	0	39	43	24	22	0	5.72
Sweeney, Brian-Brian Edward	03SeaA 04,06SDN	06-13-74	Yonkers, N.Y.		R	R	6'3	195	3	0	1.000	2	49	2	0	80	80	19	40	0	3.49
Swift, Bill-William Charles	85-86,88-91SeaA 92-94SFN 95-97ColN 98SeaA	10-27-61	Portland, Maine		R	R	6'	190	94	78	.547	27	403	220	11	1600	1688	507	767	4	3.95
Swindell, Greg-Forest Gregory	86-91CleA 92CinN 93-96HouN 96CleA 97-98MinA 98BosA 99-02AriN	01-02-65	Fort Worth, Tex.		R	L	6'2	225	123	122	.502	7	664	269	40	2233	2313	501	1542	12	3.86
Swingle, Paul-Paul Christopher	93CalA 94SJ	12-21-66	Inglewood, Cal.		R	R	6'	185	0	1	.000	0	10	0	0	10	15	6	6	0	8.38
Switzer, Jon-Jon Michael	03,05-06TBA	08-13-79	Bowling Green, Ky.		L	L	6'2	190	2	2	.500	0	47	6	0	47	56	29	30	0	5.32
Sykes, Bob-Robert Joseph	77-78DetA 79-81StLN	12-11-54	Neptune, N.J.		B	L	6'2	200	23	26	.469	2	116	61	10	457	497	190	215	5	4.65
Szuminski, Jason-Jason Ernest	04SDN	12-11-78	San Diego, Cal.		R	R	6'4	221	0	0	—	0	7	0	0	7	10	11	5	0	7.20
Tabaka, Jeff-Jeffrey Jon	94PitN 94-95SDN 95-96HouN 97CinN 98PitN 99EJ 01StLN	01-17-64	Barberton, Ohio		R	L	6'2	195	6	5	.545	2	139	0	0	148	131	82	119	0	4.31
Tadano, Kazuhito-Kazuhito Antanacio	04-05CleA	04-25-80	Tokyo, Japan		R	R	6'	180	1	1	.500	0	15	4	0	54	59	18	40	0	4.47
Takatsu, Shingo-Shinjo (Mr. Zero)	04-05ChiA 05NYN	11-25-68	Hiroshima, Japan		R	R	6'	180	8	6	.571	27	99	0	0	99	81	40	88	0	3.38
Tallet, Brian-Brian Curtis	02-03CleA 05CleA 06TorA	09-21-77	Midwest City, Okla.		L	L	6'7	206	4	2	.667	0	53	6	0	90	83	46	63	0	3.90
Tam, Jeff-Jeffrey Eugene	98NYN 99CleA 99NYN 00-02OakA 03TorA	08-19-70	Fullerton, Cal.		R	R	6'1	202	7	14	.333	9	251	0	0	271	289	98	146	0	3.91
Tanana, Frank-Frank Daryl	73-80CalA 81BosA 82-85TexA 85-92DetA 93NYN 93NYA	07-03-53	Detroit, Mich.		L	L	6'3	205	240	236	.504	1	638	616	143	4188	4063	1255	2773	34	3.66

USE NAMES - GIVEN NAMES (NICKNAMES)	TEAM BY YEAR	BIRTH DATE	BIRTHPLACE	DEATH DATE	B	T	HGT	WGT	W	L	Pct.	SV	G	GS	CG	IP	H	BB	SO	ShO	ERA
Tankersley, Dennis-Dennis Lee	02-04SDN	02-24-79	Troy, Mo.		R	R	6'2	185	1	10	.091	0	27	16	0	86	97	61	68	0	7.61
Tankersley, Taylor-Taylor Mark	06FlaN	03-07-83	Vicksburg, Miss.		L	L	6'1	220	2	1	.667	3	49	0	0	41	33	26	46	0	2.85
Tanner, Bruce-Bruce Mathew	85ChiA	12-09-61	New Castle, Pa.		R	R	6'3	220	1	2	.333	0	10	4	0	29	34	13	9	0	5.33
Tapani, Kevin-Kevin Ray	89NYN 89-95MinA 95LAN 96-98ChiA 99-01ChiN	02-18-64	Des Moines, Iowa		R	R	6'	187	143	125	.534	0	361	354	26	2265	2407	554	1482	9	4.35
Taschner, Jack-Jack Gerard	05-06SFN	04-21-78	Milwaukee, Wis.		L	L	6'3	190	2	1	.667	0	48	0	0	42	46	20	34	0	4.71
Tata, Jordan-Jordan Arthur	06DetA	09-20-81	Plano, Tex.		R	R	6'6	220	0	0	—	0	15	14	7	6	0	6.14
Tate, Randy-Randall Lee	75NYN	10-23-52	Florence, Ala.		R	R	6'3	195	5	13	.278	0	26	23	2	138	121	86	99	0	4.43
Tate, Stu-Stuart Douglas	89SFN	06-17-62	Huntsville, Ala.		R	R	6'3	205	0	0	—	0	2	0	0	3	3	0	4	0	3.38
Tatis, Ramon-Ramon Francisco [Medrano]	97ChiN 98TBA	01-05-73	Guayabin, Dom. Rep.		L	L	6'2	200	1	1	.500	0	78	0	0	67	89	45	38	0	6.82
Taubenheim-Ty-Ty Andrew	06TorA	11-17-82	Bellingham, Wash.		R	R	6'6	250	1	5	.167	0	12	7	0	35	40	18	26	0	4.89
Tavarez, Julian-Julian [Carmen]	93-96CleA 97-99SFN 00ColN 01ChiN 02FlaN 03PitN 04-05StLN 06BosA	05-22-73	Santiago, Dom. Rep.		L	R	6'2	190	77	59	.566	22	700	85	2	1180	1282	457	682	0	4.34
Taylor, Aaron-Aaron Wade	02-04SeaA	08-05-76	Valdosta, Ga.		R	R	6'5	235	0	0	—	0	20	0	0	21	30	9	19	0	8.86
Taylor, Billy-William Howell	94,96-99OakA 99NYN 00TBA 01PitN	10-16-61	Monticello, Fla.		R	R	6'8	225	16	28	.364	100	317	0	0	325	314	133	307	0	4.21
Taylor, Bruce-Bruce Bell	77-79DetA	04-16-53	Holden, Mass.		R	R	6'	180	2	2	.500	2	30	0	0	49	39	17	27	0	3.86
Taylor, Dorn-Donald Clyde	87,89PitN 90BalA	08-11-58	Abington, Pa.		R	R	6'2	195	3	5	.375	2	27	8	0	68	66	35	44	0	5.45
Taylor, Kerry-Kerry Thomas	93-94SDN	01-25-71	Bemidji, Minn.		R	R	6'2	195	0	5	.000	0	37	8	0	73	81	50	48	0	6.56
Taylor, Scott-Scott Ray	92-93BosA	08-02-67	Defiance, Ohio		L	L	6'1	190	1	2	.333	0	20	1	0	26	27	16	15	0	6.31
Taylor, Scott-Scott Michael	95TexA	10-03-66	Topeka, Kans.		R	R	6'3	200	1	2	.333	0	3	3	0	15	25	5	10	0	9.39
Taylor, Terry-Terry Derrell	88SeaA	07-28-64	Crestview, Fla.		R	R	6'1	180	0	1	.000	0	5	5	0	23	26	11	9	0	6.26
Taylor, Wade-Wade Eric	91NYA	10-19-65	Mobile, Ala.		R	R	6'1	185	7	12	.368	0	23	22	0	116	144	53	72	0	6.27
Tejeda, Robinson-Robinson Garcia	05PhiN 06TexA	03-24-82	Bani, Dom. Rep.		R	R	6'3	190	9	8	.529	0	40	27	0	159	150	83	112	0	3.90
Tejera, Michael-Michael	99FlaN 00EJ 02-04FlaN 04-05TexA	10-18-76	Havana, Cuba		L	L	5'9	185	11	13	.458	3	111	27	0	238	256	111	172	0	5.14
Tekulve, Kent-Kenton Charles	74-85PitN 85-88PhiN 89CinN	03-05-47	Cincinnati, Ohio		R	R	6'4	185	94	90	.511	184	1050	0	0	1436	1305	491	779	0	2.85
Telemaco, Amaury-Amaury [Regalado]	96-98ChiN 98-99AriN 99-01,03-05PhiN	01-19-74	Higuey, Dom. Rep.		R	R	6'4	220	23	35	.397	0	219	64	1	561	572	194	364	0	4.94
Telford, Anthony-Anthony Charles	90-91,93BalA 97-01MonN 02TexA	03-06-66	San Jose, Cal.		R	R	6'	190	22	25	.468	8	333	9	0	455	475	176	331	0	4.17
Telgheder, Dave-David William	93-95NYN 96-98OakA	11-11-66	Middletown, N.Y.		R	R	6'3	212	15	19	.441	0	81	46	1	312	372	103	158	1	5.23
Tellmann, Tom-Thomas John (Geek)	79-80SDN 83-84MilA 85OakA	03-29-54	Warren, Pa.		R	R	6'2	195	18	7	.720	13	112	2	2	227	240	83	94	0	3.05
Terlecky, Greg-Gregory John	75StLN	03-20-52	Culver City, Cal.		R	R	6'3	190	0	1	.000	0	20	0	0	30	38	12	13	0	4.50
Terpko, Jeff-Jeffrey Michael	74,76TexA 77MonN	10-16-50	Sayre, Pa.		R	R	6'	180	3	4	.429	0	48	0	0	81	76	48	41	0	3.11
Terrell, Walt-Charles Walter	82-84NYN 85-88DetA 89SDN 89NYA 90PitN 90-92DetA	05-11-58	Jeffersonville, Ind.		L	R	6'2	205	111	124	.472	0	321	294	56	1987	2090	748	929	14	4.22
Terry, Scott-Scott Ray	86CinN 87-91StLN 92SJ	11-21-59	Hobbs, N.M.		R	R	5'11	195	24	28	.462	8	236	40	2	499	491	176	262	0	3.73
Tessmer, Jay-Jay Weldon	98-00,02NYA	12-26-71	Meadville, Pa.		R	R	6'3	190	1	0	1.000	0	23	0	0	29	29	11	14	0	7.71
Teut, Nate-Nathan Mark	02FlaN	03-11-76	Newton, Iowa		R	L	6'7	220	0	1	.000	0	5	1	0	7	13	3	4	0	9.82
Tewksbury, Bob-Robert Alan	86-87NYA 87-88ChiN 89-94StLN 95TexA 96SDN 97-98MinA	11-30-60	Concord, N.H.		R	R	6'4	205	110	102	.519	1	302	277	31	1807	2043	292	782	7	3.92
Thayer, Greg-Gregory Allen (Tates)	78MinA	10-23-49	Cedar Rapids, Iowa		R	R	5'11	180	1	1	.500	2	45	40	30	30	0	3.80
Theiss, Duane-Duane Charles	77-78AtlN	11-20-53	Zanesville, Ohio		R	R	6'3	180	1	1	.500	0	20	0	0	27	29	19	10	0	5.33
Thigpen, Bobby-Robert Thomas	86-93ChiA 93PhiN 94SeaA	07-17-63	Tallahassee, Fla.		R	R	6'3	200	31	36	.463	201	448	0	0	569	537	238	376	0	3.43
Thobe, J.J.-John Joseph	95MonN	11-19-70	Covington, Ky.		R	R	6'6	200	0	0	—	0	4	0	0	4	6	3	0	9.00
Thobe, Tom-Thomas Neal	95-96AtlN	09-03-69	Covington, Ky.		L	L	6'5	195	0	1	.000	0	9	0	0	9	12	1	3	0	4.82
Thomas, Brad-Bradley Richard	01,03-04MinA 04BosA	10-22-77	Sydney, Australia		L	L	6'4	220	0	3	.000	0	11	5	0	24	33	18	8	0	9.89
Thomas, Larry-Larry Wayne	95-97ChiA	10-25-69	Miami, Fla.		L	L	6'1	195	2	3	.400	0	79	0	0	48	43	22	32	0	3.02
Thomas, Mike-Michael Steven	95MilA	09-02-69	Sacramento, Cal.		L	L	6'2	205	0	0	—	0	1	0	0	2	1	0	0	0	4.50
Thomas, Roy-Roy Justin	77HouN 78-80StLN 83-85SeaA 86EJ 87SeaA	06-22-53	Quantico, Va.		R	R	6'6	195	20	11	.645	7	182	13	0	419	385	196	289	0	3.83
Thomas, Stan-Stanley Brown	74-75TexA 76CleA 77SeaA 77NYA	07-11-49	Rumford, Maine		R	R	6'2	185	11	14	.440	9	117	17	3	266	263	110	123	0	3.69
Thomason, Erskine-Melvin Erskine	74PhiN	08-13-48	Laurens, S.C.		R	R	6'1	190	0	0	—	0	1	0	0	1	0	0	1	0	0.00
Thompson, Brad-Bradley Joseph	05-06StLN	01-31-82	Las Vegas, Nev.		R	R	6'1	190	5	2	.714	0	83	1	0	112	104	35	61	0	3.14
Thompson, Derek-Derek Ryan	05LAN	01-08-81	Tampa, Fla.		L	L	6'2	180	0	0	—	0	4	3	0	18	16	10	13	0	3.50
Thompson, Justin-Justin Willard	96-99DetA 00-01SJ 05TexA	03-08-73	San Antonio, Tex.		L	L	6'4	215	36	43	.456	0	103	101	9	649	633	235	428	0	4.72
Thompson, Mark-Mark Radford	94-98ColN 99-00StLN	04-07-71	Russellville, Ky.		R	R	6'2	210	18	24	.429	0	94	52	3	337	404	161	198	1	5.74
Thompson, Mike-Michael Paul	06SDN	11-06-80	Walsh, Colo.		R	R	6'4	200	4	5	.444	0	19	16	0	92	103	30	35	0	4.99
Thompson, Mike-Michael Wayne	71WasA 73-74StLN 74-75AtlN	09-06-49	Denver, Colo.		R	R	6'3	195	1	15	.063	0	54	29	0	165	158	128	113	0	4.85
Thompson, Rich-Richard Neil	85CleA 89-90MonN	11-01-58	New York, N.Y.		B	R	6'3	225	3	10	.231	5	77	1	0	114	123	59	45	0	5.05
Thomson, John-John Carl	97-99ColN 00SJ 01SJ 01-02ColN 02NYN 03TexA 04-06AtlN	10-01-73	Vicksburg, Miss.		R	R	6'3	195	62	84	.425	0	214	210	10	1260	1385	366	797	3	4.69
Thormodsgard, Paul-Paul Gayton (Thor)	77-79MinA	11-10-53	San Francisco, Cal.		R	R	6'2	190	12	21	.364	0	50	49	9	285	320	82	118	1	4.74
Thornton, Matt-Matthew J.	04-05SeaA 06ChiA	09-15-76	Three Rivers, Mich.		L	L	6'6	220	6	9	.400	2	137	1	0	144	130	88	136	0	4.26
Throop, George-George Lynford (Bird)	75,77-79KCA	11-24-50	Pasadena, Cal.		R	R	6'7	205	2	0	1.000	3	30	0	0	42	41	25	27	0	4.88
Thurman, Corey-Corey Lamar	02-03TorA	11-05-78	Augusta, Ga.		R	R	6'1	215	3	4	.429	0	49	8	0	83	86	54	67	0	4.75
Thurman, Mike-Michael Richard	97-01MonN 02NYA	07-22-73	Corvallis, Ore.		R	R	6'4	210	26	36	.419	0	105	87	0	494	537	190	296	0	5.05
Thurmond, Mark-Mark Anthony	83-86SDN 86-87DetA 88-89BalA 90SFN	09-12-56	Houston, Tex.		L	L	6'	190	40	46	.465	21	314	97	6	838	890	262	320	3	3.69
Tibbs, Jay-Jay Lindsey	84-85CinN 86-87MonN 88-90BalA 90PitN	01-04-62	Birmingham, Ala.		R	R	6'3	185	39	54	.419	0	158	133	13	863	887	319	448	5	4.20
Tidrow, Dick-Richard William (Dirt)	72-74CleA 74-79NYA 79-82CinN 83ChiA 84NYN	05-14-47	San Francisco, Cal.		R	R	6'4	220	100	94	.515	55	620	138	32	1748	1705	579	975	5	3.68
Timlin, Mike-Michael August	91-97TorA 97-98SeaA 99-00BalA 00-02StLN 02PhiN 03-06BosA	03-10-66	Midland, Tex.		R	R	6'4	210	69	68	.504	139	961	4	0	1100	1062	343	809	0	3.55
Tobik, Dave-David Vance	78-82DetA 83-84TexA 85SeaA	03-02-53	Euclid, Ohio		R	R	6'1	190	14	23	.378	28	196	2	0	396	355	153	256	0	3.70
Todd, Jackson-Jackson A.	77NYN 79-81TorA	11-20-51	Tulsa, Okla.		R	R	6'2	195	10	16	.385	0	64	36	7	287	302	88	138	0	4.39
Todd, Jim-James Richard	74ChiN 75-76Oak A 77ChiN 78SeaA 79OakA	09-21-47	Lancaster, Pa.		R	L	6'2	195	25	23	.521	24	270	8	0	512	541	239	194	0	3.82
Tolar, Kevin-Kevin Anthony	00-01DetA 03BosA	01-28-71	Panama City, Fla.		R	L	6'2	225	0	0	—	0	20	0	0	18	13	16	17	0	6.62
Toliver, Freddie-Freddie Lee	84CinN 85-87PhiN 88-89MinA 89SDN 93PitN	02-03-61	Natchez, Miss.		R	R	6'1	170	10	16	.385	1	78	37	0	270	288	136	180	0	4.73
Tollberg, Brian-Brian Patrick	00-03SDN	09-16-72	Tampa, Fla.		R	R	6'3	195	15	16	.484	0	53	52	1	307	356	83	182	0	4.48
Tomko, Brett-Brett Daniel	97-99CinN 00-01SeaA 02SDN 03StLN 04-05SFN 06LAN	04-07-73	Cleveland, Ohio		R	R	6'4	215	89	80	.527	2	306	231	12	1540	1601	493	1008	1	4.54
Tomlin, Dave-David Allen	72-73CinN 74-77SDN 78-80CinN 82MonN 83,85PitN 86MonN	06-22-49	Maysville, Ky.		L	L	6'2	185	25	12	.676	12	409	1	0	511	543	198	278	0	3.82
Tomlin, Randy-Randy Leon	90-94PitN	06-14-66	Bainbridge, Md.		L	L	5'11	178	30	31	.492	0	106	94	8	580	590	133	297	3	3.43
Toms, Tommy-Thomas Howard	75-77SFN	10-15-51	Charlottesville, Va.		R	R	6'4	190	3	0	1.000	0	18	0	0	23	33	9	12	0	5.48
Torrealba, Pablo-Pablo Arnaldo [Torrealba]	75-76AtlN 77OakA 78-79ChiA	04-28-48	Barquisimeto, Venez.		L	L	5'9	165	6	13	.316	5	171	13	4	240	275	104	113	2	3.26
Torres, Angel-Angel Rafael [Ruiz]	77CinN	10-24-52	Las Cienagas, Dom. Rep.		L	L	5'11	165	0	0	—	0	5	0	0	8	7	8	8	0	2.25
Torres, Dilson-Dilson Dario	95KCA	05-31-70	Sur Edo Aragua, Venez.		R	R	6'3	200	1	2	.333	0	24	2	0	44	56	17	28	0	6.09
Torres, Salomon-Salomon [Ramirez]	93-95SFN 95-97SeaA 97MonN 02-06PitN	03-11-72	San Pedro de Mac, D.R.		R	R	5'11	195	35	49	.417	17	370	64	3	715	725	299	444	1	4.32
Torrez, Mike-Michael Augustine	67-71StLN 71-74MonN 75BalA 76-77OakA 77NYA 78-82BosA 83-84NYN 84OakA	08-28-46	Topeka, Kans.		R	R	6'5	220	185	160	.536	0	494	458	117	3042	3043	1371	1404	15	3.97
Towers, Josh-Joshua Eric	01-02BalA 03-06TorA	02-26-76	Port Hueneme, Cal.		R	R	6'1	180	40	45	.471	1	112	97	4	619	752	100	311	2	4.89
Traber, Billy-William Henry	03CleA 04EJ 06WasN	09-18-79	Torrance, Cal.		L	L	6'5	205	10	12	.455	0	48	26	1	155	185	54	113	1	5.57
Tracey, Sean-Sean Patrick	06ChiA	11-14-80	Upland, Cal.		R	R	6'3	210	0	0	—	0	7	0	0	4	5	3	0	3.38
Trachsel, Steve-Stephen Christopher	93-99ChiN 00TBA 00TorA 01-06NYN	10-31-70	Oxnard, Cal.		R	R	6'3	205	134	143	.484	0	381	380	19	2303	2358	840	1519	7	4.28
Trautwein, John-John Howard	88BosA	08-07-62	Lafayette Hills, Pa.		R	R	6'3	205	0	1	.000	0	9	0	0	16	26	9	8	0	9.00
Travers, Bill-William Edward	74-80MilA 81CalA 82SJ 83CalA	10-27-52	Norwood, Mass.		L	L	6'5	200	65	71	.478	1	205	168	46	1121	1139	415	488	10	4.10
Trlicek, Ricky-Richard Alan	92TorA 93LAN 94BosA 96NYN 97BosA 97NYN	04-26-69	Houston, Tex.		R	R	6'3	200	8	8	.385	1	87	1	0	126	132	65	66	0	5.23
Troedson, Rich-Richard LaMonte	73-74SDN	05-01-50	Palo Alto, Cal.		L	L	6'2	190	8	10	.444	2	65	14	2	171	191	67	92	0	4.73
Trombley, Mike-Michael Scott	92-99MinA 00-01BalA 01LAN 02MinA	04-14-67	Springfield, Mass.		R	R	6'2	190	37	47	.440	44	509	36	0	796	800	319	672	0	4.48
Trout, Steve-Steven Russell (Rainbow)	78-82ChiA 83-87ChiN 87NYA 88-89SeaA	07-30-57	Detroit, Mich.		L	L	6'4	205	88	92	.489	4	301	236	32	1502	1665	578	656	9	4.18
Trujillo, J.J.-John	02SDN	10-09-75	Corpus Christi, Texas		R	R	6'	180	0	1	.000	0	9	0	0	6	6	3	0	0	10.12
Trujillo, Mike-Michael Andrew	85-86BosA 86-87SeaA 88-89SeaA	01-12-60	Denver, Colo.		R	R	6'1	180	12	12	.500	1	83	22	3	235	267	88	96	1	5.02
Tsamis, George-George Alex	93MinA	06-14-67	Campbell, Cal.		L	L	6'2	190	1	2	.333	1	41	0	0	69	87	27	30	0	6.19
Tsao, Chin-hui-Chin-hui	03-05ColN 06SJ	06-02-81	Hua-Lien, Taiwan		R	R	6'2	177	4	3	.571	4	29	8	0	64	71	26	44	0	5.80
Tucker, T.J.-Thomas John	02-04MonN 05WasN	06-28-78	Clearwater, Fla.		R	R	6'3	255	13	9	.591	4	171	10	0	229	263	73	140	0	4.57
Tudor, John-John Thomas	79-83BosA 84PitN 85-88StLN 88-89LAN 90StLN	02-02-54	Schenectady, N.Y.		L	L	6'	185	117	72	.619	1	281	263	50	1797	1677	475	988	16	3.12
Tufts, Bob-Robert Malcolm (BT)	81SFN 82-83KCA	11-02-55	Medford, Mass.		L	L	6'5	210	2	0	1.000	2	27	0	0	42	60	14	28	0	4.75

USE NAMES - GIVEN NAMES (NICKNAMES)	TEAM BY YEAR	BIRTH DATE	BIRTHPLACE	DEATH DATE	B	T	HGT	WGT	W	L	Pct.	SV	G	GS	CG	IP	H	BB	SO	ShO	ERA
Tunnell, Lee-Byron Lee	82-85PitN 87StLN 89MinA	10-30-60	Tyler, Tex.		R	R	6'	180	22	28	.440	1	132	66	5	483	499	200	280	3	4.23
Turnbow, Derrick-Thomas Derrick	00,03-04AnaA 05-06MilN	01-25-78	Union City, Tenn.		R	R	6'3	205	13	10	.565	63	172	1	0	183	150	109	176	0	3.78
Turner, Matt-William Matthew	93FlaN 94CleA	02-18-67	Lexington, Ky.		R	R	6'5	215	5	5	.500	1	64	0	0	81	68	33	64	0	2.79
Twitchell, Wayne-Wayne Lee	70MilA 71-77PhiN 77-78MonN 79NYN 79SeaA	03-10-48	Portland, Ore.		R	R	6'6	220	46	65	.425	2	282	133	15	1064	983	537	789	6	3.98
Twitty, Jeff-Jeffrey Dean (Bird)	80KCA	11-10-57	Lancaster, N.C.		L	L	6'2	185	2	1	.667	0	13	0	0	22	23	7	9	0	6.14
Ujdur, Jerry-Gerald Raymond	80-83DetA 84CleA	03-05-57	Duluth, Minn.		R	R	6'2	205	12	16	.429	0	53	40	7	261	268	110	118	0	4.79
Umbarger, Jim-James Harold	75-76TexA 77OakA 77-78TexA	02-17-53	Burbank, Cal.		L	L	6'6	200	25	33	.431	3	133	61	15	483	534	181	244	5	4.14
Underwood, Pat-Patrick John	78-80,82-83DetA	02-19-57	Kokomo, Ind.		L	L	6'	195	13	18	.419	8	113	34	3	344	366	92	188	0	4.42
Underwood, Tom-Thomas Gerald	74-77PhiN 77StLN 78-79TorA 80-81NYA 81-83OakA 84BalA	12-22-53	Kokomo, Ind.		R	L	5'11	185	86	87	.497	18	379	203	35	1587	1554	662	948	6	3.89
Urbani, Tom-Thomas James	93-96StLN 96DetA	01-21-68	Santa Cruz, Cal.		L	L	6'1	190	10	17	.370	0	81	36	0	260	316	86	149	0	4.98
Urbina, Uguebh-Uguetb Urtain [Villarreal]	95-01MonN 01-02BosA 03FlaN 04-05DetA 05PhiN	02-15-74	Caracas, Venez.		R	R	6'2	205	44	49	.473	237	583	21	0	697	539	307	814	0	3.45
Urdaneta, Lino-Lino	04DetA	11-20-79	Caracas, Venezuela		R	R	6'1	168	0	0	—	0	3	0	0	5	1	0	0	0	∞
Urrea, John-John Godoy	77-80StLN 81SDN	02-09-55	Los Angeles, Cal.		R	R	6'3	200	17	18	.486	9	139	27	3	364	347	160	202	1	3.73
Valdes, Marc-Marc Christopher	95-96FlaN 97-98MonN 00HouN 01AtlN	12-20-71	Dayton, Ohio		R	R	6'	180	12	15	.444	4	144	22	0	251	281	118	135	0	4.95
Valdez, Carlos-Carlos Luis [Lorenzo]	95SFN 98BosA	12-26-71	Nizao, Dom. Rep.		R	R	5'11	165	1	1	.500	2	15	0	0	18	20	13	11	0	5.00
Valdez, Efrain-Efrain Antonio	90-91CleA 98AriN	07-11-66	Nizao, Dom. Rep.		L	L	5'11	180	1	1	.500	2	26	0	0	34	32	18	16	0	2.91
Valdez, Ismael-Ismael [Alvarez] (played as Ismael Valdes 94-03)	94-99LAN 00ChiN 00LAN 01AnaA 02TexA 02SeaA 03TexA 04SDN 04-05FlaN	08-21-73	Ciudad Victoria, Mexico		R	R	6'3	220	104	105	.498	1	325	288	13	1827	1872	523	1173	6	4.09
Valdez, Rafael-Rafael	04SFN	11-05-81	San Cristobal, D.R.		R	R	6'5	208	0	0	—	0	2	0	0	2	4	3	2	0	27.00
Valdez, Rafael-Rafael Emilio [Diaz]	90SDN	12-17-67	Nizao, Dom. Rep.		R	R	5'11	175	0	1	.000	0	3	0	0	6	11	2	3	0	11.12
Valdez (Sanchez), Sergio-Sergio Sanchez [Valdez]	86MonN 89-90AtlN 90-91CleA 92-93MonN 94BosA 95SFN 96SJ	09-07-64	Elias Pina, Dom. Rep.		R	R	6'	190	12	20	.375	0	116	31	1	303	332	109	190	0	5.06
Valentine, Joe-Joseph John	03-05CinN	12-24-79	Las Vegas, Nev.		R	R	6'2	200	2	4	.333	4	42	1	0	46	46	37	39	0	6.70
Valenzuela, Fernando-Fernando [Anguamea] (El Toro, Tortilla Fats)	80-90LAN 91CalA 93BalA 94PhiN 95-97SDN 97StLN	11-01-60	Navojoa, Mexico		L	L	5'11	200	173	153	.531	2	453	424	113	2930	2718	1151	2074	31	3.54
Valera, Julio-Julio Enrique [Torres]	90-91NYN 92-93CalA 94SJ 96KCA	10-13-68	Aguadilla, P.R.		R	R	6'2	215	15	20	.429	5	85	38	4	317	361	117	179	2	4.85
Valverde, Jose-Jose Rafael	03-06AriN	07-24-79	San Pedro de Mac., D.R.		R	R	6'4	250	8	10	.444	51	188	0	0	196	148	85	253	0	3.50
Van Benschoten, John-John Wesley	04PitN	04-14-80	San Diego, Cal.		R	R	6'4	217	1	3	.250	0	6	5	0	29	33	19	18	0	6.91
Van Buren, Jermaine-Jermaine Russell	05ChiN 06BosA	07-02-80	Laurel, Miss.		R	R	6'1	220	1	2	.333	0	16	0	0	19	16	24	11	0	9.00
Vance, Cory-Cory Wade	02-03ColN	06-20-79	Dayton, Ohio		L	L	6'1	195	1	3	.250	0	11	4	0	31	35	14	13	0	5.74
Vande Berg, Ed-Edward John (Vandy)	82-85SeaA 86LAN 87CleA 88TexA	10-26-58	Redlands, Cal.		R	L	6'1	180	25	28	.472	22	413	17	2	518	572	200	314	0	3.92
VanEgmond, Tim-Timothy Layne	94-95BosA 96MilA	05-31-69	Shreveport, La.		R	R	6'2	185	5	9	.357	0	23	17	1	100	105	50	60	0	5.96
Van Hekken, Andy-Andrew William	02DetA	07-31-79	Holland, Mich.		R	L	6'3	175	1	3	.250	0	5	5	1	30	38	6	5	1	3.00
VanLandingham, William-William Joseph	94-97SFN	07-16-70	Columbia, Tenn.		R	R	6'2	210	27	26	.509	0	84	81	1	477	470	220	300	0	4.54
Van Poppel, Todd-Todd Matthew	91,93-96OakA 96DetA 98TexA 98PitN 00-01CinN 02-03TexA 03-04CinN	12-09-71	Hinsdale, Ill.		R	R	6'5	225	40	52	.435	4	359	98	2	907	944	461	711	1	5.58
VanRyn, Ben-Benjamin Ashley	96CalA 98ChiN 98SDN 98TorA	08-09-71	Fort Wayne, Ind.		L	L	6'5	185	0	2	.000	0	26	0	0	16	19	13	10	0	5.74
Vargas, Claudio-Claudio [Almonte]	03-04MonN 05WasN 05-06AriN	06-19-78	Valverde Mao, Dom. Rep.		R	R	6'3	220	32	32	.500	0	124	87	0	533	562	204	369	0	4.92
Vargas, Jason-Jason M.	05-06FlaN	02-02-83	Seattle, Wash.		L	L	6'	195	6	7	.462	0	29	18	1	117	121	61	84	0	5.25
Vasquez, Jorge-Jorge Luis	04KCA	07-16-78	Nagua, Dom. Rep.		R	R	6'1	165	0	0	—	0	2	0	0	3	4	1	4	0	8.10
Vasquez, Rafael-Rafael [Santiago]	79SeaA	06-28-58	La Romana, Dom. Rep.		R	R	5'11	165	1	0	1.000	1	9	0	0	16	23	6	9	0	5.06
Vaughn, DeWayne-DeWayne Mathew	88TexA	07-22-59	Oklahoma City, Okla.		R	R	5'11	180	0	1	.000	0	8	0	0	15	24	4	8	0	7.63
Vazquez, Javier-Javier Carlos	98-03MonN 04NYA 05AriN 06ChiA	06-25-76	Ponce, P.R.		R	R	6'2	200	100	105	.488	0	290	288	20	1846	1859	493	1602	7	4.34
Velaquez, Carlos-Carlos [Quinones]	73MilA	03-22-48	Loiza, P.R.		R	R	5'11	180	2	2	.500	2	18	0	0	38	46	10	12	0	2.58
Venafro, Mike-Michael Robert	99-01TexA 02OakA 03TBA 04LAN 06ColN	08-02-73	Takoma Park, Md.		L	L	5'10	180	15	10	.600	5	307	0	0	253	264	94	131	0	4.09
Veras, Dario-Dario Antonio	96-97SDN 98BosA	03-13-73	Santiago, Dom. Rep.		R	R	6'2	165	5	3	.625	9	53	0	0	62	64	29	46	0	4.67
Veras, Jose-Jose Enger [Romero]	06NYA	10-20-80	Santo Domingo, D.R.		R	R	6'5	230	0	0	—	0	12	0	0	11	8	5	9	0	4.09
Veres, Dave-David Scott	94-95HouN 96-97MonN 98-99ColN 00-02StLN 03ChiN	10-19-66	Montgomery, Ala.		R	R	6'2	215	36	35	.507	95	605	0	0	694	661	257	617	0	3.44
Veres, Randy-Randolph Ruhland	89-90MilA 94ChiN 95FlaN 96DetA 97KCA	11-25-65	San Francisco, Cal.		R	R	6'3	190	9	13	.409	3	135	1	0	174	179	74	116	0	4.60
Verhoeven, John-John C. (J.C.)	76-77CalA 77ChiA 80-81MinA	07-03-52	Long Beach, Cal.		R	R	6'5	200	3	8	.273	4	99	0	0	204	214	63	90	0	3.75
Verlander, Justin-Justin Brooks	05-06DetA	02-20-83	Manakin Sabot, Va.		R	R	6'5	200	17	11	.607	0	32	32	1	197	202	65	131	1	3.83
Veselic, Bob-Robert Michael	80-81MinA	09-27-55	Pittsburgh, Pa.	12-26-95	R	R	6'	180	1	1	.500	0	6	0	0	27	25	13	15	0	3.33
Villacis, Eduardo-Eduardo Enrique	04KCA	08-29-79	Caracas, Venezuela		R	R	6'2	170	0	1	.000	0	1	1	0	3	6	4	0	0	13.50
Villafuerte, Brandon-Brandon Paul	00DetA 01TexA 02-03SDN 04AriN	12-17-75	San Nicolas de los Garza, Mex.		R	R	5'11	190	1	7	.125	3	91	0	0	103	109	60	77	0	4.12
Villanueva, Carlos-Carlos Manuel [Paulino]	06MilN	11-28-83	Santiago, Dom. Rep.		R	R	6'2	190	2	2	.500	0	10	6	0	54	43	11	39	0	3.69
Villarreal, Oscar-Oscar Eduardo	03-05AriN 06AtlN	11-22-81	Monterrey, Mexico		L	R	6'	190	21	10	.677	0	172	5	0	222	209	86	157	0	3.53
Villegas, Ismael-Ismael [Diaz]	97PitN	12-08-76	Rio Piedras, P.R.		R	R	6'1	188	0	0	—	0	3	0	0	3	4	2	2	0	13.50
Villone, Ron-Ronald Thomas	95SeaA 95-96SDN 96-97MilA 98CleA 99-00CinN 01ColN 01HouN 02PitN 03HouN 04-05SeaA 05FlaN 06NYA	01-16-70	Englewood, N.J.		L	L	6'3	230	55	57	.491	6	543	93	2	1027	980	553	817	0	4.78
Vining, Ken-Kenneth Edward	01ChiA	12-05-74	Decatur, Ga.		L	L	6'	180	0	0	—	0	7	0	0	7	15	7	3	0	17.55
Viola, Frank-Frank John (Sweet Music)	82-89MinA 89-91NYN 92-94BosA 95CinN 96TorA	04-19-60	Hempstead, N.Y.		L	L	6'4	210	176	150	.540	0	421	420	74	2836	2827	864	1844	16	3.73
Vitko, Joe-Joseph John	92NYN	02-01-70	Somerville, N.J.		R	R	6'8	210	0	0	—	0	3	0	0	5	12	1	6	0	13.50
Vizcaino, Luis-Luis [Arias]	99-01OakA 02-04MilN 05ChiA 06AriN	08-06-74	Bani, Dom. Rep.		R	R	5'11	180	25	23	.521	7	408	0	0	410	371	163	369	0	4.24
Vogelsong, Ryan-Ryan Andrew	00-01SFN 01PitN 02EJ 03-06PitN	07-22-77	Charlotte, N.C.		R	R	6'3	205	10	22	.313	0	120	33	0	315	347	154	216	0	5.86
Volquez, Edinson-Edinson	05-06TexA	07-03-83	La Segunsa, Dom. Rep.		R	R	6'1	190	1	10	.091	0	14	11	0	46	77	27	26	0	9.20
Von Ohlen, Dave-David	83-84StLN 85CleA 86-87OakA	10-25-58	Queens, N.Y.		L	L	6'2	200	7	7	.500	4	127	0	0	168	185	61	59	0	3.33
Vosberg, Ed-Edward John	86SDN 90SFN 94OakA 95-97TexA 97FlaN 98SJ 99SDN 99AriN 00-01PhiN 02MonN	09-28-61	Tucson, Ariz.		L	L	6'1	200	10	15	.400	13	266	3	0	233	250	109	179	0	4.32
Voyles, Brad-Bradley Roy	01-03KCA	06-19-76	Green Bay, Wis.		R	R	6'1	195	0	4	.000	1	40	3	0	68	83	44	56	0	6.45
Vuckovich, Pete-Peter Dennis	75-76ChiA 77TorA 78-80StLN 81-83MilA 84SJ 85-86MilA	10-27-52	Johnstown, Pa.		R	R	6'4	215	93	69	.574	10	286	186	38	1455	1454	545	882	8	3.66
Waddell, Tom-Thomas David	84-85CleA 86EJ 87CleA	09-17-58	Dundee, Scotland		R	R	6'1	190	15	11	.577	15	113	9	1	215	179	83	118	0	4.30
Wade, Terrell-Hawatha Terrell	95-97AtlN 98TBA	01-25-73	Rembert, S.C.		L	L	6'3	205	8	5	.615	1	61	19	0	126	134	69	125	0	3.99
Waechter, Doug-Douglas Michael	03-06TBA	01-28-81	St. Petersburg, Fla.		R	R	6'4	210	14	25	.359	0	60	54	1	316	355	105	177	1	5.62
Wagner, Billy-William Edward	95-03HouN 04-05PhiN 06NYN	07-25-71	Tannersville, Va.		L	L	5'10	190	37	34	.521	324	654	0	0	703	468	238	934	0	2.38
Wagner (Guerrero), Hector-Hector Raul Guerrero [Wagner]	90-91KCA	11-26-68	Santo Domingo, D.R.		R	R	6'3	185	1	3	.250	0	33	48	0	33	34	14	19	0	7.83
Wagner, Matt-Matthew William	96SeaA 97SJ	04-04-72	Cedar Falls, Ia.		R	R	6'5	215	3	5	.375	0	15	14	1	80	91	38	41	0	6.86
Wagner, Paul-Paul Alan	92-97PitN 97MilN 98MilN 99CleA	11-14-67	Milwaukee, Wis.		R	R	6'1	205	29	45	.392	5	160	84	6	599	640	255	452	2	4.83
Wagner, Ryan-Ryan Scott	03-05CinN 06WasN	07-15-82	Yoakum, Texas		R	R	6'4	210	11	7	.611	0	134	0	0	150	164	71	121	0	4.69
Wainhouse, Dave-David Paul	91MonN 93SeaA 96-97PitN 98-99ColN 00StLN	11-07-67	Toronto, Canada		R	R	6'2	190	2	3	.400	0	85	0	0	105	130	61	66	0	7.37
Wainwright, Adam-Adam Parrish	05-06StLN	08-30-81	Brunswick, Ga.		R	R	6'7	205	2	1	.667	3	63	0	0	77	66	23	72	0	3.39
Waits, Rick-Michael Richard	83TexA 75-83CleA 83-85MilA	05-15-52	Atlanta, Ga.		L	L	6'3	195	79	92	.462	8	317	190	47	1426	1514	568	659	10	4.25
Wakefield, Tim-Timothy Stephen	92-93PitN 95-06BosA	08-02-66	Melbourne, Fla.		R	R	6'2	205	151	134	.530	22	480	339	29	2432	2354	948	1680	6	4.30
Walk, Bob-Robert Vernon	80PhiN 81-83AtlN 84-93PitN	11-26-56	Van Nuys, Cal.		R	R	6'4	210	105	81	.565	5	350	259	16	1666	1671	606	848	6	4.03
Walker, Jamie-James Ross	97-98KCA 02-06DetA	07-01-71	McMinnville, Tenn.		L	L	6'2	190	15	16	.484	5	383	2	0	330	334	82	244	0	3.95
Walker, Kevin-Kevin Michael	00-03SDN 04SFN 05ChiA	09-20-76	Irving, Tex.		L	L	6'4	190	7	3	.700	5	122	0	0	102	84	63	95	0	4.76
Walker, Mike-Michael Aaron	92SeaA	06-23-65	Houston, Tex.		R	R	6'3	205	0	0	—	0	5	0	0	15	21	9	5	0	7.36
Walker, Mike-Michael Charles	88,90-91CleA 95ChiN 96DetA	10-04-66	Chicago, Ill.		R	R	6'2	195	3	11	.214	2	88	12	0	161	181	95	76	0	5.09
Walker, Pete-Peter Brian	95NYN 96SDN 00ColN 01-02NYN 02-03,05-06TorA	04-08-69	Beverly, Mass.		R	R	6'2	195	20	14	.588	4	339	362	133	191	0	4.48
Walker, Tom-Robert Thomas	72-74MonN 75DetA 76StLN 77MonN 77CalA	11-07-48	Tampa, Fla.		R	R	6'1	190	18	23	.439	11	191	17	2	415	418	142	262	0	3.86
Walker, Tyler-Tyler Lanier	02NYN 04-06SFN 06TBA	05-15-76	San Francisco, Cal.		R	R	6'3	230	13	9	.591	34	150	1	0	161	175	68	128	0	4.80
Wall, Donne-Donnell Lee	95-97HouN 98-00SDN 01NYN 02AnaA	07-11-67	Potosi, Mo.		R	R	6'1	180	31	28	.525	2	234	37	2	474	468	155	322	1	4.20
Wall, Stan-Stanley Arthur	75-77LAN	06-06-51	Butler, Mo.		L	L	6'	175	6	4	.600	4	66	0	0	98	98	35	55	0	3.86
Wallace, Dave-David William	73-74PhiN 78TorA	09-07-47	Waterbury, Conn.		R	R	5'10	185	0	1	.000	0	13	0	0	21	29	16	12	0	7.84
Wallace, Derek-Derek Robert	96NYN 97SJ 99KCA	09-01-71	Van Nuys, Cal.		R	R	6'3	215	4	4	.333	3	33	36	19	20	0	3.86
Wallace, Jeff-Jeffrey Allen	97PitN 98EJ 99-00PitN 01TBA 02EJ	04-12-76	Wheeling, W.Va.		L	L	6'2	240	4	3	.500	0	119	0	0	137	119	117	120	0	4.20
Wallace, Mike-Michael Sherman	73-74PhiN 74-75NYA 75-76StLN 77TexA	02-03-51	Gastonia, N.C.		L	L	6'2	200	11	3	.786	4	117	4	1	181	188	107	105	0	3.94
Walrond, Les-Leslie Dale	03KCA 06ChiN	11-07-76	Muskogee, Okla.		L	L	6'1	190	3	3	.500	0	25	0	0	30	34	16	34	0	7.46
Walsh, Dave-David Peter	90LAN	09-25-60	Arlington, Mass.		L	L	6'1	180	1	0	1.000	1	20	0	0	16	5	6	15	0	3.86
Walter, Gene-Gene Winston	85-86SDN 87-88NYN 88SeaA 89EJ	11-22-60	Chicago, Ill.		L	L	6'4	200	4	7	.364	4	128	0	0	183	161	96	140	0	3.74

USE NAMES - GIVEN NAMES (NICKNAMES)	TEAM BY YEAR	BIRTH DATE	BIRTHPLACE	DEATH DATE	B	T	HGT	WGT	W	L	Pct.	SV	G	GS	CG	IP	H	BB	SO	ShO	ERA
Walters, Mike-Michael Charles	83-84MinA	10-18-57	St. Louis, Mo.		R	R	6'5	203	1	4	.200	4	46	0	0	88	83	34	31	0	3.99
Walton, Bruce-Bruce Kenneth	91-92OakA 93MonN 94ColN	12-25-62	Bakersfield, Cal.		R	R	6'2	195	2	0	1.000	0	27	0	0	34	45	15	18	0	8.21
Wang, Chien-Ming-Chien-Ming	05-06NYA	03-31-80	Tainan, Taiwan		R	R	6'3	200	27	11	.711	1	52	50	2	334	346	84	123	1	3.77
Wapnick, Steve-Steven Lee	90DetA 91ChiA	09-25-65	Panorama City, Cal.		R	R	6'2	200	0	1	.000	0	10	0	0	12	10	14	7	0	4.50
Ward, Bryan-Bryan Matthew	98-99ChiA 00PhiN 00AnaA	01-28-72	Bristol, Pa.		L	L	6'2	210	1	3	.250	1	95	0	0	94	115	28	66	0	5.09
Ward, Colby-Robert Colby	90CleA	01-02-64	Lansing, Mich.		R	R	6'2	185	1	3	.250	1	22	0	0	36	31	21	23	0	4.25
Ward, Colin-Colin Norval	85SFN	11-22-60	Los Angeles, Cal.		L	L	6'3	190	0	0	—	0	6	2	0	12	10	7	8	0	4.38
Ward, Duane-Roy Duane	86AtlN 86-93TorA 94SJ 95TorA	05-28-64	Park View, N.M.		R	R	6'4	220	32	37	.464	121	462	2	0	667	551	286	679	0	3.28
Wardle, Curt-Curtis Ray	84-85MinA 85CleA	11-16-60	Downey, Cal.		L	L	6'5	220	8	9	.471	1	52	12	0	119	130	62	89	0	6.13
Ware, Jeff-Jeffrey Allan	95-96TorA	11-11-70	Norfolk, Va.		R	R	6'3	190	3	6	.333	0	18	9	0	59	63	52	29	0	7.47
Warren, Mike-Michael Bruce	83-85OakA	03-26-61	Inglewood, Cal.		R	R	6'1	175	9	13	.409	0	52	27	3	205	207	100	139	1	5.06
Warthen, Dan-Gary Dean	75-77MonN 77PhiN 78HouN	12-01-52	Omaha, Neb.		B	L	6'	190	12	21	.364	3	83	41	5	308	253	198	224	1	4.30
Wasdin, John-John Truman	95-96OakA 97-00BosA 00-01ColN 01BalA 02JL 03TorA 04-06TexA	08-05-72	Fort Belvoir, Va.		R	R	6'2	195	38	38	.500	7	316	65	2	774	842	244	517	0	5.26
Washburn, Jarrod-Jarrod Michael	98-04AnaA 05LAA 06SeaA	08-13-74	La Crosse, Wis.		L	L	6'1	195	83	71	.539	0	224	214	6	1340	1320	403	802	2	4.04
Waterbury, Steve-Steven Craig	76StLN	04-06-52	Carbondale, Ill.		R	R	6'5	190	0	0	—	0	5	0	0	6	7	3	4	0	6.00
Watkins, Scott-Scott Allen	95MinA	05-15-70	Tulsa, Okla.		L	L	6'3	180	0	0	—	0	27	0	0	22	22	11	11	0	5.40
Watkins, Steve-Stephen Douglas	04SDN	07-19-78	Lubbock, Tex.		R	R	6'4	190	0	0	—	0	11	0	0	14	17	4	7	0	6.23
Watson, Allen-Allen Kenneth	93-95StLN 96SeaA 97-98AnaA 99NYN 99SeaA 99-00NYA 01SJ	11-18-70	Brooklyn, N.Y.		L	L	6'1	215	51	55	.481	1	206	137	3	892	979	351	589	0	5.03
Watson, Mark-Mark Bradford	00CleA 02SeaA 03CinN	01-23-74	Atlanta, Ga.		R	L	6'4	215	1	1	.500	0	11	0	0	12	22	7	7	0	10.95
Wayne, Gary-Gary Anthony	89-92MinA 93ColN 94LAN	11-30-62	Dearborn, Mich.		L	L	6'3	193	14	14	.500	4	231	0	0	250	237	104	164	0	3.93
Wayne, Justin-Justin Morgan	02-04FlaN	04-16-79	Honolulu, Hawaii		R	R	6'3	200	5	8	.385	0	26	8	0	62	66	36	37	0	6.13
Weathers, David-John David	91-92TorA 93-96FlaN 96-97NYA 97CleA 98CinN 98-01MilN 01CinN 02-04NYN 04HouN 04FlaN 05-06CinN	09-25-69	Lawrenceburg, Tenn.		R	R	6'3	225	63	70	.474	41	754	69	0	1167	1236	519	845	0	4.37
Weaver, Eric-James Eric	98LAN 99SeaA 00AnaA	08-04-73	Springfield, Ill.		R	R	6'5	230	2	3	.400	0	32	0	0	37	39	30	27	0	6.27
Weaver, Jeff-Jeffrey Charles	99-02DetA 02-03NYA 04-05LAN 06StLN	08-22-76	Northridge, Cal.		R	R	6'5	210	86	101	.460	2	257	240	13	1568	1672	428	1044	5	4.58
Weaver, Jered-Jered David	06LAA	10-04-82	Northridge, Cal.		R	R	6'7	205	11	2	.846	0	19	19	0	123	94	33	105	0	2.56
Weaver, Roger-Roger Edward	80DetA	10-06-54	Amsterdam, N.Y.		R	R	6'3	195	3	4	.429	0	19	6	0	64	56	34	42	0	4.08
Webb, Brandon-Brandon Tyler	03-06AriN	05-09-79	Ashland, Ky.		R	R	6'3	220	47	45	.511	0	130	129	8	853	779	296	686	4	3.28
Webb, Hank-Henry Gaylon Matthew	72-76NYN 77LAN	05-21-50	Copaigue, N.Y.		R	R	6'2	175	7	9	.438	0	53	19	3	169	159	91	71	1	4.31
Webb, John-John Floyd	04-05TBA	05-23-79	Pensacola, Fla.		R	R	6'3	220	0	1	.000	0	5	1	0	13	18	11	11	0	10.38
Weber, Ben-Benjamin Edward	00SFN 00-04AnaA 05CinN	11-17-69	Port Arthur, Tex.		R	R	6'4	195	19	8	.704	7	228	0	0	284	305	105	162	0	3.77
Weber, Neil-Neil Aaron	98AriN	12-06-72	Newport Beach, Cal.		L	L	6'5	215	0	0	—	0	4	0	0	2	5	3	4	0	11.57
Wegman, Bill-William Edward	85-95MilA	12-19-62	Cincinnati, Ohio		R	R	6'5	225	81	90	.474	2	262	216	33	1483	1567	352	696	4	4.16
Wehrmeister, Dave-David Thomas (Captain)	76-78SDN 81NYA 84PhiN 85ChiN	11-09-52	Berwyn, Ill.		R	R	6'4	195	4	9	.308	2	76	10	0	158	175	84	96	0	5.65
Welch, Bob-Robert Lynn	78-87LAN 88-94OakA	11-03-56	Detroit, Mich.		R	R	6'3	195	211	146	.591	8	506	462	61	3091	2894	1034	1969	28	3.47
Welch, Mike-Michael Paul	98CleA	08-25-72	Haverhill, Mass.		L	R	6'2	210	0	2	.000	0	10	2	0	21	26	7	15	0	8.27
Welchel, Don-Donald Ray	82-83BalA	02-03-57	Atlanta, Tex.		R	R	6'4	205	1	2	.333	0	13	0	0	31	39	12	19	0	5.81
Wellemeyer, Todd-Todd Allen	03-05ChiN 06FlaN 06KCA	08-30-78	Louisville, Ky.		R	R	6'3	200	6	7	.462	3	103	0	0	163	152	111	146	0	5.20
Wells, Bob-Robert Lee	94PhiN 94-98SeaA 99-02MinA	11-01-66	Yakima, Wash.		R	R	6'	195	40	28	.588	15	414	21	1	636	688	200	417	1	5.03
Wells, David-David Lee (Boomer)	87-92TorA 93-95DetA 95CinN 96BalA 97-98NYA 99-00TorA 01ChiA 02-03NYA 04SDN 05-06BosA 06SDN	05-20-63	Torrance, Cal.		L	L	6'3	235	230	148	.608	13	631	460	54	3282	3434	677	2119	12	4.07
Wells, Kip-Robert Kip	99-01ChiA 02-06PitN 06TexA	04-21-77	Houston, Texas		R	R	6'3	195	57	74	.435	0	197	177	3	1028	1064	467	748	2	4.46
Wells, Terry-Terry	90LAN	09-10-63	Kankakee, Ill.		L	L	6'3	205	1	2	.333	0	5	5	0	21	25	14	18	0	7.84
Welsh, Chris-Christopher Charles	81-83SDN 83MonN 85TexA 86CinN	04-14-55	Wilmington, Del.		L	L	6'2	190	22	31	.415	0	122	75	8	538	591	189	192	3	4.45
Wendell, Turk-Steven John	93-97ChiN 97-01NYN 01PhiN 02EJ 03PhiN 04ColN	05-19-67	Pittsfield, Mass.		L	R	6'2	200	36	33	.522	33	552	6	0	646	583	324	515	0	3.93
				Bats Both 93																	
Wengert, Don-Donald Paul	95-97OakA 98SDN 98ChiN 99KCA 00AtlN 01PitN	11-06-69	Sioux City, Iowa		R	R	6'2	210	14	32	.304	3	160	48	2	439	569	157	226	1	6.01
Wertz, Bill-William Charles	93-94CleA	01-15-67	Cleveland, Ohio		R	R	6'6	220	2	3	.400	0	35	0	0	64	63	33	54	0	4.08
West, David-David Lee	88-89NYN 89-92MinA 93-96PhiN 97JL 98BosA	09-01-64	Memphis, Tenn.		L	L	6'6	245	31	38	.449	3	204	78	2	569	525	311	437	0	4.66
Westbrook, Jake-Jacob Cauthen	00NYA 00-06CleA	09-29-77	Athens, Ga.		R	R	6'3	190	56	53	.514	0	170	130	11	884	959	266	471	3	4.35
Weston, Mickey-Michael Lee	89-90BalA 91TorA 92PhiN 93NYN	03-26-61	Flint, Mich.		R	R	6'1	185	1	2	.333	1	23	3	0	45	65	11	19	0	7.15
Wetteland, John-John Karl	89-91LAN 92-94MonN 95-96NYA 97-00TexA	08-21-66	San Mateo, Cal.		R	R	6'2	210	48	45	.516	330	618	17	0	765	616	252	804	0	2.93
Wever, Stefan-Stefan Matthew (Dream)	82NYA	04-22-58	Marburg, Germany		R	R	6'8	245	0	1	.000	0	1	1	0	3	6	3	2	0	27.00
Wheeler, Dan-Daniel Michael	99-01TBA 03-04NYN 04-06HouN	12-10-77	Providence, R.I.		R	R	6'3	220	11	17	.393	14	257	9	0	332	330	109	288	0	3.82
Wheelock, Gary-Gary Richard	76CalA 77,80SeaA	11-29-51	Bakersfield, Cal.		R	R	6'3	205	6	9	.400	0	20	18	2	93	104	28	50	0	5.42
Whisenant, Matt-Matthew Michael	97FlaN 97-99KCA 99-00SDN	06-08-71	Los Angeles, Cal.		R	L	6'3	215	9	8	.529	3	189	0	0	158	146	104	114	0	4.96
White, Gabe-Gabriel Allen	94-95MonN 97-00CinN 00-01ColN 02-03CinN 03-04NYA 04CinN 05StLN	11-20-71	Sebring, Fla.		L	L	6'2	200	34	26	.567	17	472	15	0	571	556	141	454	0	4.51
White, Larry-Larry David	83-84LAN	09-24-58	San Fernando, Cal.		R	R	6'5	190	0	1	.000	0	11	0	0	19	13	9	15	0	2.37
White, Matt-Matthew Joseph	03BosA 03SeaA 05WasN	08-19-77	Pittsfield, Mass.		R	L	6'1	180	0	2	.000	0	7	1	0	10	17	8	3	0	16.31
White, Rick-Richard Allen	94-95PitN 98-00TBA 00-01NYN 02ColN 02StLN 03ChiA 03HouN 04CleA 05PitN 06CinN 06PhiN	12-23-68	Springfield, Ohio		R	R	6'4	220	41	53	.436	18	584	18	0	824	883	271	524	0	4.31
Whitehouse, Len-Leonard Joseph (Whitey)	81TexA 83-85MinA	09-10-57	Burlington, Vt.		L	L	5'9	175	9	4	.692	4	97	1	0	115	119	65	68	0	4.68
Whitehurst, Wally-Walter Richard	90-92NYN 93-94SDN 96NYA	04-11-64	Shreveport, La.		R	R	6'3	195	20	37	.351	3	163	66	0	488	525	130	313	0	4.02
Whiteside, Matt-Matthew Christopher	92-97TexA 98PhiN 99-00SDN 01AtlN 05TorA	08-08-67	Charleston, Mo.		R	R	6'2	200	118	15	.545	9	286	1	0	406	455	157	259	0	5.23
Whiteside, Sean-David Sean	95DetA	04-19-71	Lakeland, Fla.		L	L	6'4	190	0	0	—	0	2	0	0	4	7	4	2	0	14.73
Whitson, Ed-Eddie Lee	77-79PitN 79-81SFN 82CleA 83-84SDN 85-86PhiN 86-91SDN 92SJ	05-19-55	Johnson City, Tenn.		R	R	6'3	200	126	123	.506	8	452	333	35	2240	2240	698	1266	12	3.79
Wickander, Kevin-Kevin Dean	89-90, 92-93CleA 93CinN 95DetA 95-96MilA	01-04-65	Fort Dodge, Iowa		L	L	6'2	200	5	1	.833	2	150	0	0	139	151	85	101	0	4.02
Wickman, Bob-Robert Joe	92-96NYA 96-97MilA 98-00MilN 00-02CleA 03EJ 04-06CleA 06AtlN	02-06-69	Green Bay, Wis.		R	R	6'1	230	60	57	.513	247	778	28	1	1009	997	411	748	1	3.57
Wiggins, Scott-Scott Joseph	02TorA	03-24-76	Fort Thomas, Ky.		L	L	6'3	205	0	0	—	0	3	0	0	5	1	3	3	0	3.37
Wihtol, Sandy-Alexander Ames	79-80,82CleA	06-01-55	Palo Alto, Cal.		R	R	6'3	210	1	0	1.000	1	28	0	0	58	54	24	34	0	3.75
Wilcox, Milt-Milton Edward	70-71CinN 72-74CleA 75ChiN 77-85DetA 86SeaA	04-20-50	Honolulu, Hawaii		R	R	6'2	210	119	113	.513	6	394	283	73	2015	1991	770	1137	10	4.08
Wiles, Randy-Randall E.	77ChiA	09-10-51	Fort Belvoir, Va.		L	L	6'1	185	1	1	.500	0	5	0	0	5	3	4	3	0	9.00
Wiley, Mark-Mark Eugene (Coyote)	75MinA 78SDN 78TorA	02-28-48	National City, Cal.		R	R	6'2	203	2	3	.400	2	21	4	1	50	64	15	18	0	5.94
Wilkins, Dean-Dean Allan	89-90ChiN 91HouN	08-24-66	Blue Island, Ill.		R	R	6'1	170	3	1	.750	2	25	0	0	31	40	26	21	0	7.84
Wilkins, Eric-Eric Lamoine	79CleA	12-09-56	St. Louis, Mo.		R	R	6'	198	2	4	.333	0	16	14	0	70	77	38	52	0	4.37
Wilkins, Marc-Marc Allen	96-01PitN	10-21-70	Mansfield, Ohio		R	R	5'11	210	19	14	.576	3	245	2	0	295	278	155	218	0	4.28
Wilkinson, Bill-William Carl	85,87-88SeaA	08-10-64	Greybull, Wyo.		R	L	5'10	165	5	8	.385	12	88	2	0	113	97	42	103	0	4.13
Williams, Al-Albert Hamilton [DeSouza] (Diablo)	80-84MinA	05-06-54	Pearl Lagoon, Nicaragua		R	R	6'4	192	35	38	.479	2	120	97	15	643	670	227	262	1	4.24
Williams, Brian-Brian O'Neal	91-94HouN 95SDN 96DetA 97BalA 98JL 99HouN 00ChiN 00CleA	02-15-69	Lancaster, S.C.		R	R	6'2	220	26	38	.406	1	256	59	2	595	655	332	397	1	5.37
Williams, Charlie-Charles Prosek	71NYN 72-78SFN	10-11-47	Queens, N.Y.		R	R	6'3	200	23	22	.511	4	268	33	2	572	581	275	257	0	3.98
Williams, David-David Aaron	01-02,04-05PitN 06CinN 06NYN	03-12-79	Anchorage, Alaska		L	L	6'2	210	22	30	.423	0	80	71	1	404	399	160	243	1	4.64
Williams, Frank-Frank Lee	84-86SFN 87-88CinN 89DetA	02-13-58	Seattle, Wash.		R	R	6'1	195	24	14	.632	9	333	1	1	472	418	227	314	1	3.00
Williams, Jeff-Jeffrey F.	99-02LAN	06-06-72	Canberra, Australia		R	L	6'	185	4	1	.800	2	37	4	0	58	65	41	30	0	7.49
Williams, Jerome-Jerome Lee	03-05SFN 05-06ChiN	12-04-81	Honolulu, Hawaii		R	R	6'3	225	23	24	.489	0	70	65	2	395	373	153	243	1	4.03
Williams, Matt-Matthew Evan	83TorA	07-25-59	Houston, Tex.		R	R	6'3	200	3	2	.600	0	11	0	0	34	33	17	27	0	5.29
Williams, Matt-Matthew Taylor	00MilN	04-12-71	Virginia Beach, Va.		B	L	6'	185	0	0	—	0	11	0	0	9	7	13	7	0	7.00
Williams, Mike-Michael Darren	92-96PhiN 97KCA 98-01PitN 01HouN 02-03PitN 03PhiN	07-29-68	Radford, Va.		R	R	6'2	200	32	54	.372	144	468	55	1	768	764	343	584	0	4.45
Williams, Mitch-Mitchell Steven (The Wild Thing)	86-88TexA 89-90ChiN 91-93PhiN 94HouN 95CalA 97KCA	11-17-64	Santa Ana, Cal.		L	L	6'4	205	45	58	.437	192	619	3	0	691	537	544	660	0	3.65
Williams, Randy-Randall Duane	04SeaA 05SDN 05ColN	11-18-75	Harlingen, Tex.		L	L	6'3	195	3	1	.750	0	38	0	0	31	38	19	25	0	6.68
Williams, Rick-Richard Allen	78-79HouN	11-09-52	Merced, Cal.		R	R	6'	180	5	9	.357	0	48	17	2	156	165	40	54	2	3.58
Williams, Shad-Shad Clayton	96CalA 97AnaA	03-10-71	Fresno, Cal.		R	R	6'	195	0	2	.000	0	14	2	0	29	43	22	26	0	8.59
Williams, Todd-Todd Michael	95LAN 98CinN 99SeaA 01NYA 04-06BalA	02-13-71	Syracuse, N.Y.		R	R	6'2	210	12	12	.500	2	213	0	0	248	241	83	107	0	4.12
Williams, Woody-Gregory Scott	93-98TorA 99-01SDN 01-04StLN 05-06SDN	08-19-66	Houston, Tex.		R	R	6'	190	124	101	.551	0	391	299	10	2028	2001	658	1379	2	4.09
Williamson, Mark-Mark Alan	87-94BalA	07-21-59	Corpus Christi, Tex.		R	R	6'	185	46	35	.568	21	365	15	2	690	701	226	397	3	3.86
Williamson, Scott-Scott Ryan	99-03CinN 03-04BosA 05-06ChiN 06SDN	02-17-76	Fort Polk, La.		R	R	6'	200	27	28	.491	55	328	10	0	425	314	236	494	0	3.32
Willis, Carl-Carl Blake	84DetA 84-86CinN 88ChiA 91-95MinA	12-28-60	Danville, Va.		R	R	6'4	210	22	16	.579	13	267	2	0	390	424	115	222	0	4.25
Willis, Dontrelle-Dontrelle Wayne (D-Train)	03-06FlaN	01-12-82	Oakland, Cal.		L	L	6'4	210	58	39	.598	0	127	127	6	817	805	257	611	8	3.44

USE NAMES - GIVEN NAMES (NICKNAMES)	TEAM BY YEAR	BIRTH DATE	BIRTHPLACE	DEATH DATE	B	T	HGT	WGT	W	L	Pct.	SV	G	GS	CG	IP	H	BB	SO	ShO	ERA
Willis, Mike-Michael Henry	77-81TorA	12-26-50	Oklahoma City, Okla.		L	L	6'2	200	7	21	.250	15	144	6	1	296	312	124	149	0	4.59
Willoughby, Jim-James Arthur	71-74SFN 75-77BosA 78ChiA	01-31-49	Salinas, Cal.		R	R	6'2	200	26	36	.419	34	238	28	8	561	568	145	250	1	3.79
Wills, Frank-Frank Lee	83-84KCA 85SeaA 86-87CleA 88-91TorA	10-26-58	New Orleans, La.		R	R	6'2	200	22	26	.458	6	154	35	1	436	438	198	281	0	5.06
Wilmet, Paul-Paul Richard	89TexA	11-08-58	Green Bay, Wis.		R	R	5'11	170	0	0	—	0	3	0	0	2	5	2	1	0	15.43
Wilshusen, Terry-Terry Wayne (Dizzy)	73CalA	03-22-49	Atascadero, Cal.	12-01-00	R	R	6'2	205	0	0	—	0	1	0	0	0.1	0	2	0	0	81.00
Wilson, Brian-Brian Patrick	06SFN	03-16-82	Londonberry, N.H.		R	R	6'1	205	2	3	.400	1	31	0	0	30	32	21	23	0	5.40
Wilson, C.J.-Christopher John	05-06TexA	11-18-80	Newport Beach, Cal.		L	L	6'2	200	3	11	.214	2	68	6	0	92	102	36	73	0	5.56
Wilson, Gary-Gary Morris	95PitN	01-01-70	Arcata, Cal.		R	R	6'3	190	0	1	.000	0	10	0	0	14	13	5	8	0	5.02
Wilson, Gary-Gary Steve	79HouN	11-21-54	Camden, Ark.		R	R	6'2	180	0	0	—	0	6	0	0	7	15	6	6	0	12.86
Wilson, Kris-Kristopher Kyle	00-03KCA 06NYA	08-06-76	Washington, D.C.		R	R	6'4	225	14	9	.609	1	95	20	0	243	305	68	142	0	5.44
Wilson, Paul-Paul Anthony	96NYN 97-98SJ 99EJ 00-02TBA 03-05CinN 06SJ	03-28-73	Orlando, Fla.		R	R	6'5	235	40	58	.408	0	170	153	3	942	1029	336	619	0	4.86
Wilson, Steve-Stephen Douglas	88TexA 89-91ChiN 91-93LAN	12-13-64	Victoria, Canada		L	L	6'4	220	13	18	.419	0	205	23	1	345	348	130	252	0	4.40
Wilson, Trevor-Trevor Kirk (T-Dub)	88-93SFN 94SJ 95SFN 96-97SJ 98AnaA	06-07-66	Torrance, Cal.		L	L	6'	200	41	46	.471	0	169	115	7	728	665	305	431	4	3.87
Winchester, Scott-Scott Joseph	97-98CinN 99SJ 00-01CinN	04-20-73	Midland, Mich.		R	R	6'2	210	3	8	.273	0	38	17	1	116	149	35	55	0	5.42
Windsor, Jason-Jason David	06OakA	07-16-82	San Bernardino, Cal.		R	R	6'2	235	0	1	.000	0	4	3	0	14	21	5	6	0	6.59
Winkelsas, Joe-Joseph	99AtlN 06MilN	09-14-73	Buffalo, N.Y.		R	R	6'3	188	0	1	.000	0	8	0	0	7	13	7	4	0	9.82
Winn, Jim-James Francis	83-86PitN 87ChiA 88MinA	09-23-59	Stockton, Cal.		R	R	6'3	215	12	17	.414	10	161	10	0	309	321	156	159	0	4.67
Winston, Darrin-Darrin Alexander	97-98PhiN	07-06-66	Passaic, N.J.		R	L	6'0	195	4	2	.667	1	34	1	0	37	39	9	19	0	5.84
Wirth, Alan-Alan Lee	78-80OakA	12-08-56	Mesa, Ariz.		R	R	6'4	200	6	6	.500	0	23	15	2	95	89	42	39	1	3.79
Wise, Matt-Matthew John	00-02AnaA 03EJ 04-06MilN	11-18-75	Montclair, Cal.		R	R	6'4	195	14	19	.424	1	145	18	0	256	227	86	195	0	4.18
Wise, Rick-Richard Charles	64,66-71PhiN 72-73StlN 74-77BosA 78-79CleA 80-82SDN	09-13-45	Jackson, Mich.		R	R	6'2	195	188	181	.509	0	506	455	138	3125	3227	804	1647	30	3.69
Witasick, Jay-Gerald Alfonse Jr.	96-98OakA 99-00KCA 00-01NYA 02SFN 03-04SDN 05ColN 05-06OakA	08-28-72	Baltimore, Md.		R	R	6'4	230	31	41	.431	5	369	56	3	700	744	337	627	1	4.62
Withem, Shannon-Shannon Bolt	98TorA	09-21-72	Ann Arbor, Mich.		R	R	6'3	185	0	0	—	0	1	0	0	3	3	2	2	0	3.00
Witt, Bobby-Robert Andrew	86-92TexA 92-94OakA 95FlaN 95-98TexA 98StLN 99TBA 00CleA 01AriN	05-11-64	Arlington, Mass.		R	R	6'2	205	142	157	.475	0	430	397	47	2465	2493	1375	1955	11	4.83
Witt, Mike-Michael Atwater	81-90CalA 90-91NYA 92EJ 93NYA	07-20-60	Fullerton, Cal.		R	R	6'7	205	117	116	.502	6	341	299	72	2108	2066	713	1373	11	3.83
Wohlers, Mark-Mark Edward	91-99AtlN 99-01CinN 01NYA 02CleA 03EJ	01-23-70	Holyoke, Mass.		R	R	6'4	207	39	29	.574	119	533	0	0	553	490	272	557	0	3.97
Wojciechowski, Steve-Steven Joseph	95-97OakA	07-29-70	Blue Island, Ill.		L	L	6'2	185	7	10	.412	0	32	24	0	139	165	57	48	0	5.65
Wojna, Ed-Edward David	85-87SDN 89CleA	08-20-60	Bridgeport, Conn.		R	R	6'1	195	4	10	.286	0	36	20	1	132	151	55	60	0	4.62
Wolcott, Bob-Robert William	95-97SeaA 98AriN 99BosA	09-08-73	Huntington Beach, Cal.		R	R	6'	190	16	21	.432	0	66	58	1	326	391	113	178	0	5.86
Wolf, Randy-Randall Christopher	99-06PhiN	08-22-76	Canoga Park, Calif.		L	L	6'	190	69	60	.535	0	194	190	11	1175	1129	437	971	7	4.21
Wood, Kerry-Kerry Lee	98ChiN 99EJ 00-06ChiN	06-16-77	Irving, Tex.		R	R	6'5	230	71	56	.559	0	189	178	11	1129	875	546	1299	5	3.68
Wood, Mike-Michael Burton	03OakA 04-06KCA	04-26-80	West Palm Beach, Fla.		R	R	6'3	190	13	20	.394	2	94	35	0	293	351	110	158	0	5.52
Woodall, Brad-Brad Bradley	94-96AtlN 98MilN 99ChiN	06-25-69	Atlanta, Ga.		B	L	6'	180	10	14	.417	0	55	27	0	190	208	67	119	0	5.31
Woodard, Steve-Steven Larry Jr.	97MilA 98-00MilN 00-01CleA 02TexA 03BosA	05-15-75	Hartselle, Ala.		L	R	6'4	225	32	36	.471	0	162	94	3	667	782	149	464	0	4.94
Woods, Jake-Jacob Thomas	05LAA 06SeaA	09-03-81	Fresno, Cal.		L	L	6'1	190	8	5	.615	1	65	8	0	133	145	61	86	0	4.27
Woodson, Kerry-Walter Browne	92SeaA 93EJ	05-18-69	Jacksonville, Fla.		R	R	6'2	190	0	1	.000	0	8	1	0	14	12	11	6	0	3.29
Woodward, Rob-Robert John	85-88BosA	09-28-62	Hanover, N.H.		R	R	6'3	210	4	4	.500	0	24	14	0	100	118	36	45	0	5.04
Woodyard, Mark-Mark Anthony	05DetA	12-19-78	Mobile, Ala.		R	R	6'4	225	0	0	—	0	3	0	0	6	4	0	3	0	1.50
Worrell, Tim-Timothy Howard	93-97SDN 98DetA 98CleA 98-99OakA 0 0BalA 00ChiN 01-03SFN 04-05PhiN 05AriN 06SFN	07-05-67	Pasadena, Cal.		R	R	6'4	225	48	59	.449	71	678	49	0	974	963	366	758	0	3.97
Worrell, Todd-Todd Roland	85-89StLN 90-91EJ 92StLN 93-97LAN	09-28-59	Arcadia, Cal.		R	R	6'5	220	50	52	.490	256	617	0	0	694	608	247	628	0	3.09
Wortham, Rich-Richard Cooper (Tex)	78-80ChiA	10-22-53	Odessa, Tex.		R	L	6'	185	21	23	.477	1	84	51	7	355	359	182	189	0	4.89
Wright, Dan-Jonathan Daniel	01-04ChiN	12-14-77	Longview, Tex.		R	R	6'3	225	20	26	.435	1	70	64	1	367	393	167	225	1	5.65
Wright, Jamey-Jamey Alan	96-99ColN 00-02MilN 02StLN 03KCA 04-05ColN 06SFN	12-24-74	Oklahoma City, Okla.		R	R	6'6	230	67	98	.406	0	260	237	6	1462	1609	723	781	3	5.14
Wright, Jaret-Jaret Samuel	97-02CleA 03SDN 03-04AtlN 05-06NYA	12-29-75	Anaheim, Cal.		R	R	6'2	230	68	57	.544	2	223	168	2	962	1034	458	687	2	5.07
Wright, Jim-James Clifton	78-79BosA	12-21-50	Reed City, Mich.		R	R	6'1	170	9	4	.692	0	35	15	5	139	141	31	71	3	3.82
Wright, Jim-James Leon	81-82KCA	03-03-55	St. Joseph, Mo.		R	R	6'5	215	2	3	.400	0	24	4	0	76	89	27	36	0	4.04
Wright, Ricky-James Richard	82-83LAN 83-86TexA	11-22-58	Paris, Tex.		L	L	6'3	190	3	3	.500	0	55	7	0	103	102	60	67	0	4.30
Wuertz, Mike-Michael James	04-06ChiN	12-15-78	Austin, Minn.		R	R	6'3	200	10	3	.769	1	147	0	0	145	117	73	161	0	3.59
Wunsch, Kelly-Kelly Douglas	00-04ChiA 05LAN	07-12-72	Houston, Tex.		L	L	6'5	220	11	6	.647	1	257	0	0	177	136	97	145	0	3.76
Yabu, Keiichi-Keiichi	05OakA	09-28-68	Mie, Japan		R	R	6'	190	2	4	.333	1	40	0	0	58	64	26	44	0	4.50
Yan, Esteban-Esteban Luis	96-97BalA 98-02TBA 03TexA 03StLN 04DetA 05-06LAA 06CinN	06-22-75	Campina del Seibo, D.R.		R	R	6'4	245	33	39	.458	51	472	23	0	695	754	270	553	0	5.14
Yarnall, Ed-Harvey Edward	99-00NYA	12-04-75	Lima, Pa.		L	L	6'3	234	1	0	1.000	0	7	3	0	20	22	13	14	0	5.40
Yates, Tyler-Tyler Kali	04NYN 06AtlN	08-07-77	Lihue, Hawaii		R	R	6'4	220	4	9	.308	1	77	7	0	97	103	56	81	0	5.12
Yett, Rich-Richard Martin	85MinA 86-89CleA 90MinA	10-06-62	Pomona, Cal.		R	R	6'2	185	22	24	.478	2	138	65	2	414	444	191	229	1	4.95
York, Jim-James Harlan	70-71KCA 72-75HouN 76NYA	08-27-47	Maywood, Cal.		R	R	6'3	200	16	17	.485	10	174	4	0	285	290	132	194	0	3.79
York, Mike-Michael David	90PitN 91CleA	09-06-64	Oak Park, Ill.		R	R	6'1	190	2	5	.286	0	18	5	0	47	58	24	23	0	5.70
Yoshii, Masato-Masato	98-99NYN 00ColN 01-02MonN	04-20-65	Osaka, Japan		R	R	6'2	210	32	47	.405	0	162	118	3	757	805	222	447	0	4.62
Youman, Shane-Shane Demond	06PitN	10-11-79	New Iberia, La.		L	L	6'4	220	4	2	.000	0	22	15	10	5	0	10	5	0	2.91
Youmans, Floyd-Floyd Everett	85-88MonN 89PhiN 90SJ	05-11-64	Tampa, Fla.		R	R	6'2	200	30	34	.469	0	94	90	10	539	428	280	424	6	3.74
Young, Anthony-Anthony Wayne	91-93NYN 94-95ChiN 96HouN	01-19-66	Houston, Tex.		R	R	6'2	200	15	48	.238	20	181	51	2	460	471	167	245	0	3.89
Young, Chris-Christopher Ryan	04-05TexA 06SDN	05-25-79	Dallas, Tex.		R	R	6'10	260	26	14	.650	0	69	69	0	380	332	124	328	0	3.93
Young, Cliff-Clifford Raphael	90-91CalA 93CleA	08-02-64	Willis, Tex.	11-04-93	L	L	6'4	205	5	4	.556	1	49	7	0	104	126	28	56	0	4.25
Young, Curt-Curtis Allen	83-91OakA 92KCA 92NYA 93OakA	04-16-60	Saginaw, Mich.		R	L	6'1	180	69	53	.566	0	251	162	15	1107	1133	366	536	3	4.31
Young, Danny-Daniel Bracy	00ChiN	11-03-71	Smyrna, Tenn.		R	R	6'4	210	0	1	.000	0	5	0	0	3	6	6	0	0	21.00
Young, Jason-Jason Kariya	03-04ColN	09-28-79	Oakland, Cal.		R	R	6'5	210	0	3	.000	0	10	5	0	30	49	14	25	0	9.71
Young, Kip-Kip Lane	78-79DetA	06-29-54	Georgetown, Ohio		R	R	5'11	175	8	9	.471	0	27	20	7	150	154	41	71	0	3.84
Young, Matt-Matthew John	83-86SeaA 87LAN 88EJ 89OakA 90SeaA 91-92BosA 93CleA	08-09-58	Pasadena, Cal.		L	L	6'3	205	55	95	.367	25	333	163	20	1190	1207	565	857	5	4.40
Young, Pete-Byran Owen	91-93MonN	03-19-68	Meadville, Miss.		R	R	6'	225	1	0	1.000	0	17	0	0	26	22	9	14	0	3.86
Young, Tim-Timothy R.	98MonN 00BosA	10-15-73	Gulfport, Miss.		L	L	5'9	170	0	0	—	0	18	0	0	13	16	6	13	0	6.23
Zachry, Pat-Patrick Paul	76-77CinN 77-82NYN 83-84LAN 85PhiN	04-24-52	Richmond, Tex.		R	R	6'2	180	69	67	.507	3	293	154	29	1179	1147	495	669	7	3.52
Zahn, Geoff-Geoffrey Clayton	73-75LAN 75-76ChiN 77-80MinA 81-85CalA	12-19-45	Baltimore, Md.		B	R	6'1	185	111	109	.505	1	304	270	79	1849	1978	526	705	20	3.74
Zambrano, Carlos-Carlos Alberto	01-06ChiN	06-01-81	Carabobo, Venezuela		R	R	6'4	250	64	42	.604	0	167	146	9	977	799	447	865	2	3.29
Zambrano, Victor-Victor Manuel	01-04TBA 04-06NYN	08-06-74	Los Teques, Venezuela		R	R	6'	195	45	41	.523	3	174	96	1	683	637	382	513	0	4.45
Zamora, Oscar-Oscar Jose [Sosa]	74-76ChiN 78HouN	09-23-44	Camaguey, Cuba		R	R	5'10	178	13	14	.481	23	158	2	0	225	256	58	99	0	4.52
Zaske, Jeff-Lloyd Jeffrey	84PitN	10-06-60	Seattle, Wash.		R	R	6'5	180	0	0	—	0	5	4	1	2	2	0	0	0	0.00
Zavaras, Clint-Clinton Wayne	89SeaA 90SJ	01-04-67	Denver, Colo.		R	R	6'1	175	1	6	.143	0	10	10	0	52	49	30	31	0	5.19
Zerbe, Chad-William Chad	00-03SFN	04-27-72	Findlay, Ohio		L	L	6'	190	6	1	.857	0	114	2	0	151	159	46	70	0	3.87
Ziem, Steve-Stephen Graeling	87AtlN	10-24-61	Milwaukee, Wis.		R	R	6'2	210	0	1	.000	0	2	0	0	2	4	1	0	0	7.71
Zimmerman, Jeff-Jeffrey Ross	99-01TexA 02-04EJ	08-09-72	Kelowna, Canada		R	R	6'2	200	17	12	.586	32	196	0	0	229	178	73	213	0	3.27
Zimmerman, Jordan-Jordan William	99SeaA	04-28-75	Kelowna, Canada		R	L	6'1	200	0	0	—	0	12	0	0	8	14	4	3	0	7.88
Zito, Barry-Barry William	00-06OakA	05-13-78	Las Vegas, Nev.		L	L	6'4	215	102	63	.618	0	222	222	9	1430	1228	560	1096	4	3.55
Zumaya, Joel-Joel Martin	06DetA	11-09-84	Chula Vista, Cal.		R	R	6'3	210	6	3	.667	1	62	0	0	83	56	42	97	0	1.94

Leaders and Features

Baseball's great magnetism has always been in the sheer numbers the sport produces. It is an attraction which no other sport can come close to matching. Although there has been repeated criticism of the lack of action of the game, no fan has ever delighted more than when a batting average is remembered and thrown up in conversation — baseball's advantage in that respect is also its disadvantage. It is a game of innings, not time, and the interest of the fan is more determined on his ability to appreciate the subtlety of play than the speed or violence present in other sports. For these reasons, it is important to realize that baseball is a season, not a single game, and that as the performance of the individuals on a team are followed, so grows the great interest in the sport.

The statistics which are part of the game of baseball are designed in a unique way as to give each man on a team a measure of his performance. It is also in this area where baseball has its great advantage over other sports. A .333 batting average, for example, tells that the player was successful one third of the time, just as an earned run average is an excellent indication of a pitcher's effectiveness. In this respect, there are statistics for every act performed on the field — a yardstick of independence not to be found in any other sport.

Baseball is by no means perfect in its representation of the individuals who perform their tasks, it is simply endowed with a greater and more accurate means for comparison than other sports. Because of the varied statistical categories available, it is possible to measure men who are separated by decades. For this reason, statistics such as Ty Cobb's lifetime batting average of .366 and Babe Ruth's hitting a home run every 11.8 times at bat are not dated numbers. The fan could, for instance, from these two percentages envision how these two immortals might fare on the playing field today. Even with playing conditions drastically altered from sixty years ago, the continuity of the sport remains uninterrupted due to its unique set of statistcal information. Along these lines the assumption could be made that even if in a hundred years from now someone was to scan through the records, he could come very close to recreating a player's performance. In the case of Tom Seaver, a few of the things which could be immediately learned is that he had an excellent fastball (number of strikeouts), good control (bases on balls vs. innings pitched), and endurance (complete games vs. games started).

On the following pages are many categories of single-season and lifetime leaders, as well as special features dealing with the World Series and other aspects of baseball. Although they do not tell the entire story of baseball, they are more than endless columns of numbers. For if they only inspire the human aspect of the people they represent, they have achieved a sound purpose.

YEARLY PENNANT WINNERS

AMERICAN LEAGUE

Year	TEAM (World Series Wins)	Manager	Won	Lost	Pct.	Games Ahead	Bat Age	Pitch Age
1901	Chicago	Clark Griffith	83	53	.610	4	30	27
1902	Philadelphia	Connie Mack	83	53	.610	5	29	26
1903	**Boston (5)**	Jimmy Collins	91	47	.659	14.5	30	28
1904	Boston	Jimmy Collins	95	59	.617	1.5	31	29
1905	Philadelphia (1)	Connie Mack	92	56	.622	2	29	25
1906	**Chicago (2)**	Fielder Jones	93	58	.616	3	30	27
1907	Detroit (0)	Hughie Jennings	92	58	.613	1.5	26	30
1908	Detroit (1)	Hughie Jennings	90	63	.588	0.5	27	27
1909	Detroit (3)	Hughie Jennings	98	54	.645	3.5	27	27
1910	**Philadelphia (4)**	Connie Mack	102	48	.680	14.5	28	27
1911	**Philadelphia (4)**	Connie Mack	101	50	.669	13.5	27	29
1912	**Boston (4)**	Jack Stahl	105	47	.691	14	27	25
1913	**Philadelphia (4)**	Connie Mack	96	57	.627	6.5	25	25
1914	Philadelphia (0)	Connie Mack	99	53	.651	8.5	26	25
1915	**Boston (4)**	Bill Carrigan	101	50	.669	2.5	27	25
1916	**Boston (4)**	Bill Carrigan	91	63	.591	2	27	26
1917	**Chicago (4)**	Pants Rowland	100	54	.649	9	26	28
1918	**Boston (4)**	Ed Barrow	75	51	.595	2.5	29	25
1919	Chicago (3)	Kid Gleason	88	52	.629	3.5	28	30
1920	**Cleveland (5)**	Tris Speaker	98	56	.636	2	29	28
1921	New York (3)	Miller Huggins	98	55	.641	4.5	28	28
1922	New York (0)	Miller Huggins	94	60	.610	1	29	27
1923	**New York (4)**	Miller Huggins	98	54	.645	16	29	29
1924	**Washington (4)**	Bucky Harris	92	62	.597	2	28	29
1925	Washington (4)	Bucky Harris	96	55	.636	8.5	30	32
1926	New York (3)	Miller Huggins	91	63	.591	3	27	30
1927	**New York (4)**	Miller Huggins	110	44	.714	19	28	31
1928	**New York (4)**	Miller Huggins	101	53	.656	2.5	28	29
1929	**Philadelphia (4)**	Connie Mack	104	46	.693	18	28	29
1930	**Philadelphia (4)**	Connie Mack	102	52	.662	8	28	32
1931	Philadelphia (3)	Connie Mack	107	45	.704	13.5	28	30
1932	**New York (4)**	Joe McCarthy	107	47	.695	13	28	29
1933	Washington (1)	Joe Cronin	99	53	.651	7	30	30
1934	Detroit (3)	Mickey Cochrane	101	53	.656	7	29	28
1935	**Detroit (4)**	Mickey Cochrane	93	58	.616	3	28	28
1936	**New York (4)**	Joe McCarthy	102	51	.667	19.5	28	30
1937	**New York (4)**	Joe McCarthy	102	52	.662	13	29	30
1938	**New York (4)**	Joe McCarthy	99	53	.651	9.5	28	30
1939	**New York (4)**	Joe McCarthy	106	45	.702	17	27	30
1940	Detroit (3)	Del Baker	90	64	.584	1	29	27
1941	**New York (4)**	Joe McCarthy	101	53	.656	17	27	29
1942	New York (1)	Joe McCarthy	103	51	.669	9	28	30
1943	**New York (4)**	Joe McCarthy	98	56	.636	13.5	29	31
1944	St. Louis (2)	Luke Sewell	89	65	.578	1	30	31
1945	**Detroit (4)**	Steve O'Neill	88	65	.575	1.5	33	29
1946	Boston (3)	Joe Cronin	104	50	.675	12	30	31
1947	**New York (4)**	Bucky Harris	97	57	.630	12	31	30
1948	**Cleveland (4)**	Lou Boudreau	97	58	.626	11	29	30
	Defeated Boston in 1 game playoff							
1949	**New York (4)**	Casey Stengel	97	58	.626	1	29	30
1950	**New York (4)**	Casey Stengel	98	56	.636	3	29	31
1951	**New York (4)**	Casey Stengel	98	56	.636	5	28	31
1952	**New York (4)**	Casey Stengel	95	59	.612	2	27	30
1953	**New York (4)**	Casey Stengel	99	52	.656	8.5	29	32
1954	Cleveland (0)	Al Lopez	111	43	.721	8	30	30
1955	New York (3)	Casey Stengel	96	58	.623	3	28	28
1956	**New York (4)**	Casey Stengel	97	57	.630	9	28	27
1957	New York (3)	Casey Stengel	98	56	.636	8	29	28
1958	**New York (4)**	Casey Stengel	92	62	.597	10	27	29
1959	Chicago (2)	Al Lopez	94	60	.610	5	30	32
1960	New York (3)	Casey Stengel	97	57	.630	8	29	29
1961	**New York (4)**	Ralph Houk	109	53	.673	8	28	27
1962	**New York (4)**	Ralph Houk	96	66	.593	5	29	28
1963	New York (0)	Ralph Houk	104	57	.646	10.5	28	27
1964	New York (3)	Yogi Berra	99	63	.611	1	29	27
1965	Minnesota (3)	Sam Mele	102	60	.630	7	27	28
1966	**Baltimore (4)**	Hank Bauer	97	63	.606	9	26	27
1967	Boston (3)	Dick Williams	92	70	.568	1	25	28
1968	**Detroit (4)**	Mayo Smith	103	59	.636	12	28	28
1969	Baltimore (1)	Earl Weaver	109	53	.673	19	28	27
	Won Championship Series over Minnessota (3 games to none)							
1970	**Baltimore (4)**	Earl Weaver	108	54	.667	15	29	29
	Won Championship Series over Minnesota (3 games to none)							

NATIONAL LEAGUE

Year	TEAM (World Series Wins)	Manager	Won	Lost	Pct.	Games Ahead	Bat Age	Pitch Age
1901	Pittsburgh	Fred Clarke	90	49	.647	1.5	29	28
1902	Pittsburgh	Fred Clarke	103	36	.741	27.5	28	29
1903	Pittsburgh (3)	Fred Clarke	91	49	.650	6.5	27	31
1904	New York	John McGraw	106	47	.693	13	29	26
1905	**New York (4)**	John McGraw	105	48	.686	9	30	27
1906	Chicago (2)	Frank Chance	116	36	.763	20	27	27
1907	**Chicago (4)**	Frank Chance	107	45	.704	17	28	29
1908	**Chicago (4)**	Frank Chance	99	55	.643	1	29	30
1909	**Pittsburgh (4)**	Fred Clarke	110	42	.724	6.5	28	30
1910	Chicago (1)	Frank Chance	104	50	.675	13	29	29
1911	New York (2)	John McGraw	99	54	.647	7.5	26	27
1912	New York (3)	John McGraw	103	48	.682	10	27	27
1913	New York (1)	John McGraw	101	51	.664	12.5	27	28
1914	**Boston (4)**	George Stallings	94	59	.614	10.5	25	24
1914 FEDERAL LEAGUE	Indianapolis	Bill Phillips	88	65	.575	1.5	29	29
1915	Philadelphia (1)	Pat Moran	90	62	.592	7	28	27
1915 FEDERAL LEAGUE	Chicago	Joe Tinker	86	66	.566	0	26	31
1916	Brooklyn (1)	Wilbert Robinson	94	60	.610	2.5	29	29
1917	New York (2)	John McGraw	98	56	.636	10	28	29
1918	Chicago (2)	Fred Mitchell	84	45	.651	10.5	29	28
1919	**Cincinnati (5)**	Pat Moran	96	44	.686	9	29	28
1920	Brooklyn (2)	Wilbert Robinson	93	61	.604	7	30	29
1921	**New York (5)**	John McGraw	94	59	.614	4	27	30
1922	**New York (4)**	John McGraw	93	61	.604	4	28	27
1923	New York (2)	John McGraw	95	58	.621	4.5	27	27
1924	New York (3)	John McGraw	93	60	.608	1.5	28	26
1925	**Pittsburgh (4)**	Bill McKechnie	95	58	.621	8.5	28	32
1926	**St. Louis (4)**	Rogers Hornsby	89	65	.578	2	27	29
1927	Pittsburgh (0)	Donie Bush	94	60	.610	1.5	28	31
1928	St. Louis (0)	Bill McKechnie	95	59	.617	2	28	31
1929	Chicago (1)	Joe McCarthy	98	54	.645	10.5	30	30
1930	St. Louis (2)	Gabby Street	92	62	.597	2	29	31
1931	**St. Louis (4)**	Gabby Street	101	53	.656	13	29	31
1932	Chicago (0)	Rogers Hornsby / Charlie Grimm	90	64	.584	4	28	31
1933	**New York (4)**	Bill Terry	91	61	.599	5	29	31
1934	**St. Louis (4)**	Frankie Frisch	95	58	.621	2	28	30
1935	Chicago (2)	Charlie Grimm	100	54	.649	4	27	27
1936	New York (2)	Bill Terry	92	62	.597	5	29	28
1937	New York (1)	Bill Terry	95	57	.625	3	28	28
1938	Chicago (0)	Charlie Grimm / Gabby Hartnett	89	63	.586	2	29	31
1939	Cincinnati (0)	Bill McKechnie	97	57	.630	4.5	29	29
1940	**Cincinnati (4)**	Bill McKechnie	100	53	.654	12	28	29
1941	Brooklyn (1)	Leo Durocher	100	54	.649	2.5	28	31
1942	**St. Louis (4)**	Billy Southworth	106	48	.688	2	26	26
1943	St. Louis (1)	Billy Southworth	105	49	.682	18	27	27
1944	**St. Louis (4)**	Billy Southworth	105	49	.682	14.5	27	28
1945	Chicago (3)	Charlie Grimm	98	66	.636	3	29	32
1946	**St. Louis (4)**	Eddie Dyer	98	58	.628	2	27	30
	Defeated Brooklyn in Playoff (2 games to none)							
1947	Brooklyn (3)	Clyde Sukeforth / Burt Shotton	94	60	.610	5	28	26
1948	Boston (2)	Billy Southworth	91	62	.595	6.5	30	31
1949	Brooklyn (1)	Burt Shotton	97	57	.630	1	27	25
1950	Philadelphia (0)	Eddie Sawyer	91	63	.591	2	27	27
1951	New York (2)	Leo Durocher	98	59	.624	1	27	29
	Defeated Brooklyn in Playoff (2 games to 1)							
1952	Brooklyn (2)	Chuck Dressen	96	57	.627	4.5	30	27
1953	Brooklyn (2)	Chuck Dressen	105	49	.682	13	29	28
1954	**New York (4)**	Leo Durocher	97	57	.630	5	28	30
1955	**Brooklyn (4)**	Walt Alston	98	55	.641	13.5	30	26
1956	Brooklyn (3)	Walt Alston	93	61	.604	1	32	27
1957	**Milwaukee (4)**	Fred Haney	95	59	.617	8	28	28
1958	Milwaukee (3)	Fred Haney	92	62	.597	8	29	29
1959	**Los Angeles (4)**	Walt Alston	88	68	.564	2	28	27
	Defeated Milwaukee in Playoff (2 games to none)							
1960	**Pittsburgh (4)**	Danny Murtaugh	95	59	.617	7	29	29
1961	Cincinnati (1)	Fred Hutchinson	93	61	.604	4	27	26
1962	San Francisco (3)	Al Dark	103	62	.624	1	27	29
	Defeated Los Angeles in Playoff (2 games to 1)							
1963	**Los Angeles (4)**	Walt Alston	99	63	.611	6	27	26
1964	**St. Louis (4)**	Johnny Keane	93	69	.574	11	27	30
1965	**Los Angeles (4)**	Walt Alston	97	65	.599	2	29	28
1966	Los Angeles 0	Walt Alston	95	67	.586	1.5	29	27
1967	**St. Louis (4)**	Red Schoendienst	101	60	.627	10.5	27	28
1968	St. Louis (3)	Red Schoendienst	97	65	.599	9	29	27
1969	**New York(4)**	Gil Hodges	100	62	.617	8	27	26
	Won Championship Series over Atlanta (3 games to none)							
1970	Cincinnati(1)	Sparky Anderson	102	60	.630	14.5	25	26
	Won Championship Series over Pittsburgh (3 games to none)							

NOTE: BOLD FACE DENOTES TEAM WINNING WORLD SERIES

YEARLY PENNANT WINNERS

AMERICAN LEAGUE

Team (World Series Wins)	Manager	Won	Lost	Pct.	Games Ahead	Bat Age	Pitch Age	Year
Baltimore(3)	Earl Weaver	101	57	.639	12	30	30	1971
Won Championship Series over Oakland (3 games to none)								
Oakland(4)	Dick Williams	93	62	.600	5.5	27	28	1972
Won Championship Series over Detroit (3 games to 2)								
Oakland(4)	Dick Williams	94	68	.580	6	28	27	1973
Won Championship Series over Baltimore (3 games to 2)								
Oakland(4)	Al Dark	90	72	.556	5	29	28	1974
Won Championship Series over Baltimore (3 games to 1)								
Boston(3)	Darrell Johnson	95	65	.594	4.5	27	29	1975
Won Championship Series over Oakland (3 games to none)								
New York(0)	Billy Martin	97	62	.610	10.5	28	30	1976
Won Championship Series over Kansas City (3 games to 2)								
New York(4)	Billy Martin	100	62	.617	2.5	29	29	1977
Won Championship Series over Kansas City (3 games to 2)								
New York(4)	Billy Martin, Dick Howser, Bob Lemon	100	63	.613	1	30	28	1978
Defeated Boston in 1 game playoff. Won Championship Series over Kansas City (3 games to 1)								
Baltimore(3)	Earl Weaver	102	57	.642	8	29	27	1979
Won Championship Series over California (3 games to 1)								
Kansas City(2)	Jim Frey	97	65	.599	14	28	29	1980
Won Championship Series over New York (3 games to none)								
New York(2)	Bob Lemon	59	48	.551		31	30	1981
Won Championship Series over Oakland (3 games to none)								
Milwaukee(3)	Bob Rodgers, Harvey Kuenn	95	67	.586	1	30	30	1982
Won Championship Series over California (3 games to 2)								
Baltimore(4)	Joe Altobelli	98	64	.605	6	30	28	1983
Won Championship Series over Chicago (3 games to 1)								
Detroit(4)	Sparky Anderson	104	58	.642	15	29	30	1984
Won Championship Series over Kansas City (3 games to none)								
Kansas City(4)	Dick Howser	91	71	.562	1	31	27	1985
Won Championship Series over Toronto (4 games to 3)								
Boston(3)	John McNamara	95	66	.590	5.5	30	29	1986
Won Championship Series over California (4 games to 3)								
Minnesota(4)	Tom Kelly	85	77	.525	2	28	32	1987
Won Championship Series over Detroit (4 games to 1)								
Oakland(1)	Tony LaRussa	104	58	.642	13	28	29	1988
Won Championship Series over Boston (4 games to none)								
Oakland(4)	Tony LaRussa	99	63	.611	7	29	29	1989
Won Championship Series over Toronto (4 games to 1)								
Oakland(0)	Tony LaRussa	103	59	.636	9	30	30	1990
Won Championship Series over Boston (4 games to 0)								
Minnesota(4)	Tom Kelly	95	67	.586	8	29	28	1991
Won Championship Series over Toronto (4 games to 1)								
Toronto(4)	Cito Gaston	96	66	.593	4	29	30	1992
Won Championship Series over Oakland (4 games to 2)								
Toronto(4)	Cito Gaston	95	67	.586	1	30	30	1993
Won Championship Series over Chicago (4 games to 2)								
								1994
Cleveland(2)	Mike Hargrove	100	44	.694	30	29	29	1995
Won Championship Series over Seattle (4 games to 2). Won Division Series over Boston (3 games to 0)								
New York(4)	Joe Torre	92	70	.568	4	31	30	1996
Won Championship Serries over Baltimore (4 games to 1). Won Division Series over Texas (3 games to 1)								
Cleveland(3)	Mike Hargrove	86	75	.534	6	31	28	1997
Won Championship Series over Baltimore (4 games to 2). Won Division Series over New York (3 games to 2)								
New York(4)	Joe Torre	114	48	.703	22	32	30	1998
Won Championship Series over Cleveland (4 games to 2). Won Division Series over Texas (3 games to 0)								
New York(4)	Joe Torre	98	64	.605	4	31	31	1999
Won Championship Series over Boston (4 games to 1). Won Division Series over Texas (3 games to 0)								
New York(4)	Joe Torre	87	74	.540	2.5	31	32	2000
Won Championship Series over Seattle (4 games to 2). Won Division Series over Oakland (3 games to 2)								
New York(3)	Joe Torre	95	65	.594	13.5	31	31	2001
Won Championship Series over Seattle (4 games to 1). Won Division Series over Oakland (3 games to 2)								
Anaheim(4)	Mike Scioscia	99	63	.611	-4	29	31	2002
Won Championship Series over Minnesota (4 games to 1). Won Division Series over New York (3 games to 1)								
New York(2)	Joe Torre	101	61	.623	6	32	34	2003
Won Championship Series over Boston (4 games to 3). Won Division Series over Minnesota (3 games to 1)								
Boston(4)	Terry Francona	98	64	.605	-3	30	32	2004
Won Championship Series over New York (4 games to 3). Won Division Series over Anaheim (3 games to 0)								
Chicago(4)	Ozzie Guillen	99	63	.611	6	29	30	2005
Won Championship Series over Los Angeles (4 games to 1). Won Division Series over Boston (3 games to 0)								
Detroit(1)	Jim Leyland	95	67	.586	-1	29	28	2006
Won Championship Series over Oakland (4 games to 0). Won Division Series over New York (3 games to 1)								

NATIONAL LEAGUE

Team (World Series Wins)	Manager	Won	Lost	Pct.	Games Ahead	Bat Age	Pitch Age	Year
Pittsburgh(4)	Danny Murtaugh	97	65	.599	7	28	28	1971
Won Championship Series over San Francisco (3 games to 1)								
Cincinnati(3)	Sparky Anderson	95	59	.617	10.5	27	25	1972
Won Championship Series over Pittsburgh (3 games to 2)								
New York(3)	Yogi Berra	82	79	.509	1.5	28	27	1973
Won Championship Series over Cincinnati (3 games to 2)								
Los Angeles(1)	Walt Alston	102	60	.630	4	27	30	1974
Won Championship Series over Pittsburgh (3 games to 1)								
Cincinnati(4)	Sparky Anderson	108	54	.667	20	28	28	1975
Won Championship Series over Pittsburgh (3 games to none)								
Cincinnati(4)	Sparky Anderson	102	60	.630	10	29	27	1976
Won Championship Series over Philadelphia (3 games to none)								
Los Angeles(2)	Tommy Lasorda	98	64	.605	10	29	28	1977
Won Championship Series over Philadelphia (3 games to 1)								
Los Angeles(2)	Tommy Lasorda	95	67	.586	2.5	30	28	1978
Won Championship Series over Philadelphia (3 games to 1)								
Pittsburgh(4)	Chuck Tanner	98	64	.605	2	30	30	1979
Won Championship Series over Cincinnati (3 games to none)								
Philadelphia(4)	Dallas Green	91	71	.562	1	31	29	1980
Won Championship Series over Houston (3 games to 2)								
Los Angeles(4)	Tommy Lasorda	63	47	.573		29	26	1981
Won Championship Series over Montreal (3 games to 2)								
St. Louis(4)	Whitey Herzog	92	70	.568	3	27	29	1982
Won Championship Series over Atlanta (3 games to none)								
Philadelphia(1)	Pat Corrales, Paul Owens	90	72	.556	6	32	30	1983
Won Championship Series over Los Angeles (3 games to 1)								
San Diego(1)	Dick Williams	92	70	.568	12	29	27	1984
Won Championship Series over Chicago (3 games to 2)								
St. Louis(3)	Whitey Herzog	101	61	.623	3	27	29	1985
Won Championship Series over Los Angeles (4 games to 2)								
New York(4)	Davey Johnson	106	54	.667	21.5	28	26	1986
Won Championship Series over Houston (4 games to 2)								
St. Louis(3)	Whitey Herzog	95	67	.586	3	28	28	1987
Won Championship Series over San Francisco (4 games to 3)								
Los Angeles(4)	Tommy Lasorda	94	67	.584	7	29	30	1988
Won Championship Series over New York (4 games to 3)								
San Francisco(0)	Roger Craig	92	70	.568	3	28	31	1989
Won Championship Series over Chicago (4 games to 1)								
Cincinnati(4)	Lou Piniella	91	71	.562	5	27	27	1990
Won Championship Series over Pittsburgh (4 games to 2)								
Atlanta(3)	Bobby Cox	94	68	.580	1	28	28	1991
Won Championship Series over Pittsburgh (4 games to 3)								
Atlanta(2)	Bobby Cox	98	64	.604	8	28	28	1992
Won Championship Series over Pittsburgh (4 games to 3)								
Philadelphia(2)	Jim Fregosi	97	65	.599	3	29	30	1993
Won Championship Series over Atlanta (4 games to 2)								
								1994
Atlanta(4)	Bobby Cox	90	54	.625	21	29	28	1995
Won Championship Series over Cincinnati (4 games to 0). Won Playoff Series over Colorado (3 games to 1)								
Atlanta(2)	Bobby Cox	96	66	.593	8	28	28	1996
Won Championship Series over St. Louis (4 games to 3). Won Division Series over Los Angeles (3 games to 0)								
Florida(4)	Jim Leyland	92	70	.568	9	29	27	1997
Won Championship Series over Atlanta (4 games to 2). Won Division Series over San Francisco (3 games to 0)								
San Diego(0)	Bruce Bochy	98	64	.604	9.5	31	30	1998
Won Championship Series over Atlanta (4 games to 2). Won Division Series over Houston (3 games to 1)								
Atlanta(0)	Bobby Cox	103	59	.636	6.5	30	28	1999
Won Championship Series over New York (4 games to 2). Won Division Series over Houston (3 games to 1)								
New York(1)	Bobby Valentine	94	68	.580	-1	30	32	2000
Won Championship Series over St. Louis (4 games to 1). Won Division Series over San Francisco (3 games to 1)								
Arizona(4)	Bob Brenly	92	70	.568	2	32	31	2001
Won Championship Series over Atlanta (4 games to 1). Won Division Series over St. Louis (3 games to 2)								
San Francisco(3)	Dusty Baker	95	66	.590	-2.5	32	29	2002
Won Championship Series over St. Louis (4 games to 1). Won Division Series over Atlanta (3 games to 2)								
Florida(4)	Jack McKeon	91	71	.562	-10	27	27	2003
Won Championship Series over Chicago (4 games to 3). Won Division Series over San Francisco (3 games to 1)								
St. Louis(0)	Tony LaRussa	105	57	.648	13	31	31	2004
Won Championship Series over Houston (4 games to 3). Won Division Series over Los Angeles (3 games to 1)								
Houston(0)	Phil Garner	89	73	.549	-11	31	31	2005
Won Championship Series over St. Louis (4 games to 2). Won Division Series over Atlanta (3 games to 1)								
St. Louis(4)	Tony LaRussa	93	78	.516	1.5	30	28	2006
Won Championship Series over New York (4 games to 3). Won Division Series over San Diego (3 games to 1)								

NOTE: BOLD FACE DENOTES TEAM WINNING WORLD SERIES

YEARLY BATTING LEADERS

AT-BATS

AMERICAN LEAGUE		Year	NATIONAL LEAGUE	
Waldron-Was. + Mil.	598	1901	Burkett-St.L.	601
Parent-Bos.	567	1902	Dolan-Bkn.	592
Dougherty-Bos.	590	1903	Beaumont-Pit.	613
Dougherty-Bos. + N.Y.	647	1904	Beaumont-Pit.	615
Stone-St.L.	632	1905	Abbaticchio-Bos.	610
Flick-Cle.	624	1906	Bennett-St.L.	595
Donahue-Chi.	609	1907	Shannon-N.Y.	585
Crawford-Det.	591	1908	Grant-Phi.	598
Hartzell-St.L.	595	1909	Grant-Phi.	631
Lajoie-Cle.	592	1910	Hoblitzell-Cin.	611
Milan-Was.	616	1911	Hoblitzell-Cin.	622
Foster-Was.	618	1912	Campbell-Bos.	624
Crawford-Det.	610	1913	Carey-Pit.	620
Foster-Was.	616	1914	Carey-Pit.	593
Foster-Was.	618	1915	Burns-N.Y.	622
Shotton-St.L.	614	1916	Burns-N.Y.	623
Cobb-Det.	588	1917	Chase-Cin.	602
Foster-Was.	519	1918	Hollocher-Chi.	509
Weaver-Chi.	571	1919	Olson-Bkn.	590
Sisler-St.L.	631	1920	Stock-St.L.	639
Tobin-St.L.	671	1921	Olson-Bkn.	652
Rice-Was.	633	1922	Maranville-Pit.	672
Dugan-N.Y.	644	1923	Statz-Chi.	655
Jamieson-Cle.	644			
Rice-Was.	646	1924	Wright-Pit.	616
Simmons-Phi.	658	1925	Adams-Chi.	627
Rice-Was.	641	1926	Adams-Chi.	624
Combs-N.Y.	648	1927	Adams-Chi.	647
Lind-Cle.	650	1928	L. Waner-Pit.	659
Johnson-Det.	640	1929	L. Waner-Pit.	662
Oliver-Bos.	646	1930	Douthit-St.L.	664
Averill-Cle.	627	1931	L. Waner-Pit.	681
Simmons-Phi.	670	1932	Critz-N.Y.	659
Cramer-Phi.	661	1933	Fullis-Phi.	647
Cramer-Phi.	649	1934	Rothrock-St.L.	647
Cramer-Phi.	644	1935	Moore-N.Y.	681
Finney-Phi.	653	1936	Jensen-Pit.	696
Lewis-Was.	668	1937	Medwick-St.L.	633
Cramer-Bos.	658	1938	McCormick-Cin.	640
Crosetti-N.Y.	656	1939	Brown-St.L.	645
Cramer-Bos.	661	1940	F. McCormick-Cin.	618
Cramer-Was.	660	1941	Rucker-N.Y.	622
Cramer-Det.	630	1942	Brown-St.L.	606
Wakefield-Det.	633	1943	Holmes-Bos.	629
Rocco-Cle.	653	1944	Williams-Cin.	653
Stirnweiss-N.Y.	632	1945	Clay-Cin.	656
Pesky-Bos.	621	1946	Musial-St.L.	624
Pesky-Bos.	638	1947	Schoendienst-St.L.	659
DiMaggio-Bos.	648	1948	Rojek-Pit.	641
Mitchell-Cle.	640	1949	Ashburn-Phi.	662
			Hamner-Phi.	662
Kell-Det.	641	1950	Schoendienst-St.L.	642
DiMaggio-Bos.	639	1951	Furillo-Bkn.	667
Fox-Chi.	648	1952	Adams-Cin.	637
Kuenn-Det.	679	1953	Dark-N.Y.	647
Kuenn-Det.	656	1954	Dark-N.Y.	644
Fox-Chi.	636	1955	Bruton-Mil.	636
Fox-Chi.	649	1956	Temple-Cin.	632
Gardner-Bal.	644	1957	Blasingame-St.L.	650
Malzone-Bos.	627	1958	Banks-Chi.	617
Fox-Chi.	624	1959	Pinson-Cin.	648
Fox-Chi.	605	1960	Pinson-Cin.	652

HITS

AMERICAN LEAGUE		Year	NATIONAL LEAGUE	
Lajoie-Phi.	229	1901	Burkett-St.L.	228
Hickman-Bos. + Cle.	194	1902	Beaumont-Pit.	194
Dougherty-Bos.	195	1903	Beaumont-Pit.	209
Lajoie-Cle.	211	1904	Beaumont-Pit.	185
Stone-St.L.	187	1905	Seymour-Cin.	219
Lajoie-Cle.	214	1906	Steinfeldt-Chi.	176
Cobb-Det.	212	1907	Beaumont-Bos.	187
Cobb-Det.	188	1908	Wagner-Pit.	201
Cobb-Det.	216	1909	Doyle-N.Y.	172
Lajoie-Cle.	227	1910	Byrne-Pit.	178
			Wagner-Pit.	178
Cobb-Det.	248	1911	Miller-Bos.	192
Cobb-Det.	227	1912	Zimmerman-Chi.	207
Jackson-Cle.	197	1913	Cravath-Phi.	179
Speaker-Bos.	193	1914	Magee-Phi.	171
Cobb-Det.	208	1915	Doyle-N.Y.	189
Speaker-Cle.	211	1916	Chase-Cin.	184
Cobb-Det.	225	1917	Groh-Cin.	182
Burns-Phi.	178	1918	Hollocher-Chi.	161
Cobb-Det.	191	1919	Olson-Bkn.	164
Veach-Det.	191			
Sisler-St.L.	257	1920	Hornsby-St.L.	218
Heilmann-Det.	237	1921	Hornsby-St.L.	235
Sisler-St.L.	246	1922	Hornsby-St.L.	250
Jamieson-Cle.	222	1923	Frisch-N.Y.	223
Rice-Was.	216	1924	Hornsby-St.L.	227
Simmons-Phi.	253	1925	Bottomley-St.L.	227
Burns-Cle.	216	1926	Brown-Bos.	201
Rice-Was.	216			
Combs-N.Y.	231	1927	P. Waner-Pit.	237
Manush-St.L.	241	1928	Lindstrom-N.Y.	231
Alexander-Det.	215	1929	O'Doul-Phi.	254
Gehringer-Det.	215			
Hodapp-Cle.	225	1930	Terry-N.Y.	254
Gehrig-N.Y.	211	1931	L. Waner-Pit.	214
Simmons-Phi.	216	1932	Klein-Phi.	226
Manush-Was.	221	1933	Klein-Phi.	223
Gehringer-Det.	214	1934	P. Waner-Pit.	217
Vosmik-Cle.	216	1935	Herman-Chi.	227
Averill-Cle.	232	1936	Medwick-St.L.	223
Bell-St.L.	218	1937	Medwick-St.L.	237
Vosmik-Bos.	201	1938	McCormick-Cin.	209
Rolfe-N.Y.	213	1939	McCormick-Cin.	209
Cramer-Bos.	200	1940	Hack-Chi.	191
McCosky-Det.	200		F. McCormick-Cin.	191
Radcliffe-St.L.	200			
Travis-Was.	218	1941	Hack-Chi.	186
Peksy-Bos.	205	1942	Slaughter-St.L.	188
Wakefield-Det.	200	1943	Musial-St.L.	220
Stirnweiss-N.Y.	205	1944	Cavarretta-Chi.	197
			Musial St.L.	197
Stirnweiss-N.Y.	195	1945	Holmes-Bos.	224
Pesky-Bos.	208	1946	Musial-St.L.	228
Pesky-Bos.	207	1947	Holmes-Bos.	191
Dillinger-St.L.	207	1948	Musial St.L.	230
Mitchell-Cle.	203	1949	Musial St.L.	207
Kell-Det.	218	1950	Snider-Bkn.	199
Kell-Det.	191	1951	Ashburn-Phi.	221
Fox-Chi.	192	1952	Musial St.L.	194
Kuenn-Det.	209	1953	Ashburn-Phi.	205
Fox-Chi.	201	1954	Mueller-N.Y.	212
Kuenn-Det.	201			
Kaline-Det.	200	1955	Kluszewski-Cin.	192
Kuenn-Det.	196	1956	Aaron-Mil.	200
Fox-Chi.	196	1957	Schoendienst-N.Y.+Mil.	200
Fox-Chi.	187	1958	Ashburn-Phi.	215
Kuenn-Det.	198	1959	Aaron-Mil.	223
Minoso-Chi.	184	1960	Mays-S.F.	190

RUNS

AMERICAN LEAGUE		Year	NATIONAL LEAGUE	
Lajoie-Phi.	145	1901	Burkett-St.L.	139
Fultz-Phi.	109	1902	Wagner-Pit.	105
Hartsel-Phi.	109			
Dougherty-Bos.	106	1903	Beaumont-Pit.	137
Dougherty-Bos. + N.Y.	113	1904	Browne-N.Y.	99
Davis-Phi.	92	1905	Donlin-N.Y.	124
Flick-Cle.	98	1906	Chance-Chi.	103
			Wagner-Pit.	103
Crawford-Det.	102	1907	Shannon-N.Y.	104
McIntyre-Det.	105	1908	Tenney-N.Y.	101
Cobb-Det.	116	1909	Leach-Pit.	126
Cobb-Det.	106	1910	Magee-Phi.	110
Cobb-Det.	147	1911	Sheckard-Chi.	121
Collins-Phi.	137	1912	Bescher-Cin.	120
Collins-Phi.	125	1913	Carey-Pit. + Leach-Chi.	99
Collins-Phi.	122	1914	Burns-N.Y.	100
Cobb-Det.	144	1915	Cravath-Phi.	89
Cobb-Det.	113	1916	Burns-N.Y.	105
Bush-Det.	112	1917	Burns-N.Y.	103
Chapman-Cle.	84	1918	Groh-Cin.	88
Ruth-Bos.	102	1919	Burns-N.Y.	86
Ruth-N.Y.	158	1920	Burns-N.Y.	115
Ruth-N.Y.	177	1921	Hornsby-St.L.	131
Sisler-St.L.	134	1922	Hornsby-St.L.	141
Ruth-N.Y.	151	1923	Youngs-N.Y.	121
Ruth-N.Y.	143	1924	Frisch-N.Y.	121
			Hornsby-St.L.	121
Mostil-Chi.	135	1925	Cuyler-Pit.	144
Ruth-N.Y.	139	1926	Cuyler-Pit.	113
Ruth-N.Y.	158	1927	Hornsby-N.Y.	133
			L. Waner-Pit.	133
Ruth-N.Y.	163	1928	P. Waner-Pit.	142
Gehringer-Det.	131	1929	Hornsby-Chi.	156
Simmons-Phi.	152	1930	Klein-Phi.	158
Gehrig-N.Y.	163	1931	Klein-Phi. + Terry-N.Y.	121
Foxx-Phi.	151	1932	Klein-Phi.	152
Gehrig-N.Y.	138	1933	Martin-St.L.	122
Gehringer-Det.	134	1934	P. Waner-Pit.	122
Gehrig-N.Y.	125	1935	Galan-Chi.	133
Gehrig-N.Y.	167	1936	Vaughan-Pit.	122
DiMaggio-N.Y.	151	1937	Medwick-St.L.	111
Greenberg-Det.	149	1938	Ott-N.Y.	116
Williams-Bos.	139	1939	Werber-Cin.	115
Williams-Bos.	134	1940	Vaughan-Pit.	113
Williams-Bos.	135	1941	Reiser-Bkn.	117
Williams-Bos.	141	1942	Ott-N.Y.	118
Case-Was.	102	1943	Vaughan-Bkn.	112
Stirnweiss-N.Y.	125	1944	Nicholson-Chi.	116
Stirnweiss-N.Y.	107	1945	Stanky-Bkn.	128
Williams-Bos.	142	1946	Musial-St.L.	124
Williams-Bos.	125	1947	Mize-N.Y.	137
Henrich-N.Y.	138	1948	Musial-St.L.	135
Williams-Bos.	150	1949	Reese-Bkn.	132
DiMaggio-Bos.	131	1950	Torgeson-Bos.	120
DiMaggio-Bos.	113	1951	Kiner-Pit.	124
			Musial-St.L.	124
Doby-Cle.	104	1952	Hemus-St.L.	105
			Musial-St.L.	105
Rosen-Cle.	115	1953	Snider-Bkn.	132
Mantle-N.Y.	129	1954	Musial-St.L.	120
			Snider-Bkn.	120
Smith-Cle.	123	1955	Snider-Bkn.	126
Mantle-N.Y.	132	1956	Robinson-Cin.	122
Mantle-N.Y.	121	1957	Aaron-Mil.	118
Mantle-N.Y.	127	1958	Mays-S.F.	121
Yost-Det.	115	1959	Pinson-Cin.	131
Mantle-N.Y.	119	1960	Bruton-Mil.	112

FEDERAL LEAGUE

AT-BATS

1914	FEDERAL LEAGUE	Swacina-Bal.	617
1915	FEDERAL LEAGUE	Tobin-St.L.	623

HITS

1914	FEDERAL LEAGUE	Kauff-Ind.	211
1915	FEDERAL LEAGUE	Tobin-St.L.	186

RUNS

1914	FEDERAL LEAGUE	Kauff-Ind.	120
1915	FEDERAL LEAGUE	Borton-St.L.	87

YEARLY BATTING LEADERS

AT-BATS

AMERICAN LEAGUE			NATIONAL LEAGUE	
Robinson-Bal.	668	1961	Wills-L.A.	613
Richardson-N.Y.	692	1962	Wills-L.A.	695
Richardson-N.Y.	630	1963	Flood-St.L.	662
Richardson-N.Y.	679	1964	Flood-St.L.	679
Versalles-Min.	666	1965	Rose-Cin.	670
Aparicio-Bal.	659	1966	F. Alou-Atl.	666
Tovar-Min.	649	1967	Brock-St.L.	689
Campaneris-Oak.	642	1968	F. Alou-Atl.	662
Clarke-N.Y.	641	1969	M. Alou-Pit.	698
Clarke-N.Y.	686	1970	M. Alou-Pit.	677
Alomar-Cal.	689	1971	Bowa-Phi.	650
Campaneris-Oak.	625	1972	Rose-Cin.	645
White-N.Y.	639	1973	Rose-Cin.	680
Money-Mil.	629	1974	Cash-Phi.	687
Brett-K.C.	634	1975	Cash-Phi.	699
Brett-K.C.	645	1976	Cash-Phi.	666
Burleson-Bos.	663	1977	Rose-Cin.	655
Rice-Bos.	677	1978	Cabell-Hou.	660
Bell-Tex.	670	1979	Moreno-Pit.	695
Wilson-K.C.	705	1980	Moreno-Pit.	676
Rice-Bos.	451	1981	Smith-S.D.	450
Molitor-Mil.	666	1982	Buckner-Chi.	657
Ripken-Bal.	663	1983	Wilson-N.Y.	638
Franco-Cle.	658	1984	Samuel-Phi.	701
Puckett-Min.	691	1985	Samuel-Phi.	663
Fernandez-Tor.	687	1986	Gwynn-S.D.	642
Sierra-Tex.	643	1987	Samuel-Phi.	655
Puckett-Min.	657	1988	Sax-L.A.	632
Carter-Cle.	651	1989	Benzinger-Cin.	628
Sax-N.Y.	651			
Reynolds-Sea.	642	1990	Carter-S.D.	634
Molitor-Mil.	665	1991	Grace-Chi.	619
Fryman-Det.	659	1992	Grissom-Mon.	653
Ripken-Bal.	641	1993	Dykstra-Phi.	637
Fryman-Det.	464	1994	Bichette-Col.	484
Johnson-Chi.	607	1995	McRae-Chi.	580
Lofton-Cle.	662	1996	Johnson-N.Y.	682
Garciaparra-Bos.	684	1997	Grudzielanek-Mon.	649
Rodriguez-Sea.	686	1998	Glanville-Phi.	678
Surhoff-Bal.	673	1999	Perez-Col.	690
Erstad-Ana.	676	2000	A. Jones-Atl.	656
Suzuki-Sea.	692	2001	Rollins-Phi.	656
Soriano-N.Y.	696	2002	Rollins-Phi.	637
Soriano-N.Y.	682	2003	Pierre-Fla.	668
Suzuki-Sea.	704	2004	Pierre-Fla.	678
Suzuki-Sea.	679	2005	Reyes-N.Y.	696
Suzuki-Sea.	695	2006	Pierre-Chi.	699

HITS

AMERICAN LEAGUE			NATIONAL LEAGUE	
Cash-Det.	193	1961	Pinson-Cin.	208
Richardson-N.Y.	209	1962	Davis-L.A.	230
Yastrzemski-Bos.	183	1963	Pinson-Cin.	204
Oliva-Min.	217	1964	Clemente-Pit.	211
			Flood-St.L.	211
Oliva-Min.	185	1965	Rose-Cin.	209
Oliva-Min.	191	1966	Alou-Atl.	218
Yastrzemski-Bos.	189	1967	Clemente-Pit.	209
Campaneris-Oak.	177	1968	Alou-Atl.	210
			Rose-Cin.	210
Oliva-Min.	197	1969	Alou-Pit.	231
Oliva-Min.	204	1970	Rose-Cin.	205
			Williams-Chi.	205
Tovar-Min.	204	1971	Torre-St.L.	230
Rudi-Oak.	181	1972	Rose-Cin.	198
Carew-Min.	203	1973	Rose-Cin.	230
Carew-Min.	218	1974	Garr-Atl.	214
Brett-K.C.	195	1975	Cash-Phi.	213
Brett-K.C.	215	1976	Rose-Cin.	215
Carew-Min.	239	1977	Parker-Pit.	215
Rice-Bos.	213	1978	Garvey-L.A.	202
Brett-K.C.	212	1979	Templeton-St.L.	211
Wilson-K.C.	230	1980	Garvey-L.A.	200
Henderson-Oak.	136	1981	Rose-Phi.	140
Yount-Mil.	210	1982	Oliver-Mon.	204
Ripken-Bal.	211	1983	Cruz-Hou.	189
			Dawson-Mon.	189
Mattingly-N.Y.	207	1984	Gwynn-S.D.	213
Boggs-Bos.	240	1985	McGee-St.L.	216
Mattingly-N.Y.	238	1986	Gwynn-S.D.	211
Puckett-Min.	207	1987	Gwynn-S.D.	218
Seitzer-K.C.	207			
Puckett-Min.	234	1988	Galarraga-Mon.	184
Puckett-Min.	215	1989	Gwynn-S.D.	203
Palmeiro-Tex.	191	1990	Butler-S.F.	192
			Dykstra-Phi.	192
Molitor-Mil.	216	1991	Pendleton-Atl.	187
Puckett-Min.	210	1992	Pendleton-Atl.	199
			Van Slyke-Pit.	199
Molitor-Tor.	211	1993	Dykstra-Phi.	194
Lofton-Cle.	160	1994	Gwynn-S.D.	165
Johnson-Chi.	186	1995	Bichette-Col.	197
			Gwynn-S.D.	197
Molitor-Min.	225	1996	Johnson-N.Y.	227
Garciaparra-Bos.	209	1997	Gwynn-S.D.	220
Rodriguez-Sea.	213	1998	Bichette-Col.	219
Jeter-N.Y.	219	1999	Gonzalez-Ari.	206
Erstad-Ana.	240	2000	Helton-Col.	216
Suzuki-Sea.	242	2001	Aurilia-S.F.	206
Soriano-N.Y.	209	2002	V. Guerrero-Mon.	206
Walls-Tor.	215	2003	Pujois-St.L.	212
Suzuki-Sea.	262	2004	Pierre-Fla.	221
Young-Tex.	221	2005	Lee-Chi.	199
Suzuki-Sea.	224	2006	Pierre-Chi.	204

RUNS

AMERICAN LEAGUE			NATIONAL LEAGUE	
Mantle-N.Y.	132	1961	Mays-S.F.	129
Maris-N.Y.	132			
Pearson-L.A.	115	1962	Robinson-Cin.	134
Allison-Min.	99	1963	Aaron-Mil.	121
Oliva-Min.	109	1964	Allen-Phi.	125
Versalles-Min.	126	1965	Harper-Cin.	126
F. Robinson-Bal.	122	1966	Alou-Atl.	122
Yastrzemski-Bos.	112	1967	Aaron-Atl.	113
			Brock-St.L.	113
McAuliffe-Det.	95	1968	Beckert-Chi.	98
Jackson-Oak.	123	1969	Bonds-S.F.	120
			Rose-Cin.	120
Yastrzemski-Bos.	125	1970	Williams-Chi.	137
Buford-Bal.	99	1971	Brock-St.L.	126
Murcer-N.Y.	102	1972	Morgan-Cin.	122
Jackson-Oak.	90	1973	Bonds-S.F.	131
Yastrzemski-Bos.	93	1974	Rose-Cin.	110
Lynn-Bos.	103	1975	Rose-Cin.	112
White-N.Y.	104	1976	Rose-Cin.	130
Carew-Min.	128	1977	Rose-Cin.	124
LeFlore-Det.	126	1978	DeJesus-Chi.	104
Baylor-Cal.	120	1979	Hernandez-St.L.	116
Wilson-K.C.	133	1980	Hernandez-St.L.	111
Henderson-Oak.	99	1981	Schmidt-Phi.	78
Molitor-Mil.	136	1982	L. Smith-St.L.	120
Ripken-Bal.	121	1983	Raines-Mon.	133
Evans-Bos.	121	1984	Sandberg-Chi.	114
Henderson-N.Y.	146	1985	Murphy-Atl.	118
Henderson-N.Y.	130	1986	Gwynn-S.D.	107
			Hayes-Phi.	107
Molitor-Mil.	114	1987	Raines-Mon.	123
Boggs-Bos.	108	1988	Butler-S.F.	109
Boggs-Bos.	113	1989	Clark-S.F.	104
Henderson-N.Y.+Oak.	113		Johnson-N.Y.	104
			Sandberg-Chi.	104
R. Henderson-Oak.	119	1990	Sandberg-Chi.	116
Molitor-Mil.	133	1991	Butler-L.A.	112
Phillips-Det.	114	1992	Bonds-Pit.	109
Palmeiro-Tex.	124	1993	Dykstra-Phi.	143
Thomas-Chi.	106	1994	Bagwell-Hou.	104
Belle-Cle.	121	1995	Biggio-Hou.	123
E. Martinez-Sea.	121			
Rodriguez-Sea.	141	1996	Burks-Col.	142
Griffey-Sea.	125	1997	Biggio-Hou.	146
Jeter-N.Y.	127	1998	Sosa-Chi.	134
R. Alomar-Cle.	138	1999	Bagwell-Hou.	143
Damon-K.C.	136	2000	Bagwell-Hou.	152
A. Rodriguez-Tex.	133	2001	Sosa-Chi.	146
Soriano-N.Y.	128	2002	Sosa-Chi.	122
Rodriguez-Tex.	123	2003	Pujois-St.L.	137
Guerrero-Ana.	124	2004	Pujols-St.L.	133
Rodriguez-N.Y.	124	2005	Pujols-St.L.	129
Sizemore-Cle.	134	2006	Utley-Phi.	131

YEARLY BATTING LEADERS

DOUBLES

American League		Year	National League	
Lajoie-Phi.	48	1901	Beckley-Cin.	39
Davis-Phi.	43	1902	Wagner-Pit.	30
Seybold-Phi.	43	1903	Clarke-Pit.	32
			Mertes-N.Y.	32
			Steinfeldt-Cin.	32
Lajoie-Cle.	50	1904	Wagner-Pit.	44
Davis-Phi.	47	1905	Seymour-Cin.	40
Lajoie-Cle.	49	1906	Wagner-Pit.	38
Davis-Phi.	37	1907	Wagner-Pit.	38
Cobb-Det.	36	1908	Wagner-Pit.	39
Crawford-Det.	35	1909	Wagner-Pit.	39
Lajoie-Cle.	53	1910	Byrne-Pit.	43
Cobb-Det.	47	1911	Konetchy-St.L.	38
Speaker-Bos.	53	1912	Zimmerman-Chi.	41
Jackson-Cle.	39	1913	Smith-Bkn.	40
Speaker-Bos.	46	1914	Magee-Phi.	39
Veach-Det.	40	1915	Doyle-N.Y.	40
Graney-Cle.	41	1916	Niehoff-Phi.	42
Speaker-Cle.	41			
Cobb-Det.	44	1917	Groh-Cin.	39
Speaker-Cle.	33	1918	Groh-Cin.	28
Veach-Det.	45	1919	Youngs-N.Y.	31
Speaker-Cle.	50	1920	Hornsby-St.L.	44
Speaker-Cle.	52	1921	Hornsby-St.L.	44
Speaker-Cle.	48	1922	Hornsby-St.L.	46
Speaker-Cle.	59	1923	Roush-Cin.	41
Heilmann-Det.	45	1924	Hornsby-St.L.	43
J. Sewell-Cle.	45			
McManus-St.L.	44	1925	Bottomley-St.L.	44
Burns-Cle.	64	1926	Bottomley-St.L.	40
Gehrig-N.Y.	52	1927	Stephenson-Chi.	46
Gehrig-N.Y.	47	1928	P. Waner-Pit.	50
Manush-St.L.	47			
Gehringer-Det.	45	1929	Frederick-Bkn.	52
Johnson-Det.	45			
Manush-St.L.	45			
Hodapp-Cle.	51	1930	Klein-Phi.	59
Webb-Bos.	67	1931	Adams-St.L.	46
McNair-Phi.	47	1932	P. Waner-Pit.	62
Cronin-Was.	45	1933	Klein-Phi.	44
Greenberg-Det.	63	1934	Allen-Phi.	42
			Cuyler-Chi.	42
Vosmik-Cle.	47	1935	Herman-Chi.	57
Gehringer-Det.	60	1936	Medwick-St.L.	64
Bell-St.L.	51	1937	Medwick-St.L.	56
Cronin-Bos.	51	1938	Medwick-St.L.	47
Rolfe-N.Y.	46	1939	Slaughter-St.L.	52
Greenberg-Det.	50	1940	F. McCormick-Cin.	44
Boudreau-Cle.	45	1941	Mize-St.L.	39
			Reiser-Bkn.	39
Kolloway-Chi.	40	1942	Marion-St.L.	38
Wakefield-Det.	38	1943	Musial-St.L.	48
Boudreau-Cle.	45	1944	Musial-St.L.	51
Moses-Chi.	35	1945	Holmes-Bos.	47
Vernon-Was.	51	1946	Musial-St.L.	50
Boudreau-Cle.	45	1947	Miller-Cin.	38
Williams-Bos.	44	1948	Musial-St.L.	46
Williams-Bos.	39	1949	Musial-St.L.	41
Kell-Det.	56	1950	Schoendienst-St.L.	43
Kell-Det.	36	1951	Dark-N.Y.	41
Mele-Was.	36			
Yost-Was.	36			
Fain-Phi.	43	1952	Musial-St.L.	42
Vernon-Was.	43	1953	Musial-St.L.	53
Vernon-Was.	33	1954	Musial-St.L.	41
Kuenn-Det.	38	1955	Aaron-Mil.	37
			Logan-Mil.	37
Piersall-Bos.	40	1956	Aaron-Mil.	34
Gardner-Bal.	36	1957	Hoak-Cin.	39
Minoso-Chi.	36			
Kuenn-Det.	39	1958	Cepeda-S.F.	38
Kuenn-Det.	42	1959	Pinson-Cin.	47
Francona-Cle.	36	1960	Pinson-Cin.	37
Kaline-Det.	41	1961	Aaron-Mil.	39
Robinson-Chi.	45	1962	Robinson-Cin.	51
Yastrzemski-Bos.	40	1963	Groat-St.L.	43
Oliva-Min.	43	1964	Maye-Mil.	44
Versalles-Bos.	45	1965	Aaron-Mil.	40
Yastrzemski-Bos.	45			
Yastrzemski-Bos.	39	1966	Callison-Phi.	40
Oliva-Min.	34	1967	Staub-Hou.	44
Smith-Bos.	37	1968	Brock-St.L.	46
Oliva-Min.	39	1969	Alou-Pit.	41
Oliva-Min.	36	1970	Parker-L.A.	47
Otis-K.C.	36			
Tovar-Min.	36			
		1914	FEDERAL LEAGUE Kauff-Ind.	44
		1915	FEDERAL LEAGUE Evans-Bkn. + Bal.	34

TRIPLES

American League		Year	National League	
Keister + Williams-Bal.	21	1901	Sheckard-Bkn.	19
Williams-Bal.	21	1902	Crawford-Cin.	23
Crawford-Det.	25	1903	Wagner-Pit.	19
Stahl-Bos.	22	1904	Lumley-Bkn.	18
Flick-Cle.	19	1905	Seymour-Cin.	21
Flick-Cle.	22	1906	Clarke-Pit., Schulte-Chi.	13
Flick-Cle.	18	1907	Alperman-Bos.	16
			Ganzel-Cin.	16
Cobb-Det.	20	1908	Wagner-Pit.	19
Baker-Phi.	19	1909	Mitchell-Cin.	17
Crawford-Det.	19	1910	Mitchell-Cin.	18
Cobb-Det.	24	1911	Doyle-N.Y.	25
Jackson-Cle.	26	1912	Wilson-Pit.	36
Crawford-Det.	23	1913	Saier-Chi.	21
Crawford-Det.	26	1914	Carey-Pit.	17
Crawford-Det.	19	1915	Long-St.L.	25
Jackson-Chi.	21	1916	Hinchman-Pit.	16
Cobb-Det.	24	1917	Hornsby-St.L.	17
Cobb-Det.	14	1918	Daubert-Bkn.	15
Veach-Det.	17	1919	Myers-Bkn.	14
			Southworth-Pit.	14
Jackson-Chi.	20	1920	Myers-Bkn.	22
Shanks-Was.	19	1921	Hornsby-St.L.	18
			Powell-Bos.	18
Sisler-St.L.	18	1922	Daubert-Cin.	22
Goslin + Rice-Was.	18	1923	Carey + Traynor-Pit.	19
Pipp-N.Y.	19	1924	Roush-Cin.	21
Goslin-Was.	20	1925	Cuyler-Pit.	26
Gehrig-N.Y.	20	1926	P. Waner-Pit.	22
Combs-N.Y.	23	1927	P. Waner-Pit.	17
Combs-N.Y.	21	1928	Bottomley-St.L.	20
Gehringer-Det.	19	1929	L. Waner-Pit.	20
Combs-N.Y.	22	1930	Comorosky-Pit.	23
Johnson-Det.	19	1931	Terry-N.Y.	20
Cronin-Was.	18	1932	Herman-Cin.	19
Manush-Was.	17	1933	Vaughan-Pit.	19
Chapman-N.Y.	13	1934	Medwick-St.L.	18
Vosmik-Cle.	20	1935	Goodman-Cin.	18
Averill-Cle., Rolfe-N.Y.	15	1936	Goodman-Cin.	14
DiMaggio-N.Y.	15			
Kreevich + Walker-Chi.	16	1937	Vaughan-Pit.	17
Heath-Cle.	18	1938	Mize-St.L.	16
Lewis-Was.	16	1939	Herman-Chi.	18
McCosky-Det.	19	1940	Vaughan-Pit.	15
Heath-Cle.	20	1941	Reiser-Bkn.	17
Spence-Wash.	15	1942	Slaughter-St.L.	17
Lindell-N.Y., Moses-Chi.	12	1943	Musial-St.L.	20
Lindell-N.Y.	16	1944	Barrett-Pit.	19
Stirnweiss-N.Y.	16			
Stirnweiss-N.Y.	22	1945	Olmo-Bkn.	13
Edwards-Cle.	16	1946	Musial-St.L.	20
Henrich-N.Y.	13	1947	Walker-St.L. + Phi.	16
Henrich-N.Y.	14	1948	Musial-St.L.	18
Mitchell-Cle.	23	1949	Musial-St.L.	13
			Slaughter-St.L.	13
DiMaggio + Doerr-Bos.	11	1950	Ashburn-Phi.	14
Evers-Det.	11			
Minoso-Cle. + Chi.	14	1951	Bell-Pit., Musial-St.L.	12
Avila-Cle.	11	1952	Thomson-N.Y.	14
Rivera-Chi.	16	1953	Gilliam-Bkn.	17
Minoso-Chi.	18	1954	Mays-N.Y.	13
Carey + Mantle-N.Y.	11	1955	Mays-N.Y.	13
Jensen-Bos., Minoso-Chi.	11	1956	Bruton-Mil.	15
Lemon-Was., Simpson-K.C.	11			
Bauer + McDougald-N.Y.	9	1957	Mays-N.Y.	20
Simpson-K.C. + N.Y.	9			
Power-K.C. + Cle.	10	1958	Ashburn-Phi.	13
Allison-Was.	9	1959	Moon + Neal-L.A.	11
Fox-Chi.	10	1960	Bruton-Mil.	13
Wood-Det.	14	1961	Altman-Chi.	12
Cimoli-K.C.	15	1962	Callison-Phi.	10
			Davis + Wills-L.A.	10
			Virdon-Pit.	10
Versalles-Min.	13	1963	Pinson-Cin.	14
Rollins-Min.	10	1964	Allen-Cin.	13
Versalles-Min.	10		Santo-Chi.	13
Campaneris-Oak.	12	1965	Callison-Phi.	16
Versalles-Min.	12			
Knoop-Cal.	11	1966	McCarver-St.L.	13
Blair-Bal.	12	1967	Pinson-Cin.	13
Fregosi-Cal.	13	1968	Brock-St.L.	14
Unser-Was.	8	1969	Clemente-Pit.	12
Tovar-Cin.	13	1970	Davis-L.A.	16
		1914	FEDERAL LEAGUE Esmond-Ind.	15
			Evans-Bkn.	15
		1915	FEDERAL LEAGUE Mann-Chi.	19

HOME RUNS

American League		Year	National League	
Lajoie-Phi.	14	1901	Crawford-Cin.	16
Seybold-Phi.	16	1902	Leach-Pit.	6
Freeman-Bos.	13	1903	Sheckard-Bkn.	9
Davis-Phi.	12	1904	Lumley-Bkn.	9
Davis-Phi.	8	1905	Odwell-Cin.	9
Davis-Phi.	12	1906	Jordan-Bkn.	12
Davis-Phi.	8	1907	Brain-Bos.	10
Crawford-Det.	7	1908	Jordan-Bkn.	12
Cobb-Det.	9	1909	Murray-N.Y.	7
Stahl-Bos.	10	1910	Beck-Bos.	10
			Schulte-Chi.	10
Baker-Phi.	11	1911	Schulte-Chi.	21
Baker-Phi.	10	1912	Zimmerman-Chi.	14
Speaker-Bos	10			
Baker-Phi.	12	1913	Cravath-Phi.	19
Baker-Phi.	9	1914	Cravath-Phi.	19
Roth-Chi. + Cle.	7	1915	Cravath-Phi.	24
Pipp-N.Y.	12	1916	Robertson-N.Y.	12
			Williams-Chi.	12
Pipp-N.Y.	9	1917	Cravath-Phi.	12
			Robertson-N.Y.	12
Ruth-Bos.	11	1918	Cravath-Phi.	8
Walker-Phi.	11			
Ruth-Bos.	29	1919	Cravath-Phi.	12
Ruth-N.Y.	54	1920	Williams-Phi.	15
Ruth-N.Y.	59	1921	Kelly-N.Y.	23
Williams-St.L.	39	1922	Hornsby-St.L.	42
Ruth-N.Y.	41	1923	Williams-Phi.	41
Ruth-N.Y.	46	1924	Fournier-Bkn.	27
Meusel-N.Y.	33	1925	Hornsby-St.L.	39
Ruth-N.Y.	47	1926	Wilson-Chi.	21
Ruth-N.Y.	60	1927	Williams-Phi.	30
			Wilson-Chi.	30
Ruth-N.Y.	54	1928	Bottomley-St.L.	31
			Wilson-Chi.	31
Ruth-N.Y.	46	1929	Klein-Phi.	43
Ruth-N.Y.	49	1930	Wilson-Chi.	56
Gehrig-N.Y.	46	1931	Klein-Phi.	31
Ruth-N.Y.	46			
Foxx-Phi.	58	1932	Klein-Phi.	38
			Ott-N.Y.	38
Foxx-Phi.	48	1933	Klein-Phi.	28
Gehrig-N.Y.	49	1934	Collins-St.L.	35
			Ott-N.Y.	35
Foxx-Phi.	36	1935	Berger-Bos.	34
Greenberg-Det.	36			
Gehrig-N.Y.	49	1936	Ott-N.Y.	33
DiMaggio-N.Y.	46	1937	Medwick-St.L.	31
			Ott-N.Y.	31
Greenberg-Det.	58	1938	Ott-N.Y.	36
Foxx-Bos.	35	1939	Mize-St.L.	28
Greenberg-Det.	41	1940	Mize-St.L.	43
Williams-Bos.	37	1941	Camilli-Bkn.	34
Williams-Bos.	36	1942	Ott-N.Y.	30
York-Det.	34	1943	Nicholson-Chi.	29
Etten-N.Y.	22	1944	Nicholson-Chi.	33
Stephens-St.L.	24	1945	Holmes-Bos.	28
Greenberg-Det.	44	1946	Kiner-Pit.	23
Williams-Bos.	32	1947	Kiner-Pit.	51
			Mize-N.Y.	51
DiMaggio-N.Y.	39	1948	Kiner-Pit.	40
			Mize-N.Y.	40
Williams-Bos.	43	1949	Kiner-Pit.	54
Rosen-Cle.	37	1950	Kiner-Pit.	47
Zernial-Chi. + Phi.	33	1951	Kiner-Pit.	42
Doby-Cle.	32	1952	Kiner-Pit.	37
			Sauer-Chi.	37
Rosen-Cle.	43	1953	Mathews-Bos.	47
Doby-Cle.	32	1954	Kluszewski-Cin.	49
Mantle-N.Y.	37	1955	Mays-N.Y.	51
Mantle-N.Y.	52	1956	Snider-Bkn.	43
Sievers-Was.	42	1957	Aaron-Mil.	44
Mantle-N.Y.	42	1958	Banks-Chi.	47
Colavito-Cle.	42	1959	Mathews-Mil.	46
Killebrew-Was.	42			
Mantle-N.Y.	40	1960	Banks-Chi.	41
Maris-N.Y.	61	1961	Cepeda-S.F.	46
Killebrew-Min.	48	1962	Mays-S.F.	49
Killebrew-Min.	45	1963	Aaron-Mil.	44
			McCovey-S.F.	44
Killebrew-Min.	49	1964	Mays-S.F.	47
Conigliaro-Bos.	32	1965	Mays-S.F.	52
F. Robinson-Bal.	49	1966	Aaron-Atl.	44
Killebrew-Min.	44	1697	Aaron-Atl.	39
Yastrzemski-Bos.	44			
Howard-Was.	44	1968	McCovey-S.F.	36
Killebrew-Min.	49	1969	McCovey-S.F.	45
Howard-Was.	44	1970	Bench-Cin.	45
		1914	FEDERAL LEAGUE Kenworthy-K.C.	15
			Zwilling-Chi.	15
		1915	FEDERAL LEAGUE Chase-Buf.	17

YEARLY BATTING LEADERS

DOUBLES

American League		Year	National League	
Smith-Bos	33	1971	Cedeno-Hou.	40
Piniella-K.C.	33	1972	Cedeno-Hou.	39
			Motanez-Phi.	39
Bando-Oak.	32	1973	Stargell-Pit.	43
Garcia-Mil.	32			
Rudi-Oak.	39	1974	Rose-Cin.	45
Lynn-Bos.	47	1975	Rose-Cin.	47
Otis-K.C.	40	1976	Rose-Cin.	42
McRae-K.C.	54	1977	Parker-Pit.	44
Brett-K.C.	45	1978	Rose-Cin.	51
Cooper-Mill.	44	1979	Hernandez-St.L.	48
Lemon-Chi.	44			
Yount-Mil.	49	1980	Rose-Phi.	42
Cooper-Mil.	35	1981	Buckner-Chi.	35
McRae-K.C.	46	1982	Oliver-Mon.	43
Yount-Mil.	46			
Ripken-Bal.	47	1983	Buckner-Chi.	38
			Oliver-Mon.	38
			Ray-Pit.	38
Mattingly-N.Y.	44	1984	Raines-Mon.	38
			Ray-Pit.	38
Mattingly-N.Y.	48	1985	Parker-Cin.	42
Mattingly-N.Y.	53	1986	Hayes-Phi.	46
Molitor-Mil.	41	1987	Wallach-Mon.	42
Boggs-Bos.	45	1988	Galarraga-Mon.	42
Boggs-Bos.	51	1989	Guerrero-St. L.	42
			Wallach-Mon.	42
Brett-K.C.	45	1990	Jefferies-N.Y.	40
Reed-Bos.	45			
Palmeiro-Tex.	49	1991	Bonilla-Pit.	44
E. Martinez-Sea.	46	1992	Van Slyke-Pit.	45
Thomas-Chi.	46			
Olerud-Tor.	54	1993	Hayes-Col.	45
Knoblauch-Mia.	45	1994	Biggio-Hou.	44
			Walker-Mon.	44
Belle-Cle.	52	1995	Grace-Chi.	51
E. Martinez-Sea.	52			
Rodriguez-Sea.	54	1996	Bagwell-Hou.	48
Valentin-Bos.	47	1997	Grudzielanek-Mon.	54
Gonzalez-Tex.	50	1998	Biggio-Hou.	51
Green-Tor.	45	1999	Biggio-Hou.	56
Delgado-Tor.	57	2000	Helton-Col.	59
Ja. Giambi-Oak.	47	2001	Berkman-Hou.	55
Anderson-Ana.	56	2002	Abreu-Phi.	50
Garciaparra-Bos.	56			
Wells-Tor.	49	2003	Pujois-St.L.	51
Anderson-Ana.	49			
Roberts-Bal.	50	2004	Overbay-Mil.	53
Tejada-Bal.	50	2005	Lee-Chi.	50
Sizemore-Cle.	53	2006	Sanchez-Pit.	53

TRIPLES

American League		Year	National League	
Patek-K.C.	11	1971	Metzger + Morgan-Hou.	11
Fisk-Bos., Rudi-Oak.	9	1972	Bowa-Phi.	13
Bumbry-Bal.	11	1973	Metzger-Hou.	14
Carew-Min.	11			
Rivers-Cal.	11	1974	Garr-Atl.	17
Brett-K.C.	13	1975	Garr-Atl.	11
Rivers-Cal.	13			
Brett-K.C.	14	1976	Cash-Phi.	12
Carew-Min.	16	1977	Templeton-St. L.	18
Rice-Bos.	15	1978	Templeton-St. L.	13
Brett-K.C.	20	1979	Templeton-St. L.	19
Griffin-Tor.	15	1980	Moreno-Pit.	13
Wilson-K.C.	15		Scott-Mon.	13
Castino-Min.	9	1981	Reynolds-Hou.	12
			Richards-S.D.	12
Wilson-K.C.	15	1982	Thon-Hou.	10
Yount-Mil.	10	1983	Butler-Atl.	13
Collins-Tor.	15	1984	Samuel-Phi.	19
Moseby-Tor.	15		Sandberg-Chi.	19
Wilson-K.C.	21	1985	McGee-St. L.	18
Butler-Cle.	14	1986	Webster-Mon.	13
Wilson-K.C.	15	1987	Samuel-Phi.	15
Reynolds-Sea.	11	1988	Van Slyke-Pit.	15
Wilson-K.C.	11			
Yount-Mil.	11			
Sierra-Tex.	14	1989	Thompson-S.F.	11
Fernandez-Tor.	17	1990	Duncan-Cin.	11
Johnson-Chi.	13	1991	Lankford-St.L.	15
Molitor-Mil.	13			
Johnson-Chi.	12	1992	Sanders-Atl.	14
Johnson-Chi.	14	1993	Finley-Hou.	13
Johnson-Chi.	14	1994	Butler-L.A.	9
			Lewis-S.F.	9
Lofton-Cle.	13	1995	Butler-N.Y.+L.A.	9
			Young-Col.	9
Knoblauch-Min.	14	1996	Johnson-N.Y.	21
Garciaparra-Bos.	11	1997	DeShields-St.L.	14
Offerman-K.C.	13	1998	Dellucci-Ari.	12
Offerman-Bos.	11	1999	Abreu-Phi.	11
			Perez-Col.	11
Guzman-Min.	20	2000	Womack-Ari.	14
Guzman-Min.	14	2001	Rollins-Phi.	12
Damon-Bos.	11	2002	Rollins-Phi.	10
Guzman-Min.	14	2003	Furcal-Atl.	10
			Finley-Ari.	10
Crawford-T.B.	19	2004	J. Wilson-Pit.	12
			Rollins-Phi.	12
			Pierre-Fla.	12
Crawford-T.B.	15	2005	Reyes-N.Y.	17
Crawford-T.B.	16	2006	Reyes-N.Y.	17

HOME RUNS

American League		Year	National League	
Melton-Chi.	33	1971	Stargell-Pitt.	48
Allen-Chi.	37	1972	Bench-Cin.	40
Jackson-Oak.	32	1973	Stargell-Pit.	44
Allen-Chi.	32	1974	Schmidt-Phi.	36
Jackson-Oak.	36	1975	Schmidt-Phi.	38
Scott-Mil.	36			
Nettles-N.Y.	32	1976	Schmidt-Phi.	38
Rice-Bos.	39	1977	Foster-Cin.	52
Rice-Bos.	46	1978	Foster-Cin.	40
Thomas-Mil.	45	1979	Kingman-Chi.	48
Jackson-N.Y.	41	1980	Schmidt-Phi.	48
Oglivie-Mil.	41			
Armas-Oak.	22	1981	Schmidt-Phi.	31
Evans-Bos.	22			
Grich-Cal.	22			
Murray-Bal.	22			
Thomas-Mil.	39	1982	Kingman-N.Y.	37
Re.Jackson-Cal.	39			
Rice-Bos.	39	1983	Schmidt-Phi.	40
Armas-Bos.	43	1984	Murphy-Atl.	36
			Schmidt-Phi.	36
Evans-Det.	40	1985	Murphy-Atl.	37
Barfield-Tor.	40	1986	Schmidt-Phi.	37
McGwire-Oak.	49	1987	Dawson-Chi.	49
Canseco-Oak.	42	1988	Strawberry-N.Y.	39
McGriff-Tor.	36	1989	Mitchell-S.F.	47
Fielder-Det.	51	1990	Sandberg-Chi.	40
Fielder-Det.	44	1991	Johnson-N.Y.	38
Canseco-Oak.	44			
Gonzalez-Tex.	43	1992	McGriff-S.D.	35
Gonzalez-Tex.	46	1993	Bonds-S.F.	46
Griffey-Sea.	40	1994	Williams-S.F.	43
Belle-Cle.	50	1995	Bichette-Col.	40
McGwire-Oak.	52	1996	Galarraga-Col.	47
Griffey-Sea.	56	1997	Walker-Col.	49
Griffey-Sea.	56	1998	McGwire-St.L.	70
Griffey-Sea.	48	1999	McGwire-St.L.	65
Glaus-Ana.	47	2000	Sosa-Chi.	50
A. Rodriguez-Tex.	52	2001	Bonds-S.F.	73
A. Rodriguez-Tex.	57	2002	Sosa-Chi.	49
Rodriguez-Tex.	47	2003	Thome-Phi.	47
Ramirez-Bos.	43	2004	Beltre-L.A.	48
Rodriguez-N.Y.	48	2005	A. Jones-Atl.	51
Ortiz-Bos.	54	2006	Howard-Phi.	58

YEARLY BATTING LEADERS

BASES ON BALLS

AMERICAN LEAGUE		Year	NATIONAL LEAGUE	
Hoy-Chi.	86	1901	Thomas-Phi.	100
Hartsel-Phi.	87	1902	Thomas-Phi.	107
Barrett-Det.	74	1903	Thomas-Phi.	107
Barrett-Det.	79	1904	Thomas-Phi.	102
Hartsel-Phi.	121	1905	Huggins-Cin.	103
Hartsel-Phi.	88	1906	Thomas-Phi.	107
Hartsel-Phi.	106	1907	Huggins-Cin.	83
			Thomas-Phi.	83
Hartsel-Phi.	93	1908	Bresnahan-N.Y.	83
Bush-Det.	88	1909	Clarke-Pit.	80
Bush-Det.	78	1910	Huggins-St.L.	116
Bush-Det.	98	1911	Sheckard-Chi.	147
Bush-Det.	117	1912	Sheckard-Chi.	122
Shotton-St.L.	99	1913	Bescher-Cin.	94
Bush-Det.	112	1914	Huggins-St.L.	105
Collins-Chi.	119	1915	Cravath-Phi.	86
Shotton-St.L.	110	1916	Groh-Cin.	84
Graney-Cle.	94	1917	Burns-N.Y.	75
Chapman-Cle	84	1918	Carey-Pit.	62
Graney-Cle.	105	1919	Burns-N.Y.	82
Ruth-N.Y.	150	1920	Burns-N.Y.	76
Ruth-N.Y.	145	1921	Burns-N.Y.	80
Witt-N.Y.	89	1922	Carey-Pit.	80
Ruth-N.Y.	170	1923	Burns-Cin.	101
Ruth-N.Y.	142	1924	Hornsby-Pit.	89
Kamm-Chi.	90	1925	Fournier-Bkn.	86
Mostil-Chi.	90			
Ruth-N.Y.	144	1926	Wilson-Chi.	69
Ruth-N.Y.	137	1927	Hornsby-N.Y.	86
Ruth-N.Y.	137	1928	Hornsby-Chi.	107
Bishop-Phi.	128	1929	Ott-N.Y.	113
Ruth-N.Y.	136	1930	Wilson-Chi.	105
Ruth-N.Y.	128	1931	Ott-N.Y.	80
Ruth-N.Y.	130	1932	Ott-N.Y.	100
Ruth-N.Y.	114	1933	Ott-N.Y.	75
Foxx-Phi.	111	1934	Vaughan-Pit.	94
Gehrig-N.Y.	132	1935	Vaughan-Pit.	97
Gehrig-N.Y.	130	1936	Vaughan-Pit.	118
Gehrig-N.Y.	127	1937	Ott-N.Y.	102
Foxx-Bos.	119	1938	Camilli-Bkn.	119
Greenberg-Det.	111	1939	Camilli-Bkn.	110
Clift-St.L.	111			
Keller-N.Y.	106	1940	Fletcher-Pit.	119
Williams-Bos.	147	1941	Fletcher-Pit.	118
Williams-Bos.	145	1942	Ott-N.Y.	109
Keller-N.Y.	106	1943	Galan-Bkn.	103
Etten-N.Y.	97	1944	Galan-Bkn.	101
Cullenbine-Cle.+Det.	112	1945	Stanky-Bkn.	148
Williams-Bos.	156	1946	Stanky-Bkn.	137
Williams-Bos.	162	1947	Greenberg-Pit.	104
			Reese-Bkn.	104
Williams-Bos.	126	1948	Elliott-Bos.	131
Williams-Bos.	162	1949	Kiner-Pit.	117
Yost-Was.	141	1950	Stanky-N.Y.	144
Williams-Bos.	144	1951	Kiner-Pit.	137
Yost-Was.	129	1952	Kiner-Pit.	110
Yost-Was.	123	1953	Musial-St.L.	105
Williams-Bos.	136	1954	Ashburn-Phi.	125
Mantle-N.Y.	113	1955	Mathews-Mil.	109
Yost-Was.	151	1956	Snider-Bkn.	99
Mantle-N.Y.	146	1957	Ashburn-Phi.	94
			Temple-Cin.	94
Mantle-N.Y.	129	1958	Ashburn-Phi.	97
Yost-Det.	135	1959	Gilliam-L.A.	96
Yost-Det.	125	1960	Ashburn-Phi.	116
Mantle-N.Y.	126	1961	Mathews-Mil.	93
Mantle-N.Y.	122	1962	Mathews-Mil.	101
Yastrzemski-Bos.	95	1963	Mathews-Mil.	124
Siebern-Bal.	106	1964	Santo-Chi.	86
Colavito-Cle.	93	1965	Morgan-Hou.	97
Killebrew-Min.	103	1966	Santo-Chi.	95
Killebrew-Min.	131	1967	Santo-Chi.	96
Yastrzemski-Bos.	119	1968	Santo-Chi.	96
Killebrew-Min.	145	1969	Wynn-Hou.	148
Howard-Was.	132	1970	McCovey-S.F.	137

STRIKEOUTS

AMERICAN LEAGUE		Year	NATIONAL LEAGUE	
		1910	Hummel-Bkn.	70
		1911	Bescher-Cin.	78
			Coulson-Bkn.	78
		1912	McDonald-Bos.	91
Moeller-Was.	103	1913	Burns-N.Y.	74
Williams-St.L.	120	1914	Merkle-N.Y.	80
Lavan-St.L.	83	1915	Baird-Pit.	88
Pipp-N.Y.	82	1916	Cravath-Phi.	89
Roth-Cle.	73	1917	Williams-Chi.	78
Ruth-Bos.	58	1918	Paskert-Chi.	49
			Youngs-N.Y.	49
Shannon-Phi.+Bos.	70	1919	Powell-Bos.	79
Ward-N.Y.	84	1920	Kelly-N.Y.	92
Meusel-N.Y.	88	1921	Powell-Bos.	85
Dykes-Phi.	98	1922	Parkinson-Phi.	93
Ruth-N.Y.	93	1923	Grantham-Chi.	92
Ruth-N.Y.	81	1924	Grantham-Chi.	63
McManus-St.L.	69	1925	Hartnett-Chi.	77
Lazzeri-N.Y.	96	1926	Friberg-Phi.	77
Ruth-N.Y.	89	1927	Wilson-Chi.	70
Ruth-N.Y.	87	1928	Wilson-Chi.	94
Foxx-Phi.	70	1929	Wilson-Chi.	83
Morgan-Cle.	66	1930	Wilson-Chi.	86
Foxx-Phi.	84	1931	Cullop-Cin.	86
Campbell-Chi.+St.L	104	1932	Wilson-Bkn.	85
Foxx-Phi.	93	1933	Berger-Bos.	77
Clift-St.L.	100	1934	Camilli-Chi. + Phi.	94
Foxx-Phi.	99	1935	Camilli-Phi.	113
Foxx-Phi.	119	1936	Brubaker-Pit.	96
Crosetti-N.Y.	105	1937	DiMaggio-Bos.	111
Crosetti-N.Y.	97	1938	DiMaggio-Bos.	134
Greenberg-Det.	95	1939	Camilli-Bkn.	107
Chapman-Phi.	96	1940	Ross-Bos.	127
Foxx-Bos.	103	1941	Camilli-Bkn.	115
Gordon-N.Y.	95	1942	DiMaggio-Pit.	87
Laabs-St.L.	105	1943	DiMaggio-Pit.	126
Seerey-Cle.	99	1944	DiMaggio-Pit.	83
Seerey-Cle.	97	1945	DiMaggio-Pit.	91
Keller-N.Y.	101	1946	Kiner-Pit.	109
Seerey-Cle.	101			
Joost-Phi.	110	1947	Nicholson-Chi.	83
Seerey-Cle. + Chi.	102	1948	Sauer-Cin.	85
Kokos-St.L.	91	1949	Snider-Bkn.	92
Zernial-Chi.	110	1950	Smalley-Chi.	114
Zernial-Chi. + Phi.	101	1951	Hodges-Bkn.	99
Doby-Cle.	111	1952	Mathews-Bos.	115
Mantle-N.Y.	111			
Doby-Cle.	121	1953	Bilko-St.L.	125
Mantle-N.Y.	107	1954	Snider-Bkn.	96
Zauchin-Bos.	105	1955	Post-Cin.	102
Lemon-Was.	138	1956	Post-Cin.	124
Lemon-Was.	94	1957	Snider-Bkn.	104
Lemon-Was.	120	1958	Anderson-Phi.	95
Mantle-N.Y.	120			
Mantle-N.Y.	126	1959	Post-Phi.	101
Mantle-N.Y.	125	1960	Herrera-Phi	136
Wood-Det.	141	1961	Stuart-Pit.	121
Killebrew-Min.	142	1962	Hubbs-Chi.	129
Nicholson-Chi.	175	1963	Clendenon-Pit.	136
Mathews-K.C.	143	1964	Allen-Phi.	138
Versalles-Min.	122	1965	Allen-Phi.	150
Scott-Bos.	152	1966	Browne-Chi.	143
Howard-Was.	155	1967	Wynn-Hou.	137
Jackson-Oak.	171	1968	Clendenon-Pit.	163
Jackson-Oak.	142	1969	Bonds-S.F.	187
Jackson-Oak.	135	1970	Bonds-S.F.	189

STOLEN BASES

AMERICAN LEAGUE		Year	NATIONAL LEAGUE	
Isbell-Chi.	52	1901	Wagner-Pit.	48
Hartsell-Phi.	47	1902	Wagner-Pit.	43
Bay-Cle.	45	1903	Chance-Chi.	67
			Sheckard-Bkn.	67
Flick-Cle.	42	1904	Wagner-Pit.	53
Hoffman-Phi.	46	1905	Devlin-N.Y.	59
			Maloney-Chi.	59
Anderson-Was.	39	1906	Chance-Chi.	57
Flick-Cle.	39			
Cobb-Det.	49	1907	Wagner-Pit.	61
Dougherty-Chi.	47	1908	Wagner-Pit.	53
Cobb-Det.	76	1909	Bescher-Cin.	54
Collins-Phi.	81	1910	Bescher-Cin.	70
Cobb-Det.	83	1911	Bescher-Cin.	81
Milan-Was.	88	1912	Bescher-Cin.	67
Milan-Was.	75	1913	Carey-Pit.	61
Maisel-N.Y.	74	1914	Burns-N.Y.	62
Cobb-Det.	96	1915	Carey-Pit.	36
Cobb-Det.	68	1916	Carey-Pit.	63
Cobb-Det.	55	1917	Carey-Pit.	46
Sisler-St.L.	45	1918	Carey-Pit.	58
Collins-Chi.	33	1919	Burns-N.Y.	40
Rice-Was.	63	1920	Carey-Pit.	52
Sisler-St.L.	35	1921	Frisch-N.Y.	49
Sisler-St.L.	51	1922	Carey-Pit.	51
Collins-Chi.	49	1923	Carey-Pit.	51
Collins-Chi.	42	1924	Carey-Pit.	49
Mostil-Chi.	43	1925	Carey-Pit.	46
Mostil-Chi.	35	1926	Cuyler-Pit.	35
Sisler-St.L.	27	1927	Frisch-St.L.	48
Myer-Bos.	30	1928	Cuyler-Chi.	37
Gehringer-Det.	27	1929	Cuyler-Chi.	43
McManus-Det.	23	1930	Cuyler-Chi.	37
Chapman-N.Y.	61	1931	Frisch-St.L.	28
Chapman-N.Y.	38	1932	Klein-Phi.	20
Chapman-N.Y.	27	1933	Martin-St.L.	26
Werber-Bos.	40	1934	Martin-St.L.	23
Werber-Bos.	29	1935	Galan-Chi.	22
Lary-St.L.	37	1936	P. Martin-St.L.	23
Chapman-Was. + Bos.	35	1937	Galan-Chi.	23
Werber-Phi.	35			
Crosetti-N.Y.	27	1938	Hack-Chi.	16
Case-Was.	51	1939	Hack-Chi.	17
			Handley-Pit.	17
Case-Was.	35	1940	Frey-Cin.	22
Case-Was.	33	1941	Murtaugh-Phi.	18
Case-Was.	44	1942	Reiser-Bkn.	20
Case-Was.	61	1943	Vaughan-Bkn.	20
Strinweiss-N.Y.	55	1944	Barnett-Pit.	28
Strinweiss-N.Y.	33	1945	Schoendienst-St.L.	26
Case-Was.	28	1946	Reiser-Bkn.	34
Dillinger-St.L.	34	1947	Robinson-Bkn.	29
Dillinger-St.L.	28	1948	Ashburn-Phi.	32
Dillinger-St.L.	20	1949	Robinson-Bkn.	37
DiMaggio-Bos.	15	1950	Jethroe-Bos.	35
Minoso-Cle. + Chi.	31	1951	Jethroe-Bos.	35
Minoso-Chi.	22	1952	Reese-Bkn.	30
Minoso-Chi.	25	1953	Bruton-Mil.	26
Jensen-Bos.	22	1954	Bruton-Mil.	34
Rivera-Chi.	25	1955	Bruton-Mil.	25
Aparicio-Chi.	21	1956	Mays-N.Y.	40
Aparicio-Chi.	28	1957	Mays-N.Y.	38
Aparicio-Chi.	29	1958	Mays-S.F.	31
Aparicio-Chi.	56	1959	Mays-S.F.	27
Aparicio-Chi.	51	1960	Wills-L.A.	50
Aparicio-Chi.	53	1961	Wills-L.A.	35
Aparicio-Chi.	31	1962	Wills-L.A.	104
Aparicio-Bal.	40	1963	Wills-L.A.	40
Aparicio-Bal.	57	1964	Wills-L.A.	53
Campaneris-Oak.	51	1965	Wills-L.A.	94
Campaneris-Oak.	52	1966	Brock-St.L.	74
Campaneris-Oak.	55	1967	Brock-St.L.	52
Campaneris-Oak.	62	1968	Brock-St.L.	62
Harper-Sea.	73	1969	Brock-St.L.	53
Campaneris-Oak.	42	1970	Tolan-Cin.	57

Federal League — Bases on Balls

Year			
1914	FEDERAL LEAGUE	Wickland-Chi.	81
1915	FEDERAL LEAGUE	Borton-St.L.	92

Federal League — Stolen Bases

Year			
1914	FEDERAL LEAGUE	Kauff-Ind.	75
1915	FEDERAL LEAGUE	Kauff-Bkn.	55

YEARLY BATTING LEADERS

BASES ON BALLS

American League		Year	National League	
Killebrew-Min.	114	1971	Mays-S.F.	112
Allen-Chi.	99	1972	Morgan-Cin.	115
White-N.Y.	99			
Mayberry-K.C.	122	1973	Evans-Atl.	124
Tenace-Oak.	110	1974	Evans-Atl.	126
Mayberry-K.C.	119	1975	Morgan-Cin.	132
Hargrove-Tex.	97	1976	Wynn-Atl.	127
Harrah-Tex.	109	1977	Tenace-S.D.	125
Hargrove-Tex.	107	1978	Burroughs-Atl.	117
Porter-K.C.	121	1979	Schmidt-Phi.	120
Randolph-N.Y.	119	1980	Driessen-Cin.	93
			Morgan-Hou.	93
Evans-Bos.	86	1981	Schmidt-Phi.	73
Henderson-Oak.	116	1982	Schmidt-Phi.	107
Henderson-Oak.	103	1983	Schmidt-Phi.	128
Murray-Bal.	107	1984	Matthews-Chi.	103
Evans-Bos.	114	1985	Murphy-Atl.	90
Boggs-Bos.	105	1986	Hernandez-N.Y.	94
Downing-Cal.	106	1987	Clark-St. L.	136
Evans-Bos.	106			
Boggs-Bos.	125	1988	Clark-S.F.	100
Henderson-N.Y.+Oak.	126	1989	Clark-S.D.	132
McGwire-Oak.	110	1990	Ja. Clark-S.D.	104
Thomas-Chi.	138	1991	Butler-L.A.	108
Tettleton-Det.	122	1992	Bonds-Pit.	127
Thomas-Chi.	122			
Phillips-Det.	132	1993	Dykstra-Phi.	129
Thomas-Chi.	109	1994	Bonds-S.F.	74
Thomas-Chi.	136	1995	Bonds-S.F.	120
Phillips-Chi.	125	1996	Bonds-S.F.	151
Thome-Cle.	120	1997	Bonds-S.F.	145
Henderson-Oak.	118	1998	McGwire-St.L.	162
Thome-Cle.	127	1999	Bagwell-Hou.	149
Ja. Giambi-Oak.	137	2000	Bonds-S.F.	117
Ja. Giambi-Oak.	129	2001	Bonds-S.F.	177
Thome-Cle.	122	2002	Bonds-S.F.	198
Giambi-N.Y.	129	2003	Bonds-S.F.	148
Chavez-Oak.	95	2004	Bonds-S.F.	232
Giambi-N.Y.	108	2005	Giles-S.D.	119
Ortiz-Bos.	119	2006	Bonds-S.F.	115

STRIKEOUTS

American League		Year	National League	
Jackson-Oak.	161	1971	Stargell-Pit.	154
Darwin-Min.	145	1972	May-Hou.	145
Darwin-Min.	137	1973	Bonds-S.F.	148
Darwin-Min.	127	1974	Schmidt-Phi.	138
Burroughs-Tex.	155	1975	Schmidt-Phi.	180
Rice-Bos.	123	1976	Schmidt-Phi.	149
Hobson-Bos.	162	1977	Luzinski-Phi.	140
Alexander-Oak.+Cle.	166	1978	Murphy-Atl.	145
Thomas-Mil.	175	1979	Kingman-Chi.	131
Thomas-Mil.	170	1980	Murphy-Atl.	133
Armas-Oak.	115	1981	Kingman-N.Y.	105
Jackson-Cal.	156	1982	Kingman-N.Y.	156
Kittle-Chi.	150	1983	Schmidt-Phi.	148
Armas-Bos.	156	1984	Schmidt-Phi.	168
Balboni-K.C.	166	1985	Murphy-Atl.	141
			Samuel-Phi.	141
Incaviglia-Tex.	185	1986	Samuel-Phi.	142
Deer-Mil.	186	1987	Samuel-Phi.	162
Deer-Mil.	153	1988	Galarraga-Mon.	153
Incaviglia-Tex.	153			
Jackson-K.C.	172	1989	Galarraga-Mon.	158
Fielder-Det.	182	1990	Galarraga-Mon.	169
Deer-Det.	175	1991	DeShields-Mon.	151
Palmer-Tex.	154	1992	Lankford-StL.	147
Deer-Det.+Bos.	169	1993	Snyder-L.A.	147
Fryman-Det.	126	1994	R. Sanders-Cin.	114
Vaughn-Bos.	150	1995	Galarraga-Col.	146
Buhner-Sea.	159	1996	Rodriguez-Mon.	160
Buhner-Sea.	175	1997	Sosa-Chi.	174
Canseco-Tor.	159	1998	Sosa-Chi.	171
Thome-Cle.	171	1999	Sosa-Chi.	171
Vaughn-Ana.	181	2000	Wilson-Fla.	187
Thome-Cle.	185	2001	Hernandez-Mil.	185
Cameron-Sea.	176	2002	Hernandez-Mil.	188
Giambi-N.Y.	140	2003	Thome-Phi.	182
Bellhorn-Bos.	177	2004	Dunn-Cin.	195
Sexson-Sea.	167	2005	Dunn-Cin.	168
Granderson-Det.	174	2006	Dunn-Cin.	194

STOLEN BASES

American League		Year	National League	
Otis-K.C.	52	1971	Brock-St. L.	64
Campaneris-Oak.	52	1972	Brock-St. L.	63
Harper-Bos.	54	1973	Brock-St. L.	70
North-Oak.	54	1974	Brock-St. L.	118
Rivers-Cal.	70	1975	Lopes-L.A.	77
North-Oak.	75	1976	Lopes-L.A.	63
Patek-K.C.	53	1977	Taveras-Pit.	70
LeFlore-Det.	68	1978	Moreno-Pit.	71
Wilson-K.C.	83	1979	Moreno-Pit.	77
Henderson-Oak.	100	1980	LeFlore-Mon.	97
Henderson-Oak.	56	1981	Raines-Mon.	71
Henderson-Oak.	130	1982	Raines-Mon.	78
Henderson-Oak.	108	1983	Raines-Mon.	90
Henderson-Oak.	66	1984	Raines-Mon.	75
Henderson-N.Y.	80	1985	Coleman-St. L.	110
Henderson-N.Y.	87	1986	Coleman-St. L.	107
Reynolds-Sea.	60	1987	Coleman-St. L.	109
Henderson-N.Y.	93	1988	Coleman-St. L.	81
Henderson-N.Y.+ Oak.	77	1989	Coleman-St. L.	65
R. Henderson-Oak.	65	1990	Coleman-St. L.	77
R. Henderson-Oak.	58	1991	Grissom-Mon.	76
Lofton-Cle.	66	1992	Grissom-Mon.	78
Lofton-Cle.	70	1993	Carr-Fla.	58
Lofton-Cle.	60	1994	Biggio-Hou.	39
Lofton-Cle.	54	1995	Veras-Fla.	56
Lofton-Cle.	75	1996	Young-Col.	53
Hunter-Det.	74	1997	Womack-Pit.	60
Henderson-Oak.	66	1998	Womack-Pit.	58
Hunter-Det.+ Sea.	44	1999	Womack-Ari.	72
Damon-K.C.	46	2000	Castillo-Fla.	62
Suzuki-Sea.	56	2001	Pierre-Col.	46
			Rollins-Phi.	46
Soriano-N.Y.	41	2002	Castillo-Fla.	48
Crawford-T.B.	55	2003	Pierre-Fla.	65
Crawford-T.B.	59	2004	Podsednik-Mil.	70
Figgins-L.A.	62	2005	Reyes-N.Y.	60
Crawford-T.B.	58	2006	Reyes-N.Y.	64

BATTING AVERAGE

AMERICAN LEAGUE		Year	NATIONAL LEAGUE	
Lajoie-Phi.	.422	1901	Burkett-St.L.	.382
Delahanty-Was.	.376	1902	Beaumont-Pit.	.357
Lajoie-Cle.	.355	1903	Wagner-Pit.	.355
Lajoie-Cle.	.381	1904	Wagner-Pit.	.349
Flick-Cle.	.306	1905	Seymour-Cin.	.377
Stone-St.L.	.358	1906	Wagner-Pit.	.339
Cobb-Det.	.350	1907	Wagner-Pit.	.350
Cobb-Det.	.324	1908	Wagner-Pit.	.354
Cobb-Det.	.377	1909	Wagner-Pit.	.339
Lajoie-Cle.	.383	1910	Magee-Phi.	.331
Cobb-Det.	.420	1911	Wagner-Pit.	.334
Cobb-Det.	.410	1912	Zimmerman-Chi.	.372
Cobb-Det.	.390	1913	Daubert-Bkn.	.350
Cobb-Det.	.368	1914	Daubert-Bkn.	.329
Cobb-Det.	.369	1915	Doyle-N.Y.	.320
Speaker-Cle.	.386	1916	Chase-Cin.	.339
Cobb-Det.	.383	1917	Roush-Cin.	.341
Cobb-Det.	.382	1918	Wheat-Bkn.	.335
Cobb-Det.	.384	1919	Roush-Cin.	.321
Sisler-St.L.	.407	1920	Hornsby-St.L.	.370
Heilmann-Det.	.394	1921	Hornsby-St.L.	.397
Sisler-St.L.	.420	1922	Hornsby-St.L.	.401
Heilmann-Det.	.403	1923	Hornsby-St.L.	.384
Ruth-N.Y.	.378	1924	Hornsby-St.L.	.424
Heilmann-Det.	.393	1925	Hornsby-St.L.	.403
Manush-Det.	.378	1926	Hargrave-Cin.	.353
Heilmann-Det.	.398	1927	P. Waner-Pit.	.380
Goslin-Was.	.379	1928	Hornsby-Bos.	.387
Fonseca-Cle.	.369	1929	O'Doul-Phi.	.398
Simmons-Phi.	.381	1930	Terry-N.Y.	.401
Simmons-Phi.	.390	1931	Hafey-St.L.	.349
Alexander-Det. + Bos.	.367	1932	O'Doul-Bkn.	.368
Foxx-Phi.	.356	1933	Klein-Phi.	.368
Gehrig-N.Y.	.363	1934	P. Waner-Pit.	.362
Myer-Was.	.349	1935	Vaughan-Pit.	.385
Appling-Chi.	.388	1936	P. Waner-Pit.	.373
Gehringer-Det.	.371	1937	Wedwick-St.L.	.374
Foxx-Bos	.349	1938	Lombardi-Cin.	.342
DiMaggio-N.Y.	.381	1939	Mize-St.L.	.349
DiMaggio-N.Y.	.352	1940	Garms-Pit.	.355
Williams-Bos.	.406	1941	Reiser-Bkn.	.343
Williams-Bos.	.356	1942	Lombardi-Bos.	.330
Appling-Chi.	.328	1943	Musial-St.L.	.357
Boudreau-Cle.	.327	1944	Walker-Bkn.	.357
Stirnweiss-N.Y.	.309	1945	Cavarretta-Chi.	.355
Vernon-Was.	.353	1946	Musial-St.L.	.365
Williams-Bos.	.343	1947	Walker-St.L. + Phi.	.363
Williams-Bos.	.369	1948	Musial-St.L.	.376
Kell-Det.	.343	1949	Robinson-Bkn.	.342
Goodman-Bos.	.354	1950	Musial-St.L.	.346
Fain-Phi.	.344	1951	Musial-St.L.	.355
Fain-Phi.	.327	1952	Musial-St.L.	.336
Vernon-Was.	.337	1953	Furillo-Bkn.	.344
Avila-Cle.	.341	1954	Mays-N.Y.	.345
Kaline-Det.	.340	1955	Ashburn-Phi.	.338
Mantle-N.Y.	.353	1956	Aaron-Mil.	.328
Williams-Bos.	.388	1957	Musial-St.L.	.351
Williams-Bos.	.328	1958	Ashburn-Phi.	.350
Kuenn-Det.	.353	1959	Aaron-Mil.	.355
Runnels-Bos.	.320	1960	Groat-Pit.	.325
Cash-Det.	.361	1961	Clemente-Pit.	.351
Runnels-Bos.	.326	1962	T. Davis-L.A.	.346
Yastrzemski-Bos.	.321	1963	T. Davis-L.A.	.326
Olive-Min.	.323	1964	Clemente-Pit.	.339
Olive-Min.	.321	1965	Clemente-Pit.	.329
F. Robinson-Bal.	.316	1966	Alou-Pit.	.342
Yastrzemski-Bos.	.326	1967	Clemente-Pit.	.357
Yastrzemski-Bos.	.301	1968	Rose-Cin.	.335
Carew-Min.	.332	1969	Rose-Cin.	.348
Johnson-Cal.	.329	1970	Carty-Atl.	.366
1914 FEDERAL LEAGUE			Kauff-Ind.	.370
1915 FEDERAL LEAGUE			Kauff-Bkn.	.342

SLUGGING AVERAGE

AMERICAN LEAGUE		Year	NATIONAL LEAGUE	
Lajoie-Phi.	.635	1901	Sheckard-Bkn.	.536
Delahanty-Was.	.590	1902	Wagner-Pit.	.467
Lajoie-Cle.	.533	1903	Clarke-Pit.	.532
Lajoie-Cle.	.554	1904	Wagner-Pit.	.520
Flick-Cle.	.466	1905	Seymour-Cin	.559
Stone-St.L.	.496	1906	Lumley-Bkn.	.477
Cobb-Det.	.473	1907	Wagner-Pit.	.513
Cobb-Det.	.475	1908	Wagner-Pit.	.542
Cobb-Det.	.517	1909	Wagner-Pit.	.489
Cobb-Det.	.549	1910	Magee-Phi.	.507
Cobb-Det.	.621	1911	Schulte-Chi.	.534
Cobb-Det.	.586	1912	Zimmerman-Chi.	.571
Jackson-Cle.	.551	1913	Cravath-Phi.	.568
Cobb-Det.	.513	1914	Magee-Phi.	.509
Fournier-Chi.	.491	1915	Cravath-Phi.	.510
Speaker-Cle.	.502	1916	Wheat-Bkn.	.461
Cobb-Det.	.570	1917	Hornsby-St.L.	.484
Ruth-Bos.	.555	1918	Roush-Cin.	.455
Ruth-Bos.	.657	1919	Myers-Bkn.	.436
Ruth-N.Y.	.847	1920	Hornsby-St.L.	.559
Ruth-N.Y.	.846	1921	Hornsby-St.L.	.639
Ruth-N.Y.	.672	1922	Hornsby-St.L.	.722
Ruth-N.Y.	.764	1923	Hornsby-St.L.	.627
Ruth-N.Y.	.739	1924	Hornsby-St.L.	.696
Williams-St.L.	.613	1925	Hornsby-St.L.	.756
Ruth-N.Y.	.737	1926	Williams-Phi.	.568
Ruth-N.Y.	.772	1927	Hafey-St.L.	.590
Ruth-N.Y.	.709	1928	Hornsby-Bos.	.632
Ruth-N.Y.	.697	1929	Hornsby-Chi.	.679
Ruth-N.Y.	.732	1930	Wilson-Chi.	.723
Ruth-N.Y.	.700	1931	Klein-Phi.	.584
Foxx-Phi.	.749	1932	Klein-Phi.	.646
Foxx-Phi.	.703	1933	Klein-Phi.	.602
Gehrig-N.Y.	.706	1934	Collins-St.L.	.615
Foxx-Phi.	.636	1935	Vaughan-Pit.	.607
Gehrig-N.Y.	.696	1936	Ott-N.Y.	.588
DiMaggio-N.Y.	.673	1937	Medwick-St.L.	.641
Foxx-Bos.	.704	1938	Mize-St.L.	.614
Foxx-Bos.	.694	1939	Mize-St.L.	.626
Greenberg-Det.	.670	1940	Mize-St.L.	.636
Williams-Bos.	.735	1941	Reiser-Bkn.	.558
Williams-Bos.	.648	1942	Mize-N.Y.	.521
York-Det.	.527	1943	Musial-St.L.	.562
Doerr-Bos.	.528	1944	Musial-St.L.	.549
Stirnweiss-N.Y.	.476	1945	Holmes-Bos.	.577
Williams-Bos.	.667	1946	Musial-St.L.	.587
Williams-Bos.	.634	1947	Kiner-Pit.	.639
Williams-Bos.	.615	1948	Musial-St.L.	.702
Williams-Bos.	.650	1949	Kiner-Pit.	.658
DiMaggio-N.Y.	.585	1950	Musial-St.L.	.596
Williams-Bos.	.556	1951	Kiner-Pit.	.627
Doby-Cle.	.541	1952	Musial-St.L.	.538
Rosen-Cle.	.613	1953	Snider-Bkn.	.627
Williams-Bos.	.635	1954	Mays-N.Y.	.667
Mantle-N.Y.	.611	1955	Mays-N.Y.	.659
Mantle-N.Y.	.705	1956	Snider-Bkn.	.598
Williams-Bos.	.731	1957	Mays-N.Y.	.626
Colavito-Cle.	.620	1958	Banks-Chi.	.614
Kaline-Det.	.530	1959	Aaron-Mil.	.636
Maris-N.Y.	.581	1960	Robinson-Cin.	.595
Mantle-N.Y.	.687	1961	Robinson-Cin.	.611
Mantle-N.Y.	.605	1962	Robinson-Cin.	.624
Killebrew-Min.	.555	1963	Aaron-Mil.	.586
Powell-Bal.	.606	1964	Mays-S.F.	.607
Yastrzemski-Bos.	.536	1965	Mays-S.F.	.645
F. Robinson-Bal.	.637	1966	Allen-Phi.	.632
Yastrzemski-Bos.	.622	1967	Aaron-Atl.	.576
Howard-Was.	.552	1968	McCovey-S.F.	.545
Jackson-Oak.	.608	1969	McCovey-S.F.	.656
Yastrzemski-Bos.	.592	1970	McCovey-S.F.	.612
1914 FEDERAL LEAGUE			Evers-Bkn.	.556
1915 FEDERAL LEAGUE			Kauff-Bkn.	.509

RUNS BATTED IN

AMERICAN LEAGUE		Year	NATIONAL LEAGUE	
Lajoie-Phi.	125	1901	Wagner-Pit.	126
Freeman-Bos.	121	1902	Wagner-Pit.	91
Freeman-Bos.	104	1903	Mertes-N.Y.	104
Lajoie-Cle.	102	1904	Dahlen-N.Y.	80
Davis-Phi.	83	1905	Seymour-Cin.	121
Davis-Phi.	96	1906	Nealon-Pit.	83
			Steinfeldt-Chi.	83
Cobb-Det.	119	1907	Magee-Phi.	85
Cobb-Det.	108	1908	Wagner-Pit.	109
Cobb-Det.	107	1909	Wagner-Pit.	100
Crawford-Det.	120	1910	Magee-Phi.	123
Cobb-Det.	127	1911	Schulte-Chi.	107
			Wilson-Pit.	107
Baker-Phi.	130	1912	Wagner-Pit.	102
Baker-Phi.	117	1913	Cravath-Phi.	128
Crawford-Det.	104	1914	Magee-Phi.	103
Crawford-Det.	112	1915	Cravath-Phi.	115
Veach-Det.	112			
Pratt-St.L.	103	1916	Zimmerman-Chi. + N.Y.	83
Veach-Det.	103	1917	Zimmerman-N.Y.	102
Veach-Det.	78	1918	Magee-Cin.	76
Ruth-Bos.	114	1919	Myers-Bkn.	73
Ruth-N.Y.	137	1920	Hornsby-St.L.	94
			Kelly-N.Y.	94
Ruth-N.Y.	171	1921	Hornsby-St.L.	126
Williams-St.L.	155	1922	Hornsby-St.L.	152
Ruth-N.Y.	131	1923	Meusel-N.Y.	125
Goslin-Was.	129	1924	Kelly-N.Y.	136
Meusel-N.Y.	138	1925	Hornsby-St.L.	143
Ruth-N.Y.	145	1926	Bottomley-St.L.	120
Gehrig-N.Y.	175	1927	P. Waner-Pit.	131
Gehrig-N.Y.	142	1928	Bottomley-St.L.	136
Ruth-N.Y.	142			
Simmons-Phi.	157	1929	Wilson-Chi.	158
Gehrig-N.Y.	174	1930	Wilson-Chi.	191
Gehrig-N.Y.	184	1931	Klein-Phi.	121
Foxx-Phi.	169	1932	Hurst-Phi.	143
Foxx-Phi.	163	1933	Klein-Phi.	120
Gehrig-N.Y.	165	1934	Ott-N.Y.	135
Greenberg-Det.	170	1935	Berger-Bos.	130
Trosky-Cle.	162	1936	Medwick-St.L.	138
Greenberg-Det.	183	1937	Medwick-St.L.	154
Foxx-Bos.	175	1938	Medwick-St.L.	122
Williams-Bos.	145	1939	McCormick-Cin.	128
Greenberg-Det.	150	1940	Mize-St.L.	137
DiMaggio-N.Y.	125	1941	Camilli-Bkn.	120
Williams-Bos.	137	1942	Mize-N.Y.	110
York-Det.	118	1943	Nicholson-Chi.	128
Stephens-St.L.	109	1944	Nicholson-Chi.	122
Etten-N.Y.	111	1945	Walker-Bkn.	124
Greenberg-Det.	127	1946	Slaughter-St.L.	130
Williams-Bos.	114	1947	Mize-N.Y.	138
DiMaggio-N.Y.	155	1948	Musial-St.L.	131
Stephens-Bos.	159	1949	Kiner-Pit.	127
Williams-Bos.	159			
Dropo-Bos.	144	1950	Ennis-Phi.	126
Stephens-Bos.	144			
Zernial-Chi. + Phi.	129	1951	Irvin-N.Y.	121
Rosen-Cle.	105	1952	Sauer-Chi.	121
Rosen-Cle.	145	1953	Campanella-Bkn.	142
Doby-Cle.	126	1954	Kluszewski-Cin.	141
Boone-Det.	116	1955	Snider-Bkn.	136
Jensen-Bos.	116			
Mantle-N.Y.	130	1956	Musial-St.L.	109
Sievers-Was.	114	1957	Aaron-Mil.	132
Jensen-Bos.	122	1958	Banks-Chi.	129
Jensen-Bos.	112	1959	Banks-Chi.	143
Maris-N.Y.	112	1960	Aaron-Mil.	126
Maris-N.Y.	142	1961	Cepeda-S.F.	142
Killebrew-Min.	126	1962	T. Davis-L.A.	153
Stuart-Bos.	118	1963	Aaron-Mil.	130
Robinson-Bal.	118	1964	Boyer-St.L.	119
Colavito-Cle.	108	1965	Johnson-Cin.	130
F. Robinson-Bal.	122	1966	Aaron-Atl.	127
Yastrzemski-Bos.	121	1967	Cepeda-St.L.	111
Harrelson-Bos.	109	1968	McCovey-S.F.	105
Killebrew-Min.	140	1969	McCovey-S.F.	126
Howard-Was.	126	1970	Bench-Cin.	148
1914 FEDERAL LEAGUE			Esmond-Ind.	107
1915 FEDERAL LEAGUE			Zwilling-Chi.	94

YEARLY BATTING LEADERS

BATTING AVERAGE

AMERICAN LEAGUE		Year	NATIONAL LEAGUE	
Oliva-Min.	.337	1971	Torre-St. L.	.363
Carew-Min.	.318	1972	Williams-Chi.	.333
Carew-Min.	.350	1973	Rose-Cin.	.338
Carew-Min.	.364	1974	Garr-Atl.	.353
Carew-Min.	.359	1975	Madlock-Chi.	.354
Brett-K.C.	.333	1976	Madlock-Chi.	.339
Carew-Min.	.388	1977	Parker-Pit.	.338
Carew-Min.	.333	1978	Parker-Pit.	.334
Lynn-Bos.	.333	1979	Hernandez-St.L.	.344
Brett-K.C.	.390	1980	Buckner-Chi.	.324
Lansford-Bos.	.336	1981	Madlock-Pit.	.341
Wilson-K.C.	.332	1982	Oliver-Mon.	.331
Boggs-Bos.	.361	1983	Madlock-Pit.	.323
Mattingly-N.Y.	.343	1984	Gwynn-S.D.	.351
Boggs-Bos.	.368	1985	McGee-St. L.	.353
Boggs-Bos.	.357	1986	Raines-Mon.	.334
Boggs-Bos.	.363	1987	Gwynn-S.D.	.370
Boggs-Bos.	.366	1988	Gwynn-S.D.	.313
Puckett-Min.	.339	1989	Gwynn-S.D.	.336
Brett-K.C.	.329	1990	McGee-St. L.	.335
Franco-Tex.	.341	1991	Pendleton-Atl.	.319
Martinez,E.-Sea.	.343	1992	Sheffield-S.D.	.330
Olerud-Tor.	.363	1993	Galarraga-Col.	.370
O'Neill-N.Y.	.359	1994	Gwynn-S.D.	.394
E. Martinez-Sea.	.356	1995	Gwynn-S.D.	.368
Rodriguez-Sea.	.358	1996	Gwynn-S.D.	.353
Thomas-Chi.	.347	1997	Gwynn-S.D.	.372
Williams-N.Y.	.339	1998	Walker-Col.	.363
Garciaparra-Bos.	.357	1999	Walker-Col.	.379
Garciaparra-Bos.	.372	2000	Helton-Col.	.372
Suzuki-Sea.	.350	2001	Walker-Col.	.350
Ramirez-Bos.	.349	2002	Bonds-S.F.	.370
Mueller-Bos.	.326	2003	Pujois-St.L.	.359
Suzuki-Sea.	.372	2004	Bonds-S.F.	.363
Young-Tex.	.331	2005	Lee-Chi.	.335
Mauer-Min.	.347	2006	Sanchez-Pit.	.344

SLUGGING AVERAGE

AMERICAN LEAGUE		Year	NATIONAL LEAGUE	
Oliva-Min.	.546	1971	Aaron-Atl.	.669
Allen-Chi.	.603	1972	Williams-Chi.	.606
Jackson-Oak.	.531	1973	Stargell-Pitt.	.646
Allen-Chi.	.563	1974	Schmidt-Phi.	.546
Lynn-Bos.	.566	1975	Parker-Pit.	.541
Jackson-Bal.	.502	1976	Morgan-Cin.	.576
Rice-Bos.	.593	1977	Foster-Cin.	.631
Rice-Bos.	.600	1978	Parker-Pit.	.585
Lynn-Bos.	.637	1979	Kingman-Chi.	.613
Brett-K.C.	.664	1980	Schmidt-Phi.	.624
Grich-Cal.	.543	1981	Schmidt-Phi.	.644
Yount-Mil.	.578	1982	Schmidt-Phi.	.547
Brett-K.C.	.563	1983	Murphy-Atl.	.540
Baines-Chi.	.541	1984	Murphy-Atl.	.547
Brett-K.C.	.585	1985	Guerrero-L.A.	.577
Mattingly-N.Y.	.573	1986	Schmidt-Phi.	.547
McGwire-Oak.	.618	1987	Clark-St. L.	.597
Canseco-Oak.	.569	1988	Strawberry-N.Y.	.545
Sierra-Tex.	.543	1989	Mitchell-S.F.	.635
Fielder-Det.	.592	1990	Bonds-Pit.	.565
Tartabull-K.C.	.593	1991	Clark-S.F.	.536
McGwire-Oak.	.585	1992	Bonds-Pit.	.624
Gonzalez-Tex.	.632	1993	Bonds-S.F.	.677
Thomas-Chi.	.729	1994	Bagwell-Hou.	.750
Belle-Cle.	.690	1995	Bichette-Col.	.620
McGwire-Oak.	.730	1996	Burks-Col.	.639
Griffey-Sea.	.646	1997	Walker-Col.	.720
Belle-Chi.	.655	1998	McGwire-St.L.	.752
M. Ramirez-Cle.	.663	1999	Walker-Col.	.710
M. Ramirez-Cle.	.697	2000	Helton-Col.	.698
Ja. Giambi-Oak.	.660	2001	Bonds-S.F.	.863
Thome-Cle.	.677	2002	Bonds-S.F.	.799
Rodriguez-Tex.	.600	2003	Bonds-S.F.	.749
Ramirez-Bos.	.613	2004	Bonds-S.F.	.812
Rodriguez-N.Y.	.610	2005	Lee-Chi.	.662
Hafner-Cle.	.659	2006	Pujols-St.L.	.671

RUNS BATTED IN

AMERICAN LEAGUE		Year	NATIONAL LEAGUE	
Killebrew-Min.	119	1971	Torre-St. L.	137
Allen-Chi.	113	1972	Bench-Cin.	125
Jackson-Oak.	117	1973	Stargell-Pit.	119
Burroughs-Tex.	118	1974	Bench-Cin.	129
Scott-Mil.	109	1975	Luzinski-Phi.	120
May-Bal.	109	1976	Foster-Cin.	121
Hisle-Min.	119	1977	Foster-Cin.	149
Rice-Bos.	139	1978	Foster-Cin.	120
Baylor-Cal.	139	1979	Winfield-S.D.	118
Cooper-Mil.	122	1980	Schmidt-Phi.	121
Murray-Bal.	78	1981	Schmidt-Phi.	91
McRae-K.C.	133	1982	Murphy-Atl.	109
			Oliver-Min.	109
Cooper-Mil.	126	1983	Murphy-Atl.	121
Armas-Bos.	123	1984	Carter-Mon.	106
			Schmidt-Phi.	106
Mattingly-N.Y.	145	1985	Parker-Cin.	125
Carter-Cle.	121	1986	Schmidt-Phi.	119
Bell-Tor.	134	1987	Dawson-Chi.	137
Canseco-Oak.	124	1988	Clark-S.F.	109
Sierra-Tex.	119	1989	Mitchell-S.F.	125
Fielder-Det.	132	1990	Williams-S.F.	122
Fielder-Det.	133	1991	Johnson-N.Y.	117
Fielder-Det.	124	1992	Daulton-Phi.	109
Belle-Cle.	129	1993	Bonds-S.F.	123
Puckett-Min.	112	1994	Bagwell-Hou.	116
Belle-Cle.	126	1995	Bichette-Col.	128
Vaughn-Bos.	126			
Belle-Cle.	148	1996	Galarraga-Col.	150
Griffey-Sea.	147	1997	Galarraga-Col.	148
Gonzalez-Tex.	157	1998	Sosa-Chi.	158
M. Ramirez-Cle.	165	1999	McGwire-St.L.	147
Martinez-Sea.	145	2000	Helton-Col.	147
Boone-Sea.	141	2001	Sosa-Chi.	160
A. Rodriguez-Tex.	142	2002	Berkman-Hou,	128
Delgado-Tor.	145	2003	Wilson-Col.	141
Tejada-Bal.	150	2004	Castilla-Col.	131
Ortiz-Bos.	148	2005	A. Jones-Atl.	128
Ortiz-Bos.	137	2006	Howard-Phi.	149

YEARLY PITCHING LEADERS

WINS

AMERICAN LEAGUE		Year	NATIONAL LEAGUE	
Young-Bos.	33	1901	Donovan-Bkn.	25
Young-Bos.	32	1902	Chesbro-Pit.	28
Young-Bos.	28	1903	McGinnity-N.Y.	31
Chesbro-N.Y.	41	1904	McGinnity-N.Y.	35
Waddell-Phi.	26	1905	Mathewson-N.Y.	32
Orth-N.Y.	27	1906	McGinnity-N.Y.	27
Joss-Cle. + White-Chi.	27	1907	Mathewson-N.Y.	24
Walsh-Chi.	40	1908	Mathewson-N.Y.	37
Mullin-Det.	29	1909	Brown-Cho.	27
Coombs-Phi.	31	1910	Mathewson-N.Y.	27
Coombs-Phi.	28	1911	Alexander-Phi.	28
Wood-Bos.	34	1912	Cheney-Chi.	26
			Marquard-N.Y.	26
Johnson-Was.	36	1913	Seaton-Phi.	27
Johnson-Was.	28	1914	Alexander-Phi.	27
Johnson-Was.	27	1915	Alexander-Phi.	31
Johnson-Was.	25	1916	Alexander-Phi.	33
Cicotte-Chi.	28	1917	Alexander-Phi.	30
Johnson-Was.	23	1918	Vaughn-Chi.	22
Cicotte-Chi.	29	1919	J. Barnes-N.Y.	25
Bagby-Cle.	31	1920	Alexander-Chi.	27
Mays-N.Y.+Shocker-St.L	27	1921	Cooper-Pit.+Grimes-Bkn.	22
Rommel-Phi.	27	1922	Rixey-Cin.	25
Uhle-Cle.	26	1923	Luque-Cin.	27
Johnson-Was.	23	1924	Vance-Bkn.	28
Lyons-Chi.+Rommell-Phi.	21	1925	Vance-Bkn.	22
Uhle-Cle.	27	1926	Donahue-Cin.+Rhem-St.L	20
			Kremer + Meadows-Pit.	20
Hoyt-N.Y.+Lyons-Chi.	22	1927	Root-Chi.	26
Grove-Phi.+Pipgras-N.Y.	24	1928	Benton-N.Y.+Grimes-Pit.	25
Earnshaw-Phi.	24	1929	Malone-Chi.	22
Grove-Phi.	28	1930	Kremer-Pit.	20
			Malone-Chi.	20
Grove-Phi.	31	1931	Elliott-Phi. + Meine-Pit.	19
			Hallahan-St.L.	19
Crowder-Was.	26	1932	Warneke-Chi.	22
Crowder-Was.+Grove-Phi.	24	1933	Hubbell-N.Y.	23
Gomez-N.Y.	26	1934	D. Dean-St.L.	30
Ferrell-Bos.	25	1935	D. Dean-St.L.	28
Bridges-Det.	23	1936	Hubbell-N.Y.	26
Gomez-N.Y.	21	1937	Hubbell-N.Y.	22
Ruffing-N.Y.	21	1938	Lee-Chi.	22
Feller-Cle.	24	1939	Walters-Cin.	27
Feller-Cle.	27	1940	Walters-Cin.	22
Feller-Cle.	25	1941	Higbe + Wyatt-Bkn.	22
Hughson-Bos.	22	1942	M. Cooper-St.L.	22
Chandler-N.Y.	20	1943	Cooper-St.L.+Riddle-Cin.	21
Trout-Det.	20		Sewell-Pit.	21
Newhouser-Det.	29	1944	Walters-Cin.	23
Newhouser-Det.	25	1945	Barrett-Bos. + St.L.	23
Feller-Cle.	26	1946	Pollet-St.L.	21
Newhouser-Det.	26			
Feller-Cle.	20	1947	Blackwell-Cin.	22
Newhouser-Det.	21	1948	Sain-Bos.	24
Parnell-Bos.	25	1949	Spahn-Bos.	21
Lemon-Cle.	23	1950	Spahn-Bos.	21
Feller-Cle.	22	1951	Jansen + Maglie-N.Y.	23
Shantz-Phi.	24	1952	Roberts-Phi.	28
Porterfield-Was.	22	1953	Roberts-Phi.+Shahn-Mil.	23
Lemon + Wynn-Cle.	23	1954	Roberts-Phi.	23
Ford-N.Y. + Lemon-Cle.	18	1955	Roberts-Phi.	23
Sullivan-Bos.	18			
Lary-Det.	21	1956	Newcombe-Bkn.	27
Bunning-Det.	20	1957	Spahn-Mil.	21
Pierce-Chi.	20			
Turley-N.Y.	21	1958	Friend-Pit. Spahn-Mil.	22
Wynn-Chi.	22	1959	Burdette + Spahn-Mil	21
			Jones-S. F.	21
Estradea-Bal.	18	1960	Broglio-St.L.	21
Perry-Cle.	18		Spahn-Mil	21
Ford-N.Y.	25	1961	Jay-Cin. + Spahn-Mil	21
Terry-N.Y.	23	1962	Drysdale-L.A.	25
Ford-N.Y.	24	1963	Koufax-L.A.	25
			Marichal-S. F.	25
Chance-L.A.+Peters-Chi.	20	1964	Jackson-St.L.	24
Grant-Min.	21	1965	Koufax-L.A.	26
Kaat-Min.	25	1966	Koufax-L.A.	27
Lonborg-Bos.	22	1967	McCormick-S.F.	22
Wilson-Det.	22			
McLain-Det.	31	1968	Marichal-S.F.	26
McLain-Det.	24	1969	Seaver-N.Y.	25
Cuellar + McNally-Bal.	24	1970	Gibson-St.L.	23
Perry-Min.	24		Perry-S. F.	23

LOSSES

AMERICAN LEAGUE		Year	NATIONAL LEAGUE	
Dowling-Mil. + Chi.	27	1901	Taylor-N.Y.	27
Dinneen-Bos.	21	1902	Yerkes-St.L.	21
Flaherty-Chi.	25	1903	Pittinger-Bos.	22
Townsend-Was.	27	1904	Jones-Bkn.+Willis-Bos.	25
Glade-St.L.	24	1905	Willis-Bos.	29
Harris + Young Bos.	21	1906	Dorner-Cin. + Bos.	26
Orth-N.Y. + Pelty-St.L.	21	1907	McGlynn-St.L.	25
Lake-N.Y.	22	1908	Raymond-St.L.	25
Groom-Was.	26	1909	Ferguson-Bos.	23
Walsh-Chi.	20	1910	Bell-Bkn.	27
Powell-St.L.	19	1911	Moore Phi.+Steele-St.L	19
Ford-N.Y.	21	1912	Tyler-Bos.	22
Scott-Chi.	20	1913	Griner-St.L.	22
Weilman-St.L.	20			
Benz-Chi.	19	1914	Ames-Cin.	23
Wyckoff-Phi.	22	1915	Rudolph-Bos.	19
			Schneider-Cin.	19
Bush-Phi.	24	1916	Meadows-St.L.	23
Groom +Sothoron-St.L.	19	1917	Barnes-Bos.	21
Cicotte-Chi.	19	1918	Marquard-Bkn.	18
Perry-Phi.	19		Oeschger-Phi.	18
Harper-Was.	21	1919	Rudolph-Bos.	18
Perry-Phi.	25	1920	Rixey-Phi.	22
Rommel-Phi.	23	1921	Smith-Phi.	20
Harris-Phi.	20	1922	Luque-Cin.	23
Pillette-Det.	19	1923	Cooper-Pit.	19
Rommel-Phi.	19			
Ehmke + Ferguson-Bos.	17	1924	Barnes-Bos.	20
Shaute-Cle.	17			
Jones-N.Y.	21	1925	Grimes-Bkn.	19
Gaston-St.L.	18	1926	Petty-Bkn.	17
Zahniser-Bos.	18		Root-Chi.	17
Harriss-Bos.	21	1927	Scott-Phi.	21
Ruffing-Bos.	25	1928	Brandt-Bos.	21
Ruffing-Bos.	22	1929	Clark-Bkn.	19
Gaston + Russell-Bos.	20	1930	French-Pit. + Frey-Cin.	18
Caraway-Chi.+Gray-St.L	24	1931	Johnson-Cin.	19
Hadley-Chi. + St.L.	21	1932	Carroll-Cin.	19
Lyons-Chi.	21	1933	Derringer-St.L. + Cin.	27
Newsom-St.L.	20	1934	Johnson-Cin.	22
Newsom-St.L. + Was.	18	1935	Cantwell-Bos.	25
Rhodes-Phi.	20	1936	Walters-Phi.	21
Kelley-Phi.	21	1937	LeMaster-Phi.	19
Caster-Phi.	20	1938	Mulcahy-Phi.	20
Kennedy-Det. + St.L.	20	1939	Butcher-Phi. + Pit.	17
			Klinger-Pit.	17
Caster-Phi.	19	1940	Mulcahy-Phi.	22
Leonard-Was.	19			
Newsom-Det.	20	1941	Sewell-Pit.	17
Smith-Chi.	20	1942	Tobin-Bos.	21
Harris-Phi.	20	1943	Andrews-Bos.	20
Dietrich-Chi.+Wynn-Was.	17	1944	Raffensberger-Phi.	20
Newsom-Phi.	20	1945	Barrett-Phi.	20
Fowler, Knerr	16	1946	Koslo-N.Y.	19
Marchildon-all Phi.	16			
Newhouser-Det.	17	1947	Schmitz-Chi.	18
Sanford-Phi.	21	1948	Leonard-Phi.	17
Calvert + Hudson-Was.	17	1949	Fox-Cin.	19
Garver-St.L.	17			
Kellner-Phi.	20	1950	Rush-Chi.	20
Gray + Trout-Det.	14	1951	Minner-Chi.	17
Kellner-Phi.+Lemon-Cle.	14		Raffensberger-Cin.	17
Pierce-Chi.+Pillette-St.L	14		Ramsdell-Cin.	17
Houtteman-Det.	20	1952	Dickson-Pit.	21
Byrd-Phi.	20	1953	Dickson-Phi.+Hacker-Chi.	19
Larsen-Bal.	21	1954	Dickson-Phi.	20
Wilson-Bal.	18	1955	Jones-Chi.	20
Ditmar-K.C.	22	1956	Kline-Pit.+Roberts-Phi.	18
Stobbs-Was.	20	1957	Roberts-Phi.	22
Ramos-Was.	18	1958	Kline-Pit.	16
Ramos-Was.	19	1959	Friend-Pit.	19
Ramos-Was.	18	1960	Hobbie-Chi.	20
Ramos-Was.	20	1961	Friend-Pit.	19
			Mahaffey-Phi.	19
Estrada-Bal.+Rakow-K.C.	17	1962	Craig-N.Y.	24
Pena-K.C.	20	1963	Craig-N.Y.	22
Segui-K.C.	17	1964	Stallard-N.Y.	20
Monboquette-Bos.	18	1965	Fisher-N.Y.	24
Morehead-Bos.	18			
Stottlemyre-N.Y.	20	1966	Ellsworth-Chi.	22
Brunet-Cal.	19	1967	Fisher-N.Y.	18
Brunet-Cal.	17	1968	Osteen-L.A.+Sadecki-S.F.	18
Tiant-Cle.	20	1969	Kirby-S.D.	20
Lolich-Det.	19	1970	Carlton-St.L.	19

WINNING PERCENTAGE

AMERICAN LEAGUE		Year	NATIONAL LEAGUE	
Griffith-Chi.	.744	1901	Chesbro-Pit.	.667
Waddell-Phi.	.744	1902	Chesbro-Pit.	.824
Young-Bos.	.757	1903	Leever-Pit.	.781
Chesbro-N.Y.	.774	1904	McGinnity-N.Y.	.814
Coakley-Phi.	.741	1905	Mathewson-N.Y.	.800
Plank-Phi.	.792	1906	Reulbach-Chi.	.826
Donovan-Det.	.862	1907	Reulbach-Chi.	.810
Walsh-Chi.	.727	1908	Reulbach-Chi.	.774
Mullin-Det.	.763	1909	Cammitz-Pit.	.806
			Mathewson-N.Y.	.806
Bender-Phi.	.821	1910	Cole-Chi.	.833
Gregg-Cle.	.767	1911	Marquard-N.Y.	.774
Wood-Bos.	.872	1912	Hendrix-Pit.	.727
Johnson-Was.	.837	1913	Humphries-Chi.	.800
Bender-Phi.	.850	1914	James-Bos.	.788
Ruth-Bos.	.750	1915	Alexander-Phi.	.756
Cicotte-Chi.	.682	1916	Hughes-Bos.	.842
Russell-Chi.	.750	1917	Schupp-N.Y.	.750
Jones-Bos.	.762	1918	Hendrix-Chi.	.741
Cicotte-Chi.	.806	1919	Ruether-Cin.	.760
Bagby-Cle.	.721	1920	Grimes-Bkn.	.676
Mays-N.Y.	.750	1921	Doak-St.L.	.714
Bush-N.Y.	.788	1922	Donohue-Cin.	.667
Pennock-N.Y.	.760	1923	Luque-Cin.	.771
Johnson-Was.	.767	1924	Yde-Pit.	.842
Coveleski-Was.	.800	1925	Sherdel-St.L.	.714
Uhle-Cle.	.711	1926	Kremer-Pit.	.769
Hoyt-N.Y.	.759	1927	Benton-Bos. + N.Y.	.708
Crowder-St.L.	.808	1928	Benton-N.Y.	.735
Grove-Phi	.769	1929	Root-Chi.	.760
Grove-Phi	.848	1930	Fitzsimmons-N.Y.	.731
Grove-Phi.	.886	1931	Derringer-St.L.	.692
Allen-Cle.	.810	1932	Warneke-Chi.	.786
Grove-Phi.	.750	1933	Cantwell-Bos.	.667
Gomez-N.Y.	.839	1934	D. Dean-St.L.	.811
Auker-Det.	.720	1935	Lee-Chi.	.769
Pearson-N.Y.	.731	1936	Hubbell-N.Y.	.813
Allen-Cle.	.938	1937	Hubbell-N.Y.	.733
Ruffing-N.Y.	.750	1938	Lee-Chi.	.710
Grove-Bos.	.789	1939	Derringer-Cin.	.781
Rowe-Det.	.842	1940	Fitzsimmons-Bkn.	.889
Gomez-N.Y.	.750	1941	Riddle-Cin.	.826
Bonham-N.Y.	.808	1942	French-Bkn.	.789
Chandler-N.Y.	.833	1943	Cooper-St.L.	.724
Hughson-Bos.	.783	1944	Wilks-St.L.	.810
Newhouser-Det.	.735	1945	Brecheen-St.L.	.789
Ferriss-Bos	.806	1946	Dickson-St.L.	.714
Reynolds-N.Y.	.704	1947	Jansen-N.Y.	.808
Kramer-Bos.	.783	1948	Brecheen-St.L.	.741
Kinder-Bos.	.793	1949	Roe-Bkn.	.714
Raschi-N.Y.	.724	1950	Maglie-N.Y.	.818
Feller-Cle.	.733	1951	Roe-Bkn.	.880
Shantz-Phi.	.774	1952	Wilhelm-N.Y.	.833
Lopat-N.Y.	.800	1953	Erskine-Bkn.	.769
Consuegra-Chi.	.842	1954	Antonelli-N.Y.	.750
Byrne-N.Y.	.762	1955	Newcombe-Bkn.	.800
Ford-N.Y.	.760	1956	Newcombe-Bkn.	.794
Donovan-Chi.	.727	1957	Buhl-Mil.	.720
Turley-N.Y.	.750	1958	Burdette-Mil.	.667
			Spahn-Mil.	.667
Shaw-Chi.	.750	1959	Face-Pit.	.947
Perry-Cle.	.643	1960	Broglio-St.L.	.700
Ford-N.Y.	.862	1961	Podres-L.A.	.783
Herbert-Chi.	.690	1962	Purkey-Cin.	.821
Ford-N.Y.	.774	1963	Perranoski-L.A.	.842
Bunker-Bal.	.792	1964	Koufax-L.A.	.792
Grant-Min.	.750	1965	Koufax-L.A.	.765
Siebert-Cle.	.667	1966	Marichal-S.F.	.806
Horlen-Chi.	.731	1967	Hughes-St.L.	.727
McLain-Det.	.838	1968	Blass-Pit.	.750
Palmer-Bal.	.800	1969	Seaver-N.Y.	.781
Cuellar-Bal.	.750	1970	Sibson-St.L.	.767

FEDERAL LEAGUE

WINS
Year			
1914	FEDERAL LEAGUE	Hendrix-Chi.	29
1915	FEDERAL LEAGUE	McConnell-Chi.	25

LOSSES
Year			
1914	FEDERAL LEAGUE	Groom-St.L.	20
1915	FEDERAL LEAGUE	Quinn-Bal.	22

WINNING PERCENTAGE
Year			
1914	FEDERAL LEAGUE	Ford-Buf.	.778
1915	FEDERAL LEAGUE	McConnell-Chi.	.714

YEARLY PITCHING LEADERS

WINS

American League	W	Year	National League	W
Lolich-Det.	25	1971	Jenkins-Chi.	24
Perry-Cle.	24	1972	Carlton-Phi.	27
Wood-Chi				
Wood-Chi.	24	1973	Bryant-S.F.	24
Hunter-Oak.	25	1974	Messersmith-L.A.	20
Jenkins-Tex.	25		P.Niekro-Atl.	20
Hunter-N.Y.	23	1975	Seaver-N.Y.	23
Palmer-Bal.	23			
Palmer-Bal.	22	1976	Jones-S.D.	22
Palmer-Bal.	20	1977	Carlton-Phi.	23
Goltz-Min.	20			
Leonard-K.C.	20			
Guidry-N.Y.	25	1978	Perry-S.D.	21
Flanagan-Bal.	23	1979	J.Niekro-Hou.	21
			P.Niekro-Atl.	21
Stone-Bal.	25	1980	Carlton-Phi.	24
McCatty-Oak.	14	1981	Seaver-Cin.	14
Hoyt-Chi.	19	1982	Carlton-Phi.	23
Hoyt-Chi.	21	1983	Denny-Phi.	19
Boddicker-Bal.	20	1984	Andujar-St.L.	20
Guidry - NY	22	1985	Gooden-N.Y.	24
Clemens-Bos.	24	1986	Valenzuela-N.Y.	21
Clemens-Bos.	20	1987	Sutcliffe-Chi.	18
Stewart-Oak.	20		Jackson - Cin.	23
Viola-Min.	24	1988	Hershiser-L.A.	23
Saberhagen-K.C.	23	1989	Scott-Hou.	20
Welch-Oak.	27	1990	Drabek-Pit.	22
Erickson-Min.	20	1991	Glavine-Atl.	20
Gullickson-Det.	20		Smiley-Pit.	20
Brown-Tex.	21	1992	Maddux-Chi.	20
Morris-Tor.	21		Glavine-Atl.	20
McDowell-Chi.	22	1993	Glavine-Atl.	22
			Burkett-S.F.	22
Key-N.Y.	17	1994	Maddux-Atl.	16
			Hill-Mon.	16
Mussina-Bal.	19	1995	Maddux-Atl.	19
Pettitte-N.Y.	21	1996	Smoltz-Atl.	24
Clemens-Tor.	21	1997	Neagle-Atl.	20
Cone-N.Y.	20	1998	Glavine-Atl.	20
Clemens-Tor.	20			
Helling-Tex.	20			
P. Martinez-Bos.	23	1999	Hampton-Hou.	22
Hudson-Oak.	20	2000	Glavine-Atl.	21
Wells-Tor.	20			
Mulder-Oak.	21	2001	Schilling-Ari.	22
			Morris-St.L.	22
Zito-Oak.	23	2002	Johnson-Ari.	24
Halladay-Tor.	22	2003	Ortiz-Atl.	21
Schilling-Bos.	21	2004	Oswalt-Hou.	20
Colon-L.A.	21	2005	Willis-Fla.	22
Santana-Min.	19	2006	Zambrano-Chi.	16
Wang-N.Y.	19		Webb-Ari.	16
			Lowe-L.A.	16
			Smoltz-Atl.	16
			Penny-L.A.	16
			Harang-Cin.	16

LOSSES

American League	L	Year	National League	L
McLain-Was.	22	1971	Arlin-S.D.	19
Dobson-Bal.	18	1972	Arlin-S.D.	21
Stottlemyre-N.Y.	18			
Bahnsen-Chi.	21	1973	Carlton-Phi.	20
Lolich-Det.	21	1974	Bonham-Chi.	22
			Jones-S.D. .	22
			Rogers - Mon.	22
Wood-Chi.	20	1975	R.Reuschel-Chi.	17
Ryan-Cal.	18	1976	Rogers-Mon.	17
			Ruthven-Atl.	17
Blue + Langford-Oak.	19	1977	P.Niekro-Atl.	20
Garland-Cle.	19		Koosman-N.Y.	20
Wise-Cle.	19	1978	P.Niekro-Atl.	18
Huffman-Tor.	18	1979	P.Niekro-Atl.	20
Kingman-Oak.	20	1980	P.Niekro-Atl.	18
Berenguer-K.C. + Tor.	13	1981	Mura-S.D.	14
Koosman- Min + Chi.	13		Zachry-N.Y.	14
Leal-Tor.	13			
Keough-Oak.	18	1982	Berenyi-Cin.	18
Gura-K.C.	18	1983	Torrez-N.Y.	17
Hoyt-Chi.	18	1984	Russell-Cin.	18
Young-Sea.	19	1985	La Point-S.F.	17
Dotson-Chi.	17	1986	Mahler-Atl.	18
Morgan-Sea.	17			
Moore-Sea.	19	1987	Knepper-Hou.	17
Blyleven-Min.	17	1988	Glavine-Atl.	17
Alexander-Det.	18	1989	Carman-Phi.	15
			Hershiser-Phi.	15
			Hill-St. L.	15
Leary-N.Y.	19	1990	DeLeon-St. L.	19
McCaskill-Cal.	19	1991	Black-S.F.	16
Hanson-Sea.	17	1992	Hershiser-L.A.	15
			Candiotti-L.A.	15
Eldred-Mil.	16	1993	Harris-S.D.+Col.	17
			Armstrong-Fla.	17
Belcher-Det.	15	1994	Benes-S.D.	14
Gross-Tex.	15	1995	Wagner-Pit.	16
Bere-Chi.	15			
Moore-Det.	15			
J. Abbott-Cal.	18	1996	Rapp-Fla.	16
			Castillo-Chi.	16
Wakefield-Bos.	15	1997	Leiter-Phi.	17
Baldwin-Chi.	15			
Eldred-Mil.	15			
Navarro-Chi.	16	1998	Kile-Col.	17
Candiotti-Oak.	16			
Moehler-Det.	16	1999	Trachsel-Chi.	18
Radke-Min.	16	2000	Daal-Ari.+Phi.	19
Mercedes-Bal.	17	2001	Jones-S.D.	19
Sturtze-T.B.	18	2002	Hernandez-S.F.	16
			Rusch-Mil.	16
			Sheets-Mil.	16
Maroth-Det.	21	2003	D'Amico-Pit.	16
May-K.C.	19	2004	Webb.Ari.	16
Greinke-K.C.	17	2005	Wells-Pit.	18
Lopez-Bal.	18	2006	Ortiz-Was.	16
			Marquis-St. L.	16

WINNING PERCENTAGE

American League	Pct.	Year	National League	Pct.
McNally-Bal.	.808	1971	Gullett-Cin.	.727
Hunter-Oak.	.750	1972	Nolan-Cin.	.750
Hunter-Oak.	.808	1973	John-L.A.	.696
Cuellar-Bal.	.688	1974	John-L.A.	.813
Moret-Bos.	.824	1975	Hrabosky-St.L.	.813
Campbell-Min.	.773	1976	Rhoden-L.A.	.800
Splittorff-K.C.	.727	1977	Candalaria-Pit.	.800
Guidry-N.Y.	.893	1978	Perry-S.D.	.778
Davis-N.Y.	.875	1979	Seaver-Cin.	.727
Stone-Bal.	.781	1980	Bibby-Pit.	.760
Vukovich-Mil.	.778	1981	Seaver-Cin.	.875
			Rijo-Cin.	.714
Palmer-Bal.	.750	1982	Niekro-Atl.	.810
Vukovich-Mil.	.750			
Dotson-Chi.	.759	1983	Denny-Phi.	.760
Alexander-Tor.	.739	1984	Sutcliffe-Chi.	.941
Guidry-N.Y.	.786	1985	Hershiser-L.A.	.864
Clemens-Bos.	.857	1986	Ojeda-N.Y.	.783
Clemens-Bos.	.690	1987	Gooden-N.Y.	.682
Viola-Min.	.774	1988	Cone-N.Y.	.870
Saberhagen-K.C.	.793	1989	Bielecki-Chi.	.720
Welch-Oak.	.818	1990	Drabek-Pit.	.786
Erickson-Min.	.714	1991	Smiley-Pit.	.714
Mussina-Bal.	.783	1992	Tewksbury-St.L.	.762
Key-N.Y.	.750	1993	Portugal-Hou.	.818
Bere-Chi.	.857	1994	Saberhagen-N.Y.	.778
Johnson-Sea.	.900	1995	Maddux-Atl.	.905
Nagy-Cle.	.773	1996	Smoltz-Atl.	.750
Johnson-Sea.	.833	1997	Maddux-Atl.	.826
Wells-N.Y.	.818	1998	Smoltz-Atl.	.850
P. Martinez-Bos.	.852	1999	Hampton-Hou.	.846
Hudson-Oak.	.769	2000	Johnson-Ari.	.731
Clemens-N.Y.	.870	2001	Schilling-Ari.	.786
Martinez-Bos.	.833	2002	Johnson-Ari.	.828
Santana-Min.	.800	2003	Schmidt-S.F.	.773
Schilling-Bos.	.778	2004	Clemens-Hou.	.818
Lee-Cle.	.783	2005	Sosa-Atl.	.813
Liriano-Min.	.800	2006	James-Atl.	.733

YEARLY PITCHING LEADERS

SHUTOUTS

American League	#	Year	National League	#
Young-Bos., Griffith-Chi.	5	1901	Chesbro-Pit. Orth-Phi. Willis-Bos.	6
Joss-Cle.	5	1902	Chesbro-Pit., Mathewson-N.Y.	8
Young-Bos.	7	1903	Leever-Pit.	7
Young-Bos.	10	1904	McGinnity-N.Y.	9
Killian-Det	8	1905	Mathewson-N.Y.	8
Walsh-Chi	10	1906	Brown-Chi.	9
Plank-Phi.	8	1907	Overall-Chi.	8
Walsh-Chi.	11	1908	Mathewson-N.Y.	11
Walsh-Chi.	8	1909	Overall-Chi.	9
Coombs-Phi.	13	1910	Brown-Chi., Mattern-Bos., Moore-Phi., Rucker-Bkn.	6
Johnson-Was., Plank-Phi	6	1911	Alexander-Phi.	7
Wood-Bos.	10	1912	Rucker-Bkn.	6
Johnson-Was.	12	1913	Alexander-Phi.	9
Johnson-Was.	10	1914	Tesreau-N.Y.	8
Johnson-Was., Scott-Chi.	7	1915	Alexander-Phi.	12
Ruth-Bos.	9	1916	Alexander-Phi.	16
Coveleski-Cle	9	1917	Alexander-Phi.	8
Johnson-Was., Mays-Bos.	8	1918	Tyler-Chi, Vaughn, Chi.	8
Johnson-Was.	7	1919	Alexander-Chi.	9
Mays-N.Y.	6	1920	Adams-Pit.	8
Jones-Bos.	5	1921	Alexander-Chi., Douglas-N.Y. Fillingim-Bos., Luque-Cin., Mitchell-Bkn., Morrison-Pit., Oeschger, Bos.	3
Uhle-Cle.	5	1922	Morrison-Pit., Vance-Bkn.	5
Coveleski-Cle.	5	1923	Luque-Cin.	6
Johnson-Was.	6	1924	Barnes-Bos. Cooper-Pit. Krenmer-Pit Rixey-Cin. Sothoren-St.L. Yde-Pit	4
Lyons-Chi	5	1925	Carlson-Phi.Luque-Cin. Vance-Bkn.	4
Wells Det.	4	1926	Donohue-Cin.	5
Lisenbee-Was.	4	1927	Haines-St.L.	6
Pennock-N.Y.	5	1928	Blake-Chi., Grimes-Pit., Lucas-Cin. McWeeney-Bkn., Vance-Bkn.	4
Blaeholder-St.L.,Gray-St.L.	4	1929	Malone-Chi.	5
Crowder-St.L., MacFayden-Bos.	4			
Earnshaw-Phi.,Pipgras-N.Y., Brown-Cle.	3	1930	Root-Chi., Vance-Bkn.	4
Grove-Phi.	4	1931	Walker-N.Y.	6
Bridges-Det., Grove-Phi	4	1932	Dean-St.L., Swetonic-Pit.,Warneke-Chi.	4
Hildebrand-Cle.	6	1933	Hubbell-N.Y.	10
Gomez-N.Y. Harder-Cle.	5	1934	D.Dean-St.L.	7
Rowe-Det.	6	1935	Blanton-Pit., Fitzaimmons-N.Y., French-Chi.,Mungo-Bkn.,Weaver-Pit.	4
Grove-Bos.	6	1936	Blanton-Pit., Carleton-Chi., French-Phi., Lee-Chi., Smith N.Y., Walters-Phi., Warneke-Chi.	4
Gomez-N.Y.	5	1937	Fette-Bos., Grissom-Cin.,Turner-Bos.	5
Gomez-N.Y.	4	1938	Lee-Chi.	9
Ruffing-N.Y.	5	1939	Fette-Bos.	6
Feller-Cle.,	4	1940	Lohrman-N.Y., Salvo-Bos., Wyatt-Bkn.	5
Lyons-Chi., Milnar-Cle.	4			
Feller-Cle.	6	1941	Wyatt-Bkn.	7
Bonham-N.Y.	5	1942	Cooper-St.L.	10
Chandler-N.Y., Trout-Det.	5	1943	Bithorn-Chi.	7
Trout-Det.	7	1944	Cooper-St.L.	7
Newhouser-Det.	8	1945	Passeau-Chi.	5
Feller-Cle.	10	1946	Blackwell-Cin.	6
Feller-Cle.	5	1947	Spahn-Bos.	7
Lemon-Cle.	10	1948	Brecheen-St.L.	7
Kinder-Bos., Trucks-Det.	6	1949	Heintzelman-Phi. Newcombe-Bkn., Pollet-St.L., Raffensberger-Cin.	5
Houtteman-Det.	4	1950	Hearn-St.L. +N.Y., Jansen-N.Y., Maglie N.Y., Roberts-Phi.	5
Reynolds-N.Y.	7	1951		
Garcia-Cle., Reynolds-N.Y.	6	1952	Raffensberger-Cin., Simmons-Phi.	5
Porterfield-Was.	9	1953	Haddix-St.L.	6
Garcia-Cle., Trucks-Chi	5	1954	Antonelli-N.Y.	6
Hoeft-Det.	7	1955	Nuxhall-Cin.	5
Score-Cle.	5	1956	Burdette-Mil.	6
Wilson-Chi.	5	1957	Podres-Bkn.	4
Ford-N.Y.	7	1958	Willey-Mil.	4
Pascual-Was.	6	1959	Antonelli-S.F., Buhl-Mil., Burdette-Mil., Craig-L.A., Drysdale-L.A.,Jones-S.F.,Spahn-Mil.	4
Ford-N.Y., Perry-Cle., Wynn-Chi.	4	1960	Sanford-S.F.	6
Barber-Bal., Pascual-Min.	8	1961	Jay-Cin., Spahn-Mil.	5
Donovan-Cle., Kaat-Min.	5	1962	Friend-Pit. Gibson-St.L.	5
Pascual-Min.				
Herbert-Chi.	7	1963	Koufax-L.A.	11
Chance-L.A.	11	1964	Koufax-L.A.	7
Grant-Min.	6	1965	Marichal-S.F.	10
John-Chi., McDowell-Cle.	5	1966	Bunning-Phi. Gibson-St.L., Jackson-Phi. Jaster-St.L., Koufax-L.A. Maloney-Cin.	5
Tiant-Cle.	5			
Hargan-Cle., Horlen-Chi., John-Chi., Lolich-Det., McGlothlin-Cal.	6	1967	Bunning-Phi.	6
Tiant-Cle.	9	1968	Gibson-St.L.	13
Mc.Lain-Det.	9	1969	Marichal-S.F.	8
Dobson-Oak., Palmer-Bal.	5	1970	Perry-S.F.	5

BASES ON BALLS

American League	#	Year	National League	#
Fraser-Phi.	132	1901	Donovan-Bkn.	152
Moore-Cle.	101	1902	Pittinger-Bos.	128
Mullin-Det.	106	1903	Pittinger-Bos.	143
Mullin-Det.	131	1904	Pittinger-Bos.	144
Mullin-Det.	138	1905	Fraser-Bos.	149
Mullin-Det.	108	1906	Scanian-Bkn.	127
Falkenberg-Was.	108			
Smith-Chi.	111	1907	McGlynn-St.L.	112
Dygert-Phi.	97	1908	Rucker-Bkn.	125
Groom-Was.	105	1909	Mattern-Bos.	108
			Moore-Phi.	108
Morgan-Phi.	117	1910	Harmon-St.L.	133
Krapp-Cle.	136	1911	Harmon-St.L.	181
Kahler-Cle.	121	1912	O'Toole-Pit.	159
Gregg-Cle.	124	1913	Seaton-Phi.	136
Shaw-Was.	137	1914	Cheney-Chi.	140
Wyckoff-Phi.	165	1915	Dale-Cin.	107
Myers-Phi.	168	1916	Mamaux-Pit.	136
Shaw-Was.	123	1917	Schneider-Cin.	119
Mogridge-N.Y.	116	1918	Schneider-Cin.	117
Ehmke-Det.	107	1919	Ruether-Cin.	83
Davis-St.L.	149	1920	Schupp-St.L.	127
Davis-St.L.	123	1921	Oeschger-Bos.	97
Collins-Bos.	103	1922	Ring-Phi.	103
Vangilder-St.L	120	1923	Ring-Phi.	115
Bush-N.Y.	109	1924	Ring-Phi.	108
Grove-Phi.	131	1925	Ring-Phi.	119
Uhle-Cle.	118	1926	Blake-Chi.	92
Whitehill-Det.	105	1927	Root-Chi.	117
Johnson-N.Y.	104	1928	McWeeney-Bkn.	114
Earnshaw-Phi.	125	1929	Blake-Chi.	130
Earnshaw-Phi.	139	1930	Hallahan-St.L	126
Ferrell-Cle.	130	1931	Hallahan-St.L	112
Hadley-Chi.+St.L	171	1932	Mungo-Bkn.	115
Hadley- St.L.	141	1933	Hallahan-St.L.	98
Newsom-St.L.	149	1934	Mungo-Bkn.	104
Cain-Phi. + St.L.	123	1935	Parmalee-N.Y.	97
Kennedy-Chi.	147	1936	Mungo-Bkn.	118
Newsom-Was.+Bos.	167	1937	Mulcahy-Phi.	97
Feller-Cle.	208	1938	Bryant-Chi.	125
Feller-Cle.	142	1939	Higbe-Chi. + Phi.	123
Chase-Was.	143	1940	Higbe- Phi.	121
Feller-Cle.	194	1941	Higbe-Bkn.	132
Marchildon-Phi.	140	1942	Melton-Phi.	114
Newhouser-Det.	111	1943	Vander Meer-Cin.	162
Gentry-Det.	108	1944	Javery-Bos.	118
			Voiselle-N.Y.	118
Reynolds-Cle.	130	1945	Gregg-Bkn.	120
Feller-Det.	153	1946	Kennedy-N.Y.	116
Marchildon-Phi.	141	1947	Higbe-Bkn. + Pit.	122
Wight-Chi.	135	1948	Vander Meer-Cin.	124
Byrne-N.Y.	179	1949	Wehmeier-Cin.	117
Byrne-N.Y.	160	1950	Wehmeier-Cin.	135
Byrne-N.Y. + St.L	150	1951	Spahn-Bos.	107
Wynn-Cle.	132	1952	Mizell-St.L.	103
			Wehmeier-Cin.	103
Parnell-Bos.	116	1953	Lindell-Pit. +Phi.	139
Turley-Bal.	181	1954	Gomez-N.Y.	109
Turley-Bal.	177	1955	Jones-Chi.	185
Foytack-Det.	142	1956	Jones-Chi.	115
Moore-Bal.	112	1957	Drott-Chi.	129
Turley-N.Y.	128	1958	Jones-St.L.	107
Wynn-Chi.	119	1959	Jones-S.F.	109
Barber-Bal.	113	1960	Buhl-Mil.	103
Estrada-Bal.	132	1961	Gibson-St.L.	119
Belinsky-L.A.	122	1962	Hamilton-Phi.	107
Wilson-Bos.	105	1963	Culp-Phi.	102
Downing-N.Y.	120	1964	Veale-Pit.	124
McDowell-Cle.	132	1965	Cloninger-Mil.	119
			Veale-Pit.	119
Chance-Cal.	114	1966	Cloninger-Atl.	116
McDowell-Cle.	123	1967	Veale-Pit.	119
McDowell-Cle.	110	1968	Veale-Pit.	94
Tiant-Cle.	129	1969	Stoneman-Mon.	123
McDowell-Cle.	131	1970	Morton-Mon.	125

STRIKEOUTS

American League	#	Year	National League	#
Young-Bos.	158	1901	Hahn-Cin.	239
Waddell-Phi.	210	1902	Willia-Bos.	225
Waddell-Phi.	302	1903	Mathewson-N.Y.	267
Waddell-Phi.	349	1904	Mathewson-N.Y.	212
Waddell-Phi.	287	1905	Mathewson-N.Y.	206
Waddell-Phi.	196	1906	Beebe-Chi. + St.L.	171
Waddell-Phi.	232	1907	Mathewson-N.Y.	178
Walsh-Cin.	269	1908	Mathewson-N.Y.	259
Smith-Cin.	177	1909	Overall-Chi.	205
Johnson-Was.	313	1910	Moore-Phi.	185
Walsh-Chi.	255	1911	Marquard-N.Y.	237
Johnson-Was.	303	1912	Alexander-Phi.	195
Johnson-Was.	243	1913	Seaton-Phi.	168
Johnson-Was.	225	1914	Alexander-Phi.	214
Johnson-Was.	203	1915	Alexander-Phi.	241
Johnson-Was.	228	1916	Alexander-Phi.	167
Johnson-Was.	188	1917	Alexander-Phi.	201
Johnson-Was.	162	1918	Vaughn-Chi.	148
Johnson-Was.	147	1919	Vaughn-Chi.	141
Coveleski-Cle.	133	1920	Vance-Bkn.	173
Johnson-Was.	143	1921	Grimes-Bkn.	136
Shocker-St.L.	149	1922	Vance-Bkn.	134
Johnson-Was.	130	1923	Vance-Bkn.	197
Johnson-Was.	158	1924	Vance-Bkn.	262
Grove-Phi.	116	1925	Vance-Bkn.	221
Grove-Phi.	194	1926	Vance-Bkn.	140
Grove-Phi.	174	1927	Vance-Bkn.	184
Grove-Phi.	183	1928	Vance-Bkn.	200
Grove-Phi.	170	1929	Malone-Chi.	166
Grove-Phi.	209	1930	Hallahan-St.L.	177
Grove-Phi.	175	1931	Hallahan-St.L.	159
Ruffing-N.Y.	190	1932	Dean-St.L.	191
Gomez-N.Y.	163	1933	Dean-St.L.	199
Gomez-N.Y.	158	1934	D. Dean-St.L.	195
Bridges-Det.	163	1935	D. Dean-St.L.	182
Bridges-Det.	175	1936	Mungo-Bkn.	238
Gomez-N.Y.	194	1937	Hubbell-N.Y.	159
Feller-Cle.	240	1938	Bryant-Chi.	135
Feller-Cle.	246	1939	Passeau-Chi. + Chi.	137
			Walters-Cin.	137
Feller-Cle.	261	1940	Higbe-Chi.	137
Feller-Cle.	260	1941	Vander Meer-Cin.	202
Hughson-Bos.	113	1942	Vander Meer-Cin.	186
Newsom-Was.	113			
Reynolds-Cle.	151	1943	Vander Meer-Cin.	174
Newhouser-Det.	187	1944	Voiselle-N.Y.	161
Newhouser-Det.	212	1945	Roe-Pit.	148
Feller-Cle.	348	1946	Schmitz-Chi.	135
Feller-Cle.	196	1947	Blackwell-Cin.	193
Feller-Cle.	164	1948	Brecheen-St.L.	149
Trucks-Bal.	153	1949	Spahn-Bos.	151
Lemon-Cle.	170	1950	Spahn-Bos.	191
Raschi-N.Y.	164	1951	Newcombe-Bkn.	164
			Spahn-Bos.	164
Reynolds-N.Y.	160	1952	Spahn-Bos.	183
Pierce-Chi.	186	1953	Roberts-Phi.	198
Turley-Bal.	185	1954	Roberts-Phi.	185
Score-Cle.	245	1955	Jones Chi.	198
Score-Cle.	263	1956	Jones-Chi.	176
Wynn-Cle.	184	1957	Sanford-Phi.	188
Wynn-Chi.	179	1958	Jones-St.L.	205
Bunning-Det.	201	1959	Drysdale-L.A.	242
Bunning-Det.	201	1960	Drysdale-L.A.	246
Pascual-Min.	221	1961	Koufax-L.A.	269
Pascual-Min.	206	1962	Drysdale-L.A.	232
Pascual-Min.	202	1963	Koufax-L.A.	306
Downing-N.Y.	217	1964	Veale-Pit.	250
McDowell-Cle.	325	1965	Koufax-L.A.	382
McDowell-Cle.	225	1966	Koufax-L.A.	317
Lonborg-Bos.	246	1967	Bunning-Phi.	253
McDowell-Cle.	283	1968	Gibson-St.L.	268
McDowell-Cle.	279	1969	Jenkins-Chi.	273
McDowell-Cle.	304	1970	Seaver-N.Y.	283

Federal League

Shutouts

1914 FEDERAL LEAGUE	Falkenberg-Ind.	9
1915 FEDERAL LEAGUE	Davenport-St.L.	10

Bases on Balls

1914 FEDERAL LEAGUE	Lafitte-Bkn.	127
1915 FEDERAL LEAGUE	Schulz-Buf.	149

Strikeouts

1914 FEDERAL LEAGUE	Falkenberg-Ind.	236
1915 FEDERAL LEAGUE	Davenport-St.L.	229

YEARLY PITCHING LEADERS

SHUTOUTS

AMERICAN LEAGUE		Year	NATIONAL LEAGUE	
Blue-Oak.	8	1971	Pappas-Chi. Downing-L.A.	5
			Blass - Pit. Gibson-St.L.	5
Ryan-Cal.	9	1972	Sutton-L.A.	9
Blyleven-Min.	9	1973	Billingham-Cin.	7
Tiant-Bos.	7	1974	Matlack-N.Y.	7
Palmer-Bal.	7	1975	Messersmith-L.A.	7
Ryan-Cal.	7	1976	Montefusco-S.F.	6
Tanana-Cal.	7	1977	Seaver-N.Y.+Cin.	7
Guidry-N.Y.	9	1978	Knepper-S.F.	6
Flanagan-Bal.	5	1979	J.Niekro-Hou.	5
Ryan-Cal.	5		Rogers-Mon.	5
Leonard-K.C.	5		Seaver-Cin.	5
John-N.Y.	6	1980	Reuss-L.A.	6
Medich-Tex.	4	1981	Valenzuela-L.A.	8
Stieb-Tor.	5	1982	Carlton-Phi.	6
Boddicker-Bal.	5	1983	Rogers-Mon.	5
Ojeda-Bos. Zahn-Cal.	5	1984	Andujar-St.L.	4
			Hershiser-L.A.	4
			Pena-L.A.	4
Blyleven-Cle.+Min.	5	1985	Tudor-St.L.	10
Morris-Det.	6	1986	Knepper-Hou.	5
			Scott-Hou.	5
Clemens-Bos.	7	1987	Reuschel-Pit.+S.F.	4
			Welch-L.A.	4
Clemens-Bos.	8	1988	Hershiser-L.A.	8
Blyleven-Cal.	5	1989	Belcher-L.A.	8
Clemens-Bos.	4	1990	Hurst-S.D.	4
Stewart-Oak.	4		Morgan-L.A.	4
Clemens-Bos.	4	1991	Martinez-Mon.	5
Clemens-Bos.	5	1992	Cone-N.Y.	5
			Glavine-Atl.	5
McDowell-Chi.	4	1993	Harnisch-Hou.	4
Johnson-Sea.	4	1994	Maddux-Atl.	3
			Gross-L.A.	3
Mussina-Bal.	4	1995	Maddux-Atl.	3
			Nomo-L.A.	3
Hentgen-Tor.	3	1996	Brown-Fla.	3
Hill-Tex.	3			
Robertson-Min.	3			
Clemens-Tor.	3	1997	Perez-Mon.	5
Hentgen-Tor.	3			
Wells-N.Y.	5	1998	Maddux-Atl.	5
Erickson-Bal.	3	1999	Ashby-S.D.	3
			Johnson-Ari.	3
			Maddux-Atl.	3
P. Martinez-Bos.	4	2000	Maddux-Atl.	3
			Vasquez-Mon.	3
Mulder-Oak.	4	2001	Burnett-Fla.	5
			Millwood-Phi.	3
			Morris-St.L.	3
			Schmidt-S.F.	3
Weaver-Det.+N.Y.	3	2002		
Halladay-Tor.	2	2003		
Hudson-Oak.	2			
Lackey-Ana.	2			
Pineiro-Sea.	2			
Mulder-Oak.	2			
Bonderman-Det.	2	2004	Lidle-Cin.+Phi.	3
Hudson-Oak.	2		Schmidt-S.F.	3
Ponson-Bal.	2			
Garland-Chi.	3	2005	Willis-Fla.	5
Westbrook-Cle.	2	2006	Webb-Ari.	3
Lackey-L.A.	2		Carpenter-St.L.	3
Sabathia-Cle.	2			
Sowers-Cle.	2			

BASES ON BALLS

AMERICAN LEAGUE		Year	NATIONAL LEAGUE	
McDowell-Cle.	153	1971	Stoneman-Mon.	146
Ryan-Cal.	157	1972	Arlin-S.D.	122
Ryan-Cal.	162	1973	Reuss-Hou.	117
Ryan-Cal.	202	1974	Carlton-Phi.	136
Torrez-Bal.	133	1975	Richard-Hou.	138
Ryan-Cal.	183	1976	Richard-Hou.	151
Ryan-Cal.	204	1977	P.Niekro-Atl.	164
Ryan-Cal.	148	1978	Richard-Hou.	141
Torrez-Bos.	121	1979	P.Niekro-Atl.	113
Clancy-Tor.	128	1980	Ryan-Hou.	98
Morris-Det.	78	1981	Berenyi-Cin.	77
Righetti-N.Y.	108	1982	Ryan-Hou.	109
Dotson-Chi.	106	1983	Torrez-N.Y.	113
Langston-Sea.	118	1984	Valenzuela-L.A.	106
P.Niekro-N.Y.	120	1985	Valenzuela-L.A.	101
Witt-Tex.	143	1986	Youmans-Mon.	118
Witt-Tex.	140	1987	Valenzuela-L.A.	124
Hough-Tex.	126	1988	K.Gross-Phi.	89
Witt-Tex.	114	1989	Hill-St. L.	99
Johnson-Sea.	120	1990	Smoltz-Atl.	90
Johnson-Sea.	152	1991	DeJesus-Phi.	128
Johnson-Sea.	144	1992	Cone-N.Y.	82
Alvarez-Chi.	122	1993	R. Martinez-L.A.	104
Moore-Det.	89	1994	Kile-Hou.	82
VanPoppel-Oak.	89			
Leiter-Tor.	108	1995	Nomo-L.A.	78
Robertson-Min.	116	1996	Leiter-Fla.	119
Eldred-Mil.	89	1997	Estes-S.F.	100
Saunders-T.B.	111	1998	Hamilton-S.D.	106
Erickson-Bal.	99	1999	Ortiz-S.F.	125
Appier-Oak.	102	2000	Clement-S.D.	125
Nomo-Bos.	96	2001	Dempster-Fla.	112
Sturtze-T.B.	89	2002	Ishii-L.A.	106
Zambrano-T.B.	106	2003	Ortiz-Atl.	102
Zambrano-T.B.	96	2004	Webb-Ari.	119
Batista-Tor.	96			
Kazmir-T.B.	100	2005	Wells-Pit.	99
Cabrera-Bal.	104	2006	Zambrano-Chi.	115

STRIKEOUTS

AMERICAN LEAGUE		Year	NATIONAL LEAGUE	
Lolich-Det.	308	1971	Seaver-N.Y.	289
Ryan-Cal.	329	1972	Carlton-Phi.	310
Ryan-Cal.	383	1973	Seaver-N.Y.	251
Ryan-Cal.	367	1974	Carlton-Phi.	240
Tanana-Cal.	269	1975	Seaver-N.Y.	243
Ryan-Cal.	327	1976	Seaver-N.Y.	235
Ryan-Cal.	341	1977	P.Niekro-Atl.	262
Ryan-Cal.	260	1978	Richard-Hou.	303
Ryan-Cal.	223	1979	Richard-Hou.	313
Barker-Cle.	187	1980	Carlton-Phi.	286
Barker-Cle.	127	1981	Valenzuela-L.A.	180
Bannister-Sea.	209	1982	Carlton-Phi.	286
Morris-Det.	232	1983	Carlton-Phi.	275
Langston-Sea.	204	1984	Gooden-N.Y.	276
Blyleven-Cle. + Min.	206	1985	Gooden-N.Y.	268
Langston-Sea.	245	1986	Scott-Hou	306
Langston-Sea.	262	1987	Ryan-Hou.	270
Clemens-Bos.	291	1988	Ryan-Hou.	228
Ryan-Tex.	301	1989	DeLeon-St. L.	201
Ryan-Tex.	232	1990	Cone-N.Y.	233
Clemens-Bos.	241	1991	Cone-N.Y.	241
Johnson-Sea.	241	1992	Smoltz-Atl.	215
Johnson-Sea.	308	1993	Rijo-Cin.	227
Johnson-Sea.	204	1994	Benes-S.D.	189
Johnson-Sea.	294	1995	Nomo-L.A.	236
Clemens-Bos.	257	1996	Smoltz-Atl.	276
Clemens-Tor.	292	1997	Schilling-Phi.	319
Clemens-Tor.	271	1998	Schilling-Phi.	300
P. Martinez-Bos.	313	1999	Johnson-Ari.	364
P. Martinez-Bos.	284	2000	Johnson-Ari.	347
Nomo-Bos.	220	2001	Johnson-Ari.	372
Matinez-Bos.	239	2002	Johnson-Ari.	334
Loaiza-Chi.	207	2003	Wood-Chi.	266
Santana-Min.	265	2004	Johnson-Ari.	290
Santana-Min.	238	2005	Peavy-S.D.	216
Santana-Min.	245	2006	Harang-Cin.	216

YEARLY PITCHING LEADERS

GAMES PITCHED

AMERICAN LEAGUE		Year	NATIONAL LEAGUE	
McGinnity-Bal.	48	1901	Donovan-Bkn.	45
			Powell-St.L.	45
			Taylor-N.Y.	45
Young-Bos.	45	1902	Willis-Bos.	51
Plank-Phi.	43	1903	McGinnity-N.Y.	55
Chesbro-N.Y.	55	1904	McGinnity-N.Y.	51
Waddell-Phi.	46	1905	McGinnity-N.Y.	46
			Pittinger-Phi.	46
Chesbro-N.Y.	49	1906	McGinnity-N.Y.	45
Walsh-Cin.	56	1907	McGinnity-N.Y.	47
Walsh-Cin.	66	1908	Mathewson-N.Y.	56
Smith-Chi.	51	1909	Brown-Chi.	50
Coombs-Phi.	45	1910	Mattern-Bos.	51
Johnson-Was.	45			
Walsh-Chi.	45			
Walsh-Chi.	56	1911	Brown-Chi.	53
Walsh-Chi.	62	1912	Benton-Chi.	50
Russell-Chi.	51	1913	Cheney-Chi.	54
Johnson-Was.	51	1914	Cheney-Chi.	50
Coveleski-Det.	50	1915	Hughes-Bos.	50
Faber-Chi.	50			
Davenport-St.L.	59	1916	Meadows-Pit.	51
Danforth-Chi.	50	1917	Douglas-Chi.	51
Bagby-Cle.	45	1918	Grimes-Bkn.	40
Mogridge-N.Y.	45			
Shaw-Was.	45	1919	Tuero-St.L.	45
Bagby-Cle.	48	1920	Haines-St.L.	47
Mays-N.Y.	49	1921	Scott-Bos.	47
Rommel-Phi.	51	1922	North-St.L.	53
Rommel-Phi.	56	1923	Jonnard-N.Y.	45
			Ryan-N.Y.	45
Marberry-Was.	50	1924	Kremer-Pit.	41
			Morrison-Pit.	41
Marberry-Was.	55	1925	Morrison-Pit.	44
Marberry-Was.	64	1926	Scott-N.Y.	50
Braxton-Was.	59	1927	Root-Chi.	48
			Scott-Phi.	48
Marberry-Was.	48	1928	Grimes-Pit.	48
Marberry-Was.	49	1929	Bush-Chi.	50
Grove-Phi.	50	1930	Elliott-Phi.	48
Hadley-Was.	55	1931	Elliott-Phi.	52
Marberry-Was.	54	1932	French-Pit.	47
Crowder-Was.	52	1933	Dean-St.L.	48
Russell-Was.	54	1934	Davis-Pit.	51
Van Atta-N.Y. + St.L.	58	1935	Jorgens-Pit.	53
Van Atta-St.L.	52	1936	D. Dean-St.L.	51
			Derringer-Cin.	51
Brown-Chi.	53	1937	Mulcahy-Phi.	56
Humphries-Cle.	45	1938	Brown-Pit.	51
			Coffman-N.Y.	51
Brown-Chi.	61	1939	Shoun-St.L.	53
Feller-Cle.	43	1940	Shoun-St.L.	40
Feller-Cle.	44	1941	Higbe-Bkn.	48
Haynes-Chi.	40	1942	Adams-N.Y.	61
Brown-Bos.	49	1943	Adams-N.Y.	70
Heving-Cle.	63	1944	Adams-N.Y.	65
Berry-Phi.	52	1945	Karl-Phi.	67
Feller-Cle.	48	1946	Trinkle-N.Y.	48
Klieman-Cle.	58	1947	Trinkle-N.Y.	62
Page-N.Y.	55	1948	Gumbert-Cin.	61
Page-N.Y.	60	1949	Wilks-St.L.	59
Harris-Was.	53	1950	Konstanty-Phi.	74
Kinder-Bos.	63	1951	Wilks-St.L. + Pit.	48
Kennedy-Bos.	47	1952	Wilhelm-N.Y.	71
Kinder-Bos.	69	1953	Wilhelm-N.Y.	68
Dixon-Was. + Phi.	54	1954	Hughes-Bkn.	60
Narleski-Cle.	60	1955	Labine-Bkn.	60
Zuverink-Bal.	62	1956	Face-Pit.	68
Zuverink-Bal.	56	1957	Lown-Chi.	67
Clevenger-Was.	55	1958	Elston-Chi.	69
Staley-Chi.	67	1959	Elston-Chi.	65
			Henry-Chi.	65
Fornieles-Bos.	70	1960	Face-Chi.	68
Arroyo-N.Y.	65	1961	Baldschun-Phi.	65
Radatz-Bos.	62	1962	Perranoski-L.A.	70
Miller-Bal.	71	1963	Perranoski-L.A.	69
Wyatt-K.C.	81	1964	Miller-L.A.	74
Fisher-Chi.	82	1965	Abernathy-Chi.	84
Fisher-Chi. + Bal.	67	1966	Carroll-Atl.	73
Locker-Chi.	77	1967	Abernathy-Cin.	70
			Perranoski-L.A.	70
Wood-Chi.	88	1968	Abernathy-Cin.	78
Wood-Chi.	76	1969	Granger-Cin.	90
Wood-Chi.	77	1970	Herbel-S.D. + N.Y.	76
1914 FEDERAL LEAGUE			Hendrix-Chi.	49
			Falkenberg-Ind.	49
1915 FEDERAL LEAGUE			Davenport-St.L.	55

EARNED RUN AVERAGE

AMERICAN LEAGUE		Year	NATIONAL LEAGUE	
Young-Bos.	1.63	1901	Tannehill-Pit.	2.18
Siever-Det.	1.91	1902	Taylor-Chi.	1.33
Moore-Cle.	1.77	1903	Leever-Pit.	2.06
Joss-Cle.	1.59	1904	McGinnity-N.Y.	1.61
Waddell-Phi	1.48	1905	Mathewson-N.Y.	1.27
White-Chi.	1.52	1906	Brown-Chi.	1.04
Walsh-Chi.	1.60	1907	Pfiester-Chi.	1.15
Joss-Cle.	1.16	1908	Mathewson-N.Y.	1.43
Krause-Phi.	1.39	1909	Mathewson-N.Y.	1.14
Walsh-Chi.	1.27	1910	McQuillan-Phi.	1.60
Gregg-Cle.	1.81	1911	Mathewson-N.Y.	1.99
Johnson-Was.	1.39	1912	Tesreau-N.Y.	1.96
Johnson-Was	1.14	1913	Mathewson-N.Y.	2.06
Leonard-Bos.	1.00	1914	Doak-St.L.	1.72
Wood-Bos.	1.49	1915	Alexander-Phi.	1.22
Ruth-Bos.	1.75	1916	Alexander-Phi.	1.55
Cicotte-Chi.	1.53	1917	Alexander-Phi.	1.86
Johnson-Was.	1.27	1918	Vaughn-Chi.	1.74
Johnson-Was.	1.49	1919	Alexander-Chi.	1.72
Shawkey-N.Y.	2.45	1920	Alexander-Chi.	1.91
Faber-Chi.	2.48	1921	Doak-St.L.	2.58
Faber-Chi.	2.80	1922	Ryan-N.Y.	3.00
S. Coveleski-Cle.	2.76	1923	Luque-Cin	1.93
Johnson-Was.	2.72	1924	Vance-Bkn.	2.16
S. Coveleski-Cle.	2.84	1925	Luque-Cin.	2.63
Grove-Phi.	2.51	1926	Kremer-Pit	2.61
Moore-N.Y.	2.28	1927	Kremer-Pit	2.47
Braxton-Was.	2.52	1928	Vance-Bkn.	2.09
Grove-Phi.	2.82	1929	Walker-N.Y.	3.08
Grove-Phi.	2.54	1930	Vance-Bkn.	2.61
Grove-Phi.	2.05	1931	Walker-N.Y.	2.26
Grove-Phi.	2.84	1932	Warneke-Chi.	2.37
Pearson-Cle.	2.33	1933	Hubbell-N.Y.	1.66
Gomez-N.Y.	2.33	1934	Hubbell-N.Y.	2.30
Grove-Bos.	2.70	1935	Blanton-Pit.	2.59
Grove-Bos.	2.81	1936	Hubbell-N.Y.	2.31
Gomez-N.Y.	2.33	1937	Turner-Bos.	2.38
Grove-Bos.	3.07	1938	Lee-Chi.	2.66
Grove-Bos.	2.54	1939	Walters-Cin.	2.29
Feller-Cle.	2.62	1940	Walters-Cin.	2.48
Lee-Chi.	2.37	1941	Riddle-Cin.	2.24
Lyons-Chi.	2.10	1942	M. Cooper-St.L.	1.77
Chandler-N.Y.	1.64	1943	Pollet-St.L.	1.75
Trout-Det.	2.12	1944	Heusser-Cin.	2.38
Newhouser-Det.	1.81	1945	Borowy-Chi.	2.14
Newhouser-Det.	1.94	1946	Pollet-St.L.	2.10
Chandler-N.Y.	2.46	1947	Spahn-Bos.	2.33
Bearden-Cle.	2.43	1948	Brecheen-St.L.	2.24
Parnell-Bos.	2.78	1949	Koslo-N.Y.	2.50
Wynn-Cle.	3.20	1950	Hearn-St.L. + N.Y.	2.49
Rogovin-Det. + Chi.	2.78	1951	Nichols-Bos.	2.88
Reynolds-N.Y.	2.07	1952	Wilhelm-N.Y.	2.43
Lopat-N.Y.	2.43	1953	Spahn-Mil.	2.10
Garcia-Cle.	2.64	1954	Antonelli-N.Y.	2.29
Pierce-Chi.	1.97	1955	Friend-Pit.	2.84
Ford-N.Y.	2.47	1956	Burdette-Mil.	2.71
Shantz-N.Y.	2.45	1957	Podres-Bkn.	2.66
Ford-N.Y.	2.01	1958	Miller-S.F.	2.47
Wilhelm-Bal.	2.19	1959	S. Jones-S.F.	2.82
Baumann-Chi.	2.68	1960	McCormick-S.F.	2.70
Donovan-Was.	2.40	1961	Spahn-Mil.	3.01
Aguirre-Det.	2.21	1962	Koufax-L.A.	2.54
Peters-Chi.	2.33	1963	Koufax-L.A.	1.88
Chance-L.A.	1.65	1964	Koufax-L.A.	1.74
McDowell-Cle.	2.18	1965	Koufax-L.A.	2.04
Peters-Chi.	1.98	1966	Koufax-L.A.	1.73
Horlen-Chi.	2.06	1967	Niekro-At.	1.87
Tiant-Cle.	1.60	1968	Gibson-St.L.	1.12
Bosman-Was.	2.19	1969	Marichal-S.F.	2.10
Segui-Oak.	2.56	1970	Seaver-N.Y.	2.81
1914 FEDERAL LEAGUE			Hendrix-Chi.	1.69
1915 FEDERAL LEAGUE			Moseley-Nwk.	1.91

SAVES

AMERICAN LEAGUE		Year	NATIONAL LEAGUE	
Hoffer-Cle.	3	1901	Donovan-Bkn.	3
McGinnity-Bal.	3		Powell-St.L.	3
Powell-St.L.	3	1902	Willis-Bos.	3
Mullin-Det.	3	1903	Lundgren-Chi., Miller-N.Y.	3
Patten-Was.	2	1904	McGinnity-N.Y.	6
Waddell-Phi.	4	1905	Elliott-N.Y.	6
Bender-Phi., Hess-Cle.,	3	1906	Ferguson-N.Y.	7
Walsh-Chi.	3			
Dinneen-St.L.	4	1907	McGinnity-N.Y.	4
Walsh-Chi.	7	1908	Brown-Chi.	5
			Mathewson-N.Y.	5
Arrellanes-Bos.	8	1909	Brown-Chi.	7
Walsh-Chi.	6	1910	Brown-Chi.,Gasper-Cin.	7
Walsh-Chi.	7	1911	Brown-Chi.	13
Walsh-Chi.	10	1912	Sallee-St.L.	6
Bender-Phi.	12	1913	Cheney-Chi.	11
Bentley + Shaw-Was.,	4	1914	Ames-St.L.	6
Dauss-Phi., Faber-Chi.,	4		Sallee-Cin.	6
Mitchell-St.L.,	4			
Leonard-Bos.	4			
Mays-Bos.	6	1915	Hughes-Bos.	9
Shawkey-N.Y.	9	1916	Ames-St.L.	8
Danforth-Chi.	11	1917	Sallee-N.Y.	4
Bagby-Cle.	6	1918	Anderson-N.Y.,	3
			Cooper-Pit.,	3
			Oeschger-Phi.,	3
			Toney-Cin. + N.Y.	3
Russell-N.Y. + Bos.	6	1919	Tuero-St.L.	4
Kerr-Chi., Shocker-St.L.	5	1920	Sherdel-St.L.	6
Mays-N.Y.	7	1921	North-St.L.	7
Uhle-Cle.	5	1922	Jonnard-N.Y.	5
Russell-Was.	9	1923	Jonnard-N.Y.	5
Marberry-Was.	15	1924	May-Cin.	6
Marberry-Was.	15	1925	Bush + Morrison-Pit.	4
Marberry-Was.	22	1926	Davies-N.Y.	6
Braxton-Was.	13	1927	Sherdel-St.L.	6
Hoyt-N.Y.	8	1928	Haid + Sherdel-St. L	5
Marberry-Was.	11	1929	Bush-Chi.	8
			Morrison-Bkn.	8
Grove-Phi.	9	1930	Bell-St.L.	8
Moore-Bos.	10	1931	Quinn-Bkn.	15
Marberry-Was.	13	1932	Quinn-Bkn.	8
Russell-Was.	13	1933	Collins-Phi.	6
Russell-Was.	7	1934	Hubbard-N.Y.	8
Knott-St.L.	7	1935	Leonard-Bkn.	8
Malone-N.Y.	9	1936	D. Dean-St.L.	11
Brown-Chi.	18	1937	Brown-Pit., Melton-N.Y.	7
Murphy-N.Y.	11	1938	Coffman-N.Y.	12
Murphy-N.Y.	19	1939	Bowman + Shoun-St.L.	9
Benton-Det.	17	1940	Beggs-Cin., Brown-N.Y.,	7
			Brown-Pit.	7
Murphy-N.Y.	15	1941	Brown-N.Y.	8
Murphy-N.Y.	11	1942	Casey-Bkn.	13
Maltzberger-Chi.	14	1943	Webber-Bkn.	10
Berry-Phi., Caster-St.L.,	12	1944	Adams-N.Y.	13
Maltzberger-Chi.	12			
Turner-N.Y.	10	1945	Adams-N.Y., Karl-Phi.	15
Klinger-Bos.	9	1946	Raffensberger-Phi.	6
Klieman-Cle., Page-N.Y.	17	1947	Casey-Bkn.	18
Christopher-Cle.	17	1948	Gumbert-Cin.	17
Page-N.Y.	27	1949	Wilks-St.L.	9
Harris-Was.	15	1950	Konstanty-Phi.	22
Kinder-Bos	14	1951	Wilks-St.L. + Pit.	13
Dorish-Chi.	11	1952	Brazle-St.L.	16
Kinder-Bos.	27	1953	Brazle-St.L.	18
Sain-N.Y.	22	1954	Hughes-Bkn.	24
Narleski-Cle.	19	1955	Meyer-Phi.	16
Zuverink-Bal.	16	1956	Labine-Bkn.	19
Grim-N.Y.	19	1957	Labine-Bkn.	17
Duren-N.Y.	20	1958	Face-Pit.	20
Lown-Chi.	15	1959	McDaniel-St.L.	15
			McMahon-Mil.	15
Fornieles-Bos.	14	1960	McDaniel-St.L.	26
Klippstein-Cle.	14			
Arroyo-N.Y.	29	1961	Miller-S.F.	17
Radatz-Bos.	24	1962	Face-Pit.	28
Miller-Bal.	27	1963	McDaniel-Chi.	22
Radatz-Bos.	29	1964	Woodshick-Hou.	23
Kline-Was.	29	1965	Abernathy-Chi.	31
Aker-K.C.	32	1966	Regan-L.A.	21
Rojas-Cal.	27	1967	Abernathy-Chi.	28
Worthington-Min.	18	1968	Regan-L.A. + Chi.	25
Perranoski-Min.	31	1969	Gladding-Hou.	29
Perranoski-Min.	34	1970	Granger-Cin.	35
1914 FEDERAL LEAGUE			Ford-Buf.	6
1915 FEDERAL LEAGUE			Bedient-Buf.	10

YEARLY PITCHING LEADERS

GAMES PITCHED

AMERICAN LEAGUE		Year	NATIONAL LEAGUE	
Sanders-Mil.	83	1971	Granger-Cin.	70
Lindblad-Tex.	66	1972	Carroll-Cin.	65
			Marshall-Mon.	65
Miller-Det.	65	1973	Marshall-Mon.	92
Fingers-Oak.	76	1974	Marshall-L.A.	106
Fingers-Oak.	75	1975	Garber-Phi.	71
Campbell-Min.	78	1976	Murray-Mon.	81
Lyle-N.Y.	72	1977	Fingers-S.D.	78
Lacey-Oak.	74	1978	Tekulve-Pit.	91
Marshall-Min.	90	1979	Tekulve-Pit.	94
Quisenberry-K.C.	75	1980	Tidrow-Chi.	84
Corbett-Min.	54	1981	Lucas-S.D.	57
Vande Berg-Sea.	78	1982	Tekulve-Pit.	85
Quisenberry-K.C.	69	1983	Campbell-Chi.	82
Hernandez-Det.	80	1984	Power-Cin.	78
Quisenberry-K.C.	84	1985	Burke-Mon.	78
Williams-Tex.	80	1986	Lefferts-S.D.	83
Eichhorn-Tor.	89	1987	Tekulve-Pit.	90
Crim-Mil.	70	1988	Murphy-Cin.	76
Crim-Mil.	76	1989	Williams-Chi.	76
Thigpen-Chi.	77	1990	Assenmacher-Chi.	74
Ward-Tor.	81	1991	Jones-Mon.	77
Rogers-Tex.	81	1992	Boever-Hou.	81
Harris-Bos.	80	1993	Jackson-S.F.	81
Wickman-N.Y.	53	1994	Reed-Col.	61
Orosco-Bal.	65	1995	Leskanic-Col.	76
Myers-Det.	83	1996	Clontz-Atl.	81
Guardado-Min.	83			
Myers-Det.	88	1997	Tavarez-S.F.	89
Runyan-Det.	88	1998	Beck-Chi.	81
Groom-Oak.	76	1999	Kline-Mon.	82
Wells-Min.	76			
Wunsch-Chi.	83	2000	Kline-Mon.	83
Quantrill-Tor.	80	2001	Kline-St.L.	89
Koch-Oak.	84	2002	Quantrill-L.A.	86
Miller-Tor.	79	2003	Quantrill-L.A.	89
Quantrill-N.Y.	86	2004	Quantrill-L.A.	89
Timlin-Bos.	81	2005	Eyre-S.F.	86
Proctor-N.Y.	83	2006	Torres-Pit.	94

EARNED RUN AVERAGE

AMERICAN LEAGUE		Year	NATIONAL LEAGUE	
Blue-Oak.	1.82	1971	Seaver-N.Y.	1.76
Tiant-Bos.	1.91	1972	Carlton-Phi.	1.98
Palmer-Bal.	2.40	1973	Seaver-N.Y.	2.08
Hunter-Oak.	2.49	1974	Capra-Atl.	2.28
Palmer-Bal.	2.09	1975	Jones-S.D.	2.24
Fidrych-Det.	2.34	1976	Denny-St.L.	2.52
Tanana-Cal.	2.54	1977	Candelaria-Pit.	2.34
Guidry-N.Y.	1.74	1978	Swan-N.Y.	2.43
Guidry-N.Y.	2.78	1979	Richard-Hou.	2.71
May-N.Y.	2.47	1980	Sutton-L.A.	2.21
McCatty-Oak.	2.32	1981	Ryan-Hou.	1.69
Sutcliffe-Cle.	2.96	1982	Rogers-Mon.	2.40
Honeycutt-Tex.	2.42	1983	Hammaker-S.F.	2.25
Boddicker-Bal.	2.79	1984	Pena-L.A.	2.48
Stieb-Tor.	2.48	1985	Gooden-N.Y.	1.53
Clemens-Bos.	2.48	1986	Scott-Hou.	2.22
Key-Tor.	2.76	1987	Ryan-Hou.	2.76
Anderson-Min	2.45	1988	Magrane-St.L.	2.18
Saberhagen-K.C.	2.16	1989	Garrelts-S.F.	2.28
Clemens-Bos.	1.93	1990	Darwin-Hou.	2.21
Clemens-Bos.	2.62	1991	Martinez-Mon.	2.39
Clemens-Bos.	2.41	1992	Swift-S.F.	2.08
Appier-K.C.	2.56	1993	Maddux-Atl.	2.36
Ontiveros-Oak.	2.65	1994	Maddux-Atl.	1.56
Johnson-Sea.	2.48	1995	Maddux-Atl.	1.63
Guzman-Tor.	2.93	1996	Brown-Fla.	1.89
Clemens-Tor.	2.05	1997	Martinez-Mon.	1.90
Clemens-Tor.	2.65	1998	Maddux-Atl.	2.22
P. Martinez-Bos.	2.07	1999	Johnson-Ari.	2.48
P. Martinez-Bos.	1.74	2000	Brown-L.A.	2.58
Garcia-Sea.	3.05	2001	Johnson-Ari.	2.49
Martinez-Bos.	2.26	2002	Johnson-Ari.	2.32
Martinez-Bos.	2.22	2003	Schmidt-S.F.	2.34
Santana-Min.	2.61	2004	Peavy-S.D.	2.27
Willwood-Cle.	2.86	2005	Clemens-Hou.	1.87
Santana-Min.	2.77	2006	Oswalt-Hou.	2.98

SAVES

AMERICAN LEAGUE		Year	NATIONAL LEAGUE	
Sanders-Mil.	31	1971	Giusti-Pit.	30
Lyle-N.Y.	35	1972	Carroll-Cin.	37
Hiller-Det.	38	1973	Marshall-Mon.	31
Forster-Chi.	24	1974	Marshall-L.A.	21
Gossage-Chi.	26	1975	Eastwick-Cin.	22
			Hrabowski - St. L.	22
Lyle-N.Y.	23	1976	Eastwick-Cin.	26
Campbell-Bos.	31	1977	Fingers-S.D.	35
Gossage-N.Y.	27	1978	Fingers-S.D.	37
Marshall-Min.	32	1979	Sutter-Chi.	37
Gossage-N.Y.	33	1980	Sutter-Chi.	28
Quissenberry-K.C.	33			
Fingers-Mil.	28	1981	Sutter-St. L.	25
Quisenberry-K.C.	35	1982	Sutter-St.L.	36
Quisenberry-K.C.	45	1983	Smith-Chi.	29
Quissenberry-K.C.	44	1984	Sutter-St.L.	45
Quissenberry-K.C.	37	1985	Reardon-Mon.	41
Righetti-N.Y.	46	1986	Worrell-St.L.	36
Henke-Tor.	34	1987	Bedrosian-Phi.	40
Eckersley-Oak.	45	1988	Franco-Cin.	39
Russell-Tex.	38	1989	Davis-S.D.	44
Thigpen-Chi.	57	1990	Franco-N.Y.	33
Harvey-Cal.	46	1991	Smith-St.L.	47
Eckersley-Oak.	51	1992	Smith-St.L.	43
Montgomery-K.C.	45	1993	Myers-Chi.	53
Ward-Tor.	45			
Smith-Bal.	33	1994	Franco-N.Y.	30
Mesa-Cle.	46	1995	Myers-Chi.	38
Wetteland-N.Y.	43	1996	Worrell-L.A.	44
			Brantley-Cin.	44
Myers-Bal.	45	1997	Shaw-Cin.	42
Gordon-Bos.	46	1998	Hoffman-S.D.	53
Rivera-N.Y.	45	1999	Urbina-Mon.	41
Jones-Det.	42	2000	Alfonseca-Fla.	45
Lowe-Bos.	42			
Rivera-N.Y.	50	2001	Nen-S.F.	45
Guardado-Mia.	45	2002	Smoltz-Atl.	55
Foulke-Oak.	43	2003	Gagne-L.A.	55
Rivera-N.Y.	53	2004	Benitez-Fla.	47
			Isringhausen-St.L.	47
Rodriguez-L.A.	45	2005	Cordero-Was.	47
Wickman-Cle.	45			
Rodriguez-L.A.	46	2006	Hoffman-S.D.	46

SINGLE SEASON LEADERS

(numbers after individual name indicates numbers of times that individual appears within a specific category)

BATTING AVERAGE

#	Player	Team	Lg	Year	Avg
1	Rogers Hornsby-1	St.L.	NL	1924	.424
2	Nap Lajoie-1	Phi.	AL	1901	.422
3	George Sisler-1	St.L.	AL	1922	.420
4	Ty Cobb-1	Det.	AL	1911	.420
5	Ty Cobb-2	Det.	AL	1912	.409
6	Joe Jackson-1	Cle.	AL	1911	.408
7	George Sisler-2	St.L.	AL	1920	.407
8	Ted Williams-1	Bos.	AL	1941	.406
9	Rogers Hornsby-2	St.L.	NL	1925	.403
10	Harry Heilmann-1	Det.	AL	1923	.403
11	Rogers Hornsby-3	St.L.	NL	1922	.401
12	Bill Terry	N.Y.	NL	1930	.401
13	Ty Cobb-3	Det.	AL	1922	.401
14	Lefty O'Doul-1	Phi.	NL	1929	.398
15	Harry Heilmann-2	Det.	AL	1927	.398
16	Rogers Hornsby-4	St.L.	NL	1921	.397
17	Joe Jackson-2	Cle.	AL	1912	.395
18	Tony Gwynn	S.D.	NL	1994	.394
19	Harry Heilmann-3	Det.	AL	1921	.394
20	Babe Ruth-1	N.Y.	AL	1923	.393
21	Harry Heilmann-4	Det.	AL	1925	.393
22	Babe Herman-1	Bkn.	NL	1930	.393
23	Al Simmons-1	Phi.	AL	1927	.392
24	Ty Cobb-4	Det.	AL	1913	.390
25	Al Simmons-2	Phi.	AL	1931	.390
26	George Brett	K.C.	AL	1980	.390
27	Tris Speaker-1	Cle.	AL	1925	.389
28	Ty Cobb-5	Det.	AL	1921	.389
29	Ted Williams-2	Bos.	AL	1957	.388
30	Rod Carew	Min.	AL	1977	.388
31	Luke Appling	Chi.	AL	1936	.388
32	Tris Speaker-2	Cle.	AL	1920	.388
33	Rogers Hornsby-5	Bos.	NL	1928	.387
34	Tris Speaker-3	Cle.	AL	1916	.386
35	Chuck Klein	Phi.	NL	1930	.386
36	Arky Vaughan	Pit.	NL	1935	.385
37	Al Simmons-3	Phi.	AL	1925	.384
38	Rogers Hornsby-6	St.L.	NL	1923	.384
39	Ty Cobb-6	Det.	AL	1919	.384
40	Nap Lajoie-3	Cle.	AL	1910	.384
41	Tris Speaker-4	Bos.	AL	1912	.383
42	Ty Cobb-7	Det.	AL	1917	.383
43	Lefty O'Doul-2	Phi.	NL	1930	.383
44	Joe Jackson-3	Chi.	AL	1920	.382
45	Ty Cobb-8	Det.	AL	1918	.382
46	Jesse Burkett	St.L.	NL	1901	.382
47	Ty Cobb-9	Det.	AL	1910	.382
48	Babe Herman-2	Bkn.	NL	1929	.381
49	Joe DiMaggio	N.Y.	AL	1939	.381
50	Nap Lajoie-4	Cle.	AL	1904	.381
51	Al Simmons-4	Phi.	AL	1930	.381
52	Paul Waner	Pit.	NL	1927	.380
53	Rogers Hornsby-7	Chi.	NL	1929	.380
54	Tris Speaker-5	Cle.	AL	1923	.380
55	Goose Goslin	Was.	AL	1928	.379
56	Fred Lindstrom	N.Y.	NL	1930	.379
57	Larry Walker	Col.	NL	1999	.379
58	Lou Gehrig	N.Y.	AL	1930	.379
59	Ty Cobb-10	Det.	AL	1925	.378
60	Babe Ruth-2	N.Y.	AL	1924	.378
61	Sam Crawford	Det.	AL	1911	.378
62	Tris Speaker-6	Cle.	AL	1922	.378
63	Earl Averill	Cle.	AL	1936	.378
64	Babe Ruth-3	N.Y.	AL	1921	.378
65	Heinie Manush-1	St.L.	AL	1928	.378
66	Heinie Manush-2	Det.	AL	1926	.378
67	Ty Cobb-11	Det.	AL	1909	.377
68	Cy Seymour	Cin.	NL	1905	.377
69	Stan Musial	St.L.	NL	1948	.376
70	Babe Ruth-4	N.Y.	AL	1920	.376
71	Ed Delahanty	Was.	AL	1902	.376
72	Zach Wheat	Bkn.	NL	1924	.375

SLUGGING AVERAGE

#	Player	Team	Lg	Year	Slg
1	Barry Bonds-1	S.F.	NL	2001	.863
2	Babe Ruth-1	N.Y.	AL	1920	.847
3	Babe Ruth-2	N.Y.	AL	1921	.846
4	Barry Bonds-2	S.F.	NL	2004	.812
5	Barry Bonds-3	S.F.	NL	2002	.799
6	Babe Ruth-3	N.Y.	AL	1927	.772
7	Lou Gehrig-1	N.Y.	AL	1927	.765
8	Babe Ruth-4	N.Y.	AL	1923	.764
9	Rogers Hornsby-1	St.L.	NL	1925	.756
10	Mark McGwire-1	St.L.	NL	1998	.752
11	Jeff Bagwell	Hou.	NL	1994	.750
12	Jimmie Foxx-1	Phi.	AL	1932	.749
	Barry Bonds-4	S.F.	NL	2003	.749
14	Babe Ruth-5	N.Y.	AL	1924	.739
15	Babe Ruth-6	N.Y.	AL	1926	.737
16	Sammy Sosa	Chi.	NL	2001	.737
17	Ted Williams-1	Bos.	AL	1941	.735
18	Babe Ruth-7	N.Y.	AL	1930	.732
19	Ted Williams-2	Bos.	AL	1957	.731
20	Mark McGwire-2	Oak.	AL	1996	.730
21	Frank Thomas	Chi.	AL	1994	.729
22	Hack Wilson	Chi.	NL	1930	.723
23	Rogers Hornsby-2	St.L.	NL	1922	.722
24	Lou Gehrig-2	N.Y.	AL	1930	.721
25	Larry Walker-1	Col.	NL	1997	.720
26	Albert Belle-1	Cle.	AL	1994	.714
27	Larry Walker-2	Col.	NL	1999	.710
28	Babe Ruth-8	N.Y.	AL	1928	.709
29	Al Simmons	Phi.	AL	1930	.708
30	Lou Gehrig-3	N.Y.	AL	1934	.706
31	Mickey Mantle-1	N.Y.	AL	1956	.705
32	Jimmie Foxx-2	Bos.	AL	1938	.704
33	Jimmie Foxx-3	Phi.	AL	1933	.703
34	Stan Musial	St.L.	NL	1948	.702
35	Babe Ruth-9	N.Y.	AL	1931	.700
36	Todd Helton-1	Col.	NL	2000	.698
37	Babe Ruth-10	N.Y.	AL	1929	.697
38	Manny Ramirez-1	Cle.	AL	2000	.697
39	Mark McGwire-3	St.L.	NL	1999	.697
40	Lou Gehrig-4	N.Y.	AL	1936	.696
41	Rogers Hornsby-3	St.L.	NL	1924	.696
42	Jimmie Foxx-4	Bos.	AL	1939	.694
43	Albert Belle-2	Cle.	AL	1995	.690
44	Luis Gonzalez	Ari.	NL	2001	.688
45	Barry Bonds-5	S.F.	NL	2000	.688
46	Mickey Mantle-2	N.Y.	AL	1961	.687
47	Chuck Klein-1	Phi.	NL	1930	.687
48	Todd Helton-2	Col.	NL	2001	.685
49	Hank Greenberg-1	Det.	AL	1938	.683
50	Kevin Mitchell	Cin.	NL	1994	.681
51	Rogers Hornsby-4	St.L.	NL	1929	.679
52	Babe Herman	Bkn.	NL	1930	.678
53	Barry Bonds-6	S.F.	NL	1993	.677
54	Jim Thome	Cle.	AL	2002	.677
55	Ken Griffey Jr.	Sea.	AL	1994	.674
56	Joe DiMaggio-1	N.Y.	AL	1937	.673
57	Babe Ruth-11	N.Y.	AL	1922	.672
58	Albert Pujols-1	St.L.	NL	2006	.671
59	Joe DiMaggio-2	N.Y.	AL	1939	.671
60	Hank Greenberg-2	Det.	AL	1940	.670
61	Hank Aaron	Atl.	NL	1971	.669
62	Hank Greenberg-3	Det.	AL	1937	.668
63	Ted Williams-3	Bos.	AL	1946	.667
64	Willie Mays-1	N.Y.	NL	1954	.667
65	Albert Pujols-2	St.L.	NL	2003	.667
66	Mickey Mantle-3	N.Y.	AL	1957	.665
67	Carlos Delgado	Tor.	AL	2000	.664
68	Vladimir Guerrero	Mon.	NL	2000	.664
69	George Brett	K.C.	AL	1980	.664
70	Manny Ramirez-2	Cle.	AL	1999	.663
71	Lou Gehrig-5	N.Y.	AL	1931	.662
72	Larry Walker-3	Col.	NL	2001	.662
73	Norm Cash	Det.	AL	1961	.662
74	Derrek Lee	Chi.	NL	2005	.662
75	Babe Ruth-12	N.Y.	AL	1932	.661
76	Jason Giambi	Oak.	AL	2001	.660
77	Ryan Howard	Phi.	NL	2006	.659
78	Willie Mays-2	N.Y.	NL	1955	.659
79	Travis Hafner	Cle.	AL	2006	.659
80	Ralph Kiner	Pit.	NL	1949	.658
81	Chuck Klein-2	Phi.	NL	1929	.657
82	Babe Ruth-13	N.Y.	AL	1919	.657
83	Albert Pujols-3	St.L.	NL	2003	.657
84	Willie McCovey	S.F.	NL	1969	.656
85	Albert Belle-3	Chi.	AL	1998	.655
86	Jimmie Foxx-5	Phi.	AL	1934	.653
87	Chick Hafey	St.L.	NL	1930	.652
88	Rudy York	Det.	AL	1937	.651
89	Ted Williams-4	Bos.	AL	1949	.650

HITS

#	Player	Team	Lg	Year	H
1	Ichiro Suzuki-1	Sea.	AL	2004	262
2	George Sisler-1	St.L.	AL	1920	257
3	Lefty O'Doul	Phi.	NL	1929	254
	Bill Terry	N.Y.	NL	1930	254
5	Al Simmons	Phi.	AL	1925	253
6	Rogers Hornsby-1	St.L.	NL	1922	250
	Chuck Klein-1	Phi.	NL	1930	250
8	Ty Cobb-1	Det.	AL	1911	248
9	George Sisler-2	St.L.	AL	1922	246
10	Ichiro Suzuki-2	Sea.	AL	2001	242
11	Heinie Manush	St.L.	AL	1928	241
	Babe Herman	Bkn.	NL	1930	241
13	Wade Boggs	Bos.	AL	1985	240
	Darin Erstad	Ana.	AL	2000	240
15	Rod Carew	Min.	AL	1977	239
16	Don Mattingly	N.Y.	AL	1986	238
17	Harry Heilmann-1	Det.	AL	1921	237
	Paul Waner	Pit.	NL	1927	237
	Joe Medwick	St.L.	NL	1937	237
20	Jack Tobin	St.L.	AL	1921	236
21	Rogers Hornsby-2	St.L.	NL	1921	235
22	Lloyd Waner	Pit.	NL	1929	234
	Kirby Puckett	Min.	AL	1988	234
24	Joe Jackson-1	Cle.	AL	1911	233
	Nap Lajoie-1	Phi.	AL	1901	232
26	Earl Averill	Cle.	AL	1936	232
27	Earle Combs	N.Y.	AL	1927	231
	Fred Lindstrom-1	N.Y.	NL	1928	231
	Fred Lindstrom-2	N.Y.	NL	1930	231
	Matty Alou	Pit.	NL	1969	231
31	Stan Musial-1	St.L.	NL	1948	230
	Tommy Davis	L.A.	NL	1962	230
	Willie Wilson	K.C.	AL	1980	230
	Joe Torre	St.L.	NL	1971	230
	Pete Rose	Cin.	NL	1973	230
	Rogers Hornsby-3	Chi.	NL	1929	229
37	Jesse Burkett	St.L.	NL	1901	228
	Kiki Cuyler	Chi.	NL	1930	228
	Stan Musial-2	St.L.	NL	1946	228
40	Nap Lajoie-2	Cle.	AL	1910	227
	Rogers Hornsby-4	St.L.	NL	1924	227
	Jim Bottomley	St.L.	NL	1925	227
	Sam Rice	Was.	AL	1925	227
	Billy Herman	Chi.	NL	1935	227
	Charlie Gehringer	Det.	AL	1936	227
	Lance Johnson	N.Y.	NL	1996	227
47	Ty Cobb-2	Det.	AL	1912	226
	Joe Jackson-2	Cle.	AL	1912	226
	Bill Terry-2	N.Y.	NL	1929	226
	Chuck Klein-2	Phi.	NL	1932	226
51	Ty Cobb-3	Det.	AL	1917	225
	Harry Heilmann-2	Det.	AL	1925	225
	Johnny Hodapp	Cle.	AL	1930	225
	Bill Terry-3	N.Y.	NL	1932	225
	Paul Molitor	Min.	AL	1996	225

DOUBLES

#	Player	Team	Lg	Year	2B
1	Earl Webb	Bos.	AL	1931	67
2	George Burns-1	Cle.	AL	1926	64
	Joe Medwick-1	St.L.	NL	1936	64
4	Hank Greenberg-1	Det.	AL	1934	63
5	Paul Waner-1	Pit.	NL	1932	62
6	Charlie Gehringer-1	Det.	AL	1936	60
7	Tris Speaker-1	Cle.	AL	1923	59
	Chuck Klein-1	Phi.	NL	1930	59
	Todd Helton-1	Col.	NL	2000	59
10	Billy Herman-1	Chi.	NL	1935	57
	Billy Herman-2	Chi.	NL	1936	57
	Carlos Delgado	Tor.	AL	2000	57
13	Joe Medwick-2	St.L.	NL	1937	56
	George Kell	Det.	AL	1950	56
	Craig Biggio-1	Hou.	NL	1999	56
	Garret Anderson	Ana.	AL	2002	56
	Nomar Garciaparra-1	Bos.	AL	2002	56
18	Gee Walker	Det.	AL	1936	55
	Lance Berkman	Hou.	NL	2001	55
20	Hal McRae	K.C.	AL	1977	54
	John Olerud	Tor.	AL	1993	54
	Alex Rodriguez	Sea.	AL	1996	54
	Mark Grudzielanek	Mon.	NL	1997	54
	Todd Helton-2	Col.	NL	2001	54
25	Nap Lajoie-1	Cle.	AL	1910	53
	Tris Speaker-2	Bos.	AL	1912	53
	Al Simmons	Phi.	AL	1926	53
	Paul Waner-2	Pit.	NL	1936	53
	Stan Musial-1	St.L.	NL	1953	53
	Don Mattingly	N.Y.	AL	1986	53
	Jeff Cirillo	Col.	NL	2000	53
	Lyle Overbay	Mil.	NL	2004	53
	Freddy Sanchez	Pit.	NL	2006	53
	Grady Sizemore	Cle.	AL	2006	53
35	Tris Speaker-3	Cle.	AL	1921	52
	Tris Speaker-4	Cle.	AL	1926	52
	Lou Gehrig	N.Y.	AL	1927	52
	Johnny Frederick	Bkn.	NL	1929	52
	Enos Slaughter	St.L.	NL	1939	52
	Edgar Martinez-1	Sea.	AL	1995	52
	Albert Belle	Cle.	AL	1995	52
	Edgar Martinez-2	Sea.	AL	1996	52
	Luis Gonzalez	Ari.	NL	2006	52
	Michael Young	Tex.	AL	2006	52
45	Baby Doll Jacobson	St.L.-Bos.	AL	1926	51
	George Burns-2	Cle.	AL	1927	51
	Johnny Hodapp	Cle.	AL	1930	51
	Beau Bell	St.L.	AL	1937	51
	Joe Cronin	Bos.	AL	1938	51
	Stan Musial-2	St.L.	NL	1944	51
	Mickey Vernon	Was.	AL	1946	51
	Frank Robinson	Cin.	NL	1962	51
	Pete Rose	Cin.	NL	1978	51
	Wade Boggs	Bos.	AL	1989	51
	Mark Grace	Chi.	NL	1995	51
	Craig Biggio-2	Hou.	NL	1998	51
	Nomar Garciaparra-2	Bos.	AL	2000	51
	Jose Vidro	Mon.	NL	2000	51
	Alfonso Soriano	N.Y.	AL	2002	51
	Albert Pujols-1	St.L.	NL	2003	51
	Albert Pujols-2	St.L.	NL	2004	51
62	Nap Lajoie-2	Cle.	AL	1904	50
	Tris Speaker-5	Cle.	AL	1920	50
	Harry Heilmann	Det.	AL	1927	50
	Paul Waner-3	Pit.	NL	1928	50
	Kiki Cuyler	Chi.	NL	1930	50
	Chuck Klein-2	Phi.	NL	1932	50
	Charlie Gehringer-2	Det.	AL	1934	50
	Ben Chapman	N.Y.-Was.	AL	1936	50
	Odell Hale	Cle.	AL	1936	50
	Hank Greenberg-2	Det.	AL	1940	50
	Stan Musial-3	St.L.	NL	1946	50
	Stan Spence	Was.	AL	1946	50
	Juan Gonzalez	Tex.	AL	1998	50
	Bobby Abreu	Phi.	NL	2002	50
	Brian Roberts	Bal.	AL	2004	50
	Derrek Lee	Chi.	NL	2005	50
	Miguel Tejada	Bal.	AL	2005	50
	Miguel Cabrera	Fla.	NL	2006	50

TRIPLES

#	Player	Team	Lg	Year	3B
1	Owen Wilson	Pit.	NL	1912	36
2	Joe Jackson-1	Cle.	AL	1912	26
	Sam Crawford-1	Det.	AL	1914	26
	Kiki Cuyler	Pit.	NL	1925	26
5	Sam Crawford-2	Det.	AL	1903	25
	Larry Doyle	N.Y.	NL	1911	25
	Tom Long	St.L.	NL	1915	25
8	Ty Cobb-1	Det.	AL	1911	24
	Ty Cobb-2	Det.	AL	1917	24
10	Sam Crawford-3	Cin.	NL	1902	23
	Ty Cobb-3	Det.	AL	1912	23
	Sam Crawford-4	Det.	AL	1913	23
	Earle Combs-1	N.Y.	AL	1927	23
	Adam Comorosky	Pit.	NL	1930	23
	Dale Mitchell	Cle.	AL	1949	23
16	Bill Bradley	Cle.	AL	1903	22
	Chick Stahl	Bos.	AL	1904	22
	Elmer Flick	Cle.	AL	1906	22
	Birdie Cree	N.Y.	AL	1911	22
	Mike Mitchell	Cin.	NL	1911	22
	Tris Speaker	Bos.	AL	1913	22
	Hy Myers	Bkn.	NL	1920	22
	Jake Daubert	Cin.	NL	1922	22
	Paul Waner	Pit.	NL	1926	22
	Earle Combs-2	N.Y.	AL	1930	22
	Stuffy Stirnweiss	N.Y.	AL	1945	22
27	Bill Keister	Bal.	AL	1901	21
	Jimmy Williams-1	Bal.	AL	1901	21
	Jimmy Williams-2	Bal.	AL	1901	21
	Buck Freeman-1	Bos.	AL	1903	21
	Cy Seymour	Cin.	NL	1905	21
	Wildfire Schulte	Chi.	NL	1911	21
	Frank Baker	Phi.	AL	1912	21
	Sam Crawford-5	Det.	AL	1912	21
	Vic Saier	Chi.	NL	1913	21
	Joe Jackson-2	Chi.	AL	1916	21
	Edd Roush	Cin.	NL	1924	21
	Willie Wilson	K.C.	AL	1985	21
	Lance Johnson	N.Y.	NL	1996	21
41	Buck Freeman-2	Bos.	AL	1902	20
	Tommy Leach	Pit.	NL	1902	20
	Ty Cobb-4	Det.	AL	1908	20
	Red Murray	N.Y.	NL	1912	20
	Honus Wagner	Pit.	NL	1912	20
	Dots Miller	Pit.	NL	1913	20
	Rogers Hornsby	St.L.	NL	1920	20
	Joe Jackson-3	Chi.	AL	1920	20
	Rabbit Maranville	Pit.	NL	1924	20
	Goose Goslin	Was.	AL	1925	20
	Lou Gehrig	N.Y.	AL	1926	20
	Curt Walker	Cin.	NL	1926	20
	Jim Bottomley	St.L.	NL	1928	20
	Heinie Manush	St.L.	AL	1928	20
	Lloyd Waner	Pit.	NL	1929	20
	Bill Terry	N.Y.	NL	1931	20
	Joe Vosmik	Cle.	AL	1935	20
	Jeff Heath	Cle.	AL	1941	20
	Stan Musial-1	St.L.	NL	1943	20
	Stan Musial-2	St.L.	NL	1946	20
	Willie Mays	N.Y.	NL	1957	20
	George Brett	K.C.	AL	1979	20
	Cristian Guzman	Min.	AL	2000	20

EXTRA BASE HITS

#	Player	Team	Lg	Year	XBH
1	Babe Ruth	N.Y.	AL	1921	119
2	Lou Gehrig-1	N.Y.	AL	1927	117
3	Chuck Klein-1	Phi.	NL	1930	107
	Barry Bonds	S.F.	NL	2001	107
5	Todd Helton-1	Col.	NL	2001	105
6	Chuck Klein-2	Phi.	NL	1932	103
	Hank Greenberg	Det.	AL	1937	103
	Stan Musial	St.L.	NL	1948	103
	Albert Belle	Cle.	AL	1995	103
	Todd Helton-2	Col.	NL	2000	103
	Sammy Sosa	Chi.	NL	2001	103
12	Rogers Hornsby	St.L.	NL	1922	102
13	Lou Gehrig-2	N.Y.	AL	1930	100
	Jimmie Foxx	Phi.	AL	1932	100
	Luis Gonzalez	Ari.	NL	2001	100

SINGLE SEASON LEADERS

(numbers after individual name indicates numbers of times that individual appears within a specific category)

HOME RUNS

Rank	Player	Team	Lg	Year	HR
1	Barry Bonds-1	S.F.	NL	2001	73
2	Mark McGwire-1	St.L.	NL	1998	70
3	Sammy Sosa-1	Chi.	NL	1998	66
4	Mark McGwire-2	St.L.	NL	1999	65
5	Sammy Sosa-2	Chi.	NL	2001	64
6	Sammy Sosa-3	Chi.	NL	1999	63
7	Roger Maris	N.Y.	AL	1961	61
8	Babe Ruth-1	N.Y.	AL	1927	60
9	Babe Ruth-2	N.Y.	AL	1921	59
10	Jimmie Foxx-1	Phi.	NL	1932	58
	Hank Greenberg	Det.	AL	1938	58
	Mark McGwire-3	Oak. AL St.L.		1997	58
	Ryan Howard	Phi.	NL	2006	58
14	Luis Gonzalez	Ari.	NL	2001	57
	Alex Rodriguez-1	Tex.	AL	2002	57
16	Hack Wilson	Chi.	NL	1930	56
	Ken Griffey Jr.-1	Sea.	AL	1997	56
	Ken Griffey Jr.-2	Sea.	AL	1998	56
19	Babe Ruth-3	N.Y.	AL	1920	54
	Babe Ruth-4	N.Y.	AL	1928	54
	Ralph Kiner-1	Pit.	NL	1949	54
	Mickey Mantle-1	N.Y.	AL	1961	54
	David Ortiz	Bos.	AL	2006	54
24	Mickey Mantle-2	N.Y.	AL	1956	52
	Willie Mays-1	S.F.	NL	1965	52
	George Foster	Cin.	NL	1977	52
	Mark McGwire-4	Oak.	AL	1996	52
	Alex Rodriguez-2	Tex.	AL	2001	52
	Jim Thome-1	Cle.	AL	2002	52
30	Ralph Kiner-2	Pit.	NL	1947	51
	Johnny Mize	N.Y.	NL	1947	51
	Willie Mays-2	N.Y.	NL	1955	51
	Cecil Fielder	Det.	AL	1990	51
	Andruw Jones	Atl.	NL	2005	51
35	Jimmie Foxx-2	Bos.	AL	1938	50
	Albert Belle-1	Cle.	AL	1995	50
	Brady Anderson	Bal.	AL	1996	50
	Greg Vaughn	S.D.	NL	1998	50
	Sammy Sosa-4	Chi.	NL	2000	50
40	Babe Ruth-5	N.Y.	AL	1930	49
	Lou Gehrig-1	N.Y.	AL	1934	49
	Lou Gehrig-2	N.Y.	AL	1936	49
	Ted Kluszewski	Cin.	NL	1954	49
	Willie Mays-3	S.F.	NL	1962	49
	Harmon Killebrew-1	Min.	AL	1964	49
	Frank Robinson	Bal.	AL	1966	49
	Harmon Killebrew-2	Min.	AL	1969	49
	Andre Dawson	Chi.	NL	1987	49
	Mark McGwire-5	Oak.	AL	1987	49
	Ken Griffey Jr.-3	Sea.	AL	1996	49
	Larry Walker	Col.	NL	1997	49
	Albert Belle-2	Chi.	AL	1998	49
	Barry Bonds-2	S.F.	NL	2000	49
	Shawn Green	L.A.	NL	2001	49
	Todd Helton	Col.	NL	2001	49
	Jim Thome-2	Cle.	AL	2001	49
	Sammy Sosa-5	Chi.	NL	2002	49
	Albert Pujols	St.L.	NL	2006	49
59	Jimmie Foxx-3	Phi.	AL	1933	48
	Harmon Killebrew-3	Min.	AL	1962	48
	Frank Howard	Was.	AL	1969	48
	Willie Stargell	Pit.	NL	1971	48
	Dave Kingman	Chi.	NL	1979	48
	Mike Schmidt	Phi.	NL	1980	48
	Albert Belle-3	Cle.	AL	1996	48
	Ken Griffey Jr.-4	Sea.	AL	1999	48
	Adrian Beltre	L.A.	NL	2004	48
	Alex Rodriguez-3	N.Y.	AL	2005	48

FEWEST AT BATS PER HOME RUN
(minimum 30 Home Runs)

Rank	Player	Team	Lg	Year	AB/HR
1	Barry Bonds-1	S.F.	NL	2001	6.52
2	Mark McGwire-1	St.L.	NL	1998	7.27
3	Mark McGwire-2	St.L.	NL	2000	7.38
4	Mark McGwire-3	St.L.	NL	1999	8.02
5	Mark McGwire-4	Oak.	AL	1995	8.13
6	Mark McGwire-5	Oak.	AL	1996	8.13
7	Barry Bonds-2	S.F.	NL	2004	8.29
8	Babe Ruth-1	N.Y.	AL	1920	8.48
9	Barry Bonds-3	S.F.	NL	2003	8.67
10	Barry Bonds-4	S.F.	NL	2002	8.76
11	Babe Ruth-2	N.Y.	AL	1927	9.00
12	Sammy Sosa-1	Chi.	NL	2001	9.02
13	Babe Ruth-3	N.Y.	AL	1921	9.15
14	Jim Thome-1	Cle.	AL	2002	9.23
15	Mark McGwire-6	Oak. AL St.L.	NL	1997	9.31
16	Mickey Mantle-1	N.Y.	AL	1961	9.52
17	Hank Greenberg	Det.	AL	1938	9.59
18	Roger Maris	N.Y.	AL	1961	9.67
19	Sammy Sosa-2	Chi.	NL	1998	9.74
20	Barry Bonds-5	S.F.	NL	2000	9.80
21	Hank Aaron-1	Atl.	NL	1973	9.80
22	Sammy Sosa-3	Chi.	NL	1999	9.92
23	Babe Ruth-4	N.Y.	AL	1928	9.93
24	Ryan Howard	Phi.	NL	2006	10.02
25	Jimmie Foxx	Phi.	NL	1932	10.09
26	Ralph Kiner	Pit.	NL	1949	10.17
27	Mickey Mantle-2	N.Y.	AL	1956	10.25
28	Kevin Mitchell	Cin.	NL	1994	10.33
29	David Ortiz	Bos.	AL	2006	10.33
30	Matt Williams	S.F.	NL	1994	10.35
31	Barry Bonds-6	S.F.	NL	1999	10.44
32	Hack Wilson	Chi.	NL	1930	10.45
33	Frank Thomas	Chi.	AL	1994	10.50
34	Babe Ruth-5	N.Y.	AL	1926	10.53
35	Hank Aaron-2	Atl.	NL	1971	10.53
36	Jim Gentile	Bal.	AL	1961	10.57
37	Barry Bonds-7	S.F.	NL	1994	10.57
38	Babe Ruth-6	N.Y.	AL	1930	10.57
39	Willie Stargell	Pit.	NL	1971	10.65
40	Luis Gonzalez	Ari.	NL	2001	10.68
41	Rudy York	Det.	AL	1937	10.71
42	Willie Mays	S.F.	NL	1965	10.73
43	Jim Thome-2	Cle.	AL	2001	10.73
44	Travis Hafner	Cle.	AL	2006	10.81
45	Ken Griffey Jr.-1	Sea.	AL	1994	10.83
46	Babe Ruth-7	N.Y.	AL	1929	10.85
47	Ken Griffey Jr.-2	Sea.	AL	1997	10.86
48	Boog Powell	Bal.	AL	1964	10.87
49	Willie McCovey	S.F.	NL	1969	10.91
50	Albert Pujols	St.L.	NL	2006	10.92
51	Albert Belle	Cle.	AL	1995	10.92
52	Alex Rodriguez	Tex.	AL	2002	10.95

RUNS BATTED IN

Rank	Player	Team	Lg	Year	RBI
1	Hack Wilson-1	Chi.	NL	1930	191
2	Lou Gehrig-1	N.Y.	AL	1931	184
3	Hank Greenberg-1	Det.	AL	1937	183
4	Lou Gehrig-2	N.Y.	AL	1927	175
	Jimmie Foxx-1	Bos.	AL	1938	175
6	Lou Gehrig-3	N.Y.	AL	1930	174
7	Babe Ruth-1	N.Y.	AL	1921	171
8	Chuck Klein-1	Phi.	NL	1930	170
	Hank Greenberg-2	Det.	AL	1935	170
10	Jimmie Foxx-2	Phi.	AL	1932	169
11	Joe DiMaggio-1	N.Y.	AL	1937	167
12	Al Simmons-1	Phi.	AL	1930	165
	Lou Gehrig-4	N.Y.	AL	1934	165
	Manny Ramirez-1	Cle.	AL	1999	165
15	Babe Ruth-2	N.Y.	AL	1927	164
16	Babe Ruth-3	N.Y.	AL	1931	163
	Jimmie Foxx-3	Phi.	AL	1933	163
18	Hal Trosky	Cle.	AL	1936	162
19	Sammy Sosa-1	Chi.	NL	2001	160
20	Hack Wilson-2	Chi.	NL	1929	159
	Lou Gehrig-5	N.Y.	AL	1937	159
	Vern Stephens	Bos.	AL	1949	159
	Ted Williams-1	Bos.	AL	1949	159
24	Sammy Sosa-2	Chi.	NL	1998	158
25	Al Simmons-2	Phi.	AL	1929	157
	Juan Gonzalez	Tex.	AL	1998	157
27	Jimmie Foxx-4	Phi.	AL	1930	156
28	Ken Williams	St.L.	AL	1922	155
	Joe DiMaggio-2	N.Y.	AL	1948	155
30	Babe Ruth-4	N.Y.	AL	1929	154
	Joe Medwick	St.L.	NL	1937	154
32	Babe Ruth-5	N.Y.	AL	1930	153
	Tommy Davis	L.A.	NL	1962	153
34	Rogers Hornsby-1	St.L.	NL	1922	152
	Lou Gehrig-6	N.Y.	AL	1936	152
	Albert Belle-1	Bal.	AL	1998	152
37	Mel Ott	N.Y.	NL	1929	151
	Lou Gehrig-7	N.Y.	AL	1932	151
	Al Simmons-3	Phi.	AL	1932	151
40	Hank Greenberg-3	Det.	AL	1940	150
	Andres Galarraga	Col.	NL	1996	150
	Miguel Tejada	Bal.	AL	2004	150
43	Rogers Hornsby-2	Chi.	NL	1929	149
	George Foster	Cin.	NL	1977	149
	Ryan Howard	Phi.	NL	2006	149
46	Johnny Bench	Cin.	NL	1970	148
	Albert Belle-2	Cle.	AL	1996	148
	Rafael Palmeiro	Tex.	AL	1999	148
	David Ortiz	Bos.	AL	2005	148
50	Ken Griffey Jr.-1	Sea.	AL	1997	147
	Mark McGwire-1	St.L.	NL	1998	147
	Mark McGwire-2	St.L.	NL	1999	147
	Todd Helton-1	Col.	NL	2000	147
54	Babe Ruth-6	N.Y.	AL	1926	146
	Hank Greenberg-4	Det.	AL	1938	146
	Ken Griffey Jr.-2	Sea.	AL	1998	146
	Todd Helton-2	Col.	NL	2001	146
58	Chuck Klein-2	Phi.	NL	1929	145
	Ted Williams-2	Bos.	AL	1939	145
	Al Rosen	Cle.	AL	1953	145
	Don Mattingly	N.Y.	AL	1985	145
	Manny Ramirez-2	Cle.	AL	1998	145
	Edgar Martinez	Sea.	AL	2000	145
	Carlos Delgado	Tor.	AL	2003	145

RUNS

Rank	Player	Team	Lg	Year	R
1	Babe Ruth-1	N.Y.	AL	1921	177
2	Lou Gehrig-1	N.Y.	AL	1936	167
3	Babe Ruth-2	N.Y.	AL	1928	163
	Lou Gehrig-2	N.Y.	AL	1931	163
5	Babe Ruth-3	N.Y.	AL	1920	158
	Babe Ruth-4	N.Y.	AL	1927	158
	Chuck Klein-1	Phi.	NL	1930	158
	Rogers Hornsby-1	Chi.	NL	1929	156
9	Kiki Cuyler-1	Chi.	NL	1930	155
10	Lefty O'Doul	Phi.	NL	1929	152
	Woody English	Chi.	NL	1930	152
	Al Simmons-1	Phi.	AL	1930	152
	Chuck Klein-2	Phi.	NL	1932	152
	Jeff Bagwell-1	Hou.	NL	2000	152
15	Babe Ruth-5	N.Y.	AL	1923	151
	Jimmie Foxx	Phi.	AL	1932	151
	Joe DiMaggio	N.Y.	AL	1937	151
18	Babe Ruth-6	N.Y.	AL	1930	150
	Ted Williams-1	Bos.	AL	1949	150
20	Lou Gehrig-3	N.Y.	AL	1927	149
	Babe Ruth-7	N.Y.	AL	1931	149
22	Ty Cobb-1	Det.	AL	1911	147
23	Hack Wilson	Chi.	NL	1930	146
	Rickey Henderson	N.Y.	AL	1985	146
	Craig Biggio	Hou.	NL	1997	146
	Sammy Sosa	Chi.	NL	2001	146
27	Nap Lajoie	Phi.	AL	1901	145
	Harlond Clift	St.L.	AL	1936	145
29	Ty Cobb-2	Det.	AL	1915	144
	Kiki Cuyler-2	Pit.	NL	1925	144
	Charlie Gehringer-1	Det.	AL	1930	144
	Al Simmons-2	Phi.	AL	1932	144
	Charlie Gehringer-2	Det.	AL	1936	144
	Hank Greenberg	Det.	AL	1938	144
35	Babe Ruth-8	N.Y.	AL	1924	143
	Lou Gehrig-4	N.Y.	AL	1930	143
	Babe Herman	Bko.	NL	1930	143
	Earle Combs	N.Y.	AL	1932	143
	Red Rolfe	N.Y.	AL	1937	143
	Len Dykstra	Phi.	NL	1993	143
	Larry Walker	Col.	NL	1997	143
	Jeff Bagwell-2	Hou.	NL	1999	143
43	Paul Waner	Pit.	NL	1928	142
	Ted Williams-2	Bos.	AL	1946	142
	Ellis Burks	Col.	NL	1996	142
46	Rogers Hornsby-2	St.L.	NL	1922	141
	Ted Williams-3	Bos.	AL	1942	141
	Alex Rodriguez	Sea.	AL	1996	141
49	Max Carey	Pit.	NL	1922	140
	Earl Averill	Cle.	AL	1931	140
	Chuck Knoblauch	Min.	AL	1996	140

TOTAL BASES

Rank	Player	Team	Lg	Year	TB
1	Babe Ruth-1	N.Y.	AL	1921	457
2	Rogers Hornsby-1	St.L.	NL	1922	450
3	Lou Gehrig-1	N.Y.	AL	1927	447
4	Chuck Klein-1	Phi.	NL	1930	445
5	Jimmie Foxx-1	Phi.	AL	1932	438
6	Stan Musial-1	St.L.	NL	1948	429
7	Sammy Sosa-1	Chi.	NL	2001	425
8	Hack Wilson	Chi.	NL	1930	423
9	Chuck Klein-2	Phi.	NL	1932	420
10	Lou Gehrig-2	N.Y.	AL	1930	419
	Luis Gonzalez	Ari.	NL	2001	419
12	Joe DiMaggio	N.Y.	AL	1937	418
13	Babe Ruth-2	N.Y.	AL	1927	417
14	Babe Herman	Bko.	NL	1930	416
	Sammy Sosa-2	Chi.	NL	1998	416
16	Barry Bonds	S.F.	NL	2001	411
17	Lou Gehrig-3	N.Y.	AL	1931	410
18	Rogers Hornsby-2	Chi.	NL	1929	409
	Lou Gehrig-4	N.Y.	AL	1934	409
	Larry Walker	Col.	NL	1997	409
21	Joe Medwick	St.L.	NL	1937	406
	Jim Rice-1	Bos.	AL	1978	406
23	Chuck Klein-3	Phi.	NL	1929	405
	Hal Trosky	Cle.	AL	1936	405
	Todd Helton-1	Col.	NL	2000	405
26	Jimmie Foxx-2	Phi.	AL	1933	403
	Lou Gehrig-5	N.Y.	AL	1936	403
28	Todd Helton-2	Col.	NL	2001	402
29	Hank Aaron	Mil.	NL	1959	400
30	George Sisler	St.L.	AL	1920	399
	Babe Ruth-3	N.Y.	AL	1923	399
	Albert Belle	Bal.	AL	1998	399
33	Jimmie Foxx-3	Bos.	AL	1938	398
34	Lefty O'Doul	Phi.	NL	1929	397
	Hank Greenberg-1	Det.	AL	1937	397
	Sammy Sosa-3	Chi.	NL	1999	397
37	Albert Pujols-1	St.L.	NL	2003	394
38	Ken Griffey Jr.-1	Sea.	AL	1997	393
	Alex Rodriguez-1	Tex.	AL	2001	393
	Derrek Lee	Chi.	NL	2005	393
41	Al Simmons-1	Phi.	AL	1925	392
	Al Simmons-2	Phi.	AL	1930	392
	Bill Terry	N.Y.	NL	1930	392
	Ellis Burks	Col.	NL	1996	392
45	Babe Ruth-4	N.Y.	AL	1924	391
46	Hank Greenberg-2	Det.	AL	1935	389
	Alex Rodriguez-2	Tex.	AL	2002	389
	Albert Pujols-2	St.L.	NL	2006	389
49	Babe Ruth-5	N.Y.	AL	1920	388
	George Foster	Cin.	NL	1977	388
	Don Mattingly	N.Y.	AL	1986	388
52	Ken Griffey Jr.-2	Sea.	AL	1998	387
53	Earl Averill	Cle.	AL	1936	385
54	Hank Greenberg-3	Det.	AL	1940	384
	Alex Rodriguez-3	Sea.	AL	1998	384
56	Mark McGwire	St.L.	NL	1998	383
	Sammy Sosa-4	Chi.	NL	2000	383
	Ryan Howard	Phi.	NL	2006	383
59	Stan Musial-2	St.L.	NL	1949	382
	Willie Mays-1	N.Y.	NL	1955	382
	Willie Mays-2	S.F.	NL	1962	382
	Jim Rice-2	Bos.	AL	1977	382
	Juan Gonzalez	Tex.	AL	1998	382
64	Rogers Hornsby-3	St.L.	NL	1925	381
	Alfonso Soriano	N.Y.	AL	2002	381
66	Babe Ruth-6	N.Y.	AL	1928	380
	Hank Greenberg-4	Det.	AL	1938	380
	Frank Robinson	Cin.	NL	1962	380
	Vinny Castilla	Col.	NL	1998	380

SINGLE SEASON LEADERS

(numbers after individual name indicates numbers of times that individual appears within a specific category)

BATTER'S BASES ON BALLS

#	Player	Team	Lg	Year	BB
1	Barry Bonds-1	S.F.	NL	2004	232
2	Barry Bonds-2	S.F.	NL	2002	198
3	Barry Bonds-3	S.F.	NL	2001	177
4	Babe Ruth-1	N.Y.	AL	1923	170
5	Ted Williams-1	Bos.	AL	1947	162
	Ted Williams-2	Bos.	AL	1949	162
	Mark McGwire-2	St.L.	NL	1998	162
8	Ted Williams-3	Bos.	AL	1946	156
9	Eddie Yost-1	Was.	AL	1956	151
	Barry Bonds-4	S.F.	NL	1996	151
11	Babe Ruth-2	N.Y.	AL	1920	150
12	Eddie Joost	Phi.	AL	1949	149
	Jeff Bagwell-1	Hou.	NL	1999	149
14	Eddie Stanky-1	Bkn.	NL	1945	148
	Jim Wynn	Hou.	NL	1969	148
	Barry Bonds-5	S.F.	NL	2003	148
17	Jimmy Sheckard	Chi.	NL	1911	147
	Ted Williams-4	Bos.	AL	1941	147
19	Mickey Mantle	N.Y.	AL	1957	146
20	Babe Ruth-3	N.Y.	AL	1921	145
	Ted Williams-5	Bos.	AL	1942	145
	Harmon Killebrew-1	Min.	AL	1969	145
	Barry Bonds-6	S.F.	NL	1997	145
24	Babe Ruth-4	N.Y.	AL	1926	144
	Eddie Stanky-2	N.Y.	NL	1950	144
	Ted Williams-6	Bos.	AL	1951	144
27	Babe Ruth-5	N.Y.	AL	1924	142
	Gary Sheffield	Fla.	NL	1996	142
29	Eddie Yost-2	Was.	AL	1950	141
30	Frank Thomas-1	Chi.	AL	1991	138
31	Babe Ruth-6	N.Y.	AL	1927	137
	Babe Ruth-7	N.Y.	AL	1928	137
	Eddie Stanky-3	Bkn.	NL	1946	137
	Roy Cullenbine	Det.	AL	1947	137
	Ralph Kiner	Pit.	NL	1951	137
	Willie McCovey	S.F.	NL	1970	137
	Jason Giambi	Oak.	AL	2000	137
38	Babe Ruth-8	N.Y.	AL	1930	136
	Ferris Fain-1	Phi.	AL	1949	136
	Ted Williams-7	Bos.	AL	1954	136
	Jack Clark-1	St.L.	NL	1987	136
	Frank Thomas-2	Chi.	AL	1995	136
43	Eddie Yost-3	Det.	AL	1959	135
	Jeff Bagwell-2	Hou.	NL	1996	135
	Brian Giles	Pit.	NL	2002	135
46	Ferris Fain-2	Phi.	AL	1950	133
	Mark McGwire-2	St.L.	NL	1999	133
48	Lou Gehrig	N.Y.	AL	1935	132
	Frank Howard	Was.	AL	1970	132
	Joe Morgan	Cin.	NL	1975	132
	Jack Clark-2	S.D.	NL	1989	132
	Tony Phillips	Det.	AL	1993	132
53	Bob Elliott	Bos.	NL	1948	131
	Eddie Yost-4	Was.	AL	1954	131
	Harmon Killebrew-2	Min.	AL	1967	131
56	Babe Ruth-9	N.Y.	AL	1932	130
	Lou Gehrig-2	N.Y.	AL	1936	130
	Barry Bonds-7	S.F.	NL	1998	130

BATTER'S STRIKEOUTS

#	Player	Team	Lg	Year	SO
1	Adam Dunn-1	Cin.	NL	2004	195
	Adam Dunn-2	Cin.	NL	2006	194
3	Bobby Bonds-1	S.F.	NL	1970	189
	Jose Hernandez-1	Mil.	NL	2002	188
5	Bobby Bonds-2	S.F.	NL	1969	187
	Preston Wilson	Fla.	NL	2000	187
7	Rob Deer-1	Mil.	AL	1987	186
8	Pete Incaviglia-1	Tex.	AL	1986	185
	Jose Hernandez-2	Mil.	NL	2001	185
	Jim Thome-1	Cle.	AL	2001	185
11	Cecil Fielder	Det.	AL	1990	182
	Jim Thome-2	Phi.	NL	2003	182
13	Mo Vaughn	Ana.	AL	2000	181
	Ryan Howard	Phi.	NL	2006	181
15	Mike Schmidt	Phi.	NL	1975	180
16	Rob Deer-2	Mil.	AL	1986	179
17	Richie Sexson-1	Mil.	AL	2001	178
18	Jose Hernandez-3	Col.-Chi.-Pit.	NL	2003	177
	Mark Bellhorn	Bos.	AL	2004	177
20	Mike Cameron	Sea.	AL	2002	176
21	Dave Nicholson	Chi.	AL	1963	175
	Gorman Thomas-1	Mil.	AL	1979	175
	Jose Canseco	Oak.	AL	1986	175
	Rob Deer-3	Det.	AL	1991	175
	Jay Buhner	Sea.	AL	1997	175
26	Sammy Sosa-1	Chi.	NL	1997	174
	Curtis Granderson	Det.	AL	2006	174
28	Jim Presley	Sea.	AL	1986	172
	Bo Jackson	K.C.	AL	1989	172
30	Reggie Jackson	Oak.	AL	1968	171
	Sammy Sosa-2	Chi.	NL	1998	171
	Sammy Sosa-3	Chi.	NL	1999	171
	Jim Thome-3	Cle.	AL	1999	171
	Jim Thome-4	Cle.	AL	2000	171
35	Gorman Thomas-2	Mil.	AL	1980	170
	Adam Dunn-3	Cin.	NL	2002	170
37	Andres Galarraga	Mon.	NL	1990	169
	Rob Deer-4	Det.-Bos.	AL	1993	169
	Craig Wilson	Pit.	NL	2004	169
40	Juan Samuel	Phi.	NL	1984	168
	Pete Incaviglia-2	Tex.	AL	1987	168
	Sammy Sosa-4	Chi.	NL	2000	168
	Corey Patterson	Chi.	NL	2004	168
	Adam Dunn-4	Cin.	NL	2005	168
45	Jim Edmonds	St.L.	NL	2000	167
	Richie Sexson-2	Sea.	AL	2005	167
47	Gary Alexander	Oak.-Cle.	AL	1978	166
	Steve Balboni	K.C.	AL	1985	166
	Cory Snyder	Cle.	AL	1987	166

STOLEN BASES

#	Player	Team	Lg	Year	SB
1	Rickey Henderson-1	Oak.	AL	1982	130
2	Lou Brock-1	St.L.	NL	1974	118
3	Vince Coleman-1	St.L.	NL	1985	110
4	Vince Coleman-2	St.L.	NL	1987	109
5	Rickey Henderson-2	Oak.	AL	1983	108
6	Vince Coleman-3	St.L.	NL	1986	107
7	Maury Wills-1	L.A.	NL	1962	104
8	Rickey Henderson-3	Oak.	AL	1980	100
9	Ron LeFlore-1	Mon.	NL	1980	97
10	Ty Cobb-1	Det.	AL	1915	96
	Omar Moreno-1	Pit.	NL	1980	96
12	Maury Wills-2	L.A.	NL	1965	94
13	Rickey Henderson-4	N.Y.	AL	1988	93
14	Tim Raines-1	Mon.	NL	1983	90
15	Clyde Milan-1	Was.	AL	1912	88
16	Rickey Henderson-5	N.Y.	AL	1986	87
17	Ty Cobb-2	Det.	AL	1911	83
	Willie Wilson	K.C.	AL	1979	83
19	Eddie Collins-1	Phi.	AL	1910	81
	Bob Bescher-1	Cin.	NL	1911	81
	Vince Coleman-4	St.L.	NL	1988	81
22	Rickey Henderson-6	N.Y.	AL	1985	80
	Eric Davis	Cin.	NL	1986	80
24	Dave Collins-5	Cin.	NL	1980	79
	Willie Wilson	K.C.	AL	1980	79
26	Ron LeFlore-2	Det.	AL	1979	78
	Tim Raines-2	Mon.	NL	1982	78
	Marquis Grissom-1	Mon.	NL	1992	78
29	Davey Lopes	L.A.	NL	1975	77
	Omar Moreno-2	Pit.	NL	1979	77
	Rudy Law	Chi.	AL	1983	77
	Rickey Henderson-7	N.Y.-Oak.	AL	1989	77
	Vince Coleman-5	St.L.	NL	1990	77
34	Ty Cobb-3	Det.	AL	1909	76
	Marquis Grissom-2	Mon.	NL	1991	76
36	Clyde Milan-2	Was.	AL	1913	75
	Benny Kauff	Ind.	FL	1914	75
	Billy North	Oak.	AL	1976	75
	Tim Raines-3	Mon.	NL	1984	75
	Kenny Lofton-1	Cle.	AL	1996	75
	Fritz Maisel	N.Y.	AL	1914	74
	Lou Brock-2	St.L.	NL	1966	74
	Brian Hunter	Det.	AL	1997	74
44	Tommy Harper	Bos.	AL	1969	73
45	Juan Samuel	Phi.	NL	1984	72
	Otis Nixon	Atl.	NL	1991	72
	Tony Womack	Ari.	NL	1999	72
48	Omar Moreno-3	Pit.	NL	1978	71
	Tim Raines-4	Mon.	NL	1981	71
50	Bob Bescher-2	Cin.	NL	1910	70
	Lou Brock-3	St.L.	NL	1973	70
	Mickey Rivers	Cal.	AL	1975	70
	Frank Taveras	Pit.	NL	1977	70
	Alan Wiggins-1	S.D.	NL	1984	70
	Tim Raines-5	Mon.	NL	1985	70
	Tim Raines-6	Mon.	NL	1986	70
	Kenny Lofton-2	Cle.	AL	1993	70
	Scott Podsednik	Mil.	NL	2004	70
59	Ty Cobb-4	Det.	AL	1916	68
	Ron LeFlore-3	Det.	AL	1978	68
	Lonnie Smith	St.L.	NL	1982	68
62	Frank Chance	Chi.	NL	1903	67
	Jimmy Sheckard	Bkn.	NL	1903	67
	Eddie Collins-2	Phi.	AL	1909	67
	Bob Bescher-3	Cin.	NL	1912	67
	Joe Morgan-1	Cin.	NL	1973	67
	Joe Morgan-2	Cin.	NL	1975	67
68	Rickey Henderson-8	Oak.	AL	1982	66
	Alan Wiggins-2	S.D.	NL	1983	66
	Kenny Lofton-3	Cle.	AL	1992	66
	Tom Goodwin	K.C.	AL	1996	66
	Rickey Henderson-9	Oak.	AL	1998	66
	Roger Cedeno	N.Y.	NL	1999	66
74	Ty Cobb-5	Det.	AL	1910	65
	Gerald Young	Hou.	NL	1988	65
	Vince Coleman-6	St.L.	NL	1989	65
	Rickey Henderson-10	Oak.	AL	1990	65
	Juan Pierre	Fla.	NL	2003	65

WINS

#	Player	Team	Lg	Year	W
1	Jack Chesbro-1	N.Y.	AL	1904	41
2	Ed Walsh	Chi.	AL	1908	40
3	Christy Mathewson-1	N.Y.	NL	1908	37
4	Walter Johnson-1	Was.	AL	1913	36
5	Joe McGinnity-1	N.Y.	AL	1904	35
6	Smokey Joe Wood	Bos.	AL	1912	34
7	Cy Young-1	Bos.	AL	1901	33
	Christy Mathewson-2	N.Y.	NL	1904	33
	Pete Alexander-1	Phi.	NL	1916	33
	Walter Johnson-2	Was.	AL	1912	33
11	Cy Young-2	Bos.	AL	1902	32
	Christy Mathewson-3	N.Y.	NL	1905	32
13	Joe McGinnity-2	N.Y.	NL	1903	31
	Jack Coombs-1	Phi.	AL	1910	31
	Pete Alexander-2	Phi.	NL	1915	31
	Jim Bagby	Cle.	AL	1920	31
	Lefty Grove-1	Phi.	AL	1931	31
	Denny McLain	Det.	AL	1968	31
19	Christy Mathewson-4	N.Y.	NL	1903	30
	Pete Alexander-3	Phi.	NL	1917	30
	Dizzy Dean-1	St.L.	NL	1934	30
22	Three Finger Brown	Chi.	NL	1908	29
	George Mullin	Det.	AL	1909	29
	Claude Hendrix	Chi.	FL	1914	29
	Eddie Cicotte-1	Chi.	AL	1919	29
	Hal Newhouser	Det.	AL	1944	29
27	Jack Chesbro-2	Pit.	NL	1902	28
	Cy Young-3	Bos.	AL	1903	28
	Pete Alexander-4	Phi.	NL	1911	28
	Jack Coombs-2	Phi.	AL	1911	28
	Walter Johnson-3	Was.	AL	1914	28
	Eddie Cicotte-2	Chi.	AL	1917	28
	Dazzy Vance	Bkn.	NL	1924	28
	Lefty Grove-2	Phi.	AL	1930	28
	Dizzy Dean-2	St.L.	NL	1935	28
	Robin Roberts	Phi.	NL	1952	28

LOSSES

#	Player	Team	Lg	Year	L
1	Vic Willis-1	Bos.	NL	1905	29
2	Pete Dowling	Mil. & Cle.	AL	1901	27
	Dummy Taylor	N.Y.	NL	1901	27
	Jack Townsend	Was.	AL	1904	27
	George Bell	Bkn.	NL	1910	27
	Paul Derringer	St.L. & Cin.	NL	1933	27
7	Gus Dorner	Cin. & Bos.	NL	1906	26
	Bob Groom	Was.	AL	1909	26
9	Patsy Flaherty	Chi.	NL	1903	25
	Oscar Jones	Bkn.	NL	1904	25
	Vic Willis-2	Bos.	NL	1904	25
	Harry McIntire	Bkn.	NL	1905	25
	Irv Young-1	Bos.	NL	1906	25
	Stony McGlynn	St.L.	NL	1907	25
	Bugs Raymond	St.L.	NL	1908	25
	Walter Johnson	Was.	AL	1909	25
	Scott Perry	Phi.	AL	1920	25
	Red Ruffling	Bos.	AL	1928	25
	Ben Cantwell	Bos.	NL	1935	25
20	Chick Fraser	Phi.	NL	1904	24
	George Mullin	Det.	AL	1904	24
	Fred Glade	St.L.	AL	1905	24
	Roger Craig	N.Y.	NL	1962	24
24	Casey Patten	Was.	AL	1903	23
	Jack Cronin	Bkn.	NL	1904	23
	Benny Jacobson	Was.	AL	1904	23
	Orvie Overall	Cin.	NL	1905	23
	Kaiser Wilhelm	Bos.	NL	1905	23
	Vive Lindaman	Bos.	NL	1906	23
	Irv Young-2	Bos.	NL	1907	23
	Cecil Ferguson	Bos.	NL	1909	23
	Buster Brown	Bos.	NL	1910	23
	Red Ames	Cin.	NL	1914	23
	Lee Meadows	St.L.	NL	1916	23
	Elmer Myers	Phi.	AL	1916	23
	Rollie Naylor	Phi.	AL	1920	23
	Eddie Rommel	Phi.	AL	1921	23
	Dolf Luque	Cin.	NL	1922	23

SINGLE SEASON LEADERS

(numbers after individual name indicates numbers of times that individual appears within a specific category)

WINNING PERCENTAGE
(Minimum 15 Wins)

#	Player	Team	Lg	Year	Pct
1	Roy Face	Pit.	NL	1959	.947
2	Johnny Allen-1	Cle.	AL	1937	.938
3	Greg Maddux-1	Atl.	NL	1995	.905
	Randy Johnson-1	Sea.	AL	1995	.900
	Ron Guidry	N.Y.	AL	1978	.893
	Freddie Fitzsimmons	Bkn.	NL	1940	.889
	Lefty Grove-1	Phi.	AL	1931	.886
	Bob Stanley	Bos.	AL	1978	.882
	Preacher Roe	Bkn.	NL	1951	.880
	Smoky Joe Wood	Bos.	AL	1912	.872
	Dave Cone	N.Y.	NL	1988	.870
	Roger Clemens-1	N.Y.	AL	2001	.870
	Orel Hershiser	L.A.	NL	1985	.864
	Wild Bill Donovan	Det.	AL	1907	.862
	Whitey Ford	N.Y.	AL	1961	.862
	Dwight Gooden	N.Y.	NL	1985	.857
	Roger Clemens-2	Bos.	AL	1986	.857
	Pedro Martinez-1	Bos.	AL	1999	.852
	Chief Bender-1	Phi.	AL	1914	.850
	John Smoltz	Atl.	NL	1998	.850
	Lefty Grove-2	Phi.	AL	1930	.848
	Mike Hampton	Hou.	NL	1999	.846
23	Tom Hughes	Bos.	NL	1916	.842
	Emil Yde	Pit.	NL	1924	.842
	Schoolboy Rowe	Det.	AL	1940	.842
	Sandy Consuegra	Chi.	AL	1954	.842
	Ralph Terry	N.Y.	AL	1961	.842
	Ron Perranoski	L.A.	NL	1963	.842
29	Lefty Gomez	N.Y.	AL	1934	.839
30	Denny McLain	Det.	AL	1968	.838
31	Walter Johnson	Was.	AL	1913	.837
32	King Cole	Chi.	NL	1910	.833
	Spud Chandler	N.Y.	AL	1943	.833
	Hoyt Wilhelm	N.Y.	AL	1952	.833
	Sandy Koufax	L.A.	NL	1963	.833
	Randy Johnson-2	Sea.	AL	1997	.833
	Pedro Martinez-2	Bos.	AL	2002	.833
38	Randy Johnson-3	Ari.	NL	2002	.828
39	Ed Reulbach-1	Chi.	NL	1906	.826
	Elmer Riddle	Cin.	NL	1941	.826
	Greg Maddux-2	Atl.	NL	1997	.826
42	Jack Chesbro	Pit.	NL	1902	.824
	Dazzy Vance	Bkn.	NL	1924	.824
44	Chief Bender-2	Phi.	AL	1910	.821
	Bob Purkey	Cin.	NL	1962	.821
	Barry Zito	Oak.	AL	2002	.821
47	Sal Maglie	N.Y.	NL	1950	.818
	Bob Welch	Oak.	AL	1990	.818
	Mark Portugal	Hou.	NL	1993	.818
	David Wells	N.Y.	AL	1998	.818
	Roger Clemens-3	N.Y.	AL	2004	.818
52	Joe McGinnity	N.Y.	NL	1904	.814
53	Three Finger Brown	Chi.	NL	1906	.813
	Russ Ford	N.Y.	AL	1910	.813
	Eddie Cicotte	Phi.	AL	1912	.813
	Carl Hubbell	N.Y.	NL	1936	.813
57	Dizzy Dean	St.L.	NL	1934	.811
58	Ed Reulbach-2	Chi.	NL	1907	.810
	Doc Crandall	N.Y.	NL	1910	.810
60	Johnny Allen-2	N.Y.	AL	1932	.810
	Ted Wilks	St.L.	NL	1944	.810
	Phil Niekro	Atl.	NL	1982	.810
	Jimmy Key	N.Y.	AL	1994	.810
	Paul Abbott	Sea.	AL	2001	.810
65	General Crowder	St.L.	AL	1928	.808
	Bobo Newsom	Det.	AL	1940	.808
	Ernie Bonham	N.Y.	AL	1942	.808
	Larry Jansen	N.Y.	NL	1947	.808
	Dave McNally	Bal.	AL	1971	.808
	Catfish Hunter	Oak.	AL	1973	.808
72	Howie Camnitz	Pit.	NL	1909	.806
	Christy Mathewson-1	N.Y.	NL	1909	.806
	Boo Ferriss	Bos.	AL	1946	.806
	Juan Marichal	S.F.	NL	1966	.806
75	Eddie Cicotte	Chi.	AL	1919	.806
76	Ed Doheny	Pit.	NL	1902	.800
	Christy Mathewson-2	N.Y.	NL	1905	.800
	Bert Humphries	Chi.	NL	1913	.800
	Stan Coveleski	Was.	AL	1925	.800
	Firpo Marberry	Was.	AL	1931	.800
	Robin Roberts	Phi.	NL	1952	.800
	Ed Lopat	N.Y.	AL	1953	.800
	Don Newcombe	Bkn.	NL	1955	.800
	Jim Palmer	Bal.	AL	1969	.800
	John Candelaria	Pit.	NL	1977	.800
	Larry Gura	K.C.	AL	1978	.800
	Tommy Greene	Phi.	NL	1993	.800
	Denny Neagle	Atl.	NL	1997	.800

STRIKEOUTS

#	Player	Team	Lg	Year	SO
	Nolan Ryan-1	Cal.	AL	1973	383
	Sandy Koufax-1	L.A.	NL	1965	382
	Randy Johnson-1	Ari.	NL	2001	372
	Nolan Ryan-2	Cal.	AL	1974	367
	Randy Johnson-2	Ari.	NL	1999	364
	Rube Waddell-1	Phi.	AL	1904	349
	Bob Feller-1	Cle.	AL	1946	348
	Randy Johnson-3	Ari.	NL	2000	347
	Nolan Ryan-3	Cal.	AL	1977	341
	Randy Johnson-4	Ari.	NL	2002	334
	Nolan Ryan-4	Cal.	AL	1972	329
	Randy Johnson-5	Sea. AL Hou.	AL	1998	329
	Nolan Ryan-5	Cal.	AL	1976	327
	Sam McDowell-1	Cal.	AL	1965	325
	Curt Schilling-1	Phi.	NL	1997	319
	Sandy Koufax-2	L.A.	NL	1966	317
	Curt Schilling-2	Ari.	NL	2002	316
	Walter Johnson-1	Was.	AL	1910	313
	J.R. Richard-1	Hou.	NL	1979	313
	Pedro Martinez-1	Bos.	AL	1999	313
	Steve Carlton-1	Phi.	NL	1972	310
22	Mickey Lolich-1	Det.	AL	1971	308
	Randy Johnson-6	Sea.	AL	1993	308
24	Sandy Koufax-3	L.A.	NL	1963	306
	Mike Scott	Hou.	NL	1986	306
26	Pedro Martinez-2	Mon.	NL	1997	305
27	Sam McDowell-2	Cle.	AL	1970	304
28	Walter Johnson-2	Was.	AL	1912	303
	J.R. Richard-2	Hou.	NL	1978	303
	Rube Waddell-2	Phi.	AL	1903	302
31	Vida Blue	Oak.	AL	1971	301
	Nolan Ryan-6	Tex.	AL	1989	301
33	Curt Schilling-3	Phi.	NL	1998	300
34	Randy Johnson-7	Sea.	AL	1995	294
35	Curt Schilling-4	Ari.	NL	2001	293
	Roger Clemens-1	Tor.	AL	1997	292
37	Roger Clemens-2	Bos.	AL	1988	291
	Randy Johnson-8	Sea.	AL	1997	291
39	Randy Johnson-9	Ari.	NL	2004	290
40	Tom Seaver-1	N.Y.	NL	1971	289
41	Rube Waddell-3	Phi.	AL	1905	287
42	Steve Carlton-2	Phi.	NL	1980	286
	Steve Carlton-3	Phi.	NL	1982	286
44	Pedro Martinez-3	Bos.	AL	2000	284
45	Sam McDowell-3	Cle.	AL	1968	283
	Tom Seaver-2	N.Y.	NL	1970	283
47	Denny McLain	Det.	AL	1968	280
48	Sam McDowell-3	Cle.	AL	1969	279
49	Bob Veale	Pit.	NL	1965	276
	Dwight Gooden-1	N.Y.	NL	1984	276
	John Smoltz	Atl.	NL	1996	276
52	Hal Newhouser	Det.	AL	1946	275
	Steve Carlton-4	Phi.	NL	1983	275
54	Bob Gibson-2	St.L.	NL	1970	274
	Ferguson Jenkins-1	Chi.	NL	1970	274
	Mario Soto	Cin.	NL	1982	274
57	Ferguson Jenkins-2	Chi.	NL	1969	273
58	Mickey Lolich-2	Det.	AL	1971	271
	Roger Clemens-3	Tor.	AL	1998	271
60	Bob Gibson-3	St.L.	NL	1965	270
	Nolan Ryan-7	Hou.	NL	1987	270
62	Ed Walsh	Chi.	AL	1908	269
	Sandy Koufax-4	L.A.	NL	1961	269
	Bob Gibson-3	St.L.	NL	1969	269
	Frank Tanana-1	Cal.	AL	1975	269
66	Jim Bunning	Phi.	NL	1965	268
	Bob Gibson-4	St.L.	NL	1968	268
	Dwight Gooden-2	N.Y.	NL	1985	268
69	Christy Mathewson	N.Y.	NL	1903	267
70	Kerry Wood	Chi.	NL	2003	266
	Jim Maloney	Cin.	NL	1963	265
	Johan Santana	Min.	AL	2004	265
	Luis Tiant	Cle.	AL	1968	264
	Ben Sheets	Mil.	NL	2004	264
75	Herb Score	Cle.	AL	1956	263
	Ferguson Jenkins-3	Chi.	NL	1971	263
77	Dazzy Vance	Bkn.	NL	1924	262
	Phil Niekro	Atl.	NL	1977	262
	Mark Langston	Sea.	AL	1987	262
80	Bob Feller-2	Cle.	AL	1940	261
	Frank Tanana-2	Cal.	AL	1976	261
	David Cone	N.Y. NL Tor.	AL	1992	261
83	Bob Feller-3	Cle.	AL	1941	260
	Ferguson Jenkins-4	Chi.	AL	1968	260
	Nolan Ryan-8	Cal.	AL	1978	260

BASES ON BALLS

#	Player	Team	Lg	Year	BB
	Bob Feller-1	Cle.	AL	1938	208
	Nolan Ryan-1	Cal.	AL	1977	204
	Nolan Ryan-2	Cal.	AL	1974	202
	Bob Feller-2	Cle.	AL	1941	194
	Bobo Newsom-1	St.L.	AL	1938	192
	Sam Jones	Chi.	NL	1955	185
	Nolan Ryan-3	Cal.	AL	1976	183
	Bob Harmon	St.L.	NL	1911	181
	Bob Turley-1	Bal.	AL	1954	181
10	Tommy Byrne-1	N.Y.	AL	1949	179
11	Bob Turley-2	N.Y.	AL	1955	177
12	Bump Hadley	Chi.& St.L.	AL	1932	171
13	Elmer Myers	Phi.	AL	1916	168
14	Bobo Newsom-2	Was.& Bos.	AL	1937	167
15	Weldon Wyckoff	Phi.	AL	1915	165
16	Earl Moore	Phi.	NL	1911	164
	Phil Niekro	Atl.	NL	1977	164
18	Johnny Vander Meer	Cin.	NL	1943	162
	Nolan Ryan-4	Cal.	AL	1973	162
20	Tommy Byrne-2	N.Y.	AL	1950	160
21	Marty O'Toole	Pit.	NL	1912	159
22	Joe Coleman	Det.	AL	1974	158
23	G. Lowdermilk	St.L.& Det.	AL	1915	157
	Nolan Ryan-5	Cal.	AL	1972	157
25	Herb Score	Cle.	AL	1955	154
26	Bob Feller-3	Cle.	AL	1946	153
	Sam McDowell	Cle.	AL	1971	153
28	Wild Bill Donovan	Bkn.	NL	1901	152
	Randy Johnson	Sea.	AL	1991	152
30	J.R. Richard	Hou.	NL	1976	151
31	Tommy Byrne-3	N.Y.& St.L.	AL	1951	150

EARNED RUN AVERAGE
(Minimum to 1950 10 Complete Games; after 1950 1 inning pitched per scheduled game)

#	Player	Team	Lg	Year	ERA
	Dutch Leonard	Bos.	AL	1914	1.00
	T.F. Brown-1	Chi.	NL	1906	1.04
	Bob Gibson	St.L.	NL	1968	1.12
	Christy Mathewson-1	N.Y.	NL	1909	1.14
	Walter Johnson-1	Was.	AL	1913	1.14
	Jack Pfeister-1	Chi.	NL	1907	1.15
	Addie Joss-1	Cle.	AL	1908	1.16
	Carl Lundgren	Chi.	NL	1907	1.17
	Pete Alexander	Phi.	NL	1915	1.22
	Cy Young-1	Bos.	AL	1908	1.26
	Christy Mathewson-2	N.Y.	NL	1905	1.27
	Ed Walsh-1	Chi.	AL	1910	1.27
	Walter Johnson-2	Was.	AL	1918	1.27
	Jack Coombs	Phi.	AL	1910	1.30
	T.F. Brown-2	Chi.	NL	1909	1.31
	Jack Taylor	Chi.	NL	1902	1.33
17	Walter Johnson-3	Was.	AL	1910	1.35
18	T.F. Brown-3	Chi.	NL	1907	1.39
	Harry Krause	Phi.	AL	1909	1.39
	Walter Johnson-4	Was.	AL	1910	1.39
	Walter Johnson-5	Was.	AL	1912	1.39
22	Ed Walsh-2	Chi.	AL	1909	1.41
23	Ed Reulbach-1	Chi.	NL	1905	1.42
	Orvie Overall	Chi.	NL	1909	1.42
	Ed Walsh-3	Chi.	AL	1909	1.42
26	Christy Mathewson-3	N.Y.	NL	1908	1.43
27	T.F. Brown-4	Chi.	NL	1908	1.47
28	Rube Waddell-1	Phi.	AL	1905	1.48
29	Smoky Joe Wood	Bos.	AL	1915	1.49
	Walter Johnson-6	Was.	AL	1919	1.49
31	Doc White	Chi.	AL	1905	1.52
	George McQuillan-1	Phi.	NL	1908	1.52
33	Eddie Cicotte	Chi.	AL	1917	1.53
	Dwight Gooden	N.Y.	NL	1985	1.53
35	Pete Alexander-2	Phi.	NL	1916	1.55
	Cy Morgan	Phi.	AL	1910	1.55
	Walter Johnson-7	Was.	AL	1915	1.55
38	Jack Pfeister-2	Chi.	NL	1906	1.56
	Howie Camnitz-1	Pit.	NL	1908	1.56
	Greg Maddux	Atl.	NL	1994	1.56
41	Fred Toney	Cin.	NL	1915	1.57
42	Chief Bender	Phi.	AL	1910	1.58
	Rube Marquard	Bkn.	NL	1916	1.58
44	Addie Joss-2	Cle.	AL	1908	1.59
	Barney Pelty	St.L.	AL	1906	1.59
46	Ed Walsh-4	Chi.	AL	1907	1.60
	George McQuillan-2	Phi.	NL	1910	1.60
	Luis Tiant	Cle.	AL	1968	1.60
49	Joe McGinnity	N.Y.	NL	1904	1.61
50	Rube Waddell-2	Phi.	AL	1904	1.62
	Howie Camnitz-2	Pit.	NL	1909	1.62
	Ray Collins	Bos.	AL	1910	1.62
53	Cy Young-2	Bos.	AL	1901	1.63
54	Ed Summers	Det.	AL	1908	1.64
	Ernie Shore	Bos.	AL	1915	1.64
	Spud Chandler	N.Y.	AL	1943	1.64
57	Ed Reulbach-2	Chi.	NL	1906	1.65
	Walter Johnson-8	Was.	AL	1908	1.65
	Rube Kroh	Chi.	NL	1909	1.65
	Russ Ford	N.Y.	AL	1910	1.65
	Rube Foster	Bos.	AL	1914	1.65

GAMES PITCHED

#	Player	Team	Lg	Year	G
	Mike Marshall-1	L.A.	NL	1974	106
	Kent Tekulve-1	Pit.	NL	1979	94
	Salomon Torres	Pit.	NL	2006	94
	Mike Marshall-2	Mon.	NL	1973	93
	Kent Tekulve-2	Pit.	NL	1978	91
	Wayne Granger	Cin.	NL	1969	90
	Mike Marshall-3	Min.	NL	1979	90
	Kent Tekulve-3	Phi.	NL	1987	90
	Mark Eichhorn	Tor.	AL	1987	89
	Julian Tavarez	S.F.	NL	1997	89
	Steve Kline-1	St.L.	NL	2001	89
	Paul Quantrill-1	L.A.	NL	2003	89
	Jim Brower	Cin.	NL	2004	89
	Wilbur Wood	Chi.	AL	1968	88
	Mike Myers-1	Det.	AL	1997	88
	Sean Runyan	Det.	AL	1998	88
17	Rob Murphy	Cin.	NL	1987	87
18	Paul Quantrill-2	L.A.	NL	2002	86
	Oscar Villarreal	Ari.	NL	2003	86
	Ray King-1	St.L.	NL	2004	86
	Paul Quantrill-3	N.Y.	AL	2004	86
	Scott Eyre-1	S.F.	NL	2005	86
23	Kent Tekulve-4	Pit.	NL	1982	85
	Frank Williams	Cin.	NL	1987	85
	Mitch Williams	Tex.	AL	1987	85
	Matt Capps	Pit.	NL	2006	85
	Jon Rauch	Was.	NL	2006	85
28	Ted Abernathy	Chi.	NL	1965	84
	Enrique Romo	Pit.	NL	1979	84
	Dick Tidrow	Chi.	NL	1980	84
	Dan Quisenberry	K.C.	AL	1985	84
	Stan Belinda	Cin.	NL	1997	84
	Graeme Lloyd	Mon.	NL	2001	84
	Billy Koch	Oak.	AL	2002	84
	Rheal Cormier	Phi.	NL	2004	84
	Chris Reitsma	Atl.	NL	2004	84
	Salomon Torres	Pit.	NL	2004	84
	Bob Howry	Chi.	NL	2006	84
39	Ken Sanders	Mil.	AL	1971	83
	Craig Lefferts	S.D.	NL	1986	83
	Eddie Guardado	Min.	AL	1996	83
	Mike Myers-2	Det.	AL	1996	83
	Steve Kline-2	Mon.	NL	2000	83
	Kelly Wunsch	Chi.	AL	2000	83
	Octavio Dotel	Hou.	NL	2002	83
	Scott Eyre-2	S.F.	NL	2004	83
	Mike Stanton	N.Y.	AL	2004	83
	Scott Proctor	N.Y.	AL	2006	83
49	Eddie Fisher	Chi.	AL	1965	82
	Bill Campbell	Chi.	NL	1983	82
	Juan Agosto	Hou.	NL	1990	82
	Paul Quantrill-4	Tor.	AL	1998	82
	Steve Kline-3	Mon.	NL	1999	82
	Jeff Fassero	Chi.	NL	2001	82
	Ray King-2	Mil.	NL	2002	82
	Mike Stanton	Was.-S.F.	NL	2006	82

SINGLE SEASON LEADERS

(numbers after individual name indicates numbers of times that individual appears within a specific category)

GAMES STARTED

#	Name	Team	Lg	Year	GS
1	Jack Chesbro	N.Y.	AL	1904	51
2	Ed Walsh	Chi.	AL	1908	49
	Wilbur Wood-1	Chi.	AL	1972	49
4	Joe McGinnity	N.Y.	NL	1903	48
	Wilbur Wood-2	Chi.	AL	1973	48
6	Vic Willis	Bos.	NL	1902	46
	Rube Waddell	Phi.	AL	1904	46
	Christy Mathewson	N.Y.	NL	1904	46
	Ed Walsh-2	Chi.	AL	1907	46
	Dave Davenport	St.L.	FL	1915	46
11	Jack Powell	N.Y.	AL	1904	45
	Pete Alexander	Phi.	NL	1916	45
	Mickey Lolich	Det.	AL	1971	45

COMPLETE GAMES

#	Name	Team	Lg	Year	CG
1	Jack Chesbro	N.Y.	AL	1904	48
2	Vic Willis	Bos.	NL	1902	45
3	Joe McGinnity	N.Y.	NL	1903	44
4	George Mullin	Det.	AL	1904	42
	Ed Walsh	Chi.	AL	1908	42
6	Noodles Hahn	Cin.	NL	1901	41
	Cy Young-1	Bos.	AL	1902	41
	Irv Young	Bos.	NL	1905	41
9	Cy Young-2	Bos.	AL	1904	40

INNINGS PITCHED

#	Name	Team	Lg	Year	IP
1	Ed Walsh-1	Chi.	AL	1908	464
2	Jack Chesbro	N.Y.	AL	1904	455
3	Joe McGinnity-1	N.Y.	NL	1903	434
4	Ed Walsh-2	Chi.	AL	1907	422
5	Vic Willis	Bos.	NL	1902	410
6	Joe McGinnity-2	N.Y.	NL	1904	408
7	Ed Walsh-3	Chi.	AL	1912	393
	Dave Davenport	St.L.	FL	1915	393
9	Christy Mathewson-1	N.Y.	NL	1908	391
10	Jack Powell	N.Y.	AL	1904	390
11	Togie Pittinger	Bos.	NL	1902	389
	Pete Alexander-1	Phi.	NL	1916	389
13	Pete Alexander-2	Phi.	NL	1917	388
14	Cy Young-1	Bos.	AL	1902	385
15	Rube Waddell	Phi.	AL	1904	383
16	Joe McGinnity-3	Bal.	AL	1901	382
	George Mullin	Det.	AL	1904	382
18	Cy Young-2	Bos.	AL	1904	380
19	Irv Young	Bos.	NL	1905	378
20	Oscar Jones	Bkn.	NL	1904	377
	Cy Falkenberg	Ind.	FL	1914	377
	Wilbur Wood	Chi.	AL	1972	377
23	Pete Alexander-3	Phi.	NL	1915	376
	Mickey Lokich	Det.	AL	1971	376
25	Noodles Hahn	Cin.	NL	1901	375
26	Walter Johnson-1	Was.	AL	1910	374
27	Walter Johnson-2	Was.	AL	1914	372
28	Cy Young-3	Bos.	AL	1901	371
	Bill Dinneen	Bos.	NL	1902	371
	Walter Johnson-3	Was.	AL	1916	371
	Bob Feller	Cle.	AL	1946	371
32	Ed Walsh-4	Chi.	AL	1910	370
33	Ed Walsh-5	Chi.	AL	1911	369
34	Christy Mathewson-2	N.Y.	NL	1904	368
	Walter Johnson-4	Was.	AL	1912	368
36	Pete Alexander-4	Phi.	NL	1911	367
37	Christy Mathewson-3	N.Y.	NL	1903	366
38	Frank Smith	Chi.	AL	1909	365
39	Pete Alexander-5	Phi.	NL	1920	363
40	Claude Hendrix	Chi.	FL	1914	362
41	George McQuillan	Phi.	NL	1908	360

FEWEST HITS ALLOWED PER 9 INNINGS PITCHED
(Minimum - 1 inning pitched per scheduled game)

#	Name	Team	Lg	Year	H/9
1	Nolan Ryan-1	Cal.	AL	1972	5.26
2	Luis Tiant	Cle.	AL	1968	5.30
3	Nolan Ryan-2	Tex.	AL	1991	5.31
4	Pedro Martinez-1	Bos.	AL	2000	5.31
5	Ed Reulbach	Chi.	NL	1906	5.33
6	Dutch Leonard	Bos.	AL	1914	5.57
7	Carl Lundgren	Chi.	NL	1907	5.65
8	Sid Fernandez-1	N.Y.	NL	1985	5.71
9	Tommy Byrne	N.Y.	AL	1949	5.74
10	Dave McNally	Bal.	AL	1968	5.77
11	Sandy Koufax-1	L.A.	NL	1965	5.79
12	Russ Ford	N.Y.	AL	1910	5.83
13	Hideo Nomo	L.A.	NL	1995	5.83
14	Al Downing	N.Y.	AL	1963	5.84
15	Herb Score	Cle.	AL	1956	5.85
16	Bob Gibson	St.L.	NL	1968	5.85
17	Sam McDowell-1	Cle.	AL	1965	5.87
18	Ed Walsh	Chi.	AL	1910	5.89
19	Pedro Martinez-2	Mon.	NL	1997	5.89
20	Mike Scott	Hou.	NL	1986	5.95
21	Mario Soto	Cin.	NL	1980	5.96
22	Floyd Youmans	Mon.	NL	1986	5.96
23	Nolan Ryan-3	Cal.	AL	1977	5.96
24	Nolan Ryan-4	Cal.	AL	1974	5.98
25	Nolan Ryan-5	Hou.	NL	1981	5.98
26	Nolan Ryan-6	Hou.	NL	1986	6.02
27	Sam McDowell-2	Cle.	AL	1966	6.02
28	Vida Blue	Oak.	AL	1971	6.03
29	Walter Johnson	Was.	AL	1913	6.03
30	Nolan Ryan-7	Tex.	AL	1990	6.04
31	Pete Alexander	Phi.	NL	1915	6.05
32	Sam McDowell-3	Cle.	AL	1968	6.06
33	Joe Horlen	Chi.	AL	1964	6.07
34	Andy Messersmith	Cal.	AL	1969	6.08
35	Nolan Ryan-8	Tex.	AL	1989	6.09
36	Stan Coveleski	Cle.	AL	1917	6.09
37	Catfish Hunter	Oak.	AL	1972	6.09
38	Nolan Ryan-9	Cal.	AL	1976	6.11
39	Sid Fernandez-2	N.Y.	NL	1988	6.11
40	Bob Turley-1	N.Y.	AL	1957	6.12
41	Bob Turley-2	N.Y.	AL	1955	6.13
42	Don Sutton	L.A.	NL	1972	6.14
43	Nolan Ryan-10	Hou.	NL	1983	6.14
44	Ron Guidry	N.Y.	AL	1978	6.15
45	Johan Santana	Min.	AL	2004	6.16
46	Three Finger Brown	Chi.	NL	1908	6.17
47	Sandy Koufax-2	L.A.	NL	1963	6.19
48	Randy Johnson	Sea.	AL	1997	6.21
49	Sandy Koufax-3	L.A.	NL	1964	6.22

MOST STRIKEOUTS PER 9 INNINGS PITCHED
(Minimum- 1 inning pitched per scheduled game)

#	Name	Team	Lg	Year	SO/9
1	Randy Johnson-1	Ari.	NL	2001	13.41
2	Pedro Martinez-1	Bos.	AL	1999	13.20
3	Kerry Wood-1	Chi.	NL	1998	12.58
4	Randy Johnson-2	Ari.	NL	2000	12.56
5	Randy Johnson-3	Sea.	AL	1995	12.35
6	Randy Johnson-4	Sea.	AL	1997	12.30
7	Randy Johnson-5	Sea. AL Hou.	NL	1998	12.12
8	Randy Johnson-6	Ari.	NL	1999	12.06
9	Pedro Martinez-2	Bos.	AL	2000	11.78
10	Randy Johnson-7	Ari.	NL	2002	11.56
11	Nolan Ryan-1	Hou.	NL	1987	11.48
12	Dwight Gooden	N.Y.	NL	1984	11.39
13	Pedro Martinez-3	Mon.	NL	1997	11.37
14	Kerry Wood-2	Chi.	NL	2003	11.35
15	Nolan Ryan-2	Tex.	AL	1989	11.32
16	Curt Schilling-1	Phi.	NL	1997	11.29
17	Kerry Wood-3	Chi.	NL	2001	11.20
18	Hideo Nomo-1	L.A.	NL	1995	11.10
19	Oliver Perez	Pit.	NL	2004	10.97
20	Curt Schilling-2	Ari.	NL	2002	10.97
21	Randy Johnson-8	Sea.	AL	1993	10.86
22	Pedro Martinez-4	Bos.	AL	2002	10.79
23	Sam McDowell-1	Cle.	AL	1965	10.71
24	Randy Johnson-9	Sea.	AL	1994	10.67
25	Randy Johnson-10	Ari.	NL	2004	10.62
26	Nolan Ryan-3	Cal.	AL	1973	10.57
27	Nolan Ryan-4	Cal.	AL	1991	10.56
28	Sandy Koufax-1	L.A.	NL	1962	10.55
29	Johan Santana	Min.	AL	2004	10.46
30	Mark Prior	Chi.	NL	2003	10.43
31	Nolan Ryan-5	Cal.	AL	1972	10.43
32	Sam McDowell-2	Cle.	AL	1966	10.42
33	Roger Clemens	Tor.	AL	1998	10.39
34	Curt Schilling-3	Ari.	NL	2003	10.39
35	Nolan Ryan-6	Cal.	AL	1976	10.35
36	Randy Johnson-11	Sea.	AL	1992	10.31
37	Curt Schilling-4	Ari.	NL	2001	10.27
38	Nolan Ryan-7	Cal.	AL	1977	10.26
39	David Cone	N.Y.	AL	1997	10.25
40	Sandy Koufax-2	L.A.	NL	1965	10.24
41	Nolan Ryan-8	Tex.	AL	1990	10.24
42	Randy Johnson-12	Sea.	AL	1991	10.19
43	Bartolo Colon	Cle.	AL	2000	10.15
44	Sandy Koufax-3	L.A.	NL	1960	10.13
45	Hideo Nomo-2	L.A.	NL	1997	10.11
46	Curt Schilling-5	Phi.	NL	1998	10.05
47	Jason Schmidt	S.F.	NL	2004	10.04
48	Ben Sheets	Mil.	NL	2004	10.03
49	Mike Scott	Hou.	NL	1986	10.00
50	Hideo Nomo-3	Bos.	AL	2001	10.00

SAVES

#	Name	Team	Lg	Year	SV
1	Bobby Thigpen	Chi.	AL	1990	57
2	John Smoltz-1	Atl.	NL	2002	55
	Eric Gagne-1	L.A.	NL	2003	55
4	Randy Myers-1	Chi.	NL	1993	53
	Trevor Hoffman-1	S.D.	NL	1998	53
	Mariano Rivera-1	N.Y.	AL	2004	53
7	Eric Gagne-2	L.A.	NL	2002	52
8	Dennis Eckersley-1	Oak.	AL	1992	51
	Rod Beck-1	Chi.	NL	1998	51
10	Mariano Rivera-2	N.Y.	AL	2001	50
11	Francisco Cordero	Tex.	AL	2004	49
12	Dennis Eckersley-2	Oak.	AL	1990	48
	Rod Beck-2	S.F.	NL	1993	48
	Jeff Shaw-1	Cin.-L.A.	NL	1998	48
15	Lee Smith-1	St.L.	NL	1991	47
	Armando Benitez-1	Fla.	NL	2004	47
	Jason Isringhausen	St.L.	NL	2004	47
	Chad Cordero	Was.	NL	2005	47
20	Francisco Rodriguez-1	L.A.	AL	2006	47
	Dave Righetti	N.Y.	AL	1986	46
	Bryan Harvey-1	Cal.	AL	1991	46
	Lee Smith-2	St.L. NL N.Y.	AL	1993	46
	Jose Mesa-1	Cle.	AL	1995	46
	Tom Gordon	Bos.	AL	1998	46
	Mike Williams	Pit.	NL	2002	46
	Trevor Hoffman-2	S.D.	NL	2006	46
25	Dan Quisenberry-1	K.C.	AL	1983	45
	Bruce Sutter	St.L.	NL	1984	45
	Dennis Eckersley-3	Oak.	AL	1988	45
	Bryan Harvey-2	Fla.	NL	1993	45
	Jeff Montgomery	K.C.	AL	1993	45
	Duane Ward	Tor.	AL	1993	45
	Randy Myers-2	Bal.	AL	1997	45
	Mariano Rivera-3	N.Y.	AL	1999	45
	Antonio Alfonseca	Fla.	NL	2000	45
	Robb Nen-1	S.F.	NL	2001	45
	Kazuhiro Sasaki	Sea.	AL	2001	45
	Eddie Guardado	Min.	AL	2002	45
	Jose Mesa-2	Phi.	NL	2002	45
	John Smoltz-2	Atl.	NL	2003	45
	Eric Gagne-3	L.A.	NL	2004	45
	Francisco Rodriguez-2	L.A.	AL	2005	45
	Bob Wickman	Cle.	AL	2005	45
42	Dan Quisenberry-2	K.C.	AL	1984	44
	Mark Davis	S.D.	NL	1989	44
	Jeff Brantley	Cin.	NL	1996	44
	Todd Worrell	L.A.	NL	1996	44
	Billy Koch	Oak.	AL	2002	44
	Billy Wagner	Hou.	NL	2003	44
	Joe Nathan-1	Min.	AL	2004	44
	John Smoltz-3	Atl.	NL	2004	44
50	Doug Jones	Cle.	AL	1990	43
	Dennis Eckersley-4	Oak.	AL	1991	43
	Lee Smith-3	St.L.	NL	1992	43
	John Wetteland-1	Mon.	NL	1993	43
	Mitch Williams	Phi.	NL	1993	43
	John Wetteland-2	N.Y.	AL	1996	43
	Mariano Rivera-4	N.Y.	AL	1997	43
	Roberto Hernandez	T.B.	AL	1999	43
	John Wetteland-3	Tex.	AL	1999	43
	Trevor Hoffman-3	S.D.	NL	2000	43
	Armando Benitez-2	N.Y.	NL	2001	43
	Trevor Hoffman-4	S.D.	NL	2001	43
	Jeff Shaw-2	L.A.	NL	2001	43
	Robb Nen-2	S.F.	NL	2002	43
	Keith Foulke	Oak.	AL	2003	43
	Jose Mesa-3	Pit.	NL	2004	43
	Trevor Hoffman-4	S.D.	NL	2005	43
	Joe Nathan-2	Min.	AL	2005	43
	Mariano Rivera-5	N.Y.	AL	2005	43

SHUTOUTS

#	Name	Team	Lg	Year	SHO
1	Pete Alexander-1	Phi.	NL	1916	16
2	Jack Coombs	Phi.	AL	1910	13
	Bob Gibson	St.L.	NL	1968	13
4	Walter Johnson-1	Was.	AL	1913	12
	Pete Alexander-2	Phi.	NL	1915	12
6	Ed Walsh-1	Chi.	AL	1908	11
	Christy Mathewson	N.Y.	NL	1908	11
	Sandy Koufax	L.A.	NL	1963	11
	Dean Chance	L.A.	AL	1964	11
10	Cy Young	Bos.	AL	1904	10
	Ed Walsh-2	Chi.	AL	1906	10
	Smokey Joe Wood	Bos.	AL	1912	10
	Walter Johnson-2	Was.	AL	1914	10
	Dave Davenport	St.L.	FL	1915	10
	Carl Hubbell	N.Y.	NL	1933	10
	Mort Cooper	St.L.	NL	1942	10
	Bob Feller	Cle.	AL	1946	10
	Bob Lemon	Cle.	AL	1948	10
	Juan Marichal	S.F.	NL	1965	10
	Jim Palmer	Bal.	AL	1975	10
	John Tudor	St.L.	NL	1985	10

LIFETIME LEADERS - BATTING
Players with lifetime BATTING AVERAGE of .300 of higher
(Minimum of 10 major league seasons and 4000 At Bats)

#		FIRST	LAST	AB	HITS	B.A.
1	Ty Cobb	1905	1928	11436	4189	.366
2	Rogers Hornsby	1915	1937	8173	2930	.358
3	Joe Jackson	1908	1920	4981	1774	.356
4	Pete Browning	1882	1894	4795	1664	.347
5	Ed Delahanty	1888	1903	7493	2593	.346
6	Willie Keeler	1892	1910	8570	2955	.345
7	Tris Speaker	1907	1928	10197	3514	.345
8	Billy Hamilton	1888	1901	6262	2157	.344
9	Ted Williams	1939	1960	7706	2654	.344
10	Dan Brouthers	1879	1904	6682	2288	.342
11	Jesse Burkett	1890	1905	8389	2872	.342
12	Babe Ruth	1914	1935	8399	2873	.342
13	Harry Heilmann	1914	1932	7787	2660	.342
14	Bill Terry	1923	1936	6428	2193	.341
15	George Sisler	1915	1930	8267	2812	.340
16	Lou Gehrig	1921	1939	8001	2721	.340
17	Nap Lajoie	1896	1916	9593	3245	.338
18	Tony Gwynn	1982	2001	9288	3141	.338
19	Riggs Stephenson	1921	1934	4508	1515	.336
20	Al Simmons	1924	1944	8761	2927	.334
21	Paul Waner	1926	1945	9459	3152	.333
22	Eddie Collins	1906	1930	9951	3315	.333
23	**Todd Helton**	**1997**		**5106**	**1700**	**.333**
24	Sam Thompson	1885	1906	5972	1984	.332
25	Cap Anson	1786	1897	9104	3012	.331
26	Stan Musial	1941	1963	10972	3630	.331
27	Heinie Manush	1923	1939	7653	2524	.330
28	Hugh Duffy	1888	1906	7026	2313	.329
29	Wade Boggs	1982	1999	9180	3010	.328
30	Rod Carew	1967	1985	9315	3053	.328
31	Honus Wagner	1897	1917	10439	3420	.328
32	Tip O'Neill	1883	1892	4254	1389	.327
33	Jimmie Foxx	1925	1945	8134	2646	.325
34	Earle Combs	1924	1935	5748	1866	.325
35	**Vladimir Guerrero**	**1996**		**5502**	**1786**	**.325**
36	Joe DiMaggio	1936	1951	6821	2214	.325
37	Babe Herman	1926	1945	5603	1818	.324
38	Joe Medwick	1932	1948	7635	2471	.324
39	Danny Lyons	1885	1897	4236	1368	.323
40	Edd Roush	1912	1931	7361	2377	.323
41	Sam Rice	1915	1934	9269	2987	.322
42	Ross Youngs	1917	1926	4627	1491	.322
43	Joe Kelley	1891	1908	6989	2245	.321
44	Kiki Cuyler	1921	1936	7161	2299	.321
45	Charlie Gehringer	1924	1942	8860	2839	.320
46	Chuck Klein	1928	1944	6486	2076	.320
47	Pie Traynor	1920	1937	7559	2416	.320
48	Mickey Cochrane	1925	1937	5169	1652	.320
49	George Van Haltren	1887	1903	8007	2558	.319
50	Ken Williams	1915	1929	4860	1552	.319
51	Roger Connor	1880	1897	7732	2460	.318
52	**Nomar Garciaparra**	**1996**		**4832**	**1537**	**.318**
53	Kirby Puckett	1984	1995	7244	2304	.318
54	Earl Averill	1929	1941	6359	2020	.318
55	Arky Vaughan	1932	1948	6622	2103	.318
56	Roberto Clemente	1955	1972	9454	3000	.317
57	Chick Hafey	1924	1937	4625	1466	.317
58	Zack Wheat	1909	1927	9106	2884	.317
59	**Derek Jeter**	**1995**		**6790**	**2150**	**.317**
60	Lloyd Waner	1927	1945	7772	2459	.316
61	Frankie Frisch	1919	1937	9112	2880	.316
62	Goose Goslin	1921	1938	8654	2735	.316
63	Elmer Flick	1898	1910	5597	1765	.315
64	**Manny Ramirez**	**1993**		**6575**	**2066**	**.314**
65	Bibb Falk	1920	1931	4656	1463	.314
66	Cecil Travis	1933	1947	4914	1544	.314
67	Mike Tieman	1887	1899	5878	1843	.314
68	Hank Greenberg	1930	1947	5193	1628	.313
69	Hughie Jennings	1891	1918	4884	1530	.313
70	Jack Fournier	1912	1927	5207	1631	.313
71	Elmer Smith	1886	1901	4675	1462	.313
72	Larry Walker	1989	2005	6907	2160	.313
73	Bill Dickey	1928	1946	6300	1969	.313
74	Cupid Childs	1888	1901	5624	1757	.312
75	Jim O'Rourke	1876	1904	7368	2300	.312
76	Johnny Mize	1936	1953	6443	2011	.312
77	Joe Sewell	1920	1933	7132	2226	.312
78	Fred Clarke	1894	1915	8584	2678	.312
79	Barney McCosky	1939	1953	4172	1301	.312
80	Bing Miller	1921	1936	6212	1937	.312
81	Edgar Martinez	1987	2004	7213	2247	.312
82	Fred Lindstrom	1924	1936	5611	1747	.311
83	Jackie Robinson	1947	1956	4877	1518	.311
84	Baby Doll Jackson	1915	1927	5507	1714	.311
85	Rip Radcliff	1934	1943	4074	1267	.311
86	Ginger Beaumont	1899	1910	5647	1754	.311
87	Irish Meusel	1914	1927	4900	1521	.310
88	Luke Appling	1930	1950	8857	2749	.310
89	Bobby Veach	1912	1925	6659	2064	.310
90	John Stone	1928	1938	4490	1391	.310
91	Jim Bottomley	1922	1937	7471	2313	.310
92	Sam Crawford	1899	1917	9579	2964	.309
93	**Mike Piazza**	**1992**		**6602**	**2042**	**.309**
94	Bob Meusel	1920	1930	5475	1693	.309
95	Jack Beckley	1888	1907	9476	2930	.309
96	Jimmy Ryan	1885	1903	8165	2524	.309
97	Ted Larkin	1884	1893	4691	1450	.309
98	Jack Tobin	1914	1927	6173	1908	.309
99	Spud Davis	1928	1945	4255	1312	.308
100	Richie Ashburn	1948	1962	8365	2574	.308
101	Steve Brodie	1890	1902	5686	1749	.308
102	Stuffy McInnis	1909	1927	7822	2406	.308
103	Don Mattingly	1982	1996	7003	2153	.307
104	Joe Vosmik	1930	1944	5472	1682	.307
105	Harry Stovey	1880	1893	6072	1866	.307
106	King Kelly	1878	1893	5901	1813	.307
107	Frank Baker	1908	1922	5985	1838	.307
108	Buck Ewing	1880	1897	5318	1633	.307
109	George Burns	1914	1929	6573	2018	.307
110	Matty Alou	1960	1974	5789	1777	.307
111	Hack Wilson	1923	1934	4760	1461	.307
112	Johnny Pesky	1942	1954	4745	1455	.307
113	Chick Stahl	1897	1906	5062	1552	.307
114	George Kell	1943	1957	6702	2054	.306
115	Paul Molitor	1978	1998	10835	3319	.306
116	Dixie Walker	1931	1949	6740	2064	.306
117	Ernie Lombardi	1931	1947	5855	1792	.306
118	Ralph Garr	1968	1980	5108	1562	.306
119	**Alex Rodriguez**	**1994**		**6767**	**2067**	**.305**
120	**Magglio Ordonez**	**1997**		**4705**	**1436**	**.305**
121	Hank Aaron	1954	1976	12364	3771	.305
122	George Brett	1973	1993	10347	3154	.305
123	**Frank Thomas**	**1990**		**7422**	**2262**	**.305**
124	Bill Madlock	1973	1987	6594	2008	.305
125	**Chipper Jones**	**1993**		**6385**	**1944**	**.304**
126	Billy Herman	1931	1947	7707	2345	.304
127	Tony Oliva	1961	1976	6301	1917	.304
128	Patsy Donovan	1890	1907	7450	2266	.304
129	Mel Ott	1926	1947	9456	2876	.304
130	Cy Seymour	1896	1913	5657	1720	.304
131	**Ivan Rodriguez**	**1991**		**7745**	**2354**	**.304**
132	Ed McKean	1887	1899	6842	2079	.304
133	Curt Walker	1919	1930	4858	1475	.304
134	Deacon White	1876	1890	5294	1607	.304
135	Will Clark	1986	2000	7173	2176	.303
136	Charlie Jamieson	1915	1932	6560	1990	.303
137	Mark Grace	1988	2003	8065	2445	.303
138	Jake Daubert	1910	1924	7673	2326	.303
139	Al Oliver	1968	1985	9049	2743	.303
140	Pete Rose	1963	1986	14053	4256	.303
141	Mike Greenwell	1985	1996	4623	1400	.303
142	Buddy Myer	1925	1941	7038	2131	.303
143	Harvey Kuenn	1952	1966	6913	2092	.303
144	George Gore	1879	1892	5324	1611	.303
145	Hal Trosky	1933	1946	5161	1561	.302
146	**Bobby Abreu**	**1996**		**5276**	**1595**	**.302**
147	George Grantham	1922	1934	4989	1508	.302
148	Ben Chapman	1930	1946	6478	1958	.302
149	**Sean Casey**	**1997**		**4414**	**1333**	**.302**
150	Carl Reynolds	1927	1939	4495	1357	.302
151	Tommy Holmes	1942	1952	4992	1507	.302
152	**Mike Sweeney**	**1995**		**4404**	**1329**	**.302**
153	Willie Mays	1951	1973	10881	3283	.302
154	Jack Doyle	1889	1905	6013	1814	.302
155	Joe Cronin	1926	1945	7577	2285	.302
156	Stan Hack	1932	1947	7278	2193	.301
157	**Jason Kendall**	**1996**		**5759**	**1735**	**.301**
158	**Moises Alou**	**1990**		**6660**	**2005**	**.301**
159	Oyster Burns	1884	1895	4615	1388	.301
160	**Jose Vidro**	**1997**		**4257**	**1280**	**.301**
161	Mike Griffin	1887	1896	5908	1775	.300
162	Paul Hines	1876	1891	6207	1864	.300
163	Roberto Alomar	1988	2004	9073	2724	.300
164	Wally Berger	1930	1940	5163	1550	.300
165	Pedro Guerrero	1978	1992	5392	1618	.300
166	Ethan Allen	1926	1938	4418	1325	.300
167	Enos Slaughter	1938	1959	7946	2383	.300
168	Hardy Richardson	1879	1892	5593	1676	.300

PLAYERS WITH 2200 or more HITS

#		FIRST	LAST	HITS
1	Pete Rose	1963	1986	4256
2	Ty Cobb	1905	1928	4189
3	Hank Aaron	1954	1976	3771
4	Stan Musial	1941	1963	3630
5	Tris Speaker	1907	1928	3514
6	Honus Wagner	1897	1917	3420
7	Carl Yastrzemski	1961	1983	3419
8	Paul Molitor	1978	1998	3319
9	Eddie Collins	1906	1930	3315
10	Willie Mays	1951	1973	3283
11	Eddie Murray	1977	1997	3255
12	Nap Lajoie	1896	1916	3245
13	Cal Ripken	1981	2001	3184
14	George Brett	1973	1993	3154
15	Paul Waner	1926	1945	3152
16	Robin Yount	1974	1993	3142
17	Tony Gwynn	1982	2001	3141
18	Dave Winfield	1973	1995	3110
19	Rickey Henderson	1979	2003	3055
20	Rod Carew	1967	1985	3053
21	Lou Brock	1961	1979	3023
22	Rafael Palmeiro	1986	2005	3020
23	Cap Anson	1876	1897	3012
24	Wade Boggs	1982	1999	3010
25	Al Kaline	1953	1974	3007
26	Roberto Clemente	1955	1972	3000
27	Sam Rice	1915	1934	2987
28	Sam Crawford	1899	1917	2964
29	Willie Keeler	1892	1910	2955
30	Frank Robinson	1956	1976	2943
31	Jack Beckley	1888	1907	2930
	Rogers Hornsby	1915	1937	2930
	Craig Biggio	**1988**		**2930**
34	Al Simmons	1924	1944	2927
35	Zack Wheat	1909	1927	2884
36	Frankie Frisch	1919	1937	2880
37	Mel Ott	1926	1947	2876
38	Babe Ruth	1914	1935	2873
39	Jesse Burkett	1890	1905	2872
40	Harold Baines	1980	2001	2866
41	Brooks Robinson	1955	1977	2848
42	**Barry Bonds**	**1986**		**2841**
43	Charlie Gehringer	1924	1942	2839
44	George Sisler	1915	1930	2812
45	Andre Dawson	1976	1996	2774
46	Vada Pinson	1958	1975	2757
47	Luke Appling	1930	1950	2749
48	Al Oliver	1968	1985	2743
49	Goose Goslin	1921	1938	2735
50	Tony Perez	1964	1986	2732
51	Roberto Alomar	1988	2004	2724
52	Lou Gehrig	1921	1939	2721
53	Rusty Staub	1963	1985	2716
54	Bill Buckner	1969	1990	2715
55	Dave Parker	1973	1991	2712
56	Billy Williams	1959	1976	2711
57	Doc Cramer	1929	1948	2705
58	George Davis	1890	1909	2683
59	Fred Clarke	1894	1915	2678
60	Luis Aparicio	1956	1973	2677
61	Max Carey	1910	1929	2665
62	Nellie Fox	1947	1965	2663
63	Harry Heilmann	1914	1932	2660
64	Ted Williams	1939	1960	2654
65	Jimmie Foxx	1925	1945	2646
66	Lave Cross	1887	1907	2645
67	Rabbit Maranville	1912	1935	2605
	Tim Raines	1979	2002	2605
69	Steve Garvey	1969	1987	2599
70	Ed Delahanty	1888	1903	2593
71	Reggie Jackson	1967	1987	2584
72	Ernie Banks	1953	1971	2583
73	Richie Ashburn	1948	1962	2574
74	**Julio Franco**	**1982**		**2566**
75	Willie Davis	1960	1979	2561
76	George Van Haltren	1887	1903	2558
77	**Steve Finley**	**1989**		**2531**
78	Jimmy Ryan	1885	1903	2524
	Heinie Manush	1923	1939	2524
80	Joe Morgan	1963	1984	2517
81	Buddy Bell	1972	1989	2514
82	Mickey Vernon	1939	1960	2495
83	Fred McGriff	1986	2004	2490
84	Bill Dahlen	1891	1911	2478
85	Ted Simmons	1968	1988	2472
	Omar Vizquel	**1989**		**2472**
87	Joe Medwick	1932	1948	2471
88	Harry Hooper	1909	1925	2466
89	Roger Connor	1880	1897	2460
	Ozzie Smith	1978	1996	2460
91	Lloyd Waner	1927	1945	2459
92	Jim Rice	1974	1989	2452
93	Red Schoendienst	1945	1963	2449
94	Dwight Evans	1972	1991	2446
95	Mark Grace	1988	2003	2445
96	Pie Traynor	1920	1937	2416
97	Mickey Mantle	1951	1968	2415
98	**Ken Griffey Jr.**	**1989**		**2412**
99	Stuffy McInnis	1909	1927	2406
100	**Gary Sheffield**	**1988**		**2390**
101	Ryne Sandberg	1981	1997	2386
102	Enos Slaughter	1938	1959	2383
103	Chili Davis	1981	1999	2380
104	Edd Roush	1912	1931	2377
105	Brett Butler	1981	1997	2375
106	**Luis Gonzalez**	**1990**		**2373**
107	Lou Whitaker	1977	1995	2369
108	Alan Trammell	1977	1996	2365
109	Carlton Fisk	1969	1993	2356
110	**Ivan Rodriguez**	**1991**		**2354**
111	Joe Judge	1915	1934	2352
112	Orlando Cepeda	1958	1974	2351
113	Billy Herman	1931	1947	2345
114	Joe Torre	1960	1977	2342
115	Barry Larkin	1986	2004	2340
116	**Bernie Williams**	**1991**		**2336**
117	Andres Galarraga	1985	2004	2333
118	Jake Daubert	1910	1924	2326
	Dave Concepcion	1970	1988	2326
	B.J. Surhoff	1987	2005	2326
121	Eddie Mathews	1952	1968	2315
122	Jeff Bagwell	1991	2005	2314
123	Hugh Duffy	1888	1906	2313
	Jim Bottomley	1922	1937	2313
125	Bobby Wallace	1894	1918	2306
126	Kirby Puckett	1984	1995	2304
	Sammy Sosa	1989	2005	2304
128	Jim O'Rourke	1876	1904	2300
129	Charlie Grimm	1916	1936	2299
	Kiki Cuyler	1921	1936	2299
131	Dan Brouthers	1879	1904	2288
132	Biddy McPhee	1882	1899	2287
133	Joe Cronin	1926	1945	2285
134	**Kenny Lofton**	**1991**		**2283**
135	Gary Gaetti	1981	2000	2280
136	Tony Fernandez	1983	2001	2276
137	Patsy Donovan	1890	1907	2266
138	**Frank Thomas**	**1990**		**2262**
139	Jimmy Dykes	1918	1939	2256
140	Ron Santo	1960	1974	2254
	Willie McGee	1982	1999	2254
142	Jose Cruz	1970	1988	2251
	Marquis Grissom	1989	2005	2251
144	Bert Campaneris	1964	1983	2249
145	Tommy Corcoran	1890	1907	2248
146	Edgar Martinez	1987	2004	2247
147	Joe Kelley	1891	1908	2245
148	Fred Tenney	1894	1911	2239
	John Olerud	1989	2005	2239
150	Mike Schmidt	1972	1989	2234
151	Willie Stargell	1962	1982	2232
152	Joe Sewell	1920	1933	2226
153	Graig Nettles	1967	1988	2225
154	Darrell Evans	1969	1989	2223
155	Joe DiMaggio	1936	1951	2214
156	Joe Kuhel	1930	1947	2212
157	Willie McCovey	1959	1980	2211
158	Willie Randolph	1975	1992	2210
159	Willie Wilson	1976	1994	2207

Players active at the end of 2006 are shown in bold face

LIFETIME LEADERS - BATTING
Players with a lifetime SLUGGING AVERAGE of .510 or higher
(Minimum of 10 major league seasons and 4000 At Bats)

#		FIRST	LAST	AB	TB	SA	#		FIRST	LAST	AB	TB	SA	#		FIRST	LAST	AB	TB	SA
1	Babe Ruth	1914	1935	8399	5793	.690	23	Ken Griffey Jr.	1989		8298	4622	.557	45	Mike Schmidt	1972	1989	8352	4404	.527
2	Ted Williams	1939	1960	7706	4884	.634	24	Mickey Mantle	1951	1968	8102	4511	.557	46	Richie Sexson	1997		4214	2218	.526
3	Lou Gehrig	1923	1939	8001	5059	.632	25	Hank Aaron	1954	1976	12364	6856	.555	47	Chick Hafey	1924	1937	4625	2433	.526
4	Jimmie Foxx	1925	1945	8134	4956	.609	26	Mike Piazza	1992		6602	3640	.551	48	Gary Sheffield	1988		8037	4221	.525
5	Barry Bonds	1986		9507	5784	.608	27	Ralph Kiner	1946	1955	5205	2852	.548	49	Brian Giles	1995		5260	2762	.525
6	Hank Greenberg	1930	1947	5193	3142	.605	28	Hack Wilson	1923	1934	4760	2593	.545	50	Mo Vaughn	1991	2003	5532	2894	.523
7	Manny Ramirez	1993		6575	3946	.600	29	Chuck Klein	1928	1944	6486	3522	.543	51	Hal Trosky	1933	1946	5161	2692	.522
8	Todd Helton	1997		5106	3029	.593	30	Chipper Jones	1993		6385	3458	.542	52	Wally Berger	1930	1940	5163	2693	.522
9	Mark McGwire	1986	2001	6187	3639	.588	31	Jason Giambi	1995		5620	3040	.541	53	Joe Jackson	1908	1920	4981	2597	.521
10	Vladimir Guerrero	1996		5502	3206	.583	32	Jeff Bagwell	1991	2005	7797	4213	.540	54	Harry Heilmann	1914	1932	7787	4053	.520
11	Rogers Hornsby	1915	1937	8137	4712	.577	33	Nomar Garciaparra	1996		4832	2610	.540	55	Dan Brouthers	1879	1904	6682	3476	.520
12	Joe DiMaggio	1936	1951	6821	3948	.579	34	Duke Snider	1947	1964	7161	3865	.540	56	Kevin Mitchell	1984	1998	4134	2149	.520
13	Alex Rodriguez	1994		6767	3875	.573	35	Jim Edmonds	1993		5907	3181	.539	57	Moises Alou	1990		6660	3438	.516
14	Frank Thomas	1990		7422	4203	.566	36	Frank Robinson	1956	1976	10006	5373	.537	58	Edgar Martinez	1987	2004	7213	3718	.515
15	Larry Walker	1989	2005	6907	3904	.565	37	Sammy Sosa	1989	2005	8401	4511	.537	59	Scott Rolen	1996		5106	2629	.515
16	Jim Thome	1991		6409	3620	.565	38	Al Simmons	1924	1944	8761	4685	.535	60	Willie McCovey	1959	1980	8197	4219	.515
17	Albert Belle	1989	2000	5853	3300	.564	39	Dick Allen	1963	1977	6332	3379	.534	61	Jose Canseco	1985	2001	7057	3631	.515
18	Johnny Mize	1936	1953	6443	3621	.562	40	Earl Averill	1929	1941	6359	3391	.533	62	Rafael Palmeiro	1986	2005	10472	5388	.515
19	Juan Gonzalez	1989	2005	6556	3676	.561	41	Mel Ott	1926	1947	9456	5041	.533	63	Magglio Ordonez	1997		4705	2414	.513
20	Stan Musial	1941	1963	10972	6134	.559	42	Babe Herman	1926	1945	5603	2980	.532	64	Ty Cobb	1905	1928	11436	5859	.512
21	Carlos Delgado	1993		6053	3376	.558	43	Ken Williams	1915	1929	4860	2579	.531	65	Ellis Burks	1987	2004	7232	3691	.510
22	Willie Mays	1951	1973	10881	6066	.557	44	Willie Stargell	1962	1982	7929	4190	.528							

Players with 1500 or more RUNS SCORED

#		FIRST	LAST	RUNS	#		FIRST	LAST	RUNS	#		FIRST	LAST	RUNS	#		FIRST	LAST	RUNS
1	Rickey Henderson	1979	2003	2295	16	Paul Molitor	1978	1998	1782	31	Cal Ripken	1981	2001	1647	46	Hugh Duffy	1888	1906	1555
2	Ty Cobb	1905	1928	2246	17	Craig Biggio	1988		1776	32	Jimmy Ryan	1885	1903	1640	47	Reggie Jackson	1967	1987	1551
3	Babe Ruth	1914	1935	2174	18	Charlie Gehringer	1924	1942	1774	33	Robin Yount	1974	1993	1632	48	George Davis	1890	1909	1546
	Hank Aaron	1954	1976	2174	19	Jimmie Foxx	1925	1945	1751	34	Eddie Murray	1977	1997	1627	49	Max Carey	1910	1929	1545
5	Pete Rose	1963	1986	2165	20	Honus Wagner	1897	1917	1739	35	Paul Waner	1926	1945	1626	50	Frankie Frisch	1919	1937	1532
6	Barry Bonds	1986		2152	21	Cap Anson	1876	1897	1722	36	Al Kaline	1953	1974	1622	51	Tom Brown	1883	1898	1524
7	Willie Mays	1951	1973	2062	22	Willie Keeler	1892	1910	1720	37	Fred Clarke	1894	1915	1622	52	Jeff Bagwell	1991	2005	1517
8	Stan Musial	1941	1963	1949	23	Jesse Burkett	1890	1905	1708	38	Lou Brock	1961	1979	1610	53	Sam Rice	1915	1934	1514
9	Lou Gehrig	1923	1939	1888	24	Billy Hamilton	1888	1901	1690	39	Roger Connor	1880	1897	1607	54	Dan Brouthers	1879	1904	1513
10	Tris Speaker	1907	1928	1882	25	Mickey Mantle	1951	1968	1677	40	Jake Beckley	1888	1907	1601		Wade Boggs	1982	1999	1513
11	Mel Ott	1926	1947	1859	26	Biddy McPhee	1882	1899	1674	41	Ed Delahanty	1888	1903	1596	56	Eddie Mathews	1952	1968	1509
12	Frank Robinson	1956	1976	1829	27	Dave Winfield	1973	1995	1669	42	Bill Dahlen	1891	1911	1594	57	Roberto Alomar	1988	2004	1508
13	Eddie Collins	1906	1930	1821	28	Rafael Palmeiro	1986	2005	1663	43	George Brett	1973	1993	1583	58	Al Simmons	1924	1944	1507
14	Carl Yastrzemski	1961	1983	1816	29	George Van Haltren	1887	1903	1650	44	Rogers Hornsby	1915	1937	1579	59	Mike Schmidt	1972	1989	1506
15	Ted Williams	1939	1960	1798		Joe Morgan	1963	1984	1650	45	Tim Raines	1979	2002	1571	60	Nap Lajoie	1896	1916	1504

Players with 1500 or more RUNS BATTED IN

#		FIRST	LAST	RBI'S	#		FIRST	LAST	RBI'S	#		FIRST	LAST	RBI'S	#		FIRST	LAST	RBI'S
1	Hank Aaron	1954	1976	2297	13	Ted Williams	1939	1960	1839	24	Goose Goslin	1921	1938	1609	35	Jake Beckley	1888	1907	1574
2	Babe Ruth	1914	1935	2213	14	Rafael Palmeiro	1986	2005	1835	25	Ken Griffey Jr.	1989		1608	36	Willie McCovey	1959	1980	1555
3	Lou Gehrig	1923	1939	1995	15	Dave Winfield	1973	1995	1833	26	Nap Lajoie	1896	1916	1599	37	Fred McGriff	1986	2004	1550
4	Stan Musial	1941	1963	1951	16	Al Simmons	1924	1944	1827	27	Mike Schmidt	1972	1989	1595	38	Willie Stargell	1962	1982	1540
5	Ty Cobb	1905	1928	1939	17	Frank Robinson	1956	1976	1812		George Brett	1973	1993	1595	39	Harry Heilmann	1914	1932	1537
6	Barry Bonds	1986		1930	18	Honus Wagner	1897	1917	1732	29	Andre Dawson	1976	1996	1591		Joe DiMaggio	1936	1951	1537
7	Jimmie Foxx	1925	1945	1921	19	Reggie Jackson	1968	1987	1702		Rogers Hornsby	1915	1937	1584	41	Jeff Bagwell	1991	2005	1529
8	Eddie Murray	1977	1997	1917	20	Cal Ripken	1981	2001	1695		Harmon Killebrew	1954	1975	1584	42	Tris Speaker	1907	1928	1527
9	Willie Mays	1951	1973	1903	21	Tony Perez	1964	1986	1652	32	Al Kaline	1953	1974	1583	43	Sam Crawford	1899	1917	1524
10	Cap Anson	1876	1897	1880	22	Ernie Banks	1953	1971	1636	33	Frank Thomas	1990		1579	44	Manny Ramirez	1993		1516
11	Mel Ott	1926	1947	1860	23	Harold Baines	1980	2001	1628	34	Sammy Sosa	1989	2005	1575	45	Mickey Mantle	1951	1968	1509
12	Carl Yastrzemski	1961	1983	1844											46	Gary Sheffield	1988		1501

Players with 5 or fewer AT BATS per RUNS BATTED IN
(Minimum of 10 Major League seasons and 4000 At Bats)

#		FIRST	LAST	AB/RBI	#		FIRST	LAST	AB/RBI	#		FIRST	LAST	AB/RBI	#		FIRST	LAST	AB/RBI
1	Babe Ruth	1914	1935	3.79	7	Mark McGwire	1986	2001	4.38	12	Frank Thomas	1990		4.70	17	Cap Anson	1876	1897	4.83
2	Lou Gehrig	1923	1939	4.01	8	Joe DiMaggio	1936	1951	4.44	13	Carlos Delgado	1993		4.70	18	Jason Giambi	1995		4.91
3	Hank Greenberg	1930	1947	4.07	9	Hack Wilson	1923	1934	4.48	14	Albert Belle	1989	2000	4.72	19	Roy Campanella	1948	1957	4.91
4	Ted Williams	1939	1960	4.19	10	Sam Thompson	1885	1906	4.60	15	Al Simmons	1924	1944	4.80	20	Jim Thome	1991		4.92
5	Jimmie Foxx	1925	1945	4.23	11	Juan Gonzalez	1989	2005	4.67	16	Johnny Mize	1936	1953	4.82	21	Barry Bonds	1986		4.93
6	Manny Ramirez	1993		4.34											22	Richie Sexson	1997		4.99

Players with 400 or more STOLEN BASES since 1898

#		FIRST	LAST	SB	#		FIRST	LAST	SB	#		FIRST	LAST	SB	#		FIRST	LAST	SB
1	Rickey Henderson	1979	2003	1406	11	Bert Campaneris	1964	1983	649	21	Paul Molitor	1978	1998	504	31	Sherry Magee	1904	1919	441
2	Lou Brock	1961	1979	938	12	Otis Nixon	1983	1999	620	22	Clyde Milan	1907	1922	495	32	Tris Speaker	1907	1928	433
3	Ty Cobb	1905	1928	892	13	Kenny Lofton	1991		599	23	Omar Moreno	1975	1986	487	33	Marquis Grissom	1989	2005	429
4	Tim Raines	1979	2002	808	14	Maury Wills	1959	1972	586	24	Jimmy Sheckard	1891	1913	474	34	Bob Bescher	1908	1918	428
5	Vince Coleman	1985	1997	752	15	Ozzie Smith	1978	1996	580		Roberto Alomar	1988	2004	474	35	Frankie Frisch	1919	1937	419
6	Eddie Collins	1906	1930	743	16	Brett Butler	1981	1997	558	26	Eric Young	1992		464	36	Craig Biggio	1988		410
7	Max Carey	1910	1929	738	17	Davey Lopes	1972	1987	557	27	Delino DeShields	1990	2002	463	37	Tommy Harper	1962	1976	408
8	Honus Wagner	1897	1917	720	18	Cesar Cedeno	1970	1986	550	28	Bobby Bonds	1968	1981	461	38	Chuck Knoblauch	1991	2002	407
9	Joe Morgan	1963	1984	689	19	Barry Bonds	1986		509	29	Ron LeFlore	1974	1982	455	39	Donie Bush	1908	1923	405
10	Willie Wilson	1976	1994	668	20	Luis Aparicio	1956	1973	506	30	Steve Sax	1981	1994	444	40	Frank Chance	1898	1914	401

Players with 2500 or more GAMES PLAYED

#		FIRST	LAST	GAMES	#		FIRST	LAST	GAMES	#		FIRST	LAST	GAMES	#		FIRST	LAST	GAMES
1	Pete Rose	1963	1986	3562	10	Dave Winfield	1973	1995	2973	19	Reggie Jackson	1967	1987	2820	28	Darrell Evans	1969	1989	2687
2	Carl Yastrzemski	1961	1983	3308	11	Rusty Staub	1963	1985	2951	20	Frank Robinson	1956	1976	2808	29	Paul Molitor	1978	1998	2683
3	Hank Aaron	1954	1976	3298	12	Brooks Robinson	1955	1977	2896	21	Honus Wagner	1897	1917	2794	30	Rabbit Maranville	1912	1935	2670
4	Rickey Henderson	1979	2003	3081	13	Barry Bonds	1986		2860	22	Tris Speaker	1907	1928	2789	31	Joe Morgan	1963	1984	2649
5	Ty Cobb	1905	1928	3034	14	Robin Yount	1974	1993	2856	23	Tony Perez	1964	1986	2777	32	Andre Dawson	1976	1996	2627
6	Stan Musial	1941	1963	3026	15	Al Kaline	1953	1974	2834	24	Mel Ott	1926	1947	2730	33	Lou Brock	1961	1979	2616
	Eddie Murray	1977	1997	3026	16	Rafael Palmeiro	1986	2005	2831	25	Craig Biggio	1988		2709	34	Dwight Evans	1972	1991	2606
8	Cal Ripken	1981	2001	3001	17	Harold Baines	1980	2001	2830	26	George Brett	1973	1993	2707	35	Luis Aparicio	1956	1973	2601
9	Willie Mays	1951	1973	2992	18	Eddie Collins	1906	1930	2826	27	Graig Nettles	1967	1988	2700					

Players with 10000 or more AT BATS

#		FIRST	LAST	AB	#		FIRST	LAST	AB	#		FIRST	LAST	AB	#		FIRST	LAST	AB
1	Pete Rose	1963	1986	14053	7	Robin Yount	1974	1993	11008	13	Brooks Robinson	1955	1977	10654	19	Luis Aparicio	1956	1973	10230
2	Hank Aaron	1954	1976	12364	8	Dave Winfield	1973	1995	11003	14	Rafael Palmeiro	1986	2005	10472	20	Tris Speaker	1907	1928	10197
3	Carl Yastrzemski	1961	1983	11988	9	Stan Musial	1941	1963	10972	15	Honus Wagner	1897	1917	10439	21	Al Kaline	1953	1974	10116
4	Cal Ripken	1981	2001	11551	10	Rickey Henderson	1979	2003	10961	16	Craig Biggio	1988		10359	22	Rabbit Maranville	1912	1935	10078
5	Ty Cobb	1905	1928	11436	11	Willie Mays	1951	1973	10881	17	George Brett	1973	1993	10349	23	Frank Robinson	1956	1976	10006
6	Eddie Murray	1977	1997	11336	12	Paul Molitor	1978	1998	10835	18	Lou Brock	1961	1979	10332					

Players active at the end of 2006 are shown in bold face

LIFETIME LEADERS - BATTING

Players with 350 or more HOME RUNS

#	Player	FIRST	LAST	HR
1	Hank Aaron	1954	1976	755
2	**Barry Bonds**	**1986**		**734**
3	Babe Ruth	1914	1935	714
4	Willie Mays	1951	1973	660
5	Sammy Sosa	1989	2005	588
6	Frank Robinson	1956	1976	586
7	Mark McGwire	1986	2001	583
8	Harmon Killebrew	1954	1975	573
9	Rafael Palmeiro	1986	2005	569
10	Reggie Jackson	1967	1987	563
11	**Ken Griffey Jr.**	**1989**		**563**
12	Mike Schmidt	1972	1989	548
13	Mickey Mantle	1951	1968	536
14	Jimmie Foxx	1925	1945	534
15	Ted Williams	1939	1960	521
16	Willie McCovey	1959	1980	521
17	Eddie Mathews	1952	1968	512
18	Ernie Banks	1953	1971	512
19	Mel Ott	1926	1947	511
20	Eddie Murray	1977	1997	504
21	Lou Gehrig	1923	1939	493
	Fred McGriff	1986	2004	493
23	**Frank Thomas**	**1990**		**487**
24	Stan Musial	1941	1963	475
	Willie Stargell	1962	1982	475
26	**Jim Thome**	**1991**		**472**
27	**Manny Ramirez**	**1993**		**470**
28	Dave Winfield	1973	1995	465
29	**Alex Rodriguez**	**1994**		**464**
30	Jose Canseco	1985	2001	462
31	**Gary Sheffield**	**1988**		**455**
32	Carl Yastrzemski	1961	1983	452
33	Jeff Bagwell	1991	2005	449
34	Dave Kingman	1971	1986	442
35	Andre Dawson	1976	1996	438
36	Juan Gonzalez	1989	2005	434
37	Cal Ripken	1981	2001	431
38	Billy Williams	1959	1976	426
39	**Mike Piazza**	**1992**		**419**
40	Darrell Evans	1969	1989	414
41	Duke Snider	1947	1964	407
	Carlos Delgado	**1993**		**407**
43	Al Kaline	1953	1974	399
	Andres Galarraga	1985	2004	399
45	Dale Murphy	1976	1993	398
46	Joe Carter	1983	1998	396
47	Graig Nettles	1967	1988	390
48	Johnny Bench	1967	1983	389
49	Dwight Evans	1972	1991	385
50	Harold Baines	1980	2001	384
51	Larry Walker	1989	2005	383
52	Frank Howard	1958	1973	382
	Jim Rice	1974	1989	382
54	Albert Belle	1989	2000	381
55	Orlando Cepeda	1958	1974	379
	Tony Perez	1964	1986	379
57	Matt Williams	1987	2003	378
58	Norm Cash	1958	1974	377
59	Carlton Fisk	1969	1993	376
60	Rocky Colavito	1955	1968	374
61	Gil Hodges	1943	1963	370
	Ralph Kiner	1946	1955	369
63	Joe DiMaggio	1936	1951	361
64	Gary Gaetti	1981	2000	360
65	Johnny Mize	1936	1953	359
	Yogi Berra	1946	1965	358
67	**Chipper Jones**	**1993**		**357**
68	Greg Vaughn	1989	2003	355
69	Lee May	1965	1982	354
70	Ellis Burks	1987	2004	352
71	Dick Allen	1963	1977	351
72	Chili Davis	1981	1999	350
	Jim Edmonds	**1993**		**350**
	Jason Giambi	**1995**		**350**

Players with 17 or fewer AT BATS per HOME RUN
(Minimum of 10 major league seasons and 4000 At Bats)

#	Player	FIRST	LAST	AB/HR
1	Mark McGwire	1986	2001	10.61
2	Babe Ruth	1914	1935	11.76
3	**Barry Bonds**	**1986**		**12.95**
4	**Jim Thome**	**1991**		**13.58**
5	**Manny Ramirez**	**1993**		**13.99**
6	Ralph Kiner	1946	1955	14.11
7	Harmon Killebrew	1954	1975	14.22
8	Sammy Sosa	1989	2005	14.29
9	**Alex Rodriguez**	**1994**		**14.58**
10	**Ken Griffey Jr.**	**1989**		**14.74**
11	Ted Williams	1939	1960	14.79
12	**Carlos Delgado**	**1993**		**14.87**
13	Juan Gonzalez	1989	2005	15.11
14	Dave Kingman	1971	1986	15.11
15	Mickey Mantle	1951	1968	15.12
16	Jimmie Foxx	1925	1945	15.23
17	Mike Schmidt	1972	1989	15.24
18	**Frank Thomas**	**1990**		**15.24**
19	Jose Canseco	1985	2001	15.27
20	Albert Belle	1989	2000	15.36
21	**Richie Sexson**	**1997**		**15.44**
22	Hank Greenberg	1930	1947	15.69
23	Willie McCovey	1959	1980	15.73
24	**Mike Piazza**	**1992**		**15.76**
25	**Jason Giambi**	**1995**		**16.06**
26	Cecil Fielder	1985	1998	16.17
27	Jay Buhner	1987	2001	16.17
28	Darryl Strawberry	1983	1999	16.17
29	Lou Gehrig	1923	1939	16.23
30	**Vladimir Guerrero**	**1996**		**16.28**
31	Hank Aaron	1954	1976	16.38
32	Willie Mays	1951	1973	16.49
33	Hank Sauer	1941	1959	16.65
34	Eddie Mathews	1952	1968	16.67
35	Willie Stargell	1962	1982	16.69
36	Mo Vaughn	1991	2003	16.87
37	**Jim Edmonds**	**1993**		**16.88**
38	Frank Howard	1958	1973	16.98

Players with 150 or more TRIPLES

#	Player	FIRST	LAST	3B
1	Sam Crawford	1899	1917	312
2	Ty Cobb	1905	1928	298
3	Honus Wagner	1897	1917	252
4	Jake Beckley	1888	1907	248
5	Roger Connor	1880	1897	227
6	Tris Speaker	1907	1928	223
7	Fred Clarke	1894	1915	220
8	Dan Brouthers	1879	1904	212
9	Paul Waner	1926	1945	190
10	Joe Kelley	1891	1908	189
11	Eddie Collins	1906	1930	187
12	Harry Stovey	1880	1893	185
13	Jesse Burkett	1890	1905	185
14	Sam Rice	1915	1934	184
15	Ed Delahanty	1888	1903	182
	Edd Roush	1913	1931	182
17	Ed Konetchy	1907	1921	181
18	Buck Ewing	1880	1897	179
19	Rabbit Maranville	1912	1935	177
	Stan Musial	1941	1963	177
21	Goose Goslin	1921	1938	173
22	Zack Wheat	1909	1927	172
23	Biddy McPhee	1882	1899	170
	Tommy Leach	1898	1918	170
25	Elmer Flick	1898	1910	169
	Rogers Hornsby	1915	1937	169
27	Joe Jackson	1908	1920	168
28	George Davis	1890	1909	167
29	Bill Dahlen	1891	1911	166
	Sherry Magee	1904	1919	166
	Roberto Clemente	1955	1972	166
32	Jake Daubert	1910	1924	165
33	George Sisler	1915	1930	164
	Pie Traynor	1920	1937	164
35	Nap Lajoie	1896	1916	163
36	Lou Gehrig	1923	1939	162
37	Harry Hooper	1909	1925	160
	Heinie Manush	1923	1939	160
39	Mike Tiernan	1887	1899	159
	George Van Haltren	1887	1903	159
	Max Carey	1910	1929	159
	Joe Judge	1915	1934	159
43	Kiki Cuyler	1921	1938	157
	Sam Thompson	1885	1906	156
	Willie Keeler	1892	1910	155
46	Kip Selbach	1894	1906	154
	Earle Combs	1924	1935	154
48	Ed McKean	1887	1899	153
	Jimmy Ryan	1885	1903	153
50	Tommy Corcoran	1890	1907	151
	Harry Heilmann	1914	1932	151
	Jim Bottomley	1922	1937	151

Players with 500 or more DOUBLES

#	Player	FIRST	LAST	2B
1	Tris Speaker	1907	1928	792
2	Pete Rose	1963	1986	746
3	Stan Musial	1941	1963	725
4	Ty Cobb	1905	1928	724
5	George Brett	1973	1993	665
6	Nap Lajoie	1896	1916	661
7	Carl Yastrzemski	1961	1983	646
8	Honus Wagner	1897	1917	643
9	**Craig Biggio**	**1988**		**637**
10	Hank Aaron	1954	1976	624
11	Paul Molitor	1978	1998	605
12	Paul Waner	1926	1945	603
	Cal Ripken	1981	2001	603
14	**Barry Bonds**	**1986**		**587**
15	Rafael Palmeiro	1986	2005	585
16	Robin Yount	1974	1993	583
17	Wade Boggs	1982	1999	578
18	Charlie Gehringer	1924	1942	574
19	Eddie Murray	1977	1997	560
20	**Luis Gonzalez**	**1990**		**547**
21	Tony Gwynn	1982	2001	543
22	Harry Heilmann	1914	1932	542
23	Rogers Hornsby	1915	1937	541
24	Joe Medwick	1932	1948	540
	Dave Winfield	1973	1995	540
26	Al Simmons	1924	1944	539
27	Lou Gehrig	1923	1939	535
28	Cap Anson	1876	1897	529
	Al Oliver	1968	1985	529
30	Frank Robinson	1956	1976	528
31	Dave Parker	1973	1991	526
32	Ted Williams	1939	1960	525
33	Willie Mays	1951	1973	523
34	Ed Delahanty	1888	1903	522
35	Joe Cronin	1926	1945	515
36	Edgar Martinez	1987	2004	514
37	Mark Grace	1988	2003	511
38	Rickey Henderson	1979	2003	510
39	Babe Ruth	1914	1935	506
40	Tony Perez	1964	1986	505
41	Roberto Alomar	1988	2004	504
42	Andre Dawson	1976	1996	503
43	**Jeff Kent**	**1992**		**501**
44	Goose Goslin	1921	1938	500
	John Olerud	1989	2005	500

Players with 1000 or more EXTRA BASE HITS

#	Player	FIRST	LAST	XBH
	Hank Aaron	1954	1976	1477
	Barry Bonds	**1986**		**1398**
	Stan Musial	1941	1963	1377
	Babe Ruth	1914	1935	1356
	Willie Mays	1951	1973	1323
	Rafael Palmeiro	1986	2005	1192
7	Lou Gehrig	1923	1939	1190
8	Frank Robinson	1956	1976	1186
9	Carl Yastrzemski	1961	1983	1157
10	Ty Cobb	1905	1928	1138
11	Tris Speaker	1907	1928	1132
12	George Brett	1973	1993	1119
13	Jimmie Foxx	1925	1945	1117
	Ted Williams	1939	1960	1117
15	Eddie Murray	1977	1997	1099
16	Dave Winfield	1973	1995	1093
17	Cal Ripken	1981	2001	1078
18	Reggie Jackson	1967	1987	1075
19	Mel Ott	1926	1947	1071
20	**Ken Griffey Jr.**	**1989**		**1048**
21	Pete Rose	1963	1986	1041
22	Andre Dawson	1976	1996	1039
23	Mike Schmidt	1972	1989	1015
24	Rogers Hornsby	1915	1937	1011
25	Ernie Banks	1952	1971	1009

Players with 4000 or more TOTAL BASES

#	Player	FIRST	LAST	TB
1	Hank Aaron	1954	1976	6856
2	Stan Musial	1941	1963	6134
3	Willie Mays	1951	1973	6066
4	Ty Cobb	1905	1928	5859
5	Babe Ruth	1914	1935	5793
6	**Barry Bonds**	**1986**		**5784**
7	Pete Rose	1963	1986	5752
8	Carl Yastrzemski	1961	1983	5539
9	Eddie Murray	1977	1998	5397
10	Rafael Palmeiro	1986	2005	5388
11	Frank Robinson	1956	1976	5373
12	Dave Winfield	1973	1995	5221
13	Cal Ripken	1981	2001	5168
14	Tris Speaker	1907	1928	5103
15	Lou Gehrig	1923	1939	5059
16	George Brett	1973	1993	5044
17	Mel Ott	1926	1947	5041
18	Jimmie Foxx	1925	1945	4956
19	Ted Williams	1939	1960	4884
20	Honus Wagner	1897	1917	4870
21	Paul Molitor	1978	1998	4854
22	Al Kaline	1953	1974	4852
23	Reggie Jackson	1967	1987	4834
24	Andre Dawson	1976	1996	4787
25	Robin Yount	1974	1993	4730
26	Rogers Hornsby	1915	1937	4712
27	Ernie Banks	1953	1971	4706
28	Al Simmons	1924	1944	4685
29	**Ken Griffey Jr.**	**1989**		**4622**
30	Harold Baines	1980	2001	4604
31	Billy Williams	1959	1976	4599
32	Rickey Henderson	1979	2003	4588
33	Tony Perez	1964	1986	4532
34	**Craig Biggio**	**1988**		**4514**
35	Mickey Mantle	1951	1968	4511
	Sammy Sosa	1989	2005	4511
37	Roberto Clemente	1955	1972	4492
38	Nap Lajoie	1896	1916	4481
39	Paul Waner	1926	1945	4474
40	Fred McGriff	1986	2004	4458
41	Dave Parker	1973	1991	4405
42	Mike Schmidt	1972	1989	4404
43	Eddie Mathews	1952	1968	4349
44	Sam Crawford	1889	1917	4334
45	Goose Goslin	1921	1938	4325
46	Brooks Robinson	1965	1977	4270
47	Eddie Collins	1906	1930	4268
48	Vada Pinson	1958	1975	4264
49	Tony Gwynn	1982	2001	4259
50	Charlie Gehringer	1924	1942	4257
51	Lou Brock	1961	1979	4238
52	Dwight Evans	1972	1991	4230
53	**Gary Sheffield**	**1988**		**4221**
54	Willie McCovey	1959	1980	4219
55	Jeff Bagwell	1991	2005	4213
56	**Frank Thomas**	**1990**		**4203**
57	Willie Stargell	1962	1982	4190
58	Rusty Staub	1963	1985	4185
59	Harmon Killebrew	1954	1975	4143
60	Jake Beckley	1888	1907	4138
61	**Steve Finley**	**1989**		**4134**
62	Jim Rice	1974	1989	4129
63	Zack Wheat	1909	1927	4100
64	Al Oliver	1968	1975	4083
65	Cap Anson	1876	1897	4080
66	Wade Boggs	1982	1999	4064
67	Harry Heilmann	1914	1932	4053
68	**Luis Gonzalez**	**1990**		**4043**
69	Andres Galarraga	1985	2004	4038
70	Roberto Alomar	1988	2004	4018

Players active at the end of 2006 are shown in bold face

LIFETIME LEADERS - BATTING

Players with 1200 or more BASES ON BALLS

#	Name	FIRST	LAST	BB
1	**Barry Bonds**	**1986**		**2426**
2	Rickey Henderson	1979	2003	2190
3	Babe Ruth	1914	1935	2062
4	Ted Williams	1939	1960	2021
5	Joe Morgan	1963	1984	1865
6	Carl Yastrzemski	1961	1983	1845
7	Mickey Mantle	1951	1968	1733
8	Mel Ott	1926	1947	1708
9	Eddie Yost	1944	1962	1614
10	Darrell Evans	1969	1989	1605
11	Stan Musial	1941	1963	1599
12	Pete Rose	1963	1986	1566
13	Harmon Killebrew	1954	1975	1559
14	**Frank Thomas**	**1990**		**1547**
15	Lou Gehrig	1923	1939	1508
16	Mike Schmidt	1972	1989	1507
17	Eddie Collins	1906	1930	1503
18	Willie Mays	1951	1973	1463
19	Jimmie Foxx	1925	1945	1452
20	Eddie Mathews	1952	1968	1444
21	Frank Robinson	1956	1976	1420
22	Wade Boggs	1982	1999	1412
23	Hank Aaron	1954	1976	1402
24	Jeff Bagwell	1991	2005	1401
25	Dwight Evans	1972	1991	1391
26	Tris Speaker	1907	1928	1381
27	Reggie Jackson	1967	1987	1375
28	**Jim Thome**	**1991**		**1364**
29	Rafael Palmeiro	1986	2005	1353
30	Willie McCovey	1959	1980	1345
31	Eddie Murray	1977	1997	1333
32	Tim Raines	1980	2002	1330
33	Tony Phillips	1982	1999	1319
34	Mark McGwire	1986	2001	1317
35	Fred McGriff	1986	2004	1305
36	Luke Appling	1930	1950	1302
37	**Gary Sheffield**	**1988**		**1293**
38	Edgar Martinez	1987	2004	1283
39	Al Kaline	1953	1974	1277
40	John Olerud	1989	2005	1275
41	Ken Singleton	1970	1984	1263
42	Jack Clark	1975	1992	1262
43	Rusty Staub	1963	1985	1255
44	Ty Cobb	1905	1928	1249
45	Willie Randolph	1975	1992	1243
46	Jim Wynn	1963	1977	1224
47	Dave Winfield	1973	1995	1216
48	Pee Wee Reese	1940	1958	1210

Players with 1500 or more STRIKEOUTS

#	Name	FIRST	LAST	SO
1	Reggie Jackson	1967	1987	2597
2	Sammy Sosa	1989	2005	2194
3	Andres Galarraga	1985	2004	2003
4	Jose Canseco	1985	2001	1942
5	Willie Stargell	1961	1982	1936
6	**Jim Thome**	**1991**		**1909**
7	Mike Schmidt	1972	1989	1883
8	Fred McGriff	1986	2004	1882
9	Tony Perez	1964	1986	1867
10	Dave Kingman	1971	1986	1816
11	Bobby Bonds	1968	1981	1757
12	Dale Murphy	1976	1993	1748
13	Lou Brock	1961	1979	1730
14	Mickey Mantle	1951	1968	1710
15	Harmon Killebrew	1954	1975	1699
16	Chili Davis	1981	1999	1698
17	Dwight Evans	1972	1991	1697
18	Rickey Henderson	1979	2003	1694
19	Dave Winfield	1973	1995	1686
20	**Craig Biggio**	**1988**		**1641**
21	Gary Gaetti	1981	2000	1602
22	**Reggie Sanders**	**1991**		**1599**
23	Mark McGwire	1986	2001	1596
24	Lee May	1965	1982	1570
25	Jeff Bagwell	1991	2005	1558
26	Dick Allen	1963	1977	1556
27	Willie McCovey	1959	1980	1550
	Ray Lankford	1990	2004	1550
29	Dave Parker	1973	1991	1537
30	Frank Robinson	1956	1976	1532
31	Lance Parrish	1977	1995	1527
32	Willie Mays	1951	1973	1526
	Devon White	1985	2001	1526
34	Eddie Murray	1977	1997	1516
35	Rick Monday	1966	1984	1513
	Greg Vaughn	1989	2003	1513
37	**Jim Edmonds**	**1993**		**1512**
38	Andre Dawson	1976	1996	1509

LIFETIME LEADERS - PITCHING

Pitchers with 200 or more WINS

#	Name	FIRST	LAST	WINS	LOSSES	PCT.
1	Cy Young	1890	1911	511	315	.619
2	Walter Johnson	1907	1927	417	279	.599
3	Christy Mathewson	1900	1916	374	188	.665
4	C.G. Pete Alexander	1911	1930	373	208	.642
5	Warren Spahn	1942	1965	363	245	.597
6	Pud Galvin	1879	1892	361	309	.539
	Kid Nichols	1890	1906	361	208	.634
8	**Roger Clemens**	**1984**		**348**	**178**	**.662**
	Tim Keefe	1880	1893	341	224	.604
10	**Greg Maddux**	**1986**		**333**	**203**	**.621**
11	Steve Carlton	1965	1988	329	244	.574
12	John Clarkson	1882	1894	327	176	.650
13	Eddie Plank	1901	1917	325	193	.627
14	Don Sutton	1965	1988	324	256	.559
	Nolan Ryan	1966	1993	324	292	.526
16	Phil Niekro	1964	1987	318	274	.537
17	Gaylord Perry	1962	1983	314	265	.542
18	Tom Seaver	1967	1986	311	205	.603
19	Mickey Welch	1880	1892	309	209	.597
20	Old Hoss Radbourn	1881	1891	308	191	.617
21	Lefty Grove	1925	1941	300	141	.680
	Early Wynn	1939	1963	300	244	.551
23	**Tom Glavine**	**1987**		**290**	**191**	**.603**
24	Tommy John	1963	1989	288	231	.555
25	Bert Blyleven	1970	1992	287	250	.534
26	Tony Mullane	1881	1894	286	213	.573
	Robin Roberts	1946	1966	286	245	.539
28	Ferguson Jenkins	1965	1983	284	226	.557
29	Jim Kaat	1959	1983	283	237	.544
30	**Randy Johnson**	**1988**		**280**	**147**	**.656**
31	Red Ruffing	1924	1947	273	225	.548
32	Burleigh Grimes	1916	1934	270	212	.560
33	Jim Palmer	1965	1984	268	152	.638
34	Gus Weyhing	1887	1901	266	229	.537
	Eppa Rixey	1912	1933	266	251	.515
	Bob Feller	1936	1956	266	162	.621
37	Jim McCormick	1878	1887	264	214	.552
38	Ted Lyons	1923	1946	260	230	.531
39	Red Faber	1914	1933	254	212	.545
	Jack Morris	1977	1994	254	186	.577
41	Carl Hubbell	1928	1943	253	154	.622
42	Bob Gibson	1959	1975	251	174	.591
43	Amos Rusie	1889	1901	248	170	.593
	Vic Willis	1898	1910	248	203	.550
	Jack Powell	1897	1912	248	255	.493
46	Joe McGinnity	1899	1908	247	142	.635
	Jack Quinn	1909	1933	247	219	.530
48	Dennis Martinez	1976	1998	245	193	.559
49	Juan Marichal	1960	1975	243	142	.631
50	Herb Pennock	1912	1934	241	161	.600
51	Frank Tanana	1973	1993	240	236	.504
52	Three Finger Brown	1903	1916	239	127	.653
	Mike Mussina	**1991**		**239**	**134**	**.641**
54	Waite Hoyt	1918	1938	237	182	.566
55	Whitey Ford	1950	1967	236	106	.690
56	Clark Griffith	1891	1914	235	143	.622
57	Charlie Buffinton	1882	1892	230	151	.604
	David Wells	**1987**		**230**	**148**	**.608**
59	George Mullin	1902	1915	229	192	.544
	Luis Tiant	1964	1982	229	172	.571
61	Sad Sam Jones	1914	1935	228	216	.514
62	Will White	1877	1886	227	167	.576
63	Jim Bunning	1955	1971	224	184	.549
	Catfish Hunter	1965	1979	224	166	.574
65	Paul Derringer	1931	1945	223	212	.513
	Mel Harder	1928	1947	223	186	.545
67	Jerry Koosman	1967	1985	222	209	.515
68	Hooks Dauss	1912	1926	221	182	.548
	Joe Niekro	1967	1988	221	204	.520
70	Jerry Reuss	1969	1990	220	191	.535
71	Earl Whitehill	1923	1939	218	185	
72	Bob Caruthers	1884	1892	217	101	
	Freddie Fitzsimmons	1925	1943	217	146	
	Mickey Lolich	1963	1979	217	191	
75	Wilbur Cooper	1912	1926	216	178	
	Stan Coveleski	1912	1928	216	143	
	Charlie Hough	1970	1994	216	216	
	Jamie Moyer	**1986**		**216**	**166**	
79	Jim Perry	1959	1975	215	174	
80	Rick Reuschel	1972	1991	214	191	
81	Bobo Newsom	1929	1953	211	222	
	Billy Pierce	1945	1964	211	169	
	Bob Welch	1978	1994	211	146	
	Kevin Brown	1986	2005	211	144	
85	Chief Bender	1903	1925	210	128	
	Jesse Haines	1918	1937	210	158	
87	Eddie Cicotte	1905	1920	209	149	
	Don Drysdale	1956	1969	209	166	
	Milt Pappas	1957	1973	209	164	
	Vida Blue	1969	1986	209	161	
91	Carl Mays	1915	1929	207	127	
	Hal Newhouser	1939	1955	207	150	
	Bob Lemon	1946	1958	207	128	
	Curt Schilling	**1988**		**207**	**138**	
	Kenny Rogers	**1989**		**207**	**139**	
96	Silver King	1886	1897	206	152	
	Pedro Martinez	**1992**		**206**	**92**	
98	Adonis Terry	1884	1897	205	197	
	Jack Stivetts	1889	1899	205	128	
100	Orel Hershiser	1983	2000	204	150	
101	Al Orth	1895	1909	203	183	
	Lew Burdette	1950	1967	203	144	
103	Rube Marquard	1908	1925	201	177	
	Charlie Root	1923	1941	201	160	
105	George Uhle	1919	1936	200	166	
	Chuck Finley	**1986**	**2002**	**200**	**173**	

Pitchers with Lifetime WINNING PERCENTAGE of .600 or higher
(Minimum of 100 Wins)

#	Name	FIRST	LAST	WINS	LOSSES	PCT.
1	Spud Chandler	1937	1947	109	43	.717
2	**Pedro Martinez**	**1992**		**206**	**92**	**.691**
3	Whitey Ford	1950	1967	236	106	.690
4	Dave Fultz	1884	1894	149	67	.690
5	Don Gullett	1970	1978	109	50	.686
6	Bob Caruthers	1884	1892	217	101	.682
7	Lefty Grove	1925	1941	300	141	.680
8	Smoky Joe Wood	1908	1920	115	57	.669
9	Vic Raschi	1945	1955	132	66	.667
10	Christy Mathewson	1900	1916	374	188	.665
11	**Tim Hudson**	**1999**		**119**	**60**	**.665**
12	**Roger Clemens**	**1984**		**348**	**178**	**.662**
13	Larry Corcoran	1880	1887	173	90	.658
14	Sam Leever	1896	1910	194	101	.658
15	Sal Maglie	1945	1958	119	62	.657
16	**Randy Johnson**	**1988**		**280**	**147**	**.656**
17	Sandy Koufax	1955	1966	165	87	.655
18	Johnny Allen	1932	1944	142	75	.654
19	Three Finger Brown	1903	1916	239	127	.653
20	Ron Guidry	1975	1988	170	91	.651
21	John Clarkson	1882	1894	327	176	.650
22	Lefty Gomez	1930	1943	189	102	.649
23	Dizzy Dean	1930	1947	150	83	.644
24	**Mark Mulder**	**2000**		**103**	**57**	**.644**
25	C.G. Pete Alexander	1911	1930	373	208	.642
26	**Andy Pettitte**	**1995**		**186**	**104**	**.641**
27	**Mike Mussina**	**1991**		**239**	**134**	**.641**
28	Fred Goldsmith	1879	1884	117	66	.639
29	Jim Palmer	1965	1984	268	152	.638
30	Joe McGinnity	1899	1908	247	142	.635
31	Kid Nichols	1890	1906	361	208	.634
32	Deacon Phillippe	1899	1911	189	109	.634
33	Dwight Gooden	1984	2000	194	112	.634
34	Ed Reulbach	1905	1917	182	106	.632
35	Juan Marichal	1960	1975	243	142	.631
36	Mort Cooper	1938	1949	128	75	.631
37	Allie Reynolds	1942	1954	182	107	.630
38	Eddie Plank	1901	1917	325	193	.627
39	Ray Kremer	1924	1933	143	85	.627
40	Addie Joss	1902	1910	159	95	.626
41	Tommy Bond	1876	1884	192	115	.625
42	Don Newcombe	1949	1960	149	90	.623
43	Firpo Marberry	1923	1936	147	89	.623
44	Doc Crandall	1908	1918	102	62	.622
45	Clark Griffith	1891	1914	235	143	.622
46	Carl Hubbell	1928	1943	253	154	.622
47	Bob Feller	1936	1956	266	162	.621
48	Chief Bender	1903	1925	210	128	.621
49	**Greg Maddux**	**1986**		**333**	**203**	**.621**
50	Mel Parnell	1947	1956	123	75	.621
51	**Freddy Garcia**	**1999**		**116**	**71**	**.620**
52	Jesse Tannehill	1894	1911	194	119	.620
53	Carl Mays	1915	1929	207	127	.620
54	John Tudor	1979	1990	117	72	.619
55	Cy Young	1890	1911	511	315	.619
56	**Barry Zito**	**2000**		**102**	**63**	**.618**
57	Bob Lemon	1946	1958	207	128	.618
58	Monte Pearson	1932	1941	100	62	.617
59	Old Hoss Radbourn	1881	1891	308	191	
60	Nig Cuppy	1892	1901	161	100	
61	**Bartolo Colon**	**1997**		**140**	**87**	
62	Urban Shocker	1916	1928	188	117	
63	Jack Stivetts	1889	1899	205	128	
64	Jeff Tesreau	1912	1918	115	72	
65	Jim Maloney	1960	1971	134	84	
66	Jimmy Key	1984	1998	186	117	
67	Lon Warneke	1930	1945	192	121	
68	Gary Nolan	1967	1977	110	70	
69	Schoolboy Rowe	1933	1949	158	101	
70	Carl Erskine	1948	1959	122	78	
71	**David Wells**	**1987**		**230**	**148**	
72	Monte Ward	1878	1894	158	102	
73	Dave McNally	1962	1975	184	119	
74	David Cone	1986	2003	194	126	
75	Ramon Martinez	1988	2001	135	88	
76	Art Nehf	1915	1929	184	120	
	Hooks Wiltse	1904	1915	138	85	
78	Charlie Buffinton	1882	1892	230	151	
79	Jack Chesbro	1899	1909	198	130	
80	Tim Keefe	1880	1893	341	224	
81	**Tom Glavine**	**1987**		**290**	**191**	
82	Tom Seaver	1967	1986	311	205	
83	Ed Walsh	1904	1917	194	128	
84	Preacher Roe	1938	1954	127	84	
85	Stan Coveleski	1912	1928	216	143	
86	Wes Farrell	1927	1941	193	128	
87	J.R. Richard	1971	1980	107	71	
88	**Curt Schilling**	**1988**		**207**	**138**	

Players active at the end of 2006 are shown in bold face

LIFETIME LEADERS - PITCHING

Pitchers with 700 or more GAMES PITCHED

#		FIRST	LAST	GAMES
1	Jesse Orosco	1979	2003	1252
2	John Franco	1984	2005	1119
3	**Mike Stanton**	**1989**		**1109**
4	Dennis Eckersley	1975	1998	1071
5	Hoyt Wilhelm	1952	1972	1070
6	Dan Plesac	1986	2003	1064
7	Kent Tekulve	1975	1989	1050
8	Lee Smith	1980	1997	1022
9	Mike Jackson	1986	2004	1005
10	Goose Gossage	1972	1994	1002
11	Lindy McDaniel	1955	1975	987
12	**Jose Mesa**	**1987**		**966**
13	**Mike Timlin**	**1991**		**961**
14	**Roberto Hernandez**	**1991**		**960**
15	Rollie Fingers	1965	1985	944
16	Gene Garber	1969	1988	931
17	Cy Young	1890	1910	906
18	Sparky Lyle	1967	1982	899
19	Jim Kaat	1959	1982	898
20	Paul Assenmacher	1986	1999	884
21	Jeff Reardon	1978	1994	880
22	Don McMahon	1957	1974	874
	Todd Jones	**1993**		**874**
24	Phil Niekro	1964	1987	864
25	Charlie Hough	1970	1994	858
26	Elroy Face	1953	1969	848
27	Doug Jones	1982	2000	846
28	Paul Quantrill	1992	2005	841
29	Steve Reed	1992	2005	833
30	Tug McGraw	1965	1984	824
31	**Trevor Hoffman**	**1993**		**821**
32	**Mike Myers**	**1995**		**811**
	Tom Gordon	**1988**		**809**
34	Nolan Ryan	1966	1993	807
35	Walter Johnson	1907	1927	802
36	**Jeff Nelson**	**1992**		**798**
37	Rick Honeycutt	1977	1997	797
38	Buddy Groom	1992	2005	786
39	**Eddie Guardado**	**1993**		**781**
40	**Bob Wickman**	**1992**		**778**
41	Gaylord Perry	1962	1983	777
42	Don Sutton	1966	1988	774
43	Darold Knowles	1965	1980	765
	Mark Guthrie	1989	2003	765
45	Tommy John	1963	1989	760
46	Jack Quinn	1909	1933	756
47	**David Weathers**	**1991**		**754**
48	Ron Reed	1966	1984	751
49	Warren Spahn	1942	1965	750
50	Tom Burgmeier	1968	1984	745
	Gary Lavelle	1974	1987	745
52	Willie Hernandez	1977	1989	744
53	Steve Carlton	1965	1988	741
54	Ron Perranoski	1961	1975	737
55	Ron Kline	1952	1970	736
56	Steve Bedrosian	1981	1995	732
	Rick Aguilera	1985	2000	732
58	Clay Carrol	1964	1978	731
59	Randy Myers	1985	2000	728
60	**Steve Kline**	**1997**		**728**
61	Mike Marshall	1965	1981	723
	Roger McDowell	1985	1997	723
63	**Kenny Rogers**	**1989**		**721**
64	**Jeff Fassero**	**1991**		**720**
	Mariano Rivera	**1995**		**720**
66	Dave Righetti	1979	1995	718
67	Danny Darwin	1978	1998	716
68	Eric Plunk	1986	1999	714
69	Johnny Klippstein	1950	1967	711
70	Greg Minton	1978	1990	710
71	**Alan Embree**	**1992**		**708**
72	Stu Miller	1952	1968	704
	Rod Beck	1991	2004	704
74	Greg Harris	1981	1995	703
75	Joe Niekro	1967	1988	702
76	Bill Campbell	1973	1987	700
	Jeff Montgomery	1987	1999	700
	Julian Tavarez	**1993**		**700**

Pitchers with 500 or more GAMES STARTED

#		FIRST	LAST	GAMES
1	Cy Young	1890	1911	816
2	Nolan Ryan	1966	1993	773
3	Don Sutton	1966	1988	756
4	Phil Niekro	1964	1987	716
5	Steve Carlton	1965	1988	709
6	Tommy John	1963	1989	700
7	Gaylord Perry	1962	1983	690
9	**Roger Clemens**	**1984**		**690**
9	Bert Blyleven	1970	1992	685
10	Pud Galvin	1879	1892	682
11	**Greg Maddux**	**1986**		**673**
12	Walter Johnson	1907	1927	667
13	Warren Spahn	1942	1965	665
14	Tom Seaver	1967	1986	647
15	**Tom Glavine**	**1987**		**635**
16	Jim Kaat	1959	1963	625
17	Frank Tanana	1973	1993	616
18	Early Wynn	1939	1963	612
19	Robin Roberts	1948	1966	609
20	G.C. Pete Alexander	1911	1930	600
21	Tim Keefe	1880	1896	594
	Ferguson Jenkins	1965	1983	594
23	Dennis Martinez	1976	1998	562
24	Kid Nichols	1890	1906	561
25	Eppa Rixey	1912	1933	553
26	Christy Mathewson	1900	1916	551
27	Mickey Welch	1880	1892	549
28	Jerry Reuss	1969	1990	547
29	**Randy Johnson**	**1988**		**546**
30	Red Ruffing	1924	1947	538
31	Eddie Plank	1901	1917	529
	Rick Reuschel	1972	1991	529
33	Jerry Koosman	1967	1985	527
	Jack Morris	1977	1994	527
35	Jim Palmer	1965	1984	521
36	Jim Bunning	1956	1971	519
37	John Clarkson	1882	1894	518
	Jamie Moyer	**1986**		**518**
39	Jack Powell	1897	1912	516
40	Tony Mullane	1881	1894	505
41	Old Hoss Radbourn	1881	1891	503
	Gus Weyhing	1887	1901	503
43	Joe Niekro	1967	1988	500

Pitchers with 300 or more COMPLETE GAMES

#		FIRST	LAST	GAMES
1	Cy Young	1890	1911	751
2	Pud Galvin	1879	1892	639
3	Tim Keefe	1880	1896	552
4	Walter Johnson	1907	1927	532
5	Kid Nichols	1890	1906	531
6	Mickey Welch	1880	1892	525
7	Old Hoss Radbourn	1881	1891	489
8	John Clarkson	1882	1894	485
9	Tony Mullane	1881	1894	469
10	Jim McCormick	1878	1887	466
11	Gus Weyhing	1887	1901	448
12	G.C. Pete Alexander	1911	1930	439
13	Christy Mathewson	1900	1916	434
14	Jack Powell	1897	1912	424
15	Eddie Plank	1901	1917	410
16	Will White	1877	1886	394
17	Amos Rusie	1889	1901	392
18	Vic Willis	1898	1910	388
19	Warren Spahn	1942	1965	382
20	Jim Whitney	1881	1890	377
21	Adonis Terry	1884	1897	358
22	Ted Lyons	1923	1946	356
23	George Mullin	1902	1915	353
24	Charlie Buffington	1882	1892	351
25	Chick Fraser	1896	1909	342
26	Clark Griffith	1891	1914	337
27	Red Ruffing	1924	1947	335
28	Silver King	1886	1897	329
29	Al Orth	1885	1909	324
30	Bill Hutchison	1889	1897	319
31	Joe McGinnity	1899	1908	314
	Burleigh Grimes	1916	1934	314
33	Red Donahue	1893	1906	312
34	Guy Hecker	1882	1890	310
35	Bill Dinneen	1898	1909	306
36	Robin Roberts	1948	1966	305
37	Gaylord Perry	1962	1983	303
38	Ted Breitenstein	1891	1901	300
	Lefty Grove	1925	1941	300

Pitchers with 4000 or more INNINGS PITCHED

#		FIRST	LAST	IP
1	Cy Young	1890	1911	7375
2	Pud Galvin	1879	1892	5941
3	Walter Johnson	1907	1927	5924
4	Phil Niekro	1964	1987	5404
5	Nolan Ryan	1966	1993	5386
6	Gaylord Perry	1962	1983	5350
7	Don Sutton	1966	1988	5282
8	Warren Spahn	1942	1965	5244
9	Steve Carlton	1965	1988	5217
10	G.C. Pete Alexander	1911	1930	5190
11	Kid Nichols	1890	1906	5061
12	Tim Keefe	1880	1893	5051
13	Bert Blyleven	1970	1992	4970
14	**Roger Clemens**	**1984**		**4818**
15	Mickey Welch	1880	1892	4791
16	Tom Seaver	1967	1986	4783
17	Christy Mathewson	1900	1916	4780
18	Tommy John	1963	1989	4710
19	Robin Roberts	1948	1966	4688
20	**Greg Maddux**	**1986**		**4616**
21	Early Wynn	1939	1963	4564
22	Tony Mullane	1881	1894	4545
23	John Clarkson	1882	1894	4536
24	Old Hoss Radbourn	1881	1891	4535
25	Jim Kaat	1959	1983	4530
26	Eddie Plank	1901	1917	4507
27	Ferguson Jenkins	1965	1983	4501
28	Eppa Rixey	1912	1933	4495
29	Jack Powell	1897	1912	4389
30	Red Ruffing	1924	1947	4344
31	Gus Weyhing	1887	1901	4324
32	Jim McCormick	1878	1887	4275
33	Frank Tanana	1973	1993	4188
34	Burleigh Grimes	1916	1934	4177
35	Ted Lyons	1923	1946	4161
36	**Tom Glavine**	**1987**		**4150**
37	Red Faber	1914	1933	4087
38	Dennis Martinez	1976	1998	4000

Players active at the end of 2006 are shown in bold face

LIFETIME LEADERS - PITCHING

Pitchers with Lifetime EARNED RUN AVERAGE of 2.50 or lower since 1893
(Minimum of 1500 Innings Pitched)

#	FIRST	LAST	ERA	#	FIRST	LAST	ERA	#	FIRST	LAST	ERA	#	FIRST	LAST	ERA
1	Ed Walsh	1904	1917	1.82	7	Orvie Overall	1905	1913	2.23	12	Ed Killian	1903	1910	2.38	17	Chief Bender	1903	1925	2.46
2	Addie Joss	1902	1910	1.88	8	Ed Reulbach	1905	1917	2.28	13	George McQuillan	1907	1918	2.38	18	Sam Leever	1898	1910	2.47
3	Three Finger Brown	1903	1916	2.06	9	Jim Scott	1909	1917	2.32	14	Doc White	1901	1913	2.38	19	Lefty Leifield	1905	1920	2.47
4	Christy Mathewson	1900	1916	2.13	10	Eddie Plank	1901	1917	2.34	15	Nap Rucker	1907	1916	2.42	20	Hooks Wiltse	1904	1915	2.47
5	Rube Waddell	1897	1910	2.16	11	Eddie Cicotte	1905	1920	2.37	16	Jeff Tesreau	1912	1918	2.43	21	Hippo Vaughn	1908	1921	2.49
6	Walter Johnson	1907	1927	2.17										22	Bob Ewing	1902	1912	2.49

Pitchers with 40 or more SHUTOUTS

#	FIRST	LAST	ShO	#	FIRST	LAST	ShO	#	FIRST	LAST	ShO	#	FIRST	LAST	ShO
1	Walter Johnson	1907	1927	110		Bob Gibson	1959	1975	56	25	Kid Nichols	1890	1906	48	37	Milt Pappas	1957	1973	43
2	G.C. Pete Alexander	1911	1930	90	14	Three Finger Brown	1903	1916	55	26	Jack Powell	1897	1912	46	38	Bucky Walters	1934	1950	42
3	Christy Mathewson	1900	1916	79		Steve Carlton	1965	1988	55		Tommy John	1963	1989	46		Catfish Hunter	1965	1979	42
4	Cy Young	1890	1911	77	16	Gaylord Perry	1962	1983	53		**Roger Clemens**	**1984**		**46**	40	Mickey Welch	1880	1892	41
5	Eddie Plank	1901	1917	69		Jim Palmer	1965	1984	53	29	Addie Joss	1902	1910	45		Hippo Vaughn	1908	1921	41
6	Warren Spahn	1942	1965	63	18	Juan Marichal	1960	1975	52		Doc White	1901	1913	45		Mickey Lolich	1963	1979	41
7	Tom Seaver	1967	1986	61	19	Rube Waddell	1897	1910	50		Red Ruffing	1924	1947	45	43	Ed Reulbach	1905	1917	40
	Nolan Ryan	1966	1993	61		Vic Willis	1898	1910	50		Robin Roberts	1946	1966	45		Chief Bender	1903	1925	40
9	Bert Blyleven	1970	1992	60	21	Early Wynn	1939	1963	49		Whitey Ford	1950	1967	45		Larry French	1929	1942	40
10	Don Sutton	1966	1988	58		Don Drysdale	1956	1969	49		Phil Niekro	1964	1987	45		Sandy Koufax	1955	1966	40
11	Ed Walsh	1904	1917	57		Luis Tiant	1964	1982	49	35	Babe Adams	1906	1926	44		Jim Bunning	1955	1971	40
12	Pud Galvin	1879	1892	56		Ferguson Jenkins	1965	1983	49		Bob Feller	1936	1958	44		Mel Stottlemyre	1964	1974	40
															Claude Osteen	1957	1975	40

Pitchers with 2000 or more STRIKEOUTS

#	FIRST	LAST	SO	#	FIRST	LAST	SO	#	FIRST	LAST	SO	#	FIRST	LAST	SO
1	Nolan Ryan	1966	1993	5714	16	Jim Bunning	1955	1971	2855	31	Jack Morris	1977	1994	2478	46	Eddie Plank	1901	1917	2246
2	**Roger Clemens**	**1984**		**4606**	17	Mickey Lolich	1963	1979	2832	32	Mark Langston	1984	1999	2464	47	Tommy John	1963	1989	2245
3	**Randy Johnson**	**1988**		**4544**	18	Cy Young	1890	1911	2803	33	Jim Kaat	1959	1983	2461	48	Jim Palmer	1965	1984	2212
4	Steve Carlton	1965	1988	4136	19	**John Smoltz**	**1988**		**2778**	34	Sam McDowell	1961	1975	2453	49	C.G. Pete Alexander	1911	1930	2199
5	Bert Blyleven	1970	1992	3701	20	Frank Tanana	1973	1993	2773	35	Luis Tiant	1964	1982	2416	50	Vida Blue	1969	1986	2175
6	Tom Seaver	1967	1986	3640	21	David Cone	1986	2003	2668	36	Dennis Eckersley	1975	1998	2401	51	Camilo Pascual	1954	1971	2167
7	Don Sutton	1966	1988	3574	22	Chuck Finley	1986	2002	2610	37	Kevin Brown	1986	2005	2397	52	Dennis Martinez	1976	1998	2149
8	Gaylord Perry	1962	1983	3534	23	Warren Spahn	1942	1965	2583	38	Sandy Koufax	1955	1966	2396	53	**David Wells**	**1987**		**2119**
9	Walter Johnson	1907	1927	3509	24	Bob Feller	1936	1956	2581	39	Charlie Hough	1970	1994	2362	54	Bobo Newsom	1929	1953	2082
10	Phil Niekro	1964	1987	3342	25	**Mike Mussina**	**1991**		**2572**	40	Robin Roberts	1948	1966	2357	55	Fernando Valenzuela	1980	1997	2074
11	Ferguson Jenkins	1965	1983	3192	26	Jerry Koosman	1967	1985	2556	41	Early Wynn	1939	1963	2334	56	Dazzy Vance	1915	1935	2045
12	**Greg Maddux**	**1986**		**3169**	27	Tim Keefe	1880	1893	2542	42	Rube Waddell	1897	1910	2316	57	Rick Reuschel	1972	1991	2015
13	Bob Gibson	1959	1975	3117	28	Christy Mathewson	1900	1916	2502	43	Juan Marichal	1960	1975	2303	58	Orel Hershiser	1983	2000	2014
14	**Curt Schilling**	**1988**		**3015**	29	Don Drysdale	1956	1969	2486	44	Dwight Gooden	1984	2000	2293	59	Catfish Hunter	1965	1979	2012
15	**Pedro Martinez**	**1992**		**2998**	30	**Tom Glavine**	**1987**		**2481**	45	Lefty Grove	1925	1941	2266	60	Andy Benes	1989	2002	2000

Pitchers with 1250 or more BASES ON BALLS

#	FIRST	LAST	BB	#	FIRST	LAST	BB	#	FIRST	LAST	BB	#	FIRST	LAST	BB
1	Nolan Ryan	1966	1993	2795	12	Bump Hadley	1926	1941	1442	23	Mike Torrez	1967	1984	1371	34	Mickey Welch	1880	1892	1297
2	Steve Carlton	1965	1988	1833	13	Warren Spahn	1942	1965	1434	24	Walter Johnson	1907	1927	1355	35	Burleigh Grimes	1916	1934	1295
3	Phil Niekro	1964	1987	1809	14	Earl Whitehill	1923	1939	1431	25	Don Sutton	1966	1988	1343	36	Mark Langston	1984	1999	1289
4	Early Wynn	1939	1963	1775	15	Tony Mullane	1881	1894	1409	26	Bob Gibson	1959	1975	1336	37	Kid Nichols	1890	1906	1268
5	Bob Feller	1936	1956	1764	16	**Randy Johnson**	**1988**		**1409**	27	Chick Fraser	1896	1909	1332	38	Joe Bush	1912	1928	1263
6	Bobo Newsom	1929	1953	1732	17	**Tom Glavine**	**1987**		**1399**		Chuck Finley	1986	2002	1332	39	Joe Niekro	1967	1988	1262
7	Amos Rusie	1889	1901	1704	18	Sad Sam Jones	1914	1935	1396	29	Bert Blyleven	1970	1992	1322	40	Allie Reynolds	1942	1954	1261
8	Charlie Hough	1970	1994	1665	19	Tom Seaver	1967	1986	1390	30	Sam McDowell	1961	1975	1312	41	Tommy John	1963	1989	1259
9	Guy Weyhing	1887	1901	1566		Jack Morris	1977	1994	1390	31	Jim Palmer	1965	1984	1311	42	Frank Tanana	1973	1993	1255
10	**Roger Clemens**	**1984**		**1549**	21	Gaylord Perry	1962	1983	1379	32	Mark Baldwin	1887	1893	1307	43	Bob Lemon	1946	1958	1251
11	Red Ruffing	1924	1947	1541	22	Bobby Witt	1986	2001	1375	33	Adonis Terry	1884	1897	1301					

Pitchers with 150 or more SAVES

#	FIRST	LAST	SAVES	#	FIRST	LAST	SAVES	#	FIRST	LAST	SAVES	#	FIRST	LAST	SAVES
1	**Trevor Hoffman**	**1993**		**482**	16	Tom Henke	1982	1995	311	31	Hoyt Wilhelm	1952	1972	227	46	**Danny Graves**	**1996**		**182**
2	Lee Smith	1980	1997	478	17	Goose Gossage	1972	1994	310	32	Gene Garber	1969	1988	218	47	Tug McGraw	1965	1984	180
3	John Franco	1984	2005	424	18	Jeff Montgomery	1987	1999	304	33	Gregg Olson	1988	2001	217	48	Ron Perranoski	1961	1973	179
4	**Mariano Rivera**	**1995**		**413**	19	Doug Jones	1982	2000	303	34	Dave Smith	1980	1992	216	49	Bryan Harvey	1987	1997	177
5	Dennis Eckersley	1975	1998	390	20	Bruce Sutter	1976	1988	300	35	Jeff Shaw	1990	2001	203	50	Lindy McDaniel	1955	1975	172
6	Jeff Reardon	1979	1994	367	21	Rod Beck	1991	2004	286	36	Bobby Thigpen	1986	1994	201		Jeff Brantley	1988	2001	172
7	Randy Myers	1985	2000	347	22	**Armando Benitez**	**1994**		**280**	37	Elroy Face	1963	1969	193	52	Billy Koch	1999	2004	163
8	Rollie Fingers	1968	1985	341	23	**Todd Jones**	**1993**		**263**		Mike Henneman	1987	1996	193	53	**Eric Gagne**	**1999**		**161**
9	John Wetteland	1989	2000	330	24	Todd Worrell	1985	1997	256	39	Mitch Williams	1986	1994	192	54	Roger McDowell	1985	1997	159
10	Roberto Hernandez	1991		326	25	Dave Righetti	1979	1995	252	40	**Keith Foulke**	**1997**		**190**	55	Dan Plesac	1986	2003	158
11	Troy Percival	1995	2005	324	26	**Jason Isringhausen**	**1995**		**249**	41	Mike Marshall	1965	1981	188	56	Jay Howell	1980	1994	155
	Billy Wagner	**1995**		**324**	27	**Bob Wickman**	**1992**		**247**	42	Jeff Russell	1983	1996	186	57	Stu Miller	1953	1968	154
13	Jose Mesa	1987		320	28	Dan Quisenberry	1979	1990	244	43	Kent Tekulve	1974	1989	184		**John Smoltz**	**1988**		**154**
14	Rick Aguilera	1985	2000	318	29	Sparky Lyle	1967	1982	238		Steve Bedrosian	1981	1995	184	59	Don McMahon	1957	1974	153
15	Robb Nen	1993	2002	314	30	Ugueth Urbina	1995	2005	237	45	**Eddie Guardado**	**1993**		**183**	60	Greg Minton	1978	1990	150
															Tom Gordon	**1988**		**150**

Pitchers with 200 or more LOSSES

#	FIRST	LAST	LOSSES	#	FIRST	LAST	LOSSES	#	FIRST	LAST	LOSSES	#	FIRST	LAST	LOSSES
1	Cy Young	1890	1911	315		Robin Roberts	1948	1966	245	22	Red Ruffing	1924	1947	225		Paul Derringer	1931	1945	212
2	Pud Galvin	1879	1892	309	13	Early Wynn	1939	1963	244	23	Tim Keefe	1880	1893	224		Mickey Welch	1880	1892	209
3	Nolan Ryan	1966	1993	292		Steve Carlton	1965	1988	244	24	Bobo Newsom	1929	1953	222		Jerry Koosman	1967	1985	209
4	Walter Johnson	1907	1927	279	15	Jim Kaat	1959	1983	237	25	Jack Quinn	1909	1933	219	33	Chick Fraser	1896	1909	208
5	Phil Niekro	1964	1987	274	16	Frank Tanana	1973	1993	236	26	Sad Sam Jones	1914	1935	216	35	G.C. Pete Alexander	1911	1930	208
6	Gaylord Perry	1962	1983	265	17	Tommy John	1963	1989	231		Charlie Hough	1970	1994	216		Kid Nichols	1890	1906	208
7	Don Sutton	1966	1988	256	18	Ted Lyons	1923	1946	230	28	Jim McCormick	1878	1887	214	38	Tom Seaver	1967	1986	205
8	Jack Powell	1897	1912	255		Bob Friend	1951	1966	230	29	Tony Mullane	1881	1894	213		Jim Whitney	1881	1890	204
9	Eppa Rixey	1912	1933	251	20	Gus Weyhing	1887	1901	229	30	Burleigh Grimes	1916	1933	212	39	Joe Niekro	1967	1988	204
10	Bert Blyleven	1970	1992	250	21	Ferguson Jenkins	1965	1983	226		Red Faber	1914	1933	212	41	Vic Willis	1888	1910	203
11	Warren Spahn	1942	1965	245											**Greg Maddux**	**1986**		**203**

Players active at the end of 2006 are shown in bold face

NO HITTERS SINCE 1901

Year	Date	H/A		Pitcher	Score
1901	July 15	A		Christy Mathewson (NY) vs. St. L.(NL)	5-0
1902	Sept. 20	H (1st game)		Jim Callahan (Chi.) vs. Det.(AL)	3-0
1903	Sept. 18	A (2nd game)		Chick Fraser (Phi.) vs. Chi.(NL)	10-0
1904	May 5	H		**Cy Young** (Bos.) vs. Phi.(AL)	3-0
	Aug. 17	H		Jesse Tannehill (Bos.) vs. Chi.(AL)	6-0
1905	June 13	A	2	Christy Mathewson (NY) vs. Chi.(NL)	1-0
	July 22	A (1st game)		Weldon Henley (Phi. vs. St. L.(AL)	6-0
	Sept. 6	A (2nd game)		Frank Smith (Chi.) vs. Det.(AL)	15-0
	Sept 27	H (1st game)		Bill Dinneen (Bos.) vs. Chi.(AL)	2-0
1906	May 1	A		John Lush (Phi.) vs. Bkn.(NL)	6-0
	July 20	A		Mal Eason (Bkn.) vs. St. L.(NL)	2-0
1907	May 8	H		Big Jeff Pfeffer (Bos.) vs. Cin.(NL)	6-0
	Sept 20	H		Nick Maddox (Pit.) vs. Bkn.(NL)	2-1
1908	June 30	A	2	Cy Young (Bos.) vs. NY(AL)	8-0
	July 4	H (A.M. game)		Hooks Wiltse (NY) vs Phi(NL)	1-0
	Sept. 5	H (2nd game)		Nap Rucker (Bkn.) vs. Bos.(NL)	6-0
	Sept. 18	H		Dusty Rhoades (Cle.) vs. Bos.(AL)	2-1
	Sept. 20	H	2	Frank Smith (Chi.) vs. Phi.(AL)	1-0
	Oct. 2	H		**Addie Joss** (Cle.) vs. Chi.(AL)	1-0
1910	Apr. 20	A	2	Addie Joss (Cle.) vs. Chi.(AL)	1-0
	May 12	H		Chief Bender (Phi.) vs. Cle(AL)	4-0
1911	Jul 20	H (1st game)		Smokey Joe Wood (Bos.) vs. St. L.(AL)	5-0
	Aug 27	H		Ed Walsh (Chi.) vs. Bos.(AL)	5-0
1912	July 4	H (P.M. game)		George Mullin (Det.) vs. St. L.(AL)	7-0
	Aug. 30	A		Earl Hamilton (St. L.) vs. Det.(AL)	5-1
	Sept. 6	A (1st game)		Jeff Tesreau (NY) vs. Phi.(NL)	3-0
1914	May 31	H		Joe Benz (Chi.) vs. Cle.(AL)	6-1
	Sept. 9	H (2nd game)		George Davis (Bos.) vs. Phi.(NL)	7-0
	Sept. 19	H		Ed Lafitte (Bkn.) vs. KC(FL)	6-2
1915	Apr. 15	H		Rube Marquard (NY) vs. Bkn.(NL)	2-0
	Apr. 24	A		Frank Allen (Pit.) vs. St. L.(FL)	2-0
	May 25	A		Claude Hendrix (Chi.) vs. Pit.(FL)	10-0
	Aug. 16	A		Alex Main (KC) vs. Buf. (FL)	5-0
	Aug. 31	A (1st game)		Jimmy Lavender (Chi.) vs. NY(NL)	2-0
	Sept. 7	H		Dave Davenport (St. L.) vs. Chi.(FL)	3-0
1916	Jun. 16	H		Tom Hughes (Bos.) vs. Pit.(NL)	2-0
	Jun. 21	H		Rube Foster (Bos.) vs. NY(AL)	2-0
	Aug. 26	H		Bullet Joe Bush (Phi.) vs. Cle.(AL)	5-0
	Aug. 30	H		Dutch Leonard (Bos.) vs. St. L.(AL)	4-0
1917	Apr. 14	A		Ed Cicotte (Chi.) vs. St. L. (AL)	11-0
	Apr. 24	A		George Mogridge (NY) vs. Bos.(AL)	2-1
	May 2			Fred Toney (Cin.) vs. Chi(NL) 10 innings	1-0
	May 5	H		Ernie Koob (St. L.) vs. Chi.(AL)	1-0
	May 6	H (2nd game)		Bob Groom (St. L.) vs. Chi.(AL)	3-0
	June 23	H (1st game)		**Ernie Shore** (Bos.) vs. Was.(AL), did not start game. Ruth walked the first batter and was ejected from the game. Shore relieved, the base runner was out stealing. Shore given credit for a perfect game facing only 26 batters.	4-0
1918	June 3	A	2	Dutch Leonard (Bos.) vs. Det.(AL)	5-0
1919	May 11	H		Hod Eller (Cin.) vs. St. L.(NL)	6-0
	Sept. 10	A (1st game)		Ray Caldwell (Cle.) vs. NY(AL)	3-0
1920	July 1	A		Walter Johnson (Was.) vs. Bos.(AL)	1-0
1922	Apr. 30	A		**Charlie Robertson** (Chi.) vs. Det.(AL)	2-0
	May 7	H		Jesse Barnes (NY) vs. Phi.(NL)	6-0
1923	Sept. 4	A		Sad Sam Jones (NY) vs. Phi.(AL)	2-0
	Sept. 7	A		Howard Ehmke (Bos.) vs. Phi.(AL)	4-0
1924	July 24	H		Jesse Haines (St. L.) vs. Bos.(NL)	5-0
1925	Sept. 13	H (1st game)		Dazzy Vance (Bkn.) vs. Phi.(NL)	10-0
1926	Aug. 21	A		Ted Lyons (Chi.) vs. Bos.(AL)	6-0
1929	May 8	H		Carl Hubbell (NY) vs. Pit.(NL)	11-0
1931	Apr. 29	H		Wes Ferrell (Cle.) vs. St. L.(AL)	9-0
	Aug. 8	H		Bob Burke (Was.) vs. Bos.(AL)	5-0
1934	Sept. 21	A (2nd game)		Paul Dean (St. L.) vs. Bkn.(NL)	3-0
1935	Aug. 31	H		Vern Kennedy (Chi.) vs. Cle.(AL)	5-0
1937	June 1	H		Bill Dietrich (Chi.) vs. St. L.(AL)	8-0
1938	June 11	H		Johnny Vander Meer (Cin.) vs. Bos.(NL)	3-0
	June 15	A	2	Johnny Vander Meer (Cin.) vs. Bkn.(NL)	6-0
	Aug. 27	H		Monte Pearson (NY) vs. Cle.(AL)	13-0
1940	Apr. 16	A		Bob Feller (Cle.) vs. Chi.(AL)	1-0
	Apr. 30	A		Tex Carleton (Bkn.) vs. Cin. (NL)	3-0
1941	Aug. 30	A		Lon Warneke (St. L.) vs. Cin.(NL)	2-0
1944	Apr. 27	H		Jim Tobin (Bos.) vs. Bkn.(NL)	2-0
	May 15	H		Clyde Shoun (Cin.) vs. Bos.(NL)	1-0
1945	Sept. 9	H (2nd game)		Dick Fowler (Phi.) vs. St. L.(AL)	1-0
1946	Apr. 23	H		Ed Head (Bkn.) vs. Bos.(NL)	5-0
	Apr. 30	A	2	Bob Feller (Cle.) vs. NY(AL)	1-0
1947	June 18	H		Ewell Blackwell (Cin.) vs. Bos.(NL)	6-0
	July 10	H (1st game)		Don Black (Cle.) vs. Phi.(AL)	3-0
	Sept 3	H		Bill McCahan (Phi.) vs. Was.(AL)	3-0
1948	June 30	A		Bob Lemon (Cle.) vs. Det.(AL)	2-0
	Sept. 9	A		Rex Barney (Bkn.) vs. NY(NL)	2-0
1950	Aug. 11	H		Vern Bickford (Bos) vs. Bkn.(NL)	7-0
1951	May 6	A (2nd game)		Cliff Chambers (Pit.) vs. Bos.(NL)	3-0
	July 1	H (1st game)	3	Bob Feller (Cle.) vs. Det.(AL)	2-1
	July 12	A		Allie Reynolds (NY) vs. Cle.(AL)	1-0
	Sept. 28	H (1st game)	2	Allie Reynolds (NY) vs.Bos.(AL)	8-0
1952	May 15	H		Virgil Trucks (Det.) vs. Was.(AL)	1-0
	June 19	H		Carl Erskine (Bkn.) vs. Chi.(NL)	5-0
	Aug. 25	A	2	Virgil Trucks (Det.) vs. NY(AL)	1-0
1953	May 6	H		Bobo Holloman (St. L.) vs. Phi.(AL)	6-0
1954	June 12			Jim Wilson (Mil. vs. Phi.(NL)	2-0
1955	May 12	H		Sam Jones (Chi.) vs. Pit.(NL)	4-0
1956	May 12	H	2	Carl Erskine (Bkn.) vs. NY(NL)	3-0
	July 14	H		Mel Parnell (Bos.) vs. Chi.(AL)	4-0
	Sept. 25	H		Sal Maglie (Bkn.) vs. Phi.(NL)	5-0
	Oct. 8	H		**Don Larsen** (NY) vs. Bkn. **World Series Game**	2-0
1957	Aug. 20	H (2nd game)		Bob Keegan (Chi.) vs. Was.(AL)	6-0
1958	July 20	A (1st game)		Jim Bunning (Det.) vs. Bos.(AL)	3-0
	Sept. 20	H		Hoyt Wilhelm (Bal.) vs. NY(AL)	1-0
1960	May 15	H (2nd game)		Don Cardwell (Chi.) vs. St. L.(NL)	4-0
	Aug. 15	H		Lew Burdette (Mil.) vs. Phi.(NL)	1-0
	Sept. 16	H		Warren Spahn (Mil.) vs. Phi.(NL)	4-0
1961	Apr. 28	H	2	Warren Spahn (Mil.) vs. SF(NL)	1-0
1962	May 5	H		Bo Belinsky (LA) vs. Bal.(AL)	2-0
	June 26	H		Earl Wilson (Bos.) vs. LA(AL)	2-0
	June 30	H		Sandy Koufax (LA) vs. NY(NL)	5-0
	Aug. 1	A		Bill Monbouquette (Bos.) vs. Chi.(AL)	1-0
	Aug. 26	H		Jack Kralick (Min.) vs. KC(AL)	1-0

NO HITTERS SINCE 1901

Year	Date	H/A		Pitcher	Score
1963	May 11	H	2	Sandy Koufax (LA) vs. SF(NL)	8-0
	May 17	H		Don Nottebart (Hou.) vs. Phi.(NL)	4-1
	June 15	H		Juan Marchal (SF) vs. Hou.(NL)	1-0
1964	Apr. 23	H		Ken Johnson (Hou.) vs. Cin.(NL)	0-1
	June 4	A	3	Sandy Koufax (LA) vs. Phi.(NL)	3-0
	June 21	A (1st game)	2	**Jim Bunning** (Phi.) vs. NY(NL)	6-0
1965	Aug. 19	A (1st game)		Jim Maloney (Cin.) vs. Chi.(NL)	1-0
	Sept. 9	H	4	**Sandy Koufax** (LA) vs. Chi.(NL)	1-0
	Sept. 16	H		Dave Morehead (Bos.) vs. Cle.(AL)	2-0
1966	June 10	H		Sonny Siebert (Cle.) vs. Was.(AL)	2-0
1967	June 18	H		Don Wilson (Hou.) vs. Atl.(NL)	2-0
	Aug. 25	A (2nd game)		Dean Chance (Min.) vs. Cle.(AL)	2-1
	Sept. 10	H (1st game)		Joe Horlen (Chi.) vs. Det.(AL)	6-0
1968	Apr. 27	H		Tom Phoebus (Bal.) vs. Bos.(AL)	6-0
	May 8	H		**Catfish Hunter** (Oak.) vs. Min.(AL)	4-0
	July 29	A (2nd game)		George Culver (Cin.) vs. Phi.(NL)	6-1
	Sept. 17	H		Gaylord Perry (SF) vs. St. L.(NL)	1-0
	Sept. 18	A		Ray Washburn (St. L.) vs. SF(NL)	2-0
1969	Apr. 17	A		Bill Stoneman (Mon.) vs. Phi.(NL)	7-0
	Apr. 30	H	2	Jim Maloney (Cin.) vs. Hou.(NL)	10-0
	May 1	A	2	Don Wilson (Hou.) vs. Cin.(NL)	4-0
	Aug. 13	H		Jim Palmer (Bal.) vs. Oak.(AL)	8-0
	Aug. 19	H		Ken Holtzman (Chi.) vs. Atl.(NL)	3-0
	Sept. 20	A		Bob Moose (Pit.) vs. NY(NL)	4-0
1970	June 20	A (1st game)		Dock Ellis (Pit.) vs. SD(NL)	2-0
	July 3	H		Clyde Wright (Cal.) vs. Oak.(AL)	4-0
	July 20	H		Bill Singer (LA) vs. Phi.(NL)	5-0
	Sept. 21	H		Vida Blue (Oak.) vs. Min.(AL)	6-0
1971	June 3	H	2	Ken Holtzman (Chi.) vs. Cin.(NL)	1-0
	June 23	A		Rick Wise (Phi.) vs. Cin.(NL)	4-0
	Aug. 14	A		Bob Gibson (St. L.) vs. Pit.(NL)	11-0
1972	Apr. 16	H		Burt Hooton (Chi.) vs. Phi.(NL)	1-0
	Sept. 2	H		Milt Pappas (Chi.) vs. SD(NL)	8-0
	Oct. 2	H	2	Bill Stoneman (Mon.) vs. NY(NL)	7-0
1973	Apr. 27	A		Steve Busby (KC) vs. Det.(AL)	3-0
	May 15	A		Nolan Ryan (Cal.) vs. KC(AL)	3-0
	July 15	A	2	Nolan Ryan (Cal.) vs. Det.(AL)	6-0
	July 30	A		Jim Bibby (Tex.) vs. Oak.(AL)	6-0
	Aug. 5	H		Phil Niekro (Atl.) vs. SD(NL)	9-0
1974	June 19	A	2	Steve Busby (KC) vs. Mil.(AL)	2-0
	July 19	H		Dick Bosman (Cle.) vs. Oak.(AL)	4-0
	Sept. 28	H	3	Nolan Ryan (Cal.) vs. Min.(AL)	4-0
1975	June 1	H	4	Nolan Ryan (Cal.) vs. Bal.(AL)	1-0
	Aug. 24	H		Ed Halicki(SF) vs. NY(NL)	6-0
1976	July 9	H		Larry Dierker (Hou.) vs. Mon.(NL)	6-0
	Aug. 9	H		John Candelaria (Pit.) vs. LA(NL)	2-0
	Sept. 29	A		John Montefusco (SF) vs. Atl.(NL)	9-0
1977	May 14	H		Jim Colborn (KC) vs. Tex.(AL)	6-0
	May 30	H		Dennis Eckersley (Cle.) vs. Cal.(AL)	2-0
	Sept. 22	A		Bert Blyleven (Tex.) vs. Cal.(AL)	9-0
1978	Apr. 16	H		Bob Forsch (St. L.) vs. Phi.(NL)	5-0
	June 16	H		Tom Seaver (Cin.) vs. St. L.(NL)	4-0
1979	Apr. 7	H		Ken Forsch (Hou.) vs. Atl.(NL)	6-0

Year	Date	H/A		Pitcher	Score
1980	June 27	A		Jerry Reuss (LA) vs. SF(NL)	8-0
1981	May 10	H		Charlie Lea (Mon.) vs. SF(NL)	4-0
	May 15	H		**Len Barker** (Cle.) vs. Tor.(AL)	3-0
	Sept. 26	H	5	Nolan Ryan (Hou.) vs. LA(NL)	5-0
1983	July 4			Dave Righetti (NY) vs. Bos (AL)	4-0
	Sept. 26	H	2	Bob Forsch (St.L.) vs. Mon (NL)	3-0
	Sept. 29	H		Mike Warren (Oak.) vs. Chi (AL)	3-0
1984	Apr. 7	A		Jack Morris (Det) vs. Chi (AL)	4-0
	Sept. 30	A		**Mike Witt** (Cal) vs. Tex (AL)	1-0
1986	Sept. 19	A		Joe Cowley (Chi) vs. Cal (AL)	7-1
	Sept. 25	H		Mike Scott (Hou) vs. SF (NL)	2-0
1987	April 15	A		Juan Nieves (Mil.) vs. Bal (AL)	7-0
1988	Sept. 16	H		**Tom Browning** (Cin.) vs. LA. (NL)	1-0
1990	June 2	A		Randy Johnson (Sea) vs Det(AL)	2-0
	June 11	A	6	Nolan Ryan (Tex) vs Oak(AL)	5-0
	June 29	H		Dave Stewart (Oak) vs Tor(AL)	5-0
	June 29	A		Fernando Valenzuela (LA) vs StL(NL)	6-0
	Aug. 15	H		Terry Mulholland (Phi) vs SF(NL)	6-0
	Sept. 2	A		Dave Stieb (Tor) vs Cle(AL)	3-0
1991	May 1	H	7	Nolan Ryan (Tex.) vs. Tor.(AL)	3-0
	May 23	A		Tommy Greene (Phi.) vs. Mon.(NL)	2-0
	July 28	A		**Dennis Martinez** (Mon.) vs. LA(NL)	2-0
	Aug. 11	A		Wilson Alvarez (Chi.) vs. Bal.(AL)	7-0
	Aug. 26	H		Bret Saberhagen (KC) vs. Chi.(AL)	7-0
1992	Aug. 17	H		Kevin Gross (LA) vs. SF(NL)	2-0
1993	Apr. 22	H		Chris Bosio (Sea.) vs. Bos.(AL)	7-0
	Sept. 4	A		Jim Abbott (NY) vs. Cle(AL)	4-0
	Sept. 8	H		Darryl Kile (Hou.) vs. NY(NL)	7-1
1994	Apr. 8	A		Kent Mercker (Atl.) vs. LA(NL)	6-0
	Apr. 27	H		Scott Erickson (Min.) vs. Mil.(AL)	6-0
	July 28	H		**Kenny Rogers** (Tex.) vs. Cal.(AL)	4-0
1995	July 14	H		Ramon Martinez (L.A.) vs. Fla.(NL)	7-0
1996	May 11	H		Al Leiter (Fla.) vs. Col.(NL)	11-0
	May 14	H		Dwight Gooden (N.Y.) vs. Sea.(AL)	2-0
	Sept. 17	A		Hideo Nomo (L.A.) vs. Col.(NL)	9-0
1997	June 10	A		Kevin Brown (Fla.) vs. S.F. (NL)	9-0
1998	May 17	H		**David Wells** (NY) vs. Min. (AL)	4-0
1999	June 25	A		Jose Jimenez (St.L.) vs. Ari.(NL)	1-0
	July 18	H		**David Cone** (NYA) vs. Mon.(NL)	6-0
	Sept. 11	H		Eric Milton (Min.) vs. Ana.(AL)	7-0
2001	Apr. 4	A		Hideo Nomo (Bos.) vs. Bal. (AL)	3-0
	May 12	A		A.J. Burnett (Fla.) vs. S.D. (NL)	3-0
	Sept. 3	A		Bud Smith (St.L.) vs. S.D. (NL)	4-0
2002	Apr. 27	H		Derek Lowe (Bos.) vs. T.B. (AL)	10-0
2003	Apr. 27	H		Kevin Millwood (Phi.) vs. S.F. (NL)	1-0
2004	May 18	A		**Randy Johnson** (Ari.) vs. Atl. (NL)	2-0
2006	Sept. 6	H		Anibal Sanchez (Fla.) vs. Ari. (NL)	2-0

Bold Number - Denotes more than one no hitter for the pitcher.

Bold Name - Denotes all pitchers who have hurled a perfect game.

TEAM LEADERS
(SINGLE SEASON)

WINNING PERCENTAGE (.700)

	Team	Lg	Year	
1	Chicago	NL	1906	.763
2	Pittsburgh	NL	1902	.741
3	Pittsburgh	NL	1909	.724
4	Cleveland	AL	1954	.721
5	Seattle	AL	2001	.716
6	New York	AL	1927	.714
7	Chicago	NL	1907	.704
	Philadelphia	AL	1931	.704
9	New York	AL	1998	.704
10	New York	AL	1939	.702

WINS (100)

	Team	Lg	Year	
1	Chicago	NL	1906	116
	Seattle	AL	2001	116
3	New York	AL	1998	114
4	Cleveland	AL	1954	111
5	Pittsburgh	NL	1909	110
	New York	AL	1927	110
7	New York	NL	1961	109
	Baltimore	AL	1969	109
9	Baltimore	AL	1970	108
	Cincinnati	NL	1975	108
	New York	NL	1986	108
12	Chicago	NL	1907	107
	Philadelphia	AL	1931	107
	New York	AL	1932	107
15	New York	AL	1904	106
	New York	AL	1939	106
	St. Louis	NL	1942	106
	Atlanta	NL	1998	106
19	New York	NL	1905	105
	Boston	AL	1912	105
	St. Louis	NL	1943	105
	St. Louis	NL	1944	105
	Brooklyn	NL	1953	105
	St. Louis	NL	2004	105
25	Chicago	NL	1909	104
	Chicago	NL	1910	104
	Philadelphia	AL	1929	104
	Brooklyn	NL	1942	104
	Boston	AL	1946	104
	New York	AL	1963	104
	Detroit	AL	1984	104
	Oakland	AL	1988	104
	Atlanta	NL	1993	104
34	Pittsburgh	NL	1902	103
	New York	NL	1912	103
	New York	AL	1942	103
	New York	AL	1954	103
	San Francisco	NL	1962	103
	Detroit	AL	1968	103
	New York	AL	1980	103
	Oakland	AL	1990	103
	San Francisco	NL	1993	103
	Atlanta	NL	1999	103
	New York	AL	2002	103
	Oakland	AL	2002	103
46	Philadelphia	AL	1910	102
	Philadelphia	AL	1930	102
	New York	AL	1936	102
	New York	AL	1937	102
	Los Angeles	NL	1962	102
	Minnesota	AL	1965	102
	Cincinnati	NL	1970	102
	Los Angeles	NL	1974	102
	Cincinnati	NL	1976	102
	Kansas City	AL	1977	102
	Baltimore	AL	1979	102
	Houston	NL	1998	102
	Oakland	AL	2001	102
59	Philadelphia	AL	1911	101
	New York	NL	1913	101
	Boston	AL	1915	101
	New York	AL	1928	101
	St. Louis	NL	1931	101
	Detroit	AL	1934	101
	New York	AL	1941	101
	Detroit	AL	1961	101
	St. Louis	NL	1967	101
	Baltimore	AL	1971	101
	Oakland	AL	1971	101
	Philadelphia	NL	1976	101
	Philadelphia	NL	1977	101
	St. Louis	NL	1985	101
	Atlanta	NL	1997	101
	Atlanta	NL	2002	101
	Atlanta	NL	2003	101
	New York	AL	2003	101
	New York	AL	2004	101
78	Detroit	AL	1915	100
	Chicago	AL	1917	100
	Chicago	NL	1935	100
	Cincinnati	NL	1940	100
	Brooklyn	NL	1941	100
	New York	NL	1969	100
	New York	AL	1977	100
	New York	AL	1978	100
	Baltimore	AL	1980	100
	New York	NL	1988	100
	Cleveland	AL	1995	100
	Arizona	NL	1999	100
	San Francisco	NL	2003	100
	St. Louis	NL	2005	100

LOSSES (106)

	Team	Lg	Year	
1	New York	NL	1962	120
2	Detroit	AL	2003	119
3	Philadelphia	AL	1916	117
4	Boston	AL	1935	115
5	Washington	AL	1904	113
6	Pittsburgh	NL	1952	112
	New York	NL	1965	112
8	Boston	AL	1932	111
	St. Louis	NL	1939	111
	Philadelphia	NL	1941	111
	New York	NL	1963	111
	Arizona	NL	2004	111
13	Washington	AL	1909	110
	Montreal	NL	1969	110
	San Diego	NL	1969	110
16	Philadelphia	AL	1915	109
	Philadelphia	AL	1928	109
	Philadelphia	AL	1942	109
	New York	NL	1964	109
	Toronto	AL	1979	109
	Detroit	AL	1996	109
22	Boston	NL	1909	108
	St. Louis	AL	1937	108
	Philadelphia	AL	1945	108
	Oakland	AL	1979	108
	Florida	NL	1998	108
27	St. Louis	AL	1910	107
	Boston	NL	1911	107
	St. Louis	AL	1911	107
	Baltimore	FL	1915	107
	Boston	AL	1926	107
	Philadelphia	AL	1961	107
	Montreal	NL	1976	107
	Toronto	AL	1977	107
	Baltimore	AL	1988	107
36	Philadelphia	AL	1920	106
	Philadelphia	NL	1939	106
	Washington	AL	1963	106
	Chicago	AL	1970	106
	Atlanta	NL	1988	106
	Detroit	AL	2002	106
	Milwaukee	NL	2002	106
	Tampa Bay	AL	2002	106
	Kansas City	AL	2005	106

SAVES (55)

	Team	Lg	Year	
1	Chicago	AL	1990	68
2	Oakland	AL	1988	64
	Oakland	AL	1990	64
4	Montreal	NL	1993	61
5	Cincinnati	NL	1970	60
	Cincinnati	NL	1972	60
	Toronto	AL	1991	60
8	Baltimore	AL	1997	59
	San Diego	NL	1998	59
	New York	AL	2004	59
11	Minnesota	AL	1970	58
	New York	AL	1986	58
	Oakland	AL	1992	58
	Los Angeles	NL	2003	58
15	Oakland	AL	1989	57
	New York	AL	2001	57
	Atlanta	NL	2002	57
	St. Louis	NL	2004	57
19	Chicago	NL	1993	56
	Chicago	NL	1998	56
	Seattle	AL	2001	56
	Los Angeles	NL	2002	56
23	San Diego	NL	1978	55
	Chicago	NL	1989	55
	Cincinnati	NL	1992	55
	Cincinnati	NL	1999	55

PITCHER'S STRIKEOUTS (1150)

	Team	Lg	Year	
1	Chicago	NL	2003	1404
2	Chicago	NL	2004	1346
3	Chicago	NL	2001	1344
4	Chicago	NL	2002	1333
5	Arizona	NL	2002	1303
6	Arizona	NL	2001	1297
7	Arizona	NL	2003	1291
8	Los Angeles	NL	2003	1289
9	Houston	NL	2004	1282
10	New York	AL	2001	1266
11	Boston	AL	2001	1259
12	Chicago	NL	2005	1256
13	Chicago	NL	2006	1250
14	Atlanta	NL	1996	1245
15	Los Angeles	NL	1997	1232
	Atlanta	NL	1998	1232
17	Houston	NL	2001	1228
18	Houston	NL	1969	1221
19	Arizona	NL	2000	1220
20	Houston	NL	2002	1219
21	Cleveland	AL	2001	1218
22	New York	NL	1990	1217
	San Diego	NL	1998	1217
24	Cleveland	AL	2000	1213
25	Los Angeles	NL	1996	1212
	Los Angeles	NL	2001	1212
27	Philadelphia	NL	1997	1209
28	Seattle	AL	1997	1207
	Chicago	NL	1998	1207
30	Montreal	NL	1996	1206
31	Houston	NL	1999	1204
32	Arizona	NL	1999	1198
33	Atlanta	NL	1999	1197
34	Atlanta	NL	1997	1196
35	San Diego	NL	1996	1194
36	New York	NL	2001	1191
37	Cleveland	AL	1967	1189
38	Florida	NL	1997	1188
39	Houston	NL	1998	1187
40	Los Angeles	NL	1998	1178
41	Philadelphia	NL	1998	1176
42	Milwaukee	NL	2005	1173
43	New York	NL	1999	1172
44	Boston	AL	1996	1165
	New York	AL	1997	1165
46	New York	NL	2000	1164
	Anaheim	AL	2004	1164
	Houston	NL	2005	1164
	Los Angeles	AL	2006	1164
	Minnesota	AL	2006	1164
51	Houston	NL	1996	1163
52	Cleveland	AL	1964	1162
53	New York	NL	2006	1161
54	Houston	NL	1986	1160
	Houston	NL	2006	1160
56	Cincinnati	NL	1997	1159
	Philadelphia	NL	2005	1159
58	Cleveland	AL	1968	1157
	New York	NL	1971	1157
	Boston	AL	2002	1157
61	Cleveland	AL	1965	1156
	Seattle	AL	1998	1156
63	Toronto	AL	1998	1154
	Los Angeles	NL	2000	1154
65	Arizona	NL	2004	1153
66	Toronto	AL	1997	1150

SHUTOUTS (25)

	Team	Lg	Year	
1	Chicago	AL	1906	32
	Chicago	NL	1907	32
	Chicago	NL	1909	32
4	Chicago	NL	1906	30
	St. Louis	NL	1968	30
6	Chicago	NL	1908	29
7	Los Angeles	NL	1964	28
	New York	NL	1969	28
9	Cleveland	AL	1906	27
	Pittsburgh	NL	1906	27
	Philadelphia	AL	1907	27
	Philadelphia	AL	1909	27
13	Chicago	AL	1904	26
	Philadelphia	AL	1904	26
	Chicago	AL	1909	26
	St. Louis	NL	1944	26
	Cleveland	AL	1948	26
18	New York	NL	1908	25
	Chicago	AL	1910	25
	Boston	AL	1918	25
	New York	NL	1968	25

EARNED RUN AVERAGE (2.25)

	Team	Lg	Year	
1	Chicago	NL	1907	1.73
2	Chicago	NL	1909	1.75
3	Chicago	NL	1906	1.76
4	Philadelphia	AL	1910	1.78
5	Philadelphia	AL	1909	1.92
6	Chicago	AL	1905	1.99
7	Chicago	AL	1910	2.01
8	Cleveland	AL	1908	2.02
9	Chicago	NL	1905	2.04
	Chicago	AL	1909	2.04
11	Pittsburgh	NL	1909	2.07
12	Cleveland	AL	1906	2.09
13	Philadelphia	AL	1908	2.10
14	Boston	AL	1904	2.12
	Pittsburgh	NL	1908	2.12
	Brooklyn	NL	1916	2.12
17	Chicago	AL	1906	2.13
18	Chicago	AL	1908	2.14
	New York	NL	1908	2.14
	Washington	AL	1918	2.14
21	St. Louis	AL	1908	2.15
22	Chicago	AL	1917	2.16
23	New York	AL	1904	2.17
	Philadelphia	AL	1915	2.17
25	Chicago	NL	1918	2.18
26	Philadelphia	AL	1905	2.19
	Boston	NL	1916	2.19
28	Boston	AL	1917	2.20
29	Chicago	NL	1902	2.21
	Pittsburgh	NL	1906	2.21
	Chicago	NL	1919	2.21
32	Cleveland	AL	1904	2.22
	Chicago	AL	1907	2.22
	Chicago	AL	1908	2.22
35	St. Louis	NL	1906	2.23
	Cincinnati	NL	1919	2.23

RUNS SCORED (900)

	Team	Lg	Year	
1	New York	AL	1931	1067
2	New York	AL	1936	1065
3	New York	AL	1930	1062
4	Boston	AL	1950	1027
5	Cleveland	AL	1999	1009
6	St. Louis	NL	1930	1004
7	New York	NL	1932	1002
8	Chicago	NL	1930	998
9	Seattle	AL	1996	993
10	Chicago	NL	1929	982
11	Philadelphia	NL	1932	981
12	New York	AL	1937	979
13	Chicago	AL	2000	978
14	New York	AL	1927	975
15	Colorado	NL	2000	968
16	New York	AL	1939	967
17	New York	AL	1938	966
18	New York	AL	1998	965
19	Colorado	NL	1996	961
	Boston	AL	2003	961
21	New York	AL	1930	959
22	Detroit	AL	1934	958
23	Brooklyn	NL	1953	955
24	Cleveland	AL	1996	952
25	Philadelphia	NL	1930	951
26	Cleveland	AL	2000	950
27	Baltimore	AL	1996	949
	Boston	AL	2004	949
29	New York	AL	1921	948
30	Oakland	AL	2000	947
31	Texas	AL	1999	945
32	Philadelphia	NL	1930	944
33	Texas	AL	1998	940
34	Houston	NL	2000	938
35	Detroit	AL	1937	935
36	New York	AL	2006	930
37	Boston	AL	1996	928
	Texas	AL	1996	928
39	New York	AL	1933	927
	Seattle	AL	2001	927
	Chicago	AL	2002	927
42	Detroit	AL	1929	926
43	Cleveland	AL	1921	925
	Seattle	AL	1997	925
	San Francisco	NL	2000	925
46	Colorado	NL	1997	923
	Colorado	NL	2001	923
48	Cleveland	AL	1936	921
	Detroit	AL	1936	921
50	Chicago	AL	1936	920
51	Detroit	AL	1935	919
52	New York	AL	1950	914
53	Pittsburgh	NL	1925	912
54	Boston	AL	2005	910
55	Arizona	NL	1999	908
56	Boston	AL	1948	907
	Seattle	AL	2000	907
	Atlanta	NL	2003	907
59	Colorado	NL	1999	906
60	Pittsburgh	NL	1929	904
61	Detroit	AL	1925	903
62	Boston	AL	1938	902
63	Philadelphia	NL	1929	901
64	New York	AL	1999	900

HITS (1640)

	Team	Lg	Year	
1	Philadelphia	NL	1930	1783
2	New York	NL	1930	1769
3	St. Louis	NL	1930	1732
4	Detroit	AL	1921	1724
5	Chicago	NL	1930	1722
6	Cleveland	AL	1936	1715
7	Pittsburgh	NL	1922	1698
8	St. Louis	AL	1922	1693
	Philadelphia	NL	1929	1693
10	Boston	AL	1997	1684
11	New York	AL	1930	1683
12	New York	AL	1936	1676
13	Detroit	AL	1929	1671
14	New York	AL	1931	1667
	Boston	AL	2003	1667
16	Boston	AL	1950	1665
	Cleveland	AL	1996	1665
18	Colorado	NL	2000	1664
19	Pittsburgh	NL	1929	1663
	Colorado	NL	2001	1663
21	New York	AL	1922	1661
22	Philadelphia	AL	1925	1659
	Pittsburgh	NL	1928	1659
24	Cleveland	AL	1921	1656
25	St. Louis	NL	1921	1655
	Chicago	NL	1929	1655
27	Brooklyn	NL	1930	1654
	Cleveland	AL	1930	1654
29	Texas	AL	1999	1653
30	Pittsburgh	NL	1925	1651
	St. Louis	NL	1920	1651
32	Pittsburgh	NL	1927	1648
33	New York	AL	1927	1644
	Detroit	AL	1934	1644
	Colorado	NL	1999	1644
	Kansas City	AL	2000	1644
37	Detroit	AL	1922	1641
38	Colorado	NL	1998	1640

TEAM LEADERS
(SINGLE SEASON)

DOUBLES (330)

	Team	Lg	Year	
1	St. Louis	NL	1930	373
	Boston	AL	1997	373
	Boston	AL	2004	373
4	Boston	AL	2003	371
5	Cleveland	AL	1930	358
6	Cleveland	AL	1936	357
	Toronto	AL	2003	357
	Texas	AL	2006	357
9	Cleveland	AL	1921	355
10	St. Louis	NL	1931	353
	Cleveland	AL	2006	351
12	Detroit	AL	1934	349
13	Boston	AL	2002	348
	Toronto	AL	2006	348
	Minnesota	AL	2002	348
16	Philadelphia	NL	1930	345
	Cleveland	AL	2004	345
18	Seattle	AL	1996	343
19	St. Louis	NL	2003	342
20	Chicago	NL	1931	340
	Cleveland	AL	1934	340
22	Detroit	AL	1929	339
	Montreal	NL	1997	339
	Boston	AL	2005	339
25	Boston	AL	1998	338
26	Toronto	AL	1999	337
	Cleveland	AL	2005	337
28	Oakland	AL	2004	336
29	Cleveland	AL	1996	335
	Cincinnati	NL	2005	335
	Kansas City	AL	2006	335
32	Cleveland	AL	1998	334
	Boston	AL	1999	334
	Oakland	AL	2001	334
35	Cleveland	AL	1926	333
	Colorado	NL	1998	333
	Anaheim	AL	2002	333
38	St. Louis	NL	1936	332
	St. Louis	NL	1939	332
	Minnesota	AL	1996	332
41	Colorado	NL	2004	331
	Arizona	NL	2006	331
43	Philadelphia	NL	1932	330
	Texas	AL	2000	330
	Colorado	NL	2003	330

TRIPLES (100)

	Team	Lg	Year	
1	Pittsburgh	NL	1912	129
2	Pittsburgh	NL	1924	122
3	Cincinnati	NL	1926	120
4	Pittsburgh	NL	1930	119
5	Pittsburgh	NL	1929	116
6	Boston	AL	1903	113
7	Baltimore	AL	1901	111
	Pittsburgh	NL	1923	111
	Cincinnati	NL	1924	111
10	Pittsburgh	NL	1903	110
	Pittsburgh	NL	1922	110
	New York	AL	1930	110
13	Philadelphia	AL	1912	108
14	Baltimore	AL	1902	107
15	Philadelphia	AL	1910	106
	Pittsburgh	NL	1911	106
	Pittsburgh	NL	1926	106
18	Boston	AL	1904	105
	Cincinnati	NL	1911	105
	St. Louis	AL	1921	105
	Pittsburgh	NL	1925	105
22	Boston	AL	1901	104
	Pittsburgh	NL	1921	104
24	New York	NL	1911	103
	New York	AL	1927	103
26	Pittsburgh	NL	1904	102
	Chicago	AL	1915	102
28	Cincinnati	NL	1905	101
	Chicago	NL	1911	101
	Detroit	AL	1913	101
	Boston	AL	1913	101
32	Chicago	AL	1916	100
	Cincinnati	NL	1917	100
	Boston	NL	1921	100
	Detroit	AL	1921	100
	Detroit	AL	1927	100
	Pittsburgh	NL	1928	100
	Washington	AL	1932	100

HOME RUNS (220)

	Team	Lg	Year	
1	Seattle	AL	1997	264
2	Texas	AL	2005	260
3	Baltimore	AL	1996	257
4	Houston	NL	2000	249
5	Texas	AL	2001	246
6	Seattle	AL	1996	245
7	Seattle	AL	1999	244
	Toronto	AL	2000	244
9	Oakland	AL	1996	243
	New York	AL	2004	243
10	Chicago	AL	2004	242
	New York	AL	2004	242
12	New York	AL	1961	240
13	Colorado	NL	1997	239
	Oakland	AL	2000	239
	Texas	AL	2003	239
16	Boston	AL	2003	238
17	Anaheim	AL	2000	236
	Chicago	AL	2006	236
19	Oakland	AL	1999	235
	St. Louis	NL	2000	235
	San Francisco	NL	2001	235
	Atlanta	NL	2003	235
	Chicago	AL	2004	235
24	Seattle	AL	1998	234
25	Texas	AL	1999	230
	Texas	AL	2002	230
	New York	AL	2003	230
28	New York	AL	2005	229
29	Texas	AL	2004	227
30	San Francisco	NL	2000	226
	Chicago	AL	2002	226
32	Minnesota	AL	1963	225
	Detroit	AL	1987	225
34	St. Louis	NL	1998	223
	Colorado	NL	1999	223
	New York	AL	2002	223
37	Boston	AL	2004	222
	Cincinnati	NL	2005	222
	Atlanta	NL	2006	222
40	New York	NL	1947	221
	Cincinnati	NL	1956	221
	Minnesota	AL	1964	221
	Texas	AL	1996	221
	Colorado	NL	1996	221
	Toronto	AL	1998	221
	Cleveland	AL	2000	221
47	Cleveland	AL	1997	220
	Chicago	AL	2003	220

BATTER'S BASES ON BALLS (700)

	Team	Lg	Year	
1	Boston	AL	1949	835
2	Boston	AL	1948	823
3	Philadelphia	AL	1949	783
4	St. Louis	AL	1941	775
	Seattle	AL	2000	775
6	Oakland	AL	1999	770
7	New York	AL	1932	766
8	Detroit	AL	1993	765
9	Detroit	AL	1947	762
10	Boston	AL	1951	756
11	Detroit	AL	1949	751
12	Oakland	AL	2000	750
13	New York	AL	1938	749
14	New York	AL	1931	748
15	Cleveland	AL	1999	743
16	Brooklyn	NL	1947	732
17	New York	AL	1949	731
18	San Francisco	NL	1970	729
19	Houston	NL	1999	728
20	Boston	AL	1956	727
21	Philadelphia	AL	1948	726
22	Cleveland	AL	1955	723
23	Detroit	AL	1950	722
24	Boston	AL	1950	719
25	New York	AL	1999	718
26	Baltimore	AL	1970	717
27	New York	NL	1999	717
28	San Francisco	NL	1969	711
29	New York	AL	1937	709
	San Francisco	NL	2000	709
31	Boston	AL	1955	707
	Oakland	AL	1992	707
33	San Francisco	NL	2004	705
34	Chicago	AL	1949	702
35	New York	AL	1939	701
	Chicago	AL	1996	701
37	New York	AL	1933	700
	New York	AL	1934	700
	New York	AL	1936	700

BATTER'S STRIKEOUTS (1150)

	Team	Lg	Year	
1	Milwaukee	NL	2001	1399
2	Cincinnati	NL	2004	1335
3	Cincinnati	NL	2003	1326
4	Cincinnati	NL	2005	1303
5	San Diego	NL	2001	1273
6	Chicago	NL	2002	1269
7	Detroit	AL	1996	1268
8	St. Louis	NL	2000	1253
9	Florida	NL	2006	1249
10	Milwaukee	NL	2000	1245
11	Arizona	NL	1998	1239
12	Milwaukee	NL	2006	1233
13	Chicago	NL	1998	1223
14	Milwaukee	NL	2003	1221
15	Cleveland	AL	2006	1204
16	New York	NL	1968	1203
	Philadelphia	NL	2006	1203
18	St. Louis	NL	1999	1202
19	Pittsburgh	NL	2006	1200
20	Pittsburgh	NL	1999	1197
21	Cincinnati	NL	2006	1192
22	St. Louis	NL	1997	1191
23	Los Angeles	NL	1996	1190
24	San Francisco	NL	1996	1189
	Boston	AL	2004	1189
26	Cincinnati	NL	2002	1188
27	Detroit	AL	1991	1185
28	Florida	NL	2000	1184
29	Oakland	AL	1997	1181
	Colorado	NL	2004	1181
31	St. Louis	NL	1998	1179
32	San Diego	NL	2000	1177
33	Cincinnati	NL	2001	1172
34	New York	NL	2003	1171
35	Chicago	NL	1999	1170
36	San Diego	NL	1999	1169
	Atlanta	NL	2006	1169
38	San Diego	NL	1970	1164
	Detroit	AL	1997	1164
40	Milwaukee	NL	2005	1162
41	Pittsburgh	NL	1997	1161
42	Atlanta	NL	1997	1160
43	Oakland	AL	2000	1159
	New York	AL	2004	1159
45	Chicago	NL	2003	1158
	Atlanta	NL	2004	1158
47	Washington	NL	2006	1156
48	Philadelphia	NL	2003	1155
49	Philadelphia	NL	1986	1154

STOLEN BASES (250)

	Team	Lg	Year	
1	New York	NL	1911	347
2	Oakland	AL	1976	341
3	New York	NL	1912	319
4	St. Louis	NL	1985	314
5	Cincinnati	NL	1910	310
6	New York	NL	1913	296
7	New York	NL	1905	291
8	Cincinnati	NL	1911	290
9	New York	NL	1906	288
	New York	AL	1910	288
11	Washington	AL	1913	287
12	New York	NL	1904	283
13	Chicago	NL	1906	283
14	New York	NL	1910	282
15	Chicago	AL	1901	280
	Detroit	AL	1909	280
	Cincinnati	NL	1909	280
18	Detroit	AL	1911	276
19	Washington	AL	1912	274
20	Brooklyn	NL	1903	273
	Indianapolis	FL	1914	273
22	New York	NL	1911	270
	Detroit	AL	1912	270
24	Chicago	NL	1905	267
25	Chicago	AL	1902	265
26	New York	NL	1903	264
	Pittsburgh	NL	1907	264
28	St. Louis	NL	1986	262
29	Pittsburgh	NL	1977	260
30	Chicago	NL	1903	259
31	Philadelphia	AL	1912	258
32	Milwaukee	AL	1992	256
33	New York	AL	1914	251

BATTING AVERAGE (.300)

	Team	Lg	Year	
1	New York	NL	1930	.319
2	Detroit	AL	1921	.316
3	Philadelphia	AL	1930	.315
4	St. Louis	NL	1930	.314
5	St. Louis	NL	1922	.313
6	New York	AL	1930	.309
7	Pittsburgh	NL	1928	.309
8	Philadelphia	NL	1929	.309
9	Chicago	NL	1930	.309
10	St. Louis	AL	1920	.308
11	St. Louis	AL	1921	.308
12	Cleveland	AL	1921	.308
13	Pittsburgh	NL	1922	.308
14	New York	AL	1927	.307
15	Pittsburgh	NL	1925	.307
16	Philadelphia	AL	1925	.307
17	Pittsburgh	NL	1927	.305
18	Detroit	AL	1922	.305
19	New York	AL	1922	.304
20	Brooklyn	NL	1930	.304
21	St. Louis	AL	1921	.304
22	Cleveland	AL	1930	.304
23	Cleveland	AL	1936	.304
24	Pittsburgh	NL	1930	.303
25	Philadelphia	AL	1927	.303
26	Cleveland	AL	1920	.303
27	Washington	AL	1925	.303
28	Pittsburgh	NL	1929	.303
29	Chicago	NL	1929	.303
30	Boston	NL	1950	.302
31	Detroit	AL	1925	.302
32	Washington	AL	1930	.302
33	Cleveland	AL	1923	.301
34	St. Louis	NL	1922	.301
35	Detroit	AL	1934	.300
36	New York	AL	1921	.300
37	New York	NL	1924	.300

SLUGGING AVERAGE (.460)

	Team	Lg	Year	
1	Boston	AL	2003	.491
2	New York	AL	1927	.489
3	New York	AL	1930	.488
4	Seattle	AL	1997	.485
5	Cleveland	AL	1994	.484
6	Seattle	AL	1996	.484
7	New York	AL	1936	.483
8	Colorado	NL	2001	.483
9	Chicago	NL	1930	.481
10	Cleveland	AL	1995	.479
11	Texas	AL	1999	.479
12	Colorado	NL	1997	.478
13	Houston	NL	2000	.477
14	Atlanta	NL	2003	.475
15	Cleveland	AL	1996	.475
16	Brooklyn	NL	1953	.474
17	New York	NL	1930	.473
18	Anaheim	AL	2000	.472
19	Colorado	NL	1996	.472
20	Boston	AL	2004	.472
21	San Francisco	NL	2000	.472
22	Baltimore	AL	1996	.472
23	Colorado	NL	1999	.472
24	St. Louis	NL	1930	.471
25	Cleveland	AL	1995	.471
26	Texas	AL	2001	.471
27	Cleveland	AL	2000	.470
28	Chicago	AL	2000	.470
29	Toronto	AL	2000	.469
30	Texas	AL	1996	.469
31	Texas	AL	2005	.469
32	Seattle	AL	1998	.468
33	Cleveland	AL	1997	.467
34	Cleveland	AL	1999	.467
35	Philadelphia	NL	1929	.467
36	Boston	AL	1977	.465
37	New York	AL	1921	.464
38	Chicago	AL	2006	.464
39	Boston	AL	1950	.464
40	Boston	AL	1997	.463
41	Toronto	AL	2006	.463
42	Boston	AL	1998	.463
43	New York	AL	1994	.462
44	Cleveland	AL	1998	.462
45	Cleveland	AL	1936	.461
46	New York	AL	2006	.461
47	Colorado	NL	1998	.461
48	New York	AL	1998	.460
49	San Francisco	NL	2001	.460

AWARDS

CHALMERS AWARD

AMERICAN LEAGUE			NATIONAL LEAGUE	
Ty Cobb-Det.	1911		Wildfire Schulte-Chi.	
Tris Speaker-Bos.	1912		Larry Doyle-N.Y.	
Walter Johnson-Was.	1913		Jack Daubert-Bkn.	
Eddie Collins-Phi.	1914		Johnny Evers-Bos.	

TRIPLE CROWN WINNERS

Year	Name-Team (league)	HR	RBI's	B.Avg.
1887	Tip O'Neill-St. L. (AA)	14*	123	.442
1894	Hugh Duffy-Bos. (NL)	18	145	.438
1901	Nap Lajoie-Phi. (AL)	14	125	.422
1909	Ty Cobb-Det. (AL)	9	107	.377
1922	Rogers Hornsby-St. L. (NL)	42	152	.401
1925	Rogers Hornsby-St. L. (NL)	39	143	.403
1933	Jimmie Foxx-Phi. (AL)	48	163	.356
1933	Chuck Klein-Phi. (NL)	28	120	.368
1934	Lou Gerhig-N.Y. (AL)	49	165	.363
1937	Joe Medwick-St. L . (NL)	31*	154	.374
1942	Ted Williams-Bos. (AL)	36	137	.356
1947	Ted Williams-Bos.(AL)	32	114	.343
1956	Mickey Mantle-N.Y. (AL)	52	130	.353
1966	Frank Robinson-Bal. (AL)	49	122	.316
1967	Carl Yastrzemski-Bos. (AL)	44*	121	.326

* = tied for lead

LEAGUE AWARDS

AMERICAN LEAGUE			NATIONAL LEAGUE
George Sisler-St. L.	1922		No selection made
Babe Ruth-N.Y.	1923		No selection made
Walter Johnson-Was.	1924		Dazzy Vance-Bkn.
Roger Peckinpaugh-Was.	1925		Rogers Hornsby-St. L.
George Burns-Cle.	1926		Bob O'Farrell-St. L.
Lou Gehrig-N.Y.	1927		Paul Waner-Pit.
Mickey Cochrane-Phi.	1928		Jim Bottomley-St. L.
No selection made	1929		Rogers Hornsby-Chi.

M.V.P. AWARDS
Selected by the Baseball Writers Association of America
(* Unanimous selection)

AMERICAN LEAGUE		Points	Year	NATIONAL LEAGUE		Points
Lefty Grove-Phi.	p	78	1931	Frankie Frisch-St.L.	2b	65
Jimmie Foxx-Phi.	1b	75	1932	Chuck Klein-Phi.	of	78
Jimmie Foxx-Phi.	1b	74	1933	Carl Hubbell-N.Y.	p	77
Mickey Cochrane-Det.	c	67	1934	Dizzy Dean-St. L.	p	78
Hank Greenberg-Det.	1b	*80	1935	Gabby Hartnett-Chi.	c	75
Lou Gehrig-N.Y.	1b	73	1936	Carl Hubbell-N.Y.	p	60
Charlie Gerhinger-Det.	2b	78	1937	Joe Medwick-St. L.	of	70
Jimmie Foxx-Bos.	1b	305	1938	Ernie Lombardi-Cin.	c	229
Joe DiMaggio-N.Y.	of	280	1939	Bucky Walters-Cin.	p	303
Hank Greenberg-Det.	of	292	1940	Frank McCormick-Cin	1b	274
Joe DiMaggio-N.Y.	of	291	1941	Dolph Camili-Bkn.	1b	300
Joe Gordon-N.Y.	2b	270	1942	Mort Cooper-St. L.	p	263
Spud Chandler-N.Y.	p	246	1943	Stan Musial-St. L.	of	267
Hal Newhouser-Det.	p	236	1944	Marty Marion-St. L.	ss	190
Hal Newhouser-Det.	p	236	1945	Phil Cavarretta-Chi.	1b	279
Ted Williams-Bos.	of	224	1946	Stan Musial-St. L.	1b	319
Joe DiMaggio-N.Y.	of	202	1947	Bob Elliot-Bos.	3b	205
Lou Boudreau-Cle.	ss	324	1948	Stan Musial-St. L.	of	303
Ted Williams-Bos.	of	272	1949	Jackie Robinson-Bkn.	2b	264
Phil Rizzuto-N.Y.	ss	284	1950	Jim Konstanty-Phi.	p	286
Yogi Berra-N.Y.	c	184	1951	Roy Campanella-Bos.	c	243
Bobby Shantz-Phi.	p	280	1952	Hank Sauer-Chi.	of	226
Al Rosen-Cle.	3b	*336	1953	Roy Campanella-Bkn.	c	297
Yogi Berra-N.Y.	c	230	1954	Willie Mays-N.Y.	of	283
Yogi Berra-N.Y.	c	218	1955	Roy Campanella-Bkn.	c	226
Mickey Mantle-N.Y.	of	*336	1956	Don Newcombe-Bkn.	p	223
Mickey Mantle-N.Y.	of	233	1957	Hank Aaron-Mil.	of	239
Jackie Jensen-Bos.	of	233	1958	Ernie Banks-Chi.	ss	283
Nellie Fox-Chi.	2b	295	1959	Ernie Banks-Chi.	ss	232.5
Roger Maris-N.Y.	of	225	1960	Dick Groat-Pit.	ss	276
Roger Maris-N.Y.	of	202	1961	Frank Robinson-Cin.	of	219
Mickey Mantle-N.Y.	of	234	1962	Maury Wills-L.A.	ss	209
Elston Howard-N.Y.	c	248	1963	Sandy Koufax-L.A.	p	237
Brooks Robinson-Bal.	3b	269	1964	Ken Boyer-St. L.	3b	243
Zoilo Versalles-Min.	ss	275	1965	Willie Mays-S.F.	of	224
Frank Robinson-Bal.	of	*280	1966	Roberto Clemente-Pit.	of	218
Carl Yastrzemski-Bos.	of	275	1967	Orlando Cepeda-St. L.	1b	*280
Denny McLain-Det.	p	*280	1968	Bob Gibson-St. L.	p	242

AMERICAN LEAGUE		Points	Year	NATIONAL LEAGUE		Points
Harmon Killebrew-Min.	1b-3b	294	1969	Willie McCovey-S.F.	1b	265
Boog Powell-Bal.	1b	234	1970	Johnny Bench-Cin.	c	326
Vida Blue-Oak.	p	268	1971	Joe Torre-St. L.	3b	318
Dick Allen-Chi.	1b	321	1972	Johnny Bench-Cin.	c	263
Reggie Jackson-Oak.	of	*336	1973	Pete Rose-Cin.	of	274
Jeff Burroughs-Tex.	of	248	1974	Steve Garvey-L.A.	1b	270
Fred Lynn-Bos.	of	326	1975	Joe Morgan-Cin.	2b	321.5
Thurman Munson-N.Y.	c	304	1976	Joe Morgan-Cin.	2b	311
Rod Carew-Min.	1b	273	1977	George Foster-Cin.	of	291
Jim Rice-Bos.	of	352	1978	Dave Parker-Pit.	of	320
Don Baylor-Cal.	of	347	1979	Willie Stargell-Pit.	1b	216
				Keith Hernandez-St. L.	1b	216
George Brett-K.C.	3b	335	1980	Mike Schmidt-Phi.	3b	*336
Rollie Fingers-Mil.	p	312	1981	Mike Schmidt-Phi.	3b	321
Robin Yount-Mil.	ss	385	1982	Dale Murphy-Atl.	of	283
Cal Ripken-Bal.	ss	322	1983	Dale Murphy-Atl.	of	318
Willie Hernandez-Det.	p	306	1984	Ryne Sandberg-Chi.	2b	326
Don Mattingly-N.Y.	1b	367	1985	Willie McGee-St. L.	of	280
Roger Clemens-Bos.	p	339	1986	Mike Schmidt-Phi.	3b	287
George Bell-Tor.	of	332	1987	Andre Dawson-Chi.	of	269
Jose Canseco-Oak.	of	*392	1988	Kirk Gibson-L.A.	of	282
Robin Yount-Mil.	of	256	1989	Kevin Mitchell-S.F.	3b	314
Rickey Henderson-Oak.	of	317	1990	Barry Bonds-Pit.	of	331
Cal Ripken-Bal.	ss	318	1991	Terry Pendleton-Atl.	3b	274
Dennis Eckersley-Oak	p	306	1992	Barry Bonds-Pit	of	304
Frank Thomas-Chi.	1b	*392	1993	Barry Bonds-S.F.	of	372
Frank Thomas-Chi.	1b	372	1994	Jeff Bagwell-Hou.	1b	*392
Mo Vaughn-Bos.	1b	308	1995	Barry Larkin-Cin.	ss	281
Juan Gonzalez-Tex.	of	290	1996	Ken Caminiti-S.D.	3b	*392
Ken Griffey-Sea.	of	392	1997	Larry Walker-Col.	of	359
Juan Gonzalez-Tex.	of	357	1998	Sammy Sosa-Chi.	of	438
Ivan Rodriguez-Tex.	c	252	1999	Chipper Jones-Atl.	3b	432
Jason Giambi-Oak.	1b	317	2000	Jeff Kent-S.F.	2b	392
Ichiro Suzuki-Sea.	of	289	2001	Barry Bonds-S.F.	of	438
Miguel Tejada-Oak.	of	356	2002	Barry Bonds-S.F.	of	*443
Alex Rodriguez-Tex.	ss	242	2003	Barry Bonds-S.F.	of	426
Vladimir Guerrero-Ana.	of	354	2004	Barry Bonds-S.F.	of	407
Alex Rodriguez-N.Y.	3b	331	2005	Albert Pujols-St.L.	1b	378
Justin Morneau-Min.	1b	320	2006	Ryan Howard-Phi.	1b	388

HANK AARON AWARDS
(Best overall hitter in each league)

AMERICAN LEAGUE		Year	NATIONAL LEAGUE	
Manny Ramirez-Cle.	of	1999	Sammy Sosa-Chi.	of
Carlos Delgago-Tor.	1b	2000	Todd Helton-Col.	1b
Alex Rodriguez-Tex.	ss	2001	Barry Bonds-S.F.	of
Alex Rodriguez-Tex.	ss	2002	Barry Bonds-S.F.	of
Alex Rodriguez-Tex.	ss	2003	Albert Pujols-St.L.	of
DavidOrtiz-Bos.	dh	2005	Andruw Jones-Atl.	of
Derek Jeter-N.Y.	ss	2006	Ryan Howard-Phi.	1b

AWARDS

Rookie of the Year Awards
(*Unanimous selection)

AMERICAN LEAGUE		Votes	Year	NATIONAL LEAGUE		Votes
Combined selection			1947	Jackie Robinson-Bkn.	1b	
Combined selection			1948	Al Dark-Bos.	ss	
Roy Sievers-St. L	of	10	1949	Don Newcombe-Bkn.	p	21
Walt Dropo-Bos.	1b	15	1950	Sam Jethroe-Bos.	of	11
Gil McDougald-N.Y.	3b	13	1951	Willie Mays-N.Y.	of	18
Harry Byrd-Phil.	p	9	1952	Joe Black-Bkn.	p	19
Harvey Kuenn-Det.	ss	23	1953	Jim Gilliam-Bkn.	2b	11
Bob Grim-N.Y.	p	15	1954	Wally Moon-St. L.	of	11
Herb Score-Cle.	p	18	1955	Bill Virdon-St. L.	of	16
Luis Aparicio-Chi.	ss	22	1956	Frank Robinson-Cin.	of	*24
Tony Kubek-N.Y.	inf-of	23	1957	Jack Sanford-Phi.	p	16
Albie Pearson-Was.	of	14	1958	Orlando Cepeda-S.F.	1b	*21
Bob Allison-Was.	of	18	1959	Willie McCovey-S.F.	1b	*24
Ron Hansen-Bal.	ss	22	1960	Frank Howard-L.A.	of	12
Don Schwall-Bos.	p	7	1961	Billy Williams-Chi.	of	10
Tommy Tresh-N.Y.	of-ss	13	1962	Ken Hubbs-Chi.	2b	19
Gary Peters-Chi.	p	10	1963	Pete Rose-Cin.	2b	17
Tony Oliva-Min.	of	19	1964	Dick Allen-Phi.	3b	18
Curt Blefary-Bal.	of	12	1965	Jim Lefebvre-L.A.	2b	13
Tommie Agee-Chi.	of	16	1966	Tommy Helms-Cin.	3b	12
Rod Carew-Min.	2b	19	1967	Tom Seaver-N.Y.	p	11
Stan Bahnsen-N.Y.	p	17	1968	Johnny Bench Cin.	c	10.5
Lou Piniella-K.C.	of	9	1969	Ted Sizemore-L.A.	2b	14
Thurman Munson-N.Y.	c	23	1970	Carl Morton-Mon.	p	11
Chris Chambliss-Cle.	1b	11	1971	Earl Williams-Atl.	c	18
Carlton Fisk-Bos.	c	*24	1972	Jon Matlack-N.Y.	p	19
Al Bumbry-Bal.	of	13.5	1973	Gary Matthews-S.F.	of	11
Mike Hargrove-Tex.	1b	16.5	1974	Bake McBride-St. L.	of	16
Fred Lynn-Bos.	of	23.5	1975	John Montefusco-S.F.	p	12
Mark Fidrych-Det.	p	22	1976	Butch Metzger-S.D.	p	11
				Pat Zachry-Cin.	p	11

AMERICAN LEAGUE		Votes	Year	NATIONAL LEAGUE		Votes
Eddie Murray-Bal.	dh	12.5	1977	Andre Dawson-Mon.	of	10
Lou Whitaker-Det.	2b	21	1978	Bob Horner-Atl.	3b	12.5
John Castino-Min.	3b	7	1979	Rick Sutcliffe-L.A.	p	20
Alfredo Griffin-Tor.	ss	7				
Joe Charboneau-Cle.	of	15	1980	Steve Howe-L.A.	p	12
Dave Righetti-N.Y.	p	23	1981	Fernando Valenzuela-L.A.	p	17.5
Cal Ripken-Bal.	ss-3b	24(130)	1982	Steve Sax-L.A.	2b	9(63)
Ron Kittle-Chi.	of	15(104)	1983	Darryl Strawberry-N.Y.	of	18(106)
Alvin Davis-Sea.	1b	25(134)	1984	Dwight Gooden-N.Y.	p	23(118)
Ozzie Guillen-Chi.	ss	16(101)	1985	Vince Coleman-St. L.	of	*24(120)
Jose Canseco-Oak.	of	16(110)	1986	Todd Worrell-St. L.	p	23(118)
Mark McGwire-Oak.	1b	*28(140)	1987	Benito Santiago-S.D.	c	*24(120)
Walt Weiss-Oak.	ss	17(103)	1988	Chris Sabo-Cin.	3b	11(79)
Gregg Olson-Bal.	p	26(136)	1989	Jerome Walton-Chi.	of	22(116)
Sandy Alomar-Cle.	c	*28(140)	1990	David Justice-Atl.	of	23(118)
Chuck Knoblauch-Min.	2b	26(136)	1991	Jeff Bagwell-Hou.	1b	23(118)
Pat Listach-Mil.	ss	20(122)	1992	Eric Karros-L.A.	1b	22(116)
Tim Salmon-Cal.	of	*28(140)	1993	Mike Piazza-L.A.	c	*28(140)
Bob Hamelin-K.C.	dh	25(134)	1994	Raul Mondesi-L.A.	of	*28(140)
Marty Cordova-Min.	of	13(105)	1995	Hideo Nomo-L.A.	p	18(118)
Derek Jeter-N.Y.	ss	*28(140)	1996	Todd Hollandsworth-L.A.	of	15(105)
Nomar Garciaparra-Bos.	ss	*28(140)	1997	Scott Rolen-Phi.	3b	*28(140)
Ben Grieve-Oak.	of	23(130)	1998	Kerry Wood-Chi.	p	16(128)
Carlos Beltran-K.C.	of	26(133)	1999	Scott Williamson-Cin.	p	17(118)
Kazuhiro Sasaki-Sea.	p	17(104)	2000	Rafael Furcal-Atl.	ss	25(144)
Ichiro Suzuki-Sea.	of	27(138)	2001	Albert Pujols-St.L.	of-3b-1b	*32(160)
Eric Hinske-Tor.	3b	19(122)	2002	Jason Jennings-Col.	p	27(150)
Angel Berroa-K.C.	ss	12(88)	2003	Dontrelle Willis-Fla.	p	17(118)
Bobby Crosby-Oak.	ss	27(138)	2004	Jason Bay-Pit.	of	25(146)
Huston Street-Oak.	p	15(97)	2005	Ryan Howard-Phi.	1b	19(109)
Justin Verlander-Det.	p	26(133)	2006	Hanley Ramerez-Fla.	ss	14(105)

CY YOUNG MEMORIAL AWARDS
(For Pitchers only)
(* Unanimous selection)

Year	MAJOR LEAGUES	
1956	Don Newcombe-Bkn.(N)	10
1957	Warren Spahn-Mil.(N)	15
1958	Bob Turley-N.Y.(A)	5
1959	Early Wynn-Chi.(A)	13
1960	Vern Law-Pit.(N)	8
1961	Whitey Ford-N.Y.(A)	9
1962	Don Drysdale-L.A.(N)	14
1963	Sandy Koufax-L.A.(N)	*20
1964	Dean Chance-L.A.(A)	17
1965	Sandy Koufax-L.A.(N)	*20
1966	Sandy Koufax-L.A.(N)	*20

AMERICAN LEAGUE	Votes	Year	NATIONAL LEAGUE	Votes
Jim Lonborg-Bos.	18	1967	Mike McCormick-S.F.	18
Denny McLain-Det.	*20	1968	Bob Gibson-St. L.	*20
Mike Cuellar-Bal.	10	1969	Tom Seaver-N.Y.	23
Denny McLain-Det.	10			
Jim Perry-Min.	55	1970	Bob Gibson-St. L.	118
Vida Blue-Oak.	98	1971	Ferguson Jenkins-Chi.	97
Gaylord Perry-Cle.	64	1972	Steve Carlton-Phi.	*120
Jim Palmer-Bal.	88	1973	Tom Seaver-N.Y.	71
Catfish Hunter-Oak.	90	1974	Mike Marshall-L.A.	96
Jim Palmer-Bal.	98	1975	Tom Seaver-N.Y.	98
Jim Palmer-Bal.	108	1976	Randy Jones-S.D.	96
Sparky Lyle-N.Y.	56.5	1977	Steve Carlton-Phi.	104
Ron Guidry-N.Y.	*140	1978	Gaylord Perry-S.D.	116
Mike Flanagan-Bal.	139	1979	Bruce Sutter-Chi.	72
Steve Stone-Bal.	100	1980	Steve Carlton-Phi.	118
Rollie Ringers-Mil.	126	1981	Fernando Valenzuela-L.A.	50
Pete Vuckovich-Mil.	87	1982	Steve Carlton-Phi.	112
LaMarr Hoyt-Chi.	116	1983	John Denny-Phi.	103
Willie Hernandez-Det.	88	1984	Rick Sutcliffe-Chi.	*120
Bret Saberhagen-K.C.	127	1985	Dwight Gooden-N.Y.	*120
Roger Clemens-Bos.	*140	1986	Mike Scott-Hou.	98
Roger Clemens-Bos.	124	1987	Steve Bedrosian-Phi.	57
Frank Viola-Min.	138	1988	Orel Hershiser-L.A.	*120
Bret Saberhagen-K.C.	138	1989	Mark Davis-S.D.	107
Bob Welch-Oak.	107	1990	Dave Drabek-Pit.	118
Roger Clemens-Bos.	119	1991	Tom Glavine-Atl.	110
Dennis Eckersley-Oak.	107	1992	Greg Maddux-Chi.	112
Jack McDowell-Chi.	124	1993	Greg Maddux-Atl.	119
David Cone-K.C.	108	1994	Greg Maddux-Atl.	*140
Randy Johnson-Sea.	136	1995	Greg Maddux-Atl.	*140
Pat Hentgen-Tor.	110	1996	John Smoltz-Atl.	136
Roger Clemens-Tor.	134	1997	Pedro Martinez-Mon.	134
Roger Clemens-Tor.	*140	1998	Tom Glavine-Atl.	99
Pedro Martinez-Bos.	*140	1999	Randy Johnson-Ari.	134
Pedro Martinez-Bos.	*140	2000	Randy Johnson-Ari.	133
Roger Clemens-N.Y.	122	2001	Randy Johnson-Ari.	156
Barry Zito-Oak.	114	2002	Randy Johnson-Ari.	*160
Roy Halladay-Tor.	136	2003	Eric Gagne-L.A.	146
Johan Santana-Min.	*140	2004	Roger Clemens-Hou.	140
Bartolo Colon-L.A.	118	2005	Chris Carpenter-St.L.	132
Johan Santana-Min.	*140	2006	Brandon Webb-Ari.	103

WORLD SERIES LEADERS

BATTING AVERAGE

(Lifetime) (Min. 50 AB)		(Individual)		(Team)	
1 Paul Molitor	.418	4g .750 Billy Hatcher-CinN 1990		4g .317 Cincinnati-N.L. 1990	
Pepper Martin	.418	5g .529 Sean Casey-DetA 2006		5g .316 Philadelphia-A.L. 1910	
3 Lou Brock	.391	6g .500 Dave Robertson-NYN 1917		6g .306 New York-A.L. 1978	
4 Marquis Grissom	.390	.500 Billy Martin-NYA 1953			
5 Thurman Munson	.373	.500 Paul Molitor-TorA 1993			
6 George Brett	.373	7g .500 Pepper Martin-StLN 1931		7g .338 New York-A.L. 1960	
7 Hank Aaron	.364	.500 Johnny Lindell-NYA 1947			
8 Frank Baker	.363	.500 Phil Garner-PitN 1979			
9 R. Clemente	.362	8g .400 Buck Herzog-NYN 1912		8g .270 New York-N.L. 1912	
10 Lou Gehrig	.361				

SLUGGING AVERAGE

(Lifetime) (Min. 50 AB)		(Individual)		(Team)	
1 Reggie Jackson	.755	4g 1.727 Lou Gehrig-NYA 1928		4g .530 New York-A.L. 1928	
2 Babe Ruth	.744	5g 1.071 Donn Clendennon-NYN 1969		5g .509 Baltimore-A.L. 1970	
3 Lou Gehrig	.731	6g 1.250 Reggie Jackson 1977		6g .510 Toronto-A.L. 1993	
4 Al Simmons	.658	7g 1.294 Barry Bonds-SFN 2002		7g .528 NewYork-A.L. 1960	
5 Lou Brock	.655	8g .600 Buck Herzog-NYN 1912		8g .401 Boston-A.L. 1903	
6 Pepper Martin	.636				
7 Hank Greenberg	.624				
8 Charlie Keller	.611				
9 Jimmie Foxx	.609				
10 Hank Aaron	.600				

HITS

(Lifetime)		(Individual)		(Team)	
1 Yogi Berra	71	4g 10 Babe Ruth-NYA 1928		4g 45 New York-A.L. 1932	
2 Mickey Mantle	59	5g 9 Eddie Collins-PhiA 1910		5g 56 Philadelphia-A.L. 1910	
3 Frankie Frisch	58	9 Frank Baker-PhiA 1910			
4 Joe DiMaggio	54	9 Frank Baker-PhiA 1913			
5 Hank Bauer	46	9 Heinie Groh-NYN 1922			
Pee Wee Reese	46	9 Jo-Jo Moore-NYN 1937			
7 Gil McDougald	45	9 Bobby Richardson-NYA 1961			
Phil Rizzuto	45	9 Paul Blair-BalA 1970			
9 Lou Gehrig	43	9 Brooks Robinson-BalA 1970			
10 Eddie Collins	42	9 Alan Trammell-DetA 1984			
Elston Howard	42	9 Derek Jeter-NYA 2000		6g 68 New York-A.L. 1978	
Babe Ruth	42	9 Paul O'Neill-NYA 2000		7g 91 New York-A.L. 1960	
		9 Sean Casey-DetA 2006			
		6g 12 Billy Martin-NYA 1953			
		12 Paul Molitor-TorA 1993			
		12 Roberto Alomar-TorA 1993			
		12 Marquis Grissom-Atl. 1996			
		7g 13 Bobby Richardson-NYA 1964			
		13 Lou Brock-StLN 1968			
		13 Marty Barrett-BosA 1986			
		8g 12 Buck Herzog-NYN 1912		8g 74 New York-N.L. 1912	
		12 Joe Jackson-ChiA 1919			

RUNS

(Lifetime)		(Individual)		(Team)	
1 Mickey Mantle	42	4g 9 Babe Ruth-NYA 1928		4g 37 New York-A.L. 1932	
2 Yogi Berra	41	9 Lou Gehrig-NYA 1932			
3 Babe Ruth	37	5g 6 Frank Baker-PhiA 1910		5g 35 Philadelphia-A.L. 1910	
4 Lou Gehrig	30	6 Danny Murphy-PhiA 1910			
5 Joe DiMaggio	27	6 Harry Hooper-BosA 1916			
Derek Jeter	27	6 Al Simmons-PhiA 1929			
7 Roger Maris	26	6 Lee May-CinN 1970			
8 Elston Howard	25	6 Boog Powell-BalA 1970			
9 Gil McDougald	23	6 Lou Whitaker-DetA 1984			
10 Jackie Robinson	22	6 Derek Jeter-NYA 2000		6g 45 Toronto-A.L. 1993	
		6g10 Reggie Jackson-NYA 1977		7g 55 New York-A.L. 1960	
		10 Paul Molitor-TorA 1993			
		7g 8 Tommy Leach-PitN 1909			
		8 Pepper Martin-StLN 1934			
		8 Billy Johnson-NYA 1947			
		8 Bobby Richardson-NYA 1960			
		8 Mickey Mantle-NYA 1960			
		8 Mickey Mantle-NYA 1964			
		8 Lou Brock-StLN 1967			
		8 Jim Thome-CleA 1997			
		8 Matt Williams-CleA 1997			
		8 Barry Bonds-SFN 2002			
		8g 8 Freddy Parent-BosA 1903		8g 39 Boston-A.L. 1903	

HOME RUNS

(Lifetime)		(Individual)		(Team)	
1 Mickey Mantle	18	4g 4 Lou Gehrig-NYA 1928		4g 9 New York-A.L. 1928	
2 Babe Ruth	15			9 Oakland-A.L. 1989	
3 Yogi Berra	12	5g 3 Donn Clendenon-NYN 1969		5g 10 Baltimore-A.L. 1970	
4 Duke Snider	11	6g 5 Reggie Jackson-NYA 1977		6g 9 New York-A.L. 1953	
5 Lou Gehrig	10			9 Los Angeles-N.L. 1977	
Reggie Jackson	10	7g 4 Babe Ruth-NYA 1926		7g 14 San Francisco-N.L. 2002	
7 Joe DiMaggio	8	4 Duke Snider-BknN 1952			
Frank Robinson	8	4 Duke Snider-BknN 1955			
Bill Skowron	8	4 Hank Bauer-NYA 1958			
10 Hank Bauer	7	4 Gene Tenace-OakA 1972			
Goose Goslin	7	4 Barry Bonds-SFN 2002		8g 2 Boston-A.L. 1903	
Gil McDougald	7	8g 2 Patsy Dougherty-BosA 1903		2 New York-A.L. 1921	
				2 New York-N.L. 1921	

RUNS BATTED IN

(Lifetime)		(Individual)		(Team)	
1 Mickey Mantle	40	4g 9 Lou Gehrig-NYA 1928		4g 36 New York-A.L. 1932	
2 Yogi Berra	39	5g 9 Danny Murphy-PhiA 1910		5g 32 Baltimore-A.L. 1970	
3 Lou Gehrig	35	6g 10 Ted Kluszewski-ChiA 1959		6g 45 Toronto-A.L. 1993	
4 Babe Ruth	33	7g 12 Bobby Richardson-NYA 1960		7g 54 New York-A.L. 1960	
5 Joe DiMaggio	30	8g 8 Pat Duncan-CinN 1919		8g 34 Boston-A.L. 1912	
6 Bill Skowron	29				
7 Duke Snider	26				
8 Hank Bauer	24				
Bill Dickey	24				
Reggie Jackson	24				
Gil McDougald	24				

DOUBLES

(Lifetime)		(Individual)		(Team)	
1 Yogi Berra	10	4g 4 Billy Hatcher-CinN 1990		4g 11 Boston-A.L. 2004	
Frankie Frisch	10	4 Bret Boone-AtlN 1999		5g 19 Philadelphia-A.L. 1910	
3 Jack Barry	9	5g 4 Eddie Collins-PhiA 1910			
Pete Fox	9	4 Rick Dempsey-BalA 1983		6g 15 Philadephia-A.L. 1911	
Carl Furillo	9	4 Chick Hafey-StLN 1930		7g 19 St. Louis-N.L. 1946	
6 Lou Gehrig	8	7g 6 Pete Fox-DetA 1934		8g 14 Boston-A.L. 1912	
Duke Snider	8	8g 6 Buck Herzog-NYN 1912		14 New York-N.L. 1912	
Lonnie Smith	8	4 Red Murray-NYN 1912			
9 15 tied with	7	4 Buck Weaver-ChiA 1919			
		4 George Burns-NYN 1921			

TRIPLES

(Lifetime)		(Individual)		(Team)	
1 Billy Jonnson	4	4g 2 Lou Gehrig-NYA 1927		4g 3 Cincinnati-N.L. 1976	
Tommy Leach	4	2 Tommy Davis-LAN 1963			
Tris Speaker	4	2 Rickey Henderson-OakA 1989			
4 Hank Bauer	3	2 Scott Podsednik-ChiA 2005			
Bobby Brown	3	5g 2 Eddie Collins-PhiA 1913		5g 2 Boston-A.L. 1916	
Buck Freeman	3	2 Bobby Brown-NYA 1949			
Frankie Frisch	3	2 Paul O'Neill-NYA 2000			
Lou Gehrig	3	6g 2 George Rohe-ChiA 1906		6g 5 Toronto-A.L. 1993	
Dan Gladden	3	2 Bob Meusel-NYA 1923			
Mark Lemke	3	2 Billy Martin-NYA 1953			
Billy Martin	3	2 Paul Molitor-TorA 1993			
Tim McCarver	3	2 Devon White-TorA 1993		7g 5 St. Louis-N.L. 1934	
Bob Meusel	3	7g 3 Mark Lemke-AtlN 1991		5 New York-A.L. 1947	
Freddy Parent	3				
Chick Stahl	3	8g 4 Tommy Leach-PitN 1903		8g 16 Boston-A.L. 1903	
Dave Concepcion	3				
Devon White	3				

AT BATS

(Lifetime)		(Individual)		(Team)	
1 Yogi Berra	259	4g 21 Johnny Damon-BosA 2004		4g 154 Chicago-A.L. 2005	
2 Mickey Mantle	230	21 Scott Podsednik-ChiA 2005			
3 Joe DiMaggio	199	5g 23 Hal Janvrin-BosA 1916		5g 179 New York-A.L. 2000	
4 Frankie Frisch	197	23 Jo-Jo Moore-NYN 1937			
5 Gil McDougald	190	23 Bobby Richardson-NYA 1961			
6 Hank Bauer	188	6g 29 Mariano Duncan-PhiN 1993		6g 222 New York-A.L. 1978	
7 Phil Rizzuto	183				
8 Elston Howard	171	7g 33 Bucky Harris-WasA 1924		7g 269 New York-A.L. 1960	
9 Pee Wee Reese	169	33 Sam Rice-WasA 1925			
10 Roger Maris	152	33 Omar Moreno-PitN 1979			
		33 Devon White-FlaN 1997			
		8g 36 Jimmy Collins-BosA 1903		8g 282 Boston-A.L. 1903	

STOLEN BASES

(Lifetime)		(Individual)		(Team)	
1 Lou Brock	14	4g 3 Rickey Henderson-OakA 1989		4g 9 Boston-N.L. 1914	
Eddie Collins	14	3 Rickey Henderson-OakA 1990			
3 Frank Chance	10	3 Derek Jeter-NYA 1999		5g 16 Chicago-N.L. 1907	
Phil Rizzuto	10	5g 6 Jimmy Slagle-ChiN 1907		6g 15 Atlanta-N.L. 1992	
Davey Lopes	10	6g 6 Kenny Lofton-CleA 1995			
6 Frankie Frisch	9			7g 18 Pittsburgh-N.L. 1909	
Honus Wagner	9	7g 7 Lou Brock-StLN 1967			
Kenny Lofton	9	7 Lou Brock-StLN 1968			
9 Johnny Evers	8	8g 4 Josh Devore-NYN 1912		8g 12 New York-N.L. 1912	
10 Pepper Martin	7				
Joe Tinker	7				
Rickey Henderson	7				
Joe Morgan	7				
Roberto Alomar	7				

BASES ON BALLS

(Lifetime)		(Individual)		(Team)	
1 Mickey Mantle	43	4g 7 Hank Thompson-NYN 1954		4g 24 Boston-A.L. 2004	
2 Babe Ruth	33	5g 7 Jimmy Sheckard-ChiN 1910		5g 25 New York-A.L. 2000	
3 Yogi Berra	32	7 Mickey Cochrane-PhiA 1929			
4 Phil Rizzuto	30	7 Joe Gordon-NYA 1941			
5 Lou Gehrig	26	6g 9 Willie Randolph-NYA 1981		6g 34 Philadelphia-N.L. 1993	
David Justice	26	7g 13 Barry Bonds-SFN 2002		7g 38 New York-A.L. 1947	
6 Mickey Cochrane	25	8g 7 Josh Devore-NYN 1912		8g 27 New York-A.L. 1921	
8 Jim Gilliam	23	7 Ross Youngs-NYN 1921			
9 Jackie Robinson	21				
10 Gil McDougald	20				
Bernie Williams	20				

STRIKEOUTS

(Lifetime)		(Individual)		(Team)	
1 Mickey Mantle	54	4g 7 Ken Caminiti-SDN 1998		4g 37 New York-A.L. 1963	
2 Elston Howard	37	7 Bob Meusel-NYA 1927		5g 50 Chicago-N.L. 1929	
3 Duke Snider	33	7 Morgan Ensberg-HouN 2005			
Derek Jeter	33	5g 9 Carmelo Martinez -SDN 1984			
5 Babe Ruth	30				
David Justice	30	6g 12 Willie Wilson-KCA 1980		6g 50 Philadelphia-N.L. 1993	
7 Gil McDougald	29	7g 11 Eddie Mathews-MilN 1958		7g 70 Arizona-N.L. 2001	
8 Bill Skowron	26	11 Wayne Garrett-NYN 1973			
Bernie Williams	26	11 Luis Gonzalez-AriN 2001			
10 Hank Bauer	25	11 Damian Miller-AriN 2001			
		8g 10 George Kelly-NYN 1921		8g 45 Pittsburgh-N.L. 1903	

WORLD SERIES LEADERS

	(Lifetime)			(Individual)				(Lifetime)			(Individual)				(Team)	

WINS / STRIKEOUTS

	(Lifetime)				(Individual)				(Lifetime)				(Individual)				(Team)	
1	Whitey Ford	10	4g	2	Bill James-BosN	1914		1	Whitey Ford	94	4g	23	Sandy Koufax-LAN	1963	4g	37	Los Angeles-N.L.	1963
2	Bob Gibson	7		2	Dick Rudolph-BosN	1914		2	Bob Gibson	92	5g	18	Christy Mathewson-NYN	1905	5g	50	Philadelphia-A.L.	1929
	Allie Reynolds	7		2	Waite Hoyt-NYA	1928		3	Allie Reynolds	62	6g	20	Chief Bender-PhiA	1911	6g	50	Toronto-A.L.	1993
	Red Ruffing	7		2	Red Ruffing-NYA	1938		4	Sandy Koufax	61								
5	Chief Bender	6		2	Sandy Koufax-LAN	1963			Red Ruffing	61	7g	35	Bob Gibson-StlN	1968	7g	70	New York-A.L.	2001
	Lefty Gomez	6		2	Jose Rijo-CinN	1990		6	Chief Bender	59	8g	28	Bill Dinneen-BosA	1903	8g	45	Boston-A.L.	1903
	Waite Hoyt	6	5g	3	Christy Mathewson-NYN	1905		7	George Earnshaw	56								
8	Three Finger Brown	5		3	Jack Coombs-PhiA	1910		8	John Smoltz	52								
	Jack Coombs	5	6g	3	Red Faber-ChiA	1917		9	Waite Hoyt	49								
	Christy Mathewson	5	7g	3	Babe Adams-PitN	1909			Roger Clemens	49								
	Herb Pennock	5		3	Stan Coveleski-CleA	1920												
	Vic Raschi	5		3	Harry Brecheen-StlN	1946												
	Catfish Hunter	5		3	Lew Burdette-MilN	1957												
				3	Bob Gibson -StlN	1967												
				3	Mickey Lolich-DetA	1968												
				3	Randy Johnson-AriN	2001												
			8g	3	Bill Dinneen-BosA	1903												
				3	Deacon Phillippe-PitN	1903												
				3	Smoky Joe Wood-BosA	1912												

GAMES PITCHED / MOST BASE ON BALLS ALLOWED

	(Lifetime)				(Individual)				(Lifetime)				(Individual)				(Team)	
1	Whitey Ford	22	4g	4	Jeff Nelson-NYA	1999		1	Whitey Ford	34	4g	8	Bob Lemon-CleA	1954	4g	24	St. Louis-N.L.	2004
2	Mike Stanton	20		4	Keith Foulke-BosA	2004		2	Art Nehf	32	5g	14	Jack Coombs-PhiA	1910	5g	25	New York-N.L.	2000
	Mariano Rivera	20		4	Neal Cotts-ChiA	2005			Allie Reynolds	32	6g	11	Lefty Tyler-ChiN	1918	6g	34	Toronto-A.L.	1993
4	Rollie Fingers	16		4	Bobby Jenks-ChiA	2005		4	Jim Palmer	31		11	Lefty Gomez-NYA	1936				
	Jeff Nelson	16	5g	5	Mike Marshall-LAN	1974		5	Bob Turley	29		11	Allie Reynolds-NYA	1951				
6	Allie Reynolds	15	6g	6	Dan Quisenberry-KCA	1980		6	Paul Derringer	27	7g	11	Walter Johnson-WasA	1924	7g	40	Florida-N.L.	1997
	Bob Turley	15	7g	7	Darold Knowles-OakA	1973			Red Ruffing	27		11	Bill Bevens-NYA	1947				
8	Clay Carroll	14	8g	8	Deacon Phillppe-PitN	1903		8	Burleigh Grimes	26	8g	13	Art Nehf-NYN	1921	8g	27	New York-N.L.	1921
9	Clem Labine	13							Don Gullett	26								
	Mark Wohlers	13						10	Vic Raschi	25								

COMPLETE GAMES / SAVES

	(Lifetime)				(Individual)				(Lifetime)				(Individual)				(Team)	
1	Christy Mathewson	10	4g	2	Dick Rudolph-BosN	1914		1	Mariano Rivera	8	4g	3	Mariano Rivera-NYA	1998	4g	3	New York-A.L.	1998
2	Chief Bender	9		2	Waite Hoyt-NYA	1928		2	Rollie Fingers	6						3	Chicago-A.L.	2005
3	Bob Gibson	8		2	Red Ruffing-NYA	1938		3	Johnny Murphy	4	5g	2	Lefty Grove-PhiA	1929	5g	3	Oakland-A.L.	1974
	Red Ruffing	8		2	Sandy Koufax-LAN	1963			Allie Reynolds	4		2	Rollie Fingers-OakA	1974				
5	Whitey Ford	7	5g	3	Christy Mathewson-NYN	1905			John Wetteland	4		2	Willie Hernandez-DetA	1984				
6	Waite Hoyt	6		3	Jack Coombs-PhiA	1910			Robb Nen	4		2	Mariano Rivera-LAN	2000				
	George Mullin	6	6g	3	Chief Bender-PhiA	1911		7	Roy Face	3	6g	4	John Wetteland-NYA	1996	6g	4	New York-N.L.	1996
	Art Nehf	6		3	Hippo Vaughn-ChiN	1918			Firpo Marberry	3	7g	3	Roy Face-PitN	1960	7g	4	Oakland-A.L.	1973
	Eddie Plank	6	7g	3	Babe Adams-PitN	1909			Herb Pennock	3		3	Kent Tekulve-PitN	1979				
10	Three Finger Brown	5		3	George Mullin-DetA	1909			Will McEnaney	3		3	Troy Percival-AnaA	2002				
	George Earnshaw	5		3	Stan Coveleski-CleA	1920			Tug McGraw	3								
	Walter Johnson	5		3	Walter Johnson-WasA	1925			Kent Tekulve	3	8g	0			8g	0		
	Carl Mays	5		3	Bobo Newsom-DetA	1940			Todd Worrell	3								
	Deacon Phillippe	5		3	Lew Burdette-MilN	1957			Troy Percival	3								
	Allie Reynolds	5		3	Bob Gibson-StlN	1967												
	Bullet Joe Bush	5		3	Bob Gibson-StlN	1968												
	Wild Bill Donovan	5		3	Mickey Lolich-DetA	1968												
			8g	5	Deacon Phillippe-PitN	1903												

INNINGS PITCHED / SHUTOUTS

	(Lifetime)				(Individual)				(Lifetime)				(Individual)				(Team)	
1	Whitey Ford	146	4g	18	Dick Rudolph-BosN	1914		1	Christy Mathewson	4	4g	1	accomplished 9 times		4g	3	Baltimore-A.L.	1966
2	Christy Mathewson	102		18	Waite Hoyt-NYA	1928		2	Three Finger Brown	3	5g	1	Christy Mathewson-NYN	1905	5g	4	New York-N.L.	1905
3	Red Ruffing	86		18	Red Ruffing-NYA	1938			Whitey Ford	3	6g	1	accomplished 12 times		6g	2	New York-N.L.	1917
4	Chief Bender	85		18	Sandy Koufax-LAN	1963		4	Lew Burdette	2						2	Chicago-A.L.	1959
5	Waite Hoyt	84	5g	27	Christy Mathewson-NYN	1905			Bill Dinneen	2					7g	3	Los Angeles-N.L.	1965
6	Bob Gibson	81		27	Jack Coombs-PhiA	1910			Bob Gibson	2	7g	2	Lew Burdette-MilN	1957				
7	Art Nehf	79	6g	27	Christy Mathewson-NYN	1911			Wild Bill Hallahan	2		2	Whitey Ford-NYA	1960				
8	Allie Reynolds	77		27	Red Faber-ChiA	1917			Sandy Koufax	2		2	Sandy Koufax-LAN	1965				
9	Andy Pettitte	66		27	Hippo Vaughn-ChiN	1918			Art Nehf	2	8g	2	Bill Dinneen-BosA	1903	8g	2	Boston-A.L.	1903
10	Jim Palmer	65	7g	32	George Mullin-DetA	1909			Allie Reynolds	2						2	Cincinnati-N.L.	1919
			8g	44	Deacon Phillippe-PitN	1903										2	New York-A.L.	1921

GAMES STARTED (Lifetime)

1	Whitey Ford	22
2	Waite Hoyt	11
	Christy Mathewson	11
	Andy Pettitte	11
4	Chief Bender	10
	Red Ruffing	10
7	Bob Gibson	9
	Art Nehf	9
	Allie Reynolds	9
	Catfish Hunter	9

LOSSES (Lifetime)

1	Whitey Ford	8
2	Bullet Joe Bush	5
	Rube Marquard	5
	Christy Mathewson	5
	Eddie Plank	5
	Schoolboy Rowe	5
7	15 tied with	4

(Individual)

6g	3	George Frazier-NYA	1981
8g	3	Lefty Williams-ChiA	1919

FEWEST HITS ALLOWED (Team)

4g	17	Baltimore-A.L.	1966
5g	23	New York-N.L.	1969
6g	32	Chicago-N.L.	1918
7g	42	New York-A.L.	1956
	42	Los Angeles-N.L.	1965
	42	Arizona-N.L.	2001
8g	50	New York-N.L.	1921

EARNED RUN AVERAGE

	(Lifetime)				(Team)	
	(Minimum 25 Innings Pitched)		4g	0.50	Baltimore-A.L.	1966
1	Jack Billingham	0.36	5g	0.00	New York-N.L.	1905
2	Henry Brecheen	0.83	6g	1.04	Chicago-N.L.	1918
3	Babe Ruth	0.87	7g	0.88	Cleveland-A.L.	1920
4	Sherry Smith	0.89	8g	1.62	Cincinnati-N.L.	1919
5	Sandy Koufax	0.95				
6	Hippo Vaughn	1.00				
7	Monte Pearson	1.01				
8	Christy Mathewson	1.06				
9	Mariano Rivera	1.16				
10	Babe Adams	1.29				

BATTER'S GAMES (Lifetime)

1	Yogi Berra	75
2	Mickey Mantle	65
3	Elston Howard	54
4	Hank Bauer	53
	Gil McDougald	53
6	Phil Rizzuto	52
7	Joe DiMaggio	51
8	Frankie Frisch	50
9	Pee Wee Reese	44
10	Roger Maris	41
	Babe Ruth	41

FEWEST BASES ON BALLS ALLOWED (Team)

4g	4	New York-A.L.	1927
5g	5	New York-N.L.	1905
6g	4	New York-N.L.	1911
7g	9	Philadelphia-A.L.	1931
8g	13	Pittsburgh-N.L.	1903

NON-PLAYING MANAGERS

Men who managed in the major leagues since 1901 and who never played major league baseball or who played in the major leagues only before 1901
(except Frank Dwyer and Biddy McPhee whose records are shown on page 10)

SE NAME-GIVEN NAMES(NICKNAMES)	TEAM BY YEAR	Birth Date	Birth Place	Death Date	B	T	Hgt	Wgt	Pos	G	HR	BA	W	L
dair, Bill-Marion Danne	M70ChiA	02-10-13	Mobile, Ala.	06-17-02			5'8	190						
rmour, Bill-William Reginald	M02-04CleA M05-06DetA	09-03-69	Homestead, Pa.	12-02-22										
ancroft, Frank-Frank Carter	M80WorN M81-82DetN M83CleN M84-85ProvN M87PhiAA M89Ind N M02CinN	05-09-46	Lancaster, Mass.	03-30-21										
arrow, Ed-Edward Grant (Cousin Ed)	M03-04DetA M18-20BosA	05-10-68	Springfield, Ill.	12-15-53										
evington, Terry-Terry Paul	M95-97ChiA	07-07-56	Akron, Ohio											
ezdek, Hugo-Hugo Francis 37-38 Head Coach in N.F.L.	M17-19PitN	04-01-83	Prague, Czech.	09-19-52										
oles, John-John	M96,99-01FlaN	08-19-48	Chicago, Ill.				5'10	165						
ristol, Dave-James David	M66-69CinN M70-72MilA M76-77AtlN M79-80SFN	06-23-33	Macon, Ga.				5'11	175						
uckenberger, Al-Albert C.	M89-90ColAA M92-94PitN M95StLN M02-04 BosN	01-31-61	Detroit, Mich.	07-01-17										
antillon, Joe-Joseph D. (Pongo Joe)	M07-09WasA	08-19-61	Janesville, Wis.	01-31-30										
ollins, Terry-Terry Lee	M94-96HouN M97-99AnaA	05-27-49	Midland, Mich.											
ogel, Horace-Horace S.	M87IndN M02NYN	03-02-61	Macungie, Pa.	11-15-28										
rey, Jim-James Gottfried	M80-81KCA M84-86ChiN	05-26-31	Cleveland, Ohio				5'9	170						
uchs, Judge-Emil Edwin	M29BosN	04-17-78	New York, N.Y.	12-05-61										
arcia, Dave-David	M77-78CalA M80-82CleA	09-15-20	East St. Louis, Ill.				6'	180						
anlon, Ned-Edward Hugh	80CleN 81-88DetN 89,M89PitN 90,M90PitP 91M91PitN92,M92-98BalN M99-05Bkn M06-07 CinN	08-22-57	Montville, Conn.	04-14-37	L	L	5'11	170	OF	1267	30	.260		
art, John-John Henry (born John Henry Reen)	M89CleA	07-21-48	Tampa, Fla.											
imsl, Vedie-Avitus Bernard	M61ChiN	04-02-17	Plevna, Mont.	03-15-04			6'1	200						
uff, George-George A.	M07BosA	06-11-72	Champaign, Ill.	10-01-36										
eane, Johnny-John Joseph	M61-64StLN M65-66NYA	11-03-11	St. Louis, Mo.	01-06-67			5'10	165						
ennedy, Kevin-Kevin Curtis	M93-94TexA M95-96BosA	05-26-54	Los Angeles, Cal.				6'3	220						
rol, Jack-John Thomas	M78,80StLN	07-05-36	Chicago, Ill.	05-30-94			5'11	175						
uehl, Karl-Karl Otto	M76MonN	09-05-37	Monterey Park, Cal.				5'10	180						
eyland, Jim-James Richard	M85-96PitN M97-98FlaN M99ColN M06DetA	12-15-44	Toledo, Ohio				5'11	170						
eyva, Nick-Nicholas Tomas	M89-91PhiN	08-16-53	Ontario, Cal.				5'11	165						
ittle, Grady-William Grady	M02-03BosA M06LAN	03-03-50	Abilene, Tex.				5'11	190						
oftus, Tom-Thomas Joseph	77StLN 83StLAA M84MilU M88CleAA 89CleN M90-91CinN MOO-01CinN M02-03WasA	11-15-56	Jefferson City, Mo.	04-16-10	R	R		168	OF	9	0	.182		
ucchesi, Frank-Frank Joseph	M70-72PhiN M75-77TexA M87ChiN	04-24-27	San Francisco, Cal.											
ack (McGillicuddy), Connie-Cornelius Alexander (The Tall Tactician)	86-89WasN 90BufP 91-96,M94-96PitN M01-50PhiA	12-22-62	East Brookfield, Ma.	02-08-56	R	R	6'2	170	C	696	5	.249		
addon, Joe-Joseph John	M06TBA	02-04-54	Hazelton, Pa.											
anning, Jim-James H.	84-85BosN 85-87DetN 89KCAA M01WasA	01-31-62	Fall River, Mass.	10-22-29	R	R	5'7	157	OF-2B	364	8	.215		
cCallister, Jack-John	M27CleA	01-19-79	Marietta, Ohio	10-18-46										
cCarthy, Joe-Joseph Vincent (Marse Joe)	M26-30ChiN M31-46NYA M48-50BosA	04-21-87	Philadelphia, Pa.	01-13-78			5'8	190						
cCloskey, John-John Joseph (Honest John)	M95-96LouN M06-08StLN	04-04-62	Louisville, Ky.	11-17-40										
cGaha, Mel-Fred Melvin 48-49 played in B.A.A.	M62CleA M64-65KCA	09-26-26	Bastrop,La.				6'2	210						
cKeon, Jack John Aloysius	M73-75KCA M77-78OakA M88-90SDN M97-00CinN M03-05FlaN	11-23-30	South Amboy, N.J.				5'8	190						
cNamara, John-John Francis	M69-70OakA M74-77SDN M79-82CinN M83-84CalA M85-88BosA M90-91CleA M96CalA	06-04-32	Sacremento, Cal.				5'10	175						
errill, Stump-Carl Harrelson	M90-91NYA	02-25-44	Brunswick, Maine				5'8	190						
iley, Dave-Dave Allen	M03-05CinN	04-03-62	Tampa, Fla.											
iller, Ray-Raymond Roger	M85-86MinA M98-99BalA	04-30-45	Takoma Park, Md.				6'3	215						
urray, Billy-William Jeremiah	M07-09PhiN	04-13-64	Peabody, Mass.	03-25-37										
'Day, Hank-Henry Francis	84TolAA 85PitAA 86-89WasN 89NYN 90NYP M12CinN M14Chi	07-08-62	Chicago, Ill.	07-02-35		R	6'	180	P	232	1	.190	70	110
wens, Paul-Paul Francis (Pope)	M72,83-84PhiN	02-07-24	Salamanca, N.Y.	12-26-03										
zark(Orzechowski), Danny-Daniel Leonard	M73-79PhiN M84SFN	11-26-23	Buffalo, N.Y.				6'3	205						
hillips, Lefty-Harold Ross	M69-72CalA	06-16-19	Los Angeles, Cal.	06-10-72			5'11	192						
opowski, Eddie-Edward Joseph	M69,73BosA	08-20-13	Sayreville, N.J.	12-04-01			5'5	145						
app, Vern-Vernon Fred	M77-78StLN M84CinN	05-11-28	St. Louis, Mo.				6'	195						
iddoch, Greg-Gregory Lee	M90-92SDN	07-17-45	Greeley, Colo.				5'11	175						
iggleman, Jim-James David	M92-94SDN M95-99ChiN	11-09-52	Fort Dix, N.J.				5'11	175						
ipken, Cal-Calvin Edwin Sr.	M85,87-88BalA	12-17-35	Aberdeen, Md.	03-25-99			5'11	170						
obison, Stanley-Matthew Stanley	M05StLN	- -57	Dubuque, Iowa	03-24-11										
owland, Pants-Clarence Henry	M15-18ChiA	02-12-79	Platteville, Wis.	05-17-69										
awyer, Eddie-Edwin Milby	M48-52,58-60PhiN	09-10-10	Westerly, R.I.	09-22-97			6'	210						
chaefer, Bob-Robert Walden	M91,05KCA	05-02-44	Putnam, Conn.											
elee, Frank-Frank Gibson	M90-01BosN M02-05ChiN	10-26-59	Amherst, N.H.	07-05-09										
hepard, Larry-Lawrence William	M68-69PitN	04-03-19	Lakewood, Ohio				5'11	180						
hettsline, Billy-William Joseph	M98-02PhiN	10-25-63	Philadelphia, Pa.	02-22-33										
howalter, Buck-William Nathaniel	M92-95NYA M98-00AriN M03-06TexA	05-23-56	DeFuniak Spr., Fla.				5'10	185						
tallings, George-Georg Tweedy (The Miracle Man, Chief)	90BknN97-98,M97-98PhiN M01DetA M09-10NYA M13-20BosN	11-17-67	Augusta, Ga.	05-13-29	R	R	5'10	180	C-OF-1B	7	0	.100		
ighe, Jack-John Thomas	M57-58DetA	08-09-13	Kearney, N.J.	08-01-02			5'8	170						
osca, Carlos-Carlos	M02-04TorA	09-29-53	Pinar Del Rio, Cuba				5'7	160						
rebelhorn, Tom-Thomas Lynn	M86-91MilA M94ChiN	01-27-48	Portand, Ore.				5'11	178						
urner, Ted-Robert Edward	M77AtlN	11-19-38	Cincinnati, Ohio				6'2	180						
eaver, Earl-Earl Sidney	M68-82, 85-86BalA	08-14-30	St. Louis, Mo.				5'7	175						
inkles, Bobby-Bobby Brooks (Winks)	M73-74CalA M77-78OakA	03-11-30	Tuckerman, Ark.				5'9	166						

HALL OF FAME

1936 B.B.W.A.A.(226):
Ty Cobb(222)
Honus Wagner(215)
Babe Ruth(215)
Christy Mathewson(205)
Walter Johnson(189)

1937 B.B.W.A.A.(201):
Nap Lajoie(168)
Tris Speaker(165)
Cy Young(153)
Centennial Commission:
*Morgan G. Bulkeley
*Ban Johnson
Connie Mack
John McGraw
George Wright

1938 B.B.W.A.A.(262):
Pete Alexander(212)
Centennial Commission:
*Alexander Cartwright
*Henry Chadwick

1939 B.B.W.A.A.(274):
George Sisler(235)
Eddie Collins(213)
Willie Keeler(207)
Lou Gehrig(by special election)

Comm. on Old-timers:
Cap Anson
Charlie Comiskey
Candy Cummings
Buck Ewing
Hoss Radbourn
Al Spalding

1942 B.B.W.A.A.(233):
Rogers Hornsby(182)

1944 Comm. on Old-timers:
*Judge Kenesaw M. Landis

1945 Comm. on Old-timers:
Roger Bresnahan
Dan Brouthers
Fred Clarke
Jimmie Collins
Ed Delahanty
Hugh Duffy
Hughie Jennings
Mike Kelly
Jim O'Rourke
Wilbert Robinson

1946 Comm. on Old-timers
Jesse Burkett
Frank Chance
Jack Chesbro
Johnny Evers
Clark Griffith
Tom McCarthy
Joe McGinnity
Eddie Plank
Joe Tinker
Rube Waddell
Ed Walsh

1947 B.B.W.A.A.(161):
Carl Hubbell(140)
Frank Frisch(136)
Mickey Cochrane(128)
Lefty Grove(123)

1948 B.B.W.A.A.(121):
Herb Pennock(94)
Pie Traynor(93)

1949 B.B.W.A.A.(187):
Charlie Gehringer(159)[R]
Comm. on Old-timers:
Three-Finger Brown
Kid Nichols

1951 B.B.W.A.A.(226):
Mel Ott(197)
Jimmie Foxx(179)

1952 B.B.W.A.A.(234):
Harry Heilmann(203)
Paul Waner(195)

1953 B.B.W.A.A.(264):
Dizzy Dean(209)
Al Simmons(199)
Comm. on Veterans:
*Ed Barrow
Chief Bender
*Tom Connolly
*Bill Klem
Bobby Wallace
*Harry Wright

1954 B.B.W.A.A.(252):
Rabbit Maranville (209)
Bill Dickey(202)
Bill Terry(195)

1955 B.B.W.A.A.(251):
Joe DiMaggio(223)
Ted Lyons(217)
Dazzy Vance(205)
Gabby Hartnett(195)
Comm. on Veterans:
Frank Baker
Ray Schalk

1956 B.B.W.A.A.(193):
Hank Greenberg(164)
Joe Cronin(152)

1957 Comm. on Veterans:
Sam Crawford
*Joe McCarthy

1959 Comm. on Veterans:
Zack Wheat

1961 Comm. on Veterans:
Max Carey
Billy Hamilton

1962 B.B.W.A.A.(160):
Bob Feller(150)
Jackie Robinson(124)
Comm. on Veterans:
*Bill McKechnie
Edd Roush

1963 Comm. on Veterans:
John Clarkson
Elmer Flick
Sam Rice
Eppa Rixey

1964 B.B.W.A.A.(225) Special runoff election:
Luke Appling(189)
Comm. on Veterans:
Red Faber
Burleigh Grimes
*Miller Huggins
Tim Keefe
Heinie Manush
John Ward

1965 Comm. on Veterans:
Pud Galvin

1966 B.B.W.A.A.(302):
Ted Williams(282)
Comm. on Veterans:
*Casey Stengel

1967 B.B.W.A.A.(306):
Red Ruffing(266)[R]
Comm. on Veterans:
*Branch Rickey
Lloyd Waner

1968 B.B.W.A.A.(283):
Joe Medwick(240)
Comm. on Veterans:
Kiki Cuyler
Goose Goslin

1969 B.B.W.A.A.(340):
Stan Musial(317)
Roy Campanella(270)
Comm. on Veterans:
Stan Coveleski
Waite Hoyt

1970 B.B.W.A.A.(300):
Lou Boudreau(232)
Comm. on Veterans:
Earle Combs
*Ford Frick
Jesse Haines

1971 Comm. on Veterans:
Jake Beckley
Dave Bancroft
Chick Hafey
Harry Hooper
Joe Kelley
Rube Marquard
*George Weiss
Special Committee on Negro Leagues:
Satchel Paige

1972 B.B.W.A.A.(396):
Sandy Koufax(344)
Yogi Berra(339)
Early Wynn(301)

Comm. on Veterans:
Lefty Gomez
*Will Harridge
Ross Youngs
Special Committee on Negro Leagues:
Josh Gibson
Buck Leonard

1973 B.B.W.A.A.(380):
Warren Spahn(316)
Comm. on Veterans:
*Billy Evans
George Kelly
Mickey Welch
Special Committee on Negro Leagues:
Monte Irvin
Special waiver of 5-year waiting period:
Roberto Clemente

HALL OF FAME

B.B.W.A.A.=Baseball Writers Association of America (75% of ballots cast necessary for election)
*Selected for the Hall of Fame as non-player.
Number in parenthesis denotes ballots cast.
[R} - Elected in runoff election.

1974 B.B.W.A.A.(365):
  Mickey Mantle(322)
  Whitey Ford(284)
  Comm. on Veterans:
  Jim Bottomley
  *Jocko Conlan
  Sam Thompson
  Special Committee on
  Negro Leagues:
  Cool Papa Bell

1975 B.B.W.A.A.(362):
  Ralph Kiner(273)
  Comm. on Veterans:
  Earl Averill
  *Bucky Harris
  Billy Herman
  Special Committee on
  Negro Leagues:
  Judy Johnson

1976 B.B.W.A.A.(388):
  Robin Roberts(337)
  Bob Lemon(305)
  Comm. on Veterans:
  Roger Connor
  Fred Lindstrom
  *Cal Hubbard
  Special Committee on
  Negro Leagues:
  Oscar Charleston

1977 B.B.W.A.A.(383):
  Ernie Banks(321)
  Comm. on Veterans:
  Amos Rusie
  Joe Sewell
  *Al Lopez
  Special Committee on
  Negro Leagues:
  Martin Dihigo
  John Henry Lloyd

1978 B.B.W.A.A.(379):
  Eddie Mathews(310)
  New Veterans Committee:
  Addie Joss
  *Larry MacPhail

1979 B.B.W.A.A.(432):
  Willie Mays(409)
  New Veterans Committee:
  *Warren Giles
  Hack Wilson

1980 B.B.W.A.A.(385)
  Al Kaline(340)
  Duke Snider(333)
  New Veterans Committee:
  Chuck Klein
  *Tom Yawkey

1981 B.B.W.A.A.(401):
  Bob Gibson(337)
  New Veterans Committee:
  Johnny Mize
  Rube Foster

1982 B.B.W.A.A.(415):
  Hank Aaron(406)
  Frank Robinson(370)
  New Veterans Committee:
  Travis Jackson
  *Happy Chandler

1983 B.B.W.A.A.(374):
  Brooks Robinson(344)
  Juan Marichal(313)
  New Veterans Committee:
  George Kell
  *Walt Alston

1984 B.B.W.A.A.(403):
  Luis Aparicio(341)
  Harmon Killebrew(335)
  Don Drysdale(316)
  New Veterans Committee:
  Rick Ferrell
  Pee Wee Reese

1985 B.B.W.A.A.(395):
  Hoyt Wilhelm(331)
  Lou Brock(315)
  New Veterans Committee:
  Enos Slaughter
  Arky Vaughan

1986 B.B.W.A.A.(425):
  Willie McCovey(346)
  New Veterans Committee:
  Bobby Doerr
  Ernie Lombardi

1987 B.B.W.A.A.(413):
  Billy Williams(354)
  Catfish Hunter(315)
  New Veterans Committee:
  Ray Dandridge

1988 B.B.W.A.A.(427):
  Willie Stargell(352)

1989 B.B.W.A.A.(447):
  Johnny Bench(431)
  Carl Yastrzemski(423)
  New Veterans Committee:
  Red Schoendienst
  *Al Barlick

1990 B.B.W.A.A.(444)
  Jim Palmer(411)
  Joe Morgan(363)

1991 B.B.W.A.A. (443)
  Rod Carew (401)
  Gaylord Perry (342)
  Ferguson Jenkins (334)
  New Veterans Committee:
  Tony Lazzeri
  *Bill Veeck

1992 B.B.W.A.A. (430)
  Tom Seaver (425)
  Rollie Fingers (349)
  New Veterans Committee:
  Hal Newhouser
  *Bill McGowan

1993 B.B.W.A.A. (423)
  Reggie Jackson (396)

1994 B.B.W.A.A. (455)
  Steve Carlton (436)
  New Veterans Committee:
  Phil Rizzuto
  *Leo Durocher

1995 B.B.W.A.A. (460)
  Mike Schmidt (444)
  New Veterans Committee:
  Richie Ashburn
  Leon Day
  *William Hulbert
  Vic Willis

1996 New Veterans Committee:
  Jim Bunning
  Bill Foster
  * Ned Hanlon
  * Earl Weaver

1997 B.B.W.A.A.(473):
  Phil Niekro(380)
  New Veterans Committee:
  Nellie Fox
  * Tommy Lasorda
  * Willie Wells

1998 B.B.W.A.A. (473)
  Don Sutton (386)
  New Veterans Committee:
  Larry Doby
  George Davis
  * Lee MacPhail
  Joe Rogan

1999 B.B.W.A.A. (497)
  Nolan Ryan (491)
  George Brett (488)
  Robin Yount (385)
  New Veterans Committee:
  Orlando Cepeda

* Frank Selee
* Nestor Chylak
  Smokey Joe Williams

2000 B.B.W.A.A. (499)
  Carlton Fisk (397)
  Tony Perez (385)
  New Veterans Committee:
  Biddy McPhee
* Sparky Anderson
  Norman "Turkey" Stearnes

2001 B.B.W.A.A. (515)
  Dave Winfield (435)
  Kirby Puckett (423)
  New Veterans Committee:
  Bill Mazeroski
  Hilton Smith

2002 B.B.W.A.A. (472)
  Ozzie Smith (433)

2003 B.B.W.A.A. (496)
  Eddie Murray (423)
  Gary Carter (387)

2004 B.B.W.A.A. (506)
  Paul Molitor (431)
  Dennis Eckersley (421)

2005 B.B.W.A.A. (516)
  Wade Boggs (474)
  Ryne Sandberg (393)

2006 B.B.W.A.A. (520)
  Bruce Sutter (400)
  Special Commitee on
  "black baseball"
  Players:
  Ray Brown
  Willard Brown
  Andy Cooper
  Frank Grant
  Pete Hill
  Biz Mackey
  Jose Mendez
  Louis Santop
  Mule Suttles
  Ben Taylor
  Cristobal Torriente
  Jud Wilson
  Executives:
  Effa Manley
  Alex Pompez
  Cum Posey
  Sol White
  J. L. Wilkinson

HALL OF FAME

Names in **bold** were elected in their first year on the ballot
Names in *italics* were not elected by the Baseball Writers Association of America
Years in **bold** are years managed

Name	Year Inducted	Career Start	Career End	Cap on plaque
Hank Aaron	1982	1954	1976	Atlanta Braves
Pete Alexander	1938	1911	1930	No insignia
Walter Alston	1983	**1954**	**1976**	Manager
Sparky Anderson	2000	**1970**	**1995**	Manager
Cap Anson	1939	1876	1897	No insignia
Luis Aparicio	1984	1956	1973	Chicago White Sox
Luke Appling	1964	1930	1950	Chicago White Sox
Richie Ashburn	1995	1948	1962	Philadelphia Phillies
Earl Averill	1975	1929	1941	Cleveland Indians
Frank Baker	1955	1908	1921	No insignia
Dave Bancroft	1971	1915	1930	No insignia
Ernie Banks	1977	1953	1971	Chicago Cubs
Al Barlick	1989			Umpire
Ed Barrow	1953			Pioneer/Executive
Jake Beckley	1971	1888	1907	No insignia
Cool Papa Bell	1974			Negro Leagues
Johnny Bench	1989	1967	1983	Cincinnati Reds
Chief Bender	1953	1903	1925	No insignia
Yogi Berra	1972	1946	1963	Head turned, insignia unseen
Wade Boggs	2005	1982	1999	Boston Red Sox
Jim Bottomley	1974	1922	1937	No insignia
Lou Boudreau	1970	1938	1952	Cleveland Indians
Roger Bresnahan	1945	1897	1915	No insignia
George Brett	1999	1973	1993	Kansas City Royals
Lou Brock	1985	1961	1979	St. Louis Cardinals
Dan Brouthers	1945	1879	1904	No hat
Three Finger Brown	1949	1903	1916	Head turned, insignia unseen
Ray Brown	2006			Negro Leagues
Willard Brown	2006			Negro Leagues
Morgan Bulkeley	1937			Pioneer/Executive
Jim Bunning	1996	1955	1971	Philadelphia Phillies
Jesse Burkett	1946	1890	1905	No hat
Roy Campanella	1969	1937	1957	Brooklyn Dodgers
Rod Carew	1991	1967	1985	Minnesota Twins
Max Carey	1961	1919	1929	Pittsburgh Pirates
Steve Carlton	1994	1965	1988	Philadelphia Phillies
Gary Carter	2003	1974	1991	Montreal Expos
Alexander Cartwright	1938			Pioneer/Executive
Orlando Cepeda	1999	1958	1974	San Francisco Giants
Henry Chadwick	1938			Pioneer/Executive
Frank Chance	1946	1898	1914	Chicago Cubs
Happy Chandler	1982			Pioneer/Executive
Oscar Charleston	1976			Negro Leagues
Jack Chesbro	1946	1899	1909	Head turned, insignia unseen
Nestor Chylak	1999			Umpire
Fred Clarke	1945	1894	1915	No insignia
John Clarkson	1963	1882	1894	No insignia
Roberto Clemente	1973	1955	1972	Pittsburgh Pirates
Ty Cobb	1936	1905	1928	Detroit Tigers
Mickey Cochrane	1947	1925	1937	Detroit Tigers
Eddie Collins	1939	1906	1930	No insignia
Jimmy Collins	1945	1895	1908	No hat
Earle Combs	1970	1924	1935	New York Yankees
Charlie Comiskey	1939	1882	1894	Pioneer/Executive
Jocko Conlan	1974			Umpire
Tom Connolly	1953			Umpire
Roger Connor	1976	1880	1897	No insignia
Andy Cooper	2006			Negro Leagues
Stan Coveleski	1969	1912	1928	Cleveland Indians
Sam Crawford	1957	1899	1917	Detroit Tigers
Joe Cronin	1956	1926	1945	Boston Red Sox
Candy Cummings	1939	1876	1876	Pioneer/Executive
Kiki Cuyler	1968	1921	1938	Chicago Cubs
Ray Dandridge	1987			Negro Leagues
George Davis	1998	1890	1909	No insignia
Leon Day	1995			Negro Leagues
Dizzy Dean	1953	1930	1947	St. Louis Cardinals
Ed Delahanty	1945	1888	1903	No hat
Bill Dickey	1954	1928	1946	New York Yankees
Martin Dihigo	1977			Negro Leagues
Joe DiMaggio	1955	1936	1951	New York Yankees
Larry Doby	1998	1942	1959	Cleveland Indians
Bobby Doerr	1986	1937	1951	Boston Red Sox
Don Drysdale	1984	1956	1969	Los Angeles Dodgers
Hugh Duffy	1945	1888	1906	No hat
Leo Durocher	1994	**1939**	**1973**	Manager
Dennis Eckersley	2004	1975	1998	Oakland A's
Billy Evans	1973			Umpire
Johnny Evers	1946	1902	1929	No insignia
Buck Ewing	1939	1880	1897	No insignia
Red Faber	1964	1914	1933	Chicago White Sox
Bob Feller	1962	1936	1956	Cleveland Indians
Rick Ferrell	1984	1929	1947	Boston Red Sox
Rollie Fingers	1992	1968	1985	Oakland A's
Carlton Fisk	2000	1969	1993	Boston Red Sox
Elmer Flick	1963	1898	1910	No insignia
Whitey Ford	1974	1950	1967	New York Yankees
Bill Foster	1996			Negro Leagues
Rube Foster	1981			Negro Leagues
Nellie Fox	1997	1947	1965	Chicago White Sox
Jimmie Foxx	1951	1925	1945	Boston Red Sox
Ford Frick	1970			Pioneer/Executive
Frankie Frisch	1947	1919	1933	No insignia
Pud Galvin	1965	1879	1892	No insignia
Lou Gehrig (special election)	1939	1923		1939 New York Yankees
Charlie Gehringer	1949	1924	1942	Head turned, insignia unseen
Bob Gibson	1981	1959	1975	St. Louis Cardinals
Josh Gibson	1972			Negro Leagues
Warren Giles	1979			Pioneer/Executive
Lefty Gomez	1972	1930	1943	New York Yankees
Goose Goslin	1968	1921	1938	Washington Senators
Frank Grant	2006			Negro Leagues
Hank Greenberg	1956	1930	1947	Detroit Tigers
Clark Griffith	1946			Pioneer/Executive
Burleigh Grimes	1964	1916	1934	Brooklyn Dodgers
Lefty Grove	1947	1925	1941	Boston Red Sox
Chick Hafey	1971	1924	1937	No insignia
Jesse Haines	1970	1918	1937	No insignia
Billy Hamilton	1961	1888	1901	Boston Beaneaters
Ned Hanlon	1996	**1889**	**1898**	Manager
Will Harridge	1972			Pioneer/Executive
Bucky Harris	1975	**1924**	**1956**	Manager
Gabby Hartnett	1955	1922	1941	Chicago Cubs
Harry Heilmann	1952	1914	1932	Detroit Tigers
Billy Herman	1975	1931	1947	Chicago Cubs
Pete Hill	2006			Negro Leagues
Harry Hooper	1971	1909	1925	No insignia
Rogers Hornsby	1942	1915	1937	Head turned, insignia unseen
Waite Hoyt	1969	1918	1938	New York Yankees
Cal Hubbard	1976			Umpire
Carl Hubbell	1947	1928	1943	New York Giants
Miller Huggins	1964	**1913**	**1929**	Manager
William Hulbert	1995			Pioneer/Executive
Catfish Hunter	1987	1965	1979	No insignia
Monte Irvin	1973			Negro Leagues
Reggie Jackson	1993	1967	1987	New York Yankees
Travis Jackson	1982	1922	1936	New York Giants
Ferguson Jenkins	1991	1965	1983	Chicago Cubs
Hughie Jennings	1945	1891	1918	Detroit Tigers
Ban Johnson	1937			Pioneer/Executive
Judy Johnson	1975			Negro Leagues
Walter Johnson	1936	1907	1927	Washington Senators
Addie Joss	1978	1902	1910	Cleveland Indians
Al Kaline	1980	1953	1974	Detroit Tigers
Tim Keefe	1964	1880	1893	No insignia
Willie Keeler	1939	1893	1910	Brooklyn Superbas
George Kell	1983	1943	1957	Detroit Tigers
Joe Kelley	1971	1891	1908	No insignia
George Kelly	1973	1915	1932	New York Giants
King Kelly	1945	1878	1893	No hat
Harmon Killebrew	1984	1954	1975	Minnesota Twins
Ralph Kiner	1975	1946	1955	Pittsburgh Pirates
Chuck Klein	1980	1928	1944	Philadelphia Phillies
Bill Klem	1953			Umpire
Sandy Koufax	1972	1956	1966	Los Angeles Dodgers
Nap Lajoie	1937	1896	1916	Cleveland Naps
Kenesaw Mountain Landis	1944			Pioneer/Executive
Tommy Lasorda	1997	**1976**	**1996**	Manager
Tony Lazzeri	1991	1926	1939	New York Yankees
Bob Lemon	1976	1946	1958	Cleveland Indians
Buck Leonard	1972			Negro Leagues
Fred Lindstrom	1976	1924	1936	New York Giants

WINS

#	Player	
1	Roger Clemens	348
2	Greg Maddux	333
3	Tom Glavine	290
4	Randy Johnson	280
5	Mike Mussina	239
6	David Wells	230
7	Jamie Moyer	216
8	Kenny Rogers	207
9	Curt Schilling	207
10	Pedro Martinez	206
11	John Smoltz	193
12	Andy Pettitte	186
13	Tim Wakefield	151
14	Aaron Sele	145
15	Scott Erickson	142
16	Bartolo Colon	140
17	Mike Hampton	138
18	Steve Trachsel	134
19	Tom Gordon	130
20	Pedro Astacio	129

LOSSES

#	Player	
1	Greg Maddux	203
2	Tom Glavine	191
3	Roger Clemens	178
4	Jamie Moyer	166
5	David Wells	148
6	Randy Johnson	147
7	Steve Trachsel	143
8	Terry Mulholland	142
9	Kenny Rogers	139
10	Curt Schilling	138
11	John Smoltz	137
12	Scott Erickson	136
13	Mike Mussina	134
14	Tim Wakefield	134
15	Pedro Astacio	124
	Jeff Fassero	124
17	Tom Gordon	119
18	Livan Hernandez	117
19	Jon Lieber	115
20	Aaron Sele	110

WINNING PERCENTAGE
(minimum 50 decisions)

#	Player	
1	Johan Santana	.716
2	Joe Nathan	.709
3	Pedro Martinez	.691
4	Roy Oswalt	.676
5	Tim Hudson	.665
6	Roy Halladay	.664
7	Roger Clemens	.662
8	Randy Johnson	.656
9	Mark Mulder	.644
10	Andy Pettitte	.641
11	Mike Mussina	.641
12	Jose Contreras	.640
13	Cliff Lee	.636
14	Greg Maddux	.621
15	Freddy Garcia	.620
16	Barry Zito	.618
17	Bartolo Colon	.617
18	David Wells	.608
19	Carlos Zambrano	.604
20	Tom Glavine	.603

EARNED RUN AVERAGE
(minimum 500 IP)

#	Player	
1	Mariano Rivera	2.29
2	Billy Wagner	2.38
3	Trevor Hoffman	2.71
4	Pedro Martinez	2.81
5	Armando Benitez	2.95
6	Roy Oswalt	3.05
7	Greg Maddux	3.07
8	Roger Clemens	3.10
9	Troy Percival	3.10
10	Johan Santana	3.20
11	Randy Johnson	3.22
12	Eric Gagne	3.27
13	John Smoltz	3.27
14	Brandon Webb	3.28
15	Carlos Zambrano	3.29
16	Keith Foulke	3.30
17	Roberto Hernandez	3.32
18	Jeff Nelson	3.41
19	Steve Kline	3.42
20	Dontrelle Willis	3.44

SAVES

#	Player	
1	Trevor Hoffman	482
2	Mariano Rivera	413
3	Roberto Hernandez	326
4	Troy Percival	324
5	Billy Wagner	324
6	Jose Mesa	320
7	Armando Benitez	280
8	Todd Jones	263
9	Jason Isringhausen	249
10	Bob Wickman	247
11	Keith Foulke	190
12	Eddie Guardado	183
13	Danny Graves	182
14	Eric Gagne	161
15	John Smoltz	154
16	Tom Gordon	150
17	Mike Timlin	139
18	Francisco Cordero	133
19	Joe Nathan	124
20	Antonio Alfonseca	121

GAMES

#	Player	
1	Mike Stanton	1109
2	Jose Mesa	966
3	Mike Timlin	961
4	Roberto Hernandez	960
5	Todd Jones	874
6	Trevor Hoffman	821
7	Mike Myers	811
8	Tom Gordon	809
9	Jeff Nelson	798
10	Eddie Guardado	781
11	Bob Wickman	778
12	David Weathers	754
13	Steve Kline	728
14	Kenny Rogers	721
15	Jeff Fassero	720
	Mariano Rivera	720
17	Alan Embree	708
18	Julian Tavarez	700
19	Armando Benitez	699
20	Roger Clemens	691

GAMES STARTED

#	Player	
1	Roger Clemens	690
2	Greg Maddux	673
3	Tom Glavine	635
4	Randy Johnson	546
5	Jamie Moyer	518
6	Mike Mussina	475
7	David Wells	460
8	Kenny Rogers	433
9	John Smoltz	429
10	Curt Schilling	412
11	Steve Trachsel	380
12	Pedro Martinez	375
13	Scott Erickson	364
14	Andy Pettitte	359
15	Aaron Sele	352
16	Pedro Astacio	343
17	Tim Wakefield	339
18	Terry Mulholland	332
19	Esteban Loaiza	323
20	Mike Hampton	321

COMPLETE GAMES

#	Player	
1	Roger Clemens	118
2	Greg Maddux	108
3	Randy Johnson	98
4	Curt Schilling	82
5	Mike Mussina	57
6	Tom Glavine	55
7	David Wells	54
8	John Smoltz	53
9	Scott Erickson	51
10	Pedro Martinez	46
	Terry Mulholland	46
12	Livan Hernandez	42
13	Kenny Rogers	36
14	Pedro Astacio	31
	Bartolo Colon	31
16	Jamie Moyer	30
17	Tim Wakefield	29
18	Sidney Ponson	28
19	Chris Carpenter	25
	Mark Mulder	25
	Andy Pettitte	25

INNINGS PITCHED

#	Player	
1	Roger Clemens	4818
2	Greg Maddux	4616
3	Tom Glavine	4150
4	Randy Johnson	3799
5	Jamie Moyer	3351
6	David Wells	3282
7	Mike Mussina	3210
8	John Smoltz	3161
9	Curt Schilling	3110
10	Kenny Rogers	3066
11	Pedro Martinez	2646
12	Terry Mulholland	2576
13	Tim Wakefield	2432
14	Scott Erickson	2361
15	Andy Pettitte	2312
16	Steve Trachsel	2303
17	Pedro Astacio	2197
18	Livan Hernandez	2167
19	Aaron Sele	2099
20	Mike Hampton	2074

SHUTOUTS

#	Player	
1	Roger Clemens	46
2	Randy Johnson	37
3	Greg Maddux	35
4	Tom Glavine	24
5	Mike Mussina	23
6	Curt Schilling	19
7	Scott Erickson	17
	Pedro Martinez	17
9	John Smoltz	16
10	Pedro Astacio	12
	Chris Carpenter	12
	David Wells	12
13	Mark Mulder	10
	Terry Mulholland	10
15	A.J. Burnett	9
	Mike Hampton	9
	Tim Hudson	9
	Jamie Moyer	9
	Kenny Rogers	9
	Jason Schmidt	9

BASES ON BALLS

#	Player	
1	Roger Clemens	1549
2	Randy Johnson	1409
3	Tom Glavine	1399
4	Kenny Rogers	1079
5	Tim Wakefield	948
6	Jamie Moyer	946
7	Tom Gordon	944
	Greg Maddux	944
9	John Smoltz	937
10	Scott Erickson	865
11	Shawn Estes	840
	Steve Trachsel	840
13	Mike Hampton	826
14	Chan Ho Park	820
15	Russ Ortiz	787
16	Aaron Sele	777
17	Jason Schmidt	766
18	Livan Hernandez	751
19	Pedro Astacio	726
20	Jeff Fassero	724

STRIKEOUTS

#	Player	
1	Roger Clemens	4604
2	Randy Johnson	4544
3	Greg Maddux	3169
4	Curt Schilling	3015
5	Pedro Martinez	2998
6	John Smoltz	2778
7	Mike Mussina	2572
8	Tom Glavine	2481
9	David Wells	2119
10	Jamie Moyer	1992
11	Tom Gordon	1870
12	Kenny Rogers	1850
13	Jason Schmidt	1728
14	Andy Pettitte	1703
15	Tim Wakefield	1680
16	Pedro Astacio	1664
17	Jeff Fassero	1643
18	Javier Vazquez	1602
19	Steve Trachsel	1519
20	Chan Ho Park	1507

FEWEST HITS PER 9IP
(Minimim 500IP)

#	Player	
1	Billy Wagner	5.99
2	Troy Percival	6.06
3	Armando Benitez	6.13
4	Pedro Martinez	6.85
5	Trevor Hoffman	6.86
6	Kerry Wood	6.98
7	Eric Gagne	6.98
8	Mariano Rivera	7.05
9	Ocatvio Dotel	7.11
10	Randy Johnson	7.14
11	Jeff Nelson	7.26
12	Johan Santana	7.31
13	Carlos Zambrano	7.36
14	Keith Foulke	7.43
15	Roger Clemens	7.63
16	Barry Zito	7.73
17	Guillermo Mota	7.79
18	A.J. Burnett	7.80
19	Bob Howry	7.84
20	John Smoltz	7.85

FEWEST BASES ON BALLS PER 9IP
(Minimim 500IP)

#	Player	
1	Josh Towers	1.45
2	Carlos Silva	1.64
3	Jon Lieber	1.71
4	Greg Maddux	1.84
5	David Wells	1.86
6	Ben Sheets	1.89
7	Roy Oswalt	1.97
8	Curt Schilling	1.99
9	Mike Mussina	2.02
10	Mark Buehrle	2.07
11	Keith Foulke	2.16
12	Danny Haren	2.21
13	Roy Halladay	2.24
14	Jose Lima	2.26
15	Paul Byrd	2.29
16	Mariano Rivera	2.31
17	Rheal Cormier	2.33
18	Terry Mulholland	2.38
19	Mike Maroth	2.38
20	Chris Reitsma	2.38

MOST STRIKEOUTS PER 9IP
(Minimim 500IP)

#	Player	
1	Billy Wagner	11.96
2	Armando Benitez	10.96
3	Ocatvio Dotel	10.79
4	Randy Johnson	10.77
5	Eric Gagne	10.38
6	Mark Prior	10.37
7	Kerry Wood	10.36
8	Troy Percival	10.30
9	Pedro Martinez	10.20
10	Trevor Hoffman	9.81
11	Oliver Perez	9.63
12	Jeff Nelson	9.51
13	Johan Santana	9.47
14	Kyle Farnsworth	9.21
15	Jake Peavy	8.85
16	Arthur Rhodes	8.84
17	Mike Remlinger	8.74
18	Curt Schilling	8.73
19	Byung-Hyun Kim	8.71
20	Roger Clemens	8.60

HALL OF FAME

Names in **bold** were elected in their first year on the ballot
Names in *italics* were not elected by the Baseball Writers Association of America
Years in **bold** are years managed

Name	Year Inducted	Career Start	Career End	Cap on plaque
Pop Lloyd	1977			Negro Leagues
Ernie Lombardi	1986	1931	1947	Cincinnati Reds
Al Lopez	1977	**1951**	**1969**	Manager
Ted Lyons	1955	1923	1942	Chicago White Sox
Connie Mack	1937	**1894**	**1950**	Manager
Biz Mackey	2006			Negro Leagues
Larry MacPhail	1978			Pioneer/Executive
Lee MacPhail	1998			Pioneer/Executive
Effa Manley	2006			Pioneer/Executive
Mickey Mantle	1974	1951	1968	New York Yankees
Heinie Manush	1964	1923	1939	Detroit Tigers
Rabbit Maranville	1954	1912	1935	Boston Braves
Juan Marichal	1983	1960	1975	San Francisco Giants
Rube Marquard	1971	1908	1925	No insignia
Eddie Mathews	1978	1952	1968	Milwaukee Braves
Christy Mathewson	1936	1900	1916	New York Giants
Willie Mays	1979	1951	1973	San Francisco Giants
Bill Mazeroski	2001	1956	1972	Pittsburgh Pirates
Joe McCarthy	1957	**1926**	**1950**	Manager
Tommy McCarthy	1946	1884	1896	Boston Beaneaters
Willie McCovey	1986	1959	1980	San Francisco Giants
Joe McGinnity	1946	1899	1908	No hat
Bill McGowan	1992			Umpire
John McGraw	1937	**1901**	**1932**	Manager
Bill McKechnie	1962	**1922**	**1946**	Manager
Biddy McPhee	2000	1882	1899	No insignia
Joe Medwick	1968	1932	1948	No insignia
Jose Mendez	2006			Negro Leagues
Johnny Mize	1981	1936	1953	No insignia
Paul Molitor	2004	1978	1998	Milwaukee Brewers
Joe Morgan	1990	1963	1984	Cincinnati Reds
Eddie Murray	2003	1977	1997	Baltimore Orioles
Stan Musial	1969	1941	1963	St. Louis Cardinals
Hal Newhouser	1992	1939	1955	Detroit Tigers
Kid Nichols	1949	1890	1906	Boston Beaneaters
Phil Niekro	1997	1964	1987	Atlanta Braves
Jim O'Rourke	1945	1876	1904	No insignia
Mel Ott	1951	1926	1947	No hat
Satchel Paige	1971			Negro Leagues
Jim Palmer	1990	1965	1984	Baltimore Orioles
Herb Pennock	1948	1912	1934	No insignia
Tony Perez	2000	1964	1986	Cincinnati Reds
Gaylord Perry	1991	1962	1983	San Francisco Giants
Eddie Plank	1946	1901	1917	No insignia
Alex Pompez	2006			Pioneer/Executive
Cum Posey	2006			Negro Leagues Executive
Kirby Puckett	2001	1984	1995	Minnesota Twins
Hoss Radbourn	1939	1880	1891	Head turned, insignia unseen
Pee Wee Reese	1984	1940	1958	Brooklyn Dodgers
Sam Rice	1963	1915	1934	Washington Senators
Branch Rickey	1967			Pioneer/Executive
Eppa Rixey	1963	1912	1933	Cincinnati Reds
Phil Rizzuto	1994	1941	1956	New York Yankees
Robin Roberts	1976	1948	1966	Philadelphia Phillies
Brooks Robinson	1983	1955	1977	Baltimore Orioles
Frank Robinson	1982	1956	1976	Baltimore Orioles
Jackie Robinson	1962	1947	1956	Brooklyn Dodgers
Wilbert Robinson	1945	**1902**	**1931**	Manager
Joe Rogan	1998			Negro Leagues
Edd Roush	1962	1913	1931	Cincinnati Reds
Red Ruffing	1967	1924	1947	New York Yankees
Amos Rusie	1977	1889	1901	No insignia
Babe Ruth	1936	1914	1935	New York Yankees
Nolan Ryan	1999	1966	1993	Texas Rangers

Name	Year Inducted	Career Start	Career End	Cap on plaque
Ryne Sandberg	2005	1981	1997	Chicago Cubs
Louis Santop	2006	1906	1926	Negro Leagues
Ray Schalk	1955	1912	1929	No insignia
Mike Schmidt	1995	1972	1989	Philadelphia Phillies
Red Schoendienst	1989	1945	1963	St. Louis Cardinals
Tom Seaver	1992	1967	1986	New York Mets
Frank Selee	1999	**1890**	**1905**	Manager
Joe Sewell	1977	1920	1933	Cleveland Indians
Al Simmons	1953	1924	1944	Philadelphia A's
George Sisler	1939	1915	1930	No hat
Enos Slaughter	1985	1938	1959	St. Louis Cardinals
Hilton Smith	2001			Negro Leagues
Ozzie Smith	2002	1978	1996	St. Louis Cardinals
Duke Snider	1980	1947	1964	Brooklyn Dodgers
Warren Spahn	1973	1942	1965	Milwaukee Braves
Al Spalding	1939			Pioneer/Executive
Tris Speaker	1937	1907	1928	Cleveland Indians
Willie Stargell	1988	1962	1982	Pittsburgh Pirates
Turkey Stearnes	2000			Negro Leagues
Casey Stengel	1966	**1934**	**1965**	Manager
Bruce Sutter	2006	**1976**	**1988**	St. Louis Cardinals
Mule Suttles	2006			Negro Leagues
Don Sutton	1998	1968	1988	Los Angeles Dodgers
Ben Taylor	2006			Negro Leagues
Bill Terry	1954	1923	1936	New York Giants
Sam Thompson	1974	1885	1906	No insignia
Joe Tinker	1946	1902	1916	Head turned, insignia unseen
Cristobal Torriente	2006			Negro Leagues
Pie Traynor	1948	1920	1937	Pittsburgh Pirates
Dazzy Vance	1955	1915	1935	Brooklyn Robins
Arky Vaughan	1985	1932	1948	Pittsburgh Pirates
Bill Veeck	1991			Pioneer/Executive
Rube Waddell	1946	1897	1910	Head turned, insignia unseen
Honus Wagner	1936	1897	1917	Head turned, insignia unseen
Bobby Wallace	1953	1894	1918	No hat
Ed Walsh	1946	1904	1917	No insignia
Lloyd Waner	1967	1927	1945	Pittsburgh Pirates
Paul Waner	1952	1926	1945	Pittsburgh Pirates
Monte Ward	1964	1878	1894	No insignia
Earl Weaver	1996	**1968**	**1986**	Manager
George Weiss	1971			Pioneer/Executive
Mickey Welch	1973	1880	1892	No insignia
Willie Wells	1997			Negro Leagues
Zack Wheat	1959	1909	1927	Brooklyn Robins
Sol White	2006			Pioneer/Executive
Hoyt Wilhelm	1985	1952	1972	New York Giants
J.L. Wilkinson	2006			Pioneer/Executive
Billy Williams	1987	1959	1976	Chicago Cubs
Joe Williams	1999			Negro Leagues
Ted Williams	1966	1939	1960	Boston Red Sox
Vic Willis	1995	1898	1910	No hat
Hack Wilson	1979	1923	1934	Chicago Cubs
Jud Wilson	2006			Negro Leagues
Dave Winfield	2001	1973	1995	San Diego Padres
George Wright	1937			Pioneer/Executive
Harry Wright	1953			Pioneer/Executive
Early Wynn	1972	1939	1963	Cleveland Indians
Carl Yastrzemski	1989	1961	1983	Boston Red Sox
Tom Yawkey	1980			Pioneer/Executive
Cy Young	1937	1890	1911	Cleveland Naps
Ross Youngs	1972	1917	1926	New York Giants
Robin Yount	1999	1974	1993	Milwaukee Brewers

ACTIVE LEADERS - BATTING

BATTING AVERAGE (minimum 2000 at bats)

1	Todd Helton	.333
2	Albert Pujols	.332
3	Ichiro Suzuki	.331
4	Vladimir Guerrero	.325
5	Nomar Garciaparra	.318
6	Derek Jeter	.317
7	Manny Ramirez	.314
8	Miguel Cabrera	.311
9	Mike Piazza	.309
10	Alex Rodriguez	.305
11	Magglio Ordonez	.305
12	Frank Thomas	.305
13	Chipper Jones	.304
14	Ivan Rodriguez	.304
15	Juan Pierre	.304
16	Juan Pierre	.303
17	Bobby Abreu	.302
18	Sean Casey	.302
19	Mike Sweeney	.302
20	Jason Kendall	.301

SLUGGING AVERAGE (minimum 2000 at bats)

1	Albert Pujols	.629
2	Barry Bonds	.608
3	Manny Ramirez	.600
4	Todd Helton	.593
5	Vladimir Guerrero	.583
6	Alex Rodriguez	.573
7	Lance Berkman	.567
8	Frank Thomas	.566
9	Jim Thome	.565
10	Carlos Delgado	.558
11	Ken Griffey Jr.	.557
12	Mike Piazza	.551
13	David Ortiz	.550
14	Chipper Jones	.542
15	Jason Giambi	.541
16	Nomar Garciaparra	.540
17	Jim Edmonds	.539
18	Miguel Cabrera	.535
19	Mark Teixeira	.534
20	Richie Sexson	.526

RUNS

1	Barry Bonds	2152
2	Craig Biggio	1776
3	Ken Griffey Jr.	1467
4	Kenny Lofton	1442
5	Steve Finley	1434
6	Gary Sheffield	1433
7	Frank Thomas	1404
8	Bernie Williams	1366
9	Alex Rodriguez	1358
10	Luis Gonzalez	1312
11	Omar Vizquel	1283
12	Julio Franco	1277
	Derek Jeter	1277
14	Jim Thome	1259
15	Manny Ramirez	1258
16	Jeff Kent	1200
17	Johnny Damon	1188
	Chipper Jones	1188
19	Ivan Rodriguez	1159
20	Ray Durham	1129

RUNS BATTED IN

1	Barry Bonds	1930
2	Ken Griffey Jr.	1608
3	Frank Thomas	1579
4	Manny Ramirez	1516
5	Gary Sheffield	1501
6	Jeff Kent	1380
7	Alex Rodriguez	1347
8	Luis Gonzalez	1324
9	Ruben Sierra	1322
10	Jim Thome	1302
11	Mike Piazza	1291
12	Carlos Delgado	1287
13	Bernie Williams	1257
14	Moises Alou	1229
15	Chipper Jones	1197
16	Julio Franco	1178
17	Steve Finley	1165
18	Jason Giambi	1144
19	Garret Anderson	1128
20	Craig Biggio	1125

HITS

1	Craig Biggio	2930
2	Barry Bonds	2841
3	Julio Franco	2566
4	Steve Finley	2531
5	Omar Vizquel	2472
6	Ken Griffey Jr.	2412
7	Gary Sheffield	2390
8	Luis Gonzalez	2373
9	Ivan Rodriguez	2354
10	Bernie Williams	2336
11	Kenny Lofton	2283
12	Frank Thomas	2262
13	Jeff Kent	2189
14	Ruben Sierra	2152
15	Derek Jeter	2150
16	Garret Anderson	2081
17	Alex Rodriguez	2067
18	Manny Ramirez	2066
19	Mike Piazza	2042
20	Moises Alou	2005

DOUBLES

1	Craig Biggio	637
2	Barry Bonds	587
3	Luis Gonzalez	547
4	Jeff Kent	501
5	Ivan Rodriguez	473
6	Frank Thomas	458
7	Ken Griffey Jr.	449
	Bernie Williams	449
9	Steve Finley	446
10	Manny Ramirez	438
11	Garret Anderson	431
12	Ruben Sierra	428
13	Gary Sheffield	418
14	Shawn Green	415
15	Carlos Delgado	414
16	Todd Helton	413
17	Julio Franco	404
18	Moises Alou	400
19	Omar Vizquel	398
20	Ray Durham	384

TRIPLES

1	Steve Finley	124
2	Kenny Lofton	110
3	Johnny Damon	85
4	Barry Bonds	77
	Ray Durham	77
6	Omar Vizquel	68
7	Cristian Guzman	67
8	Carl Crawford	65
	Luis Gonzalez	65
10	Neifi Perez	61
	Juan Pierre	61
	Jimmy Rollins	61
13	Reggie Sanders	60
14	Ruben Sierra	59
	Tony Womack	59
16	Carlos Beltran	55
	Royce Clayton	55
	Bernie Williams	55
19	Julio Franco	54
20	Craig Biggio	52
	Nomar Garciaparra	52

HOME RUNS

1	Barry Bonds	734
2	Ken Griffey Jr.	563
3	Frank Thomas	487
4	Jim Thome	472
5	Manny Ramirez	470
6	Alex Rodriguez	464
7	Gary Sheffield	455
8	Mike Piazza	419
9	Carlos Delgado	407
10	Chipper Jones	357
11	Jim Edmonds	350
	Jason Giambi	350
13	Jeff Kent	345
14	Andruw Jones	342
15	Vladimir Guerrero	338
16	Luis Gonzalez	331
17	Vinny Castilla	320
18	Moises Alou	319
19	Shawn Green	318
20	Jeromy Burnitz	315

TOTAL BASES

1	Barry Bonds	5784
2	Ken Griffey Jr.	4622
3	Craig Biggio	4514
4	Gary Sheffield	4221
5	Frank Thomas	4203
6	Steve Finley	4134
7	Luis Gonzalez	4043
8	Manny Ramirez	3946
9	Alex Rodriguez	3875
10	Jeff Kent	3815
11	Bernie Williams	3756
12	Ivan Rodriguez	3742
13	Mike Piazza	3640
14	Jim Thome	3620
15	Ruben Sierra	3616
16	Julio Franco	3594
17	Chipper Jones	3458
18	Moises Alou	3438
19	Carlos Delgado	3376
20	Shawn Green	3310

EXTRA BASE HITS

1	Barry Bonds	1398
2	Ken Griffey Jr.	1048
3	Craig Biggio	970
4	Frank Thomas	956
5	Luis Gonzalez	943
6	Manny Ramirez	924
7	Gary Sheffield	897
8	Jeff Kent	891
9	Steve Finley	873
10	Alex Rodriguez	854
11	Jim Thome	846
12	Carlos Delgado	837
13	Ruben Sierra	793
14	Ivan Rodriguez	792
15	Bernie Williams	791
16	Chipper Jones	770
17	Shawn Green	767
18	Moises Alou	757
19	Mike Piazza	753
20	Jim Edmonds	751

GAMES

1	Barry Bonds	2860
2	Craig Biggio	2709
3	Steve Finley	2540
4	Julio Franco	2472
5	Omar Vizquel	2443
6	Luis Gonzalez	2316
7	Ken Griffey Jr.	2234
8	Gary Sheffield	2229
9	Ruben Sierra	2186
10	Frank Thomas	2096
11	Bernie Williams	2076
12	Jeff Kent	2041
13	Royce Clayton	2031
14	Ivan Rodriguez	2023
15	Kenny Lofton	1967
16	Jeff Conine	1923
17	Jim Thome	1881
18	Vinny Castilla	1865
19	Moises Alou	1840
20	Mike Piazza	1829

BASES ON BALLS

1	Barry Bonds	2426
2	Frank Thomas	1547
3	Jim Thome	1364
4	Gary Sheffield	1293
5	Craig Biggio	1137
6	Jason Giambi	1089
7	Ken Griffey Jr.	1077
8	Chipper Jones	1070
9	Bernie Williams	1069
10	Luis Gonzalez	1058
11	Manny Ramirez	1054
12	Brian Giles	1006
13	Bobby Abreu	1003
14	Carlos Delgado	973
15	Julio Franco	903
16	Omar Vizquel	897
17	Kenny Lofton	889
18	Jim Edmonds	878
19	Todd Helton	864
20	Steve Finley	836

STRIKEOUTS

1	Jim Thome	1909
2	Craig Biggio	1641
3	Reggie Sanders	1599
4	Jim Edmonds	1512
5	Ken Griffey Jr.	1494
6	Barry Bonds	1485
7	Carlos Delgado	1483
8	Manny Ramirez	1451
9	Jeff Kent	1409
10	Alex Rodriguez	1404
11	Jose Hernandez	1391
12	Jeromy Burnitz	1376
13	Royce Clayton	1362
14	Mike Cameron	1340
15	Julio Franco	1318
16	Steve Finley	1295
17	Jose Valentin	1266
18	Andruw Jones	1256
19	Shawn Green	1253
20	Frank Thomas	1246

AT BATS PER HOME RUN (minimum 2000 at bats)

1	Barry Bonds	12.95
2	Jim Thome	13.58
3	Albert Pujols	13.96
4	Manny Ramirez	13.99
5	Adam Dunn	14.30
6	Alex Rodriguez	14.58
7	Ken Griffey Jr.	14.74
8	Carlos Delgado	14.87
9	Frank Thomas	15.24
10	Richie Sexson	15.44
11	Troy Glaus	15.72
12	Mike Piazza	15.76
13	David Ortiz	15.87
14	Jason Giambi	16.06
15	Vladimir Guerrero	16.28
16	Lance Berkman	16.39
17	Mark Teixeira	16.76
18	Jim Edmonds	16.88
19	Andruw Jones	17.06
20	Gary Sheffield	17.66

STOLEN BASES

1	Kenny Lofton	599
2	Barry Bonds	509
3	Eric Young	464
4	Craig Biggio	410
5	Omar Vizquel	366
6	Tony Womack	363
7	Juan Pierre	325
8	Steve Finley	320
9	Luis Castillo	306
	Johnny Damon	306
11	Reggie Sanders	304
12	Julio Franco	279
13	Bobby Abreu	271
14	Edgar Renteria	263
15	Ray Durham	255
16	Mike Cameron	254
17	Derek Jeter	249
18	Alex Rodriguez	241
19	Ichiro Suzuki	235
20	Royce Clayton	229